O'Connor's Federal Rules Civil Trials

2013 Edition Author

Michael C. Smith

Jones McClure Publishing
Houston, Texas

O'Connor's Litigation Series

Suggested cite form: *O'Connor's Federal Rules * Civil Trials* (2013)

Jones McClure Publishing
Product List

To order, visit JonesMcClure.com or call 1-800-OCONNOR

Texas Litigation Series

O'Connor's Texas Rules ★ Civil Trials

O'Connor's Texas Civil Forms*

O'Connor's Texas Civil Appeals*

Texas Expert Series

O'Connor's Texas Causes of Action

O'Connor's Texas Causes of Action Pleadings*

O'Connor's Texas Family Law Handbook

Texas Rules of Evidence Handbook

Texas Forms ★ Real Estate*

Texas Annotated Codes Series

O'Connor's Business & Commerce Code Plus

O'Connor's Business Organizations Code Plus

O'Connor's Civil Practice & Remedies Code Plus

O'Connor's Family Code Plus

O'Connor's Probate Code Plus

O'Connor's Property Code Plus

O'Connor's Texas Crimes & Consequences

O'Connor's Texas Criminal Codes Plus

O'Connor's Texas Employment Codes Plus

Federal Litigation Series

O'Connor's Federal Rules ★ Civil Trials

O'Connor's Federal Civil Forms*

Federal Annotated Codes Series

O'Connor's Federal Criminal Rules & Codes Plus

O'Connor's Federal Employment Codes Plus

O'Connor's Federal Intellectual Property Codes Plus

California Litigation Series

O'Connor's California Practice ★ Civil Pretrial

Practice Resources

Typography for Lawyers

Calculators

O'Connor's Texas Child-Support Calculator

O'Connor's Texas Pretrial Deadlines Calculator

O'Connor's Federal Deadlines Calculator

*Download forms at JonesMcClure.com

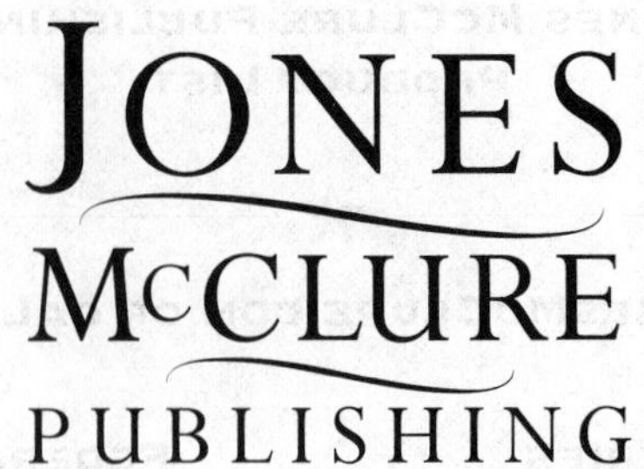

Mailing address:
P.O. Box 3348
Houston, TX 77253-3348

Shipping address:
2160 Taylor St.
Houston, TX 77007

Phone: (713) 335-8200
(800) OCONNOR (626-6667)
Fax: (713) 335-8201

www.JonesMcClure.com

Print date: November 30, 2012
Printed in the United States of America

ISBN 978-1-59839-159-6

This book is intended to provide attorneys with current information about selected federal rules and statutes. The information in this book, however, may not be sufficient in dealing with a client's particular legal problem, and Jones McClure Publishing, Michol O'Connor, and Michael C. Smith do not warrant or represent its suitability for this purpose. Attorneys using this book do so with the understanding that the information published in it should not be relied on as a substitute for independent research using original sources of authority.

Subscription Notice: This book is updated periodically to reflect current law. When you order this book, you can choose to be enrolled in our subscription program, which entitles you to a lower annual price. Before we send you an updated book, we send you a letter confirming that you want the new edition. You have the option at that time to change or cancel your order. If you do not change or cancel your order, the book will be shipped to you. If you decide to return the book, the return postage is your responsibility. If you did not purchase this book directly from Jones McClure Publishing, you are not registered as a subscriber and will not receive this update service. You can change your subscription status at any time in writing.

WHAT'S NEW IN THIS EDITION

Each year, we strive to improve the quality of our commentaries and rule annotations and to make the book more useful to practitioners. For this edition, we updated the commentaries with new case law throughout, and we made many other significant revisions and improvements.

- We revised the subchapter on subpoenas to include more in-depth discussions of who can be subpoenaed, the range of the subpoena, the notice requirements, and the manners of service permitted. See "Formal Requirements for Subpoenas," ch. 1-H, §3, p. 48.
- We added several new circuit opinions interpreting the pleading standard under ***Ashcroft v. Iqbal***, 556 U.S. 662 (2009), and ***Bell Atlantic Corp. v. Twombly***, 550 U.S. 544 (2007). See "Statement of Claim," ch. 2-B, §5, p. 80.
- We enhanced the discussion of deadlines for removing a case to federal court. See "Deadlines for Removal," ch. 4-A, §4, p. 242.
- We added several recent district-court decisions on the discoverability of electronically stored information on social-networking sites (e.g., Facebook, Twitter). See "Note," ch. 6-B, §2.2.6, p. 459.
- We revised the subchapter on electronic discovery to include a discussion of the emerging search technique of predictive coding. See "Predictive coding," ch. 6-C, §5.2, p. 491.
- We revised the discussion of the recovery of costs for exemplification and making copies under 28 U.S.C. §1920. See "Fees for exemplification & making copies," ch. 9-D, §2.1.6, p. 763.

STATUTORY CHANGES

This edition has been updated through P.L. 112-196. There were no significant legislative actions affecting civil cases in federal courts for this edition.

RULE AMENDMENTS

There were no amendments to the Federal Rules of Civil Procedure (FRCPs), Federal Rules of Evidence (FREs), or Federal Rules of Appellate Procedure (FRAPs) for this edition.

PROPOSED 2013 RULE AMENDMENTS

The Judicial Conference Committee on Rules of Practice and Procedure has approved amendments to FRCPs 37 and 45; FRE 803; FRAPs 13, 14, 24, 28, and 28.1; and FRAP Form 4. If the Supreme Court approves the amendments and Congress does not take contrary action, the amendments will take effect on December 1, 2013.

- FRCP 45 would be amended (1) to simplify the rule by making the court where the action is pending the issuing court, by permitting service throughout the United States, and by combining the provisions on the place of compliance into FRCP 45(c), (2) to address the transfer of subpoena-related motions, (3) to reject the line of cases that have compelled parties or parties' officers to travel beyond the 100-mile limit under current FRCP 45(b)(2) to testify at trial, and (4) to move the notice provision for a production subpoena to a more prominent position and require that notice include a copy of the subpoena. FRCP 37 would be amended to conform with the proposed amendments to FRCP 45.
- FRE 803 would be amended to align FRE 803(10) with the Supreme Court's ruling in ***Melendez-Diaz v. Massachusetts***, 557 U.S. 305 (2009), and would adopt a "notice-and-demand" procedure for the hearsay exception to cure constitutional issues in criminal cases when the government seeks to prove—through the introduction of a certificate—that a public record does not exist.

- FRAPs 13, 14, and 24 would be amended to address interlocutory appeals from the U.S. Tax Court under 26 U.S.C. §7482(a)(2).
- FRAPs 28 and 28.1 would be amended to remove the requirement of a separate statement of the case and statement of the facts and instead would require one "statement of the case."
- FRAP Form 4 would be amended to replace questions 10 and 11 with a single revised question to avoid requiring a person seeking to appeal in forma pauperis to provide information that may be privileged or protected and that is not necessary to rule on the request.

NOTEWORTHY CASES

Statement of Claim

In ***Khalik v. United Air Lines***, 671 F.3d 1188, 1191 & n.2 (10th Cir.2012), the Tenth Circuit addressed the continuing struggle over what constitutes sufficiently plausible facts and whether there is in fact a higher pleading standard. See "Statement of Claim," ch. 2-B, §5, p. 80.

Fraudulent Joinder

In ***Stillwell v. Allstate Ins.***, 663 F.3d 1329, 1333-34 (11th Cir.2011), the Eleventh Circuit held that the standard for establishing a valid cause of action against a nondiverse or local defendant is lower than the plausibility standard. Thus, to avoid a remand to state court based on the fraudulent joinder of a nondiverse or local defendant, the complaint only needs to establish the possibility of stating a valid cause of action under the state-law pleading standard. *Id.* See "Fraudulent joinder," ch. 4-A, §5.2.1(2)(e), p. 252.

Settlement-Negotiations Privilege

In ***In re MSTG, Inc.***, 675 F.3d 1337, 1342 & n.2 (Fed.Cir.2012), the Federal Circuit noted that the courts are divided on whether there is a settlement-negotiations privilege. The court declined to decide whether the privilege exists, but it noted that information from settlement negotiations could be protected by limiting the scope of discovery rather than creating a new privilege. *Id.* at 1346-48. See "Settlement-negotiations privilege," ch. 6-B, §3.12, p. 481.

Arbitration

In ***KPMG LLP v. Cocchi***, ___ U.S. ___, 132 S.Ct. 23, 24 (2011), the Supreme Court held that a court cannot refuse to compel arbitration because some of the claims could be resolved by the court without arbitration. Instead, the court must carefully examine the complaint to separate the arbitrable claims from the nonarbitrable claims and compel arbitration of the arbitrable claims. *Id.* at ___, 132 S.Ct. at 26. See "Dispute is arbitrable," ch. 7-E, §2.1.3(2), p. 652.

Taxable Costs

In ***Taniguchi v. Kan Pac. Saipan, Ltd.***, ___ U.S. ___, 132 S.Ct. 1997, 2000-01 (2012), the Supreme Court resolved a disagreement over whether the costs for court-appointed experts and interpreters under 28 U.S.C. §1920(6) included costs for translators (i.e., someone who translates documents but not live speech). The Court held that §1920(6) is limited to the costs of oral translation and does not include the costs for document translation. *Id.* at ___, 132 S.Ct. at 2000. See "Compensation of experts & interpreters," ch. 9-D, §2.1.8, p. 764.

In ***Race Tires Am., Inc. v. Hoosier Racing Tire Corp.***, 674 F.3d 158, 166-67 (3d Cir.2012), the Third Circuit examined the allowance for "costs of making copies" under 28 U.S.C. §1920(4). The court held that the costs for the steps leading up to the production of copies are not taxable; thus, the court did not allow recovery of costs for an e-discovery vendor locating, collecting, and reviewing electronically stored information. *Id.* at 169-70. See "Fees for exemplification & making copies," ch. 9-D, §2.1.6, p. 763.

Postjudgment Motions

In ***Blue v. International Bhd. of Elec. Workers Local Un.***, 676 F.3d 579, 584-85 (7th Cir.2012), the Seventh Circuit held that FRCPs 50(b) and 59(b) are nonjurisdictional claim-processing rules; thus, an objection to the timeliness

of a motion under FRCP 50(b) or 59 can be waived. But even though a timeliness objection can be waived, the court held that an untimely motion does not toll the time for filing an appeal. *Id.* at 582-83. See "No extension," ch. 10-B, §3.2, p. 777; "No extension," ch. 10-C, §2.2, p. 783.

In ***Obaydullah v. Obama***, ___ F.3d ___ (D.C.Cir.2012) (No. 11-5123; 8-10-12), the D.C. Circuit held that FRAP 4(a)(4) is a nonjurisdictional claims-processing rule; thus, untimely motions listed under FRAP 4(a)(4)(A) can toll the time for filing an appeal. See "Caution," ch. 10-B, §3.2, p. 777; "Caution," ch. 10-C, §2.2, p. 783; "Caution," ch. 10-D, §2.2, p. 794; "Caution," ch. 10-E, §3.2, p. 800; "Caution," ch. 10-F, §9.1.1, p. 816.

CONVENTIONS

In writing this book, we have tried to produce a plain-English reference guide that is easy for lawyers and judges to use. To this end, we should point out a few things about the book. First, the rules and statutes are in double columns so they can be instantly distinguished from the commentaries. Second, we supply page headers and side-tabs for quick reference. Third, when other sections of the book are relevant, we cross-reference them. Fourth, we include practice tips and caution notes that are separate from the main text of the commentaries so they can be easily spotted. Fifth, in the U.S.C. section, the changes since the last edition are marked with an Ⓐ or an Ⓔ button, depending on whether the code section was amended or enacted. We have also underlined the enacted or amended language. Sixth, where Congress passed two irreconcilable amendments to the same code provision, we have marked the text with a ☠ button. Finally, we include timetables for the different pretrial, post-trial, and appellate procedures.

To reduce gender-specific language, we usually refer to judges as the "court" and to most parties as "it" as though all parties were corporations, which they often are. When gender-specific language cannot be avoided, we use the feminine pronoun. To save space, we abbreviate the name of the Federal Rules of Civil Procedure to FRCP, the Federal Rules of Evidence to FRE, and the Federal Rules of Appellate Procedure to FRAP. When you cite rules in a motion or brief, we suggest you use the more traditional citation forms in *The Bluebook* (19th ed. 2010).

ABOUT THE AUTHOR

Michael C. Smith practices law with the firm of Siebman, Burg, Phillips & Smith, LLP, in Marshall, Texas, where he specializes in complex commercial and patent litigation in federal and state courts. He served as chairman of the Local Rules Advisory Committee for the U.S. District Court for the Eastern District of Texas from 2000 to 2009. He also served on the Board of Directors of the State Bar of Texas from 2005 to 2008, where he received a Presidential Citation and the Outstanding Third Year Director award. He is currently the editor of the *Eastern District of Texas Federal Court Practice* blog at www.EDTexweblog.com. He also serves as chair of the *Texas Bar Journal* Board of Editors and as chair of the Council of the Litigation Section of the State Bar of Texas, and he is a Life Fellow of the Texas Bar Foundation and an Associate member of the American Board of Trial Advocates. Mr. Smith received his master's degree in public administration from the University of Texas at Austin and his law degree from Baylor University. Mr. Smith is grateful for the support and patience of his wife, Jamie, and their sons, Grayson, Collin, and Parker.

YOUR SUGGESTIONS

We welcome your comments. If you think we should have included (or excluded) something, or if you see anything that needs to be corrected, please let us know. Send your comments to the mailing address or fax number shown on the copyright page, or by e-mail to Carrie A. Arnett, Managing Legal Editor, at carnett@JonesMcClure.com.

CAVEAT

This book provides citations to important opinions that interpret the FRCPs, FREs, FRAPs, and various statutes through November 2012. You may disagree with our explanations of the rules, statutes, and cases cited in this book. You should therefore use this book only as a research guide. Read the rules, statutes, and cases yourself and make your own evaluation of them.

EDITORIAL & PRODUCTION STAFF

As always, the staff of Jones McClure worked hard to prepare this publication, both in its substance and in its layout. The people who worked on this edition of ***O'Connor's Federal Rules * Civil Trials*** are listed below.

EXECUTIVE EDITOR
Douglas Rosenzweig, J.D.

MANAGING LEGAL EDITOR
Carrie A. Arnett, J.D.

ASSISTANT MANAGING LEGAL EDITOR
Holly R. Veselka, J.D.

DEVELOPMENT EDITORS
Gregory S. Otterson, J.D.
Jason E. Wilson, J.D.

LEGAL EDITORS
Anouchka Oppinger Bowne, J.D.
Sarah J. Cottrell, J.D.
Fiona Deshmukh, J.D.
James K. Hancock, J.D.
Amanda Pattock, J.D.
Aditi Pemmaraju, J.D.

LEGAL EDITORIAL ASSISTANTS
Wade Allison
Eric T. Bean
Cristina A. Bruce
Christy B. Bushnell, J.D.
Britney N. Cherry
Kacey M. Cox, J.D.
Sharon McCord Cozort, J.D.
Amyna Jenna Esmail, J.D.
Jessica Younger Field, J.D.
Paul T. Freeman
Rohan A. Hebbar, J.D.
Robert F. Holland, J.D.
Kacie E. Jaksa
Lindsay Kirton
Reza Manoochehri, J.D.
Caleb Ray Thornton
Nicole L. Washington, J.D.

PRODUCTION MANAGER
Jenny Sulak

PRODUCTION EDITOR
Nicole E. Hammond

PRODUCTION STAFF
Beverly B. Bellot
Danielle E. Boss
Cassandra J. Pace
Sara Y. Rhodes
Sarah M. Rutledge
Daniel Spence
Donna E. Vass
Annabelle M. Wilde

COPYEDITORS
Danielle E. Boss
Cassandra J. Pace
Kathryn A. Ritcheske, J.D.
Jenny Sulak

PROOFREADERS
Sarah M. Rutledge
Annabelle M. Wilde

MICHAEL C. SMITH
MARSHALL, TEXAS

MASTER TABLE OF CONTENTS

COMMENTARIES 1

FEDERAL RULES OF CIVIL PROCEDURE 831

FRCP FORMS.. 991

SUPPLEMENTAL RULES—ADMIRALTY & MARITIME CLAIMS.... 1001

MULTIDISTRICT LITIGATION RULES 1011

FEDERAL RULES OF EVIDENCE 1023

FEDERAL RULES OF APPELLATE PROCEDURE...................... 1089

FRAP FORMS.. 1125

ADVISORY COMMITTEE NOTES TO RULES 1133

UNITED STATES CODE 1291

U.S. CONSTITUTION 1553

THE HAGUE CONVENTION ON SERVICE ABROAD 1563

THE HAGUE CONVENTION ON TAKING EVIDENCE ABROAD...... 1566

TIMETABLES 1573

INDEX 1595

Contents
Commentaries

CHAPTER 1. INTRODUCTION

1-A Introduction to Federal Rules 3
1-B Pleading & Motion Practice 7
1-C Filing Documents 17
1-D Serving Documents 29
1-E Hearings 38
1-F Making Objections & Preserving Error 41
1-G Court Rulings 44
1-H Subpoenas Under FRCP 45 47
1-I The Attorney 58

CHAPTER 2. PLAINTIFF'S LAWSUIT

2-A General Considerations 73
2-B Plaintiff's Complaint 75
2-C Interpleader 87
2-D Injunctive Relief 93
2-E Declaratory Judgment 107
2-F Choosing the Court—Jurisdiction 112
2-G Choosing the Court—Venue 143
2-H Serving the Defendant with Process 149

CHAPTER 3. DEFENDANT'S RESPONSES & PLEADINGS

3-A Overview of Preanswer Motions & Responsive Pleadings 171
3-B Motion to Dismiss for Lack of Personal Jurisdiction—FRCP 12(b)(2) 178
3-C Motion to Dismiss for Lack of Subject-Matter Jurisdiction—FRCP 12(b)(1) 187
3-D Motion to Dismiss for Improper Venue—FRCP 12(b)(3) 192
3-E Motion to Dismiss for Forum Non Conveniens—Challenging the U.S. Forum 199
3-F Motion to Dismiss for Failure to State a Claim—FRCP 12(b)(6) 204
3-G Motion to Dismiss for Insufficient Process or Service—FRCP 12(b)(4), (b)(5) 209
3-H Motion for More Definite Statement—FRCP 12(e) 212
3-I Motion to Dismiss for Failure to Join a Party Under FRCP 19—FRCP 12(b)(7) 214
3-J Motion to Dismiss for Failure to Plead Properly—FRCP 8, 9(b) 218
3-K Motion to Transfer Venue—28 U.S.C. §1404 221
3-L The Answer—Denying Liability 230

CHAPTER 4. REMOVAL & REMAND

4-A Defendant's Notice of Removal 241
4-B Plaintiff's Motion to Remand 268

CHAPTER 5. PRETRIAL MOTIONS

5-A Scheduling Order & Pretrial Conference 289
5-B Magistrate Judges & Special Masters 297
5-C Demand for Jury Trial 309
5-D Offer of Judgment 317
5-E Motion to Recuse 321
5-F Motion to Extend Time 332
5-G Motion for Continuance 337
5-H Motion in Limine 341
5-I Motion to Amend or Supplement Pleadings—Pretrial 345
5-J Motion to Intervene 356
5-K Motion to Consolidate 362
5-L Motion for Severance or Separate Trials 366
5-M Motion for Judicial Notice 370
5-N Motion to Exclude Expert Witness 376
5-O Motion for Sanctions 384
5-P Motion for Class Certification 398

CHAPTER 6. DISCOVERY

6-A General Rules for Discovery 413
6-B Scope of Discovery 456
6-C Electronic Discovery 481
6-D Securing Discovery from Experts 515
6-E Mandatory Disclosures 532
6-F Depositions 538
6-G Interrogatories 557
6-H Requests for Admissions 563
6-I Requests for Production 569
6-J Physical & Mental Examinations of Persons 574
6-K Request for Entry on Land 579

CHAPTER 7. DISPOSITION WITHOUT TRIAL

7-A Default Judgment 583
7-B Summary Judgment 603
7-C Voluntary Dismissal 629
7-D Involuntary Dismissal 642
7-E Arbitration 650

CHAPTER 8. THE TRIAL

8-A Jury Selection 673
8-B Opening Statement 686
8-C Introducing Evidence 688
8-D Objecting to Evidence 700
8-E Offer of Proof 707
8-F Motion to Amend Pleadings—Trial & Post-trial 710
8-G Motion for Judgment as a Matter of Law 714
8-H Motion to Reopen for Additional Evidence 718
8-I Jury Charge 720
8-J Closing Argument 727

CHAPTER 9. THE JUDGMENT

9-A Entry of Judgment 735
9-B Motion for Entry of Judgment 743
9-C Motion for Attorney Fees 745
9-D Taxable Costs 761

CHAPTER 10. POSTJUDGMENT MOTIONS

10-A General 775
10-B Renewed Motion for Judgment as a Matter of Law 775
10-C Motion for New Trial 783
10-D Motion to Alter or Amend Judgment 793
10-E Motion to Add or Amend Findings of Fact 799
10-F Motion for Relief from Judgment 804
10-G Motion to Extend Time to File Notice of Appeal 817
10-H Motion to Reopen Time for Appeal 821
10-I Motion to Correct Clerical Error in Judgment 825

Contents
Rules, Codes & Appendixes

FEDERAL RULES OF CIVIL PROCEDURE

Title I. Scope of Rules; Form of Action 833
Title II. Commencing an Action; Service of Process, Pleadings, Motions, & Orders 833
Title III. Pleadings & Motions 846
Title IV. Parties 870
Title V. Disclosures & Discovery 892
Title VI. Trials 919
Title VII. Judgment 943
Title VIII. Provisional & Final Remedies 968
Title IX. Special Proceedings 978
Title X. District Courts & Clerks: Conducting Business; Issuing Orders 984
Title XI. General Provisions 987
Appendix of Forms 991
Supplemental Rules—Admiralty & Maritime Claims 1001

MULTIDISTRICT LITIGATION RULES 1011

FEDERAL RULES OF EVIDENCE

Article I. General Provisions 1028
Article II. Judicial Notice 1031
Article III. Presumptions in Civil Cases 1032
Article IV. Relevance & Its Limits 1033
Article V. Privileges 1044
Article VI. Witnesses 1047
Article VII. Opinions & Expert Testimony 1058
Article VIII. Hearsay 1064
Article IX. Authentication & Identification 1078
Article X. Contents of Writings, Recordings, & Photographs 1082
Article XI. Miscellaneous Rules 1086

FEDERAL RULES OF APPELLATE PROCEDURE

Title I. Applicability of Rules 1090
Title II. Appeal from a Judgment or Order of a District Court 1090
Title III. Review of a Decision of the United States Tax Court 1100
Title IV. Review or Enforcement of an Order of an Administrative Agency, Board, Commission, or Officer 1101
Title V. Extraordinary Writs 1103
Title VI. Habeas Corpus; Proceedings in Forma Pauperis 1104
Title VII. General Provisions 1105
Appendix of Forms 1125

ADVISORY COMMITTEE NOTES 1133

UNITED STATES CODE

TITLE 28 1301

Part I. Organization of Courts 1301
Part II. Department of Justice 1364
Part III. Court Officers & Employees 1389
Part IV. Jurisdiction & Venue 1421
Part V. Procedure 1456
Part VI. Particular Proceedings 1491

TITLE 42 1549

TITLE 50 APP. 1550

APPENDIXES

U.S. CONSTITUTION 1553

HAGUE CONVENTION—SERVICE 1563

HAGUE CONVENTION—EVIDENCE 1566

TIMETABLES 1573

1. Pleadings & Pretrial-Motions Schedule 1574
2. Pretrial Disclosures & Conferences 1577
3. Discovery Status Sheet 1579
4. Removal & Remand 1581
5. Temporary Restraining Order & Injunction 1583
6. Request to Clerk for Default Judgment 1586
7. Motion to Court for Default Judgment 1587
8. Summary Judgment 1589
9. Appeal of Civil Trial 1591

COMMENTARIES

CHAPTER 1. INTRODUCTION
TABLE OF CONTENTS

A. INTRODUCTION TO FEDERAL RULES 3
§1. FEDERAL RULES 3
§1.1 Types of federal rules 3
§1.2 Procedure for amending rules 4
§1.3 Construction of rules 4
§2. LOCAL RULES 5
§2.1 Authority 5
§2.2 Adoption & amendment 5
§2.3 Force of law 5
§2.4 Notice 6
§2.5 Construction of local rules 6
§3. STANDING ORDERS 6
§3.1 When standing orders are appropriate 6
§3.2 When standing orders are not appropriate 7

B. PLEADING & MOTION PRACTICE 7
§1. GENERAL 7
§2. PLEADING PRACTICE 7
§2.1 Drafting pleadings 7
§2.2 Amending & supplementing pleadings 12
§2.3 Defective pleadings 13
§2.4 Groundless pleadings 14
§2.5 Filing & serving pleadings 14
§2.6 Responding to pleadings 14
§2.7 Appellate review 14
§3. MOTION PRACTICE 14
§3.1 Drafting motions 14
§3.2 Serving & filing motions 16
§3.3 Responding to motions 16
§3.4 Hearing on motions 16
§3.5 Appellate review 16

C. FILING DOCUMENTS 17
§1. GENERAL 17
§2. WHAT TO FILE 17
§2.1 Redacted filing 17
§2.2 Original & copies 18
§3. WHERE TO FILE 18
§3.1 Most situations 18
§3.2 Emergency situations – courthouse closed 18
§3.3 Courtesy copies 19
§4. HOW TO FILE 19
§4.1 Mail 19
§4.2 Delivery 19
§4.3 Fax 19
§4.4 Electronic filing 20
§5. WHEN TO FILE 22
§5.1 Deadline – filing or service? 22
§5.2 Filing complete when received 23
§6. COMPUTING DEADLINES 23
§6.1 Calculating time periods 23
§6.2 Requesting more time 28
§7. FILED DOCUMENTS 28
§7.1 No refusal to accept 28
§7.2 Notation by clerk 29
§7.3 Deemed filed 29
§7.4 Withdrawing documents 29
§7.5 Lost documents 29
§8. PROOF OF FILING 29

D. SERVING DOCUMENTS 29
§1. GENERAL 29
§2. WHAT TO SERVE 30
§2.1 Most documents 30
§2.2 Documents not required to be served 30
§3. WHOM TO SERVE 30
§3.1 Party or attorney? 30
§3.2 Which attorney? 30
§3.3 How many parties? 30
§4. HOW TO SERVE 30
§4.1 Methods of service 30
§4.2 Certificate of service 33
§5. WHEN TO SERVE 33
§5.1 Deadline – filing, service, or both? 33
§5.2 Serving motions for hearing 33
§5.3 Serving affidavits with motion 33
§6. COMPUTING RESPONSE DEADLINES 33
§6.1 Determine when to begin counting 33
§6.2 Count time units 34
§6.3 Determine end of time period 34
§6.4 Determine if weekend or holiday extension applies 34
§6.5 Determine if additional three-day extension applies 34
§7. PROOF OF SERVICE 36
§7.1 Proving receipt 36
§7.2 Proving nonreceipt 37
§8. SANCTIONS FOR FAILURE TO SERVE 38

E. HEARINGS 38
§1. GENERAL 38
§2. NOTICE OF HEARING 38
§2.1 Generally 38
§2.2 Deadline 38
§3. HEARING ON MOTION 38
§3.1 Request for hearing 38
§3.2 Type of hearing 39
§3.3 Methods of conducting hearings 39
§3.4 Who conducts hearings 40
§3.5 Request for court reporter 40
§3.6 Appellate review 40
§4. COMPELLING WITNESS TO APPEAR FOR HEARING 40
§4.1 Subpoenas under FRCP 45 40
§4.2 Subpoenas under federal statute 40

F. MAKING OBJECTIONS & PRESERVING ERROR 41
§1. GENERAL 41
§2. GROUNDS FOR OBJECTION 41
§3. TYPES OF ERROR 41
§3.1 Who made error? 41
§3.2 Appealable error 42
§4. PRESERVING ERROR 42
§4.1 Make proper objection 42
§4.2 Have court rule on record 43
§4.3 Failure to preserve error 43

G. COURT RULINGS 44
§1. GENERAL 44
§2. TYPES OF RULINGS 44
§2.1 Judgment 44
§2.2 Order 45
§3. COURT'S RULING 45
§3.1 Secure ruling 45
§3.2 Second request for ruling 45

COMMENTARIES

CHAPTER 1. INTRODUCTION
TABLE OF CONTENTS

§4. RECORD OF RULING 45
§4.1 Judgment 45
§4.2 Orders 45
§5. FORM OF RULING 46
§5.1 Judgment 46
§5.2 Order on motion 46
§6. NOTICE OF RULING 46
§7. APPELLATE REVIEW 46
§7.1 Appeal after judgment 46
§7.2 Mandamus 46

H. SUBPOENAS UNDER FRCP 45 47

§1. GENERAL 47
§2. TYPES OF SUBPOENAS 47
§2.1 Production subpoena 47
§2.2 Deposition subpoena 47
§2.3 Hearing or trial subpoena 47
§3. FORMAL REQUIREMENTS FOR SUBPOENAS 48
§3.1 Form of subpoena 48
§3.2 Who should be subpoenaed 48
§3.3 Range of subpoena 49
§3.4 Who may issue subpoena 50
§3.5 Notice 50
§3.6 Manner of service 51
§3.7 Fees 52
§3.8 Proof of service 52
§4. DEADLINE TO SERVE 52
§5. PRODUCTION OF DOCUMENTS, ESI & TANGIBLE THINGS 52
§5.1 Preservation 52
§5.2 Scope 52
§5.3 Production 53
§6. RESISTING SUBPOENA TO PRODUCE OR PERMIT INSPECTION 53
§6.1 Serve objections 54
§6.2 Assert privileges 54
§7. MOTION TO COMPEL PRODUCTION OR FOR INSPECTION 55
§7.1 Motion 55
§7.2 Where to file 55
§7.3 Ruling 55
§8. MOTION TO QUASH OR MODIFY SUBPOENA 55
§8.1 Who can file 55
§8.2 Deadline to file 56
§8.3 Where to file 56
§8.4 Mandatory grounds 56
§8.5 Discretionary grounds 57
§9. ENFORCING SUBPOENA 58

I. THE ATTORNEY 58

§1. GENERAL 58
§2. APPEARING BEFORE FEDERAL COURT 59
§2.1 Application for general admission 59
§2.2 Application to appear pro hac vice 59
§2.3 Pro se representation 60
§3. COMMUNICATIONS WITH COURT 61
§3.1 Ex parte communication prohibited 61
§3.2 Ex parte communication allowed 61
§3.3 Challenging ex parte communication 61
§4. ATTORNEY IN CHARGE 61
§5. WITHDRAWAL 62
§5.1 Withdrawal by attorney 62
§5.2 Termination by client 62
§6. DISQUALIFICATION 62
§6.1 Standards for professional conduct 62
§6.2 Grounds 63
§6.3 Ruling 67
§6.4 Challenging disqualification order 67
§7. AGREEMENTS BETWEEN ATTORNEYS OR PARTIES 67
§8. ATTORNEY FEES 67
§8.1 American rule 67
§8.2 Exceptions to American rule 68
§8.3 Pleading for attorney fees 68
§9. APPELLATE REVIEW 68
§9.1 Pro hac vice 68
§9.2 Withdrawal 68
§9.3 Disqualification 68
§9.4 Attorney fees 69

1. INTRODUCTION

A. INTRODUCTION TO FEDERAL RULES

§1. FEDERAL RULES

§1.1 Types of federal rules.

1. Federal Rules of Civil Procedure (FRCPs). The Supreme Court adopted the first version of the FRCPs in 1938. The FRCPs govern all civil proceedings in the federal district courts, except as stated in FRCP 81. For the full text of the FRCPs, see p. 831.

(1) Forms. One of the purposes behind the adoption of the FRCPs was to bring about "simplicity and brevity" in pleading and motion practice. ***Keller-Dorian Colorfilm Corp. v. Eastman Kodak Co.***, 10 F.R.D. 39, 40-41 (S.D.N.Y.1950). To help accomplish this purpose, the Supreme Court adopted the Appendix of Forms in 1938. *See id.* The forms are grouped by subject areas: "special" forms as Forms 1-9; "complaint" forms as Forms 10-21; "answer" forms as Forms 30-31; "motions" forms as Forms 40-42; "discovery" forms as Forms 50-52; "condemnation" forms as Forms 60-61; "judgment" forms as Forms 70-71; and "assignment to magistrate judges" forms as Forms 80-82. *Report of the Judicial Conference: Committee on Rules of Practice & Procedure*, Agenda E-19, at Rules-Page 29 (Sept.2006), www.uscourts.gov/uscourts/RulesAndPolicies/rules/Reports/ST09-2006.pdf. These forms are cited throughout the book as "FRCP Form." For the full text of the FRCP Forms, see "Appendix of Forms," p. 991. Also, at the beginning of each section of this book, we refer to forms we publish in a companion volume titled ***O'Connor's Federal Civil Forms***.

(2) Supplemental Rules. Before 1966, civil and admiralty actions were governed by separate sets of rules of procedure. *See* 29 *Moore's Federal Practice 3d* §701.05[1] (2012). In 1966, the rules were unified, and the Supplemental Rules for Admiralty or Maritime Claims and Asset Forfeiture Actions were adopted to preserve some of the unique features of the earlier admiralty and maritime practice. *See id.* For the text of the Supplemental Rules, see p. 1001.

2. Federal Rules of Evidence (FREs). The Supreme Court adopted the first version of the FREs in 1975. P.L. 93-595, 88 Stat. 1926 (1975). The FREs govern proceedings in U.S. courts. FRE 101(a). The courts and types of proceedings that the FREs apply to are listed in FRE 1101. In diversity cases, federal courts must follow state law—not the FREs—on most issues of presumptions, privileges, and competency of witnesses. *See* FRE 501, 601; 21 Wright & Graham, *Federal Practice & Procedure 2d* §5006 (2005 & Supp.2012). For the full text of the FREs, see p. 1023.

CAUTION

On December 1, 2011, the comprehensive restyling of the FREs became effective. Use caution when citing the restyled FREs because the comprehensive restyling resulted in many changes to the wording of the rules and the arrangement of the subdivisions. The restyling was intended to clarify, simplify, and modernize the FREs without changing their substantive meaning. Summary of the Report of the Judicial Conference: Committee on Rules of Practice & Procedure, Agenda E-19, at Rules-Page 28-29 (Sept.2010), www.uscourts.gov/uscourts/RulesAndPolicies /rules/Supreme%20Court%202011/ST_Report_JC.pdf.

3. Federal Rules of Appellate Procedure (FRAPs). The Supreme Court adopted the first version of the FRAPs in 1968. Supreme Court Order, 389 U.S. 1065 (12-4-67). The reason for adopting the rules was to formulate a uniform set of rules for all the courts of appeals, which had been operating under their own rules. 16A Wright, Miller, Cooper & Struve, *Federal Practice & Procedure 4th* §3945 (2008 & Supp.2012). The scope of the FRAPs encompasses four general categories of proceedings: (1) appeals from district courts and the U.S. Tax Court, (2) appeals from bankruptcy appellate panels, (3) review or enforcement of the orders of administrative agencies, boards,

commissions, and officers, and (4) applications for writs or other relief to a court of appeals. *See* FRAP 1(a)(1). For the text of the FRAPs, see p. 1089, and for the text of the FRAP Forms, see "Appendix of Forms," p. 1125.

4. Advisory Committee Notes. The Judicial Conference Advisory Committee prepares "committee notes" that explain the purpose and intent of rule changes. 28 U.S.C. §2073(d). A plurality of the Supreme Court has stated that the Advisory Committee's notes are a "useful guide in ascertaining the meaning of the Rules." ***Tome v. U.S.***, 513 U.S. 150, 160 (1995); ***U.S. v. Orlandez-Gamboa***, 320 F.3d 328, 331 n.2 (2d Cir.2003); *see also* ***Tome***, 513 U.S. at 167 (Scalia, J., concurring) (notes are persuasive but not authoritative); ***Burnley v. City of San Antonio***, 470 F.3d 189, 193 (5th Cir.2006) (notes are not determinative but are of weight in court's construction of rule); ***Moody Nat'l Bank v. GE Life & Annuity Assur. Co.***, 383 F.3d 249, 253 (5th Cir.2004) (notes do not have force of law but are instructive in determining Congress's intent in amending rule). Because these notes are so voluminous, we generally reprint only the ones that are based on recent rule changes or that are cited in this book. For select Advisory Committee Notes, see p. 1133.

§1.2 Procedure for amending rules. Generally, Congress has delegated its rulemaking authority to the Supreme Court. *See* 28 U.S.C. §§2071-2077; FRE 1102; ***Stern v. U.S. Dist. Ct. for the Dist. of Mass.***, 214 F.3d 4, 13 (1st Cir.2000); *see also* ***Morel v. DaimlerChrysler AG***, 565 F.3d 20, 25 (1st Cir.2009) (purpose of Rules Enabling Act, 28 U.S.C. §§2071-2077, is to create system of procedure in federal courts that is uniform, comprehensive, and rational). However, Congress has expressly reserved its authority to amend a rule that creates, abolishes, or modifies an evidentiary privilege, and those amendments must be passed by an affirmative act of Congress. *See* 28 U.S.C. §2074(b).

NOTE

For a summary of the procedure to amend the federal rules, see Hogan, A Summary for the Bench & Bar (2011) Administrative Office of the U.S. Courts, www.uscourts.gov/RulesAndPolicies/FederalRulemaking/RulemakingProcess/SummaryBenchBar.aspx.

1. Judicial Conference. The procedure to amend the federal rules begins with the Judicial Conference, which has the responsibility to study the operation and effect of the rules of practice and procedure. *See* 28 U.S.C. §§331, 2073. The Judicial Conference coordinates its responsibilities through the Committee on Rules of Practice and Procedure, also known as the Standing Committee, which is assisted by five advisory committees to handle the appellate, bankruptcy, civil, criminal, and evidence rules. Hogan, *A Summary for the Bench & Bar*, at www.uscourts.gov/RulesAndPolicies/FederalRulemaking/RulemakingProcess/SummaryBenchBar.aspx. The advisory committees draft amendments and submit them to the Standing Committee for approval to publish them for public comment. *Id.* After the public-comment period, the advisory committees review the amendments, make changes if necessary, and submit them to the Standing Committee; the Standing Committee accepts, rejects, or modifies the amendments and, if accepted, submits them to the Judicial Conference; and the Judicial Conference considers the amendments and, if approved, transmits them to the Supreme Court. *Id.*

2. Supreme Court & Congress. If the Supreme Court approves the proposed amendments, it submits them to Congress by May 1 of the year in which they are to take effect. 28 U.S.C. §2074(a). Congress then has seven months to act on the proposed amendments; if Congress does nothing, the proposed amendments automatically take effect on December 1 of the same year. *See id.*; ***Henderson v. U.S.***, 517 U.S. 654, 668 (1996).

3. Application of amendments in pending cases. For cases that are pending when the amendments take effect, courts may apply the amendments if it is just and practicable and would not result in manifest injustice. ***Farmers Ins. Exch. v. RNK, Inc.***, 632 F.3d 777, 782 n.4 (1st Cir.2011); *see* 28 U.S.C. §2074(a); *see, e.g.*, ***Toth v. Grand Trunk R.R.***, 306 F.3d 335, 343 n.2 (6th Cir.2002) (court did not apply amendments to pending motions for sanctions because nearly all discovery had been completed and trial had started when amendments became effective).

§1.3 Construction of rules. The federal rules of procedure and evidence cannot be construed to abridge, enlarge, or modify any substantive right. 28 U.S.C. §2072(b); ***Shady Grove Orthopedic Assocs. v. Allstate Ins.***, ___ U.S. ___, 130 S.Ct. 1431, 1442 (2010) (plurality op.); ***Amchem Prods. v. Windsor***, 521 U.S. 591, 612-13 (1997);

James River Ins. v. Rapid Funding, LLC, 658 F.3d 1207, 1217 (10th Cir.2011); *see* FRCP 82. This limitation means that a rule must actually regulate procedure—if it governs only the manner and means by which a litigant's rights are enforced, it is valid, but if it alters the rules of decision by which the court adjudicates those rights, it is not valid. ***Shady Grove Orthopedic***, ___ U.S. at ___, 130 S.Ct. at 1442 (plurality op.). When a rule conflicts with an earlier-enacted statute, the rule prevails. *See* 28 U.S.C. §2072(b); ***Henderson v. U.S.***, 517 U.S. 654, 668 (1996); ***Local Un. No. 38, Sheet Metal Workers' Int'l v. Custom Air Sys.***, 333 F.3d 345, 348 (2d Cir.2003); *see, e.g.*, ***Owens v. Keeling***, 461 F.3d 763, 774-75 (6th Cir.2006) (parties can appeal in forma pauperis under FRAP 24(a)(5), despite conflicting earlier provision in 28 U.S.C. §1915(a)(3) that appeal cannot be taken in forma pauperis if district court certifies that appeal is not in good faith). However, when a rule conflicts with a later-enacted statute, the statute prevails. ***Custom Air***, 333 F.3d at 348.

§2. LOCAL RULES

§2.1 Authority. There are several sources of authority that allow the district courts to adopt local rules. *See* ***Stern v. U.S. Dist. Ct. for the Dist. of Mass.***, 214 F.3d 4, 13 (1st Cir.2000). The Supreme Court has authorized district courts to craft local rules to implement, or fill gaps in, national rules of practice and procedure. FRCP 83(a)(1); ***Stern***, 214 F.3d at 13. Congress has vested the lower federal courts with independent authority to prescribe local rules. *See* 28 U.S.C. §2071(a). District courts have inherent rulemaking power arising from the nature of the judicial process. *See* ***Chambers v. NASCO, Inc.***, 501 U.S. 32, 43 (1991). Several of the FRCPs permit district courts to adopt local rules. *See, e.g.*, FRCP 40 (scheduling cases for trial), FRCP 77(c) (clerk's office hours on Saturdays and legal holidays), FRCP 78 (scheduling hearing and submission dates). Some statutes also permit matters to be determined by local rule. *See* 12 Wright, Miller & Marcus, *Federal Practice & Procedure 2d* §3154 (1997 & Supp.2012); *see, e.g.*, 28 U.S.C. §1863 (plan for random jury selection), §1914(c) (advance payment of fees).

§2.2 Adoption & amendment.

1. Consistency with laws & rules. Local rules must be consistent with, but must not duplicate, federal statutes and rules adopted under 28 U.S.C. §§2072 and 2075, and they must conform to any uniform numbering system prescribed by the Judicial Conference. FRCP 83(a)(1); *see* ***Amaker v. Foley***, 274 F.3d 677, 681 (2d Cir.2001); ***Stern v. U.S. Dist. Ct. for the Dist. of Mass.***, 214 F.3d 4, 13 (1st Cir.2000); *see also* ***In re Dorner***, 343 F.3d 910, 913 (7th Cir.2003) (local rule that countermands national rule is not consistent with it); 2009 Notes to FRCP 6 at ¶1, p. 1149, this book (local rules must require that deadlines be computed consistently with FRCP 6(a)). A local rule that is inconsistent with the U.S. Constitution, a statute, or a rule of procedure is considered invalid. *See* FRCP 83(a)(1); ***Colgrove v. Battin***, 413 U.S. 149, 161 n.18 (1973); *see, e.g.*, ***Kinsley v. Lakeview Reg'l Med. Ctr. LLC***, 570 F.3d 586, 589-90 (5th Cir.2009) (when local rule allowed electronic filer to refile deficient notice of appeal beyond FRAP 4's jurisdictional deadline, local rule was invalid); *see also* ***Frazier v. Heebe***, 482 U.S. 641, 646-47 & n.7 (1987) (local rule must be both constitutional and rational, and its subject matter must be within court's regulatory power).

2. Procedure. District courts must follow certain procedures to adopt or amend local rules. ***Hollingsworth v. Perry***, 558 U.S. 183, ___, 130 S.Ct. 705, 710 (2010). Generally, local rules can be adopted or amended only after the district court gives appropriate public notice and opportunity for comment. 28 U.S.C. §2071(b); *e.g.*, ***Hollingsworth***, 558 U.S. at ___, 130 S.Ct. at 710-11 (amendment of local rule to allow broadcast of trial was invalid because court did not provide appropriate public notice when comment period was only five business days). In limited circumstances, district courts can skip the notice-and-comment period when there is an immediate need for the rule or amendment. 28 U.S.C. §2071(e); ***Hollingsworth***, 558 U.S. at ___, 130 S.Ct. at 710.

3. Effective date. A local rule takes effect on the date specified by the district court and remains in effect until amended by the district court or abrogated by the judicial council of the circuit in which the district court is located. FRCP 83(a)(1).

§2.3 Force of law. A valid local rule has the force of law. ***Hollingsworth v. Perry***, 558 U.S. 183, ___, 130 S.Ct. 705, 710 (2010); ***Weil v. Neary***, 278 U.S. 160, 169 (1929); ***Nahno-Lopez v. Houser***, 625 F.3d 1279, 1284 (10th Cir. 2010). Once local rules have been properly issued, attorneys and parties must comply with them. ***In re Jarvis***, 53

F.3d 416, 422 (1st Cir.1995). A party cannot lose rights because of an unintentional failure to comply with local rules that relate only to form. FRCP 83(a)(2); *see* 1995 Notes to FRCP 83 at ¶3, p. 1234, this book (failure to comply with rule of form should not deprive party of right to jury trial); *see also* ***Solis v. County of L.A.***, 514 F.3d 946, 955 (9th Cir.2008) (pro se P did not waive jury trial when he failed to fulfill additional procedural requirements in judge's standing order for jury trial). A district court cannot suspend the rules of procedure or evidence by its own local rules. *See* ***Carver v. Bunch***, 946 F.2d 451, 453 (6th Cir.1991). A district court cannot enforce its local rules in a way that conflicts with the FRCPs. ***NEPSK, Inc. v. Town of Houlton***, 283 F.3d 1, 7 (1st Cir.2002).

§2.4 Notice. Litigants are presumed to have notice of the local rules. ***Jetton v. McDonnell Douglas Corp.***, 121 F.3d 423, 426 (8th Cir.1997); ***Doran v. U.S.***, 475 F.2d 742, 743 (1st Cir.1973); ***Woodham v. American Cystoscope Co.***, 335 F.2d 551, 556-57 (5th Cir.1964). However, a court cannot impose sanctions for noncompliance with any requirement that was not in the federal law, the FRCPs, or the local district rules, unless the violator was furnished with actual notice of the requirement. FRCP 83(b); ***Amnesty Am. v. Town of W. Hartford***, 288 F.3d 467, 471 (2d Cir.2002). The method of publishing and distributing local rules varies from district to district. Copies of local rules can be obtained from the district clerk's office or website. *See* 1995 Notes to FRCP 83 at ¶5, p. 1234, this book.

NOTE

For links to the district courts' websites that contain local rules, see www.uscourts.gov/RulesAndPolicies/FederalRulemaking/LocalCourtRules/USDistrictCourts.aspx.

§2.5 Construction of local rules. The decision on how strictly to apply local rules is within the district court's discretion. ***NEPSK, Inc. v. Town of Houlton***, 283 F.3d 1, 7 (1st Cir.2002); ***Tobel v. City of Hammond***, 94 F.3d 360, 362 (7th Cir.1996); ***Barone v. Rich Bros. Interstate Display Fireworks Co.***, 25 F.3d 610, 611 n.2 (8th Cir.1994); *see* ***Petrolite Corp. v. Baker Hughes Inc.***, 96 F.3d 1423, 1426 (Fed.Cir.1996); *see, e.g.*, ***Phoenix Global Ventures, LLC v. Phoenix Hotel Assocs.***, 422 F.3d 72, 74 (2d Cir.2005) (district court can overlook violations of its own electronic-filing rules).

§3. STANDING ORDERS

In addition to local rules, other types of procedural rules may be implemented by court order. *See, e.g.*, ***U.S. v. Morales***, 108 F.3d 1213, 1225 n.9 (10th Cir.1997) (standing order provided that any motion filed by one D was adopted by other Ds). These court orders are referred to as standing orders, administrative orders, or general orders, and they can be applicable for an entire district or division or for an individual court. *Report & Recommended Guidelines on Standing Orders in District & Bankruptcy Courts*, at 1, www.uscourts.gov/uscourts/RulesAndPolicies/rules/Standing_Orders_Dec_2009.pdf (referred to as *Report on Standing Orders*). Standing orders should be consistent with, but must not duplicate, federal statutes, federal rules, and local rules. *See* FRCP 83(b); *Guidelines for Distinguishing Between Matters Appropriate for Standing Orders & Matters Appropriate for Local Rules & for Posting Standing Orders on a Court's Web Site*, at 4, www.uscourts.gov/uscourts/RulesAndPolicies/rules/Standing_Orders_Dec_2009.pdf (referred to as *Guidelines for Matters Appropriate for Standing Orders*). Standing orders also should not abrogate or modify a local rule. *See* FRCP 83(b); *Guidelines for Matters Appropriate for Standing Orders*, at 4-5.

CAUTION

Because standing orders are promulgated without public comment, are harder to locate than local rules, and vary significantly between and within districts, divisions, and courts, be sure to check standing orders for recent changes or any conflicts with local rules. See Report on Standing Orders, at 1.

§3.1 When standing orders are appropriate.

1. Internal administration. Standing orders are most useful and appropriate to address matters of internal administration, such as court security, planning for emergencies, directives to court personnel, referral to magistrate judges, juror wheels, PACER fees, and court staffing on or after holidays. *Guidelines for Matters Appropriate for Standing Orders*, at 1.

2. Temporary issues. Standing orders are useful to address temporary issues that will be resolved by the time a local rule could be implemented (e.g., temporarily suspending sentencing proceedings until a recent Supreme Court ruling could be analyzed). *Guidelines for Matters Appropriate for Standing Orders*, at 1-2.

3. Emergencies. Standing orders are useful to address emergency issues (e.g., unanticipated issues arising from cases involving terrorism charges). *Guidelines for Matters Appropriate for Standing Orders*, at 2.

4. Courtroom behavior. Standing orders are useful to provide rules for courtroom conduct (but not substantive rules of practice), such as eating or drinking in the courtroom, courtroom hours, and delivery of courtesy copies to chambers. *Guidelines for Matters Appropriate for Standing Orders*, at 2.

§3.2 When standing orders are not appropriate.

1. Rules on filing, pretrial practice, motion practice & other compliance issues. Standing orders are not appropriate for matters such as filing pleadings and motions, litigating motions, sealing documents, and time limits on opening statements. *See Guidelines for Matters Appropriate for Standing Orders*, at 3.

2. Rules on mediation, other forms of ADR & attorney discipline. Standing orders are not appropriate for complete sets of rules for proceedings such as alternative dispute resolution and attorney discipline. *See Guidelines for Matters Appropriate for Standing Orders*, at 4.

B. PLEADING & MOTION PRACTICE

§1. GENERAL

§1.1 Rules. FRCP 5-15, 16(b)(3), (c)(2)(B), (c)(2)(K). See FRCP 41(b)-(d).

§1.2 Purpose. Pleadings communicate the nature of the lawsuit, define and shape the issues, furnish a basis for the evidence, and provide a foundation for res judicata. Motions are applications to the court for an order on a specific issue.

§1.3 Timetable & forms. Timetable, Pleadings & Pretrial-Motions Schedule, p. 1574; ***O'Connor's Federal Civil Forms*** (2012), FORMS 1B.

§1.4 Other references. 5, 5A Wright & Miller, *Federal Practice & Procedure 3d* §§1181-1196, 1201-1204, 1215-1226, 1281-1286, 1324, 1331-1339 (2004 & Supp.2012); 6A Wright, Miller & Kane, *Federal Practice & Procedure 3d* §1493 (2010 & Supp.2012); 2, 3 *Moore's Federal Practice 3d* chs. 7, 8, 10, 15 (2012); 1 Childress & Davis, *Federal Standards of Review 4th* §§1.01-1.04 (2010 & Supp.2011); Joseph, *Sanctions: The Federal Law of Litigation Abuse 4th* ch. 2 (2008); Millner, *Notice Pleading Today*, 18 Litig. 33 (Spring 1992).

§2. PLEADING PRACTICE

Pleadings are different from motions and other papers. A pleading states either an affirmative claim for relief or a response to a claim for relief. The types of pleadings that are permitted in the federal system are the following: a complaint, an answer, a counterclaim, an answer to a counterclaim, a cross-claim, an answer to a cross-claim, a third-party complaint, an answer to a third-party complaint, and, if the court orders one, a reply to an answer. FRCP 7(a). Nothing else qualifies as a pleading under the federal rules. *See* ***Maldonado v. Dominguez***, 137 F.3d 1, 11 n.8 (1st Cir.1998) (motion to dismiss is not pleading under FRCP 7).

§2.1 Drafting pleadings.

1. Form. When drafting pleadings, the party should comply with federal and local rules. General rules on the form of pleadings can be found in FRCP 8 and 10. Local rules also have specific requirements for pleadings, such as designation of jury trial or assigned judge in the caption, paper size, paper quality, placement of the staple, number of punched holes, spacing, pagination, and binding materials. However, a party cannot lose rights because of an unintentional failure to comply with local rules that relate only to form. FRCP 83(a)(2); *see* 1995 Notes to FRCP 83 at

¶3, p. 1234, this book (failure to comply with rule of form should not deprive party of right to jury trial); *see, e.g.*, ***Cintron v. Union Pac. R.R.***, 813 F.2d 917, 920 (9th Cir.1987) (pleading presented for filing without punched holes and cover sheet should not have been dismissed as untimely).

2. Civil cover sheet. Most local rules require that a complaint be accompanied by a civil cover sheet. The cover sheet is an administrative document designed to facilitate the court's management of the case. ***Wall v. National R.R. Passenger Corp.***, 718 F.2d 906, 909 (9th Cir.1983). The cover sheet does not need to accompany any pleading other than the complaint. A copy of the cover sheet can be obtained from the court clerk's office or, in some cases, the court's website. See ***O'Connor's Federal Forms***, FORM 2B:1.

3. Caption. Every pleading must contain a caption. FRCP 10(a). The caption must include the court's name, a title with all the parties' names, a file number, and an FRCP 7(a) designation. FRCP 10(a); *see* FRCP 7(a).

(1) Parties. The caption of every pleading must contain a title with the names of the parties. FRCP 10(a); *see* ***Doe v. Megless***, 654 F.3d 404, 408 (3d Cir.2011). The original complaint must list all parties by their full names. *See* FRCP 10(a). If the suit involves multiple parties on either side, the list may be shortened in later pleadings by using the name of the first party and "et al." *See id.*; ***Bernstein Seawell & Kove v. Bosarge***, 813 F.2d 726, 730 (5th Cir.1987).

(2) File number. The caption of every pleading must contain the correct file number. FRCP 10(a). The clerk assigns a file number to a lawsuit when it is first filed. An incorrect file number may result in the document becoming lost or misplaced in the clerk's office.

(3) Designation. The caption of every pleading must contain an FRCP 7(a) designation. FRCP 10(a). The designation is the label for the pleading (e.g., "Defendant's Original Answer"). *See* FRCP 7(a), 10(a).

(a) Correct designation. The parties should designate pleadings in a manner useful for the court, clerk, and attorneys' files. The designation should be concise and direct. ***Venezolana Internacional de Aviacion, S.A. v. International Ass'n of Machinists & Aerospace Workers***, 118 F.R.D. 151, 151 (S.D.Fla.1987). The designation should always include the name of the party filing the pleading and the type of pleading (e.g., "Plaintiff's Original Complaint"). If there are multiple parties, the designation should also include an abbreviated name for the party (e.g., "Defendant Acme's Original Answer"). If a pleading has been filed before, the designation should indicate the version of the pleading (e.g., "Plaintiff's Second Amended Complaint").

(b) Incorrect designation. If a party makes an error in the designation of a pleading, the court will usually treat the pleading as if it had been properly designated. *See* FRCP 8(c)(2) (if affirmative defense is mistakenly designated as counterclaim, court must treat it as if properly designated when justice so requires); *see, e.g.*, ***McDowell v. Delaware State Police***, 88 F.3d 188, 189-91 (3d Cir.1996) (improperly designated complaint was sufficient; it was served on D and alleged sufficient facts to put D on notice). *But see* ***In re Marino***, 37 F.3d 1354, 1357 (9th Cir.1994) (because document was not properly designated as pleading and had incorrect file number, it did not satisfy complaint requirement; thus, amended complaint was untimely when it had nothing to relate back to). The court may order the pleading to be resubmitted with the correct designation.

4. Numbered paragraphs. Pleadings must be divided into separate, numbered paragraphs. FRCP 10(b); ***Schaedler v. Reading Eagle Publ'n, Inc.***, 39 F.R.D. 22, 23 (E.D.Pa.1965). The court may excuse the numbering requirement when there are only a few paragraphs and the essence of the complaint is clear. *See* ***Leon v. Hotel & Club Empls. Un.***, 26 F.R.D. 158, 159 (S.D.N.Y.1960); ***Woods v. Parsons***, 7 F.R.D. 528, 532 (D.Neb.1947). Each paragraph should be limited as far as is practicable to a single set of circumstances. FRCP 10(b); ***Schaedler***, 39 F.R.D. at 23. There is no magic formula to determine when separate paragraphs are necessary, but they are useful when the pleader has multiple claims for relief or a single claim based on more than one ground or legal theory. ***O'Donnell v. Elgin, J&E Ry.***, 338 U.S. 384, 392 (1949); ***Schexnaydre v. Travelers Ins.***, 527 F.2d 855, 856 n.1 (5th Cir.1976).

5. Statement of jurisdiction. The complaint must contain a short and plain statement of jurisdiction. FRCP 8(a)(1); ***Gardner v. First Am. Title Ins.***, 294 F.3d 991, 993 (8th Cir.2002); *see* FRCP Form 7, p. 992, this book. Other pleadings, filed after the complaint, do not require a statement of jurisdiction unless a new jurisdictional ground is necessary to support the claim. FRCP 8(a)(1).

PRACTICE TIP

FRCP 8(a) does not require that the basis for venue be alleged in the complaint. See ***Myers v. American Dental Ass'n****, 695 F.2d 716, 724 (3d Cir.1982). However, alleging the basis for venue may help eliminate unnecessary motion practice and frame discovery on the venue issue if it is contested.*

6. Factual allegations. Allegations in the pleadings must be short, plain, and direct. ***Ashcroft v. Iqbal***, 556 U.S. 662, 677-78 (2009); ***Bell Atlantic Corp. v. Twombly***, 550 U.S. 544, 555 (2007); *see* FRCP 8(d)(1); *see, e.g.*, ***Kuehl v. FDIC***, 8 F.3d 905, 908 (1st Cir.1993) (court dismissed amended complaint that did not conform to FRCP 8); *see also* FRCP 84 (FRCP forms contemplate simple and brief statements). The parties should state matters in simple, direct sentences and should avoid legalese and detailed statements of the evidence.

NOTE

The FRCP forms illustrate the "simplicity and brevity" that the rules contemplate. FRCP 84. See "Appendix of Forms," p. 991, this book. However, the complaint forms call for allegations that are far briefer than those commonly used in practice. Excerpt from the Report of the Judicial Conference: Committee on Rules of Practice & Procedure, at 12, www.uscourts.gov/uscourts/RulesAndPolicies/rules/supct1106/Excerpt_JC_Report_CV_0906.pdf.

(1) Substance of allegations.

(a) General rule – fair notice & plausibility. A complaint must (1) give the defendant fair notice of the plaintiff's claim and (2) contain sufficient factual matter that—when accepted as true—states a claim of relief that is plausible on its face. *See* FRCP 8(a); ***Iqbal***, 556 U.S. at 678; ***Twombly***, 550 U.S. at 555; ***Breaux v. American Family Mut. Ins.***, 554 F.3d 854, 862 (10th Cir.2009). For a claim to be plausible, the plaintiff must plead factual content that allows a reasonable inference that the defendant is liable for the alleged misconduct. ***Iqbal***, 556 U.S. at 678; ***Twombly***, 550 U.S. at 556; *see* 5 Wright & Miller §1216. The plaintiff is not required to plead detailed factual allegations, but the allegations must be enough to raise a right of relief above mere speculation. ***Twombly***, 550 U.S. at 555; *see* ***Iqbal***, 556 U.S. at 678 (allegations must be more than "the defendant unlawfully harmed me"). See "Standard pleadings," ch. 2-B, §5.1, p. 80.

(b) Exception – specificity. By rules, statutes, and case law, certain allegations must be pleaded with specificity. *See* FRCP 9(b). For a list of items that must be pleaded specifically, see "Particularized pleadings," ch. 2-B, §5.2, p. 82.

(2) Alternative allegations. Parties may plead alternative or inconsistent facts to support alternative theories of recovery. FRCP 8(d)(2); ***PAE Gov't Servs. v. MPRI, Inc.***, 514 F.3d 856, 860 (9th Cir.2007); ***Independent Enters. v. Pittsburgh Water & Sewer Auth.***, 103 F.3d 1165, 1175 (3d Cir.1997). If a pleading states inconsistent facts without alleging alternative theories, one or more counts may be rendered fatally defective and subject to dismissal. ***Friendship Med. Ctr., Ltd. v. Space Rentals***, 62 F.R.D. 106, 112 (N.D.Ill.1974). *But see* ***Harbor Mech., Inc. v. Arizona Elec. Power Coop.***, 496 F.Supp. 681, 685 (D.Ariz.1980) (rejecting ***Friendship*** and holding "inconsistency" to be merely pleading in alternative).

(3) Allegations based on information & belief. FRCP 11(b) permits pleading based on information and belief. A complaint in this form is appropriate when the matters are peculiarly within the knowledge of the defendant. ***Arista Records LLC v. Doe 3***, 604 F.3d 110, 120 (2d Cir.2010); *see* ***Kowal v. MCI Comms.***, 16 F.3d 1271, 1279 n.3 (D.C.Cir.1994) (securities-fraud allegations); ***Tuchman v. DSC Comms.***, 14 F.3d 1061, 1068 (5th Cir.1994) (fraudulent intent). See "Information & belief," ch. 2-B, §5.1.2(3), p. 82.

(4) Allegations adopted by reference. A statement made in one part of a pleading may be adopted by reference in a different part of the same pleading, in another pleading, or in a motion. FRCP 10(c). A pleading incorporating allegations from another document must specifically identify the statements to be incorporated. ***Fanning v. Potter***, 614 F.3d 845, 851 (8th Cir.2010); ***Lowden v. William M. Mercer, Inc.***, 903 F.Supp. 212, 216 (D.Mass.

1995); *see also* ***Swanson v. U.S. Forest Serv.***, 87 F.3d 339, 345 (9th Cir.1996) (reach of FRCP 10(c) provision, permitting adoption by reference of material from pleadings, cannot be extended by FRCP 7(b)(2) to include adoption of substantive material in "other papers").

7. Counts or defenses.

(1) Separate counts or defenses. Each claim founded on a single transaction or occurrence and each defense other than a denial must be stated in a separate count or defense whenever separation helps clarify the issue. FRCP 10(b); ***Fikes v. City of Daphne***, 79 F.3d 1079, 1082 (11th Cir.1996). Before a count is considered "separate," it must meet three tests: (1) more than one claim must be asserted, (2) the claims must arise out of separate transactions or occurrences, and (3) separate counts must help clarify the presentation of the issues. ***Insurance Consultants v. Southeastern Ins. Grp.***, 746 F.Supp. 390, 417-18 (D.N.J.1990); 5A Wright & Miller §1324; *see, e.g.*, ***Magluta v. Samples***, 256 F.3d 1282, 1284 (11th Cir.2001) (P required to replead after it filed 58-page complaint that named 14 Ds, charged all Ds in each count without making distinctions among them, and incorporated into each count allegations from another section consisting of 146 paragraphs).

(2) Alternative counts or defenses. Parties may plead alternative or inconsistent claims or defenses. FRCP 8(d)(2), (d)(3); ***Independent Enters.***, 103 F.3d at 1175; ***Henry v. Daytop Vill., Inc.***, 42 F.3d 89, 95 (2d Cir.1994); ***In re Air Disaster***, 37 F.3d 804, 821 (2d Cir.1994).

8. Prayer for relief. At the end of the pleading, the party should identify exactly what damages, order, or other relief it wants. *See* FRCP 7(b)(1)(C), 8(a)(3). A party may ask for several different types of relief or for relief in the alternative. FRCP 8(a)(3); *see also* ***American Int'l Adjustment Co. v. Galvin***, 86 F.3d 1455, 1460 (7th Cir. 1996) (FRCP 8(e)(2), now FRCP 8(d)(2) and (d)(3), abolished doctrine of election of remedies in federal court).

9. Signature. Every pleading must be signed by at least one attorney of record in the attorney's individual name. FRCP 11(a); ***Pavelic & LeFlore v. Marvel Entm't Grp.***, 493 U.S. 120, 123-24 (1989). If a party is unrepresented, the pleading must be personally signed by the party. FRCP 11(a). The pleading must include the signer's address, e-mail address, and telephone number. *Id.* The omission of a signature may be corrected if done promptly after being called to the attorney's or party's attention. ***Becker v. Montgomery***, 532 U.S. 757, 764 (2001); *see* ***Michel v. U.S.***, 519 F.3d 1267, 1271-72 (11th Cir.2008).

PRACTICE TIP

For pleadings that are filed electronically, be sure to check local rules, standing orders, and other local procedures that may provide specific signature requirements. See "Signature," ch. 1-C, §4.4.2(2), p. 21.

---

(1) Certification. The signature of an attorney or party on a pleading certifies that, to the best of the signer's knowledge, information, and belief, formed after a reasonable inquiry, all of the following are true:

(a) The pleading has not been presented for an improper purpose (e.g., to harass or to cause unnecessary delay or expense). FRCP 11(b)(1); ***Sheets v. Yamaha Motors Corp.***, 891 F.2d 533, 538 (5th Cir.1990).

(b) The claims or defenses are supported by existing law or by a good-faith argument for extension of or change in existing law. FRCP 11(b)(2); ***Zuk v. Eastern Pa. Psychiatric Inst.***, 103 F.3d 294, 299 (3d Cir. 1996).

(c) The allegations and other factual contentions have, or are likely to have after a reasonable opportunity for investigation, evidentiary support. FRCP 11(b)(3); ***O'Brien v. Alexander***, 101 F.3d 1479, 1489 (2d Cir.1996).

(d) The denials or other factual contentions are warranted by the evidence or are based on belief or a lack of information. FRCP 11(b)(4); 5A Wright & Miller §1335.

(2) Attorney in charge. Local rules may require designation of an "attorney in charge." Usually, a party designates its attorney in charge on the party's first appearance through counsel, either by personal appearance at a hearing or by signature on the first pleading. *See* Local Rules Tex. (S.D.), Rule 11.1 (by signature). Most local rules require that every document be signed by, or with the permission of, the attorney in charge. *E.g.*, Local Rules Tex. (S.D.), Rule 11.3. Some local rules require additional information about the attorney in charge under the signature line. *E.g.*, *id.*

(3) Law firm. If the attorney who signs the pleadings is a member or associate of a firm, some local rules require the firm's name to appear under the attorney's signature. *See, e.g.*, ***U.S. v. American Sur. Co.***, 25 F.Supp. 225, 226 (E.D.N.Y.1938) (motion complied with FRCP 7 and 11 even though name of law firm appeared first). Other local rules allow the firm to be listed with the designation "of counsel." *See, e.g.*, Local Rules Tex. (S.D.), Rule 11.3.B.

10. Attachments.

(1) Exhibits. Only written instruments are permitted as pleading exhibits. *See* FRCP 10(c); 2 *Moore's Federal Practice 3d* §10.05[2]. A "written instrument" is a document evidencing legal rights or duties or giving formal expression to a legal act or agreement, such as a deed, will, bond, lease, or insurance policy. ***DeMarco v. DepoTech Corp.***, 149 F.Supp.2d 1212, 1220 (S.D.Cal.2001); ***Murphy v. Cadillac Rubber & Plastics, Inc.***, 946 F.Supp. 1108, 1115 (W.D.N.Y.1996). For purposes of FRCP 10(c), written instruments usually consist of documentary evidence, specifically contracts, notes, and other writings, on which a party's action or defense is based. ***Rose v. Bartle***, 871 F.2d 331, 339 n.3 (3d Cir.1989); ***DeMarco***, 149 F.Supp.2d at 1220. Affidavits do not qualify as written instruments under FRCP 10(c). ***Rose***, 871 F.2d at 339 n.3. *But see* ***Northern Ind. Gun & Outdoor Shows, Inc. v. City of S. Bend***, 163 F.3d 449, 453 (7th Cir.1998) ("written instrument" as used in FRCP 10(c) includes affidavits). FRCP 10(c) does not require a plaintiff to adopt as true the contents of the written instrument attached to the complaint. *E.g.*, ***Gant v. Wallingford Bd. of Educ.***, 69 F.3d 669, 674 (2d Cir.1995) (libel P may attach allegedly libelous writing without risk that court will deem true all libels in it).

(a) Incorporating by reference. A copy of a written instrument attached as an exhibit to a pleading is a part of the pleading for all purposes. FRCP 10(c); *see also* ***Chambers v. Time Warner, Inc.***, 282 F.3d 147, 152-53 (2d Cir.2002) (document not incorporated by reference may still be considered when it is "integral" to complaint). If the plaintiff incorporates a document into a pleading by referring to it, the document must be attached to the pleading as an exhibit. ***Shelter Mut. Ins. v. Public Water Sup. Dist.***, 747 F.2d 1195, 1198 (8th Cir.1984). When there is a discrepancy between the language of the exhibit and the allegations in the pleading, the language of the exhibit controls. ***ALA, Inc. v. CCAIR, Inc.***, 29 F.3d 855, 859 n.8 (3d Cir.1994); *see, e.g.*, ***Nishimatsu Constr. Co. v. Houston Nat'l Bank***, 515 F.2d 1200, 1206 (5th Cir.1975) (contract showing that D was agent superseded P's claim in complaint that D was party to contract); ***Banco del Estado v. Navistar Int'l Transp.***, 942 F.Supp. 1176, 1178-79 (N.D.Ill.1996) (original Spanish documents controlled, not erroneous English translation).

(b) Attaching exhibits. FRCP 10(c) does not indicate how pleading exhibits should be attached or numbered. 2 *Moore's Federal Practice 3d* §10.05[3]. However, local rules may require the party to attach exhibits in a specific manner. *E.g.*, Local Rules Alaska, Rule 10.1(c)(3)[B] (exhibits must be "permanently attached to the pleading or document to which they apply in a manner to be easily accessible and readable without detaching from the principal document"); Local Rules Tex. (E.D.), Rule CV-5(a)(6) (exhibits must be submitted separately in electronic form, unless conventional filing allowed).

(2) Verification & affidavits. A pleading does not need to be verified or accompanied by an affidavit unless a rule or statute provides otherwise. FRCP 11(a); *see, e.g.*, FRCP 23.1 (shareholder derivative action); FRCP 65(b)(1) (application for temporary restraining order).

(a) Verification. Verification requires that a signed and notarized statement be attached to the pleading, in which a witness swears that the statements in the pleading are true and correct. *See* ***Neal v. Kelly***, 963 F.2d 453, 457 (D.C.Cir.1992) (verification is confirmation of truth by affidavit or oath).

(b) Affidavit. An affidavit is a written statement of facts, signed by the person making it and sworn to before someone who is authorized to administer oaths. ***Pfeil v. Rogers***, 757 F.2d 850, 859 (7th Cir.1985);

see ***Peters v. Lincoln Elec. Co.***, 285 F.3d 456, 475 (6th Cir.2002). The absence of a formal requirement of an affidavit, such as the notary's seal, does not invalidate a statement if it was actually sworn. ***Peters***, 285 F.3d at 475; ***Pfeil***, 757 F.2d at 859. Generally, an affidavit must be made by a person who is competent to testify and has personal knowledge of the matters stated in the affidavit. *See* FRE 601, 602. In a summary-judgment proceeding, the affidavit must also state facts that are admissible in evidence. FRCP 56(c)(4). See "Affidavits or declarations," ch. 7-B, §6.1.3, p. 610.

(c) Declaration. A written declaration made under penalty of perjury can be used instead of an affidavit or verification. 28 U.S.C. §1746; ***Peters***, 285 F.3d at 475; ***Pfeil***, 757 F.2d at 859; ***Carter v. Clark***, 616 F.2d 228, 229 (5th Cir.1980); *see* FRCP 56(c)(4) (summary-judgment proceedings). The declaration must be dated and state the following: "I declare (certify, verify, or state) under penalty of perjury that the foregoing is true and correct." 28 U.S.C. §1746(2). A written unsworn declaration cannot be used as a substitute for an affidavit in a deposition, an oath of office, or a document that must be signed before a specified official other than a notary. 28 U.S.C. §1746; ***Carter***, 616 F.2d at 230. Like an affidavit, a declaration generally must be made by a person who is competent to testify and has personal knowledge of the matters stated in the declaration; if the declaration is used in a summary-judgment proceeding, it must also state facts that are admissible in evidence. *See* FRCP 56(c)(4); FRE 601, 602. See "Affidavits or declarations," ch. 7-B, §6.1.3, p. 610.

(3) Certificate of service. All documents that must be served on the other party (except the complaint) must contain a certificate of service and be filed with the clerk within a reasonable time after service. FRCP 5(a), (d). Some local rules specify requirements for certificates of service. *E.g.*, Local Rules Tex. (E.D.), Rule CV-5(c) (must indicate date and method of service). Generally, a certificate of service should identify the document being served and state that it was served on the opposing party in a certain manner on a certain date. The certificate should also identify the name and address of each party or attorney on whom the document was served. See ***O'Connor's Federal Forms***, FORM 1D:1.

11. Notice of constitutional question. If a pleading challenges the constitutionality of a federal or state statute, the party must serve a notice of the constitutional question and a copy of the pleading on the proper attorney general. FRCP 5.1(a)(2). See ***O'Connor's Federal Forms***, FORM 1B:8. If either the United States or a state government, one of their agencies, or one of their officers or employees in an official capacity is not party to the suit, the party must also file the notice. FRCP 5.1(a)(1). Notice is required if any statute is questioned, not only those "affecting the public interest." 2006 Notes to FRCP 5.1 at ¶3, p. 1148, this book. This notice is in addition to the court's obligation to notify the U.S. Attorney General or state attorney general of a constitutional question. 2006 Notes to FRCP 5.1 at ¶1, p. 1147, this book; *see* 28 U.S.C. §2403; FRCP 5.1(b); ***Buchanan Cty. v. Blankenship***, 545 F.Supp.2d 553, 555 n.3 (W.D.Va.2008). However, if a party does not file and serve the notice to the attorney general, the party does not forfeit any timely asserted constitutional claim or defense. FRCP 5.1(d); *see* ***Oklahoma v. Pope***, 516 F.3d 1214, 1216 (10th Cir.2008) (when parties or district court does not file and serve notice, appellate court may remand to district court and order that notice be filed and served, or appellate court may notify attorney general and allow intervention on appeal).

(1) To U.S. Attorney General. The party must serve notice to the U.S. Attorney General when a pleading questions the constitutionality of any federal statute. FRCP 5.1(a)(2). A "statute" is any congressional enactment that qualifies as an "Act of Congress." 2006 Notes to FRCP 5.1 at ¶3, p. 1148, this book.

(2) To state attorney general. The party must serve notice to the state attorney general when a pleading questions the constitutionality of any state statute. FRCP 5.1(a)(2).

§2.2 Amending & supplementing pleadings. The FRCPs permit the parties to change the relevant issues by amending and supplementing the pleadings. FRCP 15(a) permits liberal amendment and supplementation. ***Nebraska v. Wyoming***, 515 U.S. 1, 8 (1995); ***Foman v. Davis***, 371 U.S. 178, 182 (1962); 5 Wright & Miller §1189.

1. Amended pleadings. Amended pleadings add or withdraw matters from previous pleadings to correct or change them. An amended pleading supersedes the previous pleading. ***Duda v. Board of Educ.***, 133 F.3d 1054,

1057 (7th Cir.1998); ***King v. Dogan***, 31 F.3d 344, 346 (5th Cir.1994); *see* ***Lacey v. Maricopa Cty.***, 693 F.3d 896, ___ (9th Cir.2012). See "Amending Pleadings – Pretrial," ch. 5-I, §3, p. 345.

2. Supplemental pleadings. Supplemental pleadings set forth transactions, occurrences, or events that have happened after the date of the pleading being supplemented. FRCP 15(d); ***Owens-Ill., Inc. v. Lake Shore Land Co.***, 610 F.2d 1185, 1188 (3d Cir.1979); *see* ***Planned Parenthood v. Neely***, 130 F.3d 400, 402 (9th Cir.1997) (supplemental pleading cannot be used to introduce separate and distinct claim). A supplemental pleading adds to—but does not replace or supersede—the previous pleading. ***Millay v. Surry Sch. Dept.***, 584 F.Supp.2d 219, 226 (D.Me.2008). Before filing a supplemental pleading, the party must file a motion in the court. *See* FRCP 15(d). The court can grant the motion and allow a supplemental pleading only on just terms and after reasonable notice to the other party. *See id.* See "Supplementing Pleadings – Pretrial," ch. 5-I, §4, p. 350.

3. Incorporating superseded pleadings by reference. Statements in a pleading can be adopted by reference in a different part of the same pleading, in another pleading, or in any motion. FRCP 10(c). An amended pleading supersedes the original pleading and renders it of no legal effect, unless it is specifically referred to and adopted or incorporated by reference. ***King***, 31 F.3d at 346. To incorporate by reference, the amended pleading must specifically identify the incorporated parts of the superseded pleading. ***Lowden v. William M. Mercer, Inc.***, 903 F.Supp. 212, 216 (D.Mass.1995). The incorporation must be specific and clear enough for the responding party to easily determine the nature and extent of the incorporation. ***Wolfe v. Charter Forest Behavioral Health Sys.***, 185 F.R.D. 225, 228-29 (W.D.La.1999).

§2.3 Defective pleadings. In general, a party cannot obtain discovery, offer proof at trial, or obtain jury findings on claims or defenses that were not pleaded. *See, e.g.*, ***Samuels v. Wilder***, 871 F.2d 1346, 1350 (7th Cir.1989) (issues raised for first time in motion for summary judgment were not considered by court).

1. Opposing party objects.

(1) Pretrial. If a party attempts discovery of an unpleaded matter before trial, the opposing party should object that the matter was not included in the pleadings. *See* FRCP 26(b)(1) (scope of discovery is anything relevant to any party's claim or defense); 2000 Notes to FRCP 26 at ¶26, p. 1181, this book (parties are not entitled to discovery of new claims or defenses that are unpleaded). If the opposing party objects, the party who filed the defective pleading should ask for leave to amend to correct the defect. *See* FRCP 15(a)(2); *see, e.g.*, ***Díaz-Rivera v. Rivera-Rodríguez***, 377 F.3d 119, 123 (1st Cir.2004) (although P had ample time to amend pleadings before trial, P did not amend; evidence on unpleaded claim was excluded at trial). In support of the motion for leave to amend, the party should argue that the other side received reasonable notice of the additional facts or issues. *See* Millner, *Notice Pleading Today*, 18 Litig. at 34; *see also* ***Sundstrand Corp. v. Standard Kollsman Indus.***, 488 F.2d 807, 812 (7th Cir.1973) (if facts were not alleged in opponent's complaint but party knew that opponent intended to prove them at trial, court could allow those issues to be raised during trial). See "Motion to Amend or Supplement Pleadings—Pretrial," ch. 5-I, p. 345.

(2) Trial & post-trial. If a party attempts to introduce evidence on an unpleaded matter at trial, the opposing party should object that the matter was not included in the pleadings. *See* FRCP 15(b)(1). When an objection is raised that no pleadings support the evidence, the court may permit the pleadings to be amended if doing so will serve the merits of the case and if the party objecting to the evidence cannot show that it will be prejudiced. *Id.* The court can grant a continuance to allow the objecting party time to respond to the evidence. *Id.*; ***Black v. J.I. Case Co.***, 22 F.3d 568, 573 (5th Cir.1994). See "Motion to Amend Pleadings—Trial & Post-trial," ch. 8-F, p. 710.

2. Opposing party consents. Unpleaded claims or defenses may be tried by express or implied consent. *See* FRCP 15(b)(2). Unpleaded claims or defenses tried by consent are treated as if they had been raised in the pleadings. *Id.*; ***Conjugal Prtshp. Comprised by Jones & Jones v. Conjugal Prtshp. Comprised of Pineda & Pineda***, 22 F.3d 391, 400 (1st Cir.1994).

(1) Express consent. Express consent to litigation of an unpleaded claim may be given by stipulation or in a pretrial order. *See* ***Cabrera v. City of Huntington Park***, 159 F.3d 374, 382 (9th Cir.1998); ***Studiengesellschaft Kohle, M.B.H. v. Shell Oil Co.***, 112 F.3d 1561, 1566 (Fed.Cir.1997); 6A Wright, Miller & Kane §1493; *see also* ***Jones v. Miles***, 656 F.2d 103, 107 n.7 (5th Cir.1981) (when opposing party raises affirmative defense, there is express consent).

(2) Implied consent. Implied consent to litigation of an unpleaded claim may arise in either of two circumstances: (1) the claim is actually introduced outside the evidence (as in a pretrial memorandum) and is then treated by the opposing party as having been pleaded, through either effective engagement of the claim or silent acquiescence, or (2) during trial, the opposing party acquiesces to the introduction of evidence that is relevant only to the unpleaded issue. ***Rodriguez v. Doral Mortg. Corp.***, 57 F.3d 1168, 1172 (1st Cir.1995); *see* ***Hardin v. Manitowoc-Forsythe Corp.***, 691 F.2d 449, 457 (10th Cir.1982); ***Miles***, 656 F.2d at 107 n.7; *see, e.g.*, ***Winger v. Winger***, 82 F.3d 140, 144 (7th Cir.1996) (D's failure to object to jury instructions and evidence of intentional misrepresentation demonstrated that issue was tried by implied consent); *see also* ***In re Cumberland Farms, Inc.***, 284 F.3d 216, 225-26 (1st Cir.2002) (courts should not presume implied consent from introduction of evidence arguably relevant to issues previously raised by pleaded claims); ***U.S. v. Ideal Elec. Sec. Co.***, 81 F.3d 240, 245-47 (D.C.Cir.1996) (same).

§2.4 Groundless pleadings. See "Motion for Sanctions," ch. 5-O, p. 384.

§2.5 Filing & serving pleadings. All pleadings must be filed in the court and served on the parties, unless a local rule provides otherwise. *See* FRCP 5(a)(1). See "Filing Documents," ch. 1-C, p. 17; "Serving Documents," ch. 1-D, p. 29; "Serving the Defendant with Process," ch. 2-H, p. 149.

§2.6 Responding to pleadings. Parties should always respond to pleadings. The failure to respond can result in the loss of substantial rights (e.g., default judgment or waiver of defenses). FRCP 12 sets out when and how a party must respond to a pleading. See "Overview of Preanswer Motions & Responsive Pleadings," ch. 3-A, p. 171.

§2.7 Appellate review.

1. Form & content. The adequacy of pleadings must be judged in light of FRCP 8(e), which provides that all pleadings must be construed to do justice. ***Almand v. DeKalb Cty.***, 103 F.3d 1510, 1514 (11th Cir.1997). Therefore, an appellate court will review de novo a district court's ruling to dismiss a case because of the form or content of a pleading. *See, e.g.*, ***Yamaguchi v. U.S. Dept. of the Air Force***, 109 F.3d 1475, 1480-81 (9th Cir.1997) (dismissal for failure to state a claim); ***Cintron v. Union Pac. R.R.***, 813 F.2d 917, 919-20 (9th Cir.1987) (dismissal for not complying with local rules on form of complaint).

2. Leave to amend. The district court's ruling granting or denying leave to amend is reviewed for abuse of discretion. ***Foman v. Davis***, 371 U.S. 178, 182 (1962). However, when the district court bases its decision to deny leave to amend on a legal conclusion that the amended pleading would not withstand a motion to dismiss, that decision may be reviewed de novo. ***Fisher v. Roberts***, 125 F.3d 974, 977 (6th Cir.1997). See "Appellate Review," ch. 5-I, §9, p. 355; "Appellate Review," ch. 8-F, §5, p. 714.

§3. MOTION PRACTICE

Motions are applications to the court for an order. FRCP 7(b)(1); *see* ***Page v. City of Southfield***, 45 F.3d 128, 133 (6th Cir.1995) (motions are what party asks court to do, not what court does on its own). Unlike with pleadings, the federal rules do not limit the types of documents that can be considered motions. *See* FRCP 7(a) (specifying what documents can be considered pleadings).

§3.1 Drafting motions.

1. Form. When drafting motions, parties should comply with both the FRCPs and the local rules. The federal rules on the form of pleadings also apply to the form of motions. FRCP 7(b)(2). See "Pleading Practice," §2, p. 7. Parties should be aware of any federal statutes and judicial precedent governing motion practice. *See, e.g.*, 28 U.S.C.

§1920 (motion to tax costs). Except in extraordinary circumstances, a court has no power to prevent a party from filing a motion or to require court approval before filing a motion. *E.g.*, ***Eisemann v. Greene***, 204 F.3d 393, 397 (2d Cir. 2000) (imposing sanctions because party filed motion against court's advice amounts to requiring court approval before filing); *see* ***Richardson Greenshields Secs., Inc. v. Lau***, 825 F.2d 647, 652 (2d Cir.1987) (history of frivolous and vexatious litigation or of failure to comply with sanctions imposed for such conduct constitutes extraordinary circumstances); *see also* FRCP 83(a)(2) (prohibiting sanctions that result in loss of rights because of unintentional failure to comply with local rules' form requirement).

2. In writing. Most motions should be in writing. FRCP 7(b)(1)(A); ***St. Mary's Hosp. Med. Ctr. v. Heckler***, 753 F.2d 1362, 1365 (7th Cir.1985); ***Wolgin v. Simon***, 722 F.2d 389, 394 (8th Cir.1983). Motions made during trial or at a recorded hearing can be made orally. FRCP 7(b)(1)(A); ***Illinois v. Peters***, 871 F.2d 1336, 1342 (7th Cir.1989). Even if a motion can be made orally, the better practice is to file a written one. ***Taragan v. Eli Lilly & Co.***, 838 F.2d 1337, 1341 (D.C.Cir.1988).

3. Caption. Every motion must contain a caption. FRCP 10(a). The caption must include the court's name, a title with the parties' names, a file number, and an FRCP 7(a) designation. FRCP 10(a); *see* FRCP 7(b)(2). See "Caption," §2.1.3, p. 8. The designation, which is the label of the motion (e.g., "Defendant's Motion to Extend Time"), should be concise and direct. ***Venezolana Internacional de Aviacion, S.A. v. International Ass'n of Machinists & Aerospace Workers***, 118 F.R.D. 151, 151 (S.D.Fla.1987). It should always include the name of the party filing the motion and the type of motion (e.g., "Plaintiff's Motion to Compel Production of Design Documents"). If there are multiple parties, the designation should use an abbreviated name for the party (e.g., "Defendant Acme's Motion for Protective Order"). If a motion is agreed or unopposed, the designation should say so (e.g., "Defendant's Agreed Motion to …"). If a party makes an error in the designation of a motion, the court will usually treat the motion as if it had been properly designated. *See* ***Armstrong v. Capshaw, Goss & Bowers, LLP***, 404 F.3d 933, 936 (5th Cir.2005) (courts should determine true nature of pleading by its substance, not its label); *see, e.g.*, ***Vasapolli v. Rostoff***, 39 F.3d 27, 36 (1st Cir.1994) (postjudgment motion under FRCP 60(b)(6) treated as motion to alter or amend judgment under FRCP 59(e)). The court may order that the motion be resubmitted with the correct designation.

4. Factual allegations & relief. A motion must state the relief sought and the grounds for the relief. FRCP 7(b)(1)(B), (b)(1)(C); ***St. Mary's***, 753 F.2d at 1365. The grounds for relief must be stated with "particularity." FRCP 7(b)(1)(B); *see* ***Registration Control Sys. v. Compusystems, Inc.***, 922 F.2d 805, 807-08 (Fed.Cir.1990) (purpose of particularity requirement is to afford notice and opportunity to respond). A motion cannot simply state that it challenges all issues. ***Snellman v. Ricoh Co.***, 836 F.2d 528, 532 (Fed.Cir.1987). A motion may incorporate by reference statements in another pleading or motion. FRCP 10(c). Local rules may provide requirements for briefs. Some courts require that parties file briefs separately from the motion; some require that any briefing be contained in the motion; and some require that a memorandum of law be filed separately from the motion. *See, e.g.*, Local Rules Fla. (M.D.), Rule 3.01(a) (one document must be filed); Local Rules Pa. (E.D.), Rule 7.1(c) (brief must be filed separately with every contested motion); Local Rules Tenn. (M.D.), Rule 7.01(a) (memorandum of law must be filed separately with every motion that may require resolution of legal issue). Some courts do not require either a brief or a memorandum of law for certain types of motions. *See, e.g.*, Local Rules Tex. (N.D.), Rule 7.1(d), (h) (brief not required for agreed motions, motion for continuance, or motions to amend, extend time, substitute counsel, or withdraw); Local Rules W.Va. (N.D.), Rule 7.02(a) (memorandum of law not required for most nondispositive motions).

5. Signature. Every motion must be signed by at least one attorney of record in the attorney's individual name. FRCP 11(a). The motion must include the signer's address, e-mail address, and telephone number. *Id.* If the party is unrepresented, the motion must be personally signed by the party. *Id.* See "Signature," §2.1.9, p. 10.

6. Exhibits. Exhibits may be attached to motions. *See* FRCP 10(c). Unlike pleading exhibits, motion exhibits can be in many forms, including written documents, photographs, maps, and charts. *See* 2 *Moore's Federal Practice 3d* §10.05[6]. See "Exhibits," §2.1.10(1), p. 11.

7. Verification & affidavits. A motion may need to be verified or accompanied by an affidavit. *See, e.g.*, 28 U.S.C. §1924 (verified bill of costs); FRCP 55(a) (affidavit in support of default judgment, proving party did not plead or defend). See "Verification & affidavits," §2.1.10(2), p. 11.

8. Certificate of service. All motions that must be served on the other party must contain a certificate of service and be filed with the clerk within a reasonable time after service. FRCP 5(a), (d). Some local rules specify requirements for certificates of service. *E.g.*, Local Rules Tex. (E.D.), Rule CV-5(c) (must indicate date and method of service). Generally, a certificate of service should identify the document and state that it was served on the opposing party in a certain manner on a certain date. The certificate should also identify the name and address of each party or attorney on whom the document was served.

9. Certificate of conference. Many local rules require the movant to include a statement that it has conferred with the opposing party and cannot agree about the disposition of the motion. *E.g.*, Local Rules Ill. (N.D.), Rule 37.2; Local Rules Tex. (S.D.), Rule 7.1.D.

10. Request for hearing. The movant may request a hearing on the motion or state that the motion may be resolved by the court on written submission without a hearing. Some local rules provide that the right to a hearing is waived if no hearing is requested. *See, e.g.*, ***Kendall v. Hoover Co.***, 751 F.2d 171, 175 (6th Cir.1984) (applying local rules of N.D. Ohio). When requesting a hearing, the movant should state whether the hearing is for argument or for the introduction of evidence. When requesting a hearing for evidence, the movant should state that a court reporter is necessary.

11. Proposed order. Some local rules require the movant, and sometimes the respondent, to file with each motion (or response) a proposed order granting the relief sought. *E.g.*, Local Rules Cal. (N.D.), Rule 7-2(c). Some local rules impose additional requirements or limitations on the proposed orders to be submitted. *E.g.*, Local Rules Tex. (E.D.), Rule CV-7(a) (proposed order must not include date or signature lines); Local Rules Tex. (S.D.), Rule 7.1.C (proposed order must set forth sufficient information stating nature of relief granted). See "Court Rulings," ch. 1-G, p. 44.

12. Notice of constitutional question. If a motion challenges the constitutionality of a statute, the party must serve notice of the constitutional question on the attorney general. FRCP 5.1(a). See "Notice of constitutional question," §2.1.11, p. 12.

§3.2 Serving & filing motions. All written motions must be served on every party that has appeared in the proceeding. *See* FRCP 5(a)(1)(D), (a)(2). See "Serving Documents," ch. 1-D, p. 29. Any motion that must be served must be filed in the court. FRCP 5(d)(1). See "Filing Documents," ch. 1-C, p. 17.

§3.3 Responding to motions. A party is not always required to file a response to a motion. ***U.S. v. Okawa***, 26 F.R.D. 384, 385-86 (D.Haw.1961). However, whenever a rule permits or requires a response, the party should file one. *See* FRCP 11(c) (motion for sanctions), FRCP 59(c) (motion for new trial). Some local rules state that the court will assume a motion is unopposed if no response is filed. *E.g.*, Local Rules Tex. (E.D.), Rule CV-7(d). Local rules may also impose time or page limits on responses and reply briefs.

§3.4 Hearing on motions. A court is not required to hold a hearing on every motion. FRCP 78(b). See "Hearings," ch. 1-E, p. 38. Although most districts have local rules that dispense with the requirement of oral arguments on motions, the decision to conduct a hearing is entirely within the court's discretion. *See, e.g.*, Local Rules Tex. (E.D.), Rule CV-7(g). If a hearing is permitted, the parties should consult the local rules for when, where, and how the hearing will be held.

§3.5 Appellate review. The appellate court reviews the district court's rulings on motions according to the law applicable to the type of motion. *See, e.g.*, ***Jarvis Christian Coll. v. Exxon Corp.***, 845 F.2d 523, 528 (5th Cir.1988) (motion to transfer reviewed for abuse of discretion).

C. FILING DOCUMENTS

§1. GENERAL

§1.1 Rule. FRCP 5(d).

§1.2 Purpose. The purpose of filing documents is to place them in the court's record of the lawsuit. *See **International Bus. Machs. Corp. v. Edelstein***, 526 F.2d 37, 45 (2d Cir.1975); ***Todd v. Nello L. Teer Co.***, 308 F.2d 397, 399 (5th Cir.1962). Filing documents should not be confused with serving documents. Documents are *filed* with the clerk; documents are *served* on other parties in the case. The rules for filing and serving are different. *Compare* FRCP 4 (serving summons) *and* FRCP 4.1 (serving other process) *with* FRCP 5(d) (filing). See "Serving Documents," ch. 1-D, p. 29. This subchapter does not discuss filing the complaint, which is covered in "Filing Requirements," ch. 2-B, §16, p. 86.

§1.3 Forms. *O'Connor's Federal Civil Forms* (2012), FORMS 1B.

§1.4 Other references. 4B Wright & Miller, *Federal Practice & Procedure 3d* §§1152-1153 (2002 & Supp.2012); 1 *Moore's Federal Practice 3d* §§5.30-5.34 (2012).

§2. WHAT TO FILE

All pleadings, motions, and other papers should be filed unless a rule or court order specifically states otherwise. FRCP 5(a)(1). Discovery should not be filed until it is used in the case, with the exception of pretrial disclosures under FRCP 26(a)(3). *See* FRCP 5(d)(1).

> **NOTE**
>
> *FRCP 5.2 requires parties to redact specific personal data from court filings. FRCP 5.2(a). The purpose of FRCP 5.2 is to address privacy and security concerns relating to electronic filing of documents and their public availability. 2007 Notes to FRCP 5.2 at ¶1, p. 1148, this book. The redaction requirement does not affect judicial procedures for sealing or any other sources of protection, such as for pretrial conferences under FRCP 16 or protective orders under FRCP 26(c). See 2007 Notes to FRCP 5.2 at ¶¶3, 7, p. 1148, this book.*

§2.1 Redacted filing. Unless the court orders otherwise, a filing must be redacted if it contains (1) a person's Social Security number or tax-identification number, (2) a person's birth date, (3) a minor's name, or (4) a financial-account number. FRCP 5.2(a). The redacted filing of the above information can only include the following: (1) the last four digits of the Social Security number and tax-identification number, (2) the year of the person's birth, (3) the minor's initials, and (4) the last four digits of the financial-account number. *Id.*

1. Additional redaction. For good cause, the court may order that additional information, such as a driver's license number, be redacted. FRCP 5.2(e)(1); *see* 2007 Notes to FRCP 5.2 at ¶3, p. 1148, this book (in certain cases, it may be necessary to prevent access to any part of account number or Social Security number); *see, e.g.*, Transcript Redaction Procedures for Attorneys (E.D.Tex.) (home addresses should be limited to only city and state).

2. Exemptions. The redaction requirement does not apply to (1) a financial-account number that identifies the property allegedly subject to forfeiture in a forfeiture action, (2) the record of an administrative or agency proceeding, (3) the official record of a state-court proceeding, (4) the record of a court or tribunal, if that record was not subject to the redaction requirement when originally filed, (5) an action for benefits under the Social Security Act, immigration cases, or filings under seal, and (6) a pro se filing in an action brought under 28 U.S.C. §2241, 2254, or 2255. FRCP 5.2(b); *see* FRCP 5.2(c), (d). District courts may provide additional exemptions from the redaction requirement.

3. Under seal. The court may order that a filing be made under seal without redaction. FRCP 5.2(d). The court may later unseal the filing or order a redacted version to be filed for the public record. *Id.* In addition to any redacted filing, a party may also file an unredacted copy under seal. FRCP 5.2(f). FRCP 5.2 does not limit or expand the

judicially developed rules that govern sealing, but rather reflects the possibility that redaction may provide an alternative to sealing in order to protect a person's specific personal information. 2007 Notes to FRCP 5.2 at ¶7, p. 1148, this book; *see* FRCP 5.2(a), (d), (f).

4. Limited access. For good cause, the court may order that a nonparty's remote electronic access to a filed document be limited or prohibited. FRCP 5.2(e)(2).

5. Trial exhibits. Trial exhibits must be redacted if they are filed in the court. 2007 Notes to FRCP 5.2 at ¶12, p. 1149, this book.

6. Waiver. A person waives protection under FRCP 5.2 for her own information by filing it without redaction and not under seal. FRCP 5.2(h); 2007 Notes to FRCP 5.2 at ¶11, p. 1149, this book. The attorney and party or nonparty making the filing must ensure that the filing is properly redacted in compliance with FRCP 5.2. 2007 Notes to FRCP 5.2 at ¶5, p. 1148, this book. If a party accidentally files an unredacted document, it may seek relief from the court. *Id.* at ¶11, p. 1148, this book.

§2.2 Original & copies. Local rules may require the parties to file the original document and a certain number of copies. *E.g.*, Local Rules Tex. (N.D.), Rule 5.1(b) (original and one copy required).

§3. WHERE TO FILE

§3.1 Most situations.

1. Clerk's office. Documents should be filed with the clerk of the court. FRCP 5(d)(2). The clerk's office, with the clerk or a deputy in attendance, must be open during business hours on all days except Saturdays, Sundays, and legal holidays. FRCP 77(c)(1). A court can require by local rule or order that the clerk's office be open for specified hours on Saturdays and some legal holidays. *Id.*

2. Courtroom or judge's chambers. Local rules may permit parties to file documents with the judge during a hearing, during the trial, or after business hours. *See, e.g.*, Local Rules Ill. (N.D.), Rule 5.4 (judge may permit filing in chambers). When a document is filed with the judge, the judge must note the filing date and promptly send the document to the clerk. FRCP 5(d)(2)(B). Although documents filed with the judge are eventually sent to the clerk's office for processing, it is better to file with the clerk, not the judge, except in unusual situations.

§3.2 Emergency situations – courthouse closed.

When a party faces a nonextendable deadline to file a document and the courthouse is closed, it is still possible to file the document on time.

1. Drop box. When the courthouse is closed, the party can file the document by depositing it in the court's drop box for after-hours filing. Check the local rules about filing in a drop box. Many drop boxes have a time clock that stamps the time of delivery. *See, e.g.*, ***Greenwood v. State of N.Y., Office of Mental Health***, 842 F.2d 636, 639 (2d Cir.1988) (document deemed filed on date and at time of stamp). Some local rules provide that if the document is not stamped, the document is deemed filed on the next day the clerk empties the drop box. *E.g.*, Local Rules Cal. (N.D.), Rule 5-4(c)(2).

2. Fax. When the courthouse is closed, the party can file the document by fax transmission. *See* FRCP 5(d)(3). See "Fax," §4.3, p. 19.

3. Electronic filing. When the courthouse is closed, the party can file the document by electronic filing. *See* FRCP 5(d)(3). See "Electronic filing," §4.4, p. 20.

4. Personal delivery. When the courthouse is closed, the party can take the document to either the clerk or the judge to have it filed. ***Casalduc v. Diaz***, 117 F.2d 915, 917 (1st Cir.1941); 4B Wright & Miller §1153; *see* FRCP 77(a) (district court always considered open for filing); *see, e.g.*, ***Greeson v. Sherman***, 265 F.Supp. 340, 342 (W.D. Va.1967) (P took complaint to deputy clerk's home). As a courtesy, the party should call the clerk or judge before delivering the document.

§3.3 Courtesy copies. Some local rules or standing orders require the parties to deliver to the office of the district judge a "courtesy copy" of the papers filed with the clerk. *See* ***Garner v. Klein***, 882 F.Supp. 66, 66 n.1 (S.D. N.Y.1995); *see, e.g.*, Local Rules Tex. (E.D.), Rule CV-5(a)(9) (paper courtesy copies required for electronic filings over five pages). *But see* Local Rules Fla. (S.D.), Rule 5.1(c) (extra courtesy copies may be delivered only when requested by judge's office).

§4. HOW TO FILE

There are four ways to file documents in the court: by mail, by delivery, by fax, or by electronic filing. Some local rules may require a particular method of filing, while others may prohibit particular methods. *See, e.g.*, Local Rules Or., Rule 5-3 (fax filing not allowed except in emergencies); Local Rules Tex. (E.D.), Rule CV-5(a) (electronic filing required in most cases).

§4.1 Mail. A party can file a document by mailing it to the office of the clerk. The party should mail the document far enough in advance to make sure it reaches the clerk by the deadline. A document is not considered filed when mailed; it is considered filed only when the clerk receives it. ***McIntosh v. Antonino***, 71 F.3d 29, 36 (1st Cir. 1995); *see* ***Raymond v. Ameritech Corp.***, 442 F.3d 600, 604-05 (7th Cir.2006). If the document reaches the clerk after the deadline, it is untimely even if it was mailed before the deadline. *E.g.*, ***Torras Herreria y Construcciones, S.A. v. M/V Timur Star***, 803 F.2d 215, 216 (6th Cir.1986) (FRCP 52(b) motion). For an imprisoned pro se litigant, a document is usually considered filed when the document is delivered to the prison authorities for mailing. ***Houston v. Lack***, 487 U.S. 266, 270 (1988). *But see* ***Smith v. Conner***, 250 F.3d 277, 278 (5th Cir.2001) (***Houston*** did not announce universal rule for all prisoner filings; if rule at issue does not clearly define "filing," then mailbox rule of ***Houston*** applies). Filing also occurs when the mailed document is placed in the clerk's post-office box. ***Torras Herreria y Construcciones***, 803 F.2d at 216.

PRACTICE TIP

Keep in mind that the complete-upon-mailing rule applies only to serving documents on the other party, not filing documents in the court. See FRCP 5(b)(2)(C). See "Date of mailing," ch. 1-D, §4.1.1(2), p. 31. If you mail a document to the clerk, you take a chance that it will not get there on time. Therefore, consider electronic filing—or hand-delivery, if electronic filing is not permitted—to make sure the document gets to the clerk before the deadline.

§4.2 Delivery. A party can file a document by delivering it to the office of the clerk. FRCP 5(d)(2)(A); *see* ***Freeman v. Giacomo Costa Fu Andrea***, 282 F.Supp. 525, 527 (E.D.Pa.1968) (delivery to clerk's office on Saturday). The requirements for filing by delivery are often spelled out in the local rules. In most cases, anyone—the attorney, the attorney's staff, or a private delivery service (e.g., FedEx, UPS)—can deliver a document to the clerk. If the local rules permit, a party can deliver documents to a drop box located outside the clerk's office or near the entrance of the federal building. The availability and location of drop boxes vary from district to district. *See, e.g.*, ***McIntosh v. Antonino***, 71 F.3d 29, 35 n.5 (1st Cir.1995) (court did not have a drop box). Leaving a notice under the door of the clerk's office after hours is not sufficient under FRCP 5(d)(2)(A). *See* ***Casalduc v. Diaz***, 117 F.2d 915, 916 (1st Cir.1941).

§4.3 Fax. A party can file a document by fax transmission if permitted by local rule. FRCP 5(d)(3); *see* ***McIntosh v. Antonino***, 71 F.3d 29, 34-35 (1st Cir.1995) (discussing 1993 version of FRCP 5(e)); 1996 Notes to FRCP 5 at ¶6, p. 1147, this book ("electronic means" includes fax transmission). Any document filed by fax in compliance with a local rule constitutes a written paper for purposes of applying the FRCPs. FRCP 5(d)(3); *see* 1996 Notes to FRCP 5 at ¶¶5, 6, p. 1147, this book.

1. When court permits fax filing. If a court has local rules for fax filing, a party may file the document by fax.

(1) File original document. Some courts may require the party to file the original document after the fax filing. *E.g.*, Local Rules Ala. (M.D.), Rule 5.3(d)(3) (original must follow by overnight mail).

(2) Transmission record. The party should keep the transmission record in case fax filing later becomes an issue. *E.g.*, Local Rules Cal. (S.D.), Rule 5.3.e.

(3) Use filing agency. Some courts require parties to use a fax-filing agency to transmit documents to the clerk. *E.g.*, Local Rules Cal. (S.D.), Rule 5.3.a. A document is considered filed when it is received by the clerk, not when it is transmitted by the filing agency. *E.g.*, Local Rules Cal. (S.D.), Rule 5.3.b.

(4) Obtain court approval. Some courts allow fax filing only when there is good cause and the party obtains court approval before filing. *E.g.*, Local Rules Haw., Rule 10.2(k); *see* Local Rules Kan., Rule 77.1(c)(1) (if party is represented, compelling circumstances); Local Rules Or., Rule 5-3 (emergency situations).

2. When court does not permit fax filing. If a court does not allow fax filing, a party may still file copies of faxed documents. *E.g.*, Local Rules Cal. (C.D.), Rule 11-2 (faxed documents may be filed if they are legible); Local Rules Okla. (E.D.), Rule 5.4(b) (faxed papers may be filed). For example, the party can fax the document to someone located near the courthouse who can deliver a copy of the faxed document to the clerk.

§4.4 Electronic filing. A party can file a document by electronic filing. FRCP 5(d)(3); 2006 Notes to FRCP 5 at ¶1, p. 1145, this book; *e.g.*, Local Rules N.Y. (E.D. & S.D.), Rule 5.2; Local Rules Tex. (E.D.), Rule CV-5(a); Admin. Order 2004-39 (S.D.Fla.), at 1. In many courts, a party must file a document by electronic means. *E.g.*, Local Rules Cal. (C.D.), Rule 5-4.1; *see, e.g.*, Elec. Case Filing Admin. Policies & Procedures Manual (D.Ariz.), ¶I.B; Local Rules Tex. (N.D.), Rule 5.1(e). But even when electronic filing is required, the court must allow for reasonable exceptions in its local rules. FRCP 5(d)(3); *see* 2006 Notes to FRCP 5 at ¶1, p. 1145, this book (local rules will define scope of reasonable exceptions); *see, e.g.*, Local Rules Cal. (C.D.), Rule 5-4.2. An electronic-filing system must accept every document, even when there is an error of form. ***Farzana K. v. Indiana Dept. of Educ.***, 473 F.3d 703, 708 (7th Cir. 2007); *see also* ***Kinsley v. Lakeview Reg'l Med. Ctr. LLC***, 570 F.3d 586, 588-89 (5th Cir.2009) (court's deficiency notice, which informs e-filer that corrected document must be refiled, did not render notice of appeal timely when request for oral argument was mistakenly filed instead of notice of appeal). See "No refusal to accept," §7.1, p. 28. Any document filed by electronic means in compliance with a local rule constitutes a written paper for purposes of applying the FRCPs. FRCP 5(d)(3); Local Rules Cal. (C.D.), Rule 5-4.1.1; Local Rules N.Y. (E.D. & S.D.), Rule 5.2; *see* 1996 Notes to FRCP 5 at ¶5, p. 1147, this book.

PRACTICE TIP

All courts now accept electronic filing, and in most cases they require it. See 2006 Notes to FRCP 5 at ¶1, p. 1145, this book; All Federal Courts Now Accepting Electronic Filing (2012), www.uscourts.gov/news/newsView/12-05-17/All_Federal_Courts_Now_Accepting_Electronic_Filing.aspx; see, e.g., Elec. Case Filing Policies & Procedures Manual (S.D.Ind.), ¶4. Because each court has its own policies and procedures for electronic filing, check the relevant local rules, standing orders, and procedure manuals for filing requirements. For links to the district courts' websites, see www.uscourts.gov/RulesAndPolicies/FederalRulemaking/LocalCourtRules/USDistrictCourts.aspx.

---

1. What to file. All complaints, petitions, motions, pleadings, memorandums of law, or other documents may be filed electronically. *E.g.*, Elec. Case Filing Procedures (D.Idaho), ¶4.A; *see, e.g.*, Supp. Rules for Elec. Case Filing (D.N.H.), ¶2.4(a) ("case opening documents and related attachments"). Attachments may be scanned and submitted electronically according to local requirements. *E.g.*, Supp. Rules for Elec. Case Filing (D.N.H.), ¶2.3(a), 2.5(a).

2. How to file – CM/ECF. The Case Management/Electronic Case Files (CM/ECF) system allows courts to accept electronic filings over the Internet and to maintain case documents in electronic format. Admin. Office of U.S. Courts, *About CM/ECF*, www.uscourts.gov/FederalCourts/CMECF/AboutCMECF.aspx; *see* ***Robinson v. Wix Filtration Corp.***, 599 F.3d 403, 406 n.1 (4th Cir.2010). The CM/ECF system was developed by the Administrative Office of the U.S. Courts as an online case-management system. Most federal courts have implemented the CM/ECF system.

For a list of courts currently using the CM/ECF system, see www.uscourts.gov/FederalCourts/CMECF/Courts.aspx. The CM/ECF system enhances the accuracy, management, and security of records; reduces delays in the flow of information; and saves money for the judiciary, bar, and litigants. *See* Admin. Office of U.S. Courts, *CM/ECF Frequently Asked Questions*, www.uscourts.gov/FederalCourts/CMECF/FAQs.aspx.

(1) Registration & training. Parties and attorneys must register with individual courts to file electronically. *See, e.g.*, Local Rules Ariz., Rule 5.5(c)-(e). Attorneys admitted to the bar of the local court, including pro hac vice attorneys and attorneys authorized to represent the United States, are eligible to register. *E.g.*, Local Rules Ariz., Rule 5.5(d); Elec. Case Filing Rules & Instructions (S.D.N.Y.), ¶2.1. Some courts may require training before an attorney is allowed to file electronically. *E.g.*, Elec. Filing Admin. Policies & Procedures (D.Alaska), ¶7 (attorney must complete either CM/ECF training session or computer-based training program).

(2) Signature. The username and password required to submit the document electronically usually constitute the registered user's signature. *E.g.*, Local Rules Ariz., Rule 5.5(g); Elec. Case Filing Admin. Policies & Procedures Manual (S.D.Cal.), ¶2.f.1.

(a) Attorney signatures. If the document requires the signature of the attorney of record, the attorney must include an electronic signature on the document. To electronically sign the document, the attorney usually must include a signature block and "/s/ (attorney's name)" on the signature line. *E.g.*, CM/ECF Admin. Policies & Procedures Manual for Civil Filings (E.D.Ark.), ¶III.C.2.a; Elec. Case Filing Admin. Policies & Procedures Manual (S.D.Cal.), ¶2.f.1; Admin. Procedures for Elec. Filing in Civil & Crim. Cases (M.D.Fla.), ¶II.C.1. The attorney may be able to sign a hard copy and then use a scanned copy of her signature. *See* ***Johnson v. Cherry***, 422 F.3d 540, 544 n.1 (7th Cir.2005). If the document requires the signatures of multiple attorneys, the filing attorney must confirm the document's contents with the other attorneys and obtain their signatures. *E.g.*, Elec. Case Filing Admin. Policies & Procedures Manual (S.D.Cal.), ¶2.f.4; Admin. Procedures for Elec. Filing in Civil & Crim. Cases (M.D.Fla.), ¶II.C.2. The other attorneys' signatures may be physical, faxed, or electronic. *E.g.*, Elec. Case Filing Admin. Policies & Procedures Manual (S.D.Cal.), ¶2.f.4; Admin. Procedures for Elec. Filing in Civil & Crim. Cases (M.D.Fla.), ¶II.C.2.

(b) Original signatures. If the document to be filed requires an original signature (e.g., an affidavit), the document may be scanned and filed electronically. *E.g.*, Elec. Case Filing Admin. Policies & Procedures Manual (S.D.Cal.), ¶2.f.2; Admin. Procedures for Elec. Filing in Civil & Crim. Cases (M.D.Fla.), ¶II.C.3.

3. When filed. If a document is electronically filed by midnight in the court's time zone, it is considered filed that day, unless a different time is set by a statute, local rule, or court order. *See* FRCP 6(a)(4)(A); ***Justice v. Town of Cicero***, 682 F.3d 662, 664 (7th Cir.2012); *see, e.g.*, Local Rules Tex. (N.D.), Rule 6.1; *see also* 2009 Notes to FRCP 6 at ¶16, p. 1150, this book (local rules may address problems that arise if a single district has clerk's offices in different time zones). Filing is not complete until a Notice of Electronic Filing is generated. *E.g.*, CM/ECF Admin. Policies & Procedures Manual for Civil Filings (W.D.Ark.), ¶III.A.1.c; *see* ***Robinson***, 599 F.3d at 406 n.1.

NOTE

If a document is not timely filed because of a technical problem, the party may be able to seek appropriate relief from the presiding judge. See 2009 Notes to FRCP 6 at ¶15, p. 1150, this book (local rules may define "inaccessibility" under FRCP 6(a)(3) to include outage of electronic-filing system); see, e.g., Elec. Case Filing Rules & Instructions (S.D.N.Y.), §11; Admin. Procedures for Elec. Filing in Civil & Crim. Cases (S.D.Tex.), ¶11. But if a document is not timely filed because of a technical problem on the filer's end and if the missed deadline is a jurisdictional one, the presiding judge may not be able to grant any relief. See, e.g., ***Justice****, 682 F.3d at 664-65 (P's deadline to file postjudgment motion was 11-22, but he electronically filed his motion at 3 a.m. on 11-23; because deadline was jurisdictional and could not be extended, district court could not deem motion filed on 11-22).*

4. Filing fees. There are no additional fees for filing documents electronically, but regular document filing fees apply. Admin. Office of U.S. Courts, *CM/ECF Frequently Asked Questions*, www.uscourts.gov/FederalCourts

/CMECF/FAQs.aspx. Some courts require the fees to be paid before a document is filed. *E.g.*, Admin. Procedures for Filing, Signing, & Verifying Documents by Elec. Means (M.D.Ga.), ¶II.A.3 (online payment of fees required to complete certain e-filing transactions).

5. Retaining electronically filed documents. Original copies of electronically filed documents should be retained until the case is closed or until all time periods for appeals expire. *E.g.*, Local Rules Idaho, Rule 5.1(e). Some courts prescribe a specific time period for retention of electronically filed documents. *E.g.*, Local Rules Kan., Rule 5.4.7 (until six years after time for appeal expires); Elec. Case Filing Rules & Instructions (S.D.N.Y.), §7 (until one year after time for appeal expires).

§5. WHEN TO FILE

Pleadings and motions must be filed within the time permitted by the rules and the court's docketing order.

§5.1 Deadline – filing or service?

Some rules have deadlines for *filing* a document with the clerk. Other rules have deadlines for *serving* a document on the other party, with filing to be accomplished soon afterward.

1. Deadline – filing. To ensure that a document is timely, the party must file the document with the clerk by the deadline stated in the specific rule. For a list of rules with only filing deadlines, see chart 1-1, below.

2. Deadline – service. To ensure that a document is timely, the party must serve the document on the other party by the deadline stated in the specific rule and file the document with the clerk within a reasonable time after service. *See* FRCP 5(d)(1) (after complaint, all papers required to be served must be filed). ***But see Blank v. Bitker***, 135 F.2d 962, 965 (7th Cir.1943) (FRCP 12(a) requires that answer be served, not filed). For a list of rules with only service deadlines, see chart 1-1, below.

(1) Exception for discovery. The following discovery is not required to be filed with the court until it is used in a proceeding or the court orders it to be filed: initial disclosures, depositions, interrogatories, requests for production, requests for admissions, requests for permission to enter land, and responses to these discovery requests. FRCP 5(d)(1).

(2) Reasonable time. The courts liberally construe "reasonable time." *See, e.g.*, ***Calhoun v. U.S.***, 647 F.2d 6, 8 (9th Cir.1981) (motion timely filed on Monday, after service on Friday); ***Claybrook Drilling Co. v. Divanco, Inc.***, 336 F.2d 697, 700 (10th Cir.1964) (motion timely filed four days after service by mail).

3. Deadline – filing & service. To ensure that a document is timely, the party must file *and* serve the document by the deadline stated in the specific rule. For a list of rules with both filing and service deadlines, see chart 1-1, below.

1-1. DEADLINE – FILING OR SERVICE?

	Action	Rule	Deadline met by filing or service?	Discussed at
1	Motion for protective order	FRCP 26(c)(1)	Filing	ch. 6-A, §12.2, p. 441
2	Notice of voluntary dismissal	FRCP 41(a)(1)(A)	Filing	ch. 7-C, §3.2, p. 631
3	Motion for attorney fees	FRCP 54(d)(2)	Filing	ch. 9-C, §4.1, p. 747
4	Renewed motion for JMOL	FRCP 50(b)	Filing	ch. 10-B, §3.1, p. 776
5	Motion for new trial	FRCP 59(b)	Filing	ch. 10-C, §2.1, p. 783
6	Motion to amend judgment	FRCP 59(e)	Filing	ch. 10-D, §2.1, p. 793
7	Motion to amend or add findings	FRCP 52(b)	Filing	ch. 10-E, §3.1, p. 800
8	Notice of appeal	FRAP 4(a)(1)	Filing	ch. 10-G, §3, p. 817

1-1. DEADLINE – FILING OR SERVICE? (CONTINUED)				
	Action	Rule	Deadline met by filing or service?	Discussed at
9	Motion for summary judgment	FRCP 56(b)	Filing	ch. 7-B, §8, p. 619
10	Answer to complaint, third-party claim, or amended complaint	FRCP 12(a), (b), 14(a)(2), 15(a)(1), (a)(2)	Service	ch. 3-A, §5, p. 174
11	Offer of judgment	FRCP 68(a)	Service	ch. 5-D, §2.2, p. 317; ch. 5-D, §2.5, p. 317
12	Discovery disclosures (initial and expert)	FRCP 26(a)(1)(A), (a)(2)(B), (a)(4)	Service	ch. 6-E, §4.1, p. 533; ch. 6-E, §4.3, p. 534; ch. 6-E, §5.1, p. 534
13	Response to discovery request	FRCP 33(b)(2), 34(b)(2)(A), 36(a)(3)	Service	ch. 6-G, §4.1, p. 562; ch. 6-H, §3, p. 564; ch. 6-I, §4, p. 572
14	Jury demand	FRCP 38(b)	Filing and service	ch. 5-C, §2.1.3, p. 309; ch. 5-C, §2.1.4, p. 309; ch. 5-C, §3, p. 310
15	Objection to magistrate's findings and recommendations	FRCP 72(a), (b)(2)	Filing and service	ch. 5-B, §2.2.7(2), p. 301
16	Pretrial disclosure and objection to trial evidence	FRCP 26(a)(3)(A), (a)(4)	Filing and service	ch. 6-E, §6, p. 536
17	Written request for jury instruction	FRCP 51(a)	Filing and service	ch. 8-I, §3.1, p. 721

§5.2 Filing complete when received. The filing of a document is complete when it is received by the clerk's office. *See, e.g.*, ***Royall v. National Ass'n of Letter Carriers***, 548 F.3d 137, 142 (D.C.Cir.2008) (notice of appeal was timely when it was electronically submitted before deadline even though notice was not docketed until two months after deadline).

§6. COMPUTING DEADLINES

FRCP 6(a) establishes the method for computing any time period found in the FRCPs, in any local rule or court order, or in any statute that does not specify a method for computing time. 2009 Notes to FRCP 6 at ¶1, p. 1149, this book. In most cases, if a party files or serves a document after a deadline, the document is not considered effective unless the party secured an extension from the opposing party or the court. Thus, correctly calculating deadlines is extremely important.

§6.1 Calculating time periods. FRCP 6(a) applies only when a time period must be computed; it does not apply to a fixed deadline. *E.g.*, 2009 Notes to FRCP 6 at ¶2, p. 1149, this book (FRCP 6(a) governs filing required to be made "within 10 days" but not filing due "no later than November 1, 2007"); *see* ***Fleischhauer v. Feltner***, 3 F.3d 148, 151 (6th Cir.1993). To calculate a deadline, a party must first identify the time unit on which the deadline is based. Most time periods are stated in days; only a few are in months and years. *See, e.g.*, FRCP 12(a)(1)(A)(i) (answer must be served within 21 days after service of complaint), FRCP 60(c)(1) (motion under FRCP 60(b)(1)-(b)(3) must be made no more than a year after judgment); Supp. FRCP F(1) (complaint from any vessel owner must be made not later than six months after receipt of claim in writing). Although the FRCPs do not include time periods stated in hours, some statutes do, as do some court orders in expedited proceedings. 2009 Notes to FRCP 6 at ¶10, p. 1150, this book. Once the time unit is determined, the party must (1) identify when to start counting (the "trigger event"), (2) count all intervening time units, (3) determine the end of the time period, and (4) determine whether any extensions apply to the time period.

COMMENTARIES
CHAPTER 1. INTRODUCTION
C. FILING DOCUMENTS

1. Days.

(1) Identify trigger event. An event (e.g., the filing of a complaint) must occur to trigger a deadline. *See* FRCP 6(a)(1)(A); *see also* 2009 Notes to FRCP 6 at ¶7, p. 1149, this book (former FRCP 6(a) referred to "act, event, or default" that triggered deadline, but now FRCP 6(a) refers simply to "event"; amended language is not intended to change meaning). Counting begins before or after the trigger event, depending on whether the time period is forward-looking or backward-looking.

(a) Forward-looking time period. A forward-looking (i.e., prospective) time period requires something to be done *after* an event. 2009 Notes to FRCP 6 at ¶18, p. 1150, this book. A forward-looking time period usually uses a phrase such as "within 30 days after" or "no later than 14 days after." *See id.*; *see, e.g.*, FRCP 59(b) (motion for new trial must be filed no later than 28 days after judgment). A deadline based on days starts to run the day after the event that triggers the deadline, so begin counting days on the day *after* the trigger event. FRCP 6(a)(1)(A); 2009 Notes to FRCP 6 at ¶6, p. 1149, this book; *see* ***Newell v. Hanks***, 283 F.3d 827, 833 (7th Cir.2002). For example, if a deadline is based on a forward-looking time period and the party is served with a motion on Friday, Friday is "day 0," Saturday is "day 1," Sunday is "day 2," and so on.

(b) Backward-looking time period. A backward-looking (i.e., retrospective) time period requires something to be done *before* an event. 2009 Notes to FRCP 6 at ¶18, p. 1150, this book. A backward-looking time period usually uses a phrase such as "at least 30 days before." *See id.*; *see, e.g.*, FRCP 26(a)(3)(B) (pretrial disclosures must be made at least 30 days before trial). A deadline based on days starts to run the day before the event that triggers the deadline, so begin counting days on the day *before* the trigger event. FRCP 6(a)(1)(A); 2009 Notes to FRCP 6 at ¶6, p. 1149, this book. For example, if a deadline is based on a backward-looking time period and the party must file its pretrial disclosures 30 days before trial (which is set for Monday, December 15), Monday is "day 0," Sunday is "day 1," Saturday is "day 2," and so on.

(2) Count days. Count the days either forward or backward, depending on the type of time period. All days in the period are counted, including intermediate Saturdays, Sundays, and legal holidays. FRCP 6(a)(1)(B); 2009 Notes to FRCP 6 at ¶6, p. 1149, this book; *see* 2009 Notes to FRCP 6 at ¶4, p. 1149, this book.

NOTE

All deadlines stated in days are now computed in the same way, regardless of length. 2009 Notes to FRCP 6 at ¶6, p. 1149, this book; see FRCP 6(a)(1). Under former FRCP 6(a), a time period of 11 days or less excluded intermediate Saturdays, Sundays, and legal holidays from the time computation. 2009 Notes to FRCP 6 at ¶5, p. 1149, this book. Because that method was unnecessarily complicated and sometimes led to counterintuitive results, the 2009 amendments to the FRCPs changed most 10-day periods to 14-day periods. See 2009 Notes to FRCP 6 at ¶¶5, 9, p. 1149, this book. The 14-day periods will usually result in the same deadline as the 10-day periods under the former time-computation method because most of those 10-day periods—with two Saturdays and two Sundays excluded—resulted in 14-day periods. See id.

---

(3) Determine end of time period. The last day of the time period is counted. FRCP 6(a)(1)(C).

(a) Electronic filing. The last day ends at midnight in the court's time zone, unless a different time is set by a statute, local rule, or court order. FRCP 6(a)(4)(A); *see* 2009 Notes to FRCP 6 at ¶16, p. 1150, this book. A local rule may, for example, address the problems that can arise if a single district has clerk's offices in different time zones. 2009 Notes to FRCP 6 at ¶16, p. 1150, this book.

(b) Filing by other means. The last day ends when the clerk's office is scheduled to close, unless a different time is set by a statute, local rule, or court order. FRCP 6(a)(4)(B); *see* 2009 Notes to FRCP 6 at ¶16, p. 1150, this book. A local rule may, for example, provide that a document filed in a drop box after the normal hours of the clerk's office is filed on the day that is date-stamped on the document by a device in the drop box. 2009 Notes to FRCP 6 at ¶16, p. 1150, this book. Although some courts have permitted after-hours filing by handing the document to an appropriate official, FRCP 6(a)(4) does not address that type of filing; instead, FRCP 6(a)(4) only addresses filing during the normal hours of the clerk's office. 2009 Notes to FRCP 6 at ¶17, p. 1150, this book.

(4) Determine if extension applies. If the time period based on days ends on a Saturday, Sunday, or legal holiday or on a day when the clerk's office is inaccessible, it continues until the end of the next day that the court is accessible and that is not a Saturday, Sunday, or legal holiday. *See* FRCP 6(a)(1)(C), (a)(3)(A); 2009 Notes to FRCP 6 at ¶¶6, 13, pp. 1149, 1150, this book.

NOTE

An extension separate from those discussed below may apply. FRCP 6(d) gives parties an additional three days to respond to a document served by any means other than personal delivery. For example, if a magistrate judge's recommendation and proposed findings of fact are served by mail and objections must be filed within 14 days under FRCP 72, the objecting party has an additional three days to file and serve the objections—the three days are added after the extensions discussed below. See "Computing Response Deadlines," ch. 1-D, §6, p. 33.

(a) Next day. When extending a deadline, the next day is determined by counting forward when the period is measured after an event and backward when measured before an event. FRCP 6(a)(5). The term "next day" is newly defined under FRCP 6(a)(5) and is important because it applies differently to time periods that are forward-looking or backward-looking. *See* 2009 Notes to FRCP 6 at ¶18, p. 1150, this book (in determining next day for forward-looking and backward-looking time periods, counting should continue in same direction—that is, forward for forward-looking periods and backward for backward-looking periods).

(b) Weekend or legal holiday.

[1] Legal holiday defined. Legal holidays are the following: (1) New Year's Day, Martin Luther King Jr.'s Birthday, Washington's Birthday, Memorial Day, Independence Day, Labor Day, Columbus Day, Veterans' Day, Thanksgiving Day, and Christmas Day, (2) any day declared a holiday by the President or Congress, and (3) for forward-looking time periods only, any other day declared a holiday by the state where the district court is located. FRCP 6(a)(6); *see, e.g.,* ***Hart v. Sheahan***, 396 F.3d 887, 891 (7th Cir.2005) (December 26 was legal holiday under executive order, so it was not counted and motion was timely); ***Prudential Oil & Minerals Co. v. Hamlin***, 261 F.2d 626, 627 (10th Cir.1958) (because federal employees were excused from work and clerk's office was locked and unattended, Utah's Pioneer Day was recognized as legal holiday).

[2] Extension for weekend or legal holiday. If the time period ends on a Saturday, Sunday, or legal holiday, it continues to run until the end of the next day that is not a Saturday, Sunday, or legal holiday. FRCP 6(a)(1)(C); 2009 Notes to FRCP 6 at ¶6, p. 1149, this book. For example, for a forward-counted deadline, if a party has 21 days to file a response and day 21 falls on Saturday, September 3, then the party's response is due on Tuesday, September 6, because of the Labor Day holiday on Monday, September 5. For a backward-counted deadline, if the plaintiff must hold the FRCP 26(f) conference at least 21 days before the scheduling conference and day 21 falls on Saturday, September 3, then the conference must be held on Friday, September 2 (and if Friday is a federal legal holiday, the conference must be held on Thursday, September 1).

NOTE

State holidays are recognized only for forward-looking time periods. FRCP 6(a)(6)(C); 2009 Notes to FRCP 6 at ¶20, p. 1151, this book. Thus, both state and federal holidays extend forward-counted deadlines. 2009 Notes to FRCP 6 at ¶20, p. 1151, this book. But for backward-counted deadlines, filing is allowed on the state holiday itself (rather than the day before). 2009 Notes to FRCP 6 at ¶20, p. 1151, this book. For example, if a filing is due 14 days ***after*** *an event and day 14 is Monday, April 21—a recognized state holiday in the relevant state—then the filing is due on Tuesday, April 22, because Monday, April 21, counts as a legal holiday. Id. But if the filing is due 14 days* ***before*** *the event and day 14 is Monday, April 21, then the filing is due on Monday, April 21 (not Friday, April 18); the fact that April 21 is a state holiday does not make it a legal holiday for purposes of computing this backward-counted deadline. Id.*

(c) Clerk's office inaccessible.

[1] Inaccessibility defined. FRCP 6(a)(3) does not define inaccessibility. FRCP 6(a) no longer refers to "weather or other conditions" as the reason for the inaccessibility of the clerk's office. 2009 Notes to FRCP 6 at ¶15, p. 1150, this book; *see* FRCP 6(a)(3).

[a] Weather. Weather can be a reason for inaccessibility. 2009 Notes to FRCP 6 at ¶15, p. 1150, this book; *e.g.*, ***Telephone & Data Sys. v. Amcell F Atl. City, Inc.***, 20 F.3d 501, 501-02 (D.C.Cir.1994) (clerk's office was closed because of bad weather; 24-hour drop box did not make court accessible); *see also* ***U.S. Leather, Inc. v. H&W Prtshp.***, 60 F.3d 222, 225-26 (5th Cir.1995) (even if clerk's office is open, office may be inaccessible; office was inaccessible because of ice storm that temporarily knocked out area's power and telephone service and made traveling dangerous, difficult, or impossible). The exception for weather may also include days when the weather in the area around the courthouse prevents access to the attorney's office or computer files. ***U.S. Leather***, 60 F.3d at 226.

[b] Other issues. Issues besides weather (e.g., an outage of an electronic-filing system) can be a reason for inaccessibility. 2009 Notes to FRCP 6 at ¶15, p. 1150, this book; *see* ***Justice v. Town of Cicero***, 682 F.3d 662, 664 (7th Cir.2012); *see, e.g.*, Local Rules Kan., Rule 5.4.11 (party whose filing is untimely because of technical failure may seek appropriate relief from court).

[2] Extension for inaccessibility. If the clerk's office is inaccessible on the last day for filing, the time period is extended to the first accessible day that is not a Saturday, Sunday, or legal holiday, unless the court orders otherwise. FRCP 6(a)(3)(A); *see* 2009 Notes to FRCP 6 at ¶13, p. 1150, this book. The court can specify an extension shorter than a full day. 2009 Notes to FRCP 6 at ¶14, p. 1150, this book; *see* FRCP 6(a)(3).

CAUTION

For a forward-looking time period, if, for example, a filing is due 21 days after an event and day 21 falls on Monday, but the court is inaccessible on that Monday, then the filing is due on Tuesday (as long as the court is accessible on that Tuesday). But for a backward-looking time period, counting does not continue in the same direction when the deadline falls on a day that the clerk's office is inaccessible. See FRCP 6(a)(3). For example, if a filing is due 21 days before an event and day 21 falls on Saturday, September 5, then the filing is due on Friday, September 4; however, if the clerk's office is inaccessible on September 4, then FRCP 6(a)(3) extends the filing deadline ***forward*** *(the opposite direction) to the next accessible day that is not a Saturday, Sunday or legal holiday—Tuesday, September 8 (because Monday, September 7, is Labor Day). 2009 Notes to FRCP 6 at ¶18, p. 1150, this book; see id. at ¶20, p. 1151, this book.*

2. Longer periods – months & years.

(1) Identify trigger event. A deadline based on months or years starts to run on either the day before or the day after the trigger event. *See* FRCP 6(a)(1)(A); 2009 Notes to FRCP 6 at ¶4, p. 1149, this book. See "Identify trigger event," §6.1.1(1), p. 24.

(2) Count units.

(a) Months. Count the months either forward or backward, depending on the type of time period. A month means a calendar month; for example, one month from February 1 is March 1, regardless of the number of days in February. *See* ***Yedwab v. U.S.***, 489 F.Supp. 717, 719 (D.N.J.1980). The directive to "count every day" does not apply to periods in months. 2009 Notes to FRCP 6 at ¶4, p. 1149, this book.

(b) Years. Count the years either forward or backward, depending on the type of time period. A year means a calendar year; for example, one year from January 1, 2008, is January 1, 2009, regardless of the fact that 2008 is a leap year. *See* ***Gammons v. Domestic Loans of Winston-Salem, Inc.***, 423 F.Supp. 819, 822 (M.D. N.C.1976). The directive to "count every day" does not apply to periods in years. 2009 Notes to FRCP 6 at ¶4, p. 1149, this book.

CAUTION

Amended FRCP 6(a)(1) specifically states that for time periods in days or "a longer unit"—that is, months or years—the day of the event that triggers the time period is excluded. FRCP 6(a)(1)(A); 2009 Notes to FRCP 6 at ¶4, p. 1149, this book. For example, if an FRCP 60(b)(1) motion is due one year after judgment and judgment is entered on Wednesday, September 30, 2009, the motion is due no later than Friday, October 1, 2010, because Wednesday, September 30, is excluded and counting starts on Thursday, October 1. Former FRCP 6(a) did not specifically address whether the day of the trigger event was excluded for time periods stated in months or years. See, e.g., ***Merriweather v. City of Memphis****, 107 F.3d 396, 399-400 (6th Cir.1997) (for one-year limitations period, when trigger event occurred on October 19, complaint had to be filed by same calendar day of next year; complaint filed on October 20 of next year was untimely).*

(3) Determine end of time period. The last day of the time period is counted. FRCP 6(a)(1)(C). For a discussion of when the last day ends, see "Determine end of time period," §6.1.1(3), p. 24.

(4) Determine if extension applies. If a deadline based on months or years ends on a Saturday, Sunday, or legal holiday or on a day when the clerk's office is inaccessible, the time period continues until the end of the next day that the court is accessible and that is not a Saturday, Sunday, or legal holiday. *See* FRCP 6(a)(1)(C), (a)(3)(A); 2009 Notes to FRCP 6 at ¶¶6, 13, pp. 1149, 1150, this book. See "Determine if extension applies," §6.1.1(4), p. 25.

3. Hours.

(1) Identify trigger event. A deadline based on hours starts to run immediately from the trigger event. FRCP 6(a)(2)(A); 2009 Notes to FRCP 6 at ¶11, p. 1150, this book. To determine if counting begins before or after the trigger event, see "Identify trigger event," §6.1.1(1), p. 24.

(2) Count hours. Count the hours either forward or backward, depending on the type of time period. Every hour is counted, including hours during intermediate Saturdays, Sundays, and legal holidays. FRCP 6(a)(2)(B). For example, a 72-hour period that begins at 10:23 a.m. on Friday, November 2, 2007, will run until 9:23 a.m. on Monday, November 5; the one-hour discrepancy results from the intervening shift from daylight-saving time to standard time. 2009 Notes to FRCP 6 at ¶12, p. 1150, this book.

(3) Determine end of time period. A deadline based on hours generally ends when the time expires. 2009 Notes to FRCP 6 at ¶11, p. 1150, this book; *see also id.* at ¶16, p. 1150, this book (FRCP 6(a)(4), which

defines when last day ends, does not apply to time periods stated in hours). Periods stated in hours are not rounded up to the next whole hour. 2009 Notes to FRCP 6 at ¶11, p. 1150, this book.

(4) Determine if extension applies. If a deadline based on hours ends on a Saturday, Sunday, or legal holiday or on a day when the clerk's office is inaccessible, the time period continues until the same time on the next day that the court is accessible and that is not a Saturday, Sunday, or legal holiday. *See* FRCP 6(a)(2)(C), (a)(3)(B); 2009 Notes to FRCP 6 at ¶¶11, 13, p. 1150, this book.

(a) Next day. Determining the "next day" for deadlines based on hours is the same as that for deadlines based on days. See "Next day," §6.1.1(4)(a), p. 25.

(b) Weekend or legal holiday. If a deadline based on hours ends on a Saturday, Sunday, or legal holiday, the time period continues to run until the same time on the next day that is not a Saturday, Sunday, or legal holiday. FRCP 6(a)(2)(C); 2009 Notes to FRCP 6 at ¶11, p. 1150, this book. For example, if the time period ends at a specific time (e.g., 12:20 p.m.) on a Saturday, Sunday, or legal holiday, then the deadline is extended to the same time (12:20 p.m.) on the next day that is not a Saturday, Sunday, or legal holiday. 2009 Notes to FRCP 6 at ¶11, p. 1150, this book. Determining an extension because of a Saturday, Sunday, or legal holiday is generally the same as that for deadlines based on days. See "Weekend or legal holiday," §6.1.1(4)(b), p. 25.

(c) Clerk's office inaccessible. If the clerk's office is inaccessible during the last hour of the filing period, the deadline is extended to the same time on the first accessible day that is not a Saturday, Sunday, or legal holiday, unless the court orders otherwise. FRCP 6(a)(3)(B); 2009 Notes to FRCP 6 at ¶13, p. 1150, this book. If the court does not want to allow a full 24-hour extension, the court can specify a shorter time. 2009 Notes to FRCP 6 at ¶14, p. 1150, this book. Determining an extension because of inaccessibility is generally the same as that for deadlines based on days. See "Clerk's office inaccessible," §6.1.1(4)(c), p. 26.

§6.2 Requesting more time. If a party needs more time to file a document, the party should ask for the extra time as soon as it becomes apparent that more time is necessary.

1. Motion to extend time. A motion to extend time is a request to extend the deadline for a party to act. FRCP 6(b) governs motions to extend time to do some act that the rules or the courts require to be done within a specified time. See "Motion to Extend Time," ch. 5-F, p. 332.

2. Agreement to extend time. The parties cannot agree to extend time without court approval. See "Agreed motion to extend time," ch. 5-F, §4.1, p. 333. However, the parties can agree to extend the time to respond to discovery if the extension does not interfere with the time set for completing discovery, for hearing a motion, or for trial. See "Agreement," ch. 6-A, §8.1.2(1), p. 422.

3. Motion for continuance. A motion for continuance is a request to postpone or delay either a case that is set for trial or a hearing on a dispositive motion. No specific rule governs motions for continuance. See "Motion for Continuance," ch. 5-G, p. 337.

§7. FILED DOCUMENTS

§7.1 No refusal to accept. The clerk cannot refuse to accept a filed document solely because it is not presented in proper form as required by the FRCPs or the local rules. FRCP 5(d)(4); ***Hooker v. Sivley***, 187 F.3d 680, 682 (5th Cir.1999); *see, e.g.*, ***GBJ, Ltd. v. Redman***, 521 F.Supp.2d 1000, 1001-02 (D.Ariz.2007) (notice of removal constructively delivered to clerk; clerk cannot refuse notice when not filed by electronic means as required by local rule); *see also* ***Farzana K. v. Indiana Dept. of Educ.***, 473 F.3d 703, 708 (7th Cir.2007) (e-filing systems must accept every document tendered for filing that clerk must accept). The effect of FRCP 5(d)(4) is that a limitations period will not expire because a clerk refuses to accept a filed document due to a defect in form. *See, e.g.*, ***U.S. v. Harvey***, 516 F.3d 553, 556 (7th Cir.2008) (notice of appeal that was filed electronically was timely even though local rules required hard copy; difference between hard copy and electronic copy is mere error of form); ***Cintron v. Union Pac. R.R.***, 813 F.2d 917, 920 (9th Cir.1987) (pleading presented for filing without punched holes and cover sheet should not have

been dismissed as untimely). *But see* ***Air Line Pilots Ass'n v. Precision Valley Aviation, Inc.***, 26 F.3d 220, 227 n.7 (1st Cir.1994) (clerk's refusal to accept motion that did not comply with local rules was supported by court's order; thus, it was as if motion had been filed and then struck).

§7.2 Notation by clerk. The clerk must endorse each document with the clerk's official name and the date and time the document was presented. If the document was filed with the judge, the judge must note the date it was presented and forward it to the clerk. FRCP 5(d)(2)(B).

§7.3 Deemed filed. A document is deemed filed when it is placed in the clerk's possession. ***Rodriguez-Roman v. INS***, 98 F.3d 416, 423 (9th Cir.1996); ***In re Toler***, 999 F.2d 140, 142 (6th Cir.1993). A document is also deemed filed when the judge accepts it. *See* 4B Wright & Miller §1153.

§7.4 Withdrawing documents. No rule specifically governs the withdrawal of filed documents. However, the rules that address withdrawal in other contexts suggest that it can be done only by motion. *See* FRCP 36(b) (withdrawing admissions by motion), FRCP 38(d) (withdrawal of demand for jury trial on consent of parties). Voluntary dismissal of actions, as opposed to withdrawal of documents, is governed by FRCP 41(a). See "Voluntary Dismissal," ch. 7-C, p. 629.

§7.5 Lost documents. The procedure governing lost or destroyed court records is described in 28 U.S.C. §1734. *See also* 28 U.S.C. §1735 (lost or destroyed record when U.S. is a party). If a party is not to blame for the lost document, the party can apply to substitute a certified copy for the original. 28 U.S.C. §1734(a); *see* ***SEC v. Worthen***, 98 F.3d 480, 483 (9th Cir.1996). If a certified copy is not available, any interested person who is not at fault may file a verified application for an order establishing the lost or destroyed record. 28 U.S.C. §1734(b). Other interested persons will then be served with a copy of the application and with a notice of hearing. *Id.* If the court is satisfied after the hearing that the statements contained in the application are true, it will enter an order reciting the substance and effect of the lost or destroyed record. *Id.*

§8. PROOF OF FILING

Proof that a document was properly filed should include actual evidence of the filing, affidavit testimony, or circumstantial evidence supporting filing. *See* ***Kinsley v. Lakeview Reg'l Med. Ctr. LLC***, 570 F.3d 586, 588-89 (5th Cir. 2009). Because many documents are now filed electronically, a party may prove proper filing with the Notice of Electronic Filing (NEF), which is automatically generated by the Case Management/Electronic Case Files system. *See* ECF Admin. Procedures Manual (N.D.Tex.), ¶II.B; *cf.* ***American Boat Co. v. Unknown Sunken Barge***, 567 F.3d 348, 353 (8th Cir.2009) (for service of order denying motion to amend judgment, D did not rebut presumption of delivery and receipt of NEF). See "When filed," §4.4.3, p. 21.

D. SERVING DOCUMENTS

§1. GENERAL

§1.1 Rule. FRCP 5(a)-(c).

§1.2 Purpose. The purpose of serving a document is to provide the other party with a copy of the document filed in the court. Serving documents should not be confused with filing documents. Documents are *served* on other parties in the case; documents are *filed* with the clerk. The rules for serving and filing are different. Two federal rules deal with the service of documents: FRCP 4, which deals exclusively with the service of the complaint, and FRCP 5, which deals exclusively with the service of other documents. This subchapter does not discuss the service of the complaint, which is covered in "Serving the Defendant with Process," ch. 2-H, p. 149.

§1.3 Forms. ***O'Connor's Federal Civil Forms*** (2012), FORMS 1D.

§1.4 Other references. 4B Wright & Miller, *Federal Practice & Procedure 3d* §§1141-1151 (2002 & Supp.2012); 1 *Moore's Federal Practice 3d* chs. 5, 6 (2012).

§2. WHAT TO SERVE

§2.1 Most documents. A party must serve on every party all of the following: (1) orders stating that service is required, (2) pleadings filed after the complaint, (3) papers relating to discovery, (4) written motions, and (5) written notices, appearances, demands, offers of judgment, or similar papers. FRCP 5(a)(1).

§2.2 Documents not required to be served.

1. Ex parte motion. It is not necessary to serve an ex parte motion on the opposing party. ***Welch v. Folsom***, 925 F.2d 666, 669 (3d Cir.1991).

2. To defaulting party. It is not necessary to serve copies of documents (after the initial complaint) on a party in default for failure to appear. But if a pleading asserts a new or additional claim for relief against the defaulting party, it must be served on that party in the manner provided in FRCP 4 for service of summons. FRCP 5(a)(2).

3. Notice of appeal. It is not necessary to serve a notice of appeal on the other parties. The court clerk is required to serve the notice on the other parties. FRAP 3(d). Most attorneys, however, send a copy of the notice to the other parties when they file it in the court.

§3. WHOM TO SERVE

§3.1 Party or attorney? If a party is represented by an attorney, all documents must be served on the attorney, unless the court orders otherwise. FRCP 5(b)(1); ***Avolio v. County of Suffolk***, 29 F.3d 50, 53 (2d Cir.1994). Only when a party is not represented should documents be served on the party. *See* FRCP 5(b)(1).

§3.2 Which attorney? If a party is represented by more than one attorney, local rules usually require that documents be served on the attorney in charge—generally the attorney who signed the first pleading. *E.g.*, Local Rules Tex. (S.D.), Rule 83.3. If there is no local rule designating an attorney in charge, documents should be served on all attorneys of record.

§3.3 How many parties? If there are multiple parties in the suit, a copy of each document should be sent to each party in the lawsuit who is not in default, unless the court orders otherwise. FRCP 5(a)(1), (a)(2). When there is an unusually large number of defendants, the court—on motion or on its own—may dispense with the requirement that the defendants' pleadings and the replies to those pleadings be served on all the defendants. FRCP 5(c)(1)(A). If the court does so, the filing and service of the defendants' pleadings on the plaintiff would constitute notice to the other parties. FRCP 5(c)(1)(C).

§4. HOW TO SERVE

§4.1 Methods of service. FRCP 5(b)(2) provides several ways to serve documents. Parties have discretion to determine which method of service to use. *See* ***Wolters Kluwer Fin. Servs. v. Scivantage***, 564 F.3d 110, 116 (2d Cir.2009).

1. Mail. A party can serve documents by mail. FRCP 5(b)(2)(C). To serve by mail, the party sends the document to the attorney's or party's last known address through the U.S. Postal Service. *Id.* Service by mail is complete upon mailing. *Id.*; ***Theede v. U.S. Dept. of Labor***, 172 F.3d 1262, 1266 (10th Cir.1999); ***Greene v. WCI Holdings Corp.***, 136 F.3d 313, 315 (2d Cir.1998); ***Russell v. Delco Remy Div. of Gen. Motors Corp.***, 51 F.3d 746, 750 (7th Cir.1995); ***Havinga v. Crowley Towing & Transp.***, 24 F.3d 1480, 1490 (1st Cir.1994); ***Vincent v. Consolidated Oper. Co.***, 17 F.3d 782, 785 n.9 (5th Cir.1994). The time of delivery is irrelevant when a document is served by mail. ***Kim v. Commandant, Def. Language Inst.***, 772 F.2d 521, 524 (9th Cir.1985). Local rules determine whether a party is required to serve documents by certified, registered, or first-class mail. Pro se prisoners can serve papers simply by depositing them with prison authorities for mailing, unless a specific statutory or regulatory scheme has different service requirements. ***Longenette v. Krusing***, 322 F.3d 758, 761-63 (3d Cir.2003).

(1) What constitutes mail. Service through the U.S. Postal Service is considered mailing. ***Prince v. Poulos***, 876 F.2d 30, 32 n.1 (5th Cir.1989). Courts have held that service by private courier (e.g., FedEx, UPS) does

not constitute service by mail for purposes of FRCP 5. *E.g.*, ***Magnuson v. Video Yesteryear***, 85 F.3d 1424, 1430-31 (9th Cir.1996) (delivery to FedEx did not satisfy requirements of FRCP 5(b)); ***Audio Enters. v. B&W Loudspeakers***, 957 F.2d 406, 409 (7th Cir.1992) (same); ***Prince***, 876 F.2d at 32 n.1 (same); *see* 4B Wright & Miller §1148. *But see* ***U.S. v. 63-29 Trimble Rd.***, 812 F.Supp. 332, 334 (E.D.N.Y.1992) (service by FedEx permitted under FRCP 5). See "Other means," §4.1.6, p. 32.

(2) Date of mailing. The date of mailing is the date the envelope is deposited at a post office or placed in a mailbox. ***Theede***, 172 F.3d at 1266; ***Greene***, 136 F.3d at 315; ***U.S. v. Kennedy***, 133 F.3d 53, 59 (D.C.Cir. 1998); ***Larez v. Holcomb***, 16 F.3d 1513, 1515 n.1 (9th Cir.1994). The date of mailing can be determined by the postmark on the envelope. The use of certified or registered mail lends credence to the genuineness of the postmark. 4B Wright & Miller §1148. See "Proof of Service," §7, p. 36.

2. Personal delivery. A party can serve documents by personal delivery. *See* FRCP 5(b)(2)(A). To serve by personal delivery, the party must send the document to the attorney or party in one of the following ways: (1) by handing the document to the attorney or party, (2) by leaving the document with a person in charge at the office of the attorney or party, (3) if there is no one in charge at the office, by leaving the document in a conspicuous place in the office, or (4) if the office is closed or if the person to be served has no office, by leaving the document at the person's house or usual place of abode with a person of suitable age and discretion who resides there. FRCP 5(b)(2)(A), (b)(2)(B). Fax transmission is not considered a form of personal delivery for purposes of service. ***Salley v. Board of Govs.***, 136 F.R.D. 417, 419 (M.D.N.C.1991).

3. Delivery to clerk's office. A party can serve documents by leaving them with the court clerk if the person to be served has no known address. FRCP 5(b)(2)(D).

4. Fax. A party can serve documents by fax if permitted by local rule. *See* ***In re Town of Amenia***, 200 F.R.D. 200, 204 (S.D.N.Y.2001); *see, e.g.*, Local Rules Conn., Rule 5(g) (parties permitted to serve pleadings by fax if copy of pleading is simultaneously served by regular mail); Local Rules Tex. (E.D.), Rule CV-5(d) (parties permitted to serve by fax or electronic means instead of by mail). Before serving by fax, the party must obtain written consent from the attorney or party to be served. FRCP 5(b)(2)(E). See ***O'Connor's Federal Forms***, FORM 1D:3. The consent must be express; it cannot be implied from conduct. 2001 Notes to FRCP 5 at ¶4, p. 1145, this book.

(1) Form of consent. The written consent to service by fax should specify all of the following:

(a) The scope and duration of the consent. 2001 Notes to FRCP 5 at ¶6, p. 1145, this book.

(b) The persons to whom service should be made. *Id.*

(c) The appropriate location for service, such as the fax number of the person to be served. *Id.*

(2) Date of delivery. The date of delivery is the date the document was transmitted by fax—that is, the date when the sender completed the last act necessary to transmit the document. 2001 Notes to FRCP 5 at ¶4, p. 1145, this book; *see* FRCP 5(b)(2)(E). Service by fax is complete on transmission, unless the party making service learns that the attempted service did not reach the person to be served. FRCP 5(b)(2)(E); *e.g.*, Local Rules Tex. (E.D.), Rule CV-5(d). Documents served by fax after 5:00 p.m. local time may be deemed served the next day. *E.g.*, Local Rules Tex. (E.D.), Rule CV-5(d). Service by an agency, such as a fax-filing agency, is complete on delivery to the designated agency. 2001 Notes to FRCP 5 at ¶4, p. 1145, this book. *But see* Local Rules Cal. (S.D.), Rule 5.3.a.1 (fax filing complete when submitted by agency and received and filed by clerk). See "Proof of Service," §7, p. 36.

5. Electronic means. A party can serve documents by electronic means if permitted by local rule. *See, e.g.*, Local Rules N.Y. (E.D. & S.D.), Rule 5.2 (parties permitted to serve by electronic means); Local Rules Tex. (E.D.), Rule CV-5(d) (parties may serve by fax or electronic means). A party may serve electronically either through the court or directly to the attorney or party. *See* FRCP 5(b)(2)(E), (b)(3).

(1) Service through court. Local rules may allow a party to serve attorneys and parties who are registered through the Case Management/Electronic Case Files (CM/ECF) system. *See* FRCP 5(b)(3). See "How to

file – CM/ECF," ch. 1-C, §4.4.2, p. 20. Receipt of the Notice of Electronic Filing (NEF) constitutes service of the attached documents on each party who is a registered user. *E.g.*, Local Rules Tex. (E.D.), Rule CV-5(a)(3)(A); Local Rules Tex. (N.D.), Rule 5.1(d).

(a) Consent. Registration as a CM/ECF user constitutes consent to electronic service under FRCP 5(b)(3). *E.g.*, Local Rules Ariz., Rule 5.5(h); Local Rules Tex. (E.D.), Rule CV-5(a)(2)(A); Admin. Procedures Guide (W.D.N.Y.), ¶1(c)(i).

(b) Delivery date. The date of delivery is the date the attorney or party being served receives the NEF. *E.g.*, General Order No. 06-07 (C.D.Cal.), ¶III.C; *see* Local Rules Tex. (E.D.), Rule CV-5(a)(3)(C) (delivery date is the "entered on" date and time stated in the NEF). Documents electronically filed after 5:00 p.m. local time may be deemed served the next day. *E.g.*, Local Rules Tex. (E.D.), Rule CV-5(a)(3)(C).

(c) E-mail address. A document is deemed delivered if the NEF is sent to the last known e-mail address given to the court. *See, e.g.*, Local Rules Tex. (E.D.), Rule CV-5(a)(2)(A).

(2) Service directly to attorney or party. If the attorney or party to be served is not a registered user of the CM/ECF system or if the document to be served is not filed in the court, the party may still serve electronically. *See* FRCP 5(b)(2)(E); *see, e.g.*, Local Rules Ariz., Rule 5.5(h) (nonregistered user will be provided notice of filing by other means in accordance with FRCPs).

(a) Consent. Before serving electronically, the party must obtain written consent from the attorney or party to be served. FRCP 5(b)(2)(E); *see* ***Calderon v. IBEW Local 47***, 508 F.3d 883, 884 (9th Cir.2007). See ***O'Connor's Federal Forms***, FORM 1D:3. Consent must be express and cannot be implied from conduct. 2001 Notes to FRCP 5 at ¶4, p. 1145, this book. The written consent to electronic service should specify all of the following:

[1] The scope and duration of the consent. 2001 Notes to FRCP 5 at ¶6, p. 1145, this book.

[2] The persons to whom service should be made. *Id.*

[3] The appropriate address or location for service, such as the e-mail address of the person to be served. *Id.*

[4] The format to be used for attachments (e.g., HTML, Microsoft Word, Corel WordPerfect, or Adobe PDF). *Id.*

(b) Delivery date. The date of delivery is the date the document was electronically transmitted—that is, the date when the sender completed the last act necessary to transmit the document. *See* FRCP 5(b)(2)(E); 2001 Notes to FRCP 5 at ¶4, p. 1145, this book. Electronic service is complete on transmission, unless the party making service learns that the attempted service did not reach the person to be served. FRCP 5(b)(2)(E). See "Proof of Service," §7, p. 36.

(3) Not complaint & summons. A complaint and summons cannot be served electronically but instead must be served according to FRCP 4. *E.g.*, Admin. Procedures for Elec. Filing in Civil & Crim. Cases (M.D.Fla.), ¶II.B.1; *see, e.g.*, CM/ECF Admin. Procedures for Filing, Signing, & Verifying Documents by Elec. Means (M.D.Ga.), ¶Civil Summonses.

6. Other means. A party can serve documents by other means, including FedEx or UPS. *See* FRCP 5(b)(2)(F); 2001 Notes to FRCP 5 at ¶4, p. 1145, this book. To serve by other means, a party must obtain written consent from the attorney or party to be served. FRCP 5(b)(2)(F). See "Consent," §4.1.5(2)(a), this page. Some local rules, however, allow service by other means without written consent. *See, e.g.*, Local Rules N.Y. (E.D. & S.D.), Rule 5.3 (overnight delivery service is deemed service by mail for purposes of FRCP 5; overnight delivery service allowed without consent). Service by other means is complete when the document is delivered to the agency designated to make delivery. FRCP 5(b)(2)(F).

§4.2 Certificate of service.

1. Generally. After the complaint, all documents served on the other party must contain a certificate of service when presented for filing. FRCP 5(d)(1). Local rules may impose additional requirements for certificates of service. *E.g.*, Local Rules Cal. (C.D.), Rule 5-3 (proof-of-service requirements). Parties using private delivery services may not know the exact date of delivery. In such cases, specifying the date of transmittal to the delivery service may be sufficient. 1991 Notes to FRCP 5 at ¶2, p. 1147, this book.

2. Electronic means. A certificate of service is required even when a party serves a document electronically. *E.g.*, ECF Admin. Procedures Manual (N.D.Tex.), ¶II.B. However, some courts do not require a certificate of service when all parties are registered CM/ECF users. *See, e.g.*, CM/ECF Admin. Procedures Manual (D.Utah), ¶II.H.4.

§5. WHEN TO SERVE

§5.1 Deadline – filing, service, or both? When filing motions, pleadings, and other documents, it is important to determine whether a party must serve the document on the other party by the deadline, file it in the court by the deadline, or both serve and file it by the deadline. To determine whether to file, serve, or both, see "Deadline – filing or service?," ch. 1-C, §5.1, p. 22. To determine how to compute a deadline to file or serve a motion, pleading, or other document, see "Computing Deadlines," ch. 1-C, §6, p. 23. And to determine how to compute a deadline to file or serve a response to a motion, pleading, or other document, see "Computing Response Deadlines," §6, this page.

§5.2 Serving motions for hearing. Motions and notices of hearing must be served at least 14 days before the time specified for the hearing, unless the motion may be heard ex parte or unless the FRCPs or the court sets a different time. FRCP 6(c)(1). For a discussion of how to compute backward-counted deadlines, see "Computing Deadlines," ch. 1-C, §6, p. 23.

§5.3 Serving affidavits with motion. Affidavits must be served with the motions they support. FRCP 6(c)(2); *see, e.g.*, FRCP 59(c) (motion for new trial). This prevents the movant from adding new facts when it is too late for the nonmovant to contest them. ***Peters v. Lincoln Elec. Co.***, 285 F.3d 456, 476 (6th Cir.2002). Unless the court orders otherwise, opposing affidavits must be served at least seven days before the hearing. FRCP 6(c)(2). For a discussion of how to compute backward-counted deadlines, see "Computing Deadlines," ch. 1-C, §6, p. 23.

§6. COMPUTING RESPONSE DEADLINES

A party should serve a response to a motion or discovery request within the deadlines established by the FRCPs, the local rules, or the court's scheduling order. If a motion or discovery request requires a response, the responding party must complete the following steps.

NOTE

The rules for computing response deadlines are generally the same as the rules for computing filing deadlines. See "Computing Deadlines," ch. 1-C, §6, p. 23.

---

§6.1 Determine when to begin counting. The responding party must compute the response date from the date of service—that is, the trigger event. *See* FRCP 6(a)(1)(A). See "Identify trigger event," ch. 1-C, §6.1.1(1), p. 24. The date that the motion or discovery request was served depends on the method of service.

1. Mail. When a party is served by mail, the party is considered served on the date the document was mailed (generally, the postmark date). *See* FRCP 5(b)(2)(C); ***Greene v. WCI Holdings Corp.***, 136 F.3d 313, 315 (2d Cir.1998). The date the document was mailed is counted as "day 0" and the first day after as "day 1." *See* FRCP 6(a)(1)(A).

2. Personal delivery. When a party is served by personal delivery, the party is considered served on the date of delivery. *See* FRCP 5(b)(2)(A), (b)(2)(B); ***Lerro v. Quaker Oats Co.***, 84 F.3d 239, 242 (7th Cir.1996). The date the document was delivered is counted as "day 0" and the first day after as "day 1." *See* FRCP 6(a)(1)(A).

3. Clerk's office. When a party with no known address is served by leaving a copy of the document with the clerk's office, the party is considered served on the date the document was left with the clerk. *See* FRCP 5(b)(2)(D). The date the document was left with the clerk is counted as "day 0" and the first day after as "day 1." *See* FRCP 6(a)(1)(A).

4. Fax. When a party is served by fax, the party is considered served on the date the sender completed the last act necessary to transmit the document. FRCP 5(b)(2)(E); 2001 Notes to FRCP 5 at ¶4, p. 1145, this book. The date the document was transmitted is counted as "day 0" and the first day after as "day 1." *See* FRCP 6(a)(1)(A).

5. Electronic means. When a party is served by electronic means (e.g., e-mail), the party is considered served on the date the sender completed the last act necessary to transmit the document. FRCP 5(b)(2)(E); 2001 Notes to FRCP 5 at ¶4, p. 1145, this book. The date the document was transmitted is counted as "day 0" and the first day after as "day 1." *See* FRCP 6(a)(1)(A).

6. Other means. When a party is served by other means—such as by FedEx or UPS—the party is considered served on the date the sender deposited the document with the agency designated for service. FRCP 5(b)(2)(F). The date the document was left with the agency is counted as "day 0" and the first day after as "day 1." *See* FRCP 6(a)(1)(A).

§6.2 Count time units. The responding party must count the intervening time units (e.g., days, months, years). *See* FRCP 6(a)(1)(B). See "Count days," ch. 1-C, §6.1.1(2), p. 24.

NOTE

Most response periods are stated in days. See, e.g., FRCP 34(b)(2)(A) (response to request for production is due 30 days after service of request). But a few response periods may be stated in months or years. See "Calculating time periods," ch. 1-C, §6.1, p. 23.

§6.3 Determine end of time period. The responding party must determine the end of the time period. *See* FRCP 6(a)(1)(C). Generally, for service by electronic means, the document should be served by midnight in that district's time zone, and for service by personal delivery or other means, the document should be served by the end of the business day. *Cf.* FRCP 6(a)(4) (deadline for filing by electronic means is midnight in court's time zone and by other means is when clerk's office is scheduled to close). But some local rules may deem service to be on the following day if the response is served after business hours. *See, e.g.*, Local Rules Tex. (E.D.), Rule CV-5(d) (for service by fax or electronic means, service after 5:00 p.m. Central Time is deemed to be served on next day).

§6.4 Determine if weekend or holiday extension applies. The responding party must determine if a weekend or legal holiday extends the deadline. If the time period ends on a Saturday, Sunday, or legal holiday, it continues to run until the end of the next day that is not a Saturday, Sunday, or legal holiday. FRCP 6(a)(1)(C). See "Determine if extension applies," ch. 1-C, §6.1.1(4), p. 25.

§6.5 Determine if additional three-day extension applies. The responding party must determine if an additional three-day extension applies.

1. Additional three days. After most methods of service, three days are added to the response period that would have otherwise expired under FRCP 6(a). FRCP 6(d).

(1) Extension applies. If a party was served by mail, through the clerk's office, by fax, by electronic means, or by any other means except for personal delivery, the responding party can add three days to the deadline to respond. FRCP 6(d); *see* ***CNPq-Conselho Nacional de Desenvolvimento Cientifico e Technologico v. Inter-Trade, Inc.***, 50 F.3d 56, 57 (D.C.Cir.1995). Intermediate Saturdays, Sundays, and legal holidays are counted in the

three days, and if the third day falls on a Saturday, Sunday, or legal holiday, the time period continues to run until the next day that is not a Saturday, Sunday, or legal holiday. 2005 Notes to FRCP 6 at ¶1, p. 1151, this book; *see* FRCP 6(a)(1)(B); 2009 Notes to FRCP 6 at ¶6, p. 1149, this book. This extension applies only to time periods triggered by service, not filing. FRCP 6(d); *see* Local Rules Tex. (E.D.), Rule CV-6(a); *see, e.g.*, ***Sea-Land Serv. v. Barry***, 41 F.3d 903, 908 (3d Cir.1994) (under statute that required action ten days after filing, FRCP 6(e), now FRCP 6(d), did not apply because action was not triggered by service).

EXAMPLE

Assume a party mails interrogatories to you on Thursday, March 26, 2009. Under FRCP 33(b)(2), the deadline to serve a response is 30 days, or Saturday, April 25. Because the deadline falls on a Saturday, it is extended until the next day that is not a Saturday, Sunday, or legal holiday, which is Monday, April 27. See FRCP 6(a)(1)(C). See "Determine if extension applies," ch. 1-C, §6.1.1(4), p. 25. FRCP 6(d) then adds three more days to respond—Tuesday, Wednesday, and Thursday. See 2005 Notes to FRCP 6 at ¶1, p. 1151, this book; 4B Wright & Miller §1171 & n.26.1. Thus, the deadline to serve a response is Thursday, April 30—35 days after the interrogatories were mailed. Or assume a party mails interrogatories to you on Tuesday, March 31, 2009. The 30-day deadline is Thursday, April 30. FRCP 6(d) adds three more days to respond—Friday, Saturday, and Sunday. Because the deadline falls on a Sunday, it is extended until the next day that is not a Saturday, Sunday, or legal holiday. Thus, the deadline to serve a response is Monday, May 4—34 days after the interrogatories were mailed.

(2) Extension does not apply.

(a) Personal delivery. The extension does not apply when a party is served by personal delivery. *See* FRCP 6(d).

CAUTION

It is unclear whether the three-day extension applies when service is by both personal delivery and another method (e.g., if interrogatories are served by personal delivery via courier and by fax). To avoid this issue, some local rules add the three days regardless of the method of service. E.g., Local Rules Tex. (E.D.), Rule CV-6(a).

(b) Service by party. The extension does not apply when the triggered deadline is for the party who is serving the document; that is, the extension does not apply to service *by* that party, only to service *on* that party. *E.g.*, ***Lewis v. School Dist. #70***, 523 F.3d 730, 739 (7th Cir.2008) (Ds served notice of removal electronically, which gave them five days to then file their answer; because service was *by* Ds—not *on* Ds—three-day extension did not apply to deadline for their answer).

(c) Act or event other than service. The extension does not apply to acts or events other than service of papers listed in FRCP 5(a)(1) that trigger a time period; therefore, the extension does not apply to time periods triggered from the entry of judgment or the filing of a notice of appeal or notice of removal. ***Palmyra Park Hosp., Inc. v. Phoebe Putney Mem'l Hosp., Inc.***, 688 F.Supp.2d 1356, 1360 (M.D.Ga.2010).

2. Motion to extend. FRCP 6(d) presumes that the document was received within three days after being served. If there is an unusual delay, the recipient should file a motion to extend time before the response is due, stating that it did not receive the document within three days and that it needs more time to respond. See "Motion to Extend Time," ch. 5-F, p. 332.

1-2. COMPUTING DEADLINES TO RESPOND

	Method of service	Deadline to respond[1]
1	Mail	Date of mailing (generally, the postmark) + time to respond + 3 days
2	Personal delivery	Date of receipt + time to respond
3	Clerk's office	Date left with clerk + time to respond + 3 days
4	Fax	Date of transmission + time to respond + 3 days
5	Electronic means	Date of transmission + time to respond + 3 days
6	FedEx, UPS, or other delivery	Date left with delivery service + time to respond + 3 days

1. For purposes of counting days, the date the document was served is counted as "day 0" and the next day as "day 1." This chart does not take into account Saturdays, Sundays, or legal holidays that may extend the deadline to respond.

§7. PROOF OF SERVICE

Proof that a document was properly sent creates a presumption that it was received by the addressee. ***Davis v. U.S. Postal Serv.***, 142 F.3d 1334, 1340 (10th Cir.1998); ***Beck v. Somerset Techs.***, 882 F.2d 993, 996 (5th Cir.1989); *see, e.g.*, ***American Boat Co. v. Unknown Sunken Barge***, 418 F.3d 910, 914 (8th Cir.2005) (presumption of delivery applied to order served by e-mail through court's Case Management/Electronic Case Files system). But this presumption of receipt can be rebutted. *See, e.g.*, ***Witt v. Roadway Express***, 136 F.3d 1424, 1429-30 (10th Cir.1998) (presumption rebutted by affidavit).

§7.1 Proving receipt.

1. Service by mail. When proving service by mail by relying on one of the cards or slips provided by the U.S. Postal Service, the card or slip should be attached to an affidavit verifying its contents.

(1) Affidavit. To prove service by mail, a party can introduce an affidavit stating (1) a description of the item, (2) that the item was properly addressed to the last known address of the recipient, (3) that the item had sufficient postage, and (4) the date the item was deposited in the mail. *See* ***Davis v. U.S. Postal Serv.***, 142 F.3d 1334, 1340 (10th Cir.1998); ***Konst v. Florida E. Coast Ry.***, 71 F.3d 850, 851 (11th Cir.1996); ***Bowers v. E.J. Rose Mfg.***, 149 F.2d 612, 613-14 (9th Cir.1945); *see, e.g.*, ***Rifkin v. U.S. Lines***, 24 F.R.D. 122, 122-23 (S.D.N.Y.1959) (proper service established by three affidavits: first stated document was served on opposing counsel, second stated counsel acknowledged receipt of document, and third stated document was served by mailing it to opposing counsel at last known address); *see also* ***Hagner v. U.S.***, 285 U.S. 427, 430 (1932) (proof that letter was deposited in post office creates presumption it was received by addressee). When relying on office routine or custom to support an inference that the document was mailed, the affidavit should describe the customary mailing practices in the attorney's office suggesting that the letter had sufficient postage and was mailed to the proper address. ***Davis***, 142 F.3d at 1340; *see* ***Wells Fargo Bus. Credit v. Ben Kozloff, Inc.***, 695 F.2d 940, 944 (5th Cir.1983).

(2) Return receipt – green card. To prove service by mail, a party can introduce a domestic return receipt—the "green card"—which establishes the date of delivery and to whom the mail was delivered. USPS Form 3811. To obtain return-receipt service, the party must send the document by certified mail—the "green and white slip"—which provides the party with a mailing receipt. USPS Form 3800. Although certified mail can be placed in a post-office mail drop, it is best to present the document to a U.S. Postal Service employee and have a date stamp applied to the "white slip" to show the date the article was accepted. *See id.* (on portion of slip retained by sender, date stamp should be made in area marked "postmark here"). The green card is returned to the party by mail after the item was received by the recipient. However, if the party does not receive the green card, there is no presumption that the item was received. ***Moya v. U.S.***, 35 F.3d 501, 504 (10th Cir.1994).

PRACTICE TIP

When sending documents through the U.S. Postal Service, make sure to use the most current postal forms.

(3) Return receipt after mailing. To prove service by mail if the green card was lost or not returned, a party can introduce a delivery confirmation receipt, which establishes the date of delivery and to whom the mail was delivered based on the post office's records. *See* USPS Form 152.

(4) Certificate of mailing – white slip. To prove service by mail, a party can introduce a U.S. Postal Service certificate of mailing (the white slip). The certificate of mailing only provides evidence that a document was presented to the U.S. Postal Service for mailing; it does not provide a record of delivery. USPS Form 3817.

2. Service by personal delivery. To prove service by personal delivery, a party should introduce the signed receipt that proves the document was delivered. Some courts require a declaration of the person who accomplished the service, including (1) the date and manner of service, (2) each person or entity served, (3) the title of each document served, and (4) the method of service employed. *E.g.*, Local Rules Cal. (C.D.), Rule 5-3.2.

3. Service by fax. To prove service by fax, a party should introduce the following documents:

(1) A copy of the written consent authorizing fax service, from the person to whom service was directed. See "Fax," §4.1.4, p. 31.

(2) An affidavit from the person attempting service, stating she had no actual knowledge that the attempted service did not reach the person to be served. *See* FRCP 5(b)(2)(E); 2001 Notes to FRCP 5 at ¶8, p. 1146, this book.

(3) A copy of the transmission confirmation statement. A transmission confirmation statement usually includes the fax number of the person to be served, the date sent, the number of pages sent, and whether the transmission was successful. Fax machines can print out transmission confirmation statements after the document has been faxed.

4. Service by electronic means. To prove service by electronic means, such as e-mail or the court's Case Management/Electronic Case Files (CM/ECF) system, a party should introduce the following documents:

(1) A copy of the written consent authorizing electronic service, from the person to whom service was directed. See "Electronic means," §4.1.5, p. 31.

(2) An affidavit from the person attempting service, stating she had no actual knowledge that the attempted service did not reach the person to be served. *See* FRCP 5(b)(2)(E); 2001 Notes to FRCP 5 at ¶8, p. 1146, this book.

(3) A copy of the transmission confirmation statement or CM/ECF's NEF. A transmission confirmation statement usually includes the e-mail address of the person to be served, the date sent, and whether the transmission was successful. Most e-mail programs have an option that allows for the creation of a delivery receipt after transmission. The NEF is automatically generated when a party files electronically; the NEF includes the date and time of filing and the registered users to whom notice was sent. *See* ***Robinson v. Wix Filtration Corp.***, 599 F.3d 403, 406 n.1 (4th Cir.2010); *see, e.g.*, Local Rules Tex. (E.D.), Rule CV-5(a)(3)(B); Local Rules Tex. (N.D.), Rule 5.1(d).

§7.2 Proving nonreceipt. To rebut a presumption of receipt of a document, a party should present specific evidence of nonreceipt. *See, e.g.*, ***Barrs v. Lockheed Martin Corp.***, 287 F.3d 202, 210-11 (1st Cir.2002) (D provided witness who testified that postcard had not been received); *see also* ***FDIC v. Schaffer***, 731 F.2d 1134, 1137 (4th Cir.1984) (when service by certified mail, evidence must be clear and convincing); *cf.* ***Nunley v. City of L.A.***, 52 F.3d 792, 796 (9th Cir.1995) (presumption of receipt under FRAP 4(a)(6) can be rebutted by specific factual denial of receipt). A party should provide evidence (1) describing the party's procedures for receiving, sorting, and distributing documents, (2) showing that the procedures were followed at the relevant time, and (3) showing that the party conducted

a thorough search for the document in the relevant locations as if it had been received. ***Schikore v. BankAmerica Supplemental Ret. Plan***, 269 F.3d 956, 964 (9th Cir.2001); *see* ***Barrs***, 287 F.3d at 211 n.10; ***Huizar v. Carey***, 273 F.3d 1220, 1223 n.3 (9th Cir.2001). The denial of receipt of a document does not rebut the presumption but creates a fact issue. ***Rosenthal v. Walker***, 111 U.S. 185, 193-94 (1884); ***Witt v. Roadway Express***, 136 F.3d 1424, 1430 (10th Cir. 1998); *see* ***Konst v. Florida E. Coast Ry.***, 71 F.3d 850, 851 n.1 (11th Cir.1996); *see also* ***American Boat Co. v. Unknown Sunken Barge***, 567 F.3d 348, 352-53 (8th Cir.2009) (court determined that P received CM/ECF notice when D's expert testified that CM/ECF system did not receive bounce-back message and P successfully received 13 other CM/ECF notices). When a document is served by certified mail, the presumption of receipt may be overcome when the return receipt is not returned to the sender. ***Moya v. U.S.***, 35 F.3d 501, 504 (10th Cir.1994); ***McPartlin v. Commissioner***, 653 F.2d 1185, 1191 (7th Cir.1981).

§8. SANCTIONS FOR FAILURE TO SERVE

If an attorney certifies that a document was served when it was not, the attorney may be subject to sanctions under FRCP 11, 28 U.S.C. §1927, or the inherent power of the court. See "Motion for Sanctions," ch. 5-O, p. 384.

E. HEARINGS

§1. GENERAL

§1.1 Rules. FRCP 6(c), 16, 77(b), 78.

§1.2 Purpose. A hearing serves the purpose of bringing the parties together before the court to argue and, sometimes, to present evidence. Because of burgeoning dockets, many local rules dispense with the requirement of oral hearings on motions. *See, e.g.*, Local Rules Fla. (S.D.), Rule 7.1(b)(1); Local Rules Miss. (N.D. & S.D.), Rule 7(b)(6)(A); *see also* ***Bath Junkie Branson, L.L.C. v. Bath Junkie, Inc.***, 528 F.3d 556, 560 (8th Cir.2008) (courts have considerable discretion in deciding whether to hold a hearing). A "hearing" can therefore mean either the court's consideration of a matter on written submission or an oral hearing for presentation of argument, evidence, or both.

§1.3 Forms. *O'Connor's Federal Civil Forms* (2012), FORMS 1E.

§1.4 Other references. 12 Wright, Miller & Marcus, *Federal Practice & Procedure 2d* §§3082, 3091 (1997 & Supp.2012); 14 *Moore's Federal Practice 3d* §77.04 & ch. 78 (2012).

§2. NOTICE OF HEARING

§2.1 Generally. District courts usually adopt their own rules governing the disposition of motions. *See* FRCP 78; *see, e.g.*, Local Rules Fla. (S.D.), Rule 7.1(b); Local Rules Miss. (N.D. & S.D.), Rule 7(b)(6); *see also* FRCP 83 (rules adopted by district courts). If a rule requires a hearing or if the court determines that a hearing is necessary, then notice of the hearing is required.

§2.2 Deadline. Unless otherwise required by a specific rule or court order, the party that schedules a hearing must serve the written motion, any supporting affidavits, and notice of the hearing on all parties at least 14 days before the hearing. FRCP 6(c). For a discussion of how to compute backward-counted deadlines, see "Computing Deadlines," ch. 1-C, §6, p. 23. The notice requirement can be set aside when the adverse party has sufficient actual knowledge of the hearing. ***Anderson v. Davila***, 125 F.3d 148, 157 (3d Cir.1997). The court may shorten the time for providing notice if a hearing needs to be expedited. FRCP 6(c)(1)(C); *see* ***Anderson***, 125 F.3d at 156-57 (court can shorten notice period when circumstances warrant expedited hearing, but this should be done sparingly); *see, e.g.*, FRCP 57 (court can order speedy hearing of application for declaratory judgment).

§3. HEARING ON MOTION

§3.1 Request for hearing. If a party wants the court to hold an oral hearing on a motion, it should make a timely request and convince the court that a hearing is necessary. *See* ***General Contracting & Trading Co. v. Interpole, Inc.***, 899 F.2d 109, 115 (1st Cir.1990) (hearing for evidence); *see, e.g.*, ***Bath Junkie Branson, L.L.C. v. Bath Junkie,***

Inc., 528 F.3d 556, 560-61 (8th Cir.2008) (Ds' request for hearing was untimely because it was made after court announced decision). The party should also comply with any local rules addressing requests for hearing. *See, e.g.*, ***Kendall v. Hoover Co.***, 751 F.2d 171, 172-73 (6th Cir.1984) (P was not entitled to hearing because he did not follow local rules). If the party does not request an oral hearing, the court does not abuse its discretion in refusing to hold one. *See* ***Vaughn v. Sexton***, 975 F.2d 498, 505 (8th Cir.1992); ***Kendall***, 751 F.2d at 172-73.

§3.2 Type of hearing. Depending on the type of motion, the court may rule on it with or without a hearing. *See* FRCP 78(b); ***Jetton v. McDonnell Douglas Corp.***, 121 F.3d 423, 427 (8th Cir.1997); ***Hill v. Porter Mem'l Hosp.***, 90 F.3d 220, 224 (7th Cir.1996). If the court holds a hearing, it may allow the parties to introduce evidence. *See* FRCP 43(c) (when motion is based on facts not appearing of record, court may decide matter on affidavits, oral testimony, or depositions); ***Gary W. v. Louisiana***, 601 F.2d 240, 244 (5th Cir.1979) (court has discretion not to hear oral testimony on motion). An attorney should not assume that every time the rules mention a hearing, an actual hearing will be held. The attorney should determine ahead of time whether the court anticipates an oral hearing and, if so, whether the court expects the presentation of evidence or only argument.

1. Submission on pleadings. The court may expedite business by adopting local rules for submission of motions and responses without an oral hearing. FRCP 78(b); ***Rose Barge Line, Inc. v. Hicks***, 421 F.2d 163, 164 (8th Cir.1970); *see* FRCP 83. A local rule that dispenses with hearings on motions does not violate due process. *See* ***U.S. Fid. & Guar. Co. v. Lawrenson***, 334 F.2d 464, 466-67 (4th Cir.1964).

> **NOTE**
>
> *If a court must resolve issues of credibility before ruling on a motion, it should give the parties an opportunity for a hearing to cross-examine the affiants.* ***Boit v. Gar-Tec Prods.***, *967 F.2d 671, 676 (1st Cir.1992). In such a case, the court may still take most of the evidence by affidavit, authenticated documents, and discovery products. Id.*

2. Hearing for argument only. When the court sets a hearing for argument only, the attorneys will simply argue the merits of the motion to the court. It is not necessary for a court reporter to record a hearing that is for argument only. The parties can, however, request that the hearing be held "on the record," or the court can determine that putting the argument on the record is in the best interest of justice.

3. Hearing for evidence. When the court sets an evidentiary hearing, a court reporter or electronic-recording operator is necessary. When a motion is based on facts that are not already of record, the court may require the matter to be heard wholly or partly on oral testimony. FRCP 43(c); ***Stewart v. M.D.F., Inc.***, 83 F.3d 247, 251 (8th Cir.1996). For example, the court may receive some evidence by affidavits, authenticated documents, and discovery products and permit the parties to present other evidence by live witnesses. *See* ***Holt v. U.S.***, 46 F.3d 1000, 1003 (10th Cir.1995) (issue of subject-matter jurisdiction); ***Boit***, 967 F.2d at 676 (issue of personal jurisdiction). If the claim is for unliquidated damages, the court normally must receive evidence at a hearing before entering a default judgment. FRCP 55(b)(2)(B); *see* ***James v. Frame***, 6 F.3d 307, 310 (5th Cir.1993) (hearing unnecessary if amount claimed is liquidated sum or capable of mathematical calculation). Before a default judgment can be entered against the United States, the court must receive evidence to support liability and damages. FRCP 55(d); ***Durant v. Husband***, 28 F.3d 12, 15 (3d Cir.1994). See "Hearing," ch. 7-A, §6.5, p. 596.

§3.3 Methods of conducting hearings.

1. In court or chambers. Most hearings on motions are held either in the courtroom or in the judge's chambers. If the court hears evidence, the hearing will probably be held in the courtroom. If the court does not hear evidence, the motion can be argued in chambers, depending on local practice.

2. By telephone. For convenience, the court can hear certain matters over the telephone. *See, e.g.*, FRCP 16(b)(1)(B) (telephone conference for scheduling order); ***In re Digital Equip. Corp.***, 949 F.2d 228, 230 (8th Cir. 1991) (telephone hearing on discovery); ***Coopers & Lybrand v. Sun-Diamond Growers***, 912 F.2d 1135, 1137 (9th

Cir.1990) (telephone hearing on party's request for stay of judgment); ***Federal S&L Ins. v. Dixon***, 835 F.2d 554, 557 (5th Cir.1987) (telephone hearing on motion for TRO and expedited discovery). Presumably, the authority to hold a hearing by telephone derives from FRCP 77(b), which allows all proceedings except trials to be held in chambers. Local rules and individual judges' practices frequently provide for hearing matters by telephone. *See, e.g.*, Local Rules Cal. (S.D.), Rule 7.1.d.2.

3. By contemporaneous transmission. Courts may receive evidence contemporaneously by transmission from another location (e.g., audio and visual transmissions). FRCP 43(a). If a witness is unable to give testimony in open court, the proponent of the evidence can request that the court allow the testimony to be presented by electronic transmission from a different location. *See id.*

§3.4 Who conducts hearings.

1. District judge. The district judge conducts hearings on motions. If a judge conducting a hearing is unable to proceed, another judge may take over after certifying familiarity with the record and determining that the proceeding may be completed without prejudice to the parties. FRCP 63; *see* ***Canseco v. U.S.***, 97 F.3d 1224, 1226 (9th Cir.1996) (certification of familiarity required, regardless of stage of proceedings). *See generally* Annotation, *Power of Successor or Substituted Judge, in Civil Case, to Render Decision or Enter Judgment on Testimony Heard by Predecessor*, 84 ALR 5th 399 (2000 & Supp.2012) (discussing power of successor or substituted judge).

2. Magistrate judge. The district court may refer certain motions to a U.S. magistrate judge for disposition or for a report and recommendation. 28 U.S.C. §636; *see* FRCP 72(a), (b)(1). On dispositive matters, the magistrate judge may conduct hearings for argument or evidence and submit to the district court proposed findings of fact and recommendations. FRCP 72(b)(1); *see* ***Provident Bank v. Manor Steel Corp.***, 882 F.2d 258, 259 (7th Cir. 1989) (hearing for evidence). On nondispositive matters, the magistrate judge issues the decision of the court. See "Magistrate Judges & Special Masters," ch. 5-B, p. 297.

3. Special master. A court-appointed special master may conduct any hearings necessary to fulfill the duties assigned by the district court. FRCP 53(c). See "Appointment of Special Master," ch. 5-B, §4, p. 302.

§3.5 Request for court reporter. A party is entitled to have the hearing recorded by a certified court reporter. 28 U.S.C. §753(b). Although the requirements of 28 U.S.C. §753(b) are mandatory, if the court refuses to have a court reporter record the proceeding, the requesting party must demonstrate on appeal that it was prejudiced by the court's refusal. *E.g.*, ***Veillon v. Exploration Servs.***, 876 F.2d 1197, 1200-01 (5th Cir.1989) (movant did not show how it was prejudiced by unrecorded conversation).

§3.6 Appellate review. The district court's decision on whether to hold a hearing on a motion is reviewed for abuse of discretion. ***Stewart v. M.D.F., Inc.***, 83 F.3d 247, 251 (8th Cir.1996); ***Mann v. Conlin***, 22 F.3d 100, 103 (6th Cir.1994).

§4. COMPELLING WITNESS TO APPEAR FOR HEARING

When a hearing for evidence is set, the parties may subpoena witnesses to attend the hearing. FRCP 45(a)(1)(A)(iii); *e.g.*, 28 U.S.C. §1785 (hearing subpoenas in multiparty, multiforum cases under 28 U.S.C. §1369); *see* ***U.S. v. Karlen***, 645 F.2d 635, 639 (8th Cir.1981). Subpoenas for hearings may be issued under FRCP 45 or under a federal statute. *See* FRCP 45(b)(2)(D), (b)(3).

§4.1 Subpoenas under FRCP 45. A party seeking to invoke the court's ability to compel a witness to attend a hearing will usually subpoena the witness under FRCP 45. See "Subpoenas Under FRCP 45," ch. 1-H, p. 47.

§4.2 Subpoenas under federal statute. In some cases, a party seeking to invoke the court's ability to compel a witness to attend a hearing can subpoena the witness under a specific federal statute. *See* FRCP 45(b)(2)(D), (b)(3); *see, e.g.*, 26 U.S.C. §7428(d) (hearing and trial subpoenas in taxpayer suits challenging IRS determination on tax-exempt status); 28 U.S.C. §1785 (hearing and trial subpoenas in multiparty, multiforum cases under 28 U.S.C.

§1369); 31 U.S.C. §3731(a) (hearing and trial subpoenas in False Claims Act qui tam actions). Unlike FRCP 45, federal statutes usually authorize subpoenas to be served anywhere within the United States. *E.g.*, 28 U.S.C. §1785 (subpoenas in multiparty, multiforum cases).

F. MAKING OBJECTIONS & PRESERVING ERROR

§1. GENERAL

§1.1 Rules. FRCP 46, 49(a), 51, 52(a)(5), (b).

§1.2 Purpose. There are two reasons for a party to make objections. The first and most important reason is to convince the court of the merits of the party's position. The second reason is to make a record of the objection so that the party can claim on appeal that the court's unfavorable ruling was erroneous.

§1.3 Forms. None.

§1.4 Other references. 9B Wright & Miller, *Federal Practice & Procedure 3d* §§2471-2473 (2008 & Supp.2012); 9 *Moore's Federal Practice 3d* ch. 46 (2012); 1 Childress & Davis, *Federal Standards of Review 4th* §6.03 (2010 & Supp.2011).

§2. GROUNDS FOR OBJECTION

Almost every rule of procedure can be the ground for an objection. Usually, when a rule requires an action from a party or the court, the beneficiary of the rule may object to nonperformance or inadequate performance. Some examples of specific rules that provide for objections include FRCP 49(a) (special verdicts and omitted fact issues), FRCP 51 (instructions to jury), and FRCP 52(a)(5) (sufficiency of evidence supporting the findings). A formal exception to the court's ruling or order is unnecessary; the party need only state its objection and the grounds at the time of the ruling or order. FRCP 46; ***Bohler-Uddeholm Am., Inc. v. Ellwood Grp.***, 247 F.3d 79, 108 (3d Cir.2001). If the party does not have the opportunity to object to the ruling or order, the lack of an objection does not prejudice the party. FRCP 46; ***Polys v. Trans-Colo. Airlines, Inc.***, 941 F.2d 1404, 1407 n.1 (10th Cir.1991).

§3. TYPES OF ERROR

The type and timing of an objection depend on the type of error committed. The first concern in making an objection is to decide who made what type of error.

§3.1 Who made error? Before making an objection, the party must determine whether the source of the error stems from the jury or the judge.

1. Role of jury. The jury is the fact-finder. The jury's task is to listen to the evidence and answer the questions the judge submits. A mistake by the jury is a mistake in evaluating the evidence.

2. Role of judge. The judge has different roles in a jury trial and a nonjury trial.

(1) In jury trial. The judge plays two roles in a jury trial. During the trial, the judge acts as an umpire and decides which facts are admissible. Once the facts are established (either by the uncontroverted evidence or by the jury) and the jury has rendered its verdict, the judge announces the winner. In neither role (as umpire or announcer) does the judge have fact-finding power. In a jury trial, the judge can make mistakes only in applying the law.

(2) In nonjury trial. The judge plays three roles in a nonjury trial. During the trial, the judge acts as an umpire and decides which facts are admissible. After the judge determines which facts are admissible, the judge resolves the factual controversies, acting as a substitute for the jury. Finally, the judge applies the appropriate law to the facts and announces the winner. In a nonjury trial, therefore, the judge can make mistakes both in applying the law and in evaluating the evidence.

§3.2 Appealable error.

1. Error in applying law. The district court errs in applying the law when it misinterprets the law, applies the wrong law, or ignores the law. The district court has no discretion on legal issues; the appellate court reviews rulings on matters of law de novo with little deference to the district court's ruling. *See, e.g.*, ***Williams v. Hanover Hous. Auth.***, 113 F.3d 1294, 1297 (1st Cir.1997) (order denying award of attorney fees); ***McKee v. Brimmer***, 39 F.3d 94, 96 (5th Cir.1994) (summary judgment).

2. Error in weighing evidence. The fact-finder—either the jury or, in a nonjury trial, the judge—errs when it clearly misevaluates the evidence. *See* ***U.S. v. 10,031.98 Acres of Land***, 850 F.2d 634, 635 (10th Cir.1988). The appellate courts show considerable deference to the fact-finder, whether jury or judge.

3. Error in deciding whether fact issue exists. The district court errs when it fails to recognize that a genuine dispute of material fact exists. A fact issue exists when a party has introduced some evidence on an issue but has not proved the issue as a matter of law.

(1) If there is fact issue. If there is a material fact issue, the court cannot grant a motion for summary judgment or a motion for judgment as a matter of law, but instead must submit the contested issue to the jury. *See* ***Celotex Corp. v. Catrett***, 477 U.S. 317, 322-23 (1986).

(2) If there is no fact issue. If no material facts are in dispute, then the facts are established conclusively. When there is no contested issue to submit to the jury, the district court must grant a motion for summary judgment or a motion for judgment as a matter of law. ***Amax Coal Co. v. United Mine Workers***, 92 F.3d 571, 575 (7th Cir.1996); ***McKee***, 39 F.3d at 96.

4. Abuse of discretion. Abuse of discretion is the most difficult type of error to reverse on appeal. Generally, a district court abuses its discretion when it renders a decision that is arbitrary and unreasonable. Appellate courts have formulated various tests for determining when to find that this has occurred. *E.g.*, ***U.S. v. Hinkson***, 585 F.3d 1247, 1263 (9th Cir.2009) (ruling on motion for new trial is reversible as abuse of discretion if court did not identify or apply correct legal standard or if court applied correct standard but application to facts was illogical, implausible, or without inferential support); ***Wimm v. Jack Eckerd Corp.***, 3 F.3d 137, 139 (5th Cir.1993) (ruling on motion for leave to amend under FRCP 15(a), which is entrusted to the sound discretion of district court, is reversible as abuse of discretion if court did not articulate "substantial reason" to deny leave to amend).

§4. PRESERVING ERROR

Preserving error is more the subject of case law than of the rules. Only FRCP 51 and FRE 103(a) deal explicitly with the preservation of error and the consequences of not objecting. FRCP 51 provides that unless the error is plain and affects substantial rights, a party may claim error based on the giving of or refusal to give an instruction to the jury if the party objected on the record before the jury was instructed. FRE 103(a) sets out the circumstances in which error may be predicated on evidentiary rulings. See "Objection to Evidence," ch. 8-D, §5, p. 703.

§4.1 Make proper objection. The procedure for making a proper objection is as follows:

1. Assert valid complaint. The party must make a valid and specific request, motion, or objection to the district court. *See* FRCP 51(c)(1); FRE 103(a)(1); ***Jimenez v. Wood Cty.***, 660 F.3d 841, 844-45 (5th Cir.2011); ***DeCaro v. Hasbro, Inc.***, 580 F.3d 55, 60-61 (1st Cir.2009); ***Dupre v. Fru-Con Eng'g***, 112 F.3d 329, 333 (8th Cir.1997). Generally, if the party does not make an objection during trial, it cannot make an objection for the first time on appeal unless there was plain error by the district court. ***Barber v. Nabors Drilling U.S.A., Inc.***, 130 F.3d 702, 710 (5th Cir.1997); ***Lightfoot v. Union Carbide Corp.***, 110 F.3d 898, 912 (2d Cir.1997); ***Stringel v. Methodist Hosp.***, 89 F.3d 415, 421 (7th Cir.1996); *see* FRE 103(e). See "Exceptions," §4.3.2, p. 43. No specific phrasing is required as long as the court is put on notice about the substance of the issue. ***Nelson v. Adams USA, Inc.***, 529 U.S. 460, 469 (2000). An objection based on one ground does not preserve review of another ground. ***Cambridge Plating Co. v. Napco, Inc.***, 85 F.3d 752, 766 (1st Cir.1996); *see* ***Prairie Band of Potawatomi Indians v. Pierce***, 253 F.3d 1234, 1249

(10th Cir.2001) (declining to consider defense not presented to district court); *see also* ***U.S. v. Seale***, 600 F.3d 473, 486 (5th Cir.2010) (to preserve objection, specific ground for stated objection must be correct one).

2. Provide proper support. The party should support its objection with evidence when necessary. For example, to preserve error when the court excludes evidence, the party must show what evidence was excluded by making an offer of proof. FRE 103(a)(2); *see* ***Dupre***, 112 F.3d at 336; ***Israel Travel Advisory Serv. v. Israel Identity Tours, Inc.***, 61 F.3d 1250, 1260 (7th Cir.1995); ***Inselman v. S&J Oper. Co.***, 44 F.3d 894, 896 (10th Cir.1995); *see, e.g.*, ***Germano v. International Profit Ass'n***, 544 F.3d 798, 801 (7th Cir.2008) (P's offer of proof, which was included in his response to D's summary-judgment motion, was sufficient to preserve error when P did not have any other opportunity to address evidentiary issue). See "Offer of Proof," ch. 8-E, p. 707.

3. Make it timely. The party must object within the time frame prescribed by rules and case law. *See* FRCP 51(c)(2). In most cases, the party must object at the opportunity provided before the jury is instructed. *See* FRCP 51(b)(2). Most objections must be made while there is still a chance to correct the error. *E.g.*, ***Holmes v. Elgin, Joliet & E. Ry.***, 18 F.3d 1393, 1397-98 (7th Cir.1994) (errors in closing argument were waived because party did not raise issue before court submitted case to jury).

§4.2 Have court rule on record. The party seeking to preserve error must get the court to (1) make a ruling on the objection and (2) make a record of the ruling either by written order or in open court. *See* ***Genmoora Corp. v. Moore Bus. Forms, Inc.***, 939 F.2d 1149, 1156 (5th Cir.1991). See "Court's Ruling," ch. 1-G, §3, p. 45.

§4.3 Failure to preserve error.

1. Generally. As a general rule, appellate courts refuse to consider an issue raised for the first time on appeal. ***Singleton v. Wulff***, 428 U.S. 106, 120 (1976); ***Vogel v. Veneman***, 276 F.3d 729, 733 (5th Cir.2002); 1 Childress & Davis §6.03; *see also* ***Scottsdale Ins. v. Flowers***, 513 F.3d 546, 552-53 (6th Cir.2008) (issue usually waived when it is raised for first time in motion for reconsideration or reply to response).

2. Exceptions. There are a number of exceptions to the rule prohibiting appellate review of errors not preserved by objection. *See* ***Lyons v. Jefferson Bank & Trust***, 994 F.2d 716, 720-22 (10th Cir.1993). These exceptions fall under the "plain error" or "manifest error" doctrine. ***Unicover World Trade Corp. v. Tri-State Mint, Inc.***, 24 F.3d 1219, 1221 (10th Cir.1994) (manifest error); ***Clausen v. Sea-3, Inc.***, 21 F.3d 1181, 1190-91 (1st Cir.1994) (plain error). The appellate courts excuse the failure to make an objection in any of the following instances: (1) when the issue is a pure question of law and refusal to consider it will result in a miscarriage of justice, (2) when the interest of substantial justice is at stake, or (3) when there was no opportunity to object to an order at the time it was issued. ***Spurlock v. FBI***, 69 F.3d 1010, 1017 (9th Cir.1995); ***National Ass'n of Soc. Workers v. Harwood***, 69 F.3d 622, 627-28 (1st Cir.1995); ***In re Novack***, 639 F.2d 1274, 1276-77 (5th Cir.1981).

NOTE

Other possible exceptions include when a new issue arises because of a change in the law while the appeal is pending or when the party had made the court aware of its concerns and further objection would have been futile. See ***Lazare Kaplan Int'l v. Photoscribe Techs.***, *628 F.3d 1359, 1372 (Fed.Cir.2010) (futility);* ***Ji v. Bose Corp.***, *626 F.3d 116, 125 (1st Cir.2010) (same);* ***In re Mercury Interactive Corp. Secs. Litig.***, *618 F.3d 988, 992 (9th Cir.2010) (change in law).*

(1) Pure question of law. When an issue presents a pure question of law, the court can consider it, even if no objection was made. ***In re Mercury Interactive Corp. Secs. Litig.***, 618 F.3d at 992; ***Wright v. Hanna Steel Corp.***, 270 F.3d 1336, 1342 (11th Cir.2001); 1 Childress & Davis §6.03. The following are examples of pure questions of law:

(a) Subject-matter jurisdiction. A party can raise an error in subject-matter jurisdiction for the first time on appeal. ***State Farm Mut. Auto. Ins. v. Powell***, 87 F.3d 93, 96 (3d Cir.1996); *see also* ***Hensgens v.***

Deere & Co., 833 F.2d 1179, 1180 (5th Cir.1987) (timeliness of objection does not matter because subject-matter jurisdiction cannot be waived).

(b) Statutory interpretation. A party can raise an argument for the first time on appeal if it is a pure issue of statutory interpretation and it is fully argued in the briefs. ***In re Mercury Interactive Corp. Secs. Litig.***, 618 F.3d at 993; ***Haroco, Inc. v. American Nat'l Bank & Trust Co.***, 38 F.3d 1429, 1439 (7th Cir.1994); *see, e.g.*, ***Wright***, 270 F.3d at 1342 (when district court improperly awarded separate ERISA penalties to P, his wife, and his children, and D did not raise separate-penalty issue in district court, miscarriage of justice would result if appellate court did not consider separate-penalty issue).

(2) Substantial justice.

(a) Integrity of trial. A party can raise an error for the first time on appeal if the error seriously affects the fairness, integrity, or public reputation of a judicial proceeding. *E.g.*, ***Glenn v. Cessna Aircraft Co.***, 32 F.3d 1462, 1464-65 (10th Cir.1994) (limit of ten minutes for opening argument was not manifest error); *see* ***Johnson v. Ashby***, 808 F.2d 676, 678-79 & n.3 (8th Cir.1987) (court can review time limits on presenting evidence under plain-error exception).

(b) Evidentiary rulings. A party can raise an error in an evidentiary ruling for the first time on appeal if the party can show that (1) there are exceptional circumstances, (2) these circumstances affect substantial rights, and (3) a miscarriage of justice will result if the plain-error doctrine is not applied. ***Kafka v. Truck Ins. Exch.***, 19 F.3d 383, 386 (7th Cir.1994); *see also* ***Douglass v. United Servs. Auto. Ass'n***, 79 F.3d 1415, 1424 (5th Cir.1996) (although FRCPs do not contain a "plain error" rule, FRCP 61 supports such a rule); ***Clausen***, 21 F.3d at 1190-91 (admission of evidence was not plain error).

(c) Jury charge. A party can challenge the jury charge for the first time on appeal if the party can show that an error in the charge affected substantial rights. FRCP 51(d)(2); *see* ***Jimenez v. Wood Cty.***, 660 F.3d 841, 845 (5th Cir.2011); 2003 Notes to FRCP 51 at ¶12, p. 1217, this book.

(3) No opportunity to object. A party can raise an error for the first time on appeal if the party had no opportunity to object to a ruling at the time it was made. *See* FRCP 46; *see, e.g.*, ***Insurance Servs. of Beaufort, Inc. v. Aetna Cas. & Sur. Co.***, 966 F.2d 847, 852 (4th Cir.1992) (P had no reason to know that hearing under Declaratory Judgment Act would not be held until court issued its damages order; objection to lack of hearing in motion for reconsideration was timely).

G. COURT RULINGS

§1. GENERAL

§1.1 Rules. FRCP 54, 55(b), 58, 60, 77(d), 79(a), (b).

§1.2 Purpose. The purpose of the court's ruling is to announce its decision on a pending matter.

§1.3 Forms. None.

§1.4 Other references. 16 Wright, Miller & Cooper, *Federal Practice & Procedure 2d* §3934 (1996 & Supp.2012); 10 Wright, Miller & Kane, *Federal Practice & Procedure 3d* §§2651-2652 (1998 & Supp.2012); 12 Wright, Miller & Marcus, *Federal Practice & Procedure 2d* §§3083-3084, 3103-3105 (1997 & Supp.2012); 10, 14 *Moore's Federal Practice 3d* §§54.01-54.03, 79.01-79.03 (2012); 1 Childress & Davis, *Federal Standards of Review 4th* §6.03 (2010 & Supp.2011); 1 *Weinstein's Federal Evidence 2d* §103.11[2][b] (2012).

§2. TYPES OF RULINGS

§2.1 Judgment. A judgment is the court's written ruling that resolves the substantive issues in the lawsuit. See "Entry of Judgment," ch. 9-A, p. 735.

§2.2 Order. An order is the court's written ruling that resolves a procedural motion or objection, not the substantive issues in the lawsuit. *See* ***MDK, Inc. v. Mike's Train House, Inc.***, 27 F.3d 116, 119 (4th Cir.1994) (discovery orders are only a stage in litigation, not final judgments on merits); ***Minority Police Officers Ass'n v. City of S. Bend***, 721 F.2d 197, 200 (7th Cir.1983) (partial summary judgment is merely an order deciding one or more issues before trial).

§3. COURT'S RULING

§3.1 Secure ruling. To preserve error on an objection or motion, the party must secure a ruling on the record. ***Libbey-Owens-Ford Co. v. Insurance Co. of N. Am.***, 9 F.3d 422, 428 (6th Cir.1993); ***Genmoora Corp. v. Moore Bus. Forms, Inc.***, 939 F.2d 1149, 1156 (5th Cir.1991); *e.g.*, FRCP 51(c)(1) (objection to jury instruction must be made on record). Most motions and objections made during a lawsuit are waived unless the district court rules on them. ***Dow v. United Bhd. of Carpenters & Joiners***, 1 F.3d 56, 61 (1st Cir.1993).

§3.2 Second request for ruling. If the court refuses to rule, the party should make a second request for a ruling and make sure the request and the court's refusal to rule appear on the record. *See* ***DesRosiers v. Moran***, 949 F.2d 15, 23 (1st Cir.1991) (when court defers ruling on objection, attorney must renew objection); *see also* 1 *Weinstein's Federal Evidence 2d* §103.11[2][b], at 103-22 (if court reserves ruling, it is proponent's obligation to raise point again). If the court merely asks the attorney to move along or tells the attorney to reurge the objection later, the court has not made a ruling.

§4. RECORD OF RULING

To be effective, all orders and rulings must be made on the record, either in writing or in open court. *See* ***Fenton v. Freedman***, 748 F.2d 1358, 1360 (9th Cir.1984).

§4.1 Judgment. Final judgments must be in writing. *See* FRCP 58(a); ***Pack v. Burns Int'l Sec. Serv.***, 130 F.3d 1071, 1072 (D.C.Cir.1997); ***Kanematsu-Gosho, Ltd. v. M/T Messiniaki Aigli***, 805 F.2d 47, 48 (2d Cir.1986). See "Requirements for Final Judgment," ch. 9-A, §2, p. 735.

§4.2 Orders. The type of record for a ruling depends on the type of motion or objection. Generally, if a motion or objection is in writing, the parties should secure a written order.

1. Written orders. The court's rulings most often take the form of written orders, memorandum opinions, or rulings, which are entered on the docket. *See* FRCP 79(a), (b).

2. Oral rulings. If the court makes an oral ruling in open court during a hearing or trial, and the ruling is transcribed by the court reporter or electronic-recording operator, then the court's ruling is preserved for appeal. If the court does not make an oral ruling on the record, the parties must secure a written order signed by the judge that reflects the ruling. *See* ***Morscott, Inc. v. City of Cleveland***, 936 F.2d 271, 272 (6th Cir.1991) (marginal entry denying D's motion for attorney fees was not sufficient).

3. Minute & docket entries.

(1) Minute entries. "Minute entries" are notes in the clerk's minutes of the court's ruling at a hearing. ***Silver Star Enters. v. M/V Saramacca***, 19 F.3d 1008, 1012 (5th Cir.1994). A minute entry is an order of the court if it (1) states that it is an order, (2) is mailed to counsel, (3) is signed by the clerk who prepared it, and (4) is entered on the docket sheet. ***Ingram v. AC&S, Inc.***, 977 F.2d 1332, 1338-39 (9th Cir.1992).

(2) Docket entries. "Docket entries" are notes the court clerk makes on the court's docket that reflect the nature of each paper filed, proof of service returned, or order issued in the case. FRCP 79(a)(3). Docket entries are not orders themselves, but only a record of orders. *See* FRCP 79(a).

§5. FORM OF RULING

§5.1 Judgment. For the form of a judgment, see "Form," ch. 9-A, §2.3, p. 736.

§5.2 Order on motion. A written order generally should include the following information.

PRACTICE TIP

Be sure to check local rules, standing orders, and other local procedures that may provide additional requirements to the form or for the submission of proposed orders. See, e.g., Local Rules Tex. (E.D.), Rule CV-7(a) (proposed order must not contain date or signature block); Local Rules Tex. (N.D.), Rule 7.1(c) (if motion is agreed, proposed order must be signed by attorneys or parties).

---

1. **Names of parties.** The order should recite the full names of the parties as stated in the pleadings.

2. **Identity of motion.** For the sake of clarity in the record, the order should (1) identify the motion and the party making the motion and (2) state whether the court held a hearing on the motion and whether the hearing was for receipt of evidence or for argument only.

3. **Disposition.** The order should resolve the issues presented by the motion.

4. **Costs.** The order should award costs as a part of the relief granted if permitted by rule or statute. *See, e.g.*, FRCP 11(c)(2) (under appropriate circumstances, court may order payment of reasonable attorney fees and other expenses to movant).

5. **Date.** The order should conclude with a line, immediately above the signature line for the judge, that reads, "SIGNED ON ____________, 20__."

6. **Signature line for judge.** The order must contain a signature line for the judge. *See* ***Woods v. Dahlberg***, 894 F.2d 187, 188 n.2 (6th Cir.1990) (if granted, order on application to proceed as pauper may be signed by magistrate judge; if denied, order must be signed by district judge).

7. **Signature block for attorneys.** Certain agreed orders, especially orders of dismissal, contain a signature block for the attorneys.

§6. NOTICE OF RULING

The clerk must serve the parties with notice of the entry of an order or judgment. FRCP 77(d)(1). It can serve the notice either by mail or, if the party has given written consent, by electronic means. *See id.*; 2001 Notes to FRCP 77 at ¶1, p. 1233, this book. Even when a party does not receive timely notice of a clerk's entry, the time to appeal is not extended, except as permitted in FRAP 4(a). FRCP 77(d)(2). Thus, the parties have a duty to monitor the progress of the case that they may want to appeal. ***Kuhn v. Sulzer Orthopedics, Inc.***, 498 F.3d 365, 371 (6th Cir.2007); ***Delaney v. Alexander***, 29 F.3d 516, 518 (9th Cir.1994); ***Latham v. Wells Fargo Bank***, 987 F.2d 1199, 1201 (5th Cir. 1993).

§7. APPELLATE REVIEW

§7.1 Appeal after judgment. Most orders can be challenged on appeal only after the entry of a final judgment. However, some orders can be challenged on appeal before then. For a list of interlocutory orders that can be appealed before the entry of a final judgment, see "Appealable orders," ch. 9-A, §3.3, p. 739.

§7.2 Mandamus. A party can challenge a nonfinal order by petition for writ of mandamus under 28 U.S.C. §1651(a) and FRAP 21. *See* 16 Wright, Miller & Cooper §3934. Generally, to be entitled to mandamus, the party must show the following:

1. A clear abuse of discretion. ***Bankers Life & Cas. Co. v. Holland***, 346 U.S. 379, 383 (1953); ***In re Jenoptik AG***, 109 F.3d 721, 722 (Fed.Cir.1997).

2. No adequate alternative means to obtain relief. ***Allied Chem. Corp. v. Daiflon, Inc.***, 449 U.S. 33, 35 (1980).

3. A clear and indisputable right to the writ. *Id.*; ***Bankers Life***, 346 U.S. at 384.

H. SUBPOENAS UNDER FRCP 45

§1. GENERAL

§1.1 Rule. FRCP 45.

§1.2 Purpose. A subpoena is a document that commands a person—usually a nonparty—to (1) appear and give testimony, (2) produce or permit inspection of documents, electronically stored information, or tangible things, or (3) permit inspection of premises. *See* FRCP 45(a)(1)(A)(iii); ***Hatcher v. Precoat Metals***, 271 F.R.D. 674, 675 (N.D.Ala.2010).

§1.3 Forms. ***O'Connor's Federal Civil Forms*** (2012), FORMS 1H, 6A:11-19.

§1.4 Other references. 9A Wright & Miller, *Federal Practice & Procedure 3d* §§2454-2466 (2008 & Supp.2012); 9 *Moore's Federal Practice 3d* ch. 45 (2012); Rothstein, et al., *Managing Discovery of Electronic Information: A Pocket Guide for Judges, Second Edition* (2012), Federal Judicial Center, www.fjc.gov (referred to as Rothstein, *Managing Discovery of Electronic Information*); *Sedona Conference Commentary on Non-Party Production & Rule 45 Subpoenas* (Sedona Conference Working Group Series, 2008), www.thesedonaconference.org/publications (referred to as *Sedona Conference Commentary on Non-Party Production & Rule 45 Subpoenas*); *Sedona Conference Cooperation Proclamation* (Sedona Conference Working Group Series, 2008), www.thesedonaconference.org/publications (referred to as *Sedona Conference Cooperation Proclamation*).

§2. TYPES OF SUBPOENAS

NOTE

The Administrative Office of the U.S. Courts provides subpoena forms in PDF format for hearing or trial (Form AO 088), deposition (Form AO 088A), and production (Form AO 088B). See www.uscourts.gov/FormsAndFees/Forms/CourtFormsByCategory.aspx.

§2.1 Production subpoena. A production subpoena (also known as a discovery subpoena) commands a person to produce documents, electronically stored information (ESI), or tangible things or to permit inspection of premises. *See* FRCP 45(a)(1)(A)(iii).

§2.2 Deposition subpoena. A deposition subpoena commands a person to appear at a deposition and testify and may command a person to produce discovery materials. *See* FRCP 45(a)(1)(A)(iii).

§2.3 Hearing or trial subpoena. A hearing or trial subpoena commands a person to appear in court at a specified time to give testimony. *See* FRCP 45(a)(1)(A)(iii). See ***O'Connor's Federal Forms***, FORM 1H:1.

NOTE

Under limited circumstances, a hearing or trial subpoena may command a person to produce materials. See ***Armenian Assembly v. Cafesjian****, 746 F.Supp.2d 55, 75 (D.D.C.2010). A hearing or trial subpoena can be used to request materials only when the materials are necessary to refresh memory, to prepare for cross-examination, or to ensure the availability at trial of original materials that were previously produced during discovery. See* ***Hatcher v. Precoat Metals****, 271 F.R.D. 674, 675 (N.D.Ala.2010);* ***Armenian Assembly****, 746 F.Supp.2d at 75;* ***Rice v. U.S.****, 164 F.R.D. 556, 558 n.1 (N.D.Okla.1995). A hearing or trial subpoena cannot be used as an untimely discovery request. See* ***Mortgage Info. Servs. v. Kitchens****, 210 F.R.D. 562, 567 (W.D.N.C.2002).*

§3. FORMAL REQUIREMENTS FOR SUBPOENAS

§3.1 Form of subpoena. All subpoenas must include the following information:

1. Issuing court. The subpoena must state the name of the court that issued it. FRCP 45(a)(1)(A)(i).

(1) Production subpoena. If a subpoena is for production or inspection and is separate from a subpoena commanding a person's attendance, the subpoena must be issued from the district where the production or inspection will be made. FRCP 45(a)(2)(C).

(2) Deposition subpoena. If a subpoena commands attendance at a deposition, the subpoena must be issued from the district where the deposition will be taken. FRCP 45(a)(2)(B); ***Hartford Fire Ins. Co. v. Transgroup Express, Inc.***, 264 F.R.D. 382, 384 (N.D.Ill.2009); ***Snoznik v. Jeld-Wen, Inc.***, 259 F.R.D. 217, 221 (W.D.N.C. 2009).

(3) Hearing or trial subpoena. If a subpoena commands attendance at a hearing or trial, the subpoena must be issued from the district where the hearing or trial will be held. FRCP 45(a)(2)(A).

2. Title & case number. The subpoena must state the title of the action, the court in which it is pending, and the civil action number. FRCP 45(a)(1)(A)(ii).

3. Action required of recipient. The subpoena must command the person to whom it is directed to do one or more of the following at a specified time and place:

(1) Give testimony. The subpoena can command a person to appear and give testimony at a deposition, hearing, or trial. *See* FRCP 45(a)(1)(A)(iii).

(2) Produce & permit inspection of documents. The subpoena can command a person to produce and permit inspection, copying, testing, or sampling of designated books, documents, ESI, or tangible things in the person's possession, custody, or control. FRCP 45(a)(1)(A)(iii). For the definition of "documents," see "Documents, ESI & tangible things," ch. 6-B, §2.2.6, p. 458; "Documents or electronically stored information," ch. 6-I, §3.4.2(1), p. 570. The subpoena can also specify the form or forms in which ESI is to be produced. FRCP 45(a)(1)(C). See "Specify form of production," ch. 6-C, §9.5.1(1), p. 500. A subpoena commanding production of or permission to inspect documents, ESI, or tangible things can be joined with a subpoena commanding a person to appear and testify at a deposition, hearing, or trial. FRCP 45(a)(1)(C); *see* ***Richardson v. Florida***, 137 F.R.D. 401, 402-03 & n.2 (M.D.Fla.1991), *aff'd*, 963 F.2d 384 (11th Cir.1992) (table case). If the subpoena for production or inspection is not joined with a subpoena for testimony, the subpoenaed person is not required to appear at the place of production or inspection. FRCP 45(c)(2)(A).

CAUTION

Determining whether a nonparty has possession, custody, or control of ESI can be a complex question because it may be unclear who actually owns the ESI and what rights (if any) the nonparty has to protect or produce the ESI. See Sedona Conference Commentary on Non-Party Production & Rule 45 Subpoenas, at 4. See "Discovery from Nonparties," ch. 6-C, §10, p. 505.

(3) Permit inspection of land. The subpoena can command a person to permit inspection of premises. FRCP 45(a)(1)(A)(iii).

4. Text of rule. The subpoena must recite the text of FRCP 45(c) and (d). FRCP 45(a)(1)(A)(iv).

5. Recording method. The subpoena must state the method for recording the testimony. FRCP 45(a)(1)(B).

§3.2 Who should be subpoenaed. Any person is subject to a subpoena. *See* FRCP 45. The term "person" includes natural persons, business associations, and governments. ***Yousuf v. Samantar***, 451 F.3d 248, 257 (D.C.Cir. 2006); *see* ***Ott v. City of Milwaukee***, 682 F.3d 552, 556-57 (7th Cir.2012) (dicta; "person" includes state agencies);

Watts v. SEC, 482 F.3d 501, 508 (D.C.Cir.2007) ("person" includes government agencies and their employees); ***In re Vioxx Prods. Liab. Litig.***, 235 F.R.D. 334, 342 (E.D.La.2006) ("person" includes federal government). *But see* ***Robinson v. City of Phila.***, 233 F.R.D. 169, 172 (E.D.Pa.2005) ("person" does not include federal government). FRCP 45 does not distinguish between nonparties and parties, but the courts do. *See* ***First Am. Corp. v. Price Waterhouse LLP***, 154 F.3d 16, 21 (2d Cir.1998).

1. Nonparty. Any person who is not a party should be subpoenaed under FRCP 45; that is, if a party seeks production from a nonparty, seeks to depose a nonparty, or seeks to compel a nonparty to attend a hearing or trial, the nonparty must be served with a subpoena. *See* ***Hobley v. Burge***, 433 F.3d 946, 949 (7th Cir.2006) (production); ***Alper v. U.S.***, 190 F.R.D. 281, 283 (D.Mass.2000) (trial); ***Trans Pac. Ins. v. Trans-Pac. Ins.***, 136 F.R.D. 385, 392 (E.D.Pa.1991) (deposition); 9A Wright & Miller §2461 & nn.1-2 (hearing or trial). FRCP 45 is the only discovery method to obtain information from a nonparty. ***Highland Tank & Mfg. v. PS Int'l***, 227 F.R.D. 374, 379 & n.7 (W.D. Pa.2005); *see* ***Fisher v. Marubeni Cotton Corp.***, 526 F.2d 1338, 1341 (8th Cir.1975).

2. Party. Depending on what is requested from the party, a party may be subpoenaed under FRCP 45.

(1) Production subpoena. Courts are divided on whether a party may be served with a production subpoena under FRCP 45. *Compare* ***Mortgage Info. Servs. v. Kitchens***, 210 F.R.D. 562, 564-65 (W.D.N.C.2002) (subpoena under FRCP 45 may be served on party), *and* ***Badman v. Stark***, 139 F.R.D. 601, 603 (M.D.Pa.1991) (same), *with* ***Alper***, 190 F.R.D. at 283 (discovery of documents in party's control is governed by FRCP 34, not FRCP 45).

(2) Deposition subpoena. A party does not need to be subpoenaed for a deposition; a notice of deposition is sufficient. ***Monks v. Marlinga***, 923 F.2d 423, 426 (6th Cir.1991) (Nelson, J., concurring); 9A Wright & Miller §2460 & n.1. See "Notice of oral deposition," ch. 6-F, §3.2, p. 540; ***O'Connor's Federal Forms***, FORMS 6F:4, 6.

(3) Hearing or trial. A party may be subpoenaed to attend hearing or trial. *See* ***Alper***, 190 F.R.D. at 283 (party can subpoena person for trial for any reason).

§3.3 Range of subpoena.

1. Generally. A person may be served in any of the following locations:

(1) Within court's district. A person may be served within the court's district. FRCP 45(b)(2)(A).

(2) Within 100 miles. A person may be served outside the court's district but within 100 miles of the place for the deposition, hearing, trial, production, or inspection. FRCP 45(b)(2)(B).

PRACTICE TIP

The proper method for measuring the 100-mile distance under FRCP 45 is a straight-line measurement. ***Palazzo v. Corio, 204 F.R.D. 639, 639 (E.D.N.Y.1998)****; cf.* ***Bellum v. PCE Constructors, Inc.****, 407 F.3d 734, 740 n.7 (5th Cir.2005) (measuring 100-mile distance under FRCP 4(k)(1)(B)). But see* ***Merchant Bank v. Grove Silk Co.****, 11 F.R.D. 439, 440 (M.D.Pa.1951) (distance determined by ordinary, usual, and shortest route of public travel). Online tools can help determine whether a subpoenaed person is located within the 100-mile radius. See, e.g., Radius Around Point Tool, www.freemaptools.com/radius-around-point.htm; cf.* ***U.S. v. Ferguson****, 432 F.Supp.2d 559, 563 & n.5 (E.D.Va.2006) (in motion to transfer venue in criminal case, court recognized distances generated by MapQuest to find that there would be substantial inconvenience for Ds to be tried in Alexandria, Virginia, rather than Connecticut).*

(a) Nonparty. If the subpoena requires a person who is neither a party nor a party's officer to appear at a place more than 100 miles from where the person lives, works, or regularly transacts business, the subpoenaed person can object by filing a motion to quash or modify the subpoena. FRCP 45(c)(3)(A)(ii).

(b) Party or party's officer. Courts disagree on whether FRCP 45(b)(2)(B) in conjunction with FRCP 45(c)(3)(A)(ii) authorizes parties and parties' officers to be subpoenaed for trial beyond the 100-mile limit. *Compare* ***Aristocrat Leisure Ltd. v. Deutsche Bank Trust Co. Ams.***, 262 F.R.D. 293, 301-02 (S.D.N.Y.2009) (parties can be subpoenaed beyond 100-mile limit), ***In re Vioxx Prods. Liab. Litig.***, 438 F.Supp.2d 664, 666-67 (E.D.La.

2006) (same), *and* ***American Fed'n of Gov't Empls. v. Ashcroft***, 354 F.Supp.2d 909, 915 (E.D.Ark.2003) (same), *with* ***Armenian Assembly v. Cafesjian***, 746 F.Supp.2d 55, 61-62 (D.D.C.2010) (FRCP 45(b)(2) defines scope of subpoenas, and 100-mile limit applies to parties and nonparties), ***Chao v. Tyson Foods, Inc.***, 255 F.R.D. 556, 559 (N.D. Ala.2009) (same), *and* ***Johnson v. Big Lots Stores, Inc.***, 251 F.R.D. 213, 215-16 (E.D.La.2008) (same).

CAUTION

Although some courts have allowed parties or parties' officers to be subpoenaed for trial beyond the 100-mile limit under FRCP 45(b)(2), the proposed amendments to FRCP 45 (scheduled to be effective December 1, 2013) reject this line of cases. Report of the Civil Rules Advisory Committee, at 3 (June 2011), www.uscourts.gov/uscourts/RulesAndPolicies/rules/Publication %20Aug%202011/CV_Report.pdf. See "Range of subpoena," §3.3, p. 49. The proposed amendments intend to make clear that all subpoenas are subject to the geographical limit in FRCP 45(b)(2). Report of the Civil Rules Advisory Committee, at 3. Thus, before serving a subpoena on a party or a party's officer beyond the 100-mile limit, consider using videotaped deposition testimony or asking the court to allow testimony by contemporaneous transmission. Id.

(3) Within state of issuing court. A person may be served within the state of the issuing court if a state statute or court rule permits a state court to serve a subpoena. FRCP 45(b)(2)(C).

(4) In place authorized by court. A person may be served in a place that the court authorizes on motion and for good cause, if provided by federal statute. FRCP 45(b)(2)(D).

2. Limited exception for trial appearance. A person can be compelled to attend trial from anywhere within the state in which the trial is held. FRCP 45(c)(3)(A)(ii); ***Mohamed v. Mazda Motor Corp.***, 90 F.Supp.2d 757, 778 (E.D.Tex.2000). If the subpoena requires a person who is neither a party nor a party's officer to incur substantial expense to travel more than 100 miles to attend trial, the court may (1) quash or modify the subpoena or (2) order a conditional appearance or production if the serving party shows a substantial need for the testimony that cannot be met without undue hardship and ensures that the subpoenaed person will be reasonably compensated. FRCP 45(c)(3)(B), (c)(3)(C). See "Motion to Quash or Modify Subpoena," §8, p. 55.

§3.4 Who may issue subpoena.

1. Clerk. The clerk may issue a subpoena. FRCP 45(a)(3). If a party requests a subpoena, the clerk must issue a subpoena that is signed but otherwise blank, and the party must complete the subpoena before service. *Id.*

2. Attorney. In most circumstances, the attorney may issue a subpoena on behalf of the court. FRCP 45(a)(3); *see* ***McGill v. Duckworth***, 944 F.2d 344, 353-54 (7th Cir.1991); *see, e.g.*, Local Rules Tex. (E.D.), Rule CV-45 (attorneys must prepare all subpoenas). The attorney may issue a subpoena on behalf of (1) a court where the attorney is authorized to practice or (2) a court for a district where a deposition or production is compelled by the subpoena if the deposition or production pertains to a case pending in a court where the attorney is authorized to practice. FRCP 45(a)(2)(B), (a)(3); *see* ***Amgen, Inc. v. Kidney Ctr., Ltd.***, 95 F.3d 562, 564 (7th Cir.1996).

§3.5 Notice.

A party may need to serve a notice along with the subpoena.

1. Production subpoena. A party who seeks production of documents, ESI, and tangible things from a nonparty or wants to inspect premises of a nonparty must first serve a notice on each party, and the notice must be served in the manner prescribed under FRCP 5(b). *See* FRCP 45(b)(1); ***Firefighters' Inst. for Racial Equal. v. City of St. Louis***, 220 F.3d 898, 903 (8th Cir.2000); ***Murphy v. Board of Educ. of the Rochester City Sch. Dist.***, 196 F.R.D. 220, 222 (W.D.N.Y.2000). See "How to Serve," ch. 1-D, §4, p. 30. That is, the notice to the parties must be served before the subpoena is served on a nonparty; the prior notice allows the parties to object to the subpoena or serve a request for additional documents, ESI, or tangible things. *See* ***Schweizer v. Mulvehill***, 93 F.Supp.2d 376, 411 (S.D. N.Y.2000); 2007 Notes to FRCP 45 at ¶2, p. 1209, this book; 9A Wright & Miller §2454 & nn.22-25. If a party does not provide proper notice, the court may impose sanctions or quash the subpoena. *See* ***Firefighters' Inst. for Racial***

Equal., 220 F.3d at 903; ***Schweizer***, 93 F.Supp.2d at 411-12 (dicta); *see, e.g.*, ***Ross v. Board of Regents***, 655 F.Supp.2d 895, 923-24 (E.D.Wis.2009) (court struck one document attached to Ds' motion for summary judgment when document was obtained from nonparty through subpoena but Ds did not provide P with notice of subpoena); ***Automotive Inspection Servs. v. Flint Auto Auction, Inc.***, No. 06-15100 (E.D.Mich.2007) (slip op.; 11-9-07) (court imposed monetary sanctions on attorney when he did not provide any notice to opposing parties).

NOTE

If the subpoena seeks production of ESI, the requesting party may specify the form or forms in which the ESI is to be produced. FRCP 45(a)(1)(C); 2006 Notes to FRCP 45 at ¶1, p. 1209, this book. See "Specify form of production," ch. 6-C, §9.5.1(1), p. 500.

2. Deposition subpoena.

(1) Nonparty. A party who seeks to depose a nonparty must serve a notice of the deposition and the subpoena on the nonparty and on each party. *See* FRCP 30(a)(1), 45(a)(1)(A)(iii); ***Westmoreland v. CBS, Inc.***, 770 F.2d 1168, 1175 (D.C.Cir.1985). See ***O'Connor's Federal Forms***, FORMS 6F:5, 7. The subpoena must state the method for recording the testimony. FRCP 45(a)(1)(B). If a party serves a deposition notice on a nonparty but does not serve a subpoena on the nonparty, and as a result, the nonparty does not attend, the court may order the party who served the deposition notice to pay the other party reasonable expenses for attending, including attorney fees. FRCP 30(g)(2).

(2) Party. A party who seeks to depose another party must serve a notice of deposition; a subpoena is not necessary. See "Deposition subpoena," §3.2.2(2), p. 49. The notice must state the method for recording the testimony. FRCP 30(b)(3)(A). See "Recording method," ch. 6-F, §3.2.6, p. 543. If a party serves a deposition notice and the party-deponent does not attend, the court may sanction the party-deponent. FRCP 37(d)(1)(A)(i). See "Deponent did not attend," ch. 6-A, §15.3.2(1)(a), p. 447

3. Hearing or trial subpoena. A party who seeks to subpoena a person to testify at a hearing or at trial must provide notice by serving the subpoena on the person and on each party.

§3.6 Manner of service. Once the subpoena is prepared, the person to be subpoenaed must be served according to the requirements in FRCP 45(b). *See* ***Snoznik v. Jeld-Wen, Inc.***, 259 F.R.D. 217, 221-22 (W.D.N.C.2009). The subpoena may be served by any person who is not a party and who is at least 18 years old. FRCP 45(b)(1); *see also* ***Ott v. City of Milwaukee***, 682 F.3d 552, 557 (7th Cir.2012) (dicta; postal employee delivering certified mail qualifies as nonparty who is at least 18 years old). Courts disagree on the manner of service required under FRCP 45(b). *See* ***OceanFirst Bank v. Hartford Fire Ins.***, 794 F.Supp.2d 752, 753-54 (E.D.Mich.2011); 9A Wright & Miller §2454 & n.4.

1. Personal delivery. Many courts require that the subpoena be delivered personally. *See* ***FTC v. Compagnie de Saint-Gobain-Pont-a-Mousson***, 636 F.2d 1300, 1312-13 (D.C.Cir.1980) (FRCP 45(b) does not permit any form of mail service; subpoena may be served "only in person"); ***Smith v. Midland Brake, Inc.***, 162 F.R.D. 683, 686 (D.Kan.1995) (service of subpoena "may not be accomplished by mail"); *see, e.g.*, ***Klockner Namasco Holdings Corp. v. Daily Access.Com, Inc.***, 211 F.R.D. 685, 687 (N.D.Ga.2002) (service on witness's wife insufficient; personal service on witness required); *see also* 9 *Moore's Federal Practice 3d* §45.21[1] (most courts have held that FRCP 45 requires personal service).

2. Certified mail or other manner for which delivery is verifiable. Some courts have allowed service by certified mail or any other manner that is reasonably calculated to result in actual delivery. *E.g.*, ***Ott***, 682 F.3d at 557 (dicta; certified mail); ***Bland v. Fairfax Cty.***, 275 F.R.D. 466, 469-70 (E.D.Va.2011) (certified mail or FedEx); ***Doe v. Hersemann***, 155 F.R.D. 630, 630 (N.D.Ind.1994) (certified mail); *see* ***Hall v. Sullivan***, 229 F.R.D. 501, 503-04 (D.Md.2005); 9A Wright & Miller §2454 & n.10; *see also* ***Firefighters' Inst. for Racial Equal. v. City of St. Louis***, 220 F.3d 898, 903 (8th Cir.2000) (although service by means other than personal delivery may be proper, service by

fax or regular mail is improper). Other courts allow an alternate manner of service only if a party first makes a diligent effort to personally serve the subpoena. *See, e.g.*, ***OceanFirst Bank***, 794 F.Supp.2d at 754-55 (because P did not establish diligent effort, P's motion for alternate service was denied).

PRACTICE TIP

Although some courts allow means other than personal delivery, personal delivery is the safest manner of service. 9A Wright & Miller §2454.

§3.7 Fees.

1. Witness fee. The attorney must tender the statutory witness fee for one day's attendance with the subpoena. FRCP 45(b)(1); ***In re Dennis***, 330 F.3d 696, 704 (5th Cir.2003); ***Tedder v. Odel***, 890 F.2d 210, 211 (9th Cir.1989); *see* 9 *Moore's Federal Practice 3d* §45.21[2][a]; 9A Wright & Miller §2454. The methods of calculating the witness fee are set out in 28 U.S.C. §1821. *See* 28 U.S.C. §1821(b) (witness must be paid $40 per day plus travel time); *see also* ***Kansas v. Colorado***, 556 U.S. 98, ___, 129 S.Ct. 1294, 1298 (2009) (for cases brought under Supreme Court's original jurisdiction, Court may have authority to award expert-witness attendance fees beyond limits of 28 U.S.C. §1821, but fees under §1821 are reasonable). The attorney does not need to tender the witness fee if the subpoena is issued on behalf of the United States or an officer or agency of the United States. FRCP 45(b)(1).

2. Mileage allowance. The attorney must tender a reasonable mileage allowance with the subpoena. *See* FRCP 45(b)(1); ***In re Dennis***, 330 F.3d at 704; ***Tedder***, 890 F.2d at 211; 9 *Moore's Federal Practice 3d* §45.21[2][a]; 9A Wright & Miller §2454. The methods of calculating the mileage allowance are set out in 28 U.S.C. §1821(c). The attorney does not need to tender the mileage allowance if the subpoena is issued on behalf of the United States or an officer or agency of the United States. FRCP 45(b)(1).

NOTE

Unless the fees are suspended by the court, a party proceeding in forma pauperis under 28 U.S.C. §1915 must still tender them. See ***Lloyd v. McKendree****, 749 F.2d 705, 706 (11th Cir.1985).*

§3.8 Proof of service. When necessary, proof of service must be made by filing in the court a statement of the date of service, the manner of service, and the names of the persons served. FRCP 45(b)(4). The proof of service must be certified by the server. *Id.*

§4. DEADLINE TO SERVE

FRCP 45 does not contain a time limit for serving a subpoena on a nonparty. *See* ***Alper v. U.S.***, 190 F.R.D. 281, 283 (D.Mass.2000). For production and deposition subpoenas, a party will usually not be allowed to serve one after the discovery deadline has passed. *Id.* at 283-84; *see also* ***Marvin Lumber & Cedar Co. v. PPG Indus.***, 177 F.R.D. 443, 443 (D.Minn.1997) (FRCP 45 subpoenas are subject to same time constraints that apply to all other methods of discovery); ***Thomas v. IEM, Inc.***, No. 06-886-B-M2 (M.D.La.2008) (slip op.; 3-12-08) (FRCP 45 subpoenas cannot be used to avoid discovery deadlines or to shorten discovery response times). For hearing or trial subpoenas, local rules may specify the time limit for service. *See, e.g.*, ***Saudi v. Northrop Grumman Corp.***, 427 F.3d 271, 279 (4th Cir.2005) (local rule from Eastern District of Virginia specified that trial subpoenas must be served at least 14 days before trial).

§5. PRODUCTION OF DOCUMENTS, ESI & TANGIBLE THINGS

§5.1 Preservation. A nonparty may have an obligation to preserve evidence; however, the obligation is not as strong as that imposed on parties. *See Sedona Conference Commentary on Non-Party Production & Rule 45 Subpoenas*, at 3, 7. Generally, a nonparty's duty to preserve arises on receipt of a subpoena. *Id.* at 7. See "Preservation," ch. 6-C, §4.2, p. 486.

§5.2 Scope. The scope of nonparty discovery under FRCP 45 is the same as that for party discovery—a party can discover any nonprivileged matter that is relevant to any party's claim or defense. *See* ***Kendrick v. Heckler***, 778 F.2d 253, 257 (5th Cir.1985); ***Coleman v. District of Columbia***, 275 F.R.D. 33, 36 (D.D.C.2011); 1991 Notes to FRCP 45 at ¶10, p. 1211, this book. See "General scope of discovery," ch. 6-B, §2.1, p. 457.

§5.3 Production.

1. Place. If the subpoenaed nonparty does not serve the requesting party with the material, the material should be produced for inspection and copying at a reasonable time and place. If the volume of material requested would make transporting and copying burdensome to the nonparty or if the distance between the parties is great, the court may order inspection to occur wherever it is convenient for the nonparty. ***Caruso v. Coleman Co.***, 157 F.R.D. 344, 349 (E.D.Pa.1994); *e.g.*, ***Gluck v. Ansett Austl. Ltd.***, 204 F.R.D. 217, 221 (D.D.C.2001) (court ordered inspection in D's Australia office rather than in D.C.).

2. Manner.

(1) Documents. A person responding to a subpoena to produce documents must produce them either as they are kept in the usual course of business or organized and labeled to correspond with the categories in the demand. FRCP 45(d)(1)(A). The documents must be complete and unredacted. See "Complete document," ch. 6-I, §4.4.4, p. 573.

(2) ESI. A person responding to a subpoena to produce ESI must produce the information either in the form requested or, if no form is specified or the person objects to the form requested, in a form in which the information is ordinarily maintained or reasonably usable. FRCP 45(d)(1)(B); 2006 Notes to FRCP 45 at ¶1, p. 1209, this book; *see Sedona Conference Commentary on Non-Party Production & Rule 45 Subpoenas*, at 6. The person responding need only produce the material in one form. FRCP 45(d)(1)(C); 2006 Notes to FRCP 45 at ¶1, p. 1209, this book. See "Requests for production," ch. 6-C, §9.5, p. 500.

3. Costs. Generally, the subpoenaed nonparty is responsible for the costs of production; however, nonparties are protected from significant expense. *See* FRCP 45(c)(1), (c)(2)(B)(ii). To protect the nonparty, the court can shift costs. *See* ***Linder v. Calero-Portocarrero***, 183 F.R.D. 314, 322-23 (D.D.C.1998) (if requesting parties are forced to pay expenses when requests for nonparty discovery are too broad, requesting parties will be more inclined to make narrowly tailored requests to balance relevance and expenses), *aff'd*, 251 F.3d 178 (D.C.Cir.2001). To determine who should bear the expense, courts should consider (1) the scope of the request, (2) the invasiveness of the request, (3) the need to separate privileged information, (4) whether the nonparty actually has an interest in the outcome of the suit, (5) whether the requesting party ultimately prevails, (6) whether the nonparty can bear the costs more readily than the requesting party, (7) the reasonableness of the expenses, and (8) whether the suit is of public importance. *Sedona Conference Commentary on Non-Party Production & Rule 45 Subpoenas*, at 7; *see* ***In re Exxon Valdez***, 142 F.R.D. 380, 383 (D.D.C.1992); ***Sound Sec., Inc. v. Sonitrol Corp.***, No. 3:08-cv-05350-RBL (W.D.Wash. 2009) (slip op.; 6-26-09); *see, e.g.*, ***Wells Fargo Bank v. Konover***, 259 F.R.D. 206, 207 (D.Conn.2009) (nonparty-entity's request to recover costs and attorney fees for complying with subpoena was denied because nonparty-entity was not disinterested party when it was controlled by Ds and had strong interest in suit). Courts may also consider the level of cooperation between the requesting party and the nonparty during the discovery process. *See* ***DeGeer v. Gillis***, 755 F.Supp.2d 909, 929 (N.D.Ill.2010); *Sedona Conference Cooperation Proclamation*, at 1-2.

NOTE

If the requesting party is seeking the discovery of ESI from a nonparty, the nonparty has additional protection under FRCP 45(d)(1)(D), which allows the nonparty to avoid production of ESI that is not reasonably accessible because of undue burden or cost. See Rothstein, Managing Discovery of Electronic Information, at 21; Sedona Conference Commentary on Non-Party Production & Rule 45 Subpoenas, at 3. See "ESI not reasonably accessible," §8.5.1(4), p. 57.

§6. RESISTING SUBPOENA TO PRODUCE OR PERMIT INSPECTION

A person commanded to produce and permit inspection, copying, testing, or sampling of materials or to permit inspection of premises may resist producing or permitting inspection by serving objections or asserting privilege. *See* FRCP 45(c)(2)(B), (d)(2).

§6.1 Serve objections.

1. Deadline to serve. Objections must be served within 14 days after service of the subpoena or before the time specified for compliance with the subpoena, whichever is earlier. FRCP 45(c)(2)(B); *see* ***Angell v. Shawmut Bank Conn.***, 153 F.R.D. 585, 590 (M.D.N.C.1994).

2. Form. A person who wants to object to a subpoena should serve a written response on the requesting party. ***U.S. v. O'Neill***, 619 F.2d 222, 225 (3d Cir.1980); ***Eastern Techs. v. Chem-Solv, Inc.***, 128 F.R.D. 74, 75 (E.D.Pa. 1989). A letter asserting the objections to the subpoena may suffice. ***Tuite v. Henry***, 98 F.3d 1411, 1416 (D.C.Cir. 1996). The objecting person must raise all objections at once, rather than in staggered batches, so that discovery does not become a "game." ***In re DG Acquisition Corp.***, 151 F.3d 75, 81 (2d Cir.1998); *see* ***Tuite***, 98 F.3d at 1416 (initial objections must be timely served, but full description of objection may be provided later at a "reasonable time").

3. Valid objections. To avoid being cited for contempt, the subpoenaed person should raise any valid objections to the subpoena. For example, if the requesting party is seeking ESI and designates in the subpoena a form for producing the information that is overly burdensome, the subpoenaed person should object to the requested form. FRCP 45(c)(2)(B); *see* 2006 Notes to FRCP 45 at ¶1, p. 1209, this book. For a list of other objections the person can raise, see "Valid objections," ch. 6-A, §8.3.1(2)(a), p. 425.

4. Effect. If an objection is made, the party serving the subpoena cannot inspect, copy, test, or sample the materials or inspect the premises without an order from the court that issued the subpoena. FRCP 45(c)(2)(B); *see* ***In re Sealed Case***, 121 F.3d 729, 741 (D.C.Cir.1997) (motion to compel was first event that could have forced disclosure of documents).

§6.2 Assert privileges.

1. Deadline to serve. If the subpoenaed person is withholding information based on a privilege, the person must assert the privilege before the 14-day deadline and, if necessary, follow up within a reasonable time with a more detailed explanation of the privilege as required by FRCP 45(d)(2). ***In re DG Acquisition Corp.***, 151 F.3d 75, 81 (2d Cir.1998); *see* ***Tuite v. Henry***, 98 F.3d 1411, 1416 (D.C.Cir.1996) (FRCP 45(d)(2) "does not alleviate the responsibility of objecting parties to assert their objections based on privilege within 14 days of service of the subpoena"). *But see* ***Universal City Dev. Partners v. Ride & Show Eng'g***, 230 F.R.D. 688, 698 (M.D.Fla.2005) ("reasonable time" is too amorphous; when determining timeliness of privilege-log submission, court should use 14-day period as guideline and decide on case-by-case basis). However, it may be permissible to assert a privilege after the time to object has passed if the basis for asserting the privilege did not exist at that time. *See* ***In re DG Acquisition***, 151 F.3d at 83 (no waiver of Fifth Amendment privilege against subpoena request when basis of privilege did not arise until after time to object); *see also* 9A Wright & Miller §2463 n.13 (district court can allow untimely objections if circumstances warrant); *cf.* ***U.S. v. Hatchett***, 862 F.2d 1249, 1252 (6th Cir.1988) (remanding for determination of whether D had reasonable fear of self-incrimination during 30-day period to answer interrogatories). *But see* ***Winchester Capital Mgmt. v. Manufacturers Hanover Trust Co.***, 144 F.R.D. 170, 175-76 (D.Mass.1992) (FRCP 45 permits assertion of attorney-client or work-product privilege at time for compliance with subpoena regardless of whether objection or motion to quash has been filed).

2. Asserting privilege before disclosure.

(1) Privilege log. If the subpoenaed person is withholding information based on privilege, the subpoenaed person must provide a privilege log. FRCP 45(d)(2)(A); *see* ***Mosley v. City of Chi.***, 252 F.R.D. 445, 449 n.5 (N.D.Ill.2008) (subpoenaed persons have same obligation to provide privilege log as parties do); *see also* ***Perry v. Schwarzenegger***, 268 F.R.D. 344, 353 (N.D.Cal.2010) (no rule prevents court from waiving privilege-log requirement to reduce nonparty's burden). See "Provide privilege log," ch. 6-A, §8.3.2(2), p. 426.

(2) Effect. If a privilege is asserted, the party serving the subpoena cannot inspect, copy, test, or sample the materials or inspect the premises without an order from the court that issued the subpoena. *See* ***Mann v. University of Cincinnati***, 824 F.Supp. 1190, 1201 (S.D.Ohio 1993), *aff'd*, 152 F.R.D. 119 (S.D.Ohio 1993), *aff'd*, 114 F.3d 1188 (6th Cir.1997); *cf.* FRCP 45(c)(2)(B) (if objection is made, requesting party must obtain court order to compel production).

3. Asserting privilege after disclosure. If the subpoenaed person produces privileged information, FRCP 45(d)(2)(B) provides a procedure for a person (either a party or another nonparty) to assert claims of attorney-client privilege and work-product protection. The procedure provides that the person claiming the privilege or protection may provide notice of the claim and the basis for it to any party that received the information. FRCP 45(d)(2)(B). After notification, the party receiving the information (1) must promptly return, sequester, or destroy the information and any copies it has, (2) must not use or disclose the information until the claim is resolved, (3) must take reasonable steps to retrieve the information if the party disclosed it before being notified, and (4) may promptly present the information to the court under seal and ask the court to determine the validity of the person's claim. *Id.* The subpoenaed person must preserve the information until the claim is resolved. *Id.* The procedure for asserting the privilege or protection after disclosure under FRCP 45(d)(2)(B) mirrors that of FRCP 26(b)(5)(B). *See* 2006 Notes to FRCP 45 at ¶4, p. 1210, this book. See "Reasonable steps to rectify error," ch. 6-A, §9.3.2(2)(c)[2][c], p. 435.

NOTE

FRE 502 provides protection against waiver of the attorney-client privilege or work-product protection after information is inadvertently produced. See "Disclosure of privileged or protected information – attorney-related privileges," ch. 6-A, §9.3.2, p. 432.

§7. MOTION TO COMPEL PRODUCTION OR FOR INSPECTION

§7.1 Motion. If the subpoenaed person or a person affected by the subpoena timely objects, the requesting party may ask the court for an order compelling production, inspection, copying, testing, or sampling (i.e., ask the court to enforce the subpoena). FRCP 45(c)(2)(B)(i); *see* ***In re Sealed Case***, 121 F.3d 729, 741 (D.C.Cir.1997). See "Motion to Compel Discovery," ch. 6-A, §14, p. 444.

§7.2 Where to file. Generally, a party seeking to enforce a subpoena should file the motion to compel in the court that issued the subpoena. *See* FRCP 45(a)(2), (c)(2)(B)(i); ***In re John Adams Assocs.***, 255 F.R.D. 7, 8 (D. D.C.2008). See "Issuing court," §3.1.1, p. 48. However, some federal statutes create an exception allowing a court that did not issue a subpoena to decide motions to compel the subpoena. ***In re Clients & Former Clients of Baron & Budd, P.C.***, 478 F.3d 670, 671 (5th Cir.2007).

§7.3 Ruling. If the court compels production and the subpoenaed person is a nonparty, the order must protect the nonparty from significant expense resulting from compliance with the subpoena. FRCP 45(c)(2)(B)(ii); ***Wells Fargo Bank v. Konover***, 259 F.R.D. 206, 207 (D.Conn.2009); ***Standard Chlorine v. Sinibaldi***, 821 F.Supp. 232, 264 (D.Del.1992); 9A Wright & Miller §2463 & n.14. Although the court can shift the expenses to the requesting party, the subpoenaed nonparty may be required to bear some or all of the expenses in certain circumstances. See "Costs," §5.3.3, p. 53.

§8. MOTION TO QUASH OR MODIFY SUBPOENA

A person may file a motion to quash if she is challenging the subpoena as a whole (e.g., the subpoena subjects the person to undue burden). A person may file a motion to modify or a written objection if she is challenging a particular provision in the subpoena (e.g., the time for compliance).

§8.1 Who can file.

1. Person subject to subpoena. A person subject to a subpoena can file a motion to quash. *See* FRCP 45(c)(3).

2. Person affected by subpoena. A person affected by a subpoena can file a motion to quash. *See* FRCP 45(c)(3)(B). The person must allege that she has standing to challenge the subpoena because it affects a personal right, proprietary interest, or claim of privilege with respect to the materials subpoenaed. ***Brown v. Braddick***, 595 F.2d 961, 967 (5th Cir.1979); ***Stevenson v. Stanley Bostitch, Inc.***, 201 F.R.D. 551, 555 n.3 (N.D.Ga.2001); *e.g.*, ***Dreyer***

v. ***GACS Inc.***, 204 F.R.D. 120, 122 n.3 (N.D.Ind.2001) (party had standing to object to subpoena because of claim of privilege over documents sought); *see* ***Johnson v. Gmeinder***, 191 F.R.D. 638, 639 n.2 (D.Kan.2000).

§8.2 Deadline to file. A motion to quash a subpoena must be timely filed. FRCP 45(c)(3)(A). Ordinarily, the motion must be filed before the time for performance. *See* ***Winchester Capital Mgmt. v. Manufacturers Hanover Trust Co.***, 144 F.R.D. 170, 175-76 (D.Mass.1992).

§8.3 Where to file. Generally, a person seeking to quash or modify a subpoena should file the motion in the court that issued the subpoena. ***SEC v. CMKM Diamonds, Inc.***, 656 F.3d 829, 832 (9th Cir.2011); *see* FRCP 45(a)(2), (c)(3)(A); ***Lefkoe v. Jos. A. Bank Clothiers, Inc.***, 577 F.3d 240, 246 (4th Cir.2009); ***In re Clients & Former Clients of Baron & Budd, P.C.***, 478 F.3d 670, 671 (5th Cir.2007). But some federal statutes create an exception allowing a court that did not issue a subpoena to decide motions to quash or modify the subpoena. ***In re Clients & Former Clients of Baron & Budd***, 478 F.3d at 671.

NOTE

A person seeking to quash or modify a subpoena can consider filing a protective order; the person should file the protective order either in the court where the action is pending or, if the challenge involves matters relating to a deposition, in the court that issued the subpoena. See FRCP 26(c)(1) (person may move for protective order in court where action is pending or, for matters related to deposition, in court where deposition will be taken), FRCP 45(c)(3)(A) (person may seek to modify or quash subpoena in court that issued subpoena); ***Lefkoe****, 577 F.3d at 246 (FRCP 26(c) and 45(c) provide flexibility for nonparty seeking protection; rules do not create contradictory jurisdictional authority);* ***In re Sealed Case****, 141 F.3d 337, 342 (D.C. Cir.1998) (same); see also 1970 Notes to FRCP 26 at ¶45, p. 1193, this book (court where deposition is being taken will often refer dispute to court where action is pending). See "Motion for Protective Order," ch. 6-A, §12, p. 440. When the challenge goes beyond matters relating to the subpoena, the protective order should typically be filed in the court where the action is pending because that court has the primary responsibility for controlling the scope of discovery. See* ***Static Control Components, Inc. v. Darkprint Imaging****, 201 F.R.D. 431, 434 & n.5 (M.D.N.C.2001);* ***Rajala v. McGuire Woods, LLP****, No. 08-2638-CM-DJW (D.Kan.2010) (slip op.; 11-12-10).*

§8.4 Mandatory grounds. A court, on a timely motion, must quash or modify a subpoena under any of the circumstances listed below. *See* FRCP 45(c)(3)(A). The proof supporting these grounds must be specific. *See* ***Association of Am. Physicians & Surgeons v. Clinton***, 837 F.Supp. 454, 458 n.2 (D.D.C.1993).

1. Unreasonable time. The subpoena does not allow reasonable time for compliance. FRCP 45(c)(3)(A)(i); *e.g.*, ***Kupritz v. Savannah Coll. of Art & Design***, 155 F.R.D. 84, 88 (E.D.Pa.1994) (subpoena served at 1:45 p.m. for 1:30 p.m. deposition on same day was not necessarily unreasonable because deponent had adequate notice under earlier defective notice, but deponent was not sanctioned for failing to appear because he timely filed motion to quash).

2. Unreasonable travel. The subpoena requires a person who is not a party or officer of a party to travel more than 100 miles from the place where the person lives, works, or regularly transacts business. FRCP 45(c)(3)(A)(ii), (c)(3)(B)(iii); ***Jackson v. Brinker***, 147 F.R.D. 189, 197 n.7 (S.D.Ind.1993). See "Range of subpoena," §3.3, p. 49.

3. Privilege. The subpoena requires disclosure of privileged or protected material, and no exemption or waiver applies. FRCP 45(c)(3)(A)(iii); *e.g.*, ***Stevenson v. Stanley Bostitch, Inc.***, 201 F.R.D. 551, 555 (N.D.Ga.2001) (psychotherapist-patient privilege); ***Raso v. CMC Equip. Rental, Inc.***, 154 F.R.D. 126, 128 (E.D.Pa.1994) (work-

product privilege defeated by showing of substantial need and undue hardship); ***RE/MAX Int'l v. Century 21 Real Estate Corp.***, 846 F.Supp. 910, 911 (D.Colo.1994) (common-law journalist's privilege).

4. Undue burden. The subpoena subjects a person to an undue burden. FRCP 45(c)(3)(A)(iv); ***Linder v. NSA***, 94 F.3d 693, 695 (D.C.Cir.1996); ***Fitzpatrick v. ARCO Mar., Inc.***, 199 F.R.D. 663, 664 (C.D.Cal.2001); ***Addamax Corp. v. Open Software Found.***, 148 F.R.D. 462, 468 (D.Mass.1993); *e.g.*, ***Miscellaneous Docket Matter No. 1 v. Miscellaneous Docket Matter No. 2***, 197 F.3d 922, 925 (8th Cir.1999) (after 9½-hour deposition in Colorado, subpoena for second deposition in Minnesota properly quashed on grounds of undue burden). It may be easier for a nonparty to show undue burden than a party. *See* ***Katz v. Batavia Mar. & Sporting Sup.***, 984 F.2d 422, 424 (Fed.Cir. 1993) (nonparty status may be considered in weighing burdens imposed); ***Whitlow v. Martin***, 263 F.R.D. 507, 512 (C.D.Ill.2009) (nonparty status is significant factor in weighing burdens imposed); *see also* ***Exxon Shipping Co. v. U.S. Dept. of Interior***, 34 F.3d 774, 779 (9th Cir.1994) (nonparties are given "special protection against the time and expense of complying with subpoenas"). Being paid only the statutory witness fee under 28 U.S.C. §1821(b) does not impose an undue burden on a subpoenaed person. ***Irons v. Karceski***, 74 F.3d 1262, 1264 (D.C.Cir.1995).

§8.5 Discretionary grounds.

1. Grant motion. A court, on a timely motion, may quash a subpoena, or it may modify a subpoena (i.e., allow discovery), under any of the circumstances listed below. *See* FRCP 45(c)(3)(B).

(1) Trade secret. The subpoena requires disclosure of a trade secret or other confidential information. FRCP 45(c)(3)(B)(i); *see* FRCP 26(c)(1)(G). The subpoenaed person bears the burden of showing that the information is a trade secret and that disclosure would be harmful. ***Centurion Indus. v. Warren Steurer & Assocs.***, 665 F.2d 323, 325 (10th Cir.1981). Once this burden has been met, the party seeking discovery must show that the information is both relevant and necessary. The court must then balance the competing interests to determine whether discovery will be allowed. ***Centurion Indus.***, 665 F.2d at 325-26; *see* ***Katz v. Batavia Mar. & Sporting Sup.***, 984 F.2d 422, 424-25 (Fed.Cir.1993).

(2) Unretained expert's opinion. The subpoena requires disclosure of an unretained expert's opinion or information not related to the case and not developed as a result of a party's request. FRCP 45(c)(3)(B)(ii). This provision is intended to protect the "intellectual property" of an unretained expert who was not compensated. ***Arkwright Mut. Ins. v. National Un. Fire Ins.***, 148 F.R.D. 552, 557 & n.11 (S.D.W.Va.1993). It does not extend to experts with knowledge of relevant facts or experts who were retained by a nonparty to conduct an investigation. *See, e.g., id.* at 557-58 (expert who was paid by nonparty insurer to investigate fire and who had personal knowledge of relevant facts could be deposed). See "Testifying expert + facts = testifying expert & fact witness," ch. 6-D, §3.1.2, p. 520; "Consulting expert + facts = fact witness," ch. 6-D, §4.1.3, p. 527. The court should consider a number of factors before determining whether to allow the discovery: (1) will the expert testify about factual knowledge or expert opinion, (2) will the expert testify about a previously formed opinion or is the expert being asked to form a new opinion, (3) is the expert a "unique" expert, (4) can the party find a comparable witness willing to testify, and (5) can the expert show "oppression" by having to testify. ***Kaufman v. Edelstein***, 539 F.2d 811, 822 (2d Cir.1976).

(3) Substantial travel expense. The subpoena requires a person who is neither a party nor a party's officer to incur substantial expense to travel more than 100 miles to attend trial. FRCP 45(c)(3)(B)(iii).

(4) ESI not reasonably accessible. The subpoena requires disclosure of ESI from sources that are not reasonably accessible because of undue burden or cost. FRCP 45(d)(1)(D); 2006 Notes to FRCP 45 at ¶2, p. 1209, this book. For a discussion of how to make this objection, see "Not reasonably accessible," ch. 6-C, §9.5.2(2)(a), p. 503. The burdens for establishing and challenging a claim of undue burden arising from a production subpoena are the same as those for a request for production between parties. *Compare* FRCP 45(d)(1)(D) *with* FRCP 26(b)(2)(B). For a discussion of these burdens, see "Motion for protective order," ch. 6-C, §11.1, p. 505.

CAUTION

It is unclear how a person should actually seek protection from a subpoena requesting ESI that is unduly burdensome. See Sedona Conference Commentary on Non-Party Production & Rule 45 Subpoenas, at 2. Under FRCP 45(c)(2)(B)(ii), a person can object that the subpoena imposes a significant expense for compliance, and under FRCP 45(d)(1)(D), a person can avoid producing ESI that is not reasonably accessible because of undue burden or cost. See "Costs," §5.3.3, p. 53. The questions of which provision must be triggered first and whether these standards are the same have not been examined. See Sedona Conference Commentary on Non-Party Production & Rule 45 Subpoenas, at 2.

(5) Improper service. The subpoena was not properly served. *See* FRCP 45(b); *see, e.g.,* ***Firefighters' Inst. for Racial Equal. v. City of St. Louis***, 220 F.3d 898, 903 (8th Cir.2000) (subpoenas were quashed when Ps did not serve Ds with prior notice of production subpoena); ***Call of the Wild Movie, LLC v. Does 1-1,062***, 770 F.Supp.2d 332, 361-62 (D.D.C.2011) (subpoena was quashed when P faxed and e-mailed subpoena but did not personally serve it); ***Chao v. Tyson Foods, Inc.***, 255 F.R.D. 556, 559-60 (N.D.Ala.2009) (subpoenas were quashed when subpoenas were served beyond geographical limits under FRCP 45(b)(2)). See "Formal Requirements for Subpoenas," §3, p. 48.

2. Deny motion. The court may deny a motion to quash and allow discovery by modifying the subpoena to require the person's appearance or production of tangible things "upon specified conditions" if the requesting party both (1) shows a substantial need for information that cannot be otherwise secured without undue hardship and (2) assures the court that the subpoenaed person will be reasonably compensated. FRCP 45(c)(3)(C); *see* ***Exxon Shipping Co. v. U.S. Dept. of Interior***, 34 F.3d 774, 779 (9th Cir.1994); ***Katz***, 984 F.2d at 425 n.1; ***R&D Bus. v. Xerox Corp.***, 152 F.R.D. 195, 196-97 (D.Colo.1993).

§9. ENFORCING SUBPOENA

If a person who was properly subpoenaed does not abide by the subpoena and does not serve objections or file a motion to quash, the court that issued the subpoena can hold the person in contempt. *See* FRCP 45(e); ***U.S. v. Karlen***, 645 F.2d 635, 639 (8th Cir.1981); *see also* ***SEC v. Hyatt***, 621 F.3d 687, 693 (7th Cir.2010) (court's power to hold person in contempt for noncompliance with subpoena is same whether subpoena is issued by court or attorney).

I. THE ATTORNEY

§1. GENERAL

§1.1 Rules. FRCP 23(h) (attorney fees in class actions), 54(d)(2) (attorney fees). See 28 U.S.C. §1654 (admission of attorneys). Attorneys should also consult the local rules concerning admission of attorneys.

§1.2 Purpose. A litigant has a constitutional right, deriving from due process, to retain counsel in a civil case. ***Texas Catastrophe Prop. Ins. v. Morales***, 975 F.2d 1178, 1180 (5th Cir.1992); ***Gray v. New England Tel. & Tel. Co.***, 792 F.2d 251, 257 (1st Cir.1986); *see also* ***Potashnick v. Port City Constr. Co.***, 609 F.2d 1101, 1118 (5th Cir.1980) (court cannot prohibit attorney from consulting with party-witness during recess). *But see* ***Hudson v. McHugh***, 148 F.3d 859, 862 n.1 (7th Cir.1998) (no right to counsel in civil cases). The right to retain counsel has been extended to certain administrative proceedings as well. ***Gray***, 792 F.2d at 257; *see* ***Goldberg v. Kelly***, 397 U.S. 254, 270-71 (1970) (in hearing to terminate welfare benefits, recipient must be allowed to retain counsel). However, there is no due-process right to appointed counsel in a civil case. *See* ***Phillips v. Jasper Cty. Jail***, 437 F.3d 791, 794 (8th Cir.2006). Such appointments are a matter of the district court's discretion. ***Zarnes v. Rhodes***, 64 F.3d 285, 288 (7th Cir.1995); *see* ***Phillips***, 437 F.3d at 794.

§1.3 Forms. *O'Connor's Federal Civil Forms* (2012), FORMS 1I.

§1.4 Other references. Restatement (3d) of the Law Governing Lawyers, ch. 2, "The Client-Lawyer Relationship" (2000 & Supp.2012); 1 Childress & Davis, *Federal Standards of Review 4th* §4.08[2] (2010 & Supp.2011); ABA Model Rules of Prof'l Conduct; ABA Model Code of Prof'l Responsibility; Hirsch & Sheehey, *Awarding Attorneys' Fees & Managing Fee Litigation* (2d ed. 2005), Federal Judicial Center, www.fjc.gov; Annotation, *Attorney's Right to Appear Pro Hac Vice in Federal Court*, 33 ALR Fed. 799 (1977 & Supp.2012-13).

§2. APPEARING BEFORE FEDERAL COURT

Admission to a state bar does not convey the automatic right to appear before a federal district court. ***Zambrano v. City of Tustin***, 885 F.2d 1473, 1483 (9th Cir.1989); *see* ***Leis v. Flynt***, 439 U.S. 438, 443-44 (1979) (attorney's interest in appearing pro hac vice does not constitute liberty or property right under U.S. Constitution); ***D.H. Overmyer, Co. v. Robson***, 750 F.2d 31, 33 (6th Cir.1984) (under local rules, decision to permit out-of-state attorney to practice in bankruptcy or district court is within sound discretion of trial judge); ***Thomas v. Cassidy***, 249 F.2d 91, 92 (4th Cir. 1957) (permission to appear pro hac vice is privilege, granting of which is within sound discretion of presiding judge). But once an attorney is admitted to a state bar, admission to a federal district court in that state is usually perfunctory. ***Zambrano***, 885 F.2d at 1483.

§2.1 Application for general admission. To practice law before a federal court, an attorney must usually be a member of either the bar of the state where the district court is located or the bar of any U.S. district court, and the attorney must be of good professional character and competence. *See* ***In re Martin***, 120 F.3d 256, 258 (Fed.Cir. 1997); ***In re Mosher***, 25 F.3d 397, 399 (6th Cir.1994); ***In re Evans***, 524 F.2d 1004, 1007 (5th Cir.1975); *see also* ***In re Desilets***, 291 F.3d 925, 930-31 (6th Cir.2002) (fact that attorney is not admitted to bar of state where district court is located cannot by itself prevent attorney from practicing in that court). The requirements for admission are governed by each district's local rules, and not all districts reciprocate membership with other federal districts.

1. Application. To be admitted to a federal bar, the attorney usually must file a written application containing information about the attorney's background and status in other courts. Local rules for each district usually provide the specific requirements for each court's application process. *E.g.*, Local Rules Fla. (M.D.), Rule 2.01(b); Local Rules Tex. (E.D.), Rule AT-1.

2. Review of application. The application is reviewed by an admissions committee, which grants or denies admission. Only the strongest evidence of unfitness will justify denying admission of a litigant's attorney. ***In re Mosher***, 25 F.3d at 400. Once an attorney is admitted to practice before a federal district court, the court has inherent power to suspend or disbar for cause. ***In re Fletcher***, 221 F.2d 477, 477 (4th Cir.1955). Federal circuit courts have subject-matter jurisdiction to review orders suspending or disbarring attorneys from practicing in federal district courts. ***In re Martin***, 400 F.3d 836, 840 (10th Cir.2005).

§2.2 Application to appear pro hac vice. An out-of-district attorney may apply for permission to appear by motion for leave to appear pro hac vice, which means "for this one particular occasion." *See Black's Law Dictionary* 1331 (9th ed. 2009). Admission to one federal court does not guarantee the right to appear pro hac vice before another federal court. ***Zambrano v. City of Tustin***, 885 F.2d 1473, 1483 (9th Cir.1989). However, admission pro hac vice is typically a formality as long as the courts of some jurisdiction have approved the attorney as having the requisite skill and integrity to practice law. ***Cole v. U.S.***, 162 F.3d 957, 958 (7th Cir.1998).

1. Application. Usually, the out-of-district attorney must file a written application stating (1) the attorney's status in other courts, (2) whether the attorney has applied for permission to practice pro hac vice before any other courts, and (3) the disposition of those requests. *See* ***Baldwin Hardware Corp. v. Franksu Enter.***, 78 F.3d 550, 561-62 (Fed.Cir.1996). In rare instances, the attorney's admission pro hac vice may be implied without an application. *See, e.g.*, ***Santa Maria v. Metro-N. Commuter R.R.***, 81 F.3d 265, 274 (2d Cir.1996) (permission was implied, given circuit's policy of permitting out-of-state attorneys who specialize in areas of federal law to work with local counsel on a P's federal claim); *see also* ***Kirkland v. National Mortg. Network, Inc.***, 884 F.2d 1367, 1370-71 (11th Cir.1989) (after court granted informal oral motion to appear pro hac vice, attorney served as counsel for five months without objection). See ***O'Connor's Federal Forms***, FORM 1I:2.

2. Standards for admission. There are no rules establishing national standards for admission pro hac vice, but an applicant who is in good standing with a state bar generally should not be denied the opportunity to appear. *See **Schlumberger Techs. v. Wiley***, 113 F.3d 1553, 1562-63 (11th Cir.1997) (applicant with state bar should not be denied opportunity to appear unless found guilty of unethical conduct justifying disbarment); ***In re Evans***, 524 F.2d 1004, 1007 (5th Cir.1975) (same). Federal courts may set reasonable standards for admission pro hac vice. *See **Zambrano***, 885 F.2d at 1483; *see, e.g.*, Local Rules Ill. (N.D.), Rule 83.14; Local Rules N.Y. (E.D. & S.D.), Rule 1.3(c). Whether an attorney is admitted pro hac vice is left to the discretion of the judge. *See* Local Rules Cal. (C.D.), Rule 83-2.3.1; *see, e.g.*, ***Roma Constr. Co. v. aRusso***, 96 F.3d 566, 577 (1st Cir.1996) (court did not need to decide whether pro hac vice rule was discretionary because, even if it were, denial of admission was abuse of discretion). What conduct justifies denial of an application varies by circuit. *See **U.S. v. Ries***, 100 F.3d 1469, 1471 (9th Cir.1996) (behavior suggesting that attorney will impede court's "orderly administration of justice" may cause court to reject application); *see, e.g.*, ***Panzardi-Alvarez v. U.S.***, 879 F.2d 975, 980-81 (1st Cir.1989) (court did not admit attorney because of potential conflict of interest and ethical violations, although court had discretion to deny application for other reasons); ***D.H. Overmyer, Co. v. Robson***, 750 F.2d 31, 34 (6th Cir.1984) (bankruptcy court did not admit attorney who had conflict of interest under state disciplinary rules). *See generally* Annotation, *Attorney's Right to Appear Pro Hac Vice in Federal Court*, 33 ALR Fed. 799 (1977 & Supp.2012-13) (discussing factors considered in permitting appearance).

3. Hearing. If the court grants permission to appear pro hac vice, a hearing is not necessary. A hearing may be necessary in the following instances:

(1) Permission denied. Before denying a pro hac vice application, some courts require that an attorney be given notice of the specific grounds for denial and an opportunity to respond. ***In re Evans***, 524 F.2d at 1008. Other courts do not require a hearing before denying a pro hac vice application. *See **U.S. v. Gonzalez-Lopez***, 399 F.3d 924, 930 n.4 (8th Cir.2005), *aff'd*, 548 U.S. 140 (2006); ***Panzardi-Alvarez***, 879 F.2d at 980.

(2) Permission revoked. Once an attorney is permitted to appear, the court cannot revoke the attorney's pro hac vice status without notice and an opportunity to respond. ***Kirkland***, 884 F.2d at 1371; ***Johnson v. Trueblood***, 629 F.2d 302, 303-04 (3d Cir.1980).

§2.3 Pro se representation.

1. Individual. A litigant has the right to represent herself without an attorney. 28 U.S.C. §1654; *see **Winkelman v. Parma City Sch. Dist.***, 550 U.S. 516, 522 (2007). Once the litigant decides to proceed pro se in a civil matter, the litigant cannot also be represented by an attorney except in unusual circumstances.

2. Not for another. A nonattorney, such as a next friend, generally cannot represent someone else pro se. ***Elustra v. Mineo***, 595 F.3d 699, 704 (7th Cir.2010); ***Powerserve Int'l v. Lavi***, 239 F.3d 508, 514 (2d Cir.2001); *see also **Winkelman***, 550 U.S. at 522, 535 (Supreme Court did not address whether nonattorney parents could litigate child's claims pro se under Individuals with Disabilities Education Act). However, there are exceptions for particular proceedings and circumstances. *See, e.g.*, ***Elustra***, 595 F.3d at 705-06 (when minor daughters had representation until judgment but were briefly without representation during ten-day period when postjudgment motion could be filed, mother was allowed to file FRCP 59(e) motion on behalf of daughters; applying former ten-day deadline); ***Machadio v. Apfel***, 276 F.3d 103, 106-07 (2d Cir.2002) (nonattorney parent may represent child pro se when parent has sufficient interest in Social Security benefits claim and meets basic standards of competence).

3. Corporations & other entities. A corporation cannot appear pro se in federal court; it must appear through licensed counsel. ***Rowland v. California Men's Colony***, 506 U.S. 194, 202-03 (1993); ***U.S. v. High Country Broad. Co.***, 3 F.3d 1244, 1245 (9th Cir.1993); ***Jones v. Niagara Frontier Transp. Auth.***, 722 F.2d 20, 22 (2d Cir. 1983). Partnerships and other organizations also must be represented by an attorney. *See **Eagle Assocs. v. Bank of Montreal***, 926 F.2d 1305, 1308-10 (2d Cir.1991) (general partner cannot represent limited partnership); ***Church of the New Testament v. U.S.***, 783 F.2d 771, 773 (9th Cir.1986) (unincorporated association must appear through counsel).

COMMENTARIES

CHAPTER 1. INTRODUCTION
I. THE ATTORNEY

§3. COMMUNICATIONS WITH COURT

§3.1 Ex parte communication prohibited. Ex parte communications involve fewer than all of the parties who are legally entitled to be present during the discussion. *See Black's Law Dictionary* 316 (9th ed. 2009). The Administrative Procedure Act defines an ex parte communication as "an oral or written communication not on the public record with respect to which reasonable prior notice to all parties is not given." 5 U.S.C. §551(14); ***Portland Audubon Soc'y v. Endangered Species Cmte.***, 984 F.2d 1534, 1539 n.9 (9th Cir.1993).

1. With party. A party or its attorney cannot communicate ex parte with the court about the merits of a pending lawsuit. ***Drobny v. Commissioner***, 113 F.3d 670, 680 (7th Cir.1997); *see* ***Guenther v. Commissioner***, 939 F.2d 758, 760-61 (9th Cir.1991) (trial brief cannot be submitted ex parte); *see also* ***Clifford v. U.S.***, 136 F.3d 144, 150 (D.C.Cir.1998) (when party conveys ex parte information to trial judge about pending case, appellate courts presume that judge can adequately determine whether communications go to merits of case). In emergency circumstances, ex parte communications about the merits may be allowed. See "Ex parte communication allowed," §3.2, this page.

2. With witness. A judge cannot communicate ex parte with a witness to gather facts outside the record. *E.g.*, ***Knop v. Johnson***, 977 F.2d 996, 1011 (6th Cir.1992) (judge's requests for additional information should have been made on the record; law clerk should not have called P's key witness). The communication will disqualify the judge if it relates to the merits or to procedures affecting the merits. ***Edgar v. K.L.***, 93 F.3d 256, 258 (7th Cir.1996).

3. With jury. Any message received from a jury must be answered in open court with an opportunity for all counsel to be heard before the court responds. *E.g.*, ***Fillippon v. Albion Vein Slate Co.***, 250 U.S. 76, 81 (1919) (judge erred in giving supplemental charge without giving litigants chance to be present or to object). A court's ex parte communication with the jury is grounds for reversal only if the substantive rights of the parties were adversely affected. *E.g.*, *id.* at 82 (supplemental charge excluded material element and was erroneous); *see* ***U.S. v. Bishawi***, 272 F.3d 458, 461-62 (7th Cir.2001) (D entitled to new trial only if ex parte communication likely affected jury's verdict); ***Miller v. American President Lines, Ltd.***, 989 F.2d 1450, 1468 (6th Cir.1993) (ex parte communication between judge and jury raises rebuttable presumption of reversible error).

4. With other nonparties. A judge cannot initiate or consider communications with nonparties about the merits, or procedures affecting the merits, of a pending or upcoming proceeding. *E.g.*, ***U.S. v. Microsoft Corp.***, 253 F.3d 34, 112-13 (D.C.Cir.2001) (judge's comments on case to reporters required disqualification; citing Code of Conduct for U.S. Judges, Canon 3A(6)). Even limited public comments about the merits of a case may require disqualification. *See, e.g.*, ***In re Boston's Children First***, 244 F.3d 164, 169-71 (1st Cir.2001) (judge's letter to newspaper commenting on decision not to certify class required disqualification); ***In re International Bus. Machs. Corp.***, 45 F.3d 641, 643-44 (2d Cir.1995) (judge's comments to newspaper about D's activities and assistant attorney general's actions required disqualification); ***U.S. v. Cooley***, 1 F.3d 985, 995 (10th Cir.1993) (judge's comments on television about abortion protesters required disqualification).

§3.2 Ex parte communication allowed. Ex parte communications between a judge and a party are permitted if they involve issues unrelated to the merits, administrative matters, or emergency circumstances. *See* ***Drobny v. Commissioner***, 113 F.3d 670, 680-81 (7th Cir.1997); ***In re School Asbestos Litig.***, 977 F.2d 764, 789 (3d Cir.1992); *cf.* ***U.S. v. Thompson***, 827 F.2d 1254, 1258-59 (9th Cir.1987) (criminal case; emergency circumstances include need to act quickly or to protect sensitive information).

§3.3 Challenging ex parte communication. The party who claims injury from an ex parte communication must demonstrate that the communication unfairly prejudiced the case. *See* ***In re School Asbestos Litig.***, 977 F.2d 764, 789 (3d Cir.1992) (complaining party must show prejudicial ex parte advocacy).

§4. ATTORNEY IN CHARGE

Local rules sometimes provide that the attorney whose signature appears on the first pleading for any party is the "attorney in charge," unless another attorney is specifically designated. For example, the local rules for the Southern District of Texas provide that the attorney who signs a party's first pleading is the attorney in charge, is responsible for the lawsuit, and must attend all court proceedings or send a fully informed attorney with authority to bind the client. Local Rules Tex. (S.D.), Rules 11.1, 11.2.

§5. WITHDRAWAL

Before withdrawing, an attorney should consult the local rules of the district and any other applicable professional rules. *See* ABA Model Rules of Prof'l Conduct, Rule 1.16; *see, e.g.*, ***Ohntrup v. Firearms Ctr., Inc.***, 802 F.2d 676, 679 (3d Cir.1986) (local rules allowed judge to deny withdrawal even though client dismissed attorney); ***Hammond v. T.J. Litle & Co.***, 809 F.Supp. 156, 159 (D.Mass.1992) (local rules required new attorney to be obtained before old attorney could withdraw). In most districts, an attorney cannot withdraw without obtaining leave of court. *E.g.*, Local Rules Ill. (N.D.), Rule 83.17; Local Rules N.Y. (E.D. & S.D.), Rule 1.4.

§5.1 Withdrawal by attorney.

1. Client agrees to withdrawal.

(1) Substitute attorney. When an attorney withdraws with the client's consent, another attorney should be simultaneously substituted for the withdrawing attorney. The proper procedure is to file a motion to withdraw and substitute. *See, e.g.*, Local Rules N.Y. (E.D. & S.D.), Rule 1.4 (motion to withdraw may be granted only on affidavit or other showing of status of case and satisfactory reasons for withdrawal). The motion to substitute should (1) identify the new attorney by name, address, telephone number, and state-bar or other identifying number, (2) state whether the client has approved of the substitution, (3) state that the substitution is not being taken for purposes of delay, and (4) be signed by both attorneys.

(2) No substitute attorney. If there is no substitute attorney, the court may deny leave to withdraw. *See, e.g.*, ***Ohntrup v. Firearms Ctr., Inc.***, 802 F.2d 676, 679 (3d Cir.1986) (court denied attorney's requests to withdraw from postjudgment collection proceedings when D did not provide for substitute attorney).

2. Client opposes withdrawal. When an attorney withdraws without the client's consent, the attorney must show that the withdrawal is for good cause and will not disrupt the lawsuit. ***Broughten v. Voss***, 634 F.2d 880, 882-83 (5th Cir.1981); *see* ***FTC v. Intellipay, Inc.***, 828 F.Supp. 33, 34 (S.D.Tex.1993); ***Darby v. City of Torrance***, 810 F.Supp. 275, 276 (C.D.Cal.1992); ***Hammond v. T.J. Litle & Co.***, 809 F.Supp. 156, 159 (D.Mass.1992).

§5.2 Termination by client. In most cases, discharge of an attorney is a matter of state law. Typically, no special formality is required for a client to discharge an attorney; any act by the client indicating an unmistakable purpose to sever the relationship is enough. ***Hanlin v. Mitchelson***, 794 F.2d 834, 842 (2d Cir.1986). A client may discharge its attorney at any time, even without cause. ***Doggett v. Deauville Corp.***, 148 F.2d 881, 882 (5th Cir.1945); ***MacLeod v. Vest Transp.***, 235 F.Supp. 369, 371 (N.D.Miss.1964); Restatement (3d) of the Law Governing Lawyers §32. *But see* 2003 Notes to FRCP 23 at ¶38, p. 1167, this book (class representatives do not have unfettered right to discharge class attorney). After being discharged, the attorney may still be entitled under state law to a reasonable payment for the services rendered. *See* ***Maksym v. Loesch***, 937 F.2d 1237, 1245 (7th Cir.1991) (under Illinois law, discharged attorney entitled to fair value of services); ***Novinger v. E.I. DuPont de Nemours & Co.***, 809 F.2d 212, 218 (3d Cir.1987) (under Pennsylvania law, discharged attorney entitled to lien for quantum meruit).

§6. DISQUALIFICATION

§6.1 Standards for professional conduct. Federal courts may adopt state or national rules of professional conduct as their ethical standards; federal law determines whether and how those rules are to be applied. ***In re American Airlines, Inc.***, 972 F.2d 605, 610 (5th Cir.1992). Without formally adopted standards of professional conduct, a court is free to regulate the conduct of attorneys appearing before it. ***Paul E. Iacono Structural Eng'r, Inc. v. Humphrey***, 722 F.2d 435, 439 (9th Cir.1983); *see* ***In re Corn Derivatives Antitrust Litig.***, 748 F.2d 157, 160 (3d Cir.1984) (simply because court has never adopted standards does not mean that attorneys appearing before it do not have ethical obligations or duties); *see also* ***In re BellSouth Corp.***, 334 F.3d 941, 959 (11th Cir.2003) (different standards for disqualification based on (1) alleged violation of ethical rule and (2) conduct disruptive of proceedings or threatening administration of laws). Generally, motions to disqualify are governed by the following:

1. Local rules. Local rules are the most immediate source of guidance for a district court because federal district courts usually adopt the rules of professional conduct promulgated either by the American Bar Association or by the state where the court is situated. ***Cole v. Ruidoso Mun. Sch.***, 43 F.3d 1373, 1383 (10th Cir.1994); *see*

In re ProEducation Int'l, 587 F.3d 296, 299 (5th Cir.2009); *see, e.g.*, ***Blair v. Armontrout***, 916 F.2d 1310, 1333 (8th Cir.1990) (district court for Western District of Missouri adopted Missouri Code of Professional Responsibility). In some circuits, the district courts may look beyond the local rules for guidance. ***In re ProEducation Int'l***, 587 F.3d at 299; *see* ***In re Dresser Indus.***, 972 F.2d 540, 543 (5th Cir.1992) (local rules are not sole authority governing motions to disqualify because local rules alone cannot regulate party's right to counsel of its choice). *But see* ***Waters v. Kemp***, 845 F.2d 260, 265-66 & n.13 (11th Cir.1988) (violation of Canon 9 of ABA's former Model Code of Professional Responsibility could not be used as ground for disqualification because district court had adopted ABA Model Rules of Professional Conduct).

2. ABA standards. The district court may consider the ethical standards established by the American Bar Association, most recently the Model Rules of Professional Conduct. ***FDIC v. U.S. Fire Ins.***, 50 F.3d 1304, 1312 (5th Cir.1995); *e.g.*, ***Humphrey***, 722 F.2d at 440 (court did not err in relying on former Model Code because California courts cited and applied it as source of ethical principles and rules governing California attorneys); *see* ***Cox v. American Cast Iron Pipe Co.***, 847 F.2d 725, 728 n.4 (11th Cir.1988) (relying on ABA's former Model Code of Professional Responsibility); *see also* ***Harker v. Commissioner***, 82 F.3d 806, 808 n.1 (8th Cir.1996) (ABA's Model Rules of Professional Conduct have been adopted by U.S. Tax Court, 36 states, and District of Columbia); ***In re Corn Derivatives Antitrust Litig.***, 748 F.2d at 160 (most courts have adopted, with variation, ABA's professional-responsibility standards); ***Fund of Funds, Ltd. v. Arthur Andersen & Co.***, 567 F.2d 225, 227 n.2 (2d Cir.1977) (former Model Code is recognized within circuit as providing appropriate guidelines for proper professional behavior).

3. State-bar standards. The federal court may consider the ethical standards announced by the bar association of the state where the court is situated. ***U.S. Fire***, 50 F.3d at 1312.

§6.2 Grounds. The following are the most common grounds for disqualifying attorneys in civil litigation:

1. Attorney as witness. A trial attorney who is likely to testify on behalf of the client about fact issues (other than uncontested issues or attorney fees) should be disqualified. ABA Model Rules of Prof'l Conduct, Rule 3.7(a); *see* ***International Woodworkers v. Chesapeake Bay Plywood Corp.***, 659 F.2d 1259, 1272-73 (4th Cir.1981); ***Fulfree v. Manchester***, 945 F.Supp. 768, 771-72 (S.D.N.Y.1996). The rationale behind this prohibition is to eliminate (1) the possibility that the attorney will appear to vouch for her own credibility in addressing the jury, (2) the unfair situation that arises when an opposing attorney has to cross-examine an attorney-adversary and seek to impeach her credibility, and (3) the appearance of impropriety (i.e., the likely implication that the testifying attorney may well be distorting the truth for the sake of her client). ***Culebras Enters. v. Rivera-Rios***, 846 F.2d 94, 99 (1st Cir.1988). Because these concerns are greatly reduced when an attorney-witness does not act as trial counsel, some courts have disqualified the attorney-witness from participating at trial while allowing her to continue as counsel in pretrial matters. *E.g.*, ***Moyer v. 1330 Nineteenth St. Corp.***, 597 F.Supp. 14, 17 (D.D.C.1984); ***Brotherhood Ry. Carmen v. Delpro Co.***, 549 F.Supp. 780, 789-90 (D.Del.1982).

2. Litigation adverse to former client. An attorney and her law firm should be disqualified if the attorney would be able to use privileged information obtained through representation of a former client in matters that are substantially related to the current litigation. ***Cromley v. Board of Educ.***, 17 F.3d 1059, 1064 (7th Cir.1994); ***Fund of Funds, Ltd. v. Arthur Andersen & Co.***, 567 F.2d 225, 235-36 (2d Cir.1977). To prove that an opposing attorney should be disqualified on this ground, the party seeking disqualification must establish the following:

(1) Attorney-client relationship. There was an attorney-client relationship between the former client and the challenged attorney. ***Cole v. Ruidoso Mun. Sch.***, 43 F.3d 1373, 1384 (10th Cir.1994); ***In re American Airlines, Inc.***, 972 F.2d 605, 614 (5th Cir.1992); ***Cox v. American Cast Iron Pipe Co.***, 847 F.2d 725, 728 (11th Cir. 1988); ***Telectronics Proprietary, Ltd. v. Medtronic, Inc.***, 836 F.2d 1332, 1336 (Fed.Cir.1988).

(2) Substantially related representations. The present litigation involves a matter that is "substantially related" to the subject of the earlier representation. ***Cole***, 43 F.3d at 1384; ***In re American Airlines***, 972 F.2d at 614; ***Borges v. Our Lady of the Sea Corp.***, 935 F.2d 436, 439-40 (1st Cir.1991); ***Atasi Corp. v. Seagate Tech.***, 847 F.2d 826, 829 (Fed.Cir.1988); ***In re Corn Derivatives Antitrust Litig.***, 748 F.2d 157, 161-62 (3d Cir.1984). There

is a substantial relationship between past work and the suit at hand if the factual contexts of the two representations are similar. ***Cole***, 43 F.3d at 1384. In other words, was the attorney so involved in the matter that her later representation could be regarded as a changing of sides in the matter in question? *See* ABA Model Rules of Prof'l Conduct, Rule 1.9 cmt. 2. To prove a substantial relationship, the party seeking disqualification should address the following issues: (1) the scope of the earlier legal representation, (2) whether it is reasonable to presume that the former client may have transmitted to the former attorney the type of confidential information allegedly given, and (3) whether the confidential information is relevant to the issues raised in the litigation pending against the former client. ***Westinghouse Elec. Corp. v. Gulf Oil Corp.***, 588 F.2d 221, 225 (7th Cir.1978); *see* ***In re American Airlines***, 972 F.2d at 614 (party seeking disqualification should specify subject matters, issues, and claims common to earlier and current representations); ***Duncan v. Merrill Lynch, Pierce, Fenner & Smith, Inc.***, 646 F.2d 1020, 1029 (5th Cir.1981) (merely pointing to superficial resemblance between present and earlier litigation is not sufficient). In proving a substantial relationship, the party seeking disqualification is not required to present a particular piece of confidential information that the challenged attorney actually received. ***LaSalle Nat'l Bank v. Lake Cty.***, 703 F.2d 252, 256 (7th Cir.1983). If the representations are substantially related, two presumptions arise—the presumption of shared confidences and the presumption of imputed knowledge. ***Panduit Corp. v. All States Plastic Mfg. Co.***, 744 F.2d 1564, 1577 (Fed.Cir.1984).

(a) Presumption of shared confidences. There is a presumption that the attorney who actually did the past work received confidences relevant to the current litigation. ***Panduit Corp. v. All States Plastic Mfg. Co.***, 744 F.2d 1564, 1577 (Fed.Cir.1984); ***Schiessle v. Stephens***, 717 F.2d 417, 420 n.2 (7th Cir.1983). The presumption may be rebutted by showing either of the following:

[1] Presumption related to earlier litigation. To rebut the presumption of shared confidences with respect to the earlier litigation, the challenged attorney must show that she had no knowledge of the information, confidences, or secrets related by the client in the earlier representation. ***Cromley***, 17 F.3d at 1065. The presumption may be rebutted using the peripheral-representation defense. *See* ***Atasi Corp.***, 847 F.2d at 829. Under this defense, an attorney previously associated with a firm that handled matters substantially related to those in which the attorney's disqualification is sought may avoid disqualification by showing that she had no personal involvement in the matters. *Id.*; *see, e.g.*, ***EZ Paintr Corp. v. Padco, Inc.***, 746 F.2d 1459, 1461-62 (Fed.Cir.1984) (although challenged attorneys did not work on earlier litigation, affidavits of former partners established that challenged attorneys received former client's confidential information). However, if the attorney actually represented and did work for the client, the presumption is virtually unrebuttable. ***Cox***, 847 F.2d at 729.

[2] Presumption related to current litigation. To rebut the presumption of shared confidences with respect to the current litigation, the challenged attorney must show that she has not passed on or is not likely to pass on to the members of her new firm the former client's confidences and secrets. ***Schiessle***, 717 F.2d at 421. One of the most common methods of challenging this presumption is by demonstrating that specific institutional mechanisms (e.g., a "Chinese Wall") have been implemented to prevent the challenged attorney's communication of confidential information to any other member of the new firm. ***Manning v. Waring, Cox, James, Sklar & Allen***, 849 F.2d 222, 225 (6th Cir.1988); ***Schiessle***, 717 F.2d at 421; *see, e.g.*, ***Blair v. Armontrout***, 916 F.2d 1310, 1333 (8th Cir.1990) (Chinese Wall could have been implemented to avoid disqualifying entire attorney general's office). *But see* ***Paul E. Iacono Structural Eng'r, Inc. v. Humphrey***, 722 F.2d 435, 442 (9th Cir.1983) (declining to adopt Chinese Wall defense). Courts consider the following factors in determining whether the former client's confidences have been adequately protected:

[a] Whether all members of the new firm have been instructed about the attorney's recusal and the ban on any exchange of information. ***Cromley***, 17 F.3d at 1065.

[b] The existence of rules that prevent the "infected" attorney from accessing relevant files or other information pertaining to the present litigation. ***Schiessle***, 717 F.2d at 421. For example, the court may inquire whether the case files are locked and whether the firm uses secret codes to limit access to case information on computers. ***Cromley***, 17 F.3d at 1065.

[c] Whether the firm prohibits sharing of fees derived from the litigation. *Id.*

[d] The size and structural divisions of the firm and the "infected" attorney's position in the firm. *Id.*

[e] The likelihood of contact between the "infected" attorney and the specific attorneys responsible for the present representation. *Id.*

[f] When the screening arrangement or other mechanism for protecting the former client's confidences was set up. *See, e.g.*, ***EZ Paintr***, 746 F.2d at 1462 (offer of Chinese Wall three months after client's former attorneys joined new firm was too late).

NOTE

The presumption of shared confidences is not rebuttable when an entire law firm changes sides. ***Cromley****, 17 F.3d at 1066;* ***Schiessle****, 717 F.2d at 420 n.2.*

(b) Presumption of imputed knowledge. There is a presumption that attorneys within a firm share each other's confidences and that those confidences will be imputed from one attorney to the other. ***Panduit Corp.***, 744 F.2d at 1577; *see* ***In re American Airlines***, 972 F.2d at 614 n.1; ***Trone v. Smith***, 621 F.2d 994, 999 (9th Cir. 1980). This presumption arises because attorneys frequently discuss the matters they are working on with other members of their firm. ***Panduit Corp.***, 744 F.2d at 1578-79. The presumption applies to partners, associates, and of-counsel attorneys. *See* ***Atasi Corp.***, 847 F.2d at 830; *cf.* ***Fund of Funds***, 567 F.2d at 234-35 (under former Canons, label of partner, cocounsel, or law clerk should not control decisions on whether disqualification is appropriate).

EXAMPLE

Under the presumption of imputed knowledge, disqualification would occur as follows: Attorney A of Firm 1 represents Client C. The receipt of confidential information is imputed to Attorney B of Firm 1, even if Attorney B did not participate in the representation. If Attorney B leaves Firm 1 and joins Firm 2, Attorney B cannot represent a party opposing Client C even though she has left Firm 1. However, Attorney D of Firm 2 could represent a party opposing Client C if Attorney D is insulated from Attorney B. See ***Panduit Corp.****, 744 F.2d at 1578 n.21; see also* ***SLC Ltd. V v. Bradford Grp. W., Inc.****, 999 F.2d 464, 467 (10th Cir.1993) (under Utah rules of professional conduct, when Attorney B becomes associated with Firm 2, Firm 2 cannot represent a client who is materially adverse to any former client of both Attorney B and Firm 1 if that former client imparted confidences to Attorney B that are material to new litigation). However, some courts have held that this presumption can be rebutted for a departing attorney if she did not acquire any confidential information from her former firm's client—that is, if Attorney B did not participate in the representation of Client C or receive any confidential information about Client C while at Firm 1, Attorney B can represent a party with an interest adverse to Client C when she joins Firm 2. See, e.g.,* ***In re ProEducation Int'l****, 587 F.3d 296, 303 (5th Cir.2009) (in bankruptcy proceeding, presumption of imputed knowledge rebutted; after attorney moved to new firm, he was allowed to represent creditor because attorney had not received any confidential information when he worked at former firm that represented another creditor in same proceeding).*

---

(3) Materially adverse interests. The interests of the challenged attorney's present client are materially adverse to the interests of the former client. ***Cole***, 43 F.3d at 1384; ***Humphrey***, 722 F.2d at 440.

(4) No consent. The former client did not consent to the adverse representation. ***In re Corn Derivatives Antitrust Litig.***, 748 F.2d at 161-62; *see* ***Manning***, 849 F.2d at 227 (consent to conflict of interest waives

objections to adverse representation). Once the party seeking disqualification asserts that the former client did not consent, the burden of proof on consent is on the party opposing disqualification. *E.g.*, ***In re Corn Derivatives Antitrust Litig.***, 748 F.2d at 162 & n.4 (attorney made no representations in affidavit or reply that former client consented).

(5) Timely objection. The party seeking disqualification moved to disqualify the attorney with reasonable promptness after it discovered the facts. ***Cox***, 847 F.2d at 729; *see* ***Redd v. Shell Oil Co.***, 518 F.2d 311, 316 (10th Cir.1975) (conflict of interest should be brought up long before date of trial); *see, e.g.*, ***Trust Corp. v. Piper Aircraft Corp.***, 701 F.2d 85, 87-88 (9th Cir.1983) (P's delay of 2½ years before filing motion to disqualify was unreasonable and amounted to waiver of its right to object).

3. Litigation adverse to current client. An attorney and her law firm should be disqualified if the attorney's independent professional judgment on behalf of a current client is likely to be adversely affected by her representation of another client. *See* ***Unified Sewerage Agency v. Jelco Inc.***, 646 F.2d 1339, 1345 (9th Cir.1981); ABA Model Rules of Prof'l Conduct, Rule 1.7(a). To prove that an attorney should be disqualified, the party seeking disqualification must establish the following:

(1) Attorney-client relationship. There was an attorney-client relationship when the attorney undertook the dual representation. *See* ***Unified Sewerage***, 646 F.2d at 1344-45 & n.4.

(2) No effective consent. The client did not give effective consent to the dual representation. ***Picker Int'l v. Varian Assocs.***, 869 F.2d 578, 582 (Fed.Cir.1989); *see* ***EEOC v. Orson H. Gygi Co.***, 749 F.2d 620, 622 (10th Cir.1984); *cf.* ***Unified Sewerage***, 646 F.2d at 1345 (discussing Oregon State Bar's disciplinary rules). Lack of consent can be established, for example, by demonstrating that the attorney obtained the consent by duress. ***Picker Int'l***, 869 F.2d at 584. In some situations, such as when a disinterested attorney would conclude that the client should not agree to the dual representation, the attorney involved cannot properly ask for consent or provide representation based on the client's consent. ABA Model Rules of Prof'l Conduct, Rule 1.7 cmt. 14.

(3) Representation adversely affected attorney's judgment. Generally, there is a presumption that the attorney's independent judgment will be adversely affected when she litigates a lawsuit against a current client. ***Picker Int'l***, 869 F.2d at 581; *see* ABA Model Rules of Prof'l Conduct, Rule 1.7(a). Even so, the party seeking disqualification should show in its motion to disqualify that the attorney could not have reasonably believed that her independent judgment would not be or was unlikely to be adversely affected by her relationship with both clients. *See* ***Shaffer v. Farm Fresh, Inc.***, 966 F.2d 142, 145-46 (4th Cir.1992) (judicial intuition is not enough to establish likelihood that independent judgment would be adversely affected); *see also* ***Unified Sewerage***, 646 F.2d at 1346 (under former Model Code, it must be obvious that attorney can adequately represent interest of each client). In determining the reasonableness of the attorney's belief, the party seeking disqualification should address the following factors:

(a) The nature of the litigation. ***Unified Sewerage***, 646 F.2d at 1350.

(b) The type of information to which the attorney may have had access. *Id.*

(c) Whether the client is in a position to protect its interests or know whether it will be disadvantaged as a result of the multiple representation. *Id.*; *see, e.g.*, ***Dunton v. County of Suffolk***, 729 F.2d 903, 909 (2d Cir.1984) (client presumably knew little about law of attorney conflicts and could not be expected to discern nature of conflict), *amended*, 748 F.2d 69 (2d Cir.1984).

(d) The questions in dispute. ***Unified Sewerage***, 646 F.2d at 1350.

(e) Whether a governmental unit is involved. *Id.*

4. Appearance of impropriety. An attorney and her law firm should be disqualified if there is a reasonable possibility that the attorney has engaged in some specifically identifiable impropriety and the likelihood of

public suspicion of such an impropriety is strong enough to outweigh the party's interest in having the attorney of its choice. ***Cox***, 847 F.2d at 731; ***McCuin v. Texas Power & Light Co.***, 714 F.2d 1255, 1265 (5th Cir.1983); *see* ***Optyl Eyewear Fashion Int'l v. Style Cos.***, 760 F.2d 1045, 1049 (9th Cir.1985). Proof of actual wrongdoing is not required, but there must be at least a reasonable possibility that some specifically identifiable impropriety occurred. ***Turner v. Orr***, 785 F.2d 1498, 1505 (11th Cir.1986); *see* ***McCuin***, 714 F.2d at 1265 (court should be concerned only with specific past improprieties); *see, e.g.*, ***Optyl Eyewear***, 760 F.2d at 1049 (party seeking disqualification did not allege any specific improprieties that would result if P's attorney testified in case). For example, an attorney's acceptance of employment solely or primarily for the purpose of disqualifying a judge creates the appearance of impropriety—namely, that for a fee the attorney is available for sheer manipulation of the judicial system. ***McCuin***, 714 F.2d at 1265.

5. Attorney as mediator in same case. An attorney who serves as a mediator in a case should be disqualified from representing a party in the same case because parties to mediation are encouraged to disclose the strengths and weaknesses of their positions without fear that the mediator will use the information against them. ***McKenzie Constr. v. St. Croix Storage Corp.***, 961 F.Supp. 857, 861-62 (D.V.I.1997). Disqualification is imputed to other members of the attorney's law firm. *Id.* at 862.

§6.3 Ruling. Courts disagree on the proper approach for ruling on disqualification motions. *See* ***In re American Airlines, Inc.***, 972 F.2d 605, 610 (5th Cir.1992); ***European Cmty. v. RJR Nabisco, Inc.***, 134 F.Supp.2d 297, 304 n.7 (E.D.N.Y.2001). Some courts have a restrained or "hands-off" approach to disqualification, under which disqualification is appropriate only on a finding that the attorney's unethical conduct would taint the trial. *See* ***Hempstead Video, Inc. v. Incorporated Vill. of Valley Stream***, 409 F.3d 127, 132-33 (2d Cir.2005); ***European Cmty.***, 134 F.Supp.2d at 303. Other courts impose a more rigid approach, under which the court must take measures against unethical conduct in any proceeding before it. ***In re ProEducation Int'l***, 587 F.3d 296, 299-300 (5th Cir.2009).

§6.4 Challenging disqualification order. An order disqualifying an attorney is not appealable as a collateral order but may be challenged by filing a petition for writ of mandamus. ***Cole v. U.S. Dist. Ct. for the Dist. of Idaho***, 366 F.3d 813, 816 (9th Cir.2004); ***In re Barnett***, 97 F.3d 181, 183-84 (7th Cir.1996); ***In re Dresser Indus.***, 972 F.2d 540, 542-43 & n.4 (5th Cir.1992). The mandamus petition must show (1) the lack of adequate alternative means for the petitioner to obtain relief and (2) a clear and indisputable right to the issuance of the writ. ***In re Barnett***, 97 F.3d at 183-84; ***In re American Airlines, Inc.***, 972 F.2d 605, 608 (5th Cir.1992); *see, e.g.*, ***In re Ford Motor Co.***, 751 F.2d 274, 276 (8th Cir.1984) (party did not show that it would be irreparably harmed or that its opportunity for meaningful appellate review would be lost unless immediate review was permitted); *see also* ***In re Sandahl***, 980 F.2d 1118, 1121 (7th Cir.1992) (litigant who seeks mandamus to set aside order of disqualification must show that order is patently erroneous). The denial of a motion to disqualify will rarely justify the issuance of a writ of mandamus. ***In re Ford Motor Co.***, 751 F.2d at 275.

§7. AGREEMENTS BETWEEN ATTORNEYS OR PARTIES

Local rules may require that all agreements between the attorneys or parties either be announced in open court or be in writing and signed. *See, e.g.*, Local Rules Tex. (S.D.), Rule 83.5 (agreements between parties are enforceable only if announced in open court or reduced to writing and signed; even so, agreements are not binding on court).

§8. ATTORNEY FEES

§8.1 American rule. In the United States, a prevailing party is not ordinarily entitled to collect attorney fees from the losing party. ***Alyeska Pipeline Serv. v. Wilderness Soc'y***, 421 U.S. 240, 247 (1975); ***In re Crescent City Estates, LLC***, 588 F.3d 822, 825 (4th Cir.2009); ***Big Yank Corp. v. Liberty Mut. Fire Ins.***, 125 F.3d 308, 313 (6th Cir. 1997). This "American rule" is distinguished from the "English rule," under which the prevailing party automatically recovers its attorney fees. *See* ***Alyeska Pipeline***, 421 U.S. at 247 & n.18.

NOTE

Under the American rule, it is presumed not only that the parties bear their own legal fees but also that the parties—not their attorneys—bear legal fees. E.g., ***In re Crescent City Estates****, 588 F.3d at 825-26 (removing party, not attorney, was liable for fee award under 28 U.S.C. §1447(c)). To overcome both presumptions, Congress must clearly express an intent to shift fees from the prevailing party to the losing party and from the prevailing party to the losing attorney. Id. at 825.*

§8.2 Exceptions to American rule. Despite the American rule, a prevailing party may be entitled to attorney fees if the fees are specifically provided for by statute or contract or if the case involves a common fund or common benefit. ***Summit Valley Indus. v. Local 112, United Bhd. of Carpenters & Joiners***, 456 U.S. 717, 721 (1982); *see* Hirsch & Sheehey, *Awarding Attorneys' Fees & Managing Fee Litigation*, at 1-2. See "Motion for Attorney Fees," ch. 9-C, p. 745.

1. Statutory exceptions. Many statutes permit the court to award attorney fees to the prevailing party. *E.g.*, 17 U.S.C. §505 (Copyright Act); 42 U.S.C. §2000e-5(k) (Civil Rights Act). See "Statutory grounds," ch. 9-C, §4.2.1, p. 749.

2. Common fund. Courts may award fees from a common fund when a suit, most often a class action, produces a recovery for persons other than the principal litigant. *See* FRCP 23(h) (attorney fees in class action); 2003 Notes to FRCP 23 at ¶56, p. 1169, this book (same). The common-fund doctrine applies to actions that create, enhance, preserve, or protect a common fund. ***Abbott, Puller & Myers v. Peyser***, 124 F.2d 524, 525 (D.C.Cir.1941). The doctrine also applies to actions that ensure access to funds. *See* ***Sprague v. Ticonic Nat'l Bank***, 307 U.S. 161, 166-67 (1939).

3. Sanctions. The court may impose attorney fees to sanction a party for misconduct. See "Motion for Sanctions," ch. 5-O, p. 384.

§8.3 Pleading for attorney fees. A party can claim attorney fees either in its complaint or by motion, depending on whether the fees are recoverable as damages or costs.

1. Attorney fees as damages. If attorney fees are recoverable as damages (i.e., substantive law requires that fees are proved as an element of damages), the party must plead for them in the complaint. ***Riordan v. State Farm Mut. Auto. Ins.***, 589 F.3d 999, 1005 (9th Cir.2009). Attorney fees as damages are special damages that must be specifically pleaded under FRCP 9(g). ***United Indus. v. Simon-Hartley, Ltd.***, 91 F.3d 762, 764 (5th Cir.1996); ***In re American Cas. Co.***, 851 F.2d 794, 802 (6th Cir.1988).

2. Attorney fees as costs. If attorney fees are recoverable as costs of suit, the party does not need to include a demand for them in the complaint. *See* FRCP 54(d)(2)(A); ***Mellon v. World Publ'g***, 20 F.2d 613, 618 (8th Cir.1927); *see also* 28 U.S.C. §1911 (fees and costs statutes). Instead, the party must file a motion requesting them. FRCP 54(d)(2)(A); ***United Indus.***, 91 F.3d at 765-66; *see also* FRCP 23(h)(1) (motion for attorney fees required in class action). See "Motion for Attorney Fees," ch. 9-C, p. 745.

§9. APPELLATE REVIEW

§9.1 Pro hac vice. The standard of review for the district court's decision whether to permit an attorney to appear in a case is de novo. ***Kirkland v. National Mortg. Network, Inc.***, 884 F.2d 1367, 1370 (11th Cir.1989).

§9.2 Withdrawal. The standard of review for the district court's denial of a motion to withdraw as attorney of record is abuse of discretion. ***Ohntrup v. Firearms Ctr., Inc.***, 802 F.2d 676, 679 (3d Cir.1986).

§9.3 Disqualification. The standard of review for disqualification is abuse of discretion. ***Harker v. Commissioner***, 82 F.3d 806, 808 (8th Cir.1996); ***FDIC v. U.S. Fire Ins.***, 50 F.3d 1304, 1310-11 (5th Cir.1995); 1 Childress & Davis §4.08[2]. In applying that standard, the appellate court reviews fact findings for clear error and performs a

"careful examination" or de novo review of the district court's application of the relevant rules of attorney conduct. ***U.S. v. Bolden***, 353 F.3d 870, 878 (10th Cir.2003); ***U.S. Fire***, 50 F.3d at 1311.

§9.4 Attorney fees. The standard of review for a district court's award of attorney fees is abuse of discretion. ***Strange v. Monogram Credit Card Bank***, 129 F.3d 943, 945 (7th Cir.1997); *see* ***Mid-Continent Cas. Co. v. Chevron Pipe Line Co.***, 205 F.3d 222, 230 (5th Cir.2000). However, any statutory interpretations or other legal conclusions that provide a basis for the award are reviewed de novo. ***Phelps v. Hamilton***, 120 F.3d 1126, 1129 (10th Cir. 1997). A district court's decision to reject a contingent-fee agreement is reviewed for abuse of discretion. ***Green v. Nevers***, 111 F.3d 1295, 1302-03 (6th Cir.1997).

COMMENTARIES

CHAPTER 2. PLAINTIFF'S LAWSUIT

COMMENTARIES

CHAPTER 2. PLAINTIFF'S LAWSUIT

TABLE OF CONTENTS

A. GENERAL CONSIDERATIONS 73

§1. GENERAL 73
§2. PREFILING CONSIDERATIONS 73
§2.1 Statute of limitations 73
§2.2 Preservation letter 73
§2.3 Notice or demand 73
§2.4 Exhaustion of administrative remedies 74
§2.5 ADR 74
§3. FILING CONSIDERATIONS 74
§3.1 Choosing the forum 74
§3.2 Filing the complaint 74
§4. MISCELLANEOUS CONSIDERATIONS 75
§4.1 Appointment of legal representative 75
§4.2 Presuit discovery 75

B. PLAINTIFF'S COMPLAINT 75

§1. GENERAL 75
§2. PARTIES 75
§2.1 Name 75
§2.2 Standing & capacity 77
§2.3 Omitted parties 78
§3. JURISDICTION 78
§3.1 Allegations in complaint 78
§3.2 Amending jurisdictional allegations 80
§4. VENUE 80
§5. STATEMENT OF CLAIM 80
§5.1 Standard pleadings 80
§5.2 Particularized pleadings 82
§5.3 Theory of recovery 84
§6. DAMAGES 84
§6.1 General damages 84
§6.2 Special damages 84
§6.3 Punitive damages 84
§7. INTEREST 85
§8. COSTS 85
§9. ATTORNEY FEES 85
§10. OTHER RELIEF 85
§11. CONDITIONS PRECEDENT 85
§12. JURY DEMAND 85
§13. SIGNATURE & ADDRESS 85
§14. VERIFICATION & AFFIDAVITS 86
§15. EXHIBITS 86
§15.1 Incorporation by attachment 86
§15.2 Excessive exhibits 86
§16. FILING REQUIREMENTS 86
§16.1 Filing fees 86
§16.2 Civil cover sheet 86
§16.3 Disclosure statement 86
§16.4 Notice of constitutional question 86

C. INTERPLEADER 87

§1. GENERAL 87
§2. PARTIES 87
§2.1 Stakeholder 87
§2.2 Claimant 87
§3. COMPLAINT 87
§3.1 General requirements 87
§3.2 Type of interpleader 88
§3.3 Request for relief 90
§4. SERVICE OF PROCESS 90
§4.1 Rule interpleader 90
§4.2 Statutory interpleader 90
§5. CHART SUMMARY OF INTERPLEADER 90
§6. RESPONSE 90
§6.1 Negate interpleader requirements 90
§6.2 Make additional allegations 91
§6.3 Request jury 91
§7. HEARING & TRIAL 91
§7.1 Hearing on right to interplead 91
§7.2 Trial on merits 92
§8. ORDER 92
§8.1 Discharge 92
§8.2 Injunctive relief 92
§8.3 Resolution of claims against stake 92
§8.4 Not binding on nonparties 93
§9. APPELLATE REVIEW 93

D. INJUNCTIVE RELIEF 93

§1. GENERAL 93
§2. GROUNDS FOR INJUNCTIVE RELIEF 94
§2.1 Equitable factors for injunctive relief 94
§2.2 Federal authority for injunctive relief 96
§2.3 State authority for injunctive relief 96
§3. TEMPORARY RESTRAINING ORDER 97
§3.1 Application 97
§3.2 Hearing 97
§3.3 Order 97
§3.4 Bond 100
§3.5 Findings of fact & conclusions of law 101
§4. PRELIMINARY INJUNCTION 101
§4.1 Parties 101
§4.2 Application 101
§4.3 Notice 102
§4.4 Hearing 102
§4.5 Order 103
§4.6 Modifying preliminary injunction 104
§4.7 Findings of fact & conclusions of law 104
§5. PERMANENT INJUNCTION 104
§5.1 Application 104
§5.2 Hearing 104
§5.3 Order 104
§5.4 Bond 105
§5.5 Modifying permanent injunction 105
§6. RESPONSE TO REQUEST FOR INJUNCTIVE RELIEF 105
§6.1 Response 105
§6.2 Motion to dissolve or modify ex parte TRO 105
§6.3 Answer to suit 105
§7. APPELLATE REVIEW 106
§7.1 TRO 106
§7.2 Preliminary injunction 106
§7.3 Permanent injunction 107
§7.4 Bond 107

E. DECLARATORY JUDGMENT 107

§1. GENERAL 107
§2. DECLARATORY JUDGMENT ACT 108
§2.1 Declaratory judgment available 108
§2.2 Declaratory judgment not available 108
§3. PROCEDURE 110
§3.1 Complaint 110
§3.2 Hearing & jury trial 110
§3.3 Burden of proof 110
§4. DECLARATORY JUDGMENT 110
§4.1 Exercising jurisdiction 110
§4.2 Judgment 111
§4.3 Amending judgment 111
§5. APPELLATE REVIEW 112

COMMENTARIES

CHAPTER 2. PLAINTIFF'S LAWSUIT

TABLE OF CONTENTS

F. CHOOSING THE COURT—JURISDICTION 112
§1. GENERAL ... 112
§2. FEDERAL-QUESTION JURISDICTION ... 113
§2.1 Authority ... 113
§2.2 Evaluating allegations of jurisdiction ... 113
§2.3 Grounds for federal-question jurisdiction ... 113
§3. DIVERSITY JURISDICTION ... 116
§3.1 Is there complete diversity? ... 116
§3.2 Who is considered for diversity jurisdiction? ... 118
§3.3 When is amount in controversy satisfied? ... 123
§3.4 When is diversity jurisdiction determined? ... 125
§3.5 When can the court decline to exercise diversity jurisdiction? ... 126
§4. ALIENAGE JURISDICTION ... 127
§4.1 Citizenship requirements ... 127
§4.2 Amount in controversy must exceed $75,000 ... 129
§5. MULTIPARTY JURISDICTION ... 129
§5.1 Interstate class actions ... 129
§5.2 Single-event mass accidents ... 133
§6. SUPPLEMENTAL JURISDICTION ... 134
§6.1 Jurisdiction over suit required ... 134
§6.2 Reach of supplemental jurisdiction ... 135
§6.3 Exercise of supplemental jurisdiction ... 136
§6.4 Loss of supplemental jurisdiction ... 137
§7. ABSTENTION ... 138
§7.1 Generally ... 138
§7.2 Substantive abstention doctrines ... 138
§7.3 Stay of related proceedings ... 139
§7.4 Anti-Injunction Act ... 141
§8. APPELLATE REVIEW ... 142
§8.1 Diversity jurisdiction ... 142
§8.2 Supplemental jurisdiction ... 142
§8.3 Abstention ... 143

G. CHOOSING THE COURT—VENUE 143
§1. GENERAL ... 143
§2. VENUE – DEFINED ... 144
§3. GENERAL VENUE STATUTE ... 144
§3.1 Civil actions – generally ... 144
§3.2 Mass tort ... 145
§3.3 Suit against United States or its agencies, officers, or employees ... 145
§3.4 Suit against foreign state ... 146
§4. SPECIAL VENUE STATUTES ... 146
§4.1 Special vs. general venue ... 146
§4.2 Examples ... 146
§5. RESIDENCE UNDER GENERAL & SPECIAL VENUE STATUTES ... 147
§5.1 Natural person ... 147
§5.2 Entity ... 147
§5.3 Nonresident defendant ... 148
§6. WHEN TO DETERMINE VENUE ... 148
§7. FORUM-SELECTION CLAUSE ... 148
§8. MULTIPLE PARTIES & CLAIMS ... 148
§8.1 Venue for each defendant & claim ... 148
§8.2 Pendent venue ... 148
§9. APPELLATE REVIEW ... 149

H. SERVING THE DEFENDANT WITH PROCESS...149
§1. GENERAL ... 149
§2. REQUESTING WAIVER OF SERVICE ... 149
§2.1 Purpose ... 149
§2.2 Types of defendants ... 149
§2.3 No summons ... 150
§2.4 Notice & request ... 150
§2.5 Filing waiver ... 150
§2.6 Response to request ... 150
§3. SECURING SUMMONS ... 151
§3.1 Requirements for summons ... 151
§3.2 Clerk's duty ... 152
§3.3 Plaintiff's duty ... 152
§4. DEADLINE FOR SERVING PROCESS ... 152
§4.1 Deadline ... 152
§4.2 Motion to extend time to serve ... 153
§5. SERVING PROCESS IN UNITED STATES ... 153
§5.1 Individual defendant ... 153
§5.2 Business defendant ... 154
§5.3 Minor or incompetent defendant ... 154
§5.4 State or local government ... 154
§5.5 U.S. government as defendant ... 154
§5.6 Nonresident additional parties ... 156
§6. SERVING PROCESS ABROAD ... 156
§6.1 Limits on foreign service ... 156
§6.2 Waiver of service ... 156
§6.3 Serving an individual abroad ... 157
§6.4 Serving foreign business abroad ... 161
§6.5 Serving minor or incompetent person abroad ... 161
§6.6 Serving foreign government ... 161
§7. WHO CAN SERVE PROCESS ... 163
§7.1 Nonparty over 18 ... 163
§7.2 U.S. marshal or specially appointed person ... 163
§7.3 Central authority ... 164
§8. TERRITORIAL LIMITS OF SERVICE ... 164
§8.1 General rules ... 164
§8.2 Federal rule ... 165
§9. PROVING SERVICE ... 165
§9.1 Affidavit by other person ... 165
§9.2 Signature of marshal ... 165
§9.3 Waiver of service ... 165
§9.4 Proof of service abroad ... 166
§9.5 Failure to make proof of service ... 166
§9.6 Amendments ... 166

2. PLAINTIFF'S LAWSUIT

A. GENERAL CONSIDERATIONS

§1. GENERAL

§1.1 Rules. FRCP 3-5, 7-11, 15, 17-20, 38, 84.

§1.2 Purpose. The plaintiff should check applicable statutes and any documents the suit is based on to determine if any action should be taken before filing suit.

§1.3 Forms. *O'Connor's Federal Civil Forms* (2012), FORMS 2A.

§1.4 Other references. 5A Wright & Miller, *Federal Practice & Procedure 3d* §§1321-1339 (2004 & Supp.2012); 2 *Moore's Federal Practice 3d* chs. 7-11 (2012).

§2. PREFILING CONSIDERATIONS

Before filing suit, the plaintiff should consider (1) the statute of limitations, (2) a preservation letter, (3) a written notice or demand, (4) exhaustion of administrative remedies, and (5) some form of alternative dispute resolution.

§2.1 Statute of limitations. The plaintiff should consider the statute of limitations. Generally, a plaintiff must file suit before the limitations period expires. *See, e.g.*, ***Patterson v. U.S.***, 451 F.3d 268, 270 (1st Cir.2006) (under Federal Tort Claims Act, tort claims against federal government are barred if not brought within two years after tortious act); *see also Black's Law Dictionary* 1546 (9th ed. 2009) (statute of limitations defined as "statute establishing a time limit for suing in a civil case"). However, if the statute of limitations is not jurisdictional, (1) the limitations period may be tolled under certain equitable circumstances or (2) a defendant's limitations defense may be subject to forfeiture or waiver. ***John R. Sand & Gravel Co. v. U.S.***, 552 U.S. 130, 133-34 (2008); *see* ***Bowles v. Russell***, 551 U.S. 205, 214 (2007); ***Valdez v. U.S.***, 518 F.3d 173, 182 (2d Cir.2008); ***Cortez v. Wal-Mart Stores***, 460 F.3d 1268, 1276-77 (10th Cir.2005); ***In re Copper Antitrust Litig.***, 436 F.3d 782, 790-91 (7th Cir.2006). See "Filing the complaint," §3.2, p. 74.

§2.2 Preservation letter. The plaintiff should consider sending a preservation letter to all persons likely to be in possession of relevant information. A preservation letter usually (1) describes the potential litigation and the parties involved, (2) asks the recipient to suspend any document-destruction policy, (3) reminds the recipient of the duty to preserve all information relevant to the lawsuit, (4) identifies the specific documents, electronically stored information, and tangible things that should be preserved, and (5) provides instructions on how to preserve those items. *See* Ball, *The Perfect Preservation Letter*, pp. 6-7 (2005), www.craigball.com/ppl.pdf. *See generally* ***Zubulake v. UBS Warburg LLC***, 220 F.R.D. 212, 217-18 (S.D.N.Y.2003) (person who anticipates being party to suit cannot destroy unique, relevant evidence that might be useful to adversary; duty extends to key players in case). See ***O'Connor's Federal Forms***, FORM 2A:4.

§2.3 Notice or demand. The plaintiff may need to send a presuit notice or demand. Provisions requiring presuit notice or demand are often included in contracts and statutes. For example, many contracts contain provisions that impose conditions precedent to filing suit, such as giving potential defendants notice of the claim and notice of intent to sue. *See, e.g.*, ***In re Colony Square Co.***, 843 F.2d 479, 481 (11th Cir.1988) (lease provision required notice of default, opportunity for cure, and suit for specific performance as prerequisites to suit for damages); ***First Nat'l Bank v. Cann***, 669 F.2d 415, 417 (6th Cir.1982) (as required by contract, bank properly notified Ds of its intent to file suit for breach of contract once it determined cause of defects). Similarly, some statutes require that a plaintiff, before filing suit, send the defendant a demand letter stating the extent of the plaintiff's damages, attorney fees, and costs. *See, e.g.*, ***Wildey v. Springs***, 47 F.3d 1475, 1484 (7th Cir.1995) (P sued D for breach of promise to marry under Illinois's Breach of Promise Act; judgment for P was reversed after court held that P's notice of intent to sue was inadequate under Illinois law).

§2.4 Exhaustion of administrative remedies. The plaintiff must exhaust all administrative remedies and submit necessary administrative claims whenever required by statute. *See, e.g.*, 28 U.S.C. §2675(a) (disputes under Federal Tort Claims Act must be submitted to appropriate federal agency before suit can be filed); ***Fair v. Norris***, 480 F.3d 865, 866 n.2 (8th Cir.2007) (employment-discrimination disputes must be submitted to EEOC before suit can be filed). If the plaintiff does not file the required administrative claim and wait for either the agency or administrative body to rule on the claim or a prescribed time to pass, the district court generally cannot acquire subject-matter jurisdiction over the dispute. *See* ***Ace Prop. & Cas. Ins. v. Federal Crop Ins.***, 440 F.3d 992, 996 (8th Cir. 2006). If the exhaustion requirement is jurisdictional, the failure to exhaust cannot be excused or waived; if it is nonjurisdictional, exhaustion is favored but can be excused under limited circumstances. *See id.*

§2.5 ADR. The plaintiff may be required to submit a dispute to some form of alternative dispute resolution (ADR) (e.g., arbitration, mediation, minitrial, early neutral evaluation) before or instead of litigation. *See* 28 U.S.C. §652(a) (court can require mediation or early neutral evaluation); *see also id.* §§651, 652 (each federal court must establish some form of ADR). One of the most common types of ADR is arbitration. See "Arbitration," ch. 7-E, p. 650.

§3. FILING CONSIDERATIONS

§3.1 Choosing the forum. When determining where to file suit, the plaintiff should do the following:

Step 1 – Forum-selection clause. The plaintiff must determine whether a forum-selection clause exists. If a suit involves a contract containing a forum-selection clause, the clause may limit the plaintiff's choice of forum. See "Forum-Selection Clause," ch. 2-G, §7, p. 148; "Forum-selection clause," ch. 3-D, §3.3.4, p. 194.

Step 2 – Subject-matter jurisdiction. The plaintiff must determine whether the court has subject-matter jurisdiction. Some suits must be filed in federal court (e.g., patent and copyright suits), some must be filed in state court, and others may be filed in either court. Federal courts are courts of limited jurisdiction—they are not presumed to have subject-matter jurisdiction. Thus, the party asserting jurisdiction bears the burden of establishing that the court has it. ***Kokkonen v. Guardian Life Ins.***, 511 U.S. 375, 377 (1994); ***Montoya v. Chao***, 296 F.3d 952, 955 (10th Cir.2002); ***Coury v. Prot***, 85 F.3d 244, 248 (5th Cir.1996); ***In re Hunter***, 66 F.3d 1002, 1005 (9th Cir. 1995). See "Choosing the Court—Jurisdiction," ch. 2-F, p. 112.

Step 3 – Personal jurisdiction. If the plaintiff determines that the court has subject-matter jurisdiction over the case, it must determine whether the court has personal jurisdiction over the defendant. See "Motion to Dismiss for Lack of Personal Jurisdiction—FRCP 12(b)(2)," ch. 3-B, p. 178.

Step 4 – Venue. If the plaintiff determines that there is both subject-matter jurisdiction and personal jurisdiction, it must decide in which federal court to file the suit. See "Choosing the Court—Venue," ch. 2-G, p. 143.

§3.2 Filing the complaint. The filing of the complaint is significant for the purpose of tolling the statute of limitations.

1. Federal-question cases. Generally, the filing of the complaint tolls the statute of limitations when jurisdiction is based solely on a federal question. ***Henderson v. U.S.***, 517 U.S. 654, 657 n.2 (1996); ***South v. Saab Cars USA, Inc.***, 28 F.3d 9, 12 & n.2 (2d Cir.1994); *see* ***West v. Conrail***, 481 U.S. 35, 38-39 (1987). Most courts hold that a complaint is deemed filed for limitations purposes when it is actually or constructively received by the court clerk, even if the required filing fee is not paid. *See* ***McDowell v. Delaware State Police***, 88 F.3d 188, 191 (3d Cir. 1996); ***Rodgers v. Bowen***, 790 F.2d 1550, 1551-52 (11th Cir.1986). *Contra* ***Wanamaker v. Columbian Rope Co.***, 713 F.Supp. 533, 538-39 (N.D.N.Y.1989), *aff'd*, 108 F.3d 462 (2d Cir.1997).

2. Diversity cases. The filing of the complaint does not necessarily toll the statute of limitations when jurisdiction is based on diversity. In diversity cases, the law of the state where the complaint is filed controls whether the statute of limitations is tolled. ***Walker v. Armco Steel Corp.***, 446 U.S. 740, 750-51 (1980); *see* ***Henderson***, 517 U.S. at 657 n.2; ***West***, 481 U.S. at 39 n.4; ***Iacobelli Constr., Inc. v. County of Monroe***, 32 F.3d 19, 27 (2d Cir.1994). Often, state law requires that the complaint be served—not merely filed—to toll the limitations period. *See, e.g.*, ***Appletree Square I, L.P. v. W.R. Grace & Co.***, 29 F.3d 1283, 1286 (8th Cir.1994) (asbestos case not tolled under state

revival statute because P did not serve D with complaint before revival deadline), *overruled in part on other grounds*, ***Bridge v. Phoenix Bond & Indem Co.***, 553 U.S. 639 (2008).

§4. MISCELLANEOUS CONSIDERATIONS

§4.1 Appointment of legal representative. Although the plaintiff generally does not have to allege a party's capacity to sue or be sued, the plaintiff's attorney should ensure that all parties have that capacity. *See* FRCP 9(a)(1)(A); *see, e.g.*, FRCP 55(b)(2) (before pursuing default judgment, attorney should ensure that minor or incompetent person has representative); ***Zaro v. Strauss***, 167 F.2d 218, 220 (5th Cir.1948) (judgment for P was voidable when D was not properly represented in suit). If a party does not have the capacity to sue or be sued, the opposing party should note that status and request that the court appoint a representative or guardian ad litem. *See* FRCP 17(c)(2); *see, e.g.*, ***Bell v. Busse***, 633 F.Supp. 628, 629 (S.D.Ohio 1986) (when P was deemed insane after psychological exam, court appointed guardian ad litem); *see also* 2 Hittner et al., *Federal Civil Procedure Before Trial, 5th Cir. Ed.* §§8:141-8:146 (2012) (common practice is to allege status of each party). See "Standing & capacity," ch. 2-B, §2.2, p. 77.

§4.2 Presuit discovery. A plaintiff can engage in discovery before filing suit. A plaintiff can file a verified petition and obtain an order to take a deposition before filing suit. FRCP 27(a). Presuit discovery functions to preserve evidence when a critical witness is elderly, infirm, or about to leave the jurisdiction. It also provides an opportunity to evaluate the legal merits of a case before filing suit, which can help avoid sanctions under FRCP 11(c). See "Deposition to Perpetuate Testimony," ch. 6-F, §6, p. 555. Presuit discovery may also be available under similar state procedure rules, and those rules may be preferable to FRCP 27. *See, e.g.*, Ariz. R. Civ. P. 27(a) (depositions before suit).

B. PLAINTIFF'S COMPLAINT

§1. GENERAL

§1.1 Rules. FRCP 3-5, 7-11, 15, 17-20, 38, 84.

§1.2 Purpose. A civil action is commenced by filing a complaint in the court. FRCP 3. The complaint should give the defendant fair notice of the essence of the plaintiff's claim. *See* ***Bell Atlantic Corp. v. Twombly***, 550 U.S. 544, 555 (2007). There is fair notice when the complaint is clear enough to enable the defendant to answer and defend the suit and to allow for a determination of res judicata. ***Simmons v. Abruzzo***, 49 F.3d 83, 86 (2d Cir.1995).

§1.3 Forms. ***O'Connor's Federal Civil Forms*** (2012), FORMS 2B.

§1.4 Other references. 5, 5A, 5B Wright & Miller, *Federal Practice & Procedure 3d* §§1259, 1286, 1321-1339, 1347-1357 (2004 & Supp.2012); 7 Wright, Miller & Kane, *Federal Practice & Procedure 3d* §1625 (2001 & Supp. 2012); 19 Wright, Miller & Cooper, *Federal Practice & Procedure 2d* §4509 (1996 & Supp.2012); 2 *Moore's Federal Practice 3d* chs. 7-11 (2012).

§2. PARTIES

§2.1 Name. The caption of the complaint must identify all parties by their names. FRCP 10(a). This requirement is relaxed in later pleadings and documents. *See id.* See "Parties," ch. 1-B, §2.1.3(1), p. 8.

1. Misspelled name. Under the rule of idem sonans, a misspelled name is adequate identification as long as it sounds practically identical to the correct name. *See* ***In re Venson***, 234 F.Supp. 271, 272 (N.D.Ga.1964), *aff'd sub nom.* ***Venson v. Housing Auth. of Atlanta***, 337 F.2d 616 (5th Cir.1964).

2. Misnomer vs. misidentification.

(1) Misnomer. If the plaintiff makes an error in naming the defendant and the person misnamed is the correct defendant, the error is misnomer—the right person has been sued under the wrong name. *See* ***Athmer v. C.E.I. Equip. Co.***, 121 F.3d 294, 296 (7th Cir.1997) ("misnomer" means P has wrong name of right party);

see, e.g., ***Datskow v. Teledyne, Inc., Cont'l Prods. Div.***, 899 F.2d 1298, 1301-02 (2d Cir.1990) (Ps identified corporate entity as "Teledyne, Inc.," but correct name was "Teledyne Industries, Inc."). This error can be corrected by an amendment that relates back to the initial filing. FRCP 15(c)(1)(C); *see* ***Athmer***, 121 F.3d at 296. See "Relation back of amendments," ch. 5-I, §3.5, p. 347.

(2) Misidentification. If the plaintiff makes an error in choosing or identifying the defendant and the person named is not the correct defendant, the error is misidentification—the wrong person has been sued. *See* ***Athmer***, 121 F.3d at 296 ("misidentification" means P has named wrong party); *see, e.g.*, ***Eison v. McCoy***, 146 F.3d 468, 471 (7th Cir.1998) (complaint that named police officers by aliases "T.C.," "Cronie," "Pac Mac," and "Crater Face" was insufficient to provide notice to individuals that they were being sued); *see also* ***Jacobsen v. Osborne***, 133 F.3d 315, 320 (5th Cir.1998) (complaint misidentified arresting officers, but because city attorney answered on behalf of city and officers and thus presumably investigated allegations, correct officers were put on notice of suit). If the plaintiff sues the wrong defendant, the statute of limitations is not tolled by the lawsuit. *See* ***Athmer***, 121 F.3d at 296 (in case of mistaken identity, P has sued wrong person and cannot prevent right person from pleading limitations). Under certain circumstances, this error may be corrected by an amendment that relates back to the initial filing. FRCP 15(c)(1)(C). See "Relation back of amendments," ch. 5-I, §3.5, p. 347.

3. "John Doe" parties. The use of fictitious names in a federal lawsuit is against public policy because the public has a legitimate right to know about the facts in a lawsuit, including the names of the parties. ***Doe v. Blue Cross & Blue Shield United***, 112 F.3d 869, 872 (7th Cir.1997); *see* ***Plaintiff B v. Francis***, 631 F.3d 1310, 1315 (11th Cir.2011). However, there are limited exceptions that allow a party to proceed anonymously. ***Sealed Plaintiff v. Sealed Defendant #1***, 537 F.3d 185, 189 (2d Cir.2008).

(1) Standard. When determining whether a party can maintain a suit under a pseudonym, the party's interest in anonymity must be balanced against the public interest in disclosure and any prejudice to the opposing party. ***Sealed Plaintiff***, 537 F.3d at 189; ***Does I thru XXIII v. Advanced Textile Corp.***, 214 F.3d 1058, 1068 (9th Cir.2000); *see* ***Doe v. Megless***, 654 F.3d 404, 408 (3d Cir.2011); ***Plaintiff B***, 631 F.3d at 1315-16. The following is a nonexhaustive list of factors the court may consider:

(a) Whether the litigation involves matters that are highly sensitive and of a personal nature. ***Sealed Plaintiff***, 537 F.3d at 189-90.

(b) Whether identification poses a risk of retaliatory physical or mental harm to the party or innocent nonparties. *Id.*; *see* ***Megless***, 654 F.3d at 409; ***Does I thru XXIII***, 214 F.3d at 1068.

(c) Whether identification presents other harms and the likely severity of those harms. ***Sealed Plaintiff***, 537 F.3d at 189-90; *see* ***Megless***, 654 F.3d at 409; ***Does I thru XXIII***, 214 F.3d at 1068.

(d) Whether the party is particularly vulnerable to the possible harms of disclosure. ***Sealed Plaintiff***, 537 F.3d at 189-90; *see* ***Does I thru XXIII***, 214 F.3d at 1068.

(e) Whether the party's fear of harm is reasonable. ***Does I thru XXIII***, 214 F.3d at 1068; *see* ***Megless***, 654 F.3d at 409.

(f) Whether the suit is challenging the actions of the government or private parties. ***Sealed Plaintiff***, 537 F.3d at 189-90.

(g) Whether the opposing party is prejudiced, whether the nature of the prejudice differs at any particular stage of the litigation, and whether any prejudice can be mitigated. *Id.*; ***Does I thru XXIII***, 214 F.3d at 1068.

(h) Whether the party's identity has been kept confidential. ***Megless***, 654 F.3d at 409; ***Sealed Plaintiff***, 537 F.3d at 189-90.

(i) Whether the public's interest in the litigation is furthered by the disclosure of the party's identity. ***Sealed Plaintiff***, 537 F.3d at 189-90; ***Does I thru XXIII***, 214 F.3d at 1068; *see* ***Megless***, 654 F.3d at 409.

(j) Whether there is an unusually weak public interest in knowing the party's identity. ***Megless***, 654 F.3d at 409; ***Sealed Plaintiff***, 537 F.3d at 189-90.

(k) Whether there is an improper motive to either use or oppose the use of a pseudonym. ***Megless***, 654 F.3d at 409.

(*l*) Whether there are any alternative mechanisms for protecting the confidentiality of the party. ***Sealed Plaintiff***, 537 F.3d at 189-90.

(2) Specific parties.

(a) Plaintiffs. In exceptional circumstances, federal courts may permit a plaintiff to proceed anonymously to protect the plaintiff's privacy or safety. ***Doe v. Frank***, 951 F.2d 320, 324 (11th Cir.1992); *see* ***Sealed Plaintiff***, 537 F.3d at 189; ***Does v. Covington Cty. Sch. Bd.***, 884 F.Supp. 462, 465 (M.D.Ala.1995); *see, e.g.*, ***Roe v. Wade***, 410 U.S. 113, 120 n.4 (1973) (pseudonyms used in constitutional challenge to criminal abortion statute); ***Doe v. C.A.R.S. Prot. Plus, Inc.***, 527 F.3d 358, 371 n.2 (3d Cir.2008) (pseudonym used in pregnancy-discrimination suit by P who was discharged because of surgical abortion). Minor embarrassment or fear of professional or economic loss, however, does not justify the use of a fictitious name. *See* ***Megless***, 654 F.3d at 408; ***Frank***, 951 F.2d at 324; 2 *Moore's Federal Practice 3d* §10.02[2][c][iii].

(b) Defendants. In certain circumstances, federal courts may permit a plaintiff to name an unknown, uncertain, or anonymous defendant as a "John Doe" defendant. In federal-question cases, the court may allow the plaintiff an opportunity, through discovery, to identify the unknown defendant, unless the discovery will not reveal the defendant's identity or the complaint will be dismissed on other grounds. ***Gillespie v. Civiletti***, 629 F.2d 637, 642 (9th Cir.1980). In diversity cases, when a state permits the use of John Doe defendants, federal courts sitting in that state must follow state practices. *E.g.*, ***Lindley v. General Elec. Co.***, 780 F.2d 797, 800 (9th Cir.1986) (California law); ***Ramski v. Sears, Roebuck & Co.***, 656 F.Supp. 963, 966-67 (N.D.Ohio 1987) (Ohio law); *see* 19 Wright, Miller & Cooper §4509. A plaintiff may prevent the statute of limitations from running by (1) filing suit against an unknown defendant and alleging that its true identity is unknown and (2) later amending the pleading to provide the true identity of that defendant. *See* 2 *Moore's Federal Practice 3d* §10.02[2][d][iii]. Whether the amendment will be allowed depends on either (1) the relation-back doctrine under FRCP 15(c) or (2) state substantive statutes addressing the statute of limitations and John Doe defendants. *See* 2 *Moore's Federal Practice 3d* §10.02[2][d][iii]; *see, e.g.*, ***Garvin v. City of Phila.***, 354 F.3d 215, 220 (3d Cir.2003) (in 42 U.S.C. §1983 suit, P's amendment identifying D-police officers did not satisfy FRCP 15(c)); ***Lindley***, 780 F.2d at 799 (in personal-injury suit under California law, statute of limitations was extended for three years from commencement of suit to discover identity of unknown D, to amend complaint, and to serve complaint on identified D). See "Relation back of amendments," ch. 5-I, §3.5, p. 347.

§2.2 Standing & capacity. The complaint must state that the plaintiff has standing and capacity to file the suit and that the correct defendant is being sued in its correct capacity.

1. Standing. A party has standing to file suit if it can demonstrate (1) an "injury in fact" (i.e., harm that is concrete and actual or imminent, not merely conjectural or hypothetical), (2) causation (i.e., a fairly traceable connection between the plaintiff's injury and the defendant's alleged conduct), and (3) redressability (i.e., likelihood that the requested relief will remedy the alleged injury). ***Summers v. Earth Island Inst.***, 555 U.S. 488, 493 (2009); ***Sprint Comms. Co. v. APCC Servs.***, 554 U.S. 269, 273-74 (2008); *see* ***Lujan v. Defenders of Wildlife***, 504 U.S. 555, 560-61 (1992); *see, e.g.*, ***W.R. Huff Asset Mgmt. Co. v. Deloitte & Touche LLP***, 549 F.3d 100, 107 (2d Cir.2008) (investment adviser did not have standing in suit for client's monetary damages against firm representing bankrupt company because injury in fact was suffered by client, not adviser). These requirements ensure that a plaintiff has a sufficiently personal stake in the outcome of the suit such that the parties are adverse. ***W.R. Huff Asset Mgmt.***, 549 F.3d at 107. Initially, the plaintiff may meet its burden of establishing standing by alleging in its complaint the nature of its injury resulting from the defendant's conduct. ***Lujan***, 504 U.S. at 561. However, whether on motion for summary judgment or at trial, the plaintiff ultimately will have to set forth specific facts necessary to support the claim. *Id.*

2. **Capacity.** A party has capacity to file or defend suit if it has the legal ability to do so. *See Black's Law Dictionary* 235 (9th ed. 2009).

(1) **Individual.** The capacity of an individual, other than one acting as a representative, to sue or be sued is determined by the law of the individual's state of domicile. FRCP 17(b)(1).

(2) **Corporation.** The capacity of a corporation to sue or be sued is determined by the law under which it was organized. FRCP 17(b)(2).

(3) **Partnership & unincorporated association.** A partnership or unincorporated association that has no capacity to sue or be sued under state law can still sue or be sued in its common name for the purpose of enforcing a substantive federal right. FRCP 17(b)(3)(A).

(4) **Receiver.** The capacity of a receiver appointed by a U.S. court to sue or be sued in a U.S. court is governed by 28 U.S.C. §§754, 959(a). FRCP 17(b)(3)(B).

(5) **Minor or incompetent person.**

(a) **Representative.** If a minor or incompetent person has a representative (e.g., general guardian, committee, conservator, other fiduciary), the representative can sue or defend on behalf of the minor or incompetent person. FRCP 17(c)(1).

(b) **No representative.** If a minor or incompetent person does not have a representative, the minor or incompetent person can sue through a next friend or guardian ad litem. FRCP 17(c)(2).

(6) **All other parties.** The capacity of all other parties to sue or be sued is determined by the law of the state in which the district court sits. FRCP 17(b)(3).

PRACTICE TIP

When suing the United States or one of its agencies, check the enabling statute to determine which entity or person to name as the correct defendant. If you cannot locate the enabling statute, call the general counsel's office for that agency and ask whom to name as the defendant.

§2.3 Omitted parties. The complaint must identify persons who are required parties under FRCP 19(a) but are not named. FRCP 19(c); 7 Wright, Miller & Kane §1625 & n.2. The complaint must state why the omitted party is not named; specifically, it must state why the person cannot be served or how joinder of the person will deprive the court of subject-matter jurisdiction. *See* FRCP 19(a)(1); FRCP Form 8, p. 993, this book. See "Motion to Dismiss for Failure to Join a Party Under FRCP 19—FRCP 12(b)(7)," ch. 3-I, p. 214.

NOTE

If the person is omitted because she cannot be served, the court can consider sending a letter or informal notice to the person that notifies her that the action is pending and offers her the opportunity to intervene. 7 Wright, Miller & Kane §1625 & nn.14-15.

§3. JURISDICTION

§3.1 Allegations in complaint. A complaint must contain a short, plain statement of the grounds for the court's jurisdiction. FRCP 8(a)(1). Conclusory allegations of jurisdiction or mere citations to federal statutes are inadequate; the complaint must clearly set out essential facts that establish jurisdiction. ***Celli v. Shoell***, 40 F.3d 324, 327 (10th Cir.1994); *see* ***Presbytery of N.J. v. Florio***, 40 F.3d 1454, 1462 (3d Cir.1994). However, if the court has jurisdiction over the suit, the failure to cite a specific ground for the court's jurisdiction does not defeat jurisdiction. *See* ***Taylor-Callahan-Coleman Cty. Dist. Adult Prob. Dept. v. Dole***, 948 F.2d 953, 956 (5th Cir.1991). See "Choosing the Court—Jurisdiction," ch. 2-F, p. 112.

NOTE

*The Appendix of Forms to the FRCPs contains a form for the statement of jurisdiction. See FRCP Form 7, p. 992, this book. The Forms in the Appendix are sufficient under the FRCPs. FRCP 84; see **Swierkiewicz v. Sorema**, 534 U.S. 506, 513 n.4 (2002); **Harris v. Rand**, 682 F.3d 846, 850 (9th Cir.2012). See **O'Connor's Federal Forms**, FORM 2B:3.*

1. Federal-question jurisdiction. Federal-question jurisdiction must be apparent on the face of a properly pleaded complaint. ***Phillips Pet. Co. v. Texaco, Inc.***, 415 U.S. 125, 127-28 (1974); ***Rice v. Office of Servicemembers' Grp. Life Ins.***, 260 F.3d 1240, 1245 (10th Cir.2001); ***Ford v. Hamilton Invs.***, 29 F.3d 255, 258 (6th Cir. 1994). The plaintiff cannot rely on an anticipated defense or a counterclaim as a basis for federal-question jurisdiction. See "Well-pleaded-complaint rule," ch. 2-F, §2.2.1, p. 113.

(1) Specific authority. The complaint should cite the specific constitutional provision, federal statute, or treaty that jurisdiction is based on. Merely referring to a federal statute does not establish federal jurisdiction if the dispute does not involve a substantial question of federal law. ***Ford***, 29 F.3d at 258. *See generally* ***LaSalle Nat'l Trust v. ECM Motor Co.***, 76 F.3d 140, 143 (7th Cir.1996) (court should not accept P's word that federal jurisdiction exists). When invoking a substantive statute as a jurisdictional ground, the plaintiff should make sure the statute contains an independent grant of jurisdiction. See "Federal-Question Jurisdiction," ch. 2-F, §2, p. 113.

(2) Supporting facts. The complaint must identify facts supporting the allegation of jurisdiction. *See* ***Spectronics Corp. v. H.B. Fuller Co.***, 940 F.2d 631, 635 (Fed.Cir.1991) (subject-matter jurisdictional facts must be pleaded and proved when challenged); *see, e.g.*, ***Luis v. Dennis***, 751 F.2d 604, 607 (3d Cir.1984) (even though P did not cite correct authority as basis for jurisdiction, complaint alleged sufficient facts to support subject-matter jurisdiction).

(3) Jurisdictional amount. Generally, the complaint does not have to state an amount in controversy when jurisdiction is based on a federal question. *See* 28 U.S.C. §1331. However, a statement of the minimum amount in controversy may be required if the statute that confers federal-question jurisdiction contains an amount-in-controversy requirement. *See, e.g.*, 28 U.S.C. §1337(a) (claim arising out of commerce and antitrust legislation must exceed $10,000).

2. Diversity jurisdiction. Diversity jurisdiction must be supported in the complaint by specific factual statements, not mere allegations. *See, e.g.*, ***Penteco Corp. v. Union Gas Sys***, 929 F.2d 1519, 1521-22 (10th Cir.1991) (allegation that "there is complete diversity of citizenship" was not sufficient). See "Diversity Jurisdiction," ch. 2-F, §3, p. 116.

(1) Specific authority. The complaint should cite the specific constitutional or federal statute provision that diversity jurisdiction is based on. See "Is there complete diversity?," ch. 2-F, §3.1, p. 116.

(2) Supporting facts. In the complaint, the plaintiff must allege each party's citizenship. Merely stating that a party is a resident of a particular state is not sufficient because diversity jurisdiction depends on citizenship, not residence. 28 U.S.C. §1332(a)(1)-(a)(3). See "Is there complete diversity?," ch. 2-F, §3.1, p. 116; "Who is considered for diversity jurisdiction?," ch. 2-F, §3.2, p. 118.

NOTE

*To establish diversity jurisdiction when a corporation is a defendant, the plaintiff must state facts showing that the corporation is not incorporated in the plaintiff's home state and does not have its principal place of business there. See **Harris**, 682 F.3d at 850; **Stafford v. Mobil Oil Corp.**, 945 F.2d 803, 804-05 (5th Cir.1991). For example, to establish diversity when the plaintiff is from Texas, the complaint must show that the corporate defendant's state of incorporation and its principal place of business are somewhere other than Texas. See, e.g., **Jones v. Petty-Ray Geophysical, Geosource, Inc.**, 954 F.2d 1061, 1064 (5th Cir.1992) (no diversity when P was citi-*

zen of Texas and D was incorporated in Delaware but had its principal place of business in Texas); see also ***American Inter-Fid. Exch. v. American Re-Ins.****, 17 F.3d 1018, 1020-21 (7th Cir.1994) (allegation that D was Delaware corporation licensed to do business in Indiana was not sufficient because it did not state D's principal place of business);* ***Hogan v. Consolidated Rail Corp.****, 961 F.2d 1021, 1027 (2d Cir.1992) (allegation that D-corporation was incorporated in "a number of states" was not sufficient). See "Corporation," ch. 2-F, §3.2.1(2)(a), p. 119.*

(3) Jurisdictional amount. The complaint must state that the amount in controversy exceeds $75,000, excluding interest and costs. 28 U.S.C. §1332(a). See "When is amount in controversy satisfied?," ch. 2-F, §3.3, p. 123.

3. Alienage jurisdiction. Alienage jurisdiction permits a federal court to hear suits between a U.S. citizen and a foreign state or one of its citizens. *See* 28 U.S.C. §1332(a)(2)-(a)(4); *see also* ***JPMorgan Chase Bank v. Traffic Stream (BVI) Infrastructure Ltd.***, 536 U.S. 88, 94-95 (2002) (alien's right to sue U.S. citizen is subcategory of diversity jurisdiction under Article 3 of U.S. Constitution). The plaintiff should specifically plead alienage jurisdiction. See "Alienage Jurisdiction," ch. 2-F, §4, p. 127.

4. Multiparty jurisdiction. Multiparty jurisdiction permits a federal court to hear certain types of multiparty cases, such as class actions, mass torts, and "single-event" actions. *See* 28 U.S.C. §§1332(d), 1369, 1453. The plaintiff should specifically plead any such basis for jurisdiction. See "Multiparty Jurisdiction," ch. 2-F, §5, p. 129.

5. Supplemental jurisdiction. Supplemental jurisdiction permits a federal court to adjudicate certain claims otherwise outside its subject-matter jurisdiction. *See* 28 U.S.C. §1367(a); ***Rosmer v. Pfizer Inc.***, 263 F.3d 110, 114 (4th Cir.2001). The plaintiff should specifically plead supplemental jurisdiction. *See* FRCP 8(a)(1). See "Supplemental Jurisdiction," ch. 2-F, §6, p. 134.

§3.2 Amending jurisdictional allegations. A party may amend defective jurisdictional allegations. 28 U.S.C. §1653. See "Motion to Amend or Supplement Pleadings—Pretrial," ch. 5-I, p. 345.

§4. VENUE

Because improper venue is a defensive issue, the plaintiff is not required to include allegations about venue in the complaint. *See* FRCP 8(a); ***Ripperger v. A.C. Allyn & Co.***, 113 F.2d 332, 334 (2d Cir.1940). But by pleading a proper basis for venue, the plaintiff may avoid having to respond to a defendant's motion to dismiss or motion to transfer. See "Choosing the Court—Venue," ch. 2-G, p. 143.

§5. STATEMENT OF CLAIM

§5.1 Standard pleadings. Generally, a plaintiff must give fair notice of a claim by providing a short and plain statement of the claim showing that the plaintiff is entitled to relief. FRCP 8(a)(2); ***Bell Atlantic Corp. v. Twombly***, 550 U.S. 544, 555 (2007); ***Erickson v. Pardus***, 551 U.S. 89, 93 (2007); *see* ***Renfro v. Unisys Corp.***, 671 F.3d 314, 320 (3d Cir.2011) (FRCP 8 requires "showing"—rather than blanket assertion—of entitlement to relief). Although the plaintiff is not required to provide detailed factual allegations, the statement of the claim must include plausible factual allegations concerning all material elements of the claim. *See* ***Ashcroft v. Iqbal***, 556 U.S. 662, 678 (2009); ***Lormand v. US Unwired, Inc.***, 565 F.3d 228, 232 (5th Cir.2009). Thus, to avoid a dismissal under FRCP 12(b)(6) for failure to state a claim, the plaintiff must (1) give the defendant fair notice of the nature of the claim and (2) provide plausible factual allegations to support the claim. ***Starr v. Baca***, 652 F.3d 1202, 1216 (9th Cir.2011); ***Ocasio-Hernandez v. Fortuño-Burset***, 640 F.3d 1, 12 (1st Cir.2011); *see* ***Iqbal***, 556 U.S. at 679; ***Erickson***, 551 U.S. at 93; ***Twombly***, 550 U.S. at 555-56 & n.3. See "Motion to Dismiss for Failure to State a Claim—FRCP 12(b)(6)," ch. 3-F, p. 204.

PRACTICE TIP

When drafting the statement of the claim, consider whether an FRCP Form applies to the claim. See, e.g., ***In re Bill of Lading Transmission & Processing Sys. Patent Litig.****, 681 F.3d 1323, 1334-35 (Fed.Cir.2012) (relying on FRCP 84 and FRCP Form 18, P's amended complaint was sufficient; to extent* ***Twombly*** *and* ***Iqbal*** *conflict with Forms and create different pleading standard, Forms control);* ***Hamilton v. Palm****, 621 F.3d 816, 818 (8th Cir.2010) (relying on FRCP 84 and FRCP Form 13, P's simple allegation that he was employed by Ds was sufficiently plausible for negligence claim; district court erred in concluding that P's allegation was insufficient, even though statement appeared to be "facially conclusory" in abstract). See "Appendix of Forms," p. 991, this book.*

1. Fair notice. The complaint must provide fair notice of the claim by including allegations that outline the elements of the claim. *See* ***Starr***, 652 F.3d at 1216; ***Brooks v. Ross***, 578 F.3d 574, 581 (7th Cir.2009); ***Brownlee v. Conine***, 957 F.2d 353, 354 (7th Cir.1992); 5B Wright & Miller §1357; *see also* ***Iqbal***, 556 U.S. at 678 (complaint must provide more than accusation that "defendant unlawfully harmed me"). That is, the plaintiff's factual allegations must be sufficient to notify the defendant of the nature and basis of the claim and the type of litigation involved. ***Burlington Indus. v. Milliken & Co.***, 690 F.2d 380, 390 (4th Cir.1982); *see* ***Erickson***, 551 U.S. at 93; ***Stanard v. Nygren***, 658 F.3d 792, 797 (7th Cir.2011). The allegations must be simple, concise, and direct. FRCP 8(d)(1); ***Stanard***, 658 F.3d at 797; ***Simmons v. Abruzzo***, 49 F.3d 83, 86 (2d Cir.1995). A complaint that provides only labels and conclusions or a formulaic recitation of the elements without sufficient supporting facts is insufficient to show "grounds" for the plaintiff to be entitled to relief. ***Iqbal***, 556 U.S. at 678; ***Twombly***, 550 U.S. at 555; ***Francis v. Giacomelli***, 588 F.3d 186, 193 (4th Cir.2009); ***Brooks***, 578 F.3d at 581; *see* ***NicSand, Inc. v. 3M Co.***, 507 F.3d 442, 451 (6th Cir.2007) (there is a key distinction between bare-bones complaint asserting only elements of claim and complaint asserting elements with supporting facts). Legal conclusions—even cast in the form of factual allegations—are not assumed to be true and, without more, do not suffice. *See* ***Iqbal***, 556 U.S. at 678; ***Moss v. U.S. Secret Serv.***, 572 F.3d 962, 969 (9th Cir.2009); *see, e.g.*, ***McTernan v. City of York***, 577 F.3d 521, 531 (3d Cir.2009) (in First Amendment case, protesters alleged ramp was public forum, but that allegation was legal conclusion and thus was not accepted as true; protesters failed to state First Amendment claim).

2. Plausibility. The factual allegations supporting the elements of the claim must be plausible; they cannot be merely conceivable, possible, or conclusory. *See* ***Iqbal***, 556 U.S. at 678-79.

NOTE

In ***Iqbal****, the Supreme Court stated that determining whether the plausibility standard has been met will be "context-specific" and will require a judge to use her experience and common sense.* ***Iqbal****, 556 U.S. at 679. After* ***Iqbal****, however, courts have struggled with what constitutes sufficiently plausible facts and whether there is in fact a higher pleading standard. See* ***Pruell v. Caritas Christi****, 678 F.3d 10, 12-13 (1st Cir.2012) (plausibility standard has been somewhat unsettled);* ***Khalik v. United Air Lines****, 671 F.3d 1188, 1191 & n.2 (10th Cir.2012) (plausibility is "new, refined" standard);* ***New Albany Tractor, Inc. v. Louisville Tractor, Inc.****, 650 F.3d 1046, 1051 (6th Cir.2011) (plausibility standard requires P to have greater knowledge of factual detail, even when facts are only within D's purview);* ***Atkins v. City of Chi.****, 631 F.3d 823, 831 (7th Cir.2011) (plausibility standard is a little unclear because plausibility, probability, and possibility overlap). To satisfy this standard, some courts and commentators have suggested that the plaintiff should be allowed to conduct limited discovery, especially when the information the plaintiff needs is within the defendant's knowledge. See* ***McCauley v. City of Chi.****, 671 F.3d 611, 619-20 n.2 (7th Cir.2011). Because of the courts' different interpretations, check the law of your circuit to determine the appropriate standard.*

(1) **Reasonable inference of liability.** A claim is plausible on its face when the plaintiff pleads factual content that allows the court to draw a reasonable inference that the defendant is liable for the alleged misconduct. *E.g.*, ***Iqbal***, 556 U.S. at 678 (P's claim of discrimination against former Attorney General and FBI Director did not cross "line from conceivable to plausible" and did not raise reasonable inference that those Ds knowingly and willfully subjected P to harsh conditions based on his protected status); *see* ***Khalik***, 671 F.3d at 1191 (plausibility refers to scope of allegations—if allegations are so general that they cover wide range of conduct, much of it innocent, Ps have not provided plausible allegations); *see, e.g.*, ***Speaker v. U.S. Dept. of H&HS Ctrs. for Disease Control & Prevention***, 623 F.3d 1371, 1384-85 (11th Cir.2010) (P's claim for Privacy Act violation crossed "line from conceivable to plausible" when P's complaint alleged the what, when, and how of CDC's violation); *see also* ***Sepú Lveda-Villarini v. Department of Educ. of P.R.***, 628 F.3d 25, 30 (1st Cir.2010) (plausibility does not mean likely success on merits). If the factual allegations do not permit an inference of more than the mere possibility of misconduct, the plaintiff has not made allegations showing that she is entitled to relief. *See* 5B Wright & Miller §1357; *see, e.g.*, ***Branham v. Dolgencorp, Inc.***, No. 6:09-CV-00037 (W.D.Va.2009) (slip op.; 8-24-09) (in slip-and-fall case, claim was not plausible when P did not allege facts showing how liquid came to be on floor, whether D should have known about liquid on floor, or how P's accident occurred). In other words, the nonconclusory factual allegations, which are generally assumed to be true, must be enough to show that the plaintiff's right to relief is more than mere speculation. ***Twombly***, 550 U.S. at 555; ***Cuvillier v. Taylor***, 503 F.3d 397, 401 (5th Cir.2007); *see* ***Iqbal***, 556 U.S. at 678-79; ***Starr***, 652 F.3d at 1216; ***Brooks***, 578 F.3d at 581.

(2) **Degree of factual specificity.** The factual allegations do not need to be detailed, but they must provide more than only labels or conclusions. ***Twombly***, 550 U.S. at 555. They also cannot be indeterminate; if they are, more factual content is required. ***Braden v. Wal-Mart Stores***, 588 F.3d 585, 594 (8th Cir.2009); *see* ***Pruell***, 678 F.3d at 15 (complaints cannot be based on generalities); ***Brooks***, 578 F.3d at 581 (factual detail cannot be sketchy). The level of specificity most likely increases as the complexity of the claim increases. ***McCauley***, 671 F.3d at 616-17; *see* ***Pruell***, 678 F.3d at 14; ***Khalik***, 671 F.3d at 1191.

CAUTION

Although the degree of factual specificity is not easily quantified, a complaint without at least some plausible factual allegations will likely be challenged by a motion to dismiss for failure to state a claim under FRCP 12(b)(6). See ***Iqbal****, 556 U.S. at 678-79;* ***Twombly****, 550 U.S. at 555-56 & n.3, 570;* ***McCauley****, 671 F.3d at 616. An FRCP 12(b)(6) challenge could result in the court dismissing the complaint or requiring the plaintiff to amend the complaint with additional factual details. See* ***Pruell****, 678 F.3d at 15.* *See "Motion to Dismiss for Failure to State a Claim—FRCP 12(b)(6)," ch. 3-F, p. 204.*

---

(3) **Information & belief.** The factual allegations can be based on information and belief. FRCP 11(b); *see* ***Arista Records LLC v. Doe 3***, 604 F.3d 110, 120 (2d Cir.2010). A complaint containing these types of allegations is appropriate when (1) the information is within the knowledge of the defendant but not the plaintiff or (2) the belief is based on factual information that makes the inference of culpability possible. ***Arista Records***, 604 F.3d at 120; *see* ***Pirelli Armstrong Tire Corp. Retiree Med. Benefits Trust v. Walgreen Co.***, 631 F.3d 436, 443 (7th Cir. 2011); ***Kowal v. MCI Comms.***, 16 F.3d 1271, 1279 n.3 (D.C.Cir.1994); ***Tuchman v. DSC Comms.***, 14 F.3d 1061, 1068 (5th Cir.1994). Factual allegations based on information and belief must still meet the plausibility requirement. *See* ***Pirelli Armstrong Tire Corp. Retiree Med. Benefits Trust***, 631 F.3d at 443; ***Arista Records***, 604 F.3d at 120; *see, e.g.*, ***Sinaltrainal v. Coca-Cola Co.***, 578 F.3d 1252, 1268 (11th Cir.2009) (Ps' vague allegations of conspiracy based on information and belief did not allow court to draw reasonable inference that D was liable for alleged misconduct), *overruled on other grounds*, ***Mohamad v. Palestinian Auth.***, ___ U.S. ___, 132 S.Ct. 1702 (2012).

§5.2 Particularized pleadings. In some cases, allegations that satisfy the requirements of FRCP 8(a) are not sufficient, and the plaintiff must satisfy a heightened requirement by pleading some matters specifically. *See* ***Bell Atlantic Corp. v. Twombly***, 550 U.S. 544, 569-70 & n.14 (2007) (greater particularity required for certain matters

that present high risk of abusive litigation); ***American Dental Ass'n v. Cigna Corp.***, 605 F.3d 1283, 1291 (11th Cir. 2010) (allegations of fraud or mistake must satisfy plausibility standard and heightened pleading standard under FRCP 9(b)). The heightened pleading requirement must be imposed by a specific statutory or rule provision; without one, only the requirements of fair notice and plausibility apply. *See* ***Ashcroft v. Iqbal***, 556 U.S. 662, 686-87 (2009); ***Swierkiewicz v. Sorema***, 534 U.S. 506, 513 (2002); *see, e.g.*, ***Jones v. Bock***, 549 U.S. 199, 211-17 (2007) (Prison Litigation Reform Act's exhaustion requirement does not impose heightened pleading requirement; normal pleading rules apply); ***In re Tower Air, Inc.***, 416 F.3d 229, 237 (3d Cir.2005) (by requiring P to allege specific facts in shareholder derivative suit, court erroneously imposed heightened pleading standard). Some of the matters that may require particularized pleading are the following:

1. Fraud or mistake. Allegations of fraud or mistake must be pleaded with particularity. FRCP 9(b); ***Swierkiewicz***, 534 U.S. at 513; ***Pirelli Armstrong Tire Corp. Retiree Med. Benefits Trust v. Walgreen Co.***, 631 F.3d 436, 441 (7th Cir.2011); *see, e.g.*, ***Shandong Yinguang Chem. Indus. Joint Stock Co. v. Potter***, 607 F.3d 1029, 1032-33 (5th Cir.2010) (P did not adequately plead fraud when P alleged only slight circumstantial evidence of fraud and those allegations did not plausibly plead fraudulent intent). To plead fraud with the necessary particularity, the plaintiff must (1) specify the statements alleged to be fraudulent, (2) identify the person who made the statements, (3) state when and where the statements were made, and (4) explain why the statements were fraudulent (i.e., what facts were misrepresented and what the person making the statements gained). ***American Dental Ass'n***, 605 F.3d at 1291; ***Williams v. WMX Techs.***, 112 F.3d 175, 177 (5th Cir.1997); ***Firestone v. Firestone***, 76 F.3d 1205, 1211 (D.C.Cir.1996). Allegations of fraud that are based on information and belief usually cannot satisfy the particularity requirement, but they can in certain circumstances if the facts constituting fraud are not accessible to the plaintiff and the plaintiff provides plausible grounds for her beliefs. ***Pirelli Armstrong Tire Corp. Retiree Med. Benefits Trust***, 631 F.3d at 442-43; *see* ***In re Burlington Coat Factory Sec. Litig.***, 114 F.3d 1410, 1418 (3d Cir.1997). See "Information & belief," §5.1.2(3), p. 82.

2. Time & place. Allegations of time and place are material and should be pleaded with particularity when the substantive nature of the case requires it. *See* FRCP 9(f); ***Huckabay v. Moore***, 142 F.3d 233, 240-41 & n.7 (5th Cir.1998); *see, e.g.*, ***Bankest Imps., Inc. v. ISCA Corp.***, 717 F.Supp 1537, 1539 (S.D.Fla.1989) (D alleged sufficient facts of time and place to survive motion to dismiss, but court ordered more definite statement when events spanned seven years); ***UD Tech. v. Phenomenex, Inc.***, No. 05-842-GMS (D.Del.2007) (slip op.; 1-4-07) (in pleading contract claim, P should have specified time when contract was signed to identify document that was subject matter of dispute). FRCP 9(f) facilitates the identification and isolation of the event at issue and provides a mechanism for the early adjudication of certain claims and defenses (e.g., statute of limitations). *See* ***Kincheloe v. Farmer***, 214 F.2d 604, 605 (7th Cir.1954); ***Jairett v. First Montauk Secs. Corp.***, 203 F.R.D. 181, 186 (E.D.Pa.2001); *see also* ***Huckabay***, 142 F.3d at 240-41 (although dates and times lend credibility to P's case and their omission may undermine it, they are not prerequisite to recovery). Allegations of time may be made with the qualification of "on or about" a certain date.

3. PSLRA suits. Allegations of federal securities fraud must be pleaded with particularity. *See* FRCP 9(b). A pleading that alleges fraud under the Private Securities Litigation Reform Act (PSLRA) must (1) specify each alleged misrepresentation and explain why it is misleading and (2) state with particularity facts giving rise to a strong inference that the defendant acted with the required scienter (i.e., intent to deceive). 15 U.S.C. §78u-4(b)(1), (b)(2)(A); ***Tellabs, Inc. v. Makor Issues & Rights, Ltd.***, 551 U.S. 308, 321 (2007); *see* FRCP 9(b). A "strong" inference is more than a reasonable or plausible one; it must be cogent and at least as compelling as any opposing inference that could be drawn from the alleged facts. ***Tellabs***, 551 U.S. at 323-24. The PSLRA does not change the scienter a plaintiff must prove to prevail at trial, but only what it must plead in its complaint to survive a motion to dismiss. ***Nathenson v. Zonagen, Inc.***, 267 F.3d 400, 409 (5th Cir.2001).

4. Civil-rights suits. Allegations in civil-rights suits generally do not have to be pleaded with particularity. In 1993, the Supreme Court held that heightened factual specificity is not required in civil-rights suits against municipalities, and in 2002, the Court held that unless a specific statute imposes a heightened pleading requirement,

FRCP 8(a)'s requirement of a "short and plain statement" applies. ***Swierkiewicz***, 534 U.S. at 513; ***Leatherman v. Tarrant Cty. Narcotics Intelligence & Coordination Unit***, 507 U.S. 163, 168 (1993). Together, ***Swierkiewicz*** and ***Leatherman*** cast doubt on any heightened pleading requirement in civil-rights cases. *See* ***Educadores Puertorriqueños en Acción v. Hernández***, 367 F.3d 61, 66-67 (1st Cir.2004) (rejecting heightened pleading standard except when required by either federal statute or specific FRCP); ***Phillip v. University of Rochester***, 316 F.3d 291, 298 (2d Cir.2003) (Title VII P does not need to specify circumstances supporting inference of discrimination to survive FRCP 12(b)(6) motion). However, when a plaintiff files a civil-rights complaint against a public official, the court may require the plaintiff to "put forward specific, nonconclusory factual allegations." *See* ***Crawford-El v. Britton***, 523 U.S. 574, 597-98 (1998); ***Goad v. Mitchell***, 297 F.3d 497, 504-05 & n.6 (6th Cir.2002). *But see* ***Randall v. Scott***, 610 F.3d 701, 709 (11th Cir.2010) (***Iqbal*** effectively overruled cases under 42 U.S.C. §1983 that involved Ds who asserted qualified immunity and that applied heightened pleading standard).

§5.3 Theory of recovery. The complaint is not required to specify the legal theory of recovery or demand specific relief. *See* ***Gilbane Bldg. Co. v. Federal Reserve Bank***, 80 F.3d 895, 900 (4th Cir.1996); ***Schott Motorcycle Sup. v. American Honda Motor Co.***, 976 F.2d 58, 62 (1st Cir.1992); *see also* ***Wynder v. McMahon***, 360 F.3d 73, 77 (2d Cir.2004) (P is not required to separate its claims by D). However, the plaintiff should identify the specific legal theories or separate them into distinct counts when doing so would assist in the clear presentation of the issues. *See* FRCP 10(b); 5A Wright & Miller §1324 & nn.18, 36; *see, e.g.*, ***Davis v. Coca-Cola Bottling Co. Consol.***, 516 F.3d 955, 979-81 (11th Cir.2008) (in employment-discrimination case, appellate court denied any attorney-fees requests when parties used "shotgun pleadings" that attempted to combine multiple claims for multiple Ps into one count). This specificity is especially important because the court is not required to fabricate a legal theory that the plaintiff does not spell out in its pleadings through factual allegations. ***Schott***, 976 F.2d at 62; 5 Wright & Miller §1286; *see* ***Davis***, 516 F.3d at 982-83. If the plaintiff identifies a legal theory but accidentally mislabels it, the complaint will not be dismissed as long as the complaint has pleaded facts supporting the claim against the defendant. ***Labram v. Havel***, 43 F.3d 918, 920 (4th Cir.1995); ***Torres Ramirez v. Bermudez Garcia***, 898 F.2d 224, 226-27 (1st Cir.1990); *see* ***Walker v. South Cent. Bell Tel. Co.***, 904 F.2d 275, 277 (5th Cir.1990) (claim may be adequate despite element's omission if element can be fairly inferred from pleadings as a whole); *see also* ***PAE Gov't Servs. v. MPRI, Inc.***, 514 F.3d 856, 860 (9th Cir.2007) (parties can file successive pleadings that include inconsistent or contradictory allegations).

§6. DAMAGES

FRCP 8 does not explicitly require that the complaint state a specific dollar amount of damages. *See* 5 Wright & Miller §1259. The demand for judgment should give the court and the defendant a general indication of the type of relief sought, but it does not need to state a specific amount of damages. *Id.*; *see* ***Avitia v. Metropolitan Club***, 49 F.3d 1219, 1226 (7th Cir.1995) (P not required to itemize damages in complaint, except for special damages). However, when the amount in controversy is a jurisdictional element, the plaintiff must at least plead that the damages exceed the jurisdictional minimum. See "When is amount in controversy satisfied?," ch. 2-F, §3.3, p. 123.

§6.1 General damages. The plaintiff does not need to specifically identify its general damages. ***Avitia v. Metropolitan Club***, 49 F.3d 1219, 1226 (7th Cir.1995). General damages are actual damages that naturally and necessarily flow from the defendant's wrongful conduct. ***M.F. Patterson Dental Sup. v. Wadley***, 401 F.2d 167, 172 (10th Cir.1968).

§6.2 Special damages. The plaintiff must specifically identify its special damages. FRCP 9(g). Special damages are those that result from the wrong but are not normally associated with the type of claim in question. ***Avitia v. Metropolitan Club***, 49 F.3d 1219, 1226 (7th Cir.1995); *see* ***PdP Parfums de Paris, S.A. v. International Designer Fragrances Inc.***, 901 F.Supp. 581, 585 (E.D.N.Y.1995) (special damages are those that are not the necessary result of the challenged act).

§6.3 Punitive damages. The plaintiff should specifically request punitive damages if the plaintiff pleads a cause of action that allows for them. *See* FRCP 9(g). In some cases, the plaintiff must allege specific facts to show it is entitled to punitive damages. For example, if the statute authorizing punitive damages requires the defendant to have

acted willfully, the plaintiff must allege willfulness and the facts supporting it. *See, e.g.,* ***New York Mar. & Gen. Ins. v. Tradeline***, 266 F.3d 112, 130 (2d Cir.2001) (claim for punitive damages properly dismissed because P did not allege facts necessary for recovery under New York law).

NOTE

For a discussion of the amount of punitive damages that can be awarded in a given case, read the Supreme Court opinion in ***State Farm Mut. Auto. Ins. v. Campbell****, 538 U.S. 408 (2003), and later cases interpreting its holding.*

§7. INTEREST

The plaintiff should specifically request prejudgment and postjudgment interest. In some cases, a request for "any other relief, both special and general, to which it may be justly entitled" has been held sufficient to plead a claim for prejudgment interest. ***Federal S&L Ins. v. Texas Real Estate Counselors, Inc.***, 955 F.2d 261, 270 (5th Cir.1992). *But see* ***Silge v. Merz***, 510 F.3d 157, 160 (2d Cir.2007) (generic request does not constitute demand for prejudgment interest).

§8. COSTS

The plaintiff should make a general request for costs. Costs should be awarded to the prevailing party unless a federal statute, the FRCPs, or a court order provides otherwise. FRCP 54(d)(1); ***Coats v. Penrod Drilling Corp.***, 5 F.3d 877, 891 (5th Cir.1993), *reh'g granted*, 20 F.3d 614 (5th Cir.1994), *aff'd*, 61 F.3d 1113 (5th Cir.1995); *see* ***McDonald v. Petree***, 409 F.3d 724, 732 (6th Cir.2005) (court has discretion to deny costs).

§9. ATTORNEY FEES

Attorney fees are considered special damages and must be specifically pleaded. ***In re American Cas. Co.***, 851 F.2d 794, 802 (6th Cir.1988); ***Atlantic Purchasers, Inc. v. Aircraft Sales, Inc.***, 705 F.2d 712, 716 n.4 (4th Cir.1983); *see* FRCP 9(g), 54(d)(2). However, the plaintiff is not required to plead the specific amount of attorney fees. *See* ***Cotton Bros. Baking Co. v. Industrial Risk Insurers***, 102 F.R.D. 964, 967 (W.D.La.1984), *aff'd*, 951 F.2d 54 (5th Cir.1992). See "Motion for Attorney Fees," ch. 9-C, p. 745.

§10. OTHER RELIEF

The complaint must demand all the relief the plaintiff seeks. FRCP 8(a)(3). For example, if the plaintiff seeks equitable relief, such as an injunction, the complaint should ask for it, along with all other relief sought. The complaint may ask for relief in the alternative or for different types of relief. *Id.*

§11. CONDITIONS PRECEDENT

The plaintiff should include a statement in the complaint that all conditions precedent have occurred or have been performed. FRCP 9(c).

§12. JURY DEMAND

The plaintiff should include a statement in the complaint requesting a jury trial unless the plaintiff wants a bench trial. *See* FRCP 38(b). The plaintiff can also make its jury demand in a separate document. *Id.* If the demand is not made in the complaint, the plaintiff should file the demand at the same time as the complaint and serve it on the defendant with the request for waiver of service of process. See "Demand for Jury Trial," ch. 5-C, p. 309. Local rules may provide additional requirements for how a jury demand must be made.

§13. SIGNATURE & ADDRESS

The plaintiff's complaint must be signed by at least one attorney of record in the attorney's individual name or by the party herself if the party is unrepresented. FRCP 11(a). See "Signature," ch. 1-B, §2.1.9, p. 10; ***O'Connor's Federal Forms***, FORM 1B:2. Local rules or procedures may require the attorney to include additional information, such as a state-bar number or a fax number. *E.g.*, Local Rules Tex. (N.D.), Rule 10.1(b) (attorney's bar number, fax number, and e-mail address).

§14. VERIFICATION & AFFIDAVITS

Generally, the plaintiff does not need to verify its complaint or attach affidavits. Verification is necessary only when specifically required by rule or statute. FRCP 11(a); *see, e.g.*, 8 U.S.C. §1445(a) (petition for naturalization); 28 U.S.C. §1734(b) (application for order establishing lost or destroyed record); FRCP 23.1(b) (complaint in derivative action), FRCP 27(a)(1) (petition for perpetuation of testimony), FRCP 65(b)(1)(A) (application for temporary restraining order).

§15. EXHIBITS

§15.1 Incorporation by attachment. A copy of any written instrument that is an exhibit to a complaint is considered a part of the complaint for all purposes. FRCP 10(c). In limited cases, the attachment of an exhibit may satisfy jurisdictional requirements not specifically pleaded in the complaint. *E.g.*, ***Flesch v. Eastern Pa. Psychiatric Inst.***, 434 F.Supp. 963, 969 n.3 (E.D.Pa.1977) (EEOC letter attached to show exhaustion of administrative remedies). Any reference to an attached exhibit must be clear and explicit. 5A Wright & Miller §1327; *see also* ***General Acc. Ins. v. Fidelity & Deposit Co.***, 598 F.Supp. 1223, 1229 & n.4 (E.D.Pa.1984) (portions of earlier pleading sought to be incorporated must be specifically identified).

§15.2 Excessive exhibits. A plaintiff should avoid attaching nonessential exhibits to a complaint. A court may strike the complaint if it has too many extraneous exhibits. *See* ***Johns-Manville Sales Corp. v. Chicago Title & Trust Co.***, 261 F.Supp. 905, 908 (N.D.Ill.1966). The better practice is to plead the substance of nonessential documents rather than attach them as exhibits. *See id.*

§16. FILING REQUIREMENTS

When filing the complaint, the plaintiff must do the following:

§16.1 Filing fees. The plaintiff must pay a filing fee when it presents the complaint to the clerk for filing. The plaintiff should check with the clerk in advance to determine the amount of the filing fee. The filing fee for a complaint and summons in district court is $350. 28 U.S.C. §1914(a).

§16.2 Civil cover sheet. The plaintiff must file a civil cover sheet (JS 44) with the complaint. The form is available on the website for the Administrative Office of the U.S. courts at www.uscourts.gov/forms/JS044.pdf. The courts use the civil cover sheet to gather statistical information about filed suits.

§16.3 Disclosure statement. If the plaintiff is a nongovernmental corporate party, it must file two copies of a statement that either (1) identifies any parent corporation and any publicly held corporation owning 10% or more of its stock or (2) states that there is no such corporation. FRCP 7.1(a). The plaintiff must promptly file a supplemental statement if any required information changes. FRCP 7.1(b)(2). See ***O'Connor's Federal Forms***, FORM 1B:9.

§16.4 Notice of constitutional question. If the plaintiff is challenging the constitutionality of a statute, it must file a notice of the constitutional question. FRCP 5.1(a)(1). See "Notice of constitutional question," ch. 1-B, §2.1.11, p. 12.

C. INTERPLEADER

§1. GENERAL

§1.1 Rule. FRCP 22. See also 28 U.S.C. §§1335, 1397, 2361.

§1.2 Purpose. Interpleader allows a party who holds property that is exposed to multiple claims to join two or more parties asserting claims to that property in one proceeding. ***Metropolitan Life Ins. v. Price***, 501 F.3d 271, 275 (3d Cir.2007); ***Commercial Un. Ins. v. U.S.***, 999 F.2d 581, 583 (D.C.Cir.1993). Interpleader protects the stakeholder from multiple lawsuits and the possibility of inconsistent or multiple determinations of liability. *See* ***State Farm Fire & Cas. Co. v. Tashire***, 386 U.S. 523, 534 (1967); ***Washington Elec. Coop. v. Paterson, Walke & Pratt***, 985 F.2d 677, 679 (2d Cir.1993). Interpleader also protects the stakeholder from liability for not only claims to the stake but also any other claims directly relating to its failure to resolve the claims at issue. *E.g.*, ***Prudential Ins. v. Hovis***, 553 F.3d 258, 265 (3d Cir.2009) (in dispute between decedent's fiancé and decedent's children over life-insurance proceeds, interpleader protection extended to fiancé's counterclaim that stakeholder failed to timely process request to change ownership of policy).

§1.3 Forms. ***O'Connor's Federal Civil Forms*** (2012), FORMS 2C.

§1.4 Other references. 7 Wright, Miller & Kane, *Federal Practice & Procedure 3d* §§1701-1721 (2001 & Supp.2012); 4 *Moore's Federal Practice 3d* ch. 22 (2012).

§2. PARTIES

§2.1 Stakeholder. A "stakeholder" is a person who holds property (i.e., the "stake") and who is or may be subject to inconsistent claims for that property. ***U.S. v. Hodgekins***, 28 F.3d 610, 614 (7th Cir.1994). The stakeholder must not be at fault for causing the dispute over its property. *See* ***Prudential Ins. v. Hovis***, 553 F.3d 258, 263 & n.4 (3d Cir.2009). The stakeholder may be (1) a plaintiff who initiates the interpleader action or (2) a defendant who defensively institutes the interpleader proceeding in an ongoing suit by filing a counterclaim or cross-claim. *See, e.g.*, ***Fleet Nat'l Bank v. Anchor Media TV, Inc.***, 45 F.3d 546, 550 (1st Cir.1995) (stakeholder filed suit as P); ***Septembertide Publ'g, B.V. v. Stein & Day, Inc.***, 884 F.2d 675, 683 (2d Cir.1989) (D1 asserted interpleader action defensively by filing counterclaim against P and cross-claim against D2). The stakeholder may be either "disinterested" or "interested." *See* ***Nationwide Mut. Ins. v. Eckman***, 555 F.Supp. 775, 781 (D.Del.1983); *see also* ***Airborne Freight Corp. v. U.S.***, 195 F.3d 238, 240 (5th Cir.1999) ("true" interpleader is when P is stakeholder but not claimant, and "in the nature of" interpleader is when P is both stakeholder and claimant).

1. Disinterested stakeholder. A disinterested stakeholder puts the stake in the possession of the court, is discharged from the proceeding, and leaves the competing claimants to litigate among themselves for ownership of the stake. ***Commercial Nat'l Bank v. Demos***, 18 F.3d 485, 487 (7th Cir.1994).

2. Interested stakeholder. An interested stakeholder claims an interest in the stake, puts the stake in the possession of the court, and litigates with the claimants for ownership of the stake. *See* ***Nationwide Mut. Ins.***, 555 F.Supp. at 781; *see also* ***First Interstate Bank v. U.S.***, 891 F.Supp. 543, 546 n.5 (D.Or.1995) (stakeholder does not need to be neutral).

§2.2 Claimant. A "claimant" is a person who asserts an interest in the stake in the possession of the stakeholder. All of the claimants must assert claims to the same stake. ***Wausau Ins. v. Gifford***, 954 F.2d 1098, 1100-01 (5th Cir.1992); ***Indianapolis Colts v. Mayor & City Council of Balt.***, 741 F.2d 954, 956 (7th Cir.1984). The claimants' interests must be adverse to each other. ***Bradley v. Kochenash***, 44 F.3d 166, 168 (2d Cir.1995).

§3. COMPLAINT

§3.1 General requirements.

1. Stake. The stakeholder must demonstrate that the stake is a single and identifiable fund, property, or disputed right. *See* ***State Farm Fire & Cas. Co. v. Tashire***, 386 U.S. 523, 530 (1967); ***Wausau Ins. v. Gifford***, 954 F.2d 1098, 1100 (5th Cir.1992). The stake can be a tangible property interest or an intangible interest in the form of

a note, bond, certificate, insurance policy, or other similar instrument of identifiable value. *See* 28 U.S.C. §1335(a); *see, e.g.*, ***Murphy v. Travelers Ins.***, 534 F.2d 1155, 1159 (5th Cir.1976) (stake was face value of disputed insurance policy). The mere existence of a fund, however, does not justify interpleader or permit the stakeholder to enjoin all potential parties to multiparty litigation arising out of a mass tort. *See* ***Tashire***, 386 U.S. at 537.

2. Multiple claimants. The stakeholder must demonstrate that there are two or more independent, adverse claimants to the same stake. 28 U.S.C. §1335(a)(1); FRCP 22(a)(1)(A); *see* ***Airborne Freight Corp. v. U.S.***, 195 F.3d 238, 240 (5th Cir.1999) (no interpleader when there is only one claimant to a stake). All necessary parties must be joined for an interpleader action to proceed. *See* ***Pentech Int'l v. Wall Street Clearing Co.***, 983 F.2d 441, 448 (2d Cir.1993).

3. Adverse claims. The stakeholder must demonstrate that there are or may be adverse claims independent of one another. 28 U.S.C. §1335(b); FRCP 22(a)(1)(A); *see* ***Metropolitan Prop. & Cas. Ins. v. Shan Trac, Inc.***, 324 F.3d 20, 23 (1st Cir.2003) (sufficient under interpleader statute if there "may be" adverse claims by interpleaded parties against stake); ***Dakota Livestock Co. v. Keim***, 552 F.2d 1302, 1308 (8th Cir.1977) (same). This requirement is not met when a stakeholder owes separate obligations to multiple claimants rather than a single obligation to multiple claimants. *See, e.g.*, ***Bradley v. Kochenash***, 44 F.3d 166, 168 (2d Cir.1995) (claimants were not adverse to each other; stakeholder could be liable to each). The claims may arise from unrelated transactions as long as they all relate to the same stake. 28 U.S.C. §1335(b); ***Ashton v. Paul Found.***, 918 F.2d 1065, 1069 (2d Cir.1990).

4. Fear of multiple liability. The stakeholder must demonstrate its real and reasonable fear of multiple liability. ***Indianapolis Colts v. Mayor & City Council of Balt.***, 741 F.2d 954, 957 (7th Cir.1984); *see also* ***Metropolitan Prop.***, 324 F.3d at 23-24 (fear of multiple liability is "relatively undemanding" jurisdictional requirement). The claims do not need to have been reduced to a judgment. ***Tashire***, 386 U.S. at 532-33.

5. Timely. The stakeholder must demonstrate that it timely filed the interpleader action after receiving notice of multiple claims. *See, e.g.*, ***Mendez v. Teachers Ins. & Annuity Ass'n***, 982 F.2d 783, 787-88 (2d Cir.1992) (interpleader action filed 11 months after notice of adverse claims was not timely).

§3.2 Type of interpleader. The stakeholder should identify the type of procedural mechanism used to interplead the parties: "rule" interpleader or "statutory" interpleader. *See* 28 U.S.C. §§1335, 1397, 2361; FRCP 22. A court can assert jurisdiction under both types of interpleader if the complaint can be construed to confer jurisdiction under one or the other. 4 *Moore's Federal Practice 3d* §22.04[1]; *see, e.g.*, ***Truck-a-Tune, Inc. v. Ré***, 23 F.3d 60, 62 (2d Cir.1994) (court converted statutory interpleader to rule interpleader).

1. Rule interpleader.

(1) Jurisdiction. FRCP 22 provides a procedural mechanism for interpleader actions, but it does not confer subject-matter jurisdiction on the federal courts. ***Commercial Un. Ins. v. U.S.***, 999 F.2d 581, 584 (D.C.Cir. 1993). Therefore, an interpleader action brought under FRCP 22 must fall within one of the general statutory grants of federal jurisdiction—diversity or federal question. *Id.*

(a) Diversity. The diversity requirement is satisfied when, at the time the suit is filed, (1) the stakeholder is diverse from each claimant and (2) the amount in controversy exceeds $75,000. *See* 28 U.S.C. §1332(a); ***Truck-a-Tune***, 23 F.3d at 62. See "Diversity Jurisdiction," ch. 2-F, §3, p. 116. If the court had diversity jurisdiction when the suit was filed, it may dismiss the stakeholder without losing jurisdiction, even if the dismissal destroys diversity. *See* ***Phoenix Mut. Life Ins. v. Adams***, 30 F.3d 554, 558 n.3 (4th Cir.1994). See "When is diversity jurisdiction determined?," ch. 2-F, §3.4, p. 125.

(b) Federal question. If there is no diversity, jurisdiction must arise from a federal statute. ***Commercial Nat'l Bank v. Demos***, 18 F.3d 485, 488 (7th Cir.1994). The requirements for federal-question jurisdiction are set out in 28 U.S.C. §1331. See "Federal-Question Jurisdiction," ch. 2-F, §2, p. 113. Because of the well-pleaded-complaint rule, few interpleader complaints qualify for federal-question jurisdiction. ***Morongo Band of Mission Indians v. California State Bd. of Equalization***, 858 F.2d 1376, 1383 (9th Cir.1988); *see* ***Metropolitan Life***

Ins. v. Price, 501 F.3d 271, 275-76 (3d Cir.2007). Interpleader is a procedural device, and the stakeholder's claim typically seeks discharge; thus, it is difficult to characterize the complaint as asserting substantive federal rights. ***Metropolitan Life Ins.***, 501 F.3d at 276; ***Morongo Band of Mission Indians***, 858 F.2d at 1383. However, several circuits have held that federal courts may exercise jurisdiction over interpleader actions that do not state a federal question on the face of the complaint if the stakeholder's right to relief necessarily depends on the resolution of a substantial question of federal law. ***Demos***, 18 F.3d at 488; *see* ***Commercial Un. Ins.***, 999 F.2d at 585; ***Morongo Band of Mission Indians***, 858 F.2d at 1384; *see, e.g.*, ***Metropolitan Life Ins.***, 501 F.3d at 277 (insurance company presented substantial federal claim when it sought to enforce ERISA provisions by ensuring that insurance funds were disbursed to proper beneficiary).

(2) Venue. Venue under FRCP 22 is governed under the general venue statute. *See* 28 U.S.C. §1391; ***State Farm Fire & Cas. Co. v. Tashire***, 386 U.S. 523, 528 n.3 (1967).

(3) Deposit of stake not required. FRCP 22 does not require the stakeholder to deposit the stake with the court clerk. ***Gelfgren v. Republic Nat'l Life Ins.***, 680 F.2d 79, 82 (9th Cir.1982); ***Murphy v. Travelers Ins.***, 534 F.2d 1155, 1159 (5th Cir.1976). However, the court has the discretion to require the stakeholder to do so. *See* Local Rules Tex. (N.D.), Rule 67.1; *see, e.g.*, ***Central Bank v. U.S.***, 838 F.Supp. 564, 566 (M.D.Fla.1993) (court ordered deposit of stake). If local rules do not require deposit of the stake but the stakeholder seeks to deposit the stake, the stakeholder should ask for leave of court to deposit the stake with the court clerk. *See* FRCP 67(a); ***John v. Sotheby's, Inc.***, 141 F.R.D. 29, 33-34 (S.D.N.Y.1992); *see also* Local Rules Cal. (E.D.), Rule 150(a) (FRCP 67) (leave of court granted to deposit stake in all interpleader actions).

2. Statutory interpleader.

(1) Jurisdiction. 28 U.S.C. §1335 confers original jurisdiction to the federal courts over some interpleader actions. 28 U.S.C. §1335; ***NYLife Distribs. v. Adherence Grp.***, 72 F.3d 371, 374 (3d Cir.1995); *see* ***Whirlpool Corp. v. Ritter***, 929 F.2d 1318, 1320-21 (8th Cir.1991) (characterizing federal interpleader as a "special brand" of diversity jurisdiction). Section 1335 is remedial and intended to be liberally construed. ***Tashire***, 386 U.S. at 533. There is no federal-question jurisdiction for statutory interpleader. *See* ***Sun Life Assur. Co. v. Thomas***, 735 F.Supp. 730, 732 (W.D.Mich.1990).

(a) Minimal diversity. The stakeholder must show that at least two of the claimants are of diverse citizenship. 28 U.S.C. §1335(a)(1); ***Correspondent Servs. v. First Equities Corp.***, 338 F.3d 119, 124 (2d Cir. 2003); ***Morongo Band of Mission Indians***, 858 F.2d at 1381. This differs from the complete diversity required for FRCP 22 interpleader jurisdiction, in which the stakeholder must be diverse from all claimants. *See* ***Truck-a-Tune***, 23 F.3d at 62. The citizenship of the plaintiff-stakeholder is generally not relevant in statutory interpleader. ***General Acc. Grp. v. Gagliardi***, 593 F.Supp. 1080, 1086 (D.Conn.1984), *aff'd*, 767 F.2d 907 (2d Cir.1985) (table case); *see* ***NYLife Distribs.***, 72 F.3d at 374; ***Selective Ins. v. Norris***, 209 F.Supp.2d 580, 582 (E.D.N.C.2002).

(b) Amount in controversy. The stakeholder meets the amount-in-controversy requirement of §1335 under any of the following conditions: (1) it has money or property worth $500 or more in its custody or possession, (2) it issued a note, bond, certificate, insurance policy, or other instrument worth $500 or more, (3) it provided for the delivery, payment, or loan of money or property worth $500 or more, or (4) it is under any written or unwritten obligation in the amount of $500 or more. 28 U.S.C. §1335(a).

(2) Venue. A statutory interpleader action may be brought in the district where one or more of the claimants reside. 28 U.S.C. §1397; ***Tashire***, 386 U.S. at 528 n.3.

(3) Deposit stake or bond with court. The stakeholder must either deposit the stake into the registry of the court or provide a bond made payable to the court clerk in an amount and with the surety that the court deems proper. 28 U.S.C. §1335(a)(2); *see* ***Gelfgren***, 680 F.2d at 81-82. The deposit of the stake is a jurisdictional prerequisite in a statutory interpleader action. ***Gelfgren***, 680 F.2d at 81-82; ***A&E TV Networks, LLC v. Pivot Point Entm't, LLC***, 771 F.Supp.2d 296, 300 (S.D.N.Y.2011); *see also* ***U.S. Fire Ins. v. Asbestospray, Inc.***, 182 F.3d 201, 210

n.4 (3d Cir.1999) (if bond is insufficient or defective, court should give stakeholder opportunity to correct error before dismissal). Without the deposit, the interpleader complaint may be dismissed.

§3.3 Request for relief. The stakeholder can ask for the following types of relief:

1. Discharge. The stakeholder can ask the court to discharge it from the suit and relieve it of all liability asserted by the claimants if it is disinterested. ***Mendez v. Teachers Ins. & Annuity Ass'n***, 982 F.2d 783, 787 (2d Cir.1992); *see* 28 U.S.C. §2361; ***General Atomic Co. v. Duke Power Co.***, 553 F.2d 53, 56 (10th Cir.1977); *see, e.g.*, ***General Elec. Capital Assur. v. Van Norman***, 209 F.Supp.2d 668, 670 (S.D.Tex.2002) (in rule interpleader, disinterested stakeholder dismissed). See "Discharge," §8.1, p. 92. If the disinterested stakeholder does not ask for discharge in the complaint, it may move to be discharged in a separate document filed after the interpleader.

2. Injunction. The stakeholder can ask the court to enter an injunction prohibiting the claimants from instituting or prosecuting any proceeding affecting the stake in another court. 28 U.S.C. §2361; *see* ***General Ry. Signal Co. v. Corcoran***, 921 F.2d 700, 706-07 (7th Cir.1991) (for rule interpleader, federal court can issue injunction directed at state court proceeding under "necessary in aid of its jurisdiction" exception to the Anti-Injunction Act). See "Injunctive relief," §8.2, p. 92; "Anti-Injunction Act," ch. 2-F, §7.4, p. 141.

3. Costs & attorney fees. The stakeholder can ask the court to award costs and attorney fees. *See* ***Perkins State Bank v. Connolly***, 632 F.2d 1306, 1311 (5th Cir.1980); ***Massachusetts Indem. & Life Ins. v. King***, 700 F.Supp. 307, 308 (M.D.La.1988). See "Costs & attorney fees," §8.3.2, p. 92.

§4. SERVICE OF PROCESS

§4.1 Rule interpleader. Service of process under FRCP 22 must be made according to FRCP 4. ***State Farm Fire & Cas. Co. v. Tashire***, 386 U.S. 523, 528 n.3 (1967).

§4.2 Statutory interpleader. Service of process under statutory interpleader allows a stakeholder to use nationwide service of process. 28 U.S.C. §2361; ***State Farm Fire & Cas. Co. v. Tashire***, 386 U.S. 523, 528 n.3 (1967).

§5. CHART SUMMARY OF INTERPLEADER

2-1. RULE INTERPLEADER VS. STATUTORY INTERPLEADER

		Rule Interpleader	Statutory Interpleader
1	Subject-matter jurisdiction	Federal-question or diversity jurisdiction. *See* 28 U.S.C. §§1331, 1332(a).	Minimal diversity (i.e., two or more claimants are diverse). 28 U.S.C. §1335(a)(1).
2	Amount in controversy	$75,000, if based on diversity jurisdiction. *See* 28 U.S.C. §1332(a).	$500. 28 U.S.C. §1335(a).
3	Venue	General venue statute. *See* 28 U.S.C. §1391.	Where one or more claimants reside. 28 U.S.C. §1397.
4	Deposit of stake	Deposit not required, but discretionary. *See* ***Central Bank v. U.S.***, 838 F.Supp. 564, 566 (M.D.Fla.1993).	Deposit required. 28 U.S.C. §1335(a)(2).
5	Service of process	Traditional service of process. *See* FRCP 4.	Nationwide service of process. 28 U.S.C. §2361.
6	Injunction	May enjoin actions against stake; limited by Anti-Injunction Act. *See* ***General Ry. Signal Co. v. Corcoran***, 921 F.2d 700, 706-07 (7th Cir.1991).	May enjoin actions against stake. 28 U.S.C. §2361.

§6. RESPONSE

The claimant should file an answer and consider other responses, such as FRCP 12(b) defenses. See "Overview of Preanswer Motions & Responsive Pleadings," ch. 3-A, p. 171.

§6.1 Negate interpleader requirements. The answer and other responses should negate the requirements for interpleader. See "Complaint," §3, p. 87. For example, the claimant can allege the following:

1. No subject-matter jurisdiction.

(1) "This is an interpleader action under FRCP 22, and this court has no jurisdiction because either the stakeholder is not diverse from the claimants or the amount in controversy does not exceed $75,000."

(2) "This is an interpleader action under FRCP 22, and there is no federal-question jurisdiction."

(3) "This is a statutory interpleader action, and this court has no jurisdiction because either there is no diversity between the claimants or the amount in controversy does not exceed $500."

2. No deposit of stake. "This is a statutory interpleader action, and the stakeholder has neither deposited the stake with the court clerk nor posted a bond." *See* 28 U.S.C. §1335(a)(2).

3. No multiple claimants. "There is only one claimant to the stake." *See* ***Airborne Freight Corp. v. U.S.***, 195 F.3d 238, 242 (5th Cir.1999).

4. No adverse interest. "There is no adverse interest between the claimants to the stake."

5. No risk of multiple liability. "There is no risk of multiple liability to the stakeholder."

6. Untimely. "The interpleader was not timely filed."

§6.2 Make additional allegations. In addition, the claimant can allege the following:

1. Interest. "The stakeholder should be required to pay interest on the money it held for the claimants before it deposited the stake with the court clerk." *See* ***Gelfgren v. Republic Nat'l Life Ins.***, 680 F.2d 79, 82 (9th Cir. 1982). See "Interest," §8.3.3, p. 93.

2. Costs & attorney fees. "The stakeholder should have costs taxed against it and be required to pay attorney fees." *See* ***Gelfgren***, 680 F.2d at 81 (if stakeholder is dilatory or otherwise guilty of bad faith, court may tax costs against it). See "Costs & attorney fees," §8.3.2, p. 92.

3. Bad faith. "The stakeholder acted in bad faith." *See, e.g.*, ***First Trust Corp. v. Bryant***, 410 F.3d 842, 855-56 (6th Cir.2005) (sophisticated corporation-stakeholder familiar with interpleader procedures was denied attorney fees from stake because of its aggressive tactics against individual beneficiary); ***Mendez v. Teachers Ins. & Annuity Ass'n***, 982 F.2d 783, 787-88 (2d Cir.1992) (stakeholder was denied discharge because of unreasonable delay and claimant's clear entitlement to stake).

§6.3 Request jury. If the claimant wants a jury trial on the merits of the claims against the stake, it should request a jury in its answer. See "Demand for Jury Trial," ch. 5-C, p. 309.

§7. HEARING & TRIAL

Courts usually dispose of interpleader actions in two steps: (1) a hearing to determine if the interpleader requirements have been met and (2) a trial to determine who owns the stake. *See* ***NYLife Distribs. v. Adherence Grp.***, 72 F.3d 371, 375 (3d Cir.1995). However, an interpleader action may be disposed of in one hearing. ***New York Life Ins. v. Connecticut Dev. Auth.***, 700 F.2d 91, 95 (2d Cir.1983).

§7.1 Hearing on right to interplead. At the first hearing on the interpleader, the court will determine whether the stakeholder (1) meets the requirements for interpleader and (2) may be relieved from liability. ***NYLife Distribs. v. Adherence Grp.***, 72 F.3d 371, 375 (3d Cir.1995). There is no right to a jury trial for this determination. *See* ***Fresh Am. Corp. v. Wal-Mart Stores***, 393 F.Supp.2d 411, 415 (N.D.Tex.2005); ***General Acc. Grp. v. Gagliardi***, 593 F.Supp. 1080, 1087 (D.Conn.1984), *aff'd*, 767 F.2d 907 (2d Cir.1985) (table case). If the stakeholder meets the requirements for interpleader, the court may enter an injunction restraining the claimants from proceeding in any other court with a suit affecting the stake, and, if the stakeholder is disinterested, it may discharge the stakeholder. *See* 28 U.S.C. §2361; ***General Ry. Signal Co. v. Corcoran***, 921 F.2d 700, 706-07 (7th Cir.1991); ***Advantage Title Agency, Inc. v. Rosen***, 297 F.Supp.2d 536, 539 (E.D.N.Y.2003). See "Injunctive relief," §8.2, p. 92.

§7.2 Trial on merits. If the requirements for interpleader are met, the case may proceed to a trial on the merits like any other suit. ***NYLife Distribs. v. Adherence Grp.***, 72 F.3d 371, 375 (3d Cir.1995). However, many interpleader actions are resolved before trial on cross-motions for summary judgment. If there is a trial on the merits, the objective is to adjudicate the claimants' adverse claims to the stake. *Id.* There may be a right to a jury depending on the classification of the issue between the adverse parties. ***Hyde Props. v. McCoy***, 507 F.2d 301, 305 (6th Cir. 1974); *see, e.g.*, ***U.S. v. Samaniego***, 345 F.3d 1280, 1282 (11th Cir.2003) (jury determined rightful owner of boxer's championship belts).

§8. ORDER

§8.1 Discharge. The court may discharge the stakeholder from further liability if the stakeholder is disinterested. ***Tittle v. Enron Corp.***, 463 F.3d 410, 424 (5th Cir.2006); *see* 28 U.S.C. §2361; ***New York Life Ins. v. Connecticut Dev. Auth.***, 700 F.2d 91, 95 (2d Cir.1983). If the stakeholder is interested, it is not discharged and continues to litigate its claim to the stake with the other claimants. *See* ***Bradley v. Kochenash***, 44 F.3d 166, 168 (2d Cir. 1995). See "Resolution of claims against stake," §8.3, this page. If there are serious charges that the stakeholder filed the suit in bad faith, the court may delay or deny the discharge of the stakeholder. ***Mendez v. Teachers Ins. & Annuity Ass'n***, 982 F.2d 783, 787 (2d Cir.1992).

§8.2 Injunctive relief. The court can enjoin other federal or state proceedings affecting interpleaded property in both statutory and rule interpleader actions. *E.g.*, 28 U.S.C. §2361 (statutory interpleader); ***General Ry. Signal Co. v. Corcoran***, 921 F.2d 700, 706-07 (7th Cir.1991) (rule interpleader, citing exception to Anti-Injunction Act); ***Ashton v. Paul Found.***, 918 F.2d 1065, 1072 (2d Cir.1990) (statutory interpleader). However, the court cannot enjoin suits outside the bounds of the interpleader proceeding (i.e., suits that do not affect the stake). *See* ***State Farm Fire & Cas. Co. v. Tashire***, 386 U.S. 523, 535 (1967). See "Injunctive Relief," ch. 2-D, p. 93.

§8.3 Resolution of claims against stake. Once the court resolves the claims against the stake, it will enter a final judgment.

1. Stake. The court will award the stake to the prevailing claimant or apportion the stake among the prevailing claimants. *See, e.g.*, ***Resolution Trust Corp. v. MacKenzie***, 60 F.3d 972, 976 (2d Cir.1995) (receiver had superior right to assets); ***Maraziti v. Thorpe***, 52 F.3d 252, 253 (9th Cir.1995) (claimant prevailed on wrongful-levy claim); ***Commercial Un. Ins. v. U.S.***, 999 F.2d 581, 589 (D.C.Cir.1993) (claimants received proportionate share of monetary judgment).

2. Costs & attorney fees.

(1) For stakeholder. The court has discretion to award costs and attorney fees to the stakeholder. *See* ***Trustees of the Dirs. Guild of Am.-Producer Pension Benefits Plans v. Tise***, 234 F.3d 415, 426 (9th Cir.2000), *amended*, 255 F.3d 661 (9th Cir.2000); ***In re Mandalay Shores Coop. Hous. Ass'n***, 21 F.3d 380, 382-83 (11th Cir. 1994); ***Corrigan Dispatch Co. v. Casa Guzman, S.A.***, 696 F.2d 359, 364 (5th Cir.1983). Attorney fees are normally awarded to a stakeholder who (1) is disinterested (i.e., claims no entitlement to any part of the stake), (2) concedes its liability in full, (3) deposits the disputed stake with the court clerk, (4) seeks discharge, and (5) is not in some way culpable with respect to the subject matter of the interpleader proceeding. *See* ***Septembertide Publ'g, B.V. v. Stein & Day, Inc.***, 884 F.2d 675, 683 (2d Cir.1989). Other relevant factors in awarding attorney fees in interpleader cases include whether (1) the case is simple or complex, (2) the stakeholder performed any unique services for the claimants or the court, (3) the stakeholder acted in good faith and with diligence, (4) the services benefited the stakeholder, and (5) the claimants improperly protracted the proceedings. *See* ***Noeller v. Metropolitan Life Ins.***, 190 F.R.D. 202, 207 (E.D.Tex.1999); 7 Wright, Miller & Kane §1719; 4 *Moore's Federal Practice 3d* §22.06 & n.22. The costs awarded to the stakeholder are most often taxed against the stake, but they may be taxed against a party whose conduct justifies it. ***Septembertide Publ'g***, 884 F.2d at 683; ***Prudential Ins. v. Boyd***, 781 F.2d 1494, 1498 (11th Cir.1986); *see, e.g.*, ***U.S. Fid. & Guar. Co. v. Sidwell***, 525 F.2d 472, 475 (10th Cir.1975) (recognized common practice of reimbursing stakeholder's litigation costs out of stake). Attorney-fee awards are typically limited to fees incurred in filing the action, not in litigating the merits of adverse claimants' positions. *See* ***Tise***, 234 F.3d at 426-27 (listing recoverable expenses).

(2) **Against stakeholder.** The court should not award costs against a stakeholder unless the stakeholder was dilatory or guilty of bad faith. ***Gelfgren v. Republic Nat'l Life Ins.***, 680 F.2d 79, 81 (9th Cir.1982); *see, e.g.*, ***Prudential Ins.***, 781 F.2d at 1498 (court abused discretion in taxing costs against stakeholder because finding of bad faith was unsupported by record).

3. Interest. The court must decide whether the stakeholder must pay interest on the money it held for the claimants. The courts do not automatically award interest on the stake to the prevailing claimant in interpleader actions under FRCP 22. ***Gelfgren***, 680 F.2d at 82; *see also* ***Unigard Mut. Ins. v. Abbott***, 732 F.2d 1414, 1419 (9th Cir. 1984) (award of interest in statutory interpleader action was in court's discretion). The courts look at a number of factors, including the following:

(1) Whether the stakeholder unreasonably delayed in instituting the action or depositing the stake with the court clerk. ***Gelfgren***, 680 F.2d at 82.

(2) Whether the stakeholder used the stake for its own benefit and would be unjustly enriched at the expense of the claimants who have a claim on the stake. *Id.*

(3) Whether the stakeholder eventually deposited the stake into the court's registry. *Id.*

§8.4 Not binding on nonparties. Interpleader actions cannot resolve the rights of nonparties. *See, e.g.*, ***Metropolitan Prop. & Cas. Ins. v. Shan Trac, Inc.***, 324 F.3d 20, 25 (1st Cir.2003) (court deleted language in interpleader judgment that purported to bind nonparties).

§9. APPELLATE REVIEW

A final order denying interpleader and dismissing the action is immediately appealable, as long as the judge makes an express determination that there is no just reason to delay entry of judgment. *See* FRCP 54(b); ***Hoornstra v. U.S.***, 969 F.2d 530, 532 n.* (7th Cir.1992); *see also* 28 U.S.C. §1291 (courts of appeals have jurisdiction over appeals from all final decisions of district courts). However, an order upholding the right to interplead is interlocutory, even when it discharges the stakeholder; the order is not appealable until all claims to the interpleaded stake have been adjudicated. *See* ***Diamond Shamrock Oil & Gas Corp. v. Commissioner of Revenues, State of Ark.***, 422 F.2d 532, 534 (8th Cir.1970). On appeal, the issue of whether the district court had jurisdiction over an interpleader suit is reviewed de novo. ***Airborne Freight Corp. v. U.S.***, 195 F.3d 238, 240 (5th Cir.1999) (applying 28 U.S.C. §1335).

D. INJUNCTIVE RELIEF

§1. GENERAL

§1.1 Rule. FRCP 65.

§1.2 Purpose. There are two general types of injunctive relief: prohibitory and mandatory. ***Tom Doherty Assocs. v. Saban Entm't, Inc.***, 60 F.3d 27, 34 (2d Cir.1995); *see* ***International Longshoremen's Ass'n v. Philadelphia Mar. Trade Ass'n***, 389 U.S. 64, 75 (1967) (mandatory injunction). Most injunctions are prohibitory—they prohibit a party from continuing certain conduct. ***Tom Doherty Assocs.***, 60 F.3d at 34. But some injunctions are mandatory—they require a party to act affirmatively rather than merely to refrain from certain conduct. *Id.*; *see* ***Texas & New Orleans R.R. v. Northside Belt Ry.***, 276 U.S. 475, 479 (1928). There are three specific types of injunctive orders: temporary restraining orders, preliminary injunctions, and permanent injunctions.

1. TRO. The purpose of a temporary restraining order (TRO) is to preserve the status quo of the subject matter of the litigation and prevent irreparable harm until a hearing can be held on a preliminary injunction. ***Granny Goose Foods, Inc. v. Brotherhood of Teamsters & Auto Truck Drivers***, 415 U.S. 423, 439 (1974); ***Hoechst Diafoil Co. v. Nan Ya Plastics Corp.***, 174 F.3d 411, 422 (4th Cir.1999); *see* FRCP 65(b). The status quo is the last actual, peaceable, noncontested status that preceded the controversy. ***LaRouche v. Kezer***, 20 F.3d 68, 74 n.7 (2d Cir. 1994).

2. Preliminary injunction. The purpose of a preliminary injunction is to preserve the status quo pending a determination of the merits. ***University of Tex. v. Camenisch***, 451 U.S. 390, 395 (1981); ***Alliance Bond Fund, Inc. v. Grupo Mexicano de Desarrollo, S.A.***, 143 F.3d 688, 692 (2d Cir.1998), *rev'd on other grounds*, 527 U.S. 308 (1999).

3. Permanent injunction. The purpose of a permanent injunction is to deter future behavior. ***Orantes-Hernandez v. Thornburgh***, 919 F.2d 549, 564 (9th Cir.1990); *see* ***Minnesota Mining & Mfg. v. Pribyl***, 259 F.3d 587, 607 (7th Cir.2001) (purpose of permanent injunction is to protect trade-secret owners from damages caused by future use of trade secrets).

§1.3 Timetable & forms. Timetable, Temporary Restraining Order & Injunction, p. 1583; ***O'Connor's Federal Civil Forms*** (2012), FORMS 2D.

§1.4 Other references. 11A Wright, Miller & Kane, *Federal Practice & Procedure 2d* §§2941-2962 (1995 & Supp.2012); 13 *Moore's Federal Practice 3d* ch. 65 (2012).

§2. GROUNDS FOR INJUNCTIVE RELIEF

Injunctive relief is authorized by general principles of equity, federal statutes, or state law. *See* ***eBay Inc. v. MercExchange, L.L.C.***, 547 U.S. 388, 391 (2006) (injunctive relief is based on well-established principles of equity); ***Grupo Mexicano de Desarrollo, S.A. v. Alliance Bond Fund, Inc.***, 527 U.S. 308, 318 (1999) (federal district courts have authority to issue injunctions under traditional principles of equity exercised by English Court of Chancery in 1789); *see, e.g.*, 11 U.S.C. §524(a) (authorizing injunction against collecting debt discharged in bankruptcy); 15 U.S.C. §1125(c)(1) (authorizing injunction to prevent dilution of distinctive and famous trademark); ***Business Records Corp. v. Lueth***, 981 F.2d 957, 959 (7th Cir.1992) (under diversity jurisdiction, federal court granted injunction based on Illinois law).

§2.1 Equitable factors for injunctive relief. A plaintiff must demonstrate the following equitable factors for granting injunctive relief: (1) irreparable injury, (2) no adequate remedy at law, (3) a likelihood of success on the merits, (4) the balance of hardships, and (5) the effect on the public interest. *See* ***Winter v. Natural Res. Def. Council, Inc.***, 555 U.S. 7, 20 (2008) (preliminary injunction); ***eBay Inc. v. MercExchange, L.L.C.***, 547 U.S. 388, 391 (2006) (permanent injunction); ***Alliance for the Wild Rockies v. Cottrell***, 632 F.3d 1127, 1135 (9th Cir.2011) (preliminary injunction); ***Asociación de Educación Privada v. García-Padilla***, 490 F.3d 1, 8 (1st Cir.2007) (permanent injunction); ***Northeast Ohio Coalition for the Homeless v. Blackwell***, 467 F.3d 999, 1009 (6th Cir.2006) (TRO).

CAUTION

Check the law of your circuit before drafting a request for injunctive relief. The circuits weigh the equitable factors differently. See ***Alliance for the Wild Rockies***, *632 F.3d at 1131-32 (under "sliding scale" approach, serious questions going to merits and balance of hardships that tips sharply toward P can satisfy preliminary injunction as long as P also shows likelihood of irreparable injury and injunction is in public interest);* ***Promatek Indus. v. Equitrac Corp.***, *300 F.3d 808, 811 (7th Cir.2002) (applying "sliding scale" approach; when P's likelihood of success is greater, balance of hardships does not need to be weighed in P's favor as much);* ***Prairie Band of Potawatomi Indians v. Pierce***, *253 F.3d 1234, 1246-47 (10th Cir.2001) (if P shows irreparable injury, balance of hardships, and effect on public interest, P does not need to show likelihood of success; instead, P must show only that there are serious questions about merits that are ripe and deserve to be litigated). The circuits also disagree on whether a flexible approach is still applicable after* ***Winter v. Natural Res. Def. Council, Inc.***, *555 U.S. 7 (2008). Compare* ***Alliance for the Wild Rockies***, *632 F.3d at 1134-35 (sliding-scale approach is still viable), and* ***Citigroup Global Mkts., Inc. v. VCG Special Opportunities Master Fund Ltd.***,

*598 F.3d 30, 36-37 (2d Cir.2010) (same), with **Real Truth About Obama, Inc. v. Federal Election Comm'n**, 575 F.3d 342, 346-47 (4th Cir.2009) (test allowing for flexibility of factors was abandoned after **Winter**), vacated & remanded, ___ U.S. ___, 130 S.Ct. 2371 (2010), reinstated in relevant part, 607 F.3d 355 (4th Cir.2010). For a good discussion of each circuit's analysis, see 13 Moore's Federal Practice 3d §65.22[5].*

1. Irreparable injury. The plaintiff should plead that it will likely suffer irreparable injury. FRCP 65(b)(1)(A) (TRO); ***Winter***, 555 U.S. at 22 (preliminary injunction); ***eBay Inc.***, 547 U.S. at 391 (permanent injunction); ***Sampson v. Murray***, 415 U.S. 61, 88-89 (1974) (TRO); ***Hoechst Diafoil Co. v. Nan Ya Plastics Corp.***, 174 F.3d 411, 417 (4th Cir.1999) (preliminary injunction); ***DSC Comms. v. DGI Techs.***, 81 F.3d 597, 600 (5th Cir.1996) (preliminary injunction); ***Performance Unlimited, Inc. v. Questar Publ'rs***, 52 F.3d 1373, 1381 (6th Cir.1995) (preliminary injunction). To satisfy the irreparable-injury requirement, the plaintiff must show that (1) it will likely suffer an imminent injury and (2) the injury would be irreparable. *See* ***Grand River Enter. Six Nations, Ltd. v. Pryor***, 481 F.3d 60, 66 (2d Cir.2007).

(1) Imminent. An irreparable injury must be actual and imminent. ***Pryor***, 481 F.3d at 66 (preliminary injunction); *see* FRCP 65(b)(1)(A) (TRO); *see, e.g.*, ***Chacon v. Granata***, 515 F.2d 922, 925 (5th Cir.1975) (harm was not imminent because request for injunction was premised on eventual passage of unconstitutional zoning ordinances). The mere possibility of irreparable injury is not sufficient; the irreparable injury must be likely. ***Winter***, 555 U.S. at 22; *see* ***Ross-Simons of Warwick, Inc. v. Baccarat, Inc.***, 102 F.3d 12, 19 (1st Cir.1996) (injunction improper if based on tenuous or overly speculative forecast of anticipated harm); *see, e.g.*, ***Acierno v. New Castle Cty.***, 40 F.3d 645, 655 (3d Cir.1994) (potential harm resulting from denial of building permit was too speculative to constitute imminent harm); ***Dan River, Inc. v. Icahn***, 701 F.2d 278, 283 (4th Cir.1983) (management's fears that company would be dismantled after acceptance of tender offer were too distant in time).

(2) Irreparable. An irreparable injury is one that cannot be prevented or fully rectified by a final judgment following a trial. ***Roland Mach. Co. v. Dresser Indus.***, 749 F.2d 380, 386 (7th Cir.1984); *see* ***Deerfield Med. Ctr. v. City of Deerfield Beach***, 661 F.2d 328, 338 (5th Cir.1981) (irreparable injury is harm that cannot be undone by award of monetary damages). An injury is irreparable if it is not accurately measurable, if the plaintiff cannot be adequately compensated in damages, or if the defendant would be unable to pay. *See* ***Ross-Simons***, 102 F.3d at 19; ***Jayaraj v. Scappini***, 66 F.3d 36, 39 (2d Cir.1995); ***Collins v. Aggreko, Inc.***, 884 F.Supp. 450, 452 (D.Utah 1995); *see, e.g.*, ***Elrod v. Burns***, 427 U.S. 347, 373 (1976) (loss of right to free speech under First Amendment); ***Doran v. Salem Inn, Inc.***, 422 U.S. 922, 932 (1975) (threat of bankruptcy); ***Basicomputer Corp. v. Scott***, 973 F.2d 507, 512 (6th Cir.1992) (loss of customer goodwill and fair competition). However, monetary loss alone is not an irreparable injury. ***Rent-A-Center v. Canyon TV & Appliance Rental, Inc.***, 944 F.2d 597, 603 (9th Cir.1991); ***Borey v. National Un. Fire Ins.***, 934 F.2d 30, 34 (2d Cir.1991); *see* ***Renegotiation Bd. v. Bannercraft Clothing Co.***, 415 U.S. 1, 24 (1974) (substantial and unrecoupable litigation expenses do not constitute irreparable injury); *see, e.g.*, ***Sampson***, 415 U.S. at 91-92 (temporary loss of income after termination from employment was not irreparable injury); ***LaForest v. Former Clean Air Holding Co.***, 376 F.3d 48, 55 (2d Cir.2004) (reduction of medical benefits was more than mere monetary harm and constituted irreparable injury). *But see* ***Hughes Network Sys. v. Interdigital Comms.***, 17 F.3d 691, 694 (4th Cir.1994) (even if loss is economic, extraordinary circumstances may permit finding of irreparable injury).

2. No adequate remedy at law. The plaintiff should plead that there is no adequate remedy at law. ***Northern Cal. Power Agency v. Grace Geothermal Corp.***, 469 U.S. 1306, 1306 (1984); *see, e.g.*, ***Crane v. Indiana High Sch. Athletic Ass'n***, 975 F.2d 1315, 1326 (7th Cir.1992) (court properly enjoined athletic association from declaring P ineligible for sporting event; P lacked adequate remedy at law). Depending on the type of injunctive relief sought, irreparable injury and no adequate remedy at law may be merged into one factor. *See* ***Kinney v. International Un. of Oper. Eng'rs***, 994 F.2d 1271, 1275 n.5 (7th Cir.1993). For the purposes of injunctive relief, there is no adequate remedy at law if (1) the legal remedy is merely illusory or (2) effective legal relief cannot be obtained without filing multiple lawsuits. *See, e.g.*, ***Wilson v. Illinois S. Ry.***, 263 U.S. 574, 576-77 (1924) (no adequate remedy at

law when multiple lawsuits would be necessary and apportioning damages would be difficult); ***Winston v. General Drivers, Warehousemen & Helpers Local Un.***, 879 F.Supp. 719, 725 (W.D.Ky.1995) (no adequate remedy at law when potential remedy of monetary damages was considered illusory because recovery of damages would be so difficult).

3. Substantial likelihood of success. The plaintiff should plead that there is a substantial likelihood that the plaintiff will succeed on the merits of the case. ***Doran***, 422 U.S. at 931 (preliminary injunction); ***Schiavo v. Schiavo***, 403 F.3d 1223, 1225-26 (11th Cir.2005) (TRO). When seeking a TRO or a preliminary injunction, the plaintiff does not need to prove that it will ultimately prevail. *See* ***Abdul Wali v. Coughlin***, 754 F.2d 1015, 1025 (2d Cir. 1985). But when seeking a permanent injunction, the plaintiff must show actual success on the merits. *See* ***Amoco Prod. v. Village of Gambell***, 480 U.S. 531, 546 n.12 (1987); ***Oglala Sioux Tribe v. C&W Enters.***, 542 F.3d 224, 229 (8th Cir.2008); ***Plummer v. American Inst. of Certified Pub. Accountants***, 97 F.3d 220, 229 (7th Cir.1996).

4. Balance of hardships. The plaintiff should plead that the injury it faces outweighs the injury that would be sustained by the defendant as a result of the injunctive relief. ***Winter***, 555 U.S. at 24; ***Yakus v. U.S.***, 321 U.S. 414, 440 (1944); ***Johnson v. California State Bd. of Accountancy***, 72 F.3d 1427, 1430 (9th Cir.1995); ***Cohen v. Brown Univ.***, 991 F.2d 888, 902 (1st Cir.1993); ***JAK Prods. v. Wiza***, 986 F.2d 1080, 1084 (7th Cir.1993); ***Virginia Carolina Tools, Inc. v. International Tool Sup.***, 984 F.2d 113, 119-20 (4th Cir.1993); *see, e.g.*, ***County Sec. Agency v. Ohio Dept. of Commerce***, 296 F.3d 477, 487 (6th Cir.2002) (P did not demonstrate that potential injury of releasing guards' names for publication outweighed reporter's First Amendment rights). When addressing this factor, the plaintiff may also have to address the effect of injunctive relief on nonparties. *See* ***Ward v. Walsh***, 1 F.3d 873, 878 (9th Cir.1993).

5. Effect on public interest. The plaintiff should plead that the injunctive relief would not adversely affect public policy or the public interest. *See* ***Hoechst Diafoil***, 174 F.3d at 417; ***DSC Comms.***, 81 F.3d at 600; ***Performance Unlimited***, 52 F.3d at 1381; *see, e.g.*, ***Winter***, 555 U.S. at 24-26 (in environmental case against Navy, public interest was harmed because of (1) burden on Navy's ability to conduct training exercises and (2) public's interest in national defense); ***Davidoff & CIE, S.A. v. PLD Int'l***, 263 F.3d 1297, 1304 (11th Cir.2001) (in trademark-infringement suit, public interest was served when injunction prevented consumer confusion in marketplace); ***ACLU v. Johnson***, 194 F.3d 1149, 1163 (10th Cir.1999) (in First Amendment suit, public interest was not harmed when injunction protected free expression of Internet users by enjoining enforcement of state statute). When addressing this factor, the plaintiff may also have to address the effect of the injunctive relief on nonparties. *See* ***Sammartano v. First Judicial Dist. Ct., in & for Cty. of Carson City***, 303 F.3d 959, 974 (9th Cir.2002); ***CSX Transp. v. Tennessee State Bd. of Equalization***, 964 F.2d 548, 551 (6th Cir.1992); *see also* ***Blackwell***, 467 F.3d at 1009 (substantial harm to others is distinct from effect on public interest).

§2.2 Federal authority for injunctive relief. When a federal statute authorizes injunctive relief, the equitable factors are suitable guidelines for determining the appropriateness of injunctive relief, but the nature of the case and purpose of the underlying statute must also be considered. *See* ***eBay Inc. v. MercExchange, L.L.C.***, 547 U.S. 388, 391 (2006); ***Maine People's Alliance & Nat. Res. Def. Council v. Mallinckrodt, Inc.***, 471 F.3d 277, 296 (1st Cir.2006). However, express statutory language may eliminate the need for showing some equitable factors. *See, e.g.*, ***EEOC v. Cosmair, Inc.***, 821 F.2d 1085, 1090 (5th Cir.1987) (in ADEA case, when statutory conditions are satisfied, P does not need to establish specific irreparable injury to obtain preliminary injunction); ***U.S. Postal Serv. v. Beamish***, 466 F.2d 804, 806 (3d Cir.1972) (postal-service statute authorizing issuance of injunction did not incorporate common-law standards); *see also* ***Weinberger v. Romero-Barcelo***, 456 U.S. 305, 313 (1982) (statute must clearly restrict court's equity jurisdiction, otherwise full scope of jurisdiction must be applied).

§2.3 State authority for injunctive relief. In diversity cases, when a state law authorizes injunctive relief, a court may consider the equitable factors. *See* ***Overholt Crop Ins. Serv. v. Travis***, 941 F.2d 1361, 1371 (8th Cir.1991). However, state law governs how the equitable factors will be applied. *See, e.g.*, ***JAK Prods. v. Wiza***, 986 F.2d 1080, 1084 (7th Cir.1993) (under state law, P was not required to prove irreparable injury in terms of dollars and cents); ***Overholt Crop Ins.***, 941 F.2d at 1371 (under state law, irreparable injury could be inferred on finding of breach of restrictive covenant).

§3. TEMPORARY RESTRAINING ORDER

§3.1 Application.

1. Complaint or motion. The application for a TRO may be filed with the complaint or as a separate motion. *See* ***Dillard v. Merrill Lynch, Pierce, Fenner & Smith, Inc.***, 961 F.2d 1148, 1155 (5th Cir.1992).

2. Grounds. The application for a TRO should plead and prove the grounds for injunctive relief. See "Grounds for Injunctive Relief," §2, p. 94.

3. Ex parte.

(1) Notice not required. A TRO may be issued without written or oral notice to the adverse party or its attorney. FRCP 65(b)(1). If the adverse party receives notice of the TRO and participates in the hearing, the application for a TRO may be treated as an application for a preliminary injunction. ***Rivera v. U.S.***, 910 F.Supp. 239, 241 (D.V.I.1996).

(2) Allegations. An ex parte TRO may be issued only if (1) specified facts in an affidavit or verified complaint clearly show that the plaintiff will suffer immediate and irreparable injury, loss, or damage if the TRO is not granted before the defendant can be heard, and (2) the plaintiff's attorney certifies in writing whether efforts were made to give notice and why notice should not be required. FRCP 65(b)(1). Notice is not required when it would be impractical or impossible (e.g., the defendant is unknown or cannot be found) or when there are no less drastic means to protect the plaintiff's interests (e.g., notice would make the plaintiff's claim moot because the defendant would destroy evidence). *See* ***First Tech. Safety Sys. v. Depinet***, 11 F.3d 641, 650 (6th Cir.1993); ***American Can Co. v. Mansukhani***, 742 F.2d 314, 323 (7th Cir.1984); ***Suppressed v. Suppressed***, 109 F.Supp.2d 902, 903-04 (N.D. Ill.2000).

4. Request for preliminary injunction. The application for a TRO does not have to include a request for a preliminary injunction. *See* ***Flying Cross Check, L.L.C. v. Central Hockey League, Inc.***, 153 F.Supp.2d 1253, 1258-59 (D.Kan.2001). However, if the need for injunctive relief extends beyond the time limits of the TRO, the application should request a preliminary injunction. *See id.*; *see also* FRCP 65(b)(3) (if TRO is ordered ex parte, hearing on preliminary injunction must be set). See "Time limit," §3.3.2, p. 98; "Preliminary Injunction," §4, p. 101.

5. Bond. The application for a TRO should state the plaintiff's willingness to post a bond. See "Bond," §3.4, p. 100.

6. Relief. The application for a TRO should identify the relief sought.

7. Evidentiary support. The application for a TRO must be accompanied by an affidavit or a verified complaint. FRCP 65(b)(1)(A). Affidavits must be based on the personal knowledge of the affiant. *See* ***In re SLK Assocs.***, 166 B.R. 985, 991 (Bankr.S.D.Fla.1994); *cf.* FRCP 56(c)(4) (motion for summary judgment). See "Affidavits or declarations," ch. 7-B, §6.1.3, p. 610.

§3.2 Hearing.

The ex parte TRO can be granted without a hearing if the requirements of FRCP 65(b) are met. *See* FRCP 65(b)(1). If there is a hearing, the plaintiff should argue that the FRCP 65(b) factors are satisfied and that the issuance of the TRO will simply preserve the status quo. The hearing may take place before the complaint is served. *See, e.g.*, ***CAP of MB, Inc. v. Champion Rock Prods.***, 111 F.Supp.2d 728, 730 (D.S.C.2000) (TRO granted before service of complaint).

§3.3 Order.

1. Form. A valid TRO must make certain specific statements, strictly following the requirements of FRCP 65(b). *See* ***American Can Co. v. Mansukhani***, 742 F.2d 314, 324 (7th Cir.1984). The TRO must do the following:

(1) State why the order was granted ex parte and without notice, if applicable. FRCP 65(b)(2); ***American Can***, 742 F.2d at 324; ***Cenergy Corp. v. Bryson Oil & Gas P.L.C.***, 657 F.Supp. 867, 870 (D.Nev.1987).

(2) State the reasons for the issuance of the TRO by describing the injury and stating why it is irreparable. FRCP 65(b)(2); ***American Can***, 742 F.2d at 324.

(3) Define in reasonable detail the act sought to be restrained. ***U.S. v. Board of Educ. of City of Chi.***, 11 F.3d 668, 672 (7th Cir.1993); ***American Can***, 742 F.2d at 332. The act sought to be restrained cannot be described by reference to the complaint or other document. FRCP 65(d)(1)(C). See "Define act restrained or required," §4.5.1(2), p. 103.

(4) State the date and hour of issuance. FRCP 65(b)(2).

(5) State the date the order expires. *See id.* See "Time limit," §3.3.2, this page.

(6) State the date for the hearing on the preliminary injunction. *See* FRCP 65(b)(3). The injunction hearing must be set at the earliest practical time and takes precedence over all other cases except older TRO matters. *Id.*

(7) Fix the amount of the TRO bond. FRCP 65(c).

(8) Be filed with the clerk's office and recorded. FRCP 65(b)(2).

2. Time limit. The court can grant a TRO for no more than 14 days. FRCP 65(b)(2); *see* ***Nutrasweet Co. v. Vit-Mar Enters.***, 112 F.3d 689, 692-94 (3d Cir.1997) (time limit applies to all TROs, even those issued with notice; applying former ten-day deadline); ***Pan Am. World Airways, Inc. v. Flight Eng'rs Int'l***, 306 F.2d 840, 842 (2d Cir. 1962) (same). See "Computing Deadlines," ch. 1-C, §6, p. 23.

CAUTION

If the TRO was issued by a state court before the case was removed to federal court, the TRO cannot remain in force for longer than it would have been under state law, but it also cannot remain in force for more than 14 days after removal. See ***Granny Goose Foods, Inc. v. Brotherhood of Teamsters & Auto Truck Drivers****, 415 U.S. 423, 439-40 (1974) (applying former ten-day deadline);* ***Carrabus v. Schneider****, 111 F.Supp.2d 204, 210-11 (E.D.N.Y.2000) (same). For example, if a state court on day 1 issues a TRO that expires in 15 days and the case is removed to federal court on day 13, the TRO will expire on day 15 as it would have under state law. See* ***Granny Goose Foods****, 415 U.S. at 440 n.15. Or, if a state court on day 1 issues a TRO that expires in 21 days and the case is removed to federal court on day 2, the TRO will expire on day 16 under FRCP 65(b)(2). See* ***Granny Goose Foods****, 415 U.S. at 440 n.15;* ***Flying Cross Check, L.L.C. v. Central Hockey League, Inc.****, 153 F.Supp.2d 1253, 1256 (D.Kan.2001). Because these examples do not necessarily take into account how to count the days, be sure to review the state and federal rules for calculating deadlines. For a discussion of how to count days under the federal rules, see "Computing Deadlines," ch. 1-C, §6, p. 23.*

3. Binding effect.

(1) Parties. An injunction (i.e., a TRO, preliminary injunction, or permanent injunction) is binding on parties to the case who receive actual notice of the order by personal service or some other method. FRCP 65(d)(2)(A); ***Blackard v. Memphis Area Med. Ctr. for Women, Inc.***, 262 F.3d 568, 574 (6th Cir.2001); 2007 Notes to FRCP 65 at ¶2, p. 1230, this book.

(2) Officers, agents, servants, employees & attorneys. An injunction is binding on the parties' officers, agents, servants, employees, and attorneys who receive actual notice of the order by personal service or some other method. FRCP 65(d)(2)(B); *e.g.*, ***ACLU v. Johnson***, 194 F.3d 1149, 1163 (10th Cir.1999) (injunction against governor and attorney general prohibiting enforcement of unconstitutional law bound state district attorneys). However, an employee of an enjoined company usually is not bound by an injunction after severing relations with the company. ***Additive Controls & Measurement Sys. v. Flowdata, Inc.***, 154 F.3d 1345, 1352 (Fed.Cir.1998); *see, e.g.*,

Alemite Mfg. v. Staff, 42 F.2d 832, 833 (2d Cir.1930) (injunction against company did not bind employee who resigned and committed infringing acts identical to those adjudicated in original suit because employee acted independently after his resignation).

(3) Persons in active concert. An injunction is binding on persons who are in active concert or participation with the parties or their officers, agents, servants, employees, or attorneys and who receive actual notice of the order by personal service or some other method. FRCP 65(d)(2)(C); ***Blackard***, 262 F.3d at 574; ***Reliance Ins. v. Mast Constr. Co.***, 84 F.3d 372, 376-77 (10th Cir.1996); 2007 Notes to FRCP 65 at ¶2, p. 1230, this book; *see* ***Additive Controls***, 154 F.3d at 1351 (nonparties may be held in contempt if they either abet D or are legally identified with D); ***G.&C. Merriam Co. v. Webster Dictionary Co.***, 639 F.2d 29, 35 (1st Cir.1980) (nonparty can be held in contempt for violating injunction if it was in active concert or participated with enjoined party in postinjunction activity); *see also* ***Doctor's Assocs. v. Reinert & Duree, P.C.***, 191 F.3d 297, 302-03 (2d Cir.1999) (Ds may not ignore court order by carrying out prohibited acts through nonparty aiders and abettors). To determine whether a person acts in concert with the enjoined party, the court must look at the actual relationship between the person and the enjoined party. ***Blackard***, 262 F.3d at 574; *see* ***Regal Knitwear Co. v. NLRB***, 324 U.S. 9, 15 (1945); 11A Wright, Miller & Kane §2956; *see, e.g.*, ***Doctor's Assocs.***, 191 F.3d at 304 & n.5 (injunction against party-agent did not bind nonparty-principal); ***Southern Elec. Health Fund v. Kelley***, 308 F.Supp.2d 847, 864-65 (M.D.Tenn.2003) (injunction against party-subcontractor bound third-party contractor who had assumed financial responsibility for subcontractor). A person is considered to act in concert with an enjoined party if she aids or abets an enjoined party in violating the injunction or if she is in privity with an enjoined party. ***Blockowicz v. Williams***, 630 F.3d 563, 567 (7th Cir.2010).

(4) Successor companies. An injunction against a corporation can survive the corporation's dissolution and continue to bind any successor in interest. ***Additive Controls***, 154 F.3d at 1351; *see* ***Walling v. James V. Reuter, Inc.***, 321 U.S. 671, 674 (1944); ***ICC v. Rio Grande Growers Coop.***, 564 F.2d 848, 849 (9th Cir.1977). This rule is necessary to prevent an enjoined defendant from nullifying a decree by carrying out prohibited acts through instrumentalities who were not parties to the original proceeding. ***Regal Knitwear***, 324 U.S. at 14; ***Additive Controls***, 154 F.3d at 1352.

4. Extending TRO.

(1) On motion. The plaintiff may ask the court to extend the TRO by filing a motion showing good cause before the TRO expires. *See* ***Geneva Assur. Syndicate, Inc. v. Medical Emerg. Servs.***, 964 F.2d 599, 600 (7th Cir.1992).

(a) Good cause. To show good cause, the plaintiff should demonstrate that (1) the grounds supporting the original TRO continue to exist and (2) the plaintiff needs more time to prepare and present its request for a preliminary injunction, the court's calendar cannot reasonably accommodate an earlier setting for the preliminary injunction, or ongoing discovery or related proceedings require an extension of time. ***Flying Cross Check***, 153 F.Supp.2d at 1260-61.

(b) One extension. The court can grant one extension of the TRO for up to an additional 14 days. FRCP 65(b)(2). If a court extends a TRO beyond this time limit, the enjoined party can treat it as a preliminary injunction and challenge it by appeal. ***Sampson v. Murray***, 415 U.S. 61, 86-88 (1974) (applying former ten-day deadline); *see also* ***Hoechst Diafoil Co. v. Nan Ya Plastics Corp.***, 174 F.3d 411, 423 (4th Cir.1999) (TRO treated as preliminary injunction). See "When TRO exceeds time limit," §7.1.2(2), p. 106.

(2) By agreement. If the defendant agrees, the TRO can be extended for a period longer than the 14-day extension allowed by the court. FRCP 65(b)(2). *But see* ***In re Arthur Treacher's Franchisee Litig.***, 689 F.2d 1150, 1153-54 (3d Cir.1982) (TRO extended for 80 days with consent of parties was more like preliminary injunction).

5. Expiring or superseding TRO. If no preliminary injunction is issued, the defendant can assume that the TRO expires after the FRCP 65(b) time limit lapses. *See* ***Granny Goose Foods***, 415 U.S. at 444-45 (applying former ten-day deadline). If the court determines that the injunctive relief provided by the TRO should continue, it can supersede the TRO with a preliminary injunction. *Id.* See "Time limit," §3.3.2, p. 98.

§3.4 Bond. A TRO (or preliminary injunction) cannot be issued unless the applicant posts a bond. FRCP 65(c). The bond provides a mechanism for reimbursing an enjoined party for harm it suffers as a result of an improperly issued TRO or injunction. ***Hoechst Diafoil Co. v. Nan Ya Plastics Corp.***, 174 F.3d 411, 421 n.3 (4th Cir.1999); *see* ***Nokia Corp. v. InterDigital, Inc.***, 645 F.3d 553, 557 (2d Cir.2011). See "Recovery against bond," §3.4.3, p. 101.

1. Posting of bond. The bond must be posted in an amount that the court considers proper. FRCP 65(c). The bond requirement is "mandatory and unambiguous," and it is reversible error when the order is completely silent on the bond amount. ***Hoechst Diafoil***, 174 F.3d at 421 & n.3.

(1) Fixed amount. The bond must be in an amount that is enough to pay the costs and damages sustained by any party found to have been wrongfully enjoined or restrained. FRCP 65(c); ***Nichols v. Alcatel USA, Inc.***, 532 F.3d 364, 379 (5th Cir.2008). The amount of the bond ordinarily depends on the gravity of the potential harm to the enjoined party and covers potential incidental and consequential costs as well as the losses the enjoined party may suffer during the period of the TRO or preliminary injunction. ***Hoechst Diafoil***, 174 F.3d at 421 n.3; *see* 11A Wright, Miller & Kane §2954. If the applicant is unable to post a bond in an amount sufficient to protect the enjoined party, the court may deny the TRO or preliminary injunction. *See* ***Nichols***, 532 F.3d at 379.

(2) No bond or nominal amount. In some circumstances, the court may not require a bond or may require only a nominal amount for the bond.

(a) U.S. government. Courts cannot require a bond from the United States, its officers, or its agencies. FRCP 65(c).

(b) Indigent. Some courts can elect to waive the bond requirement for an indigent. ***Wayne Chem., Inc. v. Columbus Agency Serv.***, 567 F.2d 692, 701 (7th Cir.1977); 11A Wright, Miller & Kane §2954 & n.21.

(c) Public-interest litigation. Some courts recognize an exception to the bond requirement for plaintiffs engaged in public-interest litigation. *E.g.*, ***Moltan Co. v. Eagle-Picher Indus.***, 55 F.3d 1171, 1176 (6th Cir.1995) (allegation of inadequate safety labeling); ***Pharmaceutical Soc'y v. New York State Dept. of Soc. Servs.***, 50 F.3d 1168, 1174-75 (2d Cir.1995) (allegation of inappropriate Medicaid copayment system); ***California v. Tahoe Reg'l Planning Agency***, 766 F.2d 1319, 1325 (9th Cir.1985) (suit to prevent development of lakefront property), *amended*, 775 F.2d 998 (9th Cir.1985). *But see* ***Habitat Educ. Ctr. v. U.S. Forest Serv.***, 607 F.3d 453, 457-58 (7th Cir.2010) (court did not exempt environmental nonprofit organization from bond requirement; language of FRCP 65(c) does not provide for such exception).

(d) Court's discretion. Some courts have held that they have discretion to waive the bond requirement or to require only a nominal bond. ***Kaepa, Inc. v. Achilles Corp.***, 76 F.3d 624, 628 (5th Cir.1996); *see* ***Habitat Educ. Ctr.***, 607 F.3d at 458; ***Connecticut Gen. Life Ins. v. New Images***, 321 F.3d 878, 882 (9th Cir.2003); ***Hoechst Diafoil***, 174 F.3d at 421 n.3. A court may require no bond or a nominal bond if (1) the bond would effectively deny judicial review, (2) the defendant does not risk any harm, (3) the plaintiff will likely succeed based on the strength of its case, and (4) the bond would place the plaintiff at financial risk. *E.g.*, ***Moltan Co.***, 55 F.3d at 1176 (P likely to succeed based on strength of case; no bond required); ***Scherr v. Volpe***, 466 F.2d 1027, 1035 (7th Cir.1972) (P likely to succeed based on strength of case; no bond required); ***Board of Educ. of Oak Park & River Forest High Sch. Dist. v. Illinois State Bd. of Educ.***, 10 F.Supp.2d 971, 981-82 (N.D.Ill.1998) (P in financial risk; nominal $10 bond ordered); *see* ***Save Our Sonoran, Inc. v. Flowers***, 408 F.3d 1113, 1126 (9th Cir.2005) (if bond would deny judicial review, court does not have to require bond). The court must conduct a hearing to consider whether a bond is necessary before it can waive the bond requirement. *See* ***Coquina Oil Corp. v. Transwestern Pipeline Co.***, 825 F.2d 1461, 1462 (10th Cir.1987).

2. Return of bond. Once any reasonable possibility of harm to the enjoined party has passed, the party may file a motion for return of the bond. ***Citizens for a Better Env't v. Village of Elm Grove***, 472 F.Supp. 1183, 1184 (E.D.Wis.1979).

3. Recovery against bond. If the enjoined party is harmed by an improperly issued TRO or injunction, the enjoined party may file a motion to recover against the bond. *See* ***Nokia Corp.***, 645 F.3d at 557. When the court determines that a party was improperly enjoined, that party is entitled to a rebuttable presumption in favor of recovery against the bond. *Id.* at 558.

§3.5 Findings of fact & conclusions of law.

1. Generally. The court is generally not required to make findings of fact and conclusions of law when issuing a TRO. ***Romer v. Green Point Sav. Bank***, 27 F.3d 12, 16 (2d Cir.1994); *see* FRCP 52(a)(2). Findings and conclusions are generally not required because (1) TROs are issued in haste, under emergency conditions, to forestall irreparable harm, and for a limited duration, and (2) TROs are usually exempt from appellate review. ***Romer***, 27 F.3d at 16.

2. Exceptions. The court should make findings of fact and conclusions of law when the TRO would be appealable because of serious consequences. *See, e.g.*, ***Romer***, 27 F.3d at 16-17 (findings necessary for appellate purposes when TRO disposed of all that was at risk in litigation). For a discussion of the appealability of TROs, see "TRO," §7.1, p. 106.

§4. PRELIMINARY INJUNCTION

§4.1 Parties. Before the court can grant preliminary injunctive relief, the plaintiff must join all required parties under FRCP 19. *See* ***Klaus v. Hi-Shear Corp.***, 528 F.2d 225, 234-35 (9th Cir.1975); *see, e.g.*, ***B. Fernandez & Hnos., Inc. v. Kellogg USA, Inc.***, 440 F.3d 541, 548 (1st Cir.2006) (in contract suit, preliminary injunction vacated when injunction would force a required party who was not adequately represented in suit to perform under contract). See "Motion to Dismiss for Failure to Join a Party Under FRCP 19—FRCP 12(b)(7)," ch. 3-I, p. 214.

§4.2 Application.

1. Motion or show-cause order. A preliminary injunction may be sought by a motion or an order to show cause. *See* ***James Luterbach Constr. Co. v. Adamkus***, 781 F.2d 599, 603 n.1 (7th Cir.1986); ***Studebaker Corp. v. Gittlin***, 360 F.2d 692, 694 (2d Cir.1966); 11A Wright, Miller & Kane §2949. If time is short, a request for preliminary injunction may be made before a complaint is filed, but the complaint must be filed before the court's hearing on the preliminary injunction. *See* ***P.K. Family Rest. v. IRS***, 535 F.Supp. 1223, 1224 (N.D.Ohio 1982) (under FRCP 3, court lacks jurisdiction to entertain request for injunctive relief when no complaint has been filed); *see, e.g.*, ***Studebaker***, 360 F.2d at 694 (show-cause order and affidavit could be filed two days before complaint). *But see* ***National Org. for the Reform of Marijuana Laws v. Mullen***, 608 F.Supp. 945, 950 n.5 (N.D.Cal.1985) (in class action, not necessary to file complaint before injunctive order is issued).

2. Grounds. The application for a preliminary injunction should plead and prove the grounds for injunctive relief. See "Grounds for Injunctive Relief," §2, p. 94.

3. Bond. The application for a preliminary injunction should state the plaintiff's willingness to post a bond. See "Bond," §3.4, p. 100.

CAUTION

A bond posted for a TRO does not automatically apply to a preliminary injunction issued later. ***Coyne-Delany Co. v. Capital Dev. Bd.**, 717 F.2d 385, 389 (7th Cir.1983).*

4. Relief. The application for a preliminary injunction should identify the relief sought.

5. Evidentiary support. The application for a preliminary injunction must be accompanied by an affidavit or a verified complaint. *See* ***Bascom Food Prods. v. Reese Finer Foods, Inc.***, 715 F.Supp. 616, 624 n.14 (D.N.J.1989). Usually, the request for a preliminary injunction is supported by affidavits. *See* ***Federal S&L Ins. v. Dixon***, 835 F.2d 554, 558 (5th Cir.1987); ***Ross-Whitney v. Smith Kline & French Labs.***, 207 F.2d 190, 198 (9th Cir.1953); *see also* ***Markowitz Jewelry Co. v. Chapal/Zenray, Inc.***, 988 F.Supp. 404, 407 (S.D.N.Y.1997) (testimonial evidence

submitted on motions must be in form of affidavits or declarations). The affidavits can be based on information and belief, hearsay, and personal knowledge. *See* ***Levi Strauss & Co. v. Sunrise Int'l Trading, Inc.***, 51 F.3d 982, 985 (11th Cir.1995); ***Dixon***, 835 F.2d at 558; ***Asseo v. Pan Am. Grain Co.***, 805 F.2d 23, 26 (1st Cir.1986).

§4.3 Notice. A preliminary injunction may be issued only after notice to the adverse party. FRCP 65(a)(1); ***U.S. v. Microsoft Corp.***, 147 F.3d 935, 943 (D.C.Cir.1998); ***Parker v. Ryan***, 960 F.2d 543, 544 (5th Cir.1992); *see* ***Weitzman v. Stein***, 897 F.2d 653, 657 (2d Cir.1990) (notice requirements apply to court's sua sponte injunction). The notice provides the opposing party with a fair opportunity to oppose the preliminary injunction. ***Granny Goose Foods, Inc. v. Brotherhood of Teamsters & Auto Truck Drivers***, 415 U.S. 423, 432 n.7 (1974). Compliance with the notice provision is mandatory. ***Parker***, 960 F.2d at 544. Preliminary injunctions issued without notice are usually dissolved. *See, e.g.*, ***Hoechst Diafoil Co. v. Nan Ya Plastics Corp.***, 174 F.3d 411, 422 (4th Cir.1999) (notice sufficient for TRO, but not injunction); ***Williams v. McKeithen***, 939 F.2d 1100, 1105-06 (5th Cir.1991) (injunction order reversed when district court did not provide notice of hearing); ***Weitzman***, 897 F.2d at 657-58 (order freezing assets given to wife vacated because wife had no notice of proceeding). *But see* ***Rosen v. Siegel***, 106 F.3d 28, 33 (2d Cir. 1997) (procedurally flawed injunction allowed to remain in place pending proper hearing on remand if equities support such disposition). Most circuits hold that the court has the discretion to determine the sufficiency of the notice. *See* ***Dominion Video Satellite, Inc. v. EchoStar Satellite Corp.***, 269 F.3d 1149, 1154 (10th Cir.2001).

§4.4 Hearing. The court should hold a hearing on a preliminary injunction. *See* 13 *Moore's Federal Practice 3d* §65.21[3].

1. Ex parte TRO issued. If the party obtains a TRO ex parte, the court automatically sets a preliminary-injunction hearing. FRCP 65(b)(3); ***Hudson v. Barr***, 3 F.3d 970, 974 (6th Cir.1993). If the party does not proceed with an application for a preliminary injunction at the hearing, the court must dissolve any TRO that was entered. FRCP 65(b)(3); ***Hudson***, 3 F.3d at 974.

2. Scope of hearing. The only issue presented at the preliminary-injunction hearing is the need for immediate relief pending a trial on the merits. Thus, the parties should focus on the factors necessary for injunctive relief. See "Equitable factors for injunctive relief," §2.1, p. 94.

3. When evidentiary hearing required. If factual disputes are involved (e.g., genuine disputes of material fact are created by the response to the preliminary injunction), the court must conduct an evidentiary hearing before issuing a preliminary injunction. ***Ty, Inc. v. GMA Accessories, Inc.***, 132 F.3d 1167, 1171 (7th Cir.1997); *see* ***Kaepa, Inc. v. Achilles Corp.***, 76 F.3d 624, 628 (5th Cir.1996). If no factual dispute is involved, an evidentiary hearing is not required, and the parties need only be given ample opportunity to present their views on the legal issues. ***Kaepa***, 76 F.3d at 628; *see* ***Campbell Soup Co. v. Giles***, 47 F.3d 467, 470 (1st Cir.1995); ***Stanley v. University of S. Cal.***, 13 F.3d 1313, 1326 (9th Cir.1994); ***Federal S&L Ins. v. Dixon***, 835 F.2d 554, 558-59 (5th Cir.1987). If a party wants an evidentiary hearing, it must persuade the court that (1) there are genuine disputes of material fact and (2) it intends to introduce evidence that, if believed, will weaken the opposing party's case enough to affect the judge's decision on whether to issue an injunction. ***Ty, Inc.***, 132 F.3d at 1171.

NOTE

If the only issues in dispute are legal and the parties have been given ample opportunity to present their cases, the court is not required to hold an oral hearing and may consider the briefs and evidence on file when making its decision. ***Kaepa****, 76 F.3d at 628; see, e.g.,* ***PCI Transp. v. Fort Worth & W. R.R.****, 418 F.3d 535, 546 (5th Cir.2005) (hearing unnecessary when P did not establish factual dispute).*

4. Burden. At the hearing, the plaintiff bears the burden of persuasion on each of the equitable factors. ***Cox v. City of Chi.***, 868 F.2d 217, 219 (7th Cir.1989). However, the plaintiff is not required to prove its case in full. ***University of Tex. v. Camenisch***, 451 U.S. 390, 395 (1981).

CAUTION

At least one circuit has held that a plaintiff must satisfy a heightened burden on three types of specifically disfavored preliminary injunctions: (1) preliminary injunctions that alter the status quo, (2) mandatory preliminary injunctions, and (3) preliminary injunctions that grant the movant all the relief recoverable after a full trial on the merits. See ***O Centro Espirita Beneficiente Uniao Do Vegetal v. Ashcroft****, 389 F.3d 973, 975 (10th Cir.2004) (en banc), aff'd sub nom.* ***Gonzales v. O Centro Espirita Benificente Uniao Do Vegetal****, 546 U.S. 418 (2006). In* ***O Centro****, the Tenth Circuit held that a plaintiff seeking any of these injunctions must make a strong showing of both the likelihood of success on the merits and the balance of hardships.* ***O Centro****, 389 F.3d at 976. But see* ***United Food & Commercial Workers Un. v. Southwest Ohio Reg'l Transit Auth.****, 163 F.3d 341, 348 (6th Cir.1998) (rejecting heightened burden for mandatory injunctive relief).*

5. Consolidation with trial. Before or after beginning the hearing, the court may advance the trial on the merits of the permanent injunction and consolidate that proceeding with the hearing for the preliminary injunction. FRCP 65(a)(2); ***Aponte v. Calderon***, 284 F.3d 184, 190 (1st Cir.2002); ***Rodriguez v. DeBuono***, 175 F.3d 227, 235 n.9 (2d Cir.1999); *see* ***Sonnier v. Crain***, 613 F.3d 436, 442 (5th Cir.2010); ***Dam Things from Den. v. Russ Berrie & Co.***, 290 F.3d 548, 566 n.27 (3d Cir.2002). When ordering consolidation, the court must preserve any party's right to a jury trial. FRCP 65(a)(2); ***Lamex Foods, Inc. v. Audeliz Lebrón Corp.***, 646 F.3d 100, 111 (1st Cir. 2011); ***Proimos v. Fair Auto. Repair, Inc.***, 808 F.2d 1273, 1278 (7th Cir.1987). The court may issue the consolidation order if the parties consent or if the parties receive timely notice allowing them to gather and present all the evidence that would be pertinent at a trial on the merits. ***Proimos***, 808 F.2d at 1277-78; *see* ***Camenisch***, 451 U.S. at 395 (courts should provide parties with clear and unambiguous notice of intent to consolidate either before hearing begins or when parties still have full opportunity to present their cases); ***Lamex Foods***, 646 F.3d at 107 (court must provide indisputably clear notice of intent to consolidate); *see also* ***Anderson v. Davila***, 125 F.3d 148, 157 n.9 (3d Cir.1997) (courts should solicit on-record responses from both parties' attorneys regarding propriety of consolidation). Any right to object to the court's timeliness in giving notice will be lost if a party does not object when the notice is actually received. ***Aponte***, 284 F.3d at 190.

§4.5 Order.

1. Form. A valid order for a preliminary injunction must make certain specific statements.

(1) Reasons for issuance. The order must state the reasons for the issuance of the injunction by defining the injury and describing why it is irreparable. FRCP 65(d)(1); *see* ***Prairie Band of Potawatomi Indians v. Pierce***, 253 F.3d 1234, 1245 (10th Cir.2001) (when issuing preliminary injunction, court must make findings of fact and conclusions of law); ***Hoechst Diafoil Co. v. Nan Ya Plastics Corp.***, 174 F.3d 411, 423 (4th Cir.1999) (FRCP 52(a) requires full, written explanation supporting preliminary injunction); ***Knapp Shoes, Inc. v. Sylvania Shoe Mfg.***, 15 F.3d 1222, 1227-28 (1st Cir.1994) (court must provide adequate level of detail, which depends on injunction's importance, complexity, depth, and evidence). If the district court does not provide reasons for the issuance of the injunction, the appellate court cannot adequately review the injunction order. ***Hoechst Diafoil***, 174 F.3d at 423; *see, e.g.*, ***Central Gulf S.S. Corp. v. International Paper Co.***, 477 F.2d 907, 907-08 (5th Cir.1973) (when district court orally stated its decision without providing reasons and parties did not request formal findings, appellate court remanded for district court to make findings).

(2) Define act restrained or required. The order must define in reasonable detail the act restrained or required. FRCP 65(d)(1)(C); *see* ***Schmidt v. Lessard***, 414 U.S. 473, 476 (1974) (specificity provisions of FRCP 65(d) are not mere technical requirements); ***Martin's Herend Imps., Inc. v. Diamond & Gem Trading U.S.***, 195 F.3d 765, 771 (5th Cir.1999) (injunction must be framed so those enjoined will know what conduct court has prohibited).

(a) Specificity required. An order must specifically state what is prohibited or required. ***City of N.Y. v. Mickalis Pawn Shop, LLC***, 645 F.3d 114, 143 (2d Cir.2011). When determining whether the order is sufficiently specific, courts look to see whether the parties understand their obligations under the order; the degree of specificity in the order depends on the nature of the subject matter. ***Planetary Motion, Inc. v. Techsplosion, Inc.***, 261 F.3d 1188, 1203-04 (11th Cir.2001); *see* ***City of N.Y.***, 645 F.3d at 143-44; ***U.S. v. Pentrack***, 428 F.3d 986, 990 (10th Cir.2005); *see also* ***Schmidt***, 414 U.S. at 476 (FRCP 65(d) was designed to prevent uncertainty and confusion for enjoined parties). However, an order generally will not be overturned unless it is so vague that it has no reasonably specific meaning. ***A&M Records, Inc. v. Napster, Inc.***, 284 F.3d 1091, 1097 (9th Cir.2002); ***Planetary Motion***, 261 F.3d at 1203; *see also* ***Martin's Herend***, 195 F.3d at 771 (mere fact that interpretation is necessary does not render injunction impermissibly vague).

(b) Narrowly tailored. An order should be narrowly tailored to fit the specific violations; it does not need to enjoin all possible violations. ***City of N.Y.***, 645 F.3d at 144.

(c) Incorporation not allowed. An order cannot describe the act to be restrained or required by reference to the complaint or other documents. FRCP 65(d)(1)(C); ***Consumers Gas & Oil, Inc. v. Farmland Indus.***, 84 F.3d 367, 370-71 (10th Cir.1996); *see* ***Marseilles Hydro Power, LLC v. Marseilles Land & Water Co.***, 299 F.3d 643, 646 (7th Cir.2002) (injunction must be self-contained); ***Dunn v. New York State Dept. of Labor***, 47 F.3d 485, 489 (2d Cir.1995) (injunction referring to order without containing copy of order is too vague). ***But see Davis v. City & Cty. of S.F.***, 890 F.2d 1438, 1450-51 (9th Cir.1989) (documents need not be attached to injunctive order when defendant already has knowledge of documents' contents); ***Perfect Fit Indus. v. Acme Quilting Co.***, 646 F.2d 800, 809 (2d Cir.1981) (same).

(3) Fixed bond amount. The order must fix the amount of the bond unless the party seeking the injunctive relief is the U.S. government. FRCP 65(c). An order that is silent on the amount of the bond is reversible error. ***Hoechst Diafoil***, 174 F.3d at 421. See "Bond," §3.4, p. 100.

2. Binding effect. See "Binding effect," §3.3.3, p. 98.

§4.6 Modifying preliminary injunction. The court can modify the preliminary injunction for reasons of equity in light of changes in the facts or for any other good reason. ***Loudner v. U.S.***, 200 F.Supp.2d 1146, 1148 (D.S.D. 2002). However, the court cannot modify the preliminary injunction if doing so would fundamentally alter the status of the parties. ***Corbin v. Texaco, Inc.***, 690 F.2d 104, 105 (6th Cir.1982).

§4.7 Findings of fact & conclusions of law. When the court issues a preliminary injunction, it must make findings of fact and conclusions of law. FRCP 52(a)(2); ***TEC Eng'g v. Budget Molders Sup.***, 82 F.3d 542, 544-45 (1st Cir.1996). However, the court's decision about a preliminary injunction is not a decision on the merits of the underlying case; its findings of fact and conclusions of law on the preliminary injunction are not binding at a trial on the merits. ***University of Tex. v. Camenisch***, 451 U.S. 390, 395 (1981); ***TEC Eng'g***, 82 F.3d at 545.

§5. PERMANENT INJUNCTION

§5.1 Application. If the plaintiff requested a TRO and a preliminary injunction, its application for a permanent injunction is merely an additional request that the court may grant after the trial on the merits. To be granted a permanent injunction, the plaintiff must have satisfied the grounds for injunctive relief. *See* ***eBay Inc. v. MercExchange, L.L.C.***, 547 U.S. 388, 391 (2006). See "Grounds for Injunctive Relief," §2, p. 94.

§5.2 Hearing. The hearing on the permanent injunction is a full trial of the issues presented for the TRO and the preliminary injunction. The plaintiff is entitled to a jury trial at the hearing on the permanent injunction. FRCP 65(a)(2). If the permanent-injunction hearing resolves the entire case, it may be the only hearing in the suit.

§5.3 Order. An order for a permanent injunction is a final judgment; it is not provisional in nature (as are TROs and preliminary injunctions). ***Plummer v. American Inst. of Certified Pub. Accountants***, 97 F.3d 220, 229 (7th Cir.1996).

1. Form. A valid order for a permanent injunction must specifically state what is being restrained or required. FRCP 65(d)(1)(C). See "Form," §4.5.1, p. 103.

2. Binding effect. See "Binding effect," §3.3.3, p. 98.

§5.4 Bond. No bond is required for a permanent injunction. ***Forest Park II v. Hadley***, 336 F.3d 724, 734 (8th Cir.2003); ***Ty, Inc. v. Publications Int'l***, 292 F.3d 512, 516 (7th Cir.2002); *see* FRCP 65(c).

§5.5 Modifying permanent injunction. The district court has continuing authority over a permanent injunction. ***In re Detroit Auto Dealers Ass'n***, 84 F.3d 787, 789 (6th Cir.1996). The court can modify the injunction if a party can show that the enjoined conduct has become lawful, the injunction has become illegal, or circumstances of law or fact have changed to make continuation of the injunction unjust. *Id.*; *see* ***Protectoseal Co. v. Barancik***, 23 F.3d 1184, 1186-87 (7th Cir.1994).

§6. RESPONSE TO REQUEST FOR INJUNCTIVE RELIEF

§6.1 Response. The defendant should file a response to the request for injunctive relief, urging any of the following:

1. Equitable factors not established. The plaintiff is not entitled to the injunctive relief because it has not established one or more of the factors supporting the need for an injunction. See "Equitable factors for injunctive relief," §2.1, p. 94.

2. Inequitable conduct. The plaintiff is not entitled to the injunctive relief because it is guilty of inequitable conduct (e.g., laches, unclean hands). ***GoTo.com, Inc. v. Walt Disney Co.***, 202 F.3d 1199, 1209 (9th Cir.2000) (laches and unclean hands); ***Original Great Am. Chocolate Chip Cookie Co. v. River Valley Cookies, Ltd.***, 970 F.2d 273, 281-82 (7th Cir.1992) (unclean hands); *see also* ***Lydo Enters. v. City of Las Vegas***, 745 F.2d 1211, 1213-14 (9th Cir.1984) (delay in seeking preliminary injunction is factor to be considered in weighing irreparable injury). *But see* ***Lyons Prtshp. v. Morris Costumes, Inc.***, 243 F.3d 789, 799 (4th Cir.2001) (if claim is for injunctive relief, laches does not apply because injunction is entered on basis of current, ongoing conduct).

3. Relief prohibited by state law. In diversity cases, the plaintiff is not entitled to the injunctive relief because state law expressly prohibits it. ***John Paul Mitchell Sys. v. Quality King Distribs.***, 106 F.Supp.2d 462, 478 (S.D.N.Y.2000); *e.g.*, ***Lauf v. E.G. Shinner & Co.***, 303 U.S. 323, 328 (1938) (state law prohibited injunction to prevent picketing); ***Sims Snowboards, Inc. v. Kelly***, 863 F.2d 643, 647 (9th Cir.1988) (state law prohibited federal-court injunction).

§6.2 Motion to dissolve or modify ex parte TRO. If a TRO was obtained ex parte, the enjoined party can move to dissolve or modify the TRO. FRCP 65(b)(4). The enjoined party must give the plaintiff at least two days' notice, unless shortened by court order, of the hearing on the motion to dissolve or modify. *Id.*

§6.3 Answer to suit. If the plaintiff requested injunctive relief in its complaint, the defendant should object to the personal-jurisdiction and venue allegations and file an answer.

1. Challenge to personal jurisdiction & venue. To avoid waiving personal jurisdiction, venue, or other FRCP 12 defenses, the defendant should (1) preserve its objections in its first pleading opposing the requested injunctive relief (e.g., defendant's response to plaintiff's application for TRO), and (2) assert the objections in its first substantive response (i.e., an FRCP 12 motion) and file that motion before the injunction hearing. ***Drayton Enters. v. Dunker***, 142 F.Supp.2d 1177, 1182 (D.N.D.2001); *see* ***Wyrough & Loser, Inc. v. Pelmor Labs.***, 376 F.2d 543, 547 (3d Cir.1967) (party waives FRCP 12 defenses if it does not raise them before hearing on preliminary injunction); *see, e.g.*, ***Marquest Med. Prods. v. EMDE Corp.***, 496 F.Supp. 1242, 1245-46 (D.Colo.1980) (D waived personal-jurisdiction defense when it stipulated to mutual injunctions at preliminary-injunction hearing). See "FRCP 12 Motion," ch. 3-A, §2, p. 171.

2. Answer. The defendant should remember to file an answer to the suit so that it avoids voluntary dismissal. See "The Answer—Denying Liability," ch. 3-L, p. 230.

PRACTICE TIP

*When involved in an injunction proceeding, remember an important lesson from **Pennzoil v. Texaco**—don't forget to file your answer. If the defendant does not file an answer or other response that prevents a voluntary dismissal, as Texaco did not, the plaintiff can dismiss the suit as a matter of right. See "Plaintiff's Notice of Dismissal," ch. 7-C, §3, p. 630. The first round of litigation in **Pennzoil v. Texaco** involved a one-month hearing for an injunction in the Delaware Chancery Court. When Pennzoil's request for injunction was denied, Pennzoil dismissed the suit and refiled it in a Texas state court. The rest is history. Texaco tried to have the Delaware case reinstated, but to no avail. **Pennzoil Co. v. Getty Oil Co.**, 473 A.2d 358, 364 (Del. Ch.1984). The Delaware Chancery Court Rule 41(a)(1)(i), which was modeled on FRCP 41(a)(1)(i) (now FRCP 41(a)(1)(A)(i)), allowed a plaintiff to dismiss without leave of court as long as the defendant had not answered. See **Pennzoil Co.**, 473 A.2d at 360-61. If the case had remained in Delaware, it would have been tried to the court without a jury, and punitive damages could not have been awarded. See id. at 364 (no right to jury in Delaware Chancery Court).*

§7. APPELLATE REVIEW

§7.1 TRO.

1. Generally. Most TROs cannot be appealed. ***Service Empls. Int'l Un. v. National Un. of Healthcare Workers***, 598 F.3d 1061, 1067 (9th Cir.2010); ***Fideicomiso de la Tierra del Caño Martín Peña v. Fortuño***, 582 F.3d 131, 132 (1st Cir.2009); ***Board of Govs. of the Fed. Reserve Sys. v. DLG Fin. Corp.***, 29 F.3d 993, 1000 (5th Cir.1994).

2. Exceptions.

(1) When TRO might have irreparable consequence. An appellate court may review the grant or denial of a TRO when the TRO might have an irreparable consequence and could be effectively challenged only by an immediate appeal. ***Carson v. American Brands, Inc.***, 450 U.S. 79, 84 (1981); ***Fideicomiso de la Tierra del Caño Martín Peña***, 582 F.3d at 133; *e.g.*, ***Romer v. Green Point Sav. Bank***, 27 F.3d 12, 15-16 (2d Cir.1994) (TRO appealable when it disposed of all that was at risk in litigation); *see* ***Ty, Inc. v. Publications Int'l***, 292 F.3d 512, 516 (7th Cir.2002).

(2) When TRO exceeds time limit. A TRO that continues beyond the time limit in FRCP 65(b)(2) will be treated as the equivalent of a preliminary injunction, thus subjecting it to appellate review. *See* ***Nutrasweet Co. v. Vit-Mar Enters.***, 112 F.3d 689, 692 (3d Cir.1997) (applying former ten-day deadline); *see, e.g.*, ***Chicago United Indus. v. City of Chi.***, 445 F.3d 940, 943 (7th Cir.2006) (after time limit for TRO expired and court modified TRO without party's consent, TRO was deemed preliminary injunction and was appealable; applying former ten-day deadline). See "Time limit," §3.3.2, p. 98.

(3) When preliminary injunction is disguised as TRO. A TRO that possesses the qualities of a preliminary injunction is reviewable by immediate appeal. ***Sampson v. Murray***, 415 U.S. 61, 86-87 (1974); ***Service Empls. Int'l Un.***, 598 F.3d at 1067.

§7.2 Preliminary injunction.

1. Appealable. An order that grants or denies either a preliminary injunction or a motion to dissolve a preliminary injunction is an appealable order. *See* 28 U.S.C. §1292(a)(1); *see also* ***Martin's Herend Imps., Inc. v. Diamond & Gem Trading U.S.***, 195 F.3d 765, 769 (5th Cir.1999) (modification of injunction immediately appealable).

2. Standard of review.

(1) Preliminary injunction. Appellate courts review the grant or denial of a preliminary injunction for abuse of discretion. ***Ashcroft v. ACLU***, 542 U.S. 656, 664 (2004); ***Schrier v. University of Colo.***, 427 F.3d 1253,

1258 (10th Cir.2005); ***Schiavo v. Schiavo***, 403 F.3d 1223, 1226 (11th Cir.2005); ***Karaha Bodas Co. v. Perusahaan Pertambangan Minyak Dan Gas Bumi Negara***, 335 F.3d 357, 363 (5th Cir.2003); ***Giovani Carandola, Ltd. v. Bason***, 303 F.3d 507, 511 (4th Cir.2002); ***Al-Fayed v. CIA***, 254 F.3d 300, 303-04 (D.C.Cir.2001); ***SG Cowen Sec. v. Messih***, 224 F.3d 79, 81 (2d Cir.2000). *But see* ***Quaak v. Klynveld Peat Marwick Goerdeler Bedrijfsrevisoren***, 361 F.3d 11, 16 (1st Cir.2004) (international antisuit injunctions subject to heightened level of appellate review). A court abuses its discretion by (1) committing an error of law, such as applying an incorrect legal standard, (2) basing the preliminary injunction on a clearly erroneous finding of fact, or (3) issuing an injunction that contains an error in form or substance. ***Quaak***, 361 F.3d at 16; ***Fun-Damental Too, Ltd. v. Gemmy Indus.***, 111 F.3d 993, 999 (2d Cir. 1997); *see, e.g.*, ***Rosen v. Cascade Int'l***, 21 F.3d 1520, 1529-30 (11th Cir.1994) (court abused its discretion when it froze D's assets pending trial for fraud because only monetary damages were sought).

(2) Findings & conclusions. Findings of fact are reviewed for plain error, and conclusions of law are reviewed de novo. ***D.L. Cromwell Invs. v. NASD Regulation, Inc.***, 279 F.3d 155, 158 (2d Cir.2002); *see* ***Karaha Bodas Co.***, 335 F.3d at 363; ***Al-Fayed***, 254 F.3d at 303-04.

(3) Consolidation order. The decision to consolidate the hearing on a preliminary injunction with a trial on the merits is reviewed for abuse of discretion. ***D.L. Cromwell Invs.***, 279 F.3d at 158; ***Associated Gen. Contractors v. Drabik***, 214 F.3d 730, 738 (6th Cir.2000); *see* ***Berry v. Bean***, 796 F.2d 713, 719 (4th Cir.1986). To overturn a consolidation order, the party opposing consolidation must demonstrate that it was prevented from presenting material evidence because of the consolidation. *See* ***D.L. Cromwell Invs.***, 279 F.3d at 160.

§7.3 Permanent injunction. A permanent injunction is appealable as a final judgment. *See* 28 U.S.C. §1291; ***Martin's Herend Imps., Inc. v. Diamond & Gem Trading U.S.***, 195 F.3d 765, 769-70 (5th Cir.1999). The grant of a permanent injunction is reviewed for abuse of discretion. ***Schlotzsky's, Ltd. v. Sterling Purchasing & Nat'l Dist. Co.***, 520 F.3d 393, 402 (5th Cir.2008); ***Doeblers' Pa. Hybrids, Inc. v. Doebler***, 442 F.3d 812, 819 (3d Cir.2006); ***Aponte v. Calderon***, 284 F.3d 184, 191 (1st Cir.2002). The court abuses its discretion by (1) relying on clearly erroneous factual findings, (2) relying on clearly erroneous legal conclusions, or (3) misapplying the factual findings or legal conclusions when fashioning the injunctive relief. *See* ***Schlotzsky's***, 520 F.3d at 402. As with preliminary injunctions, findings of fact are reviewed for clear error, and conclusions of law are reviewed de novo. ***Aponte***, 284 F.3d at 191.

§7.4 Bond. An order to post an injunction bond is generally not immediately appealable. ***Habitat Educ. Ctr. v. U.S. Forest Serv.***, 607 F.3d 453, 456 (7th Cir.2010). But an order may be immediately appealable as a collateral order if the bond is higher than necessary and beyond the plaintiff's ability to pay, thus resulting in irreparable harm without justification. *Id.*

E. DECLARATORY JUDGMENT

§1. GENERAL

§1.1 Rule. FRCP 57. See also 28 U.S.C. §§2201, 2202.

§1.2 Purpose. A suit for declaratory judgment establishes existing rights, status, or other legal relationships; it cannot be used to revise, alter, or reform the parties' rights, status, or relationships. *See* ***Burlington Ins. v. Oceanic Design & Constr., Inc.***, 383 F.3d 940, 952 (9th Cir.2004); ***Brister v. Faulkner***, 214 F.3d 675, 687 (5th Cir.2000). A declaratory judgment provides a remedy to a party that is uncertain of its rights and wants an early adjudication without having to wait for its adversary to file suit. *See* ***Wilton v. Seven Falls Co.***, 515 U.S. 277, 286 (1995); ***Phillips Plastics Corp. v. Kato Hatsujou Kabushiki Kaisha***, 57 F.3d 1051, 1053 (Fed.Cir.1995).

§1.3 Forms. ***O'Connor's Federal Civil Forms*** (2012), FORM 2E:1.

§1.4 Other references. 10B Wright, Miller & Kane, *Federal Practice & Procedure 3d* §§2751-2771 (1998 & Supp.2012); 12 *Moore's Federal Practice 3d* ch. 57 (2012).

§2. DECLARATORY JUDGMENT ACT

The Declaratory Judgment Act (28 U.S.C. §§2201-2202) does not create an independent cause of action; instead, it provides a form of relief. ***Aetna Life Ins. v. Haworth***, 300 U.S. 227, 240 (1937); ***In re Joint E.&S. Dist. Asbestos Litig.***, 14 F.3d 726, 731 (2d Cir.1993); *see* ***Countrywide Home Loans, Inc. v. Mortgage Guar. Ins.***, 642 F.3d 849, 853 (9th Cir.2011). A declaratory-judgment action is proper when the judgment will (1) serve a useful purpose in clarifying and settling legal relations at issue and (2) provide relief from the uncertainty, insecurity, and controversy giving rise to the proceeding. ***Aetna Cas. & Sur. Co. v. Sunshine Corp.***, 74 F.3d 685, 687 (6th Cir.1996); ***State Farm Fire & Cas. Co. v. Mhoon***, 31 F.3d 979, 983 (10th Cir.1994). For example, declaratory-judgment actions are often used to resolve disputes over insurance coverage. ***Nautilus Ins. v. Winchester Homes, Inc.***, 15 F.3d 371, 375-76 (4th Cir.1994), *overruled in part on other grounds*, ***Centennial Life Ins. v. Poston***, 88 F.3d 255 (4th Cir.1996).

§2.1 Declaratory judgment available. A federal court has the power to hear a declaratory-judgment action only if the case is otherwise within its subject-matter jurisdiction and involves an actual controversy. 28 U.S.C. §2201(a); ***Starter Corp. v. Converse, Inc.***, 84 F.3d 592, 594 (2d Cir.1996); ***Seattle Audubon Soc'y v. Moseley***, 80 F.3d 1401, 1405 (9th Cir.1996). The Declaratory Judgment Act is not an independent source of subject-matter jurisdiction. ***Michigan S. R.R. v. Branch & St. Joseph Cty. Rail Users Ass'n***, 287 F.3d 568, 575 (6th Cir.2002); ***Wyoming v. U.S.***, 279 F.3d 1214, 1225 (10th Cir.2002); ***In re B-727 Aircraft***, 272 F.3d 264, 270 (5th Cir.2001).

1. Subject-matter jurisdiction. A declaratory-judgment action must satisfy the well-pleaded-complaint rule—that is, the federal basis for jurisdiction must be shown on the face of the plaintiff's complaint. ***City of Huntsville v. City of Madison***, 24 F.3d 169, 172 & n.4 (11th Cir.1994); *see also* ***Skelly Oil Co. v. Phillips Pet. Co.***, 339 U.S. 667, 671-72 (1950) (mere existence of question of federal law in suit is not proof that federal law is basis of suit). See "Well-pleaded-complaint rule," ch. 2-F, §2.2.1, p. 113.

(1) Diversity jurisdiction. Jurisdiction over a declaratory-judgment action may be based on diversity jurisdiction. *See* ***Blue Ridge Ins. v. Stanewich***, 142 F.3d 1145, 1147-48 (9th Cir.1998); ***Continental Cas. Co. v. Fuscardo***, 35 F.3d 963, 965 (4th Cir.1994); *see also* ***Skelly Oil Co.***, 339 U.S. at 674 (immaterial whether declaratory remedy available in federal courts is available in state courts). See "Diversity Jurisdiction," ch. 2-F, §3, p. 116.

(2) Federal-question jurisdiction. Jurisdiction over a declaratory-judgment action may be based on federal-question jurisdiction. See "Federal-Question Jurisdiction," ch. 2-F, §2, p. 113. However, determining federal-question jurisdiction for a declaratory-judgment action can be difficult. The court must first hypothetically assume that the declaratory-judgment defendant, who normally would be the plaintiff in a traditional suit for damages, filed suit first. Then, the court must determine (1) if such a suit would arise under federal law or (2) if some element of the claim would necessarily depend on the resolution of a substantial, disputed question of federal law. *See* ***City of Huntsville***, 24 F.3d at 172. If either is true, there is federal-question jurisdiction. If the federal issue would arise only as a defense in the hypothetical suit, there is no federal-question jurisdiction. ***Franchise Tax Bd. v. Construction Laborers Vacation Trust***, 463 U.S. 1, 16 (1983); ***Fleet Bank, Nat'l Ass'n v. Burke***, 160 F.3d 883, 886 (2d Cir.1998); ***McDougald v. Jenson***, 786 F.2d 1465, 1476 (11th Cir.1986).

2. Case or controversy. Declaratory relief is available only when there is an actual, substantial case or controversy between parties who have adverse legal interests of sufficient immediacy and reality. ***MedImmune, Inc. v. Genentech, Inc.***, 549 U.S. 118, 126-27 (2007); ***Maryland Cas. Co. v. Pacific Coal & Oil Co.***, 312 U.S. 270, 273 (1941); ***Shields v. Norton***, 289 F.3d 832, 835 (5th Cir.2002). The dispute must be definite and concrete, not hypothetical or abstract. ***MedImmune***, 549 U.S. at 127; ***Babbitt v. United Farm Workers Nat'l Un.***, 442 U.S. 289, 298 (1979). The existence of an actual case or controversy is a condition precedent for a declaratory-judgment action. ***Travelers Ins. v. Obusek***, 72 F.3d 1148, 1153 (3d Cir.1995).

§2.2 Declaratory judgment not available. Generally, a declaratory judgment is not available in the following circumstances:

1. No case or controversy. A declaratory judgment is not available to resolve issues when there is no case or controversy. *E.g.*, ***S. Jackson & Son, Inc. v. Coffee, Sugar & Cocoa Exch. Inc.***, 24 F.3d 427, 431-32 (2d Cir. 1994) (no adverse dispute; thus, no case or controversy); ***Emory v. Peeler***, 756 F.2d 1547, 1552 (11th Cir.1985) (claim

based on possible future injury; thus, no case or controversy); *see also* ***Public Water Sup. Dist. v. City of Kearney***, 401 F.3d 930, 932-33 (8th Cir.2005) (case not ripe because no impending injury; declaratory judgment not appropriate).

2. Case pending in another federal court. A declaratory judgment is not usually available to resolve an issue that involves the same parties and that will be adjudicated in another federal court. ***Serco Servs. v. Kelley Co.***, 51 F.3d 1037, 1039 (Fed.Cir.1995); ***Kunkel v. Continental Cas. Co.***, 866 F.2d 1269, 1276 (10th Cir.1989). A court may, however, decide a purely legal question that arises in the context of a justiciable controversy presenting other factual issues. *E.g.*, ***Kunkel***, 866 F.2d at 1276 (court had authority to hear declaratory-judgment action on amount of coverage under insurance policy even though issue of liability under policy was pending in another federal court).

3. Case pending in state court. A declaratory judgment is usually not available to resolve state-law issues already pending before a state court. *See* ***Brillhart v. Excess Ins.***, 316 U.S. 491, 495 (1942); ***Magnolia Mar. Transp. v. LaPlace Towing Corp.***, 964 F.2d 1571, 1581 (5th Cir.1992). If the state-court case involves a state-law claim, the presumption is that the case should be tried in state court. ***Continental Cas. Co. v. Robsac Indus.***, 947 F.2d 1367, 1370-71 (9th Cir.1991), *overruled on other grounds*, ***Government Empls. Ins. v. Dizol***, 133 F.3d 1220 (9th Cir.1998); *see* ***Brillhart***, 316 U.S. at 495. See "Abstention," ch. 2-F, §7, p. 138. But if the controversy between the parties will not be resolved by the pending state suit, a declaratory judgment may be proper. *See, e.g.*, ***Sears, Roebuck & Co. v. American Mut. Liab. Ins.***, 372 F.2d 435, 438 (7th Cir.1967) (Sears asked federal court to declare coverage under insurance policy for Sears' potential liability in state-court action). The district court has substantial discretion to decide or dismiss a declaratory-judgment action when a case is pending in state court. ***Wilton v. Seven Falls Co.***, 515 U.S. 277, 286-87 (1995); *see* 28 U.S.C. §2201(a). In determining whether to dismiss, the court should consider whether (1) all of the issues raised in the declaratory complaint may be litigated in state court, (2) the majority of the issues raised are more appropriate for state-court resolution, (3) compelling federal interests are at stake, (4) the federal case is too far advanced, and (5) the declaratory-judgment plaintiff faces the danger of potentially conflicting obligations. *See* ***Travelers Ins. v. Louisiana Farm Bur. Fed'n***, 996 F.2d 774, 778 (5th Cir.1993); *see, e.g.*, ***Transamerica Occidental Life Ins. v. Digregorio***, 811 F.2d 1249, 1255 (9th Cir.1987) (no federal interest in state-law bad-faith claim against insurance company). The court may also dismiss a declaratory-judgment action in the interest of judicial economy and for the convenience of the parties and witnesses. ***American Nat'l Fire Ins. v. Hungerford***, 53 F.3d 1012, 1018 (9th Cir.1995), *overruled on other grounds*, ***Government Empls. Ins. v. Dizol***, 133 F.3d 1220 (9th Cir.1998); ***Nationwide Ins. v. Zavalis***, 52 F.3d 689, 692 (7th Cir.1995). However, the source of law, whether federal or state, is not a dispositive factor in the court's decision to dismiss. ***Transamerica Occidental Life***, 811 F.2d at 1255.

4. Criminal matters. A declaratory judgment is not available in criminal cases. *See, e.g.*, ***Younger v. Harris***, 401 U.S. 37, 44-45 (1971) (D could not challenge constitutionality of state statute under which he was being prosecuted); ***Bonner v. Circuit Ct. of St. Louis***, 526 F.2d 1331, 1336-37 (8th Cir.1975) (Ds could not challenge constitutionality of allegedly coerced guilty pleas). However, if the plaintiff can show irreparable injury that is "both great and immediate," the federal courts will intervene in state criminal proceedings. ***Younger***, 401 U.S. at 46. The threat must be one that cannot be eliminated by the state defendant's defense against a single criminal prosecution. *Id.*; *see, e.g.*, ***Dombrowski v. Pfister***, 380 U.S. 479, 490-91 (1965) (court enjoined enforcement of state criminal statutes that were being systematically used to deprive African-Americans of constitutional rights). See "Criminal proceedings," ch. 2-F, §7.2.2(1), p. 138. A prisoner seeking relief from a conviction or sentence cannot bring an action for federal declaratory relief. ***Williams v. Hill***, 74 F.3d 1339, 1340 (D.C.Cir.1996).

5. Tax matters. A declaratory judgment is not available to a taxpayer to establish tax liability. 28 U.S.C. §2201(a); ***Rebecca K. Crown Income Charitable Fund v. Commissioner***, 8 F.3d 571, 576 (7th Cir.1993); ***Warren v. U.S.***, 874 F.2d 280, 282 (5th Cir.1989).

6. Personal-injury litigation. A declaratory judgment is not available to a tortfeasor to litigate a personal-injury claim by filing a declaratory-judgment action in the forum of its choice. ***Cunningham Bros. v. Bail***, 407 F.2d 1165, 1167-68 (7th Cir.1969).

7. Barred by Anti-Injunction Act. A declaratory judgment is not available if an injunction would be barred by the Anti-Injunction Act, 28 U.S.C. §2283, because declaratory relief under 28 U.S.C. §2201 has the same effect as an injunction. ***Texas Employers' Ins. v. Jackson***, 862 F.2d 491, 506 (5th Cir.1988). See "Anti-Injunction Act," ch. 2-F, §7.4, p. 141.

§3. PROCEDURE

§3.1 Complaint. The complaint should state facts showing an actual controversy over a matter within the federal court's jurisdiction. *See* ***Volvo Constr. Equip. N. Am., Inc. v. CLM Equip. Co.***, 386 F.3d 581, 592 (4th Cir.2004). The plaintiff only needs to state facts adequate to support declaratory relief. *See* 28 U.S.C. §2201(a); FRCP 57. The complaint should generally include the following: (1) the identities of the parties to the dispute who have a claim or interest that would be affected by the declaration, (2) the facts giving rise to jurisdiction and venue, (3) the facts giving rise to the dispute, (4) the facts giving rise to the case-or-controversy requirement, (5) why declaratory relief is necessary, and (6) the relief requested. *See* ***Columbia Gas Transmission Corp. v. Drain***, 237 F.3d 366, 370 (4th Cir.2001); 10B Wright, Miller & Kane §2757. The court cannot grant declaratory relief beyond what is requested in the pleadings. *See* ***Westport Ins. v. Bayer***, 284 F.3d 489, 499 (3d Cir.2002); ***Penthouse Int'l v. Barnes***, 792 F.2d 943, 950 (9th Cir.1986); ***St. Paul Fire & Mar. Ins. v. Lawson Bros. Iron Works***, 428 F.2d 929, 931 (10th Cir.1970).

§3.2 Hearing & jury trial. The court may order a speedy hearing of a declaratory-judgment action. FRCP 57; *see* ***National Basketball Ass'n v. Williams***, 857 F.Supp. 1069, 1071 n.1 (S.D.N.Y.1994) (FRCP 57 allows for expedited treatment of declaratory-judgment actions), *aff'd*, 45 F.3d 684 (2d Cir.1995). The parties are entitled to a jury trial, as in other civil cases. FRCP 57. However, declaratory relief does not entitle a party to a jury trial when the right to a jury does not otherwise exist. ***Manning v. U.S.***, 146 F.3d 808, 811 (10th Cir.1998).

§3.3 Burden of proof. The party who moves for declaratory judgment bears the burden of establishing, by a preponderance of the evidence, that there is an actual controversy. ***Cygnus Therapeutics Sys. v. ALZA Corp.***, 92 F.3d 1153, 1159 (Fed.Cir.1996), *overruled on other grounds*, ***Nobelpharma AB v. Implant Innovations, Inc.***, 141 F.3d 1059 (Fed.Cir.1998); ***Shell Oil Co. v. Amoco Corp.***, 970 F.2d 885, 887 (Fed.Cir.1992).

§4. DECLARATORY JUDGMENT

§4.1 Exercising jurisdiction.

1. Deciding whether to hear case.

(1) Discretionary. The court's decision to exercise jurisdiction over a declaratory-judgment action is discretionary; the court may refuse to consider a declaratory-judgment action even if all the requirements are met. ***Cardinal Chem. Co. v. Morton Int'l***, 508 U.S. 83, 95 n.17 (1993); ***U.S. v. City of Las Cruces***, 289 F.3d 1170, 1180-81 (10th Cir.2002); *see* 28 U.S.C. §2201(a); ***Reno v. Catholic Soc. Servs.***, 509 U.S. 43, 57 (1993); ***Royal Indem. Co. v. Apex Oil Co.***, 511 F.3d 788, 793 (8th Cir.2008); *see also* ***Wilton v. Seven Falls Co.***, 515 U.S. 277, 286 (1995) (Declaratory Judgment Act confers on federal courts unique and substantial discretion in deciding whether to declare rights of litigants).

NOTE

Although many courts characterize a district court's discretion under the Declaratory Judgment Act as deciding whether to exercise "jurisdiction," that is an imprecise term. ***Countrywide Home Loans, Inc. v. Mortgage Guar. Ins.***, *642 F.3d 849, 852 (9th Cir.2011). The court's discretion is actually whether to exercise its remedial power under the Act, and that remedial power is separate from its jurisdiction. Id. at 852-53. See "Complaint," §3.1, this page.*

(2) Factors to consider. Although the court's discretion is broad, the court cannot refuse to hear a declaratory-judgment action on a whim or personal disinclination; it may do so only for good reason. ***Public Affairs***

Assocs. v. Rickover, 369 U.S. 111, 112 (1962); *see also* ***St. Paul Ins. v. Trejo***, 39 F.3d 585, 590-91 (5th Cir.1994) (stating relevant factors). In deciding whether to accept or decline jurisdiction, the court should evaluate the following three considerations (which have essentially the same formulation among the circuits despite differences in expression): (1) the proper allocation of decision-making between the state and federal courts, (2) fairness, and (3) efficiency. ***Sherwin-Williams Co. v. Holmes Cty.***, 343 F.3d 383, 390-91 (5th Cir.2003). For each circuit's list of the relevant factors, see ***Scottsdale Ins. v. Flowers***, 513 F.3d 546, 554 (6th Cir.2008); ***Sherwin-Williams Co.***, 343 F.3d at 389-91, ***City of Las Cruces***, 289 F.3d at 1187, ***Aetna Cas. & Sur. Co. v. Ind-Com Elec. Co.***, 139 F.3d 419, 422 (4th Cir.1998), ***Government Empls. Ins. v. Dizol***, 133 F.3d 1220, 1225 (9th Cir.1998), and ***Nationwide Ins. v. Zavalis***, 52 F.3d 689, 692 (7th Cir.1995). When addressing these factors, the court should consider whether a parallel state-court proceeding is pending; the absence of any pending related state litigation weighs strongly against dismissing the suit. *See* ***Sherwin-Williams Co.***, 343 F.3d at 394; ***Aetna Cas. & Sur. Co.***, 139 F.3d at 423; ***Government Empls. Ins.***, 133 F.3d at 1225.

2. Making ruling.

(1) Dismissal. If the court declines to exercise jurisdiction, it usually will dismiss the suit. *See, e.g.*, ***Preiser v. Newkirk***, 422 U.S. 395, 403-04 (1975) (issue moot); ***S. Jackson & Son, Inc. v. Coffee, Sugar & Cocoa Exch. Inc.***, 24 F.3d 427, 431 (2d Cir.1994) (P had no claim to litigate); ***Deveraux v. City of Chi.***, 14 F.3d 328, 331 (7th Cir.1994) (no case or controversy); ***Torch, Inc. v. LeBlanc***, 947 F.2d 193, 195 (5th Cir.1991) (case pending in state court).

(2) Stay. If the court declines to exercise jurisdiction because a related state proceeding is pending, it may choose to stay the federal suit. ***Wilton***, 515 U.S. at 288 & n.2.

(3) Proceed to judgment. If the court accepts jurisdiction, it will proceed to trial and judgment. *See* ***NUCOR Corp. v. Aceros y Maquilas de Occidente, S.A. de C.V.***, 28 F.3d 572, 578-79 (7th Cir.1994).

§4.2 Judgment. A declaratory judgment has the force and effect of a final judgment or decree. 28 U.S.C. §2201(a). A declaratory judgment can include the following:

1. Declaratory relief. The judgment can include a declaration of the rights and other legal relations of any party seeking such a declaration. 28 U.S.C. §2201(a).

2. Damages. The judgment can include an award of damages. ***BancInsure, Inc. v. BNC Nat'l Bank***, 263 F.3d 766, 772 (8th Cir.2001). The court has broad power to craft an award of damages after it has issued notice and held a hearing on the issue of damages. 28 U.S.C. §2202; ***Insurance Servs. of Beaufort, Inc. v. Aetna Cas. & Sur. Co.***, 966 F.2d 847, 852 (4th Cir.1992); *see* ***BancInsure, Inc.***, 263 F.3d at 772.

3. Attorney fees. The judgment can include an award of attorney fees.

(1) Federal-question suits. The court can award attorney fees in a suit based on federal-question jurisdiction if the underlying federal statute would provide for them. *See, e.g.*, ***May v. Cooperman***, 578 F.Supp. 1308, 1315 (D.N.J.1984) (P entitled to attorney fees under 42 U.S.C. §1983 even though it only sought declaratory relief); *see also* ***Kirchberg v. Feenstra***, 708 F.2d 991, 994-96 (5th Cir.1983) (D in declaratory suit entitled to award of attorney fees after court invalidated state statute under 28 U.S.C. §1988 because it discriminated on basis of sex).

(2) Diversity suits. The court can award attorney fees in a diversity suit when applicable state law would provide for them. ***Titan Holdings Syndicate, Inc. v. City of Keene***, 898 F.2d 265, 273-74 (1st Cir.1990); *see* 28 U.S.C. §2202. Under 28 U.S.C. §2202, it is not clear whether the court may award attorney fees in a diversity suit even when they are not allowed under the applicable state law. *Compare* ***Gant v. Grand Lodge***, 12 F.3d 998, 1002-03 (10th Cir.1993) (fees recoverable), *with* ***Utica Lloyd's v. Mitchell***, 138 F.3d 208, 210 (5th Cir.1998) (fees not recoverable).

§4.3 Amending judgment. A declaratory judgment can be amended, but only after notice and a hearing. ***Gant v. Grand Lodge***, 12 F.3d 998, 1001 (10th Cir.1993). Ordinary principles of claim preclusion do not apply to 28 U.S.C. §2202 actions. ***Gant***, 12 F.3d at 1002; ***Horn & Hardart Co. v. National Rail Passenger Corp.***, 843 F.2d 546, 549 (D.C.Cir.1988).

§5. APPELLATE REVIEW

District courts' decisions about the propriety of hearing declaratory-judgment actions are reviewed for abuse of discretion. ***Wilton v. Seven Falls Co.***, 515 U.S. 277, 289-90 (1995) (resolving circuit split); ***Sherwin-Williams Co. v. Holmes Cty.***, 343 F.3d 383, 389 (5th Cir.2003). *But see* ***Federal Express Corp. v. Air Line Pilots Ass'n***, 67 F.3d 961, 964 n.3 (D.C.Cir.1995) (***Wilton*** requires abuse-of-discretion review only when district court's decision rests on "discretionary, prudential" grounds; otherwise, review is de novo).

F. CHOOSING THE COURT—JURISDICTION

§1. GENERAL

§1.1 Rules. U.S. Const. art. 3, §2; 28 U.S.C. §§1331, 1332, 1359, 1367, 1369; FRCP 8, 9, 12-14, 19.

§1.2 Purpose. Before filing suit, the plaintiff must determine if the federal court has subject-matter jurisdiction over the suit. Lower federal courts have limited jurisdiction and are empowered to hear only those cases authorized by a federal statute, the U.S. Constitution, or a U.S. treaty. ***Kokkonen v. Guardian Life Ins.***, 511 U.S. 375, 377 (1994); ***Howery v. Allstate Ins.***, 243 F.3d 912, 916 (5th Cir.2001); ***Morrison v. Allstate Indem. Co.***, 228 F.3d 1255, 1260-61 (11th Cir.2000); *see* ***Reed Elsevier, Inc. v. Muchnick***, ___ U.S. ___, 130 S.Ct. 1237, 1243 (2010). As a result, the plaintiff must overcome an initial presumption that the federal court lacks subject-matter jurisdiction. ***Howery***, 243 F.3d at 916; *see* ***Morrison***, 228 F.3d at 1260-61. Subject-matter jurisdiction cannot be waived or conferred by agreement of the parties. ***Simon v. Wal-Mart Stores***, 193 F.3d 848, 850 (5th Cir.1999); ***Laughlin v. Kmart Corp.***, 50 F.3d 871, 873 (10th Cir.1995).

NOTE

In the Federal Courts Jurisdiction and Venue Clarification Act of 2011 (referred to as the Clarification Act), Congress made significant amendments to jurisdiction statutes in title 28. See Lamar Smith, Federal Courts Jurisdiction & Venue Clarification Act of 2011, H.R. Rep. No. 112-10 (2011). For this subchapter, the Clarification Act amended statutes on jurisdiction over certain cases involving resident aliens and corporations. See id. at 4. The Clarification Act became effective for any suit commenced in a U.S. district court on or after January 6, 2012. Federal Courts Jurisdiction & Venue Clarification Act of 2011, P.L. 112-63, §105, 125 Stat. 762 (2011) (eff. Jan. 6, 2012). For the law before the Clarification Act became effective, see ***O'Connor's Federal Rules * Civil Trials*** *(2012), "Choosing the Court—Jurisdiction," ch. 2-F, p. 106. Because of the substantive changes made by the 2011 amendments, use caution when citing cases that predate the amendments.*

§1.3 Forms. *O'Connor's Federal Civil Forms* (2012), FORM 2B:3.

§1.4 Other references. Federal Courts Jurisdiction & Venue Clarification Act of 2011, P.L. 112-63, 125 Stat. 758 (2011) (eff. Jan. 6, 2012) (referred to as Clarification Act); Lamar Smith, Federal Courts Jurisdiction & Venue Clarification Act of 2011, H.R. Rep. No. 112-10 (2011) (referred to as H.R. Rep. No. 112-10 (2011)); 6A Wright, Miller & Kane, *Federal Practice & Procedure 3d* §1588 (2010 & Supp.2012); 13D Wright, Miller, Cooper & Freer, *Federal Practice & Procedure 3d* §§3567.1, 3567.2 (2008 & Supp.2012); 13E Wright, Miller & Cooper, *Federal Practice & Procedure 3d* §§3604-3621 (2009 & Supp.2012); 14, 14A Wright, Miller & Cooper, *Federal Practice & Procedure 3d* §§3651-3700 (1998 & Supp.2012); 14AA Wright, Miller & Cooper, *Federal Practice & Procedure 4th* §3712 (2011 & Supp.2012); 14B Wright, Miller, Cooper & Steinman, *Federal Practice & Procedure 4th* §§3721-3724 (2009 & Supp.2012); 17, 17A, 17B Wright, Miller, Cooper & Amar, *Federal Practice & Procedure 3d* §§4034-4255 (2007 & Supp.2012); 15 *Moore's Federal Practice 3d* chs. 102-104 (2012); Chemerinsky, *Federal Jurisdiction* (6th ed. 2012); Beisner & Miller, *Litigating in the New Class Action World: A Practitioner's Guide to CAFA's Legislative History*, 6 BNA Class Action Litigation Report 403 (2005).

§2. FEDERAL-QUESTION JURISDICTION

§2.1 Authority. A district court has federal-question jurisdiction when an action arises under the Constitution, laws, or treaties of the United States. U.S. Const. art. 3, §2; 28 U.S.C. §1331; ***Empire Healthchoice Assur., Inc. v. McVeigh***, 547 U.S. 677, 689-90 (2006); ***Exxon Mobil Corp. v. Allapattah Servs.***, 545 U.S. 546, 552 (2005); *see* ***Bender v. Williamsport Area Sch. Dist.***, 475 U.S. 534, 541 (1986); ***Heckler v. Ringer***, 466 U.S. 602, 614-15 (1984); *see also* ***Grable & Sons Metal Prods. v. Darue Eng'g & Mfg.***, 545 U.S. 308, 312 (2005) (federal jurisdiction may be appropriate over certain state-law claims that implicate significant federal issues). Federal courts do not automatically possess the authority to hear and determine every type of action conceivably authorized by the U.S. Constitution. ***Nolan v. Boeing Co.***, 919 F.2d 1058, 1064 (5th Cir.1990). Rather, Article 3 specifies the outer limits of federal subject-matter jurisdiction. *Id.*

§2.2 Evaluating allegations of jurisdiction.

1. Well-pleaded-complaint rule. The presence or absence of a federal question is governed by the "well-pleaded-complaint rule," which provides that federal jurisdiction exists only when a federal question is presented on the face of the plaintiff's complaint. ***Rivet v. Regions Bank***, 522 U.S. 470, 475 (1998); ***Caterpillar, Inc. v. Williams***, 482 U.S. 386, 398-99 (1987); ***Wayne v. DHL Worldwide Express***, 294 F.3d 1179, 1183 (9th Cir.2002); ***Rice v. Office of Servicemembers' Grp. Life Ins.***, 260 F.3d 1240, 1245 (10th Cir.2001). The well-pleaded-complaint rule confines the search for federal-question jurisdiction to the face of the complaint. ***Franchise Tax Bd. v. Construction Laborers Vacation Trust***, 463 U.S. 1, 10 (1983); ***Lupo v. Human Affairs Int'l***, 28 F.3d 269, 272 (2d Cir.1994). As a general rule, the plaintiff is considered the master of its complaint and may avoid federal jurisdiction by relying exclusively on state law. ***Caterpillar***, 482 U.S. at 392; ***Easton v. Crossland Mortg. Corp.***, 114 F.3d 979, 982 (9th Cir. 1997). Federal courts do not have to consider responsive pleadings in determining whether a case arises under federal law. ***Vaden v. Discover Bank***, 556 U.S. 49, 60-61 (2009).

(1) Defenses not considered. A defense that raises a federal question does not give the court federal-question jurisdiction. ***Vaden***, 556 U.S. at 60; ***Rivet***, 522 U.S. at 478; ***Caterpillar***, 482 U.S. at 398-99; ***Franchise Tax Bd.***, 463 U.S. at 13-14; ***Wayne***, 294 F.3d at 1183. When the plaintiff's complaint does not raise a federal question, a defense based on federal law that only partially preempts state law does not raise a federal question. *See* ***Metropolitan Life Ins. v. Taylor***, 481 U.S. 58, 63 (1987); ***MSR Expl., Ltd. v. Meridian Oil, Inc.***, 74 F.3d 910, 912 (9th Cir.1996); ***Anderson v. American Airlines, Inc.***, 2 F.3d 590, 593 (5th Cir.1993). If the plaintiff anticipates a federal defense in its complaint, the anticipated defense does not necessarily confer federal-question jurisdiction. ***Franchise Tax Bd.***, 463 U.S. at 13-14; *see* ***Gibraltar, P.R., Inc. v. Otoki Grp.***, 914 F.Supp. 1203, 1205 (D.Md.1995), *aff'd*, 104 F.3d 616 (4th Cir.1997). See "Preemption," §2.3.4, p. 116.

(2) Counterclaims not considered. A counterclaim that raises a federal question does not give the court federal-question jurisdiction. ***Vaden***, 556 U.S. at 60; *see* ***Franchise Tax Bd.***, 463 U.S. at 10-11.

2. Artful-pleading doctrine. A corollary to the well-pleaded-complaint rule is the "artful-pleading doctrine"—a plaintiff cannot frame its suit under state law and omit federal claims that are essential to recovery. ***Franchise Tax Bd.***, 463 U.S. at 22; ***Burda v. M. Ecker Co.***, 954 F.2d 434, 438 (7th Cir.1992). The court may find that the plaintiff's claim arises under federal law even if the plaintiff has not characterized it as a federal claim. ***Burda***, 954 F.2d at 438; *see also* ***Karambelas v. Hughes Aircraft Co.***, 992 F.2d 971, 973 (9th Cir.1993) (P cannot avoid preemption by pleading purported state claim). Under the artful-pleading doctrine, removal is proper when federal law completely preempts a plaintiff's state-law claim. ***Rivet***, 522 U.S. at 475; ***Bernhard v. Whitney Nat'l Bank***, 523 F.3d 546, 551 (5th Cir.2008); *see* ***Schmeling v. NORDAM***, 97 F.3d 1336, 1339 (10th Cir.1996). See "Federal-question jurisdiction," ch. 4-A, §5.1, p. 249.

§2.3 Grounds for federal-question jurisdiction. A case arises under federal law if a well-pleaded complaint establishes that either (1) federal law creates the cause of action or (2) the plaintiff's right to relief necessarily depends on the resolution of a substantial question of federal law. ***Empire Healthchoice Assur., Inc. v. McVeigh***, 547 U.S. 677, 689-90 (2006); ***Singh v. Duane Morris LLP***, 538 F.3d 334, 337-38 (5th Cir.2008); *see* ***Grable & Sons Metal***

Prods. v. Darue Eng'g & Mfg., 545 U.S. 308, 312 (2005). For example, federal-question jurisdiction may be based on a civil action alleging a violation of the U.S. Constitution. *See* ***Bivens v. Six Unknown Named Agents***, 403 U.S. 388, 396-97 (1971). To determine whether a court has federal-question jurisdiction, it must consider the degree to which federal law is at the forefront of the case—not collateral, peripheral, or remote. *See* ***Merrell Dow Pharms. v. Thompson***, 478 U.S. 804, 813-14 & n.11 (1986); ***Howery v. Allstate Ins.***, 243 F.3d 912, 917 (5th Cir.2001).

1. Federal causes of action. For most cases brought under federal-question jurisdiction, the suit arises under the federal law that created the cause of action. ***Merrell Dow Pharms.***, 478 U.S. at 808; ***O'Conner v. Commonwealth Edison Co.***, 13 F.3d 1090, 1097 (7th Cir.1994); *see* ***Ultramar Am., Ltd. v. Dwelle***, 900 F.2d 1412, 1414 (9th Cir.1990).

(1) Nonexclusive federal jurisdiction. As a general rule, state courts have concurrent jurisdiction over federal claims with the federal courts unless (1) Congress provides that the federal courts have exclusive jurisdiction or (2) there is a clear incompatibility between the state-court jurisdiction and the federal interest. ***Gulf Offshore Co. v. Mobil Oil Corp.***, 453 U.S. 473, 478 (1981); ***Diversified Foods, Inc. v. First Nat'l Bank***, 985 F.2d 27, 29 (1st Cir.1993). When jurisdiction is concurrent, a cause of action can be pursued in either state or federal court. Some examples of actions that can be pursued in either forum are the following:

(a) Federal Employers' Liability Act (FELA) cases. 45 U.S.C. §56.

(b) Personal-injury and indemnity suits under the Outer Continental Shelf Lands Act. 43 U.S.C. §1349; ***Gulf Offshore***, 453 U.S. at 484.

(c) Civil Rights Act cases. 42 U.S.C. §1983; ***Martinez v. California***, 444 U.S. 277, 283 n.7 (1980).

(d) Age Discrimination in Employment Act (ADEA) cases. 29 U.S.C. §626(c)(1).

(e) Civil Racketeer Influenced and Corrupt Organizations Act (RICO) cases. ***Tafflin v. Levitt***, 493 U.S. 455, 458 (1990); *see* 18 U.S.C. §1964(c).

(f) Bank Holding Company Act cases. ***Diversified Foods***, 985 F.2d at 29; *see* 12 U.S.C. §1975.

(g) Fair Labor Standards Act (FLSA) cases. 29 U.S.C. §216(b).

(h) Suits under the Securities Act of 1933. 15 U.S.C. §77v(a).

(i) Jones Act cases. ***Engel v. Davenport***, 271 U.S. 33, 37 (1926); *see* 46 U.S.C. §§30104-30105.

(j) Interstate Commerce Commission Termination Act cases. 49 U.S.C. §11704(d)(1).

(k) Admiralty and maritime cases. 28 U.S.C. §1333; *see* ***Offshore Logistics, Inc. v. Tallentire***, 477 U.S. 207, 222-23 (1986) ("saving to suitors" clause allows state courts to entertain in personam maritime causes of action).

(*l*) Wiretap Act cases. *See* 18 U.S.C. §2520; ***DIRECTV, Inc. v. Bennett***, 470 F.3d 565, 568-69 (5th Cir.2006).

(2) Exclusive federal jurisdiction. Congress has vested federal courts with exclusive jurisdiction over certain actions. Some examples of actions that can be pursued only in federal court are the following:

(a) Cases in which the United States is a party. U.S. Const. art. 3, §2, cl. 1.

(b) Cases under the Securities Exchange Act of 1934. 15 U.S.C. §78aa(a).

(c) Cases under CERCLA. 42 U.S.C. §9613(a), (b), (h).

(d) Bankruptcy proceedings. 28 U.S.C. §1334.

(e) Patent, plant-variety-protection, and copyright cases. 28 U.S.C. §1338.

(f) Civil forfeiture cases. 28 U.S.C. §1355(a).

(g) Clayton Act cases. 15 U.S.C. §15(a).

(h) Certain ERISA cases. 29 U.S.C. §1132(e)(1).

(i) Federal Tort Claims Act cases. 28 U.S.C. §1346(b).

(j) Suits against foreign consuls and vice-consuls. 28 U.S.C. §1351.

(k) Suits against a foreign state. 28 U.S.C. §1441(d).

(*l*) Cases in which the FDIC is a party. 12 U.S.C. §1819(b)(2)(A).

NOTE

Congress may vest certain federal courts with jurisdiction over particular disputes and set standards for resolving those disputes. For example, Public Law 109-3 (signed on March 21, 2005) gave the federal district courts in the Middle District of Florida exclusive jurisdiction to hear arguments by Theresa Marie Schiavo's parents against certain defendants. The legislation also established a de novo standard of review and specifically directed that the doctrines of abstention and exhaustion of remedies could not be considered. Such legislative acts are sometimes referred to as "private relief bills." Although the federal courts in the ***Schiavo*** *case assumed the statute's constitutionality, it is unclear whether such legislation is in fact constitutional. See* ***Schiavo v. Schiavo****, 404 F.3d 1270, 1272 (11th Cir.2005) (Birch, J., concurring).*

(3) Exclusive state jurisdiction. Congress has, in rare cases, created a private cause of action that can be pursued only in a state court. ***Wade v. Blue***, 369 F.3d 407, 410 (4th Cir.2004); *see* ***Gulf Offshore***, 453 U.S. at 478 n.4.

2. Implied federal causes of action. Even if Congress does not specifically create a private cause of action as part of a statute, some statutes may imply a private cause of action. To determine whether to infer a private cause of action under a federal statute, courts should consider (1) whether Congress intended to create a personal right and (2) whether Congress intended to create a private remedy. *E.g.*, ***Wisniewski v. Rodale, Inc.***, 510 F.3d 294, 301 (3d Cir.2007) (no implied private cause of action under 39 U.S.C. §3009); *see* ***Alexander v. Sandoval***, 532 U.S. 275, 286-87 (2001); ***Orkin v. Taylor***, 487 F.3d 734, 739 (9th Cir.2007). The factors in ***Cort v. Ash***, 422 U.S. 66, 78 (1975), are instructive in the analysis: (1) whether the plaintiffs are part of the class for whose special benefit the statute was enacted, (2) whether there is any indication of congressional intent to create or deny a private remedy, (3) whether such a remedy is consistent with the underlying purpose of the statute, and (4) whether the matter is one traditionally relegated to the states. *See* ***Touche Ross & Co. v. Redington***, 442 U.S. 560, 575 (1979) (factors do not have equal weight; central inquiry is whether Congress intended to create private cause of action); ***Orkin***, 487 F.3d at 739 (most important factor is congressional intent; other three factors are actually indications of congressional intent); *see, e.g.*, ***Parks Sch. of Bus. v. Symington***, 51 F.3d 1480, 1484 (9th Cir.1995) (no implied private cause of action under Higher Education Act); ***In re Corestates Trust Fee Litig.***, 39 F.3d 61, 68-69 (3d Cir.1994) (no implied private cause of action under 12 U.S.C. §92a). Perhaps the most commonly invoked example of an implied private cause of action is §10(b) of the Securities Exchange Act of 1934, 15 U.S.C. §78j(b).

3. State-law claim with substantial federal question. In a few instances when state law, not federal law, created the cause of action, there may still be federal-question jurisdiction. ***Franchise Tax Bd. v. Construction Laborers Vacation Trust***, 463 U.S. 1, 13 (1983). To determine whether there is federal-question jurisdiction over a cause of action created by state law, the court must decide if (1) a federal right is an essential element of the state-law claim, (2) interpretation of the federal right is necessary to resolve the case, (3) the question of federal law is substantial, and (4) the federal forum can entertain the case without disturbing any congressionally approved balance of federal and state judicial responsibilities. *See id.*; ***Howery***, 243 F.3d at 917; *see, e.g.*, ***Grable & Sons Metal***, 545 U.S. at 314-15 (federal-question jurisdiction triggered in state-court action to quiet title when P alleged IRS did not give adequate notice of sale, requiring interpretation of federal tax provision); ***Singh***, 538 F.3d at 338-39 (no federal-question jurisdiction in state-court malpractice suit based on representation in previous trademark dispute

because substantial question of law was state malpractice law, not federal trademark law; federal law was only tangentially relevant to state claim). The mere presence of a federal issue in a state-law cause of action, however, does not automatically confer federal-question jurisdiction. ***Merrell Dow Pharms.***, 478 U.S. at 813; *e.g.*, ***Franchise Tax Bd.***, 463 U.S. at 13-14 (no federal-question jurisdiction when federal issue was presented by complaint for state declaratory judgment). Generally, if a federal law does not provide a private cause of action, a state-law cause of action based on its violation does not raise a federal question. ***Merrell Dow Pharms.***, 478 U.S. at 814; ***Mulcahey v. Columbia Organic Chems. Co.***, 29 F.3d 148, 151 (4th Cir.1994); ***City of Huntsville v. City of Madison***, 24 F.3d 169, 174 (11th Cir.1994).

4. Preemption. If Congress preempts a particular claim by statute, any complaint raising such a claim necessarily presents a federal issue. ***Metropolitan Life Ins. v. Taylor***, 481 U.S. 58, 63-64 (1987); *see also* ***Vaden v. Discover Bank***, 556 U.S. 49, 66-67 (2009) (complaint must present preempted claims; completely preempted counterclaim does not confer federal-question jurisdiction). Preemption can occur in one of three instances: (1) a federal statute expressly preempts state law, (2) federal law "occupies the field," or (3) a state law conflicts with a federal law. ***English v. General Elec. Co.***, 496 U.S. 72, 78-79 (1990); ***Wright v. Allstate Ins.***, 415 F.3d 384, 389 (5th Cir.2005); ***Air Conditioning & Refrigeration Inst. v. Energy Res. Conserv. & Dev. Comm'n***, 410 F.3d 492, 495 (9th Cir.2005); *see also* ***Wyeth v. Levine***, 555 U.S. 555, 565 (2009) (there must be "clear and manifest purpose" by Congress to preempt state-law causes of action). Usually, the issue of federal jurisdiction over a federally preempted action arises when the defendant removes the plaintiff's suit to federal court. For example, if the plaintiff's complaint does not raise a federal question on its face, the defense of federal preemption authorizes removal to federal court when the area of law has been completely preempted by Congress. ***Taylor***, 481 U.S. at 66-67; *see* ***Beneficial Nat'l Bank v. Anderson***, 539 U.S. 1, 8 (2003); *see also* ***Wayne v. DHL Worldwide Express***, 294 F.3d 1179, 1183 (9th Cir. 2002) (complete preemption occurs only when Congress intends to preempt certain state laws and to transfer jurisdiction of subject matter to federal court). The "complete preemption" doctrine is applied narrowly. *See* ***Lontz v. Tharp***, 413 F.3d 435, 439-40 (4th Cir.2005). The following are four examples in which the Supreme Court has applied the doctrine of complete preemption:

(1) ERISA. Suits covered by §502(a) of the Employee Retirement Income Security Act (ERISA) (29 U.S.C. §1132) are completely preempted by federal law. ***Aetna Health Inc. v. Davila***, 542 U.S. 200, 209-10 (2004); *see also* ***Alexander v. Electronic Data Sys.***, 13 F.3d 940, 944-45 (6th Cir.1994) (defense based on 29 U.S.C. §1132 preemption creates federal-question jurisdiction, but defense based on 29 U.S.C. §1144 preemption does not). But state insurance laws and certain types of employee benefit plans are not preempted by ERISA. *See* 29 U.S.C. §1003 (benefit plans), §1144(b)(2)(A) (state insurance laws); ***Metropolitan Life Ins. v. Massachusetts***, 471 U.S. 724, 733 (1985) (same).

(2) LMRA. Suits covered by §301 of the Labor Management Relations Act (LMRA) (29 U.S.C. §185) are completely preempted by federal law. ***Taylor***, 481 U.S. at 63-64; *see* ***Avco Corp. v. Aero Lodge***, 390 U.S. 557, 560 (1968).

(3) Usury claims against national banks. Suits covered by §30 of the National Bank Act (12 U.S.C. §§85, 86) are completely preempted by federal law. ***Beneficial Nat'l Bank***, 539 U.S. at 10-11.

(4) Indian tribe land claims. Suits involving Indian tribe land claims are completely preempted by federal law. *See* ***Oneida Indian Nation v. County of Oneida***, 414 U.S. 661, 666-67 (1974).

§3. DIVERSITY JURISDICTION

The federal courts have diversity jurisdiction when the suit involves a controversy between parties of diverse citizenship and the amount in controversy exceeds $75,000. *See* 28 U.S.C. §1332(a).

§3.1 Is there complete diversity? When a suit is based on diversity jurisdiction, the parties to the suit must be completely diverse—that is, no plaintiff can be a citizen of the same state as any defendant. ***MacGinnitie v. Hobbs Grp.***, 420 F.3d 1234, 1239 (11th Cir.2005); ***Safeco Ins. v. City of White House***, 36 F.3d 540, 545 (6th Cir.1994); *see*

Carden v. Arkoma Assocs., 494 U.S. 185, 187 (1990); ***Ravenswood Inv. Co. v. Avalon Corr. Servs.***, 651 F.3d 1219, 1223 (10th Cir.2011). The only exceptions to the complete-diversity requirement are the Federal Interpleader Act, 28 U.S.C. §1335, the Class Action Fairness Act, 28 U.S.C. §1332(d), and the Multiparty, Multiforum Trial Jurisdiction Act, 28 U.S.C. §1369(a), all of which require only minimal diversity. See "Minimal diversity," ch. 2-C, §3.2.2(1)(a), p. 89; "Minimal diversity," §5.1.2(3), p. 131; "Minimal diversity," §5.2.1, p. 134. Otherwise, for complete diversity to exist, the suit must be between the following:

1. Citizens of different U.S. states. U.S. Const. art. 3, §2, cl. 1; 28 U.S.C. §1332(a)(1).

2. Citizens of a U.S. state and citizens or subjects of a foreign state. U.S. Const. art. 3, §2, cl. 1; 28 U.S.C. §1332(a)(2). But complete diversity is lacking when citizens or subjects of a foreign state—

(1) Appear on both sides of the suit. ***U.S. Motors v. General Motors Eur.***, 551 F.3d 420, 424 (6th Cir. 2008); ***Corporacion Venezolana de Fomento v. Vintero Sales Corp.***, 629 F.2d 786, 790 (2d Cir.1980); *see* ***Allendale Mut. Ins. v. Bull Data Sys.***, 10 F.3d 425, 428 (7th Cir.1993); H.R. Rep. No. 112-10, at 6 (2011).

(2) Are lawfully admitted for permanent residence in the United States and domiciled in the same state as an opposing party. 28 U.S.C. §1332(a)(2); *see* U.S. Const. art. 3, §2; ***MB Fin. v. Stevens***, 678 F.3d 497, 499-500 (7th Cir.2012); Clarification Act, P.L. 112-63, §105, 125 Stat. 762 (2011) (eff. Jan. 6, 2012); *see also* H.R. Rep. No. 112-10, at 6-7 (2011) (28 U.S.C. §1332(a)(2) modestly restricts jurisdiction for permanent-resident aliens). See "Resident alien," §4.1.1(2), p. 127.

3. Citizens of different U.S. states and citizens or subjects of a foreign state that are additional parties on both sides of the suit. U.S. Const. art. 3, §2, cl. 1; 28 U.S.C. §1332(a)(3).

NOTE

Although the presence of aliens on both sides of the suit is fatal to the court's diversity jurisdiction under 28 U.S.C. §1332(a)(2), it is not fatal under 28 U.S.C. §1332(a)(3). ***Tango Music, LLC v. DeadQuick Music, Inc.***, *348 F.3d 244, 245-46 (7th Cir.2003);* ***Dresser Indus. v. Underwriters at Lloyd's of London***, *106 F.3d 494, 498-99 (3d Cir.1997); see* ***IGY Ocean Bay Props., Ltd. v. Ocean Bay Props. I Ltd.***, *534 F.Supp.2d 446, 449 (S.D.N.Y.2008); H.R. Rep. No. 112-10, at 6 (2011).*

---

4. A foreign state as a plaintiff and citizens of a U.S. state or of different U.S. states. U.S. Const. art. 3, §2, cl. 1; 28 U.S.C. §1332(a)(4).

Example 1: In the example below, there is complete diversity because no defendant is a citizen of the same state as Plaintiff.

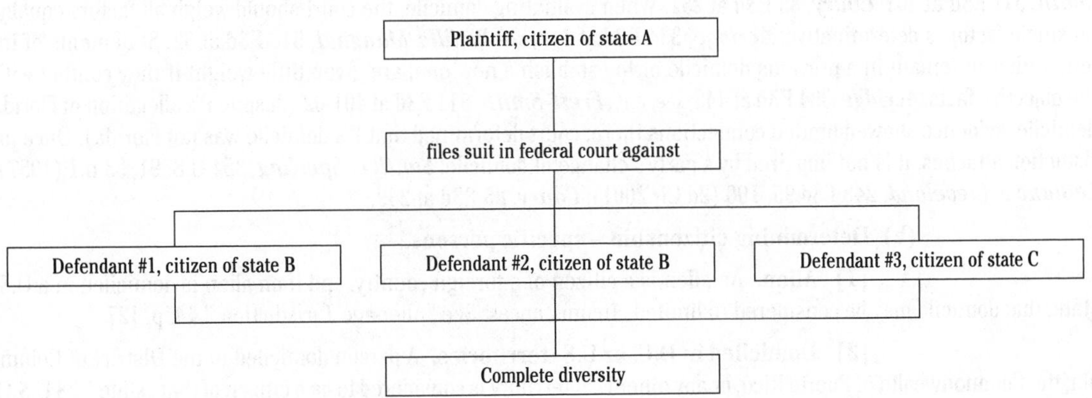

Example 2: In the example below, there is no diversity because Plaintiff #2 and Defendant #3 are citizens of the same state.

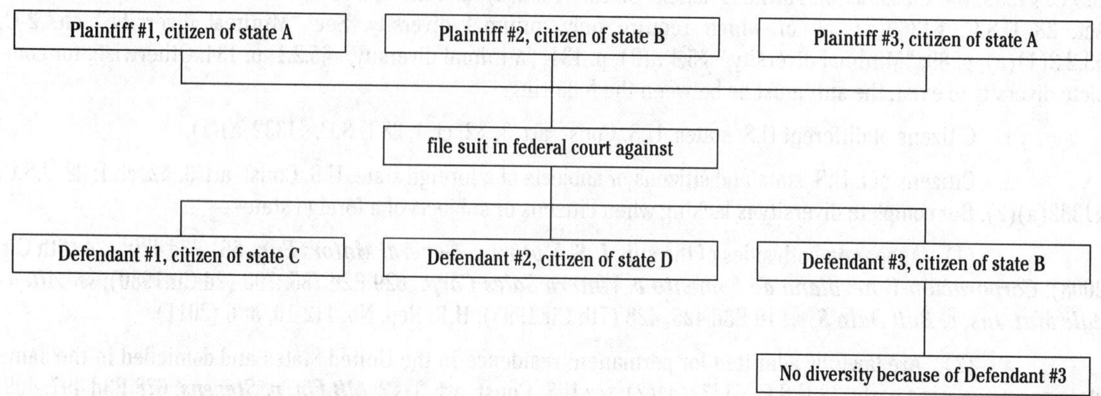

§3.2 Who is considered for diversity jurisdiction?

1. Parties considered for diversity. Diversity jurisdiction is defined in terms of the citizenship of the parties to the suit. 13E Wright, Miller & Cooper §3611; *see* 28 U.S.C. §1332(a). Parties that are often considered in determining diversity jurisdiction include the following:

(1) Natural person.

(a) Determining citizenship – domicile. A person is considered a citizen of the state where the person is domiciled—that is, where the person has established a fixed habitation or abode, intending to remain there permanently or indefinitely. ***Frett-Smith v. Vanterpool***, 511 F.3d 396, 400-01 (3d Cir.2008); ***Linardos v. Fortuna***, 157 F.3d 945, 948 (2d Cir.1998); ***Lew v. Moss***, 797 F.2d 747, 749-50 (9th Cir.1986); *see* ***Heinen v. Northrop Grumman Corp.***, 671 F.3d 669, 670 (7th Cir.2012); ***Coury v. Prot***, 85 F.3d 244, 248-50 (5th Cir.1996). Domicile is a combination of two factors: the residence of the party and the intent to remain there permanently. ***Newton v. Commissioners***, 100 U.S. 548, 562 (1879); ***Padilla-Mangual v. Pavía Hosp.***, 516 F.3d 29, 31-32 (1st Cir.2008); ***Frett-Smith***, 511 F.3d at 401; ***Acridge v. Evangelical Lutheran Good Samaritan Soc.***, 334 F.3d 444, 448 (5th Cir.2003); *see* ***Heinen***, 671 F.3d at 670. A person acquires a domicile at birth; this domicile is presumed to continue unless evidence of a new domicile is introduced. ***Acridge***, 334 F.3d at 448. Factors that courts consider in evaluating the domicile of a person include current residence, voting registration and practices, location of personal and real property, location of bank and brokerage accounts, membership in unions and other organizations, place of employment or business, driver's license and automobile registration, and payment of taxes. ***Padilla-Mangual***, 516 F.3d at 32; ***Frett-Smith***, 511 F.3d at 401; ***Coury***, 85 F.3d at 251. When evaluating domicile, the court should weigh all factors equally; no single factor is determinative. ***Acridge***, 334 F.3d at 448; *see* ***Padilla-Mangual***, 516 F.3d at 32. Statements of intent, either to remain in a previous domicile or to establish a new one, are given little weight if they conflict with the objective facts. ***Acridge***, 334 F.3d at 448; *see, e.g.*, ***Frett-Smith***, 511 F.3d at 401-02 (despite P's allegation of Florida domicile, evidence showed limited connections there; court determined that P's domicile was not Florida). Once jurisdiction attaches, it is not impaired by a party's change of domicile. ***Smith v. Sperling***, 354 U.S. 91, 93 n.1 (1957); ***LeBlanc v. Cleveland***, 248 F.3d 95, 100 (2d Cir.2001); ***Coury***, 85 F.3d at 249.

(b) Determining citizenship – specific persons.

[1] Alien. An alien is a citizen of a foreign country, and if an alien is domiciled in a U.S. state, that domicile may be considered in limited circumstances. See "Alienage Jurisdiction," §4, p. 127.

[2] Domiciled in D.C. or U.S. territories. A person domiciled in the District of Columbia, the Commonwealth of Puerto Rico, or any other U.S. territory is considered to be a citizen of that "state." 28 U.S.C. §1332(e).

[3] Living abroad. A U.S. national living abroad is a citizen of the state where the person is domiciled, if the state is one of the United States. *See* ***Coury***, 85 F.3d at 248; ***Thompson v. Deloitte & Touche LLP***, 503 F.Supp.2d 1118, 1123 (S.D.Iowa 2007). If the person is domiciled abroad, she is considered a citizen with no state for purposes of diversity jurisdiction, and thus she cannot sue or be sued in federal court. ***Coury***, 85 F.3d at 248. In other words, under 28 U.S.C. §1332(a), a U.S. national domiciled abroad is neither a citizen of a U.S. state nor a citizen of a foreign state. *See* ***Lemos v. Pateras***, 5 F.Supp.2d 164, 165 (S.D.N.Y.1998). The person's status as a dual national citizen does not change this result. *See* ***Frett-Smith***, 511 F.3d at 400; ***Coury***, 85 F.3d at 250; ***Action S.A. v. Marc Rich & Co.***, 951 F.2d 504, 507 (2d Cir.1991). See "Note," §4.1.1, p. 127.

[4] Decedent, infant, or incompetent. The citizenship of a decedent, infant, or incompetent—not the citizenship of the person's legal representative—controls. 28 U.S.C. §1332(c)(2); ***Moore v. North Am. Sports, Inc.***, 623 F.3d 1325, 1327 n.2 (11th Cir.2010); ***Gustafson v. Zumbrunnen***, 546 F.3d 398, 400 (7th Cir.2008). The purpose of 28 U.S.C. §1332(c)(2) is to prevent parties from manufacturing diversity jurisdiction by appointing an out-of-state representative or destroying it by appointing an in-state representative. ***Gustafson***, 546 F.3d at 402; *see* ***Jones v. Petty-Ray Geophysical, Geosource, Inc.***, 954 F.2d 1061, 1064 (5th Cir.1992). In wrongful-death suits, the citizenship of the plaintiff, not the decedent, generally controls. *See* ***Steinlage v. Mayo Clinic Rochester***, 435 F.3d 913, 918-19 (8th Cir.2006); ***Tank v. Chronister***, 160 F.3d 597, 601 (10th Cir.1998). *But see* ***Palmer v. Hospital Auth. of Randolph Cty.***, 22 F.3d 1559, 1562 & n.1 (11th Cir.1994) (when P brought suit in multiple representative capacities, including under wrongful-death statute, decedent's citizenship controlled); ***Wheelock v. Sport Kites, Inc.***, 839 F.Supp. 730, 734 n.3 (D.Haw.1993) (decedent's citizenship controls); ***Liu v. Westchester Cty. Med. Ctr.***, 837 F.Supp. 82, 83 (S.D.N.Y.1993) (same). Most courts hold that a represented party can make a change of domicile to meet the requirements of 28 U.S.C. §1332(c)(2). *See* ***Acridge***, 334 F.3d at 448 (person determined to be incompetent by court can change domicile as long as person understands nature and effect of act); *see also* ***Juvelis v. Snider***, 68 F.3d 648, 655 (3d Cir.1995) (incompetent person whose parents had foreign domicile could change from foreign to Pennsylvania domicile to receive state benefits after he reached age of majority). Courts are divided on whether a representative can change a party's domicile, with most holding that the representative can do so when the change is in the party's best interest. ***Acridge***, 334 F.3d at 449-50; ***Rishell v. Jane Phillips Episcopal Mem'l Med. Ctr.***, 12 F.3d 171, 173-74 (10th Cir.1993); *see also* ***Dakuras v. Edwards***, 312 F.3d 256, 258 (7th Cir.2002) (choice of domicile is within responsibility of parent or guardian). *But see* ***Long v. Sasser***, 91 F.3d 645, 647 (4th Cir. 1996) (guardian could not change domicile of incompetent, even if move was in incompetent's best interest).

[5] Class representative or party. In a class action in which jurisdiction is not based on 28 U.S.C. §1332(d), only the citizenship of the named parties or the class representative is considered. ***Snyder v. Harris***, 394 U.S. 332, 340 (1969); ***Leonhardt v. Western Sugar Co.***, 160 F.3d 631, 637 n.3 (10th Cir.1998), *overruled on other grounds*, ***Exxon Mobil Corp. v. Allapattah Servs.***, 545 U.S. 546 (2005); ***Triggs v. John Crump Toyota, Inc.***, 154 F.3d 1284, 1288 (11th Cir.1998); ***In re "Agent Orange" Prod. Liab. Litig.***, 818 F.2d 145, 162 (2d Cir.1987); *see also* ***Aetna Cas. & Sur. Co. v. Iso-Tex, Inc.***, 75 F.3d 216, 218 (5th Cir.1996) (noting and applying by analogy the rule that citizenship of unnamed class members is disregarded for jurisdictional purposes).

[6] Trustee. If the trustee is the real party in interest, the trustee's citizenship is the only one that counts. *See* ***Navarro Sav. Ass'n v. Lee***, 446 U.S. 458, 463 (1980). If the trust sues or is sued as an entity, the citizenship of the beneficiaries is considered. ***Emerald Investors Trust v. Gaunt Parsippany Partners***, 492 F.3d 192, 203 (3d Cir.2007).

(2) Business entities.

(a) Corporation. A corporation is considered a citizen of every U.S. state and foreign state where it is incorporated and the U.S. state or foreign state where it has its principal place of business. 28 U.S.C. §1332(c)(1).

NOTE

Before the Clarification Act (which applies to suits commenced before January 6, 2012), courts struggled with former §1332(c)(1) when a suit involved a U.S. corporation with foreign contacts or a foreign corporation that operated in the United States because the statute did not specify whether the term "State" included contacts with a foreign state. See Clarification Act, P.L. 112-63, §105, 125 Stat. 762 (2011) (eff. Jan. 6, 2012); H.R. Rep. No. 112-10, at 8-9 (2011). The Clarification Act resolved the confusion about the proper citizenship of U.S. corporations with foreign contacts or foreign corporations that operate in the United States. H.R. Rep. No. 112-10, at 8-9 (2011).

[1] Determining citizenship. Under the Clarification Act, the 2011 amendments to §1332(c)(1) made clear that a corporation is deemed to be a citizen of both (1) *every* U.S. state and foreign state of incorporation and (2) the U.S. state or foreign state where it has its principal place of business (i.e., its "nerve center"). *See **Bayerische Landesbank, N.Y. Branch v. Aladdin Capital Mgmt.***, 692 F.3d 42, 51 (2d Cir.2012) (dicta); H.R. Rep. No. 112-10, at 9 (2011). By deeming such corporations to be citizens of both a U.S. state and a foreign state, §1332(c)(1) prevents courts from exercising diversity jurisdiction in the following circumstances:

[a] A foreign corporation with its principal place of business in a U.S. state sues or is sued by a citizen of that same U.S. state. H.R. Rep. No. 112-10, at 9 (2011).

[b] A U.S. corporation with its principal place of business abroad sues or is sued by a citizen of a foreign state. *See id.* at 9-10.

NOTE

In these circumstances, a suit could be pursued in state court. H.R. Rep. No. 112-10, at 9 (2011).

[2] Determining principal place of business. A corporation's principal place of business is the place where the corporation's high-level officers direct, control, and coordinate the corporation's activities. ***Hertz Corp. v. Friend***, ___ U.S. ___, 130 S.Ct. 1181, 1192 (2010); ***Central W.Va. Energy Co. v. Mountain State Carbon, LLC***, 636 F.3d 101, 103-04 (4th Cir.2011). This place is often referred to as the corporation's "nerve center." ***Hertz Corp.***, ___ U.S. at ___, 130 S.Ct. at 1192. The nerve center will usually be the state where the corporation has its headquarters. *Id.*; *see **Davis v. HSBC Bank Nev.***, 557 F.3d 1026, 1028 (9th Cir.2009); ***MacGinnitie v. Hobbs Grp.***, 420 F.3d 1234, 1239 (11th Cir.2005). If a party challenges a corporation's principal place of business, the corporation must produce sufficient proof to establish its nerve center. *E.g., **Hertz Corp.***, ___ U.S. at ___, 130 S.Ct. at 1194-95 (insufficient proof to produce only Securities and Exchange Commission form that lists location of corporation's principal executive offices); *see **Harris v. Rand***, 682 F.3d 846, 851 (9th Cir.2012) (even if no motion to dismiss has been filed, court may require more specific pleading from corporation if allegations about its principal place of business are implausible). The alleged nerve center must be more than a mail drop box, a bare office with only a computer, or the location of an annual retreat. ***Hertz Corp.***, ___ U.S. at ___, 130 S.Ct. at 1195. If a corporation uses such insufficient proof in an attempt to manipulate jurisdiction, the court should determine the corporation's place of actual direction, control, and coordination. *See id.*

NOTE

*In 2010, the Supreme Court resolved a disagreement over the standard for determining a corporation's principal place of business. See **Hertz Corp.**, ___ U.S. at ___, 130 S.Ct. at 1191-92. The Court, in adopting the nerve-center test, declined to adopt the more complex "total activities" test, which determined a principal place of business by identifying the state where the corporation conducts a majority of its sales or production. See id. In adopting the less complex nerve-center test, the Court noted that in certain circumstances the test could produce counterintuitive results (e.g., when a corporation's visible business activities take place in New Jersey but*

its top officers direct those activities from New York, the principal place of business is New York) or could be difficult to apply (e.g., when a corporation divides its command and coordinating functions among officers who work at several different locations and communicate only over the Internet). See id. at ___, 130 S.Ct. at 1194. Despite these issues, the Court preferred a more uniform jurisdictional rule that focused on the location of the corporation's overall direction, control, and coordination, rather than a rule requiring the courts to evaluate and weigh corporate functions, assets, and revenues. Id.; see ***Central W.Va. Energy****, 636 F.3d at 107.*

[3] Subsidiary corporation. A subsidiary corporation may have a principal place of business in a state other than that of its parent corporation. ***Beightol v. Capitol Bankers Life Ins.***, 730 F.Supp. 190, 193 (E.D.Wis.1990); ***Armstrong v. Goldblatt Tool Co.***, 609 F.Supp. 736, 738 (D.Kan.1985). If the subsidiary is merely an alter ego or agent of the parent corporation, the parent corporation's principal place of business determines citizenship. ***Beightol***, 730 F.Supp. at 193; ***Armstrong***, 609 F.Supp. at 738.

(b) Insurance company. In a direct-action suit (i.e., a suit in which a plaintiff sues an insurance company directly, without naming as a defendant the insured whose alleged negligence gave rise to the claim) against an insurer—whether incorporated or unincorporated—of a policy or liability-insurance contract, the insurer is deemed to be a citizen of all of the following:

[1] Every U.S. state and foreign state where the insured is a citizen;

[2] Every U.S. state and foreign state where the insurer has been incorporated; and

[3] The U.S. state or foreign state where the insurer has its principal place of business. 28 U.S.C. §1332(c)(1); *see* H.R. Rep. No. 112-10, at 10-11 (2011).

NOTE

Before the Clarification Act (which applies to suits commenced before January 6, 2012), former 28 U.S.C. §1332(c)(1) did not address when insurance companies were incorporated abroad or had a foreign principal place of business. See Clarification Act, P.L. 112-63, §105, 125 Stat. 762 (2011) (eff. Jan. 6, 2012); H.R. Rep. No. 112-10, at 11 (2011). After the Clarification Act, the citizenship of an insurer in a direct-action suit is the same as what is provided for corporations; in other words, §1332(c)(1) now recognizes an insurer's foreign contacts. H.R. Rep. No. 112-10, at 10-11 (2011). *See "Corporation," §3.2.1(2)(a), p. 119.*

(c) Other business associations. The citizenship of a partnership, a limited-liability company, or an unincorporated association is determined by the citizenship of each member of the entity, not by the state where the entity was organized. ***Harvey v. Grey Wolf Drilling Co.***, 542 F.3d 1077, 1080 (5th Cir.2008); ***Safeco Ins. v. City of White House***, 36 F.3d 540, 544-45 (6th Cir.1994); *see* ***Carden v. Arkoma Assocs.***, 494 U.S. 185, 195-96 (1990) (limited partners); ***United Steelworkers v. R.H. Bouligny, Inc.***, 382 U.S. 145, 146-47 (1965) (labor-union members); ***Central W.Va. Energy***, 636 F.3d at 103 (LLC members); *see also* ***Brewer v. SmithKline Beacham Corp.***, 774 F.Supp.2d 721, 725-26 (E.D.Pa.2011) (when holding company was sole member of LLC and was nonoperating corporation that delegated its operational and business decisions to LLC, court used nerve-center test from ***Hertz*** to determine that holding company's citizenship was LLC's nerve center). This rule applies even for complex or multitiered partnerships. *See* ***Cerebus Partners v. Gadsby & Hannah***, 976 F.Supp. 119, 123 (D.R.I.1997). For a discussion of the citizenship of unincorporated associations under the Class Action Fairness Act (CAFA), see "Unincorporated associations," §5.1.2(3)(b)[2], p. 132; for a discussion of the citizenship of foreign organizations and entities, see "Other business associations," §4.1.2(2), p. 128.

(d) Banking association. A banking association is considered a citizen of the state where its main office is located as provided in its articles of association. 28 U.S.C. §1348; ***Wachovia Bank v. Schmidt***, 546 U.S. 303, 307 (2006).

(3) Real party in interest. If a nominal party sues or is being sued, the citizenship of the unnamed real party in interest should be considered. *See* ***Associated Ins. Mgmt. v. Arkansas Gen. Agency, Inc.***, 149 F.3d 794, 796 (8th Cir.1998) (diversity is tested by citizenship of real parties to controversy); *see, e.g.*, ***In re Lorazepam & Clorazepate Antitrust Litig.***, 631 F.3d 537, 540 (D.C.Cir.2011) (when health-insurance companies sued drug manufacturers for antitrust violations, unnamed customers of insurance companies should have been treated as real parties in interest for diversity-jurisdiction purposes). See "Nominal party," §3.2.2(1), this page. If the real party in interest is nondiverse, the court may be able to restore diversity if it determines that the party is not required under FRCP 19. *See* ***In re Lorazepam & Clorazepate Antitrust Litig.***, 631 F.3d at 542.

2. Parties not considered for diversity. Parties that are not considered in determining diversity jurisdiction include the following:

(1) Nominal party. The citizenship of a nominal party can be disregarded for purposes of determining diversity jurisdiction. ***Navarro***, 446 U.S. at 461; ***Brown v. Francis***, 75 F.3d 860, 865 (3d Cir.1996); 13E Wright, Miller & Cooper §3606. A party is "nominal" if it does not have a real interest in the outcome of the litigation. *See, e.g.*, ***Associated Ins. Mgmt.***, 149 F.3d at 796 (agent suing on behalf of real parties in interest was nominal party); ***U.S. Fire Ins. Co. v. Charter Fin. Grp.***, 851 F.2d 957, 958 n.3 (7th Cir.1988) (unknown tort claimants were nominal parties).

(2) Fictitious party. The courts are split on whether a person sued under a fictitious name (e.g., "John Doe" defendant), whose citizenship is never known, can be disregarded for purposes of determining diversity jurisdiction. Some courts hold that simply naming a John Doe defendant defeats diversity jurisdiction. *See* ***Howell v. Tribune Entm't Co.***, 106 F.3d 215, 218 (7th Cir.1997); ***Fifty Assocs. v. Prudential Ins.***, 446 F.2d 1187, 1191 (9th Cir.1970); ***Commonwealth Prop. Advocates, LLC v. Ocwen Loan Servicing, LLC***, No. 2:10-CV-86 (D.Utah 2010) (slip op.; 4-29-10); ***Schwarz v. Midwest Airlines, Inc.***, No. 09-CV-668 (E.D.Wis.2009) (slip op.; 7-23-09); ***Rich & Rich Prtshp. v. Poetman Records USA***, No. 08-42-ART (E.D.Ky.2008) (slip op.; 4-24-08); ***Stephens v. Halliburton Co.***, No. 3:02-CV-1442-L (N.D.Tex.2003) (slip op.; 9-5-03). Other courts hold that merely including fictitious defendants does not defeat diversity jurisdiction, but the plaintiff runs the risk of having its case dismissed if the defendant is later determined to be an indispensable, nondiverse party. *See* ***Doe I v. Ciolli***, 611 F.Supp.2d 216, 219-20 (D. Conn.2009); ***Macheras v. Center Art Galleries-Haw., Inc.***, 776 F.Supp. 1436, 1440 (D.Haw.1991); ***Johnson v. Rite Aid***, No. 10-2012 (D.N.J.2011) (slip op.; 6-28-11); ***Merrill Lynch Bus. Fin. Servs. v. Heritage Packaging Corp.***, No. CV-06-3951 (E.D.N.Y.2007) (slip op.; 9-25-07); ***W. Weber, Co. v. Kosack***, No. 96 Civ.9581 (LMM) (S.D.N.Y.1997) (slip op.; 10-24-97).

(3) Unnamed party. The citizenship of an unnamed party who is neither required under FRCP 19 nor a real party in interest can be disregarded for purposes of determining diversity jurisdiction. *See* ***F.&H.R. Farman-Farmaian Consulting Eng'rs Firm v. Harza Eng'g***, 882 F.2d 281, 284 (7th Cir.1989); ***United Tel. Co. v. Ameritech Servs.***, No. 2:10-CV-249 (S.D.Ohio 2011) (slip op.; 1-7-11); *see also* ***Lincoln Prop. Co. v. Roche***, 546 U.S. 81, 93 (2005) (if named party's interest is real, fact that other interested parties are not joined will not affect jurisdiction).

(4) Substituted defendant. The citizenship of a defendant who is later added as a substituted party under FRCP 25 can be disregarded for purposes of determining diversity jurisdiction. *E.g.*, ***Burka v. Aetna Life Ins.***, 87 F.3d 478, 480 (D.C.Cir.1996) (substitution of party under FRCP 25 did not defeat diversity); *see* ***Freeport-McMoRan, Inc. v. K N Energy, Inc.***, 498 U.S. 426, 428 (1991); *see also* ***Wichita R.R. & Light Co. v. Public Utils. Comm'n***, 260 U.S. 48, 53-54 (1922) (diversity jurisdiction was unaffected by later intervention "of a party whose presence is not essential to a decision of the controversy between the original parties"); 13E Wright, Miller & Cooper §3608 (change of parties will not defeat jurisdiction if nature of suit remains same or if there is no collusion or obvious attempt to avoid diversity).

3. Parties who cannot sue or be sued in diversity. Certain parties cannot sue or be sued based on diversity jurisdiction, so they must be dismissed from the suit. If that party is the only plaintiff or defendant or is a required party under FRCP 19, there is no diversity jurisdiction, and the case must be dismissed. *See* ***Ramada Inns, Inc. v. Rosemount Mem'l Park Ass'n***, 598 F.2d 1303, 1306 (3d Cir.1979). These parties commonly include the following:

(1) U.S. government. The U.S. government is not a citizen of a state and thus cannot sue or be sued in federal court on the basis of diversity jurisdiction. ***Texas v. Interstate Commerce Comm'n***, 258 U.S. 158, 160 (1922); ***General Ry. Signal Co. v. Corcoran***, 921 F.2d 700, 703 (7th Cir.1991).

(2) State or territory. Neither a state nor a U.S. territory is a citizen of a state and thus cannot sue or be sued in federal court on the basis of diversity jurisdiction. ***Minnesota v. Northern Secs. Co.***, 194 U.S. 48, 63 (1904) (state); ***Brown***, 75 F.3d at 865 (territory).

(3) U.S. citizen domiciled abroad. A U.S. citizen domiciled abroad is neither a citizen of any state nor a citizen of a foreign state and thus cannot sue or be sued in federal court on the basis of diversity jurisdiction. ***Coury***, 85 F.3d at 249-50; 13E Wright, Miller & Cooper §3621; *see* ***Twentieth Century-Fox Film Corp. v. Taylor***, 239 F.Supp. 913, 914 n.2 (S.D.N.Y.1965), *overruled on other grounds*, ***Gardner & Florence Call Cowles Found. v. Empire Inc.***, 754 F.2d 478 (2d Cir.1985).

(4) Stateless alien. A person who is not a citizen of any country—a stateless alien—cannot sue or be sued in federal court on the basis of diversity jurisdiction. ***Kantor v. Wellesley Galleries, Ltd.***, 704 F.2d 1088, 1092 (9th Cir.1983); ***Shoemaker v. Malaxa***, 241 F.2d 129, 129 (2d Cir.1957); 13E Wright, Miller & Cooper §3604; *see* ***Blair Holdings Corp. v. Rubinstein***, 133 F.Supp. 496, 501 (S.D.N.Y.1955). However, such a person can be sued in state court. ***Blair Holdings***, 133 F.Supp. at 501.

4. Parties added to create jurisdiction – collusive joinder. If the court finds that any party, whether by assignment or otherwise, has been improperly or collusively joined to the suit in an effort to manufacture jurisdiction, the court loses jurisdiction over the entire matter. 28 U.S.C. §1359; *see* ***Kramer v. Caribbean Mills, Inc.***, 394 U.S. 823, 827-28 (1969); ***Ambrosia Coal & Constr. Co. v. Pages Morales***, 482 F.3d 1309, 1315 (11th Cir.2007); *see, e.g.*, ***Nike, Inc. v. Comercial Iberica de Exclusivas Deportivas, S.A.***, 20 F.3d 987, 991-92 (9th Cir.1994) (court found collusive assignment when three days before filing suit, P's wholly owned subsidiary assigned its interest to P, thus creating diversity). When determining whether an assignment was made to manufacture jurisdiction, the court should focus on the consideration exchanged for the assigned claim or whether the assignor has retained an interest in the assigned claim. *See, e.g.*, ***Ambrosia Coal & Constr.***, 482 F.3d at 1315-16 (court found no collusive agreement when diverse P's wholly owned, nondiverse subsidiaries assigned their interests to P, thus creating diversity, because assignments were absolute transfers and P was real party in interest).

§3.3 When is amount in controversy satisfied? To invoke diversity jurisdiction, the plaintiff must allege facts showing that the amount in controversy exceeds $75,000, excluding interest and costs. 28 U.S.C. §1332(a); *see, e.g.*, ***Freeland v. Liberty Mut. Fire Ins.***, 632 F.3d 250, 252-53 (6th Cir.2011) (in declaratory-judgment action in which controversy concerned possible additional insurance coverage of exactly $75,000, case was remanded because amount did not exceed $75,000). The only exceptions to this rule are (1) federal statutory interpleader suits, which require an amount in controversy of at least $500, and (2) suits under the Class Action Fairness Act (CAFA), which require an amount in controversy of more than $5 million. *See* 28 U.S.C. §§1332(d)(2), 1335(a). See "Amount in controversy," ch. 2-C, §3.2.2(1)(b), p. 89; "Amount in controversy," §5.1.2(2), p. 130. Generally, a case satisfies the amount-in-controversy requirement if the complaint makes a good-faith claim for an amount above the jurisdictional amount. ***Saint Paul Mercury Indem. Co. v. Red Cab Co.***, 303 U.S. 283, 288-89 (1938); ***Kopp v. Kopp***, 280 F.3d 883, 884 (8th Cir.2002); ***Crum v. Circus Circus Enters.***, 231 F.3d 1129, 1131 (9th Cir.2000); *see* ***Esquilín-Mendoza v. Don King Prods.***, 638 F.3d 1, 4-5 (1st Cir.2011) (P's good-faith claim includes element of objective good faith; thus, amount-in-controversy requirement may not be satisfied if, despite P's good-faith claim for amount exceeding $75,000, there is legal certainty that claim is below $75,000). If a plaintiff's allegation of the amount in controversy is challenged, the plaintiff must support its contention that there is jurisdiction by a preponderance of the evidence. ***Meridian Sec. Ins. v. Sadowski***, 441 F.3d 536, 543 (7th Cir.2006); ***Kopp***, 280 F.3d at 884. The court should give the plaintiff an opportunity to present facts by affidavit or deposition or in an evidentiary hearing to prove its amount in controversy. ***Suber v. Chrysler Corp.***, 104 F.3d 578, 583-84 (3d Cir.1997). If it is apparent to a legal certainty that the plaintiff cannot recover the jurisdictional amount, either from the face of the pleadings or after submission of proof, the suit should be dismissed. ***Saint Paul Mercury Indem.***, 303 U.S. at 289; ***Esquilín-Mendoza***, 638 F.3d at 3; ***Kopp***, 280 F.3d

at 884; ***Crum***, 231 F.3d at 1131; *see* ***Indiana Hi-Rail Corp. v. Decatur Junction Ry.***, 37 F.3d 363, 366 (7th Cir.1994); *see also* 28 U.S.C. §1332(b) (if P recovers less than jurisdictional amount, court may deny P costs and even assess costs against P).

NOTE

The amount in controversy is determined when the complaint is initially filed. ***Suber***, *104 F.3d at 583. A reduction of the amount in controversy because of events occurring after the suit is filed will not divest the court of jurisdiction.* *See "When is diversity jurisdiction determined?," §3.4, p. 125.*

1. Injunction suit. In a suit seeking injunctive relief, the amount in controversy is usually measured by the value of the right sought to be protected by the equitable relief. *See* ***Hunt v. Washington State Apple Adver. Comm'n***, 432 U.S. 333, 347 (1977); ***Morrison v. Allstate Indem. Co.***, 228 F.3d 1255, 1268 (11th Cir.2000). In determining the amount in controversy, courts are divided on whether to consider the perspective of either party or only the plaintiff's perspective. ***Everett v. Verizon Wireless, Inc.***, 460 F.3d 818, 829 (6th Cir.2006); *see* ***Uhl v. Thoroughbred Tech. & Telecomms.***, 309 F.3d 978, 983 (7th Cir.2002) (P's perspective is measured by value of injunction; D's perspective is measured by cost of complying with injunction). *Compare* ***Uhl***, 309 F.3d at 983 (either perspective), ***In re Ford Motor Co.***, 264 F.3d 952, 958 (9th Cir.2001) (same), *and* ***Oklahoma Retail Grocers Ass'n v. Wal-Mart Stores***, 605 F.2d 1155, 1159 (10th Cir.1979) (same), *with* ***Cohen v. Office Depot, Inc.***, 204 F.3d 1069, 1077 (11th Cir.2000) (P's perspective), ***Burns v. Massachusetts Mut. Life Ins.***, 820 F.2d 246, 248 (8th Cir.1987) (same), *and* ***Kheel v. Port of N.Y. Auth.***, 457 F.2d 46, 48-49 (2d Cir.1972) (same). If the plaintiff does not plead a monetary value, the court may look outside the pleadings for proof of damages. ***United Food & Commercial Workers Un. v. CenterMark Props. Meriden Square, Inc.***, 30 F.3d 298, 305 (2d Cir.1994). However, courts will not speculate about value. *See, e.g., id.* at 306 (no diversity jurisdiction because court could not put monetary value on right of free speech).

2. Declaratory-judgment suit. In a suit seeking declaratory relief, the amount in controversy is measured by the value of the object of the litigation, the extent of the injury to be prevented, or the value of the right to be protected. *See* ***Hartford Ins. v. Lou-Con Inc.***, 293 F.3d 908, 910 (5th Cir.2002); ***Energy Catering Servs. v. Burrow***, 911 F.Supp. 221, 223 (E.D.La.1995).

3. Attorney fees. Attorney fees are included as part of the amount in controversy when they are recoverable by statute or contract. ***Grant v. Chevron Phillips Chem. Co.***, 309 F.3d 864, 873-74 (5th Cir.2002); ***Suber***, 104 F.3d at 585; 14AA Wright, Miller & Cooper §3712; *see also* ***Galt G/S v. JSS Scandinavia***, 142 F.3d 1150, 1156 (9th Cir. 1998) (fees included whether authorizing statute was mandatory or discretionary).

4. Aggregation of claims. Some claims can be aggregated to satisfy the amount-in-controversy requirement, while others cannot.

(1) Single plaintiff, multiple claims. When a single plaintiff sues a single defendant, the plaintiff can join as many claims, regardless of their nature, as the plaintiff has against that defendant to achieve the jurisdictional amount. ***Hunter v. United Van Lines***, 746 F.2d 635, 650 (9th Cir.1984); ***Airlines Reporting Corp. v. S&N Travel, Inc.***, 857 F.Supp. 1043, 1049 (E.D.N.Y.1994), *aff'd*, 58 F.3d 857 (2d Cir.1995); ***Assurance Alliance, Inc. v. Kujak Transp.***, 829 F.Supp. 1021, 1022 (N.D.Ill.1993); 6A Wright, Miller & Kane §1588; *see, e.g.,* ***Alberty v. Western Sur. Co.***, 249 F.2d 537, 538 (10th Cir.1957) (P could aggregate two claims against D to reach minimum amount).

(2) Multiple plaintiffs, separate claims. The claims of several plaintiffs for separate and distinct injuries cannot be aggregated to meet the minimum amount required for diversity jurisdiction. ***Snyder v. Harris***, 394 U.S. 332, 338 (1969); ***Gibson v. Chrysler Corp.***, 261 F.3d 927, 943 (9th Cir.2001); ***H&D Tire & Auto.-Hardware, Inc. v. Pitney Bowes Inc. ("H&D Tire II")***, 250 F.3d 302, 304-05 (5th Cir.2001); ***Anthony v. Security Pac. Fin. Servs.***, 75 F.3d 311, 315 (7th Cir.1996); ***In re Corestates Trust Fee Litig.***, 39 F.3d 61, 64 (3d Cir.1994); *see* ***Friedman v. New York Life Ins.***, 410 F.3d 1350, 1357 & n.7 (11th Cir.2005) (if injunctive relief protects rights that are separate and distinct, value of injunction to individual Ps cannot be aggregated).

CAUTION

For class actions not covered by the Class Action Fairness Act (CAFA), if one member of a plaintiff class meets the amount-in-controversy requirement, the court can exercise supplemental jurisdiction under 28 U.S.C. §1367 over other class members who do not meet that requirement. See ***Exxon Mobil Corp. v. Allapattah Servs.****, 545 U.S. 546, 571-72 (2005). See "Pendent-claim jurisdiction," §6.2.1, p. 135. For class actions covered by CAFA, see "Multiparty Jurisdiction," §5, p. 129.*

(3) Multiple plaintiffs, undivided claim. When the plaintiffs share a common and undivided claim and the undivided claim satisfies the minimum amount for diversity jurisdiction, the claim can be aggregated. ***Snyder***, 394 U.S. at 335; ***Gibson***, 261 F.3d at 943; ***Morrison***, 228 F.3d at 1262-63; ***Leonhardt v. Western Sugar Co.***, 160 F.3d 631, 637 (10th Cir.1998), *overruled in part on other grounds*, ***Exxon Mobil Corp. v. Allapattah Servs.***, 545 U.S. 546 (2005); ***Allen v. R&H Oil & Gas Co.***, 63 F.3d 1326, 1330 (5th Cir.1995); *see* ***Mitchell v. GEICO***, 115 F.Supp.2d 1322, 1326 (M.D.Ala.2000) (when Ps in class action seek injunctive relief to enforce common right, value of injunction must be aggregated).

(4) Multiple plaintiffs, punitive damages. Most courts hold that punitive-damages claims are not "common and undivided" and thus cannot be aggregated to meet the amount-in-controversy requirement. *See* ***Gibson***, 261 F.3d at 947; ***H&D Tire & Auto.-Hardware, Inc. v. Pitney Bowes Inc. ("H&D Tire I")***, 227 F.3d 326, 330 (5th Cir.2000); ***Cohen***, 204 F.3d at 1076-77; ***Gilman v. BHC Secs., Inc.***, 104 F.3d 1418, 1430 (2d Cir.1997); ***Anthony***, 75 F.3d at 315.

(5) Multiple plaintiffs, attorney fees. If a statute awards attorney fees to the named plaintiffs in a class action, the fees are attributed solely to the class representatives. ***H&D Tire I***, 227 F.3d at 330. If the statute does not dictate that a fee award must be attributed solely to the representative party in a class action, the fee award is attributed to the plaintiff class as a whole and is allocated pro rata among the members for purposes of determining the amount in controversy. *Id.*; *see also* ***Gibson***, 261 F.3d at 942-43 (attorney fees cannot be aggregated to reach jurisdictional amount); ***Darden v. Ford Consumer Fin. Co.***, 200 F.3d 753, 758 & n.4 (11th Cir.2000) (declining to aggregate attorney fees for jurisdictional purposes when statute entitled "any person who is injured" to attorney fees).

(6) Multiple defendants. Separate and distinct claims against several defendants cannot be aggregated even though the parties may be joined under the joinder rule. ***Jewell v. Grain Dealers Mut. Ins.***, 290 F.2d 11, 13 (5th Cir.1961). Claims against several defendants can be aggregated to meet the jurisdictional amount only if all the defendants are jointly liable. *Id.*; ***North Am. Mech. Servs. v. Hubert***, 859 F.Supp. 1186, 1189 (C.D.Ill.1994); *see* ***Chase Manhattan Bank v. Aldridge***, 906 F.Supp. 870, 874 (S.D.N.Y.1995).

§3.4 When is diversity jurisdiction determined?

1. Time-of-filing rule. Diversity jurisdiction is usually determined by the facts on the date the complaint was filed for suits initially filed in federal court; this is often referred to as the time-of-filing rule. ***Grupo Dataflux v. Atlas Global Grp.***, 541 U.S. 567, 570-71 (2004); ***Freeport-McMoRan, Inc. v. K N Energy, Inc.***, 498 U.S. 426, 428 (1991); ***Ravenswood Inv. Co. v. Avalon Corr. Servs.***, 651 F.3d 1219, 1223 (10th Cir.2011); ***ConnectU LLC v. Zuckerberg***, 522 F.3d 82, 91 (1st Cir.2008); 13E Wright, Miller & Cooper §3608. Generally, once diversity is established, it cannot be impaired (e.g., by a party's later change of domicile or by a later event that reduces the recoverable damages to below the minimum amount in controversy). ***Smith v. Sperling***, 354 U.S. 91, 93 n.1 (1957); *see* ***Saint Paul Mercury Indem. Co. v. Red Cab Co.***, 303 U.S. 283, 289-90 (1938); *see, e.g.*, ***LeBlanc v. Cleveland***, 248 F.3d 95, 99-100 (2d Cir.2001) (although P became citizen of same state as D after suit was filed, diversity jurisdiction was not destroyed); ***Wolde-Meskel v. Vocational Instruction Project Cmty. Servs.***, 166 F.3d 59, 62-63 (2d Cir.1999) (although adverse summary-judgment ruling against one of P's claims reduced amount in controversy, diversity jurisdiction was not destroyed). For suits initially filed in state court and removed to federal court based on diversity jurisdiction, see "Diversity jurisdiction," ch. 4-A, §5.2, p. 249.

2. Exceptions to time-of-filing rule. There are exceptions to the time-of-filing rule.

(1) Nondiverse party added. If diversity jurisdiction was proper at the time of filing, jurisdiction can be destroyed if a nondiverse party is later added as a required party under FRCP 19. *E.g.*, ***Estate of Alvarez v. Donaldson Co.***, 213 F.3d 993, 995-96 (7th Cir.2000) (joinder of parties under FRCP 19(b) defeated diversity); *see* ***Curry v. U.S. Bulk Transp.***, 462 F.3d 536, 540 (6th Cir.2006); ***Cobb v. Delta Exps., Inc.***, 186 F.3d 675, 676-77 (5th Cir.1999); *see, e.g.*, ***Doleac v. Michalson***, 264 F.3d 470, 476 n.5 (5th Cir.2001) (diversity lost when "John Doe" D was identified and was nondiverse). But if the later-added defendant is merely substituted, diversity is usually preserved. See "Substituted defendant," §3.2.2(4), p. 122.

(2) Nondiverse party dismissed. If diversity jurisdiction was improper at the time of filing because of the presence of a nondiverse dispensable party, jurisdiction can be preserved if the court later dismisses the party. *See* ***Grupo Dataflux***, 541 U.S. at 572; ***Newman-Green, Inc. v. Alfonzo-Larrain***, 490 U.S. 826, 836-37 (1989); ***Ravenswood Inv.***, 651 F.3d at 1223. However, if the status of the parties does not change, diversity is determined by the status of the parties at the time of filing. ***Grupo Dataflux***, 541 U.S. at 574.

(3) Parties realigned. If diversity jurisdiction was proper at the time of filing, jurisdiction can be destroyed if the court later realigns the parties according to their real interests in the dispute. ***City of Indianapolis v. Chase Nat'l Bank***, 314 U.S. 63, 69-70 (1941); ***City of Dawson v. Columbia Ave. Sav. Fund***, 197 U.S. 178, 180 (1905); ***Development Fin. Corp. v. Alpha Hous. & Health Care, Inc.***, 54 F.3d 156, 159-60 (3d Cir.1995); ***Zurn Indus. v. Acton Constr. Co.***, 847 F.2d 234, 236 (5th Cir.1988); *see* 14B Wright, Miller, Cooper & Steinman §3723 & n.68. Once the parties are realigned, the court will determine the parties' diversity based on their citizenship on the date the complaint was filed. *See* ***City of Dawson***, 197 U.S. at 180; ***Development Fin.***, 54 F.3d at 160.

§3.5 When can the court decline to exercise diversity jurisdiction? There are recognized exceptions to otherwise proper federal jurisdiction; that is, despite having diversity jurisdiction, a court may choose not to exercise it. *See* ***Marshall v. Marshall***, 547 U.S. 293, 308 (2006); ***Struck v. Cook Cty. Pub. Guardian***, 508 F.3d 858, 859 (7th Cir.2007); *see also* ***Atwood v. Fort Peck Tribal Ct. Assiniboine***, 513 F.3d 943, 947 (9th Cir.2008) (domestic-relations exception applies only to diversity jurisdiction, not federal-question jurisdiction). The rationale for these exceptions is that they are uniquely a matter of state policy and state interest, so the federal courts should not interfere. *See* ***Ankenbrandt v. Richards***, 504 U.S. 689, 703-04 (1992); ***Struck***, 508 F.3d at 859-60; 13E Wright, Miller & Cooper §3609.

1. Domestic relations. A federal court will not exercise its diversity jurisdiction to grant a divorce, determine alimony and support obligations, or settle a controversy over the custody of a child. ***Marshall***, 547 U.S. at 307-08; ***Ankenbrandt***, 504 U.S. at 703; ***Vaughan v. Smithson***, 883 F.2d 63, 64 (10th Cir.1989); *see also* ***Sutter v. Pitts***, 639 F.2d 842, 844 (1st Cir.1981) (court would not hear custody battle recharacterized as civil-rights claim). However, a federal court may hear some tort and contract suits between ex-spouses. *See, e.g.*, ***Wasserman v. Wasserman***, 671 F.2d 832, 834-35 (4th Cir.1982) (tort suit against ex-husband for removing child from ex-wife who had legal custody); ***Crouch v. Crouch***, 566 F.2d 486, 487-88 (5th Cir.1978) (contract suit to collect unpaid alimony); *see also* ***Marshall***, 547 U.S. at 308 (federal courts equipped to deal with complaints alleging commission of torts).

2. Probate. A federal court will not exercise its diversity jurisdiction over a suit that is a "pure" probate matter. ***Marshall***, 547 U.S. at 312; ***Rice v. Rice Found.***, 610 F.2d 471, 475 (7th Cir.1979); *see* ***Waterman v. Canal-La. Bank & Trust Co.***, 215 U.S. 33, 43-45 (1909); 13E Wright, Miller & Cooper §3610; *see, e.g.*, ***Struck***, 508 F.3d at 859 (court would not hear P's suit seeking to revoke appointment of guardian for P's mother). However, a federal court may entertain some collateral matters in a probate proceeding even though the court cannot disturb or affect the possession of the property in the custody of the state court. ***Marshall***, 547 U.S. at 310-11; ***Markham v. Allen***, 326 U.S. 490, 494 (1946); ***Beren v. Ropfogel***, 24 F.3d 1226, 1228 (10th Cir.1994).

§4. ALIENAGE JURISDICTION

The federal courts' power to exercise jurisdiction over foreign citizens is commonly referred to as "alienage" jurisdiction. *See* 28 U.S.C. §1332(a)(2); ***JPMorgan Chase Bank v. Traffic Stream (BVI) Infrastructure Ltd.***, 536 U.S. 88, 91 (2002); ***Coury v. Prot***, 85 F.3d 244, 248 (5th Cir.1996); ***Wilson v. Humphreys (Cayman) Ltd.***, 916 F.2d 1239, 1242 (7th Cir.1990). An alien's right to sue a U.S. citizen or a U.S. citizen's right to sue an alien in federal court arises as a subcategory of diversity jurisdiction from the explicit language of Article 3 of the U.S. Constitution. *See* ***JPMorgan Chase Bank***, 536 U.S. at 94-95. See "Diversity Jurisdiction," §3, p. 116. Persons who are not U.S. citizens can invoke federal jurisdiction by virtue of 28 U.S.C. §1332(a)(2), which provides for jurisdiction over suits between citizens of a U.S. state and citizens of a foreign state. U.S. Const. art. 3, §2, cl. 1; 13E Wright, Miller & Cooper §3621. This type of jurisdiction is intended to give the federal courts protective jurisdiction over matters implicating international relations when the national interest is paramount. ***Wilson***, 916 F.2d at 1242; *see also* ***JPMorgan Chase Bank***, 536 U.S. at 94-95 (alienage jurisdiction created as result of state courts' penchant for disrupting international relations and discouraging foreign investment).

§4.1 Citizenship requirements. Alienage jurisdiction exists in a suit between a U.S. citizen and a citizen or subject of a foreign state. 28 U.S.C. §1332(a)(2). But alienage jurisdiction does not exist if the citizen or subject of a foreign state is both a permanent resident alien and domiciled in the same state as the U.S. citizen. *Id.* There must be complete diversity before a party can invoke alienage jurisdiction. ***Depex Reina 9 Prtshp. v. Texas Int'l Pet. Corp.***, 897 F.2d 461, 465 (10th Cir.1990); ***F.&H.R. Farman-Farmaian Consulting Eng'rs Firm v. Harza Eng'g***, 882 F.2d 281, 284 (7th Cir.1989). Alienage jurisdiction does not encompass a foreign plaintiff suing a foreign defendant. ***Jain v. De Mere***, 51 F.3d 686, 689 (7th Cir.1995); ***Mutuelles Unies v. Kroll & Linstrom***, 957 F.2d 707, 711 (9th Cir. 1992); ***Iwag v. Geisel Compania Maritima, S.A.***, 882 F.Supp. 597, 602 n.2 (S.D.Tex.1995).

1. Natural person. To invoke alienage jurisdiction, an alien must be a citizen or subject of some foreign country. ***JPMorgan Chase Bank v. Traffic Stream (BVI) Infrastructure Ltd.***, 536 U.S. 88, 98-99 (2002); 13E Wright, Miller & Cooper §3621. The test for determining whether a person is a foreign citizen or subject is based on U.S. law. *See* ***JPMorgan Chase Bank***, 536 U.S. at 98-99.

NOTE

Generally, when a person has dual citizenship, only the U.S. nationality is recognized under 28 U.S.C. §1332(a). ***Frett-Smith v. Vanterpool***, *511 F.3d 396, 399-400 (3d Cir.2008);* ***Coury v. Prot***, *85 F.3d 244, 250 (5th Cir.1996);* ***Mutuelles Unies***, *957 F.2d at 711;* ***Action S.A. v. Marc Rich & Co.***, *951 F.2d 504, 507 (2d Cir.1991). Thus, the dual citizenship of a U.S. citizen does not create or destroy alienage jurisdiction.* ***Mutuelles Unies***, *957 F.2d at 711.*

---

(1) Nonresident alien. A citizen or subject of a foreign country who is not lawfully admitted for permanent residence in the United States is considered a citizen of the foreign country. *See* ***Dewan v. Walia***, No. RDB-11-02195 (D.Md.2012) (slip op.; 8-3-12); *Black's Law Dictionary* 84 (9th ed. 2009).

(2) Resident alien. A citizen or subject of a foreign country who is lawfully admitted for permanent residence in the United States (e.g., holds a green card) and is domiciled in a U.S. state is considered a citizen of the U.S. state where she is domiciled if the opposing party is a U.S. citizen who is domiciled in the same state. *See* 28 U.S.C. §1332(a)(2); ***Emekekwue v. Agwuegbo***, No. 1:12-cv-1503 (M.D.Pa.2012) (slip op.; 11-1-12); H.R. Rep. No. 112-10, at 6-7 (2011); *see also* ***Foy v. Schantz, Schatzman & Aaronson, P.A.***, 108 F.3d 1347, 1349 (11th Cir. 1997) (alien admitted for permanent residence means alien who has been given green card; applying former 28 U.S.C. §1332(a) (last paragraph)). In such cases, no alienage jurisdiction exists. *See* 28 U.S.C. §1332(a)(2). For example, there is no alienage jurisdiction when a plaintiff is a citizen of California and the defendant is a citizen of France who is lawfully admitted for permanent residence in the United States and domiciled in California.

CAUTION

Before the Clarification Act, an alien admitted to the United States for permanent residence was deemed to be a citizen of the state where the alien was domiciled; this was known as the "resident alien proviso." H.R. Rep. No. 112-10, at 6-7 (2011). Based on the proviso, courts disagreed on whether a permanent-resident alien was deemed exclusively a citizen of the state where she was domiciled or was deemed a citizen of both the domiciliary state and the foreign state. Compare ***Intec USA, LLC v. Engle****, 467 F.3d 1038, 1043-44 (7th Cir.2006) (Ds were foreign citizens and P-LLC had citizenship of all five of its members, one of whom was citizen of New Zealand and deemed permanent resident of North Carolina; court found there was no diversity when P was citizen of both U.S. state and foreign state), and* ***Saadeh v. Farouki****, 107 F.3d 52, 61 (D.C. Cir.1997) (P was foreign citizen and D was citizen of Jordan and deemed permanent resident of Maryland; court found there was no diversity when aliens were opposing parties, regardless of residency status), with* ***Singh v. Daimler-Benz AG****, 9 F.3d 303, 310 (3d Cir.1993) (P was citizen of India and deemed permanent resident of Virginia, D1 was citizen of Delaware and New Jersey, and D2 was citizen of Germany; court found there was diversity). The Clarification Act (which applies to suits commenced on or after January 6, 2012) deleted the proviso, resolving the courts' disagreement in favor of ignoring a resident alien's U.S. domicile and deeming the alien to be solely a citizen of her foreign state in nearly all diversity cases except for one: when the opposing party is a U.S. citizen domiciled in the same state as the resident alien. See 28 U.S.C. §1332(a)(2); Clarification Act, P.L. 112-63, §105, 125 Stat. 762 (2011) (eff. Jan. 6, 2012); H.R. Rep. No. 112-10, at 6-7 (2011). The amendment effectively prevents the unintended expansion of diversity jurisdiction beyond what was available in 1988, when the proviso was adopted. H.R. Rep. No. 112-10, at 7 (2011). For example, the Clarification Act now prevents a court from finding complete diversity in cases such as* ***Singh****; in that case, citizens of separate foreign states appeared as opposing parties, but P, a citizen of India, was deemed a permanent resident of Virginia and thus was considered completely diverse from D1, a citizen of Delaware and New Jersey, and D2, a citizen of Germany. See* ***Singh****, 9 F.3d at 310; H.R. Rep. No. 112-10, at 7 (2011).*

2. Business entities.

(1) Corporation. A corporation is considered a citizen of every U.S. state and foreign state where it is incorporated and the U.S. state or foreign state where it has its principal place of business. 28 U.S.C. §1332(c)(1). For diversity-jurisdiction considerations for corporations, see "Corporation," §3.2.1(2)(a), p. 119.

NOTE

The Clarification Act (which applies to suits commenced on or after January 6, 2012) amended 28 U.S.C. §1332(c)(1) to clarify how foreign contacts affect a corporation's citizenship. See Clarification Act, P.L. 112-63, §105, 125 Stat. 762 (2011) (eff. Jan. 6, 2012); H.R. Rep. No. 112-10, at 8-10 (2011).

(2) Other business associations. Other organizations may be considered a citizen or subject of a foreign country if the laws of that foreign country consider the party to be a "juridical" entity distinct from its members, regardless of corporate status. *See, e.g.,* ***Puerto Rico v. Russell & Co.***, 288 U.S. 476, 482 (1933) (*sociedad en comandita* was juridical person under Puerto Rican law); ***Autocephalous Greek-Orthodox Ch. v. Goldberg & Feldman Fine Arts, Inc.***, 917 F.2d 278, 285 (7th Cir.1990) (church, which was recognized by foreign country as a distinct juridical entity, was citizen of that country for purposes of alienage jurisdiction); ***Cohn v. Rosenfeld***, 733 F.2d 625, 629 (9th Cir.1984) (*Liechtenstein anstalt* is juridical person under law of Liechtenstein); *see also Black's Law Dictionary* 927 (9th ed. 2009) (defining "juridical" as "[of] or relating to judicial proceedings or to the administration of justice" or "[of] or relating to law; legal"). An unincorporated association is deemed a citizen of every state

where its members reside. ***Hummel v. Townsend***, 883 F.2d 367, 369 (5th Cir.1989). If the organization is an unincorporated foreign association, its citizenship is the citizenship of each of its members. *Compare* ***Certain Interested Underwriters v. Layne***, 26 F.3d 39, 41 (6th Cir.1994) (citizenship of Lloyd's of London, which consists of unincorporated groups ["syndicates"] of investors ["names"] that employ agent-underwriters, is based on citizenship of agent-underwriters), *with* ***Corfield v. Dallas Glen Hills LP***, 355 F.3d 853, 864 (5th Cir.2003) (only names that are parties to case are relevant for diversity), ***E.R. Squibb & Sons, Inc. v. Accident & Cas. Ins.***, 160 F.3d 925, 937-38 (2d Cir. 1998) (for Lloyd's of London, diversity is determined by citizenship of each potentially liable name sued in its individual capacity), *and* ***Indiana Gas Co. v. Home Ins.***, 141 F.3d 314, 317 (7th Cir.1998) (same).

§4.2 Amount in controversy must exceed $75,000. To invoke alienage jurisdiction of a federal court, the plaintiff must allege facts showing that the amount in controversy exceeds $75,000. 28 U.S.C. §1332(a). See "When is amount in controversy satisfied?," §3.3, p. 123.

§5. MULTIPARTY JURISDICTION

Federal courts have jurisdiction over certain types of multiparty cases, including interstate class actions and "single-event" mass accidents, such as aircraft or train accidents.

§5.1 Interstate class actions. In 2005, Congress passed the Class Action Fairness Act (CAFA), which expands federal jurisdiction over certain class actions. *See* P.L. 109-2, 119 Stat. 4 (2005) (codified at 28 U.S.C. §§1332, 1335, 1453, 1603, 1711-1715).

1. Effective date. CAFA applies to any action commenced on or after February 18, 2005. P.L. 109-2, §9, 119 Stat. 4, 14 (2005). Generally, an action is commenced when it is first brought in an appropriate court; removal does not affect the commencement date for purposes of CAFA. ***Pritchett v. Office Depot, Inc.***, 420 F.3d 1090, 1094 (10th Cir.2005); *see* ***Admiral Ins. v. Abshire***, 574 F.3d 267, 273 (5th Cir.2009). Courts have adopted at least three positions on how a pleading amendment may affect the commencement of an action when the initial complaint is filed before—but the amended pleading is filed after—the effective date of CAFA: (1) pleading amendments after the CAFA effective date do not affect the commencement date, (2) pleading amendments may affect the commencement date only if they do not relate back, and (3) pleading amendments may affect the commencement date if they do not relate back or if they add new defendants. ***Farina v. Nokia Inc.***, 625 F.3d 97, 110-111 (3d Cir.2010); ***Prime Care v. Humana Ins.***, 447 F.3d 1284, 1285-86 (10th Cir.2006); *see, e.g.*, ***Braud v. Transport Serv.***, 445 F.3d 801, 804 (5th Cir.2006) (following position 3 and holding that new D commenced new action); ***Plubell v. Merck & Co.***, 434 F.3d 1070, 1071 (8th Cir.2006) (following position 2 and holding that replacing class representative did not commence new action); ***Weekley v. Guidant Corp.***, 392 F.Supp.2d 1066, 1067 (E.D.Ark.2005) (following position 1 and holding that amending complaint from individual case to class-action status did not commence new action); *see also* ***Weber v. Mobil Oil Corp.***, 506 F.3d 1311, 1316 (10th Cir.2007) (intervention by additional Ps does not affect commencement date). Generally, whether a pleading amendment relates back is determined by the forum state's law. ***Prime Care***, 447 F.3d at 1286.

2. Establishing jurisdiction. The burden of establishing federal jurisdiction is on the party invoking it under CAFA. ***Westerfeld v. Independent Processing, LLC***, 621 F.3d 819, 822 (8th Cir.2010); ***Amoche v. Guarantee Trust Life Ins.***, 556 F.3d 41, 48 (1st Cir.2009); ***Strawn v. AT&T Mobility LLC***, 530 F.3d 293, 298 (4th Cir.2008); *see* ***Brill v. Countrywide Home Loans, Inc.***, 427 F.3d 446, 447-48 (7th Cir.2005) (rule that proponent of federal jurisdiction bears burden of proof applies to CAFA cases). District courts have original jurisdiction over any civil action in which the party invoking federal jurisdiction can show the following:

NOTE

Some class actions that satisfy the CAFA requirements cannot be heard in federal court if a more specific jurisdictional statute applies. See, e.g., ***Luther v. Countrywide Home Loans Servicing LP***, *533 F.3d 1031, 1034 (9th Cir.2008) (although case satisfied CAFA requirements, case was not removable under CAFA because jurisdiction was controlled by more specific anti-removal provision for certain securities cases that are originally filed in state court).*

(1) Case is class action. The case must be a "class action." 28 U.S.C. §1332(d)(1)(B), (d)(2).

(a) Generally. For purposes of CAFA, a class action is one of the following:

[1] Any civil action filed under FRCP 23 or a similar state statute or rule authorizing class-action suits. 28 U.S.C. §1332(d)(1)(B); ***Washington v. Chimei Innolux Corp.***, 659 F.3d 842, 848 (9th Cir.2011); ***College of Dental Surgeons v. Connecticut Gen. Life Ins.***, 585 F.3d 33, 39 (1st Cir.2009); *see, e.g.*, ***West Virginia v. CVS Pharm.***, 646 F.3d 169, 174-75 (4th Cir.2011) (when suit was not brought under FRCP 23 or similar state rule but rather under state statute regulating pharmacies, action was not class action under CAFA).

[2] A "mass action," which is any civil action in which monetary claims of 100 or more persons are proposed to be tried jointly on the ground that the claims involve common questions of law or fact. *See* 28 U.S.C. §1332(d)(11)(A), (d)(11)(B).

(b) Exceptions. A CAFA class action does not include any of the following:

[1] A class action in which the primary defendants are states, state officials, or other governmental entities against whom the court may be foreclosed from ordering relief. 28 U.S.C. §1332(d)(5)(A).

[2] A class action in which the total number of members of all proposed plaintiff classes is less than 100. *Id.* §1332(d)(5)(B); *see, e.g.*, ***Anderson v. Bayer Corp.***, 610 F.3d 390, 392-93 (7th Cir.2010) (five separate but factually identical cases—each with less than 100 Ps—did not satisfy CAFA's mass-action provision; cases that could be brought as mass actions can be structured to remain outside CAFA jurisdiction).

[3] A class action that solely involves claims concerning either (1) a covered security, as defined by 15 U.S.C. §77p(f)(3) and 15 U.S.C. §78bb(f)(5)(E), or (2) the rights, duties (including fiduciary duties), and obligations relating to any security defined by 15 U.S.C. §77b(a)(1) and its accompanying regulations. 28 U.S.C. §1332(d)(9)(A), (d)(9)(C); *see* ***Appert v. Morgan Stanley Dean Witter, Inc.***, 673 F.3d 609, 618-19 (7th Cir.2012); ***Greenwich Fin. Servs. Distressed Mortg. Fund 3 LLC v. Countrywide Fin. Corp.***, 603 F.3d 23, 31-32 (2d Cir.2010).

[4] A class action that solely involves claims relating to the internal affairs or governance of a business and arising under the laws of the state where the business is organized. 28 U.S.C. §1332(d)(9)(B).

[5] A mass action in which (1) all the claims arise from an event or occurrence in the state where the action was filed and (2) the claims allegedly resulted in injuries in that state or in states contiguous to that state. *Id.* §1332(d)(11)(B)(ii)(I).

[6] A mass action in which all the claims are joined on the motion of a defendant. *Id.* §1332(d)(11)(B)(ii)(II); *see* ***Tanoh v. Dow Chem. Co.***, 561 F.3d 945, 953-54 (9th Cir.2009).

[7] A mass action in which all the claims are asserted on behalf of the general public under a state statute specifically authorizing such an action. 28 U.S.C. §1332(d)(11)(B)(ii)(III).

[8] A mass action in which all the claims have been consolidated or coordinated solely for pretrial proceedings. *Id.* §1332(d)(11)(B)(ii)(IV); *see* ***Tanoh***, 561 F.3d at 954.

(2) Amount in controversy. The case must satisfy the amount-in-controversy requirement. *See* 28 U.S.C. §1332(d)(2).

(a) Class actions generally. For most cases, the amount in controversy must exceed the sum or value of $5 million, excluding interest and costs. 28 U.S.C. §1332(d)(2); *see, e.g.*, ***Strawn***, 530 F.3d at 299 (D satisfied its burden to show damages exceeding $5 million); *see also* ***Rolwing v. Nestle Holdings, Inc.***, 666 F.3d 1069, 1072 (8th Cir.2012) (binding stipulation limiting damages to amount below $5 million can be used to defeat CAFA jurisdiction). There is no requirement under CAFA that any individual plaintiff's claim exceed $75,000. ***Cappuccitti v. DirecTV, Inc.***, 623 F.3d 1118, 1122 (11th Cir.2010).

NOTE

*The circuits impose different standards of proof on removing defendants who must show that the amount-in-controversy requirement has been met; the standards may differ depending on whether the plaintiff does not plead a specific amount of damages in its complaint or pleads an amount below the $5 million jurisdictional limit. See **Frederick v. Hartford Underwriters Ins.**, 683 F.3d 1242, 1246 (10th Cir.2012); **Lewis v. Verizon Comms.**, 627 F.3d 395, 400-01 (9th Cir.2010); see, e.g., **Bell v. Hershey Co.**, 557 F.3d 953, 957, 959 n.6 (8th Cir.2009) (removing D must show by preponderance of evidence that claims exceed $5 million, regardless of whether P alleged specific amount or amount below jurisdictional limit); **Amoche**, 556 F.3d at 48-49 (removing D must show to "reasonable probability" that claims exceed $5 million if P does not plead amount of damages); **Lowdermilk v. U.S. Bank**, 479 F.3d 994, 999-1000 (9th Cir.2007) (removing D must show to "legal certainty" that claims exceed $5 million if P, in good faith, pleads amount below jurisdictional limit). Check the law of your circuit to determine the appropriate standard.*

[1] Single class action. The claims of the individual class members can be aggregated to satisfy the amount-in-controversy requirement. 28 U.S.C. §1332(d)(6); ***Marple v. T-Mobile Cent. LLC***, 639 F.3d 1109, 1110 (8th Cir.2011); ***Cappuccitti***, 623 F.3d at 1122.

[2] Multiple class actions. The claims of individual class members between class actions generally cannot be aggregated. ***Marple***, 639 F.3d at 1110. Their claims may be aggregated, however, if a plaintiff artificially structures a class action into multiple suits to avoid jurisdiction under CAFA. *See, e.g.*, ***Freeman v. Blue Ridge Paper Prods.***, 551 F.3d 405, 409 (6th Cir.2008) (Ps could not divide class claims into five separate suits covering distinct six-month time periods and allege $4.9 million in damages for each suit to avoid federal jurisdiction; Ps provided no colorable basis for division of claims, other than to avoid CAFA jurisdiction).

(b) Mass actions. For mass actions, the court must engage in a two-step process to determine whether it has jurisdiction. Beisner & Miller, *Litigating in the New Class Action World*, at 407. First, the court must determine whether all claims in the complaint exceed the sum or value of $5 million, excluding interest and costs. *See* 28 U.S.C. §1332(d)(2); Beisner & Miller, *Litigating in the New Class Action World*, at 407. Second, if the court has jurisdiction over the matter as a whole, it must determine which of the claims put more than $75,000 in controversy, and then exercise jurisdiction over those claims only. *See* 28 U.S.C. §1332(d)(11)(B)(i); Beisner & Miller, *Litigating in the New Class Action World*, at 407.

(3) Minimal diversity. The parties must be minimally diverse; they do not need to be completely diverse. *See* Beisner & Miller, *Litigating in the New Class Action World*, at 405. See "Is there complete diversity?," §3.1, p. 116.

(a) Determining diversity. The court can exercise jurisdiction over a class action when any of the following is true:

[1] Any member of a class of plaintiffs is a citizen of a state different from any defendant. 28 U.S.C. §1332(d)(2)(A); *e.g.*, ***Johnson v. Advance Am.***, 549 F.3d 932, 935-36 (4th Cir.2008) (when D-corporation was citizen of Delaware and South Carolina and P-class-members were all citizens of South Carolina, D did not satisfy its burden to establish diversity jurisdiction; Ps were not citizens of state different from D). "Class members" are the persons, named or unnamed, who fall within the definition of the proposed or certified class in a class action. 28 U.S.C. §1332(d)(1)(D); *see also* ***Dennison v. Carolina Payday Loans, Inc.***, 549 F.3d 941, 942-43 (4th Cir.2008) (class can be defined to include only citizens of particular state to avoid CAFA jurisdiction).

[2] Any member of a class of plaintiffs is a foreign state or a citizen or subject of a foreign state, and any defendant is a citizen of a state. 28 U.S.C. §1332(d)(2)(B).

[3] Any member of a class of plaintiffs is a citizen of a state, and any defendant is a foreign state or a citizen or subject of a foreign state. *Id.* §1332(d)(2)(C).

(b) Determining citizenship.

[1] Persons generally. The plaintiffs' citizenship is determined on either of the following: (1) the date of filing of the complaint or amended complaint or (2) the date of service of an amended pleading, motion, or other paper that indicates federal jurisdiction if the case was not subject to federal jurisdiction under the initial pleading. 28 U.S.C. §1332(d)(7).

[2] Unincorporated associations. The general rule that an unincorporated association is a citizen of the state of each member or partner does not apply to class actions under CAFA. Beisner & Miller, *Litigating in the New Class Action World*, at 406. See "Other business associations," §3.2.1(2)(c), p. 121. Under CAFA, an unincorporated association is deemed to be a citizen of the state where it has its principal place of business and the state under whose laws it is organized. 28 U.S.C. §1332(d)(10); *see* ***Ferrell v. Express Check Advance***, 591 F.3d 698, 699-700 (4th Cir.2010) (limited-liability company is unincorporated association under CAFA).

3. Exercising jurisdiction.

(1) Court must accept jurisdiction. If less than one-third of the members of all proposed plaintiff classes are citizens of the state where suit was filed, the court must accept jurisdiction as long as the requirements for exercising jurisdiction under CAFA have been met. *See* Beisner & Miller, *Litigating in the New Class Action World*, at 408.

(2) Court may decline jurisdiction – interests-of-justice exception. If more than one-third but fewer than two-thirds of the members of all proposed plaintiff classes and the primary defendants are citizens of the state where suit was filed, the court may decline to exercise jurisdiction. 28 U.S.C. §1332(d)(3); *see* ***Romano v. SLS Residential, Inc.***, 812 F.Supp.2d 282, 289 (S.D.N.Y.2011). In determining whether to exercise jurisdiction, the court should assess the following factors:

(a) Whether the asserted claims involve matters of national or interstate interest. 28 U.S.C. §1332(d)(3)(A); Beisner & Miller, *Litigating in the New Class Action World*, at 409.

(b) Whether the asserted claims will be governed by the laws of the state where suit was filed or by the laws of other states. 28 U.S.C. §1332(d)(3)(B); Beisner & Miller, *Litigating in the New Class Action World*, at 409.

(c) Whether the class action has been pleaded in a manner that seeks to avoid federal jurisdiction. 28 U.S.C. §1332(d)(3)(C); Beisner & Miller, *Litigating in the New Class Action World*, at 409.

(d) Whether the action was brought in a forum that has a distinct nexus with the class members, the alleged harm, or the defendants. 28 U.S.C. §1332(d)(3)(D); Beisner & Miller, *Litigating in the New Class Action World*, at 409.

(e) Whether the number of citizens of the state where suit was filed in all proposed plaintiff classes is substantially larger than the number of citizens from any other state, and whether the citizenship of the other members of the proposed classes is dispersed among a substantial number of states. 28 U.S.C. §1332(d)(3)(E); Beisner & Miller, *Litigating in the New Class Action World*, at 409.

(f) Whether one or more other class actions asserting the same or similar claims on behalf of the same or other persons have been filed in the past three years. 28 U.S.C. §1332(d)(3)(F); Beisner & Miller, *Litigating in the New Class Action World*, at 409.

(3) Court must decline jurisdiction. The court must decline to exercise jurisdiction when the controversy is primarily local or does not reach into multiple states. ***Kaufman v. Allstate N.J. Ins.***, 561 F.3d 144, 149 (3d Cir.2009); *see* ***Hollinger v. Home State Mut. Ins.***, 654 F.3d 564, 569-70 (5th Cir.2011); ***Coffey v. Freeport McMoran Copper & Gold***, 581 F.3d 1240, 1243 (10th Cir.2009); ***Johnson***, 549 F.3d at 938; Beisner & Miller, *Litigating*

in the New Class Action World, at 409-10; *see also* ***Graphic Comms. Local 1B Health & Welfare Fund "A" v. CVS Caremark Corp.***, 636 F.3d 971, 973 (8th Cir.2011) (local-controversy exceptions operate as abstention doctrine, which means court is not divested of subject-matter jurisdiction even when exception applies). If CAFA jurisdiction has been established, the burden shifts to the party resisting federal jurisdiction to show that one of the following exceptions applies. ***Hollinger***, 654 F.3d at 571; ***Westerfeld***, 621 F.3d at 822; ***Kaufman***, 561 F.3d at 153; *see* ***In re Hannaford Bros. Co. Customer Data Sec. Breach Litig.***, 564 F.3d 75, 78 (1st Cir.2009).

(a) Local-controversy exception #1 – in-state defendant. The court must decline to exercise jurisdiction if all the factors below are true. *See* ***Davis v. HSBC Bank Nev.***, 557 F.3d 1026, 1028 & n.2 (9th Cir. 2009). The party seeking remand has the burden to prove the local-controversy exception by a preponderance of the evidence. ***Preston v. Tenet Healthsystem Mem'l Med. Ctr., Inc.***, 485 F.3d 793, 797 (5th Cir.2007); *see* ***Coleman v. Estes Express Lines, Inc.***, 631 F.3d 1010, 1013 (9th Cir.2011).

[1] More than two-thirds of the members of all proposed plaintiff classes are citizens of the state where suit was filed. 28 U.S.C. §1332(d)(4)(A)(i)(I).

[2] The plaintiffs have sued at least one in-state defendant from whom they seek significant relief and whose conduct forms a significant basis of their claims. 28 U.S.C. §1332(d)(4)(A)(i)(II); ***Westerfeld***, 621 F.3d at 825; ***Kaufman***, 561 F.3d at 155-56; *see* ***Coffey***, 581 F.3d at 1243-44 (D from whom significant relief is sought does not mean D from whom significant relief may be obtained; in-state D does not have to be able to pay judgment). To determine whether the in-state defendant's conduct forms a significant basis of the claims, the court must compare the in-state defendant's alleged conduct to the alleged conduct of all the defendants. ***Kaufman***, 561 F.3d at 156.

NOTE

The circuits disagree on whether the district court may look only to the complaint when determining if the following factors have been satisfied: (1) significant relief under §1332(d)(4)(A)(i)(II)(aa) and (2) conduct forming a significant basis for the plaintiff's claims under §1332(d)(4)(A)(i)(II)(bb). Compare ***Coleman****, 631 F.3d at 1015 (when determining subsections (aa) and (bb), district court is limited to complaint), and* ***Coffey****, 581 F.3d at 1245 (when determining subsection (aa), district court is not required to make factual assessments), with* ***Evans v. Walter Indus.****, 449 F.3d 1159, 1167-68 (11th Cir.2006) (when determining subsection (bb), district court considered extrinsic evidence). If a district court cannot determine whether the requirements are satisfied, it may require or allow the complaint to be amended.* ***Coleman****, 631 F.3d at 1020-21.*

[3] The principal injuries resulting from the alleged conduct, or any related conduct, of each defendant occurred in the state where suit was filed. 28 U.S.C. §1332(d)(4)(A)(i)(III); ***Kaufman***, 561 F.3d at 158.

[4] No class action has been filed against any of the defendants alleging the same claims in the past three years. 28 U.S.C. §1332(d)(4)(A)(ii).

(b) Local-controversy exception #2 – home state. The court must decline to exercise jurisdiction if the primary defendants and at least two-thirds of the members of all proposed plaintiff classes are citizens of the state where suit was filed. 28 U.S.C. §1332(d)(4)(B); ***Hollinger***, 654 F.3d at 570; ***In re Sprint Nextel Corp.***, 593 F.3d 669, 671 (7th Cir.2010); *e.g.*, ***In re Hannaford Bros. Co. Customer Data Sec. Breach Litig.***, 564 F.3d at 77-78 (home-state exception applied when all class members were Florida citizens and corporate D had its principal place of business in Florida; court did not have to look beyond complaint for other Ps outside Florida in previous cases with same facts).

§5.2 Single-event mass accidents. The Multiparty, Multiforum Trial Jurisdiction Act (MMTJA) expands federal diversity jurisdiction over "single-event" mass accidents, such as aircraft or train accidents. *See* Multiparty, Multiforum Trial Jurisdiction Act, P.L. 107-273, §11020, 116 Stat. 1826 (2002) (codified at 28 U.S.C. §§1369, 1391, 1441,

1697, and 1785). Under the MMTJA, the district courts have jurisdiction over civil actions when (1) there is minimal diversity between adverse parties, (2) the action arises from a single accident, and (3) one defendant resides in a state where the accident did not occur, any two defendants reside in different states, or substantial parts of the accident took place in different states. 28 U.S.C. §1369(a).

1. Minimal diversity. Multiparty, multiforum jurisdiction requires only minimal diversity between adverse parties. *See* 28 U.S.C. §1369(a). Minimal diversity between adverse parties exists if any party is a citizen of a state and any adverse party is a citizen of another state, a citizen or subject of a foreign state, or a foreign state under 28 U.S.C. §1603(a). 28 U.S.C. §1369(c)(1).

(1) Citizenship of corporation. A corporation is considered a citizen of any state, and a citizen or subject of any foreign state, where it is incorporated or has its principal place of business. 28 U.S.C. §1369(c)(2).

(2) State. The term "state" includes all 50 states, plus the District of Columbia, the Commonwealth of Puerto Rico, and any territory or possession of the United States. 28 U.S.C. §1369(c)(5).

2. Single accident. Multiparty, multiforum jurisdiction is proper only when the civil action arises from a single accident. 28 U.S.C. §1369(a). The term "accident" means a sudden accident, or a natural event culminating in an accident, that results in at least 75 natural persons dying at a discrete location. *Id.* §1369(c)(4).

3. Defendant's residence or location of accident. Multiparty, multiforum jurisdiction is proper only in the following circumstances:

(1) A defendant resides in one state and a substantial part of the accident took place in another state or other location. 28 U.S.C. §1369(a)(1); *see id.* §1369(c)(5). It is irrelevant that the defendant is also a resident of the state where a substantial part of the accident took place. *Id.* §1369(a)(1). A defendant corporation is a resident of a state if it is incorporated or licensed to do business or is doing business in that state. *Id.* §1369(c)(2).

(2) Any two defendants reside in different states. *Id.* §1369(a)(2); *see id.* §1369(c)(5). It is irrelevant that the defendants are also residents of the same state or states. *Id.* §1369(a)(2).

(3) Substantial parts of the accident took place in different states. *Id.* §1369(a)(3); *see id.* §1369(c)(5).

4. Limitation of jurisdiction. Under the MMTJA, the district court must abstain from exercising jurisdiction if a substantial majority of all the plaintiffs and the primary defendants are citizens of a single state and the claims asserted will be governed primarily by the laws of that state. 28 U.S.C. §1369(b).

§6. SUPPLEMENTAL JURISDICTION

Supplemental jurisdiction extends a federal district court's jurisdiction over other claims that are within the same case or controversy, as long as the court would have original jurisdiction in the case. 28 U.S.C. §1367(a); ***Exxon Mobil Corp. v. Allapattah Servs.***, 545 U.S. 546, 558 (2005); ***Rosmer v. Pfizer Inc.***, 263 F.3d 110, 114 (4th Cir.2001); *see also* ***Arbaugh v. Y&H Corp.***, 546 U.S. 500, 514 (2006) (in case involving federal claim and state-law claims, federal district court can exercise supplemental jurisdiction over state-law claims after federal claim is dismissed for failure to state claim). Essentially, 28 U.S.C. §1367 codifies the earlier practice of pendent and ancillary jurisdiction. ***City of Chi. v. International Coll. of Surgeons***, 522 U.S. 156, 165 (1997). It is not clear whether the courts retain the power to exercise pendent or ancillary jurisdiction independent of the provisions of §1367. *See* ***Peacock v. Thomas***, 516 U.S. 349, 359 (1996) ("ancillary enforcement jurisdiction is, at its core, a creature of necessity" that should be invoked only in "extraordinary circumstances"); ***Kokkonen v. Guardian Life Ins.***, 511 U.S. 375, 379-80 (1994) (ancillary jurisdiction may be invoked "to enable a court to function successfully, that is, to manage its proceedings, vindicate its authority, and effectuate its decrees"); ***U.S. v. Cohen***, 152 F.3d 321, 324-25 (4th Cir.1998) (power is now codified in supplemental-jurisdiction statute).

§6.1 Jurisdiction over suit required. Before a federal court can exercise supplemental jurisdiction, it must first have either federal-question or diversity jurisdiction. ***Taylor v. Appleton***, 30 F.3d 1365, 1370 n.5 (11th Cir.1994); *see* ***Halmekangas v. State Farm Fire & Cas. Co.***, 603 F.3d 290, 293 (5th Cir.2010); ***Rosmer v. Pfizer Inc.***, 263 F.3d 110, 114 (4th Cir.2001); ***MCI Telecomms. Corp. v. Teleconcepts, Inc.***, 71 F.3d 1086, 1102 (3d Cir.1995).

§6.2 Reach of supplemental jurisdiction. A federal court can exercise jurisdiction over pendent claims, pendent parties, and ancillary claims when they are so related to the claims in the suit that they are part of the same case or controversy. 28 U.S.C. §1367(a); *see* ***State Nat'l Ins. v. Yates***, 391 F.3d 577, 579 (5th Cir.2004); ***Sea-Land Serv. v. Lozen Int'l***, 285 F.3d 808, 814 (9th Cir.2002); ***Stromberg Metal Works, Inc. v. Press Mech., Inc.***, 77 F.3d 928, 931-32 (7th Cir.1996); ***FDIC v. Bathgate***, 27 F.3d 850, 874 (3d Cir.1994); ***Palmer v. Hospital Auth. of Randolph Cty.***, 22 F.3d 1559, 1566-67 (11th Cir.1994). The concepts of pendent and ancillary jurisdiction are now simply called "supplemental jurisdiction," but the old terms are helpful in understanding the case law. "Pendent-claim" jurisdiction relates to a plaintiff's nonfederal (i.e., state-law) claims against a defendant when there is a federal claim that gives the court subject-matter jurisdiction. *See* ***Schlumberger Indus. v. National Sur. Corp.***, 36 F.3d 1274, 1278 n.8 (4th Cir.1994). "Pendent-party" jurisdiction relates to parties who have no independent basis for subject-matter jurisdiction but who are subject to the court's jurisdiction because of other parties who have a basis for subject-matter jurisdiction. *See id.* "Ancillary" jurisdiction relates to claims other than the plaintiff's claim, such as compulsory counterclaims. *See* ***Peacock v. Thomas***, 516 U.S. 349, 354-55 (1996); ***Ambromovage v. United Mine Workers***, 726 F.2d 972, 989 n.48 (3d Cir.1984). Although pendent and ancillary jurisdiction were conceptually distinct, they were regarded as two species of the same generic problem: under what circumstances can a federal court decide a state-law claim between citizens of the same state? ***Owen Equip. & Erection Co. v. Kroger***, 437 U.S. 365, 370 (1978).

CIRCUIT SPLIT

Congress's decision to use Article 3's "same case or controversy" language in 28 U.S.C. §1367, rather than the "common nucleus" test set out by the Supreme Court in ***United Mine Workers v. Gibbs****, 383 U.S. 715, 725 (1966), has resulted in a conflict among the circuits on whether §1367 requires a more restrictive test than* ***Gibbs****. See generally* ***Jones v. Ford Motor Credit Co.****, 358 F.3d 205, 212 n.5 (2d Cir.2004) (correct reading of §1367 "remains unsettled"). The Second, Eighth, Ninth, and Eleventh Circuits have held that §1367(c) limits the court's discretion to deny jurisdiction. See* ***Itar-Tass Russian News Agency v. Russian Kurier, Inc.****, 140 F.3d 442, 447 (2d Cir.1998);* ***McLaurin v. Prater****, 30 F.3d 982, 985 (8th Cir.1994);* ***Executive Software N. Am., Inc. v. U.S. Dist. Ct. for the Cent. Dist. of Cal.****, 24 F.3d 1545, 1556 (9th Cir.1994), overruled on other grounds,* ***California Dept. of Water Res. v. Powerex Corp.****, 533 F.3d 1087 (9th Cir.2008);* ***Palmer****, 22 F.3d at 1569. The First, Third, Fourth, Seventh, and D.C. Circuits have held that §1367(c) codifies the* ***Gibbs*** *test. See* ***Brzonkala v. Virginia Polytechnic Inst. & State Univ.****, 169 F.3d 820, 842 (4th Cir.1999), aff'd sub nom.* ***U.S. v. Morrison****, 529 U.S. 598 (2000);* ***Women Prisoners of the D.C. Dept. of Corr. v. District of Columbia****, 93 F.3d 910, 921 (D.C.Cir.1996);* ***Rodriguez v. Doral Mortg. Corp.****, 57 F.3d 1168, 1175 (1st Cir. 1995);* ***Borough of W. Mifflin v. Lancaster****, 45 F.3d 780, 788 (3d Cir.1995);* ***Brazinski v. Amoco Pet. Additives Co.****, 6 F.3d 1176, 1182 (7th Cir.1993).*

1. Pendent-claim jurisdiction. Under the doctrine of pendent-claim jurisdiction, a federal court with original jurisdiction is authorized to exercise jurisdiction over all other claims that are so related to the claim giving rise to original jurisdiction that they form part of the same case or controversy within the meaning of Article 3 of the U.S. Constitution. 28 U.S.C. §1367(a); *see* ***City of Chi. v. International Coll. of Surgeons***, 522 U.S. 156, 167 (1997). Pendent-claim jurisdiction permits the exercise of diversity jurisdiction over additional plaintiffs even when their claims do not satisfy the amount-in-controversy requirement as long as one plaintiff meets the diversity and amount-in-controversy requirements. ***Exxon Mobil Corp. v. Allapattah Servs.***, 545 U.S. 546, 549 (2005).

2. Pendent-party jurisdiction. Under the doctrine of pendent-party jurisdiction, a plaintiff who has asserted a claim against one defendant under original federal jurisdiction can seek to join a different defendant on a pendent state-law claim. *See, e.g.,* ***Ortega v. Brock***, 501 F.Supp.2d 1337, 1340-41 (M.D.Ala.2007) (court had original jurisdiction over D-officer based on 42 U.S.C. §1983 claim and had supplemental jurisdiction over other Ds based on

state-law claims). Several circuits have held that §1367(a) specifically authorizes pendent-party jurisdiction. *See* ***Stromberg Metal Works***, 77 F.3d at 930-31; ***In re Abbott Labs***, 51 F.3d 524, 527-29 (5th Cir.1995); ***Palmer***, 22 F.3d at 1567; 13D Wright, Miller, Cooper & Freer §3567.2.

NOTE

The supplemental-jurisdiction statute permits a federal court to exercise pendent-party jurisdiction in diversity class actions when at least one class member satisfies the amount-in-controversy requirement. ***Allapattah Servs.****, 545 U.S. at 566-67.*

3. Ancillary jurisdiction. Under the doctrine of ancillary jurisdiction, a federal court may permit the intervention of dependent or ancillary claims when it has jurisdiction over a cause of action. ***Aldinger v. Howard***, 427 U.S. 1, 11-12 (1976). Section 1367 provides federal courts supplemental jurisdiction to the limits of Article 3 of the U.S. Constitution. 13D Wright, Miller, Cooper & Freer §3567.1. However, the statute also protects the requirement of complete diversity by limiting the use of supplemental jurisdiction to certain instances specified in the statute. *See* 28 U.S.C. §1367(b); ***Stromberg Metal Works***, 77 F.3d at 931-32.

§6.3 Exercise of supplemental jurisdiction. Generally, the court must exercise supplemental jurisdiction over state-law claims. 28 U.S.C. §1367(a); ***McLaurin v. Prater***, 30 F.3d 982, 984-85 (8th Cir.1994); ***Palmer v. Hospital Auth. of Randolph Cty.***, 22 F.3d 1559, 1569 & n.11 (11th Cir.1994); *see* ***Blakely v. U.S.***, 276 F.3d 853, 861 (6th Cir.2002) ("default assumption" is that court will exercise supplemental jurisdiction over all related claims); *see also* ***Global NAPS, Inc. v. Verizon New England Inc.***, 603 F.3d 71, 76 (1st Cir.2010) (28 U.S.C. §1367 confers supplemental jurisdiction over compulsory counterclaims and some permissive counterclaims). Section 1367(a) requires the court to exercise supplemental jurisdiction unless (1) the exercise of supplemental jurisdiction is restricted because it will destroy diversity under 28 U.S.C. §1367(b), or (2) the exercise of supplemental jurisdiction may be declined for the reasons specified in 28 U.S.C. §1367(c).

1. Restrictions on supplemental jurisdiction. Section 1367(b) restricts the exercise of supplemental jurisdiction in certain diversity cases. ***Griffin v. Lee***, 621 F.3d 380, 386-87 (5th Cir.2010); ***Price v. Wolford***, 608 F.3d 698, 703 (10th Cir.2010); ***Rosmer v. Pfizer Inc.***, 263 F.3d 110, 115 (4th Cir.2001); ***Development Fin. Corp. v. Alpha Hous. & Health Care, Inc.***, 54 F.3d 156, 159 (3d Cir.1995). A court cannot exercise supplemental jurisdiction over the following claims when it would be inconsistent with the complete diversity required under 28 U.S.C. §1332:

(1) Claims by plaintiffs against persons made parties under FRCP 14 (impleader), FRCP 19 (necessary joinder), FRCP 20 (permissive joinder), and FRCP 24 (intervention). 28 U.S.C. §1367(b); ***State Nat'l Ins. v. Yates***, 391 F.3d 577, 579 (5th Cir.2004); ***Herrick Co. v. SCS Comms.***, 251 F.3d 315, 325 & n.7 (2d Cir.2001); ***Development Fin.***, 54 F.3d at 160. However, the statute does not bar claims by a defendant against other parties—only claims by the original plaintiff. ***Yates***, 391 F.3d at 579-81; *see also* ***United Capitol Ins. v. Kapiloff***, 155 F.3d 488, 493 (4th Cir.1998) (diversity is not destroyed by D impleading party who is not diverse with P).

(2) Claims brought by persons proposed to be joined as plaintiffs under FRCP 19. 28 U.S.C. §1367(b); *see* ***Development Fin.***, 54 F.3d at 160.

(3) Claims against persons seeking to intervene as plaintiffs under FRCP 24. 28 U.S.C. §1367(a), (b); ***Griffin***, 621 F.3d at 386-87; ***Stromberg Metal Works, Inc. v. Press Mech., Inc.***, 77 F.3d 928, 931-32 (7th Cir.1996); ***Development Fin.***, 54 F.3d at 160.

2. Declining supplemental jurisdiction.

(1) When to decline. A federal court may decline to exercise supplemental jurisdiction in the following four instances:

(a) The claim raises a novel or complex issue of state law. 28 U.S.C. §1367(c)(1); ***International Ass'n of Firefighters v. City of Ferguson***, 283 F.3d 969, 976 (8th Cir.2002); ***O'Connor v. Nevada***, 27 F.3d 357, 363 (9th Cir.1994).

(b) The state-law claim substantially predominates over any claims over which the court has original jurisdiction. 28 U.S.C. §1367(c)(2); *see* ***Garro v. Connecticut***, 23 F.3d 734, 737 (2d Cir.1994).

(c) All claims over which the federal court has original jurisdiction have been dismissed. 28 U.S.C. §1367(c)(3); *see* ***Lapides v. Board of Regents***, 535 U.S. 613, 624 (2002); ***Carnegie-Mellon Univ. v. Cohill***, 484 U.S. 343, 350 & n.7 (1988); ***Pintando v. Miami-Dade Hous. Agency***, 501 F.3d 1241, 1242 (11th Cir.2007). Generally, if the federal claims are dismissed before trial, any state claims should be dismissed or remanded as appropriate. *See* ***Blakely***, 276 F.3d at 863; ***Giordano v. City of N.Y.***, 274 F.3d 740, 754 (2d Cir.2001); ***Parker & Parsley Pet. Co. v. Dresser Indus.***, 972 F.2d 580, 585 (5th Cir.1992). However, if the dismissal of the federal claims comes late in the case and if substantial judicial resources have already been committed such that sending the case to another court will cause a duplication of effort, a belated rejection of supplemental jurisdiction may not be appropriate. ***Tomaiolo v. Mallinoff***, 281 F.3d 1, 11 (1st Cir.2002); ***Purgess v. Sharrock***, 33 F.3d 134, 138 (2d Cir.1994); ***Timm v. Mead Corp.***, 32 F.3d 273, 277 (7th Cir.1994); *see also* ***Batiste v. Island Records, Inc.***, 179 F.3d 217, 227 (5th Cir. 1999) (court may consider factors of judicial economy, convenience, fairness to litigants, and comity).

(d) The state-law claim presents exceptional circumstances, and there are other compelling reasons for the court to decline jurisdiction. 28 U.S.C. §1367(c)(4). The phrase "other compelling reasons" refers to those reasons that lead a court to conclude that declining jurisdiction best accommodates the values of judicial economy, convenience, fairness, and comity. ***Executive Software N. Am., Inc. v. U.S. Dist. Ct. for the Cent. Dist. of Cal.***, 24 F.3d 1545, 1557 (9th Cir.1994), *overruled on other grounds*, ***California Dept. of Water Res. v. Powerex Corp.***, 533 F.3d 1087 (9th Cir.2008).

(2) Statute of limitations tolled. If the plaintiff's state-law claim is dismissed under 28 U.S.C. §1367(a), the state statute of limitations is tolled for 30 days after the order of dismissal to allow the plaintiff time to file a new suit in state court, unless state law provides for a longer tolling period. 28 U.S.C. §1367(d); *see also* ***Jinks v. Richland Cty.***, 538 U.S. 456, 465 (2003) (holding §1367(d) constitutional).

§6.4 Loss of supplemental jurisdiction.

1. Federal claim omitted by plaintiff. If the plaintiff amends the complaint and omits the federal claim providing federal jurisdiction over the suit, the court cannot maintain supplemental jurisdiction. ***Pintando v. Miami-Dade Hous. Agency***, 501 F.3d 1241, 1242-43 (11th Cir.2007). *But cf.* ***Anderson v. Aon Corp.***, 614 F.3d 361, 364 (7th Cir.2010) (if case is removed and after removal P amends complaint to omit federal claim, court can maintain supplemental jurisdiction; for removed cases, jurisdiction is determined at time of removal).

2. Federal claim dismissed by court.

(1) Lack of subject-matter jurisdiction. If the court dismisses the federal claim for lack of subject-matter jurisdiction, the court cannot maintain supplemental jurisdiction. *See* ***Musson Theatrical, Inc. v. Federal Express Corp.***, 89 F.3d 1244, 1255 (6th Cir.1996). The court cannot exercise its supplemental jurisdiction because a dismissal for lack of subject-matter jurisdiction means there was never a valid federal claim to "anchor" the supplemental claims in federal court. *See id.*; ***Palmer v. Hospital Auth. of Randolph Cty.***, 22 F.3d 1559, 1570 (11th Cir. 1994); ***Ortega v. Brock***, 501 F.Supp.2d 1337, 1343 (M.D.Ala.2007); ***Trustees on Behalf of the Teamsters Benefit Trust v. Doctors Med. Ctr.***, 286 F.Supp.2d 1234, 1235 (N.D.Cal.2003).

(2) Lack of merit. If the court dismisses the federal claim for lack of merit (e.g., through an FRCP 12(b)(6) motion or a summary judgment), the court can maintain supplemental jurisdiction. *See* ***Musson Theatrical***, 89 F.3d at 1255. The court can exercise its supplemental jurisdiction because a dismissal for lack of merit means the dismissed federal claim was valid for jurisdictional purposes but was factually deficient. *See* ***Palmer***, 22 F.3d at 1570; ***Ortega***, 501 F.Supp.2d at 1343. Although the court can maintain supplemental jurisdiction after a dismissal based on FRCP 12(b)(6), there is a presumption in favor of dismissing the supplemental claims. ***Musson Theatrical***, 89 F.3d at 1255. That presumption can be overcome in unusual circumstances. *Id.*

§7. ABSTENTION

§7.1 Generally. Abstention refers to judicially created rules whereby a federal court may decline to decide some matters before it even though all jurisdictional and justiciability requirements have been met. *See* ***Barichello v. McDonald***, 98 F.3d 948, 954 (7th Cir.1996); *Black's Law Dictionary* 9 (9th ed. 2009). Under the doctrine of abstention, a court may decline to exercise, or postpone the exercise of, its jurisdiction only in extraordinary or narrow circumstances. ***Colorado River Water Conserv. Dist. v. U.S.***, 424 U.S. 800, 813 (1976); ***County of Allegheny v. Frank Mashuda Co.***, 360 U.S. 185, 188 (1959); *see* ***Quackenbush v. Allstate Ins.***, 517 U.S. 706, 727-28 (1996). If the court decides to dismiss or remand a case based on abstention principles—as opposed to staying the case—it may do so only when the relief sought is equitable or otherwise discretionary. ***Quackenbush***, 517 U.S. at 727-28. Thus, a suit for damages cannot be dismissed or remanded based on abstention principles. *See id.*

§7.2 Substantive abstention doctrines.

1. Unclear state law. Because federal courts apply state law in diversity cases, they are regularly called on to determine questions of unclear or unresolved state law. ***Erie R.R. v. Tompkins***, 304 U.S. 64, 78 (1938). There are several abstention doctrines that require the federal courts to decline jurisdiction in this circumstance.

(1) *Pullman* abstention. Abstention is appropriate when unclear questions of state law should be resolved before a federal constitutional issue is decided. ***Hawaii Hous. Auth. v. Midkiff***, 467 U.S. 229, 236 (1984); ***Nationwide Mut. Ins. v. Unauthorized Practice of Law Cmte.***, 283 F.3d 650, 652 (5th Cir.2002); *see* ***Wilbur v. Harris***, 53 F.3d 542, 545 (2d Cir.1995). When abstention is appropriate, the federal court should stay its proceedings and await a potentially dispositive pronouncement by the state courts. ***Harris Cty. Comm'rs Ct. v. Moore***, 420 U.S. 77, 88 n.14 (1975); *see* ***Railroad Comm'n v. Pullman Co.***, 312 U.S. 496, 501 (1941). A ***Pullman*** abstention is appropriate when (1) the complaint touches a sensitive area of social policy that the federal courts should not enter unless there is no alternative to adjudication, (2) a definitive ruling on the state-law issue by a state court could eliminate the need for constitutional adjudication by the federal courts, and (3) the proper resolution of a potentially determinative state-law issue is uncertain. ***Pullman Co.***, 312 U.S. at 498-500; ***Artway v. Attorney Gen.***, 81 F.3d 1235, 1270 (3d Cir.1996); ***Confederated Salish v. Simonich***, 29 F.3d 1398, 1407 (9th Cir.1994).

(2) *Thibodaux* abstention. Abstention is appropriate when litigation in a diversity suit involves state law that is unclear on some issue particularly close to the sovereign prerogatives of the state. ***Louisiana Power & Light Co. v. City of Thibodaux***, 360 U.S. 25, 27-28 (1959). Lack of clarity in state law alone is not a sufficient reason to stay a federal diversity case. ***Meredith v. Winter Haven***, 320 U.S. 228, 234-35 (1943).

(3) *Burford* abstention. Abstention is appropriate when there is a need to defer to complex state administrative procedures. *See* ***Burford v. Sun Oil Co.***, 319 U.S. 315, 331-34 (1943). A ***Burford*** abstention is appropriate when (1) the case presents a difficult issue of state law, (2) the case is in an area of important state policy, and (3) there is a unified state enforcement mechanism established to resolve the rights in question. ***New Orleans Pub. Serv. v. Council of New Orleans***, 491 U.S. 350, 361-62 (1989); *see* ***Quackenbush v. Allstate Ins.***, 517 U.S. 706, 727-28 (1996); ***Baran v. Port of Beaumont Nav. Dist.***, 57 F.3d 436, 441-42 (5th Cir.1995). Under ***Burford***, the balancing of state and federal interests "only rarely favors abstention." ***Quackenbush***, 517 U.S. at 728; ***Webb v. B.C. Rogers Poultry, Inc.***, 174 F.3d 697, 700 (5th Cir.1999).

2. *Younger* abstention.

(1) Criminal proceedings. Generally, federal courts should abstain from enjoining pending state criminal proceedings. *See* ***Younger v. Harris***, 401 U.S. 37, 53-54 (1971). Federal courts cannot provide a plaintiff with declaratory or injunctive relief when the plaintiff is subject to a pending state criminal prosecution. ***Samuels v. Mackell***, 401 U.S. 66, 72-73 (1971). Courts may disregard the ***Younger*** doctrine only when (1) the state proceeding was brought in bad faith or to harass the federal plaintiff, (2) the state statute is "flagrantly and patently violative of express constitutional prohibitions in every clause, sentence, and paragraph, and in whatever manner and against whomever an effort might be made to apply it," or (3) the doctrine was waived. ***Texas Ass'n of Bus. v. Earle***, 388 F.3d 515, 519 (5th Cir.2004); *see* ***Younger***, 401 U.S. at 53-54.

(2) Civil proceedings. Federal courts should abstain from enjoining certain pending state civil suits between private parties or suits in which the government is a party. For example, a federal court cannot enjoin civil enforcement proceedings. *See* ***Moore v. Sims***, 442 U.S. 415, 423 (1979) (child-removal proceeding); ***Trainor v. Hernandez***, 431 U.S. 434, 443-44 (1977) (suit to recover fraudulently obtained welfare benefits); ***Huffman v. Pursue, Ltd.***, 420 U.S. 592, 604 (1975) (public-nuisance statute). Moreover, a federal court cannot enjoin civil proceedings involving certain orders that are in furtherance of a state court's ability to perform its judicial functions. *See* ***Pennzoil Co. v. Texaco, Inc.***, 481 U.S. 1, 13-14 (1987) (requirement for the posting of bond pending appeal); ***Juidice v. Vail***, 430 U.S. 327, 335-36 (1977) (civil contempt order). *See generally* ***Bridges v. Kelley***, 84 F.3d 470, 476 (D.C.Cir. 1996) (application of ***Younger*** doctrine); ***Wightman v. Texas Supreme Ct.***, 84 F.3d 188, 189 (5th Cir.1996) (same).

NOTE

Most circuits agree that the ***Younger*** *abstention doctrine applies to cases involving money damages. The First, Second, Fourth, Sixth, Eighth, and Ninth Circuits have held that* ***Younger*** *applies in some fashion to damages cases.* ***Gilbertson v. Albright****, 381 F.3d 965, 978-79 & n.13 (9th Cir.2004); see* ***Kirschner v. Klemons****, 225 F.3d 227, 238 (2d Cir.2000);* ***Yamaha Motor Corp. v. Stroud****, 179 F.3d 598, 603-04 (8th Cir.1999);* ***Carroll v. City of Mount Clemens****, 139 F.3d 1072, 1075 (6th Cir.1998);* ***Kyricopoulos v. Town of Orleans****, 967 F.2d 14, 15 n.1 (1st Cir. 1992) (dicta);* ***Traverso v. Penn****, 874 F.2d 209, 212-13 (4th Cir.1989). The Fifth Circuit has held both ways—that* ***Younger*** *does and does not apply to damages cases.* ***Gilbertson****, 381 F.3d at 978 n.13. Compare* ***Lewis v. Beddingfield****, 20 F.3d 123, 125 (5th Cir.1994) (does apply to damages cases), with* ***Alexander v. Ieyoub****, 62 F.3d 709, 713 (5th Cir.1995) (does not apply to damages cases), and* ***Bishop v. State Bar of Tex.****, 736 F.2d 292, 295 (5th Cir.1984) (same). Of the circuits that do apply* ***Younger*** *to damages cases, most hold that a stay is appropriate, as opposed to a dismissal.* ***Gilbertson****, 381 F.3d at 980 n.15.*

(3) Administrative proceedings. Federal courts cannot enjoin state administrative proceedings in which important state interests are vindicated if in the course of those proceedings the federal plaintiff would have a full and fair opportunity to litigate its constitutional claim. ***Ohio Civil Rights Comm'n v. Dayton Christian Sch., Inc.***, 477 U.S. 619, 627 (1986); ***Middlesex Cty. Ethics Cmte. v. Garden State Bar Ass'n***, 457 U.S. 423, 434-35 (1982). Abstention is appropriate unless the plaintiff can show that state law clearly bars presentation of the constitutional claim. ***Squire v. Coughlan***, 469 F.3d 551, 556 (6th Cir.2006); *see* ***Stroman Rlty., Inc. v. Martinez***, 505 F.3d 658, 662 (7th Cir.2007) (abstention appropriate unless P can demonstrate exceptional circumstances requiring federal intervention).

3. *Brillhart* abstention. Abstention from exercising jurisdiction over a declaratory-judgment action is appropriate when another suit is pending in state court presenting the same issues, not governed by federal law, between the same parties. *See* ***Brillhart v. Excess Ins.***, 316 U.S. 491, 494-95 (1942); ***Black Sea Inv. v. United Heritage Corp.***, 204 F.3d 647, 652 (5th Cir.2000). In such a situation, the federal court should examine whether the questions in controversy between the parties to the federal suit can be better adjudicated in the pending state proceeding and whether necessary parties have been joined and are amenable to process in that proceeding. ***Brillhart***, 316 U.S. at 495; *see also* ***Sherwin-Williams Co. v. Holmes Cty.***, 343 F.3d 383, 389-90 & n.2 (5th Cir.2003) (listing factors used by each circuit in determining whether court should exercise jurisdiction over declaratory-judgment action). Generally, abstention from a declaratory-judgment action is proper when the state offers an alternative forum to resolve the particular dispute. ***Southwind Aviation, Inc. v. Bergen Aviation, Inc.***, 23 F.3d 948, 950 (5th Cir.1994); *see* ***Royal Indem. Co. v. Apex Oil Co.***, 511 F.3d 788, 793 (8th Cir.2008).

§7.3 Stay of related proceedings.

1. Parallel state proceeding. Generally, the pendency of parallel state and federal proceedings is not sufficient to justify a federal court declining to exercise its jurisdiction. ***Colorado River Water Conserv. Dist. v. U.S.***, 424 U.S. 800, 817 (1976); *see* ***Exxon Mobil Corp. v. Saudi Basic Indus.***, 544 U.S. 280, 292 (2005) (pending

state proceeding does not prevent federal court from exercising jurisdiction over concurrent proceeding); 17A Wright, Miller, Cooper & Amar §4247 (outlining federal courts' treatment of parallel proceedings). Only under the ***Colorado River*** "exceptional circumstances" test may a federal court abstain from exercising federal jurisdiction when the same suit has previously been filed in state court. *See* ***Moses H. Cone Mem'l Hosp. v. Mercury Constr. Corp.***, 460 U.S. 1, 15-26 (1983); *see also* ***American Guar. & Liab. Ins. v. Anco Insulations, Inc.***, 408 F.3d 248, 250-51 (5th Cir.2005) (***Colorado River*** test applies to suit seeking monetary or other relief, even if declaratory relief is also sought; court's discretion to grant stay is "narrowly circumscribed" by its obligation to hear cases within its jurisdiction). Under the exceptional-circumstances test, the court should consider six factors in determining whether to abstain: (1) the existence of a matter over which one court has established jurisdiction, (2) the relative convenience of the forums, (3) the avoidance of piecemeal litigation, (4) the priority of the cases, based more on the relative progress made in each case than simply on which one was filed first, (5) whether state or federal law controls, especially favoring the exercise of jurisdiction when federal law controls, and (6) the adequacy of the state proceeding to protect the rights of the party invoking federal jurisdiction. ***Black Sea Inv. v. United Heritage Corp.***, 204 F.3d 647, 650 (5th Cir.2000); ***U.S. Fid. & Guar. Co. v. Murphy Oil USA, Inc.***, 21 F.3d 259, 263 (8th Cir.1994). In assessing the propriety of abstention according to these factors, a federal court must keep in mind that the exercise of jurisdiction is heavily favored. ***Moses H. Cone Mem'l Hosp.***, 460 U.S. at 16; ***Colorado River***, 424 U.S. at 817; ***Bank One v. Boyd***, 288 F.3d 181, 184 (5th Cir.2002); ***FDIC v. Four Star Holding Co.***, 178 F.3d 97, 101 (2d Cir.1999); *see* ***Funkhouser v. Wells Fargo Bank***, 289 F.3d 1137, 1141 (9th Cir.2002).

(1) Declaratory-judgment action. The exceptional-circumstances test does not apply to a federal court's decision to dismiss a federal declaratory-judgment action in favor of parallel state litigation. ***Youell v. Exxon Corp.***, 74 F.3d 373, 375 (2d Cir.1996); *e.g.*, ***Royal Indem. Co. v. Apex Oil Co.***, 511 F.3d 788, 792-94 (8th Cir.2008) (although monetary damages were sought, essence of lawsuit was for declaratory judgment, so exceptional-circumstances test did not apply). For federal declaratory-judgment actions, federal courts have "broader discretion" to abstain. ***Youell***, 74 F.3d at 375; *see* ***Wilton v. Seven Falls Co.***, 515 U.S. 277, 289-90 (1995); ***Royal Indem. Co.***, 511 F.3d at 792-93; ***U.S. v. City of Las Cruces***, 289 F.3d 1170, 1181 (10th Cir.2002). However, when the parallel state proceeding is grounded in federal law, the exceptional-circumstances test still applies. ***Youell***, 74 F.3d at 376. See "Declaratory Judgment Act," ch. 2-E, §2, p. 108.

(2) Injunctive & declaratory relief. When a party seeks both injunctive and declaratory relief, the appropriateness of abstention is assessed under ***Colorado River***, unless the request for injunctive relief is either frivolous or made solely to avoid application of the ***Brillhart*** standard. ***Black Sea***, 204 F.3d at 652.

2. Parallel federal proceeding. Unlike parallel state and federal proceedings, if a plaintiff pursues two federal cases against the same party involving the same controversy at the same time, one of the two identical pending cases should be dismissed. ***Colorado River***, 424 U.S. at 817; ***Missouri v. Prudential Health Care Plan, Inc.***, 259 F.3d 949, 953-54 (8th Cir.2001); ***Serlin v. Arthur Andersen & Co.***, 3 F.3d 221, 223 (7th Cir.1993); *see* ***Zerilli v. Evening News Ass'n***, 628 F.2d 217, 222 (D.C.Cir.1980); ***Walton v. Eaton Corp.***, 563 F.2d 66, 70 (3d Cir.1977).

(1) First-to-file rule. Generally, the "first-to-file rule" determines which case should be dismissed—that is, when related cases are pending in two federal courts, the court where the suit was last filed cannot hear the case if the issues substantially overlap. ***Employers Ins. of Wausau v. Fox Entm't Grp.***, 522 F.3d 271, 274-75 (2d Cir.2008); ***Manuel v. Convergys Corp.***, 430 F.3d 1132, 1135 (11th Cir.2005); ***Cadle Co. v. Whataburger of Alice, Inc.***, 174 F.3d 599, 603 (5th Cir.1999). When the likelihood of a substantial overlap between the two cases is demonstrated, the court where the suit was first filed should determine whether later-filed suits should proceed. ***Cadle Co.***, 174 F.3d at 605.

(2) Exceptions. The first-to-file rule, however, is flexible and may be applied in the interest of justice or judicial economy. ***Certified Restoration Dry Cleaning Network, L.L.C. v. Tenke Corp.***, 511 F.3d 535, 551-52 (6th Cir.2007); ***Cedars-Sinai Med. Ctr. v. Shalala***, 125 F.3d 765, 769 (9th Cir.1997). The first-filed suit may be dismissed if (1) the first suit is based on forum shopping, bad faith, or anticipatory conduct or (2) special circumstances

weigh in favor of the forum in the later-filed suit. ***Employers Ins. of Wausau***, 522 F.3d at 275-76 (relevant factors are essentially same as those considered for motion to transfer venue).

§7.4 Anti-Injunction Act.

1. Purpose. The Anti-Injunction Act prohibits a federal court from issuing an injunction to enjoin state-court proceedings. ***Atlantic Coast Line R.R. v. Brotherhood of Locomotive Eng'rs***, 398 U.S. 281, 286 (1970); *see* 28 U.S.C. §2283; ***Smith v. Bayer Corp.***, ___ U.S. ___, 131 S.Ct. 2368, 2375 (2011). The general purpose of the Act is to prevent needless friction between state and federal courts. ***Chick Kam Choo v. Exxon Corp.***, 486 U.S. 140, 146 (1988); ***In re Diet Drugs***, 282 F.3d 220, 239 (3d Cir.2002); ***National R.R. Passenger Corp. v. Florida***, 929 F.2d 1532, 1536 (11th Cir.1991). The Act simply allows cases to proceed in a parallel fashion, and if one ends first, it has the effect of res judicata on the other proceeding. *See* ***Klay v. United Healthgroup, Inc.***, 376 F.3d 1092, 1110-11 (11th Cir.2004).

2. Exceptions. Although the Anti-Injunction Act generally allows parallel cases to proceed, the Act permits federal courts to enjoin state-court proceedings when (1) there is express statutory authority in other federal law, (2) the injunction is necessary in aid of the federal court's jurisdiction, or (3) the injunction is necessary to protect or effectuate the federal court's earlier judgment (i.e., the relitigation exception). 28 U.S.C. §2283; *see* ***McFarland v. Scott***, 512 U.S. 849, 857 (1994); ***In re Diet Drugs***, 282 F.3d at 233. These exceptions are read narrowly, and the prohibition against injunctions is read broadly. ***Smith***, ___ U.S. at ___, 131 S.Ct. at 2375; ***Chick Kam Choo***, 486 U.S. at 146; ***Great Earth Cos. v. Simons***, 288 F.3d 878, 894 (6th Cir.2002); *see* ***California v. Randtron***, 284 F.3d 969, 974 (9th Cir.2002).

(1) Other statute authorizing injunction. The Anti-Injunction Act allows a federal court to issue an injunction if one is explicitly authorized under some other statute. *E.g.*, ***Mitchum v. Foster***, 407 U.S. 225, 236-38 (1972) (42 U.S.C. §1983 actions). This requirement is met when an act of Congress has created a specific and unique federal right or remedy enforceable in a federal court that could be frustrated if the federal court were not empowered to enjoin a state-court proceeding. *Id.* at 237.

(2) Injunction in aid of jurisdiction. The injunction-in-aid-of-jurisdiction exception applies only to prevent a state court from interfering with a federal court's consideration or disposition of a case so much that the federal court's flexibility and authority to decide the case are seriously impaired. ***Atlantic Coast Line R.R.***, 398 U.S. at 295; ***Battle v. Liberty Nat'l Life Ins.***, 877 F.2d 877, 880 (11th Cir.1989). Because cases in federal and state court can proceed concurrently without interference from either court, it is not enough that the state case threatens to reach judgment before the federal case—it must interfere with the federal court's own path to judgment to justify an injunction under the Anti-Injunction Act. ***In re Diet Drugs***, 282 F.3d at 234. The requested injunction must not only relate to the jurisdiction of the court but also be necessary in aid of that jurisdiction. ***Sycuan Band of Mission Indians v. Roache***, 54 F.3d 535, 540-41 (9th Cir.1995); ***Carlough v. Amchem Prods.***, 10 F.3d 189, 202 (3d Cir.1993).

(3) Relitigation exception. The relitigation exception allows a federal court to issue an injunction to effectuate its judgment and prevent the relitigation of issues it has actually decided. ***Smith***, ___ U.S. at ___, 131 S.Ct. at 2375; ***Weyerhaeuser Co. v. Wyatt***, 505 F.3d 1104, 1109-10 (10th Cir.2007); ***Jones v. St. Paul Cos.***, 495 F.3d 888, 892-93 (8th Cir.2007); ***Great Earth Cos.***, 288 F.3d at 894; ***New York Life Ins. v. Gillispie***, 203 F.3d 384, 387 (5th Cir.2000); *see* 28 U.S.C. §2283. *But see* ***Western Sys. v. Ulloa***, 958 F.2d 864, 870 (9th Cir.1992) (relitigation exception applies not only to issues actually decided but also those that could have been decided). The relitigation exception has four requirements: (1) the parties in the later suit must be identical to, or at least in privity with, the parties in the earlier suit, (2) the judgment in the earlier suit must have been rendered by a court of competent jurisdiction, (3) the earlier suit must have concluded with a final judgment on the merits, and (4) the same claim or cause of action must be involved in both suits. ***Gillispie***, 203 F.3d at 387; *see* ***Assurance Co. v. Kirkland***, 312 F.3d 186, 189 (5th Cir.2002) (essential prerequisite for applying relitigation exception is that claims or issues actually have been decided by federal court).

NOTE

It is not clear whether one federal court can apply the relitigation exception to protect a judgment issued by another federal court. See ***Smith v. Woosley****, 399 F.3d 428, 434-36 (2d Cir.2005) (allowing federal court to protect judgment of another federal court, but noting that other case law on issue is inconclusive).*

3. Act does not apply.

(1) U.S. is party. The Anti-Injunction Act does not apply when the United States or one of its agencies seeks an injunction in federal court to prevent the frustration of superior federal interests or to protect national interests. ***NLRB v. Nash-Finch Co.***, 404 U.S. 138, 146-47 (1971); ***Leiter Minerals, Inc. v. U.S.***, 352 U.S. 220, 225-26 (1957).

(2) State administrative proceedings. The Anti-Injunction Act does not apply to state administrative proceedings. ***Entergy, Ark., Inc. v. Nebraska***, 210 F.3d 887, 900 (8th Cir.2000); ***Bud Antle, Inc. v. Barbosa***, 45 F.3d 1261, 1271-72 (9th Cir.1995); *see* ***SMA Life Assur. Co. v. Sanchez-Pica***, 960 F.2d 274, 276 (1st Cir.1992); *see also* ***Gibson v. Berryhill***, 411 U.S. 564, 573 n.12 (1973) (declining to decide whether Act applies to state administrative body).

§8. APPELLATE REVIEW

The standard of review for a dismissal for lack of subject-matter jurisdiction is de novo. *E.g.*, ***Cash v. Granville Cty. Bd. of Educ.***, 242 F.3d 219, 222 (4th Cir.2001) (federal-question jurisdiction); ***Crum v. Circus Circus Enters.***, 231 F.3d 1129, 1130 (9th Cir.2000) (diversity jurisdiction); ***Koehler v. Bank of Berm. (N.Y.) Ltd.***, 209 F.3d 130, 139 (2d Cir.2000) (alienage jurisdiction), *amended*, 229 F.3d 424 (2d Cir.2000). Subject-matter jurisdiction cannot be waived; therefore, the court can review the issue of subject-matter jurisdiction sua sponte at any stage of the proceedings. *See* ***Coury v. Prot***, 85 F.3d 244, 248 (5th Cir.1996).

§8.1 Diversity jurisdiction.

1. Party's domicile. Most courts regard the determination of a party's domicile as a mixed question of law and fact. ***Coury v. Prot***, 85 F.3d 244, 251 (5th Cir.1996). Nevertheless, in practice, the district court's determination of domicile is reviewed under the clearly-erroneous standard as a question of fact. *Id.*

2. Party's citizenship. Most courts regard the determination of a party's citizenship as a question of fact and review the findings for clear error. ***Preston v. Tenet Healthsystem Mem'l Med. Ctr., Inc.***, 485 F.3d 793, 796 (5th Cir.2007); *see* ***Sheehan v. Gustafson***, 967 F.2d 1214, 1215 (8th Cir.1992) (citizenship is mixed question of law and fact but mostly fact, and findings are reviewed for clear error).

3. Amount in controversy. Most courts regard the determination of the amount in controversy as a question of law and review the determination de novo. ***Hayes v. Equitable Energy Res.***, 266 F.3d 560, 572 (6th Cir.2001); *see* ***White v. FCI USA, Inc.***, 319 F.3d 672, 674 (5th Cir.2003).

§8.2 Supplemental jurisdiction.

A court's decision to exercise supplemental jurisdiction is reviewed for an abuse of discretion. ***Miller Aviation v. Milwaukee Cty. Bd. of Supervisors***, 273 F.3d 722, 727 (7th Cir.2001); ***Batiste v. Island Records, Inc.***, 179 F.3d 217, 226 (5th Cir.1999); ***San Pedro Hotel Co. v. City of L.A.***, 159 F.3d 470, 478 (9th Cir.1998); ***Ametex Fabrics, Inc. v. Just In Materials, Inc.***, 140 F.3d 101, 105 (2d Cir.1998). But if the underlying basis of a 28 U.S.C. §1367(c) remand is a legal question, the standard of review is de novo. ***Miller Aviation***, 273 F.3d at 727-28; ***Lazorko v. Pennsylvania Hosp.***, 237 F.3d 242, 247 (3d Cir.2000); ***Engelhardt v. Paul Revere Life Ins.***, 139 F.3d 1346, 1351 n.4 (11th Cir.1998). A court does not need to provide reasons for declining jurisdiction, unless it declines jurisdiction under the "exceptional circumstances" provision of §1367(c). ***Executive Software N. Am., Inc. v. U.S. Dist. Ct. for the Cent. Dist. of Cal.***, 24 F.3d 1545, 1560-61 (9th Cir.1994), *overruled on other grounds*, ***California Dept. of Water Res. v. Powerex Corp.***, 533 F.3d 1087 (9th Cir.2008). A number of circuits have held that once a court has the power to hear a case under §1367(a), it may exercise supplemental jurisdiction without addressing sua sponte whether it should decline to exercise jurisdiction under §1367(c). *See* ***Acri v.***

Varian Assocs., 114 F.3d 999, 1000-01 (9th Cir.1997) (noting that 7th, 9th, and D.C. Circuits follow this approach). In addition, some courts will not review the district court's decision to exercise its supplemental jurisdiction under §1367(c) if the issue is not raised at the district level. ***Acri***, 114 F.3d at 1000-01.

§8.3 Abstention. The standard of review of a court's decision to abstain from exercising jurisdiction will vary depending on the abstention doctrine applied and the circuit. For example, in ***Younger*** abstention cases, the circuits differ on whether to apply a de novo standard of review or an abuse-of-discretion standard of review. *Compare* ***Squire v. Coughlan***, 469 F.3d 551, 555 (6th Cir.2006) (de novo), ***Green v. City of Tucson***, 255 F.3d 1086, 1093 (9th Cir.2001) (same), *overruled on other grounds*, ***Gilbertson v. Albright***, 381 F.3d 965 (9th Cir.2004), ***Brooks v. New Hampshire Supreme Ct.***, 80 F.3d 633, 637 (1st Cir.1996) (same), *and* ***Trust & Inv. Advisers v. Hogsett***, 43 F.3d 290, 293-94 (7th Cir.1994) (same), *with* ***Alexander v. Ieyoub***, 62 F.3d 709, 712 (5th Cir.1995) (abuse of discretion), *and* ***Martin Marietta Corp. v. Maryland Comm'n on Human Relations***, 38 F.3d 1392, 1396 (4th Cir.1994) (same). Some circuits apply a two-part review: (1) de novo review of whether the elements for the particular abstention doctrine are present and (2) abuse-of-discretion review of the district court's decision. *See* ***Texas Ass'n of Bus. v. Earle***, 388 F.3d 515, 518 (5th Cir.2004) (applying to all abstention doctrines); ***O'Neill v. City of Phila.***, 32 F.3d 785, 790 (3d Cir. 1994) (same).

G. CHOOSING THE COURT—VENUE

§1. GENERAL

§1.1 Rules. 28 U.S.C. §§1390, 1391, 1404, 1406; FRCP 12(h)(1). Venue in federal court is governed by statute, not by the FRCPs. *See* ***Leroy v. Great W. United Corp.***, 443 U.S. 173, 183-84 (1979).

§1.2 Purpose. Once a plaintiff determines there is federal jurisdiction over the subject matter of the suit, it must decide in which federal court to file the suit. *See* 28 U.S.C. §1390. Unlike personal or subject-matter jurisdiction, both of which address a court's power to adjudicate a case between the parties, the concept of venue is designed to protect the defendant and the witnesses against a plaintiff's choice of an unfair or inconvenient forum. ***Leroy v. Great W. United Corp.***, 443 U.S. 173, 183-84 (1979); ***Daniel v. American Bd. of Emerg. Med.***, 428 F.3d 408, 432 (2d Cir.2005); 14D Wright, Miller & Cooper, *Federal Practice & Procedure 3d* §3801 (2007 & Supp.2012); *see also* ***Firstar Bank v. Faul***, 253 F.3d 982, 989-90 (7th Cir.2001) (primary purpose of venue statutes is to limit inconvenience to parties); ***Hoover Grp. v. Custom Metalcraft, Inc.***, 84 F.3d 1408, 1410 (Fed.Cir.1996) (venue requirements are for benefit of Ds).

NOTE

In the Federal Courts Jurisdiction and Venue Clarification Act of 2011 (referred to as the Clarification Act), Congress made significant amendments to venue statutes in title 28. See Lamar Smith, Federal Courts Jurisdiction & Venue Clarification Act of 2011, H.R. Rep. No. 112-10, at 17-24 (2011). For this subchapter, the Clarification Act modified venue provisions by (1) enacting new 28 U.S.C. §1390, which defines the term "venue," (2) eliminating separate sections for venue requirements for diversity and federal-question cases, (3) clarifying "residence" for venue purposes, (4) clarifying venue for aliens, and (5) repealing 28 U.S.C. §1392, which specified venue for local actions. See Lamar Smith, Federal Courts Jurisdiction & Venue Clarification Act of 2011, H.R. Rep. No. 112-10, at 17-24 (2011). The Clarification Act became effective for any suit commenced in a U.S. district court on or after January 6, 2012. Federal Courts Jurisdiction & Venue Clarification Act of 2011, P.L. 112-63, §205, 125 Stat. 764 (2011) (eff. Jan. 6, 2012). For the law before the Clarification Act became effective, see ***O'Connor's Federal Rules * Civil Trials*** *(2012), "Choosing the Court—Venue," ch. 2-G, p. 138. Because of the substantive changes made by the 2011 amendments, use caution when citing cases that predate the amendments.*

§1.3 Forms. ***O'Connor's Federal Civil Forms*** **(2012), FORM 2B:4.**

§1.4 Other references. Federal Courts Jurisdiction & Venue Clarification Act of 2011, P.L. 112-63, 125 Stat. 758 (2011) (eff. Jan. 6, 2012) (referred to as Clarification Act); Lamar Smith, Federal Courts Jurisdiction & Venue Clarification Act of 2011, H.R. Rep. No. 112-10 (2011) (referred to as H.R. Rep. No. 112-10 (2011)); 14D, 15 Wright, Miller & Cooper, *Federal Practice & Procedure 3d* §§3801-3900 (2007 & Supp.2012); 17 *Moore's Federal Practice 3d* chs. 110-111 (2012); Siegel, *Changes in Federal Jurisdiction & Practice Under the New (Dec. 1, 1990) Judicial Improvements Act*, 133 F.R.D. 61, 69-75 (1991).

§2. VENUE – DEFINED

The term "venue" is defined to refer to the geographic specification of the proper court or courts for the litigation of a civil action. 28 U.S.C. §1390(a). The term, however, is not intended to encompass geographic specifications included in statutes that grant or restrict subject-matter jurisdiction by identifying a proper forum for litigating certain types of proceedings. *Id.*; *see* H.R. Rep. No. 112-10, at 17 (2011).

NOTE

Section 1390(a) provides a general definition of venue that distinguishes venue as a geographic specification of the proper forum for litigation from venue provided in statutes that happen to provide a proper forum but are actually restrictions on subject-matter jurisdiction. H.R. Rep. No. 112-10, at 17 (2011). Although a statute restricting subject-matter jurisdiction may include geographic terms, the "venue" in those statutes cannot be waived and is not affected by amendments to the general venue rules. Id. General venue challenges (i.e., challenges to venue as a geographic specification of the proper forum for litigation) can still be waived. Id. See "Motion to Dismiss for Improper Venue—FRCP 12(b)(3)," ch. 3-D, p. 192.

§3. GENERAL VENUE STATUTE

The general venue statute applies to all civil actions filed in U.S. district courts when no other statute provides for a specific venue. *See* 28 U.S.C. §1391(a); H.R. Rep. No. 112-10, at 18 (2011).

§3.1 Civil actions – generally. 28 U.S.C. §1391(b) establishes the choice of venue when no other statute provides for a specific venue. Under §1391(b), a complaint may be filed in a district as follows:

NOTE

Under the Clarification Act (which applies to cases filed on or after January 6, 2012), the amendments to §1391(b) eliminated the venue distinction between diversity and federal-question cases in favor of a single, unified approach for determining venue. H.R. Rep. No. 112-10, at 19 (2011); see Clarification Act, P.L. 112-63, §205, 125 Stat. 764 (2011) (eff. Jan. 6, 2012).

1. Defendants in same state. A civil action can be brought in a judicial district in which any defendant resides, if all defendants are residents of the state in which the district is located. 28 U.S.C. §1391(b)(1); *see also* H.R. Rep. No. 112-10, at 19 (2011) (under Clarification Act, former §1391(a)(1) and (b)(1) were modified to make clear that venue in multiple-defendant cases is strictly limited to district of state in which all defendants reside).

2. Event or property in district. A civil action can be brought in a judicial district in which a substantial part of the events or omissions giving rise to the claim occurred, or a substantial part of property that is the subject of the action is situated. 28 U.S.C. §1391(b)(2).

NOTE

Under the Clarification Act, former §1391(a)(2) and (b)(2) were merged into new §1391(b)(2) without any change to the language. H.R. Rep. No. 112-10, at 20 (2011).

(1) **Multiple districts.** Venue may be appropriate in more than one district. *See* ***Gulf Ins. v. Glasbrenner***, 417 F.3d 353, 356 (2d Cir.2005); ***Uffner v. La Reunion Francaise, S.A.***, 244 F.3d 38, 43 (1st Cir.2001). When venue is appropriate in more than one district, the court does not ask which district among the potential forums is the "best" venue, but instead whether the district that the plaintiff chose has a substantial connection to the claim, regardless of whether other forums have great connections. *See* ***Pecoraro v. Sky Ranch for Boys, Inc.***, 340 F.3d 558, 563 (8th Cir.2003).

(2) **Substantial part.** Whether a "substantial part" of an event occurred in a district is usually determined by where the event occurred, not by whether a defendant made a deliberate contact with the forum. *See* ***First of Mich. Corp. v. Bramlet***, 141 F.3d 260, 263 (6th Cir.1998); ***Cottman Transmission Sys. v. Martino***, 36 F.3d 291, 294 (3d Cir.1994); ***Bates v. C&S Adjusters, Inc.***, 980 F.2d 865, 868 (2d Cir.1992); *see also* ***Daniel v. American Bd. of Emerg. Med.***, 428 F.3d 408, 432 (2d Cir.2005) (venue not restricted to district where "most substantial" events or omissions occurred). *But see* ***Woodke v. Dahm***, 70 F.3d 983, 985 (8th Cir.1995) (only D's acts with respect to forum are considered).

3. No other district proper. A civil action can be brought in any judicial district in which any defendant is subject to the court's personal jurisdiction with respect to the action if there is no district in which the action can otherwise be brought under 28 U.S.C. §1391. 28 U.S.C. §1391(b)(3). For example, in a suit in which the defendants reside in different states and most of the events giving rise to the suit occurred in a foreign country, the plaintiff can file the suit in a district where any defendant is subject to the court's jurisdiction. *See* H.R. Rep. No. 112-10, at 19-20 (2011) (as practical matter, §1391(b)(3) applies primarily to claims that arise abroad).

NOTE

Under the Clarification Act, the fallback provisions of former §1391(a)(3) and (b)(3) were merged in favor of more restrictive language. H.R. Rep. No. 112-10, at 20 (2011).

§3.2 Mass tort. For actions in which the court exercises diversity jurisdiction over a single-event mass accident under 28 U.S.C. §1369, venue is proper in any district in which any defendant resides or in which a substantial part of the accident giving rise to the action took place. 28 U.S.C. §1391(g).

§3.3 Suit against United States or its agencies, officers, or employees. For actions involving claims against the U.S. government or its agencies, officers, or employees, venue is governed by 28 U.S.C. §1391(e). ***Deutsch v. U.S. Dept. of Justice***, 881 F.Supp. 49, 53 (D.D.C.1995), *aff'd*, 93 F.3d 986 (D.C.Cir.1996) (table case). The purpose of §1391(e) is to provide nationwide venue for the convenience of individual plaintiffs in suits against the government, an agency, or an officer or employee. ***Stafford v. Briggs***, 444 U.S. 527, 542 (1980); *see* ***Kreines v. U.S.***, 33 F.3d 1105, 1107-08 (9th Cir.1994). However, §1391(e) does not apply to suits brought against a government official in her individual capacity; venue in such suits is covered by 28 U.S.C. §1391(b). ***Deutsch***, 881 F.Supp. at 53; *see* ***Kreines***, 33 F.3d at 1108. For actions against the United States or its agencies, officers, or employees, venue is proper in any of the following:

1. The district where a defendant in the suit resides. 28 U.S.C. §1391(e)(1)(A). Officers and agencies of the United States can have more than one residence; therefore, venue may lie in more than one forum. ***Bartman v. Cheney***, 827 F.Supp. 1, 2 (D.D.C.1993). An agency's office within a district must have a substantial connection with the complaint before it establishes the residence of the agency for venue purposes. *See* ***Davies Precision Mach., Inc. v. Defense Logistics Agency***, 825 F.Supp. 105, 107 (E.D.Pa.1993).

2. The district where a substantial part of the events or omissions giving rise to the claim occurred, or where a substantial part of property that is the subject of the suit is situated. 28 U.S.C. §1391(e)(1)(B).

3. The district where the plaintiff resides, if no real property is involved in the suit. *Id.* §1391(e)(1)(C). However, when there is more than one plaintiff, only one of the plaintiffs must reside in the district for venue to be proper. ***Institute of Certified Practitioners, Inc. v. Bentsen***, 874 F.Supp. 1370, 1372 (N.D.Ga.1994).

§3.4 Suit against foreign state. For suits against a foreign state, as defined under 28 U.S.C. §1603(a), venue is proper in any of the following:

1. A district where a substantial part of the events or omissions giving rise to the claim occurred, or where a substantial part of property that is the subject of the suit is situated. 28 U.S.C. §1391(f)(1).

2. A district where the vessel or cargo of a foreign state is situated, if the claim is asserted under 28 U.S.C. §1605(b). 28 U.S.C. §1391(f)(2).

3. A district where the agency or instrumentality is licensed to do business or is doing business, if the suit is brought against an agency or instrumentality of a foreign state as defined in 28 U.S.C. §1603(b). 28 U.S.C. §1391(f)(3).

4. The U.S. District Court for the District of Columbia, if the suit is brought against a foreign state or a political subdivision of a foreign state. *Id.* §1391(f)(4).

§4. SPECIAL VENUE STATUTES

§4.1 Special vs. general venue. When there is a special venue statute expressly identifying venue for a particular action, it controls over the general venue statute. *See* 14D Wright, Miller & Cooper §3803 & n.2. However, unless there is restrictive language in the special venue statute, the general venue statute supplements the special statute. 14D Wright, Miller & Cooper §3803 & n.3.

§4.2 Examples. The following is a nonexhaustive list of special venue statutes:

1. **Statutory interpleader.** Statutory interpleader actions under 28 U.S.C. §1335 may be brought in the district where one or more of the claimants reside. 28 U.S.C. §1397.

2. **Multidistrict litigation.** Multidistrict litigation is governed by 28 U.S.C. §1407.

3. **Bankruptcy.** Actions arising under or related to the bankruptcy statutes are governed by 28 U.S.C. §§1408 and 1409.

4. **Admiralty & maritime.** The general venue statute does not apply to admiralty and maritime actions. 28 U.S.C. §1390(b); FRCP 82; *see* H.R. Rep. No. 112-10, at 17 (2011). Rather, analysis of venue and personal jurisdiction merge, and venue is proper in any district where personal jurisdiction can be obtained over the defendant. *See* ***Sunbelt Corp. v. Noble, Denton & Assocs.***, 5 F.3d 28, 31 n.5 (3d Cir.1993); ***In re McDonnell-Douglas Corp.***, 647 F.2d 515, 516 (5th Cir.1981). However, certain remedial statutes, such as the Jones Act, 46 U.S.C. §688, have been interpreted to incorporate the general venue provisions of 28 U.S.C. §1391. *See* ***Micomonaco v. Washington***, 45 F.3d 316, 321 (9th Cir.1995).

NOTE

New §1390(b) clarifies that admiralty disputes are subject to the general transfer provisions in 28 U.S.C. §§1404-1407. 28 U.S.C. §1390(b); H.R. Rep. No. 112-10, at 17 (2011). See "Motion to Transfer Venue—28 U.S.C. §1404," ch. 3-K, p. 221.

5. **Securities.** Suits under the Securities Exchange Act of 1934 are governed by 15 U.S.C. §78aa(a).

6. **FTCA.** Suits under the Federal Tort Claims Act are governed by 28 U.S.C. §1402(b).

7. **Patent & copyright.** Patent-infringement and copyright-infringement suits are governed by 28 U.S.C. §1400. *See* ***Milwaukee Concrete Studios, Ltd. v. Fjeld Mfg. Co.***, 8 F.3d 441, 443 (7th Cir.1993). However, for purposes of patent-infringement suits, 28 U.S.C. §1391(c)(2) and (d) make a corporate defendant subject to suit in any district where it is subject to personal jurisdiction. *See* ***In re Regents of the Univ. of Cal.***, 964 F.2d 1128, 1132 (Fed. Cir.1992); ***VE Holding Corp. v. Johnson Gas Appliance Co.***, 917 F.2d 1574, 1584 (Fed.Cir.1990).

8. ERISA. Suits under the Employee Retirement Income Security Act of 1974 (ERISA) are governed by 29 U.S.C. §1132(e)(2).

9. EEOC. Suits for employment discrimination under Title VII are governed by 42 U.S.C. §2000e-5(f)(3). ***Chris v. Tenet***, 221 F.3d 648, 652 (4th Cir.2000).

10. NLRB subpoenas. Enforcement of National Labor Relations Board (NLRB) subpoenas is governed by 29 U.S.C. §161(2). *See **NLRB v. Line***, 50 F.3d 311, 314 (5th Cir.1995).

11. RICO. Suits under the Racketeer Influenced and Corrupt Organizations Act (RICO) are governed by 18 U.S.C. §1965.

12. Arbitration. Actions to confirm, vacate, or modify arbitration awards are permitted either in the district where the arbitration award was made under the Federal Arbitration Act, 9 U.S.C. §§9-11, or in any district proper under the general venue statute. *See **Cortez Byrd Chips, Inc. v. Bill Harbert Constr. Co.***, 529 U.S. 193, 203-04 (2000) (Act's venue provisions are permissive, not mandatory); ***Textile Unlimited, Inc. v. A. .BMH & Co.***, 240 F.3d 781, 784 (9th Cir.2001) (same).

§5. RESIDENCE UNDER GENERAL & SPECIAL VENUE STATUTES

Venue is based on residence, not on citizenship as with diversity jurisdiction. The residency provisions under 28 U.S.C. §1391(c) apply to all venue statutes. H.R. Rep. No. 112-10, at 20 (2011). The residency of the parties for purposes of venue is determined as follows:

§5.1 Natural person.

1. Generally. A natural person, including an alien lawfully admitted for permanent residence in the United States, is deemed to reside in the judicial district in which that person is domiciled. 28 U.S.C. §1391(c)(1).

NOTE

Under the Clarification Act, the 2011 amendments to §1391(c)(1) resolved a circuit split over the meaning of the term "resides" as it applies to natural persons. In adopting the majority view, Congress made clear that in cases in which the plaintiff seeks to sue multiple individuals domiciled in separate states, the plaintiff will have to bring suit under §1391(b)(2) (claim-based venue—that is, where the events or omissions giving rise to the claim occurred), rather than §1391(b)(1) (party-based venue). H.R. Rep. No. 112-10, at 20-21 (2011).

2. State & local officials. The residence of public officials sued for official acts is where they performed the acts, not where they live. 14D Wright, Miller & Cooper §3805 nn.21-22; *see **Butterworth v. Hill***, 114 U.S. 128, 132 (1885); ***Florida Nursing Home Ass'n v. Page***, 616 F.2d 1355, 1360 (5th Cir.1980), *rev'd on other grounds sub nom. **Florida Dept. of Health & Rehab. Servs. v. Florida Nursing Home Ass'n***, 450 U.S. 147 (1981); ***O'Neill v. Battisti***, 472 F.2d 789, 791 (6th Cir.1972). Some courts have noted that state officers may have more than one residence for venue purposes. *See **Florida Nursing Home***, 616 F.2d at 1360-61; 14D Wright, Miller & Cooper §3805 & n.25.

§5.2 Entity.

1. Generally. For an entity with the capacity to sue and be sued in its common name under applicable law, whether or not it is incorporated (e.g., corporations, partnerships, unions, LLCs), where the entity is deemed to reside depends on whether the entity is a plaintiff or defendant. *See* 28 U.S.C. §1391(c)(2); *see also* H.R. Rep. No. 112-10, at 21-22 (2011) (Clarification Act made clear that deeming provision of §1391(c)(2) applies to unincorporated associations).

(1) Entity is defendant. If the entity is a defendant, it is deemed to reside in any judicial district in which it is subject to the court's personal jurisdiction with respect to the civil action in question. 28 U.S.C. §1391(c)(2).

(2) Entity is plaintiff. If the entity is a plaintiff, it is deemed to reside only in the judicial district in which it maintains its principal place of business. 28 U.S.C. §1391(c)(2); *see* H.R. Rep. No. 112-10, at 22 (2011) (Clarification Act slightly narrowed venue option for P-entities).

2. Defendant-corporation in state with multiple districts. For purposes of venue under U.S.C. title 28, chapter 87, a defendant-corporation that is subject to personal jurisdiction when an action is commenced in a state with more than one judicial district is deemed to reside in (1) any district in the state within which the defendant's contacts would be sufficient to subject it to personal jurisdiction if that district were a separate state, or (2) if there is no such district, the district within which the defendant has the most significant contacts. 28 U.S.C. §1391(d).

§5.3 Nonresident defendant. A defendant—whether a natural person or a corporation—who is not a resident of the United States can be sued in any judicial district. 28 U.S.C. §1391(c)(3). If such a defendant is joined in the action, that defendant is disregarded when determining where the action can be brought with respect to the other defendants. *Id.*

CAUTION

Under the Clarification Act, the 2011 amendments to former §1391(d) (now §1391(c)(3)) eliminated the term "alien" in favor of "residence." H.R. Rep. No. 112-10, at 22 (2011). This amendment means that both aliens and U.S. citizens domiciled abroad are disregarded for venue purposes and that permanent-resident aliens can raise venue as a defense. Id. at 22-23.

§6. WHEN TO DETERMINE VENUE

Venue is determined when the suit is filed, not when the cause of action arose. *See* ***Tenefrancia v. Robinson Exp. & Imp. Corp.***, 921 F.2d 556, 558 n.2 (4th Cir.1990); *see also* 14D Wright, Miller & Cooper §3811 n.31 (claim arose in former district). Venue is not affected by events occurring after the suit is filed, such as the dismissal of one of the parties. ***Exxon Corp. v. FTC***, 588 F.2d 895, 899 (3d Cir.1978); *see* ***Flowers Indus. v. FTC***, 835 F.2d 775, 776 n.1 (11th Cir.1987). *But see* ***Knowlton v. Allied Van Lines, Inc.***, 900 F.2d 1196, 1200 (8th Cir.1990) (propriety of venue can be assessed on basis of current circumstances rather than circumstances when suit was filed).

§7. FORUM-SELECTION CLAUSE

Before filing suit in a controversy involving a contract, the plaintiff should check the contract for a forum-selection clause that might limit the choice of forum. Parties who execute a written contract with a mandatory forum-selection clause may waive their right to venue in another forum. ***Carnival Cruise Lines, Inc. v. Shute***, 499 U.S. 585, 590-95 (1991). Under federal law, forum-selection clauses are presumed valid and enforceable. ***Argueta v. Banco Mexicano, S.A.***, 87 F.3d 320, 325 (9th Cir.1996); ***Kevlin Servs. v. Lexington State Bank***, 46 F.3d 13, 15 (5th Cir.1995). See "Forum-selection clause," ch. 3-A, §4.3, p. 173.

§8. MULTIPLE PARTIES & CLAIMS

§8.1 Venue for each defendant & claim. In cases involving multiple parties and multiple claims, venue must be proper for each defendant and each claim. ***Sheppard v. Jacksonville Mar. Sup.***, 877 F.Supp. 260, 269 (D.S.C. 1995); *see* ***Davis v. Advantage Int'l***, 818 F.Supp. 1285, 1286 (E.D.Mo.1993); 14D Wright, Miller & Cooper §§3807, 3808.

§8.2 Pendent venue. "Pendent venue" is the exception to the rule that venue must be proper for each defendant and each claim. Pendent venue allows venue that is proper for a federal claim to be proper for other claims if all the pleaded claims arose out of the same transaction or occurrence—that is, a common nucleus of operative facts. ***Beattie v. U.S.***, 756 F.2d 91, 100-01 (D.C.Cir.1984); ***Philadelphia Musical Soc'y v. American Fed'n of Musicians***, 812 F.Supp. 509, 517 n.3 (E.D.Pa.1992). Pendent venue may support both nonfederal claims and separate federal claims with different venue requirements. ***Beattie***, 756 F.2d at 100. As with supplemental jurisdiction, the exercise of pendent venue is left to the court's discretion. *Id.* at 103.

§9. APPELLATE REVIEW

Generally, the district court's venue determination is a question of law and reviewed de novo. See "Appellate Review," ch. 3-D, §7, p. 198; "Standard of review," ch. 3-K, §7.2, p. 229.

H. SERVING THE DEFENDANT WITH PROCESS

§1. GENERAL

§1.1 Rules. FRCP 4, 4.1, 5; 28 U.S.C. §1608.

§1.2 Purpose. Service of both the summons and a copy of the complaint (together, "process") is the official method by which a plaintiff notifies a defendant that it is being sued. The purposes of service of process are (1) to give the court jurisdiction over the defendant, (2) to satisfy due-process requirements by giving the defendant notice of the suit, and (3) to give the defendant the opportunity to defend itself. *See* ***Henderson v. U.S.***, 517 U.S. 654, 672 (1996); ***Omni Capital Int'l v. Rudolf Wolff & Co.***, 484 U.S. 97, 104 (1987). Judgment cannot be rendered against a defendant unless the defendant has been served with process, has accepted or waived service, or has entered an appearance. Without valid service of process, the court does not obtain personal jurisdiction over the defendant. ***Omni***, 484 U.S. at 104; ***Adams v. AlliedSignal Gen. Aviation Avionics***, 74 F.3d 882, 885 (8th Cir.1996); ***Swaim v. Moltan Co.***, 73 F.3d 711, 719 (7th Cir.1996).

§1.3 Timetable & forms. Timetable, Pleadings & Pretrial-Motions Schedule, p. 1574; ***O'Connor's Federal Civil Forms*** (2012), FORMS 2H.

§1.4 Other references. 4, 4A, 4B Wright & Miller, *Federal Practice & Procedure 3d* §§1061-1180 (2002 & Supp.2012); 1 *Moore's Federal Practice 3d* chs. 3-6 (2012); Siegel, *The New (Dec. 1, 1993) Rule 4 of the FRCP…[Parts 1 & 2]*, 151 F.R.D. 441, 152 F.R.D. 249 (1994); Born & Vollmer, *The Effect of the Revised FRCP on Personal Jurisdiction, Service, & Discovery in International Cases*, 150 F.R.D. 221 (1993); 2 Zamora & Brand, *Basic Documents of International Economic Law* (1990); Weis, *The Federal Rules & the Hague Conventions: Concerns of Conformity & Comity*, 50 U.Pitt.L.Rev. 903 (1989); Westin, *Enforcing Foreign Commercial Judgments & Arbitral Awards in the United States, West Germany & England*, 19 Law & Pol'y in Int'l Bus. 325 (1987); Jones, *International Judicial Assistance: Procedural Chaos & a Program for Reform*, 62 Yale L.J. 515 (1953); Annotation, *Service of Process by Mail in International Civil Action as Permissible Under Hague Convention*, 112 ALR Fed. 241 (1993 & Supp.2012-13).

§2. REQUESTING WAIVER OF SERVICE

A waiver of service of process operates as a substitute for formal service of process, allowing a plaintiff to avoid the unnecessary costs of formal service while ensuring that the defendant obtains notice of the suit. ***Rogers v. Hartford Life & Acc. Ins.***, 167 F.3d 933, 937-38 (5th Cir.1999). Like formal service, a waiver of service marks the point in a suit after which the defendant must answer or risk default. *Id.* at 938.

PRACTICE TIP

Check the local rules before requesting waiver of service. Some districts have special requirements for requesting waiver.

---

§2.1 Purpose. The purpose of waiving service is to eliminate the costs of serving process on many parties and to foster cooperation among adversaries and attorneys. 1993 Notes to FRCP 4 at ¶15, p. 1140, this book. FRCP 4 imposes a duty on parties to avoid the unnecessary costs of service. FRCP 4(d)(1); ***Estate of Darulis v. Garate***, 401 F.3d 1060, 1063 (9th Cir.2005).

§2.2 Types of defendants. Waiver procedures apply to defendants who are individuals or private business entities, domestic and foreign. FRCP 4(d)(1); *see* FRCP 4(e), (f), (h). These defendants must allow the plaintiff to avoid unnecessary costs of serving process by waiving service if requested. FRCP 4(d)(1); *see* 1993 Notes to FRCP 4 at ¶15, p. 1140, this book. A plaintiff cannot ask a governmental unit, minor, or incompetent person to waive service.

1993 Notes to FRCP 4 at ¶17, p. 1140, this book; Siegel, *The New (Dec. 1, 1993) Rule 4 of the FRCPs … [Part 1]*, 151 F.R.D. at 448; *see, e.g.*, ***Lepone-Dempsey v. Carroll Cty. Comm'rs***, 476 F.3d 1277, 1281 (11th Cir.2007) (waiver inapplicable to local government).

§2.3 No summons. A summons does not need to be included in a request for waiver of service.

§2.4 Notice & request. To request waiver of service, the plaintiff must send the defendant a notice of the commencement of the suit and a request that the defendant waive service of a summons. FRCP 4(d)(1). The notice and request must meet the following requirements:

1. Be in writing. FRCP 4(d)(1)(A).

2. Be addressed directly to the defendant if the defendant is an individual, or to an officer or agent authorized to receive service of process if the defendant is a corporation or association. *Id.* The request may be addressed to the defendant wherever the plaintiff thinks the defendant can be found. There is no requirement that the request go to the defendant's residence or place of business. Siegel, *The New (Dec. 1, 1993) Rule 4 of the FRCPs … [Part 1]*, 151 F.R.D. at 451.

3. Use the text prescribed in Form 5 and inform the defendant of the consequences of both waiving and not waiving service. FRCP 4(d)(1)(D). *See* FRCP Form 5, p. 991, this book.

4. State the date that the request is sent. FRCP 4(d)(1)(E).

5. Allow the defendant a reasonable time to return the waiver. FRCP 4(d)(1)(F). For most defendants, a reasonable time is at least 30 days after the request is sent. *Id.* If defendants are outside any judicial district of the United States, a reasonable time is at least 60 days after the request is sent. *Id.*

6. Include a copy of the complaint that identifies the court where it has been filed. FRCP 4(d)(1)(B), (d)(1)(C). The plaintiff must also include two copies of the waiver for the defendant to sign. FRCP 4(d)(1)(C). *See* FRCP Form 6, p. 992, this book. The waiver is a part of the official form that FRCP 4(d) requires.

7. Provide the defendant with a prepaid means to comply with the request in writing (e.g., a self-addressed, stamped envelope). FRCP 4(d)(1)(C).

8. Send the notice and request to the defendant by first-class mail or other reliable means. FRCP 4(d)(1)(G). "Other reliable means" include registered or certified mail, private delivery service, and fax transmission. 1993 Notes to FRCP 4 at ¶25, p. 1141, this book. If the plaintiff uses electronic means such as fax transmission, it should maintain a record of the transmission to prove transmission if receipt is later denied. *Id.* A defendant cannot avoid liability for the cost of formal service if the transmission is prevented at the point of receipt. *Id.*

CAUTION

If the statute of limitations is about to run, the plaintiff must be especially careful about the time periods in the waiver procedure. The plaintiff has only 120 days after filing the complaint to serve the defendant. FRCP 4(m). The plaintiff can ask for an extension of time to serve the defendant by proving good cause. See "Motion to extend time to serve party," ch. 5-F, §4.3, p. 334. Once the plaintiff asks the defendant to waive service, a U.S. defendant has at least 30 days to agree. If the plaintiff waits the full 30 days anticipating that the defendant will waive service, but then service is not waived, the plaintiff will have lost a substantial part of its time to accomplish service. Siegel, The New (Dec. 1, 1993) Rule 4 of the FRCPs … [Part 1], 151 F.R.D. at 450.

§2.5 Filing waiver. If the defendant returns the waiver, the plaintiff must file it in the court. *See* FRCP 4(d)(4).

§2.6 Response to request.

1. Deadline to return waiver. The defendant must return the waiver within the time provided in the request for waiver. *See* FRCP 4(d)(1)(F). At the earliest, the defendant may be asked to respond 30 days after the request was sent, or 60 days after that date if the defendant is outside any judicial district of the United States. *Id.*

2. Defendant waives service. If the defendant agrees to waive formal service, it signs the waiver and mails it to the plaintiff. Although the official form does not contain a line under the signature to print the name of the person signing the waiver, the plaintiff should add such a line to protect itself from problems that could arise from an illegible signature. Siegel, *The New (Dec. 1, 1993) Rule 4 of the FRCPs … [Part 1]*, 151 F.R.D. at 452.

(1) Suit proceeds. If the defendant waives service, the suit proceeds as if the defendant had been served. The defendant does not waive objections to personal jurisdiction or venue by waiving service. FRCP 4(d)(5). All the defendant has waived is the ritual of service. Siegel, *The New (Dec. 1, 1993) Rule 4 of the FRCPs … [Part 1]*, 151 F.R.D. at 449. Obviously, when a defendant waives service, it cannot challenge the sufficiency of the process or service under FRCP 12(b)(4) and (b)(5). See "Motion to Dismiss for Insufficient Process or Service—FRCP 12(b)(4), (b)(5)," ch. 3-G, p. 209.

(2) Deadline to answer suit. When a defendant waives service, its time to respond to the suit is extended. A nongovernmental defendant ordinarily has 21 days after service to file its answer or other response. FRCP 12(a)(1)(A)(i). By signing a waiver, a domestic defendant has 60 days after the request was sent to submit its answer or other response, and a foreign defendant has 90 days. FRCP 4(d)(3), 12(a)(1)(A)(ii); 1993 Notes to FRCP 4 at ¶19, p. 1140, this book.

3. Defendant refuses to waive service. If the defendant does not agree to waive service, the plaintiff must formally serve the defendant. Once the defendant has been served and is before the court, the following apply:

(1) Fee-shifting. The court must impose the cost of service on the defendant, unless the defendant shows good cause for refusing to waive service. FRCP 4(d)(2). This subsection applies only when both the defendant and the plaintiff are located within the United States. *Id.* The cost of service includes the actual expense of formal service and the reasonable expenses, including attorney's fees, of any motion required to collect those service expenses. *Id.* The attorney fees are only for the cost of the motion and do not include the cost of arranging service. Siegel, *The New (Dec. 1, 1993) Rule 4 of the FRCPs … [Part 1]*, 151 F.R.D. at 453.

(2) Good cause. A defendant who refuses to comply with a request for waiver must be given an opportunity to show good cause for refusing to comply. If the defendant can show good cause, it can avoid paying for the costs incurred by service. FRCP 4(d)(2). For example, the defendant could establish good cause if she did not receive the request or did not understand it because she could not read English. 1993 Notes to FRCP 4 at ¶26, p. 1141, this book.

§3. SECURING SUMMONS

To accomplish formal service of process, the plaintiff must secure a summons from the clerk.

§3.1 Requirements for summons. The summons must strictly comply with FRCP 4. The clerk's office has forms for the summons.

1. Caption. When there are multiple parties, all of them must be named in the caption. *See* ***Newman v. Prior***, 518 F.2d 97, 99 (4th Cir.1975), *overruled on other grounds*, ***Newcome v. Esrey***, 862 F.2d 1099 (4th Cir.1988).

2. Court information.

(1) Identity of court. The summons must identify the court. FRCP 4(a)(1)(A).

(2) Signature & seal. The summons must be signed by the clerk and bear the seal of the court. FRCP 4(a)(1)(F), (a)(1)(G); ***Barrett v. City of Allentown***, 152 F.R.D. 46, 49 (E.D.Pa.1993); *see, e.g.*, ***Gianna Enters. v. Miss World (Jersey) Ltd.***, 551 F.Supp. 1348, 1358 (S.D.N.Y.1982) (summons, which did not have signature or seal, was not issued by court and could not be amended); *see also* ***Kramer v. Scientific Control Corp.***, 365 F.Supp. 780, 788 (E.D.Pa.1973) (in suits involving multiple defendants, copy of summons, which does not include seal, is permissible).

3. Identity of plaintiff.

(1) Name. The summons must contain the name of the plaintiff. FRCP 4(a)(1)(A).

(2) Plaintiff's attorney. The summons must contain the name and address of the plaintiff's attorney or, if the plaintiff is unrepresented, the address of the plaintiff. FRCP 4(a)(1)(C).

4. Identity of defendant.

(1) Name. The summons must contain the defendant's correct name and be directed to the defendant. FRCP 4(a)(1)(A), (a)(1)(B). If appropriate, the defendant should be identified by capacity.

(2) Defendant's agent for service. If the defendant must be served through an agent, the summons should name the agent for service and state the address. *See* FRCP 4(h)(1). However, the summons must be directed to the defendant and not to the agent. *See* FRCP 4(a)(1)(B); ***LeDonne v. Gulf Air, Inc.***, 700 F.Supp. 1400, 1412-13 & n.24 (E.D.Va.1988). If the summons is directed to the agent, it does not confer jurisdiction over the defendant. *See* ***LeDonne***, 700 F.Supp. at 1413 n.24.

(3) Multiple defendants. If there are several defendants, the plaintiff can either obtain a summons for each defendant or serve an original summons on one defendant and copies of the original on the other defendants. FRCP 4(b); *see* ***Bush v. Rauch***, 38 F.3d 842, 849 (6th Cir.1994) (each D must be served with process); 4A Wright & Miller §1085 (current FRCP 4(b) eliminates "separate and additional summons" language but retains practice of allowing additional summons).

5. Deadline to answer. The summons must state the time within which the defendant must appear and defend the allegations in the complaint. FRCP 4(a)(1)(D). For most defendants, the answer date is 21 days after service. See "Deadlines," ch. 3-A, §5, p. 174. The summons must inform the defendant that failure to appear and defend will result in a default judgment for the relief demanded in the complaint. FRCP 4(a)(1)(E).

6. Amended summons. The court may permit technical errors in the summons to be amended without requiring additional service on the parties already served. *See* FRCP 4(a)(2). When the defect is due to a minor technical error, only actual prejudice to the defendant or evidence of flagrant disregard of the rules justifies a refusal to permit amendment and a dismissal of the case. ***Libertad v. Welch***, 53 F.3d 428, 440 (1st Cir.1995); *see* ***Chan v. Society Expeditions, Inc.***, 39 F.3d 1398, 1404 (9th Cir.1994).

§3.2 Clerk's duty.

1. Sign & seal. If the summons is in proper form, the clerk must sign the summons and affix the seal of the court to it. FRCP 4(a)(1)(F), (a)(1)(G), (b).

2. Return to plaintiff. Once the summons is signed and sealed and the filing fee for the complaint is paid, the clerk must return the summons to the plaintiff or the plaintiff's attorney for service on the defendant. FRCP 4(b); ***Herrick v. Collins***, 914 F.2d 228, 230 (11th Cir.1990).

§3.3 Plaintiff's duty. The plaintiff is responsible for serving the summons and complaint on the defendant within the time allowed under FRCP 4(m). The plaintiff must furnish the person effecting service with the necessary copies of the summons and complaint. FRCP 4(c)(1). The summons and the complaint must be served together. *Id.*; *see* ***Carimi v. Royal Carribean Cruise Line, Inc.***, 959 F.2d 1344, 1345-46 (5th Cir.1992) (service of summons without complaint is invalid); ***Bolivar v. Director of the FBI***, 846 F.Supp. 163, 166 (D.P.R.1994) (service of complaint without summons is invalid), *aff'd*, 45 F.3d 423 (1st Cir.1995) (table case).

§4. DEADLINE FOR SERVING PROCESS

§4.1 Deadline. The summons and the complaint must be served on the defendant within 120 days after the filing of the complaint. FRCP 4(m); ***Lepone-Dempsey v. Carroll Cty. Comm'rs***, 476 F.3d 1277, 1281 (11th Cir.2007). This deadline does not apply to service in a foreign country under FRCP 4(f) or 4(j)(1). FRCP 4(m). The court must dismiss a suit without prejudice for the parties who are not served within 120 days or order that service be made within a specific time, unless the plaintiff shows good cause for not making service. ***Lepone-Dempsey***, 476 F.3d at 1281; ***Despain v. Salt Lake Area Metro Gang Unit***, 13 F.3d 1436, 1438 n.4 (10th Cir.1994); *see also* ***Henderson v. U.S.***, 517 U.S. 654, 656 (1996) (120-day service period under FRCP 4 is procedural and supersedes service provision in Admiralty Act for suits filed against United States); ***Cruz v. Louisiana***, 528 F.3d 375, 379 (5th Cir.2008) (dismissal under FRCP 4(m) constitutes abandonment of claim and does not toll statute of limitations).

§4.2 Motion to extend time to serve. The court may extend the time to serve the defendant. FRCP 4(m); *see* ***Coleman v. Milwaukee Bd. of Sch. Dirs.***, 290 F.3d 932, 934 (7th Cir.2002). If the plaintiff shows good cause for not serving the defendant within 120 days, the court must grant an extension. FRCP 4(m); ***Henderson v. U.S.***, 517 U.S. 654, 662 (1996); ***Espinoza v. U.S.***, 52 F.3d 838, 841 (10th Cir.1995); ***Petrucelli v. Bohringer & Ratzinger, GmbH***, 46 F.3d 1298, 1305 (3d Cir.1995). Good cause means a valid reason for delay, such as the defendant evading service. ***Coleman***, 290 F.3d at 934. But even if the plaintiff cannot show good cause, the court has discretion to grant an extension. ***Henderson***, 517 U.S. at 658 n.5; ***Zapata v. City of N.Y.***, 502 F.3d 192, 196 (2d Cir.2007); ***Horenkamp v. Van Winkle & Co.***, 402 F.3d 1129, 1132 & n.3 (11th Cir.2005); ***Thompson v. Brown***, 91 F.3d 20, 21 (5th Cir.1996); ***Adams v. AlliedSignal Gen. Aviation Avionics***, 74 F.3d 882, 887 (8th Cir.1996); ***Espinoza***, 52 F.3d at 841; ***Petrucelli***, 46 F.3d at 1305; 1993 Notes to FRCP 4 at ¶63, p. 1144, this book. *Contra* ***Mendez v. Elliot***, 45 F.3d 75, 78-79 (4th Cir.1995). See "Motion to extend time to serve party," ch. 5-F, §4.3, p. 334.

§5. SERVING PROCESS IN UNITED STATES

The method of service depends on the status of the person or entity to be served. *See* FRCP 4(e)-(j). The scheme for service in the United States is laid out in FRCP 4(e), which outlines the rules for service as they apply to individual defendants, and in FRCP 4(h)(1), which modifies those rules for business entities. Service on other parties is governed by separate subparts of FRCP 4: minors and incompetents under FRCP 4(g), state and local government under FRCP 4(j)(2), and the U.S. government and its officers or employees under FRCP 4(i).

§5.1 Individual defendant. FRCP 4(e) authorizes the plaintiff to serve process on the defendant (other than a minor or incompetent person) anywhere in the United States according to any of the methods set out in the rule. There is no priority between the choices of service in FRCP 4(e); serving by one method does not prevent an attempt to serve by another. Siegel, *The New (Dec. 1, 1993) Rule 4 of the FRCPs ... [Part 1]*, 151 F.R.D. at 459-60.

1. Service according to state law. The plaintiff may effect service of process according to the law of the state where the district court is located or the state where service is made. FRCP 4(e)(1); *see* ***Barlow v. Ground***, 39 F.3d 231, 234 (9th Cir.1994). The following are some of the methods of service authorized by the states:

(1) U.S. mail. Most states provide for service by U.S. mail. *E.g.*, Or. R. Civ. P. 7.D(2)(d)(i) (first-class and certified, registered, or express mail, with return receipt requested); Tex. R. Civ. P. 106(a)(2) (certified or registered mail, with return receipt requested); *see, e.g.*, ***Robinson v. Turner***, 15 F.3d 82, 86 (7th Cir.1994) (Indiana trial rule 4.1).

(2) Personal delivery. Most states provide for service by personal delivery. *E.g.*, Nev. R. Civ. P. 4(d).

(3) Service on agent. Most states provide for service on an agent of the defendant. *E.g.*, Fla. R. Civ. P. 1.070(i)(2)(A); *see, e.g.*, ***Robinson***, 15 F.3d at 86 (Indiana trial rule 4.16).

(4) Court order. Most states provide for alternative methods of service by court order. *E.g.*, Tex. R. Civ. P. 21a; *see* ***State Farm Fire & Cas. Co. v. Costley***, 868 S.W.2d 298, 299 (Tex.1993).

(5) Publication. Most states provide for service by publication in suits against a defendant whose residence is unknown, against unknown heirs or stockholders of defunct corporations, or against unknown owners or claimants of an interest in land. *E.g.*, Tex. R. Civ. P. 109-113. Some states also permit service by publication when authorized by court order. *E.g.*, Cal. Code Civ. Proc. §415.50.

(6) Service under long-arm statute. Most states provide some form of long-arm service on a nonresident who does business in the state. *See, e.g.*, Cal. Code Civ. Proc. §410.10 (jurisdiction may be exercised in any manner not in conflict with state or U.S. Constitution). In states that have a long-arm statute, federal courts sitting in diversity can exercise personal jurisdiction over a party to the same extent that state courts can. FRCP 4(k)(1)(A); ***Bank Brussels Lambert v. Fiddler Gonzalez & Rodriguez***, 305 F.3d 120, 124 (2d Cir.2002); *see* ***Hildebrand v. Steck Mfg. Co.***, 279 F.3d 1351, 1354 (Fed.Cir.2002); ***Indianapolis Colts, Inc. v. Metropolitan Balt. Football Club L.P.***, 34 F.3d 410, 411 (7th Cir.1994).

2. Service according to FRCP 4(e)(2). The plaintiff may effect service of process by delivering the summons and the complaint to the defendant as follows:

(1) Handing the summons and the complaint to the defendant in person. FRCP 4(e)(2)(A).

(2) Leaving the summons and the complaint at the defendant's dwelling with a person of suitable age and discretion who resides there. FRCP 4(e)(2)(B); *see, e.g.*, ***Hartford Fire Ins. v. Perinovic***, 152 F.R.D. 128, 131 (N.D.Ill.1993) (doorman at D's condominium, who had authority to sign for documents for D, was "person of suitable age and discretion").

(3) Delivering a copy of the summons and the complaint to an agent authorized by appointment or by law to receive service of process. FRCP 4(e)(2)(C); *see, e.g.*, ***U.S. v. 51 Pieces of Real Prop.***, 17 F.3d 1306, 1313 (10th Cir.1994) (delivery to attorney was not proper service because there was no showing that he was authorized to accept process).

§5.2 Business defendant. Unless otherwise provided by federal law, FRCP 4(h) authorizes the plaintiff to serve process in a judicial district in the United States on a domestic or foreign corporation, a partnership, or other unincorporated association according to the following methods:

1. In the manner prescribed by FRCP 4(e)(1) for serving individuals (i.e., according to the law of the state where the district court is located or where service is made). FRCP 4(h)(1)(A). See "Service according to state law," §5.1.1, p. 153.

2. By delivering a copy of the summons and complaint to an officer, a managing or general agent, or any other agent authorized by appointment or by law to receive service of process. FRCP 4(h)(1)(B). If the agent is authorized by statute to receive service and the statute so requires, the plaintiff must also mail a copy to the defendant. *Id.*

PRACTICE TIP

When a plaintiff serves a foreign business in the United States and the domestic service is valid under both state and federal law, no treaty is implicated. See, e.g., ***Volkswagenwerk A.G. v. Schlunk***, *486 U.S. 694, 707-08 (1988) (P properly served foreign corporation by serving its wholly owned domestic subsidiary, without reference to Hague Convention on Service, when subsidiary was considered involuntary agent for service of process under state law). For a discussion of when domestic service is not valid,* *see "Serving foreign business abroad," §6.4, p. 161.*

---

§5.3 Minor or incompetent defendant. Service on a minor or incompetent person in the United States is governed by the law of the state where the service is made. FRCP 4(g).

§5.4 State or local government. To serve a state, county, municipality, or other local government, the plaintiff must either serve a copy of the summons and complaint on the chief executive officer of the state or local government or serve the government in compliance with the laws of that state. FRCP 4(j)(2); ***Coleman v. Milwaukee Bd. of Sch. Dirs.***, 290 F.3d 932, 933 (7th Cir.2002).

§5.5 U.S. government as defendant. FRCP 4(i) provides the procedure for serving process on the United States and its agencies, corporations, officers, or employees.

1. U.S. government. To serve the federal government, the plaintiff must serve process on all the entities listed below.

(1) U.S. Attorney. The plaintiff must serve either of the following:

(a) A copy of the summons and complaint to the U.S. Attorney for the district where the suit is filed, or to a person (either an assistant U.S. Attorney or a clerical employee) designated by the U.S. Attorney in a writing filed with the court clerk. FRCP 4(i)(1)(A)(i).

(b) A copy of the summons and complaint by registered or certified mail to the "civil-process clerk" at the office of the U.S. Attorney. FRCP 4(i)(1)(A)(ii).

(2) Attorney General. The plaintiff must also send a copy of the summons and complaint by registered or certified mail to the U.S. Attorney General, Department of Justice, 950 Pennsylvania Avenue, N.W., Washington, D.C., 20530. FRCP 4(i)(1)(B); *see* ***George v. U.S. Dept. of Labor***, 788 F.2d 1115, 1116 (5th Cir.1986).

2. U.S. government – suit challenging federal order. To serve the federal government in a suit challenging the validity of an order issued by a federal agency or officer, the plaintiff must serve process on all the entities listed below.

(1) U.S. Attorney. See "U.S. Attorney," §5.5.1(1), p. 154.

(2) Attorney General. See "Attorney General," §5.5.1(2), this page.

(3) Agency or officer. The plaintiff must send a copy of the summons and complaint by registered or certified mail to the federal agency or officer. FRCP 4(i)(1)(C).

3. U.S. agency, corporation, officer, or employee – official capacity only. To serve a federal agency or corporation or a federal officer or employee sued only in her official capacity, the plaintiff must serve process on all the entities listed below.

(1) U.S. government. See "U.S. government," §5.5.1, p. 154.

(2) Agency, corporation, officer, or employee. The plaintiff must send a copy of the summons and complaint by registered or certified mail to the agency, corporation, officer, or employee. FRCP 4(i)(2).

4. U.S. officer or employee – individual capacity. To serve a federal officer or employee sued in an individual capacity for acts or omissions occurring in connection with the performance of duties on behalf of the United States, regardless of whether the officer or employee is also sued in her official capacity, the plaintiff must serve process on all the entities listed below.

(1) U.S. government. Whether the officer's or employee's connection to federal employment requires service on the United States depends on whether the individual defendant has reasonable grounds to look to the United States for assistance and whether the United States has reasonable grounds for demanding formal notice of the suit. 2000 Notes to FRCP 4 at ¶2, p. 1138, this book. Service on the United States does not depend on whether the defendant is a present or former officer or employee, and service is not required when the plaintiff's claims have no connection to the officer's or employee's governmental role. *Id.* See "U.S. government," §5.5.1, p. 154.

(2) Officer or employee. The plaintiff must serve process on the officer or employee in the manner prescribed for any of the individuals listed below.

(a) Individual defendants in the United States. FRCP 4(e), (i)(3). See "Individual defendant," §5.1, p. 153.

(b) Incompetent defendants in the United States. FRCP 4(g), (i)(3). See "Minor or incompetent defendant," §5.3, p. 154.

(c) Individual defendants abroad. FRCP 4(f), (i)(3). See "Serving an individual abroad," §6.3, p. 157.

5. Additional time for service.

(1) Suits against U.S. agency, corporation, officer, or employee in official capacity. In a suit governed by FRCP 4(i)(2), if the plaintiff has served either the U.S. Attorney or the Attorney General, but not an agency, corporation, officer, or employee in its official capacity, the court must give the plaintiff a reasonable time to serve the other entities or persons after the defect is pointed out. FRCP 4(i)(4)(A); 2000 Notes to FRCP 4 at ¶4, p. 1138, this book; *see also* 2007 Notes to FRCP 4 at ¶3, p. 1138, this book (party other than P may need reasonable time to effect service; FRCP 4(i)(4) covers any party).

(2) Suits against officer or employee in individual capacity. In a suit governed by FRCP 4(i)(3), if the plaintiff has served a federal officer or employee in her individual capacity but not the United States, the court must give the plaintiff a reasonable time to serve the United States after the defect is pointed out. FRCP 4(i)(4)(B); 2000 Notes to FRCP 4 at ¶4, p. 1138, this book.

(3) Preservation of substantive rights. FRCP 4(i)(4), regarding additional time for serving the government, should be read in connection with FRCP 15(c)(2) to prevent the loss of substantive rights against the United States or its agencies, corporations, officers, or employees resulting from a plaintiff's failure to correctly identify and serve all the appropriate persons. *See* 1993 Notes to FRCP 4 at ¶51, p. 1143, this book.

§5.6 Nonresident additional parties. When parties are added to a pending suit under FRCP 14 or 19, service is permitted within a 100-mile radius of the federal courthouse where the case is pending, even if the 100-mile radius reaches across a state line and state law does not permit such a reach. *See* FRCP 4(k)(1)(B). The 100-mile rule applies only when the nonresident will be brought into a pending suit as an additional party under FRCP 14 (third parties) or FRCP 19 (required parties). *See* FRCP 4(k)(1)(B). Personal jurisdiction may be exercised over persons who can be reached under state long-arm statutes or the Federal Interpleader Act. 28 U.S.C. §1335 (interpleader); FRCP 4(k)(1)(A) (long-arm statute); 1993 Notes to FRCP 4 at ¶54, p. 1143, this book.

§6. SERVING PROCESS ABROAD

The method of service on a defendant who is abroad depends on the defendant's status (e.g., individual, business entity). The scheme for service abroad is governed by FRCP 4(f), which outlines the rules as they apply to individual defendants, and by FRCP 4(h)(2), which modifies those rules for business entities. Service on other parties is governed by separate subparts of FRCP 4: minors and incompetents under FRCP 4(g), and foreign governments under FRCP 4(j)(1). Whether a particular type of delivery of documents in a foreign country is considered proper service is determined by the law of the country requesting service of the documents, not the country from which they are served. *See* ***Volkswagenwerk A.G. v. Schlunk***, 486 U.S. 694, 701-02 (1988). *See generally* Hague Convention on Service Abroad of Judicial & Extrajudicial Documents, p. 1563, this book (service of documents abroad).

§6.1 Limits on foreign service.

1. Comity. Comity is the extent to which the laws of one nation are allowed to operate within the territory of another nation. ***Hilton v. Guyot***, 159 U.S. 113, 163 (1895). No nation can demand that its laws have effect beyond the limits of its sovereignty. *Id.* Some countries consider service of judicial documents as requiring the performance of a judicial or "sovereign" act and thus view service from another country within their borders as offensive to their sovereignty. *See* Jones, *International Judicial Assistance*, 62 Yale L.J. at 537.

2. Constitution. The U.S. Constitution requires that before a court can exercise jurisdiction over a foreign national, the foreign national must have purposefully established minimum contacts with the United States. *See* ***Asahi Metal Indus. Co. v. Superior Ct. of Cal.***, 480 U.S. 102, 108-09 (1987) (plurality op.). Even with minimum contacts, a plaintiff's choice of forum might be so inconvenient to a foreign defendant that it would be a denial of "fair play and substantial justice" to require the defendant to defend the suit in the United States. *See, e.g., id.* at 113 (no jurisdiction over Japanese parts manufacturer selling to Taiwanese tire company with sales in U.S.); ***D'Almeida v. Stork Brabant B.V.***, 71 F.3d 50, 51 (1st Cir.1995) (no jurisdiction over European manufacturer in suit for indemnification brought by U.S. distributor). United States courts should scrupulously protect aliens who reside in foreign countries from a plaintiff's selection of a forum that would be so onerous that injustice could result. *See* ***Asahi***, 480 U.S. at 115.

§6.2 Waiver of service. Generally, a plaintiff may follow the procedures for waiver of service in the United States to ask a foreign defendant to waive service. *See* FRCP 4(d)(1); ***Brockmeyer v. May***, 383 F.3d 798, 806-07 & n.2 (9th Cir.2004). See "Requesting Waiver of Service," §2, p. 149.

1. **Purpose.** The goal of FRCP 4(d), as it relates to foreign defendants, is that its use will not offend foreign sovereignties because transmission of the notice and waiver forms is a private, nonjudicial act that does not purport to effect service and is not accompanied by any summons or directive from a court. 1993 Notes to FRCP 4 at ¶20, p. 1140, this book. The rule recognizes that no useful purpose is achieved by complying with all the formalities of service in a foreign country, including costs of translation, when, for example, a plaintiff is suing a defendant manufacturer who is fluent in English and whose products are widely distributed in the United States. 1993 Notes to FRCP 4 at ¶¶15, 21, p. 1140, this book.

2. **Differences from waiver in United States.** The procedure for waiver of service is similar to that in the United States, except for the following:

(1) **Extended time to return waiver.** Because of the additional time needed for mailing and the unreliability of some foreign mail services, a foreign defendant has at least 60 days after the request was sent to return the waiver. *See* FRCP 4(d)(1)(F); 1993 Notes to FRCP 4 at ¶19, p. 1140, this book. A domestic defendant has at least 30 days. FRCP 4(d)(1)(F).

(2) **Extended time to answer.** A foreign defendant who waives service has 90 days after the request for waiver was sent to file its answer. FRCP 4(d)(3); 1993 Notes to FRCP 4 at ¶19, p. 1140, this book. A domestic defendant ordinarily has only 21 days after service to file its answer or raise objections by motion. FRCP 12(a)(1)(A)(i).

(3) **No costs for failure to waive service.** Unlike a domestic defendant, a foreign defendant who does not agree to waiver of service is not required to pay the costs of formal service. *See* FRCP 4(d)(2).

§6.3 Serving an individual abroad. A person outside the United States may be served by the following methods: (1) a method under the Hague Convention on Service Abroad of Judicial & Extrajudicial Documents, p. 1563, this book, or any other applicable treaty, (2) if no treaty applies, any method reasonably calculated to give notice that is permitted under the law of the country where service is to be made, or (3) any other method not prohibited by international agreement as may be directed by the court. FRCP 4(f). In addition, a plaintiff can request that a defendant in a foreign country waive formal service under FRCP 4(d). See "Waiver of service," §6.2, p. 156.

PRACTICE TIP

To determine whether a country is presently a signatory to the Hague Convention or any other treaty affecting service, contact the Treaty Affairs Section, Department of State, Washington, D.C., at (202) 647-1345, www.state.gov/s/l/treaty, or refer to the Hague Conference website, www.hcch.net. For a collection of treaties and conventions that apply to international lawsuits, see 2 Zamora & Brand, Basic Documents of International Economic Law (1990).

1. **Preference for service according to international agreements.** FRCP 4(f) favors the use of internationally agreed means of service—service according to the terms of the Hague Convention or any other applicable treaty. 1993 Notes to FRCP 4 at ¶41, p. 1142, this book; *see* ***Volkswagenwerk A.G. v. Schlunk***, 486 U.S. 694, 706 (1988) (voluntary use of convention procedures may be desirable even when service could constitutionally be made in another manner). Service abroad must be made under a treaty if there is such a treaty and if the treaty requires service to be made according to its terms. FRCP 4(f)(1); 1993 Notes to FRCP 4 at ¶41, p. 1142, this book. A convention or treaty does not automatically preempt all other methods of service on a defendant who resides in a signatory country; preemption depends on the language of the treaty itself. *See* ***Kreimerman v. Casa Veerkamp***, 22 F.3d 634, 640-42 (5th Cir.1994). The Hague Convention preempts inconsistent methods of service prescribed by state law in all cases to which it applies. *See* Hague Convention on Service, art. 1, p. 1563, this book; ***Schlunk***, 486 U.S. at 699; ***Ackermann v. Levine***, 788 F.2d 830, 840 (2d Cir.1986). By contrast, the Inter-American Convention on Letters Rogatory does not preempt other methods of service. ***Kreimerman***, 22 F.3d at 647.

PRACTICE TIP

*Follow the formal procedures for service in an applicable treaty rather than resorting to a less formal method of service. When a treaty covers service, a judgment is not enforceable if process was not served according to the treaty. See **Kreimerman**, 22 F.3d at 643-44; Westin, Enforcing Foreign Commercial Judgments, 19 Law & Pol'y in Int'l Bus. at 340-41; see, e.g., Hague Convention on Service, art. 15, p. 1564, this book (judgment "shall not be given" until proper service established).*

2. Service under Hague Convention. The Hague Convention requires each signatory state to establish a "central authority" for receiving and carrying out requests for service of process from litigants in foreign states, and it provides for alternative methods of service in articles 8-10.

(1) Service through central authority. Each signatory country must designate a central authority to receive requests for service that come from other countries. Hague Convention on Service, art. 2, p. 1563, this book; ***Schlunk***, 486 U.S. at 698.

(a) Form for service. A plaintiff may obtain a "request for service" form (USM-94) from the U.S. Marshals Service. *See* U.S. Marshal Form 94 (USM-94), "Request for Service Abroad of Judicial or Extrajudicial Documents," www.usmarshals.gov/forms/usm94.pdf. There are three parts to this form, as prescribed by the Convention: the request, the certificate, and the summary. The central authority may require the document to be written in or translated into the official language, or one of the official languages, of the country where service is requested. Hague Convention on Service, art. 5, p. 1563, this book; *see, e.g.*, ***Northrup King Co. v. Compania Productora Semillas Algodoneras Selectas, S.A.***, 51 F.3d 1383, 1389 (8th Cir.1995) (Spanish central authority did not require translation).

(b) Form sent to central authority. Once Form USM-94 is completed, the plaintiff must send copies of the form and copies of the documents to be served to the central authority of the country where service is requested. Hague Convention on Service, art. 3, p. 1563, this book. To obtain the address of a country's central authority, call the Department of Justice, Foreign Litigation Office, at (202) 514-7455, or check the Service Section at www.hcch.net/index_en.php. If the central authority decides that the request does not comply with the provisions of the Convention, it must promptly inform the plaintiff and specify the objections. Hague Convention on Service, art. 4, p. 1563, this book.

(c) Service of documents. The central authority must either serve the document itself or arrange to have it served by an appropriate agency. Hague Convention on Service, art. 5, p. 1563, this book; ***Schlunk***, 486 U.S. at 699. The request, which contains a summary of the document to be served, and a copy of the document must be served by one of the following methods:

[1] A method prescribed by the country's internal law for the service of documents in domestic actions on persons within its territory. Hague Convention on Service, art. 5(a), p. 1563, this book.

[2] The method requested by the plaintiff, unless it is incompatible with the law of the country. Hague Convention on Service, art. 5(b), p. 1563, this book.

[3] Delivery to an addressee who accepts it voluntarily, unless personal service is illegal in the country. *See* Hague Convention on Service, art. 5, p. 1563, this book.

(d) No deadline for service. The Hague Convention does not specify a time within which a foreign country's central authority must effect service, but article 15 does provide that alternative methods may be used if the central authority does not respond within six months. Generally, a central authority can be expected to respond much more quickly than that, but occasionally a signatory state is dilatory or refuses to cooperate for substantive reasons. 1993 Notes to FRCP 4 at ¶43, p. 1142, this book. The plaintiff may then resort to the provision in FRCP 4(f)(3) that permits service under any other means not prohibited by international agreement, as the court orders. See "Service under court order," §6.3.4, p. 160.

(e) Certificate of service. The central authority, or its designee, must complete a certificate of service in the form approved by the Convention. Hague Convention on Service, art. 6, p. 1563, this book; ***Schlunk***, 486 U.S. at 699. The certificate must be forwarded directly to the plaintiff. Hague Convention on Service, art. 6, p. 1563, this book.

[1] Service completed. If process was served, the certificate must state that the document was served and identify the method, place, and date of service and the person to whom the document was delivered. Hague Convention on Service, art. 6, p. 1563, this book. The central authority's return of a completed certificate of service is prima facie evidence that the service was made in compliance with the Hague Convention. ***Northrup King***, 51 F.3d at 1389.

[2] Service not completed. If process was not served, the certificate must state the reasons that prevented service. Hague Convention on Service, art. 6, p. 1563, this book. The plaintiff may require that a certificate not completed by a central authority or a judicial authority be countersigned by one of those authorities. Hague Convention on Service, art. 6, p. 1563, this book.

[3] Verification before judgment. Before a default judgment can be taken against a defendant who resides in a foreign country, process must have been accomplished by one of the following: (1) a method prescribed by the internal law of the country or (2) actual delivery of the process to the defendant or its residence by some other method provided for in the Convention. Hague Convention on Service, art. 15, p. 1564, this book. *See generally* ***Schlunk***, 486 U.S. at 700 (technical meaning of "service of process"). The plaintiff must show that the notice was delivered in enough time to enable the defendant to defend the suit. Hague Convention on Service, art. 15, p. 1564, this book.

(2) Alternative service. Hague Convention article 10 provides for alternative methods of service, as long as the foreign country does not object. *See* Hague Convention on Service, art. 10(a), p. 1564, this book (freedom to send judicial documents by postal methods directly to persons abroad). Whether a particular country has authorized service by less formal methods is found in that country's declaration to the Convention. *See* Hague Convention on Service, art. 8, p. 1563, this book. For a country's declaration, see Conference (status report on Convention), www.hcch.net. Courts are split on whether a plaintiff can serve process on a foreign defendant by mail when the country has not objected to service under article 10(a). *Compare* ***Brockmeyer v. May***, 383 F.3d 798, 808-09 (9th Cir.2004) (mail service permitted, but service must also satisfy FRCP 4(f)), ***Ackermann***, 788 F.2d at 839 (mail service permitted), ***Sibley v. Alcan, Inc.***, 400 F.Supp.2d 1051, 1055 (N.D.Ohio 2005) (same), *and* ***Harvey v. Sav-U-Car Rental***, No. 2007-CV-0115 (D.V.I.2008) (no pub.; 9-22-08) (certified-mail service permitted), *with* ***Nuovo Pignone, SpA v. Storman Asia M/V***, 310 F.3d 374, 384 (5th Cir.2002) (mail service not permitted), *and* ***Bankston v. Toyota Motor Corp.***, 889 F.2d 172, 174 (8th Cir.1989) (same). *See generally* ***Air France v. Saks***, 470 U.S. 392, 396 (1985) (history of treaty, negotiations and "practical construction adopted by the parties" are important aids to courts' interpretation of Convention); Annotation, *Service of Process by Mail in International Civil Action as Permissible Under Hague Convention*, 112 ALR Fed. at 263-69 (comparing cases when Hague Convention supersedes FRCP 4).

3. Service without treaty. If no internationally agreed means of service is available, or if the applicable international agreement allows but does not specify other means of service, a plaintiff may serve an individual in another country (other than a minor or incompetent person) by a method of service reasonably calculated to give the defendant notice of the suit in the same manner as prescribed by the law of the foreign country. FRCP 4(f)(2)(A). Specifically, the plaintiff may attempt the following types of service:

(1) The plaintiff can make service as directed by a foreign authority in response to a letter rogatory or letter of request. FRCP 4(f)(2)(B). "Letter of request" is synonymous with "letter rogatory," but the term "letter of request" is preferred. 1993 Notes to FRCP 4 at ¶44, p. 1142, this book. A letter of request is a formal request from a U.S. court to a foreign court to serve process on a foreign defendant. *See Black's Law Dictionary* 988 (9th ed. 2009).

(2) The plaintiff may use the following methods of service only if they are not prohibited by the law of the foreign country:

(a) A copy of the summons and complaint can be personally delivered to an individual defendant. FRCP 4(f)(2)(C)(i). A foreign business cannot be served by personal delivery. FRCP 4(h)(2).

(b) The summons and the complaint can be sent to the defendant by the court clerk by a form of mail that requires a signed receipt. FRCP 4(f)(2)(C)(ii).

4. Service under court order. The court has authority to approve other methods of service not prohibited by international agreements. FRCP 4(f)(3). The Hague Convention on Service, for example, authorizes special forms of service in urgent circumstances if Convention methods do not permit service within the time required by the circumstances. 1993 Notes to FRCP 4 at ¶46, p. 1143, this book. The refusal of a foreign country to comply with the Convention may also justify the use of additional methods. In such a case, the court may direct a special method of service not explicitly authorized by the international agreement but not prohibited by it. *Id.* A party is not required to attempt service of process under FRCP 4(f)(2) before resorting to FRCP 4(f)(3). ***Rio Props., Inc. v. Rio Int'l Interlink***, 284 F.3d 1007, 1015-16 (9th Cir.2002). Courts have authorized a wide variety of alternative methods of service, including mail to the defendant's last known address, publication, delivery to the defendant's attorney-agent, telex, and e-mail. *See id.* at 1016-17 (court can order service by e-mail under FRCP 4(f)(3)); *see, e.g.*, ***International Controls Corp. v. Vesco***, 593 F.2d 166, 176-78 (2d Cir.1979) (throwing papers on lawn was proper service when guards made other methods impossible).

5. Service under state long-arm statute. A plaintiff may be able to use a state long-arm statute to serve a defendant in another country if the long-arm service comports with (1) due process, (2) the requirements of FRCP 4(f), (3) the principles of comity, and (4) any other applicable legal principles of domestic or international law. *See, e.g.*, ***Kreimerman***, 22 F.3d at 644 (remanded to district court to determine whether service by Texas long-arm statute was effective in Mexico).

6. Service under FRCP 4(k)(2). Any federal court may exercise personal jurisdiction over any defendant against whom a claim arising under federal law is made if that defendant is not subject to personal jurisdiction in any state. FRCP 4(k)(2); 1993 Notes to FRCP 4 at ¶55, p. 1143, this book; *see* ***Adams v. Unione Mediterranea di Sicurta***, 364 F.3d 646, 650 (5th Cir.2004); ***Glencore Grain Rotterdam B.V. v. Shivnath Rai Harnarain Co.***, 284 F.3d 1114, 1126 (9th Cir.2002); ***U.S. v. Swiss Am. Bank, Ltd.***, 191 F.3d 30, 38 (1st Cir.1999); 4B Wright & Miller §1124; Siegel, *The New (Dec. 1, 1993) Rule 4 of the FRCPs ... [Part 2]*, 152 F.R.D. at 252; *see also* ***Saudi v. Northrop Grumman Corp.***, 427 F.3d 271, 275 (4th Cir.2005) (FRCP 4(k)(2) is in essence a federal long-arm statute). The purpose of FRCP 4(k)(2) is to permit a court to consider, in federal-question cases, a defendant's national, rather than state, contacts. *See* ***Submersible Sys. v. Perforadora Cent.***, 249 F.3d 413, 420 (5th Cir.2001); 1993 Notes to FRCP 4 at ¶56, p. 1143, this book. For a court to exercise personal jurisdiction under FRCP 4(k)(2), the plaintiff should show that the claim arises under federal law, the defendant is not subject to jurisdiction in any state, and the exercise of jurisdiction comports with due process. ***Touchcom, Inc. v. Bereskin & Parr***, 574 F.3d 1403, 1412 (Fed.Cir.2009).

(1) Federal-question jurisdiction. The claim must arise under federal law. ***Touchcom, Inc.***, 574 F.3d at 1412. See "Federal-Question Jurisdiction," ch. 2-F, §2, p. 113.

(2) Defendant not subject to jurisdiction in any state. The defendant cannot be subject to the jurisdiction of any state. ***Touchcom, Inc.***, 574 F.3d at 1413. Circuits have developed different methods for determining this requirement. *See id.* at 1414-15.

(a) Burden on defendant. In many circuits, the burden is on the defendant to show that FRCP 4(k)(2) does not apply. ***Touchcom, Inc.***, 574 F.3d at 1414. If the defendant contends it cannot be sued in the forum state and refuses to identify any other state where the suit is possible, FRCP 4(k)(2) applies. ***Touchcom, Inc.***, 574

F.3d at 1414; ***ISI Int'l v. Borden Ladner Gervais LLP***, 256 F.3d 548, 552 (7th Cir.2001); ***Adams***, 364 F.3d at 651. If the defendant names a state where the suit can proceed, FRCP 4(k)(2) does not apply. ***Touchcom, Inc.***, 574 F.3d at 1414.

(b) Burden on plaintiff. In some circuits, the burden is on the plaintiff to certify that the defendant is not subject to suit in any state. ***Swiss Am. Bank***, 191 F.3d at 41; ***see Base Metal Trading, Ltd. v. OJSC "Novokuznetsky Aluminum Factory"***, 283 F.3d 208, 215 (4th Cir.2002). If the plaintiff is successful, the burden shifts to the defendant to show that it could be subject to suit in one or more states. ***Swiss Am. Bank***, 191 F.3d at 41.

(3) Due process. The exercise of jurisdiction under FRCP 4(k)(2) must comport with due process. ***Touchcom, Inc.***, 574 F.3d at 1416; *see* ***Swiss Am. Bank***, 191 F.3d at 41. See "No due process," ch. 3-B, §2.3.2, p. 178. Because jurisdiction under FRCP 4(k)(2) addresses the defendant's national contacts, the relevant scope of this requirement is the defendant's contacts with the entire United States, not just the state where the district court sits. ***Touchcom, Inc.***, 574 F.3d at 1416.

7. No time limit. The 120-day time limit for service after filing the complaint does not apply to service abroad. FRCP 4(m); ***Kim v. Frank Mohn A/S***, 909 F.Supp. 474, 479-80 (S.D.Tex.1995); ***Pennsylvania Orthopedic Ass'n v. Mercedes Benz A.G.***, 160 F.R.D. 58, 60 (E.D.Pa.1995); Siegel, *The New (Dec. 1, 1993) Rule 4 of the FRCPs ... [Part 1]*, 151 F.R.D. at 464-65; *see, e.g.*, ***Lucas v. Natoli***, 936 F.2d 432, 432-33 (9th Cir.1991) (service in foreign country 11 months after complaint was filed in court was timely). But if service is not even attempted in the foreign country, the 120-day limit has been held to justify a dismissal. ***Montalbano v. Easco Hand Tools, Inc.***, 766 F.2d 737, 740 (2d Cir.1985); *see* ***Allstate Ins. v. Funai Corp.***, 249 F.R.D. 157, 162 (M.D.Pa.2008) (P must make reasonable, good-faith effort to serve within 120-day limit); *see, e.g.*, ***Pennsylvania Orthopedic Ass'n***, 160 F.R.D. at 60-61 (when service was attempted but not successful within 120-day limit, complaint was not dismissed because time limit did not apply). *Contra* ***Cargill Ferrous Int'l v. M/V Elikon***, 154 F.R.D. 193, 195-96 (N.D.Ill.1994).

§6.4 Serving foreign business abroad. FRCP 4(h) governs service on a foreign corporation, partnership, or other unincorporated association. Unless provided otherwise by federal law, service on a foreign business may be accomplished outside the United States in any manner prescribed by FRCP 4(f) for service on individuals, except personal delivery. FRCP 4(h)(2); *see* ***Allstate Ins. v. Funai Corp.***, 249 F.R.D. 157, 161 (M.D.Pa.2008). See "Serving an individual abroad," §6.3, p. 157.

§6.5 Serving minor or incompetent person abroad. Service on a minor or incompetent person outside the United States is governed by FRCP 4(f)(2)(A), (f)(2)(B), or (f)(3). FRCP 4(g). Minors and incompetents cannot be asked to waive service. 1993 Notes to FRCP 4 at ¶17, p. 1140, this book. Thus, to serve a minor or incompetent abroad, the plaintiff must comply with one of the following procedures:

1. The law of the foreign country for service in that country. FRCP 4(f)(2)(A).

2. The directions of the foreign authority in response to a letter of request. FRCP 4(f)(2)(B).

3. A court order directing another means of service not prohibited by international agreement. FRCP 4(f)(3).

§6.6 Serving foreign government. When suing a foreign state or its political subdivision, agency, or instrumentality, the plaintiff must comply with the requirements of the Foreign Sovereign Immunities Act (FSIA), 28 U.S.C. §1608. FRCP 4(j)(1). A foreign state itself must be served according to 28 U.S.C. §1608(a). *See* ***Transaero, Inc. v. La Fuerza Aerea Boliviana***, 30 F.3d 148, 153 (D.C.Cir.1994) (armed forces are considered the foreign state itself rather than a separate "agency or instrumentality" of the state). An agent or instrumentality of a foreign state, such as a state-owned corporation, must be served according to 28 U.S.C. §1608(b). *See* ***Jim Fox Enters. v. Air France***, 705 F.2d 738, 741 & n.7 (5th Cir.1983).

PRACTICE TIP

Although technically faulty service on an instrumentality of a state may satisfy §1608(b) if it gives adequate notice to the foreign state, faulty service on the foreign state itself rarely satisfies §1608(a), even if it gives adequate notice. ***Transaero****, 30 F.3d at 153-54; see* ***Magness v. Russian Fed'n****, 247 F.3d 609, 613 & n.8 (5th Cir.2001);* ***Alberti v. Empresa Nicaraguense De La Carne****, 705 F.2d 250, 253 (7th Cir.1983). Thus, before attempting service under the FSIA, determine whether the entity to be served is part of the foreign government itself or instead is an instrumentality of the foreign government. See* ***Transaero****, 30 F.3d at 154. If the entity is part of the government itself, serve according to §1608(a); if it is merely an instrumentality of the foreign state, serve according to §1608(b).*

1. Foreign state. A plaintiff serving a foreign state or its political subdivision must attempt service according to the order of the methods as they appear in the statute. *See* 28 U.S.C. §1608(a); ***Magness***, 247 F.3d at 613 & n.8. The following are the methods and the order in which they may be attempted:

(1) The plaintiff can deliver a copy of the summons and complaint according to any special arrangement for service between the plaintiff and the foreign state. 28 U.S.C. §1608(a)(1).

(2) If there is no special arrangement, the plaintiff can deliver a copy of the summons and complaint according to an applicable international convention for service of judicial documents. *Id.* §1608(a)(2).

(3) If service cannot be made under §1608(a)(1) or (a)(2), the plaintiff can serve according to §1608(a)(3). Under subsection (a)(3), the court clerk must address and dispatch a copy of the summons, the complaint, and a notice of suit, together with a translation of each into the official language of the foreign state, by any form of mail requiring a signed receipt, to the head of the ministry of foreign affairs of the foreign state. 28 U.S.C. §1608(a)(3).

(4) If service cannot be accomplished under §1608(a)(3) within 30 days, the court clerk must address and dispatch two copies of the summons, the complaint, and a notice of suit, together with a translation of each into the official language of the foreign state, by any form of mail requiring a signed receipt, to the Secretary of State in Washington, D.C., attention Director of Special Consular Services. 28 U.S.C. §1608(a)(4). The Secretary must then transmit one copy of the papers through diplomatic channels to the foreign state and send the court clerk a certified copy of the diplomatic note indicating that the papers were forwarded. *Id.*

2. Instrumentality of foreign state. A plaintiff must use one of the following methods for properly serving an agency or instrumentality of a foreign state:

(1) The plaintiff can deliver a copy of the summons and complaint according to any special arrangement for service between the plaintiff and the agency or instrumentality. 28 U.S.C. §1608(b)(1); *see* ***General Star Nat'l Ins. v. Administratia Asigurarilor de Stat***, 289 F.3d 434, 441 (6th Cir.2002) (service-of-process provision in contracts is "special arrangement").

(2) If there is no special arrangement, the plaintiff must deliver a copy of the summons and complaint to an officer, a managing or general agent, or an authorized agent, or according to the terms of an applicable international convention on service of judicial documents. 28 U.S.C. §1608(b)(2).

(3) If service cannot be made under §1608(b)(1) or (b)(2), the plaintiff can serve according to §1608(b)(3) if such service is reasonably calculated to give actual notice. ***Richmark Corp. v. Timber Falling Consultants, Inc.***, 937 F.2d 1444, 1447-48 (9th Cir.1991). Some courts have held that substantial, rather than strict, compliance with §1608(b)(3) is sufficient. *See* ***Straub v. AP Green, Inc.***, 38 F.3d 448, 453 (9th Cir.1994) (pivotal factor is actual notice, not strict compliance); ***Sherer v. Construcciones Aeronauticas***, 987 F.2d 1246, 1250 (6th Cir.1993) (actual notice sufficient). Under subsection (b)(3), the plaintiff must deliver a copy of the summons and complaint, together with a translation of each into the official language of the foreign state, by one of the following methods:

(a) As directed by an authority of the foreign state or political subdivision in response to a letter of request. 28 U.S.C. §1608(b)(3)(A).

(b) By any form of mail requiring a signed receipt, addressed and dispatched by the court clerk to the agency or instrumentality to be served. *Id.* §1608(b)(3)(B).

(c) As directed by a court order consistent with the law of the place where service is to be made. *Id.* §1608(b)(3)(C).

3. Time to respond. The foreign state or its agency has 60 days after service to file an answer or other response. 28 U.S.C. §1608(d).

4. Default judgment. Default judgments against foreign sovereigns are disfavored. ***Commercial Bank of Kuwait v. Rafidain Bank***, 15 F.3d 238, 240 (2d Cir.1994). When a foreign government defaults, the district court must determine whether the plaintiff's allegations are supported by evidence. *Id.* at 242; *see* 28 U.S.C. §1608(e). A copy of a default judgment must be sent to the foreign state or political subdivision in the manner prescribed for service in §1608(e). 28 U.S.C. §1608(e). The circuits disagree whether notice of default must be sent to an agency or instrumentality of a foreign state. *Compare* ***Antoine v. Atlas Turner, Inc.***, 66 F.3d 105, 109 (6th Cir.1995) (notice must be sent), *with* ***Straub***, 38 F.3d at 454 (notice not required). In any event, a default judgment not served as required is considered voidable but not void. ***Antoine***, 66 F.3d at 109.

§7. WHO CAN SERVE PROCESS

Service of process must be made by a person authorized under the rules or statutes.

§7.1 Nonparty over 18. The summons and complaint can be served by any person who is not a party and who is at least 18 years old. FRCP 4(c)(2).

PRACTICE TIP

A party's attorney qualifies as "any person" and thus can serve the summons and complaint under FRCP 4(c)(2). See ***Jugolinija v. Blue Heaven Mills, Inc.***, *115 F.R.D. 13, 15 (S.D.Ga.1986). However, an attorney generally should not serve by personal delivery because if the service is attacked as improper, the attorney may have to testify as a witness. State law will determine whether a party's attorney can serve the summons and complaint when the method of service is provided by that state's law. See FRCP 4(e)(1); see, e.g., N.J. Ct. R. 4:4-3(a) (allowing plaintiff's attorney to serve summons and complaint). In addition, state law may prohibit service by persons interested in the outcome of the suit. E.g., N.J. Ct. R. 4:4-3(a); Tex. R. Civ. P. 103.*

§7.2 U.S. marshal or specially appointed person. If requested by the plaintiff, the court may order service by a U.S. marshal or a specially appointed person. FRCP 4(c)(3); ***Combs v. Nick Garin Trucking***, 825 F.2d 437, 443 n.47 (D.C.Cir.1987); *see also* 1993 Notes to FRCP 4 at ¶14, p. 1139, this book (if presence of law-enforcement officer appears to be necessary or advisable to keep peace, court should appoint a marshal, deputy, or other officer to make service); U.S. Marshals Service, www.usmarshals.gov/process/summons-complaint.htm (service by U.S. marshal may be appropriate in certain suits filed by U.S. government). When requested by the plaintiff, a U.S. marshal or a specially appointed person must serve the summons and complaint in the following type of cases:

1. Suits filed by an indigent plaintiff. FRCP 4(c)(3); *see* 28 U.S.C. §1915; ***Dumaguin v. Secretary of H&HS***, 28 F.3d 1218, 1221 (D.C.Cir.1994). The circuits disagree on whether an indigent plaintiff must submit a request that service of process be made by the U.S. marshal. *Compare* ***Nagy v. Dwyer***, 507 F.3d 161, 163 (2d Cir.2007) (without request from indigent P, court was not required to appoint U.S. marshal), *with* ***Laurence v. Wall***, 551 F.3d 92, 94 (1st Cir.2008) (indigent P does not have to request service of process by U.S. marshal, but P must cooperate with court and U.S. marshal and must provide addresses of named Ds).

2. Suits filed by seamen. FRCP 4(c)(3); *see* 28 U.S.C. §1916.

§7.3 Central authority. When process is served abroad, the central authority of the foreign country can serve process or arrange to have it served by an appropriate agency. Hague Convention on Service Abroad of Judicial & Extrajudicial Documents, art. 5, p. 1563, this book.

§8. TERRITORIAL LIMITS OF SERVICE

§8.1 General rules. FRCP 4(k) sets out the territorial limits for effective service. Under the rule, serving a summons or filing a waiver of service is effective to establish personal jurisdiction over a defendant as outlined below. See "Motion to Dismiss for Lack of Personal Jurisdiction—FRCP 12(b)(2)," ch. 3-B, p. 178.

1. State long-arm statute. A court has personal jurisdiction over a defendant who is served according to the forum state's long-arm statute. FRCP 4(k)(1)(A); ***ALS Scan, Inc. v. Digital Serv. Consultants, Inc.***, 293 F.3d 707, 710 (4th Cir.2002). Under most state long-arm statutes, a person who commits a tort or does business within a state is within the reach of that state's long-arm statute for the purpose of service in the federal court located in that state. *See* ***Indianapolis Colts, Inc. v. Metropolitan Balt. Football Club L.P.***, 34 F.3d 410, 411-12 (7th Cir.1994).

2. 100-mile rule. A court has personal jurisdiction over a defendant who is served according to the 100-mile rule. FRCP 4(k)(1)(B). This rule permits service out of state in some situations even when the state law does not permit it. The rule applies only when a nonresident will be brought in as an additional party to a pending suit. Nonresident additional parties can be served anywhere within a 100-mile radius of the federal court where the case is pending, even across a state boundary. *See id.* The types of parties that can be served within the 100-mile radius are as follows:

(1) Third-party defendants. Third-party defendants under FRCP 14 can be served within the 100-mile radius. FRCP 4(k)(1)(B).

(2) Required parties. Required parties under FRCP 19(a) can be served within the 100-mile radius. FRCP 4(k)(1)(B). A required party is a person who is needed in the suit for just adjudication and whose joinder will not destroy subject-matter jurisdiction. FRCP 19(a). See "Motion to Dismiss for Failure to Join a Party Under FRCP 19—FRCP 12(b)(7)," ch. 3-I, p. 214.

3. Federal statute. A court has personal jurisdiction over a defendant who is served according to a federal statute. FRCP 4(k)(1)(C). Some federal statutes permit nationwide service of process; however, when the suit is based on a federal statute that does not provide for nationwide service of process, the forum state's law governing personal jurisdiction applies. *See* ***Omni Capital Int'l v. Rudolf Wolff & Co.***, 484 U.S. 97, 104-05 (1987); ***Reebok Int'l v. McLaughlin***, 49 F.3d 1387, 1393 n.7 (9th Cir.1995); ***Mareno v. Rowe***, 910 F.2d 1043, 1046 (2d Cir.1990). When a federal court attempts to exercise personal jurisdiction over a defendant in a suit based on a federal statute providing for nationwide service of process, the relevant inquiry is whether the defendant has sufficient contacts with the United States as a whole. ***Adams v. Unione Mediterranea di Sicurta***, 364 F.3d 646, 650 (5th Cir.2004); ***In re Automotive Refinishing Paint Antitrust Litig.***, 358 F.3d 288, 297 (3d Cir.2004); ***Board of Trs., Sheet Metal Workers' Nat'l Pension Fund v. Elite Erectors, Inc.***, 212 F.3d 1031, 1035 (7th Cir.2000); ***In re Federal Fountain, Inc.***, 165 F.3d 600, 602 (8th Cir.1999); *see also* ***Peay v. BellSouth Med. Assistance Plan***, 205 F.3d 1206, 1211-12 (10th Cir.2000) (in federal-question cases, when jurisdiction is invoked based on nationwide service of process, Due Process Clause requires P's choice of forum to be fair and reasonable to D); ***Republic of Pan. v. BCCI Holdings S.A.***, 119 F.3d 935, 947-48 (11th Cir.1997) (to defeat jurisdiction, D must show that exercise of jurisdiction in forum will make litigation so gravely difficult and inconvenient that D would be at severe disadvantage). The following are some examples of federal statutes authorizing nationwide service of process:

(1) 15 U.S.C. §22 (Clayton Act). ***Delong Equip. Co. v. Washington Mills Abrasive Co.***, 840 F.2d 843, 848 (11th Cir.1988) (corporations only).

(2) 15 U.S.C. §78aa(a) (Securities Exchange Act). ***Busch v. Buchman, Buchman & O'Brien***, 11 F.3d 1255, 1256-57 (5th Cir.1994); ***Bourassa v. Desrochers***, 938 F.2d 1056, 1057 (9th Cir.1991).

(3) 18 U.S.C. §1965(b) or (d) (Racketeer Influenced and Corrupt Organizations Act). *See* ***Brown v. Kerkhoff***, 504 F.Supp.2d 464, 490-97 (S.D.Iowa 2007) (circuits are split over whether §1965(b) or (d) is statute authorizing nationwide service of process). When an applicable federal statute authorizes service of process over certain defendants but is silent about other defendants, a plaintiff may rely on state-law authorization for service of process on those other defendants. *See* ***Stauffacher v. Bennett***, 969 F.2d 455, 460-61 (7th Cir.1992); ***Brink's Mat Ltd. v. Diamond***, 906 F.2d 1519, 1522 (11th Cir.1990).

(4) 28 U.S.C. §1391(e)(2) (suits against federal officers). When suits are filed against federal officers and agencies, service may be accomplished by registered mail anywhere in the United States. Delivery may be made by certified mail on a defendant officer or agency that is outside the territorial limits of the district where the suit is filed. 28 U.S.C. §1391(e)(2); *see* ***Cameron v. Thornburgh***, 983 F.2d 253, 256 (D.C.Cir.1993); *see also* FRCP 4(i)(1)(C) (service by registered mail when suit attacks validity of order by officer who is not made a party); FRCP 4(i)(2) (service by registered mail when federal officer, employee, agency, or corporation is D).

(5) 28 U.S.C. §1692 (suits in which receiver is appointed for property). ***Haile v. Henderson Nat'l Bank***, 657 F.2d 816, 824 (6th Cir.1981).

(6) 28 U.S.C. §1697 (multiparty, multiforum actions).

(7) 28 U.S.C. §2361 (interpleader actions). ***State Farm Fire & Cas. Co. v. Tashire***, 386 U.S. 523, 528 n.3 (1967). See "Statutory interpleader," ch. 2-C, §4.2, p. 90.

(8) 29 U.S.C. §1132(e)(2) (ERISA). ***Cripps v. Life Ins.***, 980 F.2d 1261, 1267 (9th Cir.1992).

(9) 29 U.S.C. §1451(d) (ERISA's Multiemployer Pension Plan Amendments Act). *See* ***IUE AFL-CIO Pension Fund v. Herrmann***, 9 F.3d 1049, 1056-57 (2d Cir.1993).

(10) 42 U.S.C. §9613(e) (CERCLA).

§8.2 Federal rule. FRCP 4(k)(2) is a special-purpose long-arm law, akin to state long-arm statutes, that authorizes extraterritorial jurisdiction whenever its exercise would be consistent with the requirements of due process, as long as the defendant is not subject to the jurisdiction of the courts of general jurisdiction of any state. ***Adams v. Unione Mediterranea di Sicurta***, 364 F.3d 646, 650-51 (5th Cir.2004); *see* ***Saudi v. Northrop Grumman Corp.***, 427 F.3d 271, 275 (4th Cir.2005). See "Service under FRCP 4(k)(2)," §6.3.6, p. 160.

§9. PROVING SERVICE

FRCP 4(*l*) requires that the person serving process establish proof of service promptly—and at least by the deadline for the defendant to respond to service.

§9.1 Affidavit by other person. If the summons was served by any person other than a U.S. marshal or deputy marshal, that person must sign an affidavit verifying service. FRCP 4(*l*)(1). The affidavit for service is usually included as part of the summons form. To avoid a claim of improper service, the plaintiff should ensure that the proof of service is filed in the court. *See* FRCP 4(*l*)(1); ***U.S. v. Dimen-Pascua Constr. Co.***, 123 F.R.D. 413, 414 (D.Mass. 1988).

§9.2 Signature of marshal. The U.S. marshal who serves the summons must sign the return, state on the return when the summons was served, and identify the manner of service. *See* U.S. Marshal Form 285 (USM-285), "Process Receipt and Return," www.usmarshals.gov/process/usm-285.pdf.

§9.3 Waiver of service. If the plaintiff files a waiver of service, proof of service is not required. FRCP 4(d)(4), (*l*)(1). The waiver of service must be a written statement signed by the defendant or its attorney for proper verification. *See* FRCP 4(d)(1)(A).

§9.4 Proof of service abroad. If service abroad is made under FRCP 4(f)(1), proof must be established as required by the treaty or convention in effect. FRCP 4(*l*)(2)(A). If service is made under FRCP 4(f)(2) or (f)(3), proof must be established by a receipt signed by the addressee or other evidence satisfactory to the court. FRCP 4(*l*)(2)(B).

§9.5 Failure to make proof of service. If service is not waived, the person making service must submit proof of service to the court. FRCP 4(*l*)(1). But failure to prove service does not affect the validity of the service. FRCP 4(*l*)(3).

§9.6 Amendments. The court may allow the proof of service and the summons to be amended. FRCP 4(a)(2), (*l*)(3).

COMMENTARIES

CHAPTER 3. DEFENDANT'S RESPONSES & PLEADINGS
TABLE OF CONTENTS

A. OVERVIEW OF PREANSWER MOTIONS & RESPONSIVE PLEADINGS 171
§1. GENERAL 171
§2. FRCP 12 MOTION 171
§2.1 Purpose 171
§2.2 Types of FRCP 12 defenses 171
§2.3 Defenses raised in preanswer motion 172
§3. RESPONSIVE PLEADING 173
§3.1 Purpose 173
§3.2 Types of responsive pleadings 173
§4. CHALLENGES TO FORUM 173
§4.1 Forum non conveniens 173
§4.2 Inconvenient forum 173
§4.3 Forum-selection clause 173
§5. DEADLINES 174
§5.1 To serve preanswer motion 174
§5.2 To serve responsive pleading 175
§6. SUMMARY OF DEFENDANT'S RESPONSES & PLEADINGS 177

B. MOTION TO DISMISS FOR LACK OF PERSONAL JURISDICTION—FRCP 12(b)(2) 178
§1. GENERAL 178
§2. MOTION 178
§2.1 Form 178
§2.2 In writing or on court's initiative 178
§2.3 Grounds 178
§2.4 Affidavits 183
§2.5 Relief requested 183
§2.6 Request hearing 183
§2.7 Waiver 183
§3. RESPONSE 184
§3.1 Grounds 184
§3.2 Discovery 185
§3.3 Evidence 185
§3.4 Amended pleading 185
§4. HEARING 185
§4.1 No hearing 186
§4.2 Hearing 186
§5. RULING 186
§5.1 Denies motion 186
§5.2 Grants motion 186
§5.3 Findings of fact 186
§6. APPELLATE REVIEW 186

C. MOTION TO DISMISS FOR LACK OF SUBJECT-MATTER JURISDICTION—FRCP 12(b)(1) 187
§1. GENERAL 187
§2. MOTION 187
§2.1 Form 187
§2.2 In writing or on court's initiative 187
§2.3 Grounds 188
§2.4 Request hearing 189
§2.5 Affidavits & other evidence 189
§2.6 Request for discovery 189
§2.7 No waiver 189
§3. RESPONSE 189
§3.1 Burden 189
§3.2 Affidavits & other evidence 190
§3.3 Amended pleading 190
§4. HEARING 190
§4.1 Before most other challenges 190
§4.2 After challenge to personal jurisdiction or forum non conveniens 190
§4.3 Defer to conduct discovery or receive evidence 191
§5. RULING 191
§5.1 Standard 191
§5.2 Effect of ruling 192
§5.3 Findings of fact 192
§6. APPELLATE REVIEW 192
§6.1 Appeal 192
§6.2 Standard of review 192

D. MOTION TO DISMISS FOR IMPROPER VENUE—FRCP 12(b)(3) 192
§1. GENERAL 192
§2. VENUE CONSIDERATIONS 193
§2.1 Federal law applies 193
§2.2 When venue determined 193
§3. MOTION 193
§3.1 Form 193
§3.2 In writing or on court's initiative 193
§3.3 Grounds 193
§3.4 Discovery 196
§3.5 Affidavits 196
§3.6 Waiver 196
§4. RESPONSE 197
§4.1 Grounds 197
§4.2 Affidavits 197
§4.3 Amended pleading 197
§5. HEARING 197
§5.1 Who has burden 197
§5.2 Burden of proof 197
§6. RULING 198
§6.1 Denies motion 198
§6.2 Grants motion 198
§6.3 Curative amendment 198
§6.4 Multiple defendants 198
§6.5 Findings of fact 198
§7. APPELLATE REVIEW 198
§7.1 Appealability of order 198
§7.2 Standard of review 199

E. MOTION TO DISMISS FOR FORUM NON CONVENIENS—CHALLENGING THE U.S. FORUM 199
§1. GENERAL 199
§2. MOTION 199
§2.1 Form 199
§2.2 In writing 199
§2.3 Grounds 199
§2.4 Burden 201
§2.5 Evidence 202
§2.6 Deadline 202
§3. RESPONSE 202
§3.1 In writing 202
§3.2 Grounds 202
§3.3 Evidence 203
§4. HEARING 203
§5. RULING 203
§5.1 Denies motion 203
§5.2 Grants motion 203
§5.3 Conditionally grants motion 203
§5.4 Findings of fact 203

COMMENTARIES

CHAPTER 3. DEFENDANT'S RESPONSES & PLEADINGS

TABLE OF CONTENTS

§6. APPELLATE REVIEW 203
§6.1 Appealability 203
§6.2 Standard of review 203

F. MOTION TO DISMISS FOR FAILURE TO STATE A CLAIM—FRCP 12(b)(6) 204

§1. GENERAL 204
§2. MOTION 204
§2.1 Form 204
§2.2 In writing or on court's initiative 204
§2.3 Grounds 204
§2.4 Relief requested 205
§2.5 No affidavits or evidence 205
§2.6 Waiver 205
§3. RESPONSE 206
§3.1 Grounds 206
§3.2 Amended pleading 206
§3.3 Deadline 206
§4. HEARING 206
§4.1 No extrinsic materials 206
§4.2 Effect of considering extrinsic materials 206
§5. RULING 207
§5.1 Standard 207
§5.2 Denies motion 208
§5.3 Grants motion 208
§5.4 No findings of fact 208
§6. APPELLATE REVIEW 208
§6.1 Appealability 208
§6.2 Standard of review 208

G. MOTION TO DISMISS FOR INSUFFICIENT PROCESS OR SERVICE—FRCP 12(b)(4), (b)(5) 209

§1. GENERAL 209
§2. MOTION 209
§2.1 Form 209
§2.2 In writing 209
§2.3 Grounds 209
§2.4 Deadline 209
§2.5 Waiver 209
§2.6 Evidence 209
§3. RESPONSE 210
§3.1 In writing 210
§3.2 Grounds 210
§3.3 Amended pleading 210
§3.4 Deadline 210
§4. BURDEN OF PROOF 210
§4.1 Plaintiff's burden 210
§4.2 Defendant's burden 210
§5. HEARING 210
§6. RULING 210
§6.1 Defect in summons 211
§6.2 Defect in service 211
§7. APPELLATE REVIEW 211
§7.1 Appealability 211
§7.2 Standard of review 211

H. MOTION FOR MORE DEFINITE STATEMENT—FRCP 12(e) 212

§1. GENERAL 212
§2. MOTION 212
§2.1 Form 212
§2.2 In writing or on court's initiative 212
§2.3 Grounds 212
§2.4 Identify defects 212
§2.5 Deadline 213
§3. RESPONSE 213
§3.1 Grounds 213
§3.2 Amended pleading 213
§4. HEARING 213
§5. RULING 214
§5.1 Denies motion 214
§5.2 Grants motion 214
§6. APPELLATE REVIEW 214

I. MOTION TO DISMISS FOR FAILURE TO JOIN A PARTY UNDER FRCP 19—FRCP 12(b)(7) 214

§1. GENERAL 214
§2. MOTION 214
§2.1 Form 214
§2.2 In writing 214
§2.3 Grounds 215
§2.4 Deadline 216
§2.5 Extrinsic evidence 216
§2.6 Burden 216
§2.7 Waiver 216
§3. RESPONSE 216
§3.1 In writing 216
§3.2 Grounds 216
§3.3 Amended pleading 217
§3.4 Deadline 217
§4. HEARING 217
§5. RULING 217
§5.1 Is absent party required? 217
§5.2 Can absent party be joined? 217
§5.3 Can suit proceed in equity & good conscience? 217
§6. APPELLATE REVIEW 218
§6.1 Abuse of discretion 218
§6.2 De novo 218

J. MOTION TO DISMISS FOR FAILURE TO PLEAD PROPERLY—FRCP 8, 9(b) 218

§1. GENERAL 218
§2. MOTION 218
§2.1 Form 218
§2.2 In writing 218
§2.3 Consolidation with FRCP 12 objections 219
§2.4 Grounds 219
§3. RESPONSE 220
§3.1 Motion under FRCP 8 or 9(b) 220
§3.2 Motion under FRCP 12(b), (e), or (f) 220
§4. HEARING 220
§5. RULING 220
§6. APPELLATE REVIEW 221

K. MOTION TO TRANSFER VENUE—28 U.S.C. §1404 221

§1. GENERAL 221
§2. MOTION 221
§2.1 Form 221
§2.2 In writing or on court's initiative 221
§2.3 Deadline 221
§2.4 Grounds 222
§2.5 Evidence 225
§2.6 Discovery 225
§2.7 Burden 225

CHAPTER 3. DEFENDANT'S RESPONSES & PLEADINGS
TABLE OF CONTENTS

§3. RESPONSE 225
§3.1 In writing 225
§3.2 Grounds 225
§3.3 Deadline 227
§4. AGREED MOTION 227
§4.1 Form 228
§4.2 In writing 228
§4.3 Deadline 228
§4.4 Grounds 228
§5. HEARING 228
§6. RULING 228
§6.1 Denies motion 228
§6.2 Grants motion 228
§7. APPELLATE REVIEW 229
§7.1 Appealability 229
§7.2 Standard of review 229

L. THE ANSWER—DENYING LIABILITY 230

§1. GENERAL 230
§2. DEADLINE 230
§3. TYPES OF DENIALS 230
§3.1 General denial 230
§3.2 Specific denial 231
§3.3 Denial of knowledge 231
§3.4 Challenge to capacity 231
§3.5 Denial of conditions precedent 231
§4. AFFIRMATIVE DEFENSES 231
§4.1 Affirmative defense vs. counterclaim 232
§4.2 Affirmative defense in motion to dismiss 232
§4.3 Effect of failure to plead 232
§4.4 Affirmative defenses in FRCP 8(c) 232
§4.5 Other affirmative defenses 233
§4.6 Sufficiency of affirmative defense 234
§4.7 Inconsistent affirmative defenses 235
§5. DEFENDANT'S CLAIMS 235
§5.1 Counterclaim 235
§5.2 Cross-claim 236
§5.3 Third-party claim 236
§6. DISCLOSURE STATEMENT 237

COMMENTARIES

CHAPTER 3. DEFENDANT'S RESPONSES & PLEADINGS

3. DEFENDANT'S RESPONSES & PLEADINGS

A. OVERVIEW OF PREANSWER MOTIONS & RESPONSIVE PLEADINGS

§1. GENERAL

§1.1 Rules. FRCP 8, 9, 12-14. See also 28 U.S.C. §§1390, 1391, 1404, 1406.

§1.2 Purpose. After service of process, the defendant must file either an FRCP 12 motion or an answer to avoid default. *See* ***Breuer Elec. Mfg. v. Toronado Sys.***, 687 F.2d 182, 184 (7th Cir.1982).

§1.3 Forms. ***O'Connor's Federal Civil Forms*** (2012), FORMS ch. 3.

§1.4 Other references. 5B, 5C Wright & Miller, *Federal Practice & Procedure 3d* §§1345-1349, 1361 (2004 & Supp.2012); 14D Wright, Miller & Cooper, *Federal Practice & Procedure 3d* §3803.1 (2007 & Supp.2012); 2, 17 *Moore's Federal Practice 3d* §§12.01-12.03, 111.04 (2012).

§2. FRCP 12 MOTION

§2.1 Purpose. The objective of FRCP 12 is to eliminate unnecessary delay at the pleading stage. ***Rauch v. Day & Night Mfg.***, 576 F.2d 697, 701 & n.3 (6th Cir.1978). FRCP 12 requires that a defendant who wants to raise a defense must do so when it makes its "first defensive move," whether by an FRCP 12 motion or by a responsive pleading. ***Rauch***, 576 F.2d at 701; *see also* ***Trustees of Cent. Laborers' Welfare Fund v. Lowery***, 924 F.2d 731, 734 (7th Cir. 1991) (discussing rationale of timeliness requirement). See "Responsive Pleading," §3, p. 173. The defendant must present in a single preanswer motion or responsive pleading every available FRCP 12 defense, except those listed in FRCP 12(h)(2) or 12(h)(3), which may be raised later. *See* FRCP 12(g)(2), (h)(2), (h)(3); ***Albany Ins. v. Almacenadora Somex, S.A.***, 5 F.3d 907, 909 (5th Cir.1993); ***Marcial Ucin, S.A. v. SS GALICIA***, 723 F.2d 994, 997 (1st Cir.1983).

§2.2 Types of FRCP 12 defenses. The defendant may raise two types of defenses in a preanswer motion: defenses that terminate the lawsuit as a matter of law, and defenses that raise potentially curable procedural defects.

1. Defenses that terminate lawsuit. A defendant can terminate the lawsuit by successfully raising one of the following defenses:

(1) Lack of subject-matter jurisdiction. *See* FRCP 12(b)(1). See "Motion to Dismiss for Lack of Subject-Matter Jurisdiction—FRCP 12(b)(1)," ch. 3-C, p. 187.

(2) Lack of personal jurisdiction over the defendant. *See* FRCP 12(b)(2). See "Motion to Dismiss for Lack of Personal Jurisdiction—FRCP 12(b)(2)," ch. 3-B, p. 178.

(3) Failure to state a claim upon which relief can be granted. *See* FRCP 12(b)(6). See "Motion to Dismiss for Failure to State a Claim—FRCP 12(b)(6)," ch. 3-F, p. 204.

2. Defenses that raise procedural defects. The following defenses raise procedural defects, most of which are curable:

(1) Improper venue. *See* FRCP 12(b)(3). See "Motion to Dismiss for Improper Venue—FRCP 12(b)(3)," ch. 3-D, p. 192.

(2) Insufficient form of process. *See* FRCP 12(b)(4). See "Motion to Dismiss for Insufficient Process or Service—FRCP 12(b)(4), (b)(5)," ch. 3-G, p. 209.

(3) Insufficient service of process. *See* FRCP 12(b)(5). See "Motion to Dismiss for Insufficient Process or Service—FRCP 12(b)(4), (b)(5)," ch. 3-G, p. 209.

(4) Failure to join a party under FRCP 19. *See* FRCP 12(b)(7). See "Motion to Dismiss for Failure to Join a Party Under FRCP 19—FRCP 12(b)(7)," ch. 3-I, p. 214.

(5) Vague or ambiguous pleading. *See* FRCP 12(e). See "Motion for More Definite Statement—FRCP 12(e)," ch. 3-H, p. 212.

(6) Redundant, immaterial, impertinent, or scandalous matters. *See* FRCP 12(f). See "Motion to Dismiss for Failure to Plead Properly—FRCP 8, 9(b)," ch. 3-J, p. 218.

§2.3 Defenses raised in preanswer motion. If a defendant serves any pretrial motion under FRCP 12, it generally must include in that motion all other available defenses permitted under FRCP 12, or else it waives those defenses. FRCP 12(g)(2), (h)(1); ***American Ass'n of Naturopathic Physicians v. Hayhurst***, 227 F.3d 1104, 1106-07 (9th Cir.2000); *e.g.*, ***Albany Ins. v. Almacenadora Somex, S.A.***, 5 F.3d 907, 909-10 (5th Cir.1993) (D waived defense of improper venue based on forum-selection clause because it was not raised in D's first motion to dismiss); *see also* ***King v. Russell***, 963 F.2d 1301, 1304 (9th Cir.1992) (D does not waive FRCP 12 defense if it serves preanswer motion seeking dismissal based on rule other than FRCP 12). Some FRCP 12 defenses must be raised in a preanswer motion or responsive pleading; some FRCP 12 defenses may be raised at trial or, in the case of lack of subject-matter jurisdiction, at any time.

1. Must be included. A defendant waives the following defenses or objections unless it raises them in a preanswer motion, the answer, or an answer amended as a matter of course (i.e., an answer amended within 21 days after serving it). *See* FRCP 12(b), (h)(1), 15(a)(1)(A).

NOTE

When the defense or objection is raised only in the answer, some courts have allowed FRCP 12(b)(2), (b)(3), (b)(4), or (b)(5) motions to be filed after the answer. See 5C Wright & Miller §1361 n.7; see, e.g., ***Pope v. Elabo GmbH****, 588 F.Supp.2d 1008, 1012-13 (D.Minn.2008) (D did not waive defense of personal jurisdiction when it raised defense in answer and later argued it in motion for summary judgment, which court construed as untimely but allowable FRCP 12(b)(2) motion). But even if a defense or objection under FRCP 12(b)(2)-(b)(5) can be raised in an answer, the better practice is to file a preanswer motion. See FRCP 12(b), (h)(1)(B);* ***Pope****, 588 F.Supp.2d at 1012-13;* ***Litchfield Fin. Corp. v. Buyers Source Real Estate Grp.****, 389 F.Supp.2d 80, 84 (D.Mass.2005); 5C Wright & Miller §1361 n.3.*

---

(1) Lack of personal jurisdiction. *See* FRCP 12(b)(2), (h)(1); ***Hayhurst***, 227 F.3d at 1106-07; ***Continental Bank v. Meyer***, 10 F.3d 1293, 1296 (7th Cir.1993).

(2) Improper venue. *See* FRCP 12(b)(3), (h)(1); ***American Patriot Ins. Agency, Inc. v. Mutual Risk Mgmt.***, 364 F.3d 884, 887 (7th Cir.2004); ***King***, 963 F.2d at 1305.

(3) Insufficient form of process. *See* FRCP 12(b)(4), (h)(1); ***O'Brien v. R.J. O'Brien & Assocs.***, 998 F.2d 1394, 1399 (7th Cir.1993).

(4) Insufficient service of process. *See* FRCP 12(b)(5), (h)(1); ***Chute v. Walker***, 281 F.3d 314, 319 (1st Cir.2002); ***McCurdy v. American Bd. of Plastic Surgery***, 157 F.3d 191, 194 (3d Cir.1998); ***Resolution Trust Corp. v. Starkey***, 41 F.3d 1018, 1021 (5th Cir.1995).

(5) Vague or ambiguous pleading. *See* FRCP 12(e), (g)(2); ***In re Daboul***, 82 B.R. 657, 659 (Bankr.D. Mass.1987).

(6) Redundant, immaterial, impertinent, or scandalous matters. *See* FRCP 12(f), (g)(2).

2. May be included. A defendant can raise the following defenses in its preanswer motion, but it can also raise them in any pleading under FRCP 7(a), in a motion for judgment on the pleadings under FRCP 12(c), or at trial:

(1) Failure to state a claim upon which relief can be granted. FRCP 12(h)(2); ***Romstadt v. Allstate Ins.***, 59 F.3d 608, 611 n.1 (6th Cir.1995); *see* FRCP 12(b)(6).

(2) Failure to state a defense to a claim. FRCP 12(h)(2).

(3) Failure to join a party under FRCP 19(b). FRCP 12(h)(2); *see* FRCP 12(b)(7); ***Enterprise Mgmt. Consultants, Inc. v. U.S.***, 883 F.2d 890, 892-93 & n.2 (10th Cir.1989).

(4) Lack of subject-matter jurisdiction. FRCP 12(h)(3); ***Sault Ste. Marie Tribe of Chippewa Indians v. U.S.***, 288 F.3d 910, 915 (6th Cir.2002); ***Avitts v. Amoco Prod.***, 53 F.3d 690, 693 (5th Cir.1995); ***Hawxhurst v. Pettibone Corp.***, 40 F.3d 175, 179 (7th Cir.1994); *see* FRCP 12(b)(1).

§3. RESPONSIVE PLEADING

§3.1 Purpose. The purpose of a responsive pleading is to challenge matters alleged in the plaintiff's complaint. *See, e.g.*, ***Breuer Elec. Mfg. v. Toronado Sys.***, 687 F.2d 182, 184 (7th Cir.1982) (default judgment entered against Ds for failure to file response).

§3.2 Types of responsive pleadings. For purposes of FRCP 12, a "responsive pleading" is usually the defendant's answer to the plaintiff's complaint. *See* ***LeBoeuf, Lamb, Greene & MacRae, L.L.P. v. Worsham***, 185 F.3d 61, 66 (2d Cir.1999). However, a responsive pleading is also an answer to a counterclaim (designated as a counterclaim), an answer to a cross-claim, a third-party complaint, an answer to a third-party complaint, or a reply to an answer. FRCP 7(a); *see* ***Burns v. Lawther***, 53 F.3d 1237, 1241 (11th Cir.1995). An FRCP 12 motion is not a responsive pleading. ***Richardson v. Stanley Works, Inc.***, 597 F.3d 1288, 1297 (Fed.Cir.2010); *see, e.g.*, ***McCrary v. Poythress***, 638 F.2d 1308, 1314 (5th Cir.1981) (FRCP 12(b)(6) motion is not responsive pleading under FRCP 7(a)).

§4. CHALLENGES TO FORUM

The defendant can challenge the forum where the suit was filed in a preanswer motion or a responsive pleading.

§4.1 Forum non conveniens. If a foreign country has jurisdiction over the suit and is a more appropriate forum for resolving the parties' claims, the defendant can file a motion to dismiss the suit under the doctrine of forum non conveniens. *See* ***Piper Aircraft Co. v. Reyno***, 454 U.S. 235, 254-55 & n.22 (1981). See "Motion to Dismiss for Forum Non Conveniens—Challenging the U.S. Forum," ch. 3-E, p. 199.

§4.2 Inconvenient forum. If the forum where the suit was filed is inconvenient for the defendant or the witnesses and there is a more convenient federal district where the suit could have been brought, the defendant can file a motion to transfer venue to the more convenient forum. *See* 28 U.S.C. §1404(a). See "Motion to Transfer Venue—28 U.S.C. §1404," ch. 3-K, p. 221.

§4.3 Forum-selection clause. If a valid forum-selection clause mandates venue in a court other than the one where the suit was filed, the defendant can file a motion to dismiss, transfer venue, or remand. A forum-selection clause is a contractual provision that specifies the forum for litigation between the parties. *See* ***Marra v. Papandreou***, 216 F.3d 1119, 1123 (D.C.Cir.2000). The proper procedure depends on the forum identified in the forum-selection clause. When the forum-selection clause identifies another federal district court, a court in a different state, or a foreign court, the circuits are split on which procedural mechanism should be used for challenging venue. *See* ***Asoma Corp. v. SK Shipping Co.***, 467 F.3d 817, 822 (2d Cir.2006). In these situations, courts have dismissed cases under FRCP 12(b)(1), (b)(3), or (b)(6), under 28 U.S.C. §1406(a), or based on forum non conveniens, and they have transferred cases under 28 U.S.C. §1404(a) or §1406(a). *See* ***Slater v. Energy Servs. Grp. Int'l***, 634 F.3d 1326, 1332 (11th Cir.2011); ***Silva v. Encyclopedia Britannica Inc.***, 239 F.3d 385, 387 n.3 (1st Cir.2001); *see also* ***Haynsworth v. The Corp.***, 121 F.3d 956, 961 & n.8 (5th Cir.1997) (identifying the issue as "enigmatic"). When the forum-selection clause identifies a state court and the action has been removed from that state court, the proper procedure to challenge venue is a motion to remand. For an in-depth discussion of the different procedures, see 14D Wright, Miller & Cooper §3803.1 and 17 *Moore's Federal Practice 3d* §111.04.

CAUTION

In addition to the circuit split on which procedural mechanism should be used for challenging venue, the circuits are also split on whether federal or state law governs the enforceability of a forum-selection clause in diversity cases. See ***Wong v. PartyGaming Ltd.****, 589 F.3d 821, 826-27 (6th Cir.2009). Many circuits hold that enforceability of the forum-selection clause involves federal procedure and is thus governed by federal law. Id. at 827 & n.5; e.g.,* ***Simonoff v. Expedia, Inc.****, 643 F.3d 1202, 1205 (9th Cir.2011);* ***Fru-Con Constr. Corp. v. Controlled Air, Inc.****, 574 F.3d 527, 538 (8th Cir.2009);* ***Ginter v. Belcher, Prendergast & Laporte****, 536 F.3d 439, 441 (5th Cir.2008);* ***P&S Bus. Machs., Inc. v. Canon USA, Inc.****, 331 F.3d 804, 807 (11th Cir. 2003);* ***Jumara v. State Farm Ins.****, 55 F.3d 873, 877 (3d Cir.1995). Other circuits hold that the law governing the contract as a whole should govern enforceability of the forum-selection clause. E.g.,* ***Abbott Labs. v. Takeda Pharm. Co.****, 476 F.3d 421, 423 (7th Cir.2007);* ***Yavuz v. 61 MM, Ltd.****, 465 F.3d 418, 428 (10th Cir.2006). Therefore, always check the law of the relevant circuit before drafting a motion to enforce a forum-selection clause.*

1. Forum in another federal district court. If the forum-selection clause mandates a forum in another federal district court, the proper procedure may be dismissal or transfer, depending on whether the circuit holds that a valid forum-selection clause renders venue improper. *See* ***Kerobo v. Southwestern Clean Fuels, Corp.***, 285 F.3d 531, 534-35 (6th Cir.2002); ***Jackson v. West Telemarketing Corp. Outbound***, 245 F.3d 518, 522-23 (5th Cir.2001); 14D Wright, Miller & Cooper §3803.1. If a circuit holds that a valid forum-selection clause renders a statutorily proper venue improper, the court may transfer the case under 28 U.S.C. §1406(a) or dismiss under either FRCP 12(b)(3) or 28 U.S.C. §1406(a). *See, e.g.,* ***Muzumdar v. Wellness Int'l Network, Ltd.***, 438 F.3d 759, 760 (7th Cir.2006) (dismissal under FRCP 12(b)(3)); ***Kerobo***, 285 F.3d at 538 (§1406(a) applies only when venue is improper). If a circuit holds that a valid forum-selection clause does not render a statutorily proper venue improper, the court may transfer the case under 28 U.S.C. §1404(a) or dismiss under FRCP 12(b)(6). *See, e.g.,* ***Kerobo***, 285 F.3d at 538-39 (if venue is proper under 28 U.S.C. §1391 (2011), case cannot be dismissed for improper venue; transfer under §1404(a) is appropriate); ***Silva***, 239 F.3d at 387 (dismissal under FRCP 12(b)(6)). See "Forum-selection clause," ch. 3-D, §3.3.4, p. 194; "Grounds," ch. 3-F, §2.3.5, p. 205; "Forum-selection clause," ch. 3-K, §2.4.1(9), p. 224.

2. Forum in different state or foreign court. If the forum-selection clause mandates a forum in a different state or a foreign court, the proper procedure may be either a motion to dismiss under FRCP 12(b)(3) or 12(b)(6) or a motion to dismiss for forum non conveniens. *See* ***Salovaara v. Jackson Nat'l Life Ins.***, 246 F.3d 289, 298 (3d Cir.2001); 14D Wright, Miller & Cooper §3803.1; 17 *Moore's Federal Practice* §111.04[3][b]; *see, e.g.,* ***Sucampo Pharms. v. Astellas Pharma, Inc.***, 471 F.3d 544, 549-50 (4th Cir.2006) (forum-selection clause identified court in Japan, but suit was filed in Maryland federal court; appropriate motion was 12(b)(3)); ***Instrumentation Assocs. v. Madsen Elecs. (Canada) Ltd.***, 859 F.2d 4, 6 n.4 (3d Cir.1988) (forum-selection clause identified court in Canada, but suit was filed in Pennsylvania federal court; appropriate motion was 12(b)(6)); *see also* ***Asoma Corp.***, 467 F.3d at 822 (court will not be pigeonholed into one particular clause of FRCP 12(b); key is whether P meets burden to overcome presumption of forum-selection clause's enforceability). See "Forum-selection clause," ch. 3-D, §3.3.4, p. 194; "Private-interest factors," ch. 3-E, §2.3.2(1), p. 200; "Grounds," ch. 3-F, §2.3.5, p. 205.

3. Forum in same state. If the case was removed from a state court and the forum-selection clause mandates that the case be filed in that state court, the proper procedure may be a motion to remand. 14D Wright, Miller & Cooper §3803.1; *see, e.g.,* ***American Soda, LLP v. U.S. Filter Wastewater Grp.***, 428 F.3d 921, 927 (10th Cir.2005) (remand to state court appropriate when mandatory forum-selection clause designated state court from which case was removed). See "Plaintiff's Motion to Remand," ch. 4-B, p. 268.

§5. DEADLINES

§5.1 To serve preanswer motion. If the defendant decides to file an FRCP 12 preanswer motion, it must serve the motion within the time allowed for serving the answer. *See* FRCP 12(a)(1). Generally, a defendant must serve an answer within 21 days after service of the summons and complaint. FRCP 12(a)(1)(A)(i).

§5.2 To serve responsive pleading. The specific deadline for serving an answer or other responsive pleading depends on whether an FRCP 12 preanswer motion was filed first. *See* FRCP 12(a)(4).

CAUTION

*FRCP 6(d), which adds three days to the response period after certain methods of service, may not extend the defendant's deadline to serve its answer. See "Determine if additional three-day extension applies," ch. 1-D, §6.5, p. 34. FRCP 6(d) applies only to papers identified in FRCP 5(a) and served under FRCP 5(b). Specifically, FRCP 5(a)(1)(B) applies to service of pleadings filed **after** the summons and complaint. However, service of the summons and complaint is provided for under FRCP 4(c), not FRCP 5(a). Thus, service of the answer to the complaint is not controlled by FRCP 5(a), so the additional three days for service under FRCP 6(d) may not apply to an original answer. See **Hides v. City of Fort Wayne**, No. 1:06-CV-328 (N.D.Ind.2006) (slip op.; 12-18-06) (footnote 4); 4B Wright & Miller, Federal Practice & Procedure 3d §1171 & n.2 (2002 & Supp.2012).*

1. FRCP 12 motion filed. The filing of an FRCP 12 motion changes the deadline for serving the answer or other responsive pleading. *See* FRCP 12(a)(4). FRCP 12(a)(4) establishes the deadline for serving the answer or other responsive pleading after the court's ruling on an FRCP 12 preanswer motion, but the court or local rules can modify the FRCP 12(a)(4) deadline.

(1) Court delays ruling on motion. If the court notifies the parties that it will delay ruling on the FRCP 12 preanswer motion until trial, the defendant must serve its answer or other responsive pleading within 14 days after receiving notice of the delay. FRCP 12(a)(4)(A).

(2) Court denies motion. If the court denies the FRCP 12 motion, the defendant must serve its answer or other responsive pleading within 14 days after receiving notice of the ruling. FRCP 12(a)(4)(A).

(3) Court grants motion.

(a) Motions to dismiss. If the court grants a motion to dismiss under FRCP 12(b), it will enter an order dismissing all or part of the case. If the order dismisses the entire case, the defendant will no longer need to serve an answer or other responsive pleading. If the order dismisses only some claims, the defendant will need to serve an answer or other responsive pleading for the remaining claims within 14 days after receiving notice of the ruling. *See* FRCP 12(a)(4)(A).

(b) FRCP 12(e) motions. If the court grants a motion for a more definite statement under FRCP 12(e), the defendant must serve its answer or other responsive pleading within 14 days after the plaintiff serves its amended pleading. FRCP 12(a)(4)(B).

2. No FRCP 12 motion filed. If no FRCP 12 preanswer motion is filed, the answer must be served by the deadlines specified in FRCP 12(a)(1)-(a)(3).

(1) Deadline to answer after service.

(a) Most defendants.

[1] Answer to complaint. The answer to a complaint is due within 21 days after service of the summons and complaint on the defendant. FRCP 12(a)(1)(A)(i). FRCP 12 does not extend the time for codefendants to file an answer unless they filed FRCP 12 preanswer motions. *See* FRCP 12(a)(1)(B), (a)(4); ***Hanley v. Volpe***, 48 F.R.D. 387, 388 (E.D.Wis.1970); 5B Wright & Miller §1346 & n.13.

[2] Answer to amended complaint. The answer to an amended complaint is due within the time remaining for a response to the initial pleading or within 14 days after service of the amended pleading, whichever period is longer. FRCP 15(a)(3).

[3] Answer to counterclaim. The answer to a counterclaim is due within 21 days after service of the pleading that states the counterclaim. FRCP 12(a)(1)(B).

[4] Answer to cross-claim. The answer to a cross-claim is due within 21 days after service of the pleading that states the cross-claim. FRCP 12(a)(1)(B).

[5] Reply to answer. The reply to an answer is due within 21 days after service of an order to reply, unless the order specifies a different time. FRCP 12(a)(1)(C).

(b) U.S. government defendants.

[1] United States or its agency. The United States or one of its agencies has 60 days after service on the U.S. Attorney to serve an answer, a cross-claim, or a counterclaim. FRCP 12(a)(2); ***Gonzalez-Gonzalez v. U.S.***, 257 F.3d 31, 36 (1st Cir.2001). Various statutes relating to specific types of cases provide a shorter time for the government to answer. *See, e.g.*, 5 U.S.C. §552(a)(4)(C) (Freedom of Information Act provides 30 days to answer complaint served on U.S. or any of its officers or agencies), 5 U.S.C. §552b(h)(1) (Sunshine Act provides 30 days to answer complaint alleging violations of Act's open-meetings requirements).

[2] U.S. officer or employee – official capacity. A federal officer or employee sued in an official capacity has 60 days after service on the U.S. Attorney to serve an answer, a cross-claim, or a counterclaim. FRCP 12(a)(2).

[3] U.S. officer or employee – individual capacity. A federal officer or employee sued in an individual capacity for acts or omissions occurring in connection with the performance of official duties has 60 days after either service on the officer or employee or service on the U.S. Attorney—whichever is later—to serve an answer, a cross-claim, or a counterclaim. FRCP 12(a)(3); *see* 2000 Notes to FRCP 12 at ¶1, p. 1156, this book. See "U.S. officer or employee – individual capacity," ch. 2-H, §5.5.4, p. 155. This 60-day time period applies to both current and former federal officers and employees. 2000 Notes to FRCP 12 at ¶2, p. 1156, this book.

(2) Deadline to answer after waiver. A defendant may waive service of process. FRCP 4(d). If a defendant within the United States timely waives service, it has 60 days after the waiver request was sent to answer. FRCP 4(d)(3), 12(a)(1)(A)(ii). If a defendant outside the United States timely waives service, it has 90 days after that date to answer. FRCP 4(d)(3), 12(a)(1)(A)(ii).

(3) Deadline to answer after removal. If the defendant did not file an answer in state court before removing the case to federal court, the defendant's answer is due within the longest of the following time periods: (1) 21 days after the defendant receives a copy of the state-court pleading, (2) 21 days after service of the summons for the state-court pleading on file at the time of service, or (3) 7 days after the notice of removal is filed. FRCP 81(c)(2); *see* ***Silva v. City of Madison***, 69 F.3d 1368, 1371 (7th Cir.1995) (applying former 20-day and 5-day deadlines); *see also* ***Murphy Bros. v. Michetti Pipe Stringing, Inc.***, 526 U.S. 344, 355 (1999) (FRCP 81(c) was sensibly interpreted by court in ***Silva***). In states requiring service of the complaint along with the summons, the second time period does not apply. ***Silva***, 69 F.3d at 1375. Thus, if the defendant did not answer in state court and does not answer in federal court, default begins on either the 22nd day after the defendant received the state-court pleading and summons or the 8th day after notice of removal is filed, whichever is later. *See* FRCP 81(c)(2). See "Default Judgment," ch. 7-A, p. 583.

PRACTICE TIP

After removal, a defendant should consider filing an answer even if it is filing an FRCP 12 preanswer motion. If the defendant removes a case and files an FRCP 12 preanswer motion but not an answer, the plaintiff may be able to voluntarily dismiss the case and refile in state court with a nondiverse defendant, thus defeating diversity. See FRCP 41(a)(1)(A)(i); ***Harvey Specialty & Sup. v. Anson Flowline Equip. Inc.****, 434 F.3d 320, 324 n.15 (5th Cir.2005). The defendant can prevent unilateral voluntary dismissal under FRCP 41 simply by filing an answer or a motion for summary judgment. See FRCP 41(a)(1)(A)(i). See "Practice Tip," ch. 4-B, §2.1.1, p. 269.*

§6. SUMMARY OF DEFENDANT'S RESPONSES & PLEADINGS

Chart 3-1, below, lists the challenges a defendant can make and the procedural steps for each.

3-1. SUMMARY OF DEFENDANT'S RESPONSES & PLEADINGS

	To urge this	File this
	Challenging jurisdiction	
1	The defendant, a nonresident, does not have sufficient minimum contacts with the forum state to give the federal court jurisdiction over the defendant's person or property.	A motion to dismiss for lack of personal jurisdiction. FRCP 12(b)(2).
2	The court does not have jurisdiction over the controversy.	A motion to dismiss for lack of subject-matter jurisdiction. FRCP 12(b)(1).
3	The defendant has not been properly served.	A motion to dismiss for insufficiency of process or insufficiency of service of process and for lack of personal jurisdiction. FRCP 12(b)(2), (b)(4), (b)(5).
	Challenging court where suit was filed	
4	A more appropriate forum outside the United States has jurisdiction over the suit.	A motion to dismiss for forum non conveniens.
5	The plaintiff filed the suit in an improper district.	A motion to dismiss for improper venue or to transfer venue. 28 U.S.C. §1406(a); FRCP 12(b)(3).
6	The district where the suit was filed is too inconvenient to the defendant or witnesses.	A motion to transfer venue. 28 U.S.C. §1404(a).
7	There is a valid forum-selection clause that mandates venue in a court other than the one where the suit was filed.	A motion to transfer venue under 28 U.S.C. §1404(a) or §1406(a), a motion to dismiss under FRCP 12(b)(3) or 12(b)(6), or a motion to dismiss for forum non conveniens.
	Challenging parties	
8	All necessary parties have not been joined.	A motion to dismiss under FRCP 12(b)(7).
9	The defendant was sued in the wrong capacity.	An answer with specific negative allegations of which defendant has personal knowledge. FRCP 9(a).
10	The plaintiff sued in the wrong capacity.	An answer with specific negative allegations of which defendant has personal knowledge. FRCP 9(a).
11	The plaintiff lacks standing to sue.	A motion to dismiss under FRCP 12(b)(1).
	Challenging pleadings	
12	The complaint is vague or ambiguous and prevents the defendant from adequately responding.	A motion for more definite statement. FRCP 12(e).
13	There is an independent reason why the plaintiff cannot prevail.	An answer that includes one or more affirmative defenses. FRCP 8(c).
14	The complaint fails to state a claim upon which relief can be granted.	A motion to dismiss under FRCP 12(b)(6).
15	The complaint fails to set forth a short and plain statement of the claim for relief or is not simple, concise, and direct.	A motion to dismiss under FRCP 8(a), 8(d), or 12(b)(6).
16	The complaint does not allege fraud or mistake with sufficient particularity.	A motion to dismiss under FRCP 9(b) or 12(b)(6).
17	The complaint does not comply with the pleading requirements of the Private Securities Litigation Reform Act of 1995.	A motion to dismiss under FRCP 12(b)(6) and under §21D(b)(3)(A) of the Securities Exchange Act of 1934. *See* 15 U.S.C. §78u-4 (PSLRA); FRCP 9(b).

B. MOTION TO DISMISS FOR LACK OF PERSONAL JURISDICTION—FRCP 12(b)(2)

§1. GENERAL

§1.1 Rule. FRCP 12(b)(2).

§1.2 Purpose. A motion to dismiss for lack of personal jurisdiction permits a nonresident defendant to challenge the court's jurisdiction over the defendant's person or property.

§1.3 Forms. *O'Connor's Federal Civil Forms* (2012), FORMS 3B.

§1.4 Other references. 5B Wright & Miller, *Federal Practice & Procedure 3d* §§1347-1349, 1351 (2004 & Supp.2012); 2 *Moore's Federal Practice 3d* §§12.01-12.03, 12.31 (2012).

§2. MOTION

In an FRCP 12(b)(2) motion, a nonresident defendant alleges that it has insufficient contacts with the forum state to justify the court's exercise of jurisdiction over the defendant's person or property.

§2.1 Form. For the general requirements for the form of a motion, see "Drafting motions," ch. 1-B, §3.1, p. 14.

§2.2 In writing or on court's initiative. The defendant should submit the motion in writing. *See* FRCP 7(b)(1). However, the court may raise the issue of personal jurisdiction on its own initiative. ***System Pipe & Sup. v. M/V Viktor Kurnatovskiy***, 242 F.3d 322, 324 (5th Cir.2001). If it does, it must allow the plaintiff a reasonable opportunity to respond. *Id.* at 325.

§2.3 Grounds. The motion can allege that (1) the statute or rule relied on for service of process does not authorize service on the nonresident defendant or (2) the court's exercise of jurisdiction over the defendant would violate due process. *See* ***Omni Capital Int'l v. Rudolf Wolff & Co.***, 484 U.S. 97, 102-04 (1987); ***Wenz v. Memery Crystal***, 55 F.3d 1503, 1506-07 (10th Cir.1995); ***U.S. v. Ferrara***, 54 F.3d 825, 828 (D.C.Cir.1995).

1. No authority for service. The defendant can allege that its activities did not fall within the reach of the statute or rule authorizing service of process. *See* ***Mobile Anesthesiologists Chi., LLC v. Anesthesia Assocs.***, 623 F.3d 440, 443-44 (7th Cir.2010); ***Wenz***, 55 F.3d at 1506-07; ***Mylan Labs. v. Akzo, N.V.***, 2 F.3d 56, 60 (4th Cir.1993); ***Stuart v. Spademan***, 772 F.2d 1185, 1189 (5th Cir.1985).

(1) Nationwide service. A federal statute providing for nationwide or worldwide service of process confers personal jurisdiction on any federal district court over any defendant who has minimum contacts with the United States. See "Federal statute," ch. 2-H, §8.1.3, p. 164.

(2) Federal long-arm service. FRCP 4(k)(2) authorizes service on a defendant who is not subject to any state's courts of general jurisdiction. See "Service under FRCP 4(k)(2)," ch. 2-H, §6.3.6, p. 160.

(3) State long-arm statute. If a state long-arm statute has been construed to extend to the limits of due process, the district court can bypass analyzing the reach of the long-arm statute and proceed directly to the due-process analysis. *See, e.g.*, ***Mobile Anesthesiologists***, 623 F.3d at 443 (Illinois); ***Stroman Rlty., Inc. v. Wercinski***, 513 F.3d 476, 482 (5th Cir.2008) (Texas); ***Yahoo! Inc. v. La Ligue Contre le Racisme et L'Antisemitisme***, 433 F.3d 1199, 1205 (9th Cir.2006) (California); ***Vetrotex CertainTeed Corp. v. Consolidated Fiber Glass Prods.***, 75 F.3d 147, 150 (3d Cir.1996) (Pennsylvania). If a state long-arm statute does not extend to the limits of due process, the district court should engage in a two-part test: (1) it should decide whether the exercise of jurisdiction is permitted by the forum state's law, and if so, (2) it should decide whether the exercise of jurisdiction is consistent with due process. *See* ***Wenz***, 55 F.3d at 1506-07.

2. No due process. The defendant should allege that the court's exercise of jurisdiction will violate due process because (1) the defendant does not have minimum contacts with the forum state and (2) maintaining the suit in the forum state will offend traditional notions of fair play and substantial justice. *See* ***World-Wide Volkswagen Corp. v. Woodson***, 444 U.S. 286, 291-92 (1980); ***Johnston v. Multidata Sys. Int'l***, 523 F.3d 602, 609 (5th Cir.2008).

(1) Minimum contacts. The motion should allege that the defendant does not have minimum contacts with the state.

(a) Purposeful availment. Before a forum state can exercise personal jurisdiction over a nonresident defendant, the Due Process Clause requires that the defendant must have purposefully availed itself of the benefits and protections of the state's laws by establishing "minimum contacts" with the state. *See* ***J. McIntyre Mach., Ltd. v. Nicastro***, ___ U.S. ___, 131 S.Ct. 2780, 2787-88 (2011) (plurality op.); ***International Shoe Co. v. Washington***, 326 U.S. 310, 316 (1945). A defendant's contacts with the forum state must be such that the defendant "should reasonably anticipate being haled into court there." ***World-Wide Volkswagen***, 444 U.S. at 297; *see also* ***J. McIntyre Mach.***, ___ U.S. at ___, 131 S.Ct. at 2788 (plurality op.; principal inquiry is whether D's activities manifest intention to submit to power of forum state).

(b) Specific or general jurisdiction. There are two theories under which a defendant's contacts with the forum state are analyzed—specific jurisdiction and general jurisdiction. *See* ***Steinbuch v. Cutler***, 518 F.3d 580, 586 (8th Cir.2008). Analysis under specific jurisdiction focuses on the cause of action, the defendant, and the forum; analysis under general jurisdiction focuses only on whether there are continuous and systematic contacts between the defendant and the forum, regardless of the cause of action. ***Harlow v. Children's Hosp.***, 432 F.3d 50, 65 (1st Cir.2005); *see* ***Goodyear Dunlop Tires Opers., S.A. v. Brown***, ___ U.S. ___, 131 S.Ct. 2846, 2851 (2011). Courts apply a five-part test when measuring minimum contacts: (1) the nature and quality of the contacts, (2) the quantity of the contacts, (3) the relation of the cause of action to the contacts, (4) the interest of the forum state in providing a forum for its residents to resolve disputes, and (5) the convenience of the parties. ***Steinbuch***, 518 F.3d at 586.

[1] Specific jurisdiction.

[a] Generally. A court has specific jurisdiction when a plaintiff's cause of action arises from or is directly related to the defendant's contacts with the forum state. ***J. McIntyre Mach.***, ___ U.S. at ___, 131 S.Ct. at 2788 (plurality op.); ***Helicopteros Nacionales de Colombia, S.A. v. Hall***, 466 U.S. 408, 414 n.8 (1984); ***Avocent Huntsville Corp. v. Aten Int'l Co.***, 552 F.3d 1324, 1330 (Fed.Cir.2008); *see also* ***O'Connor v. Sandy Lane Hotel Co.***, 496 F.3d 312, 318 & n.5 (3d Cir.2007) (identifying varying interpretations of "arise out of or relate to" standard). A court has specific jurisdiction if the defendant committed at least one act in the forum state and if that act is substantially related to the suit. *See* ***Moncrief Oil Int'l v. OAO Gazprom***, 481 F.3d 309, 311 (5th Cir.2007) (single act directed at forum state can support jurisdiction if act gave rise to claim); ***Yahoo! Inc.***, 433 F.3d at 1210 (single forum-state contact can support jurisdiction if cause of action arises from that purposeful contact); *see, e.g.*, ***Chloé v. Queen Bee of Beverly Hills, LLC***, 616 F.3d 158, 170-71 (2d Cir.2010) (D's single act of shipping counterfeit purse to forum state, combined with D's employer's substantial activity in forum state that was imputed to D, was sufficient for specific jurisdiction over D); ***Carteret Sav. Bank, FA v. Shushan***, 954 F.2d 141, 149 (3d Cir.1992) (although correspondence and telephone calls alone were insufficient for minimum contacts, single meeting in forum state was "culminating event" that was sufficient). A plaintiff bringing multiple claims arising from different contacts of the defendant must establish specific jurisdiction for each claim. *See* ***Seiferth v. Helicopteros Atuneros, Inc.***, 472 F.3d 266, 274-75 (5th Cir.2006) (specific jurisdiction is a claim-specific inquiry). To challenge a claim of specific jurisdiction, an FRCP 12(b)(2) motion should allege either that the cause of action did not arise from the defendant's contacts (if any) within the forum state or that those contacts are insufficient to satisfy due process. For examples of contacts that are sufficient or insufficient to establish specific jurisdiction, see chart 3-2, below.

[b] Stream of commerce. Specific jurisdiction may be based on the movement of goods from a manufacturer through its distributors to consumers—that is, through the "stream of commerce." ***Goodyear Dunlop Tires Opers.***, ___ U.S. at ___, 131 S.Ct. at 2855; *see* ***J. McIntyre Mach.***, ___ U.S. at ___, 131 S.Ct. at 2788 (plurality op.). Typically, in stream-of-commerce cases, a nonresident defendant acting outside the forum places a product into the stream of commerce that ultimately causes harm to a plaintiff inside the forum. ***Goodyear Dunlop Tires Opers.***, ___ U.S. at ___, 131 S.Ct. at 2855. But such stream-of-commerce ties do not war-

rant a determination that based on those ties, the forum has general jurisdiction over a defendant. *Id.* at ___, 131 S.Ct. at 2855; ***Purdue Research Found. v. Sanofi-Synthelabo, S.A.***, 338 F.3d 773, 788 (7th Cir.2003); *see* ***Jackson v. Tanfoglio Giuseppe, S.R.L.***, 615 F.3d 579, 584 (5th Cir.2010) (placing product, even in substantial volume, into forum's stream of commerce, without more, does not support general jurisdiction). See "General jurisdiction," §2.3.2(1)(b)[2], p. 182.

NOTE

*In **J. McIntyre Mach., Ltd. v. Nicastro**, a majority of the Supreme Court agreed that the plaintiff's assertion of jurisdiction based on the stream of commerce was insufficient. See **J. McIntyre Mach.**, ___ U.S. at ___, 131 S.Ct. at 2785 (plurality op., Kennedy, Roberts, Scalia, Thomas, JJ.); id. at ___, 131 S.Ct. at 2791 (Breyer & Alito, JJ., concurring in the judgment). The plurality held that a defendant's placement of goods into the stream of commerce supports the exercise of jurisdiction only when the defendant targeted the forum; it would not be enough that the defendant might have predicted that its goods would reach the forum. See id. at ___, 131 S.Ct. at 2788 (plurality op.; in products-liability case in which P was injured by D's machine in New Jersey (NJ) and machine was manufactured abroad, D did not purposefully avail itself of NJ market when D's only contact with NJ was that machine ended up in NJ; D did not have NJ office, did not pay taxes or own property there, and did not advertise or send employees there). Two justices, concurring in the judgment, were critical of the plurality because that opinion did not provide a standard for the stream-of-commerce concept that is realistically applicable to modern concerns, such as how the concept will apply to a company that targets the world through the Internet. Id. at ___, 131 S.Ct. at 2792-93 (Breyer & Alito, JJ., concurring).*

[c] Internet contacts. Specific jurisdiction may be based on Internet contacts when the defendant-website operator (1) directly targets the website to the forum state, (2) knowingly conducts business with the forum state's residents through the website, or (3) has sufficient related non-Internet contacts with the forum state's residents. ***Toys "R" Us, Inc. v. Step Two, S.A.***, 318 F.3d 446, 454 (3d Cir.2003); *see* ***Neogen Corp. v. Neo Gen Screening, Inc.***, 282 F.3d 883, 890-91 (6th Cir.2002); *see also* ***AST Sports Sci., Inc. v. CLF Distrib.***, 514 F.3d 1054, 1059 (10th Cir.2008) (modern communications can eliminate need for physical presence in forum). Some courts have held that a court's ability to exercise personal jurisdiction is directly proportional to the nature and quality of the commercial activity the defendant conducts on the Internet, adopting the flexible "sliding-scale" approach first set out in ***Zippo Mfg. v. Zippo Dot Com, Inc.***, 952 F.Supp. 1119, 1124 (W.D.Pa.1997). *E.g.*, ***Toys "R" Us***, 318 F.3d at 452; ***Revell v. Lidov***, 317 F.3d 467, 470-71 (5th Cir.2002); ***ALS Scan, Inc. v. Digital Serv. Consultants, Inc.***, 293 F.3d 707, 713-14 (4th Cir.2002); ***Neogen Corp.***, 282 F.3d at 890; *see* ***Oldfield v. Pueblo De Bahia Lora, S.A.***, 558 F.3d 1210, 1219 n.26 (11th Cir.2009); ***Lakin v. Prudential Secs., Inc.***, 348 F.3d 704, 711 (8th Cir.2003); *see, e.g.*, ***Boschetto v. Hansing***, 539 F.3d 1011, 1018-19 (9th Cir.2008) (jurisdiction could not be based on Internet sale because contact involved one-time Internet sale, not broader e-commerce activity, that concerned forum state only because P-purchaser lived there). Other courts have declined to adopt a specific test for Internet-based cases. *E.g.*, ***Illinois v. Hemi Grp.***, 622 F.3d 754, 758-59 (7th Cir.2010); *see* ***Roblor Mktg. Grp. v. GPS Indus.***, 645 F.Supp.2d 1130, 1142-43 (S.D.Fla.2009). Under ***Zippo***, the more interactive a website is, the more it weighs in favor of the exercise of jurisdiction. *See* ***Zippo***, 952 F.Supp. at 1124. When the website's level of interactivity is somewhere in the middle, the court must review the "level of interactivity and commercial nature of the exchange of information" to determine whether the exercise of jurisdiction is proper. *Id.* For examples of Internet contacts that are sufficient or insufficient to establish specific jurisdiction, see chart 3-2, below. The circuits are split on whether the ***Zippo*** test applies to general jurisdiction based on Internet contacts. See "Circuit Split," §2.3.2(1)(b)[2], p. 182.

3-2. SPECIFIC JURISDICTION

	Contacts	Case
	Sufficient contacts	
1	Distributing defamatory magazines in the forum state.	***Keeton v. Hustler Mag., Inc.***, 465 U.S. 770, 773-74 (1984).
2	Making a single telephone call and mailing allegedly fraudulent materials to the forum state.	***Lewis v. Fresne***, 252 F.3d 352, 358-59 (5th Cir.2001).
3	Negotiating, consummating, and partially performing an agreement that contemplated future contacts in the forum state.	***Electrosource, Inc. v. Horizon Battery Techs.***, 176 F.3d 867, 872 (5th Cir.1999).
4	Purposefully registering someone else's trademark as one's own domain name for purposes of extorting money.	***Panavision Int'l v. Toeppen***, 141 F.3d 1316, 1322 (9th Cir.1998).
5	Knowingly acquiring an economically beneficial interest in the outcome of a lawsuit based in the forum state that involved control over property located in the forum state.	***Pritzker v. Yari***, 42 F.3d 53, 64-65 (1st Cir.1994).
6	Ordering goods from a corporation based in the forum state, traveling to the forum state to inspect the goods, and agreeing to the shipment of the goods F.O.B. in the forum state.	***Bell Paper Box, Inc. v. U.S. Kids, Inc.***, 22 F.3d 816, 819-20 (8th Cir.1994).
7	Requiring the execution of a deed of trust in the forum state as security for a debt, in addition to calls, letters, and trips to the forum state.	***Sher v. Johnson***, 911 F.2d 1357, 1363-64 (9th Cir.1990).
8	Soliciting business and negotiating, executing, and partially performing a contract in the forum state.	***Rainbow Travel Serv. v. Hilton Hotels Corp.***, 896 F.2d 1233, 1238-39 (10th Cir.1990).
9	Selling passwords to subscribers and entering into contracts with Internet access provider to provide services to subscribers and customers in the forum state.	***Zippo Mfg. v. Zippo Dot Com, Inc.***, 952 F.Supp. 1119, 1126 (W.D.Pa.1997).
	Insufficient contacts	
10	Sending cease-and-desist order and correspondence with P's attorneys.	***Stroman Rlty., Inc. v. Wercinski***, 513 F.3d 476, 484-85 (5th Cir.2008).
11	Contracting to nonspecific location for P's unilateral performance, which happened to take place in the forum state.	***Moncrief Oil Int'l v. OAO Gazprom***, 481 F.3d 309, 312-13 (5th Cir.2007).
12	Advertising on third-party websites accessible by the forum state's residents when D had no responsibility for the advertising.	***Trintec Indus. v. Pedre Promotional Prods.***, 395 F.3d 1275, 1281-82 (Fed.Cir.2005).
13	Maintaining a passive website that does no more than provide information about the company and its products to the forum state.	***Jennings v. AC Hydraulic A/S***, 383 F.3d 546, 549-50 (7th Cir.2004).
14	Operating an interactive website accessible by the forum state's residents but designed solely for foreign customers.	***Toys "R" Us, Inc. v. Step Two, S.A.***, 318 F.3d 446, 454 (3d Cir.2003).
15	Providing bandwidth to codefendant to create website and transmit photographs over Internet to the forum state.	***ALS Scan, Inc. v. Digital Serv. Consultants, Inc.***, 293 F.3d 707, 714-15 (4th Cir.2002).
16	Having subsidiary companies that have sufficient contacts with the forum state.	***Doe v. Unocal Corp.***, 248 F.3d 915, 925-26 (9th Cir.2001).
17	Registering someone else's trademark as a domain name and posting a website.	***Cybersell, Inc. v. Cybersell, Inc.***, 130 F.3d 414, 419 (9th Cir.1997).
18	Contracting to deliver cargo to a port in the forum state.	***Francosteel Corp. v. M/V Charm***, 19 F.3d 624, 629 (11th Cir.1994).
19	Making telephone calls and sending correspondence to the forum state.	***Market/Media Research, Inc. v. Union-Tribune Publ'g***, 951 F.2d 102, 105-06 (6th Cir.1991).

[2] General jurisdiction. A court has general jurisdiction when the defendant has engaged in "continuous and systematic" activities within the forum state, even if the cause of action is unrelated to the defendant's contacts. ***Goodyear Dunlop Tires Opers.***, ___ U.S. at ___, 131 S.Ct. at 2853; ***Helicopteros Nacionales***, 466 U.S. at 414-16; ***Metropolitan Life Ins. v. Robertson-Ceco Corp.***, 84 F.3d 560, 568 (2d Cir.1996); ***Vetrotex CertainTeed Corp.***, 75 F.3d at 151 n.3; *see* ***Tuazon v. R.J. Reynolds Tobacco Co.***, 433 F.3d 1163, 1172 (9th Cir.2006) (factors include longevity, continuity, volume, economic impact, physical presence, and integration). To challenge a claim of general jurisdiction, the defendant should allege that any contacts it may have had with the forum state were not continuous or systematic enough to justify the exercise of personal jurisdiction. *See* ***Johnston***, 523 F.3d at 609-10. General jurisdiction can be assessed by evaluating the defendant's contacts with the forum state over a reasonable number of years, up to the date the suit was filed. *See id.* at 610; ***Metropolitan Life***, 84 F.3d at 569. The test for general jurisdiction is considerably more stringent than the test for specific jurisdiction. ***Avocent Huntsville Corp.***, 552 F.3d at 1330; ***Platten v. HG Bermuda Exempted Ltd.***, 437 F.3d 118, 138 (1st Cir.2006); *see* ***Johnston***, 523 F.3d at 609 (test is difficult to meet and requires extensive contacts between D and forum). For examples of contacts that are sufficient or insufficient to establish general jurisdiction, see chart 3-3, below.

CIRCUIT SPLIT

In some circuits, a defendant may be subject to general jurisdiction through continuous and systematic Internet contacts. See ***Gorman v. Ameritrade Holding Corp.****, 293 F.3d 506, 513 (D.C. Cir.2002). The courts are split on whether and how the* ***Zippo*** *sliding-scale test for specific jurisdiction applies to claims of general jurisdiction. Compare* ***Mavrix Photo, Inc. v. Brand Techs.****, 647 F.3d 1218, 1227 (9th Cir.2011) (sliding scale provides limited help for general jurisdiction; general jurisdiction based only on accessibility of interactive website is likely inconsistent with constitutional requirements),* ***Lakin****, 348 F.3d at 711-12 (sliding scale alone insufficient for general jurisdiction; "nature and quality" as well as quantity of contacts must be considered), and* ***Revell****, 317 F.3d at 471 (sliding scale not well adapted to general jurisdiction because doing business with forum, but not in forum, may not meet the requirement for substantial, continuous, and systematic contacts), with* ***Gorman****, 293 F.3d at 513 (dicta; sliding scale applicable to general jurisdiction), and* ***Soma Med. Int'l v. Standard Chartered Bank****, 196 F.3d 1292, 1296 (10th Cir.1999) (sliding scale applicable to general jurisdiction).* *See "Internet contacts," §2.3.2(1)(b)[1][c], p. 180.*

3-3. GENERAL JURISDICTION

	Contacts	Case
	Sufficient contacts	
1	Maintaining a temporary office in the forum state, keeping the business's files in the forum state, and maintaining two active bank accounts carrying substantial balances in the forum state.	***Perkins v. Benguet Consol. Mining Co.***, 342 U.S. 437, 447-49 (1952).
2	Employing salesmen who live in the forum state but limiting their authority to exhibiting samples of merchandise and soliciting orders from prospective buyers.	***International Shoe Co. v. Washington***, 326 U.S. 310, 320 (1945).
3	Soliciting business and selling products through dealers in the forum state.	***Metropolitan Life Ins. v. Robertson-Ceco Corp.***, 84 F.3d 560, 573 (2d Cir.1996).

3-3. GENERAL JURISDICTION (CONTINUED)

	Contacts	Case
	Sufficient contacts (continued)	
4	Appointing a registered agent for service of process in the forum state.	***Knowlton v. Allied Van Lines, Inc.***, 900 F.2d 1196, 1200 (8th Cir.1990). *But see* ***Wenche Siemer***, row 8, below.
5	Maintaining a highly interactive Internet store, advertising on a well-known Internet search engine and other websites, making substantial sales as an electronic retailer in the forum state, and purchasing products from vendors in the forum state.	***Coremetrics, Inc. v. AtomicPark.com LLC***, 370 F.Supp.2d 1013, 1021-24 (N.D.Cal.2005).
	Insufficient contacts	
6	Having some tires, which were made abroad by foreign subsidiaries, reach the forum state through stream of commerce.	***Goodyear Dunlop Tires Opers., S.A. v. Brown***, ___ U.S. ___, 131 S.Ct. 2846, 2851 (2011).
7	Selling $140,000 worth of goods (approximately 3% of business), advertising in national trade journal, and having employees periodically attend trade conventions.	***Johnston v. Multidata Sys. Int'l***, 523 F.3d 602, 611 (5th Cir.2008).
8	Designating a corporate agent for service of process under the forum state's registration act.	***Wenche Siemer v. Learjet Acquisition Corp.***, 966 F.2d 179, 183 (5th Cir.1992). *But see* ***Knowlton***, row 4, above.
9	Contacting a member of an unincorporated association.	***Donatelli v. National Hockey League***, 893 F.2d 459, 470 (1st Cir.1990).
10	Providing health coverage under a group policy to a plaintiff and other company employees who were residents of the forum state.	***Hirsch v. Blue Cross, Blue Shield***, 800 F.2d 1474, 1478 (9th Cir.1986).

(2) Fair play & substantial justice. The motion should also allege that the court's exercise of jurisdiction will offend traditional notions of fair play and substantial justice. *See* ***International Shoe***, 326 U.S. at 316. The motion should focus on (1) the burden on the defendant, (2) the interests of the forum state in adjudicating the dispute, (3) the plaintiff's interest in obtaining convenient and effective relief, (4) the efficient resolution of controversies between the states, and (5) the shared interests of the states in furthering fundamental, substantive social policies. ***Asahi Metal Indus. Co. v. Superior Ct. of Cal.***, 480 U.S. 102, 113 (1987); ***uBID, Inc. v. GoDaddy Grp.***, 623 F.3d 421, 432 (7th Cir.2010); ***Johnston***, 523 F.3d at 615; ***O'Connor***, 496 F.3d at 324. Although the Supreme Court has not applied the five factors in a general-jurisdiction case, some lower courts have done so. *E.g.*, ***Metropolitan Life***, 84 F.3d at 573 (issue of fair play and substantial justice applies to all questions of personal jurisdiction).

§2.4 Affidavits. The motion should be supported by affidavits that deny all or part of the jurisdictional facts pleaded by the plaintiff. *See* ***Theunissen v. Matthews***, 935 F.2d 1454, 1458-59 (6th Cir.1991).

§2.5 Relief requested. The motion should request that the court dismiss the plaintiff's claims against the defendant because the court lacks jurisdiction. *See* ***Theunissen v. Matthews***, 935 F.2d 1454, 1458 (6th Cir.1991).

§2.6 Request hearing. If the defendant alleges facts to defeat jurisdiction, it should request an evidentiary hearing. *See* ***Theunissen v. Matthews***, 935 F.2d 1454, 1458 (6th Cir.1991); ***Serras v. First Tenn. Bank***, 875 F.2d 1212, 1214 (6th Cir.1989). If there is an evidentiary hearing, the plaintiff has the burden to prove its grounds for personal jurisdiction by a preponderance of the evidence. See "Hearing," §4.2, p. 186. If there is not an evidentiary hearing, the plaintiff need only make a prima facie showing of personal jurisdiction. See "No hearing," §4.1, p. 186.

§2.7 Waiver. The defense of lack of personal jurisdiction can be waived in the following circumstances:

1. Untimely challenge. If the defendant does not file an FRCP 12(b)(2) motion and does not challenge personal jurisdiction in its first responsive pleading or in an amendment to its first responsive pleading allowed as a matter of course (i.e., amendment allowed within 21 days after the responsive pleading is served), the defense is waived. FRCP 12(h)(1); *see* FRCP 12(g)(2), 15(a)(1)(A); *see, e.g.*, ***American Ass'n of Naturopathic Physicians v.***

Hayhurst, 227 F.3d 1104, 1106-07 (9th Cir.2000) (D did not challenge personal jurisdiction in FRCP 55 motion to set aside default judgment, which in essence was FRCP 12 motion); *see also* ***Insurance Corp. of Ir., Ltd. v. Compagnie des Bauxites de Guinee***, 456 U.S. 694, 703 (1982) (personal jurisdiction, like other individual rights, can be waived). See "Defenses raised in preanswer motion," ch. 3-A, §2.3, p. 172; "Waiver," §3.1.1, this page.

2. Implied consent. If the defendant impliedly consents to the court's jurisdiction, the defense is waived. *See* ***Gerber v. Riordan***, 649 F.3d 514, 517-18 (6th Cir.2011); *see, e.g.*, ***Victory Transp. v. Comisaria General de Abástecimientos y Transportes***, 336 F.2d 354, 363 (2d Cir.1964) (because D agreed to arbitrate in New York, D consented to personal jurisdiction of New York court that could compel arbitration).

3. Conduct negating challenge. Even when the defendant makes a timely challenge to personal jurisdiction, the defense may be waived if the defendant's conduct leading up to the challenge is inconsistent with its claim that personal jurisdiction is lacking. *See* ***PaineWebber Inc. v. Chase Manhattan Private Bank***, 260 F.3d 453, 460 (5th Cir.2001); ***Peterson v. Highland Music, Inc.***, 140 F.3d 1313, 1318 (9th Cir.1998); *see, e.g.*, ***Blockowicz v. Williams***, 630 F.3d 563, 566 (7th Cir.2010) (Ds waived challenge to personal jurisdiction when they participated in proceeding through briefing and oral arguments on merits; without more, Ds' single footnote reference to personal jurisdiction in its first filing was insufficient to preserve issue on appeal); *see also* ***Patin v. Thoroughbred Power Boats Inc.***, 294 F.3d 640, 653-54 (5th Cir.2002) (waiver of personal jurisdiction by predecessor corporation can be imputed to its successor corporation or individual alter ego).

§3. RESPONSE

Once a defendant files a motion to dismiss for lack of personal jurisdiction, the plaintiff bears the burden of establishing that the court has jurisdiction over the defendant. ***Boschetto v. Hansing***, 539 F.3d 1011, 1015 (9th Cir.2008); ***Adelson v. Hananel***, 510 F.3d 43, 48 (1st Cir.2007); ***Neogen Corp. v. Neo Gen Screening, Inc.***, 282 F.3d 883, 887 (6th Cir.2002); ***Soma Med. Int'l v. Standard Chartered Bank***, 196 F.3d 1292, 1295 (10th Cir.1999); ***Gundle Lining Constr. Corp. v. Adams Cty. Asphalt, Inc.***, 85 F.3d 201, 204 (5th Cir.1996). The plaintiff cannot rely on its pleadings but must, by affidavit or otherwise, set forth specific facts demonstrating that the court has jurisdiction. ***Theunissen v. Matthews***, 935 F.2d 1454, 1458 (6th Cir.1991); *see* ***Foster-Miller, Inc. v. Babcock & Wilcox Canada***, 46 F.3d 138, 145 (1st Cir.1995).

§3.1 Grounds.

1. Waiver. The plaintiff may allege that the defendant waived its challenge to personal jurisdiction because it did not object to personal jurisdiction in an FRCP 12(b) motion, in its first responsive pleading, or in an amendment to its first responsive pleading allowed as a matter of course (i.e., amendment allowed within 21 days after the responsive pleading is served). FRCP 12(h)(1); *see* FRCP 12(g)(2), 15(a)(1)(A); ***Reynolds v. International Amateur Athletic Fed'n***, 23 F.3d 1110, 1120 (6th Cir.1994); ***McDermott v. FedEx Ground Sys.***, 520 F.Supp.2d 254, 256-57 (D.Mass.2007). See "Amending as matter of course," ch. 5-I, §3.1, p. 345. The plaintiff may also allege that the defendant waived its challenge to personal jurisdiction by participating in litigation and seeking affirmative relief. *See* ***Continental Bank v. Meyer***, 10 F.3d 1293, 1296-97 (7th Cir.1993). See "Waiver," §2.7, p. 183.

2. Responsive allegations. The plaintiff should challenge the defendant's factual grounds for denying jurisdiction and the defendant's legal interpretation of the factors that determine jurisdiction over a nonresident.

(1) Minimum contacts. The plaintiff should allege that the court has specific or general jurisdiction over the defendant because the defendant purposefully availed itself of the laws or privileges of the forum state. *See* ***Electrosource, Inc. v. Horizon Battery Techs.***, 176 F.3d 867, 871 (5th Cir.1999); ***Metropolitan Life Ins. v. Robertson-Ceco Corp.***, 84 F.3d 560, 567 (2d Cir.1996); ***Vetrotex CertainTeed Corp. v. Consolidated Fiber Glass Prods.***, 75 F.3d 147, 150 (3d Cir.1996).

(a) Specific jurisdiction. To establish specific jurisdiction, the plaintiff should allege and offer evidence that its claims arose from or are related to the nonresident defendant's contact with the forum state. ***Electrosource***, 176 F.3d at 871.

(b) General jurisdiction. To establish general jurisdiction, the plaintiff should allege and offer evidence that even though the litigation is not specifically based on the defendant's forum-state contacts, the defendant engaged in continuous and systematic activities in the forum state. ***Metropolitan Life***, 84 F.3d at 568.

(2) Fair play. The plaintiff should also argue that the court's exercise of jurisdiction over the defendant and its property will not offend traditional notions of fair play and substantial justice. ***Gundle Lining Constr. Corp. v. Adams Cty. Asphalt, Inc.***, 85 F.3d 201, 205 (5th Cir.1996) (specific jurisdiction); ***Metropolitan Life***, 84 F.3d at 573 (general jurisdiction).

§3.2 Discovery.

1. Appropriate. Discovery of jurisdictional facts is appropriate when the existing record is inadequate to support personal jurisdiction and the plaintiff demonstrates that it can supplement its jurisdictional allegations through discovery. ***Trintec Indus. v. Pedre Promotional Prods.***, 395 F.3d 1275, 1283 (Fed.Cir.2005). The court should give the plaintiff an opportunity to discover jurisdictional facts so it can establish jurisdiction over the defendant. *See* ***Steinbuch v. Cutler***, 518 F.3d 580, 589 (8th Cir.2008); ***Toys "R" Us, Inc. v. Step Two, S.A.***, 318 F.3d 446, 456 (3d Cir.2003); ***Gorman v. Ameritrade Holding Corp.***, 293 F.3d 506, 513 (D.C.Cir.2002); ***First City v. Rafidain Bank***, 150 F.3d 172, 175 (2d Cir.1998); ***Williamson v. Tucker***, 645 F.2d 404, 414 (5th Cir.1981). If discovery is granted, the court does not have to defer a ruling on a jurisdictional question until the discovery is complete. ***Patterson v. Dietze, Inc.***, 764 F.2d 1145, 1147 n.4 (5th Cir.1985).

2. Not appropriate. Discovery of jurisdictional facts is inappropriate when the plaintiff does not have a good-faith belief that the court has jurisdiction. *See* ***Caribbean Broad. Sys. v. Cable & Wireless P.L.C.***, 148 F.3d 1080, 1090 (D.C.Cir.1998); *see also* ***Fielding v. Hubert Burda Media, Inc.***, 415 F.3d 419, 429 (5th Cir.2005) (Ps did not make preliminary showing of jurisdiction and did not prove prejudice resulting from court's refusal to permit discovery). If the plaintiff does not allege the type of jurisdiction for which it is seeking discovery, the court can deny a request for jurisdictional discovery. *See, e.g.*, ***Seiferth v. Helicopteros Atuneros, Inc.***, 472 F.3d 266, 276-77 (5th Cir.2006) (when P alleged only specific jurisdiction, court denied request for further discovery that would disclose contacts supporting general jurisdiction).

§3.3 Evidence. The plaintiff may include affidavits, interrogatories, or depositions as evidence for the court to consider in determining jurisdiction over the defendant. *See, e.g.*, ***Steinbuch v. Cutler***, 518 F.3d 580, 589 (8th Cir. 2008) (court remanded to allow P an opportunity to conduct discovery on D's contacts); ***Metropolitan Life Ins. v. Robertson-Ceco Corp.***, 84 F.3d 560, 575-76 (2d Cir.1996) (court allowed discovery on D's contacts over six-year period).

§3.4 Amended pleading. The plaintiff should consider filing an amended pleading in addition to—or possibly instead of—a response. If the plaintiff has not already amended once as a "matter of course" (i.e., 21 days after serving its complaint), the plaintiff can amend—without the court's leave or the opposing party's consent—within the earlier of 21 days after the defendant's answer or FRCP 12(b)(2) motion is served. *See* FRCP 15(a)(1)(B). See "Deadline," ch. 5-I, §3.1.1, p. 345. When leave is necessary, the plaintiff's response should request that, if the court grants the motion to dismiss, it should also grant the plaintiff leave to amend. See "Motion for Leave to Amend," ch. 5-I, §5, p. 351.

§4. HEARING

District courts have discretion to decide a motion to dismiss for lack of personal jurisdiction before ruling on objections to subject-matter jurisdiction under FRCP 12(b)(1) or objections based on forum non conveniens. *See* ***Sinochem Int'l Co. v. Malaysia Int'l Shipping Corp.***, 549 U.S. 422, 425 (2007); ***Ruhrgas AG v. Marathon Oil Co.***, 526 U.S. 574, 588 (1999). A court facing multiple grounds for dismissal should consider the complexity of the jurisdictional issues raised by the case, as well as concerns of undue expense and judicial economy. *See* ***Sinochem Int'l***, 549 U.S. at 435; ***Alpine View Co. v. Atlas Copco AB***, 205 F.3d 208, 213 (5th Cir.2000). If a court can readily determine that it lacks subject-matter jurisdiction, it should dismiss on that ground. ***Sinochem Int'l***, 549 U.S. at 436. But

if subject-matter jurisdiction is difficult to determine, the court may first decide personal jurisdiction or forum non conveniens, which may be less burdensome. *See id.* at 435. See "After challenge to personal jurisdiction or forum non conveniens," ch. 3-C, §4.2, p. 190. The court may decide a motion to dismiss for lack of personal jurisdiction on written submissions or at a hearing.

§4.1 No hearing. The court is not required to hold an evidentiary hearing on a motion challenging personal jurisdiction. If there is no evidentiary hearing, the plaintiff need only make a prima facie showing of personal jurisdiction through affidavits or discovery materials. ***Walk Haydel & Assocs. v. Coastal Power Prod.***, 517 F.3d 235, 241 (5th Cir.2008); ***Bird v. Parsons***, 289 F.3d 865, 871 (6th Cir.2002); ***Rio Props., Inc. v. Rio Int'l Interlink***, 284 F.3d 1007, 1019 (9th Cir.2002); ***Soma Med. Int'l v. Standard Chartered Bank***, 196 F.3d 1292, 1295 (10th Cir.1999); *see* ***Metropolitan Life Ins. v. Robertson-Ceco Corp.***, 84 F.3d 560, 566-67 (2d Cir.1996) (prima facie showing must include averment of facts); *see also* ***Trintec Indus. v. Pedre Promotional Prods.***, 395 F.3d 1275, 1282 (Fed.Cir.2005) (if no discovery on jurisdictional issue, P need only make prima facie showing of jurisdiction). A prima facie case is established if the plaintiff presents enough evidence to defeat a motion for judgment as a matter of law (formerly a motion for directed verdict). ***Meier v. Sun Int'l Hotels, Ltd.***, 288 F.3d 1264, 1269 (11th Cir.2002). See "Motion for Judgment as a Matter of Law," ch. 8-G, p. 714. When considering the motion challenging personal jurisdiction, the court will accept as true the plaintiff's uncontroverted allegations and resolve all factual disputes in favor of the plaintiff. ***Nuovo Pignone, SpA v. Storman Asia M/V***, 310 F.3d 374, 378 (5th Cir.2002); ***Pinker v. Roche Holdings Ltd.***, 292 F.3d 361, 368 (3d Cir.2002); ***Meier***, 288 F.3d at 1269; ***AT&T v. Compagnie Bruxelles Lambert***, 94 F.3d 586, 588 (9th Cir.1996); *see* ***Trintec Indus.***, 395 F.3d at 1282-83 (court must construe all pleadings and affidavits in light most favorable to P). However, the court is not required to give credit to conclusory allegations, even if they are uncontroverted. ***Panda Brandywine Corp. v. Potomac Elec. Power Co.***, 253 F.3d 865, 869 (5th Cir.2001); ***Massachusetts Sch. of Law v. American Bar Ass'n***, 142 F.3d 26, 34 (1st Cir.1998).

§4.2 Hearing. If there are issues of fact or credibility, the court may require an evidentiary hearing. ***Sher v. Johnson***, 911 F.2d 1357, 1361 (9th Cir.1990). If there is an evidentiary hearing (or if the case proceeds to trial), the plaintiff must prove grounds for personal jurisdiction by a preponderance of the evidence. ***Metropolitan Life Ins. v. Robertson-Ceco Corp.***, 84 F.3d 560, 567 (2d Cir.1996); ***Mylan Labs. v. Akzo, N.V.***, 2 F.3d 56, 59-60 (4th Cir.1993); *see* ***Walk Haydel & Assocs. v. Coastal Power Prod.***, 517 F.3d 235, 241 (5th Cir.2008). If the court holds a hearing for argument only or limits the presentation of evidence, the plaintiff need only meet the prima facie test. *See* ***Walk Haydel & Assocs.***, 517 F.3d at 241-42; ***Rano v. Sipa Press, Inc.***, 987 F.2d 580, 587 n.3 (9th Cir.1993).

§5. RULING

§5.1 Denies motion. If the court denies the FRCP 12(b)(2) motion to dismiss for lack of personal jurisdiction, it should enter an order noting the ruling and continue with the trial of the case. The defendant's participation in the trial is not a waiver of its objection to personal jurisdiction if the objection has been properly preserved. ***Serras v. First Tenn. Bank***, 875 F.2d 1212, 1214 (6th Cir.1989).

§5.2 Grants motion. If the court grants the FRCP 12(b)(2) motion, it will dismiss the claims against the movant without prejudice to refiling the suit in another jurisdiction. *See* FRCP 41(b); ***Intera Corp. v. Henderson***, 428 F.3d 605, 620-21 (6th Cir.2005). If there are other defendants in the case, the suit will continue against them. *See* ***Screen v. Equifax Info. Sys.***, 303 F.Supp.2d 685, 690-91 (D.Md.2004) (when court lacks personal jurisdiction over one D, court can dismiss that D and retain case over remaining D or transfer entire jurisdiction under 28 U.S.C. §1406(a) to forum that would be proper for both Ds).

§5.3 Findings of fact. If there are disputed fact issues, the court should make findings of fact. *See* ***Rano v. Sipa Press, Inc.***, 987 F.2d 580, 587 (9th Cir.1993).

§6. APPELLATE REVIEW

Whether personal jurisdiction may be exercised over a defendant is a question of law that is reviewed de novo. ***Moncrief Oil Int'l v. OAO Gazprom***, 481 F.3d 309, 311 (5th Cir.2007); ***Daniel v. American Bd. of Emerg. Med.***, 428

F.3d 408, 422 (2d Cir.2005); ***Bird v. Parsons***, 289 F.3d 865, 871 (6th Cir.2002); ***Meier v. Sun Int'l Hotels, Ltd.***, 288 F.3d 1264, 1268 (11th Cir.2002); ***Soma Med. Int'l v. Standard Chartered Bank***, 196 F.3d 1292, 1295 (10th Cir.1999). Any factual findings made by the district court are reviewed only for clear error. ***Lolavar v. de Santibañes***, 430 F.3d 221, 224 (4th Cir.2005); ***Mario Valente Collezioni, Ltd. v. Confezioni Semeraro Paolo, S.R.L.***, 264 F.3d 32, 36 (2d Cir.2001); ***Vetrotex CertainTeed Corp. v. Consolidated Fiber Glass Prods.***, 75 F.3d 147, 150 (3d Cir.1996). A court's decision to rule without allowing additional discovery will not be set aside unless the court abused its discretion. *See* ***Steinbuch v. Cutler***, 518 F.3d 580, 588 (8th Cir.2008); ***Caribbean Broad. Sys. v. Cable & Wireless P.L.C.***, 148 F.3d 1080, 1089 (D.C.Cir.1998).

C. MOTION TO DISMISS FOR LACK OF SUBJECT-MATTER JURISDICTION—FRCP 12(b)(1)

§1. GENERAL

§1.1 Rule. FRCP 12(b)(1).

§1.2 Purpose. A motion to dismiss for lack of subject-matter jurisdiction seeks dismissal of the lawsuit because the court lacks the authority to hear the dispute. *See* ***Holloway v. Pagan River Dockside Seafood, Inc.***, 669 F.3d 448, 452 (4th Cir.2012). *See generally* ***U.S. v. Morton***, 467 U.S. 822, 828 (1984) (subject-matter jurisdiction defines court's authority to hear given types of cases).

NOTE

In the Federal Courts Jurisdiction and Venue Clarification Act of 2011 (referred to as the Clarification Act), Congress made significant amendments to the jurisdiction statutes in title 28. See Lamar Smith, Federal Courts Jurisdiction & Venue Clarification Act of 2011, H.R. Rep. No. 112-10 (2011). See "Choosing the Court—Jurisdiction," ch. 2-F, p. 112. The Clarification Act became effective for any suit commenced in a U.S. district court on or after January 6, 2012, and for removed cases, the Clarification Act became effective for any suit commenced—within the meaning of state law—in state court on or after January 6, 2012. Federal Courts Jurisdiction & Venue Clarification Act of 2011, P.L. 112-63, §105, 125 Stat. 762 (2011) (eff. Jan. 6, 2012). For the law before the Clarification Act became effective, see ***O'Connor's Federal Rules * Civil Trials*** *(2012), "Motion to Dismiss for Lack of Subject-Matter Jurisdiction—FRCP 12(b)(1)," ch. 3-C, p. 183. Because of the substantive changes made by the 2011 amendments, use caution when citing cases that predate the amendments.*

§1.3 Forms. ***O'Connor's Federal Civil Forms*** (2012), FORMS 3C.

§1.4 Other references. 5B, 5C Wright & Miller, *Federal Practice & Procedure 3d* §§1350, 1363 (2004 & Supp.2012); 2 *Moore's Federal Practice 3d* §12.30 (2012).

§2. MOTION

§2.1 Form. For the general requirements for the form of a motion, see "Drafting motions," ch. 1-B, §3.1, p. 14.

§2.2 In writing or on court's initiative. The motion must be in writing. *See* FRCP 7(b)(1)(A). If the issue is not raised by the parties, the court has a duty to raise it sua sponte. FRCP 12(h)(3); ***United Investors Life Ins. v. Waddell & Reed Inc.***, 360 F.3d 960, 967 (9th Cir.2004).

§2.3 Grounds.

NOTE

FRCP 12(b)(1) covers a wide variety of different challenges to subject-matter jurisdiction. ***Valentin v. Hospital Bella Vista****, 254 F.3d 358, 362-63 (1st Cir.2001). Most often, an FRCP 12(b)(1) motion alleges the absence of federal-question or diversity jurisdiction, but it can also challenge, for example, supplemental jurisdiction, ripeness, mootness, sovereign immunity, or standing. See* ***Valentin****, 254 F.3d at 362-63; 5B Wright & Miller §1350 & nn.4-8, 10-13. In the Second Circuit, an FRCP 12(b)(1) motion has been recognized as an appropriate mechanism to dismiss based on a forum-selection clause. See* ***TradeComet.com LLC v. Google, Inc.****, 647 F.3d 472, 475 (2d Cir.2011). However, this use of an FRCP 12(b)(1) motion has been criticized as (1) impractical because the issue would have to be raised sua sponte by the court, (2) inefficient because the issue may be raised at any time, even on appeal, and (3) doctrinally inappropriate because bringing a suit in a particular forum is unrelated to the actual basis of subject-matter jurisdiction. See* ***Slater v. Energy Servs. Grp. Int'l****, 634 F.3d 1326, 1332-33 (11th Cir. 2011);* ***Sucampo Pharms. v. Astellas Pharma, Inc.****, 471 F.3d 544, 548-49 (4th Cir.2006). For a discussion of a circuit split on the proper procedure for challenging venue based on a forum-selection clause, see "Forum-selection clause," ch. 3-A, §4.3, p. 173; for the factors used to determine the enforceability of a forum-selection clause, see "Forum-selection clause," ch. 3-D, §3.3.4, p. 194.*

1. Challenging jurisdiction to hear case. To challenge the court's jurisdiction over the case, the defendant should argue that the court does not have federal-question jurisdiction, diversity jurisdiction, or supplemental jurisdiction.

(1) Federal-question jurisdiction. If the plaintiff's allegation of federal jurisdiction is based on a federal question, the motion to dismiss should allege that the plaintiff's suit does not involve the Constitution, laws, or treaties of the United States. *See* 28 U.S.C. §1331. See "Federal-Question Jurisdiction," ch. 2-F, §2, p. 113.

(2) Diversity jurisdiction. If the plaintiff's allegation of federal jurisdiction is based on diversity of citizenship, the motion to dismiss should allege that there is not "complete diversity" at the time of filing or that the amount in controversy does not exceed $75,000 (excluding interest and costs). *See* 28 U.S.C. §1332. See "Diversity Jurisdiction," ch. 2-F, §3, p. 116.

(3) Supplemental jurisdiction. If the plaintiff's allegation of federal jurisdiction is based on supplemental jurisdiction, the motion to dismiss should allege that one of the factors in 28 U.S.C. §1367(c) favors dismissal. *See* ***Shekoyan v. Sibley Int'l***, 409 F.3d 414, 423-24 (D.C.Cir.2005); ***Flores v. County of Hardeman***, 124 F.3d 736, 739 (5th Cir.1997); 5B Wright & Miller §1350 n.9. See "Declining supplemental jurisdiction," ch. 2-F, §6.3.2, p. 136.

2. Challenging standing. To challenge the plaintiff's standing to bring the suit, the defendant should argue that the plaintiff does not have standing to complain of the alleged acts and to seek the requested relief. *See* ***Steel Co. v. Citizens for a Better Env't***, 523 U.S. 83, 102 (1998); ***Lujan v. Defenders of Wildlife***, 504 U.S. 555, 560 (1992). See "Standing," ch. 2-B, §2.2.1, p. 77.

3. Abstention. To challenge the court's discretionary jurisdiction over the case, the defendant should argue that exceptional circumstances allow the court to abstain from exercising its jurisdiction. *See* ***Nissan N. Am., Inc. v. Andrew Chevrolet, Inc.***, 589 F.Supp.2d 1036, 1039 (E.D.Wis.2008); *see, e.g.*, ***Loch v. Watkins***, 337 F.3d 574, 578-79 (6th Cir.2003) (based on the ***Younger*** abstention doctrine, federal court abstained from hearing P's §1983 claim because P's quasi-criminal forfeiture action was pending in state court). See "Abstention," ch. 2-F, §7, p. 138.

NOTE

Whether dismissal based on abstention should be brought in a motion to dismiss for lack of subject-matter jurisdiction or a motion to dismiss for failure to state a claim is unclear. See ***Carter v. Doyle****, 95 F.Supp.2d 851, 855 n.8 (N.D.Ill.2000);* ***Discovery House, Inc. v. Consolidated City of Indianapolis****, 970 F.Supp. 655, 657-58 (S.D.Ind.1997). See "Motion to Dismiss for Failure to State a Claim—FRCP 12(b)(6)," ch. 3-F, p. 204.*

§2.4 Request hearing. If a defendant alleges facts to support its motion, it should submit supporting evidence and request an evidentiary hearing. *See* ***Holt v. U.S.***, 46 F.3d 1000, 1003 (10th Cir.1995).

§2.5 Affidavits & other evidence. If the court must resolve factual issues before it decides the jurisdictional question, the defendant should attach affidavits or other evidence to support its allegations. *See* ***Robb v. U.S.***, 80 F.3d 884, 891 n.9 (4th Cir.1996); ***Moran v. Kingdom of Saudi Arabia***, 27 F.3d 169, 172 (5th Cir.1994); *see, e.g.*, ***Apex Digital, Inc. v. Sears, Roebuck & Co.***, 572 F.3d 440, 444 (7th Cir.2009) (in breach-of-contract suit, D attached letter to motion that indicated P lacked standing because P had sold and assigned all its contractual rights to another company).

§2.6 Request for discovery. If factual issues cannot be resolved by affidavits, the defendant may request permission to engage in limited discovery. *See* ***Rivera-Flores v. Puerto Rico Tel. Co.***, 64 F.3d 742, 748 (1st Cir.1995); ***Moran v. Kingdom of Saudi Arabia***, 27 F.3d 169, 172 (5th Cir.1994).

§2.7 No waiver. A party cannot inadvertently or intentionally (e.g., by agreement) waive its right to object to the court's lack of subject-matter jurisdiction. ***Insurance Corp. of Ir., Ltd. v. Compagnie des Bauxites de Guinee***, 456 U.S. 694, 702 (1982); ***Herrick Co. v. SCS Comms.***, 251 F.3d 315, 321 (2d Cir.2001); ***Coury v. Prot***, 85 F.3d 244, 248 (5th Cir.1996); ***Laughlin v. Kmart Corp.***, 50 F.3d 871, 873 (10th Cir.1995). As a result, defects in the court's subject-matter jurisdiction can be raised at any time, including on appeal, by any party or the court. FRCP 12(h)(3); ***Arbaugh v. Y&H Corp.***, 546 U.S. 500, 506 (2006); ***Baca v. King***, 92 F.3d 1031, 1034 (10th Cir.1996).

NOTE

If a party challenges subject-matter jurisdiction on appeal, the appellate court must satisfy itself of both its own jurisdiction and that of the lower court. ***Steel Co. v. Citizens for a Better Env't****, 523 U.S. 83, 95 (1998); see also* ***Herrick Co.****, 251 F.3d at 322 (court must address threshold question of jurisdiction whenever it arises). If the appellate court finds the jurisdictional allegations defective, the party opposing the jurisdictional challenge can cure those defects on appeal. 28 U.S.C. §1653. But to do so, the party may need to enlarge the appellate record. See* ***America's Best Inns, Inc. v. Best Inns****, 980 F.2d 1072, 1073 (7th Cir.1992). For example, if a district court's subject-matter jurisdiction is challenged on the ground that the parties were not completely diverse, the appellate record should be enlarged to show the citizenship of each party as of the date the complaint was filed. See, e.g., id. (parties filed affidavits after oral argument on appeal to establish complete diversity).*

§3. RESPONSE

§3.1 Burden. Once a defendant files a motion to dismiss for lack of subject-matter jurisdiction, the plaintiff bears the burden of establishing that the court has subject-matter jurisdiction over the dispute. ***Lujan v. Defenders of Wildlife***, 504 U.S. 555, 561 (1992); ***Thomson v. Gaskill***, 315 U.S. 442, 446 (1942); ***Luckett v. Bure***, 290 F.3d 493, 496-97 (2d Cir.2002).

1. Jurisdiction.

(1) Federal question. If the motion alleges a lack of federal-question jurisdiction, the plaintiff must demonstrate that its claim is based on the Constitution, laws, or treaties of the United States. *See* 28 U.S.C. §1331.

(2) Diversity. If the motion attacks diversity, the plaintiff must show that at the time of filing there was complete diversity and that the amount in controversy exceeded $75,000. *See* ***City of Indianapolis v. Chase Nat'l Bank***, 314 U.S. 63, 69 (1941).

(3) Supplemental jurisdiction. If the motion alleges that the court should decline supplemental jurisdiction over state-law claims, the plaintiff must show that the factors in 28 U.S.C. §1367(c) favor exercising jurisdiction. *See* ***Shekoyan v. Sibley Int'l***, 409 F.3d 414, 423-24 (D.C.Cir.2005). See "Supplemental Jurisdiction," ch. 2-F, §6, p. 134.

2. Standing. If the motion alleges a lack of standing, the plaintiff must establish the three elements of standing: injury in fact, causation, and redressability. ***Steel Co. v. Citizens for a Better Env't***, 523 U.S. 83, 103-04 (1998). See "Standing," ch. 2-B, §2.2.1, p. 77.

3. Abstention. If the motion alleges that the court should abstain from exercising its jurisdiction, the plaintiff must show that no extraordinary circumstances justify abstention. *See* ***Loch v. Watkins***, 337 F.3d 574, 578 (6th Cir.2003); ***Nissan N. Am., Inc. v. Andrew Chevrolet, Inc.***, 589 F.Supp.2d 1036, 1039 (E.D.Wis.2008).

§3.2 Affidavits & other evidence. If the court must resolve factual issues before it decides the question of jurisdiction, the plaintiff should attach affidavits or other evidence to support its response. *See* ***Madison-Hughes v. Shalala***, 80 F.3d 1121, 1130 (6th Cir.1996).

§3.3 Amended pleading. The plaintiff should consider filing an amended pleading in addition to—or possibly instead of—a response. If the plaintiff has not already amended once as a "matter of course" (i.e., 21 days after serving its complaint), the plaintiff can amend—without the court's leave or the opposing party's consent—within the earlier of 21 days after the defendant's answer or FRCP 12(b)(1) motion is served. *See* FRCP 15(a)(1)(B). See "Deadline," ch. 5-I, §3.1.1, p. 345. When leave is necessary, the plaintiff's response should request that, if the court grants the motion to dismiss, it should also grant the plaintiff leave to amend. See "Motion for Leave to Amend," ch. 5-I, §5, p. 351.

§4. HEARING

A court may decide a motion to dismiss for lack of subject-matter jurisdiction on written submissions or at a hearing. *See* FRCP 12(i); ***Padilla-Mangual v. Pavía Hosp.***, 516 F.3d 29, 33-34 (1st Cir.2008). The court may require an evidentiary hearing when there is a factual attack on jurisdiction. ***Kerns v. U.S.***, 585 F.3d 187, 192 (4th Cir.2009); *see, e.g.*, ***Apex Digital, Inc. v. Sears, Roebuck & Co.***, 572 F.3d 440, 445-46 (7th Cir.2009) (court was not required to conduct evidentiary hearing when P did not attach any evidence to its response to motion to dismiss; there was no factual dispute because only one set of facts had been alleged); ***Padilla-Mangual***, 516 F.3d at 33-34 (in diversity case, court should have held evidentiary hearing to assess P's credibility about his intent to change his domicile). See "Factual attack," §5.1.2, p. 191.

§4.1 Before most other challenges. The court should resolve an FRCP 12(b)(1) motion before most of the defendant's other challenges because the court must find that it has subject-matter jurisdiction before it can determine any other issues. ***Moran v. Kingdom of Saudi Arabia***, 27 F.3d 169, 172 (5th Cir.1994); *see* ***Deniz v. Municipality of Guaynabo***, 285 F.3d 142, 149-50 (1st Cir.2002).

§4.2 After challenge to personal jurisdiction or forum non conveniens. District courts have discretion to avoid ruling on objections to subject-matter jurisdiction when the case may be decided on the less burdensome issues of (1) lack of personal jurisdiction under FRCP 12(b)(2) or (2) forum non conveniens. *See, e.g.*, ***Sinochem Int'l Co. v. Malaysia Int'l Shipping Corp.***, 549 U.S. 422, 435 (2007) (deciding forum non conveniens first); ***Ruhrgas AG v. Marathon Oil Co.***, 526 U.S. 574, 588 (1999) (deciding personal jurisdiction first); *see also* ***Tenet v. Doe***, 544 U.S. 1, 6 n.4 (2005) (dicta; Court assumed question of whether public policy barred spies from suing United States to enforce purported secret espionage agreements was threshold issue that might be resolved before addressing subject-matter jurisdiction). A court facing multiple grounds for dismissal should consider the complexity of the jurisdictional issues raised by the case, as well as concerns of undue expense and judicial economy. *See* ***Sinochem***

Int'l, 549 U.S. at 435-36; ***Alpine View Co. v. Atlas Copco AB***, 205 F.3d 208, 213 (5th Cir.2000). If a court can readily determine that it lacks subject-matter jurisdiction, it should dismiss on that ground; however, if subject-matter jurisdiction is difficult to determine, it may first decide personal jurisdiction or forum non conveniens, which may be less burdensome. *See* ***Sinochem Int'l***, 549 U.S. at 436.

NOTE

Some courts have held that district courts have discretion to decide a motion to transfer under 28 U.S.C. §1404(a), in addition to deciding issues of personal jurisdiction and forum non conveniens, before ruling on objections to subject-matter jurisdiction. ***In re LimitNone, LLC, 551 F.3d 572, 576 (7th Cir.2008); Public Employees' Ret. Sys. v. Stanley****, 605 F.Supp.2d 1073, 1075 (C.D.Cal.2009).*

§4.3 Defer to conduct discovery or receive evidence. The court may defer ruling on the FRCP 12(b)(1) motion to allow the parties to present additional materials or engage in limited discovery, or the court may defer until evidence is offered at trial. *See* ***Sizova v. National Inst. of Stds. & Tech.***, 282 F.3d 1320, 1326 (10th Cir.2002); ***Moran v. Kingdom of Saudi Arabia***, 27 F.3d 169, 172 (5th Cir.1994); *see also* ***Kerns v. U.S.***, 585 F.3d 187, 193 (4th Cir.2009) (when jurisdictional facts are inextricably intertwined with merits, court should resolve factual issues only after appropriate discovery). The court has broad authority to order discovery, consider extrinsic evidence, hold an evidentiary hearing, or hear testimony. ***Padilla-Mangual v. Pavía Hosp.***, 516 F.3d 29, 34 (1st Cir.2008); *see* ***Kerns***, 585 F.3d at 193; ***Moran***, 27 F.3d at 172.

§5. RULING

§5.1 Standard. The court can dismiss for lack of subject-matter jurisdiction based on (1) the complaint alone, (2) the complaint supplemented by undisputed facts evidenced in the record, or (3) the complaint supplemented by undisputed facts plus the court's resolution of disputed facts. ***Walch v. Adjutant General's Dept. of Tex.***, 533 F.3d 289, 293 (5th Cir.2008); ***McElmurray v. Consolidated Gov't of Augusta-Richmond Cty.***, 501 F.3d 1244, 1251 (11th Cir.2007); *see* ***Apex Digital, Inc. v. Sears, Roebuck & Co.***, 572 F.3d 440, 444 (7th Cir.2009). In resolving the question of subject-matter jurisdiction, courts look at whether the motion to dismiss for lack of subject-matter jurisdiction is either a facial attack or a factual attack.

1. Facial attack. If an FRCP 12(b)(1) motion challenges the sufficiency of the allegations of jurisdiction (i.e., the complaint does not allege sufficient facts on which subject-matter jurisdiction can be based), then it is a facial attack. ***Kerns v. U.S.***, 585 F.3d 187, 192 (4th Cir.2009); ***Apex Digital***, 572 F.3d at 443. In a facial attack, the court will accept all material allegations in the complaint as true and construe them in the light most favorable to the nonmovant. ***Scheuer v. Rhodes***, 416 U.S. 232, 236 (1974), *overruled on other grounds*, ***Harlow v. Fitzgerald***, 457 U.S. 800 (1982); ***McElmurray***, 501 F.3d at 1251; ***U.S. v. Ritchie***, 15 F.3d 592, 598 (6th Cir.1994); *see* ***Kerns***, 585 F.3d at 192. The court will not look beyond the allegations in the complaint. ***Apex Digital***, 572 F.3d at 443-44.

2. Factual attack. If an FRCP 12(b)(1) motion denies or controverts the allegations of jurisdiction (i.e., the facts alleged in the complaint are not true), then it is a factual attack. ***Kerns***, 585 F.3d at 192; ***Apex Digital***, 572 F.3d at 444; ***Ritchie***, 15 F.3d at 598; *see* ***Trentacosta v. Frontier Pac. Aircraft Indus.***, 813 F.2d 1553, 1558-59 (9th Cir.1987); *see, e.g.*, ***McElmurray***, 501 F.3d at 1251 (when court did not decide any issues of disputed fact, court properly granted motion to dismiss as facial attack based on complaint and attached exhibits). In a factual attack, the allegations in the complaint are not controlling. *See* ***Kerns***, 585 F.3d at 192; ***Sizova v. National Inst. of Stds. & Tech.***, 282 F.3d 1320, 1324 (10th Cir.2002); ***Reynolds v. Army & Air Force Exch. Serv.***, 846 F.2d 746, 747 (Fed.Cir.1988). Only uncontroverted factual allegations are accepted as true. ***Cedars-Sinai Med. Ctr. v. Watkins***, 11 F.3d 1573, 1583 (Fed.Cir.1993); *see* ***Ohio Nat'l Life Ins. v. U.S.***, 922 F.2d 320, 325 (6th Cir.1990). Thus, in resolving a factual attack on jurisdiction, the court can refer to evidence outside the pleadings, such as testimony or affidavits. ***Apex Digital***,

572 F.3d at 444; *see* ***Kerns***, 585 F.3d at 193; 5C Wright & Miller §1363. See "Defer to conduct discovery or receive evidence," §4.3, p. 191. When a defendant makes a factual attack, the plaintiff must establish subject-matter jurisdiction by a preponderance of the evidence. ***Irwin v. Veterans Admin.***, 874 F.2d 1092, 1096 (5th Cir.1989), *aff'd sub nom.* ***Irwin v. Department of Veterans Affairs***, 498 U.S. 89 (1990).

NOTE

Unlike with a motion for failure to state a claim under FRCP 12(b)(6), the attachment of exhibits to an FRCP 12(b)(1) motion does not convert it into a motion for summary judgment. ***Gonzalez v. U.S.****, 284 F.3d 281, 288 (1st Cir.2002). But see* ***Sizova****, 282 F.3d at 1324 (conversion occurs when jurisdictional question is intertwined with merits of case). See "Conversion to summary-judgment motion," ch. 3-F, §4.2.1, p. 206.*

§5.2 Effect of ruling.

1. Denies motion. If the court denies the motion, the case continues.

2. Grants motion. If the court grants the motion, it must dismiss the suit without prejudice to refiling in the proper court. *See* FRCP 41(b); ***Robinson v. Overseas Military Sales Corp.***, 21 F.3d 502, 507 n.4 (2d Cir.1994).

§5.3 Findings of fact. If the court grants the motion on the basis of the complaint, alone or supplemented by undisputed facts in the record, findings of fact are not necessary. *See* ***Williamson v. Tucker***, 645 F.2d 404, 413 (5th Cir.1981). However, if the court also resolved disputed facts, it should file findings of fact as part of its ruling. *See id.* at 413-14; *see also* ***Eaton v. Dorchester Dev., Inc.***, 692 F.2d 727, 732-33 (11th Cir.1982) (review of court's dismissal under FRCP 12(b)(1) was difficult because court did not give reasons for decision or make specific findings of fact).

§6. APPELLATE REVIEW

§6.1 Appeal. If the district court grants an FRCP 12(b)(1) motion to dismiss, the court's order is a final ruling and is immediately appealable. *See* ***Logistics Mgmt. v. One Pyramid Tent Arena***, 86 F.3d 908, 911 (9th Cir.1996). If the district court denies an FRCP 12(b)(1) motion to dismiss, the court's order is not a final ruling and is not immediately appealable. *See* ***Hospitality House, Inc. v. Gilbert***, 298 F.3d 424, 429 n.5 (5th Cir.2002).

§6.2 Standard of review. The court of appeals reviews a dismissal for lack of subject-matter jurisdiction de novo. ***Corfield v. Dallas Glen Hills LP***, 355 F.3d 853, 857 (5th Cir.2003); ***Crum v. Circus Circus Enters.***, 231 F.3d 1129, 1130 (9th Cir.2000); ***Joelson v. U.S.***, 86 F.3d 1413, 1416 (6th Cir.1996); ***Olcott v. Delaware Flood Co.***, 76 F.3d 1538, 1544 (10th Cir.1996); ***Region 8 Forest Serv. Timber Purchasers Council v. Alcock***, 993 F.2d 800, 806 (11th Cir.1993). If the district court resolved disputed facts while determining its jurisdiction, the court of appeals will not set aside the district court's findings unless they are clearly erroneous. ***Drevlow v. Lutheran Ch., Mo. Synod***, 991 F.2d 468, 470 (8th Cir.1993); *see* ***Crum***, 231 F.3d at 1130; ***Olcott***, 76 F.3d at 1544.

D. MOTION TO DISMISS FOR IMPROPER VENUE—FRCP 12(b)(3)

§1. GENERAL

§1.1 Rule. FRCP 12(b)(3). See also 28 U.S.C. §§1390, 1391, 1406.

§1.2 Purpose. If a plaintiff files a lawsuit in a district that is improper under the applicable venue statutes, the defendant can file a motion challenging the venue under FRCP 12(b)(3), asking the court either to dismiss the lawsuit or to transfer it to a proper district under 28 U.S.C. §1406(a). A motion based on *improper* venue should not be confused with one based on *inconvenient* venue. If a suit is filed in a proper but inconvenient district, the defendant should file a motion asking the court to transfer the case to a more convenient venue under 28 U.S.C. §1404(a). See "Motion to Transfer Venue—28 U.S.C. §1404," ch. 3-K, p. 221.

NOTE

In the Federal Courts Jurisdiction and Venue Clarification Act of 2011 (referred to as the Clarification Act), Congress made significant amendments to venue statutes in title 28. See Lamar Smith, Federal Courts Jurisdiction & Venue Clarification Act of 2011, H.R. Rep. No. 112-10 (2011). See "Choosing the Court—Venue," ch. 2-G, p. 143. The Clarification Act became effective for any suit commenced in a U.S. district court on or after January 6, 2012, and for removed cases, the Clarification Act became effective for any suit commenced—within the meaning of state law—in state court on or after January 6, 2012. Federal Courts Jurisdiction & Venue Clarification Act of 2011, P.L. 112-63, §205, 125 Stat. 764 (2011) (eff. Jan. 6, 2012). For the law before the Clarification Act became effective, see ***O'Connor's Federal Rules * Civil Trials*** *(2012), "Motion to Dismiss for Improper Venue—FRCP 12(b)(3)," ch. 3-D, p. 189. Because of the substantive changes made by the 2011 amendments, use caution when citing cases that predate the amendments.*

§1.3 Forms. *O'Connor's Federal Civil Forms* (2012), FORMS 3D.

§1.4 Other references. Federal Courts Jurisdiction & Venue Clarification Act of 2011, P.L. 112-63, 125 Stat. 758 (2011) (eff. Jan. 6, 2012) (referred to as Clarification Act); 5B Wright & Miller, *Federal Practice & Procedure 3d* §1352 (2004 & Supp.2012); 14D, 15 Wright, Miller & Cooper, *Federal Practice & Procedure 3d* §§3803.1, 3805, 3826-3827, 3846 (2007 & Supp.2012); 2, 17 *Moore's Federal Practice 3d* §§12.32, 110.01, 111.04 (2012).

§2. VENUE CONSIDERATIONS

§2.1 Federal law applies. Issues about venue are resolved under federal law, even in cases based on diversity jurisdiction, because these issues are essentially procedural rather than substantive. ***Jumara v. State Farm Ins.***, 55 F.3d 873, 877 (3d Cir.1995); *see also* ***Stewart Org. v. Ricoh Corp.***, 487 U.S. 22, 28 (1988) (federal law applied to motion to transfer based on forum-selection clause); ***Jones v. Weibrecht***, 901 F.2d 17, 19 (2d Cir.1990) (federal law applies in diversity cases, regardless of ***Erie R.R. v. Tompkins***, 304 U.S. 64 (1938)).

§2.2 When venue determined. Venue is determined when the suit is filed. See "When to Determine Venue," ch. 2-G, §6, p. 148.

§3. MOTION

§3.1 Form. For the general requirements for the form of a motion, see "Drafting motions," ch. 1-B, §3.1, p. 14.

§3.2 In writing or on court's initiative. The motion to dismiss is usually made by the defendant in writing. *See* FRCP 7(b)(1). Whether the issue can be raised on the court's own initiative depends on the circuit. Some circuits hold that the court errs if it dismisses for improper venue without a motion. *See* 5B Wright & Miller §1352 n.12; 14D Wright, Miller & Cooper §3826; *see, e.g.*, ***CPL, Inc. v. Fragchem Corp.***, 512 F.3d 389, 392 (7th Cir.2008); ***Concession Consultants, Inc. v. Mirisch***, 355 F.2d 369, 371-72 (2d Cir.1966). Other circuits permit the court to raise the issue on its own, but only if the court acts before the defendant waives the defense of improper venue. *See, e.g.*, ***Stjernholm v. Peterson***, 83 F.3d 347, 349 (10th Cir.1996); ***Lipofsky v. New York State Workers Comp. Bd.***, 861 F.2d 1257, 1259 (11th Cir.1988). When a court raises the issue sua sponte, it must first give notice of the potential dismissal to the parties and then give them the opportunity to brief or argue the issue. *See* ***Moore v. Rohm & Haas Co.***, 446 F.3d 643, 647 (6th Cir.2006); ***Stjernholm***, 83 F.3d at 349; *see, e.g.*, ***Algodonera de las Cabezas, S.A. v. American Suisse Capital, Inc.***, 432 F.3d 1343, 1345-46 (11th Cir.2005) (court abused its discretion when it dismissed for lack of venue without giving parties opportunity to present their views on issue).

§3.3 Grounds. The defendant should argue that venue in the district is improper under the applicable statute. If no special venue statute expressly identifies venue for a particular claim, either 28 U.S.C. §1391 or a valid forum-selection clause governs venue. See "General Venue Statute," ch. 2-G, §3, p. 144; "Special Venue Statutes," ch. 2-G,

§4, p. 146. If venue is based on 28 U.S.C. §1391 or a forum-selection clause, venue is improper if (1) the defendant does not reside in the district where the suit is brought, (2) a substantial part of the claim did not occur in the district where the suit is brought, (3) a substantial part of the property that is the subject of the action is not situated where the suit is brought, or (4) the plaintiff's choice of venue does not comply with a valid forum-selection clause.

1. Defendant does not reside in district. If all the defendants reside in the same state, the suit can be brought in a district where any defendant resides. 28 U.S.C. §1391(b)(1). To challenge venue based on §1391(b)(1), the defendant can argue that it does not reside in the forum district. For a discussion of determining a party's residence for venue purposes, see "Residence Under General & Special Venue Statutes," ch. 2-G, §5, p. 147.

2. Substantial part of claim did not occur in district. The suit can be brought in a district where a substantial part of the events or omissions giving rise to the claim occurred. 28 U.S.C. §1391(b)(2). If venue is based on 28 U.S.C. §1391(b)(2), the defendant can argue that a substantial part of the events or omissions giving rise to the plaintiff's claim did not occur in the district the plaintiff chose. To determine whether a "substantial" part of the claim's activities occurred in a particular venue, the court may look to the entire sequence of events underlying the claim, not just a single triggering event prompting the action. *See, e.g.*, ***Uffner v. La Reunion Francaise, S.A.***, 244 F.3d 38, 42-43 (1st Cir.2001) (diversity claim against insurance company for losses caused by damage to yacht could be brought in district where damage occurred); *see also* ***Gulf Ins. v. Glasbrenner***, 417 F.3d 353, 356-57 (2d Cir.2005) ("substantial" part means that significant events or omissions material to P's claim occurred in district). In making its determination, the court does not ask which district among potential forums is the "best" venue. ***Bates v. C&S Adjusters, Inc.***, 980 F.2d 865, 867 (2d Cir.1992). Instead, the court asks whether the district the plaintiff chose had a substantial connection to the claim, regardless of whether other districts had greater connections. *See* ***Pecoraro v. Sky Ranch for Boys, Inc.***, 340 F.3d 558, 563 (8th Cir.2003); ***Bates***, 980 F.2d at 867; *see also* ***Uffner***, 244 F.3d at 42 (when events underlying claim have taken place in different places, venue may be proper in several districts). Merely showing that another district has a more substantial connection to the plaintiff's claim is not enough to defeat the plaintiff's choice of venue. *See* ***First of Mich. Corp. v. Bramlet***, 141 F.3d 260, 264 (6th Cir.1998).

3. Substantial part of property is not situated in district. The suit can be brought in a district where a substantial part of the property that is the subject of the action is situated. 28 U.S.C. §1391(b)(2). If venue is based on 28 U.S.C. §1391(b)(2), the defendant can argue that a substantial part of the property that is the subject of the action is situated in a different district. *See* ***Bassili v. Chu***, 242 F.Supp.2d 223, 231 (W.D.N.Y.2002); ***Hicklin Eng'g, L.C. v. Bartell***, 116 F.Supp.2d 1107, 1112-13 (S.D.Iowa 2000); *see also* ***Falcoal, Inc. v. Turkiye Komur Isletmeleri Kurumu***, 660 F.Supp. 1536, 1543 (S.D.Tex.1987) (property clause refers to suits involving property disputes or in rem actions).

4. Forum-selection clause. A suit can be brought in a district that complies with a valid forum-selection clause. If there is a valid forum-selection clause, the defendant can argue that the plaintiff's choice of venue does not comply with the forum-selection clause. *See* ***Slater v. Energy Servs. Grp. Int'l***, 634 F.3d 1326, 1330-31 (11th Cir. 2011); *see also* ***Simonoff v. Expedia, Inc.***, 643 F.3d 1202, 1206 (9th Cir.2011) (forum-selection clause that specifies "courts of" a state limits jurisdiction to state courts, but clause that specifies "courts in" a state includes both state and federal courts). To determine whether a forum-selection clause should be enforced, the court will then consider (1) whether the clause was reasonably communicated to the party resisting its enforcement, (2) whether the clause is mandatory, and (3) whether the clause applies to the claims and parties involved in the suit. ***Phillips v. Audio Active Ltd.***, 494 F.3d 378, 383 (2d Cir.2007). If those three factors are satisfied, the clause is presumptively enforceable, and the court will then consider whether the party resisting the clause can show that enforcement is otherwise unreasonable. *See id.* at 383-84.

CIRCUIT SPLIT

The circuits are split on the proper procedure for challenging venue based on a forum-selection clause. See "Forum-selection clause," ch. 3-A, §4.3, p. 173. The Second, Fourth, Fifth, Seventh, Ninth, Tenth, Eleventh, and D.C. Circuits have identified FRCP 12(b)(3) as an appropriate mechanism to dismiss based on a forum-selection clause. See ***Slater****, 634 F.3d at 1333;* ***Doe 1 v. AOL LLC****, 552 F.3d 1077, 1081 (9th Cir.2009);* ***Phillips****, 494 F.3d at 384;* ***Sucampo Pharms. v. Astellas Pharma, Inc.****, 471 F.3d 544, 550 (4th Cir.2006);* ***Muzumdar v. Wellness Int'l Network, Ltd.****, 438 F.3d 759, 760 (7th Cir.2006);* ***Lim v. Offshore Specialty Fabricators, Inc.****, 404 F.3d 898, 902 (5th Cir.2005);* ***K&V Sci. Co. v. Bayerische Motoren Werke A.G.****, 314 F.3d 494, 497 (10th Cir.2002);* ***Commerce Consultants Int'l v. Vetrerie Riunite, S.p.A.****, 867 F.2d 697, 698 (D.C.Cir.1989). But see* ***Kerobo v. Southwestern Clean Fuels, Corp.****, 285 F.3d 531, 535 (6th Cir.2002) (use of FRCP 12(b)(3) motion is inappropriate because forum-selection clause should be enforced as matter of contract, not venue). Because most circuits have identified FRCP 12(b)(3) as an appropriate mechanism, this subchapter addresses the factors used to determine the enforceability of a forum-selection clause. These factors apply regardless of which mechanism a circuit requires.*

(1) Reasonably communicated. To be enforceable, a forum-selection clause must be reasonably communicated to the parties. ***D.H. Blair & Co. v. Gottdiener***, 462 F.3d 95, 103 (2d Cir.2006); *see* ***Carnival Cruise Lines, Inc. v. Shute***, 499 U.S. 585, 590 (1991); *see, e.g.*, ***Harris v. comScore, Inc.***, 825 F.Supp.2d 924, 927 (N.D.Ill. 2011) (clause was not "reasonably communicated" when it was in online, click-through agreement, but hyperlink for agreement was obscured and was not readily available to user); ***O'Brien v. Okemo Mountain, Inc.***, 17 F.Supp.2d 98, 103 (D.Conn.1998) (clause was not "reasonably communicated" when it was located on the back of ticket near bottom in small typeface and there was no instruction to read the back).

(2) Mandatory vs. permissive. To be enforceable, a forum-selection clause must be mandatory, not permissive. *See* ***M/S Bremen v. Zapata Off-Shore Co.***, 407 U.S. 1, 15 (1972); ***Rivera v. Centro Médico de Turabo, Inc.***, 575 F.3d 10, 17 (1st Cir.2009); ***AAR Int'l v. Nimelias Enters. S.A.***, 250 F.3d 510, 525 (7th Cir.2001).

(a) Mandatory. A mandatory clause states that a suit must be brought in an exclusive forum. ***Slater***, 634 F.3d at 1330; ***Rivera***, 575 F.3d at 17; *see, e.g.*, ***Alliance Health Grp. v. Bridging Health Options, LLC***, 553 F.3d 397, 399-400 (5th Cir.2008) (forum-selection clause was mandatory when it required suit to be filed in specific county even though suit could be filed in state or federal court within that county); *see also* ***American Soda, LLP v. U.S. Filter Wastewater Grp.***, 428 F.3d 921, 926-27 (10th Cir.2005) (when venue is specified and language is mandatory, clause is enforced; when only jurisdiction is specified, clause may be enforced if there is intent for exclusive venue).

(b) Permissive. A permissive clause states that a suit may be brought in a designated forum (i.e., the clause does not require that the suit be brought in that forum). ***Rivera***, 575 F.3d at 17; ***AAR Int'l***, 250 F.3d at 525. A forum-selection clause may be disregarded when the language in the clause is permissive. *See, e.g.*, ***K&V Sci. Co.***, 314 F.3d at 500-01 (when clause did not use term "exclusive," "sole," or "only," clause was not mandatory); ***McDonnell Douglas Corp. v. Islamic Republic of Iran***, 758 F.2d 341, 346 (8th Cir.1985) (rejecting contention that "should" in clause makes it mandatory); ***Scott v. Guardsmark Sec.***, 874 F.Supp. 117, 120-21 (D.S.C.1995) (when parties merely consented to jurisdiction and venue of court, clause was not mandatory).

(3) Applicable to claims & parties. To be enforceable, a forum-selection clause must by its terms apply to the claims and parties involved in the case. *See* ***Roby v. Corporation of Lloyd's***, 996 F.2d 1353, 1358-61 (2d Cir.1993). A forum-selection clause may apply to a nonsignatory party when that party is so closely related to the dispute that it is foreseeable that the party will be bound. *See* ***Marano Enters. v. Z-Teca Rests., L.P.***, 254 F.3d 753, 757 (8th Cir.2001).

(4) Unreasonable. If the forum-selection clause is unreasonable, it may be disregarded. ***M/S Bremen***, 407 U.S. at 15; *see* ***Rivera***, 575 F.3d at 18; ***Calix-Chacon v. Global Int'l Mar., Inc.***, 493 F.3d 507, 514 (5th Cir. 2007). The party resisting enforcement of the forum-selection clause bears a "heavy" burden of proof that the contractual forum should be avoided. ***M/S Bremen***, 407 U.S. at 17; ***Slater***, 634 F.3d at 1331; *see* ***Asoma Corp. v. SK Shipping Co.***, 467 F.3d 817, 822 (2d Cir.2006) (dicta; party must make strong showing to defeat contractual commitment); ***Blanco v. Banco Indus. de Venezuela, S.A.***, 997 F.2d 974, 979 (2d Cir.1993) (standards for disregarding mandatory clause are higher).

(a) Fraud or overreaching. A forum-selection clause may be unreasonable and therefore disregarded if transfer to the forum would be based on fraud or overreaching because (1) the forum was selected by the other party as a bad-faith tactic to discourage the pursuit of legitimate claims by the movant or (2) the other party used fraud or overreached in securing the movant's consent to the clause. *See* ***Carnival Cruise Lines***, 499 U.S. at 595; ***Wong v. PartyGaming Ltd.***, 589 F.3d 821, 828 (6th Cir.2009); ***Rivera***, 575 F.3d at 20-21; ***Marano Enters.***, 254 F.3d at 757; ***Effron v. Sun Line Cruises, Inc.***, 67 F.3d 7, 9-10 (2d Cir.1995). The fraudulent conduct must be specifically aimed at the forum-selection clause. *See* ***Scherk v. Alberto-Culver Co.***, 417 U.S. 506, 519 n.14 (1974); ***Marano Enters.***, 254 F.3d at 757; ***Haynsworth v. The Corp.***, 121 F.3d 956, 963 (5th Cir.1997). Allegations of fraudulent conduct involving the contract as a whole or other parts of it are insufficient to invalidate the clause. ***Haynsworth***, 121 F.3d at 963. Allegations of overreaching should be based on more than the mere fact that the forum-selection clause was a boilerplate provision printed on the back of a form contract or that there was unequal bargaining power between the parties. ***Rivera***, 575 F.3d at 21.

(b) Serious inconvenience. A forum-selection clause may be unreasonable and therefore disregarded if transfer to the forum would be so "gravely difficult and inconvenient" that the complaining party would "for all practical purposes be deprived of its day in court." ***M/S Bremen***, 407 U.S. at 18; ***Phillips***, 494 F.3d at 392; ***Servewell Plumbing, LLC v. Federal Ins.***, 439 F.3d 786, 790 (8th Cir.2006); ***Argueta v. Banco Mexicano, S.A.***, 87 F.3d 320, 325 (9th Cir.1996); *see* ***Wong***, 589 F.3d at 829-30.

(c) Unfairness. A forum-selection clause may be unreasonable and therefore disregarded if transfer to the forum would be fundamentally unfair and deprive the plaintiff of a remedy. *See* ***M/S Bremen***, 407 U.S. at 18; ***Wong***, 589 F.3d at 829.

(d) Public policy. A forum-selection clause may be unreasonable and therefore disregarded if transfer to the forum would contravene a strong public policy. ***M/S Bremen***, 407 U.S. at 15; ***Pee Dee Health Care, P.A. v. Sanford***, 509 F.3d 204, 213-14 (4th Cir.2007); ***Servewell Plumbing***, 439 F.3d at 790; ***Argueta***, 87 F.3d at 325; *see, e.g.*, 46 U.S.C. §30509(a) (vessels carrying passengers between ports cannot enforce forum-selection clauses in contracts with passengers); ***Red Bull Assocs. v. Best W. Int'l***, 862 F.2d 963, 966-67 (2d Cir.1988) (refusing to enforce forum-selection clause because of strong federal public policy of civil-rights law); *see also* ***U.S. v. St. Paul Mercury Ins.***, 70 F.3d 1115, 1118 (10th Cir.1995) (refusing to enforce choice of state forum because Miller Act grants federal court exclusive jurisdiction).

§3.4 Discovery. If the complaint and evidence presented are insufficient to determine proper venue, discovery on that issue may be necessary. *See* ***Home Ins. v. Thomas Indus.***, 896 F.2d 1352, 1358 (11th Cir.1990). If discovery is needed, the parties may ask the court either to limit initial discovery to venue facts or to defer ruling on the motion until certain discovery relating to venue can be completed. *See id.*

§3.5 Affidavits. All factual statements in an FRCP 12(b)(3) motion should be supported by sworn proof, usually affidavits. *See* ***Argueta v. Banco Mexicano, S.A.***, 87 F.3d 320, 323-24 (9th Cir.1996). The pleadings are not accepted as true under FRCP 12(b)(3), as they are under other provisions of FRCP 12(b). ***Argueta***, 87 F.3d at 324.

§3.6 Waiver. Venue is waived if not timely raised. ***Wachovia Bank v. Schmidt***, 546 U.S. 303, 316 (2006). See "Defenses raised in preanswer motion," ch. 3-A, §2.3, p. 172. The defendant will waive improper venue if it does not raise the issue in an FRCP 12(b) motion, in its first responsive pleading, or in an amendment to its first responsive pleading allowed as a matter of course (i.e., amendment allowed within 21 days after the responsive pleading is

served). FRCP 12(h)(1); *see* FRCP 12(g)(2), 15(a)(1)(A); ***Stjernholm v. Peterson***, 83 F.3d 347, 349 (10th Cir.1996); ***Costlow v. Weeks***, 790 F.2d 1486, 1488 (9th Cir.1986); *see also* ***Hillis v. Heineman***, 626 F.3d 1014, 1018 (9th Cir.2010) (if improper venue is asserted in answer, filing of counterclaim or third-party complaint does not constitute waiver). A defendant can also waive improper venue by statements or conduct inconsistent with challenging venue. *See* ***American Patriot Ins. Agency, Inc. v. Mutual Risk Mgmt.***, 364 F.3d 884, 887-88 (7th Cir.2004) (traditional principles of waiver and equitable estoppel apply to venue). A motion to extend time to file a responsive pleading does not constitute a waiver of venue. ***Manchester Knitted Fashions, Inc. v. Amalgamated Cotton Garment & Allied Indus. Fund***, 967 F.2d 688, 692 n.6 (1st Cir.1992). See "Motion to Extend Time," ch. 5-F, p. 332.

§4. RESPONSE

§4.1 Grounds. The plaintiff can respond by making either of the following allegations:

1. Venue proper. The plaintiff can allege that venue is proper in the district where the suit was filed. The response should (1) identify the statute that permits the plaintiff to file suit in the district and (2) allege facts sufficient to satisfy the statute's requirements. *See* 28 U.S.C. §§1390, 1391; ***NLRB v. Line***, 50 F.3d 311, 314 (5th Cir. 1995). If necessary, the plaintiff should seek leave to file an amended complaint correcting any defect in the pleadings.

2. Waiver. The plaintiff can allege that even if venue is not proper in the district where the suit was filed, the defendant waived its opportunity to move for a dismissal based on venue because it did not include the issue in an FRCP 12(b) motion, in its first responsive pleading, or in an amendment to its first responsive pleading allowed as a matter of course (i.e., amendment allowed within 21 days after the responsive pleading is served). FRCP 12(h)(1); *see* FRCP 12(g)(2), 15(a)(1)(A).

§4.2 Affidavits. All factual statements in the response should be supported by sworn proof, usually affidavits. *See* ***Argueta v. Banco Mexicano, S.A.***, 87 F.3d 320, 323-24 (9th Cir.1996).

§4.3 Amended pleading. The plaintiff should consider filing an amended pleading in addition to—or possibly instead of—a response. If the plaintiff has not already amended once as a "matter of course" (i.e., 21 days after serving its complaint), the plaintiff can amend—without the court's leave or the opposing party's consent—within the earlier of 21 days after the defendant's answer or FRCP 12(b)(3) motion is served. *See* FRCP 15(a)(1)(B). See "Deadline," ch. 5-I, §3.1.1, p. 345. When leave is necessary, the plaintiff's response should request that, if the court grants the motion to dismiss, it should also grant the plaintiff leave to amend. *See* 5B Wright & Miller §1352 & n.19; *see, e.g.*, ***Moore v. Coats Co.***, 270 F.2d 410, 411-12 (3d Cir.1959) (P was allowed to amend complaint to cure venue defect). See "Motion for Leave to Amend," ch. 5-I, §5, p. 351.

§5. HEARING

The court may decide a motion challenging venue on written submissions or at a hearing. If the court holds a hearing, it may receive and consider live testimony. *See* FRCP 12(i).

§5.1 Who has burden. Courts and commentators disagree about which party has the burden to prove proper venue once it has been challenged. *Compare* ***Gulf Ins. v. Glasbrenner***, 417 F.3d 353, 355 (2d Cir.2005) (P's burden), ***Bartholomew v. Virginia Chiropractors Ass'n***, 612 F.2d 812, 816 (4th Cir.1979) (same), *and* 14D Wright, Miller & Cooper §3826 & n.24 (same), *with* ***Myers v. American Dental Ass'n***, 695 F.2d 716, 724-25 (3d Cir.1982) (D's burden), ***Time, Inc. v. Manning***, 366 F.2d 690, 698 (5th Cir.1966) (same), *and* 17 *Moore's Federal Practice 3d* §110.01[5][c] (same).

§5.2 Burden of proof. If the court relies only on pleadings and affidavits, the party with the burden of proof satisfies its burden with a prima facie showing. ***Mitrano v. Hawes***, 377 F.3d 402, 405 (4th Cir.2004); *see* ***Gulf Ins. v. Glasbrenner***, 417 F.3d 353, 355 (2d Cir.2005); *see also* ***Dearth v. Gonzales***, No. 2:06-cv-1012 (S.D.Ohio 2007) (slip op.; 4-10-07) (dicta; when D has burden of proof, same standard applies as when P has burden). If the court holds an evidentiary hearing, the party with the burden of proof satisfies its burden with a showing of a preponderance of the evidence. ***Gulf Ins.***, 417 F.3d at 355.

§6. RULING

§6.1 Denies motion. If the court denies the motion, the case continues.

§6.2 Grants motion. If the court grants the motion, the court may dismiss the case or, in the interest of justice, transfer it under 28 U.S.C. §1406(a) to a district where it could have been brought. The decision to dismiss or transfer is within the court's discretion. ***Minnette v. Time Warner***, 997 F.2d 1023, 1026 (2d Cir.1993); ***Naartex Consulting Corp. v. Watt***, 722 F.2d 779, 789 (D.C.Cir.1983).

1. Dismissal. If the court grants the motion and dismisses the suit, the dismissal is without prejudice and is not an adjudication on the merits. FRCP 41(b); ***In re Hall, Bayoutree Assocs.***, 939 F.2d 802, 804 (9th Cir. 1991).

2. Transfer. If the court grants the motion and transfers the suit, the entire case is transferred to a district of proper venue. *See* 28 U.S.C. §1406(a). After a §1406(a) transfer, the transferee court should apply the law it would have applied if the action had been initially filed there. ***Schaeffer v. Village of Ossining***, 58 F.3d 48, 50 (2d Cir.1995); ***Muldoon v. Tropitone Furniture Co.***, 1 F.3d 964, 967 (9th Cir.1993); ***Tel-Phonic Servs. v. TBS Int'l***, 975 F.2d 1134, 1141 (5th Cir.1992); 15 Wright, Miller & Cooper §3846 & n.27. Some of the reasons a court may choose to transfer rather than dismiss are the following:

(1) Limitations. Generally, the court should transfer if dismissal would result in a statute of limitations barring the plaintiff from refiling its claim. ***Goldlawr, Inc. v. Heiman***, 369 U.S. 463, 466-67 (1962); ***Daniel v. American Bd. of Emerg. Med.***, 428 F.3d 408, 435 (2d Cir.2005). *But see* ***Nichols v. G.D. Searle & Co.***, 991 F.2d 1195, 1201-02 (4th Cir.1993) (even though limitations period had run, court dismissed because P's attorney made obvious error regarding venue).

(2) Judicial economy. The court should transfer if it would advance the timely disposition of the case on the merits. *See* ***Minnette***, 997 F.2d at 1027.

§6.3 Curative amendment. The court may permit the plaintiff to file an amended complaint to cure a venue defect. *See* ***Moore v. Coats Co.***, 270 F.2d 410, 411-12 (3d Cir.1959).

§6.4 Multiple defendants. If venue is proper for one defendant but not for another, and if dismissal is inappropriate, the court may (1) transfer the entire case to another district that is proper for both defendants or (2) sever the claims, retaining jurisdiction over one defendant and transferring the case for the other defendant. ***Cottman Transmission Sys. v. Martino***, 36 F.3d 291, 296 (3d Cir.1994); 14D Wright, Miller & Cooper §3827. However, if a defendant is so involved in the controversy that granting a partial transfer would require the same issue to be litigated in two places, the case should not be severed. ***Sunbelt Corp. v. Noble, Denton & Assocs.***, 5 F.3d 28, 33-34 (3d Cir. 1993).

§6.5 Findings of fact. The court may make findings of fact to support its ruling granting the motion. *See* ***Peteet v. Dow Chem. Co.***, 868 F.2d 1428, 1436 (5th Cir.1989) (courts are not required to file written orders explaining their decisions, but it is better practice).

§7. APPELLATE REVIEW

§7.1 Appealability of order.

1. Order denying motion. An order denying a motion to dismiss for improper venue is an interlocutory order and is not immediately appealable. *See* ***Lauro Lines S.R.L. v. Chasser***, 490 U.S. 495, 498 (1989); ***Turi v. Main St. Adoption Servs.***, 633 F.3d 496, 502 (6th Cir.2011).

2. Order granting motion.

(1) Dismissal. An order granting a motion to dismiss for improper venue is appealable. *See* ***Argueta v. Banco Mexicano, S.A.***, 87 F.3d 320, 323 (9th Cir.1996); ***Cook v. Fox***, 537 F.2d 370, 371 (9th Cir.1976).

(2) Order granting transfer. An order granting a motion to transfer under 28 U.S.C. §1406(a) is not an adjudication on the merits and is not appealable. ***In re Joint E.&S. Dists. Asbestos Litig.***, 22 F.3d 755, 761-64 & n.14 (7th Cir.1994); ***Ukiah Adventist Hosp. v. FTC***, 981 F.2d 543, 546 (D.C.Cir.1992); ***Fischer v. First Nat'l Bank***, 466 F.2d 511, 511 (8th Cir.1972); *see* ***Sunbelt Corp. v. Noble, Denton & Assocs.***, 5 F.3d 28, 30 (3d Cir.1993). Mandamus is the appropriate mechanism for reviewing an improper transfer order. ***Sunbelt Corp.***, 5 F.3d at 30.

§7.2 Standard of review.

1. Factual issues. The court's determination of factual disputes in a motion to dismiss for improper venue is reviewed for abuse of discretion. ***Milwaukee Concrete Studios, Ltd. v. Fjeld Mfg. Co.***, 8 F.3d 441, 445 (7th Cir.1993). *But see* ***Gulf Ins. v. Glasbrenner***, 417 F.3d 353, 355 (2d Cir.2005) (factual findings reviewed for clear error). The determination of whether to dismiss or to transfer is also reviewed for abuse of discretion. ***Kerobo v. Southwestern Clean Fuels, Corp.***, 285 F.3d 531, 533 (6th Cir.2002).

2. Legal issues. If the facts are undisputed and the venue determination involves only the application or interpretation of a venue statute, the court's determination is reviewed de novo. *See* ***Gulf Ins.***, 417 F.3d at 355; ***Kerobo***, 285 F.3d at 533; ***Milwaukee Concrete Studios***, 8 F.3d at 445.

3. Forum-selection clause. If the facts are undisputed and the venue determination involves only the interpretation or enforceability of a forum-selection clause, the court's determination is reviewed de novo. ***Slater v. Energy Servs. Grp. Int'l***, 634 F.3d 1326, 1329-30 (11th Cir.2011); *see* ***Kochert v. Adagen Med. Int'l***, 491 F.3d 674, 677 (7th Cir.2007); ***Silva v. Encyclopedia Britannica Inc.***, 239 F.3d 385, 387 (1st Cir.2001); *see also* ***Lipcon v. Underwriters at Lloyd's, London***, 148 F.3d 1285, 1290-91 (11th Cir.1998) (de novo for international agreements). If a venue determination under a forum-selection clause depends on the credibility of extrinsic evidence, the court's determination is reviewed for abuse of discretion. *See* ***Doe 1 v. AOL LLC***, 552 F.3d 1077, 1081 (9th Cir.2009).

E. MOTION TO DISMISS FOR FORUM NON CONVENIENS—CHALLENGING THE U.S. FORUM

§1. GENERAL

§1.1 Rule. None.

§1.2 Purpose. A motion to dismiss for forum non conveniens asks the court to dismiss the suit because a court in a foreign country is the more appropriate and convenient forum for adjudicating the case. ***Sinochem Int'l Co. v. Malaysia Int'l Shipping Corp.***, 549 U.S. 422, 425 (2007). The doctrine of forum non conveniens applies only when the alternative forum is abroad. *Id.* When the alternative forum is another U.S. federal court, the defendant should file a motion to transfer venue. See "Motion to Transfer Venue—28 U.S.C. §1404," ch. 3-K, p. 221.

§1.3 Forms. *O'Connor's Federal Civil Forms* (2012), FORMS 3E.

§1.4 Other references. 5B Wright & Miller, *Federal Practice & Procedure 3d* §1352 (2004 & Supp.2012); 14D Wright, Miller & Cooper, *Federal Practice & Procedure 3d* §§3803.1, 3828.2, 3828.4 (2007 & Supp.2012); 17 *Moore's Federal Practice 3d* §§111.70-111.95 (2012).

§2. MOTION

§2.1 Form. For the general requirements for the form of a motion, see "Drafting motions," ch. 1-B, §3.1, p. 14.

§2.2 In writing. The motion should be in writing. *See* FRCP 7(b)(1).

§2.3 Grounds. The defendant must show that (1) the claim can be heard in an available and adequate alternative forum that has jurisdiction over the dispute and (2) the balance of certain private and public interests favors dismissal. *See* ***Piper Aircraft Co. v. Reyno***, 454 U.S. 235, 254-55 & n.22 (1981); ***Gulf Oil Corp. v. Gilbert***, 330 U.S. 501, 508-09 (1947); ***Wong v. PartyGaming Ltd.***, 589 F.3d 821, 830 (6th Cir.2009).

1. Available & adequate alternative forum. The defendant must first demonstrate that there is an available and adequate foreign forum for resolving the dispute. ***Piper Aircraft***, 454 U.S. at 254 n.22; *see* ***Iragorri v. United Techs.***, 274 F.3d 65, 72 (2d Cir.2001); ***Kamel v. Hill-Rom Co.***, 108 F.3d 799, 802 (7th Cir.1997). A foreign forum is "available" when the entire case and all parties can come within the forum's jurisdiction. ***Alpine View Co. v. Atlas Copco AB***, 205 F.3d 208, 221 (5th Cir.2000). A foreign forum is "adequate" when the parties will not be deprived of all remedies or treated unfairly, even though they might not enjoy the same benefits they would have in a U.S. court. *Id.*; *see also* ***Piper Aircraft***, 454 U.S. at 254 n.22 (alternative forum not appropriate if it does not permit litigation of subject matter of dispute); ***El-Fadl v. Central Bank***, 75 F.3d 668, 677-78 (D.C.Cir.1996) (court erred in finding adequate foreign forum when D did not address potentially dispositive provisions in foreign forum's laws), *overruled on other grounds*, ***Samantar v. Yousuf***, ___ U.S. ___, 130 S.Ct. 2278 (2010). Generally, the requirement of an available and adequate alternative forum is satisfied if the defendant can be served with process in the foreign jurisdiction. ***Piper Aircraft***, 454 U.S. at 254 n.22; ***Ceramic Corp. v. Inka Maritime Corp.***, 1 F.3d 947, 949 (9th Cir. 1993); ***Mercier v. Sheraton Int'l***, 935 F.2d 419, 424 (1st Cir.1991). Some courts include a "return jurisdiction" clause in a forum non conveniens dismissal, which provides that the parties can return to the dismissing court if the lawsuit becomes impossible in the foreign forum. *See* ***Vasquez v. Bridgestone/Firestone, Inc.***, 325 F.3d 665, 675 (5th Cir.2003) (failure to include "return jurisdiction" clause is abuse of discretion).

2. Balance of interests. The plaintiff's choice of forum is presumed to be convenient. ***Piper Aircraft***, 454 U.S. at 255-56; *see* ***Koster v. Lumbermens Mut. Cas. Co.***, 330 U.S. 518, 524 (1947). To overcome this presumption, the defendant must show that certain private and public interests outweigh the deference given to the plaintiff's choice of forum under the analysis first set forth in ***Gulf Oil***, 330 U.S. at 508-09. *See* ***American Dredging Co. v. Miller***, 510 U.S. 443, 448-49 (1994); ***Iragorri***, 274 F.3d at 73-74; ***Kamel***, 108 F.3d at 802; ***Mercier***, 935 F.2d at 423-24; 14D Wright, Miller & Cooper §3828.4. The balance of these interests must clearly point toward the alternative forum. ***Piper Aircraft***, 454 U.S. at 255; *see* ***Gulf Oil***, 330 U.S. at 508 (unless balance is strongly in favor of D, P's choice of forum should not be disturbed).

(1) Private-interest factors. There are several private-interest factors that should be considered by the court. ***Gulf Oil***, 330 U.S. at 508. The private-interest factors include the following:

(a) Convenience of the forum for litigants and witnesses. ***Lueck v. Sundstrand Corp.***, 236 F.3d 1137, 1145 (9th Cir.2001). The court should focus on the precise issues that are likely to actually be tried. ***Iragorri***, 274 F.3d at 74. If a forum-selection clause is at issue, the clause may affect the convenience of the parties. *See* ***Wong***, 589 F.3d at 833 (forum-selection clause weighs heavily as private-interest factor favoring enforcement of clause); ***Northwestern Nat'l Ins. v. Donovan***, 916 F.2d 372, 378 (7th Cir.1990) (signing valid forum-selection clause is waiver of right to seek change of venue on ground of inconvenience); *see also* ***Royal Bed & Spring Co. v. Famossul Industria e Comercio de Moveis Ltda.***, 906 F.2d 45, 51 (1st Cir.1990) (forum-selection clause is just one factor to be considered under traditional forum non conveniens principles). However, if a mandatory forum-selection clause is at issue, the stricter standard under ***M/S Bremen v. Zapata Off-Shore Co.***, 407 U.S. 1 (1972), may apply, rather than the traditional two-step analysis for forum non conveniens. ***AAR Int'l v. Nimelias Enters. S.A.***, 250 F.3d 510, 524-25 (7th Cir.2001). See "Mandatory," ch. 3-D, §3.3.4(2)(a), p. 195.

CIRCUIT SPLIT

The circuits are split on the proper procedure for challenging venue based on a forum-selection clause. For the factors used to determine the enforceability of a forum-selection clause, see "Forum-selection clause," ch. 3-D, §3.3.4, p. 194.

(b) Relative ease of access to sources of proof. ***Gulf Oil***, 330 U.S. at 508; ***Lueck***, 236 F.3d at 1145.

(c) Cost and feasibility of bringing willing and unwilling witnesses to trial. ***Gulf Oil***, 330 U.S. at 508; ***Lueck***, 236 F.3d at 1145.

(d) Possibility of the jury viewing the premises involved in the case. ***Gulf Oil***, 330 U.S. at 508.

(e) Enforceability of the alternative forum's judgment. *See* ***Lueck***, 236 F.3d at 1145; *see, e.g.*, ***Contact Lumber Co. v. P.T. Moges Shipping Co.***, 918 F.2d 1446, 1450 (9th Cir.1990) (court considered question of P's ability to collect judgment in its inquiry into adequacy of alternative forum). When enforceability is in doubt, dismissal might still be permissible if it is conditioned on a letter of guarantee from the defendant. *See* ***Contact Lumber***, 918 F.2d at 1450.

(f) All other practical issues that make trial of a case easy, expeditious, and inexpensive. ***Gulf Oil***, 330 U.S. at 508; ***Lueck***, 236 F.3d at 1145; *see, e.g.*, ***Henderson v. Metropolitan Bank & Trust Co.***, 502 F.Supp.2d 372, 376 (S.D.N.Y.2007) (court considered $5 million filing fee in Philippines to tilt balance of private-interest factors toward chosen U.S. forum).

(2) Public-interest factors. There are several public-interest factors that should be considered by the court. The public-interest factors are generally less important than the private-interest factors. ***Leon v. Millon Air, Inc.***, 251 F.3d 1305, 1311 (11th Cir.2001). The public-interest factors include the following:

(a) Administrative difficulties arising from congested courts. ***Gulf Oil***, 330 U.S. at 508; ***Windt v. Qwest Comms. Int'l***, 529 F.3d 183, 189 (3d Cir.2008); *see* ***Lueck***, 236 F.3d at 1147.

(b) Imposition of jury duty on people of a community with no relation to the litigation. ***Gulf Oil***, 330 U.S. at 508-09; ***Leetsch v. Freedman***, 260 F.3d 1100, 1105 (9th Cir.2001); *see* ***Windt***, 529 F.3d at 189.

(c) Local interest in having localized controversies decided at home. ***Gulf Oil***, 330 U.S. at 508-09; *see* ***Piper Aircraft***, 454 U.S. at 260; ***Liquidation Comm'n of Banco Intercontinental, S.A. v. Renta***, 530 F.3d 1339, 1356-57 (11th Cir.2008).

(d) Interest in having the trial of a diversity case in a forum that is "at home" with the law that governs the case. ***Gulf Oil***, 330 U.S. at 508-09; ***Clerides v. Boeing Co.***, 534 F.3d 623, 628 (7th Cir.2008); ***Windt***, 529 F.3d at 189.

(e) Avoidance of unnecessary problems in conflicts of law or the application of foreign law. ***Gulf Oil***, 330 U.S. at 509; *see* ***Piper Aircraft***, 454 U.S. at 259-60 & n.29; ***Windt***, 529 F.3d at 189.

§2.4 Burden. The defendant has the burden of persuasion on all elements necessary for the court to dismiss a claim based on forum non conveniens. ***Northrup King Co. v. Compania Productora Semillas Algodoneras Selectas, S.A.***, 51 F.3d 1383, 1390 (8th Cir.1995); ***Lacey v. Cessna Aircraft Co.***, 862 F.2d 38, 43-44 (3d Cir.1988); ***In re Air Crash Disaster Near New Orleans***, 821 F.2d 1147, 1164 (5th Cir.1987), *vacated & remanded sub nom.* ***Pan Am. World Airways, Inc. v. Lopez***, 490 U.S. 1032 (1989), *reinstated in relevant part*, 883 F.2d 17 (5th Cir.1989). The defendant ordinarily bears a heavy burden to disturb the plaintiff's choice of forum. ***Sinochem Int'l Co. v. Malaysia Int'l Shipping Corp.***, 549 U.S. 422, 430 (2007); *see* ***Piper Aircraft Co. v. Reyno***, 454 U.S. 235, 255 (1981); ***Gulf Oil Corp. v. Gilbert***, 330 U.S. 501, 508 (1947).

1. Plaintiff chooses home forum. If the plaintiff chooses its home forum, the defendant's burden is heightened. *See* ***Adelson v. Hananel***, 510 F.3d 43, 53 (1st Cir.2007) (court recognizes strong presumption for U.S. forum when U.S. Ps select forum); *see, e.g.*, ***Duha v. Agrium, Inc.***, 448 F.3d 867, 873-74 (6th Cir.2006) (court erred when it did not apply heightened standard of deference to U.S. P's choice of U.S. as forum but instead applied lower standard normally given to foreign Ps); *see also* ***U.S.O. Corp. v. Mizuho Holding Co.***, 547 F.3d 749, 752 (7th Cir.2008) (central purpose of forum non conveniens is convenience, not nationalism or protectionism; deference to P's choice of forum is based on P's relationship to forum, and the more tenuous the relationship, the weaker the case for litigating there).

2. Plaintiff does not choose home forum. If the plaintiff does not choose its home forum (i.e., a foreign plaintiff), the deference ordinarily given to it applies with "less force" because the assumption that the chosen forum is appropriate is less reasonable. ***Sinochem Int'l***, 549 U.S. at 430; ***Piper Aircraft***, 454 U.S. at 255-56; ***Bhatnagar v. Surrendra Overseas Ltd.***, 52 F.3d 1220, 1226 n.4 (3d Cir.1995). The degree of deference given to the plaintiff's choice of forum when suit is brought outside the plaintiff's home district depends on whether the choice was

motivated by legitimate reasons, including the plaintiff's convenience or tactical considerations. ***Iragorri v. United Techs.***, 274 F.3d 65, 73 (2d Cir.2001); *see* 14D Wright, Miller & Cooper §3828.2.

3. Forum-selection clause. If the parties have agreed to a forum-selection clause, the plaintiff's choice of forum is given less deference. ***Wong v. PartyGaming Ltd.***, 589 F.3d 821, 833 (6th Cir.2009); *see also* ***Evolution Online Sys. v. Koninklijke PTT Nederland N.V.***, 145 F.3d 505, 510-11 (2d Cir.1998) (if parties contemplated forum-selection clause but did not memorialize it in final agreement, court should apply private- and public-interest factors evenly, rather than heavily favoring P's choice of forum). See "Private-interest factors," §2.3.2(1)(a), p. 200.

§2.5 Evidence. The defendant must support its factual allegations in the motion with evidence. *See* ***Rivendell Forest Prods. v. Canadian Pac. Ltd.***, 2 F.3d 990, 993 (10th Cir.1993). The defendant may rely on affidavits, discovery, or stipulations. *See* ***El-Fadl v. Central Bank***, 75 F.3d 668, 677 (D.C.Cir.1996), *overruled on other grounds*, ***Samantar v. Yousuf***, ___ U.S. ___, 130 S.Ct. 2278 (2010); ***Linton v. Airbus Industrie***, 30 F.3d 592, 594-95 (5th Cir. 1994); ***Rivendell Forest Prods.***, 2 F.3d at 993.

§2.6 Deadline. No rule or statute provides a deadline for filing a motion to dismiss for forum non conveniens. However, the defendant must file its motion within a reasonable time after it learns or reasonably should have learned of facts that support the motion. ***In re Air Crash Disaster Near New Orleans***, 821 F.2d 1147, 1165 (5th Cir.1987), *vacated & remanded sub nom.* ***Pan Am. World Airways, Inc. v. Lopez***, 490 U.S. 1032 (1989), *reinstated in relevant part*, 883 F.2d 17 (5th Cir.1989).

NOTE

Unlike some defenses under FRCP 12, a defense based on forum non conveniens is not waived if the defendant does not raise it in the first responsive pleading or preanswer motion. ***Yavuz v. 61 MM, Ltd.***, *576 F.3d 1166, 1173 (10th Cir.2009); see* ***In re Air Crash Disaster Near New Orleans***, *821 F.2d at 1165 (although D does not waive objection to forum by filing untimely motion, untimeliness weighs heavily against granting motion).*

§3. RESPONSE

§3.1 In writing. The plaintiff's response should be in writing.

§3.2 Grounds. The response to a motion to dismiss for forum non conveniens should argue that another forum is unavailable or inadequate and should rebut the defendant's analysis of the private and public interests.

1. Other forum unavailable or inadequate. The plaintiff should argue that the other forum will deprive it of a remedy or treat it unfairly. ***Piper Aircraft Co. v. Reyno***, 454 U.S. 235, 254 (1981). The plaintiff should allege not only that the other forum is less favorable but also that the other forum imposes such an extreme burden on the plaintiff that the forum is inadequate. *See* ***Bhatnagar v. Surrendra Overseas Ltd.***, 52 F.3d 1220, 1227-28 (3d Cir.1995) (as a matter of law, delay of up to 25 years in resolving dispute in other forum renders forum inadequate); ***Mercier v. Sheraton Int'l***, 935 F.2d 419, 424-27 (1st Cir.1991) (prohibition on affidavit or deposition testimony of P would render forum inadequate).

2. Private & public interests do not favor dismissal. The plaintiff should address each of the private and public interests set out in ***Gulf Oil*** and explain why the factors do not support dismissal for refiling in another country.

3. Delay. The plaintiff may argue that the defendant's delay in making the motion should weigh against granting it because the delay caused the parties to incur unnecessary costs that the forum non conveniens doctrine was meant to prevent. *See* ***Lony v. E.I. DuPont de Nemours & Co.***, 935 F.2d 604, 614 (3d Cir.1991); ***In re Air Crash Disaster Near New Orleans***, 821 F.2d 1147, 1165 (5th Cir.1987), *vacated & remanded sub nom.* ***Pan Am. World Airways, Inc. v. Lopez***, 490 U.S. 1032 (1989), *reinstated in relevant part*, 883 F.2d 17 (5th Cir.1989).

§3.3 Evidence. The plaintiff should attach evidence to support all the factual allegations in its response. *See* ***Rivendell Forest Prods. v. Canadian Pac. Ltd.***, 2 F.3d 990, 993 (10th Cir.1993).

§4. HEARING

District courts have discretion to decide a motion to dismiss for forum non conveniens before ruling on objections to subject-matter jurisdiction under FRCP 12(b)(2) or personal jurisdiction under FRCP 12(b)(3). ***Sinochem Int'l Co. v. Malaysia Int'l Shipping Corp.***, 549 U.S. 422, 425 (2007). A court facing multiple grounds for dismissal should consider the complexity of the jurisdictional issues, as well as concerns of undue expense and judicial economy. *See id.* at 435-36. If a court can readily determine that it lacks subject-matter or personal jurisdiction, it should dismiss on either of those grounds; however, if the jurisdictional issues are difficult to determine, it may first decide the issue of forum non conveniens, which may be less burdensome. *Id.* at 436. Although the court will typically decide a forum non conveniens motion based on the written record, it may conduct an evidentiary hearing if necessary. *See* ***Boone v. Sulphur Creek Resort, Inc.***, 749 F.Supp. 195, 196 (S.D.Ind.1990). If the court decides the motion on written submission, it may consider discovery, stipulations, or admissions. *See* ***In re Air Crash Disaster Near New Orleans***, 821 F.2d 1147, 1166 (5th Cir.1987), *vacated & remanded sub nom.* ***Pan Am. World Airways, Inc. v. Lopez***, 490 U.S. 1032 (1989), *reinstated in relevant part*, 883 F.2d 17 (5th Cir.1989).

§5. RULING

§5.1 Denies motion. If the court denies the motion, the case will proceed. No interlocutory appeal is allowed. ***Van Cauwenberghe v. Biard***, 486 U.S. 517, 527 (1988).

§5.2 Grants motion. If the court grants the motion, it will enter an order dismissing the case. The order is immediately appealable. ***In re Joint E.&S. Dists. Asbestos Litig.***, 22 F.3d 755, 762 n.13 (7th Cir.1994).

§5.3 Conditionally grants motion. To prevent prejudice to the plaintiff, the court may condition the granting of the motion on the defendant's agreement to submit to the jurisdiction of the alternative forum. *See* ***Constructora Spilimerg, C.A. v. Mitsubishi Aircraft Co.***, 700 F.2d 225, 226 (5th Cir.1983); ***Farmanfarmaian v. Gulf Oil Corp.***, 437 F.Supp. 910, 928 (S.D.N.Y.1977), *aff'd*, 588 F.2d 880 (2d Cir.1978). The conditional granting should allow the plaintiff to reinstate the suit in a U.S. court if the defendant evades the jurisdiction of the alternative forum. *See* ***Yavuz v. 61 MM, Ltd.***, 576 F.3d 1166, 1182 (10th Cir.2009); ***Baris v. Sulpicio Lines, Inc.***, 932 F.2d 1540, 1551 (5th Cir.1991).

§5.4 Findings of fact. The court must make findings of fact, either written or transcribed in the record, to support its ruling. ***In re Air Crash Disaster Near New Orleans***, 821 F.2d 1147, 1166 (5th Cir.1987), *vacated & remanded sub nom.* ***Pan Am. World Airways, Inc. v. Lopez***, 490 U.S. 1032 (1989), *reinstated in relevant part*, 883 F.2d 17 (5th Cir.1989); *see, e.g.*, ***La Seguridad v. Transytur Line***, 707 F.2d 1304, 1308 (11th Cir.1983) (vacating lower court's decision on forum non conveniens because of incomplete record supporting decision).

§6. APPELLATE REVIEW

§6.1 Appealability. An order granting a motion to dismiss for forum non conveniens is immediately appealable. ***King v. Cessna Aircraft Co.***, 562 F.3d 1374, 1378 (11th Cir.2009). An order denying the motion, however, is not. ***Van Cauwenberghe v. Biard***, 486 U.S. 517, 527 (1988); ***King***, 562 F.3d at 1378.

§6.2 Standard of review. The district court's ruling on a motion to dismiss for forum non conveniens is generally reviewed for abuse of discretion. *See* ***Piper Aircraft Co. v. Reyno***, 454 U.S. 235, 257 (1981) (if court's balancing of factors is reasonable, its decision deserves substantial deference); ***Adelson v. Hananel***, 510 F.3d 43, 52 (1st Cir.2007) (abuse of discretion); ***Duha v. Agrium, Inc.***, 448 F.3d 867, 873 (6th Cir.2006) (clear abuse of discretion); ***Gonzalez v. Chrysler Corp.***, 301 F.3d 377, 379 (5th Cir.2002) (same); ***Iragorri v. United Techs.***, 274 F.3d 65, 72 (2d Cir.2001) (same). The court abuses its discretion if it (1) does not address and balance the relevant private and public interests, (2) clearly errs in evaluating the relevant factors, or (3) does not hold the defendant to its burden of persuasion. *See* ***Adelson***, 510 F.3d at 52; ***El-Fadl v. Central Bank***, 75 F.3d 668, 677 (D.C.Cir.1996), *overruled on* *other grounds*, ***Samantar v. Yousuf***, ___ U.S. ___, 130 S.Ct. 2278 (2010); ***In re Air Crash Disaster Near New Orleans***, 821 F.2d 1147, 1166 (5th Cir.1987), *vacated & remanded sub nom.* ***Pan Am. World Airways, Inc. v. Lopez***, 490 U.S. 1032 (1989), *reinstated in relevant part*, 883 F.2d 17 (5th Cir.1989). Errors of law are reviewed de novo. ***Adelson***, 510 F.3d at 52.

F. MOTION TO DISMISS FOR FAILURE TO STATE A CLAIM—FRCP 12(b)(6)

§1. GENERAL

§1.1 Rule. FRCP 12(b)(6).

§1.2 Purpose. A motion to dismiss for failure to state a claim upon which relief can be granted tests the formal sufficiency of the plaintiff's statement of its claim for relief in its complaint. *See* ***Republican Party v. Martin***, 980 F.2d 943, 952 (4th Cir.1992). The motion cannot be used to resolve factual issues or the merits of the case. *Id.* A motion to dismiss under FRCP 12(b)(6) is appropriate only if the plaintiff has not provided fair notice of its claim and factual allegations that—when accepted as true—are plausible and rise above mere speculation. *See* ***Ashcroft v. Iqbal***, 556 U.S. 662, 678 (2009); ***Bell Atlantic Corp. v. Twombly***, 550 U.S. 544, 555-56 (2007). *See generally* 5B Wright & Miller, *Federal Practice & Procedure 3d* §§1356-1357 (2004 & Supp.2012) (discussing purpose of FRCP 12(b)(6) motion). See "Statement of Claim," ch. 2-B, §5, p. 80. Generally, motions to dismiss for failure to state a claim are viewed with disfavor. ***Collins v. Morgan Stanley Dean Witter***, 224 F.3d 496, 498 (5th Cir.2000); *see* 5B Wright & Miller §1357 & n.34.

§1.3 Forms. ***O'Connor's Federal Civil Forms*** (2012), FORMS 3F.

§1.4 Other references. 5B, 5C Wright & Miller, *Federal Practice & Procedure 3d* §§1355-1358 (2004 & Supp.2012); 2 *Moore's Federal Practice 3d* §12.34 (2012).

§2. MOTION

§2.1 Form. For the general requirements for the form of a motion, see "Drafting motions," ch. 1-B, §3.1, p. 14.

§2.2 In writing or on court's initiative. The motion to dismiss must be in writing. FRCP 7(b)(1). If the defendant does not raise the defense of failure to state a claim upon which relief can be granted, the court may dismiss a complaint on its own initiative if the plaintiff cannot possibly win relief. ***Carroll v. Fort James Corp.***, 470 F.3d 1171, 1177 (5th Cir.2006); ***Best v. Kelly***, 39 F.3d 328, 331 (D.C.Cir.1994). However, sua sponte dismissals are generally disfavored and are appropriate only in limited circumstances. *See* ***Chute v. Walker***, 281 F.3d 314, 319 (1st Cir.2002); ***Stewart Title Guar. Co. v. Cadle Co.***, 74 F.3d 835, 836 (7th Cir.1996). The court should give the plaintiff notice and an opportunity to respond before dismissing the case on its own initiative. ***Carroll***, 470 F.3d at 1177; ***Stewart Title Guar.***, 74 F.3d at 836; *see also* ***American United Life Ins. v. Martinez***, 480 F.3d 1043, 1057 (11th Cir.2007) (sua sponte dismissals are prohibited when D does not file answer and P has right to amend complaint, has brought claim in good faith, and has not been given notice and opportunity to respond). Notice and an opportunity to respond may not be required if the claim is frivolous, the defect cannot be cured by amendment, or the plaintiff cannot prevail based on the facts alleged in the complaint. *See* ***Clorox Co. P.R. v. Proctor & Gamble Commercial Co.***, 228 F.3d 24, 30-31 (1st Cir.2000); ***Smith v. Boyd***, 945 F.2d 1041, 1043 (8th Cir.1991).

§2.3 Grounds. A motion to dismiss for failure to state a claim admits the facts alleged in the complaint but challenges the plaintiff's right to any relief based on those facts. ***Crowe v. Henry***, 43 F.3d 198, 203 (5th Cir.1995). The issue is not whether the plaintiff will ultimately prevail but whether the plaintiff will be able to offer evidence to support its claims. ***Semerenko v. Cendant Corp.***, 223 F.3d 165, 173 (3d Cir.2000); *see* ***Scheuer v. Rhodes***, 416 U.S. 232, 236 (1974), *overruled on other grounds*, ***Harlow v. Fitzgerald***, 457 U.S. 800 (1982); ***Gorski v. New Hampshire Dept. of Corr.***, 290 F.3d 466, 473 (1st Cir.2002). Some examples of successful FRCP 12(b)(6) motions are the following:

1. The plaintiff did not allege facts of specific instances of unlawful discrimination. ***Coyne v. City of Somerville***, 972 F.2d 440, 442-45 (1st Cir.1992); *see* ***New Albany Tractor, Inc. v. Louisville Tractor, Inc.***, 650 F.3d 1046, 1051-52 (6th Cir.2011) (claim of discriminatory pricing under Robinson-Patman Act).

2. The plaintiff pleaded claims of fraud but did not identify any false or misleading disclosure made by the defendant. ***Royal Bus. Grp. v. Realist, Inc.***, 933 F.2d 1056, 1065-66 (1st Cir.1991).

3. The municipal defendants were entitled to immunity under state law. ***Carter v. Cornwell***, 983 F.2d 52, 54-55 (6th Cir.1993).

4. The plaintiff did not respond to the defendant's motion to dismiss, which alleged that the plaintiff's claim had no basis in law. ***Kirksey v. R.J. Reynolds Tobacco Co.***, 168 F.3d 1039, 1041-42 (7th Cir.1999).

5. The plaintiff filed suit in a district other than the venue mandated by a valid forum-selection clause. *See* ***Silva v. Encyclopedia Britannica Inc.***, 239 F.3d 385, 386-87 (1st Cir.2001).

CIRCUIT SPLIT

The circuits are split on the proper procedure for challenging venue based on a forum-selection clause. See "Forum-selection clause," ch. 3-A, §4.3, p. 173. The First, Second, and Third Circuits have identified FRCP 12(b)(6) as an appropriate mechanism to dismiss based on a forum-selection clause. See ***Rivera v. Centro Médico de Turabo, Inc.****, 575 F.3d 10, 15 (1st Cir.2009);* ***Salovaara v. Jackson Nat'l Life Ins.****, 246 F.3d 289, 298 (3d Cir.2001);* ***Evolution Online Sys. v. Koninklijke PTT Nederland N.V.****, 145 F.3d 505, 508 n.6 (2d Cir.1998); see also* ***Langley v. Prudential Mortg. Capital Co.****, 546 F.3d 365, 369 (6th Cir.2008) (appellate court remanded to allow for consideration of enforceable forum-selection clause under either FRCP 12(b)(6) motion to dismiss or motion to transfer venue). However, the use of an FRCP 12(b)(6) motion has been criticized as (1) inefficient because it may be raised anytime before adjudication on the merits and (2) doctrinally inappropriate because the pleadings based on a forum-selection clause cannot be accepted as true as required under FRCP 12(b)(6). See* ***Sucampo Pharms. v. Astellas Pharma, Inc.****, 471 F.3d 544, 549 (4th Cir.2006). For the factors used to determine the enforceability of a forum-selection clause, see "Forum-selection clause," ch. 3-D, §3.3.4, p. 194.*

---

§2.4 Relief requested. The defendant may request dismissal with or without leave to amend. Generally, a court will not dismiss without leave to amend on the first challenge to the plaintiff's complaint. ***Curley v. Perry***, 246 F.3d 1278, 1281-82 (10th Cir.2001); *see, e.g.*, ***Welch v. Laney***, 57 F.3d 1004, 1009 (11th Cir.1995) (court should not have dismissed P's civil-rights claim without leave to amend because county commissioners were potentially liable for sheriff's acts); *see also* ***Grayson v. Mayview State Hosp.***, 293 F.3d 103, 108 (3d Cir.2002) (court must inform P of right to amend unless amendment would be inequitable or futile). A court is more likely to dismiss without leave to amend if the plaintiff has had opportunities to state a claim upon which relief can be granted but has not succeeded. *See, e.g.*, ***Kuehl v. FDIC***, 8 F.3d 905, 908 (1st Cir.1993) (complaint was dismissed because Ps never properly amended complaint despite order to conform to concise-pleading requirements of FRCP 8(a)).

§2.5 No affidavits or evidence. The defendant should not attach affidavits, evidence, or other extrinsic materials to the motion. Generally, the motion must be decided solely on the allegations in the plaintiff's complaint. ***Speaker v. U.S. Dept. of H&HS Ctrs. for Disease Control & Prevention***, 623 F.3d 1371, 1379 (11th Cir.2010); *see* FRCP 12(d). Under most circumstances, if the court considers extrinsic evidence, the FRCP 12(b)(6) motion must be converted into a motion for summary judgment. ***Speaker***, 623 F.3d at 1379; *see* FRCP 12(d); ***Weise v. Casper***, 507 F.3d 1260, 1267 (10th Cir.2007). See "Hearing," §4, p. 206.

§2.6 Waiver. A defendant does not waive its right to challenge the legal sufficiency of the complaint by filing an FRCP 12(b) motion that does not include an FRCP 12(b)(6) challenge. A defendant may raise an FRCP 12(b)(6) defense in any pleading permitted under FRCP 7(a), in a motion for judgment on the pleadings, or at any time up to

and including, but not beyond, the trial on the merits. FRCP 12(h)(2); ***Arbaugh v. Y&H Corp.***, 546 U.S. 500, 507 (2006); *see, e.g.*, ***Ennenga v. Starns***, 677 F.3d 766, 773 (7th Cir.2012) (because failure-to-state-claim defense cannot be waived and does not have to be consolidated with other defenses, D could raise statute-of-limitations defense for first time in second motion to dismiss).

§3. RESPONSE

§3.1 Grounds. The response should demonstrate that the complaint provides fair notice of the plaintiff's claims and that the facts alleged sufficiently show a plausible claim for relief. *See* ***Ashcroft v. Iqbal***, 556 U.S. 662, 678 (2009); ***Bell Atlantic Corp. v. Twombly***, 550 U.S. 544, 555-56 (2007). See "Statement of Claim," ch. 2-B, §5, p. 80. The response should emphasize that the court must assume that all material facts contained in the complaint are true and resolve all inferences in the plaintiff's favor, and that FRCP 12(b)(6) motions are disfavored in light of the liberal pleading policies of the FRCPs. See "Standard," §5.1, p. 207.

§3.2 Amended pleading. The plaintiff should consider filing an amended pleading in addition to—or possibly instead of—a response. If the plaintiff has not already amended once as a "matter of course" (i.e., 21 days after serving its complaint), the plaintiff can amend—without the court's leave or the opposing party's consent—within the earlier of 21 days after the defendant's answer or FRCP 12(b)(6) motion is served. *See* FRCP 15(a)(1)(B). See "Deadline," ch. 5-I, §3.1.1, p. 345. When leave is necessary, the plaintiff's response should request that, if the court grants the motion to dismiss, it should also grant the plaintiff leave to amend. See "Motion for Leave to Amend," ch. 5-I, §5, p. 351.

§3.3 Deadline. The FRCPs do not contain a deadline for filing a response. The plaintiff should check the local rules of the district and the standing orders of the court where the case is pending.

§4. HEARING

The court may hold a hearing to receive oral arguments on an FRCP 12(b)(6) motion, but a hearing is not necessary. ***Cline v. Rogers***, 87 F.3d 176, 184 (6th Cir.1996).

§4.1 No extrinsic materials. Generally, in deciding a motion to dismiss for failure to state a claim, the court limits its inquiry to facts stated in the complaint. *See* FRCP 12(d); ***Gee v. Pacheco***, 627 F.3d 1178, 1186 (10th Cir. 2010); ***Tackett v. M&G Polymers, USA, LLC***, 561 F.3d 478, 487 (6th Cir.2009). But if a document is central to the claim and is attached to or incorporated by reference into the complaint, it is not considered "outside the pleading" and can be considered by the court. *See* ***Gee***, 627 F.3d at 1186; ***DiFolco v. MSNBC Cable L.L.C.***, 622 F.3d 104, 111 (2d Cir.2010); ***SFM Holdings, Ltd. v. Banc of Am. Secs., LLC***, 600 F.3d 1334, 1337 (11th Cir.2010); ***Scanlan v. Texas A&M Univ.***, 343 F.3d 533, 536 (5th Cir.2003); 5B Wright & Miller §1357 & n.1; *see, e.g.*, ***Beddall v. State St. Bank & Trust Co.***, 137 F.3d 12, 17 (1st Cir.1998) (agreement attached to motion was considered when its authenticity was not challenged and it was central to Ps' allegations).

§4.2 Effect of considering extrinsic materials. The court is sometimes asked to consider materials outside the complaint in support of or in opposition to an FRCP 12(b)(6) motion. *See* ***Lovelace v. Software Spectrum, Inc.***, 78 F.3d 1015, 1017-18 (5th Cir.1996). If the court decides it will not consider the materials, they are in essence excluded, but the court is not required take any formal steps to do so. ***Harper v. Lawrence Cty.***, 592 F.3d 1227, 1232 (11th Cir.2010).

1. Conversion to summary-judgment motion. Under most circumstances, if the court decides to consider extrinsic materials, the motion must be converted into a motion for summary judgment. *See* FRCP 12(d); ***Ashanti v. City of Golden Valley***, 666 F.3d 1148, 1150-51 (8th Cir.2012); ***Michigan Paytel Jt.V. v. City of Detroit***, 287 F.3d 527, 533 (6th Cir.2002); *see, e.g.*, ***Doss v. Clearwater Title Co.***, 551 F.3d 634, 639-40 (7th Cir.2008) (court should not have considered deed attached to motion and taken by judicial notice without converting motion under FRCP 12(d) when ownership of deed was subject to reasonable dispute). Conversion to a summary-judgment motion takes place at the court's discretion, when the court affirmatively decides to consider extrinsic materials. ***Finley Lines Joint Prot. Bd. v. Norfolk S. Corp.***, 109 F.3d 993, 996-97 (4th Cir.1997); ***Aamot v. Kassel***, 1 F.3d 441, 444-45

(6th Cir.1993); *see also* ***Tackett v. M&G Polymers, USA, LLC***, 561 F.3d 478, 487 (6th Cir.2009) (court may convert motion sua sponte, but that conversion should be exercised with great caution). If the court converts the motion, the parties must be given notice to prevent unfair surprise and allowed an opportunity to take reasonable discovery. *See* ***E.I. du Pont de Nemours & Co. v. Kolon Indus.***, 637 F.3d 435, 448 (4th Cir.2011); ***Sahu v. Union Carbide Corp.***, 548 F.3d 59, 67 (2d Cir.2008); ***In re Rockefeller Ctr. Props., Inc. Secs. Litig.***, 184 F.3d 280, 287-88 (3d Cir. 1999); ***Arnold v. Air Midwest, Inc.***, 100 F.3d 857, 859 n.2 (10th Cir.1996). *But see* ***Maldonado v. Dominguez***, 137 F.3d 1, 5-6 (1st Cir.1998) (not giving notice is harmless if opponent has received materials, has had opportunity to respond, and has not controverted their accuracy).

2. Exception. Under limited circumstances, the court can consider extrinsic materials without converting the motion. *See* ***Rivera v. Centro Médico de Turabo, Inc.***, 575 F.3d 10, 15 (1st Cir.2009); *see, e.g.*, ***Little Gem Life Sci. LLC v. Orphan Med., Inc.***, 537 F.3d 913, 916 (8th Cir.2008) (court could consider public records without converting motion under FRCP 12(d) when records were background facts, did not contradict complaint, and were not critical to outcome of motion); ***Lovelace***, 78 F.3d at 1017-18 (in securities-fraud claim, court could consider public-disclosure documents filed with SEC without converting motion under FRCP 12(d)); *see also* ***Geinosky v. City of Chi.***, 675 F.3d 743, 745 n.1 (7th Cir.2012) (P opposing FRCP 12(b)(6) motion has more flexibility with extrinsic materials to illustrate facts it expects to be able to prove). The court may be able to consider extrinsic materials such as exhibits, affidavits, matters of public record, or matters taken by judicial notice. *See* ***Lovelace***, 78 F.3d at 1017-18; 5B Wright & Miller §1357 & n.1; *see also* ***Halebian v. Berv***, 644 F.3d 122, 130 n.7 (2d Cir.2011) (court can consider documents that either are in P's possession or P had knowledge of and that P relied on in bringing suit).

§5. RULING

§5.1 Standard. The court should dismiss under FRCP 12(b)(6) if the plaintiff has not provided both fair notice of the nature of the claim and plausible factual allegations to support the claim. *See* ***Ashcroft v. Iqbal***, 556 U.S. 662, 678 (2009); ***Erickson v. Pardus***, 551 U.S. 89, 93 (2007); ***Bell Atlantic Corp. v. Twombly***, 550 U.S. 544, 555-56 & n.3 (2007); ***Sinaltrainal v. Coca-Cola Co.***, 578 F.3d 1252, 1268 (11th Cir.2009), *overruled on other grounds*, ***Mohamad v. Palestinian Auth.***, ___ U.S. ___, 132 S.Ct. 1702 (2012). See "Statement of Claim," ch. 2-B, §5, p. 80. In ruling on an FRCP 12(b)(6) motion, the court must (1) identify allegations that, because they are merely conclusions, are not entitled to an assumption of truth and (2) consider the factual allegations to determine if they plausibly suggest a claim for relief. ***Iqbal***, 556 U.S. at 679; ***Moss v. U.S. Secret Serv.***, 572 F.3d 962, 970 (9th Cir.2009).

NOTE

The Supreme Court formerly held that a complaint should not be dismissed for failure to state a claim unless it appeared beyond doubt that the plaintiff could prove no set of facts to support a claim for relief. ***Conley v. Gibson****, 355 U.S. 41, 45-46 (1957). The Court retired the "no set of facts" language from* ***Conley*** *and now requires a pleading to have enough facts to state a claim for relief that is "plausible on its face."* ***Twombly****, 550 U.S. at 562-63, 570. Although detailed factual allegations are not required, a complaint may be dismissed when (1) it does not show a right to relief beyond mere speculation or (2) it sets forth a claim for relief from which no more than a mere possibility of misconduct can be inferred. See* ***Iqbal****, 556 U.S. at 678;* ***Twombly****, 550 U.S. at 555. Defendants should pay particular attention to the* ***Iqbal*** *and* ***Twombly*** *decisions when determining whether a plaintiff has pleaded sufficient facts.*

1. Conclusory allegations. Conclusory allegations of law, inferences unsupported by facts, or a formulaic recitation of the elements in a complaint will not defeat an FRCP 12(b)(6) motion. ***Iqbal***, 556 U.S. at 678; ***Twombly***, 550 U.S. at 555; ***Brooks v. Ross***, 578 F.3d 574, 581 (7th Cir.2009); ***Browning v. Clinton***, 292 F.3d 235, 242 (D.C.Cir.2002); ***Fernandez-Montes v. Allied Pilots Ass'n***, 987 F.2d 278, 284 (5th Cir.1993); *see* ***Nemet Chevrolet, Ltd. v. Consumeraffairs.com, Inc.***, 591 F.3d 250, 255 (4th Cir.2009) (unwarranted inferences, unreasonable conclusions, and arguments are not considered).

2. Plausible factual allegations. When there are nonconclusory factual allegations, the court must assume that they are true and then determine whether they plausibly give rise to an entitlement to relief. ***Iqbal***, 556 U.S. at 679; *see, e.g.*, ***Brooks***, 578 F.3d at 581-82 (P's allegations were too vague to provide notice to Ds of §1983 claim; P's allegations of Ds' actions were just as consistent with lawful conduct as with wrongdoing). See "Plausibility," ch. 2-B, §5.1.2, p. 81. The court must indulge all inferences in favor of the plaintiff. ***Collins v. Morgan Stanley Dean Witter***, 224 F.3d 496, 498 (5th Cir.2000); ***Jones v. General Elec. Co.***, 87 F.3d 209, 211 (7th Cir.1996); *see, e.g.*, ***Casanova v. Ulibarri***, 595 F.3d 1120, 1125-26 (10th Cir.2010) (in §1983 case, district court erred when it did not indulge inferences in favor of P-prisoner because, by improperly relying on start date in D's answer, court assumed that undated allegations in P's complaint necessarily occurred before D-warden started working at prison). If the factual allegations are plausible, the court cannot decide disputed fact issues—that is, the court must assume that all plausible facts contained in the complaint are true. *See* ***Tellabs, Inc. v. Makor Issues & Rights, Ltd.***, 551 U.S. 308, 322 (2007); ***Twombly***, 550 U.S. at 555-56; *see also* ***Neitzke v. Williams***, 490 U.S. 319, 326-27 (1989) (FRCP 12(b)(6) does not permit dismissal based on judge's disbelief of complaint's factual allegations). The court, however, cannot assume that the plaintiff can prove facts it has not alleged. ***Cline v. Rogers***, 87 F.3d 176, 184 (6th Cir.1996).

§5.2 Denies motion. If the court denies the motion to dismiss, the case continues.

§5.3 Grants motion. If the court grants the motion to dismiss, it will enter an order dismissing all or part of the case. If the order grants the plaintiff leave to amend, the plaintiff may do so, and the case continues. Leave to amend should ordinarily be granted before dismissal with prejudice. *See* ***EEOC v. Concentra Health Servs.***, 496 F.3d 773, 782 (7th Cir.2007) (dicta); ***ArthroCare Corp. v. Smith & Nephew, Inc.***, 406 F.3d 1365, 1370 (Fed.Cir. 2005); ***Shane v. Fauver***, 213 F.3d 113, 116 (3d Cir.2000). If the court enters an order dismissing the case without leave to amend, the order bars relitigation of the claim. *See* ***Gasho v. U.S.***, 39 F.3d 1420, 1438 n.17 (9th Cir.1994). A dismissal under FRCP 12(b)(6) is considered a decision on the merits. *See* ***Nowak v. Ironworkers Local 6 Pension Fund***, 81 F.3d 1182, 1187-88 (2d Cir.1996).

§5.4 No findings of fact. The court should not make findings of fact or conclusions of law when ruling on an FRCP 12(b)(6) motion. *See* FRCP 52(a)(3); ***Roth v. Jennings***, 489 F.3d 499, 509 (2d Cir.2007).

§6. APPELLATE REVIEW

§6.1 Appealability.

1. Motion denied. A defendant generally cannot immediately appeal an order denying an FRCP 12(b)(6) motion. ***Jackson v. City of Atlanta***, 73 F.3d 60, 62 (5th Cir.1996); ***Foster Wheeler Energy Corp. v. Metropolitan Knox Solid Waste Auth., Inc.***, 970 F.2d 199, 202 (6th Cir.1992); *see also* ***In re Text Messaging Antitrust Litig.***, 630 F.3d 622, 625-26 (7th Cir.2010) (in antitrust case, interlocutory appeal under 28 U.S.C. §1292(b) allowed on controlling question of law about adequacy of amended complaint under ***Twombly*** standard).

2. Motion granted. A plaintiff generally can immediately appeal an order granting an FRCP 12(b)(6) motion. *See* ***Cousins v. Lockyer***, 568 F.3d 1063, 1067 (9th Cir.2009); ***In re Merck & Co., Inc. Secs. Litig.***, 432 F.3d 261, 266 (3d Cir.2005).

PRACTICE TIP

On appeal from a dismissal based on FRCP 12(b)(6), a plaintiff may be allowed to supplement the complaint with additional facts to show that the dismissal was improper; the additional facts are allowed as long as they are consistent with the complaint. ***Reynolds v. CB Sports Bar, Inc.****, 623 F.3d 1143, 1146-47 (7th Cir.2010). The Seventh Circuit has held that this after-the-fact supplementation is still permissible after* ***Twombly*** *and* ***Iqbal****. Id. at 1147.*

---

§6.2 Standard of review. On appeal, the court reviews a dismissal under FRCP 12(b)(6) de novo. ***Carroll v. Fort James Corp.***, 470 F.3d 1171, 1173 (5th Cir.2006); ***Michigan Paytel Jt.V. v. City of Detroit***, 287 F.3d 527, 533 (6th Cir.2002). No deference is given to the district court's original decision. *See* ***Frey v. City of Herculaneum***, 44 F.3d 667, 671 (8th Cir.1995); ***Peloza v. Capistrano Unified Sch. Dist.***, 37 F.3d 517, 521 (9th Cir.1994).

G. MOTION TO DISMISS FOR INSUFFICIENT PROCESS OR SERVICE—FRCP 12(b)(4), (b)(5)

§1. GENERAL

§1.1 Rule. FRCP 12(b)(4), (b)(5). See also FRCP 4(*l*).

§1.2 Purpose. The purpose of a motion under FRCP 12(b)(4) or 12(b)(5) is to dismiss because of insufficient process or service of process. A motion to dismiss for insufficient process allows a party to challenge the form of the summons. ***Buck Mtn. Cmty. Org. v. Tennessee Valley Auth.***, 629 F.Supp.2d 785, 792 n.5 (M.D.Tenn.2009). A motion to dismiss for insufficient service allows a party to challenge the method of service. *Id.* A court cannot constitutionally exercise jurisdiction over a defendant who was not properly served because of insufficient form or method of service.

§1.3 Forms. *O'Connor's Federal Civil Forms* (2012), FORMS 3G.

§1.4 Other references. 4A, 4B Wright & Miller, *Federal Practice & Procedure 3d* §§1082-1105, 1137 (2002 & Supp.2012); 5B Wright & Miller, *Federal Practice & Procedure 3d* §1353 (2004 & Supp.2012); 2 *Moore's Federal Practice 3d* §12.33 (2012).

§2. MOTION

§2.1 Form. For the general requirements for the form of a motion, see "Drafting motions," ch. 1-B, §3.1, p. 14.

§2.2 In writing. The motion should be in writing. *See* FRCP 7(b)(1).

§2.3 Grounds. To challenge the form of the summons, the defendant should file a motion to dismiss for insufficient process under FRCP 12(b)(4). 5B Wright & Miller §1353. To challenge the method of service attempted by the plaintiff, the defendant should file a motion to dismiss for insufficient service under FRCP 12(b)(5). 5B Wright & Miller §1353; *see also* ***Adams v. AlliedSignal Gen. Aviation Avionics***, 74 F.3d 882, 884 n.2 (8th Cir.1996) (because of confusion between the two insufficiencies, it is appropriate to present service issues under both FRCP 12(b)(4) and (b)(5)). The defendant must make specific objections and explain how the attempted service did not satisfy the requirements of service. ***O'Brien v. R.J. O'Brien & Assocs.***, 998 F.2d 1394, 1400 (7th Cir.1993); ***Photolab Corp. v. Simplex Specialty Co.***, 806 F.2d 807, 810 (8th Cir.1986).

§2.4 Deadline. The defendant must raise objections to the sufficiency of process or service in either the answer or a preanswer motion. FRCP 12(b)(4), (b)(5), (h)(1); ***Chute v. Walker***, 281 F.3d 314, 319 (1st Cir.2002); ***McCurdy v. American Bd. of Plastic Surgery***, 157 F.3d 191, 194 (3d Cir.1998); ***Resolution Trust Corp. v. Starkey***, 41 F.3d 1018, 1021 (5th Cir.1995); ***O'Brien v. R.J. O'Brien & Assocs.***, 998 F.2d 1394, 1399 (7th Cir.1993); ***FDIC v. Oaklawn Apts.***, 959 F.2d 170, 175 (10th Cir.1992); ***Sanderford v. Prudential Ins.***, 902 F.2d 897, 900 (11th Cir.1990); *see also* 5B Wright & Miller §1353 (objection to sufficiency of process or service may be made in answer if no other FRCP 12(b) motion has been filed).

§2.5 Waiver. The defense of insufficient service of process or service is waived unless it is made in the FRCP 12(b) motion, in the first responsive pleading, or in an amendment to the first responsive pleading allowed as a matter of course (i.e., amendment allowed within 21 days after the responsive pleading is served). FRCP 12(h)(1); *see* FRCP 12(g)(2), 15(a)(1)(A); ***U.S. v. Ligas***, 549 F.3d 497, 501 (7th Cir.2008). See "Defenses raised in preanswer motion," ch. 3-A, §2.3, p. 172; "Amending as matter of course," ch. 5-I, §3.1, p. 345. The defendant should still object to the sufficiency of process despite the language of FRCP 4(m), which states that a court must dismiss a case if service is not made on the defendant within 120 days after the complaint is filed. *See* 4B Wright & Miller §1137 & n.24. A defendant waives its objection to improper service if it participates in pretrial proceedings without raising the issue. *See* ***Datskow v. Teledyne, Inc., Cont'l Prods. Div.***, 899 F.2d 1298, 1302-03 (2d Cir.1990); ***Allied Semi-Conductors Int'l v. Pulsar Components Int'l***, 907 F.Supp. 618, 623 (E.D.N.Y.1995).

§2.6 Evidence. The defendant may attach affidavits and other evidence to support its allegations. ***Trustees of Cent. Laborers' Welfare Fund v. Lowery***, 924 F.2d 731, 732 n.2 (7th Cir.1991) (dicta); *see, e.g.*, ***Davis v. Musler***, 713 F.2d 907, 910-11 (2d Cir.1983) (D submitted affidavit and other evidence to prove insufficient service).

§3. RESPONSE

§3.1 In writing. The plaintiff's response to a motion challenging the sufficiency of process or service should be in writing. *See* FRCP 7(b)(1).

§3.2 Grounds. The plaintiff's response should negate the allegations in the defendant's motion.

1. **Defective process.** If the defendant is challenging the form of process under FRCP 12(b)(4), the plaintiff should either argue that the form of process was proper or, if process was defective, ask the court for leave to serve again.

2. **Defective service.** If the defendant is challenging the service of process under FRCP 12(b)(5), the plaintiff should either argue that the service was proper or, if it was not, file a motion to extend time to serve. See "Motion to extend time to serve," ch. 2-H, §4.2, p. 153; "Motion to extend time to serve party," ch. 5-F, §4.3, p. 334.

§3.3 Amended pleading. If it will help resolve the dispute about the sufficiency of process or service of process, the plaintiff may consider filing an amended pleading in addition to—or possibly instead of—a response. If the plaintiff has not already amended once as a "matter of course" (i.e., 21 days after serving its complaint), the plaintiff can amend—without the court's leave or the opposing party's consent—within the earlier of 21 days after the defendant's answer or motion under FRCP 12(b)(4) or 12(b)(5) is served. *See* FRCP 15(a)(1)(B). See "Deadline," ch. 5-I, §3.1.1, p. 345. When leave is necessary, the plaintiff's response should request that, if the court grants the motion to dismiss, it should also grant the plaintiff leave to amend. See "Motion for Leave to Amend," ch. 5-I, §5, p. 351.

§3.4 Deadline. The FRCPs do not provide a deadline for filing a response to an FRCP 12(b)(4) or (b)(5) motion. The plaintiff should check the local rules of the district court where the case is pending.

§4. BURDEN OF PROOF

§4.1 Plaintiff's burden. Once the defendant makes a timely objection to the sufficiency of service of process, the plaintiff has the burden to establish proper service of process. *See* ***Northrup King Co. v. Compania Productora Semillas Algodoneras Selectas, S.A.***, 51 F.3d 1383, 1387 (8th Cir.1995); ***Saez Rivera v. Nissan Mfg.***, 788 F.2d 819, 821 n.2 (1st Cir.1986); ***Norlock v. City of Garland***, 768 F.2d 654, 656 (5th Cir.1985); 5B Wright & Miller §1353. The plaintiff can meet this burden by introducing the process server's return of service as prima facie evidence that the form and manner of service were proper. ***O'Brien v. R.J. O'Brien & Assocs.***, 998 F.2d 1394, 1398 (7th Cir.1993); 5B Wright & Miller §1353 & n.34.

§4.2 Defendant's burden. If the plaintiff meets its burden of showing proper service of process, the burden shifts to the defendant to present strong and convincing proof of insufficient service. ***O'Brien v. R.J. O'Brien & Assocs.***, 998 F.2d 1394, 1398 (7th Cir.1993); ***Nikwei v. Ross Sch. of Aviation, Inc.***, 822 F.2d 939, 941 (10th Cir.1987). The defendant must either establish that there is a defect in service, as shown on the face of the return, or produce affidavits or other admissible evidence proving that service was improper. *See* ***O'Brien***, 998 F.2d at 1398; ***Nikwei***, 822 F.2d at 941-42. The mere denial of receipt of service is insufficient to overcome the presumption of validity of the process server's affidavit. ***New York v. Operation Rescue Nat'l***, 69 F.Supp.2d 408, 416 (W.D.N.Y.1999).

§5. HEARING

The court may hold an evidentiary hearing to determine whether the defendant was properly served. FRCP 12(i); *see* ***Nikwei v. Ross Sch. of Aviation, Inc.***, 822 F.2d 939, 941 (10th Cir.1987).

§6. RULING

If the court grants a motion to dismiss for insufficient process or insufficient service, it may either dismiss the suit or retain the suit and quash the service, giving the plaintiff an opportunity to re-serve the defendant. ***Adams v. AlliedSignal Gen. Aviation Avionics***, 74 F.3d 882, 886 (8th Cir.1996); ***Montalbano v. Easco Hand Tools, Inc.***, 766 F.2d 737, 740 (2d Cir.1985).

§6.1 Defect in summons. Usually, the court will not dismiss if there are defects in the form of the summons. If the summons substantially complies with the requirements of FRCP 4(a), the defendant must show actual prejudice before the court will dismiss. *See **Sanderford v. Prudential Ins.***, 902 F.2d 897, 900-01 (11th Cir.1990); ***U.S. v. Carney***, 796 F.Supp. 700, 704 (E.D.N.Y.1992). But if the summons does not substantially comply with FRCP 4(a), the court can dismiss even if there is no actual prejudice to the defendant. For the requirements of the summons, see "Requirements for summons," ch. 2-H, §3.1, p. 151.

§6.2 Defect in service. If there is a defect in the service, the court can either dismiss the suit or quash the defective service and permit the plaintiff to re-serve the defendant. Dismissal for failure to serve is generally without prejudice. *See **Saez Rivera v. Nissan Mfg.***, 788 F.2d 819, 821 (1st Cir.1986). But dismissal with prejudice may be appropriate if the plaintiff has repeatedly failed to cure service defects or has been lax in trying to serve the defendant. *Cf. **Betty K Agencies, Ltd. v. M/V Monada***, 432 F.3d 1333, 1340-41 (11th Cir.2005) (dismissal with prejudice under FRCP 41(b) for defect in service under FRCP 4(m) is appropriate only when there is clear pattern of delay or willful contempt and lesser sanctions are inadequate).

1. Defective service. If the service was defective but curable, the court will quash service with leave to re-serve. *See **Umbenhauer v. Woog***, 969 F.2d 25, 30 (3d Cir.1992); ***Gregory v. U.S.***, 942 F.2d 1498, 1500 (10th Cir. 1991). Not all circuits are this lenient; some treat defective service as a matter for the court's discretion. *See **Adams v. AlliedSignal Gen. Aviation Avionics***, 74 F.3d 882, 886 (8th Cir.1996).

2. Late service. If the plaintiff shows good cause for late service, the court must grant the plaintiff an extension of time. FRCP 4(m); ***Panaras v. Liquid Carbonic Indus.***, 94 F.3d 338, 340 (7th Cir.1996); ***Adams***, 74 F.3d at 887; 1993 Notes to FRCP 4 at ¶63, p. 1144, this book; *see also **MCI Telecomms. Corp. v. Teleconcepts, Inc.***, 71 F.3d 1086, 1097 (3d Cir.1995) (absence of prejudice cannot by itself be good cause for late service). If the plaintiff cannot show good cause for late service, the court may extend the time to serve. FRCP 4(m); ***Henderson v. U.S.***, 517 U.S. 654, 662 (1996); 1993 Notes to FRCP 4 at ¶63, p. 1144, this book. The court may either dismiss the suit without prejudice or direct that service be made within a specified time. FRCP 4(m); ***Henderson***, 517 U.S. at 662-63 & n.10; ***Panaras***, 94 F.3d at 340; ***Adams***, 74 F.3d at 887. See "Motion to extend time to serve," ch. 2-H, §4.2, p. 153; "Motion to extend time to serve party," ch. 5-F, §4.3, p. 334.

§7. APPELLATE REVIEW

On appeal, the court reviews a dismissal under FRCP 12(b)(4) or 12(b)(5) for abuse of discretion. *See **George v. U.S. Dept. of Labor***, 788 F.2d 1115, 1116 (5th Cir.1986).

§7.1 Appealability.

1. Orders quashing service. An order quashing service of process is not a final order and is not appealable until a final judgment is entered. ***Stevens v. Security Pac. Nat'l Bank***, 538 F.2d 1387, 1388 (9th Cir.1976).

2. Dismissal orders.

(1) Single defendant. If the case is dismissed based on the motion of the only defendant in the case, the order is appealable.

(2) Multiple defendants. If a case is dismissed for all served defendants and only unserved defendants remain in the suit, the order may be final and appealable under 28 U.S.C. §1291. ***Patchick v. Kensington Publ'g***, 743 F.2d 675, 677 (9th Cir.1984). But if there are other defendants who have been served but have not answered, the dismissal order is not appealable. *E.g., id.* (when D1 and D2 were dismissed for lack of personal jurisdiction but D3 had been served and claimed service was improper, order dismissing D1 and D2 was not appealable until service dispute was resolved in favor of D3 or case was dismissed for D3).

§7.2 Standard of review. The district court's ruling on a motion to dismiss for insufficient process or service is generally reviewed for abuse of discretion. ***Nafziger v. McDermott Int'l***, 467 F.3d 514, 521 (6th Cir.2006); ***Thompson v. Maldonado***, 309 F.3d 107, 110 (2d Cir.2002); *see **Millan v. USAA Gen. Indem. Co.***, 546 F.3d 321, 326 (5th

Cir.2008). However, when a suit is dismissed without prejudice and the statute of limitations likely bars refiling the suit—effectively resulting in a dismissal with prejudice—a heightened standard of review may apply. ***Millan***, 546 F.3d at 326. The heightened standard limits the court's discretion and allows dismissal only when there is a clear record of delay or "contumacious conduct" by the plaintiff and lesser sanctions are inadequate. *See id.* See "Statute of limitations has run," ch. 7-D, §6.4.2(1), p. 649.

H. MOTION FOR MORE DEFINITE STATEMENT—FRCP 12(e)

§1. GENERAL

§1.1 Rule. FRCP 12(e).

§1.2 Purpose. If a plaintiff files a complaint so vague or ambiguous that the defendant cannot frame a responsive pleading, the defendant (instead of attempting to respond to the suit) may file a motion asking the court to require the plaintiff to amend its complaint with a more definite statement. ***Havens Rlty. Corp. v. Coleman***, 455 U.S. 363, 383 (1982) (Powell, J., concurring). However, motions for a more definite statement are not favored by the courts. ***Guess?, Inc. v. Chang***, 912 F.Supp. 372, 381 (N.D.Ill.1995); ***Taylor v. Cox***, 912 F.Supp. 140, 143 (E.D.Pa.1995). *But see* ***Davis v. Coca-Cola Bottling Co. Consol.***, 516 F.3d 955, 983-84 (11th Cir.2008) (motion for more definite statement should be made in response to "shotgun" pleadings).

§1.3 Forms. ***O'Connor's Federal Civil Forms*** (2012), FORMS 3H.

§1.4 Other references. 5C Wright & Miller, *Federal Practice & Procedure 3d* §§1374-1379 (2004 & Supp.2012); 2 *Moore's Federal Practice 3d* §12.36 (2012).

§2. MOTION

In a motion for a more definite statement, the defendant must identify the defects in the complaint and the details it wants the plaintiff to include. FRCP 12(e).

§2.1 Form. For the general requirements for the form of a motion, see "Drafting motions," ch. 1-B, §3.1, p. 14.

§2.2 In writing or on court's initiative. The motion should be in writing. *See* FRCP 7(b)(1). However, the court may strike a complaint and order a more definite statement on its own initiative. *See* ***Davis v. Coca-Cola Bottling Co. Consol.***, 516 F.3d 955, 984 (11th Cir.2008).

§2.3 Grounds. A motion for a more definite statement is appropriate only when the complaint is so unintelligible that a responsive pleading cannot be framed. ***Bureerong v. Uvawas***, 922 F.Supp. 1450, 1461 (C.D.Cal.1996); ***Taylor v. Cox***, 912 F.Supp. 140, 143 (E.D.Pa.1995). In the motion, the defendant can assert the following arguments.

NOTE

Whether and to what extent the ***Iqbal*** *and* ***Twombly*** *decisions have affected the FRCP 12(e) standard is an open question.* ***Williamson v. Munsen Paving, LLC****, No. 09-cv-736-AC (D.Or. 2009) (slip op.; 11-6-09) (footnote 1).*

1. **Not able to answer.** The defendant is not able to frame a response to the plaintiff's complaint because the complaint is too vague or ambiguous. FRCP 12(e); ***Sisk v. Texas Parks & Wildlife Dept.***, 644 F.2d 1056, 1059 (5th Cir.1981); *see* FRCP 8(a)(2); ***Martin v. Malhoyt***, 830 F.2d 237, 261 n.74 (D.C.Cir.1987).

2. **Particularized pleading.** The plaintiff is required to plead the matters in its complaint specifically and cannot rely on fair-notice allegations for the type of claims the plaintiff is alleging against the defendant. See "Particularized pleadings," ch. 2-B, §5.2, p. 82.

§2.4 Identify defects. FRCP 12(e) requires the defendant to identify the defects in the complaint and the details it wants to be included. *See* ***Pits, Ltd. v. American Express Bank Int'l***, 911 F.Supp. 710, 720 (S.D.N.Y.1996).

PRACTICE TIP

*If a specific fact is not included in a complaint and it may be dispositive (e.g., a specific date for the defense of limitations or exhaustion of administrative remedies), the defendant should file a motion for a more definite statement asking for that specific fact. See **Casanova v. Ulibarri**, 595 F.3d 1120, 1125 (10th Cir.2010); 5C Wright & Miller §1376.*

§2.5 Deadline.

1. Within time to answer. The defendant should make a motion for a more definite statement within the time limits prescribed for the answer. *See* FRCP 12(e). See "Deadlines," ch. 3-A, §5, p. 174. Because the purpose of this motion is to require the plaintiff to file an intelligible complaint, the motion must be filed before any other responsive pleading. FRCP 12(e).

2. Tolls time for other responses. While the motion is pending, the defendant's time to file responsive pleadings is tolled. FRCP 12(a)(4)(B). See "FRCP 12 motion filed," ch. 3-A, §5.2.1, p. 175.

§3. RESPONSE

§3.1 Grounds.

1. Fair notice & plausibility. The plaintiff should argue that the complaint provides fair notice of its claim and that the facts alleged sufficiently show a plausible claim for relief. *See **Ashcroft v. Iqbal***, 556 U.S. 662, 678 (2009); ***Bell Atlantic Corp. v. Twombly***, 550 U.S. 544, 555-56 (2007). See "Statement of Claim," ch. 2-B, §5, p. 80.

2. Substitute for discovery. The plaintiff may argue that the defendant is improperly attempting to use FRCP 12(e) as a substitute for discovery. If the information sought by the defendant is obtainable through the discovery process, a motion for more definite statement is inappropriate and should be denied. *See **Sagan v. Apple Computer, Inc.***, 874 F.Supp. 1072, 1077 (C.D.Cal.1994); ***Moore v. Fidelity Fin. Serv.***, 869 F.Supp. 557, 560 (N.D.Ill.1994).

3. Failure to identify defects. The plaintiff may argue that the defendant did not meet the requirements of FRCP 12(e)—that is, the defendant did not identify the defects in the complaint or the details desired. *See **Pits, Ltd. v. American Express Bank Int'l***, 911 F.Supp. 710, 720 (S.D.N.Y.1996).

4. Disfavored motion. The plaintiff should emphasize that motions for a more definite statement are disfavored and are granted only when the challenged complaint is so unintelligible that a responsive pleading cannot be framed. ***Guess?, Inc. v. Chang***, 912 F.Supp. 372, 381 (N.D.Ill.1995); ***Taylor v. Cox***, 912 F.Supp. 140, 143 (E.D. Pa.1995); ***Delta Educ., Inc. v. Langlois***, 719 F.Supp. 42, 50 (D.N.H.1989); *see **One Indus. v. Jim O'Neal Distrib.***, 578 F.3d 1154, 1160 (9th Cir.2009); 5C Wright & Miller §1376. The plaintiff should explain why its complaint is sufficient—that is, a responsive pleading can be framed because the defendant can either admit or deny the complaint's allegations.

§3.2 Amended pleading. The plaintiff should consider filing an amended pleading in addition to—or possibly instead of—a response. If the plaintiff has not already amended once as a "matter of course" (i.e., 21 days after serving its complaint), the plaintiff can amend—without the court's leave or the opposing party's consent—within the earlier of 21 days after the defendant's answer or FRCP 12(e) motion is served. *See* FRCP 15(a)(1)(B). See "Deadline," ch. 5-I, §3.1.1, p. 345. When leave is necessary, the plaintiff's response should request that, if the court grants the motion to dismiss, it should also grant the plaintiff leave to amend. See "Motion for Leave to Amend," ch. 5-I, §5, p. 351.

§4. HEARING

The motion and response will probably be considered based on the written submissions, without a hearing.

§5. RULING

§5.1 Denies motion. If the court denies the motion, the defendant must file its responsive pleading. See "The Answer—Denying Liability," ch. 3-L, p. 230.

§5.2 Grants motion. If the court grants the motion, the plaintiff must replead within 14 days after notice of the order or as scheduled by the court. FRCP 12(e). If the plaintiff does not obey the order by the 14-day deadline, the court may strike the complaint. FRCP 12(e).

§6. APPELLATE REVIEW

A ruling on an FRCP 12(e) motion for a more definite statement is reviewed for abuse of discretion. ***Old Time Enters. v. International Coffee Corp.***, 862 F.2d 1213, 1217 (5th Cir.1989).

I. MOTION TO DISMISS FOR FAILURE TO JOIN A PARTY UNDER FRCP 19—FRCP 12(b)(7)

§1. GENERAL

§1.1 Rules. FRCP 12(b)(7), 19.

§1.2 Purpose. The purpose of an FRCP 12(b)(7) motion to dismiss is to challenge the plaintiff's failure to join a required party under FRCP 19. The purpose of FRCP 19, which requires joinder of a party whose absence would prevent the existing parties from being granted complete relief, is to protect the legitimate interests of absent parties and to discourage duplicate litigation. ***Askew v. Sheriff of Cook Cty.***, 568 F.3d 632, 634 (7th Cir.2009); ***U.S. v. Rose***, 34 F.3d 901, 908 (9th Cir.1994).

NOTE

In 2007, as part of the restyling amendments, FRCP 19(b) was amended to delete the word "indispensable" as redundant. 2007 Notes to FRCP 19 at ¶1, p. 1164, this book. This style amendment did not change the substantive meaning of the rule. ***Republic of the Phil. v. Pimentel****, 553 U.S. 851, 855-56 (2008); see 2007 Notes to FRCP 1 at ¶1, p. 1137, this book. The term "indispensable" was imprecise because a supposedly indispensable person could be dispensable—that is, after evaluating a suit under FRCP 19(b), the suit could proceed without that person.* ***Pimentel****, 553 U.S. at 863; see* ***Schlumberger Indus. v. National Sur. Corp.****, 36 F.3d 1274, 1285-86 (4th Cir.1994) (all indispensable parties are necessary, but not all necessary parties are indispensable); see also* ***Jiménez v. Rodríguez-Pagán****, 597 F.3d 18, 25 n.3 (1st Cir.2010) (despite change to rule language, court continues to use term "necessary" because it is term of art);* ***CP Solutions PTE, Ltd. v. General Elec. Co.****, 553 F.3d 156, 159 n.2 (2d Cir.2009) (despite change to rule language, court continues to use term "indispensable" for convenience). The term "required" is similarly imprecise.* ***Pimentel****, 553 U.S. at 863. In this subchapter, we use the term "required" instead of "necessary" or "indispensable" because of the amendments to the rule; cases issued before the amendment are still cited when the substance of the proposition remains unchanged.*

---

§1.3 Forms. *O'Connor's Federal Civil Forms* (2012), FORMS 3I.

§1.4 Other references. 5C Wright & Miller, *Federal Practice & Procedure 3d* §1359 (2004 & Supp.2012); 7 Wright, Miller & Kane, *Federal Practice & Procedure 3d* §§1601-1626 (2001 & Supp.2012); 2 *Moore's Federal Practice 3d* §12.35 (2012).

§2. MOTION

§2.1 Form. For the general requirements for the form of a motion, see "Drafting motions," ch. 1-B, §3.1, p. 14.

§2.2 In writing. The motion to dismiss should be in writing. *See* FRCP 7(b)(1).

§2.3 Grounds. FRCP 19(a) provides the test to determine when a person is required—that is, when the person must be joined if feasible. *See* FRCP 19; ***Republic of the Phil. v. Pimentel***, 553 U.S. 851, 862 (2008). When joinder of a required person is not feasible, FRCP 19(b) provides the test to determine whether the suit should proceed without that person or should be dismissed. *See* ***Pimentel***, 553 U.S. at 862. The court's determination under FRCP 19(a) and (b) is flexible. *See* ***Picciotto v. Continental Cas. Co.***, 512 F.3d 9, 14-15 (1st Cir.2008). The defendant's motion to dismiss for failure to join a required party must allege that (1) the absent party is required for the suit to proceed, (2) the absent party cannot be joined, and (3) the suit cannot proceed in equity and good conscience without the absent party. FRCP 19(a), (b).

1. Absent party is required. An absent party is required for the litigation in either of the following instances:

(1) Complete relief is not possible among the existing parties. FRCP 19(a)(1)(A); ***School Dist. of Pontiac v. Secretary of the U.S. Dept. of Educ.***, 584 F.3d 253, 265 (6th Cir.2009); ***City of Marietta v. CSX Transp.***, 196 F.3d 1300, 1305 (11th Cir.1999); *e.g.*, ***Dawavendewa v. Salt River Project Agric. Imprv. & Power Dist.***, 276 F.3d 1150, 1155 (9th Cir.2002) (P sought injunctive relief to prevent enforcement of Navajo hiring preferences as required by lease with Navajo Nation; absent nation-party could enforce hiring preferences, so complete relief was not possible); ***Janney Montgomery Scott, Inc. v. Shepard Niles, Inc.***, 11 F.3d 399, 405-06 (3d Cir.1993) (because both obligors were jointly and severally liable under contract, complete relief could be granted when only one obligor was party to suit).

(2) The absent party has a legally protected interest related to the subject of the suit. FRCP 19(a)(1)(B); ***Dawavendewa***, 276 F.3d at 1155. The "interest" requirement of FRCP 19(a)(1)(B) is not limited to a legal interest; it is determined from a practical perspective not limited by strict legal definitions and technicalities. ***Aguilar v. Los Angeles Cty.***, 751 F.2d 1089, 1093 (9th Cir.1985); *see* ***Huber v. Taylor***, 532 F.3d 237, 249-50 (3d Cir. 2008). The defendant must allege that disposition of the suit without the absent party would do one of the following:

(a) Impair or impede, as a practical matter, the absent party's ability to protect its interest in the suit. FRCP 19(a)(1)(B)(i); ***School Dist. of Pontiac***, 584 F.3d at 266; ***Dawavendewa***, 276 F.3d at 1155; ***City of Marietta***, 196 F.3d at 1305; ***Janney Montgomery Scott, Inc.***, 11 F.3d at 406.

(b) Leave an existing party subject to a substantial risk of incurring double, multiple, or otherwise inconsistent obligations because of the interest. FRCP 19(a)(1)(B)(ii); ***School Dist. of Pontiac***, 584 F.3d at 266-67; ***City of Marietta***, 196 F.3d at 1305; ***U.S. v. Rose***, 34 F.3d 901, 908 (9th Cir.1994); ***Janney Montgomery Scott, Inc.***, 11 F.3d at 411-12.

2. Absent party cannot be joined. If the absent party is required, the court must determine whether the party can be joined in the litigation. ***Janney Montgomery Scott, Inc.***, 11 F.3d at 404. The party cannot be joined if (1) it cannot be served (i.e., it is beyond the personal jurisdiction of the court), (2) its presence would deprive the court of subject-matter jurisdiction, or (3) it has a valid objection to venue. *See* FRCP 19(a)(1), (a)(3); ***Askew v. Sheriff of Cook Cty.***, 568 F.3d 632, 634-35 (7th Cir.2009).

3. Suit cannot proceed in equity & good conscience. Once the court has determined that the absent party is required but cannot feasibly be joined in the litigation, it must determine whether in equity and good conscience the suit should proceed with the existing parties or should be dismissed. FRCP 19(b). Whether a suit should proceed without the required party is determined by the factors in FRCP 19(b). ***Pimentel***, 553 U.S. at 862. But the FRCP 19(b) factors are nonexclusive. *See* ***Pimentel***, 553 U.S. at 862-63 (appropriate factors are determined on case-by-case basis); ***CP Solutions PTE, Ltd. v. General Elec. Co.***, 553 F.3d 156, 159 (2d Cir.2009) (standard for FRCP 19(b) is flexible).

(1) A judgment rendered in the party's absence will be prejudicial to that party or to the existing parties. FRCP 19(b)(1); ***Pimentel***, 553 U.S. at 865; ***Schlumberger Indus. v. National Sur. Corp.***, 36 F.3d 1274, 1287 (4th Cir.1994); ***Pit River Home & Agric. Coop. v. U.S.***, 30 F.3d 1088, 1101 (9th Cir.1994). The likelihood of a future

event does not necessarily make all parties who might be affected by that event required parties under FRCP 19. ***McLaughlin v. International Ass'n of Mach.***, 847 F.2d 620, 621 (9th Cir.1988).

(2) The prejudice to the absent party cannot be lessened or avoided by protective provisions in the judgment, by shaping the relief, or by any other measures. FRCP 19(b)(2); ***Pimentel***, 553 U.S. at 869; ***Schlumberger Indus.***, 36 F.3d at 1287; ***Pit River***, 30 F.3d at 1101.

(3) A judgment rendered in the party's absence will not be adequate. FRCP 19(b)(3); ***Pimentel***, 553 U.S. at 870; ***Schlumberger Indus.***, 36 F.3d at 1287; ***Pit River***, 30 F.3d at 1101. Adequacy refers to the public interest in settling a dispute in its entirety, thus avoiding multiple litigation. ***Pimentel***, 553 U.S. at 870.

(4) The plaintiff will have an adequate remedy if the suit is dismissed for nonjoinder. FRCP 19(b)(4); ***Pimentel***, 553 U.S. at 871; ***Schlumberger Indus.***, 36 F.3d at 1287; ***Pit River***, 30 F.3d at 1101. However, the lack of an alternative forum does not automatically prevent dismissal of the suit. ***Pimentel***, 553 U.S. at 872; ***Pit River***, 30 F.3d at 1102.

§2.4 Deadline. The defendant should assert an objection under FRCP 19(a) (i.e., to the absence of a required party whose joinder is feasible) in its answer or in a preanswer motion. *See* FRCP 12(h)(2). The defendant may assert the defense of failure to join a required party under FRCP 19(b) (i.e., to the absence of a required party who cannot feasibly be joined) in any pleading permitted under FRCP 7(a), in a motion for judgment on the pleadings, or at trial. FRCP 12(h)(2); *see* FRCP 12(b); ***Symes v. Harris***, 472 F.3d 754, 760 (10th Cir.2006); ***Manning v. Energy Conversion Devices, Inc.***, 13 F.3d 606, 609 (2d Cir.1994); *see also* ***Bowling Transp. v. NLRB***, 352 F.3d 274, 281 (6th Cir. 2003) (appellate court can raise issue sua sponte). Dismissals based on FRCP 19(b) are rarely appropriate, however, when the objection is first made at the end of the case. ***National Ass'n of Chain Drug Stores v. New England Carpenters Health Benefits Fund***, 582 F.3d 30, 43 (1st Cir.2009).

§2.5 Extrinsic evidence. In ruling on a motion to dismiss for failure to join a required party, a court may go outside the pleadings and look to extrinsic evidence such as affidavits or documents. ***Davis Cos. v. Emerald Casino, Inc.***, 268 F.3d 477, 480 n.4 (7th Cir.2001); *see* ***McShan v. Sherrill***, 283 F.2d 462, 463-64 (9th Cir.1960).

§2.6 Burden. The defendant has the burden of producing evidence identifying the scope and nature of the absent party's interest in the litigation and showing that the protection of that interest will be impaired by the party's absence. ***American Gen. Life & Acc. Ins. v. Wood***, 429 F.3d 83, 92 (4th Cir.2005); ***Citizen Band Potawatomi Indian Tribe v. Collier***, 17 F.3d 1292, 1293 (10th Cir.1994).

§2.7 Waiver. Although a defendant can raise the defense under FRCP 19(b) (i.e., to the absence of a required party who cannot feasibly be joined) as late as at trial, the defendant waives the defense under FRCP 19(a) (i.e., to the absence of a required party whose joinder is feasible) if it does not raise the objection in its answer or in a preanswer motion. *See* FRCP 12(b), (h)(2); ***Manning v. Energy Conversion Devices, Inc.***, 13 F.3d 606, 609 (2d Cir. 1994); ***State Farm Mut. Auto. Ins. v. Mid-Continent Cas. Co.***, 518 F.2d 292, 294 (10th Cir.1975); *see also* 7 Wright, Miller & Kane §1609 (noting that FRCP 19(a) objection can be waived, but criticizing waiver as inconsistent with FRCP 19's objective). See "Deadline," §2.4, this page. However, the court on its own initiative at any time can consider the absence of a required party who cannot be feasibly joined under FRCP 19(b). *See* ***Republic of the Phil. v. Pimentel***, 553 U.S. 851, 861 (2008); ***National Ass'n of Chain Drug Stores v. New England Carpenters Health Benefits Fund***, 582 F.3d 30, 43 (1st Cir.2009).

§3. RESPONSE

§3.1 In writing. The plaintiff's response should be in writing. *See* FRCP 7(b)(1).

§3.2 Grounds. In addition to negating the allegations in the defendant's motion, the plaintiff may challenge an FRCP 12(b)(7) motion on several grounds.

1. Public-rights litigation. If the suit seeks to vindicate a public right, the plaintiff may argue that third persons who could be adversely affected by a decision favorable to the plaintiff are not required parties. ***Kickapoo Tribe of Indians of the Kickapoo Reservation in Kan. v. Babbitt***, 43 F.3d 1491, 1500 (D.C.Cir.1995); *see* ***National***

Licorice Co. v. NLRB, 309 U.S. 350, 362-63 (1940). Public-rights litigation generally involves issues of public concern and requires joinder of a large number of people. ***Kickapoo Tribe***, 43 F.3d at 1500.

2. Impleader. An absent party who can be impleaded by the defendant is never considered a required party. ***EEOC v. Peabody W. Coal Co.***, 610 F.3d 1070, 1086-87 (9th Cir.2010); ***Pasco Int'l (London) v. Stenograph Corp.***, 637 F.2d 496, 505 n.20 (7th Cir.1980). Therefore, the plaintiff may challenge a defendant's FRCP 12(b)(7) motion on the ground that the absent party can be impleaded. See "Third-party claim," ch. 3-L, §5.3, p. 236.

§3.3 Amended pleading. The plaintiff should consider filing an amended pleading in addition to—or possibly instead of—a response. If the plaintiff has not already amended once as a "matter of course" (i.e., 21 days after serving its complaint), the plaintiff can amend—without the court's leave or the opposing party's consent—within the earlier of 21 days after the defendant's answer or FRCP 12(b)(7) motion is served. *See* FRCP 15(a)(1)(B). See "Deadline," ch. 5-I, §3.1.1, p. 345. When leave is necessary, the plaintiff's response should request that, if the court grants the motion to dismiss, it should also grant the plaintiff leave to amend. See "Motion for Leave to Amend," ch. 5-I, §5, p. 351.

§3.4 Deadline. The FRCPs do not provide a deadline for filing a response to an FRCP 12(b)(7) motion. The plaintiff should check the local rules of the district court where the case is pending.

§4. HEARING

The motion and response will probably be considered based on the written submissions, without a hearing.

§5. RULING

The court must make the following determinations before issuing its ruling:

§5.1 Is absent party required? If a party is required for the litigation under FRCP 19(a)(1), the party should be joined, if joinder is possible. *See* FRCP 19(a)(2); ***Salt River Project Agric. Imprv. & Power Dist. v. Lee***, 672 F.3d 1176, 1179 (9th Cir.2012); ***Askew v. Sheriff of Cook Cty.***, 568 F.3d 632, 635 (7th Cir.2009). If the party is not required for the litigation, the court should deny the motion to dismiss. See "Absent party is required," §2.3.1, p. 215.

§5.2 Can absent party be joined?

1. Required party can be joined. If the required party would not deprive the court of subject-matter jurisdiction and is subject to service, the party can be joined; thus, the court must order the party to be joined and deny the motion to dismiss. *See* FRCP 19(a); ***Salt River Project Agric. Imprv. & Power Dist. v. Lee***, 672 F.3d 1176, 1179 (9th Cir.2012); ***Askew v. Sheriff of Cook Cty.***, 568 F.3d 632, 635 (7th Cir.2009).

(1) Required party refuses to join. If the required party can be joined but refuses to be joined as a plaintiff, the court can make the required party either a defendant or an involuntary plaintiff. FRCP 19(a)(2); ***Askew***, 568 F.3d at 635; *see* ***Abbott Labs. v. Diamedix Corp.***, 47 F.3d 1128, 1133 (Fed.Cir.1995).

(2) Required party has valid objection to venue. If the required party objects to venue and joinder would render venue improper, the court must dismiss the required party. FRCP 19(a)(3); ***Askew***, 568 F.3d at 635.

2. Required party cannot be joined. If the required party would deprive the court of subject-matter jurisdiction or is not subject to service, the party cannot be joined and the court must determine whether the suit can proceed in equity and good conscience. FRCP 19(a), (b).

§5.3 Can suit proceed in equity & good conscience? If the required party cannot be joined in the litigation but the suit can proceed in equity and good conscience, the court must deny the motion to dismiss. *See* FRCP 19(b); ***Salt River Project Agric. Imprv. & Power Dist. v. Lee***, 672 F.3d 1176, 1179 (9th Cir.2012). See "Suit cannot proceed in equity & good conscience," §2.3.3, p. 215. If the suit cannot proceed in equity and good conscience without the required party, the court must dismiss the suit. *See* FRCP 19(b). As an alternative to dismissal, however, the court can order the plaintiff to amend its pleadings by restructuring the requested relief, thus changing the status of the absent party to that of a required party under FRCP 19(a). 7 Wright, Miller & Kane §1609; *see* ***Jota v. Texaco Inc.***,

157 F.3d 153, 162 (2d Cir.1998) (P can restructure relief to lessen or avoid prejudice to absent party under FRCP 19(b), now FRCP 19(b)(2)). When the party's status is changed, the court is required to join the party only if feasible; therefore, dismissal is not necessary. *See* ***Jota***, 157 F.3d at 162.

§6. APPELLATE REVIEW

§6.1 Abuse of discretion. Generally, the district court's ruling on a motion to dismiss for failure to join a required party is reviewed for abuse of discretion. ***Cachil Dehe Band of Wintun Indians of the Colusa Indian Cmty. v. California***, 547 F.3d 962, 969 (9th Cir.2008); ***Dixon v. Edwards***, 290 F.3d 699, 710 (4th Cir.2002); ***Jota v. Texaco Inc.***, 157 F.3d 153, 161 (2d Cir.1998); ***Kickapoo Tribe of Indians of the Kickapoo Reservation in Kan. v. Babbitt***, 43 F.3d 1491, 1495 (D.C.Cir.1995); *see also* ***Republic of the Phil. v. Pimentel***, 553 U.S. 851, 864 (2008) (Supreme Court declined to specify standard of review under FRCP 19(b) but noted that review should provide some degree of deference to district court); ***Askew v. Sheriff of Cook Cty.***, 568 F.3d 632, 634 (7th Cir.2009) (7th Circuit is undecided on whether standard of review under FRCP 19 is de novo or for abuse of discretion).

§6.2 De novo. To the extent that dismissal under FRCP 12(b)(7) and FRCP 19 involves conclusions of law, the court of appeals reviews the decision de novo. ***Cachil Dehe Band of Wintun Indians of the Colusa Indian Cmty. v. California***, 547 F.3d 962, 970 (9th Cir.2008); ***Janney Montgomery Scott, Inc. v. Shepard Niles, Inc.***, 11 F.3d 399, 404 (3d Cir.1993). Any subsidiary findings of fact are reviewed only for clear error. ***Janney Montgomery Scott, Inc.***, 11 F.3d at 404.

J. MOTION TO DISMISS FOR FAILURE TO PLEAD PROPERLY—FRCP 8, 9(b)

§1. GENERAL

§1.1 Rules. FRCP 8(a), 8(d)(1), 9(b), 12(e), (f).

§1.2 Purpose.

1. **FRCP 8.** Under FRCP 8(a), pleadings must include a "short and plain" statement of the grounds for jurisdiction, the claims presented, and the relief sought. *See* ***Swierkiewicz v. Sorema***, 534 U.S. 506, 512 (2002). Under FRCP 8(d)(1), pleadings must be "simple, concise, and direct." *See* ***Swierkiewicz***, 534 U.S. at 512. The purpose of a motion to dismiss under either of these rules is to ensure that the defendant is given at least minimal notice of the plaintiff's claims. ***Vicom, Inc. v. Harbridge Merchant Servs.***, 20 F.3d 771, 775 (7th Cir.1994); *see also* ***Swierkiewicz***, 534 U.S. at 514 (FRCP 8 is starting point of simplified pleading system adopted to focus litigation on merits of claim); ***Jennings v. Emry***, 910 F.2d 1434, 1436 (7th Cir.1990) (complaint must be presented with enough clarity to avoid requiring D to sift through pages searching for what P asserts).

2. **FRCP 9(b).** Under FRCP 9(b), allegations of fraud or mistake must state the circumstances constituting the fraud or mistake "with particularity." FRCP 9(b) ensures that the defendant can effectively respond to the plaintiff's allegations, prevents the filing of baseless complaints, and protects defendants from unfounded allegations of wrongdoing that might injure their reputations. ***Hernandez v. Ciba-Geigy Corp.***, 200 F.R.D. 285, 290 (S.D.Tex. 2001); *see* ***U.S. v. Medco Health Solutions, Inc.***, 671 F.3d 1217, 1222 (11th Cir.2012). The pleading requirements under FRCP 9(b) are more rigorous than those under FRCP 8. ***Leatherman v. Tarrant Cty. Narcotics Intelligence & Coordination Unit***, 507 U.S. 163, 168 (1993).

§1.3 Forms. *O'Connor's Federal Civil Forms* (2012), FORMS 3J.

§1.4 Other references. 5, 5A Wright & Miller, *Federal Practice & Procedure 3d* §§1281, 1296-1301.1 (2004 & Supp.2012); 2 *Moore's Federal Practice 3d* chs. 8, 9 (2012).

§2. MOTION

§2.1 Form. For the general requirements for the form of a motion, see "Drafting motions," ch. 1-B, §3.1, p. 14.

§2.2 In writing. The motion should be in writing. *See* FRCP 7(b)(1); *see also* FRCP 12(f)(1) (court may strike redundant, immaterial, impertinent, or scandalous matters on its own initiative).

§2.3 Consolidation with FRCP 12 objections.

1. FRCP 8 objections. The defendant may consolidate objections under FRCP 8 with objections under FRCP 12(e) (motion for more definite statement) or FRCP 12(f) (motion to strike redundant material), or the defendant may serve the FRCP 8 objections separately. *See* ***McHenry v. Renne***, 84 F.3d 1172, 1179 (9th Cir.1996) (FRCP 8(d) applies to good claims as well as bad and is basis for dismissal independent of FRCP 12(b)(6)); ***Salahuddin v. Cuomo***, 861 F.2d 40, 42 (2d Cir.1988) (when complaint does not comply with FRCP 8, court may strike any redundant or immaterial portions under FRCP 12(f) or dismiss complaint); ***Security First Bank v. Burlington N. & Santa Fe Ry.***, 213 F.Supp.2d 1087, 1093 (D.Neb.2002) (usual procedure for raising FRCP 8(a) objection is by motion for more definite statement under FRCP 12(e)); ***Smith v. Oppenheimer & Co.***, 635 F.Supp. 936, 938-39 (W.D.Mich.1985) (complaint that is "prolix" and "amorphous" and does not meet standards of pleading under FRCP 8(a) and 8(d)(1) may justify motion to strike under FRCP 12(f)); *see also* ***BJC Health Sys. v. Columbia Cas. Co.***, 478 F.3d 908, 917 (8th Cir.2007) (court has liberal discretion to strike pleading under FRCP 12(f)); ***Ohio Cas. Ins. v. Continental Cas. Co.***, 279 F.Supp.2d 1281, 1283 (S.D.Fla.2003) (reciting standards of review for motions to dismiss under FRCP 8(a)). See "Motion for More Definite Statement—FRCP 12(e)," ch. 3-H, p. 212. If the grounds are consolidated under FRCP 12(f), the motion must be made before responding to the plaintiff's complaint. *See* FRCP 12(f)(2).

2. FRCP 9(b) objections. Because the standards of review are identical, the defendant may consolidate objections under FRCP 9(b) with objections under FRCP 12(b)(6) (motion for failure to state a claim), or the defendant may serve the FRCP 9 objections separately. *See* ***Vess v. Ciba-Geigy Corp. USA***, 317 F.3d 1097, 1107-08 (9th Cir. 2003) (dismissal under FRCP 9(b) is treated the same as dismissal under FRCP 12(b)(6)); ***Lovelace v. Software Spectrum, Inc.***, 78 F.3d 1015, 1017 (5th Cir.1996) (same); ***Seattle-First Nat'l Bank v. Carlstedt***, 800 F.2d 1008, 1011 (10th Cir.1986) (same); *see also* 5A Wright & Miller §1300 (FRCP 9(b) does not explicitly provide for motion challenging insufficient particularity; thus, challenge is usually included in motion to dismiss for failure to state a claim, motion for more definite statement, or motion to strike). See "Standard," ch. 3-F, §5.1, p. 207.

§2.4 Grounds.

1. FRCP 8(a)(1). A motion under FRCP 8(a)(1) should allege that the complaint does not include a "short and plain" statement of the grounds supporting jurisdiction and that nothing else in the complaint reveals a proper basis for jurisdiction. *See* ***Williams v. U.S.***, 405 F.2d 951, 954 (9th Cir.1969); ***Hardy v. National Kinney***, 565 F.Supp. 1027, 1029 (N.D.Cal.1983).

2. FRCP 8(a)(2). A motion under FRCP 8(a)(2) should allege that the complaint does not include a "short and plain" statement of the plaintiff's claims. *See* ***Stanard v. Nygren***, 658 F.3d 792, 797-98 (7th Cir.2011); ***Cafasso v. General Dynamics C4 Sys.***, 637 F.3d 1047, 1058-59 (9th Cir.2011). A defendant should not file a motion to dismiss under FRCP 8 on the ground that the complaint contains extraneous matters unless the additional matters are actually prejudicial to the defendant's defense. *See* ***Davis v. Ruby Foods, Inc.***, 269 F.3d 818, 821 (7th Cir.2001) (dicta); *see also* ***Hearns v. San Bernardino Police Dept.***, 530 F.3d 1124, 1131 (9th Cir.2008) (verbosity or length by itself is not basis for dismissal under FRCP 8(a)).

3. FRCP 8(a)(3). A motion under FRCP 8(a)(3) should allege that the complaint does not include a demand for relief or damages. *See* ***Seven Words LLC v. Network Solutions***, 260 F.3d 1089, 1097-98 (9th Cir.2001).

4. FRCP 8(d)(1). A motion under FRCP 8(d)(1) should allege that the plaintiff's allegations are not "simple, concise, and direct." *See, e.g.,* ***McPhee v. Simonds Saw & Steel Co.***, 294 F.Supp. 779, 783 (W.D.Wis.1969) (motion to dismiss under FRCP 8(e)(1), now FRCP 8(d)(1), stated that complaint was "verbose, confusing and redundant").

5. FRCP 9(b). A motion under FRCP 9(b) should allege that the plaintiff did not plead the circumstances constituting fraud or mistake "with particularity." *See* ***In re Stac Elecs. Secs. Litig.***, 89 F.3d 1399, 1405 (9th Cir. 1996); ***J. Geils Band Empl. Benefit Plan v. Smith Barney Shearson, Inc.***, 76 F.3d 1245, 1255 (1st Cir.1996); *see also* ***U.S. v. Columbia/HCA Healthcare Corp.***, 125 F.3d 899, 901 (5th Cir.1997) (motion to dismiss under FRCP 9(b)

is in essence a motion to dismiss under FRCP 12(b)(6)). The motion should allege that the plaintiff's allegations of fraud do not include the who, what, when, where, and how of the false representations. ***In re Healthcare Compare Corp. Sec. Litig.***, 75 F.3d 276, 281 (7th Cir.1996); *see* ***U.S. v. Medco Health Solutions, Inc.***, 671 F.3d 1217, 1222 (11th Cir.2012). Because the circuits apply different standards for specificity under FRCP 9(b), the plaintiff should consult the law of the forum circuit. *Compare* ***In re Stac Elecs.***, 89 F.3d at 1404 (in securities-fraud cases, P can simply state that there was scienter), *with* ***Greebel v. FTP Software, Inc.***, 194 F.3d 185, 196 (1st Cir.1999) (scienter must be supported by factual pleadings), *and* ***San Leandro Emerg. Med. Grp. Profit Sharing Plan v. Philip Morris Cos.***, 75 F.3d 801, 813 (2d Cir.1996) (same).

NOTE

In a suit alleging violations of federal securities laws, a motion to dismiss under FRCP 9(b) can also allege that the plaintiff did not plead the circumstances constituting fraud as required by the Private Securities Litigation Reform Act of 1995. See 15 U.S.C. §78u-4(b)(1), (b)(2). Legislative history suggests that Congress intended for the Act to impose a higher standard for pleading fraud than courts have used for FRCP 9(b). ***Florida State Bd. of Admin. v. Green Tree Fin. Corp.***, *270 F.3d 645, 657 (8th Cir.2001).*

§3. RESPONSE

§3.1 Motion under FRCP 8 or 9(b). When the plaintiff's complaint is challenged by a motion to dismiss under FRCP 8 or 9(b), the plaintiff may either concede and amend or object.

1. Leave to amend. If the grounds in the motion to dismiss are well founded and the plaintiff cannot amend as a matter of course, the plaintiff should ask the court for permission to amend its complaint. *See* ***Vess v. Ciba-Geigy Corp. USA***, 317 F.3d 1097, 1107-08 (9th Cir.2003) (leave to amend should be granted if it appears P can correct defect); ***Firestone v. Firestone***, 76 F.3d 1205, 1209 (D.C.Cir.1996) (leave to amend is almost always granted to cure deficient fraud allegations under FRCP 9(b)); ***Salahuddin v. Cuomo***, 861 F.2d 40, 42 (2d Cir.1988) (before court dismisses for failure to comply with FRCP 8, it normally grants leave to file amended pleading). See "Motion to Amend or Supplement Pleadings—Pretrial," ch. 5-I, p. 345.

2. Objection to motion. If the complaint is sufficient under FRCP 8 or 9(b), the plaintiff should file a response to defend its complaint. *See, e.g.,* ***Firestone***, 76 F.3d at 1207-08 (opposition to motion argued that complaint properly pleaded fraud under FRCP 9(b)).

§3.2 Motion under FRCP 12(b), (e), or (f). When the plaintiff's complaint is challenged by a motion to dismiss under FRCP 8 or 9(b) and under FRCP 12(b), (e), or (f), the plaintiff should consider filing an amended pleading in addition to—or possibly instead of—a response. If the plaintiff has not already amended once as a "matter of course" (i.e., 21 days after serving its complaint), the plaintiff can amend—without the court's leave or the opposing party's consent—within the earlier of 21 days after the defendant's answer or motion under FRCP 12(b), (e), or (f) is served. *See* FRCP 15(a)(1)(B). See "Deadline," ch. 5-I, §3.1.1, p. 345. When leave is necessary, the plaintiff's response should request that, if the court grants the motion to dismiss, it should also grant the plaintiff leave to amend. See "Motion for Leave to Amend," ch. 5-I, §5, p. 351.

§4. HEARING

The motion and response will probably be considered based on the written submissions, without a hearing.

§5. RULING

The court should not dismiss a plaintiff's complaint that violates FRCP 8 or 9(b) unless the plaintiff has already been given the opportunity to amend. *See* ***Salahuddin v. Cuomo***, 861 F.2d 40, 42 (2d Cir.1988); 5 Wright & Miller §1281; *see, e.g.,* ***Gold v. Morrison-Knudsen Co.***, 68 F.3d 1475, 1476 (2d Cir.1995) (court denied FRCP 9(b) motion but ordered P to replead); ***Kuehl v. FDIC***, 8 F.3d 905, 908-09 (1st Cir.1993) (case was dismissed because Ps filed long, redundant complaint after being ordered to replead under FRCP 8(a)). Dismissal under FRCP 8 is usually reserved for

cases in which the complaint is so confusing, ambiguous, vague, or otherwise unintelligible that its true substance is well disguised. ***Salahuddin***, 861 F.2d at 42; ***Gillibeau v. City of Richmond***, 417 F.2d 426, 431 (9th Cir.1969).

§6. APPELLATE REVIEW

The district court's order striking allegations or dismissing pleadings that violate FRCP 8 is reviewed for abuse of discretion. *See* ***Kuehl v. FDIC***, 8 F.3d 905, 908 (1st Cir.1993) (motion under FRCP 8(a)(2)). The court's order dismissing pleadings for violating FRCP 9(b) is reviewed de novo. ***Carroll v. Fort James Corp.***, 470 F.3d 1171, 1173 (5th Cir.2006).

K. MOTION TO TRANSFER VENUE—28 U.S.C. §1404

§1. GENERAL

§1.1 Rule. None. See 28 U.S.C. §1404(a).

§1.2 Purpose. If a plaintiff files a lawsuit in a district of proper venue that is inconvenient for the defendant or the witnesses and there is a more convenient federal court where the lawsuit could have been brought, the defendant may file a motion to transfer venue under 28 U.S.C. §1404(a). *See* ***In re TS Tech USA Corp.***, 551 F.3d 1315, 1319 (Fed.Cir.2008). A motion to transfer venue under §1404(a) is appropriate when the more convenient forum is another federal court and both the original and requested venues are proper. If a defendant seeks a transfer to another division within the same district based on local rules, the standards of 28 U.S.C. §1404 may apply. *See* 14D Wright, Miller & Cooper, *Federal Practice & Procedure 3d* §3809 & n.31 (2007 & Supp.2012). When the more convenient forum is abroad, the defendant should file a motion to dismiss for forum non conveniens. *See* ***Quackenbush v. Allstate Ins.***, 517 U.S. 706, 722 (1996). See "Motion to Dismiss for Forum Non Conveniens—Challenging the U.S. Forum," ch. 3-E, p. 199. When the original venue is improper, and not merely inconvenient, the defendant should file a motion to dismiss for improper venue. *See* ***Jumara v. State Farm Ins.***, 55 F.3d 873, 878 (3d Cir.1995). See "Motion to Dismiss for Improper Venue—FRCP 12(b)(3)," ch. 3-D, p. 192.

§1.3 Forms. *O'Connor's Federal Civil Forms* (2012), FORMS 3K.

§1.4 Other references. Federal Courts Jurisdiction & Venue Clarification Act of 2011, P.L. 112-63, 125 Stat. 758 (2011) (eff. Jan. 6, 2012) (referred to as Clarification Act); Lamar Smith, Federal Courts Jurisdiction & Venue Clarification Act of 2011, H.R. Rep. No. 112-10 (2011) (referred to as H.R. Rep. 112-10 (2011)); 14D, 15 Wright, Miller & Cooper, *Federal Practice & Procedure 3d* §§3801, 3841-3855 (2007 & Supp.2012); 17 *Moore's Federal Practice 3d* ch. 111 (2012).

§2. MOTION

§2.1 Form. For the general requirements for the form of a motion, see "Drafting motions," ch. 1-B, §3.1, p. 14.

§2.2 In writing or on court's initiative. A defendant should request a transfer of venue in writing and in a motion separate from its answer. *See* FRCP 7(b)(1). If appropriate, the motion to transfer can be included as an alternative ground either in an FRCP 12(b)(3) motion to dismiss for improper venue or in a motion to transfer for improper venue. The court may order transfer on its own, but it should advise the parties it is considering such an action so they may present their views. *See* ***Mills v. Beech Aircraft Corp.***, 886 F.2d 758, 761 (5th Cir.1989). Sua sponte transfers are generally reserved for exceptional circumstances and are strongly disfavored. ***In re Chatman-Bey***, 718 F.2d 484, 487 (D.C.Cir.1983).

§2.3 Deadline. There is no deadline for a motion to transfer venue under 28 U.S.C. §1404. ***Martin-Trigona v. Meister***, 668 F.Supp. 1, 3 (D.D.C.1987). However, a party seeking a transfer should act with "reasonable promptness." ***Peteet v. Dow Chem. Co.***, 868 F.2d 1428, 1436 (5th Cir.1989). The motion should be filed early enough to avoid prejudice to the parties. *See* ***McGraw-Edison Co. v. Van Pelt***, 350 F.2d 361, 363-64 (8th Cir.1965); ***Mohamed v. Mazda Motor Corp.***, 90 F.Supp.2d 757, 760 (E.D.Tex.2000); ***Martin-Trigona***, 668 F.Supp. at 3.

§2.4 Grounds. A court has two broad categories of factors to consider when deciding a 28 U.S.C. §1404(a) motion to transfer: (1) the convenience of the parties and witnesses and (2) the interests of justice. The "interests of justice" factors are public-interest factors traditionally related to the efficient administration of the court system. *E.g.*, ***Coffey v. Van Dorn Iron Works***, 796 F.2d 217, 220-21 (7th Cir.1986) (P's attempt to transfer case to Ohio in order to reach merits of her case was not in interests of justice). The statutory factors have been called "placeholders" for the broad interests that the court should consider, and there is no statutory indication of what weight they should be given. *Id.* at 219 n.3. When ruling on a §1404(a) motion to transfer, the court is not limited to these factors, but rather must engage in a case-by-case consideration of convenience and fairness. *See* ***Stewart Org. v. Ricoh Corp.***, 487 U.S. 22, 29 (1988); ***Research Automation, Inc. v. Schrader-Bridgeport Int'l***, 626 F.3d 973, 978 (7th Cir.2010); 15 Wright, Miller & Cooper §3847. Most courts have used the "private-interest" and "public-interest" factors set out in ***Gulf Oil Corp. v. Gilbert***, 330 U.S. 501, 508-09 (1947), a forum non conveniens case, when deciding motions to transfer under §1404(a). ***Mohamed v. Mazda Motor Corp.***, 90 F.Supp.2d 757, 771 (E.D.Tex.2000). The following are the factors courts have considered in ruling on motions to transfer, though none of the factors should be given dispositive weight. ***In re Volkswagen AG***, 371 F.3d 201, 203 (5th Cir.2004).

1. Private-interest factors. There are nine private-interest factors that the court can consider when ruling on a §1404(a) motion to transfer: (1) plaintiff's choice of forum, (2) convenience of the parties, (3) convenience of key witnesses, (4) cost of obtaining witnesses, (5) location of counsel, (6) ability to compel the attendance of witnesses, (7) accessibility and location of sources of proof, (8) possibility of jury view of evidence located in the proposed forum, and (9) existence of a forum-selection clause.

(1) Plaintiff's choice of forum. The plaintiff's choice of forum is typically given great weight and generally should not be disturbed unless it is clearly outweighed by other considerations. ***Robinson v. Giarmarco & Bill, P.C.***, 74 F.3d 253, 260 (11th Cir.1996); ***Scheidt v. Klein***, 956 F.2d 963, 965 (10th Cir.1992); *see also* 15 Wright, Miller & Cooper §3848 (discussing varying degrees of emphasis courts place on P's choice of forum); *cf.* ***Gulf Oil***, 330 U.S. at 508 (forum non conveniens; "unless the balance is strongly in favor of the defendant, the plaintiff's choice of forum should rarely be disturbed"). *But see* ***In re TS Tech USA Corp.***, 551 F.3d 1315, 1320 (Fed.Cir.2008) (P's choice of venue is not distinct factor in §1404(a) analysis; rather, it corresponds to D's burden that transferee forum is clearly more convenient). The defendant can argue, however, that any deference given to the plaintiff's choice of forum should be reduced or eliminated because the forum does not have any meaningful ties to the controversy or the plaintiff is not a resident of the district where it filed suit and has no particular connection to that district. *See* ***Neil Bros. v. World Wide Lines, Inc.***, 425 F.Supp.2d 325, 333 (E.D.N.Y.2006); ***Devaughn v. Inphonic, Inc.***, 403 F.Supp.2d 68, 72 (D.D.C.2005); *cf.* ***Piper Aircraft Co. v. Reyno***, 454 U.S. 235, 255-56 (1981) (forum non conveniens; greater deference given to P's choice of forum when forum is also P's home district).

(2) Convenience of parties. The fact that the plaintiff's choice of forum is inconvenient to the defendant is usually not sufficient to warrant changing the venue of the suit. ***Van Dusen v. Barrack***, 376 U.S. 612, 633-34 (1964). The defendant must show that it is not simply shifting the inconvenience to the plaintiff. *See* ***Scheidt***, 956 F.2d at 966; ***Sorrels Steel Co. v. Great Sw. Corp.***, 651 F.Supp. 623, 630 (S.D.Miss.1986); 15 Wright, Miller & Cooper §3849. When making its determination, the court can assume that the convenience of the defendant's employees is less significant than that of nonparty witnesses. ***In re Triton Ltd. Secs. Litig.***, 70 F.Supp.2d 678, 690 (E.D. Tex.1999).

(3) Convenience of key witnesses. The defendant can assert that the present forum is inconvenient for key witnesses—those who will actually be called to testify—and state why the proposed forum is more convenient for those witnesses. *See* ***In re Volkswagen of Am., Inc.***, 545 F.3d 304, 317 (5th Cir.2008).

(a) Key witnesses. Key witnesses include testifying witnesses involved in the original complaint as well as any witnesses with claims or controversies properly joined to the original complaint. *E.g.*, ***In re Volkswagen AG***, 371 F.3d at 204 (convenience of third-party witnesses joined as parties is proper consideration). The defendant should avoid making a general allegation that witnesses will be necessary; instead, the defendant should specify the identity and location of potential key witnesses and provide a description of their testimony—enough to

show that each witness has relevant and material information. *See* ***Laumann Mfg. v. Castings USA, Inc.***, 913 F.Supp. 712, 720 (E.D.N.Y.1996); ***Young v. Armstrong World Indus.***, 601 F.Supp. 399, 401-02 (N.D.Tex.1984); *see, e.g.*, ***Scheidt***, 956 F.2d at 966 (D did not show quality or materiality of witnesses' testimony, unwillingness of witnesses to travel, deposition testimony as unsatisfactory, or necessity of compulsory process). *But see* ***In re Genentech, Inc.***, 566 F.3d 1338, 1343 (Fed.Cir.2009) (although party must show that potential witnesses' testimony will be relevant and material, party does not need to determine who will be key witnesses). By focusing on key witnesses, the defendant can avoid the "battle of the numbers" problem—that is, when the parties argue the merits of a transfer based solely on who has the longer list of possible witnesses. *See* ***Dupre v. Spanier Mar. Corp.***, 810 F.Supp. 823, 826 (S.D. Tex.1993); 15 Wright, Miller & Cooper §3851.

(b) Expert witnesses. Experts are generally not considered key witnesses, and their convenience is given little consideration. *See* ***Houston Trial Reports, Inc. v. LRP Publ'ns, Inc.***, 85 F.Supp.2d 663, 669 (S.D.Tex.1999) (convenience of expert witnesses given little weight); ***Babbidge v. Apex Oil Co.***, 676 F.Supp. 517, 520 (S.D.N.Y.1987) (same).

(c) Travel burden. Generally, witnesses are more inconvenienced the farther they have to travel to attend trial. ***In re TS Tech USA Corp.***, 551 F.3d at 1320. When the distance between the existing and proposed venues exceeds 100 miles, the inconvenience to the witnesses increases in direct relationship to the additional distance to be traveled. ***In re Volkswagen AG***, 371 F.3d at 204-05. But even when there is an increased burden on the witnesses, the burden may be insufficient to outweigh the plaintiff's right to choose the forum. *See, e.g.*, ***Jarvis Christian Coll. v. Exxon Corp.***, 845 F.2d 523, 528 (5th Cir.1988) (travel of 203 miles a "minor inconvenience"); ***Mohamed***, 90 F.Supp.2d at 776 (additional 150 miles "negligible"); ***Crystal Semiconductor Corp. v. OPTi, Inc.***, 44 U.S.P.Q.2d 1497, 1504 (W.D.Tex.1997) ("measly three-hour plane ride" insufficient to justify transfer).

(4) Cost of obtaining witnesses. The defendant can assert that the cost of obtaining the attendance of witnesses will be substantially less in the forum it proposes. *See* ***Bevil v. Smit Americas, Inc.***, 883 F.Supp. 168, 171 (S.D.Tex.1995) (rarely is chosen forum least expensive venue for every individual affiliated with dispute).

(5) Location of counsel. Although the defendant can assert that the proposed forum will be more convenient for counsel, the location of counsel is generally given little or no weight. 15 Wright, Miller & Cooper §3850; *see* ***In re Horseshoe Entm't***, 337 F.3d 429, 434 (5th Cir.2003) (factor is irrelevant and improper for consideration).

(6) Ability to compel attendance of witnesses. The defendant can assert that there are unwilling material witnesses whose presence cannot be compelled by the court under FRCP 45. *See* ***In re Genentech, Inc.***, 566 F.3d at 1345; *see also* ***In re Hoffmann-La Roche Inc.***, 587 F.3d 1333, 1337-38 (Fed. Cir.2009) (transfer is favored if transferee court has "absolute" subpoena power over substantial number of witnesses; court has absolute subpoena power when it can subpoena witnesses for both deposition and trial). See "Compelling Witness to Appear for Hearing," ch. 1-E, §4, p. 40. Because FRCP 45 has several overlapping grants of subpoena authority, the defendant must determine whether its witnesses are covered by any of them. The defendant must identify the witnesses who are actually unwilling to travel to the plaintiff's choice of forum, state their proposed testimony, and state why they are material. The parties can be compelled to present their employees regardless of where they are located. *See* ***DEV Indus. v. NPC, Inc.***, 763 F.Supp. 313, 315 (N.D.Ill.1991).

CAUTION

One of the main purposes of the 1991 revisions to FRCP 45 was to enable courts to compel the attendance of a witness found within the state where the court sits. ***Mohamed****, 90 F.Supp.2d at 778; 1991 Notes to FRCP 45 at ¶1, p. 1210, this book; see* ***Chung v. Chrysler Corp.****, 903 F.Supp. 160, 164-65 (D.D.C.1995). Do not make the mistake of arguing that a witness who is outside the district and not within 100 miles of the courthouse cannot be compelled to attend trial when that witness is present in the state where the court sits. See FRCP 45(c)(3)(A)(ii);* ***Mohamed****, 90 F.Supp.2d at 778. While a trial subpoena may be subject to a motion to quash under FRCP*

45(c)(3)(B)(iii) when it requires a person who is neither a party nor a party's officer to incur substantial expense to travel more than 100 miles to attend trial, the court does not need to quash the subpoena if the party issuing it shows a substantial need for the testimony and assures the court that the witness will be reasonably compensated. FRCP 45(c)(3)(C). See "Discretionary grounds," ch. 1-H, §8.5, p. 57.

(7) Accessibility & location of evidence. The defendant can assert that evidence is not located in the present forum and is particularly bulky or difficult to transport. *See* ***In re Genentech, Inc.***, 566 F.3d at 1345-46. The defendant must identify the location of documents or other sources of proof and show why they are important and more accessible in the proposed forum. *See* ***Scheidt***, 956 F.2d at 966. Access to documents has been given decreasing emphasis due to advances in copying technology and information storage. ***Mohamed***, 90 F.Supp.2d at 778.

(8) Possibility of jury view. The defendant can assert that the jury will need to observe evidence located in the proposed forum and should assert with particularity why the jury view is necessary, including how the evidence cannot be reasonably brought to or satisfactorily reproduced in the courtroom. *See* ***Southern Ry. v. Madden***, 235 F.2d 198, 200-01 (4th Cir.1956); ***Mohamed***, 90 F.Supp.2d at 778-79; ***Resorts Int'l v. Liberty Mut. Ins.***, 813 F.Supp. 289, 292 (D.N.J.1992); *see also* ***Clemente v. Carnicon-P.R. Mgmt. Assocs., L.C.***, 52 F.3d 383, 386 (1st Cir. 1995) (within court's discretion to allow jury view). Courts disagree on the weight to be given to this factor. *See* 15 Wright, Miller & Cooper §3854 nn.29-31. *Compare* ***Ramsey v. Fox News Network, LLC***, 323 F.Supp.2d 1352, 1358 (N.D.Ga.2004) (factor given greater weight in favor of transfer if jury view would be impossible in original venue), *with* ***Mohamed***, 90 F.Supp.2d at 778 (jury views are now disfavored and should rarely be used, so factor should be given little weight).

(9) Forum-selection clause. If the parties contractually agreed to the proposed forum, the defendant can assert that there is a valid and enforceable forum-selection clause. *See* ***Slater v. Energy Servs. Grp. Int'l***, 634 F.3d 1326, 1330 (11th Cir.2011); ***Jumara v. State Farm Ins.***, 55 F.3d 873, 880 (3d Cir.1995). When a court is ruling on a motion to transfer, a valid forum-selection clause is not decisive. *See* ***Stewart Org.***, 487 U.S. at 29-31 (forum-selection clause does not compel transfer if factors listed in §1404(a) weigh against transfer); ***Kerobo v. Southwestern Clean Fuels, Corp.***, 285 F.3d 531, 535 (6th Cir.2002) (forum-selection clauses do not dictate forum); ***Terra Int'l v. Mississippi Chem. Corp.***, 119 F.3d 688, 695 (8th Cir.1997) (forum-selection clause is one factor, but a very important one); *see also* ***Brock v. Baskin-Robbins USA Co.***, 113 F.Supp.2d 1078, 1086 (E.D.Tex.2000) (in diversity cases, forum-selection clause does not render venue improper, but it does require analysis under §1404(a)). The forum-selection clause usually affects only one factor in the §1404(a) analysis: the convenience of the parties. *See* ***Northwestern Nat'l Ins. v. Donovan***, 916 F.2d 372, 378 (7th Cir.1990) (signing valid forum-selection clause is waiver of right to move for change of venue on ground of inconvenience). Thus, the remaining private-interest factors must still be weighed and may require the court to deny the motion to transfer despite the agreement. *See* ***Stewart Org.***, 487 U.S. at 29; ***Jones v. GNC Franchising, Inc.***, 211 F.3d 495, 499 (9th Cir.2000); ***White v. ABCO Eng'g***, 199 F.3d 140, 143 (3d Cir.1999).

CIRCUIT SPLIT

The circuits are split on the proper procedure for challenging venue based on a forum-selection clause. For factors used to determine the enforceability of a forum-selection clause, see "Forum-selection clause," ch. 3-D, §3.3.4, p. 194.

2. Public-interest factors. The public-interest factors traditionally relate to the efficient administration of the court system. *See* ***Research Automation***, 626 F.3d at 978. Courts have identified three public-interest factors that should be considered in a motion to transfer: (1) administrative difficulties caused by court congestion, (2) local interest in the controversy and the burden of jury duty, and (3) the proposed forum's familiarity with the governing law.

(1) Administrative difficulties caused by court congestion. Using federal-court-management statistics, the defendant can assert that the parties will receive a speedier trial in the proposed forum because the present forum's docket is too congested. *See* ***Coffey***, 796 F.2d at 221; ***Solomon v. Continental Am. Life Ins.***, 472 F.2d 1043, 1047 (3d Cir.1973); *see, e.g.*, ***Mohamed***, 90 F.Supp.2d at 779 (comparing time to trial and number of cases pending); ***Hernandez v. Graebel Van Lines***, 761 F.Supp. 983, 991 (E.D.N.Y.1991) (comparing time to trial). The traditionally used statistic is the median time to trial as stated in the annual *Federal Court Management Statistics*. *See* ***Mohamed***, 90 F.Supp.2d at 779; 15 Wright, Miller & Cooper §3854 & n.16. More information on the district courts' dockets is contained in tables appended to the federal courts' annual report, which is available on the federal courts' website at www.uscourts.gov/judbususc/judbus.html. A court cannot, however, transfer a case merely to reduce its own docket congestion. *See* ***Mazinski v. Dight***, 99 F.Supp. 192, 194 (W.D.Pa.1951); 15 Wright, Miller & Cooper §3854 & n.15.

(2) Local interest & jury duty. The defendant can assert that a transfer will serve the local interest in adjudicating localized controversies and will avoid the unfairness of burdening citizens in an unrelated forum with jury duty. *See* ***In re TS Tech USA Corp.***, 551 F.3d at 1321; *cf.* ***Gulf Oil***, 330 U.S. at 508-09 (forum non conveniens).

(3) Forum's familiarity with governing law. In a diversity case, the defendant can assert that the proposed forum will be more "at home" with the law governing the controversy. *See, e.g.*, ***Regents of the Univ. of Cal. v. Eli Lilly & Co.***, 119 F.3d 1559, 1565 (Fed.Cir.1997) (transfer was proper when court was already familiar with case's highly technical factual issues). The defendant should demonstrate that the law of the proposed forum will apply to the controversy and is either unclear or will be difficult to apply. *See* ***Vandeveld v. Christoph***, 877 F.Supp. 1160, 1169 (N.D.Ill.1995) (court will disregard factor if it is unclear which state's law will apply); *see, e.g.*, ***Action Indus. v. U.S. Fid. & Guar. Co.***, 358 F.3d 337, 340 (5th Cir.2004) (D did not establish that court was either unable or unwilling to apply another state's law); ***Emrick v. Calcasieu Kennel Club, Inc.***, 800 F.Supp. 482, 484 (E.D.Tex. 1992) (court believed it was capable of being educated on applicable law); ***Sorrels Steel***, 651 F.Supp. at 630 (Ds did not contend that applicable law was unclear or difficult to apply).

§2.5 Evidence. The defendant must support the motion to transfer with discovery, affidavits, or other proof containing detailed factual statements supporting the grounds in the motion. *See* ***Plum Tree, Inc. v. Stockment***, 488 F.2d 754, 756-57 & n.2 (3d Cir.1973) (finding no evidence to support transfer and giving examples of evidence that would have been appropriate); *see, e.g.*, ***Simon v. Ward***, 80 F.Supp.2d 464, 471 (E.D.Pa.2000) (Ds did not provide any evidence in support of decision to transfer). Mere conclusory assertions of inconvenience will not justify a transfer. ***Scheidt v. Klein***, 956 F.2d 963, 966 (10th Cir.1992).

§2.6 Discovery. If discovery is necessary, the parties may ask the court either to limit initial discovery to venue facts or to defer ruling on the motion until certain discovery relating to venue can be completed. *Cf.* ***Home Ins. v. Thomas Indus.***, 896 F.2d 1352, 1358-59 (11th Cir.1990) (reversing dismissal for improper venue and allowing case to proceed on assumption that facts relevant to venue determination would become clearer as discovery in case progressed).

§2.7 Burden. The defendant has the burden of establishing that a transfer is warranted. ***Terra Int'l v. Mississippi Chem. Corp.***, 119 F.3d 688, 695 (8th Cir.1997); ***Scheidt v. Klein***, 956 F.2d 963, 965 (10th Cir.1992); ***Time, Inc. v. Manning***, 366 F.2d 690, 698 (5th Cir.1966). When a defendant alleges that venue is controlled by a forum-selection clause *and* that the case should be transferred for convenience under 28 U.S.C. §1404(a), some courts hold that the burden of persuasion shifts to the plaintiff to prove that its chosen forum is more convenient than the one designated in the forum-selection clause. *See* ***Jumara v. State Farm Ins.***, 55 F.3d 873, 880 (3d Cir.1995); ***In re Ricoh Corp.***, 870 F.2d 570, 573 (11th Cir.1989).

§3. RESPONSE

§3.1 In writing. The plaintiff's response should be in writing. *See* FRCP 7(b)(1).

§3.2 Grounds. The response should call the court's attention to any failure by the defendant to carry its burden to justify, under the ***Gulf Oil*** factors, a transfer from the plaintiff's chosen forum.

1. Private-interest factors.

(1) Plaintiff's choice of forum. The plaintiff should argue that its choice of forum should not be disturbed because it is not clearly outweighed by other considerations. ***Robinson v. Giarmarco & Bill, P.C.***, 74 F.3d 253, 260 (11th Cir.1996); ***Scheidt v. Klein***, 956 F.2d 963, 965 (10th Cir.1992); ***Time, Inc. v. Manning***, 366 F.2d 690, 698 (5th Cir.1966); *see, e.g.*, ***In re Nat'l Presto Indus.***, 347 F.3d 662, 665 (7th Cir.2003) (despite limited subpoena power of chosen court, lighter docket of transferee court, and location of documents in transferee forum, balance of inconvenience was not so askew as to justify transfer); *cf.* ***Gulf Oil Corp. v. Gilbert***, 330 U.S. 501, 508 (1947) (forum non conveniens). The plaintiff should state that the chosen forum is its home district or explain how the choice of forum has meaningful ties to the controversy and relates to the plaintiff's legitimate and rational concerns. *See* ***Neil Bros. v. World Wide Lines, Inc.***, 425 F.Supp.2d 325, 333 (E.D.N.Y.2006); ***Devaughn v. Inphonic, Inc.***, 403 F.Supp.2d 68, 72 (D.D.C.2005); *cf.* ***Piper Aircraft Co. v. Reyno***, 454 U.S. 235, 255-56 (1981) (forum non conveniens); ***Koster v. Lumbermens Mut. Cas. Co.***, 330 U.S. 518, 524 (1947) (derivative action).

(2) Convenience of parties. The plaintiff should argue that the defendant's proposed forum merely shifts the inconvenience from one party to the other. *See* ***Scheidt***, 956 F.2d at 966. The plaintiff should attach sworn proof factually demonstrating the convenience of its chosen forum for the parties. If the defendant is asserting that the forum is inconvenient for the plaintiff, the plaintiff should note that the purpose of the venue statutes is to protect a defendant against a plaintiff's choice of an unfair or inconvenient forum, not the other way around. *See* ***Leroy v. Great W. United Corp.***, 443 U.S. 173, 183-84 (1979); 14D Wright, Miller & Cooper §3801. In other words, the defendant cannot assert the plaintiff's inconvenience as a reason to transfer. ***American Can Co. v. Crown Cork & Seal Co.***, 433 F.Supp. 333, 338 (E.D.Wis.1977); 15 Wright, Miller & Cooper §3849.

(3) Convenience of key witnesses. The plaintiff should identify which witnesses will actually be called to testify, not just those who have been identified as persons with knowledge of relevant information. *See* ***Scheidt***, 956 F.2d at 966 n.2. The plaintiff should also attach sworn proof from those witnesses stating that the trial in the chosen forum will not be inconvenient for them. If the defendant is claiming that the forum is inconvenient based on distance, the plaintiff should assert that the burden of travel does not outweigh the plaintiff's right to choose the forum. *See, e.g.*, ***Jarvis Christian Coll. v. Exxon Corp.***, 845 F.2d 523, 528 (5th Cir.1988) (travel of 203 miles a "minor inconvenience"); ***Mohamed v. Mazda Motor Corp.***, 90 F.Supp.2d 757, 776 (E.D.Tex.2000) (additional 150 miles "negligible"); ***Crystal Semiconductor Corp. v. OPTi, Inc.***, 44 U.S.P.Q.2d 1497, 1504 (W.D.Tex.1997) ("measly three-hour plane ride" insufficient to justify transfer). If the defendant is claiming that the forum is inconvenient for the plaintiff's witnesses, the plaintiff should note that the defendant cannot rely on that inconvenience as a reason for transfer. *See* ***Sun Oil Co. v. Lederle***, 199 F.2d 423, 424 (6th Cir.1952); ***American Can Co.***, 433 F.Supp. at 338.

(4) Cost of obtaining witnesses. The plaintiff should argue that the cost of obtaining the attendance of witnesses in the chosen forum will not be substantially greater than in the defendant's proposed forum. *See* ***Bevil v. Smit Americas, Inc.***, 883 F.Supp. 168, 171 (S.D.Tex.1995) (rarely is chosen forum least expensive for every individual affiliated with dispute).

(5) Location of counsel. The plaintiff should argue that the location of defense counsel should not be a factor, or at least not a significant one, in the court's decision on the motion to transfer. 15 Wright, Miller & Cooper §3850; *see* ***In re Horseshoe Entm't***, 337 F.3d 429, 434 (5th Cir.2003) (factor is irrelevant and should not be considered).

(6) Ability to compel attendance of witnesses. The plaintiff can argue that a transfer is unnecessary because the court's subpoena power under FRCP 45 is sufficient to compel the attendance of any unwilling material witnesses the defendant may call. *See* FRCP 45(c)(3)(C) (subpoena requiring nonparty to incur substantial expense to travel more than 100 miles to attend trial is still valid if the issuing party shows substantial need for the testimony and assures court that witness will be reasonably compensated). Even if the chosen court has limited subpoena power over some of the potential witnesses, the plaintiff should still assert that the balance of factors favors its choice of forum. *See* ***In re Nat'l Presto Indus.***, 347 F.3d at 665.

(7) Accessibility & location of sources of proof. The plaintiff should assert that, because of advances in copying technology and information storage, any requested documents can be easily transported to the chosen forum. ***Mohamed***, 90 F.Supp.2d at 778; *see* ***In re Horseshoe Entm't***, 337 F.3d at 434. The plaintiff should, if necessary, attach affidavits stating that proof will be readily available in the chosen forum. Even if the location of some of the evidence favors transfer, the plaintiff should still assert that the balance of factors favors its choice of forum. *See* ***In re Nat'l Presto Indus.***, 347 F.3d at 665.

(8) Possibility of jury view. The plaintiff should argue that (1) the defendant has not demonstrated that a jury view is necessary to adequately present its evidence and (2) the evidence can be brought to and reasonably reproduced in the chosen forum. *See* ***Mohamed***, 90 F.Supp.2d at 779; ***Resorts Int'l v. Liberty Mut. Ins.***, 813 F.Supp. 289, 292 (D.N.J.1992); *see, e.g.*, ***Decker Coal Co. v. Commonwealth Edison Co.***, 805 F.2d 834, 843 (9th Cir. 1986) (jury view of damaged plants in two different states was unnecessary for breach of contract that occurred in Montana); ***Marbury-Pattillo Constr. Co. v. Bayside Whs. Co.***, 490 F.2d 155, 158 (5th Cir.1974) (jury view of damaged grain-storage tanks, while potentially helpful, was not proved necessary by movant); ***Gdovin v. Catawba Rental Co.***, 596 F.Supp. 1325, 1326 (N.D.Ohio 1984) (photographs of accident site could be used instead of jury view); ***Culbertson v. Ford Motor Co.***, 531 F.Supp. 406, 408 (E.D.Pa.1982) (65-mile trip from courtroom to possible jury-view site was not so onerous as to require transfer to court 12 miles from site).

(9) Forum-selection clause. The plaintiff should assert that in diversity cases a forum-selection clause is not decisive. *See* ***Stewart Org. v. Ricoh Corp.***, 487 U.S. 22, 31 (1988); ***Kerobo v. Southwestern Clean Fuels, Corp.***, 285 F.3d 531, 537-38 (6th Cir.2002). The plaintiff should argue specifically how the other §1404(a) factors outweigh the enforcement of the agreement. *See* ***Stewart Org.***, 487 U.S. at 30-31; ***Kerobo***, 285 F.3d at 537-38.

2. Public-interest factors.

(1) Administrative difficulties caused by court congestion. The plaintiff should argue that judicial economy alone is insufficient to support a transfer of venue. *E.g.*, ***In re Warrick***, 70 F.3d 736, 740 & n.6 (2d Cir.1995) (transfer denied because documents and potential witnesses were available in current forum and related cases in transferee forum had already reached final judgment). Even when docket congestion is not the only factor favoring transfer, the court can still preserve the plaintiff's choice of forum. *See* ***In re Nat'l Presto Indus.***, 347 F.3d at 665.

(2) Local interest & jury duty. The plaintiff should argue that there is more of a significant local interest in adjudicating the controversy in the plaintiff's chosen forum than in the defendant's proposed forum. *Cf.* ***Gulf Oil***, 330 U.S. at 509 (forum non conveniens). The plaintiff should also argue that the burden of jury duty is no more unfair in the plaintiff's chosen forum than in the defendant's proposed forum. *Cf. id.* (forum non conveniens).

(3) Forum's familiarity with governing law. The plaintiff should argue that the court in the plaintiff's chosen forum either is sufficiently familiar with the law governing the case or can learn what it needs to know to adequately decide the case. *See, e.g.*, ***In re Vistaprint Ltd.***, 628 F.3d 1342, 1346 (Fed.Cir.2010) (transfer was properly denied when court (1) was already familiar with asserted patent and related technology from earlier litigation and (2) had on its docket pending litigation involving same patent and related technology). The plaintiff should also state that the applicable state law is clear and the defendant did not demonstrate otherwise. *See* ***Sorrels Steel Co. v. Great Sw. Corp.***, 651 F.Supp. 623, 630 (S.D.Miss.1986); *see, e.g.*, ***Action Indus. v. U.S. Fid. & Guar. Co.***, 358 F.3d 337, 340 (5th Cir.2004) (D did not establish that court was either unable or unwilling to apply another state's law). The court may disregard this factor if it is not clear which state's law will apply. *See* ***Vandeveld v. Christoph***, 877 F.Supp. 1160, 1169 (N.D.Ill.1995).

§3.3 Deadline. The FRCPs do not provide a deadline for filing a response to a motion to transfer venue. The plaintiff should check the local rules of the district court where the case is pending for the deadline.

§4. AGREED MOTION

The parties can submit an agreed motion to transfer under 28 U.S.C. §1404(a). See ***O'Connor's Federal Forms***, FORM 3K:3.

NOTE

In the Federal Courts Jurisdiction and Venue Clarification Act of 2011 (referred to as the Clarification Act), Congress made significant amendments to venue statutes in title 28. See H.R. Rep. No. 112-10 (2011). The Clarification Act amended 28 U.S.C. §1404(a) to allow a court to transfer a case to a district court agreed on by all parties. The authority for these transfers became effective for cases (1) commenced in a U.S. district court on or after January 6, 2012, or (2) commenced—within the meaning of state law—in state court on or after January 6, 2012, and then removed to a district court. See Clarification Act, P.L. 112-63, §205, 125 Stat. 764 (2011) (eff. Jan. 6, 2012).

§4.1 Form. For the general requirements for the form of a motion, see "Drafting motions," ch. 1-B, §3.1, p. 14.

§4.2 In writing. The parties should request a transfer of venue in writing. *See* FRCP 7(b)(1).

§4.3 Deadline. There is no deadline for a motion to transfer venue under 28 U.S.C. §1404. However, the parties generally should seek a transfer early in the suit. See "Deadline," §2.3, p. 221.

§4.4 Grounds. The parties must identify the district or division to which they agree to transfer the suit. The parties should identify why the transfer is for the convenience of the parties and witnesses and is in the interest of justice. H.R. Rep. No. 112-10, at 24 (2011). The parties can agree to transfer the suit to any district or division that all parties have consented to, even if the suit could not have been brought in that district or division originally. *Id.* But the parties can only agree to a transfer between Article 3 courts. *See* 28 U.S.C. §1404(d). See "Where all parties have consented," §6.2.1(2), this page.

§5. HEARING

The motion and any response will probably be considered based on the written submissions, without a hearing.

§6. RULING

Although an order explaining the reasons for the court's decision is the better practice, the court can grant or deny a motion to transfer with no explanation at all. ***Peteet v. Dow Chem. Co.***, 868 F.2d 1428, 1436 (5th Cir.1989).

NOTE

*Some courts have held that district courts have discretion to decide a motion to transfer under 28 U.S.C. §1404(a) before ruling on an objection to subject-matter jurisdiction under FRCP 12(b)(1). See **In re LimitNone, LLC**, 551 F.3d 572, 576 (7th Cir.2008); **Public Employees' Ret. Sys. v. Stanley**, 605 F.Supp.2d 1073, 1075 (C.D.Cal.2009). See "Hearing," ch. 3-C, §4, p. 190.*

§6.1 Denies motion. If the court denies the motion, the case will proceed.

§6.2 Grants motion. If the court grants a motion under 28 U.S.C. §1404, it can transfer the case.

1. Transferee court. The court is restricted to transferring a case to a district where it might have been brought initially or to any district or division that all parties have consented to. 28 U.S.C. §1404(a).

(1) Where case might have been brought. When transferring a case to "where it might have been brought," the court is limited to transferring the case to a district in which subject-matter jurisdiction, personal jurisdiction, and venue are proper. *See* ***Hoffman v. Blaski***, 363 U.S. 335, 343-44 (1960); ***Chrysler Credit Corp. v. Country Chrysler, Inc.***, 928 F.2d 1509, 1515 (10th Cir.1991); ***Washington Pub. Utils. Grp. v. U.S. Dist. Ct. for the W. Dist. of Wash.***, 843 F.2d 319, 327-28 (9th Cir.1987); ***International Patent Dev. Corp. v. Wyomont Partners***, 489 F.Supp. 226, 229 (D.Nev.1980).

(2) Where all parties have consented. When transferring a case to where all parties have consented, the court is limited to transfers between Article 3 courts. *See* 28 U.S.C. §1404(a); H.R. Rep. No. 112-10, at 24 (2011). Specifically, the court cannot transfer the case to any of the following districts:

(a) The District Court of Guam. 28 U.S.C. §1404(d).

(b) The District Court for the Northern Mariana Islands. *Id.*

(c) The District Court of the Virgin Islands. *Id.*

2. Choice-of-law rules. In diversity cases, the "***Van Dusen*** rule" states that the transferee court will apply the same state law, choice-of-law rules, and statutes of limitations that the transferor court would have applied. *See* ***Ferens v. John Deere Co.***, 494 U.S. 516, 524-25 (1990); ***Van Dusen v. Barrack***, 376 U.S. 612, 633-37 (1964). Appellate courts disagree, however, about which court's law applies in federal-question cases. The ***Van Dusen*** rule has been rejected for federal questions by some courts of appeals. *See, e.g.*, ***In re Korean Air Lines Disaster***, 829 F.2d 1171, 1174-75 (D.C.Cir.1987) (court decided that ***Van Dusen*** did not apply to transfer under multidistrict-litigation rules when claims arose under federal law rather than state law), *aff'd*, 490 U.S. 122 (1989). *But see* ***In re Rospatch Sec. Litig.***, 760 F.Supp. 1239, 1256-57 (W.D.Mich.1991) (in determining statute of limitations for federal claims, court looked to law of district where transferor court was located).

3. Stay of transfer order. To permit appellate review of transfer orders, some courts have local rules or other procedures that stay the transfer order for a period of time after its entry. *See* ***In re Nine Mile Ltd.***, 673 F.2d 242, 243 (8th Cir.1982) (although no local rule requires stay of transfer, the better procedure is to hold up transferring files for reasonable time pending possible appellate review); 15 Wright, Miller & Cooper §3846 (same). When there is no such local rule, a party seeking reconsideration or other appeal of the order should immediately move for a stay of the transfer order to permit proper reconsideration or appellate review. *See* ***Chrysler Credit Corp.***, 928 F.2d at 1516-17 (filing appeal of transfer order after case has been transferred is futile); 15 Wright, Miller & Cooper §3844 (motion for transfer can be made at any time; party opposing motion should be heard). The plaintiff must also immediately take steps to stay the physical transfer of the papers to the transferee court because the transferor court loses jurisdiction over the case once the papers are docketed with the transferee court. ***In re Nine Mile Ltd.***, 673 F.2d at 243; *see* ***Wilson-Cook Med., Inc. v. Wilson***, 942 F.2d 247, 250 (4th Cir.1991) (general rule is that jurisdiction transfers when record is physically transferred).

§7. APPELLATE REVIEW

§7.1 Appealability.

1. Generally. The grant or denial of a 28 U.S.C. §1404(a) request is interlocutory and not immediately appealable. ***SongByrd, Inc. v. Estate of Grossman***, 206 F.3d 172, 176 (2d Cir.2000); ***In re Joint E.&S. Dists. Asbestos Litig.***, 22 F.3d 755, 762 n.14 (7th Cir.1994); ***Louisiana Ice Cream Distribs. v. Carvel Corp.***, 821 F.2d 1031, 1033 (5th Cir.1987). A transfer order is also not appealable as a "collateral order." *Cf.* ***FDIC v. McGlamery***, 74 F.3d 218, 221 (10th Cir.1996) (transfer under 28 U.S.C. §1631).

2. Errors of law. A court of appeals has the authority to review by mandamus an order transferring venue under §1404(a) if the district court made an error of law. ***Van Dusen v. Barrack***, 376 U.S. 612, 615 n.3 (1964); *see* ***Fort Knox Music Inc. v. Baptiste***, 257 F.3d 108, 112 (2d Cir.2001) (mandamus available, but 2d Circuit is reluctant to grant writ); ***Sunbelt Corp. v. Noble, Denton & Assocs.***, 5 F.3d 28, 30 (3d Cir.1993) (mandamus is appropriate remedy); ***Hustler Mag., Inc. v. U.S. Dist. Ct. for the Dist. of Wyo.***, 790 F.2d 69, 70 (10th Cir.1986) (same); ***Codex Corp. v. Milgo Elec. Corp.***, 553 F.2d 735, 737 (1st Cir.1977) (mandamus available, but granted only in "really extraordinary situations"); *see also* ***In re Volkswagen of Am., Inc.***, 545 F.3d 304, 319 (5th Cir.2008) (mandamus appropriate if district court clearly abused its discretion, producing "patently erroneous" result).

§7.2 Standard of review.

1. Ruling on motion to transfer. District courts have great discretion when deciding a motion to transfer under 28 U.S.C. §1404. ***Research Automation, Inc. v. Schrader-Bridgeport Int'l***, 626 F.3d 973, 979 (7th Cir. 2010). An appellate court will not disturb the district court's ruling unless the district court abused its discretion. ***Casarez v. Burlington N./Santa Fe Co.***, 193 F.3d 334, 339 (5th Cir.1999); ***Scheidt v. Klein***, 956 F.2d 963, 965 (10th

Cir.1992); *see also* ***SongByrd, Inc. v. Estate of Grossman***, 206 F.3d 172, 179 (2d Cir.2000) (to obtain reversal of transfer order after final judgment has been entered, party urging transfer must show that different result would have been reached if suit had been transferred; party opposing transfer must show it lost case because of handicap caused by transfer).

2. Rulings on forum-selection clause. The district court's ruling on the enforceability of a forum-selection clause is reviewed for abuse of discretion. ***Servewell Plumbing, LLC v. Federal Ins.***, 439 F.3d 786, 788 (8th Cir.2006); ***Kukje Hwajae Ins. Co. v. M/V Hyundai Liberty***, 408 F.3d 1250, 1254 (9th Cir.2005). *But see* ***Hugel v. Corporation of Lloyd's***, 999 F.2d 206, 207 (7th Cir.1993) (enforceability of forum-selection clause reviewed de novo). The district court's ruling on the contractual interpretation of the forum-selection clause, including its meaning, scope, and applicability, is reviewed de novo. ***Servewell Plumbing***, 439 F.3d at 788; ***Northern Cal. Dist. Council of Laborers v. Pittsburg-Des Moines Steel Co.***, 69 F.3d 1034, 1036 n.3 (9th Cir.1995); ***Milk 'N' More, Inc. v. Beavert***, 963 F.2d 1342, 1345 (10th Cir.1992); *see* ***Jumara v. State Farm Ins.***, 55 F.3d 873, 880-81 (3d Cir.1995).

L. THE ANSWER—DENYING LIABILITY

§1. GENERAL

§1.1 Rules. FRCP 8, 9, 12-14.

§1.2 Purpose. The purpose of the answer is to challenge matters alleged in the plaintiff's complaint and to avoid a default judgment. *See* ***Williams v. Life S&L***, 802 F.2d 1200, 1203 (10th Cir.1986).

§1.3 Forms. ***O'Connor's Federal Civil Forms*** (2012), FORMS 3L.

§1.4 Other references. 5, 5B Wright & Miller, *Federal Practice & Procedure 3d* §§1261-1280, 1357 (2004 & Supp.2012); 6, 6A Wright, Miller & Kane, *Federal Practice & Procedure 3d* §§1412, 1431, 1554 (2010 & Supp.2012); 2 *Moore's Federal Practice 3d* §§8.06-8.08 (2012).

§2. DEADLINE

Generally, if no FRCP 12 motion is filed, the answer to a complaint is due within 21 days after the defendant is served with the summons and complaint. See "Deadlines," ch. 3-A, §5, p. 174.

§3. TYPES OF DENIALS

If the defendant does not deny the allegations in the plaintiff's complaint, the allegations are treated as if the defendant has admitted them. FRCP 8(b)(6); ***Burlington N. R.R. v. Huddleston***, 94 F.3d 1413, 1415 (10th Cir.1996); ***Lockwood v. Wolf Corp.***, 629 F.2d 603, 611 (9th Cir.1980). There are, however, two exceptions to this rule: a defendant does not need to deny (1) allegations of the amount of damages or (2) allegations in a pleading to which no response is required. FRCP 8(b)(6); 5 Wright & Miller §1279.

PRACTICE TIP

The defendant should be careful to deny each of the plaintiff's allegations that it can legitimately deny and admit only the allegations that good faith requires it to admit. If the defendant cannot respond to the plaintiff's complaint at all because it is so vague or ambiguous, the defendant should consider filing a motion for a more definite statement. See FRCP 12(e); ***Davis v. Coca-Cola Bottling Co. Consol.****, 516 F.3d 955, 983-84 (11th Cir.2008). See "Motion for More Definite Statement—FRCP 12(e)," ch. 3-H, p. 212.*

§3.1 General denial. A general denial is proper only if the defendant intends in good faith to deny all of the complaint's allegations, including the jurisdictional grounds. FRCP 8(b)(3). Rarely, if ever, should a defendant in federal court file a general denial. *See* 5 Wright & Miller §1265.

§3.2 Specific denial. The defendant must state in short and plain terms its defenses to each claim and must admit or deny the plaintiff's allegations. FRCP 8(b)(1). Denials must fairly meet the substance of the allegations that are denied. FRCP 8(b)(2). If the defendant, in good faith, can deny only part of an allegation, the defendant must specify the part that it admits is true and deny only the remainder. FRCP 8(b)(4); *see* ***Mann v. Smith***, 796 F.2d 79, 86 (5th Cir.1986).

§3.3 Denial of knowledge. If the defendant lacks knowledge or information sufficient to form a belief about the truth of an allegation, the defendant must so state. FRCP 8(b)(5); ***Hewlett-Packard Co. v. Olympus Corp.***, 931 F.2d 1551, 1554 (Fed.Cir.1991); ***Ingersoll-Rand Fin. Corp. v. Anderson***, 921 F.2d 497, 501 n.4 (3d Cir.1990). Such a statement has the effect of a denial. FRCP 8(b)(5); 5 Wright & Miller §1262. The defendant should track the exact language of FRCP 8(b)(5) when asserting lack of knowledge or information. *See* ***Wilshin v. Allstate Ins.***, 212 F.Supp.2d 1360, 1369 (M.D.Ga.2002).

§3.4 Challenge to capacity. If the defendant wants to challenge the legal existence of a party, the capacity of a party to sue or be sued, or the representative capacity of a party, the defendant must make a specific denial, stating any supporting facts that are peculiarly within the defendant's knowledge. FRCP 9(a); *see* ***Wagner Furniture Interiors, Inc. v. Kemner's Georgetown Manor, Inc.***, 929 F.2d 343, 345 (7th Cir.1991); ***Marston v. American Empls. Ins.***, 439 F.2d 1035, 1041 (1st Cir.1971). If the defendant does not challenge the plaintiff's lack of capacity, it waives the defense. ***Howerton v. Designer Homes by Georges, Inc.***, 950 F.2d 281, 283 (5th Cir.1992).

NOTE

The defendant must raise a real-party-in-interest defense when it becomes evident that the plaintiff does not have the right to pursue the claim. ***Gogolin & Stelter v. Karn's Auto Imports, Inc.****, 886 F.2d 100, 102 (5th Cir.1989); see FRCP 17(a). The defense is waived, however, if it is asserted late in the proceedings.* ***Gogolin & Stelter****, 886 F.2d at 102; see also 6A Wright, Miller & Kane §1554 & nn.2-10 (defense should be raised in responsive pleadings or at least with reasonable promptness).*

§3.5 Denial of conditions precedent. If the plaintiff alleged that "all conditions precedent were performed or occurred," the defendant must deny "with particularity" any conditions that were not performed or did not occur. FRCP 9(c); ***EEOC v. Service Temps Inc.***, 679 F.3d 323, 331 (5th Cir.2012); ***Myers v. Central Fla. Invs.***, 592 F.3d 1201, 1224 (11th Cir.2010); ***Walton v. Nalco Chem. Co.***, 272 F.3d 13, 21 (1st Cir.2001); ***Carroll v. Acme-Cleveland Corp.***, 955 F.2d 1107, 1115 (7th Cir.1992). If the defendant states the denial with particularity, the plaintiff then has the burden of proving that the conditions precedent have been satisfied. ***Myers***, 592 F.3d at 1224. If the defendant does not state the denial with particularity, the plaintiff's allegations of the conditions precedent are deemed admitted. *Id.* A denial of a condition precedent is not an affirmative defense. ***Mellon Bank v. Aetna Bus. Credit, Inc.***, 619 F.2d 1001, 1008 n.6 (3d Cir.1980); *see* ***Myers***, 592 F.3d at 1224-25.

NOTE

It is unclear whether the denial of a condition precedent can be raised in a motion for summary judgment if it was not first raised in the answer. Compare ***EEOC****, 679 F.3d at 332-33 (FRCP 9(c) limited to pleadings; denial of condition precedent cannot be raised for first time in summary-judgment motion), with* ***Associated Mech. Contractors, Inc. v. Martin K. Eby Constr. Co.****, 271 F.3d 1309, 1317 (11th Cir.2001) (denial of conditions precedent can be raised by motion or answer; D did not waive denial when D challenged denial in summary-judgment motion but had only pleaded denial as affirmative defense in its answer).*

§4. AFFIRMATIVE DEFENSES

An affirmative defense permits a defendant to avoid liability even if the allegations in the plaintiff's complaint are true. By pleading an affirmative defense, the defendant avoids the truth of the complaint by alleging another matter that prevents liability. *See Black's Law Dictionary* 482 (9th ed. 2009).

§4.1 Affirmative defense vs. counterclaim. The defendant can raise the same types of allegations in an affirmative defense as in a counterclaim. The test to determine whether the allegation is an affirmative defense or a counterclaim is whether the defendant asks for affirmative relief: if affirmative relief is requested, the defense is a counterclaim; if affirmative relief is not requested, the defense is an affirmative defense. *See* ***Resolution Trust Corp. v. Midwest Fed. Sav. Bank***, 36 F.3d 785, 791-92 (9th Cir.1993). For example, if a defendant alleges fraud but does not request damages, fraud is an affirmative defense; if the defendant asks for damages as part of its fraud allegation, fraud is a counterclaim. When a party mistakenly designates an affirmative defense as a counterclaim or a counterclaim as an affirmative defense, the court must, if justice requires, treat the pleading as if it had been correctly designated. FRCP 8(c)(2); ***Reiter v. Cooper***, 507 U.S. 258, 263 (1993); ***Resolution Trust Corp.***, 36 F.3d at 791-92; *cf.* ***National Un. Fire Ins. v. City Sav.***, 28 F.3d 376, 394 (3d Cir.1994) (parties cannot avoid statute's jurisdictional bar against counterclaim by labeling it as affirmative defense).

§4.2 Affirmative defense in motion to dismiss. Affirmative defenses can also be raised in a motion to dismiss. ***Cedars-Sinai Med. Ctr. v. Shalala***, 177 F.3d 1126, 1128-29 (9th Cir.1999); *see* 5B Wright & Miller §1357.

§4.3 Effect of failure to plead.

1. Generally. If a defendant intends to rely on an affirmative defense at trial, it generally must plead the defense in its answer or else the defense is waived. *See* FRCP 8(c); ***John R. Sand & Gravel Co. v. U.S.***, 552 U.S. 130, 133 (2008); ***Day v. McDonough***, 547 U.S. 198, 202 (2006); ***In re Cumberland Farms, Inc.***, 284 F.3d 216, 225 (1st Cir.2002). A defendant cannot introduce evidence in support of an affirmative defense that is not pleaded in its answer. ***Prinz v. Greate Bay Casino Corp.***, 705 F.2d 692, 694 (3d Cir.1983). But if the defendant does not initially assert an affirmative defense, it may be able to amend its answer to include it. *See* FRCP 15(a)(1), (a)(2); 5 Wright & Miller §1278. See "Motion to Amend or Supplement Pleadings—Pretrial," ch. 5-I, p. 345.

2. Exceptions.

(1) Raised early & no prejudice. An unpleaded affirmative defense is not waived if the defense is raised at the earliest possible time and it would not prejudice or unfairly surprise the opposing party. ***American Fed. Grp. v. Rothenberg***, 136 F.3d 897, 909-10 (2d Cir.1998); *see* ***First Un. Nat'l Bank v. Pictet Overseas Trust Corp.***, 477 F.3d 616, 622 & n.5 (8th Cir.2007); ***Cedars-Sinai Med. Ctr. v. Shalala***, 177 F.3d 1126, 1128-29 (9th Cir.1999); *see, e.g.*, ***Creative Consumer Concepts, Inc. v. Kreisler***, 563 F.3d 1070, 1076-77 (10th Cir.2009) (D could introduce evidence on unpleaded affirmative defense raised just before trial; even though defense could have been raised earlier, there was no error because P received informal notice of defense during discovery and thus was not prejudiced); ***Steger v. General Elec. Co.***, 318 F.3d 1066, 1077 (11th Cir.2003) (D could introduce evidence on unpleaded affirmative defense raised during pretrial conference). Many courts allow unpleaded defenses to be raised for the first time in a pretrial dispositive motion. ***Brinkley v. Harbour Recreation Club***, 180 F.3d 598, 612 (4th Cir.1999); *e.g.*, ***Blaney v. U.S.***, 34 F.3d 509, 512 (7th Cir.1994) (affirmative defense raised in FRCP 12(b)(1) motion to dismiss); *see* 5 Wright & Miller §1278 & n.25.

(2) Tried by express or implied consent. An unpleaded affirmative defense is not waived if it is tried by express or implied consent. *See* FRCP 15(b)(2); ***Steger***, 318 F.3d at 1077.

(3) Mistakenly designated. An unpleaded affirmative defense is not waived if it is mistakenly designated as a counterclaim. *See* FRCP 8(c)(2). If justice requires, the court must treat the pleading as correctly designated and may impose terms for doing so. *Id.*

(4) Included in joint pretrial order. An unpleaded affirmative defense is not waived if it is included in a final pretrial order because a final pretrial order supersedes all previous pleadings. *See* FRCP 16(e); ***Rockwell Int'l v. U.S.***, 549 U.S. 457, 474 (2007); ***Wilson v. Muckala***, 303 F.3d 1207, 1215 (10th Cir.2002).

§4.4 Affirmative defenses in FRCP 8(c). The purpose of FRCP 8(c) is to give the court and the adverse parties fair notice that the defendant will pursue a particular defense. ***Williams v. Ashland Eng'g Co.***, 45 F.3d 588, 593 (1st Cir.1995), *overruled on other grounds*, ***Carpenters Local Un. v. U.S. Fid. & Guar. Co.***, 215 F.3d 136 (1st Cir.2000). The following affirmative defenses are specifically listed in FRCP 8(c).

1. Accord and satisfaction. ***Macurdy v. Sikov & Love, P.A.***, 894 F.2d 818, 824 (6th Cir.1990).

2. Arbitration and award. *See* ***Hill v. Ricoh Americas Corp.***, 603 F.3d 766, 771 (10th Cir.2010) (affirmative defense of arbitration and award is appropriate when claim has already been arbitrated and award has been obtained, not when claim should be arbitrated); ***Thyssen, Inc. v. Calypso Shipping Corp., S.A.***, 310 F.3d 102, 106 (2d Cir.2002) (same).

3. Assumption of risk. ***Coleman v. Ramada Hotel Oper. Co.***, 933 F.2d 470, 474-75 (7th Cir.1991).

4. Contributory negligence. ***Marino v. Otis Eng'g***, 839 F.2d 1404, 1406 & n.3 (10th Cir.1988); *see also* ***Coleman***, 933 F.2d at 475 (defense of contributory negligence encompasses defense of assumption of risk).

5. Duress. *See* ***Harsco Corp. v. Zlotnicki***, 779 F.2d 906, 911 (3d Cir.1985).

6. Estoppel. ***Bechtold v. City of Rosemount***, 104 F.3d 1062, 1068 (8th Cir.1997).

7. Failure of consideration. ***Overholt Crop Ins. Serv. v. Travis***, 941 F.2d 1361, 1368 (8th Cir.1991).

8. Fraud. *See* ***Olympia Hotels Corp. v. Johnson Wax Dev. Corp.***, 908 F.2d 1363, 1370 (7th Cir.1990).

9. Illegality. ***Development Fin. Corp. v. Alpha Hous. & Health Care, Inc.***, 54 F.3d 156, 163 n.3 (3d Cir. 1995).

10. Injury by fellow servant. ***American Smelting & Ref. Co. v. Sutyak***, 175 F.2d 123, 127 (10th Cir.1949).

11. Laches. ***White v. Daniel***, 909 F.2d 99, 102 (4th Cir.1990).

12. License. *See* ***Kansas Jack, Inc. v. Kuhn***, 719 F.2d 1144, 1148 (Fed.Cir.1983).

13. Payment. ***Bank Leumi Le-Israel, B.M. v. Lee***, 928 F.2d 232, 235 (7th Cir.1991).

14. Release. ***Melanson v. Browning-Ferris Indus.***, 281 F.3d 272, 276 (1st Cir.2002).

15. Res judicata. ***Energy Dev. Corp. v. St. Martin***, 296 F.3d 356, 361 (5th Cir.2002); ***Garry v. Geils***, 82 F.3d 1362, 1367 n.8 (7th Cir.1996).

16. Statute of frauds. *See* ***Anglada v. Sprague***, 822 F.2d 1035, 1037 (11th Cir.1987).

17. Statute of limitations. ***Kropelnicki v. Siegel***, 290 F.3d 118, 130 n.7 (2d Cir.2002); ***Ray v. Kertes***, 285 F.3d 287, 292 (3d Cir.2002); ***In re Cumberland Farms, Inc.***, 284 F.3d 216, 225 (1st Cir.2002).

18. Waiver. ***Melanson***, 281 F.3d at 276.

§4.5 Other affirmative defenses.

1. Catchall provision. FRCP 8(c) contains a catchall provision requiring the defendant to plead "any avoidance or affirmative defense." Although the FRCPs do not identify what constitutes an "avoidance or affirmative defense," when a defendant seeks to raise a point about an issue that is not an element the plaintiff must establish for a prima facie showing of liability, the defendant generally must plead that point as an affirmative defense. ***Estate of Hamilton v. City of N.Y.***, 627 F.3d 50, 57 (2d Cir.2010).

2. Applicable law. In deciding what constitutes an affirmative defense in a diversity case, courts will apply state law. ***Roskam Baking Co. v. Lanham Mach. Co.***, 288 F.3d 895, 901 (6th Cir.2002); ***Brunswick Leasing Corp. v. Wisconsin Cent., Ltd.***, 136 F.3d 521, 530 (7th Cir.1998); 5 Wright & Miller §1271 & n.7. However, when and how the defense must be raised and when waiver occurs are governed by federal rules. ***Troxler v. Owens-Ill., Inc.***, 717 F.2d 530, 532 (11th Cir.1983).

3. Examples. Some examples of other affirmative defenses are the following:

(1) Absolute immunity. ***Cozzo v. Tangipahoa Parish Council—President Gov't***, 279 F.3d 273, 283 (5th Cir.2002).

(2) Arbitration agreement. ***American Recovery Corp. v. Computerized Thermal Imaging, Inc.***, 96 F.3d 88, 96 (4th Cir.1996); *see* ***Wilson Wear, Inc. v. United Merchs. & Mfrs.***, 713 F.2d 324, 326-27 (7th Cir.1983) (affirmative defense of arbitration agreement can be raised either in answer or in motion to compel or stay). *But see* ***Demsey & Assocs. v. S.S. Sea Star***, 461 F.2d 1009, 1017 (2d Cir.1972) (although "arbitration and award" is itemized affirmative defense under FRCP 8(c), mere existence of arbitration clause is not a defense; party should move for stay of action pending arbitration or ask to sever claim to be arbitrated). See "Affirmative defenses in FRCP 8(c)," §4.4.2, p. 233.

(3) Borrowed-servant doctrine. ***Green v. U.S.***, 709 F.2d 1158, 1164 n.7 (7th Cir.1983).

(4) Comparative fault of phantom party. ***O'Gilvie v. International Playtex, Inc.***, 821 F.2d 1438, 1445 (10th Cir.1987).

(5) Defensive use of issue preclusion. ***Terrell v. DeConna***, 877 F.2d 1267, 1270 (5th Cir.1989).

(6) Exemption. If a federal law bars a class or category of individuals from recovery, a defendant must affirmatively plead the exemptions created under that federal law. *See* ***Renfro v. City of Emporia***, 948 F.2d 1529, 1539 (10th Cir.1991).

(7) Failure to mitigate damages. ***Travellers Int'l v. Trans World Airlines, Inc.***, 41 F.3d 1570, 1580 (2d Cir.1994).

(8) Invalid patent. ***Cornwall v. U.S. Constr. Mfg.***, 800 F.2d 250, 252 (Fed.Cir.1986).

(9) Mutual mistake. ***Landmark Bank v. Saettele***, 784 F.Supp. 1434, 1440 (E.D.Mo.1992).

(10) Novation. ***Union Mut. Life Ins. v. Chrysler Corp.***, 793 F.2d 1, 13 (1st Cir.1986).

(11) Patent misuse. ***Bio-Rad Labs. v. Nicolet Instr. Corp.***, 739 F.2d 604, 617 (Fed.Cir.1984), *overruled on other grounds*, ***Markman v. Westview Instrs. Inc.***, 52 F.3d 967 (Fed.Cir.1995).

(12) Penalty. *See, e.g.*, ***Pace Comms. v. Moonlight Design, Inc.***, 31 F.3d 587, 593-94 (7th Cir.1994) (dicta; argument that liquidated-damages provision is unenforceable because it is a penalty clause is affirmative defense).

(13) Preemption. ***Williams v. Ashland Eng'g Co.***, 45 F.3d 588, 593 n.7 (1st Cir.1995).

(14) Qualified or good-faith immunity. A defendant-official must affirmatively plead the defense of qualified or good-faith immunity. ***Harlow v. Fitzgerald***, 457 U.S. 800, 815 (1982); *see* ***Gagan v. Norton***, 35 F.3d 1473, 1477 (10th Cir.1994).

(15) Rescission. ***National Un. Fire Ins. v. City Sav.***, 28 F.3d 376, 394 (3d Cir.1994).

(16) Sovereign immunity. *See* ***Charpentier v. Godsil***, 937 F.2d 859, 863 (3d Cir.1991).

§4.6 Sufficiency of affirmative defense. Because an affirmative defense is a pleading, it must set forth a short and plain statement of the defense. FRCP 8(b)(1)(A); ***Heller Fin., Inc. v. Midwhey Powder Co.***, 883 F.2d 1286, 1294 (7th Cir.1989). The court may strike an affirmative defense that is insufficient on its face. ***Heller Fin.***, 883 F.2d at 1294. When fraud or mistake is asserted as a defense, the circumstances constituting the fraud or mistake must be stated with particularity. FRCP 9(b).

NOTE

Courts disagree on whether the standard under ***Iqbal*** *and* ***Twombly*** *applies to pleading affirmative defenses. Compare* ***Racick v. Dominion Law Assocs.***, *270 F.R.D. 228, 233-34 (E.D. N.C.2010) (standard applies), and* ***Hayne v. Green Ford Sales, Inc.***, *263 F.R.D. 647, 649-50 (D.Kan.2009) (same), with* ***Lane v. Page***, *272 F.R.D. 581, 589-91 & nn.5-6 (D.N.M.2011) (standard does not apply), and* ***Odyssey Imaging, LLC v. Cardiology Assocs.***, *752 F.Supp.2d 721, 725-26 (W.D.Va.2010) (same).* *See "Plausibility," ch. 2-B, §5.1.2, p. 81.* *Check the law of the relevant circuit or district to determine whether the* ***Iqbal*** *and* ***Twombly*** *standard applies to affirmative defenses.*

§4.7 Inconsistent affirmative defenses. Just as a plaintiff can assert inconsistent theories of recovery in its complaint, a defendant can assert inconsistent affirmative defenses in its answer. FRCP 8(d)(3).

§5. DEFENDANT'S CLAIMS

FRCP 13 permits parties to file counterclaims and cross-claims; FRCP 14 permits parties to bring suit against, or "implead," another person who is not a party to the suit.

§5.1 Counterclaim. A defendant may file a claim against the plaintiff by alleging a counterclaim. FRCP 13. A counterclaim is a claim for relief filed against an opposing party who first asserted a claim. *Black's Law Dictionary* 402 (9th ed. 2009).

1. Assert in answer. A defendant generally should assert a counterclaim in the answer. However, if the defendant does not raise the counterclaim in its answer, it may be able to amend the answer to include the counterclaim (1) once as "a matter of course" (i.e., within 21 days after serving it), (2) by leave of court, or (3) with the plaintiff's consent. *See* FRCP 15(a)(1), (a)(2). For an amendment to relate back to the original pleading, the defendant must satisfy FRCP 15(c). 2009 Notes to FRCP 13 at ¶1, p. 1156, this book; *see* 2009 Notes to FRCP 15 at ¶7, p. 1157, this book. See "Amending Pleadings – Pretrial," ch. 5-I, §3, p. 345.

2. Inconsistent with affirmative defense. A counterclaim may be inconsistent with an affirmative defense raised in the same answer. FRCP 8(d)(3); ***Keebler Co. v. Rovira Biscuit Corp.***, 624 F.2d 366, 373 n.7 (1st Cir. 1980).

3. Compulsory or permissive. Counterclaims are either compulsory or permissive.

(1) Compulsory counterclaim.

(a) Generally. A counterclaim is compulsory if it arises out of the transaction or occurrence that is the subject of the plaintiff's claim and if its adjudication does not require the presence of another party over whom the court cannot acquire jurisdiction. FRCP 13(a)(1); ***Nippon Credit Bank, Ltd. v. Matthews***, 291 F.3d 738, 755 (11th Cir.2002); *see, e.g.*, ***Kane v. Magna Mixer Co.***, 71 F.3d 555, 561-62 (6th Cir.1995) (third-party D's counterclaim for indemnity was compulsory because claim arose from same transaction asserted in third-party complaint and resolution did not depend on any events that might arise after judgment). A compulsory counterclaim must be pleaded in the present suit; if not, the defendant is barred from asserting it in a later suit. ***Hydranautics v. FilmTec Corp.***, 70 F.3d 533, 536 (9th Cir.1995); *see* FRCP 13(a); ***Nippon Credit***, 291 F.3d at 755; ***Kane***, 71 F.3d at 562. A counterclaim is compulsory only if it meets the following criteria:

[1] Mature claim. The counterclaim must be mature at the time it is served. ***Eon Labs. v. SmithKline Beecham Corp.***, 298 F.Supp.2d 175, 181-82 (D.Mass.2003); ***Jupiter Aluminum Corp. v. Home Ins. Co.***, 181 F.R.D. 605, 608 (N.D.Ill.1998); *see* FRCP 13(a)(1); ***In re Ark-La-Tex Timber Co.***, 482 F.3d 319, 332 (5th Cir. 2007).

[2] Not filed elsewhere. The counterclaim must not be the subject of a pending case in another court when the suit is commenced. *See* FRCP 13(a)(2)(A).

[3] Same transaction or occurrence. The counterclaim must arise out of the same transaction or occurrence as the opposing claim. FRCP 13(a)(1)(A); ***Kane***, 71 F.3d at 561-62; ***Hydranautics***, 70 F.3d at 536. The phrase "transaction or occurrence" may include a series of occurrences, depending on their logical relationship. ***Costello, Porter, Hill, Heisterkamp & Bushnell v. Providers Fid. Life Ins.***, 958 F.2d 836, 839 n.4 (8th Cir.1992).

[4] Same capacity. The counterclaim must be against the plaintiff in the same capacity in which the plaintiff sued the defendant. ***In re Williams Contract Furniture, Inc.***, 148 B.R. 799, 803 (Bankr.E.D. Va.1992); *see* ***Bender v. Williamsport Area Sch. Dist.***, 475 U.S. 534, 543 & n.6 (1986). For example, a defendant cannot bring a counterclaim against the plaintiff in its individual capacity when the plaintiff sued only in its representative capacity. ***In re Williams Contract Furniture***, 148 B.R. at 803.

[5] All parties available. The counterclaim must not require the presence of additional parties over whom the court cannot acquire personal jurisdiction. FRCP 13(a)(1)(B).

[6] Logical relationship. Some circuits require the court to determine whether there is a "logical relationship" between the claim and the counterclaim and whether substantially the same evidence would support or refute both claims. ***Transamerica Occidental Life Ins. v. Aviation Office***, 292 F.3d 384, 389-90 (3d Cir. 2002); ***Underwriters at Interest on Cover Note JHB92M10582079 v. Nautronix, Ltd.***, 79 F.3d 480, 483 n.2 (5th Cir.1996); ***Adam v. Jacobs***, 950 F.2d 89, 92 (2d Cir.1991); ***Sanders v. First Nat'l Bank & Trust Co.***, 936 F.2d 273, 277 (6th Cir.1991). Some circuits break this analysis down into a four-part test: (1) Is there a logical relationship between the two claims? (2) Are the issues of fact and law raised by the claim and counterclaim largely the same? (3) Would res judicata bar a later suit on the counterclaim if the court did not take jurisdiction? (4) Would substantially the same evidence support or refute both the claim and the counterclaim? ***FDIC v. Hulsey***, 22 F.3d 1472, 1487 (10th Cir.1994); ***Maddox v. Kentucky Fin. Co.***, 736 F.2d 380, 382 (6th Cir.1984).

(b) Exceptions.

[1] Declaratory or injunctive claims. If the plaintiff's claim seeks only declaratory or injunctive relief, the defendant is not barred from asserting the claim in a later suit. *See* ***Andrew Robinson Int'l v. Hartford Fire Ins.***, 547 F.3d 48, 58-59 (1st Cir.2008); ***Allan Block Corp. v. County Materials Corp.***, 512 F.3d 912, 916-17 (7th Cir.2008); ***U.S. v. Snider***, 779 F.2d 1151, 1156 (6th Cir.1985); 6 Wright, Miller & Kane §1412.

[2] Two pending suits. When there are two pending suits, the defendant does not have to assert its compulsory counterclaim in the suit with the first responsive pleading; instead, the defendant may assert its counterclaim in the second suit. ***Southern Constr. Co. v. Pickard***, 371 U.S. 57, 60-61 (1962); 6 Wright, Miller & Kane §1412 & nn.18-19.

(2) Permissive counterclaim. A counterclaim is permissive if it may be pleaded against the plaintiff even if it does not arise out of the transaction or occurrence that is the subject matter of the plaintiff's claim. *See* FRCP 13(b). Any counterclaim that does not satisfy the compulsory-counterclaim test is a permissive counterclaim. ***Employers Ins. v. U.S.***, 764 F.2d 1572, 1576 (Fed.Cir.1985). A permissive counterclaim can be filed in the same suit, but if it is not, the compulsory-counterclaim bar will not prevent it from being asserted in a later suit. ***Mercoid Corp. v. Mid-Continent Inv.***, 320 U.S. 661, 671 (1944).

4. After-acquired counterclaim. With the court's permission, a defendant can amend its pleadings to add a counterclaim that has matured or was acquired by the defendant after serving a pleading. FRCP 13(e); ***Harbor Ins. v. Continental Bank Corp.***, 922 F.2d 357, 360 (7th Cir.1990). Before allowing the defendant to amend, the court must determine whether the counterclaim is compulsory, allowing the court to exercise ancillary jurisdiction over the claim, or whether the counterclaim is permissive, requiring the court to find an independent basis for jurisdiction. ***Harbor Ins.***, 922 F.2d at 360-61.

5. Dismissal of counterclaim. If the court dismisses the claim that gave rise to the counterclaim, the court may also dismiss the counterclaim. ***Scott v. Long Island Sav. Bank***, 937 F.2d 738, 742-43 (2d Cir.1991) (compulsory counterclaim); ***Harris v. Steinem***, 571 F.2d 119, 124-25 (2d Cir.1978) (permissive counterclaim).

§5.2 Cross-claim. A cross-claim is an affirmative claim for relief filed by a party against a coparty. *See Black's Law Dictionary* 433 (9th ed. 2009). A party may file a cross-claim against a coparty if the claim arises out of the transaction or occurrence that is the subject matter of the original action or counterclaim, or if the claim relates to any property that is the subject matter of the original action. FRCP 13(g); *see* ***Cam-Ful Indus. v. Fidelity & Deposit Co.***, 922 F.2d 156, 160 (2d Cir.1991). Cross-claims are always permissive, and a party's failure to assert a cross-claim will not prevent the party from asserting that claim in a later suit. *See* ***U.S. v. Confederate Acres Sanitary Sewage & Drainage Sys.***, 935 F.2d 796, 799 (6th Cir.1991); 6 Wright, Miller & Kane §1431.

§5.3 Third-party claim. Third-party practice allows a defendant to bring an additional party into the lawsuit. FRCP 14(a). Under third-party practice, or "impleader," a defendant, as a third-party plaintiff, may bring into the suit any third party who may be liable to the defendant or to the plaintiff for all or part of the plaintiff's claim against the

defendant. FRCP 14(a)(1); ***Discovery Grp. v. Chapel Dev., LLC***, 574 F.3d 986, 989 n.* (8th Cir.2009); ***FDIC v. Bathgate***, 27 F.3d 850, 873 (3d Cir.1994); *see also* ***Coons v. Industrial Knife Co.***, 620 F.3d 38, 43 (1st Cir.2010) (FRCP 14 addresses when P can assert claims against third-party D, but it does not address whether those claims are timely). The scope of federal impleader is narrow.

1. Claims must be derivative. A defendant may implead a third-party defendant only when the third-party claim is derivative of the plaintiff's claim. ***Israel Disc. Bank, Ltd. v. Entin***, 951 F.2d 311, 314 n.6 (11th Cir. 1992). A third-party complaint depends at least in part on the resolution of the primary lawsuit. The most common example of a third-party claim is a claim for contribution or indemnity if the defendant is found liable to the plaintiff. *See* ***Washington Hosp. Ctr. Nat'l Rehab. Hosp. v. Collier***, 947 F.2d 1498, 1501 (D.C.Cir.1991). If the defendant is not found liable to the original plaintiff, there is no underlying liability to be shifted to the third-party defendant. *See* ***First Golden Bancorp. v. Weiszmann***, 942 F.2d 726, 731 (10th Cir.1991).

2. Adverse to plaintiff. Like the third-party plaintiff (i.e., the defendant), the impleaded party is adverse to the plaintiff. ***McLaughlin v. Pernsley***, 876 F.2d 308, 313 (3d Cir.1989).

3. Timing of complaint. The defendant may file a third-party complaint without leave of court within 14 days after serving its answer. FRCP 14(a)(1). To file a third-party complaint more than 14 days after serving its answer, the defendant must secure leave of court. *Id.*

4. Jurisdiction. To determine jurisdiction in an impleader action, FRCP 14 must be read in conjunction with 28 U.S.C. §1367. Section 1367 provides for supplemental jurisdiction over certain kinds of claims. A claim that is proper under FRCP 14 will generally fall within the scope of 28 U.S.C. §1367(a). Thus, the district court will have jurisdiction over that claim. See "Supplemental Jurisdiction," ch. 2-F, §6, p. 134.

§6. DISCLOSURE STATEMENT

If the defendant is a nongovernmental corporate party, it must file with its answer two copies of a statement that either (1) identifies any parent corporation and any publicly held corporation that owns 10% or more of its stock or (2) states that there is no such corporation. FRCP 7.1(a); *see* FRCP 7.1(b)(1) (statement must be filed with defendant's first appearance, pleading, petition, response, or other request to court). The defendant must promptly file a supplemental statement if any of the information in the earlier statement changes. FRCP 7.1(b)(2). See ***O'Connor's Federal Forms***, FORM 1B:9.

COMMENTARIES

CHAPTER 4. REMOVAL & REMAND
TABLE OF CONTENTS

A. DEFENDANT'S NOTICE OF REMOVAL 241
§1. GENERAL 241
§2. REASONS FOR REMOVAL 241
§2.1 Avoiding local prejudice 241
§2.2 Different judge 241
§2.3 Expertise with federal questions 241
§2.4 Delaying trial 242
§2.5 Favorable procedural rules 242
§2.6 Different voir dire procedures 242
§2.7 Different juries 242
§2.8 Smaller verdicts & judgments 242
§2.9 Settlement advantages 242
§2.10 Arbitration clauses 242
§3. CHECKLIST FOR REMOVAL 242
§3.1 Are there grounds for removal? 242
§3.2 Is it too late to remove? 242
§3.3 Will all codefendants agree to remove? 242
§3.4 Has anything new developed since earlier unsuccessful removal? 242
§4. DEADLINES FOR REMOVAL 242
§4.1 Suit removable at time initial pleading filed 243
§4.2 Suit becomes removable later 245
§4.3 Particular cases 247
§4.4 Extension of deadline 248
§4.5 Revival exception 248
§5. GROUNDS FOR REMOVAL 249
§5.1 Federal-question jurisdiction 249
§5.2 Diversity jurisdiction 249
§5.3 Special removal statutes 257
§5.4 Alienage jurisdiction 260
§5.5 Supplemental jurisdiction 260
§6. PROHIBITIONS AGAINST REMOVAL 260
§6.1 Suits against railroads 260
§6.2 Suits against common carriers 260
§6.3 Workers' compensation suits 260
§6.4 Jones Act suits 260
§6.5 Admiralty & maritime suits 260
§6.6 Securities Act suits 260
§6.7 Proceedings from state agency 261
§7. NOTICE OF REMOVAL 261
§7.1 Who can file notice 261
§7.2 Deadline to file notice 261
§7.3 Contents of notice 261
§7.4 Filing & serving notice 263
§7.5 Amending notice 263
§8. CONSENT TO REMOVAL 263
§8.1 Consent required 263
§8.2 Form of consent 264
§8.3 Time for consent 265
§9. NO ORDER REQUIRED FOR REMOVAL 265
§9.1 Ancillary orders 265
§9.2 Federal & local rules 265
§9.3 Defendant's answer 265
§10. WHEN REMOVAL IS EFFECTIVE 266
§10.1 After notice filed in state court 266
§10.2 Before notice filed in state court 266
§11. WAIVER OF REMOVAL 266
§11.1 Late notice of removal 266
§11.2 Contract 266
§11.3 Conduct in state court 266

B. PLAINTIFF'S MOTION TO REMAND 268
§1. GENERAL 268
§2. AMENDING PLEADINGS AFTER REMOVAL 268
§2.1 Removal based on diversity 268
§2.2 Removal based on federal question 270
§3. MOTION 270
§3.1 Grounds 271
§3.2 Verification 273
§3.3 Hearing request 273
§3.4 Costs & fees 273
§3.5 Deadlines for remand 273
§4. HEARING 275
§4.1 Evidence or argument? 275
§4.2 Jurisdictional issues 275
§5. RESPONSE 275
§6. RULING 276
§6.1 Remand on court's initiative 276
§6.2 Remand mandatory 276
§6.3 Denial of remand mandatory 277
§6.4 Remand discretionary 277
§6.5 Award of costs, expenses & attorney fees 277
§6.6 Procedure after remand 279
§6.7 Findings of fact 279
§7. APPELLATE REVIEW 279
§7.1 Standard of review 279
§7.2 When reviewable 279

COMMENTARIES

CHAPTER 4. REMOVAL & REMAND

4. REMOVAL & REMAND

A. DEFENDANT'S NOTICE OF REMOVAL

§1. GENERAL

§1.1 Rules. FRCP 81(c); 28 U.S.C. §§1441-1454.

§1.2 Purpose. Removal is the procedure by which a defendant can transfer a case from state court to federal court. In general, any case that could have been originally filed in federal court can be removed, but there are significant exceptions.

NOTE

In the Federal Courts Jurisdiction and Venue Clarification Act of 2011 (referred to as the Clarification Act), Congress made significant amendments to removal statutes in title 28. See Lamar Smith, Federal Courts Jurisdiction & Venue Clarification Act of 2011, H.R. Rep. No. 112-10 (2011). For this subchapter, the Clarification Act modified removal procedure in these situations: (1) when federal claims are joined with nonremovable claims, (2) when there are multiple defendants, (3) when removal is sought after one year and the plaintiff acted in bad faith, and (4) when the amount in controversy is not specified in the complaint. See id. at 11-17. For removed cases, the Clarification Act became effective for any suit commenced—within the meaning of state law—in state court on or after January 6, 2012. Federal Courts Jurisdiction & Venue Clarification Act of 2011, P.L. 112-63, §105, 125 Stat. 762 (2011) (eff. Jan. 6, 2012). For the law before the Clarification Act became effective, see ***O'Connor's Federal Rules * Civil Trials*** *(2012), "Defendant's Notice of Removal," ch. 4-A, p. 237. Because of the substantive changes made by the 2011 amendments, use caution when citing cases that predate the amendments.*

§1.3 Timetable & forms. Timetable, Removal & Remand, p. 1581; ***O'Connor's Federal Civil Forms*** (2012), FORMS 4A.

§1.4 Other references. Federal Courts Jurisdiction & Venue Clarification Act of 2011, P.L. 112-63, 125 Stat. 758 (2011) (eff. Jan. 6, 2012) (referred to as Clarification Act); Lamar Smith, Federal Courts Jurisdiction & Clarification Act of 2011, H.R. Rep. No. 112-10 (2011) (referred to as H.R. Rep. No. 112-10 (2011)); 14A Wright, Miller & Cooper, *Federal Practice & Procedure 3d* §3674 (1998 & Supp.2012); 14B, 14C Wright, Miller, Cooper & Steinman, *Federal Practice & Procedure 4th* §§3721-3740 (2009 & Supp.2012); 16 *Moore's Federal Practice 3d* ch. 107 (2012); Beisner & Miller, *Litigating in the New Class Action World: A Guide to CAFA's Legislative History*, 6 BNA Class Action Litig. Rep. 403 (2005); Annotation, *When Does Period for Filing Petition for Removal of Civil Action from State Court to Federal District Court Begin to Run Under 28 USCS §1446(b)*, 139 ALR Fed. 331 (1997 & Supp.2012-13); Annotation, *Effect [of Removal] on Jurisdiction of State Court, of 28 USCS §1446(e), Relating to Removal of Civil Case to Federal Court*, 38 ALR Fed. 824 (1978 & Supp.2012-13).

§2. REASONS FOR REMOVAL

Many defense lawyers believe that federal courts are more favorable to defendants than state courts are, so they will try to remove cases whenever possible. By removing a case to federal court, the defendant may benefit from the following:

§2.1 Avoiding local prejudice. The defendant can avoid any local prejudice it might encounter in a state court.

§2.2 Different judge. The defendant can avoid a state-court judge who is perceived to be unfavorable.

§2.3 Expertise with federal questions. For a case involving a federal question, the defendant can present its claim to a judge who may be more familiar with federal law.

§2.4 Delaying trial. The defendant may be able to delay the trial. In some areas of the country, federal courts are slower than state courts because of the high number of criminal prosecutions in federal drug cases. Some defense lawyers prefer courts with slow dockets, hoping the delay will encourage a favorable settlement from the plaintiff or make testimony less credible because of fading memories.

§2.5 Favorable procedural rules. The defendant can avail itself of federal rules of procedure or evidence that are perceived to be more advantageous than the corresponding state rules.

§2.6 Different voir dire procedures. The defendant may be able to prevent the plaintiff's attorney from conducting an extensive voir dire. In many federal courts, the judge conducts a more limited form of voir dire than what the attorneys conduct in state court.

§2.7 Different juries. The defendant may be able to select a jury that is considered more favorable and that is less likely to contain jurors known to the plaintiff's attorney. The jury pools for federal courts are usually drawn from larger geographic areas than jury pools for state courts, which are often limited to a county or parish. In federal court, civil juries consist of six or more jurors (in most state courts, juries consist of 12), and federal juries must be unanimous in reaching a verdict (in some state courts, unanimity is not a requirement).

§2.8 Smaller verdicts & judgments. The defendant may be able to avoid a large verdict. Many defense attorneys believe that federal juries award smaller verdicts than state juries do and that federal judges are more willing than state judges to reduce large verdicts.

§2.9 Settlement advantages. The defendant can place the plaintiff's attorney in a possibly unfamiliar court system, which can encourage a settlement more favorable to the defendant.

§2.10 Arbitration clauses. The defendant may be able to require that the matter be submitted to arbitration. Federal courts are more receptive than state courts to enforcing arbitration agreements. See "Arbitration," ch. 7-E, p. 650.

§3. CHECKLIST FOR REMOVAL

Any case can be removed to federal court. But unless certain criteria are met, the case will be summarily remanded to state court, and costs and expenses may be assessed against the defendant for "improvident" removal. *See* 28 U.S.C. §1447(c). To remove a case to federal court and keep it there, the defendant must consider the following:

§3.1 Are there grounds for removal? Generally, removal is proper if there is (1) federal-question jurisdiction, (2) diversity jurisdiction, (3) a statute that authorizes removal, or (4) alienage jurisdiction. See "Grounds for Removal," §5, p. 249. However, some federal statutes prohibit removal of certain claims. See "Prohibitions Against Removal," §6, p. 260.

§3.2 Is it too late to remove? In most cases, the defendant must file a notice of removal within 30 days after receiving notice of the suit. See "Deadlines for Removal," §4, this page.

§3.3 Will all codefendants agree to remove? When removal is based on 28 U.S.C. §1441(a) (i.e., federal-question or diversity jurisdiction when no other statute authorizing removal would apply), all defendants who have been properly joined and served in the suit must join in the notice of removal or consent to the removal. 28 U.S.C. §1446(b)(2)(A). See "Notice of Removal," §7, p. 261; "Consent to Removal," §8, p. 263.

§3.4 Has anything new developed since earlier unsuccessful removal? If there has been a new development since an earlier unsuccessful removal that renders the case removable, a second removal is proper. ***Knudsen v. Liberty Mut. Ins.***, 435 F.3d 755, 757 (7th Cir.2006); *see* 28 U.S.C. §1446(b)(3), (c). See "Suit becomes removable later," §4.2, p. 245.

§4. DEADLINES FOR REMOVAL

There are two mutually exclusive 30-day windows during which a case can be removed. The first window is 30 days after the defendant receives the initial pleading. *See* 28 U.S.C. §1446(b)(1); ***Harris v. Bankers Life & Cas. Co.***, 425

F.3d 689, 692 (9th Cir.2005). This window "opens" only if the case is clearly removable on the basis of jurisdictional facts apparent from the face of the complaint. *See* ***Harris***, 425 F.3d at 694. The second window is 30 days after the defendant receives a paper from which it can first ascertain that the case is removable or that the case has become removable if the case stated in the initial pleading was not removable. *See* 28 U.S.C. §1446(b)(3); ***Harris***, 425 F.3d at 692. This window applies when the case is clearly not removable on the basis of jurisdictional facts apparent from the face of the initial pleading or when it is unclear from the initial pleading whether the case is removable (i.e., an "indeterminate pleading"). *See* ***Harris***, 425 F.3d at 694.

NOTE

Before the Clarification Act, the two 30-day windows were commonly known as first-paragraph and second-paragraph removals. Although the Clarification Act has made these designations obsolete, the substance of the removal procedures based on the two windows has not been affected; thus, earlier case law discussing first- and second-paragraph removals is still applicable.

§4.1 Suit removable at time initial pleading filed.

1. Determining removability. If a suit is removable at the time the initial pleading is filed, the defendant must file the notice of removal within 30 days after receiving the initial pleading. *See* 28 U.S.C. §1446(b)(1); ***Murphy Bros. v. Michetti Pipe Stringing, Inc.***, 526 U.S. 344, 354 (1999); ***Board of Regents v. Nippon Tel. & Tel. Corp.***, 478 F.3d 274, 278 (5th Cir.2007). This deadline is triggered by (1) actual receipt of the summons, the complaint, or both, *and* (2) the existence of jurisdictional facts on the face of the initial pleading.

(1) Receipt of summons & initial pleading. The start of the 30-day period varies depending on when the defendant receives the summons and the initial pleading. Under 28 U.S.C. §1446(b)(1), there are a few ways for the deadline to be triggered, and the deadline will always run from the earliest triggering event.

(a) Summons & initial pleading served together. If the summons and pleading are served together, the 30-day removal period begins immediately. ***Murphy Bros.***, 526 U.S. at 354; *see* 28 U.S.C. §1446(b)(1); *see, e.g.*, ***Tucci v. Hartford Fin. Servs. Grp.***, 600 F.Supp.2d 630, 632-33 (D.N.J.2009) (30-day period begins to run when D actually receives summons and complaint; period does not run from service on D's statutory agent); ***Anderson v. Ford Motor Co.***, 303 F.Supp.2d 1253, 1258 (W.D.Okla.2004) (P served summons and complaint on D 1½ years after filing suit; D had 30 days after service to file notice of removal).

(b) Summons before initial pleading. If the summons is served first but the defendant does not receive a copy of the initial pleading until later, the 30-day removal period begins on the date the complaint is received or made available through filing. *See* ***Murphy Bros.***, 526 U.S. at 354; ***Sikirica v. Nationwide Ins.***, 416 F.3d 214, 223 (3d Cir.2005); ***Riggs v. Fling Irrigation, Inc.***, 535 F.Supp.2d 572, 577-78 (W.D.N.C.2008). The Second Circuit, however, has refused to interpret ***Murphy Bros.*** so narrowly, holding that a summons with only notice can serve as the "initial pleading" for purposes of triggering the 30-day deadline. ***Whitaker v. American Telecasting, Inc.***, 261 F.3d 196, 205 (2d Cir.2001).

CAUTION

In jurisdictions where the plaintiff can serve the summons before filing the initial pleading, some district courts have held that the 30 days may begin to run from the receipt of the summons if (1) state procedure specifies that an action can "commence" when the summons is served, (2) state procedure grants the defendant the right to compel the plaintiff to file an initial pleading after service of the summons, and (3) the defendant does not exercise that right within one year after receiving the summons. See, e.g., ***Namey v. Malcolm****, 534 F.Supp.2d 494, 497-98 (M.D.Pa.2008).*

(c) Initial pleading before summons. If the initial pleading is filed before the summons is served, the 30-day removal period begins on the date the summons is served. ***Murphy Bros.***, 526 U.S. at 354; *see* 28 U.S.C. §1446(b)(1).

(2) Existence of jurisdictional facts. The start of the 30-day period depends on whether jurisdictional facts revealing a basis for removal are apparent from the face of the initial pleading. In other words, the grounds for removal must be ascertainable from an examination of the four corners of the initial pleading and not through the defendant's subjective knowledge or duty to make a further inquiry. ***Carvalho v. Equifax Info. Servs.***, 629 F.3d 876, 886 (9th Cir.2010); ***Chapman v. Powermatic, Inc.***, 969 F.2d 160, 163 (5th Cir.1992); *see* ***Moltner v. Starbucks Coffee Co.***, 624 F.3d 34, 38 (2d Cir.2010) (time for removal on diversity grounds does not begin to run until P serves D with paper explicitly specifying amount of monetary damages sought); ***In re Willis***, 228 F.3d 896, 897 (8th Cir.2000) (same); ***Akin v. Ashland Chem. Co.***, 156 F.3d 1030, 1036 (10th Cir.1998) (first-paragraph removal requires clear and unequivocal notice from initial pleading); *see, e.g.*, ***Lovern v. General Motors Corp.***, 121 F.3d 160, 162 (4th Cir. 1997) (case was not removable when jurisdictional details were obscured, omitted, or misstated in initial pleading). For example, a pre-complaint document (e.g., demand letter) that contains a jurisdictional "clue," such as an amount in controversy, cannot operate in tandem with an indeterminate pleading to trigger the 30-day deadline. ***Carvalho***, 629 F.3d at 886.

2. Cases involving multiple defendants. If removal is based on 28 U.S.C. §1441(a) (i.e., federal-question or diversity jurisdiction when no other statute authorizing removal would apply) and the suit is removable at the time it is filed, all defendants who have been properly joined and served in the suit must join in the notice of removal or consent to the removal. 28 U.S.C. §1446(b)(2)(A); *see* ***Balazik v. County of Dauphin***, 44 F.3d 209, 213 (3d Cir.1995); ***Roe v. O'Donohue***, 38 F.3d 298, 301 (7th Cir.1994), *overruled on other grounds*, ***Murphy Bros. v. Michetti Pipe Stringing, Inc.***, 526 U.S. 344 (1999); ***Hewitt v. City of Stanton***, 798 F.2d 1230, 1232 (9th Cir.1986). See "Consent to Removal," §8, p. 263. If all defendants are served on the same day, the deadline for filing the notice of removal or consent to removal is the same for all defendants—that is, all defendants must have filed the notice or consent to removal within 30 days of service. ***Barbour v. International Un.***, 640 F.3d 599, 605-06 (4th Cir.2011). See "Suit removable at time initial pleading filed," §4.1, p. 243. But if defendants are served on different days, the deadline for filing the notice of removal or consent to removal will be different for each defendant.

(1) Deadline to file notice. Each defendant has 30 days from the date it is served to file a notice of removal. 28 U.S.C. §1446(b)(2)(B); H.R. Rep. No. 112-10, at 14 (2011). See "Receipt of summons & initial pleading," §4.1.1(1), p. 243.

NOTE

Before the Clarification Act became effective, courts were divided on whether a defendant who is served after another defendant (i.e., a later-served defendant) has 30 days to remove from the date it was served or from the date the first defendant was served. See ***Pietrangelo v. Alvas Corp.***, *686 F.3d 62, 64-65 (2d Cir.2012). The Clarification Act adopted the later-served-defendant rule. H.R. Rep. No. 112-10, at 14 (2011).*

(2) Deadline to consent.

(a) Earlier-served defendant. If a later-served defendant files a notice of removal, any earlier-served defendant can consent to the removal even though that defendant did not previously initiate or consent to removal. 28 U.S.C. §1446(b)(2)(C); H.R. Rep. No. 112-10, at 14 (2011). The earlier-served defendant must consent before the later-served defendant's deadline to file a notice of removal. *See* 28 U.S.C. §1446(b)(2)(C). See "Consent to Removal," §8, p. 263.

(b) Later-served defendant. The Clarification Act did not specifically address the deadline for a later-served defendant to consent to an earlier-served defendant's notice of removal. Because each defendant

under the Clarification Act has 30 days from the date it is served to file a notice of removal, it seems to follow that a later-served defendant would also have 30 days to consent to an earlier-filed notice of removal. If not, the later-served defendant could simply file its own notice of removal within 30 days and have the earlier-served defendant consent to its notice. *See* 28 U.S.C. §1446(b)(2)(C).

§4.2 Suit becomes removable later. If a suit is not removable at the time it is initially filed, the suit must remain in state court unless a voluntary act by the plaintiff brings about a change that makes the suit removable. ***Great N. Ry. v. Alexander***, 246 U.S. 276, 282 (1918); ***California v. Keating***, 986 F.2d 346, 348 (9th Cir.1993); *see* ***Higgins v. E.I. DuPont de Nemours & Co.***, 863 F.2d 1162, 1166 (4th Cir.1988); *see also* ***Insinga v. La Bella***, 845 F.2d 249, 254 (11th Cir.1988) (fraudulent joinder is well-established exception to rule that only P's voluntary act can make case removable). See "Grounds for Removal," §5, p. 249.

1. Determining removability. If the suit is not removable at the time of filing but becomes removable later, the suit can be removed if the defendant files the notice of removal within 30 days after the defendant's receipt, "through service or otherwise," of a copy of an amended pleading, motion, order, or other paper from which the defendant can ascertain that the case has become removable. 28 U.S.C. §1446(b)(3); ***Caterpillar Inc. v. Lewis***, 519 U.S. 61, 68-69 (1996); ***Dahl v. R.J. Reynolds Tobacco Co.***, 478 F.3d 965, 968 (8th Cir.2007); ***Crockett v. R.J. Reynolds Tobacco Co.***, 436 F.3d 529, 532 (5th Cir.2006); *cf.* ***Durham v. Lockheed Martin Corp.***, 445 F.3d 1247, 1251-52 (9th Cir.2006) (suit was removable—but not removed—based on diversity when filed; suit later became removable—and was considered timely removed—based on federal-officer grounds under 28 U.S.C. §1442, which did not become apparent until after D received interrogatory responses). A suit usually is not removable at the time of filing because either the case is clearly not removable on the basis of jurisdictional facts apparent from the face of the initial pleading or the initial pleading is indeterminate as to removability. *See* ***Harris v. Bankers Life & Cas. Co.***, 425 F.3d 689, 692-93 (9th Cir.2005). For example, the plaintiff, a California resident, files suit in California state court against defendant A, a California resident, and defendant B, a Connecticut resident. If, six months after filing the suit, defendant B receives a paper showing that the plaintiff settled with defendant A and dismissed A from the suit, then defendant B has 30 days after receipt to remove based on diversity jurisdiction. The information supporting removal in an amended pleading, motion, order, or other paper must be "unequivocal" to start the time limit for a notice of removal under 28 U.S.C. §1446(b)(3). ***Bosky v. Kroger Tex., LP***, 288 F.3d 208, 211 (5th Cir.2002); *see* ***Harris v. Bankers Life & Cas. Co.***, 425 F.3d 689, 694 (9th Cir.2005) (grounds for removal must be apparent from four corners of initial pleading or later paper); ***Lovern v. General Motors Corp.***, 121 F.3d 160, 162 (4th Cir.1997) (same); ***DeBry v. Transamerica Corp.***, 601 F.2d 480, 489-90 (10th Cir.1979) (unequivocal requirement means that it "should not be an ambiguous statement that requires an extensive investigation to determine the truth"); ***Soto v. Apple Towing***, 111 F.Supp.2d 222, 226 (E.D.N.Y.2000) (same).

(1) Other papers sufficient for removal. The term "other paper" in 28 U.S.C. §1446(b)(3) has not been helpful in determining what the defendant can use to ascertain that a case has become removable. *See* ***Movie Gallery US, LLC v. Smith***, 574 F.Supp.2d 1244, 1248 (M.D.Ala.2008). But the Clarification Act amended §1446 to provide that "other paper" includes information relating to the amount in controversy that is found in the records of the state proceeding or in discovery responses. 28 U.S.C. §1446(c)(3)(A); *see* H.R. Rep. No. 112-10, at 16 (2011). Apart from this amendment, courts developed certain criteria for determining whether something qualifies as "other paper." Generally, for something to be considered "other paper," it must be in writing, it must come from the plaintiff, and it must be received by the defendant after the initial complaint has been filed. *See* ***Carvalho v. Equifax Info. Servs.***, 629 F.3d 876, 885-86 (9th Cir.2010) (paper must be received after initial complaint filed); ***Lowery v. Alabama Power Co.***, 483 F.3d 1184, 1221 (11th Cir.2007) (paper must come from P); ***Entrekin v. Fisher Sci. Inc.***, 146 F.Supp.2d 594, 613 (D.N.J.2001) (paper usually must be in writing). Based on these criteria, courts have found that the following qualify as "other paper" to determine that a case has become removable under §1446(b)(3).

NOTE

Courts have recognized two exceptions to the in-writing requirement. ***Entrekin****, 146 F.Supp.2d at 613. Even though deposition testimony and statements made in open court are made orally, they can qualify as "other paper." See, e.g.,* ***Carvalho****, 629 F.3d at 886-87 (deposition testimony);* ***Peters v. Lincoln Elec. Co.****, 285 F.3d 456, 466 (6th Cir.2002) (deposition testimony);* ***Huffman v. Saul Holdings L.P.****, 194 F.3d 1072, 1078 (10th Cir.1999) (deposition testimony);* ***S.W.S. Erectors, Inc. v. Infax, Inc.****, 72 F.3d 489, 494 (5th Cir.1996) (deposition testimony);* ***Hessler v. Armstrong World Indus.****, 684 F.Supp. 393, 395 (D.Del.1988) (oral statements made in open court). At least one court has held that for deposition testimony, the 30-day period begins to run from the date of the testimony, not from the date the transcript is received.* ***Huffman****, 194 F.3d at 1079.*

(a) Discovery obtained from plaintiff. A discovery response obtained from the plaintiff qualifies as "other paper." *See* 28 U.S.C. §1446(c)(3)(A) (discovery responses); ***Lovern***, 121 F.3d at 161-62 (other documents may include answers to interrogatories); *see, e.g.*, ***Ritchie v. Williams***, 395 F.3d 283, 287 n.2 (6th Cir.2005) (agreement produced in discovery); ***Chapman v. Powermatic, Inc.***, 969 F.2d 160, 164 (5th Cir.1992) (answers to interrogatories); ***Riggs v. Continental Baking Co.***, 678 F.Supp. 236, 238 (N.D.Cal.1988) (statements in deposition).

(b) Post-complaint correspondence from plaintiff. Post-complaint correspondence received from the plaintiff qualifies as "other paper." *See* ***Addo v. Globe Life & Acc. Ins.***, 230 F.3d 759, 762 (5th Cir.2000) (post-complaint demand letter); ***Vermande v. Hyundai Motor Am., Inc.***, 352 F.Supp.2d 195, 200 (D.Conn.2004) (post-complaint settlement offer). The correspondence does not have to be filed with the court to constitute "other paper." ***Addo***, 230 F.3d at 761; ***Vermande***, 352 F.Supp.2d at 200.

(c) Court orders in related cases. Some courts have held that a court order in a related case can qualify as "other paper." *See, e.g.*, ***Green v. R.J. Reynolds Tobacco Co.***, 274 F.3d 263, 267-68 (5th Cir.2001); ***Doe v. American Red Cross***, 14 F.3d 196, 202-03 (3d Cir.1993). The order must come from a higher court in the same judicial hierarchy, the defendant must be the same in both cases, the cases must involve similar factual situations, and the order must have expressly authorized removal. *See* ***Green***, 274 F.3d at 267-68; ***Doe***, 14 F.3d at 202-03.

(2) Other papers not sufficient for removal. Courts have found that the following do not qualify as "other paper" to determine that a suit has become removable under §1446(b)(3).

(a) Documents created by defendant. A document created by the defendant does not qualify as "other paper." ***Lowery***, 483 F.3d at 1221; *see* ***Pretka v. Kolter City Plaza II, Inc.***, 608 F.3d 744, 763 (11th Cir.2010) (distinguishing ***Lowery*** from removal cases brought under first paragraph of former §1446(b)); *see, e.g.*, ***S.W.S. Erectors***, 72 F.3d at 494 (affidavit created by D did not qualify as "other paper").

(b) Documents received before initial pleading filed. A document received from the plaintiff before the initial complaint is filed does not qualify as "other paper." ***Carvalho***, 629 F.3d at 885-86; *see, e.g.*, ***Chapman***, 969 F.2d at 164 (prefiling demand letter).

(c) Court orders in unrelated cases. A court order in an unrelated case does not qualify as "other paper." ***Dahl***, 478 F.3d at 969-70; ***Green***, 274 F.3d at 266; ***Morsani v. Major League Baseball***, 79 F.Supp.2d 1331, 1333-34 (M.D.Fla.1999); ***Kocaj v. Chrysler Corp.***, 794 F.Supp. 234, 235-36 (E.D.Mich.1992); *see* ***Wisconsin v. Amgen, Inc.***, 516 F.3d 530, 533 (7th Cir.2008) ("other paper" refers to document filed in suit to be removed, not some other suit).

(d) Information obtained through silence or inaction. Information obtained through silence or inaction by the plaintiff does not qualify as "other paper." *See* ***Jhohman, LLC v. U.S. Sec. Assocs.***, 513 F.Supp.2d 913, 919 (E.D.Mich.2007) (deemed admissions did not qualify as other papers).

2. Limitation for diversity cases.

(1) One-year limit. If the suit is not removable at the time of filing but becomes removable later when the plaintiff brings about a change that creates diversity jurisdiction, the suit can be removed if the defendant

files the notice of removal within one year from the commencement of the suit. *See* 28 U.S.C. §1446(c)(1); ***Price v. Wyeth Holdings Corp.***, 505 F.3d 624, 630-31 & n.6 (7th Cir.2007); ***Burns v. Windsor Ins.***, 31 F.3d 1092, 1094 n.4 (11th Cir.1994). That is, under the one-year limit, if the plaintiff creates diversity, the defendant may remove the suit if it files a notice of removal within 30 days after the amended pleading was received but no later than one year after the initial pleading commenced the suit. *See* 28 U.S.C. §1446(b), (c)(1); *see also* ***Berbig v. Sears Roebuck & Co.***, 568 F.Supp.2d 1033, 1035-36 (D.Minn.2008) (when case was dismissed by one state court and same case was later filed in different state court, one-year limit did not run from filing in first state court; removal deadline ran from filing of initial pleading in second state court). Continuing with the example in §4.2.1, above, if the plaintiff dismisses defendant A, the California resident, 50 weeks after filing the suit in California state court, then defendant B, the Connecticut resident, has two weeks to file a notice of removal. But if the plaintiff dismisses defendant A 13 months after commencing the suit, it is too late for defendant B to remove. *See* ***Caterpillar***, 519 U.S. at 75 & n.12; ***Ritchey v. Upjohn Drug Co.***, 139 F.3d 1313, 1316 (9th Cir.1998); ***Jones Mgmt. Servs. v. KES, Inc.***, 296 F.Supp.2d 892, 894 (E.D.Tenn.2003); ***Beisel v. Aid Ass'n for Lutherans***, 843 F.Supp. 616, 619 (C.D.Cal.1994).

CAUTION

The one-year limit on diversity removal runs from the commencement of the suit in state court, not from the time of service. 28 U.S.C. §1446(c)(1); see ***Service Asset Mgmt. v. Hibernia Corp.****, 80 F.Supp.2d 626, 628-29 (E.D.Tex.2000);* ***Green Point Sav. Bank v. Hidalgo****, 910 F.Supp. 89, 91 (E.D.N.Y.1995). The date of commencement is the file-stamp date on the state-court pleading.* ***Robinson v. General Motors Corp.****, 601 F.Supp.2d 833, 837 (N.D.Tex.2008).*

(2) Exceptions.

(a) Bad faith. The one-year time limit does not apply if the court finds that the plaintiff acted in bad faith to prevent the defendant from removing the suit. 28 U.S.C. §1446(c)(1); *see* H.R. Rep. No. 112-10, at 15 (2011). Based on the phrase "to prevent a defendant from removing the action," the bad-faith exception is intended to be limited in scope. H.R. Rep. No. 112-10, at 15 (2011). A finding that the plaintiff deliberately failed to disclose the actual amount in controversy to prevent removal is considered bad faith. 28 U.S.C. §1446(c)(3)(B).

NOTE

The Clarification Act amended §1446 to add the bad-faith exception to the one-year time limit to file a notice of removal in diversity cases. See H.R. Rep. No. 112-10, at 15 (2011). The exception applies to suits commenced—within the meaning of state law—in state court on or after January 6, 2012. See Clarification Act, P.L. 112-63, §105, 125 Stat. 762 (2011) (eff. Jan. 6, 2012). For suits commenced before January 6, 2012, only the Fifth Circuit had recognized an equitable exception to the one-year time limit when a plaintiff attempted to manipulate the rules and prevent a defendant from exercising its removal rights. See ***Tedford v. Warner-Lambert Co.****, 327 F.3d 423, 427-28 (5th Cir.2003).*

(b) Class actions. The one-year time limit to file a notice of removal in diversity cases under 28 U.S.C. §1446(c)(1) does not apply to class actions. 28 U.S.C. §1453(b). See "Class actions," §5.3.1, p. 257.

§4.3 Particular cases.

1. Fraudulent-joinder cases. When there is a claim that a defendant has been fraudulently joined to prevent removal based on diversity jurisdiction, a defendant has 30 days after the time it learns or should have learned of the fraudulent joinder to file a notice of removal. *See* ***Beasley v. Goodyear Tire & Rubber Co.***, 835 F.Supp. 269, 272-73 (D.S.C.1993); 14C Wright, Miller, Cooper & Steinman §3731 & nn.79-81; *see, e.g.*, ***Ayres v. Sears***, 571 F.Supp.2d 768, 772-73 (W.D.Tex.2008) (remand granted for untimely removal when Ds did not identify specific date or event for learning about fraudulent joinder but rather created ambiguity and doubt about date, which made removal improper); ***Clingan v. Celtic Life Ins.***, 244 F.Supp.2d 1298, 1308 (M.D.Ala.2003) (remand granted for untimely removal

when D should have ascertained removability from complaint, not from later deposition); *see also* ***United Computer Sys. v. AT&T Corp.***, 298 F.3d 756, 762-63 (9th Cir.2002) (30-day deadline did not commence from service on fraudulently joined D when that D was the first D served). Most courts hold that the one-year limit applies to fraudulent-joinder cases. *See* ***Caudill v. Ford Motor Co.***, 271 F.Supp.2d 1324, 1327 (N.D.Okla.2003) (one-year limit applies to fraudulent-joinder cases); ***Russaw v. Voyager Life Ins.***, 921 F.Supp. 723, 724-25 (M.D.Ala.1996) (same); *see also* ***Lovern v. General Motors Corp.***, 121 F.3d 160, 163 (4th Cir.1997) (dicta; one-year limit is absolute bar to removal for diversity cases). *But see* ***Hardy v. Ajax Magnathermic Corp.***, 122 F.Supp.2d 757, 759 (W.D.Ky.2000) (one-year limit does not apply to fraudulent-joinder cases). See "Fraudulent joinder," §5.2.1(2)(e), p. 252.

2. FDIC cases. When the FDIC is a party, it has 90 days to remove a case from either the date the suit is filed against it or the date it is substituted as a party. 12 U.S.C. §1819(b)(2)(B); ***Casey v. FDIC***, 583 F.3d 586, 591 (8th Cir.2009); ***Buczkowski v. FDIC***, 415 F.3d 594, 595 (7th Cir.2005); ***Bullion Servs. v. Valley State Bank***, 50 F.3d 705, 708 (9th Cir.1995). The 90-day period begins when the FDIC is served. ***Costin Eng'g Consultants, Inc. v. Latham***, 905 F.Supp. 861, 864 (D.Colo.1995). *But see* ***CML-AZ Blue Ridge, LLC v. Sterling Plaza W., LLC***, No. CV 11-01122-PHX-FJM (D.Ariz.2011) (slip op.; 9-12-11) (90-day period begins on date suit is filed).

3. FTCA cases. When a tort action is brought against a federal employee under the Federal Tort Claims Act (FTCA), the suit can be removed at any time before trial if the Attorney General or the U.S. Attorney certifies that the conduct alleged by the plaintiff satisfies the requirements of an FTCA claim and that the defendant was acting within the scope of her employment at the time of the incident. *See* 28 U.S.C. §2679(d)(1), (d)(2); 42 U.S.C. §233(c); *see, e.g.*, ***Celestine v. Mount Vernon Neighborhood Health Ctr.***, 403 F.3d 76, 82 (2d Cir.2005) (notice of removal filed before trial by U.S. Attorney was timely). See "Removal under FTCA," §5.3.2(2), p. 258.

4. Certain cases or proceedings under 28 U.S.C. §1442(a). When a civil action that is removable under 28 U.S.C. §1442(a) is a proceeding in which a judicial order for testimony or documents is sought or issued, the United States, a federal agency, a federal officer, or any other person permitted to remove has 30 days to remove after receiving notice of the proceeding through service. *See* 28 U.S.C. §1446(g). When a proceeding within an otherwise nonremovable civil action in which a judicial order for testimony or documents is sought or issued or the enforcement of such an order is sought, only that proceeding—not the entire action—is removable by the United States, a federal agency, a federal officer, or any other person permitted to remove 30 days after receiving notice of the proceeding through service. *See* 28 U.S.C. §§1442(c), 1446(g). See "Removal under 28 U.S.C. §1442," §5.3.2(1), p. 257.

§4.4 Extension of deadline.

1. Generally – no extension. In most cases, the statutory time limit for removing a case is mandatory and cannot be extended by order of the court or consent of the parties. ***Cook v. Travelers Cos.***, 904 F.Supp. 841, 842 (N.D.Ill.1995); ***Godman v. Sears, Roebuck & Co.***, 588 F.Supp. 121, 123 (E.D.Mich.1984).

2. Exceptions.

(1) Foreign state actions. When an action is brought against a foreign state, the time limit for filing a notice of removal under 28 U.S.C. §1446(b) can be extended for cause. 28 U.S.C. §1441(d). See "Suits against foreign states," §5.3.8, p. 259.

(2) Patent, plant-variety-protection & copyright actions. When a party asserts a claim for relief arising under federal law relating to patents, plant variety protection, or copyrights, the time limit for filing a notice of removal under 28 U.S.C. §1446(b) can be extended for cause. 28 U.S.C. §1454(b)(2). See "Patent, plant-variety-protection & copyright actions," §5.3.9, p. 259.

§4.5 Revival exception.

Some courts permit revival of a lapsed right to remove an initially removable case if the complaint is so substantially amended as to alter the character of the action and essentially constitute a new lawsuit. ***Johnson v. Heublein Inc.***, 227 F.3d 236, 241 (5th Cir.2000); ***Wilson v. Intercollegiate (Big Ten) Conf. Athletic Ass'n***, 668 F.2d 962, 965 (7th Cir.1982); 16 *Moore's Federal Practice 3d* §107.30[3][a][i][B].

§5. GROUNDS FOR REMOVAL

The party removing the case has the burden to establish facts showing federal jurisdiction. ***Wilson v. Republic Iron & Steel Co.***, 257 U.S. 92, 97 (1921); ***Estate of Martineau v. ARCO Chem. Co.***, 203 F.3d 904, 910 (5th Cir.2000). Whether a case may be removed is a question of federal law to be decided by federal courts. ***Kansas Pub. Empls. Ret. Sys. v. Reimer & Koger Assocs.***, 4 F.3d 614, 618 (8th Cir.1993). The removal statutes are strictly construed. ***Syngenta Crop Prot., Inc. v. Henson***, 537 U.S. 28, 32 (2002). Any doubt about the propriety of removal is construed against removal. ***Diaz v. Sheppard***, 85 F.3d 1502, 1505 (11th Cir.1996); ***Duncan v. Stuetzle***, 76 F.3d 1480, 1485 (9th Cir.1996); ***Brown v. Francis***, 75 F.3d 860, 865 (3d Cir.1996); 16 *Moore's Federal Practice 3d* §107.05. *But see* ***Durham v. Lockheed Martin Corp.***, 445 F.3d 1247, 1253 (9th Cir.2006) (court liberally construed federal-officer removal statute to protect government's right of removal). There are several grounds for removal jurisdiction.

§5.1 Federal-question jurisdiction. Suits that raise a federal question can usually be removed. *See* 28 U.S.C. §§1331, 1441(a).

1. Federal question. A federal question can arise in two instances: (1) when a plaintiff's right to relief is created by federal law and (2) when the plaintiff's right to relief is created by state law but the resolution of the case necessarily depends on a substantial question of federal law. ***Dixon v. Coburg Dairy, Inc.***, 369 F.3d 811, 816 (4th Cir.2004); *see* ***Franchise Tax Bd. v. Construction Laborers Vacation Trust***, 463 U.S. 1, 9 (1983). For a federal question to arise when a plaintiff's right to relief is created by state law, the district court must conclude that (1) the state-law claim necessarily raises an explicit federal issue, (2) the federal issue is actually disputed and substantial, and (3) a federal forum can entertain the issue without disturbing any congressionally approved balance of federal and state judicial responsibilities. ***Grable & Sons Metal Prods. v. Darue Eng'g & Mfg.***, 545 U.S. 308, 314 (2005). For a discussion of how to determine if a complaint has raised a federal question, see "Federal-Question Jurisdiction," ch. 2-F, §2, p. 113.

2. Particular suits.

(1) Only federal question. If a suit involves only a federal question, the suit is removable. *See* 28 U.S.C. §§1331, 1441(a).

(2) Federal question brought with nonremovable claim. If a suit involves both a federal question and an otherwise nonremovable claim (i.e., a claim not within the court's original or supplemental jurisdiction or a claim statutorily barred from being removed), the entire suit is removable. 28 U.S.C. §1441(c). For a discussion of the court's power to remand the otherwise nonremovable claim to state court under §1441(c), see "Certain claims removed under §1441(c)," ch. 4-B, §6.2.1(2)(b), p. 276.

§5.2 Diversity jurisdiction. Suits that could have been brought in federal court based on diversity jurisdiction can usually be removed. *See* 28 U.S.C. §1332(a). Federal courts have diversity jurisdiction when the suit involves a controversy between parties of diverse citizenship and an amount in controversy that exceeds $75,000. *See id.* See "Diversity Jurisdiction," ch. 2-F, §3, p. 116.

NOTE

For suits initially filed in state court, the time to determine diversity is by the facts on both the date the complaint was filed in state court and the date the notice of removal was filed in federal court. ***Petrop v. Lassen Art Publ'ns, Inc.***, *939 F.Supp. 742, 744 (D.Haw.1995);* ***Atlanta Shipping Corp. v. International Modular Hous., Inc.***, *547 F.Supp. 1356, 1360 (S.D.N.Y. 1982); see* ***Thomas v. Guardsmark, Inc.***, *381 F.3d 701, 704 (7th Cir.2004); see also 14B Wright, Miller, Cooper & Steinman §3723 & nn.15-17 (must have diversity at both times to prevent nondiverse D from acquiring new domicile after complaint is filed and then removing based on diversity). But see* ***Curry v. U.S. Bulk Transp.***, *462 F.3d 536, 540 (6th Cir.2006) (court can consider citizenship of parties after removal based on amended complaint that includes names of previously unidentified Ds).*

COMMENTARIES
CHAPTER 4. REMOVAL & REMAND
A. DEFENDANT'S NOTICE OF REMOVAL

1. Parties are diverse. The defendant must establish that the parties are diverse.

(1) Establishing diversity of citizenship. To be removable on the basis of diversity jurisdiction, a suit must involve a controversy between the following: (1) citizens of different states, (2) citizens of a state and citizens or subjects of a foreign state (except when the suit is between a citizen of a state and a citizen or subject of a foreign state admitted for permanent residence that is domiciled in the same state), (3) citizens of different states when citizens or subjects of a foreign state are additional parties, or (4) a foreign state as a plaintiff and citizens of a state or of different states. 28 U.S.C. §1332(a); *see* U.S. Const. art. 3, §2. Below are some examples of whether a case is removable based on the parties' citizenship.

NOTE

The Clarification Act made significant amendments to 28 U.S.C. §1332(a) involving diversity jurisdiction and foreign parties. For a complete discussion of those amendments, see "Choosing the Court—Jurisdiction," ch. 2-F, p. 112. For removed cases, the Clarification Act became effective for any suit commenced—within the meaning of state law—in state court on or after January 6, 2012. Clarification Act, P.L. 112-63, §105, 125 Stat. 762 (2011) (eff. Jan. 6, 2012).

Example 1: In the example below, the case is removable because there is diversity jurisdiction—no defendant is a citizen of the same state as the plaintiffs.

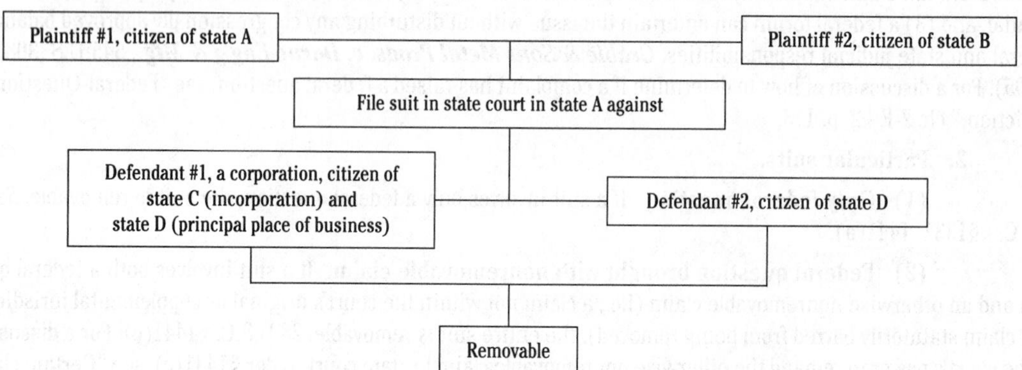

Example 2: In the example below, the case is not removable because one of the defendants is nondiverse—Plaintiff #2 and Defendant #3 are citizens of the same state.

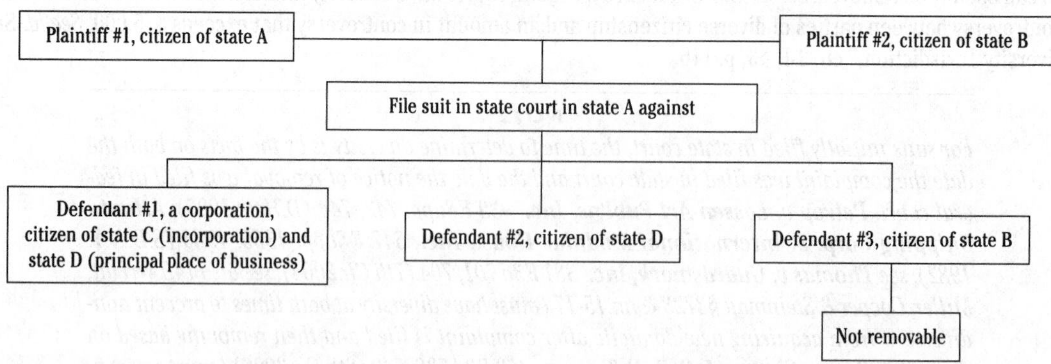

(2) Determining citizenship of parties. For a complete discussion of determining the citizenship of parties for diversity purposes, see "Who is considered for diversity jurisdiction?," ch. 2-F, §3.2, p. 118. But for removal cases only, there are certain parties that can and cannot be disregarded.

CAUTION

When seeking removal based on diversity jurisdiction, be sure to refer to the parties' citizenship, not their residency, because citizenship and residency are not synonymous. See ***Corporate Mgmt. Advisors, Inc. v. Artjen Complexus, Inc.****, 561 F.3d 1294, 1295-96 (11th Cir.2009);* ***Seven Resorts, Inc. v. Cantlen****, 57 F.3d 771, 774 (9th Cir.1995). A case may be remanded if the defendant alleged the residency of the parties but not their citizenship. See, e.g.,* ***Meltzer v. Continental Ins.****, 163 F.Supp.2d 523, 526 (E.D.Pa.2001) (court remanded case when complaint and notice of removal referred only to P's residency); see also* ***Blockbuster, Inc. v. Galeno****, 472 F.3d 53, 59 (2d Cir.2006) (dicta; in class-action suit, complaint alleged named P's residency, not citizenship, and that "thousands" of customers in state were class members; court inferred that at least one class member was a citizen of diverse state). If residency was alleged, the defendant should amend—or ask for leave to amend—its notice of removal to include an allegation of citizenship. See* ***Corporate Mgmt. Advisors****, 561 F.3d at 1297.* *See "Amending notice," §7.5, p. 263.*

(a) Local defendants.

[1] Generally. Under the no-local-defendant rule, a suit cannot be removed if one of the defendants, who is properly joined *and* served, is a citizen of the state where the suit was filed even though there is complete diversity between the parties. 28 U.S.C. §1441(b)(2); *see* ***Hurley v. Motor Coach Indus.***, 222 F.3d 377, 380 (7th Cir.2000); ***Hurt v. Dow Chem. Co.***, 963 F.2d 1142, 1145 (8th Cir.1992); ***WRS Motion Picture & Video Lab. v. Post Modern Edit, Inc.***, 33 F.Supp.2d 876, 876 (C.D.Cal.1999). This is also referred to as the forum-defendant rule or in-state-defendant barrier. *See* ***Crockett v. R.J. Reynolds Tobacco Co.***, 436 F.3d 529, 532 (5th Cir.2006) (in-state-defendant barrier); ***Hurley***, 222 F.3d at 380 (forum-defendant rule); ***WRS Motion Picture***, 33 F.Supp.2d at 877 (no-local-defendant rule).

Example 3: In the example below, the case is not removable despite complete diversity because one of the defendants is a local defendant—Defendant #1 is a citizen of the state where the suit was filed.

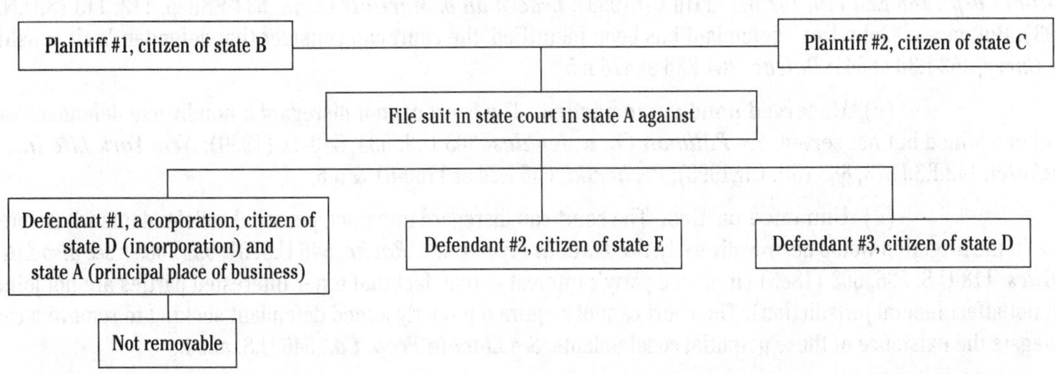

[2] Joined but not served. The court can disregard a diverse local defendant if that defendant has been joined but not served. *See* 28 U.S.C. §1441(b)(2); ***McCall v. Scott***, 239 F.3d 808, 813 n.2 (6th Cir. 2001) (dicta), *amended*, 250 F.3d 997 (6th Cir.2001); ***Clawson v. FedEx Ground Package Sys.***, 451 F.Supp.2d 731, 735-36 (D.Md.2006); ***Stan Winston Creatures, Inc. v. Toys "R" Us, Inc.***, 314 F.Supp.2d 177, 180-81 (S.D.N.Y.2003); ***Ott v. Consolidated Freightways Corp.***, 213 F.Supp.2d 662, 665 & n.3 (S.D.Miss.2002); *see, e.g.*, ***North v. Precision Airmotive Corp.***, 600 F.Supp.2d 1263, 1270 (M.D.Fla.2009) (in case filed in Florida by Vermont P, Washington D could remove action even though P had joined, but not yet served, local Florida D). Some courts, however, have disregarded the plain meaning of 28 U.S.C. §1441(b)—which applies only when a local defendant is joined *and* served—when the application of the statute would lead to "absurd" results and be inconsistent with congressional

intent. *See, e.g.*, ***Sullivan v. Novartis Pharms.***, 575 F.Supp.2d 640, 645-47 (D.N.J.2008) (removal was improper when local D removed case after suit was filed but before it was served, because when statute was adopted, Congress could not have foreseen technological development that allows Ds to electronically monitor state-court dockets); ***Vivas v. Boeing Co.***, 486 F.Supp.2d 726, 733-34 (N.D.Ill.2007) (to allow local D to remove case before P has chance to serve it would permit D to manipulate removal statutes).

CAUTION

*Despite the "properly joined and served" qualification, many courts incorrectly interpret 28 U.S.C. §1441(b)(2) as a limit on a court's original diversity jurisdiction; in other words, these courts hold that the presence of a local defendant—regardless of whether it has been served—defeats diversity jurisdiction. E.g., **Grizzly Mountain Aviation, Inc. v. McTurbine, Inc.**, 619 F.Supp.2d 282, 286 n.5 (S.D.Tex.2008) (regardless of whether local D was properly served at time of removal, §1441(b) still bars removal because of D's local citizenship). Many of these courts rely on **Pecherski v. General Motors Corp.**, 636 F.2d 1156, 1160-61 & n.6 (8th Cir.1981), for the proposition that the mere failure to serve a local defendant who would defeat diversity jurisdiction does not permit a court to ignore that defendant when determining the propriety of removal. But the **Pecherski** court did not actually find that the presence of an unserved local defendant defeated jurisdiction; rather, the court remanded the case to state court because the removing defendant had not shown that the unserved defendant was, in fact, diverse. See **Pecherski**, 636 F.2d at 1161 (removal improper because D failed to establish diversity of citizenship between P and "Jane Doe" D). Thus, when reviewing this line of cases, pay close attention to the citizenship of the parties at the time of removal and make sure the parties were actually diverse before relying on the court's analysis.*

(b) Fictitious parties. The court can disregard a party sued under a fictitious name (e.g., a "John Doe" defendant) whose name and citizenship are unknown. 28 U.S.C. §1441(b)(1); *see* ***McPhail v. Deere & Co.***, 529 F.3d 947, 951 (10th Cir.2008); ***Doleac v. Michalson***, 264 F.3d 470, 475 (5th Cir.2001); ***Wilson v. General Motors Corp.***, 888 F.2d 779, 782 n.3 (11th Cir.1989); ***Lederman v. Marriott Corp.***, 834 F.Supp. 112, 113 (S.D.N.Y. 1993). But once a "John Doe" defendant has been identified, the court can consider that defendant's citizenship. *See* ***Curry***, 462 F.3d at 541; ***Doleac***, 264 F.3d at 476 n.5.

(c) Unserved nondiverse parties. The court cannot disregard a nondiverse defendant who has been joined but not served. *See* ***Pullman Co. v. Jenkins***, 305 U.S. 534, 540-41 (1939); ***New York Life Ins. v. Deshotel***, 142 F.3d 873, 883 (5th Cir.1998); ***Pecherski***, 636 F.2d at 1160-61 & n.6.

(d) Unnamed parties. The court can disregard unnamed potential codefendants whose presence in the litigation would destroy diversity. *See* ***Lincoln Prop. Co. v. Roche***, 546 U.S. 81, 93 (2005); *see also* ***Little v. Giles***, 118 U.S. 596, 603 (1886) (if named party's interest is real, fact that other interested parties are not joined will not affect federal jurisdiction). The court cannot require a properly joined defendant seeking to remove a case to negate the existence of these potential codefendants. *See* ***Lincoln Prop. Co.***, 546 U.S. at 94.

(e) Fraudulent joinder.

[1] When fraudulent joinder applies. Under the doctrine of "fraudulent joinder," the court can disregard a nondiverse or local defendant when (1) the plaintiff has fraudulently pleaded jurisdictional facts to add the nondiverse or local defendant, (2) the plaintiff has no possibility of establishing a cause of action against the nondiverse or local defendant, or (3) the claims against the nondiverse or local defendant have no real connection to the claims against the other defendants. *See* ***Salazar v. Allstate Tex. Lloyd's, Inc.***, 455 F.3d 571, 574 (5th Cir.2006); ***Triggs v. John Crump Toyota, Inc.***, 154 F.3d 1284, 1287 (11th Cir.1998); ***Pampillonia v. RJR Nabisco, Inc.***, 138 F.3d 459, 461 (2d Cir.1998); ***Hoosier Energy Rural Elec. Coop. v. Amoco Tax Leasing IV Corp.***, 34 F.3d 1310, 1315 (7th Cir.1994).

NOTE

The term "fraudulent joinder" is something of a misnomer because the plaintiff's intent or motive in choosing a defendant is immaterial and joinder is not required. ***Schur v. L.A. Weight Loss Ctrs., Inc.****, 577 F.3d 752, 763 n.9 (7th Cir.2009); see* ***Triggs****, 154 F.3d at 1291;* ***Wells' Dairy, Inc. v. American Indus. Refrigeration, Inc.****, 157 F.Supp.2d 1018, 1037 (N.D.Iowa 2001); 16 Moore's Federal Practice 3d §107.14[2][c][iv][A]; see also* ***Smallwood v. Illinois Cent. R.R.****, 385 F.3d 568, 571 & n.1 (5th Cir.2004) (in 5th Circuit, term "improper joinder" is used instead of "fraudulent joinder").*

[a] Fraud in pleading jurisdictional facts. A nondiverse or local defendant can be disregarded under the fraudulent-joinder doctrine if the plaintiff knowingly or mistakenly pleads that the defendant is a citizen of the same state as the plaintiff or that the defendant is a citizen of the state where the suit is filed, even though the defendant is in fact a citizen of a different state. *See* ***Smallwood***, 385 F.3d at 573; ***Triggs***, 154 F.3d at 1287; ***Pampillonia***, 138 F.3d at 461. In these cases, discovery may be necessary to determine the jurisdictional facts concerning the nondiverse or local defendant's citizenship. ***Wells' Dairy***, 157 F.Supp.2d at 1036-37.

[b] No cause of action against nondiverse or local defendant. A nondiverse or local defendant can be disregarded under the fraudulent-joinder doctrine if there is no possibility the plaintiff can establish a cause of action against that defendant under applicable state law. ***Schur***, 577 F.3d at 764; ***Wells' Dairy***, 157 F.Supp.2d at 1037; *see* ***Hunter v. Philip Morris USA***, 582 F.3d 1039, 1043 (9th Cir.2009) (no possibility of recovery by P must be "obvious" under state law); *see, e.g.*, ***Cuevas v. BAC Home Loans Servicing, LP***, 648 F.3d 242, 249-50 (5th Cir.2011) (in suit for wrongful foreclosure and other state-law claims, Ps had no possibility of recovery against local D when local D did not originate or service Ps' home loan). This type of fraudulent joinder may consist of (1) not pleading a factual basis for an element of the plaintiff's claim against the nondiverse or local defendant, (2) pleading only a legally insufficient factual basis for an element of the claim against the nondiverse or local defendant, or (3) pleading a status of the nondiverse or local defendant when in fact the defendant lacks that status (e.g., alleging that the defendant is the plaintiff's employer when in fact the defendant is not). ***Wells' Dairy***, 157 F.Supp.2d at 1037-38; *see, e.g.*, ***Morris v. Princess Cruises, Inc.***, 236 F.3d 1061, 1067-68 (9th Cir.2001) (nondiverse D was fraudulently joined when P's negligent-misrepresentation claim against nondiverse D was based on representations that were not actionable as matter of law and when pleadings were obviously inadequate to support claim).

NOTE

The standard for establishing a valid cause of action against a nondiverse or local defendant is not the same as the plausibility standard necessary to avoid a motion to dismiss under FRCP 12(b)(6). ***Stillwell v. Allstate Ins.****, 663 F.3d 1329, 1333 (11th Cir.2011). The proper standard is lower; the complaint only needs to establish the possibility of stating a valid cause of action under the state-law pleading standard. See id. at 1333-34.*

[c] No real connection to claims of nondiverse or local defendant. A nondiverse or local defendant can be disregarded under the fraudulent-joinder doctrine if (1) there is no joint, several, or alternative liability between the diverse defendant and the nondiverse or local defendant and (2) the claim against the diverse defendant has no real connection to the claim against the nondiverse or local defendant. ***Triggs***, 154 F.3d at 1287; *see* ***In re Prempro Prods. Liab. Litig.***, 591 F.3d 613, 620 (8th Cir.2010). Some courts refer to this as "fraudulent misjoinder." ***Wakeland v. Brown & Williamson Tobacco Corp.***, 996 F.Supp. 1213, 1217 n.4 (S.D.Ala.1998).

NOTE

Only the Eleventh Circuit and some district courts have adopted the fraudulent-misjoinder doctrine. ***In re Prempro Prods. Liab. Litig.****, 591 F.3d at 620 & nn.4-5. The Fifth and Ninth Circuits have acknowledged the doctrine but have not expressly adopted it. Id. at 620 n.4.*

[2] **When fraudulent joinder does not apply.** Some courts have held that the doctrine of fraudulent joinder does not apply in the following circumstances:

[a] The nondiverse or local defendant could have, but did not, raise a valid defense to its joinder in the lawsuit (e.g., lack of personal jurisdiction or improper service). *See* ***Seguros Comercial Am., S.A. de C.V. v. American President Lines, Ltd.***, 934 F.Supp. 243, 245 (S.D.Tex.1996).

[b] The joinder of a nondiverse defendant occurred after removal. ***Borden v. Allstate Ins.***, 589 F.3d 168, 171 (5th Cir.2009); *see also* ***Mayes v. Rapoport***, 198 F.3d 457, 463 (4th Cir.1999) (doctrine does not directly apply after removal, but it can be element of court's discretionary approach to resolving postremoval question of whether nondiverse D should be joined under §1447(e)).

[c] The plaintiff has no reasonable basis for recovery against the nondiverse or local defendant under state law, and such a showing is equally dispositive for all defendants, not just the nondiverse or local defendant. *See* ***Smallwood***, 385 F.3d at 574-76 (holding is narrow and applies only to limited range of cases); *see, e.g.*, ***Hunter***, 582 F.3d at 1044-45 (diverse Ds' use of affirmative defense of preemption to assert fraudulent joinder of nondiverse D was improper; preemption argument applied to merits of entire case, not fraudulent joinder of single D). This is referred to as the common-defense doctrine. *See* ***Frisby v. Lumbermens Mut. Cas. Co.***, 500 F.Supp.2d 697, 700 (S.D.Tex.2007) (discussing paradox created by common-defense doctrine).

[3] **Hearing.** The defendant assumes a heavy burden of proving a claim of fraudulent joinder because it must show there is no possibility the plaintiff would be able to establish a cause of action against the nondiverse defendant in state court. ***Pampillonia***, 138 F.3d at 461; *see also* ***Smallwood***, 385 F.3d at 573 (D must show there is no reasonable basis for court to predict that P might be able to recover against in-state D). To resolve this issue, the court may use a summary-judgment-like procedure and consider affidavits and other evidence outside the pleadings. ***Hart v. Bayer Corp.***, 199 F.3d 239, 246-47 (5th Cir.2000); *see* ***Ritchey v. Upjohn Drug Co.***, 139 F.3d 1313, 1318 (9th Cir.1998); ***Pampillonia***, 138 F.3d at 461-62. At least one court has cautioned that a summary inquiry is appropriate only to identify discrete and undisputed facts that would prevent the plaintiff's recovery against the nondiverse defendant, that discovery be limited to that issue, and that the inquiry should not entail substantial hearings. ***Smallwood***, 385 F.3d at 573-74 (court's inability to make decision in summary manner suggests inability of removing party to carry its burden). The court must resolve all disputed questions of fact and all ambiguities in the controlling state law in favor of the nonremoving party. ***Hart***, 199 F.3d at 246; ***De Perez v. AT&T Co.***, 139 F.3d 1368, 1380 (11th Cir.1998).

2. **Amount in controversy.** The defendant must establish the amount in controversy exceeds $75,000, excluding interest and costs. 28 U.S.C. §1332(a); *e.g.*, ***Freeland v. Liberty Mut. Fire Ins.***, 632 F.3d 250, 252-53 (6th Cir.2011) (in declaratory-judgment action in which controversy concerned possible additional insurance coverage of exactly $75,000, case was remanded because amount did not exceed $75,000). The amount in controversy is the estimate of the damages that will be put at issue, not the amount the plaintiff will actually recover. ***McPhail***, 529 F.3d at 956; *see* ***Back Doctors Ltd. v. Metropolitan Prop. & Cas. Ins.***, 637 F.3d 827, 829-30 (7th Cir.2011) (CAFA case).

(1) **Claims of single plaintiff.** The burden of proof necessary to establish the amount in controversy for a single plaintiff varies depending on whether the plaintiff made a specific claim for monetary relief.

(a) **Amount specified exceeds $75,000.** If the plaintiff seeks monetary relief and demands an amount that exceeds the minimum jurisdictional amount of $75,000 (excluding interest and costs), the defendant can rely on that demand to meet the jurisdictional requirement. 28 U.S.C. §1446(c)(2); *see* ***S.W.S. Erectors, Inc. v. Infax, Inc.***, 72 F.3d 489, 492 (5th Cir.1996); *see also* ***Smith v. American Gen. Life & Acc. Ins. Co.***, 337 F.3d 888, 892 (7th Cir.2003) (amount alleged is presumed correct on assumption that P would not fabricate amount in controversy to meet jurisdictional requirement, file suit in state court, and rely on D to remove to federal court). The defendant can remove based on the amount in the complaint even if the defendant has a complete or partial defense to the suit. ***Saint Paul Mercury Indem. Co. v. Red Cab Co.***, 303 U.S. 283, 292 (1938).

(b) Amount specified below $75,000. If the plaintiff seeks monetary relief and demands a specific amount that is $75,000 or less or alleges that damages do not exceed $75,000 (excluding interest and costs), the plaintiff can usually defeat removal to federal court. *See* 28 U.S.C. §1446(c)(2); ***Saint Paul Mercury Indem.***, 303 U.S. at 294. But the defendant may be able to remove the case if it can establish that the amount in controversy was not alleged in good faith. *See* 28 U.S.C. §1446(c)(2) (sum demanded in "good faith" in initial pleading shall be deemed to be amount in controversy). To show a lack of good faith, the defendant will most likely have to prove to a legal certainty that the plaintiff's claim exceeds $75,000. *See* ***Frederico v. Home Depot***, 507 F.3d 188, 196 (3d Cir. 2007) (CAFA case); ***Lowdermilk v. U.S. Bank***, 479 F.3d 994, 998-99 (9th Cir.2007) (CAFA case); ***Burns v. Windsor Ins.***, 31 F.3d 1092, 1095-96 & n.6 (11th Cir.1994) (single-P case); *cf.* ***Saint Paul Mercury Indem.***, 303 U.S. at 288-89 (sum claimed by P controls if claim made in good faith; to justify dismissal for lack of subject-matter jurisdiction, D must show to legal certainty that claim is actually less than jurisdictional amount). This standard is objective; that is, the plaintiff's subjective intent in alleging the amount of the claim is not at issue. ***Burns***, 31 F.3d at 1096; *see, e.g.*, ***Esquilín-Mendoza v. Don King Prods.***, 638 F.3d 1, 4 (1st Cir.2011) (on motion to dismiss for lack of subject-matter jurisdiction, P's good faith in claiming amount of damages is trumped by objective legal certainty that claim is actually less than jurisdictional amount). To satisfy this standard, the defendant should support the notice of removal with summary-judgment-type evidence (e.g., testimony, published precedent) establishing that the claim is greater than $75,000. *See, e.g.*, ***Rogers v. Wal-Mart Stores***, 230 F.3d 868, 871 (6th Cir.2000) (applying "more likely than not" rather than "legal certainty" standard, court considered complaint, discovery responses, and other evidence that P claimed higher damages in earlier suit for same injuries); ***De Aguilar v. Boeing Co.***, 11 F.3d 55, 58 (5th Cir.1993) (applying "preponderance of the evidence" rather than "legal certainty" standard, court considered testimonial evidence, published precedent, and evidence that Ps claimed higher damages in other courts for same injuries).

(c) Amount not specified. If either (1) the plaintiff seeks nonmonetary relief or (2) the plaintiff seeks monetary relief but state practice does not allow the plaintiff to demand a specific sum or allows the plaintiff to recover damages in excess of the amount demanded, the defendant can remove by specifying the amount in controversy in the notice of removal and establishing the amount in controversy by a preponderance of the evidence. 28 U.S.C. §1446(c)(2); *see* ***Proctor v. Swifty Oil Co.***, No. 3:12-CV-00490-TBR (W.D.Ky.2012) (slip op.; 10-1-12); *see also* ***De Aguilar v. Boeing Co.***, 47 F.3d 1404, 1410 (5th Cir.1995) (noting that many states prohibit plaintiffs from pleading specific amounts in cases involving unliquidated damages).

NOTE

The Clarification Act amended removal procedure to allow the defendant to specify the amount in controversy in the notice of removal when it was not specified in the complaint. For removed cases, the Clarification Act became effective for any suit commenced—within the meaning of state law—in state court on or after January 6, 2012. Clarification Act, P.L. 112-63, §105, 125 Stat. 762 (2011) (eff. Jan. 6, 2012). Because of the substantive changes made by the 2011 amendments, use caution when citing cases that predate the amendments.

[1] Defendant's burden. To establish the amount in controversy, the defendant must do the following:

[a] Specify amount in controversy. The defendant must assert the amount in controversy in the notice of removal. *See* 28 U.S.C. §1446(c)(2)(A).

[b] Establish amount in controversy. The defendant must establish that the amount in controversy exceeds $75,000 by a preponderance of the evidence. 28 U.S.C. §1446(c)(2)(B); ***Roe v. Michelin N. Am., Inc.***, 613 F.3d 1058, 1061 (11th Cir.2010); ***McPhail***, 529 F.3d at 953; ***Luckett v. Delta Airlines, Inc.***, 171 F.3d 295, 298 (5th Cir.1999); 14C Wright, Miller, Cooper & Steinman §3725.1 & n.25; *see* H.R. Rep. No. 112-10, at 16 (2011). The defendant should provide evidence beyond the complaint to support its claim. ***Pretka v. Kolter City Plaza II, Inc.***, 608 F.3d 744, 754 (11th Cir.2010); ***Singer v. State Farm Mut. Auto. Ins.***, 116 F.3d 373, 377 (9th Cir.

1997); *see* ***St. Paul Reinsurance Co. v. Greenberg***, 134 F.3d 1250, 1253-54 (5th Cir.1998). The defendant can rely on various sources to establish the amount in controversy.

PRACTICE TIP

If the defendant does not have enough information to support removal within 30 days after the suit was commenced, it can take discovery in state court to help determine the amount. H.R. Rep. No. 112-10, at 16 (2011); see 28 U.S.C. §1446(c)(3)(A); ***Ramsey v. Kearns****, No. 12-06-ART (E.D.Ky.2012) (slip op.; 2-23-12). Under the Clarification Act, information that appears in the record of the state proceeding or in responses to discovery qualifies as "other paper," which allows removal based on those papers when the information indicates that the amount in controversy is greater than $75,000. 28 U.S.C. §1446(c)(3)(A). See "Suit becomes removable later," §4.2, p. 245. The defendant's burden of proof for that information remains the same—the defendant must establish the amount in controversy by a preponderance of the evidence. H.R. Rep. No. 112-10, at 16 (2011).*

{1} Allegations in complaint. The defendant may rely on an estimation of damages calculated from the allegations in the complaint. ***McPhail***, 529 F.3d at 955; ***Meridian Sec. Ins. v. Sadowski***, 441 F.3d 536, 541 (7th Cir.2006); *see, e.g.*, ***Luckett***, 171 F.3d at 298 (even though complaint did not state specific amount, it was evident that damages were over jurisdictional amount when complaint sought recovery for property damage, travel expenses, medical bills, pain and suffering, and humiliation).

{2} Evidence outside complaint. The defendant may rely on the notice of removal, affidavits, stipulations, interrogatories, or other evidence (e.g., settlement demand) that was submitted in either state or federal court. *See* ***Pretka***, 608 F.3d at 755; ***Meridian Sec. Ins.***, 441 F.3d at 541-42; ***Marcel v. Pool Co.***, 5 F.3d 81, 84-85 (5th Cir.1993); *see, e.g.*, ***McPhail***, 529 F.3d at 956-57 (removal proper when, in addition to complaint, Ds submitted attorney correspondence discussing value of claim in which P's attorney stated amount in controversy "may very well be" over jurisdictional amount).

CAUTION

If a suit is removable when it is filed, the defendant can rely on its own affidavits or other evidence to establish the amount in controversy. See ***Pretka****, 608 F.3d at 767-68. See "Suit removable at time initial pleading filed," §4.1, p. 243. But if a suit is not initially removable, the defendant may be limited to evidence received from the plaintiff; that is, the defendant may not be able to create its own evidence (e.g., by affidavit) to show that a suit has become removable.* ***Pretka****, 608 F.3d at 760-61. See "Suit becomes removable later," §4.2, p. 245.*

{3} Substantive law. In limited circumstances, the defendant may rely on substantive law that sets the damages amount; for example, in a breach-of-contract suit, the contract may be valued over the jurisdictional amount. *See* ***McPhail***, 529 F.3d at 956; ***Movie Gallery US, LLC v. Smith***, 574 F.Supp.2d 1244, 1248 (M.D.Ala.2008).

[2] Plaintiff's burden. If the defendant satisfies its burden and the plaintiff wants the suit to be remanded to state court, the plaintiff must prove to a legal certainty that, if successful, it would not be able to recover more than the jurisdictional amount. *See* ***McPhail***, 529 F.3d at 955.

(2) Claims of multiple plaintiffs.

(a) Generally. Generally, damages claims of multiple plaintiffs cannot be aggregated; each plaintiff must independently meet the minimum amount in controversy for diversity jurisdiction. *See* ***H&D Tire & Auto.-Hardware, Inc. v. Pitney Bowes Inc.***, 250 F.3d 302, 304-05 (5th Cir.2001); ***Kirkland v. Midland Mortg. Co.***, 243 F.3d 1277, 1280 (11th Cir.2001). However, if the damages present a united claim for a common and undivided

interest, they can be aggregated to meet the minimum amount. ***Kirkland***, 243 F.3d at 1280; *see* ***Allen v. R&H Oil & Gas Co.***, 63 F.3d 1326, 1334 (5th Cir.1995). See "Aggregation of claims," ch. 2-F, §3.3.4, p. 124.

NOTE

Most circuits hold that plaintiffs cannot aggregate punitive damages in class-action suits. E.g., ***Martin v. Franklin Capital Corp.****, 393 F.3d 1143, 1148 (10th Cir.2004), aff'd, 546 U.S. 132 (2005);* ***Crawford v. F. Hoffman-La Roche Ltd.****, 267 F.3d 760, 765 (8th Cir.2001);* ***In re Ford Motor Co.****, 264 F.3d 952, 963 (9th Cir.2001);* ***H&D Tire****, 250 F.3d at 304;* ***Ayres v. General Motors Corp.****, 234 F.3d 514, 517 (11th Cir.2000);* ***Gilman v. BHC Secs., Inc.****, 104 F.3d 1418, 1430 (2d Cir.1997).*

(b) Class actions. For the requirements on determining the amount in controversy for interstate class actions under the CAFA, see "Amount in controversy," ch. 2-F, §5.1.2(2), p. 130.

§5.3 Special removal statutes. A defendant can remove a case if a special removal statute applies. These statutes provide direct and independent grants of jurisdiction. The following are some examples of special removal statutes:

1. Class actions. A defendant can remove certain types of class actions to federal court even if a defendant is a citizen of the forum state. Beisner & Miller, *Litigating in the New Class Action World*, 6 BNA Class Action Litig. Rep. at 412; *see* 28 U.S.C. §1453(b). The Class Action Fairness Act (CAFA) of 2005, P.L. 109-2, 119 Stat. 4, is a broad removal provision applicable to many class actions. For a more extensive discussion of jurisdiction under CAFA, see "Interstate class actions," ch. 2-F, §5.1, p. 129. However, CAFA removal differs from traditional removal in the following ways:

(1) Class actions are exempt from the one-year limit for removal under 28 U.S.C. §1446(c)(1). 28 U.S.C. §1453(b); ***Blockbuster, Inc. v. Galeno***, 472 F.3d 53, 56 (2d Cir.2006). See "Limitation for diversity cases," §4.2.2, p. 246.

(2) Removal is allowed even if a defendant is a citizen of the state where the suit was filed (i.e., the no-local-defendant rule does not apply). 28 U.S.C. §1453(b); ***Blockbuster***, 472 F.3d at 56. See "Local defendants," §5.2.1(2)(a), p. 251.

(3) The removing defendant is not required to obtain the consent of all the other defendants. 28 U.S.C. §1453(b); ***United Steel v. Shell Oil Co.***, 549 F.3d 1204, 1208 (9th Cir.2008); ***Blockbuster***, 472 F.3d at 56; ***Miedema v. Maytag Corp.***, 450 F.3d 1322, 1327 (11th Cir.2006). See "Consent required," §8.1, p. 263.

(4) CAFA authorizes discretionary appellate review of remand orders issued in cases removed under the statute. 28 U.S.C. §1453(c)(1), (c)(2). See "Interstate class actions," ch. 4-B, §7.2.3(1), p. 281.

2. Suits against federal agencies, officers & employees.

(1) Removal under 28 U.S.C. §1442.

(a) Persons or entities that can remove. A civil action that is against or directed to any of the following persons or entities can be removed to federal court. 28 U.S.C. §1442(a); *see* Lamar Smith, Removal Clarification Act of 2011, H.R. Rep. No. 112-17, pt. 1, at 1 (2011) (any individual brought into state proceeding based on her status as federal officer has right to remove).

[1] The United States, a federal agency, or a federal officer (or any person acting under that officer) in an official or individual capacity for or relating to any act under color of office. 28 U.S.C. §1442(a)(1); *see also* ***Isaacson v. Dow Chem. Co.***, 517 F.3d 129, 135-36 (2d Cir.2008) (person can include private corporation).

[2] Property holders whose title is derived from a federal officer when the civil action affects the validity of any U.S. law. 28 U.S.C. §1442(a)(2).

[3] Officers of the U.S. courts for or relating to any act under color of office or in the performance of their duties. *Id.* §1442(a)(3).

[4] Officers of either House of Congress for or relating to any act in the discharge of their official duty under an order of that House. *Id.* §1442(a)(4).

(b) Colorable federal defense. For the action to be removable, the United States or federal party must assert a "colorable" federal defense. *See* ***Mesa v. California***, 489 U.S. 121, 129 (1989); ***Isaacson***, 517 F.3d at 138; ***Faulk v. Owens-Corning Fiberglass Corp.***, 48 F.Supp.2d 653, 659 (E.D.Tex.1999); *see also Black's Law Dictionary* 301 (9th ed. 2009) (defining "colorable" as "appearing to be true, valid, or right").

(c) Cases or proceedings when judicial order is sought or issued. Under 28 U.S.C. §1442, removal is permitted for a civil action or a proceeding (whether or not ancillary to another proceeding) within a civil action in which a judicial order, including a subpoena for testimony or documents, is sought or issued. 28 U.S.C. §1442(c); *see* Lamar Smith, Removal Clarification Act of 2011, H.R. Rep. No. 112-17, pt. 1, at 6 (2011) (state proceedings for presuit discovery qualify as civil actions). But if a civil action involves more than the proceeding for a judicial order and if there is no other basis for removal, only the specific proceeding related to the judicial order is removable. 28 U.S.C. §1442(c).

(2) Removal under FTCA. Any civil action for money damages brought under the Federal Tort Claims Act (FTCA) against a federal employee for injury to person or property resulting from the employee's negligent or wrongful conduct must be removed to federal court, as long as the federal employee was acting within the scope of employment at the time of the incident. 28 U.S.C. §2679(d)(2). Once the Attorney General certifies that the federal employee was acting within the scope of employment, the United States must be substituted as the defendant and the case must be removed. *Id.* §2679(d)(1), (d)(2); ***Green v. Hall***, 8 F.3d 695, 698 (9th Cir.1993); *see* ***McLaurin v. U.S.***, 392 F.3d 774, 780-81 (5th Cir.2004) (no time limit on removal under FTCA). The removal provisions in the FTCA are not identical to those in 28 U.S.C. §1442(a)(1), but they do overlap. ***Jamison v. Wiley***, 14 F.3d 222, 237-38 (4th Cir.1994). See "Removal under 28 U.S.C. §1442," §5.3.2(1), p. 257.

3. Suits against member of armed forces. A member of the armed forces can remove to federal court any civil or criminal case arising out of an act (1) under color of the member's office or status, (2) for which the member claims any right, title, or authority under federal law regarding the armed forces, or (3) under the law of war. 28 U.S.C. §1442a.

4. Foreclosures against United States. In a case brought to quiet title, to foreclose a mortgage or other lien, or to partition or condemn real or personal property on which the United States has or claims a mortgage or other lien, the United States can remove the suit to federal court. *See* 28 U.S.C. §1444.

5. Civil-rights cases. A defendant can remove a civil or criminal case to federal court (1) if the defendant was denied or cannot enforce a right under any law that provides for equal civil rights of U.S. citizens or of all persons within the jurisdiction of the United States or (2) for any act done under color of authority derived from a law providing for equal rights, or for refusing to do any act on the ground that it would be inconsistent with a law providing for equal rights. 28 U.S.C. §1443; *see* ***Charter Sch. of Pine Grove, Inc. v. St. Helena Parish Sch. Bd.***, 417 F.3d 444, 446 (5th Cir.2005).

6. Bankruptcy cases. Under the bankruptcy removal statute, any party can remove. *See* 28 U.S.C. §§1334(c)(2), 1452(a). Before removing, a party should check Federal Rule of Bankruptcy Procedure 9027 for the procedure and the time requirements. Local district and bankruptcy court rules should also be consulted for any specific requirements.

7. FDIC removal. The FDIC can remove any case in which it is a party, whether as a plaintiff or a defendant. ***FDIC v. S&I 85-1, Ltd.***, 22 F.3d 1070, 1073 (11th Cir.1994); *see* 12 U.S.C. §1819(b)(2)(B); ***Destfino v. Reiswig***, 630 F.3d 952, 957-58 (9th Cir.2011). The FDIC can remove even if the state court has already entered judgment and the case is awaiting appeal. ***Resolution Trust Corp. v. BVS Dev., Inc.***, 42 F.3d 1206, 1211 (9th Cir.1994);

FDIC v. Keating, 12 F.3d 314, 316 (1st Cir.1993). The FDIC, like other federal agencies, must present a "colorable" federal defense. *See* ***Lazuka v. FDIC***, 931 F.2d 1530, 1534-35 (11th Cir.1991); *see also Black's Law Dictionary* 301 (9th ed. 2009) (defining "colorable" as "appearing to be true, valid, or right").

8. Suits against foreign states. A foreign state has an absolute right to remove any suit to which it is a party. 28 U.S.C. §§1441(d), 1602 (Foreign Sovereign Immunities Act); ***In re Delta Am.***, 900 F.2d 890, 893 (6th Cir. 1990); *see* ***USX Corp. v. Adriatic Ins.***, 345 F.3d 190, 207 (3d Cir.2003). A foreign state includes the political subdivisions of the foreign state, any agency or instrumentality of the foreign state, and entities in which the foreign state has a majority interest. 28 U.S.C. §1603(a), (b); ***California Dept. of Water Res. v. Powerex Corp.***, 533 F.3d 1087, 1097 (9th Cir.2008); ***In re Texas E. Transmission Corp. PCB Contamination Ins. Coverage Litig.***, 15 F.3d 1230, 1238 n.8 (3d Cir.1994); *see* ***Delgado v. Shell Oil Co.***, 231 F.3d 165, 175-76 (5th Cir.2000) (indirect or tiered ownership sufficient). If a foreign state seeks removal, the case is removable without regard to the amount in controversy, the citizenship of the parties, or the existence of a federal question. *See* 14C Wright, Miller, Cooper & Steinman §3728.1 & nn.6-8. In the removal of a suit against a foreign state, the following principles apply:

(1) The foreign state does not need to obtain the consent of the other defendants to remove. See "Foreign state," §8.1.2(1), p. 264.

(2) All claims will be litigated in federal court. 28 U.S.C. §1441(d).

(3) The trial in federal court will be to the court, without a jury. *Id.*; ***In re Delta Am.***, 900 F.2d at 893.

(4) The time limits under 28 U.S.C. §1446(b) for removing suits against a foreign state may be extended for "cause shown." 28 U.S.C. §1441(d); ***Big Sky Network Canada, Ltd. v. Sichuan Provincial Gov't***, 533 F.3d 1183, 1185 (10th Cir.2008); ***In re Delta Am.***, 900 F.2d at 893.

NOTE

The Foreign Sovereign Immunities Act is the sole basis for obtaining jurisdiction over a foreign state in U.S. courts. ***Saudi Arabia v. Nelson****, 507 U.S. 349, 355 (1993);* ***Argentine Republic v. Amerada Hess Shipping Corp.****, 488 U.S. 428, 434 (1989);* ***In re Air Crash Disaster Near Roselawn****, 96 F.3d 932, 936 (7th Cir.1996). Sections 1604 and 1330(a) of title 28 work in tandem: §1604 bars federal and state courts from exercising jurisdiction when a foreign state is entitled to immunity, and §1330(a) confers jurisdiction on federal district courts to hear suits brought by U.S. citizens and aliens when a foreign state is not entitled to immunity.* ***Argentine Republic****, 488 U.S. at 434.*

9. Patent, plant-variety-protection & copyright actions. Any party can remove an action in which a party has asserted a claim for relief under federal law relating to patents, plant variety protection, or copyrights. 28 U.S.C. §1454(a), (b)(1). Removal of such actions is governed by the requirements under 28 U.S.C. §1446, except that any party—not just a defendant—can seek removal and the deadline to file notice of removal can be extended for cause. 28 U.S.C. §1454(b).

10. Securities Act class actions. A defendant can remove class actions involving a "covered security" (i.e., a nationally traded security). *See* 15 U.S.C. §77p(c); ***Kircher v. Putnam Funds Trust***, 547 U.S. 633, 642-43 (2006). However, other actions under the Securities Act are generally not removable. See "Securities Act suits," §6.6, p. 260.

11. Multiparty, multiforum actions. A defendant can remove a civil action filed in state court to federal court if (1) the action could have been brought in federal court under 28 U.S.C. §1369 (jurisdiction for actions arising from single accident in which at least 75 people died at discrete location), or (2) the defendant is a party to another action that is or could have been brought in federal court under 28 U.S.C. §1369 and arises from the same accident as the action filed in state court. 28 U.S.C. §1441(e)(1).

§5.4 Alienage jurisdiction. A defendant can remove if there is alienage jurisdiction. *See* ***Coury v. Prot***, 85 F.3d 244, 248-51 (5th Cir.1996). Persons who are not U.S. citizens can invoke federal jurisdiction under 28 U.S.C. §1332(a)(2) or (a)(3), which provide for jurisdiction over suits between aliens and U.S. citizens. See "Alienage Jurisdiction," ch. 2-F, §4, p. 127.

§5.5 Supplemental jurisdiction. A defendant can remove otherwise nonremovable state-law claims under supplemental jurisdiction if there is an independent basis for original jurisdiction (e.g., federal-question or diversity jurisdiction). ***Halmekangas v. State Farm Fire & Cas. Co.***, 603 F.3d 290, 293 (5th Cir.2010); *see* 28 U.S.C. §§1367, 1441. The supplemental-jurisdiction statute on its own, however, does not provide a basis for original jurisdiction. *E.g.*, ***Halmekangas***, 603 F.3d at 294 (after P filed suit against insurer in federal court and then against another insurer and agent in state court, state-court D sought to remove based on supplemental jurisdiction of already-pending federal case; case was remanded because federal court did not have original jurisdiction over state claims). See "Supplemental Jurisdiction," ch. 2-F, §6, p. 134.

§6. PROHIBITIONS AGAINST REMOVAL

The following suits cannot be removed to federal court:

§6.1 Suits against railroads. A civil action arising under 45 U.S.C. §§51-60 filed in state court against a railroad, its receivers, or its trustees cannot be removed. 28 U.S.C. §1445(a); *see* ***Edmonds v. Norfolk & W. Ry.***, 883 F.Supp. 89, 93 (S.D.W.Va.1995).

§6.2 Suits against common carriers. A civil action arising under 49 U.S.C. §11706 filed in state court against a common carrier, its receivers, or its trustees cannot be removed unless the amount in controversy exceeds $10,000, excluding interest and costs. 28 U.S.C. §1445(b).

§6.3 Workers' compensation suits. A civil action arising under the workers' compensation laws of the state where the suit was filed cannot be removed. 28 U.S.C. §1445(c); ***Reed v. Heil Co.***, 206 F.3d 1055, 1058 (11th Cir. 2000); ***Armistead v. C&M Transp.***, 49 F.3d 43, 46 (1st Cir.1995). *But see* ***Patin v. Allied Signal, Inc.***, 77 F.3d 782, 789 (5th Cir.1996) (claims "related to" compensation claim are removable). However, a suit based on another state's workers' compensation laws is removable. *See* 28 U.S.C. §1445(c); ***Jackson v. Diamond M. Co.***, 575 F.Supp. 995, 996 (S.D.Miss.1983).

§6.4 Jones Act suits. A civil action based on a Jones Act claim cannot be removed because the Jones Act incorporates the antiremoval provisions from FELA. ***Lackey v. Atlantic Richfield Co.***, 990 F.2d 202, 207 (5th Cir.1993); *see* 46 U.S.C. §30104; ***Burchett v. Cargill, Inc.***, 48 F.3d 173, 175 (5th Cir.1995).

§6.5 Admiralty & maritime suits. A civil action based on an admiralty or maritime claim generally cannot be removed. Admiralty claims do not arise under the Constitution, treaties, or laws of the United States. ***Tennessee Gas Pipeline v. Houston Cas. Ins.***, 87 F.3d 150, 153 (5th Cir.1996). Thus, an admiralty claim does not present a federal question. *Id.* at 155. The removal of an admiralty claim is possible only when the action would be removable on some ground other than its admiralty nature. *Id.* at 153; ***Servis v. Hiller Sys.***, 54 F.3d 203, 207 (4th Cir.1995).

CAUTION

Removal in admiralty suits is extremely confusing. Before attempting to remove this type of suit, refer to 14A Wright, Miller & Cooper §3674.

§6.6 Securities Act suits. A civil action arising under the Securities Act of 1933 cannot be removed, except for class actions involving a "covered security." *See* 15 U.S.C. §77v(a); ***Luther v. Countrywide Home Loans Servicing LP***, 533 F.3d 1031, 1033 & n.1 (9th Cir.2008). See "Securities Act class actions," §5.3.10, p. 259. Courts disagree, however, on whether securities class actions (other than those involving a covered security) can avoid the antiremoval provision by removing under the Class Action Fairness Act (CAFA). *Compare* ***Katz v. Gerardi***, 552 F.3d

558, 562 (7th Cir.2009) (removal allowed under CAFA), *with **Luther***, 533 F.3d at 1034 (no removal under CAFA because CAFA cannot trump Securities Act's more specific antiremoval provision). See "Class actions," §5.3.1, p. 257.

§6.7 Proceedings from state agency. A proceeding from a state agency cannot be removed; an action can only be removed from a state "court." ***Oregon Bur. of Labor & Indus. v. U.S. W. Comms.***, 288 F.3d 414, 417-18 (9th Cir.2002); *e.g.*, ***Porter Trust v. Rural Water Sewer & Solid Waste Mgmt. Dist.***, 607 F.3d 1251, 1254-55 (10th Cir. 2010) (removal was improper from board of county commissioners adjudicating deannexation proceeding). *But see **Floeter v. C.W. Transp.***, 597 F.2d 1100, 1101-02 (7th Cir.1979) (removal was allowed from state agency when employment-relations commission functioned substantially similarly to a state court).

§7. NOTICE OF REMOVAL

§7.1 Who can file notice.

1. Original defendants.

(1) Removal under §1441(a). When removal is based on 28 U.S.C. §1441(a) (i.e., federal-question or diversity jurisdiction when no other statute authorizing removal would apply), only a defendant can remove a case. ***First Nat'l Bank v. Curry***, 301 F.3d 456, 463 (6th Cir.2002). The majority of courts have interpreted the term "defendant" narrowly under §1441(a) to mean the party against whom the original plaintiff asserted a claim. ***First Nat'l Bank***, 301 F.3d at 462-63; ***Hamilton v. Aetna Life & Cas. Co.***, 5 F.3d 642, 643 (2d Cir.1993); ***American Int'l Underwriters, (Phil.), Inc. v. Continental Ins.***, 843 F.2d 1253, 1260 (9th Cir.1988). Thus, only original defendants—not counterclaim defendants, cross-claim defendants, or third-party defendants—can remove a case under §1441(a). *See **Westwood Apex v. Contreras***, 644 F.3d 799, 807 (9th Cir.2011); ***Palisades Collections LLC v. Shorts***, 552 F.3d 327, 333 (4th Cir.2008); ***First Nat'l Bank***, 301 F.3d at 463; ***Federal Ins. v. Tyco Int'l***, 422 F.Supp.2d 357, 372-73 (S.D.N.Y.2006); 14C Wright, Miller, Cooper & Steinman §3730 & nn.1-6. *But see **Texas v. Walker***, 142 F.3d 813, 816 (5th Cir.1998) (counterclaim D can remove separate and independent claim under former 28 U.S.C. §1441(c)).

(2) Removal under §1453(b). When removal is based on 28 U.S.C. §1453(b) (i.e., class action under CAFA), only an original defendant can remove a case. *See **In re Mortgage Elec. Registration Sys.***, 680 F.3d 849, 854 (6th Cir.2012). See "Class actions," §5.3.1, p. 257. Courts have interpreted the term "any defendant" under §1453(b) to mean the same as the term "defendant" under §1441(a). *See **In re Mortgage Elec. Registration Sys.***, 680 F.3d at 854; ***Westwood Apex***, 644 F.3d at 806-07; ***First Bank v. DJL Props., LLC***, 598 F.3d 915, 917-18 (7th Cir. 2010); ***Palisades Collections LLC***, 552 F.3d at 334-36.

2. Other parties.

Some statutes do not limit removal to "original" defendants. *See, e.g.*, 12 U.S.C. §1819(b)(2)(B) (FDIC can remove any action); 28 U.S.C. §1452(a) ("[a] party" can remove any claims or causes of action in bankruptcy); 28 U.S.C. §1454(b)(1) ("any party" can remove a patent, plant-variety-protection, or copyright case). Under these statutes, parties other than original defendants (i.e., plaintiffs, counterclaim defendants, cross-claim defendants, and third-party defendants) may be allowed to seek removal. *See, e.g.*, ***California Pub. Employees' Ret. Sys. v. WorldCom, Inc.***, 368 F.3d 86, 103 (2d Cir.2004) (P or D can seek removal under §1452); ***EIE Guam Corp. v. Long Term Credit Bank of Japan, Ltd.***, 322 F.3d 635, 649 (9th Cir.2003) (under §1441(d), foreign states that are named as third-party Ds or who voluntarily join as Ds can seek removal); ***FDIC v. S&I 85-1, Ltd.***, 22 F.3d 1070, 1073 (11th Cir.1994) (FDIC as P or D can seek removal under 12 U.S.C. §1819). See "Special removal statutes," §5.3, p. 257.

§7.2 Deadline to file notice.

For a discussion of the deadline for filing notice, see "Deadlines for Removal," §4, p. 242.

§7.3 Contents of notice.

The defendant must file a notice of removal with the federal district court. 28 U.S.C. §1446(a). The notice must contain a short and plain statement of the grounds for removal and must be signed as required by FRCP 11. 28 U.S.C. §1446(a); *see **Ellenburg v. Spartan Motors Chassis, Inc.***, 519 F.3d 192, 199 (4th Cir. 2008) (pleading standard for notice of removal is same as for initial complaint).

COMMENTARIES
CHAPTER 4. REMOVAL & REMAND
A. DEFENDANT'S NOTICE OF REMOVAL

PRACTICE TIP

Always check the local rules of the federal court to which the case is being removed. Often, the local rules impose additional requirements for removal, including documents to be attached, filing fees, cover sheets, etc.

1. Grounds for removal. The defendant must identify the grounds for removal in the notice.

(1) Federal-question jurisdiction. If removal is based on federal-question jurisdiction, the notice must state that removal is based on a claim arising under federal law, identify the specific statute, and explain why the claim arises under federal law. *See* 28 U.S.C. §§1441(a), 1446(a); *see, e.g.*, ***Barringer v. Parker Bros. Empl. Ret. Fund***, 877 F.Supp. 358, 360 (S.D.Tex.1995) (P's motion to remand was granted when D's notice of removal was vague and included only conclusory contentions of federal-question jurisdiction). See "Federal-question jurisdiction," §5.1, p. 249.

(2) Diversity jurisdiction. If removal is based on diversity jurisdiction, the notice must state facts establishing both the citizenship of the parties and the amount in controversy. ***Booty v. Shoney's Inc.***, 872 F.Supp. 1524, 1528 (E.D.La.1995). See "Diversity jurisdiction," §5.2, p. 249.

(3) Special removal statute. If removal is based on a special removal statute, the notice must state that removal is based on a specific federal statute, identify the statute, and if necessary, establish any statutory requirements. *See, e.g.*, ***Charter Sch. of Pine Grove, Inc. v. St. Helena Parish Sch. Bd.***, 417 F.3d 444, 448 (5th Cir. 2005) (D did not establish its right to removal under 28 U.S.C. §1443 when D provided only conclusory allegations as its basis for removal). See "Special removal statutes," §5.3, p. 257.

(4) Alienage jurisdiction. If removal is based on alienage jurisdiction, the notice must state the applicable requirements under 28 U.S.C. §1332(a). See "Diversity Jurisdiction," ch. 2-F, §3, p. 116; "Alienage Jurisdiction," ch. 2-F, §4, p. 127.

2. Identify state proceeding. The defendant should identify the parties and the state-court suit being removed.

3. Describe suit. The defendant should describe the nature of the suit and state when it was commenced.

4. Attach state-court documents. The defendant must attach to the notice of removal all state-court pleadings, processes, or orders served on the defendant, and any other document required by local rules. 28 U.S.C. §§1446(a), 1447(b), 1449.

5. Jury demand. The defendant must state whether a jury demand was made in state court.

(1) Demand made in state court. If a party wants a jury trial and a demand was made in state court, the party does not need to renew its demand after removal. FRCP 81(c)(3)(A).

(2) Demand not required in state court. If the state law did not require an express demand for a jury trial, a party does not need to make a demand after removal unless the federal court orders the parties to do so within a specified time. FRCP 81(c)(3)(A). See "Demand for Jury Trial," ch. 5-C, p. 309. When a party does not make a demand within the time ordered by the federal court, it waives the right to a jury trial. FRCP 81(c)(3)(A).

(3) No demand made in state court. If all necessary pleadings have been served at the time of removal and no demand was made in state court, a party entitled to a jury trial under FRCP 38 can make a demand in federal court. FRCP 81(c)(3)(B). If a party wants a jury, it must serve a demand within 14 days after (1) it files a notice of removal or (2) it is served with a notice of removal filed by another party. *Id.*; *see* FRCP 38(b). See "Demand for Jury Trial," ch. 5-C, p. 309.

6. Compliance with deadline. The defendant should state when it was served with the complaint and summons and that the notice of removal was filed before the applicable deadline. *See* ***Murphy Bros. v. Michetti Pipe Stringing, Inc.***, 526 U.S. 344, 347-48 (1999). See "Deadlines for Removal," §4, p. 242.

7. Consent from other defendants. If consent from other defendants is required, the notice should be signed by all defendants who join in the notice or written consent from each defendant should be attached to the notice. See "Consent to Removal," §8, this page. If consent is not unanimous at the time of removal—and the consent period has not expired—the removing defendant does not have to explain why all the defendants have not yet consented. ***City of Cleveland v. Deutsche Bank Trust Co.***, 571 F.Supp.2d 807, 811-12 (N.D.Ohio 2008). But if the consent period has expired, to avoid remand, the removing defendant should explain why the other defendants do not need to consent. *Id.* at 812 n.3.

8. Signature. The defendant or its attorney must sign the notice of removal. *See* FRCP 11(a).

§7.4 Filing & serving notice.

1. Filing.

(1) In federal court. The defendant must file the original notice of removal with its attachments in the proper federal district court. The proper court is the one located in the federal district and the division where the state-court action was pending. 28 U.S.C. §1446(a). If the defendant attempts to remove the case to the wrong federal district, the mistake does not require remand. Instead, the case will be transferred to the district court of proper venue. ***S.W.S. Erectors, Inc. v. Infax, Inc.***, 72 F.3d 489, 493 n.3 (5th Cir.1996). Removal to the wrong district does not deprive the federal district court of subject-matter jurisdiction. ***Peterson v. BMI Refractories***, 124 F.3d 1386, 1394 (11th Cir.1997).

(2) In state court. The defendant must file a copy of the removal notice and attachments in the state court. 28 U.S.C. §1446(d). Most courts hold that notice to the state court effectuates the removal and terminates the state court's jurisdiction. *See* ***Anthony v. Runyon***, 76 F.3d 210, 213 (8th Cir.1996). However, some courts treat removal as effective when the notice of removal is filed in federal court. *Id.* at 213-14; *see* ***Resolution Trust Corp. v. Bayside Developers***, 43 F.3d 1230, 1238 (9th Cir.1994).

2. Service. The defendant must serve a copy of the removal notice and attachments on all adverse parties. 28 U.S.C. §1446(d). The defendant must give the other parties notice of the removal "promptly" after filing the notice. *Id.*; *see* ***Adler v. Adler***, 862 F.Supp. 70, 72 (S.D.N.Y.1994); ***La Maina v. Brannon***, 804 F.Supp. 607, 613-14 (D.N.J. 1992).

§7.5 Amending notice. Once the case has been removed, the defendant can amend its notice of removal within the original 30-day time limit for removal. ***Energy Catering Servs. v. Burrow***, 911 F.Supp. 221, 222-23 (E.D.La. 1995); *see* ***Countryman v. Farmers Ins. Exch.***, 639 F.3d 1270, 1273 (10th Cir.2011). After the 30-day period expires, the defendant can amend the notice only to correct a defective allegation of jurisdiction; it cannot amend to add a missing allegation of jurisdiction. ***Energy Catering***, 911 F.Supp. at 223; *see* 28 U.S.C. §1653; ***Lowery v. Alabama Power Co.***, 483 F.3d 1184, 1214 n.66 (11th Cir.2007); *see, e.g.*, ***Countryman***, 639 F.3d at 1272-73 (when Ds did not attach one co-D's summons to joint notice of removal, Ds were able to cure procedural defect after removal by supplementing notice with summons; P had not been prejudiced and progress of case had not been materially impaired by omission); ***Tech Hills II Assocs. v. Phoenix Home Life Mut. Ins.***, 5 F.3d 963, 969 (6th Cir.1993) (D permitted to file affidavits, which were treated as amendment, to clarify diversity allegations).

§8. CONSENT TO REMOVAL

§8.1 Consent required.

1. Removal under §1441(a). Generally, when removal is based on 28 U.S.C. §1441(a) (i.e., federal-question or diversity jurisdiction when no other statute authorizing removal would apply), all defendants who have been properly joined and served in the suit must join in the notice of removal or consent to the removal. 28 U.S.C. §1446(b)(2)(A); *see* ***Esposito v. Home Depot U.S.A., Inc.***, 590 F.3d 72, 75 (1st Cir.2009); ***Pritchett v. Cottrell, Inc.***, 512 F.3d 1057, 1062 (8th Cir.2008); ***Balazik v. County of Dauphin***, 44 F.3d 209, 213 (3d Cir.1995); ***Roe v. O'Donohue***, 38 F.3d 298, 301 (7th Cir.1994), *overruled on other grounds*, ***Murphy Bros. v. Michetti Pipe Stringing, Inc.***, 526 U.S. 344 (1999); ***Penson Fin. Servs. v. Golden Summit Investors Grp.***, No. 3:12-CV-300-B (N.D.Tex.2012)

(slip op.; 7-5-12); H.R. Rep. No. 112-10, at 13 (2011). In other words, when there are multiple defendants, the removing defendant must secure consent to remove from the other served defendants. *See* ***Pritchett***, 512 F.3d at 1062; *see also* ***Esposito***, 590 F.3d at 75 (referred to as "unanimity" requirement). If one of the defendants refuses to or does not consent, the removal is procedurally defective, and the case should be remanded if the plaintiff timely seeks remand. *See* ***Doe v. Kerwood***, 969 F.2d 165, 169 (5th Cir.1992). The exceptions to the requirement that all defendants must consent under 28 U.S.C. §1441(a) are the following:

(1) Federal question brought with nonremovable claim. If a case involves both a federal question and a nonremovable claim (i.e., a claim not within the court's original or supplemental jurisdiction or a claim statutorily barred from being removed), only the defendants against whom the federal question is asserted are required to join in the notice of removal or consent to removal. 28 U.S.C. §1441(c)(2). See "Certain claims removed under §1441(c)," ch. 4-B, §6.2.1(2)(b), p. 276.

(2) Nominal defendant. A defendant can remove without the consent of a defendant who is merely a nominal party. ***Balazik***, 44 F.3d at 213 n.4; ***O'Donohue***, 38 F.3d at 301; *see* ***Acosta v. Master Maint. & Constr. Inc.***, 452 F.3d 373, 379 (5th Cir.2006) (D is considered nominal if court can enter final judgment without D and that judgment is not unfair to P).

NOTE

Before the Clarification Act, the unanimity requirement had been based on case law, and courts had recognized another exception to the unanimity requirement: that a defendant could remove without the consent of another defendant who had not been served. ***O'Donohue****, 38 F.3d at 301;* ***Lewis v. Rego Co.****, 757 F.2d 66, 68 (3d Cir.1985); see, e.g.,* ***Cachet Residential Builders, Inc. v. Gemini Ins.****, 547 F.Supp.2d 1028, 1029-30 (D.Ariz.2007) (D1 was not required to obtain D2's consent to remove when D2 was served only by FedEx, which did not constitute proper service under state law). But when the Clarification Act codified the unanimity requirement, that exception was incorporated into the statute. See 28 U.S.C. §1446(b)(2)(A) ("defendants who have been properly joined and served must join in or consent to removal").*

---

2. Removal under other statutes. When removal is based on a special removal statute (i.e., authority other than §1441(a)), consent of all defendants may not be necessary. See "Special removal statutes," §5.3, p. 257. Many removal statutes give a defendant an independent right to remove without the need to obtain consent from other defendants. Situations in which unanimity is not required include the following:

(1) Foreign state. A foreign state can remove a case under 28 U.S.C. §1441(d) without the consent of the other defendants. *See* ***Arango v. Guzman Travel Advisors Corp.***, 621 F.2d 1371, 1375-76 (5th Cir.1980); 14C Wright, Miller, Cooper & Steinman §3728.1 & n.8; *see also* ***Admiral Ins. v. L'Union des Assurances de Paris Incendie Accs.***, 758 F.Supp. 293, 295 (E.D.Pa.1991) (after removal by foreign state, court remanded Ds other than foreign state when court did not have independent basis of jurisdiction over other Ds).

(2) Class actions. A defendant can remove a class action under 28 U.S.C. §1453(b) without the consent of the other defendants. See "Class actions," §5.3.1(3), p. 257.

(3) Suits against federal agencies, officers & employees. A federal officer or agency can remove a case under 28 U.S.C. §1442 without the consent of the other defendants. ***Durham v. Lockheed Martin Corp.***, 445 F.3d 1247, 1253 (9th Cir.2006).

§8.2 Form of consent.

1. Written. The consent should be written and show that all necessary defendants have consented to removal. *See* ***Christiansen v. West Branch Cmty. Sch. Dist.***, 674 F.3d 927, 932 (8th Cir.2012); ***Esposito v. Home Depot U.S.A., Inc.***, 590 F.3d 72, 76-77 (1st Cir.2009); ***Loftis v. United Parcel Serv.***, 342 F.3d 509, 516 (6th Cir.2003). *But see* ***Colin K. v. Schmidt***, 528 F.Supp. 355, 358-59 (D.R.I.1981) (oral statement satisfies unanimity requirement).

2. Sign notice or file separate notice. Generally, a consenting defendant can sign the notice of removal or file a separate form agreeing to the notice of removal. *See* ***Esposito***, 590 F.3d at 76; *see, e.g.*, ***Pritchett v. Cottrell, Inc.***, 512 F.3d 1057, 1062 (8th Cir.2008) (written consent attached to removal notice as exhibit was sufficient). However, some courts require each consenting defendant to submit a timely written notice of consent, while other courts allow one defendant to sign the notice of removal, certifying with the signature that the other defendants consent. *Compare* ***Proctor v. Vishay Intertechnology Inc.***, 584 F.3d 1208, 1225 (9th Cir.2009) (unanimity requirement satisfied if notice of removal includes signature of filing defendant and certification that other defendants consent), ***Cook v. Randolph Cty.***, 573 F.3d 1143, 1150-51 (11th Cir.2009) (same), *and* ***Harper v. AutoAlliance Int'l***, 392 F.3d 195, 201-02 (6th Cir.2004) (same), *with* ***Roe v. O'Donohue***, 38 F.3d 298, 301 (7th Cir.1994) (each D must submit timely written notice of consent), *overruled on other grounds*, ***Murphy Bros. v. Michetti Pipe Stringing, Inc.***, 526 U.S. 344 (1999), *and* ***Getty Oil Corp. v. Insurance Co. of N. Am.***, 841 F.2d 1254, 1262 n.11 (5th Cir. 1988) (same).

PRACTICE TIP

To avoid any confusion as to consent, the best practice is to contact all the other defendants before filing a notice of removal to determine if they will consent and then file written consent from each defendant at the same time as the notice of removal. See ***Esposito***, *590 F.3d at 77.*

3. Other actions as consent. Under certain circumstances, conduct other than signing the notice of removal or filing a separate notice of consent can satisfy the consent requirement. *See, e.g.*, ***Esposito***, 590 F.3d at 76-77 (even though D had not explicitly consented to removal and did not technically satisfy unanimity requirement by filing answer in federal court, remand was not necessary because D subsequently cured defective consent by opposing P's remand motion). An answer that does not refer to removal and is from the defendant who has not explicitly consented may also satisfy the consent requirement. *See, e.g.*, ***Glover v. W.R. Grace & Co.***, 773 F.Supp. 964, 965 (E.D.Tex.1991) (co-D consented to removal by filing its answer in federal court; remand not required). *But see* ***Unicom Sys. v. National Louis Univ.***, 262 F.Supp.2d 638, 642-43 & n.6 (E.D.Va.2003) (answer that is silent on removal is not affirmative and unambiguous manifestation of consent; remand required).

§8.3 Time for consent. For a discussion of the deadline to consent, see "Cases involving multiple defendants," §4.1.2, p. 244.

§9. NO ORDER REQUIRED FOR REMOVAL

Once a notice of removal is filed, it confers jurisdiction on the federal court. The federal court does not need to sign an order to effectuate removal.

§9.1 Ancillary orders. Once a notice of removal is filed in federal court, the court has the authority to "issue all necessary orders and process to bring before it all proper parties whether served by process issued by the State court or otherwise." 28 U.S.C. §1447(a). If service of process was not completed in the state-court action, service may be accomplished in the same manner as if the case had been originally filed in federal court. *Id.* §1448.

§9.2 Federal & local rules. The FRCPs apply to cases removed to federal court. FRCP 81(c)(1); ***Alonzi v. Budget Constr. Co.***, 55 F.3d 331, 333 (7th Cir.1995). Many districts also have local rules that govern procedures after removal, such as rules for which pending motions must be refiled to be considered. *See, e.g.*, Local Rules N.H., Rule 81.1(b).

§9.3 Defendant's answer. If the removing defendant did not file an answer in the state-court action, the defendant's answer is due within the longest of the following time periods: (1) 21 days after the defendant receives a copy of the state-court pleading, (2) 21 days after service of the summons for the state-court pleading on file at the time of service, or (3) 7 days after the notice of removal is filed. FRCP 81(c)(2). *See generally* ***Silva v. City of Madison***, 69 F.3d 1368, 1375-76 (7th Cir.1995) (analysis of FRCP 81(c) when D has not been properly served; applying

former 20-day and 5-day deadlines). See "Deadline to answer after removal," ch. 3-A, §5.2.2(3), p. 176. If the removing defendant did file an answer in the state-court action, repleading is unnecessary unless the court orders it. FRCP 81(c)(2).

§10. WHEN REMOVAL IS EFFECTIVE

Once a case is removed, the state court does not have the power to take any action in the case.

§10.1 After notice filed in state court. The removal is effective after the notice of removal is filed in the state court. ***Anthony v. Runyon***, 76 F.3d 210, 214 (8th Cir.1996); *see also* ***Sweeney v. Resolution Trust Corp.***, 16 F.3d 1, 4 (1st Cir.1994) (state-court judgment issued after notice of removal was void); ***Tarbell v. Jacobs***, 856 F.Supp. 101, 104 (N.D.N.Y.1994) (state court's default judgment, signed after notice of removal filed in state court, was void). Orders rendered by the state court before removal remain in effect unless they are altered by the federal court. ***Alonzi v. Budget Constr. Co.***, 55 F.3d 331, 333 (7th Cir.1995); *see also* ***Burroughs v. Palumbo***, 871 F.Supp. 870, 872 (E.D. Va.1994) (default judgment entered by state court before removal was treated as if entered by federal court).

§10.2 Before notice filed in state court. During the period after the notice of removal is filed in federal court but before it is filed in state court, the state court and the federal court have concurrent jurisdiction. ***Burroughs v. Palumbo***, 871 F.Supp. 870, 872 (E.D.Va.1994); ***Tarbell v. Jacobs***, 856 F.Supp. 101, 104 (N.D.N.Y.1994); *see* Annotation, *Effect [of Removal] on Jurisdiction of State Court, of 28 USCS §1446(e)...*, 38 ALR Fed. at 858-59.

§11. WAIVER OF REMOVAL

§11.1 Late notice of removal. A defendant waives its right to remove if it does not file a timely notice of removal. ***Brown v. Demco, Inc.***, 792 F.2d 478, 481 (5th Cir.1986). See "Deadlines for Removal," §4, p. 242.

§11.2 Contract. A party can waive removal rights by contract. ***Ensco Int'l v. Certain Underwriters at Lloyd's***, 579 F.3d 442, 443 (5th Cir.2009); *see* ***Global Satellite Comm. v. Starmill U.K. Ltd.***, 378 F.3d 1269, 1272 (11th Cir.2004) (contractual waiver determined by ordinary contract principles); ***Milk 'N' More, Inc. v. Beavert***, 963 F.2d 1342, 1345-46 (10th Cir.1992) (waiver must be "clear and unequivocal"). In a contract, a party can waive removal rights by (1) explicitly stating that it is doing so, (2) allowing the other party the right to choose the venue, or (3) establishing an exclusive venue (e.g., under a forum-selection clause). ***Ensco Int'l***, 579 F.3d at 443-44. A contractual waiver of removal can also waive the right to consent to removal. *See* ***Medtronic, Inc. v. Endologix, Inc.***, 530 F.Supp.2d 1054, 1057-58 (D.Minn.2008).

§11.3 Conduct in state court. A defendant may waive its right to remove if it proceeds to defend the suit in state court. ***Schmitt v. Insurance Co. of N. Am.***, 845 F.2d 1546, 1551 (9th Cir.1988); ***Brown v. Demco, Inc.***, 792 F.2d 478, 481 (5th Cir.1986); *see* 14B Wright, Miller, Cooper & Steinman §3721 nn.144-45; 16 *Moore's Federal Practice 3d* §107.18[3]. The key factor in determining whether the defendant's actions in state court constitute a waiver of its right to remove is the defendant's intent to seek a disposition on the merits in state court rather than to maintain the status quo. ***Bolivar Sand Co. v. Allied Equip., Inc.***, 631 F.Supp. 171, 173 (W.D.Tenn.1986). A defendant's intent to waive the right to remove must be "clear and unequivocal." *See* ***Beighley v. FDIC***, 868 F.2d 776, 782 (5th Cir.1989); *see also* ***Grubb v. Donegal Mut. Ins.***, 935 F.2d 57, 59 (4th Cir.1991) (waiver should be found only in "extreme situations"); ***Rothner v. City of Chi.***, 879 F.2d 1402, 1416 (7th Cir.1989) (same).

1. Seeking disposition on merits. A defendant cannot "experiment" with rulings in the state court and then remove the case if it does not like the result. ***Moore v. Permanente Med. Grp.***, 981 F.2d 443, 447 (9th Cir.1992); ***Bolivar Sand***, 631 F.Supp. at 172; *see* ***Alley v. Nott***, 111 U.S. 472, 476 (1884). If a defendant seeks a disposition on the merits of the case in state court, it may be held to have waived its removal rights. ***Fate v. Buckeye State Mut. Ins.***, 174 F.Supp.2d 876, 881-82 (N.D.Ind.2001); *see* ***Heafitz v. Interfirst Bank***, 711 F.Supp. 92, 96 (S.D.N.Y.1989) (if D's motion seeks disposition, in whole or in part, of state-court action, D cannot try to remove after losing motion); *see, e.g.*, ***Johnson v. Heublein Inc.***, 227 F.3d 236, 244 (5th Cir.2000) (dicta; Ds waived right to remove by filing motions to dismiss and for summary judgment in state court). *But see* ***Cogdell v. Wyeth***, 366 F.3d 1245, 1249 (11th Cir. 2004) (in 11th Circuit, D must take substantial offensive or defensive actions in state court to waive right to remove);

Tedford v. Warner-Lambert Co., 327 F.3d 423, 428 (5th Cir.2003) (in 5th Circuit, right to remove is not lost by participating in state-court proceedings that do not seek adjudication on merits); ***In re Bridgestone/Firestone, Inc.***, 128 F.Supp.2d 1198, 1201 (S.D.Ind.2001) (in 7th Circuit, right to remove cannot be waived without some "extreme situation," such as trying case on merits). Citing the requirement that a waiver of rights be both clear and unequivocal, some courts have refused to find a waiver when the defendant filed a dispositive motion in state court but never obtained a ruling on it. *See* ***Beighley***, 868 F.2d at 782.

2. Filing permissive claims. The filing of permissive cross-claims, counterclaims, or third-party claims may waive the right to remove. ***Bolivar Sand***, 631 F.Supp. at 173; *see, e.g.*, ***Virginia Beach Resort & Conf. Ctr. Hotel Ass'n Condo. v. Certain Interested Underwriters at Lloyd's***, 812 F.Supp.2d 762, 765-66 (E.D.Va.2011) (D waived its right to remove when it filed its notice of removal 8 days after filing its answer and permissive counterclaim in state court and 20 days after becoming aware case was removable). However, the filing of a purely defensive pleading, such as an answer containing a general denial, an affirmative defense, or a compulsory counterclaim, will not result in a waiver. *See* ***Miami Herald Publ'g v. Ferre***, 606 F.Supp. 122, 124 (S.D.Fla.1984) (no waiver for filing answer and affirmative defenses in state court).

3. Seeking injunctive relief. Seeking a temporary restraining order or injunction in state court may waive the right to remove. ***Zbranek v. Hofheinz***, 727 F.Supp. 324, 325 (E.D.Tex.1989). However, opposing or seeking to dissolve an injunctive order is a defensive action that does not constitute a waiver. *See* ***Rothner***, 879 F.2d at 1418-19; ***Rose v. Giamatti***, 721 F.Supp. 906, 922 (S.D.Ohio 1989). *See generally* Annotation, *Opposing Injunction or Restraining Order in State Court Action …*, 58 ALR Fed. 732 (1982 & Supp.2012-13) (comparing cases in which these actions do and do not constitute waiver).

4. Moving to compel arbitration. A motion seeking to compel arbitration may waive the right to remove. *See* ***McKinnon v. Doctor's Assocs.***, 769 F.Supp. 216, 220 (E.D.Mich.1991). However, defending against an attempt to stay arbitration will not result in a waiver. *See* ***Morgan v. Nikko Secs. Co. Int'l***, 691 F.Supp. 792, 799-800 (S.D. N.Y.1988).

5. Moving for new trial after default. Filing a motion for new trial to set aside a default judgment does not waive a defendant's right to remove. ***Beighley***, 868 F.2d at 782.

6. Conducting discovery. The extent to which a defendant can participate in discovery without waiving the right to remove is uncertain. Some actions, such as noticing the plaintiff's deposition, serving interrogatories, or obtaining an order staying discovery, have been held not to constitute a waiver. *See* ***California Republican Party v. Mercier***, 652 F.Supp. 928, 931-32 (C.D.Cal.1986) (obtaining order staying discovery); ***Estevez-Gonzalez v. Kraft Inc.***, 606 F.Supp. 127, 128-29 (S.D.Fla.1985) (serving interrogatories); ***Markantonatos v. Maryland Drydock Co.***, 110 F.Supp. 862, 864 (S.D.N.Y.1953) (noticing P's deposition).

7. Conduct before case becomes removable. If a case is not initially removable but later becomes removable, the defendant's conduct before the case became removable cannot amount to waiver. *See* ***Grubb***, 935 F.2d at 58-59 (D's waiver of 30-day right to removal should be found only in "extreme situations").

B. PLAINTIFF'S MOTION TO REMAND

§1. GENERAL

§1.1 Rule. 28 U.S.C. §1447(c)-(e) (procedure for remand). See also FRCP 81(c).

§1.2 Purpose. The purpose of a motion to remand is to transfer a removed case from federal court back to state court.

NOTE

*In the Federal Courts Jurisdiction and Venue Clarification Act of 2011 (referred to as the Clarification Act), Congress made significant amendments to removal statutes in title 28. See Lamar Smith, Federal Courts Jurisdiction & Venue Clarification Act of 2011, H.R. Rep. No. 112-10 (2011). For this subchapter, the Clarification Act modified removal procedure in these situations: (1) when federal claims are joined with nonremovable claims, (2) when there are multiple defendants, (3) when removal is sought after one year and the plaintiff acted in bad faith, and (4) when the amount in controversy is not specified in the complaint. See id. at 11-17. For removed cases, the Clarification Act became effective for any suit commenced—within the meaning of state law—in state court on or after January 6, 2012. Federal Courts Jurisdiction & Venue Clarification Act of 2011, P.L. 112-63, §105, 125 Stat. 762 (2011) (eff. Jan. 6, 2012). For the law before the Clarification Act became effective, see **O'Connor's Federal Rules * Civil Trials** (2012), "Plaintiff's Motion to Remand," ch. 4-B, p. 263. Because of the substantive changes made by the 2011 amendments, use caution when citing cases that predate the amendments.*

§1.3 Timetable & forms. Timetable, Removal & Remand, p. 1581; ***O'Connor's Federal Civil Forms*** (2012), FORMS 4B.

§1.4 Other references. Lamar Smith, Federal Courts Jurisdiction & Venue Clarification Act of 2011, H.R. Rep. No. 112-10 (2011) (referred to as H.R. Rep. No. 112-10 (2011)); 14C Wright, Miller, Cooper & Steinman, *Federal Practice & Procedure 4th* §§3739-3740 (2009 & Supp.2012); 16 *Moore's Federal Practice 3d* §107.41[1] (2012); Beisner & Miller, *Litigating in the New Class Action World: A Guide to CAFA's Legislative History*, 6 BNA Class Action Litig. Rep. 403 (2005); Cesarano & Vega, *So You Thought a Remand Was Imminent? Post-Removal Litigation & the Waiver of the Right to Seek a Remand Grounded on Removal Defects*, 74 Fla. B.J. 22, 24-28 (Feb.2000); Annotation, *When Does Period for Filing Petition for Removal of Civil Action from State Court to Federal District Court Begin to Run Under 28 USCS §1446(b)*, 139 ALR Fed. 331 (1997 & Supp.2012-13); Annotation, *When Is Order, Remanding Case ... Reviewable by Court of Appeals ...*, 104 ALR Fed. 864 (1991 & Supp.2012-13).

§2. AMENDING PLEADINGS AFTER REMOVAL

§2.1 Removal based on diversity. If the case was removed based on diversity jurisdiction and the plaintiff wants to remand to state court, it can consider amending its pleadings to join a defendant whose presence would destroy diversity jurisdiction (i.e., a nondiverse defendant). *See* 28 U.S.C. §1447(e); *see also* ***Spencer v. U.S. Dist. Ct. for the N. Dist. of Cal.***, 393 F.3d 867, 870 (9th Cir.2004) (adding local, but completely diverse, D after removal does not require remand to state court because addition of local D does not destroy diversity jurisdiction). See "Parties are diverse," ch. 4-A, §5.2.1, p. 250. Once a nondiverse defendant is added, the court's diversity jurisdiction is destroyed, and the case must be remanded, not dismissed. ***Cobb v. Delta Exps., Inc.***, 186 F.3d 675, 677 (5th Cir. 1999); *see* 28 U.S.C. §1447(e); *see also* ***Curry v. U.S. Bulk Transp.***, 462 F.3d 536, 541 (6th Cir.2006) (case must be remanded when "John Doe" parties are identified after removal and they are nondiverse).

1. Amending as matter of course. Early in the litigation, the plaintiff may amend its pleading once as "a matter of course" to join a nondiverse defendant. FRCP 15(a)(1). The plaintiff may amend its pleading (1) within 21 days after serving it or (2) within 21 days after service of a responsive pleading or a motion under FRCP 12(b),

(e), or (f), whichever is earlier. FRCP 15(a)(1); *see* 2009 Notes to FRCP 15 at ¶¶3-6, p. 1157, this book. See "Amending as matter of course," ch. 5-I, §3.1, p. 345. Although leave of court is not required, a court may have the authority to reject a postremoval joinder that destroys diversity jurisdiction under 28 U.S.C. §1447(e). *See* ***Bevels v. American States Ins.***, 100 F.Supp.2d 1309, 1312 (M.D.Ala.2000); 14C Wright, Miller, Cooper & Steinman §3739 & n.27; *see, e.g.*, ***Mayes v. Rapoport***, 198 F.3d 457, 461-62 & n.11 (4th Cir.1999) (neither party raised issue that added D was nondiverse; even though leave was not required to add nondiverse D, court could properly invoke its authority when determining whether that nondiverse D was an appropriate party).

PRACTICE TIP

Instead of amending to add a nondiverse defendant, a plaintiff can (1) voluntarily dismiss the case and (2) refile it in state court with a defendant whose presence would prevent removal—either a nondiverse defendant or a local defendant. See FRCP 41(a)(1)(A)(i); ***Harvey Specialty & Sup. v. Anson Flowline Equip. Inc.****, 434 F.3d 320, 324 & n.15 (5th Cir.2005). A plaintiff, however, cannot voluntarily dismiss the case if a defendant has filed either an answer or a motion for summary judgment. See FRCP 41(a)(1)(A)(i);* ***Harvey Specialty & Sup.****, 434 F.3d at 324 & n.15. See "Plaintiff's Notice of Dismissal," ch. 7-C, §3, p. 630.*

2. Amending by consent or leave. If the plaintiff cannot file an amended pleading as a matter of course, the plaintiff can amend its pleading only by obtaining the defendant's written consent or the court's leave. FRCP 15(a)(2); ***McPhail v. Deere & Co.***, 529 F.3d 947, 951 & n.1 (10th Cir.2008).

(1) Amendment by consent. The plaintiff should first ask the defendant for its written consent to allow an amendment. See "Amendment by consent," ch. 5-I, §3.2.1, p. 346.

(2) Amendment by leave of court.

(a) Plaintiff's request for leave. Because many defendants in a removed suit will not agree to an amendment to join a nondiverse defendant, the plaintiff must usually file a written motion asking for leave to amend and submit the amended pleading along with the motion. See "Amendment by leave of court," ch. 5-I, §3.2.2, p. 346. If the plaintiff asks the court for leave to join a nondiverse defendant, the court will scrutinize that amendment more closely than an ordinary amendment. ***Bailey v. Bayer CropScience L.P.***, 563 F.3d 302, 309 (8th Cir.2009); ***Hensgens v. Deere & Co.***, 833 F.2d 1179, 1182 (5th Cir.1987).

PRACTICE TIP

When seeking to add a nondiverse additional defendant, the plaintiff should inform the court that the proposed defendant will destroy diversity jurisdiction. If the plaintiff does not inform the court, the court can reconsider its decision whether to allow joinder of the additional defendant. See, e.g., ***Bailey****, 563 F.3d at 307 (when P knew that proposed Ds would destroy diversity jurisdiction but did not inform court, court reversed its previous decision that had allowed joinder, denied reconsidered motion to amend, dismissed nondiverse Ds, and denied motion to remand).*

(b) Defendant's response. To avoid an amendment that would require that the case be remanded to state court, the defendant should file a response asking the court to deny leave. If the primary purpose of the plaintiff's amendment is to defeat jurisdiction, the defendant can consider the argument that (1) the plaintiff has no possibility of establishing a cause of action against the nondiverse party the plaintiff is seeking to join or (2) the plaintiff has fraudulently pleaded jurisdictional facts to add the nondiverse party. *See* ***Cobb***, 186 F.3d at 677-78; *cf.* ***Henderson v. Washington Nat'l Ins.***, 454 F.3d 1278, 1281 (11th Cir.2006) (fraudulent joinder). Although the fraudulent-joinder doctrine does not apply in a case already removed, the court may consider it when determining whether to allow joinder of a nondiverse party. ***Schur v. L.A. Weight Loss Ctrs., Inc.***, 577 F.3d 752, 764 (7th Cir. 2009); ***Mayes***, 198 F.3d at 463. See "Fraudulent joinder," ch. 4-A, §5.2.1(2)(e), p. 252.

(c) Court's ruling. The court may grant joinder of the additional nondiverse defendant and remand the case to state court, or it may decide the additional nondiverse defendant is not required, deny joinder, and proceed with the suit. 28 U.S.C. §1447(e); ***Schur***, 577 F.3d at 759; ***Bailey***, 563 F.3d at 307-08. In deciding whether to permit the plaintiff to amend its pleading to add a diversity-destroying defendant, the court can consider (1) whether the primary purpose of the amendment is to defeat federal jurisdiction, (2) whether the plaintiff was diligent in requesting the amendment, (3) whether the plaintiff will be prejudiced if the amendment is denied, and (4) any other factors bearing on the equities. ***Wilson v. Bruks-Klockner, Inc.***, 602 F.3d 363, 367 (5th Cir.2010); ***Mayes***, 198 F.3d at 462; *e.g.*, ***Schur***, 577 F.3d at 759 (although there was extensive delay between removal and P's motion to amend in tort case, remand was proper when P sought leave only after learning of new Ds' role in events that formed basis of suit); *see* ***Bailey***, 563 F.3d at 309. The court should not apply the factors mechanically but should seek to balance the defendant's interest in a federal forum against the possibility that judicial resources would be wasted if joinder were denied. ***Mammano v. American Honda Motor Co.***, 941 F.Supp. 323, 325 (W.D.N.Y.1996).

NOTE

Some courts address FRCP 19 when deciding whether to permit an amendment to join a nondiverse defendant. See ***Bailey***, *563 F.3d at 308. But see 14C Wright, Miller, Cooper & Steinman §3739 & n.29 (courts generally do not limit postremoval joinder of nondiverse parties to those who satisfy FRCP 19(a) requirements). Specifically, the court may consider (1) whether the new defendant is required for the full resolution of the suit and (2) if the defendant is required but joinder is not feasible, whether the suit should proceed without the required defendant. See* ***Bailey***, *563 F.3d at 308. See "Motion to Dismiss for Failure to Join a Party Under FRCP 19—FRCP 12(b)(7)," ch. 3-I, p. 214. If the party is required and the suit should not proceed, the court must dismiss the suit under FRCP 19(b). See* ***McPhail***, *529 F.3d at 951. In not allowing the joinder, a court may also consider FRCP 21, which allows a court to drop a dispensable nondiverse party at any time. See* ***Bailey***, *563 F.3d at 308. If the party is not required, the court must consider whether permissive joinder under FRCP 20 is appropriate. See* ***McPhail***, *529 F.3d at 951-52.*

§2.2 Removal based on federal question. If the case was removed based on federal-question jurisdiction and the plaintiff wants to remand to state court, it can consider amending its pleadings to delete the federal claim. *See* 28 U.S.C. §1441(a), (c).

1. Amending as matter of course. Early in the litigation, the plaintiff may amend its pleading once as "a matter of course" to delete the federal-question claims. FRCP 15(a)(1); *see* ***Naples v. New Jersey Sports & Exposition Auth.***, 102 F.Supp.2d 550, 552 (D.N.J.2000); ***Grynberg Prod. v. British Gas, P.L.C.***, 149 F.R.D. 135, 137 (E.D.Tex.1993). See "Amending as matter of course," §2.1.1, p. 268.

2. Amending by consent or leave. If the plaintiff cannot file an amended pleading as a matter of course, the plaintiff can amend its pleading only by obtaining the defendant's written consent or the court's leave. FRCP 15(a)(2). See "Amending by consent or leave," §2.1.2, p. 269. If the plaintiff asks the court for leave, the court may allow the amendment and remand to state court if the plaintiff has a "substantive and meritorious reason" for deleting the federal claims; the reason must be more than simply to defeat federal jurisdiction. *See* ***Carnegie-Mellon Univ. v. Cohill***, 484 U.S. 343, 357 (1988); ***Harless v. CSX Hotels, Inc.***, 389 F.3d 444, 448 (4th Cir.2004).

§3. MOTION

If the defendant removes the case but the plaintiff still wants to try the case in state court, the plaintiff must file a motion to remand. ***Hurley v. Motor Coach Indus.***, 222 F.3d 377, 380 (7th Cir.2000); *see also* ***H&H Terminals, LC v. R. Ramos Family Trust, LLP***, 634 F.Supp.2d 770, 776-77 (W.D.Tex.2009) (third-party D cannot move for remand).

COMMENTARIES
CHAPTER 4. REMOVAL & REMAND
B. PLAINTIFF'S MOTION TO REMAND

CAUTION

*A plaintiff's affirmative conduct in federal court can cause it to waive its right to seek remand. See, e.g., **Koehnen v. Herald Fire Ins.**, 89 F.3d 525, 528 (8th Cir.1996) (P sought leave to file supplemental complaint); **Johnson v. Odeco Oil & Gas Co.**, 864 F.2d 40, 42 (5th Cir.1989) (P participated in discovery and filed amended complaint). See generally Cesarano & Vega, So You Thought a Remand Was Imminent?, 74 Fla. B.J. at 25-27 (discussing removal concerns and explaining that federal courts disagree about specifics of what constitutes waiver of right to seek remand). A plaintiff who intends to seek a remand should make sure its actions cannot be construed as a waiver.*

§3.1 Grounds. The courts strictly construe the removal statutes in favor of remand and against removal. ***Bosky v. Kroger Tex., LP***, 288 F.3d 208, 211 (5th Cir.2002); *see **Diaz v. Sheppard***, 85 F.3d 1502, 1505 (11th Cir.1996); ***Duncan v. Stuetzle***, 76 F.3d 1480, 1485 (9th Cir.1996); ***Brown v. Francis***, 75 F.3d 860, 864-65 (3d Cir.1996). A motion to remand must respond to the grounds asserted by the defendant in its notice of removal and indicate why the grounds do not apply. The grounds for remand will generally be based on jurisdictional or procedural grounds under 28 U.S.C. §1447(c).

NOTE

*Outside of remands under 28 U.S.C. §1447(c), remand orders can also be based on the refusal to grant supplemental jurisdiction, on an abstention doctrine, or on a forum-selection clause. **Kamm v. ITEX Corp.**, 568 F.3d 752, 756 (9th Cir.2009). If a removed case involves claims with independent federal jurisdiction and state-law claims, the plaintiff can argue that the court should refuse to exercise supplemental jurisdiction over the state-law claims. 14C Wright, Miller, Cooper & Steinman §3739 & nn.117-121; see, e.g., **Anderson v. Aon Corp.**, 614 F.3d 361, 364-65 (7th Cir.2010) (after P voluntarily dismissed federal claim, court properly denied remand and exercised supplemental jurisdiction over state-law claims because state-law securities claims arose from same transaction as federal RICO claims); **In re Prairie Island Dakota Sioux**, 21 F.3d 302, 304-05 (8th Cir.1994) (after federal claim was dismissed for lack of federal-question jurisdiction, court properly remanded supplemental state-law claims). See "Supplemental Jurisdiction," ch. 2-F, §6, p. 134. If the court can abstain from exercising its jurisdiction over the removed case, the plaintiff should state why the court should decline jurisdiction in the case. See **Larsen v. CIGNA HealthCare Mid-Atl., Inc.**, 224 F.Supp.2d 998, 1006-07 (D.Md.2002); 14C Wright, Miller, Cooper & Steinman §3739 & nn.126-132. See "Abstention," ch. 2-F, §7, p. 138. If a removed case involves a forum-selection clause, the plaintiff can argue that the court should remand in accordance with the parties' forum-selection clause. See **Kamm**, 568 F.3d at 754-55. See "Contract," ch. 4-A, §11.2, p. 266.*

1. Jurisdictional grounds. Generally, jurisdictional grounds for remand are defects in the defendant's allegations of subject-matter jurisdiction. *See **In re Methyl Tertiary Butyl Ether Prods. Liab. Litig.***, 522 F.Supp.2d 557, 562 (S.D.N.Y.2007). See "Lack of jurisdiction," §3.5.1, p. 273. When there is no subject-matter jurisdiction, remand is mandatory. 28 U.S.C. §1447(c); ***International Primate Prot. League v. Administrators of Tulane Educ. Fund***, 500 U.S. 72, 89 (1991); ***Anusbigian v. Trugreen/Chemlawn, Inc.***, 72 F.3d 1253, 1254 (6th Cir.1996). Whether the court has subject-matter jurisdiction is determined at the time of removal; post-removal events generally do not deprive a court of jurisdiction. ***Bank One Tex. v. Morrison***, 26 F.3d 544, 547 (5th Cir.1994); *see* 28 U.S.C. §1447(e) (after removal, if P wants to join additional Ds that would destroy diversity jurisdiction, court has discretion to deny joinder; if joinder is allowed, court must remand action).

(1) No federal-question jurisdiction. If the defendant removed the case based on federal-question jurisdiction and the case does not "arise under" federal law, the plaintiff should move to remand. *See **In re Hot-Hed***

Inc., 477 F.3d 320, 323 (5th Cir.2007). In the motion for remand, the plaintiff should specifically state that "the federal court lacks subject-matter jurisdiction." *See* ***Tillman v. CSX Transp.***, 929 F.2d 1023, 1026-27 (5th Cir.1991). See "Federal-Question Jurisdiction," ch. 2-F, §2, p. 113.

(2) No jurisdiction over certain claims removed under §1441(c). If an otherwise nonremovable claim (i.e., a claim not within the court's original or supplemental jurisdiction or a claim statutorily barred from being removed) is removed under 28 U.S.C. §1441(c)(1) because the case also involved a federal question, the plaintiff can assert that the nonremovable claim should be remanded to state court because the federal court lacks jurisdiction over the claim. *See* 28 U.S.C. §1441(c). See "Certain claims removed under §1441(c)," §6.2.1(2)(b), p. 276.

(3) No diversity jurisdiction. If the defendant removed the case on grounds of diversity, the plaintiff should argue there is no diversity jurisdiction for one or more of the following reasons:

(a) The parties are not diverse. For example, the plaintiff and the defendant are citizens of the same state or a diversity-destroying defendant is added after removal. See "Parties are diverse," ch. 4-A, §5.2.1, p. 250; "Removal based on diversity," §2.1, p. 268.

(b) The case does not meet the required amount in controversy. See "Amount in controversy," ch. 4-A, §5.2.2, p. 254.

(c) There is no "fraudulent joinder." If the defendant removed the case on fraudulent-joinder grounds, the plaintiff should argue that the defendant has not met its burden of proving the plaintiff has absolutely no possibility of recovering against the defendant whose presence would prevent removal. See "Fraudulent joinder," ch. 4-A, §5.2.1(2)(e), p. 252.

(4) No special removal statute. If the defendant removed the case under the authority of a special statute permitting removal, the plaintiff should state why that statute does not apply. See "Special removal statutes," ch. 4-A, §5.3, p. 257.

(5) No alienage jurisdiction. If the defendant removed the case because of alienage jurisdiction, the plaintiff should state why the court has no such jurisdiction. See "Alienage Jurisdiction," ch. 2-F, §4, p. 127.

(6) Waiver by contract. If the defendant signed a contract specifying the state court as the forum to settle disputes, the plaintiff should state that, by doing so, the defendant waived its right to removal. See "Contract," ch. 4-A, §11.2, p. 266.

(7) Waiver by defending in state court. If the defendant proceeded to defend the suit in the state court, the plaintiff should state that, by doing so, the defendant waived its right to removal. See "Conduct in state court," ch. 4-A, §11.3, p. 266.

2. Procedural grounds. Generally, procedural grounds for remand are defects other than defects in the defendant's allegations of subject-matter jurisdiction. *See* ***Advanced Bodycare Solutions, LLC v. Thione Int'l***, 524 F.3d 1235, 1237 n.1 (11th Cir.2008); ***Ellenburg v. Spartan Motors Chassis, Inc.***, 519 F.3d 192, 199 (4th Cir.2008); ***Lively v. Wild Oats Mkts., Inc.***, 456 F.3d 933, 939 (9th Cir.2006); ***In re Methyl***, 522 F.Supp.2d at 563-64; *see also* ***Corporate Mgmt. Advisors, Inc. v. Artjen Complexus, Inc.***, 561 F.3d 1294, 1297 (11th Cir.2009) (court cannot remand sua sponte based on procedural defect). See "Procedural defects," §3.5.2, p. 274.

(1) Residence alleged instead of citizenship. If the defendant alleged the residence of the parties but not their citizenship, the plaintiff should state that only the citizenship of parties determines diversity. *See* ***Heinen v. Northrop Grumman Corp.***, 671 F.3d 669, 670 (7th Cir.2012). See "Is there complete diversity?," ch. 2-F, §3.1, p. 116; "Who is considered for diversity jurisdiction?," ch. 2-F, §3.2, p. 118; "Parties are diverse," ch. 4-A, §5.2.1, p. 250.

(2) Notice not timely filed. If the defendant did not timely file notice, the plaintiff should state that the notice was not timely filed. *See* 28 U.S.C. §1446(b), (c)(1). See "Deadlines for Removal," ch. 4-A, §4, p. 242.

NOTE

Under the Clarification Act, a defendant can remove a diversity suit more than one year after it is filed if the plaintiff acted in bad faith to prevent the defendant from removing it. 28 U.S.C. §1446(c)(1). See "Bad faith," ch. 4-A, §4.2.2(2)(a), p. 247. If the defendant removed after one year based on the plaintiff's alleged bad faith, the plaintiff should state that it did not act in bad faith and thus the notice was not timely filed.

(3) Not all defendants timely consented. If any served defendant that was required to consent to removal did not timely consent, the plaintiff should state that the defendant did not obtain the consent required by the removal statute. *See* 28 U.S.C. §1446(a), (b)(2); ***Esposito v. Home Depot U.S.A., Inc.***, 590 F.3d 72, 75 (1st Cir.2009); ***Doe v. Kerwood***, 969 F.2d 165, 169 (5th Cir.1992). See "Consent to Removal," ch. 4-A, §8, p. 263.

(4) Presence of local defendant. If one of the properly joined and served defendants is a citizen of the state where the suit was filed (i.e., local defendant), the plaintiff should state that the case cannot be removed. 28 U.S.C. §1441(b)(2). See "Local defendants," ch. 4-A, §5.2.1(2)(a), p. 251.

(5) Improper party filed notice. If an improper party filed the notice of removal, the plaintiff should state that the party cannot seek removal. *See* 28 U.S.C. §1441(a), (c)(2); ***Palisades Collections LLC v. Shorts***, 552 F.3d 327, 333 (4th Cir.2008); ***First Nat'l Bank v. Curry***, 301 F.3d 456, 461 (6th Cir.2002); 16 *Moore's Federal Practice 3d* §107.11[1][b][iv]. See "Who can file notice," ch. 4-A, §7.1, p. 261.

§3.2 Verification. Although nothing in 28 U.S.C. §1447 requires it, any supporting statement not included in the record should be verified.

§3.3 Hearing request. If an evidentiary hearing is necessary to develop facts supporting the propriety of the removal, the plaintiff should request a hearing. *See* ***Jerguson v. Blue Dot Inv.***, 659 F.2d 31, 35 (5th Cir.1981). If the impropriety of the removal is apparent from the face of the pleadings, a hearing may not be necessary. ***Bell v. Taylor***, 509 F.2d 808, 810 (5th Cir.1975); *see* 14C Wright, Miller, Cooper & Steinman §3739 & n.74.

§3.4 Costs & fees. The plaintiff can ask for court costs, expenses, and attorney fees in the motion to remand under 28 U.S.C. §1447(c). See "Award of costs, expenses & attorney fees," §6.5, p. 277.

§3.5 Deadlines for remand. The deadlines for filing a motion for remand depend on whether the motion is based on the lack of subject-matter jurisdiction, which can be raised at any time, or on any defect other than the lack of subject-matter jurisdiction (i.e., a procedural defect), which must be raised within 30 days after the filing of the notice of removal. *See* 28 U.S.C. §1447(c). There is no bright-line rule, however, for whether an argument is based on subject-matter jurisdiction or a procedural defect. ***Behrazfar v. Unisys Corp.***, 687 F.Supp.2d 999, 1002 (C.D.Cal. 2009).

PRACTICE TIP

Because the distinction between a lack of subject-matter jurisdiction and a procedural defect is tricky, a plaintiff should file a motion for remand within 30 days after the defendant's notice of removal—regardless of the grounds for remand. ***Behrazfar****, 687 F.Supp.2d at 1002; see, e.g.,* ***Orange Cty. Water Dist. v. Unocal Corp.****, 584 F.3d 43, 49-51 (2d Cir.2009) (because bankruptcy removal statute, which was grounds for P's motion to remand, provided only procedural mechanism for removal and not subject-matter jurisdiction, P waived objections under that statute for improper removal when motion was filed more than 30 days after notice of removal).*

1. Lack of jurisdiction. If the court lacks subject-matter jurisdiction, the plaintiff may file a motion to remand at any time before the district court or appellate court renders a final judgment. 28 U.S.C. §1447(c); ***Page v. City of Southfield***, 45 F.3d 128, 133 (6th Cir.1995); *see* ***Corporate Mgmt. Advisors, Inc. v. Artjen Complexus, Inc.***, 561 F.3d 1294, 1296 (11th Cir.2009) (court can remand for lack of subject-matter jurisdiction on its own initiative at

any time). In such a case, remand is mandatory, not discretionary. But if the defendant can cure the jurisdictional defect before judgment is rendered, the erroneous denial of a motion to remand will not be grounds for reversal. *E.g.*, ***Moffitt v. Residential Funding Co.***, 604 F.3d 156, 159-60 (4th Cir.2010) (even though removal may have been improper at time of removal, P filed amended complaint after removal that provided independent ground for federal jurisdiction under CAFA; court properly denied P's motion to remand); *see* ***Caterpillar Inc. v. Lewis***, 519 U.S. 61, 76-77 (1996). A plaintiff may also file a motion to remand even after a court has rendered a final judgment. *See* ***Gould v. Mutual Life Ins.***, 790 F.2d 769, 772 (9th Cir.1986) (treated as motion to vacate and remand). A remand is necessary even after final judgment if the court never had subject-matter jurisdiction. ***American Fire & Cas. Co. v. Finn***, 341 U.S. 6, 18-19 (1951).

(1) Lack of federal-question, diversity, or alienage jurisdiction. If remand is based on the lack of federal-question, diversity, or alienage jurisdiction, the plaintiff can move to remand at any time. *See* 28 U.S.C. §1447(c).

(2) Forum-selection clause. If remand is based on a forum-selection clause, the plaintiff does not need to seek remand within 30 days after removal. ***Kamm v. ITEX Corp.***, 568 F.3d 752, 756-57 (9th Cir.2009). The plaintiff must, however, seek remand within a reasonable time. *Id.* at 757.

2. Procedural defects. If the defendant's notice of removal was defective in any way other than a lack of subject-matter jurisdiction, the plaintiff must move for remand within 30 days after the notice of removal was filed. 28 U.S.C. §1447(c); ***Caterpillar***, 519 U.S. at 69; *see* ***Orange Cty. Water Dist.***, 584 F.3d at 49-50 & n.13; ***Pavone v. Mississippi Riverboat Amusement Corp.***, 52 F.3d 560, 566 (5th Cir.1995); *see also* ***Phoenix Global Ventures, LLC v. Phoenix Hotel Assocs.***, 422 F.3d 72, 76 (2d Cir.2005) (if P attempted to file motion to remand electronically but did not comply with requirements of court's electronic-filing system, court may deem motion timely as if it had been physically filed on same day).

CAUTION

FRCP 6(d), which adds three days to service by any method other than hand delivery, does not extend the 30-day period for the plaintiff to file a motion to remand. ***Pavone****, 52 F.3d at 566. FRCP 6(d) applies only when a party is required to act within a prescribed period after service, not after filing.* ***Pavone****, 52 F.3d at 566. But see* ***New Jersey Dept. of Env'tl Prot. v. Exxon Mobil Corp.****, 381 F.Supp.2d 398, 402 (D.N.J.2005) (additional three days applies to any situation when opposing party triggers response period, and thus applies to remand).*

(1) Incurable defects. If the procedural defect is not curable, the federal court should remand the case to state court.

(2) Curable defects. If the procedural defect is curable, the federal court may permit the defendant to amend its notice of removal. See "Amending notice," ch. 4-A, §7.5, p. 263.

PRACTICE TIP

To prevent the defendant from curing a defect by adding a new ground for removal, the plaintiff can consider filing the motion to remand after the defendant's time to remove expires. See ***O'Halloran v. University of Wash.****, 856 F.2d 1375, 1381 (9th Cir.1988). But see* ***ARCO Env'tl Remediation, L.L.C. v. Department of Health & Env'tl Quality****, 213 F.3d 1108, 1117 (9th Cir.2000) (amendment allowed after 30-day removal deadline to correct defective allegation of jurisdiction).* *See "Deadlines for Removal," ch. 4-A, §4, p. 242.*

(3) Waiver. If the plaintiff does not seek remand within 30 days after removal, it generally waives all defects except subject-matter jurisdiction. *See* ***Patin v. Allied Signal, Inc.***, 77 F.3d 782, 786 (5th Cir.1996); ***Northern Cal. Dist. Council of Laborers v. Pittsburg-Des Moines Steel Co.***, 69 F.3d 1034, 1037-38 (9th Cir.1995). If the plaintiff does not timely object to the following defects, it may waive its right to remand.

(a) Defects in removal notice. If the plaintiff does not timely object to a defect in the defendant's notice of removal, the plaintiff waives its right to remand on that ground. *E.g.*, ***Coury v. Prot***, 85 F.3d 244, 252 (5th Cir.1996) (although D could not properly remove state suit to federal court when D was citizen of state where suit was filed, P waived defect when it did not file for remand within 30 days after removal).

(b) Late notice of removal. If the plaintiff does not timely object to the defendant's untimely notice of removal, the plaintiff may have waived its right to remand. *E.g.*, ***Music v. Arrowood Indem. Co.***, 632 F.3d 284, 286-87 (6th Cir.2011) (even though D removed case after one-year limit, P waived right to remand because motion to remand was filed more than 30 days after removal); *see* ***Belser v. St. Paul Fire & Mar. Ins.***, 965 F.2d 5, 8 (5th Cir.1992). See "Deadlines for Removal," ch. 4-A, §4, p. 242. Most courts hold that the defendant's removal deadlines are not jurisdictional, and the defects may be waived if they are not timely raised. *See* ***Music***, 632 F.3d at 287-88; ***Ariel Land Owners, Inc. v. Dring***, 351 F.3d 611, 614-15 (3d Cir.2003); ***Maniar v. FDIC***, 979 F.2d 782, 785 (9th Cir.1992); ***Barnes v. Westinghouse Elec. Corp.***, 962 F.2d 513, 516 (5th Cir.1992); ***Wilson v. General Motors Corp.***, 888 F.2d 779, 781 n.1 (11th Cir.1989) (dicta). However, some courts have held that the defendant's removal deadlines are jurisdictional. *See* ***Rashid v. Schenck Constr. Co.***, 843 F.Supp. 1081, 1086-88 (S.D.W.Va.1993); ***Perez v. General Packer, Inc.***, 790 F.Supp. 1464, 1470-71 (C.D.Cal.1992).

(c) Late consent to removal. If the plaintiff does not timely object to a defendant's untimely consent to removal, the plaintiff waives its right to remand on that ground. ***Getty Oil Corp. v. Insurance Co. of N. Am.***, 841 F.2d 1254, 1263 (5th Cir.1988). See "Cases involving multiple defendants," ch. 4-A, §4.1.2, p. 244. Although the removal statute requires all defendants to join in the removal, the requirement is not jurisdictional, and if the plaintiff does not object, it waives that defect. *See* ***Johnson v. Helmerich & Payne, Inc.***, 892 F.2d 422, 423 (5th Cir. 1990).

(d) Local-defendant rule. If the plaintiff does not timely object to the presence of a defendant that is a citizen of the state where the suit was filed (i.e., the local defendant), the plaintiff may have waived its right to remand on that ground. *See* 28 U.S.C. §1447(c) (P must move to remand within 30 days after notice of removal is filed). *But see* 28 U.S.C. §1453(b) (local-defendant rule does not apply to class-action removal statute). See "Local defendants," ch. 4-A, §5.2.1(2)(a), p. 251. Most courts hold that the local-defendant rule is not jurisdictional and the defect is waived if it is not timely raised. *See* ***Samaan v. St. Joseph Hosp.***, 670 F.3d 21, 28 (1st Cir.2012); ***Lively v. Wild Oats Mkts., Inc.***, 456 F.3d 933, 935-36 (9th Cir.2006); ***Hurley v. Motor Coach Indus.***, 222 F.3d 377, 379-80 (7th Cir.2000); ***Handelsman v. Bedford Vill. Assocs.***, 213 F.3d 48, 50 n.2 (2d Cir.2000); *see also* ***In re 1994 Exxon Chem. Fire***, 558 F.3d 378, 392-93 (5th Cir.2009) (identifying that local-defendant rule is procedural in certain circumstances). *But see* ***Horton v. Conklin***, 431 F.3d 602, 605 (8th Cir.2005) (local-defendant rule is jurisdictional and not waivable); ***Balzer v. Bay Winds Fed. Credit Un.***, 622 F.Supp.2d 628, 630-31 (W.D.Mich.2009) (local-defendant rule is not necessarily procedural and waivable).

§4. HEARING

§4.1 Evidence or argument? The court does not need to conduct a hearing to receive evidence if the lack of removal jurisdiction is apparent from the face of the pleadings. ***Bell v. Taylor***, 509 F.2d 808, 810 (5th Cir.1975). But if it is necessary to develop facts on the propriety of the removal, the court should conduct an evidentiary hearing.

§4.2 Jurisdictional issues. A hearing on a motion to remand is limited to jurisdictional issues. The court should not litigate the substantive issues in the case as part of its inquiry into jurisdiction. ***Green v. Amerada Hess Corp.***, 707 F.2d 201, 204 (5th Cir.1983).

§5. RESPONSE

The defendant responding to the plaintiff's motion to remand should reiterate and provide support for the grounds stated in its notice of removal. See "Grounds for removal," ch. 4-A, §7.3.1, p. 262. If appropriate, the defendant should also argue that the plaintiff waived its right to remand because the motion to remand was based on a procedural defect and was untimely. See "Deadlines for remand," §3.5, p. 273.

§6. RULING

§6.1 Remand on court's initiative. The court can remand a case for lack of subject-matter jurisdiction without a motion by the plaintiff. ***Page v. City of Southfield***, 45 F.3d 128, 133 (6th Cir.1995); *see* ***In re Allstate Ins.***, 8 F.3d 219, 223 (5th Cir.1993). But the court cannot remand a case for procedural defects in the removal without a motion by the plaintiff. ***Corporate Mgmt. Advisors, Inc. v. Artjen Complexus, Inc.***, 561 F.3d 1294, 1296 (11th Cir. 2009); ***Ellenburg v. Spartan Motors Chassis, Inc.***, 519 F.3d 192, 198 (4th Cir.2008); ***Lively v. Wild Oats Mkts., Inc.***, 456 F.3d 933, 936 (9th Cir.2006); ***Page***, 45 F.3d at 133-34; ***In re Continental Cas. Co.***, 29 F.3d 292, 294-95 (7th Cir.1994); ***In re Allstate Ins.***, 8 F.3d at 223. *Contra* ***Cassara v. Ralston***, 832 F.Supp. 752, 753 (S.D.N.Y.1993).

§6.2 Remand mandatory.

1. Lack of subject-matter jurisdiction. The court must grant a remand if the court lacks subject-matter jurisdiction. 28 U.S.C. §1447(c).

(1) Remand entire case. If the court lacks subject-matter jurisdiction over the entire case, the court must remand all claims. *See* 28 U.S.C. §1447(c).

(2) Partial remand.

(a) Generally. If the court lacks subject-matter jurisdiction over some claims, the court can grant a partial remand. *See, e.g.*, 28 U.S.C. §1454(d)(1) (court must remand all claims not within court's original or supplemental jurisdiction that are removed with patent, plant-variety-protection, or copyright claim).

(b) Certain claims removed under §1441(c). If a suit involves both a federal question and an otherwise nonremovable claim (i.e., a claim not within the court's original or supplemental jurisdiction or a claim statutorily barred from being removed), the court must sever the otherwise nonremovable claim. *See* 28 U.S.C. §1441(c); ***Bivins v. Glanz***, No. 12-CV-103-TCK-FHM (N.D.Okla.2012) (slip op.; 8-1-12). The court must then remand the severed claim to state court. 28 U.S.C. §1441(c)(2). For a list of some claims that are statutorily barred from being removed, see "Prohibitions Against Removal," ch. 4-A, §6, p. 260.

NOTE

Before the Clarification Act became effective, if a suit involved an otherwise nonremovable claim and a federal question, the court could remand the nonremovable claim to state court if the claim was separate and independent from the federal question and involved a matter in which state law predominates. See ***Eastus v. Blue Bell Creameries, L.P.****, 97 F.3d 100, 104 (5th Cir.1996). Former §1441(c) had been criticized as unconstitutional for allowing federal courts to decide state-law claims for which they did not have jurisdiction. See H.R. Rep. No. 112-10, at 12 (2011). The amendments to §1441(c) under the Clarification Act are intended to cure the constitutional problems. See H.R. Rep. No. 112-10, at 12 (2011). The sever-and-remand approach now provides jurisdiction that is equal to—and not greater than—what is provided under Article 3 of the U.S. Constitution. See H.R. Rep. No. 112-10, at 12 (2011).*

2. Procedural defect. Generally, the court should grant a remand if there is a defect in the removal procedure (e.g., consent of all defendants is not obtained, notice is untimely filed). *See* ***Thompson v. Louisville Ladder Corp.***, 835 F.Supp. 336, 339-40 (E.D.Tex.1993) (remand is mandatory for procedural defects); ***Catalina Corp. v. Pauma Band of Luiseno Indians***, No. 10cv1404-WQH-BLM (S.D.Cal.2010) (slip op.; 10-12-10) (same). *But see* ***Scoular Co. v. DJCB Farm Prtshp.***, No. 2:09cv00061-WRW (E.D.Ark.2009) (slip op.; 7-24-09) (remand for procedural defects is discretionary; noting that 8th Circuit has not addressed issue). But some courts may deny remand if the defect can be cured and the procedural defect does not affect the court's authority to hear the removed suit. *See, e.g.*, ***Countryman v. Farmers Ins. Exch.***, 639 F.3d 1270, 1272-73 (10th Cir.2011) (not attaching state-court summons was curable procedural defect); ***Young v. Community Assessment & Treatment Servs.***, No. 1:07cv1797 (N.D.Ohio

2007) (slip op.; 11-6-07) (same); *see also* ***Yellow Transp. v. Apex Digital, Inc.***, 406 F.Supp.2d 1213, 1217-18 (D.Kan. 2005) (dicta; defects in filing timely notice or obtaining consent of all Ds may not be curable).

3. Certain class actions. The court must grant a remand of a class action that meets one of the exceptions under 28 U.S.C. §1332(d)(4). For a discussion of those exceptions, see "Court must decline jurisdiction," ch. 2-F, §5.1.3(3), p. 132.

§6.3 Denial of remand mandatory. Generally, unless there is basis for the court to decline to exercise its jurisdiction (e.g., abstention), the court must deny a remand if it possesses original jurisdiction over a removed claim. *See* ***Cuevas v. BAC Home Loans Servicing, LP***, 648 F.3d 242, 248 (5th Cir.2011) (no discretion to remand claim when court had subject-matter jurisdiction; jurisdiction could not be destroyed by parties' waiver); ***Gaming Corp. v. Dorsey & Whitney***, 88 F.3d 536, 542 (8th Cir.1996) (no discretion to remand claim that states federal question); ***Brockman v. Merabank***, 40 F.3d 1013, 1017 (9th Cir.1994) (same); ***Woods Corporate Assocs. v. Signet Star Holdings, Inc.***, 910 F.Supp. 1019, 1027 (D.N.J.1995) (no discretion to remand claim based on diversity jurisdiction), *aff'd*, 96 F.3d 1437 (3d Cir.1996) (table case). See "Abstention," ch. 2-F, §7, p. 138.

§6.4 Remand discretionary.

1. Supplemental jurisdiction. The court has discretion to remand claims over which it has supplemental jurisdiction. *See* 28 U.S.C. §1454(d)(2) (court can remand claims within court's supplemental jurisdiction that were removed with patent, plant-variety-protection, or copyright claim); *see, e.g.*, ***City of New Rochelle v. Town of Mamaroneck***, 111 F.Supp.2d 353, 369-70 (S.D.N.Y.2000) (in suit involving federal and state-law claims, court remanded state-law claims because they raised novel and complex state-law questions of first impression, which federal courts should decline to hear based on interests of comity and federalism); *see also* 28 U.S.C. §1367(c) (basis for declining to exercise supplemental jurisdiction). See "Supplemental Jurisdiction," ch. 2-F, §6, p. 134. Generally, if all claims that supported removal are dismissed, the court should remand any remaining pendent state-law claims, but the decision to remand is still discretionary. ***Carnegie-Mellon Univ. v. Cohill***, 484 U.S. 343, 350-51 (1988); ***Harrell v. 20th Century Ins.***, 934 F.2d 203, 205 (9th Cir.1991); *see* ***Valencia v. Lee***, 316 F.3d 299, 305-06 (2d Cir.2003) (noting circumstances in which it is appropriate for court to exercise supplemental jurisdiction even after claims supporting original jurisdiction have been dismissed).

2. Abstention. The court has discretion to grant a remand based on abstention when the relief sought in federal court is equitable or otherwise discretionary. ***Quackenbush v. Allstate Ins.***, 517 U.S. 706, 730 (1996). See "Abstention," ch. 2-F, §7, p. 138.

3. Bankruptcy cases. The court has discretion to remand on any equitable ground any claim or cause of action that is removed based on a court's bankruptcy jurisdiction under 28 U.S.C. §1334. 28 U.S.C. §1452(b).

NOTE

In the alternative to remand, a party can ask the court to abstain from hearing any claim or cause of action that is removed based on a court's bankruptcy jurisdiction under 28 U.S.C. §1334. 28 U.S.C. §1334(c) provides both a permissive and a mandatory basis for abstention.

4. Certain class actions. The court has discretion to remand a class action if more than one-third but less than two-thirds of the members of all proposed plaintiff classes in the aggregate and the primary defendants are citizens of the state where the action was originally filed. 28 U.S.C. §1332(d)(3).

§6.5 Award of costs, expenses & attorney fees.

1. Against defendant. If the federal court grants a motion to remand, the court's order may require payment of costs, expenses, and attorney fees incurred if removal was unreasonable or improper. 28 U.S.C. §1447(c); ***Martin v. Franklin Capital Corp.***, 546 U.S. 132, 141 (2005); *see* FRCP 11(c)(1); ***Garcia v. Amfels, Inc.***, 254 F.3d 585, 587 (5th Cir.2001).

(1) Award under 28 U.S.C. §1447(c). Under the fee-shifting provisions of 28 U.S.C. §1447(c), a court can award attorney fees when the removing party lacked an "objectively reasonable basis" for seeking removal. ***Martin***, 546 U.S. at 141; ***Knop v. Mackall***, 645 F.3d 381, 382 (D.C.Cir.2011); ***Valdes v. Wal-Mart Stores***, 199 F.3d 290, 293 (5th Cir.2000); *see* ***MB Fin. v. Stevens***, 678 F.3d 497, 498 (7th Cir.2012); *see, e.g.*, ***Porter Trust v. Rural Water Sewer & Solid Waste Mgmt. Dist.***, 607 F.3d 1251, 1254-55 (10th Cir.2010) (removal was not objectively reasonable when D removed based on federal-question jurisdiction from board of county commissioners' deannexation proceeding; removal permitted only from state "court"); ***Warthman v. Genoa Township Bd. of Trs.***, 549 F.3d 1055, 1059-60 (6th Cir.2008) (removal was not objectively reasonable when complaint included single mention of U.S. Constitution and was carefully drafted to plead only state-law claims; remanded to determine if attorney fees were appropriate); ***Lussier v. Dollar Tree Stores***, 518 F.3d 1062, 1065-66 (9th Cir.2008) (removal was objectively reasonable when sought under CAFA and statute's meaning of when action "commenced" had not been determined at time of removal; attorney fees denied). The party—not the attorney—is liable for the attorney fees. *See* ***In re Crescent City Estates, LLC***, 588 F.3d 822, 825-26 (4th Cir.2009). *But see* ***Wisconsin v. Missionaries to the Preborn***, 798 F.Supp. 542, 543-44 (E.D.Wis.1992) (imposing joint and several responsibility on attorneys and Ds for award under §1447(c)).

(a) Scope of fees & costs. The court typically limits an award to the plaintiff's fees and costs associated with opposing the removal and seeking a remand, and any other expenses incurred because of the improper removal. ***Avitts v. Amoco Prod.***, 111 F.3d 30, 32 (5th Cir.1997); *see also* ***Simenz v. Amerihome Mortg. Co.***, 544 F.Supp.2d 743, 746 (E.D.Wis.2008) (fees and costs allowed even if P has not actually incurred costs because of contingency-fee agreement with attorney). Ordinary litigation expenses that would have been incurred if the case had remained in state court cannot be awarded. ***Avitts***, 111 F.3d at 32; *see* ***Simenz***, 544 F.Supp.2d at 747.

(b) Unusual circumstances – award denied. If there are unusual circumstances (e.g., the plaintiff delayed seeking remand or did not disclose facts that were necessary to determine jurisdiction), the court can deny an award of fees even if the removing party lacked an objectively reasonable basis for seeking removal. ***Martin***, 546 U.S. at 141. When the court denies an award of fees because of unusual circumstances, it must remain faithful to the purpose of awarding fees under §1447(c)—to deter removals sought for the purposes of prolonging litigation and imposing costs on the opposing party. *See* ***Martin***, 546 U.S. at 140-41.

(2) Award under FRCP 11. Under FRCP 11, the court can award sanctions for improper removal. ***In re Crescent City Estates***, 588 F.3d at 831. Sanctions are required if the motion to remove is filed for an "improper purpose," such as to harass the plaintiff or to delay the trial. ***Unanue-Casal v. Unanue-Casal***, 898 F.2d 839, 841 (1st Cir.1990). Sanctions can be imposed against the attorney rather than the party. ***In re Crescent City Estates***, 588 F.3d at 831. See "Motion for Sanctions," ch. 5-O, p. 384.

2. Against plaintiff.

(1) Award under 28 U.S.C. §1447(c). Generally, the plaintiff is not subject to 28 U.S.C. §1447(c) sanctions, but §1447(c) is not limited to a particular party. *See* ***Micrometl Corp. v. Tranzact Techs.***, 656 F.3d 467, 470 (7th Cir.2011); ***Ramotnik v. Fisher***, 568 F.Supp.2d 598, 601 (D.Md.2008). A plaintiff, for example, can be sanctioned under §1447(c) if she concealed facts necessary to determine jurisdiction or otherwise acted in bad faith to delay removal. ***Micrometl Corp.***, 656 F.3d at 470. If the defendant is entitled to an award under §1447(c), the costs and expenses cannot be merely associated with removal (e.g., when a defendant properly removes a case, but after removal the plaintiff omits the claim creating federal-question jurisdiction), but rather, the costs and expenses awarded under 28 U.S.C. §1447(c) must be incurred as a result of removal. *See* ***Ramotnik***, 568 F.Supp.2d at 601 & n.7.

(2) Award under FRCP 11. Generally, the plaintiff is not subject to FRCP 11 sanctions for the pleadings it signed and filed in state court before removal. ***Griffen v. City of Okla. City***, 3 F.3d 336, 339 (10th Cir.1993). But the federal court has the power, even after remand, to sanction the plaintiff for improper conduct following removal and may do so even if the plaintiff is successful in its motion to remand. *See* ***Willy v. Coastal Corp.***, 503 U.S. 131, 138 (1992). In ***Willy***, the district court sanctioned the plaintiff for filing large amounts of unorganized documents and citing nonexistent rules of law. *Id.* at 133.

§6.6 Procedure after remand.

1. Federal procedure. The federal district clerk must send a certified copy of the remand order to the state-court clerk. 28 U.S.C. §1447(c). If the reasons for the remand are based on §1447(c), the federal court is divested of jurisdiction, including the jurisdiction to reconsider or modify its remand order, when the federal clerk mails the certified copy of the order to the state clerk. ***Shapiro v. Logistec USA Inc.***, 412 F.3d 307, 312 (2d Cir.2005); ***Arnold v. Garlock, Inc.***, 278 F.3d 426, 437-38 (5th Cir.2001); *see* 28 U.S.C. §1447(c), (d); ***Bender v. Mazda Motor Corp.***, 657 F.3d 1200, 1204 (11th Cir.2011). *But see* ***In re Lowe***, 102 F.3d 731, 736 (4th Cir.1996) (federal court loses jurisdiction when it enters remand order, even if certified copy is not mailed). If the reasons for the remand are not based on §1447(c), the mailing of the remand order to the state clerk does not divest the federal court of jurisdiction. ***Shapiro***, 412 F.3d at 312; *see* ***Hudson United Bank v. LiTenda Mortg. Corp.***, 142 F.3d 151, 158 (3d Cir.1998).

2. State procedure. Once the federal clerk sends a certified copy of the remand order to the state clerk, or once the certified copy is hand-delivered to the state clerk, jurisdiction is transferred from federal court to state court and the state's rules of procedure take over. *See* ***Gonzalez v. Guilbot***, 315 S.W.3d 533, 537-38 (Tex.2010). Some states have additional requirements after their clerk receives the certified copy of the order before the case is actually reinstated on the state's docket. *See* Tex. R. Civ. P. 237a (P must file certified copy of remand order with state clerk and send notice of filing to adverse parties before state court reacquires jurisdiction); ***HBA E., Ltd. v. JEA Boxing Co.***, 796 S.W.2d 534, 537 (Tex.App.—Houston [1st Dist.] 1990, writ denied) (same).

§6.7 Findings of fact. The district court should make findings of fact to support its order on the motion to remand. *See* ***McDermott Int'l v. Lloyds Underwriters***, 944 F.2d 1199, 1201 n.1 (5th Cir.1991). If the appellate court cannot determine the exact reason for the remand to state court, it can remand the order to the district court for an explanation. *E.g.*, ***Van Meter v. State Farm Fire & Cas. Co.***, 1 F.3d 445, 451 (6th Cir.1993) (appellate court remanded to district court for limited purpose of supplementing record), *overruled on other grounds*, ***Blackburn v. Oaktree Capital Mgmt.***, 511 F.3d 633 (6th Cir.2008); ***Getty Oil Corp. v. Insurance Co. of N. Am.***, 841 F.2d 1254, 1264 (5th Cir.1988) (appellate court remanded to district court to determine relevant jurisdictional and removal issues). Most courts hold that findings in a remand order have no preclusive effect and may be relitigated in state court. *See* ***Nutter v. Monongahela Power Co.***, 4 F.3d 319, 322 (4th Cir.1993); ***Baldridge v. Kentucky-Ohio Transp.***, 983 F.2d 1341, 1350 (6th Cir.1993); ***Whitman v. Raley's Inc.***, 886 F.2d 1177, 1181 (9th Cir.1989). *But see* ***Transit Cas. Co. v. Certain Underwriters at Lloyd's of London***, 119 F.3d 619, 624 n.10 (8th Cir.1997) (if district court has pendent jurisdiction over remanded state-law claim, its adjudication of preemption issue is binding).

§7. APPELLATE REVIEW

§7.1 Standard of review. Because removal is a matter of statutory construction, the appellate court reviews the district court's orders on removal and remand using the de novo standard. ***McLaurin v. U.S.***, 392 F.3d 774, 777 (5th Cir.2004); ***Crawford Country Homeowners Ass'n v. Delta S&L***, 77 F.3d 1163, 1165 (9th Cir.1996). The district court's decision whether to award attorney fees for improper removal is reviewed for abuse of discretion. ***Porter Trust v. Rural Water Sewer & Solid Waste Mgmt. Dist.***, 607 F.3d 1251, 1253 (10th Cir.2010); ***Gibson v. Chrysler Corp.***, 261 F.3d 927, 950 (9th Cir.2001); ***Garcia v. Amfels, Inc.***, 254 F.3d 585, 587 (5th Cir.2001).

§7.2 When reviewable. Whenever a party asks the appellate court to review the district court's remand order, the first question the court must address is whether it has jurisdiction to consider the issue. ***In re International Paper Co.***, 961 F.2d 558, 561 (5th Cir.1992).

1. Remand granted. Even though 28 U.S.C. §1447(d) clearly states that remand orders (except for those under 28 U.S.C. §1442 or §1443) are not reviewable on appeal or otherwise, the Supreme Court has held they are reviewable under certain circumstances. *See* ***Carlsbad Tech. v. HIF Bio, Inc.***, 556 U.S. 635, 638 (2009); ***Thermtron Prods. v. Hermansdorfer***, 423 U.S. 336, 351-52 (1976), *overruled on other grounds*, ***Quackenbush v. Allstate Ins.***, 517 U.S. 706 (1996); 14C Wright, Miller, Cooper & Steinman §3740. An appellate court's ability to review the remand order depends on the district court's stated reasons for remand. *See* 28 U.S.C. §1447(d); ***Powerex Corp. v. Reliant***

Energy Servs., 551 U.S. 224, 232-33 (2007). *See generally* Annotation, *When Is Order, Remanding Case ... Reviewable by Court of Appeals ...*, 104 ALR Fed. 864 (discussing ***Thermtron*** and later federal cases).

(1) Not reviewable. The appellate court cannot review the remand order, by appeal or otherwise, if the district court intended to remand on the grounds listed in 28 U.S.C. §1447(c), which are a defect in the removal procedure or a lack of subject-matter jurisdiction. ***Powerex***, 551 U.S. at 233-34; ***Kircher v. Putnam Funds Trust***, 547 U.S. 633, 640 (2006); *see* ***Alvarez v. Uniroyal Tire Co.***, 508 F.3d 639, 641 (11th Cir.2007) (appellate court will not review remand order even if subject-matter jurisdiction is lost after removal); ***Schexnayder v. Entergy La., Inc.***, 394 F.3d 280, 283 (5th Cir.2004) (appellate court will review remand order only if district court affirmatively states a non-§1447(c) ground for remand). Any remand order issued on a ground listed in §1447(c) is not reviewable regardless of whether the case was removed under the general removal statute or a special removal statute or whether an appellate court deems the order erroneous. *See* ***Kircher***, 547 U.S. at 641-42 (appeal of remand for lack of jurisdiction vacated even though case removed under Securities Litigation Standards Act of 1998 (15 U.S.C. §77p(c)); ***Smith v. Texas Children's Hosp.***, 172 F.3d 923, 925-26 (5th Cir.1999) (even when court incorrectly concludes it does not have jurisdiction, order cannot be reviewed if it affirmatively states it is under §1447(c)).

NOTE

It is unclear to what extent, if any, an appellate court may look beyond the "label" used by the district court in its remand order to determine if the removal was in fact based on a §1447(c) ground. See ***Powerex****, 551 U.S. at 233-34 (review of district court's characterization of its remand for lack of subject-matter jurisdiction should be limited to confirming that such characterization was "colorable");* ***Kircher****, 547 U.S. at 641 n.9 (declining to address whether appellate court can look beyond district court's label);* ***Townsquare Media, Inc. v. Brill****, 652 F.3d 767, 775-76 (7th Cir.2011) (what must be "colorable" is that district court's ground for dismissal was lack of subject-matter jurisdiction, even though district court may be mistaken);* ***Atlantic Nat'l Trust LLC v. Mt. Hawley Ins.****, 621 F.3d 931, 938 (9th Cir.2010) (if district court's remand is purportedly based on ground in §1447(c), appellate court can look beyond district court's characterization of its basis for remand only to determine if ground was "colorable").*

(2) Reviewable. If the district court remands a case for reasons other than those listed in §1447(c), the remand may be reviewed by the appellate court. ***In re City of Mobile***, 75 F.3d 605, 607 (11th Cir.1996); ***Hamilton v. Aetna Life & Cas. Co.***, 5 F.3d 642, 644 (2d Cir.1993); *see* ***Flores v. Long***, 110 F.3d 730, 732 (10th Cir.1997). Some examples of what a court may review include the following:

(a) A remand order based on a substantive decision on the merits of a collateral issue, as opposed to matters of jurisdiction. ***Russell Corp. v. American Home Assur. Co.***, 264 F.3d 1040, 1045-46 (11th Cir. 2001); ***Niehaus v. Greyhound Lines, Inc.***, 173 F.3d 1207, 1211 (9th Cir.1999); ***Regis Assocs. v. Rank Hotels (Mgmt.)***, 894 F.2d 193, 194 (6th Cir.1990).

(b) A remand order based on a forum-selection clause in a contract. ***Kamm v. ITEX Corp.***, 568 F.3d 752, 754-55 (9th Cir.2009); ***Global Satellite Comm. v. Starmill U.K. Ltd.***, 378 F.3d 1269, 1271 (11th Cir.2004); ***Cruthis v. Metropolitan Life Ins.***, 356 F.3d 816, 818 n.1 (7th Cir.2004); ***Autoridad de Energia Eléctrica de P.R. v. Ericsson Inc.***, 201 F.3d 15, 16-17 (1st Cir.2000); ***SBKC Serv. v. 1111 Prospect Partners***, 105 F.3d 578, 580-81 (10th Cir.1997); *see* ***McDermott Int'l v. Lloyds Underwriters***, 944 F.2d 1199, 1203-04 (5th Cir.1991). *But see* ***Travelers Ins. v. Keeling***, 996 F.2d 1485, 1489 (2d Cir.1993) (if district court did not select forum under forum-selection clause, remand not reviewable).

(c) The defects in an untimely filed remand motion. ***Ellenburg v. Spartan Motors Chassis, Inc.***, 519 F.3d 192, 197 (4th Cir.2008); ***In re Bethesda Mem'l Hosp., Inc.***, 123 F.3d 1407, 1409-10 (11th Cir.1997); *see* ***Maniar v. FDIC***, 979 F.2d 782, 784-85 (9th Cir.1992) (defects in untimely sua sponte order).

(d) An untimely motion to amend. ***Ariel Land Owners, Inc. v. Dring***, 351 F.3d 611, 616 (3d Cir. 2003).

(e) The award of costs and attorney fees in an order of remand. ***Porter Trust v. Rural Water Sewer & Solid Waste Mgmt. Dist.***, 607 F.3d 1251, 1253 (10th Cir.2010); ***Hornbuckle v. State Farm Lloyds***, 385 F.3d 538, 541 (5th Cir.2004); ***Stuart v. UNUM Life Ins.***, 217 F.3d 1145, 1148 (9th Cir.2000).

(f) An abstention-based remand. ***Quackenbush v. Allstate Ins.***, 517 U.S. 706, 714 (1996).

(g) A remand order based on the court's decision declining to exercise supplemental jurisdiction over state-law claims under 28 U.S.C. §1367. ***Carlsbad Tech.***, 556 U.S. at 637-38; ***Brookshire Bros. Holding, Inc. v. Dayco Prods.***, 554 F.3d 595, 600-01 (5th Cir.2009); ***California Dept. of Water Res. v. Powerex Corp.***, 533 F.3d 1087, 1091 (9th Cir.2008); ***Lindsey v. Dillard's, Inc.***, 306 F.3d 596, 598-99 (8th Cir.2002).

(h) A remand order based on the court's decision to decline jurisdiction under the Declaratory Judgment Act. ***Snodgrass v. Provident Life & Acc. Ins.***, 147 F.3d 1163, 1165-66 (9th Cir.1998).

(i) A remand order based on the court's own motion. ***In re Allstate Ins.***, 8 F.3d 219, 221 (5th Cir.1993); *see* ***Ellenburg***, 519 F.3d at 197-98; ***In re Continental Cas. Co.***, 29 F.3d 292, 294 (7th Cir.1994); *see, e.g.*, ***Corporate Mgmt. Advisors, Inc. v. Artjen Complexus, Inc.***, 561 F.3d 1294, 1295-96 (11th Cir.2009) (court's own remand order, which was based on perceived lack of subject-matter jurisdiction when Ds alleged residency rather than citizenship, was reviewable because failure to establish citizenship at time of removal is procedural defect).

(j) A remand order based on the defendant's alleged waiver of its right to remove. ***Cogdell v. Wyeth***, 366 F.3d 1245, 1249 (11th Cir.2004).

(k) A remand order based on 28 U.S.C. §1445, which forbids removal of certain actions (e.g., action under workers' compensation laws). ***In re Norfolk S. Ry.***, 592 F.3d 907, 912 (8th Cir.2010).

(*l*) A magistrate judge's remand order based on lack of subject-matter jurisdiction. ***Williams v. Beemiller, Inc.***, 527 F.3d 259, 264 (2d Cir.2008); ***Vogel v. U.S. Office Prods.***, 258 F.3d 509, 519 (6th Cir.2001); ***In re U.S. Healthcare***, 159 F.3d 142, 145-46 (3d Cir.1998).

2. Remand denied. An order denying remand cannot be appealed until after judgment is entered in the federal case. ***Caterpillar Inc. v. Lewis***, 519 U.S. 61, 74 (1996); *see* ***Pope v. MCI Telecomm. Corp.***, 937 F.2d 258, 262 (5th Cir.1991). The order denying remand will be upheld if the district court had jurisdiction when it entered judgment; therefore, a jurisdictional defect at the time the court denied the motion to remand is irrelevant if it is cured before judgment. *See* ***Lexecon Inc. v. Milberg Weiss Bershad Hynes & Lerach***, 523 U.S. 26, 43 (1998); ***Caterpillar***, 519 U.S. at 64; ***H&D Tire & Auto.-Hardware, Inc. v. Pitney Bowes Inc.***, 227 F.3d 326, 328 (5th Cir.2000); ***Huffman v. Saul Holdings L.P.***, 194 F.3d 1072, 1080 (10th Cir.1999).

3. By statute. Remand orders in certain types of cases are appealable by statute. The following are some examples:

(1) Interstate class actions.

NOTE

Some circuits have held that a party seeking to appeal the grant or denial of remand under CAFA must follow the permissive-appeal procedures of FRAP 5. ***Froud v. Anadarko E&P Co.***, *607 F.3d 520, 522 (8th Cir.2010);* ***Amalgamated Transit Un. v. Laidlaw Transit Servs.***, *435 F.3d 1140, 1145 (9th Cir.2006).*

(a) Reviewable. Although the general rule is that an order to remand is not appealable, CAFA expanded appellate jurisdiction to allow review of orders granting or denying a motion to remand. 28 U.S.C. §1453(c)(1); ***BP Am., Inc. v. Oklahoma***, 613 F.3d 1029, 1030-31 (10th Cir.2010); ***Greenwich Fin. Servs. Distressed Mortg. Fund 3 LLC v. Countrywide Fin. Corp.***, 603 F.3d 23, 26-27 (2d Cir.2010); *see, e.g.*, ***Anderson v. Bayer Corp.***, 610 F.3d 390, 394 (7th Cir.2010) (when remanded cases did not meet CAFA's definition of class action, remand order was not reviewable; appellate jurisdiction under §1453(c) applies only when cases are class actions as defined by

CAFA); *see also* ***Nevada v. Bank of Am. Corp.***, 672 F.3d 661, 672-73 (9th Cir.2012) (appellate court can consider non-CAFA issue along with CAFA issue when order is appealable under §1453(c)(1)). The appellate court has discretion to accept or refuse a timely filed appeal. ***BP Am.***, 613 F.3d at 1033. When determining whether to accept an appeal, the court can consider the following:

[1] The presence of an important CAFA-related question. *Id.* at 1034; ***College of Dental Surgeons v. Connecticut Gen. Life Ins.***, 585 F.3d 33, 38 (1st Cir.2009).

[2] Whether the question is unsettled. ***BP Am.***, 613 F.3d at 1034; *see* ***College of Dental Surgeons***, 585 F.3d at 38.

[3] Whether the question appears to be either incorrectly decided or at least fairly debatable. ***BP Am.***, 613 F.3d at 1034.

[4] Whether the question is consequential to the resolution of the particular case. *Id.*; ***College of Dental Surgeons***, 585 F.3d at 38.

[5] Whether the question is likely to evade effective review if left for consideration only after final judgment. ***BP Am.***, 613 F.3d at 1034; ***College of Dental Surgeons***, 585 F.3d at 38.

[6] Whether the question is likely to recur. ***BP Am.***, 613 F.3d at 1034; ***College of Dental Surgeons***, 585 F.3d at 38.

[7] Whether the application arises from a decision or order that is sufficiently final to position the case for intelligent review. ***BP Am.***, 613 F.3d at 1034; ***College of Dental Surgeons***, 585 F.3d at 38.

[8] Whether the probable harm to the applicant if the appeal is refused outweighs the probable harm to the other parties if the appeal is accepted. ***BP Am.***, 613 F.3d at 1034; ***College of Dental Surgeons***, 585 F.3d at 39.

(b) Not reviewable. 28 U.S.C. §1453(d) sets out three exceptions when appellate review of a remand order is barred. A remand order cannot be reviewed if the class action solely involves (1) a claim about a covered security under 15 U.S.C. §78p(f)(3) or §78bb(f)(5)(E), (2) a claim that relates to the internal affairs or governance of a corporation or other business enterprise and arises under the law of the state in which it is incorporated or organized, or (3) a claim that relates to the rights, duties, and obligations relating to, created by, or pursuant to any security. 28 U.S.C. §1453(d); ***Greenwich Fin. Servs. Distressed Mortg. Fund 3***, 603 F.3d at 27 & n.2.

(c) Deadline.

[1] To appeal. An appellate court may review a remand order under CAFA if a plaintiff makes a request within ten days after the order is entered. 28 U.S.C. §1453(c)(1); Beisner & Miller, *Litigating in the New Class Action World*, 6 BNA Class Action Litig. Rep. at 412.

[2] For ruling. If the appellate court accepts an appeal, it must issue a ruling within 60 days after the appeal was filed; if the ruling is not made within that time, the appeal will be denied. 28 U.S.C. §1453(c)(2), (c)(4); ***Miedema v. Maytag Corp.***, 450 F.3d 1322, 1326-27 & n.2 (11th Cir.2006). Because the appellate court has discretion to accept or reject the appeal, the appeal is considered filed when it is accepted; thus, the 60-day period begins when the appellate court accepts the appeal. *See* ***In re Mortgage Elec. Registration Sys.***, 680 F.3d 849, 852-53 (6th Cir.2012); ***Lewis v. Verizon Comms.***, 627 F.3d 395, 396-97 (9th Cir.2010). The court may extend the 60-day time period (1) for any length of time the parties agree to or (2) for up to ten days in the interest of justice and after good cause is shown. 28 U.S.C. §1453(c)(3).

(2) Civil-rights suits. An order remanding a case is reviewable on appeal if the suit is a civil-rights case removed under 28 U.S.C. §1443. 28 U.S.C. §1447(d); *see* ***Kircher***, 547 U.S. at 640 n.7.

(3) Suits against United States, federal agencies & officers. An order remanding a case is reviewable on appeal if the suit is removed under 28 U.S.C. §1442. 28 U.S.C. §1447(d). See "Removal under 28 U.S.C. §1442," ch. 4-A, §5.3.2(1), p. 257.

(4) FDIC. The FDIC can appeal an order of remand. 12 U.S.C. §1819(b)(2)(C); ***Heaton v. Monogram Credit Card Bank***, 297 F.3d 416, 420 (5th Cir.2002).

4. By mandamus. The district court's remand order may be reviewable by mandamus in the following instances:

(1) If the district court had no authority to remand. *E.g.*, ***Thermtron***, 423 U.S. at 353 (district court could not remand because of its crowded docket); ***In re City of Mobile***, 75 F.3d at 607-08 (district court cannot remand properly removed federal claims based on pendent claims that may be remanded to state court).

(2) If the district court remanded for lack of removal jurisdiction. ***FDIC v. Loyd***, 955 F.2d 316, 319-20 (5th Cir.1992); ***In re Shell Oil Co.***, 932 F.2d 1518, 1520 (5th Cir.1991).

(3) If the district court remanded for untimely removal. ***Air-Shields, Inc. v. Fullam***, 891 F.2d 63, 66 (3d Cir.1989).

(4) If the district court's remand error was of "sufficient magnitude." ***Jamison v. Wiley***, 14 F.3d 222, 239 (4th Cir.1994). *But see* ***Angelides v. Baylor Coll. of Med.***, 117 F.3d 833, 836 (5th Cir.1997) (purposefully declining to follow ***Jamison***; courts cannot review erroneous remand orders based on 28 U.S.C. §1447(c)).

PRACTICE TIP

To request review of the district court's order granting remand, file a notice of appeal and, at the same time, file a petition for writ of mandamus in the alternative. This procedure was used in ***Balazik v. County of Dauphin****, 44 F.3d 209, 211 (3d Cir.1995), and* ***In re International Paper****, 961 F.2d at 560. However, keep in mind that it is considerably more difficult to obtain a writ of mandamus.* ***California Dept. of Water Res.****, 533 F.3d at 1092.*

CHAPTER 5

COMMENTARIES

CHAPTER 5. PRETRIAL MOTIONS
TABLE OF CONTENTS

A. SCHEDULING ORDER & PRETRIAL CONFERENCE....289

§1. GENERAL....289
§2. CASE-MANAGEMENT CONFERENCE & DISCOVERY PLAN....289
§3. SCHEDULING CONFERENCE & ORDER....289
§3.1 Purpose....289
§3.2 Deadline....289
§3.3 Contents of order....289
§3.4 Modification....290
§4. PRETRIAL CONFERENCE & ORDER....290
§4.1 Purposes of pretrial conference....290
§4.2 Scheduling....290
§4.3 Attendance....291
§4.4 Scope....291
§4.5 Pretrial order....293
§4.6 Enforceability of order....294
§4.7 Modification of pretrial order....295
§5. EXPERT & PRETRIAL DISCLOSURE UNDER FRCP 26(a)(2), (a)(3)....296
§6. FINAL PRETRIAL CONFERENCE....296
§6.1 Purpose....296
§6.2 Scheduling....296
§6.3 Attendance....296
§6.4 Scope....296
§6.5 Final pretrial order....296
§6.6 Modification of final pretrial order....296
§7. APPELLATE REVIEW....297
§7.1 Exclusion of witness not listed in pretrial order....297
§7.2 Order dismissing suit as sanction....297

B. MAGISTRATE JUDGES & SPECIAL MASTERS....297

§1. GENERAL....297
§2. TRANSFER OF PRETRIAL MATTERS TO MAGISTRATE JUDGE....298
§2.1 Nondispositive pretrial matters for determination....298
§2.2 Dispositive pretrial matters for recommendations....299
§3. REFERRAL OF TRIAL TO MAGISTRATE JUDGE BY CONSENT....301
§3.1 Scope of authority....301
§3.2 Obtaining consent....302
§3.3 Vacating a referral....302
§4. APPOINTMENT OF SPECIAL MASTER....302
§4.1 Types of special masters....303
§4.2 Appointing special master....304
§4.3 Special master's orders, reports, or recommendations....306
§4.4 Paying special master....306
§5. APPELLATE REVIEW....307
§5.1 Magistrate judge....307
§5.2 Special master....308

C. DEMAND FOR JURY TRIAL....309

§1. GENERAL....309
§2. DEMAND....309
§2.1 Procedure....309
§2.2 Other party....310
§3. DEADLINES....310
§3.1 Most cases....311
§3.2 Defendant files counterclaim....311
§3.3 Multiple defendants jointly liable....311
§3.4 Amended complaint....311
§3.5 Second demand....311
§3.6 After removal....311
§4. RIGHT TO JURY TRIAL....311
§4.1 Legal vs. equitable claims....311
§4.2 Statutory rights....312
§4.3 Suits involving United States....312
§4.4 Bankruptcy matters....313
§4.5 Limitations on right to jury....313
§5. MOTION TO STRIKE JURY DEMAND....314
§5.1 Form....314
§5.2 Sua sponte....314
§5.3 Deadline....314
§5.4 Grounds....314
§5.5 Proposed order....314
§6. MOTION FOR JURY TRIAL....314
§6.1 Form....314
§6.2 Deadline....314
§6.3 Grounds....314
§6.4 Standard....315
§6.5 Proposed order....315
§7. MOTION FOR TRIAL BY ADVISORY JURY....315
§7.1 Motion....315
§7.2 Form....315
§7.3 Grounds....315
§7.4 Proposed order....315
§7.5 Notice....315
§7.6 Verdict....316
§8. APPELLATE REVIEW....316
§8.1 Court denies jury demand under FRCP 38....316
§8.2 Court grants or denies motion for jury under FRCP 39....316
§8.3 Court rejects advisory jury's verdict....316

D. OFFER OF JUDGMENT....317

§1. GENERAL....317
§2. OFFER....317
§2.1 In writing....317
§2.2 Served on all parties....317
§2.3 Not filed....317
§2.4 Unconditional....317
§2.5 Deadline....317
§2.6 Amount of offer....318
§2.7 Revoking offer....319
§3. RESPONSE TO OFFER....319
§3.1 Notice of acceptance....319
§3.2 No response....319
§4. ACCEPTED OFFER....319
§4.1 Filing accepted offer....319
§4.2 Entry of judgment....319
§5. EFFECT OF NOT ACCEPTING OFFER....319
§5.1 Judgment less favorable than offer....319
§5.2 Monetary damages....320
§5.3 Injunctive relief....320
§6. DETERMINING COSTS....320
§6.1 Costs included....321
§6.2 Costs not included....321
§7. APPELLATE REVIEW....321
§7.1 Interlocutory orders....321
§7.2 Final consent judgment....321

E. MOTION TO RECUSE....321

§1. GENERAL....321
§2. STATUTES GOVERNING RECUSAL....322
§2.1 Section 144....322
§2.2 Section 455....322

COMMENTARIES

CHAPTER 5. PRETRIAL MOTIONS

TABLE OF CONTENTS

§3. MOTION ... 322
§3.1 Form ... 322
§3.2 In writing ... 322
§3.3 Affidavit ... 322
§3.4 Attorney's certificate ... 322
§3.5 Notice ... 322
§3.6 Number of motions allowed ... 322
§3.7 Grounds ... 322
§3.8 Deadline ... 328
§3.9 Proposed order ... 329
§3.10 Waiver ... 329
§4. RESPONSE ... 329
§5. RULINGS ... 329
§5.1 By challenged judge ... 329
§5.2 By assigned judge ... 330
§6. APPELLATE REVIEW ... 330
§6.1 Interlocutory ... 330
§6.2 Appeal ... 330
§6.3 Mandamus ... 330
§6.4 Relief ... 331

F. MOTION TO EXTEND TIME ... 332
§1. GENERAL ... 332
§2. EXTENDING DEADLINES ... 332
§2.1 Most deadlines ... 332
§2.2 No extensions permitted ... 332
§3. REQUESTS TO EXTEND TIME WITHOUT MOTION ... 333
§4. MOTIONS TO EXTEND TIME ... 333
§4.1 Agreed motion to extend time ... 333
§4.2 Most motions to extend time ... 333
§4.3 Motion to extend time to serve party ... 334
§4.4 Motion to extend time for discovery ... 336
§4.5 Motion to extend time to substitute party ... 336
§5. APPELLATE REVIEW ... 336

G. MOTION FOR CONTINUANCE ... 337
§1. GENERAL ... 337
§2. MOTION ... 337
§2.1 Form ... 337
§2.2 In writing ... 337
§2.3 Affidavits ... 337
§2.4 Notice ... 337
§2.5 When to file ... 337
§2.6 Proposed order ... 337
§3. GROUNDS ... 337
§3.1 Agreed continuance ... 337
§3.2 Additional time for discovery ... 337
§3.3 Witness or party unavailable for trial ... 339
§3.4 Attorney unavailable for trial ... 340
§3.5 Surprise evidence ... 340
§3.6 Response to motion for summary judgment ... 340
§4. RESPONSE ... 340
§5. APPELLATE REVIEW ... 340
§5.1 *Flynt* factors ... 340
§5.2 Other factors ... 341

H. MOTION IN LIMINE ... 341
§1. GENERAL ... 341
§2. MOTION ... 341
§2.1 Form ... 341
§2.2 Procedure ... 341
§2.3 Grounds ... 341
§2.4 Deadline ... 343
§2.5 Proposed order ... 343
§2.6 Agreed motions ... 343
§3. RESPONSE ... 343
§4. HEARING ... 343
§5. RULING ... 343
§5.1 Preliminary ruling ... 343
§5.2 Ruling on admissibility ... 344
§6. OFFER & OBJECTION AT TRIAL ... 344
§6.1 Motion denied ... 344
§6.2 Motion granted ... 344
§6.3 Violation of motion – preserving error ... 344
§7. RULING ON OFFER ... 344
§8. APPELLATE REVIEW ... 344

I. MOTION TO AMEND OR SUPPLEMENT PLEADINGS—PRETRIAL ... 345
§1. GENERAL ... 345
§2. GENERAL RULES FOR AMENDING PLEADINGS ... 345
§3. AMENDING PLEADINGS – PRETRIAL ... 345
§3.1 Amending as matter of course ... 345
§3.2 Amending by consent or leave ... 346
§3.3 Amending when ordered ... 347
§3.4 Amending after complaint dismissed ... 347
§3.5 Relation back of amendments ... 347
§4. SUPPLEMENTING PLEADINGS – PRETRIAL ... 350
§4.1 Original pleading defective ... 350
§4.2 Adding new claim ... 350
§4.3 Relation back ... 350
§4.4 Jurisdiction & venue ... 350
§5. MOTION FOR LEAVE TO AMEND ... 351
§5.1 Form ... 351
§5.2 In writing ... 351
§5.3 Notice ... 351
§5.4 Grounds ... 351
§5.5 Proposed amended pleading ... 351
§5.6 Deadline ... 351
§5.7 Proposed order ... 351
§6. RESPONSE ... 351
§6.1 Grounds ... 352
§6.2 Proposed order ... 352
§6.3 Request continuance ... 352
§7. RULING ... 353
§7.1 Standard ... 353
§7.2 Factors ... 353
§8. DEADLINE FOR RESPONSIVE PLEADING ... 355
§9. APPELLATE REVIEW ... 355
§9.1 Standard of review ... 355
§9.2 Failure to give reasons ... 355

J. MOTION TO INTERVENE ... 356
§1. GENERAL ... 356
§2. MOTION TO INTERVENE ... 356
§2.1 Form ... 356
§2.2 In writing ... 356
§2.3 Grounds ... 356
§2.4 Pleading ... 360
§2.5 File & serve ... 360
§2.6 Proposed order ... 360
§2.7 Notice of constitutional question ... 360
§3. DEADLINE ... 360
§3.1 Motion must be timely ... 360
§3.2 Postjudgment application to intervene ... 361

COMMENTARIES

CHAPTER 5. PRETRIAL MOTIONS
TABLE OF CONTENTS

§4. ORDER....361
§4.1 Ruling....361
§4.2 Conditions imposed on intervenor....361
§5. APPELLATE REVIEW....361
§5.1 Applicant's right to appeal denial of motion....361
§5.2 Intervenor's right to appeal suit....361
§5.3 Standard of review....362

K. MOTION TO CONSOLIDATE....362
§1. GENERAL....362
§2. MOTION TO CONSOLIDATE....362
§2.1 Form....362
§2.2 In writing....362
§2.3 Sua sponte....363
§2.4 Grounds....363
§2.5 Deadline....364
§2.6 Proposed order....364
§3. RESPONSE....364
§3.1 In writing....364
§3.2 Grounds....364
§3.3 Waiver....364
§3.4 Proposed order....364
§4. ORDER OF CONSOLIDATION....364
§4.1 Order....364
§4.2 Effect of consolidation....365
§5. APPELLATE REVIEW....365
§5.1 Standard of review....365
§5.2 No interlocutory appeal....365
§5.3 Mandamus....365

L. MOTION FOR SEVERANCE OR SEPARATE TRIALS....366
§1. GENERAL....366
§2. SEVERANCE VS. SEPARATE TRIALS....366
§2.1 Severance – different suits....366
§2.2 Separate trials – same suit....366
§3. MOTION FOR SEVERANCE....366
§3.1 Form....366
§3.2 In writing....366
§3.3 Grounds....366
§3.4 Proposed order....367
§4. MOTION FOR SEPARATE (BIFURCATED) TRIALS....367
§4.1 Form....367
§4.2 In writing....367
§4.3 Sua sponte....367
§4.4 Deadline....367
§4.5 Grounds under FRCP 42(b)....367
§4.6 Grounds under FRCP 20(b)....368
§4.7 Proposed order....368
§5. RESPONSE....368
§5.1 In writing....368
§5.2 Grounds – general....368
§5.3 Response to motion for severance....368
§5.4 Response to FRCP 42(b) motion for separate trials....368
§5.5 Response to FRCP 20(b) motion for separate trials....369
§5.6 Proposed order....369
§6. RULING....369
§6.1 Rule....369
§6.2 Scope of division....369
§6.3 Effect....369
§7. APPELLATE REVIEW....369
§7.1 Appeal of severance....369
§7.2 Appeal of separate trials....370

M. MOTION FOR JUDICIAL NOTICE....370
§1. GENERAL....370
§2. TYPES OF JUDICIAL NOTICE....370
§2.1 Adjudicative facts....370
§2.2 Foreign law....372
§3. MOTION....372
§3.1 Form....372
§3.2 In writing....372
§3.3 Evidence....372
§3.4 Proposed order....373
§3.5 Notice of motion....373
§4. DEADLINE....373
§4.1 Adjudicative facts....373
§4.2 Foreign law....373
§5. RESPONSE....374
§5.1 Adjudicative facts....374
§5.2 Foreign law....374
§6. HEARING....374
§6.1 Adjudicative facts....374
§6.2 Foreign law....374
§7. RULING....374
§7.1 Adjudicative facts....374
§7.2 Foreign law....375
§8. APPELLATE REVIEW....375
§8.1 Judicial notice of adjudicative facts....375
§8.2 Determination of foreign law....375

N. MOTION TO EXCLUDE EXPERT WITNESS....376
§1. GENERAL....376
§2. PRETRIAL ORDER....376
§3. MOTION....376
§3.1 Form....376
§3.2 Grounds....376
§3.3 Affidavits....379
§3.4 Request hearing....379
§3.5 Request special proceedings....379
§3.6 Proposed order....379
§3.7 Deadline....379
§4. RESPONSE....379
§4.1 Burden....379
§4.2 Grounds....380
§4.3 Not trial on merits....381
§4.4 Affidavits....382
§4.5 Proposed order....382
§4.6 Deadline....382
§5. HEARING....382
§5.1 Proceedings determined by court....382
§5.2 Standard of admissibility....383
§6. RULING....383
§6.1 Definitive ruling....383
§6.2 Tentative ruling....383
§7. APPELLATE REVIEW....384
§7.1 Expert's qualifications....384
§7.2 Application of ***Daubert*** factors....384
§7.3 Evidentiary ruling....384
§7.4 Determination of reliability....384

O. MOTION FOR SANCTIONS....384
§1. GENERAL....384
§2. WHO CAN BE SANCTIONED....384

COMMENTARIES

CHAPTER 5. PRETRIAL MOTIONS
TABLE OF CONTENTS

§3. SANCTIONS JUSTIFIED 385
§3.1 Frivolous or improper purpose – FRCP 11 385
§3.2 Violation of pretrial order 387
§3.3 Discovery abuse 387
§3.4 Filing bad-faith affidavit or declaration 388
§3.5 Failure to prosecute 388
§3.6 Failure to comply with court order 388
§3.7 Improper removal 388
§3.8 Multiplying proceedings unreasonably 388
§3.9 Bad-faith conduct 389
§3.10 Conduct sanctionable under local rules 390
§4. SANCTIONS NOT JUSTIFIED 391
§4.1 Pleadings & motions 391
§4.2 Discovery 391
§4.3 Oral argument 391
§4.4 Settlement 391
§4.5 Court orders 391
§4.6 Violation by both parties 391
§4.7 Appeals 391
§4.8 Other cases 391
§5. MOTION FOR SANCTIONS 391
§5.1 Motion by party 391
§5.2 Motion on court's initiative 392
§5.3 Proposed order 393
§6. RESPONSE 393
§6.1 Withdraw or correct 393
§6.2 File response 394
§6.3 Request hearing 394
§7. NOTICE & OPPORTUNITY TO RESPOND 394
§8. TYPES OF SANCTIONS 395
§8.1 Compensatory vs. punitive sanctions 395
§8.2 Authorized sanctions under FRCP 11 395
§8.3 Authorized sanctions under court's inherent power 396
§8.4 Authorized sanctions under FRCP 16(f) 396
§8.5 Authorized sanctions for discovery abuse 396
§8.6 Authorized sanctions for bad-faith affidavits 396
§8.7 Authorized sanctions for multiplying proceedings unreasonably 396
§8.8 Unauthorized sanctions 396
§9. ORDER 396
§9.1 Order under FRCP 11 396
§9.2 Order under court's inherent power 397
§9.3 Order under FRCP 16(f) & 37 397
§9.4 Order under FRCP 26(g) 397
§9.5 Order under FRCP 41 397
§10. APPELLATE REVIEW 397
§10.1 Appealability 397
§10.2 Standard of review 397

P. MOTION FOR CLASS CERTIFICATION 398
§1. GENERAL 398
§2. MOTION 398
§2.1 Form 398
§2.2 Deadline to file 398
§2.3 Burden of proof 398
§2.4 Grounds 399
§2.5 Proposed order 402
§3. RESPONSE 402
§3.1 Considerations before filing 402
§3.2 Opposing the motion 403
§4. PRECERTIFICATION DISCOVERY & INTERIM COUNSEL 403
§4.1 Discovery 403
§4.2 Interim counsel 403
§5. RULING 403
§5.1 Hearing 403
§5.2 Analysis 403
§5.3 Deadline 404
§5.4 Order 404
§5.5 Altering or amending order 406
§6. APPELLATE REVIEW 406
§6.1 Appealability 406
§6.2 Standard of review 408

5. PRETRIAL MOTIONS

A. SCHEDULING ORDER & PRETRIAL CONFERENCE

§1. GENERAL

§1.1 Rule. FRCP 16; see also FRCP 26(a), (f).

§1.2 Purpose. FRCP 16 gives the court the power to control pretrial matters and facilitate settlement. *See **In re Arizona***, 528 F.3d 652, 657 (9th Cir.2008); ***Olcott v. Delaware Flood Co.***, 76 F.3d 1538, 1555 (10th Cir.1996). The purpose of FRCP 16 is to clarify the nature of the dispute and aid the parties and the court in preparing for and conducting the trial. ***Wilson v. Kelkhoff***, 86 F.3d 1438, 1442 n.6 (7th Cir.1996); *see **Olcott***, 76 F.3d at 1555.

§1.3 Timetable & forms. Timetable, Pretrial Disclosures & Conferences, p. 1577; ***O'Connor's Federal Civil Forms*** (2012), FORMS 5A.

§1.4 Other references. 6A Wright, Miller & Kane, *Federal Practice & Procedure 3d* §§1521-1531 (2010 & Supp.2012); 3 *Moore's Federal Practice 3d* §§16.01-16.16, 16.78 (2012).

§2. CASE-MANAGEMENT CONFERENCE & DISCOVERY PLAN

After a suit is filed and the defendant has appeared, the parties must conduct a case-management conference to discuss their claims and defenses and the possibility of settlement, to arrange for initial disclosures, to discuss issues about preserving discoverable information, and to develop a proposed discovery plan. FRCP 26(f)(2). The case-management conference should be completed before the scheduling conference to ensure that the court has the parties' proposals before it enters a scheduling order. For the deadlines for the case-management conference and the contents of the discovery plan, see "FRCP 26(f) Conference," ch. 6-A, §4, p. 416.

§3. SCHEDULING CONFERENCE & ORDER

§3.1 Purpose. The purpose of the scheduling conference and order is to set deadlines for completing the principal pretrial steps, motions, and orders. ***Hoffman-La Roche, Inc. v. Sperling***, 493 U.S. 165, 172 (1989); *see also* ***Parker v. Columbia Pictures Indus.***, 204 F.3d 326, 339-40 (2d Cir.2000) (FRCP 16 is designed to offer measure of certainty in pretrial proceedings, ensuring that at some point parties and pleadings will be fixed). Once the court has issued a pretrial scheduling order under FRCP 16, the order controls the case unless the court modifies it. ***Johnson v. Mammoth Recreations, Inc.***, 975 F.2d 604, 608 (9th Cir.1992); *see* FRCP 16(b)(4).

§3.2 Deadline. In most cases, once the court receives the FRCP 26(f) discovery plan from the parties, or after it consults with the parties' attorneys and unrepresented parties at a scheduling conference or by telephone, mail, or other means, the court must issue a scheduling order. FRCP 16(b)(1). *But see* ***Dodson v. Runyon***, 86 F.3d 37, 41 (2d Cir.1996) (judge's failure to enter scheduling order did not relieve attorney of duty to conduct discovery). The court must issue the scheduling order as soon as possible, but no later than 90 days after the appearance of any defendant or 120 days after the complaint has been served on any defendant, whichever is earlier. FRCP 16(b)(2); ***Parker v. Columbia Pictures Indus.***, 204 F.3d 326, 339 (2d Cir.2000).

§3.3 Contents of order.

1. Mandatory items. In all cases except those exempted by local rule, the court must enter a scheduling order that limits the time to do the following:

(1) Join other parties. FRCP 16(b)(3)(A).

(2) Amend the pleadings. *Id.*; ***Campania Mgmt. v. Rooks, Pitts & Poust***, 290 F.3d 843, 848 n.1 (7th Cir.2002).

(3) Complete discovery. FRCP 16(b)(3)(A).

(4) File motions. *Id.*

2. **Permissive items.** The scheduling order may also do the following:

(1) Modify the timing of disclosures under FRCP 26(a) and FRCP 26(e)(1). FRCP 16(b)(3)(B)(i). See "Supplementing Discovery," ch. 6-A, §11, p. 438; "Mandatory Disclosures," ch. 6-E, p. 532.

(2) Modify the extent of discovery. FRCP 16(b)(3)(B)(ii).

(3) Provide for the disclosure or discovery of electronically stored information. FRCP 16(b)(3)(B)(iii); *see also* FRCP 34(a)(1)(A) (electronically stored information includes writings and other data stored in any medium from which information can be obtained). See "FRCP 16 Conference & Order," ch. 6-C, §8, p. 498.

(4) Include any agreements the parties make for asserting claims of privilege or work-product protection after material is inadvertently produced. *See* FRCP 16(b)(3)(B)(iv); *see also* 2006 Notes to FRCP 16 at ¶2, p. 1158, this book (parties can agree that if privileged information is produced, producing party can give timely notice and have materials returned without waiving privilege). See "FRCP 16 Conference & Order," ch. 6-C, §8, p. 498.

(5) Set dates for pretrial conferences and for trial. FRCP 16(b)(3)(B)(v).

(6) Include any other appropriate matters. FRCP 16(b)(3)(B)(vi).

§3.4 Modification. A scheduling order can be modified by the parties only on a showing of good cause and with the court's consent. FRCP 16(b)(4); ***S&W Enters. v. SouthTrust Bank***, 315 F.3d 533, 535 (5th Cir.2003); ***Inge v. Rock Fin. Corp.***, 281 F.3d 613, 625 (6th Cir.2002); ***Parker v. Columbia Pictures Indus.***, 204 F.3d 326, 340 (2d Cir. 2000). The moving party's diligence in meeting the order's requirements is often the primary factor in determining if there is good cause. ***Alioto v. Town of Lisbon***, 651 F.3d 715, 720 (7th Cir.2011); *e.g.*, ***Sherman v. Winco Fireworks, Inc.***, 532 F.3d 709, 717 (8th Cir.2008) (D was not diligent in seeking leave to amend its answer when it did not seek leave until 2½ years after suit was filed, 18 months after deadline to amend pleadings had passed, and 8 months after it became aware of defense); *see also* ***S&W Enters.***, 315 F.3d at 535 (good cause requires showing that deadlines cannot reasonably be met despite party's diligence); ***Parker***, 204 F.3d at 340 (court may modify pretrial order if party cannot reasonably meet schedule despite diligence in attempting to comply); 1983 Notes to FRCP 16 at ¶16, p. 1161, this book (changes in court's calendar may oblige judge to modify scheduling order). In some courts, another relevant consideration is possible prejudice to the party opposing the modification. ***Inge***, 281 F.3d at 625; *see* ***Sherman***, 532 F.3d at 717 (prejudice to party opposing modification is considered only if moving party was diligent in meeting deadlines); ***Dag Enters. v. Exxon Mobil Corp.***, 226 F.R.D. 95, 110 (D.D.C.2005) (prejudice to party opposing modification is consideration, but it is not relevant to movant's diligence and does not show good cause). *But see* ***Leviton Mfg. Co. v. Nicor, Inc.***, 245 F.R.D. 524, 528 (D.N.M.2007) (prejudice is not relevant consideration).

§4. PRETRIAL CONFERENCE & ORDER

CAUTION

District courts vary widely in how they use FRCP 16. Many districts and individual judges within districts have adopted local rules, standing orders, and judge-specific procedures regulating pretrial conferences. Thus, in preparing for a pretrial conference, make sure to comply not only with FRCP 16 but also with any applicable local procedures.

§4.1 Purposes of pretrial conference. The purposes of a pretrial conference are to narrow the issues, to obtain admissions and stipulations, and to foster settlement. ***Wellmore Coal Corp. v. Stiltner***, 81 F.3d 490, 496 n.8 (4th Cir.1996); *see* ***Marschand v. Norfolk & W. Ry.***, 81 F.3d 714, 716 (7th Cir.1996); *see also* ***Dawson v. U.S.***, 68 F.3d 886, 897 (5th Cir.1995) (judges have considerable power to encourage and facilitate early settlement of cases).

§4.2 Scheduling. In most cases, the court will schedule a pretrial conference on its own. *See* FRCP 16(a). To request a pretrial conference, a party may file a motion stating its reasons for requesting the conference. If the court decides to hold a pretrial conference, the conference cannot be waived by consent of the parties. ***Wellmore Coal Corp. v. Stiltner***, 81 F.3d 490, 496 n.8 (4th Cir.1996).

§4.3 Attendance. The court can require the parties or their representatives, the parties' attorneys, and unrepresented parties to attend a pretrial conference. FRCP 16(a), (c)(1); *see* ***Lucien v. Breweur***, 9 F.3d 26, 28 (7th Cir. 1993). At least one attorney who attends must have the authority to enter into stipulations and make admissions about all matters that can reasonably be anticipated for discussion at a pretrial conference. FRCP 16(c)(1); *see, e.g.*, ***Ergo Sci., Inc. v. Martin***, 73 F.3d 595, 598 n.4 (5th Cir.1996) (attorney could not contend that it lacked authority to waive interest in interpleaded funds). The conference may be held by telephone, by mail, in the judge's chambers, in the courtroom, or by other means. *See* FRCP 16(b)(1), (c)(1); ***Lucien***, 9 F.3d at 28.

§4.4 Scope. FRCP 16(c)(2) lists the matters the court can schedule for consideration at a pretrial conference. The rule authorizes the court to make appropriate orders to provide for an efficient and economical trial. 1993 Notes to FRCP 16 at ¶6, p. 1159, this book. At the pretrial conference, the court may consider and take appropriate action on any of the following matters:

1. Identification of proper issues.

(1) Formulation & simplification of issues. The court may require the parties to identify the claims and defenses they intend to present at trial. 1983 Notes to FRCP 16 at ¶21, p. 1162, this book; *see* FRCP 16(c)(2)(A); ***McLean Contracting Co. v. Waterman S.S. Corp.***, 277 F.3d 477, 479-80 (4th Cir.2002); ***Marschand v. Norfolk & W. Ry.***, 81 F.3d 714, 716 (7th Cir.1996). Attorneys at a pretrial conference must make a full and fair disclosure of their views on what the real issues of the trial will be. ***Youren v. Tintic Sch. Dist.***, 343 F.3d 1296, 1304 (10th Cir.2003). Some local rules require the parties to provide a statement of the issues that excludes uncontroverted issues in the pleadings and includes all issues of law and ultimate issues of fact from the standpoint of each party. *E.g.*, Local Rules Ill. (N.D.), Rule 16.1(a) (Standing Order Establishing Pretrial Procedure, ¶6(b)).

(2) Elimination of frivolous claims & defenses. The court may identify frivolous claims and defenses and eliminate them through procedures such as partial summary judgment. *See* FRCP 16(c)(2)(A), (c)(2)(E); ***Aetna Cas. Sur. Co. v. P&B Autobody***, 43 F.3d 1546, 1568 (1st Cir.1994); 1993 Notes to FRCP 16 at ¶8, p. 1159, this book.

2. Pleading amendments. The court may consider amending the pleadings if necessary or desirable. FRCP 16(c)(2)(B).

3. Stipulations & admissions. The court may consider obtaining admissions and stipulations about facts and documents to avoid unnecessary proof, and ruling in advance on the admissibility of evidence. FRCP 16(c)(2)(C); *see* ***FDIC v. Stahl***, 89 F.3d 1510, 1521 (11th Cir.1996). At the pretrial conference, the parties do not have to offer proof of any matters stipulated to in the pretrial order. ***Alberty-Vélez v. Corporación de P.R. Para la Difusión Pública***, 242 F.3d 418, 423 (1st Cir.2001).

4. Limits on evidence & expert testimony. The court may consider ways to avoid both unnecessary proof and cumulative evidence. FRCP 16(c)(2)(D). The court may also consider limiting the use of expert testimony under FRE 702. FRCP 16(c)(2)(D); ***Robinson v. Missouri Pac. R.R.***, 16 F.3d 1083, 1089 n.6 (10th Cir.1994). See "Motion to Exclude Expert Witness," ch. 5-N, p. 376. Many courts establish early deadlines for filing motions to exclude expert testimony.

5. Nontrial disposition.

(1) Settlement. When authorized by statute or local rule, the court may require the parties to consider settling the case or using special procedures to assist in resolving the dispute. FRCP 16(c)(2)(I); ***In re Munford, Inc.***, 97 F.3d 449, 454-55 (11th Cir.1996); ***In re Continental Gen. Tire, Inc.***, 81 F.3d 1089, 1092 (Fed.Cir.1996); *see also* ***In re Atlantic Pipe Corp.***, 304 F.3d 135, 145 (1st Cir.2002) (court has inherent power to order nonbinding mediation in appropriate circumstances). Some of the special procedures the court can require are minitrials, summary jury trials, mediation, neutral evaluation, and nonbinding arbitration. 1993 Notes to FRCP 16 at ¶10, p. 1159, this book. *But see* ***In re Continental Gen. Tire***, 81 F.3d at 1092 (court cannot require party to participate in potentially expensive proceeding that party chooses not to pursue); ***In re Ashcroft***, 888 F.2d 546, 547 (8th Cir.1989) (pretrial conference discussion about settlement is not designed to impose settlement on unwilling litigants).

CAUTION

If your client is not interested in settling the dispute, alert the court before the entry of an order for a pretrial settlement conference. The court cannot coerce an offer or settlement through the threat of sanctions. ***Dawson v. U.S.****, 68 F.3d 886, 897 (5th Cir.1995). But sanctions may be awarded against a party or its attorney for violating a court order for mediation and settlement. E.g.,* ***Scaife v. Associated Air Ctr. Inc.****, 100 F.3d 406, 411-12 (5th Cir.1996) (under its inherent powers, court sanctioned party for failure to appear at mediation as ordered).*

(2) Summary judgment. The court should consider the appropriateness and timing of summary judgment under FRCP 56. FRCP 16(c)(2)(E); 1993 Notes to FRCP 16 at ¶8, p. 1159, this book. See "Summary Judgment," ch. 7-B, p. 603.

6. Discovery. The court may consider the control and scheduling of discovery, including orders affecting disclosures and discovery under FRCP 26 and FRCPs 29 through 37. FRCP 16(c)(2)(F); *see* 1993 Notes to FRCP 16 at ¶9, p. 1159, this book; *see, e.g.,* ***Barrett v. Atlantic Richfield Co.***, 95 F.3d 375, 379 (5th Cir.1996) (court entered scheduling order setting discovery cutoff and expert-designation deadline).

NOTE

FRCP 16(b) includes provisions that are designed to alert courts to the possible need for the scheduling order to address how discovery of electronically stored information will be handled. 2006 Notes to FRCP 16 at ¶1, p. 1158, this book. Thus, parties should discuss discovery of electronically stored information before the pretrial conference. Id.; see FRCP 16(b)(3)(B)(iii), 26(f). See "Electronic Discovery," ch. 6-C, p. 481.

7. Witness list. The court may require the parties to identify witnesses who will be called to testify. FRCP 16(c)(2)(G); ***Hill v. Porter Mem'l Hosp.***, 90 F.3d 220, 224 (7th Cir.1996); *e.g.*, Local Rules Cal. (C.D.), Rule 16-2.4; *see also* ***D'Onofrio v. SFX Sports Grp.***, 247 F.R.D. 43, 53-54 (D.D.C.2008) (party not required to disclose witnesses until final pretrial statement).

8. Exhibits. The court may require the parties to identify exhibits. *See* FRCP 16(c)(2)(G).

9. Pretrial briefs. The court may require the parties to file and exchange pretrial briefs. FRCP 16(c)(2)(G).

10. Trial date & schedule. The court may set dates for further conferences and for trial. FRCP 16(c)(2)(G).

11. Magistrate judge or master. The court may consider referring certain issues or the entire case to a magistrate judge, or referring the case to a special master for findings to be used as evidence in a jury trial. *See* FRCP 16(c)(2)(H). See "Magistrate Judges & Special Masters," ch. 5-B, p. 297.

12. Pending motions. The court may resolve pending motions. FRCP 16(c)(2)(K). For example, the court may rule on a pending motion for summary judgment that is ripe for decision at the time of the conference. 1993 Notes to FRCP 16 at ¶8, p. 1159, this book.

13. Special rules for complex cases. The court may adopt special procedures for managing potentially difficult or protracted cases that involve (1) complex issues, (2) multiple parties, (3) difficult legal questions, or (4) unusual proof problems. FRCP 16(c)(2)(L). The four factors in FRCP 16(c)(2)(L) are for illustration only and are not exhaustive. 1983 Notes to FRCP 16 at ¶29, p. 1162, this book. FRCP 16(c) does not list any techniques for managing complex litigation. Some local rules require the parties in complex cases to file a scheduling order that proposes the use of the *Manual for Complex Litigation*. *See, e.g.*, Local Rules Fla. (S.D.), Rule 16.1(b)(3)(G); Local Rules Ill. (N.D.), Rule 16.1(a) (Standing Order Establishing Pretrial Procedure, ¶3(a)). *See generally Manual for Complex Litigation, Fourth* (2004), Federal Judicial Center, www.fjc.gov.

14. Separate trials. The court may order a separate trial under FRCP 42(b) of a claim, counterclaim, cross-claim, third-party claim, or particular issue. FRCP 16(c)(2)(M). See "Motion for Severance or Separate Trials," ch. 5-L, p. 366.

15. Resolution of limited issues. The court may order the presentation of evidence early in the trial on a manageable issue that might, on the evidence, be the basis for judgment as a matter of law under FRCP 50(a) or the basis for judgment on partial findings under FRCP 52(c). FRCP 16(c)(2)(N); ***Dick v. Department of Veterans Affairs***, 290 F.3d 1356, 1364 n.5 (Fed.Cir.2002), *overruled on other grounds*, ***Garcia v. Department of Homeland Sec.***, 437 F.3d 1322 (Fed.Cir.2006).

16. Time limit to present evidence. The court may establish a reasonable limit on the time allowed to present evidence. FRCP 16(c)(2)(O); *see, e.g.*, ***General Signal Corp. v. MCI Telecomms.***, 66 F.3d 1500, 1508 (9th Cir.1995) (14-day limit for trial was not unreasonable). Before entering an order limiting time, the court should ask the parties to submit a plan outlining the nature of the anticipated testimony and the expected duration of direct and cross-examination. 1993 Notes to FRCP 16 at ¶14, p. 1160, this book.

17. Other ways. The court may consider other ways to facilitate the just, speedy, and inexpensive disposition of the case. FRCP 16(c)(2)(P); *see, e.g.*, ***Olcott v. Delaware Flood Co.***, 76 F.3d 1538, 1556 (10th Cir.1996) (court could enforce provision in stipulated pretrial order requiring an accounting of Ds' financial affairs). The court may require the parties to present and file proposed jury questions, instructions, definitions, and objections to the opposing party's submissions. ***Senra v. Cunningham***, 9 F.3d 168, 170-71 (1st Cir.1993).

§4.5 Pretrial order. The court should issue an order reciting any action taken at the conference. FRCP 16(d). This order controls the case unless the court modifies it. *Id.*; ***Rockwell Int'l v. U.S.***, 549 U.S. 457, 474 (2007); ***Hamburger v. State Farm Mut. Auto. Ins.***, 361 F.3d 875, 887 (5th Cir.2004). *See generally* ***Marschand v. Norfolk & W. Ry.***, 81 F.3d 714, 716 (7th Cir.1996) (discussing importance of pretrial order). See "Modification of pretrial order," §4.7, p. 295.

NOTE

Be sure to check local rules, standing orders, and other local procedures that may have specific requirements for submitting and objecting to pretrial orders. See, e.g., Local Rules Or., Rule 16-5(c) (P must serve proposed final pretrial order on D; D must serve objections, additions, and changes on P; and proposed final pretrial order must note all areas of disagreement, be signed by P and D, and be filed by P).

1. In writing. The pretrial order must be in writing. *See* FRCP 16(d). Some local rules make the plaintiff's attorney responsible for drafting the pretrial order, some allow the court to appoint one of the attorneys to perform the task, and some leave the task to the court. 1983 Notes to FRCP 16 at ¶36, p. 1163, this book. It may not be necessary to have the judge's signature on the pretrial order. *See, e.g.*, ***U.S. v. First Nat'l Bank***, 652 F.2d 882, 886 n.3 (9th Cir.1981) (pretrial order was never signed by judge but was signed by both attorneys, docketed by clerk, and treated as valid order).

2. Notice. Although not expressly required by the FRCPs, the court clerk usually sends a copy of the pretrial order to the attorney in charge for each party, unless the order requires one of the parties to serve it on the others.

3. Number of orders. Because the court may hold more than one pretrial conference, it may need to issue additional pretrial orders to recite the rulings made in those conferences. *See* FRCP 16(d); 1983 Notes to FRCP 16 at ¶34, p. 1163, this book.

4. Waiver. Once the pretrial order is entered, it supersedes all earlier pleadings and governs the issues and evidence to be presented at trial. ***Rockwell Int'l***, 549 U.S. at 474; ***Elvis Presley Enters. v. Capece***, 141 F.3d 188, 206 (5th Cir.1998); ***Wilson v. Kelkhoff***, 86 F.3d 1438, 1442 (7th Cir.1996). Claims and issues not included in the final pretrial order are waived, even if they appeared in the complaint. ***Wilson v. Muckala***, 303 F.3d 1207, 1215 (10th

Cir.2002); ***McLean Contracting Co. v. Waterman S.S. Corp.***, 277 F.3d 477, 480 (4th Cir.2002); ***Kona Tech. v. Southern Pac. Transp.***, 225 F.3d 595, 604 (5th Cir.2000); ***Marschand***, 81 F.3d at 716; ***Correa v. Hospital S.F.***, 69 F.3d 1184, 1195 (1st Cir.1995). Exhibits or witnesses not listed in the pretrial order are also typically excluded. *See* ***R.M.R. v. Muscogee Cty. Sch. Dist.***, 165 F.3d 812, 818 (11th Cir.1999); *see also* ***Youren v. Tintic Sch. Dist.***, 343 F.3d 1296, 1304 (10th Cir.2003) (issue not included in pretrial report was not part of case before court). See "Sanctions for disobedience," §4.6.3(1), this page.

§4.6 Enforceability of order. The court has broad powers to enforce its orders. ***Tower Ventures, Inc. v. City of Westfield***, 296 F.3d 43, 46 (1st Cir.2002); ***Olcott v. Delaware Flood Co.***, 76 F.3d 1538, 1555-56 (10th Cir.1996); *see* FRCP 16(f). See "Motion for Sanctions," ch. 5-O, p. 384.

1. Limiting evidence. At trial, the fact-finder should consider only those claims or theories raised in the pretrial order, unless the court modifies the pretrial order or an issue is tried by consent. *See* ***Marschand v. Norfolk & W. Ry.***, 81 F.3d 714, 716 (7th Cir.1996); ***Rios v. Bigler***, 67 F.3d 1543, 1549 (10th Cir.1995); ***Arsement v. Spinnaker Expl. Co.***, 400 F.3d 238, 245 (5th Cir.2005). Thus, with a pretrial order, the court can limit the evidence and restrict the issues submitted to the jury. *See* ***Gorlikowski v. Tolbert***, 52 F.3d 1439, 1443-44 (7th Cir.1995). But a pretrial order should be liberally construed to permit evidence and theories at trial that can be fairly inferred from the language of the order. ***U.S. v. First Nat'l Bank***, 652 F.2d 882, 886 (9th Cir.1981); *see also* ***Morton Int'l v. A.E. Staley Mfg.***, 343 F.3d 669, 685 (3d Cir.2003) (purpose of rule is to minimize prejudicial surprise).

2. Disobeying order. The court may impose sanctions on disobedient parties, their attorneys, or both whenever the following conduct occurs:

(1) A party or its attorney does not appear at a scheduling or other pretrial conference. FRCP 16(f)(1)(A); *see, e.g.*, ***Nascimento v. Dummer***, 508 F.3d 905, 909 (9th Cir.2007) (court dismissed case because party did not appear at scheduled final pretrial conference); *see also* ***Ackra Direct Mktg. Corp. v. Fingerhut Corp.***, 86 F.3d 852, 856 (8th Cir.1996) (court entered default judgment because party did not comply with discovery orders, attend final pretrial settlement conference, or comply with other pretrial requirements).

(2) A party or its attorney is substantially unprepared to participate in the conference. FRCP 16(f)(1)(B); *see* ***Lillie v. U.S.***, 40 F.3d 1105, 1110 (10th Cir.1994).

(3) A party or its attorney does not participate in good faith in the conference. FRCP 16(f)(1)(B); ***Guillory v. Domtar Indus.***, 95 F.3d 1320, 1334 (5th Cir.1996); *see* ***Lillie***, 40 F.3d at 1110.

(4) A party or its attorney does not obey scheduling or other pretrial orders. FRCP 16(f)(1)(C); *see* ***Barrett v. Atlantic Richfield Co.***, 95 F.3d 375, 380 (5th Cir.1996) (court may exclude expert testimony as sanction under FRCP 37(b)(2)(B), now FRCP 37(b)(2)(A)(ii)).

NOTE

Before the court can impose sanctions under FRCP 16(f), a party or its attorney must have violated a court order. ***Lillie****, 40 F.3d at 1110. But the court cannot impose sanctions under FRCP 16(f) if the order was ambiguous. E.g.,* ***Ashlodge, Ltd. v. Hauser****, 163 F.3d 681, 683-84 (2d Cir. 1998) (sanctions could not be predicated on court's letter stating that particular action "should" be performed by certain date, rather than "must"). Sanctions for other kinds of discovery misconduct must be addressed under other sanction provisions, such as FRCP 26(g)(3).* ***Lillie****, 40 F.3d at 1110; see* ***Salahuddin v. Harris****, 782 F.2d 1127, 1133 (2d Cir.1986).*

3. Sanctions for disobedience. Some of the sanctions available to the court are the following:

(1) Excluding exhibits or testimony of witnesses not listed before trial as required by the pretrial order. ***Hill v. Porter Mem'l Hosp.***, 90 F.3d 220, 224 (7th Cir.1996); *see* ***R.M.R. v. Muscogee Cty. Sch. Dist.***, 165 F.3d 812, 818 (11th Cir.1999); ***Admiral Theatre Corp. v. Douglas Theatre Co.***, 585 F.2d 877, 889 (8th Cir.1978). In ruling on a party's motion to call a witness not included on the pretrial witness list, the court should consider all the following factors:

(a) Prejudice or surprise to the party against whom the excluded witness would testify. ***Barrett***, 95 F.3d at 380.

(b) The ability of that party to cure the prejudice. *Id.*

(c) The extent to which waiver of the rule against calling unlisted witnesses would disrupt the orderly and efficient trial of the case or other cases in the court. ***Rapco, Inc. v. Commissioner***, 85 F.3d 950, 953 (2d Cir.1996).

(d) Bad faith or willful noncompliance with the court's order. *Id.*; ***Burks v. Oklahoma Publ'g***, 81 F.3d 975, 979 (10th Cir.1996).

(2) Issuing a preclusion order. 1983 Notes to FRCP 16 at ¶39, p. 1163, this book. See "Prevent party from supporting or opposing claims," ch. 6-A, §15.5.1(2), p. 448.

(3) Striking the party's pleadings. 1983 Notes to FRCP 16 at ¶39, p. 1163, this book. See "Strike pleadings, stay proceedings, dismiss case, or render default," ch. 6-A, §15.5.1(3), p. 449.

(4) Staying the proceedings. 1983 Notes to FRCP 16 at ¶39, p. 1163, this book. See "Strike pleadings, stay proceedings, dismiss case, or render default," ch. 6-A, §15.5.1(3), p. 449.

(5) Entering default judgment. 1983 Notes to FRCP 16 at ¶39, p. 1163, this book; *see* ***Ackra Direct Mktg.***, 86 F.3d at 856-57. See "Strike pleadings, stay proceedings, dismiss case, or render default," ch. 6-A, §15.5.1(3), p. 449.

(6) Holding the party in contempt. 1983 Notes to FRCP 16 at ¶39, p. 1163, this book. See "Find person in contempt of court," ch. 6-A, §15.5.1(4), p. 450.

(7) Charging the party or its attorney with expenses and attorney fees caused by its noncompliance with the pretrial order. 1983 Notes to FRCP 16 at ¶39, p. 1163, this book. See "Award attorney fees & expenses," ch. 6-A, §15.5.1(5), p. 451.

(8) Dismissing the case with prejudice. ***Link v. Wabash R.R.***, 370 U.S. 626, 633 (1962); ***Tower Ventures***, 296 F.3d at 46.

4. Factors to consider before dismissal. Before the court dismisses a party's case as a sanction for violating the pretrial order, the court should consider the following factors:

(1) The severity of the violation. ***Robson v. Hallenbeck***, 81 F.3d 1, 2 (1st Cir.1996).

(2) The legitimacy of the party's excuse. *See* ***Tower Ventures***, 296 F.3d at 47.

(3) Repetition of violations. ***Robson***, 81 F.3d at 2. Repeated violations indicating a general unwillingness to comply with a scheduling order may be enough to justify dismissal. *Id.* at 4.

(4) Whether there is a clear record of delay or deliberate misconduct by the party. *See* ***Culwell v. City of Fort Worth***, 468 F.3d 868, 871 (5th Cir.2006); ***Robson***, 81 F.3d at 2.

(5) Prejudice to the other side and to the operations of the court. ***Robson***, 81 F.3d at 2.

(6) The adequacy of lesser sanctions. *Id.* The court cannot dismiss a case unless it finds that lesser sanctions would not serve the interests of justice. ***Culwell***, 468 F.3d at 871.

§4.7 Modification of pretrial order. The court has broad discretion to modify a pretrial order. ***Jones v. Potter***, 488 F.3d 397, 411 (6th Cir.2007); *see* FRCP 16(d). A pretrial order should not be changed lightly, but total inflexibility is undesirable. 1983 Notes to FRCP 16 at ¶35, p. 1163, this book. FRCP 16 provides standards for modifying scheduling orders and final pretrial orders, but it does not provide standards for modifying other types of pretrial orders. *See* FRCP 16(b)(4) (scheduling order can be modified only for good cause and with court's consent), FRCP 16(e) (final pretrial order can be modified only to prevent manifest injustice); *see, e.g.*, ***Petersen v. Elmhurst An-***

esthesiologists, P.C., No. 93 C 1468 (N.D.Ill.1993) (no pub.; 10-6-93) (when no final pretrial order was entered, standard for modifying preliminary pretrial scheduling order was for good cause shown). By not limiting the modification of pretrial orders, FRCP 16 reflects the reality that in the continuous management of a case, what is done at one conference may be changed at the next. 1983 Notes to FRCP 16 at ¶35, p. 1163, this book. See "Modification," §3.4, p. 290; "Modification of final pretrial order," §6.6, this page.

PRACTICE TIP

Remember that under FRCP 15(b), a pretrial order can be amended after the trial if an issue that was not raised in either the pleadings or the pretrial order is tried by consent. ***United Phosphorus, Ltd. v. Midland Fumigant, Inc.****, 205 F.3d 1219, 1236 (10th Cir.2000);* ***Hardin v. Manitowoc-Forsythe Corp.****, 691 F.2d 449, 456 (10th Cir.1982); see* ***Kirkland v. District of Columbia****, 70 F.3d 629, 634-35 (D.C.Cir.1995) (court must use FRCP 15(b) standards to analyze trial of issue by implied consent even if issue was omitted from pleading or pretrial order).*

§5. EXPERT & PRETRIAL DISCLOSURE UNDER FRCP 26(a)(2), (a)(3)

See "Expert Disclosures," ch. 6-E, §5, p. 534; "Final Pretrial Disclosures," ch. 6-E, §6, p. 536.

§6. FINAL PRETRIAL CONFERENCE

§6.1 Purpose. The purpose of the final pretrial conference is to formulate a plan for trial, including a program to facilitate the admission of evidence. FRCP 16(e).

§6.2 Scheduling. A final pretrial conference must be held as close to the start of the trial as is reasonable. FRCP 16(e). However, the exact timing of the final pretrial conference, unless set by local rule, is left to the court's discretion. 1983 Notes to FRCP 16 at ¶31, p. 1163, this book.

§6.3 Attendance. Each party must send to the conference at least one attorney who will be trying the case; unrepresented parties must attend in person. FRCP 16(e).

§6.4 Scope. The court may address any of the topics listed in "Scope," §4.4, p. 291.

§6.5 Final pretrial order. After the final pretrial conference, the court should prepare a final pretrial order reflecting any action taken or direct one of the parties to prepare it.

§6.6 Modification of final pretrial order. After the final pretrial conference, the court can modify the final pretrial order only to prevent manifest injustice. FRCP 16(e); ***Hoffman v. Tonnemacher***, 593 F.3d 908, 913 (9th Cir. 2010); ***Jones v. Potter***, 488 F.3d 397, 411 (6th Cir.2007); ***Gorlikowski v. Tolbert***, 52 F.3d 1439, 1444 (7th Cir.1995). "Manifest injustice" is a stringent standard that fits the purpose of the final pretrial order, which is to promote efficiency and conserve judicial resources by identifying real issues before trial. ***Gorlikowski***, 52 F.3d at 1444; 1983 Notes to FRCP 16 at ¶35, p. 1163, this book; *see* ***Schmitt v. Beverly Health & Rehab. Servs.***, 993 F.Supp. 1354, 1365 (D. Kan.1998) (standard imposes some restraint on court's normally broad discretion to amend pleadings); 3 *Moore's Federal Practice 3d* §16.78[4][a] (although intensity of standard varies, standard for modifying final pretrial order is more stringent than that imposed on earlier pretrial orders). *But see* ***Manley v. AmBase Corp.***, 337 F.3d 237, 249 (2d Cir.2003) (pretrial order is not legal "straitjacket" binding parties and court to unwavering course at trial). The party seeking the modification has the burden of showing manifest injustice. ***Koch v. Koch Indus.***, 203 F.3d 1202, 1222 (10th Cir.2000). The courts have considered different factors when determining whether modification is necessary to prevent manifest injustice:

1. The degree of prejudice to the moving party if the pretrial order is not modified. ***Rapco, Inc. v. Commissioner***, 85 F.3d 950, 953 (2d Cir.1996); ***U.S. v. First Nat'l Bank***, 652 F.2d 882, 887 (9th Cir.1981).

2. The degree of prejudice or surprise to the party opposing the modification. ***Galdamez v. Potter***, 415 F.3d 1015, 1020 (9th Cir.2005); ***Palace Expl. Co. v. Petroleum Dev. Co.***, 316 F.3d 1110, 1117 (10th Cir.2003); ***Alberty-Vélez v. Corporación de P.R. Para la Difusión Pública***, 242 F.3d 418, 423 (1st Cir.2001); ***Ryan v. Illinois Dept. of Children & Family Servs.***, 185 F.3d 751, 763 (7th Cir.1999); ***Rapco***, 85 F.3d at 953; *see* ***U.S. v. $84,615 in U.S. Currency***, 379 F.3d 496, 499 (8th Cir.2004).

3. The opposing party's ability to cure the prejudice. ***Galdamez***, 415 F.3d at 1020; ***Palace Expl.***, 316 F.3d at 1117; ***Ryan***, 185 F.3d at 763.

4. The impact of the modification on the orderly and efficient conduct of the case at the present stage of the litigation. ***Galdamez***, 415 F.3d at 1020; ***Palace Expl.***, 316 F.3d at 1117; ***Ryan***, 185 F.3d at 763; ***Rapco***, 85 F.3d at 953.

5. The degree of the moving party's willfulness, bad faith, or excusable neglect. ***Galdamez***, 415 F.3d at 1020; ***Palace Expl.***, 316 F.3d at 1117; ***Ryan***, 185 F.3d at 763; ***Rapco***, 85 F.3d at 953.

6. Whether the party timely moved for the modification. ***Koch***, 203 F.3d at 1223.

§7. APPELLATE REVIEW

A pretrial conference order may be appealed after the entry of a final judgment. The district court has broad discretion to supervise pretrial litigation, and its decisions on the preclusive effect of a pretrial order will not be disturbed on appeal unless the court clearly abused its discretion. *See* ***Culwell v. City of Fort Worth***, 468 F.3d 868, 870 (5th Cir.2006); ***Manley v. AmBase Corp.***, 337 F.3d 237, 249 (2d Cir.2003); ***McLean Contracting Co. v. Waterman S.S. Corp.***, 277 F.3d 477, 479 (4th Cir.2002); ***Alberty-Vélez v. Corporación de P.R. Para la Difusión Pública***, 242 F.3d 418, 423 (1st Cir.2001); ***United Phosphorus, Ltd. v. Midland Fumigant, Inc.***, 205 F.3d 1219, 1236 (10th Cir.2000); ***Gorlikowski v. Tolbert***, 52 F.3d 1439, 1444 (7th Cir.1995).

§7.1 Exclusion of witness not listed in pretrial order. A district court's decision to exclude a witness not listed in the pretrial order is reviewable only for abuse of discretion. ***R.M.R. v. Muscogee Cty. Sch. Dist.***, 165 F.3d 812, 818 (11th Cir.1999). An appellate court reviewing the decision to exclude a witness should consider the following: (1) the importance of the testimony, (2) the offering party's reason for not disclosing the witness earlier, and (3) the prejudice to the opposing party if the witness had been allowed to testify. *Id.*

§7.2 Order dismissing suit as sanction. A sanction order dismissing a suit should address all explanations offered by the sanctioned party so the appellate court can perform an effective review; if the order does not address all offered explanations, the appellate court may remand for further proceedings. *See* ***Robson v. Hallenbeck***, 81 F.3d 1, 5 (1st Cir.1996).

B. MAGISTRATE JUDGES & SPECIAL MASTERS

§1. GENERAL

§1.1 Rules. FRCP 53, 72, 73; see 28 U.S.C. §§631-639.

§1.2 Purpose. Federal magistrate judges are judicial officers who assist the federal district judges with their caseloads. *See* 28 U.S.C. §636. Unlike district judges, circuit judges, and Supreme Court judges, magistrate judges are not Article 3 judges. *See* U.S. Const. art. 3, §1; ***Powershare, Inc. v. Syntel, Inc.***, 597 F.3d 10, 13 (1st Cir.2010). Special masters are nonjudicial personnel who are appointed by the court to assist the court in complicated cases. *See* FRCP 53(a).

§1.3 Forms. ***O'Connor's Federal Civil Forms*** (2012), FORMS 5B.

§1.4 Other references. 9C Wright & Miller, *Federal Practice & Procedure 3d* §§2601-2615 (2008 & Supp.2012); 12 Wright, Miller & Marcus, *Federal Practice & Procedure 2d* §§3071-3073 (1997 & Supp.2012); 29 Wright & Gold, *Federal Practice & Procedure* §6304 (1997 & Supp.2012); 9, 14 *Moore's Federal Practice 3d* ch. 53, §§72.01-72.12 (2012); Willging et al., *Special Masters' Incidence & Activity: Report to the Judicial Conference's Advisory Committee on Civil Rules & Its Subcommittee on Special Masters* (2000), Federal Judicial Center, www.fjc.gov; Feinberg, *Creative Use of ADR: The Court-Appointed Special Settlement Master*, 59 Alb.L.Rev. 881 (1996); Smith, *United States Magistrates in the Federal Courts: Subordinate Judges* (1990); Wald, *'Some Exceptional Condition'—The Anatomy of a Decision Under Federal Rule of Civil Procedure 53(b)*, 62 St. John's L.Rev. 405, 412 (1988); Brazil, *Special Masters in Complex Cases: Extending the Judiciary or Reshaping Adjudication?*, 53 U.Chi.L.Rev. 394 (1986).

NOTE

Some districts have a separate set of local rules for magistrate judges and special masters. See, e.g., Local Rules Tex. (E.D.), Appendix B: Local Rules of Court for the Assignment of Duties to United States Magistrate Judges.

§2. TRANSFER OF PRETRIAL MATTERS TO MAGISTRATE JUDGE

The district court may transfer certain pretrial matters to a magistrate judge without the parties' consent. *See* 28 U.S.C. §636(b)(1); FRCP 72. When the court transfers nondispositive pretrial matters (i.e., matters that do not dispose of a party's claim or defense), the magistrate judge may hear, determine, and enter orders resolving them. *See* ***Arista Records LLC v. Doe 3***, 604 F.3d 110, 116 (2d Cir.2010); 14 *Moore's Federal Practice 3d* §72.02[2]. When the court transfers dispositive pretrial matters (i.e., matters that terminate or dispose of a party's claim or defense), the magistrate judge may hear them, make recommendations for resolving them, and file a report with proposed findings of fact to the court. *See* ***Arista Records***, 604 F.3d at 116; 14 *Moore's Federal Practice 3d* §72.02[2]. The jurisdiction of magistrate judges is limited by statute and cannot be expanded by the federal courts. ***Beazer E., Inc. v. Mead Corp.***, 412 F.3d 429, 437 (3d Cir.2005); *see* ***Thomas v. Whitworth***, 136 F.3d 756, 758 (11th Cir.1998); ***NLRB v. A-Plus Roofing, Inc.***, 39 F.3d 1410, 1415 (9th Cir.1994).

§2.1 Nondispositive pretrial matters for determination.

1. Authority to hear & determine. The district court may transfer nondispositive pretrial matters not covered by Article 3 to a magistrate judge for a hearing and a determination. *See* 28 U.S.C. §636(b)(1)(A); ***Schur v. L.A. Weight Loss Ctrs., Inc.***, 577 F.3d 752, 760 (7th Cir.2009); ***Estate of Conners v. O'Connor***, 6 F.3d 656, 658 (9th Cir.1993); 14 *Moore's Federal Practice 3d* §72.02[2]. Rulings on nondispositive matters, which include most pretrial and discovery issues, are "self-operating"—that is, a ruling does not require the district court's approval to be effective. ***U.S. v. Brown***, 79 F.3d 1499, 1503 (7th Cir.1996); ***U.S. v. Ecker***, 923 F.2d 7, 9 (1st Cir.1991).

2. What may be heard & determined under FRCP 72(a). The district court may transfer any nondispositive pretrial matter to a magistrate judge for a determinative hearing, except the matters specifically listed in 28 U.S.C. §636(b)(1)(A). A magistrate judge may hear and determine the following nondispositive pretrial matters:

(1) Matters that the local rules permit a magistrate judge to hear. *E.g.*, Local Rules Nev., Rule IB 1-9.

(2) Discovery motions. *See* ***Arista Records LLC v. Doe 3***, 604 F.3d 110, 116 (2d Cir.2010) (motion to quash subpoena); ***Commodity Futures Trading Comm'n v. Noble Metals Int'l***, 67 F.3d 766, 770 (9th Cir.1995) (motion to compel); ***ICA Constr. Corp. v. Reich***, 60 F.3d 1495, 1499 n.10 (11th Cir.1995) (motion for protective order).

(3) Sanctions. ***Gomez v. Martin Marietta Corp.***, 50 F.3d 1511, 1519-20 (10th Cir.1995). Whether the issue of sanctions is dispositive or nondispositive controls the scope of the magistrate judge's authority. *See* ***Retired Chi. Police Ass'n v. City of Chi.***, 76 F.3d 856, 868 (7th Cir.1996) (district judge cannot refer dispute about sanctions to magistrate judge under §636(b)(1)(A) because grant or denial of request for sanctions is dispositive matter). If the motion for sanctions asks for dispositive sanctions but the magistrate judge does not grant them, the referral is governed by FRCP 72(a); if the magistrate judge grants them, the referral is governed by FRCP 72(b). ***Gomez***, 50 F.3d at 1519-20.

NOTE

Whether a magistrate judge can determine FRCP 11 sanctions is unclear. See ***Kiobel v. Millson***, *592 F.3d 78, 85-86 (2d Cir.2010) (Cabranes, J., concurring). Compare* ***Alpern v. Lieb***, *38 F.3d 933, 936 (7th Cir.1994) (magistrate judge can recommend FRCP 11 sanctions), with* ***Maisonville v. F2 Am., Inc.***, *902 F.2d 746, 748 (9th Cir.1990) (magistrate judge can determine FRCP 11 sanctions).*

(4) Motions in limine. *See* ***Brock v. Caterpillar, Inc.***, 94 F.3d 220, 223 (6th Cir.1996).

(5) Motions to realign the parties. ***Green Constr. Co. v. Kansas Power & Light Co.***, 1 F.3d 1005, 1011 (10th Cir.1993).

(6) Supervision of settlement negotiations. ***Maywalt v. Parker & Parsley Pet. Co.***, 67 F.3d 1072, 1075 (2d Cir.1995).

(7) Motions for self-representation and to substitute counsel. ***U.S. v. Schultz***, 565 F.3d 1353, 1357-58 (11th Cir.2009).

(8) Motions to stay litigation pending arbitration. ***Powershare, Inc. v. Syntel, Inc.***, 597 F.3d 10, 14 (1st Cir.2010). *But see* ***Flannery v. Tri-State Div.***, 402 F.Supp.2d 819, 821 (E.D.Mich.2005) (motions to stay considered dispositive because practical effect is allowing case to proceed in different forum).

(9) Motions to transfer venue. *See* ***Meier v. Premier Wine & Spirits, Inc.***, 371 F.Supp.2d 239, 244 (E.D.N.Y.2005) (dicta); ***Holmes v. TV-3, Inc.***, 141 F.R.D. 697, 697 (W.D.La.1991). *But see* ***Payton v. Saginaw Cty. Jail***, 743 F.Supp.2d 691, 692-93 (E.D.Mich.2010) (when P is deprived of chosen forum and forced to litigate elsewhere, order is functional equivalent of dismissal and thus is considered dispositive; magistrate judge could not enter order to transfer venue).

3. Deadline for hearing. The magistrate judge must hear nondispositive motions promptly. FRCP 72(a).

4. Order. Generally, the magistrate judge's order should be in writing and entered into the record. *See* FRCP 72(a); 1983 Notes to FRCP 72 at ¶1, p. 1231, this book. However, an oral order read into the record by the magistrate judge is sufficient. 1983 Notes to FRCP 72 at ¶1, p. 1231, this book.

5. Objection to order. The parties must file and serve any objections within 14 days after being served a copy of the magistrate judge's order. FRCP 72(a). A party cannot wait until the end of the trial before deciding to object to a ruling by the magistrate judge. ***Green Constr.***, 1 F.3d at 1011.

6. District court's consideration of order. If a party objects to the magistrate judge's order, the district court must determine whether the order is clearly erroneous or contrary to law. FRCP 72(a); ***Powershare, Inc.***, 597 F.3d at 14. If any part of the order is clearly erroneous or contrary to law, the district court can modify or set aside the objectionable part. FRCP 72(a); *see* 28 U.S.C. §636(b)(1)(A); ***Osband v. Woodford***, 290 F.3d 1036, 1041 (9th Cir. 2002); ***Castillo v. Frank***, 70 F.3d 382, 385-86 (5th Cir.1995). If a party does not object, the district court still has discretion to review the order on its own initiative to determine if the order was clearly erroneous or contrary to law. ***Schur***, 577 F.3d at 760.

§2.2 Dispositive pretrial matters for recommendations.

1. Authority to hear & recommend. The district court may refer certain dispositive matters covered by Article 3 to a magistrate judge for the purpose of holding a hearing, receiving evidence, and submitting recommendations and proposed findings of fact. *See* 28 U.S.C. §636(b)(1)(B); ***Arista Records LLC v. Doe 3***, 604 F.3d 110, 116 (2d Cir.2010); ***Schur v. L.A. Weight Loss Ctrs., Inc.***, 577 F.3d 752, 760 (7th Cir.2009); 14 *Moore's Federal Practice 3d* §72.02[2]. Rulings on dispositive matters, such as motions to dismiss, for summary judgment, or for injunctive relief, are "non-self-operating"—that is, a ruling does not take effect until the district court accepts the magistrate judge's report and recommendation and enters a corresponding order or judgment. *See* ***Stripling v. Jordan Prod. Co.***, 234 F.3d 863, 868 (5th Cir.2000); ***U.S. v. Brown***, 79 F.3d 1499, 1503 (7th Cir.1996); ***U.S. v. Ecker***, 923 F.2d 7, 9 (1st Cir.1991).

2. What may be referred for recommendations under FRCP 72(b). The district court may designate a magistrate judge to hear and submit recommendations on dispositive matters. 28 U.S.C. §636(b)(1)(B). Dispositive matters include those listed in 28 U.S.C. §636(b)(1)(A), but that list is nonexhaustive; the list is a guide to help courts determine if a matter is dispositive or nondispositive. ***Powershare, Inc. v. Syntel, Inc.***, 597 F.3d 10, 13

(1st Cir.2010); *see* ***Williams v. Beemiller, Inc.***, 527 F.3d 259, 265 (2d Cir.2008). A magistrate judge may hear and submit recommendations for the following dispositive matters:

(1) Motions for injunctive relief. 28 U.S.C. §636(b)(1)(A), (b)(1)(B). See "Injunctive Relief," ch. 2-D, p. 93.

(2) Motions for judgment on the pleadings. 28 U.S.C. §636(b)(1)(A), (b)(1)(B).

(3) Motions for summary judgment. *Id.* §636(b)(1)(A), (b)(1)(B). See "Summary Judgment," ch. 7-B, p. 603.

(4) Motions to dismiss or to permit maintenance of a class action. 28 U.S.C. §636(b)(1)(A), (b)(1)(B).

(5) Motions to dismiss for failure to state a claim upon which relief can be granted. *Id.* §636(b)(1)(A), (b)(1)(B). See "Motion to Dismiss for Failure to State a Claim—FRCP 12(b)(6)," ch. 3-F, p. 204.

(6) Motions to involuntarily dismiss a case. 28 U.S.C. §636(b)(1)(A), (b)(1)(B). See "Involuntary Dismissal," ch. 7-D, p. 642. This includes a motion for default judgment. *See* ***Callier v. Gray***, 167 F.3d 977, 981 (6th Cir. 1999) (motion for default judgment treated same as motion for involuntary dismissal); ***Conetta v. National Hair Care Ctrs., Inc.***, 186 F.R.D. 262, 267-68 (D.R.I.1999) (magistrate judge can hear evidence on amount of default judgment but cannot enter judgment), *aff'd*, 236 F.3d 67 (1st Cir.2001).

(7) Motions for dispositive sanctions. *See* ***Bambu Sales, Inc. v. Ozak Trading Inc.***, 58 F.3d 849, 852 (2d Cir.1995) (default judgment).

NOTE

Whether a magistrate judge can determine FRCP 11 sanctions is unclear. See "Note," §2.1.2(3), p. 298.

---

(8) Motions to stay litigation and compel arbitration under an arbitration agreement. *See* ***Nielsen v. Piper, Jaffray & Hopwood, Inc.***, 66 F.3d 145, 146 (7th Cir.1995). See "Compelling Arbitration," ch. 7-E, §2, p. 650.

(9) Motions to remand. *See* ***Williams***, 527 F.3d at 265-66 (remand order is functional equivalent of dismissal order); ***Vogel v. U.S. Office Prods.***, 258 F.3d 509, 517 (6th Cir.2001) (same); ***First Un. Mortg. Corp. v. Smith***, 229 F.3d 992, 996 (10th Cir.2000) (same); ***In re U.S. Healthcare***, 159 F.3d 142, 145 (3d Cir.1998) (same). *But see* ***Meier v. Premier Wine & Spirits, Inc.***, 371 F.Supp.2d 239, 243 (E.D.N.Y.2005) (magistrate judges have authority to hear and determine motions to remand); ***Johnson v. Wyeth***, 313 F.Supp.2d 1272, 1272-73 (N.D.Ala.2004) (same). See "Plaintiff's Motion to Remand," ch. 4-B, p. 268.

3. Deadline for hearing. The magistrate judge must hear the dispositive motion promptly. FRCP 72(b)(1); *see also* ***Cline v. Commissioner of Soc. Sec.***, 96 F.3d 146, 150 (6th Cir.1996) (although FRCP 72(b), now FRCP 72(b)(1), allows magistrate judge to hold oral argument, it does not require oral argument).

4. Record of hearing. If the magistrate judge holds an evidentiary hearing on the motion, a record of the proceedings must be made. FRCP 72(b)(1). A party may request that a record be made of any other necessary hearing before the magistrate judge. *See id.*

5. Magistrate judge's recommendations. The magistrate judge must enter into the record its recommendations for the disposition of the motion. 28 U.S.C. §636(b)(1)(C); FRCP 72(b)(1). If appropriate, the magistrate judge must enter proposed findings of fact. FRCP 72(b)(1).

6. Notice. The clerk must promptly mail a copy of the recommendations and proposed findings to each party. 28 U.S.C. §636(b)(1)(C); FRCP 72(b)(1).

7. Objection to recommended disposition & proposed findings.

(1) Form. A party who objects to the magistrate judge's recommendations and proposed findings must file and serve specific, written objections to the recommendations and the proposed findings. FRCP 72(b)(2);

Habets v. Waste Mgmt., 363 F.3d 378, 381 (5th Cir.2004); ***Page v. Lee***, 337 F.3d 411, 416 n.3 (4th Cir.2003); ***U.S. v. One Parcel of Real Prop.***, 73 F.3d 1057, 1059 (10th Cir.1996). The objections must be specific enough to preserve the issue for appellate review. ***Page***, 337 F.3d at 416 n.3; ***One Parcel***, 73 F.3d at 1060. The word "specific," as used in FRCP 72(b), requires a party only "to specify each issue for which review is sought and not the factual or legal basis of the objection." ***Johnson v. Zema Sys.***, 170 F.3d 734, 741 (7th Cir.1999). However, local rules may require more specificity. *Id.* at 742.

(2) Deadline. After being served a copy of the magistrate judge's recommendations and proposed findings, a party has 14 days to file and serve objections and ask the district court to reconsider the magistrate judge's recommendations and proposed findings. 28 U.S.C. §636(b)(1)(C); FRCP 72(b)(2). If the magistrate judge serves the recommendations and proposed findings by mail, the complaining party has an additional three days to object. FRCP 6(d); *see* ***Lerro v. Quaker Oats Co.***, 84 F.3d 239, 242 (7th Cir.1996) (applying former ten-day deadline to file and serve objections). See "Computing Response Deadlines," ch. 1-D, §6, p. 33.

(3) Record. The party objecting to the magistrate judge's recommended disposition must promptly arrange for the transcription of the entire record, or the portions of the record that the parties agree are necessary or that the magistrate judge considers sufficient. FRCP 72(b)(2).

8. Response to objections. The prevailing party may respond to the objections within 14 days after being served with a copy of them. FRCP 72(b)(2).

9. District court's consideration of recommendations & proposed findings.

(1) Timely objection. If a party timely objects to the magistrate judge's recommendations and proposed findings, the district court must make a de novo determination of the objectionable portions. 28 U.S.C. §636(b)(1); FRCP 72(b)(3). The term "de novo" signifies two things: (1) a second hearing for evidence is not required, and (2) the magistrate judge's findings are not protected by the clearly-erroneous standard of review. 1983 Notes to FRCP 72 at ¶6, p. 1232, this book. Although the district court is not required to do so, it may either hold a second evidentiary hearing to receive additional evidence or return the matter to the magistrate judge with instructions. 28 U.S.C. §636(b)(1); FRCP 72(b)(3); *see* 1983 Notes to FRCP 72 at ¶6, p. 1232, this book. When deciding whether to accept additional evidence, the district court may consider (1) the reasons the evidence was not originally submitted, (2) the importance of the omitted evidence, (3) whether the evidence was previously available, and (4) the likelihood of unfair prejudice if the evidence is accepted. ***Performance Autoplex II Ltd. v. Mid-Continent Cas. Co.***, 322 F.3d 847, 862 (5th Cir.2003). One circuit has held that when conducting a de novo review, the district court is required to consider all arguments, even if they were not raised before the magistrate judge. ***U.S. v. George***, 971 F.2d 1113, 1118 (4th Cir.1992). Other circuits have rejected this view. ***Williams v. McNeil***, 557 F.3d 1287, 1291-92 (11th Cir.2009); ***U.S. v. Howell***, 231 F.3d 615, 621 (9th Cir.2000); *see* ***Performance Autoplex***, 322 F.3d at 862 (litigants cannot use magistrate judge as mere sounding board for sufficiency of evidence); ***Paterson-Leitch Co. v. Massachusetts Mun. Wholesale Elec. Co.***, 840 F.2d 985, 991 (1st Cir.1988) (litigants cannot use appearance before magistrate judge as dress rehearsal).

(2) No timely objection. If no objection is timely made, the district court should make sure that there is no clear error on the face of the record before accepting the magistrate judge's recommendations. 1983 Notes to FRCP 72 at ¶6, p. 1232, this book. The district court is not required to conduct any kind of review of the magistrate judge's report if there is no objection. ***Thomas v. Arn***, 474 U.S. 140, 150-53 (1985).

(3) District court's order. The district court may accept, reject, or modify the magistrate judge's recommendations or findings in whole or in part. 28 U.S.C. §636(b)(1); FRCP 72(b)(3). The district court is not required to wait a certain period of time before ruling on the objections. ***Habets***, 363 F.3d at 381-82.

§3. REFERRAL OF TRIAL TO MAGISTRATE JUDGE BY CONSENT

§3.1 Scope of authority. A civil action or proceeding, including a jury or nonjury trial, may be referred to a magistrate judge if all parties consent to the magistrate judge's jurisdiction. 28 U.S.C. §636(c)(1); FRCP 73(a); ***Reiter v. Honeywell, Inc.***, 104 F.3d 1071, 1073 (8th Cir.1997); ***Colorado Bldg. & Constr. Trades Council v. B.B.***

Andersen Constr. Co., 879 F.2d 809, 811 (10th Cir.1989). If the parties do not consent, a magistrate judge cannot conduct a trial. *See* 28 U.S.C. §636(c)(1); *see, e.g.*, ***Beazer E., Inc. v. Mead Corp.***, 412 F.3d 429, 437 n.11 (3d Cir. 2005) (equitable-allocation proceeding under CERCLA, 42 U.S.C. §9613(f)(1), constituted a "trial," which magistrate judge could not conduct without consent). Even if the parties consent, a magistrate judge lacks jurisdiction if the district court does not enter an order of reference or special designation. *See, e.g.*, ***Hill v. City of Seven Points***, 230 F.3d 167, 168-69 (5th Cir.2000) (district court had not signed order of reference).

§3.2 Obtaining consent. When a magistrate judge is specifically designated under 28 U.S.C. §636(c)(1), the court clerk must notify the parties of the magistrate judge's availability to exercise jurisdiction over the case. 28 U.S.C. §636(c)(2). For the parties' consent to be proper, the following requirements must be met:

1. Written notice. The court clerk must give all parties written notice of their opportunity to consent to the magistrate judge's exercise of civil jurisdiction over the case. FRCP 73(b)(1); ***New York Chinese TV Programs, Inc. v. U.E. Enters.***, 996 F.2d 21, 23-24 (2d Cir.1993). Many districts send a consent form to the parties when they make an appearance in the case. *E.g.*, Form AO 85, Notice, Consent, and Reference of a Civil Action to a Magistrate Judge, www.uscourts.gov/uscourts/FormsAndFees/Forms/AO085.pdf.

2. All parties consent. All parties to the litigation must consent. ***Reiter v. Honeywell, Inc.***, 104 F.3d 1071, 1073 (8th Cir.1997); ***Caprera v. Jacobs***, 790 F.2d 442, 444-45 (5th Cir.1986). Without the consent of all parties, the magistrate judge cannot render a final, appealable decision. *See* ***New York Chinese TV***, 996 F.2d at 24; ***Fowler v. Jones***, 899 F.2d 1088, 1092 (11th Cir.1990). A district judge or the magistrate judge may be informed of a party's response to the clerk's notice only if all parties have consented to referral. FRCP 73(b)(1).

(1) Clerk to obtain consent. The court clerk must obtain the consent of all the parties. FRCP 73(b)(1); *see* ***Gairola v. Commonwealth Dept. of Gen. Servs.***, 753 F.2d 1281, 1284-85 (4th Cir.1985); 1983 Notes to FRCP 73 at ¶2, p. 1232, this book. An applicant for intervention is not a party for the purpose of consenting to a magistrate judge. ***People Who Care v. Rockford Bd. of Educ.***, 171 F.3d 1083, 1089 (7th Cir.1999).

(2) Implied consent. Consent to trial before a magistrate judge is implied when the party was made aware of the right to trial before a district judge but still voluntarily appeared to try the case before the magistrate judge. ***Roell v. Withrow***, 538 U.S. 580, 590 (2003); *see also* ***Beazer E., Inc. v. Mead Corp.***, 412 F.3d 429, 437 n.11 (3d Cir.2005) (brief lapse in time between district court's order of referral to magistrate judge and D's objection after magistrate judge's scheduling order did not constitute waiver).

3. Signed consent forms. Each party must jointly or separately file a statement consenting to have the magistrate judge conduct the civil action or proceeding. FRCP 73(b)(1); ***New York Chinese TV***, 996 F.2d at 24. *But see* ***Mark I, Inc. v. Gruber***, 38 F.3d 369, 370 (7th Cir.1994) (written consent not required, but consent must be on record and be unequivocal). An attorney may give consent on behalf of a client; a party does not need to consent personally. ***U.S. v. Muhammad***, 165 F.3d 327, 331 (5th Cir.1999).

§3.3 Vacating a referral. The district court may vacate a referral on its own initiative for good cause or when a party shows extraordinary circumstances. 28 U.S.C. §636(c)(4); FRCP 73(b)(3); ***Fulton v. Robinson***, 289 F.3d 188, 199 (2d Cir.2002); *e.g.*, ***Manion v. American Airlines, Inc.***, 251 F.Supp.2d 171, 173 (D.D.C.2003) (magistrate judge's purported bias was not considered to be extraordinary circumstance); *see also* 12 Wright, Miller & Marcus §3071.3 (court should vacate referral only when extraordinary questions of law are at issue and decision is likely to be significant).

§4. APPOINTMENT OF SPECIAL MASTER

In complex cases, courts may seek the assistance of a special master. *See* ***In re Hanford Nuclear Reservation Litig.***, 292 F.3d 1124, 1138 (9th Cir.2002) (court can appoint master and decide extent of duties). A special master is usually a nonjudicial officer who helps courts handle complicated cases more effectively. *See* Willging et al., *Special Masters' Incidence & Activity*, at 40. *But see* 2003 Notes to FRCP 53 at ¶¶13, 14, p. 1219, this book (in special circumstances, magistrate judge may be available for special-master assignments). Although the principal source of

authority for appointing special masters is FRCP 53, some statutes permit appointment as well. *See* FRCP 53(a)(1); 9C Wright & Miller §2607 & n.13; *see, e.g.*, 42 U.S.C. §300aa-12(c) (appointment of special masters under National Vaccine Injury Compensation Program).

§4.1 Types of special masters.

1. Consent master. A consent master is a special master who has been appointed to perform duties consented to by the parties. FRCP 53(a)(1)(A); 2003 Notes to FRCP 53 at ¶4, p. 1218, this book. The parties' consent to appoint a special master is not binding on the district court, which retains discretion to refuse the appointment. 2003 Notes to FRCP 53 at ¶4, p. 1218, this book.

2. Trial master. A trial master is a special master who has been appointed to hold trial proceedings and make or recommend findings of fact in bench trials. FRCP 53(a)(1)(B).

(1) Grounds for appointment. A trial master can be appointed if the appointment is warranted by (1) some exceptional condition or (2) the need to perform an accounting or resolve a difficult computation of damages. FRCP 53(a)(1)(B).

(a) Exceptional condition. FRCP 53 does not define "exceptional condition," but the Supreme Court has stated that calendar congestion, complex issues, and a lengthy trial are not exceptional conditions justifying the appointment of a trial master. ***La Buy v. Howes Leather Co.***, 352 U.S. 249, 259 (1957); *see* 9C Wright & Miller §2605 & nn.18-20; Wald, *'Some Exceptional Condition,'* 62 St. John's L.Rev. at 412; *see also* ***Sierra Club v. Clifford***, 257 F.3d 444, 447 (5th Cir.2001) (voluminous filings and technical subject matter about compliance with regulations are not exceptional condition); ***U.S. v. Microsoft Corp.***, 147 F.3d 935, 956 (D.C.Cir.1998) (reversing referral because no exceptional condition was present).

(b) Accounting or difficult computation. When a trial master is appointed to perform an accounting or assist in computing damages, the appointment is usually made because the determination requires mastery of a great deal of detailed information but does not require extensive determinations of credibility. *See* 2003 Notes to FRCP 53 at ¶6, p. 1219, this book.

(2) Scope of appointment.

(a) Issues decided by jury. A trial master can be appointed to consider matters to be decided by a jury only with the parties' consent. *See* 2003 Notes to FRCP 53 at ¶7, p. 1219, this book. Even if the parties consent, a trial master should be appointed to consider these matters only when the parties waive a jury trial on the issues submitted to the master or when the master's findings will be submitted to the jury as evidence in the manner provided by former FRCP 53(e)(3). *See* 2003 Notes to FRCP 53 at ¶8, p. 1219, this book. Former FRCP 53(e)(3) allowed the master's findings to be read to the jury, subject to the court's ruling on any objections to the findings. *See* FRCP 53(e)(3) (former FRCP 53(e)(3), deleted 2003). A trial master cannot be appointed to preside at a jury trial. 2003 Notes to FRCP 53 at ¶8, p. 1219, this book.

(b) Issues decided by court. A trial master can be appointed to preside over an evidentiary hearing on the merits of the claims or defenses in the case. 2003 Notes to FRCP 53 at ¶9, p. 1219, this book. A trial master can also be appointed to assist the court in discharging trial duties other than conducting an evidentiary hearing. *Id.* at ¶11, p. 1219, this book.

3. Pretrial & post-trial masters. A pretrial master or post-trial master is a special master appointed to handle matters that cannot be effectively and timely addressed by the court. FRCP 53(a)(1)(C); 2003 Notes to FRCP 53 at ¶12, p. 1219, this book. Ordinarily, when a magistrate judge is available, these functions should be referred to a magistrate judge. 2003 Notes to FRCP 53 at ¶13, p. 1219, this book.

(1) Pretrial master. A pretrial master should be appointed only when the need for one is clear. 2003 Notes to FRCP 53 at ¶16, p. 1219, this book. The following are examples of the matters that a pretrial master can be appointed to address:

(a) **Discovery.** A pretrial master can be appointed in complex cases to handle discovery disputes. *See* ***In re Wilson***, 451 F.3d 161, 164 (3d Cir.2006).

(b) **Dispositive motions.** A pretrial master can be appointed to handle dispositive or other motions, including motions to exclude experts. *See* ***Jack Walters & Sons Corp. v. Morton Bldg., Inc.***, 737 F.2d 698, 712-13 (7th Cir.1984) (motion for summary judgment).

(c) **Settlement.** A pretrial master can be appointed to handle settlement negotiations. *See* 9C Wright & Miller §2602; Feinberg, *Creative Use of ADR*, 59 Alb.L.Rev. at 881; *see also* 2003 Notes to FRCP 53 at ¶12, p. 1219, this book (settlement negotiations not suitable for judge).

(d) **Complex issues.** A pretrial master can be appointed to assist the court with complex issues of law, such as interpreting patent claims or making determinations of foreign law. 2003 Notes to FRCP 53 at ¶17, p. 1219, this book. Courts also have authority under FRE 706 to appoint an impartial expert to provide guidance on complex or confusing matters, but such appointments are rare. *See* ***Monolithic Power Sys. v. 02 Micro Int'l***, 558 F.3d 1341, 1346-47 (Fed.Cir.2009); 29 Wright & Gold §6304.

(2) **Post-trial master.** A post-trial master can be appointed to assist the court in handling complex decrees. 2003 Notes to FRCP 53 at ¶18, p. 1220, this book. In certain types of litigation, post-trial masters are useful in formulating remedial orders or supervising compliance with court orders. *See* ***Apex Fountain Sales, Inc. v. Kleinfeld***, 818 F.2d 1089, 1097 (3d Cir.1987) (appointment of master appropriate when implementing court's order would be complex and involve monitoring and detailed enforcement mechanisms); 2003 Notes to FRCP 53 at ¶¶18, 19, p. 1220, this book (same); Brazil, *Special Masters in Complex Cases*, 53 U.Chi.L.Rev. at 414 (master given power to investigate, conduct hearings, find facts, analyze solutions, and draft proposed remedies in form of injunctions).

§4.2 Appointing special master.

1. Notice & hearing. Before the court can appoint a special master, it must give the parties notice and an opportunity to be heard. FRCP 53(b)(1). Any party can suggest candidates for the appointment. *Id.* Unless oral testimony is necessary, the court can consider the parties' arguments by written submission. 2003 Notes to FRCP 53 at ¶24, p. 1220, this book.

2. Motion to appoint special master. The court can appoint a special master on motion of a party, by joint motion, or on its own initiative. The motion should indicate the purpose of and grounds for the appointment. See "Types of special masters," §4.1, p. 303. A party seeking to appoint a special master should also show that the appointment would not create unreasonable expense or delay. FRCP 53(a)(3).

3. Affidavit of special master. Before the court can issue the order appointing a special master, the proposed special master must file an affidavit disclosing whether there are any grounds for disqualification. FRCP 53(b)(3)(A). If grounds for disqualification are disclosed and the parties waive disqualification, the court must approve the waiver. FRCP 53(b)(3)(B).

4. Factors for consideration.

(1) **Use of master limited.** In determining whether to appoint a special master, the court must consider the policy behind FRCP 53: special masters should be appointed only in limited circumstances. 2003 Notes to FRCP 53 at ¶¶1, 3, p. 1218, this book; *see, e.g.*, FRCP 53(a)(1)(B) (court can appoint trial master for trial proceedings only if appointment is warranted by some exceptional condition or need to perform accounting or computation of damages).

(2) **Grounds for disqualification.** In determining whether to appoint a special master, the court must consider whether there are any grounds for disqualifying a proposed special master. *See* 2003 Notes to FRCP 53 at ¶21, p. 1220, this book (careful inquiry into grounds for disqualification should be made at time of appointment). A special master cannot have a relationship to the parties, attorneys, action, or court that would require disqualification of a judge under 28 U.S.C. §455, unless the parties and the court consent after disclosure of the relationship.

FRCP 53(a)(2); *see* 2003 Notes to FRCP 53 at ¶22, p. 1220, this book (disqualification issue arises when master, who is attorney, represents client before judge who appointed attorney as master). The court can make an appointment only after the proposed special master has filed an affidavit disclosing whether there is any ground for disqualification. FRCP 53(b)(3). See "Affidavit of special master," §4.2.3, p. 304.

(3) Expense or delay. In determining whether to appoint a special master, the court must consider the fairness of imposing the likely expense of a master on the parties and protect against unreasonable expense or delay. FRCP 53(a)(3).

5. Order. If the court decides to appoint a special master, the court must enter an order appointing her. *See* FRCP 53(b). The order referring a case to a special master is the source of the special master's duties and powers. ***U.S. v. Clifford Matley Family Trust***, 354 F.3d 1154, 1159 (9th Cir.2004). The initial order appointing a special master must state the following:

(1) Duties. The order must state the special master's duties, including any investigation or enforcement duties, and any limits on the special master's authority under FRCP 53(c). FRCP 53(b)(2)(A). If the order does not limit the special master's authority, the special master can do the following:

(a) Regulate all proceedings and take all appropriate measures to perform the assigned duties fairly and efficiently. FRCP 53(c)(1)(A), (c)(1)(B).

(b) Compel, take, and record evidence. FRCP 53(c)(1)(C).

(c) Impose noncontempt sanctions against a party. FRCP 53(c)(2).

(d) Recommend contempt sanctions against a party. *Id.*

(e) Recommend sanctions against a nonparty. *Id.*

(2) Contact with court & parties.

(a) Ex parte communications. The order must state the circumstances in which the special master may communicate ex parte with the court or the parties. FRCP 53(b)(2)(B). The court may determine whether ex parte communications are permitted or prohibited. *See* ***Texas v. New Mexico***, 485 U.S. 388, 393 (1988) (contact with parties), *amended*, 502 U.S. 903 (1991); ***Edgar v. K.L.***, 93 F.3d 256, 261 (7th Cir.1996) (contact with court); *see also* 2003 Notes to FRCP 53 at ¶¶26, 27, p. 1220, this book (ex parte contact should ordinarily be prohibited).

(b) Appearances before court. The order may prohibit the special master from appearing before the court if the special master is an attorney who represents a client with a case pending before the judge who appointed the attorney as special master. 2003 Notes to FRCP 53 at ¶22, p. 1220, this book.

(3) Time limits. The order must state the time limits for performing the assigned duties and any other relevant procedures. FRCP 53(b)(2)(D); *see* 2003 Notes to FRCP 53 at ¶25, p. 1220, this book.

(4) Filing the record. The order must state the nature of the materials to be preserved and filed as the record of the special master's activities and the method of filing that record. FRCP 53(b)(2)(C), (b)(2)(D); 2003 Notes to FRCP 53 at ¶28, p. 1221, this book. If there is a possibility that the appointment will require the special master to make or recommend evidence-based findings of fact, the order should state that the special master must make and file a complete record of the evidence considered. 2003 Notes to FRCP 53 at ¶28, p. 1221, this book. The parties may seek the court's permission to supplement the record with additional evidence. *Id.* at ¶36, p. 1221, this book.

(5) Standards of review. The order must state the standards of review for the special master's orders, findings, and recommendations. FRCP 53(b)(2)(D). See "Standards of review," §4.3.3(2), p. 306.

(6) Compensation. The order must state how the special master is to be compensated. FRCP 53(b)(2)(E). The special master's compensation "should be liberal, but not exorbitant." ***Newton v. Consolidated Gas Co.***, 259 U.S. 101, 105 (1922). The basis and terms of compensation may be modified by the court after the parties have been given notice and an opportunity to be heard. FRCP 53(g)(1).

(7) Proceed with diligence. The order must direct the special master to proceed with reasonable diligence. FRCP 53(b)(2).

(8) Magistrate judge as special master. A magistrate judge is subject to the requirements of FRCP 53 only when the order of appointment expressly states that the appointment is made under FRCP 53. FRCP 53(h).

6. Amending order of appointment. The order of appointment may be amended after the parties have been given notice and an opportunity to be heard. FRCP 53(b)(4). Unless oral testimony is necessary, the court can consider the parties' arguments by written submission. 2003 Notes to FRCP 53 at ¶32, p. 1221, this book.

§4.3 Special master's orders, reports, or recommendations.

1. Filing & serving. The special master must file in the court and promptly serve the parties with copies of all orders, reports, and recommendations. FRCP 53(d) (orders), FRCP 53(e) (reports); *see* FRCP 53(f)(2) (language of rule suggests recommendations must be served).

2. Party's response.

(1) Objecting. A party may file objections to the special master's order, report, or recommendation. FRCP 53(f)(2). Unless the court sets a different time, the objections must be filed within 21 days after the order, report, or recommendation was served. *Id.*; *see also* ***Wallace v. Skadden, Arps, Slate, Meagher & Flom, LLP***, 362 F.3d 810, 816 n.7 (D.C.Cir.2004) (time limit is not jurisdictional).

(2) Motion to adopt or modify. A party may file a motion to adopt or modify the special master's order, report, or recommendation. FRCP 53(f)(2). Unless the court sets a different time, the objections must be filed within 21 days after the order, report, or recommendation was served. *Id.*

3. Court's action.

(1) Opportunity to be heard. The court cannot act on the special master's order, report, or recommendation unless the parties have been given an opportunity to be heard. FRCP 53(f)(1). Unless oral testimony is necessary, the court can consider the parties' arguments by written submission. 2003 Notes to FRCP 53 at ¶38, p. 1222, this book.

(2) Standards of review.

(a) Factual findings. The court must review de novo all objections to findings of fact made or recommended by the special master, unless the parties stipulated, with the court's approval, that the court would review only for clear error or that the findings of a pretrial, post-trial, or consent master would be final. FRCP 53(f)(3); *see* ***AgGrow Oils, L.L.C. v. National Un. Fire Ins.***, 420 F.3d 751, 753 n.2 (8th Cir.2005); ***Summers v. Howard Univ.***, 374 F.3d 1188, 1195 n.6 (D.C.Cir.2004).

(b) Legal conclusions. The court must review the special master's legal conclusions de novo. FRCP 53(f)(4); ***Wallace***, 362 F.3d at 816-17.

(c) Procedural matters. Unless the order of appointment provided otherwise, the special master's rulings on procedural matters are reviewed only for abuse of discretion. FRCP 53(f)(5).

(3) Action. In acting on the special master's order, report, or recommendation, the court may do any of the following: (1) adopt, (2) affirm, (3) modify, (4) wholly reject or reverse, (5) partly reject or reverse, or (6) resubmit to the special master with instructions. FRCP 53(f)(1).

§4.4 Paying special master. The special master must be paid on the basis and terms stated in the order of appointment. *See* FRCP 53(g)(1).

1. Who pays. The special master's compensation must be paid (1) by a party or parties or (2) from a fund or the subject matter (e.g., property) that is related to the case and within the court's control. FRCP 53(g)(2); *see* 2003 Notes to FRCP 53 at ¶45, p. 1222, this book.

2. Allocating compensation. The special master's compensation must be allocated among the parties. FRCP 53(g)(3). In determining the proper allocation, the court must consider the nature and amount of the controversy, the parties' means, and the extent to which any party is more responsible than the other parties for the reference to a master. *Id.*

§5. APPELLATE REVIEW

§5.1 Magistrate judge.

1. Appealing magistrate judge's exercise of jurisdiction. An appellate court reviews de novo the magistrate judge's exercise of jurisdiction. *E.g.*, ***Anderson v. Woodcreek Venture Ltd.***, 351 F.3d 911, 915 (9th Cir.2003) (case remanded to determine whether party had voluntarily consented to proceed to judgment before magistrate judge). Objections to a magistrate judge's authority are jurisdictional and can be raised at any time, including for the first time on appeal. ***Government of V.I. v. Williams***, 892 F.2d 305, 309-10 (3d Cir.1989).

2. Appealing district court's review of magistrate judge's recommendations or findings. The parties may appeal a judgment entered by the district court that accepted, rejected, or modified, in whole or in part, the magistrate judge's recommendations or findings. *See* ***Guillory v. PPG Indus.***, 434 F.3d 303, 307 (5th Cir.2005); ***Wingerter v. Chester Quarry Co.***, 185 F.3d 657, 661 (7th Cir.1998).

(1) Failure to timely object. Depending on the circuit, the failure to timely object may make the complaining party's appellate burden more onerous.

(a) Waiver of review of findings & conclusions. The First, Second, Fourth, Fifth, Sixth, Seventh, and Tenth Circuits hold that if a party is properly informed of the consequences of failing to object and does not file an objection to both findings of fact and conclusions of law, it waives review by the district court and the court of appeals. ***Douglass v. United Servs. Auto. Ass'n***, 79 F.3d 1415, 1422-23 (5th Cir.1996); ***FDIC v. Hillcrest Assocs.***, 66 F.3d 566, 569 (2d Cir.1995); ***Lorentzen v. Anderson Pest Control***, 64 F.3d 327, 330 (7th Cir.1995); ***Miller v. Currie***, 50 F.3d 373, 380 (6th Cir.1995); ***Henley Drilling Co. v. McGee***, 36 F.3d 143, 150-51 (1st Cir.1994); ***Moore v. U.S.***, 950 F.2d 656, 658-59 (10th Cir.1991); ***U.S. v. Schronce***, 727 F.2d 91, 93-94 (4th Cir.1984).

[1] No appellate review at all. At least three of the circuits listed above (First, Second, and Fourth) have indicated that unless the party objects to the magistrate judge's report, no appellate review is available, even for plain error. *See* ***Hillcrest Assocs.***, 66 F.3d at 569; ***U.S. v. George***, 971 F.2d 1113, 1118 n.7 (4th Cir.1992); ***Park Motor Mart, Inc. v. Ford Motor Co.***, 616 F.2d 603, 604-05 (1st Cir.1980).

[2] Review for plain error. Several circuits review findings of fact and conclusions of law for plain error even if the appellant did not object. Error is plain when it is clear and obvious, affects substantial rights, or seriously affects the fairness, integrity, or public reputation of the judicial proceedings. *See* ***U.S. v. Schultz***, 565 F.3d 1353, 1356-57 (11th Cir.2009); *see also* ***Douglass***, 79 F.3d at 1424-28 (discussing standards used by different circuits).

NOTE

The appellate-waiver rule has been applied with equal force to 28 U.S.C. §636(b)(1)(A) pretrial orders and 28 U.S.C. §636(b)(1)(B) dispositive motions. See ***U.S. v. Brown***, *79 F.3d 1499, 1504 n.4 (7th Cir.1996) (party who does not challenge magistrate judge's pretrial ruling under §636(b)(1)(A) to district court waives right to attack rulings on appeal); see also* ***Simpson v. Lear Astronics Corp.***, *77 F.3d 1170, 1174 & n.1 (9th Cir.1996) (party who does not challenge magistrate judge's nondispositive order to district judge forfeits right to appellate review).*

(b) Waiver of review of findings but not conclusions. The Third, Eighth, Ninth, and Eleventh Circuits hold that a failure to object does not waive a party's right to appeal, but simply limits the scope of appellate review of factual findings to plain error. ***Nara v. Frank***, 488 F.3d 187, 194 (3d Cir.2007); ***Flaten v. Secretary***

of H&HS, 44 F.3d 1453, 1458 (9th Cir.1995); ***Resolution Trust Corp. v. Hallmark Builders, Inc.***, 996 F.2d 1144, 1149 (11th Cir.1993); *see* ***Burgess v. Moore***, 39 F.3d 216, 218 (8th Cir.1994). There is no resulting limit on the right to review legal conclusions accepted by the district court. *See* ***Burgess***, 39 F.3d at 218.

(c) Limited exceptions to waiver of review. The failure to object will not limit a party's right to appeal when (1) a pro se litigant is not informed of the time period for and the consequences of not objecting to findings and recommendations or (2) the interests of justice require review. ***Morales-Fernandez v. INS***, 418 F.3d 1116, 1119 (10th Cir.2005); *see* ***Thomas v. Arn***, 474 U.S. 140, 155 (1985) (court may excuse waiver in interest of justice); ***Small v. Secretary of H&HS***, 892 F.2d 15, 16 (2d Cir.1989) (magistrate's report must notify party of both time limit and effect of failing to object); ***U.S. v. Valencia-Copete***, 792 F.2d 4, 6 (1st Cir.1986) (same); ***Wright v. Collins***, 766 F.2d 841, 846 (4th Cir.1985) (same); *see also* ***Caidor v. Onondaga Cty.***, 517 F.3d 601, 605 (2d Cir.2008) (exception applies only to magistrate's order on dispositive matter). The "interests of justice" analysis is similar to the analysis for plain error. ***Morales-Fernandez***, 418 F.3d at 1120; ***Douglass***, 79 F.3d at 1428. See "Review for plain error," §5.1.2(1)(a)[2], p. 307. Although this exception is an elusive concept, factors that may be considered include the party's effort to comply, the force and plausibility of the explanation for the failure to comply, and the importance of the issues raised. ***Morales-Fernandez***, 418 F.3d at 1119-20.

(2) District court's failure to conduct de novo review. If the appellant can show that the district court did not perform the required de novo review, the district court's order will be reversed and remanded so that the district court can conduct the proper review. ***Hernandez v. Estelle***, 711 F.2d 619, 620 (5th Cir.1983); ***Hill v. Duriron Co.***, 656 F.2d 1208, 1215 (6th Cir.1981).

NOTE

Circuits differ on exactly what de novo review means when challenging a magistrate judge's recommendations. The Fourth Circuit holds that the district court can consider both new evidence and new legal arguments that were not presented to the magistrate judge. ***George****, 971 F.2d at 1118. The Fifth and Ninth Circuits, however, hold that the district court can consider new evidence but not new legal arguments. See* ***U.S. v. Howell****, 231 F.3d 615, 621 (9th Cir.2000);* ***Freeman v. County of Bexar****, 142 F.3d 848, 852-53 (5th Cir.1998).*

3. Appealing magistrate judge's order directly to court of appeals. If the parties consented to allow a magistrate judge to conduct the proceeding and enter judgment, the magistrate judge's order of judgment can be appealed directly to the court of appeals. *See* 28 U.S.C. §636(c)(3); FRCP 73(c); ***Barber v. Shinseki***, 660 F.3d 877, 878-79 (5th Cir.2011). For the purpose of appeal, the magistrate judge's order of judgment is treated like any other district-court judgment. 28 U.S.C. §636(c)(3); FRCP 73(c); 1983 Notes to FRCP 73 at ¶5, p. 1232, this book.

§5.2 Special master.

1. Challenging district court's appointment of special master.

(1) Mandamus. A district court's appointment of a special master can be challenged by mandamus. ***La Buy v. Howes Leather Co.***, 352 U.S. 249, 250-51 (1957); *see, e.g.,* ***U.S. v. Microsoft Corp.***, 147 F.3d 935, 956 (D.C.Cir.1998) (mandamus granted because court had no discretion to impose "surrogate judge" on parties against their will). The district court's decision is reviewed for abuse of discretion. *See* ***Microsoft Corp.***, 147 F.3d at 954; ***Williams v. Lane***, 851 F.2d 867, 884 (7th Cir.1988). The denial of a mandamus petition does not prevent a later appeal. ***Stauble v. Warrob, Inc.***, 977 F.2d 690, 693 (1st Cir.1992); ***Key v. Wise***, 629 F.2d 1049, 1054-55 (5th Cir.1980).

(2) Appeal. A district court's appointment of a special master can be appealed after judgment if the challenging party timely objected to the appointment or sought revocation of the referral. ***Jenkins v. Sterlacci***, 849 F.2d 627, 628 (D.C.Cir.1988); *see* ***Fajardo Shopping Ctr., S.E. v. Sun Alliance Ins. Co.***, 167 F.3d 1, 5-6 (1st Cir.1999). The district court's decision is generally reviewed for abuse of discretion. *See* ***Beazer E., Inc. v. Mead Corp.***, 412 F.3d 429, 440 (3d Cir.2005); ***Reynolds v. McInnes***, 380 F.3d 1303, 1305 n.3 (11th Cir.2004); ***Sierra Club v. Clifford***,

257 F.3d 444, 446 (5th Cir.2001); ***U.S. v. Suquamish Indian Tribe***, 901 F.2d 772, 774 (9th Cir.1990). *But see* ***Stauble***, 977 F.2d at 693 (exercise of court's power to refer cases to masters is question of law and reviewed de novo).

2. Appealing district court's review of special master's recommendations. On appeal, the complaining party must show that the district court abused its discretion in determining that the master's report was or was not clearly erroneous. ***Williams***, 851 F.2d at 884-85.

3. Appealing district court's allowance of fees to special master. On appeal, the complaining party must show that the district court abused its discretion in determining the amount of fees for the special master's compensation. ***Stonesifer v. Swanson***, 146 F.2d 671, 673 (7th Cir.1945).

C. DEMAND FOR JURY TRIAL

§1. GENERAL

§1.1 Rules. FRCP 38, 39; see also U.S. Const. amend. 7.

§1.2 Purpose. The purpose of a jury demand is to invoke the party's right to a jury trial.

§1.3 Forms. ***O'Connor's Federal Civil Forms*** (2012), FORMS 5C.

§1.4 Other references. 9 Wright & Miller, *Federal Practice & Procedure 3d* §§2318-2322 (2008 & Supp.2012); 8 *Moore's Federal Practice 3d* ch. 38 (2012).

§2. DEMAND

§2.1 Procedure. Once a party demands a jury trial under FRCP 38, the action must be designated a jury action, and the trial must be by jury unless the parties stipulate otherwise or there is no federal right to a jury. FRCP 39(a); *see* ***Solis v. County of L.A.***, 514 F.3d 946, 955 (9th Cir.2008). To be entitled to a jury trial as a matter of right, the party must comply with FRCP 38. *See* ***Solis***, 514 F.3d at 955.

1. In writing. The jury demand must be in writing. FRCP 38(b)(1); *see* ***Fuller v. City of Oakland***, 47 F.3d 1522, 1530-31 (9th Cir.1995) (not filing jury demand constitutes waiver). The demand may be included in the plaintiff's complaint, the defendant's answer, or a separate instrument. Merely checking the jury-demand box on the civil cover sheet is not a proper demand for a jury. ***Wall v. National R.R. Passenger Corp.***, 718 F.2d 906, 909 (9th Cir.1983). *But see* ***Wright v. Lewis***, 76 F.3d 57, 59 (2d Cir.1996) (jury demand made on civil cover sheet is sufficient to meet FRCP 38(b) as long as cover sheet is served in timely manner).

> **NOTE**
>
> *Many local rules require the parties to include in the title of the pleading a notation that a jury demand has been made. E.g., Local Rules Ind. (S.D.), Rule 38-1. However, omitting the notation does not waive the party's right to a jury.* ***Partee v. Buch****, 28 F.3d 636, 638 (7th Cir.1994).*

2. Scope of demand. The jury demand should state that the party "demands a trial by jury."

(1) Some issues. The party may demand a jury trial on only some of the issues. FRCP 38(c).

(2) All issues. If the party does not limit its demand to certain issues, there is a presumption that the demand is for a jury trial on all issues. FRCP 38(c).

3. Served on other parties. The party requesting a jury trial must serve a written demand on the other parties within the deadlines in FRCP 38. See "Deadlines," §3, p. 310.

4. Filed with clerk. The party making the demand must file it with the court clerk as required by FRCP 5(d). FRCP 38(b)(2).

5. Waiver.

(1) Failure to file & serve demand. A party waives its right to a jury trial if it does not properly file and serve a jury demand. FRCP 38(d); ***Kletzelman v. Capistrano Unified Sch. Dist.***, 91 F.3d 68, 71 (9th Cir. 1996). Because the jury as fact-finder is important to the judicial system, the courts will carefully scrutinize any waiver. ***Dimick v. Schiedt***, 293 U.S. 474, 486 (1935); ***Garcia-Ayala v. Lederle Parenterals, Inc.***, 212 F.3d 638, 645 (1st Cir.2000); ***Tray-Wrap, Inc. v. Six L's Packing Co.***, 984 F.2d 65, 67-68 (2d Cir.1993); *see* ***California Scents v. Surco Prods.***, 406 F.3d 1102, 1108 (9th Cir.2005) (courts must use every reasonable presumption against waiver of jury demand); ***Jennings v. McCormick***, 154 F.3d 542, 545 (5th Cir.1998) (same). The waiver of the right to a jury before the time to demand a jury has begun must be based on an affirmative representation to the court by the party or its attorney that the matter has been discussed and the party has decided not to exercise its right to a jury trial. ***Heyman v. Kline***, 456 F.2d 123, 129-30 (2d Cir.1972).

(2) Participation in bench trial. A party waives its right to a jury trial by participating, without objection, in a bench trial. ***Fillmore v. Page***, 358 F.3d 496, 503 (7th Cir.2004); ***McAfee v. Martin***, 63 F.3d 436, 437-38 (5th Cir.1995); ***Haynes v. W.C. Caye & Co.***, 52 F.3d 928, 929-30 (11th Cir.1995); *see, e.g.*, ***Bostic v. Goodnight***, 443 F.3d 1044, 1047-48 (8th Cir.2006) (D waived right when D's objection was to potential double recovery and not to bench trial of specific claim); *see also* ***Solis***, 514 F.3d at 955 (waiver by participation is narrow and applies only when party claiming right to jury purposefully participates in bench trial and later asserts it did not consent to bench trial after outcome is unfavorable).

(3) By stipulation. A party may waive its right to a jury trial through either a written stipulation or an oral stipulation on the record. FRCP 39(a)(1).

(4) By contract. A party may contractually waive its right to a jury trial. *See* ***IFC Credit Corp. v. United Bus. & Indus. Fed. Credit Un.***, 512 F.3d 989, 994 (7th Cir.2008); ***Tracinda Corp. v. DaimlerChrysler AG***, 502 F.3d 212, 221 (3d Cir.2007); ***Paracor Fin., Inc. v. General Elec. Capital Corp.***, 96 F.3d 1151, 1166 (9th Cir.1996). But the jury waiver may be invoked only by a party to the contract. ***Paracor Fin.***, 96 F.3d at 1166; *see also* ***Tracinda Corp.***, 502 F.3d at 225 (contractual jury-waiver provision made by corporation applies to its nonsignatory directors and officers as agents of corporation).

6. Withdrawal. A proper demand for a jury trial may be withdrawn only if the parties consent. FRCP 38(d); ***Bennett v. Pippin***, 74 F.3d 578, 586-87 (5th Cir.1996); ***Fuller***, 47 F.3d at 1531. *But see* ***Kramer v. Banc of Am. Sec., LLC***, 355 F.3d 961, 968 (7th Cir.2004) (consent of all parties not required to withdraw demand for jury trial that is not of right under FRCP 39). To withdraw a jury demand, the parties must either file a written stipulation in the court or make an oral stipulation on the record. FRCP 39(a)(1); ***Fuller***, 47 F.3d at 1531.

7. Conversion to bench trial. Once a jury trial has been timely demanded, the court cannot convert it to a bench trial on its own initiative, unless the court finds that there is no federal right to a jury trial on some or all of the issues. *See* FRCP 39(a)(2); ***Fuller***, 47 F.3d at 1533.

§2.2 Other party.

1. Rely on demand. Once one party files a demand for a jury trial, all other parties are entitled to rely on that demand for the issues covered and do not need to file their own demands. ***California Scents v. Surco Prods.***, 406 F.3d 1102, 1106 (9th Cir.2005); ***Bennett v. Pippin***, 74 F.3d 578, 586 (5th Cir.1996). Whether the initial demand covers issues raised by other parties depends on whether the issues involve the same "matrix of facts" and the same general area of dispute. ***California Scents***, 406 F.3d at 1109.

2. Make own demand. If one party demands a jury trial on only some issues, the other party must make its own demand to be entitled to a jury trial on any other issues. FRCP 38(c).

§3. DEADLINES

A party may demand a jury trial by serving a demand anytime after the commencement of the suit, but no later than 14 days after service of the last pleading directed to the issue on which the jury is demanded. FRCP 38(b)(1); *see,*

e.g., ***Irvin v. Airco Carbide***, 837 F.2d 724, 727 (6th Cir.1987) (amended complaint that introduced no new issues did not extend deadline; applying former ten-day deadline). The term "last pleading" in FRCP 38(b) includes pleadings listed in FRCP 7(a): a complaint, an answer to a complaint, an answer to a counterclaim, an answer to a cross-claim, a third-party complaint, an answer to a third-party complaint, and, if necessary, a reply to an answer. ***Burns v. Lawther***, 53 F.3d 1237, 1241 (11th Cir.1995); *see* ***Richardson v. Stanley Works, Inc.***, 597 F.3d 1288, 1297 (Fed.Cir.2010).

§3.1 Most cases. A party's jury demand is timely if it is served within 14 days after the defendant's answer to the complaint. FRCP 38(b)(1).

§3.2 Defendant files counterclaim. A party's jury demand is timely if it is served within 14 days after the plaintiff's answer to a counterclaim. FRCP 38(b)(1).

§3.3 Multiple defendants jointly liable. When there are multiple defendants who are jointly liable, a party's jury demand is timely if it is served within 14 days after the last answer served by any defendant. *See* ***Bentler v. Bank of Am. Nat'l Trust & Sav. Ass'n***, 959 F.2d 138, 141 (9th Cir.1992) (applying former ten-day deadline); ***In re Kaiser Steel Corp.***, 911 F.2d 380, 388 (10th Cir.1990) (same).

§3.4 Amended complaint. A party's jury demand is timely if it is served within 14 days after a defendant's answer to an amended complaint that adds new fact issues. *See* ***Lutz v. Glendale Un. High Sch.***, 403 F.3d 1061, 1066-67 (9th Cir.2005) (applying former ten-day deadline). To revive a party's previously waived right to a jury trial, the amended complaint must add new fact issues. ***Shelton v. Consumer Prods. Safety Comm'n***, 277 F.3d 998, 1011 (8th Cir.2002); ***Communications Maint., Inc. v. Motorola, Inc.***, 761 F.2d 1202, 1208 (7th Cir.1985); ***Guajardo v. Estelle***, 580 F.2d 748, 752-53 (5th Cir.1978). If the amended complaint only adds additional claims based on the same facts as those in the original complaint, the amended complaint does not revive the right to demand a jury. ***Irvin v. Airco Carbide***, 837 F.2d 724, 727 (6th Cir.1987); *e.g.*, ***Westchester Day Sch. v. Village of Mamaroneck***, 504 F.3d 338, 356 (2d Cir.2007) (D's right to demand jury was not revived by amended answer that only asserted new defenses based on same facts as original answer).

§3.5 Second demand. If a party demands a jury trial on only some issues, a second demand by the other party on any other issues must be filed and served within 14 days after service of the first demand, unless the court requires it to be filed earlier. FRCP 38(c).

§3.6 After removal. The deadline for a jury demand in a case removed from state court depends on whether a demand was made in state court and whether state law requires an express demand for a jury trial. *See* FRCP 81(c)(3). See "Jury demand," ch. 4-A, §7.3.5, p. 262.

§4. RIGHT TO JURY TRIAL

The Seventh Amendment to the U.S. Constitution provides that in "suits at common law," the right to trial by jury is preserved. U.S. Const. amend. 7; ***City of Monterey v. Del Monte Dunes at Monterey, Ltd.***, 526 U.S. 687, 708 (1999); *see* FRCP 38(a); *see also* ***Pavey v. Conley***, 544 F.3d 739, 741 (7th Cir.2008) (not every factual issue is triable to jury as matter of right). FRCP 38(a) provides that the right to trial by jury can also be preserved by a federal statute. The following are some circumstances when the parties do and do not have the right to a jury trial.

§4.1 Legal vs. equitable claims.

1. Legal claims. When the issues are legal in nature (e.g., a suit for money damages), the entire suit may be tried to a jury. ***Heyman v. Kline***, 456 F.2d 123, 130 (2d Cir.1972); *see* ***Simplot v. Chevron Pipeline Co.***, 563 F.3d 1102, 1115 (10th Cir.2009). The phrase "suits at common law" in the Seventh Amendment refers to suits in which legal rights, not equitable rights, are to be determined. ***Granfinanciera, S.A. v. Nordberg***, 492 U.S. 33, 41 (1989); ***Cass Cty. Music Co. v. C.H.L.R., Inc.***, 88 F.3d 635, 641 (8th Cir.1996).

2. Equitable claims. If the suit is in equity (e.g., an injunction, mandamus, restitution), there is no right to a jury. ***Curtis v. Loether***, 415 U.S. 189, 192-93 (1974); *see* ***Dexia Crédit Local v. Rogan***, 629 F.3d 612, 625 (7th Cir.2010); ***Vodusek v. Bayliner Mar. Corp.***, 71 F.3d 148, 152-53 (4th Cir.1995).

3. Mixed legal & equitable claims. When an issue of fact is common to both the legal and equitable claims, determination of which issues should be tried to the jury and which should be tried to the court is problematic. *See* ***Ross v. Bernhard***, 396 U.S. 531, 537-38 (1970) (shareholder derivative suits have legal and equitable aspects).

(1) Equity rule. When a case involves both a jury and a bench trial, any essential factual issues that are central to both the legal and equitable claims must be first tried to the jury so the litigants' Seventh Amendment jury-trial rights are not foreclosed on common factual issues. ***Ross***, 396 U.S. at 537-38; ***Shum v. Intel Corp.***, 499 F.3d 1272, 1276-77 (Fed.Cir.2007); ***Tidwell v. Fort Howard Corp.***, 989 F.2d 406, 412 (10th Cir.1993); *see* ***Pavey v. Conley***, 544 F.3d 739, 742 (7th Cir.2008). The jury's factual findings on common issues will be binding on the district court if equitable relief is granted. ***Lebow v. American Trans Air, Inc.***, 86 F.3d 661, 672 (7th Cir.1996).

(2) Admiralty rule. When a suit arises out of a single accident involving legal and admiralty claims, both claims may be decided by the jury. ***Ghotra v. Bandila Shipping, Inc.***, 113 F.3d 1050, 1057 (9th Cir.1997); *see* ***Fitzgerald v. U.S. Lines Co.***, 374 U.S. 16, 18-20 (1963). *But see* ***St. Paul Fire & Mar. Ins. v. Lago Canyon, Inc.***, 561 F.3d 1181, 1188 (11th Cir.2009) (when P asserts both admiralty and diversity jurisdiction in same complaint, complaint constitutes choice to proceed in admiralty alone without jury); ***Durden v. Exxon Corp.***, 803 F.2d 845, 848-49 (5th Cir.1986) (same).

§4.2 Statutory rights. Legal rights created by statute may give the parties a right to a jury trial if Congress specifically provided for that right when enacting the statute. *See* ***Cass Cty. Music Co. v. C.H.L.R., Inc.***, 88 F.3d 635, 640-41 (8th Cir.1996); *see, e.g.*, 42 U.S.C. §1981a(c)(1) (providing right to jury in employment-discrimination cases); 46 U.S.C. §30104 (providing right to jury for seamen in Jones Act cases). If the statute does not imply a congressional intent to grant the parties the right to a jury trial, the court must decide whether a jury trial is constitutionally required under the Seventh Amendment. *See* ***City of Monterey v. Del Monte Dunes at Monterey, Ltd.***, 526 U.S. 687, 707 (1999); ***Chauffeurs, Teamsters & Helpers v. Terry***, 494 U.S. 558, 564 n.3 (1990). A jury trial is available if the court finds that the cause of action was, or is analogous to, an issue tried at law in England in 1791, when the Seventh Amendment was adopted. ***Terry***, 494 U.S. at 565; ***Granfinanciera, S.A. v. Nordberg***, 492 U.S. 33, 42 (1989); ***Entergy Ark., Inc. v. Nebraska***, 358 F.3d 528, 541 (8th Cir.2004); ***In re Air Crash Disaster Near Roselawn***, 96 F.3d 932, 943 (7th Cir.1996). To determine whether a statutory action is more analogous to cases tried at law than at equity, the court must examine the nature of both the action and the remedy sought. ***Tull v. U.S.***, 481 U.S. 412, 417 (1987). Characterizing the relief sought is more important than finding a precisely analogous common-law cause of action. ***Id.*** at 421; ***Spinelli v. Gaughan***, 12 F.3d 853, 855 (9th Cir.1993).

1. Nature of action. The court must compare modern and 18th-century law and practices when deciding whether issues were historically determined by the court or the jury. ***Markman v. Westview Instrs., Inc.***, 517 U.S. 370, 376-77 (1996); *see* ***City of Monterey***, 526 U.S. at 708 (comparing suit for legal relief under 42 U.S.C. §1983 with common-law tort claims); ***Terry***, 494 U.S. at 567-69 (comparing violations of duty of fair representation under Labor Management Relations Act to claim for breach of fiduciary duty and attorney malpractice); ***Tull***, 481 U.S. at 422 (comparing government's suit under Clean Water Act to action in debt); ***Lebow v. American Trans Air, Inc.***, 86 F.3d 661, 668-69 (7th Cir.1996) (comparing P's unlawful-discharge claim under federal statute with common-law breach-of-contract claim).

2. Nature of remedy. If the cause of action can be characterized as an action at law, the court must then determine whether the particular remedy sought is legal or equitable in nature. ***Tull***, 481 U.S. at 424-25; ***Curtis v. Loether***, 415 U.S. 189, 195-96 (1974). For example, money damages generally are considered a legal remedy, but remedies intended to provide restitutionary relief or restore the status quo are considered equitable. *See* ***City of Monterey***, 526 U.S. at 710; ***Tull***, 481 U.S. at 422.

§4.3 Suits involving United States.

1. Suit against United States. Generally, there is no right to a jury trial in a suit against the federal government or its officers in their official capacities. ***Wilson v. Big Sandy Health Care, Inc.***, 576 F.3d 329, 333 (6th Cir.2009); *see* ***Lehman v. Nakshian***, 453 U.S. 156, 160 (1981); ***Crawford v. Runyon***, 79 F.3d 743, 744 (8th Cir.

1996). However, a jury trial in a suit against the United States is required if a statute provides for one expressly or by fair implication. ***Austin v. Shalala***, 994 F.2d 1170, 1175 (5th Cir.1993); *see* ***Wilson***, 576 F.3d at 333.

2. Suit brought by United States. If the United States brings the suit, the right to a jury trial is determined in the same manner as if the suit were between private parties. ***Austin***, 994 F.2d at 1175.

§4.4 Bankruptcy matters.

1. Core & noncore proceedings. Generally, a bankruptcy court can hold a jury trial on a core proceeding if it is designated by the district court to conduct jury trials and has the consent of all parties; a bankruptcy court cannot hold a jury trial on a noncore proceeding. *See* 28 U.S.C. §157(e); 17 Wright, Miller, Cooper & Amar, *Federal Practice & Procedure 3d* §4106 (2007 & Supp.2012). Proceedings "arising under" the bankruptcy laws are considered core, and proceedings "related to" the bankruptcy laws are considered noncore. ***Herrans v. Mender***, 364 B.R. 463, 468 (Bankr.D.P.R.2007), *aff'd sub nom.* ***In re Barroso-Herrans***, 524 F.3d 341 (1st Cir.2008); *see* ***In re OCA, Inc.***, 551 F.3d 359, 367 (5th Cir.2008); ***In re Methyl Tertiary Butyl Ether Prods. Liab. Litig.***, 522 F.Supp.2d 557, 560 (S.D.N.Y.2007); *see also* 28 U.S.C. §157(b)(2) (nonexhaustive list of core proceedings). The Seventh Amendment's Reexamination Clause—"no fact tried by a jury, shall be otherwise re-examined in any Court of the United States, than according to the rules of the common law"—prohibits jury trials in bankruptcy courts for noncore proceedings because of the district court's de novo review of these proceedings. ***In re Orion Pictures Corp.***, 4 F.3d 1095, 1101 (2d Cir.1993).

2. Claim adjustments. A creditor brings itself within the equitable jurisdiction of the bankruptcy court by submitting claims against the estate, so it is not entitled to a jury trial on any issue that can be characterized as a claim adjustment. ***Langenkamp v. Culp***, 498 U.S. 42, 44-45 (1990).

3. Adversary proceedings. The Seventh Amendment does not confer a right to a jury trial to a debtor who voluntarily files for bankruptcy and then becomes a defendant in an adversary proceeding. ***In re McLaren***, 3 F.3d 958, 960 (6th Cir.1993).

4. Dischargeability. There is no constitutional right to a jury trial on the issue of dischargeability itself; the only issues that may be tried to a jury are factual issues related to the question of dischargeability. ***In re Maurice***, 21 F.3d 767, 773 (7th Cir.1994).

§4.5 Limitations on right to jury. In some situations, the courts and Congress have limited the right to a trial by jury.

1. Public-rights doctrine. The Seventh Amendment does not entitle the litigant to a jury trial if (1) the statutory claim asserts a "public right" and (2) Congress assigns the adjudication of the claim to a non-Article 3 court (e.g., Tax Court, Court of Federal Claims). ***Granfinanciera, S.A. v. Nordberg***, 492 U.S. 33, 42 n.4 (1989). The Seventh Amendment protects a litigant's right to a jury trial only if a claim is legal in nature and involves a matter of "private right." ***Granfinanciera***, 492 U.S. at 42 n.4. Under the public-rights doctrine, there is no right to a jury trial for statutory claims (1) closely integrated into a public regulatory scheme enacted by Congress and (2) involving a right that neither belongs to nor exists against the federal government. *See id.* at 54.

2. Complex case. One court has said the Seventh Amendment does not guarantee the right to a jury if the lawsuit is too complex for the jury to make rational decisions and a jury trial would thus deprive the parties of their Fifth Amendment right to due process. *See* ***In re Japanese Elec. Prods. Antitrust Litig.***, 631 F.2d 1069, 1084-86 (3d Cir.1980). Other courts have refused to make an exception for complex cases. *See, e.g.*, ***Green Constr. Co. v. Kansas Power & Light Co.***, 1 F.3d 1005, 1011 (10th Cir.1993) (court denied motion to strike jury demand, rejecting argument that lawsuit would be too confusing for jury).

3. Damages. If the plaintiff seeks common-law damages in a suit brought under a federal statute, the plaintiff has a right to a jury trial if Congress has provided for it. *See, e.g.*, ***Townsend v. Indiana Univ.***, 995 F.2d 691, 693-94 (7th Cir.1993) (right to jury in Title VII action). However, a party does not have a constitutional right to a jury trial when Congress has delegated to the district court the responsibility for determining the amount of the plaintiff's damages. ***Tull v. U.S.***, 481 U.S. 412, 425-27 (1987).

§5. MOTION TO STRIKE JURY DEMAND

If an improper jury demand is made, the objecting party should file a motion to strike the demand. *See* ***Akin v. PAFEC Ltd.***, 991 F.2d 1550, 1555 (11th Cir.1993).

§5.1 Form. For the general requirements for the form of a motion, see "Drafting motions," ch. 1-B, §3.1, p. 14.

§5.2 Sua sponte. The court may strike the jury demand on its own initiative if it finds that there is no federal right to a jury trial on some or all of the issues. FRCP 39(a)(2).

§5.3 Deadline. A motion to strike can be made anytime before trial. *See* ***Jones-Hailey v. Corporation of the Tenn. Valley Auth.***, 660 F.Supp. 551, 553 (E.D.Tenn.1987).

§5.4 Grounds. A party should include the grounds for its objection in a motion to strike a jury demand. The motion can include the following procedural and substantive grounds:

1. The demand was made too late. *See* FRCP 38(b)(1) (14-day deadline); ***Irvin v. Airco Carbide***, 837 F.2d 724, 727 (6th Cir.1987) (jury demand must be made within deadline; applying former ten-day deadline); ***Blau v. Del Monte Corp.***, 748 F.2d 1348, 1357 (9th Cir.1984) (same). See "Deadlines," §3, p. 310. The movant should identify the date of the deadline and the date of the demand.

2. The demand was not served on the parties or filed with the clerk as required by FRCP 38(b).

3. There is no federal right to a jury trial in the case. FRCP 39(a)(2); *see, e.g.*, ***Sullivan v. LTV Aerospace & Def. Co.***, 82 F.3d 1251, 1257-58 (2d Cir.1996) (no right to jury for ERISA claim); ***SEC v. Rind***, 991 F.2d 1486, 1493 (9th Cir.1993) (Securities Act did not include right to jury). See "Statutory rights," §4.2, p. 312.

4. The party's plea for damages is actually a plea for restitution or other equitable remedies. *See* ***U.S. v. Balistrieri***, 981 F.2d 916, 927-28 (7th Cir.1992).

5. The parties consented to a bench trial by a written stipulation filed in the court or an oral stipulation on the record. FRCP 39(a)(1); *see* ***Sewell v. Jefferson Cty. Fiscal Ct.***, 863 F.2d 461, 464-65 (6th Cir.1988).

6. The right to a jury trial was waived by contract between the parties. *See* ***Tracinda Corp. v. Daimler-Chrysler AG***, 502 F.3d 212, 221 (3d Cir.2007); *see, e.g.*, ***IFC Credit Corp. v. United Bus. & Indus. Fed. Credit Un.***, 512 F.3d 989, 994 (7th Cir.2008) (lease agreement waiving jury trial and providing for bench trial was enforceable without additional evidence supporting waiver clause).

§5.5 Proposed order. Some districts require the movant to submit a proposed order with the motion. In those districts, the movant should prepare a written order for the court's signature and submit it with the motion. See "Proposed order," ch. 1-B, §3.1.11, p. 16.

§6. MOTION FOR JURY TRIAL

Even if a party did not make a timely jury demand under FRCP 38(b), it can still file and serve a motion for jury trial on any or all issues. FRCP 39(b); ***Kletzelman v. Capistrano Unified Sch. Dist.***, 91 F.3d 68, 71 (9th Cir.1996). The party requesting a jury trial under FRCP 39(b) should explain why it did not timely demand one under FRCP 38(b). ***Parrott v. Wilson***, 707 F.2d 1262, 1267-68 (11th Cir.1983); *see* ***Blau v. Del Monte Corp.***, 748 F.2d 1348, 1357 (9th Cir.1984).

§6.1 Form. For the general requirements for the form of a motion, see "Drafting motions," ch. 1-B, §3.1, p. 14.

§6.2 Deadline. FRCP 39(b) does not set a deadline for a motion for jury trial. The motion can be made anytime after the FRCP 38(b)(1) deadline has passed. *See* ***Pierce v. Underwood***, 487 U.S. 552, 562 (1988); ***Daniel Int'l v. Fischbach & Moore, Inc.***, 916 F.2d 1061, 1064 (5th Cir.1990).

§6.3 Grounds. In its motion, the party should allege the following:

1. The case involves issues that are best tried to a jury. ***Parrott v. Wilson***, 707 F.2d 1262, 1267 (11th Cir. 1983).

2. Granting the motion will not result in a disruption of the court's or adverse party's schedule. *Id.*

3. Granting the motion will not prejudice the adverse party. ***Rowlett v. Anheuser-Busch, Inc.***, 832 F.2d 194, 200 (1st Cir.1987); ***Parrott***, 707 F.2d at 1267.

4. Granting the motion will not result in a delay of the trial. ***Rowlett***, 832 F.2d at 200; *see* ***Daniel Int'l v. Fischbach & Moore, Inc.***, 916 F.2d 1061, 1064 (5th Cir.1990); ***Parrott***, 707 F.2d at 1267.

5. The adverse party has not been unfairly surprised. ***Rowlett***, 832 F.2d at 200.

6. The failure to make a timely demand under FRCP 38 was the result of an honest mistake. ***Pawlak v. Metropolitan Life Ins.***, 87 F.R.D. 717, 719 n.3 (D.Mass.1980); 9 Wright & Miller §2334; *see* ***SEC v. Infinity Grp.***, 212 F.3d 180, 195 (3d Cir.2000); ***Kletzelman v. Capistrano Unified Sch. Dist.***, 91 F.3d 68, 71 (9th Cir.1996).

§6.4 Standard. The standard for granting an untimely motion for jury trial varies widely. In the Fifth Circuit, district courts are directed to grant a jury trial in the absence of "strong and compelling reasons to the contrary." ***Daniel Int'l v. Fischbach & Moore, Inc.***, 916 F.2d 1061, 1064 (5th Cir.1990). A motion for trial by jury "should be favorably received unless there are persuasive reasons to deny it." *Id.*; *see* 9 Wright & Miller §2334 ("technical insistence upon imposing a penalty for failing to follow the demand procedure by denying a jury trial is not in the spirit of the Federal Rules"). In other circuits, however, the standard is much stricter, and many courts hold that the motion should not be granted unless there are special circumstances excusing the oversight or default. *See* ***Pacific Fisheries Corp. v. HIH Cas. & Gen. Ins.***, 239 F.3d 1000, 1002 (9th Cir.2001) (some cause beyond mere inadvertence or oversight must be shown); ***General Tire & Rubber Co. v. Watkins***, 331 F.2d 192, 197 (4th Cir.1964) (exceptional circumstances must be shown). The court should approach each application for relief from waiver under FRCP 39 "with an open mind and an eye to the factual situation of the particular case, rather than with a fixed policy." ***Members v. Paige***, 140 F.3d 699, 703 (7th Cir.1998).

§6.5 Proposed order. Some districts require the movant to submit a proposed order with the motion. In those districts, the movant should prepare a written order for the court's signature and submit it with the motion. See "Proposed order," ch. 1-B, §3.1.11, p. 16.

§7. MOTION FOR TRIAL BY ADVISORY JURY

§7.1 Motion. In a case in which the plaintiff does not have the right to a jury trial (e.g., an equitable suit), the court may try any issue with an advisory jury. FRCP 39(c)(1); ***Alexander v. Gerhardt Enters.***, 40 F.3d 187, 192 (7th Cir.1994). The court can submit an issue to an advisory jury on its own initiative or on a party's motion. FRCP 39(c)(1). If an advisory jury is empaneled, the court is not bound by the advisory verdict. ***Goodgame v. American Cast Iron Pipe Co.***, 75 F.3d 1516, 1520 (11th Cir.1996); *see also* ***DeFelice v. American Int'l Life Assur. Co.***, 112 F.3d 61, 65 (2d Cir.1997) (district court retains ultimate responsibility for findings of fact and conclusions of law).

§7.2 Form. For the general requirements for the form of a motion, see "Drafting motions," ch. 1-B, §3.1, p. 14.

§7.3 Grounds. The motion for a trial by advisory jury should allege the following grounds:

1. The party does not have a constitutional right to a jury trial on one or more of its claims. ***Gragg v. City of Omaha***, 20 F.3d 357, 358 (8th Cir.1994).

2. The empaneling of an advisory jury would be helpful to the court and would serve the interests of justice. ***Cudmore v. Smith***, 260 F.Supp. 760, 760 (D.Conn.1966).

§7.4 Proposed order. Some districts require the movant to submit a proposed order with the motion. In those districts, the movant should prepare a written order for the court's signature and submit it with the motion. See "Proposed order," ch. 1-B, §3.1.11, p. 16.

§7.5 Notice. The court should notify the parties in advance that it will treat the jury as advisory. ***Merex A.G. v. Fairchild Weston Sys.***, 29 F.3d 821, 827 (2d Cir.1994); ***Thompson v. Parkes***, 963 F.2d 885, 889 (6th Cir.1992). The court abuses its discretion if it declares the jury advisory only after the jury has returned its verdict. ***Thompson***, 963 F.2d at 890.

CIRCUIT SPLIT

Several circuits hold that the district court's failure to provide notice to treat the jury as advisory is reversible error because the parties might have engaged in a different trial strategy if they had known of the jury's merely advisory role. See ***Thompson****, 963 F.2d at 888;* ***Bereda v. Pickering Creek Indus. Park, Inc.****, 865 F.2d 49, 53 (3d Cir.1989);* ***Pradier v. Elespuru****, 641 F.2d 808, 811 (9th Cir.1981). At least two circuits, however, hold that the lack of notice is reversible error only if the complaining party shows demonstrable prejudice.* ***Ed Peters Jewelry Co. v. C&J Jewelry Co.****, 215 F.3d 182, 188 (1st Cir.2000);* ***Merex****, 29 F.3d at 827.*

§7.6 Verdict. The court is free to accept or reject the jury's advisory verdict in making its findings. ***Goodgame v. American Cast Iron Pipe Co.***, 75 F.3d 1516, 1520 (11th Cir.1996); *see also* ***Sullivan v. LTV Aerospace & Def. Co.***, 82 F.3d 1251, 1261 (2d Cir.1996) (court adopted findings but made no explanation of how it arrived at them). In rejecting the advisory verdict, the court should enter its own contrary findings under FRCP 52(a). *See* ***Dilley v. Super-Valu, Inc.***, 296 F.3d 958, 965-66 (10th Cir.2002); ***Gragg v. City of Omaha***, 20 F.3d 357, 358-59 (8th Cir.1994).

§8. APPELLATE REVIEW

§8.1 Court denies jury demand under FRCP 38. The right to a jury trial is a question of law reviewed de novo. ***Richardson v. Stanley Works, Inc.***, 597 F.3d 1288, 1296 (Fed.Cir.2010); ***Entergy Ark., Inc. v. Nebraska***, 358 F.3d 528, 540 (8th Cir.2004); ***Mile High Indus. v. Cohen***, 222 F.3d 845, 855 (10th Cir.2000). If the district court erroneously refuses to grant a jury trial under FRCP 38, the error is harmful unless no reasonable jury could have found for the losing party. ***California Scents v. Surco Prods.***, 406 F.3d 1102, 1109 (9th Cir.2005); *see* ***Burns v. Lawther***, 53 F.3d 1237, 1241-42 (11th Cir.1995); ***Partee v. Buch***, 28 F.3d 636, 639 (7th Cir.1994). Mandamus is available to correct the improper denial of a jury trial. ***Dairy Queen, Inc. v. Wood***, 369 U.S. 469, 472 (1962); *see* ***Wilmington Trust v. U.S. Dist. Ct. for the Dist. of Haw.***, 934 F.2d 1026, 1028 (9th Cir.1991) (mandamus proper even if no "clear and indisputable right" shown); ***First Nat'l Bank v. Warren***, 796 F.2d 999, 1006 (7th Cir.1986) (normal mandamus standards must be met).

§8.2 Court grants or denies motion for jury under FRCP 39. The court of appeals reviews the grant or denial of an FRCP 39(b) motion for abuse of discretion. ***Richardson v. Stanley Works, Inc.***, 597 F.3d 1288, 1297 (Fed. Cir.2010); ***Mile High Indus. v. Cohen***, 222 F.3d 845, 855 n.8 (10th Cir.2000); ***SEC v. Infinity Grp.***, 212 F.3d 180, 195 (3d Cir.2000). However, given the fundamental right to a jury in the Seventh Amendment, at least one circuit holds that the review is somewhat less deferential. ***Daniel Int'l v. Fischbach & Moore, Inc.***, 916 F.2d 1061, 1064 (5th Cir.1990).

§8.3 Court rejects advisory jury's verdict. If the case was tried to an advisory jury and the district court rejected the jury's verdict, the court of appeals will review the district court's contrary findings for clear error, as if there had been no jury. ***EEOC v. Clear Lake Dodge***, 60 F.3d 1146, 1151 (5th Cir.1995). *But see* ***Goodgame v. American Cast Iron Pipe Co.***, 75 F.3d 1516, 1520 (11th Cir.1996) (court of appeals reviews district court's application of FRCP 39(c) de novo). See "Standard of review," ch. 10-E, §8.3, p. 803.

D. OFFER OF JUDGMENT

§1. GENERAL

§1.1 Rule. FRCP 68.

§1.2 Purpose. The purpose of an offer of judgment is to encourage the party asserting a claim (usually the plaintiff) to settle the case when the party defending it (usually the defendant) makes a reasonable offer. ***Marek v. Chesny***, 473 U.S. 1, 10-11 (1985); ***Payne v. Milwaukee Cty.***, 288 F.3d 1021, 1024 (7th Cir.2002); ***Louisiana Power & Light Co. v. Kellstrom***, 50 F.3d 319, 333 (5th Cir.1995); *see also* **Association of Disabled Americans v. Neptune Designs, Inc.**, 469 F.3d 1357, 1360 n.4 (11th Cir.2006) (FRCP 68 is designed to "discourage litigiousness and unnecessarily prolonged litigation"). When the defendant makes an offer of judgment, the plaintiff runs the risk of being taxed for costs if it refuses the offer and that offer later proves to be more favorable than the final judgment. FRCP 68(d); ***King v. Rivas***, 555 F.3d 14, 15 (1st Cir.2009); ***Herrington v. County of Sonoma***, 12 F.3d 901, 907 (9th Cir. 1993).

§1.3 Forms. *O'Connor's Federal Civil Forms* (2012), FORMS 5D.

§1.4 Other references. 12 Wright, Miller & Marcus, *Federal Practice & Procedure 2d* §§3001-3007 (1997 & Supp.2012); 15A Wright, Miller & Cooper, *Federal Practice & Procedure 2d* §3902 (1992 & Supp.2012); 13 *Moore's Federal Practice 3d* ch. 68 (2012); Bone, *"To Encourage Settlement": Rule 68, Offers of Judgment, and the History of the Federal Rules of Civil Procedure*, 102 Nw.U.L.Rev. 1561 (2008).

§2. OFFER

§2.1 In writing. The offer must be in writing. *See* FRCP 68(a); ***Clark v. Sims***, 28 F.3d 420, 424 (4th Cir.1994). Settlement proposals merely discussed between the parties do not meet the requirements of FRCP 68. ***Clark***, 28 F.3d at 424.

§2.2 Served on all parties. The offer of judgment must be served on every party to the litigation, and service must be in accordance with FRCP 5(b). *See* FRCP 68(a); ***Clark v. Sims***, 28 F.3d 420, 424 (4th Cir.1994); 12 Wright, Miller & Marcus §3002 & n.9. See "Serving Documents," ch. 1-D, p. 29.

PRACTICE TIP

The offer should be served separately from other documents—it should not be buried among pleadings or motions. See, e.g., ***U.S. v. Jim Cooley Constr., Inc.***, *572 F.Supp.2d 1276, 1280 (D. N.M.2008) (offer was void because it was served ambiguously on P when D attached it to another document).*

---

§2.3 Not filed. Generally, the offer should not be filed. *See* FRCP 68(a); ***Berberena-Garcia v. Aviles***, 258 F.R.D. 39, 40 (D.P.R.2009). The offer should be filed only if it is (1) accepted or (2) used by the offering party to later prove costs; if the offer is improperly filed, the court should strike it. *See* FRCP 68(a); ***Berberena-Garcia***, 258 F.R.D. at 40; 12 Wright, Miller & Marcus §3002 & nn.10-11.

§2.4 Unconditional. The offer of judgment must be unconditional. ***Herrington v. County of Sonoma***, 12 F.3d 901, 907 (9th Cir.1993). *But see* ***Lang v. Gates***, 36 F.3d 73, 75 (9th Cir.1994) (offer conditioned on joint acceptance by all Ps is proper under FRCP 68).

§2.5 Deadline.

1. **After suit commenced.** An offer of judgment must be made after the suit has been commenced. ***Clark v. Sims***, 28 F.3d 420, 424 (4th Cir.1994).

2. **Before trial.** An offer of judgment may be made anytime until 14 days before the date set for trial. FRCP 68(a); *see* 2009 Notes to FRCP 68 at ¶1, p. 1231, this book. For a discussion of how to compute backward-counted deadlines, see "Computing Deadlines," ch. 1-C, §6, p. 23.

NOTE

When a trial date is reset, a new 14-day deadline for serving an offer is triggered. See 2009 Notes to FRCP 68 at ¶¶1, 2, p. 1231, this book. The same occurs if a hearing for determining liability is reset. See id. at ¶1. See "After liability determined," §2.5.4, this page.

3. Second offer. A second offer of judgment may be made even if an earlier one was rejected. FRCP 68(b).

4. After liability determined. The defendant may make an offer of judgment after it has been found liable but before the hearing to determine the amount or extent of liability. FRCP 68(c); ***Guerrero v. Cummings***, 70 F.3d 1111, 1114 (9th Cir.1995). The defendant has until 14 days before the date set for the hearing to make the offer. FRCP 68(c). See "Before trial," §2.5.2, p. 317. For a discussion of how to compute backward-counted deadlines, see "Computing Deadlines," ch. 1-C, §6, p. 23.

§2.6 Amount of offer. The offer must specify either a definite sum for which judgment can be entered or a particular action to be completed. *See* ***Clark v. Sims***, 28 F.3d 420, 423-24 (4th Cir.1994); ***Herrington v. County of Sonoma***, 12 F.3d 901, 907 (9th Cir.1993); *see, e.g.*, ***Basha v. Mitsubishi Motor Credit***, 336 F.3d 451, 454-55 (5th Cir. 2003) (offer was invalid when it purported to settle all claims but did not quantify damages); *see also* ***Garrity v. Sununu***, 752 F.2d 727, 731 (1st Cir.1984) (questioning whether FRCP 68 applies to cases involving complex injunctive remedies). When determining the amount of the offer, the defendant may consider an amount that provides the plaintiff with an incentive to end the litigation rather than risk incurring the defendant's costs. *See* ***Payne v. Milwaukee Cty.***, 288 F.3d 1021, 1024 (7th Cir.2002). A party should consider the following when determining the amount of the offer:

1. Accrued costs. The offer should provide for "costs now accrued." ***Grissom v. Mills Corp.***, 549 F.3d 313, 319 (4th Cir.2008); ***Utility Automation 2000, Inc. v. Choctawhatchee Elec. Coop.***, 298 F.3d 1238, 1241 (11th Cir.2002); *see* ***Thompson v. Southern Farm Bur. Cas. Ins.***, 520 F.3d 902, 904 (8th Cir.2008). This phrase limits costs to those that accrued before the offer. ***Holland v. Roeser***, 37 F.3d 501, 504 & n.1 (9th Cir.1994). Although an offer can include the accrued costs as part of a lump-sum amount, the offer cannot explicitly exclude costs. ***Marek v. Chesny***, 473 U.S. 1, 6 (1985); ***Thompson***, 520 F.3d at 904; ***Utility Automation 2000***, 298 F.3d at 1241.

2. Attorney fees. The offer should state clearly that attorney fees are included as part of the total sum for which judgment can be entered if the underlying statute or other relevant authority does not define costs to include attorney fees. *See* ***Utility Automation 2000***, 298 F.3d at 1243. If the underlying statute or other relevant authority defines costs to include attorney fees, the attorney fees are included as costs under FRCP 68; thus, the phrase "costs now accrued" would limit the attorney fees to those that accrued before the offer. *See* ***Utility Automation 2000***, 298 F.3d at 1243-44; ***Holland***, 37 F.3d at 503-04 & n.1. See "Accrued costs," §2.6.1, this page. But if the offer provides for "costs now accrued and reasonable attorney fees as determined by the court," the offer may be construed to include attorney fees not yet accrued at the time of the offer. *See, e.g.*, ***Holland***, 37 F.3d at 504 (D was liable for attorney fees after offer, which were necessary to prepare post-offer petition for attorney fees).

CAUTION

Because offers of judgment are essentially offers to enter into a contract, courts apply general contract principles to interpret them. See ***Basha****, 336 F.3d at 453;* ***Hennessy v. Daniels Law Office****, 270 F.3d 551, 553 (8th Cir.2001). One general contract principle is that ambiguous terms are construed against the offeror.* ***Hennessy****, 270 F.3d at 553-54. Therefore, to avoid fees in addition to the offer, an offer of judgment should make it clear that attorney fees are included as part of the total sum for which judgment can be entered. See* ***Nusom v. Comh Woodburn, Inc.****, 122 F.3d 830, 834 (9th Cir.1997); see, e.g.,* ***Garcia v. Oasis Legal Fin. Oper. Co.****, 608 F.Supp.2d 975, 978-79 (N.D.Ill.2009) (P was awarded attorney fees in addition to offer of judgment when*

*offer was silent on fees and did not include language that it was covering P's entire relief requested); see also **Lima v. Newark Police Dept.**, 658 F.3d 324, 330 (3d Cir.2011) (when offer is silent on attorney fees and costs, extrinsic evidence is not admissible to determine whether offer includes fees and costs; district court erred when it denied fees and costs based on Ds' e-mail and affidavits stating their intent to include fees and costs in offer).*

§2.7 Revoking offer. Once the defendant makes an offer of judgment, the plaintiff has 14 days to consider it. FRCP 68(a). During that 14-day period, the offer of judgment is generally not revocable. *See* ***Webb v. James***, 147 F.3d 617, 620-21 (7th Cir.1998) (applying former ten-day period); ***Richardson v. National R.R. Passenger Corp.***, 49 F.3d 760, 765 (D.C.Cir.1995) (same). However, some courts have held that an offer can be revoked in exceptional circumstances, such as fraud or mistake. *See* ***Colonial Penn Ins. v. Coil***, 887 F.2d 1236, 1240 (4th Cir.1989) (offer can be revoked when procured by fraud); ***Cesar v. Rubie's Costume Co.***, 219 F.R.D. 257, 259-60 (E.D.N.Y.2004) (offer can be revoked under general contract principles when mistake is made); *see, e.g.*, ***Hawkins v. Johnston Mem'l Hosp., Inc.***, 267 F.R.D. 483, 485-86 (W.D.Va.2010) (D was allowed to withdraw offer when P did not disclose that he was receiving pain medication from four doctors and D had relied on P's representation that he received pain medication from only one doctor). Even if the offer is not revocable and a judgment is entered based on the offer, the defendant can still attack the judgment under FRCP 60(b). *See* ***Webb***, 147 F.3d at 621-22; *see, e.g.*, ***Richardson***, 49 F.3d at 765 (D entitled to relief under FRCP 60(b) if offer was induced by P's actual misconduct). See "Motion for Relief from Judgment," ch. 10-F, p. 804.

§3. RESPONSE TO OFFER

§3.1 Notice of acceptance. The plaintiff is free to accept or reject the offer. ***Clark v. Sims***, 28 F.3d 420, 423 (4th Cir.1994). To accept the offer, the plaintiff must do the following:

1. **Give notice in writing.** The plaintiff must give notice of acceptance in writing. *See* FRCP 68(a).

2. **Served on all parties.** The notice of acceptance must be served on every party to the litigation, and service must be in accordance with FRCP 5(b). *See* FRCP 68(a); *see, e.g.*, ***Ortiz-Moss v. New York City Dept. of Transp.***, 623 F.Supp.2d 404, 407-08 (S.D.N.Y.2008) (P did not properly serve notice of acceptance when (1) she served notice by e-mail and fax but parties had not agreed to service by electronic means and (2) she attempted in-person service on attorney but improperly served security guard at attorney's building).

3. **Accept by deadline.** The plaintiff must accept the offer within 14 days after the offer is served. FRCP 68(a); *see* ***Richardson v. National R.R. Passenger Corp.***, 49 F.3d 760, 765 (D.C.Cir.1995) (applying former ten-day deadline).

§3.2 No response. If the plaintiff does not accept the offer, the offer is considered withdrawn. FRCP 68(b). An unaccepted offer does not prohibit a later offer. *Id.* Evidence of an unaccepted offer is not admissible except in a proceeding to determine costs. *Id.*; ***Atonio v. Wards Cove Packing Co.***, 10 F.3d 1485, 1504 n.18 (9th Cir.1993).

§4. ACCEPTED OFFER

§4.1 Filing accepted offer. Either party may file the offer and notice of acceptance, plus proof of service. FRCP 68(a).

§4.2 Entry of judgment. Once the notice of acceptance is filed, the court clerk must enter judgment according to the offer's terms. FRCP 68(a). The clerk generally has no discretion whether to enter the judgment. ***Webb v. James***, 147 F.3d 617, 621 (7th Cir.1998); ***Perkins v. U.S. W. Comms.***, 138 F.3d 336, 338 (8th Cir.1998); *see* ***Ramming v. Natural Gas Pipeline Co.***, 390 F.3d 366, 370-71 (5th Cir.2004) (noting exceptions for class actions and injunctive relief); *see also* ***Mallory v. Eyrich***, 922 F.2d 1273, 1279 (6th Cir.1991) (court has no discretion to alter or modify parties' agreement).

§5. EFFECT OF NOT ACCEPTING OFFER

§5.1 Judgment less favorable than offer. If the plaintiff rejects the offer and then wins a judgment less favorable than the offer, the plaintiff must pay any costs incurred after the offer was made. FRCP 68(d); ***Pittari v. American Eagle Airlines, Inc.***, 468 F.3d 1056, 1064 (8th Cir.2006); ***Louisiana Power & Light Co. v. Kellstrom***, 50

F.3d 319, 333 (5th Cir.1995); *see also* ***Le v. University of Pa.***, 321 F.3d 403, 411 (3d Cir.2003) (in civil-rights suit, whether D can recover attorney fees under FRCP 68 depends on the underlying statute and its interpretation and how "costs" are determined). The term "judgment" includes the termination of litigation resolved by a later settlement between the parties. ***Lang v. Gates***, 36 F.3d 73, 76 (9th Cir.1994). *But see* ***Good Timez, Inc. v. Phoenix Fire & Mar. Ins. Co.***, 754 F.Supp. 459, 462-63 (D.V.I.1991) (applying FRCP 68 when litigation is resolved by later settlement is likely to frustrate rule's primary objective; P is less inclined to accept later settlement offer because P's interim costs may not be compensable). FRCP 68(d) does not apply to cases in which the plaintiff refuses an offer of judgment and the defendant later obtains judgment against the plaintiff. ***Delta Air Lines, Inc. v. August***, 450 U.S. 346, 352 (1981); *see* ***Kellstrom***, 50 F.3d at 333-34 (exception is created so that nonsettling P does not run risk of suffering additional burden if P loses).

CAUTION

Check the law of your circuit before drafting an offer of judgment from multiple defendants. FRCP 68 does not explain how a joint offer by multiple defendants should be treated, and courts disagree on how to apply FRCP 68 to joint offers. ***King v. Rivas***, *555 F.3d 14, 17-18 (1st Cir. 2009). For example, if five defendants make a joint offer of $10,000, the plaintiff rejects the offer, the plaintiff dismisses two of the five defendants, and at trial the plaintiff recovers $5,000, it is unclear if the judgment is actually less favorable than the offer because it is against only three of the five defendants. Some courts require joint offers to allocate an amount for each defendant. See* ***Harbor Motor Co. v. Arnell Chevrolet-Geo, Inc.***, *265 F.3d 638, 648-49 (7th Cir.2001). Other courts allow unapportioned offers to trigger FRCP 68 and shift costs when the joint offer exceeds the judgment. See* ***Le***, *321 F.3d at 408; see also* ***King***, *555 F.3d at 19 (court looks to see if unapportioned offer exceeds plaintiff's total recovery, including judgment plus any relief from settling Ds).*

§5.2 Monetary damages. To determine whether the judgment is less favorable than the offer, the court must compare two clearly defined figures—the FRCP 68 offer and the amount awarded by the judgment. ***Johnston v. Penrod Drilling Co.***, 803 F.2d 867, 870 (5th Cir.1986). The following are examples of this comparison:

- A $225,000 offer was compared with both $250,000 in damages and $226,608.91, which was the plaintiff's damages minus the defendant's damages under its counterclaim. ***Bright v. Land O'Lakes, Inc.***, 844 F.2d 436, 443 (7th Cir.1988). The defendant was required to pay the plaintiff's costs. *Id.*

- A $26,000 offer was compared with $5,010 in damages. ***Crossman v. Marcoccio***, 806 F.2d 329, 330-31 (1st Cir.1986). The plaintiff was required to pay the defendant's postoffer costs. *Id.* at 333.

§5.3 Injunctive relief. To determine whether the judgment is less favorable than the offer, the court must compare the FRCP 68 offer and the relief awarded in the judgment. ***Reiter v. MTA N.Y. City Transit Auth.***, 457 F.3d 224, 229 (2d Cir.2006). Because of the difficulty in comparing monetary damages with equitable relief, the question of whether the judgment is more favorable than the offer is determined by the facts of the case. *See, e.g.*, ***Andretti v. Borla Performance Indus.***, 426 F.3d 824, 837 (6th Cir.2005) (offer included both damages and permanent injunction; judgment included only injunction; thus, judgment less favorable); *see also* ***Reiter***, 457 F.3d at 231 (nothing in FRCP 68 suggests that either equitable relief or monetary damages are more favorable); ***Leach v. Northern Telecom, Inc.***, 141 F.R.D. 420, 428 (E.D.N.C.1991) (same). *See generally* Cubbage, Note, *Federal Rule 68 Offers of Judgment & Equitable Relief: Where Angels Fear to Tread*, 70 Tex.L.Rev. 465, 470-75 (1991) (discussing application of FRCP 68 to equitable relief). In determining the value of relief, the offering party bears the burden of showing that the FRCP 68 offer was more favorable than the judgment. ***Reiter***, 457 F.3d at 231.

§6. DETERMINING COSTS

Because FRCP 68 does not define "costs," courts should use the definition of costs that would normally apply to the case. ***Marek v. Chesny***, 473 U.S. 1, 9 n.2 (1985).

§6.1 Costs included. The definition of costs includes the following:

1. Filing fees. ***U.S. v. American Commercial Barge Line Co.***, 988 F.2d 860, 864 (8th Cir.1993).

2. Witness fees. 28 U.S.C. §1821(b); ***Aceves v. Allstate Ins.***, 68 F.3d 1160, 1167 (9th Cir.1995); ***American Commercial***, 988 F.2d at 864.

3. Attorney fees, if the underlying statute includes them. ***Marek v. Chesny***, 473 U.S. 1, 9 (1985); ***U.S. v. Trident Seafoods Corp.***, 92 F.3d 855, 860 (9th Cir.1996); ***Clark v. Sims***, 28 F.3d 420, 423 (4th Cir.1994); ***Fegley v. Higgins***, 19 F.3d 1126, 1134 (6th Cir.1994); *see, e.g.*, ***Haworth v. Nevada***, 56 F.3d 1048, 1052 (9th Cir.1995) (FRCP 68 does not bar recovery of attorney fees in Fair Labor Standards Act case).

4. Costs allowable under 28 U.S.C. §1920. ***Sea Coast Foods, Inc. v. Lu-Mar Lobster & Shrimp, Inc.***, 260 F.3d 1054, 1060-61 (9th Cir.2001); ***Knight v. Snap-On Tools Corp.***, 3 F.3d 1398, 1404 (10th Cir.1993); ***Parkes v. Hall***, 906 F.2d 658, 660 (11th Cir.1990). See "Taxable Costs," ch. 9-D, p. 761.

§6.2 Costs not included. The definition of costs does not include the following:

1. Prejudgment interest. ***U.S. v. American Commercial Barge Line Co.***, 988 F.2d 860, 864 (8th Cir.1993).

2. Attorney fees for work done on a postoffer fee petition, if the offer of judgment is specifically limited to "costs now accrued." ***Guerrero v. Cummings***, 70 F.3d 1111, 1113 (9th Cir.1995).

3. Attorney fees, if the underlying statute does not include them. ***Sea Coast Foods, Inc. v. Lu-Mar Lobster & Shrimp, Inc.***, 260 F.3d 1054, 1059 (9th Cir.2001); *see* ***Fletcher v. City of Fort Wayne***, 162 F.3d 975, 977 (7th Cir.1998).

§7. APPELLATE REVIEW

§7.1 Interlocutory orders. A party must specifically reserve its right to appeal any interlocutory orders or other claims included in the final FRCP 68 judgment. ***Shores v. Sklar***, 885 F.2d 760, 762 (11th Cir.1989); *see* ***Dugas v. Trans Un. Corp.***, 99 F.3d 724, 729 (5th Cir.1996); ***Blair v. Shanahan***, 795 F.Supp. 309, 315-16 (N.D.Cal.1992).

§7.2 Final consent judgment. A party to a consent judgment is deemed to waive any objection it has to matters within the scope of the judgment. ***Wrightsell v. Cook Cty.***, 599 F.3d 781, 783-84 (7th Cir.2010); ***Mallory v. Eyrich***, 922 F.2d 1273, 1280 (6th Cir.1991); 15A Wright, Miller & Cooper §3902 & n.59; *see* 13 *Moore's Federal Practice 3d* §68.05[5]. The court of appeals, however, may review de novo a district court's interpretation and application of FRCP 68. ***Andretti v. Borla Performance Indus.***, 426 F.3d 824, 837 (6th Cir.2005); ***Ramming v. Natural Gas Pipeline Co.***, 390 F.3d 366, 370 (5th Cir.2004); ***U.S. v. Trident Seafoods Corp.***, 92 F.3d 855, 859 (9th Cir.1996). The district court's findings on the factual circumstances of FRCP 68 offers and acceptances are reviewed for clear error. ***Andretti***, 426 F.3d at 837; ***Basha v. Mitsubishi Motor Credit***, 336 F.3d 451, 453 (5th Cir.2003).

E. MOTION TO RECUSE

§1. GENERAL

§1.1 Rules. 28 U.S.C. §§144, 455; see U.S. Const. amend. 14.

§1.2 Purpose. A motion to recuse asks a judge to remove herself from the case so another judge can hear it. The Due Process Clause of the U.S. Constitution entitles a person to an impartial and disinterested tribunal in both civil and criminal cases, and it may serve as the basis for recusal. *See* ***Caperton v. A.T. Massey Coal Co.***, 556 U.S. 868, 889 (2009); ***Marshall v. Jerrico, Inc.***, 446 U.S. 238, 242 (1980). The Due Process Clause, however, provides only the "outer boundaries" of judicial disqualification, and Congress and the states can impose more rigorous standards. ***Caperton***, 556 U.S. at 889; ***Aetna Life Ins. v. Lavoie***, 475 U.S. 813, 828 (1986).

§1.3 Forms. ***O'Connor's Federal Civil Forms*** (2012), FORMS 5E.

§1.4 Other references. 13D Wright, Miller, Cooper & Freer, *Federal Practice & Procedure 3d* §§3541-3553 (2008 & Supp.2012); 12 *Moore's Federal Practice 3d* §§63.60-63.63 (2012); Code of Conduct for United States Judges (CCUSJ), 150 F.R.D. 307 (1992).

§2. STATUTES GOVERNING RECUSAL

There are significant differences between recusals under 28 U.S.C. §144 and recusals under 28 U.S.C. §455(a).

§2.1 Section 144. Recusal under §144 is limited to district judges, the grounds must be asserted in a motion, the grounds are waivable, and the party can make only one motion.

§2.2 Section 455. Recusal under §455 includes all federal judges, the grounds in subsection (a) are waivable only after full disclosure on the record, the grounds in subsection (b) are not waivable, and the party is not limited to one motion.

§3. MOTION

§3.1 Form. For the general requirements for the form of a motion, see "Drafting motions," ch. 1-B, §3.1, p. 14.

§3.2 In writing. A motion to recuse should be in writing. *See* FRCP 7(b)(1)(A).

§3.3 Affidavit. A motion to recuse under 28 U.S.C. §144 must be accompanied by the party's affidavit stating the facts and reasons for the belief that there is bias or prejudice. The affidavit is strictly construed against the affiant. ***U.S. v. Burger***, 964 F.2d 1065, 1070 (10th Cir.1992). Although there is no prescribed procedure for a motion to recuse under 28 U.S.C. §455, a party should file an affidavit because the motion questions the integrity of a judicial officer.

§3.4 Attorney's certificate. A motion to recuse under §144 must be accompanied by a certificate by the attorney of record that the motion was made in good faith. Although a certificate is not required under §455, the attorney should file a certificate because the motion questions the integrity of a judicial officer.

§3.5 Notice. The party moving for recusal must file and serve copies of the motion on all parties or their attorneys. *See* FRCP 5.

§3.6 Number of motions allowed.

1. Section 144. A party can file only one §144 motion per case. If a party makes a successful motion alleging bias or prejudice and a new judge is assigned to the case, that party cannot make another §144 motion. However, each separate party is entitled to make its own §144 motion.

2. Section 455. A party is not limited in the number of §455 recusal motions it can make.

§3.7 Grounds.

1. Bias or prejudice. If the judge has a personal bias or prejudice against a party or about the subject matter of the suit, the judge must recuse herself. 28 U.S.C. §§144, 455(b)(1). The standard is whether a reasonable person would be convinced the judge was biased. ***Hook v. McDade***, 89 F.3d 350, 355 (7th Cir.1996). Recusal is required only if actual bias or prejudice is proved by compelling evidence. *Id.*

(1) Allegations. If a party moves to recuse a judge on the grounds of bias or prejudice, the party must allege the following:

(a) Directed against party. The bias or prejudice must be directed against the party itself, not the party's attorney. ***Gilbert v. City of Little Rock***, 722 F.2d 1390, 1398-99 (8th Cir.1983).

(b) Stems from extrajudicial source. The bias or prejudice must be from an "extrajudicial source" (i.e., a source outside the official proceedings, such as a letter written to a newspaper). ***U.S. v. Grinnell Corp.***, 384 U.S. 563, 583 (1966); ***Selkridge v. United of Omaha Life Ins.***, 360 F.3d 155, 167 (3d Cir.2004); ***Andrade v. Chojnacki***, 338 F.3d 448, 455 (5th Cir.2003); ***Thomas v. Tenneco Packaging Co.***, 293 F.3d 1306, 1329 (11th Cir.

2002); ***Hook***, 89 F.3d at 355; *cf.* ***Liteky v. U.S.***, 510 U.S. 540, 554 (1994) (criminal case). Bias arising from the litigation itself is generally not sufficient to require recusal. *See* ***Berger v. U.S.***, 255 U.S. 22, 31 (1921); ***Loranger v. Stierheim***, 10 F.3d 776, 780 (11th Cir.1994); ***Pau v. Yosemite Park & Curry Co.***, 928 F.2d 880, 885 (9th Cir.1991). However, opinions formed by the judge on the basis of facts introduced or events occurring during the proceedings may constitute a basis for bias or prejudice if the opinions display a deep-seated favoritism or antagonism that would prevent fair judgment. ***Liteky***, 510 U.S. at 555; ***LoCascio v. U.S.***, 473 F.3d 493, 495 (2d Cir.2007); ***Selkridge***, 360 F.3d at 167; ***Andrade***, 338 F.3d at 455.

(c) Casts doubt on judge's impartiality. A reasonable person must have doubts about the judge's impartiality. ***Maez v. Mountain States Tel. & Tel., Inc.***, 54 F.3d 1488, 1508 (10th Cir.1995).

(2) Improper factors. The following factors should not be considered in a motion to recuse under 28 U.S.C. §§144 and 455(b)(1):

(a) A judge's ruling in the case. ***Berger***, 255 U.S. at 31; ***Loranger***, 10 F.3d at 780; *see* ***LoCascio***, 473 F.3d at 495 (rulings alone almost never constitute basis for recusal); ***Andrade***, 338 F.3d at 455 (same); ***Glass v. Pfeffer***, 849 F.2d 1261, 1268 (10th Cir.1988) (same).

(b) An earlier antagonistic trial relationship between the judge and a party's attorney. ***Yagman v. Republic Ins.***, 987 F.2d 622, 626-27 (9th Cir.1993).

(c) Rumor, speculation, beliefs, conclusions, innuendo, suspicion, opinion, or similar nonfactual matters. ***U.S. v. Burger***, 964 F.2d 1065, 1070 (10th Cir.1992); ***Glass***, 849 F.2d at 1267; *see, e.g.*, ***Moideen v. Gillespie***, 55 F.3d 1478, 1482 (9th Cir.1995) (recusal unwarranted for judge who stated his concerns about unfunded benefit plans).

(d) The judge's previously expressed opinion on a point of law. ***U.S. v. Bray***, 546 F.2d 851, 857 (10th Cir.1976).

(e) The judge's expressed dedication to upholding the law or her determination to impose severe punishment within the limits of the law on those found guilty of a particular offense. ***U.S. v. Gigax***, 605 F.2d 507, 513 (10th Cir.1979); ***U.S. v. Haldeman***, 559 F.2d 31, 134 n.302 (D.C.Cir.1976).

(f) Mere familiarity with the defendant, the type of charge, or the kind of defense presented. ***U.S. v. Ayala***, 289 F.3d 16, 27 (1st Cir.2002); ***Maez***, 54 F.3d at 1508; *see* ***Frates v. Weinshienk***, 882 F.2d 1502, 1506 (10th Cir.1989); *see also* ***U.S. v. Bremers***, 195 F.3d 221, 226 (5th Cir.1999) (opinions judge forms based on information acquired in earlier proceedings are not biased or prejudiced).

(g) A party's earlier personal attacks against the judge. ***Bray***, 546 F.2d at 858.

(h) Threats or other attempts to intimidate the judge. ***U.S. v. Studley***, 783 F.2d 934, 940 (9th Cir. 1986).

(i) The judge's religious beliefs. ***Feminist Women's Health Ctr. v. Codispoti***, 69 F.3d 399, 400-01 (9th Cir.1995).

(j) A factor created by the party or attorney seeking recusal. *E.g.*, ***Sullivan v. Conway***, 157 F.3d 1092, 1095-96 (7th Cir.1998) (P showed judge letter written by D's attorney praising judge; no basis for recusal because judge would not have known about letter if not for P).

2. Impartiality might be questioned. If the judge's impartiality might reasonably be questioned, the judge must recuse herself. 28 U.S.C. §455(a); ***ISC Holding AG v. Nobel Biocare Fin. AG***, 688 F.3d 98, 107 (2d Cir. 2012); ***In re Kensington Int'l***, 368 F.3d 289, 301 (3d Cir.2004); ***Andrade***, 338 F.3d at 454; ***U.S. v. Microsoft Corp.***, 253 F.3d 34, 114 (D.C.Cir.2001). Because the goal of §455(a) is to "exact the appearance of impartiality," recusal may be required even when there is no actual partiality. *See* ***In re Basciano***, 542 F.3d 950, 956 (2d Cir.2008); ***In re Kensington Int'l***, 368 F.3d at 303; ***Moran v. Clarke***, 296 F.3d 638, 648 (8th Cir.2002); ***Bremers***, 195 F.3d at 226. In determining whether the judge must recuse herself under §455(a), the question is whether a reasonable person perceives

a significant risk that the judge will resolve the case on a basis other than the merits; this is an objective standard viewed from the perspective of a well-informed, thoughtful observer rather than an unduly sensitive person. ***Liljeberg v. Health Servs. Acquisition Corp.***, 486 U.S. 847, 865 (1988); *see* ***ISC Holding AG***, 688 F.3d at 107; ***U.S. v. Ruff***, 472 F.3d 1044, 1046 (8th Cir.2007); ***In re Kensington Int'l***, 368 F.3d at 303; ***U.S. v. DeTemple***, 162 F.3d 279, 287 (4th Cir.1998). Section 455(a) requires judicial recusal only if a reasonable person, knowing all the circumstances, would expect that the judge would have actual knowledge of her interest or bias in the case. ***Sao Paulo State v. American Tobacco Co.***, 535 U.S. 229, 232-33 (2002). Doubts must be resolved in favor of recusal. ***Murray v. Scott***, 253 F.3d 1308, 1310 (11th Cir.2001); *see also* ***Bryce v. Episcopal Ch. in the Diocese of Colo.***, 289 F.3d 648, 659 (10th Cir. 2002) (if issue is close, judge must recuse herself). There is no requirement that the judge have knowledge of the disqualifying circumstance. ***Liljeberg***, 486 U.S. at 860. Each §455(a) case must be decided on its unique facts and circumstances rather than by comparison to similar situations considered in prior cases. ***Bremers***, 195 F.3d at 226.

(1) Allegations. If a party moves to recuse a judge on the ground that the judge's impartiality might reasonably be questioned, the party should allege the following:

(a) There is a reasonable factual basis for calling the judge's impartiality into question. *See, e.g.*, ***In re Kensington Int'l***, 368 F.3d at 303 (recusal warranted when advisers appointed by judge simultaneously served as advocates in another asbestos-related bankruptcy); ***U.S. v. Avilez-Reyes***, 160 F.3d 258, 259 (5th Cir.1998) (judge erred by not recusing himself after D's attorney had recently testified against judge in judicial disciplinary proceeding); ***U.S. v. Anderson***, 160 F.3d 231, 233 (5th Cir.1998) (public defender successfully challenged judge against whom he had testified in judicial disciplinary proceedings); ***Nichols v. Alley***, 71 F.3d 347, 352 (10th Cir.1995) (criminal D successfully challenged judge whose chambers were damaged by D's alleged bombing of federal courthouse); ***Hamid v. Price Waterhouse***, 51 F.3d 1411, 1416-17 (9th Cir.1995) (relationship between judge's law clerk and attorney could have compromised impartiality of judge's decisions in which law clerk participated).

(b) The judge has outwardly exhibited partiality. ***U.S. v. Cooley***, 1 F.3d 985, 995 (10th Cir.1993).

(c) The question about the judge's impartiality stems from an extrajudicial source and not from conduct or rulings made during the course of the proceedings. ***Selkridge***, 360 F.3d at 167; ***Thomas***, 293 F.3d at 1329. But the fact that a judge's opinion derives from an extrajudicial source is not alone a sufficient basis to show impartiality. *See* ***Liteky***, 510 U.S. at 554; ***ISC Holding AG***, 688 F.3d at 107-08.

(d) The public's confidence in the judiciary will be irreparably harmed if the case is allowed to proceed before a judge who appears to be tainted. ***Alexander v. Primerica Holdings, Inc.***, 10 F.3d 155, 162 (3d Cir. 1993).

(e) A reasonable person knowing all the relevant facts would harbor doubts about the judge's impartiality. ***Cooley***, 1 F.3d at 993; ***Pope v. Federal Express Corp.***, 974 F.2d 982, 985 (8th Cir.1992). For example, a reasonable person could harbor doubts about a judge's impartiality when the judge recuses herself, without explanation, from presiding over one group of cases, yet refuses to recuse herself from presiding over a separate but nearly identical group of cases. *See* ***Selkridge***, 360 F.3d at 170.

(2) Improper factors. The following factors should not be considered in a motion to recuse under 28 U.S.C. §455(a):

(a) The judge's actual state of mind, purity of heart, incorruptibility, or lack of partiality. ***Cooley***, 1 F.3d at 993.

(b) The judge's previously expressed opinion on factual or legal issues related to the case. ***Leaman v. Ohio Dept. of Mental Retardation & Dev. Disabilities***, 825 F.2d 946, 949 n.1 (6th Cir.1987); ***Bray***, 546 F.2d at 857.

(c) Earlier rulings in the case or a different case, when the motion is made solely on the grounds that the rulings were adverse. ***Trust Co. of La. v. N.N.P. Inc.***, 104 F.3d 1478, 1491 (5th Cir.1997); ***Taylor v. Regents of the Univ. of Cal.***, 993 F.2d 710, 712 (9th Cir.1993). *But see* ***Moran***, 296 F.3d at 649 (although earlier unfavorable rulings do not raise inference of bias, these rulings may be part of relevant facts showing bias).

(d) A party's or attorney's testimony supporting or opposing the judge's judicial nomination. ***Denardo v. Municipality of Anchorage***, 974 F.2d 1200, 1201 (9th Cir.1992); ***U.S. v. Helmsley***, 760 F.Supp. 338, 342-43 (S.D.N.Y.1991), *aff'd*, 963 F.2d 1522 (2d Cir.1992).

(e) The judge's membership in one party's bar association. ***Denardo***, 974 F.2d at 1201.

(f) The judge's support of one party's dismissed attorney in a grievance action filed by the party, when the judge's affidavit in support was restrained in tone, was confined to the judge's personal observations of the attorney's courtroom behavior, and did not display deep-seated favoritism toward either party. ***In re Adams***, 31 F.3d 389, 396 (6th Cir.1994).

(g) The judge's spouse being employed as an attorney in a firm that represents the opposing party in litigation, but not the present case. ***In re Billedeaux***, 972 F.2d 104, 106 (5th Cir.1992).

(h) A controversy between the judge and one party's attorney, without proof of bias or prejudice against the parties. ***Gilbert***, 722 F.2d at 1399; *see also* ***Liteky***, 510 U.S. at 555-56 (expressions of impatience, dissatisfaction, annoyance, and even anger are not sufficient to require recusal).

(i) The judge's social relationship with a party. *See, e.g.*, ***U.S. v. Lovaglia***, 954 F.2d 811, 816 (2d Cir.1992) (past social relationship between judge and crime victim did not create appearance of bias). *But see* ***Moran***, 296 F.3d at 649 (social relationship raised concerns about denial of recusal).

(j) The judge's religious beliefs. ***Bryce***, 289 F.3d at 660; ***Feminist Women's Health Ctr.***, 69 F.3d at 400.

(k) The judge's membership in a particular group. ***Bryce***, 289 F.3d at 660.

(*l*) The judge's involvement in litigation with a party when the litigation was frivolous or brought to compel recusal. ***Lyons v. Sheetz***, 834 F.2d 493, 495 n.1 (5th Cir.1987); *see* ***In re Taylor***, 417 F.3d 649, 652 (7th Cir. 2005) (suits against public officials are common; judge would likely not harbor bias against party simply because party named judge in meritless civil suit).

(m) The judge's friendship with a witness. ***Fletcher v. Conoco Pipe Line Co.***, 323 F.3d 661, 665 (8th Cir.2003). *But see* ***U.S. v. Kelly***, 888 F.2d 732, 744-45 (11th Cir.1989) (recusal might be warranted if court, not jury, were to decide fact issue and if close friend were involved in case).

(n) Threats or other attempts to intimidate the judge. *See* ***In re Basciano***, 542 F.3d at 956-57. *But see* ***U.S. v. Greenspan***, 26 F.3d 1001, 1006 (10th Cir.1994) (when D allegedly conspired to kill trial judge and D's actions were more than mere threats to obtain different judge, judge should have recused himself).

3. Personal knowledge. If the judge is the fact-finder and has personal knowledge of a disputed fact, the judge must recuse herself. 28 U.S.C. §455(b)(1); *see* ***Murray***, 253 F.3d at 1313. The knowledge in question must come from outside the lawsuit; knowledge of facts gained from the lawsuit itself or from a similar lawsuit is not grounds for recusal. ***Omega Eng'g v. Omega, S.A.***, 432 F.3d 437, 447-48 (2d Cir.2005).

4. Involvement during private practice.

(1) Judge served as attorney or material witness. If the judge served as the attorney in the matter in controversy or was a material witness in the matter in controversy, the judge must recuse herself. 28 U.S.C. §455(b)(2); *see also* ***Baker & Hostetler LLP v. U.S. Dept. of Commerce***, 471 F.3d 1355, 1357-58 (D.C.Cir.2006) ("associational" rule for recusal based on prior law-firm employment).

(2) Former associate served as attorney or material witness. If an attorney with whom the judge previously practiced law served as an attorney in the matter in controversy during their association or was a material witness in the matter in controversy, the judge must recuse herself. 28 U.S.C. §455(b)(2).

5. Participation during governmental employment.

(1) Judge served as attorney, adviser, or material witness. If the judge participated as an attorney, adviser, or material witness in the proceeding in her capacity during governmental employment, the judge

must recuse herself. 28 U.S.C. §455(b)(3); ***Murray***, 253 F.3d at 1312; *see also* ***Baker & Hostetler***, 471 F.3d at 1357-58 ("personal-participation" rule for recusal based on previous governmental employment is narrower than "associational" rule based on previous employment in private practice). The judge must have personally participated in the proceeding to require recusal. ***Baker & Hostetler***, 471 F.3d at 1357-58. A proceeding includes pretrial, trial, appellate review, and other stages of litigation. 28 U.S.C. §455(d)(1); ***Baker & Hostetler***, 471 F.3d at 1357.

(2) Judge expressed opinion. If the judge expressed an opinion on the merits of the particular case in her judicial capacity during governmental employment, the judge must recuse herself. 28 U.S.C. §455(b)(3); ***U.S. v. Ruzzano***, 247 F.3d 688, 695 (7th Cir.2001).

6. Financial interest. If the judge (individually or as a fiduciary), her spouse, or her minor child residing in her household has a financial interest in the subject of the controversy or in a party to the proceeding or any other interest that would be substantially affected by the outcome of the proceeding, the judge must recuse herself. 28 U.S.C. §455(b)(4); *see* ***Shell Oil Co. v. U.S.***, 672 F.3d 1283, 1289 (Fed.Cir.2012); ***In re Kansas Pub. Empls. Ret. Sys.***, 85 F.3d 1353, 1362 (8th Cir.1996); *see also* ***Caperton v. A.T. Massey Coal Co.***, 556 U.S. 868, 886-87 (2009) (under due process, judge on state supreme court should have recused himself when (1) corporation's chairperson had contributed $3 million to judge's election campaign and (2) case involving $50 million judgment against corporation was to be reviewed by state supreme court).

(1) Elements of financial interest. For the purpose of recusal, a financial interest includes the following:

(a) Any type of legal or equitable ownership. 28 U.S.C. §455(d)(4); ***Shell Oil***, 672 F.3d at 1289; ***First Nat'l Bank v. Lustig***, 96 F.3d 1554, 1574 n.18 (5th Cir.1996); ***Hook***, 89 F.3d at 356. *But see* ***In re Kansas Pub. Empls.***, 85 F.3d at 1362 (refusing to create rule requiring judges to recuse themselves from all cases that might remotely affect nonparty companies in which they own stock; judge owned stock in parent company of D); ***In re Drexel Burnham Lambert, Inc.***, 861 F.2d 1307, 1314-17 (2d Cir.1988) (no recusal required even though party to suit was retained by firm that had contract with judge's wife for sale of her family business from which she was to receive $30 million; on denial of en banc review, four judges dissented).

(b) A relationship as a director, adviser, or other active participant in the affairs of one of the parties. 28 U.S.C. §455(d)(4); *see* ***In re Drexel Burnham***, 861 F.2d at 1313 (judge's financial interest must be direct, not remote or speculative).

(2) What is not financial interest. For purposes of recusal, a financial interest does not include the following:

(a) Ownership interest in a mutual or common investment fund that holds securities, unless the judge participates in the management of the fund. 28 U.S.C. §455(d)(4)(i).

(b) Securities held by an educational, religious, charitable, fraternal, or civic organization in which the judge maintains an office. *Id.* §455(d)(4)(ii).

(c) The proprietary interest of a policyholder in a mutual-insurance company, of a depositor in a mutual savings association, or a similar proprietary interest, unless the outcome of the proceeding could substantially affect the value of the interest. *Id.* §455(d)(4)(iii).

(d) Ownership of government securities, unless the outcome of the proceeding could substantially affect their value. *Id.* §455(d)(4)(iv).

(e) Status the judge shares with the public at large, unless a reasonable person knowing all relevant facts would harbor doubts about the judge's impartiality. *See* ***In re New Mexico Nat. Gas Antitrust Litig.***, 620 F.2d 794, 796-97 (10th Cir.1980) (judge's status as natural-gas consumer); ***U.S. v. Zuger***, 602 F.Supp. 889, 892 (D.Conn.1984) (judge's status as employee of United States), *aff'd*, 755 F.2d 915 (2d Cir.1984) (table case).

(3) Judge divests financial interest. If the financial interest is discovered after the judge has devoted substantial judicial time to the case and the interest would not be substantially affected by the outcome, the judge is not required to recuse herself as long as she divests herself of the financial interest. 28 U.S.C. §455(f); ***In re Certain Underwriter***, 294 F.3d 297, 303 (2d Cir.2002); ***Baldwin Hardware Corp. v. Franksu Enter.***, 78 F.3d 550, 556 (Fed.Cir.1996). "Substantial judicial time" means the amount of judicial work the case has required, not the time the case has been on the court's calendar. ***In re Certain Underwriter***, 294 F.3d at 304.

(4) Judge's duty to keep informed. Judges should make reasonable efforts to remain informed about their personal and fiduciary financial interests, as well as those of their spouses and minor children residing in their household. 28 U.S.C. §455(c).

7. Relationship to person in case. If the judge, her spouse, a person within the third degree of relationship to either of them, or that person's spouse is a party, an attorney, a material witness, or has an interest in the litigation, the judge must recuse herself. 28 U.S.C. §455(b)(5); ***Hook***, 89 F.3d at 353-54; ***Pashaian v. Eccleston Props., Ltd.***, 88 F.3d 77, 83 (2d Cir.1996); ***Harris v. Champion***, 15 F.3d 1538, 1571 (10th Cir.1994); *see* ***In re Kansas Pub. Empls.***, 85 F.3d at 1364 (employment relationship between party and judge's son or daughter does not always necessitate judge's disqualification); *see, e.g.*, ***McCuin v. Texas Power & Light Co.***, 714 F.2d 1255, 1259-60 (5th Cir.1983) (judge's brother-in-law's involvement in case and substantial interest in outcome necessitated judge's disqualification). The interests declared in §455(b)(5) include noneconomic (e.g., reputation) as well as economic interests. ***In re Kansas Pub. Empls.***, 85 F.3d at 1359; *see* ***Potashnick v. Port City Constr. Co.***, 609 F.2d 1101, 1113 (5th Cir.1980).

CIRCUIT SPLIT

The Fifth Circuit holds that when a law-firm partner is related to a judge within the third degree, that partner will always be known by the judge to have an interest that could be substantially affected by the outcome of a proceeding involving the law firm. ***Potashnick****, 609 F.2d at 1113. The Second Circuit has rejected the Fifth Circuit's rule of automatic recusal. See* ***Pashaian****, 88 F.3d at 83 (§455(b)(5)(iii) requires a showing of bias-in-fact, not simply an objective appearance of bias).*

(1) Who are relatives. People are related by consanguinity (i.e., blood) or affinity (i.e., marriage). A person has two groups of relatives by affinity: (1) people married to her blood relatives and (2) people related to her spouse by blood. Other people who are considered relatives by either consanguinity or affinity include the following:

(a) Adopted relatives, who have the same status as natural children.

(b) Half-blood relatives, who have the same status as full-blood relatives.

(c) Step-relatives, who likely have the same status as other relatives by affinity as long as the marriage that created the relationship still exists.

(2) Degree of relationship. Degree of relationship is determined by the civil-law system of computing degrees of kinship. 28 U.S.C. §455(d)(2); *see, e.g.*, ***Pashaian***, 88 F.3d at 83 (relationship to judge was within third-degree when wife of partner in law firm representing Ds was sister of judge's wife); ***Oriental Fin. Grp. v. Federal Ins. Co.***, 467 F.Supp.2d 176, 179 (D.P.R.2006) (relationship to judge was not within third-degree when director of P-corporation was judge's son-in-law's father). In this system, each generation counts as one degree. To determine the degree of relationship, start with the judge, count up to the nearest common ancestor and then down to the relative. The number you count is the number of degrees (e.g., a judge is related to her sister in the second degree). All relatives listed in chart 5-1, below, are within the third degree.

5-1. Degrees of Relationship[1]

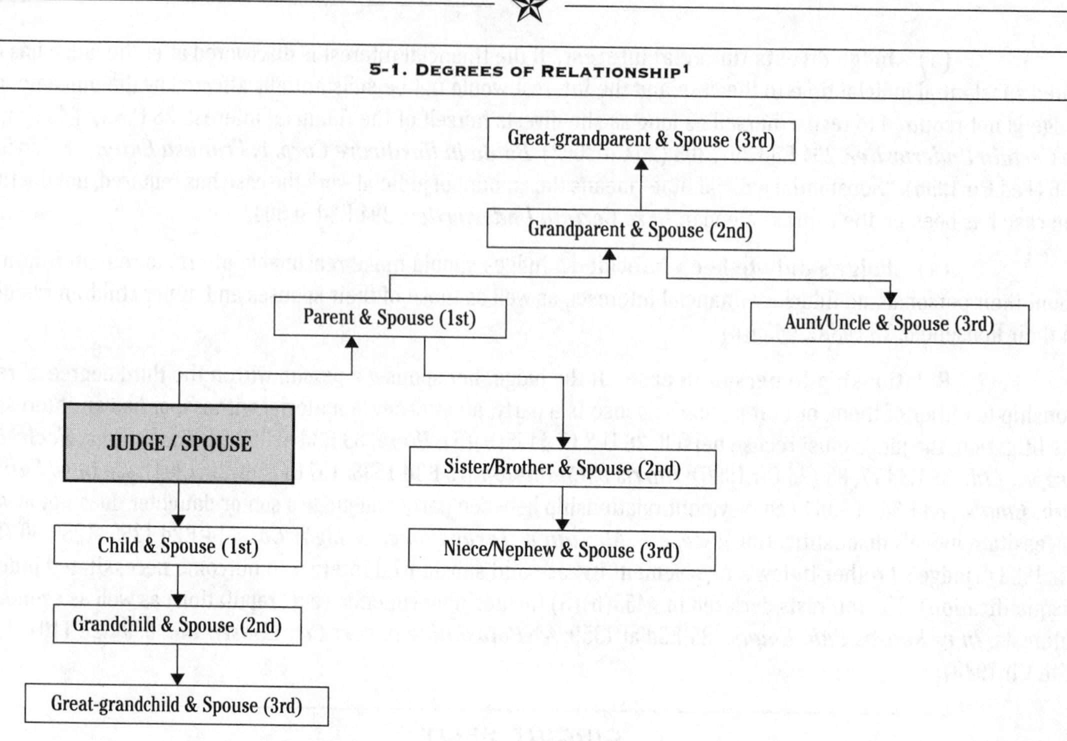

1. This chart also applies to adopted relatives, half-blood relatives, and step-relatives.

(3) Death. The death of a relative does not end a relationship, and recusal may still be required. *See* ***Harris***, 15 F.3d at 1570-71 (recusal was required when judge's late uncle had been party to prisoners' habeas corpus action).

§3.8 Deadline.

1. Section 144. A motion to recuse under §144 must be filed at least ten days before the trial or other hearing. 28 U.S.C. §144; ***U.S. v. Sibla***, 624 F.2d 864, 867 (9th Cir.1980).

2. Section 455. There is no express deadline under §455, but some courts impose a timeliness requirement. 13D Wright, Miller, Cooper & Freer §3550 & n.9; *see* ***LoCascio v. U.S.***, 473 F.3d 493, 497 (2d Cir.2007); ***Andrade v. Chojnacki***, 338 F.3d 448, 459 n.5 (5th Cir.2003); ***Summers v. Singletary***, 119 F.3d 917, 920 (11th Cir. 1997); ***Davies v. Commissioner***, 68 F.3d 1129, 1131 (9th Cir.1995); ***Schurz Comms. v. FCC***, 982 F.2d 1057, 1060 (7th Cir.1992). Courts consider the following factors in determining whether a motion is timely: (1) whether the party seeking recusal participated in trial or pretrial proceedings, (2) whether granting the motion would waste judicial resources, (3) whether the motion was filed after judgment, and (4) whether the party seeking recusal can show good cause for any delay in filing the motion. ***Omega Eng'g v. Omega, S.A.***, 432 F.3d 437, 448 (2d Cir.2005).

NOTE

Filing a timely motion to recuse serves many purposes. One is to meet the timeliness requirement imposed by some circuits. See ***In re Kansas Pub. Empls. Ret. Sys.***, *85 F.3d 1353, 1360 (8th Cir.1996). Another is to give the judge an opportunity to assess the merits before taking any steps that may be inappropriate if recusal is necessary.* ***LoCascio***, *473 F.3d at 497. A third is to dispel the argument that the moving party was motivated to file the motion by an adverse ruling. Id.;* ***In re Kansas Pub. Empls.***, *85 F.3d at 1360.*

§3.9 Proposed order. Some districts require the movant to submit a proposed order with the motion. In those districts, the movant should prepare a written order for the court's signature and submit it with the motion. See "Proposed order," ch. 1-B, §3.1.11, p. 16.

§3.10 Waiver.

1. When proper. Waiver of recusal is not addressed under 28 U.S.C. §144. If a recusal is based on the ground that the judge's impartiality might reasonably be questioned, the recusal can be waived by the parties only after the ground is fully disclosed on the record. 28 U.S.C. §455(e); ***In re Cargill, Inc.***, 66 F.3d 1256, 1261 (1st Cir. 1995).

2. When prohibited. The parties cannot agree to waive a recusal that is based on the grounds listed in §455(b). 28 U.S.C. §455(e); *e.g.*, ***Edgar v. K.L.***, 93 F.3d 256, 258 (7th Cir.1996) (parties could not consent to private investigation of case by judge).

§4. RESPONSE

The nonmovant should file a response to the motion to recuse. In preparing the response (or the response to the appeal or mandamus), the nonmovant should not communicate ex parte about the recusal with the challenged judge; such a communication could become another reason to recuse.

§5. RULINGS

§5.1 By challenged judge.

1. Motion under §144. When a motion to recuse is filed under 28 U.S.C. §144, the challenged judge may either (1) recuse herself or (2) not recuse herself and determine whether the §144 affidavit is timely and states facts and reasons for believing that there is prejudice. *See* 28 U.S.C. §144.

(1) Judge recuses self. If the challenged judge grants the motion, the case will be assigned to another judge. *See* 28 U.S.C. §144.

(2) Judge declines recusal.

(a) Motion is proper. If the challenged judge does not recuse herself but determines that the motion is proper, she must refer the motion to another judge for resolution on the merits. The reviewing judge must assess the legal sufficiency of the affidavit. *See* ***Sine v. International Bhd. of Teamsters***, 882 F.2d 913, 914 (4th Cir.1989); ***Hepperle v. Johnston***, 590 F.2d 609, 613 (5th Cir.1979). The reviewing judge must assume the facts stated in the affidavit are true, even if the reviewing judge knows they are false. ***U.S. v. Balistrieri***, 779 F.2d 1191, 1199 (7th Cir.1985).

(b) Motion is improper. If the challenged judge does not recuse herself and determines that the motion is improper, she can deny the motion and continue presiding over the case. *See, e.g.*, ***Omega Eng'g v. Omega, S.A.***, 432 F.3d 437, 448 (2d Cir.2005) (untimely motion; judge continued to preside over case); ***SEC v. Loving Spirit Found.***, 392 F.3d 486, 492 (D.C.Cir.2004) (same).

2. Motion under §455. There is no provision under 28 U.S.C. §455 for referring the recusal issue to another judge. ***U.S. v. Sibla***, 624 F.2d 864, 868 (9th Cir.1980). If the motion to recuse is made under §455(a), the challenged judge may determine both the sufficiency and the merits of the motion. *See* ***Aronson v. Brown***, 14 F.3d 1578, 1581-82 (Fed.Cir.1994). The judge must document the reasons for her decision so that it can be reviewed by an appellate court. ***U.S. v. Greenspan***, 26 F.3d 1001, 1007 (10th Cir.1994).

3. No further orders. Once challenged on grounds of recusal, the judge cannot take any further action in the case. 28 U.S.C. §144; *see* ***U.S. v. Feldman***, 983 F.2d 144, 145 (9th Cir.1992). If a judge determines that recusal is appropriate, she does not have discretion to recuse herself on only some issues; recusal must be from the whole

proceeding. ***Feldman***, 983 F.2d at 145. *But see* ***Ellis v. U.S.***, 313 F.3d 636, 641-42 (1st Cir.2002) (criminal case; if appropriate, judge may recuse herself for some issues but decide others). A judge who recuses herself cannot reconsider the recusal order, even if the motion to recuse was deficient. ***El Fenix v. M/Y Johanny***, 36 F.3d 136, 141-42 (1st Cir.1994).

§5.2 By assigned judge.

1. Grants motion. If the judge assigned to hear the motion to recuse grants the motion, the presiding judge must appoint another judge to hear the case on the merits. *See* ***El Fenix v. M/Y Johanny***, 36 F.3d 136, 142 (1st Cir.1994).

2. Denies motion. If the judge assigned to hear the motion to recuse denies the motion, the case will be returned to the challenged judge for a trial on the merits.

3. Sanctions. If a motion to recuse was brought solely for the purpose of delay or without sufficient cause, the judge may impose any sanctions authorized by FRCP 11. See "Motion for Sanctions," ch. 5-O, p. 384.

§6. APPELLATE REVIEW

PRACTICE TIP

When challenging a judge on impartiality in the appellate court, the party should also raise the issue of reassignment of the case. *See "Reassign case," §6.4.3, p. 331.*

§6.1 Interlocutory. An order denying a motion to recuse is interlocutory and not immediately appealable. ***Wyatt v. Rogers***, 92 F.3d 1074, 1080 (11th Cir.1996); ***Nichols v. Alley***, 71 F.3d 347, 350 (10th Cir.1995).

§6.2 Appeal. When the appellate court reviews an order on a motion to recuse after a trial on the merits, the standard of review depends on whether the party raised the issue of recusal in the district court.

1. Objection raised. The circuits are split on the standard of review for an order on a motion to recuse when the party raised the issue of recusal in the district court. *Compare* ***LoCascio v. U.S.***, 473 F.3d 493, 495 (2d Cir. 2007) (abuse of discretion), ***U.S. v. Ruff***, 472 F.3d 1044, 1046 (8th Cir.2007) (same), ***In re Kensington Int'l***, 368 F.3d 289, 301 (3d Cir.2004) (same), ***Andrade v. Chojnacki***, 338 F.3d 448, 454 (5th Cir.2003) (same), ***U.S. v. Ayala***, 289 F.3d 16, 27 (1st Cir.2002) (same), ***Murray v. Scott***, 253 F.3d 1308, 1310 (11th Cir.2001) (same), *and* ***Baldwin Hardware Corp. v. Franksu Enter.***, 78 F.3d 550, 556 (Fed.Cir.1996) (same), *with* ***Hook v. McDade***, 89 F.3d 350, 353-54 & n.3 (7th Cir.1996) (de novo), *and* ***People Helpers Found. v. City of Richmond***, 12 F.3d 1321, 1325 (4th Cir.1993) (same).

2. Objection not raised. If a party wants the appellate court to consider a motion to disqualify under 28 U.S.C. §144 for the first time on appeal, the party must show good cause for not objecting in the district court, allege exceptional circumstances why the court of appeals should consider the motion, and show that the judge's not recusing herself was plain error. ***Weiss v. Sheet Metal Workers***, 719 F.2d 302, 304 (9th Cir.1983).

§6.3 Mandamus. Mandamus is appropriate to challenge the judge's refusal to recuse herself. ***In re Kensington Int'l***, 353 F.3d 211, 219 (3d Cir.2003); ***Wyatt v. Rogers***, 92 F.3d 1074, 1081 (11th Cir.1996); ***In re Kansas Pub. Empls. Ret. Sys.***, 85 F.3d 1353, 1358 (8th Cir.1996); ***Nichols v. Alley***, 71 F.3d 347, 350 (10th Cir.1995); *see* ***In re United States***, 572 F.3d 301, 307 (7th Cir.2009).

1. Petition for mandamus. The petition for mandamus should allege the following:

(1) The petitioner has no other adequate means of relief, such as direct appeal. ***In re Cement Antitrust Litig.***, 688 F.2d 1297, 1301 (9th Cir.1982), *aff'd sub nom.* ***Arizona v. U.S. Dist. Ct. for the Dist. of Ariz.***, 459 U.S. 1191 (1983).

(2) The petitioner will be damaged or prejudiced in a way that is not correctable on appeal. *Id.*

(3) The district court's order is clearly erroneous as a matter of law—that is, the petitioner has a clear and indisputable right to relief. ***In re International Bus. Machs. Corp.***, 45 F.3d 641, 643 (2d Cir.1995); ***In re Drexel Burnham Lambert, Inc.***, 861 F.2d 1307, 1312-13 (2d Cir.1988); ***In re Cement Antitrust Litig.***, 688 F.2d at 1301; *see* ***In re Kansas Pub. Empls.***, 85 F.3d at 1358.

(4) There is an indication that the district court's order is a frequently repeated error or manifests a persistent disregard for federal rules. ***In re Cement Antitrust Litig.***, 688 F.2d at 1301.

(5) There is an indication that the district court's order raises new and important problems or legal issues. *Id.*

2. Response.

(1) Real party in interest. The real party in interest (the nonmovant) should file a response to the petition for mandamus. The real party in interest should not communicate ex parte about the recusal with the challenged judge; such a communication could become another reason to recuse. The real party in interest should object if the facts suggest that the petitioner is "judge-shopping." *See, e.g.*, ***In re Cargill, Inc.***, 66 F.3d 1256, 1262-63 (1st Cir.1995) (petitioner delayed attempt to retract waiver of disqualification ground until after the ruling on motion to dismiss); ***Schurz Comms. v. FCC***, 982 F.2d 1057, 1060 (7th Cir.1992) (P petitioned for mandamus only after judge issued major ruling against him).

(2) Not judge. A judge should not participate in a mandamus action that challenges her refusal to recuse herself. ***Rapp v. Van Dusen***, 350 F.2d 806, 810 (3d Cir.1965); ***U.S. v. Craig***, 875 F.Supp. 816, 818 (S.D.Fla. 1994). A judge who is challenged by a motion to recuse should not hire her own attorney, designate the attorney for the real party in interest as her attorney, or file her own response to the petition for mandamus. ***Rapp***, 350 F.2d at 813; ***Craig***, 875 F.Supp. at 818. By filing a response, a judge makes an appearance in the case and becomes aligned with the party opposing recusal. ***Craig***, 875 F.Supp. at 818. The judge should not communicate with either party about the petition for mandamus. *E.g.*, ***Alexander v. Primerica Holdings, Inc.***, 10 F.3d 155, 166 (3d Cir.1993) (judge should not have written letter to P objecting to statements in P's petition for mandamus).

§6.4 Relief.

1. Order recusal. The appellate court can order that the judge recuse herself. *See* ***U.S. v. Feldman***, 983 F.2d 144, 145 (9th Cir.1992).

2. Vacate acts. The appellate court can make the disqualification retroactive and vacate the judge's prior acts. *See* ***Shell Oil Co. v. U.S.***, 672 F.3d 1283, 1294 (Fed.Cir.2012); *see, e.g.*, ***U.S. v. Microsoft Corp.***, 253 F.3d 34, 116 (D.C.Cir.2001) (partial retroactive disqualification appropriate).

3. Reassign case. The appellate court can reassign the case. *See* ***Feldman***, 983 F.2d at 145. The appellate court has supervisory authority over district courts, and that authority allows the appellate court to reassign a case. *See* 28 U.S.C. §2106; ***Liteky v. U.S.***, 510 U.S. 540, 554 (1994); *see also* ***Wyler Summit Prtshp. v. Turner Broad. Sys.***, 235 F.3d 1184, 1196 (9th Cir.2000) (appellate court has statutory authorization and inherent authority to reassign case to different judge on remand when there are unusual circumstances). To reassign a case under §2106, the appellate court does not need to find actual bias or prejudice, but only that the facts "might reasonably cause an objective observer to question" the judge's impartiality. ***U.S. v. Microsoft Corp.***, 56 F.3d 1448, 1463 (D.C.Cir.1995); *see* ***Liljeberg v. Health Servs. Acquisition Corp.***, 486 U.S. 847, 865 (1988); ***In re International Bus. Machs. Corp.***, 45 F.3d 641, 643-45 (2d Cir.1995). In determining whether to reassign a case, the appellate court should consider the following:

(1) Whether the original judge would reasonably be expected to have substantial difficulty putting her previous views and findings aside. ***Armco, Inc. v. United Steelworkers***, 280 F.3d 669, 683 (6th Cir.2002).

(2) Whether reassignment is appropriate to preserve the appearance of justice. *Id.*

(3) Whether reassignment would entail waste and duplication out of proportion to any gains realized from reassignment. *Id.*

(4) Whether the case is stalemated because of the district judge's stubbornness. *Cf.* ***U.S. v. Remillong***, 55 F.3d 572, 577 & n.12 (11th Cir.1995) (criminal case; reassignment was proper when district judge did not follow appellate court's directives after second remand on sentencing).

F. MOTION TO EXTEND TIME

§1. GENERAL

§1.1 Rule. FRCP 6(b).

§1.2 Purpose. A motion to extend time (sometimes called a motion to "enlarge" time) is a request to extend the deadline for a party to act. FRCP 6(b)(1). By comparison, a motion for continuance is a request to delay or postpone a case that has been set for trial or for hearing on a summary-judgment motion. See "Motion for Continuance," ch. 5-G, p. 337.

NOTE

FRCP 6(b)(1) governs extensions of time limits imposed by the rules or by the court. ***Argentine Republic v. National Grid PLC****, 637 F.3d 365, 368 (D.C.Cir.2011). But FRCP 6(b)(1) does not govern extensions of statutory time limits. E.g.,* ***Argentine Republic****, 637 F.3d at 368 (FRCP 6(b) could not be used to extend deadline to serve motion to vacate arbitration award under 9 U.S.C. §12).*

§1.3 Forms. *O'Connor's Federal Civil Forms* (2012), FORMS 5F.

§1.4 Other references. 4B Wright & Miller, *Federal Practice & Procedure 3d* §§1165-1168 (2002 & Supp.2012); 1 *Moore's Federal Practice 3d* §§6.06-6.08 (2012).

§2. EXTENDING DEADLINES

§2.1 Most deadlines. Most deadlines can be extended by the court. *See* ***McIntosh v. Antonino***, 71 F.3d 29, 38 (1st Cir.1995); ***Hetzel v. Bethlehem Steel Corp.***, 50 F.3d 360, 367 (5th Cir.1995). When a party needs more time to file a document, it should ask for the extra time in advance. Some examples of motions to extend time under FRCP 6(b)(1) are the following:

1. Motion to extend the time to file objections to the magistrate judge's findings. ***Patterson v. Mintzes***, 717 F.2d 284, 286-87 (6th Cir.1983).

2. Motion to extend the 90-day requirement in FRCP 25(a)(1) for substituting the proper party after a party's death. ***Continental Bank v. Meyer***, 10 F.3d 1293, 1297 (7th Cir.1993); 1963 Notes to FRCP 25 at ¶2, p. 1171, this book.

3. Motion to extend the time to file a motion for attorney fees under FRCP 54(d)(2). *See* ***Planned Parenthood v. Attorney Gen. of N.J.***, 297 F.3d 253, 259 (3d Cir.2002).

§2.2 No extensions permitted. FRCP 6(b)(2) prohibits the court from granting extensions to take any action under the following rules:

1. FRCP 50(b), renewed motion for judgment as a matter of law. ***Rodick v. City of Schenectady***, 1 F.3d 1341, 1346 (2d Cir.1993); *see* ***In re Kontrick***, 295 F.3d 724, 731 (7th Cir.2002), *aff'd sub nom.* ***Kontrick v. Ryan***, 540 U.S. 443 (2004). See "No extension," ch. 10-B, §3.2, p. 777.

2. FRCP 50(d), motion for new trial. See "No extension," ch. 10-C, §2.2, p. 783.

3. FRCP 52(b), motion to amend findings. ***In re Texas Extrusion Corp.***, 836 F.2d 217, 220 (5th Cir.1988). See "No extension," ch. 10-E, §3.2, p. 800.

4. FRCP 59(b), motion for new trial. ***Tarlton v. Exxon***, 688 F.2d 973, 977-78 (5th Cir.1982). See "No extension," ch. 10-C, §2.2, p. 783.

5. FRCP 59(d), order for new trial on the court's own initiative. See "On court's initiative," ch. 10-C, §6.4, p. 787.

6. FRCP 59(e), motion to amend judgment. ***Albright v. Virtue***, 273 F.3d 564, 571 (3d Cir.2001); ***Hertz Corp. v. Alamo Rent-a-Car, Inc.***, 16 F.3d 1126, 1128 (11th Cir.1994); ***Collard v. U.S.***, 10 F.3d 718, 719 (10th Cir. 1993). See "No extension," ch. 10-D, §2.2, p. 794.

7. FRCP 60(b), motion for relief from judgment. ***Toolasprashad v. Bureau of Prisons***, 286 F.3d 576, 582 (D.C.Cir.2002). See "No extension," ch. 10-F, §2.1.1(2), p. 805.

§3. REQUESTS TO EXTEND TIME WITHOUT MOTION

A party may ask the court to extend the time to do an act before that time expires. FRCP 6(b)(1)(A) permits the court to grant an extension of time for "good cause," with or without a motion or notice. ***Jenkins v. Commonwealth Land Title Ins.***, 95 F.3d 791, 795 (9th Cir.1996). Even though FRCP 6(b)(1)(A) does not require a written motion when a party seeks additional time before the deadline, a party should always file a written motion or make the request on the record in open court in the presence of the court reporter. If the court denies an unwritten, unrecorded request, the request will not preserve error for appeal. The best practice is to file a motion that includes all the elements of the motion to extend time.

§4. MOTIONS TO EXTEND TIME

§4.1 Agreed motion to extend time. Generally, the parties' agreement to extend time is insufficient without a court order. *See* ***In re Sonoma V***, 703 F.2d 429, 431 (9th Cir.1983). *But see* FRCP 29(b) (parties can extend time for discovery deadlines without court approval if extension would not interfere with time set for completing discovery, for hearing, or for trial). Thus, the parties should file an agreed motion to extend time.

§4.2 Most motions to extend time. If a party needs additional time to act or respond to the other party's motion, the party should ask for an extension as soon as it realizes it needs additional time. The longer the party waits to ask for an extension, the more difficult it becomes to get one.

1. Form. For the general requirements for the form of a motion, see "Drafting motions," ch. 1-B, §3.1, p. 14.

2. In writing. If the motion is made before the deadline, the motion should be made in writing, but it can also be made orally in open court on the record. FRCP 7(b)(1)(A); *see* FRCP 6(b)(1). If the motion is made after the deadline, the motion must be made in writing. FRCP 6(b)(1)(B); *e.g.*, ***Drippe v. Tobelinski***, 604 F.3d 778, 784-85 (3d Cir.2010) (court's granting of D's third motion for summary judgment was reversed because motion was made seven months after deadline and without formal motion).

3. Affidavits. The party should attach affidavits to the motion to support all factual allegations. *Cf.* ***Sablan v. Department of Fin.***, 856 F.2d 1317, 1321 (9th Cir.1988) (assistant attorney general's affidavit attached to support motion for continuance).

4. Grounds. The motion to extend time should state the following:

(1) Deadline. The motion should identify the deadline it seeks to extend.

(2) Excusable neglect. The motion should state whether the request for an extension is being filed before or after the deadline. If the party asks for additional time after the deadline, FRCP 6(b)(1)(B) requires that the party show good cause and that the failure to act be the result of "excusable neglect." ***Donald v. Cook Cty. Sheriff's Dept.***, 95 F.3d 548, 558 (7th Cir.1996); *see* ***Huggins v. FedEx Ground Package Sys.***, 592 F.3d 853, 856 (8th Cir. 2010). In ***Pioneer Inv. Servs. v. Brunswick Assocs.***, 507 U.S. 380 (1993), a bankruptcy case, the Supreme Court expanded the definition of excusable neglect; thus, when determining what constitutes excusable neglect, avoid cases

that predate ***Pioneer***. *See* ***Committee for Idaho's High Desert, Inc. v. Yost***, 92 F.3d 814, 825 n.4 (9th Cir.1996) (***Pioneer***'s analysis of excusable neglect applies to FRCP 6(b)). A determination of excusable neglect takes into account all relevant circumstances surrounding the party's omission. ***Pioneer Inv.***, 507 U.S. at 395; ***Virella-Nieves v. Briggs & Stratton Corp.***, 53 F.3d 451, 454 (1st Cir.1995). In ***Pioneer***, the Supreme Court identified a nonexclusive list of factors the district court should consider when determining excusable neglect: (1) the danger of prejudice to the nonmovant, (2) the length of the delay and its potential impact on judicial proceedings, (3) the reason for the delay, including whether it was within the reasonable control of the movant, and (4) whether the movant acted in good faith. ***Pioneer Inv.***, 507 U.S. at 395; ***Yesudian v. Howard Univ.***, 270 F.3d 969, 971 (D.C.Cir.2001); *see* ***MCI Telecomms. Corp. v. Teleconcepts, Inc.***, 71 F.3d 1086, 1097 (3d Cir.1995) (excusable neglect requires demonstration of good faith by party seeking extension and some reasonable basis for noncompliance within time specified in rules). The motion to extend time should address the ***Pioneer*** factors:

(a) No prejudice. The motion should state that the other party will not be prejudiced by the extension and give reasons why.

(b) Length of delay & impact. The motion should identify the length of the delay and state that its potential impact on judicial proceedings is insignificant. *See* ***Fowler v. Jones***, 899 F.2d 1088, 1094 (11th Cir. 1990). If possible, the motion should explain how the court's schedule can be rearranged to eliminate or minimize any inconvenience that may be caused by the delay.

(c) Reason for delay. The motion should identify the reason for the delay. Excusable neglect will excuse delays caused by circumstances beyond the movant's control and may excuse the mistake, inadvertence, or carelessness of the party or its attorney. ***Pioneer Inv.***, 507 U.S. at 396; ***Panis v. Mission Hills Bank***, 60 F.3d 1486, 1494 (10th Cir.1995); *see, e.g.*, ***Steel v. Alma Pub. Sch. Dist.***, 162 F.Supp.2d 1083, 1084 (W.D.Ark.2001) (court granted attorney's motion to extend time for responding to motions to dismiss because delay in receiving motions was caused by attorney's change of address). Although ***Pioneer*** construed excusable neglect to include an attorney's negligence, the circuits seldom permit a party to escape the effects of its attorney's negligence. *See, e.g.*, ***Hawks v. J.P. Morgan Chase Bank***, 591 F.3d 1043, 1047-48 (8th Cir.2010) (fact that attorney was occupied with other hearings was not excusable neglect); ***Yost***, 92 F.3d at 824 (attorney's unfamiliarity with amended local and federal rules was not excusable neglect); ***McIntosh v. Antonino***, 71 F.3d 29, 38 & n.8 (1st Cir.1995) (fact that attorney was suddenly called out of town on other business on last day of extension period was not excusable neglect); ***Kyle v. Campbell Soup Co.***, 28 F.3d 928, 931-32 (9th Cir.1994) (attorney's miscalculation of time after service was not excusable neglect). *But see* ***Benjamin v. Aroostook Med. Ctr., Inc.***, 57 F.3d 101, 108 (1st Cir.1995) (court of appeals changed order of dismissal with prejudice to dismissal without prejudice after attorney missed hearing because of serious illness).

(d) Good faith. The motion should state that the movant acted in good faith and should relate facts supporting that statement. *See* ***MCI Telecomms.***, 71 F.3d at 1097.

5. Proposed order. Some districts require the movant to submit a proposed order with the motion. In those districts, the movant should prepare a written order for the court's signature and submit it with the motion. See "Proposed order," ch. 1-B, §3.1.11, p. 16.

6. Response. If the nonmovant objects to the motion to extend time, it can file a response that challenges the facts stated in the motion and the movant's application of the ***Pioneer*** factors.

§4.3 Motion to extend time to serve party. If the plaintiff needs additional time to complete service of the complaint and summons on the defendant, it should move to extend time. See "Motion to extend time to serve," ch. 2-H, §4.2, p. 153; "Failure to serve defendant with suit," ch. 7-D, §3.4, p. 645. When requesting additional time to serve a party with the complaint and summons, a party should file a motion to extend time that meets the following requirements:

1. Identity of movant. Although FRCP 4(m) considers the plaintiff to be the party seeking service and the defendant to be the party being served, the term "plaintiff" is used generically to include a defendant who asserts claims against nonparties under FRCP 13(h), 14, 19, 20, or 21. 1993 Notes to FRCP 4 at ¶64, p. 1144, this book. Thus, the movant should identify whether it is the plaintiff or defendant in the motion.

2. Form. For the general requirements for the form of a motion, see "Drafting motions," ch. 1-B, §3.1, p. 14.

3. In writing. A motion to extend the time to serve the defendant should be in writing, but it may be made orally in open court on the record. FRCP 6(b)(1), 7(b)(1)(A).

4. Affidavits. The motion should be supported by affidavits presenting the facts about the inability to timely serve the defendant.

5. Grounds. FRCP 4(m) requires the court to extend the time to serve the defendant if the movant shows good cause and permits the court to extend the time even if the movant does not show good cause. ***Kurka v. Iowa Cty.***, 628 F.3d 953, 957 (8th Cir.2010); ***Lemoge v. U.S.***, 587 F.3d 1188, 1198 (9th Cir.2009); ***Zapata v. City of N.Y.***, 502 F.3d 192, 196 (2d Cir.2007); 1993 Notes to FRCP 4 at ¶63, p. 1144, this book. The motion should state facts (and attach documents, if possible) that support the statement of good cause or the reason for the delay. *See* ***Kurka***, 628 F.3d at 959 (reason for delay is generally key factor).

(1) Good cause. If the plaintiff shows good cause for the delay in serving the defendant, the court must extend the time to serve the defendant beyond the 120 days permitted under FRCP 4(m). ***Lemoge***, 587 F.3d at 1198; ***Laurence v. Wall***, 551 F.3d 92, 94 (1st Cir.2008); *see* ***Kurka***, 628 F.3d at 958 (focus is on whether there is good cause for failure to serve, not whether there is good cause for extension of time). FRCP 4(m) does not define good cause, but it at least requires a showing of good faith and some reasonable basis for the delay in service. ***Kurka***, 628 F.3d at 957. Acceptable reasons for service being delayed beyond the 120 days permitted under FRCP 4(m) include the following:

(a) The defendant consciously evaded service. ***Kurka***, 628 F.3d at 957; 1993 Notes to FRCP 4 at ¶63, p. 1144, this book.

(b) The delay was a result of the conduct of a third person, usually the process server. ***Kurka***, 628 F.3d at 957.

(c) The defendant is the U.S. government. Under FRCP 4(i)(4), the court is explicitly directed to grant additional time to complete service on all the multiple officers and agencies required when the United States is a defendant. 1993 Notes to FRCP 4 at ¶63, p. 1144, this book.

(d) The plaintiff is pro se, is presently incarcerated, and is forced to rely on the U.S. Marshal's Office for service. *See* ***Fowler v. Jones***, 899 F.2d 1088, 1093-94 (11th Cir.1990) (pre-1993-amendment case).

(2) No good cause. Even if the plaintiff cannot show good cause for the delay in serving the defendant, the court has the discretion to extend the time to serve the defendant beyond the 120 days permitted under FRCP 4(m). ***Henderson v. U.S.***, 517 U.S. 654, 662 (1996); ***Kurka***, 628 F.3d at 957; ***Lemoge***, 587 F.3d at 1198; ***Zapata***, 502 F.3d at 196; 1993 Notes to FRCP 4 at ¶63, p. 1144, this book. For the court to grant an extension when the plaintiff does not show good cause, the plaintiff should establish excusable neglect. ***Kurka***, 628 F.3d at 957; ***Lemoge***, 587 F.3d at 1198.

NOTE

To establish excusable neglect, a plaintiff should show (1) the possibility of prejudice to the defendant, (2) the length of the delay and the potential impact on the proceedings, (3) the reason for the delay, including whether the delay was within the plaintiff's reasonable control, and (4) whether the plaintiff acted in good faith. ***Kurka****, 628 F.3d at 959. These factors, however, overlap with the factors for good cause. See id. at 957 (showing of good cause requires, at a minimum, showing of excusable neglect);* ***Lemoge****, 587 F.3d at 1198 n.3 (same). Because of the overlap, a plaintiff should be sure to show additional factors, such as diligence, usefulness, lack of prejudice, and harm to the plaintiff. See* ***Lemoge****, 587 F.3d at 1198 n.3. See "Additional factors," §4.3.6, p. 336.*

6. Additional factors. The motion should address the following:

(1) Diligence. The plaintiff was diligent in attempting service and requesting the extension. *See **Lab Crafters, Inc. v. Flow Safe, Inc.***, 233 F.R.D. 282, 284 (E.D.N.Y.2005).

(2) Usefulness of extension. The extension will make service possible. The plaintiff should ask the court for an extension of a specific number of days to complete service on the defendant.

(3) No inconvenience or prejudice. The extension will not prejudice the unserved defendant and will not be an inconvenience to the court, opposing parties, or witnesses. *See **Cardenas v. City of Chi.***, 646 F.3d 1001, 1006 (7th Cir.2011) (court should consider relative hardships of parties); ***Zapata***, 502 F.3d at 197 (court should weigh impact of dismissal or extension on all parties).

NOTE

*While the running of the statute of limitations is one factor for an extension, that factor alone does not establish prejudice to a defendant. **Boley v. Kaymark**, 123 F.3d 756, 759 (3d Cir.1997); see **Cardenas**, 646 F.3d at 1006.*

(4) Harm to plaintiff. The plaintiff will suffer harm if the court denies the extension. The motion should describe the harm the plaintiff will suffer. *See **Lemoge***, 587 F.3d at 1198. For example, the plaintiff will not be able to refile the suit because the statute of limitations will have run. The running of the statute of limitations, however, does not require the court to extend the time to serve the defendant. ***Kurka***, 628 F.3d at 959; ***Petrucelli v. Bohringer & Ratzinger, GmbH***, 46 F.3d 1298, 1306 (3d Cir.1995); *see, e.g.*, ***Zapata***, 502 F.3d at 199 (when P made no effort to effect service, did not ask for extension in reasonable time, and provided no excuse for delay, court denied extension even though statute of limitations would bar refiling).

7. Proposed order. Some districts require the movant to submit a proposed order with the motion. In those districts, the movant should prepare a written order for the court's signature and submit it with the motion. See "Proposed order," ch. 1-B, §3.1.11, p. 16.

8. Order. If the court grants the extension, it must order the plaintiff to complete service on the defendant within a specified time. If the court denies the extension, it must dismiss the suit against the unserved defendant without prejudice. FRCP 4(m).

§4.4 Motion to extend time for discovery. If the party needs additional time to conduct or complete discovery, it should move for an extension. *See **U.S. v. $100,375 in U.S. Currency***, 70 F.3d 438, 440 (6th Cir.1995). In most cases, a motion to extend the time for discovery involves a continuance of the trial date. See "Additional time for discovery," ch. 5-G, §3.2, p. 337.

§4.5 Motion to extend time to substitute party. If family members of a deceased party have difficulty identifying the party's legal representative, they should move for an extension of the time to file a motion for substitution under FRCP 25. ***Jones Inlet Marina, Inc. v. Inglima***, 204 F.R.D. 238, 240 (E.D.N.Y.2001).

§5. APPELLATE REVIEW

The standard for reviewing the district court's ruling on a motion to extend time is abuse of discretion. ***Lujan v. National Wildlife Fed'n***, 497 U.S. 871, 895-96 & n.5 (1990); ***Allen v. Murph***, 194 F.3d 722, 724 (6th Cir.1999); ***Ellis v. University of Kan. Med. Ctr.***, 163 F.3d 1186, 1193 (10th Cir.1998); ***Smith v. Severn***, 129 F.3d 419, 424 (7th Cir.1997); ***Jenkins v. Commonwealth Land Title Ins.***, 95 F.3d 791, 795 (9th Cir.1996); ***Petrucelli v. Bohringer & Ratzinger, GmbH***, 46 F.3d 1298, 1306 (3d Cir.1995).

G. MOTION FOR CONTINUANCE

§1. GENERAL

§1.1 Rule. None. See FRCP 15(b); see also FRCP 56(d)(2).

§1.2 Purpose. A motion for continuance is a request to postpone or delay a case that has been set for trial or is in trial or that has been set for hearing on a summary-judgment motion. By comparison, a motion to extend time is a request to extend the deadline for a party to act. See "Motion to Extend Time," ch. 5-F, p. 332.

§1.3 Forms. *O'Connor's Federal Civil Forms* (2012), FORMS 5G.

§1.4 Other references. 9 Wright & Miller, *Federal Practice & Procedure 3d* §2352 (2008 & Supp.2012); 8 *Moore's Federal Practice 3d* §40.02[5] (2012).

§2. MOTION

§2.1 Form. For the general requirements for the form of a motion, see "Drafting motions," ch. 1-B, §3.1, p. 14.

§2.2 In writing. A motion for continuance should be in writing. *See* FRCP 7(b)(1)(A).

§2.3 Affidavits. The motion should be supported by affidavits presenting the facts that create the need for the continuance. The motion should include affidavits of both the party and the attorney so the court is assured that the client is aware of the requested delay.

§2.4 Notice. The movant must serve notice of the filing of a motion for continuance on opposing counsel. *See* FRCP 5(a)(1)(D).

§2.5 When to file. A party may file a motion for continuance anytime after the defendant files an answer, subject to any filing deadlines established by the scheduling order or court order. *See, e.g.*, Judge Stengel's Policies & Procedures (E.D.Pa.), ¶II.B (motions for continuance of trial date, discovery deadline, or dispositive-motion deadline must be made early enough to allow court time to consider motion); Judge Fish's Specific Requirements (N.D.Tex.), ¶II.A.3 (motions for continuance of trial date must be made before deadline for completion of discovery). Even after the scheduling-order deadline has passed, a party may need to file a motion for continuance if the opposing party is granted leave to amend its pleadings. *See* FRCP 16(b).

§2.6 Proposed order. Some districts require the movant to submit a proposed order with the motion. In those districts, the movant should prepare a written order for the court's signature and submit it with the motion. See "Proposed order," ch. 1-B, §3.1.11, p. 16.

§3. GROUNDS

§3.1 Agreed continuance. Before the final pretrial conference, an agreed motion for continuance signed by all parties can be filed in the court. All parties should be present at the final pretrial conference to explain the reasons for the requested continuance.

§3.2 Additional time for discovery. In most cases, a motion for continuance to conduct discovery involves an extension of the trial date. *See* ***Martel v. County of L.A.***, 56 F.3d 993, 995 (9th Cir.1995); ***Daniel J. Hartwig Assocs. v. Kanner***, 913 F.2d 1213, 1222 (7th Cir.1990). When a party needs additional time to complete discovery and the extension of the discovery deadlines will affect the date set for trial, the party should ask in one motion to extend the time for discovery and to continue the date for trial. The motion for continuance should state the following:

1. Discovery deadline & trial setting. The motion should identify the discovery deadline that needs to be extended and the date the case is set for trial.

2. Extend trial setting. The motion should ask the court to extend the trial setting and grant additional time for discovery; it should state why additional time is necessary and exactly how much time is necessary to complete discovery. For example, if the other party recently amended its pleadings, the motion can state that additional

time for discovery is needed to respond to the amended matters. *See, e.g.*, ***Menendez v. Perishable Distribs., Inc.***, 763 F.2d 1374, 1379-80 (11th Cir.1985) (court should not have permitted Ds to add affirmative defenses without giving P additional time for discovery).

3. Identify necessary discovery. The motion should identify what specific discovery must be completed or what new discovery needs to be undertaken. *See* ***Employers Teamsters Local Nos. 175 & 505 Pension Trust Fund v. Clorox Co.***, 353 F.3d 1125, 1129 (9th Cir.2004) (burden is on party seeking additional discovery to present sufficient facts to show existence of evidence sought). The party should identify the witnesses it wants to depose, the specific documents it wants to examine, or the specific interrogatories it wants answered. *See, e.g.*, ***Perkins v. American Elec. Power Fuel Sup.***, 246 F.3d 593, 605-06 (6th Cir.2001) (no showing of what information or discovery was needed); ***Stevens v. Bangor & Aroostook R.R.***, 97 F.3d 594, 600 n.6 (1st Cir.1996) (D's motion stated only that it needed to investigate further, not that it needed to locate expert witness).

4. Relevant & material. The motion must show that the discovery needed by the movant is relevant and material. *See* ***Perkins***, 246 F.3d at 605-06; ***U.S. v. Antioch Found.***, 822 F.2d 693, 697 (7th Cir.1987); *see also* ***Kozikowski v. Toll Bros.***, 354 F.3d 16, 26 (1st Cir.2003) (motion must state plausible basis for believing that specified facts will influence outcome of pending motion); ***Employers Teamsters***, 353 F.3d at 1129-30 (party must show that additional evidence sought would prevent summary judgment).

5. Substantial prejudice. The motion must show that the movant will suffer actual and substantial prejudice if it is not permitted to get the evidence. ***Martel***, 56 F.3d at 995. The prejudice that must be shown to justify a continuance to obtain additional discovery is substantially greater because of the court's unusually broad discretion to control discovery. *See* ***U.S. v. Mejia***, 69 F.3d 309, 318 n.11 (9th Cir.1995).

6. Diligence. The motion must show that the party has been reasonably diligent in securing discovery. *See* ***Kozikowski***, 354 F.3d at 26; ***Antioch Found.***, 822 F.2d at 697. When a party cannot show diligence, the court is not likely to grant a continuance. ***Reeg v. Shaughnessy***, 570 F.2d 309, 316 (10th Cir.1978); *see, e.g.*, ***Nidds v. Schindler Elevator Corp.***, 113 F.3d 912, 921 (9th Cir.1996) (second motion for continuance refused after party did not take depositions within time permitted under first continuance).

(1) Statement of diligence. The motion must state why the party was not able to get the evidence earlier even though it diligently used the discovery procedures. A party who does not diligently use the discovery procedures can seldom prove reversible error if the court refuses a continuance. *See, e.g.*, ***McKenzie Constr., Inc. v. Maynard***, 823 F.2d 43, 48 (3d Cir.1987) (no reversible error for refusal to allow continuance after party ignored order setting time for discovery).

(2) Description of diligence. The motion must describe the attempts to secure the evidence.

7. Not for delay. The motion must show that the continuance is not just for delay but so that justice may be done.

8. No undue inconvenience to court. If the party is in a position to explain how the court's schedule can be arranged to eliminate or minimize inconvenience, the motion should include that information. *See, e.g.*, ***Fowler v. Jones***, 899 F.2d 1088, 1094 (11th Cir.1990) (court faced considerable delay by granting continuance to serve new Ds after jury had been selected).

9. No prejudice to opposing party. The motion should explain why the other party will not suffer prejudice as a result of the continuance. For example, when a request for additional time for discovery is the result of the other party's late pleading amendment, misconduct, or surprise evidence, that party will not be prejudiced by the extension. *See, e.g.*, ***Menendez***, 763 F.2d at 1379-80 (trial amendment added affirmative defenses); ***Szeliga v. General Motors Corp.***, 728 F.2d 566, 568 (1st Cir.1984) (D did not list films as potential exhibits in pretrial memorandum); ***Conway v. Chemical Leaman Tank Lines, Inc.***, 687 F.2d 108, 112 (5th Cir.1982) (unidentified witness called at trial).

10. Affidavits. The motion must include affidavits that support all factual allegations in the motion. *See, e.g.*, ***Sablan v. Department of Fin.***, 856 F.2d 1317, 1321 (9th Cir.1988) (assistant attorney general attached affidavit in support of motion for continuance).

§3.3 Witness or party unavailable for trial. If a witness or party is unavailable for trial and the party cannot proceed to trial without the witness, the party should move for a continuance. *See, e.g.*, ***Mraovic v. Elgin, Joliet & E. Ry.***, 897 F.2d 268, 271 (7th Cir.1990) (P requested continuance because medical experts were unavailable). The party should file a motion for continuance that includes the following information:

1. Identity of witness or party. The motion should provide the witness's or party's name and address (street, county, and state of residence).

2. Unavailability of witness or party. The motion should state why the witness or party is not available to testify at trial. *See, e.g.*, ***Johnston v. Harris Cty. Flood Control Dist.***, 869 F.2d 1565, 1570 (5th Cir.1989) (party unavailable because he had suffered heart attack). The most convincing reason for a continuance based on the unavailability of a witness or party is that the circumstances have changed, as with a sudden illness. ***Daniel J. Hartwig Assocs. v. Kanner***, 913 F.2d 1213, 1222-23 (7th Cir.1990); *see, e.g.*, ***Johnston***, 869 F.2d at 1570 (heart attack). If a witness or party is unavailable because of illness, the movant should attach to the motion the affidavit of a doctor for the witness or party. *See* ***Command-Aire Corp. v. Ontario Mech. Sales & Serv.***, 963 F.2d 90, 96 (5th Cir.1992) (court not required to delay case indefinitely when it is unknown if witness would ever be able to appear); *see, e.g.*, ***Weisman v. Alleco, Inc.***, 925 F.2d 77, 79 (4th Cir.1991) (no evidence of medical condition that necessitated hospitalization); ***Schneider Nat'l Carriers, Inc. v. Carr***, 903 F.2d 1154, 1158 (7th Cir.1990) (P made no effort to show that doctors would have forbidden him to attend trial). The doctor's affidavit should state the following:

(1) The nature and severity of the illness. ***Weisman***, 925 F.2d at 79.

(2) The witness or party is too ill to testify at trial, or the witness's or party's health will be jeopardized if the person is forced to attend the trial. *See, e.g.*, ***Amarin Plastics, Inc. v. Maryland Cup Corp.***, 946 F.2d 147, 152 (1st Cir.1991) (doctor certified that witness was in poor health and that testifying might endanger witness's health).

(3) If and when the witness or party might be able to attend the trial. *See, e.g.*, ***Command-Aire***, 963 F.2d at 96 (doctor's letter said party could not leave home but did not explain when he could attend trial; continuance denied); ***Johnston***, 869 F.2d at 1570 (party's doctor did not state when party would be able to appear; continuance denied).

3. Description of testimony. The motion must describe the witness's anticipated testimony and what it is expected to prove. *See, e.g.*, ***Gardner v. Federated Dept. Stores***, 907 F.2d 1348, 1354 (2d Cir.1990) (description of proposed testimony showed that it was speculative in nature).

4. Materiality. The motion must show that the witness's testimony is material. *See, e.g.*, ***Gardner***, 907 F.2d at 1354 (movant did not demonstrate that excluded witness's testimony was material); ***Sturgeon v. Airborne Freight Corp.***, 778 F.2d 1154, 1158-59 (5th Cir.1985) (movant did not explain how absent witness's testimony would have been anything other than expert testimony).

5. Substantial prejudice. The motion must show that the party will be substantially prejudiced if it is not permitted to present the evidence. *See, e.g.*, ***Johnston***, 869 F.2d at 1570-71 (movant did not show that absence of D created prejudice); ***Harbor Tug & Barge, Inc. v. Belcher Towing Co.***, 733 F.2d 823, 827 (11th Cir.1984) (movant did not suffer prejudice when court did not continue case for purpose of introducing cumulative evidence). The absence of a witness or party from trial is not enough to prove prejudice and justify a continuance when the testimony is available by deposition. *See, e.g.*, ***Command-Aire***, 963 F.2d at 96 (court not required to delay case indefinitely because of witness's incapacity). However, the movant may still argue that the deposition testimony of the absent party or witness is substantially and materially different from what live testimony would reveal. ***Wells v. Rushing***, 755 F.2d 376, 381 (5th Cir.1985).

6. Diligence. The motion must show that the party used diligence to procure the testimony of the absent party or witness. *See, e.g.*, ***Havee v. Belk***, 775 F.2d 1209, 1223 (4th Cir.1985) (party had over a year to prepare its case and submit expert's valuation opinion).

§3.4 Attorney unavailable for trial. If a party's attorney is unavailable for trial and the party cannot proceed to trial without the attorney, the party should move for a continuance. The motion for continuance should include the following information:

1. Attorney necessary. The motion should state that the attorney's presence is necessary for the proper presentation of the case.

2. Attorney unavailable. The motion must state why the attorney is not available for trial. *See, e.g.*, ***Laborers Clean-Up Contract Admin. Trust Fund v. Uriarte Clean-Up Serv.***, 736 F.2d 516, 520 (9th Cir.1984) (D's attorney was involved in another trial); ***Smith-Weik Mach. Corp. v. Murdock Mach. & Eng'g***, 423 F.2d 842, 844 (5th Cir.1970) (D's attorney became ill just before trial).

3. No substitute possible. The motion must state why another attorney in the same firm or another attorney named in the pleadings, if any, could not handle the case. *See, e.g.*, ***Smith-Weik Mach.***, 423 F.2d at 844-45 (local attorney was not sufficiently informed about facts and pertinent law to conduct trial by himself on short notice).

4. No fault of party. The motion should state that the lack of representation is not the party's fault. *See, e.g.*, ***Falcon Trading Grp. v. SEC***, 102 F.3d 579, 581 (D.C.Cir.1996) (client who knew of attorney's unpreparedness for hearing should have retained other attorney rather than allowing hearing to pass); ***Northeast Women's Ctr., Inc. v. McMonagle***, 939 F.2d 57, 68 (3d Cir.1991) (continuance denied because party requested that his attorney withdraw so he could represent himself).

5. Order. The court should grant a continuance for the party to secure an attorney if the party was not at fault for being without one. ***McMonagle***, 939 F.2d at 68.

§3.5 Surprise evidence. If a party needs additional time to respond to either surprise evidence presented during trial or evidence that was beyond the scope of the pleadings, the party should ask for a continuance. *See* FRCP 15(b)(1); ***Tobin v. Astra Pharm.***, 993 F.2d 528, 541 (6th Cir.1993); ***In re Control Data Corp. Sec. Litig.***, 933 F.2d 616, 621-22 (8th Cir.1991); ***Johnson v. H.K. Webster, Inc.***, 775 F.2d 1, 8-9 (1st Cir.1985); ***Hardin v. Manitowoc-Forsythe Corp.***, 691 F.2d 449, 456-57 (10th Cir.1982). The motion may be made orally on the record at the time of the surprise, but if possible, it should be reduced to writing and filed with the court.

§3.6 Response to motion for summary judgment. A party may request time to obtain affidavits or declarations or conduct discovery in order to respond to a motion for summary judgment. See "Motion for Continuance," ch. 7-B, §9, p. 620.

§4. RESPONSE

A party opposing a motion for continuance should file a response and challenge the factors established by the movant—that is, diligence, relevance, materiality, and prejudice. The respondent should argue that the motion for continuance is solely for the purpose of delay. If the response contains evidence outside the record, it should be supported by an affidavit.

§5. APPELLATE REVIEW

The standard for reviewing the district court's ruling on a motion for continuance is abuse of discretion. ***Ungar v. Sarafite***, 376 U.S. 575, 589 (1964); ***Research Sys. v. IPSOS Publicite***, 276 F.3d 914, 919 (7th Cir.2002); ***Beard v. Flying J, Inc.***, 266 F.3d 792, 802 (8th Cir.2001); ***FTC v. Gill***, 265 F.3d 944, 954-55 (9th Cir.2001); ***Dorsey v. Scott Wetzel Servs.***, 84 F.3d 170, 171 (5th Cir.1996); ***Loinaz v. EG&G, Inc.***, 910 F.2d 1, 6 (1st Cir.1990).

§5.1 *Flynt* factors. In determining whether the district court abused its discretion in denying a motion for continuance, the appellate court may consider the factors listed in ***U.S. v. Flynt***, 756 F.2d 1352, 1358-59 (9th Cir.1985), *amended*, 764 F.2d 675 (9th Cir.1985):

1. The movant's diligence in attempting to prepare its case for the originally scheduled trial date. *Id.* at 1359.

2. The likelihood that the grant of a continuance would have resolved the problem that led the movant to seek a continuance. *Id.*

3. The inconvenience that a continuance would have caused the court and the opposing party. *Id.*

4. The extent to which the movant might have suffered harm as a result of the district court's denial. *Id.* Most courts hold that the movant must demonstrate actual prejudice as a result of the denial of the continuance. *E.g.*, ***U.S. v. Chiappetta***, 289 F.3d 995, 998 (7th Cir.2002); ***Perkins v. American Elec. Power Fuel Sup.***, 246 F.3d 593, 605-06 (6th Cir.2001); ***HC Gun & Knife Shows, Inc. v. City of Houston***, 201 F.3d 544, 550 (5th Cir.2000).

§5.2 Other factors. The appellate court may consider other factors to determine whether the district court abused its discretion in denying a motion for continuance. *See* 9 Wright & Miller §2352. The following are some of the other factors courts have considered:

1. Changed circumstances that a party cannot reasonably be expected to adjust to without an extension of time. ***Daniel J. Hartwig Assocs. v. Kanner***, 913 F.2d 1213, 1222-23 (7th Cir.1990).

2. Whether the district judge's ruling violates a local rule for establishing trial settings. *See* ***Martel v. County of L.A.***, 56 F.3d 993, 1000-01 (9th Cir.1995) (Kleinfeld, Fletcher, Reinhardt, JJ., dissenting).

3. How much time was requested. ***FDIC v. Houde***, 90 F.3d 600, 608 (1st Cir.1996).

4. Whether the movant contributed to the circumstance. *Id.*

5. Whether alternative relief was granted. ***Star Fin. Servs. v. AASTAR Mortg. Corp.***, 89 F.3d 5, 12 (1st Cir.1996).

H. MOTION IN LIMINE

§1. GENERAL

§1.1 Rule. None. See FRE 103 (rulings on evidence).

§1.2 Purpose. A motion in limine permits a party to identify before trial certain evidentiary rulings that the court may be asked to make. The purpose of a motion in limine is to prevent the other party from asking prejudicial questions or introducing prejudicial evidence in front of the jury. *See Black's Law Dictionary* 1109 (9th ed. 2009).

§1.3 Timetable & forms. Timetable, Pleadings & Pretrial-Motions Schedule, p. 1574; ***O'Connor's Federal Civil Forms*** (2012), FORMS 5H.

§1.4 Other references. 21 Wright & Graham, *Federal Practice & Procedure 2d* §§5037.10-5037.12, 5042 (2005 & Supp.2012); 22A Wright & Graham, *Federal Practice & Procedure* §5224 (2012 & Supp.2012); 3 *Moore's Federal Practice 3d* §16.77[4][d] (2012).

§2. MOTION

Because no rule or statute provides a procedure for a motion in limine, the movant should look to the local rules or case law.

§2.1 Form. For the general requirements for the form of a motion, see "Drafting motions," ch. 1-B, §3.1, p. 14.

§2.2 Procedure. A party should file a motion in limine and serve copies on all parties. FRCP 5(a)(1)(D), (d).

§2.3 Grounds. The motion should include the following information:

1. The evidence or question the party anticipates its opponent will attempt to introduce or ask in front of the jury.

PRACTICE TIP

In addition to identifying potential evidentiary issues, motions in limine can also be a useful tool for ascertaining an opponent's trial strategy. For example, if the nonmovant objects to the movant's request to exclude unrelated drug or alcohol use or references to current events, the movant can assume that the nonmovant intends to raise those issues. Motions in limine are also frequently used as a trial-management tool because they allow the movant to ask the court to prohibit objectionable trial tactics or procedures. Common examples of objectionable tactics are improper requests in the jury's presence or references to the size or location of an attorney's firm.

2. Why the evidence or question is inadmissible. Any evidence that the rules of evidence classify as inadmissible may be made the subject of a motion in limine. The following are examples of inadmissible evidence that may be addressed in a motion in limine:

(1) Evidence of other crimes, wrongs, or acts that is not admissible to prove the person's character to show that on a particular occasion the person acted in accordance with the character. FRE 404(b)(1).

(2) Evidence of a subsequent remedial measure to prove negligence. FRE 407; ***Wood v. Morbark Indus.***, 70 F.3d 1201, 1206 (11th Cir.1995); ***Mehojah v. Drummond***, 56 F.3d 1213, 1214-15 (10th Cir.1995).

(3) Settlement negotiations. FRE 408; ***Affiliated Mfrs. v. Aluminum Co.***, 56 F.3d 521, 526-30 (3d Cir. 1995); ***Cassino v. Reichhold Chems., Inc.***, 817 F.2d 1338, 1342-43 (9th Cir.1987); ***Olin Corp. v. Insurance Co. of N. Am.***, 603 F.Supp. 445, 449 (S.D.N.Y.1985). *But see* ***Maryland Cas. Co. v. Knight***, 96 F.3d 1284, 1293-94 (9th Cir. 1996) (settlement negotiations were relevant to suit for emotional distress because P benefited from settlement).

(4) Liability insurance coverage. FRE 411; ***Higgins v. Hicks Co.***, 756 F.2d 681, 684-85 (8th Cir.1985).

(5) Evidence protected by a privilege. *See* FRE 501.

(6) Criminal convictions. FRE 609; ***U.S. v. Carter***, 528 F.2d 844, 846-47 (8th Cir.1975).

(7) Evidence of a party's earlier antitrust violations. ***Sullivan v. National Football League***, 34 F.3d 1091, 1113 (1st Cir.1994).

(8) An expert's opinions that are not supported by admissible facts. ***Guillory v. Domtar Indus.***, 95 F.3d 1320, 1331 (5th Cir.1996); ***Tyger Constr. Co. v. Pensacola Constr. Co.***, 29 F.3d 137, 142 (4th Cir.1994).

(9) Testimony of experts who are not identified in responses to interrogatories and not designated by the time specified in the pretrial order or local rule. ***Coastal Fuels v. Caribbean Pet. Corp.***, 79 F.3d 182, 202-03 (1st Cir.1996); ***Alldread v. City of Grenada***, 988 F.2d 1425, 1435-36 (5th Cir.1993).

(10) Expert testimony outside the scope of the expert's written opinion produced during pretrial discovery. ***Thudium v. Allied Prods.***, 36 F.3d 767, 769-70 (8th Cir.1994).

(11) A party's secondary evidence in support of its claim because it did not make a sufficiently diligent search for material requested during discovery. ***Cartier v. Jackson***, 59 F.3d 1046, 1048 (10th Cir.1995).

(12) Evidence supporting an issue not contained in the final pretrial order. ***Life Care Ctrs., Inc. v. Charles Town Assocs.***, 79 F.3d 496, 507 (6th Cir.1996).

(13) Computer-animated videotape evidence purporting to re-create events at issue, but not substantially similar to the actual events. ***Hinkle v. City of Clarksburg***, 81 F.3d 416, 424-25 (4th Cir.1996).

(14) In the damages stage of a bifurcated trial, evidence characterizing the defendant's misconduct. ***Pescatore v. Pan Am. World Airways, Inc.***, 97 F.3d 1, 16 (2d Cir.1996).

3. Why a trial objection would not protect the movant if the evidence were offered or the question asked in front of the jury.

4. Why the opposing attorney should be required to approach the bench before introducing the evidence or asking the question.

PRACTICE TIP

If you want a pretrial ruling that definitively excludes evidence, the motion should not be called a motion in limine. Instead, you should file a motion to exclude evidence, asking the court to hold a hearing and enter an order excluding the evidence. For example, if a party asks the court to conduct a ***Daubert*** *"gatekeeper" hearing and exclude the other party's scientific expert, the court could make a final ruling excluding the testimony, instead of making just a preliminary ruling. See* ***Daubert v. Merrell Dow Pharms.****, 509 U.S. 579, 592 (1993); see, e.g.,* ***U.S. v. Malik****, 345 F.3d 999, 1001 (8th Cir.2003) (motion was in limine, but context of ruling made clear that it was a "definitive" ruling);* ***Sylla-Sawdon v. Uniroyal Goodrich Tire Co.****, 47 F.3d 277, 283 (8th Cir.1995) (motion was called in limine, but because order excluded expert's testimony, motion acted as motion to exclude). See "Motion to Exclude Expert Witness," ch. 5-N, p. 376.*

§2.4 Deadline. A motion in limine should be filed by any deadline set in the court's scheduling order, and certainly in time for a response to be filed and for the court to make its ruling before voir dire begins. *See* Local Rules Ill. (N.D.), Rule 16.1(a) (Standing Order Establishing Pretrial Procedure, ¶6(e)) (motion should be brought to court's attention no later than date of submission of final pretrial order).

§2.5 Proposed order. Some districts require the movant to submit a proposed order with the motion. In those districts, the movant should prepare a written order for the court's signature and submit it with the motion. See "Proposed order," ch. 1-B, §3.1.11, p. 16.

§2.6 Agreed motions. Frequently, a motion in limine is only a precautionary device to ensure that an opposing party does not go into clearly impermissible and highly prejudicial areas without warning. It protects a party from prejudicial questions that, despite an instruction from the judge to disregard, will nonetheless be heard by the jury. In many cases, the parties can and should note that they agree on most, if not all, of the topics raised in a motion in limine.

§3. RESPONSE

In most cases, it is not necessary to file a response to a motion in limine, although a party may want to submit a brief on some of the evidentiary issues. Attorneys should check the local rules and the individual judge's operating procedures to determine whether a response is required.

§4. HEARING

If the court holds a hearing on a motion in limine, it may be either for taking evidence or for the attorneys' argument. *See* ***United Auto, Aerospace & Agric. Implement Workers v. R.E. Dietz Co.***, 996 F.2d 592, 598 (2d Cir.1993) (hearing for oral argument). Generally, the court will schedule a hearing on a motion in limine to coincide with the final pretrial conference. If the court conducts a hearing on the admissibility of evidence and a record is made of the evidence offered and the objections to it, the court's ruling is probably a pretrial ruling on the admissibility of the evidence, not a ruling on a motion in limine. If the court makes a definitive ruling on the admissibility of the evidence, any claim of error is preserved for appeal.

§5. RULING

The party presenting a motion in limine should ask the court to make a ruling on the motion before trial. The order should clearly state whether the ruling is a preliminary ruling or a definitive ruling on admissibility.

§5.1 Preliminary ruling. If the court rules that the party offering the evidence must first approach the bench and ask for a ruling, the order granting the motion in limine should include this instruction. See "Motion granted," §6.2, p. 344. The court may also include a statement that the ruling is not a ruling on admissibility and that the parties must offer and object to the evidence at trial. *See* ***Hendrix v. Raybestos-Manhattan, Inc.***, 776 F.2d 1492, 1504 (11th Cir.1985) (court's grant or denial of motion in limine is not ruling that admits or excludes evidence).

§5.2 Ruling on admissibility. If the court rules definitively on the record, a party does not need to renew an objection or offer of proof to preserve a claim of error for appeal. FRE 103(b); ***Olson v. Ford Motor Co.***, 481 F.3d 619, 629 n.7 (8th Cir.2007); ***Fuesting v. Zimmer, Inc.***, 448 F.3d 936, 940 (7th Cir.2006); ***Zachar v. Lee***, 363 F.3d 70, 75 (1st Cir.2004); *see also* ***Mathis v. Exxon Corp.***, 302 F.3d 448, 459 (5th Cir.2002) (pretrial objection is sufficient to preserve error for appellate review). But renewal is still required when the court has reserved its ruling, made a preliminary or conditional ruling, or changed a previously definitive ruling. *See* FRE 103(b); ***U.S. v. Harris***, 471 F.3d 507, 513 (3d Cir.2006); *see also* ***U.S. v. Gajo***, 290 F.3d 922, 927 (7th Cir.2002) (whether D waived objection to admission of evidence depends on whether court's order definitively settled issue of admissibility).

§6. OFFER & OBJECTION AT TRIAL

§6.1 Motion denied. By denying a motion in limine, the court has refused to require the party offering the evidence to first approach the bench before presenting the evidence. But the party offering the evidence must still offer it at trial; the court's ruling does not automatically admit the evidence. *See* ***Polk v. Yellow Freight Sys.***, 876 F.2d 527, 532 (6th Cir.1989); ***Petty v. Ideco***, 761 F.2d 1146, 1150 (5th Cir.1985). When the evidence is offered at trial, the party objecting to it must object when it is offered. ***Judd v. Rodman***, 105 F.3d 1339, 1342 (11th Cir.1997); *see* ***Guides, Ltd. v. Yarmouth Grp. Prop. Mgmt.***, 295 F.3d 1065, 1075 (10th Cir.2002). The making of a motion in limine generally does not preserve error in the admission of the evidence at trial. *See* ***U.S. v. Kelly***, 204 F.3d 652, 655-56 (6th Cir.2000); ***Huff v. Heckendorn Mfg. Co.***, 991 F.2d 464, 466 (8th Cir.1993). However, a formal objection at trial may not be necessary to preserve error if the court and the other parties knew either what action the losing party wanted the court to take or what action the losing party opposed. See "Objections before trial," ch. 8-D, §2.1, p. 700; "Objection to Evidence," ch. 8-D, §5, p. 703.

CAUTION

If the court sustains the objection to the evidence at trial, the party whose evidence was excluded must make an offer of proof. If not, any potential error is not preserved. See ***Moran v. Clarke****, 296 F.3d 638, 649 (8th Cir.2002);* ***Holst v. Countryside Enters.****, 14 F.3d 1319, 1323 (8th Cir.1994). But see* ***Favala v. Cumberland Eng'g****, 17 F.3d 987, 991 (7th Cir.1994) (party was not required to call witness after motion in limine excluding witness was granted). See "Offer of Proof," ch. 8-E, p. 707.*

§6.2 Motion granted. By granting a motion in limine, the court has ruled that the party must first approach the bench for a ruling on the admissibility of the evidence before presenting it. When an objection to evidence in a motion in limine has been sustained, the party seeking to introduce the evidence must make an offer of proof at trial. *See* ***Palmieri v. Defaria***, 88 F.3d 136, 140-41 (2d Cir.1996); ***Fusco v. General Motors Corp.***, 11 F.3d 259, 262-63 (1st Cir.1993). See "Offer of Proof," ch. 8-E, p. 707. When the evidence is offered at trial, the party who does not want the evidence introduced must object when the offer is made. ***Star Fin. Servs. v. AASTAR Mortg. Corp.***, 89 F.3d 5, 12 (1st Cir.1996); ***Kostelec v. State Farm Fire & Cas. Co.***, 64 F.3d 1220, 1229 (8th Cir.1995); ***Collins v. Wayne Corp.***, 621 F.2d 777, 784 (5th Cir.1980).

§6.3 Violation of motion – preserving error. If one party violates the motion in limine and prejudicial information is revealed to the jury, the other party—to preserve error—must make a number of objections in sequential order until the court makes an adverse ruling. This is called "pursuing an adverse ruling." For the procedure for pursuing an adverse ruling, see "Instruction to Disregard & Motion for Mistrial," ch. 8-D, §8, p. 705.

§7. RULING ON OFFER

Once the party offers the evidence and the opposing party makes an objection, the opposing party should ensure that the court makes a ruling on the record by either admitting or excluding the evidence. Without an adverse ruling on the record made during trial, no error is preserved.

§8. APPELLATE REVIEW

The district court's ruling on a motion in limine is reviewed for abuse of discretion. ***Hinkle v. City of Clarksburg***, 81 F.3d 416, 424 (4th Cir.1996); ***Cartier v. Jackson***, 59 F.3d 1046, 1048 (10th Cir.1995); *see* ***Moran v. Clarke***, 296

F.3d 638, 650 (8th Cir.2002). If the court errs in granting or denying the motion, the error is not reversible unless (1) the questions were asked or the evidence was introduced and (2) the party that presented the motion objected in time to preserve the complaint. *See* ***Collins v. Wayne Corp.***, 621 F.2d 777, 784 (5th Cir.1980). An erroneous evidentiary ruling must affect a party's "substantial rights." ***Haun v. Ideal Indus.***, 81 F.3d 541, 547 (5th Cir.1996). An error is harmless if the court of appeals is sure, after reviewing the entire record, that the error did not influence the jury or had only a very slight effect on its verdict. *Id.*

I. MOTION TO AMEND OR SUPPLEMENT PLEADINGS—PRETRIAL

§1. GENERAL

§1.1 Rule. FRCP 15.

§1.2 Purpose. A party can amend its pleadings before trial to correct errors and defects in the pleadings. *See* ***Schacht v. Brown***, 711 F.2d 1343, 1352 (7th Cir.1983). A party can supplement its pleadings before trial to add any transaction, occurrence, or event that happened *after* the date of the original pleading. *See* ***ConnectU LLC v. Zuckerberg***, 522 F.3d 82, 90 (1st Cir.2008). An amended pleading supersedes the earlier pleading. *See id.* at 91; ***King v. Dogan***, 31 F.3d 344, 346 (5th Cir.1994). A supplemental pleading adds to—but does not replace or supersede—the earlier pleading. ***Millay v. Surry Sch. Dept.***, 584 F.Supp.2d 219, 226 (D.Me.2008). Even though amended and supplemental pleadings are different, mislabeling is common, and courts may treat a pleading as amended or supplemental as necessary. *See* 6A Wright, Miller & Kane, *Federal Practice & Procedure 3d* §1504 & nn.14-15 (2010 & Supp.2012).

§1.3 Timetable & forms. Timetable, Pleadings & Pretrial-Motions Schedule, p. 1574; ***O'Connor's Federal Civil Forms*** (2012), FORMS 5I.

§1.4 Other references. 6, 6A Wright, Miller & Kane, *Federal Practice & Procedure 3d* §§1471-1510 (2010 & Supp.2012); 3 *Moore's Federal Practice 3d* ch. 15 (2012).

§2. GENERAL RULES FOR AMENDING PLEADINGS

The rules for amending pleadings vary significantly depending on what stage the case is in when the amendment occurs. This subchapter discusses motions to amend the pleadings before trial. For a discussion of motions to amend the pleadings during and after trial, see "Motion to Amend Pleadings—Trial & Post-trial," ch. 8-F, p. 710.

§3. AMENDING PLEADINGS – PRETRIAL

§3.1 Amending as matter of course. Early in the litigation, a party can amend its pleading once as "a matter of course." *See* FRCP 15(a)(1); 2009 Notes to FRCP 15 at ¶1, p. 1157, this book.

1. Deadline.

(1) Responsive pleading required. If the pleading is one to which a responsive pleading is required, a party may amend the pleading within (1) 21 days after serving it or (2) 21 days after service of the responsive pleading or a motion under FRCP 12(b), (e), or (f), whichever is earlier. FRCP 15(a)(1); *see* FRCP 7(a) (defining responsive pleading). See "FRCP 12 Motion," ch. 3-A, §2, p. 171; "Responsive Pleading," ch. 3-A, §3, p. 173. The 21-day period to amend after service of a responsive pleading or a designated FRCP 12 motion is not cumulative—that is, there is only one 21-day period. *See* 2009 Notes to FRCP 15 at ¶5, p. 1157, this book. For example, if a defendant files its answer after filing a motion for failure to state a claim under FRCP 12(b)(6), the 21-day amendment period begins when the FRCP 12 motion is filed; filing the answer does not trigger a new 21-day period. *See* 2009 Notes to FRCP 15 at ¶5, p. 1157, this book.

NOTE

Before the 2009 amendments to FRCP 15, the right to amend as a matter of course ended when a responsive pleading was served; FRCP 12 motions did not affect the right to amend because those motions are not pleadings under FRCP 7(a). 2009 Notes to FRCP 15 at ¶¶2, 4, p. 1157, this book. Thus, under former FRCP 15, the right to amend remained available—potentially late into the litigation—if a party filed an FRCP 12 motion but not an answer. See 2009 Notes to FRCP 15 at ¶2, p. 1157, this book. Under current FRCP 15, the right to amend cannot remain open late into the litigation because the right now ends 21 days after service of the responsive

pleading or a motion under FRCP 12(b), (e), or (f), whichever is earlier. The current deadline gives the pleader time to consider the responsive pleading or the FRCP 12 motion and allows her 21 days to amend the original pleading in response if necessary. 2009 Notes to FRCP 15 at ¶¶3, 4, p. 1157, this book. The current deadline may also expedite the determination of—or even avoid—many FRCP 12 motions. See 2009 Notes to FRCP 15 at ¶3, p. 1157, this book. For example, if an FRCP 12 motion is well founded, the pleader can consider simply filing (1) an amended complaint that corrects the defects alleged in the motion and (2) a response asserting that the motion has become moot.

(2) Responsive pleading not required. If the pleading is one to which no responsive pleading is required (e.g., a defendant's answer), a party may amend the pleading within 21 days after serving it. *See* FRCP 15(a)(1)(A); *see also* 2009 Notes to FRCP 15 at ¶6, p. 1157, this book (FRCP 15 no longer refers to actions "not yet on the trial calendar"; parties should rely on scheduling orders and pretrial directions that may otherwise allow amendments as matter of course).

2. Absolute right to amend. During the period in which a party can amend as a matter of course, the party has an absolute right to amend; even if the proposed amendment is futile, the court lacks the discretion to reject an amended pleading that is filed as a matter of course. *See* ***Williams v. Board of Regents***, 477 F.3d 1282, 1292 & n.6 (11th Cir.2007) (applying former FRCP 15(a), under which amending as matter of course ended on service of responsive pleading); ***Gaming Mktg. Solutions, Inc. v. Cross***, 528 F.Supp.2d 403, 406 & n.5 (S.D.N.Y.2007) (same). *But see* ***Foster v. DeLuca***, 545 F.3d 582, 584 (7th Cir.2008) (court has discretion to deny amendment as matter of course when proposed complaint clearly does not cure original complaint's deficiencies or would not survive motion to dismiss).

NOTE

If a party can amend as a matter of course but chooses to file a motion to amend instead, the party waives its absolute right to amend and invites the district court to review the amendment. See ***Coventry First, LLC v. McCarty***, *605 F.3d 865, 869-70 (11th Cir.2010) (applying former FRCP 15(a), under which amending as matter of course ended on service of responsive pleading).*

§3.2 Amending by consent or leave. If a party cannot file an amended complaint as a matter of course, the party can amend its pleading only by obtaining the opposing party's written consent or the court's leave. FRCP 15(a)(2); ***Bylin v. Billings***, 568 F.3d 1224, 1229 (10th Cir.2009); ***U.S. v. Cervantes***, 132 F.3d 1106, 1111 (5th Cir. 1998); ***Perrian v. O'Grady***, 958 F.2d 192, 193-94 (7th Cir.1992). Generally, an amended complaint filed without consent of the adverse party or leave of court is a nullity. ***Friedman v. Village of Skokie***, 763 F.2d 236, 239 (7th Cir.1985). However, local rules may provide a procedure that allows a party to file an amended complaint and motion for leave concurrently. *See, e.g.*, Local Rules Tex. (E.D.), Rule CV-7(k) (motion for leave must be accompanied by document the party is seeking to file; if leave is granted, document is deemed filed as of original date of its filing). See "Proposed amended pleading," §5.5, p. 351.

1. Amendment by consent. To request an amendment, the party should first ask the opposing party for written consent to an amendment. FRCP 15(a)(2); *see* ***Lowrey v. Texas A&M Univ. Sys.***, 117 F.3d 242, 246 & n.2 (5th Cir.1997) (under express terms of FRCP 15(a), agreement eliminates court's discretion to deny motion to amend).

2. Amendment by leave of court. Generally, if the adverse party will not agree to an amendment, the party must file a written motion for leave to amend and submit the proposed amended pleading with the motion. *See* ***Averbach v. Rival Mfg.***, 879 F.2d 1196, 1202 (3d Cir.1989); ***Wolgin v. Simon***, 722 F.2d 389, 394 (8th Cir.1983). See "Motion for Leave to Amend," §5, p. 351. However, courts must issue a scheduling order containing a deadline for

amending the pleadings, and in some courts, a party who wants to amend its pleadings before that deadline does not have to file a motion for leave. *See* FRCP 16(b)(3)(A); ***Campania Mgmt. v. Rooks, Pitts & Poust***, 290 F.3d 843, 848 n.1 (7th Cir.2002). Thus, before filing a motion, the attorney should check the court's scheduling order to see if a motion is required.

§3.3 Amending when ordered. A party must replead if ordered to do so by the court. FRCP 81(c)(2). When the court orders the plaintiff to replead after removal from state to federal court, it does not automatically deprive the plaintiff of its one-time option to amend without leave under FRCP 15(a)(1). ***Kuehl v. FDIC***, 8 F.3d 905, 908 (1st Cir.1993).

§3.4 Amending after complaint dismissed. If the court dismisses a complaint, the plaintiff can file an amended complaint with the court's leave under FRCP 15(a)(2) as long as the court has not entered judgment. *See* ***Newland v. Dalton***, 81 F.3d 904, 906-07 (9th Cir.1996). If judgment has been entered, the plaintiff must first move to have the judgment set aside under FRCP 59(e) or 60(b) before filing a motion to amend. ***Fisher v. Kadant, Inc.***, 589 F.3d 505, 508-09 (1st Cir.2009); ***Sparrow v. Heller***, 116 F.3d 204, 205 (7th Cir.1997); *see, e.g.*, ***Firestone v. Firestone***, 76 F.3d 1205, 1208 (D.C.Cir.1996) (after complaint was dismissed with prejudice, P could amend complaint only by filing FRCP 59(e) motion to alter or amend judgment, combined with FRCP 15(a) motion for leave to amend complaint).

§3.5 Relation back of amendments. FRCP 15(c) governs the "relation back" of amendments to the original pleading. ***Krupski v. Costa Crociere S.p.A.***, ___ U.S. ___, 130 S.Ct. 2485, 2489 (2010). The relation-back doctrine allows a plaintiff to amend its complaint to add a new party to an otherwise untimely claim and treats the amended complaint as if it had been filed when the original complaint was filed. *See* ***Krupski***, ___ U.S. at ___, 130 S.Ct. at 2489; ***Springman v. AIG Mktg., Inc.***, 523 F.3d 685, 688 (7th Cir.2008); ***Mandacina v. U.S.***, 328 F.3d 995, 1000 (8th Cir.2003); *see also* ***Vélez-Díaz v. U.S.***, 507 F.3d 717, 719 (1st Cir.2007) (amended pleading must relate back to original pleading in same action, not different case). When an amended complaint relates back, the plaintiff avoids the preclusive effect of a statute-of-limitations defense that would otherwise bar the claims added in the amended complaint. *See* ***Krupski***, ___ U.S. at ___, 130 S.Ct. at 2489; ***ConnectU LLC v. Zuckerberg***, 522 F.3d 82, 90 (1st Cir. 2008). For an amended pleading to relate back for limitations purposes, FRCP 15(c) necessarily requires that there be an earlier pleading to which the amendment relates. *E.g.*, ***Kansa Reinsurance Co. v. Congressional Mortg. Corp.***, 20 F.3d 1362, 1367 (5th Cir.1994) (cross-claim did not relate back to D's amended answer); *see* ***Bularz v. Prudential Ins.***, 93 F.3d 372, 379 (7th Cir.1996) (relation back is permitted when amended complaint asserts new claim on same core of facts but involves different legal theory). FRCP 15(c)(1) allows a plaintiff to correct its complaint to ensure that it has (1) stated all claims against the defendant arising out of the same facts and (2) named all proper defendants. *See, e.g.*, ***Edwards v. Occidental Chem. Corp.***, 892 F.2d 1442, 1446 (9th Cir.1990) (new D named); ***Percy v. San Francisco Gen. Hosp.***, 841 F.2d 975, 979 (9th Cir.1988) (new claims added). An amended pleading relates back to the date of the original pleading when any of the three conditions in FRCP 15(c)(1) are met.

NOTE

An amended pleading relates back to the original pleading if (1) the law imposing the statute of limitations permits relation back, (2) the amended pleading arose from the same conduct, transaction, or occurrence set out in the original pleading, or (3) the amended pleading changes the party against whom a claim is asserted. FRCP 15(c)(1); ***Makro Capital v. UBS AG****, 543 F.3d 1254, 1258 (11th Cir.2008). If the plaintiff is seeking to change the identity or name of the defendant under FRCP 15(c)(1)(C), the plaintiff must satisfy the requirements of FRCP 15(c)(1)(C) in addition to the "same conduct, transaction, or occurrence" requirement under FRCP 15(c)(1)(B). FRCP 15(c)(1)(C);* ***Makro Capital****, 543 F.3d at 1258; see* ***Sanders-Burns v. City of Plano****, 594 F.3d 366, 372-73 (5th Cir.2010).*

1. As permitted by law. Under FRCP 15(c)(1)(A), relation back is proper if the law that provides the applicable statute of limitations allows relation back. ***Arendt v. Vetta Sports, Inc.***, 99 F.3d 231, 236-37 (7th Cir.1996);

Lovelace v. O'Hara, 985 F.2d 847, 851-52 (6th Cir.1993); *see also* ***Morel v. DaimlerChrysler AG***, 565 F.3d 20, 24-25 (1st Cir.2009) (relation back proper when state law provides statute of limitations); ***Lundy v. Adamar of N.J., Inc.***, 34 F.3d 1173, 1181 (3d Cir.1994) (same). FRCP 15(c)(1)(A) operates to save a plaintiff's claim if the law providing the statute of limitations has a more forgiving relation-back provision than the one in FRCP 15(c). ***Coons v. Industrial Knife Co.***, 620 F.3d 38, 42 (1st Cir.2010); ***Nelson v. County of Allegheny***, 60 F.3d 1010, 1014 n.4 (3d Cir.1995).

2. Claim arises out of same transaction. Under FRCP 15(c)(1)(B), a new substantive claim or defense that would otherwise be time-barred relates back to the date of the original pleading as long as the new claim or defense arose out of the same conduct, transaction, or occurrence set out or attempted to be set out in the original pleading. ***Arthur v. Maersk, Inc.***, 434 F.3d 196, 203 (3d Cir.2006), *overruled on other grounds*, ***Krupski v. Costa Crociere, S.p.A.***, ___ U.S. ___, 130 S.Ct. 2485 (2010); ***Bularz***, 93 F.3d at 379; *see* ***Eaglesmith v. Ward***, 73 F.3d 857, 860 (9th Cir.1995); *see, e.g.*, ***Jones v. Bernanke***, 557 F.3d 670, 675 (D.C.Cir.2009) (when amended discrimination claims differed in time and type, they did not relate back). Thus, relation back is proper when an amended complaint asserts a new claim or defense that is based on the same core facts contained in the original pleading but involves a different substantive legal theory than what was originally asserted. ***Bularz***, 93 F.3d at 379; ***Alpern v. Utilicorp United, Inc.***, 84 F.3d 1525, 1543 (8th Cir.1996); ***Kern Oil & Ref. Co. v. Tenneco Oil Co.***, 840 F.2d 730, 736 (9th Cir. 1988). Relation back applies even when the amendment states a new ground for subject-matter jurisdiction. ***Carney v. Resolution Trust Corp.***, 19 F.3d 950, 954 (5th Cir.1994); ***Berkshire Fashions, Inc. v. M.V. Hakusan II***, 954 F.2d 874, 887 (3d Cir.1992).

3. Identity of proper party discovered after limitations. Under FRCP 15(c)(1)(C), a plaintiff is protected when it mistakenly names a party and then, after the statute of limitations has run, discovers the identity of the proper party. *See* ***Krupski***, ___ U.S. at ___, 130 S.Ct. at 2494; ***Donald v. Cook Cty. Sheriff's Dept.***, 95 F.3d 548, 556-57 (7th Cir.1996). If the amendment changes the identity or name of the party, relation back is proper if FRCP 15(c)(1)(B) is satisfied and if the party brought in by amendment (1) received enough notice of the suit that it will not be prejudiced in defending on the merits and (2) knew or should have known that the suit would have been brought against it but for a mistake in identifying the proper party. FRCP 15(c)(1)(C); ***Krupski***, ___ U.S. at ___, 130 S.Ct. at 2493; ***Joseph v. Elan Motorsports Techs. Racing Corp.***, 638 F.3d 555, 559-60 (7th Cir.2011); ***Skoczylas v. Federal Bur. of Prisons***, 961 F.2d 543, 545 (5th Cir.1992). *But see* ***Eaglesmith***, 73 F.3d at 860 (amendment changing capacity in which D was sued was properly denied because P did not serve D again within limitations period).

NOTE

A typical FRCP 15(c)(1)(C) case involves a plaintiff filing an amended complaint that adds a new defendant. ***Krupski***, *___ U.S. at ___, 130 S.Ct. at 2493 n.3. But FRCP 15(c)(1)(C) is not limited to a plaintiff adding a new defendant; new plaintiffs can be added as well. See* ***Krupski***, *___ U.S. at ___, 130 S.Ct. at 2493 n.3 (because rule says "pleading" that changes "the party against whom a claim is asserted," rule is not limited to P filing amended complaint to add new D);* ***In re Community Bank of N. Va.***, *622 F.3d 275, 297 (3d Cir.2010) (dicta; despite rule language, courts have allowed addition of new Ps); see also* ***Asher v. Unarco Material Handling, Inc.***, *596 F.3d 313, 318-19 (6th Cir.2010) (amendments changing identities of Ps are limited to misnomers or misdescriptions; amendment that adds—rather than substitutes—new party creates new cause of action and cannot relate back for limitations purposes).*

(1) Sufficient notice. The party being substituted must have received sufficient notice of the suit within the 120 days permitted under FRCP 4(m) for service of the complaint and summons, such that the party being substituted will not be prejudiced in defending the suit. *See* FRCP 15(c)(1)(C); ***Joseph***, 638 F.3d at 559-60; ***Cox v. Treadway***, 75 F.3d 230, 240 (6th Cir.1996). *But see* ***Urrutia v. Harrisburg Cty. Police Dept.***, 91 F.3d 451, 453-54 (3d Cir.1996) (120-day period is tolled when court makes in forma pauperis determination under 28 U.S.C. §1915). The notice requirement in FRCP 15(c)(1)(C)(i) is satisfied if the party learns of the suit informally. ***Krupski***, ___

U.S. at ___, 130 S.Ct. at 2497 n.5; *see* ***Berndt v. Tennessee***, 796 F.2d 879, 884 (6th Cir.1986) (notice requirement satisfied if D received constructive notice); *see, e.g.*, ***Donald***, 95 F.3d at 560 (individual Ds on notice when pro se P sued their department). The prejudice to the party being substituted cannot be manufactured by that party. *E.g.*, ***Joseph***, 638 F.3d at 560-61 (when D to be substituted (1) knew P intended to sue it but P mistakenly sued affiliate and (2) did nothing for six years, D to be substituted could not allege that it was prejudiced by delay because delay was brought about by its own inaction).

(2) Knowledge. The party being substituted must have known or should have known that the suit would have been brought against it but for the mistake. FRCP 15(c)(1)(C)(ii); *e.g.*, ***Krupski***, ___ U.S. at ___, 130 S.Ct. at 2497-98 (P made mistake when complaint clearly intended to sue entity that owned and operated ship on which P was injured but P misunderstood which entity was in charge of ship; based on similar names of entities and shared counsel, D should have known of P's mistake); *see* ***Robinson v. Clipse***, 602 F.3d 605, 609-10 (4th Cir.2010). Relation back is not permitted when the proper party has no knowledge of the suit. FRCP 15(c)(1)(C)(ii); ***Cox***, 75 F.3d at 240; ***Wilson v. U.S.***, 23 F.3d 559, 563 (1st Cir.1994). If the plaintiff has a ground to assert liability against a party named in the complaint and if another party who potentially could be substituted has no reason to believe that the plaintiff did anything other than make a deliberate choice between potential defendants, the knowledge requirement has not been met. ***Lundy***, 34 F.3d at 1183; ***Lovelace***, 985 F.2d at 850-51; *see* ***Krupski***, ___ U.S. at ___, 130 S.Ct. at 2494.

NOTE

The "knowledge" requirement under FRCP 15(c)(1)(C)(ii) depends not on what the plaintiff knew or should have known at the time of filing her original complaint but rather on what the prospective defendant knew or should have known during the FRCP 4(m) period. ***Krupski***, *___ U.S. at ___, 130 S.Ct. at 2493; see* ***Joseph***, *638 F.3d at 560 (P's carelessness is no longer independent ground to deny relation back). A plaintiff can make a mistake about a party's identity even if she knows of that party.* ***Krupski***, *___ U.S. at ___, 130 S.Ct. at 2494. For example, P may know that prospective D1 exists but may mistakenly believe that prospective D1 has the status of prospective D2, or P may know generally what prospective D1 does but may misunderstand the roles that prospective D1 and D2 played in the transaction giving rise to the claim. Id. If prospective D1 is the proper defendant but P sues prospective D2, P has made a mistake under FRCP 15(c)(1)(C)(ii) even though she had knowledge of both prospective Ds.* ***Krupski***, *___ U.S. at ___, 130 S.Ct. at 2494. If, however, the original complaint and P's conduct demonstrate that P made a fully informed decision about the proper defendant's identity, she has not made a mistake under FRCP 15(c)(1)(C)(ii).* ***Krupski***, *___ U.S. at ___, 130 S.Ct. at 2494. Thus, if the prospective defendant knew or should have known the suit would have been brought against it but for a mistake, the amendment will relate back if the other requirements of FRCP 15(c) are satisfied. See* ***Krupski***, *___ U.S. at ___, 130 S.Ct. at 2494. In addition to the plaintiff's knowledge, the speed with which the plaintiff moves to amend is also not relevant, and the district court must find that the amendment relates back if the rule's requirements are met. Id. at ___, 130 S.Ct. at 2496.*

(3) Examples. Relation back was allowed in the following circumstances:

(a) Mistake in naming or describing a party. ***Joseph***, 638 F.3d at 560-61; ***U.S. v. Bill Harbert Int'l Constr., Inc.***, 608 F.3d 871, 883 (D.C.Cir.2010). However, relation back will generally not be allowed if a complaint is amended to add a "John Doe" defendant's real name; most John Doe parties will be protected either because they were prejudiced or because they did not receive proper notice. *See* ***Goodman v. Praxair, Inc.***, 494 F.3d 458, 471 (4th Cir.2007). See "'John Doe' parties," ch. 2-B, §2.1.3, p. 76.

(b) Mistake in capacity. *See* ***Sanders-Burns***, 594 F.3d at 373; *see, e.g.*, ***Goodman v. U.S.***, 298 F.3d 1048, 1054 (9th Cir.2002) (P allowed to amend complaint to substitute P, in his individual capacity, for P, as personal

representative of estate, when state law required that only relatives of victim, in individual capacity, could bring wrongful-death action); *see also* ***Sanders-Burns***, 594 F.3d at 375-77 (reviewing circuit decisions on whether amendments that change suit against someone in their official capacity to their individual capacity relate back).

(c) Mistake of law. *E.g.*, ***Woods v. Indiana Univ.-Purdue Univ. at Indianapolis***, 996 F.2d 880, 887 (7th Cir.1993) (attorney's decision to sue university, rather than university employees in their individual capacities, was mistake of law that would justify relation back).

§4. SUPPLEMENTING PLEADINGS – PRETRIAL

On a motion and reasonable notice, the court may, on just terms, permit a party to serve a supplemental pleading setting out any transaction, occurrence, or event that happened *after* the date of the original pleading. FRCP 15(d); ***ConnectU LLC v. Zuckerberg***, 522 F.3d 82, 90 (1st Cir.2008); ***Black v. Secretary of H&HS***, 93 F.3d 781, 789 (Fed. Cir.1996); *see* ***U.S. v. Hicks***, 283 F.3d 380, 385 (D.C.Cir.2002) (intervening judicial decisions are not "occurrences or events" under FRCP 15(d)); *see, e.g.*, ***Quaratino v. Tiffany & Co.***, 71 F.3d 58, 66 (2d Cir.1995) (in discrimination suit, P allowed to add claim alleging she was unlawfully retaliated against for filing discrimination charge with EEOC). Generally, a supplemental pleading deals with events that are additional to or continuations of the original pleading. *See* ***Hicks***, 283 F.3d at 385-86; 6A Wright, Miller & Kane §1504. Although an amended pleading can be filed as a matter of course, a supplemental pleading cannot; a party must obtain leave of court. *See* ***ConnectU LLC***, 522 F.3d at 90. If a party seeks leave, the court determines whether and on what terms the filing should be permitted. 1963 Notes to FRCP 15 at ¶2, p. 1158, this book; *see* ***Quaratino***, 71 F.3d at 66 (leave to file supplemental pleading should be freely given when supplemental facts connect supplemental pleading to original pleading). If the court allows a supplemental pleading, it may order that the opposing party respond to the supplemental pleading within a specified time. FRCP 15(d).

§4.1 Original pleading defective. The court may permit supplementation even when the original pleading is defective in stating a claim or defense. FRCP 15(d); *see* ***Black v. Secretary of H&HS***, 93 F.3d 781, 789-90 (Fed.Cir. 1996) (jurisdictional defect may be cured by supplemental pleading under FRCP 15(d)). *But see* ***Innovative Therapies, Inc. v. Kinetic Concepts, Inc.***, 599 F.3d 1377, 1383-84 (Fed.Cir.2010) (even though supplemental pleading showed actual controversy in declaratory-judgment action, case was dismissed because neither supplemental pleading nor original pleading showed that there was actual controversy at time of original pleading).

§4.2 Adding new claim. The court may permit supplementation that in effect states a new claim, even though supplemental pleadings usually provide additional facts about the claims already asserted. ***Rowe v. U.S. Fid. & Guar. Co.***, 421 F.2d 937, 943 (4th Cir.1970); *see* ***Keith v. Volpe***, 858 F.2d 467, 473-74 (9th Cir.1988). In determining whether to allow a new claim, the court should consider the following factors: (1) the likelihood that the claim is being added in a desperate effort to protract the litigation and complicate the defense, (2) the claim's probable merit, (3) whether the claim should have been added earlier, and (4) the burden on the defendant of having to defend against the claim. ***Glatt v. Chicago Park Dist.***, 87 F.3d 190, 194 (7th Cir.1996); *see* ***Rowe***, 421 F.2d at 943; *see also* 6A Wright, Miller & Kane §1506 (courts can allow new claim if it is convenient to litigate all claims between parties at same time). The court cannot allow a new claim if it is based on facts that are different from those underlying the original claims. ***U.S. v. Hicks***, 283 F.3d 380, 388-89 (D.C.Cir.2002); *see* ***Planned Parenthood v. Neely***, 130 F.3d 400, 402 (9th Cir. 1997) (supplementation cannot be used to introduce "separate, distinct, and new" claim).

§4.3 Relation back. Unlike amended pleadings, the circumstances in which supplemental pleadings may relate back have not been codified. *See* 6A Wright, Miller & Kane §1508; 1963 Notes to FRCP 15 at ¶2, p. 1158, this book. Most courts apply the relation-back principles for amended pleadings to supplemental pleadings. ***U.S. v. Hicks***, 283 F.3d 380, 385 (D.C.Cir.2002); ***FDIC v. Knostman***, 966 F.2d 1133, 1138-39 (7th Cir.1992); ***Davis v. Piper Aircraft Corp.***, 615 F.2d 606, 609 n.3 (4th Cir.1980); *see* ***Finnerty v. Wireless Retail, Inc.***, 624 F.Supp.2d 642, 651-52 (E.D. Mich.2009); 6A Wright, Miller & Kane §1508. See "Relation back of amendments," §3.5, p. 347.

§4.4 Jurisdiction & venue. The movant should allege facts that support personal jurisdiction and venue. *See* ***Frank v. U.S. West, Inc.***, 3 F.3d 1357, 1365 (10th Cir.1993); ***Gilbert v. DaGrossa***, 756 F.2d 1455, 1459 (9th Cir.1985).

§5. MOTION FOR LEAVE TO AMEND

§5.1 Form. For the general requirements for the form of a motion, see "Drafting motions," ch. 1-B, §3.1, p. 14.

§5.2 In writing. The motion for leave to amend should be in writing. FRCP 7(b)(1)(A). But under certain circumstances, the courts will treat an action as an amendment of the pleadings even without a formal motion to amend under FRCP 15. *See, e.g.*, ***999 v. C.I.T. Corp.***, 776 F.2d 866, 870 n.2 (9th Cir.1985) (affirmative defense included for first time in pretrial order had effect of amending pleadings); ***Johnson v. Mateer***, 625 F.2d 240, 242 (9th Cir.1980) (when affidavit was filed in response to motion for summary judgment and raised factual allegations for first time, district court should have construed affidavit as request to amend pleadings under FRCP 15(b)).

§5.3 Notice. The movant must serve the motion for leave to amend on all parties. FRCP 5(a)(1)(D).

§5.4 Grounds. The movant should state why the amendment is appropriate and necessary. See "Factors," §7.2, p. 353.

§5.5 Proposed amended pleading. The proposed amended pleading should be submitted with the motion for leave to amend. ***Roskam Baking Co. v. Lanham Mach. Co.***, 288 F.3d 895, 906 (6th Cir.2002); 6 Wright, Miller & Kane §1485.

PRACTICE TIP

The best practice is to attach the proposed amended pleading to the motion for leave to amend. E.g., ***In re 2007 Novastar Fin. Inc., Secs. Litig.****, 579 F.3d 878, 884-85 (8th Cir.2009) (leave to amend was denied when P did not include proposed amended complaint and did not file motion for leave but merely included footnote requesting leave in its response to D's motion to dismiss); see* ***Fletcher-Harlee Corp. v. Pote Concrete Contractors, Inc.****, 482 F.3d 247, 252 (3d Cir.2007). Many local rules expressly require that a copy of the proposed amended pleading be attached. E.g., Local Rules Md., Rule 103.6(a); Local Rules Tex. (N.D.), Rule 15.1(a). Local rules may also add further requirements. See, e.g., Local Rules Tex. (N.D.), Rule 15.1(a) (two copies of proposed pleading, including signed original, must be included with motion but not attached).*

---

§5.6 Deadline. FRCP 15 does not set an absolute deadline for a motion for leave to amend. If the court issues a pretrial order that requires all pleadings to be amended by a certain date, the parties must abide by that order. *See* FRCP 16(b)(3)(A). However, if a party discovers evidence needed to prove its new claim after the scheduling order's amendment deadline, it may still amend its pleadings. *See* ***Haddock v. Nationwide Fin. Servs.***, 514 F.Supp.2d 267, 271 (D.Conn.2007) (P may amend even after end of discovery period if legal theory evolved during discovery); ***Forstmann v. Culp***, 114 F.R.D. 83, 86 n.1 (M.D.N.C.1987) (P has good cause for modifying scheduling order when it uncovers facts during discovery that support additional claim); *see, e.g.*, ***Sweetheart Plastics, Inc. v. Detroit Forming, Inc.***, 743 F.2d 1039, 1044-45 (4th Cir.1984) (court abused its discretion by denying amendment when evidence for amendment was discovered shortly before trial). See "Standard," §7.1, p. 353.

§5.7 Proposed order. Some districts require the movant to submit a proposed order with the motion. In those districts, the movant should prepare a written order for the court's signature and submit it with the motion. See "Proposed order," ch. 1-B, §3.1.11, p. 16.

§6. RESPONSE

A party opposing a motion for leave to amend pleadings should carefully read ***Foman v. Davis***, 371 U.S. 178 (1962), in which the Supreme Court directed the district court to grant leave to amend unless there was a good reason to deny leave, such as undue delay, bad faith, dilatory motive, repeated failure to cure deficiencies by amendments previously allowed, or undue prejudice to the other party. *See* ***Campania Mgmt. v. Rooks, Pitts & Poust***, 290 F.3d 843, 848-49 (7th Cir.2002); ***Kropelnicki v. Siegel***, 290 F.3d 118, 130-31 (2d Cir.2002); ***In re Burlington Coat Factory***

Sec. Litig., 114 F.3d 1410, 1434 (3d Cir.1997); ***Executive Leasing Corp. v. Banco Popular***, 48 F.3d 66, 71 (1st Cir. 1995); ***Engstrom v. First Nat'l Bank***, 47 F.3d 1459, 1464 (5th Cir.1995).

§6.1 Grounds. The party opposing the motion to amend should make the following allegations, as appropriate:

1. Prejudice. The opposing party should allege that the amendment would prejudice its claim or defense on the merits. Prejudice may exist if the new claim or defense (1) requires the opponent to expend significant additional resources to conduct discovery and prepare for trial, (2) significantly delays the resolution of the dispute, or (3) prevents the plaintiff from timely bringing suit in another jurisdiction. ***Phelps v. McClellan***, 30 F.3d 658, 662-63 (6th Cir.1994); *see* ***AEP Energy Servs. Gas Holding Co. v. Bank of Am.***, 626 F.3d 699, 725-26 (2d Cir.2010); *see, e.g.*, ***U.S. v. Casino Magic Corp.***, 293 F.3d 419, 426 (8th Cir.2002) (court did not abuse discretion in denying attempt to add new D two and a half years into litigation due to concerns of delay and burden of additional discovery). Prejudice also exists if a party being added would not have a sufficient opportunity to respond. *See* ***Nelson v. Adams USA, Inc.***, 529 U.S. 460, 466 (2000).

2. Futility. The opposing party may allege that the amendment is futile and, if granted, would not withstand a motion to dismiss. ***National Wrestling Coaches Ass'n v. Department of Educ.***, 366 F.3d 930, 945 (D.C.Cir. 2004); *see* ***Brunt v. Service Empls. Int'l Un.***, 284 F.3d 715, 720 (7th Cir.2002); ***Walton v. Mental Health Ass'n***, 168 F.3d 661, 665 (3d Cir.1999).

3. Undue delay. The opposing party may allege that the party seeking the amendment unduly delayed in securing it. *See* ***In re Southmark Corp.***, 88 F.3d 311, 315-16 (5th Cir.1996) (court may consider unexplained delay following original complaint and whether facts in amended complaint were known to party when original complaint was filed).

CIRCUIT SPLIT

The courts of appeals are split on the showing necessary to establish "undue delay" as a ground for denying a pretrial motion to amend. The Second, Third, Fourth, Fifth, Sixth, Seventh, Eighth, Ninth, and D.C. Circuits hold that an amendment may be denied for undue delay only if the court also finds prejudice, bad faith, futility, or a substantial burden on the court. E.g., ***Bjorgung v. Whitetail Resort, LP****, 550 F.3d 263, 266 (3d Cir.2008);* ***Doe v. Cassel****, 403 F.3d 986, 990-91 (8th Cir.2005);* ***Mayeaux v. Louisiana Health Serv. & Indem. Co.****, 376 F.3d 420, 427 (5th Cir.2004);* ***Wade v. Knoxville Utils. Bd.****, 259 F.3d 452, 458-59 (6th Cir.2001);* ***Bowles v. Reade****, 198 F.3d 752, 758 (9th Cir.1999);* ***Edwards v. City of Goldsboro****, 178 F.3d 231, 242 (4th Cir. 1999);* ***King v. Cooke****, 26 F.3d 720, 723 (7th Cir.1994);* ***Block v. First Blood Assocs.****, 988 F.2d 344, 350 (2d Cir.1993); see* ***Atchinson v. District of Columbia****, 73 F.3d 418, 426 (D.C.Cir. 1996) (undue delay is sufficient reason for denying leave to amend, but determination of whether delay is undue involves factors such as prejudice). The First, Tenth, and Eleventh Circuits hold that an amendment may be denied based solely on the lack of an adequate explanation for the delay. E.g.,* ***Minter v. Prime Equip. Co.****, 451 F.3d 1196, 1206 (10th Cir.2006);* ***Hayes v. New England Millwork Distribs.****, 602 F.2d 15, 19-20 (1st Cir.1979); see, e.g.,* ***Andrx Pharms. v. Elan Corp.****, 421 F.3d 1227, 1237 (11th Cir.2005).*

---

4. Fraudulent joinder. The opposing party may allege that the primary purpose of the amendment is to add a nondiverse defendant to defeat diversity jurisdiction. See "Fraudulent joinder," ch. 4-A, §5.2.1(2)(e), p. 252.

§6.2 Proposed order. Some local rules require the responding party to submit a proposed order denying the relief requested in the motion. *E.g.*, Local Rules Tex. (S.D.), Rule 7.4.D. In those districts, the nonmovant should prepare a written order for the court's signature and file it with the motion. The proposed order denying leave to amend must include the reasons justifying denial. ***Foman v. Davis***, 371 U.S. 178, 182 (1962).

§6.3 Request continuance. If the court permits a late amendment to the pleadings and the party opposing the amendment needs additional time for discovery, that party should request a continuance. See "Motion for Continuance," ch. 5-G, p. 337.

§7. RULING

§7.1 Standard. The court should freely grant leave to amend when justice requires it. FRCP 15(a)(2); ***Foman v. Davis***, 371 U.S. 178, 182 (1962); ***New York City Employees' Ret. Sys. v. Jobs***, 593 F.3d 1018, 1025 (9th Cir.2010), *overruled on other grounds*, ***Lacey v. Maricopa Cty.***, 693 F.3d 896 (9th Cir.2012); ***Sibley v. Lando***, 437 F.3d 1067, 1073 (11th Cir.2005); ***Park v. City of Chi.***, 297 F.3d 606, 612 (7th Cir.2002); ***Lyn-Lea Travel Corp. v. American Airlines, Inc.***, 283 F.3d 282, 286 (5th Cir.2002). While there is a "bias" in favor of granting leave to amend, courts will not automatically do so. ***Price v. Pinnacle Brands, Inc.***, 138 F.3d 602, 608 (5th Cir.1998); *see also* ***Arreola v. Godinez***, 546 F.3d 788, 796 (7th Cir.2008) (even if all factors are met, discretion is not "one-way street"; it applies equally to decisions to grant or deny leave). Most circuits have ruled that the FRCP 16(b)(4) "good cause" standard, rather than the more liberal standard of FRCP 15(a)(2), governs a motion to amend filed after the deadline for amending the pleadings set in the court's scheduling order. *E.g.*, ***Alioto v. Town of Lisbon***, 651 F.3d 715, 719 (7th Cir.2011); ***Pressure Prods. Med. Sups. v. Greatbatch Ltd.***, 599 F.3d 1308, 1319 (Fed.Cir.2010); ***Romero v. Drummond Co.***, 552 F.3d 1303, 1318-19 (11th Cir.2008); ***Nourison Rug Corp. v. Parvizian***, 535 F.3d 295, 298 (4th Cir.2008); ***Sherman v. Winco Fireworks, Inc.***, 532 F.3d 709, 716 (8th Cir.2008); *see also* ***Eastern Minerals & Chems. Co. v. Mahan***, 225 F.3d 330, 340 (3d Cir.2000) (affirming denial of leave to amend more than six months after deadline for amending pleadings under FRCP 16). See "Scheduling Conference & Order," ch. 5-A, §3, p. 289. In those circuits, before the court can consider whether a party satisfied the FRCP 15(a)(2) standard, the party must show good cause under FRCP 16(b)(4) for not meeting the scheduling-order deadline. ***Alioto***, 651 F.3d at 719; *see* ***Fahim v. Marriott Hotel Servs.***, 551 F.3d 344, 348 (5th Cir.2008). Under the good-cause standard, the court generally will consider the following factors: (1) the explanation for not timely moving to amend, (2) the importance of the amendment, (3) potential prejudice in allowing the amendment, and (4) the availability of a continuance to cure the prejudice. ***Fahim***, 551 F.3d at 348.

NOTE

*Because of the uncertainty in pleading standards resulting from the **Iqbal** and **Twombly** decisions, courts may be more inclined to grant leave to amend. See **Independent Trust Corp. v. Stewart Info. Servs.**, 665 F.3d 930, 943 (7th Cir.2012).* *See "Plausibility," ch. 2-B, §5.1.2, p. 81.*

§7.2 Factors. Before granting leave to amend, the court should consider the following factors:

1. Undue delay. ***Foman v. Davis***, 371 U.S. 178, 182 (1962); ***Smith v. EMC Corp.***, 393 F.3d 590, 595 (5th Cir.2004); *see, e.g.*, ***Hom v. Squires***, 81 F.3d 969, 973 (10th Cir.1996) (court denied request to amend complaint to add new claim two months before trial and three years after suit filed); ***John Hancock Mut. Life Ins. v. Amerford Int'l***, 22 F.3d 458, 462 (2d Cir.1994) (court denied request to amend answer to add counterclaim four months after deadline to amend). *But see* ***Parker v. Columbia Pictures Indus.***, 204 F.3d 326, 339 (2d Cir.2000) (mere delay is not sufficient to justify denial of leave to amend); ***Harrison v. Rubin***, 174 F.3d 249, 250 (D.C.Cir.1999) (without showing of prejudice, delay is not basis for denying leave to amend requested merely to clarify legal theories); ***King v. Cooke***, 26 F.3d 720, 723-24 (7th Cir.1994) (court granted request to amend answer to deny liability and raise new affirmative defenses even though request was made three years after answer date). If the movant filed the amendment as soon as it realized the amendment was necessary, the court should permit the amendment. ***Auster Oil & Gas, Inc. v. Stream***, 764 F.2d 381, 391 (5th Cir.1985); *see* ***ACA Fin. Guar. Corp. v. Advest, Inc.***, 512 F.3d 46, 57 (1st Cir. 2008) (the longer P delays, the more likely it is that the motion for leave will be denied). But if the movant had earlier opportunities to amend or if the delay places an unwarranted burden on the court, the court should not permit the amendment. ***Goldfish Shipping, S.A. v. HSH Nordbank AG***, 623 F.Supp.2d 635, 640 (E.D.Pa.2009).
2. Bad faith or dilatory motive by the movant. ***Foman***, 371 U.S. at 182; ***EMC Corp.***, 393 F.3d at 595.
3. Repeated failure to cure deficiencies by previous amendments. ***Foman***, 371 U.S. at 182; ***EMC Corp.***, 393 F.3d at 595; ***Price v. Pinnacle Brands, Inc.***, 138 F.3d 602, 608 (5th Cir.1998); *see, e.g.*, ***De Jesus v. Sears, Roebuck & Co.***, 87 F.3d 65, 72 (2d Cir.1996) (Ps' claims were dismissed after Ps were given four opportunities to properly plead them).

4. Undue prejudice to opposing party. ***Foman***, 371 U.S. at 182; ***Pressure Prods. Med. Sups. v. Greatbatch Ltd.***, 599 F.3d 1308, 1320 (Fed.Cir.2010); ***EMC Corp.***, 393 F.3d at 595; ***Garner v. Kinnear Mfg.***, 37 F.3d 263, 269 (7th Cir.1994); *see also* 6 Wright, Miller & Kane §1487 & nn.19-22 (prejudice to nonparties or litigants other than opposing party is appropriate consideration that may justify denial of leave). Leave to amend should not be granted if a party would not have an opportunity to respond to the amendment. ***Nelson v. Adams USA, Inc.***, 529 U.S. 460, 466 (2000); *see* ***Bylin v. Billings***, 568 F.3d 1224, 1229 (10th Cir.2009) (prejudice usually shown only when amendment unfairly affects opposing party's ability to prepare response to amendment).

5. Futility of amendment. ***Foman***, 371 U.S. at 182; ***Nourison Rug Corp. v. Parvizian***, 535 F.3d 295, 298 (4th Cir.2008); ***EMC Corp.***, 393 F.3d at 595; ***National Wrestling Coaches Ass'n v. Department of Educ.***, 366 F.3d 930, 945 (D.C.Cir.2004); ***Brunt v. Service Empls. Int'l Un.***, 284 F.3d 715, 720 (7th Cir.2002); ***Reeder v. American Econ. Ins.***, 88 F.3d 892, 896 (10th Cir.1996).

NOTE

An amendment to a complaint is futile if the amended complaint would not survive a motion to dismiss for failure to state a claim under FRCP 12(b)(6). ***Great W. Mining & Mineral Co. v. Fox Rothschild LLP****, 615 F.3d 159, 175 (3d Cir.2010);* ***Sweaney v. Ada Cty.****, 119 F.3d 1385, 1393 (9th Cir.1997); see* ***Sibley v. Lando****, 437 F.3d 1067, 1073 (11th Cir.2005). In making this determination, the court must decide whether the factual allegations in the complaint plausibly state a claim for relief. See* ***Great W. Mining & Mineral****, 615 F.3d at 175-76. See "Standard," ch. 3-F, §5.1, p. 207.*

6. Frivolity of claims or defenses. ***Gamma-10 Plastics, Inc. v. American President Lines, Ltd.***, 32 F.3d 1244, 1255-56 (8th Cir.1994).

7. Timing of amendment. ***Laber v. Harvey***, 438 F.3d 404, 426-27 (4th Cir.2006); *see* ***Block v. First Blood Assocs.***, 988 F.2d 344, 350 (2d Cir.1993) (if movant delays filing amendment, opposing party's burden to show prejudice lessens).

8. Nature of amendment. ***Laber***, 438 F.3d at 426-27.

(1) *Amendment corrects.* If the amendment merely clarifies or corrects allegations made in the pleadings, it is less likely to cause surprise and should be permitted. *See, e.g.*, ***Associated Musicians v. Parker Meridien Hotel***, 145 F.3d 85, 89-90 (2d Cir.1998) (correcting typographical error would not cause delay or undue prejudice); ***Wilwording v. Swenson***, 502 F.2d 844, 847 n.4 (8th Cir.1974) (court may assist pro se litigant by allowing clarification as long as new facts are not added).

(2) *Amendment subtracts.* If the amendment deletes an allegation, the amendment should usually be permitted. *See, e.g.*, ***Allen v. National Video, Inc.***, 610 F.Supp. 612, 621 (S.D.N.Y.1985) (amendment deleted references to common law).

(3) *Amendment adds.* If the amendment raises additional theories of recovery, raises additional defenses, or adds new parties, it is more likely to cause surprise or prejudice. *See, e.g.*, ***Nelson***, 529 U.S. at 466 (added party had no opportunity to respond); ***Orix Credit Alliance, Inc. v. Taylor Mach. Works, Inc.***, 125 F.3d 468, 480-81 (7th Cir.1997) (by adding prospect of punitive damages, new counts added element of surprise). In such a case, the court will be within its discretion to deny leave to file the amended pleading. ***Jenkins v. Union Pac. R.R.***, 22 F.3d 206, 213 (9th Cir.1994). *But see* ***Lowrey v. Texas A&M Univ. Sys.***, 117 F.3d 242, 246 n.2 (5th Cir.1997) (amendment merely stated alternative theories for recovery on same facts, so amendment should have been allowed). A party should not present its claims or defenses in a series—that is, the party should not present claims or defenses individually and expect to try different claims or defenses by motions for leave after an individual claim or defense is unsuccessful. *See, e.g.*, ***Southern Constructors Grp. v. Dynalectric Co.***, 2 F.3d 606, 612 (5th Cir.1993) (P attempted to add another ground for recovery after losing at arbitration).

9. Fraudulent joinder. ***Mayes v. Rapoport***, 198 F.3d 457, 463 (4th Cir.1999). See "Fraudulent joinder," ch. 4-A, §5.2.1(2)(e), p. 252.

§8. DEADLINE FOR RESPONSIVE PLEADING

The responsive pleading to an amended pleading must be filed either within the time remaining to respond to the original pleading or within 14 days after service of the amended pleading, whichever is later, unless the court orders otherwise. FRCP 15(a)(3). If the proposed amended pleading was attached to the motion for leave, local rules may deem the amended pleading served on the date the court grants leave for its filing. *E.g.*, Local Rules Md., Rule 103.6(a).

NOTE

Under FRCP 12(a)(4), the filing of a preanswer motion tolls the deadline to serve a responsive pleading until the court takes action on the motion by notifying the parties that it is either denying the preanswer motion or delaying ruling on the motion. See "FRCP 12 motion filed," ch. 3-A, §5.2.1, p. 175. But if an amended complaint is filed before the defendant responds to the original complaint, the FRCP 12(a)(4) tolling provision may not apply. See ***General Mills, Inc. v. Kraft Foods Global, Inc.****, 495 F.3d 1378, 1380 (Fed.Cir.2007). The deadline for a responsive pleading after an amended complaint is determined by the longer of two time periods under FRCP 15(a)(3). When "the time remaining to respond to the original pleading" is the longer of the two time periods under FRCP 15(a)(3) (e.g., the plaintiff amends her complaint as a matter of right before serving the defendant, thus giving the defendant at least 21 days to respond), the FRCP 12(a)(4) tolling provision applies and the defendant can file an FRCP 12(b) preanswer motion without having to file an answer until the court takes action on the motion. See* ***General Mills****, 495 F.3d at 1379. But when the time period of "14 days after service of the amended pleading" is the longer of the two time periods under FRCP 15(a)(3) (e.g., the plaintiff amends her complaint as a matter of right the day before the defendant's deadline to file its original answer), the defendant should file its answer in addition to an FRCP 12(b) preanswer motion within the FRCP 15(a)(3) 14-day deadline because the FRCP 12(a)(4) tolling provision may not apply. See* ***General Mills****, 495 F.3d at 1380.*

§9. APPELLATE REVIEW

§9.1 Standard of review. The denial of a motion to amend pleadings will generally be reversed only if the district court abused its discretion. ***Foman v. Davis***, 371 U.S. 178, 182 (1962); ***AEP Energy Servs. Gas Holding Co. v. Bank of Am.***, 626 F.3d 699, 725 (2d Cir.2010); ***Carroll v. Fort James Corp.***, 470 F.3d 1171, 1174 (5th Cir.2006); ***Inge v. Rock Fin. Corp.***, 281 F.3d 613, 625 (6th Cir.2002); ***Harrison v. Rubin***, 174 F.3d 249, 252 (D.C.Cir.1999). But if the denial is based on a legal interpretation, the review is de novo. *See* ***AEP Energy Servs.***, 626 F.3d at 725; *see, e.g.*, ***Inge***, 281 F.3d at 625 (denial of leave to amend complaint because of futility is reviewed de novo); ***Coghlan v. Wellcraft Mar. Corp.***, 240 F.3d 449, 451-52 (5th Cir.2001) (question of whether alleged facts state justiciable controversy is reviewed de novo).

§9.2 Failure to give reasons. The outright refusal to grant leave to amend without any justifiable reason is an abuse of discretion. ***Foman v. Davis***, 371 U.S. 178, 182 (1962); ***Manzarek v. St. Paul Fire & Mar. Ins.***, 519 F.3d 1025, 1034 (9th Cir.2008); ***Jin v. Metropolitan Life Ins.***, 310 F.3d 84, 101 (2d Cir.2002); ***Firestone v. Firestone***, 76 F.3d 1205, 1209 (D.C.Cir.1996). *But see* ***Riley Stoker Corp. v. Fidelity & Guar. Ins. Underwriters, Inc.***, 26 F.3d 581, 591-92 (5th Cir.1994) (although court did not give specific reasons for denial, no abuse of discretion).

J. MOTION TO INTERVENE

§1. GENERAL

§1.1 Rule. FRCP 24.

§1.2 Purpose. FRCP 24 permits a party to voluntarily join a pending lawsuit by filing a motion to intervene. FRCP 24 is intended to prevent multiple lawsuits when common questions of law or fact are involved. ***Deus v. Allstate Ins.***, 15 F.3d 506, 525 (5th Cir.1994); ***Washington Elec. Coop. v. Massachusetts Mun. Wholesale Elec. Co.***, 922 F.2d 92, 97 (2d Cir.1990); *see* ***Bridges v. Department of Md. State Police***, 441 F.3d 197, 207-08 (4th Cir.2006). FRCP 24 does not permit the creation of a whole new lawsuit by an intervenor. ***Deus***, 15 F.3d at 525; ***Washington Elec.***, 922 F.2d at 97.

§1.3 Timetable & forms. Timetable, Pleadings & Pretrial-Motions Schedule, p. 1574; *O'Connor's Federal Civil Forms* (2012), FORMS 5J.

§1.4 Other references. 7C Wright, Miller & Kane, *Federal Practice & Procedure 3d* §§1901-1923 (2007 & Supp.2012); 6 *Moore's Federal Practice 3d* ch. 24 (2012).

§2. MOTION TO INTERVENE

§2.1 Form. For the general requirements for the form of a motion, see "Drafting motions," ch. 1-B, §3.1, p. 14.

§2.2 In writing. A motion to intervene must be in writing. *See* FRCP 24(c).

§2.3 Grounds. The motion to intervene must state the grounds for intervention. FRCP 24(c); ***Beckman Indus. v. International Ins.***, 966 F.2d 470, 474 (9th Cir.1992); ***In re Beef Indus. Antitrust Litig.***, 589 F.2d 786, 788-89 (5th Cir.1979).

1. Intervention as matter of right. FRCP 24(a) provides for intervention as a matter of right. Courts generally construe FRCP 24(a) broadly in favor of intervenors. ***U.S. v. City of L.A.***, 288 F.3d 391, 397-98 (9th Cir. 2002); *see* ***John Doe No. 1 v. Glickman***, 256 F.3d 371, 375 (5th Cir.2001) (intervention should be allowed when no one would be hurt and greater justice could be attained). When an applicant alleges and proves it has a right to intervene under FRCP 24(a), it generally is not required to plead and prove an independent ground for jurisdiction. ***Smith Pet. Serv. v. Monsanto Chem. Co.***, 420 F.2d 1103, 1115 (5th Cir.1970); *see also* 7C Wright, Miller & Kane §1917 (discussing difficult question of jurisdiction and intervention when court has jurisdiction over original action but applicant, if suing or being sued alone, would not present basis for federal jurisdiction). To intervene as a matter of right, the applicant must show that (1) a federal statute confers a right to intervene or (2) the applicant has an interest in the suit. *See* FRCP 24(a).

NOTE

It is unclear whether an applicant must satisfy the requirements of standing, in addition to the requirements of FRCP 24(a), at the time it seeks to intervene. ***U.S. v. Metropolitan St. Louis Sewer Dist.****, 569 F.3d 829, 833 n.2 (8th Cir.2009);* ***Mangual v. Rotger-Sabat****, 317 F.3d 45, 61 & n.5 (1st Cir.2003); 7C Wright, Miller & Kane §1908 & nn.8-9. See "Standing," ch. 2-B, §2.2.1, p. 77. Some courts require an applicant to have standing. E.g.,* ***Metropolitan St. Louis Sewer Dist.****, 569 F.3d at 833;* ***U.S. v. Philip Morris USA Inc.****, 566 F.3d 1095, 1146 (D.C.Cir. 2009); see* ***Bond v. Utreras****, 585 F.3d 1061, 1069-70 (7th Cir.2009). Some courts do not require an applicant to have standing. E.g.,* ***Ruiz v. Estelle****, 161 F.3d 814, 832 (5th Cir.1998);* ***U.S. Postal Serv. v. Brennan****, 579 F.2d 188, 190 (2d Cir.1978); see* ***City of Colo. Springs v. Climax Molybdenum Co.****, 587 F.3d 1071, 1079 (10th Cir.2009) (allowing "piggybacking" standing, in which applicant's standing is satisfied by another party who already satisfied standing and remains in case);* ***Dillard v. Chilton Cty. Comm'n****, 495 F.3d 1324, 1330 (11th Cir.2007) (same).*

And some courts have not decided the issue. ***American Auto. Ins. v. Murray****, 658 F.3d 311, 318 n.4 (3d Cir.2011);* ***Perry v. Proposition 8 Official Proponents****, 587 F.3d 947, 950 n.2 (9th Cir. 2009);* ***Mangual****, 317 F.3d at 61-62. It is clear that an applicant must have standing to continue a suit if the parties who had established standing and were on the same side as the intervenor are no longer in the suit.* ***Diamond v. Charles****, 476 U.S. 54, 68 (1986); see* ***Mangual****, 317 F.3d at 61. When standing must be shown, courts disagree on how the interest requirement under FRCP 24(a)(2) relates to the interest required for standing. Compare* ***Flying J, Inc. v. Van Hollen****, 578 F.3d 569, 571 (7th Cir.2009) (interest requirement under FRCP 24(a)(2) requires more than interest requirement for standing), with* ***Philip Morris USA****, 566 F.3d at 1146 (interest requirement under FRCP 24(a)(2) is met if intervenor establishes standing).*

---

(1) Statute confers right. Under FRCP 24(a)(1), the applicant can show that a federal statute gives it an unconditional right to intervene. *See, e.g.*, 33 U.S.C. §1365(c)(2) (EPA administrator may intervene in citizen's suit under Clean Water Act). The applicant must show that the motion to intervene was timely. See "Deadline," §3, p. 360.

(2) Interest in suit. Under FRCP 24(a)(2), the applicant can show that it has an interest in the subject matter of the pending suit and that disposition of the suit may impair its interest. ***Davis v. Butts***, 290 F.3d 1297, 1300 (11th Cir.2002); ***In re Troutman Enters.***, 286 F.3d 359, 363 (6th Cir.2002); ***John Doe No. 1***, 256 F.3d at 375; ***Utah Ass'n of Cty. v. Clinton***, 255 F.3d 1246, 1249 (10th Cir.2001); *see, e.g.*, ***Westchester Fire Ins. v. Mendez***, 585 F.3d 1183, 1188 (9th Cir.2009) (airline, whose plane was damaged by insured, sought to intervene in suit in which insurer sought declaration that insured forfeited his insurance coverage; airline-intervenor's interest was obvious because it wanted to collect judgment against insured under his insurance policy with insurer). The applicant must show (1) timeliness of the motion to intervene, (2) an interest relating to the action, (3) that the interest would be impaired or impeded by the case, and (4) that the interest is not adequately represented by existing parties. ***U.S. v. Albert Inv. Co.***, 585 F.3d 1386, 1391 (10th Cir.2009); ***R&G Mortg. Corp. v. Federal Home Loan Mortg. Corp.***, 584 F.3d 1, 7 (1st Cir.2009); ***In re Lease Oil Antitrust Litig.***, 570 F.3d 244, 247 (5th Cir.2009); ***Philip Morris USA***, 566 F.3d at 1146.

(a) Timeliness. The applicant must show that the motion to intervene was timely. See "Deadline," §3, p. 360.

(b) Interest related to suit. The applicant must show it has an interest in the suit that is direct, substantial, and legally protectable. ***In re Lease Oil Antitrust Litig.***, 570 F.3d at 250; ***Loyd v. Alabama Dept. of Corr.***, 176 F.3d 1336, 1340 (11th Cir.1999); ***U.S. v. Union Elec. Co.***, 64 F.3d 1152, 1161 (8th Cir.1995). *But see* ***San Juan Cty. v. U.S.***, 503 F.3d 1163, 1192-93 (10th Cir.2007) (rejecting "direct, substantial, and legally protectable" test and instead adopting "legally protectable interest" test). The applicant does not need to have an interest in every part of the suit; it is entitled to intervene as long as its interest is significantly protectable. *See* ***Mountain Top Condo. Ass'n v. Dave Stabbert Master Builder, Inc.***, 72 F.3d 361, 366 (3d Cir.1995). The applicant must demonstrate the following:

[1] The interest is a legal interest, as distinguished from a general or indefinite interest. ***Mountain Top Condo.***, 72 F.3d at 366; ***U.S. v. AT&T Co.***, 642 F.2d 1285, 1292 (D.C.Cir.1980); *see, e.g.*, ***Medical Liab. Mut. Ins. v. Alan Curtis LLC***, 485 F.3d 1006, 1008-09 (8th Cir.2007) (applicant was denied intervention in declaratory-judgment action between insurer and insureds who were being sued by applicant; applicant's interests were too indirect because they were contingent not only on obtaining judgment against insureds but also on her inability to satisfy judgment against any of insureds). *But see* ***Forest Conserv. Council v. U.S. Forest Serv.***, 66 F.3d 1489, 1493 (9th Cir.1995) ("[n]o specific legal or equitable interest need be established"), *overruled on other grounds*, ***Wilderness Soc'y v. U.S. Forest Serv.***, 630 F.3d 1173 (9th Cir.2011). Mere economic interest in the outcome of the litiga-

tion is insufficient. ***Medical Liab. Mut. Ins.***, 485 F.3d at 1008; ***In re Lease Oil Antitrust Litig.***, 570 F.3d at 251; ***Mountain Top Condo.***, 72 F.3d at 366. Interest in a specific fund, however, is sufficient in a case affecting that fund. ***Mountain Top Condo.***, 72 F.3d at 366; *see* ***Gaines v. Dixie Carriers, Inc.***, 434 F.2d 52, 54 (5th Cir.1970).

[2] There is a tangible threat to a legally cognizable interest. ***Mountain Top Condo.***, 72 F.3d at 366; ***Development Fin. Corp. v. Alpha Hous. & Health Care, Inc.***, 54 F.3d 156, 162 (3d Cir.1995); *see also* ***Union Elec.***, 64 F.3d at 1162 (applicant does not have to wait until it has suffered irreparable harm).

[3] The interest is recognized as one belonging to or owned by the proposed applicant. ***In re Lease Oil Antitrust Litig.***, 570 F.3d at 250; ***Mountain Top Condo.***, 72 F.3d at 366; *see* ***WildEarth Guardians v. National Park Serv.***, 604 F.3d 1192, 1198 (10th Cir.2010) (applicant's interest is measured by its relationship to property or transaction in suit, not by particular issue before court).

(c) Interest may be impaired. The applicant must show that its interest may be impaired by an unfavorable disposition of the case. ***WildEarth Guardians***, 604 F.3d at 1199; ***Michigan State AFL-CIO v. Miller***, 103 F.3d 1240, 1247 (6th Cir.1997). Generally, the burden of establishing impairment of the interest is minimal. ***WildEarth Guardians***, 604 F.3d at 1199. The applicant must show practical impairment of its interest, not just that it will be bound by the disposition of the case. ***U.S. v. Texas E. Transmission Corp.***, 923 F.2d 410, 413 (5th Cir.1991); *see* ***Coalition of Ariz./N.M. Cty. for Stable Econ. Growth v. Department of Interior***, 100 F.3d 837, 844 (10th Cir. 1996); ***Union Elec.***, 64 F.3d at 1161. The applicant must show only that, without its intervention, its interest may—not would—be impaired by the operation of res judicata, collateral estoppel, or stare decisis. ***Union Elec.***, 64 F.3d at 1161; *see* ***WildEarth Guardians***, 604 F.3d at 1199. For example, the applicant can show that its ability to obtain effective remedies in later litigation may be impaired if the court does not consider its contentions in the pending suit. ***U.S. v. Oregon***, 839 F.2d 635, 638 (9th Cir.1988).

(d) Inadequate representation. The applicant must show that its interest may not be adequately represented by the present parties. ***Trbovich v. United Mine Workers***, 404 U.S. 528, 538 n.10 (1972); ***Kane Cty. v. U.S.***, 597 F.3d 1129, 1134 (10th Cir.2010); ***Michigan State***, 103 F.3d at 1247; ***Union Elec.***, 64 F.3d at 1168; *see also* ***Clark v. Putnam Cty.***, 168 F.3d 458, 461 (11th Cir.1999) (there is a weak presumption that representation is adequate when present party seeks same objectives as intervenors).

[1] Factors. The applicant may satisfy the requirement by showing the following:

[a] A present party will not make all of the applicant's arguments because its interest in the suit is different from the applicant's interest. ***Forest Conserv. Council***, 66 F.3d at 1498-99; ***Oregon***, 839 F.2d at 638.

[b] The present party is either not capable or not willing to make the arguments. ***Forest Conserv. Council***, 66 F.3d at 1499.

[c] The applicant would offer necessary elements to the proceedings that other parties would neglect. *Id.*

[d] There is collusion between the representative and an opposing party. ***Coalition***, 100 F.3d at 844; ***Purnell v. City of Akron***, 925 F.2d 941, 949 (6th Cir.1991).

[e] The representative has an interest adverse to the applicant. ***Coalition***, 100 F.3d at 844; ***Purnell***, 925 F.2d at 950.

[f] The representative did not fulfill its duty to represent the applicant's interest. ***Coalition***, 100 F.3d at 844-45; ***Purnell***, 925 F.2d at 949-50.

[2] Burden. Generally, the burden of establishing the inadequacy of representation is minimal. ***WildEarth Guardians***, 604 F.3d at 1200; ***Prete v. Bradbury***, 438 F.3d 949, 956 (9th Cir.2006).

NOTE

If the applicant claims that the government or another similarly situated party is the party who will inadequately represent the applicant's interest, the applicant's burden is to show that (1) its interest is separate from the shared interest between the government and its citizens, or (2) if the interest is shared, the applicant has compelling reasons why the government will not adequately represent the shared interest. See ***WildEarth Guardians****, 604 F.3d at 1200;* ***Prete****, 438 F.3d at 956;* ***Union Elec.****, 64 F.3d at 1168-70;* ***Environmental Def. Fund, Inc. v. Higginson****, 631 F.2d 738, 740 (D.C.Cir.1979); see, e.g.,* ***City of Houston v. American Traffic Solutions, Inc.****, 668 F.3d 291, 294 (5th Cir.2012) (applicant was not required to prove "meaningful probability" of inadequate representation by City; district court should have allowed intervention when City's financial motives and conduct in litigation were questionable).*

2. Permissive intervention. FRCP 24(b) provides for permissive intervention. To intervene permissively, the applicant must show that the intervention will not unduly delay or prejudice the adjudication of the original parties' rights. FRCP 24(b)(3); *see* ***City of L.A.***, 288 F.3d at 403. Permissive intervention requires the applicant to plead and prove an independent ground for jurisdiction. ***Perry***, 587 F.3d at 955; ***Union Elec.***, 64 F.3d at 1170 n.9. See "Choosing the Court—Jurisdiction," ch. 2-F, p. 112. The applicant must show that the motion to intervene was timely and should allege at least one of the following reasons why the court should permit the intervention. *See* FRCP 24(b). See "Deadline," §3, p. 360.

NOTE

It is unclear whether an applicant must satisfy the requirements of standing, in addition to the requirements under FRCP 24(b), at the time it seeks to intervene. ***Bond****, 585 F.3d at 1069;* ***Metropolitan St. Louis Sewer Dist.****, 569 F.3d at 833 n.2; see* ***Mangual****, 317 F.3d at 61 & n.5. See "Standing," ch. 2-B, §2.2.1, p. 77. Some courts require an applicant to have standing. E.g.,* ***Metropolitan St. Louis Sewer Dist.****, 569 F.3d at 833. Some courts do not require an applicant to have standing. E.g.,* ***Pope v. Hunt****, 154 F.3d 161, 165 (4th Cir.1998); see* ***City of Colo. Springs v. Climax Molybdenum Co.****, 587 F.3d 1071, 1079 (10th Cir.2009) (allowing "piggybacking" standing, in which applicant's standing is satisfied by another party who already satisfied standing and remains in case);* ***Newby v. Enron Corp.****, 443 F.3d 416, 422 (5th Cir.2006) (applicant does not need to have standing if standing has already been established and applicant is seeking the same relief as that sought by at least one of parties). And some courts have not decided the issue.* ***Bond****, 585 F.3d at 1070-71 & n.7;* ***Mangual****, 317 F.3d at 61-62. It is clear that an applicant must have standing to continue a suit if the parties who had established standing and were on the same side as the intervenor are no longer in the suit.* ***Diamond v. Charles****, 476 U.S. 54, 68 (1986); see* ***Mangual****, 317 F.3d at 61.*

(1) Statute confers right. A federal statute gives the applicant a conditional right to intervene. FRCP 24(b)(1)(A).

(2) Common questions of law or fact. The applicant's claim or defense shares common questions of law or fact with the main suit. FRCP 24(b)(1)(B); ***Perry v. Schwarzenegger***, 630 F.3d 898, 905 (9th Cir.2011); *see also* ***Lower Ark. Valley Water Conservancy Dist. v. U.S.***, 252 F.R.D. 687, 690-91 (D.Colo.2008) (after applicant establishes common-questions requirement, applicant can assert that (1) applicant's input adds value to litigation, (2) applicant's interests are not adequately represented by parties, and (3) adequate remedy is not available in another action).

(3) Suit involves statute or executive order. A party's claim or defense in the main suit is based on (1) a statute or executive order or (2) any regulation, order, requirement, or agreement issued or made under the statute or executive order; thus, the officer or agency responsible for administering the statute or executive order may be permitted to intervene. FRCP 24(b)(2).

§2.4 Pleading. Along with the motion to intervene, the applicant should file and serve the pleading by which it seeks to intervene. FRCP 24(c); ***U.S. v. Metropolitan St. Louis Sewer Dist.***, 569 F.3d 829, 834 (8th Cir.2009). The pleading must state the claim or defense for which intervention is sought. FRCP 24(c). If the applicant does not file a pleading, it should file a document that provides the court and parties with sufficient notice of the applicant's interests. *E.g.*, ***Metropolitan St. Louis Sewer Dist.***, 569 F.3d at 834 (applicant's statement of interest explaining reasons for intervention satisfied FRCP 24(c)); *see* ***Arizonans for Official English v. Arizona***, 520 U.S. 43, 57 (1997) (absence of pleading not critical deficiency); ***Westchester Fire Ins. v. Mendez***, 585 F.3d 1183, 1188 (9th Cir.2009) (pleading requirement is purely technical defect, which does not result in disregard of substantial right).

§2.5 File & serve. An applicant must file and serve the motion to intervene and the pleading in intervention on the parties to the suit, as provided in FRCP 5. FRCP 24(c).

§2.6 Proposed order. Some districts require the movant to submit a proposed order with the motion. In those districts, the movant should prepare a written order for the court's signature and submit it with the motion. See "Proposed order," ch. 1-B, §3.1.11, p. 16.

§2.7 Notice of constitutional question. See "Notice of constitutional question," ch. 1-B, §2.1.11, p. 12.

§3. DEADLINE

§3.1 Motion must be timely. Whether intervention of right or permissive intervention is requested, the applicant's motion must be timely filed. ***NAACP v. New York***, 413 U.S. 345, 365-66 (1973); *see* ***In re Lease Oil Antitrust Litig.***, 570 F.3d 244, 248 (5th Cir.2009); ***Davis v. Butts***, 290 F.3d 1297, 1300 (11th Cir.2002); ***In re Troutman Enters.***, 286 F.3d 359, 363 (6th Cir.2002); ***Utah Ass'n of Cty. v. Clinton***, 255 F.3d 1246, 1249 (10th Cir.2001). The court must determine from all the circumstances whether the intervention is timely. *See* ***United Airlines, Inc. v. McDonald***, 432 U.S. 385, 394-95 (1977); ***NAACP***, 413 U.S. at 366-67; ***R&G Mortg. Corp. v. Federal Home Loan Mortg. Corp.***, 584 F.3d 1, 7 (1st Cir.2009). The timeliness requirement is usually applied less strictly to an intervention of right. ***R&G Mortg.***, 584 F.3d at 8. There is no bright-line rule about how quickly an applicant must move to intervene; rather, the inquiry focuses on how diligently the applicant acted once she received actual or constructive notice of the impending threat. *Id.* To determine whether a motion has been timely filed, the court may consider the following factors:

1. The point to which the suit has progressed. ***Blount-Hill v. Zelman***, 636 F.3d 278, 284 (6th Cir.2011); ***U.S. v. Washington***, 86 F.3d 1499, 1503 (9th Cir.1996); *see* ***R&G Mortg.***, 584 F.3d at 7 (status of litigation at time of application is "highly relevant"); *see, e.g.*, ***Zbaraz v. Madigan***, 572 F.3d 370, 377 (7th Cir.2009) (intervention denied when intervenors waited until district court had already denied two motions for reconsideration, defendants had filed notice of appeal, and litigation had been ongoing for almost 25 years).

2. The purpose for which intervention is sought. ***Blount-Hill***, 636 F.3d at 284.

3. The length of time preceding the application during which the proposed intervenor knew, or reasonably should have known, of its interest in the case. ***Blount-Hill***, 636 F.3d at 284; ***Oklahoma v. Tyson Foods, Inc.***, 619 F.3d 1223, 1232 (10th Cir.2010); ***R&G Mortg.***, 584 F.3d at 7; ***In re Lease Oil Antitrust Litig.***, 570 F.3d at 247. Some circuits measure the time from the point when the applicant was on notice that its interest may not be protected by a party already in the suit, not from the point when it learned of its interest. ***Oklahoma***, 619 F.3d at 1232; *see* ***Washington***, 86 F.3d at 1503.

4. The prejudice to the original parties because of the proposed intervenor's failure to file a motion, after it knew or reasonably should have known of its interest in the case. ***Blount-Hill***, 636 F.3d at 284; ***Oklahoma***, 619 F.3d at 1232; ***R&G Mortg.***, 584 F.3d at 7; ***In re Lease Oil Antitrust Litig.***, 570 F.3d at 247.

5. Unusual circumstances weighing in favor of or against intervention. ***Blount-Hill***, 636 F.3d at 284; ***Oklahoma***, 619 F.3d at 1232; ***R&G Mortg.***, 584 F.3d at 7; ***In re Lease Oil Antitrust Litig.***, 570 F.3d at 247-48.

6. The resulting prejudice to the applicant if the motion is denied. ***Oklahoma***, 619 F.3d at 1232; ***R&G Mortg.***, 584 F.3d at 7; ***In re Lease Oil Antitrust Litig.***, 570 F.3d at 247-48; *see, e.g.*, ***Zbaraz***, 572 F.3d at 377 (when two state's attorneys and a pro-life center sought to intervene in suit involving constitutionality of abortion law, denial of intervention did not prejudice proposed intervenors because existing parties—attorney general and another state's attorney—adequately represented intervenors' interests).

§3.2 Postjudgment application to intervene. A postjudgment application for intervention is timely if it is filed within the time a party to the suit could have filed a notice of appeal, and if the intervenor has taken some other step to protect its interest. *E.g.*, ***U.S. v. Northrop Corp.***, 25 F.3d 715, 719-20 (9th Cir.1994) (government permitted to intervene in qui tam action). But postjudgment applications are generally disfavored, and they are granted only on a strong showing of entitlement and justification for not filing the application earlier. *See* ***Planned Parenthood of the Heartland v. Heineman***, 664 F.3d 716, 718 (8th Cir.2011).

§4. ORDER

§4.1 Ruling. Courts should construe FRCP 24 liberally and resolve any doubts in favor of the proposed intervenor. ***In re Lease Oil Antitrust Litig.***, 570 F.3d 244, 248 (5th Cir.2009); ***Turn Key Gaming, Inc. v. Oglala Sioux Tribe***, 164 F.3d 1080, 1081 (8th Cir.1999).

§4.2 Conditions imposed on intervenor.

1. **Intervention as matter of right.** Historically, courts have held that conditions cannot be imposed on an intervenor of right. ***Columbus-Am. Discovery Grp. v. Atlantic Mut. Ins.***, 974 F.2d 450, 469 (4th Cir.1992); *see* 7C Wright, Miller & Kane §1922. However, several courts have allowed reasonable conditions to be imposed on an intervenor of right. ***Columbus-Am.***, 974 F.2d at 470; 7C Wright, Miller & Kane §1922; *see* ***Harris v. Pernsley***, 820 F.2d 592, 599 & n.11 (3d Cir.1987) (limiting intervention of right to separate phases of litigation may be necessary in some cases).

2. **Permissive intervention.** The court can impose almost any condition when it grants a permissive intervention. ***Columbus-Am.***, 974 F.2d at 469; *see, e.g.*, ***Stringfellow v. Concord Neighbors in Action***, 480 U.S. 370, 377-78 (1987) (court restricted discovery and intervenor's right to request additional relief).

§5. APPELLATE REVIEW

§5.1 Applicant's right to appeal denial of motion.

1. **Denial of intervention of right.** The denial of a motion to intervene as a matter of right is a final, appealable order. ***U.S. v. Albert Inv. Co.***, 585 F.3d 1386, 1389 (10th Cir.2009); ***Purcell v. BankAtlantic Fin. Corp.***, 85 F.3d 1508, 1511 n.2 (11th Cir.1996); ***Northwest Forest Res. Council v. Glickman***, 82 F.3d 825, 828 (9th Cir.1996); *see, e.g.*, ***Heaton v. Monogram Credit Card Bank***, 297 F.3d 416, 422 (5th Cir.2002) (denial of intervention was appealable collateral order).

2. **Denial of permissive intervention.** The denial of a motion for permissive intervention is subject to provisional appellate jurisdiction to determine if the denial is correct. ***Lucas v. McKeithen***, 102 F.3d 171, 173 (5th Cir.1996). If the district court did not abuse its discretion in denying the motion, the court of appeals must dismiss the appeal for lack of jurisdiction. *Id.* at 173 n.6; *see* ***Grilli v. Metropolitan Life Ins. Co.***, 78 F.3d 1533, 1538 (11th Cir.1996). If the district court abused its discretion, the court of appeals retains jurisdiction and must reverse. ***Edwards v. City of Houston***, 78 F.3d 983, 992 (5th Cir.1996).

§5.2 Intervenor's right to appeal suit. Permission to intervene does not automatically confer standing to appeal. ***Diamond v. Charles***, 476 U.S. 54, 68 (1986). Generally, the intervenor can appeal only if an original party to the suit appeals. *See id.* at 64. To pursue its own appeal, an intervenor must have standing as required by Article 3 of the U.S. Constitution. ***Arizonans for Official English v. Arizona***, 520 U.S. 43, 65 (1997).

§5.3 Standard of review.

1. Timeliness of motion to intervene. A district court's ruling on the timeliness of an FRCP 24(a) or (b) motion to intervene is reviewed for abuse of discretion. ***NAACP v. New York***, 413 U.S. 345, 366 (1973); ***Zbaraz v. Madigan***, 572 F.3d 370, 377 (7th Cir.2009); ***John Doe No. 1 v. Glickman***, 256 F.3d 371, 376 (5th Cir.2001). If the court does not articulate reasons for the ruling, it will be reviewed de novo. ***Blount-Hill v. Zelman***, 636 F.3d 278, 283 (6th Cir.2011); ***John Doe No. 1***, 256 F.3d at 376.

2. Denial of intervention of right. Different circuits apply different standards of review to denials of FRCP 24(a) motions to intervene of right.

(1) Abuse of discretion. The First, Second, Third, and Fourth Circuits review the district court's denial of an FRCP 24(a) motion for abuse of discretion. ***Ungar v. Arafat***, 634 F.3d 46, 51 (1st Cir.2011); ***Safety-Kleen, Inc. v. Wyche***, 274 F.3d 846, 867 (4th Cir.2001); ***Harris v. Pernsley***, 820 F.2d 592, 597 (3d Cir.1987); ***U.S. v. Hooker Chems. & Plastics Corp.***, 749 F.2d 968, 990 (2d Cir.1984); *see also* ***Cotter v. Massachusetts Ass'n of Minority Law Enforcement Officers***, 219 F.3d 31, 34 (1st Cir.2000) (phrase "abuse of discretion" is misleading; decisions on abstract issues of law are always reviewed de novo, and standards under FRCP 24(a)(2) considerably restrict district court's discretion).

(2) Clearly erroneous. The D.C. Circuit reviews the district court's denial of an FRCP 24(a) motion under the clearly-erroneous standard. ***Foster v. Gueory***, 655 F.2d 1319, 1324 (D.C.Cir.1981).

(3) De novo. The Fifth, Sixth, Seventh, Eighth, Ninth, Tenth, and Eleventh Circuits review the district court's denial of an FRCP 24(a) motion de novo. ***Blount-Hill***, 636 F.3d at 283; ***Perry v. Schwarzenegger***, 630 F.3d 898, 903 (9th Cir.2011); ***U.S. v. Albert Inv. Co.***, 585 F.3d 1386, 1390 (10th Cir.2009); ***Sierra Club, Inc. v. Leavitt***, 488 F.3d 904, 909-10 (11th Cir.2007); ***Armstrong v. Capshaw, Goss & Bowers, LLP***, 404 F.3d 933, 937 (5th Cir. 2005); ***Turn Key Gaming, Inc. v. Oglala Sioux Tribe***, 164 F.3d 1080, 1081 (8th Cir.1999); ***People Who Care v. Rockford Bd. of Educ.***, 68 F.3d 172, 175 (7th Cir.1995).

3. Denial of permissive intervention. A denial of permissive intervention is reviewed for abuse of discretion. ***City of Stillwell v. Ozarks Rural Elec. Coop.***, 79 F.3d 1038, 1042 (10th Cir.1996); ***Winbush v. Iowa***, 66 F.3d 1471, 1478 (8th Cir.1995); ***Hopwood v. Texas***, 21 F.3d 603, 606 (5th Cir.1994); ***H.L. Hayden Co. v. Siemens Med. Sys.***, 797 F.2d 85, 89 (2d Cir.1986). A denial of permissive intervention is rarely reversed. ***New York News, Inc. v. Kheel***, 972 F.2d 482, 487 (2d Cir.1992).

K. MOTION TO CONSOLIDATE

§1. GENERAL

§1.1 Rule. FRCP 42.

§1.2 Purpose. Courts have broad discretion to consolidate civil actions when they involve common questions of law and fact, when the parties would not be prejudiced by consolidation, and when consolidation would serve the interests of judicial economy. *See* FRCP 42(a); ***Enterprise Bank v. Saettele***, 21 F.3d 233, 235 (8th Cir.1994); 9A Wright & Miller, *Federal Practice & Procedure 3d* §2383 (2008 & Supp.2012).

§1.3 Forms. ***O'Connor's Federal Civil Forms*** (2012), FORMS 5K.

§1.4 Other references. 9A Wright & Miller, *Federal Practice & Procedure 3d* §§2381-2386 (2008 & Supp.2012); 8 *Moore's Federal Practice 3d* §§42.10-42.15 (2012).

§2. MOTION TO CONSOLIDATE

§2.1 Form. For the general requirements for the form of a motion, see "Drafting motions," ch. 1-B, §3.1, p. 14.

§2.2 In writing. The motion to consolidate should be in writing. *See* FRCP 7(b)(1)(A).

§2.3 Sua sponte. The court can order consolidation on its own initiative, even if the parties object. ***Devlin v. Transportation Comms. Int'l Un.***, 175 F.3d 121, 130 (2d Cir.1999); ***Cantrell v. GAF Corp.***, 999 F.2d 1007, 1011 (6th Cir.1993).

§2.4 Grounds. The party moving for consolidation bears the burden of showing that the cases should be consolidated. ***In re Repetitive Stress Injury Litig.***, 11 F.3d 368, 373 (2d Cir.1993); ***Single Chip Sys. v. Intermec IP Corp.***, 495 F.Supp.2d 1052, 1057 (S.D.Cal.2007); ***Servants of the Paraclete, Inc. v. Great Am. Ins.***, 866 F.Supp. 1560, 1572 (D.N.M.1994). The motion for consolidation should allege the following:

1. Two or more cases. The cases proposed for consolidation are pending either before the same court for all purposes or before two different courts within the same judicial district. *See* FRCP 42(a)(2); ***Investors Research Co. v. U.S. Dist. Ct. for the Cent. Dist. of Cal.***, 877 F.2d 777, 777 (9th Cir.1989).

2. Common question of law or fact. The cases involve a common question of law or fact. *See* FRCP 42(a)(2); ***Young v. City of Augusta***, 59 F.3d 1160, 1168-69 (11th Cir.1995); ***Cantrell v. GAF Corp.***, 999 F.2d 1007, 1010-11 (6th Cir.1993); ***Frazier v. Garrison ISD***, 980 F.2d 1514, 1531 (5th Cir.1993). When the suits to be consolidated involve a large number of plaintiffs who claim a common injury (e.g., asbestos poisoning), the court should consider additional factors, and the movant should address them in its motion to consolidate. ***In re Repetitive Stress Injury Litig.***, 11 F.3d at 373. These factors include the following:

(1) Whether the claims involve a common work site. *Id.*

(2) Whether the claims involve a similar occupation. *Id.*

(3) Whether the claims involve a similar time of exposure. *Id.*

(4) The type of disease. *Id.*

(5) The status of discovery in each case. *Id.*

(6) Whether all plaintiffs are represented by the same attorney. *Id.*

3. Balancing test. The benefits of consolidation outweigh the burdens. ***Arnold v. Eastern Air Lines, Inc.***, 681 F.2d 186, 193 (4th Cir.1982); ***Takeda v. Turbodyne Techs.***, 67 F.Supp.2d 1129, 1133 (C.D.Cal.1999); 9A Wright & Miller §2383 & nn.4-4.3; *see* ***Hanson v. District of Columbia***, 257 F.R.D. 19, 21 (D.D.C.2009) (courts should weigh considerations of convenience and economy against confusion and prejudice); ***Single Chip***, 495 F.Supp.2d at 1057 (court should weigh saving time and effort against inconvenience, delay, or expense). To show the benefits of consolidation, the motion can allege the following:

(1) There is no risk of prejudice or possible confusion if the cases are consolidated. If there is any risk, it is outweighed by the risk of inconsistent adjudication of common factual and legal issues if the cases are tried separately. *See* ***Cantrell***, 999 F.2d at 1011; ***Hendrix v. Raybestos-Manhattan, Inc.***, 776 F.2d 1492, 1495 (11th Cir. 1985); ***Arnold***, 681 F.2d at 193; ***Hailey v. City of Camden***, 631 F.Supp.2d 528, 553 (D.N.J.2009). The risks of prejudice and confusion can be reduced by the use of cautionary jury instructions and verdict sheets outlining the claims of each plaintiff. ***Johnson v. Celotex Corp.***, 899 F.2d 1281, 1285 (2d Cir.1990).

(2) Consolidation will not burden the parties or witnesses. *See* ***Cantrell***, 999 F.2d at 1011; ***Hendrix***, 776 F.2d at 1495; ***Arnold***, 681 F.2d at 193.

(3) Consolidation will conserve judicial resources. *See* ***Cantrell***, 999 F.2d at 1011; ***Hendrix***, 776 F.2d at 1495; ***Arnold***, 681 F.2d at 193.

(4) Consolidation will resolve the cases in less time than if they were tried separately. *E.g.*, ***Hendrix***, 776 F.2d at 1497 (consolidation saved Ps from wasteful relitigation); *see* ***Arnold***, 681 F.2d at 193.

(5) Consolidation will be less expensive than trying the cases separately. *See* ***Cantrell***, 999 F.2d at 1011; ***Hendrix***, 776 F.2d at 1495; ***Arnold***, 681 F.2d at 193; *see, e.g.*, ***In re Prudential Secs. Inc.***, 158 F.R.D. 562, 570 (S.D.N.Y.1994) (using consolidated complaint for pretrial purposes avoided unnecessary paperwork and costs of service of separate complaints).

§2.5 Deadline. There is no time limit for filing a motion to consolidate; however, the motion should be filed as soon as the party determines consolidation is proper.

§2.6 Proposed order. Some districts require the movant to submit a proposed order with the motion. In those districts, the movant should prepare a written order for the court's signature and submit it with the motion. See "Proposed order," ch. 1-B, §3.1.11, p. 16.

§3. RESPONSE

§3.1 In writing. The response to a motion to consolidate should be in writing.

§3.2 Grounds. The party objecting to the consolidation should state the opposite of what the moving party alleged. For example, a party may include the following objections in its response:

1. The cases contain no, or only a few, common questions of law or fact. ***Werner v. Satterlee, Stephens, Burke & Burke***, 797 F.Supp. 1196, 1211 (S.D.N.Y.1992); *see* ***Star Ins. v. Risk Mktg. Grp.***, 561 F.3d 656, 660-61 (7th Cir.2009); 9A Wright & Miller §2382 & n.17.

2. The potential for prejudice, delay, and confusion outweighs the judicial resources conserved by consolidation. *See* ***Malcolm v. National Gypsum Co.***, 995 F.2d 346, 350 (2d Cir.1993); ***Werner***, 797 F.Supp. at 1211.

3. Consolidating the cases will confuse the jury. ***Werner***, 797 F.Supp. at 1210.

4. One case is ready for trial, but the other is not. ***Mills v. Beech Aircraft Corp.***, 886 F.2d 758, 762 (5th Cir.1989).

5. The consolidation will increase the defendants' costs by forcing the defendants to participate in discovery and other proceedings not relevant to their own case. The defendants will be forced to settle baseless claims to avoid the costs. *See* ***In re Repetitive Stress Injury Litig.***, 11 F.3d 368, 373-74 (2d Cir.1993).

6. The cases cannot be tried to the same fact-finder; one case must be tried to the court and the other to a jury. ***EPA v. City of Green Forest***, 921 F.2d 1394, 1402-03 (8th Cir.1990).

§3.3 Waiver. If a party does not either object to the consolidation or move for a severance, it waives any error the court may have committed in ordering the consolidation. ***Cantrell v. GAF Corp.***, 999 F.2d 1007, 1011 (6th Cir. 1993).

§3.4 Proposed order. In districts that require the party responding to a motion to submit a proposed order, the movant should prepare a written order for the court's signature and submit it with the response. See "Proposed order," ch. 1-B, §3.1.11, p. 16.

§4. ORDER OF CONSOLIDATION

§4.1 Order. The order of consolidation should identify the scope of the consolidation and issue any other orders to avoid unnecessary costs or delay. FRCP 42(a)(3); *see* ***Road Sprinkler Fitters Local Un. v. Continental Sprinkler Co.***, 967 F.2d 145, 149-50 (5th Cir.1992) (appellate court looks to intention of district court to determine nature of consolidation).

1. Complete consolidation. The court can order that the cases be consolidated for all purposes. ***Huene v. U.S.***, 743 F.2d 703, 704-05 (9th Cir.1984); ***Ivanov-McPhee v. Washington Nat'l Ins.***, 719 F.2d 927, 930 (7th Cir. 1983). If the separate suits could originally have been brought as one suit, they can be consolidated and treated as a single case for the purposes of trial, judgment, and appeal. ***Ringwald v. Harris***, 675 F.2d 768, 769 (5th Cir.1982); *see* ***Hageman v. City Investing Co.***, 851 F.2d 69, 71 (2d Cir.1988).

2. Partial consolidation.

(1) Consolidate stages of procedure. Courts sometimes consolidate cases for pretrial purposes so that discovery proceedings can be joined. *See* ***In re Prudential Secs. Inc.***, 158 F.R.D. 562, 570 (S.D.N.Y.1994). The parties then conduct joint discovery but try their cases separately.

(2) Consolidate issues for trial. Courts sometimes consolidate cases for joint trial on common issues but order separate trials on issues that are not common. *See, e.g.*, ***Lewis Charters, Inc. v. Huckins Yacht Corp.***, 871 F.2d 1046, 1049 (11th Cir.1989) (consolidation was for limited purposes only; first case would be tried by jury, and court would decide remaining case). A common form of partial consolidation is for the court to consolidate cases for the determination of liability but not damages. The court then holds a trial on the liability issues, and if the plaintiffs prevail, the parties try the damages issues separately.

§4.2 Effect of consolidation.

1. Merger?

(1) Yes. The Ninth, Tenth, and Federal Circuits hold that the consolidated cases merge, and no appeal can be taken until there is a judgment disposing of all claims. *E.g.*, ***Trinity Broad. Corp. v. Eller***, 827 F.2d 673, 675 (10th Cir.1987), *supplemented*, 832 F.2d 245 (10th Cir.1987); ***Huene v. U.S.***, 743 F.2d 703, 705 (9th Cir.1984); *see* ***Spraytex, Inc. v. DJS&T***, 96 F.3d 1377, 1382 (Fed.Cir.1996).

(2) No. The First and Sixth Circuits hold that consolidation of two or more cases does not merge them into one. *E.g.*, ***Advey v. Celotex Corp.***, 962 F.2d 1177, 1180 (6th Cir.1992); ***Albert v. Maine Cent. R.R.***, 898 F.2d 5, 6-7 (1st Cir.1990). Therefore, a final judgment entered in one case is appealable even if no final judgment has been entered in the other cases. ***Albert***, 898 F.2d at 6-7.

(3) Maybe. Other circuits take a case-by-case approach and hold that consolidation can merge two or more cases into one. *E.g.*, ***U.S. v. Columbia/HCA Healthcare Corp.***, 318 F.3d 214, 216 (D.C.Cir.2003); ***Doe v. Howe Military Sch.***, 227 F.3d 981, 986 (7th Cir.2000); ***Road Sprinkler Fitters Local Un. v. Continental Sprinkler Co.***, 967 F.2d 145, 149 (5th Cir.1992); ***Bergman v. City of Atl. City***, 860 F.2d 560, 566 (3d Cir.1988); *see* ***Hageman v. City Investing Co.***, 851 F.2d 69, 71 (2d Cir.1988) (case-by-case analysis is needed to determine whether judgment that does not dispose of all claims is appealable). These circuits explain that contrary opinions rely on a Supreme Court decision predating the FRCPs. ***Road Sprinkler***, 967 F.2d at 149. To determine the effect of the consolidation, these circuits inquire into the nature and extent of consolidation intended by the district court. *Id.* See "Consolidated cases," ch. 9-A, §3.2.2, p. 739.

2. No change in rights. Consolidation does not change the rights of the parties. ***U.S. v. Tippett***, 975 F.2d 713, 716 (10th Cir.1992). Consolidation does not deprive a party of rights or defenses it had before consolidation. ***Werner v. Satterlee, Stephens, Burke & Burke***, 797 F.Supp. 1196, 1212 (S.D.N.Y.1992).

§5. APPELLATE REVIEW

§5.1 Standard of review. The appellate court will not disturb the district court's decision to grant or deny a motion to consolidate unless the district court abused its discretion. ***Enterprise Bank v. Saettele***, 21 F.3d 233, 235 (8th Cir.1994); ***Frazier v. Garrison ISD***, 980 F.2d 1514, 1531 (5th Cir.1993).

§5.2 No interlocutory appeal. An order of consolidation is not a final judgment. ***In re Repetitive Stress Injury Litig.***, 11 F.3d 368, 372 (2d Cir.1993). Thus, it cannot be appealed before final judgment. *Id.* at 372-73.

§5.3 Mandamus. If the district court's decision to grant or deny consolidation was a sufficiently clear abuse of discretion, the appellate court can review it by mandamus. ***In re Repetitive Stress Injury Litig.***, 11 F.3d 368, 373 (2d Cir.1993).

L. MOTION FOR SEVERANCE OR SEPARATE TRIALS

§1. GENERAL

§1.1 Rules. FRCP 13(i), 20(b), 21, 42(b).

§1.2 Purpose. The rules permit the court to divide one lawsuit into separate lawsuits or separate parts.

§1.3 Forms. *O'Connor's Federal Civil Forms* (2012), FORMS 5L.

§1.4 Other references. 9A Wright & Miller, *Federal Practice & Procedure 3d* §§2387-2392 (2008 & Supp.2012); 8 *Moore's Federal Practice 3d* §§42.20-42.24 (2012); Landes, *Sequential Versus Unitary Trials: An Economic Analysis*, 22 J. Legal Stud. 99 (1993).

§2. SEVERANCE VS. SEPARATE TRIALS

The court may either sever a claim into a separate suit or divide up issues for separate trials. FRCP 20(b), 21, 42(b); *see* ***Hydrite Chem. Co. v. Calumet Lubricants Co.***, 47 F.3d 887, 891 (7th Cir.1995); ***Sanford v. Johns-Manville Sales Corp.***, 923 F.2d 1142, 1146 n.7 (5th Cir.1991). Courts sometimes confuse the names of the two procedures, using the term "separate trial" to mean a case that has been severed under FRCP 21 and "severance" to mean a case that has been divided for separate trials under FRCP 20(b) or 42(b). ***Houseman v. U.S. Aviation Underwriters***, 171 F.3d 1117, 1122 n.5 (7th Cir.1999); ***U.S. v. O'Neil***, 709 F.2d 361, 366 (5th Cir.1983). There are important differences between severance under FRCP 21 and separate trials under FRCP 20(b) or 42(b). Before a party asks the court to "sever" a case or "separate" an issue for trial, it should know the differences between the procedures. *See* 9A Wright & Miller §2387.

§2.1 Severance – different suits. Severance creates two suits out of one. ***Allied Elevator, Inc. v. East Tex. State Bank***, 965 F.2d 34, 36 (5th Cir.1992); ***Chrysler Credit Corp. v. Country Chrysler, Inc.***, 928 F.2d 1509, 1519 n.8 (10th Cir.1991). If a claim is severed out of a suit, it proceeds as a discrete, independent suit with its own pleadings, discovery, trial, judgment, and appeal. ***DirecTV, Inc. v. Leto***, 467 F.3d 842, 846 (3d Cir.2006); ***Gaffney v. Riverboat Servs.***, 451 F.3d 424, 441 (7th Cir.2006); ***Allied Elevator***, 965 F.2d at 36; ***Chrysler Credit Corp.***, 928 F.2d at 1519 n.8.

§2.2 Separate trials – same suit. Splitting a case into separate issues for trial divides one case into two or more parts but results in only one judgment. ***Chrysler Credit Corp. v. Country Chrysler, Inc.***, 928 F.2d 1509, 1519 n.8 (10th Cir.1991); *see* ***Brooks v. District Hosp. Partners***, 606 F.3d 800, 805 (D.C.Cir.2010). The court may bifurcate, trifurcate, or further subdivide a case at whatever point the division will promote economy and accuracy in adjudication. ***Hydrite Chem. Co. v. Calumet Lubricants Co.***, 47 F.3d 887, 891 (7th Cir.1995).

§3. MOTION FOR SEVERANCE

§3.1 Form. For the general requirements for the form of a motion, see "Drafting motions," ch. 1-B, §3.1, p. 14.

§3.2 In writing. The motion for severance must be in writing. *See* FRCP 7(b)(1)(A).

§3.3 Grounds. If a party wants to sever one lawsuit into two, it should request a motion for severance of claims or parties under FRCP 21. The party moving for severance of claims or parties under FRCP 21 may allege the following:

1. The claims or parties have been inappropriately joined (e.g., claims are distinct and separable). *See* FRCP 21; ***American Fid. Fire Ins. v. Construcciones Werl, Inc.***, 407 F.Supp. 164, 190 (D.V.I.1975).

2. The claims or parties should be tried separately in the interest of justice. *See* FRCP 21; ***American Fid. Fire Ins.***, 407 F.Supp. at 189-90.

3. The claim to be severed is a pendent state-law claim. *See* ***Dixon v. CSX Transp.***, 990 F.2d 1440, 1443 (4th Cir.1993).

§3.4 Proposed order. Some districts require the movant to submit a proposed order with the motion. In those districts, the movant should prepare a written order for the court's signature and submit it with the motion. See "Proposed order," ch. 1-B, §3.1.11, p. 16.

§4. MOTION FOR SEPARATE (BIFURCATED) TRIALS

§4.1 Form. For the general requirements for the form of a motion, see "Drafting motions," ch. 1-B, §3.1, p. 14.

§4.2 In writing. The motion for separate trials must be in writing. *See* FRCP 7(b)(1)(A).

§4.3 Sua sponte. The court may order separate trials on its own initiative to expedite the trial and conserve resources. ***In re Paoli R.R. Yard PCB Litig.***, 113 F.3d 444, 452 n.5 (3d Cir.1997); ***Saxion v. Titan-C-Mfg.***, 86 F.3d 553, 556 (6th Cir.1996).

§4.4 Deadline. Generally, one of the parties will move for bifurcation before trial starts. ***Saxion v. Titan-C-Mfg.***, 86 F.3d 553, 556 (6th Cir.1996). This is not a formal requirement, however, and the court in an appropriate case may separate issues of liability and damages during trial. *See id.*; *see, e.g.*, ***Berry v. Deloney***, 28 F.3d 604, 609-10 (7th Cir.1994) (motion to bifurcate made after trial started).

§4.5 Grounds under FRCP 42(b). If a party wants to try one or more claims or defenses separately, it should move for separate trials under FRCP 42(b). The party moving for separate trials should show that separate trials will do justice, avoid prejudice, and further the convenience of the parties and the court. *See* ***Saxion v. Titan-C-Mfg.***, 86 F.3d 553, 556 (6th Cir.1996). The motion should state the following:

1. The issues are clearly separable and can be tried separately without confusing the jury. ***Angelo v. Armstrong World Indus.***, 11 F.3d 957, 964-65 (10th Cir.1993); *see* ***Athridge v. Aetna Cas. & Sur. Co.***, 604 F.3d 625, 635 (D.C.Cir.2010); *see, e.g.*, ***Castle v. Cohen***, 840 F.2d 173, 176 (3d Cir.1988) (contract claim separated from securities-fraud issues).

2. Bifurcating the issues will avoid prejudice to the parties. *See* ***Athridge***, 604 F.3d at 635; ***Westchester Specialty Ins. Servs. v. U.S. Fire Ins.***, 119 F.3d 1505, 1512 n.14 (11th Cir.1997); *see, e.g.*, ***Quintanilla v. City of Downey***, 84 F.3d 353, 356 (9th Cir.1996) (risk of prejudice and confusion by introducing evidence of police-dog attacks on people other than P); ***Barr Labs. v. Abbott Labs.***, 978 F.2d 98, 115 (3d Cir.1992) (bifurcated issue of relevant product market). The court cannot bifurcate claims in such a way that the same issue is reexamined by different juries. ***In re Rhone-Poulenc Rorer Inc.***, 51 F.3d 1293, 1303 (7th Cir.1995). *But see* ***Valentino v. Carter-Wallace, Inc.***, 97 F.3d 1227, 1233 (9th Cir.1996) (9th Circuit may certify different classes in products-liability cases).

3. Prejudice and confusion will be avoided by first trying certain claims without introducing evidence that is prejudicial to those claims but is necessary for the other claims. *E.g.*, ***Angelo***, 11 F.3d at 965 (reverse bifurcation, tried damages before liability); ***Mattison v. Dallas Carrier Corp.***, 947 F.2d 95, 110 (4th Cir.1991) (bifurcated liability and compensatory damages from amount of punitive damages).

4. Bifurcation will enhance juror comprehension of complex issues. ***Barr Labs.***, 978 F.2d at 115.

5. Bifurcation will eliminate or reduce the presentation of lengthy evidence. *Id.*; *see, e.g.*, ***Angelo***, 11 F.3d at 964 (asbestos litigation).

6. The controversy involves more than one claim or defense, and a separate trial of one issue might render trial of the other issues unnecessary. ***Athridge***, 604 F.3d at 635; *see* ***Jinro Am. Inc. v. Secure Invs.***, 266 F.3d 993, 998 (9th Cir.2001) (bifurcation would permit deferral of costly and possibly unnecessary proceedings pending resolution of potentially dispositive preliminary issues), *amended*, 272 F.3d 1289 (9th Cir.2001); ***Rose v. A.C.&S., Inc.***, 796 F.2d 294, 298 n.2 (9th Cir.1986) (court can try limitations issue first); ***Stewart v. RCA Corp.***, 790 F.2d 624, 629 (7th Cir.1986) (same); ***Triplett v. Heckler***, 767 F.2d 210, 212 n.2 (5th Cir.1985) (same); *see, e.g.*, ***In re Innotron Diagnostics***, 800 F.2d 1077, 1085 (Fed.Cir.1986) (court separated patent claims from antitrust claims).

7. Separate trials of the issues will be more convenient for the parties and the court. ***In re Innotron Diagnostics***, 800 F.2d at 1085.

8. Separate trials will preserve the party's right to a jury. ***Shum v. Intel Corp.***, 499 F.3d 1272, 1276 (Fed. Cir.2007).

§4.6 Grounds under FRCP 20(b). The party moving for separate trials under FRCP 20(b) may allege the following:

1. The movant is not adverse to a party joined to the suit. *See, e.g.*, ***Herder Truck Lines v. U.S.***, 335 F.2d 261, 263 (5th Cir.1964) (under FRCP 20(b), court should have ordered separate trials of P's two issues when second count sought relief only against government and not remaining two Ds).

2. The movant will suffer embarrassment, delay, expense, or other prejudice by including a person who asserts no claim against the movant or against whom the movant asserts no claim. FRCP 20(b); ***Dillard v. Crenshaw Cty.***, 640 F.Supp. 1347, 1371 (M.D.Ala.1986). *But see* ***Ward v. Johns Hopkins Univ.***, 861 F.Supp. 367, 378-79 (D.Md.1994) (court could have ordered separate trials to prevent prejudice, but chose to give limiting jury instruction instead).

§4.7 Proposed order. Some districts require the movant to submit a proposed order with the motion. In those districts, the movant should prepare a written order for the court's signature and submit it with the motion. See "Proposed order," ch. 1-B, §3.1.11, p. 16.

§5. RESPONSE

§5.1 In writing. The response to a motion for severance or separate trials should be in writing. *See* FRCP 7(b)(1)(A).

§5.2 Grounds – general. A party opposing the motion for severance or separate trials should state the opposite of what the movant alleged. The opposing party should allege that alternative methods (e.g., special jury instructions or interrogatory verdict forms) are available to protect the movant from prejudice or harm. *See* ***Ward v. Johns Hopkins Univ.***, 861 F.Supp. 367, 379 (D.Md.1994) (any undue prejudice in denying motion to sever can be eliminated at trial by giving jury instruction); *see, e.g.*, ***Duke v. Uniroyal Inc.***, 928 F.2d 1413, 1421 (4th Cir.1991) (court instructed jury that each of P's claims should be considered separately).

§5.3 Response to motion for severance. A party objecting to the severance of claims or parties under FRCP 21 may allege the following:

1. The claims and parties are appropriately joined and should be tried together. *See* FRCP 21; ***American Fid. Fire Ins. v. Construcciones Werl, Inc.***, 407 F.Supp. 164, 189-90 (D.V.I.1975). Any prejudice in trying the cases together can be eliminated by a limiting instruction to the jury. ***Ward v. Johns Hopkins Univ.***, 861 F.Supp. 367, 379 (D.Md.1994).

2. Multiple trials will substantially duplicate the time and work in each case. ***Avitia v. Metropolitan Club***, 49 F.3d 1219, 1224 (7th Cir.1995).

3. The party that would be severed is required. FRCP 19(b); ***Sta-Rite Indus. v. Allstate Ins.***, 96 F.3d 281, 287 (7th Cir.1996).

§5.4 Response to FRCP 42(b) motion for separate trials. A party objecting to the separate trial of issues under FRCP 42(b) may allege the following:

1. The issues are so interwoven that they cannot be submitted to the jury independently without confusing the jury. *See* ***Shum v. Intel Corp.***, 499 F.3d 1272, 1276-77 (Fed.Cir.2007); ***Martin v. Heideman***, 106 F.3d 1308, 1311-12 (6th Cir.1997); ***York v. AT&T Co.***, 95 F.3d 948, 958 (10th Cir.1996).

2. Inconsistent jury verdicts may result if the suit is divided for separate trials.

3. The movant did not ask for separate trials at the pretrial conference, and it is now too late. ***McLaughlin v. State Farm Mut. Auto. Ins.***, 30 F.3d 861, 870 (7th Cir.1994).

4. If the court bifurcates the issues, both juries will have to examine the same issue. ***In re Rhone-Poulenc Rorer Inc.***, 51 F.3d 1293, 1303 (7th Cir.1995). *But see* ***Valentino v. Carter-Wallace, Inc.***, 97 F.3d 1227, 1232-33 (9th Cir.1996) (9th Circuit may certify different classes in products-liability cases).

5. The bifurcation will adversely affect judicial efficiency and strain judicial resources. ***York***, 95 F.3d at 958.

6. The objecting party will be prejudiced by bifurcation. *Id.*; ***Bath & Body Works, Inc. v. Luzier Personalized Cosmetics, Inc.***, 76 F.3d 743, 747 (6th Cir.1996).

7. The bifurcation does not preserve a party's right to a jury. *See, e.g.*, ***Shum***, 499 F.3d at 1276-77 (trial bifurcated into bench trial for equitable claim and later jury trial for legal claim did not preserve P's right to jury on legal issues when there were facts common to both claims).

§5.5 Response to FRCP 20(b) motion for separate trials. A party objecting to the separate trial of issues under FRCP 20(b) may allege the following:

1. The movant is adverse to a party joined to the suit, and a separate trial under FRCP 20(b) would not be appropriate.

2. Even if the movant is not adverse to the joined party, the movant will not suffer embarrassment, delay, expense, or other prejudice by including a party who asserts no claim against it. *See* FRCP 20(b).

§5.6 Proposed order. In districts that require the responding party to submit a proposed order, the nonmovant should prepare a written order denying relief sought for the court's signature and file it with the motion. *See* Local Rules Tex. (S.D.), Rule 7.4.D. See "Proposed order," ch. 1-B, §3.1.11, p. 16.

§6. RULING

Because there can be much confusion about whether the court's order is meant to sever or separate issues, the order should include the following information:

§6.1 Rule. The order should specifically state the rule under which the motion for severance or separate trials is granted. *See, e.g.*, ***Chrysler Credit Corp. v. Country Chrysler, Inc.***, 928 F.2d 1509, 1519 (10th Cir.1991) (order could not be construed as FRCP 21 severance; order did not refer to FRCP 21 or imply that two different suits were being created).

NOTE

Under FRCP 21, the court can dismiss a misjoined party—rather than severing the party—only if the party will not be prejudiced by the dismissal. E.g., ***Strandlund v. Hawley****, 532 F.3d 741, 745-46 (8th Cir.2008) (court should have severed Ds' claim rather than dismissing Ds when dismissal prevented Ds from refiling because of statute of limitations); see* ***DirecTV, Inc. v. Leto****, 467 F.3d 842, 845 (3d Cir.2006);* ***Elmore v. Henderson****, 227 F.3d 1009, 1012 (7th Cir.2000).*

§6.2 Scope of division. The order should specifically identify which claims, defenses, issues, or parties are being separated.

§6.3 Effect. The order should provide information to specifically answer the following three questions:

1. Will the cases be joined for some purposes and not others? For example, will the parties conduct discovery in the cases together, but try the liability and damages issues separately?

2. Will the resolution of one part of the case result in a final, appealable judgment? If so, the order is one of severance and must be under FRCP 21. If the court orders a separate trial under FRCP 20(b) or 42(b), the order should specifically state that the judgment will not be final and appealable until all issues are adjudicated.

3. Will separate parts of the case be tried by different fact-finders (i.e., judge and jury)?

§7. APPELLATE REVIEW

§7.1 Appeal of severance.

1. **Time to appeal.** If claims have been severed into two different lawsuits and a final judgment has been rendered disposing of one of the suits, the time to appeal that suit runs from the date that judgment is entered. The unadjudicated claims in the other lawsuit cannot be appealed until that suit is resolved by a final judgment. Even if

the order severing the lawsuits was erroneous, the time for appeal runs from the date the final judgment is entered. ***Hofmann v. De Marchena Kaluche & Asociados***, 642 F.3d 995, 998 (11th Cir.2011); ***Gomez v. Department of Air Force***, 869 F.2d 852, 859 (5th Cir.1989).

2. Standard of review. The appellate court will not disturb the district court's decision to grant a severance unless the district court abused its discretion. ***Conkling v. Turner***, 18 F.3d 1285, 1293 (5th Cir.1994); ***New York v. Hendrickson Bros.***, 840 F.2d 1065, 1082 (2d Cir.1988).

§7.2 Appeal of separate trials.

1. Time to appeal. If claims have been separated or bifurcated (but not severed), and an order has been rendered disposing of one part of the suit, the time to appeal the resolved part does not begin until a final judgment is entered in the whole case. Issues separated or bifurcated are not appealable before a final judgment is entered unless the court makes an FRCP 54(b) certification. ***Brooks v. District Hosp. Partners***, 606 F.3d 800, 805 (D.C.Cir. 2010); ***Chrysler Credit Corp. v. Country Chrysler, Inc.***, 928 F.2d 1509, 1519 n.8 (10th Cir.1991). Before the court can order a separate appeal of a part of the case under FRCP 54(b), the judgment must be final for one or more claims. See "Judgments covering fewer than all claims or parties," ch. 9-A, §3.2, p. 738.

2. Standard of review. The ruling on a motion to separate is reviewed for abuse of discretion. ***Thabault v. Chait***, 541 F.3d 512, 529 (3d Cir.2008); ***Shum v. Intel Corp.***, 499 F.3d 1272, 1276 (Fed.Cir.2007); ***Wilson v. Morgan***, 477 F.3d 326, 339 (6th Cir.2007); ***Jinro Am. Inc. v. Secure Invs.***, 266 F.3d 993, 998 (9th Cir.2001), *amended*, 272 F.3d 1289 (9th Cir.2001); ***Alexander v. Fulton Cty.***, 207 F.3d 1303, 1325 (11th Cir.2000), *overruled on other grounds*, ***Manders v. Lee***, 338 F.3d 1304 (11th Cir.2003). Denial of a motion for severance is an abuse of discretion only if it deprives the movant of a fair trial. ***Person v. Miller***, 854 F.2d 656, 665 (4th Cir.1988).

M. MOTION FOR JUDICIAL NOTICE

§1. GENERAL

§1.1 Rule. FRE 201; see also FRCP 44, 44.1.

§1.2 Purpose. Judicial notice dispenses with the need to provide formal proof of a fact that is easily determinable from reliable sources. It is a rule of convenience that saves time by eliminating the need for proof of facts about which there is no real controversy. *See* FRE 201.

§1.3 Forms. ***O'Connor's Federal Civil Forms*** (2012), FORMS 5M.

§1.4 Other references. 9A Wright & Miller, *Federal Practice & Procedure 3d* §§2444-2446 (2008 & Supp.2012); 21B Wright & Graham, *Federal Practice & Procedure 2d* §§5101-5111.1 (2005 & Supp.2012); 7, 18, 20 *Moore's Federal Practice 3d* §§32.24[3][c], 131.52[2], 310.10[5][b] (2012); Broun, *McCormick on Evidence* §§328-335 (6th ed. 2006 & Supp.2010).

§2. TYPES OF JUDICIAL NOTICE

Matters that can be judicially noticed are conveniently divided into two categories—adjudicative facts and foreign law.

§2.1 Adjudicative facts.

1. Defined. The court may take judicial notice of a fact that is not subject to reasonable dispute because it (1) is generally known within the court's territorial jurisdiction or (2) can be accurately and readily determined from sources whose accuracy cannot reasonably be questioned. FRE 201(b); ***U.S. v. Boyd***, 289 F.3d 1254, 1258 (10th Cir.2002); ***LaSalle Nat'l Bank v. First Conn. Holding Grp.***, 287 F.3d 279, 290 (3d Cir.2002); *see* ***Cantrell v. Knoxville Cmty. Dev. Corp.***, 60 F.3d 1177, 1180 (6th Cir.1995) (mental instability is not capable of accurate and ready determination by resort to sources whose accuracy cannot reasonably be questioned); *see, e.g.*, ***Wooden v. Missouri***

Pac. R.R., 862 F.2d 560, 563 (5th Cir.1989) (because of presence of controverted issues, proposition that working in silicon dust leads to increased risk of contracting lung cancer is not self-evident enough to be subject to judicial notice).

NOTE

FRE 201 covers judicial notice of only adjudicative facts, not legislative facts. FRE 201(a); ***Hargis v. Access Capital Funding, LLC****, 674 F.3d 783, 792 (8th Cir.2012). Adjudicative facts are simply the facts of the particular case, and legislative facts are those that are relevant to legal reasoning and the lawmaking process. 1972 Notes to FRE 201 at ¶2, p. 1242, this book; see* ***U.S. v. Hernandez-Fundora****, 58 F.3d 802, 812 (2d Cir.1995) (adjudicative facts are developed in a particular case, while legislative facts are established truths that do not change from case to case). Because of the differences, legislative facts are not covered by the FREs or FRCPs; thus, judicial notice of legislative facts does not have the same limitations as judicial notice of adjudicative facts under FRE 201. See 1972 Notes to FRE 201 at ¶¶1, 2, p. 1242, this book.*

2. Examples. The following are examples of judicial notice of adjudicative facts.

5-2. EXAMPLES OF JUDICIAL NOTICE OF ADJUDICATIVE FACTS

	Fact	Authority
1	Stock price on a certain day.	***Lanfear v. Home Depot, Inc.***, 679 F.3d 1267, 1282 n.17 (11th Cir.2012).
2	General location of home, based on Google map and satellite image.	***U.S. v. Perea-Rey***, 680 F.3d 1179, 1182 n.1 (9th Cir.2012).
3	Consumer Price Index.	***Pickett v. Sheridan Health Care Ctr.***, 664 F.3d 632, 648 (7th Cir.2011).
4	Matters of public record, including filing date of complaint.	***Deicher v. City of Evansville***, 545 F.3d 537, 541-42 (7th Cir.2008).
5	Commercial Internet sites.	***O'Toole v. Northrup Grumman Corp.***, 499 F.3d 1218, 1225 (10th Cir.2007); ***Laborers' Pension Fund v. Blackmore Sewer Constr.***, 298 F.3d 600, 607 (7th Cir.2002).
6	Proceedings in other courts, but not findings of fact of other courts.	***Gray v. Beverly Enters.-Miss., Inc.***, 390 F.3d 400, 407 n.7 (5th Cir.2004); ***Liberty Mut. Ins. v. Rotches Pork Packers, Inc.***, 969 F.2d 1384, 1388 (2d Cir.1992); *see* ***Bias v. Moynihan***, 508 F.3d 1212, 1225 (9th Cir.2007).
7	Government data and publications.	***Nebraska v. EPA***, 331 F.3d 995, 998 & n.3 (D.C.Cir.2003); ***Barron v. Reich***, 13 F.3d 1370, 1377 (9th Cir.1994).
8	Historical information contained in authoritative publications.	***Hotel Empls. & Rest. Empls. Un. v. City of N.Y. Dep't of Parks & Recreation***, 311 F.3d 534, 540 n.1 (2d Cir.2002).
9	Time of sunrise.	***U.S. v. Bervaldi***, 226 F.3d 1256, 1266 n.9 (11th Cir.2000).
10	In securities cases, public-disclosure documents required by law to be filed, and actually filed, with the SEC, but not other forms of public disclosure such as press releases and announcements at shareholder meetings.	***Lovelace v. Software Spectrum Inc.***, 78 F.3d 1015, 1018 n.1 (5th Cir.1996).
11	A matter of law can be judicially noticed as a matter of fact—that is, the court can look at a law (e.g., OSHA regulation) not as a rule governing the case before it, but as a social fact with evidentiary consequences.	***City of Wichita v. U.S. Gypsum Co.***, 72 F.3d 1491, 1496 (10th Cir.1996).
12	Definitions of words.	***Cose v. Getty Oil Co.***, 4 F.3d 700, 705 (9th Cir.1993).

5-2. EXAMPLES OF JUDICIAL NOTICE OF ADJUDICATIVE FACTS (CONTINUED)

	Fact	Authority
13	Fact that television station is operated by the state's public broadcasting affiliate.	***Vote Choice, Inc. v. Distefano***, 4 F.3d 26, 41 n.19 (1st Cir.1993).
14	Distance between one hospital and eight others.	***Coffey v. Healthtrust, Inc.***, 1 F.3d 1101, 1103 (10th Cir.1993).
15	Traditional features of a snowman.	***Eden Toys, Inc. v. Marshall Field & Co.***, 675 F.2d 498, 500 n.1 (2d Cir.1982).

§2.2 Foreign law. The court may make a determination on the use of foreign law if the party who intends to raise an issue about a foreign country's law gives notice by a pleading or other writing. FRCP 44.1; ***DP Aviation v. Smiths Indus. Aerospace & Def. Sys.***, 268 F.3d 829, 846 (9th Cir.2001); ***Weidner Comms. v. Al Faisal***, 859 F.2d 1302, 1308 n.9 (7th Cir.1988). The court, in determining foreign law, may consider any relevant material or source, including testimony, regardless of whether it is submitted by a party or is admissible under the FREs. ***Pittway Corp. v. U.S.***, 88 F.3d 501, 504 (7th Cir.1996); ***Reebok Int'l v. McLaughlin***, 49 F.3d 1387, 1392 n.4 (9th Cir.1995); *see* ***Carlisle Ventures, Inc. v. Banco Español de Crédito***, 176 F.3d 601, 604 (2d Cir.1999); *see also* 9A Wright & Miller §§2444-2446 (procedures for making foreign-law determinations).

§3. MOTION

§3.1 Form. For the general requirements for the form of a motion, see "Drafting motions," ch. 1-B, §3.1, p. 14.

§3.2 In writing. Generally, the request should be in writing. *See* FRCP 7(b)(1)(A).

1. Adjudicative facts. Even though a written motion is not required when asking the court to take judicial notice of adjudicative facts, the better procedure is to file and serve one. The court may take judicial notice on its own initiative. FRE 201(c)(1).

2. Foreign law. If a party intends to raise an issue about foreign law, it must give notice by a pleading or other writing. FRCP 44.1; ***In re Griffin Trading Co.***, 683 F.3d 819, 822 (7th Cir.2012); 1966 Notes to FRCP 44.1 at ¶2, p. 1208, this book; *see* ***Whirlpool Fin. Corp. v. Sevaux***, 96 F.3d 216, 221 (7th Cir.1996). The notice must be written but does not need to be incorporated into the party's complaint or answer. 1966 Notes to FRCP 44.1 at ¶2, p. 1208, this book; *see* ***In re Griffin Trading Co.***, 683 F.3d at 822.

§3.3 Evidence.

1. Adjudicative facts. For judicial notice of adjudicative facts, the party must supply the court with the necessary information before the court is required to take judicial notice. FRE 201(c)(2).

2. Foreign law. If a party wants to rely on foreign law, the party must present the court with clear proof of the relevant foreign legal principles. ***Banque Libanaise Pour Le Commerce v. Khreich***, 915 F.2d 1000, 1006 (5th Cir.1990). Because the court is not required to conduct its own research into foreign law, the movant should provide the court with (1) copies and translations of the foreign law, (2) expert testimony or affidavits of attorneys familiar with the foreign law stating their opinion about its application in the present case, and (3) any other secondary sources that might be helpful to the court. *See* ***Pittway Corp. v. U.S.***, 88 F.3d 501, 504 (7th Cir.1996) (court may do its own research and consider any relevant material found); ***McGhee v. Arabian Am. Oil Co.***, 871 F.2d 1412, 1424 n.10 (9th Cir.1989) (court not required to do own research); ***Carey v. Bahama Cruise Lines***, 864 F.2d 201, 205-06 (1st Cir.1988) (court not required to apply foreign law); *see, e.g.*, ***Khreich***, 915 F.2d at 1006 (party failed to meet its burden to prove foreign law; did not present expert testimony or affidavits). If the party presents expert testimony, the expert does not have to meet any special qualifications or be admitted to practice in the country whose laws are at issue. ***In re Grand Jury Proceedings***, 40 F.3d 959, 964 (9th Cir.1994); *see, e.g.*, ***BCCI Holdings (Lux.), S.A. v. Khalil***, 184 F.R.D. 3, 9 (D.D.C.1999) (for declaration on English law, expert did not need to comply with disclosure requirements under FRCP 26(a)(2)).

§3.4 Proposed order. Some districts require the movant to submit a proposed order with the motion. In those districts, the movant should prepare a written order for the court's signature and submit it with the motion. See "Proposed order," ch. 1-B, §3.1.11, p. 16.

§3.5 Notice of motion.

1. Adjudicative facts. FRE 201(e) does not provide any procedure for giving notice of a request for judicial notice of adjudicative facts. 1972 Notes to FRE 201 at ¶26, p. 1244, this book. In fact, FRE 201(e) recognizes that a party may not receive advance notice that a fact has been judicially noticed by the court. When a party does not get advance notice, it may request an opportunity to be heard on the propriety of taking judicial notice. FRE 201(e).

2. Foreign law. The party relying on foreign law must give the court and the other party written notice that it intends to ask for judicial notice of the foreign country's law. FRCP 44.1; *see* ***DP Aviation v. Smiths Indus. Aerospace & Def. Sys.***, 268 F.3d 829, 846 (9th Cir.2001); ***Whirlpool Fin. Corp. v. Sevaux***, 96 F.3d 216, 221 (7th Cir. 1996). The notice may be included in the party's pleading (i.e., complaint or answer) or in a separate document. FRCP 44.1; 1966 Notes to FRCP 44.1 at ¶2, p. 1208, this book.

§4. DEADLINE

§4.1 Adjudicative facts. The court can take judicial notice of adjudicative facts at any stage of the proceeding as long as it is not unfair to a party and does not undermine the court's fact-finding authority. ***In re Indian Palms Assocs.***, 61 F.3d 197, 205 (3d Cir.1995); *see also* ***Victaulic Co. v. Tieman***, 499 F.3d 227, 236 (3d Cir.2007) (court should rarely take judicial notice at pleading stage). Therefore, a party may file a motion at any time, even for the first time on appeal. ***Christopher v. Cutter Labs.***, 53 F.3d 1184, 1197 n.4 (11th Cir.1995) (Barkett, J., concurring); *see* FRE 201(d); *see, e.g.*, ***Lynnbrook Farms v. SmithKline Beecham Corp.***, 79 F.3d 620, 629 n.7 (7th Cir.1996) (judicial notice of effect of agency letter on tort claims).

§4.2 Foreign law. The court can make a determination on the use of foreign law at any time before or during trial. *See* 1966 Notes to FRCP 44.1 at ¶3, p. 1208, this book. But a party who wants to raise the issue of foreign law must provide notice in a pleading or other document. FRCP 44.1; ***APL Co. Pte. Ltd. v. UK Aerosols Ltd.***, 582 F.3d 947, 955 (9th Cir.2009).

1. Party's notice of foreign law.

(1) Generally. FRCP 44.1 does not provide a definite deadline for a party to provide notice that it will raise the issue of foreign law, but the notice should be provided as soon as possible after suit is filed. ***DP Aviation v. Smiths Indus. Aerospace & Def. Sys.***, 268 F.3d 829, 847 (9th Cir.2001); *see* ***Northrop Grumman Ship Sys. v. Ministry of Def. of the Republic of Venez.***, 575 F.3d 491, 496-97 (5th Cir.2009); 1966 Notes to FRCP 44.1 at ¶3, p. 1208, this book. The notice should generally be given before or during the pretrial conference. ***DP Aviation***, 268 F.3d at 847.

(2) Reasonableness. If the foreign-law issue is not apparent until later in the proceedings, the timing of the notice must be reasonable. ***Northrop Grumman Ship***, 575 F.3d at 496-97; *see* 1966 Notes to FRCP 44.1 at ¶3, p. 1208, this book. The reasonable-notice requirement is intended to avoid unfair surprise for the opposing party. ***APL Co. Pte.***, 582 F.3d at 955; ***Northrop Grumman Ship***, 575 F.3d at 496-97. To determine whether the notice is reasonable, the court can consider (1) the stage the case has reached at the time of the notice, (2) the reason given by the party for not providing earlier notice, and (3) the importance of the foreign-law issue in the entire case. ***APL Co. Pte.***, 582 F.3d at 955; 1966 Notes to FRCP 44.1 at ¶3, p. 1208, this book; *e.g.*, ***Northrop Grumman Ship***, 575 F.3d at 497 (even though D filed its FRCP 44.1 notice 18 months after suit was filed, notice was reasonable because P was not prejudiced when P had at least 5 months to research and respond to D's version of foreign law).

2. Waiver. Although an appellate court is free to review questions of foreign law on appeal, the party raising the foreign law still has the burden to prove the applicability of the foreign law at trial. ***Banque Libanaise Pour Le Commerce v. Khreich***, 915 F.2d 1000, 1006 (5th Cir.1990). Thus, if a party does not plead or otherwise give notice of its intent to argue the applicability of foreign law at the district-court level, the party will be deemed on appeal to have waived its right to the application of any law other than that of the forum. *See id.*; ***Carey v. Bahama Cruise Lines***, 864 F.2d 201, 205-06 (1st Cir.1988).

§5. RESPONSE

If the motion was written and served, the response should be as well. *See* FRCP 5(a).

§5.1 Adjudicative facts. The following are objections to the judicial notice of adjudicative facts:

1. Facts not generally known.

(1) The facts are subject to reasonable dispute within the court's territorial jurisdiction. The court may take notice of adjudicative facts only if the facts are beyond reasonable dispute and are generally known within the court's territorial jurisdiction. FRE 201(b)(1); ***U.S. v. Boyd***, 289 F.3d 1254, 1258 (10th Cir.2002); ***LaSalle Nat'l Bank v. First Conn. Holding Grp.***, 287 F.3d 279, 290 (3d Cir.2002); *see* ***Carley v. Wheeled Coach***, 991 F.2d 1117, 1126 (3d Cir.1993).

(2) The facts are commonly known only by a specially informed class of people. *See* ***Carley***, 991 F.2d at 1126 (most people probably do not know that vehicles with high centers of gravity are more prone to rolling over).

2. Facts cannot be accurately & readily determined.

(1) The facts cannot be accurately and readily determined. FRE 201(b)(2); ***Boyd***, 289 F.3d at 1258; ***LaSalle Nat'l Bank***, 287 F.3d at 290; *see, e.g.*, ***Bias v. Moynihan***, 508 F.3d 1212, 1225 (9th Cir.2007) (deposition excerpts that were not available to district court were not capable of accurate and ready determination); ***Storm Plastics, Inc. v. U.S.***, 770 F.2d 148, 155 (10th Cir.1985) (judge's personal appraisal of quality and reputation of fishing lures was not capable of accurate and ready determination).

(2) The facts were not presented with sufficient information. *See, e.g.*, ***U.S. v. Husein***, 478 F.3d 318, 337 (6th Cir.2007) (no judicial notice when government only offered "westlaw.com" without guidance on where within Westlaw database information was located); ***Haavistola v. Community Fire Co.***, 6 F.3d 211, 218 (4th Cir.1993) (court's judicial notice of facts was unsupported by any direct evidence).

§5.2 Foreign law. The following are objections to the judicial notice of foreign law:

1. Lack of notice. The movant did not give the requisite notice of intent to use foreign law under FRCP 44.1. *See* ***DP Aviation v. Smiths Indus. Aerospace & Def. Sys.***, 268 F.3d 829, 846 (9th Cir.2001); ***Carey v. Bahama Cruise Lines***, 864 F.2d 201, 205-06 (1st Cir.1988); ***Weidner Comms. v. Al Faisal***, 859 F.2d 1302, 1308 n.9 (7th Cir. 1988).

2. Lack of evidence. The movant did not produce sufficient evidence to support the foreign legal principles. *See* ***Banque Libanaise Pour Le Commerce v. Khreich***, 915 F.2d 1000, 1006 (5th Cir.1990).

§6. HEARING

§6.1 Adjudicative facts. When a party makes a request for judicial notice, it can request a hearing. FRE 201(e). When the court takes judicial notice of a fact on its own, it should notify the parties that it is doing so and give them an opportunity to be heard. ***Cooperativa de Ahorro v. Kidder, Peabody & Co.***, 993 F.2d 269, 273 (1st Cir.1993); ***U.S. v. Garcia***, 672 F.2d 1349, 1356 n.9 (11th Cir.1982); *see* FRE 201(e); ***Barr Rubber Prods. v. Sun Rubber Co.***, 425 F.2d 1114, 1125-26 (2d Cir.1970); *see also* ***Pickett v. Sheridan Health Care Ctr.***, 664 F.3d 632, 648 (7th Cir.2011) (because websites have varying degrees of reliability, permanence, and accessibility, court should ensure that parties are provided opportunity to be heard before court takes judicial notice of websites).

§6.2 Foreign law. Although a hearing is not required, the court should inform the parties of any material it has found that diverges substantially from the material they have presented. *See* 1966 Notes to FRCP 44.1 at ¶6, p. 1208, this book. Generally, the court should give the parties an opportunity to analyze the new material and raise new points on which each party proposes to rely. *Id.*

§7. RULING

§7.1 Adjudicative facts.

1. Order. After the hearing, if any, the court should determine whether the matter requested can be judicially noticed. Even though there is no requirement that the court sign a written order, the party should ask the court to sign an order to preserve error.

(1) **Mandatory.** The court must take judicial notice of adjudicative facts when the party properly requests it and the court is supplied with the necessary information. FRE 201(c)(2).

(2) **Discretionary.** The court may take judicial notice of adjudicative facts at any time, whether or not notice is provided. *See* FRE 201(c)(1), (d).

2. Jury instruction. Once the court has judicially noticed an adjudicative fact, the court must instruct the jury in a civil case to accept the fact as conclusive. FRE 201(f).

3. Effect of judicial notice. Once the court has judicially noticed an adjudicative fact, the fact is established as a matter of law. *See* FRE 201(f); 1972 Notes to FRE 201 at ¶31, p. 1245, this book. In other words, judicially noticing a fact has the same effect as directing a verdict against a party on the noticed fact. ***U.S. v. Boyd***, 289 F.3d 1254, 1258 (10th Cir.2002); *see* ***Werner v. Werner***, 267 F.3d 288, 295 (3d Cir.2001); ***General Elec. Capital Corp. v. Lease Resolution Corp.***, 128 F.3d 1074, 1083 (7th Cir.1997).

§7.2 Foreign law.

1. Order. After the hearing, if any, the court should make a determination on the use of foreign law. *See* ***Sunstar, Inc. v. Alberto-Culver Co.***, 586 F.3d 487, 494 (7th Cir.2009); 1966 Notes to FRCP 44.1 at ¶9, p. 1209, this book. Even though there is no requirement that the court sign a written order, the party should ask the court to sign an order to preserve error.

2. Jury instruction. Once the court has judicially noticed the foreign law, the court must instruct the jury on the meaning of the foreign law. ***Sunstar, Inc.***, 586 F.3d at 494.

3. Effect of foreign law. Once the court has judicially noticed the foreign law, the foreign law is established as a matter of law and the requesting party can rely on it. *See* ***Baloco v. Drummond Co.***, 640 F.3d 1338, 1349 n.13 (11th Cir.2011).

§8. APPELLATE REVIEW

§8.1 Judicial notice of adjudicative facts. The district court's ruling on a request to take judicial notice of an adjudicative fact will be reversed only if the court abused its discretion. ***In re NAHC, Inc. Sec. Litig.***, 306 F.3d 1314, 1323 (3d Cir.2002); ***York v. AT&T Co.***, 95 F.3d 948, 958 (10th Cir.1996); ***Ritter v. Hughes Aircraft Co.***, 58 F.3d 454, 458-59 (9th Cir.1995).

§8.2 Determination of foreign law. The district court's determination on the use of foreign law is treated as a ruling on a question of law. FRCP 44.1; ***McGee v. Arkel Int'l***, 671 F.3d 539, 546 (5th Cir.2012); ***Pittway Corp. v. U.S.***, 88 F.3d 501, 504 (7th Cir.1996). This determination is subject to a de novo review. ***APL Co. Pte. Ltd. v. UK Aerosols Ltd.***, 582 F.3d 947, 955 (9th Cir.2009); ***Karim v. Finch Shipping Co.***, 265 F.3d 258, 271 (5th Cir.2001); ***SEC v. Dunlap***, 253 F.3d 768, 777 (4th Cir.2001); ***Carlisle Ventures, Inc. v. Banco Español de Crédito***, 176 F.3d 601, 604 (2d Cir.1999). But the district court's determination of whether reasonable notice of foreign law was given is reviewed for abuse of discretion. ***APL Co. Pte.***, 582 F.3d at 955; ***Northrop Grumman Ship Sys. v. Ministry of Def. of the Republic of Venez.***, 575 F.3d 491, 496 (5th Cir.2009). The court of appeals may consider information not available to or considered by the district court. ***Kilbarr Corp. v. Business Sys.***, 990 F.2d 83, 88 n.5 (3d Cir.1993).

N. MOTION TO EXCLUDE EXPERT WITNESS

§1. GENERAL

§1.1 Rules. FRE 104, 401-403, 702-706; see also FRCP 16(c)(2)(D), (c)(2)(F), 26(a)(2).

§1.2 Purpose. The court may make pretrial rulings on the admissibility of expert testimony. FRCP 16(c)(2)(D); *see also* FRE 104(a) (court may hold preliminary hearing on admissibility of evidence). In ***Daubert v. Merrell Dow Pharms.***, 509 U.S. 579 (1993), and ***Kumho Tire Co. v. Carmichael***, 526 U.S. 137 (1999), the Supreme Court directed district judges to act as "gatekeepers" for all expert testimony by evaluating whether the offered testimony satisfies the requirements of FRE 702 and thus can be presented to the jury. By acting as gatekeepers, the judges prevent unqualified opinion testimony from reaching the jury. ***Schneider v. Fried***, 320 F.3d 396, 404 (3d Cir.2003).

§1.3 Forms. *O'Connor's Federal Civil Forms* (2012), FORMS 5N.

§1.4 Other references. 29 Wright & Gold, *Federal Practice & Procedure* §§6241-6246 (1997 & Supp.2012); *Reference Manual on Scientific Evidence* (3d ed. 2011), Federal Judicial Center, www.fjc.gov.

§2. PRETRIAL ORDER

Early disclosure of experts, their opinions, and the methodologies they used in arriving at those opinions will help promptly resolve ***Daubert*** challenges. If a party anticipates the use of expert testimony at trial, it should make sure the pretrial order specifically addresses the timing and sequence of FRCP 26(a) disclosures about the experts and the subject matter of their testimony. *See* FRCP 16(c)(2)(D), (c)(2)(F), 26(a)(2)(B)-(a)(2)(D). For the scope and timing of pretrial disclosures under FRCP 16 and 26, see "Discovery," ch. 5-A, §4.4.6, p. 292, and "Mandatory Disclosures," ch. 6-E, p. 532.

§3. MOTION

On motion, the court can make a pretrial evaluation of whether an expert's opinion is inadmissible under FRE 702. ***Daubert v. Merrell Dow Pharms.***, 509 U.S. 579, 592-93 (1993); *see* FRE 104(a). To object to an expert's opinion offered under FRE 702, a party should file a pretrial motion to exclude the expert. *See* ***McCullock v. H.B. Fuller Co.***, 61 F.3d 1038, 1041 (2d Cir.1995); ***Bradley v. Brown***, 42 F.3d 434, 436 (7th Cir.1994).

§3.1 Form. For the general requirements for the form of a motion, see "Drafting motions," ch. 1-B, §3.1, p. 14.

§3.2 Grounds. For an expert's opinion to be admissible, the expert must first be qualified. *See* FRE 702; ***Hendrix v. Evenflo Co.***, 609 F.3d 1183, 1194 (11th Cir.2010). If an expert is qualified, the court must determine whether the expert's opinion is (1) reliable (i.e., whether the expert's opinion has a reliable basis in knowledge of and experience in the particular field) and (2) relevant (i.e., whether the expert's opinion has a valid connection to the specific inquiry and is helpful to the jury). *See* ***Daubert v. Merrell Dow Pharms.***, 509 U.S. 579, 590-91 (1993); ***Hendrix***, 609 F.3d at 1194; ***North Am. Specialty Ins. v. Britt Paulk Ins. Agency, Inc.***, 579 F.3d 1106, 1112 (10th Cir. 2009); ***Wintz v. Northrop Corp.***, 110 F.3d 508, 512 (7th Cir.1997). Thus, the motion can challenge the expert's qualifications as well as the reliability and relevance of the expert's opinion. *See* ***Hendrix***, 609 F.3d at 1194.

1. Expert not qualified. An expert must be qualified by knowledge, skill, experience, training, or education. FRE 702. The party seeking to exclude expert testimony because the expert is not qualified should show that the expert does not possess a higher level of knowledge, skill, experience, training, or education than an ordinary person. *See* FRE 104(a), 702; ***Mukhtar v. California State Univ.***, 299 F.3d 1053, 1065 n.9 (9th Cir.2002), *amended*, 319 F.3d 1073 (9th Cir.2003); ***McCullock v. H.B. Fuller Co.***, 61 F.3d 1038, 1043 (2d Cir.1995); ***In re Paoli R.R. Yard PCB Litig.***, 35 F.3d 717, 741 (3d Cir.1994). For example, the movant can assert that the expert does not have the practical experience and necessary academic training to support the opinion. *See* ***Bogosian v. Mercedes-Benz, Inc.***, 104 F.3d 472, 477 (1st Cir.1997); ***McCullock***, 61 F.3d at 1043.

NOTE

A lack of specialization does not affect the admissibility of the expert opinion, only the weight to be given to that opinion. ***Pagés-Ramírez v. Ramírez-González****, 605 F.3d 109, 114 (1st Cir. 2010);* ***Compton v. Subaru, Inc.****, 82 F.3d 1513, 1518 (10th Cir.1996), overruled on other grounds,* ***Kumho Tire Co. v. Carmichael****, 526 U.S. 137 (1999); see* ***Pineda v. Ford Motor Co.****, 520 F.3d 237, 244 (3d Cir.2008) (abuse of discretion to exclude testimony simply because court does not believe proposed expert is best qualified or has most appropriate specialization); see also* ***U.S. v. Roach****, 644 F.3d 763, 764 (8th Cir.2011) (FRE 702 does not rank academic training over demonstrated practical experience). But lack of specialization goes to weight rather than admissibility only if the expert's opinion stays within the reasonable confines of her expertise. E.g.,* ***Avila v. Willits Env'tl Remediation Trust****, 633 F.3d 828, 839 (9th Cir.2011) (expert properly excluded for lack of qualifications because, despite having degrees in chemistry, he did not have special knowledge regarding metalworking industries).*

2. Expert's opinion not reliable. An expert's opinion must be sufficiently reliable. *See* FRE 702. The purpose of the reliability analysis is to ensure that the expert uses the same level of intellectual rigor as other experts in the same field. ***Kumho Tire Co. v. Carmichael***, 526 U.S. 137, 152 (1999). FRE 702 requires that (1) the expert's testimony be based on sufficient facts or data, (2) the expert's testimony be the product of reliable principles and methods, and (3) the expert apply the principles and methods reliably to the facts of the case. FRE 702(b)-(d); ***U.S. v. Conn***, 297 F.3d 548, 555 (7th Cir.2002); *see also* ***Hendrix***, 609 F.3d at 1194 (expert's opinion cannot be connected to facts by *ipse dixit* of expert, i.e., because expert said so); ***Minix v. Canarecci***, 597 F.3d 824, 835 (7th Cir. 2010) (expert's testimony must offer more than "bottom line"). In assessing the reliability requirement, practitioners should look to the factors developed by the courts examining whether an expert's opinions are sufficiently reliable under ***Daubert***, beginning with the ***Daubert*** factors themselves. In ***Daubert***, the Supreme Court provided several "general observations" or factors for the court to consider when evaluating the reasoning or methodology underlying the expert's testimony. ***Daubert***, 509 U.S. at 593. In ***Kumho Tire***, the Court noted that while these factors should be considered when they are "reasonable measures" of reliability, they are not exclusive, and the district court is given broad latitude to determine when they apply. ***Kumho Tire***, 526 U.S. at 152-53; *see* ***Pineda***, 520 F.3d at 248 (***Daubert*** factors are neither exhaustive nor applicable in every case); ***Pipitone v. Biomatrix, Inc.***, 288 F.3d 239, 244 (5th Cir.2002) (***Daubert*** factors are starting point for analysis). The factors the court should consider when evaluating reliability are the following:

(1) Testing. The court should consider whether the theory or technique underlying the expert's testimony can be or has been tested. ***Daubert***, 509 U.S. at 593; ***Raynor v. Merrell Pharms.***, 104 F.3d 1371, 1375 (D.C. Cir.1997); ***Deimer v. Cincinnati Sub-Zero Prods.***, 58 F.3d 341, 344 (7th Cir.1995). For example, the movant might object that the expert has not conducted any studies or analyses to substantiate the opinion. *See* ***Braun v. Lorillard Inc.***, 84 F.3d 230, 235 (7th Cir.1996); ***Deimer***, 58 F.3d at 344; ***Wheat v. Pfizer, Inc.***, 31 F.3d 340, 343 (5th Cir.1994).

(2) Potential rate of error. The court should consider the technique's known or potential rate of error and the existence and maintenance of standards controlling the technique's operation. ***Daubert***, 509 U.S. at 594; ***Raynor***, 104 F.3d at 1375. For some techniques, such as polygraph, voice identification, and psychological evaluations, the known or potential rate of error may be helpful in determining its validity. ***U.S. v. Posado***, 57 F.3d 428, 433 (5th Cir.1995). For others, such as product design, the known or potential rate of error may not be helpful. *See, e.g.*, ***Pestel v. Vermeer Mfg.***, 64 F.3d 382, 384 (8th Cir.1995) (rate of error not relevant to whether safety bar was necessary on stump cutter).

(3) Peer review & publication. The court should consider whether the theory or technique has been subjected to peer review and publication. ***Daubert***, 509 U.S. at 593. Peer review is important because it helps expose any substantive flaws in a particular methodology. *Id.*; *see* ***Nelson v. Tennessee Gas Pipeline Co.***, 243 F.3d 244, 251 (6th Cir.2001); ***Peitzmeier v. Hennessey Indus.***, 97 F.3d 293, 297 (8th Cir.1996).

(4) General acceptance. The court should consider whether the expert's theory or technique has gained "general acceptance" within a relevant scientific community. ***Daubert***, 509 U.S. at 594. General acceptance can be an important factor in ruling certain evidence admissible, and a known technique that has attracted only minimal support within the community may properly be viewed with skepticism. *Id.* In addition, the movant might object that the expert's opinion contains only unsupported assertions that she has used methods generally and reasonably accepted by those in her discipline. *See* ***Daubert v. Merrell Dow Pharms.***, 43 F.3d 1311, 1316 (9th Cir.1995); *see, e.g.*, ***Braun***, 84 F.3d at 235 (whether report adhered to customary methods for conducting particular kind of scientific inquiry is relevant); *see also* ***Rushing v. Kansas City S. Ry.***, 185 F.3d 496, 507 (5th Cir.1999) (when applicable law mandates use of particular test, proponent should not have to establish its reliability; instead, its reliability should be irrebuttably presumed).

(5) Sufficiency of facts. The court should consider whether the expert's testimony is based on sufficient facts or data. FRE 702(b); *see, e.g.*, ***Ervin v. Johnson & Johnson, Inc.***, 492 F.3d 901, 904-05 (7th Cir.2007) (expert excluded when he could not provide data or valid explanation of theory). This requirement is quantitative and imposes a "floor" on the amount of facts or data an expert must have to support an opinion. *See* ***Rudd v. General Motors Corp.***, 127 F.Supp.2d 1330, 1339 (M.D.Ala.2001); *see, e.g.*, ***Milward v. Acuity Specialty Prods. Grp.***, 639 F.3d 11, 22 (1st Cir.2011) (district court overstepped role as gatekeeper when it repeatedly challenged expert's facts and data and took sides on questions of fact; exclusion was reversed because expert had provided sufficient support for his conclusion).

(6) Other factors. In ***Kumho Tire***, the Supreme Court made it clear that the district court can consider other factors when appropriate to ensure that the expert "employs in the courtroom the same level of intellectual rigor that characterizes the practice of an expert in the relevant field." ***Kumho Tire***, 526 U.S. at 152; ***Pipitone***, 288 F.3d at 244. The Advisory Committee has identified several of these factors. 2000 Notes to FRE 702 at ¶¶4, 5, p. 1260, this book. These factors include the following:

(a) Whether the expert's opinion was developed expressly for the purpose of testifying or as a result of independent research. *See* ***Clausen v. M/V New Carissa***, 339 F.3d 1049, 1056 (9th Cir.2003); ***Nelson***, 243 F.3d at 252; ***Braun***, 84 F.3d at 235. *But see* ***Daubert***, 43 F.3d at 1317 n.5 (some expert disciplines closely associated with law enforcement are primarily used in courtroom, so "the fact that the expert has developed an expertise principally for purposes of litigation will obviously not be a substantial consideration").

(b) Whether the expert has unjustifiably extrapolated from an accepted premise to an unfounded conclusion. *See* ***General Elec. Co. v. Joiner***, 522 U.S. 136, 146 (1997) (court "may conclude that there is simply too great an analytical gap between the data and the opinion proffered"); *see, e.g.*, ***Junk v. Terminix Int'l Co.***, 628 F.3d 439, 448 (8th Cir.2010) (expert excluded when he did not follow his own general practice and when his reliance on unfounded assumptions created impermissible analytical gap).

(c) Whether the expert has adequately accounted for alternative explanations. *See* ***Claar v. Burlington N. R.R.***, 29 F.3d 499, 502 (9th Cir.1994); *see also* ***Muñoz v. Orr***, 200 F.3d 291, 301 (5th Cir.2000) (expert must consider possible variables); ***Tagatz v. Marquette Univ.***, 861 F.2d 1040, 1045 (7th Cir.1988) (failure to control for other explanatory variables made expert's table "essentially worthless"). *But see* ***Bazemore v. Friday***, 478 U.S. 385, 400 (1986) (failure to include variables will normally affect probativeness of analysis, not admissibility); ***Tyler v. Union Oil Co.***, 304 F.3d 379, 393 (5th Cir.2002) (same); ***Conwood Co. v. U.S. Tobacco Co.***, 290 F.3d 768, 794 (6th Cir.2002) (expert's testimony does not need to eliminate all other possible causes of injury); ***Jahn v. Equine Servs. PSC***, 233 F.3d 382, 390 (6th Cir.2000) (same); ***Ambrosini v. Labarraque***, 101 F.3d 129, 140 (D.C.Cir.1996) (possibility of some unexplained causes presents a question of weight, as long as expert has considered the most obvious causes).

(d) Whether the expert "is being as careful as he would be in his regular professional work outside his paid litigation consulting." ***Sheehan v. Daily Racing Form, Inc.***, 104 F.3d 940, 942 (7th Cir.1997); *see* ***Kumho Tire***, 526 U.S. at 152.

(e) Whether the field of expertise claimed by the expert is known to reach reliable results for the type of opinion the expert will give. *See **Kumho Tire***, 526 U.S. at 151 (disciplines such as astrology and necromancy lack reliability).

3. Expert's opinion not relevant. FRE 702(a) requires that the expert's opinion help the trier of fact to understand the evidence or determine a fact in issue—that is, the opinion must be relevant. *See **Pipitone***, 288 F.3d at 245; ***Westberry v. Gislaved Gummi AB***, 178 F.3d 257, 260 (4th Cir.1999); *see also **Boca Raton Cmty. Hosp., Inc. v. Tenet Health Care Corp.***, 582 F.3d 1227, 1232 (11th Cir.2009) (there must be a valid scientific connection to specific issue, i.e., testimony must "fit" the issue). The party seeking to exclude expert testimony may attempt to show that the expert's opinion will not help the trier of fact understand the evidence or determine a fact at issue. FRE 702(a); ***Daubert***, 43 F.3d at 1321 n.17; *see* FRE 401; ***Buckner v. Sam's Club, Inc.***, 75 F.3d 290, 293 (7th Cir.1996); ***Tuli v. Brigham & Women's Hosp., Inc.***, 592 F.Supp.2d 208, 211-12 & n.4 (D.Mass.2009); *see, e.g.*, ***North Am. Specialty Ins.***, 579 F.3d at 1112 (expert testimony was not helpful because jury was capable of resolving case without expert's assistance). The motion should argue that the evidence supporting the expert's opinion is not sufficient to allow a reasonable juror to conclude that the proposition is more likely to be true than false. ***Pipitone***, 288 F.3d at 245; ***Glaser v. Thompson Med. Co.***, 32 F.3d 969, 972 (6th Cir.1994). For example, the party may argue that (1) the expert's opinion is based on scientific studies dissimilar to the facts of the case and the expert has not offered reasons for drawing such conclusions from the studies, or (2) the expert's opinion is only providing the jurors with a conclusion about what the outcome should be rather than providing them with a framework to consider what the outcome should be. *See **Joiner***, 522 U.S. at 144-45 (dissimilarity); ***Tuli***, 592 F.Supp.2d at 211 & n.3 (conclusory).

§3.3 Affidavits. If facts outside the record must be relied on, the movant should verify the motion with affidavits. For example, the party could attach excerpts from the expert's deposition and verify them by affidavit.

§3.4 Request hearing. The movant should request a hearing on the motion. *E.g.*, ***Gruca v. Alpha Therapeutic Corp.***, 51 F.3d 638, 643 (7th Cir.1995) (because court did not conduct preliminary assessment of expert, case was remanded with directions to evaluate expert testimony under ***Daubert***); *see also **Hose v. Chicago Nw. Transp.***, 70 F.3d 968, 973 n.3 (8th Cir.1995) (challenges to scientific reliability of expert testimony should be addressed before trial). Although a hearing is not necessary to preserve error, the failure to request a pretrial ruling may result in waiver of the challenge on appeal. *See **Marbled Murrelet v. Babbitt***, 83 F.3d 1060, 1067 (9th Cir.1996).

§3.5 Request special proceedings. The movant should allege that there is good reason for questioning the expert's reliability and that gatekeeper proceedings (e.g., special briefing, hearings) are necessary. See "Proceedings determined by court," §5.1, p. 382.

§3.6 Proposed order. Some districts require the movant to submit a proposed order with the motion. In those districts, the movant should prepare a written order for the court's signature and submit it with the motion. See "Proposed order," ch. 1-B, §3.1.11, p. 16.

§3.7 Deadline. The pretrial order often provides a deadline for motions challenging the sufficiency of expert testimony. When it does not, the parties must object to an expert's testimony in a timely manner. ***Feliciano-Hill v. Principi***, 439 F.3d 18, 24 (1st Cir.2006); *see **Club Car, Inc. v. Club Car (Quebec) Import, Inc.***, 362 F.3d 775, 780 (11th Cir.2004) (***Daubert*** objection not raised before trial may be rejected as untimely); *see also **Alfred v. Caterpillar, Inc.***, 262 F.3d 1083, 1087 (10th Cir.2003) (untimely ***Daubert*** motions should be considered "only in rare circumstances").

§4. RESPONSE

The responding party (i.e., the proponent of the expert) should initially argue that full gatekeeper proceedings are not required because this is an "ordinary" case in which the reliability of an expert's methods can be properly taken for granted and the expert's reliability has not been "called sufficiently into question." ***Kumho Tire Co. v. Carmichael***, 526 U.S. 137, 149-52 (1999). See "Proceedings determined by court," §5.1, p. 382.

§4.1 Burden. The responding party has the burden of establishing the admissibility of the expert's testimony under FRE 702 by a preponderance of the evidence. *See **Barrett v. Rhodia, Inc.***, 606 F.3d 975, 980 (8th Cir.2010); ***U.S. v. Nacchio***, 555 F.3d 1234, 1244 (10th Cir.2009); ***Mathis v. Exxon Corp.***, 302 F.3d 448, 459-60 (5th Cir.2002);

In re Paoli R.R. Yard PCB Litig., 35 F.3d 717, 743-44 (3d Cir.1994); 2000 Notes to FRE 702 at ¶7, p. 1261, this book. The responding party does not, however, have the burden of proving that the expert's opinions are correct. ***Tanner v. Westbrook***, 174 F.3d 542, 547 (5th Cir.1999); ***In re Paoli R.R. Yard PCB Litig.***, 35 F.3d at 744; *see* ***Oddi v. Ford Motor Co.***, 234 F.3d 136, 155-56 (3d Cir.2000) (evidentiary requirement for reliability is lower than standard for proving case). In other words, the responding party does not have to show that it will win its case on the merits; it must show only that the requirements of the Federal Rules of Evidence have been met. ***In re Paoli R.R. Yard PCB Litig.***, 35 F.3d at 744.

§4.2 Grounds. The response should negate the grounds stated in the motion to exclude. See "Grounds," §3.2, p. 376.

1. Expert qualified. The party offering the expert testimony must show that the expert has the proper educational background or requisite experience to be qualified as a person with specialized knowledge. ***McCullock v. H.B. Fuller Co.***, 61 F.3d 1038, 1042-43 (2d Cir.1995); *see* ***Rushing v. Kansas City S. Ry.***, 185 F.3d 496, 507 (5th Cir.1999) (as long as reasonable indication of qualifications is offered, qualifications become issue for trier of fact, not court).

2. Expert's opinion reliable. The party offering the expert testimony should show that each of the reliability factors either supports admission of the evidence or does not apply.

(1) Expert's testimony has been tested. The party offering the expert's opinion should show that the expert has tested the theory, technique, or concept. *See, e.g.,* ***Pestel v. Vermeer Mfg.***, 64 F.3d 382, 384 (8th Cir. 1995) (in products-liability suit, expert had not tested safety-bar guard design for stump cutter). The party is not required to show that the expert performed the most elaborate tests or studies imaginable. ***Oddi v. Ford Motor Co.***, 234 F.3d 136, 160 (3d Cir.2000). This factor does not apply when the expert did not perform original research but instead only surveyed the available literature and arrived at different conclusions from those presented by the scientists who performed the original work. *See* ***Lust v. Merrell Dow Pharms.***, 89 F.3d 594, 597 (9th Cir.1996).

(2) Potential rate of error is low. The party offering the expert's opinion should show that the potential rate of error for the theory, technique, or concept is low. *See, e.g.,* ***Gier v. Educational Serv. Unit***, 66 F.3d 940, 943-44 (8th Cir.1995) (party did not show that its experts' use of psychological evaluations resulted in low rate of error). If the analysis of the potential rate of error does not apply to the expert's opinion, the party should state this in its response. *See, e.g.,* ***Pipitone v. Biomatrix, Inc.***, 288 F.3d 239, 246 (5th Cir.2002) (rate of error and standards not particularly relevant when expert's testimony derived mainly from firsthand observations and professional experience in translating observations into medical diagnoses); ***Pestel***, 64 F.3d at 384 (rate of error not relevant to whether safety bar was required for stump cutter); *see also* ***Lust***, 89 F.3d at 597 (if expert has not done original research, potential rate of error does not apply).

(3) Expert's methodology published or subjected to peer review. The party offering the expert's opinion should show that the theory, technique, or concept is supported by objective empirical studies. *See* ***Sappington v. Skyjack, Inc.***, 512 F.3d 440, 454 (8th Cir.2008); *see, e.g.,* ***Glaser v. Thompson Med. Co.***, 32 F.3d 969, 972 (6th Cir.1994) (expert provided several articles to support theory). Any articles or empirical data that are damaging to the expert's methodology should be specifically addressed, distinguished, and discredited. ***Glaser***, 32 F.3d at 974-75. In some instances, well-grounded or novel theories or theories of limited interest will not have been published or subjected to peer review. ***Daubert v. Merrell Dow Pharms.***, 509 U.S. 579, 593 (1993); ***Pipitone***, 288 F.3d at 246; *see* ***Kannankeril v. Terminix Int'l***, 128 F.3d 802, 809 (3d Cir.1997) (lack of peer review not dispositive if expert's opinion supported by "widely accepted scientific knowledge"); *see also* ***Bonner v. ISP Techs.***, 259 F.3d 924, 929 (8th Cir.2001) (no requirement that epidemiological studies supporting expert's opinion be published for opinion to be admissible). Citations to published authorities may be unnecessary when the issue involved is not novel or complex. *See* ***Feliciano-Hill v. Principi***, 439 F.3d 18, 25 (1st Cir.2006).

(4) Expert's testimony generally accepted. The party offering the expert's opinion should show that the theory, technique, or concept has gained general acceptance in the expert's discipline. *See* ***Sappington***, 512

F.3d at 454. Even if the scientific evidence is not generally accepted in the relevant scientific community, ***Daubert*** allows for the admission of the evidence as long as its reliability has other independent support. ***Borawick v. Shay***, 68 F.3d 597, 610 (2d Cir.1995). Experts may properly rely on a wide variety of sources of information and may use a similarly wide choice of methodologies in developing an expert opinion. *See* ***Cooper v. Carl A. Nelson & Co.***, 211 F.3d 1008, 1020 (7th Cir.2000) (doctor can consider physical history related by patient); *see also* ***Smith v. BMW N. Am., Inc.***, 308 F.3d 913, 919 (8th Cir.2002) (fact that experts in other fields would base opinions on other factors does not require exclusion of expert whose testimony is helpful to jury).

(5) Sufficiency of underlying facts or data. The party offering the expert's opinion should show that the theory, technique, or concept is supported by sufficient facts or data. FRE 702(b); *see* ***Hartley v. Dillard's, Inc.***, 310 F.3d 1054, 1061 (8th Cir.2002) (expert's opinion should be excluded if opinion is so fundamentally unsupported that it can offer no assistance to jury). "Sufficient facts or data" may include inadmissible evidence, hypothetical facts, and other experts' opinions. ***Rudd v. General Motors Corp.***, 127 F.Supp.2d 1330, 1343 (M.D.Ala.2001). When reviewing the sufficiency of the underlying facts, the court must determine whether the expert considered enough facts to support the opinion. *See* ***Pipitone***, 288 F.3d at 249. Because experts can reach different conclusions based on competing versions of the facts, the court should not exclude an expert's opinion simply because the court believes another version of the facts or considers the evidence doubtful or tenuous. ***In re Scrap Metal Antitrust Litig.***, 527 F.3d 517, 529-30 (6th Cir.2008); ***Olson v. Ford Motor Co.***, 481 F.3d 619, 626 (8th Cir.2007); *see* ***Micro Chem., Inc. v. Lextron, Inc.***, 317 F.3d 1387, 1392 (Fed.Cir.2003); ***Pipitone***, 288 F.3d at 249. The factual basis of an expert's opinion generally relates to the weight a jury should give that opinion and the expert's credibility, not to the testimony's admissibility. ***In re Scrap Metal Antitrust Litig.***, 527 F.3d at 531-32; ***Olson***, 481 F.3d at 627; *see* ***Primrose Oper. Co. v. National Am. Ins.***, 382 F.3d 546, 562 (5th Cir.2004) (questions about bases and sources of expert's opinion generally affect weight to be assigned to that opinion rather than its admissibility, and should be left for jury's consideration).

(6) Other factors. The party offering the expert's opinion should, in addition to explaining why some or all of the factors in ***Daubert*** do not apply, address any other factors raised by the movant and explain what other factors would be appropriate based on the facts and expertise at issue in the case. ***Pipitone***, 288 F.3d at 247. The principal focus is the expert's methodology, which should show the same level of intellectual rigor as that of other experts in the field of practice. ***Kumho Tire Co. v. Carmichael***, 526 U.S. 137, 152 (1999); ***Pipitone***, 288 F.3d at 244; *see* 2000 Notes to FRE 702 at ¶4, p. 1260, this book.

3. Expert's opinion relevant. The party offering the expert's opinion must show that the reasoning and methodology can be properly applied to the facts and can assist the trier of fact in resolving an issue. FRE 702(a); ***Daubert***, 509 U.S. at 592-93; *see* ***Ambrosini v. Labarraque***, 101 F.3d 129, 134 (D.C.Cir.1996) (if expert's testimony "fits" an issue in the case, it is admissible under FRE 702); *see, e.g.*, ***General Elec. Co. v. Joiner***, 522 U.S. 136, 144 (1997) (expert's studies were too dissimilar to facts presented in case); ***Tanner v. Westbrook***, 174 F.3d 542, 548 (5th Cir.1999) (medical expert did not have specialization needed to testify about causation); ***Daubert v. Merrell Dow Pharms.***, 43 F.3d 1311, 1321-22 (9th Cir.1995) (experts' testimony that drug could "possibly" have caused Ps' injuries was not helpful in determining causation issue). An expert's testimony does not need to relate directly to the ultimate issue that is to be resolved by the trier of fact; it only needs to be relevant to evaluating a factual matter. *See* ***Smith v. Ford Motor Co.***, 215 F.3d 713, 720 (7th Cir.2000).

§4.3 Not trial on merits. In addition to negating the movant's grounds, the responding party should object to any challenges that go only to the weight and credibility of the expert's testimony and not to its admissibility. *See* ***In re Scrap Metal Antitrust Litig.***, 527 F.3d 517, 531-32 (6th Cir.2008); *see, e.g.*, ***Cruz-Vázquez v. Mennonite Gen. Hosp., Inc.***, 613 F.3d 54, 59-60 (1st Cir.2010) (expert's bias); ***McCullock v. H.B. Fuller Co.***, 61 F.3d 1038, 1043 (2d Cir.1995) (caliber of expert's training, education, or experience); ***Glaser v. Thompson Med. Co.***, 32 F.3d 969, 975 (6th Cir.1994) (differences in opinions among experts in testifying expert's discipline). The responding party should emphasize that the focus of the gatekeeper analysis is "on principles and methodology, not on the conclusions that they generate." ***Daubert v. Merrell Dow Pharms.***, 509 U.S. 579, 595 (1993); ***Guy v. Crown Equip. Corp.***, 394 F.3d

320, 325 (5th Cir.2004); ***Smith v. BMW N. Am., Inc.***, 308 F.3d 913, 919 n.9 (8th Cir.2002); *see* ***Milward v. Acuity Specialty Prods. Grp.***, 639 F.3d 11, 15 (1st Cir.2011). Whether the expert could have done a better job is similarly irrelevant. ***Oddi v. Ford Motor Co.***, 234 F.3d 136, 156 (3d Cir.2000). The responding party should also argue that under FRE 702, the court's role as gatekeeper is not intended to replace the adversary system, and that the Supreme Court stated in ***Daubert*** that vigorous cross-examination, presentation of contrary evidence, and careful instruction on the burden of proof are the traditional and appropriate means of attacking shaky but admissible evidence. ***Olson v. Ford Motor Co.***, 481 F.3d 619, 626 (8th Cir.2007); ***Micro Chem., Inc. v. Lextron, Inc.***, 317 F.3d 1387, 1392 (Fed.Cir.2003); ***Pipitone v. Biomatrix, Inc.***, 288 F.3d 239, 250 (5th Cir.2002). The ultimate credibility determination and the testimony's accorded weight are for the jury to decide. *See* ***Cruz-Vázquez***, 613 F.3d at 59; ***Olson***, 481 F.3d at 626.

§4.4 Affidavits. Because the responding party bears the burden of proving that its expert's opinion is both reliable and relevant, it may support its response with the expert's affidavit. *See, e.g.*, ***Ambrosini v. Labarraque***, 101 F.3d 129, 131-32 (D.C.Cir.1996) (D's response included affidavit discussing its expert's opinion). If the expert has already been deposed, a supplemental affidavit may be offered to clarify any ambiguous or confusing deposition testimony. ***Buckner v. Sam's Club, Inc.***, 75 F.3d 290, 292 (7th Cir.1996). To the extent that the expert's report and deposition testimony are insufficient, the affidavit should specifically state the following information:

1. The expert's opinions.

2. An explanation of precisely how the expert reached her conclusions. ***Navarro v. Fuji Heavy Indus.***, 117 F.3d 1027, 1032 (7th Cir.1997); *see* ***Daubert v. Merrell Dow Pharms.***, 43 F.3d 1311, 1319 (9th Cir.1995); ***Claar v. Burlington N. R.R.***, 29 F.3d 499, 500-02 (9th Cir.1994); *see, e.g.*, ***Turpin v. Merrell Dow Pharms.***, 959 F.2d 1349, 1360 (6th Cir.1992) (analytical gap between evidence presented and inferences to be drawn was too wide). The basis for the expert's conclusions must be explained and supported; an expert vouching for her own method of analysis is not sufficient. *See* ***General Elec. Co. v. Joiner***, 522 U.S. 136, 146 (1997) (opinion evidence that is connected to existing data only by expert's unsupported assertion is insufficient); ***U.S. v. Hermanek***, 289 F.3d 1076, 1094 (9th Cir.2002) (presenting expert's qualifications, conclusions, and assurances of reliability is not enough); *see also* ***Rudd v. General Motors Corp.***, 127 F.Supp.2d 1330, 1344 (M.D.Ala.2001) (expert explained how his experience led to his conclusions).

3. Evidence that the opinions are the result of the same level of intellectual rigor as would be used in the expert's relevant field. ***Kumho Tire Co. v. Carmichael***, 526 U.S. 137, 152 (1999); ***Pipitone v. Biomatrix, Inc.***, 288 F.3d 239, 244 (5th Cir.2002). If applicable, the expert should show that the same method has been followed by at least a recognized minority of experts in the field. ***Daubert***, 43 F.3d at 1319; *see* ***Claar***, 29 F.3d at 500-02. This should be supported by a list of objective sources, such as learned treatises, policy statements of a professional association, or published articles in a reputable scientific journal demonstrating the accepted methods in that field.

§4.5 Proposed order. In districts that require the respondent to submit a proposed order with the response, the response should include an order denying the motion to exclude the expert. See "Proposed order," ch. 1-B, §3.1.11, p. 16.

§4.6 Deadline. The proponent of the expert should file a response within the deadline imposed by a court order or local rule and before any hearing on the motion.

§5. HEARING

§5.1 Proceedings determined by court. In ***Kumho Tire***, the Supreme Court indicated that full gatekeeper proceedings are unnecessary in "ordinary" cases when the reliability of an expert's methods is properly taken for granted, but are necessary when reliability is "called sufficiently into question." ***Kumho Tire Co. v. Carmichael***, 526 U.S. 137, 149-52 (1999); 2000 Notes to FRE 702 at ¶6, p. 1261, this book; *see* ***Rodriguez v. Sports, Inc.***, 242 F.3d 567, 581 (5th Cir.2001) (party must call testimony sufficiently into question to trigger ***Daubert*** inquiry); *see also* ***Schneider v. Fried***, 320 F.3d 396, 404 (3d Cir.2003) (by acting as gatekeeper, court prevents unqualified opinion testimony from reaching jury). It is not clear what the movant must show to call the reliability of the expert's opinions

into question. *Compare* ***Tanner v. Westbrook***, 174 F.3d 542, 546 (5th Cir.1999) (experts' opinions sufficiently called into question by providing conflicting medical literature and expert testimony), *with* ***Brooks v. Outboard Mar. Corp.***, 234 F.3d 89, 91 (2d Cir.2000) (rebuttal expert not necessary to call expert's testimony into question), *and* ***U.S. v. Velarde***, 214 F.3d 1204, 1209 (10th Cir.2000) (invocation of ***Daubert/Kumho*** probably sufficient to require a reliability determination). The court has discretion to determine what proceedings are needed to investigate reliability and when the reliability of an expert's methods can properly be taken for granted. ***Kumho Tire***, 526 U.S. at 152-53; ***U.S. v. Turner***, 285 F.3d 909, 913 (10th Cir.2002); *see* ***Millenkamp v. Davisco Foods Int'l***, 562 F.3d 971, 979 (9th Cir.2009); ***In re Scrap Metal Antitrust Litig.***, 527 F.3d 517, 532 (6th Cir.2008); *see also* ***Nelson v. Tennessee Gas Pipeline Co.***, 243 F.3d 244, 249 (6th Cir.2001) (hearing not required for ***Daubert*** inquiry); ***U.S. v. Alatorre***, 222 F.3d 1098, 1105 (9th Cir.2000) (court may evaluate relevance and reliability after voir dire, rather than at pretrial hearing).

NOTE

Because the court's gatekeeper function is to keep unreliable expert testimony from the jury, the timing and extent of the ***Daubert*** *analysis may be different in a bench trial. See* ***Metavante Corp. v. Emigrant Sav. Bank***, *619 F.3d 748, 760 (7th Cir.2010). For example, in a bench trial, the reliability and relevancy determinations do not need to be made before evidence is presented. Id. But the court must provide more than conclusory statements of admissibility; if the court provides only conclusory statements, the appellate court will review the admissibility ruling de novo rather than for abuse of discretion. Id. See "Appellate Review," §7, p. 384.*

§5.2 Standard of admissibility. In determining admissibility, the court is not bound by evidence rules except those on privilege. FRE 104(a).

§6. RULING

§6.1 Definitive ruling. If the court makes a definitive ruling on the admissibility of the expert, the parties have probably preserved error in the pretrial hearing. *See* FRCP 16(c)(2)(D).

1. Expert excluded. If the expert is excluded, the party who offered the expert can rely on the pretrial ruling excluding the expert to preserve error. *See* FRE 103(b). See "After definitive ruling excluding evidence," ch. 8-E, §2.2.2, p. 708. If the party is unsure whether the court actually excluded the expert or merely made a tentative ruling, the party should follow the procedure as if the expert is only tentatively excluded. See "Expert tentatively excluded," §6.2.1, this page.

2. Expert admitted. If the expert is admitted, the party who objected to the expert should object when the expert is offered at trial and refer (1) to the pretrial proceeding in support of its objection and (2) to any differences in the factual record at trial compared to the facts the court reviewed when it denied the motion to exclude the expert. *See* FRE 103(a)(1).

§6.2 Tentative ruling. If the court makes only a tentative ruling and does not either admit or exclude the evidence, the ruling is like a ruling on a motion in limine. To preserve error, the parties must offer the evidence at trial and make objections on the record. See "Motion in Limine," ch. 5-H, p. 341; "Objections before trial," ch. 8-D, §2.1, p. 700.

1. Expert tentatively excluded. If the court made a tentative ruling that the expert would be excluded, the party who offered the expert should, at trial, approach the bench and, out of the hearing of the jury but within the hearing of the court reporter, formally offer the expert. If the court excludes the expert, the party should make an offer of proof. See "Offer of Proof," ch. 8-E, p. 707. If the evidence was fully developed at the pretrial hearing, the party may offer the transcript of the hearing as the offer of proof. The offer should include evidence about the qualifications of the expert, the opinion that the expert would give if permitted to testify at trial, evidence of the relevance and reliability of the opinion, and a statement of how and why the exclusion of the opinion affected a substantial right of the party. *See* FRE 103(a).

2. Expert tentatively admitted. If the court made a tentative ruling that the expert would be admitted, the party who offered the expert should offer the expert during trial. The party who objected to the expert should object when the expert is offered and refer to the pretrial hearing in support of its objection.

§7. APPELLATE REVIEW

§7.1 Expert's qualifications. The district court's ruling on an expert's qualifications are reviewed for abuse of discretion. *See* ***General Elec. Co. v. Joiner***, 522 U.S. 136, 141 (1997); ***Allen v. Brown Clinic, P.L.L.P.***, 531 F.3d 568, 573 (8th Cir.2008); ***U.S. v. Garcia***, 7 F.3d 885, 889 (9th Cir.1993). The district court has broad discretion in determining whether an expert's qualifications are sufficient. *See* ***Correa v. Cruisers***, 298 F.3d 13, 24 (1st Cir.2002).

§7.2 Application of *Daubert* factors. The court of appeals will review de novo the applicability of the ***Daubert*** factors to the district court's evaluation of expert testimony. ***Chapman v. Maytag Corp.***, 297 F.3d 682, 686 (7th Cir.2002); ***Compton v. Subaru, Inc.***, 82 F.3d 1513, 1517 (10th Cir.1996), *overruled on other grounds*, ***Kumho Tire Co. v. Carmichael***, 526 U.S. 137 (1999); *see* ***Claar v. Burlington N. R.R.***, 29 F.3d 499, 500 (9th Cir.1994).

§7.3 Evidentiary ruling. The district court's decision to admit or exclude expert testimony is reviewed for abuse of discretion. ***Kumho Tire Co. v. Carmichael***, 526 U.S. 137, 152 (1999); ***Olson v. Ford Motor Co.***, 481 F.3d 619, 626 (8th Cir.2007); ***Hochen v. Bobst Grp.***, 290 F.3d 446, 452 (1st Cir.2002); ***Hollander v. Sandoz Pharms. Corp.***, 289 F.3d 1193, 1204 (10th Cir.2002); ***Metabolife Int'l v. Wornick***, 264 F.3d 832, 839 (9th Cir.2001); ***Nelson v. Tennessee Gas Pipeline Co.***, 243 F.3d 244, 248 (6th Cir.2001); ***Cavallo v. Star Enter.***, 100 F.3d 1150, 1153-54 (4th Cir. 1996); *see* ***Smith v. Goodyear Tire & Rubber Co.***, 495 F.3d 224, 226-27 (5th Cir.2007) (appellate court will not find abuse of discretion unless ruling is "manifestly erroneous").

§7.4 Determination of reliability. The district court's decision on how to determine the issue of reliability is reviewed for abuse of discretion. ***Kumho Tire Co. v. Carmichael***, 526 U.S. 137, 152 (1999); ***Nelson v. Tennessee Gas Pipeline Co.***, 243 F.3d 244, 248 (6th Cir.2001); ***U.S. v. Alatorre***, 222 F.3d 1098, 1100-01 (9th Cir.2000); ***U.S. v. Velarde***, 214 F.3d 1204, 1208-09 (10th Cir.2000). This allows the district court to determine when special briefings or other proceedings are needed to investigate reliability and when the reliability of an expert's methods is properly taken for granted. ***Kumho Tire***, 526 U.S. at 152-53; *see* 2000 Notes to FRE 702 at ¶6, p. 1261, this book.

O. MOTION FOR SANCTIONS

§1. GENERAL

§1.1 Rules. FRCP 11, 16(f), 26(g), 30(g), 37, 41(b), 56(h); see also 28 U.S.C. §1927.

§1.2 Purpose. A motion for sanctions is a request that the district court impose sanctions on the other party. The purpose of sanctions is to secure the parties' compliance with the rules and to deter and punish those who violate them.

§1.3 Forms. ***O'Connor's Federal Civil Forms*** (2012), FORMS 5O.

§1.4 Other references. 5A Wright & Miller, *Federal Practice & Procedure 3d* §§1331-1339 (2004 & Supp.2012); 6A Wright, Miller & Kane, *Federal Practice & Procedure 3d* §1531 (2010 & Supp.2012); 8A Wright, Miller & Marcus, *Federal Practice & Procedure 3d* §§2050, 2052 (2010 & Supp.2012); 9 Wright & Miller, *Federal Practice & Procedure 3d* §2370 (2008 & Supp.2012); 3, 6, 7 *Moore's Federal Practice 3d* §§16.93, 26.06, 26.154, 37.23-37.122 (2012); Joseph, *Sanctions: The Federal Law of Litigation Abuse 4th* (2008); Rauma & Willging, *Report of a Survey of United States District Judges' Experiences & Views Concerning Rule 11, Federal Rules of Civil Procedure* (2005), Federal Judicial Center, www.fjc.gov.

§2. WHO CAN BE SANCTIONED

Depending on the authority for the sanctions, parties, their attorneys, the attorneys' firms, and even nonparties can be sanctioned. *See* FRCP 11(c)(1), 37(b); ***United Stars Indus. v. Plastech Engineered Prods.***, 525 F.3d 605, 610 (7th Cir.2008); ***MacDraw, Inc. v. CIT Grp. Equip. Fin., Inc.***, 73 F.3d 1253, 1259 n.5 (2d Cir.1996); ***Corder v. Howard Johnson & Co.***, 53 F.3d 225, 232 (9th Cir.1994).

§3. SANCTIONS JUSTIFIED

§3.1 Frivolous or improper purpose – FRCP 11. The court can impose sanctions if a pleading, written motion, or other paper is signed, filed, submitted, or later advocated to the court in violation of FRCP 11(b). *See* ***Ali v. Tolbert***, 636 F.3d 622, 626-27 & n.5 (D.C.Cir.2011). For the representations made by the signer of a document under FRCP 11(b), see "Certification," ch. 1-B, §2.1.9(1), p. 10. To impose FRCP 11 sanctions, there must be a showing of at least "culpable carelessness" and a showing of more than just a claim that ultimately proved unsuccessful. ***CitiBank Global Mkts., Inc. v. Rodríguez Santana***, 573 F.3d 17, 32 (1st Cir.2009); *see* ***Ario v. Underwriting Members of Syndicate 53 at Lloyds for the 1998 Year of Account***, 618 F.3d 277, 297 (3d Cir.2010).

1. Objective test. The standard for deciding whether sanctionable conduct has occurred is objective: did the attorney make a reasonable inquiry into the facts and law before signing and presenting the offending document? FRCP 11(b); ***ATSI Comms. v. Shaar Fund, Ltd.***, 579 F.3d 143, 150 (2d Cir.2009); ***Lichtenstein v. Consolidated Servs.***, 173 F.3d 17, 23 (1st Cir.1999); ***Sheets v. Yamaha Motors Corp.***, 891 F.2d 533, 538 (5th Cir.1990); ***Zaldivar v. City of L.A.***, 780 F.2d 823, 831 (9th Cir.1986), *overruled in part on other grounds*, ***Cooter & Gell v. Hartmarx Corp.***, 496 U.S. 384 (1990). To decide whether the inquiry was reasonable, the court looks to the circumstances and facts available to the attorney when the document was filed. *See* ***Townsend v. Holman Consulting Corp.***, 929 F.2d 1358, 1365 (9th Cir.1990) (FRCP 11 calls for intensely fact-bound inquiry). Courts may consider a variety of factors when evaluating prefiling conduct, including the following:

(1) The time available for investigation. ***Lichtenstein***, 173 F.3d at 23; ***Thornton v. General Motors Corp.***, 136 F.3d 450, 454 (5th Cir.1998); ***Adams v. Pan Am. World Airways, Inc.***, 828 F.2d 24, 32 (D.C.Cir.1987).

(2) Whether the attorney has to rely on the client for facts. ***Thornton***, 136 F.3d at 454; *see* ***Hendrix v. Naphtal***, 971 F.2d 398, 400 & n.3 (9th Cir.1992) (reliance on the client's statements must be reasonable); ***S.A. Auto Lube, Inc. v. Jiffy Lube Int'l***, 842 F.2d 946, 949 (7th Cir.1988) (listing factors for determining when exclusive reliance is reasonable); *see also* ***Thomas v. Tenneco Packaging Co.***, 293 F.3d 1306, 1327 (11th Cir.2002) (attorney should not be passive and allow unchecked opinions or desires of client or witness into filings).

(3) Whether the attorney relied on an expert's opinion. ***Coffey v. Healthtrust, Inc.***, 1 F.3d 1101, 1104 (10th Cir.1993).

(4) Whether the attorney depended on another attorney. *See* ***Unioil, Inc. v. E.F. Hutton & Co.***, 809 F.2d 548, 558 (9th Cir.1986) (attorney cannot delegate duty of reasonable inquiry into facts of case to cocounsel who referred P); *see, e.g.*, ***S.A. Auto Lube***, 842 F.2d at 949 (attorney did not need to rely on cocounsel because information was matter of public record).

(5) The factual or legal complexity of the case. ***Lichtenstein***, 173 F.3d at 23; ***Thornton***, 136 F.3d at 454; ***Brown v. Federation of State Med. Bds.***, 830 F.2d 1429, 1435 (7th Cir.1987).

(6) Whether the opposing party controls the relevant facts or the allegations are of an opposing party's knowledge, purpose, intent, or state of mind. *See* ***Nassau-Suffolk Ice Cream v. Integrated Res.***, 114 F.R.D. 684, 689 (S.D.N.Y.1987) (attorney should not rely on others for information available in public domain).

(7) The feasibility of investigation. ***Thornton***, 136 F.3d at 454; ***Szabo Food Serv. v. Canteen Corp.***, 823 F.2d 1073, 1083 (7th Cir.1987).

(8) The attorney's level of experience. ***Huettig & Schromm, Inc. v. Landscape Contractors Council***, 790 F.2d 1421, 1426 (9th Cir.1986); *see also* ***Cabell v. Petty***, 810 F.2d 463, 466 (4th Cir.1987) ("inexperience and incompetence" may result in sanctions).

(9) Whether the law is in flux. ***Nieto v. L&H Packing Co.***, 108 F.3d 621, 624 n.9 (5th Cir.1997).

(10) Postfiling developments. *E.g.*, ***Jones v. International Riding Helmets, Ltd.***, 49 F.3d 692, 695 (11th Cir.1995) (formulation of discovery request revealed that attorney did not believe complaint against D was well grounded when signed).

(11) Whether discovery is necessary. ***Thornton***, 136 F.3d at 454.

2. FRCP 11(b) grounds.

(1) Filing for improper purpose. The court can impose sanctions if a document has been presented for an improper purpose (e.g., to harass or to cause unnecessary delay or expense). FRCP 11(b)(1); ***Mercury Air Grp. v. Mansour***, 237 F.3d 542, 548 (5th Cir.2001); ***Sheets***, 891 F.2d at 538; *see, e.g.*, ***Union Planters Bank v. L&J Dev. Co.***, 115 F.3d 378, 385 (6th Cir.1997) (presentation of false deposition testimony to defeat summary judgment was sanctionable).

(a) Paper nonfrivolous but intent improper. Most courts hold that sanctions should not be imposed if the pleading is nonfrivolous on its face, even if the signer's subjective intent was improper. ***Sussman v. Bank of Israel***, 56 F.3d 450, 458-59 (2d Cir.1995); ***Burkhart v. Kinsley Bank***, 852 F.2d 512, 515 (10th Cir.1988); ***National Ass'n of Gov't Empls., Inc. v. National Fed'n of Fed. Empls.***, 844 F.2d 216, 223 (5th Cir.1988); ***Golden Eagle Distrib. Corp. v. Burroughs Corp.***, 801 F.2d 1531, 1538 (9th Cir.1986). *But see* ***Whitehead v. Food Max of Miss., Inc.***, 332 F.3d 796, 805 (5th Cir.2003) (representation sanctionable when it is objectively ascertainable that nonfrivolous paper was submitted for improper purpose); ***Zaldivar***, 780 F.2d at 832 n.10 (filing of excessive motions, even if nonfrivolous, may rise to level of harassment).

(b) Part of paper improper. The court can impose sanctions even if only a part of the paper does not meet the FRCP 11 certification requirement. ***Patterson v. Aiken***, 841 F.2d 386, 387 (11th Cir.1988). Some courts decline to impose sanctions when the improper claims have little effect on the litigation. ***Burull v. First Nat'l Bank***, 831 F.2d 788, 790 (8th Cir.1987). The presence of an improper alternative legal theory will not be sanctionable when a supportable legal basis is also asserted. ***Townsend***, 929 F.2d at 1363.

(2) Claims & defenses not warranted by law. The court can impose sanctions if the claims or defenses of the signer are not warranted either by existing law or by a nonfrivolous argument for extending, modifying, or reversing existing law or for establishing new law. FRCP 11(b)(2); ***Truesdell v. Southern Cal. Permanente Med. Grp.***, 293 F.3d 1146, 1153 (9th Cir.2002); ***Zuk v. Eastern Pa. Psychiatric Inst.***, 103 F.3d 294, 299 (3d Cir.1996); ***Knipe v. Skinner***, 19 F.3d 72, 77 (2d Cir.1994); *see* 1993 Notes to FRCP 11 at ¶11, p. 1154, this book.

(a) Legal contention unjustified. The court can impose sanctions if a legal contention has absolutely no chance of success under the existing precedent. ***Corroon v. Reeve***, 258 F.3d 86, 92 (2d Cir.2001); ***In re Sargent***, 136 F.3d 349, 352 (4th Cir.1998).

(b) Frivolous argument for change. The court can impose sanctions if a competent attorney could not reasonably believe that the paper was warranted by a good-faith argument for a change in the law. ***Eastway Constr. Corp. v. City of N.Y.***, 762 F.2d 243, 253-54 (2d Cir.1985); *see* ***Roger Edwards, LLC v. Fiddes & Son Ltd.***, 437 F.3d 140, 142 (1st Cir.2006) (some degree of fault required, but need not be wicked or subjectively reckless state of mind); *cf.* ***Procter & Gamble Co. v. Amway Corp.***, 280 F.3d 519, 531-32 (5th Cir.2002) (party that predicates its legal claim on controversial and unsettled legal theory should not face sanctions under 28 U.S.C. §1927 or 15 U.S.C. §1117(a) when court ultimately rejects claim).

(c) Ignoring unfavorable precedent. The court can impose sanctions if a party or attorney, instead of acknowledging unfavorable precedent and seeking to overturn it, simply ignores it. *See* ***Szabo Food Serv.***, 823 F.2d at 1081-82 ("pretending that potentially dispositive authority against a litigant's contention does not exist" is sanctionable); *see also* ***Brunt v. Service Empls. Int'l Un.***, 284 F.3d 715, 721 (7th Cir.2002) (court could not impose sanctions when party attempted to distinguish facts in present case from those in contrary precedent).

(d) Being unfamiliar with law. Depending on the resources available, the court can sanction an attorney for being unfamiliar with cases decided between six weeks and six months before a paper is filed. *E.g.*, ***Rush v. McDonald's Corp.***, 966 F.2d 1104, 1123 (7th Cir.1992) (no reasonable inquiry was conducted). In some cases, the attorney may be required to obtain or retain additional expertise in an unfamiliar area of the law. ***Hays v. Sony Corp.***, 847 F.2d 412, 419 (7th Cir.1988).

(3) Lack of evidentiary support. The court can impose sanctions if the factual contentions lack evidentiary support or are unlikely to have evidentiary support after a reasonable opportunity for investigation or

discovery. FRCP 11(b)(3); ***Mercury Air Grp.***, 237 F.3d at 548; ***O'Brien v. Alexander***, 101 F.3d 1479, 1489 (2d Cir. 1996); ***Zaldivar***, 780 F.2d at 829; *see* ***Bradgate Assocs. v. Fellows, Read & Assocs.***, 999 F.2d 745, 752 (3d Cir.1993); *see, e.g.*, ***Ortho Pharm. v. Sona Distribs.***, 847 F.2d 1512, 1518 (11th Cir.1988) (court sanctioned attorney for filing motion to dismiss almost immediately after suit was filed, without first investigating claim). A factual contention is sanctionable only when the specific allegation is utterly lacking in support. ***Kiobel v. Millson***, 592 F.3d 78, 81 (2d Cir.2010). A factual contention may be supported by an inference (i.e., circumstantial evidence) or a fact (i.e., direct evidence). *E.g.*, ***Lucas v. Duncan***, 574 F.3d 772, 777-78 (D.C.Cir.2009) (court reversed sanctions on attorney for disguising inferences as fact because nothing in FRCP 11 requires attorney to distinguish between direct and circumstantial evidence). Under certain circumstances, an isolated factual misrepresentation may serve as the basis for sanctions. *E.g.*, ***Jenkins v. Methodist Hosps.***, 478 F.3d 255, 265 (5th Cir.2007) (erroneous inclusion of racially charged word in brief and two-month delay in correcting error warranted sua sponte sanctions).

(4) Denials not warranted. The court can impose sanctions if the signer's denials of factual contentions are neither warranted by the evidence nor based on belief or a lack of information. FRCP 11(b)(4); *see* 5A Wright & Miller §1335.

3. Who can be sanctioned. The court can impose monetary sanctions on a party, the party's attorneys, or the attorneys' firms. *See* FRCP 11(c)(1).

(1) Parties. Although courts generally decline to impose sanctions on parties, sanctions may be imposed when the party misrepresents key facts during a deposition or at trial. ***Rentz v. Dynasty Apparel Indus.***, 556 F.3d 389, 398 (6th Cir.2009); *see* 1993 Notes to FRCP 11 at ¶15, p. 1154, this book. A party cannot, however, be sanctioned under FRCP 11(b)(2) for unwarranted legal contentions. ***Rentz***, 556 F.3d at 398; *see* FRCP 11(c)(1), (c)(5)(A). Even though courts are lenient with pro se pleadings, a court may impose FRCP 11 sanctions on pro se litigants. *See* ***Saunders v. Bush***, 15 F.3d 64, 68 (5th Cir.1994).

(2) Attorneys. Attorneys of any experience level or position are equally subject to FRCP 11 sanctions. ***Rentz***, 556 F.3d at 401; *see* FRCP 11(c)(1).

(3) Firms. When an attorney is sanctioned for an FRCP 11 violation, the attorney's law firm must be held jointly responsible unless there are exceptional circumstances. FRCP 11(c)(1); *e.g.*, ***Rentz***, 556 F.3d at 396-97 (court declined to impose sanctions against law firm because firm was formed after sanctionable case had been ongoing and there was understanding at firm's formation that two sanctioned attorneys would be solely responsible for case).

§3.2 Violation of pretrial order. The court can sanction the party or its attorney for not complying with pretrial conference orders. FRCP 16(f)(1)(C); 6A Wright, Miller & Kane §1531. For example, the court can impose sanctions if a party or its attorney does not participate in a settlement conference in good faith. ***Smith v. Northwest Fin. Acceptance, Inc.***, 129 F.3d 1408, 1419 (10th Cir.1997). For the types of sanctionable conduct, see "Disobeying order," ch. 5-A, §4.6.2, p. 294. For a list of factors the court should consider before dismissing a suit under FRCP 16(f), see "Factors," ch. 7-D, §3.3.3, p. 645.

§3.3 Discovery abuse.

1. False signatures. The court can impose sanctions for a discovery disclosure, request, response, or objection that is in violation of FRCP 26(g)(1). FRCP 26(g)(3); ***Mancia v. Mayflower Textile Servs.***, 253 F.R.D. 354, 357 (D.Md.2008); 6 *Moore's Federal Practice 3d* §26.154[1]; *see* **Cherrington Asia Ltd. v. A&L Underground, Inc.**, 263 F.R.D. 653, 657 (D.Kan.2010) (FRCP 26(g) sanctions apply only to written discovery). The person who signed the document, the party on whose behalf the signer was acting, or both can be sanctioned under FRCP 26(g). FRCP 26(g)(3). For the representations certified by the signer of discovery, see "Disclosures," ch. 6-A, §6.1, p. 420; for sanctions for not properly certifying discovery, see "Not properly certifying under FRCP 26(g)," ch. 6-A, §15.3.8, p. 448.

2. Failure to serve deposition notice or subpoena. The court can sanction a party noticing a deposition if the party (1) did not attend and proceed with the deposition or (2) did not serve a subpoena on a nonparty, who consequently did not attend. FRCP 30(g). See "Noticing party did not attend or serve subpoena," ch. 6-A, §15.3.2(1)(b), p. 447.

3. Violation of court order. The court can sanction a person for not obeying a court order compelling disclosures or responses to discovery. FRCP 37. For a list of factors the court should consider before dismissing a suit under FRCP 37, see "Factors," ch. 7-D, §3.3.3, p. 645.

§3.4 Filing bad-faith affidavit or declaration. The court can sanction a party or its attorney for submitting in bad faith affidavits or declarations either supporting or opposing summary judgment. FRCP 56(h). See "Sanctions for bad-faith affidavit or declaration," ch. 7-B, §6.1.3(3), p. 612.

§3.5 Failure to prosecute. The court can dismiss a case for a party's failure to prosecute an action diligently. ***Link v. Wabash R.R.***, 370 U.S. 626, 630 (1962); *see* FRCP 41(b). For a list of factors the court must consider before dismissing the plaintiff's suit, see "Failure to prosecute," ch. 7-D, §3.1, p. 643.

§3.6 Failure to comply with court order. The court can dismiss a case for a party's failure to comply with court rules or orders. FRCP 41(b). For a list of factors the court must consider before dismissing the plaintiff's suit, see "Failure to comply with court rule or order," ch. 7-D, §3.2, p. 644.

§3.7 Improper removal. The court can sanction a defendant for improper removal. See "Award of costs, expenses & attorney fees," ch. 4-B, §6.5, p. 277.

§3.8 Multiplying proceedings unreasonably. The court may require an attorney who multiplies the proceedings unreasonably and vexatiously to pay the excess costs, expenses, and attorney fees incurred because of the conduct. 28 U.S.C. §1927; ***In re Schaefer Salt Recovery, Inc.***, 542 F.3d 90, 101 (3d Cir.2008); ***Trulis v. Barton***, 107 F.3d 685, 691-92 (9th Cir.1995); ***FDIC v. Conner***, 20 F.3d 1376, 1384 (5th Cir.1994). Unlike FRCP 11 sanctions, 28 U.S.C. §1927 sanctions cover only the multiplication of proceedings that prolong the litigation of a case; they do not cover the initial pleading because proceedings cannot be multiplied until a case has been ongoing. ***Jensen v. Phillips Screw Co.***, 546 F.3d 59, 65 (1st Cir.2008); ***In re Schaefer Salt Recovery***, 542 F.3d at 101; *see* ***Peer v. Lewis***, 606 F.3d 1306, 1314 (11th Cir.2010); *see also* ***Carr v. Tillery***, 591 F.3d 909, 919 (7th Cir.2010) (28 U.S.C. §1927 sanctions do not cover misconduct that occurred before case was in federal court).

NOTE

The circuits disagree on whether sanctions under 28 U.S.C. §1927 are intended only to compensate victims of dilatory practices or to both compensate victims and punish offending attorneys. Compare ***Shales v. General Chauffeurs, Sales Drivers & Helpers Local Un.****, 557 F.3d 746, 749 (7th Cir.2009) (§1927 sanctions are compensatory, not punitive),* ***Hamilton v. Boise Cascade Express****, 519 F.3d 1197, 1205 (10th Cir.2008) (§1927 sanctions are to compensate for abusive litigation practices, not to punish offenders; statute is "victim-centered"), and* ***In re Prudential Ins. Co. Am. Sales Practice Litig. Agent Actions****, 278 F.3d 175, 188 (3d Cir.2002) (principal purpose of §1927 sanctions is deterrence of intentional and unnecessary delay in proceedings, but only costs and expenses that result from misconduct can be awarded), with* ***Lamboy-Ortiz v. Ortiz-Velez****, 630 F.3d 228, 247 (1st Cir.2010) (§1927 sanctions serve both to deter frivolous litigation and abusive practices and to ensure that those who create unnecessary costs bear them),* ***Norelus v. Denny's, Inc.****, 628 F.3d 1270, 1281 (11th Cir.2010) (§1927 sanctions are punitive in nature), and* ***Red Carpet Studios Div. of Source Advantage, Ltd. v. Sater****, 465 F.3d 642, 646-47 (6th Cir.2006) (§1927 sanctions serve both to deter dilatory practices and to punish abusive tactics; §1927 sanctions are punitive).*

1. Standard. The imposition of attorney fees and costs under 28 U.S.C. §1927 is reserved for egregious behavior that violates recognized standards of litigation conduct. ***Baker Indus. v. Cerberus Ltd.***, 764 F.2d 204, 208 (3d Cir.1985); *see* ***Rosselló-González v. Acevedo-Vilá***, 483 F.3d 1, 7 (1st Cir.2007); *see also* ***United Stars Indus. v. Plastech Engineered Prods.***, 525 F.3d 605, 610 (7th Cir.2008) (§1927 sanctions set higher standard than sanctions under FRCPs); ***McMahan v. Toto***, 256 F.3d 1120, 1129 (11th Cir.2001) (something more than lack of merit is required for sanctions under §1927), *modified on other grounds*, 311 F.3d 1077 (11th Cir.2002). The circuits, however,

disagree on the standard for imposing §1927 sanctions. *Compare* ***Rentz v. Dynasty Apparel Indus.***, 556 F.3d 389, 396 (6th Cir.2009) (bad faith not required; conduct, viewed objectively, can be something less than subjective bad faith but more than negligence or incompetence), ***Jensen***, 546 F.3d at 64 (bad faith is not essential element; conduct, viewed objectively, must add up to reckless breach of attorney's obligations as officer of court), ***Hamilton***, 519 F.3d at 1202 (bad faith not required; conduct, viewed objectively, that manifests either intentional or reckless disregard of duties is sanctionable), *and* ***Amlong & Amlong, P.A. v. Denny's, Inc.***, 500 F.3d 1230, 1240-42 (11th Cir.2007) (bad faith not required; conduct, viewed objectively, that shows attorney knowingly or recklessly pursued frivolous claim is sanctionable), *with* ***Dal Pozzo v. Basic Mach. Co.***, 463 F.3d 609, 614 (7th Cir.2006) (objective bad faith and, under some circumstances, subjective bad faith is required), *and* ***LaSalle Nat'l Bank v. First Conn. Holding Grp.***, 287 F.3d 279, 289 (3d Cir.2002) (bad faith required, rather than misunderstanding, bad judgment, or well-intentioned zeal). *See generally* Joseph, *Sanctions: The Federal Law of Litigation Abuse 4th*, §23(B)(1) (2008) (discussion of "unreasonable and vexatious" standard). One type of conduct that can be sanctioned under §1927 is when an attorney makes a baseless contention for an ulterior purpose, such as harassment or delay. ***Ford v. Temple Hosp.***, 790 F.2d 342, 347 (3d Cir.1986); *see, e.g.*, ***Hamilton***, 519 F.3d at 1202-03 (§1927 sanction was imposed when motion from P's attorney clearly mischaracterized D's position and P's attorney did not amend or withdraw motion even after being put on notice that statement was incorrect); *see also* ***Cook v. American S.S. Co.***, 134 F.3d 771, 774 (6th Cir.1998) (§1927 sanction was imposed when attorney assaulted opposing attorney after day's proceedings had adjourned).

NOTE

Because the standard of review for arbitration awards is extremely narrow, and because arbitration is intended to expedite dispute resolution, sanctions under 28 U.S.C. §1927 can be particularly appropriate when an argument to vacate an arbitration award is meritless. See ***DMA Int'l v. Qwest Comms. Int'l****, 585 F.3d 1341, 1345-46 (10th Cir.2009).* *See "Arbitration," ch. 7-E, p. 650.*

2. Who can be sanctioned. Generally, only the attorney, not the client or law firm, can be sanctioned under 28 U.S.C. §1927. ***Sneller v. City of Bainbridge Island***, 606 F.3d 636, 640 (9th Cir.2010); ***BDT Prods. v. Lexmark Int'l***, 602 F.3d 742, 750-51 (6th Cir.2010); ***Maguire Oil Co. v. City of Houston***, 143 F.3d 205, 208 (5th Cir.1998); *see* ***United Stars***, 525 F.3d at 609; *see also* ***Carr***, 591 F.3d at 919 (attorney who represents herself can be sanctioned). The courts disagree on whether a pro se litigant can be sanctioned under 28 U.S.C. §1927. *Compare* ***Sassower v. Field***, 973 F.2d 75, 80 (2d Cir.1992) (§1927 sanctions do not apply to pro se litigants), *with* ***Wages v. IRS***, 915 F.2d 1230, 1235-36 (9th Cir.1990) (§1927 sanctions apply to pro se litigants).

§3.9 Bad-faith conduct.

1. Standard. The court has inherent power to sanction a person for certain conduct. But because of the "very potency" of a court's inherent powers, the court must exercise them "with restraint and discretion." ***Chambers v. NASCO, Inc.***, 501 U.S. 32, 44 (1991); *see* ***Thomas v. Tenneco Packaging Co.***, 293 F.3d 1306, 1320 (11th Cir. 2002); ***In re First City Bancorporation of Tex. Inc.***, 282 F.3d 864, 867 (5th Cir.2002).

(1) Sanctionable conduct. Under the court's inherent power, it can sanction a person for reasons that include the following:

(a) For bad faith, willful disobedience of a court order, or fraud on the court. ***Chambers***, 501 U.S. at 43-45; ***Gomez v. Vernon***, 255 F.3d 1118, 1133-34 (9th Cir.2001); *see* ***Ali v. Tolbert***, 636 F.3d 622, 627 (D.C.Cir.2011); *see, e.g.*, ***Sahyers v. Prugh, Holliday & Karatinos, P.L.***, 560 F.3d 1241, 1245-46 & n.9 (11th Cir.2009) (based on its inherent power, court denied attorney fees to prevailing P in Fair Labor Standards Act suit when (1) P's attorney provided no notice of suit to Ds and did not meaningfully attempt to resolve dispute and (2) such conduct rose to level of bad faith); *see also* ***Eisemann v. Greene***, 204 F.3d 393, 396 (2d Cir.2000) (bad faith interpreted restrictively, requiring clear evidence and high degree of specificity).

NOTE

There is disagreement and confusion about a district court's power to sanction under its inherent powers, including whether a showing of bad faith is required. ***U.S. v. Seltzer****, 227 F.3d 36, 41 (2d Cir.2000). Compare* ***Maguire Oil Co. v. City of Houston****, 143 F.3d 205, 209 (5th Cir. 1998) (specific finding of bad faith required), and* ***In re Keegan Mgmt. Co., Secs. Litig.****, 78 F.3d 431, 436 (9th Cir.1996) (same), with* ***Republic of the Phil. v. Westinghouse Elec. Corp.****, 43 F.3d 65, 74 n.11 (3d Cir.1994) (finding of bad faith not required in every case; bad faith is required for sanctions of attorney fees). Therefore, when requesting sanctions under the court's inherent power, check the law of the relevant circuit.*

(b) For an attorney's negligent or reckless failure to perform her responsibilities as an officer of the court. ***Seltzer***, 227 F.3d at 41-42; *see* ***Chambers***, 501 U.S. at 43.

(c) When necessary for the court to regulate its docket, promote judicial efficiency, and deter frivolous filings. ***Mann v. Boatright***, 477 F.3d 1140, 1150 (10th Cir.2007).

(2) Notice required. Before a person can be sanctioned under the court's inherent power, the court must provide the person with (1) notice of precisely what conduct is potentially sanctionable and (2) an opportunity to respond. ***Methode Elecs., Inc. v. Adam Techs.***, 371 F.3d 923, 928 (7th Cir.2004); *see* ***Fellheimer, Eichen & Braverman, P.C. v. Charter Techs.***, 57 F.3d 1215, 1225 (3d Cir.1995); *see also* ***Mendez v. County of San Bernardino***, 540 F.3d 1109, 1132 (9th Cir.2008) (there must be something in local rules or standards of professional conduct to put attorney on reasonable notice that conduct was improper).

(3) Conduct sanctionable under FRCP or statute. While the court can authorize sanctions under its inherent power even when there are procedural rules or statutes that sanction the same conduct, the court should not rely on its inherent power if the conduct can be adequately sanctioned under an FRCP or a statute. ***Chambers***, 501 U.S. at 49-50; *see* ***ClearValue, Inc. v. Pearl River Polymers, Inc.***, 560 F.3d 1291, 1309 (Fed.Cir.2009); ***Methode Elecs.***, 371 F.3d at 927; ***Toon v. Wackenhut Corr. Corp.***, 250 F.3d 950, 952 (5th Cir.2001).

2. Who can be sanctioned. A party, its attorney, or both can be sanctioned under the court's inherent power. ***In re Sunshine Jr. Stores***, 456 F.3d 1291, 1304 (11th Cir.2006); *see* ***Chambers***, 501 U.S. at 45-47. In certain circumstances, a nonparty can be sanctioned under the court's inherent power. ***Corder v. Howard Johnson & Co.***, 53 F.3d 225, 232 (9th Cir.1994); *see* ***Helmac Prods. v. Roth (Plastics) Corp.***, 150 F.R.D. 563, 568 (E.D.Mich.1993) (nonparty can be sanctioned if it is subject to court order or is real party in interest). *But see* ***Natural Gas Pipeline Co. v. Energy Gathering, Inc.***, 2 F.3d 1397, 1411 & n.39 (5th Cir.1993) (unclear whether nonparty can be sanctioned).

§3.10 Conduct sanctionable under local rules. The courts' local rulemaking authority includes the power to sanction. *See* FRCP 83(b); *see, e.g.*, ***Libel v. Adventure Lands***, 482 F.3d 1028, 1032-33 (8th Cir.2007) (when P repeatedly did not correct her statement of undisputed facts to comply with local rule, court sanctioned P by deeming as admitted each noncompliant disputed fact); Local Rules La. (W.D.), Rule 7.4.1 (for certain motions, such as extension of time, court may impose sanctions on nonmovant if nonmovant does not have good-faith reason for not consenting to motion). However, the local rules cannot be inconsistent with federal law. FRCP 83(a)(1); *see* ***Zambrano v. City of Tustin***, 885 F.2d 1473, 1479-82 (9th Cir.1989) (sanctions for mere negligent violation of local rules is inconsistent with congressional intent for federal court authority); *see, e.g.*, ***Standing Cmte. on Discipline v. Yagman***, 55 F.3d 1430, 1436-38 (9th Cir.1995) (sanctions under local rule cannot infringe on attorney's right to free speech). The court must follow local procedures created to discipline attorneys. *See, e.g.*, ***Willhite v. Collins***, 459 F.3d 866, 871 (8th Cir.2006) (suspension sanction remanded when court did not follow local rules for suspending attorneys). The court cannot sanction a person for violating an individual judge's procedural requirement unless the person had actual notice of the requirement. FRCP 83(b).

§4. SANCTIONS NOT JUSTIFIED

§4.1 Pleadings & motions. Sanctions should not be imposed in the following circumstances: • A court cannot impose FRCP 11 sanctions based on documents filed in state court before removal, unless the documents are advocated later in federal court. ***Brown v. Capitol Air, Inc.***, 797 F.2d 106, 108 (2d Cir.1986); *see* ***Buster v. Greisen***, 104 F.3d 1186, 1190 n.4 (9th Cir.1997); ***Kirby v. Allegheny Bev. Corp.***, 811 F.2d 253, 256-57 (4th Cir.1987); *see also* ***Tompkins v. Cyr***, 202 F.3d 770, 787 (5th Cir.2000) (FRCPs do not apply to pleading filed in state court before removal, but court can apply state's sanctions rules to those pleadings). *But see* ***Herron v. Jupiter Transp.***, 858 F.2d 332, 335-36 & n.6 (6th Cir.1988) (party and attorney are under continuing obligation after removal to review pleadings or risk FRCP 11 sanctions). • A court should not impose sanctions on a party for filing a motion even though the party was advised by the judge's law clerk that the grounds for the motion were inappropriate. *See* ***Eisemann v. Greene***, 204 F.3d 393, 396 (2d Cir.2000). • A court should not impose sanctions for asserting nonfrivolous claims even though one of the purposes for asserting those claims may have been improper. *E.g.*, ***Sussman v. Bank of Israel***, 56 F.3d 450, 459 (2d Cir.1995) (party's warnings of intention to file complaint to exert pressure on Ds through negative publicity was not improper purpose). • A court should not impose sanctions for repleading a dismissed claim if the grant of leave to replead was ambiguous about whether the claim was sanctionable or simply defective as originally pleaded. *See* ***Anderson v. Smithfield Foods, Inc.***, 353 F.3d 912, 916 (11th Cir.2003). • A court should not impose sanctions for asserting an allegation in an amended complaint that is contrary to an allegation in an earlier pleading. *See* ***PAE Gov't Servs. v. MPRI, Inc.***, 514 F.3d 856, 859-60 (9th Cir.2007). • A court should not impose sanctions for technical errors that are traditionally allowed to be corrected. *E.g.*, ***Montrose Chem. Corp. v. American Motorists Ins.***, 117 F.3d 1128, 1136 (9th Cir.1997) (P's failure to allege D's citizenship did not provide independent grounds for imposing sanctions). • A court should not impose sanctions when the law of the case is unsettled. ***Nieto v. L&H Packing Co.***, 108 F.3d 621, 624 n.9 (5th Cir.1997); ***Smith Int'l v. Texas Commerce Bank***, 844 F.2d 1193, 1201 (5th Cir.1988).

§4.2 Discovery. Sanctions should not be imposed in the following circumstances: • A court cannot impose FRCP 11 sanctions for disclosures and discovery filings. FRCP 11(d); 5A Wright & Miller §1331. • A court should not impose FRCP 11 sanctions when the preliminary inquiry is inadequate but later-acquired evidence supports the complaint. ***In re Keegan Mgmt. Co., Secs. Litig.***, 78 F.3d 431, 434-35 & n.1 (9th Cir.1996). *But see* ***Lichtenstein v. Consolidated Servs.***, 173 F.3d 17, 23 (1st Cir.1999) ("shot in the dark" allegations sanctionable); ***Garr v. U.S. Healthcare, Inc.***, 22 F.3d 1274, 1279 (3d Cir.1994) (same).

§4.3 Oral argument. Sanctions should not be imposed for representations made for the first time during an oral presentation. ***In re Bees***, 562 F.3d 284, 289 (4th Cir.2009); 1993 Notes to FRCP 11 at ¶6, p. 1153, this book.

§4.4 Settlement. Sanctions should not be imposed on an attorney or a party for refusing to settle a case. *See* ***Insurance Benefit Adm'rs, Inc. v. Martin***, 871 F.2d 1354, 1361 (7th Cir.1989).

§4.5 Court orders. Sanctions should not be imposed for violating a directive of the court stated in terms of "should" rather than "must." ***Ashlodge, Ltd. v. Hauser***, 163 F.3d 681, 684 (2d Cir.1998).

§4.6 Violation by both parties. Sanctions should not be imposed if both sides are equally guilty. *See* ***Associated Indem. Corp. v. Fairchild Indus.***, 961 F.2d 32, 36 (2d Cir.1992) ("defendants who live in glass pleadings ought not to throw Rule 11 stones"); *see, e.g.*, ***Fayemi v. Hambrecht & Quist, Inc.***, 174 F.R.D. 319, 326 (S.D.N.Y.1997) (no sanctions because moving party had "unclean hands").

§4.7 Appeals. Sanctions should not be imposed by the district court for a frivolous interlocutory appeal. ***Conner v. Travis Cty.***, 209 F.3d 794, 801 (5th Cir.2000).

§4.8 Other cases. Sanctions should not be imposed in one suit for an attorney's or party's action in other suits. *E.g.*, ***Woodward v. STP Corp.***, 170 F.3d 1043, 1045 (11th Cir.1999) (court attempted to reserve jurisdiction to assess sanctions if case was refiled in another court).

§5. MOTION FOR SANCTIONS

§5.1 Motion by party. The motion for sanctions must identify the specific conduct that deserves sanction and the rule, statute, or order the person violated. If the motion includes facts that are not apparent in the record, the

movant must attach affidavits. Any additional rules, statutes, or orders under which the conduct is sanctionable must also be referenced. ***Ted Lapidus, S.A. v. Vann***, 112 F.3d 91, 97 (2d Cir.1997).

1. Comply with FRCP 11. The motion for sanctions is itself subject to FRCP 11; the movant must comply with the certification requirements of FRCP 11(b). ***Bond v. American Med. Ass'n***, 764 F.Supp. 122, 126 n.3 (N.D.Ill.1991); 1993 Notes to FRCP 11 at ¶22, p. 1155, this book.

2. Form. An FRCP 11 motion must be made separately from any other motion. FRCP 11(c)(2); *see* ***Travelers Ins. v. St. Jude Med. Office Bldg. L.P.***, 154 F.R.D. 143, 144 n.4 (E.D.La.1994) (FRCP 11 and 28 U.S.C. §1927 motions for sanctions must be filed separately). It must be an actual motion, rather than a letter or other notice. ***Roth v. Green***, 466 F.3d 1179, 1192 (10th Cir.2006); *cf.* ***In re Pratt***, 524 F.3d 580, 586-87 & n.25 (5th Cir.2008) (interpreting Bankruptcy Rule 9011, which is substantially identical to FRCP 11). *But see* ***Nisenbaum v. Milwaukee Cty.***, 333 F.3d 804, 808 (7th Cir.2003) (letter can constitute substantial compliance with former FRCP 11(c)(1)(A), now FRCP 11(c)(2)).

3. Deadline to serve & file.

(1) Generally. The motion for sanctions should be served and filed reasonably soon after the discovery of sanctionable conduct or, in the case of some FRCP 11 sanctions, after an adequate time for discovery. *See* ***Brandt v. Vulcan, Inc.***, 30 F.3d 752, 756 (7th Cir.1994) (unreasonable delay in filing motion for sanctions under FRCP 37(b)(2) renders motion untimely); 1993 Notes to FRCP 11 at ¶18, p. 1155, this book (motion should be served promptly after paper is filed or after reasonable time for discovery). Some courts hold that a motion for sanctions must be filed before the entry of final judgment. *E.g.*, ***Prosser v. Prosser***, 186 F.3d 403, 405-06 (3d Cir.1999). *But see* ***Smith v. CB Commercial Real Estate Grp.***, 947 F.Supp. 1282, 1285 (S.D.Ind.1996) (timeliness requirement in FRCP 11 does not apply to motion under 28 U.S.C. §1927).

(2) When to serve FRCP 11 motion for sanctions. A motion for sanctions under FRCP 11 can be served on the person charged with sanctionable conduct anytime after the challenged paper is "presented" to a federal court. *See* 1993 Notes to FRCP 11 at ¶18, p. 1155, this book (motion should be served promptly after paper is filed or after reasonable time for discovery). A challenged paper is presented to a federal court when the person signs it, files it, submits it, or later advocates it. FRCP 11(b); ***Buster v. Greisen***, 104 F.3d 1186, 1190 n.4 (9th Cir.1997); *see* 1993 Notes to FRCP 11 at ¶6, p. 1153, this book (papers are not presented only at time of filing; party can violate FRCP 11 if it later advocates position in paper after learning that paper does not have any merit). The movant cannot, however, wait until after judgment or dismissal to serve the motion for sanctions. ***Roth***, 466 F.3d at 1193; *see* ***Brickwood Contractors, Inc. v. Datanet Eng'g***, 369 F.3d 385, 389 (4th Cir.2004) (sanctions cannot be sought after summary judgment has been granted); ***In re Pennie & Edmonds LLP***, 323 F.3d 86, 89 (2d Cir.2003) (motion is untimely if filed too late to permit correction or withdrawal); ***Barber v. Miller***, 146 F.3d 707, 710 (9th Cir.1998) (party must serve motion before dismissal).

(3) When to file FRCP 11 motion for sanctions – "safe harbor" provision. A motion for sanctions under FRCP 11 cannot be filed in the court until 21 days after it has been served on the party. FRCP 11(c)(2); *see* ***Truesdell v. Southern Cal. Permanente Med. Grp.***, 293 F.3d 1146, 1152 (9th Cir.2002). The purpose of this mandatory safe-harbor provision is to formalize procedural due-process considerations (i.e., to provide notice to the accused party) and to provide ample time for a party to withdraw or correct the challenged paper before court involvement. ***Roth***, 466 F.3d at 1192; ***In re Pennie & Edmonds***, 323 F.3d at 89; *see* ***Truesdell***, 293 F.3d at 1151; 1993 Notes to FRCP 11 at ¶20, p. 1155, this book.

§5.2 Motion on court's initiative.

1. FRCP 11. Under FRCP 11, a court can order an attorney, law firm, or party to show cause why FRCP 11(b) has not been violated. FRCP 11(c)(3).

(1) Standard under FRCP 11. Courts have held that sua sponte FRCP 11 sanctions are proper only in response to the most egregious conduct. *See* ***In re Bees***, 562 F.3d 284, 287 (4th Cir.2009) (sua sponte sanctions

should be imposed only in situations similar to contempt of court); ***Kaplan v. DaimlerChrysler, A.G.***, 331 F.3d 1251, 1255 (11th Cir.2003) (same). *But see* ***Young v. City of Providence***, 404 F.3d 33, 39 (1st Cir.2005) (sua sponte sanctions do not require more than FRCP 11(b) breach of duty). Because sua sponte sanctions are only appropriate for serious misconduct, the safe-harbor provision in FRCP 11(c)(2) does not apply to sanctions ordered on the court's own motion. *See* ***Young***, 404 F.3d at 39-40; ***Brickwood Contractors, Inc. v. Datanet Eng'g***, 369 F.3d 385, 389 n.2 (4th Cir.2004); ***Elliott v. Tilton***, 64 F.3d 213, 216 (5th Cir.1995); 1993 Notes to FRCP 11 at ¶23, p. 1155, this book. See "When to file FRCP 11 motion for sanctions – 'safe harbor' provision," §5.1.3(3), p. 392.

NOTE

Most circuits apply the objective standard to sua sponte sanctions. ***Jenkins v. Methodist Hosps.****, 478 F.3d 255, 264 (5th Cir.2007); see* ***Young****, 404 F.3d at 39-40. See "Objective test," §3.1.1, p. 385. But at least one court has held that sua sponte sanctions require a showing of subjective bad faith if the sanctions are imposed long after the attorney had an opportunity to correct the sanctionable conduct.* ***In re Pennie & Edmonds LLP****, 323 F.3d 86, 91 (2d Cir.2003).*

(2) Show-cause order under FRCP 11. Under FRCP 11, the court cannot impose monetary sanctions on its own initiative unless it issues a show-cause order before voluntary dismissal or settlement. FRCP 11(c)(5)(B); ***Johnson v. Waddell & Reed, Inc.***, 74 F.3d 147, 151 (7th Cir.1996). The show-cause order must describe the specific conduct that allegedly violates FRCP 11 and the types of sanctions under consideration. FRCP 11(c)(3); ***Margo v. Weiss***, 213 F.3d 55, 64 (2d Cir.2000); *see* ***In re Tutu Wells Contamination Litig.***, 120 F.3d 368, 379 (3d Cir.1997).

2. Violation of pretrial order. Under FRCP 16, a court generally can impose sanctions on its own, without a motion, for violation of a pretrial order. FRCP 16(f)(1). See "Violation of pretrial order," §3.2, p. 387.

3. False signatures. Under FRCP 26, a court generally can impose sanctions on its own, without a motion, for false signatures. FRCP 26(g)(3). See "False signatures," §3.3.1, p. 387.

4. Failure to serve deposition notice or subpoena. Under FRCP 30(g), a court generally can impose sanctions on its own, without a motion, for failure to serve a deposition notice or subpoena. *See* ***U.S. v. Lot 9, Block 2 of Donnybrook Place, Harris Cty., Tex.***, 919 F.2d 994, 997 n.2 (5th Cir.1990). See "Failure to serve deposition notice or subpoena," §3.3.2, p. 387.

5. Violation of court order. Under FRCP 37, a court generally can impose sanctions on its own, without a motion, for violation of a court order. *See* ***Chambers v. NASCO, Inc.***, 501 U.S. 32, 42 n.8 (1991). See "Violation of court order," §3.3.3, p. 388.

6. Filing bad-faith affidavit or declaration. Under FRCP 56(h), a court generally can impose sanctions on its own, without a motion, when an affidavit or declaration is filed in bad faith. *See* ***Chambers***, 501 U.S. at 42 n.8. See "Filing bad-faith affidavit or declaration," §3.4, p. 388.

7. Bad-faith conduct. Under its inherent power, a court generally can impose sanctions on its own, without a motion, for certain conduct. ***Chambers***, 501 U.S. at 42-45; ***In re Itel Sec. Litig.***, 791 F.2d 672, 675 (9th Cir.1986). See "Bad-faith conduct," §3.9, p. 389.

§5.3 Proposed order. Some districts require the movant to submit a proposed order with the motion. In those districts, the movant should prepare a written order for the court's signature and submit it with the motion. See "Proposed order," ch. 1-B, §3.1.11, p. 16.

§6. RESPONSE

When a person is notified that a motion for sanctions is pending against her, she should take the following steps.

§6.1 Withdraw or correct. If a motion for sanctions under FRCP 11 has been served but not filed, the person charged with sanctionable conduct should withdraw or appropriately correct the challenged paper, claim, defense, contention, or denial. FRCP 11(c)(2); *see, e.g.*, ***Sneller v. City of Bainbridge Island***, 606 F.3d 636, 639-40 (9th Cir.

2010) (P properly withdrew challenged claims by filing motion for leave to amend under FRCP 15). The person may formally withdraw the challenged paper or informally advise by letter that the challenged paper is abandoned. These actions do not concede an FRCP 11 violation. *See* FRCP 11(c)(2); ***Photocircuits Corp. v. Marathon Agents, Inc.***, 162 F.R.D. 449, 451-52 (E.D.N.Y.1995).

§6.2 File response. If the motion for sanctions has been served and filed, the person charged with sanctionable conduct should file a response. If the person does not timely respond to the motion for sanctions, any defense raised may be considered waived. *See* ***DiPaolo v. Moran***, 407 F.3d 140, 144-45 (3d Cir.2005) (response filed six months after sanctions granted; defense waived).

1. No sanctionable conduct. The person charged should inform the court, under oath, why sanctions should not be imposed. The person should attach as many affidavits as necessary.

2. No safe-harbor period. The person charged should assert that the court must deny the motion for sanctions because the movant violated the mandatory safe-harbor provision of FRCP 11. *See* ***Ridder v. City of Springfield***, 109 F.3d 288, 294 (6th Cir.1997) (sanctions inappropriate when motion filed less than 21 days after service); *see also* ***Radcliffe v. Rainbow Constr. Co.***, 254 F.3d 772, 789 (9th Cir.2001) (although D filed motion for sanctions and court did not grant motion until three months later, sanctions were inappropriate because P had not been served with motion). If a violation of the safe-harbor provision is not raised in the response, the person charged may waive the argument on appeal. *See* ***DiPaolo***, 407 F.3d at 145; ***Brickwood Contractors, Inc. v. Datanet Eng'g***, 369 F.3d 385, 392 (4th Cir.2004). The Fourth Circuit has held, however, that imposition of FRCP 11 sanctions when a party failed to comply with the safe-harbor provision is an error that can be corrected even if it is raised for the first time on appeal. ***Brickwood Contractors***, 369 F.3d at 398. The court has discretion on a case-by-case basis to correct an error if (1) there is an error, (2) it is plain, (3) it affects the appellant's substantial rights, and (4) it seriously affects the fairness, integrity, or public reputation of judicial proceedings. *Id.* at 397; *see* ***Taylor v. Virginia Un. Univ.***, 193 F.3d 219, 239-40 (4th Cir.1999) (applying ***Olano*** to civil cases); *cf.* ***U.S. v. Olano***, 507 U.S. 725, 732 (1993) (interpreting Fed. R. Crim. P. 52). See "Motion on court's initiative," §5.2, p. 392.

3. No ability to pay. The person charged with sanctionable conduct should inform the court of her potential inability to pay the sanctions. *See* ***Landscape Props., Inc. v. Whisenhunt***, 127 F.3d 678, 685 (8th Cir.1997); *see, e.g.*, ***Willhite v. Collins***, 459 F.3d 866, 870 (8th Cir.2006) (district court did not investigate attorney's ability to pay sanction when attorney did not raise issue to court). If the issue is raised, the court should consider the person's ability to pay in determining the amount of the sanction. ***White v. General Motors Corp.***, 908 F.2d 675, 684-85 (10th Cir.1990); *cf.* ***Roth v. Green***, 466 F.3d 1179, 1194 (10th Cir.2006) (in civil-rights case, nonprevailing P's ability to pay is not factor in determining whether to award attorney fees against P but may be factor in determining amount of attorney fees). The assertion of the inability to pay is similar to an affirmative defense, with the burden on the party asserting the inability. ***White***, 908 F.2d at 685.

§6.3 Request hearing. The person charged with sanctionable conduct should request a hearing for oral argument or, if necessary, for presenting evidence. *See* 1993 Notes to FRCP 11 at ¶17, p. 1155, this book (whether hearing for argument or evidence is necessary depends on circumstances).

§7. NOTICE & OPPORTUNITY TO RESPOND

The person threatened with sanctions is entitled to receive specific notice of the allegedly sanctionable conduct and the standard by which that conduct will be assessed, and the person must have an opportunity to be heard on the matter. *See* ***Nuwesra v. Merrill Lynch, Fenner & Smith, Inc.***, 174 F.3d 87, 92 (2d Cir.1999) (FRCP 11); ***Johnson v. Waddell & Reed, Inc.***, 74 F.3d 147, 151 (7th Cir.1996) (same); ***Baulch v. Johns***, 70 F.3d 813, 817-18 (5th Cir.1995) (28 U.S.C. §1927); ***Kirshner v. Uniden Corp.***, 842 F.2d 1074, 1082 (9th Cir.1988) (local rules); *see, e.g.*, ***Marlin v. Moody Nat'l Bank***, 533 F.3d 374, 378-79 (5th Cir.2008) (FRCP 11 sanctions awarded sua sponte and without notice were abuse of discretion). *But see* ***Merriman v. Security Ins.***, 100 F.3d 1187, 1191 (5th Cir.1996) (mere existence of FRCP 11 is sufficient notice to attorney who files court papers with no basis in fact). See "Notice under FRCP 16(f) & 37(b)," ch. 7-D, §5.2, p. 647. However, sanctions are not criminal proceedings, so criminal procedural protections

are not required. ***Margo v. Weiss***, 213 F.3d 55, 62 (2d Cir.2000). *But see* ***Mackler Prods. v. Cohen***, 146 F.3d 126, 129 (2d Cir.1998) (criminal procedural protections required when sanctions are explicitly punitive, not compensatory, and are payable to court, not to opposing party).

§8. TYPES OF SANCTIONS

§8.1 Compensatory vs. punitive sanctions. The court can order compensatory or punitive sanctions. Compensatory sanctions (generally monetary) are intended to compensate a party for a wrong committed by the opposing party; punitive sanctions (either monetary or nonmonetary) are intended to punish a party for a wrong committed. *See* ***Fleming & Assocs. v. Newby & Tittle***, 529 F.3d 631, 639 (5th Cir.2008); ***Hamilton v. Boise Cascade Express***, 519 F.3d 1197, 1205 (10th Cir.2008); ***Clark Equip. Co. v. Lift Parts Mfg. Co.***, 972 F.2d 817, 819 (7th Cir.1992); *see also* ***Rentz v. Dynasty Apparel Indus.***, 556 F.3d 389, 399-400 (6th Cir.2009) (primary purpose of FRCP 11 is deterrence; however, to effectively deter, court may need to compensate opposing party for attorney fees). The court can order monetary sanctions payable to the court or to the opposing party, or the court can order nonmonetary sanctions. *See* ***Fleming & Assocs.***, 529 F.3d at 639; ***Clark Equip.***, 972 F.2d at 819. During settlement negotiations, parties can agree to bargain away compensatory sanctions; parties cannot, however, bargain away punitive sanctions. *See, e.g.*, ***Fleming & Assocs.***, 529 F.3d at 640 (court vacated attorney fees as moot based on parties' settlement; court did not vacate sanction order that described sanctioned party's misconduct); ***Kleiner v. First Nat'l Bank***, 751 F.2d 1193, 1199-1200 (11th Cir.1985) (court vacated attorney fees and costs as moot based on parties' settlement; court did not vacate attorney's disqualification or fine payable to court).

§8.2 Authorized sanctions under FRCP 11. If the court finds that a person presented a paper in violation of FRCP 11, the court can impose nonmonetary or monetary sanctions.

1. Nonmonetary sanctions. The court can impose nonmonetary sanctions, including striking the offending document, imposing disciplinary actions, requiring attendance at continuing-legal-education courses, or other "creative" sanctions. FRCP 11(c)(4); ***Thomas v. Capital Sec. Servs.***, 836 F.2d 866, 878 (5th Cir.1988); *see* 1993 Notes to FRCP 11 at ¶12, p. 1154, this book (admonition, reprimand, censure, or referral to disciplinary authorities); 5A Wright & Miller §1336.3 & nn.60-71 (reprimand, continuing legal education, suspension, disbarment); *see, e.g.*, ***Willhite v. Collins***, 459 F.3d 866, 870 (8th Cir.2006) (appellate court recommended that sanctioned attorney should be required to attend continuing-legal-education classes rather than law-school course on federal jurisdiction).

2. Monetary sanctions.

(1) Payment.

(a) To court. If the court imposes a monetary sanction on its own initiative, the payment must be made as a penalty to the court, not to the other party. FRCP 11(c)(4); ***United Stars Indus. v. Plastech Engineered Prods.***, 529 F.3d 1199, 1199 (7th Cir.2008); ***Johnson v. Waddell & Reed, Inc.***, 74 F.3d 147, 152 n.3 (7th Cir.1996); *see* ***Willhite***, 459 F.3d at 870 (attorney fees under FRCP 11 cannot be awarded for sanction imposed sua sponte); ***Methode Elecs., Inc. v. Adam Techs.***, 371 F.3d 923, 926 (7th Cir.2004) (same).

(b) To opposing party. Monetary sanctions paid to the opposing party are proper only under "unusual circumstances" when deterrence is ineffective. ***Rentz v. Dynasty Apparel Indus.***, 556 F.3d 389, 395 (6th Cir.2009); 1993 Notes to FRCP 11 at ¶13, p. 1154, this book. Any award under FRCP 11 to the opposing party must have been requested in a motion and is limited to attorney fees and expenses directly resulting from the violation. FRCP 11(c)(4); ***Cooter & Gell v. Hartmarx Corp.***, 496 U.S. 384, 406-07 (1990); *see* FRCP 11(c)(2); ***United Stars***, 529 F.3d at 1199; ***Methode Elecs.***, 371 F.3d at 926. The requesting party must prove the fees and expenses using, for example, attorney timesheets. *See* ***Lockary v. Kayfetz***, 974 F.2d 1166, 1177 (9th Cir.1992).

(2) Apportionable. The court can apportion monetary sanctions according to the results achieved. ***Divane v. Krull Elec. Co.***, 319 F.3d 307, 315-16 (7th Cir.2003). For example, if a plaintiff brings distinct claims and one of those claims is sanctionable, the plaintiff can be ordered to pay fees incurred by the defendant in defending the frivolous claim but not those for the nonsanctionable claims. *Cf.* ***Wade v. Soo Line R.R.***, 500 F.3d 559, 562 (7th Cir.2007) (sanctions under FRCP 37).

§8.3 Authorized sanctions under court's inherent power. The court can impose sanctions that include the following: (1) contempt citations, (2) fines, (3) attorney fees and costs, (4) dismissal, and (5) default judgment. ***Ali v. Tolbert***, 636 F.3d 622, 627 (D.C.Cir.2011); *see* ***Chambers v. NASCO, Inc.***, 501 U.S. 32, 46 (1991); ***Micron Tech. v. Rambus Inc.***, 645 F.3d 1311, 1326 (Fed.Cir.2011). Which particular sanction to impose is within the court's discretion. ***Micron Tech.***, 645 F.3d at 1326.

§8.4 Authorized sanctions under FRCP 16(f). See "Sanctions for disobedience," ch. 5-A, §4.6.3, p. 294.

§8.5 Authorized sanctions for discovery abuse. See "Motion for Discovery Sanctions," ch. 6-A, §15, p. 446; "Motion for sanctions," ch. 6-G, §5.2, p. 562; "Failure to Timely Respond – Deemed Admissions," ch. 6-H, §5, p. 566.

§8.6 Authorized sanctions for bad-faith affidavits. See "Attorney fees as sanctions for bad-faith affidavit or declaration," ch. 7-B, §3.1.3(2), p. 605.

§8.7 Authorized sanctions for multiplying proceedings unreasonably. The court can award excess costs, expenses, and attorney fees incurred because of conduct that multiplies the proceedings. 28 U.S.C. §1927. See "Note," §3.8, p. 388. "Excess costs" include only those enumerated in 28 U.S.C. §1920, which lists the items ordinarily taxed to a losing party. ***Roadway Express, Inc. v. Piper***, 447 U.S. 752, 757-61 (1980). Sanctions under 28 U.S.C. §1927 cannot be based on the court's wasted time or judicial resources. *See* ***Blue v. U.S. Dept. of Army***, 914 F.2d 525, 548 (4th Cir.1990).

§8.8 Unauthorized sanctions.

1. No monetary sanctions under FRCP 11(c)(5). The court cannot impose a monetary sanction on a party represented by an attorney for a violation of FRCP 11(b)(2) (claims warranted under existing law). FRCP 11(c)(5)(A); *see* ***Larez v. Holcomb***, 16 F.3d 1513, 1522 (9th Cir.1994) (court must exercise caution when sanctioning attorney under FRCP 11 when sanctions emerge from attorney's effort to secure new rights).

2. No award to attorney's client. The court cannot order an attorney to pay sanctions to her own client. ***Mark Indus. v. Sea Captain's Choice, Inc.***, 50 F.3d 730, 732 (9th Cir.1995).

3. No award to nonparty. The court cannot order payment of sanctions to a nonparty. ***In re Tutu Wells Contamination Litig.***, 120 F.3d 368, 383 (3d Cir.1997).

§9. ORDER

The order should identify the source of authority for awarding the sanctions because the different sources of authority require different standards of proof and permit different types of sanctions against different parties. ***Willhite v. Collins***, 459 F.3d 866, 870 (8th Cir.2006).

§9.1 Order under FRCP 11. The court is not required to assess sanctions for an FRCP 11 violation unless otherwise provided by statute. *See* FRCP 11(c)(1); 5A Wright & Miller §§1331, 1335, 1336.1; *see, e.g.*, ***CitiBank Global Mkts., Inc. v. Rodríguez Santana***, 573 F.3d 17, 32 (1st Cir.2009) (under Private Securities Litigation Reform Act, court is required to make findings regarding parties' compliance with FRCP 11(b), and if noncompliant, court must impose sanctions). However, the court should rule on a motion for FRCP 11 sanctions before or at the same time the final judgment is entered so that any appeal of the sanctions ruling can be included with the appeal of the ruling on the merits. ***Gary v. Braddock Cemetery***, 517 F.3d 195, 201 (3d Cir.2008).

1. Impose least severe sanction to deter. If the court imposes sanctions, it should impose the least severe sanction that is sufficient to serve the purposes of the sanction. FRCP 11(c)(4); ***Mercury Air Grp. v. Mansour***, 237 F.3d 542, 548 (5th Cir.2001); ***Barrett v. Tallon***, 30 F.3d 1296, 1302-03 (10th Cir.1994). The purpose of sanctions is to deter repetition of the offending conduct or comparable conduct by others who are similarly situated. FRCP 11(c)(4); *see* ***Willhite v. Collins***, 459 F.3d 866, 869 (8th Cir.2006).

2. Explain grounds for sanctions. If the court imposes sanctions, it must state in sufficient detail why it concluded that sanctions should be imposed. FRCP 11(c)(6). The court should identify, either in its order for sanctions or on the record, the objectionable conduct by specific reference to the offending document or the statement

in the document, and it should give the reasons why the conduct is sanctionable. *See id.* Sanctions resulting in the dismissal of a suit must be accompanied by specific reasons why lesser sanctions were rejected. *See* ***Halaco Eng'g v. Costle***, 843 F.2d 376, 381 (9th Cir.1988).

NOTE

The court is not required to explain its reasons for denying a motion for sanctions. See 1993 Notes to FRCP 11 at ¶17, p. 1155, this book. But if the requesting party makes a strong showing that violations of FRCP 11 have occurred, the court should explain why it disregarded the showing. ***Trulis v. Barton****, 107 F.3d 685, 695-96 (9th Cir.1995); e.g.,* ***S. Bravo Sys. v. Containment Techs.****, 96 F.3d 1372, 1375-76 (Fed.Cir.1996) (court abused discretion by denying FRCP 11 motion without adequate explanation).*

§9.2 Order under court's inherent power. If the court imposes sanctions under its inherent power, it should describe the conduct that constituted a violation and state in sufficient detail the factual and legal reasons supporting the sanctions. *See* ***First Bank v. Hartford Underwriters Ins.***, 307 F.3d 501, 522-23 (6th Cir.2002). If the court imposes dismissal or default judgment, it should state why lesser sanctions are not sufficient. *See* ***Webb v. District of Columbia***, 146 F.3d 964, 971 (D.C.Cir.1998).

§9.3 Order under FRCP 16(f) & 37. If the court imposes sanctions under FRCP 16(f) or 37, it should describe the conduct that constituted a violation and state in sufficient detail the factual and legal reasons supporting the sanctions. 3 *Moore's Federal Practice 3d* §16.93[3]; *see* ***Connecticut Gen. Life Ins. v. New Images***, 482 F.3d 1091, 1096 (9th Cir.2007) (explicit findings are preferred but not required).

§9.4 Order under FRCP 26(g). If the court imposes discovery sanctions under FRCP 26(g), it should describe the conduct that constituted a violation and state in sufficient detail the factual and legal reasons supporting the sanctions. *See* ***Shepherd v. ABC, Inc.***, 62 F.3d 1469, 1480 (D.C.Cir.1995); ***Insurance Benefit Adm'rs, Inc. v. Martin***, 871 F.2d 1354, 1361-63 (7th Cir.1989); 6 *Moore's Federal Practice 3d* §26.155.

§9.5 Order under FRCP 41. See "Order of Dismissal," ch. 7-D, §6, p. 647.

§10. APPELLATE REVIEW

§10.1 Appealability. Generally, sanction orders are neither appealable final decisions nor appealable collateral orders. ***Williams v. Midwest Empls. Cas. Co.***, 243 F.3d 208, 209 (5th Cir.2001). *But see* ***Riverhead Sav. Bank v. National Mortg. Equity Corp.***, 893 F.2d 1109, 1113-14 (9th Cir.1990) (appeal permitted if sanctions threaten to render postjudgment review ineffective). For example, a sanction order issued against an attorney is not appealable until the underlying case is over, even if the attorney no longer represents a party in the case. ***Cunningham v. Hamilton Cty.***, 527 U.S. 198, 209 (1999); *see also* ***Grider v. Keystone Health Plan Cent., Inc.***, 580 F.3d 119, 131-32 (3d Cir.2009) (sanction orders were final and appealable for sanctioned attorneys, even though order did not quantify amount of sanctions, because parties had settled and court had dismissed all claims with prejudice). However, when the enforcement of a sanction order results in exceptional hardship, mandamus may be available to determine whether the district court's decision to enforce the sanction was an abuse of discretion. ***Cunningham***, 527 U.S. at 211 (Kennedy, J., concurring).

§10.2 Standard of review. The court's ruling on a motion for sanctions is reviewed for abuse of discretion. ***Cooter & Gell v. Hartmarx Corp.***, 496 U.S. 384, 405 (1990) (FRCP 11); ***Rentz v. Dynasty Apparel Indus.***, 556 F.3d 389, 395 (6th Cir.2009) (FRCP 11 and 28 U.S.C. §1927); ***Connecticut Gen. Life Ins. v. New Images***, 482 F.3d 1091, 1096 (9th Cir.2007) (FRCP 37); ***Jenkins v. Methodist Hosps.***, 478 F.3d 255, 263 (5th Cir.2007) (FRCP 11); ***Roth v. Green***, 466 F.3d 1179, 1187 (10th Cir.2006) (FRCP 11 and 28 U.S.C. §1927); ***Willhite v. Collins***, 459 F.3d 866, 869 (8th Cir.2006) (FRCP 11); ***Methode Elecs., Inc. v. Adam Techs.***, 371 F.3d 923, 925-26 (7th Cir.2004) (FRCP 11 and court's inherent power); ***Thomas v. Tenneco Packaging Co.***, 293 F.3d 1306, 1319 (11th Cir.2002) (court's inherent power); ***Eisemann v. Greene***, 204 F.3d 393, 396 (2d Cir.2000) (court's inherent power and 28 U.S.C. §1927); ***Blue v.***

U.S. Dept. of Army, 914 F.2d 525, 538-39 (4th Cir.1990) (FRCP 11 and 16 and 28 U.S.C. §1927). If the sanctions are imposed sua sponte, the ruling is generally reviewed with "particular stringency." ***In re Pennie & Edmonds LLP***, 323 F.3d 86, 90 (2d Cir.2003); ***Hunter v. Earthgrains Co. Bakery***, 281 F.3d 144, 153 (4th Cir.2002); ***United Nat'l Ins. v. R&D Latex Corp.***, 242 F.3d 1102, 1115 (9th Cir.2001); *see* ***Lucas v. Duncan***, 574 F.3d 772, 775 (D.C.Cir.2009) (appellate court should engage in "careful appellate review"). The court abuses its discretion to impose sanctions when a ruling is based on an erroneous view of the law or a clearly erroneous assessment of the evidence. ***Cooter & Gell***, 496 U.S. at 405; ***Roth***, 466 F.3d at 1187.

P. MOTION FOR CLASS CERTIFICATION

§1. GENERAL

§1.1 Rule. FRCP 23.

§1.2 Purpose. A motion for class certification under FRCP 23 asks the court to permit one or more members of a class to sue (or be sued) as representative parties. *See* ***Wal-Mart Stores v. Dukes***, ___ U.S. ___, 131 S.Ct. 2541, 2550 (2011) (class action is exception to general rule that suit is conducted by and on behalf of only individually named parties). Although rare, defendant class actions are permitted and generally have the same certification requirements as plaintiff class actions. ***Tilley v. TJX Cos.***, 345 F.3d 34, 37 (1st Cir.2003); *see* ***Califano v. Yamasaki***, 442 U.S. 682, 701 (1979); ***In re Broadhollow Funding Corp.***, 66 B.R. 1005, 1007 (Bankr.E.D.N.Y.1986).

§1.3 Forms. ***O'Connor's Federal Civil Forms*** (2012), FORMS 5P.

§1.4 Other references. 7A, 7AA Wright, Miller & Kane, *Federal Practice & Procedure 3d* §§1751-1790 (2005 & Supp.2012); 5 *Moore's Federal Practice 3d* ch. 23 (2012); 1 Rubenstein et al., *Newberg on Class Actions* ch. 3 (5th ed. 2011); 3 Rubenstein et al., *Newberg on Class Actions* ch. 7 (4th ed. 2002 & Supp.2012); *Manual for Complex Litigation, Fourth*, §21 (2004), Federal Judicial Center, www.fjc.gov; Hensler et al., *Class Action Dilemmas: Pursuing Public Goals for Private Gain*, Rand Institute for Civil Justice (2000); Partridge & Miller, *Some Practical Considerations for Defending & Settling Products Liability & Consumer Class Actions*, 74 Tul.L.Rev. 2125 (2000).

§2. MOTION

The party seeking class certification—usually the proposed class representative—must file a motion to certify the class.

NOTE

Although the standard procedure is a motion for class certification, a party seeking to avoid class certification—usually the defendant—can file a preemptive motion to deny certification. See ***Vinole v. Countrywide Home Loans, Inc.***, *571 F.3d 935, 939 (9th Cir.2009).*

§2.1 Form. For the general requirements for the form of a motion, see "Drafting motions," ch. 1-B, §3.1, p. 14.

§2.2 Deadline to file. The motion for class certification should be filed as soon as possible and within any deadlines imposed by the court. *See* FRCP 23(c)(1)(A) (court must determine class certification "at an early practicable time").

§2.3 Burden of proof. The party filing the motion has the burden of proving the propriety of establishing a class under FRCP 23. ***Wal-Mart Stores v. Dukes***, ___ U.S. ___, 131 S.Ct. 2541, 2551 (2011); ***Madison v. Chalmette Ref., L.L.C.***, 637 F.3d 551, 554-55 (5th Cir.2011). Generally, at the certification stage, the party is not required to prove the merits of the class claim or even to establish a probability that the action will be successful. ***Eisen v. Carlisle & Jacquelin***, 417 U.S. 156, 177-78 (1974). But to make the certification ruling, the court may look beyond the pleadings and inquire into the merits; thus, the party should be prepared to provide some evidence favoring the underlying class claim. *See* ***Wal-Mart Stores***, ___ U.S. at ___, 131 S.Ct. at 2551-52; ***Madison***, 637 F.3d at 555. See "Analysis," §5.2, p. 403.

§2.4 Grounds. A motion for class certification must assert that all the requirements of FRCP 23(a) are met and that the class falls within one of the three categories of FRCP 23(b). ***Wal-Mart Stores v. Dukes***, ___ U.S. ___, 131 S.Ct. 2541, 2548 (2011); ***Amchem Prods. v. Windsor***, 521 U.S. 591, 614 (1997); ***Maldonado v. Ochsner Clinic Found.***, 493 F.3d 521, 523 (5th Cir.2007); *see also* ***Shady Grove Orthopedic Assocs. v. Allstate Ins.***, ___ U.S. ___, 130 S.Ct. 1431, 1442 (2010) (FRCP 23 authorizes any P in any federal civil proceeding to maintain class action if FRCP 23 requirements are met). Except for the manageability requirement under FRCP 23(b)(3)(D), the requirements for certifying trial classes and settlement classes are the same. *See* ***Amchem Prods.***, 521 U.S. at 620.

NOTE

In 2010, the Supreme Court held that FRCP 23 conflicted with a New York state law prohibiting class actions for statutory penalties and that, based on 28 U.S.C. §2072, FRCP 23 prevailed over the New York law; thus, the class action could proceed in federal court. ***Shady Grove Orthopedic***, *___ U.S. at ___, 130 S.Ct. at 1442. Although a majority agreed on the outcome, a majority did not agree on the rationale for the decision. See id. at ___, 130 S.Ct. at 1442-44, 1447-48 (plurality op., Roberts, C.J., Scalia, Thomas, Sotomayor, JJ.) (when FRCP 23 and New York law conflicted, New York law had to give way to FRCP 23 because FRCP 23 "really regulates procedure"; it was irrelevant that the rule may incidentally affect party's substantive right); id. at ___, 130 S.Ct. at 1448-60 (Stevens, J., concurring) (in certain diversity-jurisdiction cases—but not in this case—state law could trump federal procedure rule if state law, although procedural in ordinary sense, still defines a substantive right). See "Construction of rules," ch. 1-A, §1.3, p. 4. It is unclear what effect the decision will have on other state laws that limit class actions, especially considering the splintered rationale.*

1. FRCP 23(a) requirements. FRCP 23(a) imposes four threshold requirements applicable to all class actions. ***Ortiz v. Fibreboard Corp.***, 527 U.S. 815, 828 n.6 (1999).

(1) Numerosity. The class must be so numerous that joinder of all members is "impracticable." FRCP 23(a)(1). The proposed class representative needs to show only that joining all class members would be extremely difficult or inconvenient. 7A Wright, Miller & Kane §1762 & n.7. The proposed class representative does not need to prove the exact number or identity of class members. *See* ***Pederson v. Louisiana State Univ.***, 213 F.3d 858, 868 & n.11 (5th Cir.2000); 3 Rubenstein et al., *Newberg on Class Actions* §7:22.

(2) Commonality. There must be questions of law or fact common to the class. FRCP 23(a)(2); ***Wal-Mart Stores***, ___ U.S. at ___, 131 S.Ct. at 2550-51; ***Vega v. T-Mobile USA, Inc.***, 564 F.3d 1256, 1268 (11th Cir.2009); ***Robinson v. Metro-N. Commuter R.R.***, 267 F.3d 147, 155 (2d Cir.2001). To satisfy the commonality requirement, the class members must have suffered the same injury; however, that does not mean merely that they have suffered a violation of the same law (e.g., commonality is not met by claims that all class members suffered a Title VII injury). ***Wal-Mart Stores***, ___ U.S. at ___, 131 S.Ct. at 2551. The requirement can be met by a single contention common to the class. *Id.* at ___, 131 S.Ct. at 2556; ***Ross v. RBS Citizens***, 667 F.3d 900, 908 (7th Cir.2012), *cert. filed*, ___ S.Ct. ___ (2012) (No. 12-165; 8-1-12). But that contention's truth or falsity must resolve a central issue in each of the class members' claims. ***Wal-Mart Stores***, ___ U.S. at ___, 131 S.Ct. at 2551; ***M.D. v. Perry***, 675 F.3d 832, 840 (5th Cir. 2012); *see* ***Williams v. Mohawk Indus.***, 568 F.3d 1350, 1355 (11th Cir.2009). That is, the key to determining commonality is not whether the class raises common questions, but whether the class generates common answers that are capable of resolving the suit. *E.g.*, ***Wal-Mart Stores***, ___ U.S. at ___, 131 S.Ct. at 2551-52 (class claiming employment discrimination did not satisfy commonality when there was no "glue" holding alleged reasons for particular employment decisions together; thus, there was no common answer to question of why each individual class member was disfavored); ***Ross***, 667 F.3d at 908-09 (class claiming violations of Fair Labor Standards Act satisfied commonality when "glue" holding class together was alleged unlawful overtime policy that prevented Ps from collecting lawfully earned overtime pay).

NOTE

Before ***Wal-Mart Stores v. Dukes****, the commonality requirement was described as generally "not demanding."* ***M.D.****, 675 F.3d at 839; see* ***Vega****, 564 F.3d at 1268 (commonality requirement is "relatively light burden"); 1 Rubenstein et al., Newberg on Class Actions §3:18 (commonality requirement is "easily met in most cases"); see also* ***Wal-Mart Stores****, ___ U.S. at ___, 131 S.Ct. at 2565 (Ginsburg, Breyer, Sotomayor, Kagan, JJ., concurring in part and dissenting in part) (blending commonality requirement under FRCP 23(a)(2) and more-demanding predominance requirement under FRCP 23(b)(3) elevates commonality requirement so that it is no longer easily satisfied). After* ***Wal-Mart Stores****, at least one circuit has held that the commonality standard has been heightened because the standard is no longer met by merely establishing that the resolution of at least one issue will affect all or a significant number of the class members. See* ***M.D.****, 675 F.3d at 839-40.*

(3) Typicality. The proposed class representative must have claims or defenses that are typical of the class. FRCP 23(a)(3). The test for typicality is whether the claims or defenses of the class and the proposed class representative (1) arise from the same event, pattern, or practice and (2) are based on the same legal theories. ***Williams***, 568 F.3d at 1356-57; ***Robinson***, 267 F.3d at 155; *see* ***Stirman v. Exxon Corp.***, 280 F.3d 554, 562 (5th Cir.2002). Even if there are substantial factual differences, typicality may be satisfied if the legal theories are substantially similar. ***Williams***, 568 F.3d at 1357. The test for typicality is not demanding. ***Stirman***, 280 F.3d at 562. In practice, the typicality test tends to merge with the commonality test. ***Wal-Mart Stores***, ___ U.S. at ___, 131 S.Ct. at 2551 n.5; ***General Tel. Co. v. Falcon***, 457 U.S. 147, 157 n.13 (1982). As long as the proposed class representative is a member of the class and has the same interests and generally the same injury as the other class members, the representative's claims do not need to be identical to the claims of the rest of the putative class. ***General Tel.***, 457 U.S. at 156; *see* ***De La Fuente v. Stokely-Van Camp, Inc.***, 713 F.2d 225, 232 (7th Cir.1983) (when claims arise from same event, practice, or course of conduct and are based on same legal theory, test may be satisfied even if there are factual distinctions between claims). The court may define multiple classes or subclasses if there are differences in class members' positions that could cause conflicts and if the class members can be placed in categories. *See* ***Eisenberg v. Gagnon***, 766 F.2d 770, 786 (3d Cir.1985); ***Kerrigan v. Philadelphia Bd. of Election***, 248 F.R.D. 470, 477 (E.D.Pa.2008).

(4) Adequacy of representation. The proposed class representative must show that it will fairly and adequately protect the interests of the class. FRCP 23(a)(4). The adequacy inquiry serves to uncover conflicts of interest between the proposed class representative and the class it seeks to represent. ***Amchem Prods.***, 521 U.S. at 625. In other words, the proposed class representative must assure the court that its interests are aligned with those of the class members. *See* ***Marcus v. Kansas Dept. of Revenue***, 206 F.R.D. 509, 512 (D.Kan.2002). The court cannot presume the adequacy of the proposed class representative; adequacy must be proved. ***Berger v. Compaq Computer Corp.***, 257 F.3d 475, 481-82 (5th Cir.2001); *see also* ***London v. Wal-Mart Stores***, 340 F.3d 1246, 1254 (11th Cir.2003) (court must carry out stringent examination of adequacy of representation by representative when class representative has close relationship with attorney and attorney fees will "far exceed" representative's recovery). To prove adequacy under FRCP 23(a)(4), the proposed class representative must show the following:

(a) Member of class. The representative is a member of the class. ***East Tex. Motor Freight Sys. v. Rodriguez***, 431 U.S. 395, 403 (1977).

(b) No conflict. The representative has the same interest as the class members and does not have a conflict of interest with the class members. *See* ***East Tex. Motor Freight***, 431 U.S. at 403; ***Sosna v. Iowa***, 419 U.S. 393, 403 (1975); ***Ward v. Dixie Nat'l Life Ins.***, 595 F.3d 164, 179-80 (4th Cir.2010); ***Rutter & Wilbanks Corp. v. Shell Oil Co.***, 314 F.3d 1180, 1187-88 (10th Cir.2002); ***Mullen v. Treasure Chest Casino, L.L.C.***, 186 F.3d 620, 625-26 (5th Cir.1999); ***Hanlon v. Chrysler Corp.***, 150 F.3d 1011, 1020 (9th Cir.1998); 1 Rubenstein et al., *Newberg on Class Actions* §3:58. If there is a conflict of interest related to the specific issues being litigated, the proposed

class representative cannot adequately represent the class. ***Warren v. City of Tampa***, 693 F.Supp. 1051, 1061 (M.D. Fla.1988), *aff'd*, 893 F.2d 347 (11th Cir.1989) (table case); *see* ***Randall v. Rolls-Royce Corp.***, 637 F.3d 818, 824 (7th Cir.2011). The conflict of interest must be fundamental, not merely speculative or hypothetical. ***Ward***, 595 F.3d at 180.

(c) Same injury. The representative suffered generally the same injury as the class members. ***East Tex. Motor Freight***, 431 U.S. at 403.

(d) Competent counsel. The representative has competent counsel. ***Amchem Prods.***, 521 U.S. at 626 n.20; *see* FRCP 23(g); ***Mullen***, 186 F.3d at 625; 1 Rubenstein et al., *Newberg on Class Actions* §3:72. FRCP 23(g)(1) establishes both mandatory and discretionary criteria for determining whether the proposed class counsel is competent.

[1] Mandatory criteria. The court must consider the following criteria: (1) the work that counsel has done in identifying or investigating potential claims in the action, (2) counsel's experience in handling class actions, complex litigation, and the types of claims asserted in the action, (3) counsel's knowledge of the applicable law, and (4) the resources that counsel will commit to representing the class. FRCP 23(g)(1)(A); ***Sheinberg v. Sorensen***, 606 F.3d 130, 132 (3d Cir.2010).

[2] Discretionary criteria. The court may consider any other matter pertinent to counsel's ability to fairly and adequately represent the interests of the class. FRCP 23(g)(1)(B); ***Sheinberg***, 606 F.3d at 132-33. For example, the representative's counsel should not have any conflicts of interest with the class members. *See* ***Amchem Prods.***, 521 U.S. at 626 n.20.

2. FRCP 23(b) categories. In addition to the four requirements of FRCP 23(a), a class action must also satisfy the requirements of one of the three categories under FRCP 23(b). ***Wal-Mart Stores***, ___ U.S. at ___, 131 S.Ct. at 2548.

(1) FRCP 23(b)(1) class action. A class action is permitted if the prosecution of separate suits would create one of the following two risks:

(a) Inconsistent or varying adjudications for individual class members. FRCP 23(b)(1)(A); ***Amchem Prods.***, 521 U.S. at 614.

(b) Adjudications for individual class members that (1) would as a practical matter be dispositive of the interests of the other members who are not parties to the suits or (2) would substantially impair or impede the other members' ability to protect their interests. FRCP 23(b)(1)(B); ***Amchem Prods.***, 521 U.S. at 614. This is also known as the "limited fund" theory. Under this theory, the movant must show that the "fund" available to satisfy all the liquidated claims is inadequate and that the class must be certified to allow for an equitable, pro rata distribution of the entire fund to plaintiffs who have liquidated claims based on a common theory of liability. *See* ***Ortiz***, 527 U.S. at 838-41; ***In re Katrina Canal Breaches Litig.***, 628 F.3d 185, 192-93 (5th Cir.2010); ***Zinser v. Accufix Research Inst.***, 253 F.3d 1180, 1196-97 (9th Cir.2001), *amended*, 273 F.3d 1266 (9th Cir.2001).

NOTE

The lower courts disagree on the standard in mass-tort cases for determining whether a fund is in fact limited. ***Ortiz****, 527 U.S. at 848 n.26; see* ***In re Bendectin Prods. Liab. Litig.****, 749 F.2d 300, 306 (6th Cir.1984). Compare* ***In re Dalkon Shield IUD Prods. Liab. Litig.****, 693 F.2d 847, 852 (9th Cir.1982) (class proponents must demonstrate that allowing adjudication of individual claims will "inescapably compromise" claims of absent class members), with* ***In re "Agent Orange" Prod. Liab. Litig.****, 100 F.R.D. 718, 726 (E.D.N.Y.1983) (requiring only "substantial probability—that is, less than a preponderance but more than a mere possibility—that if damages are awarded, the claims of earlier litigants would exhaust the defendants' assets"), aff'd, 818 F.2d 145 (2d Cir.1987).*

(2) FRCP 23(b)(2) class action. A class action is permitted if the defendant has acted or refused to act on grounds generally applicable to the class, such that injunctive or declaratory relief is appropriate for the entire class. FRCP 23(b)(2); ***Wal-Mart Stores***, ___ U.S. at ___, 131 S.Ct. at 2557; ***M.D.***, 675 F.3d at 845; ***Williams***, 568 F.3d at 1359; *see also* ***DG v. Devaughn***, 594 F.3d 1188, 1199-1200 (10th Cir.2010) (class-wide injunctive relief must satisfy FRCP 65(d)(1) elements).

(a) Defendant's conduct. The defendant's conduct does not need to have injured all class members in exactly the same way—it is enough if the defendant has adopted a pattern of activity that is likely to affect all class members similarly. ***Rodriguez v. Hayes***, 591 F.3d 1105, 1125 (9th Cir.2010); ***Baby Neal v. Casey***, 43 F.3d 48, 63-64 (3d Cir.1994).

(b) Injunctive or declaratory relief. A class is appropriate only when a single injunction or declaratory judgment would provide relief to each member of the class. ***Wal-Mart Stores***, ___ U.S. at ___, 131 S.Ct. at 2557; ***Gates v. Rohm & Haas Co.***, 655 F.3d 255, 263-64 (3d Cir.2011). Thus, class certification under FRCP 23(b)(2) is inappropriate if each class member would be entitled to a different injunction or declaratory judgment. ***Wal-Mart Stores***, ___ U.S. at ___, 131 S.Ct. at 2557. If the relief sought involves individualized monetary damages, class certification is also inappropriate. *Id.*

NOTE

Some courts have held that monetary damages can be awarded under FRCP 23(b)(2) if they are merely "incidental" to the claims for injunctive or declaratory relief. ***Randall****, 637 F.3d at 825;* ***Williams****, 568 F.3d at 1359; see* ***Allison v. Citgo Pet. Corp.****, 151 F.3d 402, 415 (5th Cir.1998) (monetary damages are incidental when they flow directly from liability to class as a whole on claims that form basis of injunctive or declaratory relief). But in* ***Wal-Mart Stores v. Dukes****, the Supreme Court declined to answer whether there are any forms of incidental monetary relief that are consistent with FRCP 23(b)(2) and the Due Process Clause.* ***Wal-Mart Stores****, ___ U.S. at ___, 131 S.Ct. at 2560; see* ***Ellis v. Costco Wholesale Corp.****, 657 F.3d 970, 986 (9th Cir. 2011). The Court held that when individualized monetary damages are involved, certification should proceed under FRCP 23(b)(3).* ***Wal-Mart Stores****, ___ U.S. at ___, 131 S.Ct. at 2558. See "FRCP 23(b)(3) class action," §2.4.2(3), this page.*

(3) FRCP 23(b)(3) class action. A class action is permitted if two criteria are met: (1) common questions of law or fact predominate over individual issues and (2) a class action is superior to other available methods for fairly and efficiently adjudicating the controversy. FRCP 23(b)(3); ***Amchem Prods.***, 521 U.S. at 615; ***United Steel, Paper & Forestry, Rubber, Mfg. Energy, Allied Indus. & Serv. Workers Int'l Union v. ConocoPhillips Co.***, 593 F.3d 802, 807 (9th Cir.2010); ***In re New Motor Vehicles Canadian Exp. Antitrust Litig.***, 522 F.3d 6, 18 (1st Cir.2008). FRCP 23(b)(3) sets out four nonexhaustive factors for the court to consider when determining whether a case meets these criteria: (1) the class members' interest in individually controlling the prosecution or defense of separate actions, (2) the extent and nature of any litigation on the controversy already begun by or against class members, (3) the desirability or undesirability of concentrating the litigation of the claims in the particular forum, and (4) the likely difficulties in managing a class action. FRCP 23(b)(3); ***Amchem Prods.***, 521 U.S. at 615-16.

§2.5 Proposed order. Some districts require the movant to submit a proposed order with the motion for class certification. In those districts, the movant should prepare a written order for the court's signature and submit it with the motion. See "Proposed order," ch. 1-B, §3.1.11, p. 16.

§3. RESPONSE

§3.1 Considerations before filing.

1. Is class treatment preferable? A defendant presented with a motion for class certification should first consider whether class treatment of the claims being asserted is preferable. In some cases, certification of a class may actually be advantageous because res judicata binds class members—that is, the class action enables the

defendant to dispose of all related litigation against it in a single action. *See* ***Randall v. Rolls-Royce Corp.***, 637 F.3d 818, 820-21 (7th Cir.2011). In other cases, such as when the potential class members have numerous small claims that would not justify bringing individual suits, the defendant should probably oppose class certification.

2. Can certification be used to defendant's advantage? In some cases, a defendant can use the certification process strategically to define the size and shape of the class to its advantage. *See* Hensler et al., *Class Action Dilemmas*, at 484-85. For example, the defendant can persuade the court to certify a class consisting only of members who have claims that would be individually viable, and excluding members whose claims are so small they would likely not sue separately.

§3.2 Opposing the motion. If the defendant believes that a class action is inappropriate or that it should be restricted to certain issues or classes, the defendant should respond to the plaintiff's allegations by arguing that the FRCP 23 requirements are not met. *See* Partridge & Miller, *Some Practical Considerations for Defending & Settling Products Liability & Consumer Class Actions*, 74 Tul.L.Rev. at 2133. See "Grounds," §2.4, p. 399.

§4. PRECERTIFICATION DISCOVERY & INTERIM COUNSEL

§4.1 Discovery. The court may allow discovery and conduct hearings on the issue of class certification, as well as decide whether discovery on the merits should proceed, before determining whether to certify the class. *See* ***Washington v. Brown & Williamson Tobacco Corp.***, 959 F.2d 1566, 1570-71 (11th Cir.1992); ***Sirota v. Solitron Devices, Inc.***, 673 F.2d 566, 571-72 (2d Cir.1982); ***Stewart v. Winter***, 669 F.2d 328, 331 (5th Cir.1982); 2003 Notes to FRCP 23 at ¶48, p. 1168, this book; *Manual for Complex Litigation, Fourth*, §21.14; *see also* ***Blair v. Equifax Check Servs.***, 181 F.3d 832, 835 (7th Cir.1999) (disputes about class certification cannot be separated from the merits). In most cases, a certain amount of discovery is necessary because the party must make a preliminary exploration of some of the elements contained in the allegations so the court can determine if the prerequisites of class certification are present. *See* ***Pittman v. E.I. duPont de Nemours & Co.***, 552 F.2d 149, 150 (5th Cir.1977); ***Blackie v. Barrack***, 524 F.2d 891, 901 n.17 (9th Cir.1975). The discovery should be limited to information required to identify the nature of the issues that will be presented at trial; the discovery should not entail an evaluation of the probable outcome on the merits. 2003 Notes to FRCP 23 at ¶3, p. 1164, this book; *see* ***Madison v. Chalmette Ref., L.L.C.***, 637 F.3d 551, 554-55 (5th Cir.2011).

§4.2 Interim counsel. The court may designate interim counsel to act on behalf of the proposed class before determining whether to certify the class. FRCP 23(g)(3). The interim counsel's duties may include taking action to prepare for the certification decision (e.g., conducting discovery and making and responding to motions) and discussing settlement possibilities. 2003 Notes to FRCP 23 at ¶48, p. 1168, this book.

§5. RULING

§5.1 Hearing. A hearing is not required under FRCP 23, but most courts hold one because of the significance of class certification. *See Manual for Complex Litigation, Fourth*, §21.21.

§5.2 Analysis. The court must perform a rigorous analysis to determine whether the FRCP 23 requirements have been met. ***Wal-Mart Stores v. Dukes***, ___ U.S. ___, 131 S.Ct. 2541, 2551-52 (2011); ***Madison v. Chalmette Ref., L.L.C.***, 637 F.3d 551, 554 (5th Cir.2011). This analysis will often require the court to look beyond the pleadings and inquire into—and make a preliminary resolution of—disputed factual issues, even if those facts are relevant to the ultimate merits of the case. ***Wal-Mart Stores***, ___ U.S. at ___, 131 S.Ct. at 2551-52; *see* ***Madison***, 637 F.3d at 554-55 (while class-certification hearing should not be minitrial, court must understand claims, defenses, relevant facts, and applicable substantive law to make meaningful determination of certification issues). The court may look to the record and any completed discovery to make the certification decision. *See* ***Castano v. American Tobacco Co.***, 84 F.3d 734, 744 (5th Cir.1996). If the court is not satisfied that the FRCP 23 requirements have been met, it should refuse certification until they are. ***Oscar Private Equity Invs. v. Allegiance Telecom, Inc.***, 487 F.3d 261, 267 (5th Cir.2007); 2003 Notes to FRCP 23 at ¶6, p. 1164, this book.

NOTE

When an expert's report or testimony is critical to determining class certification, the court must rule on any challenges to the expert before making the certification decision. ***American Honda Motor Co. v. Allen****, 600 F.3d 813, 815-16 (7th Cir.2010); see* ***Wal-Mart Stores****, ___ U.S. at ___, 131 S.Ct. at 2553-54 (dicta; questioning district court's assessment that* ***Daubert*** *does not apply at certification stage); see also* ***In re Zurn Pex Plumbing Prods. Liab. Litig.****, 644 F.3d 604, 612 & n.5 (8th Cir.2011) (district court should apply* ***Daubert*** *by conducting "tailored" inquiry into expert reliability based on evidence available at certification stage). See "Motion to Exclude Expert Witness," ch. 5-N, p. 376.*

§5.3 Deadline. The court should make its class-certification determination at an "early practicable time" after a person sues or is sued as a class representative. FRCP 23(c)(1)(A); *see* 2003 Notes to FRCP 23 at ¶2, p. 1164, this book. This standard is intended to be more lenient than the former "as soon as practicable" standard and allow for circumstances that may justify deferring the certification decision until after a thorough evaluation of the FRCP 23 factors. *See* ***In re Hydrogen Peroxide Antitrust Litig.***, 552 F.3d 305, 318-19 (3d Cir.2008); ***In re New Motor Vehicles Canadian Exp. Antitrust Litig.***, 522 F.3d 6, 26-27 (1st Cir.2008); 2003 Notes to FRCP 23 at ¶2, p. 1164, this book. Circumstances that may delay the court's ruling include the following:

1. Discovery. The time needed to gather information necessary to make the certification decision may delay the court's ruling. *See* 2003 Notes to FRCP 23 at ¶3, p. 1164, this book. See "Discovery," §4.1, p. 403.

2. Designation of class counsel. The time needed to explore designating class counsel under FRCP 23(g) may delay the court's ruling. *See* 2003 Notes to FRCP 23 at ¶4, p. 1164, this book.

3. Dismissal or summary judgment. The time taken by a defendant in attempting to obtain a dismissal of the plaintiff's complaint or a summary judgment may delay the court's ruling. 2003 Notes to FRCP 23 at ¶4, p. 1164, this book.

§5.4 Order. If the court grants the motion, the court (1) must issue a written order certifying the class and appointing class counsel, (2) may direct notice of certification to the proposed class members, and (3) may make other appropriate orders. *See* FRCP 23(c)(1)(B), (c)(2), (d).

1. Order certifying class & appointing class counsel.

(1) Certifying class. The court must issue an order that defines the class and the class claims, issues, or defenses. FRCP 23(c)(1)(B); ***Ross v. RBS Citizens***, 667 F.3d 900, 905 (7th Cir.2012), *cert. filed*, ___ S.Ct. ___ (2012) (No. 12-165; 8-1-12); ***In re Pharmaceutical Indus. Average Wholesale Price Litig.***, 588 F.3d 24, 39 (1st Cir.2009).

(a) Classes & subclasses. The court may define multiple classes or subclasses if there are differences in class members' positions that could cause conflicts. FRCP 23(c)(5); ***In re Insurance Brokerage Antitrust Litig.***, 579 F.3d 241, 271 (3d Cir.2009).

(b) Particular issues. The court may limit the certification to particular issues. FRCP 23(c)(4); *see* ***Robinson v. Metro-N. Commuter R.R.***, 267 F.3d 147, 167 (2d Cir.2001) (courts should take full advantage of this provision to reduce range of disputed issues in complex litigation and to achieve judicial efficiency); *see, e.g.*, ***Jenkins v. Raymark Indus.***, 782 F.2d 468, 471-72 (5th Cir.1986) (class certified to determine viability of "state of the art" defense).

(2) Appointing class counsel. In the order certifying the class, the court must appoint class counsel. FRCP 23(c)(1)(B). An attorney appointed to serve as class counsel must fairly and adequately represent the interests of the class. FRCP 23(g)(4).

(a) Appointment criteria. Before making an appointment, the court must consider the criteria in FRCP 23(g)(1). For a list of the criteria, see "Competent counsel," §2.4.1(4)(d), p. 401.

(b) Single & multiple applicants. If there is only one applicant for appointment as class counsel, the court may appoint that applicant only if the applicant satisfies the requirements of FRCP 23(g)(1) and (g)(4). FRCP 23(g)(2); ***Sheinberg v. Sorensen***, 606 F.3d 130, 133 (3d Cir.2010). If there are multiple adequate applicants seeking approval, the court must appoint the applicant best able to represent the interests of the class. FRCP 23(g)(2); ***Sheinberg***, 606 F.3d at 133.

(c) Contents of order. In addition to the name of the attorney appointed as class counsel, the appointment order may include any of the following:

[1] A directive to class counsel to provide the court with information pertinent to the appointment. FRCP 23(g)(1)(C).

[2] Provisions for the award of attorney fees and nontaxable costs under FRCP 23(h). FRCP 23(g)(1)(D).

[3] Any further orders in connection with the appointment. FRCP 23(g)(1)(E).

2. Notice of certification. Once the court has certified a class, notice of certification may need to be sent to the proposed class members.

NOTE

Generally, the plaintiff must initially bear the cost of notice to the class. ***Eisen v. Carlisle & Jacquelin****, 417 U.S. 156, 178 (1974);* ***Hunt v. Imperial Merch. Servs.****, 560 F.3d 1137, 1143 (9th Cir.2009). In certain circumstances, however, a court may shift the cost of notification to the defendant. E.g.,* ***Hunt****, 560 F.3d at 1143-44 (court shifted notification costs to D after Ps' partial summary judgment on liability was granted).*

(1) Class certified under FRCP 23(b)(1) or (b)(2). For a class certified under FRCP 23(b)(1) or (b)(2), the court may, but is not required to, send appropriate notice to the class. FRCP 23(c)(2)(A).

(2) Class certified under FRCP 23(b)(3). For a class certified under FRCP 23(b)(3), the court must send to the class members the best notice practicable under the circumstances, including individual notice to all members who can be identified through reasonable effort. FRCP 23(c)(2)(B). The notice must concisely state the following in easily understood language:

(a) The nature of the action. FRCP 23(c)(2)(B)(i).

(b) The definition of the class certified. FRCP 23(c)(2)(B)(ii).

(c) The class claims, issues, or defenses. FRCP 23(c)(2)(B)(iii).

(d) That a class member may appear through an attorney. FRCP 23(c)(2)(B)(iv).

(e) That the court will exclude from the class any member who requests exclusion. FRCP 23(c)(2)(B)(v).

(f) The time and manner for requesting exclusion. FRCP 23(c)(2)(B)(vi).

(g) The binding effect of a class judgment on class members under FRCP 23(c)(3). FRCP 23(c)(2)(B)(vii).

NOTE

The Federal Judicial Center has developed several illustrative notices of proposed class-action certification. The notices are designed to show how attorneys and judges can comply with the "plain, easily understood language" requirement of FRCP 23(c)(2)(B). For copies of these notices, visit the Federal Judicial Center's website at www.fjc.gov.

3. Other orders. In addition to the certification and appointment order and the notice order, the court may make any of the orders listed below. The orders may be combined with an FRCP 16 pretrial order and may be altered or amended. FRCP 23(d)(2).

(1) Judicial economy. The court may make orders that determine the course of proceedings or prescribe measures to prevent undue repetition or complication in presenting evidence or argument. FRCP 23(d)(1)(A).

(2) Notice. To protect class members and fairly conduct the class action, the court may issue orders requiring that appropriate notice be given to some or all of the class members. FRCP 23(d)(1)(B). The orders may direct notice of the following:

(a) Any step in the action. FRCP 23(d)(1)(B)(i).

(b) The proposed extent of the judgment. FRCP 23(d)(1)(B)(ii).

(c) The members' opportunity to signify whether they consider the representation fair and adequate. FRCP 23(d)(1)(B)(iii).

(d) The members' opportunity to intervene and present claims or defenses or otherwise come into the action. *Id.*

(3) Class representatives & intervenors. The court may issue orders imposing conditions on the representative parties or on intervenors. FRCP 23(d)(1)(C).

(4) Pleadings. The court may issue orders requiring the pleadings to be amended to eliminate allegations about the representation of absent persons. FRCP 23(d)(1)(D).

(5) Procedural matters. The court may issue orders dealing with procedural matters. FRCP 23(d)(1)(E).

§5.5 Altering or amending order. The court's order may be altered or amended before final judgment. FRCP 23(c)(1)(C); *see also* ***Prado-Steiman v. Bush***, 221 F.3d 1266, 1274 (11th Cir.2000) (emphasizing importance of court's ability to fine-tune its class-certification order); ***Waste Mgmt. Holdings, Inc. v. Mowbray***, 208 F.3d 288, 294 (1st Cir.2000) (same). The concept of "final judgment" is not the same as that used for appeal purposes, but instead should be flexible, particularly in protracted litigation. 2003 Notes to FRCP 23 at ¶6, p. 1164, this book. See "Final judgments," ch. 9-A, §3.1, p. 737. For example, under FRCP 23(c)(1)(C), a court may amend the class definition or subdivide the class after a finding of liability but before a determination of damages. *See* 2003 Notes to FRCP 23 at ¶6, p. 1164, this book.

§6. APPELLATE REVIEW

§6.1 Appealability. An order granting or denying class certification can be appealed. FRCP 23(f); ***Richardson Elecs., Ltd. v. Panache Broad., Inc.***, 202 F.3d 957, 957 (7th Cir.2000). FRCP 23(f) permits appeal only on the issue of class certification; no other issues can be raised. ***McKowan Lowe & Co. v. Jasmine, Ltd.***, 295 F.3d 380, 390 (3d Cir.2002); ***Bertulli v. Independent Ass'n of Cont'l Pilots***, 242 F.3d 290, 294 (5th Cir.2001). A court may, however, review a legal or factual issue that addresses the merits of the case if the issue also involves the merits of the class certification. *See* ***Regents of Univ. of Cal. v. Credit Suisse First Boston (USA), Inc.***, 482 F.3d 372, 380 (5th Cir. 2007).

1. Deadline.

(1) Generally. The appeal must be made within 14 days after the order granting or denying class certification is entered. FRCP 23(f); ***Fleischman v. Albany Med. Ctr.***, 639 F.3d 28, 30 (2d Cir.2011); *see also* ***Richardson Elecs.***, 202 F.3d at 958 (although FRCP 23(f) deadline does not apply if district judge grants permission for immediate appeal under 28 U.S.C. §1292(b), appellate court may refuse application as "inexcusably dilatory"; applying former ten-day deadline). A party cannot extend the 14-day deadline by making another motion for class certification. *See* ***Asher v. Baxter Int'l***, 505 F.3d 736, 739 (7th Cir.2007) (applying former ten-day deadline).

(2) Exceptions.

(a) Motion to reconsider – within 14 days. If a party files a motion for reconsideration within 14 days after the order granting or denying class certification is issued, the 14-day deadline to appeal may be postponed until the court rules on the motion. *See* ***McNair v. Synapse Grp.***, 672 F.3d 213, 222 n.8 (3d Cir.2012); ***In re DC Water & Sewer Auth.***, 561 F.3d 494, 495-96 (D.C.Cir.2009) (applying former ten-day deadline); ***Gutierrez v. Johnson & Johnson***, 523 F.3d 187, 193 (3d Cir.2008) (same); ***McNamara v. Felderhof***, 410 F.3d 277, 281 (5th Cir. 2005) (same).

(b) Material alteration of certification order. An order that materially alters an earlier order granting or denying class certification may be appealable under FRCP 23(f). *E.g.*, ***Matz v. Household Int'l Tax Reduction Inv. Plan***, 687 F.3d 824, 825-26 (7th Cir.2012) (appellate court had jurisdiction over appeal from district-court order that partially decertified class); *see* ***Gary v. Sheahan***, 188 F.3d 891, 893 (7th Cir.1999).

2. No stay unless ordered. The interlocutory appeal does not stay proceedings in the district court unless the district judge or the circuit court orders a stay. FRCP 23(f); ***Bacon v. Stiefel Labs.***, 837 F.Supp.2d 1280, 1282 (S.D.Fla.2011); *see* ***Blair v. Equifax Check Servs.***, 181 F.3d 832, 835 (7th Cir.1999) (stays of pending FRCP 23(f) appeals should not be routinely granted).

3. Standard for determining appealability. The circuit court is given "unfettered discretion" in deciding whether to permit the appeal and may base its decision on "any consideration that the court of appeals finds persuasive." ***Vallario v. Vandehey***, 554 F.3d 1259, 1262 (10th Cir.2009); ***Gutierrez***, 523 F.3d at 192; 1998 Notes to FRCP 23 at ¶¶1, 3, pp. 1170, 1171, this book. The circuits that have decided the issue differ on the precise formulation of the standard for reviewing requests to appeal class-certification orders.

(1) 7th Circuit. The Seventh Circuit has held that an appeal should be permitted (1) when denial of class status effectively ends the case (i.e., a "death-knell" situation), (2) when the grant of class status raises the stakes of the litigation so substantially that the defendant will likely feel irresistible pressure to settle (i.e., the opposite of a "death-knell" situation), and (3) when the appeal will lead to clarification of a fundamental issue of law. ***Blair***, 181 F.3d at 834-35. An appeal under the first two categories must also show that the district court's ruling on class certification is questionable; under the third category, the court's focus is on the importance of the issue to be resolved. *Id.* at 835.

(2) 1st & 2d Circuits. The First and Second Circuits have agreed with much of ***Blair***'s analysis, but with one important caveat. The First Circuit has emphasized that "interlocutory appeals should be the exception, not the rule" and has held that the third category should be restricted "to those instances in which an appeal will permit the resolution of an unsettled legal issue that is important to the particular litigation as well as important in itself and likely to escape effective review if left hanging until the end of the case." ***Waste Mgmt. Holdings, Inc. v. Mowbray***, 208 F.3d 288, 294 (1st Cir.2000); *see also* ***In re Sumitomo Copper Litig.***, 262 F.3d 134, 139-40 (2d Cir. 2001) (indicating approval of approach in ***Mowbray***).

(3) 3d, 4th & 11th Circuits. In ***Prado-Steiman v. Bush***, 221 F.3d 1266, 1276 (11th Cir.2000), the Eleventh Circuit added two nonexhaustive factors to the ***Mowbray*** analysis: (1) the nature and status of the litigation before the district court and (2) the likelihood that future events may make immediate appellate review more or less appropriate. *See* ***Lienhart v. Dryvit Sys.***, 255 F.3d 138, 145-46 (4th Cir.2001) (adopting ***Prado-Steiman*** test). Following the Eleventh and Fourth Circuits' decisions, the Third Circuit identified four categories of cases in which FRCP 23(f) would be appropriate: the three established by the Seventh Circuit in ***Blair*** and by the advisory committee's note, plus the Eleventh and Fourth Circuits' inclusion of a category of likely erroneous class-certification decisions. ***Newton v. Merrill Lynch, Pierce, Fenner & Smith, Inc.***, 259 F.3d 154, 164 (3d Cir.2001).

(4) 9th, 10th & D.C. Circuits. The Ninth, Tenth, and D.C. Circuits have held that interlocutory appeal is appropriate when (1) there is a "death-knell" situation—that is, a questionable class-certification order is likely to force a party to resolve the case based on considerations independent of the merits, (2) the certification de-

cision presents an unsettled and fundamental issue of law relating to class actions that is important both to the specific litigation and in general and is likely to evade end-of-the-case review, or (3) the district court's class-certification decision is manifestly erroneous. ***Vallario***, 554 F.3d at 1263-64; ***Chamberlan v. Ford Motor Co.***, 402 F.3d 952, 959 (9th Cir.2005); ***In re Lorazepam & Clorazepate Antitrust Litig.***, 289 F.3d 98, 99-100 (D.C.Cir.2002). The Tenth and D.C. Circuits may also grant interlocutory review in "special circumstances," although such review is intended to be rare. ***Vallario***, 554 F.3d at 1264; ***In re Veneman***, 309 F.3d 789, 794 (D.C.Cir.2002).

§6.2 Standard of review. District courts have broad power and discretion in certifying and managing class actions. *See* ***Reiter v. Sonotone Corp.***, 442 U.S. 330, 345 (1979); ***Maldonado v. Ochsner Clinic Found.***, 493 F.3d 521, 523 (5th Cir.2007); ***Kern v. Siemens Corp.***, 393 F.3d 120, 123-24 (2d Cir.2004); ***Staton v. Boeing Co.***, 327 F.3d 938, 953 (9th Cir.2003); ***Coleman v. General Motors Acceptance Corp.***, 296 F.3d 443, 446 (6th Cir.2002); ***Rutstein v. Avis Rent-A-Car Sys.***, 211 F.3d 1228, 1233 (11th Cir.2000). The court's ruling on a class certification is reviewed for abuse of discretion. ***In re New Motor Vehicles Canadian Exp. Antitrust Litig.***, 522 F.3d 6, 17 (1st Cir.2008); ***Regents of Univ. of Cal. v. Credit Suisse First Boston (USA), Inc.***, 482 F.3d 372, 380 (5th Cir.2007); *see* ***In re Salomon Analyst Metromedia Litig.***, 544 F.3d 474, 480 (2d Cir.2008) (granting of class certification is given more deference than denial of certification). The court's application of legal standards used in ruling on class certification is reviewed de novo. ***Regents of Univ. of Cal.***, 482 F.3d at 380; ***In re Nassau Cty. Strip Search Cases***, 461 F.3d 219, 224 (2d Cir.2006). However, because it is improper for a district court to certify a class action without first demonstrating that the plaintiff has satisfied each of the FRCP 23 requirements, an order that certifies a class without any findings of fact, legal analysis, or reference to the requirements will typically be vacated. *See* ***Narouz v. Charter Comms.***, 591 F.3d 1261, 1266 (9th Cir.2010); ***Vizena v. Union Pac. R.R.***, 360 F.3d 496, 503 (5th Cir.2004).

COMMENTARIES
CHAPTER 6. DISCOVERY
TABLE OF CONTENTS

A. GENERAL RULES FOR DISCOVERY 413
§1. GENERAL 413
§2. METHODS OF DISCOVERY 413
§2.1 Mandatory disclosures 415
§2.2 Deposition 415
§2.3 Deposition by written questions 415
§2.4 Interrogatories 415
§2.5 Request for admissions 415
§2.6 Request for production 415
§2.7 Motion for physical or mental examination 416
§2.8 Request for entry on land 416
§3. PRESERVATION 416
§4. FRCP 26(f) CONFERENCE 416
§4.1 When required 416
§4.2 Meet & confer 416
§4.3 Deadline for conference 416
§4.4 Objectives of conference 416
§4.5 Written report of discovery plan 418
§4.6 Scheduling order 419
§5. MODIFYING DISCOVERY PROCEDURES & LIMITS 419
§5.1 Modifying discovery by stipulation 419
§5.2 Modifying discovery by court order 420
§5.3 Modifying discovery by local rule or standing order 420
§6. DISCOVERY CERTIFICATES 420
§6.1 Disclosures 420
§6.2 Requests, responses, or objections 420
§6.3 Failure to sign 420
§6.4 Improper certification 420
§7. OBTAINING DISCOVERY 421
§7.1 When discovery begins 421
§7.2 How to obtain discovery 421
§8. RESPONDING TO DISCOVERY 422
§8.1 Deadline to respond 422
§8.2 Producing written discovery 423
§8.3 Resisting discovery 424
§9. WAIVER OF DISCOVERY, OBJECTIONS & PRIVILEGES 429
§9.1 Waiver of discovery 429
§9.2 Waiver of objections & privileges – before disclosure 429
§9.3 Waiver of privilege or protection – by disclosure 430
§10. FILING DISCOVERY 438
§10.1 Discovery to be filed 438
§10.2 Discovery not to be filed 438
§10.3 Exceptions 438
§11. SUPPLEMENTING DISCOVERY 438
§11.1 Supplementation required 438
§11.2 Supplementation not required 439
§11.3 Types of discovery requiring supplementation 439
§11.4 Time to supplement 439
§11.5 In writing & signed 439
§11.6 Failure to supplement disclosures 439
§11.7 Failure to supplement discovery responses 440
§12. MOTION FOR PROTECTIVE ORDER 440
§12.1 Power to protect 440
§12.2 Time to file motion 441
§12.3 Grounds 441
§12.4 Certificate of conference 442
§12.5 Order 442
§13. MOTION TO QUASH SUBPOENA 444
§14. MOTION TO COMPEL DISCOVERY 444
§14.1 Proper court 444
§14.2 Time to file motion 444
§14.3 Grounds 444
§14.4 Certificate of conference 445
§14.5 Order 445
§14.6 Standard of review 446
§15. MOTION FOR DISCOVERY SANCTIONS 446
§15.1 Purposes of sanctions 446
§15.2 Due-process concerns 446
§15.3 Grounds 446
§15.4 Certificate of conference 448
§15.5 Sanctions available 448
§15.6 Order 454
§16. REVIEW OF DISCOVERY ORDERS 454
§16.1 Review by appeal 454
§16.2 Review by mandamus 455

B. SCOPE OF DISCOVERY 456
§1. GENERAL 456
§2. WHAT IS DISCOVERABLE? 457
§2.1 General scope of discovery 457
§2.2 Types of discoverable information 458
§3. WHAT IS NOT DISCOVERABLE? 460
§3.1 Irrelevant information 460
§3.2 Privileged & protected information – generally 460
§3.3 Attorney-client privilege 463
§3.4 Work-product protection 467
§3.5 Privilege against self-incrimination 471
§3.6 Psychotherapist-patient privilege 472
§3.7 Clergy-communicant privilege 474
§3.8 Journalist's privilege 475
§3.9 Government privileges 476
§3.10 Trade-secret protection 480
§3.11 Spousal privileges 481
§3.12 Settlement-negotiations privilege 481

C. ELECTRONIC DISCOVERY 481
§1. GENERAL 481
§2. WHAT IS ESI? 482
§3. DIFFERENCES BETWEEN ESI & CONVENTIONAL DISCOVERY 483
§3.1 Volume 483
§3.2 Location 483
§3.3 Format 483
§3.4 Indestructibility 483
§3.5 Dimensions 483
§3.6 Dynamic nature 483
§4. PREPARING FOR ELECTRONIC DISCOVERY 483
§4.1 Understanding electronic discovery 483
§4.2 Preservation 486
§4.3 Waiver of privilege 490
§4.4 Costs 490
§5. ESI SEARCH TECHNIQUES 490
§5.1 Keyword searches 491
§5.2 Predictive coding 491
§5.3 Targeted searches 493
§5.4 Testing & sampling 493
§5.5 Other restrictions 493
§6. SCOPE OF ESI DISCOVERY 493
§6.1 ESI is reasonably accessible 493
§6.2 ESI is not reasonably accessible 494
§7. FRCP 26(f) CONFERENCE 495
§7.1 Responsibilities – before FRCP 26(f) conference 496
§7.2 Discussion topics – at FRCP 26(f) conference 496
§7.3 Discovery report – after FRCP 26(f) conference 498

COMMENTARIES
CHAPTER 6. DISCOVERY
TABLE OF CONTENTS

§8. FRCP 16 CONFERENCE & ORDER 498
§9. ESI & SPECIFIC TYPES OF DISCOVERY 498
§9.1 Initial disclosures 498
§9.2 Depositions 499
§9.3 Interrogatories 499
§9.4 Requests for admissions 499
§9.5 Requests for production 500
§10. DISCOVERY FROM NONPARTIES 505
§11. RESOLVING ESI DISPUTES 505
§11.1 Motion for protective order 505
§11.2 Motion to compel 510
§12. SANCTIONS FOR LOST ESI 513
§12.1 Avoiding sanctions – good-faith defense 514
§12.2 Types of sanctions available 515

D. SECURING DISCOVERY FROM EXPERTS 515

§1. GENERAL 515
§2. TYPES OF EXPERTS 516
§3. TESTIFYING EXPERTS 516
§3.1 Retained 516
§3.2 Nonretained 522
§4. CONSULTING EXPERTS 525
§4.1 Retained 525
§4.2 Nonretained 527
§5. SUPPLEMENTING EXPERT DISCOVERY 527
§5.1 Supplementing retained-expert discovery 528
§5.2 Supplementing nonretained-expert discovery 528
§6. DEADLINES FOR SECURING DISCOVERY FROM EXPERTS 528
§6.1 Deadlines to disclose testifying experts 528
§6.2 Deadlines to depose testifying experts 528
§6.3 Deadlines to supplement 528
§7. EXPERT'S REPORT 529
§7.1 Form of report 529
§7.2 Contents of report 529
§8. PAYING THE EXPERT 530
§8.1 Who must pay 530
§8.2 How much must be paid 530
§8.3 When payment is made 532
§8.4 Review 532

E. MANDATORY DISCLOSURES 532

§1. GENERAL 532
§2. STAGES OF DISCLOSURES 532
§2.1 Initial disclosures 532
§2.2 Expert disclosures 532
§2.3 Final pretrial disclosures 532
§3. FORM OF DISCLOSURES 532
§3.1 In writing & served 532
§3.2 Signed 532
§3.3 No filing 533
§4. INITIAL DISCLOSURES 533
§4.1 Deadline 533
§4.2 Contents 533
§4.3 No excuses 534
§4.4 Modification of initial-disclosures requirement 534
§4.5 Proceedings exempt from initial disclosures 534
§5. EXPERT DISCLOSURES 534
§5.1 Procedure 534
§5.2 Contents 535
§6. FINAL PRETRIAL DISCLOSURES 536
§6.1 Deadline 536
§6.2 Contents 536
§6.3 Objections to pretrial disclosures 537
§7. SANCTIONS 537
§7.1 Barring evidence 537
§7.2 Other sanctions 538

F. DEPOSITIONS 538

§1. GENERAL 538
§2. TYPES OF DEPOSITIONS 538
§2.1 Oral deposition 538
§2.2 Deposition by written questions 538
§2.3 Deposition to perpetuate testimony 538
§3. PROCEDURE FOR ORAL DEPOSITION 538
§3.1 Deposition of any person 538
§3.2 Notice of oral deposition 540
§3.3 Taking deposition before authorized officer 544
§3.4 Attendance at deposition 545
§3.5 Modifying deposition procedure 546
§3.6 Examination & cross-examination 546
§3.7 Exhibits 548
§3.8 Officer's certification 548
§3.9 Terminating or limiting deposition 548
§3.10 Reviewing & changing deposition transcript 549
§3.11 Signing deposition 550
§3.12 Sending deposition to attorney 551
§3.13 Officer retains notes or copy 551
§4. USING DEPOSITION IN COURT PROCEEDINGS 551
§4.1 Filing & notice 551
§4.2 General use 551
§4.3 Restrictions on use 552
§4.4 Waiver of errors & irregularities 553
§4.5 Form of presentation 553
§4.6 Objections to admissibility 554
§5. DEPOSITION BY WRITTEN QUESTIONS 554
§5.1 Deposition of any person 554
§5.2 Notice of deposition by written questions 554
§5.3 Cross-questions 555
§5.4 Redirect questions 555
§5.5 Recross-questions 555
§5.6 Objections to questions 555
§5.7 Procedure for deposition by written questions 555
§5.8 Notify parties after deposition 555
§6. DEPOSITION TO PERPETUATE TESTIMONY 555
§6.1 Deposition before suit is filed 555
§6.2 Deposition pending appeal 557
§6.3 Not exclusive 557

G. INTERROGATORIES 557

§1. GENERAL 557
§2. INTERROGATORIES 557
§2.1 Serve on party 557
§2.2 Time to serve 558

COMMENTARIES
CHAPTER 6. DISCOVERY
TABLE OF CONTENTS

§2.3 No filing....558
§2.4 Number of interrogatories....558
§2.5 Scope....558
§2.6 Standard interrogatories....558
§3. RESPONDING TO INTERROGATORIES....559
§3.1 Deadline....559
§3.2 Who must answer....560
§3.3 Form of answers....560
§3.4 Option to produce business records....561
§3.5 Time to supplement answers....561
§3.6 No filing....561
§4. OBJECTING TO INTERROGATORIES....562
§4.1 When to serve....562
§4.2 Specificity....562
§4.3 Signature....562
§4.4 Timeliness....562
§4.5 No objections....562
§4.6 Deferral....562
§5. SANCTIONS....562
§5.1 Motion to compel....562
§5.2 Motion for sanctions....562
§6. USING INTERROGATORIES....563
§6.1 Trial....563
§6.2 Summary judgment....563

H. REQUESTS FOR ADMISSIONS....563
§1. GENERAL....563
§2. REQUESTS FOR ADMISSIONS....564
§2.1 Serve on party....564
§2.2 Time to serve....564
§2.3 No filing....564
§2.4 Number of requests....564
§2.5 Form....564
§2.6 Scope....564
§3. RESPONDING TO REQUESTS....564
§3.1 Deadline....564
§3.2 Changing deadline to respond....564
§3.3 No filing....565
§3.4 Response must be signed....565
§3.5 Contents of response....565
§4. CHALLENGING SUFFICIENCY OF RESPONSE....565
§4.1 Motion....566
§4.2 Order....566
§5. FAILURE TO TIMELY RESPOND – DEEMED ADMISSIONS....566
§6. SETTING ASIDE DEEMED ADMISSIONS....566
§6.1 Procedure for setting aside admissions....567
§6.2 Permitting late answers....567
§7. SANCTIONS....567
§8. USING ADMISSIONS....568
§8.1 Effect of admissions....568
§8.2 By whom & against whom....568
§8.3 No denials....568
§8.4 No contradictory proof....568
§8.5 Summary judgment....569
§8.6 Trial....569
§8.7 Pending suit only....569
§9. APPELLATE REVIEW....569
§9.1 Standard on appeal....569
§9.2 No mandamus....569

I. REQUESTS FOR PRODUCTION....569
§1. GENERAL....569
§2. REQUEST VS. SUBPOENA....569
§2.1 From party....569
§2.2 From nonparty....569
§3. MAKING REQUESTS....570
§3.1 Time to serve....570
§3.2 No filing....570
§3.3 Number of requests & sets....570
§3.4 Request....570
§4. RESPONDING TO REQUESTS....572
§4.1 Deadline....572
§4.2 Changing deadline to respond....572
§4.3 Response....572
§4.4 Production....573
§4.5 Supplementing or amending responses....573
§5. MOTION TO COMPEL....574
§6. MOTION FOR SANCTIONS....574

J. PHYSICAL & MENTAL EXAMINATIONS OF PERSONS....574
§1. GENERAL....574
§2. MOTION TO EXAMINE PERSON....574
§2.1 Examinee....574
§2.2 Motion....575
§2.3 Response....576
§2.4 Examiner....577
§2.5 Hearing not required....577
§2.6 Sanctions....577
§2.7 Presence of other persons or recording devices....577
§3. EXAMINER'S REPORT....577
§3.1 Report....577
§3.2 Waiver of privilege....578
§3.3 Examinations by agreement....578
§3.4 Other discovery methods not prohibited....578

K. REQUEST FOR ENTRY ON LAND....579
§1. GENERAL....579
§2. REQUEST FOR ENTRY....579
§2.1 Time to serve....579
§2.2 Scope of request....579
§2.3 Form of request....579
§2.4 Subpoena for nonparty....579
§2.5 No filing....579
§3. RESPONDING TO REQUEST....579
§3.1 Response to request....579
§3.2 Response to subpoena....580
§3.3 Objections to request....580
§4. CHALLENGING RESPONSE....580
§5. APPELLATE REVIEW....580

COMMENTARIES

CHAPTER 6. DISCOVERY

6. DISCOVERY

A. GENERAL RULES FOR DISCOVERY

§1. GENERAL

§1.1 Rules. FRCP 26-37, 45.

§1.2 Purpose. Modern discovery—the pretrial disclosure of facts, documents, and other information relevant to the lawsuit—serves many purposes: • To avoid prejudicial surprise. ***Brown Badgett, Inc. v. Jennings***, 842 F.2d 899, 902 (6th Cir.1988). • To narrow the parties' theories of liability and defense. ***O2 Micro Int'l v. Monolithic Power Sys.***, 467 F.3d 1355, 1365 (Fed.Cir.2006); *see* ***Nutt v. Black Hills Stage Lines, Inc.***, 452 F.2d 480, 483 (8th Cir.1971). • To give all parties full knowledge of the facts so they can prepare for trial. ***Gary Plastic Packaging Corp. v. Merrill Lynch, Pierce, Fenner & Smith, Inc.***, 756 F.2d 230, 236 (2d Cir.1985); *see* ***O2 Micro Int'l***, 467 F.3d at 1365; ***Computer Task Grp. v. Brotby***, 364 F.3d 1112, 1117 (9th Cir.2004); ***Pro-Football, Inc. v. Harjo***, 191 F.Supp.2d 77, 80 (D.D.C.2002). • To prevent delays at trial and conserve scarce judicial resources. ***Burns v. Thiokol Chem. Corp.***, 483 F.2d 300, 304 (5th Cir.1973); *see also* ***Mancia v. Mayflower Textile Servs.***, 253 F.R.D. 354, 357-58 (D.Md.2008) (discovery also requires that attorneys cooperate to identify and fulfill legitimate discovery needs and avoid costs and burdens disproportionate to what is at stake in litigation).

§1.3 Timetable & forms. Timetable, Discovery Status Sheet, p. 1579; ***O'Connor's Federal Civil Forms*** (2012) for each specific type of discovery: disclosures, FORMS 6E; depositions, FORMS 6F; interrogatories, FORMS 6G; requests for admissions, FORMS 6H; requests for production, FORMS 6I; motions to examine persons, FORMS 6J; and requests for entry on land, FORMS 6K.

§1.4 Other references. 8, 8A, 8B Wright, Miller & Marcus, *Federal Practice & Procedure 3d* §§2001-2293 (2010 & Supp.2012); 23 Wright & Graham, *Federal Practice & Procedure* §5442 (1980 & Supp.2012); 6, 7 *Moore's Federal Practice 3d* §§26.01-26.155, 37.90-37.121 (2012).

PRACTICE TIP

Before engaging in discovery, prepare a draft of the jury charge based on all the pleadings. Only when you know what questions the jury will be asked can you design an intelligent discovery plan.

---

§2. METHODS OF DISCOVERY

The discovery rules provide the permissible methods for obtaining information from parties and nonparties. *See* FRCP 26-36, 45. However, the parties can use discovery methods (e.g., interviews of witnesses or other informal discovery) besides those provided in the rules. *See, e.g.*, ***Los Angeles News Serv. v. CBS Broad., Inc.***, 305 F.3d 924, 932-33 (9th Cir.2002) (P was entitled to conduct its own fact-finding; request for videotape from third-party television station was not formal discovery under FRCPs), *amended*, 313 F.3d 1093 (9th Cir.2002). Unless the court orders otherwise, the methods of discovery can be used in any sequence, and discovery by one party does not require any other party to delay its own discovery. FRCP 26(d)(2). Chart 6-1, below, compares the available methods of discovery; each is discussed in detail later in the chapter.

COMMENTARIES
CHAPTER 6. DISCOVERY
A. GENERAL RULES FOR DISCOVERY

6-1. METHODS OF DISCOVERY

	Type of discovery	Need court order?	Discovery signed by	Under oath?	Failure to respond	Discussed at
Party Discovery						
1	Deposition	No	Party (if requested)	Yes	Possible sanctions	ch. 6-F, §3, p. 538
2	Deposition before lawsuit	Yes	Party (if requested)	Yes	Possible sanctions	ch. 6-F, §6, p. 555
3	Interrogatories	No	Party (attorney signs objections)	Yes	Waive objections and possible sanctions	ch. 6-G, p. 557
4	Request for admissions	No	Party or attorney	No	Deemed admissions and possible sanctions	ch. 6-H, p. 563
5	Request to produce documents, electronically stored information, and tangible things	No	Attorney	No	Waive objections and possible sanctions	ch. 6-I, p. 569
6	Deposition by written questions	No	Party (if requested)	Yes	Possible sanctions	ch. 6-F, §5, p. 554
7	Motion for physical or mental examination	Yes	Attorney	No	Waive objections and possible sanctions	ch. 6-J, p. 574
8	Request for entry on land	No	Attorney	No	Waive objections and possible sanctions	ch. 6-K, p. 579
9	FRCP 26(a)(1) disclosures	No	Attorney	No	Possible sanctions	ch. 6-E, §4, p. 533
10	FRCP 26(a)(2)(A) disclosures identifying testifying experts	No	Attorney	No	Possible sanctions	ch. 6-E, §5.2.1, p. 535
11	FRCP 26(a)(2)(B) expert reports from retained testifying experts	No	Witness	No	Possible sanctions	ch. 6-E, §5.2.2(1), p. 535
12	FRCP 26(a)(2)(C) disclosures about nonretained testifying experts	No	Attorney	No	Possible sanctions	ch. 6-E, §5.2.2(2), p. 536
13	FRCP 26(a)(3) disclosures	No	Attorney	No	Possible sanctions	ch. 6-E, §6, p. 536
Nonparty Discovery						
14	Deposition	No, just subpoena	Witness (if requested)	Yes	Possible contempt	ch. 6-F, §3, p. 538
15	Deposition before lawsuit	Yes, and subpoena	Witness (if requested)	Yes	Possible contempt	ch. 6-F, §6, p. 555
16	Deposition by written questions	No, just subpoena	Witness (if requested)	Yes	Possible contempt	ch. 6-F, §5, p. 554

6-1. Methods of Discovery (continued)

	Type of discovery	Need court order?	Discovery signed by	Under oath?	Failure to respond	Discussed at
Nonparty Discovery (continued)						
17	Request to produce documents, electronically stored information, and tangible things	No, just subpoena	Witness (if requested)	No	Waive objections and possible contempt	ch. 1-H, §5, p. 52; ch. 6-C, §10, p. 505
18	Request for entry on land	No, just subpoena	Witness (if requested)	No	Waive objections and possible contempt	ch. 6-K, p. 579
19	Deposition of witness in prison	Yes	Witness (if requested)	Yes	Possible contempt	ch. 6-F, §3.1.2(5), p. 539

§2.1 Mandatory disclosures. Mandatory disclosures allow a party to obtain specific types of information from another party without a discovery request. *See* FRCP 26(a)(1)(A). Mandatory disclosures accelerate the exchange of basic information about the case and eliminate the paperwork involved in requesting the information. 1993 Notes to FRCP 26 at ¶2, p. 1182, this book. See "Mandatory Disclosures," ch. 6-E, p. 532.

§2.2 Deposition. An oral deposition allows a party to take the testimony of any person, whether a party or not, under oath before trial. *See* FRCP 30. Depositions are expensive and time-consuming and should ordinarily be used only after a party is familiar with the facts of the case. Oral depositions are a good way to probe the depth of a witness's knowledge about the case. The number of oral and written depositions is limited to ten per side, but this limit can be increased by leave of court or by stipulation of the parties. FRCP 26(b)(2)(A), 30(a)(2)(A)(i); *see* 8A Wright, Miller & Marcus §§2104, 2132 (depositions by written questions under FRCP 31 are counted against limit). A deposition is limited to seven hours in one day, unless extended by stipulation or court order. FRCP 30(d)(1). See "Oral deposition," ch. 6-F, §2.1, p. 538.

§2.3 Deposition by written questions. A deposition by written questions allows a party to present written questions to a witness, who then answers orally under oath. *See* FRCP 31. Depositions by written questions can be used to acquire information from any person, whether a party or not. These depositions are ordinarily used to obtain records from a nonparty and authenticate them, usually as business records. Depositions by written questions are included with oral depositions in the ten-deposition limit of FRCP 30 and 31, but this limit can be increased by leave of court or by stipulation of the parties. FRCP 26(b)(2)(A), 31(a)(2)(A)(i). See "Deposition by written questions," ch. 6-F, §2.2, p. 538.

§2.4 Interrogatories. Interrogatories are written questions used to acquire information from another party. *See* FRCP 33. The other party must answer the interrogatories in writing and under oath. FRCP 33(b)(1), (b)(3). Interrogatories are a relatively inexpensive form of discovery and are normally used to narrow the issues and identify witnesses who should be deposed. The number of questions a party can submit is limited to 25, but this limit can be increased by leave of court or by stipulation of the parties. FRCP 26(b)(2)(A), 33(a)(1). See "Interrogatories," ch. 6-G, p. 557.

§2.5 Request for admissions. A party may request that another party admit the truth of any relevant, nonprivileged matter. FRCP 36(a). Requests for admissions may refer to factual matters, ultimate legal issues, or the genuineness of documents. FRCP 36(a)(1). Requests for admissions are often used to narrow the issues for trial. FRCP 36 does not limit the number of requests for admissions, but a court can impose a limit by order or local rule. FRCP 26(b)(2)(A). See "Requests for Admissions," ch. 6-H, p. 563.

§2.6 Request for production. A party may request the production of documents, electronically stored information, and tangible things in another party's possession, custody, or control. FRCP 34(a)(1). The request must describe with "reasonable particularity" each item or category of items requested. FRCP 34(b)(1)(A). A nonparty may

be required to produce documents, electronically stored information, and tangible things through service of a subpoena. FRCP 45(a)(1)(A)(iii). See "Requests for production," ch. 6-C, §9.5, p. 500; "Requests for Production," ch. 6-I, p. 569.

§2.7 Motion for physical or mental examination. A party may ask the court for an order requiring another party or someone in the other party's custody or legal control to submit to a physical or mental examination, but only when the person's physical or mental condition is in dispute. FRCP 35(a)(1). See "Physical & Mental Examinations of Persons," ch. 6-J, p. 574.

§2.8 Request for entry on land. A party may request permission to enter land or other property possessed or controlled by another party to inspect, measure, survey, photograph, test, or sample the land or anything on it. FRCP 34(a)(2). A party may seek entry and inspection of land owned by a nonparty through service of a subpoena. FRCP 45(a)(1)(A)(iii). See "Request for Entry on Land," ch. 6-K, p. 579.

§3. PRESERVATION

To prepare for discovery, a party should take steps to ensure that all relevant evidence—including documents, electronically stored information, and tangible things—is preserved. See "Preservation plan," §4.4.4, p. 417; "Preservation," ch. 6-C, §4.2, p. 486.

§4. FRCP 26(f) CONFERENCE

An FRCP 26(f) conference expedites the disposition of the case by exploring the possibility of settlement and planning for discovery.

§4.1 When required. FRCP 26(f) conferences are required for all civil cases except those that are exempt from initial disclosures under FRCP 26(a)(1)(B) or by court order. FRCP 26(f)(1). For a list of cases exempt under FRCP 26(a)(1)(B), see "Proceedings exempt from initial disclosures," ch. 6-E, §4.5, p. 534.

§4.2 Meet & confer. The parties and their attorneys must confer and formulate a plan for conducting discovery, including electronic discovery. FRCP 26(f)(2); *see* ***Beecham v. Socialist People's Libyan Arab Jamahiriya***, 424 F.3d 1109, 1111 (D.C.Cir.2005). See "FRCP 26(f) Conference," ch. 6-C, §7, p. 495. Although the parties and their attorneys are not required to meet face-to-face, the court can order any of them to attend an FRCP 26(f) conference in person. FRCP 26(f)(2); 2000 Notes to FRCP 26 at ¶32, p. 1181, this book; *see, e.g.*, ***Warfield v. AlliedSignal TBS Holdings, Inc.***, 267 F.3d 538, 543 (6th Cir.2001) (attorneys conducted FRCP 26(f) conference by telephone).

§4.3 Deadline for conference. The deadline for the FRCP 26(f) conference depends on whether an FRCP 16(b) scheduling (case-management) conference will be held. *See* FRCP 26(f)(1). The deadline can be modified by a court order. *See* FRCP 26(f)(1). See "Case-Management Conference & Discovery Plan," ch. 5-A, §2, p. 289.

1. Scheduling conference to be held.

(1) 21-day deadline. The parties must hold an FRCP 26(f) conference as soon as possible, but no later than 21 days before a scheduling conference is held or a scheduling order is due under FRCP 16(b). FRCP 26(f)(1).

(2) Expedited deadline. If the court has adopted an expedited schedule for the FRCP 16(b) scheduling conference, the court may by local rule require the FRCP 26(f) conference to occur less than 21 days before the scheduling conference is held or the scheduling order is due. FRCP 26(f)(4).

2. No scheduling conference to be held. If no scheduling conference is held, the FRCP 26(f) conference ordinarily must be held within 75 days after a defendant first appears in the case. 1993 Notes to FRCP 26 at ¶12, p. 1183, this book.

§4.4 Objectives of conference. The parties must do the following at the FRCP 26(f) conference:

1. Claims & defenses. The parties must discuss the nature of their claims and defenses, and the grounds for them. FRCP 26(f)(2).

2. Settlement. The parties must discuss the possibilities for promptly settling or resolving the case. FRCP 26(f)(2).

3. FRCP 26(a)(1) disclosures. The parties must make or arrange for the disclosures required by FRCP 26(a)(1). FRCP 26(f)(2). The parties should also discuss what other information can be made available informally, without the need for discovery requests. 1993 Notes to FRCP 26 at ¶49, p. 1187, this book.

4. Preservation plan. The parties must discuss any issues relating to preserving discoverable information. FRCP 26(f)(2); 2006 Notes to FRCP 26 at ¶22, p. 1177, this book. This provision encourages the parties to anticipate and address preservation-of-evidence issues early in the discovery process to avoid uncertainty about what information must be preserved and to reduce the risk of future disputes. *See* 2006 Notes to FRCP 26 at ¶¶22, 23, p. 1177, this book; *see, e.g.*, ***Danis v. USN Comms.***, No. 98 C 7482 (N.D.Ill.2000) (no pub.; 10-23-00) (D was sanctioned for not implementing clear procedures and standards concerning preservation of electronically stored information and for not ensuring that procedures and standards were disseminated and followed). Although this provision applies to any type of discoverable information, it is particularly important for electronically stored information—the volume and dynamic nature of this information can complicate preservation obligations. 2006 Notes to FRCP 26 at ¶22, p. 1177, this book (ordinary operation of computers involves both automatic creation and automatic deletion or overwriting of certain information); *see, e.g.*, ***Antioch Co. v. Scrapbook Borders, Inc.***, 210 F.R.D. 645, 651-52 (D.Minn.2002) (court granted P's motion to appoint neutral expert in computer forensics based in part on expert's affidavit stating that data deleted from computer is retained on hard drive but is constantly being overwritten by new data through normal use of computer). See "Preservation," ch. 6-C, §4.2, p. 486.

PRACTICE TIP

A party who anticipates litigation might consider using a preservation letter to remind potential parties and witnesses of their duty to preserve evidence, including electronically stored information, that may be relevant to the potential case. See "Preservation letter," ch. 2-A, §2.2, p. 73.

5. Discovery plan. The parties must develop a proposed discovery plan. FRCP 26(f)(2). The plan should include proposals on the following:

(1) Initial disclosures. The plan should include any changes to the timing, form, or requirement for disclosures under FRCP 26(a), including a statement of when the initial disclosures were made or will be made. FRCP 26(f)(3)(A).

(2) Scope of discovery. The plan should identify all subjects on which discovery may be needed, the date when the discovery should be completed, and whether discovery should be limited to or focused on certain issues. FRCP 26(f)(3)(B); *see* FRCP Form 52, p. 998, this book.

(3) Electronically stored information. The plan should address any issues about disclosure or discovery of electronically stored information, including the form or forms in which it should be produced. FRCP 26(f)(3)(C); 2006 Notes to FRCP 26 at ¶21, p. 1176, this book. The parties' proposal should include such topics as what types of information will be produced, how searches for the information will be conducted (e.g., by names of individuals or business organizations, date ranges, or specific search terms), and the various forms in which the information can be produced (e.g., in print, native electronic format, or both). *See Summary of the Report of the Judicial Conference*, Agenda E-18, at Rules App. C-24 (parties should discuss disclosure and discovery issues to avoid future disputes before costly and time-consuming searches and production occur). See "Discussion topics – at FRCP 26(f) conference," ch. 6-C, §7.2, p. 496; "Requests for production," ch. 6-C, §9.5, p. 500.

(4) Asserting claims of privilege & protection. The plan should address any issues about claims of privilege or protection of trial-preparation material, including whether to ask the court to include in an order any agreement on a procedure for asserting claims after material has been produced. FRCP 26(f)(3)(D); *see* FRCP

16(b)(3)(B)(iv); *see also* 2008 Explanatory Note on FRE 502 at ¶¶15, 16, pp. 1254, 1255, this book (party agreements can limit prohibitive costs of privilege and protection review); 2006 Notes to FRCP 16 at ¶¶2, 3, p. 1158, this book (same). The protection of trial-preparation material includes attorney-client privilege and work-product protection. *Summary of the Report of the Judicial Conference: Committee on Rules of Practice & Procedure*, Agenda E-18, at Rules App. C-25 (Sept. 2005), www.uscourts.gov/uscourts/RulesAndPolicies/rules/Reports/ST09-2005.pdf. Given the extensive amount of time and money that can be spent reviewing large volumes of data for privilege or protection—particularly electronically stored information—FRCP 26(f) encourages the parties to develop a plan that reduces the producing party's time and cost for privilege review and speeds up the requesting party's access to the materials. *See* 2006 Notes to FRCP 26 at ¶¶25, 28, p. 1177, this book; *Summary of the Report of the Judicial Conference*, Agenda E-18, at Rules App. C-25. Generally, the parties' agreement will control if they adopt a procedure different from that specified in FRCP 26(b)(5)(B), and a party who receives privileged information that is inadvertently disclosed under such an agreement cannot assert waiver of the privilege or protection claim. 2006 Notes to FRCP 16 at ¶2, p. 1158, this book; 2006 Notes to FRCP 26 at ¶14, p. 1176, this book; *see* FRE 502(e); 2008 Explanatory Note on FRE 502 at ¶19, p. 1255, this book. If the parties want the agreement to be binding on nonparties and in other state and federal proceedings, the agreement must be incorporated into a court order. *See* FRE 502(d), (e); 2008 Explanatory Note on FRE 502 at ¶¶16, 19, p. 1255, this book. See "Limits on waiver," §9.3.2(5), p. 437. Types of agreements include the following:

(a) Quick-peek agreement. To facilitate discovery, the parties can make a "quick-peek" agreement. 2006 Notes to FRCP 26 at ¶27, p. 1177, this book; *see* 2008 Explanatory Note on FRE 502 at ¶16, p. 1255, this book. Under this type of agreement, the responding party provides information to the requesting party without waiving any claims of privilege, the requesting party reviews the information and designates specific material for production, and the responding party conducts its privilege review of only those specified documents. 2006 Notes to FRCP 16 at ¶2, p. 1158, this book; 2006 Notes to FRCP 26 at ¶27, p. 1177, this book.

(b) Clawback agreement. To facilitate discovery, the parties can make a "clawback" agreement. 2006 Notes to FRCP 26 at ¶27, p. 1177, this book; *see* 2008 Explanatory Note on FRE 502 at ¶16, p. 1255, this book. Under this type of agreement, if privileged or protected material is produced, the responding party can, with timely notice, assert the claim and have the material returned without waiving the claim. 2006 Notes to FRCP 16 at ¶2, p. 1158, this book; 2006 Notes to FRCP 26 at ¶27, p. 1177, this book; *see* ***Rajala v. McGuire Woods, LLP***, No. 08-2638-CM-DJW (D.Kan.2010) (slip op.; 7-22-10) (clawback provisions essentially "undo" document production).

(5) Discovery limits. The plan should identify any discovery limits that should be set or amended. FRCP 26(f)(3)(E). A party can object in the discovery plan that initial disclosures are not appropriate in the case. FRCP 26(a)(1)(C).

(6) Other orders. The plan should request any other orders the court should issue under FRCP 26(c), 16(b), or 16(c). FRCP 26(f)(3)(F); *see, e.g.*, ***In re Atlantic Pipe Corp.***, 304 F.3d 135, 146 (1st Cir.2002) (court has power under FRCP 26(f) to issue pretrial cost-sharing orders for mediation in complex litigation).

§4.5 Written report of discovery plan. The parties must submit a written report outlining the proposed discovery plan. FRCP 26(f)(2).

1. Deadline.

(1) 14-day deadline. The parties must submit the report to the court within 14 days after the parties' FRCP 26(f) conference. FRCP 26(f)(2).

(2) Expedited deadline. If the court has adopted an expedited schedule for the FRCP 16(b) scheduling conference, the court may by local rule require the written report to be filed less than 14 days after the parties' FRCP 26(f) conference or excuse the parties from submitting a written report and permit them to report orally on the discovery plan at the scheduling conference. FRCP 26(f)(4)(B).

2. Contents. The parties can use FRCP Form 52 for guidance in preparing the report. FRCP Form 52, p. 998, this book. See ***O'Connor's Federal Forms***, FORM 6A:1. The parties must state their views and proposals

on the items listed in FRCP 26(f)(3). See "Discovery plan," §4.4.5, p. 417. Local rules may provide a form for the report that requires additional content. *See, e.g.*, Joint Discovery/Case Management Plan Under Rule 26(f) Federal Rules of Civil Procedure (S.D.Tex.).

§4.6 Scheduling order. The court can include the parties' agreements in the scheduling order. FRCP 16(b)(3)(B)(iv). See "Contents of order," ch. 5-A, §3.3, p. 289.

§5. MODIFYING DISCOVERY PROCEDURES & LIMITS

The 2000 amendments to FRCP 26 were primarily intended to restore national uniformity to disclosure practice and other areas of discovery procedure, such as case-management conferences, depositions, and interrogatory requests. *See* 2000 Notes to FRCP 26 at ¶6, p. 1178, this book. Thus, most of the opt-out language in the former rule was eliminated. *See id.* at ¶¶6, 7, p. 1178, this book. The discovery rules maintain some flexibility, however, allowing parties to modify discovery procedures and limits by stipulation and allowing courts to control discovery by case-specific court orders, by local rules, or by standing orders. Chart 6-2, below, summarizes the various ways that discovery procedures and limits can be modified.

6-2. MODIFYING DISCOVERY PROCEDURES & LIMITS

	Type of discovery	Can be modified by—				FRCP
		Stipulation?	Case order?	Local rule?	Standing order?	
1	Timing of FRCP 26(f) conference and discovery plan	No	Yes	Yes	No	26(f); 2000 Notes to FRCP 26 at ¶¶31, 32, p. 1181, this book
2	Disclosures	Yes	Yes	No	No	26(a)(1); 2000 Notes to FRCP 26 at ¶7, p. 1178, this book
3	Deposition	Yes	Yes	No	No	26(b)(2)(A); 2000 Notes to FRCP 26 at ¶29, p. 1181, this book
4	Deposition by written questions	Yes	Yes	No	No	26(b)(2)(A); 2000 Notes to FRCP 26 at ¶29, p. 1181, this book
5	Interrogatories	Yes	Yes	No	No	26(b)(2)(A); 2000 Notes to FRCP 26 at ¶29, p. 1181, this book
6	Request for production	Yes	Yes	Yes	Yes	34(b); *see* 2000 Notes to FRCP 26 at ¶29, p. 1181, this book
7	Request for admissions	Yes	Yes	Yes	Yes	26(b)(2)(A), 36(a); 2000 Notes to FRCP 26 at ¶29, p. 1181, this book
8	Request for entry on land	Yes	Yes	Yes	Yes	34(b); *see* 2000 Notes to FRCP 26 at ¶29, p. 1181, this book

§5.1 Modifying discovery by stipulation. The parties may agree to modify discovery procedures and limits if the FRCPs do not specifically prohibit the modification. *See* FRCP 29(b) (modification must have court approval if it

would interfere with time set for completing discovery); 2000 Notes to FRCP 26 at ¶29, p. 1181, this book (limits can be modified by agreement). To compare what the parties can change by agreement and what the court can change by case-specific order, local rule, or standing order, see chart 6-2, above.

1. In writing. To be enforceable, the stipulation must be in writing. ***Petrucelli v. Bohringer & Ratzinger, GmbH***, 46 F.3d 1298, 1310-11 (3d Cir.1995); ***Angell v. Shawmut Bank Conn.***, 153 F.R.D. 585, 590 n.5 (M.D. N.C.1994); *see* FRCP 29. See "Agreements Between Attorneys or Parties," ch. 1-I, §7, p. 67. Oral agreements modifying discovery are not binding on the parties. ***Smith v. Conway Org.***, 154 F.R.D. 73, 76 (S.D.N.Y.1994).

2. Court approval. Some stipulations require court approval. Stipulations extending the deadline for responses to interrogatories, requests for production, and requests for admissions must be approved by the court if the extension will interfere with the time set for completing discovery, for hearing a motion, or for trial. FRCP 29(b); ***Rogerson v. Xidex Corp.***, 110 F.R.D. 412, 413 (D.Mass.1986). See "Modifying time to respond," §8.1.2, p. 422.

§5.2 Modifying discovery by court order. The court can modify discovery procedures and limits by case-specific orders. FRCP 26(b)(2)(A), (d); 2000 Notes to FRCP 26 at ¶¶7, 29, pp. 1178, 1181, this book. See chart 6-2, above.

§5.3 Modifying discovery by local rule or standing order. The court cannot use local rules or standing orders to modify the presumptive limit on the number and length of depositions and the number of interrogatories. 2000 Notes to FRCP 26 at ¶29, p. 1181, this book; *see* FRCP 26(b)(2)(A). Other forms of discovery, such as requests for admissions, can be modified by local rule or standing order. *See* 2000 Notes to FRCP 26 at ¶29, p. 1181, this book (FRCP 26(b)(2) was amended to remove permission for local rules to establish different presumptive limits for depositions and interrogatories only). See chart 6-2, above.

§6. DISCOVERY CERTIFICATES

All written discovery—including disclosures, requests, responses, and objections—must be signed by the attorney or pro se party, but expert reports under FRCP 26(a)(2)(B) must be signed by the expert witness. FRCP 26(a)(2)(B), (g)(1); ***Legault v. Zambarano***, 105 F.3d 24, 27 (1st Cir.1997). If signed by an attorney, the signature must be in the attorney's own name (not the name of a law firm) and must state the attorney's address, e-mail address, and telephone number. FRCP 26(g)(1). If signed by a pro se party, the signature must be in the party's name and must state the party's address, e-mail address, and telephone number. *Id.*

§6.1 Disclosures. By signing a disclosure, an attorney or pro se party certifies that, to the best of the signer's knowledge, information, and belief formed after a reasonable inquiry, the disclosure is complete and correct at the time it is made. FRCP 26(g)(1)(A); ***Mancia v. Mayflower Textile Servs.***, 253 F.R.D. 354, 357 (D.Md.2008).

§6.2 Requests, responses, or objections. By signing discovery materials, an attorney or pro se party certifies that, to the best of the signer's knowledge, information, and belief formed after a reasonable inquiry, the request, response, or objection (1) is consistent with the FRCPs and warranted by existing law or by a nonfrivolous argument for extending, modifying, or reversing existing law, or for establishing new law, (2) is not made for any improper purpose, such as to harass, cause unnecessary delay, or needlessly increase the cost of litigation, and (3) is neither unreasonable nor unduly burdensome or expensive, considering the needs of the case, previous discovery, the amount in controversy, and the importance of the issues at stake. FRCP 26(g)(1)(B); ***Mancia v. Mayflower Textile Servs.***, 253 F.R.D. 354, 357 (D.Md.2008).

§6.3 Failure to sign. Unsigned disclosures, requests, responses, and objections will be struck unless remedied by signature as soon as the omission is called to the attention of the party who served them unsigned. FRCP 26(g)(2). A party who receives an unsigned request is not required to respond to it. *Id.*

§6.4 Improper certification. A party can be sanctioned for improperly certifying discovery. See "Not properly certifying under FRCP 26(g)," §15.3.8, p. 448.

§7. OBTAINING DISCOVERY

§7.1 When discovery begins. Discovery usually begins after the plaintiff has filed suit, the defendant has answered, and the parties have completed the FRCP 26(f) conference. *See* FRCP 26(d)(1). However, discovery can begin earlier in some instances.

1. Before suit. A party can obtain discovery before suit by filing a verified petition asking the court's permission to perpetuate the testimony of certain persons by deposition. *See* FRCP 27; *see also* ***In re I-35W Bridge Collapse Site Inspection***, 243 F.R.D. 349, 351-52 (D.Minn.2007) (FRCP 27 may allow for presuit discovery beyond depositions). See "Deposition to Perpetuate Testimony," ch. 6-F, §6, p. 555.

2. Before FRCP 26(f) conference. A party can obtain discovery before the case-management conference by court order. *See* ***Yokohama Tire Corp. v. Dealers Tire Sup.***, 202 F.R.D. 612, 613-14 (D.Ariz.2001).

NOTE

Courts apply different standards to determine whether expedited discovery should be permitted; the standard may be good cause, reasonableness, or an inquiry similar to that for a preliminary injunction. See ***Momenta Pharms. v. Teva Pharms. Indus.***, *765 F.Supp.2d 87, 88-89 (D.Mass. 2011);* ***Stern v. Cosby***, *246 F.R.D. 453, 457 (S.D.N.Y.2007);* ***Sheridan v. Oak St. Mortg., LLC***, *244 F.R.D. 520, 521-22 (E.D.Wis.2007). See "Grounds for Injunctive Relief," ch. 2-D, §2, p. 94. Because of the varying standards, check the law of the relevant district or circuit when requesting expedited discovery.*

3. Proceedings with no discovery restrictions. Several types of proceedings usually do not require much discovery and thus have no restrictions on when discovery can begin. *See* FRCP 26(a)(1)(B); 2000 Notes to FRCP 26 at ¶15, p. 1179, this book. See "Proceedings exempt from initial disclosures," ch. 6-E, §4.5, p. 534.

§7.2 How to obtain discovery.

1. By disclosure. Parties can obtain certain information by disclosure throughout the course of the litigation without having to make a discovery request. *See* FRCP 26(a)(1)(A). See "Mandatory Disclosures," ch. 6-E, p. 532.

2. By request. Parties can obtain most discovery by request and without a motion or court order. Express court approval is not necessary to take the oral or written deposition of a party or witness, to serve interrogatories, to request admissions, to serve a request or subpoena for production of documents or tangible things, or to request entry on land or other property. FRCP 30(a)(1), 31(a)(1), 33(a)(1), 34(a), 36(a)(1); ***Holloway v. Lockhart***, 813 F.2d 874, 880 & n.3 (8th Cir.1987). See "Methods of Discovery," §2, p. 413.

3. By court order. A party must seek court approval before obtaining some forms of discovery. These include the following:

(1) Certain depositions. A party must secure a court order to take a deposition to (1) perpetuate testimony before suit is filed, (2) perpetuate testimony before the FRCP 26(f) conference, (3) take more than ten depositions, unless the parties stipulate to the additional depositions in writing, or (4) depose a person who has already been deposed in the case, unless the parties stipulate to the deposition in writing. See "Leave of court required," ch. 6-F, §3.1.2, p. 539.

(2) Examination. A party must secure a court order to obtain a physical or mental examination of a party or a person in a party's custody. FRCP 35(a)(1); ***Schlagenhauf v. Holder***, 379 U.S. 104, 115-16 (1964). See "Physical & Mental Examinations of Persons," ch. 6-J, p. 574.

4. By stipulation. The parties are encouraged to make agreements that will efficiently dispose of the case. *See* ***Angell v. Shawmut Bank Conn.***, 153 F.R.D. 585, 590 (M.D.N.C.1994). The parties can agree by stipulation on less expensive and less time-consuming methods to obtain information, such as voluntarily exchanging documents or conducting interviews instead of depositions. 1993 Notes to FRCP 29 at ¶1, p. 1196, this book. See "Modifying discovery by stipulation," §5.1, p. 419.

§8. RESPONDING TO DISCOVERY

§8.1 Deadline to respond.

1. Generally. For the rules for computing deadlines, see "Computing Deadlines," ch. 1-C, §6, p. 23.

(1) To serve response. The responding party must serve its response (answers, objections, and assertions of privilege) on the requesting party before the discovery deadline. When parties are served with requests for written discovery, the discovery request must provide at least 30 days to respond. FRCP 33(b)(2) (interrogatories), FRCP 34(b)(2)(A) (requests for production and entry on land), FRCP 36(a)(3) (requests for admissions). Depending on the type of service (mail or personal delivery), the party may have additional time to respond. See "Computing Response Deadlines," ch. 1-D, §6, p. 33.

NOTE

*It is unclear whether a pending motion for protective order excuses a party from providing a timely written response to discovery. See **Enron Corp. Sav. Plan v. Hewitt Assocs.**, 258 F.R.D. 149, 157-58 (S.D.Tex.2009). See "Motion for Protective Order," §12, p. 440. To avoid the possibility of waiving objections or claims of privilege, the better practice is to serve a timely written response to discovery even if there is a pending motion for protective order.*

(2) To disclose experts. See "Procedure," ch. 6-E, §5.1, p. 534.

2. Modifying time to respond. To extend the time to respond to discovery, a party must secure either an agreement from the other parties or a court order.

(1) Agreement. The parties can agree by stipulation to shorten or extend the time to respond, but any extension cannot interfere with the time set for completing discovery, for hearing a motion, or for trial. *See* FRCP 29(b) (parties must have court approval if modification would interfere with time for discovery), FRCP 33(b)(2) (parties can shorten or extend time to respond to interrogatories), FRCP 34(b)(2)(A) (same for requests for production or entry on land), FRCP 36(a)(3) (same for requests for admissions). Local rules may impose specific requirements on the parties' stipulation. *See, e.g.*, Local Rules Ariz., Rule 29.1 (stipulation must state reasons for extension and whether there is court-ordered discovery deadline). See "Modifying discovery by stipulation," §5.1, p. 419.

(2) Court order before deadline. Before the discovery is due, a party may ask the court to extend the time for good cause with or without motion or notice. FRCP 6(b)(1)(A); *see also* FRCP 26(c)(1)(B) (protective orders), FRCP 33(b)(2) (interrogatories), FRCP 34(b)(2)(A) (requests for production), FRCP 36(a)(3) (requests for admissions). A request for an extension is normally made by motion to create a record showing that the request was filed before the deadline to answer. *See* FRCP 6(b)(1)(A). The court's decision whether to grant an extension is discretionary. ***Lujan v. National Wildlife Fed'n***, 497 U.S. 871, 894-98 (1990). An extension normally should be granted unless the requesting party is acting in bad faith or the other party would be prejudiced. ***Bryant v. Smith***, 165 B.R. 176, 182 (Bankr.W.D.Va.1994); *see* ***Cia. Petrolera Caribe, Inc. v. Arco Caribbean, Inc.***, 754 F.2d 404, 409 (1st Cir.1985).

(3) Court order after deadline. If a party does not meet a discovery deadline because of "excusable neglect," it may file a motion requesting an extension of time for good cause. FRCP 6(b)(1)(B); *see* ***Lujan***, 497 U.S. at 896-97. The court's determination of excusable neglect is discretionary. ***Davidson v. Keenan***, 740 F.2d 129, 132 (2d Cir.1984). Although inadvertence, ignorance of the rules, and mistake usually do not suffice, excusable neglect is not limited strictly to omissions caused by circumstances beyond the movant's control. ***Pioneer Inv. Servs. v. Brunswick Assocs.***, 507 U.S. 380, 392 (1993). To obtain an extension, the movant should show that (1) the danger of prejudice to the nonmovant is not great, (2) the proceedings will not be delayed or adversely impacted, (3) the movant has a reasonable basis for the delay, and (4) the movant acted in good faith when it did not comply with the deadline. *See* ***Pioneer Inv.***, 507 U.S. at 395; ***Lewis v. Herrman's Excavating, Inc.***, 200 F.R.D. 657, 659 (D.Kan.2001);

see, e.g., ***Cornelius v. La Croix***, 631 F.Supp. 610, 622 (E.D.Wis.1986) (affidavit stating that attorney missed deadline was insufficient), *rev'd in part on other grounds*, 838 F.2d 207 (7th Cir.1988).

§8.2 Producing written discovery.

1. Form of response.

(1) In writing. The party must provide written answers to discovery requests. FRCP 33(b)(3) (interrogatories), FRCP 34(b)(2)(A) (requests for production), FRCP 36(a)(3) (requests for admissions). An answer, objection, or other response should directly follow the specific request to which it applies. *See* 7 *Moore's Federal Practice 3d* §33.101 (local rules often require responding party to first set forth each question before answering or objecting to it).

(2) Signed. Depending on the type of discovery, the responses to written discovery must be signed by the attorney, represented party, pro se party, or person making the response. See "Discovery Certificates," §6, p. 420; "Methods of Discovery," chart 6-1, p. 414. For example, answers to interrogatories must be signed by the person making them; objections to interrogatories must be signed by the attorney or pro se party making them. *See* FRCP 33(b)(5). See "Signed," ch. 6-G, §3.3.5, p. 561.

(3) Verification. Most responses to written discovery do not need to be verified. See "Methods of Discovery," chart 6-1, p. 414. However, the party must verify its answers to interrogatories. See "Verified," ch. 6-G, §3.3.4, p. 560.

2. Service on all parties. Discovery responses must be served on all parties, unless the court orders otherwise. FRCP 5(a)(1)(C); *see* 1970 Notes to FRCP 5 at ¶1, p. 1147, this book. However, the service requirement may be changed by court order if discovery responses are voluminous or the parties are numerous. 1970 Notes to FRCP 5 at ¶1, p. 1147, this book.

3. Timely. A party must timely respond to discovery requests. Discovery responses must be served within the time permitted by the rules, ordered by the court, or agreed to by the parties. See "Deadline to respond," §8.1, p. 422.

4. Discovery that must be produced. A party must produce all of the requested information unless the party serves timely objections or assertions of privilege. See "Burden to partially comply," §8.3.6, p. 428.

(1) Information relevant to claims or defenses. A party must produce information that is relevant to the claims or defenses involved in the action. FRCP 26(b)(1); *see* 2000 Notes to FRCP 26 at ¶¶10, 25, 26, pp. 1179, 1180, 1181, this book.

(2) Documents in possession. A party must produce documents in its possession, custody, or control. FRCP 34(a)(1). A party has possession, custody, or control of a document if it has either physical possession of the document or a legal right to obtain it. See "Possession, custody, or control," ch. 6-I, §3.4.2(3), p. 571.

(3) Electronically stored information that is reasonably accessible. A party must produce electronically stored information that is reasonably accessible. *See* FRCP 26(b)(2)(B); 2006 Notes to FRCP 26 at ¶5, p. 1174, this book. See "Scope of ESI Discovery," ch. 6-C, §6, p. 493.

5. Discovery not required to be produced. A party who makes a proper and timely objection or assertion of privilege does not have to produce certain information.

(1) All discovery types.

(a) Information beyond parties' claims or defenses. A party who makes a proper objection does not have to produce information in response to a discovery request seeking information beyond the scope of the parties' claims or defenses. *See* FRCP 26(b)(1); ***In re Sealed Case (Med. Records)***, 381 F.3d 1205, 1214-15 (D.C.Cir.2004). If the discovery request seeks information that is beyond the parties' claims or defenses—but that is still relevant to the subject matter of the lawsuit—a party must produce responsive information only if the court

finds good cause to permit the broader discovery. FRCP 26(b)(1); ***In re Sealed Case***, 381 F.3d at 1214-15; *see* ***Sallis v. University of Minn.***, 408 F.3d 470, 477-78 (8th Cir.2005); 2000 Notes to FRCP 26 at ¶24, p. 1180, this book.

(b) Information subject to privilege. A party who makes a proper assertion of privilege does not have to produce information that is subject to the asserted privilege. *See* FRCP 26(b)(1). See "Burden to partially comply," §8.3.6, p. 428; "Privileges recognized," ch. 6-B, §3.2.2(2), p. 461.

(c) Electronically stored information that is not reasonably accessible. A party who makes a proper objection does not have to provide electronically stored information from sources that the party identifies as not reasonably accessible because of undue burden or cost. *See* FRCP 26(b)(2)(B). See "Scope of ESI Discovery," ch. 6-C, §6, p. 493.

(2) Initial disclosures – information not reasonably available. When making initial disclosures, a party does not have to disclose information that is not reasonably available to it at the time of the disclosure. FRCP 26(a)(1)(E); *see* ***Malozienc v. Pacific Rail Servs.***, 572 F.Supp.2d 939, 943 (N.D.Ill.2008). See "No excuses," ch. 6-E, §4.3, p. 534.

(3) Requests for admissions – information insufficient. When responding to a request for admissions, a party does not have to admit or deny the request if it states that after a reasonable inquiry the current information is insufficient to enable the party to admit or deny the request. FRCP 36(a)(4).

6. Organize discovery documents. Discovery must be produced either (1) as the material is kept in the usual course of business or (2) organized and labeled to correspond with the categories in the request. FRCP 34(b)(2)(E)(i). See "Manner," ch. 6-I, §4.4.3, p. 573.

§8.3 Resisting discovery.

1. Burden to object. The party resisting discovery has the burden to plead its objections. *See* FRCP 33(b)(1), (b)(4) (interrogatories), FRCP 34(b)(2)(A), (b)(2)(C) (requests for production), FRCP 36(a)(1), (a)(5) (requests for admissions). No matter how improper the discovery request, the party to whom the request is addressed must object, or else it waives any objections. ***In re U.S.***, 864 F.2d 1153, 1156 (5th Cir.1989); *see* FRCP 33(b)(4) (interrogatories).

(1) Timely objection. The party resisting discovery must object at or before the time to respond to the discovery request, or the objection is waived. ***Marx v. Kelly, Hart & Hallman, P.C.***, 929 F.2d 8, 12 (1st Cir.1991); ***Davis v. Fendler***, 650 F.2d 1154, 1160 (9th Cir.1981); ***U.S. v. 58.16 Acres of Land***, 66 F.R.D. 570, 572 (E.D.Ill.1975).

(a) Depositions.

[1] Parties. Objections to the taking of a party's deposition must be made before the deposition. See "Time to file motion," §12.2, p. 441.

[2] Nonparties. Objections to the taking of a nonparty's deposition must be made before the time specified for compliance with the subpoena. See "Resisting Subpoena to Produce or Permit Inspection," ch. 1-H, §6, p. 53.

(b) Interrogatories. Objections to interrogatories must be made within the time allowed for the answers, ordinarily 30 days. FRCP 33(b)(2); ***Willner v. University of Kan.***, 848 F.2d 1023, 1027 (10th Cir.1988). An untimely objection is waived unless the court excuses the failure for good cause shown. FRCP 33(b)(4). *But see* ***U.S. v. Hatchett***, 862 F.2d 1249, 1252 (6th Cir.1988) (remanding for determination of whether D had reasonable fear of self-incrimination during 30-day period to answer interrogatories).

(c) Requests for admissions. Objections to requests for admissions must be made within the time allowed for a response, ordinarily 30 days. FRCP 36(a)(3). If a party does not timely object to or answer a specific request for admission, the matter will be deemed admitted. *Id.*; ***Hulsey v. Texas***, 929 F.2d 168, 171 (5th Cir. 1991). The court may allow a deemed admission to be withdrawn or amended if it will further the purposes of deciding the case on the merits and if the discovering party cannot show that withdrawal or amendment will be prejudicial

to its claim or defense. FRCP 36(b); ***Pleasant Hill Bank v. U.S.***, 60 F.R.D. 1, 3 (W.D.Mo.1973). Withdrawal or amendment may take the form of permitting a late response. *See **Gutting v. Falstaff Brewing Corp.***, 710 F.2d 1309, 1313-14 (8th Cir.1983) (courts should allow late filing if no prejudice).

(d) Requests for production.

[1] Parties. Objections to requests for production served on a party must be made within the time allowed for a response, ordinarily 30 days. FRCP 34(b)(2)(A), (b)(2)(B); *see **Poulos v. Naas Foods, Inc.***, 959 F.2d 69, 74 (7th Cir.1992); ***Marx***, 929 F.2d at 12.

[2] Nonparties. Objections to a subpoena duces tecum served on a nonparty to produce documents or tangible things must be made before the time specified for compliance or 14 days after the subpoena is served, whichever is earlier. FRCP 45(c)(2)(B). See "Resisting Subpoena to Produce or Permit Inspection," ch. 1-H, §6, p. 53.

(e) Request for entry on land. Objections to requests for entry on land must be made within the time allowed for a response, ordinarily 30 days. FRCP 34(b)(2)(A), (b)(2)(B). See "Response to request," ch. 6-K, §3.1, p. 579.

(2) Specific objection. The party objecting to discovery must state a specific objection or assert an appropriate privilege for each item it wants to exclude from discovery. *See **Panola Land Buyers Ass'n v. Shuman***, 762 F.2d 1550, 1559 (11th Cir.1985). A party cannot make a blanket objection that all documents requested are covered by a privilege. *See, e.g., **SEC v. First Fin. Grp.***, 659 F.2d 660, 668 (5th Cir.1981) (party could not make blanket assertion claiming Fifth Amendment privilege in response to request for documents).

(a) Valid objections. A party can object to a discovery request for the following reasons:

[1] Not relevant. The discovery request asks for information that is not relevant to the claim or defense of any party. FRCP 26(b)(1).

[2] Not permissible form of discovery. The discovery request asks for discovery in a form not permitted by the rules or agreed to by stipulation. *See generally* FRCP 26, 29-31, 33-36 (identifying permissible discovery methods).

[3] Cumulative or duplicative. The discovery request is unreasonably cumulative or duplicative, or the information can be obtained from another source that is more convenient, less burdensome, or less expensive. FRCP 26(b)(2)(C)(i); ***In re Malev Hungarian Airlines***, 964 F.2d 97, 102 (2d Cir.1992); *see also **Thompson v. Department of Hous. & Urban Dev.***, 199 F.R.D. 168, 171 (D.Md.2001) (all discovery is subject to limits imposed by FRCP 26(b)(2), now FRCP 26(b)(2)(C)); 2000 Notes to FRCP 26 at ¶28, p. 1181, this book (same).

[4] Ample opportunity to discover. The discovery request asks for information that the requesting party has had ample opportunity to discover on its own. FRCP 26(b)(2)(C)(ii); ***Avirgan v. Hull***, 932 F.2d 1572, 1580 (11th Cir.1991); *see also **Thompson***, 199 F.R.D. at 171 (all discovery is subject to limits imposed by FRCP 26(b)(2), now FRCP 26(b)(2)(C)); 2000 Notes to FRCP 26 at ¶28, p. 1181, this book (same).

[5] Undue burden. The discovery request places a burden or expense on the party that outweighs its likely benefit. FRCP 26(b)(2)(C)(iii). A court weighing the burdens and benefits should take into account the needs of the case, the amount in controversy, the parties' resources, the importance of the issues at stake in the litigation, and the importance of the proposed discovery in resolving the case. *Id.*; *see **Nugget Hydroelectric, L.P. v. Pacific Gas & Elec. Co.***, 981 F.2d 429, 438-39 (9th Cir.1992); ***Graham v. Casey's Gen. Stores***, 206 F.R.D. 251, 254 (S.D.Ind.2002). All discovery is subject to the limits imposed by FRCP 26(b)(2)(C). *See **Thompson***, 199 F.R.D. at 171 (discussing FRCP 26(b)(2), now FRCP 26(b)(2)(C)); 2000 Notes to FRCP 26 at ¶28, p. 1181, this book (same).

[6] Overbroad request. The discovery request is overly broad—it inquires into matters that go beyond what is relevant to the parties' claims or defenses. *See* FRCP 26(b)(1); *see **Mack v. Great Atl. & Pac. Tea Co.***, 871 F.2d 179, 187 (1st Cir.1989). A party cannot plead its allegations in entirely indefinite terms and then

base massive discovery requests on those nebulous allegations in the hope of finding particular evidence of wrongdoing. ***Koch v. Koch Indus.***, 203 F.3d 1202, 1238 (10th Cir.2000).

[7] **Improper procedure.** The discovery request is improper. If a party makes an improper discovery request, the other party may file either an objection or a motion for protective order before the response is due, stating why the request is improper. *See, e.g.*, ***Rahn v. Hawkins***, 464 F.3d 813, 821-22 (8th Cir.2006) (Ds filed first motion to quash deposition by written questions based on improper notice and improper questions and second motion to quash oral deposition based on unreasonable notice).

(b) **Invalid objections.** The following objections to discovery are not valid.

[1] **Not admissible.** Inadmissibility is not a ground for objection to discovery. As long as information appears "reasonably calculated" to lead to the discovery of admissible evidence, it is discoverable. FRCP 26(b)(1); ***Oppenheimer Fund, Inc. v. Sanders***, 437 U.S. 340, 351-52 (1978).

[2] **Fishing expedition.** An objection that a request is a "fishing expedition" is not sufficient. However, the objection may be sufficient if it is tied to a valid objection, usually relevance. ***Hofer v. Mack Trucks, Inc.***, 981 F.2d 377, 380 (8th Cir.1992); ***Micro Motion, Inc. v. Kane Steel Co.***, 894 F.2d 1318, 1327-28 (Fed. Cir.1990).

(c) **Seek protective order.** The party may request a protective order to clarify its rights and duties until the discoverability of the information is resolved. *See* FRCP 26(b)(2)(B) (party can seek protective order if electronically stored information is not reasonably accessible because of undue burden or cost); *see, e.g.*, ***LaFleur v. Teen Help***, 342 F.3d 1145, 1152-53 (10th Cir.2003) (protective order was granted to postpone depositions until motion to dismiss was resolved); ***Haka v. Lincoln Cty.***, 246 F.R.D. 577, 578-79 (W.D.Wis.2007) (protective order was granted to limit P's broad request for electronically stored information). See "Motion for Protective Order," §12, p. 440.

(d) **Signature.** The attorney or pro se party must sign the objections. FRCP 26(g)(1). See "Discovery Certificates," §6, p. 420.

2. **Burden to assert privilege.** The party resisting discovery must notify the other parties that it is withholding information subject to a claim of privilege or work product. *See* FRCP 26(b)(5)(A); 1993 Notes to FRCP 26 at ¶33, p. 1186, this book. Withholding information without notice to the other parties is sanctionable conduct under FRCP 37(b)(2) and may result in waiver of a privilege or protection. ***Dorf & Stanton Comms. v. Molson Breweries***, 100 F.3d 919, 923 (Fed.Cir.1996); 1993 Notes to FRCP 26 at ¶33, p. 1186, this book. A privilege against written discovery must be asserted as follows:

(1) **Withhold information.** The party must withhold the privileged information from the discovery it produces. *See* FRCP 26(b)(5)(A). A party can withhold only the information sought to be protected; it cannot withhold other nonprivileged information requested. See "Burden to partially comply," §8.3.6, p. 428.

(2) **Provide privilege log.** The party must serve a response that includes information sufficient to allow the requesting party to evaluate the applicability of the claimed privilege or protection. *See* FRCP 26(b)(5)(A)(ii); 1993 Notes to FRCP 26 at ¶34, p. 1186, this book.

(a) **Assert privilege.** The party must assert a specific privilege for each item or group of items withheld. *See* FRCP 26(b)(5)(A)(i) (party must make claim "expressly").

(b) **Identify privileged information withheld.**

[1] **Description of privileged information.** In the privilege log, the party must describe the nature of the documents, communications, or tangible things withheld, without revealing the privileged information itself. FRCP 26(b)(5)(A)(ii); *see* ***Horton v. U.S.***, 204 F.R.D. 670, 673 (D.Colo.2002) (privilege log must state specific reasons why each document or communication is subject to asserted privilege). Cursory descriptions and comments about the documents are not sufficient to support a claim of privilege. *See* ***U.S. v. Construction Prods. Research, Inc.***, 73 F.3d 464, 473 (2d Cir.1996).

[2] Specific information to be included. Although FRCP 26(b)(5)(A)(ii) does not specify what information must be provided, the privilege log should generally include a document number ("Bates number"), author or source, recipient, persons receiving copies, date, document title, document type, number of pages, and any other relevant nonprivileged information. *See **Alleyne v. New York State Educ. Dept.***, 248 F.R.D. 383, 386 (N.D.N.Y.2008) (information provided in privilege log must be sufficient to enable court to determine whether each element of asserted privilege is satisfied); ***Horton***, 204 F.R.D. at 673 (same); *see also **Gerber v. Down E. Cmty. Hosp.***, 266 F.R.D. 29, 36 (D.Me.2010) (courts disagree whether privilege log must identify names of each witness from whom party seeks a statement; Ps could categorically identify communications with witnesses without including witnesses' names). In rare circumstances, some of the information affecting the applicability of the privilege claim (e.g., the identity of the client) may itself be privileged; if so, that information does not have to be disclosed. 1993 Notes to FRCP 26 at ¶35, p. 1186, this book. The privilege log should not include irrelevant or duplicate information. For an example of a privilege log, see ***O'Connor's Federal Forms***, FORM 6A:10.

NOTE

*When privileged e-mails are at issue, courts disagree on whether a privilege log should include separate entries for multiple e-mails within the same e-mail chain. Compare **Muro v. Target Corp.**, 250 F.R.D. 350, 362-63 (N.D.Ill.2007) (each part of e-mail chain does not need to be itemized separately; even though one e-mail is not privileged, second e-mail that forwards the prior e-mail might be privileged in its entirety), aff'd, 580 F.3d 485 (7th Cir.2009), with **In re Universal Serv. Fund Tel. Billing Practices Litig.**, 232 F.R.D. 669, 674 (D.Kan.2005) (each part of e-mail chain should be itemized separately).*

[3] Failure to properly describe privileged information. If the privileged documents are not listed or are misrepresented as cumulative or duplicative, the privilege may be waived. *See **Ritacca v. Abbott Labs.***, 203 F.R.D. 332, 335-36 (N.D.Ill.2001); ***Grossman v. Schwarz***, 125 F.R.D. 376, 386-87 (S.D.N.Y.1989); *see also **U.S. v. British Am. Tobacco (Invs.)***, 387 F.3d 884, 890-91 (D.C.Cir.2004) (if party reasonably believes that its objections apply, waiver of privilege is not automatic when party does not include document in privilege log).

(3) Seek protective order. The party must request a protective order if compiling the information for the privilege log would impose an unreasonable burden. 1993 Notes to FRCP 26 at ¶35, p. 1186, this book; *see* FRCP 26(b)(2)(B) (party can seek protective order if electronically stored information is not reasonably accessible because of undue burden or cost).

(4) Signature. The attorney or pro se party must sign the response. FRCP 26(g)(1). See "Discovery Certificates," §6, p. 420.

3. Burden to resolve dispute without court action. Before asking the court to resolve claims of privilege or objection and before filing a motion for protective order or motion to compel, the parties must in good faith confer or attempt to confer in an effort to resolve the dispute. FRCP 26(c)(1), 37(a)(1); *see* 2006 Notes to FRCP 26 at ¶8, p. 1175, this book (party must confer before bringing motion for protective order or to compel electronically stored information from sources identified as not reasonably accessible). "Confer" means to make a genuine effort to resolve the dispute by determining (1) what the requesting party is actually seeking, (2) what the responding party is reasonably capable of producing that is responsive to the request, and (3) what specific genuine issues cannot be resolved without judicial intervention. ***Cotracom Commodity Trading Co. v. Seaboard Corp.***, 189 F.R.D. 456, 459 (D.Kan.1999). The conferencing requirement is meant to encourage the parties to communicate on discovery disputes and to conserve judicial resources. ***Taylor v. Florida Atl. Univ.***, 132 F.R.D. 304, 305 (S.D.Fla.1990), *aff'd sub nom. **Taylor v. Popovich***, 976 F.2d 743 (11th Cir.1992) (table case). Many local rules also contain a conferencing requirement. *E.g.*, Local Rules Cal. (S.D.), Rule 26.1(a); Local Rules Fla. (S.D.), Rule 7.1(a)(3); *see, e.g.*, Local Rules N.Y. (S.D.), Rule 37.2 (before court will hear discovery dispute, moving party must first request informal conference with court). The court can deny the motion if the movant has not conferred properly. ***Kidwiler v. Progressive Paloverde Ins.***, 192 F.R.D. 193, 196-97 (N.D.W.Va.2000) (motion to compel).

4. Burden to secure hearing & ruling. Either party may ask for a hearing on objections, on claims of privilege, or on motions for protective orders or to compel automatic disclosures under FRCP 26(a). *See* FRCP 26(c)(1) (protective orders), FRCP 37(a)(3)(A) (motion to compel disclosures). However, only the requesting party can bring a motion to compel answers to specific discovery requests or subpoenas. *See* FRCP 37(a)(3)(B) (motion to compel discovery), FRCP 45(c)(2)(B)(i) (motion to compel production after subpoena); ***Payne v. Exxon Corp.***, 121 F.3d 503, 509-10 (9th Cir.1997) (motion to compel answers to discovery requests).

(1) Most discovery. If neither party asks for a hearing, the party who sent the discovery request waives the requested discovery. *See, e.g.*, ***Bruce v. Weekly World News, Inc.***, 310 F.3d 25, 30-31 (1st Cir.2002) (P was not awarded damages because of insufficient evidence; P should have moved to compel production of evidence necessary to prove damages). Thus, once objections or claims of privilege have been served, the party seeking discovery must secure a hearing on a discovery dispute. *See* FRCP 37(a)(3)(B); ***Calderon v. Presidio Valley Farmers Ass'n***, 863 F.2d 384, 389 (5th Cir.1989).

(2) Nonparty objections to discovery after subpoena. When one party seeks discovery from a nonparty, the procedure for the other party to object depends on whether the nonparty also objects to the discovery. If the nonparty objects, the objecting party and the nonparty can coordinate their efforts. If the nonparty does not object, the objecting party must file a motion to quash the subpoena, set the motion for a hearing, and get a ruling before the nonparty produces the requested information. *See* FRCP 45(c)(3)(B) (court may quash or modify subpoena to protect affected person); 1991 Notes to FRCP 45 at ¶¶24, 26, p. 1212, this book (court is authorized to protect all persons from undue burden imposed by use of subpoena power). Once the nonparty produces the discovery, most objections by an affected party are moot.

5. Burden to provide evidence. Once a hearing is set, the party resisting discovery must produce any evidence necessary to support the objection or claim of privilege. *See* ***Roesberg v. Johns-Manville Corp.***, 85 F.R.D. 292, 297 (E.D.Pa.1980); 7 *Moore's Federal Practice 3d* §33.172. Evidence at the hearing can include the following:

(1) Affidavits. In most cases, affidavits are used to establish the applicability of an objection or a claim of privilege. *See, e.g.*, ***Rabushka v. Crane Co.***, 122 F.3d 559, 565 (8th Cir.1997) (D met its burden by producing detailed privilege log stating basis of claimed privilege for each document in question, along with its general counsel's explanatory affidavit); ***Mervin v. FTC***, 591 F.2d 821, 826 (D.C.Cir.1978) (in camera inspection of documents was not required because affidavit established that material was attorney work product).

(2) Deposition testimony. Deposition testimony may be used to help establish a claim of privilege. *See, e.g.*, ***Motley v. Marathon Oil Co.***, 71 F.3d 1547, 1551 (10th Cir.1995) (court did not abuse its discretion in finding attorney-client privilege based on privilege log, attorney's affidavit, and deposition testimony).

(3) Documents for inspection. When a party asserts a privilege, the documents themselves may be the only adequate evidence of the privilege. *See* ***Bogosian v. Gulf Oil Corp.***, 738 F.2d 587, 595-96 (3d Cir.1984) (documents alleged to contain legal theories might require in camera inspection if adversary is not satisfied with attorney's claim of work-product protection); *see, e.g.*, ***Schreiber v. Society for Sav. Bancorp, Inc.***, 11 F.3d 217, 221 (D.C.Cir.1993) (court should have reviewed documents to determine applicability of bank examiner's privilege); ***United Coal Cos. v. Powell Constr. Co.***, 839 F.2d 958, 966-67 (3d Cir.1988) (court should have reviewed documents in camera to determine applicability of attorney-client privilege and work-product protection). The party resisting discovery should produce the documents—marking each one with the claimed privilege—in a sealed wrapper and file them in the court for an in camera inspection.

6. Burden to partially comply. In most instances, a person who objects to discovery or seeks a protective order must respond to the discovery request by producing some of the information sought.

(1) Partial compliance necessary – parties. A party is required to comply with written discovery to the extent that no objection is made. FRCP 33(b)(3) (interrogatories), FRCP 34(b)(2)(B) (requests for production).

(2) No compliance necessary – nonparties. A nonparty is not required to partially comply if it timely objects to the subpoena. *See* FRCP 45(c)(2)(B)(ii) (once objection is made, requesting party is not entitled to information except by court order).

§9. WAIVER OF DISCOVERY, OBJECTIONS & PRIVILEGES

§9.1 Waiver of discovery.

1. Discovery proponent. If a party seeking discovery does not ask for a hearing on the other party's objections or motion for protective order or on its own motion to compel, it waives its right to the requested discovery. *See* 1970 Notes to FRCP 33 at ¶9, p. 1201, this book (interrogating party must move for court order compelling responding party to answer questions it has objected to); *see, e.g.*, ***Calderon v. Presidio Valley Farmers Ass'n***, 863 F.2d 384, 389 (5th Cir.1989) (party seeking discovery waived claim that interrogatory response was defective because it did not move to compel more specific answers).

2. Discovery opponent. A party resisting discovery does not need to request a ruling to preserve its own objections or claims of privilege. Thus, once objections or claims of privilege have been served, the requesting party must secure a hearing on a discovery dispute. *See* FRCP 37(a)(3)(B); 1970 Notes to FRCP 33 at ¶9, p. 1201, this book (interrogating party must move for court order compelling responding party to answer questions it has objected to).

§9.2 Waiver of objections & privileges – before disclosure.

1. Failure to timely object. If a party resisting discovery does not timely object, it may waive its objections and claims of privilege. ***Marx v. Kelly, Hart & Hallman, P.C.***, 929 F.2d 8, 12 (1st Cir.1991); ***Davis v. Fendler***, 650 F.2d 1154, 1160 (9th Cir.1981); ***Enron Corp. Sav. Plan v. Hewitt Assocs.***, 258 F.R.D. 149, 156 (S.D.Tex.2009); *see* FRCP 33(b)(4) (interrogatories); *see, e.g.*, ***SEC v. First Fin. Grp.***, 659 F.2d 660, 668-69 (5th Cir.1981) (party attempted to invoke Fifth Amendment). However, objections and claims of privilege are not waived if the court finds that the responding party had good cause for not timely asserting them. *See* FRCP 33(b)(4) (interrogatories); *see, e.g.*, ***Drexel Heritage Furnishings, Inc. v. Furniture USA, Inc.***, 200 F.R.D. 255, 258-59 (M.D.N.C.2001) (court excused D's delay, which was less than 30 days); ***Greer v. Lowes Home Ctrs., Inc.***, No. 05-0322 (W.D.La.2006) (slip op.; 1-26-06) (court excused P's four-day delay; D did not show prejudice); *see also* ***U.S. v. Hatchett***, 862 F.2d 1249, 1252 (6th Cir.1988) (D did not raise Fifth Amendment privilege within 30-day response period because his alleged fear of incrimination only arose after later grand-jury investigation; court remanded to determine why D believed his answers were incriminating).

NOTE

When determining whether there is good cause for failure to timely respond, the court may consider the following factors: (1) the length of delay or failure to particularize, (2) the reason for the delay or failure to particularize, (3) whether the party resisting discovery acted in bad faith, (4) whether the party seeking discovery was prejudiced, (5) whether the discovery request was properly framed and not excessively burdensome, and (6) whether waiver would impose an excessively harsh result on the party resisting discovery. ***Enron Corp. Savings Plan***, *258 F.R.D. at 157. The good-cause factors can also be applied when the party resisting discovery does not object with a specific claim of privilege or does not describe the documents claimed to be privileged. See id. See "Failure to specifically object," §9.2.2, this page.*

2. Failure to specifically object. If a party resisting discovery does not object to a discovery request with an express claim of a specific privilege or describe the documents or things claimed to be privileged, the party waives the privilege. *See* FRCP 26(b)(5)(A); ***Clarke v. American Commerce Nat'l Bank***, 974 F.2d 127, 129 (9th Cir. 1992); ***Ritacca v. Abbott Labs.***, 203 F.R.D. 332, 336 (N.D.Ill.2001).

3. Withholding materials. If a party resisting discovery withholds materials responsive to a discovery request and does not give notice to the other parties, it may waive any claims of privilege or protection. *See* ***Dorf &***

Stanton Comms. v. Molson Breweries, 100 F.3d 919, 923 (Fed.Cir.1996); 1993 Notes to FRCP 26 at ¶33, p. 1186, this book.

4. Misrepresenting nature of materials. If a party resisting discovery misrepresents privileged documents as merely cumulative or duplicative, it may waive any claims of privilege. ***Ritacca***, 203 F.R.D. at 336.

CAUTION

Before representing privileged electronically stored information as merely cumulative or duplicative, verify that the information does not include hidden data, such as metadata or editorial notes, that may change the contents of the information. See "Metadata," ch. 6-C, §4.1.9, p. 485.

§9.3 Waiver of privilege or protection – by disclosure.

1. Disclosure of privileged or protected information – generally. If a party discloses a communication or other information that is privileged or protected and the party does not assert the privilege or protection under FRCP 26(b)(5), it usually waives the privilege or protection. *See* ***Rhoads Indus. v. Building Materials Corp.***, 254 F.R.D. 216, 221 (E.D.Pa.2008), *clarified on other grounds*, 254 F.R.D. 238 (E.D.Pa.2008).

NOTE

FRE 502 provides the standards for determining the consequences of disclosing information protected by the attorney-client privilege or work-product protection. See 2008 Explanatory Note on FRE 502 at ¶2, p. 1253, this book. See "Disclosure of privileged or protected information – attorney-related privileges," §9.3.2, p. 432. Federal common law continues to apply to all other testimonial and evidentiary privileges. See 2008 Explanatory Note on FRE 502 at ¶¶3, 23, pp. 1253, 1255, this book.

(1) Types of disclosure. Disclosure of a communication or other information that is privileged or protected can be voluntary, involuntary, or inadvertent.

(a) Voluntary. A privilege or protection can be waived voluntarily, either expressly or impliedly.

[1] Express disclosure. Privileged or protected information is expressly disclosed when the holder of the privilege or protection knowingly and intentionally releases the information to a third party. *See, e.g.*, ***City of Va. Beach v. U.S. Dept. of Commerce***, 995 F.2d 1247, 1253 (4th Cir.1993) (D-agency could waive Freedom of Information Act exemption for documents protected by deliberative-process privilege through voluntary, authorized release of documents to nongovernmental recipient).

[2] Implied disclosure. Privileged or protected information can be impliedly disclosed when the holder of the privilege or protection intentionally acts in a manner inconsistent with preserving the privilege or protection. *See* ***Sedco Int'l, S.A. v. Cory***, 683 F.2d 1201, 1206 (8th Cir.1982); ***In re Sealed Case***, 676 F.2d 793, 818 (D.C.Cir.1982); ***AHF Cmty. Dev., LLC. v. City of Dallas***, 258 F.R.D. 143, 148-49 (N.D.Tex.2009); *see, e.g.*, ***Nguyen v. Excel Corp.***, 197 F.3d 200, 207-08 (5th Cir.1999) (Ds waived attorney-client privilege when they relied on advice-of-counsel defense for communications relevant to defense); ***Alexander v. Holden***, 66 F.3d 62, 68 n.4 (4th Cir.1995) (Ds, county commissioners, waived legislative privilege by voluntarily testifying about their motives for eliminating P's position as secretary); ***U.S. v. Bilzerian***, 926 F.2d 1285, 1292 (2d Cir.1991) (D waived attorney-client privilege by putting communications with attorney at issue); ***Preferred Care Partners Holding Corp. v. Humana, Inc.***, 258 F.R.D. 684, 696 (S.D.Fla.2009) (Ds waived attorney-client privilege when they volunteered details about document as essential part of defense to P's motion for sanctions); ***Whitman v. U.S.***, 108 F.R.D. 5, 8 (D.N.H.1985) (D waived peer-review privilege by revealing certain information during deposition testimony); ***Byers v. Burleson***, 100 F.R.D. 436, 440 (D.D.C.1983) (P waived attorney-client privilege by alleging legal malpractice).

NOTE

Implied disclosure is a misnomer because privileged or protected information is not actually disclosed. The more precise term is "waiver by implication." E.g., ***Sedco Int'l****, 683 F.2d at 1206 (waiver by implication of attorney-client privilege). The effect of the party's actions, however, is the same as if the party expressly disclosed the information.*

(b) Involuntary. A privilege or protection usually cannot be waived involuntarily because the disclosure is considered beyond the control of the holder of the privilege or protection. ***American Nat'l Bank & Trust Co. v. Equitable Life Assur. Soc'y***, 406 F.3d 867, 877 n.5 (7th Cir.2005); *see* ***SEC v. Lavin***, 111 F.3d 921, 930 (D.C. Cir.1997) (disclosures are involuntary when made by third parties over whom holder of privilege has no control); *see, e.g.*, ***Transamerica Computer Co. v. International Bus. Machs. Corp.***, 573 F.2d 646, 651 (9th Cir.1978) (under accelerated discovery schedule, party's production of privileged documents was "compelled" because party did not have adequate opportunity to claim privilege); *see also* ***In re Fannie Mae Secs. Litig.***, 552 F.3d 814, 823-24 (D.C.Cir. 2009) (nonparty who was held in contempt for not complying with court-ordered deadline was ordered to produce documents being withheld on basis of privilege; contempt order required disclosure only to Ds' attorneys and included procedure for nonparty to later recover documents actually covered by privilege). However, the holder can be found to have waived the privilege or protection if it did not take steps reasonably designed to preserve the confidentiality of the information before the disclosure occurred. ***SEC***, 111 F.3d at 930; *e.g.*, ***Gomez v. Vernon***, 255 F.3d 1118, 1131-32 (9th Cir.2001) (prisoners took reasonable steps to preserve confidentiality of legal files by marking binders with case names, placing them in library, and establishing sign-out procedures).

(c) Inadvertent. For privileges and protections other than those protecting attorney-client communications and attorney work product ("attorney-related privileges"), it is not clear whether the privilege or protection can be waived by inadvertent disclosure of information. *See, e.g.*, ***Redland Soccer Club, Inc. v. Department of Army***, 55 F.3d 827, 856 (3d Cir.1995) (court held that government's disclosure of five documents subject to deliberative-process privilege was inadvertent and not voluntary). This uncertainty is because the federal common law on the effect of inadvertent waiver of privileged or protected information has developed almost exclusively in the context of attorney-related privileges. Although FRE 502 now governs the effect of inadvertent waiver for attorney-related privileges, the federal common law may still offer some guidance on dealing with other testimonial and evidentiary privileges and protections, despite the differences in public policies among them. *Cf.* ***Gray v. Bicknell***, 86 F.3d 1472, 1483-84 (8th Cir.1996) (discussing three approaches courts took to determine whether inadvertent disclosure of attorney-related privileges would result in waiver); ***Hopson v. Mayor & City Council of Baltimore***, 232 F.R.D. 228, 235-36 (D.Md.2005) (same).

(2) Effect of disclosure.

(a) Specific information. In some cases, the disclosure may waive the privilege or protection only for the specific information disclosed. *See* ***In re Sealed Case***, 121 F.3d 729, 741 (D.C.Cir.1997) (executive privileges); ***Mobil Oil Corp. v. U.S. E.P.A.***, 879 F.2d 698, 700-01 (9th Cir.1989) (Freedom of Information Act exemption).

(b) Subject matter. In some cases, the disclosure may waive the privilege or protection for all information (disclosed or undisclosed) related to the same subject matter. *See, e.g.*, ***Young v. U.S.***, 149 F.R.D. 199, 205 (S.D.Cal.1993) (tax-return privilege). For a discussion of the effect of disclosure of attorney-related privileges, see "Effect of disclosure," §9.3.2(4), p. 436.

(c) Parties. In some cases, the disclosure may waive the privilege or protection only for particular parties—that is, "selective waiver" allows a party to voluntarily disclose privileged information to one person but assert the privilege against another person. ***Dellwood Farms, Inc. v. Cargill, Inc.***, 128 F.3d 1122, 1126 (7th Cir. 1997). Most circuits, however, view an express waiver as a complete waiver of the privilege or protection and have declined to adopt a selective-waiver exception. *See* ***In re Pacific Pictures Corp.***, 679 F.3d 1121, 1127-28 (9th Cir. 2012); ***In re Qwest Comms. Int'l***, 450 F.3d 1179, 1186-91 (10th Cir.2006); ***In re Columbia/HCA Healthcare Corp.***

Billing Practices Litig., 293 F.3d 289, 295-97 (6th Cir.2002); *see also* ***Bittaker v. Woodford***, 331 F.3d 715, 720 n.5 (9th Cir.2003) (law on selective waiver is not settled). Selective waiver is different from inadvertent disclosure, which requires a finding that a party mistakenly disclosed information it had intended to keep secret. ***Dellwood Farms***, 128 F.3d at 1126-27.

2. Disclosure of privileged or protected information – attorney-related privileges. If a party discloses a communication or other information protected by the attorney-client privilege or work-product protection ("attorney-related privileges") and the party does not assert the privilege or protection under FRCP 26(b)(5), it usually waives the privilege or protection. *See* ***Grace United Methodist Ch. v. City of Cheyenne***, 451 F.3d 643, 668 (10th Cir.2006); ***Rhoads Indus.***, 254 F.R.D. at 221. Whether a particular disclosure actually results in waiver, however, is governed in part by federal common law and in part by FRE 502. To determine whether an attorney-related privilege is waived (and to what extent) by disclosure, a party seeking protection must determine (1) whether FRE 502 applies, (2) the type of disclosure made, (3) where the disclosure occurred, (4) the effect of the disclosure, and (5) whether any agreement or court order limits the effect of the waiver.

NOTE

FRE 502 applies to all cases filed after September 19, 2008, and it may apply to cases filed before that date if the application would be "just and practicable." P.L. 110-322, 122 Stat. 3537, 3538 (2008). Before the enactment of FRE 502, the effect of disclosing—without objection—information subject to an attorney-related privilege was governed exclusively by federal common law. FRE 502 was enacted to address two major problems with federal common law: (1) the circuits' disagreement about the effect of certain disclosures of information protected by attorney-related privileges and (2) the complaint that protecting against waiver of attorney-related privileges had become prohibitively expensive because of the risk that an inadvertent disclosure could operate as a subject-matter waiver (i.e., waiver of privilege for both disclosed and undisclosed information). See 2008 Explanatory Note on FRE 502 at ¶1, p. 1253, this book; see also 23 Wright & Graham §5442 (FRE 502 is a "special waiver rule[] for the wealthy"; people of modest means do not make so many communications to attorneys that mistaken disclosure is an issue). See generally Report of the Advisory Committee on Evidence Rules, at 2 (May 2007), www.uscourts.gov/uscourts/RulesAndPolicies/rules/Reports/2007-05-Committee_Report-Evidence.pdf (discussing problems with federal common law governing waiver of attorney-client privilege and work-product protection).

(1) Application of FRE 502. FRE 502 applies to disclosures of information protected by the attorney-client privilege or work-product protection. FRE 502(a); 2008 Explanatory Note on FRE 502 at ¶23, p. 1255, this book; *see* FRE 502(g); ***Heriot v. Byrne***, 257 F.R.D. 645, 655-56 (N.D.Ill.2009); 23 Wright & Graham §§5443, 5445. FRE 502 does not apply to any initial determination of whether a communication or other information is protected, under either federal or state law, by the attorney-client privilege or work-product protection. 2008 Explanatory Note on FRE 502 at ¶3, p. 1253, this book. To determine whether a document is protected under the attorney-client privilege or work-product protection, see "Attorney-client privilege," ch. 6-B, §3.3, p. 463; "Work-product protection," ch. 6-B, §3.4, p. 467.

(a) Disclosures. FRE 502 applies to a disclosure that is voluntary or inadvertent and is made in a federal or state proceeding, to a federal office or agency, or under a court order or the parties' agreement. *See* FRE 502(a)-(e); *see, e.g.*, ***Alpert v. Riley***, 267 F.R.D. 202, 210 (S.D.Tex.2010) (when disclosure was made before court proceedings, FRE 502 did not apply); *see also* 23 Wright & Graham §5443 (questioning whether disclosure made "in" federal or state proceeding carries temporal meaning, i.e., disclosure made when proceeding is in progress, or functional meaning, e.g., disclosure made during settlement discussions related to that proceeding). FRE 502 does not apply to findings of waiver of an attorney-related privilege when no disclosure has been made. 2008 Explanatory Note on FRE 502 at ¶¶3, 4, p. 1253, this book. See "Types of disclosure," §9.3.2(2), p. 433.

(b) Attorney-related privileges. For purposes of FRE 502, "attorney-client privilege" means the protection that applicable law (either federal or state) provides for confidential attorney-client communications. FRE 502(g)(1). See "Attorney-client privilege," ch. 6-B, §3.3, p. 463. Likewise, "work-product protection" means the protection that applicable law provides for tangible material (or its intangible equivalent) prepared in anticipation of litigation or for trial. FRE 502(g)(2); *see* 2008 Explanatory Note on FRE 502 at ¶24, p. 1255, this book. See "Work-product protection," ch. 6-B, §3.4, p. 467.

(c) Federal & state proceedings. FRE 502 applies to (1) federal proceedings, including court-annexed and court-mandated arbitration proceedings, and (2) state proceedings. FRE 502(f); *see* 23 Wright & Graham §§5443, 5445. FRE 502 does not apply to a disclosure made in one state-court proceeding and later offered in another state-court proceeding. *See* Report to Congress Transmitting FRE 502, at 4 (Sept.2007), www.uscourts.gov/uscourts/RulesAndPolicies/rules/Hill_Letter_re_EV_502.pdf.

CAUTION

FRE 502's application to state proceedings has not yet been challenged. It is debatable whether Congress has the authority to federalize the attorney-client privilege and work-product protection by enacting a rule of evidence that preempts state law. See 23 Wright & Graham §5444 & n.10; Noyes, Federal Rule of Evidence 502: Stirring the State Law of Privilege & Professional Responsibility with a Federal Stick, 66 Wash. & Lee L.Rev. 673, 701 (2009); Mitchell, Note, Preserving the Privilege: Codification of Selective Waiver & the Limits of Federal Power over State Courts, 86 B.U.L.Rev. 691, 726 (2006); Glynn, Federalizing Privilege, 52 Am.U.L.Rev. 59, 156 (2002); see also Report of the Advisory Committee on Evidence Rules, at 9 (in draft of Explanatory Note to then-proposed FRE 502, Advisory Committee acknowledged that rule of evidence cannot bind state courts unless Congress enacts rule directly under authority of Commerce Clause).

(2) Types of disclosure. Disclosure of a communication or other information protected by an attorney-related privilege can be voluntary, involuntary, or inadvertent.

(a) Voluntary. An attorney-related privilege can be waived voluntarily, either expressly or impliedly. *See* FRE 502(a); ***In re Qwest Comms. Int'l***, 450 F.3d at 1185-86; ***PaineWebber Grp. v. Zinsmeyer Trusts Prtshp.***, 187 F.3d 988, 992 (8th Cir.1999).

[1] Express disclosure. Information protected by an attorney-related privilege is expressly disclosed when the holder of the privilege knowingly and intentionally releases the information to a third party. *See* ***Cavallaro v. U.S.***, 284 F.3d 236, 246-47 (1st Cir.2002); ***Montgomery Cty. v. MicroVote Corp.***, 175 F.3d 296, 304 (3d Cir.1999); *see, e.g.*, ***Permian Corp. v. U.S.***, 665 F.2d 1214, 1219 (D.C.Cir.1981) (attorney-client privilege was waived after documents were produced to SEC); ***Urban Outfitters, Inc. v. DPIC Cos.***, 203 F.R.D. 376, 380 (N.D. Ill.2001) (attorney-client privilege was waived when client faxed documents to opposing counsel). *But see* ***Shields v. Sturm, Ruger & Co.***, 864 F.2d 379, 382 (5th Cir.1989) (work-product protection cannot be waived by mere disclosure to third person; protection is waived only when attorney voluntarily discloses information to court by directing witness to disclose information or failing to object when it is offered); ***U.S. v. AT&T Co.***, 642 F.2d 1285, 1299 (D.C. Cir.1980) (work-product protection cannot be waived by mere disclosure to third person).

[2] Implied disclosure. Information protected by an attorney-related privilege can be impliedly disclosed when the holder of the privilege intentionally acts in a manner inconsistent with preserving the privilege. See "Implied disclosure," §9.3.1(1)(a)[2], p. 430.

(b) Involuntary. An attorney-related privilege usually cannot be waived by the involuntary disclosure of privileged information. See "Involuntary," §9.3.1(1)(b), p. 431.

(c) Inadvertent. An attorney-related privilege can be waived by the inadvertent disclosure of privileged information. But the waiver may not be automatic. ***In re Grand Jury (Impounded)***, 138 F.3d 978, 981 (3d Cir.1998); *see* FRE 502(b).

NOTE

*Before the enactment of FRE 502, courts disagreed on the approach for determining when an inadvertent disclosure resulted in waiver of privilege or protection. See **Gray v. Bicknell**, 86 F.3d 1472, 1483-84 (8th Cir.1996); 2008 Explanatory Note on FRE 502 at ¶¶8, 9, p. 1254, this book. FRE 502 adopted the middle approach. 2008 Explanatory Note on FRE 502 at ¶9, p. 1254, this book.*

[1] Burden. Under FRE 502, the disclosing party has the burden to prove that it has not waived the privilege or protection. *See* ***Peterson v. Bernardi***, 262 F.R.D. 424, 428 (D.N.J.2009); ***Amobi v. District of Columbia Dept. of Corrs.***, 262 F.R.D. 45, 53 (D.D.C.2009); ***Heriot***, 257 F.R.D. at 658. Before reaching the FRE 502(b) elements, the disclosing party must show that the disclosure is protected by the attorney-client privilege or as work product. *E.g.*, ***Peterson***, 262 F.R.D. at 427-28 (P did not satisfy burden when he did not attempt to establish that documents were privileged or protected; P only attached privilege log and expected court to assume privilege or protection); *see* ***Heriot***, 257 F.R.D. at 655. See "Application of FRE 502," §9.3.2(1), p. 432. If the disclosure is not privileged or protected, the FRE 502(b) inquiry ends. ***Heriot***, 257 F.R.D. at 655. If the disclosure is privileged or protected, it will not operate as a waiver in a federal (or state) proceeding if the FRE 502 elements are met.

[2] FRE 502 elements. To prevent a privileged or protected disclosure from operating as a waiver in a federal (or state) proceeding, the holder of the privilege must show that (1) the disclosure was inadvertent, (2) the holder took reasonable steps to prevent disclosure, and (3) the holder promptly took reasonable steps to rectify the error. FRE 502(b); ***Peterson***, 262 F.R.D. at 427; ***Preferred Care Partners Holding Corp.***, 258 F.R.D. at 690; *see* 2008 Explanatory Note on FRE 502 at ¶¶8, 9, p. 1254, this book.

[a] Inadvertent. The disclosure must be inadvertent. FRE 502(b)(1); *see* ***Laethem Equip. Co. v. Deere & Co.***, 261 F.R.D. 127, 135 (E.D.Mich.2009). A disclosure is inadvertent if the disclosing party did not intend a privileged or work-product-protected document to be produced or if the production was a mistake. ***Amobi***, 262 F.R.D. at 53; ***Coburn Grp. v. Whitecap Advisors LLC***, 640 F.Supp.2d 1032, 1038 (N.D.Ill.2009); *see* 23 Wright & Graham §5445 & n.26 ("inadvertent" likely was intended to mean mistaken or unintentional disclosure); *see also* ***Heriot***, 257 F.R.D. at 658-59 (to determine whether disclosure is inadvertent, courts may look to total number of documents reviewed, procedures used for review, and action of disclosing party after discovering documents had been produced).

[b] Reasonable steps to prevent disclosure. Before information is disclosed, the holder of the privilege must take reasonable steps to prevent inadvertent disclosure of privileged or protected information. FRE 502(b)(2); ***Heriot***, 257 F.R.D. at 660-61. The reasonableness standard is not "all reasonable means"; it is simply reasonable steps taken to prevent disclosure. ***Coburn Grp.***, 640 F.Supp.2d at 1040; *see* ***Rhoads Indus.***, 254 F.R.D. at 226 (reasonableness standard should be applied objectively). In determining whether reasonable steps were taken to prevent disclosure, a court may consider the following factors:

- The reasonableness of precautions taken. ***Eden Isle Marina, Inc. v. U.S.***, 89 Fed.Cl. 480, 502 (Fed.Cl.2009); 2008 Explanatory Note on FRE 502 at ¶10, p. 1254, this book; *see, e.g.*, ***Williams v. District of Columbia***, 806 F.Supp.2d 44, 49-50 (D.D.C.2011) (privilege was waived when D did not provide any details for reviewing and producing documents; D's conclusory statement that material was reviewed by experienced litigation paralegal under supervision of attorney was insufficient); ***Peterson***, 262 F.R.D. at 428-31 (for most of 135 inadvertently produced documents, privilege was waived when P took only minimal steps to protect against disclosure (dicta), but for nine documents, it was the rare case that privilege was not waived because documents were so obviously work product that injustice would result if privilege was waived).

• The scope of discovery. ***Eden Isle Marina***, 89 Fed.Cl. at 502; 2008 Explanatory Note on FRE 502 at ¶10, p. 1254, this book. The scope of discovery may be a logical starting point in many cases because when discovery is extensive, mistakes are inevitable; thus, claims of inadvertence will generally be allowed as long as appropriate precautions are taken. ***Coburn Grp.***, 640 F.Supp.2d at 1039.

• The extent of disclosure. ***Eden Isle Marina***, 89 Fed.Cl. at 502; 2008 Explanatory Note on FRE 502 at ¶10, p. 1254, this book.

• The overriding issue of fairness. ***Eden Isle Marina***, 89 Fed.Cl. at 502; 2008 Explanatory Note on FRE 502 at ¶10, p. 1254, this book.

• The number of documents to be reviewed. ***Eden Isle Marina***, 89 Fed.Cl. at 502; 2008 Explanatory Note on FRE 502 at ¶10, p. 1254, this book; Statement of Congressional Intent Regarding FRE 502 at ¶7, p. 1256, this book; *see* ***Williams***, 806 F.Supp.2d at 50.

• The time constraints for production. ***Eden Isle Marina***, 89 Fed.Cl. at 502; 2008 Explanatory Note on FRE 502 at ¶10, p. 1254, this book; *see* ***Williams***, 806 F.Supp.2d at 50.

• The use of advanced analytical software applications and linguistic tools in screening for privilege and work product. ***Eden Isle Marina***, 89 Fed.Cl. at 502; 2008 Explanatory Note on FRE 502 at ¶10, p. 1254, this book.

• The implementation of efficient systems of records management before litigation. ***Eden Isle Marina***, 89 Fed.Cl. at 502; 2008 Explanatory Note on FRE 502 at ¶10, p. 1254, this book.

• The experience and training of the people who conduct the document review; however, the use of paralegals and nonlawyers is not unreasonable in every case. ***Heriot***, 257 F.R.D. at 660 & n.10; *e.g.*, ***Coburn Grp.***, 640 F.Supp.2d at 1039 (document review by experienced paralegals who were supervised by lead attorney was not unreasonable).

NOTE

Because FRE 502 is a flexible rule, the reasonableness factors are actually nondeterminative guidelines that courts may evaluate on a case-by-case basis. 2008 Explanatory Note on FRE 502 at ¶10, p. 1254, this book; see ***Amobi****, 262 F.R.D. at 54;* ***Heriot****, 257 F.R.D. at 655 & n.7. Therefore, before drafting a motion to compel the return of inadvertently disclosed documents, check the law of your circuit to determine which factors are considered.*

[c] Reasonable steps to rectify error. The holder of the privilege must take reasonable steps to rectify the error. FRE 502(b)(3). In determining whether reasonable steps were taken to rectify the error, a court may consider the same factors used to determine whether reasonable steps were taken to prevent disclosure. *See* 2008 Explanatory Note on FRE 502 at ¶10, p. 1254, this book. When and how the disclosing party discovers and rectifies the disclosure is also critical. ***Heriot***, 257 F.R.D. at 662; *see, e.g.*, ***Coburn Grp.***, 640 F.Supp.2d at 1040-41 (when D discovered, at deposition, that documents had been inadvertently disclosed four months earlier, D objected, requested return of documents the next day, and after P's refusal, filed motion to compel five weeks later; D's actions were reasonable). Although the holder is not required to engage in a postproduction review to determine whether any privileged information has been mistakenly produced, the holder must follow up on any obvious indications of inadvertent disclosure. 2008 Explanatory Note on FRE 502 at ¶11, p. 1254, this book; *see* ***Coburn Grp.***, 640 F.Supp.2d at 1040; *see, e.g.*, ***Williams***, 806 F.Supp.2d at 52 (D waived privilege when D requested return of privileged communication from P but P did not respond and then D waited two years and eight months before following up with P or involving court); ***Preferred Care Partners Holding Corp.***, 258 F.R.D. at 700 (D waived privilege when it took no action for almost two months after disclosure, including three-week delay after P used privileged document in its motion for sanctions; D should have acted more quickly after P's use of document). In taking reasonable steps to rectify the error, the disclosing party may need to follow the procedure in FRCP 26(b)(5)(B). FRE 502(b)(3); *see also*

Williams, 806 F.Supp.2d at 53 (mere compliance with FRCP 26(b)(5)(B), without more, may not constitute reasonable steps to rectify error). The disclosing party should do so when, for example, the receiving party has relied on the inadvertently disclosed information. *See* Statement of Congressional Intent Regarding FRE 502 at ¶7, p. 1256, this book. The procedure in FRCP 26(b)(5)(B) is as follows:

• **Notice of claim.** The disclosing party generally must give written notice of the claim of privilege and the basis for it to any party that received the information. *See* FRCP 26(b)(5)(B); 2006 Notes to FRCP 26 at ¶15, p. 1176, this book. However, written notice may sometimes be impractical, such as during a deposition. 2006 Notes to FRCP 26 at ¶15, p. 1176, this book. The notice must be specific enough to allow the receiving party and the court to understand the basis of the claim and to determine whether the privilege has been waived. *Id.*

• **Information returned.** The receiving party must promptly return, sequester, or destroy the information and any copies it has. FRCP 26(b)(5)(B); 2006 Notes to FRCP 26 at ¶16, p. 1176, this book. The receiving party should certify that it no longer has any copies of the information. It cannot use or disclose the information until the privilege claim is resolved. FRCP 26(b)(5)(B); 2006 Notes to FRCP 26 at ¶16, p. 1176, this book. If the receiving party disclosed the information to third parties before it received notice of the privilege claim, the receiving party must take reasonable steps to retrieve the information. FRCP 26(b)(5)(B).

• **Challenging claim.** To challenge the privilege claim, the receiving party must sequester the information, promptly present it to the court under seal, and ask the court to determine whether the claim, as stated in the disclosing party's notice, is valid or has been waived. FRCP 26(b)(5)(B); *see* 2006 Notes to FRCP 26 at ¶16, p. 1176, this book.

• **Preserve information.** The disclosing party must preserve the information pending the court's ruling on whether the claim of privilege is valid or has been waived. FRCP 26(b)(5)(B); 2006 Notes to FRCP 26 at ¶18, p. 1176, this book.

(3) Where disclosure occurred.

(a) In federal proceeding. If the disclosure occurred in a federal proceeding, the disclosure constitutes a waiver of an attorney-related privilege to the extent allowed by federal common law and FRE 502. *See* FRE 502(a).

(b) To federal agency or office. If the disclosure was made to a federal agency or office, the disclosure constitutes a waiver of an attorney-related privilege to the extent allowed by federal common law and FRE 502. *See* FRE 502(a).

(c) In state proceeding. If the disclosure occurred in a state proceeding and was not the subject of a state-court order, the disclosure constitutes a waiver of an attorney-related privilege to the extent allowed by FRE 502 or the law of the state where the disclosure occurred, whichever provides greater protection for the privilege. FRE 502(c); 2008 Explanatory Note on FRE 502 at ¶13, p. 1254, this book; *see* 2008 Explanatory Note on FRE 502 at ¶18, p. 1255, this book. See "Federal & state proceedings," §9.3.2(1)(c), p. 433.

(4) Effect of disclosure.

(a) Voluntary disclosure.

[1] Waiver of disclosed information. A voluntary disclosure generally results in a waiver of privilege for the disclosed information only. *See* FRE 502(a); 2008 Explanatory Note on FRE 502 at ¶5, p. 1253, this book; *see, e.g.*, ***Chevron Corp. v. Pennzoil Co.***, 974 F.2d 1156, 1162 (9th Cir.1992) (waiver only of tax matters actually disclosed to auditor, not of all information about anticipated tax deferral). FRE 502 does not allow the parties to agree to a selective waiver of the privilege, such as to a federal agency conducting an investigation, while preserving the privilege as against other parties seeking the information. Statement of Congressional Intent Regarding FRE 502 at ¶11, p. 1256, this book. See "Parties," §9.3.1(2)(c), p. 431.

[2] **Waiver of subject matter.** A voluntary disclosure can result in a "subject-matter waiver"—that is, waiver of privilege for both disclosed and undisclosed information. 2008 Explanatory Note on FRE 502 at ¶5, p. 1253, this book; *see* FRE 502(a). Subject-matter waiver of an attorney-related privilege occurs only when (1) the waiver is intentional, (2) the disclosed and undisclosed privileged information concern the same subject matter, and (3) the disclosed and undisclosed privileged information should in fairness be considered together. *See* FRE 502(a); ***Trustees of the Elec. Workers Local No. 26 Pension Trust Fund v. Trust Fund Advisors, Inc.***, 266 F.R.D. 1, 11 (D.D.C.2010); ***Eden Isle Marina***, 89 Fed.Cl. at 503; *cf.* ***Wi-Lan, Inc. v. LG Elecs., Inc.***, 684 F.3d 1364, 1369-70 (Fed.Cir.2012) (when privileged document was intentionally disclosed before suit—meaning that FRE 502 did not apply—district court was required to apply fairness considerations to question of whether prelitigation disclosure would result in subject-matter waiver). A finding of subject-matter waiver should be limited to situations in which a party intentionally discloses privileged information in a selective, misleading, and unfair manner. 2008 Explanatory Note on FRE 502 at ¶5, p. 1253, this book; *see* ***US Airline Pilots Ass'n v. Pension Benefit Guar. Corp.***, 274 F.R.D. 28, 32-33 (D.D.C.2011); ***Eden Isle Marina***, 89 Fed.Cl. at 503.

NOTE

FRE 502 limits subject-matter waiver, but FRE 502 does not define "same subject matter" or elaborate on considerations for "fairness." See 23 Wright & Graham §5444. Although there is no bright-line test for determining what constitutes the subject matter of a waiver, the court can consider the circumstances of the disclosure, the nature of the legal advice sought, and the prejudice to the parties if further disclosure is allowed or denied. ***Fort James Corp. v. Solo Cup Co.***, *412 F.3d 1340, 1349-50 (Fed.Cir.2005); e.g.,* ***Eden Isle Marina***, *89 Fed.Cl. at 503 (P did not demonstrate that D selectively disclosed documents to gain advantage; court did not extend scope of waiver to fact work product of same subject matter).*

(b) Inadvertent disclosure. An inadvertent disclosure of information protected by an attorney-related privilege cannot result in a subject-matter waiver. *See* FRE 502(b); 2008 Explanatory Note on FRE 502 at ¶5, p. 1253, this book.

(5) Limits on waiver.

(a) Parties' agreement. The parties can enter into an agreement to limit the effect of waiver by disclosure between them. 2008 Explanatory Note on FRE 502 at ¶19, p. 1255, this book. The agreement is binding only on the parties to it unless it is incorporated into a court order. FRE 502(e); 2008 Explanatory Note on FRE 502 at ¶19, p. 1255, this book; Statement of Congressional Intent Regarding FRE 502 at ¶14, p. 1256, this book; *see* 2006 Notes to FRCP 26 at ¶14, p. 1176, this book (in determining whether privilege is waived, court should consider any agreement by parties); *see also* 23 Wright & Graham §5446 & nn.9-19 (questioning meaning of "incorporated" and when court can make order). However, if the parties agree to a selective waiver of the privilege, such as to a federal agency conducting an investigation, the agreement will not be binding on third parties even if it is incorporated into a court order. *See* Statement of Congressional Intent Regarding FRE 502 at ¶11, p. 1256, this book.

(b) Court order. The court can order that an attorney-related privilege is not waived by a disclosure connected to the litigation pending before the court. FRE 502(d); ***S2 Automation LLC v. Micron Tech.***, No. CIV 11-0884 JB/WDS (D.N.M.2012) (slip op.; 7-23-12); Statement of Congressional Intent Regarding FRE 502 at ¶11, p. 1256, this book; *see also* ***Rajala v. McGuire Woods, LLP***, No. 08-2638-CM-DJW (D.Kan.2010) (slip op.; 7-22-10) (under FRCP 26(c), court can order clawback provision even if not all parties agree to one). FRE 502(d) allows the parties to reduce the prohibitive costs of reviewing for and retaining privileged information and work product without the fear of waiver. 2008 Explanatory Note on FRE 502 at ¶16, p. 1255, this book; *see* Statement of Congressional Intent Regarding FRE 502 at ¶11, p. 1256, this book. For example, an order can provide for the return of documents without waiver regardless of the care taken by the disclosing party. 2008 Explanatory Note on FRE 502 at ¶16, p. 1255, this book. The court has discretion to include conditions it deems appropriate. *See* Statement of Congressional Intent Regarding FRE 502 at ¶12, p. 1256, this book.

[1] Without parties' agreement. The order is enforceable regardless of whether it memorializes an agreement between the parties—that is, the parties' agreement should not be a condition of enforceability of the court's order. ***S2 Automation***, No. CIV 11-0884 JB/WDS (slip op.); 2008 Explanatory Note on FRE 502 at ¶17, p. 1255, this book.

[2] Other federal & state proceedings. The order is enforceable against nonparties in any federal or state proceeding. FRE 502(d); *see* 2008 Explanatory Note on FRE 502 at ¶15, p. 1254, this book. The order can provide that a disclosure made "in connection with" a federal proceeding does not result in waiver; however, the order cannot determine the effect of a separate disclosure made in another federal or state proceeding. 2008 Explanatory Note on FRE 502 at ¶18, p. 1255, this book.

§10. FILING DISCOVERY

Most discovery is filed in the court only when needed. *See* 2000 Notes to FRCP 5 at ¶1, p. 1146, this book.

§10.1 Discovery to be filed. The following discovery materials must be filed in the court:

1. Pretrial disclosures and objections to those disclosures under FRCP 26(a)(3)(A). FRCP 26(a)(3)(A); 2000 Notes to FRCP 5 at ¶1, p. 1146, this book.
2. Filings in connection with a physical or mental examination under FRCP 35. 2000 Notes to FRCP 5 at ¶1, p. 1146, this book; *see* FRCP 5(d)(1).
3. Motions and responses to motions on discovery issues. *See* FRCP 5(d)(1).

§10.2 Discovery not to be filed. The following discovery materials must not be filed in the court:

1. Initial and expert disclosures, depositions, deposition notices, and discovery requests. FRCP 5(d)(1); 2000 Notes to FRCP 5 at ¶1, p. 1146, this book.
2. Responses and objections to discovery requests. 2000 Notes to FRCP 5 at ¶1, p. 1146, this book; *see* FRCP 5(d)(1).
3. Documents and tangible things produced in discovery. FRCP 5(d)(1).

§10.3 Exceptions. The following are exceptions to the do-not-file rule of FRCP 5(d)(1):

1. The court may order that discovery materials be filed. *See* FRCP 5(d)(1).
2. A person may file discovery materials supporting or opposing a motion or for other use in a court proceeding. FRCP 5(d)(1); *see* 2000 Notes to FRCP 5 at ¶4, p. 1146, this book (another use might include materials used in connection with pretrial conference under FRCP 16). The exception is not triggered by the use of discovery materials in other activities such as depositions. 2000 Notes to FRCP 5 at ¶4, p. 1146, this book. Once this exception is triggered, only the parts of voluminous materials that are actually used should be filed. *Id.* at ¶5, p. 1146, this book.

§11. SUPPLEMENTING DISCOVERY

A party has a duty to supplement its disclosures and discovery responses—including those covering electronically stored information—if they are incomplete or incorrect. FRCP 26(e)(1). The duty applies whenever a party learns that an earlier disclosure or response is incomplete or incorrect; the duty is not limited to situations where the failure to supplement would constitute a "knowing concealment." *See* ***Reed v. Iowa Mar. & Repair Corp.***, 16 F.3d 82, 84-85 (5th Cir.1994) (rule no longer requires "knowing concealment"). Supplementation, however, cannot be used to extend deadlines—that is, to provide information that should have been included in the original disclosure or response. ***Sierra Club v. Cedar Point Oil Co.***, 73 F.3d 546, 571 (5th Cir.1996).

§11.1 Supplementation required. The burden to supplement is on the party responding to discovery, not the party requesting discovery. *See* ***Harriman v. Hancock Cty.***, 627 F.3d 22, 29 (1st Cir.2010) (obligation to supplement is continuing one). A party must supplement a disclosure or discovery response in the following instances:

1. The party is so ordered by the court. FRCP 26(e)(1)(B).

2. The party learns that an earlier disclosure is incomplete or incorrect in some material respect, and the additional or corrective information has not otherwise been made known to the other parties during the discovery process or in writing. FRCP 26(e)(1)(A); ***Southern States Rack & Fixture, Inc. v. Sherwin-Williams Co.***, 318 F.3d 592, 595-96 (4th Cir.2003); *see* ***Klonoski v. Mahlab***, 156 F.3d 255, 268 (1st Cir.1998) (FRCP 26 provides no exception for documents found after discovery deadlines have passed).

3. The party learns that an earlier response to an interrogatory, request for production, or request for admissions is incomplete or incorrect in some material respect, and the additional or corrective information has not otherwise been made known to the other parties during the discovery process or in writing. FRCP 26(e)(1)(A); ***Colón-Millín v. Sears Roebuck***, 455 F.3d 30, 37 (1st Cir.2006).

4. The party learns that information included in an expert report or given during an expert's deposition is incomplete or incorrect. *See* FRCP 26(e)(2). See "Supplementing Expert Discovery," ch. 6-D, §5, p. 527.

§11.2 Supplementation not required. Supplementation is not required if the information has otherwise been made known to the other parties during the discovery process or in writing. *See* FRCP 26(e)(1)(A); ***Kapche v. Holder***, 677 F.3d 454, 468 (D.C.Cir.2012); ***Ferrara & DiMercurio v. St. Paul Mercury Ins.***, 240 F.3d 1, 10 (1st Cir. 2001); *see also* 8A Wright, Miller & Marcus §2049.1 (no need to submit supplemental disclosure to include information already revealed by witness in deposition or otherwise through formal discovery).

§11.3 Types of discovery requiring supplementation.

1. Mandatory disclosures. FRCP 26(e) requires supplementation of all mandatory disclosures required by FRCP 26(a).

2. Most formal discovery requests. The duty to supplement responses to formal discovery applies to interrogatories, requests for production, and requests for admissions, but not to deposition testimony. 1993 Notes to FRCP 26 at ¶41, p. 1187, this book.

3. Expert reports & depositions. The duty to supplement applies to information included in an expert report and given in an expert's deposition. FRCP 26(e)(2); ***Southern States Rack & Fixture, Inc. v. Sherwin-Williams Co.***, 318 F.3d 592, 595-96 (4th Cir.2003). See "Supplementing retained-expert discovery," ch. 6-D, §5.1, p. 528.

§11.4 Time to supplement. Disclosures and discovery responses must be supplemented in a timely manner or as ordered by the court. FRCP 26(e)(1); *see, e.g.*, ***Hancock v. Hobbs***, 967 F.2d 462, 468 (11th Cir.1992) (identification of expert five months after he was retained and three months after close of discovery was not timely); ***Havenfield Corp. v. H&R Block, Inc.***, 509 F.2d 1263, 1272 (8th Cir.1975) (waiting 2½ months until close of discovery and another five to six weeks before supplementing was not timely); ***R&R Sails Inc. v. Insurance Co. of Pa.***, 251 F.R.D. 520, 526 (S.D.Cal.2008) (production of additional portions of insurance claim log one month after D represented that P had entire log was not timely). For expert reports and depositions, see "Supplementing Expert Discovery," ch. 6-D, §5, p. 527.

§11.5 In writing & signed. The rules contemplate that the parties will supplement discovery in writing and in the same form as the original discovery. *See, e.g.*, ***Knights Armament Co. v. Optical Sys. Tech.***, 254 F.R.D. 463, 466-67 (M.D.Fla.2008) (amended or supplemented interrogatory responses must be verified), *aff'd*, 254 F.R.D. 470 (M.D.Fla.2008). Oral supplementation does not satisfy the requirement that every disclosure or response be signed by the attorney or pro se party. *See* FRCP 26(g).

§11.6 Failure to supplement disclosures. If a party does not timely supplement or correct disclosures, the party cannot use that information or witness to supply evidence, unless the failure to supplement was substantially justified or is harmless. FRCP 37(c)(1); *see* ***Finley v. Marathon Oil Co.***, 75 F.3d 1225, 1230 (7th Cir.1996); *see, e.g.*, ***Patterson v. State Auto. Mut. Ins.***, 105 F.3d 1251, 1252 (8th Cir.1997) (failure to disclose additional inspection and

testing by expert justified exclusion of expert's testimony on those subjects). The district court's decision to exclude evidence or a witness is reviewed only for abuse of discretion. ***Miksis v. Howard***, 106 F.3d 754, 760 (7th Cir.1997). Courts may consider many factors in deciding whether to exclude evidence, including the prejudice or surprise to the party against whom the evidence is offered, the party's ability to cure the prejudice, the extent to which introducing the evidence would disrupt the trial, the importance of the evidence, the possibility of granting a continuance, and the movant's bad faith or willfulness. ***Southern States Rack & Fixture, Inc. v. Sherwin-Williams Co.***, 318 F.3d 592, 597 (4th Cir.2003); ***Woodworker's Sup. v. Principal Mut. Life Ins.***, 170 F.3d 985, 993 (10th Cir.1999); ***U.S. v. $9,041,598.68***, 163 F.3d 238, 252 (5th Cir.1998). The court, on motion and hearing, may impose other sanctions besides exclusion of evidence. FRCP 37(c)(1). The permitted sanctions include the following:

1. An order providing payment of reasonable expenses, including attorney fees, caused by the nondisclosure. FRCP 37(c)(1)(A).

2. A statement informing the jury of the party's nondisclosure. FRCP 37(c)(1)(B).

3. An order that the nondisclosed matters are deemed established in favor of the party seeking sanctions. FRCP 37(b)(2)(A)(i); *see* FRCP 37(c)(1)(C); *see, e.g.*, ***Commodity Futures Trading Comm'n v. Noble Metals Int'l***, 67 F.3d 766, 770-71 (9th Cir.1995) (allegations were deemed established when Ds willfully refused to designate deposition representative and court had considered lesser sanctions).

4. An order prohibiting the nondisclosing party from supporting or opposing claims or defenses related to the undisclosed material or from introducing the undisclosed material into evidence. FRCP 37(b)(2)(A)(ii); *see* FRCP 37(c)(1)(C); *see, e.g.*, ***Braun v. Lorillard Inc.***, 84 F.3d 230, 236 (7th Cir.1996) (court refused to permit party to call witness not listed in pretrial order).

5. An order striking pleadings in whole or in part. FRCP 37(b)(2)(A)(iii); *see* FRCP 37(b)(1)(C).

6. An order staying further proceedings until the order to disclose is obeyed. FRCP 37(b)(2)(A)(iv); *see* FRCP 37(b)(1)(C).

7. An order dismissing the action or proceeding in whole or in part. FRCP 37(b)(2)(A)(v); *see* FRCP 37(b)(1)(C).

8. An order rendering a default judgment against the nondisclosing party. FRCP 37(b)(2)(A)(vi); *see* FRCP 37(b)(1)(C).

§11.7 Failure to supplement discovery responses. The court can award the same sanctions for not supplementing discovery responses as it can for not supplementing disclosures. FRCP 37(c)(1); 2000 Notes to FRCP 37 at ¶2, p. 1205, this book; *see* ***Campbell Indus. v. M/V Gemini***, 619 F.2d 24, 27 (9th Cir.1980). See "Failure to supplement disclosures," §11.6, p. 439. Thus, the failure to timely supplement discovery responses may result in the imposition of sanctions, including the exclusion of evidence or testimony. *See* ***Ortiz-Lopez v. Sociedad Espanola de Auxilio Mutuo y Beneficiencia de P.R.***, 248 F.3d 29, 33 (1st Cir.2001); ***Holiday Inns, Inc. v. Robertshaw Controls Co.***, 560 F.2d 856, 858 (7th Cir.1977). When faced with accusations that a party has not properly supplemented a discovery response, a court may look at the conduct of the trial, the importance of the evidence to the nonsupplementing party, the opposing party's ability to formulate a response, and the reason for not timely supplementing. ***Thibeault v. Square D Co.***, 960 F.2d 239, 244 (1st Cir.1992).

§12. MOTION FOR PROTECTIVE ORDER

Instead of filing an objection to a discovery request, a party may seek a protective order narrowing the scope of discovery or limiting the dissemination of privileged or confidential materials. *See* ***Covad Comms. v. Revonet, Inc.***, 258 F.R.D. 5, 11 (D.D.C.2009). A motion for protective order may also be filed in response to a motion to compel.

§12.1 Power to protect. In a standard motion for protective order, the party asks the court to enter an order protecting it from certain discovery requests. FRCP 26(c)(1). For good cause, the court may issue an order to protect

a party or person from annoyance, embarrassment, oppression, or undue burden or expense. *Id.* But the court's discretion to enter a protective order is "limited by the careful dictates of [FRCP] 26." ***Procter & Gamble Co. v. Bankers Trust Co.***, 78 F.3d 219, 227 (6th Cir.1996); *see, e.g.*, ***Pierson v. Indianapolis Power & Light Co.***, 205 F.R.D. 646, 647 (S.D.Ind.2002) (in approving parties' agreement to joint protective order, court would not allow parties carte blanche to seal or protect whatever they desired).

§12.2 Time to file motion. A motion for protective order should be filed before the time to respond to the discovery request. ***Drexel Heritage Furnishings, Inc. v. Furniture USA, Inc.***, 200 F.R.D. 255, 259 (M.D.N.C.2001); *e.g.*, ***In re Coordinated Pretrial Proceedings in Pet. Prods. Antitrust Litig.***, 669 F.2d 620, 622 n.2 (10th Cir.1982) (motion made four days before date set for production). For a deposition, a party should secure the protective order before the date of the deposition (i.e., before the time specified in the notice). For example, a deposition cannot be used at trial against a party who received less than 14 days' notice of the deposition and who promptly filed a motion for protective order under FRCP 26(c)(1)(B) if the deposition was taken while the motion was pending. FRCP 32(a)(5)(A). See "Party seeking protective order," ch. 6-F, §4.3.2, p. 552.

§12.3 Grounds.

1. For most discovery requests.

(1) Producing party's burden. The producing party must show good cause for a protective order. FRCP 26(c)(1); ***In re Roman Catholic Archbishop of Portland***, 661 F.3d 417, 424 (9th Cir.2011); ***Shingara v. Skiles***, 420 F.3d 301, 305-06 (3d Cir.2005); *see also* ***In re Violation of Rule 28(d)***, 635 F.3d 1352, 1358 (Fed.Cir.2011) (even with agreed protective order, good cause must be shown). The producing party must support its claim for good cause through specific facts rather than conclusory or stereotypical statements. *See* ***Shingara***, 420 F.3d at 306; ***In re Terra Int'l***, 134 F.3d 302, 306 (5th Cir.1998); ***Cipollone v. Liggett Grp.***, 785 F.2d 1108, 1121 (3d Cir.1986); ***Drexel Heritage Furnishings, Inc. v. Furniture USA, Inc.***, 200 F.R.D. 255, 259 (M.D.N.C.2001).

(2) Good-cause standard.

(a) Generally. The standard of proof for good cause will vary with the type of information and protective order sought. For example, when seeking a protective order to limit both the people who can have access to the requested information and how they can use it, a producing party might establish good cause by showing that it will suffer a clearly defined and serious injury if the requested information is disclosed. *See, e.g.*, ***Drexel Heritage Furnishings***, 200 F.R.D. at 262 (production of D's supplier list was restricted to eyes of P's outside counsel only, because of possible harm resulting from P's predatory motives); ***Brittain v. Stroh Brewery Co.***, 136 F.R.D. 408, 415 (M.D.N.C.1991) (production of D's commercial information could cause harm if released); *see also* ***Spencer Trask Software & Info. Servs. v. RPost Int'l***, 206 F.R.D. 367, 368 (S.D.N.Y.2002) (to obtain order temporarily staying discovery, party may establish good cause by showing that it has filed dispositive motion, that requested stay is for short period of time, and that opposing party will not be prejudiced by stay).

(b) Factors. The following is a nonexhaustive list of factors the producing party may have to address when seeking to establish good cause:

[1] Whether the disclosure will violate any privacy interests. ***Glenmede Trust Co. v. Thompson***, 56 F.3d 476, 483 (3d Cir.1995).

[2] Whether the information is being sought for a legitimate purpose. *Id.*

[3] Whether disclosure of the information will cause a party embarrassment. *Id.*

[4] Whether confidentiality is being sought over information important to public health and safety. *Id.*

[5] Whether the sharing of information among litigants will promote fairness and efficiency. *Id.*

[6] Whether a party benefiting from the confidentiality order is a public entity or official. *Id.*

[7] Whether the case involves issues important to the public. *Id.*

[8] The danger of abuse if a protective order is granted. ***Brittain***, 136 F.R.D. at 415.

[9] The good faith of each party's position. *Id.*

[10] The adequacy of the protective measures provided by the protective order. *Id.*

[11] The availability of other means of proof. *Id.*

(3) Court's balancing test. If good cause has been established, the court must still determine whether the producing party's burden of production and its privacy interests outweigh the right of the opposing party and the public to obtain the information sought. ***Phillips v. General Motors Corp.***, 307 F.3d 1206, 1212-13 (9th Cir. 2002); *see* ***Seattle Times Co. v. Rhinehart***, 467 U.S. 20, 34-36 (1984); ***Coleman v. American Red Cross***, 979 F.2d 1135, 1139 (6th Cir.1992); ***Drexel Heritage Furnishings***, 200 F.R.D. at 259. If the court determines that the information sought should be protected, the court can still consider whether redacting portions of the information sought would allow for disclosure. ***In re Roman Catholic Archbishop of Portland***, 661 F.3d at 425.

2. For requests seeking electronically stored information. If the party wants a protective order for a discovery request seeking electronically stored information, the party must show that the information is not reasonably accessible because of undue burden or cost. FRCP 26(b)(2)(B). See "Motion for protective order," ch. 6-C, §11.1, p. 505.

§12.4 Certificate of conference. The producing party must attach a certificate to the motion stating that it conferred or attempted to confer with the other parties in a good-faith effort to resolve the dispute without court action. FRCP 26(c)(1). See "Burden to resolve dispute without court action," §8.3.3, p. 427.

§12.5 Order. The court has broad discretion to issue a protective order. *See* FRCP 26(c); ***Seattle Times Co. v. Rhinehart***, 467 U.S. 20, 36 (1984).

1. Types of protective relief. The court may order, but is not limited to, the protections listed below:

(1) Block discovery. The court may forbid the disclosure or discovery. FRCP 26(c)(1)(A); *see* ***Degen v. U.S.***, 517 U.S. 820, 826 (1996) (court may enter protective order to prevent parties from using civil suit to discover information that could not be discovered in pending criminal suit); *see, e.g.*, ***Reed v. AMAX Coal Co.***, 971 F.2d 1295, 1301 (7th Cir.1992) (affirmed order barring further discovery when, after close of discovery, party conducted oral depositions without notice to D and served three additional discovery requests, each containing more than 200 questions); ***Elvis Presley Enters. v. Elvisly Yours, Inc.***, 936 F.2d 889, 894 (6th Cir.1991) (upheld order blocking deposition of Priscilla Presley on showing that she had no personal knowledge and that deposition was primarily intended to harass and annoy her).

(2) Set terms & conditions of discovery. The court may specify the terms, including time and place, for the disclosure or discovery. FRCP 26(c)(1)(B). This provision allows a court to order a party seeking discovery to pay part of the cost of obtaining discoverable materials. *E.g.*, ***Penk v. Oregon State Bd. of Higher Educ.***, 816 F.2d 458, 468 (9th Cir.1987) (affirmed order that Ps pay half the cost of updating database for trial). A court can also use this provision to set discovery deadlines. *E.g.*, ***Transamerica Computer Co. v. International Bus. Machs. Corp.***, 573 F.2d 646, 652-53 (9th Cir.1978) (affirmed imposition of strict discovery deadline and order providing that inadvertent disclosure of privileged materials would not waive privilege).

(3) Set method of discovery. The court may prescribe a discovery method other than the one selected by the party seeking discovery. FRCP 26(c)(1)(C); *see, e.g.*, ***Rolex Watch U.S.A., Inc. v. Crowley***, 74 F.3d 716, 722 (6th Cir.1996) (court could prohibit deposition when affidavits already filed were sufficient on issues of attorney fees and expenses); ***Alex v. Jasper Wyman & Son***, 115 F.R.D. 156, 159 (D.Me.1986) (production of certified copies of all disclosable, relevant documents was adequate alternative to burdensome deposition of government official).

(4) Set conditions for discovery of electronically stored information. The court may specify conditions for the discovery of electronically stored information. FRCP 26(b)(2)(B); ***Rodríguez-Torres v. Government Dev. Bank of P.R.***, 265 F.R.D. 40, 43 (D.P.R.2010). See "Set terms & conditions of discovery," ch. 6-C, §11.1.5(2), p. 508.

(5) Limit scope of discovery. The court may order the parties not to inquire into certain matters, or it may limit the scope of disclosure or discovery to certain matters. FRCP 26(c)(1)(D); *see* ***Coleman v. American Red Cross***, 979 F.2d 1135, 1139 (6th Cir.1992).

(6) Limit persons present for discovery. The court may designate the persons who may be present while the discovery is conducted. FRCP 26(c)(1)(E); ***Galella v. Onassis***, 487 F.2d 986, 997 (2d Cir.1973); *e.g.*, ***Tolbert-Smith v. Bodman***, 253 F.R.D. 2, 4-5 (D.D.C.2008) (in discrimination suit, court barred P's former supervisors from attending her deposition when P had bipolar disorder, she feared her former supervisors, and her psychiatrist believed their presence would very likely result in severe and catastrophic harm to P). See "Other witnesses," ch. 6-F, §3.4.2, p. 545. The courts disagree on whether FRCP 26(c)(1)(E) permits exclusion of a party. *Compare* ***In re Shell Oil Refinery***, 136 F.R.D. 615, 616-17 & n.1 (E.D.La.1991) (allowed exclusion under a more lenient standard), *with* ***Kerschbaumer v. Bell***, 112 F.R.D. 426, 426-27 (D.D.C.1986) (denied motion because movant did not show that exclusion was required by fundamental fairness; noted that other courts impose lower threshold).

(7) Seal depositions. The court may order that a deposition be sealed and opened only by court order. FRCP 26(c)(1)(F); *see, e.g.*, ***Hawley v. Hall***, 131 F.R.D. 578, 581 (D.Nev.1990) (public officials did not make showing of good cause necessary to seal their depositions in civil-rights suit).

(8) Restrict disclosure of trade secrets. The court may order that a trade secret or other confidential research, development, or commercial information not be revealed or be revealed only in a specified way. FRCP 26(c)(1)(G); *see* ***Sega Enters. v. Accolade, Inc.***, 977 F.2d 1510, 1532 (9th Cir.1993) (court can restrict disclosure to only opposing counsel or independent experts); *see also* ***Brown Bag Software v. Symantec Corp.***, 960 F.2d 1465, 1470-72 (9th Cir.1992) (affirmed protective order allowing outside counsel access to trade secrets but shielding in-house counsel from knowledge of them). The most common type of protection for trade secrets is an order that limits the persons who have access to the information and how those persons may use the information. 8A Wright, Miller & Marcus §2043 & n.20; *see* ***Pansy v. Borough of Stroudsburg***, 23 F.3d 772, 787 (3d Cir.1994); ***Julius M. Ames Co. v. Bostitch, Inc.***, 235 F.Supp. 856, 857 (S.D.N.Y.1964); 4 Milgrim, *Milgrim on Trade Secrets* §14.02[4] (2012); Miller, *Confidentiality, Protective Orders, and Public Access to the Courts*, 105 Harv.L.Rev. 427, 432-36 (1991); Annotation, *Construction … of FRCP 26(c) Providing for the Filing of … Confidential Documents …*, 19 ALR Fed. 970, 973-76 (1974 & Supp.2012-13). *See generally* 26 Wright & Graham, *Federal Practice & Procedure* §§5641-5652 (1992 & Supp.2012) (discussing history, policy, and elements of trade-secrets privilege).

(9) Order simultaneous filing under seal. The court may require the parties to simultaneously file documents or information under seal, to be opened as the court directs. FRCP 26(c)(1)(H). This provision is mainly used in patent litigation involving disputes over invention date and assertions of prior art. *See, e.g.*, ***Friction Div. Prods. v. E.I. DuPont de Nemours & Co.***, 658 F.Supp. 998, 1002-03 (D.Del.1987) (denied motion because parties had been exchanging information for more than two years and simultaneous exchange would serve no purpose), *aff'd*, 883 F.2d 1027 (Fed.Cir.1989) (table case).

(10) Restrict use of discovered information. The court may restrict the use of discovered materials to the case in which they are discovered. *See* ***Jepson, Inc. v. Makita Elec. Works, Ltd.***, 30 F.3d 854, 858 (7th Cir.1994). Ordinarily, parties may freely disseminate materials obtained in discovery. *Id.*; *see* ***Zapata v. IBP, Inc.***, 160 F.R.D. 625, 627-28 (D.Kan.1995).

2. Duration of order. A protective order that survives the underlying litigation continues to have full force and effect even after final resolution of the case. ***Yates v. Applied Performance Techs.***, 205 F.R.D. 497, 500-01 (S.D.Ohio 2002); ***Tucker v. Ohtsu Tire & Rubber Co.***, 191 F.R.D. 495, 499 (D.Md.2000); *see also* ***United Nuclear Corp. v. Cranford Ins.***, 905 F.2d 1424, 1427 (10th Cir.1990) (as long as protective order remains in effect, court that entered it retains power to modify it even if underlying suit has been dismissed).

§13. MOTION TO QUASH SUBPOENA

See "Motion to Quash or Modify Subpoena," ch. 1-H, §8, p. 55.

§14. MOTION TO COMPEL DISCOVERY

A party may ask the court for an order compelling disclosure or discovery. FRCP 37(a)(1). See "Burden to secure hearing & ruling," §8.3.4, p. 428.

§14.1 Proper court. When a party seeks to compel discovery from a party, a motion to compel must be made in the court where the action is pending. FRCP 37(a)(2). When a party seeks to compel discovery from a nonparty, a motion to compel must be made in the district where the discovery is or will be taken. *Id.*; ***In re Sealed Case***, 141 F.3d 337, 341 (D.C.Cir.1998); *see also* ***Angell v. Shawmut Bank Conn.***, 153 F.R.D. 585, 589 (M.D.N.C.1994) (court issuing subpoena has authority to resolve controversies about subpoena because that court has most direct interest).

§14.2 Time to file motion. Ordinarily, a motion to compel should be filed either when a party does not complete the disclosures required by FRCP 26(a) or when a party or person does not properly respond to a discovery request. *See* FRCP 37(a)(3). A party should not wait until the discovery deadline passes. *See* ***Kinetic Concepts, Inc. v. ConvaTec Inc.***, 268 F.R.D. 226, 246 (M.D.N.C.2010).

§14.3 Grounds. A party may file a motion to compel discovery in the following instances:

1. Failure to disclose. If a party does not make a required disclosure, any other party may file a motion to compel. FRCP 37(a)(3)(A). See "Burden to secure hearing & ruling," §8.3.4, p. 428.

2. Failure to respond to discovery. If a party does not respond to discovery requests, the requesting party may file a motion to compel. FRCP 37(a)(3)(B). The following are some examples:

(1) Refusal to answer deposition questions. If a party or witness does not answer questions at a deposition, the asking party may move for an order compelling answers. FRCP 37(a)(3)(B)(i); ***R.W. Int'l v. Welch Foods, Inc.***, 937 F.2d 11, 15 (1st Cir.1991); ***Bank One v. Abbe***, 916 F.2d 1067, 1077-78 (6th Cir.1990).

(2) Failure to designate representative. If a party does not designate an organizational representative, the requesting party may move for an order compelling a designation. FRCP 37(a)(3)(B)(ii); ***Cates v. LTV Aerospace Corp.***, 480 F.2d 620, 624 (5th Cir.1973).

(3) Failure to answer interrogatory. If a party does not answer an interrogatory, the requesting party may move for an order compelling an answer. FRCP 37(a)(3)(B)(iii); ***Toma v. City of Weatherford***, 846 F.2d 58, 60 (10th Cir.1988); ***Schleper v. Ford Motor Co.***, 585 F.2d 1367, 1370-71 (8th Cir.1978).

(4) Failure to produce or permit inspection. If a party does not produce or permit inspection, the requesting party may move for an order compelling production or inspection. FRCP 37(a)(3)(B)(iv); ***R.W. Int'l***, 937 F.2d at 17-19 (motion to compel is necessary first step before seeking sanctions). The requesting party must demonstrate that the requested documents exist and are being withheld. ***Alexander v. FBI***, 194 F.R.D. 305, 311 (D.D.C. 2000); *see* ***Hubbard v. Potter***, 247 F.R.D. 27, 29 (D.D.C.2008) (if requesting party contends that producing party is withholding additional production, already-produced discovery must suggest that there is additional discovery to produce or that the discovery has been destroyed). FRCP 37(a)(3)(B) applies only to requests for production served on a party under FRCP 30(b)(2) and 34, not to a subpoena duces tecum under FRCP 45(a)(1)(A)(iii). *See* ***Fisher v. Marubeni Cotton Corp.***, 526 F.2d 1338, 1341-42 (8th Cir.1975) (contempt under FRCP 45(e) is proper remedy for nonparty's failure to produce). A party moving to hold a nonparty in contempt under FRCP 45(e) must show, by clear and convincing evidence, that the nonparty has violated the subpoena. ***Food Lion, Inc. v. United Food & Commercial Workers Int'l Un.***, 103 F.3d 1007, 1016 (D.C.Cir.1997). A showing of bad faith is not necessary. *Id.*

(5) Evasive or incomplete responses. If a party does not provide adequate responses to discovery requests, the requesting party may move for an order compelling adequate responses. *See* ***GMAC Bank v. HTFC Corp.***, 248 F.R.D. 182, 193 (E.D.Pa.2008). For purposes of a motion to compel, an evasive or incomplete disclosure,

answer, or response must be treated as a failure to disclose, answer, or respond. FRCP 37(a)(4); *see* ***Beard v. Braunstein***, 914 F.2d 434, 446 (3d Cir.1990); *see, e.g.*, ***Continental Ins. v. McGraw***, 110 F.R.D. 679, 681-82 & n.2 (D.Colo. 1986) (improperly signed answers to interrogatories were treated as failure to answer, but sanctions were not appropriate without FRCP 37(a) motion to compel).

(6) Incomplete production of electronically stored information. If a party does not provide an adequate response to a request for electronically stored information, the requesting party may move for an order compelling a more complete production of the information. *See* ***John B. v. Goetz***, 531 F.3d 448, 459 (6th Cir.2008). See "ESI production incomplete," ch. 6-C, §11.2.2(2)(a)[1], p. 510.

3. After objection to discovery. If a party or nonparty timely files an objection in response to a discovery request or a subpoena duces tecum, the requesting party may move to compel production.

(1) Objections to interrogatories. A party may move for an order compelling answers to interrogatories after the answering party has objected to them. ***Fox v. Studebaker-Worthington, Inc.***, 516 F.2d 989, 995 (8th Cir.1975); *see* FRCP 37(a)(3)(B)(iii). See "Valid objections," §8.3.1(2)(a), p. 425. A motion to compel is the proper method to attack objections to interrogatories. *See* ***Pan-Islamic Trade Corp. v. Exxon Corp.***, 632 F.2d 539, 552 (5th Cir.1980) (court will not rule on objection without motion to compel under FRCP 37(a)).

(2) Objections to requests for production. A party may move for an order compelling production after the responding party has objected. *See* FRCP 37(a)(3)(B)(iv); ***Peat, Marwick, Mitchell & Co. v. West***, 748 F.2d 540, 541-42 (10th Cir.1984). See "Valid objections," §8.3.1(2)(a), p. 425.

(3) Objections to requests for admissions. A party may move to determine the sufficiency of objections made to requests for admissions. FRCP 36(a)(6). See "Valid objections," §8.3.1(2)(a), p. 425. The court may order that an amended answer be served or may deem the matter admitted. FRCP 36(a)(6); ***Thalheim v. Eberheim***, 124 F.R.D. 34, 35 (D.Conn.1988). These motions are almost always titled "Motion to Deem Requests Admitted."

(4) Objections to subpoena. A party may move to compel production or inspection after a nonparty objects to the inspection or copying of designated materials or the inspection of premises. FRCP 45(c)(2)(B)(i). See "Motion to Compel Production or for Inspection," ch. 1-H, §7, p. 55; "Valid objections," §8.3.1(2)(a), p. 425.

4. After electronically stored information declared inaccessible. A party may move to compel discovery after a producing party objects that electronically stored information is not reasonably accessible. See "Objections that ESI not reasonably accessible," ch. 6-C, §11.2.2(2)(b)[2], p. 512.

§14.4 Certificate of conference. The requesting party must attach a certificate to the motion stating that it conferred or attempted to confer with the other parties in a good-faith effort to resolve the dispute without court action. FRCP 37(a)(1). See "Burden to resolve dispute without court action," §8.3.3, p. 427.

§14.5 Order.

1. Motion granted. If the court grants the motion, it will order the responding party to produce the requested information. The court must also award the movant reasonable expenses, including attorney fees, unless (1) the movant filed the motion before attempting in good faith to obtain the disclosure or discovery without court action, (2) the respondent's position was substantially justified, or (3) other circumstances make an award of expenses unjust. FRCP 37(a)(5)(A); *see* ***Devaney v. Continental Am. Ins.***, 989 F.2d 1154, 1159 (11th Cir.1993) (1970 amendments mandated award of expenses unless conduct was substantially justified); *see also* ***Westmoreland v. CBS, Inc.***, 770 F.2d 1168, 1173 (D.C.Cir.1985) (court cannot grant motion for sanctions without first ruling on motion to compel). Expenses may be charged against the party or deponent whose conduct made the motion necessary, the party or attorney advising the conduct, or both. FRCP 37(a)(5)(A); *see* ***Devaney***, 989 F.2d at 1161-62 (attorney may be sanctioned for willful blindness or acquiescence to client's malfeasance); *see, e.g.*, ***GMAC Bank v. HTFC Corp.***, 248 F.R.D. 182, 198-99 (E.D.Pa.2008) (D and D's attorney were jointly and severally liable for P's expenses when D repeatedly did not answer questions at deposition and D's attorney did not take any steps to curb D's misconduct).

2. Motion granted in part, denied in part. If the court grants the motion in part and denies it in part, the court (1) will order the responding party to produce some of the requested information, (2) may issue a protective order under FRCP 26(c), and (3) may, after giving the parties an opportunity to be heard, apportion the reasonable expenses for the motion. *See* FRCP 37(a)(5)(C); ***Smith v. Conway Org.***, 154 F.R.D. 73, 78 (S.D.N.Y.1994). See "Order," §12.5, p. 442.

3. Motion denied. If the court denies the motion, it may issue a protective order under FRCP 26(c). FRCP 37(a)(5)(B). After a hearing, the court must award the responding party reasonable expenses, including attorney fees, unless the movant's position was substantially justified or other circumstances make an award of expenses unjust. *Id.*; *see also* ***Westmoreland***, 770 F.2d at 1173 (court cannot grant motion for sanctions without first ruling on motion to compel). Expenses may be charged against the movant, the attorney filing the motion, or both. FRCP 37(a)(5)(B); *see* ***Devaney***, 989 F.2d at 1161-62 (attorney may be sanctioned for willful blindness or acquiescence to client's malfeasance).

§14.6 Standard of review. The district court's ruling on a motion to compel discovery will be reviewed only for abuse of discretion. ***Regan-Touhy v. Walgreen Co.***, 526 F.3d 641, 647 (10th Cir.2008); *see, e.g.*, ***Commercial Un. Ins. v. Westrope***, 730 F.2d 729, 731-32 (11th Cir.1984) (refusal to review deposition questions was abuse of discretion). The party seeking review may need to prove prejudice to demonstrate an abuse of discretion. *See* ***Hastings v. North E. ISD***, 615 F.2d 628, 631 (5th Cir.1980).

§15. MOTION FOR DISCOVERY SANCTIONS

§15.1 Purposes of sanctions. A court imposes discovery sanctions to (1) secure compliance with the rules of discovery, (2) deter others from violating them, and (3) punish those who do violate them. *See* ***National Hockey League v. Metropolitan Hockey Club, Inc.***, 427 U.S. 639, 643 (1976). See "Motion for Sanctions," ch. 5-O, p. 384.

§15.2 Due-process concerns. Due process limits a court's power to impose discovery sanctions. ***Wyle v. R.J. Reynolds Indus.***, 709 F.2d 585, 589 (9th Cir.1983). A court can impose sanctions only to the extent that the party's conduct is based on bad faith, obstructiveness, or failure to produce material evidence. *See, e.g.*, ***Hammond Packing Co. v. Arkansas***, 212 U.S. 322, 349-54 (1909) (striking pleadings and entering default judgment did not violate due process because party's conduct justified presumption that its claim lacked merit). The party's conduct must be related to the merits of the case. ***Phoceene Sous-Marine v. U.S. Phosmarine, Inc.***, 682 F.2d 802, 806 (9th Cir.1982). The provision in FRCP 37(a)(5) permitting a court to impose expenses on an attorney does not violate due process. *See* ***Devaney v. Continental Am. Ins.***, 989 F.2d 1154, 1159-60 (11th Cir.1993) (FRCP 37 requires notice to attorney that motion for sanctions has been filed against client).

§15.3 Grounds.

1. Not obeying court order. A party may move for sanctions if the other party or its representative does not obey a specific order to provide or permit discovery, including an order made under FRCP 26(f), 35, or 37(a). FRCP 37(b)(2)(A); *see* ***Salahuddin v. Harris***, 782 F.2d 1127, 1131 (2d Cir.1986) (language of FRCP 37(b)(2) requires earlier order).

(1) Earlier order. Sanctions under FRCP 37(b) are not available until the court has issued a specific discovery order instructing a party to submit to discovery. ***Shepherd v. ABC, Inc.***, 62 F.3d 1469, 1474 (D.C.Cir. 1995); ***Salahuddin***, 782 F.2d at 1131; *see, e.g.*, ***Schempp v. Reniker***, 809 F.2d 541, 542 (8th Cir.1987) (court ordered mental and physical examination of P; case was dismissed without prejudice because mother would not permit physical examination of daughter unless mother was in room); *see also* ***Unigard Sec. Ins. v. Lakewood Eng'g & Mfg.***, 982 F.2d 363, 368 (9th Cir.1992) (earlier discovery order is not necessary when sanctions are based on court's inherent power to sanction). The requirement of an earlier discovery order (1) serves to alert the offending party to the seriousness of its noncompliance, (2) permits judicial scrutiny of the discovery request, (3) functions as a final warning that sanctions are imminent, and (4) informs the party resisting discovery of its obligations. ***Daval Steel Prods. v. M/V Fakredine***, 951 F.2d 1357, 1364-65 (2d Cir.1991). Sanctions cannot be based on discovery requests or

subpoenas. *See **Daval Steel***, 951 F.2d at 1364-65 (trial subpoena is not order that FRCP 37(b) sanctions can be based on, although noncompliance can be punished by contempt); ***R.W. Int'l v. Welch Foods, Inc.***, 937 F.2d 11, 15 & n.2 (1st Cir.1991) (general commands of scheduling order are not sufficiently specific to support FRCP 37(b) sanctions); ***Fisher v. Marubeni Cotton Corp.***, 526 F.2d 1338, 1341 (8th Cir.1975) (subpoena duces tecum will not support FRCP 37(b) sanctions).

(2) Oral or written. The order does not need to be formal, written, or signed. *E.g.*, ***Halas v. Consumer Servs.***, 16 F.3d 161, 164 (7th Cir.1994) (oral directive from court was sufficient basis for FRCP 37(b) sanctions); ***Jones v. Uris Sales Corp.***, 373 F.2d 644, 647-48 (2d Cir.1967) (oral order requiring compliance with subpoena was sufficient basis for FRCP 37(b) sanction striking answer).

2. Not responding to discovery. A party may move for sanctions for a failure to respond to discovery under FRCP 37(d) in the following circumstances: (1) a party or its representative does not attend a deposition after service of proper notice or (2) a party does not serve answers, objections, or a written response to properly served interrogatories or a request for inspection. FRCP 37(d)(1)(A). A motion under FRCP 37(d)(1)(A)(ii) must include a certificate of conference. FRCP 37(d)(1)(B).

CIRCUIT SPLIT

The circuits are split on whether FRCP 37(d) requires a total failure to respond. ***Badalamenti v. Dunham's, Inc.****, 896 F.2d 1359, 1363 (Fed.Cir.1990). Some courts allow for sanctions when the response is so evasive or misleading that it amounts to no response at all. See* ***Coane v. Ferrara Pan Candy Co.****, 898 F.2d 1030, 1031 n.1 (5th Cir.1990);* ***Airtex Corp. v. Shelley Radiant Ceiling Co.****, 536 F.2d 145, 155 (7th Cir.1976);* ***Bell v. Automobile Club****, 80 F.R.D. 228, 232 (E.D.Mich.1978). Other courts require a total failure to respond before sanctions can be awarded.* ***Fox v. Studebaker-Worthington, Inc.****, 516 F.2d 989, 995 (8th Cir.1975); see* ***Fjelstad v. American Honda Motor Co.****, 762 F.2d 1334, 1339-40 (9th Cir.1985).*

(1) Not attending deposition.

(a) Deponent did not attend. A party may move for sanctions under FRCP 37(d) if a party or its representative does not attend a deposition after service of proper notice. FRCP 37(d)(1)(A)(i). The failure to appear does not need to have been in bad faith. ***Telluride Mgmt. Solutions, Inc. v. Telluride Inv.***, 55 F.3d 463, 466 (9th Cir.1995). Sanctions for not attending a deposition are permitted only when the deponent does not appear at the deposition session. ***SEC v. Research Automation Corp.***, 521 F.2d 585, 588-89 (2d Cir.1975). This strict construction distinguishes this sanction from FRCP 37(a)(3)(C) and (b)(2), which permit both a motion to compel and sanctions for not answering a question in an oral or written deposition. ***R.W. Int'l***, 937 F.2d at 15 & n.2.

(b) Noticing party did not attend or serve subpoena. A party who attends a deposition, expecting it to be taken, may recover reasonable expenses, including attorney fees, for attending if the noticing party (1) did not attend and proceed with the deposition or (2) did not serve a subpoena on a nonparty, who consequently did not attend. FRCP 30(g).

(c) Unprepared witness. If the deponent appears at the deposition but is unprepared to answer any questions, the appearance may be considered no appearance at all. ***Black Horse Lane Assocs. v. Dow Chem. Corp.***, 228 F.3d 275, 304 (3d Cir.2000); ***Resolution Trust Corp. v. Southern Un. Co.***, 985 F.2d 196, 197 (5th Cir.1993); ***Cherrington Asia Ltd. v. A&L Underground, Inc.***, 263 F.R.D. 653, 658 (D.Kan.2010).

(2) Not serving answers or objections to interrogatories. A party may move for sanctions if another party or its representative does not serve answers or objections to properly served interrogatories. FRCP 37(d)(1)(A)(ii); ***Oklahoma Federated Gold & Numismatics, Inc. v. Blodgett***, 24 F.3d 136, 139 (10th Cir.1994).

(3) Not serving response to request for inspection. A party may move for sanctions if another party does not respond to a properly served request for inspection. FRCP 37(d)(1)(A)(ii). Unless the party filed a motion for protective order, failure to respond is not excused on the ground that the discovery is objectionable. ***Badalamenti***, 896 F.2d at 1362.

3. Not participating in framing discovery plan. A party may move for sanctions if the other party or its attorney does not participate in good faith in the development and submission of a discovery plan. FRCP 37(f); *see **Apex Oil Co. v. Belcher Co.***, 855 F.2d 1009, 1014 (2d Cir.1988).

4. Refusing to disclose. A party may move for sanctions if the other party refuses to disclose information required by FRCP 26(a) or (e) without substantial justification. FRCP 37(c)(1); *see **Morrison Knudsen Corp. v. Fireman's Fund Ins.***, 175 F.3d 1221, 1229 (10th Cir.1999); ***McClain v. Metabolife Int'l***, 193 F.Supp.2d 1252, 1258-59 (N.D.Ala.2002).

5. Not supplementing. A party may move for sanctions if the other party does not supplement an earlier response to discovery as required by FRCP 26(e) without substantial justification. FRCP 37(c)(1).

6. Refusing to admit. A party may move for sanctions if a party responding to requests for admissions does not admit the genuineness of a document or the truth of a matter and the requesting party later proves the document to be genuine or the matter to be true. FRCP 37(c)(2). See "Sanctions," ch. 6-H, §7, p. 567.

7. Losing electronically stored information. A party may move for sanctions if the other party did not operate its electronic information system in a routine, good-faith manner and as a result was unable to provide electronically stored information. *See* FRCP 37(e). See "Sanctions for Lost ESI," ch. 6-C, §12, p. 513.

8. Not properly certifying under FRCP 26(g). A party may move for sanctions if the other party or its representative did not properly certify its discovery or disclosure as required by FRCP 26(g). FRCP 26(g)(3); ***Oregon RSA No. 6, Inc. v. Castle Rock Cellular L.P.***, 76 F.3d 1003, 1007 (9th Cir.1996); ***Cache La Poudre Feeds, LLC v. Land O'Lakes, Inc.***, 244 F.R.D. 614, 637 (D.Colo.2007); *see **Mancia v. Mayflower Textile Servs.***, 253 F.R.D. 354, 357 (D.Md.2008); *see also **In re Chester Cty. Elec., Inc.***, 208 F.R.D. 545, 548 (E.D.Pa.2002) (person seeking deposition to perpetuate testimony under FRCP 27 is not considered a party for purposes of FRCP 26(g)). A party does not properly certify its discovery or disclosure unless it makes a reasonable inquiry into the factual basis of its request, response, or objection. ***Mancia***, 253 F.R.D. at 357. See "Discovery Certificates," §6, p. 420.

9. Inherent power to sanction. When a party's deplorable conduct is not effectively sanctionable under an existing rule or statute, a court may rely on its inherent power to impose sanctions. *See **Chambers v. NASCO, Inc.***, 501 U.S. 32, 50 (1991); ***Carroll v. Jaques Admiralty Law Firm, P.C.***, 110 F.3d 290, 292-93 (5th Cir.1997). See "Bad-faith conduct," ch. 5-O, §3.9, p. 389; "Authorized sanctions under court's inherent power," ch. 5-O, §8.3, p. 396.

§15.4 Certificate of conference. A motion for sanctions based on failure to respond to interrogatories or requests for production must include a certificate that the movant conferred or attempted to confer in a good-faith effort to obtain the response without court action. FRCP 37(d)(1)(B). See "Burden to resolve dispute without court action," §8.3.3, p. 427.

§15.5 Sanctions available. Whether to impose discovery sanctions is a matter within the court's discretion. *E.g.*, ***Gomez v. Martin Marietta Corp.***, 50 F.3d 1511, 1519 (10th Cir.1995) (court declined to impose sanctions against party who destroyed evidence subject to discovery when evidence was summary of evidence already produced and party requesting sanctions was not prejudiced).

1. Sanctions for not complying with order. The courts may enforce discovery orders by providing strong and specific sanctions for not complying. *See* FRCP 37(b). Imposition of sanctions under FRCP 37(b)(2) is left to the court's discretion, but each sanction must be just and must relate to the claim to which the discovery order was addressed. ***Insurance Corp. of Ir., Ltd. v. Compagnie des Bauxites de Guinee***, 456 U.S. 694, 707 (1982).

(1) Order facts deemed established. A court may order that matters relating to the violated discovery order, or other designated facts, be deemed established for purposes of the action as the prevailing party claims. FRCP 37(b)(2)(A)(i). This may include jurisdictional facts. *See **Insurance Corp.***, 456 U.S. at 706-07 (sanction applied to facts that form basis for personal jurisdiction over D).

(2) Prevent party from supporting or opposing claims. A court may refuse to allow a party to support or oppose claims or to introduce evidence. FRCP 37(b)(2)(A)(ii). This sanction is generally used to prevent

the introduction of evidence that the party refused to produce in discovery. ***Carroll v. Acme-Cleveland Corp.***, 955 F.2d 1107, 1115-16 (7th Cir.1992); ***Navarro de Cosme v. Hospital Pavia***, 922 F.2d 926, 932 (1st Cir.1991). The court should not exclude evidence unless it finds that the party's noncompliance was both unjustified and harmful to the opposing party. ***Grajales-Romero v. American Airlines, Inc.***, 194 F.3d 288, 297 (1st Cir.1999); ***Newman v. GHA Osteopathic, Inc.***, 60 F.3d 153, 156 (3d Cir.1995).

(3) Strike pleadings, stay proceedings, dismiss case, or render default. A court may make an order striking pleadings in whole or in part, staying proceedings until the order is obeyed, dismissing the case in whole or in part, or rendering a default judgment. FRCP 37(b)(2)(A)(iii)-(b)(2)(A)(vi); *see* ***Degen v. U.S.***, 517 U.S. 820, 827 (1996); ***Lee v. Max Int'l***, 638 F.3d 1318, 1320-21 (10th Cir.2011); ***Banco del Atlantico, S.A. v. Woods Indus.***, 519 F.3d 350, 354 (7th Cir.2008); ***Poole v. Textron, Inc.***, 192 F.R.D. 494, 506 n.14 (D.Md.2000). Because this sanction prevents the resolution of claims on their merits, it is disfavored, and due-process concerns are heightened whenever it is used. ***Sentis Grp. v. Shell Oil Co.***, 559 F.3d 888, 899 (8th Cir.2009); ***Brinkmann v. Abner***, 813 F.2d 744, 749 (5th Cir.1987); *see* ***Lee***, 638 F.3d at 1321 (public policy strongly favors disposition of cases on merits); ***Sun v. Board of Trs.***, 473 F.3d 799, 811 (7th Cir.2007) (same). The courts have used a variety of factors to determine whether a court may impose this sanction, including the following:

(a) Willfulness. A court may impose a severe sanction when a party's recalcitrance is due to willfulness or bad faith. ***National Hockey League v. Metropolitan Hockey Club, Inc.***, 427 U.S. 639, 643 (1976); ***Brown v. Columbia Sussex Corp.***, 664 F.3d 182, 190-91 (7th Cir.2011); ***Lee***, 638 F.3d at 1321. When a party has the ability to comply with the court's order, a willful or bad-faith refusal to comply will justify dismissal. ***Regional Refuse Sys. v. Inland Reclamation Co.***, 842 F.2d 150, 153-54 (6th Cir.1988); *e.g.*, ***Lee***, 638 F.3d at 1321 (dismissal was appropriate when Ps had materials in their control that were responsive to D's discovery request, but Ps did not respond to D's request and then disobeyed two court orders to produce materials); *see also* ***Poole***, 192 F.R.D. at 506 (in cases of bad faith, courts have ordinarily found direct and often repeated violations of court orders).

NOTE

A court may consider a party's action in a related case to determine whether a party acted willfully or in bad faith. ***Smith v. Smith****, 145 F.3d 335, 344 (5th Cir.1998). But see* ***Atchison, Topeka & Santa Fe Ry. v. Hercules Inc.****, 146 F.3d 1071, 1073 (9th Cir.1998) (FRCP 37(b) does not "authorize dismissal of an entirely separate action for violations in a related action").*

(b) Interference with truth. A court may impose a severe sanction when the violation (1) threatens to interfere with the "rightful decision" of the case and (2) makes it impossible to be confident that the parties will ever have access to the true facts. *See* ***Connecticut Gen. Life Ins. v. New Images***, 482 F.3d 1091, 1097 (9th Cir.2007).

(c) Delay & public interest. A court may impose a severe sanction based on the public's interest in the expeditious resolution of litigation when a party's actions create unjustified delays. ***Connecticut Gen. Life Ins.***, 482 F.3d at 1096; *see* ***Coane v. Ferrara Pan Candy Co.***, 898 F.2d 1030, 1032 (5th Cir.1990).

(d) Court's need to manage its docket. A court may impose a severe sanction based on the need to manage its docket when a party's actions create unmanageable delays. *See* ***Connecticut Gen. Life Ins.***, 482 F.3d at 1096; ***Procter & Gamble Co. v. Haugen***, 427 F.3d 727, 738 (10th Cir.2005).

(e) Violation attributable to client. A court ordinarily may dismiss a party's claim or defense on the merits only when the violation of the discovery order is attributable to the client and not the attorney. ***Coane***, 898 F.2d at 1032; ***Lolatchy v. Arthur Murray, Inc.***, 816 F.2d 951, 953 (4th Cir.1987); ***Carter v. Albert Einstein Med. Ctr.***, 804 F.2d 805, 807-08 (3d Cir.1986). *But see* ***Comiskey v. JFTJ Corp.***, 989 F.2d 1007, 1010 (8th Cir.1993) (party may be held responsible for its attorney's actions).

(f) Substantial prejudice. A court may impose a severe sanction only when the party's conduct has substantially prejudiced the opposing party. ***Coane***, 898 F.2d at 1032; *see* ***Haugen***, 427 F.3d at 738 (court should consider degree of actual prejudice to opposing party); *see, e.g.*, ***Bass v. Jostens, Inc.***, 71 F.3d 237, 242 (6th

Cir.1995) (complete refusal to answer interrogatories for over a year hindered other party's ability to conduct discovery); ***FDIC v. Conner***, 20 F.3d 1376, 1381 (5th Cir.1994) (violation of order compelling answers to interrogatories did not prejudice opposing party enough to justify dismissal of claims); *see also* ***Schoffstall v. Henderson***, 223 F.3d 818, 823 (8th Cir.2000) (dismissal requires both substantial prejudice and willfulness); ***Wilson v. Volkswagen***, 561 F.2d 494, 503-04 (4th Cir.1977) (amount of prejudice necessarily includes inquiry into materiality of evidence not produced). *But see* ***Southern New England Tel. Co. v. Global NAPs, Inc.***, 251 F.R.D. 82, 90 (D.Conn.2008) (showing of prejudice is not a requirement for dismissal under FRCP 37; it is only a consideration in weighing appropriateness of sanction).

(g) Warning of severe sanctions. A court should not dismiss or render default unless it has warned the party that failure to cooperate will lead to severe sanctions. ***Brown***, 664 F.3d at 192; ***Haugen***, 427 F.3d at 738; ***Bass***, 71 F.3d at 242. The warning does not necessarily have to come from the court, however; a party can be put on notice of possible dismissal if the opposing party requests that as a sanction. ***Brown***, 664 F.3d at 192.

NOTE

In certain circumstances, a warning of severe sanctions may not be necessary. See ***Brown***, *664 F.3d at 192 (dicta; although Ps were sufficiently warned, warning may not have been necessary because Ps missed five discovery deadlines, violated two court orders, and completely failed to respond to interrogatories).*

(h) Lesser sanctions not available. A court should not impose a severe sanction if a lesser sanction would provide adequate deterrence. ***Haugen***, 427 F.3d at 738; ***Coane***, 898 F.2d at 1032; ***Founding Ch. of Scientology v. Webster***, 802 F.2d 1448, 1459 (D.C.Cir.1986); *see* ***Connecticut Gen. Life Ins.***, 482 F.3d at 1096; ***Wilson***, 561 F.2d at 503-04. The court is not required to explicitly state that it has considered lesser sanctions and found them inappropriate. ***Phipps v. Blakeney***, 8 F.3d 788, 790 (11th Cir.1993). However, an appellate court may be reluctant to affirm if the district court's findings of fact do not adequately detail the culpable conduct and do not explain why lesser sanctions would be ineffective. ***Ocelot Oil Corp. v. Sparrow Indus.***, 847 F.2d 1458, 1465 (10th Cir.1988).

(4) Find person in contempt of court. A court may find a person in contempt of court for not obeying any order, except an order to submit to a physical or mental examination. FRCP 37(b)(2)(A)(vii), (b)(2)(B), 45(e); *see* 18 U.S.C. §401 (criminal contempt). A court may impose criminal or civil contempt sanctions. *See* ***Lamar Fin. Corp. v. Adams***, 918 F.2d 564, 566-67 (5th Cir.1990). When imposing contempt sanctions, the court should distinguish between criminal and civil contempt because the standards of proof and notice requirements are different. ***Buffington v. Baltimore Cty.***, 913 F.2d 113, 133 (4th Cir.1990). The distinction is based on the substance of the proceeding and the character of the relief sought. ***Hicks v. Feiock***, 485 U.S. 624, 631-32 (1988).

(a) Criminal contempt. Criminal contempt is meant to punish the person in contempt for disobedience and to deter future litigants' misconduct. ***Bradley v. American Household Inc.***, 378 F.3d 373, 378 (4th Cir.2004); *see* ***Hicks***, 485 U.S. at 631; ***U.S. v. Straub***, 508 F.3d 1003, 1009 (11th Cir.2007); ***Falstaff Brewing Corp. v. Miller Brewing Co.***, 702 F.2d 770, 778 (9th Cir.1983). When a court orders criminal contempt, it must observe applicable procedural safeguards, such as notifying the person in contempt that the contempt proceedings are criminal in nature. ***Lamar Fin. Corp.***, 918 F.2d at 567; *see* ***Romero v. Drummond Co.***, 480 F.3d 1234, 1242-43 (11th Cir. 2007); *see also* ***Fonar Corp. v. Magnetic Resonance Plus, Inc.***, 128 F.3d 99, 102 (2d Cir.1997) (court does not have to specifically warn attorney of contempt sanction when attorney is fully apprised of court's sanctioning authority under FRCP 37(b)). When imposing criminal contempt sanctions, a court must consider whether there was a lawful and reasonably specific order that the defendant willfully violated. ***Romero***, 480 F.3d at 1242; *see* ***Straub***, 508 F.3d at 1011-12; *see, e.g.*, ***In re Katz***, 476 F.Supp.2d 572, 577 (W.D.Va.2007) (attorney-D was guilty of criminal contempt when he willfully violated court order by calling witnesses "liars" during closing argument).

(b) Civil contempt. Civil contempt is meant to compel obedience to a court order or to compensate the complainant for losses sustained. ***U.S. v. United Mine Workers***, 330 U.S. 258, 303-04 (1947); ***In re Bradley***, 588 F.3d 254, 263 (5th Cir.2009); *see* ***Hicks***, 485 U.S. at 631; ***Straub***, 508 F.3d at 1009; *see, e.g.*, ***In re Fannie Mae***

Secs. Litig., 552 F.3d 814, 823-24 (D.C.Cir.2009) (court sanctioned nonparty for noncompliance with production deadline by ordering nonparty to provide documents withheld on basis of privilege; because contempt sanction allowed for later recovery of privileged documents, it was proper and not punitive). When imposing civil contempt sanctions, a court must consider the following factors: (1) harm from noncompliance, (2) probable effectiveness of the sanction, (3) financial resources of the party being sanctioned and the burden the sanctions may impose, and (4) willfulness of the party's conduct in disregarding the court's order. ***United Mine Workers***, 330 U.S. at 303-04. The record should reflect the court's consideration of these factors. *See* ***In re Chase & Sanborn Corp.***, 872 F.2d 397, 401 (11th Cir.1989); ***General Signal Corp. v. Donallco, Inc.***, 787 F.2d 1376, 1380 (9th Cir.1986).

NOTE

If a deponent refuses to be sworn or to answer a question after the court's instruction, the deponent may be punished by contempt either by the court where the case is pending or by a court in the district where the deposition is being taken. See FRCP 37(b)(1), (b)(2)(A)(vii). However, at least one court has suggested that FRCP 37(b)(1) should not be applied against parties outside the district where the case is pending. ***Miller v. Transamerican Press, Inc.****, 709 F.2d 524, 531 (9th Cir.1983).*

(5) Award attorney fees & expenses. Besides any of the other sanctions in FRCP 37(b)(2)(A), a court must require the party violating a discovery order, the attorney advising the party, or both to pay the moving party's reasonable expenses, including attorney fees, caused by the violation. FRCP 37(b)(2)(C); ***O'Neill v. AGWI Lines***, 74 F.3d 93, 96 (5th Cir.1996); ***Jankins v. TDC Mgmt.***, 21 F.3d 436, 444 (D.C.Cir.1994); ***Toth v. Trans World Airlines, Inc.***, 862 F.2d 1381, 1386 (9th Cir.1988); *see* ***Novak v. Wolpoff & Abramson LLP***, 536 F.3d 175, 177-78 (2d Cir.2008) (dicta). The court does not need to award expenses if the violation was substantially justified or if other circumstances make the award unjust. FRCP 37(b)(2)(C); *see* ***Novak***, 536 F.3d at 178. The burden of showing substantial justification and special circumstances is on the party being sanctioned. ***Falstaff Brewing Corp.***, 702 F.2d at 784. A court imposing expenses on an organization's attorney may require the attorney to pay the sanction personally without seeking reimbursement. ***Conner***, 20 F.3d at 1382.

(a) Calculating fees. When calculating the award of attorney fees, the court should consider all of the following:

[1] The reasonableness of the requested attorney fees. ***Cherrington Asia Ltd. v. A&L Underground, Inc.***, 263 F.R.D. 653, 662 (D.Kan.2010); ***Poole***, 192 F.R.D. at 508. In determining the reasonableness of the fees, the court should (1) review contemporaneous timesheets to ensure that time spent was not excessive and (2) consider the hourly rate charged in the legal community for similar services. ***Poole***, 192 F.R.D. at 508.

[2] The minimum amount of attorney fees needed to deter future litigation abuse. ***Cherrington Asia***, 263 F.R.D. at 662; ***Poole***, 192 F.R.D. at 508.

[3] The sanctioned party's ability to pay the attorney fees. ***Cherrington Asia***, 263 F.R.D. at 662; ***Poole***, 192 F.R.D. at 508; *e.g.*, ***ClearValue, Inc. v. Pearl River Polymers, Inc.***, 560 F.3d 1291, 1305-06 (Fed. Cir.2009) (joint and several liability for sanctions award against attorney and party was improper as to attorney because award was four times attorney's net income).

[4] The severity of the sanctionable conduct. ***Poole***, 192 F.R.D. at 508.

(b) Calculating expenses. When calculating expenses, the court should review the documentation supporting the claimed expenses and consider objections raised by the sanctioned party. *See* ***Poole***, 192 F.R.D. at 510 & n.22.

2. Sanctions for refusing to disclose. The court can impose a number of sanctions against a party who does not disclose information required by FRCP 26(a) or (e). *See* FRCP 37(c)(1). Under FRCP 37(c)(1), an attorney cannot be sanctioned. ***Grider v. Keystone Health Plan Cent., Inc.***, 580 F.3d 119, 141 (3d Cir.2009). *But see*

Tom v. S.B., Inc., 280 F.R.D. 603, 612 (D.N.M.2012) (monetary sanctions under FRCP 37(c) can be imposed on attorney). The sanctions are mandatory, unless the violation was substantially justified or is harmless. ***Bessemer & Lake Erie R.R. v. Seaway Mar. Transp.***, 596 F.3d 357, 370 (6th Cir.2010); *see* FRCP 37(c)(1); ***Ortiz-Lopez v. Sociedad Espanola de Auxilio Mutuo y Beneficiencia de P.R.***, 248 F.3d 29, 33 (1st Cir.2001). When deciding whether the refusal to disclose was harmless, the court should consider the following: (1) the prejudice or surprise to the opposing party, (2) the opposing party's ability to cure that prejudice, (3) the extent to which the introduction of the undisclosed evidence would disrupt the trial, and (4) the bad faith or willfulness of the party seeking to introduce the evidence. ***Tribble v. Evangelides***, 670 F.3d 753, 759-60 (7th Cir.2012); ***Eugene S. v. Horizon Blue Cross Blue Shield***, 663 F.3d 1124, 1129-30 (10th Cir.2011). The court may also need to consider the availability of lesser sanctions. *See, e.g.*, ***R&R Sails, Inc. v. Insurance Co. of Pa.***, 673 F.3d 1240, 1247 (9th Cir.2012) (when P did not include invoices in initial disclosures and did not supplement disclosures, district court excluded invoices; because exclusion amounted to dismissal of P's claim, court was required to consider lesser sanction first).

(1) Bar evidence. If a party does not make a disclosure required by FRCP 26(a) or (e), the court may order that the party cannot use the undisclosed information or witness on a motion, at a hearing, or at trial. FRCP 37(c)(1); *see* FRCP 37(b)(2)(A)(ii) (court can prohibit party from supporting or opposing claims or defenses); ***Esposito v. Home Depot U.S.A., Inc.***, 590 F.3d 72, 77 (1st Cir.2009) (court can exclude expert if expert disclosure is untimely unless untimeliness is substantially justified or harmless); ***Kotes v. Super Fresh Food Mkts., Inc.***, 157 F.R.D. 18, 19 (E.D.Pa.1994) (undisclosed witness should be excluded unless nondisclosure is substantially justified or harmless or evidence is offered solely for impeachment); *see, e.g.*, ***Heidtman v. County of El Paso***, 171 F.3d 1038, 1040 (5th Cir.1999) (experts were properly excluded for failure to designate); ***A.J. v. Kierst***, 56 F.3d 849, 860 (8th Cir.1995) (undesignated expert could not testify about report); ***Wachtel v. Health Net, Inc.***, 239 F.R.D. 81, 104-05 (D.N.J.2006) (court granted Ps' motion to strike evidence when Ds did not notify Ps of plan to rely on documents not produced in discovery, but instead produced documents when impact would be most severe). In deciding whether to exclude a witness who was not properly disclosed, the court should consider (1) the explanation for not identifying the witness, (2) the importance of the testimony, (3) the potential prejudice in allowing the testimony, and (4) the availability of a continuance to cure the prejudice. *E.g.*, ***Hamburger v. State Farm Mut. Auto. Ins.***, 361 F.3d 875, 883-84 (5th Cir.2004) (expert witnesses not properly designated were excluded); *see* ***Harriman v. Hancock Cty.***, 627 F.3d 22, 30 (1st Cir.2010).

(2) Declare facts established. If a party does not make a disclosure required by FRCP 26(a) or (e), the court may, after a motion and hearing, order the undisclosed evidence to be taken as established in favor of the moving party. FRCP 37(b)(2)(A)(i), (c)(1)(C); *see, e.g.*, ***Compaq Computer Corp. v. Ergonome Inc.***, 387 F.3d 403, 413-14 (5th Cir.2004) (court found alter-ego status as sanction against D for not providing requested disclosure).

(3) Strike pleadings, stay proceedings, dismiss case, or render default. If a party does not make a disclosure required by FRCP 26(a) or (e), the court may, after a motion and hearing, strike all or part of the party's pleadings, stay the proceedings, dismiss all or part of the party's case, or render a default judgment against the party. FRCP 37(b)(2)(A)(iii)-(b)(2)(A)(vi), (c)(1)(C).

(4) Instruct the jury. If a party does not make a disclosure required by FRCP 26(a) or (e), the court may, after a motion and hearing, inform the jury of the party's failure to disclose. FRCP 37(c)(1)(B). If a party does not disclose evidence in time for use at trial, a party may seek an "adverse-inference instruction." *See* ***In re Oracle Corp. Secs. Litig.***, 627 F.3d 376, 386-87 (9th Cir.2010); ***Residential Funding Corp. v. DeGeorge Fin. Corp.***, 306 F.3d 99, 107 (2d Cir.2002). To be entitled to an adverse-inference instruction, the party seeking the instruction must show the following:

(a) The party having control over the discoverable evidence had an obligation to timely produce it or preserve it when it was destroyed. ***Residential Funding***, 306 F.3d at 107.

(b) The party had a culpable state of mind when it destroyed or did not timely produce the discoverable evidence. *Id.* Some courts require bad faith of the party destroying the discoverable evidence and will not apply an adverse inference for mere negligence. *See* ***Aramburu v. Boeing Co.***, 112 F.3d 1398, 1407 (10th Cir.1997);

Vick v. Texas Empl. Comm'n, 514 F.2d 734, 737 (5th Cir.1975). However, the Second Circuit has held that the requirement of a culpable state of mind can be met by showing that the producing party was negligent—rather than grossly negligent or acting in bad faith—or "purposely sluggish" in producing the discoverable evidence. ***Residential Funding***, 306 F.3d at 112-13; *see also* ***Stevenson v. Union Pac. R.R.***, 354 F.3d 739, 750 (8th Cir.2004) (explicit bad-faith finding is not required for adverse-inference instruction).

(c) The missing evidence was relevant to the moving party's claim or defense such that a reasonable trier of fact could find that it would support the claim or defense. ***Residential Funding***, 306 F.3d at 107; *see* ***Stevenson***, 354 F.3d at 748 (court must make finding of prejudice to opposing party before imposing sanction for destruction of evidence).

NOTE

If an adverse-inference instruction is given, the party against whom it is given should be permitted to offer a reasonable rebuttal to the inference. ***Stevenson****, 354 F.3d at 750;* ***Webb v. District of Columbia****, 146 F.3d 964, 974 n.20 (D.C.Cir.1998). However, the court does not need to permit a complete retrial of the sanctions hearing.* ***Stevenson****, 354 F.3d at 750; see* ***Webb****, 146 F.3d at 974 n.20.*

(5) Pay expenses & attorney fees. If a party does not make a disclosure required by FRCP 26(a) or (e), the court may, after a motion and hearing, require the party to pay reasonable expenses, including attorney fees, caused by the party's nondisclosure. FRCP 37(c)(1)(A).

(6) Impose other sanctions. If a party does not make a disclosure required by FRCP 26(a) or (e), the court may, after a motion or hearing, impose other appropriate sanctions. FRCP 37(c)(1)(C); *see* ***Gay v. Stonebridge Life Ins.***, 660 F.3d 58, 62 (1st Cir.2011) (rather than exclude nondisclosed witness, appropriate lesser sanction can be continuance to allow party who will be cross-examining that witness more preparation time). See "Sanctions for not complying with order," §15.5.1, p. 448.

3. Sanctions for failure to respond. A court can impose sanctions for a complete failure to respond to discovery under FRCP 37(d). See "Not responding to discovery," §15.3.2, p. 447. If a party or its representative does not respond to discovery requests, the court, on motion, may impose any just sanctions, including those authorized by FRCP 37(b)(2)(A)(i)-(b)(2)(A)(vi). FRCP 37(d)(3). Unlike FRCP 37(b), FRCP 37(d) does not require an earlier discovery order before the court can impose sanctions. ***Coane***, 898 F.2d at 1031. Besides any sanction provided in FRCP 37(d)(3), the court must order the party, the attorney advising the party, or both to pay the reasonable expenses, including attorney fees, caused by its failure to respond unless the failure was substantially justified or other circumstances make an award of expenses unjust. FRCP 37(d)(3); *see* ***Cherrington Asia***, 263 F.R.D. at 658. The burden of showing substantial justification and special circumstances is on the party being sanctioned. ***Hyde & Drath v. Baker***, 24 F.3d 1162, 1171 (9th Cir.1994).

4. Sanctions for failure to participate in discovery plan. A court may impose sanctions on a party or attorney for not participating in good faith in developing and submitting a proposed discovery plan. FRCP 37(f); *see* ***Apex Oil Co. v. Belcher Co.***, 855 F.2d 1009, 1014 (2d Cir.1988). After giving the parties an opportunity to be heard, a court may order the party or attorney to pay another party the reasonable expenses, including attorney fees, caused by the failure. FRCP 37(f).

5. Sanctions for failure to supplement. The refusal to supplement earlier discovery responses required by FRCP 26(e) will result in a mandatory sanction prohibiting the use of the undisclosed witness or information as evidence on a motion, at a hearing, or at trial, unless the failure was substantially justified or is harmless. FRCP 37(c)(1). The court may also order other appropriate sanctions, including those under FRCP 37(b)(2)(A)(i)-(b)(2)(A)(vi). FRCP 37(c)(1)(C).

6. Sanctions for refusal to admit. A court may award reasonable expenses to a party who proves the truth of a matter or the genuineness of a document after an opposing party refuses to admit the truth of the matter or the genuineness of the document in response to a request under FRCP 36. FRCP 37(c)(2).

7. Sanctions for losing electronically stored information. A court may impose sanctions on a party for not properly handling discovery of electronically stored information. The available sanctions depend on the grounds asserted in the motion. See "Types of sanctions available," ch. 6-C, §12.2, p. 515.

8. Sanctions for certifying in violation of FRCP 26(g). A court may impose appropriate sanctions for making a certification in violation of FRCP 26(g), including an order to pay the reasonable expenses and attorney fees caused by the violation. FRCP 26(g)(3); ***Mancia v. Mayflower Textile Servs.***, 253 F.R.D. 354, 357 (D.Md. 2008); *see* ***Cache La Poudre Feeds, LLC v. Land O'Lakes, Inc.***, 244 F.R.D. 614, 637 (D.Colo.2007) (FRCP 26(g)(3) gives court discretion to impose appropriate sanctions, which may not necessarily include award of attorney fees and costs).

§15.6 Order. The order granting sanctions should identify how the particular requirements for imposing sanctions have been satisfied. *See* ***Sentis Grp. v. Shell Oil Co.***, 559 F.3d 888, 899 (8th Cir.2009). If the order includes multiple sources of authority for imposing sanctions, the order should separate the analysis for each source of authority. *E.g.*, *id.* at 899-900 (district court should have addressed structured analysis under FRCP 37, and then, as alternative, it should have addressed relatively unstructured analysis of court's inherent power). See "Order," ch. 5-O, §9, p. 396.

§16. REVIEW OF DISCOVERY ORDERS

§16.1 Review by appeal.

1. Discovery from parties. Discovery orders are ordinarily interlocutory and may be reviewed on appeal only after a final judgment. *See* ***Cunningham v. Hamilton Cty.***, 527 U.S. 198, 204-05 (1999); ***Church of Scientology v. U.S.***, 506 U.S. 9, 18 n.11 (1992); ***Piratello v. Philips Elecs. N. Am. Corp.***, 360 F.3d 506, 508 (5th Cir. 2004); ***In re Flat Glass Antitrust Litig.***, 288 F.3d 83, 87 (3d Cir.2002). A party who wants to immediately appeal a discovery order must first refuse compliance, be held in contempt, and then appeal the contempt order. ***Mohawk Indus. v. Carpenter***, 558 U.S. 100, ___, 130 S.Ct. 599, 608 (2009); ***Church of Scientology***, 506 U.S. at 18 n.11; ***Piratello***, 360 F.3d at 508. On rare occasions, courts may permit interlocutory review of a discovery order under the collateral-order doctrine or 28 U.S.C. §1292(b). *See* ***Perry v. Schwarzenegger***, 591 F.3d 1147, 1154-56 (9th Cir.2010) (discussing collateral-order doctrine). See "Appealable orders," ch. 9-A, §3.3, p. 739.

NOTE

Disclosure orders adverse to the attorney-client privilege cannot be appealed under the collateral-order doctrine. ***Mohawk Indus.***, *558 U.S. at ___, 130 S.Ct. at 603. See "Collateral orders," ch. 9-A, §3.3.2(1), p. 741. The combination of postjudgment appeals, appeals under 28 U.S.C. §1292(b), mandamus, and contempt appeals provide adequate protection to parties who are ordered to disclose allegedly privileged materials.* ***Mohawk Indus.***, *558 U.S. at ___, 130 S.Ct. at 609.*

2. Discovery from nonparties. Generally, a nonparty cannot appeal a pretrial discovery order because it is not a final, appealable order. ***Hooker v. Continental Life Ins.***, 965 F.2d 903, 904 (10th Cir.1992); ***Minpeco, S.A. v. Conticommodity Servs.***, 844 F.2d 856, 859 (D.C.Cir.1988). But in certain circumstances, an order may be immediately appealable.

(1) Order from ancillary court. When an ancillary district court—a court other than the one where the main action is pending—denies discovery against a nonparty, the order is appealable. ***Hooker***, 965 F.2d at 904 n.1; ***Minpeco***, 844 F.2d at 859.

(2) Order of contempt. When a court grants discovery against a nonparty, the nonparty can refuse to comply with the discovery order and submit to a contempt proceeding; if the nonparty is held in contempt, the contempt order may be appealed. ***In re Flat Glass Antitrust Litig.***, 288 F.3d at 88; ***Connaught Labs. v. SmithKline Beecham P.L.C.***, 165 F.3d 1368, 1370 (Fed.Cir.1999); ***MDK, Inc. v. Mike's Train House, Inc.***, 27 F.3d 116, 121 (4th Cir. 1994); ***FTC v. Alaska Land Leasing, Inc.***, 778 F.2d 577, 578 (10th Cir.1985).

(3) Order appealed by another nonparty. When a court grants discovery against a nonparty, the order may be appealable by another nonparty, if the appealing nonparty is the privilege holder of the discovery that is in the custody of the nonparty subject to the order. *See* ***Holt-Orsted v. City of Dickson***, 641 F.3d 230, 238-40 (6th Cir.2011); ***U.S. v. Krane***, 625 F.3d 568, 572 (9th Cir.2010); *see, e.g.*, ***SEC v. CMKM Diamonds, Inc.***, 656 F.3d 829, 830-31 (9th Cir.2011) (in suit in which SEC sought to collect judgment against D and D had wired $25,000 to his attorney—who was nonparty—attorney could immediately appeal denial of motion to quash subpoena directed at attorney's bank—who was also nonparty—for records of attorney's entire client trust account). The rationale for allowing the privilege holder's appeal is that the nonparty custodian of the discovery may not have any stake in the outcome of the privilege claim and should not be expected to be held in contempt to help the privilege holder obtain an appealable order. ***CMKM Diamonds***, 656 F.3d at 830-31; *see* ***Burden-Meeks v. Welch***, 319 F.3d 897, 899-900 (7th Cir. 2003).

3. Discovery sanctions. Generally, a party cannot appeal a pretrial order imposing discovery sanctions because it is not a final, appealable order. ***Law v. NCAA***, 134 F.3d 1025, 1029 (10th Cir.1998); *see, e.g.*, ***SEC v. Kirkland***, 533 F.3d 1323, 1325 (11th Cir.2008) (order of civil contempt was not immediately appealable). See "Appealability," ch. 5-O, §10.1, p. 397.

4. Discovery suit. If the application for discovery comprises the entire proceeding (e.g., a petition to perpetuate testimony before litigation under FRCP 27, an application to compel discovery for use in a proceeding in a foreign or international tribunal), the discovery order may be appealable as a final order. *See* ***Heraeus Kulzer, GmbH v. Biomet, Inc.***, 633 F.3d 591, 593 (7th Cir.2011); *see, e.g.*, ***In re Deiulemar Compagnia Di Navigazione S.p.A.***, 198 F.3d 473, 476-77 (4th Cir.1999) (court permitted appeal of FRCP 27(a) petition granted to preserve evidence of ship's condition that was crucial to expected arbitration); ***In re Gianoli Aldunate***, 3 F.3d 54, 57 (2d Cir.1993) (court permitted appeal of discovery order granted under 28 U.S.C. §1782 allowing foreign guardians to discover incompetent's assets in United States); *see also* ***Ash v. Cort***, 512 F.2d 909, 911-12 (3d Cir.1975) (court permitted appeal from discovery order denying motion to perpetuate testimony pending appeal on merits under FRCP 27(b); order on FRCP 27(b) motion is final and appealable for same reasons as order on FRCP 27(a) petition). See "Discovery for proceeding in foreign tribunal," ch. 6-B, §2.2.14, p. 460; "Deposition to Perpetuate Testimony," ch. 6-F, §6, p. 555.

§16.2 Review by mandamus. Discovery orders are not normally reviewable by mandamus. ***In re Sims***, 534 F.3d 117, 128-29 (2d Cir.2008); ***In re U.S.***, 878 F.2d 153, 158 (5th Cir.1989); ***Diversified Indus. v. Meredith***, 572 F.2d 596, 599 (8th Cir.1977). Mandamus in the federal courts has traditionally been reserved for extraordinary circumstances. ***In re Whirlpool Corp.***, 597 F.3d 858, 860 (7th Cir.2010); ***Perry v. Schwarzenegger***, 591 F.3d 1147, 1156 (9th Cir.2010). However, some courts are more willing to grant it. ***In re Reyes***, 814 F.2d 168, 170-71 (5th Cir. 1987); *see, e.g.*, ***John B. v. Goetz***, 531 F.3d 448, 456-57 (6th Cir.2008) (mandamus was granted when district court's order for forensic duplication of state computers was unnecessarily intrusive and there was no evidence of intentional destruction of electronically stored information).

1. Standard. There is no single standard by which federal courts determine a petition for writ of mandamus. Although approaches among the circuits are similar, each circuit has its own set of considerations. These considerations include the following:

(1) The party seeking the writ has no other adequate means, such as direct appeal, to attain the relief desired. ***Hernandez v. Tanninen***, 604 F.3d 1095, 1099 (9th Cir.2010); ***John B.***, 531 F.3d at 457; *see* ***U.S. v. Victoria-21***, 3 F.3d 571, 575 (2d Cir.1993).

(2) The petitioner will be damaged or prejudiced in a way that is not correctable on appeal. ***John B.***, 531 F.3d at 457; *e.g.*, ***Hernandez***, 604 F.3d at 1099 (district court's order of blanket waiver of attorney-client privilege and work-product protection was particularly injurious to P; waiver should have been limited to communication and subject matter actually disclosed); *see* ***In re Sims***, 534 F.3d at 128-29 (petitioner's privilege will be lost if review must wait until after final judgment).

(3) The district court's order is clearly erroneous as a matter of law. ***Hernandez***, 604 F.3d at 1099; ***John B.***, 531 F.3d at 457; ***Sporck v. Peil***, 759 F.2d 312, 314 (3d Cir.1985). Some circuits have stated this requirement more strictly, permitting mandamus only in exceptional circumstances amounting to a judicial usurpation of power. *See, e.g.*, ***In re Ford Motor Co.***, 751 F.2d 274, 275 (8th Cir.1984).

(4) The district court's order is an oft-repeated error or manifests a persistent disregard of the federal rules. ***Hernandez***, 604 F.3d at 1099; ***John B.***, 531 F.3d at 457.

(5) The district court's order raises either new and important problems or legal issues of first impression. ***Hernandez***, 604 F.3d at 1099; ***John B.***, 531 F.3d at 457; *see* ***In re Sims***, 534 F.3d at 128-29.

(6) Immediate resolution will avoid the development of discovery practices or doctrines undermining a discovery privilege. ***In re Sims***, 534 F.3d at 128-29.

2. Findings of fact. To determine whether a writ of mandamus is proper for a court's discovery order, the appellate court must scrutinize the petitioner's claims in light of the required findings of fact and the statement of the court's legal reasoning. Mandamus is not an appropriate remedy for a discovery order when the record is so incomplete that it prevents making findings of fact. ***Thornton v. Corcoran***, 407 F.2d 695, 698 (D.C.Cir.1969).

3. Orders denying discovery. Unlike an order compelling disclosure, an order denying discovery may be reviewed on appeal from the final judgment and, if erroneous, may be remedied by granting a new trial. Thus, an order denying discovery is not reviewable by mandamus. ***Westinghouse Elec. Corp. v. Philippines***, 951 F.2d 1414, 1422 (3d Cir.1991).

4. Orders granting discovery. For orders granting discovery, mandamus is appropriate only when adequate review on appeal would be difficult or effectively unobtainable (e.g., when discovery of privileged documents is ordered). ***Victoria-21***, 3 F.3d at 575. When a discovery order involves a claim of privilege, mandamus is appropriate only when the disclosure renders any meaningful appellate review of the claim impossible and the disclosure involves questions of substantial importance to the administration of justice. ***U.S. v. Winner***, 641 F.2d 825, 830 (10th Cir.1981). Mandamus may also be appropriate to review the following discovery orders:

(1) Mandamus is appropriate to review orders compelling the production of trade secrets in the form of confidential business information. ***In re Remington Arms Co.***, 952 F.2d 1029, 1031 (8th Cir.1991).

(2) Mandamus is sometimes available to review a discovery order when a claim of attorney-client privilege has been raised in and rejected by a district court. ***In re Bieter Co.***, 16 F.3d 929, 931 (8th Cir.1994); *see* ***In re Avantel***, 343 F.3d 311, 317 & n.5 (5th Cir.2003); ***Haines v. Liggett Grp.***, 975 F.2d 81, 89-91 (3d Cir.1992).

B. SCOPE OF DISCOVERY

§1. GENERAL

§1.1 Rule. FRCP 26(b).

§1.2 Purpose. The scope of discovery determines what information can and cannot be discovered. This subchapter deals with the scope of discovery, not with the specific methods of discovery.

§1.3 Forms. *O'Connor's Federal Civil Forms* (2012), FORM 6A:10 for privilege log, and for each specific type of discovery: disclosures, FORMS 6E; depositions, FORMS 6F; interrogatories, FORMS 6G; requests for admissions, FORMS 6H; requests for production, FORMS 6I; motions to examine persons, FORMS 6J; and requests for entry on land, FORMS 6K.

§1.4 Other references. 26 Wright & Graham, *Federal Practice & Procedure* §§5641-5652 (1992 & Supp.2012); 25 Wright & Graham, *Federal Practice & Procedure* §§5521-5602 (1989 & Supp.2012); 8, 8A Wright, Miller & Marcus, *Federal Practice & Procedure 3d* §§2001-2034 (2010 & Supp.2012); 6 *Moore's Federal Practice 3d* §§26.40-26.52 (2012); *Rules of Evidence for the U.S. Courts & Magistrates*, 56 F.R.D. 183 (1973) [*Proposed Rules of Evidence*].

§2. WHAT IS DISCOVERABLE?

FRCP 26(b) sets out the general scope of discovery in federal civil cases.

§2.1 General scope of discovery. A party can discover any nonprivileged matter that is relevant to any party's claim or defense. FRCP 26(b)(1); ***In re Sealed Case (Med. Records)***, 381 F.3d 1205, 1214 (D.C.Cir.2004). Relevant information does not have to be admissible at trial as long as it appears reasonably calculated to lead to the discovery of admissible evidence. FRCP 26(b)(1); ***Degen v. U.S.***, 517 U.S. 820, 825-26 (1996). But a request for information that has no conceivable bearing on the case will usually not be allowed. ***Food Lion, Inc. v. United Food & Commercial Workers Int'l Un.***, 103 F.3d 1007, 1012-13 (D.C.Cir.1997); *see* FRCP 26(b)(1); *see, e.g.*, ***Miscellaneous Docket Matter No. 1 v. Miscellaneous Docket Matter No. 2***, 197 F.3d 922, 925-26 (8th Cir.1999) (in "sex for stock" suit, inquiries into former legal publisher's voluntary romantic relationships were irrelevant to subject matter). See "Discovery not required to be produced," ch. 6-A, §8.2.5, p. 423. There are five main questions relating to the scope of discovery:

1. *Is the information relevant to the suit?* As long as the information is relevant, it is discoverable. FRCP 26(b)(1). Without court approval, the scope of discovery is limited to matters relevant to the claims and defenses asserted in the case. FRCP 26(b)(1); *see also* ***NLRB v. New England Newspapers, Inc.***, 856 F.2d 409, 414 & n.4 (1st Cir.1988) (standard for discovery relevancy under FRCP 26(b)(1) is different from trial relevancy under FRE 401, which requires evidence to be probative of consequential fact). If the court finds good cause, it can expand the scope of discovery to matters relevant to the subject matter involved in the case. FRCP 26(b)(1); ***In re Cooper Tire & Rubber Co.***, 568 F.3d 1180, 1188 (10th Cir.2009).

2. *Will the information lead to the discovery of admissible evidence?* If the information is reasonably calculated to lead to the discovery of admissible evidence, it is discoverable. FRCP 26(b)(1). A party cannot object to discovery on the ground that the information sought is not admissible at trial. *See id.* See "Not admissible," ch. 6-A, §8.3.1(2)(b)[1], p. 426.

3. *Is there an exemption that prevents the discovery of the information?* If there is an exemption from discovery, the information is not discoverable. See "What Is Not Discoverable?," §3, p. 460.

4. *Do the discovery rules permit the type of discovery procedure necessary to secure the information?* If no discovery rule permits the type of discovery method involved, the information is probably not discoverable unless the court orders or the parties agree to the discovery procedure. *See* FRCP 26(c)(1)(C) (court can issue protective order requiring that discovery be conducted by specific method); FRCP 29 (parties can agree to modify procedures governing discovery); ***Wisconsin Real Estate Inv. Trust v. Weinstein***, 530 F.Supp. 1249, 1253 (E.D.Wis.1982) (court has broad discretion under FRCP 26 to require that certain discovery methods be used to obtain information), *rev'd in part on other grounds*, 712 F.2d 1095 (7th Cir.1983); *see also* ***In re Subpoena Issued to Friedman***, 350 F.3d 65, 69 (2d Cir.2003) (FRCPs generally do not place any initial burden on parties to justify discovery requests). *But see* ***Amarin Plastics, Inc. v. Maryland Cup Corp.***, 116 F.R.D. 36, 38 (D.Mass.1987) (court cannot issue protective order preventing informal witness interviews, which are not covered by FRCP 26).

5. *Should the court limit discovery?* FRCP 26(b)(2)(C) expressly states the court's power to limit discovery based on the needs and circumstances of the case. Courts should limit discovery only to prevent unwarranted delay and expense, as stated in the rule. *See* 1993 Notes to FRCP 26 at ¶29, p. 1185, this book; *see, e.g.*, ***Thompson v. U.S. Dept. of Hous. & Urban Dev.***, 219 F.R.D. 93, 97 (D.Md.2003) (because of possible burdens associated with discovering electronic records, courts acknowledge need to use cost-benefit analysis under FRCP 26(b)(2), now FRCP 26(b)(2)(C)); *see also* ***Crawford-El v. Britton***, 523 U.S. 574, 598 (1998) (under FRCP 26, court has broad discretion to tailor discovery narrowly and to dictate sequence of discovery). See "Valid objections," ch. 6-A, §8.3.1(2)(a), p. 425 (discussing permissible objections to discovery). The court can also limit discovery by issuing a protective order. *See* FRCP 26(c)(1). See "Motion for Protective Order," ch. 6-A, §12, p. 440.

§2.2 Types of discoverable information. The following are some common types of discoverable information:

1. Party opinions & contentions. A party's opinions and contentions about a fact or the application of law to a fact are generally discoverable. *See* FRCP 26(b)(1), 36(a)(1)(A). A party may request that another party admit facts, the application of law to facts, opinions about either law or facts, or the genuineness of a document. FRCP 36(a)(1).

2. Party statement. A party may discover any statement it has made about the lawsuit without having to show substantial need or undue hardship. *See* FRCP 26(b)(3)(C). For purposes of this rule, a statement is (1) a written statement that the person has signed or otherwise adopted or approved or (2) a contemporaneous recording of an oral statement that is substantially verbatim. *Id.*

3. Nonparty statement. A nonparty may obtain a copy of any statement it has made about the lawsuit or its subject matter by making a request from the party who has the statement. *See* FRCP 26(b)(3)(C).

4. Fact witnesses. A party may discover information about all fact witnesses. *See* FRCP 26(b)(1). Fact witnesses include all persons with relevant information, whether or not their testimony supports the position of the disclosing party. ***Scheetz v. Bridgestone/Firestone, Inc.***, 152 F.R.D. 628, 631 n.3 (D.Mont.1993).

(1) Discovery of fact witnesses.

(a) Potential fact witnesses.

[1] Witnesses to be used in litigation. A party must disclose the name and, if known, the address and telephone number of each individual who might have discoverable information that the party may use in the litigation process. FRCP 26(a)(1)(A)(i); ***Gluck v. Ansett Austl. Ltd.***, 204 F.R.D. 217, 221-22 (D.D.C.2001); *see **In re Theragenics Corp. Secs. Litig.***, 205 F.R.D. 631, 634 (N.D.Ga.2002). See "Witnesses," ch. 6-E, §4.2.1, p. 533.

[2] Other fact witnesses. A party may be able to discover the names, addresses, and telephone numbers of potential fact witnesses other than those used to support a party's claim or defense. *See* FRCP 26(b)(1); ***In re Theragenics Corp.***, 205 F.R.D. at 634; *see, e.g.*, ***American Floral Servs. v. Florists' Transworld Delivery Ass'n***, 107 F.R.D. 258, 260-61 (N.D.Ill.1985) (Ps were compelled to identify which two witnesses out of list of 200 had inculpatory information).

(b) Trial witnesses. The parties must disclose the following information about trial witnesses:

[1] The name, address, and telephone number of each person who may be called as a witness. FRCP 26(a)(3)(A)(i). See "Witness identity," ch. 6-E, §6.2.1, p. 536.

[2] The identity of each witness whose testimony is expected to be presented by deposition. FRCP 26(a)(3)(A)(ii). See "Deposition witness identity," ch. 6-E, §6.2.2, p. 536.

(2) Cost of witnesses. A witness is entitled to receive $40 for each day of attendance at court proceedings or depositions, reimbursement of travel expenses, and, when an overnight stay is required, a subsistence allowance. 28 U.S.C. §1821. For a discussion of reimbursements to experts, see "Paying the Expert," ch. 6-D, §8, p. 530.

5. Expert witnesses. See "Testifying Experts," ch. 6-D, §3, p. 516; "Consulting Experts," ch. 6-D, §4, p. 525.

6. Documents, ESI & tangible things. A party may discover the existence, description, nature, custody, condition, and location of relevant documents, electronically stored information (ESI), or tangible things within the possession, custody, or control of another party or nonparty. FRCP 26(b)(1), 34(a)(1), 45(a)(1)(A)(iii); *see* 2006 Notes to FRCP 34 at ¶¶1, 2, p. 1203, this book. Documents and ESI include writings, drawings, graphs, charts, photographs, sound recordings, images, and other data or data compilations from which information can be obtained. FRCP 34(a)(1)(A). See "What Is ESI?," ch. 6-C, §2, p. 482. "Possession, custody, or control" includes not only actual

physical possession but also constructive possession and the right to obtain possession from a third party, such as an agent or representative. A party has constructive possession when it has a legal right to compel production of the document. See "Possession, custody, or control," ch. 6-I, §3.4.2(3), p. 571.

NOTE

A party may discover ESI on social-networking sites (e.g., Facebook, Twitter) from the opposing party when the content is relevant to the suit; however, because social-networking sites provide a fairly new context for discovery, courts are developing the extent to which public and private content is considered relevant and thus discoverable. See ***EEOC v. Simply Storage Mgmt.****, 270 F.R.D. 430, 434 (S.D.Ind.2010);* ***Mailhot v. Home Depot U.S.A., Inc.****, No. CV 11-03892 DOC CSSx (C.D.Cal.2012) (slip op.; 9-7-12); see, e.g.,* ***Tompkins v. Detroit Metro. Airport****, 278 F.R.D. 387, 388-89 (E.D.Mich.2012) (D's request to access P's entire Facebook account was denied; based on public content of P's Facebook account, D did not show that access to private content would lead to discovery of admissible evidence). ESI on social-networking sites generally should be requested from the opposing party because, based on privacy concerns, the Stored Communications Act limits access to ESI when it is requested from the opposing party's Internet service provider. See* ***Crispin v. Christian Audigier, Inc.****, 717 F.Supp.2d 965, 971-72 (C.D.Cal. 2010). See generally 18 U.S.C. §2702 (electronic-communication service cannot knowingly divulge content of communication while communication is in service's electronic storage).*

7. Financial information. A party may discover the financial information of an individual or business organization if it is relevant to the issues in the lawsuit. ***Yancey v. Hooten***, 180 F.R.D. 203, 215 (D.Conn.1998). Depending on the circumstances of the case, discoverable financial information may include income statements, balance sheets, tax returns, and other forms of information that demonstrate a party's financial condition. *See* ***City of Newport v. Fact Concerts, Inc.***, 453 U.S. 247, 270 (1981) (information on net worth and financial condition is relevant in determining punitive damages). *But see* ***John Does I-VI v. Yogi***, 110 F.R.D. 629, 633 (D.D.C.1986) (discovery of financial status should not take place until it is necessary to prove punitive damages). Although tax returns are not privileged, some courts have suggested that relevant tax returns should be disclosed only if the information is not available from other sources. *See* ***Terwilliger v. York Int'l***, 176 F.R.D. 214, 216-17 (W.D.Va.1997); ***Hawkins v. South Plains Int'l Trucks, Inc.***, 139 F.R.D. 679, 681-82 (D.Colo.1991); ***U.S. v. Bonanno Organized Crime Family of La Cosa Nostra***, 119 F.R.D. 625, 627 (E.D.N.Y.1988); *see also* **Poulos v. Naas Foods, Inc.**, 959 F.2d 69, 74-75 (7th Cir.1992) (declining to decide whether public policy provides protection for disclosure of tax returns, but noting that tax returns in taxpayer's possession are not privileged); ***U.S. v. Certain Real Prop. Known as & Located at 6469 Polo Pointe Way, Delray Beach, Fla.***, 444 F.Supp.2d 1258, 1262-64 (S.D.Fla.2006) (discussing disagreement on whether tax returns are entitled to enhanced protection).

8. Insurance. A party may discover any insurance agreement that would either satisfy all or part of a possible judgment or indemnify or reimburse the party for payments made to satisfy the judgment. FRCP 26(a)(1)(A)(iv); ***Wegner v. Cliff Viessman, Inc.***, 153 F.R.D. 154, 160 (N.D.Iowa 1994).

9. Damages. A party may discover a computation of each type of damages. FRCP 26(a)(1)(A)(iii).

10. Trial-preparation materials. A party may discover certain materials prepared in anticipation of litigation by a party or its representative. FRCP 26(b)(3)(A). If documents and other tangible things that would normally be discoverable are prepared in anticipation of litigation by a party or its representative, then another party may discover those items only on a showing of both a substantial need for the materials and an inability to obtain substantially equivalent materials without undue hardship. *Id.*; ***Toledo Edison Co. v. G A Techs.***, 847 F.2d 335, 339 (6th Cir.1988). If a court orders production of work product, it must protect against disclosure of the mental impressions, conclusions, opinions, or legal theories of an attorney or representative. FRCP 26(b)(3)(B).

11. Land. A party may discover information about land by requesting to inspect, measure, survey, photograph, test, or sample the property or any object or operation on it. FRCP 34(a)(2); *see* FRCP 45(a)(1)(A)(iii). See "Request for Entry on Land," ch. 6-K, p. 579.

12. Medical condition. If the mental or physical condition (including blood type) of a party or a person in the party's custody or legal control is in dispute, the person may be compelled to submit to an examination on proof of good cause. FRCP 35(a). See "Physical & Mental Examinations of Persons," ch. 6-J, p. 574.

13. Waiver. A party is entitled to discover anything it requests from the other party if that other party has waived its objections. See "Waiver of objections & privileges – before disclosure," ch. 6-A, §9.2, p. 429.

14. Discovery for proceeding in foreign tribunal. A federal district court may allow discovery from a party for use in a proceeding in a foreign or international tribunal. 28 U.S.C. §1782(a); *see* ***Intel Corp. v. Advanced Micro Devices, Inc.***, 542 U.S. 241, 253 (2004); ***Brandi-Dohrn v. IKB Deutsche Industriebank AG***, 673 F.3d 76, 80 (2d Cir.2012); ***Heraeus Kulzer, GmbH v. Biomet, Inc.***, 633 F.3d 591, 594 (7th Cir.2011). 28 U.S.C. §1782 does not require that information sought for use in a foreign tribunal be discoverable or admissible in that tribunal. ***Intel***, 542 U.S. at 253 (discoverability); ***Brandi-Dohrn***, 673 F.3d at 82 (discoverability and admissibility). 28 U.S.C. §1782 is available to interested persons who are not litigants in the foreign proceeding, and that a proceeding before a foreign tribunal does not need to be pending or even imminent to invoke §1782. ***Intel***, 542 U.S. at 253-54. But because discovery in federal district courts is typically broader than that in most foreign tribunals, a federal district court should make sure that applications under 28 U.S.C. §1782 are not sought in bad faith or for harassment. *See* ***Heraeus Kulzer***, 633 F.3d at 594-95.

§3. WHAT IS NOT DISCOVERABLE?

Some information is not discoverable because it is irrelevant, privileged, or protected from discovery. *See* ***U.S. v. Farley***, 11 F.3d 1385, 1389-91 (7th Cir.1993).

§3.1 Irrelevant information. Information is not discoverable if it is not relevant. *See* FRCP 26(b)(1); ***Haroco, Inc. v. American Nat'l Bank & Trust Co.***, 38 F.3d 1429, 1439 (7th Cir.1994); *see, e.g.*, ***Nugget Hydroelectric, L.P. v. Pacific Gas & Elec. Co.***, 981 F.2d 429, 438-39 (9th Cir.1992) (request was overly broad because only a fraction of millions of requested documents was relevant). Information is discoverable only if it is relevant to the claims or defenses of a party. FRCP 26(b)(1); ***Thompson v. Department of Hous. & Urban Dev.***, 199 F.R.D. 168, 171 (D.Md. 2001). On a showing of good cause, the court can order discovery relevant to not only the claims or defenses but also the broader subject matter of the case. FRCP 26(b)(1); *see* ***Sanyo Laser Prods. v. Arista Records, Inc.***, 214 F.R.D. 496, 501-02 (S.D.Ind.2003); 2000 Notes to FRCP 26 at ¶¶24, 25, p. 1180, this book.

§3.2 Privileged & protected information – generally. Information is not discoverable if it is privileged. *See* FRCP 26(b)(1).

1. Federal vs. state privilege law. In diversity cases, state law governs privileges. ***In re Sealed Case (Med. Records)***, 381 F.3d 1205, 1212 (D.C.Cir.2004); ***Favala v. Cumberland Eng'g***, 17 F.3d 987, 989 (7th Cir.1994); *see* FRE 501; Notes of Cmte. on Jud., House Rpt. No. 93-650, to FRE 501 at ¶¶2-3, p. 1252, this book. Federal privilege law governs when the court's jurisdiction is premised on a federal question, even if the witness's testimony is relevant to a pendent state-law claim that may be controlled by a contrary state law of privilege. ***Virmani v. Novant Health Inc.***, 259 F.3d 284, 286 n.3 (4th Cir.2001); ***Pearson v. Miller***, 211 F.3d 57, 66 (3d Cir.2000); ***Hancock v. Hobbs***, 967 F.2d 462, 467 (11th Cir.1992); ***Hancock v. Dodson***, 958 F.2d 1367, 1373 (6th Cir.1992); ***von Bulow v. von Bulow***, 811 F.2d 136, 141 (2d Cir.1987); ***Memorial Hosp. v. Shadur***, 664 F.2d 1058, 1061 & n.3 (7th Cir.1981). *But see* ***Motley v. Marathon Oil Co.***, 71 F.3d 1547, 1551 (10th Cir.1995) (even though federal and state causes of action were asserted, state privilege law governs state causes of action). But even if federal privilege law controls, the court can look to state privilege law and the 1974 proposed Federal Rules of Evidence—which were rejected by Congress—for guidance. ***Tennenbaum v. Deloitte & Touche***, 77 F.3d 337, 340 (9th Cir.1996).

NOTE

Although many of the privileges defined in the proposed FREs—such as the clergy-communicant privilege—were never adopted by Congress, federal courts continue to use the proposed rules as a guide to determine whether and how to apply a privilege. ***In re Grand Jury Investigation****, 918 F.2d 374, 379-80 (3d Cir.1990).*

2. Identifying privileges. Federal privileges are governed by common-law principles unless the U.S. Constitution, a federal statute, or rules prescribed by the Supreme Court provide otherwise. FRE 501; ***Jaffee v. Redmond***, 518 U.S. 1, 8-9 (1996); ***In re Sealed Case***, 381 F.3d at 1211-12; ***Goodyear Tire & Rubber Co. v. Chiles Power Sup.***, 332 F.3d 976, 979-80 (6th Cir.2003).

(1) New privileges. Federal courts are given flexibility to develop the rules of privilege and to identify new privileges on a case-by-case basis. ***University of Pa. v. EEOC***, 493 U.S. 182, 189 (1990); ***Trammel v. U.S.***, 445 U.S. 40, 47 (1980); *see* FRE 501. When identifying a new privilege, the courts have considered whether it (1) protects a private relationship requiring confidence and trust, (2) protects a public interest sufficiently important to outweigh the need for probative evidence, and (3) is identified in common law by a majority of states or in the 1974 draft of FRE 501. *See* ***Jaffee***, 518 U.S. at 10-12 (considering all three factors and identifying psychotherapist-patient privilege); ***University of Pa.***, 493 U.S. at 189 (considering factors 2 and 3 but refusing to identify peer-review privilege); ***U.S. v. Arthur Young & Co.***, 465 U.S. 805, 817-18 (1984) (considering factor 1 but refusing to identify accountant-client privilege because of public relationship); ***Upjohn Co. v. U.S.***, 449 U.S. 383, 389 (1981) (considering factor 2 and expanding attorney-client privilege); ***Trammel***, 445 U.S. at 51 (considering all three factors and further defining spousal privilege); ***Barton v. U.S. Dist. Ct. for the Cent. Dist. of Cal.***, 410 F.3d 1104, 1111 (9th Cir. 2005) (considering factor 3 and expanding attorney-client privilege); ***Goodyear Tire***, 332 F.3d at 980 (considering all three factors and identifying settlement-negotiations privilege). When asking the court to identify a new privilege, a party should explain how the new privilege meets all three factors. *See* ***In re Subpoena Duces Tecum Issued to Commodity Futures Trading Comm'n WD Energy Servs.***, 439 F.3d 740, 751 (D.C.Cir.2006) (proponent of privilege must identify particular contextual basis for privilege). *See generally* Lauderdale, *A New Trend in the Law of Privilege: The Federal Settlement Privilege & the Proper Use of Federal Rule of Evidence 501 for the Recognition of New Privileges*, 35 U. Mem. L.Rev. 255 (2005) (discussing process for recognizing new privileges under FRE 501).

(2) Privileges recognized. The following are some of the privileges recognized in federal civil cases:

(a) Accounting-oversight privilege. See "Accounting oversight," §3.9.9(4), p. 480.

(b) Attorney-client privilege. See "Attorney-client privilege," §3.3, p. 463.

(c) Bank-examination privilege. See "Bank-examination privilege," §3.9.8, p. 480.

(d) Census privilege. See "Census," §3.9.9(3), p. 480.

(e) Clergy-communicant privilege. See "Clergy-communicant privilege," §3.7, p. 474.

(f) Deliberative-process privilege. See "Deliberative-process privilege," §3.9.1, p. 476.

(g) Informant privilege. See "Informant privilege," §3.9.3(1), p. 479.

(h) Investigatory privilege. See "Investigatory privilege," §3.9.3(2), p. 479.

(i) Journalist's privilege. See "Journalist's privilege," §3.8, p. 475.

(j) Judicial privilege. See "Judicial privilege," §3.9.6, p. 480.

(k) Legislative privilege. See "Legislative privilege," §3.9.5, p. 480.

(*l*) Litigation privilege. See "Litigation privilege," §3.9.7, p. 480.

(m) Marital confidential-communications privilege. See "Spousal privileges," §3.11, p. 481.

(n) Patent-application privilege. See "Patent application," §3.9.9(1), p. 480.

(o) Privilege against self-incrimination. See "Privilege against self-incrimination," §3.5, p. 471.

(p) Psychotherapist-patient privilege. See "Psychotherapist-patient privilege," §3.6, p. 472.

(q) Settlement-negotiations privilege. See "Settlement-negotiations privilege," §3.12, p. 481.

(r) Spousal testimonial privilege. See "Spousal privileges," §3.11, p. 481.

(s) State-secrets privilege. See "State-secrets privilege," §3.9.2, p. 478.

(t) Tax-return privilege. See "Tax return," §3.9.9(2), p. 480.

(u) Trade-secret protection. See "Trade-secret protection," §3.10, p. 480.

(v) Work-product protection. See "Work-product protection," §3.4, p. 467.

(3) Privileges not recognized. The following privileges are generally not recognized in federal civil cases, but they may apply in diversity cases under state law:

(a) Accountant-client. Federal courts do not recognize an accountant-client privilege. ***Arthur Young***, 465 U.S. at 817; ***Couch v. U.S.***, 409 U.S. 322, 335 (1973). However, the attorney-client privilege can protect communications between a client and its accountant when the accountant's role is to clarify communications between the client and its attorney. ***U.S. v. Ackert***, 169 F.3d 136, 139 (2d Cir.1999); *see, e.g.*, 26 U.S.C. §7525(a)(1) (in noncriminal tax matters, communication involving tax advice between taxpayer and tax practitioner is privileged under attorney-client privilege to extent that communication would be considered privileged if it were between taxpayer and attorney). Unless the accountant's role meets the requirements of the attorney-client privilege, the accountant's presence as a third-party witness to an attorney-client communication will destroy the attorney-client privilege. *See* ***Cavallaro v. U.S.***, 284 F.3d 236, 246 (1st Cir.2002). See "Accountants," §3.3.2(1)(a), p. 464.

(b) Banker-client. Federal courts do not recognize a banker-client privilege. ***Rosenblatt v. Northwest Airlines, Inc.***, 54 F.R.D. 21, 22 (S.D.N.Y.1971); *see* ***Young v. U.S. Dept. of Justice***, 882 F.2d 633, 642 (2d Cir.1989).

(c) Insurer-insured. Federal courts do not recognize an insurer-insured privilege. ***Linde Thomson Langworthy Kohn & Van Dyke, P.C. v. Resolution Trust Corp.***, 5 F.3d 1508, 1514 (D.C.Cir.1993).

(d) Ombudsman. Federal courts do not recognize a privilege for communications between corporate ombudsmen and employees. ***Carman v. McDonnell Douglas Corp.***, 114 F.3d 790, 793-94 (8th Cir.1997).

(e) Parent-child. Federal courts generally do not recognize a parent-child privilege. ***In re Grand Jury***, 103 F.3d 1140, 1146-56 (3d Cir.1997); ***In re Erato***, 2 F.3d 11, 16 (2d Cir.1993); ***Grand Jury Proceedings of John Doe v. U.S.***, 842 F.2d 244, 246 (10th Cir.1988); ***U.S. v. Davies***, 768 F.2d 893, 899-900 (7th Cir.1985); ***Port v. Heard***, 764 F.2d 423, 429 (5th Cir.1985); ***In re Grand Jury Subpoena of Santarelli***, 740 F.2d 816, 817 (11th Cir.1984). *But see* ***In re Agosto***, 553 F.Supp. 1298, 1325 (D.Nev.1983) (court recognized parent-child privilege).

(f) Peer review. Federal courts do not recognize a privilege against disclosure of medical or academic peer-review material. ***University of Pa.***, 493 U.S. at 189 (academic peer review); ***Adkins v. Christie***, 488 F.3d 1324, 1329-30 (11th Cir.2007) (medical peer review in federal employment-discrimination cases); ***Virmani***, 259 F.3d at 293 (same).

(g) Physician-patient. Federal courts do not recognize a general physician-patient privilege. ***Whalen v. Roe***, 429 U.S. 589, 602 n.28 (1977); ***Patterson v. Caterpillar, Inc.***, 70 F.3d 503, 506 (7th Cir.1995); ***Dodson***, 958 F.2d at 1373; *see also* 25 Wright & Graham §§5521-5553 (discussing history, policy, and elements of patient privilege). But federal common law does recognize a patient's limited right to privacy regarding medical records. ***Whalen***, 429 U.S. at 599-600; ***Doe v. Southeastern Pa. Transp. Auth.***, 72 F.3d 1133, 1137 (3d Cir.1995). *But see* ***Jarvis v. Wellman***, 52 F.3d 125, 126 (6th Cir.1995) (disclosure of medical records is not breach of fundamental rights under Constitution). The privacy interest is neither an absolute right nor dispositive in all circumstances, and it must

be weighed against any competing interests. ***Doe***, 72 F.3d at 1138; *see, e.g.*, 45 C.F.R. §164.512(f)(1)(ii)(B) (patient's right to privacy under Health Insurance Portability and Accountability Act is subject to relevant grand-jury subpoenas).

(h) Political consultant. Federal courts do not recognize a privilege for communications between a client and a political consultant when the advice was not intended to assist an attorney in providing legal advice. *See* ***Blumenthal v. Drudge***, 186 F.R.D. 236, 243 (D.D.C.1999) (court did not address whether communications were protected as work product).

(i) Probation officer. Federal courts do not recognize a privilege for communications between a probation officer and a parolee. ***U.S. v. Holmes***, 594 F.2d 1167, 1171 (8th Cir.1979).

(j) Self-evaluation. Federal appellate courts do not recognize a privilege for self-evaluation, also known as the self-critical-analysis privilege. ***In re Kaiser Aluminum & Chem. Co.***, 214 F.3d 586, 593 (5th Cir. 2000); ***Dowling v. American Haw. Cruises, Inc.***, 971 F.2d 423, 425-26 & n.1 (9th Cir.1992); ***Coates v. Johnson & Johnson***, 756 F.2d 524, 551-52 (7th Cir.1985).

NOTE

Some federal district courts, however, do recognize the self-evaluation privilege. E.g., ***Melhorn v. New Jersey Transit Rail Opers., Inc.****, 203 F.R.D. 176, 178-79 (E.D.Pa.2001);* ***Reichhold Chems., Inc. v. Textron, Inc.****, 157 F.R.D. 522, 524-26 (N.D.Fla.1994); see* ***Hoffman v. United Telecomms.****, 117 F.R.D. 440, 442-43 (D.Kan.1987). The privilege protects candid self-assessments of compliance with laws and regulations, such as materials resulting from a corporation's review of compliance with federal government regulations or a peer-review committee's review of medical records. See* ***Lara v. Tri-State Drilling, Inc.****, 504 F.Supp.2d 1323, 1325-26 (N.D.Ga.2007); Black's Law Dictionary 1319 (9th ed. 2009); Note, The Privilege of Self-Critical Analysis, 96 Harv.L.Rev. 1083, 1083 (1983). Under this privilege, information is protected if (1) the information results from a critical self-analysis undertaken by the party seeking protection, (2) the public has a strong interest in preserving the free flow of the type of information sought, (3) the information is of the type whose flow would be curtailed if discovery were allowed, and (4) the information was prepared with the expectation of confidentiality and has in fact been kept confidential.* ***Dowling****, 971 F.2d at 425-26.*

(k) Stockbroker-client. The federal courts do not recognize a stockbroker-client privilege. ***King v. E.F. Hutton & Co.***, 117 F.R.D. 2, 8 (D.D.C.1987).

§3.3 Attorney-client privilege. The purpose of the attorney-client privilege is to encourage full and frank communication between attorneys and their clients, thus promoting broader public interest in the observance of law and the administration of justice. ***Upjohn Co. v. U.S.***, 449 U.S. 383, 389 (1981); ***U.S. v. BDO Seidman, LLP***, 492 F.3d 806, 815 (7th Cir.2007); ***In re Keeper of Records***, 348 F.3d 16, 22 (1st Cir.2003); *see* ***Wachtel v. Health Net, Inc.***, 482 F.3d 225, 231 (3d Cir.2007) (when purpose ends, so does protection of privilege). The privilege rests on the need for the attorney to know everything that relates to the client's reasons for seeking representation. ***Trammel v. U.S.***, 445 U.S. 40, 51 (1980). Thus, the privilege exists to promote full disclosure by the client and to foster a relationship of trust. *See* ***Commodity Futures Trading Comm'n v. Weintraub***, 471 U.S. 343, 348 (1985).

1. What privilege protects. The attorney-client privilege protects from discovery certain communications among the attorney, the client, and their representatives.

(1) Attorney-client communication. The attorney-client privilege generally protects communications between only the attorney and the client. *See* ***In re Grand Jury Subpoena 92-1(SJ)***, 31 F.3d 826, 829 (9th Cir. 1994) (privilege protects communications between client seeking legal advice and attorney providing advice). But in certain circumstances, the privilege may extend to communications involving the attorney's and client's representatives, including secretaries, paralegals, accountants, and investigators. See "Who is included," §3.3.2, p. 464.

(2) Confidential communication. The attorney-client privilege protects only communications made in confidence for the purpose of obtaining legal advice from the attorney. ***In re Application of Chevron Corp.***, 650 F.3d 276, 289 (3d Cir.2011); ***In re Keeper of Records***, 348 F.3d at 22; ***U.S. v. El Paso Co.***, 682 F.2d 530, 538 (5th Cir. 1982). A communication is confidential only if it is not intended to be disclosed to third persons. The privilege is waived through disclosure of any significant part of a confidential communication to a third person who is not a representative of either the client or the attorney. *See, e.g.*, **Permian Corp. v. U.S.**, 665 F.2d 1214, 1219 (D.C.Cir.1981) (when confidential communications voluntarily disclosed to one person, privilege waived for all others). See "Waiver of privilege," §3.3.6, p. 466.

(3) Legal advice. The attorney-client privilege protects information from discovery only if the communication was made for the purpose of securing legal advice. ***In re Bieter Co.***, 16 F.3d 929, 936 (8th Cir.1994); ***U.S. v. Kovel***, 296 F.2d 918, 922 (2d Cir.1961); ***In re Vioxx Prods. Liab. Litig.***, 501 F.Supp.2d 789, 797 (E.D.La.2007); *see, e.g.*, ***In re Air Crash Disaster***, 133 F.R.D. 515, 522-23 (N.D.Ill.1990) (purpose of document written by general manager and distributed to employees through in-house counsel was not to seek legal advice; document dealt more with safety and litigation in general rather than specific litigation).

2. Who is included. The attorney-client privilege protects certain communications between the attorney and the client, or among their representatives. ***In re Bieter***, 16 F.3d at 936.

(1) Generally. The possible pairings of persons whose communications are protected include the following: (1) the client or its representative with the attorney or the attorney's representative, (2) the attorney with the attorney's representative, (3) the client or its attorney with an attorney representing another client on a matter of common interest, and (4) the client with a representative of the client. ***In re Bieter***, 16 F.3d at 935. Also protected are (5) communications between the client's representatives and (6) communications between the client's attorneys. *See id.* Communications with accountants, patent agents, public-relations firms, and trial consultants may also be protected under the attorney-client privilege.

(a) Accountants. An accountant-client communication is privileged under the attorney-client privilege if (1) the accountant, whether hired by the attorney or by the client, is the attorney's agent, (2) the accountant is necessary, or at least highly useful, to facilitate attorney-client communication, and (3) the communication was made to obtain legal advice from the attorney. ***Cavallaro v. U.S.***, 284 F.3d 236, 247 (1st Cir.2002); ***Kovel***, 296 F.2d at 922; *see* ***U.S. v. Ackert***, 169 F.3d 136, 139 (2d Cir.1999). There is a privilege if (1) the communication is legal advice, not just an accounting service, or (2) the advice is the attorney's, rather than the accountant's. ***Cavallaro***, 284 F.3d at 247; ***In re Grand Jury Proceedings***, 220 F.3d 568, 571 (7th Cir.2000). For example, the preparation of a tax return is not privileged because it is an accounting service (i.e., not legal advice); however, information transmitted to an attorney or to the attorney's agent is privileged if it was not intended to appear on a tax return but was given to the attorney for the sole purpose of seeking legal advice. ***In re Grand Jury Proceedings***, 220 F.3d at 571; *see* ***U.S. v. Davis***, 636 F.2d 1028, 1043 (5th Cir.1981). *But see* **Colton v. U.S.**, 306 F.2d 633, 637 (2d Cir.1962) (tax advice and preparation of tax returns are matters sufficiently within attorney's professional competence to make them subject to attorney-client privilege).

(b) Patent agents. Some courts hold that the attorney-client privilege extends to communications between an attorney and a patent agent acting under the attorney's authority and control if the communications relate to the prosecution of a patent application in the United States. **Gorman v. Polar Electro, Inc.**, 137 F.Supp.2d 223, 227 (E.D.N.Y.2001); ***In re Ampicillin Antitrust Litig.***, 81 F.R.D. 377, 391 (D.D.C.1978); ***Hercules, Inc. v. Exxon Corp.***, 434 F.Supp. 136, 146 (D.Del.1977). *But see* **Joh. A. Benckiser, G.m.b.H. v. Hygrade Food Prods.**, 253 F.Supp. 999, 1000 (D.N.J.1966) (privilege denied); ***U.S. v. United Shoe Mach. Corp.***, 89 F.Supp. 357, 360-61 (D. Mass.1950) (same).

(c) Public-relations firms. Some courts hold that the attorney-client privilege extends to communications between an attorney and a public-relations firm if the communications relate to the client's litigation or legal strategies. *See* ***FTC v. GlaxoSmithKline***, 294 F.3d 141, 148 (D.C.Cir.2002); *see, e.g.*, ***In re Grand Jury Subpoenas***, 265 F.Supp.2d 321, 330-31 (S.D.N.Y.2003) (communication about client's grand-jury investigation protected).

(d) Trial consultants. It is not clear whether the attorney-client privilege protects communications between a client and a trial consultant. *See* ***In re Cendant Corp. Secs. Litig.***, 343 F.3d 658, 661 n.4 (3d Cir. 2003) (communications protected under work product; issue of attorney-client privilege was not reached); *see also id.* at 668 (Garth, J., concurring) (communications protected by attorney-client privilege).

(2) Corporate clients. The attorney-client privilege protects certain communications between a corporation and its attorney. ***In re Vioxx***, 501 F.Supp.2d at 796. Because a corporation acts through its agents, the protected communications generally occur between a corporation's officer, director, or employee and the corporation's attorney. *See* ***U.S. v. Graf***, 610 F.3d 1148, 1156 (9th Cir.2010).

NOTE

When the interests of a corporation's agent become adverse to the interests of the corporation, it can be a complex issue to determine who the "client" actually is and what is protected by the attorney-client privilege. See ***Graf***, *610 F.3d at 1156.*

(a) Current corporate employees. The attorney-client privilege protects communications by any corporate employee, regardless of position, when the communications concern matters within the scope of the employee's corporate duties and the employee is aware the information is being furnished to enable the attorney to provide legal advice to the corporation. ***Upjohn Co.***, 449 U.S. at 394.

(b) Former corporate employees. Former corporate employees may possess relevant information needed by an attorney to advise a corporate client. Thus, certain communications with former corporate employees are protected by the attorney-client privilege. ***In re Coordinated Pretrial Proceedings***, 658 F.2d 1355, 1361 n.7 (9th Cir.1981).

(c) Nonemployee representatives. The attorney-client privilege protects certain communications with nonemployees who are significantly connected to the client and the client's involvement in the transaction that is the subject of legal services. ***In re Bieter***, 16 F.3d at 937-38; ***Horton v. U.S.***, 204 F.R.D. 670, 672 (D.Colo. 2002). To claim the privilege, the party must make a detailed factual showing that the nonemployee is the functional equivalent of an employee and the information sought from the nonemployee would be subject to the attorney-client privilege if she were an employee. ***Horton***, 204 F.R.D. at 672.

(3) Parties who share common interest. The attorney-client privilege protects certain communications between parties who undertake a joint effort for a common legal interest. ***BDO Seidman***, 492 F.3d at 815-16; ***HSH Nordbank AG N.Y. Branch v. Swerdlow***, 259 F.R.D. 64, 71 (S.D.N.Y.2009); *see* ***In re Grand Jury Subpoena: Under Seal***, 415 F.3d 333, 341 (4th Cir.2005); *see also* ***In re Commercial Money Ctr., Inc., Equip. Lease Litig.***, 248 F.R.D. 532, 536 (N.D.Ohio 2008) (protection applies to Ps or Ds in civil cases as well as potential coparties in prospective litigation). The protection is limited to communications made in furtherance of the common interest. ***BDO Seidman***, 492 F.3d at 816; *see* ***In re Teleglobe Comms.***, 493 F.3d 345, 364-65 (3d Cir.2007) (privilege is for communications between attorneys, not between clients). The common-interest doctrine is an exception to the rule of no disclosure to third parties. ***BDO Seidman***, 492 F.3d at 815. See "By disclosure," §3.3.6(1), p. 466.

3. Privilege belongs to client. The attorney-client privilege belongs to the client, not to the attorney. ***U.S. v. Doe***, 429 F.3d 450, 452 (3d Cir.2005); ***In re Sarrio, S.A.***, 119 F.3d 143, 147 (2d Cir.1997). The attorney may claim the privilege, but only on behalf of the client. ***Haines v. Liggett Grp.***, 975 F.2d 81, 90 (3d Cir.1992); *see* ***In re Sarrio, S.A.***, 119 F.3d at 147. The attorney's authority to claim the privilege for the client should be presumed if there is no evidence to the contrary. *Cf.* Tex. R. Evid. 503(c) (attorney is presumed to have authority to claim privilege on client's behalf).

4. Duration of privilege. The attorney-client privilege continues for as long as the client asserts it. It does not terminate at the conclusion of the employment or at the end of the dispute for which the client hired the attorney. *See* ***U.S. v. Kleifgen***, 557 F.2d 1293, 1297 (9th Cir.1977). The privilege survives the client's death. *E.g.*, ***Swidler & Berlin v. U.S.***, 524 U.S. 399, 408-11 (1998) (independent prosecutor could not obtain notes taken by D's attorney days before D's death).

5. Exceptions.

(1) Crime/fraud exception. The privilege does not extend to communications that solicit or offer advice for the commission of a crime or fraud. ***In re Green Grand Jury Proceedings***, 492 F.3d 976, 979 (8th Cir. 2007); ***In re Napster, Inc. Copyright Litig.***, 479 F.3d 1078, 1090 (9th Cir.2007), *overruled on other grounds*, ***Mohawk Indus. v. Carpenter***, 558 U.S. 100 (2009). The crime/fraud exception applies to communications between an attorney and client made in furtherance of a continuing or future crime or fraud, regardless of who initiated the communication. ***In re Grand Jury Investigation***, 445 F.3d 266, 274 (3d Cir.2006); *see* ***U.S. v. Zolin***, 491 U.S. 554, 562-63 (1989); ***BDO Seidman***, 492 F.3d at 818. The crime/fraud exception applies only to cases in which there is probable cause to believe the communication was intended to facilitate or conceal criminal or fraudulent activity. ***In re Richard Roe, Inc.***, 68 F.3d 38, 40 (2d Cir.1995); *see also* ***In re Napster, Inc. Copyright Litig.***, 479 F.3d at 1093-94 (courts differ on standard for what constitutes probable cause to believe). The court may order an in camera review to determine whether the party seeking discovery made a threshold showing that the communication revealed plans for a crime or fraud. ***Zolin***, 491 U.S. at 568-72; *see* ***BDO Seidman***, 492 F.3d at 819.

(2) Fiduciary exception. The privilege does not extend to communications provided to certain fiduciaries about the execution of their fiduciary obligations when the communications are sought by their beneficiaries. ***U.S. v. Jicarilla Apache Nation***, ___ U.S. ___, 131 S.Ct. 2313, 2318 (2011); *see* ***Solis v. Food Empls. Labor Relations Ass'n***, 644 F.3d 221, 226-27 (4th Cir.2011); ***Wachtel***, 482 F.3d at 226. The exception applies to many fiduciary relationships. *See* ***Stephan v. Unum Life Ins.***, ___ F.3d ___ (9th Cir.2012) (No. 10-16840; 9-12-12) (exception may apply to insurance companies serving as ERISA fiduciaries); ***Garner v. Wolfinbarger***, 430 F.2d 1093, 1103-04 (5th Cir.1970) (exception may apply to communications between corporation and its attorneys when corporation's stockholders seek to discover communications in shareholder derivative actions).

6. Waiver of privilege.

(1) By disclosure. The party may waive the attorney-client privilege by disclosing privileged communications to third parties. ***In re Qwest Comms. Int'l***, 450 F.3d 1179, 1185 (10th Cir.2006); *see* FRE 502(a); ***Jenkins v. Bartlett***, 487 F.3d 482, 490 (7th Cir.2007). See "Disclosure of privileged or protected information – attorney-related privileges," ch. 6-A, §9.3.2, p. 432. For example, the privilege can be waived if a client refers to the communication during testimony. ***In re County of Erie***, 546 F.3d 222, 228 (2d Cir.2008); *see* ***Baker v. General Motors Corp.***, 209 F.3d 1051, 1055 (8th Cir.2000).

(2) By claim or defense. The party may waive the privilege by asserting a claim (e.g., legal-malpractice action) or defense (e.g., advice-of-counsel defense) that puts the subject matter of the privileged communication or the attorney's advice at issue. ***Baker***, 209 F.3d at 1055; ***Rhone-Poulenc Rorer Inc. v. Home Indem. Co.***, 32 F.3d 851, 863 (3d Cir.1994); *see* ***In re County of Erie***, 546 F.3d at 228; *see, e.g.*, ***Chevron Corp. v. Pennzoil Co.***, 974 F.2d 1156, 1162-63 (9th Cir.1992) (in securities case, corporation waived privilege when it put reasonableness of attorney's tax advice at issue); ***Anchondo v. Anderson, Crenshaw, & Assocs.***, 256 F.R.D. 661, 671-72 (D.N.M. 2009) (in Fair Debt Collection Practices Act case, debt collector waived privilege for legal research it performed when debt collector raised bona-fide-error defense).

NOTE

Courts disagree on whether a party must actually rely on privileged communication for there to be a waiver of the privilege. See ***Union Cty. v. Piper Jaffray & Co.***, *248 F.R.D. 217, 221 (S.D.Iowa 2008). Compare* ***In re County of Erie***, *546 F.3d at 229 (party must rely on privileged communication as part of claim or defense; mere relevance of communication is insufficient), with* ***Home Indem. Co. v. Lane Powell Moss & Miller***, *43 F.3d 1322, 1326 (9th Cir.1995) (party does not have to rely on privileged communication; privilege may be waived if use of privilege would be manifestly unfair to opposing party).*

§3.4 Work-product protection. An attorney's "work product" is protected from discovery. FRCP 26(b)(3)(A); *see **U.S. v. Deloitte LLP***, 610 F.3d 129, 136 (D.C.Cir.2010) (documents and tangible things are protected under FRCP 26(b)(3), and attorney's mental impressions are protected under doctrine announced in ***Hickman v. Taylor***); *see, e.g.*, FRCP 26(b)(4)(B), (b)(4)(C) (drafts of expert reports and most attorney-expert communications are protected as work product); *see also* ***United Coal Cos. v. Powell Constr. Co.***, 839 F.2d 958, 966 (3d Cir.1988) (unlike attorney-client privilege, work-product protection is governed, even in diversity cases, by FRCP 26(b)(3)). The work-product protection was created to protect trial-preparation materials that could reveal an attorney's evaluations and strategy about the case. ***Hickman v. Taylor***, 329 U.S. 495, 510-11 (1947). Exempting work product from discovery protects the privacy of an attorney's thought processes and prevents parties from trying lawsuits by borrowing the wits of their adversaries. *Id.* at 516 (Jackson, J., concurring); *see* ***U.S. v. Adlman***, 68 F.3d 1495, 1501 (2d Cir.1995) (work-product protection is intended to "establish a zone of privacy for strategic litigation planning and to prevent one party from piggybacking on the adversary's preparation"). The work-product rule is not a privilege but a qualified immunity protecting from discovery (1) work product (2) prepared in anticipation of litigation (3) by a party or its representative. ***Admiral Ins. v. U.S. Dist. Ct., Dist. Ariz.***, 881 F.2d 1486, 1494 (9th Cir.1989); *see* ***In re Grand Jury Subpoena Dated July 6, 2005***, 510 F.3d 180, 183 (2d Cir.2007). The work-product protection is broader than the attorney-client privilege. ***In re Cendant Corp. Secs. Litig.***, 343 F.3d 658, 666 (3d Cir.2003). The party asserting work-product protection has the burden of establishing its applicability. ***In re Grand Jury Subpoena Dated July 6, 2005***, 510 F.3d at 183; *see* ***Kartman v. State Farm Mut. Auto. Ins.***, 247 F.R.D. 561, 565 (S.D.Ind.2007) (applicability must be shown on document-by-document basis).

1. Work product. There are two general types of work product: opinion work product and ordinary work product.

(1) Opinion work product. Opinion work product consists of the mental impressions, conclusions, opinions, or legal theories of an attorney or other representative of a party. FRCP 26(b)(3)(B); ***In re Grand Jury Subpoena Dated July 6, 2005***, 510 F.3d at 183; ***In re Green Grand Jury Proceedings***, 492 F.3d 976, 980 (8th Cir. 2007); *see also* ***Garcia v. City of El Centro***, 214 F.R.D. 587, 591 (S.D.Cal.2003) (opinion work product may protect certain factual information when facts inherently reveal attorney's mental impressions). Examples of opinion work product include the following:

(a) Attorney notes. Attorney notes are the prime example of opinion work product. ***Upjohn Co. v. U.S.***, 449 U.S. 383, 399-400 (1981); *see* ***Hickman***, 329 U.S. at 510-11. Even purely factual attorney notes may reflect an opinion since an attorney reveals her view of the case in deciding what to write and what to omit. ***Director, Office of Thrift Supervision v. Vinson & Elkins, LLP***, 124 F.3d 1304, 1308 (D.C.Cir.1997).

(b) Documents. Documents reflecting strategy discussions and evaluation of cases are opinion work product. *See* ***In re San Juan Dupont Plaza Hotel Fire Litig.***, 859 F.2d 1007, 1015 (1st Cir.1988); ***US Airline Pilots Ass'n. v. Pension Benefit Guar. Corp.***, 274 F.R.D. 28, 30 (D.D.C.2011); ***Ideal Elec. Co. v. Flowserve Corp.***, 230 F.R.D. 603, 609 (D.Nev.2005).

(c) Compilations. Some compilations of documents may be protected as opinion work product because even acknowledging them will disclose the attorney's mental impressions and thought processes. ***Shelton v. American Motors Corp.***, 805 F.2d 1323, 1328-29 (8th Cir.1986); ***Sporck v. Peil***, 759 F.2d 312, 316-17 (3d Cir. 1985). *But see* ***Audiotext Comms. Network v. US Telecom, Inc.***, 164 F.R.D. 250, 252 (D.Kan.1996) (selecting and grouping documents does not transform discoverable documents into work product).

(d) Litigation file. The organization of the file, as well as the decision about what to include in it, is opinion work product because it necessarily reveals the attorney's thought processes about the case. *See* ***Hickman***, 329 U.S. at 511-12; ***Kartman***, 247 F.R.D. at 564.

(2) Ordinary work product. Ordinary work product consists of other trial-preparation materials that do not disclose impressions or opinions. *See* ***In re Grand Jury Subpoena Dated July 6, 2005***, 510 F.3d at 183; ***In re Doe***, 662 F.2d 1073, 1076 n.2 (4th Cir.1981). Examples of ordinary work product include the following:

(a) Raw, factual information. Raw, factual information is ordinary work product. ***In re Green Grand Jury Proceedings***, 492 F.3d at 980; ***In re Doe***, 662 F.2d at 1076 n.2.

(b) Nonparty witness statements. Nonparty witness statements to an attorney are ordinary work product. ***Hickman***, 329 U.S. at 509-12; ***Institute for the Dev. of Earth Awareness v. People for the Ethical Treatment of Animals***, 272 F.R.D. 124, 125 (S.D.N.Y.2011); *see* ***Gerber v. Down E. Cmty. Hosp.***, 266 F.R.D. 29, 33 (D.Me.2010) (e-mail correspondence between attorney and potential witnesses can be protected as work product; e-mail correspondence can be similar to shorthand or stenographic recording of witness statement or interview); *see also* ***Murphy v. Kmart Corp.***, 259 F.R.D. 421, 428 (D.S.D.2009) (addressing disagreement in district courts over whether nonparty witness's affidavit that is drafted by attorney after attorney interviews witness is protected as work product; court followed majority view and held that affidavits were not protected).

NOTE

On request, a witness may obtain a copy of any statement she made without having to show substantial need or undue hardship. See FRCP 26(b)(3)(C). But the fact that the witness can obtain a copy of her statement does not prevent the statement from being covered as work product. ***Gerber****, 266 F.R.D. at 33.*

(c) Certain information. A computer tape reflecting an attorney's selection of certain information is ordinary work product. ***In re Chrysler Motors Corp. Overnight Evaluation Program Litig.***, 860 F.2d 844, 846 (8th Cir.1988). Collection of evidence, without any creative or analytic input by the attorney or agent, does not qualify as work product. *E.g.*, ***Riddell Sports Inc. v. Brooks***, 158 F.R.D. 555, 559 (S.D.N.Y.1994) (transcript of tape was not work product).

(d) Exhibit lists. Forcing premature production of an exhibit list reveals attorney thought processes; treating the lists as ordinary work product safeguards the legitimate privacy concerns at stake. ***In re San Juan***, 859 F.2d at 1018-19.

2. Prepared in anticipation of litigation. To determine whether documents were prepared in anticipation of litigation, most circuits ask whether the documents were prepared or obtained because of the prospect of litigation (rather than for an ordinary business purpose) and whether that belief of prospective litigation was objectively reasonable. *See* ***U.S. v. Roxworthy***, 457 F.3d 590, 593-94 (6th Cir.2006); ***In re Grand Jury Subpoena (Torf)***, 357 F.3d 900, 907 (9th Cir.2004); ***In re Sealed Case***, 146 F.3d 881, 884 (D.C.Cir.1998); ***U.S. v. Adlman***, 134 F.3d 1194, 1202 (2d Cir.1998); 8 Wright, Miller & Marcus §2024 & n.12. *But see* ***U.S. v. El Paso Co.***, 682 F.2d 530, 542 (5th Cir. 1982) (documents must have been prepared primarily to assist in litigation). In applying the "because of" standard, courts must consider the totality of the circumstances and determine whether the documents would not have been created in substantially similar form but for the prospect of litigation. ***U.S. v. Richey***, 632 F.3d 559, 568 (9th Cir.2011). The documents must actually be prepared in anticipation of litigation; it is not enough that the subject matter of a document is related to an issue that might conceivably be litigated or that materials were prepared by attorneys. *E.g.*, ***U.S. v. Textron Inc. & Subsidiaries***, 577 F.3d 21, 29-30 (1st Cir.2009) (tax-accrual work papers, which were prepared to support financial filings and audit and to comply with securities law, were not protected as work product because papers were prepared in ordinary course of business).

NOTE

A party who is seeking to withhold a document has the burden to show that the document was prepared in anticipation of litigation. ***Biegas v. Quickway Carriers, Inc.****, 573 F.3d 365, 381 (6th Cir.2009). To satisfy that burden, the party should produce specific and detailed evidence, such as affidavits, deposition excerpts, answers to interrogatories, or equivalent proof. Id. at 381-82. If the party does not produce evidence, the court can reject the work-product claim and order that the document be disclosed. See, e.g., id.*

(1) Current litigation. Parties often anticipate litigation and begin preparation before a suit is formally commenced. *See, e.g.*, ***Equal Rights Ctr. v. Post Props., Inc.***, 247 F.R.D. 208, 210-11 (D.D.C.2008) (before complaint was filed, D-developer hired attorney to perform compliance reviews; reviews were created in anticipation of litigation when suits had already been filed against similarly situated developers). Materials created in the ordinary course of business, to comply with regulatory requirements, or for other nonlitigation reasons are not prepared in anticipation of litigation. ***Martin v. Bally's Park Place Hotel & Casino***, 983 F.2d 1252, 1260-61 (3d Cir.1993); ***National Un. Fire Ins. v. Murray Sheet Metal Co.***, 967 F.2d 980, 984 (4th Cir.1992); 1970 Notes to FRCP 26 at ¶23, p. 1191, this book; *see, e.g.*, ***In re Grand Jury Subpoena (Torf)***, 357 F.3d at 909-10 (protection applied when litigation purpose permeated nonlitigation purpose so that the two purposes could not be discretely separated); ***Simon v. G.D. Searle & Co.***, 816 F.2d 397, 401-02 (8th Cir.1987) (protection did not apply when aggregate-reserve information in risk-management documents served many business-planning functions but did not enhance defense of lawsuit).

(2) Later litigation. The work-product protection covers work product prepared in anticipation of earlier litigation but used in later litigation. *See* ***Frontier Ref., Inc. v. Gorman-Rupp Co.***, 136 F.3d 695, 703 (10th Cir.1998); ***In re Grand Jury Proceedings***, 43 F.3d 966, 971 (5th Cir.1994); *see also* ***Duplan Corp. v. Moulinage et Retorderie de Chavanoz***, 509 F.2d 730, 732 (4th Cir.1974) (work-product protection covers attorneys' mental impressions and opinions even after suit for which it was prepared has ended). The courts are split on whether the work-product protection extends to all later litigation or only to later litigation that is closely related to the earlier litigation. *Compare* ***In re Grand Jury Proceedings***, 604 F.2d 798, 803 (3d Cir.1979) (only closely related litigation), *with* ***In re Murphy***, 560 F.2d 326, 335 (8th Cir.1977) (all later litigation), *and* ***Duplan Corp. v. Moulinage et Retorderie de Chavanoz***, 487 F.2d 480, 484 & n.15 (4th Cir.1973) (same). Some courts have declined to decide whether the work-product protection extends only to later litigation that is closely related. *See, e.g.*, ***Frontier Ref.***, 136 F.3d at 703; ***In re Grand Jury Proceedings***, 43 F.3d at 971.

3. Prepared by party or representative. The work-product protection extends to materials prepared by the party or its representative, including an attorney, consultant, surety, indemnitor, insurer, or agent. FRCP 26(b)(3)(A); *see* ***United Coal***, 839 F.2d at 966 (materials prepared by or for party's insurer or agents of insurer qualify for work-product protection); *see, e.g.*, ***In re Cendant Corp.***, 343 F.3d at 667-68 (trial consultant's advice to client was protected); ***Holmgren v. State Farm Mut. Auto. Ins.***, 976 F.2d 573, 576 (9th Cir.1992) (documents prepared by representative of insurer qualified for work-product protection); ***In re Int'l Sys. & Controls Corp. Secs. Litig.***, 693 F.2d 1235, 1238 (5th Cir.1982) (work of independent accounting firm hired to investigate possibility of improper payments was protected); ***Sprague v. Director, Office of Workers' Comp. Programs***, 688 F.2d 862, 868-70 (1st Cir. 1982) (letter written by doctor for attorney was protected).

4. Who holds protection. Unlike the attorney-client privilege, the work-product protection belongs to both the client and the attorney, and either may assert it. ***In re Green Grand Jury Proceedings***, 492 F.3d at 980. Thus, the client's waiver will not waive the attorney's work-product protection, and vice versa. ***In re Grand Jury Proceedings***, 43 F.3d at 972; ***In re Sealed Case***, 676 F.2d 793, 812 n.75 (D.C.Cir.1982). *But see* ***Rhone-Poulenc Rorer Inc. v. Home Indem. Co.***, 32 F.3d 851, 866 (3d Cir.1994) (protection belongs to professional, not client). But when the interests of the client and the attorney are not aligned, the client's interests in protecting the work product will likely prevail. *See* ***SEC v. McNaul***, 271 F.R.D. 661, 666 (D.Kan.2010).

5. Overcoming protection. There are two tiers of protection for attorney work product, based on whether the work product is opinion work product or ordinary work product. ***In re Cendant Corp.***, 343 F.3d at 663. Protection for opinion work product is generally greater than protection for ordinary work product. ***In re Green Grand Jury Proceedings***, 492 F.3d at 980; *see* ***In re Cendant Corp.***, 343 F.3d at 664 (to be discoverable, opinion work product requires heightened showing of extraordinary circumstances).

(1) Opinion work product. Some circuits have held that protection for opinion work product is not absolute and may be overcome in extraordinary circumstances. *See* ***In re Cendant Corp.***, 343 F.3d at 664; ***Baker v. General Motors Corp.***, 209 F.3d 1051, 1054 (8th Cir.2000); ***Cox v. Administrator U.S. Steel & Carnegie***, 17 F.3d

1386, 1422 (11th Cir.1994), *modified on other grounds*, 30 F.3d 1347 (11th Cir.1994). *But see* ***Duplan Corp.***, 509 F.2d at 735 (protection of opinion work product is absolute). A party may overcome the protection for opinion work product by establishing (1) the crime/fraud exception or (2) a compelling need for the material. *See* ***In re Cendant Corp.***, 343 F.3d at 666 n.8 (crime/fraud exception); ***Cox***, 17 F.3d at 1422 (same); ***Holmgren***, 976 F.2d at 577 (compelling need for material). The Supreme Court has intentionally avoided deciding whether the protection for opinion work product is absolute. ***Upjohn Co.***, 449 U.S. at 401.

(a) Crime/fraud exception. Under the crime/fraud exception, opinion work product may be discovered when it is made to further continuing or future criminal or fraudulent activity. ***In re Green Grand Jury Proceedings***, 492 F.3d at 980-81; ***In re Burlington N., Inc.***, 822 F.2d 518, 524 (5th Cir.1987); *cf.* ***U.S. v. Zolin***, 491 U.S. 554, 562-63 (1989) (discussing crime/fraud exception in context of attorney-client privilege). A client who uses an attorney's assistance to perpetrate a crime or fraud cannot assert work-product protection for opinion work product; however, an attorney who does not knowingly participate in the client's crime or fraud may be able to assert work-product protection for her own opinion work product. ***In re Green Grand Jury Proceedings***, 492 F.3d at 980; ***In re Grand Jury Proceedings #5 Empanelled Jan. 28, 2004***, 401 F.3d 247, 252 (4th Cir.2005); ***In re Grand Jury Proceedings***, 867 F.2d 539, 541 (9th Cir.1989). The party seeking discovery of protected material under the crime/fraud exception has the initial burden to show that the legal advice was obtained in furtherance of the criminal or fraudulent activity and was closely related to it. ***In re BankAmerica Corp. Secs. Litig.***, 270 F.3d 639, 642 (8th Cir.2001). If the requesting party satisfies its burden, the court must determine whether the client consulted the attorney or used the material for the purpose of committing a crime or fraud. ***In re Sealed Case***, 223 F.3d 775, 778 (D.C.Cir.2000); ***In re Sealed Case***, 107 F.3d 46, 51 (D.C.Cir.1997).

(b) Compelling need. Under the compelling-need exception, opinion work product may be discovered when mental impressions are at issue in a case and the need for the material is compelling. ***Holmgren***, 976 F.2d at 577; *see* ***In re Sealed Case***, 676 F.2d at 809-10; ***Handgards, Inc. v. Johnson & Johnson, Corp.***, 413 F.Supp. 926, 933 (N.D.Cal.1976); *see, e.g.*, ***Conoco Inc. v. Boh Bros. Constr. Co.***, 191 F.R.D. 107, 119 (W.D.La.1998) (in suit seeking contractual indemnification, Ds satisfied compelling-need exception when Ps' attorneys' assessment of Ps' potential liability was focus of suit).

(2) Ordinary work product. A party may overcome the protection for ordinary work product by establishing either (1) the crime/fraud exception or (2) a substantial need for the material and an inability to otherwise obtain the substantial equivalent of the material without undue hardship. *See* FRCP 26(b)(3)(A)(ii) (substantial need and undue hardship); ***In re Green Grand Jury Proceedings***, 492 F.3d at 979-80 (crime/fraud exception); ***In re Cendant Corp.***, 343 F.3d at 663 (substantial need and undue hardship); ***PepsiCo v. Baird, Kurtz & Dobson LLP***, 305 F.3d 813, 817 (8th Cir.2002) (same); *see also* ***In re Harmonic, Inc. Secs. Litig.***, 245 F.R.D. 424, 429 (N.D. Cal.2007) (when case involves work product of minimal substantive content, such as identity of confidential witnesses, showing of substantial need and undue hardship is comparatively lower).

(a) Crime/fraud exception. Under the crime/fraud exception, ordinary work product may be discovered when it is made to further continuing or future criminal or fraudulent activity. ***In re Green Grand Jury Proceedings***, 492 F.3d at 979-80; *cf.* ***Zolin***, 491 U.S. at 562-63 (discussing crime/fraud exception in context of attorney-client privilege). Neither the client who uses an attorney's assistance to perpetrate a crime or fraud nor the attorney herself—even an attorney who does not knowingly participate in her client's crime or fraud—can assert work-product protection for ordinary work product. *See* ***In re Green Grand Jury Proceedings***, 492 F.3d at 981; ***In re Grand Jury Proceedings #5***, 401 F.3d at 252. For a discussion of the parties' burden for the crime/fraud exception, see "Crime/fraud exception," §3.4.5(1)(a), this page.

(b) Substantial need & undue hardship. Under the exception for substantial need and undue hardship, ordinary work product may be discovered when a party shows that (1) it has a substantial need for the materials to prepare its case and (2) it cannot, without undue hardship, obtain the substantial equivalent of the materials any other way. FRCP 26(b)(3)(A)(ii); *see, e.g.*, ***Baker***, 209 F.3d at 1054-55 (no substantial need or undue hard-

ship for documents sought to counter testimony of witness when party already had substantial countering evidence); ***Vinson & Elkins***, 124 F.3d at 1307-08 (no substantial need or undue hardship when documents sought would merely reinforce already-known inconsistencies).

6. Waiver of work-product protection.

(1) By untimely assertion or intentional disclosure. A party may waive the work-product protection by failing to timely assert it or by intentionally disclosing the materials to third parties. ***Eagle Compressors, Inc. v. HEC Liquidating Corp.***, 206 F.R.D. 474, 479 (N.D.Ill.2002); *see* FRE 502(a) (intentional disclosure); ***In re Qwest Comms. Int'l***, 450 F.3d 1179, 1186 (10th Cir.2006) (disclosure); ***Norton v. Caremark, Inc.***, 20 F.3d 330, 339 (8th Cir.1994) (same);***Marx v. Kelly, Hart & Hallman, P.C.***, 929 F.2d 8, 12 (1st Cir.1991) (untimely assertion). See "Disclosure of privileged or protected information – attorney-related privileges," ch. 6-A, §9.3.2, p. 432; "Waiver of privilege," §3.3.6, p. 466.

(2) By claim or defense. A party may waive the work-product protection by asserting a claim or defense that puts the subject matter of the attorney's work product at issue. ***Davidson v. Goord***, 215 F.R.D. 73, 78 (W.D.N.Y.2003); ***Buford v. Holladay***, 133 F.R.D. 487, 494-95 (S.D.Miss.1990); *see* ***Nicholas v. Bituminous Cas. Corp.***, 235 F.R.D. 325, 333 (N.D.W.Va.2006); *see, e.g.*, ***Conoco Inc.***, 191 F.R.D. at 119 (protection of Ps' attorneys' assessment of case was waived when that assessment was placed at issue). A client's waiver of the attorney-client privilege does not automatically waive the work-product protection. ***Eagle Compressors***, 206 F.R.D. at 479; ***Handgards***, 413 F.Supp. at 929. But if the client voluntarily waives the attorney-client privilege by asserting a defense that puts the attorney's advice at issue, it may be deemed to have waived the work-product protection as well. *Compare* ***Novartis Pharms. v. EON Labs Mfg.***, 206 F.R.D. 396, 398 (D.Del.2002) (advice-of-counsel defense waives both attorney-client privilege and work-product protection), *with* ***Thorn EMI v. Micron Tech.***, 837 F.Supp. 616, 622 (D.Del.1993) (party's assertion of reliance on advice of counsel does not necessarily put attorney's work product at issue). See "Implied disclosure," ch. 6-A, §9.3.1(1)(a)[2], p. 430.

§3.5 Privilege against self-incrimination. A person cannot be compelled to give evidence that tends to incriminate the person in a criminal matter. U.S. Const. amend. 5; ***Bank One v. Abbe***, 916 F.2d 1067, 1074 (6th Cir. 1990). The privilege may be asserted during civil as well as criminal proceedings. ***SEC v. Smart***, 678 F.3d 850, 854 (10th Cir.2012); ***SEC v. Graystone Nash, Inc.***, 25 F.3d 187, 190 (3d Cir.1994). This privilege must be asserted in response to specific questions or requests, not in blanket fashion. ***Anglada v. Sprague***, 822 F.2d 1035, 1037 (11th Cir. 1987).

1. Answer tends to incriminate. If a person has a reasonable apprehension that an answer might tend to be incriminating, the person may invoke the Fifth Amendment. ***Hoffman v. U.S.***, 341 U.S. 479, 486-87 (1951).

2. Timeliness. The privilege against self-incrimination, like other privileges, may be lost if not timely asserted. *See* ***Roberts v. U.S.***, 445 U.S. 552, 559 (1980); ***Maness v. Meyers***, 419 U.S. 449, 466 (1975); ***U.S. v. Rivas-Macias***, 537 F.3d 1271, 1280 (10th Cir.2008); ***U.S. v. Hatchett***, 862 F.2d 1249, 1251-52 (6th Cir.1988); ***Davis v. Fendler***, 650 F.2d 1154, 1160 (9th Cir.1981). But some courts have suggested that untimeliness alone cannot justify a waiver of the Fifth Amendment privilege because the privilege is qualitatively distinct from other discovery objections. ***In re DG Acquisition Corp.***, 151 F.3d 75, 81 (2d Cir.1998); ***Brock v. Gerace***, 110 F.R.D. 58, 64 (D.N.J.1986).

3. Who may claim privilege. Any person involved in a criminal or civil proceeding may claim the privilege. *See Black's Law Dictionary* 1438 (9th ed. 2009) (defining right against self-incrimination). A collective entity, like a corporation or partnership, or a person appearing in a representative capacity who is not subject to prosecution, cannot invoke the privilege. ***Braswell v. U.S.***, 487 U.S. 99, 104-05 (1988).

4. May apply to document production. Business records are ordinarily not privileged, but if producing them has a testimonial effect, the privilege may be invoked in response to a request for production. *E.g.*, ***U.S. v. Hubbell***, 530 U.S. 27, 43-45 (2000) (producing documents in response to subpoena had compelled testimonial effect); ***U.S. v. Teeple***, 286 F.3d 1047, 1049-50 (8th Cir.2002) (producing documents is not testimonial because requesting party already knows of documents and information requested); *see* ***U.S. v. Doe***, 465 U.S. 605, 610-13 (1984); ***In re J.W.O.***, 940 F.2d 1165, 1167 (8th Cir.1991).

5. Effect of privilege.

(1) For plaintiff. A plaintiff waives the privilege for any information disclosed in its complaint. A plaintiff who attempts to invoke the privilege will be estopped from continuing the suit if the information is needed to prosecute or defend against the plaintiff's claims. ***Zenith Radio Corp. v. U.S.***, 764 F.2d 1577, 1579 (Fed.Cir.1985). Although a party cannot be sanctioned for a valid invocation of the privilege, a fact-finder may draw an adverse inference from the invocation of the Fifth Amendment in civil cases. ***Graystone Nash***, 25 F.3d at 190; *e.g.*, ***Aptix Corp. v. Quickturn Design Sys.***, 269 F.3d 1369, 1374 (Fed.Cir.2001) (court could draw adverse inference against P who asserted Fifth Amendment privilege in contempt proceedings to determine whether P submitted fraudulent discovery material to court); ***Cerro Gordo Charity v. Fireman's Fund Am. Life Ins.***, 819 F.2d 1471, 1480-82 (8th Cir.1987) (employee's claim of privilege was treated as vicarious admission against employer); ***Campbell v. Gerrans***, 592 F.2d 1054, 1058 (9th Cir.1979) (refusal to answer interrogatories about assault could result in negative inference); *see* ***Baxter v. Palmigiano***, 425 U.S. 308, 318 (1976).

(2) For defendant. A defendant who claims Fifth Amendment protection does not waive its defense. ***National Acceptance Co. v. Bathalter***, 705 F.2d 924, 930-32 (7th Cir.1983); *see* ***Graystone Nash***, 25 F.3d at 191. That is, the invocation of the privilege is not a deemed admission of liability, and the plaintiff must still present proof. ***National Acceptance Co.***, 705 F.2d at 932. However, a fact-finder may draw an adverse inference from the invocation of the Fifth Amendment in civil cases.

6. Invocation & later retraction. If a party properly invokes the privilege, she may or may not be allowed to later retract the privilege. *See* ***Nationwide Life Ins. v. Richards***, 541 F.3d 903, 910 (9th Cir.2008); *see, e.g.*, ***Smart***, 678 F.3d at 855-56 (court denied request to withdraw assertion of privilege when owner of D-LLC invoked privilege during discovery and requested withdrawal only when he needed to respond to P's summary-judgment motion and after discovery deadline had passed); ***Gutierrez-Rodriguez v. Cartagena***, 882 F.2d 553, 576-77 (1st Cir.1989) (court barred P from testifying at trial because of P's earlier refusal to testify during discovery). To determine whether a party who invokes the privilege may later retract it, the court should consider (1) how and when the privilege was invoked, (2) how and when it was retracted, (3) the nature of the proceedings, and (4) any resulting prejudice to the opposing party. *See* ***Nationwide Life Ins.***, 541 F.3d at 910; ***U.S. v. Certain Real Prop. & Premises Known as 4003-4005 5th Ave., Brooklyn, N.Y.***, 55 F.3d 78, 84 (2d Cir.1995); ***SEC v. Merrill Scott & Assocs.***, 505 F.Supp.2d 1193, 1209 (D.Utah 2007).

§3.6 Psychotherapist-patient privilege. A person has a limited privilege to refuse to disclose, and to prevent another person from disclosing, confidential communications made to a psychotherapist, or persons who are participating in the diagnosis or treatment under the direction of the psychotherapist, for the purposes of diagnosis or treatment of a mental or emotional condition, including drug addiction. ***Jaffee v. Redmond***, 518 U.S. 1, 15 (1996); ***In re Sealed Case (Med. Records)***, 381 F.3d 1205, 1213 (D.C.Cir.2004); ***In re Doe***, 964 F.2d 1325, 1328 (2d Cir.1992); *see* ***In re Zuniga***, 714 F.2d 632, 640 (6th Cir.1983).

1. Distinguished from physician-patient privilege. Courts have distinguished communications with psychotherapists from ordinary doctor-patient communications because communications between a psychotherapist and a patient usually consist of far more intensely personal information than communications with other kinds of doctors. ***In re Doe***, 964 F.2d at 1328; *see* ***Stevenson v. Stanley Bostitch, Inc.***, 201 F.R.D. 551, 557-58 (N.D.Ga.2001) (privilege protects only psychotherapy records, not general medical records).

2. Who is a psychotherapist.

(1) Generally. A psychotherapist can be any of the following: (1) a person authorized, or reasonably believed by the patient to be authorized, to practice medicine in any state or nation while engaged in the diagnosis or treatment of a mental or emotional condition, including drug addiction, or (2) a person licensed or certified as a psychiatrist or psychologist under the laws of any state or nation, while similarly engaged. *Proposed Rules of Evidence*, 56 F.R.D. at 240 (proposed FRE 504(a)(2)); *see also* 25 Wright & Graham §5525 (calling this definition problematic). A clinical social worker also qualifies as a psychotherapist in most jurisdictions. ***Jaffee***, 518 U.S. at 16-17.

(2) Unlicensed counselors. The privilege may extend to certain unlicensed counselors. *See, e.g.*, ***Oleszko v. State Comp. Ins. Fund***, 243 F.3d 1154, 1157 (9th Cir.2001) (privilege extended to unlicensed counselors employed by company's employment-assistance program); ***U.S. v. Lowe***, 948 F.Supp. 97, 99 (D.Mass.1996) (privilege extended to unlicensed rape-crisis counselors). *But see* ***Jane Student 1 v. Williams***, 206 F.R.D. 306, 310 (S.D.Ala. 2002) (privilege does not extend to unlicensed social workers or unlicensed professional counselors). Factors used to determine whether the privilege should extend to unlicensed counselors include whether the persons (1) had backgrounds in psychology or social work, including relevant clinical or field experience, (2) regularly participated in ongoing training and education, or (3) were trained as counselors, were held out as counselors in the workplace, and, like psychotherapists, their job was to extract personal and often painful information from persons in order to determine how best to assist them. *See* ***Oleszko***, 243 F.3d at 1156-57; ***U.S. v. Schwensow***, 151 F.3d 650, 657 (7th Cir.1998).

3. Limited to confidential communications. The privilege is limited to confidential communications made in the course of diagnosis or treatment. ***Jaffee***, 518 U.S. at 15; ***U.S. v. Ghane***, 673 F.3d 771, 780 (8th Cir.2012). Facts like the patient's identity, the date and time of treatment, the type of medications prescribed, or the patient's billing records are not protected. *E.g.*, ***In re Zuniga***, 714 F.2d at 640 (patient's identity not protected); ***Jane Student 1***, 206 F.R.D. at 311 (billing records not protected); ***Stevenson***, 201 F.R.D. at 557-58 (billing statements and date of therapy not protected). A communication is confidential if it was not intended to be disclosed to third persons other than (1) persons who were present to further the patient's interest in the consultation, examination, or interview, (2) persons reasonably necessary for the transmission of the communication, or (3) persons who were participating in the diagnosis and treatment under the direction of the psychotherapist. ***Tesser v. Board of Educ.***, 154 F.Supp.2d 388, 392 (E.D.N.Y.2001).

4. Exceptions.

(1) Examination by court order. If the court orders an examination of the patient's mental condition, communications made during the examination are not privileged for the particular purpose for which the examination is ordered. *See* FRCP 35(b)(4).

(2) Crime/fraud exception. At least one circuit has held that the privilege is subject to the crime/fraud exception, under the theory that communications intended to further crime or fraud are rarely allied with bona fide psychotherapy. ***In re Grand Jury Proceedings Violette***, 183 F.3d 71, 76-77 (1st Cir.1999). Similarly, the significant evidentiary problems in locating relevant evidence in prosecutions for sexual abuse of a child has led another court to declare that it will not recognize a psychotherapist-client privilege in a criminal case involving such abuse. ***U.S. v. Burtrum***, 17 F.3d 1299, 1302 (10th Cir.1994).

(3) Dangerous patient. At least one circuit has recognized an exception allowing a psychotherapist to disclose in federal court psychotherapist-patient communications of serious threats of harm to the patient or third persons. *See* ***U.S. v. Glass***, 133 F.3d 1356, 1360 (10th Cir.1998) (recognizing exception if threat was serious when stated and disclosure was only way to avoid harm). Other circuits, however, hold that the psychotherapist-patient privilege is not subject to such an exception. *See* ***Ghane***, 673 F.3d at 785; ***U.S. v. Chase***, 340 F.3d 978, 985 (9th Cir.2003); ***U.S. v. Hayes***, 227 F.3d 578, 579 (6th Cir.2000); *see also* ***U.S. v. Auster***, 517 F.3d 312, 316-20 (5th Cir. 2008) (discussing disagreement among circuits).

5. Waiver of privilege. A party can expressly or impliedly waive the psychotherapist-patient privilege. ***In re Sims***, 534 F.3d 117, 131 (2d Cir.2008). For example, a party may waive the psychotherapist-patient privilege by (1) basing her claim on the psychotherapist's communications with her, (2) selectively disclosing part of a privileged communication to gain an advantage in the litigation, or (3) suing the therapist for malpractice. ***In re Sims***, 534 F.3d at 133-34; *see* ***Koch v. Cox***, 489 F.3d 384, 390-91 (D.C.Cir.2007). A party may also waive the privilege if she places her mental condition at issue. ***Schoffstall v. Henderson***, 223 F.3d 818, 823 (8th Cir.2000).

(1) Mental condition placed at issue. Courts have adopted a narrow, broad, or middle-ground approach to determine whether a party has placed her mental condition at issue. ***Koch***, 489 F.3d at 390.

(a) Narrow approach – affirmative reliance on communications waives privilege. Some courts adopt a narrow approach and hold that a party must affirmatively rely on the psychotherapist-patient communications in support of a claim or defense before the privilege is waived. *E.g.*, ***Fitzgerald v. Cassil***, 216 F.R.D. 632, 638 (N.D.Cal.2003); ***Hucko v. City of Oak Forest***, 185 F.R.D. 526, 532 (N.D.Ill.1999); ***Vanderbilt v. Town of Chilmark***, 174 F.R.D. 225, 228-30 (D.Mass.1997).

(b) Broad approach – simple allegation in complaint waives privilege. Some courts adopt a broad approach and find that a simple allegation of emotional distress in a complaint constitutes waiver. *E.g.*, ***Dixon v. City of Lawton***, 898 F.2d 1443, 1450-51 (10th Cir.1990); ***Tesser***, 154 F.Supp.2d at 395 n.4; ***Doe v. City of Chula Vista***, 196 F.R.D. 562, 569 (S.D.Cal.1999); ***Sarko v. Penn-Del Directory Co.***, 170 F.R.D. 127, 130 (E.D.Pa.1997).

(c) Middle-ground approach – allegation of more than incidental distress waives privilege. Some courts adopt a moderate approach under which the plaintiff must allege more than "garden variety" or incidental emotional distress to waive the privilege. *E.g.*, ***Ruhlmann v. Ulster Cty. Dept. of Soc. Servs.***, 194 F.R.D. 445, 450 (N.D.N.Y.2000); *see* ***Koch***, 489 F.3d at 390-91; *see, e.g.*, ***In re Sims***, 534 F.3d at 134 (P did not waive privilege when he testified about emotional distress only at his deposition and did not seek damages for emotional distress).

(2) No waiver. A party can avoid waiver by withdrawing or formally abandoning all claims for emotional distress. ***In re Sims***, 534 F.3d at 134; *see* ***Koch***, 489 F.3d at 391. The privilege is also not waived if the defendant puts the plaintiff's mental state at issue. ***Koch***, 489 F.3d at 391.

§3.7 Clergy-communicant privilege. A person has a privilege to refuse to disclose, and to prevent another from disclosing, a confidential communication made by the person (the "communicant") to a member of the clergy as spiritual adviser. *See* ***In re Grand Jury Investigation***, 918 F.2d 374, 384 (3d Cir.1990); *Proposed Rules of Evidence*, 56 F.R.D. at 247(proposed FRE 506); *see also* ***Trammel v. U.S.***, 445 U.S. 40, 51 (1980) (dicta; priest-penitent privilege recognizes human need to disclose to spiritual counselor, in total and absolute confidence, what are believed to be flawed acts or thoughts and to receive priestly consolation and guidance in return); ***Totten v. U.S.***, 92 U.S. 105, 107 (1875) (dicta; as general principle, public policy forbids maintaining suit if trial would inevitably lead to disclosure of confidences of the confessional); ***Mullen v. U.S.***, 263 F.2d 275, 277-80 (D.C.Cir.1959) (Fahy, J., concurring) (recognizing priest-penitent privilege and discussing its history). This privilege has been referred to as the priest-penitent, clergyman-penitent, and clergy-communicant privilege. ***In re Grand Jury Investigation***, 918 F.2d at 377 n.2.

1. Who qualifies as clergy. A clergy member is a minister, priest, rabbi, or other similar functionary of a religious organization, or an individual reasonably believed to be so by the communicant. ***In re Grand Jury Investigation***, 918 F.2d at 380 (citing proposed FRE 506); *Proposed Rules of Evidence*, 56 F.R.D. at 247 (proposed FRE 506(a)(1)); *see, e.g.*, ***Eckmann v. Board of Educ.***, 106 F.R.D. 70, 72 (E.D.Mo.1985) (Catholic nun); ***In re Verplank***, 329 F.Supp. 433, 436 (C.D.Cal.1971) (reverend's counseling staff).

2. Who may claim privilege. The privilege may be claimed by the clergy member, by the communicant, by the communicant's guardian or conservator, or, if the communicant is deceased, by her personal representative. *Proposed Rules of Evidence*, 56 F.R.D. at 247 (proposed FRE 506(c)); *see* ***In re Grand Jury Investigation***, 918 F.2d at 385 n.15 (clergy member can invoke privilege on behalf of communicant); *see, e.g.*, ***Eckmann***, 106 F.R.D. at 72 (Catholic nun could invoke privilege); ***In re Verplank***, 329 F.Supp. at 436 (minister of United Presbyterian Church could invoke privilege against subpoena); *see also* ***Seidman v. Fishburne-Hudgins Educ. Found.***, 724 F.2d 413, 415 (4th Cir.1984) (in diversity cases, state statutes vary, but most explicitly prohibit clergy members from disclosing confidential communication).

3. Communication. To be protected, the communication must be confidential and must be made to the clergy member in her capacity as spiritual adviser.

(1) Confidential. A communication is "confidential" if made privately and not intended for further disclosure except to third parties present in furtherance of or essential to the purpose of the communication. ***In re***

Grand Jury Investigation, 918 F.2d at 380; *e.g.*, ***U.S. v. Webb***, 615 F.2d 828, 828 (9th Cir.1980) (confession to minister in presence of security officer destroyed confidentiality necessary to invoke privilege); ***U.S. v. Wells***, 446 F.2d 2, 4 (2d Cir.1971) (letter to cleric not privileged because there was no indication it was intended to be confidential or its purpose was to obtain religious or other counsel, advice, solace, absolution, or ministration).

(2) Made to clergy member as spiritual adviser. The communication must be made to the clergy member in her professional capacity as spiritual adviser. ***In re Grand Jury Investigation***, 918 F.2d at 380 (citing proposed FRE 506(b)); *Proposed Rules of Evidence*, 56 F.R.D. at 247 (proposed FRE 506(b)); *e.g.*, ***U.S. v. Dube***, 820 F.2d 886, 889-90 (7th Cir.1987) (privilege did not apply to communications made to cleric to obtain assistance in avoiding taxes); ***U.S. v. Gordon***, 655 F.2d 478, 486 (2d Cir.1981) (D's business communications to priest he employed in nonreligious capacity were not protected); ***In re Verplank***, 329 F.Supp. at 435-36 (counseling services provided by reverend in course of his duties as clergyman were within scope of privilege).

§3.8 Journalist's privilege. In some circuits, a journalist may assert a qualified First Amendment privilege to protect against the disclosure of facts acquired in the course of gathering news. ***U.S. v. Cuthbertson***, 630 F.2d 139, 147 (3d Cir.1980); *see* ***Branzburg v. Hayes***, 408 U.S. 665, 702-04 (1972); ***Chevron Corp. v. Berlinger***, 629 F.3d 297, 306-07 (2d Cir.2011); *see also* ***In re Grand Jury Subpoena, Miller***, 397 F.3d 964, 972-73 (D.C.Cir.2005) (no First Amendment privilege, but declined to decide whether there is common-law privilege); ***McKevitt v. Pallasch***, 339 F.3d 530, 532 (7th Cir.2003) (whether privilege exists remains open question in 7th Circuit); ***In re Grand Jury Subpoena Duces Tecum***, 112 F.3d 910, 918 n.8 (8th Cir.1997) (whether privilege exists remains open question in 8th Circuit). The privilege is intended to protect the integrity of the news-gathering process and ensure the free flow of information to the public. *See* ***Shoen v. Shoen***, 48 F.3d 412, 416 (9th Cir.1995) (***Shoen II***).

1. Who may claim privilege. The privilege belongs to the journalist; it cannot be asserted by a witness. ***Cuthbertson***, 630 F.2d at 147. The person claiming the privilege does not need to be a credentialed reporter working for an established press entity; however, the person must intend to gather information for the purpose of dissemination and usually should independently seek the information (as opposed to serving or promoting the interests of another). ***Chevron Corp.***, 629 F.3d at 307-08; *see, e.g.*, ***In re Madden***, 151 F.3d 125, 128-30 (3d Cir.1998) (employee of professional-wrestling promoter engaged primarily in marketing and promotional activities was not journalist). Courts have applied the privilege to the following: • Documentary filmmakers. ***Silkwood v. Kerr-McGee Corp.***, 563 F.2d 433, 436-37 (10th Cir.1977). • Authors of technical publications. ***Apicella v. McNeil Lab.***, 66 F.R.D. 78, 84-85 (E.D.N.Y.1975). • Professional investigative-book authors. ***Shoen v. Shoen***, 5 F.3d 1289, 1292-94 (9th Cir.1993) (***Shoen I***).

2. What information is protected.

(1) Confidential information. The privilege protects a journalist's confidential sources. ***Gonzales v. NBC, Inc.***, 194 F.3d 29, 32-33 (2d Cir.1999); ***Cuthbertson***, 630 F.2d at 147; *e.g.*, ***In re Petroleum Prods. Antitrust Litig.***, 680 F.2d 5, 7-8 (2d Cir.1982) (document containing names of confidential sources was privileged); *see also* ***Cusumano v. Microsoft Corp.***, 162 F.3d 708, 715 (1st Cir.1998) (determinations of whether particular disclosures are confidential and degree of protection that attaches to them is based on totality of circumstances).

(2) Nonconfidential information. The privilege may protect a journalist's nonconfidential sources. *E.g.*, ***In re Application to Quash Subpoena to NBC, Inc.***, 79 F.3d 346, 353 (2d Cir.1996) (subpoena seeking outtakes from NBC's *Dateline* program quashed). Whether nonconfidential sources are protected depends on the circuit and on the nature of the proceedings in which the privilege is invoked. *Compare* ***Gonzales***, 194 F.3d at 32 (privilege in civil case), ***Shoen II***, 48 F.3d at 416 (same), ***U.S. v. LaRouche Campaign***, 841 F.2d 1176, 1182 (1st Cir.1988) (privilege in criminal case), *and* ***Stickels v. General Rental Co.***, 750 F.Supp. 729, 731-32 (E.D.Va.1990) (privilege in civil case), *with* ***U.S. v. Smith***, 135 F.3d 963, 972 (5th Cir.1998) (no privilege in criminal case), *and* ***In re Shain***, 978 F.2d 850, 852 (4th Cir.1992) (same).

3. Asserting privilege. The party claiming the journalist's privilege has the initial burden to prove that at the beginning of an investigation, she had intended to disseminate to the public the information obtained through the investigation. ***Shoen I***, 5 F.3d at 1293; ***von Bulow v. von Bulow***, 811 F.2d 136, 142 (2d Cir.1987). The party must

do more than merely assert the privilege; she must provide the court with particularized allegations or facts that support the claim of privilege. *See* ***Silkwood***, 563 F.2d at 438; ***Continental Cablevision, Inc. v. Storer Broad. Co.***, 583 F.Supp. 427, 435-36 (E.D.Mo.1984).

4. Overcoming privilege. Because the journalist's privilege is qualified, a court must weigh the First Amendment concerns against the opposing need for disclosure in light of the surrounding facts. ***Shoen I***, 5 F.3d at 1292-93; ***Farr v. Pitchess***, 522 F.2d 464, 468 (9th Cir.1975); *see* ***Branzburg***, 408 U.S. at 710 (Powell, J., concurring). In making this determination, many courts follow a three-part test suggested by Justice Powell in his concurring opinion in ***Branzburg***: (1) whether the information is relevant to the underlying cause of action, (2) whether the information can be obtained by alternative means, and (3) whether there is a compelling interest in the information (i.e., the information goes to the heart of the matter). *E.g.*, ***Gonzales***, 194 F.3d at 33; ***U.S. v. Caporale***, 806 F.2d 1487, 1504 (11th Cir.1986); ***LaRouche v. NBC, Inc.***, 780 F.2d 1134, 1139 (4th Cir.1986); ***Miller v. Transamerican Press, Inc.***, 621 F.2d 721, 726 (5th Cir.1980), *modified on other grounds*, 628 F.2d 932 (5th Cir.1980); ***Riley v. City of Chester***, 612 F.2d 708, 717 (3d Cir.1979); ***Silkwood***, 563 F.2d at 438. *But see* ***In re Grand Jury Proceedings***, 810 F.2d 580, 584-86 (6th Cir.1987) (refusing to adopt ***Branzburg*** test).

NOTE

The Ninth Circuit has formulated a separate test for nonconfidential information. See ***Shoen II***, *48 F.3d at 415-16. In* ***Shoen II***, *the court stated that a party to a civil suit is entitled to nonconfidential information if the material is (1) unavailable despite exhaustion of all reasonable alternative sources, (2) noncumulative, and (3) clearly relevant to an important issue in the case. Id. at 416.*

§3.9 Government privileges. The government as a party to a lawsuit generally has the same rights and duties regarding evidentiary privileges as a private party. *See* ***U.S. v. Procter & Gamble Co.***, 356 U.S. 677, 681 (1958); *see, e.g.*, ***Green v. IRS***, 556 F.Supp. 79, 85 (N.D.Ind.1982) (government could invoke attorney-client privilege), *aff'd*, 734 F.2d 18 (7th Cir.1984) (table case). But a number of special privileges are available only to the government.

NOTE

The Freedom of Information Act (FOIA) allows a private party to bring a suit directly against a governmental agency for the release of documents possessed by the agency. See 5 U.S.C. §552(a)(4)(B). FOIA is not designed to supplement or displace the civil rules of discovery. ***John Doe Agency v. John Doe Corp.***, *493 U.S. 146, 153 (1989); see* ***U.S. v. Weber Aircraft Corp.***, *465 U.S. 792, 801-02 (1984). Although government privileges often are at issue in FOIA proceedings, the Act itself does not create, expand, or limit the availability of privileges that otherwise exist in civil discovery.* ***Association for Women in Sci. v. Califano***, *566 F.2d 339, 342 (D.C. Cir.1977). Thus, a party who files suit under FOIA has neither greater nor lesser access to governmental documents than in other civil actions. See 5 U.S.C. §552(b)(5) (information is not discoverable in FOIA suit if it would be privileged under FREs); see also* ***Weber Aircraft***, *465 U.S. at 801-02 (FOIA cannot be used to circumvent discovery privileges);* ***Kerr v. U.S. Dist. Ct. for N. Dist. of Cal.***, *511 F.2d 192, 197 (9th Cir.1975) (exceptions to disclosure in FOIA were not intended to create evidentiary privileges), aff'd, 426 U.S. 394 (1976).*

1. Deliberative-process privilege. The deliberative-process privilege, also known as the official-information privilege, protects documents that reflect the opinions, recommendations, and deliberations comprising the decision-making process of a governmental agency. ***First E. Corp. v. Mainwaring***, 21 F.3d 465, 468 (D.C. Cir.1994); *see also* ***Loving v. Department of Def.***, 550 F.3d 32, 38 (D.C.Cir.2008) (privilege does not always protect documents in their entirety; if privileged information can be segregated, government must do so and disclose non-privileged factual information). It is a form of the executive privilege and is intended to encourage frank and honest

decision-making in governmental agencies. *See* ***Department of Interior v. Klamath Water Users Prot. Ass'n***, 532 U.S. 1, 8-9 (2001); ***Marriott Int'l Resorts, L.P. v. U.S.***, 437 F.3d 1302, 1305 n.3 (Fed.Cir.2006); ***Tax Analysts v. IRS***, 117 F.3d 607, 616 (D.C.Cir.1997).

(1) Who may claim privilege. The head of the department that has control over the matter at issue may assert the privilege. ***Landry v. FDIC***, 204 F.3d 1125, 1135 (D.C.Cir.2000). Some courts allow the department head to delegate the authority to invoke the privilege on the department's behalf. *See* ***Marriott Int'l Resorts***, 437 F.3d at 1308; *see, e.g.*, ***Landry***, 204 F.3d at 1135-36 (regional director, rather than head, of FDIC was allowed to assert privilege). *But see* ***U.S. v. O'Neill***, 619 F.2d 222, 225 (3d Cir.1980) (privilege was denied when not invoked by department head).

(2) Privilege may cover nongovernmental materials. The privilege may extend to a document prepared for an agency by outside experts because the government may have a special need for the opinions and recommendations of temporary consultants, and those individuals should be able to give their judgments freely, without fear of publicity. ***Soucie v. David***, 448 F.2d 1067, 1078 n.44 (D.C.Cir.1971). The privilege is not limited to information prepared by consultants working directly for the government; the privilege may include materials generated at the agency's request. *See* ***Ryan v. Department of Justice***, 617 F.2d 781, 789-91 (D.C.Cir.1980).

(3) Asserting privilege. For information to be protected under the deliberative-process privilege, the government has the initial burden to prove that the material is both predecisional and deliberative. ***Grand Cent. Prtshp. v. Cuomo***, 166 F.3d 473, 482 (2d Cir.1999); *see* ***Renegotiation Bd. v. Grumman Aircraft Eng'g***, 421 U.S. 168, 184-85 (1975).

(a) Predecisional. A document is "predecisional" if it was prepared to assist an agency decision-maker in arriving at a decision, and it was prepared before the decision was made. ***Renegotiation Bd.***, 421 U.S. at 184-85; ***Senate of P.R. v. U.S. Dept. of Justice***, 823 F.2d 574, 585 (D.C.Cir.1987); *see* 5 U.S.C. §552(a)(2)(A) (under FOIA, agency must disclose "final" opinions). Some courts hold that a document is predecisional only if it relates to and can be identified with a specific agency decision. *Compare* ***Maricopa Audubon Soc'y v. U.S. Forest Serv.***, 108 F.3d 1089, 1094 (9th Cir.1997) (agency must identify specific policy that document relates to), *and* ***Senate of P.R.***, 823 F.2d at 585 (document is predecisional only if court can pinpoint agency decision or policy that document contributed to), *with* ***City of Va. Beach v. U.S. Dept. of Commerce***, 995 F.2d 1247, 1253 (4th Cir.1993) (rejecting specific-decision requirement for deliberative-process privilege), *and* ***Schell v. U.S. Dept. of H&HS***, 843 F.2d 933, 941 (6th Cir.1988) (same).

(b) Deliberative. A document is "deliberative" if it was related to the process by which policies are formulated (i.e., part of the agency give-and-take in making decisions). ***Cuomo***, 166 F.3d at 482; ***Hinckley v. U.S.***, 140 F.3d 277, 284 (D.C.Cir.1998); ***National Wildlife Fed'n v. U.S. Forest Serv.***, 861 F.2d 1114, 1117 (9th Cir. 1988). A document is deliberative if (1) it formed an essential link in a specified consultative process, (2) it reflects the personal opinions of the writer rather than the policy of the agency, and (3) if released, it would inaccurately reflect or prematurely disclose the views of the agency. ***Providence Journal Co. v. U.S. Dept. of Army***, 981 F.2d 552, 559 (1st Cir.1992); ***National Wildlife Fed'n***, 861 F.2d at 1118-19; *see* ***Maricopa Audubon Soc'y***, 108 F.3d at 1094-95 (9th Cir.1997) (release of document would expose agency's decision-making process and thus discourage candid discussion within agency and undermine agency's ability to perform its functions).

(4) Overcoming privilege. The deliberative-process privilege is a qualified privilege that can be overcome by showing that the need for discovery of the information outweighs the reasons for confidentiality. ***Hinckley***, 140 F.3d at 285; ***U.S. v. Farley***, 11 F.3d 1385, 1389 (7th Cir.1993); ***FTC v. Warner Comms.***, 742 F.2d 1156, 1161 (9th Cir.1984). Courts look to the following factors to determine whether the privilege should be overcome: (1) the relevance of the evidence sought to be protected, (2) the availability of other evidence, (3) the seriousness of the litigation and the issues involved, (4) the role of the government in the litigation, and (5) the possibility of future timidity by government employees who will be forced to recognize the violability of their secrets. ***First E. Corp.***, 21 F.3d at 468 n.5; ***In re Subpoena Served upon Comptroller of Currency***, 967 F.2d 630, 634 (D.C.Cir.1992).

2. State-secrets privilege. The state-secrets privilege allows the government to withhold information or prevent another from disclosing it when disclosure would be harmful to national security. ***U.S. v. Reynolds***, 345 U.S. 1, 6-7 (1953); ***Mohamed v. Jeppesen Dataplan, Inc.***, 614 F.3d 1070, 1081 (9th Cir.2010); *see* ***Tenet v. Doe***, 544 U.S. 1, 3 (2005) (privilege prohibits suits against U.S. based on covert espionage agreements). The privilege is intended to prevent the impairment of the nation's defense capabilities, disclosure of intelligence-gathering methods or capabilities, and disruption of diplomatic relations with foreign governments. ***Ellsberg v. Mitchell***, 709 F.2d 51, 57 (D.C.Cir.1983). The privilege is available only in a very narrow set of circumstances. ***General Dynamics Corp. v. U.S.***, ___ U.S. ___, 131 S.Ct. 1900, 1910 (2011).

(1) Who may claim privilege. The state-secrets privilege may be asserted by the government only through the head of the department that has control over the material at issue. ***Reynolds***, 345 U.S. at 7-8; ***Mohamed***, 614 F.3d at 1080; ***Zuckerbraun v. General Dynamics Corp.***, 935 F.2d 544, 546 (2d Cir.1991). The privilege cannot be claimed or waived by a private party. ***Mohamed***, 614 F.3d at 1080.

(2) When privilege should be claimed. The state-secrets privilege may be claimed at any time. ***Mohamed***, 614 F.3d at 1080. The privilege may be raised at the pleading stage, and the government does not need to wait for an evidentiary dispute to arise during discovery or at trial. *Id.* at 1081.

(3) Privilege may cover nongovernmental party. The state-secrets privilege may protect documents in the possession of a private party. For example, a governmental department may intervene in litigation and assert the state-secrets privilege to prevent a litigant from obtaining sensitive governmental information in discovery. ***Bareford v. General Dynamics Corp.***, 973 F.2d 1138, 1141 (5th Cir.1992); *e.g.*, ***Crater Corp. v. Lucent Techs.***, 255 F.3d 1361, 1370 (Fed.Cir.2001) (in patent-infringement suit between manufacturers, government intervened and asserted state-secrets privilege on D's behalf); ***Fitzgerald v. Penthouse Int'l***, 776 F.2d 1236, 1243 (4th Cir.1985) (in libel suit for alleged espionage, government intervened and asserted that P's claim was founded on state secret; court dismissed suit under state-secrets privilege).

(4) Asserting privilege. The department head must formally assert the privilege after actual personal consideration by that officer. ***Reynolds***, 345 U.S. at 7-8; ***Al-Haramain Islamic Found. v. Bush***, 507 F.3d 1190, 1202 (9th Cir.2007). After asserting the privilege, the government must give the court some form of detailed public explanation of the kinds of harm to national security it seeks to avoid and the reason those harms would result from disclosure of the requested information, or indicate why such an explanation would itself endanger national security. ***Ellsberg***, 709 F.2d at 58-59. If necessary, the court may examine in camera the material or affidavits describing the material. ***Black v. U.S.***, 62 F.3d 1115, 1119 (8th Cir.1995).

(5) Privilege is absolute. The state-secrets privilege is absolute, not qualified. ***Ellsberg***, 709 F.2d at 57; *see* ***Al-Haramain Islamic Found.***, 507 F.3d at 1204.

(6) Effect of privilege. If the court determines the material at issue is privileged, it may (1) dismiss the case on the pleadings or (2) exclude the privileged evidence. ***Mohamed***, 614 F.3d at 1077.

(a) Dismiss case on pleadings. If the subject matter of the suit is a state secret (e.g., a contract to perform espionage), the court may dismiss the plaintiff's suit on the pleadings. ***Mohamed***, 614 F.3d at 1077-78; *see* ***General Dynamics Corp.***, ___ U.S. at ___, 131 S.Ct. at 1906; ***Reynolds***, 345 U.S. at 11 n.26.

(b) Exclude privileged evidence.

[1] Case can proceed. If some evidence is a state secret, the court may exclude the privileged evidence and allow the case to proceed. ***Mohamed***, 614 F.3d at 1082; *see* ***General Dynamics Corp.***, ___ U.S. at ___, 131 S.Ct. at 1907 n.*; ***Bareford***, 973 F.2d at 1141.

[2] Case must be dismissed. If some evidence is a state secret and excluding the privileged evidence results in any of the following, the case may not proceed and must be dismissed:

[a] The plaintiff cannot prove the elements of its claim with other, nonprivileged evidence. ***Mohamed***, 614 F.3d at 1083; *see* ***General Dynamics Corp.***, ___ U.S. at ___, 131 S.Ct. at 1907; ***Halkin v. Helms***, 690 F.2d 977, 997-98 (D.C.Cir.1982).

[b] The defendant is deprived of information that would otherwise give it a valid defense. ***Mohamed***, 614 F.3d at 1083; ***Bareford***, 973 F.2d at 1141; ***In re U.S.***, 872 F.2d 472, 476 (D.C.Cir.1989); *see* ***General Dynamics Corp.***, ___ U.S. at ___, 131 S.Ct. at 1907.

[c] Proceeding with the case would present an unacceptable risk of disclosing state secrets because the privileged evidence cannot be separated from the nonprivileged evidence. ***Mohamed***, 614 F.3d at 1083; *see* ***Bareford***, 973 F.2d at 1143.

3. Law-enforcement privileges. Federal courts recognize the following privileges relating to law enforcement:

(1) Informant privilege. The government has a qualified privilege to prevent disclosure of the identity of informants and their communications. ***Roviaro v. U.S.***, 353 U.S. 53, 59-60 (1957). The privilege is intended to prevent reprisal or retaliation against the informant. ***Dole v. Local 1942, IBEW***, 870 F.2d 368, 372 (7th Cir.1989). Although this privilege ordinarily arises in criminal proceedings, it also applies in civil cases. ***Holman v. Cayce***, 873 F.2d 944, 946 (6th Cir.1989); *see, e.g.*, ***Usery v. Local Un. 720, Laborers' Int'l Un.***, 547 F.2d 525, 527 (10th Cir.1977) (court recognized qualified privilege to protect identity of informants in actions under Fair Labor Standards Act).

(a) Who may claim privilege. The privilege belongs to the government to withhold from disclosure the identity of persons who furnish information about violations of law to officers who must enforce that law. ***Roviaro***, 353 U.S. at 59; ***Simmons v. City of Racine***, 37 F.3d 325, 328 (7th Cir.1994).

(b) Party may overcome privilege. A party can overcome the informant privilege by demonstrating a need for the information that outweighs the public's interest or the government's entitlement to the privilege. ***U.S. v. Bender***, 5 F.3d 267, 270 (7th Cir.1993); ***Dole***, 870 F.2d at 372-73; *see* ***U.S. v. Bagley***, 473 U.S. 667, 682-83 (1985); *see also* ***U.S. v. Lindsey***, 284 F.3d 874, 877 (8th Cir.2002) (party must establish beyond mere speculation that informant's testimony will be material to determination of case).

(2) Investigatory privilege. The investigatory privilege protects information gathered by law-enforcement officers. *See* ***In re City of N.Y.***, 607 F.3d 923, 948 (2d Cir.2010); ***In re U.S. Dept. of Homeland Sec.***, 459 F.3d 565, 569 & n.2 (5th Cir.2006). The privilege preserves the integrity of law-enforcement techniques and confidential sources, protects witnesses and law-enforcement personnel, safeguards the privacy of individuals under investigation, and prevents interference with investigations. ***In re City of N.Y.***, 607 F.3d at 944; ***Tuite v. Henry***, 181 F.R.D. 175, 176-77 (D.D.C.1998), *aff'd*, 203 F.3d 53 (D.C.Cir.1999) (table case); *see* ***In re U.S. Dept. of Homeland Sec.***, 459 F.3d at 569 n.2 (purpose of privilege is to protect from release documents relating to ongoing criminal investigation). To assert the privilege, (1) the head of the department having control over the requested information must make a formal claim of privilege, (2) assertion of the privilege must be based on actual personal consideration by that official, and (3) the information for which the privilege is claimed must be specified, with an explanation of why it properly falls within the scope of the privilege. ***In re Sealed Case***, 856 F.2d 268, 271 (D.C.Cir.1988); *see also* ***Landry***, 204 F.3d at 1135 (officials other than department head may be able to invoke claim of privilege). The privilege is qualified and can be overcome by a compelling need for the privileged materials. ***In re City of N.Y.***, 607 F.3d at 945; *see* ***Tuite v. Henry***, 98 F.3d 1411, 1417 (D.C.Cir.1996); *see also* ***Friedman v. Bache Halsey Stuart Shields, Inc.***, 738 F.2d 1336, 1342-43 (D.C.Cir.1984) (listing ten factors to determine whether to override investigatory privilege).

4. Executive privileges. Executive officials may assert a number of privileges to protect against discovery of information crucial to the fulfillment of the executive branch's unique role and responsibilities. ***In re Sealed Case***, 121 F.3d 729, 736 (D.C.Cir.1997). These include the deliberative-process privilege, the state-secrets privilege, and various law-enforcement privileges. *Id.* at 736-37; *see* ***Marriott Int'l Resorts***, 437 F.3d at 1305 n.3; Wetlaufer, *Justifying Secrecy: An Objection to the General Deliberative Privilege*, 65 Ind. L.J. 845, 845 n.3 (1990). The President also has a broad communications privilege and absolute immunity from civil liability for official acts. *See* ***Nixon v. Fitzgerald***, 457 U.S. 731, 749 (1982); ***Loving***, 550 F.3d at 37-38; ***Marriott Int'l Resorts***, 437 F.3d at 1305 n.3.

5. Legislative privilege. The legislative privilege protects acts that occur in the regular course of the legislative process. U.S. Const. art. 1, §6; ***U.S. v. Johnson***, 383 U.S. 169, 179-80 (1966); *see* ***Tenney v. Brandhove***, 341 U.S. 367, 376-77 (1951) (privilege extends to state decision-makers acting within sphere of legitimate legislative activity). Generally, a legislator may be required to testify about legislative activity only in cases involving constitutional challenges that require an examination of a statute's legislative purpose, such as discrimination cases, establishment-of-religion cases, challenges to statutes that on their face directly inhibit or have the inevitable effect of inhibiting freedom of speech or related constitutional rights, and criminal actions. ***U.S. v. O'Brien***, 391 U.S. 367, 383-84 (1968); ***South Carolina Educ. Ass'n v. Campbell***, 883 F.2d 1251, 1259 (4th Cir.1989); *see, e.g.*, ***U.S. v. Gillock***, 445 U.S. 360, 373 & n.11 (1980) (no legislative privilege for state legislators in federal criminal prosecution).

6. Judicial privilege. Judges and their staffs may assert a qualified judicial privilege protecting their confidential communications made in the performance of their judicial duties. ***In re Matter of Certain Complaints Under Investigation***, 783 F.2d 1488, 1520 (11th Cir.1986).

7. Litigation privilege. Attorneys, witnesses, judges, and other participants in judicial proceedings may have a qualified litigation privilege that protects communications made during the course of the proceedings and makes the participants immune from suit. *See* ***Imbler v. Pachtman***, 424 U.S. 409, 439 (1976) (White, J., concurring); ***Jones v. Cannon***, 174 F.3d 1271, 1281-82 (11th Cir.1999); *see, e.g.*, ***Steffes v. Stepan Co.***, 144 F.3d 1070, 1077 (7th Cir.1998) (court refused to recognize absolute litigation privilege because it would interfere with antiretaliation provisions of Title VII and ADA).

8. Bank-examination privilege. The bank-examination privilege is a qualified privilege that may protect reports and records generated by a federal bank examiner. ***In re Bankers Trust Co.***, 61 F.3d 465, 471 (6th Cir. 1995); *see* ***Bank of Am. Nat'l Trust & Sav. Ass'n v. Douglas***, 105 F.2d 100, 103 (D.C.Cir.1939). It is similar to the deliberative-process privilege. *See* ***In re Subpoena Duces Tecum***, 145 F.3d 1422, 1424-25 (D.C.Cir.1998); ***Redland Soccer Club, Inc. v. Department of Army***, 55 F.3d 827, 853 n.18 (3d Cir.1995). See "Deliberative-process privilege," §3.9.1, p. 476.

9. Statutory privileges. The following statutes protect from discovery material possessed by the government:

(1) Patent application. The Patent & Trademark Office cannot release information contained in a patent application. 35 U.S.C. §122(a). But this privilege does not extend to the same information possessed by a private party. *See* ***James B. Clow & Sons v. U.S. Pipe & Foundry Co.***, 313 F.2d 46, 51 (5th Cir.1963).

(2) Tax return. The government cannot release tax-return information to the public. *See* 26 U.S.C. §6103(a). In fact, inappropriate release of the information is a felony. 26 U.S.C. §7213. But this privilege does not extend to the same information possessed by a private party. *See id.*

(3) Census. The government cannot release information in census reports. 13 U.S.C. §9(a).

(4) Accounting oversight. The government generally cannot release any documents or information prepared or received by or for the Public Accounting Oversight Board. 15 U.S.C. §7215(b)(5)(A) (Sarbanes-Oxley Act of 2002).

§3.10 Trade-secret protection. A person has a qualified privilege to protect trade secrets or similar confidential information. ***Federal Open Mkt. Cmte. of the Fed. Reserve Sys. v. Merrill***, 443 U.S. 340, 362 (1979); ***Centurion Indus. v. Warren Steurer & Assocs.***, 665 F.2d 323, 325 (10th Cir.1981); *see* ***Drexel Heritage Furnishings, Inc. v. Furniture USA, Inc.***, 200 F.R.D. 255, 260 (M.D.N.C.2001). To resist disclosure of a trade secret, a party must file a motion under FRCP 26(c)(1) showing good cause to prevent the disclosure. *See* FRCP 26(c)(1)(G). The party must establish the information as a trade secret and then demonstrate the harmfulness of the disclosure. ***Centurion Indus.***, 665 F.2d at 325; *see* ***Chicago Tribune Co. v. Bridgestone/Firestone, Inc.***, 263 F.3d 1304, 1313-14 (11th Cir.2001). If the party seeking protection of its trade secrets meets these requirements, the burden then shifts to the party seeking discovery to establish the relevance and necessity of disclosing the trade secrets. ***Centurion***

Indus., 665 F.2d at 325. The court must balance the need for the trade secret against the claim of injury resulting from its disclosure. 1970 Notes to FRCP 26 at ¶47, p. 1194, this book; *see* ***Pansy v. Borough of Stroudsburg***, 23 F.3d 772, 787 (3d Cir.1994).

§3.11 Spousal privileges. Federal common law generally recognizes two types of spousal privileges: the marital confidential-communications privilege and the spousal testimonial privilege. *See* ***Trammel v. U.S.***, 445 U.S. 40, 49-51 (1980); ***U.S. v. Miller***, 588 F.3d 897, 904 (5th Cir.2009); ***U.S. v. Singleton***, 260 F.3d 1295, 1297 (11th Cir.2001). These privileges usually apply only in criminal proceedings. *See* 25 Wright & Graham §§5571-5602 (discussing family privileges). *See generally* Annotation, *Marital Privilege Under Rule 501 of Federal Rules of Evidence*, 46 ALR Fed 735, 745-46 (1980 & Supp.2012-13) (collecting and analyzing cases construing or applying FRE 501). *But see* ***U.S. v. Sriram***, No. 00 C 4988 (N.D.Ill.2001) (no pub.; 1-23-01) (in civil action for Medicare fraud brought concurrently with criminal action, D could invoke spousal testimonial privilege in civil action if his wife's testimony could be adversely used against him in criminal action).

§3.12 Settlement-negotiations privilege. At least one circuit has recognized a privilege for confidential settlement negotiations. *See* ***Goodyear Tire & Rubber Co. v. Chiles Power Sup.***, 332 F.3d 976, 983 (6th Cir.2003); *see also* ***In re MSTG, Inc.***, 675 F.3d 1337, 1342 & n.1 (Fed.Cir.2012) (district courts are divided on whether there is a settlement-negotiations privilege). Other circuits have declined to decide whether there is such a privilege. *E.g.*, ***In re Subpoena Duces Tecum Issued to Commodity Futures Trading Comm'n WD Energy Servs.***, 439 F.3d 740, 750 (D.C.Cir.2006); *see, e.g.*, ***In re MSTG, Inc.***, 675 F.3d at 1347-48 (declining to decide whether privilege exists, but noting that rather than protecting such information under new privilege, information could be protected by limiting scope of discovery).

C. ELECTRONIC DISCOVERY

§1. GENERAL

§1.1 Rules. FRCP 16, 26, 33, 34, 37, 45.

NOTE

Be aware that electronic discovery is applicable in the other subchapters in this chapter covering discovery in general (chs. 6-A and 6-B) and specific forms of discovery (chs. 6-D through 6-K). This subchapter discusses some of the issues that are unique to electronic discovery.

§1.2 Purpose. Electronic discovery (or "e-discovery") involves the process of collecting, preparing, reviewing, and producing discoverable information that is stored electronically. *See Sedona Conference Glossary: E-Discovery & Digital Information Management (Third Edition)*, at 18 (Sedona Conference Working Group Series, 2010), www.thesedonaconference.org/publications. The FRCPs refer to this information as "electronically stored information" (ESI). *E.g.*, FRCP 34. The discovery of ESI is on equal footing with conventional discovery of paper documents and tangible things. *See* 2006 Notes to FRCP 34 at ¶1, p. 1203, this book. But unlike documents and tangible things, ESI is dynamic, which complicates its discovery. *See* Rosenthal, *A Few Thoughts on Electronic Discovery After December 1, 2006*, 116 Yale L.J. Pocket Part 167, 168 (2006).

§1.3 Timetable & forms. Timetable, Discovery Status Sheet, p. 1579; ***O'Connor's Federal Civil Forms*** (2012), FORM 2A:4 for preservation letter, FORM 6A:1 for joint discovery plan, FORM 6A:3 for stipulated preservation plan, FORM 6A:4 for stipulated discovery plan, and for each specific type of discovery: disclosures, FORMS 6E; depositions, FORMS 6F; interrogatories, FORMS 6G; requests for admissions, FORMS 6H; requests for production of documents, FORMS 6I; motions to examine persons, FORMS 6J; and requests for entry on land, FORMS 6K.

§1.4 Other references.

1. Sedona Conference. *Sedona Conference Commentary on Proportionality in Electronic Discovery* (Sedona Conference Working Group Series, 2010), www.thesedonaconference.org/publications (referred to as *Sedona*

Conference Commentary on Proportionality); *Sedona Conference Cooperation Proclamation* (Sedona Conference Working Group Series, 2008), www.thesedonaconference.org/publications (referred to as *Sedona Conference Cooperation Proclamation*); *Sedona Principles Addressing Electronic Document Production, Second Edition* (Sedona Conference Working Group Series, 2007), www.thesedonaconference.org/publications (referred to as *Sedona Principles, Second Edition*); *Sedona Conference Glossary: E-Discovery & Digital Information Management (Third Edition)* (Sedona Conference Working Group Series, 2010), www.thesedonaconference.org/publications (referred to as *Sedona Conference Glossary*).

NOTE

Courts cite the Sedona Principles and other Sedona references as the leading authority on electronic discovery. E.g., ***Ford Motor Co. v. Edgewood Props., Inc.****, 257 F.R.D. 418, 424 (D.N.J. 2009); see* ***Aguilar v. Immigration & Customs Enforcement Div. of U.S. Dept. of Homeland Sec.****, 255 F.R.D. 350, 355 (S.D.N.Y.2008).*

2. Local rules & procedures. Local Rules Ark. (E.D.), Rule 26.1(4); Local Rules N.J., Rule 26.1(d); Local Rules Ohio (N.D.), App. K (Default Standard for Discovery of Electronically Stored Information ("E-Discovery")); Local Rules Pa. (M.D.), Rule 26.1; Default Standard for Discovery, Including Discovery of Electronically Stored Information ("ESI") – U.S. Dist. Judge Sue Robinson (D.Del.); Guidelines for Discovery of Electronically Stored Information (ESI) (D.Kan.).

3. Additional references. 8, 8B Wright, Miller & Marcus, *Federal Practice & Procedure 3d* §§2003.1, 2218, 2284.1 (2010 & Supp.2012); 6, 7 *Moore's Federal Practice 3d* §§26.53, 37A (2011); Diamond, *Six Critical Steps to Managing Electronically Stored Information Under FRCP*, www.metrocorpcounsel.com/pdf/2008/April/55.pdf (referred to as Diamond, *Six Critical Steps*); Fuchs & Wolinsky, *Understand Predictive Coding Options*, Tex. Lawyer, 8 (9-3-12); Hedges, *Discovery of Electronically Stored Information: Surveying the Legal Landscape* (BNA Books, 2007) (referred to as Hedges, *Discovery of Electronically Stored Information*); *Manual for Complex Litigation, Fourth* (2004), Federal Judicial Center, www.fjc.gov; Peck, *Search, Forward: Will manual document review & keyword searches be replaced by computer-assisted coding?*, Law Technology News (2011), www.law.com/jsp/lawtechnologynews/index.jsp (referred to as Peck, *Search, Forward*); Rosenthal, *A Few Thoughts on Electronic Discovery After December 1, 2006*, 116 Yale L.J. Pocket Part 167 (2006) (referred to as Rosenthal, *A Few Thoughts on Electronic Discovery*); Rothstein et al., *Managing Discovery of Electronic Information: A Pocket Guide for Judges, Second Edition* (2012), Federal Judicial Center, www.fjc.gov (referred to as Rothstein, *Managing Discovery of Electronic Information*); Scheindlin, *The Ten Most FAQ's in the Post-December 1, 2006 World of E-Discovery* (2006), In Camera (Fed. Judges Ass'n), www.fjc.gov/public/pdf.nsf/lookup/FAQEDisc.pdf/$file/FAQEDisc.pdf (referred to as Scheindlin, *The Ten Most FAQ's*); Shah, *Use of "Predictive Coding" to Limit Cost & Improve Efficiency in Healthcare E-discovery: The Light Is Green, But Proceed With Caution*, AHLA (2012), www.ebglaw.com/articles.aspx (referred to as Shah, *Use of "Predictive Coding" to Limit Cost & Improve Efficiency*).

§2. WHAT IS ESI?

ESI is information that is stored in an electronic medium and retrievable in viewable form. *See* ***Columbia Pictures, Inc. v. Bunnell***, 245 F.R.D. 443, 447 (C.D.Cal.2007); National Conference of Commissioners on Uniform State Laws, *Uniform Rules Relating to the Discovery of Electronically Stored Information*, Rule 1(3) (2007). In the FRCPs, the term "electronically stored information" is intended to be read expansively to include all current and future electronic-storage media. ***Columbia Pictures***, 245 F.R.D. at 447; 2006 Notes to FRCP 34 at ¶2, p. 1203, this book. ESI includes the following: (1) voice-mail messages and files, (2) e-mail messages and files, (3) deleted files, programs, or e-mails, (4) data files, (5) program files, (6) backup and archival tapes, (7) temporary files, (8) system-history files, (9) website information stored in textual, graphical, or audio format, (10) website log files, (11) cache files, and (12) cookies. ***Thompson v. U.S. Dept. of Hous. & Urban Dev.***, 219 F.R.D. 93, 96 (D.Md.2003); ***Kleiner v. Burns***, No. 00-2160-JWL (D.Kan.2000) (no pub.; 12-22-00); *see* ***Flagg v. City of Detroit***, 252 F.R.D. 346, 352-53 (E.D.Mich.

2008) (archived text messages); ***Columbia Pictures***, 245 F.R.D. at 446 (data stored in RAM); ***Lorraine v. Markel Am. Ins.***, 241 F.R.D. 534, 538 & n.4 (D.Md.2007) (Internet postings); ***Antioch Co. v. Scrapbook Borders, Inc.***, 210 F.R.D. 645, 652 (D.Minn.2002) (deleted files); ***Rowe Entm't, Inc. v. William Morris Agency, Inc.***, 205 F.R.D. 421, 428 (S.D.N.Y.2002) (e-mail); *Sedona Principles, Second Edition*, at 1 (virtually anything stored on computing device); *see also* ***Armstrong v. Bush***, 139 F.R.D. 547, 550-51 (D.D.C.1991) (Ps entitled to seek discovery on oral training given to employees about types of communications that could be sent using computer system and on how to use computer to save, delete, and manipulate information).

§3. DIFFERENCES BETWEEN ESI & CONVENTIONAL DISCOVERY

ESI differs from conventional paper documents and tangible things in several ways:

§3.1 Volume. The volume of ESI is almost always much greater than the amount of paper documents. Rothstein, *Managing Discovery of Electronic Information*, at 2; *Sedona Principles, Second Edition*, at 2.

§3.2 Location. ESI can be located in multiple places—for example, one draft of an electronic document may be located on the drafter's, reviewer's, and recipient's hard drives, on the company's and other network servers, on a laptop or home computer, and on backup tapes. Rothstein, *Managing Discovery of Electronic Information*, at 2; *see Sedona Principles, Second Edition*, at 2 & n.5. See "Backup data," §4.1.3, p. 484.

§3.3 Format. ESI, unlike words on paper, may be incomprehensible when separated from the system and software that created it. Rosenthal, *A Few Thoughts on Electronic Discovery*, 116 Yale L.J. Pocket Part at 170-71; Rothstein, *Managing Discovery of Electronic Information*, at 3; *Sedona Principles, Second Edition*, at 4. The way that ESI is created, maintained, stored, and accessed introduces new obstacles for parties seeking to discover it. *See* Rosenthal, *A Few Thoughts on Electronic Discovery*, 116 Yale L.J. Pocket Part at 171. See "Form of production," §7.2.5, p. 497.

§3.4 Indestructibility. Deletion of ESI does not necessarily get rid of the information (as shredding a paper document does). Rothstein, *Managing Discovery of Electronic Information*, at 4. See "Deleted data," §4.1.5, p. 484.

§3.5 Dimensions. ESI presents new dimensions of discovery—that is, some types of ESI have no counterparts in documents or tangible things. *See* Rothstein, *Managing Discovery of Electronic Information*, at 3. For example, metadata is part of ESI, but it is not readily apparent on a computer screen. *Sedona Principles, Second Edition*, at 3; *see* Rothstein, *Managing Discovery of Electronic Information*, at 3. See "Metadata," §4.1.9, p. 485.

§3.6 Dynamic nature. ESI has a dynamic, mutable nature. Rothstein, *Managing Discovery of Electronic Information*, at 3; *see Sedona Principles, Second Edition*, at 3. A distinctive feature of ESI is that normal computer use may include routine modifying, overwriting, and deleting. *See* 2006 Notes to FRCP 37 at ¶1, p. 1204, this book; Rosenthal, *A Few Thoughts on Electronic Discovery*, 116 Yale L.J. Pocket Part at 174. As a result, normal computer use creates a risk that a party may lose potentially discoverable information without any culpable conduct on its part. 2006 Notes to FRCP 37 at ¶1, p. 1204, this book.

§4. PREPARING FOR ELECTRONIC DISCOVERY

A party should prepare for electronic discovery before litigation begins. *See* Rothstein, *Managing Discovery of Electronic Information*, at 5 (court should encourage parties to identify potential problems with discovery of ESI in earliest stages of litigation); *Sedona Principles, Second Edition*, Principle 1, at 11 (organizations must properly preserve ESI that can be reasonably anticipated to be relevant to litigation). See "Responsibilities – before FRCP 26(f) conference," §7.1, p. 496.

§4.1 Understanding electronic discovery. In preparing for electronic discovery, a party should have both a general understanding of electronic discovery and a specific understanding of its own ESI systems. *See* Hedges, *Discovery of Electronically Stored Information*, at 146. To understand electronic discovery, a party should familiarize itself with the terminology.

NOTE

Understanding the terminology of electronic discovery will help with drafting precise discovery requests, dealing with electronic-discovery vendors, and communicating effectively with clients, opposing parties, and the court. See Hedges, Discovery of Electronically Stored Information, at 146. The following definitions are important for a basic understanding of electronic discovery; the list is not intended to be comprehensive. For more terms used in electronic discovery, see the Sedona Conference Glossary.

1. Active data. "Active data" is data that is currently being created, received, or processed, or that needs to be accessed frequently and quickly. Rothstein, *Managing Discovery of Electronic Information*, at 14; *see* ***Zubulake v. UBS Warburg LLC***, 217 F.R.D. 309, 318 (S.D.N.Y.2003) (data on hard drives is active data). Active data is usually immediately accessible and does not have to be restored or reconstructed. *Sedona Conference Glossary*, at 2.

2. Archival data. "Archival data" is data maintained for long-term storage and record-keeping purposes. Rothstein, *Managing Discovery of Electronic Information*, at 35; *Sedona Conference Glossary*, at 4. Archival data is not immediately accessible. Rothstein, *Managing Discovery of Electronic Information*, at 35; *Sedona Conference Glossary*, at 4; *see* ***Zubulake***, 217 F.R.D. at 319.

3. Backup data. "Backup data" is an exact copy of electronic data that serves as a source of recovery of that data in the event of a system problem or disaster. Rothstein, *Managing Discovery of Electronic Information*, at 35; *Sedona Conference Glossary*, at 5; *see* ***Zubulake***, 217 F.R.D. at 319 (backup data is not organized for retrieval of individual files); *Manual for Complex Litigation, Fourth* §11.446 (backup data is created and maintained for short-term disaster recovery, not for retrieving particular files, data, or programs). Backup data is often stored on magnetic backup tapes or removable disk drives. *See* Rothstein, *Managing Discovery of Electronic Information*, at 35; *Sedona Conference Glossary*, at 5. Because backup tapes must be restored, recovery of information stored on them may involve substantial costs. *See* Rothstein, *Managing Discovery of Electronic Information*, at 4.

4. Backup tape recycling. "Backup tape recycling" is the process by which an organization's backup tapes are overwritten with new data, usually on a fixed schedule. Rothstein, *Managing Discovery of Electronic Information*, at 36; *Sedona Conference Glossary*, at 5. See "Routine operation," §12.1.1, p. 514.

5. Deleted data. "Deleted data" is data that was on a computer but has been deleted by the computer system or computer user. Rothstein, *Managing Discovery of Electronic Information*, at 36; *Sedona Conference Glossary*, at 14. Generally, deletion does not actually erase the data from the computer; rather, deletion makes the data inaccessible with normal software but still leaves it on the computer. *See* ***Zubulake***, 217 F.R.D. at 313 n.19; Rothstein, *Managing Discovery of Electronic Information*, at 4, 36; *Sedona Conference Glossary*, at 15. Deleted data may remain on the computer until it is overwritten, "wiped," or "scrubbed." *See* Rothstein, *Managing Discovery of Electronic Information*, at 36; *Sedona Conference Glossary*, at 14.

6. Forensic inspection. "Forensic inspection" is an examination of data stored on or retrieved from ESI that can be used as evidence in court. *See Sedona Conference Glossary*, at 23.

7. Form of production. "Form of production" is the manner in which requested ESI is produced. ***Covad Comms. v. Revonet, Inc.***, 260 F.R.D. 5, 6 (D.D.C.2009); Rothstein, *Managing Discovery of Electronic Information*, at 38; *Sedona Conference Glossary*, at 23. The term refers to both the file format (e.g., native format vs. static format) and the media used (e.g., paper vs. electronic). Rothstein, *Managing Discovery of Electronic Information*, at 38; *Sedona Conference Glossary*, at 23. ESI can be produced in a variety of forms. Rothstein, *Managing Discovery of Electronic Information*, at 3. The form of production determines whether the information can be electronically searched (e.g., searchable PDF files), whether relevant information is obscured (e.g., Word document with metadata deleted or scrubbed), and whether confidential or privileged information is disclosed (e.g., Word document with

all metadata intact). *See* Rothstein, *Managing Discovery of Electronic Information*, at 3. See "Requests for production," §9.5, p. 500.

8. Legacy data. "Legacy data" is data that was created and is stored with software or hardware that has become obsolete. Rothstein, *Managing Discovery of Electronic Information*, at 38. Recovery of legacy data may involve substantial costs. *Id.*

9. Metadata. "Metadata," commonly referred to as "data about data," is information about a particular data set that describes how, when, and by whom ESI was collected, created, accessed, or modified and how it was formatted. ***Autotech Techs. v. Automationdirect.com, Inc.***, 248 F.R.D. 556, 557 n.1 (N.D.Ill.2008); ***Williams v. Sprint/United Mgmt.***, 230 F.R.D. 640, 646 (D.Kan.2005); *see* Rothstein, *Managing Discovery of Electronic Information*, at 38; *Sedona Principles, Second Edition*, at 3; *see also* Scheindlin, *The Ten Most FAQ's*, at question 8 (metadata is electronic equivalent of DNA, ballistics, and fingerprint evidence). Although it is not routinely accessed or viewed, metadata is generated automatically and is linked to the source document. *See* ***Williams***, 230 F.R.D. at 646-47. Metadata includes all the contextual, processing, and usage information needed to identify and certify the scope, authenticity, and integrity of active or archival electronic information or records. ***Latimer v. Roaring Toyz, Inc.***, 574 F.Supp.2d 1265, 1269 n.6 (M.D.Fla.2008), *rev'd in part on other grounds*, 601 F.3d 1224 (11th Cir.2010). Metadata may be important to the facts of the case or to the usability and searchability of ESI. *Sedona Principles, Second Edition*, at 60. Examples of metadata include (1) a file's name, (2) a file's location (e.g., directory structure or path name), (3) a file format or file type, (4) a file size, (5) file dates (e.g., creation date, date of last data modification, date of last data access, and date of last metadata modification), and (6) file permissions (e.g., who can read the data, who can write to it, and who can run it). ***Latimer***, 574 F.Supp.2d at 1269 n.6. There are various types of metadata—two in particular are embedded and file-system metadata. *See Sedona Conference Glossary*, at 34 (other types include application, document, e-mail, user-added, and vendor-added metadata).

(1) Embedded metadata. Embedded metadata includes numbers, data, draft language, editorial comments, and other information that typically is not visible on the output display. *See* ***Aguilar v. Immigration & Customs Enforcement Div. of U.S. Dept. of Homeland Sec.***, 255 F.R.D. 350, 354-55 (S.D.N.Y.2008); 2006 Notes to FRCP 26 at ¶26, p. 1177, this book; Rothstein, *Managing Discovery of Electronic Information*, at 37; *Sedona Conference Glossary*, at 19. Specific examples include spreadsheet formulas, hidden columns, hyperlinks, and database information. ***Aguilar***, 255 F.R.D. at 355; *see* Rothstein, *Managing Discovery of Electronic Information*, at 37. While some metadata is routinely extracted during processing and conversion for electronic discovery, embedded data may not be and may only be available in the native format. *Sedona Conference Glossary*, at 19. However, because embedded data is often crucial to understanding certain electronic documents (e.g., a complicated spreadsheet is difficult to understand without embedded formulas hidden in each cell), it is generally discoverable and should be produced for those electronic documents. ***Aguilar***, 255 F.R.D. at 355.

(2) File-system metadata. File-system metadata includes information about the name, size, location, and usage of an electronic file. *See* ***Aguilar***, 255 F.R.D. at 354; 2006 Notes to FRCP 26 at ¶26, p. 1177, this book; *Sedona Conference Glossary*, at 22. Specific examples include the author of a document and the date a document was modified. ***Aguilar***, 255 F.R.D. at 354. File-system metadata is not embedded within ESI but rather is stored separately from it. *Sedona Conference Glossary*, at 22. Although file-system metadata is usually not relevant, it may be if the electronic document's authenticity is questioned or if there is a question of "who received what information and when." ***Aguilar***, 255 F.R.D. at 354.

10. Mirror imaging. "Mirror imaging," also known as forensic imaging or forensic duplication, is the creation of an exact, bit-by-bit copy of the entire physical hard drive of a computer system. *See* ***Equity Analytics, LLC v. Lundin***, 248 F.R.D. 331, 334 (D.D.C.2008); *Sedona Conference Glossary*, at 34.

(1) Use by parties. Parties can choose to preserve ESI with mirror imaging. ***John B. v. Goetz***, 531 F.3d 448, 459 (6th Cir.2008).

(2) Use by court. Courts can order mirror imaging of a party's computer for searching and retrieving ESI. *See* ***John B.***, 531 F.3d at 459; ***Covad Comms. v. Revonet, Inc.***, 258 F.R.D. 5, 9-10 (D.D.C.2009). After a mirror image is made, the copied data can then be secured and searched while the original data is returned to routine use. *See* ***Covad Comms.***, 258 F.R.D. at 12. See "Conduct justifying mirror imaging," §11.2.2(2)(a)[3][a], p. 511.

11. Native format. "Native format" is the form in which ESI is originally created or normally kept (e.g., Microsoft Excel produces native files with an .xls extension, Microsoft Word produces native files with a .doc extension). *See* ***Covad Comms. v. Revonet, Inc.***, 254 F.R.D. 147, 148 (D.D.C.2008); ***Autotech Techs.***, 248 F.R.D. at 557; Rothstein, *Managing Discovery of Electronic Information*, at 22. Native data may include additional data or features. For example, an Excel spreadsheet may contain mathematical formulas, but an image of the spreadsheet may show only the final numbers resulting from the formulas.

12. Static format. "Static format" is ESI that has been captured as an image capable of being viewed on a standard computer system. ***O'Bar v. Lowe's Home Ctrs., Inc.***, No. 5:04-cv-00019-W (W.D.N.C.2007) (no pub.; 5-2-07). In a static format (e.g., PDF, TIFF), the ESI cannot be manipulated and metadata cannot be viewed. *Sedona Conference Glossary*, at 35; *see* ***O'Bar***, No. 5:04-cv-00019-W (no pub.); *see also* Rothstein, *Managing Discovery of Electronic Information*, at 22 (PDF and TIFF files are essentially photographs of electronic documents).

(1) PDF. PDF ("Portable Document Format") is a file format that captures formatting information (e.g., margins, spacing, fonts) from the original software program so that the information can be viewed and printed as it was intended to be seen, regardless of whether the viewer has access to the software used to create it. *Sedona Conference Glossary*, at 39; *see* Rothstein, *Managing Discovery of Electronic Information*, at 39.

(2) TIFF. TIFF ("Tagged Image File Format") is a file format for storing images, including photographs. *See Sedona Conference Glossary*, at 50. The images can be black-and-white, grayscale, or color. *Id.*

§4.2 Preservation. In preparing for electronic discovery, a party should take steps to ensure that relevant evidence, including not only ESI but also documents and tangible things, is preserved.

1. Identifying sources of duty of preservation. A party should identify sources that impose a duty of preservation. Although the FRCPs themselves do not impose this duty, it can arise from many sources, including the common law, statutes and regulations, or a court order or the parties' agreement. *See* 2006 Notes to FRCP 37 at ¶3, p. 1205, this book; 8B Wright, Miller & Marcus §2284.1 & n.4.

NOTE

Although the FRCPs do not currently address the duty of preservation, in 2011 the Discovery Subcommittee of the Advisory Committee on Civil Rules considered a potential new FRCP on preservation and sanctions for failure to preserve. See Dallas Conference on Preservation/Sanctions (9/9/11), www.uscourts.gov/RulesAndPolicies/FederalRulemaking/Overview/DallasMiniConfSept2011.aspx. The potential rule includes the following elements: (1) the trigger—that is, the point in time when the obligation to preserve information accrues, (2) the scope of the duty to preserve, (3) the duration of the duty to preserve, (4) the requirement of a litigation hold, (5) to what extent, if any, preservation actions are protected as work product, (6) the consequences for not fulfilling preservation responsibilities, and (7) the options for judicial resolution of preservation issues. For materials produced by the Discovery Subcommittee, including an extensive brief on the elements of the potential rule, see www.uscourts.gov/RulesAndPolicies/FederalRulemaking/Overview/DallasMiniConfSept2011.aspx. As of this book's publication, the Advisory Committee continues to work on the potential rule, but there is some uncertainty where that work will lead. Report of the Judicial Conference: Committee on Rules of Practice & Procedure, Agenda E-19, at Rules-Pages 24-25 (Sept.2012), www.uscourts.gov/RulesAndPolicies/rules/archives/reports-judicial-conference.aspx.

(1) Common law. A party may be required to preserve evidence based on common law.

(a) Trigger. The duty to preserve evidence, including ESI, arises when a party knows or should have known that evidence may be relevant in current or future litigation. *See* ***John B. v. Goetz***, 531 F.3d 448, 459 (6th Cir.2008); ***Stevenson v. Union Pac. R.R.***, 354 F.3d 739, 746 (8th Cir.2004); ***Zubulake v. UBS Warburg LLC***, 220 F.R.D. 212, 216-18 (S.D.N.Y.2003); *see, e.g.*, ***Covad Comms. v. Revonet, Inc.***, 258 F.R.D. 5, 14-15 (D.D.C.2009) (when one of D's e-mail servers crashed after D was on notice of litigation and D did not try to recover e-mails, court ordered D to bear costs of imaging and searching all of D's servers). In some cases, the duty is triggered when a suit is filed. ***Cache La Poudre Feeds, LLC v. Land O'Lakes, Inc.***, 244 F.R.D. 614, 621 (D.Colo.2007). In other cases, the duty may be triggered before suit, when litigation is reasonably anticipated. ***Goodman v. Praxair Servs.***, 632 F.Supp.2d 494, 511 (D.Md.2009); ***Cache La Poudre Feeds***, 244 F.R.D. at 621; *see, e.g.*, ***Trask-Morton v. Motel 6 Oper., L.P.***, 534 F.3d 672, 681 (7th Cir.2008) (duty arose when litigation was imminent based on D's receipt of demand letter from P's attorney); ***Doe v. Norwalk Cmty. Coll.***, 248 F.R.D. 372, 377 (D.Conn.2007) (duty arose at meeting about alleged sexual harassment, even before receipt of intent-to-sue letter); *see also* Rothstein, *Managing Discovery of Electronic Information*, at 4 (litigation may be reasonably anticipated well before complaint is filed and answer served).

NOTE

Although the mere possibility of litigation usually does not trigger the preservation duty, courts consider the facts of each case to determine when litigation becomes "reasonably anticipated." ***Cache La Poudre Feeds****, 244 F.R.D. at 621; see* ***Micron Tech. v. Rambus Inc.****, 645 F.3d 1311, 1320 (Fed.Cir.2011) (although duty is not triggered by mere existence of potential claim or distant possibility of claim, litigation does not need to be imminent or certain). But see* ***Goodman****, 632 F.Supp.2d at 509 & n.7 (rejecting line of cases requiring more than mere possibility; duty arises when party reasonably should know that evidence may be relevant to litigation).*

(b) Scope. The duty does not extend to all potential evidence; instead, a party must preserve evidence that is reasonably likely to be the subject of a discovery request even before a request is actually received. ***Best Buy Stores v. Developers Diversified Rlty. Corp., DDR GLH, LLC***, 247 F.R.D. 567, 570 (D.Minn.2007); *see* ***Zubulake***, 220 F.R.D. at 218. See "*Zubulake* steps," §4.2.3(1), p. 488.

(c) Duration. The duty is ongoing, and a party must ensure that relevant evidence is preserved on a continuing basis. *See* ***Cache La Poudre Feeds***, 244 F.R.D. at 629; ***Zubulake v. UBS Warburg LLC***, 229 F.R.D. 422, 431 (S.D.N.Y.2004).

(d) Requirements. The duty to preserve ESI requires reasonable and good-faith efforts to retain it. *Sedona Principles, Second Edition*, Principle 5, at 28. A reasonable balance must be struck between (1) a party's duty to preserve relevant ESI and (2) a party's need, in good faith, to continue its day-to-day operations. *Sedona Principles, Second Edition*, at 28. See "Routine computer operations," §7.2.3(2), p. 497.

(2) Statutes & regulations. A party may be required to preserve evidence under certain statutes and regulations. *See, e.g.*, 17 C.F.R. §240.17a-4 (records must be preserved by certain exchange members, brokers, and dealers); 29 C.F.R. §1602.14 (in employment disputes under Title VII, employment records must be preserved by employer).

(3) Court order or parties' agreement. The court may order or the parties may agree to certain preservation requirements. *See* FRCP 16(b)(3)(B)(iii); ***Treppel v. Biovail Corp.***, 233 F.R.D. 363, 368 (S.D.N.Y.2006); 2006 Notes to FRCP 16 at ¶1, p. 1158, this book. A preservation order can clearly define the parties' obligations and can (1) minimize the risk that relevant evidence will be deliberately or inadvertently destroyed, (2) help ensure that ESI is retrieved when it is most accessible (i.e., before it has been deleted or removed from active data), and (3) pro-

tect the producing party from spoliation allegations. Rothstein, *Managing Discovery of Electronic Information*, at 28-29; *see* ***Treppel***, 233 F.R.D. at 368.

NOTE

During the comment period for the 2006 amendments to FRCP 26(f), concerns were raised about the routine entry of preservation orders following the case-management conference. See Summary of the Report of the Judicial Conference: Committee on Rules of Practice & Procedure, Agenda E-18, at Rules App. C-24 (Sept.2005), www.uscourts.gov/uscourts/RulesAndPolicies/rules/Reports/ST09-2005.pdf. In response, the Advisory Committee revised its Note to state that the amended rule does not imply that courts should routinely enter preservation orders, and if a preservation order is entered, it should be narrowly tailored and rarely issued ex parte. See 2006 Notes to FRCP 26 at ¶24, p. 1177, this book; Rothstein, Managing Discovery of Electronic Information, at 29; see also ***Valdez v. Town of Brookhaven****, No. CV 05-4323 (E.D.N.Y.2007) (no pub.; 7-5-07) (preservation orders are burdensome and expensive, and if no clear need is shown they should not be "lightly entered"). See generally* ***Treppel****, 233 F.R.D. at 370-71 (reviewing various standards for issuance of preservation orders, and applying three-part balancing test).*

2. Communicating duty to potential parties & nonparties. A party should send a letter to potential parties and nonparties with relevant information to put them on notice of the duty of preservation. The letter should outline the types of information to be preserved and should specifically provide notice of the party's intention to discover ESI. *See* ***Cache La Poudre Feeds***, 244 F.R.D. at 623 & n.10; *Sedona Principles, Second Edition*, at 32. See "Preservation letter," ch. 2-A, §2.2, p. 73. The party should consider following up with the recipients of the preservation letter, reiterating the duty to preserve, and attempting to reach an agreement in writing about their respective duties to preserve.

3. Preserving own evidence. A party should ensure that it preserves its own evidence, or it risks being sanctioned. *See* FRCP 37(e); ***Rimkus Consulting Grp. v. Cammarata***, 688 F.Supp.2d 598, 612-13 (S.D.Tex.2010); ***Zubulake***, 229 F.R.D. at 436-37. See "Sanctions available," ch. 6-A, §15.5, p. 448; "Sanctions for Lost ESI," §12, p. 513. To fulfill its preservation duty, a party should (1) follow the steps outlined in ***Zubulake v. UBS Warburg LLC***, 229 F.R.D. 422 (S.D.N.Y.2004), and (2) contact an electronic-discovery vendor.

(1) *Zubulake* steps. The scope of what is necessary to preserve evidence will differ for each case. *See* ***Rimkus Consulting***, 688 F.Supp.2d at 613. The ***Zubulake*** steps, however, provide basic guidelines for preservation. *See* Hedges, *Discovery of Electronically Stored Information*, at 9; *Sedona Principles, Second Edition*, at 31.

(a) Determine scope of preservation.

[1] Identify subject matter – relevant information. When litigation is commenced or a party reasonably anticipates litigation, the party should suspend its routine document-retention-and-destruction policy to ensure the preservation of relevant information. ***Cache La Poudre Feeds***, 244 F.R.D. at 625; ***Zubulake***, 229 F.R.D. at 431; *see* ***In re Seroquel Prods. Liab. Litig.***, 244 F.R.D. 650, 663 (M.D.Fla.2007); Hedges, *Discovery of Electronically Stored Information*, at 143; *see, e.g.*, ***Doe***, 248 F.R.D. at 378 & n.9 (Ds were sanctioned when they did not suspend routine deletion even though Ds claimed they had no choice but to continue deletion because P was Jane Doe).

[2] Identify individuals with relevant information. A party should identify employees or other individuals who may have relevant information and determine how they stored their information. *See* ***Cache La Poudre Feeds***, 244 F.R.D. at 625; ***Zubulake***, 229 F.R.D. at 432.

CAUTION

Make sure to identify all employees or other individuals who had involvement with the issues raised in the litigation or anticipated litigation; the failure to collect records from key players could constitute gross negligence, and the failure to collect records from all other employees could constitute negligence. See ***Pension Cmte. of the Univ. of Montreal Pension Plan v. Banc of Am. Secs., LLC****, 685 F.Supp.2d 456, 465 (S.D.N.Y.2010); see also* ***Orbit One Comms. v. Numerex Corp.****, 271 F.R.D. 429, 441-42 (S.D.N.Y.2010) (before court finds negligence or gross negligence for uncollected or lost records, information should be shown to be at least minimally relevant).*

(b) Learn document-retention policies & computer systems. A party should become fully aware of its document-retention policies and data-retention systems. ***Cache La Poudre Feeds***, 244 F.R.D. at 625; ***Zubulake***, 229 F.R.D. at 432.

(c) Issue litigation hold. A party should issue a litigation hold. ***Cache La Poudre Feeds***, 244 F.R.D. at 625; ***Zubulake***, 229 F.R.D. at 431; *see also* ***Chin v. Port Auth. of N.Y. & N.J.***, 685 F.3d 135, 162 (2d Cir.2012) (failure to issue litigation hold is factor courts can consider when determining whether discovery sanctions are appropriate). An effective litigation hold requires (1) identifying and preserving relevant information, (2) issuing written notice of the hold to the individuals most likely to have relevant information, and (3) monitoring compliance. Scheindlin, *The Ten Most FAQ's*, at question 3; *see also Sedona Conference Glossary*, at 31 (defining "legal hold" as communication that suspends normal disposition or processing of records because of current or reasonably anticipated litigation). The litigation-hold process should be documented in case the party's compliance is challenged.

CAUTION

Whether the litigation hold should specifically cover ESI that is not available from reasonably accessible sources could be a difficult decision. See "Scope of ESI Discovery," §6, p. 493. Some sources suggest that the ESI's relevance—not the difficulty of retrieving it—is the litmus test for preservation. See Scheindlin, The Ten Most FAQ's, at question 4 (if ESI is likely to be discoverable, it should be preserved); see also 2006 Notes to FRCP 26 at ¶6, p. 1174, this book (party's identification of ESI as not reasonably accessible does not necessarily relieve party of its preservation duty). Other sources, however, suggest that the test is more flexible. Sedona Principles, Second Edition, at 28 (parties do not need to preserve every e-mail, electronic document, or backup tape). In the end, the decision to specifically address such data in the litigation hold is probably a matter of good judgment and risk tolerance. See Scheindlin, The Ten Most FAQ's, at questions 3-4.

(d) Communicate & discuss litigation hold. A party should communicate and discuss the litigation hold with the key players in the litigation. ***Cache La Poudre Feeds***, 244 F.R.D. at 625; ***Zubulake***, 229 F.R.D. at 432; *see* ***In re Seroquel Prods.***, 244 F.R.D. at 663; Hedges, *Discovery of Electronically Stored Information*, at 143; *see also* ***Treppel v. Biovail Corp.***, 249 F.R.D. 111, 120-21 (S.D.N.Y.2008) (any backup tapes containing key players' documents must be preserved).

(e) Monitor litigation hold & preserve relevant information. A party should take reasonable steps to monitor compliance with the litigation hold so that all sources of discoverable information are identified and searched. ***Cache La Poudre Feeds***, 244 F.R.D. at 625; ***Zubulake***, 229 F.R.D. at 432; *see* ***In re Seroquel Prods.***, 244 F.R.D. at 663-64; *see, e.g.*, Hedges, *Discovery of Electronically Stored Information*, at 143 (party should preserve chain of custody to prevent inadvertent changing or obscuring of metadata when accessing files and should consider using software tools to extract certain files, including deleted information). A litigation hold, without more, does not satisfy the reasonable-inquiry requirement. ***Cache La Poudre Feeds***, 244 F.R.D. at 630; *see* FRCP 26(g).

After having identified all sources of potentially relevant information, a party is under a duty to preserve that information and produce responsive information. ***Cache La Poudre Feeds***, 244 F.R.D. at 625; ***Zubulake***, 229 F.R.D. at 432-33.

(2) Electronic-discovery vendor. A party should consider hiring an electronic-discovery vendor to assist in preserving ESI. *See* Hedges, *Discovery of Electronically Stored Information*, at 143; *Sedona Principles, Second Edition*, at 40. However, the party—not the vendor—is ultimately responsible for ensuring that ESI is preserved. *Sedona Principles, Second Edition*, at 40; *see* ***Residential Funding Corp. v. DeGeorge Fin. Corp.***, 306 F.3d 99, 113 (2d Cir.2002) (party can be sanctioned when its vendor adds to "purposeful sluggishness" during discovery). Thus, a party's evaluation of vendor software and services should include the defensibility of the vendor's process in the litigation context, the costs, and the vendor's experience and expertise. *Sedona Principles, Second Edition*, at 40.

§4.3 Waiver of privilege. In preparing for electronic discovery, a party should develop a plan to reduce the risks of waiving privileged or protected ESI. *See* 2008 Explanatory Note on FRE 502 at ¶9, p. 1254, this book; *Sedona Principles, Second Edition*, at 8-9. Unlike with traditional paper information, identifying and segregating privileged and protected ESI is more difficult and costly, increasing the possibility of inadvertent disclosures. *See* Rosenthal, *A Few Thoughts on Electronic Discovery*, 116 Yale L.J. Pocket Part at 181-82; Rothstein, *Managing Discovery of Electronic Information*, at 24. To reduce this risk, the party should consider (1) entering into an agreement with the opposing party, such as a quick-peek or clawback agreement, that allows the party to belatedly assert a privilege or protection for inadvertently produced ESI, and (2) whether such an agreement should be incorporated into a court order. *See* FRCP 26(b)(5)(B); FRE 502(b), (e); 2006 Notes to FRCP 26 at ¶¶26-28, p. 1177, this book; Rothstein, *Managing Discovery of Electronic Information*, at 24-25; *see, e.g.*, ***Victor Stanley, Inc. v. Creative Pipe, Inc.***, 250 F.R.D. 251, 256-57 (D.Md.2008) (Ds' privilege claims were considered waived when Ds had abandoned clawback agreement and their keyword search was unreasonable); *see also* Local Rules Ohio (N.D.), App. K ¶8 (Default Standard for Discovery of Electronically Stored Information ("E-Discovery")) (ESI that contains privileged or protected information must be immediately returned if documents appear on their face to have been inadvertently produced or if there is notice of inadvertent production within 30 days; in other circumstances, FRCP 26(b)(5)(B) applies). See "Asserting claims of privilege & protection," ch. 6-A, §4.4.5(4), p. 417; "Disclosure of privileged or protected information – attorney-related privileges," ch. 6-A, §9.3.2, p. 432; "Claims of privilege & protection," §7.2.7, p. 498.

§4.4 Costs. In preparing for electronic discovery, a party should consider the costs of electronic discovery and any possibilities of sharing or shifting those costs.

1. Amount. A party should consider the costs of electronic discovery, including the technological feasibility and realistic costs of preserving, retrieving, reviewing, and producing ESI, as well as the nature of the litigation and the amount in controversy. *Sedona Principles, Second Edition*, Principle 2, at 17; *see* Rothstein, *Managing Discovery of Electronic Information*, at 7-8; *see, e.g.*, ***Haka v. Lincoln Cty.***, 246 F.R.D. 577, 579 (W.D.Wis.2007) (in suit in which damages were low, court ordered only limited search for ESI); *see also* ***Spieker v. Quest Cherokee, LLC***, No. 07-1225-EFM (D.Kan.2008) (no pub.; 10-30-08) (parties should consider FRE 502 when assessing cost of privilege review).

2. Cost-shifting. A party should consider the possibility of sharing or shifting the costs of producing ESI. *See* FRCP 26(b)(2)(B); ***Zubulake v. UBS Warburg LLC***, 217 F.R.D. 309, 316 (S.D.N.Y.2003); 2006 Notes to FRCP 26 at ¶11, p. 1175, this book; Rothstein, *Managing Discovery of Electronic Information*, at 18. Court-ordered cost-shifting is usually only considered when electronic discovery imposes an undue burden or costs on the producing party. ***D'Onofrio v. SFX Sports Grp.***, 254 F.R.D. 129, 134 (D.D.C.2008); *see* Rothstein, *Managing Discovery of Electronic Information*, at 17-18. See "Shifting costs," §11.1.5(2)(b), p. 509.

§5. ESI SEARCH TECHNIQUES

The parties must consider how to conduct searches to locate responsive ESI within sources identified as likely to contain relevant material (e.g., an e-mail database). Aside from a traditional, manual review of ESI, the parties can consider the following search techniques.

PRACTICE TIP

If the parties intend to use a new or complex search technique, they should consider having a representative from the electronic-discovery vendor that will perform the searches attend any conferences or hearings that address the search technique. See, e.g., ***Da Silva Moore v. Publicis Groupe****, No. 11 Civ. 1279 (ALC) (AJP) (S.D.N.Y.2012) (slip op.; 2-24-12) (court stated that it was "very helpful" when vendors were present and spoke at hearing about ESI protocol involving predictive coding), aff'd, No. 11 Civ. 1279 (ALC) (AJP) (S.D.N.Y.2012) (slip op.; 4-25-12).*

§5.1 Keyword searches. The parties can consider keyword searches to locate relevant ESI. ***Victor Stanley, Inc. v. Creative Pipe, Inc.***, 250 F.R.D. 251, 256-57 (D.Md.2008); *see* ***William A. Gross Constr. Assocs. v. American Mfrs. Mut. Ins.***, 256 F.R.D. 134, 135 (S.D.N.Y.2009); ***Rhoads Indus. v. Building Materials Corp.***, 254 F.R.D. 216, 220 (E.D.Pa.2008), *clarified on other grounds*, 254 F.R.D. 238 (E.D.Pa.2008); ***In re Seroquel Prods. Liab. Litig.***, 244 F.R.D. 650, 662 (M.D.Fla.2007); *see, e.g.*, Local Rules Ohio (N.D.), App. K ¶5 (Default Standard for Discovery of Electronically Stored Information ("E-Discovery")) (parties should agree on method of search, including words, terms, and phrases to be searched); *see also* ***In re Fannie Mae Secs. Litig.***, 552 F.3d 814, 818-19 (D.C.Cir.2009) (under agreed order, Ds had sole discretion to specify search terms, and Ds submitted 400 search terms that yielded 660,000 documents; producing nonparty's objection to search terms was denied because of agreed order). Keyword searches are currently the most common search technique used to cull an entire set of ESI. *See* ***Da Silva Moore v. Publicis Groupe***, No. 11 Civ. 1279 (ALC) (AJP) (S.D.N.Y.2012) (slip op.; 2-24-12), *aff'd*, No. 11 Civ. 1279 (ALC) (AJP) (S.D.N.Y.2012) (slip op.; 4-25-12).

1. Process. The process of using keyword searches usually includes the following steps: (1) attorneys develop a list of keywords, (2) the list of keywords is applied to all of the ESI, and (3) the parties manually review only the ESI that contains the keywords. *See* ***Da Silva Moore***, No. 11 Civ. 1279 (ALC) (AJP) (slip op.). Especially in cases involving a high volume of ESI, keyword searches may be necessary to narrow the amount of ESI because traditional manual review of all of the ESI is virtually impossible. *See id.* To improve the effectiveness of keyword searches, the parties can consider seeking expert assistance to develop the list of keywords. *See* ***Victor Stanley***, 250 F.R.D. at 259-60; ***Equity Analytics, LLC v. Lundin***, 248 F.R.D. 331, 333 (D.D.C.2008). To enhance keyword searches, the parties can use more advanced search techniques such as Boolean connectors, elimination of duplicate documents, grouping of "near duplicates," and threading e-mail chains. Peck, *Search, Forward*.

NOTE

If a keyword search is challenged, the court applies a reasonableness test to determine the adequacy of the search. ***Eurand, Inc. v. Mylan Pharms.****, 266 F.R.D. 79, 85 (D.Del.2010). A search is adequate if it could have been expected to produce the information requested. Id.*

2. Limitations. Courts have become increasingly critical of keyword searches. *See* ***Victor Stanley***, 250 F.R.D. at 260-62; ***Equity Analytics***, 248 F.R.D. at 333. Keyword searches are limited because the people who originally created the ESI may describe the same concept using different words, may misspell words, or may use abbreviations and acronyms for certain terms. *See* Peck, *Search, Forward*. Without cooperation from all the parties, the attorneys who develop the list of keywords are essentially guessing what words will produce relevant information; thus, the list of keywords is often overinclusive, resulting in a high return of irrelevant ESI. *See* ***Da Silva Moore***, No. 11 Civ. 1279 (ALC) (AJP) (slip op.); Peck, *Search, Forward*.

§5.2 Predictive coding. The parties can consider predictive coding to locate relevant ESI. *See* ***Da Silva Moore v. Publicis Groupe***, No. 11 Civ. 1279 (ALC) (AJP) (S.D.N.Y.2012) (slip op.; 2-24-12), *aff'd*, No. 11 Civ. 1279 (ALC) (AJP) (S.D.N.Y.2012) (slip op.; 4-25-12). Predictive coding, also referred to as computer-assisted review, is an emerging ESI search tool that requires a person (usually a senior attorney or team of attorneys) to review a small amount

of ESI to "train" the predictive-coding software to identify relevant ESI; the software then applies what it learns from the human review to predict the relevancy of the remaining ESI. *See id.*; Fuchs & Wolinsky, *Understand Predictive Coding Options*, Tex. Lawyer at 8; Shah, *Use of "Predictive Coding" to Limit Cost & Improve Efficiency*, at 9. To determine whether predictive coding is an appropriate search technique, courts may consider the following factors: (1) the parties' agreement, (2) the amount of ESI, (3) the reasonableness of predictive coding compared to other available search techniques, (4) the need for cost-effectiveness and proportionality under FRCP 26(b)(2)(C), and (5) the transparency of the discovery process. *See* ***Da Silva Moore***, No. 11 Civ. 1279 (ALC) (AJP) (slip op.).

CAUTION

Predictive coding is a relatively new technology, and only a handful of cases have addressed whether it is an appropriate way to conduct discovery. See ***Da Silva Moore****, No. 11 Civ. 1279 (ALC) (AJP) (slip op.) (court approved use of predictive coding when parties agreed to its use);* ***In re Actos (Pioglitazone) Prods. Liab. Litig.****, No. 6:11-md-2299 (W.D.La.2012) (case mgmt. order; 7-27-12) (same); see also* ***National Day Laborer Org. Network v. U.S. Immigration & Customs Enforcement Agency****, No. 10 Civ. 3488 (SAS) (S.D.N.Y.2012) (slip op.; 7-13-12) (court was critical of keyword searching in FOIA case and identified predictive coding as better alternative). Also, because of its relative newness, it is unclear to what extent predictive coding can handle privilege determinations. See Shah, Use of "Predictive Coding" to Limit Cost & Improve Efficiency, at 10. At a minimum, if a party seeks to use predictive coding, it should address the topic early in the litigation, usually at the FRCP 26(f) conference, and it should raise any unresolved issues related to the topic at the FRCP 16 pretrial conference. See FRCP 16, 26(b)(2)(C), 26(f); see also* ***Da Silva Moore****, No. 11 Civ. 1279 (ALC) (AJP) (slip op.) (discussing predictive coding and proportionality analysis under FRCP 26(b)(2)(C)).* *See "FRCP 26(f) Conference," §7, p. 495; "FRCP 16 Conference & Order," §8, p. 498.*

1. Process. Although the specific process for predictive coding may differ depending on the software used, the process usually includes the following steps:

(1) Attorneys code "seed" set. Attorneys review and code a small amount of the ESI—known as a "seed" set—to train the predictive-coding software. *See* ***Da Silva Moore***, No. 11 Civ. 1279 (ALC) (AJP) (slip op.) (attorneys typically need to review only a few thousand documents).

(2) Software predicts. The software applies the principles it learned from the seed set to predict how the attorneys would code ESI outside of the seed set. ***Da Silva Moore***, No. 11 Civ. 1279 (ALC) (AJP) (slip op.).

(3) Software codes all ESI. The coding and predicting continues until the software is able to accurately predict how the attorneys would code the ESI, at which point the software codes all of the ESI. ***Da Silva Moore***, No. 11 Civ. 1279 (ALC) (AJP) (slip op.).

(4) Random sample selected. When the software completes the coding, it selects a random sample of the coded ESI for quality control. Shah, *Use of "Predictive Coding" to Limit Cost & Improve Efficiency*, at 9.

(5) Attorneys review sample. Attorneys assess the sample of coded ESI for both the percentage of relevant ESI identified (called "completeness" or "recall") and the percentage of the identified ESI that is actually relevant (called "accuracy" or "precision"). Shah, *Use of "Predictive Coding" to Limit Cost & Improve Efficiency*, at 9; *see* ***Da Silva Moore***, No. 11 Civ. 1279 (ALC) (AJP) (slip op.).

(6) Additional seed set may be chosen. If the attorneys find errors, additional seed ESI is chosen, reviewed, and coded until the software reaches acceptable levels of completeness and accuracy. Shah, *Use of "Predictive Coding" to Limit Cost & Improve Efficiency*, at 9.

2. **Benefits.** The benefits of predictive coding include the following:

(1) **Minimal human review.** Predictive coding requires minimal input from human reviewers. *See* Peck, *Search, Forward*; Shah, *Use of "Predictive Coding" to Limit Cost & Improve Efficiency*, at 9.

(2) **Lower costs.** Predictive coding potentially lowers costs. *See* Peck, *Search, Forward*. Predictive coding may offer the potential for lower costs because it requires fewer attorneys and fewer review hours. *See* Shah, *Use of "Predictive Coding" to Limit Cost & Improve Efficiency,* at 10.

(3) **Greater accuracy.** Predictive coding may provide greater accuracy. *See* Peck, *Search, Forward*; *see also* ***Da Silva Moore***, No. 11 Civ. 1279 (ALC) (AJP) (slip op.) (statistics have shown that predictive coding is at least as accurate as traditional manual review, which has been considered "gold standard" in document review). Predictive coding provides greater accuracy than keyword searches because it does not rely on attorneys to develop the list of keywords and it is not based on particular keywords or Boolean operators. *See* ***Da Silva Moore***, No. 11 Civ. 1279 (ALC) (AJP) (slip op.); Peck, *Search, Forward*. See "Limitations," §5.1.2, p. 491.

§5.3 Targeted searches. The parties can consider targeted searches to locate relevant ESI. Targeted searches are limited and reasonably well-defined searches in likely sources. *See* ***Oracle Corp. v. SAP AG***, 566 F.Supp.2d 1010, 1014 (N.D.Cal.2008).

§5.4 Testing & sampling. The parties can consider testing or sampling to locate relevant ESI contained in sources identified as not reasonably accessible. *See* ***Hopson v. Mayor & City Council of Baltimore***, 232 F.R.D. 228, 245 (D.Md.2005); Rothstein, *Managing Discovery of Electronic Information*, at 16. Sampling can help refine the search parameters and determine the benefits and burdens associated with a more complete search. Rothstein, *Managing Discovery of Electronic Information*, at 16. See "Request manner of production," §9.5.1(2), p. 501.

§5.5 Other restrictions. The parties can consider other restrictions on searches for ESI, such as limiting (1) the time period for discovery or (2) the amount of hours the producing party must spend searching, compiling, and reviewing ESI. *See* ***Hopson v. Mayor & City Council of Baltimore***, 232 F.R.D. 228, 245 (D.Md.2005).

§6. SCOPE OF ESI DISCOVERY

The scope of ESI discovery is the same as that for paper documents and tangible things—a party can discover any nonprivileged matter that is relevant to any party's claim or defense. *See* FRCP 26(b)(1); ***Zubulake v. UBS Warburg LLC***, 217 F.R.D. 309, 316 (S.D.N.Y.2003); Rothstein, *Managing Discovery of Electronic Information*, at 14; *see, e.g.*, ***SEC v. Collins & Aikman Corp.***, 256 F.R.D. 403, 417-18 (S.D.N.Y.2009) (SEC could not refuse to produce e-mails simply because of cost; parties ordered to meet and confer to negotiate reasonable search protocol). This scope of discovery, however, is limited by a two-tiered approach. *See* FRCP 26(b)(2)(B); ***Best Buy Stores v. Developers Diversified Rlty. Corp., DDR GLH, LLC***, 247 F.R.D. 567, 569 (D.Minn.2007); *Summary of the Report of the Judicial Conference: Committee on Rules of Practice & Procedure*, Agenda E-18, at Rules App. C-42 (Sept.2005), www.uscourts.gov/uscourts/RulesAndPolicies/rules/Reports/ST09-2005.pdf. Under the first tier, a party must produce ESI that is reasonably accessible, as long as it is relevant and not privileged; under the second tier, a party may not need to produce ESI that is not reasonably accessible. *See* FRCP 26(b)(1), (b)(2)(B); 2006 Notes to FRCP 26 at ¶5, p. 1174, this book; *Sedona Principles, Second Edition*, at 7.

§6.1 ESI is reasonably accessible. Before producing any ESI, a party must determine (1) whether the ESI is relevant, nonprivileged, and reasonably accessible, and if so, (2) whether the factors listed in FRCP 26(b)(2)(C) would limit the production of that ESI. *See* FRCP 26(b)(1), (b)(2)(B); 2006 Notes to FRCP 26 at ¶¶5, 12, pp. 1174, 1175, this book; Rothstein, *Managing Discovery of Electronic Information*, at 13-14; Rosenthal, *A Few Thoughts on Electronic Discovery*, 116 Yale L.J. Pocket Part at 177; *Sedona Principles, Second Edition*, at 7. Reasonable accessibility is best understood in terms of whether the ESI is kept in an accessible or inaccessible form, which is a distinction that corresponds closely to the expense of the production. ***Best Buy Stores v. Developers Diversified Rlty. Corp., DDR GLH, LLC***, 247 F.R.D. 567, 569-70 (D.Minn.2007); *see* ***Zubulake v. UBS Warburg LLC***, 217 F.R.D. 309, 318 (S.D.N.Y.2003); Rothstein, *Managing Discovery of Electronic Information*, at 14-15.

1. Reasonably accessible. A party must produce ESI that is reasonably accessible. *See* FRCP 26(b)(2)(B). The primary source of reasonably accessible ESI should be active data. *Sedona Principles, Second Edition*, Principle 8, at 45; *see* ***Zubulake***, 217 F.R.D. at 318; Rothstein, *Managing Discovery of Electronic Information*, at 13-14. See "Active data," §4.1.1, p. 484. Examples of sources that are reasonably accessible include files that are available on a computer's desktop or on a company's network in the ordinary course of operation. *Sedona Principles, Second Edition*, at 18.

2. FRCP 26(b)(2)(C) factors. A party should address the FRCP 26(b)(2)(C) factors and determine if those factors support not producing the reasonably accessible ESI. See "Cumulative or duplicative," ch. 6-A, §8.3.1(2)(a)[3], p. 425; "Ample opportunity to discover," ch. 6-A, §8.3.1(2)(a)[4], p. 425; "Undue burden," ch. 6-A, §8.3.1(2)(a)[5], p. 425.

3. Costs. Costs for reasonably accessible ESI are generally covered by the producing party; a party is not relieved of its obligation to produce reasonably accessible ESI merely because it may take time and effort to find what is necessary. *E.g.*, ***Peskoff v. Faber***, 240 F.R.D. 26, 31 (D.D.C.2007) (D ordered to search sources where one may reasonably expect to find e-mails to P, from P, or in which P's name appears); *see* ***Zubulake v. UBS Warburg LLC***, 216 F.R.D. 280, 283-84 (S.D.N.Y.2003) (when ESI is readily accessible, it is typically inappropriate to consider cost-shifting). Some courts, however, have held that cost-shifting can apply to reasonably accessible ESI to enforce the proportionality limits of FRCP 26(b)(2)(C). *See* ***Thompson v. U.S. Dept. of Hous. & Urban Dev.***, 219 F.R.D. 93, 97-99 (D.Md.2003); Rosenthal, *A Few Thoughts on Electronic Discovery*, 116 Yale L.J. Pocket Part at 180-81; Rothstein, *Managing Discovery of Electronic Information*, at 18 & n.16. For a discussion of factors the court must consider when shifting costs, see "Shifting costs," §11.1.5(2)(b), p. 509.

§6.2 ESI is not reasonably accessible. Before producing any ESI, a party must determine what ESI is not reasonably accessible. *See* FRCP 26(b)(2)(B). The party is not required to assess whether the sources of that ESI contain relevant or privileged information, but the party must identify those sources. *See id.*; *see also* Rosenthal, *A Few Thoughts on Electronic Discovery*, 116 Yale L.J. Pocket Part at 178 (producing party may not know what information is contained in a source or whether it is even relevant or privileged because of cost and time needed to make assessment). If the opposing party wants the not reasonably accessible ESI, the parties must meet and confer on whether and how the ESI should be produced. 2006 Notes to FRCP 26 at ¶7, p. 1175, this book.

PRACTICE TIP

If a large organization does not maintain e-discovery software that would allow it to easily conduct centralized e-mail searches, a later argument by the organization that e-mails are not reasonably accessible may be unsuccessful. See ***Capital Records, Inc. v. MP3tunes, LLC****, 261 F.R.D. 44, 51-52 (S.D.N.Y.2009).*

---

1. Not reasonably accessible. A party does not initially need to produce ESI that is not reasonably accessible because of undue burden or cost. FRCP 26(b)(2)(B); ***Best Buy Stores v. Developers Diversified Rlty. Corp., DDR GLH, LLC***, 247 F.R.D. 567, 569 (D.Minn.2007); ***Peskoff v. Faber***, 240 F.R.D. 26, 31 (D.D.C.2007); *see Sedona Principles, Second Edition*, at 46 (accessibility limitation is specific invocation of limitations under FRCP 26(b)(2)(C)). But a party must identify, by category and types, the sources containing potentially responsive ESI that it is neither searching nor producing. 2006 Notes to FRCP 26 at ¶6, p. 1174, this book; *see* ***Cache La Poudre Feeds, LLC v. Land O'Lakes, Inc.***, 244 F.R.D. 614, 628 (D.Colo.2007). However, a party still has the duty of preservation even though it does not need to produce ESI that is not reasonably accessible. See "Scope," §4.2.1(1)(b), p. 487. Examples of sources that are not reasonably accessible include the following:

(1) Backup tapes intended for disaster-recovery purposes that are not indexed, organized, or susceptible to electronic searching. *Sedona Principles, Second Edition*, at 18; *Summary of the Report of the Judicial Conference: Committee on Rules of Practice & Procedure*, Agenda E-18, at Rules App. C-42 (Sept.2005), www.uscourts.gov

/uscourts/RulesAndPolicies/rules/Reports/ST09-2005.pdf; *see* ***W.E. Aubuchon Co. v. BeneFirst, LLC***, 245 F.R.D. 38, 42-43 (D.Mass.2007). See "Backup data," §4.1.3, p. 484.

(2) Legacy data left over from obsolete systems that cannot be retrieved on the successor systems. *Summary of the Report of the Judicial Conference*, Agenda E-18, at Rules App. C-42; *see Sedona Principles, Second Edition*, at 18. See "Legacy data," §4.1.8, p. 485.

(3) Deleted data remaining in fragmented form that requires some type of forensic inspection to restore and retrieve it. *Sedona Principles, Second Edition*, at 18; *Summary of the Report of the Judicial Conference*, Agenda E-18, at Rules App. C-42; *see* ***W.E. Aubuchon Co.***, 245 F.R.D. at 42-43. See "Deleted data," §4.1.5, p. 484.

(4) Databases that were designed to create information in certain ways and that cannot readily create different kinds or forms of information. *Summary of the Report of the Judicial Conference*, Agenda E-18, at Rules App. C-42.

2. Meet & confer.

(1) Topics to discuss. If a party continues to seek discovery of not reasonably accessible ESI even after reviewing production of reasonably accessible ESI, the parties must meet and confer about (1) the burdens and costs of accessing and retrieving the ESI, (2) the needs that may establish good cause for requiring production of all or part of the ESI, and (3) any appropriate conditions for obtaining and producing the ESI. 2006 Notes to FRCP 26 at ¶7, p. 1175, this book.

(2) No agreement reached. If, after meeting and conferring, the parties cannot agree on whether or how sources identified as not reasonably accessible should be searched and discoverable information produced, the party seeking the not reasonably accessible ESI may raise the issue in a motion to compel, or the party resisting production of the not reasonably accessible ESI may raise the issue in a motion for protective order. *See* 2006 Notes to FRCP 26 at ¶8, p. 1175, this book. See "Resolving ESI Disputes," §11, p. 505.

3. Costs. Costs for ESI that is not reasonably accessible may be shifted to the party seeking the ESI. *See* Rothstein, *Managing Discovery of Electronic Information*, at 18. For a discussion of factors the court must consider when shifting costs, see "Shifting costs," §11.1.5(2)(b), p. 509.

§7. FRCP 26(f) CONFERENCE

Under FRCP 26(f), the parties are required to meet and confer about electronic discovery. The parties have a duty to develop a plan for appropriate discovery of ESI. *See* ***Aguilar v. Immigration & Customs Enforcement Div. of U.S. Dept. of Homeland Sec.***, 255 F.R.D. 350, 358 (S.D.N.Y.2008); ***Hopson v. Mayor & City Council of Baltimore***, 232 F.R.D. 228, 245 (D.Md.2005); Hedges, *Discovery of Electronically Stored Information*, at 146. Specifically, the parties must discuss issues relating to disclosure or discovery of ESI, including the form of production, preservation of evidence, and claims of privilege or protection. *See* FRCP 26(f)(2); ***In re Seroquel Prods. Liab. Litig.***, 244 F.R.D. 650, 655 (M.D.Fla.2007); ABA, *Civil Discovery Standards*, pp. 66-70 (2004); Hedges, *Discovery of Electronically Stored Information*, at 24-25; Rothstein, *Managing Discovery of Electronic Information*, at 7-8; *Sedona Principles, Second Edition*, Principle 3, at 21; *see also* Rosenthal, *A Few Thoughts on Electronic Discovery*, 116 Yale L.J. Pocket Part at 175-76 (in complex cases, parties may need several FRCP 26(f) conferences). Local rules, standing orders, or other local procedures may impose additional or specific requirements at the FRCP 26(f) conference. *See* Rothstein, *Managing Discovery of Electronic Information*, at 7, 9; *see, e.g.*, Local Rules N.J, Rule 26.1(d)(3) (parties must confer and attempt to agree on preservation and production of digital information; procedures for inadvertent production of privileged information; whether restoration of deleted digital information may be necessary; whether backup or legacy data is within the scope of discovery; the media, format, and procedures for producing digital information; and who will bear the costs of preservation, production, and restoration, if necessary, of any digital discovery).

CAUTION

Even if a court does not impose specific requirements for the FRCP 26(f) conference (e.g., a certification that the parties have met and conferred), parties should genuinely attempt to resolve the dispute on their own. ***Newman v. Borders, Inc.****, 257 F.R.D. 1, 3 n.3 (D.D.C.2009);* ***Aguilar****, 255 F.R.D. at 358-59; Sedona Conference Cooperation Proclamation, at 1; see, e.g.,* ***Covad Comms. v. Revonet, Inc.****, 254 F.R.D. 147, 149 (D.D.C.2008) (dispute would have been avoided if parties would have discussed form of production as required under FRCP 26(f));* ***Surplus Source Grp. v. Mid Am. Engine, Inc.****, No. 4:08-cv-049 (E.D.Tex.2009) (slip op.; 4-8-09) (when ESI sought was critical to resolution of material issue but Ps delayed in communicating search terms, costs of search were shifted to Ps).*

§7.1 Responsibilities – before FRCP 26(f) conference. Before the FRCP 26(f) conference takes place, a party should become familiar with sources of ESI relevant to the litigation and what is entailed in retrieving ESI. ***U&I Corp. v. Advanced Med. Design, Inc.***, 251 F.R.D. 667, 674 (M.D.Fla.2008); 2006 Notes to FRCP 26 at ¶20, p. 1176, this book; *see* Local Rules N.J., Rule 26.1(d)(1); Local Rules Pa. (M.D.), Rule 26.1(a); Guidelines for Discovery of Electronically Stored Information (ESI) (D.Kan.), ¶1. At a minimum, the parties should be prepared to identify (1) what sources of ESI are likely to be most helpful, (2) how ESI is preserved, stored, and retrieved, and (3) any policies on document retention or destruction. *See* ***Zubulake v. UBS Warburg LLC***, 229 F.R.D. 422, 432 (S.D.N.Y.2004); ***Zubulake v. UBS Warburg LLC***, 220 F.R.D. 212, 218 (S.D.N.Y.2003); Rosenthal, *A Few Thoughts on Electronic Discovery*, 116 Yale L.J. Pocket Part at 176; Rothstein, *Managing Discovery of Electronic Information*, at 8-9.

§7.2 Discussion topics – at FRCP 26(f) conference. At the FRCP 26(f) conference, the parties must discuss ESI issues and identify potential problems. Rosenthal, *A Few Thoughts on Electronic Discovery*, 116 Yale L.J. Pocket Part at 175; Rothstein, *Managing Discovery of Electronic Information*, at 7-8; *see* Hedges, *Discovery of Electronically Stored Information*, at 25-32. The primary goals of the conference are to determine the nature and location of ESI, narrow the scope of ESI discovery, and address issues of accessibility and production costs. *See* ***Cason-Merenda v. Detroit Med. Ctr.***, No. 06-15601 (E.D.Mich.2008) (no pub.; 7-7-08). At the conference, the parties should discuss the following issues.

NOTE

In cases involving extensive discovery of ESI, the FRCP 26(f) conference should be viewed as an ongoing process. Rothstein, Managing Discovery of Electronic Information, at 10. In such cases, rather than a single conference, the court may require the parties to hold a series of conferences to deal with different aspects of discovery. Id. The expanded conference can help to identify and resolve discovery disputes before they become more complicated and difficult. Id.

1. Involvement of ESI. The parties should discuss if there will be discovery of ESI at all. Rothstein, *Managing Discovery of Electronic Information*, at 7. If a party intends on seeking discovery of ESI, that party should identify categories of information that it may seek, including, for example, what substantive allegations directly involve ESI. *See* Local Rules N.J., Rule 26.1(d)(2); Guidelines for Discovery of Electronically Stored Information (ESI) (D.Kan.), ¶3; 7 *Moore's Federal Practice 3d* §37A.20[1]. The parties should identify what methods of discovery (e.g., interrogatories, depositions, requests for production) will best address the need to discover ESI. *See* Hedges, *Discovery of Electronically Stored Information*, at 31.

2. Sources of ESI.

(1) Sources. The parties should discuss what sources should be searched for ESI (e.g., centralized repositories of ESI; asking employees about what relevant ESI they have on specific topics). *See* ***Oracle Corp. v. SAP AG***, 566 F.Supp.2d 1010, 1014 (N.D.Cal.2008); ***Hopson v. Mayor & City Council of Baltimore***, 232 F.R.D. 228, 245 (D.Md.2005); 2006 Notes to FRCP 26 at ¶21, p. 1176, this book; Rothstein, *Managing Discovery of Electronic Information*, at 7-8.

(2) Accessibility. The parties should discuss the accessibility of the identified sources. *See* ***Hopson***, 232 F.R.D. at 245; 2006 Notes to FRCP 26 at ¶21, p. 1176, this book; Rothstein, *Managing Discovery of Electronic Information*, at 7-8. See "Scope of ESI Discovery," §6, p. 493.

(3) Search techniques. The parties should consider how to conduct searches for relevant ESI in the identified sources. See "ESI Search Techniques," §5, p. 490.

3. Preservation. The parties should discuss how to preserve ESI, including terms that will best preserve relevant ESI without imposing undue burdens. *See* FRCP 26(f)(2); *Manual for Complex Litigation, Fourth* §11.442; *see also* ***Treppel v. Biovail Corp.***, 233 F.R.D. 363, 369-70 (S.D.N.Y.2006) (preservation order may protect party producing ESI because order can clearly define extent of obligation). See "Preservation," §4.2, p. 486.

(1) Scope. The parties should discuss the responsibilities of each party to preserve reasonably accessible ESI as well as sources that are not reasonably accessible that may contain responsive ESI. *See* 2006 Notes to FRCP 26 at ¶¶6, 22, pp. 1174, 1177, this book. For example, the parties should discuss the need to preserve any sources that would require recovery, restoration, or translation to locate, retrieve, review, or produce potentially responsive information. *See Summary of the Report of the Judicial Conference: Committee on Rules of Practice & Procedure*, Agenda E-18, at Rules App. C-42 (Sept.2005), www.uscourts.gov/uscourts/RulesAndPolicies/rules/Reports/ST09-2005.pdf.

(2) Routine computer operations. The parties should discuss the appropriate balance between the need to preserve relevant evidence and the need to avoid disruptions of routine computer operations. *See Manual for Complex Litigation, Fourth* §11.442 (blanket preservation order may be prohibitively expensive); 2006 Notes to FRCP 26 at ¶23, p. 1177, this book (complete or broad cessation of party's routine computer operations could paralyze its activities); *see, e.g.*, ***Pueblo of Laguna v. U.S.***, 60 Fed.Cl. 133, 140 (Fed.Cl.2004) (P's request to review all records before they are transferred from one governmental agency to another would unduly burden agencies' day-to-day operations). Because it is impractical to preserve all ESI, the parties should consider what ESI can continue to be recycled, overwritten, deleted, or discarded. Rosenthal, *A Few Thoughts on Electronic Discovery*, 116 Yale L.J. Pocket Part at 189; *see* FRCP 37(e). See "Avoiding sanctions – good-faith defense," §12.1, p. 514.

(3) Court order. The parties should discuss whether to ask the court to incorporate the parties' preservation responsibilities into a court order. See "FRCP 16 Conference & Order," §8, p. 498.

4. Knowledgeable persons. The parties should discuss whether to identify or take early discovery from individuals with special knowledge of a party's computer systems. 2006 Notes to FRCP 26 at ¶20, p. 1176, this book; *see, e.g.*, Local Rules Ohio (N.D.), App. K ¶7 (Default Standard for Discovery of Electronically Stored Information ("E-Discovery")) (to avoid later accusation of spoliation, FRCP 30(b)(6) deposition of each party's retention coordinator may be appropriate); *see also* Rothstein, *Managing Discovery of Electronic Information*, at 9 (parties should consider having knowledgeable persons attend FRCP 26(f) conference).

5. Form of production. The parties should discuss the form or forms in which ESI should be produced. *See* FRCP 26(f)(3)(C); ***Ford Motor Co. v. Edgewood Props., Inc.***, 257 F.R.D. 418, 426 (D.N.J.2009); Guidelines for Discovery of Electronically Stored Information (ESI) (D.Kan.), ¶4(f); Rothstein, *Managing Discovery of Electronic Information*, at 8; *see, e.g.*, ***White v. Graceland Coll. Ctr. for Prof'l Dev. & Lifelong Learning, Inc.***, 586 F.Supp.2d 1250, 1264-65 (D.Kan.2008) (D was compelled to produce ESI again in different form; if parties had adequately conferred at FRCP 26(f) conference, discovery dispute could have been avoided). For example, the parties should discuss whether to produce information automatically included in ESI but not apparent to the reader, such as embedded or file-system metadata. 2006 Notes to FRCP 26 at ¶26, p. 1177, this book. See "Metadata," §4.1.9, p. 485; "Requests for production," §9.5, p. 500.

6. Costs. The parties should discuss the costs of producing ESI and the possibility of sharing or shifting costs. *See* Hedges, *Discovery of Electronically Stored Information*, at 25 & n.16; Rothstein, *Managing Discovery of Electronic Information*, at 8. See "Costs," §4.4, p. 490.

7. Claims of privilege & protection. The parties should discuss any issues about claims of privilege or protection and develop a plan for asserting claims of privilege or protection for ESI after inadvertent production. FRCP 26(f)(3)(D); *see* FRCP 26(b)(5)(B); Rothstein, *Managing Discovery of Electronic Information*, at 8; 2006 Notes to FRCP 26 at ¶14, p. 1176, this book. If the parties agree on a plan (e.g., a quick-peek or clawback agreement), they should discuss whether to ask the court to include their agreement in the scheduling order. *See* FRCP 26(f)(3)(D); 2008 Explanatory Note on FRE 502 at ¶10, p. 1254, this book; 2006 Notes to FRCP 16 at ¶2, p. 1158, this book; 2006 Notes to FRCP 26 at ¶27, p. 1177, this book; Rothstein, *Managing Discovery of Electronic Information*, at 8, 24-25. See "Waiver of privilege," §4.3, p. 490. If the parties cannot agree on a plan, a party may be able to assert a specific privilege or protection after producing privileged or protected information. *See* FRCP 26(b)(5)(B); FRE 502(b). See "Disclosure of privileged or protected information – attorney-related privileges," ch. 6-A, §9.3.2, p. 432.

8. Other problem areas. The parties should discuss any other problems or issues involving ESI (e.g., the need for an electronic-discovery vendor or expert).

§7.3 Discovery report – after FRCP 26(f) conference. After the FRCP 26(f) conference, the parties must submit a discovery report that reflects the parties' views and proposals on ESI issues, including the form or forms in which ESI should be produced and any issues about asserting claims of privilege or protection after inadvertent production. *See* FRCP 26(f)(3)(C), (f)(3)(D); ***In re Celexa & Lexapro Prods. Liab. Litig.***, No. MDL 1736 (E.D.Mo. 2006) (no pub.; 11-13-06); *see, e.g.*, ***R&R Sails Inc. v. Insurance Co. of Pa.***, 251 F.R.D. 520, 524-25 (S.D.Cal.2008) (FRCP 26(f) report did not mention ESI; D was later sanctioned for failing to timely produce ESI); *see also* Local Rules Pa. (M.D.), Rule 26.1(d) (report must identify disagreements over ESI issues so court can address them during FRCP 16 conference). See "Waiver of privilege," §4.3, p. 490.

§8. FRCP 16 CONFERENCE & ORDER

At the initial FRCP 16 pretrial conference, the court and parties should address the need for court involvement in the discovery of ESI. *See* FRCP 16(a)(1)-(a)(3); 2006 Notes to FRCP 16 at ¶1, p. 1158, this book. The parties should identify unresolved electronic-discovery issues and ask the court to help avoid difficulties that might otherwise arise. *See* 2006 Notes to FRCP 16 at ¶1, p. 1158, this book. The court and parties should also discuss whether any agreements reached by the parties, including agreements about preservation or minimizing the risk of waiver of privilege or protection, should be incorporated into the scheduling order. 2006 Notes to FRCP 16 at ¶2, p. 1158, this book; *see* FRCP 16(b)(3)(B)(iii), (b)(3)(B)(iv), 26(b)(5)(B); 2008 Explanatory Note on FRE 502 at ¶¶15, 19, pp. 1254, 1255, this book. See "Pretrial Conference & Order," ch. 5-A, §4, p. 290; "Waiver of privilege," §4.3, p. 490.

§9. ESI & SPECIFIC TYPES OF DISCOVERY

ESI, or information about it, can be requested using any discovery method. Because of the unique nature of ESI, discovery requests involving ESI should be as clear as possible, and responses should clearly identify the scope and limits of what is being produced. *Sedona Principles, Second Edition*, Principle 4, at 25.

§9.1 Initial disclosures. The parties must disclose the identities of individuals likely to have discoverable information and produce all evidence that may be used to support their claims or defenses. FRCP 26(a)(1)(A)(i), (a)(1)(A)(ii); *see* Local Rules Pa. (M.D.), Rule 26.1(b) (parties must disclose ESI to same extent they would disclose information, files, or documents stored by any other means). See "Initial Disclosures," ch. 6-E, §4, p. 533.

1. Individuals. A party should consider whether to disclose individuals who are knowledgeable about the party's ESI systems. *See* FRCP 26(a)(1)(A)(i); *see also* Hedges, *Discovery of Electronically Stored Information*, at 35 (open question whether individuals most knowledgeable about party's ESI are subject to disclosure under FRCP 26(a)(1)(A)(i)).

2. ESI. A party must disclose reasonably accessible ESI that may be used to support its claims or defenses. *See* FRCP 26(a)(1)(A)(ii); ***In re Bristol-Myers Squibb Secs. Litig.***, 205 F.R.D. 437, 440-41 (D.N.J.2002). At a minimum, a party should identify the nature of its computer systems, including the backup system, network system, e-mail system, and software applications. Rothstein, *Managing Discovery of Electronic Information*, at 12; *see* FRCP

26(a)(1)(A)(ii) (party must provide copy or description by category and location of ESI). But in general, a party does not need to search through and disclose ESI that is not reasonably accessible. *See* Hedges, *Discovery of Electronically Stored Information*, at 36 (FRCP 26(a)(1) requires disclosure of ESI that party may "use," and usable ESI is presumably reasonably accessible); 7 *Moore's Federal Practice 3d* §37A.20[2] (disclosing party should not be required to search backup systems or retrieve deleted data); Rothstein, *Managing Discovery of Electronic Information*, at 12 (FRCP 26(a)(1) is not intended to require exhaustive review of ESI in party's possession). *But see* Guidelines for Discovery of Electronically Stored Information (ESI) (D.Kan.), ¶2 (under FRCP 26(a)(1), parties should review ESI, including current, backup, archival, and legacy computer files). See "Scope of ESI Discovery," §6, p. 493.

§9.2 Depositions. A party seeking information about an organization's sources of ESI should consider deposing an information-technology employee or other person who knows about the organization's ESI system. *See* FRCP 30(b)(6); ***Newman v. Borders, Inc.***, 257 F.R.D. 1, 3 (D.D.C.2009); *see also* Diamond, *Six Critical Steps*, at 55 (organization should designate person in information-technology department who understands data). The party noticing the deposition under FRCP 30(b)(6) should clearly define any ESI topics for the deposition. *See, e.g.*, ***Newman***, 257 F.R.D. at 3 (when P's deposition notice included detailed topics about retention policies and search protocol for documents but did not include words "e-mail" or "electronically stored information," it was not unreasonable that D did not include e-mail retention policy and searching as deposition topics). See "Naming organization," ch. 6-F, §3.2.2(2), p. 540.

§9.3 Interrogatories.

1. Request. A party may request information about the opposing party's ESI in an interrogatory. *See* FRCP 33(a)(2). Interrogatories can be useful in determining the extent of the opposing party's discoverable ESI (e.g., ask for identity of opposing party's computer-network specialist, ask about document-retention-and-destruction policy) or the opposing party's compliance with its preservation duty (e.g., ask for dates and actions taken to preserve ESI, ask about recipients of any litigation holds). *See* Hedges, *Discovery of Electronically Stored Information*, at 44-45; 7 *Moore's Federal Practice 3d* §37A.22.

2. Response. In response to an interrogatory, a party may produce ESI. *See* FRCP 33(d). If the answer to an interrogatory may be determined by business records in the form of ESI, the responding party is not required to give a narrative answer and may instead produce the responsive ESI. *See id.* See "Specify records," ch. 6-G, §3.4.1, p. 561. If the responding party opts to produce ESI, the responding party may have to provide technical support, software, or other assistance. 2006 Notes to FRCP 33 at ¶2, p. 1199, this book; *see* 8B Wright, Miller & Marcus §2219 & n.13. However, before giving the requesting party an opportunity to search the responding party's ESI systems, the responding party should determine whether any confidential or private information could be compromised. 2006 Notes to FRCP 33 at ¶2, p. 1199, this book; *see* ***Covad Comms. v. Revonet, Inc.***, 258 F.R.D. 5, 11 (D.D.C.2009); *see also* ***John B. v. Goetz***, 531 F.3d 448, 460-61 (6th Cir.2008) (discussing confidentiality and privacy concerns for mirror imaging). If confidentiality cannot be ensured, the responding party should provide a narrative answer rather than produce the ESI. *See* 2006 Notes to FRCP 33 at ¶2, p. 1199, this book.

PRACTICE TIP

To avoid disputes over producing ESI responsive to an interrogatory, the parties should discuss during the FRCP 26(f) conference the accessibility of electronically stored business records, how those records will be produced, and how confidential or private information will be protected. See "FRCP 26(f) Conference," §7, p. 495.

§9.4 Requests for admissions. A party may request that the opposing party admit the truth of matters relating to (1) facts, the application of law to fact, or opinions about either involving ESI, and (2) the genuineness of any known or described ESI. FRCP 36(a)(1); *see* ***Lorraine v. Markel Am. Ins.***, 241 F.R.D. 534, 562 (D.Md.2007) (to prepare to properly authenticate ESI, attorneys should consider filing request for admission of genuineness of ESI). See "Scope," ch. 6-H, §2.6, p. 564. A party may respond by admitting, denying, or stating why it cannot truthfully admit or

deny each matter. *See* FRCP 36(a)(4); *see, e.g.*, ***John B. v. Goetz***, No. 3:98-0168 (M.D.Tenn.2007) (no pub.; 11-26-07) (in response to request for admission, party stated that he was unaware of destruction or loss of any responsive materials and had produced all responsive documents). See "Contents of response," ch. 6-H, §3.5, p. 565.

§9.5 Requests for production.

1. Request. A party may request that the opposing party produce and permit inspection, copying, testing, or sampling of ESI that is in the opposing party's possession, custody, or control. *See* FRCP 34(a). See "Making Requests," ch. 6-I, §3, p. 570.

(1) Specify form of production. The request may specify the form or forms in which ESI is to be produced. FRCP 34(b)(1)(C); ***D'Onofrio v. SFX Sports Grp.***, 247 F.R.D. 43, 47 (D.D.C.2008); 2006 Notes to FRCP 34 at ¶9, p. 1203, this book. The requesting party should clearly identify the requested form or forms (e.g., by using bold typeface) and avoid using boilerplate instructions. *See* ***Bray & Gillespie Mgmt. v. Lexington Ins.***, 259 F.R.D. 568, 582 (M.D.Fla.2009); ***Covad Comms. v. Revonet, Inc.***, 254 F.R.D. 147, 149 (D.D.C.2008). The requesting party can specify multiple forms because a single form may not be appropriate for all the requested ESI. 2006 Notes to FRCP 34 at ¶9, p. 1203, this book; *see* 8B Wright, Miller & Marcus §2219 & n.6. In general, when determining what form or forms to specify, the requesting party should consider (1) the forms most likely to provide the information needed to establish the relevant facts of the case, (2) the need for metadata to organize and search the ESI produced, (3) whether the ESI sought is reasonably accessible in the forms requested, and (4) the requesting party's own ability to effectively manage and use the ESI in the forms requested. *Sedona Principles, Second Edition*, at 63. Although the necessary form or forms of production will depend on the facts of the case, the requesting party will generally need to address whether ESI should be produced in native or static format and whether metadata should be included.

(a) Native format. The request may specify that ESI be produced in its native format. See "Native format," §4.1.11, p. 486. For example, the requesting party may want to specify that certain types of ESI—such as word-processing documents, electronic spreadsheets, text-messaging logs, image files, and sound files—be produced in their native format. 2006 Notes to FRCP 34 at ¶9, p. 1203, this book; *see Sedona Principles, Second Edition*, at 62 (certain types of ESI, such as databases, cannot be converted from native format without significant loss of information and functionality).

(b) Static format. The request may specify that ESI be produced as static images. See "Static format," §4.1.12, p. 486. For example, the requesting party may want to specify that certain types of ESI—such as e-mail kept on the Internet through services like Google or Yahoo—be converted to a reasonably usable format (e.g., download online e-mail messages and save as PDF file). *See* 2006 Notes to FRCP 34 at ¶9, p. 1203, this book; *Sedona Principles, Second Edition*, at 63.

(c) Metadata. The request may specify that ESI be produced with all metadata intact. ***Ford Motor Co. v. Edgewood Props., Inc.***, 257 F.R.D. 418, 424-25 (D.N.J.2009); *see* ***Autotech Techs. v. Automationdirect.com, Inc.***, 248 F.R.D. 556, 559 (N.D.Ill.2008) (courts will not compel production of metadata when party did not include it in request). See "Mirror imaging," §4.1.10, p. 485. When requesting metadata, a party should consider (1) what metadata is ordinarily maintained, (2) the potential relevance of the metadata to the dispute (e.g., is the metadata needed to prove a claim or defense, such as the transmittal of an incriminating statement), and (3) the importance of reasonably accessible metadata to facilitating review, production, and use of the requested ESI. ***Aguilar v. Immigration & Customs Enforcement Div. of U.S. Dept. of Homeland Sec.***, 255 F.R.D. 350, 356 (S.D.N.Y. 2008); *Sedona Principles, Second Edition*, at 61. There is a modest legal presumption against the production of metadata. ***Williams v. Sprint/United Mgmt.***, 230 F.R.D. 640, 651 (D.Kan.2005); *see* ***Dahl v. Bain Capital Partners***, 655 F.Supp.2d 146, 149 (D.Mass.2009); *Sedona Principles, Second Edition*, at 4; *see also* ***Wyeth v. Impax Labs.***, 248 F.R.D. 169, 171 (D.Del.2006) (most metadata is of limited evidentiary value and reviewing it can waste litigation resources). But if a party can show a particular need for metadata, the presumption can be overcome. *See* Scheindlin, *The Ten Most FAQ's*, at question 8 (depending on circumstances of case, metadata may be highly relevant); *see, e.g.*, ***White v. Graceland Coll. Ctr. for Prof'l Dev. & Lifelong Learning, Inc.***, 586 F.Supp.2d 1250, 1264 (D.Kan.

2008) (in FMLA case, P showed need for metadata when timing of decision to terminate P was critical to case and metadata would show timing and modification of e-mails about termination).

PRACTICE TIP

If the requesting party intends to request metadata, it should do so in its initial request for production because courts are more likely to order production of metadata when the producing party has not yet produced discovery in any form. ***Ford Motor Co.****, 257 F.R.D. at 425;* ***Aguilar****, 255 F.R.D. at 357. If the requesting party seeks metadata after discovery has been ongoing, it will have trouble convincing the court to compel production of metadata. E.g.,* ***Aguilar****, 255 F.R.D. at 359 (when Ps did not request metadata until three months after their request for production, court ordered second production of only some of the already-disclosed discovery and at Ps' cost).*

(2) Request manner of production. The request may ask for an opportunity to inspect, copy, test, or sample ESI sources to search for or retrieve any relevant evidence. FRCP 34(a)(1); 2006 Notes to FRCP 34 at ¶6, p. 1203, this book; *see* Hedges, *Discovery of Electronically Stored Information*, at 146. See "Items to be tested," ch. 6-I, §3.4.2(5), p. 571. Such a request may allow the requesting party direct access to the producing party's electronic-information systems. 8B Wright, Miller & Marcus §2218; *see* ***Henderson v. U.S. Bank***, No. 08C0839 (E.D. Wis.2009) (slip op.; 4-29-09) (direct access may be appropriate if responding party does not have expertise necessary to search and retrieve all data, including metadata); 2006 Notes to FRCP 34 at ¶6, p. 1203, this book (right to test or sample does not create routine right of direct access, which is allowed only in certain circumstances); Scheindlin, *The Ten Most FAQ's*, at question 7 (direct access may be appropriate when computer itself is subject of suit); *see, e.g.*, ***Covad Comms. v. Revonet, Inc.***, 258 F.R.D. 5, 12-13 (D.D.C.2009) (when database itself, and not just information in it, was exhibit in case, court allowed forensic inspection of database servers because there was no other way to seek information and it would advance resolution of case). See "Forensic inspection," §4.1.6, p. 484; "Mirror imaging," §4.1.10, p. 485. However, direct access is rarely allowed as part of a discovery request because of confidentiality and privacy issues. ***Covad Comms.***, 258 F.R.D. at 11; *see* ***U&I Corp. v. Advanced Med. Design, Inc.***, 251 F.R.D. 667, 674 (M.D.Fla.2008) (direct access available only after court makes factual finding of some noncompliance with discovery rules). See "ESI withheld, concealed, or destroyed," §11.2.2(2)(a)[3], p. 511.

2. Response.

(1) Form of production. The responding party should produce ESI in a form or forms agreed to by the parties, ordered by the court, or specified by the requesting party, or if no form is agreed to or specified, in a form or forms in which ESI is ordinarily maintained or that is reasonably usable. FRCP 34(b)(2)(E)(ii). Thus, there is a distinction between conventional document discovery and electronic discovery in terms of the form of production. *Cf.* ***U.S. v. O'Keefe***, 537 F.Supp.2d 14, 23 (D.D.C.2008) (criminal case applying FRCP 34). *Compare* FRCP 34(b)(2)(E)(i) (documents must be produced as they are kept in ordinary course of business or organized and labeled to correspond to categories in request) *with* FRCP 34(b)(2)(E)(ii) (if no form of production is specified, ESI must be produced in ordinarily maintained or reasonably usable form).

(a) Agreed form. If the parties agreed to a specific form or forms of production, the responding party must produce the ESI according to the terms of the agreement. *See* FRCP 34(b)(2)(E). See "Form of production," §7.2.5, p. 497.

(b) Court-ordered form.

[1] Case-specific order. If the court, by case-specific order, ordered a specific form or forms of production, the responding party must produce the ESI according to the terms of the court order. *See* FRCP 34(b)(2)(E). See "Specific form of production," §11.1.5(2)(a)[1], p. 508.

[2] Local rule or procedure. If the court, by local rule or procedure, ordered a specific form or forms of production as a default when parties cannot agree, the responding party must produce the ESI according to the terms of the local rule or procedure. *See, e.g.*, Default Standard for Discovery, Including Discovery of

Electronically Stored Information ("ESI") – U.S. Dist. Judge Sue Robinson (D.Del.), ¶5.c (as default, ESI must be produced as text-searchable image files (e.g., PDF, TIFF) and integrity of underlying ESI must be preserved).

PRACTICE TIP

If the parties have not agreed to or the court has not ordered a specific form or forms of production, the responding party generally should not simply produce the ESI in a form of its choice. 2006 Notes to FRCP 34 at ¶11, p. 1204, this book. Rather, the responding party should specify a form or forms in advance and allow time to resolve any potential disputes before production occurs. Id.; see ***Ford Motor Co.****, 257 F.R.D. at 425. The responding party's process for determining an appropriate form may require that the requesting party give the responding party more than the standard 30 days to prepare the response. See FRCP 34(b)(2)(A); 2006 Notes to FRCP 34 at ¶11, p. 1204, this book. See "Modifying time to respond," ch. 6-A, §8.1.2, p. 422.*

(c) Form specified by requesting party. If the requesting party specified a form or forms of production, the responding party should produce the ESI in the specified form or forms. *See* FRCP 34(b)(2)(D); ***In re Porsche Cars N. Am., Inc.***, 279 F.R.D. 447, 449-50 (S.D.Ohio 2012). If the responding party objects to the requested form or forms, the responding party must object and identify the form or forms it intends to use. FRCP 34(b)(2)(D). The intended form must be one in which the ESI is ordinarily maintained or that is reasonably usable. *See* FRCP 34(b)(2)(E); 2006 Notes to FRCP 34 at ¶13, p. 1204, this book.

PRACTICE TIP

If the responding party objects to the requesting party's specified form or forms of production, the requesting party should promptly respond to the objection; if the requesting party does not respond in a reasonable time, it may waive its own objection to the responding party's chosen form of production. See, e.g., ***Ford Motor Co.****, 257 F.R.D. at 425-26 (after D requested production in native format, P objected to specified form and produced complete discovery in alternative form; D's motion to compel production in native format was denied because D waited eight months to raise objection to P's alternative form).*

(d) No form specified by requesting party. If the requesting party did not specify a form or forms of production and the parties did not agree to or the court did not order a specific form or forms of production, the responding party must produce the ESI in a form (1) in which it is ordinarily maintained or (2) that is reasonably usable. FRCP 34(b)(2)(E)(ii); ***Autotech Techs.***, 248 F.R.D. at 558; 2006 Notes to FRCP 34 at ¶13, p. 1204, this book; *see Sedona Principles, Second Edition*, Principle 12, at 60; *see, e.g.*, ***D'Onofrio***, 247 F.R.D. at 47-48 (when party's instruction was to produce ESI as it is maintained in normal course of business, court did not consider instruction to be request that production of ESI be in native format with metadata intact); ***Perfect Barrier LLC v. Woodsmart Solutions Inc.***, No. 3:07-CV-103 JVB (N.D.Ind.2008) (no pub.; 5-27-08) (when P did not specify form and D produced e-mail as it was ordinarily maintained in native format on disk, court would not compel production in static format with Bates numbers). The responding party is not required to produce the ESI in a form in which it is ordinarily maintained as long as it is produced in a reasonably usable form. 2006 Notes to FRCP 34 at ¶13, p. 1204, this book; *see, e.g.*, ***Covad Comms. v. Revonet, Inc.***, 260 F.R.D. 5, 8-9 (D.D.C.2009) (dicta; D did not produce document as ordinarily maintained or in reasonably usable form when D produced spreadsheet in hard-copy format with information running horizontally across several pages without labels or headings). The responding party must provide notice to the requesting party of the form it intends to use. FRCP 34(b)(2)(D); 2006 Notes to FRCP 34 at ¶11, p. 1204, this book.

[1] Ordinarily maintained. ESI is often ordinarily maintained in native format; however, ordinarily maintained is not necessarily synonymous with native format. *See Sedona Principles, Second Edition*, at 8; 8B Wright, Miller & Marcus §2219; *see also* ***Daimler Truck N. Am. LLC v. Younessi***, No. 08-MC-5011RBL

(W.D.Wash.2008) (no pub.; 6-20-08) (ordinarily maintained is in original state, e.g., actually copying and producing hard drives). See "Native format," §4.1.11, p. 486. Because of the variety of sources where ESI can be maintained and stored, there may be a difference between the form in which ESI is preserved and that in which it is produced for use, and the responding party can choose between those forms of production. *See* FRCP 34(b)(2)(E)(ii); *Sedona Principles, Second Edition*, at 8; 8B Wright, Miller & Marcus §2219.

[2] Reasonably usable. Whether ESI is reasonably usable will depend on the circumstances of the case and may require the responding party to ascertain what would be reasonably usable for the requesting party. *See* ***Covad Comms. v. Revonet, Inc.***, 267 F.R.D. 14, 20 (D.D.C.2010); *Sedona Principles, Second Edition*, at 63; 8B Wright, Miller & Marcus §2219. If the ESI is ordinarily maintained in a form that is **not** reasonably usable (e.g., legacy data that can only be accessed by outmoded computer systems), the responding party should object under FRCP 26(b)(2)(B) and follow that procedure for resolving the objection. *See* 2006 Notes to FRCP 34 at ¶14, p. 1204, this book. See "Legacy data," §4.1.8, p. 485; "Not reasonably accessible," §9.5.2(2)(a), this page.

[a] Convert to reasonably usable form. The responding party may have to convert the ESI into a reasonably usable form. 2006 Notes to FRCP 34 at ¶13, p. 1204, this book; *see* FRCP 34(a)(1)(A) (party may have to "translate" ESI to reasonably usable form); ***D'Onofrio***, 247 F.R.D. at 47 (same); *see also* 2006 Notes to FRCP 34 at ¶5, p. 1203, this book (translation of ESI into reasonably usable form is not translation from one human language to another). In choosing this option, the party may need to provide technical support, software information, or other reasonable assistance to enable the requesting party to use the ESI. 2006 Notes to FRCP 34 at ¶13, p. 1204, this book.

[b] Convert to not reasonably usable form. Although the responding party can convert ESI into a different form, the responding party does not have the right to convert the ESI from the form in which it is ordinarily maintained to a different form that makes it more difficult or burdensome for the requesting party to use. 2006 Notes to FRCP 34 at ¶13, p. 1204, this book; *e.g.*, ***White***, 586 F.Supp.2d at 1263-64 (Ds' conversion of e-mails to PDF files was not producing them as they were ordinarily maintained or in reasonably usable form). For example, if the responding party ordinarily maintains the ESI in a way that makes it electronically searchable, the information should not be produced in a form that removes or significantly degrades that feature. ***Covad Comms.***, 260 F.R.D. at 9; 2006 Notes to FRCP 34 at ¶13, p. 1204, this book.

CAUTION

Unless there is a good reason for doing so, the responding party generally should not convert ESI into a form different from how it is ordinarily maintained. Without the requesting party's agreement or a court order allowing the use of a different form, the responding party could be at risk of having to produce the ESI again at its expense and in a form demanded by the requesting party. See 2006 Notes to FRCP 34 at ¶11, p. 1204, this book; see, e.g., ***Jannx Med. Sys. v. Methodist Hosps., Inc.***, *No. 2:08-CV-286-PRC (N.D.Ind.2010) (slip op.; 11-17-10) (although D did not specify form of production, P's production of information that had been converted from searchable ESI to PDF files was improper; P was ordered to produce ESI again in reasonably usable form); see also* ***Covad Comms.***, *260 F.R.D. at 8 (requesting party should not be punished because producing party did not maintain discovery in organized fashion).*

(2) Objections. The responding party can object to the production of ESI. As with conventional discovery of documents and tangible things, a party must state a specific objection or assert an appropriate privilege for each item it wants to exclude from discovery. *See* FRCP 34(b)(2)(B). The responding party can assert any objection that would be appropriate for conventional discovery. See "Specific objection," ch. 6-A, §8.3.1(2), p. 425. But the responding party can also assert the following objections that are unique to electronic discovery:

(a) Not reasonably accessible. The responding party can object if the discovery request seeks ESI from sources that are not reasonably accessible because of undue burden or cost. FRCP 26(b)(2)(B); *see* ***Cache***

La Poudre Feeds, LLC v. Land O'Lakes, Inc., 244 F.R.D. 614, 628 (D.Colo.2007); 2006 Notes to FRCP 26 at ¶4, p. 1174, this book; *see also Summary of the Report of the Judicial Conference: Committee on Rules of Practice & Procedure*, Agenda E-18, at Rules App. C-43 (Sept.2005), www.uscourts.gov/uscourts/RulesAndPolicies/rules/Reports/ST09-2005.pdf (objection is based on burden and cost of locating, restoring, and retrieving potentially responsive information from electronic sources).

[1] Responding party's burden. After making the objection, the responding party must identify, by category or type, the sources of ESI that were not searched or are not being produced. ***Cache La Poudre Feeds***, 244 F.R.D. at 628; 2006 Notes to FRCP 26 at ¶5, p. 1174, this book. The identification of sources not searched should provide enough detail to enable the requesting party to evaluate the burdens and costs of providing the ESI and the likelihood of finding responsive information in the identified sources. 2006 Notes to FRCP 26 at ¶5, p. 1174, this book; *see also* Rosenthal, *A Few Thoughts on Electronic Discovery*, 116 Yale L.J. Pocket Part at 178 (party can consider providing "not-reasonably-accessible log," similar to privilege log, to address identification requirement; however, log itself could be source of cost and delay). To show that ESI is not reasonably accessible, the responding party should consider providing (1) the number of inaccessible sources to be searched, (2) the different methods the responding party uses to store ESI, (3) the responding party's document-retention-and-destruction policy, (4) the extent to which ESI stored in inaccessible sources overlaps with ESI stored in more accessible sources, and (5) the extent to which the responding party has searched ESI that is accessible. ***Mikron Indus. v. Hurd Windows & Doors, Inc.***, No. C07-532RSL (W.D.Wash.2008) (no pub.; 4-21-08). If the parties cannot agree on what sources are not reasonably accessible, the responding party can file a motion for protective order. See "Motion for protective order," §11.1, p. 505. If the responding party shows that the ESI is not reasonably accessible, the court may consider cost-shifting or other options to alleviate the responding party's burden. *See* ***Mikron Indus.***, No. C07-532RSL (no pub.). See "Shifting costs," §11.1.5(2)(b), p. 509.

PRACTICE TIP

A party objecting that ESI is not reasonably accessible should consider retaining an electronic-discovery consultant or vendor to identify the ESI by category, type, or source and to certify that the ESI is not reasonably accessible. See Sedona Principles, Second Edition, at 40. See "Electronic-discovery vendor," §4.2.3(2), p. 490.

---

[2] Requesting party's response. After receiving an objection that the ESI is not reasonably accessible but before pursuing a motion to compel, the requesting party may need discovery to test the responding party's assertion that the ESI is not reasonably accessible. This discovery may involve (1) taking depositions of people knowledgeable about the responding party's information systems, (2) inspecting the data sources, or (3) requiring the responding party to conduct a sampling of ESI contained in the sources identified as not reasonably accessible. Rothstein, *Managing Discovery of Electronic Information*, at 16. If the parties cannot agree on what sources are not reasonably accessible, the requesting party can file a motion to compel. See "Motion to compel," §11.2, p. 510.

PRACTICE TIP

If, during the litigation, the responding party converted ESI from a reasonably accessible form to one that is not reasonably accessible, the requesting party can move for sanctions. See ***Quinby v. WestLB AG****, 245 F.R.D. 94, 104 (S.D.N.Y.2006) (if responding party creates own burden by converting ESI to inaccessible form, responding party should not be entitled to shift costs to requesting party);* ***Treppel v. Biovail Corp.****, 233 F.R.D. 363, 372 n.4 (S.D.N.Y.2006) (downgrading ESI to a less accessible form is violation of preservation duty). See "Motion for Discovery Sanctions," ch. 6-A, §15, p. 446; "Sanctions for Lost ESI," §12, p. 513.*

(b) Not in more than one form. The responding party can object that the requesting party wants the same information in more than one form. *See* FRCP 34(b)(2)(E)(iii). A responding party generally does

not need to produce ESI in more than one form. *Id.*; *e.g.*, ***Autotech Techs.***, 248 F.R.D. at 559 (court denied production of metadata when requesting party did not ask for it until after production in different form); *see* ***Wyeth***, 248 F.R.D. at 171. However, if production is in a form different than what was agreed to or if the ESI is not produced as it is ordinarily maintained or in a reasonably usable form, a party may have to produce the ESI again in a different form. *See* FRCP 34(b)(2)(E); 2006 Notes to FRCP 34 at ¶11, p. 1204, this book; *see, e.g.*, ***White***, 586 F.Supp.2d at 1264 (when P showed need for metadata, D was ordered to produce e-mails again in native format when D's conversion of e-mails to PDFs in paper format was not reasonably usable form); ***PSEG Power N.Y., Inc. v. Alberici Constructors, Inc.***, No. 1:05-CV-657 (N.D.N.Y.2007) (no pub.; 9-7-07) (P was ordered to produce ESI again at P's cost when P initially did not produce e-mails as kept in ordinary course of business because e-mails were "divorced" from their attachments); *see also Sedona Principles, Second Edition*, at 66 (if party is ordered to produce ESI again in different form because of unclear or untimely request, court should consider shifting costs to requesting party). To avoid having to produce ESI in a second form, the responding party should provide advance notice and secure an agreement from the requesting party. *See* 2006 Notes to FRCP 34 at ¶11, p. 1204, this book; 8B Wright, Miller & Marcus §2219 & n.15.

§10. DISCOVERY FROM NONPARTIES

A party may request production of ESI from a nonparty. *See* FRCP 34(c), 45(a)(1)(A)(iii), (a)(1)(C); 2006 Notes to FRCP 45 at ¶1, p. 1209, this book. The obligations and protections provided in FRCPs 26 and 34 generally apply to nonparties. *See* FRCP 45; 2006 Notes to FRCP 45 at ¶¶1-4, p. 1209, this book; Rothstein, *Managing Discovery of Electronic Information*, at 21-22; *Sedona Principles, Second Edition*, at 9; *see, e.g.*, ***Guy Chem. Co. v. Romaco AG***, 243 F.R.D. 310, 313 (N.D.Ind.2007) (when requesting party showed good cause for production of ESI from nonparty, court compelled nonparty to produce ESI on condition that requesting party reimburse nonparty for all production costs); ***Daimler Truck N. Am. LLC v. Younessi***, No. 08-MC-5011RBL (W.D.Wash.2008) (no pub.; 6-20-08) (court denied nonparty's motion to quash, but rather than order forensic duplication of nonparty's hard drive, nonparty was ordered to search its own computer and show why any relevant discovery identified was not produced); *see also* ***Mintel Int'l Grp. v. Neergheen***, 636 F.Supp.2d 677, 694 (N.D.Ill.2009) (nonparties are entitled to somewhat greater protection on discovery issues than parties are). However, because of the potentially enormous burdens involved with nonparty discovery of ESI, requests to nonparties should be narrowly focused to avoid mandatory cost-shifting to the requesting party. *Sedona Principles, Second Edition*, at 69; *see* FRCP 45(c)(1) (party must take reasonable steps to avoid undue burden or expense on nonparty served with discovery subpoena). See "Subpoenas Under FRCP 45," ch. 1-H, p. 47.

NOTE

Although FRCP 45 does not require a procedure similar to the FRCP 26(f) conference, local procedures may require the party and the nonparty to informally meet and confer to discuss issues about the production of ESI. E.g., Guidelines for Discovery of Electronically Stored Information (ESI) (D.Kan.), ¶5; see Rothstein, Managing Discovery of Electronic Information, at 21; Sedona Principles, Second Edition, at 69. See "FRCP 26(f) Conference," §7, p. 495.

§11. RESOLVING ESI DISPUTES

A party can ask the court for an order (either for protection or to compel) to resolve discovery disputes about ESI.

§11.1 Motion for protective order. A producing party can seek a protective order on issues involving potentially relevant ESI located in sources that are not reasonably accessible because of undue burden or cost. *See* FRCP 26(b)(2)(B). See "ESI is not reasonably accessible," §6.2, p. 494. These issues can include whether the sources should be searched for discoverable information, to what extent the ESI must be preserved until the discovery dispute is resolved, and in what form the ESI should be produced (e.g., should it be converted to a usable form). *See* 2006 Notes to FRCP 26 at ¶8, p. 1175, this book; 2006 Notes to FRCP 34 at ¶14, p. 1204, this book; *Summary of the Report of the Judicial Conference: Committee on Rules of Practice & Procedure*, Agenda E-18, at Rules App. C-43 (Sept.2005), www.uscourts.gov/uscourts/RulesAndPolicies/rules/Reports/ST09-2005.pdf.

1. Before filing – meet & confer. The producing party should confer with the requesting party before filing a motion for protective order. *See* 2006 Notes to FRCP 26 at ¶¶7, 8, p. 1175, this book. During this conference, the parties should discuss the following:

(1) The burdens and costs of accessing and retrieving the ESI. *Id.*

(2) The needs that may establish good cause for requiring all or part of the requested discovery even if the ESI sought is not reasonably accessible. *Id.*

(3) The appropriate conditions for obtaining and producing the ESI. *Id.*

2. Motion.

(1) Deadline. A motion for protective order can be filed as soon as the producing party has identified sources of ESI that are not reasonably accessible or are in a form that is not reasonably usable; the party does not have to wait to receive a discovery request. *See Summary of the Report of the Judicial Conference*, Agenda E-18, at Rules App. C-43. If the motion is not filed earlier, it should be filed before the time to respond to the discovery request at issue. See "Motion for Protective Order," ch. 6-A, §12, p. 440.

(2) Grounds. To obtain a protective order, the producing party must show that the ESI is not reasonably accessible because of undue burden or cost required to search for, retrieve, and produce the discovery. *See* FRCP 26(b)(2)(B); ***Mikron Indus. v. Hurd Windows & Doors, Inc.***, No. C07-532RSL (W.D.Wash.2008) (no pub.; 4-21-08); Rothstein, *Managing Discovery of Electronic Information*, at 15; *see also Sedona Principles, Second Edition*, Principle 9, at 49 (deleted, shadowed, fragmented, or residual ESI generally does not need to be preserved, reviewed, or produced without a showing of good cause).

(a) Undue burden. The producing party should provide specific information about the undue burden the producing party would incur. ***Mikron Indus.***, No. C07-532RSL (no pub.); *see* Hedges, *Discovery of Electronically Stored Information*, at 146 (because case law on discovery disputes is fact-specific, party should make complete record of steps taken to discover ESI). This showing should, at least, include the following:

[1] The amount of backup data to be searched. *See* ***Mikron Indus.***, No. C07-532RSL (no pub.).

[2] The different methods the producing party uses to store ESI. *See id.*

[3] The producing party's document-retention-and-destruction policy. *See id.*

[4] The extent to which the ESI stored in sources that are not reasonably accessible overlaps with ESI stored in more accessible formats. *See id.*

[5] The extent to which the producing party has searched ESI that remains accessible. *See id.*

(b) Costs. The producing party should provide estimated costs of producing or converting the ESI.

(3) Supporting evidence. The producing party should attach to the motion any affidavits, deposition transcripts, discovery responses, business records, other documents, and items that can be judicially noticed to support all factual allegations about ESI, including, for example, how it was determined that the ESI at issue is not reasonably accessible or how a particular form of production is as it is ordinarily maintained or reasonably usable. *See* ***Equity Analytics, LLC v. Lundin***, 248 F.R.D. 331, 333 (D.D.C.2008); ***Peskoff v. Faber***, 240 F.R.D. 26, 31 (D.D.C. 2007); Rothstein, *Managing Discovery of Electronic Information*, at 15. The producing party should ensure that any affidavit testimony is not only accurate but also comprehensible to individuals with little technical knowledge. *Sedona Principles, Second Edition*, at 20. Generalized or conclusory statements about costs and burdens will not be sufficient. Rothstein, *Managing Discovery of Electronic Information*, at 15.

(4) **Form.** A motion for protective order should be in writing and in the same form as motions generally. See "Drafting motions," ch. 1-B, §3.1, p. 14. The producing party must attach a certificate stating that it conferred or attempted to confer with the other parties in a good-faith effort to resolve the dispute without court action. FRCP 26(c)(1); *see, e.g.*, ***Mikron Indus.***, No. C07-532RSL (no pub.) (motion for protective order denied when D did not comply with conference requirement). See "Burden to resolve dispute without court action," ch. 6-A, §8.3.3, p. 427.

(5) **Request for hearing.** The producing party should request a hearing if necessary to provide testimony or evidence on the ESI issues. See "Request for hearing," §11.2.2(6), p. 513.

3. Response. If the producing party satisfies its burden to show that the ESI is not reasonably accessible, the requesting party must challenge the producing party's allegations and show that there is good cause for denying the protective order. FRCP 26(b)(2)(B); ***Best Buy Stores v. Developers Diversified Rlty. Corp., DDR GLH, LLC***, 247 F.R.D. 567, 569 (D.Minn.2007); 2006 Notes to FRCP 26 at ¶¶9, 10, p. 1175, this book; *e.g.*, ***Disability Rights Council v. Washington Metro. Transit Auth.***, 242 F.R.D. 139, 147-48 (D.D.C.2007) (P showed good cause when D did not stop automatic deletion of e-mails and did not impose litigation hold after suit had been filed; D was ordered to restore and produce not reasonably accessible ESI). To establish good cause, the requesting party must do the following:

(1) Make particularized arguments and not generalized objections. ***Best Buy Stores***, 247 F.R.D. at 571.

(2) Demonstrate that need and relevance outweigh the costs and burdens of retrieving and processing the ESI, such as the disruption of the requesting party's business and information-management activities. *Sedona Principles, Second Edition*, Principle 8, at 45.

(3) Address the following nonexhaustive list of factors:

(a) The specificity of the discovery request. ***Best Buy Stores***, 247 F.R.D. at 571; ***W.E. Aubuchon Co. v. BeneFirst, LLC***, 245 F.R.D. 38, 43 (D.Mass.2007); 2006 Notes to FRCP 26 at ¶9, p. 1175, this book; *see* ***Haka v. Lincoln Cty.***, 246 F.R.D. 577, 578 (W.D.Wis.2007); *see also* **Autotech Techs. v. Automationdirect.com, Inc.**, 248 F.R.D. 556, 559 (N.D.Ill.2008) (courts will not compel production of metadata when party did not include it in its request); *Sedona Principles, Second Edition*, Principle 4, at 25 (request should target particular ESI that requesting party contends is important to resolve case).

(b) The quantity of information available from other, more easily accessed sources. ***Best Buy Stores***, 247 F.R.D. at 571; ***W.E. Aubuchon Co.***, 245 F.R.D. at 43-44; 2006 Notes to FRCP 26 at ¶9, p. 1175, this book; *see* FRCP 26(b)(2)(C)(i); ***Treppel v. Biovail Corp.***, 249 F.R.D. 111, 117 (S.D.N.Y.2008); *Sedona Conference Commentary on Proportionality*, at 293.

(c) The likelihood of finding relevant, responsive information that cannot be obtained from more easily accessed sources. ***Best Buy Stores***, 247 F.R.D. at 571; 2006 Notes to FRCP 26 at ¶9, p. 1175, this book; *see* FRCP 26(b)(2)(C)(i); *Sedona Conference Commentary on Proportionality*, Principle 2, at 296-98.

(d) The responding party's failure to produce relevant information that seems likely to have existed but is no longer available from more easily accessed sources. ***Best Buy Stores***, 247 F.R.D. at 571; ***W.E. Aubuchon Co.***, 245 F.R.D. at 43-44; 2006 Notes to FRCP 26 at ¶9, p. 1175, this book.

(e) The requesting party's lack of opportunity to otherwise obtain the same information through discovery. *See* FRCP 26(b)(2)(C)(ii); *Sedona Conference Commentary on Proportionality*, at 293.

(f) The predicted importance and usefulness of the additional information. ***Best Buy Stores***, 247 F.R.D. at 571; ***W.E. Aubuchon Co.***, 245 F.R.D. at 43-44; 2006 Notes to FRCP 26 at ¶9, p. 1175, this book.

(g) The requesting party's willingness to share or bear the access costs. 2006 Notes to FRCP 26 at ¶11, p. 1175, this book.

(h) The needs of the case. FRCP 26(b)(2)(C)(iii); ***Best Buy Stores***, 247 F.R.D. at 571 n.4; *see* ***Haka***, 246 F.R.D. at 579; 2006 Notes to FRCP 26 at ¶12, p. 1175, this book; *Sedona Conference Commentary on Proportionality*, Principle 5, at 300-01.

(i) The amount in controversy. FRCP 26(b)(2)(C)(iii); ***Best Buy Stores***, 247 F.R.D. at 571 n.4; *see* 2006 Notes to FRCP 26 at ¶12, p. 1175, this book; *Sedona Conference Commentary on Proportionality*, at 294-95.

(j) The parties' resources. FRCP 26(b)(2)(C)(iii); ***Best Buy Stores***, 247 F.R.D. at 571 & n.4; ***W.E. Aubuchon Co.***, 245 F.R.D. at 43-44; 2006 Notes to FRCP 26 at ¶9, p. 1175, this book; *see* 2006 Notes to FRCP 26 at ¶12, p. 1175, this book; *Sedona Conference Commentary on Proportionality*, at 294-95.

(k) The importance of the issues at stake in the case. FRCP 26(b)(2)(C)(iii); ***Best Buy Stores***, 247 F.R.D. at 571 & n.4; ***W.E. Aubuchon Co.***, 245 F.R.D. at 43-44; 2006 Notes to FRCP 26 at ¶9, p. 1175, this book; *see* 2006 Notes to FRCP 26 at ¶12, p. 1175, this book; *Sedona Conference Commentary on Proportionality*, Principle 5, at 300-01.

(*l*) The importance of the proposed discovery in resolving the issues. FRCP 26(b)(2)(C)(iii); ***Best Buy Stores***, 247 F.R.D. at 571 n.4; *see* 2006 Notes to FRCP 26 at ¶12, p. 1175, this book; *Sedona Conference Commentary on Proportionality*, at 294-95.

4. Ruling. The court must determine whether the producing party and the requesting party have met their respective burdens of proof, and if so, the court must determine whether the benefits of the discovery outweigh its potential costs. *See* FRCP 26(b)(2)(B), (b)(2)(C); 2006 Notes to FRCP 26 at ¶¶9, 11, 12, p. 1175, this book. *See generally Sedona Conference Commentary on Proportionality* (discussing key issues to consider when conducting proportionality analysis under FRCP 26(b)(2)(C)).

5. Order. The court has broad discretion to issue protective orders. *See* FRCP 26(c); ***Packman v. Chicago Tribune Co.***, 267 F.3d 628, 646 (7th Cir.2001). The court may order, but is not limited to, the following protections:

(1) Block discovery. The court may forbid the discovery of ESI. FRCP 26(c)(1)(A). See "Block discovery," ch. 6-A, §12.5.1(1), p. 442.

(2) Set terms & conditions of discovery.

(a) Limiting amount, type, or sources. The court may set conditions for the discovery of ESI, including limiting the amount, type, or sources of ESI the responding party will be required to access and produce. *See* FRCP 26(b)(2)(B), (c); ***U&I Corp. v. Advanced Med. Design, Inc.***, 251 F.R.D. 667, 674 (M.D.Fla.2008); 2006 Notes to FRCP 26 at ¶11, p. 1175, this book. For example, the court may order the following:

[1] Specific form of production. The court may order that the ESI be produced in a specific form. *See* FRCP 34(b)(2)(E); 2006 Notes to FRCP 34 at ¶12, p. 1204, this book. When making its order, the court is not limited to the forms chosen by the requesting party, stated by the responding party in its answer, or specified in FRCP 34(b). 2006 Notes to FRCP 34 at ¶12, p. 1204, this book.

[2] Reasonably accessible ESI first. The court may order the parties to examine the ESI that is available from reasonably accessible sources before requiring discovery into sources that are identified as not reasonably accessible. *See* Rothstein, *Managing Discovery of Electronic Information*, at 15.

[3] Specific & tailored discovery requests. The court may order the requesting party to modify its discovery requests to be more specific and tailored. *See* Rothstein, *Managing Discovery of Electronic Information*, at 15.

[4] Discovery on costs & burdens. The court may order limited discovery into the costs and burdens of accessing the information from the sources identified as not reasonably accessible and into the reasons for believing that those sources do, or do not, contain information likely to be important to the case and to be

unavailable from other, accessible sources. *See* Rothstein, *Managing Discovery of Electronic Information*, at 15. For example, the court may (1) require the responding party to conduct a sampling of information contained in the sources identified as not reasonably accessible, (2) allow some form of inspection of the sources, or (3) allow the requesting party to take depositions of witnesses who know about the responding party's information system. *See* 2006 Notes to FRCP 26 at ¶10, p. 1175, this book; Rothstein, *Managing Discovery of Electronic Information*, at 16. This type of focused discovery allows the parties to learn more about what burdens and costs are involved in accessing the information, what the information consists of, and how valuable the information is to the litigation. *See* 2006 Notes to FRCP 26 at ¶10, p. 1175, this book.

[5] Sampling & testing. The court may order sampling and testing or limited discovery of the sources identified as not reasonably accessible to assess the likelihood of finding responsive information and its usefulness to the litigation. *See* Rothstein, *Managing Discovery of Electronic Information*, at 16; *see, e.g.*, ***Haka***, 246 F.R.D. at 579 (court ordered limited discovery of e-mails stored on particular hard drives); ***ClearOne Comms. v. Chiang***, No. 2:07 CV 37 TC (D.Utah 2008) (no pub.; 4-1-08) (court ordered keyword search, which in effect may be sampling and may reveal need for more, fewer, or different keyword searches).

(b) Shifting costs. The court can require the requesting party to pay all or part of the reasonable costs of obtaining the ESI from sources that are not reasonably accessible. 2006 Notes to FRCP 26 at ¶11, p. 1175, this book; *see* ***Zubulake v. UBS Warburg LLC***, 216 F.R.D. 280, 283-84 (S.D.N.Y.2003); ***Rowe Entm't, Inc. v. William Morris Agency, Inc.***, 205 F.R.D. 421, 428 (S.D.N.Y.2002); Rothstein, *Managing Discovery of Electronic Information*, at 17-18; *see, e.g.*, ***Haka***, 246 F.R.D. at 579 (court ordered parties to split costs 50-50 to perform search for e-mails); *see also Sedona Principles, Second Edition*, Principle 13, at 67 (if ESI is not reasonably available in ordinary course of business, costs may be shifted or shared). Some courts have held that cost-shifting can apply for ESI that is reasonably accessible. See "Costs," §6.1.3, p. 494. When shifting or allocating costs, the court should consider the factors listed below.

CAUTION

When the producing party's actions created the additional expense of converting inaccessible ESI to accessible ESI, the producing party will probably not be able to shift the conversion costs to the requesting party. See ***Quinby v. WestLB AG****, 245 F.R.D. 94, 104-05 (S.D.N.Y.2006).*

[1] The extent to which the discovery request is specifically tailored to discover relevant information. ***Zubulake v. UBS Warburg LLC***, 217 F.R.D. 309, 322 (S.D.N.Y.2003); *see* ***Rowe Entm't***, 205 F.R.D. at 429.

[2] The availability of the information from other sources. ***Zubulake***, 217 F.R.D. at 322; ***Rowe Entm't***, 205 F.R.D. at 429.

[3] The total cost of production, compared to the amount in controversy. ***Zubulake***, 217 F.R.D. at 322; *see* ***Rowe Entm't***, 205 F.R.D. at 429.

[4] The total cost of production, compared to the resources available to each party. ***Zubulake***, 217 F.R.D. at 322; *see* ***Rowe Entm't***, 205 F.R.D. at 429.

[5] The relative ability of each party to control costs and its incentive to do so. ***Zubulake***, 217 F.R.D. at 322; ***Rowe Entm't***, 205 F.R.D. at 429; *see also* Rosenthal, *A Few Thoughts on Electronic Discovery*, 116 Yale L.J. Pocket Part at 181 (even if requesting party is willing to pay costs to retrieve not reasonably accessible ESI, that is only one factor in determining good cause to shift costs).

[6] The importance of the issues at stake in the litigation. ***Zubulake***, 217 F.R.D. at 322.

[7] The relative benefits to the parties of obtaining the information. ***Zubulake***, 217 F.R.D. at 322.

(3) Appoint special master or expert. The court may order appointment of a special master or neutral expert to resolve the issues or to provide expert assistance to the parties, if the volume or complexity of the ESI issues is substantial. *See Manual for Complex Litigation, Fourth* §11.446; *see, e.g.*, ***U&I Corp.***, 251 F.R.D. at 676-77 (court ordered forensic inspection and sampling of P's computers by independent third-party examiner); ***Maggette v. BL Dev. Corp.***, No. 2:07CV182-M-A (N.D.Miss.2009) (slip op.; 11-24-09) (court ordered that third-party expert was needed to determine whether Ds responded to discovery in good faith; Ds were responsible for all costs related to expert); ***Inventory Locator Serv. v. Partsbase, Inc.***, No. 02-2695 Ma/V (W.D.Tenn.2006) (no pub.; 6-14-06) (court appointed special master to determine whether D fabricated electronic evidence).

§11.2 Motion to compel. The requesting party can file a motion to compel asking for an order compelling disclosure or discovery of ESI. *See* FRCP 26(b)(2)(B), 37(a)(1); 2006 Notes to FRCP 26 at ¶8, p. 1175, this book.

1. Before filing – meet & confer. The requesting party should confer with the producing party before filing a motion to compel when (1) the ESI is found in sources the producing party claims are not reasonably accessible, or (2) the producing party objected to the form of production demanded by the requesting party. *See* FRCP 26(b)(2)(B), 34(b)(2)(E); 2006 Notes to FRCP 26 at ¶8, p. 1175, this book; 2006 Notes to FRCP 34 at ¶12, p. 1204, this book. During this conference, the parties should discuss the same issues as they would before filing a motion for protective order. See "Before filing – meet & confer," §11.1.1, p. 506.

2. Motion.

(1) Deadline. A motion to compel should be filed either when a party does not complete the disclosures required by FRCP 26(a) or when a party or person does not properly respond to a discovery request. *See* FRCP 37(a)(3). Before filing a motion to compel ESI from sources the producing party claims are not reasonably accessible, the requesting party should obtain and evaluate information from all reasonably accessible sources. 2006 Notes to FRCP 26 at ¶7, p. 1175, this book.

(2) Grounds. The requesting party can file a motion to compel discovery of ESI based on the following:

(a) Failure to respond to discovery. If a party does not respond to discovery requests, the requesting party may file a motion to compel. FRCP 37(a)(3)(B). For the purpose of the motion to compel, an evasive or incomplete disclosure, answer, or response must be treated as a failure to disclosure, answer, or respond. FRCP 37(a)(4). See "Evasive or incomplete responses," ch. 6-A, §14.3.2(5), p. 444. The following are some examples:

[1] ESI production incomplete. If the producing party does not provide ESI in its initial disclosures or does not provide an adequate response to a request for ESI, the requesting party may move to compel adequate production of ESI. *See* FRCP 37(a)(3)(B), (a)(4); *see, e.g.*, ***Treppel v. Biovail Corp.***, 249 F.R.D. 111, 117 (S.D.N.Y.2008) (P moved to compel production of backup tapes). To obtain relief, the requesting party must show (1) a reasonable basis (i.e., beyond mere speculation) that there likely is other ESI or there was ESI and it has been destroyed, (2) the responding party's steps to produce or preserve relevant ESI were inadequate, and (3) additional efforts by the responding party to produce relevant ESI are warranted. *See Sedona Principles, Second Edition*, at 43; *see, e.g.*, ***Hubbard v. Potter***, 247 F.R.D. 27, 29-30 (D.D.C.2008) (motion to compel denied when P only alleged theoretical possibility that there was more ESI); ***Disability Rights Council v. Washington Metro. Transit Auth.***, 242 F.R.D. 139, 145-46 (D.D.C.2007) (motion to compel granted when P showed D did not properly instruct employees to retain relevant ESI and did nothing to stop automatic destruction of e-mails); *see also* ***John B. v. Goetz***, 531 F.3d 448, 460 (6th Cir.2008) (mere skepticism that party has not produced all relevant information is not sufficient to warrant drastic electronic-discovery measures). If the ESI has been destroyed and will need to be restored, the requesting party will also need to address the FRCP 26(b)(2) factors and demonstrate how the balance of those factors supports an order compelling restoration of the ESI. *See* ***Disability Rights Council***, 242 F.R.D. at 147-48. See "Response," §11.1.3, p. 507.

[2] **ESI production in improper form.** If the producing party does not produce ESI in a form in which it is ordinarily maintained or is reasonably usable, the requesting party may move to compel production of the ESI in the proper form. *See* FRCP 34(b)(2)(E)(ii). See "Form of production," §9.5.2(1), p. 501.

[3] **ESI withheld, concealed, or destroyed.** If the producing party's conduct suggests that it may be withholding, concealing, or destroying discoverable ESI, the requesting party may move to compel production of ESI through mirror imaging. *See* ***John B.***, 531 F.3d at 459; ***Covad Comms. v. Revonet, Inc.***, 258 F.R.D. 5, 13 (D.D.C.2009); ***Simon Prop. Grp. v. mySimon, Inc.***, 194 F.R.D. 639, 640-41 (S.D.Ind.2000); *see also* 2006 Notes to FRCP 34 at ¶6, p. 1203, this book (addition of testing and sampling requests to FRCP 34(a) was not meant to create routine right of access to party's electronic information, but access may be justified in some circumstances). If the requesting party seeks mirror imaging of the producing party's computers, the motion to compel should do the following:

[a] **Conduct justifying mirror imaging.** The requesting party should show that the producing party's conduct makes the order to compel mirror imaging necessary. *See* ***Genworth Fin. Wealth Mgmt. v. McMullan***, 267 F.R.D. 443, 447-48 (D.Conn.2010). This showing requires that the requesting party's claims of withheld, concealed, or destroyed ESI have a sufficient nexus to the need for mirror imaging. *See id.* at 448. In some cases, this showing may require proof of willful withholding, concealment, or destruction of potentially relevant ESI. *See id.* at 447-48; Scheindlin, *The Ten Most FAQ's*, at question 7; *see, e.g.*, ***John B.***, 531 F.3d at 460-61 (when there was no evidence that Ds intentionally destroyed relevant ESI in past or would refuse to preserve and produce relevant ESI in future, court abused its discretion by ordering forensic imaging); *see also* ***In re Ford Motor Co.***, 345 F.3d 1315, 1317 (11th Cir.2003) (party may need to perform its own examination of opposing party's computer systems "due to improper conduct on the part of the responding party"). Mere skepticism that all relevant ESI was not produced does not justify a forensic inspection. ***John B.***, 531 F.3d at 460. In the following cases, the court ordered a forensic inspection of a party's data:

- ***Genworth Fin. Wealth Mgmt.***, 267 F.R.D. at 447-48 (court ordered mirror imaging because Ps produced evidence that Ds used computer to retrieve confidential information and one D admitted to spoliation of incriminating evidence).

- ***RKI, Inc. v. Grimes***, 177 F.Supp.2d 859, 869-70 (N.D.Ill.2001) (court ordered forensic inspection because D deleted data from computers during litigation and defragmented hard drives before court-ordered inspections).

- ***Simon Prop. Grp.***, 194 F.R.D. at 641 (court allowed forensic duplication of D's hard drive following "troubling discrepancies" in D's document production).

- ***Playboy Enters. v. Welles***, 60 F.Supp.2d 1050, 1053 (S.D.Cal.1999) (court ordered mirror imaging of D's hard drive because D did not produce computer used for business and personal matters and D continued to delete potentially relevant e-mails after demand to produce).

[b] **Examination to reveal discoverable information.** The requesting party should show that the examination of the ESI will yield further discoverable information. *See* ***John B.***, 531 F.3d at 459-60. This showing requires, at a minimum, that the discovery request is narrowly tailored and seeks ESI relevant to the allegations in the suit. *See id.*; *see, e.g.*, ***Playboy Enters.***, 60 F.Supp.2d at 1053-54 (court allowed forensic duplication of D's hard drive when P showed that D used computer for business and personal use and e-mails could provide evidence supporting P's trademark and dilution claims and P's defense to D's counterclaim); ***Diepenhorst v. City of Battle Creek***, No. 1:05-CV-734 (W.D.Mich.2006) (no pub.; 6-30-06) (court denied mirror imaging of hard drive because D did not identify any category of relevant discovery material that would be uncovered by investigation); ***Balboa Threadworks, Inc. v. Stucky***, No. 05-1157-JTM-DWB (D.Kan.2006) (no pub.; 3-24-06) (court allowed forensic duplication of D's computers and peripheral drives in copyright-infringement case when P showed that D used his computers for business and alleged infringement was claimed to have occurred through use of computers).

[c] FRCP 26(b)(2) factors support order. The requesting party should address the FRCP 26(b)(2) factors and demonstrate how the balance of those factors supports an order compelling mirror imaging of the ESI. *See* ***Thompson v. U.S. Dept. of Hous. & Urban Dev.***, 219 F.R.D. 93, 97-98 (D.Md.2003); ***Powers v. Thomas M. Cooley Law Sch.***, No. 5:05-CV-117 (W.D.Mich.2006) (no pub.; 9-21-06). For a discussion of these factors, see "Response," §11.1.3, p. 507.

[d] Propose protocol. The requesting party should propose a protocol for duplicating and producing the ESI. *See* ***Genworth Fin. Wealth Mgmt.***, 267 F.R.D. at 447; ***Antioch Co. v. Scrapbook Borders, Inc.***, 210 F.R.D. 645, 651 (D.Minn.2002); ***Advante Int'l v. Mintel Learning Tech.***, No. C 05-01022 JW (RS) (N.D.Cal.2006) (slip op.; 6-29-06). See "Protocol for production," §11.2.2(4), this page.

(b) After objection to discovery. If a party or nonparty timely files an objection to a discovery request or a subpoena duces tecum seeking ESI, the requesting party may file a motion to compel.

[1] Objections to form of production. If the responding party objects to the requesting party's form of production, the requesting party may move to compel production in the form requested. *See* FRCP 34(b)(2)(B).

[2] Objections that ESI not reasonably accessible. If the responding party objects to the request by arguing that the ESI is not reasonably accessible, the requesting party may move to compel production of the ESI. FRCP 26(b)(2)(B); *see* ***U&I Corp. v. Advanced Med. Design, Inc.***, 251 F.R.D. 667, 674 (M.D.Fla. 2008). The burdens for challenging and defending the objection are the same as if the issues were raised in a motion for protective order—that is, the responding party must show undue burden or cost and the requesting party must show good cause for the discovery. *See* FRCP 26(b)(2)(B); ***Rodríguez-Torres v. Government Dev. Bank of P.R.***, 265 F.R.D. 40, 44 (D.P.R.2010); ***Peskoff v. Faber***, 240 F.R.D. 26, 31 (D.D.C.2007); *see, e.g.*, ***U&I Corp.***, 251 F.R.D. at 674 (D showed good cause for limited inspection of hard drives of certain employees of P); ***Treppel***, 249 F.R.D. at 117 (burden on D to produce discovery from backup tapes outweighed likely benefit to P when tapes covered time period after litigation began and discovery would likely duplicate what was already produced); ***W.E. Aubuchon Co. v. BeneFirst, LLC***, 245 F.R.D. 38, 43-45 (D.Mass.2007) (P showed good cause for discovery of inaccessible data when P narrowed its request and D caused inaccessibility). See "Motion for protective order," §11.1, p. 505.

(3) Supporting evidence. The requesting party should attach to the motion any affidavits, deposition transcripts, discovery responses, business records, other documents, and items that can be judicially noticed to support all factual allegations about ESI, including, for example, how it was determined that the ESI at issue is reasonably accessible or how a particular form of production is not as it is ordinarily maintained or not reasonably usable. *See* ***Equity Analytics, LLC v. Lundin***, 248 F.R.D. 331, 333 (D.D.C.2008); ***Peskoff***, 240 F.R.D. at 31. The requesting party should also ensure that any affidavit testimony is not only accurate but also comprehensible to individuals with little technical knowledge. *Sedona Principles, Second Edition*, at 20.

(4) Protocol for production. If appropriate, the requesting party should propose a protocol for dealing with the production of ESI. *See* ***D'Onofrio v. SFX Sports Grp.***, 254 F.R.D. 129, 130-31 (D.D.C.2008); ***Victor Stanley, Inc. v. Creative Pipe, Inc.***, 250 F.R.D. 251, 254-55 (D.Md.2008); ***Advante Int'l***, No. C 05-01022 JW (RS) (slip op.); *see, e.g.*, ***Antioch Co.***, 210 F.R.D. at 651 (P suggested protocol for duplication and production of computer files). The protocol can include the following:

PRACTICE TIP

Because the appropriate protocol will depend on the facts of the case, the requesting party should review the following cases for their fact-specific protocols: ***D'Onofrio****, 254 F.R.D. at 132-34;* ***Disability Rights Council****, 242 F.R.D. at 151;* ***Antioch Co.****, 210 F.R.D. at 653-54;* ***Rowe Entm't, Inc. v. William Morris Agency, Inc.****, 205 F.R.D. 421, 432-33 (S.D.N.Y.2002);* ***Simon Prop. Grp.****, 194 F.R.D. at 641-44;* ***Playboy Enters.****, 60 F.Supp.2d at 1054-55.*

(a) Appoint an expert. The protocol can identify an expert to be appointed to perform ESI-related tasks. *See **Equity Analytics, LLC***, 248 F.R.D. at 333; *see, e.g.*, ***Simon Prop. Grp.***, 194 F.R.D. at 641 (order required P to select and pay expert to inspect computers and create mirror image of hard drives); ***Playboy Enters.***, 60 F.Supp.2d at 1055 (order required appointment of expert in field of electronic discovery). Electronic-discovery vendors can offer a variety of software and services to assist with the electronic-discovery process. *Sedona Principles, Second Edition*, at 40.

(b) Protecting privileged & confidential information. The protocol can outline the procedures designed to protect privileged and confidential information. *See **John B.***, 531 F.3d at 460 (when party seeks mirror imaging, protocol must account for any privacy and confidentiality concerns); *see, e.g.*, ***Antioch Co.***, 210 F.R.D. at 653-54 (court ordered one copy of forensic duplicate be sent to D to fulfill production request and one copy be sent to court in case D's privilege log was reviewed); ***Balboa Threadworks***, No. 05-1157-JTM-DWB (no pub.) (court ordered no electronic search of forensic duplicate until search terms designed to protect privileged and personal information were agreed to); *see also **Covad Comms.***, 258 F.R.D. at 11 (confidentiality is not basis for withholding information, but protective order can restrict access to and use of confidential information).

(c) Minimize burden on responding party. The protocol should be designed to protect the responding party from undue burden or expense. *See **Playboy Enters.***, 60 F.Supp.2d at 1053; *see, e.g.*, ***Antioch Co.***, 210 F.R.D. at 653 (court ordered expert to avoid unnecessarily disrupting D's normal activities or business operations); ***Simon Prop. Grp.***, 194 F.R.D. at 641 (court intended for production procedure to minimize burden on D's business); *see also **Daimler Truck N. Am. LLC v. Younessi***, No. 08-MC-5011RBL (W.D.Wash.2008) (no pub.; 6-20-08) (rather than order forensic duplication, court ordered nonparty to search its own computers to protect nonparty's privileged information and trade secrets).

(5) Form. A motion to compel should be in writing and in the same form as motions generally. See "Drafting motions," ch. 1-B, §3.1, p. 14. The requesting party must attach a certificate stating that it conferred or attempted to confer with the other parties in a good-faith effort to resolve the dispute without court action. FRCP 37(a)(1). See "Burden to resolve dispute without court action," ch. 6-A, §8.3.3, p. 427.

(6) Request for hearing. The requesting party should request a hearing if necessary to provide testimony or evidence on the ESI issues. *See, e.g.*, ***Peskoff***, 240 F.R.D. at 31 (court ordered evidentiary hearing to take testimony about person who conducted ESI search, that person's qualifications, how search was conducted, and why search was adequate).

3. Response. The producing party should file a response to the motion challenging the requesting party's grounds for relief. It should also consider filing a motion for protective order. See "Motion for protective order," §11.1, p. 505.

4. Ruling. The court must determine whether the requesting party has met its burden of proof, and if so, the court must determine whether the benefits of the discovery outweigh its potential costs. *See* FRCP 26(b)(2)(B), (b)(2)(C); 2006 Notes to FRCP 26 at ¶¶9, 11, 12, p. 1175, this book. *See generally Sedona Conference Commentary on Proportionality* (discussing key issues to consider when conducting proportionality analysis under FRCP 26(b)(2)(C)).

5. Order. The court has broad discretion to issue orders compelling production. *See* FRCP 26(c); ***Packman v. Chicago Tribune Co.***, 267 F.3d 628, 646 (7th Cir.2001). For the scope of the court's order on a motion to compel, see "Order," ch. 6-A, §14.5, p. 445.

§12. SANCTIONS FOR LOST ESI

A party can seek the same sanctions against an opposing party for violating the rules governing discovery of ESI as it can for violating the rules governing discovery of paper documents or other tangible things. *See, e.g.*, ***R&R Sails***

Inc. v. Insurance Co. of Pa., 251 F.R.D. 520, 524-25 (S.D.Cal.2008) (D was liable for sanctions under FRCP 26(e) and (g) for failing to supplement initial disclosures and making incorrect certifications for discovery responses when D incorrectly claimed that it did not have electronic records); ***Southern New England Tel. Co. v. Global NAPs, Inc.***, 251 F.R.D. 82, 93 (D.Conn.2008) (P was granted default judgment because D willfully violated court's discovery order, including intentionally deleting computer files); ***In re Seroquel Prods. Liab. Litig.***, 244 F.R.D. 650, 664 (M.D. Fla.2007) (D was liable for sanctions under FRCP 37(b)(2) for not complying with court order when D's effort to prevent and solve ESI problems was deficient); ***Keithley v. Home Store.com, Inc.***, No. C-03-04447 SI (N.D.Cal.2008) (no pub.; 8-12-08) (Ds sanctioned for over $1 million when they did not "even come close to making reasonable efforts" to fulfill preservation and discovery obligations). See "Grounds," ch. 6-A, §15.3, p. 446. However, in certain circumstances, the opposing party may be able to avoid sanctions.

§12.1 Avoiding sanctions – good-faith defense. If the requesting party's grounds for sanctions are based on an allegation that the responding party lost ESI, the responding party can avoid sanctions if (1) its inability to provide the ESI was the result of the routine, good-faith operation of an electronic information system, and (2) there are no exceptional circumstances to justify the imposition of sanctions. *See* FRCP 37(e); Rosenthal, *A Few Thoughts on Electronic Discovery*, 116 Yale L.J. Pocket Part at 189; 8B Wright, Miller & Marcus §2284.1; *see also* ***Nucor Corp. v. Bell***, 251 F.R.D. 191, 196 n.3 (D.S.C.2008) (under plain language of FRCP 37(e), good-faith exception applies only to sanctions under FRCPs, not to sanctions under court's inherent power). Whether a party acted in good faith is determined on a case-by-case basis. *See* 2006 Notes to FRCP 37 at ¶4, p. 1205, this book.

1. Routine operation. The responding party should show that there is an actual, consistent, and routine operation of a system in place. *See* ***Phillip M. Adams & Assocs. v. Dell, Inc.***, 621 F.Supp.2d 1173, 1192 (D.Utah 2009); 2006 Notes to FRCP 37 at ¶2, p. 1205, this book; *see, e.g.*, ***Doe v. Norwalk Cmty. Coll.***, 248 F.R.D. 372, 378 (D. Conn.2007) (Ds did not have consistent, routine system in place when some e-mails were backed up for one year but others were only retained for six months). The phrase "routine operation of an electronic information system" refers to the ways computer systems are generally designed, programmed, and implemented to meet the party's technical and business needs. 2006 Notes to FRCP 37 at ¶2, p. 1205, this book; *see* FRCP 37(e); *see also* 8B Wright, Miller & Marcus §2284.1 & n.3 (FRCP 37(e) raises question about particular designs that are not for technical or business needs but for litigation needs). The routine operation of an electronic information system includes the alteration and overwriting of information, often without the operator's specific direction or awareness. 2006 Notes to FRCP 37 at ¶2, p. 1205, this book.

2. Good faith. The responding party should show that it affirmatively acted in good faith to prevent a system from destroying or altering relevant information, even if this destruction or alteration would occur in the regular course of business. ***Doe***, 248 F.R.D. at 378. To do so, the responding party should comply with any duty to preserve ESI or follow a litigation hold. *See* 2006 Notes to FRCP 37 at ¶3, p. 1205, this book; 8B Wright, Miller & Marcus §2284.1. See "Preservation," §4.2, p. 486. For example, if the responding party has a duty to preserve ESI, that party should determine whether it must intervene to modify or suspend certain features of its electronic information system to prevent the loss of relevant information. *See* 2006 Notes to FRCP 37 at ¶3, p. 1205, this book. The party should also comply with the requirement to discuss any ESI issues at the FRCP 26(f) conference and follow any ESI agreement that results from the conference. See "FRCP 26(f) Conference," §7, p. 495. FRCP 37(e) does not exempt a party who does not stop the operation of a system that destroys potentially discoverable ESI. ***Disability Rights Council v. Washington Metro. Transit Auth.***, 242 F.R.D. 139, 146 (D.D.C.2007); *see* Rothstein, *Managing Discovery of Electronic Information*, at 31; Scheindlin, *The Ten Most FAQ's*, at question 2; *see, e.g.*, ***Doe***, 248 F.R.D. at 378 (good-faith exception did not apply to D because D did not suspend its system).

NOTE

The practical effect of FRCP 37(e) is that it will likely require a party to suspend some or all daily or weekly backup programs and systems to prevent them from deleting or altering potentially relevant ESI. Balancing business needs with the duty to preserve may be difficult. When weighing the options, the party must make a judgment call on whether it foresees the backed-up ESI (which may become "not reasonably accessible" after the routine operation of the computer system) will be needed in the litigation; that is, whether the opposing party will be able to get the same information from reasonably accessible ESI. See 8B Wright, Miller & Marcus §2284.1. At a minimum, the party should contact the opposing party as early as possible to discuss these concerns. See Sedona Principles, Second Edition, at 21.

3. Exceptional circumstances. The responding party should challenge any allegation that there are exceptional circumstances justifying sanctions even though the ESI was lost as a result of routine, good-faith operation of a system. *See* FRCP 37(e); Rothstein, *Managing Discovery of Electronic Information*, at 31; 8B Wright, Miller & Marcus, §2284.1. A finding of exceptional circumstances should be rare. 8B Wright, Miller & Marcus §2284.1.

§12.2 Types of sanctions available. If the requesting party seeks sanctions based on an allegation that the responding party lost ESI, the available sanctions will depend on the specific ground asserted in the motion. See "Sanctions available," ch. 6-A, §15.5, p. 448. The court may order, but is not limited to, the following sanctions:

1. Dismissal. Dismissal or a default judgment may be an appropriate sanction if the court finds that a party lost ESI. *See* ***Southern New England Tel. Co. v. Global NAPs, Inc.***, 251 F.R.D. 82, 96 (D.Conn.2008); ***Arista Records, L.L.C. v. Tschirhart***, 241 F.R.D. 462, 465-66 (W.D.Tex.2006); *see, e.g.*, ***Leon v. IDX Sys.***, 464 F.3d 951, 958-60 (9th Cir.2006) (dismissal was proper when P was under duty to preserve information but intentionally destroyed data on laptop).

2. Adverse inference. An adverse inference may be an appropriate sanction if the court finds that a party lost ESI. *E.g.*, ***Doe v. Norwalk Cmty. Coll.***, 248 F.R.D. 372, 381 (D.Conn.2007) (P entitled to adverse inference when D did not preserve certain key individuals' hard drives and e-mails); ***Teague v. Target Corp.***, No. 3:06CV191 (W.D. N.C.2007) (slip op.; 4-4-07) (D entitled to adverse inference when P discarded personal computer that had crashed). See "Instruct the jury," ch. 6-A, §15.5.2(4), p. 452.

3. Other remedies. Other remedies may be appropriate if the court finds that a party lost ESI. *See, e.g.*, ***Treppel v. Biovail Corp.***, 249 F.R.D. 111, 124 (S.D.N.Y.2008) (court denied adverse inference but ordered forensic inspection of D's laptop at D's expense when D did not preserve evidence); ***Cache La Poudre Feeds, LLC v. Land O'Lakes, Inc.***, 244 F.R.D. 614, 636-37 (D.Colo.2007) (court denied adverse findings and dispositive sanctions but ordered monetary sanctions when D did not preserve evidence).

D. SECURING DISCOVERY FROM EXPERTS

§1. GENERAL

§1.1 Rules. FRCP 26, 37(c)(1), 45(c)(3)(B).

§1.2 Purpose. An expert is a person with scientific, technical, or other specialized knowledge who forms helpful opinions for a party in anticipation of litigation or in preparation for trial. *See* FRCP 26(a)(2), (b)(4); FRE 702, 703, 705. This subchapter discusses discovery about and from expert witnesses.

§1.3 Forms. *O'Connor's Federal Civil Forms* (2012), FORMS 5N, 6E:3.

§1.4 Other references. 8A Wright, Miller & Marcus, *Federal Practice & Procedure 3d* §2029 (2010 & Supp.2012); 6 *Moore's Federal Practice 3d* §26.80 (2012).

§2. TYPES OF EXPERTS

There are two general types of experts: (1) testifying experts and (2) consulting experts. *See* ***Ager v. Jane C. Stormont Hosp. & Training Sch. for Nurses***, 622 F.2d 496, 500-01 (10th Cir.1980) (testifying, consulting, and informally consulted); ***Construction Indus. Servs. v. Hanover Ins.***, 206 F.R.D. 43, 52 (E.D.N.Y.2001) (expert can be both consulting and testifying expert); 1970 Notes to FRCP 26 at ¶¶33, 34, 41, pp. 1192, 1193, this book (testifying, consulting, and informally consulted).

§3. TESTIFYING EXPERTS

A testifying expert is an expert who may be used at trial to present evidence under FRE 702, 703, or 705. *See* FRCP 26(a)(2)(A). When selected by the parties, testifying experts are either retained or nonretained. *See* FRCP 26(a)(2)(B).

NOTE

Under FRE 706, the court may appoint an independent expert to testify about complex or confusing matters, but such appointments are rare. ***Monolithic Power Sys. v. 02 Micro Int'l****, 558 F.3d 1341, 1346 (Fed.Cir.2009); 29 Wright & Gold, Federal Practice & Procedure §6305 (1997 & Supp.2012).*

§3.1 Retained. A retained testifying expert is a testifying expert who is retained or specially employed to provide testimony or whose duties as a party's employee regularly involve giving expert testimony. *See* FRCP 26(a)(2)(B); *see, e.g.*, ***Kranis v. Scott***, 178 F.Supp.2d 330, 335-36 (E.D.N.Y.2002) (court ordered P to designate legal expert, stating in order that D could depose P's legal expert); ***Duluth Lighthouse for the Blind v. C.G. Bretting Mfg.***, 199 F.R.D. 320, 324 (D.Minn.2000) (employee-expert was lay witness under FRE 701 and thus not subject to FRCP 26(a)(2)(A) disclosures); *see also* ***KW Plastics v. U.S. Can Co.***, 199 F.R.D. 687, 690 (M.D.Ala.2000) (although D's employee did not regularly testify as expert, D "specially employed" him when it designated him as testifying expert). For the distinction between retained and nonretained testifying experts, see "Note," §3.2, p. 523. A testifying expert is retained or specially employed if she has agreed to give expert testimony in exchange for consideration that is different from the witness fees and allowances provided under 28 U.S.C. §1821. ***Smith v. State Farm Fire & Cas. Co.***, 164 F.R.D. 49, 56 (S.D.W.Va.1995); *see* ***Downey v. Bob's Discount Furniture Holdings, Inc.***, 633 F.3d 1, 6 (1st Cir.2011) (retained or specially employed expert is one who does not have prior knowledge of facts involved in litigation and is recruited to provide expert testimony). A testifying expert is a party's employee who regularly gives expert testimony if she is providing expert testimony (not lay testimony) and her normal employee duties include giving expert testimony (e.g., employees of automobile or tire manufacturers who are on staff to provide expert-witness services because their employers are often involved in litigation). *See* ***Greenhaw v. City of Cedar Rapids***, 255 F.R.D. 484, 488 (N.D.Iowa 2009); ***Phillip M. Adams & Assocs. v. Fujitsu Ltd.***, No. 1:05-CV-64 (D.Utah 2010) (slip op.; 3-22-10).

1. Testifying-only expert. A testifying-only expert is a testifying expert who has acquired facts or developed opinions solely in anticipation of litigation or for trial. *See* ***Ager v. Jane C. Stormont Hosp. & Training Sch. for Nurses***, 622 F.2d 496, 500 (10th Cir.1980); ***Nelco Corp. v. Slater Elec. Inc.***, 80 F.R.D. 411, 414 (E.D.N.Y. 1978).

(1) What can be discovered. The parties are entitled to full discovery of each other's testifying-only experts, except for drafts of the expert reports and most attorney-expert communications. *See* FRCP 26(a)(2)(A), (a)(2)(B), (b)(4)(A)-(b)(4)(C). See "What cannot be discovered," §3.1.1(2), p. 518. The list below identifies some of the discoverable information about testifying-only experts. More detailed information can be secured by a deposition, but only after the expert's report is produced. *See* FRCP 26(b)(4)(A); 2010 Notes to FRCP 26 at ¶11, p. 1173, this book. Local rules may require that additional information be disclosed. *E.g.*, Local Rules Tex. (E.D.), Rule CV-26(b)(1) (disclosure of earlier testimony must include case styles, courts, cause numbers, and whether testimony was at trial or by deposition).

(a) Identity. A party is entitled to discover the identity of the testifying-only expert. *See* FRCP 26(a)(2)(A). This information is provided through the expert disclosures. FRCP 26(a)(2)(A); ***Hamburger v. State Farm Mut. Auto. Ins.***, 361 F.3d 875, 882 (5th Cir.2004). See "Expert Disclosures," ch. 6-E, §5, p. 534. FRCP 26(a)(2)(A) does not require the parties to disclose the names of persons who may testify as a lay witness under FRE 701. ***Wilburn v. Maritrans GP Inc.***, 139 F.3d 350, 356 (3d Cir.1998). If a witness is originally designated as a lay witness, that witness will not be allowed to make expert-opinion statements based on generalized knowledge. *See* ***Harms v. Laboratory Corp.***, 155 F.Supp.2d 891, 903-04 (N.D.Ill.2001).

(b) Written report. A party is entitled to discover the report prepared by the testifying-only expert. FRCP 26(a)(2)(B). FRCP 26(b), however, extends work-product protection to drafts of expert reports. FRCP 26(b)(4)(B); 2010 Notes to FRCP 26 at ¶1, p. 1172, this book. See "Drafts of report," §3.1.1(2)(a), p. 518. The report prepared by a testifying-only expert is provided through the expert disclosures. *See* FRCP 26(a)(2)(B). See "Expert's Report," §7, p. 529.

(c) Subject of testimony. A party is entitled to discover the subject matter on which the testifying-only expert will testify. *See* FRCP 26(a)(2)(B). This information is provided in the expert's report and produced with the expert disclosures. *See* FRCP 26(a)(2)(B). See "Expert's Report," §7, p. 529.

(d) Opinions. A party is entitled to discover the opinions of the testifying-only expert and the bases and reasons for them. FRCP 26(a)(2)(B)(i). This information is provided in the expert's report and produced with the expert disclosures. *See* FRCP 26(a)(2)(B). See "Expert's Report," §7, p. 529.

NOTE

Discovery of the expert's opinions or the development, foundation, or basis of those opinions is unaffected by work-product protection for drafts of expert reports and for most attorney-expert communications under FRCP 26(b)(4)(B) and (b)(4)(C). 2010 Notes to FRCP 26 at ¶12, p. 1173, this book. For example, the expert's testing of material involved in litigation, and notes from any such testing, would not be protected as work product. Id. Similarly, inquiry into communications the expert had with anyone other than the party's attorney about the opinions expressed is unaffected. Id. Opposing counsel can also question the expert about alternative analyses, testing methods, or approaches to the issues the expert is testifying about, whether or not the expert considered those analyses, methods, or approaches in forming her opinions. Id.

(e) Information considered. A party is entitled to discover the facts or data considered by the testifying-only expert in forming the expert's opinions. FRCP 26(a)(2)(B)(ii). This information is provided in the expert's report and produced with the expert disclosures. *See* FRCP 26(a)(2)(B). See "Expert's Report," §7, p. 529.

(f) Materials used. A party is entitled to discover any exhibits to be used as a summary of or support for the testifying-only expert's opinions. FRCP 26(a)(2)(B)(iii); ***Miller v. Corrections Corp.***, 375 F.Supp.2d 889, 896 (D.Alaska 2005); ***Intercargo Ins. v. Burlington N. Santa Fe R.R.***, 185 F.Supp.2d 1103, 1106 (C.D.Cal.2001). This information is provided in the expert's report and produced with the expert disclosures. *See* FRCP 26(a)(2)(B). See "Expert's Report," §7, p. 529.

(g) Résumé & bibliography. A party is entitled to discover the current résumé and bibliography for the testifying-only expert's previous ten years. *See* FRCP 26(a)(2)(B)(iv). This information is provided in the expert's report and produced with the expert disclosures. *See* FRCP 26(a)(2)(B). See "Expert's Report," §7, p. 529.

(h) List of other cases. A party is entitled to discover a list of all other cases, during the previous four years, in which the testifying-only expert has testified at trial or by deposition. FRCP 26(a)(2)(B)(v). This information is provided in the expert's report and produced with the expert disclosures. *See* FRCP 26(a)(2)(B). See "Expert's Report," §7, p. 529.

(i) Compensation. A party is entitled to discover information about the amount of compensation to be paid to the testifying-only expert for the study and testimony. FRCP 26(a)(2)(B)(vi); ***Smith***, 164 F.R.D. at 55. This information is provided in the expert's report and produced with the expert disclosures. *See* FRCP 26(a)(2)(B). See "Expert's Report," §7, p. 529.

(2) What cannot be discovered. A party is not entitled to discover drafts of the expert report or most attorney-expert communications. FRCP 26(b)(4)(B), (b)(4)(C); *see* 2010 Notes to FRCP 26 at ¶¶9, 10, p. 1172, this book.

(a) Drafts of report.

[1] Generally. All drafts of an expert report required under FRCP 26(a)(2)(B) are protected as work product. FRCP 26(b)(4)(B). See "Work-product protection," ch. 6-B, §3.4, p. 467. The drafts are protected regardless of the form in which they are recorded, whether written, electronic, or otherwise. FRCP 26(b)(4)(B); 2010 Notes to FRCP 26 at ¶9, p. 1172, this book. The drafts of any supplementation under FRCP 26(e) are also protected. 2010 Notes to FRCP 26 at ¶9, p. 1172, this book. See "Supplementing Expert Discovery," §5, p. 527.

[2] Exception for substantial need & undue hardship. Under FRCP 26(b)(3)(A)(ii), drafts of the expert report may be discovered when a party shows that (1) it has a substantial need for the materials to prepare its case and (2) it cannot, without undue hardship, obtain the substantial equivalent of the materials any other way. *See* 2010 Notes to FRCP 26 at ¶18, p. 1173, this book. See "Substantial need & undue hardship," ch. 6-B, §3.4.5(2)(b), p. 470. A party will rarely be able to make such a showing given the broad disclosure and discovery otherwise allowed for experts. *See* 2010 Notes to FRCP 26 at ¶18, p. 1173, this book. The requirements of the exception are not satisfied merely because a party does not provide the required disclosure or discovery; remedies for not disclosing or producing discovery are provided under FRCP 37. 2010 Notes to FRCP 26 at ¶18, p. 1173, this book. In the rare case in which a party does make the showing of substantial need and undue hardship, the court must protect against disclosure of the attorney's mental impressions, conclusions, opinions, or legal theories under FRCP 26(b)(3)(B). 2010 Notes to FRCP 26 at ¶19, p. 1173, this book. But this protection does not extend to the expert's own development of the opinions to be presented; those are subject to questioning during deposition or at trial. *Id.*

(b) Attorney-expert communications. Communications between the attorney and the expert are protected as work product—with three specific exceptions. FRCP 26(b)(4)(C). FRCP 26(b)(4)(C) is designed to protect an attorney's work product and to ensure that attorneys can interact with retained testifying experts without fear of having to disclose or produce the communications to the opposing party. 2010 Notes to FRCP 26 at ¶10, p. 1172, this book. See "Work-product protection," ch. 6-B, §3.4, p. 467.

CAUTION

The protection does not apply to discovery of opinions to be offered by the expert or discovery of the development, foundation, or basis of those opinions. 2010 Notes to FRCP 26 at ¶12, p. 1173, this book. See "Opinions," §3.1.1(1)(d), p. 517.

---

[1] Generally.

[a] What is protected. The protection covers all forms of the communications, whether oral, written, electronic, or otherwise. FRCP 26(b)(4)(C); 2010 Notes to FRCP 26 at ¶10, p. 1172, this book. The protection includes any "preliminary" expert opinions communicated to the attorney. 2010 Notes to FRCP 26 at ¶10, p. 1172, this book.

[b] Who is included. The protection applies to communications between an expert who is required to provide an expert report and the attorney for the party who designated the testifying-only expert. FRCP 26(b)(4)(C); 2010 Notes to FRCP 26 at ¶10, p. 1172, this book. The protection includes communications between the attorney and the expert's assistants. 2010 Notes to FRCP 26 at ¶10, p. 1172, this book.

NOTE

The concept of the "party's attorney" usually should not be limited to communications with a single attorney or a single law firm. 2010 Notes to FRCP 26 at ¶13, p. 1173, this book. For example, a party may be involved in a number of suits about a given product or service, and that party can retain a particular expert to testify on its behalf in several of the suits. Id. In those situations, the protection applies to communications between the expert and the attorneys representing the party in any of those cases. Id. Similarly, communications with in-house counsel for the party would often be protected even if that in-house attorney is not the attorney of record in the suit. Id. Other situations may also justify a pragmatic application of the "party's attorney" concept. Id.

[2] Exceptions. There are three specific exceptions under FRCP 26(b)(4)(C) and one general exception under FRCP 26(b)(3)(A)(ii) to the protection of attorney-expert communications. 2010 Notes to FRCP 26 at ¶¶14, 18, p. 1173, this book.

[a] Specific exceptions. The scope of the FRCP 26(b)(4)(C) exceptions is narrow; the discovery allowed does not extend beyond those specific topics. *See* 2010 Notes to FRCP 26 at ¶14, p. 1173, this book (when excepted topics are included in a communication, protection applies to all aspects of communication beyond excepted topics). Attorney-expert communications that identify the following are discoverable:

- **Compensation.** Attorney-expert communications related to compensation for the expert's study or testimony are discoverable. FRCP 26(b)(4)(C)(i). The objective of this exception is to permit full discovery into potential sources of bias. 2010 Notes to FRCP 26 at ¶15, p. 1173, this book. Thus, the exception is not limited to compensation for work forming the expert's opinions, but rather extends to all compensation for the study and testimony related to the suit. *Id.* Any communications about additional benefits to the expert (e.g., further work if there is a successful outcome in the present case) are also discoverable. *Id.* In addition, compensation for work performed by a person or organization associated with the expert is also discoverable. *Id.* The discovery allowed may go beyond the requirement to include a statement about compensation in the expert report. *Id.*; *see* FRCP 26(a)(2)(B)(vi). See "Compensation," §3.1.1(1)(i), p. 518.

- **Facts or data.** Attorney-expert communications that identify facts or data the attorney provided and the expert considered in forming her opinions are discoverable. FRCP 26(b)(4)(C)(ii). See "Opinions," §3.1.1(1)(d), p. 517; "Information considered," §3.1.1(1)(e), p. 517. The exception applies only to communications "identifying" the facts or data provided by the attorney; further communications about the potential relevance of the facts or data are protected. 2010 Notes to FRCP 26 at ¶16, p. 1173, this book.

- **Assumptions.** Attorney-expert communications that identify assumptions the attorney provided and the expert relied on in forming her opinions are discoverable. FRCP 26(b)(4)(C)(iii); *e.g.*, 2010 Notes to FRCP 26 at ¶17, p. 1173, this book (attorney may tell expert to assume the truth of certain testimony or evidence or the correctness of another expert's conclusions). See "Opinions," §3.1.1(1)(d), p. 517; "Information considered," §3.1.1(1)(e), p. 517. The exception is limited to assumptions that the expert actually relied on in forming her opinions. 2010 Notes to FRCP 26 at ¶17, p. 1173, this book. More general attorney-expert communications about hypotheticals, or exploring possibilities based on hypothetical facts, are not discoverable. *Id.*

[b] General exception – substantial need & undue hardship. Under FRCP 26(b)(3)(A)(ii), attorney-expert communications beyond the three specific exceptions may be discoverable through a court order when a party shows that (1) it has a substantial need for the materials to prepare its case and (2) it cannot, without undue hardship, obtain the substantial equivalent of the materials any other way. *See* 2010 Notes to FRCP 26 at ¶18, p. 1173, this book. See "Exception for substantial need & undue hardship," §3.1.1(2)(a)[2], p. 518.

(3) Procedures for securing discovery. The discovery procedures available to secure information relating to testifying-only experts depend on whether the discovery is sought from the party or the expert.

(a) Discovery from party. From the party who designated the testifying-only expert, a party may secure information through the following discovery procedures: (1) expert-witness disclosures (identity of witness, expert report, materials considered, résumé and bibliography, etc.), (2) interrogatories (names of expert trial witnesses, subject of testimony, substance of opinion), and (3) requests for production (materials provided to expert). *See* FRCP 26(a)(2)(B) (expert disclosures); ***Alper v. U.S.***, 190 F.R.D. 281, 283 (D.Mass.2000) (party can use request for production to obtain documents considered by other party's retained testifying expert); ***Jayne H. Lee, Inc. v. Flagstaff Indus.***, 173 F.R.D. 651, 653 (D.Md.1997) (party can use interrogatories to have other party identify expert witnesses who will offer trial testimony); *see, e.g.*, ***Chakales v. Hertz Corp.***, 152 F.R.D. 240, 245-46 (N.D.Ga.1993) (interrogatory seeking identity of all experts expected to testify required disclosure of all retained and nonretained testifying experts). See "Expert Disclosures," ch. 6-E, §5, p. 534.

(b) Discovery from testifying-only expert. From the testifying-only expert, a party may secure information through the following discovery procedures: (1) oral deposition or deposition by written questions (e.g., facts known, substance and bases of opinions, qualifications, bias), and (2) subpoena duces tecum or request for production (things used or prepared by the expert in anticipation of testimony and other relevant information not provided in the expert disclosures, such as draft reports). *See* FRCP 30 (oral deposition), FRCP 31 (deposition by written questions), FRCP 34 (requests for production), FRCP 45 (subpoena); ***Brown v. Ringstad***, 142 F.R.D. 461, 465 (S.D.Iowa 1992) (if expert is designated as trial witness, expert may be deposed); *see also* 2010 Notes to FRCP 26 at ¶11, p. 1173, this book (although depositions are the most frequent method for discovery of information about an expert, 2010 amendments to FRCP 26(b) apply to all forms of discovery).

2. Testifying expert + facts = testifying expert & fact witness. A testifying expert who obtained factual knowledge about the case before litigation was anticipated or pending is also discoverable as a fact witness. *See* 1970 Notes to FRCP 26 at ¶33, p. 1192, this book. These experts are often considered "actors" or "viewers." *See* ***Ager***, 622 F.2d at 503; ***Nelco Corp.***, 80 F.R.D. at 414; 1970 Notes to FRCP 26 at ¶33, p. 1192, this book. An example is the defendant's in-house experts. *E.g.*, ***Nelco Corp.***, 80 F.R.D. at 414 (employee expert); ***Virginia Elec. & Power Co. v. Sun Shipbuilding & Dry Dock Co.***, 68 F.R.D. 397, 408 (E.D.Va.1975) (in-house experts).

(1) What can be discovered. A party is entitled to obtain the same information about a testifying expert who has knowledge of facts as it can obtain about a fact witness. *See* ***Quarantillo v. Consolidated Rail Corp.***, 106 F.R.D. 435, 437 (W.D.N.Y.1985); ***Nelco Corp.***, 80 F.R.D. at 414. The following is a list of the information discoverable about testifying experts with facts.

NOTE

When a retained testifying expert obtained factual knowledge about the case before the litigation, the expert is discoverable as a fact witness as well as a testifying expert. Thus, in addition to the information below, a party is also entitled to the discoverable information for testifying-only experts. See "What can be discovered," §3.1.1(1), p. 516.

(a) Identity. A party is entitled to discover the name, address, and telephone number of each testifying expert witness who has firsthand knowledge of facts. FRCP 26(a)(1)(A)(i). This information should be provided in the initial disclosures. *Id.*

(b) Connection with case. A party is entitled to obtain a brief description identifying the general topics on which the expert has information. FRCP 26(a)(1)(A)(i); 1993 Notes to FRCP 26 at ¶6, p. 1182, this book. This information should be provided in the initial disclosures. FRCP 26(a)(1)(A)(i). A more detailed form of this information may be obtained from the party through interrogatories or requests for admissions, or from the expert through an oral deposition or a deposition by written questions. *See* FRCP 30 (oral deposition), FRCP 31 (deposition by written questions), FRCP 33 (interrogatories), FRCP 36 (requests for admissions).

(c) Facts. A party is entitled to discover what facts the testifying expert knew before becoming involved with the litigation. ***Atari Corp. v. Sega of Am.***, 161 F.R.D. 417, 421-22 (N.D.Cal.1994); ***Nelco Corp.***, 80 F.R.D. at 414. This information may be obtained from the party through interrogatories or requests for admissions, or from

the expert through an oral deposition or a deposition by written questions. *See* FRCP 30 (oral deposition), FRCP 31 (deposition by written questions), FRCP 33 (interrogatories), FRCP 36 (requests for admissions).

(d) "Fact opinion." A party is entitled to obtain the retained testifying expert's opinions held before the expert's involvement in the underlying litigation. ***Atari Corp.***, 161 F.R.D. at 421-22; ***Nelco Corp.***, 80 F.R.D. at 414. For example, the "fact opinions" of a treating physician might include opinions about the causation, diagnosis, prognosis, and extent of a disability or injury. ***Ngo v. Standard Tools & Equip., Co.***, 197 F.R.D. 263, 267 (D.Md. 2000); *cf.* ***Young v. U.S.***, 181 F.R.D. 344, 346-47 (W.D.Tex.1997) (nonretained treating physician may be asked questions implicating his expertise). If the opinion is based on information learned after the expert became involved in the litigation, the opinion is usually beyond "fact opinion" and thus not discoverable through initial disclosures but rather expert disclosures. *See* ***Ngo***, 197 F.R.D. at 267. See "What can be discovered," §3.1.1(1), p. 516. The "fact opinion" information may be obtained from the party through interrogatories or requests for admissions, or from the expert through an oral deposition or a deposition by written questions. *See* FRCP 30 (oral deposition), FRCP 31 (deposition by written questions), FRCP 33 (interrogatories), FRCP 36 (requests for admissions).

(2) Procedures for securing discovery. The discovery procedures available to secure information about a testifying expert with firsthand knowledge of facts are the same as those for securing information about testifying expert witnesses and fact witnesses. *See* FRCP 26(b)(1); *see, e.g.*, FRCP 26(a)(1)(A) (initial disclosures), FRCP 30 (oral deposition), FRCP 31 (deposition by written questions), FRCP 33 (interrogatories), FRCP 34 (requests for production), FRCP 36 (requests for admissions). For procedures used to secure discovery about the witness's expert testimony, see "Procedures for securing discovery," §3.1.1(3), p. 519. The discovery procedures available to secure information relating to the testifying expert's firsthand knowledge of facts depend on whether the discovery is sought from the party or the expert.

(a) From party. From the party who designated the testifying expert as a person with factual knowledge, a party may secure information through the following discovery procedures: (1) initial disclosures (identity and general topics of knowledge), (2) interrogatories (identity of persons with knowledge of relevant facts and detailed topics of knowledge), and (3) other types of discovery (e.g., oral deposition of party) to obtain other discoverable information known to the party about the testifying expert's factual knowledge. *See* FRCP 26(a)(1)(A) (initial disclosures), FRCP 30 (oral deposition), FRCP 31 (deposition by written questions), FRCP 33 (interrogatories), FRCP 34 (requests for production), FRCP 36 (requests for admissions).

(b) From testifying expert with facts. From the testifying expert with facts, a party may secure information through the following discovery procedures: (1) oral deposition or deposition by written questions (facts known, fact opinions, and bases for fact opinions), and (2) subpoena duces tecum (things used or prepared by the expert relating to testimony on firsthand knowledge of facts). *See* FRCP 30 (oral deposition), FRCP 31 (deposition by written questions), FRCP 45 (subpoena).

3. Testifying expert + de-designation = consulting expert. An expert who is first designated as a testifying expert but later de-designated (i.e., will not be called as a witness) is considered a consulting-only expert if, before the de-designation, no discovery of the expert was conducted and the expert did not conduct a physical or mental examination of a party under FRCP 35. *See* ***Durflinger v. Artiles***, 727 F.2d 888, 891 (10th Cir.1984); ***Hartford Fire Ins. Co. v. Transgroup Express, Inc.***, 264 F.R.D. 382, 384 (N.D.Ill.2009); ***FMC Corp. v. Vendo Co.***, 196 F.Supp.2d 1023, 1045-46 (E.D.Cal.2002). See "Consulting-only expert," §4.1.1, p. 525. Courts disagree about whether the exceptional-circumstances standard for consulting-only experts determines whether a de-designated expert can be deposed or called by the opposing party. *E.g.*, ***House v. Combined Ins.***, 168 F.R.D. 236, 240 (N.D.Iowa 1996) (identifying two other standards: (1) discretionary standard—court balances parties' interests and prejudice to party who de-designated expert, and (2) entitlement standard—opposing party is entitled to call de-designated expert; court used discretionary standard and allowed deposition of de-designated expert); *see* ***Hartford Fire Ins. Co.***, 264 F.R.D. at 384; ***FMC Corp.***, 196 F.Supp.2d at 1042-43; *see also* FRCP 26(b)(4)(D)(ii) (exceptional-circumstances standard). To ensure that a de-designated expert is protected as a consulting-only expert (i.e., no discovery of expert), any designation change should take place before the expert submits a written report or is deposed. *See* ***CP Kelco U.S. Inc.***

v. Pharmacia Corp., 213 F.R.D. 176, 179 (D.Del.2003); ***Ross v. Burlington N. R.R.***, 136 F.R.D. 638, 639 (N.D.Ill. 1991). See "Changing designation," ch. 6-E, §5.1.2, p. 535.

(1) What can be discovered. A party is entitled to obtain the same information about a retained expert who was de-designated as it can obtain about a consulting-only expert. *See* ***Durflinger***, 727 F.2d at 891. See "What can be discovered," §4.1.1(1), p. 525.

(2) Procedures for securing discovery. The discovery procedures available to secure information about a retained expert who has been de-designated are the same as those used to obtain information about a consulting-only expert. *See* ***Durflinger***, 727 F.2d at 891 (de-designated expert treated as consulting expert). See "Procedures for securing discovery," §4.1.1(2), p. 526. However, a party should be able to conduct limited discovery of the expert using oral depositions and subpoenas if, before de-designation, the facts known and opinions held by the expert were disclosed or the expert conducted a physical or mental examination of a party under FRCP 35. *See* ***Ross***, 136 F.R.D. at 638-39.

4. Testifying expert + consultant = testifying expert. An expert who is retained both to give expert testimony and to consult on other matters outside the scope of the expert's testimony is discoverable as a retained testifying expert. *See* ***Construction Indus. Servs. v. Hanover Ins.***, 206 F.R.D. 43, 52-53 (E.D.N.Y.2001). See "What can be discovered," §3.1.1(1), p. 516. The scope of discovery, however, can be limited if a clear distinction is drawn between the expert's anticipated trial testimony and the consulting advice. *See* ***Employees Committed for Justice v. Eastman Kodak Co.***, 251 F.R.D. 101, 104 (W.D.N.Y.2008); ***B.C.F. Oil Ref., Inc. v. Consolidated Edison Co.***, 171 F.R.D. 57, 61-62 (S.D.N.Y.1997). Any ambiguity about which function was served by the expert when creating a document must be resolved in favor of discovery. ***Employees Committed for Justice***, 251 F.R.D. at 104; ***B.C.F. Oil Ref.***, 171 F.R.D. at 62.

(1) What can be discovered. When there is no clear distinction between the work done for an expert's trial testimony and that done as a consultant, a party is entitled to obtain the same information about that expert as it can obtain about a testifying-only expert. *See* ***Construction Indus. Servs.***, 206 F.R.D. at 52-53. See "Testifying-only expert," §3.1.1, p. 516. When there is a clear distinction between the work done for the expert's trial testimony and that done as a consultant, a party is entitled to obtain the same information about that expert's trial testimony as it can obtain about a testifying-only expert, but the party is not entitled to obtain the work performed by the expert in her consulting capacity. *See* ***Construction Indus. Servs.***, 206 F.R.D. at 52-53. See "Consulting-only expert," §4.1.1, p. 525.

(2) Procedures for securing discovery. The discovery procedures available to secure information about an expert retained to provide expert testimony and consulting advice are the same as those used to obtain information about a retained testifying-only expert. See "Procedures for securing discovery," §3.1.1(3), p. 519.

§3.2 Nonretained. A nonretained testifying expert is a testifying expert who is not retained or specially employed to provide testimony and who usually has firsthand factual knowledge about the case. *See* ***Young v. U.S.***, 181 F.R.D. 344, 346 (W.D.Tex.1997); *see, e.g.*, ***Downey v. Bob's Discount Furniture Holdings, Inc.***, 633 F.3d 1, 6-7 (1st Cir.2011) (exterminator was not retained when he was part of ongoing sequence of events involved in litigation and he arrived at his causation opinion during treatment); ***Fielden v. CSX Transp.***, 482 F.3d 866, 869 (6th Cir.2007) (treating physician was not retained when he formed opinions at time of treatment and was not asked by attorney to form expert opinion for litigation purposes). Nonretained testifying experts with knowledge of facts are discoverable as fact witnesses. *See* ***Ngo v. Standard Tools & Equip., Co.***, 197 F.R.D. 263, 266-67 (D.Md.2000); ***Young***, 181 F.R.D. at 346; 2010 Notes to FRCP 26 at ¶7, p. 1172, this book; 1970 Notes to FRCP 26 at ¶33, p. 1192, this book. These experts are often considered "actors" or "viewers" or lay experts under FRE 701. *See* ***Downey***, 633 F.3d at 6; ***Ager v. Jane C. Stormont Hosp. & Training Sch. for Nurses***, 622 F.2d 496, 501 (10th Cir.1980); ***Duluth Lighthouse for the Blind v. C.G. Bretting Mfg.***, 199 F.R.D. 320, 324 (D.Minn.2000); ***Ngo***, 197 F.R.D. at 266-67; 1970 Notes to FRCP 26 at ¶33, p. 1192, this book. Examples include the plaintiff's treating physician, an accident investigator for a governmental entity, and an employee-expert who does not regularly provide expert testimony. *E.g.*, ***Goodman v. Staples***

the Office Superstore, LLC, 644 F.3d 817, 824 (9th Cir.2011) (treating physician); ***Brandt Distrib. Co. v. Fed. Ins.***, 247 F.3d 822, 825-26 (8th Cir.2001) (fire captain for city fire department); ***Duluth Lighthouse***, 199 F.R.D. at 324 (employee-expert); *see* ***Wreath v. U.S.***, 161 F.R.D. 448, 450 (D.Kan.1995); 2010 Notes to FRCP 26 at ¶7, p. 1172, this book; *see also* ***In re Snyder***, 115 F.R.D. 211, 215 (D.Ariz.1987) (witness was not truly involuntary expert witness because he had firsthand factual knowledge of historical events related to litigation).

NOTE

Most courts distinguish a retained expert from a nonretained expert based on the role the expert played in the case. ***Downey****, 633 F.3d at 7 n.3. That is, a retained expert is one who does not have prior knowledge of the facts involved in the litigation and is recruited in preparation for trial to provide expert testimony; a nonretained expert is one who has ground-level involvement with the events giving rise to the litigation and whose opinion of causation is based on personal knowledge and observations made during that involvement. See id. at 6-7. But some courts have made the distinction based on the timing of the causation opinion; if the expert's causation opinion was made outside of or after the ground-level involvement, the expert is considered retained and must file an expert report. See* ***Goodman****, 644 F.3d at 819-20 (treating physician becomes witness hired to render expert opinion when opinions go beyond usual scope of treating physician's testimony);* ***Meyers v. National R.R. Passenger Corp.****, 619 F.3d 729, 734-35 (7th Cir.2010) (treating physician who does not make causation determination during treatment should be deemed retained testifying expert). See "Retained," §3.1, p. 516. It is unclear whether courts will continue to make this distinction when applying FRCP 26(a)(2) as amended December 1, 2010. See 2010 Notes to FRCP 26 at ¶6, p. 1172, this book (amendment resolved disagreement that had prompted some courts to require expert reports from experts who were actually exempt from report requirement; expert report is required only from witness described in FRCP 26(a)(2)(B)); see also* ***Downey****, 633 F.3d at 7 n.4 (although court's opinion was based on version of FRCP 26(a) before amendments, court acknowledged disagreement has been resolved by those amendments). Regardless, check the local rules to determine whether a witness may be exempt from the expert-report requirement. See 1993 Notes to FRCP 26 at ¶19, p. 1184, this book (local rule can waive report requirement for particular experts); see, e.g., Local Rules Md., Rule 104.10 (excluding hybrid fact/expert witnesses, such as treating physicians, from report requirement).*

1. What can be discovered. A party is entitled to obtain the same information about a nonretained testifying expert who has knowledge of facts as it can about a fact witness. *See* ***Ngo***, 197 F.R.D. at 266-67; 2010 Notes to FRCP 26 at ¶7, p. 1172, this book; 1970 Notes to FRCP 26 at ¶33, p. 1192, this book. For the type of information discoverable about these experts, see "Testifying expert + facts = testifying expert & fact witness," §3.1.2, p. 520. A nonretained expert is not required to submit an expert report under FRCP 26(a)(2)(B); however, the subject matter on which the expert is expected to present evidence and a summary of facts and opinions to be offered must be disclosed. *See* FRCP 26(a)(2)(C); 2010 Notes to FRCP 26 at ¶5, p. 1172, this book. See "FRCP 26(a)(2)(C) disclosure," §3.2.3(1)(a)[2], p. 524. For example, a nonretained treating physician who is deposed or called to testify at trial need only provide an FRCP 26(a)(2)(C) disclosure. *See* 2010 Notes to FRCP 26 at ¶7, p. 1172, this book; 1993 Notes to FRCP 26 at ¶19, p. 1184, this book.

2. What cannot be discovered.

(1) Generally. A party is not entitled to drafts of the FRCP 26(a)(2)(C) disclosure. FRCP 26(b)(4)(B); 2010 Notes to FRCP 26 at ¶¶1, 9, p. 1172, this book. The drafts are protected regardless of the form in which they are recorded, whether written, electronic, or otherwise. FRCP 26(b)(4)(B); 2010 Notes to FRCP 26 at ¶9, p. 1172, this book. The drafts of any supplementation under FRCP 26(e) are also protected. 2010 Notes to FRCP 26 at ¶9, p. 1172, this book. See "Supplementing Expert Discovery," §5, p. 527.

NOTE

Work-product protection applies to most communications between an attorney and a retained testifying expert. FRCP 26(b)(4)(C); 2010 Notes to FRCP 26 at ¶¶1, 10, p. 1172, this book. See "Attorney-expert communications," §3.1.1(2)(b), p. 518. This protection, however, does not apply to nonretained testifying experts. 2010 Notes to FRCP 26 at ¶10, p. 1172, this book. Even though the protection under FRCP 26(b)(4)(C) does not apply to these experts, protection may be available under other doctrines, such as privilege or independent development of the work-product doctrine. 2010 Notes to FRCP 26 at ¶10, p. 1172, this book. See "What Is Not Discoverable?," ch. 6-B, §3, p. 460.

(2) Exception for substantial need & undue hardship. Under FRCP 26(b)(3)(A)(ii), drafts of the FRCP 26(a)(2)(C) disclosure may be discovered when a party shows that (1) it has a substantial need for the materials to prepare its case and (2) it cannot, without undue hardship, obtain the substantial equivalent of the materials any other way. *See* 2010 Notes to FRCP 26 at ¶18, p. 1173, this book. See "Exception for substantial need & undue hardship," §3.1.1(2)(a)[2], p. 518.

3. Procedures for securing discovery. The discovery procedures available to secure information relating to nonretained testifying experts depends on whether the discovery is being sought from the party or the expert.

(1) Discovery from party. From the party who designated the nonretained testifying expert, a party may secure information through the following discovery procedures.

(a) Expert disclosures.

[1] Identity. A party is entitled to disclosure of the identity of each nonretained testifying expert witness who has firsthand knowledge of facts. *See* FRCP 26(a)(2)(A); 2010 Notes to FRCP 26 at ¶7, p. 1172, this book. This information is provided through the expert disclosures. *See* FRCP 26(a)(2)(A); 2010 Notes to FRCP 26 at ¶7, p. 1172, this book. Because these experts have firsthand knowledge of facts, the party should also disclose the expert's name, address, and telephone number in the initial disclosures. *See* FRCP 26(a)(1)(A)(i), (a)(2)(A); 2010 Notes to FRCP 26 at ¶7, p. 1172, this book.

[2] FRCP 26(a)(2)(C) disclosure. A party is entitled to the FRCP 26(a)(2)(C) disclosure. FRCP 26(a)(2)(C); *see* 2010 Notes to FRCP 26 at ¶7, p. 1172, this book. Unless otherwise stipulated or ordered by the court, an FRCP 26(a)(2)(C) disclosure must contain the following information:

[a] The subject matter the expert is expected to testify on under FRE 702, 703, or 705. FRCP 26(a)(2)(C).

[b] A summary of the facts and opinions on which the expert is expected to testify. *Id.* The disclosure, however, does not include facts unrelated to the expert's opinions that may be presented. 2010 Notes to FRCP 26 at ¶7, p. 1172, this book.

NOTE

The FRCP 26(a)(2)(C) disclosure is considerably less extensive than the full expert report required under FRCP 26(a)(2)(B). 2010 Notes to FRCP 26 at ¶5, p. 1172, this book. See "Expert's Report," §7, p. 529. This disclosure avoids requiring undue detail from the experts who have not been retained and who may not be as responsive to attorneys as those experts who have been retained. 2010 Notes to FRCP 26 at ¶5, p. 1172, this book.

(b) Deposition. A party is entitled to depose an opposing party to obtain discoverable information known to the opposing party about the nonretained testifying expert. *See* FRCP 30.

(c) Interrogatories. A party is entitled to discovery through interrogatories (names of expert trial witnesses, subject of testimony, substance of opinion). *See* FRCP 33; ***Jayne H. Lee, Inc. v. Flagstaff Indus.***, 173 F.R.D. 651, 652 (D.Md.1997); ***Chakales v. Hertz Corp.***, 152 F.R.D. 240, 245-46 (N.D.Ga.1993).

(2) Discovery from nonretained expert. From the nonretained testifying expert, a party may secure information through the following discovery procedures: (1) oral deposition or deposition by written questions (e.g., facts known, substance and bases of opinions, qualifications, bias), and (2) subpoena duces tecum (things used or prepared by the expert in anticipation of testimony and the expert's résumé and bibliography). *See* FRCP 30 (oral deposition), FRCP 31 (deposition by written questions), FRCP 45 (subpoena); ***Brown v. Best Foods, Inc.***, 169 F.R.D. 385, 387 (N.D.Ala.1996) (party is entitled to take deposition of nonretained expert).

§4. CONSULTING EXPERTS

A consulting expert is an expert who has been consulted, retained, or specially employed by a party in anticipation of litigation or to prepare for trial, but who will not testify at trial. *See* FRCP 26(b)(4)(D); ***Ager v. Jane C. Stormont Hosp. & Training Sch. for Nurses***, 622 F.2d 496, 500 (10th Cir.1980); *see also* ***Hermsdorfer v. American Motors Corp.***, 96 F.R.D. 13, 15 (W.D.N.Y.1982) (FRCP 26(b)(4)(B), now FRCP 26(b)(4)(D), protects experts hired for dual purpose of preparing for pending litigation and for litigation expected on basis of logical probability). Consulting experts are usually consulted to educate the attorney about the whole case or some facet of it, who and what kind of trial experts should be consulted and retained, how to best present evidence to the court or jury, or to discover, compile, and assimilate data for a testifying expert. ***Bergeson v. Dilworth***, 132 F.R.D. 277, 284 (D.Kan.1990), *vacated on other grounds*, 749 F.Supp. 1555 (D.Kan.1990). Consulting experts can be classified as either retained or nonretained.

§4.1 Retained.

1. Consulting-only expert. A consulting-only expert is a consulting expert (1) who has no firsthand factual knowledge about the case and no secondhand knowledge except for knowledge acquired through the consultation and (2) whose work product, opinions, or mental impressions have not been reviewed by a testifying expert. *See* FRCP 26(b)(4)(D); ***Delcastor, Inc. v. Vail Assocs.***, 108 F.R.D. 405, 408 (D.Colo.1985); ***Heitmann v. Concrete Pipe Mach.***, 98 F.R.D. 740, 742-43 (E.D.Mo.1983); 1970 Notes to FRCP 26 at ¶¶33, 41, pp. 1192, 1193, this book; *see also* ***House v. Combined Ins.***, 168 F.R.D. 236, 245 (N.D.Iowa 1996) (under FRCP 26(b)(4), party has "free consultation privilege" for experts who were consulted but never designated). *See generally* 6 *Moore's Federal Practice 3d* §26.80[2] (discussing discovery of facts and opinions of specially retained consulting experts). Generally, information about consulting-only experts is not discoverable. *See* FRCP 26(b)(4)(D).

PRACTICE TIP

To protect the status of a consulting-only expert, do not let the consulting expert view the site of the accident or examine the physical evidence in the case; do not let the consulting expert's work be reviewed by the testifying expert; and do not let the consulting expert interact with the testifying expert. Keep separate files for each expert, and keep a log of all documents reviewed by each expert.

---

(1) What can be discovered.

(a) General rule – no discovery. Generally, no information about a consulting-only expert is discoverable; thus, there are no discovery tools that can be used to secure information about them. *See* FRCP 26(b)(4)(D); ***USM Corp. v. American Aerosols, Inc.***, 631 F.2d 420, 424 (6th Cir.1980); ***Ager v. Jane C. Stormont Hosp. & Training Sch. for Nurses***, 622 F.2d 496, 503 (10th Cir.1980).

(b) Exceptions.

[1] Identifying relationship. A party may need to reveal its relationship with any consulting-only experts and provide a privilege log for any documents being withheld that were generated as a result of the consultation. *See* FRCP 26(b)(5)(A); ***Eisai Co. v. Teva Pharms. USA, Inc.***, 247 F.R.D. 440, 442 (D.N.J. 2007); ***Queen's Univ. v. Kinedyne Corp.***, 161 F.R.D. 443, 446-47 (D.Kan.1995). The courts disagree over the requisite showing for the requesting party to obtain access to the consulting-only expert's identity. *See* ***In re Welding Fume***

Prods. Liab. Litig., 534 F.Supp.2d 761, 767 (N.D.Ohio 2008). *Compare* ***Eisai Co.***, 247 F.R.D. at 442 (consulting-only expert's identity can be obtained on simple showing of relevance), *and* ***Baki v. B.F. Diamond Constr. Co.***, 71 F.R.D. 179, 182 (D.Md.1976) (consulting-only expert's identity can be obtained without showing of exceptional circumstances), *with* ***Ager***, 622 F.2d at 503 (consulting-only expert's identity can be obtained on showing of exceptional circumstances), *and* ***In re Sinking of Barge "Ranger I"***, 92 F.R.D. 486, 488 (S.D.Tex.1981) (same).

[2] Facts & opinions. If the requesting party can prove exceptional circumstances, it is entitled to obtain the facts known and opinions held by the consulting-only expert through interrogatories, oral depositions, or depositions by written questions. *See* FRCP 26(b)(4)(D)(ii). An exceptional circumstance is the requesting party's basic lack of ability to discover the equivalent information. ***Delcastor***, 108 F.R.D. at 409; *see* FRCP 26(b)(4)(D). The following are examples of exceptional circumstances that allowed for the discovery of consulting-only experts:

- The requesting party showed that the object at issue had been destroyed or had deteriorated after the consulting-only expert observed it but before the requesting party's expert had an opportunity to observe it. ***Ager***, 622 F.2d at 503 n.8; ***Spearman Indus. v. St. Paul Fire & Mar. Ins.***, 128 F.Supp.2d 1148, 1152 (N.D.Ill.2001); ***Disidore v. Mail Contractors, Inc.***, 196 F.R.D. 410, 417 (D.Kan.2000).

- The requesting party showed that there were no other available experts in the same field or subject area. ***Ager***, 622 F.2d at 503 n.8; ***Spearman Indus.***, 128 F.Supp.2d at 1152; ***Bailey v. Meister Brau, Inc.***, 57 F.R.D. 11, 14 (N.D.Ill.1972).

- The requesting party showed that the withholding party had been "shopping" for expert opinions and thus tying up a number of experts with consulting agreements. *See* ***Coates v. AC&S, Inc.***, 133 F.R.D. 109, 110-11 (E.D.La.1990). *But see* ***Dominguez v. Syntax Labs.***, 149 F.R.D. 158, 163 (S.D.Ind.1993) (visiting two consulting experts for purpose of litigation is not expert-shopping).

(2) Procedures for securing discovery. Because no information about a consulting-only expert is usually discoverable, there are no formal or informal discovery tools available to secure information about them. *See* ***Durflinger v. Artiles***, 727 F.2d 888, 891 (10th Cir.1984) (party cannot circumvent discovery rules and contact consulting expert directly and request his report without going to court first). However, if a party establishes exceptional circumstances under FRCP 26(b)(4)(D)(ii), it can conduct limited discovery of the expert using interrogatories and depositions. FRCP 26(b)(4)(D). The discovery will probably be limited to facts known and opinions held by the expert and any reports or notes generated by the expert. *See* ***Disidore***, 196 F.R.D. at 418; *see, e.g.*, ***Braun v. Lorillard Inc.***, 84 F.3d 230, 235-36 (7th Cir.1996) (finding exceptional circumstances, court granted D's request that P's consulting-only expert produce test results).

2. Consulting expert + work reviewed = testifying expert. If a consulting expert's factual knowledge and opinions are considered by a testifying expert for purposes of forming an opinion, the facts and opinions are discoverable. *See* ***Dominguez***, 149 F.R.D. at 162; ***Delcastor***, 108 F.R.D. at 408; ***Eliasen v. Hamilton***, 111 F.R.D. 396, 399 (N.D.Ill.1986); ***Heitmann***, 98 F.R.D. at 742-43; 6 *Moore's Federal Practice 3d* §26.80[2].

(1) What can be discovered. A party is entitled to obtain any reports, notes, or other records created by a consulting expert and considered by a testifying expert. ***Johnson v. Gmeinder***, 191 F.R.D. 638, 647 (D.Kan. 2000); ***Delcastor***, 108 F.R.D. at 408; ***Eliasen***, 111 F.R.D. at 399; ***Heitmann***, 98 F.R.D. at 742-43; 6 *Moore's Federal Practice 3d* §26.80[2]. This information should be provided in the expert disclosures from the testifying expert. *See* FRCP 26(a)(2). See "Procedures for securing discovery," §4.1.2(2), this page. Because discovery is limited to the facts and opinions actually considered by the testifying expert (whether relied on or not), the consulting expert still retains the protections of FRCP 26(b)(4)(D) for all other facts known or opinions held that were not considered. ***Eliasen***, 111 F.R.D. at 399.

(2) Procedures for securing discovery. If a consulting expert's work has been considered by a retained testifying expert, that information will usually be secured through the testifying expert's disclosures under FRCP 26(a)(2)(B)(ii). See "Information considered," §3.1.1(1)(e), p. 517.

3. Consulting expert + facts = fact witness. A consulting expert who obtained knowledge about the case either firsthand or in some way other than in consultation about the case (i.e., not in anticipation of litigation or preparation for trial) is discoverable as a fact witness. *See* ***Rocky Mountain Nat. Gas Co. v. Cooper Indus.***, 166 F.R.D. 481, 482 (D.Colo.1996); ***Sullivan v. Sturm, Ruger & Co.***, 80 F.R.D. 489, 491 (D.Mont.1978); ***Barkwell v. Sturm Ruger Co.***, 79 F.R.D. 444, 446-47 (D.Alaska 1978). Examples include consultants who investigated the scene of an accident or who were present at the scene of an accident as it occurred. *See* ***Battle v. Memorial Hosp.***, 228 F.3d 544, 551-52 (5th Cir.2000); ***Delcastor***, 108 F.R.D. at 408; 1970 Notes to FRCP 26 at ¶33, p. 1192, this book. However, if the consulting expert merely examined a photograph of the accident site at the party's request, that expert is not discoverable as a fact witness. *Cf.* ***Agron v. Trustees of Columbia Univ.***, 176 F.R.D. 445, 448 (S.D.N.Y.1997) (testifying expert does not become fact witness merely because he learned facts and formed opinions through personal observations).

(1) What can be discovered. A party is entitled to obtain the same information from a consulting expert who has knowledge of facts as it can obtain from a fact witness. ***Rocky Mountain***, 166 F.R.D. at 482; ***Sullivan***, 80 F.R.D. at 491; ***Barkwell***, 79 F.R.D. at 446. See "What can be discovered," §3.1.2(1), p. 520.

(2) Procedures for securing discovery. The discovery procedures available to secure information from a consulting expert who has firsthand knowledge of facts are the same as those for securing information from retained testifying-only experts with knowledge of facts. See "Procedures for securing discovery," §3.1.2(2), p. 521.

§4.2 Nonretained. A nonretained consulting expert (also called an "informally consulted" expert) is an expert who has been consulted in preparation for trial but has not been retained or specially employed in anticipation of litigation. ***Ager v. Jane C. Stormont Hosp. & Training Sch. for Nurses***, 622 F.2d 496, 500-01 (10th Cir.1980); *see* ***Eisai Co. v. Teva Pharms. USA, Inc.***, 247 F.R.D. 440, 442 (D.N.J.2007). The status of an expert as "informally consulted" must be determined on a case-by-case basis, and the courts consider the following factors when making that determination: (1) the manner in which the consultation was initiated, (2) the nature, type, and extent of information or material provided to, or determined by, the expert in connection with her review, (3) the duration and intensity of the consultative relationship, and (4) the terms of the consultation, if any, such as payment, confidentiality of test data, or opinions. ***Ager***, 622 F.2d at 501; ***Ngo v. Standard Tools & Equip., Co.***, 197 F.R.D. 263, 266 (D. Md.2000); ***Healy v. Counts***, 100 F.R.D. 493, 496 (D.Colo.1984).

1. What can be discovered. No information about an informally consulted expert is discoverable from a party—not the expert's identity, mental impressions, opinions, or work product. ***Ager***, 622 F.2d at 501; *see* ***Eisai Co.***, 247 F.R.D. at 442.

2. Procedures for securing discovery. The discovery procedures available to secure information relating to nonretained consulting experts depend on whether the discovery is sought from the party or the expert.

(1) Discovery from party. Because no information about a nonretained consulting expert is discoverable from a party, there are no discovery tools available to secure information about them.

(2) Discovery from nonretained consulting expert. Although nonretained consulting experts cannot be discovered from a party, they can be discovered using independent investigative methods. ***Procter & Gamble Co. v. Haugen***, 184 F.R.D. 410, 413 (D.Utah 1999). Once discovered, a party can use the same discovery procedures used to obtain information from nonretained testifying experts. See "Nonretained," §3.2, p. 522.

§5. SUPPLEMENTING EXPERT DISCOVERY

The party must supplement expert disclosures when required under FRCP 26(e). FRCP 26(a)(2)(E); ***Morel v. Daimler-Chrysler Corp.***, 259 F.R.D. 17, 20 (D.P.R.2009). See "Supplementing Discovery," ch. 6-A, §11, p. 438. A party must supplement expert discovery by supplementing or correcting information if any of the previously disclosed information was incomplete or incorrect. *See* FRCP 26(e); ***English v. District of Columbia***, 651 F.3d 1, 12 (D.C.Cir. 2011). The party cannot, however, offer new expert opinions by alleging that they are supplementation. *See* ***Sierra Club v. Cedar Point Oil Co.***, 73 F.3d 546, 571 (5th Cir.1996); ***Solaia Tech. v. ArvinMeritor, Inc.***, 361 F.Supp.2d 797, 806 (N.D.Ill.2005).

NOTE

Drafts of expert reports and FRCP 26(a)(2)(C) disclosures are protected as work product under FRCP 26(b)(4)(B). 2010 Notes to FRCP 26 at ¶¶1, 9, p. 1172, this book. See "Drafts of report," §3.1.1(2)(a), p. 518; "Generally," §3.2.2(1), p. 523. This protection applies to drafts of any supplementation of those reports or disclosures. 2010 Notes to FRCP 26 at ¶9, p. 1172, this book.

§5.1 Supplementing retained-expert discovery.

1. Expert report. A party must supplement an expert report by the time the party's pretrial disclosures are due, which is usually at least 30 days before trial. FRCP 26(e)(2); *see* FRCP 26(a)(2)(B), (a)(3)(B); ***Reid v. Lockheed Martin Aeronautics Co.***, 205 F.R.D. 655, 662 (N.D.Ga.2001). For a discussion of how to compute backward-counted deadlines, see "Computing Deadlines," ch. 1-C, §6, p. 23. An expert's deposition testimony either concerning matters not disclosed in her report or correcting information contained in the report may qualify as an FRCP 26(e)(1) supplementation. ***Ways v. City of Lincoln***, 206 F.Supp.2d 978, 988-89 (D.Neb.2002); ***Tucker v. Ohtsu Tire & Rubber Co.***, 49 F.Supp.2d 456, 460 (D.Md.1999); 1993 Notes to FRCP 26 at ¶42, p. 1187, this book.

2. Deposition testimony. A party must supplement an expert's deposition by the time the party's pretrial disclosures are due, which is normally at least 30 days before trial. FRCP 26(e)(2); *see* FRCP 26(a)(3)(B); ***Reid***, 205 F.R.D. at 662. For a discussion of how to compute backward-counted deadlines, see "Computing Deadlines," ch. 1-C, §6, p. 23.

3. Response to challenge. A party should supplement its expert's report in response to any assertions by opposing experts that there are gaps in the expert's logic. ***Miller v. Pfizer, Inc.***, 356 F.3d 1326, 1332 (10th Cir. 2004).

§5.2 Supplementing nonretained-expert discovery. Generally, a party's duty to supplement written discovery about a nonretained expert is the same as for supplementing written discovery about fact witnesses. *See* FRCP 26(e)(1); *see, e.g.*, ***Duluth Lighthouse for the Blind v. C.G. Bretting Mfg.***, 199 F.R.D. 320, 324 (D.Minn.2000) (party timely supplemented interrogatories on lay-expert testimony by court-ordered discovery deadline). Therefore, a party must supplement any written discovery, including any FRCP 26(a)(2)(C) disclosures, in a timely manner or as ordered by the court. *See* FRCP 26(e)(1). See "Supplementation required," ch. 6-A, §11.1, p. 438. But a party is not required to supplement the deposition testimony of a nonretained testifying expert. ***Sullivan v. Glock, Inc.***, 175 F.R.D. 497, 502 (D.Md.1997). Even though FRCP 26(a)(2)(C) disclosures are to be supplemented in a timely manner, a party should supplement those disclosures by the time the party's pretrial disclosures are due, which is usually at least 30 days before trial. *See* FRCP 26(a)(3)(B); *cf.* FRCP 26(e)(2) (deadline for supplementing expert report under FRCP 26(a)(2)(B)). For a discussion of how to compute backward-counted deadlines, see "Computing Deadlines," ch. 1-C, §6, p. 23.

§6. DEADLINES FOR SECURING DISCOVERY FROM EXPERTS

§6.1 Deadlines to disclose testifying experts. See "Deadlines for expert disclosures," ch. 6-E, §5.1.1(2), p. 535.

§6.2 Deadlines to depose testifying experts.

1. Retained testifying experts. The deposition of a retained testifying expert cannot be taken until after the expert's report has been provided. FRCP 26(b)(4)(A).

2. Nonretained testifying experts. The deposition of a nonretained testifying expert may be taken according to the same rules as for deposing other nonparties. *See* FRCP 26(b)(4)(A). See "Notice of oral deposition," ch. 6-F, §3.2, p. 540.

§6.3 Deadlines to supplement. See "Supplementing Expert Discovery," §5, p. 527.

§7. EXPERT'S REPORT

Only a retained testifying expert must submit an expert report. FRCP 26(a)(2)(B); 2010 Notes to FRCP 26 at ¶6, p. 1172, this book; *see* ***Peña-Crespo v. Puerto Rico***, 408 F.3d 10, 13 (1st Cir.2005); ***Hamburger v. State Farm Mut. Auto. Ins.***, 361 F.3d 875, 882 (5th Cir.2004). By local rule, order, or written stipulation, the requirement of a written report may be waived for particular experts or imposed on additional persons who will provide opinions under FRE 702. 1993 Notes to FRCP 26 at ¶19, p. 1184, this book; *see* FRCP 26(a)(2)(B).

NOTE

Nonretained experts are not required to submit an expert report. See 2010 Notes to FRCP 26 at ¶6, p. 1172, this book (2010 amendment to FRCP 26 resolved disagreement that had prompted some courts to require reports from experts who were actually exempt from report requirement). See "Nonretained," §3.2, p. 522. These experts must make an FRCP 26(a)(2)(C) disclosure. See "FRCP 26(a)(2)(C) disclosure," §3.2.3(1)(a)[2], p. 524.

§7.1 Form of report.

1. Prepared by expert. The report must be prepared by the expert. FRCP 26(a)(2)(B). The report should be written in a manner that reflects the testimony to be given by the expert. ***Smith v. State Farm Fire & Cas. Co.***, 164 F.R.D. 49, 53 (S.D.W.Va.1995). Although the attorney who retained the expert can help in preparing the report so it complies with the requirements of FRCP 26(a)(2)(B), the attorney cannot write the report. ***Trigon Ins. v. U.S.***, 204 F.R.D. 277, 291-92 (E.D.Va.2001); *e.g.*, ***Bekaert Corp. v. City of Dyersburg***, 256 F.R.D. 573, 578-79 (W.D.Tenn. 2009) (expert testimony struck because expert did not substantially participate in preparation of report); *see* ***Butera v. District of Columbia***, 235 F.3d 637, 661 (D.C.Cir.2001).

2. Signed by expert. The report must be signed by the expert. FRCP 26(a)(2)(B).

§7.2 Contents of report.

1. Opinions & bases. The report must include a complete statement of all opinions the expert will express and the bases and reasons for them. FRCP 26(a)(2)(B)(i); *e.g.*, ***Smith v. State Farm Fire & Cas. Co.***, 164 F.R.D. 49, 53-54 (S.D.W.Va.1995) (expert reports that were a page or two long and referred to bases for opinions in vague terms, with few specific references, were insufficient); *see* ***Fiber Optic Designs, Inc. v. New England Pottery, LLC***, 262 F.R.D. 586, 595 (D.Colo.2009). A "preliminary" report is not sufficient. ***Smith***, 164 F.R.D. at 53-54; *see* ***Salgado v. General Motors Corp.***, 150 F.3d 735, 741 n.6 (7th Cir.1998).

2. Information considered. The report must include the facts or data considered by the expert in forming the opinions. FRCP 26(a)(2)(B)(ii); *see also* 2010 Notes to FRCP 26 at ¶¶3, 4, p. 1172, this book (2010 amendment to FRCP 26 changed rule's language to read "facts or data" instead of "data or other information"; amendment was intended to refocus expert disclosures toward materials of factual nature and away from theories or mental impressions of counsel). Generally, facts or data are "considered" when they have been received, reviewed, read, or authored by the expert before or in connection with forming her opinions. *See* ***Employees Committed for Justice v. Eastman Kodak Co.***, 251 F.R.D. 101, 104 (W.D.N.Y.2008); *see also* 2010 Notes to FRCP 26 at ¶4, p. 1172, this book (disclosure obligation extends to any facts or data "considered" in forming expert opinion, not only those "relied on"). In the report, the expert should include all materials considered, regardless of whether she ultimately relied on all the materials in forming her opinion. *See* ***In re Pioneer Hi-Bred Int'l***, 238 F.3d 1370, 1375 (Fed.Cir.2001); ***Employees Committed for Justice***, 251 F.R.D. at 104; ***Trigon Ins. v. U.S.***, 204 F.R.D. 277, 282-83 (E.D.Va.2001).

3. Exhibits. The report must include any exhibits that will be used to summarize or support the expert's opinion. FRCP 26(a)(2)(B)(iii); *see, e.g.*, ***Smith***, 164 F.R.D. at 54 (report was unsatisfactory because no exhibits were provided to support report's already vague opinions).

4. Résumé & bibliography. The report must include the expert's qualifications, including a list of all publications authored in the previous ten years. FRCP 26(a)(2)(B)(iv).

5. List of other cases. The report must include a list of other cases in which the expert testified as an expert at trial or by deposition during the previous four years. FRCP 26(a)(2)(B)(v). The list should include enough information for the opposing party to identify and locate each case, such as the case name and number and the court, county, and state where the case was filed. *See* ***Griffith v. General Motors Corp.***, 303 F.3d 1276, 1282-83 (11th Cir. 2002). The party does not need to produce copies of the expert's reports and transcripts of the expert's previous testimony as part of the disclosure. ***All W. Pet Sup. Co. v. Hill's Pet Prods. Div.***, 152 F.R.D. 634, 640 (D.Kan.1993).

6. Compensation. The report must include a statement of compensation to be paid to the expert for the study and testimony. FRCP 26(a)(2)(B)(vi).

§8. PAYING THE EXPERT

§8.1 Who must pay.

1. Retained testifying expert. The court may require a party seeking discovery from the opposing party's retained testifying expert to pay a reasonable fee for time spent responding to discovery. FRCP 26(b)(4)(E)(i); *see* ***Knight v. Kirby Inland Mar. Inc.***, 482 F.3d 347, 356 (5th Cir.2007); ***Research Sys. v. IPSOS Publicite***, 276 F.3d 914, 920 (7th Cir.2002); ***Rock River Comms. v. Universal Music Grp.***, 276 F.R.D. 633, 634-35 (C.D.Cal.2011); ***Schmidt v. Solis***, 272 F.R.D. 1, 2 (D.D.C.2010).

NOTE

Fees under FRCP 26(b)(4)(E) are limited to the discovery context and do not apply to expenses related to ***Daubert*** *hearings.* ***Knight****, 482 F.3d at 356.*

2. Nonretained testifying expert. A party seeking discovery from the opposing party's nonretained expert will generally be required to pay that expert for time spent responding to discovery. *See* 28 U.S.C. §1821; FRCP 26(b)(4)(E)(i); *see also* ***Rogers v. Penland***, 232 F.R.D. 581, 583 (E.D.Tex.2005) (when request for fees was made after final judgment, court determined it would be manifestly unjust to require party to pay fees for expert who was not called and who was excluded as unreliable under FRE 702). The courts are split on how much the expert must be paid. See "Nonretained expert," §8.2.2, p. 531.

3. Retained consulting expert. If a party is entitled to discover facts and opinions from an opposing party's consulting-only expert under FRCP 26(b)(4)(D), the court may require the party seeking discovery to pay a fair portion of the fees and expenses reasonably incurred by the opposing party in obtaining those facts and opinions. FRCP 26(b)(4)(E)(ii); *see* ***Research Sys.***, 276 F.3d at 920; ***S.A. Healy Co. v. Milwaukee Metro. Sewerage Dist.***, 154 F.R.D. 212, 213 (E.D.Wis.1994).

§8.2 How much must be paid.

NOTE

How much an expert is paid is resolved under federal law, even in cases based on diversity jurisdiction, because the issue is procedural rather than substantive. See ***First Nat'l Mortg. Co. v. Federal Rlty. Inv. Trust****, 631 F.3d 1058, 1070 (9th Cir.2011).*

1. Retained expert. FRCP 26(b)(4)(E)(i) allows for payment to an expert of a "reasonable fee" from a party seeking discovery from the expert.

(1) Payment for time spent. The expert can be paid for time spent doing the following:

(a) Responding to discovery. The expert can be paid for the actual time spent responding to discovery, including testifying at a deposition. *See* FRCP 26(b)(4)(E)(i); ***Rock River Comms. v. Universal Music Grp.***, 276 F.R.D. 633, 634 (C.D.Cal.2011).

(b) Traveling to deposition. The expert can be paid for time spent traveling to and from a deposition. *See* FRCP 26(b)(4)(E)(i); ***Haarhuis v. Kunnan Enters.***, 177 F.3d 1007, 1015-16 (D.C.Cir.1999); ***Rock River Comms.***, 276 F.R.D. at 637; ***Rogers v. Penland***, 232 F.R.D. 581, 582 (E.D.Tex.2005); 8A Wright, Miller & Marcus §2034 & n.22.

(c) Preparing for deposition. Courts disagree on whether the expert can be paid for time spent preparing for a deposition. ***Rock River Comms.***, 276 F.R.D. at 635; ***Fiber Optic Designs, Inc. v. New England Pottery, LLC***, 262 F.R.D. 586, 591 (D.Colo.2009); ***Rhee v. Witco Chem. Corp.***, 126 F.R.D. 45, 47 (N.D.Ill.1989). Some courts do not allow fees for preparation time. *E.g.*, ***Rock River Comms.***, 276 F.R.D. at 635; ***Benjamin v. Gloz***, 130 F.R.D. 455, 457 (D.Colo.1990). Some courts allow these fees. *E.g.*, ***Borel v. Chevron U.S.A. Inc.***, 265 F.R.D. 275, 277-78 (E.D.La.2010); ***Fiber Optic Designs***, 262 F.R.D. at 594; *see* ***Schmidt v. Solis***, 272 F.R.D. 1, 3-4 (D.D.C.2010) (court can consider whether parties had agreement about payment of fees for preparation time). And some courts allow fees for preparation time only when there are extenuating circumstances, such as a complex case in which there has been a considerable lapse of time between the expert's work on the case and the date of the deposition. ***M.T. McBrian, Inc. v. Liebert Corp.***, 173 F.R.D. 491, 493 (N.D.Ill.1997).

NOTE

Most courts do not allow fees for time spent reviewing or correcting the deposition transcript. See ***Rock River Comms.***, *276 F.R.D. at 635.*

(2) Reasonable fee. In evaluating whether a proposed expert fee is reasonable, courts have considered the following factors:

(a) The witness's area of expertise. ***Borel***, 265 F.R.D. at 276; ***Fiber Optic Designs***, 262 F.R.D. at 589; ***Coleman v. Dydula***, 190 F.R.D. 320, 324 (W.D.N.Y.1999).

(b) The education and training required to provide the expert insight sought. ***Borel***, 265 F.R.D. at 276; ***Fiber Optic Designs***, 262 F.R.D. at 589; ***Coleman***, 190 F.R.D. at 324.

(c) The prevailing rates for other comparably respected available experts. ***Borel***, 265 F.R.D. at 276; ***Fiber Optic Designs***, 262 F.R.D. at 589; ***Coleman***, 190 F.R.D. at 324.

(d) The nature, quality, and complexity of the discovery responses provided. ***Borel***, 265 F.R.D. at 276; ***Fiber Optic Designs***, 262 F.R.D. at 589; ***Coleman***, 190 F.R.D. at 324.

(e) The cost of living in the particular geographic area. ***Coleman***, 190 F.R.D. at 324.

(f) The fee being charged by the expert to the party who retained her. ***Borel***, 265 F.R.D. at 276; ***Coleman***, 190 F.R.D. at 324; *see also* ***Fiber Optic Designs***, 262 F.R.D. at 589-91 (except in extraordinary cases, surcharge from expert-witness agency should not be recoverable under FRCP 26(b)(4)(E)).

(g) The fees traditionally charged by the expert on similar matters. ***Borel***, 265 F.R.D. at 276; ***Fiber Optic Designs***, 262 F.R.D. at 589; ***Coleman***, 190 F.R.D. at 324.

(h) Any other factor likely to help the court balance the interests implicated by FRCP 26. ***Borel***, 265 F.R.D. at 276; ***Fiber Optic Designs***, 262 F.R.D. at 589; ***Coleman***, 190 F.R.D. at 324.

2. Nonretained expert. The courts are split on whether a nonretained testifying expert is entitled to a reasonable fee under FRCP 26(b)(4)(E)(i) or to the statutory witness fee under 28 U.S.C. §1821. *Compare* ***Mock v. Johnson***, 218 F.R.D. 680, 682-83 (D.Haw.2003) (nonretained expert witness is entitled to reasonable fee under FRCP 26(b)(4)(C)(i), now FRCP 26(b)(4)(E)(i)), *and* ***Grant v. Otis Elevator Co.***, 199 F.R.D. 673, 675-76 (N.D.Okla.2001) (same), *with* ***McDermott v. FedEx Ground Sys.***, 247 F.R.D. 58, 60-61 (D.Mass.2007) (nonretained expert witness is "fact witness" and should be compensated under 28 U.S.C. §1821), ***Demar v. U.S.***, 199 F.R.D. 617, 619-20 (N.D.Ill. 2001) (same), *and* ***Mangla v. University of Rochester***, 168 F.R.D. 137, 139 (W.D.N.Y.1996) (same). For a discussion of the statutory witness fee, see "Fees," ch. 1-H, §3.7, p. 52.

3. Consulting expert. FRCP 26(b)(4)(E)(ii) allows for the payment of a "fair portion" of the fees and expenses reasonably incurred by the party who retained the consulting expert in obtaining facts and opinions from the expert. No cases have defined what "fair portion" means in this context. *See, e.g.*, ***Williams v. E.I. du Pont de Nemours & Co.***, 119 F.R.D. 648, 651 (W.D.Ky.1987) (parties ordered to agree on what fair portion would be); ***Fauteck v. Montgomery Ward & Co.***, 91 F.R.D. 393, 399 (N.D.Ill.1980) (if P wanted electronic database, it would have to share D's expenses incurred in creating it).

§8.3 When payment is made. FRCP 26(b)(4)(E) does not specify when a party must demand payment of expert fees. *Compare* ***Ellis v. United Airlines, Inc.***, 73 F.3d 999, 1011-12 (10th Cir.1996) (motion for fees was untimely because it was filed 4½ months after court had entered final judgment and ordered each party to bear its own costs), *with* ***Louisiana Power & Light Co. v. Kellstrom***, 50 F.3d 319, 336 (5th Cir.1995) (application for costs filed nine months after original application for taxation of costs was timely). The court may either order the payment of fees as a condition of discovery or delay the payment of fees until after discovery is completed. 1970 Notes to FRCP 26 at ¶43, p. 1193, this book.

§8.4 Review. The district court's ruling on FRCP 26(b)(4)(E) fees is reviewed for abuse of discretion. ***Knight v. Kirby Inland Mar. Inc.***, 482 F.3d 347, 355 (5th Cir.2007).

E. MANDATORY DISCLOSURES

§1. GENERAL

§1.1 Rule. FRCP 26(a), (f).

§1.2 Purpose. The purpose of mandatory disclosures is to accelerate the exchange of basic information about the case and to eliminate the paperwork involved in requesting that information. 1993 Notes to FRCP 26 at ¶2, p. 1182, this book.

§1.3 Timetable & forms. Timetable, Discovery Status Sheet, p. 1579; ***O'Connor's Federal Civil Forms*** (2012), FORMS 6E.

§1.4 Other references. 8B Wright, Miller & Marcus, *Federal Practice & Procedure 3d* §§2281-2293 (2010 & Supp.2012); 7 *Moore's Federal Practice 3d* §§37.01-37.76 (2012); ABA, *Civil Discovery Standards* (2004).

§2. STAGES OF DISCLOSURES

FRCP 26(a) requires that certain information be voluntarily disclosed without a discovery request. Disclosures must be made in three distinct stages.

§2.1 Initial disclosures. Initial disclosures require the parties to exchange information about potential witnesses, documentary evidence, damages, and insurance early in the case. 1993 Notes to FRCP 26 at ¶1, p. 1182, this book; *see* FRCP 26(a)(1)(A). See "Initial Disclosures," §4, p. 533.

§2.2 Expert disclosures. Expert disclosures identify expert witnesses and provide a detailed written statement of the testimony that may be offered at trial through specially retained experts. 1993 Notes to FRCP 26 at ¶1, p. 1182, this book; *see* FRCP 26(a)(2). See "Expert Disclosures," §5, p. 534.

§2.3 Final pretrial disclosures. Final pretrial disclosures, which are made as the trial date approaches, identify the particular evidence that may be offered at trial. 1993 Notes to FRCP 26 at ¶1, p. 1182, this book; *see* FRCP 26(a)(3)(A). See "Final Pretrial Disclosures," §6, p. 536.

§3. FORM OF DISCLOSURES

§3.1 In writing & served. All discovery disclosures must be in writing and served. FRCP 26(a)(4).

§3.2 Signed. All discovery disclosures must be signed by an attorney of record or the party if pro se. *See* FRCP 26(a)(4), (g)(1). See "Discovery Certificates," ch. 6-A, §6, p. 420.

§3.3 No filing. Although final pretrial disclosures under FRCP 26(a)(3) are filed in the court, initial and expert disclosures under FRCP 26(a)(1) and (a)(2) must not be filed until they are used in the proceeding or unless the court orders filing. FRCP 5(d)(1). See "Filing Discovery," ch. 6-A, §10, p. 438.

§4. INITIAL DISCLOSURES

§4.1 Deadline. The initial disclosures ordinarily must be made within 14 days after the case-management conference required by FRCP 26(f), unless (1) a different time is set by stipulation or court order or (2) a party objects during the FRCP 26(f) conference, arguing that initial disclosures are not appropriate in the case, and states its objection in the proposed discovery plan. FRCP 26(a)(1)(C); *see* ***R&R Sails, Inc. v. Insurance Co. of Pa.***, 673 F.3d 1240, 1246 (9th Cir.2012). See "Case-Management Conference & Discovery Plan," ch. 5-A, §2, p. 289.

1. Deadline after party objects. The 14-day deadline does not apply if a party objects to disclosure during the case-management conference and states the objection in the discovery plan. 2000 Notes to FRCP 26 at ¶18, p. 1179, this book. When an objection is made, the court's ruling on the objection, which normally will be included in the FRCP 16(b) scheduling order, will determine what disclosures are to be made and will set the time for them. FRCP 26(a)(1)(C); *see* 2000 Notes to FRCP 26 at ¶18, p. 1179, this book.

2. Deadline for party joined after FRCP 26(f) conference. A party served or joined after the FRCP 26(f) conference must make its initial disclosures within 30 days after being served or joined, unless a different time is set by stipulation or court order. FRCP 26(a)(1)(D).

§4.2 Contents. FRCP 26(a)(1)(A) is the functional equivalent of court-ordered interrogatories and requires early disclosure, without the need for any request, of four types of information that were traditionally secured through formal discovery. *See* ***Harriman v. Hancock Cty.***, 627 F.3d 22, 29 (1st Cir.2010).

1. Witnesses. A party must provide the names and, if known, addresses and telephone numbers of certain potential witnesses. FRCP 26(a)(1)(A)(i). The party must also identify the subject matter of the information known to disclosed potential witnesses. *Id.* FRCP 26(a) limits required disclosure to individuals with discoverable information supporting a party's claims or defenses, and it specifically does not require disclosure of potential witnesses whose information is solely for impeachment purposes. FRCP 26(a)(1)(A)(i); *e.g.*, ***Gluck v. Ansett Austl. Ltd.***, 204 F.R.D. 217, 221-22 (D.D.C.2001) (essential inquiry was whether disclosing party intended to use witness; motion to compel was denied when P did not show that D intended to call any undisclosed individuals as witnesses); *see* ***Searles v. Van Bebber***, 251 F.3d 869, 877 (10th Cir.2001).

2. Documents, electronically stored information & tangible things. A party must disclose all documents, electronically stored information, and tangible things in its possession, custody, or control that may be used to support its claims or defenses, unless they would be used solely for impeachment purposes. FRCP 26(a)(1)(A)(ii); *see* 2006 Notes to FRCP 26 at ¶1, p. 1174, this book. See "Initial disclosures," ch. 6-C, §9.1, p. 498. FRCP 26(a)(1)(A)(ii) permits the parties to disclose documentary information in either of two ways:

(1) Produce copies. In cases involving a small amount of discovery, the disclosing party will probably prefer to produce copies of the discovery rather than describe it. However, if the party plans to assert a privilege, the discovery should be withheld and described in a privilege log. See "Provide privilege log," ch. 6-A, §8.3.2(2), p. 426.

(2) Describe by category & location. In cases involving a large amount of discovery, the disclosing party will probably prefer to describe the discovery by category and location. Once a description has been provided, the other party can proceed under FRCP 34 or by informal request to secure the documents. 1993 Notes to FRCP 26 at ¶8, p. 1183, this book.

3. Damages. The party must produce for inspection and copying any document or other material used in computing each category of damages claimed by the disclosing party, including those on the nature and extent of the damages, unless they are protected from disclosure. FRCP 26(a)(1)(A)(iii).

4. Insurance. The party must produce for inspection and copying any insurance agreements under which an insurance business may be liable either to satisfy all or part of a judgment or to indemnify or reimburse for payments made to satisfy the judgment. FRCP 26(a)(1)(A)(iv); *see* ***Gluck***, 204 F.R.D. at 222; ***Wegner v. Cliff Viessman, Inc.***, 153 F.R.D. 154, 160 (N.D.Iowa 1994).

§4.3 No excuses. A party must make disclosures even if (1) it has not finished investigating the case, (2) the other party's initial disclosures are insufficient, or (3) the other party has not made initial disclosures. FRCP 26(a)(1)(E). The party must make these disclosures based on the information then reasonably available after conducting an inquiry. FRCP 26(a)(1)(E); ***Sender v. Mann***, 225 F.R.D. 645, 650 (D.Colo.2004); *see* FRCP 26(g)(1); *see, e.g.*, ***In re Independent Serv. Orgs. Antitrust Litig.***, 168 F.R.D. 651, 653 (D.Kan.1996) (P did not meet its disclosure obligations when it did not perform a sufficient inquiry and did not disclose its employees who had discoverable information). The inquiry should be reasonable under the circumstances and should focus on the facts alleged in the pleadings. ***Sender***, 225 F.R.D. at 651; ***Dixon v. CertainTeed Corp.***, 164 F.R.D. 685, 691 (D.Kan.1996). The inquiry does not require an exhaustive search. ***Sender***, 225 F.R.D. at 651; ***Dixon***, 164 F.R.D. at 691. *But see* ***In re Independent Serv. Orgs.***, 168 F.R.D. at 654 (court remanded for P to complete exhaustive inquiry or file affidavit explaining noncompliance).

§4.4 Modification of initial-disclosures requirement. A district cannot opt out of the initial-disclosure requirement by local rule or by informal standing orders from an individual judge or court. 2000 Notes to FRCP 26 at ¶7, p. 1178, this book; *see* FRCP 26(a). However, the court can enter a case-specific order to exclude or modify initial disclosures, or the parties can agree to forgo disclosures. 2000 Notes to FRCP 26 at ¶7, p. 1178, this book.

§4.5 Proceedings exempt from initial disclosures. The following categories of proceedings are exempt from the initial-disclosure requirement: (1) an action for review on an administrative record, (2) a forfeiture action in rem arising from a federal statute, (3) a habeas corpus petition or other challenge to a criminal conviction or sentence, (4) an action by a pro se prisoner, (5) an action to enforce or quash an administrative summons or subpoena, (6) an action by the United States to recover benefit payments, (7) an action by the United States to collect on a federally guaranteed student loan, (8) a proceeding ancillary to a proceeding in another court, and (9) an action to enforce an arbitration award. FRCP 26(a)(1)(B). The court, however, can order the exchange of information similar to the initial-disclosure requirement in the scheduling order. 2000 Notes to FRCP 26 at ¶7, p. 1178, this book.

§5. EXPERT DISCLOSURES

§5.1 Procedure. The disclosure of testifying experts is accomplished by furnishing the information about the experts, including identifying the expert and providing either a written report of a retained testifying expert's opinions or a summary disclosure of a nonretained testifying expert's opinions. *See* FRCP 26(a)(2)(A)-(a)(2)(C); ***Reese v. Herbert***, 527 F.3d 1253, 1265 (11th Cir.2008). See "Testifying Experts," ch. 6-D, §3, p. 516.

1. Making disclosure. FRCP 26(a)(2)(D) establishes a schedule for making initial disclosures about testifying experts. The sequence of the expert disclosures and the deadlines for making them may be directed by court order. If the FRCP 16(b) scheduling order does not address the sequence and timing of expert disclosures, a party must designate its testifying experts and supply the information required under FRCP 26(a)(2)(A), (a)(2)(B), and (a)(2)(C) in the following sequence and within the following time periods:

(1) Sequence of expert disclosures. FRCP 26(a)(2)(D) provides for simultaneous disclosure of testifying experts. *See* ***Pfohl Bros. Landfill Site Steering Cmte. v. Pfohl Enters.***, 187 F.R.D. 462, 465 (W.D.N.Y. 1999); *see also* ***Sierra Club v. Cedar Point Oil Co.***, 73 F.3d 546, 569-70 & n.39 (5th Cir.1996) (court order setting discovery schedule that tracked language of FRCP 26(a)(2)(C), now FRCP 26(a)(2)(D), appeared to call for simultaneous disclosure of reports because it did not direct one party to submit reports first). The court may enter an FRCP 16(b) scheduling order that requires the party with the burden of proof on an issue to disclose its expert testimony

before other parties are required to make their disclosures about the issue. 1993 Notes to FRCP 26 at ¶15, p. 1184, this book; *see also* ABA, *Civil Discovery Standards*, at 42 (P should disclose expert first, followed by D's disclosure, followed by P's rebuttal).

(2) Deadlines for expert disclosures.

(a) Expert disclosures. Expert disclosures under FRCP 26(a)(2) must be made by the date set by the court or stipulated by the parties, or at least 90 days before the date set for trial or for the case to be ready for trial. FRCP 26(a)(2)(D)(i); ***Robinson v. Missouri Pac. R.R.***, 16 F.3d 1083, 1089 n.6 (10th Cir.1994); *see, e.g.*, ***Sherrod v. Lingle***, 223 F.3d 605, 612-13 (7th Cir.2000) (court order setting deadline for "all discovery" included deadline for disclosure of expert reports). For a discussion of how to compute backward-counted deadlines, see "Computing Deadlines," ch. 1-C, §6, p. 23.

NOTE

Until the court sets a date by which the parties must identify their trial experts, the parties are entitled to the protection of FRCP 26(b)(4)(D), under which no information about the expert is discoverable. See ***Moore U.S.A. Inc. v. Standard Register Co.***, *206 F.R.D. 72, 75 (W.D.N.Y. 2001). See "Consulting-only expert," ch. 6-D, §4.1.1, p. 525.*

(b) Rebuttal experts. If the expert testimony is for rebuttal only, the party must disclose the testimony within 30 days after disclosure of the other party's witness on the same subject matter. FRCP 26(a)(2)(D)(ii); ***Hester v. CSX Transp.***, 61 F.3d 382, 388 n.11 (5th Cir.1995). The deadline applies to experts providing full expert reports under FRCP 26(a)(2)(B) and experts providing FRCP 26(a)(2)(C) disclosures. 2010 Notes to FRCP 26 at ¶8, p. 1172, this book.

2. Changing designation. An expert who has been designated as a testifying expert can be redesignated as a consulting expert. *See* ***Durflinger v. Artiles***, 727 F.2d 888, 891 (10th Cir.1984); *see also* ***In re Shell Oil Refinery***, 132 F.R.D. 437, 440 (E.D.La.1990) (party can change expert's designation anytime before deadline to exchange witness lists), *modified on other grounds*, 134 F.R.D. 148 (E.D.La.1990). For a discussion of the effect of changing the designation, see "Testifying expert + de-designation = consulting expert," ch. 6-D, §3.1.3, p. 521.

§5.2 Contents. The expert disclosures include (1) the identity of the testifying experts and (2) for each expert, either a written report or an FRCP 26(a)(2)(C) disclosure. *See* FRCP 26(a)(2)(A)-(a)(2)(C).

1. Identity. The expert disclosure should identify each expert who may be used at trial to present evidence under FRE 702, 703, or 705. FRCP 26(a)(2)(A); *see* 2010 Notes to FRCP 26 at ¶7, p. 1172, this book. See "Identity," ch. 6-D, §3.1.1(1)(a), p. 517; "Identity," ch. 6-D, §3.2.3(1)(a)[1], p. 524.

NOTE

If an expert is only going to testify at a hearing (e.g., a ***Daubert*** *hearing), the expert does not need to be identified in the expert disclosures. See* ***Arble v. State Farm Mut. Ins.***, *272 F.R.D. 604, 607 (D.N.M.2011) (FRCP 26(a)(2)(A) applies only when expert is testifying at trial). But if the expert is not identified in the expert disclosures, the expert cannot later testify at trial. Id.*

2. Report or disclosure. The expert disclosure should include a full written report or an FRCP 26(a)(2)(C) disclosure. FRCP 26(a)(2)(B), (a)(2)(C). The purpose of requiring a report or a disclosure is to eliminate unfair surprise to the opposing party. *See* ***Sylla-Sawdon v. Uniroyal Goodrich Tire Co.***, 47 F.3d 277, 284 (8th Cir.1995) (written report).

(1) Written report – retained expert. Unless otherwise stipulated or ordered by the court, each party must produce a report prepared and signed by each retained testifying expert and containing the following information:

(a) A complete statement of all opinions the expert will express and the bases and reasons for them. FRCP 26(a)(2)(B)(i). See "Subject of testimony," ch. 6-D, §3.1.1(1)(c), p. 517; "Opinions," ch. 6-D, §3.1.1(1)(d), p. 517.

(b) The facts or data considered by the expert in forming the opinions. FRCP 26(a)(2)(B)(ii). See "Information considered," ch. 6-D, §3.1.1(1)(e), p. 517; "Information considered," ch. 6-D, §7.2.2, p. 529.

(c) Any exhibits that will be used to summarize or support the opinions. FRCP 26(a)(2)(B)(iii). See "Materials used," ch. 6-D, §3.1.1(1)(f), p. 517.

(d) The expert's qualifications, including a list of all publications authored in the previous ten years. FRCP 26(a)(2)(B)(iv). See "Résumé & bibliography," ch. 6-D, §3.1.1(1)(g), p. 517.

(e) A list of other cases in which the witness has testified as an expert at trial or by deposition during the previous four years. FRCP 26(a)(2)(B)(v). See "List of other cases," ch. 6-D, §3.1.1(1)(h), p. 517.

(f) A statement of the compensation to be paid for the study and testimony in the case. FRCP 26(a)(2)(B)(vi). See "Compensation," ch. 6-D, §3.1.1(1)(i), p. 518.

(2) FRCP 26(a)(2)(C) disclosure – nonretained testifying expert. Unless otherwise stipulated or ordered by the court, each party must produce an FRCP 26(a)(2)(C) disclosure for each expert who is not required to provide a written report under FRCP 26(a)(2)(B). The FRCP 26(a)(2)(C) disclosure must contain the following information:

(a) The subject matter the expert is expected to testify on under FRE 702, 703, or 705. FRCP 26(a)(2)(C)(i). See "FRCP 26(a)(2)(C) disclosure," ch. 6-D, §3.2.3(1)(a)[2][a], p. 524.

(b) A summary of the facts and opinions the expert is expected to testify on. FRCP 26(a)(2)(C)(ii). See "FRCP 26(a)(2)(C) disclosure," ch. 6-D, §3.2.3(1)(a)[2][b], p. 524.

§6. FINAL PRETRIAL DISCLOSURES

§6.1 Deadline. The parties must make their final pretrial disclosures at least 30 days before trial, unless the evidence is to be used solely for impeachment purposes. FRCP 26(a)(3)(B); ***Hernandez-Torres v. Intercontinental Trading, Inc.***, 158 F.3d 43, 49 (1st Cir.1998). For a discussion of how to compute backward-counted deadlines, see "Computing Deadlines," ch. 1-C, §6, p. 23. These disclosures must be promptly filed in the court. FRCP 26(a)(3)(A); 2000 Notes to FRCP 26 at ¶20, p. 1180, this book.

§6.2 Contents. FRCP 26(a)(3)(A) requires disclosure of the following:

1. Witness identity. The name, address, and telephone number of (1) each person the party expects to call as a witness and (2) each person the party might call as a witness if the need arises. FRCP 26(a)(3)(A)(i); *see* ***D'Onofrio v. SFX Sports Grp.***, 247 F.R.D. 43, 53 (D.D.C.2008).

2. Deposition witness identity. The designation of witnesses whose testimony is expected to be presented by deposition. FRCP 26(a)(3)(A)(ii). If the deposition was not taken stenographically, the party must provide a transcript of the pertinent portions of the deposition testimony. *Id.*; *see* ***Tilton v. Capital Cities/ABC, Inc.***, 115 F.3d 1471, 1478 (10th Cir.1997).

3. Document identity. An identification of each document or exhibit, including summaries of other evidence, that (1) the party expects to offer as evidence and (2) the party might offer if the need arises. FRCP 26(a)(3)(A)(iii).

4. Not impeachment evidence. A party does not need to disclose evidence if the material is to be used at trial solely for impeachment purposes. FRCP 26(a)(3)(A); ***DeBiasio v. Illinois Cent. R.R.***, 52 F.3d 678, 686 (7th Cir.1995).

CAUTION

*Although FRCP 26(a)(3)(A) does not require disclosure of evidence to be used solely for impeachment purposes, disclosure of such evidence may be required by local rule. 1993 Notes to FRCP 26 at ¶20, p. 1184, this book; e.g., Local Rules Tex. (E.D.), Appendix D, §H (exhibits used solely for impeachment purposes must be identified in pretrial order). Also, there is a risk that the court will determine that the evidence is not solely for impeachment purposes and exclude it. E.g., **Wilson v. AM Gen. Corp.**, 167 F.3d 1114, 1122 (7th Cir.1999) (court denied motion to add allegedly impeachment-only witnesses to trial witness list when witnesses could testify to primary part of D's defense).*

§6.3 Objections to pretrial disclosures. To expedite the presentation of evidence at trial and eliminate the need for trial witnesses to provide foundation testimony for uncontested documentary evidence, objections to some types of pretrial disclosures must be filed and served before trial. FRCP 26(a)(3)(B); *see* ***Drexel Heritage Furnishings, Inc. v. Furniture USA, Inc.***, 200 F.R.D. 255, 258 (M.D.N.C.2001); 1993 Notes to FRCP 26 at ¶25, p. 1185, this book.

1. Deadline for objections. Objections to the opposing party's pretrial disclosures must be served and promptly filed within 14 days after the disclosures are made, unless the court orders otherwise. FRCP 26(a)(3)(B).

2. Required objections. Each party must serve and promptly file the following objections:

(1) Objections to the use under FRCP 32(a) of a deposition designated by another party under FRCP 26(a)(3)(A)(ii). FRCP 26(a)(3)(B).

(2) Objections (and the grounds for them) that may be made to the admissibility of documents, exhibits, or other materials identified under FRCP 26(a)(3)(A)(iii). FRCP 26(a)(3)(B).

3. Preserves right to object. The list of objections neither constitutes the making of objections nor requires the court to rule on them. 1993 Notes to FRCP 26 at ¶25, p. 1185, this book. The list simply preserves the party's right to make the objections at trial. *Id.* However, the court may treat the objections as a motion in limine and rule on them before trial. *Id.*

4. Waiver of objection. An objection not made, except for one under FRE 402 or 403, is waived unless the omission is excused by the court for good cause. FRCP 26(a)(3)(B); *see* 1993 Notes to FRCP 26 at ¶25, p. 1185, this book.

§7. SANCTIONS

A party may move to compel disclosure and seek sanctions for nondisclosure. See "Motion to Compel Discovery," ch. 6-A, §14, p. 444; "Sanctions for refusing to disclose," ch. 6-A, §15.5.2, p. 451.

§7.1 Barring evidence. If a party does not provide information or identify a witness as required by FRCP 26(a) or (e), the party cannot use that information or testimony in a motion, at a hearing, or at trial, unless the party was substantially justified or the nondisclosure is harmless. FRCP 37(c)(1); ***R&R Sails, Inc. v. Insurance Co. of Pa.***, 673 F.3d 1240, 1246 (9th Cir.2012); *see, e.g.*, ***Morel v. Daimler-Chrysler Corp.***, 259 F.R.D. 17, 20-21 (D.P.R.2009) (D's post-discovery-deadline motion to substitute expert after original expert's death was substantially justified; late substitution was harmless because Ps were not prejudiced when they had been on notice for a year that original expert was ill and there was possible need for substitution). This prohibition should be automatic, without the need for a motion. 1993 Notes to FRCP 37 at ¶9, p. 1206, this book; 7 *Moore's Federal Practice 3d* §37.60[2][a]; *see* ***Hoffman v. Construction Prot. Servs.***, 541 F.3d 1175, 1180 (9th Cir.2008). However, when a party attempts to introduce information or a witness that was not disclosed, the opposing party should bring the nondisclosure to the court's attention by filing a motion in limine, a motion to exclude the evidence or testimony, or a motion to exclude in combination with a motion to compel. 7 *Moore's Federal Practice 3d* §37.60[2][a]; *see, e.g.*, ***Hamburger v. State Farm Mut.***

Auto. Ins., 361 F.3d 875, 879 (5th Cir.2004) (motion to exclude expert witness); ***Sommer v. Davis***, 317 F.3d 686, 691-92 (6th Cir.2003) (motion in limine); ***Derby v. Godfather's Pizza, Inc.***, 45 F.3d 1212, 1214-15 (8th Cir.1995) (same).

§7.2 Other sanctions. In addition to or instead of barring evidence, the court may, after a motion and a hearing, (1) order payment of the reasonable expenses, including attorney fees, caused by the nondisclosure, (2) inform the jury of the party's nondisclosure, and (3) impose other appropriate sanctions under FRCP 37(b)(2)(A)(i)-(b)(2)(A)(vi). FRCP 37(c)(1). See "Sanctions for refusing to disclose," ch. 6-A, §15.5.2, p. 451.

F. DEPOSITIONS

§1. GENERAL

§1.1 Rules. FRCP 26-32.

§1.2 Purpose. A deposition may be used to learn about and preserve sworn testimony before trial for use in court. Both parties and nonparties may be deposed.

§1.3 Timetable & forms. Timetable, Discovery Status Sheet, p. 1579; ***O'Connor's Federal Civil Forms*** (2012), FORMS 6F.

§1.4 Other references. 8A Wright, Miller & Marcus, *Federal Practice & Procedure 3d* §§2071-2084, 2101-2157 (2010 & Supp.2012); 6 *Moore's Federal Practice 3d* §§27.10-27.52 (2012); ABA, *Civil Discovery Standards* (2004); Dickerson, *Deposition Dilemmas: Vexatious Scheduling & Errata Sheets*, 12 Geo. J. Legal Ethics 1 (1998).

§2. TYPES OF DEPOSITIONS

§2.1 Oral deposition. An oral deposition is a discovery device that allows one party to ask questions orally of another party or of a witness. *Black's Law Dictionary* 505 (9th ed. 2009); *see* FRCP 30. The person who is deposed is called the deponent. *Black's Law Dictionary* 504 (9th ed. 2009). The deposition is conducted under oath outside the courtroom—usually in an attorney's office—and either a word-for-word transcript, a video recording, or both are made of the deposition. *See id.* at 505; *see also* ABA, *Civil Discovery Standards*, at 30 (depositions are normally held in nonpublic settings, such as attorney's or deponent's office).

§2.2 Deposition by written questions. A deposition by written questions is a discovery device that allows one party to ask questions in writing of another party or of a witness. *Black's Law Dictionary* 505 (9th ed. 2009); *see* FRCP 31. As with the oral deposition, the person being deposed is called the deponent and the deposition is conducted under oath outside the courtroom—usually at the deponent's place of business. A deposition by written questions is most commonly used to avoid the time, travel, and money constraints of an oral deposition. *See* ***DBMS Consultants Ltd. v. Computer Assocs.***, 131 F.R.D. 367, 370 (D.Mass.1990); *see, e.g.*, ***B&L Drilling Elec. v. Totco***, 87 F.R.D. 543, 545 (W.D.Okla.1978) (because of expense of taking oral depositions in Canada, court ordered D to conduct discovery first by deposition by written questions). See "Deposition by Written Questions," §5, p. 554.

§2.3 Deposition to perpetuate testimony. A deposition to perpetuate testimony is an examination by oral or written questions taken either before a lawsuit is filed or while a lawsuit is pending on appeal. *See* FRCP 27(a), (b). The purpose of a deposition to perpetuate testimony is to preserve any testimony that might be lost before suit is filed or before further postjudgment proceedings can be held. See "Deposition to Perpetuate Testimony," §6, p. 555.

§3. PROCEDURE FOR ORAL DEPOSITION

§3.1 Deposition of any person. Generally, a party may take the oral deposition of any person or party. FRCP 30(a)(1); ***Founding Ch. of Scientology v. Webster***, 802 F.2d 1448, 1451 (D.C.Cir.1986).

1. Leave of court not required. Ordinarily, a party does not need leave of court to take an oral deposition. FRCP 30(a)(1); ***Holloway v. Lockhart***, 813 F.2d 874, 880 n.3 (8th Cir.1987). Each side in the lawsuit (not each party) may take ten depositions. FRCP 30(a)(2)(A)(i). The ten-deposition limit includes both oral and written depositions.

FRCP 30(a)(2)(A)(i), 31(a)(2)(A)(i). In a multiparty case, the parties on each side are expected to confer and agree on the depositions to be taken. 1993 Notes to FRCP 30 at ¶5, p. 1197, this book.

2. Leave of court required. Leave of court to take a deposition is required in the following instances:

(1) Before filing suit. A party must obtain leave of court to take a deposition before filing suit or while an appeal is pending in anticipation of further proceedings in the district court. FRCP 27(a)(1), (b)(2). See "Deposition before suit is filed," §6.1, p. 555.

(2) Exceeding limit. A party must obtain leave of court to take more than ten oral or written depositions, unless the parties stipulate to additional depositions. FRCP 30(a)(2)(A)(i), 31(a)(2)(A)(i); ***Advanced Sterilization Prods. v. Jacob***, 190 F.R.D. 284, 286 & n.2 (D.Mass.2000); *see* FRCP 26(b)(2)(A) (limit may be changed by court order); *see, e.g.*, ***Andrews v. Fowler***, 98 F.3d 1069, 1080 (8th Cir.1996) (court did not abuse its discretion in denying leave for additional depositions). See "Modifying Discovery Procedures & Limits," ch. 6-A, §5, p. 419. If a party seeks leave, it should show why the depositions are necessary and that they are sought in good faith. *See* ***San Francisco Health Plan v. McKesson Corp.***, 264 F.R.D. 20, 21 (D.Mass.2010). If the court grants leave, it can place conditions on the additional depositions, including shifting the costs to the party taking the additional depositions. *See, e.g., id.* (when D sought leave for additional 11 depositions beyond already-stipulated-to 30 depositions, court denied leave for 2, granted leave for additional 9, and ordered that if D chose to take more than 5 of the additional depositions, D would pay reasonable costs for the additional 4).

(3) Deponent already deposed.

(a) Individual. A party must obtain leave of court to take the deposition of a person who has already been deposed in the case, unless the parties stipulate to another deposition of that person. FRCP 30(a)(2)(A)(ii), 31(a)(2)(A)(ii); ***Melhorn v. New Jersey Transit Rail Opers., Inc.***, 203 F.R.D. 176, 180 (E.D.Pa. 2001); *see, e.g.*, ***Polycarpe v. E&S Landscaping Serv.***, 275 F.R.D. 700, 701 (S.D.Fla.2011) (when parties cross-noticed second round of depositions of Ps and D, court held that parties impliedly stipulated to second depositions); *see also* ***Christy v. Pennsylvania Tpk. Comm'n***, 160 F.R.D. 51, 53 (E.D.Pa.1995) (burden is on person seeking to block deposition); ***Deines v. Vermeer Mfg.***, 133 F.R.D. 46, 48 (D.Kan.1990) (person who has already been deposed is not automatically entitled to protective order).

(b) Organization. A party generally must obtain leave of court to take the deposition of an organization or other business entity that has already been deposed under FRCP 30(b)(6). *See* ***Ameristar Jet Charter, Inc. v. Signal Composites, Inc.***, 244 F.3d 189, 192 (1st Cir.2001); ***State Farm Mut. Auto. Ins. v. New Horizont, Inc.***, 254 F.R.D. 227, 234-35 (E.D.Pa.2008). *But see* ***Quality Aero Tech. v. Telemetrie Elektronik, GmbH***, 212 F.R.D. 313, 319 (E.D.N.C.2002) (because FRCP 30(b)(6) depositions are different from depositions of individuals, leave of court is not always required for second deposition under FRCP 30(b)(6)). See "Naming organization," §3.2.2(2), p. 540.

(4) Before case-management conference. A party must obtain leave of court to take a deposition before the FRCP 26(f) case-management conference, unless the parties stipulate to a premature deposition or the deposing party certifies in the notice with supporting facts that the deponent is expected to leave the United States and will be unavailable for examination after that time. FRCP 30(a)(2)(A)(iii); *see* FRCP 31(a)(2)(A)(iii).

(5) Prisoner. A party must obtain leave of court if the deponent is confined in prison. FRCP 30(a)(2)(B), 31(a)(2)(B); *see* ***Moon v. Newsome***, 863 F.2d 835, 837 (11th Cir.1989).

3. Leave of court should not be granted. In most cases, the court should grant leave to depose a witness. The party seeking to block the deposition has the burden to show why leave should not be granted. *See, e.g.*, ***Christy***, 160 F.R.D. at 53 (party seeking to stop opponent from redeposing him did not show good cause for protective order under FRCP 26(b)(2), now FRCP 26(b)(2)(C)). The following circumstances justify the court denying leave to take a deposition:

(1) Deposition is unreasonably cumulative. The court should not permit the deposition if it determines that the deposition will be unreasonably cumulative or duplicative, or that the same information can be

obtained from some other source that is more convenient, less burdensome, or less expensive. FRCP 26(b)(2)(C)(i). Often, a court will allow a duplicative deposition but limit it to subjects not already covered. ***Christy***, 160 F.R.D. at 53.

(2) Ample opportunity for discovery. The court should not permit the deposition if the party seeking the deposition has had ample opportunity to obtain the information by discovery in the action. FRCP 26(b)(2)(C)(ii).

(3) Burden outweighs benefit. The court should not permit the deposition if it determines that the burden or expense of the deposition outweighs its likely benefit, considering the needs of the case, the amount in controversy, the parties' resources, the importance of the issues at stake, and the importance of the deposition in resolving the issues. FRCP 26(b)(2)(C)(iii); *see, e.g.*, ***Moore v. Armour Pharm.***, 927 F.2d 1194, 1198 (11th Cir.1991) (considering "cumulative impact" of repeated requests for testimony of federal AIDS researchers in upholding decision to quash subpoena under FRCP 45).

(4) Discovery deadline has passed. The court should not permit the deposition if it cannot be completed before the discovery deadline has passed. *See* ***In re Sulfuric Acid Antitrust Litig.***, 230 F.R.D. 527, 531 (N.D. Ill.2005).

§3.2 Notice of oral deposition. To take an oral deposition, the party must give reasonable written notice to every other party in the suit. FRCP 30(b)(1); *e.g.*, ***Lauson v. Stop-N-Go Foods, Inc.***, 133 F.R.D. 92, 94 (W.D.N.Y.1990) (notice must be written; even acknowledged oral notice is insufficient). The notice must state the time and place for the deposition and, if known, the name and address of each person to be deposed. The notice requirement is not mandatory if the attorney is not conducting a deposition but instead is taking interviews sworn under oath with a court reporter present to assist in trial preparation and investigation. ***Corley v. Rosewood Care Ctr., Inc.***, 142 F.3d 1041, 1052-53 (7th Cir.1998). If the party giving the notice fails to attend the deposition, a party that did attend may seek a court order compelling the noticing party to pay the reasonable expenses incurred by the attending party, including attorney fees. FRCP 30(g)(1). See "Noticing party did not attend or serve subpoena," ch. 6-A, §15.3.2(1)(b), p. 447.

1. No filing. The notice must not be filed until it is used in the proceeding or the court orders filing. *See* FRCP 5(d)(1). See "Filing Discovery," ch. 6-A, §10, p. 438.

2. Naming deponent.

(1) Naming person. When naming a person as the deponent, the party noticing the deposition must provide either the deponent's name and address or, if the deponent's name is unknown, a general description sufficient to identify the person or the particular class or group to which the person belongs. FRCP 30(b)(1).

(2) Naming organization. When naming a corporation, partnership, association, governmental agency, or other entity as the deponent, the party noticing the deposition may describe the subject matter for examination and allow the organization to designate one or more officers, directors, managing agents, or other consenting persons who are familiar with that subject matter. FRCP 30(b)(6). Alternatively, the party noticing the deposition may designate a specific officer, director, or managing agent of the corporate deponent. ***Sugarhill Records Ltd. v. Motown Record Corp.***, 105 F.R.D. 166, 169 (S.D.N.Y.1985); *see* FRCP 30(b)(6) (rule "does not preclude a deposition by any other procedure" allowed by FRCPs).

(a) Designating subject matter of testimony. If a party chooses to allow the organization to designate a representative, the party must describe with reasonable specificity the subject matter of the questions to be asked. FRCP 30(b)(6); ***Murphy v. Kmart Corp.***, 255 F.R.D. 497, 505-06 (D.S.D.2009). The party should include the following in its deposition notice:

[1] A concise identification of the designated areas of requested testimony. ***U.S. v. Taylor***, 166 F.R.D. 356, 360 (M.D.N.C.1996), *aff'd*, 166 F.R.D. 367 (M.D.N.C.1996); ***Mitsui & Co. v. Puerto Rico Water Res. Auth.***, 93 F.R.D. 62, 66 (D.P.R.1981); ABA, *Civil Discovery Standards*, at 37.

[2] A request that the organization (1) provide the names and titles of the persons designated to give testimony and (2) identify the subject matter on which each designated person will testify. FRCP 30(b)(6); ***Taylor***, 166 F.R.D. at 360; ***Mitsui & Co.***, 93 F.R.D. at 66; *see also* ABA, *Civil Discovery Standards*, at 37 (designations should be made by reasonable date before deposition). If the organization is a nonparty, the subpoena accompanying the deposition notice must inform the organization of its duty to make this designation. FRCP 30(b)(6).

(b) Designating representative. If a party chooses to designate a specific deponent as the representative of the organization, the party must determine whether the named deponent is an officer, director, or managing agent of the organization because the organization cannot be deposed through ordinary employees. *See* ***Moore v. Pyrotech Corp.***, 137 F.R.D. 356, 357 (D.Kan.1991); ***Sugarhill Records***, 105 F.R.D. at 169; ***Williams v. Lehigh Valley R.R.***, 19 F.R.D. 285, 286 (S.D.N.Y.1956); *see also* ***GTE Prods. v. Gee***, 115 F.R.D. 67, 68 (D.Mass.1987) (named employee who is officer, director, or managing agent of organization is regarded as representative). If the named deponent is not an officer, director, or managing agent but merely an employee, the examining party must treat the employee as an ordinary nonparty witness whose testimony cannot be regarded as that of the organization. *See* ***Sugarhill Records***, 105 F.R.D. at 169-171. Whether a person is an officer or director is usually clear by her title. *See id.* at 170. To determine whether a person is a managing agent, the courts have weighed the following factors:

[1] Does the individual possess general powers to exercise judgment and discretion in the organization's matters? *Id.*; 7 *Moore's Federal Practice 3d* §30.03[2].

[2] Can the individual be relied on to give testimony, at the organization's request, in response to the demand of the examining party? ***Sugarhill Records***, 105 F.R.D. at 170; 7 *Moore's Federal Practice 3d* §30.03[2].

[3] Does any person employed by the organization have more authority than the individual in the area of the information sought by the examining party? ***Sugarhill Records***, 105 F.R.D. at 170; *see also* ***In re Honda Am. Motor Co.***, 168 F.R.D. 535, 541 (D.Md.1996) (former employees cannot be managing agents of corporation).

[4] What are the general responsibilities of the individual for the matters involved in the litigation? ***Sugarhill Records***, 105 F.R.D. at 170.

[5] Can the individual be expected to identify with the interests of the organization? *Id.*; 7 *Moore's Federal Practice 3d* §30.03[2].

(c) Duties of organization. In response to the deposition notice, the organization must do all of the following:

[1] Designate person to testify. If a party chooses to allow the organization to designate a representative, the organization must identify and designate one or more people to testify about each subject area listed in the notice. FRCP 30(b)(6); ***Reilly v. NatWest Mkts. Grp.***, 181 F.3d 253, 268 (2d Cir.1999); ***FCC v. Mizuho Medy Co.***, 257 F.R.D. 679, 681 (S.D.Cal.2009); ***Poole v. Textron, Inc.***, 192 F.R.D. 494, 504 (D.Md.2000); *see* ***Murphy***, 255 F.R.D. at 506-07 (organization must identify person; it cannot allege that documents state its position). The persons designated must testify to the knowledge of the organization, not to their own knowledge. ***Calzaturficio S.C.A.R.P.A. v. Fabiano Shoe Co.***, 201 F.R.D. 33, 37 (D.Mass.2001); ***Poole***, 192 F.R.D. at 504; ***Taylor***, 166 F.R.D. at 361. The purpose of designating an organizational representative is to prevent "bandying," which is the practice of presenting for deposition employees who disclaim knowledge of facts that are clearly known by other employees and thus to the organization itself. ***Brazos River Auth. v. GE Ionics, Inc.***, 469 F.3d 416, 432-33 (5th Cir.2006); ***Cherrington Asia Ltd. v. A&L Underground, Inc.***, 263 F.R.D. 653, 661 (D.Kan.2010); ***Murphy***, 255 F.R.D. at 504. An organization can be sanctioned if it refuses to designate a person or if it designates someone without knowledge of the matters about which the organization will testify. ***Resolution Trust Corp. v. Southern Un. Co.***, 985 F.2d 196, 197 (5th Cir.1993); *see* ***Cherrington Asia***, 263 F.R.D. at 658; *cf.* ***Ecclesiastes 9:10-11-12, Inc. v. LMC Holding Co.***, 497 F.3d 1135, 1142 n.9, 1148 (10th Cir.2007) (under FRCP 41(b), case was dismissed as sanction when P willfully

avoided scheduling FRCP 30(b)(6) deposition for four months and when designated deponent died without being deposed). See "Not attending deposition," ch. 6-A, §15.3.2(1), p. 447.

NOTE

Whether an organization must produce a witness prepared to testify about its parent or subsidiary company depends on the control the deponent-organization has over the parent or subsidiary. See, e.g., ***Murphy****, 255 F.R.D. at 508-09 (organization required to produce witness because it had control over parent and sister companies; parent was created when organization merged with sister, and board of all three entities was identical). For a discussion of control, see "Possession, custody, or control," ch. 6-I, §3.4.2(3), p. 571. If an organization does not have an employee who is sufficiently knowledgeable of a parent or subsidiary, the organization can designate any person familiar with the relevant topics.* ***Murphy****, 255 F.R.D. at 509.*

[2] Identify areas of testimony. The organization may set out the matters on which each designated person will testify. FRCP 30(b)(6).

[3] Prepare witnesses. The organization must prepare the witnesses so they will give complete, knowledgeable, and binding answers on behalf of the organization. ***Poole***, 192 F.R.D. at 504; ***SEC v. Morelli***, 143 F.R.D. 42, 44 (S.D.N.Y.1992); ***Marker v. Union Fidelity Life Ins.***, 125 F.R.D. 121, 126 (M.D.N.C.1989); *see also* ***State Farm Mut. Auto. Ins. v. New Horizont, Inc.***, 250 F.R.D. 203, 212 (E.D.Pa.2008) (answers given during FRCP 30(b)(6) deposition are admissible against organization, but they are not judicial admissions absolutely binding on organization). The designated witness must be able to testify about facts within the organization's knowledge and about the organization's subjective beliefs and opinions. ***Paul Revere Life Ins. v. Jafari***, 206 F.R.D. 126, 127 (D.Md.2002); ***Taylor***, 166 F.R.D. at 361. The designated witness must review all documentation relating to the deposition topics. ***Prokosch v. Catalina Lighting, Inc.***, 193 F.R.D. 633, 639 (D.Minn.2000); *see* ***Fabiano Shoe***, 201 F.R.D. at 37 (organization must prepare deponents by having them review earlier fact-witness testimony as well as documents).

(d) Limits on scope of deposition. Whether an FRCP 30(b)(6) deposition requires a party to limit its cross-examination to the matters designated in the notice is an unsettled question. *Compare* ***FCC***, 257 F.R.D. at 682 (cross-examination not limited to matters identified in deposition notice), ***Cabot Corp. v. Yamulla Enters.***, 194 F.R.D. 499, 500 (M.D.Pa.2000) (cross-examination limited only by FRCP 26), *and* ***King v. Pratt & Whitney***, 161 F.R.D. 475, 476 (S.D.Fla.1995) (same), *aff'd*, 213 F.3d 646 (11th Cir.2000) (table case), *with* ***Paparelli v. Prudential Ins.***, 108 F.R.D. 727, 730 (D.Mass.1985) (cross-examination limited to matters identified in deposition notice).

3. Place for deposition. Generally, the person noticing the deposition selects the place for the deposition. ***Riley v. Murdock***, 156 F.R.D. 130, 131-32 (E.D.N.C.1994). If necessary, the court can specify the time and place for any deposition. *See* ***Redland Soccer Club, Inc. v. Department of Army***, 55 F.3d 827, 853 n.17 (3d Cir.1995); *see, e.g.*, ***Custom Form Mfg. v. Omron Corp.***, 196 F.R.D. 333, 336-37 (N.D.Ind.2000) (court ordered foreign corporation's agent to appear for deposition in United States).

(1) For specific parties.

(a) Plaintiff. The plaintiff's deposition should take place in the district where the litigation is pending, unless special circumstances are shown. ***Abdullah v. Sheridan Square Press, Inc.***, 154 F.R.D. 591, 592 (S.D.N.Y.1994); *see* 6 *Moore's Federal Practice 3d* §26.105[3][b].

(b) Defendant. The defendant's deposition should take place in the district of the defendant's residence, unless special circumstances are shown. ***Six W. Retail Acquisition, Inc. v. Sony Theatre Mgmt.***, 203 F.R.D. 98, 107 (S.D.N.Y.2001).

(c) Witness. The deposition of a witness should take place where the witness is located, unless special circumstances are shown. ***Work v. Bier***, 107 F.R.D. 789, 792 n.4 (D.D.C.1985).

(d) Organization. The deposition of an organizational representative should take place in the district of the organization's principal place of business, unless justice requires otherwise. ***Rapoca Energy Co. v. AMCI Exp. Corp.***, 199 F.R.D. 191, 193 (W.D.Va.2001); *see* ***Thomas v. International Bus. Machs.***, 48 F.3d 478, 483 (10th Cir.1995); ***Salter v. Upjohn Co.***, 593 F.2d 649, 651 (5th Cir.1979).

(2) By telephone or remote electronic means. To take a deposition by telephone or other remote electronic means, the party should secure a stipulation or a court order. FRCP 30(b)(4). Under FRCP 30(b)(4), a remote deposition takes place where the deponent answers the questions, which presents at least two problems. First, the oath should be administered to the deponent in person. FRCP 28(a)(1)(A); *see* ***Aquino v. Automotive Serv. Indus.***, 93 F.Supp.2d 922, 923-24 (N.D.Ill.2000) (officer must administer oath in person and be in presence of deponent during deposition); ***Jahr v. IU Int'l***, 109 F.R.D. 429, 433 (M.D.N.C.1986) (officer must administer oath in person unless parties stipulate or court orders otherwise). Second, if there is a problem with the deponent in another district, the deposing party must go to that district to compel answers or seek sanctions. FRCP 37(a)(1), (b)(1). FRCP 30(b)(4) contains no reference to FRCP 28(b), leading some courts to conclude that foreign depositions cannot be taken by telephone. *See* ***Jahr***, 109 F.R.D. at 432 n.3. *But see* ***U.S. v. Ruiz-Castro***, 92 F.3d 1519, 1532-33 (10th Cir.1996) (assuming that telephone deposition could be taken in Mexico, but holding that applicant had not satisfied requirements), *overruled on other grounds*, ***U.S. v. Flowers***, 464 F.3d 1127 (10th Cir.2006).

NOTE

If a party seeks leave to have a deposition conducted by telephone or other remote electronic means, the motion will usually be granted unless the party opposing leave can show that it will suffer prejudice if leave is granted. ***Rehau, Inc. v. Colortech, Inc.***, *145 F.R.D. 444, 446-47 (W.D.Mich.1993). But if the party seeking leave is a plaintiff-deponent who wants to be deposed by telephone or other remote electronic means, courts disagree on whether the party opposing leave still has the burden to show prejudice. See* ***Clinton v. California Dept. of Corr.***, *No. CIV S-05-1600-LKK-CMK-P (E.D.Cal.2009) (slip op.; 1-20-09). Compare* ***Clem v. Allied Van Lines Int'l***, *102 F.R.D. 938, 939-40 (S.D.N.Y.1984) (P-deponent had to show extreme hardship to explain why he should not have to appear for his deposition in forum where he filed suit), with* ***Rehau, Inc.***, *145 F.R.D. at 446-47 (P-deponents did not have to show extraordinary need for telephonic deposition; because opposing party did not show prejudice, P-deponents could be deposed by telephone).*

4. Reasonable notice. The rules require only reasonable notice, not a specific number of days, and reasonableness depends on the particular circumstances of each case. ***Hart v. U.S.***, 772 F.2d 285, 286 (6th Cir.1985); *see, e.g.*, ***FAA v. Landy***, 705 F.2d 624, 634-35 (2d Cir.1983) (four days' notice was reasonable when witness was discovered ten days before trial and opposing counsel did not make use of effective procedures available to block deposition); ***Lloyd v. Cessna Aircraft Co.***, 430 F.Supp. 25, 26 (E.D.Tenn.1976) (two workdays' notice to parties in Tennessee and Washington, D.C., of depositions scheduled to take place in California was not reasonable).

5. Subpoena. For the requirements for issuing subpoenas to compel nonparties to give testimony, see "Subpoenas Under FRCP 45," ch. 1-H, p. 47.

6. Recording method. The deposition notice must state the method for recording the testimony. FRCP 30(b)(3)(A). If the deponent is a nonparty, the subpoena must also state the method for recording the testimony. FRCP 45(a)(1)(B). The deposing party may select the recording method. *See* FRCP 30(b)(3). The deposing party pays the recording costs. ***Bogan v. Northwestern Mut. Life Ins.***, 152 F.R.D. 9, 11 (S.D.N.Y.1993). Any party may arrange to transcribe a deposition. FRCP 30(b)(3)(A).

(1) Audio or stenographic. A deposition may be recorded by audio or stenographic means. FRCP 30(b)(3)(A); ***Cherry v. Champion Int'l***, 186 F.3d 442, 448-49 (4th Cir.1999).

(2) Video. Video depositions are particularly appropriate if the witness will not be available to testify in court. *See* FRCP 30(b)(3)(A); ***Greenidge v. Ruffin***, 927 F.2d 789, 793 (4th Cir.1991). Video depositions are

now the preferred form of deposition. *See **Riley***, 156 F.R.D. at 131. They are superior to stenographic depositions because they convey the witness's full message in a way that helps the fact-finder assess the witness's credibility. *Id.*

(3) Additional recording methods. Any party may, on notice to the deponent and the other parties, designate another method for recording the testimony in addition to what is specified in the original notice. FRCP 30(b)(3)(B). For example, if a deposition notice states that the deposition is to be recorded by audio only, another party may give notice that the deposition will also be recorded by video. The party requesting the additional recording method pays the additional cost unless the court directs otherwise. *Id.*; ***Barber v. Ruth***, 7 F.3d 636, 645 (7th Cir.1993).

7. Production of documents.

(1) Notice to party. A deposition notice to a party may be accompanied by a request for production of documents and tangible things at the deposition. FRCP 30(b)(2); *see, e.g.*, ***Devaney v. Continental Am. Ins.***, 989 F.2d 1154, 1156 (11th Cir.1993) (P filed request for production along with deposition notice). The parties should agree ahead of time to have any requested documents or other information made available long enough before the deposition so they can be reviewed. ABA, *Civil Discovery Standards*, at 31.

NOTE

A party who wants a party-deponent to produce electronically stored information at the deposition must serve a separate request under FRCP 34. See FRCP 34(a)(1). FRCP 45, however, allows a party to combine a subpoena for a nonparty's attendance at a deposition with a request for production of electronically stored information. See FRCP 45(a)(1)(C).

(2) Notice to nonparty. A deposition notice to a nonparty may be accompanied by a subpoena for production of documents, electronically stored information, and tangible things under FRCP 45. *See* FRCP 30(b)(2), 45(c)(2)(A). If a subpoena for production is to be served on the deponent, the materials designated for production must be listed in the notice or in an attachment. FRCP 30(b)(2); *see* FRCP 45(a)(1)(C). For the requirements for issuing subpoenas to compel nonparties to produce documents, see "Subpoenas Under FRCP 45," ch. 1-H, p. 47.

§3.3 Taking deposition before authorized officer. Generally, a deposition must be taken before an authorized officer, but who the officer will be depends on whether the deposition is taken in the United States or in a foreign country. FRCP 28(a), (b).

1. In United States. A deposition in the United States must be taken before any of the following persons:

(1) An officer authorized to administer oaths by federal law. FRCP 28(a)(1)(A); *see **Jahr v. IU Int'l***, 109 F.R.D. 429, 433 (M.D.N.C.1986).

(2) An officer authorized to administer oaths by the law in the place of the deposition. FRCP 28(a)(1)(A); ***Hale v. U.S.***, 406 F.2d 476, 480 (10th Cir.1969).

(3) A person appointed by the court where the action is pending to administer oaths and take testimony. FRCP 28(a)(1)(B); ***Rice's Toyota World, Inc. v. Southeast Toyota Distrib.***, 114 F.R.D. 647, 651 (M.D. N.C.1987). This includes persons appointed by the court through a letter rogatory or a request from a foreign or international tribunal under 28 U.S.C. §1782.

2. In foreign country. A deposition in a foreign country may be taken in any of the following ways:

(1) Under any applicable treaty or convention. FRCP 28(b)(1)(A). When a letter of request or any other device is used according to a treaty or convention, it must be captioned in the form prescribed by the treaty or convention. FRCP 28(b)(3). An example of an applicable convention is the Hague Convention on the Taking of Evidence Abroad for Civil or Commercial Matters, p. 1566, this book. *See generally **Societe Nationale Industrielle Aerospatiale v. U.S. Dist. Ct.***, 482 U.S. 522, 529-30 (1987) (Hague Convention establishes procedures for taking of evidence abroad). The party should identify the treaty or convention that it relies on. *See **U.S. v. Ruiz-Castro***, 92 F.3d 1519, 1533 (10th Cir.1996).

PRACTICE TIP

Many foreign judicial systems are openly hostile to American discovery requests. If there is a treaty between the United States and a foreign country, it will almost certainly be the cheapest and quickest means of discovery.

(2) Under a letter of request. FRCP 28(b)(1)(B). The court may issue a letter of request on appropriate terms after an application and notice. FRCP 28(b)(2)(A); ***DBMS Consultants Ltd. v. Computer Assocs.***, 131 F.R.D. 367, 369 (D.Mass.1990) (before issuing letter of request, court ordinarily will not weigh evidence to be elicited or decide whether witness will be able to give requested testimony). A party applying for a letter of request does not need to show that another manner of taking the deposition is impractical or inconvenient. FRCP 28(b)(2)(B). A letter of request may be addressed "To the appropriate authority in [name of country]." FRCP 28(b)(3). Evidence obtained in response to a letter of request does not need to be excluded merely because (1) it is not a verbatim transcript, (2) the testimony was not taken under oath, or (3) the evidence may have departed from the requirements for depositions taken within the United States. FRCP 28(b)(4); *see, e.g.*, ***U.S. v. Salim***, 855 F.2d 944, 951-52 (2d Cir. 1988) (deposition taken in France under French law was admissible).

(3) On notice, before a person authorized to administer oaths either by federal law or by the law of the place where the deposition will occur. FRCP 28(b)(1)(C); *see* ***U.S. v. Sturman***, 951 F.2d 1466, 1481 (6th Cir.1991) (Swiss law allowing prosecutor to administer oaths in case would govern, even though inconsistent with U.S. law). A deposition notice must designate by name or descriptive title the person before whom the deposition is to be taken. FRCP 28(b)(3). The notice should probably state that the deponent will testify before a person authorized to administer oaths. *See* FRCP 28(b)(1)(D); ***Ruiz-Castro***, 92 F.3d at 1533.

(4) Before a person commissioned by the court to administer the oath and take the testimony. FRCP 28(b)(1)(D); ***Pain v. United Techs.***, 637 F.2d 775, 788 n.64 (D.C.Cir.1980). The court may issue a commission on appropriate terms after an application and notice. FRCP 28(b)(2)(A). However, a court is not likely to issue an open commission to depose many unnamed persons without a strong showing of need. ***Branyan v. Koninklijke Luchtvaart Maatschappij***, 13 F.R.D. 425, 430 (S.D.N.Y.1953). The applying party does not need to show that another manner of taking the deposition is impractical or inconvenient. FRCP 28(b)(2)(B). A commission must designate by name or descriptive title the person before whom the deposition is to be taken. FRCP 28(b)(3).

3. No interest in litigation. A person cannot act as an authorized officer if the person is (1) any party's relative, employee, or attorney, (2) related to or employed by any party's attorney, or (3) financially interested in the case. FRCP 28(c). An attorney in the case cannot administer oaths at depositions or take official stenographic notes of depositions. *See* ***Sheppard v. Beerman***, 822 F.Supp. 931, 941 (E.D.N.Y.1993), *vacated in part on other grounds*, 18 F.3d 147 (2d Cir.1994); ***Rice's Toyota World***, 114 F.R.D. at 651. It is not clear whether an attorney in the case can operate an audio recorder or stationary video recorder at a deposition. *Compare* ***Pioneer Drive, LLC v. Nissan Diesel Am., Inc.***, 262 F.R.D. 552, 555 (D.Mont.2009) (yes, because video recording was in addition to stenographic recording by authorized officer), *and* ***Rice's Toyota World***, 114 F.R.D. at 651 (yes, because video recording does not involve any interpretation by attorney, thus diminishing concern of conflict of interest), *with* ***Sheppard***, 822 F.Supp. at 941 (no, because attorney was party to suit and was acting pro se).

§3.4 Attendance at deposition.

1. Who should attend. Attendance should be limited to the persons who have a direct relationship to the case, giving them a legitimate reason for being at the deposition to hear firsthand what the witness has to say. ABA, *Civil Discovery Standards*, at 31. These persons include a party, the party's attorney, and the witness's attorney, as well as any expert who could assist in questioning or understanding the witness's testimony. *Id.*

2. Other witnesses. Other witnesses are not automatically excluded from a deposition simply by the request of a party. *See* 1993 Notes to FRCP 30 at ¶15, p. 1198, this book. But a court may order exclusion under FRCP 26(c)(1)(E) when appropriate. 1993 Notes to FRCP 30 at ¶15, p. 1198, this book. See "Limit persons present for discovery," ch. 6-A, §12.5.1(6), p. 443. If exclusion is ordered, the court should consider whether the excluded witness

should be prohibited from reading or being otherwise informed about the testimony given in earlier depositions. 1993 Notes to FRCP 30 at ¶15, p. 1198, this book. FRCP 26(c)(1)(E) addresses only the attendance by potential deponents and does not attempt to resolve issues about attendance by others, such as members of the public or the press. 1993 Notes to FRCP 30 at ¶15, p. 1198, this book.

§3.5 Modifying deposition procedure. Parties may modify the deposition procedure by stipulation and arrange to take the deposition before any person, at any time or place, on any notice, and in any manner specified. FRCP 29(a). If the modification is properly stipulated, a deposition taken under modified procedures can be used like any other deposition. See "By stipulation," ch. 6-A, §7.2.4, p. 421.

§3.6 Examination & cross-examination.

1. Getting started. Unless otherwise agreed to by the parties, a deposition begins with a statement on the record by the officer before whom the deposition is to be taken. If the deposition is not recorded stenographically, the officer must repeat the first three items at the beginning of each unit of the recording medium. FRCP 30(b)(5)(B). The statement includes the following:

(1) The officer's name and business address. FRCP 30(b)(5)(A)(i).

(2) The date, time, and place of the deposition. FRCP 30(b)(5)(A)(ii).

(3) The deponent's name. FRCP 30(b)(5)(A)(iii).

(4) The officer's administration of the oath or affirmation to the deponent. FRCP 30(b)(5)(A)(iv).

(5) The identity of all persons present. FRCP 30(b)(5)(A)(v).

2. Recording deposition. After putting the deponent under oath or affirmation, the officer must record the testimony by the method designated in FRCP 30(b)(3)(A). FRCP 30(c)(1). The testimony must be recorded by the officer personally or by a person acting in the presence and under the direction of the officer. *Id.* The deponent's and attorneys' appearance or demeanor must not be distorted through recording techniques. FRCP 30(b)(5)(B).

3. Questioning. The examination and cross-examination of a deponent proceed as they would at trial under the FREs, except for (1) FRE 103, which deals with rulings on evidence, and (2) FRE 615, which deals with excluding witnesses. FRCP 30(c)(1); *see* FRE 103, 615.

NOTE

*In multiparty suits, one party can notice the deposition and the coparties can attend the deposition and cross-examine the deponent without having to notice the deposition. **FCC v. Mizuho Medy Co.**, 257 F.R.D. 679, 682 (S.D.Cal.2009).*

---

(1) Objections. The officer before whom the deposition is taken must note all objections, whether to evidence, to a party's conduct, to the officer's qualifications, to the manner of taking the deposition, or to any other aspect of the deposition. FRCP 30(c)(2). An objection must be stated concisely in a nonargumentative and nonsuggestive manner. *Id.*; *see* ABA, *Civil Discovery Standards*, at 33 (in most cases, short-form objection such as "leading," "argumentative," "asked and answered," or "nonresponsive" will suffice). The attorney should state the objection on the record and then permit the witness to answer the question. ***Eggleston v. Chicago Journeymen Plumbers***, 657 F.2d 890, 902 (7th Cir.1981); ***GMAC Bank v. HTFC Corp.***, 248 F.R.D. 182, 191 (E.D.Pa.2008); *see* FRCP 30(c)(2) (testimony is taken subject to any objection). Objections during a deposition should be kept to a minimum and preferably should be limited to those under FRCP 32(d)(3). ***Quantachrome Corp. v. Micromeritics Instr. Corp.***, 189 F.R.D. 697, 701 (S.D.Fla.1999).

(2) Instructing deponent not to answer. Generally, a person should refrain from instructing a deponent not to answer questions during a deposition. ***Wilson v. Martin Cty. Hosp. Dist.***, 149 F.R.D. 553, 555 (W.D. Tex.1993).

(a) When proper. A person can instruct a deponent not to answer a question only for the following reasons: (1) to preserve a privilege, (2) to enforce a limitation ordered by the court, or (3) to present a motion to terminate or limit the deposition because it is being conducted in bad faith or in a manner that unreasonably annoys, embarrasses, or oppresses the deponent or party. FRCP 30(c)(2), (d)(3)(A); ***GMAC Bank***, 248 F.R.D. at 191 & n.10; ***Riddell Sports Inc. v. Brooks***, 158 F.R.D. 555, 557 (S.D.N.Y.1994); ABA, *Civil Discovery Standards*, at 33-34; *see* ***Wilson***, 149 F.R.D. at 555 (attorney has duty to move for protective order when she instructs her witness not to answer). See "Terminating or limiting deposition," §3.9, p. 548. These restrictions apply to both parties and nonparties. 2000 Notes to FRCP 30 at ¶2, p. 1196, this book.

(b) When improper. A person cannot instruct a deponent not to answer a question because it is irrelevant, calls for speculation, or calls for a legal opinion. *See* ***Resolution Trust Corp. v. Dabney***, 73 F.3d 262, 266 (10th Cir.1995); ***Castillo v. St. Paul Fire & Mar. Ins.***, 938 F.2d 776, 778-79 (7th Cir.1991); ***Eggleston***, 657 F.2d at 902-03. Such instructions may expose the attorney and the client to sanctions. *See* ***Dabney***, 73 F.3d at 266-67; ***Castillo***, 938 F.2d at 779; *see also* ***Ralston Purina Co. v. McFarland***, 550 F.2d 967, 973 (4th Cir.1977) (action of P's attorney in directing witness not to answer questions "was indefensible and utterly at variance with the discovery provisions" of FRCPs).

(3) Coaching. Some courts severely limit communications between a deponent and the attorney during a deposition. An attorney should not attempt to coach a witness with suggestive and narrative objections. ***McDonough v. Keniston***, 188 F.R.D. 22, 24 (D.N.H.1998); ***Hall v. Clifton Precision***, 150 F.R.D. 525, 530-31 (E.D.Pa. 1993); *see, e.g.*, ***Calzaturficio S.C.A.R.P.A. v. Fabiano Shoe Co.***, 201 F.R.D. 33, 39-40 (D.Mass.2001) (attorney improperly interpreted questions for witness, coached witness on answers, and engaged in lengthy speaking objections). An attorney should avoid coaching a witness by interrupting to "clarify" a question, unless the witness asks for clarification. ***Hall***, 150 F.R.D. at 530 n.10. An attorney should not confer privately with a witness during a deposition about the testimony other than to decide whether to assert a privilege. *Id.* at 531-32; *see, e.g.*, ***Dabney***, 73 F.3d at 266 (sanctions against attorney were proper when attorney prohibited witness from answering factual inquiries and instructed witness not to answer questions unless attorney gave permission to answer). However, an attorney should be allowed to confer privately with a client-witness when the conference is initiated by the client or there is a recess from the deposition. ABA, *Civil Discovery Standards*, at 34-35; *e.g.*, ***Odone v. Croda Int'l***, 170 F.R.D. 66, 68-69 (D.D.C.1997) (client-initiated conference with attorney during deposition that resulted in client changing answer was not sanctionable event).

(4) Written questions. Instead of participating in the oral examination of a witness, a party may serve written questions in a sealed envelope on the party noticing the deposition. FRCP 30(c)(3). The party noticing the deposition must deliver the envelope to the officer conducting the deposition. *Id.* The officer must ask the deponent those questions and record the answers verbatim. *Id.*

(5) Time limit. A deposition is limited to one day of seven hours. FRCP 30(d)(1). For purposes of this seven-hour limit, the deposition of each person designated under FRCP 30(b)(6) is considered a separate deposition. 2000 Notes to FRCP 30 at ¶3, p. 1196, this book; *see, e.g.*, ***Miller v. Waseca Med. Ctr.***, 205 F.R.D. 537, 540 (D.Minn.2002) (acknowledging rule that person may be deposed both as individual and as FRCP 30(b)(6) witness with each part subject to separate seven-hour limit, but holding that this distinction must be made on case-by-case basis). See "Naming deponent," §3.2.2, p. 540. The rule contemplates that a single day is preferable to a deposition extending over multiple days, and that there will be reasonable breaks during the day for lunch and other reasons. 2000 Notes to FRCP 30 at ¶¶3, 5, pp. 1196, 1197, this book. However, the only time to be counted against the seven-hour limit is the time spent on the actual deposition. *Id.* at ¶3, p. 1196, this book. This presumptive limit can be extended by stipulation or by court order. FRCP 30(d)(1).

(a) Extension by stipulation. The parties can agree by stipulation to extend or otherwise modify the time limit. FRCP 30(d)(1); *see* 2000 Notes to FRCP 30 at ¶¶3-5, p. 1196, this book. For example, instead of a single day, the parties could agree to conduct the deposition over multiple days. *See* 2000 Notes to FRCP 30 at ¶5, p. 1197, this book.

(b) Extension by court order. A party can ask the court to extend the length of a deposition. FRCP 26(b)(2)(A). The court must allow additional time if it is needed to fairly examine the deponent or if the deponent, another person, or any other circumstance impedes or delays the examination. FRCP 30(d)(1). When a party asks for additional time, the court may consider a number of factors—such as the length of time being covered in the deposition, whether the witness is familiar with documentary exhibits, and whether multiple parties need to question the witness—and should permit additional time except in the following instances:

[1] The additional interrogation is unreasonably cumulative or duplicative, or the information can be obtained from some other source. FRCP 26(b)(2)(C)(i). See "Deposition is unreasonably cumulative," §3.1.3(1), p. 539.

[2] The party seeking the additional interrogation has had ample opportunity to obtain the information. FRCP 26(b)(2)(C)(ii). See "Ample opportunity for discovery," §3.1.3(2), p. 540.

[3] The burden or expense of the additional interrogation outweighs its likely benefit. FRCP 26(b)(2)(C)(iii). See "Burden outweighs benefit," §3.1.3(3), p. 540.

(c) Sanctions for delay. The court may impose an appropriate sanction on a person—the deponent, a party, or any other person involved in the deposition—who impedes, delays, or frustrates the fair examination of the deponent. FRCP 30(d)(2); 2000 Notes to FRCP 30 at ¶8, p. 1197, this book; *see, e.g.*, ***GMAC Bank***, 248 F.R.D. at 193-94 (court ordered that D and D's attorney were jointly and severally liable for P's expenses when D's deposition lasted nearly 12 hours and most answers were useless). Sanctions may include reasonable expenses and attorney fees incurred by any party as a result of the delay. FRCP 30(d)(2). Sanctions are usually not appropriate if the court finds that some other circumstance, not the parties or the deponent, has caused the delay. 2000 Notes to FRCP 30 at ¶8, p. 1197, this book.

4. Winding up. At the end of a deposition, the officer must state on the record that the deposition is complete and must set out any stipulations made by the attorneys about custody of the transcript or recording and of the exhibits, or about any other pertinent matters. FRCP 30(b)(5)(C).

§3.7 Exhibits. Documents and tangible things produced for inspection during the deposition should be marked for identification and attached to the deposition. FRCP 30(f)(2)(A); *see* ***C.P.C. Prtshp. Bardot Plastics, Inc. v. P.T.R., Inc.***, 96 F.R.D. 184, 185 (E.D.Pa.1982). Any party may inspect and copy the exhibits. FRCP 30(f)(2)(A).

1. Retaining originals. If the person who produced the documents and tangible things wants to keep the originals, the person may do one of the following:

(1) Offer the copies to be marked, attached to the deposition, and then used as originals. FRCP 30(f)(2)(A)(i). The offering party must give all parties a fair opportunity to verify the copies by comparing them with the originals. *Id.*

(2) Give all parties a fair opportunity to inspect and copy the originals after they are marked, and then the originals may be used as if attached to the deposition. FRCP 30(f)(2)(A)(ii).

2. Including originals with deposition. Any party may move for an order that the originals be attached to the deposition pending final disposition of the case. FRCP 30(f)(2)(B).

§3.8 Officer's certification. The officer must certify in writing that the witness was duly sworn and that the deposition accurately records the witness's testimony. FRCP 30(f)(1). The certificate must accompany the record of the deposition. *Id.*

§3.9 Terminating or limiting deposition. A party or deponent who refuses to answer can move to terminate or limit the deposition and seek a protective order to prevent further examination. *See* FRCP 26(c)(1), 30(c)(2), (d)(3)(A); *see, e.g.*, ***Redwood v. Dobson***, 476 F.3d 462, 467-68 (7th Cir.2007) (when questions were designed to harass rather than obtain information, attorney should have sought protective order after instructing deponent not to answer). *But see* ***Neuberger Berman Real Estate Income Fund, Inc. v. Lola Brown Trust No. 1B***, 230 F.R.D. 398,

421 (D.Md.2005) (burden is on opposing attorney to file motion to compel when witness refuses to answer). See "Motion for Protective Order," ch. 6-A, §12, p. 440. The deposition must be suspended for the time necessary to obtain a court order if the objecting party so demands. FRCP 30(d)(3)(A).

1. Protective order. A party or deponent can move to terminate or limit a deposition and seek a protective order because the deposition is being conducted in bad faith or in a manner that unreasonably annoys, embarrasses, or oppresses the party or deponent. *See* FRCP 26(c)(1), 30(d)(3)(A); ***FCC v. Mizuho Medy Co.***, 257 F.R.D. 679, 681 (S.D.Cal.2009). A party can also seek a protective order to (1) protect a privilege or (2) enforce a limitation ordered by the court. *See* FRCP 26(c)(1), 30(c)(2). The motion may be filed in either the court where the suit is pending or the court in the district where the deposition is being taken. FRCP 30(d)(3)(A).

2. Resuming deposition. If the court orders the deposition terminated or limited, the deposition may be resumed only by order of the court where the action is pending. *See* FRCP 30(d)(3)(B). If the court grants the protective order, the court can order the deposition to be terminated or it can prohibit questioning of certain matters or otherwise limit the scope of the deposition. *See* ***McClelland v. Blazin' Wings, Inc.***, 675 F.Supp.2d 1074, 1081 (D. Colo.2009).

3. Award of expenses. If the motion for protective order is granted, the court must, after giving an opportunity to be heard, require the party, attorney, or both to pay the moving party the reasonable expenses incurred in making the motion, including attorney fees. FRCP 30(d)(3)(C), 37(a)(5)(A); ***Riddell Sports Inc. v. Brooks***, 158 F.R.D. 555, 558 (S.D.N.Y.1994). The party or deponent whose conduct necessitated the motion, the party or attorney advising the conduct, or both may be responsible for the expenses awarded. FRCP 30(d)(3)(C), 37(a)(5)(A). The court must not award expenses if (1) the motion was filed before attempting in good faith to resolve the matter without court action, (2) the party's or deponent's conduct was substantially justified, or (3) other circumstances make an award of expenses unjust. FRCP 37(a)(5)(A).

§3.10 Reviewing & changing deposition transcript. After the deposition transcript (or deposition recording) is completed, the deponent may be able to review it and make changes. *See* FRCP 30(e)(1).

1. Request for review. If the deponent wants to review the transcript, she must make that request before the deposition is completed. FRCP 30(e)(1); ***EBC, Inc. v. Clark Bldg. Sys.***, 618 F.3d 253, 265 (3d Cir.2010). The deponent or a party may make the request. FRCP 30(e)(1). The officer, usually a court reporter, certifies that the request was made. FRCP 30(e)(2); *see* ***EBC, Inc.***, 618 F.3d at 265 (without court reporter's certification, court cannot determine whether request requirement was satisfied). If the request is not made, the deponent waives the right to make changes to the transcript. *See* ***Rios v. Bigler***, 67 F.3d 1543, 1551 (10th Cir.1995); ***Agrizap, Inc. v. Woodstream Corp.***, 232 F.R.D. 491, 493 (E.D.Pa.2006).

2. Notification of transcript's availability. The officer notifies the deponent when the transcript is available. FRCP 30(e)(1); *see* ***Parkland Ventures, LLC v. City of Muskego***, 270 F.R.D. 439, 441 (E.D.Wis.2010). The officer is only required to notify the deponent that the transcript is available; the officer can notify the deponent that she can purchase a copy of the transcript, but the officer is not required to automatically provide the deponent with a copy for review. *See, e.g.*, ***Parkland Ventures***, 270 F.R.D. at 441 (court reporter complied with notification requirement when she notified deponents that they could come to her office and review transcripts). If the deponent or a party pays reasonable charges, the officer must provide a copy of the transcript. *See* FRCP 30(f)(3); ***Kinan v. City of Brockton***, 112 F.R.D. 206, 207 (D.Mass.1986).

3. Deadline to review & make changes. The deponent has 30 days to review the transcript and submit a statement of changes. FRCP 30(e)(1); ***Holland v. Cedar Creek Mining, Inc.***, 198 F.R.D. 651, 652-53 (S.D. W.Va.2001); *see* ***Delaware Valley Floral Grp. v. Shaw Rose Nets, LLC***, 597 F.3d 1374, 1379 (Fed.Cir.2010).

(1) Start of review period. The 30-day period starts when the deponent receives notice from the officer, not when the deponent actually receives the transcript. ***EBC, Inc.***, 618 F.3d at 266; *see* FRCP 30(e)(1).

(2) Untimely changes. If the deponent does not submit the statement of changes within the 30-day period, the court can strike the statement. ***EBC, Inc.***, 618 F.3d at 266. But the court may allow a deponent additional time to submit changes beyond the 30-day period. *See id.* at 266 n.12 (dicta; FRCP 30(e) gives courts discretion to allow additional changes in appropriate circumstances); ***U.S. v. Boeing Co.***, No. 05-1073-WEB (D.Kan.2011) (slip op.; 2-10-11) (court can allow additional time if party shows good cause or excusable neglect under FRCP 6(b)).

4. Changes to deposition transcript. If there are changes in form or substance to the deposition, the deponent must sign a statement of changes (sometimes referred to as an errata sheet) listing the changes and the reasons for making them. FRCP 30(e)(1)(B); ***EBC, Inc.***, 618 F.3d at 265-66; ***Podell v. Citicorp Diners Club, Inc.***, 112 F.3d 98, 103 (2d Cir.1997); *see also* ***Wigg v. Sioux Falls Sch. Dist. 49-5***, 274 F.Supp.2d 1084, 1091-92 (D.S.D. 2003) (to determine if errata sheet is proper, courts must consider whether deponent was cross-examined, whether she had access to pertinent evidence, and whether she was confused during earlier testimony), *rev'd in part on other grounds*, 382 F.3d 807 (8th Cir.2004); ***DeLoach v. Philip Morris Cos.***, 206 F.R.D. 568, 573 (M.D.N.C.2002) (errata sheets are proper if given to clarify, to correct misstatement resulting from inaccurate recollections, or to correct response because deponent did not understand question). If the deponent does not include the reasons for the changes, the court can strike the changes. ***EBC, Inc.***, 618 F.3d at 266.

(1) Types of changes. The courts are split on the scope of permissible changes. ***EBC, Inc.***, 618 F.3d at 267; ***Harden v. Wicomico Cty.***, 263 F.R.D. 304, 307-08 (D.Md.2009).

(a) Nonsubstantive changes. Some courts allow only nonsubstantive changes (e.g., typographical or spelling corrections) and do not allow changes to the meaning of the answers. *See* ***Hambleton Bros. Lumber Co. v. Balkin Enters.***, 397 F.3d 1217, 1225-26 (9th Cir.2005); ***Burns v. Board of Cty. Comm'rs of Jackson Cty.***, 330 F.3d 1275, 1282 (10th Cir.2003); ***EEOC v. Skanska USA Bldg., Inc.***, 278 F.R.D. 407, 410 (W.D.Tenn. 2012); *see, e.g.*, ***Thorn v. Sundstrand Aerospace Corp.***, 207 F.3d 383, 389 (7th Cir.2000) (change that contradicts transcript is impermissible unless it is correction of error in transcription); ***E.I. du Pont de Nemours & Co. v. Kolon Indus.***, 277 F.R.D. 286, 297 (E.D.Va.2011) (only corrections to transcriptional or typographical errors are permitted); ***Greenway v. International Paper Co.***, 144 F.R.D. 322, 325 (W.D.La.1992) (someone cannot alter what was said under oath; deposition is not "a take home examination").

(b) Substantive changes. Other courts allow any type of change—either in form or in substance. *See* ***EBC, Inc.***, 618 F.3d at 267-68 (FRCP 30(e) allows substantive changes if party provides sufficient justification; adopting flexible approach for deciding when to allow substantive changes); ***Podell***, 112 F.3d at 103 (FRCP 30(e) does not limit types of changes that can be made); ***Cultivos Yadran S.A. v. Rodriguez***, 258 F.R.D. 530, 533 (S.D.Fla.2009) (FRCP 30(e) allows change in substance because it furthers purpose of discovery, which is to determine true facts); ***Reilly v. TXU Corp.***, 230 F.R.D. 486, 490 (N.D.Tex.2005) (FRCP 30(e) allows changes in substance made for legitimate reasons, such as to correct misstatement or honest mistake); ***Glenwood Farms, Inc. v. Ivey***, 229 F.R.D. 34, 35 (D.Me.2005) (FRCP 30(e) allows deponent to make change in substance). If the deponent is allowed to make substantive changes to her testimony, she may be redeposed and cross-examined on those changes. ***Foutz v. Town of Vinton***, 211 F.R.D. 293, 295 (W.D.Va.2002); *see also* ***EBC, Inc.***, 618 F.3d at 267 (if deponent is redeposed about changes, amending party may be required to pay costs).

(2) Effect of changes. The changes do not completely supersede the original answers because the original answers remain part of the record and can be read at trial. ***Podell***, 112 F.3d at 103; ***Lugtig v. Thomas***, 89 F.R.D. 639, 641 (N.D.Ill.1981).

(3) Challenging changes. A party may challenge the accuracy and reasonableness of the changes to the court (and the jury). *See* ***Thorn***, 207 F.3d at 389.

§3.11 Signing deposition. A deponent is required to sign the deposition only if she requests a review of the deposition and makes changes. 1993 Notes to FRCP 30 at ¶21, p. 1199, this book. Use of an unsigned deposition in violation of FRCP 30(e) is harmless error unless the party can show that there are inaccuracies in the deposition or that the party would be prejudiced by its use. ***Vukadinovich v. Zentz***, 995 F.2d 750, 754 (7th Cir.1993).

§3.12 Sending deposition to attorney. Unless the court orders otherwise, the officer must do the following: (1) seal the deposition in an envelope or package bearing the title of the case and marked "Deposition of [witness's name]" and (2) promptly send it to the attorney who arranged for the transcript or recording. FRCP 30(f)(1). The attorney must store it under conditions that will protect it against loss, destruction, tampering, or deterioration. *Id.*

§3.13 Officer retains notes or copy. The officer must retain the stenographic notes or a copy of the deposition recording, unless otherwise stipulated by the parties or ordered by the court. FRCP 30(f)(3); *see* ***Bogan v. Northwestern Mut. Life Ins.***, 152 F.R.D. 9, 11 (S.D.N.Y.1993).

§4. USING DEPOSITION IN COURT PROCEEDINGS

§4.1 Filing & notice. The party who intends to use a deposition at a hearing or trial must file it with the court and promptly notify all other parties of the filing. *See* FRCP 5(d), 30(f)(4), 31(c)(2). See "Filing Discovery," ch. 6-A, §10, p. 438.

§4.2 General use. At a hearing or trial, all or part of a deposition may be used against a party under the following conditions: (1) the party was present or represented at the taking of the deposition or had reasonable notice of it, (2) the deposition is used to the extent it would be admissible under the FREs if the deponent were present and testifying, and (3) the use is allowed by one of the conditions set out in FRCP 32(a)(2)-(a)(8). FRCP 32(a)(1); ***In re Ashley***, 903 F.2d 599, 603 (9th Cir.1990); *see* ***Ikerd v. Lapworth***, 435 F.2d 197, 205-06 (7th Cir.1970). FRCP 32(a)(1)(B) essentially acts as an exception to the hearsay rule. ***Southern Ind. Broad., Ltd. v. FCC***, 935 F.2d 1340, 1342 (D.C.Cir.1991). The party seeking to use the deposition at trial bears the burden of showing that these conditions were met. ***Allgeier v. U.S.***, 909 F.2d 869, 876 (6th Cir.1990); *see* ***Jauch v. Corley***, 830 F.2d 47, 50 (5th Cir.1987).

PRACTICE TIP

Because FRCP 32(a) is essentially an independent exception to the hearsay rule, a deposition admitted under that rule does not also need to meet the admissibility requirements under FRE 804(b). ***Nationwide Life Ins. v. Richards****, 541 F.3d 903, 914 (9th Cir.2008). Under FRE 802, hearsay is admissible when allowed by the FREs or "other rules prescribed by the Supreme Court"; FRCP 32(a) is one of those other rules.* ***Nationwide Life Ins.****, 541 F.3d at 914.*

---

1. Impeachment & other uses. Any party may use a deposition to contradict or impeach the testimony of the deponent as a witness or for any other purpose permitted by the FREs. FRCP 32(a)(2); ***Davis v. Freels***, 583 F.2d 337, 342 (7th Cir.1978). The "other purpose" provision is intended to allow admission of a deposition to show a prior inconsistent statement in accordance with FRE 801(d)(1)(A).

2. Party or organizational representative. An adverse party may use the deposition of a party or organizational representative for any purpose. FRCP 32(a)(3); *see* ***Founding Ch. of Scientology v. Webster***, 802 F.2d 1448, 1451 (D.C.Cir.1986). An organizational representative is a person who, when deposed, was an officer, director, managing agent, or person designated under FRCP 30(b)(6) or 31(a)(4) to testify on behalf of a corporation, partnership, association, governmental agency, or other entity. *See* FRCP 32(a)(3); ***King & King Enters. v. Champlin Pet. Co.***, 657 F.2d 1147, 1163-64 (10th Cir.1981). There is no requirement for a managing agent to hold any formal office or position in the organization; she need only exercise de facto supervisory control over the organization. *See* ***Founding Ch. of Scientology***, 802 F.2d at 1452-53. Although an adverse party may use the deposition of a party or organizational representative for any purpose, a court order limiting its use is probably harmless if the witness is available at trial. ***Dhyne v. Meiners Thriftway, Inc.***, 184 F.3d 983, 989-90 (8th Cir.1999); *see* ***Brazos River Auth. v. GE Ionics, Inc.***, 469 F.3d 416, 434 (5th Cir.2006).

3. Unavailable witness. A party may use the deposition of a party or nonparty witness for any purpose if the court finds one of the following:

(1) The witness is dead. FRCP 32(a)(4)(A); ***Allgeier***, 909 F.2d at 876.

(2) The witness is more than 100 miles from the place of hearing or trial, or is outside the United States, unless it appears the witness's absence was caused by the party offering the deposition. FRCP 32(a)(4)(B);

Nationwide Life Ins., 541 F.3d at 914; ***Tatman v. Collins***, 938 F.2d 509, 511 (4th Cir.1991); ***Mazloum v. District of Columbia Metro. Police Dept.***, 248 F.R.D. 725, 726 (D.D.C.2008). FRCP 32(a)(4)(B) does not distinguish between fact witnesses and expert witnesses. *See, e.g.*, ***Alfonso v. Lund***, 783 F.2d 958, 960-61 (10th Cir.1986) (no abuse of discretion when court permitted P to admit deposition testimony of his own expert who was abroad at time of trial). Given the historical preference for live testimony and the desire to limit aggressive examination of opposing experts at depositions, a court may require live expert testimony under appropriate circumstances despite an expert being unavailable under FRCP 32(a)(4)(B). *See, e.g.*, ***Polys v. Trans-Colo. Airlines, Inc.***, 941 F.2d 1404, 1410 (10th Cir. 1991) (court not automatically required to admit expert deposition testimony when opposing party is unfairly surprised).

(3) The witness cannot attend or testify because of age, illness, infirmity, or imprisonment. FRCP 32(a)(4)(C); ***Delgado v. Pawtucket Police Dept.***, 668 F.3d 42, 48 (1st Cir.2012); *see* ***Bonner v. City of Prichard***, 661 F.2d 1206, 1213 (11th Cir.1981) (deposition of inmate may be used as substitute for live testimony at trial); *see, e.g.*, ***Jones v. U.S.***, 720 F.Supp. 355, 366 (S.D.N.Y.1989) (unavailable because of infirmity). The party seeking to use the deposition must explain why the witness's age, illness, infirmity, or imprisonment makes the witness unable to provide live testimony. *E.g.*, ***Delgado***, 668 F.3d at 48-49 (when Ps did not establish why witness's imprisonment prevented him from testifying in person, court denied admission of deposition testimony).

(4) The party offering the deposition could not procure the witness's attendance by subpoena. FRCP 32(a)(4)(D); ***Angelo v. Armstrong World Indus.***, 11 F.3d 957, 963 (10th Cir.1993). The party offering the deposition should show that it used reasonable diligence to get the witness to attend. ***Thomas v. Cook Cty. Sheriff's Dept.***, 604 F.3d 293, 308 (7th Cir.2010).

4. Substituting parties. Substituting a party under FRCP 25 does not affect the right to use a deposition previously taken. FRCP 32(a)(7).

5. Deposition taken in earlier related case. A deposition lawfully taken and, if required, filed in any federal- or state-court case may be used in a later case involving the same subject matter between the same parties, or their representatives or successors in interest, to the same extent as if taken in the later case. FRCP 32(a)(8). The primary inquiry is whether the party-opponent in the earlier case had the same motive and opportunity to cross-examine the deponent as the present opponent. ***Minyen v. American Home Assur., Co.***, 443 F.2d 788, 791 (10th Cir.1971); ***Ikerd***, 435 F.2d at 205-06.

6. Deposition taken in unrelated case. A deposition previously taken may be used as allowed by the FREs. FRCP 32(a)(8); *see* ***Angelo***, 11 F.3d at 963 (deposition may be independently admissible under FREs).

7. Exceptional circumstances. On motion and notice, there may be exceptional circumstances, in the interest of justice and with due regard to the importance of live testimony in open court, that permit the deposition to be used. FRCP 32(a)(4)(E). In determining whether there are exceptional circumstances, the court should examine the party's need for the evidence in the deposition and the reasons why the deponent is unavailable. *See, e.g.*, ***Griman v. Makousky***, 76 F.3d 151, 153-54 (7th Cir.1996) (disappearance of witness released from jail is not exceptional circumstance); *see also* ***Allgeier***, 909 F.2d at 876 (doctors are not "automatically unavailable").

§4.3 Restrictions on use.

1. Not party at time of deposition. A deposition cannot be used against a party joined after the deposition was taken, unless the later-joined party had a reasonable opportunity to redepose the deponent but did not do so. *See* FRCP 32(a)(1)(A); ***Mid-West Nat'l Life Ins. v. Breton***, 199 F.R.D. 369, 371 (N.D.Fla.2001). *But see* ***Ikerd v. Lapworth***, 435 F.2d 197, 205-06 (7th Cir.1970) (deposition may be used against party not present at deposition if another party with same motive to cross-examine and to identify issues is present).

2. Party seeking protective order. A deposition cannot be used against a party when (1) the party received less than 14 days' notice of the deposition, (2) the party promptly moved for a protective order under FRCP 26(c)(1)(B) requesting that the deposition not be taken or that it be taken at a different time or place, and (3) the

motion was still pending when the deposition was taken. FRCP 32(a)(5)(A). For a discussion of how to compute backward-counted deadlines, see "Computing Deadlines," ch. 1-C, §6, p. 23.

3. Party not represented at preconference deposition. A deposition taken without leave of court before the FRCP 26(f) conference cannot be used against a party who shows that it could not, despite diligent efforts, obtain counsel to represent it at the deposition, unless the deposing party certified in the deposition notice that the deponent is expected to leave the United States and be unavailable for examination after that time. FRCP 32(a)(5)(B); *see* FRCP 30(a)(2)(A)(iii).

§4.4 Waiver of errors & irregularities.

1. In writing. An objection to an error or irregularity in the deposition is waived unless a written objection is promptly served on the party giving notice. FRCP 32(d)(1); *see* ***Brown Badgett, Inc. v. Jennings***, 842 F.2d 899, 902 (6th Cir.1988) (by prohibiting objections to technical errors at trial, FRCP 32(d)(1) "enhances judicial efficiency and promotes substantial justice").

2. Disqualification of officer. An objection based on the disqualification of the officer conducting the deposition is waived if not made (1) before the deposition begins or (2) promptly after the basis for disqualification becomes known or, with reasonable diligence, could have been known. FRCP 32(d)(2); *see* ***Hale v. U.S.***, 406 F.2d 476, 480 (10th Cir.1969).

3. Competence, relevance, or materiality. An objection to the competence of a witness or the competence, relevance, or materiality of testimony is waived if (1) the objection was not made before or during the deposition and (2) the ground for the objection might have been corrected at that time. *See* FRCP 32(d)(3)(A); ***Jordan v. Medley***, 711 F.2d 211, 217-18 (D.C.Cir.1983).

4. Form or manner of deposition. An objection to the manner of taking the deposition, the form of the questions or answers, the oath or affirmation, a party's conduct, or other matters that might have been corrected during the deposition is waived if the objection was not raised during the deposition. FRCP 32(d)(3)(B); *see* ***Kirschner v. Broadhead***, 671 F.2d 1034, 1037 (7th Cir.1982). The goal is to require the parties to make objections at a time in the proceedings when the error can be remedied. ***Bahamas Agric. Indus. v. Riley Stoker Corp.***, 526 F.2d 1174, 1181 (6th Cir.1975).

5. Errors in completion & return of deposition. An objection to how the officer transcribed the testimony or prepared, signed, certified, sealed, endorsed, sent, or otherwise dealt with the deposition is waived unless a motion to suppress is made promptly after the error or irregularity becomes known or, with reasonable diligence, could have been known. FRCP 32(d)(4); ***Brown v. ASD Computing Ctr.***, 519 F.Supp. 1096, 1098 (S.D.Ohio 1981), *aff'd sub nom.* ***Brown v. Mark***, 709 F.2d 1499 (6th Cir.1983) (table case). FRCP 32(d)(4) applies only to errors committed by the court reporter and does not concern changes made to the testimony through errata sheets. ***Holland v. Cedar Creek Mining, Inc.***, 198 F.R.D. 651, 652 (S.D.W.Va.2001).

§4.5 Form of presentation. Unless the court orders otherwise, a party must provide a transcript of any deposition testimony that the party offers. FRCP 32(c); *see also* ***Morrison v. Reichhold Chems., Inc.***, 97 F.3d 460, 465 n.4 (11th Cir.1996) (transcript of videotape deposition is express obligation, not for "convenience of counsel"). The party may also provide the court with the testimony in nontranscript form. FRCP 32(c).

1. Nontranscript presentation. On any party's request, deposition testimony offered in a jury trial must be presented in nontranscript form, if available, unless the court for good cause orders otherwise. FRCP 32(c). This requirement does not apply to deposition testimony offered for impeachment purposes. *Id.*

2. Optional completeness. If a party offers only part of a deposition, an adverse party may require the offering party to introduce other parts that in fairness should be considered with the part introduced, and any party may introduce any other part. FRCP 32(a)(6); ***Lentomyynti Oy v. Medivac, Inc.***, 997 F.2d 364, 371 (7th Cir.1993); *see also* ***Mid-West Nat'l Life Ins. v. Breton***, 199 F.R.D. 369, 371-72 (N.D.Fla.2001) (if party introduces part of deposition as substantive evidence, party waives objection based on not having been present, represented, or noticed for deposition). Even under this rule, however, deposition testimony is admissible only in accordance with the FREs. ***Reeg v. Shaughnessy***, 570 F.2d 309, 316 (10th Cir.1978).

§4.6 Objections to admissibility. A party may object at a hearing or trial to the admission of any deposition testimony that would be inadmissible if the witness were present and testifying. FRCP 32(b); *see* ***Huddleston v. Herman & MacLean***, 640 F.2d 534, 553 (5th Cir.1981), *rev'd in part on other grounds*, 459 U.S. 375 (1983). Objections to admissibility are subject to the requirements of FRCP 28(b) and 32(d)(3). *See* FRCP 32(b). See "In foreign country," §3.3.2, p. 544; "Competence, relevance, or materiality," §4.4.3, p. 553; "Form or manner of deposition," §4.4.4, p. 553.

§5. DEPOSITION BY WRITTEN QUESTIONS

Depositions by written questions are a useful and relatively inexpensive way to get limited testimony from certain witnesses, like a custodian of business records. *See* ***Burnham v. Superior Ct. of Cal.***, 495 U.S. 604, 639 n.13 (1990) (Brennan, J., concurring). But there are two important drawbacks of depositions by written questions: (1) they do not permit the probing follow-up questions necessary in most litigation, and (2) they do not give the attorneys a chance to observe the demeanor and credibility of the witness before trial. *See* ***National Life Ins. v. Hartford Acc. & Indem. Co.***, 615 F.2d 595, 600 n.5 (3d Cir.1980).

§5.1 Deposition of any person. A party may depose any person or party by written questions. FRCP 31(a)(1); ***National Life Ins. v. Hartford Acc. & Indem. Co.***, 615 F.2d 595, 599-600 (3d Cir.1980); ***Peterson v. Nadler***, 452 F.2d 754, 756-57 (8th Cir.1971), *overruled on other grounds*, ***Mallard v. U.S. Dist. Ct. for the S. Dist. of Iowa***, 490 U.S. 296 (1989).

1. Without leave of court. Ordinarily, a party does not need leave of court to depose any person or party by written questions. FRCP 31(a)(1). Each side to the lawsuit (not each party) may take ten depositions. FRCP 31(a)(2)(A)(i); 1993 Notes to FRCP 30 at ¶3, p. 1197, this book. The ten-deposition limit includes both written and oral depositions. FRCP 30(a)(2)(A)(i), 31(a)(2)(A)(i).

2. Leave of court required. A party must secure leave of court to depose by written questions in certain instances. See "Leave of court required," §3.1.2, p. 539.

3. Leave should be granted. In most cases, the court should grant leave to take a deposition, but in some instances, it should deny leave. See "Leave of court should not be granted," §3.1.3, p. 539.

§5.2 Notice of deposition by written questions. To depose by written questions, the party must serve the questions and a deposition notice on every other party. FRCP 31(a)(3). A notice of deposition by written questions must not be filed in the court until it is used in the proceeding or the court orders filing. FRCP 5(d)(1).

1. Name & address of deponent. The notice must state the deponent's name and address, if known. FRCP 31(a)(3). If the name and address are unknown (e.g., if the deponent is a custodian of records), the notice must provide a general description sufficient to identify the person or the particular class or group to which the person belongs. *Id.*

2. Name & address of officer. The notice must state the name or descriptive title and the address of the officer before whom the deposition will be taken. FRCP 31(a)(3).

3. Organizational deponent. A corporation, partnership, association, or governmental agency may be deposed by written questions. FRCP 31(a)(4); *cf.* FRCP 30(b)(6) ("other entity" is an additional organization that may be deposed by oral examination). The named organization must designate one or more officers, directors, or managing agents or other persons who consent to testify on its behalf, and it may set out the matters on which each person will testify. FRCP 30(b)(6). If the organization is not a party, the subpoena must instruct the organization to make that designation. *Id.* A person produced for deposition under FRCP 30(b)(6) must testify about matters known or reasonably available to the organization. This rule does not prohibit a party from taking a deposition of any person not designated by the organization, although third-party employees must be served with a subpoena under FRCP 45. ***U.S. v. Afram Lines (USA), Ltd.***, 159 F.R.D. 408, 413 (S.D.N.Y.1994).

4. Nonparty. To depose a nonparty, the party should compel the person's attendance by serving a subpoena. FRCP 31(a)(1), 45. If the nonparty-deponent is required to produce documents, the party should serve a subpoena duces tecum. For the requirements for issuing subpoenas to compel nonparties to give testimony and produce documents, see "Subpoenas Under FRCP 45," ch. 1-H, p. 47.

§5.3 Cross-questions. Within 14 days after being served with the notice and direct questions, any other party may serve cross-questions on all other parties. FRCP 31(a)(5).

§5.4 Redirect questions. The party noticing the deposition may serve redirect questions within seven days after being served with cross-questions. FRCP 31(a)(5).

§5.5 Recross-questions. A party may serve recross-questions within seven days after being served with redirect questions. FRCP 31(a)(5).

§5.6 Objections to questions. An objection to the form of a written question is waived if it is not served in writing on the party submitting the question within the time for serving responsive questions or, if the question is a recross-question, within seven days after being served with the question. FRCP 32(d)(3)(C); *see* ***Baranowski v. National Un. Fire Ins.***, 141 F.R.D. 55, 56 (N.D.Tex.1992) (applying former five-day deadline).

§5.7 Procedure for deposition by written questions. The procedure for a deposition by written questions is much like that for an oral deposition. See "Procedure for Oral Deposition," §3, p. 538. A deposition by written questions must proceed in the manner of an oral deposition as provided in FRCP 30(c), (e), and (f). *See* FRCP 31(b). The party who noticed the deposition by written questions must deliver to the officer a copy of the notice and all the questions. FRCP 31(b). After delivery, the officer must promptly do the following:

1. Take the deponent's testimony in response to the questions. FRCP 31(b)(1).
2. Prepare and certify the deposition. FRCP 31(b)(2).
3. Send the deposition to the party with a copy of the questions and notice attached. FRCP 31(b)(3).

§5.8 Notify parties after deposition.

1. When completed. The party who noticed the deposition must notify all other parties when it is completed. FRCP 31(c)(1). A deposition is completed once it is recorded and the deponent has reviewed or waived its right to review the deposition under FRCP 30(e)(1). 2007 Notes to FRCP 31 at ¶1, p. 1199, this book. See "Reviewing & changing deposition transcript," §3.10, p. 549.

2. When filed. A party who files the deposition must promptly notify all other parties of the filing. FRCP 31(c)(2). See "No filing," §3.2.1, p. 540.

§6. DEPOSITION TO PERPETUATE TESTIMONY

A deposition to perpetuate testimony is an examination by oral or written questions taken before a lawsuit is filed or for further use in proceedings on remand from an appeal. *See* FRCP 27. An FRCP 27 deposition cannot be used as a mechanism to conduct pretrial discovery. ***Ash v. Cort***, 512 F.2d 909, 912 (3d Cir.1975); ***In re Chester Cty. Elec., Inc.***, 208 F.R.D. 545, 547 (E.D.Pa.2002). Courts disagree about whether a party can use FRCP 27 to learn enough about a claim to satisfy its FRCP 11 obligations. *Compare* ***In re I-35W Bridge Collapse Site Inspection***, 243 F.R.D. 349, 353 (D.Minn.2007) (FRCP 27 cannot be used to satisfy FRCP 11), *and* ***In re Landry-Bell***, 232 F.R.D. 266, 267 (W.D. La.2005) (same), *with* ***In re Alpha Indus.***, 159 F.R.D. 456, 456-57 (S.D.N.Y.1995) (FRCP 27 can be used to satisfy FRCP 11). See "Certification," ch. 1-B, §2.1.9(1), p. 10. The scope of a deposition to perpetuate testimony is not as broad as that of a deposition taken under FRCP 30. *See* ***Nevada v. O'Leary***, 63 F.3d 932, 935-36 (9th Cir.1995); ***In re Chester Cty. Elec.***, 208 F.R.D. at 548 n.4.

§6.1 Deposition before suit is filed.

1. Petition. A person who wants to perpetuate testimony about any matter cognizable in a federal court can file a verified petition in the court where any expected adverse party resides. FRCP 27(a)(1); ***De Wagenknecht v. Stinnes***, 250 F.2d 414, 417-18 (D.C.Cir.1957). The petition must be titled in the petitioner's name and must show the following:

(1) The petitioner expects to be a party to a suit cognizable in a federal court. FRCP 27(a)(1)(A); ***In re Price***, 723 F.2d 1193, 1194 (5th Cir.1984); *see* ***Nevada v. O'Leary***, 63 F.3d 932, 935 (9th Cir.1995) (FRCP 27 deposition proper if petitioner expects to be party to suit in federal court, but not proper if intent is merely to make deposition testimony part of administrative record). The petitioner does not need to provide an independent basis for federal jurisdiction, but it must show that the anticipated suit will be within federal jurisdiction. ***In re Deiulemar***

Compagnia Di Navigazione S.p.A., 198 F.3d 473, 484 (4th Cir.1999); ***In re I-35W Bridge Collapse Site Inspection***, 243 F.R.D. 349, 352 (D.Minn.2007). The petitioner does not need to prove that litigation is an absolute certainty. ***In re Deiulemar***, 198 F.3d at 484-85; *e.g.*, ***Penn Mut. Life Ins. v. U.S.***, 68 F.3d 1371, 1374-75 (D.C.Cir.1995) (risk that 80-year-old retired IRS agent would not be available for trial justified FRCP 27 deposition).

(2) The petitioner cannot presently bring the suit or cause it to be brought. FRCP 27(a)(1)(A); ***In re I-35W Bridge Collapse***, 243 F.R.D. at 352; *e.g.*, ***Shore v. Acands, Inc.***, 644 F.2d 386, 388 (5th Cir.1981) (party who had already brought suit could not use FRCP 27(a) to obtain deposition).

(3) The subject matter of the expected suit and the petitioner's interest. FRCP 27(a)(1)(B); ***In re Delta Quarries & Disposal, Inc.***, 139 F.R.D. 68, 69 (M.D.Pa.1991).

(4) The facts the petitioner wants to establish by the proposed testimony and the reasons to perpetuate the testimony. FRCP 27(a)(1)(C). A petition to perpetuate testimony will ordinarily be granted only when a witness is elderly or gravely ill or injured and in danger of dying. *See, e.g.*, ***Texaco, Inc. v. Borda***, 383 F.2d 607, 609 (3d Cir.1967) (permitted deposition of 71-year-old witness); ***In re Delta Quarries***, 139 F.R.D. at 70 (permitted deposition when deponent's condition was serious and only deponent had knowledge of activities at landfill before physical records were kept).

(5) The names or a description of the persons whom the petitioner expects to be adverse parties and their addresses, if known. FRCP 27(a)(1)(D).

(6) The name, address, and expected substance of each deponent's testimony. FRCP 27(a)(1)(E).

(7) A request for a court order authorizing the depositions. FRCP 27(a)(1); *see* ***In re Delta Quarries***, 139 F.R.D. at 69.

2. Notice. The petitioner must provide each expected adverse party with notice of the time and place of the hearing. FRCP 27(a)(2); *see* ***In re Letters Rogatory from the Tokyo Dist. Prosecutor's Office***, 16 F.3d 1016, 1020 (9th Cir.1994).

3. Service. The petitioner must serve a copy of the petition and notice on each expected adverse party at least 21 days before the hearing. FRCP 27(a)(2). For a discussion of how to compute backward-counted deadlines, see "Computing Deadlines," ch. 1-C, §6, p. 23. The notice may be served in the manner provided under FRCP 4, whether within or outside the district or state. FRCP 27(a)(2). It is not clear whether the court may dispense with the notice period on the application of a party. *Compare* ***In re Deiulemar Di Navigazione S.p.A.***, 153 F.R.D. 592, 593 (E.D.La.1994) (yes), *with* ***In re Jacobs***, 110 F.R.D. 422, 424 (N.D.Ind.1986) (no). See "Serving the Defendant with Process," ch. 2-H, p. 149. If service cannot be made with reasonable diligence on an expected adverse party, the court may order service by publication or otherwise. FRCP 27(a)(2).

(1) Attorney appointed for party not served. The court must appoint an attorney to represent an expected adverse party not served with a request for waiver of service under FRCP 4(d). FRCP 27(a)(2). If that party is not otherwise represented, the appointed attorney must cross-examine the deponent. *Id.*

(2) Ad litem for minor or incompetent party. If any expected adverse party is a minor or is incompetent, the court must appoint a guardian ad litem to represent that party. FRCP 17(c), 27(a)(2).

4. Order. If the court is satisfied that perpetuating the testimony may prevent a failure or delay of justice, it must issue an order that the deposition be taken. FRCP 27(a)(3). FRCP 27 is not a substitute for general discovery; it properly applies only in that special category of cases where it is necessary to prevent testimony from being lost. ***In re Deiulemar***, 198 F.3d at 484-85; ***Ash v. Cort***, 512 F.2d 909, 912 (3d Cir.1975). A showing that the evidence is unique is not necessary, but there must be a reasonable showing that the testimony may be lost if it is not preserved. ***In re Bay Cty. Middlegrounds Landfill Site***, 171 F.3d 1044, 1047 (6th Cir.1999). The court's order must state the following:

(1) The name or description of the person to be deposed. FRCP 27(a)(3).

(2) The subject matter of the examination. *Id.*

(3) The manner of the deposition, whether oral or written. *Id.*

5. Deposition. The rules for other depositions apply. FRCP 27(a)(3). For purposes of FRCP 27, a reference in the FRCPs to "the court where an action is pending" means the court where the petition for the deposition was filed. *Id.* The court may also order (1) documents to be produced under FRCP 34 or (2) a physical or mental examination under FRCP 35. FRCP 27(a)(3).

6. Using deposition. A deposition to perpetuate testimony may be used under FRCP 32(a) in any later-filed action in court involving the same subject matter if the deposition either (1) was taken under the FRCPs or (2) would be admissible in evidence in the courts of the state where it was taken. FRCP 27(a)(4).

§6.2 Deposition pending appeal. If an appeal has been taken or may still be taken, the court where a judgment has been rendered may permit a party to depose witnesses to perpetuate their testimony for use in the event of further proceedings in that court (e.g., on remand). FRCP 27(b)(1); *see* ***Shore v. Acands, Inc.***, 644 F.2d 386, 389 (5th Cir.1981) (available only if case is on appeal). The party wanting to perpetuate testimony can ask the district court for leave to take the depositions. FRCP 27(b)(2).

1. Notice & service. A deposition to perpetuate testimony pending appeal has the same notice and service requirements as if the action were pending in the district court. FRCP 27(b)(2).

2. Motion. The motion must show (1) the name and address of each deponent, (2) the expected substance of each deponent's testimony, and (3) the reasons for perpetuating the testimony. FRCP 27(b)(2); *e.g.*, ***Lombards, Inc. v. Prince Mfg.***, 753 F.2d 974, 976 (11th Cir.1985) (court denied deposition pending appeal when party did not show why testimony needed to be perpetuated); *see* ***In re City of El Paso***, 887 F.2d 1103, 1105 (D.C.Cir.1989) (FRCP 27(b) requires "a real showing of need" for preservation of evidence).

3. Order. If the court finds that perpetuating the testimony may prevent a lack or delay of justice, the court may permit the deposition to be taken. FRCP 27(b)(3). The court may also order (1) the production of documents under FRCP 34 or (2) a physical or mental examination under FRCP 35. FRCP 27(b)(3); *see* FRCP 34, 35.

4. Use of deposition. The deposition may be taken and used as would any other deposition in a pending district-court action. FRCP 27(b)(3).

§6.3 Not exclusive. FRCP 27 does not limit a court's power to entertain an action to perpetuate testimony. FRCP 27(c). While FRCP 27(c) creates no separate ancillary or auxiliary proceeding, it does recognize that FRCP 27(a) did not abolish the power of a federal district court to entertain an action to perpetuate testimony, such as the former bill in equity. ***Shore v. Acands, Inc.***, 644 F.2d 386, 389 (5th Cir.1981).

G. INTERROGATORIES

§1. GENERAL

§1.1 Rule. FRCP 33.

§1.2 Purpose. Interrogatories are written questions served on a party to the lawsuit. They require answers written under oath. Interrogatories are often the first form of discovery in a lawsuit. They are used to obtain a party's contentions under oath, to narrow the issues, and to identify the witnesses and documents. ***Duncan v. Paragon Publ'g***, 204 F.R.D. 127, 129 (S.D.Ind.2001).

§1.3 Timetable & forms. Timetable, Discovery Status Sheet, p. 1579; ***O'Connor's Federal Civil Forms*** (2012), FORMS 6G.

§1.4 Other references. 8B Wright, Miller & Marcus, *Federal Practice & Procedure 3d* §§2161-2182 (2010 & Supp.2012); 7 *Moore's Federal Practice 3d* ch. 33 (2012); 10A *Federal Procedure, Lawyer's Ed.* ch. 26 (2007 & Supp.2011-12).

§2. INTERROGATORIES

§2.1 Serve on party. Interrogatories can be served only on another party. FRCP 33(a)(1); ***Newman-Green, Inc. v. Alfonzo-Larrain R.***, 854 F.2d 916, 923 (7th Cir.1988), *rev'd on other grounds*, 490 U.S. 826 (1989). Parties do not have to be adverse to one another to seek discovery by interrogatories. ***Andrulonis v. U.S.***, 96 F.R.D. 43, 45

(N.D.N.Y.1982); ***U.S. v. Burczyk***, 68 F.R.D. 465, 466 (E.D.Wis.1975). A party cannot serve interrogatories on nonparty witnesses. ***University of Tex. v. Vratil***, 96 F.3d 1337, 1340 (10th Cir.1996); ***Ellison v. Runyan***, 147 F.R.D. 186, 188-89 (S.D.Ind.1993).

§2.2 Time to serve. Interrogatories cannot be served before the FRCP 26(f) conference unless the parties stipulate or the court orders otherwise. FRCP 26(d)(1).

§2.3 No filing. Interrogatories must not be filed until they are used in the proceeding or the court orders filing. FRCP 5(d)(1).

§2.4 Number of interrogatories. Each party is limited to 25 written interrogatories, including all discrete subparts. FRCP 33(a)(1); *see* ***Duncan v. Paragon Publ'g***, 204 F.R.D. 127, 128 (S.D.Ind.2001).

1. Subparts. Interrogatories often contain subparts, which can be explicit and separately numbered or implicit and not separately numbered. For example, a question asking about communications of a particular type often contains subparts because it will ask the responding party to identify the time, place, persons present, and contents separately. Questions like this are usually treated as a single interrogatory for purposes of the numerical limit because they seek details about a common theme. *See* ***Williams v. Board of Cty. Comm'rs***, 192 F.R.D. 698, 701 (D. Kan.2000); 1993 Notes to FRCP 33 at ¶3, p. 1200, this book. *But see* ***Valdez v. Ford Motor Co.***, 134 F.R.D. 296, 298 (D.Nev.1991) (all subparts should be counted as separate interrogatories). To determine whether a subpart should be counted as a separate interrogatory, the court should decide if the question could be asked separately from the primary question—that is, whether it is logically or factually subsumed within and necessarily related to the primary question. ***Kendall v. GES Exposition Servs.***, 174 F.R.D. 684, 685-86 (D.Nev.1997); *see* ***Nyfield v. Virgin Islands Tel. Corp.***, 200 F.R.D. 246, 247-48 (D.V.I.2001).

2. Limiting or expanding number of interrogatories.

(1) Limiting. The number of interrogatories may be limited by stipulation or court order. *See* FRCP 26(b)(2)(A), 33(a)(1); *see, e.g.*, ***Capacchione v. Charlotte-Mecklenburg Sch.***, 182 F.R.D. 486, 492 (W.D.N.C.1998) (cases on "standard track" are limited to 20 interrogatories). See "Modifying Discovery Procedures & Limits," ch. 6-A, §5, p. 419.

(2) Expanding. The number of interrogatories may be expanded by stipulation or court order. *See* FRCP 26(b)(2)(A), 33(a)(1); *see, e.g.*, ***Atkinson v. Denton Publ'g***, 84 F.3d 144, 147-48 (5th Cir.1996) (court did not abuse discretion in refusing to expand number of interrogatories beyond what was permitted by local rule). See "Modifying Discovery Procedures & Limits," ch. 6-A, §5, p. 419. To expand the number of interrogatories allowed, the party should file a motion for leave to serve additional interrogatories showing the following:

(a) Why the additional interrogatories are necessary. *See* ***Duncan***, 204 F.R.D. at 128.

(b) Why the information sought cannot be secured from any other source. *See id.*

(c) Why the use of interrogatories is more convenient than other forms of discovery. *See id.*

(d) How the interrogatories are carefully construed and are not unreasonably cumulative or duplicative. *See id.*

(e) How the interrogatories do not create an annoyance or significant expense to the responding party. *See id.*

§2.5 Scope. The scope of discovery for interrogatories is governed by FRCP 26(b). FRCP 33(a)(2); ***Ryan v. Board of Police Comm'rs***, 96 F.3d 1076, 1083 (8th Cir.1996); *see* ***Trevino v. Celanese Corp.***, 701 F.2d 397, 406 (5th Cir.1983) (scope of discovery through interrogatories is limited only by relevance and burden); ***Rich v. Martin Marietta Corp.***, 522 F.2d 333, 343 (10th Cir.1975) (same). See "Scope of Discovery," ch. 6-B, p. 456.

§2.6 Standard interrogatories. Since the mandatory-disclosure provisions of FRCP 26(a) require certain discoverable information to be offered without a request, some of the standard interrogatories are no longer necessary. See "Initial Disclosures," ch. 6-E, §4, p. 533. The following are standard interrogatories that should still be included in the first set of questions:

1. Persons providing information for answers. Ask the other party to identify the persons answering the interrogatories, supplying information, or in any way assisting with the preparation of the answers.

2. Defendant's capacity. Ask the defendant to identify whether it has been sued in the correct name and, if not, to state its correct name.

3. Potential parties. Ask the other party to identify potential parties to the suit, and ask for their names, addresses, and telephone numbers. The list of potential parties, like the list of fact witnesses, can be a good source of information.

4. Fact witnesses. Ask the other party to identify persons with knowledge of any discoverable matter, other than those individuals used to support claims or defenses, and ask for the witnesses' names, addresses, and telephone numbers. *See* FRCP 26(a)(1)(A)(i), (b)(1). But the other party cannot be asked to identify the witnesses it intends to call at trial. ***D'Onofrio v. SFX Sports Grp.***, 247 F.R.D. 43, 53 (D.D.C.2008); *see* ***Brock v. R.J. Auto Parts & Serv.***, 864 F.2d 677, 679 (10th Cir.1988). *But see* **Scholl v. U.S.**, 69 Fed.Cl. 393, 394-95 (Fed.Cl.2005) (court compelled interrogatory answer for names of each witness that party intended to call at trial); ***U.S. EEOC v. Metropolitan Museum of Art***, 80 F.R.D. 317, 318 (S.D.N.Y.1978) (same). The identity of trial witnesses must be disclosed in the final pretrial disclosures. See "Witness identity," ch. 6-E, §6.2.1, p. 536.

5. Existence & location of documents, electronically stored information & tangible things. Ask the other party to identify and give the location of documents, electronically stored information, and tangible things, other than those used to support claims or defenses, that are relevant or will lead to relevant evidence. *See* FRCP 26(a)(1)(A)(ii). Ask the other party the names, addresses, and telephone numbers of persons who have possession of the documents, electronically stored information, and tangible things. *See* FRCP 26(a)(1)(A)(i). See "Request," ch. 6-C, §9.3.1, p. 499. The party should also serve a request for production asking for the documents, electronically stored information, and tangible things. FRCP 34(a)(1). See "Request," ch. 6-C, §9.5.1, p. 500.

6. Opinions or contentions. Ask the other party to identify its opinions or contentions. A party may ask for another party's opinions or contentions that relate to facts or the application of law to facts. FRCP 33(a)(2); *see* ***Ackerman v. Northwestern Mut. Life Ins.***, 172 F.3d 467, 469 (7th Cir.1999) (D can get all the information it needs by filing contention interrogatories); *see also* ***O2 Micro Int'l v. Monolithic Power Sys.***, 467 F.3d 1355, 1365 (Fed. Cir.2006) (contention interrogatories allow parties to discover their opponent's theories of liability). But a party cannot ask about another party's contentions on pure matters of law (i.e., legal issues unrelated to the facts of the case). 1970 Notes to FRCP 33 at ¶15, p. 1202, this book. Examples of proper contention interrogatories include asking a party to (1) state its contentions or clarify whether it is making a contention, (2) articulate the facts underlying a contention, (3) assert a position or explain a position in relation to how the law applies to the facts, and (4) explain the legal or theoretical basis behind a contention. ***Capacchione v. Charlotte-Mecklenburg Sch.***, 182 F.R.D. 486, 489 (W.D.N.C.1998).

§3. RESPONDING TO INTERROGATORIES

§3.1 Deadline. Answers and any objections must be served on the requesting party within 30 days after service of the interrogatories, unless the parties agree or the court orders otherwise. FRCP 33(b)(2); ***Smith v. Principal Cas. Ins.***, 131 F.R.D. 104, 105 (S.D.Miss.1990); *see* FRCP 33(a)(2); ***Kartman v. State Farm Mut. Auto. Ins.***, 247 F.R.D. 561, 566 (S.D.Ind.2007). Not timely responding can subject a party to a motion to compel and to sanctions. FRCP 37(a)(3)(B)(iii), (a)(4), (d)(1)(A)(ii). See "Computing Deadlines," ch. 1-C, §6, p. 23.

1. Changing deadline to respond.

(1) By agreement. The parties may stipulate to a shorter or longer time for answering interrogatories. FRCP 33(b)(2); *see* FRCP 29; *see also* ***Smith v. Conway Org.***, 154 F.R.D. 73, 76 (S.D.N.Y.1994) (oral agreements to extend are not binding). The parties must obtain court approval if the stipulation extending the time would interfere with the discovery deadline, a hearing on a motion, or trial. FRCP 29(b). See "Modifying Discovery Procedures & Limits," ch. 6-A, §5, p. 419.

(2) By leave of court. The responding party may ask the court to extend the time for responding to the interrogatories. *See* FRCP 6(b)(1), 33(b)(2). See "Motion to Extend Time," ch. 5-F, p. 332. The party should ask for the extension before the time to answer expires; if a response is not timely served, any objections may be waived. FRCP 33(b)(4); ***Davis v. Fendler***, 650 F.2d 1154, 1160 (9th Cir.1981). See "When to serve," §4.1, p. 562.

2. Answers needing time for discovery. When an interrogatory asks for an opinion or contention that relates to fact or the application of law to fact, the court may order that the interrogatory be suspended until (1) the specific discovery is complete, (2) a pretrial conference is held, or (3) some later time. FRCP 33(a)(2); *see* ***Kartman***, 247 F.R.D. at 566; ***B. Braun Med., Inc. v. Abbott Labs.***, 155 F.R.D. 525, 527 (E.D.Pa.1994). Answers to contention interrogatories are often postponed until the close of discovery or are amended during the discovery period as the party develops its case. ***O2 Micro Int'l v. Monolithic Power Sys.***, 467 F.3d 1355, 1365 (Fed.Cir.2006); *see* ***In re Convergent Techs. Secs. Litig.***, 108 F.R.D. 328, 336 (N.D.Cal.1985).

§3.2 Who must answer.

1. Natural person. If the party is a natural person, the interrogatories must be answered by the party to whom they are directed. FRCP 33(b)(1)(A); ***McDougall v. Dunn***, 468 F.2d 468, 472 (4th Cir.1972). This is not a hard-and-fast rule, especially when interrogatories ask for legal opinions. *See* ***Greene v. U.S.***, 447 F.Supp. 885, 890 n.2 (N.D.Ill.1978). A "natural person" is an individual human being. *See* ***U.S. v. Consumer Ins.***, 318 F.3d 1199, 1208 (10th Cir.2003).

2. Organization. If the party is a corporation, partnership, association, or governmental agency, the interrogatories must be answered by an officer or agent of the organization. FRCP 33(b)(1)(B). The officer or agent must furnish all available requested discoverable information to the producing party. *Id.*; ***Brunswick Corp. v. Suzuki Motor Co.***, 96 F.R.D. 684, 686 (E.D.Wis.1983). The organization may designate its attorney to answer interrogatories, and the attorney may sign and verify the interrogatory answers as the organization's agent. ***Wilson v. Volkswagen***, 561 F.2d 494, 508 (4th Cir.1977).

§3.3 Form of answers. To properly respond to interrogatories, the party should make its answers in the form required by FRCP 33(b).

1. In writing. The party must respond to interrogatories in writing. FRCP 33(b)(3); ***Dykes v. Morris***, 85 F.R.D. 373, 375 (N.D.Ill.1980).

2. Separate answers. Each interrogatory must be answered separately. FRCP 33(b)(3). If an interrogatory asks a question already answered in response to another interrogatory, the party may refer to the other answer. Multiple parties cannot file joint or consolidated interrogatory answers. ***Nagler v. Admiral Corp.***, 167 F.Supp. 413, 415 (S.D.N.Y.1958).

3. Sufficient answers. Each interrogatory must be answered fully. FRCP 33(b)(3). The party answering an interrogatory must furnish all discoverable information requested. *See* ***Martin v. Brown***, 151 F.R.D. 580, 593-94 (W.D.Pa.1993) (party answering must promptly furnish responsive information available through reasonable efforts). Ordinarily, a party cannot answer an interrogatory simply by referring to statements in a pleading. ***Sempier v. Johnson & Higgins***, 45 F.3d 724, 733-34 (3d Cir.1995); ***Dipietro v. Jefferson Bank***, 144 F.R.D. 279, 281-82 (E.D.Pa. 1992). The sufficiency of the answers is decided on a case-by-case basis. An evasive or incomplete answer may be treated as a failure to answer, possibly subjecting the party to sanctions. FRCP 37(a)(4), (d)(1)(A)(ii); *see* FRCP 37(a)(3)(B)(iii); ***Wilson v. Bradlees, Inc.***, 250 F.3d 10, 19 n.18 (1st Cir.2001). See "Not responding to discovery," ch. 6-A, §15.3.2, p. 447. If the interrogatory asks for information permitted by the rules of discovery, the information must be disclosed. If, however, the interrogatory asks for more information than the rules permit, the party must object. See "Objecting to Interrogatories," §4, p. 562.

4. Verified. The answers must be made under oath, with a sworn affidavit. FRCP 33(b)(3); ***Sempier***, 45 F.3d at 736; ***Rayman v. American Charter Fed. S&L Ass'n***, 148 F.R.D. 647, 651 (D.Neb.1993). The affidavit verifying the answers cannot be made on information and belief. ***Nagler***, 167 F.Supp. at 415.

5. Signed. The person making the answers must sign them. FRCP 33(b)(5); ***Rayman***, 148 F.R.D. at 651. If the party is a corporation or other organization, an officer or agent may sign the interrogatory answers. *See* FRCP 33(b)(1)(B). For example, an attorney can sign the answers on behalf of a corporation. ***Wilson v. Volkswagen***, 561 F.2d 494, 508 (4th Cir.1977); ***U.S. v. 42 Jars, More or Less***, 264 F.2d 666, 670 (3d Cir.1959). Although the representative does not need to have personal knowledge of every response, the representative must have a basis for signing the responses and for stating on the organization's behalf that the responses are accurate. ***Shepherd v. ABC, Inc.***, 62 F.3d 1469, 1482 (D.C.Cir.1995).

§3.4 Option to produce business records. If the answer to an interrogatory can be determined by examining, auditing, compiling, abstracting, or summarizing a party's business records, including electronically stored information, and if the burden of deriving the answer will be substantially the same for either party, the responding party is not required to give a narrative answer to the interrogatory but may instead produce the records. *See* FRCP 33(d). It is not clear whether the term "business records" is limited to records produced for commercial business or whether it includes documents that are records of a regularly conducted activity under FRE 803(6). ***SEC v. Elfindepan***, 206 F.R.D. 574, 577 n.6 (M.D.N.C.2002). However, pleadings, depositions, and exhibits are not business records under FRCP 33. ***Continental Ill. Nat'l Bank & Trust Co. v. Caton***, 136 F.R.D. 682, 687 (D.Kan.1991).

1. Specify records. For business records, the responding party may (1) specify the records that must be reviewed and (2) give the requesting party a reasonable opportunity to examine and audit the records and to make copies, compilations, abstracts, or summaries. FRCP 33(d); ***Oppenheimer Fund, Inc. v. Sanders***, 437 U.S. 340, 357 (1978). The responding party must provide enough detail to enable the requesting party to locate and identify the records as readily as the responding party. FRCP 33(d)(1); *see* 2006 Notes to FRCP 33 at ¶2, p. 1199, this book. For business records that are electronically stored, see "Response," ch. 6-C, §9.3.2, p. 499.

2. Request for narrative answer. If the requesting party insists on a narrative answer, it must prove that the FRCP 33(d) procedure is inadequate for answering the discovery because the information is not fully contained in the documents, is too difficult to extract, or cannot be derived for other similar reasons. *See* ***Elfindepan***, 206 F.R.D. at 576. If the requesting party satisfies this burden, the producing party must justify its actions under FRCP 33(d) by proving the following:

(1) A review of the documents will reveal answers to the interrogatories. ***Elfindepan***, 206 F.R.D. at 576; ***Oleson v. Kmart Corp.***, 175 F.R.D. 560, 564 (D.Kan.1997). To satisfy this burden, the producing party must specify for each interrogatory the actual documents where information responsive to the request will be found. ***Elfindepan***, 206 F.R.D. at 576; *see* FRCP 33(d); ***O'Connor v. Boeing, Inc.***, 185 F.R.D. 272, 277-78 (C.D.Cal.1999). "Document dumps" or vague references to documents are not sufficient answers. ***Elfindepan***, 206 F.R.D. at 576. Also, the producing party cannot (1) point to documents if the proper answer cannot be ascertained from those documents or (2) tell the requesting party that it must find the answer by searching the producing party's records. ***EEOC v. General Dynamics Corp.***, 999 F.2d 113, 118 (5th Cir.1993); *see* ***Govas v. Chalmers***, 965 F.2d 298, 302 (7th Cir.1992).

(2) The burden of deriving or ascertaining the answer is substantially the same for the requesting party as it is for the producing party. FRCP 33(d); ***Govas***, 965 F.2d at 302; ***Elfindepan***, 206 F.R.D. at 577. Appellate courts generally defer to the district court's determination of the relative burdens of sifting through documents under FRCP 33(d). *See* ***Al Barnett & Son, Inc. v. Outboard Mar. Corp.***, 611 F.2d 32, 35 (3d Cir.1979), *overruled on other grounds*, ***Alexander v. Gino's, Inc.***, 621 F.2d 71 (3d Cir.1980).

§3.5 Time to supplement answers. Unless the court orders otherwise, interrogatory answers should be supplemented in a timely manner if the party learns that an answer is incomplete or incorrect in some material respect and if the additional or corrective information has not otherwise been made known to the other parties during the discovery process or in writing. FRCP 26(e)(1)(A); ***O'Donnell v. Georgia Osteopathic Hosp., Inc.***, 748 F.2d 1543, 1548 (11th Cir.1984), *overruled on other grounds*, ***Lindsey v. American Cast Iron Pipe Co.***, 810 F.2d 1094 (11th Cir.1987); ***Bunch v. U.S.***, 680 F.2d 1271, 1282 (9th Cir.1982).

§3.6 No filing. Interrogatory answers must not be filed until they are used in the proceeding or the court orders filing. FRCP 5(d)(1). See "Filing Discovery," ch. 6-A, §10, p. 438.

§4. OBJECTING TO INTERROGATORIES

§4.1 When to serve. Objections to interrogatories must be served within 30 days after being served with the interrogatories. FRCP 33(b)(2). Objections are waived if not timely served, unless (1) the court, for good cause, excuses the failure or (2) the parties stipulate to or the court orders a longer response time. FRCP 33(b)(2), (b)(4); ***Davis v. Fendler***, 650 F.2d 1154, 1160 (9th Cir.1981); *see* ***Drexel Heritage Furnishings, Inc. v. Furniture USA, Inc.***, 200 F.R.D. 255, 258-59 (M.D.N.C.2001); *see also* ***Cahela v. James D. Bernard, D.O., P.C.***, 155 F.R.D. 221, 227 (N.D. Ga.1994) (although original objection was timely but "insufficient," objection was not waived, and court allowed party to supplement objection).

§4.2 Specificity. An objection to an interrogatory must be stated with specificity. FRCP 33(b)(4); ***Puricelli v. Borough of Morrisville***, 136 F.R.D. 393, 396 (E.D.Pa.1991). The objecting party must justify its objections. ***Leksi, Inc. v. Federal Ins. Co.***, 129 F.R.D. 99, 105 (D.N.J.1989); *see* ***Chubb Integrated Sys. v. National Bank of Wash.***, 103 F.R.D. 52, 59-60 (D.D.C.1984) (objecting party must specifically show how interrogatory is overly broad, burdensome, or oppressive by submitting affidavits or offering evidence that reveals nature of burden). A party cannot simply invoke the familiar litany of boilerplate or general interrogatory objections (i.e., privileged, beyond the scope of discovery, and not calculated to lead to admissible evidence). ***Walker v. Lakewood Condo. Owners Ass'n***, 186 F.R.D. 584, 587 (C.D.Cal.1999); ***Puricelli***, 136 F.R.D. at 396. General objections asserted without specific support may be waived. ***Puricelli***, 136 F.R.D. at 396.

§4.3 Signature. Objections to interrogatories must be signed by the attorney making them. FRCP 33(b)(5); ***Hindmon v. National-Ben Franklin Life Ins.***, 677 F.2d 617, 619 n.1 (7th Cir.1982).

§4.4 Timeliness. If the party does not timely object to an interrogatory, the objection may be waived. ***Walker v. Lakewood Condo. Owners Ass'n***, 186 F.R.D. 584, 587 (C.D.Cal.1999); ***Boselli v. Southeastern Pa. Transp. Auth.***, 108 F.R.D. 723, 726 (E.D.Pa.1985). However, even if untimely, some objections may not be waived if the request does not have any relevance to the subject matter of the suit or is otherwise patently improper. *See* ***Boselli***, 108 F.R.D. at 726.

§4.5 No objections. The party must answer all unobjected-to interrogatories by the answer deadline. *See* ***Martin v. Brown***, 151 F.R.D. 580, 593-94 (W.D.Pa.1993) (objection that interrogatories are burdensome does not permit party to respond with nothing).

§4.6 Deferral. When a party objects to an interrogatory, the court will not rule on the objection unless the interrogating party files a motion to compel an answer under FRCP 37(a). ***Pan-Islamic Trade Corp. v. Exxon Corp.***, 632 F.2d 539, 552 (5th Cir.1980).

§5. SANCTIONS

§5.1 Motion to compel. A party may file a motion to compel if interrogatories are not answered or if the answers are evasive or incomplete. FRCP 37(a)(3)(B)(iii), (a)(4); ***Pan-Islamic Trade Corp. v. Exxon Corp.***, 632 F.2d 539, 552 (5th Cir.1980); *see also* 1970 Notes to FRCP 33 at ¶9, p. 1201, this book (although requesting party has burden of seeking motion to compel, objecting party still has burden of justifying objections). See "Motion to Compel Discovery," ch. 6-A, §14, p. 444. If the motion to compel is granted, the court must award reasonable expenses, including attorney fees, incurred in making the motion, unless (1) the moving party filed the motion before attempting in good faith to resolve the dispute without court action, (2) the failure to properly answer was substantially justified, or (3) other circumstances make an award of expenses unjust. FRCP 37(a)(5)(A). An action is substantially justified if there is a genuine dispute or if reasonable people could differ on the appropriateness of the contested action. ***Pierce v. Underwood***, 487 U.S. 552, 565 (1988); ***Devaney v. Continental Am. Ins.***, 989 F.2d 1154, 1163 (11th Cir.1993).

§5.2 Motion for sanctions. If a party completely fails to serve answers, objections, or a written response to interrogatories, the court may order more severe sanctions. *See* FRCP 37(d)(1)(A)(ii); ***Oklahoma Federated Gold & Numismatics, Inc. v. Blodgett***, 24 F.3d 136, 139-40 (10th Cir.1994). The court does not need to compel answers

from the offending party under FRCP 37(a). ***Charter House Ins. Brokers, Ltd. v. New Hampshire Ins.***, 667 F.2d 600, 604 (7th Cir.1981). Instead, the court may order the following:

1. That matters relating to the interrogatories be deemed established as the requesting party claims. FRCP 37(b)(2)(A)(i); *see* FRCP 37(d)(3).

2. That certain evidence be excluded, or that the party be prevented from supporting or opposing designated claims or defenses. FRCP 37(b)(2)(A)(ii); ***Blodgett***, 24 F.3d at 139-40; *see* FRCP 37(d)(3).

3. That pleadings be struck in whole or in part. FRCP 37(b)(2)(A)(iii); *see* FRCP 37(d)(3).

4. That proceedings be stayed until the order is obeyed. FRCP 37(b)(2)(A)(iv); *see* FRCP 37(d)(3).

5. That the action be dismissed in whole or in part. FRCP 37(b)(2)(A)(v); *see* FRCP 37(d)(3).

6. That a default judgment be entered against the party. FRCP 37(b)(2)(A)(vi); *see* FRCP 37(d)(3); *see also* ***Govas v. Chalmers***, 965 F.2d 298, 301 (7th Cir.1992) (dismissal is authorized when party does not serve answers or objections to interrogatories).

7. That the party failing to act, the attorney advising the party, or both pay the reasonable expenses, including attorney fees, caused by the failure. FRCP 37(d)(3). The court must not award expenses if the failure was substantially justified or if other circumstances make an award of expenses unjust. *Id.*

§6. USING INTERROGATORIES

§6.1 Trial.

1. **To extent permitted by FREs.** An answer to an interrogatory may be used to the extent allowed by the FREs. FRCP 33(c). Answers to interrogatories are admissible for any purpose. ***Gridiron Steel Co. v. Jones & Laughlin Steel Corp.***, 361 F.2d 791, 794 (6th Cir.1966). Answers to interrogatories may be used as admissions. ***Continental Cas. Co. v. U.S.***, 308 F.2d 846, 849 (5th Cir.1962). Answers may also be used to impeach a witness in the same or another lawsuit. *See, e.g.*, ***Carter v. Casa Cent.***, 849 F.2d 1048, 1050 n.2 (7th Cir.1988) (same lawsuit); ***Kesmarki v. Kisling***, 400 F.2d 97, 102 (6th Cir.1968) (different lawsuit).

2. **Must be offered & admitted into evidence.** Answers to interrogatories, even if on file with the clerk, are not considered evidence until they are formally offered and admitted into evidence by a ruling of the court. ***White v. Vathally***, 732 F.2d 1037, 1041 (1st Cir.1984); ***Jones v. Diamond***, 519 F.2d 1090, 1098 & n.13 (5th Cir.1975). Answers to interrogatories may be excluded after proper objection if during trial it appears that the answers are not material or relevant. 10A *Federal Procedure, Lawyer's Ed.* §26.592.

§6.2 Summary judgment. Interrogatory answers can be used in a summary-judgment proceeding. *See* ***Lujan v. National Wildlife Fed'n***, 497 U.S. 871, 884 (1990). See "Interrogatories," ch. 7-B, §6.1.6, p. 613.

H. REQUESTS FOR ADMISSIONS

§1. GENERAL

§1.1 Rule. FRCP 36.

§1.2 Purpose. The main purpose of requests for admissions is to simplify trials by eliminating matters about which there is no real controversy. *See* ***Kelly v. McGraw-Hill Cos.***, 279 F.R.D. 470, 472 (N.D.Ill.2012); ***Gluck v. Ansett Austl. Ltd.***, 204 F.R.D. 217, 218 (D.D.C.2001).

§1.3 Timetable & forms. Timetable, Discovery Status Sheet, p. 1579; ***O'Connor's Federal Civil Forms*** (2012), FORMS 6H.

§1.4 Other references. 8B Wright, Miller & Marcus, *Federal Practice & Procedure 3d* §§2251-2265 (2010 & Supp.2012); 7 *Moore's Federal Practice 3d* §§36.10-36.13 (2012).

§2. REQUESTS FOR ADMISSIONS

§2.1 Serve on party. Requests for admissions can be served only on another party. FRCP 36(a)(1).

§2.2 Time to serve. Requests for admissions cannot be served before the FRCP 26(f) conference unless the parties stipulate or the court orders otherwise. FRCP 26(d)(1).

CAUTION

A few district courts disagree on whether requests for admissions are "tools for discovery" and thus subject to discovery cutoff dates specified in scheduling orders. Compare ***Kelly v. McGraw-Hill Cos.****, 279 F.R.D. 470, 472-73 (N.D.Ill.2012) (requests for admissions are not subject to discovery cutoff dates when they seek admission of facts already learned through discovery),* ***O'Neill v. Medad****, 166 F.R.D. 19, 21 (E.D.Mich.1996) (requests for admissions are distinct from general discovery and not subject to discovery cutoff dates), and* ***Hurt v. Coyne Cylinder Co.****, 124 F.R.D. 614, 615 (W.D.Tenn.1989) (requests for admissions are not covered by general cutoff for discovery in scheduling order), with* ***Gluck v. Ansett Austl. Ltd.****, 204 F.R.D. 217, 219 (D.D.C.2001) (requests for admissions are subject to discovery cutoff dates), and* ***Kershner v. Beloit Corp.****, 106 F.R.D. 498, 499 (D.Me.1985) (general deadline for completing discovery applies to requests for admissions).*

§2.3 No filing. Requests for admissions must not be filed until they are used in the proceeding or the court orders filing. FRCP 5(d)(1).

§2.4 Number of requests. FRCP 36 does not limit the number of requests or the number of sets of requests a party may serve. But a court may limit the number of requests by order or local rule. FRCP 26(b)(2)(A). See "Modifying Discovery Procedures & Limits," ch. 6-A, §5, p. 419.

§2.5 Form. The requests should be stated in simple and concise terms allowing for admission or denial with a minimum of explanation. ***United Coal Cos. v. Powell Constr. Co.***, 839 F.2d 958, 967-68 (3d Cir.1988). Poorly drafted requests produce responses that are not helpful.

§2.6 Scope. The scope of discovery by requests for admissions is governed by FRCP 26(b)(1). FRCP 36(a)(1); *see* ***U.S. v. One Tract of Real Prop.***, 95 F.3d 422, 427 (6th Cir.1996) (party may seek admission of any relevant matter). See "Scope of Discovery," ch. 6-B, p. 456. Requests for admissions may be used to request that a party admit the truth of matters relating to (1) facts, the application of law to facts, or opinions about either, and (2) the genuineness of any described documents. FRCP 36(a)(1); *see* ***Kelly v. McGraw-Hill Cos.***, 279 F.R.D. 470, 472-73 (N.D.Ill.2012); ***Gluck v. Ansett Austl. Ltd.***, 204 F.R.D. 217, 218-19 (D.D.C.2001). A request involving a "pure matter of law" is improper. ***Reliance Ins. v. Marathon LeTourneau Co.***, 152 F.R.D. 524, 525 n.2 (S.D.W.Va.1994).

§3. RESPONDING TO REQUESTS

§3.1 Deadline. Answers and objections must be served on the requesting party within 30 days after the requests are served on the responding party, unless the parties agree or the court orders otherwise. *See* FRCP 36(a)(3); ***Gutting v. Falstaff Brewing Corp.***, 710 F.2d 1309, 1312 (8th Cir.1983). See "Computing Deadlines," ch. 1-C, §6, p. 23.

§3.2 Changing deadline to respond.

1. By agreement. The parties may stipulate to a shorter or longer time for responding to the requests for admissions. FRCP 36(a)(3); *see* FRCP 29; *see also* ***Smith v. Conway Org.***, 154 F.R.D. 73, 76 (S.D.N.Y.1994) (oral agreements to extend are not binding). The parties must obtain court approval if the stipulation extending the time would interfere with the discovery deadline, a hearing on a motion, or trial. FRCP 29(b). See "Modifying Discovery Procedures & Limits," ch. 6-A, §5, p. 419.

2. By leave of court. The responding party may ask the court to extend the time for responding to the requests for admissions. *See* FRCP 6(b)(1), 36(a)(3); ***Gutting v. Falstaff Brewing Corp.***, 710 F.2d 1309, 1312 (8th Cir.1983). See "Motion to Extend Time," ch. 5-F, p. 332. The party should ask for the extension before the time to answer expires; if a response is not timely served, the matters in the request will be deemed admitted. See "Failure to Timely Respond – Deemed Admissions," §5, p. 566.

§3.3 No filing. The response must not be filed until it is used in the proceeding or the court orders filing. FRCP 5(d)(1).

§3.4 Response must be signed. The response to the requests for admissions must be signed by either the party or its attorney. FRCP 36(a)(3); *see* ***Apex Oil Co. v. Belcher Co.***, 855 F.2d 1009, 1014-15 (2d Cir.1988).

§3.5 Contents of response. The response to the requests for admissions must admit the matter, deny the matter, or if the responding party cannot truthfully admit or deny a matter, state in detail why the matter cannot be admitted or denied. FRCP 36(a)(4). Instead of answering, the responding party may object to specific requests for admissions. *See* FRCP 36(a)(3).

1. Admit. A responding party should admit relevant matters of fact or opinion that are true. *See* FRCP 36(a)(4). When an answer does not comply with FRCP 36 (e.g., it is evasive), the request may be deemed admitted. FRCP 36(a)(6); *see* ***Southern Ry. v. Crosby***, 201 F.2d 878, 880 (4th Cir.1953) (without specific denial or detailed reasons why party cannot truthfully admit or deny, response is equivalent to admission).

2. Deny. A responding party should deny relevant matters of fact or opinion that are not true. *See* FRCP 36(a)(4). A denial must be specific and must "fairly respond to the substance of the matter." FRCP 36(a)(4). When a party requests the admission of an issue genuinely in dispute, the word "denied" is ordinarily sufficient to deny the request. ***United Coal Cos. v. Powell Constr. Co.***, 839 F.2d 958, 967 (3d Cir.1988). When good faith requires a party to qualify an answer or deny only part of a matter, the answer must specify the part admitted and qualify or deny the rest. FRCP 36(a)(4); *see* ***Apex Oil Co. v. Belcher Co.***, 855 F.2d 1009, 1015 (2d Cir.1988) (party cannot entirely deny request when only part of it is untrue).

3. Cannot admit or deny. If a responding party cannot admit or deny a matter, it must state in detail why the matter cannot truthfully be admitted or denied. FRCP 36(a)(4). The responding party may assert lack of knowledge or information if it cannot admit or deny the matter. *Id.* When asserting lack of knowledge or information, the party must state that it has made a reasonable inquiry and that the information it knows or can readily obtain is insufficient to enable it to admit or deny. *Id.*; *see, e.g.*, ***Brown v. Arlen Mgmt.***, 663 F.2d 575, 580 (5th Cir.1981) (no reasonable inquiry when party had a year to get answers from former employees who eventually testified at trial for party); *see also* ***Radian Asset Assur., Inc. v. College of the Christian Bros.***, No. 09-0885 JB/DJS (D.N.M.2010) (slip op.; 11-11-10) (courts disagree on whether party must assert its reasonable inquiry in detail or if it may simply state that it has made reasonable inquiry; court held party can simply make statement but it must explain in detail why it cannot admit or deny).

4. Object. The party must file objections within 30 days after service unless the parties stipulate or the court orders otherwise. FRCP 36(a)(3); *see* FRCP 29. Objections must be specific, and the grounds for them must be stated. FRCP 36(a)(5); ***Southern Ry.***, 201 F.2d at 880. A party must not object on the sole ground that the request presents a genuine issue for trial. FRCP 36(a)(5). If an objection is not justifiable, the court must order that an answer be served. FRCP 36(a)(6). The party cannot serve both objections and answers to the same question; it must choose one or the other. ***Poole v. Textron, Inc.***, 192 F.R.D. 494, 499 (D.Md.2000).

§4. CHALLENGING SUFFICIENCY OF RESPONSE

If the responding party does not provide a sufficient response, the requesting party may move to determine the sufficiency of the responding party's answers or objections. FRCP 36(a)(6); ***Apex Oil Co. v. Belcher Co.***, 855 F.2d 1009, 1015 (2d Cir.1988).

§4.1 Motion. A motion challenging responses to requests for admissions (i.e., a motion to deem matters admitted) should clearly state why the responses are objectionable or insufficient. *See* ***United Coal Cos. v. Powell Constr. Co.***, 839 F.2d 958, 967 (3d Cir.1988) (responding party was never informed what requesting party objected to in responses). See ***O'Connor's Federal Forms***, FORM 6H:33.

1. Unjustified objection. "The question is not confusing; therefore, it is not objectionable." If the request is not confusing, the court must order that an answer be served. *See* FRCP 36(a)(6). If that answer is not sufficient, the court can deem the matter admitted or order an amended answer. *See id.*

2. Failure to make reasonable inquiry. "The responding party refused to answer only on the ground that it did not have sufficient information. The responding party did not state that it had made a reasonable effort to ascertain the matter." *See* ***Brown v. Arlen Mgmt.***, 663 F.2d 575, 578-79 (5th Cir.1981). Unless the responding party states that it made a reasonable effort to ascertain the requested matters, the refusal to answer is not valid and the court can deem the matter admitted. *See* FRCP 26(g)(1), 36(a)(4); ***Brown***, 663 F.2d at 580.

3. Nonresponsive answer. "The answer does not specifically admit or deny the request." If the answer is evasive, the court can deem the matter admitted. *See* ***Southern Ry. v. Crosby***, 201 F.2d 878, 880 (4th Cir.1953) (denying "accuracy of a statement" or refusing to admit does not deny truth of statement and is equivalent to admission).

4. Quibbling. "The answer quibbles over the meaning of simple words." If an answer quibbles over the meaning of a word, the court can deem the matter admitted. *See* ***Marchand v. Mercy Med. Ctr.***, 22 F.3d 933, 938 (9th Cir.1994) (parties should not seek to evade disclosure by quibbling and objection).

5. Not in good faith. "The qualified answers were not made in good faith." If the qualified answer or partial denial is not made in good faith, the court can deem the matter admitted. *See* FRCP 36(a)(4); ***Flanders v. Claydon***, 115 F.R.D. 70, 71-72 (D.Mass.1987).

§4.2 Order. On a finding that an objection is not justified, the court must order that an answer—rather than an objection—be served. *See* FRCP 36(a)(6). On a finding that an answer does not comply with FRCP 36, the court may order either that the matter is admitted or that an amended answer be served. FRCP 36(a)(6); ***Apex Oil Co. v. Belcher Co.***, 855 F.2d 1009, 1015 (2d Cir.1988); *see also* ***Asea, Inc. v. Southern Pac. Transp.***, 669 F.2d 1242, 1247 (9th Cir.1981) (court may deem matter admitted if responding party intentionally disregarded its FRCP 36(a) obligations).

1. Deferring decision. The court may defer its final decision on challenges to the response until a pretrial conference or a specified time before trial. FRCP 36(a)(6).

2. Expenses. An award of expenses may be ordered for the prevailing party on a motion challenging the sufficiency of an answer or objection. FRCP 36(a)(6); *see* FRCP 37(a)(5)(A).

§5. FAILURE TO TIMELY RESPOND – DEEMED ADMISSIONS

If the responding party does not timely serve answers or objections to the request, the matters in the request are admitted as a matter of law. FRCP 36(a)(3); ***Gabbanelli Accordians & Imps., L.L.C. v. Ditta Gabbanelli Ubaldo di Elio Gabbanelli***, 575 F.3d 693, 696 (7th Cir.2009); ***Sonoda v. Cabrera***, 255 F.3d 1035, 1039 (9th Cir.2001). It is no excuse that the same matters were covered in other discovery. *E.g.*, ***U.S. v. Kasuboski***, 834 F.2d 1345, 1349-50 (7th Cir.1987) (deposition); ***Mangan v. Broderick & Bascom Rope Co.***, 351 F.2d 24, 28 (7th Cir.1965) (interrogatories). The requesting party does not need to ask the court to deem the matters admitted; they are deemed automatically. *See* FRCP 36(a)(3).

§6. SETTING ASIDE DEEMED ADMISSIONS

A party may move that the court permit withdrawal or amendment of admissions deemed against it. FRCP 36(b). See ***O'Connor's Federal Forms***, FORM 6H:36. In many cases, a party first realizes that the requests for admissions were deemed admitted when the requesting party files a motion for summary judgment based on them.

§6.1 Procedure for setting aside admissions.

1. Motion for continuance. If a motion for summary judgment or any other motion that depends on the deemed admissions is pending, the party against whom the admissions were deemed should file a motion to continue the hearing on that motion. The movant should state that it needs additional time to challenge the deemed admissions before responding to the pending motion. See "Motion for Continuance," ch. 5-G, p. 337; "Motion for Continuance," ch. 7-B, §9, p. 620.

2. Motion to withdraw or amend deemed admissions. The party seeking to set aside admissions should file a motion to withdraw or amend the deemed admissions. ***Quasius v. Schwan Food Co.***, 596 F.3d 947, 951 (8th Cir.2010); *see also* ***U.S. v. Petroff-Kline***, 557 F.3d 285, 293 (6th Cir.2009) (formal motion to withdraw is not always required; withdrawal may be imputed from party's actions, such as filing late response to request for admissions). The court should not order withdrawal of admissions sua sponte. ***American Auto. Ass'n v. AAA Legal Clinic of Jefferson Crooke, P.C.***, 930 F.2d 1117, 1120 (5th Cir.1991).

(1) Before final pretrial order. If a final pretrial order has not been issued, the court may allow an admission to be withdrawn or amended when (1) the movant shows that the presentation of the merits will be promoted and (2) the nonmovant—the party who obtained the admissions—does not show that withdrawal or amendment will prejudice it in maintaining or defending the suit on the merits. FRCP 36(b); ***Conlon v. U.S.***, 474 F.3d 616, 621-22 (9th Cir.2007); ***Kerry Steel, Inc. v. Paragon Indus.***, 106 F.3d 147, 154 (6th Cir.1997); *see also* ***Pritchard v. Dow Agro Sci.***, 255 F.R.D. 164, 171-72 (W.D.Pa.2009) (excusable-neglect standard under FRCP 6(b)(2) for extending time after period has expired does not apply to withdrawal of admissions that were deemed admitted because of failure to timely respond). A court must consider both factors; however, even if both factors are satisfied, the court is not required to withdraw or amend the deemed admissions. *See* ***Conlon***, 474 F.3d at 621.

(a) Movant's burden – presentation of merits. The movant must show that the presentation of the merits of the case will be promoted by allowing the admissions to be withdrawn or amended. *See* FRCP 36(b); ***Sonoda v. Cabrera***, 255 F.3d 1035, 1039 (9th Cir.2001). If the admission is material, this requirement will be easy to satisfy. *See* ***Hadley v. U.S.***, 45 F.3d 1345, 1348 (9th Cir.1995) (requirement satisfied "when upholding the admissions would practically eliminate any presentation of the merits of the case").

(b) Nonmovant's burden – prejudice. If the movant shows that the presentation of the merits will be promoted, the nonmovant must show that withdrawal or amendment will prejudice its case. ***Sonoda***, 255 F.3d at 1039; *see* FRCP 36(b); ***Gutting v. Falstaff Brewing Corp.***, 710 F.2d 1309, 1313 (8th Cir.1983). Prejudice may occur when a party faces special difficulties caused by a sudden need to obtain evidence after the withdrawal or amendment of an admission. ***Hadley***, 45 F.3d at 1348; ***American Auto. Ass'n***, 930 F.2d at 1120; *see, e.g.*, ***Sonoda***, 255 F.3d at 1039-40 (nonmovant would not be hindered by pretrial withdrawal of deemed admissions). The nonmovant does not demonstrate prejudice merely by showing that it will have to convince the fact-finder of the withdrawn admission's truth. ***Brook Village N. Assocs. v. General Elec. Co.***, 686 F.2d 66, 70 (1st Cir.1982).

(2) After final pretrial order. If the movant does not move to withdraw or amend its admissions until after the entry of the final pretrial order, the court may permit withdrawal or amendment only to prevent manifest injustice. FRCP 16(e), 36(b); *see* ***Conlon***, 474 F.3d at 623 n.5.

§6.2 Permitting late answers. It is unclear whether, under FRCP 36, a court may permit a party to file a late answer to a request for admissions. Ordinarily, the court will treat a request to allow a late answer as a motion to withdraw or amend deemed admissions. *See* ***Gutting v. Falstaff Brewing Corp.***, 710 F.2d 1309, 1312-13 (8th Cir. 1983); ***French v. U.S.***, 416 F.2d 1149, 1152 (9th Cir.1969); ***Moosman v. Joseph P. Blitz, Inc.***, 358 F.2d 686, 688 (2d Cir.1966). *But see* ***Nguyen v. CNA Corp.***, 44 F.3d 234, 242-43 (4th Cir.1995) (allowing answers one day late).

§7. SANCTIONS

A party may ask the court to award sanctions in the form of reasonable expenses, including attorney fees, if a party responding to requests for admissions does not admit what is requested and the requesting party later proves a document to be genuine or the matter true. FRCP 37(c)(2); *see* ***Kelly v. McGraw-Hill Cos.***, 279 F.R.D. 470, 472 (N.D.Ill.

2012). See "Motion for Discovery Sanctions," ch. 6-A, §15, p. 446. Expenses may also be awarded for not properly qualifying a denial. ***Holmgren v. State Farm Mut. Auto. Ins.***, 976 F.2d 573, 579-80 (9th Cir.1992). The court must award expenses unless (1) the request was objectionable, (2) the admission was not substantially important, (3) the responding party had a reasonable ground to believe it might prevail, or (4) there was good reason not to admit. FRCP 37(c)(2); ***Marchand v. Mercy Med. Ctr.***, 22 F.3d 933, 936 (9th Cir.1994); *e.g.*, ***Harolds Stores v. Dillard Dept. Stores***, 82 F.3d 1533, 1554-55 (10th Cir.1996) (expenses properly denied because party had good reason to deny statement even though it was ultimately admitted at trial); *see, e.g.*, ***EEOC v. E.J. Sacco, Inc.***, 102 F.Supp.2d 413, 416-17 (E.D.Mich.2000) (expenses granted when party did not justify lack of adequate response). A court cannot award as expenses any amount that was not incurred as a result of proving the matter. ***Holmgren***, 976 F.2d at 581; *see* ***Stillman v. Edmund Sci. Co.***, 522 F.2d 798, 801 & n.8 (4th Cir.1975) (sanctions cannot be awarded under FRCP 37 for expenses incurred outside discovery process). A court cannot award sanctions under FRCP 37(c)(2) against a party's attorney. ***Apex Oil Co. v. Belcher Co.***, 855 F.2d 1009, 1013-14 (2d Cir.1988). *But see* ***Tom v. S.B., Inc.***, 280 F.R.D. 603, 612 (D.N.M.2012) (monetary sanctions under FRCP 37(c) can be imposed on attorney).

NOTE

Even if the requesting party did not challenge the sufficiency of an answer or objection, sanctions can still be awarded under FRCP 37(c)(2). ***Apex Oil****, 855 F.2d at 1015;* ***House v. Giant of Md., LLC****, 232 F.R.D. 257, 260 (E.D.Va.2005); see* ***Marchand****, 22 F.3d at 938 (challenge to objection is not necessary; it would be unduly burdensome to require that every objection be challenged before sanctions could be imposed). But see* ***Russo v. Baxter Healthcare Corp.****, 51 F.Supp.2d 70, 78-79 (D.R.I.1999) (court should not award attorney fees when motion to challenge sufficiency of objection was not filed).*

§8. USING ADMISSIONS

§8.1 Effect of admissions. A matter admitted under FRCP 36 is conclusively established unless withdrawn or amended. FRCP 36(b); ***U.S. v. Kasuboski***, 834 F.2d 1345, 1350 (7th Cir.1987); *see* ***Airco Indus. Gases, Inc. v. Teamsters Health & Welfare Pension Fund***, 850 F.2d 1028, 1037 (3d Cir.1988) (admission is "unassailable statement of fact that narrows the triable issues in the case"). However, giving conclusive effect to an admission may not be appropriate when the request or the response is ambiguous. *E.g.*, ***Rolscreen Co. v. Pella Prods.***, 64 F.3d 1202, 1210 (8th Cir.1995) (manufacturer's admission that it had "terminated" distribution agreement was sufficiently ambiguous that court did not err in declining to give strict legal interpretation to the word).

§8.2 By whom & against whom.

1. Use admissions only against answering party. Answers to requests for admissions can be used only against the party that made the answer. ***Walsh v. McCain Foods Ltd.***, 81 F.3d 722, 726 (7th Cir.1996); 8B Wright, Miller & Marcus §2264 & n.9; *see also* ***Becerra v. Asher***, 105 F.3d 1042, 1048 (5th Cir.1997) (deemed admissions are binding only on nonresponding party, not coparties).

2. Cannot use own admissions. The answering party cannot use its own self-serving answers. *See* ***In re Air Crash at Charlotte***, 982 F.Supp. 1060, 1067 (D.S.C.1996).

§8.3 No denials. A party cannot read into evidence another party's denial of or refusal to admit a fact. ***Stockdale v. Stockdale***, No. 4:08-CV-1773 CAS (E.D.Mo.2009) (slip op.; 12-30-09). A denial or refusal to answer is not evidence of any fact. *Id.*

§8.4 No contradictory proof. A specific request for admission, once admitted or deemed, is a judicial admission, and a party cannot introduce testimony to controvert it. ***American Auto. Ass'n v. AAA Legal Clinic of Jefferson Crooke, P.C.***, 930 F.2d 1117, 1120 (5th Cir.1991); *see* ***Praetorian Ins. v. Site Inspection, LLC***, 604 F.3d 509, 514 (8th Cir.2010). If the admitting party attempts to offer controverting evidence, the other party should object to the evidence as immaterial. The subject of the admission is no longer an issue because the party admitted it.

§8.5 Summary judgment. A party can rely on the other party's admissions to support a motion for summary judgment. See "Admissions," ch. 7-B, §6.1.5, p. 612.

§8.6 Trial. Admissions are subject to the limitations on hearsay evidence and must fit within a hearsay exception to be properly admitted at trial. ***Walsh v. McCain Foods Ltd.***, 81 F.3d 722, 726 (7th Cir.1996).

1. No need to introduce. Admissions made by parties in response to requests for admissions on file in the court do not need to be introduced into evidence to be properly before the trial and appellate courts.

2. Waiver. Even though admissions are judicial admissions, a party can waive its right to rely on them. When the admitting party attempts to offer evidence contradicting the admissions, the opposing party must object, or it waives its right to rely on the admissions. If controverting evidence is allowed to be introduced without objection, the admissions are no longer conclusive.

§8.7 Pending suit only. An admission is not an admission for any other purpose and cannot be used against the party in any other proceeding. FRCP 36(b); *see also* ***Kohler v. Leslie Hindman, Inc.***, 80 F.3d 1181, 1185 (7th Cir. 1996) (admission is a judicial admission only in the pending suit, but it can be evidence in another suit).

§9. APPELLATE REVIEW

§9.1 Standard on appeal. The district court has broad discretion to grant or refuse leave to withdraw deemed admissions and to substitute answers. The district court's decision will be set aside on appeal only on a showing of a clear abuse of discretion. ***Sonoda v. Cabrera***, 255 F.3d 1035, 1039 (9th Cir.2001); ***Brown v. Arlen Mgmt.***, 663 F.2d 575, 580 (5th Cir.1981).

§9.2 No mandamus. Mandamus relief is generally not available to review a district court's withdrawal of deemed admissions. See "Review by mandamus," ch. 6-A, §16.2, p. 455.

I. REQUESTS FOR PRODUCTION

§1. GENERAL

§1.1 Rule. FRCP 34.

§1.2 Purpose. FRCP 34 provides for discovery of documents, electronically stored information, and tangible things. *See* FRCP 34(a)(1). FRCP 34 applies to information that is fixed in a tangible form and information that is stored in an electronic form from which it can be retrieved and examined. 2006 Notes to FRCP 34 at ¶1, p. 1203, this book. See "Electronic Discovery," ch. 6-C, p. 481.

§1.3 Timetable & forms. Timetable, Discovery Status Sheet, p. 1579; ***O'Connor's Federal Civil Forms*** (2012), FORMS 6I.

§1.4 Other references. 8B Wright, Miller & Marcus, *Federal Practice & Procedure 3d* §§2201-2219 (2010 & Supp.2012); 7 *Moore's Federal Practice 3d* ch. 34 (2012).

§2. REQUEST VS. SUBPOENA

§2.1 From party. To obtain documents, electronically stored information, or tangible things from a party, the party seeking them should serve the other party with a request for production. FRCP 34(a)(1); ***Wilson v. City of Zanesville***, 954 F.2d 349, 352-53 (6th Cir.1992). A party is not required to file a motion or subpoena, ask for a hearing, or get a court order to obtain these items from another party. *See* FRCP 34(a), (b).

§2.2 From nonparty. To obtain documents, electronically stored information, or tangible things from a nonparty, the party seeking them should obtain and serve a subpoena duces tecum on the nonparty under FRCP 45(a)(1)(A)(iii). *See* FRCP 34(c), 45(a)(1)(A)(iii); ***Thomas v. FAG Bearings Corp.***, 846 F.Supp. 1382, 1399 (W.D. Mo.1994). See "Subpoenas Under FRCP 45," ch. 1-H, p. 47.

PRACTICE TIP

Although the parties will discuss a preservation plan after the suit has been filed, either party should consider using a preservation letter before the suit is filed to remind potential parties and witnesses of their duty to preserve evidence, including electronically stored information, relevant to the upcoming case. See "Preservation letter," ch. 2-A, §2.2, p. 73.

§3. MAKING REQUESTS

§3.1 Time to serve. Requests for production to parties cannot be served before the FRCP 26(f) conference unless the parties stipulate or the court orders otherwise. FRCP 26(d)(1).

§3.2 No filing. The request must not be filed until it is used in the proceeding or the court orders filing. FRCP 5(d)(1).

§3.3 Number of requests & sets. FRCP 34 does not limit the number of items a party can ask to have produced or the number of sets of requests a party can serve.

§3.4 Request. A party may serve on any other party a request to produce any designated documents, electronically stored information, or tangible things in the responding party's possession, custody, or control for inspection, copying, testing, or sampling. FRCP 34(a)(1); ***Wilson v. City of Zanesville***, 954 F.2d 349, 352-53 (6th Cir.1992); ***Japan Halon Co. v. Great Lakes Chem. Corp.***, 155 F.R.D. 626, 626 n.1 (N.D.Ind.1993).

1. **In writing.** The request for production must be in writing. *See* FRCP 34(a).

2. **Scope of discovery.** The party is entitled to inspect, copy, test, or sample any designated documents, electronically stored information, or tangible things discoverable under FRCP 26(b). FRCP 34(a)(1). The items must be discoverable and in the responding party's possession, custody, or control. *Id.*

(1) Documents or electronically stored information. The term "documents or electronically stored information" in FRCP 34(a)(1)(A) is extremely broad and includes writings, drawings, graphs, charts, photographs, sound recordings, images, and any other data or data compilations stored in any medium from which information can be obtained. *See* ***Simon Prop. Grp. v. mySimon, Inc.***, 194 F.R.D. 639, 640 (S.D.Ind.2000) (computer records, including deleted records, are documents under FRCP 34); 2006 Notes to FRCP 34 at ¶2, p. 1203, this book ("images" could be hard-copy documents or electronically stored information). See "Documents, ESI & tangible things," ch. 6-B, §2.2.6, p. 458.

(2) Discoverable documents, information & tangible things. A party may seek production of any document, electronically stored information, or tangible thing within the scope of FRCP 26(b)—that is, anything relevant and not privileged. FRCP 34(a)(1); ***Gile v. United Airlines, Inc.***, 95 F.3d 492, 495 (7th Cir.1996); ***Camden Iron & Metal, Inc. v. Marubeni Am. Corp.***, 138 F.R.D. 438, 441 (D.N.J.1991). See "Scope of Discovery," ch. 6-B, p. 456; "Scope of ESI Discovery," ch. 6-C, §6, p. 493.

NOTE

A party cannot use a request for production to compel an opposing party to sign an authorization for the release of medical records. ***Klugel v. Clough****, 252 F.R.D. 53, 55 (D.D.C.2008);* ***Clark v. Vega Wholesale, Inc.****, 181 F.R.D. 470, 471 (D.Nev.1998). But see* ***Doe v. District of Columbia****, 231 F.R.D. 27, 35 (D.D.C.2005) (court ordered P to comply with production request and to produce copies of medical records or authorize release of records). To obtain relevant medical records, the party can either request a physical or medical examination under FRCP 35 or subpoena the records under FRCP 45.* ***Klugel****, 252 F.R.D. at 55 n.2. See "Subpoenas Under FRCP 45," ch. 1-H, p. 47; "Physical & Mental Examinations of Persons," ch. 6-J, p. 574.*

(3) Possession, custody, or control. A party seeking production of documents bears the burden of establishing the opposing party's control over them. ***U.S. v. International Un. of Pet. & Indus. Workers***, 870 F.2d 1450, 1452 (9th Cir.1989).

(a) Production required. A party is only required to produce documents, electronically stored information, and tangible things within its possession, custody, or control. FRCP 34(a)(1); *see also* ***Transamerica Life Ins. v. Lincoln Nat'l Life Ins.***, 255 F.R.D. 645, 652 (N.D.Iowa 2009) (party must produce documents even if they are publicly available). Legal ownership is not necessary to make documents discoverable. *E.g.*, ***In re Bankers Trust Co.***, 61 F.3d 465, 469 (6th Cir.1995) (documents in party's possession are within definition of FRCP 34 despite Federal Reserve's ownership and regulations restricting disclosure).

(b) Control. "Control" is defined as the legal right to obtain documents on demand. ***Cochran Consulting, Inc. v. Uwatec USA, Inc.***, 102 F.3d 1224, 1229-30 (Fed.Cir.1996); ***Searock v. Stripling***, 736 F.2d 650, 653 (11th Cir.1984); ***Linde v. Arab Bank, PLC***, 262 F.R.D. 136, 141 (E.D.N.Y.2009). If the party has a legal right to obtain the documents, it has control of the documents even if they are in the possession of a nonparty. ***Flagg v. City of Detroit***, 252 F.R.D. 346, 355 (E.D.Mich.2008); ***Tomlinson v. El Paso Corp.***, 245 F.R.D. 474, 476-77 (D.Colo.2007); ***Riddell Sports Inc. v. Brooks***, 158 F.R.D. 555, 558 (S.D.N.Y.1994); *see* ***Poole v. Textron, Inc.***, 192 F.R.D. 494, 501 (D.Md.2000) (documents in possession, custody, or control of party's attorney or former attorney are within party's control for FRCP 34 purposes); *see, e.g.*, ***Chaveriat v. Williams Pipe Line Co.***, 11 F.3d 1420, 1426-27 (7th Cir.1993) (even though unrelated third party would have given tangible things to P, P did not have authority to order third party to turn them over; P was not considered to have control of tangible things); ***Columbia Pictures, Inc. v. Bunnell***, 245 F.R.D. 443, 453 (C.D.Cal.2007) (D had control of electronically stored information routed to third-party entity who was under contract to D); *see also* ***Hanson v. Gartland S.S. Co.***, 34 F.R.D. 493, 496 (N.D.Ohio 1964) (determination of whether documents in possession of party's attorney are under party's control depends on origin of documents).

NOTE

Some courts have held that a parent corporation has control over documents in its subsidiary corporation's physical possession if the subsidiary is wholly owned or controlled by the parent. See ***Gerling Int'l Ins. v. Commissioner***, *839 F.2d 131, 140 (3d Cir.1988). Control may also run from a subsidiary to a parent company under an alter-ego theory, which allows piercing of the corporate veil, or on a showing that the subsidiary has access to the documents and the ability to obtain them (e.g., documents flow freely between subsidiary and parent). E.g., id. at 140-41 (alter ego); Linde, 262 F.R.D. at 141 (access to and ability to obtain documents).*

(4) Items to be produced. The request for production must describe with reasonable particularity each item or category of items to be produced. FRCP 34(b)(1)(A); ***Parsons v. Jefferson-Pilot Corp.***, 141 F.R.D. 408, 412 (M.D.N.C.1992); ***In re Kolinsky***, 140 B.R. 79, 87 (Bankr.S.D.N.Y.1992); *see* ***Kidwiler v. Progressive Paloverde Ins.***, 192 F.R.D. 193, 202 (N.D.W.Va.2000); ***Nexxus Prods. v. CVS N.Y., Inc.***, 188 F.R.D. 11, 20 (D.Mass.1999). A request for production does not require a party to create documents. *See* ***Washington v. Garrett***, 10 F.3d 1421, 1437 (9th Cir.1993). A document request is not reasonably particular if it merely asks for documents related to a claim or defense in the litigation. ***Kidwiler***, 192 F.R.D. at 202; *see, e.g.*, ***Holland v. Muscatine Gen. Hosp.***, 971 F.Supp. 385, 392 (S.D.Iowa 1997) (request asking for "all papers" relied on in answering set of interrogatories did not describe documents with reasonable particularity).

(5) Items to be tested. If the requesting party intends to test or sample a requested item, the party should specify the procedure for testing or sampling. *See, e.g.*, ***Quinn v. Chrysler Corp.***, 35 F.R.D. 34, 35 (W.D.Pa. 1964) (court granted D's request for "functional test" on allegedly defective braking system, conducted by installing system in another car of same make, model, and year as P's car). The requesting party should identify to what extent, if any, the testing or sampling will alter or harm the item. *See, e.g.*, ***Diepenhorst v. City of Battle Creek***, No. 1:05-CV-734 (W.D.Mich.2006) (no pub.; 6-30-06) (expert submitted affidavit stating that test was nondestructive).

(6) State time, place, manner & form of production. The request for production must specify a reasonable time (generally 30 days after service of the request), place (generally the attorney's office), and manner (organized as kept in the ordinary course of business or organized and labeled to correspond to each particular request) for the production. FRCP 34(b)(1)(B); *e.g.*, ***Resolution Trust Corp. v. North Bridge Assocs.***, 22 F.3d 1198, 1201 (1st Cir.1994) (30 days' notice was reasonable). The request may also specify the form or forms in which electronically stored information is to be produced. FRCP 34(b)(1)(C); 2006 Notes to FRCP 34 at ¶9, p. 1203, this book. See "Specify form of production," ch. 6-C, §9.5.1(1), p. 500.

§4. RESPONDING TO REQUESTS

§4.1 Deadline. A party served with a request for production must serve a response on the requesting party within 30 days after being served, unless the parties agree or the court orders otherwise. FRCP 34(b)(2)(A).

§4.2 Changing deadline to respond.

1. By agreement. The parties may stipulate to a shorter or longer time for responding to the request for production. FRCP 34(b)(2)(A); *see* FRCP 29; *see also* ***Smith v. Conway Org.***, 154 F.R.D. 73, 76 (S.D.N.Y.1994) (oral agreements to extend are not binding). The parties must obtain court approval if the stipulation changing the time would interfere with the discovery deadline, a hearing on a motion, or trial. FRCP 29(b). See "Modifying Discovery Procedures & Limits," ch. 6-A, §5, p. 419.

2. By leave of court. The responding party may ask the court to extend the time for responding to the request for production. *See* FRCP 6(b)(1), 34(b)(2)(A). See "Motion to Extend Time," ch. 5-F, p. 332. The party should ask for the extension before the time to answer expires; if a response is not timely served, any objections may be waived. See "Waiving," §4.3.3(2)(b), this page.

§4.3 Response.

1. In writing. The response to a request for production must be in writing and served on the requesting party. FRCP 34(b)(2)(A).

2. No filing. The response must not be filed until it is used in the proceeding or the court orders filing. FRCP 5(d)(1).

3. Answers. For each item or category, the answer must either (1) state that inspection and related activities will be permitted as requested or (2) state an objection to the request, including the reasons. FRCP 34(b)(2)(B); *see* ***Kinetic Concepts, Inc. v. ConvaTec Inc.***, 268 F.R.D. 226, 240-41 (M.D.N.C.2010) (answer can be hybrid by objecting to part of request and permitting inspection for unobjectionable part).

(1) Request permitted. The responding party may state that inspection and related activities will be permitted as requested. FRCP 34(b)(2)(B); ***Mirak v. McGhan Med. Corp.***, 142 F.R.D. 34, 39 (D.Mass.1992).

(2) Objection. The responding party may state an objection to the request. FRCP 34(b)(2)(B).

(a) Making. If the responding party does not plan to comply, it must state the objection and include the reasons. FRCP 34(b)(2)(B); *see* ***Gile v. United Airlines, Inc.***, 95 F.3d 492, 495 (7th Cir.1996); ***Kansas-Neb. Nat. Gas Co. v. Marathon Oil Co.***, 109 F.R.D. 12, 24 (D.Neb.1985). See "Valid objections," ch. 6-A, §8.3.1(2)(a), p. 425. If a party objects to part of a request, the objection must specify the objectionable part, and the party must produce the remaining parts not specifically covered by the objection. FRCP 34(b)(2)(C); *see* ***Peat, Marwick, Mitchell & Co. v. West***, 748 F.2d 540, 541 (10th Cir.1984). A party asserting an objection has the burden of establishing its claim of privilege or protection; a blanket assertion is inadequate. ***Biliske v. American Live Stock Ins.***, 73 F.R.D. 124, 126 (W.D.Okla.1977).

(b) Waiving. If the responding party does not object to a request for production within the 30-day time limit of FRCP 34(b)(2)(A), its objections are waived unless it obtains an extension from the court or the other party before the deadline. ***Krewson v. City of Quincy***, 120 F.R.D. 6, 7 (D.Mass.1988); *see* ***Drexel Heritage Furnishings, Inc. v. Furniture USA, Inc.***, 200 F.R.D. 255, 258-59 (M.D.N.C.2001); ***Day v. Boston Edison Co.***, 150 F.R.D.

16, 21 (D.Mass.1993). This waiver rule has not been universally applied, however, and a party may argue that a particular objection was not waived even though it was not timely asserted. *See, e.g.*, ***Godsey v. U.S.***, 133 F.R.D. 111, 113 (S.D.Miss.1990) (more prudent course was to sanction P for failure to timely respond in light of late privilege objection); ***Brock v. Gerace***, 110 F.R.D. 58, 60 (D.N.J.1986) (Fifth Amendment privilege not waived). There is some authority to support an attempt to assert late objections under the excusable-neglect standard. ***General Elec. Co. v. Lehnen***, 974 F.2d 66, 67 (8th Cir.1992).

§4.4 Production. A party is required to produce all requested and discoverable items in its possession.

1. Duty to search. The responding party must search its own records for the relevant documents, electronically stored information, and tangible things. *E.g.*, ***In re Ford Motor Co.***, 345 F.3d 1315, 1317 (11th Cir.2003) (FRCP 34(a) does not give requesting party the right to search responding party's records). The responding party's attorney must make a reasonable effort to ensure that the client has produced all the documents responsive to the discovery request. ***Poole v. Textron, Inc.***, 192 F.R.D. 494, 503 (D.Md.2000).

2. Filing or service. Produced items do not need to be served on other parties or filed in the court. ***Mirak v. McGhan Med. Corp.***, 142 F.R.D. 34, 38-39 (D.Mass.1992).

3. Manner.

(1) Organization. The documents must be produced either (1) as they are kept in the ordinary course of business or (2) organized and labeled to correspond to the categories in the request. FRCP 34(b)(2)(E)(i); *see* ***Pass & Seymour, Inc. v. Hubbell Inc.***, 255 F.R.D. 331, 333-34 (N.D.N.Y.2008); ***Rowlin v. Alabama DPS***, 200 F.R.D. 459, 462 (M.D.Ala.2001); ***Pack v. Beyer***, 157 F.R.D. 226, 233 (D.N.J.1994). The producing party generally has the right to choose between the two manners of production, unless the requesting party has identified a specific form of production for electronically stored information or the parties have agreed or the court ordered otherwise. *See* FRCP 34(b)(2)(E)(i); ***Pass & Seymour, Inc.***, 255 F.R.D. at 334; ***In re Adelphia Comms.***, 338 B.R. 546, 553 (Bankr.S.D.N.Y.2005); 8B Wright, Miller & Marcus §2213. See "Requests for production," ch. 6-C, §9.5, p. 500. To show that documents are produced as they are kept in the ordinary course of business, the responding party can (1) allow the requesting party to inspect the documents where they are maintained and inspect how they are organized or (2) organize, label, and, if appropriate, index the documents and then produce them just as they are maintained. *E.g.*, ***Pass & Seymour, Inc.***, 255 F.R.D. at 335-36 (responding party improperly produced documents when it did not organize, label, or index 405,367 electronic pages of documents that were produced in 202 unlabeled folders and did not provide any additional information about how documents were maintained). If the responding party does not allow an inspection, it should also disclose information about how the documents are ordinarily kept so the requesting party can make use of the production. *Id.* at 337. The disclosure can include (1) where the documents were maintained, (2) whether they came from a single source or file or from multiple ones, (3) the identity of the record custodians, and (4) how the documents were organized. *Id.* at 334, 337.

(2) Translated. If necessary, the responding party may have to translate the documents into a reasonably usable form. FRCP 34(a)(1)(A); *see* FRCP 34(b)(2)(E)(ii) (form of electronically stored information); ***Crown Life Ins. v. Craig***, 995 F.2d 1376, 1383 (7th Cir.1993) (includes electronic data). But the responding party is required to produce only those documents already in existence. ***Alexander v. FBI***, 194 F.R.D. 305, 310 (D.D.C.2000); ***Rockwell Int'l v. H. Wolfe Iron & Metal Co.***, 576 F.Supp. 511, 513 (W.D.Pa.1983); *see* ***Washington v. Garrett***, 10 F.3d 1421, 1437 (9th Cir.1993). The party is not required to prepare or have someone else prepare new documents for the sole purpose of production. ***Alexander***, 194 F.R.D. at 310; ***Rockwell Int'l***, 576 F.Supp. at 513.

4. Complete document. A party producing documents cannot delete part of a document and produce only the redacted copy. *See* ***U.S. v. Owatonna Recognition, Inc.***, 196 F.Supp.2d 1315, 1319-20 (Ct.Int'l Trade 2002). If any part of a document is redacted, the producing party must object to the request, explain what was redacted, and identify the privilege or immunity that protects it from discovery. *See* ***Riddell Sports Inc. v. Brooks***, 158 F.R.D. 555, 560 (S.D.N.Y.1994) (party must carry its burden on redacted portion).

§4.5 Supplementing or amending responses. See "Supplementing Discovery," ch. 6-A, §11, p. 438.

§5. MOTION TO COMPEL

The requesting party must ask the court to compel production if the responding party objects to a request, does not respond to a request, or does not permit inspection as requested. *See* FRCP 37(a)(3)(B)(iv); ***GFI Computer Indus. v. Fry***, 476 F.2d 1, 3 (5th Cir.1973). See "Motion to Compel Discovery," ch. 6-A, §14, p. 444; "Motion to compel," ch. 6-C, §11.2, p. 510. Before the requesting party files a motion to compel, the parties should meet and confer. 2006 Notes to FRCP 34 at ¶12, p. 1204, this book; *see* FRCP 34(b). See "Burden to resolve dispute without court action," ch. 6-A, §8.3.3, p. 427.

§6. MOTION FOR SANCTIONS

If the responding party does not serve a written response at all, the requesting party can move for sanctions. FRCP 37(d)(1)(A)(ii); ***Marx v. Kelly, Hart & Hallman, P.C.***, 929 F.2d 8, 11 (1st Cir.1991); *see* ***Fonseca v. Regan***, 734 F.2d 944, 947 (2d Cir.1984). See "Motion for Discovery Sanctions," ch. 6-A, §15, p. 446.

J. PHYSICAL & MENTAL EXAMINATIONS OF PERSONS

§1. GENERAL

§1.1 Rule. FRCP 35.

§1.2 Purpose. One of the purposes of FRCP 35 is to level the playing field between two parties in a case where a party's physical or mental condition has become an issue. ***Favale v. Roman Catholic Diocese of Bridgeport***, 235 F.R.D. 553, 557 (D.Conn.2006); ***Womack v. Stevens Transp.***, 205 F.R.D. 445, 446 (E.D.Pa.2001); ***Ragge v. MCA/Univ'l Studios, Corp.***, 165 F.R.D. 605, 608 (C.D.Cal.1995). Because of the sensitive nature of physical and mental examinations and the potential for their abuse, FRCP 35 provides additional procedural protections to a proposed examinee by requiring court approval of any proposed examination. ***Schlagenhauf v. Holder***, 379 U.S. 104, 118 (1964).

§1.3 Timetable & forms. Timetable, Discovery Status Sheet, p. 1579; *O'Connor's Federal Civil Forms* (2012), FORMS 6J.

§1.4 Other references. 8B Wright, Miller & Marcus, *Federal Practice & Procedure 3d* §§2231-2239 (2010 & Supp.2012); 7 *Moore's Federal Practice 3d* ch. 35 (2012).

§2. MOTION TO EXAMINE PERSON

Unlike other discovery mechanisms, a party must file a motion asking the court to order the examination of a person. ***Herrera v. Lufkin Indus.***, 474 F.3d 675, 689 (10th Cir.2007); *see also* ***In re Oil Spill by the Oil Rig "Deepwater Horizon" in the Gulf of Mex.***, No. MDL No. 2179 SECTION: J (E.D.La.2012) (slip op.; 2-24-12) (formal motion may not be required if, for example, request for FRCP 35 exam is implicitly raised in another filing).

§2.1 Examinee.

1. Who can be examined. A court can order a party whose physical or mental condition is in controversy to submit to a physical or mental examination by a suitably licensed or certified examiner. FRCP 35(a)(1); *see* ***Schlagenhauf v. Holder***, 379 U.S. 104, 118-19 (1964). A court can also order a physical or mental examination of a person who is in a party's custody or legal control. FRCP 35(a)(1).

2. Who cannot be examined. A court has no authority beyond FRCP 35 to order a person to submit to a physical or mental examination. ***Caban v. 600 E. 21st St. Co.***, 200 F.R.D. 176, 181 (E.D.N.Y.2001). Examples of persons who could not be ordered to submit to an FRCP 35 exam include the following:

(1) Party's parents. *E.g.*, ***Dulles v. Quan Yoke Fong***, 237 F.2d 496, 499 (9th Cir.1956) (court erred by ordering blood tests of party's parents, who were not parties); ***Caban***, 200 F.R.D. at 180-81 (court refused to order mother representing infant-P to submit to IQ test).

(2) Party's employee. *E.g.*, ***Lewis v. Herrman's Excavating, Inc.***, 200 F.R.D. 657, 660-61 (D.Kan. 2001) (employee is not in employer-D's legal control for purposes of ordering FRCP 35 exam).

§2.2 Motion.

1. Grounds. A physical or mental examination can be ordered only when (1) the physical or mental condition of the proposed examinee is in controversy and (2) good cause is shown for the examination. FRCP 35(a)(1), (a)(2)(A); *see* ***Schlagenhauf v. Holder***, 379 U.S. 104, 118-19 (1964); ***Winters v. Travia***, 495 F.2d 839, 841 (2d Cir. 1974); ***Ricks v. Abbott Labs.***, 198 F.R.D. 647, 648 (D.Md.2001).

(1) Condition in controversy. The motion must allege that the party's condition is genuinely in controversy. ***Schlagenhauf***, 379 U.S. at 118. To be "in controversy" for purposes of a physical or mental examination, the condition must be ongoing; an examination cannot be ordered for a past injury from which the party has recovered. ***Coca-Cola Bottling Co. v. Torres***, 255 F.2d 149, 153 (1st Cir.1958).

NOTE

Generally, the party to be examined is the plaintiff, but a defendant can also be required to submit to an examination. See 8B Wright, Miller & Marcus §2233 nn.3-4 (FRCP 35 applies to every party—plaintiff or defendant). For example, a plaintiff can be required to submit to a physical examination by claiming physical injuries as a result of an automobile collision with a defendant; the defendant can be required to submit to a physical examination by admitting during discovery to an eye condition that could have contributed to the collision.

(a) Physical condition. A party's physical condition is usually in controversy when the plaintiff alleges that the defendant's conduct caused the plaintiff physical injury or the defendant asserts a defense that rests on the plaintiff's physical condition. *E.g.*, ***Beach v. Beach***, 114 F.2d 479, 481-82 (D.C.Cir.1940) (court ordered blood tests of P-mother and P-child because D's defense of nonpaternity required determination of Ps' blood types); ***Bennett v. White Labs.***, 841 F.Supp. 1155, 1157-58 (M.D.Fla.1993) (court ordered physical examination of P because she alleged that D's drug caused her in utero injuries); *see* FRCP 35(a)(1) (physical condition includes blood group).

(b) Mental condition. A party's mental condition is usually in controversy when the alleged emotional distress is unusually severe, requires an expert to explain, or is described in medical terms. ***Ricks***, 198 F.R.D. at 649. Less-serious emotional distress, such as the grief, anxiety, anger, and frustration that people experience when bad things happen, is generally not sufficiently in controversy. *Id.*; *see, e.g.*, ***Acosta v. Tenneco Oil Co.***, 913 F.2d 205, 209 (5th Cir.1990) (allegations of age discrimination do not justify examination); ***Stevenson v. Stanley Bostitch, Inc.***, 201 F.R.D. 551, 553 (N.D.Ga.2001) (party does not place her mental condition in controversy merely by claiming damages for mental anguish or "garden variety" emotional distress). *But see* ***Nuskey v. Lambright***, 251 F.R.D. 3, 7 (D.D.C.2008) (employee who seeks compensatory damages for emotional pain based on employer's action places mental condition in controversy). The party's mental condition may be in controversy when one or more of the following factors are present:

[1] The party puts the condition in issue by pleading it in support of its position. *E.g.*, ***Schlagenhauf***, 379 U.S. at 119 (P in negligence action who asserts mental injury places that injury in controversy); ***Gattegno v. PricewaterhouseCoopers, LLP***, 204 F.R.D. 228, 231-32 (D.Conn.2001) (P alleged ongoing mental injury in every count); ***Jefferys v. LRP Publ'ns, Inc.***, 184 F.R.D. 262, 262 (E.D.Pa.1999) (P alleged disability discrimination); *see* ***Stevenson***, 201 F.R.D. at 551-54 (mental exam is warranted when tort claim is asserted for infliction of emotional distress, specific mental or psychiatric injury or disorder, or unusually severe emotional distress).

[2] The party intends to offer expert testimony in support of a claim for emotional-distress damages. ***Stevenson***, 201 F.R.D. at 554; ***Ricks***, 198 F.R.D. at 650; ***Turner v. Imperial Stores***, 161 F.R.D. 89, 98 (S.D. Cal.1995).

[3] The party concedes that her mental condition is in controversy within the meaning of FRCP 35. ***Stevenson***, 201 F.R.D. at 554; ***Turner***, 161 F.R.D. at 98.

(2) Good cause. The motion must allege that there is good cause for the examination. ***Schlagenhauf***, 379 U.S. at 118. To prove good cause, the requesting party must show that the examination could lead to the

discovery of specific facts relevant to the cause of action and is necessary to the requesting party's case. ***Womack v. Stevens Transp.***, 205 F.R.D. 445, 447 (E.D.Pa.2001); *see, e.g.*, ***Gattegno***, 204 F.R.D. at 233 (D needed mental exam to assess injuries alleged in P's complaint). The factors supporting the in-controversy requirement are often used to determine whether there is good cause for the examination. ***Schlagenhauf***, 379 U.S. at 118-19; ***Bethel v. Dixie Homecrafters, Inc.***, 192 F.R.D. 320, 322 (N.D.Ga.2000).

2. Notice. The party seeking the examination must give notice to all parties and to the proposed examinee. FRCP 35(a)(2)(A).

3. Time, place & manner. The motion should provide the court with information allowing it to specify the time, place, manner, conditions, and scope of the examination. *See* FRCP 35(a)(2)(B); ***Gattegno***, 204 F.R.D. at 233; *see, e.g.*, ***Calderon v. Reederei Claus-Peter Offen GmbH & Co.***, 258 F.R.D. 523, 526 (S.D.Fla.2009) (when D did not sufficiently identify scope of examination, court did not deny examination but redefined scope).

4. Examiner. The motion should identify the person (or persons) who would be a suitable examiner, including specialization if necessary. *See* FRCP 35(a)(1), (a)(2)(B); ***Calderon***, 258 F.R.D. at 526.

5. Waiver. Physical or mental examinations are often arranged by stipulation of the parties. ***Herrera v. Lufkin Indus.***, 474 F.3d 675, 689 (10th Cir.2007). If a plaintiff voluntarily submits to an examination by a doctor selected by a defendant, the plaintiff waives the right to insist on an order for examination under FRCP 35(a). ***Herrera***, 474 F.3d at 689.

6. Deadline. FRCP 35 does not include a deadline to file the motion. ***Furlong v. Circle Line Statue of Liberty Ferry, Inc.***, 902 F.Supp. 65, 70 (S.D.N.Y.1995); 8B Wright, Miller & Marcus §2234 nn.4-5.

NOTE

Although there is no deadline under FRCP 35, district courts disagree on whether the FRCP 26(a)(2) deadline for expert disclosures applies to motions for an FRCP 35 examination. Compare ***Diaz v. Con-Way Truckload, Inc.****, 279 F.R.D. 412, 418 (S.D.Tex.2012) (FRCP 26 and 35 should be read in conjunction; motion under FRCP 35 must be made before FRCP 26(a)(2) expert-disclosure deadline), and* ***Shumaker v. West****, 196 F.R.D. 454, 456-57 (S.D.W.Va.2000) (if party intends to call FRCP 35 examiner as expert witness, FRCP 35 report must be produced by FRCP 26(a)(2) expert-disclosure deadline), with* ***Waggoner v. Ohio Cent. R.R.****, 242 F.R.D. 413, 414 (S.D.Ohio 2007) (FRCP 26 expert-disclosure deadline does not apply to FRCP 35 examination report). To ensure a timely motion, a party should file the motion early enough before the discovery deadline to allow time for (1) the examination to be conducted and (2) the party against whom the examination is ordered to receive and review the report and depose the examiner. See* ***Miksis v. Howard****, 106 F.3d 754, 759 (7th Cir.1997);* ***Bush v. Pioneer Human Servs.****, No. C09-0518 RSM (W.D.Wash.2010) (slip op.; 1-21-10).*

§2.3 Response. The proposed examinee can make the following arguments in her response to deny or limit the examination.

1. Condition not in controversy. The motion for an FRCP 35 examination should be denied because the proposed examinee's condition is not in controversy. *See, e.g.*, ***Acosta v. Tenneco Oil Co.***, 913 F.2d 205, 208-09 (5th Cir.1990) (in age-discrimination suit, P's mental or physical condition was not in controversy because P was not seeking emotional or mental damages; D's defense that P failed to mitigate damages by not finding comparable work also did not place P's condition in controversy).

2. No good cause. The motion for an FRCP 35 examination should be denied because it did not establish good cause for the examination. *E.g.*, ***Kunstler v. City of N.Y.***, 242 F.R.D. 261, 263 (S.D.N.Y.2007) (in case under 42 U.S.C. §1983, no good cause to order examinations because Ps were not claiming ongoing or serious psychological damages).

3. **Examination oppressive or burdensome.** The motion for an FRCP 35 examination should be denied or limited because it will be oppressive, too burdensome, or too costly. *See* ***Favale v. Roman Catholic Diocese of Bridgeport***, 235 F.R.D. 553, 555 (D.Conn.2006); ***Romano v. Interstate Express, Inc.***, No. CV408-121 (S.D.Ga. 2009) (slip op.; 1-28-09); *see, e.g.*, ***Bennett v. White Labs.***, 841 F.Supp. 1155, 1159 (M.D.Fla.1993) (motion granted with condition that examinee could be examined in Jacksonville, where case was pending, rather than having her travel to Miami because examination was going to cause her severe discomfort and pain). The proposed examinee can ask for a protective order under FRCP 26(c)(1). See "Motion for Protective Order," ch. 6-A, §12, p. 440. To obtain the protective order, the proposed examinee must prove good cause. *E.g.*, ***Favale***, 235 F.R.D. at 555 (no good cause to exclude specific test from examination; examinee's claim that test would not adequately gauge her emotional condition was insufficient to show that test would be burdensome or harmful).

§2.4 Examiner. The examination must be conducted by a certified or licensed professional, normally a physician or a psychologist. ***Jefferys v. LRP Publ'ns, Inc.***, 184 F.R.D. 262, 263 (E.D.Pa.1999). The movant has no absolute right to have the examination conducted by a particular doctor. ***Peters v. Nelson***, 153 F.R.D. 635, 637 (N.D.Iowa 1994). However, the examination should usually be conducted by a physician of the movant's choosing unless the proposed examinee has a valid objection to the selection. ***Liechty v. Terrill Trucking Co.***, 53 F.R.D. 590, 591 (E.D. Tenn.1971).

§2.5 Hearing not required. An evidentiary hearing is not required in every case. ***Schlagenhauf v. Holder***, 379 U.S. 104, 119 (1964); ***Gattegno v. PricewaterhouseCoopers, LLP***, 204 F.R.D. 228, 230 (D.Conn.2001). A hearing may not be required when the movant provides sufficient information through affidavits, deposition excerpts, pleadings, or other methods not requiring a hearing showing both that the proposed examinee's physical or mental condition is in controversy and that there is good cause for the examination. ***Schlagenhauf***, 379 U.S. at 118-19; ***Gattegno***, 204 F.R.D. at 230.

§2.6 Sanctions. If a party does not comply with an order requiring it to produce a person for examination, the court may issue any of the sanctions orders in FRCP 37(b)(2)(A)(i)-(b)(2)(A)(vi) unless the disobedient party shows it cannot produce the person. FRCP 37(b)(2)(B). See "Sanctions for not complying with order," ch. 6-A, §15.5.1, p. 448.

§2.7 Presence of other persons or recording devices. Although a party can request the presence of other persons or recording devices during the examination, there is a presumption against the presence of third persons or things, such as attorneys, court reporters, or audio or video recorders, in an examination because they are considered distractions that can compromise the accuracy of the examination and turn a neutral examination into an adversarial event. *See* ***Favale v. Roman Catholic Diocese of Bridgeport***, 235 F.R.D. 553, 557 (D.Conn.2006); ***Bethel v. Dixie Homecrafters, Inc.***, 192 F.R.D. 320, 323-24 (N.D.Ga.2000); ***Hertenstein v. Kimberly Home Health Care, Inc.***, 189 F.R.D. 620, 634 (D.Kan.1999). Thus, courts routinely deny such requests. *See, e.g.*, ***Calderon v. Reederei Claus-Peter Offen GmbH & Co.***, 258 F.R.D. 523, 527-28 (S.D.Fla.2009) (court denied P's request for attorney and recording device to be present during examination because allegation that P needed reassurance of safety was not sufficient); ***Hertenstein***, 189 F.R.D. at 634 (court denied P's requests for a "familiar face" and recording device to be present during examination because P did not show any special circumstances justifying her requests). ***But see Bennett v. White Labs.***, 841 F.Supp. 1155, 1159 (M.D.Fla.1993) (court granted P's request for her personal physician to be present because physical examination was going to cause her discomfort and pain); ***T.B. v. Chico Unified Sch. Dist.***, No. S-07-0926-GEB-CMK (E.D.Cal.2009) (no pub.; 3-26-09) (court allowed examining doctor to videotape examination when examinee was child and use of camera was unobtrusive). The party requesting the presence of a third party has the burden to show that the third party's presence is necessary and that there are special circumstances justifying her presence. ***Calderon***, 258 F.R.D. at 526.

§3. EXAMINER'S REPORT

§3.1 Report. The examiner must prepare a written report that sets out in detail the examiner's findings, including diagnoses, conclusions, and the results of any tests. FRCP 35(b)(2).

1. Request by party or person examined. On request by either the party against whom the examination was ordered or the person examined, the party who moved for the examination must deliver to the requesting party or examinee a copy of the examiner's report, together with similar reports of all earlier examinations of the same condition. FRCP 35(b)(1); *see* ***Buffington v. Wood***, 351 F.2d 292, 296 (3d Cir.1965). Discovery of the report is permitted without a showing of good cause. *See* FRCP 35(b). The report must be produced early enough before trial to give the party ample preparation time. ***Shapiro v. Win-Sum Ski Corp.***, 95 F.R.D. 38, 38-39 (W.D.N.Y.1982).

2. Request by examining party. After the party who moved for the examination delivers a copy of the examiner's report, that party, on request, is entitled to receive from the party against whom the examination was ordered similar reports of all earlier or later examinations of the same condition. FRCP 35(b)(3); ***Ewing v. Ayres Corp.***, 129 F.R.D. 137, 139 (N.D.Miss.1989). The party with custody or control of the person examined does not need to deliver the reports to the requesting party if it could not obtain them. FRCP 35(b)(3).

3. Not delivering report. On motion, the court may order a party to deliver the report on just terms. FRCP 35(b)(5); *see* ***Salvatore v. American Cyanamid Co.***, 94 F.R.D. 156, 158 (D.R.I.1982) (party cannot tell doctor not to prepare report if it does not like examination results). If the report is not provided, the court may exclude the examiner's testimony at trial. FRCP 35(b)(5).

§3.2 Waiver of privilege. By requesting and obtaining a copy of the examiner's report, or by deposing the examiner, the party against whom an examination was ordered waives any privilege it may have for testimony about all examinations of the same condition. FRCP 35(b)(4); ***Buffington v. Wood***, 351 F.2d 292, 296 (3d Cir.1965). Thus, the trade-off for obtaining discovery of the examiner's report or deposing the examiner is a waiver of any privilege for any other relevant personal medical reports. *See* FRCP 35(b)(4). The privilege is waived in that case and any other case involving the same controversy. *Id.*

§3.3 Examinations by agreement. The requirements of FRCP 35(b) also apply to examinations conducted according to the parties' agreement. FRCP 35(b)(6); *see* ***Grajales-Romero v. American Airlines, Inc.***, 194 F.3d 288, 298 n.12 (1st Cir.1999).

§3.4 Other discovery methods not prohibited.

1. Discovery by examined party. The provisions for production of the examiner's report do not prohibit obtaining an examiner's report or deposing an examiner under other rules. FRCP 35(b)(6). The report may be discovered under FRCP 34 without waiving any privilege for other personal medical records. *See* ***Buffington v. Wood***, 351 F.2d 292, 297 (3d Cir.1965) (party should be free to move under FRCP 34 to discover report). Because the examiner will ordinarily be considered an expert witness, discovery from the examiner will be permitted only when the examining party intends to use the examiner as a trial witness. FRCP 26(b)(4)(D); *e.g.*, ***Brown v. Ringstad***, 142 F.R.D. 461, 463 (S.D.Iowa 1992) (deposition of nontestifying examiner would have been allowed only under FRCP 26(b)(4)(B), now FRCP 26(b)(4)(D)). See "Securing Discovery from Experts," ch. 6-D, p. 515.

(1) Examiner expected to testify. If the examiner is expected to testify, the party retaining or employing the examiner must make full disclosure about the examiner. FRCP 26(a)(2). The party seeking discovery may depose the examiner. FRCP 26(b)(4)(A); ***Brown***, 142 F.R.D. at 463.

(2) Examiner not expected to testify. If the examiner is not expected to testify, the only information automatically discoverable will be the examiner's report. *See* ***Marine Pet. Co. v. Champlin Pet. Co.***, 641 F.2d 984, 989 n.11 (D.C.Cir.1979) (FRCP 35(b) relates only to physicians' reports). Facts known or opinions held by the examiner are discoverable only when a party shows exceptional circumstances that prevent discovery of facts or opinions on the same subject by other means. FRCP 26(b)(4)(D)(ii); *e.g.*, ***Brown***, 142 F.R.D. at 463 (deposition of nontestifying examiner would have been allowed only under FRCP 26(b)(4)(B), now FRCP 26(b)(4)(D)). See "Facts & opinions," ch. 6-D, §4.1.1(1)(b)[2], p. 526.

2. Discovery by examining party. FRCP 35 does not limit a party's ability to discover another party's medical condition through other discovery provisions. *E.g.*, ***Buffington***, 351 F.2d at 296-97 (FRCP 35(b) did not bar discovery of other medical reports under FRCP 34).

K. REQUEST FOR ENTRY ON LAND

§1. GENERAL

§1.1 Rules. FRCP 34, 45.

§1.2 Purpose. A party may serve on any other party a request within the scope of FRCP 26(b) to permit entry on land to inspect, measure, survey, photograph, test, or sample the property or any designated object or operation on it. FRCP 34(a)(2). FRCP 34 also permits inspection of land belonging to nonparties. FRCP 34(c). Formerly, inspection of land not belonging to a party could be obtained only by an independent lawsuit in the nature of an equitable bill of discovery. ***Lubrin v. Hess Oil V.I. Corp.***, 109 F.R.D. 403, 405 (D.V.I.1986); ***Home Ins. Co. v. First Nat'l Bank***, 89 F.R.D. 485, 488-89 (N.D.Ga.1980).

NOTE

To discourage parties from circumventing the purpose of FRCP 34(a)(2), courts will usually declare inadmissible any evidence gathered through informal investigations on a party's real property. See ***Baugus v. CSX Transp.***, *223 F.R.D. 469, 471 (N.D.Ohio 2004). But see* ***McNierney v. Long Island R.R.***, *215 F.R.D. 458, 459 (S.D.N.Y.2003) (evidence gathered before suit and without request for inspection was admitted because it would have inevitably been discovered).*

§1.3 Timetable & forms. Timetable, Discovery Status Sheet, p. 1579; ***O'Connor's Federal Civil Forms*** (2012), FORMS 6K.

§1.4 Other references. 8B Wright, Miller & Marcus, *Federal Practice & Procedure 3d* §§2201-2217 (2010 & Supp.2012); 7 *Moore's Federal Practice 3d* ch. 34 (2012).

§2. REQUEST FOR ENTRY

To gain access to the land of another party, a party may serve a request for entry on land. FRCP 34(a)(2).

§2.1 Time to serve. A request to permit entry on land cannot be served before the FRCP 26(f) conference unless the parties stipulate or the court orders otherwise. FRCP 26(d)(1).

§2.2 Scope of request. FRCP 34(a) specifically sets forth the scope of entry on land and requires compliance with the scope of FRCP 26(b). ***Eirhart v. Libbey-Owens-Ford Co.***, 93 F.R.D. 370, 371 (N.D.Ill.1981).

§2.3 Form of request. The request should state (1) that the party would like access to the property for the purpose of inspecting, measuring, surveying, photographing, testing, or sampling the property or any object or operation on it and (2) the reasons why access is necessary. *See* FRCP 34(a)(2). The request must describe with reasonable particularity each item or category of items to be inspected. FRCP 34(b)(1)(A); *e.g.*, ***Belcher v. Bassett Furniture Indus.***, 588 F.2d 904, 907-08 (4th Cir.1978) (motion to compel inspection was improperly granted when motion contained "skeletal" request). The request must also specify a reasonable time, place, and manner for the inspection. FRCP 34(b)(1)(B). See "State time, place, manner & form of production," ch. 6-I, §3.4.2(6), p. 572.

§2.4 Subpoena for nonparty. If a party requests access to the land of a nonparty, the party must also serve a subpoena on the person in possession or control of the land. FRCP 34(c), 45(a)(1)(A)(iii). See "Subpoenas Under FRCP 45," ch. 1-H, p. 47.

§2.5 No filing. The request must not be filed until it is used in the proceeding or the court orders filing. FRCP 5(d)(1).

§3. RESPONDING TO REQUEST

§3.1 Response to request. A party who has been served with a request for entry on land must serve a written response within 30 days after the request is served. FRCP 34(b)(2)(A). The response must not be filed until it is used in the proceeding or the court orders filing. FRCP 5(d)(1). The parties may stipulate to or the court may order a shorter

or longer response time. FRCP 34(b)(2)(A); *see* FRCP 29. The response must state whether the party consents to the entry. FRCP 34(b)(2)(B). If the party objects to the request, the response must state an objection and the reasons for it. *Id.* An objection to part of a request must specify the objectionable part and permit inspection of the rest. FRCP 34(b)(2)(C).

§3.2 Response to subpoena. A nonparty who has been served with a subpoena to inspect the premises must serve written objections before the time specified for compliance or 14 days after the subpoena is served, whichever is earlier. FRCP 45(c)(2)(B). It is not necessary for the nonparty to appear at the site for the inspection. FRCP 45(c)(2)(A).

§3.3 Objections to request.

1. Outside scope of permitted inspection. A party should object to a request for entry on land that is being used to obtain interviews with or depositions of persons on the land. *See, e.g.*, ***Belcher v. Bassett Furniture Indus.***, 588 F.2d 904, 908-09 (4th Cir.1978) (court could not permit P's expert to roam D's plant and interrogate employees); ***Curry v. Allan S. Goodman, Inc.***, No. 3:02CV1149 (D.Conn.2003) (no pub.; 5-22-03) (court limited P's expert's visit to measurements and observations and would not allow him to informally question D's employees).

2. Oppressive & burdensome. A party should object to a request for entry on land if the degree to which the proposed inspection will aid the search for truth is outweighed by the burdens and dangers created by the inspection. ***New York Ass'n for Retarded Children, Inc. v. Carey***, 706 F.2d 956, 961 (2d Cir.1983). For example, a request that hampers a company's ability to conduct its business or creates a safety hazard can be disallowed. ***Belcher***, 588 F.2d at 909.

3. Not reasonably particular. A party should object to a request for entry on land that does not particularly describe the items to be inspected. ***Belcher***, 588 F.2d at 911.

4. Protection of trade secrets. A party, and especially a nonparty, should object to a request for inspection if it has a legitimate interest in maintaining its trade secrets. *E.g.*, ***Bio-Vita, Ltd. v. Biopure Corp.***, 138 F.R.D. 13, 17-18 (D.Mass.1991) (court denied request for entry to observe testing of new drug on property when nonparty had legitimate and strong interest in protecting commercial secrets).

5. No possession or control. A party should object to a request for entry on land if the party does not have possession or control of the land. *See* FRCP 34(a)(2); ***Peterson v. Union Pac. R.R.***, No. 06-3084 (C.D.Ill.2007) (slip op.; 11-1-07).

§4. CHALLENGING RESPONSE

If the party or person served with a request or subpoena for entry on land asserts objections, the party seeking discovery may ask the court to compel entry on land. FRCP 37(a)(3)(B)(iv), 45(c)(2)(B)(i). See "Motion to Compel Discovery," ch. 6-A, §14, p. 444. If, in the response to the motion to compel, the party asks the court to allow her attorney to be present during the inspection, the party seeking the inspection should object on the grounds of work-product protection. *See* ***Teer v. Law Eng'g & Env'tl Servs.***, 176 F.R.D. 206, 207 (E.D.N.C.1997) (dicta); *see, e.g.*, ***Mancuso v. D.R.D. Towing Co.***, No. 05-2441 (E.D.La.2006) (no pub.; 3-10-06) (court denied respondent's request for its attorney to shadow opposing counsel during inspection on grounds that it would violate work-product doctrine).

§5. APPELLATE REVIEW

Ordinarily, a court's order on a request for entry on land is challenged by appeal. Granting or denying a request to inspect land under FRCP 34 is a matter within the district court's discretion and "will be reversed only if the action taken was improvident and affected substantial rights." ***Belcher v. Bassett Furniture Indus.***, 588 F.2d 904, 907 (4th Cir.1978). Mandamus relief is generally not available. See "Review by mandamus," ch. 6-A, §16.2, p. 455.

COMMENTARIES

CHAPTER 7. DISPOSITION WITHOUT TRIAL

TABLE OF CONTENTS

A. DEFAULT JUDGMENT 583

§1. GENERAL 583
§2. ENTRY OF DEFAULT VS. DEFAULT JUDGMENT 583
§2.1 Different effect 583
§2.2 Different authority 583
§2.3 Different standards of review 584
§2.4 Different requests 584
§3. REQUEST TO CLERK FOR ENTRY OF DEFAULT 584
§3.1 Parties 584
§3.2 Request for entry of default 584
§3.3 No notice required 586
§3.4 Defendant's objections to entry of default 586
§3.5 Clerk's entry of default 587
§4. MOTION TO SET ASIDE ENTRY OF DEFAULT UNDER FRCP 55(c) 588
§4.1 Motion 588
§4.2 Proposed pleading & motion for leave 590
§4.3 Response 590
§5. REQUEST TO CLERK FOR DEFAULT JUDGMENT 590
§5.1 Entry of default judgment by clerk 590
§5.2 Request for default judgment 591
§5.3 Affidavits & attachments 592
§5.4 No notice required 592
§5.5 Defendant's objections to clerk's entry of default judgment 592
§5.6 Clerk's default judgment 593
§6. MOTION TO COURT FOR DEFAULT JUDGMENT 593
§6.1 Motion for default judgment 593
§6.2 Affidavits & attachments 594
§6.3 Notice of hearing 594
§6.4 Defendant's objections to court's entry of default judgment 595
§6.5 Hearing 596
§6.6 Ruling 597
§7. NOTICE OF DEFAULT JUDGMENT 598
§8. MOTION TO VACATE DEFAULT JUDGMENT UNDER FRCP 60(b) 598
§8.1 Form 598
§8.2 Grounds 598
§8.3 Proposed answer or other responsive pleading 601
§8.4 Deadline 601
§8.5 Response 602
§8.6 Ruling 602
§9. APPELLATE REVIEW 602
§9.1 Entry of default 602
§9.2 Default judgment 602

B. SUMMARY JUDGMENT 603

§1. GENERAL 603
§2. COMPARISON WITH OTHER NONTRIAL DISPOSITIONS 603
§2.1 FRCP 12(b)(6) motion to dismiss 603
§2.2 FRCP 12(c) motion for judgment on the pleadings 603
§2.3 Motion for judgment as a matter of law (JMOL) 603
§2.4 FRCP 12(b)(1) motion to dismiss for lack of subject-matter jurisdiction 604
§3. MOTION FOR SUMMARY JUDGMENT 604
§3.1 Motion 604
§3.2 Supporting proof 606
§3.3 Point-counterpoint statement of undisputed facts 606
§3.4 Brief or memorandum 606
§3.5 Proposed order 606
§4. RESPONSE TO MOTION FOR SUMMARY JUDGMENT 606
§4.1 Response 606
§4.2 Supporting proof 609
§4.3 Point-counterpoint statement of genuine disputes 609
§4.4 Brief or memorandum 609
§4.5 Proposed order 609
§4.6 Motion to extend & motion for continuance 609
§4.7 Leave to amend pleadings 609
§5. REPLY BRIEF 609
§5.1 No fact disputes 610
§5.2 Objections 610
§5.3 Supporting proof 610
§6. SUMMARY-JUDGMENT PROOF 610
§6.1 Types of SJ proof 610
§6.2 Proper SJ proof 614
§6.3 Citing SJ proof 614
§6.4 Placing SJ proof in the record 614
§6.5 Organizing SJ proof 614
§7. BURDEN OF PROOF 615
§7.1 Generally 615
§7.2 When defendant moves for SJ on plaintiff's claim 616
§7.3 When defendant moves for SJ on its affirmative defense 617
§7.4 When defendant moves for SJ on its counterclaim 617
§7.5 When plaintiff moves for SJ on its claim 618
§7.6 When plaintiff moves for SJ on defendant's affirmative defense 618
§7.7 When both parties move for SJ 618
§8. DEADLINES 619
§8.1 When to move for SJ 619
§8.2 When to respond to motion for SJ 619
§8.3 When to reply to nonmovant's response 620
§9. MOTION FOR CONTINUANCE 620
§9.1 Procedure 620
§9.2 Grounds 620
§9.3 Response 622
§9.4 Ruling 622
§10. HEARING 623
§10.1 Hearing vs. submission 623
§10.2 Request for hearing 623
§11. SUMMARY-JUDGMENT RULING 623
§11.1 Review of SJ proof 623
§11.2 Review when nonmovant cannot present facts to justify response 624
§11.3 Review of party's SJ motion 625
§11.4 Review on court's own initiative 626
§11.5 Order & judgment 627
§11.6 Motion for reconsideration 627
§12. APPELLATE REVIEW 628
§12.1 Standard of review 628
§12.2 SJ granted 628
§12.3 SJ denied 628
§12.4 Costs & attorney fees under FRCP 56(h) 629

COMMENTARIES

CHAPTER 7. DISPOSITION WITHOUT TRIAL
TABLE OF CONTENTS

C. VOLUNTARY DISMISSAL 629
§1. GENERAL 629
§2. TYPES OF VOLUNTARY DISMISSALS 629
§2.1 Parties 629
§2.2 Types of dismissals 629
§2.3 Partial dismissal of parties & claims 630
§3. PLAINTIFF'S NOTICE OF DISMISSAL 630
§3.1 Form 630
§3.2 Deadline 631
§3.3 Effect 631
§3.4 Response 631
§4. PARTIES' STIPULATION OF DISMISSAL 631
§4.1 Form 631
§4.2 Deadline 632
§4.3 Effect 632
§4.4 Response 632
§5. PLAINTIFF'S MOTION FOR COURT-ORDERED DISMISSAL 632
§5.1 Form 633
§5.2 Deadline 633
§5.3 Response 633
§5.4 Proposed order denying relief 635
§6. ORDER OF DISMISSAL 635
§6.1 In writing 635
§6.2 Dismissal under FRCP 41(a)(1) 635
§6.3 Dismissal under FRCP 41(a)(2) 636
§6.4 FRCP 11 order after dismissal 638
§7. EFFECT OF DISMISSAL 638
§7.1 Without prejudice 638
§7.2 With prejudice 638
§8. CHALLENGING DISMISSAL IN DISTRICT COURT 639
§8.1 Challenging notice of dismissal under FRCP 41(a)(1)(A)(i) 639
§8.2 Challenging stipulation of dismissal under FRCP 41(a)(1)(A)(ii) 639
§8.3 Challenging dismissal on motion under FRCP 41(a)(2) 640
§9. APPELLATE REVIEW 640
§9.1 Standard of review 640
§9.2 Appeal 640

D. INVOLUNTARY DISMISSAL 642
§1. GENERAL 642
§2. MOTION 642
§2.1 Party's motion 642
§2.2 Sua sponte 643
§3. GROUNDS 643
§3.1 Failure to prosecute 643
§3.2 Failure to comply with court rule or order 644
§3.3 Sanctions 645
§3.4 Failure to serve defendant with suit 645
§3.5 Indigent's frivolous suit 646
§3.6 Other grounds 646
§4. RESPONSE 646
§4.1 Deadline 646
§4.2 Objections 647
§4.3 Affidavits 647
§4.4 Proposed order denying relief 647
§5. NOTICE OF INTENT TO DISMISS 647
§5.1 Notice under FRCP 41(b) 647
§5.2 Notice under FRCP 16(f) & 37(b) 647
§5.3 Notice to indigent 647
§5.4 Notice under FRCP 4(m) 647
§6. ORDER OF DISMISSAL 647
§6.1 Findings 647
§6.2 Types of dismissal 648
§6.3 Scope of order 648
§6.4 Options after dismissal 649
§7. APPELLATE REVIEW 649

E. ARBITRATION 650
§1. GENERAL 650
§2. COMPELLING ARBITRATION 650
§2.1 Motion to compel 650
§2.2 Response 653
§2.3 Ruling 658
§3. MODIFYING OR VACATING ARBITRATION AWARD 659
§3.1 Motion 659
§3.2 Response 662
§3.3 District court's review of arbitration award 663
§4. CONFIRMING ARBITRATION AWARD 663
§4.1 Motion to confirm domestic award 663
§4.2 Motion to confirm foreign award 664
§5. APPELLATE REVIEW 666
§5.1 Appealable order 666
§5.2 Standard of review 667
§5.3 Waiver 668

7. DISPOSITION WITHOUT TRIAL

A. DEFAULT JUDGMENT

§1. GENERAL

§1.1 Rule. FRCP 55. See also FRCP 5(a)(2), 16(f), 37(b)(2)(A)(vi), 54(c), 60(b); FRAP 4(a)(4)(A)(vi); 50 U.S.C. app. §521.

§1.2 Purpose. When a party defaults (i.e., does not answer or defend against a claim), the court or clerk may enter a final judgment without conducting a trial on liability. FRCP 55. The threat of a default judgment encourages parties to timely file responsive pleadings and discourages the use of delay as a litigation tactic. *See* ***Enron Oil Corp. v. Diakuhara***, 10 F.3d 90, 95-96 (2d Cir.1993). Because courts prefer to resolve disputes on the merits, they disfavor default judgments and grant them sparingly. ***Rogers v. Hartford Life & Acc. Ins.***, 167 F.3d 933, 936 (5th Cir.1999); ***Security Ins. v. Schipporeit, Inc.***, 69 F.3d 1377, 1381 (7th Cir.1995); ***Whelan v. Abell***, 48 F.3d 1247, 1258 (D.C.Cir. 1995); *see* ***Weiss v. St. Paul Fire & Mar. Ins.***, 283 F.3d 790, 795 (6th Cir.2002) (trials on merits favored in federal courts); ***Powerserve Int'l v. Lavi***, 239 F.3d 508, 514 (2d Cir.2001) (same); *see also* ***Stewart v. Astrue***, 552 F.3d 26, 28 (1st Cir.2009) (disfavor against default judgments is especially strong when defendant is U.S. government).

§1.3 Timetables & forms. Timetable, Request to Clerk for Default Judgment, p. 1586; Timetable, Motion to Court for Default Judgment, p. 1587; ***O'Connor's Federal Civil Forms*** (2012), FORMS 7A.

§1.4 Other references. 10A Wright, Miller & Kane, *Federal Practice & Procedure 3d* §§2681-2702 (1998 & Supp.2012); 10 *Moore's Federal Practice 3d* ch. 55 (2012); Annotation, *What Constitutes "Appearance" Under Rule 55(b)(2)* ..., 139 ALR Fed. 603 (1997 & Supp.2012-13); Annotation, *Default Judgments Against the U.S. Under Rule 55(e)* ..., 55 ALR Fed. 190 (1981 & Supp.2012-13); Annotation, *What Constitutes "Good Cause" ... Under Rule 55(c)* ..., 29 ALR Fed. 7 (1976 & Supp.2012-13).

§2. ENTRY OF DEFAULT VS. DEFAULT JUDGMENT

Securing a default judgment is a three-step procedure involving the defendant's default, the entry of default, and the entry of default judgment. ***New York Life Ins. v. Brown***, 84 F.3d 137, 141 (5th Cir.1996); ***Eitel v. McCool***, 782 F.2d 1470, 1471 (9th Cir.1986); *see* ***City of N.Y. v. Mickalis Pawn Shop, LLC***, 645 F.3d 114, 128 (2d Cir.2011). A "default" occurs when the defendant does not plead or otherwise respond to the complaint. ***New York Life***, 84 F.3d at 141. An "entry of default" is the notation the clerk makes after the default is established by affidavit. *Id.*; *see* ***City of N.Y.***, 645 F.3d at 128. An "entry of default judgment" is the entry of the judgment based on the entry of default. ***City of N.Y.***, 645 F.3d at 128; ***New York Life***, 84 F.3d at 141. The entry of default is different from the entry of default judgment in several respects:

§2.1 Different effect. The entry of default is an acknowledgment that a default has occurred; it merely permits the plaintiff to move for entry of a default judgment under FRCP 55(b). ***U.S. v. $23,000 in U.S. Currency***, 356 F.3d 157, 163 (1st Cir.2004); ***U.S. v. DiMucci***, 879 F.2d 1488, 1490 n.3 (7th Cir.1989); *see* ***Johnson v. Dayton Elec. Mfg.***, 140 F.3d 781, 783 (8th Cir.1998) (entry of default must precede grant of default judgment). It is an interlocutory order and is not appealable. ***$23,000 in U.S. Currency***, 356 F.3d at 163; ***Ackra Direct Mktg. Corp. v. Fingerhut Corp.***, 86 F.3d 852, 855 (8th Cir.1996). *But see* ***Dayton Elec.***, 140 F.3d at 783 (interlocutory review of entry of default granted under 28 U.S.C. §1292(b)). By comparison, the default judgment is a final adjudication of liability and can be appealed immediately. ***Ackra Direct Mktg.***, 86 F.3d at 855 n.3.

§2.2 Different authority. The request for entry of default should be directed to the clerk but may be directed to the court. ***Breuer Elec. Mfg. v. Toronado Sys.***, 687 F.2d 182, 185 (7th Cir.1982). See "Request to Clerk for Entry of Default," §3, p. 584. The motion for default judgment should be addressed to the court but may sometimes be addressed to the clerk. See "Request to Clerk for Default Judgment," §5, p. 590; "Motion to Court for Default Judgment," §6, p. 593.

§2.3 Different standards of review. The courts apply different standards of review to a motion to set aside an entry of default and a motion to vacate a default judgment. ***Weiss v. St. Paul Fire & Mar. Ins.***, 283 F.3d 790, 794 (6th Cir.2002); ***Pretzel & Stouffer v. Imperial Adjusters, Inc.***, 28 F.3d 42, 44-45 (7th Cir.1994). For a motion to set aside an entry of default, courts apply the more lenient good-cause standard of review. FRCP 55(c); ***U.S. v. $23,000 in U.S. Currency***, 356 F.3d 157, 164 (1st Cir.2004). For a motion to vacate a default judgment, courts apply the more stringent excusable-neglect standard of review. FRCP 60(b)(1); ***$23,000 in U.S. Currency***, 356 F.3d at 164; ***U.S. v. Timbers Preserve***, 999 F.2d 452, 454 (10th Cir.1993).

§2.4 Different requests. A party moving for a default judgment may either request the entry of default separately from the default judgment or ask for them in the same document. There is an advantage to asking for the entry of default and the default judgment in the same document. If the plaintiff asks for the entry of default first, the defendant may file its answer before the plaintiff asks for the entry of the default judgment. *See, e.g.*, ***U.S. v. Harre***, 983 F.2d 128, 130 (8th Cir.1993) (party's late answer was an appearance). Even though untimely, the answer would entitle the defendant to notice of a motion for entry of default judgment. *Id.* By comparison, if the plaintiff asks for the entry of default and the default judgment in the same document, the clerk may enter the default and the default judgment before the defendant files its answer. ***Direct Mail Specialists, Inc. v. Eclat Computerized Techs.***, 840 F.2d 685, 689 (9th Cir.1988). A defaulting party is not guaranteed the right to set aside a clerk's entry of default before a default judgment is entered. ***Ackra Direct Mktg. Corp. v. Fingerhut Corp.***, 86 F.3d 852, 855 (8th Cir.1996).

§3. REQUEST TO CLERK FOR ENTRY OF DEFAULT

PRACTICE TIP

Even though FRCP 55 provides for the entry of default by the clerk without notice or hearing, in some districts only the court will enter default. Sometimes, the clerk or court will not enter default until after the defendant is notified of the pending request for entry of default. Contact the clerk about the court's procedure before filing a request for entry of default. See Civil Forms – Default Judgment Package (E.D.Tenn.), Step One.

§3.1 Parties. Any party who has requested affirmative relief may request entry of default against the defaulting party. In most cases the movant is the plaintiff, but if the defendant files a counterclaim, cross-claim, or third-party claim, the movant may be the defendant. *See* FRCP 55(a); *see also* ***Johnson v. Gudmundsson***, 35 F.3d 1104, 1111 (7th Cir.1994) (as sanction against P, default judgment granted to D on its counterclaim). Any party from whom another party has requested affirmative relief may be a defaulting party.

NOTE

Because the party seeking default is almost always a plaintiff and the defaulting party is almost always a defendant, for the sake of simplicity we will refer to the moving party as the plaintiff and the defaulting party as the defendant.

§3.2 Request for entry of default. The plaintiff must request that the clerk (or the court) enter the default. *See* ***City of N.Y. v. Mickalis Pawn Shop, LLC***, 645 F.3d 114, 128 (2d Cir.2011); ***New York Life Ins. v. Brown***, 84 F.3d 137, 141 (5th Cir.1996). *But see* ***McMahan v. CCC Express Corp.***, 153 F.R.D. 633, 634 (N.D.Ind.1994) (clerk could have entered default on its own). The request for entry of default is sometimes called an "affidavit of default."

1. **Grounds.** The request must show the following:

(1) **Suit filed.** The plaintiff filed a complaint (or other pleading) seeking affirmative relief on a certain date.

(2) **Defendant served.** The summons and complaint were served on the defendant on a certain date. The plaintiff must show that the defendant was properly served with the complaint. ***O'Brien v. R.J. O'Brien &***

Assocs., 998 F.2d 1394, 1398 (7th Cir.1993); *see* FRCP 4(*l*). The process server's affidavit under FRCP 4(*l*) is prima facie proof of service. ***O'Brien***, 998 F.2d at 1398; *see* FRCP 4(*l*)(1).

(3) Defendant's status. The request for entry of default should include the following statements about the defendant:

(a) Minor or incompetent. Whether the defendant is a minor or an incompetent person. *See* FRCP 55(b); ***Hutton v. Fisher***, 359 F.2d 913, 915 (3d Cir.1966).

(b) Military servicemember. Whether the defendant is currently in military service. 50 U.S.C. app. §521(b)(1).

NOTE

While the clerk cannot enter a default judgment against the U.S. government, she can enter a default. See ***Alameda v. Secretary of Health, Educ. & Welfare****, 622 F.2d 1044, 1048 (1st Cir. 1980). See "Entry of Default vs. Default Judgment," §2, p. 583. Only the court can enter a default judgment against the U.S. government. See "Liability of United States," §6.5.1(2), p. 596.*

(4) No defense. The defendant did not file a pleading or otherwise defend. FRCP 55(a). Generally, default is entered because a defendant did not timely file an answer. ***City of N.Y.***, 645 F.3d at 129. The request for entry of default must show the following:

(a) No answer. The defendant did not file an answer or other required pleading, including a response to an amended pleading, counterclaim, or cross-claim. *E.g.*, ***New York Life***, 84 F.3d at 141 (D defaulted when it did not timely file answer); ***Pretzel & Stouffer v. Imperial Adjusters, Inc.***, 28 F.3d 42, 44 (7th Cir.1994) (same).

(b) Not otherwise defended. The defendant did not take any action that indicated the defendant's intent to defend the suit (e.g., filing a motion under FRCP 12 or a motion for summary judgment). *See* FRCP 55(a); ***City of N.Y.***, 645 F.3d at 129.

NOTE

The circuits disagree on what circumstances constitute a failure to "otherwise defend" under FRCP 55(a). See ***City of N.Y.****, 645 F.3d at 129-31; 10A Wright, Miller & Kane §2682 nn.14-19. Many circuits interpret the phrase broadly; these circuits can find a failure to defend when, for example, the defendant does not meet deadlines, does not appear at trial, or uses obstructionist litigation tactics—even if the defendant has filed an answer. See* ***Hoxworth v. Blinder, Robinson & Co.****, 980 F.2d 912, 917-18 (3d Cir.1992); see, e.g.,* ***City of N.Y.****, 645 F.3d at 129-30 (after motions to dismiss were filed and varying amounts of discovery were conducted, entry of default was proper when Ds affirmatively confirmed their intent to stop participating in case, one of D's attorneys withdrew without substitute, and Ds indicated their understanding that conduct would likely result in default). A few circuits interpret the phrase more narrowly; these circuits do not find a failure to defend when the defendant files an answer and only later does not appear or defend. See* ***Solaroll Shade & Shutter Corp. v. Bio-Energy Sys.****, 803 F.2d 1130, 1134 (11th Cir.1986);* ***Seven Elves, Inc. v. Eskenazi****, 635 F.2d 396, 400 n.2 (5th Cir.1981). For a discussion of actions that may show an intent to defend, see "Otherwise defend," §3.4.2, p. 586.*

(5) Time to defend expired. The time allowed to file a response to the suit expired on a certain date. *See* FRCP 12(a)(1)(A) (general deadline), FRCP 12(a)(1)(B) (counterclaim or cross-claim), FRCP 15(a) (amended pleading). See "Deadlines," ch. 3-A, §5, p. 174.

2. Affidavits & supporting documentation. Along with the request for entry of default, the plaintiff should file the following:

(1) Affidavit for entry of default. The request for entry of default must be accompanied by an affidavit or otherwise demonstrate that the defendant has defaulted. FRCP 55(a); ***Enron Oil Corp. v. Diakuhara***, 10 F.3d 90, 95 (2d Cir.1993). The affidavit must verify both the facts supporting the allegations of default and the attachments to the request.

(2) Military affidavit. The request for entry of default should include a military affidavit stating whether the defendant is in military service. The Servicemembers Civil Relief Act (formerly the Soldiers' & Sailors' Civil Relief Act of 1940) provides members of the armed forces with certain protections against default judgments in civil litigation. *See* 50 U.S.C. app. §521. If the defendant is in the military, or if the plaintiff is not certain whether the defendant is in the military, the court may appoint a lawyer to represent the defendant. *Id.* §521(b)(2); *see id.* §521(b)(3). It is a federal misdemeanor to knowingly make a false military affidavit. *See id.* §521(c).

(a) When required. Although the affidavit is not required when requesting entry of default, the clerk will not be able to enter a default judgment until the plaintiff files the affidavit. 50 U.S.C. app. §521(b)(1).

(b) Supporting facts. The affidavit must show necessary facts to support the affidavit. 50 U.S.C. app. §521(b)(1)(A).

(c) In writing. The affidavit must be in writing. *See* 50 U.S.C. app. §521(b)(4) (affidavit requirement satisfied by statement, declaration, verification, or certificate).

(d) Verified. The affidavit must be subscribed and certified, or declared to be true under penalty of perjury. 50 U.S.C. app. §521(b)(4); *see* ***U.S. v. Simmons***, 508 F.Supp. 552, 552 n.* (E.D.Tenn.1980) (courts will reject affidavit based on information and belief).

(3) Supporting documentation. The request for entry of default should include copies of all documents that prove the defendant is in default. For example, even though the complaint and return of service are in the clerk's file, the plaintiff should attach copies of those documents to the request for entry of default. The documents should also be attached as exhibits to an affidavit that verifies them by reference.

§3.3 No notice required. The FRCPs do not require the clerk to give notice of the entry of default. ***Hawaii Carpenters' Trust Funds v. Stone***, 794 F.2d 508, 512 (9th Cir.1986). But local rules may require the plaintiff or the clerk to notify the defaulting party of the entry of default. *E.g.*, Local Rules P.R., Rule 55(a) (moving party must give notice); *see* FRCP 5(a), 55(a); *see also* ***Blanchard v. Cortés-Molina***, 453 F.3d 40, 47 (1st Cir.2006) (even if P did not notify D as required by local rule, D must still show why D was not at fault for delay under FRCP 60(b)(6)).

§3.4 Defendant's objections to entry of default. The clerk cannot enter default if the defendant has answered or taken some action to otherwise defend or if the defendant was not properly served. *See* FRCP 55(a).

NOTE

*An appearance alone will not prevent the entry of default. See FRCP 55(a) (party must "plead or otherwise defend"); **Martinez v. Picker Int'l**, 635 F.Supp. 658, 659 (D.P.R.1986) (party must file defensive pleading or suffer default). But a notice of appearance will prevent the clerk from entering a default judgment. See "When clerk cannot enter default judgment," §5.1.2, p. 590.*

1. File answer. If the defendant learns that entry of default has been requested, it can prevent the entry of default by filing an answer. *See, e.g.*, ***Mason & Hanger-Silas Mason Co. v. Metal Trades Council***, 726 F.2d 166, 168 (5th Cir.1984) (court denied motion for default judgment after D filed answer).

2. Otherwise defend. If the defendant learns that entry of default has been requested, it can prevent the entry of default by showing that it took some action to otherwise defend. *See* FRCP 55(a). Although a notice of appearance or a request for extension of time to file an answer are not defensive moves that will prevent the entry

of default, a motion to dismiss under FRCP 12(b) is always sufficient to prevent entry of default. *See* FRCP 55(a); ***U.S. v. 51 Pieces of Real Prop.***, 17 F.3d 1306, 1314 (10th Cir.1994); ***Sun Bank v. Pelican Homestead & Sav. Ass'n***, 874 F.2d 274, 277 (5th Cir.1989); ***Patton Elec. Co. v. Rampart Air, Inc.***, 777 F.Supp. 704, 712-13 (N.D.Ind.1991). Other actions that may show an intent to defend include the following:

(1) A late answer raising affirmative defenses filed after the plaintiff filed an affidavit of default but before the entry of default. ***U.S. v. Harre***, 983 F.2d 128, 129-30 (8th Cir.1993).

(2) Letters or conversations about the lawsuit between attorneys for the parties. *See* ***Lacy v. Sitel Corp.***, 227 F.3d 290, 292-93 (5th Cir.2000); ***Key Bank v. Tablecloth Textile Co.***, 74 F.3d 349, 353-54 & n.6 (1st Cir. 1996).

(3) Settlement negotiations after the complaint was filed. ***Key Bank***, 74 F.3d at 353-54; ***Eitel v. McCool***, 782 F.2d 1470, 1472 (9th Cir.1986).

(4) A claim and cost bond filed with the IRS to transfer jurisdiction of a forfeiture case to district court. ***U.S. v. One 1966 Chevrolet Pickup Truck***, 56 F.R.D. 459, 462 (E.D.Tex.1972).

(5) Stipulations extending the time to answer that have been filed in the court. ***U.S. v. Melichar***, 56 F.R.D. 49, 50 (E.D.Wis.1972).

(6) A motion to transfer venue. ***Pikofsky v. Jem Oil***, 607 F.Supp. 727, 734 (E.D.Wis.1985).

(7) A motion to dismiss, even though it did not meet the requirements in the local rules and was returned to the defendant by the clerk. ***Sun Bank***, 874 F.2d at 277.

(8) The defendant's letter, sent to the court, labeled "special appearance." ***U.S. v. McCoy***, 954 F.2d 1000, 1003 (5th Cir.1992).

(9) Participating in a conference before the court. ***New York Life Ins. v. Brown***, 84 F.3d 137, 141-42 (5th Cir.1996).

(10) A motion for summary judgment. ***Rashidi v. Albright***, 818 F.Supp. 1354, 1356 (D.Nev.1993), *aff'd*, 39 F.3d 1188 (9th Cir.1994) (table case).

3. Object to service. If the defendant was not properly served, the clerk cannot enter default. ***Pinaud v. County of Suffolk***, 52 F.3d 1139, 1152 n.11 (2d Cir.1995); ***Martinez***, 635 F.Supp. at 659.

§3.5 Clerk's entry of default. When the clerk receives the request for entry of default together with proof of default, the clerk must enter the default. FRCP 55(a), (b)(1); *see* Civil Forms – Default Judgment Package (E.D.Tenn.). The entry of default is merely a docket entry noting that one party is in default. *See* ***Dow Chem. Pac. Ltd. v. Rascator Maritime S.A.***, 782 F.2d 329, 335 (2d Cir.1986). The plaintiff should check the docket to make sure the clerk made the entry as requested. *See, e.g.,* ***Taylor v. City of Ballwin***, 859 F.2d 1330, 1332 (8th Cir.1988) (clerk did not act on request for over 13 months); ***Meehan v. Snow***, 652 F.2d 274, 276 (2d Cir.1981) (clerk did not make docket entry).

1. Effect of entry of default. The entry of default against a defendant cuts off the defendant's right to appear in the case with respect to liability issues. *See* ***Greyhound Exhibitgroup, Inc. v. E.L.U.L. Rlty. Corp.***, 973 F.2d 155, 160 (2d Cir.1992); ***Taylor***, 859 F.2d at 1333 n.7. Once default is entered, the defendant's only recourse is to file a motion to set aside the entry of default. *See* FRCP 55(c); ***New York Life Ins. v. Brown***, 84 F.3d 137, 143 (5th Cir.1996). However, the defendant can contest on appeal the sufficiency of the complaint to state a claim for relief. ***Black v. Lane***, 22 F.3d 1395, 1399 (7th Cir.1994); ***Alan Neuman Prods. v. Albright***, 862 F.2d 1388, 1392 (9th Cir. 1988).

(1) Right to jury. After default, the right to a jury is limited by FRCP 55(b)(2). Generally, neither party has a right to demand a jury trial on damages. 10A Wright, Miller & Kane §2688 & n.27. The court may, however, order a jury trial on damages if it determines that a jury trial is the best means of assessing damages. ***Bonilla v. Trebol Motors Corp.***, 150 F.3d 77, 82 (1st Cir.1998).

(a) Failure to answer. FRCP 55(b)(2) provides that the court must preserve any federal statutory right to a jury trial. Most courts interpret FRCP 55(b)(2) as cutting off the right to a jury trial unless a specific statute requires it. *See* ***Bonilla***, 150 F.3d at 82-83 (right to jury is ordinarily lost when litigant does not appear); ***In re Dierschke***, 975 F.2d 181, 185 (5th Cir.1992) (right to jury is waived when party purposefully chooses not to answer). *But see* ***Comdyne I, Inc. v. Corbin***, 908 F.2d 1142, 1146 n.2 (3d Cir.1990) (court mentioned that D, who had not answered, was "arguably" entitled to jury trial on damages under FRCP 55(b)(2)). One treatise suggests that the only relevant statute is 28 U.S.C. §1874 (suits on bonds). 10A Wright, Miller & Kane §2688.

(b) Default as sanction. If the court enters a default as a sanction under FRCP 37(b)(2)(A)(vi), the defendant is not entitled to a jury trial on damages. ***Goldman, Antonetti, Ferraiuoli, Axtmayer & Hertell v. Medfit Int'l***, 982 F.2d 686, 692 n.15 (1st Cir.1993); ***Adriana Int'l v. Thoeren***, 913 F.2d 1406, 1414 (9th Cir.1990).

(2) Right to defend. If there is a hearing on damages, a defaulting party is entitled to contest and participate in the hearing. ***Bonilla***, 150 F.3d at 82.

2. Not appealable. The entry of default, whether by the clerk or by the court, is not an appealable order because it is not an adjudication of the issues in the complaint. ***Ackra Direct Mktg. Corp. v. Fingerhut Corp.***, 86 F.3d 852, 855 (8th Cir.1996); ***Enron Oil Corp. v. Diakuhara***, 10 F.3d 90, 95 (2d Cir.1993). The entry of default is merely an interim order officially recognizing that (1) the defendant is in default and (2) the plaintiff's well-pleaded factual allegations (except damages) are deemed admitted and cannot be contested. *See* ***Black***, 22 F.3d at 1399; ***Broadcast Music, Inc. v. R Bar, Inc.***, 919 F.Supp. 656, 658 (S.D.N.Y.1996); *see also* FRCP 8(b)(6) (allegations requiring response are deemed admitted if not denied in responsive pleading). A defendant cannot appeal the entry of default until after the default judgment is entered. ***Dow Chem.***, 782 F.2d at 335-36. *But see* ***Johnson v. Dayton Elec. Mfg.***, 140 F.3d 781, 783 (8th Cir.1998) (interlocutory review of entry of default granted under 28 U.S.C. §1292(b)).

§4. MOTION TO SET ASIDE ENTRY OF DEFAULT UNDER FRCP 55(c)

If the defendant learns about the entry of default before the default judgment is entered, it should immediately file a motion to set aside the entry of default, before the clerk (or the court) enters the default judgment. *See* FRCP 55(c); ***Pretzel & Stouffer v. Imperial Adjusters, Inc.***, 28 F.3d 42, 45 (7th Cir.1994); ***EEOC v. Mike Smith Pontiac GMC, Inc.***, 896 F.2d 524, 527-29 (11th Cir.1990). District courts are more willing to set aside an entry of default than a default judgment. *See* ***Frontier Ins. v. Blaty***, 454 F.3d 590, 595 (6th Cir.2006) (once judgment has been entered, court's discretion to set aside judgment is limited by public policy favoring finality of judgments). For a discussion of how to challenge a default judgment, see "Motion to Vacate Default Judgment Under FRCP 60(b)," §8, p. 598.

§4.1 Motion.

1. Form. The defendant should file a formal, written motion addressed to the court, even if the entry of default was made by the clerk. ***Gray v. John Jovino Co.***, 84 F.R.D. 46, 47 (E.D.Tenn.1979). The motion should be supported by an affidavit verifying the facts. Some courts also require the defendant to provide evidence of its alleged meritorious defense. ***Augusta Fiberglass Coatings, Inc. v. Fodor Contracting Corp.***, 843 F.2d 808, 812 (4th Cir.1988); *see* ***Teamsters, Chauffeurs, Warehousemen & Helpers Un. v. Superline Transp.***, 953 F.2d 17, 21 (1st Cir.1992) (conclusory allegation that meritorious claim exists is insufficient).

2. Sua sponte. The court may have the authority to set aside an entry of default on its own initiative. *See* ***Judson Atkinson Candies, Inc. v. Latini-Hohberger Dhimantec***, 529 F.3d 371, 385-86 (7th Cir.2008); ***Anheuser Busch v. Philpot***, 317 F.3d 1264, 1267 (11th Cir.2003).

3. Grounds.

(1) Defendant did not default. If the defendant filed an answer or other pleading or took any action indicating its intent to defend the suit, the defendant should state that the entry of default violated FRCP 55(a). See "Otherwise defend," §3.4.2, p. 586.

(2) Improper service. If service of process was improper, the court must set aside the entry of default. ***O.J. Distrib. v. Hornell Brewing Co.***, 340 F.3d 345, 353 (6th Cir.2003). See "Defendant served," §3.2.1(2), p. 584; "Object to service," §3.4.3, p. 587.

(3) Good cause. If the defendant shows good cause, the court may set aside the entry of default. FRCP 55(c); ***Franchise Holding II, LLC. v. Huntington Rests. Grp.***, 375 F.3d 922, 925 (9th Cir.2004); ***O.J. Distrib.***, 340 F.3d at 353; ***Enron Oil Corp. v. Diakuhara***, 10 F.3d 90, 96 (2d Cir.1993). Because FRCP 55(c) does not define "good cause," the courts generally rely on the same three factors—prejudice to the plaintiff, meritorious defense, and culpable conduct—used to evaluate a motion to vacate a default judgment for excusable neglect. *See* ***Indigo Am., Inc. v. Big Impressions, LLC***, 597 F.3d 1, 3 (1st Cir.2010); ***Enron***, 10 F.3d at 96; ***In re Dierschke***, 975 F.2d 181, 183 (5th Cir.1992); *see also* Annotation, *What Constitutes "Good Cause" ... Under Rule 55(c) ...*, 29 ALR Fed. at 14 (most courts recognize that good-cause standard exclusively governs relief from entry of default). Although the same factors are considered to set aside an entry of default or to vacate a default judgment, the courts apply the factors more liberally to an entry of default. ***Weiss v. St. Paul Fire & Mar. Ins.***, 283 F.3d 790, 794 (6th Cir.2002); ***American Alliance Ins. Co. v. Eagle Ins.***, 92 F.3d 57, 59 (2d Cir.1996); *see* ***Colleton Preparatory Acad., Inc. v. Hoover Univ'l, Inc.***, 616 F.3d 413, 420 (4th Cir.2010) (because setting aside entry of default does not involve final judgment, standard is more forgiving); ***Sims v. EGA Prods.***, 475 F.3d 865, 868 (7th Cir.2007) (same). See "Excusable neglect," §8.2.1, p. 598.

(a) Prejudice to plaintiff. The first good-cause factor is whether setting aside the entry of default would prejudice the plaintiff. ***O'Connor v. Nevada***, 27 F.3d 357, 364 (9th Cir.1994); ***Enron***, 10 F.3d at 96. The court uses this factor to consider whether the defendant took quick action to correct the default. *See* ***Pretzel & Stouffer v. Imperial Adjusters, Inc.***, 28 F.3d 42, 45 (7th Cir.1994).

(b) Meritorious defense. The second good-cause factor is whether the defendant has a prima facie meritorious defense. ***O'Connor***, 27 F.3d at 364; ***Enron***, 10 F.3d at 96. The mere denial of the plaintiff's claim is not sufficient for a meritorious defense. ***Pretzel & Stouffer***, 28 F.3d at 46.

(c) Culpable conduct. The third good-cause factor is whether the default was willful. ***O'Connor***, 27 F.3d at 364; ***Enron***, 10 F.3d at 96. A default should not be set aside if it was willful. ***Brien v. Kullman Indus.***, 71 F.3d 1073, 1078 (2d Cir.1995).

CAUTION

The defendant is responsible for bringing the correct standard of review to the court's attention. If in a motion to set aside entry of default the defendant inadvertently urges the court to apply the more stringent excusable-neglect standard rather than the good-cause standard, the defendant may be held to the higher standard. See ***EEOC v. Mike Smith Pontiac GMC, Inc.****, 896 F.2d 524, 528 (11th Cir.1990).*

(4) Other factors. The courts may also consider other factors when reviewing a motion to set aside the entry of default, including whether the entry of default would lead to a harsh or unfair result, whether the defendant is pro se, whether the public interest is implicated, and whether the defendant acted expeditiously to correct the default. *See* ***In re OCA, Inc.***, 551 F.3d 359, 369 (5th Cir.2008); ***Enron***, 10 F.3d at 96.

4. Deadline to file motion to set aside. FRCP 55(c) does not provide a deadline for filing a motion to set aside the entry of default. The courts generally require reasonable promptness. ***Dow Chem. Pac. Ltd. v. Rascator Maritime S.A.***, 782 F.2d 329, 336 (2d Cir.1986); *see* ***Pretzel & Stouffer***, 28 F.3d at 45 ("quick action"). The defendant should file the motion to set aside the entry of default immediately after learning of it and, if possible, before the court grants the default judgment. *See* ***Merrill Lynch Mortg. Corp. v. Narayan***, 908 F.2d 246, 252 (7th Cir. 1990). Once the court grants the default judgment, it is less likely to set aside the default.

5. Deadline to set aside entry of default. The entry of default is interlocutory; the court may set it aside at any time. ***Titus v. Smith***, 51 F.R.D. 224, 226 (E.D.Pa.1970).

§4.2 Proposed pleading & motion for leave. Along with the motion to set aside the entry of default, the defendant should file a proposed answer or motion to dismiss and a motion for leave to file it late. Certain FRCP 12(b) defenses (e.g., personal jurisdiction) not raised in the motion to set aside the entry of default or not filed in a motion to dismiss may be waived. *See* ***American Ass'n of Naturopathic Physicians v. Hayhurst***, 227 F.3d 1104, 1107-08 (9th Cir.2000). See "Defendant's Responses & Pleadings," ch. 3, p. 167; "Judgment is void," §8.2.2, p. 600. The filing of the proposed pleading should be conditioned on the granting of the motion to set aside the default. The proposed pleading should include allegations that, if found to be true, would amount to a meritorious defense. General denials, without allegations supporting a meritorious defense, are not sufficient. ***Sony Corp. v. Elm State Elecs., Inc.***, 800 F.2d 317, 320-21 (2d Cir.1986); ***Breuer Elec. Mfg. v. Toronado Sys.***, 687 F.2d 182, 186 (7th Cir.1982); ***Chandler Leasing Corp. v. UCC, Inc.***, 91 F.R.D. 81, 84 (N.D.Ill.1981).

§4.3 Response. If the defendant made allegations in the motion to set aside the entry of default that the plaintiff does not believe are true, the plaintiff should file a response to the motion. If the response contains facts outside the record, it should be verified by affidavit.

§5. REQUEST TO CLERK FOR DEFAULT JUDGMENT

PRACTICE TIP

Even though FRCP 55 permits a clerk to enter default judgments under certain circumstances, some districts require that only the court enter default judgments. If the district requires entry by the court, make sure to direct the request to the court, not the clerk. See ***U.S. v. Rainbolt***, *543 F.Supp. 580, 580 (E.D.Tenn.1982). This issue is seldom covered by local rules. Call the clerk before filing a request for default judgment.*

§5.1 Entry of default judgment by clerk. In some cases, the plaintiff should address the request for entry of default judgment to the clerk. *See* ***City of N.Y. v. Mickalis Pawn Shop, LLC***, 645 F.3d 114, 129 n.17 (2d Cir.2011).

1. When clerk can enter default judgment. The clerk can enter a default judgment only when (1) the defendant has defaulted for failure to appear, (2) the defendant is not a minor, an incompetent person, a member of the military, the U.S. government, or a federal officer or agency, and (3) the damages are liquidated or capable of being ascertained from figures contained in the documentary evidence or in detailed affidavits. *See* FRCP 55(b)(1), (d); 50 U.S.C. app. §521(b)(1); ***Franchise Holding II, LLC. v. Huntington Rests. Grp.***, 375 F.3d 922, 927-28 (9th Cir.2004).

2. When clerk cannot enter default judgment. In some cases, the clerk cannot enter a default judgment. In these cases, the plaintiff must file a motion for default judgment in the court. See "Motion to Court for Default Judgment," §6, p. 593.

(1) Defendant made appearance. The clerk cannot enter a default judgment if the defendant has made an appearance. FRCP 55(b)(1); ***Eitel v. McCool***, 782 F.2d 1470, 1471 (9th Cir.1986). Any doubt whether an action by the defendant constitutes an appearance should be resolved in favor of finding that the defendant made an appearance. ***In re Roxford Foods, Inc.***, 12 F.3d 875, 881 (9th Cir.1993); *see* ***Rogers v. Hartford Life & Acc. Ins.***, 167 F.3d 933, 936 (5th Cir.1999) (expansive view of what constitutes appearance); ***Key Bank v. Tablecloth Textile Co.***, 74 F.3d 349, 353 n.6 (1st Cir.1996) (listing actions sufficient to constitute appearance); 10A Wright, Miller & Kane §2686 & n.14 (court will usually try to find that there has been appearance by D). To qualify as an appearance, the defendant's actions only need to give the plaintiff a clear indication that the defendant intends to pursue a defense. *See* ***Philos Techs. v. Philos & D, Inc.***, 645 F.3d 851, 858 (7th Cir.2011); ***Rogers***, 167 F.3d at 937. A notice of appearance is sufficient to prevent the clerk from entering a default judgment. ***Eitel***, 782 F.2d at 1471.

(2) Defendant defaulted after answer. The clerk cannot enter a default judgment if the defendant filed a timely answer but defaulted in some later proceeding. *See, e.g.*, ***Hoxworth v. Blinder, Robinson & Co.***,

980 F.2d 912, 917-18 (3d Cir.1992) (D refused to cooperate in discovery, obtain new attorney, or appear for trial); ***Ringgold Corp. v. Worrall***, 880 F.2d 1138, 1140-41 (9th Cir.1989) (D refused to obtain new attorney and appear for pretrial conference); ***Mutual Fed. S&L Ass'n v. Richards & Assocs.***, 872 F.2d 88, 93 (4th Cir.1989) (D refused to cooperate in discovery).

(3) Defendant is prohibited party. The clerk cannot enter a default judgment against a minor, an incompetent person, a member of the military, the U.S. government, or a federal officer or agency. *See* FRCP 55(b)(1), (d); 50 U.S.C. app. §521(b)(1); ***Alameda v. Secretary of Health, Educ. & Welfare***, 622 F.2d 1044, 1048 (1st Cir. 1980).

(4) Claim is unliquidated. The clerk cannot enter a default judgment if the claim for relief does not meet the FRCP 55(b)(1) test for a sum certain. ***Durant v. Husband***, 28 F.3d 12, 15 (3d Cir.1994); *see, e.g.*, ***CSXT Intermodal, Inc. v. Mercury Cartage, LLC***, 271 F.R.D. 400, 401 (D.Me.2010) (FRCP 55(b)(1) was not satisfied when P submitted single affidavit from employee stating D owed certain amount but provided no other documentation). See "When proof of damages required," §6.5.2, p. 596.

§5.2 Request for default judgment. The request for default judgment must be in writing, unless made during a hearing or trial. FRCP 7(b)(1)(A). Once the clerk enters a default, the plaintiff should file a request for the clerk to enter a default judgment, alleging the following:

1. Default was entered. The clerk entered a default, and the plaintiff now requests the entry of a default judgment. If the default has not already been entered, the clerk can enter the default and the default judgment at the same time.

2. Defendant did not appear. The defendant did not answer, appear, or take any action showing an intent to defend. FRCP 55(a), (b)(1); ***Franchise Holding II, LLC. v. Huntington Rests. Grp.***, 375 F.3d 922, 927-28 (9th Cir.2004).

3. Claim is for sum certain. The claim in the complaint is for a sum certain or can be reliably computed. FRCP 55(b)(1); *see* ***Franchise Holding II***, 375 F.3d at 929 (default judgment proper when there is no doubt about amount owed); ***CSXT Intermodal, Inc. v. Mercury Cartage, LLC***, 271 F.R.D. 400, 401 (D.Me.2010) (action is typically for sum certain when it involves money judgment, negotiable instruments, or damages that can be determined without extrinsic proof). For example, the clerk can enter a default judgment if the claim includes the following:

(1) Liquidated damages. Liquidated damages qualify as a sum certain. ***Dundee Cement Co. v. Howard Pipe & Concrete Prods.***, 722 F.2d 1319, 1323 (7th Cir.1983).

(2) Attorney fees. The clerk can award attorney fees as long as the plaintiff is entitled to a specific amount of attorney fees based on a contract or statute. However, if the plaintiff is entitled only to "reasonable" attorney fees, the amount is not a sum certain and therefore can be awarded only by the court and after a hearing. ***Hunt v. Inter-Globe Energy, Inc.***, 770 F.2d 145, 148 (10th Cir.1985).

(3) Interest. The clerk can enter a default judgment for the principal amount plus interest at the legal rate as long as it is a sum that, by computation, could be made certain. *See* ***Design & Dev., Inc. v. Vibromatic Mfg.***, 58 F.R.D. 71, 74 (E.D.Pa.1973). However, if the complaint asks for prejudgment interest, the clerk cannot enter a default judgment because the allowance of prejudgment interest is generally within the court's discretion. ***U.S. v. Rainbolt***, 543 F.Supp. 580, 580 n.* (E.D.Tenn.1982).

(4) Costs. The clerk can award costs. FRCP 55(b)(1).

4. Not against prohibited defendant. The defendant in the case is not a minor, an incompetent, a member of the military, the U.S. government, or a federal officer or agency. *See* FRCP 55(b)(1), (d); 50 U.S.C. app. §521(b)(1). See "Defendant is prohibited party," §5.1.2(3), this page.

§5.3 Affidavits & attachments. Along with the request for default judgment, the plaintiff should file the following:

1. Affidavit for entry of default judgment. The request for default judgment must be accompanied by an affidavit. FRCP 55(b)(1). The affidavit must verify the attachments to the request and the amount due, excluding costs. *See id.* The clerk then computes the costs. *Id.*

2. Military affidavit. If the defendant is in military service, the clerk cannot enter a default judgment, so the plaintiff must include a sworn statement proving that the defendant is not currently in military service. 50 U.S.C. app. §521(b)(1). See "Military affidavit," §3.2.2(2), p. 586.

3. Attachments. The request for default judgment should include copies of all documents proving the amount of damages. For example, to prove liquidated damages in a suit on a promissory note, the plaintiff should attach a copy of the note. The attachments should be exhibits to the affidavit.

§5.4 No notice required. The defendant is not entitled to notice before the clerk enters the default judgment. *See* FRCP 55(b)(1); ***Key Bank v. Tablecloth Textile Co.***, 74 F.3d 349, 352-53 (1st Cir.1996).

§5.5 Defendant's objections to clerk's entry of default judgment. If the defendant learns about the request to enter a default judgment, it should respond as follows:

1. File answer or motion to dismiss. Technically, the entry of default cuts off the defendant's right to file any document other than a motion to set aside the entry of default. *See* ***New York Life Ins. v. Brown***, 84 F.3d 137, 143 (5th Cir.1996). Nonetheless, if the defendant has not filed an answer, it should immediately file one before the clerk enters the default judgment. *See* ***U.S. v. Harre***, 983 F.2d 128, 130 (8th Cir.1993). Along with the answer, the defendant should file a motion for leave to file the answer and a motion to set aside the entry of default.

2. Show intent to defend. If after the complaint was filed the defendant took any action that showed its intent to defend, it should file an objection to the request for entry of default judgment and identify the action. See "Otherwise defend," §3.4.2, p. 586.

3. No entry of default made. If the plaintiff moved for a default judgment without first obtaining an entry of default, the defendant should file an objection. *See* ***Johnson v. Dayton Elec. Mfg.***, 140 F.3d 781, 783 (8th Cir.1998).

4. Claim not sum certain. If the plaintiff's claim is for unliquidated damages or for damages that cannot be calculated from the complaint, the defendant should object to the entry of default judgment by the clerk. *See* FRCP 55(b)(1).

5. Against prohibited defendant. If the defendant is a minor, an incompetent, a member of the military, the U.S. government, or a federal officer or agency, the defendant should object to the entry of default judgment by the clerk. *See* 50 U.S.C. app. §521(b)(1); FRCP 55(b)(1), (d).

6. Complaint does not support judgment. The defendant can always complain, even after default, that the allegations in the complaint are legally insufficient to support a judgment. ***Bonilla v. Trebol Motors Corp.***, 150 F.3d 77, 80 (1st Cir.1998); ***Black v. Lane***, 22 F.3d 1395, 1399 (7th Cir.1994); *see* FRCP 54(c) (default judgment cannot be different from one prayed for in demand for judgment). A defendant's default is nothing more than a concession of the well-pleaded liability allegations in the complaint. ***Black***, 22 F.3d at 1399; ***Greyhound Exhibitgroup, Inc. v. E.L.U.L. Rlty. Corp.***, 973 F.2d 155, 158 (2d Cir.1992).

(1) Claims. Claims that are legally insufficient cannot be established by default. ***Cripps v. Life Ins.***, 980 F.2d 1261, 1267 (9th Cir.1992). If the complaint does not allege the facts necessary to support the plaintiff's claim for relief, the default judgment should be set aside. *See id.* at 1268; *see, e.g.*, ***Alan Neuman Prods. v. Albright***, 862 F.2d 1388, 1392 (9th Cir.1988) (complaint did not properly allege Racketeer Influenced and Corrupt Organizations Act claim).

(2) **Relief.** If the relief awarded is more than or different from the relief requested by the plaintiff, the default judgment should be set aside. *See* FRCP 54(c); ***Scala v. Moore McCormack Lines***, 985 F.2d 680, 683 (2d Cir.1993).

§5.6 Clerk's default judgment. Once the plaintiff files the request to enter a default judgment, the clerk should enter the judgment as long as it is a proper case for the clerk to do so. A default judgment entered by the clerk is a final, appealable judgment. The plaintiff should check the clerk's record to make sure the clerk entered the default judgment. *See, e.g.*, ***Arango v. Guzman Travel Advisors***, 761 F.2d 1527, 1530-31 (11th Cir.1985) (at trial of nondefaulting D, Ps discovered that clerk had not entered default judgment against defaulting Ds). For a discussion of how to challenge the clerk's entry of default judgment, see "Motion to Vacate Default Judgment Under FRCP 60(b)," §8, p. 598.

§6. MOTION TO COURT FOR DEFAULT JUDGMENT

When the default judgment cannot be resolved on the pleadings and a hearing is necessary, or when the default judgment would not resolve the entire case, the motion must be directed to the court, not the clerk. *See* ***City of N.Y. v. Mickalis Pawn Shop, LLC***, 645 F.3d 114, 129 n.17 (2d Cir.2011). The court can enter a default judgment in all cases. *See id.*

§6.1 Motion for default judgment. A motion for default judgment must be in writing unless it is made during a hearing or trial. FRCP 7(b)(1)(A). The motion should allege the following:

1. **Default was entered.** The clerk entered a default, and the plaintiff now requests the entry of a default judgment. If the clerk has not already entered a default, the court can enter the default and the default judgment at the same time.

2. **Defendant did or did not appear.** The plaintiff should identify whether the defendant appeared, filed an appearance, filed an answer, filed a motion to dismiss or any other motion, or took any action showing its intent to defend. *See* FRCP 55(a).

3. **Amount of claim.** Generally, the amount of the claim should be limited to the damages alleged in the complaint. *See, e.g.*, ***Silge v. Merz***, 510 F.3d 157, 160 (2d Cir.2007) (P was not awarded prejudgment interest when he did not specifically plead for it or include it in demand clause).

(1) **Sum certain.** If the claim is for a sum certain, the motion should state the amount due. If the amount of the judgment can be reliably computed from the record, a default judgment can be entered without a hearing. ***James v. Frame***, 6 F.3d 307, 310 (5th Cir.1993); ***Action S.A. v. Marc Rich & Co.***, 951 F.2d 504, 508-09 (2d Cir.1991); ***HMG Prop. Investors, Inc. v. Parque Indus. Rio Canas, Inc.***, 847 F.2d 908, 919 (1st Cir.1988). However, the court cannot simply accept a pleaded estimate of damages as true; it must ensure there is a basis for the damages. ***Transatlantic Mar. Claims Agency, Inc. v. Ace Shipping Corp.***, 109 F.3d 105, 111 (2d Cir.1997).

(2) **Not sum certain.** If the claim is not for a sum certain, the plaintiff should state that the amount is not a sum certain and request a hearing to determine damages. *See* FRCP 55(b)(2). See "Hearing," §6.5, p. 596.

(3) **Default as sanction.** If a default is entered as a sanction after the suit has been pending, the court may award damages without a hearing because it is familiar with the record. ***HMG Prop. Investors***, 847 F.2d at 919. See "Default entered as sanction," §6.3.1(2), p. 594.

4. **Military status.** The plaintiff must state whether the defendant is a person currently in military service. 50 U.S.C. app. §521(b)(1). See "Military affidavit," §3.2.2(2), p. 586.

5. **If defendant is minor or incompetent.** If the defendant is a minor or an incompetent person, the plaintiff must show that the defendant is represented in the suit by a general guardian, conservator, or other fiduciary who appeared in the suit. FRCP 55(b)(2).

6. **If defendant is United States.** Before the court can enter a default judgment against the U.S. government or a federal officer or agency, the court must be satisfied that the plaintiff proved through satisfactory evidence its right to relief. FRCP 55(d); ***Ledo Fin. Corp. v. Summers***, 122 F.3d 825, 827 (9th Cir.1997); ***Alameda v.***

Secretary of Health, Educ. & Welfare, 622 F.2d 1044, 1047-48 (1st Cir.1980). The rationale for the limitation on the entry of a default judgment against the U.S. government is that taxpayers should not have to pay for a windfall judgment resulting from a procedural default against a government official. ***Durant v. Husband***, 28 F.3d 12, 16 (3d Cir.1994); *e.g.*, ***Campbell v. Eastland***, 307 F.2d 478, 491 (5th Cir.1962) (default judgment entered against U.S. for discovery sanctions under FRCP 37(b)).

7. If defendant is foreign sovereign. Before the court can enter a default judgment against a foreign sovereign, the court must be satisfied that the plaintiff established its right to relief by evidentiary support. 28 U.S.C. §1608(e). The plaintiff must provide sufficient evidence in support of its claim, and the court must consider the evidence before default can be entered. ***Compania Interamericana Exp.-Imp. v. Compania Dominicana de Aviacion***, 88 F.3d 948, 951 (11th Cir.1996); ***Commercial Bank of Kuwait v. Rafidain Bank***, 15 F.3d 238, 242-43 (2d Cir. 1994).

8. Request for hearing. If a hearing is necessary to establish the truth of any statement in the motion or to make an investigation of any other matter, the plaintiff should request a hearing. *See* FRCP 55(b)(2). If a trial by jury is required by any federal statute, either party may request a jury. *See id.*

§6.2 Affidavits & attachments. Along with the motion for default judgment, the plaintiff should file the following:

1. Affidavit of amount due. If the damages meet the sum-certain requirement, the plaintiff should file an affidavit of the amount due. FRCP 55(b)(1); *see* ***Dundee Cement Co. v. Howard Pipe & Concrete Prods.***, 722 F.2d 1319, 1323 (7th Cir.1983). See "Claim is for sum certain," §5.2.3, p. 591. If the damages are not certain, the plaintiff must request a hearing to determine the amount of damages.

2. Military affidavit. The plaintiff must include a sworn statement stating whether the defendant currently serves in the military or stating that the plaintiff is unable to make this determination. 50 U.S.C. app. §521(b)(1). See "Military affidavit," §3.2.2(2), p. 586.

3. Attachments. The motion for default judgment should include copies of all documents proving the defendant is in default and the amount of damages. For example, to prove liquidated damages in a suit on a promissory note, the plaintiff should attach a copy of the note.

§6.3 Notice of hearing.

1. Notice not required. If the defendant did not appear or otherwise indicate an intent to defend, the defendant is not entitled to notice of the motion for entry of default judgment. FRCP 55(b)(2); *see* ***Key Bank v. Tablecloth Textile Co.***, 74 F.3d 349, 352-53 (1st Cir.1996). However, the court may require the plaintiff to give notice even if the defendant has not appeared. Even when notice is not required, the plaintiff should probably give the defendant notice to avoid a postjudgment attack on the default judgment. In addition, a defendant is not entitled to notice in the following circumstances:

(1) Default entered sua sponte. When the court enters a default judgment on its own initiative, it may dispense with the notice requirement in FRCP 55(b)(2). ***Goldman, Antonetti, Ferraiuoli, Axtmayer & Hertell v. Medfit Int'l***, 982 F.2d 686, 692 (1st Cir.1993).

(2) Default entered as sanction. When default is entered as a sanction, the court does not have to comply with the notice requirement in FRCP 55(b)(2). ***Ringgold Corp. v. Worrall***, 880 F.2d 1138, 1141 (9th Cir. 1989); *see, e.g.*, ***Brock v. Unique Racquetball & Health Clubs, Inc.***, 786 F.2d 61, 65 (2d Cir.1986) (no notice required when default was entered as sanction for failure to attend trial; court was entitled to proceed with scheduled trial).

2. Notice required. If the defendant appeared in the case, it is entitled to written notice of the motion for default judgment at least seven days before the hearing on the motion. FRCP 55(b)(2); *see* ***U.S. v. $23,000 in U.S. Currency***, 356 F.3d 157, 163-64 (1st Cir.2004) (applying former three-day notice period); ***In re Roxford Foods, Inc.***, 12 F.3d 875, 879 (9th Cir.1993) (same); *see also* ***Florida Physician's Ins. Co. v. Ehlers***, 8 F.3d 780, 784 (11th

Cir.1993) (notice was sufficient when it was sent to D's address on file with court; default judgment could be entered when D made himself impossible to contact); ***U.S. v. Harre***, 983 F.2d 128, 130 (8th Cir.1993) (D who filed late answer was entitled to notice). For a discussion of how to compute backward-counted deadlines, see "Computing Deadlines," ch. 1-C, §6, p. 23.

(1) Defendant made appearance. If the defendant answered, appeared, or took some action that can be construed as showing an intent to defend, the defendant is entitled to notice of the hearing on the motion. FRCP 55(b)(2); ***Key Bank***, 74 F.3d at 352-53; *see* ***New York Life Ins. v. Brown***, 84 F.3d 137, 141 (5th Cir.1996). See "Defendant made appearance," §5.1.2(1), p. 590. The acceptance of formal service of process or the waiver of service is not an appearance for the purpose of requiring notice of the default judgment. ***Rogers v. Hartford Life & Acc. Ins.***, 167 F.3d 933, 937-38 (5th Cir.1999).

(2) Postanswer default. A party who has answered the suit is entitled to notice of the hearing on the motion, even after a later default. *See, e.g.*, ***Bambu Sales, Inc. v. Ozak Trading Inc.***, 58 F.3d 849, 853 (2d Cir. 1995) (P's motion seeking default judgment was adequate notice); ***U.S. v. McCoy***, 954 F.2d 1000, 1005 (5th Cir.1992) (show-cause order was sufficient to meet notice requirements).

3. Modification of notice requirement. FRCP 81(a)(5) allows courts, under certain circumstances, to modify the rules of procedure, including the seven-day notice requirement of FRCP 55(b)(2). *See* ***McCoy***, 954 F.2d at 1004-05 (applying former three-day notice period). As long as the court's modification is permissible, the seven-day period can be changed. *See, e.g.*, *id.* at 1005 (show-cause order, which informed D of her need to appear in court, was sufficient notice to forgo procedural requirements of FRCP 55(b)(2)).

§6.4 Defendant's objections to court's entry of default judgment. If the defendant learns about the motion to enter a default judgment before the court enters the judgment, the defendant should respond as follows:

1. File answer or motion to dismiss. Technically, the entry of default cuts off the defendant's right to file any document other than a motion to set aside the entry of default. *See* ***New York Life Ins. v. Brown***, 84 F.3d 137, 143 (5th Cir.1996). Nonetheless, if the defendant has not filed an answer, it should immediately file an answer, a motion for leave to file, and a motion to vacate the entry of default before the court enters the default judgment. The defendant's right to contest subject-matter jurisdiction is never lost, so a motion to dismiss for lack of subject-matter jurisdiction should be considered, if appropriate. ***Transatlantic Mar. Claims Agency, Inc. v. Ace Shipping Corp.***, 109 F.3d 105, 107-08 (2d Cir.1997).

2. Show intent to defend. If after the complaint was filed the defendant took any action regarding the suit that showed its intent to defend, it should file an objection to the request for entry of default and identify the action. *See* ***Key Bank v. Tablecloth Textile Co.***, 74 F.3d 349, 352-53 (1st Cir.1996) (D should identify the nature of its contacts with P). See "Otherwise defend," §3.4.2, p. 586.

3. Claim not sum certain. If the plaintiff's claim is for unliquidated damages or for damages that cannot be calculated from the complaint, the defendant should object to the entry of default judgment without a hearing. *See* ***KPS & Assocs. v. Designs by FMC, Inc.***, 318 F.3d 1, 17-18 (1st Cir.2003).

4. Against prohibited defendant. If the defendant is a minor, an incompetent, a member of the military, the U.S. government, or a federal officer or agency, the defendant should object to the entry of default judgment. *See* FRCP 55(b)(1), (d); 50 U.S.C. app. §521(b)(1). A defendant in military service can also request a stay of the proceedings for at least 90 days if the defendant can provide the following:

(1) Letter from defendant. The defendant's application for stay must include a letter or other communication showing that current military duty materially affects the defendant's ability to appear, and a date when the defendant will be available to appear. 50 U.S.C. app. §522(b).

(2) Letter from defendant's commanding officer. The defendant's application for stay must also include a letter or other communication from the defendant's commanding officer stating that the defendant's current military duty prevents appearance and that military leave is not authorized for the defendant. 50 U.S.C. app. §522(b).

5. Notice required. If the defendant was entitled to receive notice of the request for entry of default (not default judgment) because the defendant had appeared, the defendant should state that the initial default was entered in violation of FRCP 55(a).

6. Complaint does not support judgment. The defendant can always complain, even after default, that the allegations in the complaint are legally insufficient to support a judgment. See "Complaint does not support judgment," §5.5.6, p. 592.

7. Request hearing. If the defendant filed an answer, appeared, or took any action showing an intent to defend, or if the damages are unliquidated, the defendant is entitled to a hearing and should request one.

§6.5 Hearing. The court may hold a hearing to conduct an accounting, to determine the amount of damages, to establish the truth of any allegation by evidence, or to investigate any other matter. FRCP 55(b)(2); *see* ***Finkel v. Romanowicz***, 577 F.3d 79, 87 (2d Cir.2009). But when there are no disputed facts, the court is not required to hold a hearing, and it can make its determination based on the motion, response, and attached evidence. *See, e.g.*, ***Finkel***, 577 F.3d at 87 (no hearing necessary because P did not ask for hearing and there were no disputed facts); ***James v. Frame***, 6 F.3d 307, 310 (5th Cir.1993) (no hearing necessary because default was entered after answer and court was familiar with case). When there is a hearing, it is sometimes called an inquest. *See* ***Greyhound Exhibitgroup, Inc. v. E.L.U.L. Rlty. Corp.***, 973 F.2d 155, 158 (2d Cir.1992). The court may conduct the hearing itself or refer the hearing to a magistrate judge or special master. FRCP 55(b)(2); *see* ***Greyhound Exhibitgroup***, 973 F.2d at 156. See "Magistrate Judges & Special Masters," ch. 5-B, p. 297.

1. When proof of liability required. Even though the entry of default generally establishes the defendant's liability, additional proof of liability is required in certain situations.

(1) Indefinite allegation. The court may require proof of any uncertain or indefinite allegation in the complaint. *See, e.g.*, ***Alan Neuman Prods. v. Albright***, 862 F.2d 1388, 1390 (9th Cir.1988) (hearing held to determine damages, capacity to sue, and prima facie showing of liability). FRCP 55(b)(2) gives the court broad discretion to "establish the truth of any allegation" by evidence or to investigate any other matter. ***Pacheco v. Morales***, 953 F.2d 15, 16 (1st Cir.1992).

(2) Liability of United States. Before entering a default judgment against the U.S. government or a federal officer or agency, the plaintiff must prove it is entitled to recover "by evidence that satisfies the court." FRCP 55(d); ***Alameda v. Secretary of Health, Educ. & Welfare***, 622 F.2d 1044, 1047 (1st Cir.1980). In Social Security cases, this requirement is relaxed. *See* ***Giampaoli v. Califano***, 628 F.2d 1190, 1195-96 (9th Cir.1980).

2. When proof of damages required. When the claim for relief is for money and is not liquidated or capable of mathematical computation, in most cases the court must hold a hearing to determine damages. ***e360 Insight v. Spamhaus Project***, 500 F.3d 594, 602 (7th Cir.2007); ***James***, 6 F.3d at 310; ***HMG Prop. Investors, Inc. v. Parque Indus. Rio Canas, Inc.***, 847 F.2d 908, 919 (1st Cir.1988); *see* ***Silge v. Merz***, 510 F.3d 157, 158 (2d Cir.2007). If damages are awarded in the default judgment and the defendant does not appear at the hearing on damages, it cannot question the damages for the first time on appeal. ***Bonanza Int'l v. Corceller***, 480 F.2d 613, 614 (5th Cir. 1973).

(1) Punitive damages. When the party seeks punitive damages, a hearing is normally required. ***Flaks v. Koegel***, 504 F.2d 702, 707 (2d Cir.1974). *But see* ***James***, 6 F.3d at 310-11 (no hearing required).

(2) Causal connection to injuries. The plaintiff must prove that the compensation it seeks is related to the damages that naturally resulted from the injuries. ***Greyhound Exhibitgroup***, 973 F.2d at 159. This does not mean the plaintiff must prove proximate cause, which is different from proving the causal connection to the damages. *Id.* When proximate cause is pleaded, it is established by the entry of the default. *Id.*

(3) Prejudgment interest. If an award of prejudgment interest is not determined by statute, the court may hold a hearing to determine the amount of prejudgment interest. *See* ***U.S. v. Rainbolt***, 543 F.Supp. 580,

580 n.* (E.D.Tenn.1982); *see also* ***Silge***, 510 F.3d at 160 (P must specifically plead for prejudgment interest or include it in demand clause).

(4) Attorney fees. A plaintiff seeking attorney fees must prove both the amount of the fees (just like any other unliquidated damages) and the reasonableness of the fees. Therefore, attorney fees are subject to court inquiry at a hearing. ***Hunt v. Inter-Globe Energy, Inc.***, 770 F.2d 145, 148 (10th Cir.1985).

§6.6 Ruling. The court has the discretion to grant or deny the motion for entry of default judgment. ***Eitel v. McCool***, 782 F.2d 1470, 1471 (9th Cir.1986). Thus, a party is not entitled to a default judgment as a matter of right, even when the defendant technically is in default. ***Ganther v. Ingle***, 75 F.3d 207, 212 (5th Cir.1996). In making its decision on the motion for default judgment, the court may consider the possibility of prejudice to the plaintiff, the merits of the plaintiff's substantive claim, the sufficiency of the complaint, the sum of money at stake in the suit, the possibility of a dispute about material facts, whether the default was due to excusable neglect, and the strong policy of favoring decisions on the merits. ***Eitel***, 782 F.2d at 1471-72; *see* 10A Wright, Miller & Kane §2685.

1. Multiple defendants. In a multiple-defendant case, when one or more defendants default and other defendants contest the suit, the court generally should enter a default (but not necessarily a default judgment) against the defaulting defendants. However, the courts are split on whether to delay the entry of default judgment and the assessment of damages when one or more—but fewer than all—defendants have defaulted. *See* ***Jefferson v. Briner, Inc.***, 461 F.Supp.2d 430, 434-35 & nn.6, 7 (E.D.Va.2006).

(1) Delay entering default judgment. Some courts delay entering a default judgment and assessing damages against the defaulting defendants until the plaintiff resolves its claim against the nondefaulting defendants, whether the defendants are jointly liable, jointly and severally liable, or otherwise closely interrelated. ***Jefferson***, 461 F.Supp.2d at 435; *see* ***Pfanenstiel Architects, Inc. v. Chouteau Pet. Co.***, 978 F.2d 430, 433 (8th Cir.1992) (when Ds may be jointly and severally liable, court should stay determination of damages against defaulting Ds until P's claim against nondefaulting Ds is resolved). Courts should delay entry of judgment to avoid inconsistent judgments among multiple defendants. ***Jefferson***, 461 F.Supp.2d at 435 n.7; *see* ***Farzetta v. Turner & Newall, Ltd.***, 797 F.2d 151, 154 (3d Cir.1986) (if facts exonerate certain nondefaulting Ds and would have also precluded liability against defaulting Ds, P should be collaterally estopped from obtaining judgment against defaulting Ds); ***Gulf Coast Fans, Inc. v. Midwest Elecs. Imps., Inc.***, 740 F.2d 1499, 1512 (11th Cir.1984) (when Ds are similarly situated but not jointly liable, judgment should not be entered against defaulting D if other D prevails on merits); *see also* ***Frow v. De La Vega***, 82 U.S. 552, 554 (1872) (if suit decided on merits against P, complaint should be dismissed against all Ds, including defaulting Ds).

(2) No delay entering default judgment. Other courts enter a default judgment and assess damages against the defaulting defendants before resolving the suit against the other defendants unless all the defendants are truly jointly liable. *See* ***In re Uranium Antitrust Litig.***, 617 F.2d 1248, 1258 (7th Cir.1980) (when different results for different parties are not logically inconsistent or contradictory, judgment may be entered against defaulting Ds before adjudication of merits against remaining Ds); *see, e.g.*, ***McMillian/McMillian, Inc. v. Monticello Ins.***, 116 F.3d 319, 321 (8th Cir.1997) (when Ds shared closely related interests but were not sued on theory of joint liability, default judgment was entered before dispute was tried); ***Arango v. Guzman Travel Advisors***, 761 F.2d 1527, 1531 n.1 (11th Cir.1985) (because liability was not joint, court could enter default judgment against defaulting Ds even though nondefaulting Ds prevailed on merits).

2. Defendant in military service. Depending on the court's determination of the defendant's military status and other considerations, there are several ways the court can protect a defendant in military service.

(1) Appoint attorney. If the court finds that the defendant is in military service, it cannot enter default judgment until after appointing an attorney to represent the defendant. 50 U.S.C. app. §521(b)(2).

(2) Stay proceedings. The court must grant a stay of at least 90 days if, on motion by the appointed attorney or the court, the court determines that (1) there may be a defense that cannot be presented without the de-

fendant, or (2) after due diligence, the appointed attorney has been unable to contact the defendant or otherwise determine whether there is a meritorious defense. 50 U.S.C. app. §521(d).

(3) Require bond. If the court cannot determine whether the defendant is in military service, it may require the plaintiff to file a bond to indemnify the defendant in the event that the defendant is in military service and suffers loss or damage as a result of the judgment. 50 U.S.C. app. §521(b)(3).

3. Effect of court's entry of default judgment. If the court grants the motion for default judgment, the judgment is final and appealable. ***Ackra Direct Mktg. Corp. v. Fingerhut Corp.***, 86 F.3d 852, 855 n.3 (8th Cir. 1996); ***Enron Oil Corp. v. Diakuhara***, 10 F.3d 90, 95 (2d Cir.1993).

§7. NOTICE OF DEFAULT JUDGMENT

Once a default judgment is entered, the defendant is not entitled to the same notice as an appearing party against whom a final judgment is entered. FRCP 77(d)(1). *But see* 28 U.S.C. §1608(e) (copy of default judgment must be served on defaulting foreign state or subsidiary). See "Notice of Judgment," ch. 9-A, §4, p. 741. It is not necessary to serve parties who have defaulted for not appearing. FRCP 5(a)(2).

§8. MOTION TO VACATE DEFAULT JUDGMENT UNDER FRCP 60(b)

A motion under FRCP 60(b) is required in order to vacate a default judgment. FRCP 55(c). For a general discussion of FRCP 60(b) motions, see "Motion for Relief from Judgment," ch. 10-F, p. 804. A motion to vacate a default judgment necessarily challenges both the entry of default and the entry of default judgment. *See* ***Enron Oil Corp. v. Diakuhara***, 10 F.3d 90, 95 (2d Cir.1993); ***Hawaii Carpenters' Trust Funds v. Stone***, 794 F.2d 508, 512 (9th Cir. 1986).

§8.1 Form. The defendant should file a formal, written motion to vacate the default judgment, whether the judgment was entered by the clerk or the court. *Cf.* ***Gray v. John Jovino Co.***, 84 F.R.D. 46, 47 (E.D.Tenn.1979) (motion to set aside default). The motion should be supported by an affidavit verifying the facts stated in the motion and any supporting documents. *See* ***Sloss Indus. v. Eurisol***, 488 F.3d 922, 935 (11th Cir.2007). The affidavit must contain more than sworn conclusory statements. ***Sony Corp. v. Elm State Elecs., Inc.***, 800 F.2d 317, 320-21 (2d Cir.1986); *see, e.g.*, ***Sloss Indus.***, 488 F.3d at 935 (when D's affidavit did not include any dates for D's knowledge of default judgment or other actions taken by D, court affirmed default judgment). For the general requirements for the form of a motion, see "Drafting motions," ch. 1-B, §3.1, p. 14.

CIRCUIT SPLIT

The circuits are split on whether the court has authority to grant relief under FRCP 60(b) on its own initiative. See "Sua sponte," ch. 10-F, §3.3, p. 806.

§8.2 Grounds. The reasons for vacating a default judgment are stated in FRCP 60(b). See "Motion for Relief from Judgment," ch. 10-F, p. 804.

1. Excusable neglect. Most of the time, a defendant seeks to vacate a default judgment on the grounds of "mistake, inadvertence, surprise, or excusable neglect" under FRCP 60(b)(1); the court then applies the three-factor test of prejudice, meritorious defense, and culpable conduct to decide whether to grant the defendant's request. ***Powerserve Int'l v. Lavi***, 239 F.3d 508, 514 (2d Cir.2001); ***Al-Torki v. Kaempen***, 78 F.3d 1381, 1384-85 (9th Cir. 1996); *see* ***Swaim v. Moltan Co.***, 73 F.3d 711, 722 (7th Cir.1996). The mistake or inadvertence may be on the part of the judge. ***Kingvision Pay-Per-View Ltd. v. Lake Alice Bar***, 168 F.3d 347, 350 (9th Cir.1999). The court may consider other factors, including the amount of money at stake, whether the motion was made within a reasonable time, whether the interest in deciding the case outweighs the interest in the finality of the judgment, and whether the public interest is implicated. *See* ***Sloss Indus. v. Eurisol***, 488 F.3d 922, 935 (11th Cir.2007); ***Sims v. EGA Prods.***, 475 F.3d 865, 868-69 (7th Cir.2007); ***Hibernia Nat'l Bank v. Administracion Central***, 776 F.2d 1277, 1280 (5th Cir. 1985).

NOTE

Although the same factors are considered in vacating a default judgment and in setting aside an entry of default, the excusable-neglect standard for a motion to vacate is more onerous because the motion involves a final judgment. ***Colleton Preparatory Acad., Inc. v. Hoover Univ'l, Inc.****, 616 F.3d 413, 420 (4th Cir.2010); see* ***Johnson v. Dayton Elec. Mfg.****, 140 F.3d 781, 785 (8th Cir.1998); see also* ***In re Dierschke****, 975 F.2d 181, 184 (5th Cir.1992) (essentially same standard applies to both motion to set aside default and motion to vacate default judgment). See "Good cause," §4.1.3(3), p. 589.*

(1) Prejudice to plaintiff. The court may refuse to vacate a default judgment if it would pose too great a burden on the plaintiff to litigate the case on the merits because of lost evidence, increased problems with discovery, or greater potential for fraud. ***Home Port Rentals, Inc. v. Ruben***, 957 F.2d 126, 132 (4th Cir.1992); ***Action S.A. v. Marc Rich & Co.***, 951 F.2d 504, 507-08 (2d Cir.1991); ***Berthelsen v. Kane***, 907 F.2d 617, 621 (6th Cir. 1990); *see* ***Whelan v. Abell***, 48 F.3d 1247, 1258-59 (D.C.Cir.1995) (having to try claim twice would prejudice P). Delaying a plaintiff's collection of a judgment or requiring a plaintiff to litigate the merits of the claim is not sufficient. ***U.S. v. One Parcel of Real Prop.***, 763 F.2d 181, 183 (5th Cir.1985). The mere possibility of prejudice from delay, which is inherent in every case, is not sufficient. ***Hibernia***, 776 F.2d at 1280; *see* ***Weiss v. St. Paul Fire & Mar. Ins.***, 283 F.3d 790, 795 (6th Cir.2002); ***Cody v. Mello***, 59 F.3d 13, 16 (2d Cir.1995).

(2) Meritorious defense. Courts do not decide whether the defendant is likely to succeed on the merits, but instead whether the allegations, if proved, would constitute a complete defense. ***Whelan***, 48 F.3d at 1259; ***Enron Oil Corp. v. Diakuhara***, 10 F.3d 90, 98 (2d Cir.1993); *see also* ***Federal Sav. & Loan Ins. v. Kroenke***, 858 F.2d 1067, 1069 (5th Cir.1988) (dicta; defendant must show that there is fair probability of success on merits). When deciding whether to vacate the default judgment, the court does not have to find that the defense will ultimately be persuasive. ***American Alliance Ins. Co. v. Eagle Ins.***, 92 F.3d 57, 61 (2d Cir.1996). The court must decide only whether the trier of fact has some determination to make based on the defendant's version of events. *See id.*; *see also* ***Augusta Fiberglass Coatings, Inc. v. Fodor Contracting Corp.***, 843 F.2d 808, 812 (4th Cir.1988) (court requires proffer of evidence sufficient to "permit a finding for the defaulting party"). The requirement of a meritorious defense is intended only to ensure that the court's order vacating the judgment is not an exercise in futility. ***Owens-Ill., Inc. v. T&N Ltd.***, 191 F.R.D. 522, 526 (E.D.Tex.2000).

(3) Culpable conduct. FRCP 60(b)(1) excuses some situations where the defendant's failure to respond is due to its own negligence. *See* ***Pioneer Inv. Servs. v. Brunswick Assocs.***, 507 U.S. 380, 394 (1993). Because Congress provided no guideposts for determining which categories of neglect are excusable, the ***Pioneer*** Court emphasized an equitable inquiry, "taking account of all relevant circumstances surrounding the party's omission." *Id.* at 395. Although the concept of excusable neglect is "somewhat elastic," it generally excludes gross carelessness, ignorance of the rules, or ignorance of the law. *See id.* at 392. Some courts have held that a litigant's or attorney's carelessness suggesting an absence of minimal internal procedural safeguards is not excusable neglect. *See, e.g.*, ***Rogers v. Hartford Life & Acc. Ins.***, 167 F.3d 933, 939 (5th Cir.1999) (D's agent for process received complaint but never forwarded it to D's claim office); ***Johnson v. Gudmundsson***, 35 F.3d 1104, 1117 (7th Cir.1994) (attorney's continued absences and missed deadlines); ***Gibbs v. Air Canada***, 810 F.2d 1529, 1537-38 (11th Cir.1987) (complaint sent through intercompany mail was "misplaced"). *But see* ***Owens-Ill.***, 191 F.R.D. at 527-28 (mislaid complaint was product of isolated human error, rather than lack of minimum procedural safeguards; default judgment set aside). The courts will not vacate a default judgment if the default was willful. ***Swaim***, 73 F.3d at 721; ***Brien v. Kullman Indus.***, 71 F.3d 1073, 1078 (2d Cir.1995); ***Information Sys. & Networks Corp. v. U.S.***, 994 F.2d 792, 796 (Fed.Cir. 1993); *see* ***Employee Painters' Trust v. Ethan Enters.***, 480 F.3d 993, 1000 (9th Cir.2007) (for court to grant relief, actions leading to default must not be devious, deliberate, willful, or in bad faith). A default is "willful" when the defendant actively evades service, ignores court orders, or intentionally violates court rules. *See* ***Swaim***, 73 F.3d at 721-22; ***Action***, 951 F.2d at 507; ***Berthelsen***, 907 F.2d at 622; *see, e.g.*, ***Employee Painters' Trust***, 480 F.3d at 1000 (Ds'

default was willful when Ds provided Ps with incorrect address and thus prevented normal service of process). However, gross negligence by the attorney may constitute "extraordinary circumstances" that justify setting aside a default judgment under FRCP 60(b)(6). ***Community Dental Servs. v. Tani***, 282 F.3d 1164, 1170 n.12 (9th Cir.2002).

CIRCUIT SPLIT

Many courts balance the three factors in determining whether to grant relief under FRCP 60(b)(1), but some courts consider the three factors separately. Compare ***Brandt v. American Bankers Ins.***, *653 F.3d 1108, 1111-12 (9th Cir.2011) (balanced factors),* ***Information Sys.***, *994 F.2d at 796 (same), and* ***Jackson v. Beech***, *636 F.2d 831, 836 (D.C.Cir.1980) (same), with* ***Manufacturers' Indus. Relations Ass'n v. East Akron Casting Co.***, *58 F.3d 204, 210 (6th Cir.1995) (absence of culpable conduct must be demonstrated before addressing other factors), and* ***In re Dierschke***, *975 F.2d at 183-84 (factors are disjunctive). Also, the Second, Third, and Sixth Circuits are much more likely than the Fifth, Seventh, Tenth, and Eleventh Circuits to find excusable neglect when a party or attorney has been careless. See* ***American Alliance***, *92 F.3d at 60-61 (comparing and contrasting various holdings of Third, Fifth, Sixth, Seventh, Tenth, and Eleventh Circuits with Second Circuit's determination that some types of neglect are by definition "excusable," particularly neglect that does not approach gross negligence).*

2. Judgment is void. The defendant can seek to vacate a default judgment if the judgment is void. FRCP 60(b)(4); ***New York Life Ins. v. Brown***, 84 F.3d 137, 142 (5th Cir.1996). A judgment is void if the court did not have personal or subject-matter jurisdiction or if it acted inconsistently with due process. *See* ***e360 Insight v. Spamhaus Project***, 500 F.3d 594, 598 (7th Cir.2007); ***Precision Etchings & Findings, Inc. v. LGP Gem, Ltd.***, 953 F.2d 21, 23 (1st Cir.1992). However, a judgment may not be void if a defendant waived its right to raise certain defenses (e.g., improper service of process or venue) that would be grounds for vacating the judgment. *See* ***Rogers***, 167 F.3d at 942; *see, e.g.,* ***Democratic Republic of Congo v. FG Hemisphere Assocs.***, 508 F.3d 1062, 1064-65 (D.C.Cir.2007) (D waived personal-jurisdiction defense after engaging in 13 months of postdefault litigation before raising defense); ***e360 Insight***, 500 F.3d at 599-600 (D waived personal-jurisdiction argument when it raised but intentionally withdrew defense and then abandoned case). The following are grounds for vacating a default judgment because it is void:

(1) No personal jurisdiction. The plaintiff did not establish personal jurisdiction over the defendant. *See, e.g.,* ***Precision Etchings & Findings***, 953 F.2d at 23 (P did not properly serve D); *see also* ***City of N.Y. v. Mickalis Pawn Shop, LLC***, 645 F.3d 114, 133 (2d Cir.2011) (noting that in some circuits, before entering default judgment, court must determine whether it has personal jurisdiction over D).

NOTE

Although the plaintiff generally has the burden to establish jurisdiction, the defendant has the burden to prove that service did not occur when she had actual notice of the original proceeding but is seeking to vacate a default judgment based on improper service. ***SEC v. Internet Solutions for Bus.***, *509 F.3d 1161, 1165 (9th Cir.2007);* ***Burda Media, Inc. v. Viertel***, *417 F.3d 292, 299 (2d Cir.2005); see also* ***On Track Transp. v Lakeside Whs. & Trucking Inc.***, *245 F.R.D. 213, 223 (E.D.Pa.2007) (identifying courts' disagreement over which party has burden after default judgment is entered). But see* ***Morris v. B.C. Olympiakos, SFP***, *721 F.Supp.2d 546, 556-57 (S.D.Tex.2010) (P, not D, bears burden to establish personal jurisdiction).*

(2) No subject-matter jurisdiction. The court did not have subject-matter jurisdiction over the case. ***On Track Transp.***, 245 F.R.D. at 215.

(3) Complaint does not support judgment. The allegations in the complaint were legally insufficient to support the judgment. See "Complaint does not support judgment," §5.5.6, p. 592.

(4) No notice of hearing on default judgment. The defendant filed an answer before entry of default or made a sufficient appearance and did not receive the notice required by FRCP 55(b)(2). *See **Key Bank v. Tablecloth Textile Co.***, 74 F.3d 349, 352-53 (1st Cir.1996); ***In re Roxford Foods, Inc.***, 12 F.3d 875, 879 (9th Cir. 1993). See "Defendant made appearance," §5.1.2(1), p. 590; "Notice required," §6.3.2, p. 594.

(5) Defendant in military service. The judgment was improperly entered against a servicemember defendant. If a default judgment was entered against a servicemember defendant during or within 60 days after the defendant's period of military service, on timely motion by the defendant, the court must reopen the judgment if (1) the defendant was materially affected in defending the suit because of military service and (2) the defendant has a meritorious or legal defense to at least some part of the suit. 50 U.S.C. app. §521(g)(1).

(6) Defendant is minor or incompetent. The judgment was entered against a minor or an incompetent person who was not represented by a guardian, conservator, or other similar representative. *See* FRCP 55(b)(2); ***Zaro v. Strauss***, 167 F.2d 218, 220 (5th Cir.1948).

3. Other FRCP 60(b) grounds. The defendant can seek to vacate a default judgment based on the other grounds listed in FRCP 60(b). *See* FRCP 60(b)(2), (b)(3), (b)(5); *see, e.g.*, ***State St. Bank & Trust Co. v. Inversiones Errazuriz Limitada***, 374 F.3d 158, 175-76 (2d Cir.2004) (FRCP 60(b)(3)); *see also* 10A Wright, Miller & Kane §2695 (FRCP 60(b)(1), (b)(4), and (b)(6) grounds are most commonly applied to motions to vacate default judgment, but other sections may apply in appropriate cases). See "Grounds," ch. 10-F, §3.4, p. 806.

4. Catchall provision. The defendant can seek to vacate a default judgment on the ground that there are extraordinary circumstances justifying relief from the judgment. FRCP 60(b)(6); ***Frontier Ins. v. Blaty***, 454 F.3d 590, 597-98 (6th Cir.2006); *e.g.*, ***Lowe v. McGraw-Hill Cos.***, 361 F.3d 335, 342-43 (7th Cir.2004) (when no parties knew about earlier default judgment and P did not rely on judgment, judgment was vacated under catchall provision); *see also* ***Ungar v. Palestine Liberation Org.***, 599 F.3d 79, 84 (1st Cir.2010) (no absolute bar to relief for party that willfully defaults and later seeks relief under FRCP 60(b)(6)). FRCP 60(b)(6) should only be applied in unusual and extreme situations where equity demands relief. ***Frontier Ins.***, 454 F.3d at 597.

§8.3 Proposed answer or other responsive pleading. If the defendant does not have an answer or other responsive pleading on file when it files the motion to vacate the default judgment, the defendant should file a proposed answer or other responsive pleading when it files the motion. The meritorious defense in the answer should mirror the allegations of a meritorious defense in the motion to vacate the default judgment. See "Proposed pleading & motion for leave," §4.2, p. 590.

§8.4 Deadline.

1. For motion. The deadline to file a motion to vacate the default judgment depends on whether the grounds asserted in the motion are under FRCP 60(b)(1)-(b)(3) or FRCP 60(b)(4)-(b)(6) and whether a military servicemember is involved.

(1) Deadline under FRCP 60(b)(1)-(b)(3). A party must file a motion to vacate based on the grounds under FRCP 60(b)(1)-(b)(3) within a reasonable time but no more than one year after the judgment or order is entered or the date of the proceeding. FRCP 60(c)(1); *see* ***Home Port Rentals, Inc. v. Ruben***, 957 F.2d 126, 132 (4th Cir.1992). See "Deadline under FRCP 60(b)(1)-(b)(3)," ch. 10-F, §2.1.1, p. 804. For a discussion of how to compute deadlines stated in years, see "Computing Deadlines," ch. 1-C, §6, p. 23. The one-year deadline for filing a motion to vacate under FRCP 60(b)(1)-(b)(3) is jurisdictional and cannot be extended by the court or the parties. See "No extension," ch. 10-F, §2.1.1(2), p. 805.

(2) Deadline under FRCP 60(b)(4)-(b)(6). A party must file a motion to vacate based on the grounds under FRCP 60(b)(4)-(b)(6) within a "reasonable time." *See* FRCP 60(c)(1); *see, e.g.*, ***Days Inns Worldwide, Inc. v. Patel***, 445 F.3d 899, 906 (6th Cir.2006) (11 months not reasonable time). See "Deadline under FRCP 60(b)(4)-(b)(6)," ch. 10-F, §2.1.2, p. 805. A party should not base its motion to vacate on the catchall provision in FRCP 60(b)(6) in an attempt to circumvent the time limits under other subsections of FRCP 60(b). ***Home Port***, 957 F.2d at 132-33.

(3) For judgment against military servicemember. If the party filing a motion to vacate the default judgment is a military servicemember and the default judgment was entered against her during her military service or within 60 days after her service ended, the military servicemember has 90 days after the end of her service to file the motion to vacate. *See* 50 U.S.C. app. §521(g).

2. To toll time for appeal. If the defendant learns of the default judgment when it is entered or soon after it is entered, the defendant should file the motion to vacate within 28 days after the entry. When the defendant challenges a default judgment with an FRCP 60 motion filed within 28 days, the motion tolls the time for appeal until the date the court overrules the motion. FRAP 4(a)(4)(A)(vi); *see* ***Swaim v. Moltan Co.***, 73 F.3d 711, 716 (7th Cir.1996) (applying former ten-day deadline). See "Deadline," ch. 10-F, §9.1, p. 815. Thus, by filing the motion within 28 days, the defendant secures appellate review of both the default judgment and the order on the motion to vacate. *See* ***Swaim***, 73 F.3d at 716.

§8.5 Response. If the plaintiff opposes the motion to vacate the default judgment, it should file a response objecting to all grounds in the motion. See "Objections," ch. 10-F, §4.1, p. 811. If the response contains facts outside the record, they should be verified by affidavit.

§8.6 Ruling.

1. Standard. The court should resolve any doubt in favor of setting aside the default judgment. ***Weiss v. St. Paul Fire & Mar. Ins.***, 283 F.3d 790, 795 (6th Cir.2002); ***Powerserve Int'l v. Lavi***, 239 F.3d 508, 514 (2d Cir.2001).

2. Findings. The court should make express findings explaining the reasons for its ruling. ***Enron Oil Corp. v. Diakuhara***, 10 F.3d 90, 96-97 (2d Cir.1993); ***Emcasco Ins. v. Sambrick***, 834 F.2d 71, 74 (3d Cir.1987). The findings should cover the three good-cause factors for excusable neglect. ***Enron***, 10 F.3d at 96; *see, e.g.*, ***Sun Bank v. Pelican Homestead & Sav. Ass'n***, 874 F.2d 274, 277 (5th Cir.1989) (district court gave no explanation for its finding of culpable conduct; appellate court reversed default judgment). See "Excusable neglect," §8.2.1, p. 598.

3. Imposition of conditions. If the court vacates a default judgment under FRCP 60(b), the court may order that the defaulting party pay costs. *See* ***Powerserve Int'l***, 239 F.3d at 515 (court may condition vacating default or default judgment on posting security for amount of judgment); ***Nilsson, Robbins, Dalgarn, Berliner, Carson & Wurst v. Louisiana Hydrolec***, 854 F.2d 1538, 1546-47 (9th Cir.1988) (court may condition vacating default judgment on payment of sanction); *see also* 10A Wright, Miller & Kane §2700 (discussing use of terms and conditions, including payment of costs). However, the defaulting party cannot be assessed costs if the motion to vacate is denied. ***Brien v. Kullman Indus.***, 71 F.3d 1073, 1078 (2d Cir.1995).

§9. APPELLATE REVIEW

§9.1 Entry of default. A defendant cannot appeal the entry of default or an order denying a motion to set aside the entry of default until after a default judgment is entered. *See* ***Ackra Direct Mktg. Corp. v. Fingerhut Corp.***, 86 F.3d 852, 855 (8th Cir.1996).

§9.2 Default judgment. A defendant can appeal a default judgment because it is a final, appealable judgment.

NOTE

In an appeal from a default judgment, the appellate court can review both the interlocutory entry of default and the final default judgment. ***City of N.Y. v. Mickalis Pawn Shop, LLC***, *645 F.3d 114, 129 (2d Cir.2011).*

1. Types of challenges. On appeal, a default judgment can be challenged in two ways: direct appeal and collateral attack. Because default judgments are disfavored, doubts about whether a default judgment should have been entered are usually resolved against the default judgment. ***Enron Oil Corp. v. Diakuhara***, 10 F.3d 90, 96 (2d Cir.1993); ***Information Sys. & Networks Corp. v. U.S.***, 994 F.2d 792, 795 (Fed.Cir.1993); ***In re Hammer***, 940 F.2d 524, 525 (9th Cir.1991).

(1) Direct appeal. A default judgment, like any other final judgment, can be appealed. The notice of appeal must be filed with the district clerk within 30 days after the entry of the default judgment (60 days if the U.S. government is a party). FRAP 4(a)(1)(A), (a)(1)(B).

(2) Collateral attack. In rare cases, a party may collaterally attack the validity of a default judgment in a separate suit. A collateral attack on a default judgment is usually limited to challenges to the court's jurisdiction or to the constitutionality of the default judgment. ***Hugel v. McNell***, 886 F.2d 1, 3 n.3 (1st Cir.1989); ***Practical Concepts, Inc. v. Republic of Bolivia***, 811 F.2d 1543, 1547 (D.C.Cir.1987); *see* 10 *Moore's Federal Practice 3d* §55.84.

2. Standard of review. In the appeal of a default judgment, the standard of review is abuse of discretion. ***City of N.Y.***, 645 F.3d at 128; ***Rogers v. Hartford Life & Acc. Ins.***, 167 F.3d 933, 936 (5th Cir.1999); ***Swaim v. Moltan Co.***, 73 F.3d 711, 716 (7th Cir.1996); ***Whelan v. Abell***, 48 F.3d 1247, 1258 (D.C.Cir.1995). The same standard governs the appeal of the denial of a motion to vacate a default judgment. ***Weiss v. St. Paul Fire & Mar. Ins.***, 283 F.3d 790, 794 (6th Cir.2002); ***Claremont Flock Corp. v. Alm***, 281 F.3d 297, 299 (1st Cir.2002); ***Powerserve Int'l v. Lavi***, 239 F.3d 508, 514 (2d Cir.2001); *see* ***City of N.Y.***, 645 F.3d at 128.

B. SUMMARY JUDGMENT

§1. GENERAL

§1.1 Rule. FRCP 56.

§1.2 Purpose. The purpose of summary judgment is to pierce the pleadings and to assess the proof to determine whether there is a genuine need for trial. ***Matsushita Elec. Indus. Co. v. Zenith Radio Corp.***, 475 U.S. 574, 587 (1986). Summary-judgment procedure is designed to isolate and dispose of factually unsupported claims or defenses. ***Celotex Corp. v. Catrett***, 477 U.S. 317, 323-24 (1986); *see* FRCP 56(a), (c).

§1.3 Timetable & forms. Timetable, Summary Judgment, p. 1589; *O'Connor's Federal Civil Forms* (2012), FORMS 7B.

§1.4 Other references. 10A, 10B Wright, Miller & Kane, *Federal Practice & Procedure 3d* §§2711-2742 (1998 & Supp.2012); 11 *Moore's Federal Practice 3d* ch. 56 (2012); Knight, *Rule 56 Revisited: The Effect of Seeking or Opposing Summary Judgment on the Basis of Unpleaded Claims or Defenses*, 43:8 Federal Lawyer 15 (Sept.1996); Schwarzer et al., *The Analysis & Decision of Summary Judgment Motions*, 139 F.R.D. 441 (1992).

§2. COMPARISON WITH OTHER NONTRIAL DISPOSITIONS

Summary judgment is similar to other types of dispositive motions.

§2.1 FRCP 12(b)(6) motion to dismiss. The FRCP 12(b)(6) motion to dismiss for failure to state a claim upon which relief can be granted is a challenge to the legal sufficiency of the plaintiff's pleadings before the defendant's answer is due. See "Motion to Dismiss for Failure to State a Claim—FRCP 12(b)(6)," ch. 3-F, p. 204. If an FRCP 12(b)(6) motion is based on evidence, it must be converted to a motion for summary judgment. FRCP 12(d). See "Effect of considering extrinsic materials," ch. 3-F, §4.2, p. 206.

§2.2 FRCP 12(c) motion for judgment on the pleadings. A summary-judgment motion that depends entirely on the pleadings and the exhibits functions as an FRCP 12(c) motion for judgment on the pleadings. ***Dyal v. Union Bag-Camp Paper Corp.***, 263 F.2d 387, 391 (5th Cir.1959); *see* ***Commercial Money Ctr., Inc. v. Illinois Un. Ins.***, 508 F.3d 327, 335-36 (6th Cir.2007) (for motion for judgment on pleadings, court can consider documents attached to pleadings and matters of public record). When an FRCP 12(c) motion is based on extrinsic evidence, it must be converted to a motion for summary judgment. FRCP 12(d).

§2.3 Motion for judgment as a matter of law (JMOL). The main difference between a summary-judgment motion and a motion for JMOL (formerly called a motion for directed verdict) is procedural. See "Motion for Judgment as a Matter of Law," ch. 8-G, p. 714. A summary judgment is a pretrial procedure that depends on written evidence; a motion for JMOL is a trial procedure that depends on evidence admitted at trial. The issue, however, is the same for both: does the evidence present a sufficient dispute to require submission to a jury, or is it so one-sided

that one party must prevail as a matter of law? ***Anderson v. Liberty Lobby, Inc.***, 477 U.S. 242, 251-52 (1986); ***Glenn Distribs. v. Carlisle Plastics, Inc.***, 297 F.3d 294, 299 (3d Cir.2002).

§2.4 FRCP 12(b)(1) motion to dismiss for lack of subject-matter jurisdiction. An FRCP 12(b)(1) motion challenges the court's subject-matter jurisdiction; thus, an order granting an FRCP 12(b)(1) motion is not a decision on the merits. See "Motion to Dismiss for Lack of Subject-Matter Jurisdiction—FRCP 12(b)(1)," ch. 3-C, p. 187. As a general rule, a party should not raise lack of jurisdiction in a motion for summary judgment because if the court lacks jurisdiction, it lacks the power to grant the summary judgment. When a motion for summary judgment asserts lack of jurisdiction, the court may treat it as a "suggestion" under FRCP 12(h)(3) of lack of subject-matter jurisdiction. *See* ***State Farm Mut. Auto. Ins. v. Dyer***, 19 F.3d 514, 518 (10th Cir.1994).

§3. MOTION FOR SUMMARY JUDGMENT

To move for summary judgment, the movant must file (1) a motion for summary judgment that identifies (a) the grounds for summary judgment, including citations to summary-judgment proof that supports the factual assertions, (b) the relief sought (i.e., final or partial summary judgment), and (c) if appropriate, a request for attorney fees, and (2) the necessary summary-judgment proof (if it is not already in the record). Depending on local rules, the movant may also need to file (3) a "point-counterpoint" statement of undisputed facts, (4) a brief or memorandum, or (5) a proposed order granting the motion for summary judgment.

§3.1 Motion. The motion for summary judgment must be in writing. ***National Fire Ins. v. Bartolazo***, 27 F.3d 518, 520 (11th Cir.1994); ***In re Hailey***, 621 F.2d 169, 171 (5th Cir.1980); *see* ***Hanson v. Polk Cty. Land, Inc.***, 608 F.2d 129, 131 (5th Cir.1979) (FRCP 56 does not authorize oral SJ motions). The court may, however, consider summary judgment on its own initiative. FRCP 56(f)(3). See "Review on court's own initiative," §11.4, p. 626.

NOTE

FRCP 56 does not limit the number of summary-judgment motions that can be filed. ***Hoffman v. Tonnemacher****, 593 F.3d 908, 911 (9th Cir.2010). Local rules, however, may determine whether a party can file more than one motion for summary judgment. Compare Local Rules Tex. (N.D.), Rule 56.2(b) (party can file only one SJ motion, unless court orders otherwise) with Local Rules Tex. (E.D.), Rule CV-7(a)(3) (party can file more than one SJ motion). A renewed or successive motion for summary judgment may be appropriate after facts are further developed.* ***Hoffman****, 593 F.3d at 911.*

1. **Grounds.** In the motion, the movant should state all reasonable grounds for summary judgment.

(1) No fact disputes. Summary judgment is proper if the movant shows that there are no genuine disputes of material fact and that the movant is entitled to judgment as a matter of law. FRCP 56(a); *see* ***Celotex Corp. v. Catrett***, 477 U.S. 317, 322 (1986); ***Policastro v. Northwest Airlines, Inc.***, 297 F.3d 535, 538 (6th Cir.2002); ***Baton Rouge Oil & Chem. Workers Un. v. ExxonMobil Corp.***, 289 F.3d 373, 375 (5th Cir.2002); *see also* 2010 Notes to FRCP 56 at ¶2, p. 1225, this book (2010 amendments to FRCP 56 changed genuine "issue" to genuine "dispute"; term "dispute" better reflects focus of SJ determination). See "Burden of Proof," §7, p. 615. To show that the asserted facts are not genuinely disputed, the movant must cite specific parts of the summary-judgment materials (i.e., depositions, documents, electronically stored information, affidavits or declarations, stipulations, admissions, interrogatory answers, or other materials). *See* FRCP 56(c)(1)(A); ***Celotex Corp.***, 477 U.S. at 323. See "Summary-Judgment Proof," §6, p. 610.

NOTE

FRCP 56(c)(1) requires parties to cite materials in the record for statements of fact or disputes of fact. See 2010 Notes to FRCP 56 at ¶¶8, 10, p. 1225, this book. See "Citing SJ proof," §6.3, p. 614. If the movant does not properly support its assertions of fact, the court has several options. See FRCP 56(e). See "Review of SJ proof," §11.1, p. 623.

(2) Legal issues. Summary judgment is particularly appropriate when the questions to be decided are issues of law. ***Flath v. Garrison Pub. Sch. Dist.***, 82 F.3d 244, 246 (8th Cir.1996). However, the line between legal issues and fact disputes can be difficult to draw. ***Pullman-Std. v. Swint***, 456 U.S. 273, 288 (1982). For example, when the application of a rule of law depends on the resolution of disputed facts, the motion presents a mixed question of law and fact. In this situation, summary judgment might not be appropriate. *See, e.g.*, ***Lujan v. National Wildlife Fed'n***, 497 U.S. 871, 889 (1990) (P's standing to sue depended on disputed activities of P). The following are some examples of purely legal issues that can be resolved by summary judgment:

(a) Interpretation of constitutions and statutes. *See, e.g.*, ***Edwards v. Aguillard***, 482 U.S. 578, 595-96 (1987) (despite affidavits, decision could be made using plain language of statute).

(b) Legal sufficiency of documents. *See, e.g.*, ***Lund v. Albrecht***, 936 F.2d 459, 463 (9th Cir.1991) (review of letter alleged to be agreement was dispositive).

(c) Interpretation of unambiguous contract. ***Hanson v. McCaw Cellular Comms.***, 77 F.3d 663, 667 (2d Cir.1996); ***United Bhd. of Carpenters & Joiners of Am., Lathers Local 42-L v. United Bhd. of Carpenters & Joiners***, 73 F.3d 958, 961 (9th Cir.1996); *see* ***Constitution State Ins. v. Iso-Tex Inc.***, 61 F.3d 405, 407 (5th Cir.1995).

(d) Statute of limitations. If there are no fact disputes about when the limitations period began to run, the defense of limitations is appropriate for summary judgment. ***BellSouth Telecomms. v. W.R. Grace & Co.***, 77 F.3d 603, 609 (2d Cir.1996); *see* ***McIntosh v. Antonino***, 71 F.3d 29, 33 (1st Cir.1995).

(e) Qualified immunity. *See* ***Behrens v. Pelletier***, 516 U.S. 299, 305-07 (1996) (examining ability to immediately appeal denial of SJ on defense of qualified immunity).

2. Relief – final SJ vs. partial SJ.

(1) Moving for final SJ. If the movant seeks final summary judgment, it should ask the court to dispose of the entire case (i.e., all disputes and all parties under all theories of recovery). *See* FRCP 56(a); 2010 Notes to FRCP 56 at ¶3, p. 1225, this book.

(2) Moving for partial SJ. If the movant seeks a partial summary judgment, it should ask the court to dispose of a claim, a defense, or part of a claim or defense. 2010 Notes to FRCP 56 at ¶3, p. 1225, this book; *see* FRCP 56(a). A partial summary judgment is the disposition of less than the entire case, regardless of whether the order grants all the relief requested. 2010 Notes to FRCP 56 at ¶3, p. 1225, this book; *see* ***Norton v. Assisted Living Concepts, Inc.***, 786 F.Supp.2d 1173, 1187 (E.D.Tex.2011) (after December 1, 2010 amendments, courts recognize motions for SJ that are directed toward matters of law that are less than all of a particular claim). The granting of a partial summary judgment is a pretrial ruling that certain issues are deemed established for the trial. ***FDIC v. Massingill***, 24 F.3d 768, 774 (5th Cir.1994), *supplemented*, 30 F.3d 601 (5th Cir.1994); 1946 Notes to FRCP 56 at ¶3, p. 1228, this book. This ruling is similar to the preliminary order under FRCP 16(c)(2)(N) and speeds up litigation by eliminating, before trial, the issues for which there is no genuine dispute of fact. 1946 Notes to FRCP 56 at ¶3, p. 1228, this book. See "Deny motion & order FRCP 16(c)(2)(N) presentation," §11.3.1(2), p. 625.

3. Attorney fees. The movant may request attorney fees (1) as damages under substantive law for the claim or defense, (2) as sanctions under FRCP 56(h) for an affidavit or declaration submitted in bad faith, and (3) as costs under FRCP 54(d)(2).

(1) Attorney fees as damages. If the movant is entitled to attorney fees as an element of damages, the movant must request attorney fees both in its complaint and in its motion for summary judgment. See "Attorney fees as damages," ch. 1-I, §8.3.1, p. 68; "Fees as damages," ch. 9-C, §2.3, p. 746. To support its claim for attorney fees, the movant must prove the amount and reasonableness of the fees with summary-judgment proof, generally by affidavits.

(2) Attorney fees as sanctions for bad-faith affidavit or declaration. The court may order payment of reasonable expenses, including attorney fees, if a party submits a summary-judgment affidavit or de-

claration in bad faith or solely for delay. FRCP 56(h). See "Sanctions for bad-faith affidavit or declaration," §6.1.3(3), p. 612.

PRACTICE TIP

When requesting sanctions under FRCP 56(h), consider whether sanctions would be appropriate under FRCP 11 or 28 U.S.C. §1927. See ***U.S. Indus. v. Touche Ross & Co.****, 854 F.2d 1223, 1243 (10th Cir.1988);* ***Stewart v. RCA Corp.****, 790 F.2d 624, 632-33 (7th Cir.1986). But see* ***Zaldivar v. City of L.A.****, 780 F.2d 823, 830 (9th Cir.1986) (inappropriate affidavits should be challenged under FRCP 56, not FRCP 11), overruled in part on other grounds,* ***Cooter & Gell v. Hartmarx Corp.****, 496 U.S. 384 (1990). See "Motion for Sanctions," ch. 5-O, p. 384.*

(3) Attorney fees as costs. To recover attorney fees as costs, the movant must request them. FRCP 54(d)(2)(A); *see* 28 U.S.C. §1920. See "Attorney fees as costs," ch. 1-I, §8.3.2, p. 68; "Motion for Attorney Fees," ch. 9-C, p. 745.

§3.2 Supporting proof. A movant seeking summary judgment on factual grounds should present supporting proof in the form of depositions, documents, electronically stored information, affidavits or declarations, stipulations, admissions, interrogatory answers, or other materials. *See* FRCP 56(c)(1)(A). See "Summary-Judgment Proof," §6, p. 610.

§3.3 Point-counterpoint statement of undisputed facts. Under some local rules, the movant must file a "point-counterpoint" statement of undisputed facts with the motion. *See, e.g.*, Local Rules Fla. (S.D.), Rule 56.1(a); Local Rules Ill. (N.D.), Rule 56.1(a)(3). In the statement of undisputed facts, the movant identifies the material facts that it contends are undisputed and therefore entitle it to summary judgment. *See, e.g.*, Local Rules Fla. (S.D.), Rule 56.1(a); Local Rules Ill. (N.D.), Rule 56.1(a)(3). The statement of undisputed facts should include specific citations to the summary-judgment proof. ***Waldridge v. American Hoechst Corp.***, 24 F.3d 918, 922 (7th Cir.1994); *see* ***Jackson v. Finnegan, Henderson, Farabow, Garrett & Dunner***, 101 F.3d 145, 150-51 (D.C.Cir.1996) (function of statement of undisputed facts is to define material facts and relevant portions of record for court). See "Summary-Judgment Proof," §6, p. 610. If a statement of undisputed facts is required, the court may deny a motion for summary judgment if the movant does not file the statement. ***Zeno v. Cropper***, 650 F.Supp. 138, 139 (S.D.N.Y.1986).

§3.4 Brief or memorandum. Under some local rules, the movant must file a brief or memorandum of law in support of the motion for summary judgment, stating the reasons that support the motion with citations to legal authority. *E.g.*, Local Rules Fla. (S.D.), Rule 7.1(c) (memorandum of law); Local Rules Ill. (N.D.), Rule 56.1(a)(2) (same); Local Rules Pa. (E.D.), Rule 7.1(c) (brief).

§3.5 Proposed order. Under some local rules, the movant must attach to its motion a proposed order with the reasons supporting the summary judgment. *See, e.g.*, Local Rules Cal. (C.D.), Rule 56-1 (movant must lodge proposed judgment if seeking SJ or proposed order if seeking partial SJ). See "Reasons for SJ," §11.5.2, p. 627.

§4. RESPONSE TO MOTION FOR SUMMARY JUDGMENT

To respond to a motion for summary judgment, the nonmovant must file (1) a response that identifies (a) the objections to the motion and summary-judgment proof and (b) the grounds for the response, including citations to any summary-judgment proof that supports the nonmovant's factual assertions, and (2) any necessary summary-judgment proof to support the response (if the proof is not already in the record). Depending on local rules, the nonmovant may also need to file (3) a "point-counterpoint" statement of genuine disputes, (4) a brief or memorandum, and (5) a proposed order denying the motion for summary judgment. When appropriate, the nonmovant may also need to file (6) a motion to extend time or a motion for continuance and (7) a motion for leave to amend its pleadings.

§4.1 Response. The nonmovant must be given an opportunity to file a response, but it is not required to do so. *See* ***Members v. Paige***, 140 F.3d 699, 701 (7th Cir.1998). If the nonmovant does not file a response, the motion will

not automatically result in summary judgment for the movant. ***Champion v. Artuz***, 76 F.3d 483, 486 (2d Cir.1996); ***Anchorage Assocs. v. Virgin Islands Bd. of Tax Rev.***, 922 F.2d 168, 175 (3d Cir.1990); 2010 Notes to FRCP 56 at ¶18, p. 1226, this book. When the nonmovant does not file a response, the court can grant summary judgment only if the movant satisfied its summary-judgment burden. *See* FRCP 56(e)(3); ***Champion***, 76 F.3d at 486; 2010 Notes to FRCP 56 at ¶20, p. 1226, this book; *see, e.g.*, ***Johnson v. Gudmundsson***, 35 F.3d 1104, 1112 (7th Cir.1994) (when nonmovant did not file response, facts became undisputed but nonmovant did not waive legal issues). See "Review of SJ proof," §11.1, p. 623. By failing to respond to the motion for summary judgment, the nonmovant admits there are no disputed facts for trial but does not waive legal arguments based on the undisputed facts. ***Flynn v. Sandahl***, 58 F.3d 283, 288 (7th Cir.1995). Even when a local rule equates the failure to file a response with consent to a motion for summary judgment, the motion must still satisfy the requirements of FRCP 56. *See* 2010 Notes to FRCP 56 at ¶¶18, 20, p. 1226, this book; *see, e.g.*, ***Ramsdell v. Bowles***, 64 F.3d 5, 7 (1st Cir.1995) (applying local rule of Maine, SJ affirmed); ***Cristobal v. Siegel***, 26 F.3d 1488, 1489 (9th Cir.1994) (applying local rule of Guam, SJ reversed); *see also* ***U.S. v. One Piece of Real Prop. Located at 5800 SW 74th Ave.***, 363 F.3d 1099, 1102 (11th Cir.2004) (local rule cannot allow SJ to be granted by default).

1. Objections. In the response, the nonmovant can object to any procedural defects in the movant's pleadings, motion, factual assertions, or proof. To preserve error, the nonmovant must assert all its challenges to the motion for summary judgment in the response. *See, e.g.*, ***Wiley v. U.S.***, 20 F.3d 222, 226 (6th Cir.1994) (nonmovant's objection that movant's affidavit did not comply with FRCP 56(e), now FRCP 56(c)(4), was made after court's ruling and thus was untimely); ***Oberg v. Allied Van Lines, Inc.***, 11 F.3d 679, 684 (7th Cir.1993) (objection to SJ on counterclaims was waived because it was not made until appeal). FRCP 56 defects are waived if not raised in the response. ***In re Unisys Sav. Plan Litig.***, 74 F.3d 420, 437 n.12 (3d Cir.1996).

(1) Challenge pleadings. The nonmovant should object if the movant's complaint or answer does not allege all the elements of its claims or defenses. As a general rule, the movant's pleadings must support its motion for summary judgment. *See* ***National Treasury Empls. Un. v. Helfer***, 53 F.3d 1289, 1295 (D.C.Cir.1995); *see also* ***Law Co. v. Mohawk Constr. & Sup. Co.***, 577 F.3d 1164, 1171 (10th Cir.2009) (movant's pretrial order must support its motion for SJ). Some courts, however, will grant summary judgment on claims or affirmative defenses that were not pleaded. *See* Knight, *Rule 56 Revisited*, 43:8 Federal Lawyer at 15; *see, e.g.*, ***Apex Oil Co. v. Archem Co.***, 770 F.2d 1353, 1356 n.3 (5th Cir.1985) (although waiver was not pleaded, SJ was proper on that issue).

(2) Challenge motion. The nonmovant should object to any legal or procedural shortcomings of the motion for summary judgment (e.g. the motion was filed too late, the movant did not properly support or address a fact). See "Citing SJ proof," §6.3, p. 614; "When to move for SJ," §8.1, p. 619.

(3) Challenge SJ proof.

(a) Objectionable proof. The nonmovant should object that the materials cited to support a fact cannot be presented in a form that would be admissible in evidence or that the materials cited are otherwise objectionable. *See* FRCP 56(c)(2); ***Allen v. Scribner***, 812 F.2d 426, 435 n.18 (9th Cir.1987), *amended*, 828 F.2d 1445 (9th Cir.1987); *see, e.g.*, ***EBC, Inc. v. Clark Bldg. Sys.***, 618 F.3d 253, 271 (3d Cir.2010) (court properly refused to consider errata sheet that contained impermissible substantive changes to deposition); ***Akin v. Q-L Invs.***, 959 F.2d 521, 530-31 (5th Cir.1992) (court properly struck false statements in affidavit). An objection to admissibility functions much like an objection at trial but is adjusted for the pretrial setting. 2010 Notes to FRCP 56 at ¶12, p. 1225, this book. See "Objecting to Evidence," ch. 8-D, p. 700. When objecting to an affidavit, the nonmovant should ask the court to strike only the objectionable parts of the affidavit; it should not ask the court to strike the entire affidavit. ***Akin***, 959 F.2d at 530-31; ***Perma Research & Dev. Co. v. Singer Co.***, 410 F.2d 572, 579 (2d Cir.1969); *see* ***Gore v. GTE S., Inc.***, 917 F.Supp. 1564, 1569-70 nn.4-5 (M.D.Ala.1996); *see, e.g.*, ***Evans v. Technologies Applications & Serv.***, 80 F.3d 954, 962 (4th Cir.1996) (court properly struck only parts of affidavit actually containing inadmissible evidence).

NOTE

The burden is on the movant to show that the cited materials are admissible as presented or to explain the admissible form that is anticipated. 2010 Notes to FRCP 56 at ¶12, p. 1225, this book. If at trial the movant attempts to admit materials that the nonmovant did not challenge at the summary-judgment stage, the nonmovant can still raise an admissibility objection (i.e., the nonmovant does not forfeit admissibility objections). Id.

(b) Form of objection. The nonmovant can challenge the proof in its response to the motion for summary judgment or in a separate motion to strike. *See* ***Desrosiers v. Hartford Life & Acc. Ins.***, 515 F.3d 87, 91 (1st Cir.2008) (inadmissible affidavit can be challenged by motion to strike, objection, or memorandum); ***Dragon v. I.C. Sys.***, 241 F.R.D. 424, 426 (D.Conn.2007) (defects in summary-judgment evidence should be raised in summary-judgment brief, but motion to strike is also appropriate); 2010 Notes to FRCP 56 at ¶12, p. 1225, this book (nonmovant does not need to make separate motion to strike to object to inadmissible summary-judgment proof). See ***O'Connor's Federal Forms***, FORM 7B:12.

PRACTICE TIP

Although the advisory committee's note states that motions to strike inadmissible summary-judgment proof are not necessary, parties should always check the local rules to determine whether the court has specific requirements for challenging summary-judgment proof. E.g., Local Rules Ind. (N.D.), Rule 56.1(e) (dispute about admissibility of evidence should be addressed in separate motion); Local Rules Or., Rule 56-1(b) (dispute about admissibility of evidence should not be addressed in motion to strike; evidentiary objections should be asserted in response or reply); see 2010 Notes to FRCP 56 at ¶12, p. 1225, this book; see, e.g., Local Rules Wash. (W.D.), Rule CR 7(g) (requests to strike evidence should not be addressed in separate motion to strike but should be included in responsive brief).

2. Grounds. In the response, the nonmovant should state all reasonable grounds for denying summary judgment.

(1) Fact disputes. Summary judgment is not proper if the nonmovant shows that there are genuine disputes of material fact and that the movant is not entitled to judgment as a matter of law. FRCP 56(a); *see* ***Celotex Corp. v. Catrett***, 477 U.S. 317, 322 (1986). See "Burden of Proof," §7, p. 615. To show that the asserted facts are genuinely disputed, the nonmovant must show that (1) the materials cited by the movant do not establish the absence of a genuine dispute or (2) the movant cannot produce admissible evidence to support the material fact. *See* FRCP 56(c)(1)(B). To make this showing, the nonmovant should cite specific parts of its own summary-judgment materials (i.e., depositions, documents, electronically stored information, affidavits or declarations, stipulations, admissions, interrogatory answers, or other materials). *See* FRCP 56(c)(1)(A); ***Nahno-Lopez v. Houser***, 625 F.3d 1279, 1283 (10th Cir.2010); *see, e.g.*, ***Thomason v. Aetna Life Ins.***, 9 F.3d 645, 646 n.1 (7th Cir.1993) (lack of affidavit supporting motion for SJ allowed court to assume nonmovant's assertion in affidavit was true). See "Summary-Judgment Proof," §6, p. 610. But the nonmovant does not always need to cite its own materials; it may be sufficient that the nonmovant—citing only the movant's materials—shows that those materials do not establish the absence of a genuine dispute. 2010 Notes to FRCP 56 at ¶11, p. 1225, this book; *see* FRCP 56(c)(1)(B).

NOTE

FRCP 56(c)(1) requires parties to cite materials in the record for statements of fact or disputes of fact. See 2010 Notes to FRCP 56 at ¶¶8, 10, p. 1225, this book. See "Citing SJ proof," §6.3, p. 614. If the nonmovant does not properly support its assertions of fact or properly address the movant's assertions of fact, the court has several options. See FRCP 56(e). See "Review of SJ proof," §11.1, p. 623.

(2) Legal issues. Summary judgment may not be appropriate when legal issues are intertwined with fact disputes. See "Legal issues," §3.1.1(2), p. 605.

§4.2 Supporting proof. A nonmovant seeking denial of summary judgment on factual grounds should present supporting proof in the form of depositions, documents, electronically stored information, affidavits or declarations, stipulations, admissions, interrogatory answers, or other materials. *See* FRCP 56(c)(1)(A). See "Summary-Judgment Proof," §6, p. 610.

§4.3 Point-counterpoint statement of genuine disputes. Under some local rules, the nonmovant must file a "point-counterpoint" statement of genuine disputes with the response. *See, e.g.*, Local Rules Cal. (C.D.), Rule 56-2; Local Rules Ill. (N.D.), Rule 56.1(b)(3); *see* ***Moro v. Shell Oil Co.***, 91 F.3d 872, 874-75 (7th Cir.1996). In the statement of genuine disputes, the nonmovant identifies the material facts that it contends are disputed, thus making summary judgment inappropriate. *See* ***Moro***, 91 F.3d at 874-75. If the nonmovant is required to include the statement of genuine disputes and does not do so, the movant's version of the facts may be deemed admitted. ***Jackson v. Finnegan, Henderson, Farabow, Garrett & Dunner***, 101 F.3d 145, 154 (D.C.Cir.1996); ***Midwest Imps., Ltd. v. Coval***, 71 F.3d 1311, 1316-17 (7th Cir.1995); ***Gaspard v. Amerada Hess Corp.***, 13 F.3d 165, 166 n.1 (5th Cir.1994). The court may also no longer construe facts in favor of the nonmovant. ***Feliberty v. Kemper Corp.***, 98 F.3d 274, 277 (7th Cir. 1996); *see also* ***Corder v. Lucent Techs.***, 162 F.3d 924, 927 (7th Cir.1998) (court can rely on movant's version of facts when nonmovant did not comply with local rule on verification). However, the decision whether to strictly enforce the local rule, or to overlook a breach of the rule, is within the court's discretion. *See* ***Little v. Cox's Supermkts.***, 71 F.3d 637, 641 (7th Cir.1995); ***Texas Instrs., Inc. v. Hyundai Elecs. Indus., Co.***, 42 F.Supp.2d 660, 670 (E.D.Tex. 1999).

§4.4 Brief or memorandum. Under some local rules, the nonmovant must file a brief or memorandum of points and authorities with the response, while others require the legal authority to be incorporated into the response. *E.g.*, Local Rules Ill. (N.D.), Rule 56.1(b)(2) (memorandum of law); Local Rules Pa. (E.D.), Rule 7.1(c) (brief). The brief or memorandum should address the legal issues raised by the movant and any significant legal issue raised by the record.

§4.5 Proposed order. Under some local rules, the nonmovant must attach a proposed order to its response.

§4.6 Motion to extend & motion for continuance. If the nonmovant cannot respond to the motion for summary judgment because the motion is premature, the nonmovant should ask that the court defer ruling on the motion (i.e., ask the court to extend the time to respond). *See* FRCP 56(d)(1); 2010 Notes to FRCP 56 at ¶¶7, 17, pp. 1225, 1226, this book; 2009 Notes to FRCP 56 at ¶1, p. 1227, this book; *see also* FRCP 6(b) (motion to extend time). See "Extending Deadlines," ch. 5-F, §2, p. 332; "Note," §8.1.1, p. 619. If the nonmovant cannot respond to the motion for summary judgment because it cannot present facts to justify its opposition, the nonmovant should request that the court allow time for the nonmovant to obtain affidavits or declarations or to conduct discovery (i.e., ask for a continuance). *See* FRCP 56(d)(2); ***Celotex Corp. v. Catrett***, 477 U.S. 317, 326 & n.6 (1986). See "Motion for Continuance," §9, p. 620. Depending on the stage of litigation, a party may need to make one or both requests.

§4.7 Leave to amend pleadings. The nonmovant should request leave to amend its pleadings if the motion for summary judgment shows that the nonmovant did not plead its case adequately. *See* FRCP 15(a); ***Dunn v. J.P. Stevens & Co.***, 192 F.2d 854, 856 (2d Cir.1951). See "Motion to Amend or Supplement Pleadings—Pretrial," ch. 5-I, p. 345. The court may deny leave to amend and grant summary judgment if it finds that the nonmovant unreasonably delayed seeking an amendment or if the amendment would not cure the problem. ***In re Southmark Corp.***, 88 F.3d 311, 316 (5th Cir.1996); ***Barber v. Hawaii***, 42 F.3d 1185, 1197-98 (9th Cir.1994). Some courts do not require a formal motion for leave to amend; in these courts, the summary-judgment process can effectively amend the pleadings. *See, e.g.*, ***Ganther v. Ingle***, 75 F.3d 207, 211-12 (5th Cir.1996) (court should have treated nonmovant's response as motion to amend complaint).

§5. REPLY BRIEF

If allowed by the local rules or required by the pretrial order, the movant should file a reply brief responding to the allegations raised in the nonmovant's response.

§5.1 No fact disputes. As in the motion for summary judgment, the movant must show that there are no genuine disputes of material fact. See "No fact disputes," §3.1.1(1), p. 604. To show that the asserted facts are not genuinely disputed, the movant must show that (1) the materials cited by the nonmovant do not establish a genuine dispute or (2) the nonmovant cannot produce admissible evidence to support the allegedly disputed fact. *See* FRCP 56(c)(1)(B). See "Citing SJ proof," §6.3, p. 614. Asserted facts must be supported by citing specific parts of the summary-judgment materials. *See* FRCP 56(c)(1)(A). But in the reply, the movant may not need to cite additional materials; it may be sufficient that the movant—citing only the nonmovant's materials—shows that those materials do not establish a genuine dispute. 2010 Notes to FRCP 56 at ¶11, p. 1225, this book; *see* FRCP 56(c)(1)(B).

§5.2 Objections.

1. Challenge response. The movant should object to any legal or procedural shortcoming of the response to the motion for summary judgment (e.g., the response was filed too late).

2. Challenge SJ proof. The movant should object to any inadmissible or otherwise objectionable summary-judgment proof. See "Challenge SJ proof," §4.1.1(3), p. 607.

§5.3 Supporting proof. A movant seeking summary judgment on factual grounds should present supporting proof. See "Supporting proof," §3.2, p. 606. Affidavits and declarations may accompany a reply brief when they relate to new disputes that have arisen during briefing. ***Graning v. Sherburne Cty.***, 172 F.3d 611, 614 n.2 (8th Cir.1999); *see* ***Alaska Wildlife Alliance v. Jensen***, 108 F.3d 1065, 1068 n.5 (9th Cir.1997).

§6. SUMMARY-JUDGMENT PROOF

§6.1 Types of SJ proof. To provide support for a factual assertion in a motion for summary judgment, the response, or the reply, a party can cite depositions, documents, electronically stored information (ESI), affidavits or declarations, stipulations, admissions, interrogatory answers, or other materials as proof. FRCP 56(c)(1)(A).

1. Depositions. A party can cite deposition testimony to support a factual assertion. FRCP 56(c)(1)(A).

2. Documents or ESI. A party can cite documents or ESI to support a factual assertion. FRCP 56(c)(1)(A).

3. Affidavits or declarations. A party can cite affidavits or declarations as support for a factual assertion. FRCP 56(c)(1)(A), (c)(4); *see* 2010 Notes to FRCP 56 at ¶15, p. 1226, this book (party can provide formal affidavit or written unsworn declaration).

(1) Requirements for affidavit or declaration.

(a) Form.

[1] Affidavit. An affidavit must be sworn and made under penalty of perjury. ***Pfeil v. Rogers***, 757 F.2d 850, 859 (7th Cir.1985); *see* ***Hayes v. Marriott***, 70 F.3d 1144, 1147-48 (10th Cir.1995).

[2] Declaration. A declaration must be verified as true under penalty of perjury. 28 U.S.C. §1746; 2010 Notes to FRCP 56 at ¶15, p. 1226, this book. A declaration does not need to be sworn. 2010 Notes to FRCP 56 at ¶15, p. 1226, this book.

(b) FRCP 56(c)(4) requirements. The affidavit or declaration must be made on personal knowledge, set out facts that would be admissible in evidence, and show that the affiant or declarant is competent to testify on the matters stated. FRCP 56(c)(4). A court must not consider parts of an affidavit or declaration that do not meet the requirements of FRCP 56(c)(4) when determining a motion for summary judgment. *See* ***Cooper-Schut v. Visteon Auto. Sys.***, 361 F.3d 421, 429 (7th Cir.2004).

[1] Personal knowledge.

[a] Generally. The facts stated in the affidavit or declaration must be based on the affiant's or declarant's personal knowledge. FRCP 56(c)(4); *see* ***Cooper-Schut***, 361 F.3d at 429; ***Evans v. Technolo-***

gies Applications & Serv., 80 F.3d 954, 962 (4th Cir.1996); ***Sellers v. M.C. Floor Crafters, Inc.***, 842 F.2d 639, 643 (2d Cir.1988); *see also* ***Velázquez-García v. Horizon Lines***, 473 F.3d 11, 18 (1st Cir.2007) (self-serving affidavit may be competent SJ evidence as long as it contains relevant information based on affiant's personal knowledge). The affiant or declarant should state the basis for her personal knowledge. However, an affiant's or declarant's personal knowledge may be inferred from the contents of the affidavit or declaration as a whole; explicit assertions that the affiant or declarant has personal knowledge of each statement are unnecessary. *See* ***Barthelemy v. Air Lines Pilots Ass'n***, 897 F.2d 999, 1018 (9th Cir.1990); ***Credentials Plus, LLC v. Calderone***, 230 F.Supp.2d 890, 904 (N.D.Ind. 2002); ***Reddy v. Good Samaritan Hosp. & Health Ctr.***, 137 F.Supp.2d 948, 956 (S.D.Ohio 2000). For example, personal knowledge may be inferred from the affiant's or declarant's position within a company. *See* ***In re Kaypro***, 218 F.3d 1070, 1075 (9th Cir.2000); *see, e.g.*, ***Self-Realization Fellowship Ch. v. Ananda Ch. of Self-Realization***, 206 F.3d 1322, 1330 (9th Cir.2000) (corporate officer could be expected to know employees' identities and tasks). An affidavit or declaration made on "information and belief" does not meet the FRCP 56(c)(4) requirement of personal knowledge. *See* ***Automatic Radio Mfg. Co. v. Hazeltine Research, Inc.***, 339 U.S. 827, 831 (1950), *overruled on other grounds*, ***Lear, Inc. v. Adkins***, 395 U.S. 653 (1969); ***Columbia Pictures Indus. v. Professional Real Estate Investors, Inc.***, 944 F.2d 1525, 1529 (9th Cir.1991), *aff'd*, 508 U.S. 49 (1993); ***Reddy***, 137 F.Supp.2d at 956.

[b] Experts. The facts stated in an affidavit or declaration submitted by an expert do not have to be based on the expert's personal knowledge. *See* ***City of Chanute v. Williams Nat. Gas Co.***, 743 F.Supp. 1437, 1444 (D.Kan.1990), *aff'd*, 955 F.2d 641 (10th Cir.1992). However, the affidavit or declaration must include the expert's opinion as well as the facts and reasoning that the opinion is based on. *See* ***Dolihite v. Maughon***, 74 F.3d 1027, 1047 (11th Cir.1996); ***Iacobelli Constr., Inc. v. County of Monroe***, 32 F.3d 19, 25 (2d Cir.1994); ***Hayes v. Douglas Dynamics, Inc.***, 8 F.3d 88, 92 (1st Cir.1993); *see, e.g.*, ***Guidroz-Brault v. Missouri Pac. R.R.***, 254 F.3d 825, 830-31 (9th Cir.2001) (expert affidavit excluded because opinion not sufficiently based on facts).

[2] Admissible facts. The facts stated in the affidavit or declaration must be specific and must constitute admissible evidence. FRCP 56(c)(4); *see* ***Lujan v. National Wildlife Fed'n***, 497 U.S. 871, 888 (1990); *see, e.g.*, ***Evans***, 80 F.3d at 962 (inadmissible hearsay cannot be considered). Bare allegations of fact, ultimate or conclusory facts, and legal conclusions are not sufficient. ***BellSouth Telecomms. v. W.R. Grace & Co.***, 77 F.3d 603, 615 (2d Cir.1996); *see* ***Cooper-Schut***, 361 F.3d at 429 (conclusory statements unsupported by evidence of record are insufficient to avoid summary judgment); ***TIG Ins. v. Sedgwick James***, 276 F.3d 754, 759 (5th Cir.2002) (conclusory allegations, speculation, unsubstantiated assertions, and legalistic argumentation are no substitute for specific facts showing genuine dispute of material fact).

[3] Competence. The affidavit or declaration must affirmatively show that the affiant or declarant is competent to testify on the matters in the affidavit or declaration. FRCP 56(c)(4); *see* ***Gell v. Town of Aulander***, 252 F.R.D. 297, 304 (E.D.N.C.2008) (competence goes to matters in affidavit, not affiant's age or recall ability). Generally, an affiant or declarant is competent to testify when her testimony is grounded in observation or other personal experience and is not based on speculation, intuition, or rumors about matters remote from that personal experience. *See* ***Visser v. Packer Eng'g Assocs.***, 924 F.2d 655, 659 (7th Cir.1991); *see, e.g.*, ***Ruffin v. Shaw Indus.***, 149 F.3d 294, 302 (4th Cir.1998) (without factual basis for conclusory comments, affiant would not be competent to testify about defect in carpet); ***Maietta v. United Parcel Serv.***, 749 F.Supp. 1344, 1369 (D.N.J.1990) (layman may have been able to testify about fact of his elevated blood pressure, but he was not competent to testify about medical determination of why it was elevated), *aff'd*, 932 F.2d 960 (3d Cir.1991) (table case).

(2) Sham affidavit or declaration. A "sham" affidavit or declaration is one that contradicts the affiant's or declarant's earlier testimony for the sole purpose of creating a fact dispute to prevent summary judgment. *See* ***Rojas v. Roman Catholic Diocese of Rochester***, 660 F.3d 98, 105-06 (2d Cir.2011); ***Law Co. v. Mohawk Constr. & Sup. Co.***, 577 F.3d 1164, 1169 (10th Cir.2009); ***Bank of Ill. v. Allied Signal Safety Restraint Sys.***, 75 F.3d 1162, 1168-69 (7th Cir.1996).

NOTE

Not all affidavits or declarations that are inconsistent with earlier testimony are sham affidavits or declarations. See ***Nelson v. City of Davis****, 571 F.3d 924, 928 (9th Cir.2009);* ***Jiminez v. All Am. Rathskeller, Inc.****, 503 F.3d 247, 254 (3d Cir.2007);* ***State Farm Mut. Auto. Ins. v. New Horizont, Inc.****, 250 F.R.D. 203, 212-13 (E.D.Pa.2008). The court may consider the affidavit if, for example, (1) the affiant was confused at the deposition, the affiant explains those aspects of the deposition testimony, and the affiant provides independent evidence of that explanation, or (2) the affiant did not have access to material facts and the affidavit sets out newly discovered evidence. See* ***Jiminez****, 503 F.3d at 254; see, e.g.,* ***U.S. v. Torres****, 142 F.3d 962, 968 (7th Cir. 1998) (affidavits that contradicted earlier sworn statements could not create fact dispute when they were not based on newly discovered evidence);* ***S.W.S. Erectors, Inc. v. Infax, Inc.****, 72 F.3d 489, 495-96 (5th Cir.1996) (contradictory affidavit did not "supplement" earlier deposition testimony).*

(a) Effect on SJ. A party cannot defeat a motion for summary judgment by filing an affidavit or declaration that impeaches, without explanation, earlier sworn testimony of the same affiant or declarant. *See* ***Rojas***, 660 F.3d at 106; ***In re Family Dollar FLSA Litig.***, 637 F.3d 508, 512 (4th Cir.2011). The court can simply disregard the sham affidavit or declaration. *See* ***In re Family Dollar FLSA Litig.***, 637 F.3d at 513; ***Buttry v. General Signal Corp.***, 68 F.3d 1488, 1493 (2d Cir.1995).

(b) Sanctions. The court can impose sanctions when a party's affidavit or declaration is inconsistent with the party's earlier statements and there is direct proof of the earlier statement. *See, e.g.,* ***Margo v. Weiss***, 213 F.3d 55, 65 (2d Cir.2000) (sanctions under FRCP 11 awarded when affidavits, delayed errata sheets, and supplemental interrogatory responses contradicted deposition testimony).

(3) Sanctions for bad-faith affidavit or declaration. If a party submits an affidavit or declaration in bad faith or solely for delay, the court can impose sanctions on that party. FRCP 56(h); *see, e.g.,* ***Acrotube, Inc. v. J.K. Fin. Grp.***, 653 F.Supp. 470, 478 (N.D.Ga.1987) (sanctions granted when affidavit was at odds with facts within party's knowledge); *see also* 2010 Notes to FRCP 56 at ¶25, p. 1227, this book (2010 amendments to FRCP 56(h) made sanctions discretionary, not mandatory, as courts rarely used FRCP 56 authority to impose sanctions).

(a) Notice & reasonable time to respond. Before ordering sanctions for an affidavit or declaration submitted in bad faith or solely for delay, the court must give the offending party notice and allow a reasonable time to respond. FRCP 56(h).

(b) Sanctions available. If the court finds that an affidavit or declaration was submitted in bad faith or solely for delay, the court can order (1) the submitting party to pay the other party the reasonable expenses, including attorney fees, that the other party incurred as a result, (2) that the submitting party or its attorney be held in contempt, or (3) other appropriate sanctions against the submitting party or its attorney. FRCP 56(h).

4. Stipulations. A party can cite stipulations (including those made only for purposes of the motion) to support a factual assertion. FRCP 56(c)(1)(A); *see* ***U.S. v. De Witt***, 265 F.2d 393, 399-400 (5th Cir.1959).

5. Admissions. A party can cite admissions to support a factual assertion. FRCP 56(c)(1)(A); *see* ***Hulsey v. Texas***, 929 F.2d 168, 171 (5th Cir.1991); ***Donovan v. Carls Drug Co.***, 703 F.2d 650, 651-52 (2d Cir.1983). A party cannot cite its own admissions; it can cite only the other party's admissions. *See* ***Anchorage Assocs. v. Virgin Islands Bd. of Tax Rev.***, 922 F.2d 168, 176 n.7 (3d Cir.1990); ***H.B. Zachry Co. v. O'Brien***, 378 F.2d 423, 425 (10th Cir.1967). See "By whom & against whom," ch. 6-H, §8.2, p. 568.

NOTE

A party cannot rebut admissions through affidavits or other summary-judgment proof. See ***Praetorian Ins. v. Site Inspection, LLC****, 604 F.3d 509, 514 (8th Cir.2010);* ***U.S. v. Kasuboski****, 834 F.2d 1345, 1350 (7th Cir.1987).*

6. Interrogatories. A party can cite interrogatory answers to support a factual assertion. FRCP 56(c)(1)(A); *see* ***Lujan***, 497 U.S. at 884; ***Bradley v. Allstate Ins.***, 620 F.3d 509, 527 n.21 (5th Cir.2010). A party can cite interrogatory answers, even its own answers, as long as the content of the answers would be admissible at trial. *See* ***Hardrick v. City of Bolingbrook***, 522 F.3d 758, 761 (7th Cir.2008); ***H.B. Zachry Co.***, 378 F.2d at 425; 10A Wright, Miller & Kane §2722 & nn.16-17; *see also* ***Garside v. Osco Drug, Inc.***, 895 F.2d 46, 49-50 (1st Cir.1990) (interrogatory answers are treated like affidavits; answers must be made on personal knowledge, set out facts that would be admissible in evidence, and show that answering party is competent to testify on matters in answers).

7. Other materials. A party can cite other materials to support a factual assertion. FRCP 56(c)(1)(A). Any properly authenticated (and otherwise admissible) material may be used as summary-judgment proof. *See id.*; ***Bias v. Moynihan***, 508 F.3d 1212, 1224 (9th Cir.2007); *see, e.g.*, ***Law Co.***, 577 F.3d at 1170 (letters, faxes, and memorandums that were attached to D's SJ response and were on P's letterhead should not have been disregarded without authentication analysis under FRE 901; because they were on P's letterhead, no authentication affidavit was required). An affidavit or declaration authenticating the materials should be made by a person through whom the materials would be introduced at trial. *See* ***Orr v. Bank of Am.***, 285 F.3d 764, 773-74 (9th Cir.2002); ***Zoslaw v. MCA Distrib.***, 693 F.2d 870, 883 (9th Cir.1982); *see, e.g.*, ***Bias***, 508 F.3d at 1224 (application for emergency psychiatric detention should have been authenticated by officer's declaration rather than by his attorney's declaration).

(1) Pleadings. Pleadings and legal memorandums generally cannot be used as summary-judgment proof. *See* ***Wallace v. Texas Tech Univ.***, 80 F.3d 1042, 1047 (5th Cir.1996); ***Orson, Inc. v. Miramax Film Corp.***, 79 F.3d 1358, 1372 (3d Cir.1996); ***Lipton v. Nature Co.***, 71 F.3d 464, 469 (2d Cir.1995). However, statements of fact in a pleading, a motion for summary judgment, or a response to a motion for summary judgment can be used as summary-judgment proof if the document qualifies as an "affidavit." For example, a verified complaint can be competent summary-judgment proof under FRCP 56(c)(4). *See* ***Huckabay v. Moore***, 142 F.3d 233, 240 n.6 (5th Cir.1998); ***Hayes***, 70 F.3d at 1148. See "Affidavits or declarations," §6.1.3, p. 610.

(2) Public records. Authenticated or certified public records can be used as summary-judgment proof. *See* FRE 902(4).

(3) Judicial notice. Judicially noticed facts can be used as summary-judgment proof. *See* FRE 201; ***Soley v. Star & Herald Co.***, 390 F.2d 364, 367 (5th Cir.1968). Matters that the court can take judicial notice of include adjudicative facts (such as court records and pleadings) and other facts that are not subject to reasonable dispute because they either are generally known or can be accurately and readily determined from sources whose accuracy cannot reasonably be questioned. *See* FRE 201(a), (b). See "Motion for Judicial Notice," ch. 5-M, p. 370.

(4) Testimony.

(a) Oral testimony. Although FRCP 56 does not say whether oral testimony can be received at a hearing on a motion for summary judgment, some courts have suggested that FRCP 43(c), which permits oral testimony on motions in general, allows oral testimony at summary-judgment hearings. *See* ***Waskovich v. Morgano***, 2 F.3d 1292, 1295-96 (3d Cir.1993); ***Utah v. Marsh***, 740 F.2d 799, 801 n.2 (10th Cir.1984). The better practice, however, is to use either a transcribed deposition or an affidavit.

(b) Expert-witness testimony. A party may establish facts using the testimony of an expert witness. For the requirements for an expert's affidavit, see "Requirements for affidavit or declaration," §6.1.3(1), p. 610. The expert's testimony must meet the requirements for admissibility under FRE 702. *See* ***Williams Nat. Gas***, 743 F.Supp. at 1444. See "Motion to Exclude Expert Witness," ch. 5-N, p. 376.

(c) Interested-witness testimony. A party may establish facts using the testimony of an interested witness if the witness's testimony relates to specific facts and is undisputed and unchallenged by the other party. *See* ***Pelphrey v. U.S.***, 674 F.2d 243, 247 (4th Cir.1982).

NOTE

If the summary-judgment proof involves the credibility of a witness's testimony, the court usually cannot grant summary judgment because weighing the credibility of witnesses raises a factual dispute. See ***Alspaugh v. McConnell****, 643 F.3d 162, 168 (6th Cir.2011);* ***Schoonejongen v. Curtiss-Wright Corp.****, 143 F.3d 120, 129-30 (3d Cir.1998).*

§6.2 Proper SJ proof. To support a fact asserted in a motion for summary judgment, the response, or the reply, the summary-judgment proof must be admissible at trial, but at the summary-judgment stage, it does not need to be in admissible form and can be opposed by any evidentiary materials listed in FRCP 56(c)(1)(A). *See* ***Celotex Corp. v. Catrett***, 477 U.S. 317, 324 (1986); ***Law Co. v. Mohawk Constr. & Sup. Co.***, 577 F.3d 1164, 1170 (10th Cir. 2009); ***Alexander v. Caresource***, 576 F.3d 551, 558 (6th Cir.2009). See "Introducing Evidence," ch. 8-C, p. 688.

§6.3 Citing SJ proof. A party asserting that a fact cannot be disputed or is genuinely disputed must cite a specific part of the record that supports the assertion. *See* FRCP 56(c)(1); 2010 Notes to FRCP 56 at ¶10, p. 1225, this book. A party should include specific, not general, citations to the summary-judgment proof. *See, e.g.*, ***Smith v. U.S.***, 391 F.3d 621, 625 (5th Cir.2004) (SJ proof not properly before court because party did not specifically refer to expert's opinion in responding to motion). For example, deposition testimony that supports the party's position should be identified by deponent, date, page, and line rather than just by deponent. Also, when relying on summary-judgment proof, the party should state precisely how the submitted evidence supports its claim. *Id.*

PRACTICE TIP

Although FRCP 56(c)(1)(A) imposes a citation requirement, the rule does not address how or where to cite summary-judgment proof. 2010 Notes to FRCP 56 at ¶9, p. 1225, this book. To determine how and where to cite summary-judgment proof, be sure to check the local rules or any court order that may impose specific requirements. See, e.g., Local Rules Tex. (E.D.), Rule CV-56(d) (attorneys should cite SJ materials by page and, if possible, by line; attorneys are strongly encouraged to highlight or underline cited portions, unless citation covers entire page). By local rule or court order, the court may require that the proof be included in the motion, made part of a separate statement of facts, included in the body of a brief or memorandum, or provided in a separate statement of facts included in a brief or memorandum. 2010 Notes to FRCP 56 at ¶9, p. 1225, this book.

§6.4 Placing SJ proof in the record. A party citing summary-judgment proof must ensure that the materials are in the court's record or, if not, that the materials will be placed in the record. 2010 Notes to FRCP 56 at ¶10, p. 1225, this book; *see* FRCP 56(c)(1)(A). When a party relies on materials that are not in the record (e.g., affidavits, declarations, most discovery), the party must attach copies of the materials to its motion, response, or reply. *See* 2010 Notes to FRCP 56 at ¶10, p. 1225, this book; *see, e.g.*, Local Rules Tex. (S.D.), Rule 7.7 (if motion requires consideration of facts not in record, proof by affidavit or other documentary evidence must be filed with motion). If the materials are already on file, a party may cite the materials without attaching them. *See* FRCP 56(c)(1)(A); ***McLaughlin v. Liu***, 849 F.2d 1205, 1206 n.3 (9th Cir.1988).

§6.5 Organizing SJ proof. A party should check local rules, standing orders, and other local procedures that may have specific requirements for organizing and presenting summary-judgment proof.

1. Appendix. Generally, if a party has only a few materials for summary-judgment proof, they can be attached directly to the motion, response, or reply if they are not already on file. If the party cites a large assortment of materials, it should organize the materials in an appendix. *See* 2010 Notes to FRCP 56 at ¶10, p. 1225, this book. Once

the materials are in the record, a party may voluntarily submit an appendix, the parties may submit a joint appendix, or the court, by local rule or case-specific court order, may order the parties to submit an appendix. *Id.* A party can organize the appendix as follows:

NOTE

Citation to a specific location in an appendix satisfies the citation requirement under FRCP 56(c)(1). 2010 Notes to FRCP 56 at ¶10, p. 1225, this book. Local rules, however, may establish different or additional procedures for the appendix. See id. See "Citing SJ proof," §6.3, p. 614.

(1) Table of contents. The appendix should include a table of contents of the evidence with reference to the tabs where the different items are located.

(2) Separate tabs & numbers. The appendix should have separate tabs and page numbers for each item included. *See, e.g.*, Motion Practice – U.S. Dist. Judge Avern Cohn (E.D.Mich.), ¶III (requiring exhibits to be indexed and tabbed in three-ring binder filed with court). In the motion or response, the party should refer to the appendix by tab and page number to make the court's task of reviewing the materials easier.

(3) Incorporation by reference. The appendix should include a statement that all the summary-judgment proof in the appendix is incorporated by reference into the motion or response. Likewise, the motion or response should include a similar statement.

(4) Verification. The appendix should include an affidavit by a person with knowledge stating that all copies of discovery and documents in the appendix are true copies of the originals. If necessary, the party should attach additional affidavits to overcome hearsay objections to documents.

2. Voluminous record. Once the materials are in the record, if the record is voluminous, the court can order that a party help the court locate materials in the record. 2010 Notes to FRCP 56 at ¶10, p. 1225, this book.

§7. BURDEN OF PROOF

§7.1 Generally. The burden of proof in a summary-judgment proceeding is on the same party who would bear the burden of proof at trial. ***Celotex Corp. v. Catrett***, 477 U.S. 317, 325 (1986). The court may grant summary judgment against a party who cannot establish an element essential to that party's case and on which that party will bear the burden of proof at trial. *Id.* at 322-23; ***Policastro v. Northwest Airlines, Inc.***, 297 F.3d 535, 538 (6th Cir.2002); ***Baton Rouge Oil & Chem. Workers Un. v. ExxonMobil Corp.***, 289 F.3d 373, 375 (5th Cir.2002); *see* FRCP 56(a). When the movant has carried its burden under FRCP 56(a), the nonmovant must demonstrate that there is a genuine dispute of material fact and not merely allege that there is a factual dispute. *See* ***Scott v. Harris***, 550 U.S. 372, 380 (2007). The court must examine the record as a whole and make reasonable inferences about the facts in favor of the nonmovant. *Id.* at 378-80; ***Cooper Tire & Rubber Co. v. Farese***, 423 F.3d 446, 456 (5th Cir.2005); ***Garcia v. Pueblo Country Club***, 299 F.3d 1233, 1236-37 (10th Cir.2002); ***Policastro***, 297 F.3d at 538; ***Pocchia v. NYNEX Corp.***, 81 F.3d 275, 277 (2d Cir.1996). *But see* ***Corder v. Lucent Techs.***, 162 F.3d 924, 927 (7th Cir.1998) (court can rely on movant's version of facts when nonmovant did not comply with local rule on verification). When there are two opposing versions of the facts and one is blatantly contradicted by the record, the court cannot adopt that version for summary-judgment purposes. *E.g.*, ***Scott***, 550 U.S. at 380 (court declined to adopt nonmovant's version of facts because they were so contradicted by videotape that no reasonable jury could have believed them). Therefore, the court "shall" render summary judgment if there is no genuine dispute about any material fact and the movant is entitled to judgment as a matter of law. FRCP 56(a); *see* ***Irby v. Bittick***, 44 F.3d 949, 953 (11th Cir.1995); ***Campbell v. Hewitt, Coleman & Assocs.***, 21 F.3d 52, 55 (4th Cir.1994).

NOTE

The 2010 amendments to FRCP 56 restored the word "shall" to the statement about the court rendering summary judgment if there is no genuine dispute about any material fact. 2010 Notes to FRCP 56 at ¶¶2, 4, p. 1225, this book. As part of the 2007 restyling amendments, the word "shall" was replaced by "should." Id. at ¶4, p. 1225, this book. But the phrasing of FRCP 56(a), including the word "shall," had become a term of art that the Advisory Committee thought should not be changed for stylistic reasons without risking change to the substantive meaning. See Report of the Judicial Conference: Committee on Rules of Practice & Procedure, Agenda E-19, at Rules-p.17 (Sept.2009), www.uscourts.gov/uscourts/RulesAndPolicies/rules/Supreme%20 Court%202009/ST_Report_Sept_2009.pdf. Thus, the word "shall" was restored to allow the courts—which, on different occasions, have interpreted "shall" to mean "must" and "should"—to continue to develop the term. See id.

1. Genuine dispute. A genuine dispute is one that can be determined only by a trier of fact because it may be resolved in favor of either party. ***Anderson v. Liberty Lobby, Inc.***, 477 U.S. 242, 248-49 (1986); *see* ***Matsushita Elec. Indus. Co. v. Zenith Radio Corp.***, 475 U.S. 574, 586-87 (1986); *see also* 2010 Notes to FRCP 56 at ¶2, p. 1225, this book (2010 amendments to FRCP 56 changed genuine "issue" to genuine "dispute"; term "dispute" better reflects focus of SJ determination). A genuine dispute exists when a reasonable jury could resolve the disputed fact in favor of, or in the manner described by, the nonmovant. ***New Par v. City of Saginaw***, 301 F.3d 390, 394 (6th Cir.2002); ***Jenkins v. Wood***, 81 F.3d 988, 990 (10th Cir.1996); ***Meadowbriar Home for Children, Inc. v. Gunn***, 81 F.3d 521, 533 (5th Cir.1996); *see* ***Matsushita Elec. Indus.***, 475 U.S. at 587.

2. Material fact. A material fact is one that can affect the outcome of the suit under the governing substantive law. ***Anderson***, 477 U.S. at 248. The substantive law determines which facts are material. *Id.*; ***Boyle v. County of Allegheny Pa.***, 139 F.3d 386, 393 (3d Cir.1998); ***Douglass v. United Servs. Auto. Ass'n***, 79 F.3d 1415, 1423 n.11 (5th Cir.1996).

§7.2 When defendant moves for SJ on plaintiff's claim. Most summary judgments are granted to a defendant based on the insufficiency of the plaintiff's claim.

1. Defendant's motion. When a defendant moves for summary judgment on the plaintiff's claim, it may satisfy its summary-judgment burden in one of two ways:

(1) The defendant may submit summary-judgment evidence that negates the existence of an essential element of the plaintiff's claim. ***Lavespere v. Niagara Mach. & Tool Works, Inc.***, 910 F.2d 167, 178 (5th Cir. 1990); *see* ***Celotex Corp. v. Catrett***, 477 U.S. 317, 323-25 (1986).

(2) The defendant may show there is no evidence to support an essential element of the plaintiff's claim. *See* ***Celotex Corp.***, 477 U.S. at 325; ***J. Geils Band Empl. Benefit Plan v. Smith Barney Shearson, Inc.***, 76 F.3d 1245, 1251 (1st Cir.1996); ***Buck v. FDIC***, 75 F.3d 1285, 1289 (8th Cir.1996). It is not necessary for the defendant to introduce evidence that negates the plaintiff's claim. ***Celotex Corp.***, 477 U.S. at 323; ***Wallace v. Texas Tech Univ.***, 80 F.3d 1042, 1047 (5th Cir.1996). If there has been sufficient time for discovery, in its motion for summary judgment the defendant should review the pleadings, the discovery products, and any other relevant parts of the record to show that the plaintiff cannot prove at least one element of its claim.

2. Plaintiff's response. If the defendant makes the required showing, the burden shifts to the plaintiff to show there is a genuine dispute of fact for trial. ***Anderson v. Liberty Lobby, Inc.***, 477 U.S. 242, 250 (1986); ***Hysten v. Burlington N. & Santa Fe Ry.***, 296 F.3d 1177, 1180 (10th Cir.2002); ***Bratton v. Roadway Package Sys.***, 77 F.3d 168, 173 (7th Cir.1996); ***Buck***, 75 F.3d at 1289. The plaintiff may defeat the motion for summary judgment only if it shows there are issues that are genuinely in dispute and advances convincing theories supporting their materiality. ***Anderson***, 477 U.S. at 247-48; *see* ***FDIC v. Elder Care Servs.***, 82 F.3d 524, 526-27 (1st Cir.1996); ***BellSouth Telecomms. v. W.R. Grace & Co.***, 77 F.3d 603, 615 (2d Cir.1996). The plaintiff must do one of the following:

(1) rehabilitate the evidence attacked in the motion, (2) produce evidence showing the existence of a genuine dispute for trial, or (3) submit an FRCP 56(d) affidavit or declaration explaining why further discovery is necessary. *See* 10A Wright, Miller & Kane §2727. See "Motion for Continuance," §9, p. 620.

3. Defendant's reply. The defendant may reply to the plaintiff's response by attempting to demonstrate the inadequacy of the plaintiff's evidence. *See, e.g.*, ***Beck v. Board of Regents***, 75 F.3d 1130, 1134 n.* (7th Cir.1996) (D's affidavit in SJ reply brief properly considered by court). Because FRCP 56 neither authorizes nor forbids the use of reply briefs, a party should look to the local rules for permission to file one. ***Beaird v. Seagate Tech.***, 145 F.3d 1159, 1164 (10th Cir.1998). Affidavits may be produced at the reply stage if they respond to new issues that have arisen during briefing. ***Graning v. Sherburne Cty.***, 172 F.3d 611, 614 n.2 (8th Cir.1999); ***Alaska Wildlife Alliance v. Jensen***, 108 F.3d 1065, 1068 n.5 (9th Cir.1997).

4. Plaintiff's surreply. If the court permits the defendant to file a reply, the plaintiff may be able to file a surreply. ***Beaird***, 145 F.3d at 1164. But before filing a surreply, the plaintiff should look to the local rules. *See, e.g.*, Local Rules Md., Rule 105.2(a) (unless otherwise ordered, surreplies are not permitted); Local Rules Wash. (W.D.), Rule CR 7(g) (surreply allowed only to request that court strike objectionable materials in response). If the defendant raises new reasons or evidence in its reply, the plaintiff should be given an opportunity to respond. ***Beaird***, 145 F.3d at 1164. However, the court is not required to permit the plaintiff to file a surreply; if the court can make its ruling without relying on the defendant's new reasons or evidence, it does not abuse its discretion by denying a surreply. *Id.* at 1164-65.

§7.3 When defendant moves for SJ on its affirmative defense.

1. Defendant's motion. When a defendant moves for summary judgment on its affirmative defense, it must show the absence of a genuine dispute of material fact and establish each element of its defense as a matter of law. *See* ***Buttry v. General Signal Corp.***, 68 F.3d 1488, 1492 (2d Cir.1995); *see, e.g.*, ***Crescent Towing & Salvage Co. v. M/V Anax***, 40 F.3d 741, 744 (5th Cir.1994) (affirmative defense of judicial sale); ***Fox v. Citicorp Credit Servs.***, 15 F.3d 1507, 1514 (9th Cir.1994) (affirmative defense of bona fide error). Unless the defendant produces evidence establishing its defense as a matter of law, it is not entitled to summary judgment. *See* ***Fox***, 15 F.3d at 1514.

2. Plaintiff's response. If the defendant meets its burden, the plaintiff must then produce significant, probative evidence demonstrating the existence of a triable dispute of fact on at least one element of the defendant's defense. ***Reynolds v. School Dist.***, 69 F.3d 1523, 1531 (10th Cir.1995); ***Irby v. Bittick***, 44 F.3d 949, 953 (11th Cir. 1995); ***Kansa Reinsurance Co. v. Congressional Mortg. Corp.***, 20 F.3d 1362, 1371 (5th Cir.1994); *see* ***McIntosh v. Antonino***, 71 F.3d 29, 33 (1st Cir.1995) (when D moves for SJ on defense that suit is time-barred, burden of identifying triable dispute falls on P). To defeat the defendant's motion for summary judgment, the plaintiff may (1) submit summary-judgment proof that negates the existence of some material element of the defendant's defense, (2) demonstrate that the summary-judgment proof in the record is not sufficient to support an essential element of the defendant's defense, or (3) submit an FRCP 56(d) affidavit or declaration explaining why further discovery is necessary. See "Motion for Continuance," §9, p. 620.

§7.4 When defendant moves for SJ on its counterclaim.

1. Defendant's motion. When a defendant moves for summary judgment on its counterclaim, it has the same burden as a plaintiff who moves for summary judgment on its own claim—the defendant must show there are no genuine disputes of material fact and establish its counterclaim as a matter of law. *See, e.g.*, ***Gasaway v. Northwestern Mut. Life Ins.***, 26 F.3d 957, 959 (9th Cir.1994) (D counterclaimed for rescission of contract); ***Topalian v. Ehrman***, 954 F.2d 1125, 1137 (5th Cir.1992) (Ds counterclaimed for unpaid notes).

2. Plaintiff's response. If the defendant meets its burden, the plaintiff must then produce evidence that could support a jury verdict in the plaintiff's favor. *See* ***Gasaway***, 26 F.3d at 959. This requires the plaintiff to show by affidavits, depositions, answers to interrogatories, or admissions on file that there is a material fact dispute on the defendant's counterclaim. *Id.*; *see, e.g.*, ***Topalian***, 954 F.2d at 1137 (Ps did not negate Ds' proof on unpaid notes).

If the plaintiff has pleadings to support an affirmative defense to the defendant's counterclaim, when the defendant moves for summary judgment, the plaintiff may attempt to produce summary-judgment evidence to raise a material fact dispute on each element of its affirmative defense. See "Defendant's response," §7.5.2, this page.

§7.5 When plaintiff moves for SJ on its claim.

1. Plaintiff's motion. To be entitled to summary judgment on its claim, the plaintiff must show there are no genuine disputes of material fact and establish each element of its claim as a matter of law. ***Fontenot v. Upjohn Co.***, 780 F.2d 1190, 1194 (5th Cir.1986); *see* ***San Pedro v. U.S.***, 79 F.3d 1065, 1068 (11th Cir.1996). That is, the plaintiff must show that no reasonable trier of fact could find other than for the plaintiff. ***Calderone v. U.S.***, 799 F.2d 254, 259 (6th Cir.1986). The court should grant the plaintiff's motion for summary judgment only if, viewing the evidence in the light most favorable to the defendant, there are no genuine disputes of material fact and no jury could find in favor of the defendant. *See* ***Chlorine Inst. v. California Hwy. Patrol***, 29 F.3d 495, 496 (9th Cir.1994).

2. Defendant's response. If the plaintiff meets its burden, the defendant must produce significant, probative evidence demonstrating the existence of a triable dispute of fact on at least one element of the plaintiff's claim. *See* ***Irby v. Bittick***, 44 F.3d 949, 953 (11th Cir.1995). If the defendant has an affirmative defense to the plaintiff's claim, when the plaintiff moves for summary judgment, the defendant should produce sufficient evidence to raise a genuine dispute of material fact on each element of its affirmative defense. *See* ***Continental Airlines, Inc. v. Intra Brokers, Inc.***, 24 F.3d 1099, 1103-04 (9th Cir.1994). As an alternative, the defendant may file an FRCP 56(d) affidavit or declaration explaining why further discovery is necessary.

§7.6 When plaintiff moves for SJ on defendant's affirmative defense.

1. Plaintiff's motion. A plaintiff moving for summary judgment on a defendant's affirmative defense may satisfy its burden by (1) submitting evidence that negates an essential element of the defendant's defense or (2) showing that the defendant's evidence is insufficient to establish an essential element of its defense. ***FDIC v. Giammettei***, 34 F.3d 51, 54 (2d Cir.1994). The plaintiff is not required to produce evidence negating the defendant's affirmative defense. *Id.*

2. Defendant's response. If the plaintiff meets its burden, the defendant must either (1) produce summary-judgment evidence that demonstrates the existence of a genuine dispute of material fact on the challenged issue or (2) submit an FRCP 56(d) affidavit or declaration requesting additional time for discovery. *Cf.* ***Chambers v. American Trans Air, Inc.***, 17 F.3d 998, 1001-02 (7th Cir.1994) (nonmovant was P). If the defendant does not produce sufficient evidence to support its affirmative defense, the court may grant a partial summary judgment for the plaintiff and strike the defendant's affirmative defense. *See* ***Transmatic, Inc. v. Gulton Indus.***, 53 F.3d 1270, 1274-75 (Fed.Cir.1995).

§7.7 When both parties move for SJ.

1. Burdens. When both parties move for summary judgment, each party must carry its own burden as the movant for its motion and as the nonmovant in response to the other party's motion. *See* ***Wells Real Estate Inv. Trust II, Inc. v. Chardon/Hato Rey Prtshp., S.E.***, 615 F.3d 45, 51 (1st Cir.2010). The motions are determined independently of each other. ***Monumental Paving & Excavating, Inc. v. Pennsylvania Mfrs. Ass'n Ins.***, 176 F.3d 794, 797 (4th Cir.1999); ***Blackie v. Maine***, 75 F.3d 716, 721 (1st Cir.1996); 10A Wright, Miller & Kane §2720 & n.12. All justifiable inferences must still be made in favor of the nonmovant. ***Murphy Expl. & Prod. v. Oryx Energy Co.***, 101 F.3d 670, 673 (Fed.Cir.1996).

2. Ruling. When both parties file cross-motions for summary judgment, the court does not have to grant one of the motions; it may be that neither party can establish grounds for summary judgment. ***Heublein, Inc. v. U.S.***, 996 F.2d 1455, 1461 (2d Cir.1993). The filing of cross-motions is not a waiver of trial. ***Miller v. LeSea Broad., Inc.***, 87 F.3d 224, 230 (7th Cir.1996).

NOTE

The court should usually consider cross-motions for summary judgment at the same time. ***Puerto Rico Am. Ins. v. Rivera-Vázquez****, 603 F.3d 125, 133 (1st Cir.2010). If the court considers the motions at different times, it must ensure that it applies the same standards to both. E.g., id. at 133-34 (on cross-SJ motions, court abused its discretion when it entered two conflicting SJ orders after inconsistently applying local rule to each motion without good cause).*

3. Stipulations. If the parties file cross-motions for summary judgment and stipulate to all the material facts, the court may treat the case as a trial on a stipulated record. ***Vetter v. Frosch***, 599 F.2d 630, 632 (5th Cir.1979). Because the scope of a trial on a stipulated record is severely limited, the parties' consent to one should not be implied lightly. *See* ***Miller***, 87 F.3d at 229-30 (filing of cross-motions for SJ does not automatically waive trial).

§8. DEADLINES

§8.1 When to move for SJ.

1. Motion deadline. Unless a local rule sets a different deadline or the court orders otherwise, any party—the plaintiff or the defendant—may file a motion for summary judgment at any time until 30 days after the close of all discovery. FRCP 56(b); *see* 2010 Notes to FRCP 56 at ¶7, p. 1225, this book; 2009 Notes to FRCP 56 at ¶1, p. 1227, this book. Thus, a party can move for summary judgment at any time before the deadline, even as early as the commencement of the suit. *See* 2010 Notes to FRCP 56 at ¶7, p. 1225, this book (timing provisions under former FRCP 56(a) were superseded).

NOTE

Although FRCP 56(b) allows a summary-judgment motion to be filed at the commencement of a suit, in many cases the motion will be premature until the nonmovant has had time to file a responsive pleading or conduct discovery. See 2010 Notes to FRCP 56 at ¶7, p. 1225, this book. See "Motion to extend & motion for continuance," §4.6, p. 609.

(1) Local rule. Local rules may provide a different deadline for the motion. *E.g.*, Local Rules Tex. (N.D.), Rule 56.2(a) (motion cannot be filed within 90 days of trial setting, unless otherwise ordered).

(2) Court order. A scheduling order may provide a different deadline (e.g., a fixed deadline) for the motion. *See* 2010 Notes to FRCP 56 at ¶7, p. 1225, this book (scheduling order or other pretrial orders can change deadline to fit needs of case); *see also* FRCP 16(b) (court must enter scheduling order that contains deadlines to file motions). A scheduling order may be adjusted to adopt the parties' agreement on timing or may require that discovery and motions occur in stages (e.g., separating expert-witness discovery from other discovery). 2009 Notes to FRCP 56 at ¶2, p. 1227, this book.

2. Discovery considerations. The movant should file supporting affidavits and declarations and other summary-judgment proof with its motion, unless the evidence is already on file. *See* FRCP 6(c)(2), 56(c)(1)(A). See "Summary-Judgment Proof," §6, p. 610. The motion and evidence should be filed early in the litigation if the dispute involves only legal issues and little or no discovery is required. But if the motion is based on facts, it should not be filed until after the parties have had adequate time to investigate the case and conduct discovery. Courts are reluctant to grant fact-based summary-judgment motions before discovery is completed. *See* ***Evans v. Technologies Applications & Serv.***, 80 F.3d 954, 961 (4th Cir.1996). However, the fact that discovery is not completed—or has not even begun—does not prevent the granting of a motion for summary judgment. ***U.S. v. Bloom***, 112 F.3d 200, 205 n.17 (5th Cir.1997); *see* ***Chambers v. American Trans Air, Inc.***, 17 F.3d 998, 1002 (7th Cir.1994).

§8.2 When to respond to motion for SJ.

1. Response deadline. FRCP 56 does not contain a deadline for the response to a motion for summary judgment; however, the response should be filed by the deadline set by the case-specific court order or by local rule. *See* 2010 Notes to FRCP 56 at ¶7, p. 1225, this book (timing provisions under former FRCP 56(c) were superseded);

see, e.g., Local Rules Ariz., Rule 56.1(d) (response due 30 days after service of motion for SJ). See "Court order," §8.1.1(2), p. 619.

2. Discovery considerations. Generally, the nonmovant should file opposing affidavits and declarations and other summary-judgment proof with its response, unless the evidence is already on file. *See* FRCP 6(c)(2), 56(c)(1)(A). See "Summary-Judgment Proof," §6, p. 610. If a hearing is scheduled, any opposing affidavits or declarations must be filed at least seven days before the hearing unless otherwise ordered. *See* FRCP 6(c)(2), 56(c)(1)(A). See "Hearing," §10, p. 623. However, the deadline for filing opposing affidavits and declarations will usually be controlled by local rule or the scheduling order. *See, e.g.*, Local Rules Fla. (N.D.), Rule 56.1(B) (affidavits are due before court takes motion under advisement, which is 21 days after motion is filed or 7 days after response is filed, whichever is later). If the motion is filed prematurely, the nonmovant should request that the court extend the time to respond; if the nonmovant cannot respond to the motion and needs additional time for discovery, it should request a continuance. See "Motion to extend & motion for continuance," §4.6, p. 609.

§8.3 When to reply to nonmovant's response. FRCP 56 does not contain a deadline for the reply to a response to a motion for summary judgment; however, the reply should be filed by the deadline set by the case-specific court order or by local rule. *See* 2010 Notes to FRCP 56 at ¶7, p. 1225, this book (timing provisions under former FRCP 56(c) were superseded); *see, e.g.*, Local Rules Ariz., Rule 56.1(d) (reply due 15 days after service of response to motion for SJ). See "Court order," §8.1.1(2), p. 619.

§9. MOTION FOR CONTINUANCE

If a party is unable to respond to a motion for summary judgment, it should request additional time to obtain affidavits or declarations or to conduct discovery. FRCP 56(d)(2); *see* ***Celotex Corp. v. Catrett***, 477 U.S. 317, 326 (1986); ***Culwell v. City of Fort Worth***, 468 F.3d 868, 871 (5th Cir.2006); ***Evans v. Technologies Applications & Serv.***, 80 F.3d 954, 961 (4th Cir.1996). See "Motion for Continuance," ch. 5-G, p. 337.

NOTE

The 2010 amendments to FRCP 56 changed the language that a court may "order a continuance" for additional discovery to the court may "allow time" for additional discovery. See 2010 Notes to FRCP 56 at ¶16, p. 1226, this book (former FRCP 56(f) was redesignated as FRCP 56(d) without substantial change). In this subchapter, we continue to use the phrase "motion for continuance" for the request under FRCP 56(d)(2). This request to "allow time" is distinct from a request under FRCP 56(d)(1), which allows a party to seek an order deferring the time to respond to the motion for summary judgment. See 2010 Notes to FRCP 56 at ¶17, p. 1226, this book. See "Motion to extend & motion for continuance," §4.6, p. 609.

§9.1 Procedure. The party unable to respond to the motion for summary judgment should present a motion for continuance in writing, support it by affidavits or declarations, file it in the court, and serve it on the summary-judgment movant. *See* FRCP 56(d)(2); ***Trask v. Franco***, 446 F.3d 1036, 1042 (10th Cir.2006). *But see* ***Byrd v. Guess***, 137 F.3d 1126, 1135 (9th Cir.1998) (oral motion acceptable).

§9.2 Grounds. Generally, courts review a motion for continuance according to the following requirements: authoritativeness, timeliness, diligence, and utility and materiality. *See* ***Resolution Trust Corp. v. North Bridge Assocs.***, 22 F.3d 1198, 1203 (1st Cir.1994). The requirements are flexible, and courts have considerable discretion in applying them. *Id.*

PRACTICE TIP

Because the circuits rely on different combinations of factors, check the substantive law of your circuit before drafting a motion for continuance. See, e.g., ***Jones v. Secord***, *684 F.3d 1, 6 (1st Cir.2012) (factors are whether party seeking continuance provides affidavit explaining inability to provide material facts for response to SJ motion, plausible basis for believing that sought-*

after facts can be determined within reasonable time, and how those facts would influence outcome of SJ motion); ***CenTra, Inc. v. Estrin****, 538 F.3d 402, 420 (6th Cir.2008) (factors are when party seeking continuance learned of additional discovery sought, whether discovery would affect SJ ruling, how long discovery lasted, whether party seeking continuance was dilatory in seeking discovery, and whether SJ movant was responsive to discovery requests of party seeking continuance);* ***Family Home & Fin. Ctr., Inc. v. Federal Home Loan Mortg. Corp.****, 525 F.3d 822, 827 (9th Cir.2008) (factors are whether party seeking continuance provides affidavit with specific facts sought by additional discovery, whether facts sought exist, and whether facts are essential to response to SJ motion).*

1. Authoritativeness – affidavit or declaration. Most courts hold that the motion for continuance must be supported by an affidavit or declaration, which must be filed in the court and served on the summary-judgment movant. *See* FRCP 56(d); ***Marksmeier v. Davie***, 622 F.3d 896, 903 (8th Cir.2010); ***McKissick v. Yuen***, 618 F.3d 1177, 1190 (10th Cir.2010); ***Bradley v. U.S.***, 299 F.3d 197, 206-07 (3d Cir.2002). Other courts have not required an affidavit or declaration when the party seeking a continuance adequately informed the court that the summary-judgment motion was premature and that more discovery was necessary. *See* ***Harrods Ltd. v. Sixty Internet Domain Names***, 302 F.3d 214, 244 (4th Cir.2002). If an affidavit or declaration is submitted, it must be signed by a person who has firsthand knowledge and who is competent to address the specifics of the matters discussed. *See, e.g.*, ***North Bridge***, 22 F.3d at 1204 (affidavit signed by attorney). Some courts hold that a motion not supported by an affidavit or declaration can be denied on that ground alone. *See* ***McKissick***, 618 F.3d at 1190; *see, e.g.*, ***Dowling v. City of Phila.***, 855 F.2d 136, 140 (3d Cir.1988) (dispute over D's motion for protective order did not relieve P of burden of filing affidavit); ***Micro-Sparc, Inc. v. Weinstock***, 758 F.2d 790, 793 (1st Cir.1985) (letter to clerk was not substitute for affidavit); *see also* ***Gettings v. Building Laborers Local 310 Fringe Benefits Fund***, 349 F.3d 300, 305 (6th Cir.2003) (in absence of affidavit, court did not abuse its discretion in staying discovery pending resolution of SJ motion).

2. Timeliness. There is no fixed time limit in the FRCPs for filing a motion for continuance under FRCP 56(d)(2) and the supporting affidavit or declaration. The party seeking a continuance must file them at least within a "reasonable time" after receiving the motion for summary judgment. ***North Bridge***, 22 F.3d at 1204. As a general rule, the motion for continuance and affidavit or declaration should be filed before the deadline to file the response to the motion for summary judgment, or at the latest, they should accompany the response. *See* ***McKissick***, 618 F.3d at 1190 (motion under FRCP 56(f), now FRCP 56(d), must be made before court decides SJ motion); *see also* ***Massachusetts Sch. of Law v. American Bar Ass'n***, 142 F.3d 26, 44 (1st Cir.1998) (parties may be allowed to file at later time when there are extenuating circumstances, such as when party does not realize until time for oral argument that it needs additional time for discovery). The party seeking the continuance has the burden to raise the issue of the need for additional time, and failure to do so will result in waiver of that issue on appeal. ***White Consol. Indus. v. Westinghouse Elec. Corp.***, 179 F.3d 403, 411-12 (6th Cir.1999); *see* ***Jones***, 684 F.3d at 6.

3. Diligence. The party seeking a continuance must (1) briefly explain why it does not have the evidence it needs to oppose the summary judgment, (2) show how it diligently pursued discovery, and (3) explain why those efforts have not yielded the necessary evidence. *See* ***Culwell v. City of Fort Worth***, 468 F.3d 868, 872-73 (5th Cir. 2006); ***Plott v. General Motors Corp.***, 71 F.3d 1190, 1196-97 (6th Cir.1995); ***Paddington Partners v. Bouchard***, 34 F.3d 1132, 1138 (2d Cir.1994). The party may need to explain why it did not conduct discovery earlier. *See* ***Berkeley v. Home Ins.***, 68 F.3d 1409, 1414-15 (D.C.Cir.1995); ***Resolution Trust Corp. v. Gold***, 30 F.3d 251, 254 n.1 (1st Cir.1994). If the party has outstanding discovery requests that the summary-judgment movant has not responded to, the party should attach those requests to the motion for continuance. If the party has no outstanding discovery requests, it should attach copies of proposed discovery requests to the motion.

4. Utility & materiality. The party seeking a continuance must explain (1) what discoverable material it believes exists and why additional discovery is needed and (2) how that discovery will reasonably create a genu-

ine dispute of material fact and thus defeat summary judgment. *See **Adams v. Travelers Indem. Co.***, 465 F.3d 156, 162 (5th Cir.2006); ***Maljack Prods. v. GoodTimes Home Video Corp.***, 81 F.3d 881, 888 (9th Cir.1996); ***Allen v. Bridgestone/Firestone, Inc.***, 81 F.3d 793, 797-98 (8th Cir.1996); ***North Bridge***, 22 F.3d at 1206-07. To present a plausible basis for a belief that additional discoverable material exists, the party must present reasons that rise above mere speculation. *See **North Bridge***, 22 F.3d at 1206; ***Carney v. U.S. Dept. of Justice***, 19 F.3d 807, 813 (2d Cir.1994). To show that additional discovery will create a genuine dispute of material fact, the party must show how that additional discovery will lead to a genuine dispute; the party cannot simply argue that some additional discovery is needed or that additional discovery will produce needed but unspecified facts. ***Adams***, 465 F.3d at 162; *see **Hackworth v. Progressive Cas. Ins.***, 468 F.3d 722, 732 (10th Cir.2006). Conclusory allegations that are not supported by factual data will not create a genuine dispute. ***Carpenter v. Federal Nat'l Mortg. Ass'n***, 174 F.3d 231, 237 (D.C.Cir.1999); ***Bauer v. Albemarle Corp.***, 169 F.3d 962, 968 (5th Cir.1999).

(1) Type of discovery needed. In the affidavit or declaration, the party seeking a continuance should specifically identify the types of discovery it needs to conduct (e.g., deposition of a certain witness, request for documents, request for interrogatory answers). *See **Allen***, 81 F.3d at 797-98; ***Paddington Partners***, 34 F.3d at 1138; *see also **Hackworth***, 468 F.3d at 732 (affidavit must identify steps taken to obtain probable but unavailable facts). If the party started discovery before the motion for summary judgment was filed, it should identify the types of discovery and the dates it began the discovery, state that the summary-judgment movant has not responded to the discovery, and attach copies of the discovery requests. If the party seeking a continuance did not start discovery before the motion for summary judgment was filed, the party should identify the discovery it needs to conduct and attach copies of the proposed discovery requests.

(2) Evidence likely to be uncovered. The party seeking a continuance should specifically describe the information it expects to find through discovery. *See **Ikossi v. Department of Navy***, 516 F.3d 1037, 1045-46 (D.C.Cir.2008); ***Jarrow Formulas, Inc. v. Nutrition Now, Inc.***, 304 F.3d 829, 842 (9th Cir.2002); ***Schaffer v. A.O. Smith Harvestore Prods.***, 74 F.3d 722, 732 (6th Cir.1996); ***Mattoon v. City of Pittsfield***, 980 F.2d 1, 8 (1st Cir.1992). A motion that merely asserts that necessary evidence is solely in the summary-judgment movant's possession, or that vaguely refers to ongoing discovery, is insufficient. ***Pasternak v. Lear Pet. Expl., Inc.***, 790 F.2d 828, 833 (10th Cir. 1986); *see **California v. Campbell***, 138 F.3d 772, 779-80 (9th Cir.1998) (denial of continuance is proper when evidence sought is almost certainly nonexistent or subject of pure speculation).

§9.3 Response. In response to a motion for a continuance under FRCP 56(d)(2), the summary-judgment movant can argue that the request is merely a delay tactic. To support this argument, the summary-judgment movant can point out (as appropriate) that (1) the party seeking a continuance had ample time for discovery, (2) the motion for summary judgment involves pure questions of law or incontrovertible facts, (3) further discovery is unlikely to uncover evidence of material fact disputes, or (4) the requests from the party seeking a continuance contain only conclusory allegations. *See **Ray v. American Airlines, Inc.***, 609 F.3d 917, 923-24 (8th Cir.2010); ***Baker v. American Airlines, Inc.***, 430 F.3d 750, 756 (5th Cir.2005); ***Barfield v. Brierton***, 883 F.2d 923, 932 (11th Cir.1989).

§9.4 Ruling. Motions for continuance are generally favored and should be liberally granted. ***Culwell v. City of Fort Worth***, 468 F.3d 868, 871 (5th Cir.2006); *see* 10B Wright, Miller & Kane §2740 & nn.12-13 (rulings based on technicalities have no place under FRCP 56(f), now FRCP 56(d)).

1. Court's options. If the court agrees with the motion for continuance, it can grant the continuance and allow the party seeking a continuance time to obtain affidavits or declarations or to conduct discovery. FRCP 56(d)(2); *see **Liquid Drill, Inc. v. U.S. Turnkey Expl., Inc.***, 48 F.3d 927, 930 (5th Cir.1995). If the court disagrees with the motion for continuance, it can deny that motion and grant the motion for summary judgment. *See **Carney v. U.S. Dept. of Justice***, 19 F.3d 807, 812-13 (2d Cir.1994).

2. Standard of review.

(1) Expressly denied. If the court denies the motion in writing or on the record, the denial is reviewed for abuse of discretion. *See **Adams v. Travelers Indem. Co.***, 465 F.3d 156, 161 (5th Cir.2006); ***Carpenter v.***

Federal Nat'l Mortg. Ass'n, 174 F.3d 231, 238 (D.C.Cir.1999); ***Maljack Prods. v. GoodTimes Home Video Corp.***, 81 F.3d 881, 887 (9th Cir.1996); ***Allen v. Bridgestone/Firestone, Inc.***, 81 F.3d 793, 797 (8th Cir.1996).

(2) Impliedly denied. If the court does not rule on the motion before granting summary judgment, the motion is presumed denied, and the denial is reviewed de novo. ***Byrd v. Guess***, 137 F.3d 1126, 1135 (9th Cir. 1998).

§10. HEARING

§10.1 Hearing vs. submission. Although the court has discretion to hold a hearing on a motion for summary judgment, a hearing is not required. *See* ***Himes v. U.S.***, 645 F.3d 771, 784 (6th Cir.2011); ***L.S.T., Inc. v. Crow***, 49 F.3d 679, 684 n.9 (11th Cir.1995). If the court considers the written evidence and arguments supporting and opposing the motion for summary judgment by submission rather than by oral argument, the court satisfies the requirements of FRCP 56. ***Himes***, 645 F.3d at 784; ***Anchorage Assocs. v. Virgin Islands Bd. of Tax Rev.***, 922 F.2d 168, 176 (3d Cir.1990); *see, e.g.*, ***Hamman v. Southwestern Gas Pipeline, Inc.***, 721 F.2d 140, 142 (5th Cir.1983) (court was not required to give separate notice of date it would rule on motion for SJ; under local rules, motion could be determined without oral argument at any time after response was due); *see also* FRCP 78(b) (courts generally have power to decide motions without hearing).

§10.2 Request for hearing. If either party wants a hearing on the motion for summary judgment, it should make a timely request in writing. *See* FRCP 6(c)(1); *see, e.g.*, ***Yamaha Corp. v. Stonecipher's Baldwin Pianos & Organs, Inc.***, 975 F.2d 300, 301 (6th Cir.1992) (local rule required timely application for hearing). The form of the request is generally governed by local rule. The court is more likely to grant a hearing if the case involves numerous or complex issues or if the arguments supporting the motion and response need clarification.

NOTE

FRCP 56 no longer includes a requirement that a motion for summary judgment be served at least ten days before the summary-judgment hearing. See ***Himes v. U.S.***, *645 F.3d 771, 784 n.10 (6th Cir.2011); 2009 Notes to FRCP 56 at ¶1, p. 1227, this book. If a party is requesting a hearing on the motion, it should follow the general rule for motions and hearings under FRCP 6(c) and, if appropriate, local rules. Under FRCP 6(c), the motion and notice of hearing must be served at least 14 days before the hearing. FRCP 6(c)(1). Some local rules, however, may require more than 14 days' notice. See, e.g., Local Rules Minn., Rule 7.1(c)(1) (dispositive motions, including motions for SJ, must be filed and served at least 42 days before hearing). For a discussion of how to compute backward-counted deadlines, see "Computing Deadlines," ch. 1-C, §6, p. 23.*

§11. SUMMARY-JUDGMENT RULING

§11.1 Review of SJ proof. The court must determine whether the movant properly supported its assertions of fact and whether the nonmovant properly addressed the movant's assertions of fact as required under FRCP 56(c)(1). 2010 Notes to FRCP 56 at ¶18, p. 1226, this book; *see* FRCP 56(e). See "No fact disputes," §3.1.1(1), p. 604; "Fact disputes," §4.1.2(1), p. 608. During its review, the court is only required to consider the cited materials; thus, the court can make a summary-judgment ruling without performing an independent search of the record for factual support. *See* FRCP 56(c)(3); ***Forsyth v. Barr***, 19 F.3d 1527, 1537 (5th Cir.1994); 2010 Notes to FRCP 56 at ¶13, p. 1225, this book. But the court can also consider materials in the record that the parties did not cite. FRCP 56(c)(3); 2010 Notes to FRCP 56 at ¶13, p. 1225, this book. If a party does not properly support or address a fact, the court can do the following: (1) give the party the opportunity to properly support or address the fact, (2) consider the fact undisputed, (3) grant the motion, or (4) issue any other appropriate order. FRCP 56(e).

NOTE

If a party does not properly support or address the asserted facts, or even if a party does not file a response or a reply, summary judgment cannot be granted or denied by default. 2010 Notes to FRCP 56 at ¶18, p. 1226, this book. Thus, when a party does not support or address a fact, the court's preference will generally be to give the party an opportunity to properly support or address the fact. Id.

1. **Give opportunity to support or address fact.** The court can give the party the opportunity to properly support or address the fact. FRCP 56(e)(1); 2010 Notes to FRCP 56 at ¶18, p. 1226, this book.

2. **Consider fact undisputed.** The court can consider the fact undisputed for purposes of the motion. FRCP 56(e)(2). This approach reflects the "deemed admitted" provision in many local rules. 2010 Notes to FRCP 56 at ¶19, p. 1226, this book; *see* ***Puerto Rico Am. Ins. v. Rivera-Vázquez***, 603 F.3d 125, 130-31 (1st Cir.2010). Under this approach, the fact is considered undisputed only for purposes of the motion; if summary judgment is denied, the party that did not make a proper response or reply can dispute the fact in later proceedings. 2010 Notes to FRCP 56 at ¶19, p. 1226, this book. The court, however, can choose to not consider the fact undisputed, especially when the court knows of materials in the record that show grounds for a genuine dispute. *Id.*; *see* FRCP 56(c)(3) (court can consider other materials in record even if party did not cite them).

3. **Grant motion.** The court can grant summary judgment if the motion and the supporting materials—including the facts considered undisputed under FRCP 56(e)(2)—show that the movant is entitled to it. FRCP 56(e)(3); 2010 Notes to FRCP 56 at ¶20, p. 1226, this book. See "Grant motion," §11.3.2, p. 625. Considering some facts undisputed, however, does not by itself allow for summary judgment. 2010 Notes to FRCP 56 at ¶20, p. 1226, this book. If there is a proper response or reply as to some facts, the court cannot grant summary judgment without determining whether those facts can be genuinely disputed. *Id.* Once the court has determined the set of facts—those considered undisputed because the party did not properly respond or reply and those that cannot be genuinely disputed despite a procedurally proper response or reply—it must determine the legal consequences of the facts and the permissible inferences from them before granting summary judgment. *Id.*

4. **Issue other order.** The court can issue any other appropriate order. FRCP 56(e)(4); 2010 Notes to FRCP 56 at ¶21, p. 1226, this book. Any orders should be designed to encourage the proper presentation of the record. 2010 Notes to FRCP 56 at ¶21, p. 1226, this book.

NOTE

Many courts are more lenient with pro se litigants, advising them of the need to respond and the risk of losing by summary judgment if an adequate response is not filed. 2010 Notes to FRCP 56 at ¶21, p. 1226, this book. The court may carefully examine the record before granting summary judgment against a pro se litigant. Id.

§11.2 Review when nonmovant cannot present facts to justify response.

1. **Defer considering SJ motion.** If the nonmovant cannot present facts necessary to oppose the motion, the court can extend the time to respond to the summary-judgment motion and defer considering the motion. *See* FRCP 56(d)(1); 2010 Notes to FRCP 56 at ¶17, p. 1226, this book. See "Motion to extend & motion for continuance," §4.6, p. 609.

NOTE

If the nonmovant can present facts but does not properly support or address a fact as required under FRCP 56(c), the court can give the nonmovant an opportunity to properly support or address the fact. See FRCP 56(e)(1); 2010 Notes to FRCP 56 at ¶18, p. 1226, this book. See "Review of SJ proof," §11.1, p. 623.

2. Deny SJ motion. If the nonmovant cannot present facts necessary to oppose the motion, the court may still deny the motion for summary judgment. FRCP 56(d)(1). See "Deny motion," §11.3.1, this page.

3. Grant continuance. If the nonmovant cannot present facts necessary to oppose the motion, the court can grant a continuance to allow the nonmovant time to obtain affidavits or declarations or to conduct discovery. FRCP 56(d)(2). See "Motion for Continuance," §9, p. 620.

4. Issue other order. If the nonmovant cannot present facts necessary to oppose the motion, the court can issue any other appropriate order. FRCP 56(d)(3).

§11.3 Review of party's SJ motion.

1. Deny motion. On a party's motion for summary judgment, the court can (1) deny summary judgment and continue the case or (2) deny summary judgment and order an FRCP 16(c)(2)(N) presentation.

(1) Generally. If the movant did not meet its summary-judgment burden, the court "shall" deny the motion for summary judgment and continue with the case. *See* FRCP 56(a). See "Note," §7.1, p. 616. Even if the movant met its burden, the court may deny the motion. ***Andrew v. Clark***, 561 F.3d 261, 271 (4th Cir.2009); *see* 2010 Notes to FRCP 56 at ¶4, p. 1225, this book; *Report of the Judicial Conference: Committee on Rules of Practice & Procedure*, Agenda E-19, at Rules-pp.15-17 (Sept.2009), www.uscourts.gov/uscourts/RulesAndPolicies/rules/Supreme%20Court%202009/ST_Report_Sept_2009.pdf. An order denying the motion is generally not appealable. ***Robson v. Hallenbeck***, 81 F.3d 1, 4 (1st Cir.1996); ***Mick v. Brewer***, 76 F.3d 1127, 1133 (10th Cir.1996). For the exceptions to this rule, see "Appealable orders," ch. 9-A, §3.3, p. 739.

(2) Deny motion & order FRCP 16(c)(2)(N) presentation. If the court is not sure whether to grant a motion for summary judgment, it may simplify the trial using the following procedure. The court can (1) deny the motion, (2) schedule the jury trial to begin with a presentation on the essential element that the plaintiff (i.e., the summary-judgment nonmovant) seems least likely to be able to maintain, and (3) if the plaintiff cannot maintain that element, grant judgment as a matter of law for the defendant (i.e., the summary-judgment movant) as soon as the plaintiff has been fully heard. *See* FRCP 16(c)(2)(N); 1991 Notes to FRCP 50 at ¶5, p. 1215, this book. See "Resolution of limited issues," ch. 5-A, §4.4.15, p. 293.

2. Grant motion. On a party's motion for summary judgment, the court can grant final or partial summary judgment. *See* FRCP 56(a).

(1) Grant motion for movant & enter final SJ. If the movant met its burden, the court "shall" enter a final summary judgment. FRCP 56(a); *see* 2010 Notes to FRCP 56 at ¶4, p. 1225, this book. See "Note," §7.1, p. 616. To be final and appealable, the judgment must dispose of all parties and issues. *See **Maynard v. Williams***, 72 F.3d 848, 851 (11th Cir.1996); ***Midlantic Nat'l Bank v. Hansen***, 48 F.3d 693, 698 (3d Cir.1995).

(2) Grant motion for movant & enter partial SJ. If the movant met its burden on a claim, a defense, or part of a claim or defense, the court "shall" enter a partial summary judgment. FRCP 56(a); *see* 2010 Notes to FRCP 56 at ¶4, p. 1225, this book. See "Relief – final SJ vs. partial SJ," §3.1.2, p. 605; "Note," §7.1, p. 616.

(a) Order on facts not genuinely in dispute. If the court does not grant all the relief requested in the motion, it can enter an order identifying material facts (including an item of damages or other relief) that are not genuinely in dispute. FRCP 56(g); *see* 2010 Notes to FRCP 56 at ¶23, p. 1226, this book; *see also **URI Cogeneration Partners v. Board of Govs. for Higher Educ.***, 915 F.Supp. 1267, 1279 (D.R.I.1996) (purpose of FRCP 56(d), now FRCP 56(g), is to salvage constructive results of attempt to resolve case by SJ). The facts identified in the order are treated as established in the case. FRCP 56(g). The court, however, can enter the order only after it has applied the summary-judgment standard in FRCP 56(a) to each claim, defense, or part of a claim or defense identified in the motion. 2010 Notes to FRCP 56 at ¶23, p. 1226, this book. When the court considers whether some facts should be treated as established, it must ensure that the determination does not interfere with a party's ability to accept a fact only for purposes of the motion. *Id.* A nonmovant, for example, may be confident that a genuine dispute

about one or a few facts will defeat a summary-judgment motion and may prefer to avoid the cost of a detailed response that addresses all the facts stated by the movant. *Id.* The nonmovant should be able to address only one or a few facts without risking that the unaddressed facts be taken as established under FRCP 56(g) or otherwise found to have been accepted for other purposes. 2010 Notes to FRCP 56 at ¶23, p. 1226, this book. Local rules, however, may require that the nonmovant specifically state that it does not agree with the unaddressed facts from the motion. *See, e.g.*, Local Rules Ill. (N.D.), Rule 56.1(b)(3)(C) (all material facts set forth in movant's statement of material facts are deemed admitted unless controverted by statement of nonmovant).

NOTE

If the court cannot grant all the relief requested in the motion, it is not required to enter an order on facts not genuinely in dispute. See 2010 Notes to FRCP 56 at ¶24, p. 1226, this book. The court may decide that the cost of determining whether some potential fact disputes could be eliminated is greater than the cost of resolving those disputes by other means, including trial. Id. Even if the court believes that some facts are not genuinely in dispute, it may decide that they should be addressed at trial. See id.

(b) Effect of partial SJ. If the court renders a partial summary judgment, the parties are entitled to rely on the partial summary judgment at trial and are not required to introduce evidence on the disputes that were resolved. ***Leddy v. Standard Drywall, Inc.***, 875 F.2d 383, 386 (2d Cir.1989). A partial summary judgment is an interlocutory order, subject to revision by the district court, with no res judicata effect. ***FDIC v. Massingill***, 24 F.3d 768, 774 (5th Cir.1994), *supplemented*, 30 F.3d 601 (5th Cir.1994). If, during trial, the court revises its ruling on the partial summary judgment, it must give the parties an opportunity to present evidence on the affected disputes. *Id.*

(c) Making partial SJ final & appealable. A partial summary judgment can be made final and appealable in the following ways:

[1] Severance of unadjudicated claims. The parties can move to sever the claims resolved by partial summary judgment from the unadjudicated claims. *See* FRCP 21; ***U.S. v. O'Neil***, 709 F.2d 361, 367-68 (5th Cir.1983); *see, e.g.*, ***Allied Elevator, Inc. v. East Tex. State Bank***, 965 F.2d 34, 36 (5th Cir.1992) (on D's motion, court severed partial SJ on counterclaim). When a single claim is severed from a suit, the claim proceeds as an independent suit, and the court may render a final, appealable judgment in either of the two suits. ***Allied Elevator***, 965 F.2d at 36. See "Motion for Severance or Separate Trials," ch. 5-L, p. 366.

[2] Dismissal under FRCP 41. The plaintiff can stipulate to dismissal of the remaining claims or move to dismiss them, making the partial summary judgment final and appealable. *See* FRCP 41(a). See "Voluntary Dismissal," ch. 7-C, p. 629; "Final judgments," ch. 9-A, §3.1, p. 737.

[3] Certification for permissive interlocutory appeal. A party who loses a motion for partial summary judgment can convince the court that the matter satisfies the requirements for a permissive interlocutory appeal under 28 U.S.C. §1292(b).

[4] Entry of final SJ on certain claims or parties. A party can convince the court to enter a final summary judgment on some of the claims or parties under FRCP 54(b). To do this, the court must expressly (1) direct the entry of final judgment on one or more, but fewer than all, of the claims or parties and (2) determine there is no just reason to delay appellate review. FRCP 54(b); ***General Acquisition, Inc. v. GenCorp, Inc.***, 23 F.3d 1022, 1026 (6th Cir.1994). See "Judgments covering fewer than all claims or parties," ch. 9-A, §3.2, p. 738.

§11.4 Review on court's own initiative. On its own initiative, the court may (1) grant summary judgment for the nonmovant, (2) grant a motion on legal or factual grounds not raised by the parties, or (3) consider summary judgment after identifying facts that may not be genuinely in dispute. *See* FRCP 56(f); 2010 Notes to FRCP 56 at ¶22, p. 1226, this book.

1. **Grant SJ for nonmovant.** If summary judgment should be granted for the nonmovant, the court may do so after giving the parties notice and a reasonable time to respond. FRCP 56(f)(1); *see* ***Ramsey v. Coughlin***, 94 F.3d 71, 73 (2d Cir.1996) (motion for SJ may lead to sua sponte grant of SJ for nonmovant, even without formal cross-motion).

2. **Grant SJ on grounds not raised.** If summary judgment should be granted on factual or legal grounds not raised by a party, the court may do so after giving the parties notice and a reasonable time to respond. FRCP 56(f)(2); 2010 Notes to FRCP 56 at ¶22, p. 1226, this book; *see* ***Turco v. Hoechst Celanese Corp.***, 101 F.3d 1090, 1093 (5th Cir.1996) (court may grant summary judgment on any ground supported by entire record, even if not briefed by movant, as long as nonmovant has notice of ground).

3. **Consider SJ on its own.** If summary judgment should be granted but a motion for summary judgment has not been filed, the court may consider summary judgment on its own initiative after (1) identifying for the parties material facts that may not be genuinely in dispute and (2) giving the parties notice and a reasonable time to respond. *See* FRCP 56(f)(3); ***Nationwide Mut. Ins. v. Mortensen***, 606 F.3d 22, 28 (2d Cir.2010); ***Gibson v. Mayor & Council of Wilmington***, 355 F.3d 215, 222-23 (3d Cir.2004); ***Berkovitz v. Home Box Office, Inc.***, 89 F.3d 24, 29 & n.5 (1st Cir.1996); 2010 Notes to FRCP 56 at ¶22, p. 1226, this book. The notice should include the grounds that the court will consider. *See* ***Rogan v. Menino***, 175 F.3d 75, 79 (1st Cir.1999).

NOTE

In many cases, before giving notice of a sua sponte summary judgment, the court should first ask for a motion for summary judgment; the motion will then trigger the regular procedures of FRCP 56(c). 2010 Notes to FRCP 56 at ¶22, p. 1226, this book.

§11.5 Order & judgment. An order granting the motion for summary judgment is not itself a judgment. Because an appeal can be taken only from a judgment, the judgment must be a separate document that is signed by the judge and entered on the docket. *See* FRCP 58(a). See "Entry of Judgment," ch. 9-A, p. 735.

1. **Form of order.** The form of the order on the summary judgment is within the court's discretion. *See* 2010 Notes to FRCP 56 at ¶5, p. 1225, this book.

2. **Reasons for SJ.** A court should state its reasons for granting or denying the summary judgment. FRCP 56(a); *see* ***Brewster of Lynchburg, Inc. v. Dial Corp.***, 33 F.3d 355, 366-67 (4th Cir.1994); *see also* 2010 Notes to FRCP 56 at ¶5, p. 1225, this book (detail of reasons is at court's discretion). The court's reasons can facilitate later district-court proceedings or an appeal; thus, including the reasons is particularly important when the court grants summary judgment. 2010 Notes to FRCP 56 at ¶5, p. 1225, this book. If the court denies summary judgment, the court does not need to address every possible reason; however, the reasons should identify the central issues, which can help the parties to focus later proceedings. *Id.* at ¶6, p. 1225, this book.

NOTE

Although the court should state its reasons, it is not actually required to state its findings or conclusions when ruling on a motion for summary judgment. FRCP 52(a)(3).

§11.6 Motion for reconsideration. A party can challenge a summary judgment by filing a motion for reconsideration under either FRCP 59(e) or FRCP 60(b). ***Backlund v. Barnhart***, 778 F.2d 1386, 1388 (9th Cir.1985); *see* ***PaineWebber Income Props. Three L.P. v. Mobil Oil Corp.***, 902 F.Supp. 1514, 1521 (M.D.Fla.1995).

1. **Motion to alter or amend SJ under FRCP 59(e).** If a party wants to correct something stated in the summary judgment, it must file a motion to alter or amend the judgment under FRCP 59(e). *See* ***Committee for the First Amendment v. Campbell***, 962 F.2d 1517, 1523 (10th Cir.1992); *see also* ***Templet v. HydroChem Inc.***, 367 F.3d 473, 479 (5th Cir.2004) (reconsidering judgment after entry is extraordinary remedy that should be used sparingly). See "Motion to Alter or Amend Judgment," ch. 10-D, p. 793.

2. Motion for relief from SJ under FRCP 60(b). A motion for reconsideration can be brought under FRCP 60(b) if the party can show (1) mistake, inadvertence, surprise, or excusable neglect, (2) newly discovered evidence, (3) fraud, misinterpretation, or misconduct, (4) that the judgment is void, (5) that the judgment was satisfied, released, or discharged, or (6) any other reason that justifies relief. ***Backlund***, 778 F.2d at 1388. See "Motion for Relief from Judgment," ch. 10-F, p. 804.

PRACTICE TIP

If a party asks for leave to file supplementary material in a motion for reconsideration, the party must (1) provide a legitimate justification for not filing the affidavit or exhibit with the motion for summary judgment (or the response) and (2) cite and direct the court's attention to the specific factual evidence in the supplemental affidavit or exhibit that tends to create a material fact dispute. See ***Wallace v. Texas Tech Univ.***, *80 F.3d 1042, 1052 (5th Cir.1996);* ***Davidson & Schaaff, Inc. v. Liberty Nat'l Fire Ins.***, *69 F.3d 868, 871 (8th Cir.1995);* ***Cray Comms. v. Novatel Computer Sys.***, *33 F.3d 390, 395 (4th Cir.1994); see also* ***Templet***, *367 F.3d at 479 (motion for reconsideration can be denied if movant does not provide legitimate excuse for failing to present evidence earlier).*

§12. APPELLATE REVIEW

§12.1 Standard of review. The standard of review for the grant or denial of summary judgment is de novo. ***Templet v. HydroChem Inc.***, 367 F.3d 473, 477 (5th Cir.2004); ***Gettings v. Building Laborers Local 310 Fringe Benefits Fund***, 349 F.3d 300, 305 (6th Cir.2003); ***Garcia v. Pueblo Country Club***, 299 F.3d 1233, 1236 (10th Cir. 2002); ***Corder v. Lucent Techs.***, 162 F.3d 924, 927 (7th Cir.1998); ***Saelee v. Chater***, 94 F.3d 520, 521 (9th Cir.1996); ***Ramsey v. Coughlin***, 94 F.3d 71, 74 (2d Cir.1996); ***Roe v. Doe***, 28 F.3d 404, 406 (4th Cir.1994).

§12.2 SJ granted.

1. Affirm. The appellate court will affirm the summary judgment if it determines that there is no genuine dispute of material fact and that the movant is entitled to judgment as a matter of law. ***Johnson v. Weld Cty.***, 594 F.3d 1202, 1207 (10th Cir.2010); ***C.B. v. Driscoll***, 82 F.3d 383, 386 (11th Cir.1996). The appellate court can affirm the summary judgment on any legal ground supported in the record and is not limited to the reasons stated in the district court's order. ***Bombard v. Fort Wayne Newspapers, Inc.***, 92 F.3d 560, 562 (7th Cir.1996); ***Phillips v. Marist Soc'y***, 80 F.3d 274, 275 (8th Cir.1996); ***Resolution Trust Corp. v. District of Columbia***, 78 F.3d 606, 608 (D.C.Cir. 1996).

2. Reverse. The appellate court will reverse the summary judgment if it determines that there was a genuine dispute of material fact or that the movant was not entitled to judgment as a matter of law. *See* ***Thornton, Summers, Biechlin, Dunham & Brown, Inc. v. Cook Paint & Varnish***, 82 F.3d 114, 116 (5th Cir.1996).

3. Remand. When the summary judgment does not include the reasons supporting the district court's decision, the appellate court may remand the case and direct the district court to enter the reasons. ***Brewster of Lynchburg, Inc. v. Dial Corp.***, 33 F.3d 355, 366-67 (4th Cir.1994).

§12.3 SJ denied. The denial of summary judgment is an interlocutory order and is generally not appealable. ***Ortiz v. Jordan***, ___ U.S. ___, 131 S.Ct. 884, 891 (2011); ***Robson v. Hallenbeck***, 81 F.3d 1, 4 (1st Cir.1996); ***Mick v. Brewer***, 76 F.3d 1127, 1133 (10th Cir.1996). However, there are the following exceptions:

1. Appealable orders. Some interlocutory orders are appealable. *See* ***Ortiz***, ___ U.S. at ___, 131 S.Ct. at 891 (denial of SJ on qualified immunity is appealable when appeal presents pure issue of law but not when determination involves fact disputes). To be appealable, an interlocutory order must be made appealable by a specific statute or by a case-law exception. See "Appealable Judgments & Orders," ch. 9-A, §3, p. 737.

2. Severed claims. The court may sever any claim against a party. FRCP 21. Therefore, severance may be used to create finality for the purpose of appeal. ***U.S. v. O'Neil***, 709 F.2d 361, 369 (5th Cir.1983); *see* ***Hebel v. Ebersole***, 543 F.2d 14, 16-17 (7th Cir.1976).

3. Cross-motions for SJ. When both parties move for summary judgment and the district court grants one motion and denies the other, the result is a final judgment. *See* ***Podberesky v. Kirwan***, 38 F.3d 147, 157 (4th Cir.1994), *amended*, 46 F.3d 5 (4th Cir.1994). The party that did not prevail may appeal both the summary judgment granted against it and its own denied motion for summary judgment. ***North River Ins. v. CIGNA Reinsurance Co.***, 52 F.3d 1194, 1203 (3d Cir.1995); ***Podberesky***, 38 F.3d at 157; ***National Fire Ins. v. Bartolazo***, 27 F.3d 518, 519 (11th Cir.1994).

§12.4 Costs & attorney fees under FRCP 56(h). The award of costs and attorney fees as a sanction under FRCP 56(h) is an interlocutory order and thus is not appealable until final judgment. *See* ***Alart Assocs. v. Aptaker***, 402 F.2d 779, 780-81 (2d Cir.1968). The decision denying an award of costs and attorney fees will be reversed only if the appellate court finds an abuse of discretion. *See* ***Stewart v. RCA Corp.***, 790 F.2d 624, 633 (7th Cir.1986). See "Appealability," ch. 5-O, §10.1, p. 397; "Sanctions for bad-faith affidavit or declaration," §6.1.3(3), p. 612.

C. VOLUNTARY DISMISSAL

§1. GENERAL

§1.1 Rule. FRCP 41(a). See also FRCP 23(e) (dismissal of class action), FRCP 66 (dismissal of suit after receiver appointed).

§1.2 Purpose. The purpose of a voluntary dismissal under FRCP 41(a) is to terminate all or part of a lawsuit during the early stages of the proceeding, leaving open the possibility of refiling another lawsuit with the same claims.

§1.3 Timetable & forms. Timetable, Pleadings & Pretrial-Motions Schedule, p. 1574; *O'Connor's Federal Civil Forms* (2012), FORMS 7C.

§1.4 Other references. 9 Wright & Miller, *Federal Practice & Procedure 3d* §§2361-2368, 2374-2376 (2008 & Supp.2012); 8 *Moore's Federal Practice 3d* §§41.10-41.40 (2012); Annotation, *Effect of Nonsuit, Dismissal, or Discontinuance of Action on Previous Orders*, 11 ALR 2d 1407, 1411-12, 1420-24 (1950).

§2. TYPES OF VOLUNTARY DISMISSALS

§2.1 Parties. In most cases, the party moving for dismissal is the plaintiff. However, a defendant can be the party moving for dismissal of a counterclaim.

NOTE

Because the party seeking voluntary dismissal is almost always the plaintiff, we will refer to the party moving for dismissal as the plaintiff and the party objecting to dismissal as the defendant throughout this subchapter.

§2.2 Types of dismissals. There are three types of voluntary dismissals under FRCP 41: (1) the plaintiff's notice of dismissal filed before the defendant serves either an answer or a motion for summary judgment, (2) the parties' stipulation of dismissal, and (3) the plaintiff's motion for court-ordered dismissal. FRCP 41(a)(1), (a)(2). Certain types of dismissals require court approval.

1. Class actions. The court must approve any voluntary dismissal of the claims, issues, or defenses of a certified class. FRCP 23(e). The court may approve the dismissal only after (1) the court has directed reasonable notice to all the members of the class who would be bound, (2) the parties seeking dismissal have filed a statement identifying any agreement made about the proposed dismissal, and (3) the court has conducted a hearing and has found that the dismissal is "fair, reasonable, and adequate." FRCP 23(e)(1)-(e)(3). Any of the class members may object to a proposed voluntary dismissal that requires court approval under FRCP 23(e), but any objection can be withdrawn only with the court's approval. FRCP 23(e)(5).

2. Receiverships. A plaintiff cannot dismiss a suit in which a receiver has been appointed except by court order. FRCP 66.

§2.3 Partial dismissal of parties & claims. The plaintiff is allowed to voluntarily dismiss an "action." FRCP 41(a)(1)(A). The term "action" has led the courts to disagree about exactly what can be dismissed under FRCP 41(a)(1). It is important, especially in cases with multiple defendants, to distinguish between dismissal of a defendant and dismissal of a claim.

1. Dismiss some defendants. If the plaintiff wants to dismiss some of the defendants, and all the requirements in FRCP 41(a)(1) have been met, the plaintiff may dismiss by filing a notice of dismissal or a stipulation by the parties. ***Pedrina v. Chun***, 987 F.2d 608, 609-10 (9th Cir.1993); *see* ***Baker v. America's Mortg. Servicing, Inc.***, 58 F.3d 321, 324 n.2 (7th Cir.1995) (FRCP 41(a)(1) can be used to dismiss fewer than all Ds).

2. Dismiss some claims. If the plaintiff wants to dismiss some of its claims against a defendant, it should follow the procedure for amending pleadings in FRCP 15(a), not the procedure in FRCP 41. *See* ***Gobbo Farms & Orchards v. Poole Chem. Co.***, 81 F.3d 122, 123 (10th Cir.1996); ***General Signal Corp. v. MCI Telecomms.***, 66 F.3d 1500, 1513 (9th Cir.1995). See "Motion to Amend or Supplement Pleadings—Pretrial," ch. 5-I, p. 345.

§3. PLAINTIFF'S NOTICE OF DISMISSAL

Before the defendant serves either an answer or a motion for summary judgment, the plaintiff has an absolute right to voluntarily dismiss its case without a court order or the defendant's consent. FRCP 41(a)(1)(A)(i); ***Marques v. Federal Reserve Bank***, 286 F.3d 1014, 1017 (7th Cir.2002).

§3.1 Form. Because the plaintiff has a right to dismiss under FRCP 41(a)(1)(A)(i), the plaintiff is not required to file a motion—a simple notice of dismissal is sufficient. ***Williams v. Clarke***, 82 F.3d 270, 272 (8th Cir.1996); ***Aamot v. Kassel***, 1 F.3d 441, 443-44 (6th Cir.1993); *see* ***In re Bath & Kitchen Fixtures Antitrust Litig.***, 535 F.3d 161, 165 (3d Cir.2008); ***Smith v. Potter***, 513 F.3d 781, 782-83 (7th Cir.2008). In a suit with multiple defendants, the service of an answer by one defendant does not prevent the plaintiff from dismissing a defendant who has not answered. ***Aggregates, Inc. v. Kruse***, 134 F.R.D. 23, 25 (D.P.R.1991).

1. In writing. The plaintiff's notice of dismissal should be in writing. *See* FRCP 41(a)(1)(A) (dismiss by "filing" notice of dismissal).

2. Filed. The plaintiff's notice of dismissal must be filed in the court. *See* ***Wilson v. City of San Jose***, 111 F.3d 688, 692 (9th Cir.1997) (dismissal effective on filing).

3. Grounds. The plaintiff's notice of dismissal should contain the following information:

(1) The date the complaint was filed.

(2) Whether the defendant was served.

(3) A statement that the defendant has not served either an answer or a motion for summary judgment. *See* FRCP 41(a)(1)(A)(i).

NOTE

The defendant's filing of a motion to dismiss under FRCP 12(b) generally does not affect the plaintiff's right to a voluntary dismissal under FRCP 41(a)(1)(A)(i). ***Finley Lines Joint Prot. Bd. v. Norfolk S. Corp.****, 109 F.3d 993, 996 (4th Cir.1997);* ***Aamot****, 1 F.3d at 444; 9 Wright & Miller §2363. But if the court converts the motion to dismiss into a motion for summary judgment because evidence outside the pleadings is attached and not excluded, the plaintiff no longer has the right to a voluntary dismissal under FRCP 41(a)(1)(A)(i). See FRCP 12(d);* ***In re Bath & Kitchen Fixtures****, 535 F.3d at 166; see, e.g.,* ***Swedberg v. Marotzke****, 339 F.3d 1139, 1142-43 (9th Cir.2003) (voluntary dismissal allowed when party filed notice of dismissal before court considered converting motion to dismiss into motion for SJ);* ***Exxon Corp. v. Maryland Cas. Co.****, 599 F.2d 659, 661 (5th Cir.1979) (voluntary dismissal not allowed when FRCP 12(b)(6)*

motion was converted into motion for SJ); see also ***Wilson-Cook Med., Inc. v. Wilson***, *942 F.2d 247, 252 (4th Cir.1991) (dicta; if court had considered affidavits supporting FRCP 12(b)(6) motion, motion would have been converted to motion for SJ). See "Effect of considering extrinsic materials," ch. 3-F, §4.2, p. 206.*

(4) A statement that the plaintiff files the notice of dismissal with the intention of dismissing the case under FRCP 41(a)(1)(A)(i) without prejudice to refiling. *See* ***Williams***, 82 F.3d at 272.

4. Second dismissal. If the plaintiff's notice of dismissal is the second notice, the plaintiff should consider the effect of the two-dismissal rule. See "Two-dismissal rule," §7.2.4, p. 638.

5. Proposed order granting relief. Although no order is required to effect a voluntary dismissal under FRCP 41(a)(1)(A)(i), courts generally enter some type of order to close the case on their computer docketing system. In some districts, the clerk will automatically enter an order dismissing a case when the plaintiff files a notice of voluntary dismissal under FRCP 41(a)(1)(A)(i); in others, the clerk will not enter an order of dismissal until the court signs one. Before filing a notice of voluntary dismissal, the plaintiff should ask the clerk if a proposed order should be filed with the notice. See "Order of Dismissal," §6, p. 635.

§3.2 Deadline. The plaintiff's deadline for filing the notice of dismissal is anytime before the defendant serves either an answer or a motion for summary judgment on the plaintiff, not when the defendant files either in the court. FRCP 41(a)(1)(A)(i); ***Cooter & Gell v. Hartmarx Corp.***, 496 U.S. 384, 394 (1990); *see* ***Nelson v. Napolitano***, 657 F.3d 586, 588-89 (7th Cir.2011); *see, e.g.*, ***In re Bath & Kitchen Fixtures Antitrust Litig.***, 535 F.3d 161, 166-67 (3d Cir.2008) (P could file notice of dismissal because D had not served answer or motion for SJ; it was irrelevant that court granted P's motion to amend complaint and extension to amend); ***Follette v. Wal-Mart Stores***, 41 F.3d 1234, 1238 n.2 (8th Cir.1994) (P could not file notice of dismissal after D moved for SJ), *supplemented*, 47 F.3d 311 (8th Cir.1995).

§3.3 Effect. The dismissal is self-executing and effective at the moment the notice is filed with the clerk. ***Finley Lines Joint Prot. Bd. v. Norfolk S. Corp.***, 109 F.3d 993, 995 (4th Cir.1997); *see* ***ISC Holding AG v. Nobel Biocare Fin. AG***, 688 F.3d 98, 111 (2d Cir.2012); ***University of S. Ala. v. American Tobacco Co.***, 168 F.3d 405, 408 (11th Cir.1999). The filing of the dismissal automatically terminates the suit against the defendants listed in the notice and is generally without prejudice. FRCP 41(a)(1)(B); *see* ***Wilson v. City of San Jose***, 111 F.3d 688, 692 (9th Cir.1997) (dismissal effective on filing). Such a dismissal leaves the situation as if the suit had never been filed. ***City of S. Pasadena v. Mineta***, 284 F.3d 1154, 1157 (9th Cir.2002). Neither the court nor the defendant has any role to play once the notice of dismissal has been filed—the case is closed. ***American Soccer Co. v. Score First Enters.***, 187 F.3d 1108, 1110 (9th Cir.1999); *see* ***In re Bath & Kitchen Fixtures Antitrust Litig.***, 535 F.3d 161, 165-66 (3d Cir.2008). A judgment on the merits is void if it is entered after the plaintiff has filed a proper notice of dismissal. ***Marques v. Federal Reserve Bank***, 286 F.3d 1014, 1018 (7th Cir.2002).

§3.4 Response. In most cases, the defendant does not have the opportunity to respond to a notice of dismissal because (1) the notice must be filed before the defendant serves either an answer or a motion for summary judgment, and (2) the dismissal becomes effective immediately upon filing. Thus, to claim that a voluntary dismissal was improper in some way, the defendant should file a motion to vacate the dismissal. See "Challenging notice of dismissal under FRCP 41(a)(1)(A)(i)," §8.1, p. 639.

§4. PARTIES' STIPULATION OF DISMISSAL

The plaintiff can dismiss its suit if all parties who have appeared sign a stipulation of dismissal. FRCP 41(a)(1)(A)(ii).

§4.1 Form. Because the plaintiff has a right to dismiss under FRCP 41(a)(1)(A)(ii), a motion is not required—a stipulation signed by all parties is sufficient. *See* ***Garber v. Chicago Mercantile Exch.***, 570 F.3d 1361, 1365-66 (Fed. Cir.2009).

1. In writing. The stipulated dismissal should be in writing. *See* FRCP 41(a)(1)(A)(ii); ***Camacho v. Mancuso***, 53 F.3d 48, 51 (4th Cir.1995); ***Morris v. City of Hobart***, 39 F.3d 1105, 1109 (10th Cir.1994). Some courts per-

mit the stipulation to be made orally on the record. *See, e.g.*, ***Broadcast Music, Inc. v. M.T.S. Enters.***, 811 F.2d 278, 279 n.1 (5th Cir.1987) (stipulation made orally in open court was valid); ***Eitel v. McCool***, 782 F.2d 1470, 1472 n.3 (9th Cir.1986) (oral stipulation during telephone conference with judge was valid). *But see* ***Negron v. City of Miami Beach***, 113 F.3d 1563, 1571 (11th Cir.1997) (suggesting that oral motion is insufficient). Even if the stipulation may be made orally, the better practice is to file a written stipulation.

2. Signed by all parties. The stipulated dismissal must be signed by all parties who have appeared in the case. FRCP 41(a)(1)(A)(ii). If the stipulation is not signed by all parties, it is not effective as a dismissal under FRCP 41(a)(1)(A)(ii). *See* ***Camacho***, 53 F.3d at 52; ***Morris***, 39 F.3d at 1109.

3. Filed. The stipulated dismissal must be filed in the court. FRCP 41(a)(1)(A)(ii); ***Orsini v. Kugel***, 9 F.3d 1042, 1045 (2d Cir.1993); ***McCall-Bey v. Franzen***, 777 F.2d 1178, 1185 (7th Cir.1985). An unfiled stipulated dismissal is not effective. ***Orsini***, 9 F.3d at 1045.

4. Proposed order granting relief. Generally, a voluntary dismissal by stipulation is effective on filing and does not require the court's approval. ***SmallBizPros, Inc. v. MacDonald***, 618 F.3d 458, 461 (5th Cir.2010); *see* ***Garber***, 570 F.3d at 1364-65. But courts generally enter some type of order to close the case on their computer docketing system. Before filing a stipulated dismissal, the plaintiff should ask the clerk if a proposed order should be filed with the stipulated dismissal. See "Order of Dismissal," §6, p. 635.

§4.2 Deadline. A stipulated dismissal may be filed at any time after all parties to the dismissal have appeared in the case. ***Republic of the Phil. v. Westinghouse Elec. Corp.***, 43 F.3d 65, 81 n.21 (3d Cir.1994); *see* FRCP 41(a)(1)(A)(ii).

§4.3 Effect. The stipulation is self-executing and effective at the moment the notice is filed with the clerk. ***Anago Franchising, Inc. v. Shaz, LLC***, 677 F.3d 1272, 1277-78 (11th Cir.2012); ***SmallBizPros, Inc. v. MacDonald***, 618 F.3d 458, 461 (5th Cir.2010); *see* ***Gambale v. Deutsche Bank AG***, 377 F.3d 133, 139 (2d Cir.2004). The filing of the stipulation automatically terminates the suit and is generally without prejudice. FRCP 41(a)(1)(B); ***Anago Franchising***, 677 F.3d at 1276.

§4.4 Response.

1. Defendant. The defendant ordinarily should have no reason to respond to a stipulation of dismissal, having already agreed to it and signed it. But if the stipulated dismissal does not reflect the terms of the agreement, the defendant should move either to vacate or to correct the dismissal. Because the stipulation of dismissal under FRCP 41(a)(1)(A)(ii) is self-executing, a motion to vacate the dismissal is the best way to challenge the dismissal. See "Challenging stipulation of dismissal under FRCP 41(a)(1)(A)(ii)," §8.2, p. 639.

2. Third party. A third party generally cannot prevent a stipulated dismissal. *See* ***Alternative Research & Dev. Found. v. Veneman***, 262 F.3d 406, 411 (D.C.Cir.2001); ***Eli Lilly & Co. v. Synthon Labs.***, 538 F.Supp.2d 944, 947 (E.D.Va.2008); ***GMAC Commercial Mortg. Corp. v. LaSalle Bank Nat'l Ass'n***, 213 F.R.D. 150, 150-51 (S.D. N.Y.2003); 8 *Moore's Federal Practice 3d* §41.34[4][b]. However, under certain equitable circumstances, an intervening third party can stop the stipulated dismissal because of prejudice to the third party. *See, e.g.*, ***Eli Lilly & Co.***, 538 F.Supp.2d at 947 (potential intervenor could not stop stipulating parties' dismissal when potential intervenor was not prejudiced).

§5. PLAINTIFF'S MOTION FOR COURT-ORDERED DISMISSAL

Unless the plaintiff can file a notice of dismissal or the parties agree to a stipulation of dismissal, the plaintiff can move to dismiss its suit only by court order. FRCP 41(a)(2); *see* ***Bridgeport Music, Inc. v. Universal-MCA Music Publ'g***, 583 F.3d 948, 953 (6th Cir.2009). The main purpose of requiring court approval for a dismissal under FRCP 41(a)(2) is to protect the defendant from unfair treatment and to permit the imposition of curative conditions. ***Elbaor v. Tripath Imaging, Inc.***, 279 F.3d 314, 317 (5th Cir.2002); ***Phillips USA, Inc. v. Allflex USA, Inc.***, 77 F.3d 354, 357 (10th Cir.1996); *see* ***Bridgeport Music***, 583 F.3d at 953-54; *see also* ***ITV Direct, Inc. v. Healthy Solutions, LLC***, 445 F.3d 66, 70 (1st Cir.2006) (third-party intervenor's interests should also be considered). The plaintiff should

file a motion to voluntarily dismiss as soon as it perceives dismissal as desirable because delay may result in a denial of the dismissal or the imposition of unfavorable conditions. *See* ***D'Alto v. Dahon Cal., Inc.***, 100 F.3d 281, 283 (2d Cir.1996).

§5.1 Form.

1. In writing. The motion to dismiss should be in writing. *See* ***Taragan v. Eli Lilly & Co.***, 838 F.2d 1337, 1340-41 (D.C.Cir.1988). The motion may be made orally at a hearing, but the better practice is to file a written motion. *Id.*

2. Grounds. The motion to dismiss should state the following:

(1) The reason for dismissal. *See, e.g.*, ***Davis v. USX Corp.***, 819 F.2d 1270, 1272 (4th Cir.1987) (P planned to pursue common-law claims in state court). An inadequate explanation can cause the dismissal to be denied. *See* ***D'Alto v. Dahon Cal., Inc.***, 100 F.3d 281, 283-84 (2d Cir.1996).

(2) That the defendant refused to stipulate to a dismissal. *See* FRCP 41(a)(1)(A)(ii).

(3) That the request is for dismissal without prejudice to refiling the suit. *See* FRCP 41(a)(2) (unless otherwise stated, dismissal is without prejudice). The plaintiff should state sufficient reasons why the dismissal should be without prejudice. *See, e.g.*, ***Phillips USA, Inc. v. Allflex USA, Inc.***, 77 F.3d 354, 358 (10th Cir.1996) (party was not permitted to avoid adverse decision on dispositive motion when "little explanation" was offered for decision to dismiss); ***Ratkovich v. Smith Kline***, 951 F.2d 155, 158-59 (7th Cir.1991) (court held P's reason for dismissal without prejudice was meritless).

(4) Whether the defendant filed a counterclaim. If the defendant files a counterclaim before the motion to dismiss is served on the defendant, the court cannot dismiss the suit over the defendant's objection unless the court severs the counterclaim for independent adjudication. FRCP 41(a)(2).

(5) That the defendant and any third party will not be prejudiced. When ruling on a motion to dismiss, the court must determine whether the defendant or a third party will suffer "plain legal prejudice" as a result of the dismissal. *See* ***ITV Direct, Inc. v. Healthy Solutions, LLC***, 445 F.3d 66, 70 (1st Cir.2006); ***Westlands Water Dist. v. U.S.***, 100 F.3d 94, 96 (9th Cir.1996).

3. Certificate of conference. Some local rules require a party filing an opposed motion to include a statement that the party conferred with the respondent and no agreement about the disposition of the motion could be reached. *E.g.*, Local Rules Tex. (S.D.), Rule 7.1.D.

4. Affidavits. If the motion contains facts outside the record, the plaintiff should support the motion with affidavits.

5. Request for hearing. If the motion presents contested fact issues, or if oral argument will help the court resolve the motion, the plaintiff should request a hearing. The plaintiff should comply with any requirements in the local rules for securing a hearing.

6. Proposed order granting relief. Some districts require the party filing a motion to submit a proposed order with it. See "Proposed order," ch. 1-B, §3.1.11, p. 16.

§5.2 Deadline. A motion to dismiss may be filed at any time after the defendant has answered or filed a motion for summary judgment, whichever is done first. *See* FRCP 41(a)(2).

§5.3 Response. The defendant's response to a motion to dismiss is generally to either (1) object to the dismissal or (2) agree to the dismissal, but with terms.

1. Object to dismissal. The defendant can ask the court to deny the motion to dismiss. If the defendant does not specifically object to the motion, it cannot urge new grounds on appeal. ***Hamilton v. Firestone Tire & Rubber Co.***, 679 F.2d 143, 146 (9th Cir.1982). The defendant can argue that the court should deny the motion to dismiss for any of the following reasons:

(1) The defendant or a third party will suffer legal prejudice if the motion to dismiss is granted. *See* ***Highway Equip. Co. v. FECO, Ltd.***, 469 F.3d 1027, 1034 (Fed.Cir.2006) (prejudice can be D's loss of success in first case); ***Westlands Water Dist. v. U.S.***, 100 F.3d 94, 97 (9th Cir.1996) (suggesting factors that demonstrate legal prejudice, including loss of federal forum, right to jury trial, or limitations defense); ***Phillips USA, Inc. v. Allflex USA, Inc.***, 77 F.3d 354, 358 (10th Cir.1996) (P should not be able to avoid adverse decision by dismissal with prejudice); *see, e.g.*, ***Hyde v. Hoffmann-La Roche, Inc.***, 511 F.3d 506, 509 (5th Cir.2007) (D was prejudiced when D would be effectively stripped of statute-of-repose defense); ***ITV Direct, Inc. v. Healthy Solutions, LLC***, 445 F.3d 66, 70-71 (1st Cir.2006) (motion to dismiss denied because third-party intervenor's rights would be prejudiced); *see also* ***In re FEMA Trailer Formaldahyde Prods. Liab. Litig.***, 628 F.3d 157, 163 (5th Cir.2010) (prejudice to co-P can also be considered). Expense alone does not constitute legal prejudice because the dismissal may be conditioned on the plaintiff's payment of appropriate costs. ***Westlands***, 100 F.3d at 97. The uncertainty caused by the prospect of future litigation is also insufficient to constitute legal prejudice. *Id.* at 96-97. Dismissal for the purpose of refiling in another forum that will apply a different body of substantive law is disfavored. ***Horton v. T.W.A. Corp.***, 169 F.R.D. 11, 17 (E.D.N.Y.1996).

PRACTICE TIP

The circuits have adopted different standards for determining "legal prejudice" when considering a motion to dismiss. Before responding to a motion, check the law of your circuit to argue and prove the correct standard.

---

(2) The defendant has a counterclaim that was pending when the motion to dismiss was filed and served, and the counterclaim cannot be independently adjudicated if the plaintiff's suit is dismissed. FRCP 41(a)(2); ***Smith v. Dowden***, 47 F.3d 940, 943 (8th Cir.1995). The court should not dismiss the plaintiff's suit over the defendant's objection unless the court severs the counterclaim for independent adjudication. FRCP 41(a)(2); *see* ***Schwarzkopf Dev. Corp. v. Ti-Coating, Inc.***, 800 F.2d 240, 244 (Fed.Cir.1986). However, if the defendant's objection is based on an improper counterclaim, the court may enter a dismissal because the improper counterclaim is not entitled to independent adjudication. *See* ***Sams v. Beech Aircraft Corp.***, 625 F.2d 273, 277 (9th Cir.1980).

(3) The court should rule on the defendant's pending motion for summary judgment instead of granting the plaintiff's motion to dismiss without prejudice. ***Grover v. Eli Lilly & Co.***, 33 F.3d 716, 718 (6th Cir.1994); *see also* ***Phillips USA***, 77 F.3d at 358 (court did not err in denying motion to dismiss filed after motion for SJ).

(4) The plaintiff is not entitled to dismiss one of several claims against the defendant under FRCP 41. ***Gobbo Farms & Orchards v. Poole Chem. Co.***, 81 F.3d 122, 123 (10th Cir.1996). To dismiss a particular claim, the plaintiff must file a motion for leave to amend its complaint under FRCP 15(a). ***Ethridge v. Harbor House Rest.***, 861 F.2d 1389, 1392 (9th Cir.1988); *see* ***Gronholz v. Sears, Roebuck & Co.***, 836 F.2d 515, 518 (Fed.Cir.1987). See "Motion to Amend or Supplement Pleadings—Pretrial," ch. 5-I, p. 345.

2. Agree to dismissal with terms. The defendant can ask the court to impose terms on the dismissal. *See* FRCP 41(a)(2). The court may impose only those terms that will alleviate the harm to the defendant. ***American Nat'l Bank & Trust Co. v. Bic Corp.***, 931 F.2d 1411, 1412 (10th Cir.1991). Thus, the defendant's response should clearly identify the harm to the defendant that will result from the dismissal.

(1) The defendant can ask the court to dismiss the suit with prejudice. *See* ***Burnette v. Lockheed Missiles & Space Co.***, 72 F.3d 766, 767 (9th Cir.1995). See "With prejudice," §7.2, p. 638.

(2) The defendant can ask the court to require the plaintiff to pay the defendant's reasonable attorney fees and costs incurred in defending the suit. *See* ***Cone v. West Va. Pulp & Paper Co.***, 330 U.S. 212, 217 (1947); ***Belle-Midwest, Inc. v. Missouri Prop. & Cas. Ins. Guar. Ass'n***, 56 F.3d 977, 978-79 (8th Cir.1995). The court may order the attorney fees and costs to be payable as a term of the dismissal or the refiling of the case. *See* ***Belle-Midwest***, 56 F.3d at 978-79 (payable before refiling case); ***EMPO Corp. v. J.D. Benefits, Inc.***, No. Civ.03-

2480(RHK/AJB) (D.Minn.2003) (no pub.; 6-26-03) (payable before dismissal). *But see* ***Woodward v. STP Corp.***, 170 F.3d 1043, 1045 (11th Cir.1999) (improper to condition P's request to dismiss suit on court's ability to impose attorney fees against P if he refiles in another forum). Only potentially duplicative attorney fees and costs can be awarded. *See* ***Cauley v. Wilson***, 754 F.2d 769, 772 (7th Cir.1985). Thus, in seeking attorney fees and costs, the defendant must distinguish between the amount incurred for work that will be useless after the dismissal and the amount incurred for work that might be useful if the case is refiled. *See* ***Koch v. Hankins***, 8 F.3d 650, 652 (9th Cir.1993); ***Taragan v. Eli Lilly & Co.***, 838 F.2d 1337, 1340 (D.C.Cir.1988); ***Cauley***, 754 F.2d at 772.

(3) The defendant can ask the court to impose any other terms that will alleviate the harm to the defendant. *See, e.g.*, ***McCants v. Ford Motor Co.***, 781 F.2d 855, 859-60 (11th Cir.1986) (D wanted to retain benefits it had in first suit under discovery order).

3. Affidavits. If the response contains facts outside the record, the defendant should support the response with affidavits. For example, if the defendant asks for attorney fees and costs as a term of dismissal, the defendant should attach affidavits to prove the amount of attorney fees and verify the attached invoices.

4. Request for hearing. If the response presents contested fact issues, or if oral argument will help the court resolve the motion, the defendant should request a hearing. For example, if the defendant requests substantial attorney fees and costs as a term of dismissal, it should probably ask for a hearing. The defendant should comply with any requirements in the local rules for securing a hearing.

§5.4 Proposed order denying relief. Some districts require the party responding to a motion to submit a proposed order with its response. See "Proposed order," ch. 1-B, §3.1.11, p. 16. In those districts, the defendant should submit an order that (1) denies the motion to dismiss or (2) grants the dismissal with terms and includes a statement of the reasons for the terms. See "Findings on terms," §6.3.3, p. 637.

§6. ORDER OF DISMISSAL

§6.1 In writing. The order of dismissal should be in writing and meet the separate-document requirement of FRCP 58. ***Bolivar v. Pocklington***, 975 F.2d 28, 30 n.5 (1st Cir.1992). See "Separate document," ch. 9-A, §2.2, p. 735.

§6.2 Dismissal under FRCP 41(a)(1).

1. Effective without court order. FRCP 41(a)(1)(A) provides that a plaintiff may voluntarily dismiss its lawsuit "without a court order." Courts have interpreted this phrase to mean that no order is necessary to effectuate a notice of dismissal or stipulation of dismissal. *See* ***Garber v. Chicago Mercantile Exch.***, 570 F.3d 1361, 1364-65 (Fed.Cir.2009); ***Ramming v. Natural Gas Pipeline Co.***, 390 F.3d 366, 369 n.1 (5th Cir.2004); ***Williams v. Clarke***, 82 F.3d 270, 272 (8th Cir.1996); ***Marex Titanic, Inc. v. Wrecked & Abandoned Vessel***, 2 F.3d 544, 546 (4th Cir.1993); *see also* 9 Wright & Miller §2363 (discussing dismissal as matter of right under FRCP 41(a)(1)). However, courts generally enter some type of order to close the file on their computer docketing system. *See* ***Baker v. America's Mortg. Servicing, Inc.***, 58 F.3d 321, 324 (7th Cir.1995) (under local rules, deputy clerks enter minute orders dismissing case when P files notice of dismissal under FRCP 41(a)(1)). Before filing a request for voluntary dismissal under FRCP 41(a)(1), the plaintiff should ask the clerk if a proposed order should be filed with the notice of dismissal or the stipulation.

2. No court-imposed terms. The court has no authority to place terms on a voluntary dismissal under FRCP 41(a)(1)(A)(ii). ***Kokkonen v. Guardian Life Ins.***, 511 U.S. 375, 381 (1994); ***Hospitality House, Inc. v. Gilbert***, 298 F.3d 424, 430 n.6 (5th Cir.2002). Doing so would deprive the plaintiff of its unconditional right to an FRCP 41(a)(1) dismissal. *See* ***Gardiner v. A.H. Robins Co.***, 747 F.2d 1180, 1190 (8th Cir.1984) (stipulated dismissal). *But see* ***Green v. Nevers***, 111 F.3d 1295, 1301 (6th Cir.1997) (court may decline to permit stipulated dismissal if necessary to avoid manipulation of judicial system or safeguard persons entitled to protection).

3. Agreed terms by parties. If the parties agree to terms for a settlement, they can ask the court to enter a dismissal order that explicitly incorporates the terms of the settlement agreement. *See* ***Kokkonen***, 511 U.S. at 381-82; ***Anago Franchising, Inc. v. Shaz, LLC***, 677 F.3d 1272, 1279-80 (11th Cir.2012); ***SmallBizPros, Inc. v. MacDonald***, 618 F.3d 458, 462-63 (5th Cir.2010). By incorporating the terms into the court's dismissal order, the parties

allow for the court to retain jurisdiction to enforce the settlement agreement. *See* ***Anago Franchising***, 677 F.3d at 1280; ***SmallBizPros, Inc.***, 618 F.3d at 462-63. But to do so, the court must explicitly state in its order that it is retaining jurisdiction. *See* ***Kokkonen***, 511 U.S. at 381-82; ***Anago Franchising***, 677 F.3d at 1280; ***SmallBizPros, Inc.***, 618 F.3d at 462-63; ***Lipman v. Dye***, 294 F.3d 17, 20 (1st Cir.2002). If the court retains jurisdiction, a party's violation of the settlement agreement would be a violation of the court's order; thus, the court would have jurisdiction to enforce the agreement. ***SmallBizPros, Inc.***, 618 F.3d at 464.

NOTE

For a district court to retain jurisdiction, some circuits require that the district court enter its order retaining jurisdiction before the stipulated dismissal becomes effective; in those circuits, a post-dismissal order is not effective because the earlier-filed voluntary dismissal was effective on filing and the court automatically lost jurisdiction. See ***SmallBizPros, Inc.****, 618 F.3d at 464; see, e.g.,* ***Anago Franchising****, 677 F.3d at 1280-81 (although parties agreed to extend court's jurisdiction in their stipulated dismissal, district court did not retain jurisdiction when it did not issue order explicitly retaining jurisdiction before stipulated dismissal). Other circuits might allow a district court to retain jurisdiction through a post-dismissal order based on ancillary jurisdiction, which allows jurisdiction over some matters that are incidental to other matters properly before the court. See* ***Bond v. Utreras****, 585 F.3d 1061, 1078 (7th Cir.2009) (dicta). To avoid any jurisdictional question, the parties should ensure that either (1) the court issues the order retaining jurisdiction before the parties file the stipulated dismissal or (2) the parties condition the effectiveness of the stipulated dismissal on the court's entry of an order retaining jurisdiction.* ***Anago Franchising****, 677 F.3d at 1280;* ***SmallBizPros, Inc.****, 618 F.3d at 463.*

§6.3 Dismissal under FRCP 41(a)(2).

1. Court order necessary. A court order is necessary to effect a dismissal under FRCP 41(a)(2). ***Parker v. Freightliner Corp.***, 940 F.2d 1019, 1023 (7th Cir.1991). Thus, the motion to dismiss does not become effective until an order of dismissal is entered. Before filing a motion to dismiss under FRCP 41(a)(2), the plaintiff should ask the clerk if a proposed order should be filed with the motion.

2. Types of dismissal.

(1) Without prejudice. The decision whether to permit the plaintiff to dismiss without prejudice is within the court's discretion. ***Tolle v. Carroll Touch, Inc.***, 23 F.3d 174, 177 (7th Cir.1994). The court should grant the plaintiff's motion for voluntary dismissal under FRCP 41(a)(2) without prejudice to refiling, unless it would cause substantial legal prejudice to the defendant. *See* ***Grover v. Eli Lilly & Co.***, 33 F.3d 716, 718 (6th Cir.1994) ("plain legal prejudice"); ***Ratkovich v. Smith Kline***, 951 F.2d 155, 158 (7th Cir.1991) ("legal prejudice"); *see also* ***Ohlander v. Larson***, 114 F.3d 1531, 1537 (10th Cir.1997) (court abuses its discretion when it denies motion to dismiss based on its own inconvenience). To determine whether the defendant would suffer prejudice from a dismissal, the court may consider the following factors:

(a) The defendant's effort and expense in preparing for trial. ***D'Alto v. Dahon Cal., Inc.***, 100 F.3d 281, 283 (2d Cir.1996); ***Phillips USA, Inc. v. Allflex USA, Inc.***, 77 F.3d 354, 358 (10th Cir.1996); ***Grover***, 33 F.3d at 718; ***Ratkovich***, 951 F.2d at 158. However, the inconvenience of defending another lawsuit or the fact that the defendant has already begun trial preparations does not constitute prejudice. *See* ***Elbaor v. Tripath Imaging, Inc.***, 279 F.3d 314, 317-18 (5th Cir.2002); ***Pontenberg v. Boston Sci. Corp.***, 252 F.3d 1253, 1256 (11th Cir.2001); ***Hyde & Drath v. Baker***, 24 F.3d 1162, 1169 (9th Cir.1994).

(b) Excessive delay and lack of diligence by the plaintiff in seeking dismissal. ***D'Alto***, 100 F.3d at 283; ***Phillips USA***, 77 F.3d at 358; ***Unida v. Levi Strauss & Co.***, 986 F.2d 970, 974 (5th Cir.1993); ***Ratkovich***, 951 F.2d at 158. *But see* ***Pontenberg***, 252 F.3d at 1256 (fact that P's attorney was negligent in prosecuting case does not establish plain legal prejudice).

(c) Insufficient explanation for the need to take a dismissal. ***D'Alto***, 100 F.3d at 283; ***Phillips USA***, 77 F.3d at 358; ***Ratkovich***, 951 F.2d at 158.

(d) Whether the defendant filed a motion for summary judgment. ***Phillips USA***, 77 F.3d at 358; ***Unida***, 986 F.2d at 974. *But see* ***Pontenberg***, 252 F.3d at 1258 (fact that case had proceeded to summary-judgment stage or party's mere attempt to avoid adverse summary-judgment ruling did not constitute plain legal prejudice).

(e) Whether the defendant will lose any substantive rights. *See* ***Hyde v. Hoffmann-La Roche, Inc.***, 511 F.3d 506, 509 (5th Cir.2007) (loss of statute-of-repose defense); ***Phillips v. Illinois Cent. Gulf R.R.***, 874 F.2d 984, 987 (5th Cir.1989) (loss of limitations defense); *see also* ***Horton v. T.W.A. Corp.***, 169 F.R.D. 11, 17 (E.D. N.Y.1996) (dismissal to permit refiling in another forum that might apply different body of substantive law is disfavored). *But see* ***McCants v. Ford Motor Co.***, 781 F.2d 855, 858 (11th Cir.1986) (potential loss of limitations defense alone does not prevent dismissal).

(f) The present stage of the litigation. ***Ohlander***, 114 F.3d at 1537.

(2) With prejudice. The court may convert a plaintiff's motion to dismiss without prejudice into a dismissal with prejudice if the court gives the plaintiff notice and an opportunity to withdraw the motion. ***Michigan Surgery Inv. v. Arman***, 627 F.3d 572, 575 (6th Cir.2010); ***Elbaor***, 279 F.3d at 320; ***Jaramillo v. Burkhart***, 59 F.3d 78, 79 (8th Cir.1995). As a term of dismissal, the court may require the plaintiff to accept a dismissal with prejudice to refiling the suit. ***Michigan Surgery Inv.***, 627 F.3d at 576; ***Marlow v. Winston & Strawn***, 19 F.3d 300, 304 (7th Cir.1994).

(3) Other court-imposed terms. The court's order on a motion to dismiss under FRCP 41(a)(2) may be conditioned on the plaintiff's fulfilling certain terms to offset prejudice to the defendant from the dismissal. ***In re FEMA Trailer Formaldahyde Prods. Liab. Litig.***, 628 F.3d 157, 162-63 (5th Cir.2010); ***Davis v. USX Corp.***, 819 F.2d 1270, 1273 (4th Cir.1987). The terms are the quid pro quo for allowing the plaintiff to dismiss its suit without being barred by res judicata from filing the same suit. ***McCall-Bey v. Franzen***, 777 F.2d 1178, 1184 (7th Cir. 1985). The court may impose any terms on the dismissal it deems proper. ***Ratkovich***, 951 F.2d at 158.

(a) Costs & attorney fees. If the dismissal is without prejudice, the court may require the plaintiff to pay the defendant's costs and attorney fees in defending the first suit. ***Belle-Midwest, Inc. v. Missouri Prop. & Cas. Ins. Guar. Ass'n***, 56 F.3d 977, 978-79 (8th Cir.1995); *see* ***Bridgeport Music, Inc. v. Universal-MCA Music Publ'g***, 583 F.3d 948, 954 (6th Cir.2009) (terms often involve payment of costs incurred by D). The purpose of awarding costs and attorney fees is to compensate the defendant for the unnecessary expense that the litigation has caused. However, if the dismissal is with prejudice, the court cannot award costs and attorney fees to a defendant unless there are exceptional circumstances. *See* ***Aerotech, Inc. v. Estes***, 110 F.3d 1523, 1528 (10th Cir.1997) (habitually bringing claims and then dismissing them with prejudice may constitute an exceptional circumstance).

[1] The defendant may recover costs and attorney fees only for its work product that is rendered useless by the dismissal of the plaintiff's case. ***Westlands Water Dist. v. U.S.***, 100 F.3d 94, 97 (9th Cir.1996); ***Koch v. Hankins***, 8 F.3d 650, 652-53 (9th Cir.1993); ***Taragan v. Eli Lilly & Co.***, 838 F.2d 1337, 1340 (D.C.Cir.1988). The court must distinguish between fees incurred for work that will be useless after the dismissal and fees incurred for work that might be useful if the case is refiled. ***Koch***, 8 F.3d at 652-53.

[2] If the court awards costs and attorney fees as a term of the dismissal without prejudice, the record must contain evidence that supports the award. ***Taragan***, 838 F.2d at 1340.

(b) Other terms. The court may enter an order of dismissal on terms that the court considers proper. FRCP 41(a)(2). The court may consider any terms that will alleviate the harm to the defendant. *See, e.g.*, ***Versa Prods. v. Home Depot, USA, Inc.***, 387 F.3d 1325, 1328 (11th Cir.2004) (P ordered to refile any future complaint in specific district); ***McCants***, 781 F.2d at 859-60 (D wanted to retain benefits it had in first suit under limitations defense).

3. Findings on terms. The court should dismiss only on the terms it deems proper. FRCP 41(a)(2). Although findings of fact are not necessary, the court should include in its order the reasons for imposing or refusing to impose terms. If there are no reasons stated in the order, and if the appellate court cannot evaluate the district

court's discretion in making its ruling, the appellate court may remand the case to the district court and require it to include a statement of reasons. *E.g.*, ***DWG Corp. v. Granada Invs.***, 962 F.2d 1201, 1202 (6th Cir.1992) (district court did not explain why it did not award costs and expenses requested by D); ***Taragan***, 838 F.2d at 1339 (same); ***McCants***, 781 F.2d at 860 (same).

4. Opportunity to withdraw motion. When the court imposes terms on the dismissal, it must give the plaintiff an opportunity to withdraw the motion to dismiss. ***Marlow***, 19 F.3d at 305; ***Gravatt v. Columbia Univ.***, 845 F.2d 54, 56 (2d Cir.1988); ***Andes v. Versant Corp.***, 788 F.2d 1033, 1037 (4th Cir.1986). The "terms" clause of FRCP 41(a)(2) gives the plaintiff the choice of either (1) accepting the terms and obtaining a dismissal or (2) withdrawing the motion and proceeding to trial. ***Gravatt***, 845 F.2d at 56; ***Lau v. Glendora Unified Sch. Dist.***, 792 F.2d 929, 930 (9th Cir.1986); ***Andes***, 788 F.2d at 1037.

§6.4 FRCP 11 order after dismissal. The court may impose FRCP 11 sanctions on the plaintiff after an FRCP 41(a) voluntary dismissal. *See* ***Cooter & Gell v. Hartmarx Corp.***, 496 U.S. 384, 396 (1990); ***Bolivar v. Pocklington***, 975 F.2d 28, 31 (1st Cir.1992). See "Motion for Sanctions," ch. 5-O, §5, p. 391.

§7. EFFECT OF DISMISSAL

§7.1 Without prejudice. If the notice, stipulation, or order of dismissal does not mention whether the case is dismissed with prejudice, the dismissal is without prejudice to refiling. FRCP 41(a)(1)(B), (a)(2); ***Meinecke v. H&R Block***, 66 F.3d 77, 82 n.3 (5th Cir.1995); ***Jaramillo v. Burkhart***, 59 F.3d 78, 79 (8th Cir.1995). If a suit is dismissed without prejudice, the dismissal renders the proceedings in that case a nullity and puts the plaintiff in the same legal position it would be in if it had not filed the suit. ***Williams v. Clarke***, 82 F.3d 270, 273 (8th Cir.1996); ***Beck v. Caterpillar, Inc.***, 50 F.3d 405, 407 (7th Cir.1995); ***Brown v. Hartshorne Pub. Sch. Dist.***, 926 F.2d 959, 961 (10th Cir.1991).

1. No res judicata. A dismissal without prejudice is not a final judgment on the merits, and refiling the same suit does not invoke the doctrine of res judicata. ***Cooter & Gell v. Hartmarx Corp.***, 496 U.S. 384, 396 (1990); *see* ***National R.R. Passenger Corp. v. International Ass'n of Mach.***, 915 F.2d 43, 48 (1st Cir.1990).

2. Limitation on refiling. If the statute of limitations has not run when the plaintiff secures a voluntary dismissal without prejudice under FRCP 41(a), the plaintiff can refile the suit. If the statute of limitations has run, the plaintiff cannot refile the suit. ***Beck***, 50 F.3d at 407.

§7.2 With prejudice. If the suit is dismissed with prejudice, the dismissal is a final adjudication on the merits. ***Warfield v. AlliedSignal TBS Holdings, Inc.***, 267 F.3d 538, 542 (6th Cir.2001); ***Chase Manhattan Bank v. Celotex Corp.***, 56 F.3d 343, 345 (2d Cir.1995); ***Clark v. Haas Grp.***, 953 F.2d 1235, 1238 (10th Cir.1992).

1. Res judicata. If the suit is dismissed with prejudice, it is a final judgment, and the doctrine of res judicata bars a later suit based on the same facts and claims. ***Warfield***, 267 F.3d at 542; ***Clark***, 953 F.2d at 1238; ***Brooks v. Barbour Energy Corp.***, 804 F.2d 1144, 1146 (10th Cir.1986).

2. Collateral estoppel. A dismissal with prejudice also bars a plaintiff from bringing, in a later suit, new allegations relating to the same underlying facts. ***Catz v. Chalker***, 142 F.3d 279, 287 (6th Cir.1998), *amended*, 243 F.3d 234 (6th Cir.2001).

3. No refiling. If the suit is dismissed with prejudice, it cannot be refiled.

4. Two-dismissal rule. Once a plaintiff dismisses a suit by notice under FRCP 41(a)(1)(A)(i), a second notice of dismissal of the same claims operates as an adjudication on the merits. FRCP 41(a)(1)(B); ***Cooter & Gell v. Hartmarx Corp.***, 496 U.S. 384, 394 (1990); ***City of S. Pasadena v. Mineta***, 284 F.3d 1154, 1157 n.2 (9th Cir. 2002). This is called the "two-dismissal rule." The plaintiff cannot refile the suit after the second dismissal because it will be barred by res judicata. ***Lake at Las Vegas Investors Grp. v. Pacific Malibu Dev. Corp.***, 933 F.2d 724, 728 (9th Cir.1991). The two-dismissal rule does not apply to suits dismissed by the court on the plaintiff's motion under FRCP 41(a)(2), by stipulation of the parties, or by involuntary dismissal. ***ASX Inv. v. Newton***, 183 F.3d 1265, 1267-68

(11th Cir.1999); ***Sutton Place Dev. Co. v. Abacus Mortg. Inv.***, 826 F.2d 637, 640 (7th Cir.1987); ***Burnett v. Perry Mfg.***, 151 F.R.D. 398, 404 (D.Kan.1993); 9 Wright & Miller §2368 & nn.4-7; *see also* ***Brown v. Hartshorne Pub. Sch. Dist.***, 926 F.2d 959, 961 (10th Cir.1991) (two-dismissal rule did not apply when first dismissal was on D's motion, second was by court order, and only third was voluntary dismissal by P).

§8. CHALLENGING DISMISSAL IN DISTRICT COURT

If a motion to challenge the dismissal is filed within 28 days after the dismissal, it should be a motion to alter or amend the judgment under FRCP 59(e). See "Motion to Alter or Amend Judgment," ch. 10-D, p. 793. If a motion is filed more than 28 days after the dismissal, it should be a motion for relief from the order of dismissal under FRCP 60(b). See "Motion for Relief from Judgment," ch. 10-F, p. 804. The following are some of the grounds a party can assert when challenging a dismissal in the district court and later on appeal.

§8.1 Challenging notice of dismissal under FRCP 41(a)(1)(A)(i).

1. By plaintiff. The court should modify or vacate the dismissal because of the following:

(1) The court dismissed the suit with prejudice even though the plaintiff filed a notice to dismiss before the defendant served either an answer or a motion for summary judgment. Under these circumstances, dismissal is self-effectuating and effective immediately. Thus, the court exceeds its power in ordering a dismissal with prejudice. FRCP 41(a)(1)(B); ***Marex Titanic, Inc. v. Wrecked & Abandoned Vessel***, 2 F.3d 544, 547 (4th Cir.1993); ***Aamot v. Kassel***, 1 F.3d 441, 444 (6th Cir.1993); ***Safeguard Bus. Sys. v. Hoeffel***, 907 F.2d 861, 864 (8th Cir.1990).

(2) The court did not have the authority to enter the order of dismissal. *E.g.*, ***Pedrina v. Chun***, 987 F.2d 608, 610 (9th Cir.1993) (court could not order Ps to file motion for dismissal); *see also* ***Netwig v. Georgia-Pac. Corp.***, 375 F.3d 1009, 1010 (10th Cir.2004) (when P's case was voluntarily dismissed without prejudice, court did not have jurisdiction to reinstate case and dismiss it with prejudice).

2. By defendant. The court should modify or vacate the dismissal because of the following:

(1) The defendant served its answer or motion for summary judgment on the plaintiff before the plaintiff filed the notice of dismissal, which terminated the plaintiff's right to a voluntary dismissal under FRCP 41(a). ***Barr Lab. v. Abbott Lab.***, 867 F.2d 743, 747-48 (2d Cir.1989) (motion for SJ).

(2) The defendant served an FRCP 12(b)(6) motion to dismiss on the plaintiff before the plaintiff filed a notice of dismissal, and the FRCP 12(b)(6) motion could have been considered as a motion for summary judgment because it contained extraneous materials. *See* ***Wilson-Cook Med., Inc. v. Wilson***, 942 F.2d 247, 251 (4th Cir.1991). *But see* ***Aamot***, 1 F.3d at 444-45 (voluntary dismissal not barred by FRCP 12(b)(6) motion with extraneous material, regardless of amount of time spent in preparation).

(3) It is the second notice of dismissal for the same claim. *E.g.*, ***Bolivar v. Pocklington***, 975 F.2d 28, 30 n.5 (1st Cir.1992) (second notice of voluntary dismissal included same claims). See "Two-dismissal rule," §7.2.4, p. 638. The court should enter a dismissal with prejudice because the second notice of dismissal of the same claim operates as an adjudication on the merits. FRCP 41(a)(1)(B); ***Cooter & Gell v. Hartmarx Corp.***, 496 U.S. 384, 394 (1990); *cf.* ***Brown v. Hartshorne Pub. Sch. Dist.***, 926 F.2d 959, 961 (10th Cir.1991) (two-dismissal rule did not apply when first dismissal was on D's motion, second was by court order, and only third was voluntary by P).

§8.2 Challenging stipulation of dismissal under FRCP 41(a)(1)(A)(ii). The parties may ask the court to modify or vacate the dismissal because of the following:

1. The court dismissed with prejudice even though the parties stipulated to a dismissal without prejudice.

2. The court imposed terms on the dismissal that were not part of the parties' stipulation. The court has no authority to place terms on a voluntary dismissal under FRCP 41(a)(1). ***Republic of the Phil. v. Westinghouse Elec. Corp.***, 43 F.3d 65, 81 n.21 (3d Cir.1994); ***Gardiner v. A.H. Robins Co.***, 747 F.2d 1180, 1190 (8th Cir.1984).

§8.3 Challenging dismissal on motion under FRCP 41(a)(2).

1. By plaintiff. The court should modify or vacate the dismissal because of the following:

(1) The court converted a requested dismissal without prejudice into a dismissal with prejudice without giving the plaintiff an opportunity to withdraw its motion to dismiss. ***Marlow v. Winston & Strawn***, 19 F.3d 300, 305 (7th Cir.1994); ***Gravatt v. Columbia Univ.***, 845 F.2d 54, 56 (2d Cir.1988); ***Lau v. Glendora Unified Sch. Dist.***, 792 F.2d 929, 930-31 (9th Cir.1986).

(2) The court imposed unreasonable terms on the voluntary dismissal. *E.g.*, ***LeCompte v. Mr. Chip, Inc.***, 528 F.2d 601, 604-05 (5th Cir.1976) (P appealed and showed prejudice); *see, e.g.*, ***Parker v. Freightliner Corp.***, 940 F.2d 1019, 1023-24 (7th Cir.1991) (insufficient showing of prejudice to P).

(3) The court awarded costs and attorney fees to the defendant without differentiating between the work product that was rendered useless by the dismissal and the work product that might be useful in a refiled suit. ***Koch v. Hankins***, 8 F.3d 650, 652-53 (9th Cir.1993).

2. By defendant. The court should modify or vacate the dismissal because of the following:

(1) The court should have ruled on the defendant's motion for summary judgment instead of granting a motion to dismiss without prejudice. ***Phillips USA, Inc. v. Allflex USA, Inc.***, 77 F.3d 354, 358 (10th Cir.1996); ***Grover v. Eli Lilly & Co.***, 33 F.3d 716, 718 (6th Cir.1994).

(2) The defendant was legally prejudiced by the dismissal. ***Phillips USA***, 77 F.3d at 358.

(3) The court did not state its reasons for denying the defendant's request for costs and attorney fees as a term of the dismissal. ***DWG Corp. v. Granada Invs.***, 962 F.2d 1201, 1202 (6th Cir.1992); ***Taragan v. Eli Lilly & Co.***, 838 F.2d 1337, 1339 (D.C.Cir.1988).

(4) Other reasons. See "Response," §5.3, p. 633.

§9. APPELLATE REVIEW

§9.1 Standard of review. The decision to grant or deny a voluntary dismissal under FRCP 41(a)(2) is reviewed for abuse of discretion. ***Camilli v. Grimes***, 436 F.3d 120, 123 (2d Cir.2006); ***Eagles, Ltd. v. American Eagle Found.***, 356 F.3d 724, 730 (6th Cir.2004); ***Elbaor v. Tripath Imaging, Inc.***, 279 F.3d 314, 318 (5th Cir.2002); ***Pontenberg v. Boston Sci. Corp.***, 252 F.3d 1253, 1256 (11th Cir.2001); ***Phillips USA, Inc. v. Allflex USA, Inc.***, 77 F.3d 354, 357 (10th Cir.1996); ***Metropolitan Fed. Bank v. W.R. Grace & Co.***, 999 F.2d 1257, 1262 (8th Cir.1993). An order setting terms for an FRCP 41(a)(2) dismissal is also reviewed for abuse of discretion. ***Versa Prods. v. Home Depot, USA, Inc.***, 387 F.3d 1325, 1327 (11th Cir.2004); ***Elbaor***, 279 F.3d at 319-20; *see* ***Eagles***, 356 F.3d at 730 (court's decision to include certain terms in FRCP 41(a)(2) voluntary dismissal is appealable only if unreasonable).

§9.2 Appeal.

NOTE

This section addresses the appealability of a suit when all the claims in the suit are voluntarily dismissed. For a discussion of the appealability of a suit involving multiple claims (either multiple claims by the plaintiff or counterclaims, cross-claims, or third-party claims) when some of the claims are dismissed or disposed of by the court (e.g., for failure to state a claim, on summary judgment) and the remaining claims are voluntarily dismissed without prejudice, see "Circuit Split," ch. 9-A, §3.1, p. 737.

1. Dismissal with prejudice. A voluntary dismissal with prejudice is not usually appealable because it is not an involuntary adverse judgment. ***Laczay v. Ross Adhesives***, 855 F.2d 351, 351 (6th Cir.1988). There are exceptions to this general rule if the order imposes a prejudicial term for dismissal or is designed to expedite appellate review.

(1) Prejudicial term. The plaintiff may appeal a voluntary dismissal with prejudice that does not result from a settlement agreement if the dismissal imposes a term that is prejudicial in the legal sense. *See, e.g.*, ***Versa Prods. v. Home Depot, USA, Inc.***, 387 F.3d 1325, 1328 (11th Cir.2004) (term that P must refile any future complaint in specific district did not constitute legal prejudice). For example, if the court dismissed the suit with prejudice when the plaintiff requested a dismissal without prejudice, the plaintiff may appeal. *See, e.g.*, ***Lau v. Glendora Unified Sch. Dist.***, 792 F.2d 929, 930-31 (9th Cir.1986) (court did not give P opportunity to agree to dismissal with prejudice).

(2) Expedite appellate review. The plaintiff may appeal a voluntary dismissal with prejudice designed to expedite appellate review of jurisdictional or procedural rulings. ***Libbey-Owens-Ford v. Blue Cross & Blue Shield***, 982 F.2d 1031, 1034 (6th Cir.1993); ***Raceway Props., Inc. v. Emprise Corp.***, 613 F.2d 656, 657 (6th Cir.1980).

2. Dismissal without prejudice. A voluntary dismissal without prejudice is usually not appealable because the order does not act as an adjudication adverse to the plaintiff's claims barring further proceedings and is not considered a final judgment. *See* ***Dearth v. Mukasey***, 516 F.3d 413, 415 (6th Cir.2008); ***Marshall v. Kansas City S. Ry.***, 378 F.3d 495, 500 (5th Cir.2004); ***Madsen v. Audrain Health Care, Inc.***, 297 F.3d 694, 697-98 (8th Cir.2002); ***Concha v. London***, 62 F.3d 1493, 1506-07 (9th Cir.1995); ***Libbey-Owens-Ford***, 982 F.2d at 1034. *But see* ***University of S. Ala. v. American Tobacco Co.***, 168 F.3d 405, 408 n.1 (11th Cir.1999) (appeal allowed because court's order effectively terminated litigation). The rationale for not allowing these appeals is that (1) the plaintiff is placed in the same legal position it would be in if it had not filed the suit and (2) the plaintiff has the right to bring a later suit on the same claim. ***Dearth***, 516 F.3d at 415. There are exceptions to this general rule if the order imposes a prejudicial term or can be treated by the court as a dismissal with prejudice.

(1) Appealability of conditional dismissal. Some circuits hold that a party can appeal a conditional, voluntary dismissal without prejudice if the decision of the district court results in "plain legal prejudice" to that party. *See, e.g.*, ***Belle-Midwest, Inc. v. Missouri Prop. & Cas. Ins. Guar. Ass'n***, 56 F.3d 977, 978 (8th Cir.1995) (P appealed; did not show prejudice); ***Grover v. Eli Lilly & Co.***, 33 F.3d 716, 718 (6th Cir.1994) (D appealed; showed prejudice); ***LeCompte v. Mr. Chip, Inc.***, 528 F.2d 601, 604 (5th Cir.1976) (P appealed; showed prejudice).

(2) Appealability of award of costs & attorney fees. The circuits disagree on whether the plaintiff can appeal the award of costs and attorney fees to the defendant after the plaintiff accepts a conditional dismissal. *Compare* ***Belle-Midwest***, 56 F.3d at 978 (if term of costs and attorney fees is reasonable, there is no legal prejudice), *and* ***Unioil, Inc. v. E.F. Hutton & Co.***, 809 F.2d 548, 556 (9th Cir.1986) (same), *with* ***Cauley v. Wilson***, 754 F.2d 769, 771 (7th Cir.1985) (P can appeal award of attorney fees after it accepts conditional dismissal if it disagrees with amount awarded), *and* ***Yoffe v. Keller Indus.***, 580 F.2d 126, 131 (5th Cir.1978) (P can appeal dismissal conditioned on payment of costs and attorney fees if term is "clearly unreasonable" and amounts to legal prejudice).

(3) Treated as final order. If the party cannot refile the lawsuit because of procedural problems (e.g., limitations), or if the refiling would place the party in the same position it was in before the dismissal, the court may treat a dismissal without prejudice as a final and appealable order. *See, e.g.*, ***LeBlang Motors, Ltd. v. Subaru***, 148 F.3d 680, 690 (7th Cir.1998) (limitations); ***Concha***, 62 F.3d at 1508-09 (Ps would be in same position).

D. INVOLUNTARY DISMISSAL

§1. GENERAL

§1.1 Rule. FRCP 41(b). See also FRCP 4(m), 12, 25(a), 37, 52(c), 59(e), 60(b).

§1.2 Purpose. An involuntary dismissal disposes of the case without a trial. Depending on the grounds, the dismissal can operate either as a final adjudication on the merits or as a method for returning the parties to the positions they were in before the suit was filed.

§1.3 Forms. *O'Connor's Federal Civil Forms* (2012), FORMS 7D.

§1.4 Other references. 9 Wright & Miller, *Federal Practice & Procedure 3d* §§2369-2376 (2008 & Supp.2012); 8 *Moore's Federal Practice 3d* §§41.50-41.53, 41.60 (2012).

§2. MOTION

§2.1 Party's motion.

1. Form. For the general requirements for the form of a motion, see "Drafting motions," ch. 1-B, §3.1, p. 14.

2. In writing. The motion for involuntary dismissal should be in writing, filed in the court, and served on the other party. *See* FRCP 7(b)(1).

3. Movant. The motion may be made by a defendant on a plaintiff's complaint, by a plaintiff on a defendant's counterclaim, by a defendant on another defendant's cross-claim, or by a third-party defendant on a third-party plaintiff's complaint. FRCP 41(b) (motion by D), FRCP 41(c) (motion against counterclaimant or cross-claimant).

NOTE

Because the party seeking involuntary dismissal is almost always a defendant, we will refer to the party moving for dismissal as the defendant and the party objecting to dismissal as the plaintiff throughout this subchapter.

4. Grounds for dismissal. The motion should specifically state the grounds for dismissal. *See* FRCP 7(b)(1)(B). If dismissal is sought under FRCP 12, the requirements of that rule must be observed.

5. Request for relief.

(1) Dismissal with prejudice. As a general rule, if a motion permits a dismissal with prejudice, the defendant should ask the court to dismiss with prejudice. The motion should also ask the court to dismiss the suit, not just the complaint. See "Dismissal with prejudice," §6.2.1, p. 648.

(2) Dismissal without prejudice. Some types of motions to dismiss authorize the court to dismiss only without prejudice. For example, a court must dismiss a claim without prejudice on any of the following grounds: failure to timely serve a complaint and summons, lack of jurisdiction, improper venue, and failure to join a party under FRCP 19. FRCP 4(m), 41(b).

(3) Conditional dismissal. If the defendant wants to force the plaintiff to comply with discovery or with some court order, the defendant may request that the court enter a conditional order of dismissal that becomes effective if the plaintiff does not comply with the order. See "Conditional dismissals," §6.3.2, p. 648.

6. Affidavits. If the motion contains facts outside the record, the defendant should support the motion with affidavits.

7. Request for hearing. If the motion presents contested fact issues, or if oral argument will help the court in resolving the motion, the defendant should request a hearing. The defendant should comply with any requirements in the local rules for securing a hearing on the motion.

8. **Proposed order granting relief.** Some districts require the movant to submit a proposed order with the motion. See "Proposed order," ch. 1-B, §3.1.11, p. 16. In those districts, the defendant should submit an order granting the motion that includes the factors relevant to that type of dismissal. See "Order of Dismissal," §6, p. 647.

§2.2 Sua sponte. The court may enter an involuntary dismissal on its own initiative. ***Link v. Wabash R.R.***, 370 U.S. 626, 629-33 (1962); ***Bowling v. Hasbro, Inc.***, 403 F.3d 1373, 1375 (Fed.Cir.2005); ***Long v. Simmons***, 77 F.3d 878, 879 (5th Cir.1996); ***In re Bluestein & Co.***, 68 F.3d 1022, 1025 (7th Cir.1995). Before the court enters an involuntary dismissal, it should determine whether (1) the defendant was served with the complaint, (2) the parties were notified of the court's intent to dismiss, (3) the plaintiff was given a chance to amend the complaint or respond to the court's reasons for dismissing sua sponte, and (4) the defendant was given a chance to respond or file an answer or motion. ***Catz v. Chalker***, 142 F.3d 279, 285 (6th Cir.1998), *amended*, 243 F.3d 234 (6th Cir.2001); *see* ***Briscoe v. Klaus***, 538 F.3d 252, 258 (3d Cir.2008). If the court dismisses the claim sua sponte, it should state its reasons for dismissal in the order. ***Catz***, 142 F.3d at 285.

§3. GROUNDS

§3.1 Failure to prosecute. If the plaintiff does not actively pursue the lawsuit, the court may dismiss the case for failure to prosecute. FRCP 41(b); ***Link v. Wabash R.R.***, 370 U.S. 626, 630 (1962); ***Larson v. Scott***, 157 F.3d 1030, 1031 (5th Cir.1998); ***Baker v. Latham Sparrowbrush Assocs.***, 72 F.3d 246, 252-53 (2d Cir.1995); ***In re Bluestein & Co.***, 68 F.3d 1022, 1025 (7th Cir.1995); ***GCIU Empl. Ret. Fund v. Chicago Tribune Co.***, 8 F.3d 1195, 1199 (7th Cir.1993); *see also* ***Chamorro v. Puerto Rican Cars, Inc.***, 304 F.3d 1, 4 (1st Cir.2002) (courts' inherent power to dismiss cases for failure to prosecute is reinforced and augmented by FRCP 41(b)). Dismissal for failure to prosecute is a harsh sanction that should be used only in extreme situations, such as when there is a clear record of delay or contempt or when less drastic sanctions are unavailable. ***Grun v. Pneumo Abex Corp.***, 163 F.3d 411, 425 (7th Cir.1998); *see* ***Ecclesiastes 9:10-11-12, Inc. v. LMC Holding Co.***, 497 F.3d 1135, 1143 (10th Cir. 2007); *see also* ***Emerson v. Thiel Coll.***, 296 F.3d 184, 190 (3d Cir.2002) (dismissal with prejudice is appropriate only in limited circumstances, and doubts should be resolved in favor of reaching decision on merits). Unless intentional or willful conduct is present, the dismissal should be without prejudice. *See* ***Mann v. Lewis***, 108 F.3d 145, 147 (8th Cir.1997) (recognizing power to dismiss with prejudice, but reversing "extreme sanction" of dismissal with prejudice as abuse of discretion). Typically, the appellate courts require the district courts to consider certain factors when deciding whether to dismiss a case for failure to prosecute. *See* ***Emerson***, 296 F.3d at 190 (six factors); ***Lucas v. Miles***, 84 F.3d 532, 535 (2d Cir.1996) (five factors); ***Al-Torki v. Kaempen***, 78 F.3d 1381, 1384 (9th Cir.1996) (five factors); ***Berry v. CIGNA/RSI-CIGNA***, 975 F.2d 1188, 1191 (5th Cir.1992) (two regular factors plus three aggravating factors). Some of the factors that the district courts must consider before dismissing the plaintiff's suit are listed below.

PRACTICE TIP

Because the circuits rely on different combinations of the factors listed below, check the substantive law of your circuit before drafting a motion to dismiss or a response.

---

1. The extent of the plaintiff's personal responsibility for the conduct. ***Emerson***, 296 F.3d at 190; ***Mann***, 108 F.3d at 147; ***Berry***, 975 F.2d at 1191; *see* ***Betty K Agencies, Ltd. v. M/V Monada***, 432 F.3d 1333, 1337-38 (11th Cir.2005) (prejudice more appropriate when party, not attorney, is culpable).

2. Whether there is a clear record of delay. *See* ***Emerson***, 296 F.3d at 190; ***Al-Torki***, 78 F.3d at 1384; ***In re Bluestein***, 68 F.3d at 1025; ***Berry***, 975 F.2d at 1191.

3. The risk of prejudice to the defendant. ***Emerson***, 296 F.3d at 190; ***Al-Torki***, 78 F.3d at 1384; ***Berry***, 975 F.2d at 1191. Unreasonable delay in the prosecution of the case creates a rebuttable presumption of prejudice to the defendant. ***In re Eisen***, 31 F.3d 1447, 1452-53 (9th Cir.1994). The plaintiff may rebut the presumption of prejudice by showing a nonfrivolous reason for the delay. *Id.* at 1453. If the plaintiff satisfies its burden, the defendant must show at least some actual prejudice. *Id.* If the defendant shows actual prejudice, the plaintiff must convince the court that the claims of prejudice are either illusory or relatively insignificant compared with the reason for the delay. *Id.*

4. Whether the conduct was willful or in bad faith. ***Emerson***, 296 F.3d at 190; *see also* ***Dorsey v. Scott Wetzel Servs.***, 84 F.3d 170, 171-72 (5th Cir.1996) (contempt); ***In re Bluestein***, 68 F.3d at 1025 (same).

5. The court's need to manage its docket as opposed to the party's right to due process and a fair chance to be heard. *See* ***Al-Torki***, 78 F.3d at 1384.

6. The public policy that favors disposition of cases on their merits rather than on procedural defaults. *Id.*

7. Whether the court could impose an effective sanction that is less drastic than dismissal. ***Emerson***, 296 F.3d at 190; ***Dorsey***, 84 F.3d at 172; ***Al-Torki***, 78 F.3d at 1384; *see* ***Smith v. Gold Dust Casino***, 526 F.3d 402, 406 (8th Cir.2008) (court should consider this factor first). If the pattern of a plaintiff's dilatory conduct is clear, the court does not need to impose graduated sanctions before dismissing the case. ***Dickerson v. Board of Educ.***, 32 F.3d 1114, 1117 (7th Cir.1994).

8. The public interest in expeditious resolution of litigation. ***Al-Torki***, 78 F.3d at 1384. Before dismissing a case for failure to prosecute, the court must find an unreasonable delay. *Id.* Many local rules specify that inactivity for three to six months is evidence that a case is not being diligently prosecuted. *E.g.*, Local Rules Cal. (S.D.), Rule 41.1.a (six months); Local Rules Fla. (N.D.), Rule 41.1(A) (90 days).

9. The probable merits of the suit. ***Emerson***, 296 F.3d at 190.

10. Whether the court warned the plaintiff that the case might be dismissed as a sanction for the plaintiff's conduct. *See* ***In re Bluestein***, 68 F.3d at 1025-26 (although court should normally warn P before dismissing its case for failure to prosecute, decision to warn is within court's discretion; any warning given must be direct and explicit); ***Ball v. City of Chi.***, 2 F.3d 752, 755 (7th Cir.1993) (explicit warning required).

§3.2 Failure to comply with court rule or order. The court may dismiss a plaintiff's suit (or a defendant's counterclaim) as a sanction for violating a court rule or order. FRCP 41(b); *see* ***Degen v. U.S.***, 517 U.S. 820, 827-28 (1996); ***Long v. Simmons***, 77 F.3d 878, 879 (5th Cir.1996); *see also* ***Chamorro v. Puerto Rican Cars, Inc.***, 304 F.3d 1, 4 (1st Cir.2002) (courts' inherent power to dismiss cases for disregard of judicial orders is reinforced and augmented by FRCP 41(b)). *But see* ***Wynder v. McMahon***, 360 F.3d 73, 80 (2d Cir.2004) (court cannot dismiss for failure to comply with court-ordered heightened pleading standards in excess of FRCP 8). To determine whether to dismiss a case for this conduct, courts generally use the same types of factors as those used to decide whether to dismiss a case for failure to prosecute. See "Failure to prosecute," §3.1, p. 643.

1. Whether the plaintiff's failure to comply with the court's order was willful. ***Hutchins v. A.G. Edwards & Sons, Inc.***, 116 F.3d 1256, 1260 (8th Cir.1997).

2. The duration of the plaintiff's failure to comply with the court's order. ***Lucas v. Miles***, 84 F.3d 532, 535 (2d Cir.1996). The court must determine that the failures were those of the plaintiff and were of significant duration. *Id.*

3. Whether the plaintiff was notified that further delays would result in dismissal. *Id.*; ***Robson v. Hallenbeck***, 81 F.3d 1, 3 (1st Cir.1996).

4. Whether the defendant would be prejudiced by the delay. ***Lucas***, 84 F.3d at 535; ***Robson***, 81 F.3d at 2.

5. Whether the court balanced the need to manage its docket against the need to protect a party's right to due process and a fair chance to be heard. ***Lucas***, 84 F.3d at 535.

6. Whether the court imposed lesser sanctions before the ultimate sanction of dismissal. ***McHenry v. Renne***, 84 F.3d 1172, 1178 (9th Cir.1996); ***Lucas***, 84 F.3d at 535; ***Robson***, 81 F.3d at 2; *see* ***Long***, 77 F.3d at 880.

7. Whether the record reflects contempt by the plaintiff. ***Robson***, 81 F.3d at 2; ***Long***, 77 F.3d at 880.

8. The strength of the plaintiff's case. ***McHenry***, 84 F.3d at 1179.

§3.3 Sanctions. The court may dismiss a suit as a sanction under FRCP 16(f) and 37(b). Because dismissal is a harsh sanction, courts should limit its use. ***Ladien v. Astrachan***, 128 F.3d 1051, 1057 (7th Cir.1997).

1. Dismissal under FRCP 16(f). The court may dismiss a suit if a party or its attorney (1) does not attend a scheduling or other pretrial conference, (2) is substantially unprepared to participate in the conference, (3) does not participate in good faith in the conference, or (4) does not obey a scheduling or other pretrial order. FRCP 16(f)(1). See "Enforceability of order," ch. 5-A, §4.6, p. 294.

2. Dismissal under FRCP 37. The court may dismiss a suit if a party does not comply with discovery. FRCP 37(b)(2), (c). See "Motion for Discovery Sanctions," ch. 6-A, §15, p. 446.

3. Factors. Before dismissing a suit as a sanction under FRCP 16(f) or 37(b), the court should consider factors similar to those outlined for FRCP 41(b) dismissals. See "Failure to prosecute," §3.1, p. 643. These factors include the following:

(1) The degree of actual prejudice to the defendant. ***Bass v. Jostens, Inc.***, 71 F.3d 237, 241 (6th Cir. 1995); ***Archibeque v. Atchison, Topeka & Santa Fe Ry.***, 70 F.3d 1172, 1174 (10th Cir.1995); ***Harris v. City of Phila.***, 47 F.3d 1311, 1330 n.18 (3d Cir.1995).

(2) The amount of interference with the judicial process. ***Archibeque***, 70 F.3d at 1174.

(3) The culpability of the litigant. ***Archibeque***, 70 F.3d at 1174; ***Harris***, 47 F.3d at 1330 n.18.

(4) Whether the court warned the party in advance that dismissal would be a likely sanction for noncompliance. ***Bass***, 71 F.3d at 241; ***Archibeque***, 70 F.3d at 1174.

(5) The effectiveness of lesser sanctions. ***Bass***, 71 F.3d at 241; ***Archibeque***, 70 F.3d at 1174; ***Harris***, 47 F.3d at 1330 n.18.

(6) The history of delay. ***Harris***, 47 F.3d at 1330 n.18.

(7) Whether the conduct of the party or the attorney was willful or in bad faith. ***Bass***, 71 F.3d at 241; ***Harris***, 47 F.3d at 1330 n.18.

(8) The merit of the claim. ***Harris***, 47 F.3d at 1330 n.18.

§3.4 Failure to serve defendant with suit. Under FRCP 4(m), the plaintiff must serve the defendant with the complaint and summons within 120 days after the suit is filed. ***Cardenas v. City of Chi.***, 646 F.3d 1001, 1004 (7th Cir.2011). If the plaintiff does not timely serve the defendant, the court may dismiss the suit without prejudice. FRCP 4(m); ***Espinoza v. U.S.***, 52 F.3d 838, 841 (10th Cir.1995). Before dismissing under FRCP 4(m), the court should determine whether the plaintiff showed good cause for late service. ***Espinoza***, 52 F.3d at 841; *see* ***Adams v. Allied-Signal Gen. Aviation Avionics***, 74 F.3d 882, 887 (8th Cir.1996). See "Grounds," ch. 5-F, §4.3.5, p. 335.

1. Good cause. When the plaintiff shows good cause for not serving the defendant within the 120 days, the plaintiff is entitled to a mandatory extension. FRCP 4(m); ***Lemoge v. U.S.***, 587 F.3d 1188, 1198 (9th Cir.2009); ***Millan v. USAA Gen. Indem. Co.***, 546 F.3d 321, 325 (5th Cir.2008); ***Adams***, 74 F.3d at 887; ***Espinoza***, 52 F.3d at 841; *see* 1993 Notes to FRCP 4 at ¶63, p. 1144, this book. A showing of good cause requires "excusable neglect," which is good faith and some reasonable basis for noncompliance with the rules. ***Adams***, 74 F.3d at 887. In addition to excusable neglect, the plaintiff should show that the party to be served received actual notice of the suit, the defendant would suffer no prejudice, and the plaintiff would be severely prejudiced if the complaint were dismissed. ***Lemoge***, 587 F.3d at 1198 n.3.

2. No good cause. When the plaintiff cannot show good cause, the court still has the discretion to grant an extension. FRCP 4(m); ***Henderson v. U.S.***, 517 U.S. 654, 662 (1996); ***Millan***, 546 F.3d at 325; ***Adams***, 74 F.3d at 887; ***Espinoza***, 52 F.3d at 841.

NOTE

*Generally, dismissals under FRCP 4(m) are without prejudice. See "Dismissal without prejudice," §6.2.2, p. 648. But even if the case is dismissed without prejudice, an FRCP 4(m) dismissal may effectively be a dismissal with prejudice when it happens after the statute of limitations has run. See **Millan**, 546 F.3d at 325-26. See "Dismissal with prejudice," §6.2.1, p. 648. In these situations, rather than reviewing under the good-cause standard, the court may review an FRCP 4(m) dismissal under the heightened standard that is usually applied to dismissals with prejudice; under that heightened standard, dismissals with prejudice are usually appropriate only when there is a clear record of delay or contumacious conduct and a lesser sanction is not available. **Millan**, 546 F.3d at 325-26. See "Failure to prosecute," §3.1, p. 643.*

§3.5 Indigent's frivolous suit. The court may dismiss an indigent's suit if (1) the allegations of poverty in the indigent's affidavit supporting the suit are false or (2) the indigent's suit is frivolous or malicious, fails to state a claim on which relief may be granted, or seeks monetary relief against a defendant who is immune from such relief. 28 U.S.C. §1915(e)(2); *see **Neitzke v. Williams***, 490 U.S. 319, 324 (1989); ***Cochran v. Morris***, 73 F.3d 1310, 1315-16 (4th Cir.1996); ***Hidalgo-Disla v. INS***, 52 F.3d 444, 446-47 (2d Cir.1995). A complaint is frivolous under 28 U.S.C. §1915 when it lacks an arguable basis in fact or law. ***Hamilton v. Lyons***, 74 F.3d 99, 102 (5th Cir.1996); ***Cochran***, 73 F.3d at 1316; ***Cato v. U.S.***, 70 F.3d 1103, 1106 (9th Cir.1995); *see **Neitzke***, 490 U.S. at 331 (complaint is not automatically frivolous when it does not state a claim). Most indigents file complaints pro se. When making a determination under 28 U.S.C. §1915(d), the courts must liberally construe the complaint of a pro se indigent. *See **Boag v. MacDougall***, 454 U.S. 364, 365 (1982); ***Nasim v. Warden, Md. House of Corr.***, 64 F.3d 951, 961 (4th Cir.1995).

§3.6 Other grounds. Most requests for involuntary dismissal are based on the argument that the plaintiff cannot maintain the suit as filed. The defendant must prove there is a bar to the plaintiff's suit or a defect in the pleadings as to the court, the parties, or the claim of liability. For example, the court can dismiss a suit if it determines any of the following:

1. The plaintiff's complaint is subject to dismissal under any of the grounds in FRCP 12(b). See "Types of FRCP 12 defenses," ch. 3-A, §2.2, p. 171.

2. A foreign court, rather than a U.S. federal court, is a more appropriate forum for the lawsuit. See "Motion to Dismiss for Forum Non Conveniens—Challenging the U.S. Forum," ch. 3-E, p. 199.

3. The plaintiff's complaint is excessively long, confused, or vague, in violation of FRCP 8(a)(2). *See **Hearns v. San Bernardino Police Dept.***, 530 F.3d 1124, 1130-31 (9th Cir.2008); ***Wynder v. McMahon***, 360 F.3d 73, 80 (2d Cir.2004). *But see **Davis v. Ruby Foods, Inc.***, 269 F.3d 818, 821 (7th Cir.2001) (presence of unnecessary or extraneous matter in complaint does not warrant dismissal unless it is actually prejudicial to defense). See "Motion to Dismiss for Failure to Plead Properly—FRCP 8, 9(b)," ch. 3-J, p. 218.

4. The complaint does not satisfy the pleading requirements of FRCP 9(b). *See **U.S. v. Bahler Med., Inc.***, 619 F.3d 104, 115-16 (1st Cir.2010). See "Motion to Dismiss for Failure to Plead Properly—FRCP 8, 9(b)," ch. 3-J, p. 218.

5. The plaintiff lacks standing to bring the suit. *See **U.S. v. Tribal Dev. Corp.***, 49 F.3d 1208, 1211 (7th Cir. 1995).

6. The case is moot. *Cf. **Murphy v. Hunt***, 455 U.S. 478, 481-82 (1982) (declaratory-judgment suit over pretrial bail was moot once D was convicted).

§4. RESPONSE

§4.1 Deadline. The plaintiff should file a response within the deadline imposed by court order or local rules and before the motion is submitted to the court for resolution.

§4.2 Objections. If the plaintiff opposes the motion, it should file a response negating the grounds asserted in the motion and argue the facts in favor of retaining the case. See "Grounds," §3, p. 643.

§4.3 Affidavits. If the response contains facts outside the record, the plaintiff should support the response with affidavits. Generally, if the defendant attached affidavits to its motion to dismiss, the plaintiff should attach affidavits to its response.

§4.4 Proposed order denying relief. Some districts require the respondent to submit a proposed order with the response. *E.g.*, Local Rules Tex. (S.D.), Rule 7.4.D. In those districts, the plaintiff should submit an order denying the motion. See "Order of Dismissal," §6, this page.

§5. NOTICE OF INTENT TO DISMISS

§5.1 Notice under FRCP 41(b).

1. Defendant files motion to dismiss. If the defendant files a motion to dismiss and serves it on the plaintiff, the court is not required to warn the plaintiff about the possibility of dismissal. ***Curtis v. Bembenek***, 48 F.3d 281, 286-88 (7th Cir.1995); ***In re Eisen***, 31 F.3d 1447, 1455 (9th Cir.1994).

2. Court enters dismissal sua sponte. If the dismissal is sua sponte, the court must give the plaintiff explicit notice and an opportunity to respond before dismissing its case. ***Stewart Title Guar. Co. v. Cadle Co.***, 74 F.3d 835, 836 (7th Cir.1996). The notice can be written or oral and must specify a date by which the parties must respond. ***Catz v. Chalker***, 142 F.3d 279, 286 (6th Cir.1998), *amended*, 243 F.3d 234 (6th Cir.2001); *see also* ***Ecclesiastes 9:10-11-12, Inc. v. LMC Holding Co.***, 497 F.3d 1135, 1149-50 (10th Cir. 2007) (notice can be constructive—that is, notice without express warning and objectively based on totality of circumstances). However, if the plaintiff disobeys a court order or does not prosecute the case, the court is not required to give the plaintiff express notice before it dismisses the case sua sponte. *See* ***Link v. Wabash R.R.***, 370 U.S. 626, 631 (1962); ***In re Bluestein & Co.***, 68 F.3d 1022, 1025-27 (7th Cir.1995).

§5.2 Notice under FRCP 16(f) & 37(b). Generally, before the court can impose sanctions under FRCP 16(f) or 37(b), the court must give the offending party an opportunity to show why the sanctions are inappropriate. *See, e.g.*, ***Martin v. Brown***, 63 F.3d 1252, 1262-63 (3d Cir.1995) (monetary sanctions imposed under FRCP 37(b)(2)); ***Newton v. A.C. & S., Inc.***, 918 F.2d 1121, 1127 (3d Cir.1990) (monetary sanctions imposed under FRCP 16(f)).

§5.3 Notice to indigent. If an indigent plaintiff's complaint is irreparably frivolous or malicious, the court can dismiss the suit without notice to the indigent. ***Boyce v. Alizaduh***, 595 F.2d 948, 950-51 (4th Cir.1979); *see* 28 U.S.C. §1915(e) (statute does not address whether court must give indigent notice before dismissing suit). If the complaint is reparable, the court should permit the indigent plaintiff to amend it. ***Street v. Fair***, 918 F.2d 269, 273 (1st Cir.1990); ***Boyce***, 595 F.2d at 951; *see* ***Neitzke v. Williams***, 490 U.S. 319, 330 (1989) (indigent P must be given same opportunity as nonindigent P to amend complaint before dismissal for failure to state a claim under FRCP 12(b)(6)). In a suit with more than one defendant, if the complaint is irreparably frivolous or malicious against a particular defendant, the court should dismiss the suit against that defendant and permit the suit to continue against the remaining defendants. ***Boyce***, 595 F.2d at 951.

§5.4 Notice under FRCP 4(m). If the plaintiff does not timely serve the defendant, the court can dismiss the suit on the defendant's motion or on the court's own initiative "after notice to the plaintiff." FRCP 4(m). The notice requirement gives the plaintiff the opportunity to show good cause for not timely serving the defendant. ***Sanders v. Southwestern Bell Tel., L.P.***, 544 F.3d 1101, 1111 (10th Cir.2008); *see* ***Meilleur v. Strong***, 682 F.3d 56, 61 (2d Cir. 2012).

§6. ORDER OF DISMISSAL

§6.1 Findings. The court is not required under the FRCPs to make specific findings of the reasons for the dismissal in its order. ***Al-Torki v. Kaempen***, 78 F.3d 1381, 1384 (9th Cir.1996). However, by addressing the relevant factors for dismissal in the order, the district court will help the court of appeals conduct a meaningful review of the

district court's decision. *See* ***Davis v. Bayless***, 70 F.3d 367, 376 (5th Cir.1995); ***Mobley v. McCormick***, 40 F.3d 337, 341 (10th Cir.1994); ***Ash v. Cvetkov***, 739 F.2d 493, 496 (9th Cir.1984). If a meaningful review is not possible, the case will be remanded for further explanation. *See* ***Davis***, 70 F.3d at 376. Even though the FRCPs do not require specific findings, some circuits require them by circuit rule. *E.g.*, ***Pasquino v. Prather***, 13 F.3d 1049, 1051 (7th Cir.1994) (Circuit Rule 50).

§6.2 Types of dismissal.

1. Dismissal with prejudice. An order of dismissal under FRCP 41(b) for failure to prosecute is an adjudication on the merits and a dismissal with prejudice, unless the order states otherwise. ***Edwards v. City of Houston***, 78 F.3d 983, 994 (5th Cir.1996); ***Proctor v. Millar Elevator Serv.***, 8 F.3d 824, 825 (D.C.Cir.1993); *see* ***Semtek Int'l v. Lockheed Martin Corp.***, 531 U.S. 497, 503 (2001). *But see* Local Rules Cal. (S.D.), Rule 41.1.a (if no proceeding or discovery occurs for six months, suit is dismissed without prejudice, unless otherwise ordered). A dismissal with prejudice is a final adjudication on the merits; therefore, relitigation of the same suit is barred by res judicata. ***Proctor***, 8 F.3d at 825-26; ***Nagle v. Lee***, 807 F.2d 435, 442-43 (5th Cir.1987). But a dismissal with prejudice cannot be ordered, even as a sanction, when the court lacks subject-matter jurisdiction. ***Hernandez v. Conriv Rlty. Assocs.***, 182 F.3d 121, 123 (2d Cir.1999).

2. Dismissal without prejudice. Some types of motions to dismiss authorize only a dismissal without prejudice to refiling the suit. For example, FRCP 4(m) expressly states that a dismissal for failing to timely serve a complaint and summons must be without prejudice. FRCP 41(b) states that a dismissal for lack of jurisdiction, improper venue, or failure to join a party under FRCP 19 is not an "adjudication on the merits," which means these dismissals are without prejudice. *See* ***Costello v. U.S.***, 365 U.S. 265, 285 (1961) ("lack of jurisdiction" encompasses failure to comply with preconditions for going forward with merits of substantive claim). If a suit is dismissed without prejudice, it renders the proceedings in that case a nullity and puts the plaintiff in the same legal position it would be in if it had not filed the suit. ***Williams v. Clarke***, 82 F.3d 270, 273 (8th Cir.1996); ***Beck v. Caterpillar, Inc.***, 50 F.3d 405, 407 (7th Cir.1995); ***Brown v. Hartshorne Pub. Sch. Dist.***, 926 F.2d 959, 961 (10th Cir.1991). The suit may be refiled if the statute of limitations has not run.

§6.3 Scope of order.

1. Dismissal of complaint vs. dismissal of suit. There is a distinction between an order that dismisses the plaintiff's complaint and an order that dismisses the plaintiff's suit. An order that dismisses the complaint does not necessarily dismiss the suit. ***Telluride Mgmt. Solutions, Inc. v. Telluride Inv.***, 55 F.3d 463, 466 (9th Cir. 1995).

(1) Dismissal of suit. If the order dismisses the suit, the order is appealable. ***Sanford v. Motts***, 258 F.3d 1117, 1119 (9th Cir.2001).

(2) Dismissal of complaint. If the order dismisses the complaint, the order is generally not appealable. ***Telluride***, 55 F.3d at 466; ***Mobley v. McCormick***, 40 F.3d 337, 339 (10th Cir.1994); ***Domino Sugar Corp. v. Sugar Workers Local Un. 392***, 10 F.3d 1064, 1066-67 (4th Cir.1993). *But see* ***Whitaker v. City of Houston***, 963 F.2d 831, 836 (5th Cir.1992) (order dismissing complaint is final and appealable, but if P files motion to amend, finality is destroyed unless motion is denied). However, when no amendment could cure the defect, the order dismissing the complaint is a final, appealable order. ***Telluride***, 55 F.3d at 466; ***Domino Sugar***, 10 F.3d at 1066; *see* ***Elfenbein v. Gulf & W. Indus.***, 590 F.2d 445, 448-49 & n.1 (2d Cir.1978) (because P cannot amend complaint after dismissal, order dismissing complaint without further comment is appealable). To determine whether the order dismissing the complaint is appealable, the appellate court focuses on the intent of the district court in issuing its order of dismissal. ***Mobley***, 40 F.3d at 339.

2. Conditional dismissals. Rather than immediately dismissing a case, the court may order a conditional dismissal. *See* ***Otis v. City of Chi.***, 29 F.3d 1159, 1163 (7th Cir.1994). For example, the court may dismiss the

case but give the plaintiff a deadline to comply with the terms of the order before making the dismissal final. *See, e.g., id.* (court could have conditioned dismissal on P's failure to timely provide answers to discovery). If the court grants a conditional dismissal and the plaintiff does not meet the condition within the prescribed time period, the dismissal automatically becomes final and appealable on the day the time period expires. *Id.* at 1165. *But see* ***WMX Techs. v. Miller***, 104 F.3d 1133, 1136 (9th Cir.1997) (dismissal with leave to amend does not become final merely because P chooses not to amend; separate order must be entered).

§6.4 Options after dismissal.

1. Case dismissed with prejudice. If the court dismisses the plaintiff's case with prejudice, the plaintiff cannot refile the suit. *See* ***Asset Allocation & Mgmt. v. Western Empls. Ins.***, 892 F.2d 566, 571 (7th Cir.1989). *But see* ***Semtek Int'l v. Lockheed Martin Corp.***, 531 U.S. 497, 505-06 (2001) (dismissal bars refiling in same court but is not necessarily claim-preclusive in other courts). However, the plaintiff has the following options after dismissal:

(1) File postjudgment motion in district court. The plaintiff can move for reconsideration under FRCP 59(e) or for relief from judgment under FRCP 60(b). The motion for reconsideration must be filed within 28 days after the order of dismissal. *See* FRCP 59(e). See "Motion to Alter or Amend Judgment," ch. 10-D, p. 793. Courts seldom grant relief under FRCP 60(b), which requires "exceptional circumstances." See "Motion for Relief from Judgment," ch. 10-F, p. 804.

(2) File appeal. The plaintiff can appeal the order of dismissal and the denial of the motion for reconsideration. *See* ***McHenry v. Renne***, 84 F.3d 1172, 1177 (9th Cir.1996).

2. Case dismissed without prejudice.

(1) Statute of limitations has run. If the court dismisses the plaintiff's case without prejudice after the statute of limitations has run, the dismissal operates as a dismissal with prejudice, and the plaintiff cannot refile the suit. ***Lambert v. U.S.***, 44 F.3d 296, 298 (5th Cir.1995). The plaintiff should treat the order as if it were an order dismissing the suit with prejudice. See "Case dismissed with prejudice," §6.4.1, this page. A dismissal without prejudice after the limitations period has run must meet the same requirements as a dismissal with prejudice. *See, e.g.,* ***Long v. Simmons***, 77 F.3d 878, 880 (5th Cir.1996) (when dismissing without prejudice after limitations period has run, court should have determined whether P's failure to comply with court order was result of purposeful delay or contempt and whether lesser sanctions could have been imposed first).

(2) Statute of limitations has not run. If the court dismisses the plaintiff's case without prejudice and the statute of limitations has not run, the plaintiff has the following options:

(a) Refile suit. The plaintiff can refile the suit.

(b) Challenge order in district court. The plaintiff can move for reconsideration under FRCP 59(e) or for relief from judgment under FRCP 60(b). See "File postjudgment motion in district court," §6.4.1(1), this page.

(c) File appeal. The plaintiff can appeal the order of dismissal. *E.g.,* ***L.E.A. Dynatech, Inc. v. Allina***, 49 F.3d 1527, 1529 (Fed.Cir.1995) (counterclaim P appealed dismissal, attorney fees, and amount of fee award).

§7. APPELLATE REVIEW

The grant or denial of a dismissal is reviewed for abuse of discretion. ***National Hockey League v. Metropolitan Hockey Club, Inc.***, 427 U.S. 639, 642 (1976); ***Link v. Wabash R.R.***, 370 U.S. 626, 633 (1962); ***Doe v. Cassel***, 403 F.3d 986, 990 (8th Cir.2005); *see also* ***Emerson v. Thiel Coll.***, 296 F.3d 184, 190 (3d Cir.2002) (although standard is abuse of discretion, dismissal with prejudice is appropriate only in limited circumstances, and doubts should be resolved in favor of reaching decision on merits).

E. ARBITRATION

§1. GENERAL

§1.1 Rule. None. See Federal Arbitration Act (FAA), 9 U.S.C. §§1-16.

§1.2 Purpose. Arbitration is one form of alternative dispute resolution. Through an arbitration agreement, parties can limit the issues they choose to arbitrate, agree on rules under which the arbitration will proceed, specify with whom they choose to arbitrate their disputes, and choose who will resolve the specific disputes. ***Stolt-Nielsen S.A. v. AnimalFeeds Int'l***, ___ U.S. ___, 130 S.Ct. 1758, 1774 (2010). To be considered "arbitration" under the FAA, there must be an agreement for an independent arbitrator who (1) applies substantive legal standards, (2) considers evidence and argument from each party, and (3) renders a decision that resolves the rights and duties of the parties, generally awarding damages or equitable relief. ***Advanced Bodycare Solutions, LLC v. Thione Int'l***, 524 F.3d 1235, 1239 (11th Cir.2008); *see* ***Salt Lake Tribune Publ'g Co. v. Management Planning, Inc.***, 390 F.3d 684, 690-91 (10th Cir.2004).

§1.3 Forms. ***O'Connor's Federal Civil Forms*** (2012), FORMS 7E.

§1.4 Other references. Bland, Jr. et al., *Consumer Arbitration Agreements: Enforceability & Other Topics* (6th ed.2011); Annotation, *Construction & Application of §10(a)(4) of Federal Arbitration Act … Providing for Vacating of Arbitration Awards Where Arbitrators Exceed or Imperfectly Execute Powers*, 136 ALR Fed. 183, §26b (1997 & Supp.2012-13); Annotation, *Pre-emption by Federal Arbitration Act … of State Laws Prohibiting or Restricting Formation or Enforcement of Arbitration Agreements*, 108 ALR Fed. 179 (1992 & Supp.2012-13); Annotation, *Defendant's Participation in Action as Waiver of Right to Arbitration of Dispute Involved Therein*, 98 ALR 3d 767, 773-74 (1980 & Supp.2012).

§2. COMPELLING ARBITRATION

§2.1 Motion to compel. If a plaintiff brings a suit in federal court that is subject to mandatory binding arbitration, either party can file a motion to compel arbitration. *See* 9 U.S.C. §4. If no suit has been filed in federal court, a party can file a complaint in federal court to compel arbitration. *See id.* The complaint must assert an independent basis for jurisdiction, such as diversity or a federal question, because the FAA does not provide one. *See id.*; ***Vaden v. Discover Bank***, 556 U.S. 49, 59 (2009); ***Moses H. Cone Mem'l Hosp. v. Mercury Constr. Corp.***, 460 U.S. 1, 25 n.32 (1983); ***Northport Health Servs. v. Rutherford***, 605 F.3d 483, 486 (8th Cir.2010). For federal-question jurisdiction, a court can "look through" the complaint and examine the parties' underlying dispute to determine whether it involves federal-question jurisdiction. *See, e.g.*, ***Vaden***, 556 U.S. at 66 (no federal-question jurisdiction when Court looked through complaint and determined jurisdiction was based only on counterclaim). See "Evaluating allegations of jurisdiction," ch. 2-F, §2.2, p. 113. For diversity jurisdiction, the court looks at the citizenship of the parties named in the complaint plus any parties required under FRCP 19 to determine whether there is diversity of citizenship, and it can "look through" the complaint and examine the value at stake in the arbitration to determine whether the amount in controversy is over $75,000. ***Northport Health Servs.***, 605 F.3d at 486-87, 491. See "Diversity Jurisdiction," ch. 2-F, §3, p. 116.

1. Where to file. Most circuits hold that a motion to compel must be filed in a district court located in the forum where the parties agreed to arbitrate their dispute, and only that court can order the parties to arbitrate in that forum. ***Ansari v. Qwest Comms.***, 414 F.3d 1214, 1219-20 (10th Cir.2005); *see* ***Inland Bulk Transfer Co. v. Cummins Engine Co.***, 332 F.3d 1007, 1018 (6th Cir.2003); ***Merrill Lynch, Pierce, Fenner & Smith, Inc. v. Lauer***, 49 F.3d 323, 327 (7th Cir.1995). The Fifth Circuit goes further, holding that its district courts can hear a motion to compel and order the parties to arbitrate in the forum specified in the agreement, even if the forum is outside the circuit. *See* ***Dupuy-Busching Gen. Agency, Inc. v. Ambassador Ins.***, 524 F.2d 1275, 1277-78 (5th Cir.1975). The Ninth Circuit goes the furthest, holding that its district courts can hear a motion to compel and order the parties to arbitrate in the Ninth Circuit, even if the forum specified in the agreement is different. *See* ***Textile Unlimited, Inc.***

v. A. .BMH & Co., 240 F.3d 781, 783 (9th Cir.2001). In reaching this holding, the Ninth Circuit relied on ***Cortez Byrd Chips, Inc. v. Bill Harbert Constr. Co.***, 529 U.S. 193, 195 (2000), which held that the venue provisions of 9 U.S.C. §§9-11—concerning motions to confirm, vacate, or modify an arbitration award—are permissive and allow motions to be brought in any district court where venue is proper. The Ninth Circuit reasoned that ***Cortez Byrd Chips*** should apply to the entire FAA, thus making the venue provisions of 9 U.S.C. §4 permissive, not mandatory. ***Textile Unlimited***, 240 F.3d at 784.

2. Form. For the general requirements for the form of a motion, see "Drafting motions," ch. 1-B, §3.1, p. 14.

PRACTICE TIP

*When asking the court to compel arbitration, a party should not bury the grounds to compel in a motion to dismiss. See **Conrad v. Phone Directories Co.**, 585 F.3d 1376, 1385-86 (10th Cir. 2009). The better practice is to (1) identify in the caption that arbitration should be compelled or (2) make the grounds plainly apparent within the motion. Id. at 1385. If the party does not do so and the motion is denied, the appellate court may not have jurisdiction over an interlocutory appeal of the denial of arbitration. See, e.g., id. at 1386 (appellate court lacked jurisdiction over denial of motion to dismiss, which was partly premised on existence of arbitration agreement but did not explicitly move to stay litigation or compel arbitration under FAA).*

---

3. Grounds. A party seeking to enforce a contractual provision requiring arbitration of a dispute should file a motion alleging that (1) the parties agreed to arbitration and (2) the claim is arbitrable. ***Dealer Computer Servs. v. Old Colony Motors, Inc.***, 588 F.3d 884, 886 (5th Cir.2009).

(1) Agreement to arbitrate. The motion should state that the parties contractually agreed to arbitrate. *See* ***Covington v. Aban Offshore Ltd.***, 650 F.3d 556, 558 (5th Cir.2011); *see also* ***Banks v. Mitsubishi Motors Credit***, 435 F.3d 538, 539-40 (5th Cir.2005) (existence of written arbitration agreement may be proved by affidavit); ***Rojas v. TK Comms.***, 87 F.3d 745, 748 (5th Cir.1996) (FAA requires arbitration clause to be in writing). For there to be a contractual agreement to arbitrate, the court must find that there is a valid agreement to arbitrate and the dispute falls within the scope of that agreement. ***Dealer Computer Servs.***, 588 F.3d at 886; ***Telectronics Pacing Sys. v. Guidant Corp.***, 143 F.3d 428, 433 (8th Cir.1998).

(a) Valid agreement. The motion should state that the agreement is a valid agreement to arbitrate. ***Dealer Computer Servs.***, 588 F.3d at 886. The validity of a contractual agreement to arbitrate is determined by the relevant state's law governing the formation of contracts generally. ***First Options v. Kaplan***, 514 U.S. 938, 944 (1995). See "Contractual defenses," §2.2.2(9), p. 655. When an arbitration agreement is valid, parties to the agreement—and, in certain circumstances, nonsignatories—can compel arbitration or be compelled to arbitrate.

[1] General rule – parties agreed. The court cannot require a party to arbitrate a dispute unless the party has entered into a valid contractual agreement to do so. *See* ***Howsam v. Dean Witter Reynolds, Inc.***, 537 U.S. 79, 83 (2002); ***First Options***, 514 U.S. at 943; ***Banks***, 435 F.3d at 540; ***R.J. Griffin & Co. v. Beach Club II Homeowners Ass'n***, 384 F.3d 157, 160 (4th Cir.2004); ***InterGen N.V. v. Grina***, 344 F.3d 134, 142 (1st Cir.2003); ***Bratt Enters. v. Noble Int'l***, 338 F.3d 609, 612 (6th Cir.2003); ***Specht v. Netscape Comms.***, 306 F.3d 17, 26 (2d Cir. 2002); ***Penn v. Ryan's Family Steak Houses, Inc.***, 269 F.3d 753, 758 (7th Cir.2001); ***Brown v. ITT Consumer Fin. Corp.***, 211 F.3d 1217, 1221 (11th Cir.2000).

[2] Exception – party is not signatory. A nonsignatory to a contract can compel arbitration or be compelled to arbitrate in some situations. *See* ***Todd v. Steamship Mut. Underwriting Ass'n (Bermuda) Ltd.***, 601 F.3d 329, 333-34 (5th Cir.2010); ***Ross v. American Express Co.***, 547 F.3d 137, 143 (2d Cir.2008); ***R.J. Griffin & Co.***, 384 F.3d at 161.

NOTE

Whether a nonsignatory can compel arbitration or be compelled to arbitrate may depend on whether the party resisting arbitration is the nonsignatory. E.g., ***Covington****, 650 F.3d at 561 (nonsignatory-president and nonsignatory-V.P. of signatory-corporation could not be compelled to arbitrate in their individual capacities because they were not personally bound to arbitration agreement based only on their positions in corporation).*

[a] Equitable estoppel. A nonsignatory can compel arbitration or be compelled to arbitrate under the doctrine of equitable estoppel in the following situations:

- **Party relies on terms of contract.** A party can be prevented from claiming the benefits of a contract while simultaneously seeking to avoid an arbitration clause in the contract. *See* ***Comer v. Micor, Inc.***, 436 F.3d 1098, 1101 (9th Cir.2006). For example, a nonsignatory can compel arbitration when a signatory to a written contract containing an arbitration clause relies on the terms of the contract as the basis for its claims against the nonsignatory. ***Weingarten Rlty. Investors v. Miller***, 661 F.3d 904, 912 (5th Cir.2011); ***Brantley v. Republic Mortg. Ins.***, 424 F.3d 392, 395-96 (4th Cir.2005); ***MS Dealer Serv. v. Franklin***, 177 F.3d 942, 947 (11th Cir. 1999); *see also* ***Comer***, 436 F.3d at 1101-02 (nonsignatory was not compelled to arbitration when his claims were not based on contract). Similarly, a nonsignatory can be compelled to arbitrate when it claims benefits under a contract that includes an arbitration clause. ***Washington Mut. Fin. Grp. v. Bailey***, 364 F.3d 260, 267 (5th Cir.2004).

- **Signatory alleges concerted action.** A nonsignatory can compel arbitration when a signatory to a written contract containing an arbitration clause alleges that the nonsignatory and another signatory engaged in interdependent and concerted misconduct relating to the contract. ***Brantley***, 424 F.3d at 396; ***MS Dealer Serv.***, 177 F.3d at 947; *see* ***Grigson v. Creative Artists Agency, L.L.C.***, 210 F.3d 524, 530-31 (5th Cir. 2000). However, some courts have required a relationship between the nonsignatory and the signatory party being ordered to arbitrate that justifies a conclusion that the signatory consented to extend the agreement to the nonsignatory. *See, e.g.,* ***Ross***, 547 F.3d at 145-46 (D1, nonsignatory credit-card company, could not compel arbitration even though P-cardholders, who held cards with D2, signatory credit-card company, but not with D1, alleged conspiracy between D1 and D2; insufficient relationship between D1 and Ps to show that Ps intended to arbitrate with D1).

[b] Nonsignatory is third-party beneficiary. A third-party beneficiary of a contract containing an arbitration clause can be subject to that clause and compelled to arbitrate. ***InterGen***, 344 F.3d at 146; *see* ***Bridas S.A.P.I.C. v. Government of Turkmenistan***, 345 F.3d 347, 355-56 (5th Cir.2003); *see also* ***R.J. Griffin & Co.***, 384 F.3d at 161 (nonsignatory estopped from refusing to comply with arbitration clause when it seeks or receives direct benefit from contract containing clause).

[c] Nonsignatory is principal. An agent can commit its nonsignatory principal to an arbitration agreement. ***InterGen***, 344 F.3d at 147; *see also* ***Comer***, 436 F.3d at 1104 n.10 (contract and agency principles can bind nonsignatories to arbitration agreements); ***Bridas S.A.P.I.C.***, 345 F.3d at 356 (under alter-ego and agency theories, nonsignatory can be required to arbitrate).

(b) Dispute within scope of agreement. The motion should state that the dispute falls within the scope of the arbitration agreement. ***Dealer Computer Servs.***, 588 F.3d at 886; ***Century Indem. Co. v. Certain Underwriters at Lloyd's***, 584 F.3d 513, 523 (3d Cir.2009). Whether a dispute falls within the scope of an agreement is determined by federal law on arbitrability. ***Century Indem.***, 584 F.3d at 524; ***Donaldson Co. v. Burroughs Diesel, Inc.***, 581 F.3d 726, 731 (8th Cir.2009). See "Questions of arbitrability," §2.3.2, p. 658.

(2) Dispute is arbitrable.

(a) All claims are arbitrable. If all the claims are arbitrable, the motion should state that the claims are arbitrable and there is no other legal constraint, such as a federal statute or policy, that renders the claims nonarbitrable. *See* ***Mitsubishi Motors Corp. v. Soler Chrysler-Plymouth, Inc.***, 473 U.S. 614, 628 (1985); ***Dealer***

Computer Servs., 588 F.3d at 886. See "Dispute not arbitrable," §2.2.2(2), this page. Claims under some federal statutes are arbitrable. *See, e.g.*, ***Guyden v. Aetna Inc.***, 544 F.3d 376, 383-84 (2d Cir.2008) (retaliation claims under Sarbanes-Oxley Act are subject to arbitration under FAA); ***Landis v. Pinnacle Eye Care, LLC***, 537 F.3d 559, 562-63 (6th Cir.2008) (claims under Uniformed Services Employment and Reemployment Rights Act are subject to arbitration under FAA); ***Bautista v. Star Cruises***, 396 F.3d 1289, 1299-1300 (11th Cir.2005) (FAA exemption for seamen's employment contracts does not apply to certain foreign arbitration agreements).

(b) Some claims are arbitrable. If only some of the claims are arbitrable, the motion should state which claims are arbitrable and that those arbitrable claims must be sent to arbitration, even if it results in piecemeal litigation. ***KPMG LLP v. Cocchi***, ___ U.S. ___, 132 S.Ct. 23, 26 (2011).

4. Request stay. The motion should request a stay of the lawsuit pending resolution of the arbitration proceedings. *See* 9 U.S.C. §3 (stay of suit that raises arbitrable issues); ***Lloyd v. Hovensa, LLC***, 369 F.3d 263, 269 (3d Cir.2004) (stay required if requested); *see also* ***Mendez v. Puerto Rican Int'l Cos.***, 553 F.3d 709, 711 (3d Cir. 2009) (stay applies only to parties who are compelled to arbitration; federal-court litigation continues for noncompelled parties); ***Halim v. Great Gatsby's Auction Gallery***, 516 F.3d 557, 561 (7th Cir.2008) (when party moves to compel arbitration, court should stay proceedings rather than dismiss).

NOTE

By requesting a stay, the movant ensures that the order directing the arbitration to proceed is interlocutory and thus not appealable. 9 U.S.C. §16(b)(1), (b)(2); see ***Lloyd****, 369 F.3d at 270-71;* ***Apache Bohai Corp., LDC v. Texaco China, B.V.****, 330 F.3d 307, 309 (5th Cir.2003). However, if the court orders the parties to arbitration and also dismisses the suit, the order can be appealed.* ***Green Tree Fin. Corp. v. Randolph****, 531 U.S. 79, 89 (2000). But see* ***Dees v. Billy****, 394 F.3d 1290, 1294 (9th Cir.2005) (administrative order closing case following order compelling arbitration is not final, appealable order under FAA). See "Appellate Review," §5, p. 666.*

---

§2.2 Response.

1. In writing. The response should be in writing. *See* FRCP 7(b)(1)(A).

2. Grounds. When appropriate, the party seeking to avoid arbitration should allege the following in its response:

(1) No agreement to arbitrate. The responding party should allege that there was no agreement to arbitrate. The presumption in favor of arbitration disappears when the parties dispute the existence of a valid arbitration agreement. *See* ***First Options v. Kaplan***, 514 U.S. 938, 944-45 (1995); ***American Heritage Life Ins. v. Lang***, 321 F.3d 533, 537-38 (5th Cir.2003); ***Dumais v. American Golf Corp.***, 299 F.3d 1216, 1220 (10th Cir.2002); *see also* ***EEOC v. Waffle House, Inc.***, 534 U.S. 279, 294 (2002) (because FAA favors enforcement of private contractual agreements, court first looks at whether parties agreed to arbitrate, not at general policy goals). When the dispute is whether a party agreed to enter into an arbitration agreement in the first place, and not simply whether the dispute is within the scope of the arbitration agreement, some courts have held that any ambiguities must be resolved against the drafter. *See* ***Kristian v. Comcast Corp.***, 446 F.3d 25, 35 (1st Cir.2006). Some courts will not order arbitration if the arbitration clause is impermissibly vague. *See, e.g.*, ***Marks 3-Zet-Ernst Marks GmbH v. Presstek, Inc.***, 455 F.3d 7, 9-10 (1st Cir.2006) (arbitration clause did not adequately identify arbitration body and required application of nonexistent set of arbitral rules).

(2) Dispute not arbitrable. The responding party should allege that a federal statute or policy renders the dispute nonarbitrable under the FAA. *See, e.g.*, ***American Bankers Ins. v. Inman***, 436 F.3d 490, 493-94 (5th Cir.2006) (under McCarran-Ferguson Act, 15 U.S.C. §1012(b), state insurance law preempts FAA); ***Brown v. Nabors Offshore Corp.***, 339 F.3d 391, 392 (5th Cir.2003) (FAA exempts seamen's employment contracts from arbitration). Courts typically consider three factors in determining whether Congress intended to prohibit the application of the

FAA to a particular statutory right: (1) the statute's text, (2) its legislative history, and (3) whether there is an inherent conflict between arbitration and the statute's underlying purposes. ***Landis v. Pinnacle Eye Care, LLC***, 537 F.3d 559, 562 (6th Cir.2008); ***Davis v. Southern Energy Homes, Inc.***, 305 F.3d 1268, 1273 (11th Cir.2002); ***Walton v. Rose Mobile Homes LLC***, 298 F.3d 470, 473-74 (5th Cir.2002).

(3) Claim not arbitrable. The responding party should allege that one or more of the claims is not arbitrable. *See* ***KPMG LLP v. Cocchi***, ___ U.S. ___, 132 S.Ct. 23, 26 (2011). If a dispute involves multiple claims and only some of those claims are arbitrable, the court can compel arbitration only for those claims that are arbitrable. *Id.*

PRACTICE TIP

If there are both arbitrable and nonarbitrable claims involved in a suit and a plaintiff wants to avoid being compelled to arbitrate, the plaintiff can amend the complaint, drop the arbitrable claims, and proceed with the nonarbitrable claims in court. See, e.g., ***French v. Wachovia Bank***, *574 F.3d 830, 835 (7th Cir.2009). But if the plaintiff wants to later assert the arbitrable claims, it may have to defend against arguments that it waived the arbitrable claims or is estopped from asserting them. Id. at 835-36.* *See "Waiver," §2.2.2(11), p. 657.*

---

(4) Interstate commerce not involved. The responding party should allege that the contract containing the arbitration clause does not involve interstate commerce. *See* 9 U.S.C. §§1, 2; *see, e.g.,* ***Jenkins v. First Am. Cash Advance***, 400 F.3d 868, 874 (11th Cir.2005) (contract satisfied interstate-commerce requirement).

(5) Arbitration will not provide same relief available in court.

(a) Deprivation of substantive rights. The responding party should allege that arbitration will not offer remedies equal to those available in court because the party will be deprived of substantive rights. *See* ***Gilmer v. Interstate/Johnson Lane Corp.***, 500 U.S. 20, 26 (1991) (by agreeing to arbitrate statutory claim, party is not relinquishing substantive rights provided by statute; party is only submitting its case for resolution in arbitral, rather than judicial, forum); ***Morrison v. Circuit City Stores***, 317 F.3d 646, 653 (6th Cir.2003) (same). If an arbitration agreement strips the party of substantive rights that it would have had in court, the court can refuse to enforce the agreement. *See* ***Bradford v. Rockwell Semiconductor Sys.***, 238 F.3d 549, 555-56 (4th Cir.2001); ***Graham Oil Co. v. ARCO Prods.***, 43 F.3d 1244, 1247-48 (9th Cir.1994); ***Parrett v. City of Connersville***, 737 F.2d 690, 697 (7th Cir.1984); *see, e.g.,* ***In re American Express Merchants' Litig.***, 667 F.3d 204, 217-18 (2d Cir.2012) (class-action waiver was unenforceable because pursuing individual arbitrations would be cost-prohibitive, effectively depriving Ps of statutory rights under antitrust laws), *cert. granted*, ___ S.Ct. ___ (2012) (No. 12-133; 11-9-12); ***Kristian***, 446 F.3d at 52-53 (limitation on recovery of fees and expenses was unenforceable); ***Hadnot v. Bay, Ltd.***, 344 F.3d 474, 478 n.14 (5th Cir.2003) (limitation on remedies in Title VII case was unenforceable); ***McCaskill v. SCI Mgmt.***, 298 F.3d 677, 680 (7th Cir.2002) (arbitration agreement that required employee to pay her own attorney fees regardless of outcome of dispute was unenforceable in Title VII case). *But see* ***Jenkins***, 400 F.3d at 877-78 (arbitration provision was enforceable although it prevented participation in class action); ***Investment Partners v. Glamour Shots Licensing, Inc.***, 298 F.3d 314, 318 (5th Cir.2002) (arbitration provision prohibiting punitive damages was enforceable); ***Larry's United Super, Inc. v. Werries***, 253 F.3d 1083, 1085 (8th Cir.2001) (provision prohibiting punitive damages does not make entire arbitration agreement unenforceable).

(b) Burden. The responding party has the burden to show that the arbitration will not provide the same relief available in court. *See* ***In re Cotton Yarn Antitrust Litig.***, 505 F.3d 274, 286-87 (4th Cir.2007) (burden is substantial).

(c) Severance of invalid provisions. Some courts will sever invalid provisions of an otherwise enforceable arbitration agreement rather than void the entire agreement. *E.g.,* ***Kristian***, 446 F.3d at 62-63 (court severed agreement's prohibition on class actions); ***Booker v. Robert Half Int'l***, 413 F.3d 77, 83 (D.C.Cir.2005) (court

severed provision banning award of punitive damages); ***Spinetti v. Service Corp.***, 324 F.3d 212, 214 (3d Cir.2003) (court severed provisions on attorney fees and arbitration costs); ***Morrison***, 317 F.3d at 677 (court severed cost-splitting provision); ***Gannon v. Circuit City Stores***, 262 F.3d 677, 681 (8th Cir.2001) (court severed punitive-damages cap). But if the invalid provisions of the arbitration agreement are too prevalent, the court may be reluctant to sever them. *See, e.g.*, ***Alexander v. Anthony Int'l***, 341 F.3d 256, 271 (3d Cir.2003) (when offensive provisions "permeated" arbitration agreement, provisions were not severed); ***Ingle v. Circuit City Stores***, 328 F.3d 1165, 1180 (9th Cir.2003) (court declined to sever unconscionable provisions because there was "insidious pattern" that favored one side); *see also* ***Iberia Credit Bur., Inc. v. Cingular Wireless LLC***, 379 F.3d 159, 171 (5th Cir.2004) (court refused to save agreement by adding language requiring both sides to arbitrate); ***McMullen v. Meijer, Inc.***, 355 F.3d 485, 496 (6th Cir.2004) (case remanded to determine whether agreement could be enforced without impermissible arbitrator-selection provision).

(6) Movant can modify or ignore rules. The responding party should allege that the moving party can unilaterally modify or ignore the rules of the arbitration agreement. *See* ***Floss v. Ryan's Family Steak Houses, Inc.***, 211 F.3d 306, 315-16 (6th Cir.2000) (ability to choose nature of forum and alter arbitration without notice or consent renders arbitration agreement illusory); ***Hooters, Inc. v. Phillips***, 173 F.3d 933, 939 (4th Cir.1999) (employer's ability to modify rules without notice to employee renders arbitration agreement illusory). A party who has the unilateral right to alter the scope of an arbitration agreement cannot enforce it. ***Dumais***, 299 F.3d at 1219.

(7) Party was not signatory to arbitration agreement. The responding party should allege that it was not a signatory to the arbitration agreement. *See, e.g.*, ***Fleetwood Enters. v. Gaskamp***, 280 F.3d 1069, 1074 (5th Cir.2002) (children not obligated under arbitration agreement signed by parents), *supplemented*, 303 F.3d 570 (5th Cir.2002); *see also* ***InterGen N.V. v. Grina***, 344 F.3d 134, 150 (1st Cir.2003) (federal policy favoring arbitration does not extend to situations in which identity of parties is in dispute). See "Exception – party is not signatory," §2.1.3(1)(a)[2], p. 651.

(8) Movant can select arbitrator. The responding party should allege that the arbitration agreement is unenforceable because it gives the moving party either the exclusive right to select the pool of potential arbitrators from whom the ultimate arbitrators will be chosen or the discretion to disregard the result of the arbitration if the result is against that party. *See* ***McMullen***, 355 F.3d at 494; ***Murray v. United Food & Commercial Workers Int'l Un.***, 289 F.3d 297, 302-03 (4th Cir.2002).

(9) Contractual defenses. The responding party should raise any contractual defenses that would invalidate the arbitration agreement. 9 U.S.C. §2; ***AT&T Mobility LLC v. Concepcion***, ___ U.S. ___, 131 S.Ct. 1740, 1746 (2011) (contractual defenses, such as fraud, duress, or unconscionability, may invalidate arbitration agreement); ***Doctor's Assocs. v. Casarotto***, 517 U.S. 681, 687 (1996) (same); *see also* ***Faber v. Menard, Inc.***, 367 F.3d 1048, 1052 (8th Cir.2004) (whether arbitration agreement is valid is matter of state contract law). The validity of a contractual agreement to arbitrate is determined by the relevant state's law governing the formation of contracts generally. ***First Options***, 514 U.S. at 944; ***Hadnot***, 344 F.3d at 476 n.2; ***Ingle***, 328 F.3d at 1170; ***Specht v. Netscape Comms.***, 306 F.3d 17, 26 (2d Cir.2002); ***Ferguson v. Countrywide Credit Indus.***, 298 F.3d 778, 782 (9th Cir.2002); ***Blair v. Scott Specialty Gases***, 283 F.3d 595, 603 (3d Cir.2002); ***Penn v. Ryan's Family Steak Houses, Inc.***, 269 F.3d 753, 758-59 (7th Cir.2001). But if the state law conflicts with the FAA, the FAA preempts the conflicting state law. *See, e.g.*, ***AT&T Mobility***, ___ U.S. at ___, 131 S.Ct. at 1748 (state law that required availability of class-action arbitration was preempted by FAA because state law interfered with fundamental purposes of arbitration and thus was inconsistent with FAA). For a comprehensive discussion of the defenses used to defeat arbitration, see Bland, Jr. et al., *Consumer Arbitration Agreements: Enforceability & Other Topics*, ch. 6 (6th ed. 2011).

(a) Types of contractual defenses. The following are some contractual defenses that courts have used to invalidate arbitration agreements:

[1] Unconscionability. An arbitration agreement may be invalidated on the ground of unconscionability. ***Doctor's Assocs.***, 517 U.S. at 687; ***Jenkins***, 400 F.3d at 875; ***Iberia Credit Bur.***, 379 F.3d at 166; ***Parilla v. IAP Worldwide Servs., VI, Inc.***, 368 F.3d 269, 276 (3d Cir.2004); ***Morrison***, 317 F.3d at 666. For example,

some states will not enforce contracts of adhesion (i.e., contracts in which bargaining power is clearly unequal). *E.g.*, ***Ticknor v. Choice Hotels Int'l***, 265 F.3d 931, 941 (9th Cir.2001) (Montana law).

[2] Inadequate consideration. An arbitration agreement may be invalidated on the ground of inadequate consideration. ***Morrison***, 317 F.3d at 667. A mutual obligation to arbitrate claims or of continued at-will employment is generally adequate consideration for an arbitration agreement. *See, e.g., id.* at 667-68 (employer's limited right to alter agreement and notice requirement sufficient under Ohio law); ***Michalski v. Circuit City Stores***, 177 F.3d 634, 636-37 (7th Cir.1999) (mutual promise to arbitrate sufficient under Wisconsin law).

[3] No meeting of the minds. An arbitration agreement may be invalidated on the ground that the parties did not have a meeting of the minds on the agreement to arbitrate. *E.g.*, ***American Heritage Life Ins.***, 321 F.3d at 537-38 (agreement to arbitrate signed by illiterate person was invalidated because there was no meeting of the minds).

(b) Applicability of contractual defenses. To attempt to invalidate the arbitration provisions, the responding party must show the following:

[1] The state-law contractual defense applies to all contracts generally and is not limited to determining the enforceability of arbitration provisions. *See* ***Doctor's Assocs.***, 517 U.S. at 686; ***Jenkins***, 400 F.3d at 875; ***Iberia Credit Bur.***, 379 F.3d at 166; ***Ting v. AT&T***, 319 F.3d 1126, 1147-48 (9th Cir.2003). *See generally* Annotation, *Pre-emption by Federal Arbitration Act ... of State Laws Prohibiting or Restricting Formation or Enforcement of Arbitration Agreements*, 108 ALR Fed. 179 (1992 & Supp.2012-13) (discussing when FAA preempts state contract law). In other words, the state law cannot use generally applicable contractual principles in a way that subjects arbitration clauses to special scrutiny. *See* ***Iberia Credit Bur.***, 379 F.3d at 166.

[2] The state-law contractual defense relates specifically to the validity or enforceability of the arbitration provision, not to the contract as a whole. *See* ***Primerica Life Ins. v. Brown***, 304 F.3d 469, 471-72 (5th Cir.2002) (unless defense relates specifically to arbitration agreement, it must be submitted to arbitrator as part of underlying dispute); *see, e.g.*, ***Prima Paint Corp. v. Flood & Conklin Mfg.***, 388 U.S. 395, 404 (1967) (court could not address fraudulent-inducement claim with regard to entire contract).

(10) Arbitration is too expensive. The responding party should allege that the arbitration agreement is unenforceable because it will require the party to pay arbitration fees so expensive that the party effectively will be denied access to the arbitration forum. *See* ***Green Tree Fin. Corp. v. Randolph***, 531 U.S. 79, 90 (2000); ***In re Cotton Yarn Antitrust Litig.***, 505 F.3d at 285. The responding party has the burden of showing the likelihood of incurring prohibitive costs. ***Green Tree Fin.***, 531 U.S. at 92; ***In re American Express Merchants' Litig.***, 667 F.3d at 216; ***In re Cotton Yarn Antitrust Litig.***, 505 F.3d at 285; ***Faber***, 367 F.3d at 1053; ***Spinetti***, 324 F.3d at 217; ***Morrison***, 317 F.3d at 659-60; ***American Heritage Life Ins. v. Orr***, 294 F.3d 702, 711 (5th Cir.2002). Several courts have held that an offer to pay all arbitration costs defeats any claim that the responding party may incur prohibitive costs. ***Carter v. Countrywide Credit Indus.***, 362 F.3d 294, 300 (5th Cir.2004); ***Livingston v. Associates Fin., Inc.***, 339 F.3d 553, 557 (7th Cir.2003); ***Large v. Conseco Fin. Servicing Corp.***, 292 F.3d 49, 56-57 (1st Cir.2002); *see also* ***Anders v. Hometown Mortg. Servs.***, 346 F.3d 1024, 1029 (11th Cir.2003) (offer to pay any costs that arbitrator deems responding party cannot afford prevents attack on costs of arbitration).

(a) Proof of prohibitive costs. The responding party must provide some evidence that it likely will face prohibitive costs in the arbitration and that it is financially unable to pay those costs. *See* ***Livingston***, 339 F.3d at 557 (bare assertion of prohibitive costs insufficient). An affidavit of indigency, by itself, is probably insufficient to demonstrate financial inability to pay the cost of arbitration. *See* ***Blair***, 283 F.3d at 608. Instead, the party claiming indigency should support the allegations in its affidavit with proof of income and expenses, such as W-2 forms or bank statements, demonstrating that the party has limited financial means. *See id.* The party should also factually support the cost of arbitration by showing proof of the filing fees, the arbitrator's rates, and the typical length of an arbitration. *See* ***Faber***, 367 F.3d at 1054; ***Blair***, 283 F.3d at 610; *see, e.g.*, ***Kristian***, 446 F.3d at 52 (costs of pro-

ceeding supported by detailed affidavits). This showing can be made either by obtaining the arbitrator's records or by obtaining information about similar arbitrations from the party seeking arbitration. *See* ***Blair***, 283 F.3d at 609 (discovery should be available on issue of estimated cost of arbitration and claimant's ability to pay). The proof of the party's financial status and the cost of arbitration should be for the time period recognized under the applicable federal or state law. *See, e.g.*, ***Overstreet v. Contigroup Cos.***, 462 F.3d 409, 412 (5th Cir.2006) (under Georgia law, unconscionability analyzed by looking at party's financial status at time contract was made, not at time of dispute).

(b) Fee-splitting provision. Most courts hold that an arbitration agreement is not necessarily unenforceable even though the responding party is required to pay some of the arbitration costs. *E.g.*, ***Morrison***, 317 F.3d at 677 (cost-splitting provision was not interwoven with rest of agreement and could be deleted without affecting agreement's arbitration provisions); ***Bradford***, 238 F.3d at 558 (fee-splitting does not automatically render arbitration agreement unenforceable; appellant not deterred from attempting to vindicate his rights by means of full and fair arbitration proceeding); *see also* ***Faber***, 367 F.3d at 1053 (fee-shifting provisions reviewed on case-by-case basis). *But see* ***Ferguson***, 298 F.3d at 785-86 (fee-allocation scheme that requires employee to split arbitrator's fees with employer renders arbitration agreement substantively unconscionable).

(11) Waiver. The responding party should allege that the moving party was aware of an existing right to arbitrate and waived that right. *See* ***Hooper v. Advance Am., Cash Advance Ctrs.***, 589 F.3d 917, 920 (8th Cir. 2009).

(a) Presumption against waiver. There is a strong presumption against finding that a party waived its contractual right to arbitrate, and any doubts must be resolved in favor of arbitration. ***Texaco Expl. & Prod. v. AmClyde Engineered Prods.***, 243 F.3d 906, 911 (5th Cir.2001); *see* ***Hill v. Ricoh Americas Corp.***, 603 F.3d 766, 775 (10th Cir.2010).

(b) Grounds. A party waives its right to arbitrate by (1) initially pursuing litigation and not diligently attempting to compel arbitration or (2) substantially invoking the judicial process, rather than demonstrating a desire to resolve the dispute through arbitration. *See* ***Zuckerman Spaeder, LLC v. Auffenberg***, 646 F.3d 919, 921-22 (D.C.Cir.2011); ***Forrester v. Penn Lyon Homes, Inc.***, 553 F.3d 340, 343 (4th Cir.2009); ***Texaco Expl. & Prod.***, 243 F.3d at 911; *see, e.g.*, ***Hooper***, 589 F.3d at 921 (when D filed extensive motion to dismiss asking for judgment on merits, D waived right to compel); ***Nicholas v. KBR, Inc.***, 565 F.3d 904, 907 (5th Cir.2009) (when P pursued her case for more than ten months before seeking to compel arbitration, P waived right to compel); *see also* ***Halim v. Great Gatsby's Auction Gallery***, 516 F.3d 557, 562 (7th Cir.2008) (party can expressly or impliedly waive right to arbitrate). What constitutes waiver generally depends on the facts of each case. ***In re Mirant Corp.***, 613 F.3d 584, 589 (5th Cir. 2010); ***Hill***, 603 F.3d at 772. To show the moving party waived its right to arbitration, the responding party can consider addressing the following nonexclusive factors. *See* ***Hill***, 603 F.3d at 772-73.

[1] Whether the moving party's actions were inconsistent with the right to arbitration. *Id.* at 772.

[2] Whether the judicial process has been invoked and whether the parties had already prepared for litigation before the moving party sought arbitration. *Id.*

[3] Whether the moving party requested arbitration close to trial or delayed for a long period before seeking a stay. *Id.*

[4] Whether the moving party filed a counterclaim without asking for a stay. *Id.*

[5] Whether important intervening steps (e.g., discovery that is not available in arbitration) have taken place. *Id.*

[6] Whether the responding party has been prejudiced. *Id.* at 772-73.

NOTE

In many circuits, the responding party must show prejudice resulting from the moving party's conduct that was inconsistent with the existing right to arbitrate. See ***In re Mirant Corp.****, 613 F.3d at 591;* ***Hooper****, 589 F.3d at 922-23 & n.8;* ***U.S. v. Park Place Assocs.****, 563 F.3d 907, 921 (9th Cir.2009);* ***Forrester****, 553 F.3d at 343. But see* ***Khan v. Parsons Global Servs.****, 521 F.3d 421, 425 (D.C.Cir.2008) (prejudice is not required, but court may consider prejudice as relevant factor).*

[7] Whether the moving party is improperly manipulating the judicial process. ***Hill***, 603 F.3d at 774.

[8] The need to maintain the combined efficiency of the public and private dispute-resolution systems. *Id.*; *see, e.g.*, ***Menorah Ins. Co. v. INX Reinsurance Corp.***, 72 F.3d 218, 223 (1st Cir.1995) (inefficiency would result if party were allowed to invoke its right to arbitrate after earlier refusing to do so; party waived right to arbitrate when party sought to invoke arbitration agreement only after default judgment had been rendered and judgment-holder was seeking judicial enforcement of that judgment).

(c) "No waiver" clause. Several courts have held that despite the inclusion of a "no waiver" clause in a contract, a district court can still exercise its inherent power over its docket and find that a party waived its right to arbitration when the party actively participated in litigation rather than pursuing arbitration. *See* ***Republic Ins. v. PAICO Receivables, LLC***, 383 F.3d 341, 348 (5th Cir.2004); ***S&R Co. v. Latona Trucking, Inc.***, 159 F.3d 80, 85-86 (2d Cir.1998).

§2.3 Ruling.

1. Arbitration agreements favored. The FAA applies to all contracts involving interstate commerce and was enacted to overcome courts' reluctance to enforce arbitration agreements. *See* 9 U.S.C. §2; ***Allied-Bruce Terminix Cos. v. Dobson***, 513 U.S. 265, 270-71 (1995). The FAA establishes a strong federal policy in favor of enforcing arbitration agreements. ***Howsam v. Dean Witter Reynolds, Inc.***, 537 U.S. 79, 83 (2002); ***Gilmer v. Interstate/Johnson Lane Corp.***, 500 U.S. 20, 25 (1991); *see also* ***Allied-Bruce Terminix***, 513 U.S. at 276-77 (language of FAA should be interpreted to provide for enforcement of arbitration agreements within full reach of Commerce Clause). Thus, the court should resolve any doubts about the arbitrability of claims in favor of arbitration when deciding whether to grant or deny the motion to compel. ***Tittle v. Enron Corp.***, 463 F.3d 410, 418 (5th Cir.2006); ***Dockser v. Schwartzberg***, 433 F.3d 421, 425 (4th Cir.2006); ***Sink v. Aden Enters.***, 352 F.3d 1197, 1200 (9th Cir.2003); *see* ***InterGen N.V. v. Grina***, 344 F.3d 134, 142 (1st Cir.2003) (as long as parties are bound to arbitrate and court has personal jurisdiction over them, court is under "unflagging, nondiscretionary duty" to grant timely motion to compel arbitration); *see also* ***Turi v. Main St. Adoption Servs.***, 633 F.3d 496, 507 (6th Cir.2011) (narrowly tailored arbitration agreement may not have same presumption of arbitrability as a broader agreement).

2. Questions of arbitrability. In ruling on the motion to compel, courts may decide "questions of arbitrability"—that is, questions relating to whether the parties to a dispute have agreed to submit the dispute to arbitration. ***Howsam***, 537 U.S. at 83; ***In re Van Dusen***, 654 F.3d 838, 844 (9th Cir.2011); ***Tittle***, 463 F.3d at 418; ***Anders v. Hometown Mortg. Servs.***, 346 F.3d 1024, 1027 (11th Cir.2003); *see* ***Granite Rock Co. v. International Bhd. of Teamsters***, ___ U.S. ___, 130 S.Ct. 2847, 2857-58 (2010) (before sending dispute to arbitration, court must be satisfied that formation of arbitration agreement and its enforceability or applicability to dispute are not at issue). Generally, a court, not an arbitrator, will decide the question of arbitrability. *See* ***Howsam***, 537 U.S. at 83. If there is doubt over whether an issue is a question of arbitrability, the presumption in favor of arbitration should make the issue one for the arbitrator. ***United Steelworkers of Am. v. Saint Gobain Ceramics & Plastics, Inc.***, 505 F.3d 417, 420 (6th Cir.2007).

(1) Questions for court. Questions for the court can include the following:

• Whether the parties are bound by an arbitration clause in a contract. ***Howsam***, 537 U.S. at 84.

• Whether an arbitration clause applies to a particular type of controversy. ***Howsam***, 537 U.S. at 84; *see* ***Anders***, 346 F.3d at 1027; *see, e.g.*, ***Stolt-Nielsen S.A. v. AnimalFeeds Int'l***, ___ U.S. ___, 130 S.Ct. 1758, 1775 (2010) (arbitrators improperly interpreted arbitration agreement to allow for class-action arbitration when agreement was silent on that issue; arbitrators' ruling was not procedural question that arbitrators could answer).

• Whether the parties actually entered into an arbitration agreement. ***DK Jt. V. 1 v. Weyand***, 649 F.3d 310, 317 (5th Cir.2011).

• Whether the arbitration clause itself is valid. *See* ***Preston v. Ferrer***, 552 U.S. 346, 353 (2008); ***Buckeye Check Cashing, Inc. v. Cardegna***, 546 U.S. 440, 445-46 (2006); ***Bridge Fund Capital Corp. v. Fastbucks Franchise Corp.***, 622 F.3d 996, 1000 (9th Cir.2010).

NOTE

The parties can agree to submit questions of arbitrability to an arbitrator, but only if there is "clear and unmistakable" evidence that the parties agreed to do so. ***First Options v. Kaplan***, *514 U.S. 938, 944 (1995); see* ***In re Van Dusen***, *654 F.3d at 843; see, e.g.,* ***Fallo v. High-Tech Inst.***, *559 F.3d 874, 877-78 (8th Cir.2009) (parties clearly intended to submit arbitrability question to arbitrator because parties incorporated AAA rules into arbitration agreement and those rules expressly give arbitrator power to rule on her own jurisdiction).*

(2) Questions for arbitrator. Questions for the arbitrator can include the following:

• Procedural issues such as whether time limits, notice, laches, estoppel, and other conditions precedent to an obligation to arbitrate have been met. ***Howsam***, 537 U.S. at 84-85; *see* ***Stolt-Nielsen S.A.***, ___ U.S. at ___, 130 S.Ct. at 1775; ***Lumbermens Mut. Cas. Co. v. Broadspire Mgmt. Servs.***, 623 F.3d 476, 480-81 (7th Cir. 2010); ***United Steelworkers***, 505 F.3d at 422; *see, e.g.*, ***Green Tree Fin. Corp. v. Bazzle***, 539 U.S. 444, 452-53 (2003) (whether class-action claims are permissible in arbitration contracts is question for arbitrator); ***Dockser***, 433 F.3d at 425 (issue about number of arbitrators is question for arbitrator).

• Whether the entire contract is valid. *See* ***Rent-A-Center, W., Inc. v. Jackson***, ___ U.S. ___, 130 S.Ct. 2772, 2778 (2010); ***Preston***, 552 U.S. at 353; ***Buckeye Check Cashing***, 546 U.S. at 445-46; ***Bridge Fund Capital Corp.***, 622 F.3d at 1000.

§3. MODIFYING OR VACATING ARBITRATION AWARD

The FAA permits any party to an arbitration to modify or vacate an arbitration award. *See* 9 U.S.C. §§10, 11. Applications to modify or vacate an arbitration award are generally not governed by the FRCPs and are treated procedurally as motions. *See* 9 U.S.C. §6; FRCP 81(a)(6)(B); ***IFC Interconsult, AG v. Safeguard Int'l Partners***, 438 F.3d 298, 308-09 (3d Cir.2006); *see, e.g.*, ***Webster v. A.T. Kearney, Inc.***, 507 F.3d 568, 570-71 & n.1 (7th Cir.2007) (party seeking to vacate arbitration award erroneously titled document "complaint"; document should have been titled "motion" and should not have been treated as new civil litigation).

§3.1 Motion.

1. Where to file. The FAA does not confer subject-matter jurisdiction; therefore, a party seeking to modify or vacate an arbitration award in federal court must present an independent basis for jurisdiction, such as diversity or a federal question. ***Moses H. Cone Mem'l Hosp. v. Mercury Constr. Corp.***, 460 U.S. 1, 25 n.32 (1983). Subject-matter jurisdiction and venue are the same as for a motion to confirm a domestic award. See "Where to file," §4.1.1(1), p. 663.

2. In writing. A motion to modify or vacate must be in writing. *See* 9 U.S.C. §§10, 11 (court may vacate, modify, or correct award on application of any party).

3. Limitations period. A motion to modify or vacate must be served within three months after the arbitration award was filed or delivered by the arbitrator. 9 U.S.C. §12.

NOTE

A party has one year after the award was made to file a motion to confirm, but only three months to serve a motion to modify or vacate. See 9 U.S.C. §§9, 12; ***Taylor v. Nelson****, 788 F.2d 220, 225 (4th Cir.1986) (after three-month limitations period ends, party cannot move to modify or vacate arbitration award, not even as response to motion to confirm);* ***Florasynth, Inc. v. Pickholz****, 750 F.2d 171, 174-75 (2d Cir.1984) (same).*

(1) Limitations period begins. The three-month limitations period begins when the award is filed or delivered. 9 U.S.C. §12. Courts disagree on the meaning of "delivered" and on when the limitations period actually begins to run. *See, e.g.,* ***Webster v. A.T. Kearney, Inc.***, 507 F.3d 568, 573-74 (7th Cir.2007) (limitations period begins to run when award is placed in mail); ***Sargent v. Paine Webber Jackson & Curtis, Inc.***, 882 F.2d 529, 531 (D.C.Cir.1989) (limitations period begins to run when award is received); ***Tokura Constr. Co. v. Corporacion Raymond, S.A.***, 533 F.Supp. 1274, 1278 (S.D.Tex.1982) (limitations period begins to run when award is made).

(2) Limitations period ends. The three-month limitations period ends when the motion is served on the adverse party—not when the motion is filed in the court. ***Webster***, 507 F.3d at 571-72; *see* 9 U.S.C. §12.

4. Modifying – grounds. Under the FAA, the exclusive grounds for modifying an arbitration award are stated in 9 U.S.C. §11. ***Hall St. Assocs. v. Mattel, Inc.***, 552 U.S. 576, 584 (2008). The court can modify an arbitration award in the following circumstances:

NOTE

Grounds for modification besides those in 9 U.S.C. §11 may be available when the arbitration award is authorized under the common law or by a different statute. ***Hall St. Assocs.****, 552 U.S. at 590.* *See "Grounds outside FAA," §3.1.5(2), p. 662.*

(1) Evident material miscalculation or mistake. An arbitration award can be modified when there was an evident material miscalculation of figures or an evident material mistake in the description of any person, thing, or property referred to in the award. 9 U.S.C. §11(a). An evident material miscalculation occurs when (1) the record that was before the arbitrator demonstrates an unambiguous and undisputed mistake of fact and (2) when there was strong reliance on that mistake by the arbitrator in making the award. ***Prestige Ford v. Ford Dealer Computer Servs.***, 324 F.3d 391, 396 (5th Cir.2003), *overruled on other grounds*, ***Hall St. Assocs. v. Mattel, Inc.***, 552 U.S. 576 (2008). Generally, only an arbitrator's mistake—not a party's—will result in a modification of the award. *E.g.*, ***AIG Baker Sterling Heights, LLC v. American Multi-Cinema, Inc.***, 508 F.3d 995, 999 (11th Cir.2007) (court cannot modify award when party made mistake in stipulating tax payment at issue). *But see* ***Transnitro, Inc. v. M/V Wave***, 943 F.2d 471, 474 (4th Cir.1991) (court may have power to modify award when mistake is attributable to one or both parties).

(2) Award on unsubmitted matter. An arbitration award can be modified when it is based on a matter that was not submitted to the arbitrator. 9 U.S.C. §11(b); *see* ***Kansas City Luggage & Novelty Workers Un. v. Neevel Luggage Mfg.***, 325 F.2d 992, 994 (8th Cir.1964); ***Orion Shipping & Trading Co. v. Eastern States Pet. Corp.***, 312 F.2d 299, 300-01 (2d Cir.1963).

(3) Imperfect form of award. An arbitration award can be modified when the form of the award is imperfect and the imperfection does not affect the merits of the controversy. 9 U.S.C. §11(c); *see, e.g.*, ***Atlantic Aviation, Inc. v. EBM Grp.***, 11 F.3d 1276, 1284 (5th Cir.1994) (arbitration panel's failure to award balance remaining under contract was clerical error that could be corrected without disturbing merits of decision).

5. Vacating – grounds.

(1) Grounds under FAA. Under the FAA, the exclusive grounds for vacating an arbitration award are stated in 9 U.S.C. §10(a). ***Hall St. Assocs.***, 552 U.S. at 584. The court can vacate an arbitration award in the following circumstances:

NOTE

The Supreme Court has determined that "manifest disregard of the law" is not an independent ground for vacating an arbitration award. ***Hall St. Assocs.****, 552 U.S. at 584-85. After* ***Hall Street****, courts have disagreed on what role that phrase continues to play in FAA cases. Compare* ***Frazier v. CitiFinancial Corp.****, 604 F.3d 1313, 1323-24 (11th Cir.2010) (manifest disregard is not independent ground to vacate; arbitration awards under FAA can be vacated only for reasons in 9 U.S.C. §10), and* ***Citigroup Global Mkts., Inc. v. Bacon****, 562 F.3d 349, 353 (5th Cir. 2009) (same), with* ***Wachovia Secs., LLC v. Brand****, 671 F.3d 472, 483 (4th Cir.2012) (manifest disregard continues either as independent ground for review or as "judicial gloss" on 9 U.S.C. §10), and* ***Comedy Club, Inc. v. Improv W. Assocs.****, 553 F.3d 1277, 1290 (9th Cir.2009) (manifest disregard remains valid ground to vacate because it is part of, or shorthand for, 9 U.S.C. §10(a)(4)). In 2010, the Supreme Court refused to rule on this disagreement. See* ***Stolt-Nielsen S.A. v. AnimalFeeds Int'l****, ___ U.S. ___, 130 S.Ct. 1758, 1768 n.3 (2010). In* ***Hall Street****, the Supreme Court left open the question of whether the parties can contractually agree to different grounds for review—independent of the FAA—that the district court can enforce as part of its inherent power to manage cases under FRCP 16.* ***Hall St. Assocs.****, 552 U.S. at 591-92; see* ***Johnson v. Wells Fargo Home Mortg., Inc.****, 635 F.3d 401, 415-16 (9th Cir.2011).*

(a) Corruption, fraud, or undue means. An arbitration award can be vacated if the award was procured by corruption, fraud, or undue means. 9 U.S.C. §10(a)(1). A party seeking to vacate an award on this ground must demonstrate that the improper conduct influenced the outcome of the arbitration. ***Delta Mine Holding Co. v. AFC Coal Props., Inc.***, 280 F.3d 815, 822 (8th Cir.2001). In other words, there must be a causal connection between the improper conduct and the arbitration award. *See* ***PaineWebber Grp. v. Zinsmeyer Trusts Prtshp.***, 187 F.3d 988, 994 (8th Cir.1999).

(b) Partiality. An arbitration award can be vacated if there is evidence of partiality or corruption by an arbitrator. 9 U.S.C. §10(a)(2). Because an arbitrator must disclose any dealings that might create an impression of possible bias, the arbitrator's nondisclosure of certain facts can lead to a finding of evident partiality. *See* ***Commonwealth Coatings Corp. v. Continental Cas. Co.***, 393 U.S. 145, 149-50 (1968). However, the circuits are divided on the standard of proof required to make this finding. The Fifth, Eighth, and Ninth Circuits hold that an arbitrator displays evident partiality when the undisclosed facts would create a reasonable impression of the arbitrator's partiality. ***New Regency Prods. v. Nippon Herald Films, Inc.***, 501 F.3d 1101, 1106 (9th Cir.2007); ***Olson v. Merrill Lynch, Pierce, Fenner & Smith, Inc.***, 51 F.3d 157, 159-60 (8th Cir.1995); *see* ***Positive Software Solutions, Inc. v. New Century Mortg. Corp.***, 476 F.3d 278, 283 (5th Cir.2007) ("reasonable impression of bias" standard should be interpreted practically; thus, nondisclosure of trivial or insubstantial prior relationship between arbitrator and parties does not require award to be vacated). The Second, Fourth, Sixth, Tenth, and Eleventh Circuits have adopted a stricter standard and hold that an arbitrator displays evident partiality only when a reasonable person would conclude that the arbitrator was partial to one of the parties; in other words, the alleged partiality must be direct, definite, and capable of demonstration. ***University Commons-Urbana, Ltd. v. Universal Constructors Inc.***, 304 F.3d 1331, 1339 (11th Cir.2002); ***ANR Coal Co. v. Cogentrix of N.C., Inc.***, 173 F.3d 493, 500 (4th Cir.1999); ***Apperson v. Fleet Carrier Corp.***, 879 F.2d 1344, 1358 (6th Cir.1989); ***Morelite Constr. Corp. v. New York City Dist. Council Carpenters Benefit Funds***, 748 F.2d 79, 84 (2d Cir.1984); ***Ormsbee Dev. Co. v. Grace***, 668 F.2d 1140, 1147 (10th Cir.1982). A party seeking to vacate an award on the ground of partiality must have raised the objection to the arbitration panel, or else the objection is waived. ***Delta Mine Holding***, 280 F.3d at 821; ***Apperson***, 879 F.2d at 1358-59.

(c) Misconduct. An arbitration award can be vacated if the arbitrators were guilty of misconduct by refusing to postpone the hearing, by not allowing evidence pertinent and material to the controversy, or by engaging in any other misbehavior that prejudiced the rights of any party. 9 U.S.C. §10(a)(3); ***U.S. Life Ins. v. Superior Nat'l Ins.***, 591 F.3d 1167, 1174 (9th Cir.2010). A party seeking to vacate an award on this ground must demonstrate that the misconduct influenced the outcome of the arbitration. ***Delta Mine Holding***, 280 F.3d at 822. In other words, there must be a causal connection between the misconduct and the arbitration award. *See* ***PaineWebber Grp.***, 187 F.3d at 994.

(d) Powers exceeded. An arbitration award can be vacated if the arbitrators exceeded their powers or so imperfectly executed them that a mutual, final, and definite award was not made. 9 U.S.C. §10(a)(4); *see* ***U.S. Life Ins.***, 591 F.3d at 1177 (arbitrator does not exceed authority if she makes plausible interpretation of arbitration agreement); *see, e.g.*, ***Stolt-Nielsen S.A.***, ___ U.S. at ___, 130 S.Ct. at 1767 (arbitrators exceeded powers when they inferred from arbitration agreement that parties agreed to class-action arbitration even though agreement was silent on that issue); *see also* ***Smith v. Transport Workers Un.***, 374 F.3d 372, 375 (5th Cir.2004) (arbitrators exceeded authority by modifying award in manner not permitted by agreement). The arbitrators' powers and authority depend on the contractual provisions under which they were appointed. ***Szuts v. Dean Witter Reynolds, Inc.***, 931 F.2d 830, 831 (11th Cir.1991); *see* ***Smith***, 374 F.3d at 374-75. *But see* ***Kergosien v. Ocean Energy, Inc.***, 390 F.3d 346, 354 (5th Cir.2004) (arbitrator's authority is defined by scope of submissions provided to arbitrator, as well as contract), *overruled on other grounds*, ***Citigroup Global Mkts., Inc. v. Bacon***, 562 F.3d 349 (5th Cir.2009). Thus, the court can vacate an arbitration award under 9 U.S.C. §10(a)(4) if the arbitrator who granted the award was appointed in violation of the terms of the arbitration agreement. ***R.J. O'Brien & Assoc. v. Pipkin***, 64 F.3d 257, 263 (7th Cir.1995); ***Cargill Rice, Inc. v. Empresa Nicaraguense Dealimentos Basicos***, 25 F.3d 223, 226 (4th Cir.1994); *see also* ***Avis Rent A Car Sys. v. Garage Empls. Un.***, 791 F.2d 22, 25 (2d Cir.1986) (courts generally enforce selection clauses strictly). *But see* ***Bulko v. Morgan Stanley DW Inc.***, 450 F.3d 622, 626 (5th Cir.2006) (dicta; even assuming that arbitrator's selection did not comply with parties' agreement, selection was trivial departure from agreement and did not justify award being vacated).

(2) Grounds outside FAA. Other grounds besides those in 9 U.S.C. §10 may be available when the arbitration award is authorized under the common law or by a different statute. ***Hall St. Assocs.***, 552 U.S. at 590; *see, e.g.*, ***Ramos-Santiago v. United Parcel Serv.***, 524 F.3d 120, 124-25 & n.3 (1st Cir.2008) (arbitration award under collective-bargaining agreement was evaluated under standard of manifest disregard of law); ***International Un., United Mine Workers v. Marrowbone Dev. Co.***, 232 F.3d 383, 389-90 (4th Cir.2000) (arbitration award under collective-bargaining agreement was vacated because party was denied fair hearing); ***Stroehmann Bakeries, Inc. v. Local 776, Int'l Bhd. of Teamsters***, 969 F.2d 1436, 1441-42 (3d Cir.1992) (arbitration award under collective-bargaining agreement was vacated because award was against public policy); *see also* ***Saturn Telecomms. Servs. v. Covad Comms.***, 560 F.Supp.2d 1278, 1282 (S.D.Fla.2008) (parties may contractually specify rules under which arbitration will be conducted, but there must be express provision to proceed outside FAA).

§3.2 Response.

1. In writing. The response to a motion to modify or vacate must be in writing. *See* 9 U.S.C. §§10, 11 (court may vacate, modify, or correct award on application of any party).

2. Grounds. The responding party should file a response objecting to all the grounds in the motion. See "Modifying – grounds," §3.1.4, p. 660; "Vacating – grounds," §3.1.5, p. 661. The responding party may be able to argue that the party seeking to modify or vacate the award waived its objection by not filing a clear and timely written objection during the arbitration proceeding. *See, e.g.*, ***Environmental Barrier Co. v. Slurry Sys.***, 540 F.3d 598, 606-07 (7th Cir.2008) (D waived arbitrability objection when it did not challenge absence of agreement to arbitrate during arbitration proceeding).

PRACTICE TIP

In addition to the response, the responding party can consider filing a motion for sanctions based on 28 U.S.C. §1927 if the motion to vacate an arbitration award is meritless; 28 U.S.C. §1927 allows sanctions when an attorney multiplies the proceedings unreasonably and vexatiously. See ***DMA Int'l v. Qwest Comms. Int'l****, 585 F.3d 1341, 1345-46 (10th Cir.2009). See "Multiplying proceedings unreasonably," ch. 5-O, §3.8, p. 388.*

§3.3 District court's review of arbitration award. The district court's power to review an arbitration award is extremely narrow. ***Kyocera Corp. v. Prudential-Bache Trade Servs.***, 341 F.3d 987, 998 (9th Cir.2003); *see* ***Major League Baseball Players Ass'n v. Garvey***, 532 U.S. 504, 510 (2001) (labor arbitration decision could not be overturned even if "serious error" shown); *see, e.g.*, ***Positive Software Solutions, Inc. v. New Century Mortg. Corp.***, 619 F.3d 458, 461-62 (5th Cir.2010) (district court exceeded authority when it sanctioned attorney for her actions during arbitration; court has no authority to interfere with arbitration proceeding); *see also* ***IDS Life Ins. v. Royal Alliance Assocs.***, 266 F.3d 645, 651 (7th Cir.2001) (lack of clarity or logical consistency in arbitrator's ruling does not justify vacating award). Although the district court has a narrow standard of review, when it is presented with a motion to modify or vacate, it must consider and rule on the motion. *See* ***Johnson v. Wells Fargo Home Mortg., Inc.***, 635 F.3d 401, 411-12 (9th Cir.2011) (district court cannot decline to consider motion). Even when the arbitrator's award is vacated or deemed unenforceable, the appropriate remedy is not a judicial determination but rather a remand of the case for further arbitration proceedings. ***Garvey***, 532 U.S. at 511.

§4. CONFIRMING ARBITRATION AWARD

Applications to confirm an arbitration award are generally not governed by the FRCPs and are treated procedurally as motions. *See* 9 U.S.C. §6; FRCP 81(a)(6)(B); ***IFC Interconsult, AG v. Safeguard Int'l Partners***, 438 F.3d 298, 308-09 (3d Cir.2006); *cf.* ***Webster v. A.T. Kearney, Inc.***, 507 F.3d 568, 570-71 & n.1 (7th Cir.2007) (party seeking to vacate arbitration award erroneously titled document "complaint"; document should have been titled "motion" and should not have been treated as new civil litigation).

§4.1 Motion to confirm domestic award. The FAA permits any party to an arbitration to confirm an award made in a U.S. arbitration proceeding. *See* 9 U.S.C. §9. Once confirmed and entered by a district court, the award has the same force and effect as a judgment, and it can be enforced as a judgment rendered in the court where it is entered. *Id.* §13.

1. Motion.

(1) Where to file.

(a) Subject-matter jurisdiction. A motion to confirm a domestic arbitration award can be brought in a district court only if there is an independent ground for subject-matter jurisdiction. ***Moses H. Cone Mem'l Hosp. v. Mercury Constr. Corp.***, 460 U.S. 1, 25 n.32 (1983); ***Perpetual Secs., Inc. v. Tang***, 290 F.3d 132, 140 (2d Cir.2002). An independent ground for subject-matter jurisdiction exists when a complaint establishes federal-question or diversity jurisdiction. *See* ***Perpetual Secs.***, 290 F.3d at 136-37; *see also* ***U.S. v. American Soc'y of Composers, Authors & Publ'rs***, 32 F.3d 727, 731 (2d Cir.1994) (consent judgment that provided for continuing jurisdiction by district court constituted independent source of jurisdiction for motion to modify or vacate arbitration award). See "Choosing the Court—Jurisdiction," ch. 2-F, p. 112.

(b) Venue. A motion to confirm a domestic arbitration award can be brought in the district specified in the agreement, in the district where the award was made, or in any proper district under the general venue statute. *See* 9 U.S.C. §9; 28 U.S.C. §1391; ***Cortez Byrd Chips, Inc. v. Bill Harbert Constr. Co.***, 529 U.S. 193, 195 (2000). See "General Venue Statute," ch. 2-G, §3, p. 144; "Arbitration," ch. 2-G, §4.2.12, p. 147.

(2) Limitations period. Any party can file a motion to confirm a domestic arbitration award within one year after the award was made. 9 U.S.C. §9. Courts are divided on whether this provision imposes a one-year

statute of limitations on filing motions to confirm. *Compare* ***Photopaint Techs. v. Smartlens Corp.***, 335 F.3d 152, 158 (2d Cir.2003) (provision imposes one-year statute of limitations), ***FIA Card Servs. v. Gachiengu***, 571 F.Supp.2d 799, 804 (S.D.Tex.2008) (same), ***General Elec. Co. v. Anson Stamping Co.***, 426 F.Supp.2d 579, 591 (W.D.Ky.2006) (same), *and* ***In re Consolidated Rail Corp.***, 867 F.Supp. 25, 28 (D.D.C.1994) (same), *with* ***Val-U Constr. Co. v. Rosebud Sioux Tribe***, 146 F.3d 573, 581 (8th Cir.1998) (provision is permissive, not mandatory, allowing confirmation beyond one-year period), *and* ***Sverdrup Corp. v. WHC Constructors, Inc.***, 989 F.2d 148, 156 (4th Cir.1993) (same).

(3) Prerequisite to filing. Before filing a motion to confirm a domestic arbitration award, the parties must show they have provided in their arbitration agreement that a judgment will be entered on the arbitration award. 9 U.S.C. §9.

(4) Attachments. When the motion and arbitration award are filed for entry of judgment, the party seeking confirmation must attach the following documents:

(a) The arbitration agreement. 9 U.S.C. §13(a).

(b) Any selection or appointment of an additional arbitrator or umpire. *Id.*

(c) Any written extension of the time to make the award. *Id.*

(d) The arbitration award. *Id.* §13(b).

(e) Each notice, affidavit, or other paper used in an application to confirm, modify, or correct the award, and a copy of each court order ruling on the application. *Id.* §13(c).

2. Response. A party can challenge the motion to confirm by showing that the award should be vacated, modified, or corrected. *See* 9 U.S.C. §§10, 11; ***Taylor v. Nelson***, 788 F.2d 220, 226 (4th Cir.1986). See "Modifying or Vacating Arbitration Award," §3, p. 659. A motion to vacate, modify, or correct must be served within three months after the arbitration award was filed or delivered. 9 U.S.C. §12. See "Limitations period," §3.1.3, p. 660.

3. Ruling. Once the motion and proposed order confirming the domestic arbitration award are filed, the court must confirm the award unless there is a response seeking to vacate, modify, or correct the award. *See* 9 U.S.C. §9; ***Taylor***, 788 F.2d at 225; *see also* 9 U.S.C. §10 (grounds and procedure for vacating arbitration award), §11 (grounds and procedure for modifying or correcting arbitration award); ***Pfizer Inc. v. Uprichard***, 422 F.3d 124, 130 (3d Cir. 2005) (court cannot condition enforcement of arbitration award on party's compliance with new substantive requirement).

§4.2 Motion to confirm foreign award. By implementing provisions of the U.N. Convention on the Recognition and Enforcement of Foreign Arbitral Awards (commonly referred to as the New York Convention), chapter 2 of the FAA (9 U.S.C. §§201-208) permits any party to request confirmation of an award made in a foreign arbitration proceeding. *See* 9 U.S.C. §207; Convention on the Recognition and Enforcement of Foreign Arbitral Awards, art. IV, *opened for signature* June 10, 1958, 21 U.S.T. 2517, 330 U.N.T.S. 38 [N.Y. Convention]; ***Phoenix A.G. v. Ecoplas, Inc.***, 391 F.3d 433, 435-36 (2d Cir.2004); *see also* ***Industrial Risk Insurers v. M.A.N. Gutehoffnungshütte GmbH***, 141 F.3d 1434, 1440 (11th Cir.1998) (FAA ch. 2 covers the enforcement of New York Convention in U.S. courts). The New York Convention applies to (1) awards made in a different country than where confirmation is sought and (2) awards "not considered domestic" in the country where confirmation is sought. N.Y. Convention, art. I.1; ***Industrial Risk Insurers***, 141 F.3d at 1440. Under the FAA, an award is considered nondomestic when it (1) is not entirely between citizens of the United States, (2) involves property located outside the United States, (3) involves contractual performance outside the United States, or (4) has some other reasonable relation to one or more foreign countries. *See* 9 U.S.C. §202; ***Industrial Risk Insurers***, 141 F.3d at 1440-41 & n.6; *see also* ***Bergesen v. Joseph Muller Corp.***, 710 F.2d 928, 932 (2d Cir.1983) (awards not considered domestic are made within legal framework of another country).

1. Motion. Confirmation of a foreign arbitration award is proper if the party seeking confirmation complies with the requirements of the New York Convention and the party opposing confirmation does not prove any grounds to bar the confirmation. *See* 9 U.S.C. §10(a); N.Y. Convention, art. V; ***Geotech Lizenz AG v. Evergreen Sys.***, 697 F.Supp. 1248, 1252 (E.D.N.Y.1988).

(1) Where to file.

(a) Subject-matter jurisdiction. A motion to confirm a foreign arbitration award is deemed to arise under the laws and treaties of the United States, and the federal district courts have original jurisdiction over such a motion, regardless of the amount in controversy. *See* 9 U.S.C. §203.

(b) Venue. A motion to confirm a foreign arbitration award can be brought (1) in any federal court where a suit or proceeding involving the controversy between the parties could be brought, if not for the arbitration agreement, or (2) in the court for the district and division of the place designated in the agreement as the place of arbitration, if it is within the United States. 9 U.S.C. §204; *see* ***Cortez Byrd Chips, Inc. v. Bill Harbert Constr. Co.***, 529 U.S. 193, 202 n.3 (2000) (noting liberal choices for venue in confirmation actions under FAA ch. 2).

(2) Limitations period. Any party can file a motion to confirm a foreign arbitration award within three years after the award was made. 9 U.S.C. §207; ***China Minmetals Materials Imp. & Exp. Co. v. Chi Mei Corp.***, 334 F.3d 274, 279 (3d Cir.2003); ***Seetransport Wiking Trader Schiffarhtsgesellschaft MBH & Co. v. Navimpex Centrala Navala***, 989 F.2d 572, 581 (2d Cir.1993).

(3) No prerequisite to filing. Before filing a motion to confirm a foreign arbitration award, the parties do not have to provide in an agreement that a judgment will be entered on the award. *See* 9 U.S.C. §207; ***Phoenix A.G.***, 391 F.3d at 436-37.

(4) Attachments. When the motion is filed for entry of judgment, the party seeking confirmation must attach (1) the duly authenticated original award or a duly certified copy, (2) the original arbitration agreement or a duly certified copy, and (3) if the award or agreement is in a language different from the official language of the country where the award is relied on, a duly certified translation of the award or agreement. N.Y. Convention, art. IV.

2. Response. A party can challenge the motion to confirm a foreign arbitration award.

(1) Applicable law. The extent of FAA applicability to nondomestic arbitration awards depends on whether (1) the award was rendered in a foreign country or under a foreign country's law or (2) the award was rendered in the United States or under U.S. law. *See* ***Yusuf Ahmed Alghanim & Sons, W.L.L. v. Toys "R" Us, Inc.***, 126 F.3d 15, 23 (2d Cir.1997), *overruled in part on other grounds*, ***Hall St. Assocs. v. Mattel, Inc.***, 552 U.S. 576 (2008); ***International Std. Elec. Corp. v. Bridas Sociedad Anonima Petrolera, Industrial y Comercial***, 745 F.Supp. 172, 177 (S.D.N.Y.1990).

(a) Award rendered outside United States. If the nondomestic arbitration award was rendered outside the United States, the party challenging the motion to confirm is limited to the grounds for refusing or deferring the award's confirmation under article V of the New York Convention. *See* ***China Minmetals***, 334 F.3d at 283; ***Ministry of Def. & Support for the Armed Forces of the Islamic Republic of Iran v. Cubic Def. Sys.***, 29 F.Supp.2d 1168, 1171-72 (S.D.Cal.1998); *see, e.g.*, ***M&C Corp. v. Erwin Behr GmbH & Co., KG***, 87 F.3d 844, 851 (6th Cir.1996) (in U.S. confirmation proceeding, only the grounds in the New York Convention, not the FAA, applied because award was rendered under international arbitration law and involved two foreign parties).

NOTE

If the award was rendered outside the United States, the response to the motion to confirm cannot seek to modify or vacate the foreign arbitration award; the responding party can only object to the confirmation. See ***Yusuf Ahmed Alghanim & Sons****, 126 F.3d at 21;* ***M&C Corp.****, 87 F.3d at 848-49. If the responding party seeks to modify or vacate the award, those issues must be heard by a court in the country where the award was made or whose procedural law controlled the making of the award. See N.Y. Convention, arts. V.1.(e), VI;* ***Yusuf Ahmed Alghanim & Sons****, 126 F.3d at 21;* ***M&C Corp.****, 87 F.3d at 848-49;* ***International Std. Elec. Corp.****, 745 F.Supp. at 178.*

(b) **Award rendered in United States.** If the nondomestic arbitration award was rendered in the United States, the party challenging the motion to confirm (1) can allege grounds for refusing or deferring the award's confirmation under article V of the New York Convention and (2) may be able to allege grounds for modifying or vacating the award under chapter 1 of the FAA. *See* N.Y. Convention, art. V; ***In re Halcot Navigation L.P.***, 491 F.Supp.2d 413, 419-20 (S.D.N.Y.2007); *see, e.g.*, ***Yusuf Ahmed Alghanim & Sons***, 126 F.3d at 23 (in U.S. confirmation proceeding, FAA chs. 1 and 2 and New York Convention applied to foreign award because award was rendered under U.S. law and involved two foreign parties, U.S. corporation, and contractual performance in Middle East); *see also* ***Admart AG v. Stephen & Mary Birch Found.***, 457 F.3d 302, 308 (3d Cir.2006) (more flexibility for challenging award is available when arbitration location and confirmation proceedings are in same country). *But see* ***Industrial Risk Insurers***, 141 F.3d at 1440-41 (in U.S. confirmation proceeding of nondomestic award rendered in United States, FAA ch. 1 was not applied). See "Modifying or Vacating Arbitration Award," §3, p. 659. If FAA chapter 1 applies, the provisions of chapter 1 (9 U.S.C. §§1-16) apply to the confirmation of foreign awards except to the extent that they conflict with chapter 2 (9 U.S.C. §§201-208). 9 U.S.C. §208; *see* ***Certain Underwriters at Lloyd's London v. Argonaut Ins.***, 500 F.3d 571, 577 (7th Cir.2007) (sections under FAA ch. 1 fill in gaps left by New York Convention).

(2) **Refusing to confirm.**

(a) **Grounds under New York Convention.** For nondomestic awards rendered inside or outside the United States, the party responding to a motion to confirm should allege that the award should not be confirmed for the following reasons:

[1] The arbitration agreement is invalid. N.Y. Convention, art. V.1.(a).

[2] The responding party was unable to present its case. *Id.* art. V.1.(b).

[3] The award exceeds the scope of the arbitration agreement. *Id.* art. V.1.(c); ***Ministry of Def.***, 29 F.Supp.2d at 1171-72.

[4] The arbitration procedures were not in accordance with the arbitration agreement or the law of the country where the arbitration award was rendered. N.Y. Convention, art. V.1.(d).

[5] The award is not yet binding on the parties or has been set aside or suspended by a court in the country where the award was made or whose procedural law controlled the making of the award. *Id.* art. V.1.(e).

[6] The subject matter was not arbitrable. *Id.* art. V.2.(a).

[7] The recognition or enforcement of the arbitration award would be contrary to public policy. *Id.* art. V.2.(b); ***Admart AG***, 457 F.3d at 308; ***Indocomex Fibres Pte., Ltd. v. Cotton Co. Int'l***, 916 F.Supp. 721, 727 (W.D.Tenn.1996).

(b) **Grounds under FAA ch. 1.** For nondomestic awards rendered inside the United States, the party responding to a motion to confirm should allege grounds for modifying or vacating the arbitration award. See "Modifying or Vacating Arbitration Award," §3, p. 659.

3. **Ruling.** Once the motion and proposed order confirming the foreign arbitration award are filed, the court must confirm the award unless there are grounds for refusing or deferring the recognition or enforcement of the award under the New York Convention or FAA chapter 1. *See* 9 U.S.C. §207; ***Admart AG***, 457 F.3d at 307; ***Yusuf Ahmed Alghanim & Sons***, 126 F.3d at 19.

§5. APPELLATE REVIEW

§5.1 Appealable order. An appeal can be taken from a final decision that grants or denies arbitration or from certain interlocutory orders that are hostile to arbitration; however, an appeal cannot be taken from interlocutory orders that are favorable to arbitration. *See* 9 U.S.C. §16; ***Sourcing Unlimited, Inc. v. Asimco Int'l***, 526 F.3d 38, 44 (1st Cir.2008); ***Apache Bohai Corp., LDC v. Texaco China, B.V.***, 330 F.3d 307, 309 (5th Cir.2003); ***McCaskill v. SCI Mgmt.***, 298 F.3d 677, 678 (7th Cir.2002).

1. Final order. A final decision that grants or denies arbitration is appealable. *See* 9 U.S.C. §16(a)(3); ***Green Tree Fin. Corp. v. Randolph***, 531 U.S. 79, 89 (2000). A final decision is a decision that ends the litigation on the merits and leaves nothing more for the court to do but execute the judgment. *E.g.*, ***Green Tree Fin.***, 531 U.S. at 86-89 (order compelling arbitration and dismissing all other claims with prejudice was reviewable); *see, e.g.*, ***McCaskill***, 298 F.3d at 678-79 (order compelling arbitration and dismissing case without prejudice was reviewable); *see also* ***Blair v. Scott Specialty Gases***, 283 F.3d 595, 602 (3d Cir.2002) (possible anomaly of different jurisdictional results depending on whether district court dismisses or stays case).

2. Interlocutory order.

(1) Hostile to arbitration. Certain interlocutory orders that are hostile to arbitration are appealable. ***Wabtec Corp. v. Faiveley Transp. Malmo AB***, 525 F.3d 135, 138-39 (2d Cir.2008); *see* 9 U.S.C. §16(a)(1), (a)(2); ***Iberia Credit Bur., Inc. v. Cingular Wireless LLC***, 379 F.3d 159, 165 (5th Cir.2004); *see, e.g.*, ***Arthur Andersen LLP v. Carlisle***, 556 U.S. 624, 627-29 (2009) (order denying stay pending arbitration was appealable; underlying merits are irrelevant to appellate jurisdiction, so that even denial of frivolous motion to stay is appealable under 9 U.S.C. §16(a)(1)(A)); ***Advanced Bodycare Solutions, LLC v. Thione Int'l***, 524 F.3d 1235, 1238 (11th Cir.2008) (order denying stay pending arbitration, coupled with "colorable" argument to arbitrate, was reviewable). Parties who are nonsignatories to a written arbitration agreement may also be able to appeal certain interlocutory orders. *See* ***Arthur Andersen LLP***, 556 U.S. at 631 (nonsignatory may be able to appeal order denying stay if agreement is enforceable against or for benefit of nonsignatory under state contract law); *see, e.g.*, ***Sourcing Unlimited***, 526 F.3d at 44-45 (nonsignatory to international arbitration agreement could appeal order denying application to compel arbitration).

CIRCUIT SPLIT

The circuits are split on whether a district court is divested of jurisdiction once an interlocutory order has been appealed and thus is required to stay the case pending the appeal. Compare ***Levin v. Alms & Assocs.****, 634 F.3d 260, 266 (4th Cir.2011) (stay required unless appeal is frivolous),* ***Ehleiter v. Grapetree Shores, Inc.****, 482 F.3d 207, 215 n.6 (3d Cir.2007) (same),* ***McCauley v. Halliburton Energy Servs.****, 413 F.3d 1158, 1160 (10th Cir.2005) (same),* ***Blinco v. Green Tree Servicing, LLC****, 366 F.3d 1249, 1253 (11th Cir.2004) (same), and* ***Bradford-Scott Data Corp. v. Physician Computer Network, Inc.****, 128 F.3d 504, 506 (7th Cir.1997) (same), with* ***Weingarten Rlty. Investors v. Miller****, 661 F.3d 904, 907-08 (5th Cir.2011) (stay not required),* ***Motorola Credit Corp. v. Uzan****, 388 F.3d 39, 54 (2d Cir.2004) (same), and* ***Britton v. Co-op Banking Grp.****, 916 F.2d 1405, 1412 (9th Cir.1990) (same).*

---

(2) Favorable to arbitration. Interlocutory orders that grant a stay of an action or that direct arbitration to proceed are not appealable. 9 U.S.C. §16(b); *see, e.g.*, ***ConArt, Inc. v. Hellmuth, Obata + Kassabaum, Inc.***, 504 F.3d 1208, 1210 (11th Cir.2007) (no appellate jurisdiction over order refusing to enjoin arbitration on D's counterclaims when P's original claims remained pending in district court). This is true even if the interlocutory order is accompanied by an administrative order closing the case. ***Dees v. Billy***, 394 F.3d 1290, 1294 (9th Cir.2005); ***Mire v. Full Spectrum Lending Inc.***, 389 F.3d 163, 167 (5th Cir.2004); ***ATAC Corp. v. Arthur Treacher's, Inc.***, 280 F.3d 1091, 1099 (6th Cir.2002).

§5.2 Standard of review.

1. Order on motion to compel arbitration.

(1) Ruling on motion. A district court's ruling on a motion to compel arbitration is reviewed de novo. ***Terrebonne v. K-Sea Transp. Corp.***, 477 F.3d 271, 277 (5th Cir.2007); ***Kristian v. Comcast Corp.***, 446 F.3d 25, 31 (1st Cir.2006); ***Ansari v. Qwest Comms.***, 414 F.3d 1214, 1218 (10th Cir.2005); ***Jenkins v. First Am. Cash Advance***, 400 F.3d 868, 873 (11th Cir.2005); ***Al-Safin v. Circuit City Stores***, 394 F.3d 1254, 1257 (9th Cir.2005); ***Faber v. Menard, Inc.***, 367 F.3d 1048, 1051 (8th Cir.2004); ***Bratt Enters. v. Noble Int'l***, 338 F.3d 609, 612 (6th Cir.2003).

(2) Findings on scope. A district court's determination of the scope of an arbitration agreement is reviewed de novo. ***Specht v. Netscape Comms.***, 306 F.3d 17, 26 (2d Cir.2002).

(3) Findings on waiver. A district court's determination that a party's conduct amounts to a waiver of arbitration is reviewed de novo, but any factual findings underlying the waiver determination are reviewed for plain error. ***Halim v. Great Gatsby's Auction Gallery***, 516 F.3d 557, 561-62 (7th Cir.2008); ***Republic Ins. v. PAICO Receivables, LLC***, 383 F.3d 341, 344 (5th Cir.2004).

2. Order confirming or vacating arbitration award. A district court's findings of fact in an order confirming or vacating an arbitration award are reviewed for plain error, and conclusions of law are reviewed de novo. ***First Options v. Kaplan***, 514 U.S. 938, 947-48 (1995); ***Bridas S.A.P.I.C. v. Government of Turkmenistan***, 345 F.3d 347, 353 (5th Cir.2003); ***Boise Cascade Corp. v. Paper Allied-Indus., Chem. & Energy Workers***, 309 F.3d 1075, 1080 (8th Cir.2002).

§5.3 Waiver. Although a district court's rulings on arbitration agreements are generally appealable, the parties may waive appellate review. *See* ***Uhl v. Komatsu Forklift Co.***, 512 F.3d 294, 301-02 (6th Cir.2008); ***MACTEC, Inc. v. Gorelick***, 427 F.3d 821, 830 (10th Cir.2005). The waiver language must be clear and unequivocal. *E.g.*, ***MACTEC, Inc.***, 427 F.3d at 830 (term "final" by itself would be insufficient to waive appellate review; adding term "nonappealable" was sufficient); *see, e.g.*, ***Uhl***, 512 F.3d at 301 (language that award would be "exclusive, final, and binding," without language that award was completely "nonappealable," was not clear and unequivocal waiver of appellate review).

COMMENTARIES
CHAPTER 8. THE TRIAL
TABLE OF CONTENTS

A. JURY SELECTION 673
§1. GENERAL 673
§2. AUTHORITY FOR JURY TRIAL 673
§2.1 Constitutional 673
§2.2 Statutory 673
§3. ASSEMBLING THE JURY PANEL 673
§3.1 Jury Selection & Service Act 673
§3.2 Jury plan of district 674
§3.3 Master jury wheel 674
§3.4 Juror-qualification form 674
§3.5 Qualified jury wheel 674
§3.6 Number of jurors 674
§3.7 Challenging selection process 674
§4. QUALIFICATIONS & EXEMPTIONS OF JURORS 675
§4.1 Qualifications 675
§4.2 Statutory disqualifications 675
§4.3 Mandatory exemptions 676
§4.4 Permissive exemptions 676
§4.5 Exclusions 676
§5. VOIR DIRE 677
§5.1 Prepare voir dire questions 677
§5.2 Request permission to use questionnaire forms 677
§5.3 Actual examination 677
§5.4 Scope of examination 677
§5.5 Length of voir dire 678
§5.6 Preserving error 678
§5.7 Proper subjects of inquiry 678
§5.8 Improper questions & comments 679
§6. CHALLENGES FOR CAUSE 679
§6.1 Purpose 679
§6.2 Grounds 679
§6.3 Making challenge 680
§6.4 Timing 681
§6.5 Objecting to challenge 681
§7. PEREMPTORY CHALLENGES 681
§7.1 Purpose 681
§7.2 Number of challenges 681
§7.3 Objecting to peremptory challenge – ***Batson*** 681
§8. JUROR NOTE-TAKING 684
§8.1 Motion 685
§8.2 Instruction 685
§8.3 Objection 685
§9. JUROR MISCONDUCT 685
§10. APPELLATE REVIEW 685
§10.1 Voir dire procedure 685
§10.2 Seating or excusing jurors 685

B. OPENING STATEMENT 686
§1. GENERAL 686
§2. OPPORTUNITY TO OPEN & CLOSE 686
§2.1 Traditional rule – plaintiff opens & closes 686
§2.2 Exception – defendant opens & closes 686
§2.3 Multiple parties 686
§3. MOTION TO OPEN & CLOSE 686
§3.1 Motion 686
§3.2 Deadline 687
§3.3 Response 687
§3.4 Ruling 687
§4. NATURE OF OPENING STATEMENT 687
§4.1 Time limit 687
§4.2 Brief statement of case 687
§4.3 Improper opening 687
§5. OBJECTING TO OPENING STATEMENT & PRESERVING ERROR 687
§5.1 Specific & timely objection 687
§5.2 Pursue adverse ruling 687
§6. APPELLATE REVIEW 687
§6.1 Objection – abuse of discretion 687
§6.2 No objection – plain error 688
§6.3 Choice of party to open 688

C. INTRODUCING EVIDENCE 688
§1. GENERAL 688
§2. RIGHT TO OPEN EVIDENCE 688
§3. SCOPE OF EXAMINATION 688
§3.1 Direct examination 688
§3.2 Cross-examination 689
§3.3 Rebuttal 689
§3.4 Questions from jurors 689
§4. INTRODUCING EVIDENCE 689
§4.1 Types of testimony 689
§4.2 Discovery products 689
§4.3 Subpoenaed witness 689
§4.4 Expert testimony 690
§4.5 Learned treatise, periodical, or pamphlet 690
§4.6 Opinion testimony from lay witness 690
§4.7 Prior or subsequent bad acts 691
§4.8 Dying declaration 691
§4.9 Audio or video recording 692
§4.10 Demonstrative evidence 692
§5. IMPEACHING WITNESSES 692
§5.1 Impeaching by reputation 692
§5.2 Impeaching by prior inconsistent statement 693
§5.3 Impeaching by bias 693
§5.4 Impeaching by conviction 693
§6. REHABILITATING WITNESSES 694
§6.1 Proving character or reputation for truthfulness 694
§6.2 Rebutting charge of recent fabrication or improper influence 694
§7. INTRODUCING DOCUMENTS 694
§7.1 Original required 694
§7.2 Authentication 694
§8. APPELLATE REVIEW 699

D. OBJECTING TO EVIDENCE 700
§1. GENERAL 700
§2. TIMING & SPECIFICITY OF OBJECTIONS 700
§2.1 Objections before trial 700
§2.2 Trial objections 700
§2.3 Timing 700
§2.4 Specificity 701
§2.5 No general objections 701
§3. OBJECTION TO WITNESS 701
§3.1 Taking witness on voir dire 701
§3.2 Objection to expert testimony 702
§3.3 Objection to witness who violated sequestration order 702
§3.4 Objection to undisclosed witness 703
§4. OBJECTION TO QUESTION 703
§5. OBJECTION TO EVIDENCE 703
§5.1 Multiple parties 703
§5.2 Repeating the objection 703
§5.3 Running objection 704
§5.4 Different forms of same evidence 704

COMMENTARIES

CHAPTER 8. THE TRIAL

TABLE OF CONTENTS

§6. RULING ON OBJECTION 704
§6.1 Ruling 704
§6.2 Nonruling 705
§7. PRESERVING ERROR WHEN EVIDENCE IS EXCLUDED 705
§8. INSTRUCTION TO DISREGARD & MOTION FOR MISTRIAL 705
§9. APPELLATE REVIEW 706
§9.1 Admissibility 706
§9.2 Standards of review 706

E. OFFER OF PROOF 707
§1. GENERAL 707
§2. TIMING OF OFFER 707
§2.1 General rule 707
§2.2 Exceptions 707
§3. OFFER OF PROOF 708
§3.1 Attempt to introduce 708
§3.2 Make an objection 708
§3.3 Offer the evidence 708
§4. RESPONSE 709
§5. RULING 709
§6. APPELLATE REVIEW 709
§6.1 Record 709
§6.2 Standard of review 709

F. MOTION TO AMEND PLEADINGS—TRIAL & POST-TRIAL 710
§1. GENERAL 710
§2. MOTION TO AMEND 710
§2.1 Form 710
§2.2 Motion 710
§2.3 Trial by express or implied consent 711
§2.4 Amended pleading 711
§2.5 Deadline 712
§3. RESPONSE 712
§3.1 Response 712
§3.2 Request continuance 713
§3.3 Motion for additional discovery 713
§3.4 Affidavit 713
§4. RULING 713
§5. APPELLATE REVIEW 714

G. MOTION FOR JUDGMENT AS A MATTER OF LAW 714
§1. GENERAL 714
§2. DIVERSITY CASES & MOTION FOR JMOL 714
§3. TIME TO MAKE MOTION 715
§3.1 After presenting evidence 715
§3.2 After opportunity to cure 715
§4. MOTION 715
§4.1 Oral or written 715
§4.2 Grounds 715
§4.3 Burden on movant 716
§5. RESPONSE 716
§5.1 Form 716
§5.2 Grounds 716
§5.3 Additional evidence 717
§6. RENEWING MOTION 717
§7. RULING 717
§7.1 Standard 717
§7.2 Written judgment 718
§8. MOTION FOR JUDGMENT IN NONJURY CASE 718
§8.1 Standard 718
§8.2 Findings of fact & conclusions of law 718
§9. APPELLATE REVIEW 718

H. MOTION TO REOPEN FOR ADDITIONAL EVIDENCE 718
§1. GENERAL 718
§2. MOTION 718
§2.1 Form 718
§2.2 Grounds 719
§2.3 Court's initiative 719
§3. RESPONSE 719
§4. RULING 719
§4.1 Factors 719
§4.2 Jury trial 719
§4.3 Nonjury trial 719
§5. DEADLINE 719
§6. APPELLATE REVIEW 720

I. JURY CHARGE 720
§1. GENERAL 720
§2. TYPES OF VERDICTS 720
§2.1 Special verdict 720
§2.2 General verdict 721
§3. PREPARING PROPOSED INSTRUCTIONS 721
§3.1 Deadline 721
§3.2 Draft of charge 722
§4. CHARGE CONFERENCE 722
§5. OBJECTIONS 722
§5.1 Opportunity to object 722
§5.2 Multiple parties 722
§5.3 Form of objection 723
§5.4 Timing of objection 723
§5.5 Preserving error 723
§6. FINAL CHARGE 723
§6.1 Responsibility for charge 723
§6.2 Comment on evidence 723
§6.3 Timing of charge 724
§7. VERDICT-URGING INSTRUCTIONS 724
§7.1 Origin of ***Allen*** charge 724
§7.2 Propriety of charge 724
§7.3 Factors determining coercive effect 724
§7.4 Objecting to ***Allen*** charge 725
§8. REQUEST TO POLL JURY 725
§9. APPELLATE REVIEW 725
§9.1 Standard of review 725
§9.2 Preservation of error 726
§9.3 Harmful error 726

J. CLOSING ARGUMENT 727
§1. GENERAL 727
§2. MANAGEMENT OF ARGUMENT 727
§2.1 Federal law 727
§2.2 Court's supervisory responsibility 727
§2.3 Order of argument 727
§2.4 Nonjury trial 727
§2.5 Time limit 727
§3. LIMITS OF ARGUMENT 727
§3.1 Permitted argument 727
§3.2 Prohibited argument 728
§4. OBJECTING TO IMPROPER ARGUMENT 729
§4.1 Make proper objection 729
§4.2 Make timely objection 730

Table of Contents

§4.3 Secure ruling 730
§4.4 Repeat objection 730
§5. ERROR IN ARGUMENT 730
§5.1 Curable 730
§5.2 Incurable 731
§6. APPELLATE REVIEW 731
§6.1 Record 731
§6.2 Standard of review 731

8. THE TRIAL

A. JURY SELECTION

§1. GENERAL

§1.1 Rules. FRCP 38, 39, 47, 48; 28 U.S.C. §§1861-1878; see also U.S. Const. amends. 5, 7.

§1.2 Purpose. Jury selection includes assembling the jury panel and conducting voir dire. The main purpose of voir dire is to probe each panelist's state of mind so the attorney can accurately assess suspected bias or prejudice. ***Scott v. Lawrence***, 36 F.3d 871, 874 (9th Cir.1994). Voir dire gives the parties sufficient information to exercise their challenges for cause and their peremptory strikes. ***Darbin v. Nourse***, 664 F.2d 1109, 1113 (9th Cir.1981).

§1.3 Forms. ***O'Connor's Federal Civil Forms*** (2012), FORMS 8A.

§1.4 Other references. 9B Wright & Miller, *Federal Practice & Procedure 3d* §§2481-2486 (2008 & Supp.2012); 9 *Moore's Federal Practice 3d* ch. 47 (2012); ForsterLee & Horowitz, *The Effects of Jury-Aid Innovations on Juror Performance in Complex Civil Trials*, 86 Judicature 184, 187-89 (2003); Fried, *Fulfilling the Promise of Batson: Protecting Jurors from the Use of Race-Based Peremptory Challenges by Defense Counsel*, 64 U.Chi.L.Rev. 1311 (1997); Larrabee & Drucker, *Adieu Voir Dire: The Jury Questionnaire*, 21 Litig. 37 (Fall 1994); Annotation, *Effect of Juror's False or Erroneous Answer on Voir Dire Regarding Previous Claims or Actions Against Himself or His Family*, 66 ALR 4th 509 (1988 & Supp.2012); Annotation, *Propriety & Prejudicial Effect of Federal Court's Refusal on Voir Dire in Civil Action to Ask or Permit Questions Submitted by Counsel*, 72 ALR Fed. 638 (1985 & Supp.2012-13); Annotation, *Taking & Use of Trial Notes by Jury*, 36 ALR 5th 255 (1996 & Supp.2012).

§2. AUTHORITY FOR JURY TRIAL

§2.1 Constitutional. The right to an impartial jury trial in civil cases is inherent in the Seventh Amendment's preservation of a "right to trial by jury" and the Fifth Amendment's guarantee that "no person shall be … deprived of life, liberty or property, without due process." ***McCoy v. Goldston***, 652 F.2d 654, 657 (6th Cir.1981); *see, e.g.*, ***Hernandez v. City of Hartford***, 959 F.Supp. 125, 134 (D.Conn.1997) (Seventh Amendment protected P's right to trial under Rehabilitation Act and Americans with Disabilities Act). The Due Process Clause entitles a person to an impartial and disinterested tribunal in both civil and criminal cases. ***Marshall v. Jerrico, Inc.***, 446 U.S. 238, 242 (1980). A fair trial in a fair tribunal is a basic requirement of due process. ***In re Murchison***, 349 U.S. 133, 136 (1955); ***Baran v. Port of Beaumont Nav. Dist.***, 57 F.3d 436, 444 (5th Cir.1995). For a discussion of which civil matters fall within the constitutional right to a jury trial, see "Right to Jury Trial," ch. 5-C, §4, p. 311.

NOTE

Many of the cases cited in this subchapter are criminal cases. These cases are cited for their reliance on the Fifth and Seventh Amendments and related statutes, not on the Sixth Amendment, which applies only to criminal cases.

---

§2.2 Statutory. All litigants have the right to a trial jury randomly selected from a fair cross-section of the community in the district or division where the court is located. 28 U.S.C. §1861; *see* ***U.S. v. Ovalle***, 136 F.3d 1092, 1099 (6th Cir.1998).

§3. ASSEMBLING THE JURY PANEL

§3.1 Jury Selection & Service Act. The Jury Selection & Service Act (JSS Act) governs the procedures for calling people to serve on juries in federal courts. The policy of the federal courts is for all citizens to have the opportunity to be considered for service on grand and petit (i.e., trial) juries. 28 U.S.C. §1861. The JSS Act prohibits exclusion from federal jury service based on race, color, religion, sex, national origin, or economic status. *Id.* §1862; *see* ***U.S. v. Davis***, 546 F.2d 583, 589 (5th Cir.1977).

§3.2 Jury plan of district. Each district must devise and implement a written plan for selecting jurors. 28 U.S.C. §1863(a); ***U.S. v. McKinney***, 53 F.3d 664, 670 (5th Cir.1995); *e.g.*, Plan for Random Selection of Grand & Petit Jurors (N.D.Ala.); Plan for the Random Selection of Jurors (E.D.Tex.); *see also* 28 U.S.C. §1866(a) (clerk or jury commission must post in office and on website notice explaining process of drawing names). The court must decide whether it will select jurors from the voter-registration lists or from lists of actual voters from the political subdivisions in the court's district. 28 U.S.C. §1863(b)(2). The plan must specify the method to be used and prescribe a source of additional names, when necessary, to provide a fair cross-section of the community. *Id.*; *see, e.g.*, ***U.S. v. Bailey***, 76 F.3d 320, 321-22 (10th Cir.1996) (Colorado voter-registration and driver's-license lists); ***McKinney***, 53 F.3d at 669-70 (Texas voter-registration and driver's-license lists); ***U.S. v. Lewis***, 10 F.3d 1086, 1090 (4th Cir.1993) (South Carolina voter-registration list). The plan must also establish a jury commission or authorize the court clerk to manage the jury-selection process. 28 U.S.C. §1863(b)(1); *e.g.*, Amended Plan ... for the Random Selection of Grand & Petit Jurors (N.D.Ga.), §III (court clerk). Before the plan can be implemented, it must be approved by the judicial council of the circuit. 28 U.S.C. §1863(a); *see* ***In re Jury Plan***, 61 F.3d 119, 120 (2d Cir.1995).

§3.3 Master jury wheel. Once selected according to the district's jury plan, the names of the prospective jurors are placed in a master jury wheel or similar device. 28 U.S.C. §1863(b)(4). The jury wheel may be in an electronic format. 28 U.S.C. §1869(g); *see, e.g.*, Plan for Random Selection of Grand & Petit Jurors (N.D.Ala.), §IV.A (records must be in form of electronic database media); Plan for the Random Selection of Jurors (E.D.Tex.), §6 (records may be magnetic tapes or magnetic-disk files).

§3.4 Juror-qualification form. The court clerk draws the names of as many people as may be needed for jury service from the master jury wheel. Those people are sent a juror-qualification form to be completed and returned within ten days. 28 U.S.C. §1864(a); *see* ***U.S. v. McKinney***, 53 F.3d 664, 670 (5th Cir.1995); ***U.S. v. Pion***, 25 F.3d 18, 24 (1st Cir.1994). The completed forms are not provided to the parties for voir dire unless the district's jury-selection plan requires them to be disclosed. 28 U.S.C. §1867(f). A party can obtain copies of the juror-qualification forms to support a motion to stay the proceedings because the clerk did not comply with the proper jury-selection procedures. *See id.*; ***U.S. v. Gray***, 47 F.3d 1359, 1367-68 (4th Cir.1995).

§3.5 Qualified jury wheel. The names of people who are qualified to serve as jurors, and who are not exempt or excused, are kept in a qualified jury wheel. 28 U.S.C. §1866(a). The court clerk will draw from the qualified jury wheel the names of people needed for assignment to a grand or petit jury. *Id.* If selected, those people are sent a summons for jury duty. *Id.* §1866(b). See "Qualifications & Exemptions of Jurors," §4, p. 675.

§3.6 Number of jurors. A jury must begin with a minimum of 6 and a maximum of 12 jurors in a civil case. FRCP 48(a). Unless the parties stipulate otherwise, the verdict must be unanimous and must be rendered by at least six jurors. FRCP 48(b). During trial or deliberation, the court may excuse a juror for good cause. FRCP 47(c). Because alternate jurors were abolished by the 1991 revision of FRCP 47, the court will seat more than six jurors in most cases. 1991 Notes to FRCP 48 at ¶3, p. 1213, this book. All seated jurors will participate in the verdict, and a sufficient number will remain to render a unanimous verdict of six or more. *Id.* at ¶4, p. 1213, this book. If a jury is depleted beyond the minimum during trial, the parties may agree to be bound by a verdict rendered by fewer than six jurors. *Id.* at ¶5, p. 1213, this book. Barring exceptional circumstances, the parties should not be encouraged to waive the right to a jury of six, not only because of the constitutional nature of the right, but also because smaller juries are more erratic and less effective. *Id.*

§3.7 Challenging selection process. The only method for challenging jury selection is a motion to stay under 28 U.S.C. §1867. *See* ***U.S. v. Ovalle***, 136 F.3d 1092, 1098-99 (6th Cir.1998); ***Morro v. City of Birmingham***, 117 F.3d 508, 518-19 (11th Cir.1997); ***U.S. v. Flores-Rivera***, 56 F.3d 319, 326 (1st Cir.1995); ***U.S. v. Young***, 38 F.3d 338, 342 (7th Cir.1994). Strict compliance with the statute's procedural requirements is essential. *See, e.g.*, ***U.S. v. Phillips***, 239 F.3d 829, 841 (7th Cir.2001) (failure to make timely motion and provide sworn statement of evidence prevented statutory challenge); ***Young***, 38 F.3d at 342 (statutory challenge waived because no timely objection); *see also* ***U.S. v. Contreras***, 108 F.3d 1255, 1266 (10th Cir.1997) (procedural requirements are designed to give courts opportunity to evaluate alleged noncompliance and correct it before wasting judicial resources).

1. Deadline. A motion to stay the proceeding because the jury was improperly selected must be made before voir dire or within seven days after the party either discovered or could have discovered the noncompliance, whichever is earlier. 28 U.S.C. §1867(c); ***Morro***, 117 F.3d at 518-19. In most cases, the motion must be made before voir dire, or else it is waived. *See* ***Morro***, 117 F.3d at 519; ***Young***, 38 F.3d at 342; ***Dawson v. Wal-Mart Stores***, 978 F.2d 205, 209 (5th Cir.1992).

2. Form. The motion must be in writing and include a sworn statement of facts that, if true, would constitute a substantial failure to comply with the provisions of the statute. 28 U.S.C. §1867(d); *see* ***Contreras***, 108 F.3d at 1267-68. *But see* ***U.S. v. Calabrese***, 942 F.2d 218, 222 (3d Cir.1991) (oral motion sufficient because D presented clerk's sworn testimony about exclusionary practices).

3. Grounds. The motion must state that the district's jury-selection plan does not comply with statutory or constitutional requirements either in its substance or in its application. *See* 28 U.S.C. §1867(c). A party objecting to the selection process usually alleges a systematic exclusion of a distinctive group in the community. Groups based on race, color, religion, sex, national origin, or economic status are distinctive groups in the community. *See* 28 U.S.C. §1862; ***Lockhart v. McCree***, 476 U.S. 162, 175 (1986). A prima facie case consists of the following elements:

(1) The excluded group is a distinctive group in the community. ***U.S. v. Hardwell***, 80 F.3d 1471, 1486 (10th Cir.1996), *modified on other grounds*, 88 F.3d 897 (10th Cir.1996); *see, e.g.*, ***U.S. v. Cannady***, 54 F.3d 544, 546-47 (9th Cir.1995) (African-Americans, Hispanics, and Asians recognized as distinctive groups); ***U.S. v. McKinney***, 53 F.3d 664, 671 (5th Cir.1995) (African-Americans recognized as distinctive group); ***U.S. v. Purdy***, 946 F.Supp. 1094, 1100 (D.Conn.1996) (while noting that African-Americans and Hispanics are distinctive groups, court declined to consider underrepresentation of African-Americans and Hispanics combined into single group), *aff'd*, 144 F.3d 241 (2d Cir.1998).

(2) The group is not represented fairly in relation to its numbers in the community. ***Hardwell***, 80 F.3d at 1486; ***Cannady***, 54 F.3d at 546-47.

(3) Underrepresentation of the group is due to systematic exclusion in the jury-selection process. ***U.S. v. Miller***, 116 F.3d 641, 657 (2d Cir.1997); ***Hardwell***, 80 F.3d at 1486; ***Floyd v. Garrison***, 996 F.2d 947, 949 (8th Cir.1993); *see, e.g.*, ***U.S. v. Cooke***, 110 F.3d 1288, 1301 (7th Cir.1997) (party's observation that there were no African-Americans on panel drawn from population containing African-Americans was not enough to demonstrate systematic exclusion); *see also* ***Cannady***, 54 F.3d at 547 (violation occurs when group excluded because of "gerrymandering" of divisions); *cf.* ***Duren v. Missouri***, 439 U.S. 357, 364 (1979) (review of state jury-selection process).

4. Hearing. The party is entitled to a hearing on the motion. *See* 28 U.S.C. §1867(d). The party can present any relevant evidence, which may include the testimony of the jury commissioner or clerk and any records and papers used by the commissioner or clerk. *Id.*

5. Burden. To successfully challenge the selection process, the party must show a substantial failure to comply with the U.S. Constitution or the JSS Act. *See* ***Floyd***, 996 F.2d at 949; ***Timmel v. Phillips***, 799 F.2d 1083, 1085-86 (5th Cir.1986).

6. Remedy. If the party successfully challenges the selection process, the proceedings will be stayed until a jury that complies with the statute is selected. 28 U.S.C. §1867(d). This is the only remedy; the statute does not provide for a new trial. ***Dawson***, 978 F.2d at 209.

§4. QUALIFICATIONS & EXEMPTIONS OF JURORS

§4.1 Qualifications. All people are qualified as jurors unless they are disqualified by statute. *See* 28 U.S.C. §1861.

§4.2 Statutory disqualifications. A person is disqualified under any of the following conditions:

1. The person is not a U.S. citizen, at least 18 years old, and a resident of the judicial district for at least one year. 28 U.S.C. §1865(b)(1).

2. The person is unable to read, write, and understand the English language with enough proficiency to complete the juror-qualification form. *Id.* §1865(b)(2). If a panelist satisfactorily completed the juror-qualification form, the panelist is considered proficient in English. ***U.S. v. Gray***, 47 F.3d 1359, 1367 (4th Cir.1995); *see* 28 U.S.C. §1865(b)(2). If there are questions about a panelist's proficiency, the attorney should request that the court ask each juror during voir dire whether she can read, write, and understand English. ***Gray***, 47 F.3d at 1368.

3. The person is unable to speak the English language. 28 U.S.C. §1865(b)(3); *see* ***U.S. v. Flores-Rivera***, 56 F.3d 319, 326 (1st Cir.1995).

4. The person is incapable of rendering satisfactory jury service because of a mental or physical infirmity. 28 U.S.C. §1865(b)(4).

5. The person is charged with or has been convicted of a state or federal crime punishable by imprisonment of more than one year, and the person's civil rights have not been restored. *Id.* §1865(b)(5); *see* ***U.S. v. Greene***, 995 F.2d 793, 795-96 (8th Cir.1993).

§4.3 Mandatory exemptions. The following people are exempt from jury service:

1. A member of the U.S. military in active service. 28 U.S.C. §1863(b)(6)(A).

2. A member of the fire or police department of any state, city, municipality, district, territory, possession, or subdivision of a state. *Id.* §1863(b)(6)(B).

3. A public officer actively engaged in the performance of official duties in the executive, legislative, or judicial branch of the United States or of any state, district, territory, possession, or subdivision of a state. *Id.* §1863(b)(6)(C). "Public officer" means a person elected to public office or someone who is directly appointed by a person elected to public office. *Id.* §1869(i).

§4.4 Permissive exemptions.

1. On individual request, a member of a volunteer safety organization who works in an official capacity, without compensation, as a firefighter, member of a rescue squad, or member of an ambulance crew is exempt from jury service. 28 U.S.C. §1863(b)(5)(B).

2. In any two-year period, a person is not required to (1) serve, or appear for prospective jury service, as a trial juror for more than 30 days except when necessary to complete service in a particular case, (2) serve on more than one grand jury, or (3) serve as both a grand juror and a trial juror. *Id.* §1866(e).

3. The court can exempt additional groups of people or occupational classifications from jury service. *See id.* §1866(c)(1). These groups or classes may be excused only if the court finds that service would entail undue hardship or extreme inconvenience and that the excuse is consistent with the citizens' rights and antidiscrimination policies of 28 U.S.C. §§1861 and 1862. *See* 28 U.S.C. §1866(c)(1).

§4.5 Exclusions. The court can exclude people from jury service in the following circumstances:

1. If the person would be disruptive or unable to render impartial jury service. 28 U.S.C. §1866(c)(2); *see, e.g.*, ***U.S. v. Amerson***, 938 F.2d 116, 118 (8th Cir.1991) (when case turned on credibility of police witnesses, court abused its discretion in refusing to remove panelists who admitted they were more inclined to believe police than other witnesses).

2. On a peremptory challenge. 28 U.S.C. §1866(c)(3).

3. On a challenge for good cause shown. *Id.* §1866(c)(4).

4. If the inclusion of the person would threaten the secrecy of the proceedings or the integrity of the jury deliberations. *Id.* §1866(c)(5). Before the court may exclude a person under §1866(c)(5), it must hold a hearing to determine whether the exclusion is consistent with the citizens' rights and antidiscrimination policies of 28 U.S.C. §§1861 and 1862. *See* 28 U.S.C. §1866(c).

§5. VOIR DIRE

Voir dire examination is necessary for selecting an impartial jury. Voir dire provides both the means to discover actual or implied bias and the grounds on which the parties may intelligently exercise their peremptory challenges and challenges for cause. ***J.E.B. v. Alabama***, 511 U.S. 127, 143-44 (1994); ***Cimino v. Raymark Indus.***, 151 F.3d 297, 323 (5th Cir.1998); ***Darbin v. Nourse***, 664 F.2d 1109, 1113 (9th Cir.1981). During voir dire, the court must test the qualifications and competency of the panelists to sit on a jury in a trial of the case. ***Vasey v. Martin Marietta Corp.***, 29 F.3d 1460, 1467-68 (10th Cir.1994); *see* ***U.S. v. Bedonie***, 913 F.2d 782, 795 (10th Cir.1990). A magistrate judge can conduct voir dire, but only with the consent of the parties. ***Stockler v. Garratt***, 974 F.2d 730, 732 (6th Cir.1992); *see* ***Olympia Hotels Corp. v. Johnson Wax Dev. Corp.***, 908 F.2d 1363, 1368-69 (7th Cir.1990).

§5.1 Prepare voir dire questions. Some local rules require the parties to submit proposed voir dire questions along with the pretrial orders. *See, e.g.*, Local Rules Ill. (N.D.), Rule 16.1 (Form LR 16.1.1 – Final Pretrial Order Form (2)(h)(iii)). Even if not specified by local rule, the parties should prepare proposed questions for the court to submit to the prospective jurors after the court conducts the initial voir dire. *See* FRCP 47(a) (party may propose additional questions to supplement court-conducted voir dire). Proposed questions should be objective and probe for potential bias and prejudice. ***U.S. v. Quiroz-Hernandez***, 48 F.3d 858, 869 (5th Cir.1995); *e.g.*, ***Pitasi v. Stratton Corp.***, 968 F.2d 1558, 1563 (2d Cir.1992) (P submitted questions concerning bias and whether panelists had been employees of D); *see, e.g.*, ***U.S. v. Phibbs***, 999 F.2d 1053, 1071-72 (6th Cir.1993) (questions directed at personal habits and activities of panel members are not necessary to select fair-minded jury); ***King v. Jones***, 824 F.2d 324, 326 (4th Cir. 1987) (argumentative, nonobjective questions are not necessary for proper voir dire by court). The court has no duty to sort through a collection of argumentative questions to determine which ones should be asked. *See, e.g.*, ***King***, 824 F.2d at 326 (appellant submitted 90 argumentative questions).

§5.2 Request permission to use questionnaire forms. In a case that can support the extra cost, the parties should consider asking the court to submit written questions to the panel to supplement the oral voir dire. *See* Larrabee & Drucker, *Adieu Voir Dire: The Jury Questionnaire*, 21 Litig. at 37-38. Panelists are more likely to respond candidly to questions in writing than to questions asked orally in front of the entire panel. *See id.* at 37. The court has the discretion to deny this type of request because individualized examination of the panel is not constitutionally required. ***U.S. v. Phibbs***, 999 F.2d 1053, 1071 (6th Cir.1993).

§5.3 Actual examination. The court may either perform the voir dire itself or allow the parties to do it. FRCP 47(a); ***Hicks v. Mickelson***, 835 F.2d 721, 725 (8th Cir.1987); *see, e.g.*, ***U.S. v. Sherwood***, 98 F.3d 402, 407 (9th Cir. 1996) (court denied request for attorney voir dire, but allowed individual voir dire by attorney at sidebar regarding pretrial publicity). In most federal courts, the judge conducts the entire voir dire. ***Hicks***, 835 F.2d at 725. A judge who chooses to conduct the examination has a duty to uncover actual bias. ***U.S. v. Rowe***, 106 F.3d 1226, 1227 (5th Cir. 1997). If the court performs the voir dire, the parties should be prepared to supplement the examination with additional questions. *See* FRCP 47(a).

§5.4 Scope of examination. The court has broad discretion to determine the questions to ask the panel during voir dire. ***U.S. v. Adams***, 305 F.3d 30, 35 (1st Cir.2002); ***Jones v. Wellham***, 104 F.3d 620, 630 (4th Cir.1997); ***U.S. v. Quiroz-Hernandez***, 48 F.3d 858, 868 (5th Cir.1995). But the court's discretion is limited by each party's due-process right to an impartial jury. ***Britz v. Thieret***, 940 F.2d 226, 232 (7th Cir.1991); *see, e.g.*, ***U.S. v. Rowe***, 106 F.3d 1226, 1230 (5th Cir.1997) (judge's intimidation of panelists cut off vital flow of information and deprived Ds of impartial jury); ***Tyus v. Urban Search Mgmt.***, 102 F.3d 256, 262 (7th Cir.1996) (court's questions about racial composition of panelist's residence injected prejudice into trial that party could not overcome).

1. Reasonable limits. The court may limit the type of questions asked as long as each party's right to effectively select a jury is not impaired. ***Langley v. Turner's Express, Inc.***, 375 F.2d 296, 297 (4th Cir.1967). The court has no obligation to ask the questions proposed by the parties or use the language submitted by counsel. ***Sasaki v. Class***, 92 F.3d 232, 238-40 (4th Cir.1996); ***Darbin v. Nourse***, 664 F.2d 1109, 1113 (9th Cir.1981). The decisive issue

is whether the court adequately tests the panel for bias or prejudice. *See* ***Cimino v. Raymark Indus.***, 151 F.3d 297, 323 (5th Cir.1998); ***U.S. v. Lancaster***, 96 F.3d 734, 742 (4th Cir.1996); ***Waldorf v. Shuta***, 3 F.3d 705, 710 (3d Cir. 1993).

2. Cannot impair right to select jury. A court cannot restrict the voir dire in a way that destroys a party's ability to exercise its peremptory challenges. ***Knox v. Collins***, 928 F.2d 657, 661 (5th Cir.1991); ***Langley***, 375 F.2d at 297. It is reversible error for the court to restrict the voir dire to "stock questions" that merely establish the identity of the panelists and do not permit the discovery of potential bias or prejudice. ***Art Press, Ltd. v. Western Printing Mach. Co.***, 791 F.2d 616, 618-19 (7th Cir.1986). Similarly, a catchall question asking panelists whether they know of any reason why their impartiality might be impaired is not sufficient to protect the parties' rights. ***U.S. v. Gillis***, 942 F.2d 707, 710-11 (10th Cir.1991).

3. Questions required by state law. In federal court, the content of voir dire is controlled by FRCP 47(a) and is not subject to the requirements of contrary state law. *E.g.*, ***Smith v. Vicorp, Inc.***, 107 F.3d 816, 818 (10th Cir. 1997) (court was not required to ask questions on voir dire that are required by state law in tort cases).

§5.5 Length of voir dire. The court has broad discretion over the length of voir dire. *See, e.g.*, ***Ratliff v. Schiber Truck Co.***, 150 F.3d 949, 955-56 (8th Cir.1998) (limiting voir dire to 20 minutes per party was not plain error). The court's discretion in conducting voir dire will not be disturbed unless the appellate court finds that the voir dire did not probe the panelists for bias and prejudice. ***U.S. v. Shannon***, 21 F.3d 77, 82 (5th Cir.1994); ***Pitasi v. Stratton Corp.***, 968 F.2d 1558, 1563 (2d Cir.1992); ***U.S. v. Gillis***, 942 F.2d 707, 709-10 (10th Cir.1991).

§5.6 Preserving error. To preserve error during voir dire, the party must do the following:

1. Make a record. The party should ensure that the court reporter records the complete voir dire, including all objections and all bench conferences. *See* ***Hicks v. Mickelson***, 835 F.2d 721, 724 (8th Cir.1987).

CAUTION

Always make sure that any discussion with the court about the procedure for voir dire or the qualifications of panelists is made on the record—that is, the court reporter hears the discussion and transcribes it. If the discussion or any objection is not on the record, the appellate court cannot review the error. E.g., ***Hicks****, 835 F.2d at 724 (party waived error on limits of voir dire).*

2. Make a timely objection. Any objection must be timely to preserve error. *See* FRCP 46; ***U.S. v. Carter***, 236 F.3d 777, 788 n.7 (6th Cir.2001). If the party considers additional questions so essential that not asking them would constitute reversible error, the party must inform the court before the end of the court-conducted examination of the panel. ***King v. Jones***, 824 F.2d 324, 326 (4th Cir.1987). The party must explain why the questions are necessary to a proper voir dire. *See* ***Horsey v. Mack Trucks, Inc.***, 882 F.2d 844, 847-49 (3d Cir.1989); ***King***, 824 F.2d at 326.

§5.7 Proper subjects of inquiry. The following are proper subjects of inquiry during voir dire:

NOTE

Even though the subjects listed below are acceptable during voir dire, the court has complete control over the process and may prohibit inquiry into any of them.

1. The panelists' bias or prejudice regarding the facts of the case and the nature of the controversy. ***U.S. v. Beckner***, 69 F.3d 1290, 1291-92 (5th Cir.1995); ***Art Press, Ltd. v. Western Printing Mach. Co.***, 791 F.2d 616, 619 (7th Cir.1986); ***Darbin v. Nourse***, 664 F.2d 1109, 1113 (9th Cir.1981).

2. The panelists' bias or prejudice regarding the parties. *See, e.g.*, ***U.S. v. Lancaster***, 96 F.3d 734, 741-42 (4th Cir.1996) (bias favoring law-enforcement personnel); ***U.S. v. Kyles***, 40 F.3d 519, 524 (2d Cir.1994) (racial or ethnic prejudice); ***Darbin***, 664 F.2d at 1113 (bias favoring law-enforcement personnel); *cf.* ***U.S. v. Okoronkwo***, 46 F.3d 426, 433-34 (5th Cir.1995) (questioning jurors about racial and ethnic bias not required, except in special circumstances).

3. The panelists' relationship to the parties. *E.g.*, ***Pitasi v. Stratton Corp.***, 968 F.2d 1558, 1563 (2d Cir. 1992) (whether any panelist had been D's employee). No attorney can try a case in which a panelist has an interest in the outcome. ***In re Murchison***, 349 U.S. 133, 136 (1955). There is, however, no constitutional prohibition against jurors simply knowing the parties or knowing about the case. ***U.S. v. Davis***, 306 F.3d 398, 419 (6th Cir.2002).

4. The panelists' relationship with the attorneys. *See* ***Richardson v. City of Indianapolis***, 658 F.2d 494, 503 (7th Cir.1981).

5. The panelists' acquaintance with potential witnesses. *Cf.* ***U.S. v. Licavoli***, 725 F.2d 1040, 1052 (6th Cir. 1984) (in middle of trial, juror discovered he knew witness).

6. The panelists' financial interest in the litigation. *E.g.*, ***Getter v. Wal-Mart Stores***, 66 F.3d 1119, 1122 (10th Cir.1995) (juror owned stock in D, and his wife was employed by D); ***Horsey v. Mack Trucks, Inc.***, 882 F.2d 844, 845-47 (3d Cir.1989) (juror owned stock in insurance company); ***Gladhill v. General Motors Corp.***, 743 F.2d 1049, 1050-51 (4th Cir.1984) (juror owned stock in D). *But see* ***Vasey v. Martin Marietta Corp.***, 29 F.3d 1460, 1468 (10th Cir.1994) (employee of consultant to D was not presumptively biased).

7. The panelists' ability to set aside feelings of sympathy or guilt when considering a proper verdict. ***Morrissey v. Welsh Co.***, 821 F.2d 1294, 1306 (8th Cir.1987).

8. The panelists' ability to award whatever damages the evidence justifies. ***Hoffman v. Sterling Drug, Inc.***, 374 F.Supp. 850, 859 (M.D.Pa.1974).

9. The panelists' education. ***U.S. v. Moeller***, 80 F.3d 1053, 1060 (5th Cir.1996).

§5.8 Improper questions & comments. The following matters are improper during voir dire:

1. Discussing evidence that will be inadmissible at trial. *See* FRE 402.

2. Discussing the wrong legal standard. *See* ***Jewell v. Arctic Enters.***, 801 F.2d 11, 12 (1st Cir.1986).

3. Attempting to convince a juror to commit to certain views or conclusions. ***Soria v. Johnson***, 207 F.3d 232, 243-44 (5th Cir.2000).

4. Pleas for sympathy. ***Morrissey v. Welsh Co.***, 821 F.2d 1294, 1303 n.4 (8th Cir.1987).

§6. CHALLENGES FOR CAUSE

§6.1 Purpose. A challenge for cause alleges some fact that by law disqualifies the panelist from serving as a juror or renders the panelist unfit for jury service because of bias or prejudice. *See* ***Getter v. Wal-Mart Stores***, 66 F.3d 1119, 1122 (10th Cir.1995); ***Darbin v. Nourse***, 664 F.2d 1109, 1113 (9th Cir.1981). See "Bias or prejudice," §6.2.2, this page. The challenge for cause permits the parties to eliminate any panelists who are disqualified from serving on the jury in that case.

§6.2 Grounds. A juror can be disqualified for cause if she is not qualified to serve as a juror or if she is biased or prejudiced.

1. **Not qualified.** See "Qualifications & Exemptions of Jurors," §4, p. 675.

2. **Bias or prejudice.** If a panelist is biased or prejudiced, the panelist cannot serve as a juror. *See* 28 U.S.C. §1866(c)(2). The party making the challenge must make a prima facie showing that the juror is biased. *See* ***Fuller v. Johnson***, 114 F.3d 491, 499-500 (5th Cir.1997); ***Cox v. Treadway***, 75 F.3d 230, 239 (6th Cir.1996); ***U.S. v. Chandler***, 996 F.2d 1073, 1102 (11th Cir.1993). Jurors are most often dismissed for cause because they are "unwilling or unable to follow the applicable law." ***U.S. v. Nelson***, 277 F.3d 164, 203 (2d Cir.2002). The district court is in the best position to observe and make a firsthand evaluation of the panelist's ability to be fair. ***Getter v. Wal-Mart Stores***, 66 F.3d 1119, 1122 (10th Cir.1995); *see* ***Nelson***, 277 F.3d at 202.

(1) Actual bias. Actual bias is a state of mind prejudicial to a party's interest. ***Skaggs v. Otis Elevator Co.***, 164 F.3d 511, 517 (10th Cir.1998). Actual bias requires express proof, such as a panelist's admission of the

requisite state of mind. *Id.* Generally, a court must grant a challenge for cause if the panelist's actual bias or prejudice is shown. ***U.S. v. McCullah***, 76 F.3d 1087, 1100 (10th Cir.1996). Doubts about the existence of actual bias should be resolved against permitting the juror to serve, unless the prospective panelist unequivocally states she has set aside a preconception. ***Nelson***, 277 F.3d at 202; ***Bailey v. Board of Cty. Comm'rs***, 956 F.2d 1112, 1128 (11th Cir.1992).

(2) Implied bias. Implied bias exists when there is such a close connection between the juror's experiences and the facts at trial that bias can be presumed as a matter of law. ***Skaggs***, 164 F.3d at 516 n.3. Implied bias can be proved by showing that the juror has a personal connection to the parties or the circumstances of the trial, or that there are similarities between the personal experiences of the juror and the issues being litigated. *Id.* at 517. Implied bias may be found even when the juror denies any partiality, and a juror's dishonesty during voir dire may be considered in determining whether bias may be implied. *Id.* For example, courts presume bias if the panelist has a direct financial interest in the trial's outcome. *E.g.*, ***Getter***, 66 F.3d at 1122 (juror owned stock in D); ***Gladhill v. General Motors Corp.***, 743 F.2d 1049, 1050-51 (4th Cir.1984) (same). But not all relationships between a panelist and a party create implied bias. *See, e.g.*, ***U.S. v. Parmley***, 108 F.3d 922, 924 (8th Cir.1997) (fact that 18 members of jury panel had participated in voir dire—but not as jurors—at earlier trial for same offense did not create a presumption of bias); ***Vasey v. Martin Marietta Corp.***, 29 F.3d 1460, 1468 (10th Cir.1994) (panelist who was employee of company serving as consultant to D was not presumed to be biased); ***Poynter v. Ratcliff***, 874 F.2d 219, 222 (4th Cir.1989) (panelist who was patient of D-doctor in medical malpractice case was not presumed to be biased).

§6.3 Making challenge.

1. Make record. The party should make a record of the challenge for cause, along with the reasons supporting it and the court's ruling.

2. Ask for additional questions. The party may request that the court allow it to ask the challenged juror additional questions in an attempt to convince the court to grant the challenge for cause. ***Hopkins v. County of Laramie***, 730 F.2d 603, 605 (10th Cir.1984).

3. If challenge unsuccessful. If the challenge for cause is unsuccessful, the party should proceed as follows:

(1) The party must inform the court that it will be forced to use one of its peremptory challenges against the panelist. *See* ***Hopkins***, 730 F.2d at 605. The party must tell the court that this use of a peremptory challenge will prevent it from striking another specific juror who is undesirable. *See* ***Bright v. Coastal Lumber Co.***, 962 F.2d 365, 370 (4th Cir.1992). See "Peremptory Challenges," §7, p. 681.

(2) The party should ask the court for an additional peremptory challenge as compensation. If the court refuses the request but the party does not use all of its original peremptory challenges, the party cannot claim on appeal that the court erred in refusing to increase them. ***Mills v. GAF Corp.***, 20 F.3d 678, 679 n.2 (6th Cir.1994); *see* ***Connecticut Mut. Life Ins. v. Hillmon***, 188 U.S. 208, 212 (1903).

(3) The party should strike the challenged juror using a peremptory challenge.

(4) After exhausting its peremptory challenges, the party must contest the impartiality of the jury actually seated by the court. ***Ross v. Oklahoma***, 487 U.S. 81, 83-86 (1988).

NOTE

In ***U.S. v. Martinez-Salazar***, *528 U.S. 304, 317 (2000), the Supreme Court held that the defendant's Fifth Amendment due-process right was not violated when a trial judge erroneously refused to strike a juror for cause and the defendant was forced to use one of his peremptory challenges. However, the defendant did not seek additional strikes or complain about the final jury seated.* ***Martinez-Salazar***, *528 U.S. at 315-16. The Court did not decide whether reversal is required when the district court erroneously refuses to excuse a juror for cause, forcing a party to exhaust its peremptory challenges before it can strike another objectionable juror. Id. at 316. Compare* ***Kirk v. Raymark Indus.***, *61 F.3d 147, 157, 162 (3d Cir.1995) (reversal required), with* ***Getter v. Wal-Mart Stores***, *66 F.3d 1119, 1122-23 (10th Cir.1995) (reversal not required).*

§6.4 Timing. A party must make a challenge for cause during voir dire and before making its peremptory challenges. A challenge for cause cannot be made for the first time in a motion for new trial. ***Atlas Roofing Mfg. v. Parnell***, 409 F.2d 1191, 1193 (5th Cir.1969).

§6.5 Objecting to challenge. If the court grants a challenge for cause, the other party can object to the dismissal of the panelist and contest the impartiality of the jury actually selected. *See* ***U.S. v. Gonzalez-Balderas***, 11 F.3d 1218, 1222 (5th Cir.1994).

§7. PEREMPTORY CHALLENGES

§7.1 Purpose. A peremptory challenge (or "strike") is a challenge to a panelist made as a matter of right, without showing any cause. In addition to striking those who are unqualified or clearly biased, each party can seek an impartial jury by using peremptory challenges to eliminate panelists it does not want. *See* ***U.S. v. Brown***, 34 F.3d 569, 571 (7th Cir.1994); ***Burks v. Borg***, 27 F.3d 1424, 1429 n.3 (9th Cir.1994); ***Darbin v. Nourse***, 664 F.2d 1109, 1113 (9th Cir.1981). The U.S. Constitution does not require that Congress grant parties the use of peremptory challenges. ***U.S. v. Martinez-Salazar***, 528 U.S. 304, 311 (2000). Thus, a procedure that impairs the exercise of peremptory challenges is not unconstitutional per se; the issue is whether a party received a fair trial by an impartial jury. *See id.*; *see, e.g.*, ***Rivera v. Illinois***, 556 U.S. 148, 157-58 (2009) (criminal D's constitutional right to fair trial by impartial jury was not violated when state-court judge, in good faith, erroneously denied peremptory challenge; automatic reversal not required).

§7.2 Number of challenges.

1. Most cases – three. Each party is permitted three peremptory challenges in a civil case. 28 U.S.C. §1870; *see* FRCP 47(b).

2. Motion to equalize in multiparty cases. In a multiparty case, the court may consider several plaintiffs or defendants as a single party for the purpose of making peremptory challenges or may allow additional peremptory challenges and permit them to be exercised either jointly or separately. 28 U.S.C. §1870. See ***O'Connor's Federal Forms***, FORMS 8A:6-8. When a defendant shows, for example, that its interests are adverse and hostile to another defendant's, the court should grant the defendant additional peremptory challenges. *See* ***John Long Trucking, Inc. v. Greear***, 421 F.2d 125, 127-28 (10th Cir.1970). The decision to grant extra challenges to adverse parties on one side does not necessarily mean the opposing side must also be given extra challenges. ***Rogers v. De Vries & Co.***, 236 F.Supp. 110, 111 (S.D.Tex.1964); *see* 9B Wright & Miller §2483 & n.18.

3. Objections. To preserve error when the court refuses to realign or erroneously realigns the parties, a party must object to the allocation of challenges after voir dire but before it exercises its challenges. *See* ***Rahn v. Hawkins***, 464 F.3d 813, 819 (8th Cir.2006).

§7.3 Objecting to peremptory challenge – *Batson*. The objection that a panelist was excluded because of some protected classification is called a ***Batson*** challenge, named after the first criminal case that held racially based challenges unconstitutional. *See* ***Batson v. Kentucky***, 476 U.S. 79, 100 (1986). ***Batson*** challenges have since been allowed in civil suits. ***Avichail v. St. John's Mercy Health Sys.***, 686 F.3d 548, 551 (8th Cir.2012). Thus, a party to a civil suit can object to another party's use of a peremptory challenge that excludes a prospective juror because of the juror's race. ***Edmonson v. Leesville Concrete Co.***, 500 U.S. 614, 628-31 (1991); ***Great Plains Equip., Inc. v. Koch Gathering Sys.***, 45 F.3d 962, 964 (5th Cir.1995). Both the litigants and the potential jurors have an equal-protection right to jury-selection procedures that are not impermissibly discriminatory. ***J.E.B. v. Alabama***, 511 U.S. 127, 140 (1994); ***Edmonson***, 500 U.S. at 629-30; ***U.S. v. Huey***, 76 F.3d 638, 640 (5th Cir.1996); ***Shaw v. Hahn***, 56 F.3d 1128, 1130-31 (9th Cir.1995). The U.S. Supreme Court has held that racial discrimination in jury selection harms the litigants, racial minorities, and the integrity of the courts. ***Miller-El v. Dretke***, 545 U.S. 231, 237-38 (2005); *see* ***Johnson v. California***, 545 U.S. 162, 172 (2005) (harm from discriminatory jury selection touches entire community).

1. Protected classifications. Litigants cannot use peremptory challenges to exclude a panelist solely based on the following characteristics:

(1) Race. Race-based peremptory challenges are unconstitutional. ***Dretke***, 545 U.S. at 237-38; ***Batson***, 476 U.S. at 100.

(2) Ethnicity. Ethnicity-based peremptory challenges are unconstitutional. ***Hernandez v. New York***, 500 U.S. 352, 355 (1991) (Hispanic); ***U.S. v. Munoz***, 15 F.3d 395, 399 (5th Cir.1994) (same).

(3) Gender. Gender-based peremptory challenges are unconstitutional. ***J.E.B.***, 511 U.S. at 141. Challenges based on characteristics that are disproportionately associated with one gender are not necessarily prohibited. *See, e.g., id.* at 143 n.16 (challenges to all nurses are not gender-based, even though they would disproportionately affect women).

(4) Religion. Although the Supreme Court has not yet decided whether religion-based peremptory challenges are unconstitutional, several circuits have held that while strikes based on religious affiliation are not permissible, strikes based on religious activity or specific beliefs are permissible. *See, e.g.,* ***U.S. v. Brown***, 352 F.3d 654, 669-70 (2d Cir.2003) (strike based on degree of juror's religious activities permissible); ***U.S. v. DeJesus***, 347 F.3d 500, 510-11 (3d Cir.2003) (strike based on juror's heightened religious involvement permissible); ***U.S. v. Stafford***, 136 F.3d 1109, 1114 (7th Cir.1998) (strike based on specific religious beliefs permissible), *modified on other grounds*, 136 F.3d 1115 (7th Cir.1998); *see also* ***U.S. v. Somerstein***, 959 F.Supp. 592, 595 (E.D.N.Y.1997) (***Batson*** applied in the case, whether Jews are considered members of religion or race or both).

NOTE

Before applying ***Batson*** *to a peremptory challenge on religious grounds, the court must determine whether the juror's religion is relevant to the issues of the case. If the* ***Batson*** *challenge is proper, the inquiry into purposeful discrimination should involve only the juror and not the juror's family or friends.* ***Somerstein****, 959 F.Supp. at 596.*

(5) Other groups. Other "cognizable groups" under ***Batson*** include the following:

(a) Native Americans. *See* ***U.S. v. Joe***, 8 F.3d 1488, 1499 (10th Cir.1993); ***U.S. v. Childs***, 5 F.3d 1328, 1337 (9th Cir.1993).

(b) Italian-Americans. *See* ***Rico v. Leftridge-Byrd***, 340 F.3d 178, 183 (3d Cir.2003). *But see* ***U.S. v. Bucci***, 839 F.2d 825, 833 (1st Cir.1988) (whether Italian-Americans are cognizable group is question of fact). For a list of cases involving ***Batson*** challenges to Italian-Americans, see ***U.S. v. Campione***, 942 F.2d 429, 432 (7th Cir. 1991).

(c) Asian-Americans. *See* ***U.S. v. Canoy***, 38 F.3d 893, 897-98 (7th Cir.1994); ***U.S. v. Sneed***, 34 F.3d 1570, 1578-79 (10th Cir.1994).

NOTE

The moving party and the struck panelist do not need to be members of the same cognizable group. A party may contest a peremptory challenge that violates any panelist's equal-protection rights. ***Powers v. Ohio****, 499 U.S. 400, 411-14 (1991);* ***Great Plains Equip.****, 45 F.3d at 964.*

2. *Batson* procedure. The following is an outline of the procedure for making a ***Batson*** challenge (i.e., challenging an improper peremptory strike):

(1) Challenge use of peremptory strike as discriminatory. The party must object that its opponent used a peremptory strike to exclude a panelist based on a protected classification (i.e., race, ethnicity, gender, religion, or another cognizable group). *See* ***Avichail***, 686 F.3d at 551.

(a) Timely object. The party must make a ***Batson*** challenge before the court completes voir dire (i.e., empanels the jury and dismisses the excluded panelists). ***Brown***, 352 F.3d at 662; ***Garcia v. Excel Corp.***, 102 F.3d 758, 759 (5th Cir.1997); ***U.S. v. Parham***, 16 F.3d 844, 847 (8th Cir.1994); ***U.S. v. Chandler***, 12 F.3d 1427, 1431 (7th Cir.1994).

(b) Make prima facie case. The movant must make a prima facie showing that (1) the challenged attorney exercised peremptory strikes to remove from the panel members of a cognizable protected group and (2) the totality of the relevant facts gives rise to an inference that the attorney excluded people from the panel with a discriminatory purpose. *See* ***Johnson***, 545 U.S. at 168.

(c) Introduce supporting evidence. A prima facie case of discrimination can be established by offering a wide variety of evidence, as long as the totality of the facts gives rise to an inference of discriminatory purpose. *See* ***Johnson***, 545 U.S. at 170. Evidence supporting an inference of discrimination may include a comparative analysis of the panel demonstrating that a disproportionate number of strikes were used against members of a cognizable protected group. *See* ***Miller-El v. Cockrell***, 537 U.S. 322, 331 (2003); *see, e.g.*, ***Williams v. Woodford***, 384 F.3d 567, 584 (9th Cir.2004) (statistical facts such as high proportion of African-Americans successfully struck and disproportionate rate of strikes made against African-Americans can establish pattern of exclusion on basis of race that gives rise to prima facie ***Batson*** violation). Other relevant evidence includes racially disparate questioning and a pattern and practice of exercising strikes in a discriminatory fashion. *See* ***Cockrell***, 537 U.S. at 333-34; ***Holloway v. Horn***, 355 F.3d 707, 722 (3d Cir.2004). The fact that other members of the same protected classification are not struck does not excuse using a strike against a panelist on the basis of the characteristic. *See* ***Holloway***, 355 F.3d at 720; ***Harris v. Kuhlmann***, 346 F.3d 330, 346 (2d Cir.2003); ***Lancaster v. Adams***, 324 F.3d 423, 434 (6th Cir.2003). Likewise, the fact that one strike was used against a panelist who was not in a protected classification, or that the attorney denies a discriminatory motive, does not excuse using a strike against a panelist on the basis of the characteristic. ***Holloway***, 355 F.3d at 722-23. The court should consider all relevant circumstances in assessing whether a prima facie showing of discrimination has been made. ***Batson***, 476 U.S. at 96-97; ***Holloway***, 355 F.3d at 723-24; *see* ***Dretke***, 545 U.S. at 239.

(d) Make record. The movant must make a record of the ***Batson*** challenge by describing on the record the overall composition of the panel and identifying the panelists (by name and position on the panel) who were excluded because of the protected characteristic. *See* ***Williams***, 384 F.3d at 584. The court must allow the challenging party to make a full record so that the court can make an informed decision about whether the challenge was discriminatory. *See* ***Jordan v. Lefevre***, 206 F.3d 196, 201-02 (2d Cir.2000) (rejecting court's summary ruling on ***Batson*** challenge to save "an awful lot of time"). For example, the attorney could state that the panel was composed of 24 people—16 white, 5 African-American, and 3 Mexican-American—and the following people were excluded: panelist number 3, Ms. Smith, who is African-American, etc. *E.g.*, ***Williams***, 384 F.3d at 584 (because there was no record of facts showing how many African-Americans sat on jury, how many were in panel, and how large panel was, it was impossible to know if there was any statistical disparity to support inference of discrimination); *cf.* ***Dretke***, 545 U.S. at 241 (court considered side-by-side analysis of African-American panelists who were struck and white panelists who were allowed to serve when deciding whether prosecutor purposefully discriminated against African-American panelists).

(2) Rebut inference with facially neutral reason. Once the movant has made a prima facie showing, the burden shifts to the challenged attorney to adequately explain the reasons for the strike. *See* ***Johnson***, 545 U.S. at 168; ***Avichail***, 686 F.3d at 551. The reasons for the strike should be facially neutral, clear, reasonably specific, and related to the case to be tried. ***Gibson v. Bowersox***, 78 F.3d 372, 374 (8th Cir.1996); ***Great Plains Equip.***, 45 F.3d at 965; *see* ***Dretke***, 545 U.S. at 252 (attorney does not need to think up rational reason, but instead only needs to state neutral explanation). A neutral explanation is one based on something other than the race, gender, or other protected characteristic of the panelist. *See, e.g.*, ***Felkner v. Jackson***, ___ U.S. ___, 131 S.Ct. 1305, 1306 (2011) (panelist had master's degree in social work, and another panelist had animosity toward police officers); ***Thaler v. Haynes***, ___ U.S. ___, 130 S.Ct. 1171, 1172 (2010) (panelist had acted "somewhat humorous" and not serious); ***U.S. v. Evans***, 192 F.3d 698, 700-01 (7th Cir.1999) (panelist had been convicted of felony); ***U.S. v. Moeller***, 80 F.3d 1053, 1060 (5th Cir.1996) (panelist lacked high-school education); ***Polk v. Dixie Ins.***, 972 F.2d 83, 85-86 (5th Cir.1992) (panelist was reluctant to make eye contact with attorney). The explanation does not need to be persuasive or even plausible; it simply must be neutral. ***Purkett v. Elem***, 514 U.S. 765, 767-68 (1995); *see* ***U.S. v. James***, 113 F.3d 721, 730 (7th Cir.1997) (***Batson*** requires a prosecutor to give race-neutral reason every time she wants to peremptorily

challenge an African-American person, no matter how many African-Americans remain); *see also* ***Dretke***, 545 U.S. at 251-52 (judge assesses plausibility of explanation in light of all evidence). If the challenged attorney admits that discriminatory characteristics played the only role in making the peremptory strike, the strike is constitutionally defective. When the attorney asserts that there were dual motives for the strike, she must affirmatively demonstrate that she would have acted the same way regardless of the improper motive. ***Brown***, 352 F.3d at 662 n.5.

NOTE

Generally, the challenged attorney will be the only witness at a ***Batson*** *hearing. Before stating reasons for the strike, the attorney should be sworn.*

(3) Challenge neutral reason as pretext for discrimination. Once the attorney explains the strikes, the movant must show that the reason given was "pretextual" or otherwise inadequate. *See* ***U.S. v. Copeland***, 321 F.3d 582, 599 (6th Cir.2003); ***Great Plains Equip.***, 45 F.3d at 965. Implausible or fantastic justifications may be pretextual. *See* ***Cockrell***, 537 U.S. at 339 (comparative analysis of panel, racially disparate modes of examination, and evidence of pattern and practice of exercising strikes in discriminatory fashion can be considered when weighing credibility of challenged attorney's explanations); *see, e.g.*, ***Turner v. Marshall***, 121 F.3d 1248, 1251-52 (9th Cir.1997) (prosecutor's concern about potential African-American juror hesitant to view gruesome photographs was facially race-neutral, but she also seated white juror hesitant to view photographs). The movant bears the burden of proving purposeful discrimination after a neutral explanation for the contested strike is offered. ***Johnson***, 545 U.S. at 171; ***Copeland***, 321 F.3d at 599; ***U.S. v. Gibson***, 105 F.3d 1229, 1232 (8th Cir.1997).

(4) Court decides whether explanation is pretext for discrimination. After both parties present their positions, the court must decide whether the movant proved purposeful discrimination. ***Johnson***, 545 U.S. at 171; ***Avichail***, 686 F.3d at 551; *see* ***Murray v. Groose***, 106 F.3d 812, 814-15 (8th Cir.1997) (court must determine if explanation was neutral or merely pretext for discriminatory strikes). The issue is whether the court finds the challenged attorney's neutral explanations to be credible. *See* ***Cockrell***, 537 U.S. at 339; ***U.S. v. Thomas***, 320 F.3d 315, 320 (2d Cir.2003); ***U.S. v. Perkins***, 105 F.3d 976, 978 (5th Cir.1997). The court may consider the attorney's demeanor, how reasonable or improbable the explanations are, and whether the offered rationale has some basis in accepted trial strategy. ***Cockrell***, 537 U.S. at 339; *see also* ***Thaler***, ___ U.S. at ___, 130 S.Ct. at 1175 (best evidence of attorney's intent in exercising strike is often attorney's demeanor). The court may also consider the prospective juror's demeanor; however, there is no bright-line rule that the judge must actually observe or recall the juror's demeanor. *E.g.*, ***Thaler***, ___ U.S. at ___, 130 S.Ct. at 1175 (one judge presided over voir dire and another judge presided over challenges; even though juror's demeanor was not personally observed by judge ruling on challenge, demeanor-based challenge was sufficient). The proper inquiry is whether the protected characteristic was the main reason the attorney made the peremptory strike, not whether it was the sole factor motivating the strike. ***Murray***, 106 F.3d at 814. In making its decision, the court must assess the plausibility of the explanation in light of all of the evidence. ***Dretke***, 545 U.S. at 251-52; ***Purkett***, 514 U.S. at 768; ***Holloway***, 355 F.3d at 723-24.

(5) Remedies. If the court decides a panelist was improperly excluded, it may either reinstate the panelist or dismiss the entire panel and call a new one. *See* ***Batson***, 476 U.S. at 99 n.24.

§8. JUROR NOTE-TAKING

Historically, jurors were prohibited from taking notes, but today the trend is to allow it. Most of the federal circuits permit jurors to take notes, subject to the trial judge's discretion. *See* ***U.S. v. Maclean***, 578 F.2d 64, 66 (3d Cir.1978); ***U.S. v. Riebold***, 557 F.2d 697, 705-06 (10th Cir.1977); ***U.S. v. Bertolotti***, 529 F.2d 149, 159 (2d Cir.1975); ***U.S. v. Braverman***, 522 F.2d 218, 224 (7th Cir.1975); ***U.S. v. Pollack***, 433 F.2d 967, 967-68 (5th Cir.1970); ***Toles v. U.S.***, 308 F.2d 590, 594 (9th Cir.1962); ***Goodloe v. U.S.***, 188 F.2d 621, 621-22 (D.C.Cir.1950); ***Chicago & N.W. Ry. v. Kelly***, 84 F.2d 569, 576-77 (8th Cir.1936); ForsterLee & Horowitz, *The Effects of Jury-Aid Innovations on Juror Performance in Complex Civil Trials*, 86 Judicature at 187-89; Annotation, *Taking & Use of Trial Notes by Jury*, 36 ALR 5th at 275-76.

§8.1 Motion. A party may file a motion asking the court to allow juror note-taking. The motion should state that the case is long and complex and that note-taking will be a valuable method for the jurors to refresh their memories. *See* ***U.S. v. Maclean***, 578 F.2d 64, 66 (3d Cir.1978). See ***O'Connor's Federal Forms***, FORMS 8A:12, 15, 16.

§8.2 Instruction. If the jurors are permitted to take notes, they should be instructed that their notes are not evidence and should not take precedence over their independent recollections of the proceedings. ***U.S. v. Wild***, 47 F.3d 669, 672 (4th Cir.1995); ***U.S. v. Maclean***, 578 F.2d 64, 66 (3d Cir.1978); ***U.S. v. Bertolotti***, 529 F.2d 149, 160 (2d Cir.1975). The jury should be told that if there is a disagreement about the evidence, they should inform the court and request that the portion of disputed testimony be read from the official transcript. See ***O'Connor's Federal Forms***, FORMS 8A:13, 14.

§8.3 Objection. If the jurors are permitted to take notes but are not instructed that the notes are not evidence, a party must object and request an instruction to preserve error. *See* ***U.S. v. Polowichak***, 783 F.2d 410, 413 (4th Cir. 1986).

§9. JUROR MISCONDUCT

If a party claims that a juror intentionally concealed information during voir dire, the court should hold an evidentiary hearing and apply the two-part ***McDonough*** analysis: (1) did the juror conceal information in response to a material question on voir dire, and (2) did the withheld information prevent the party from exercising a valid challenge for cause? ***McDonough Power Equip., Inc. v. Greenwood***, 464 U.S. 548, 556 (1984). A new trial is warranted only when a truthful answer would have provided grounds for a challenge for cause. ***Zerka v. Green***, 49 F.3d 1181, 1184 (6th Cir.1995). If a truthful answer would not have provided grounds for a challenge for cause, the court will deny the motion for new trial, even if the truthful answer would have permitted the attorney to make a more intelligent peremptory challenge. *Id.* at 1186-87. A juror's motive for concealing information is relevant but not dispositive. *Id.* at 1185.

§10. APPELLATE REVIEW

§10.1 Voir dire procedure. The district court's conduct during voir dire is reviewed for abuse of discretion. ***Cimino v. Raymark Indus.***, 151 F.3d 297, 323 (5th Cir.1998); ***U.S. v. Sherwood***, 98 F.3d 402, 407 (9th Cir.1996); ***Waldorf v. Shuta***, 3 F.3d 705, 710 (3d Cir.1993). The court's discretion in conducting voir dire will not be disturbed unless the voir dire was not sufficient to determine the qualifications and impartiality of the panelists. *See* ***Waldorf***, 3 F.3d at 710; ***Pitasi v. Stratton Corp.***, 968 F.2d 1558, 1563 (2d Cir.1992); ***Darbin v. Nourse***, 664 F.2d 1109, 1113-14 (9th Cir.1981). The court abuses its discretion if the scope of voir dire is inadequate to discover bias or deprives a party of the opportunity to make reasonably intelligent use of its peremptory challenges. ***Cimino***, 151 F.3d at 323. If the error was not preserved by an objection, the standard of review is plain error—that is, whether the error was so prejudicial that it caused a miscarriage of justice. ***Ratliff v. Schiber Truck Co.***, 150 F.3d 949, 956 (8th Cir.1998).

§10.2 Seating or excusing jurors. The district court has the discretion to decide the seating or excusing of jurors, and the appellate court will not reverse those decisions unless the district court abused its discretion. ***Palmer v. Lares***, 42 F.3d 975, 979-80 (5th Cir.1995); ***Robinson v. Missouri Pac. R.R.***, 16 F.3d 1083, 1091 (10th Cir.1994).

1. Untruthful answer by juror. The district court's ruling on a motion for new trial based on the untruthful answer of a panelist during voir dire is reversible only for an abuse of discretion or for a clear error of law in the exercise of this discretion. ***Zerka v. Green***, 49 F.3d 1181, 1184 (6th Cir.1995); ***Artis v. Hitachi Zosen Clearing, Inc.***, 967 F.2d 1132, 1141 (7th Cir.1992).

2. Challenge for cause. The district court's ruling on a challenge for cause is reviewed for abuse of discretion. ***Wilson v. Morgan***, 477 F.3d 326, 346 (6th Cir.2007); ***U.S. v. Nelson***, 277 F.3d 164, 201 (2d Cir.2002); ***U.S. v. Tucker***, 137 F.3d 1016, 1029 (8th Cir.1998); ***U.S. v. Miguel***, 111 F.3d 666, 673 (9th Cir.1997); ***Kirk v. Raymark Indus.***, 61 F.3d 147, 153 (3d Cir.1995); ***Vasey v. Martin Marietta Corp.***, 29 F.3d 1460, 1467 (10th Cir.1994). *But see* ***Skaggs v. Otis Elevator Co.***, 164 F.3d 511, 517 (10th Cir.1998) (determination of implied bias is question of law reviewed de novo).

3. *Batson* ruling. The district court's ruling on a ***Batson*** challenge is reviewed under the "clearly erroneous" standard. ***Miller-El v. Cockrell***, 537 U.S. 322, 340 (2003); *see* ***Felkner v. Jackson***, ___ U.S. ___, 131 S.Ct. 1305, 1307 (2011). Most circuits review untimely ***Batson*** objections for plain error. *E.g.*, ***U.S. v. Brown***, 352 F.3d 654, 663 (2d Cir.2003); ***Hidalgo v. Fagen, Inc.***, 206 F.3d 1013, 1020 (10th Cir.2000). *But see* ***James v. Bowersox***, 187 F.3d 866, 869 n.4 (8th Cir.1999) (noting in dicta that plain-error review does not apply to untimely ***Batson*** challenges).

4. Interpretation of JSS Act. The district court's decisions about the jury-selection process are reviewed de novo to determine whether the process complied with the JSS Act, 28 U.S.C. ch. 121. ***U.S. v. Contreras***, 108 F.3d 1255, 1265 (10th Cir.1997). See "Jury Selection & Service Act," §3.1, p. 673.

B. OPENING STATEMENT

§1. GENERAL

§1.1 Rule. None.

§1.2 Purpose. In opening statements, the parties briefly tell the jury about their claims or defenses, the relief sought, and what they expect to prove. Although most courts permit the parties to make an opening statement, no federal rule requires it. *See* ***Clark Adver. Agency, Inc. v. Tice***, 490 F.2d 834, 836-37 (5th Cir.1974) (matter of court's discretion). An opening statement is a privilege that the court may grant or deny, depending on the circumstances of the case. ***U.S. v. Salovitz***, 701 F.2d 17, 20 (2d Cir.1983); *see* ***Defenders of Wildlife, Inc. v. Endangered Species Sci. Auth.***, 659 F.2d 168, 182 (D.C.Cir.1981).

§1.3 Forms. ***O'Connor's Federal Civil Forms*** (2012), FORMS 8B.

§1.4 Other references. 75 Am.Jur.2d *Trial* §§429-442 (2007 & Supp.2012).

§2. OPPORTUNITY TO OPEN & CLOSE

The opportunity to make the opening statement and closing argument is valuable. The party that opens and closes summarizes its case to the jury before its opponent and has the final word after its opponent.

§2.1 Traditional rule – plaintiff opens & closes. The party with the burden of proof on the case as a whole—usually the plaintiff—is permitted to open and close the argument and the evidence. ***Hall v. Weare***, 92 U.S. 728, 732 (1875); ***Anheuser-Busch, Inc. v. John Labatt Ltd.***, 89 F.3d 1339, 1344 (8th Cir.1996); *cf.* ***Martin v. Chesebrough-Pond's, Inc.***, 614 F.2d 498, 501 (5th Cir.1980) (when Ds file claims against each other, court has discretion to determine order of arguments among them). The test to determine who has the burden of proof is this: if no evidence is introduced, which party would the judgment be rendered against?

§2.2 Exception – defendant opens & closes. If the defendant has the burden of proof on the case as a whole, it should be permitted to open and close. *E.g.*, ***Moylan v. Meadow Club, Inc.***, 979 F.2d 1246, 1251 (7th Cir.1992) (only issue for trial was D's affirmative defense); ***Montwood Corp. v. Hot Springs Theme Park Corp.***, 766 F.2d 359, 364 (8th Cir.1985) (only issue was whether rents were included in purchase price, and D had burden of proof); ***John Hancock Mut. Life Ins. v. Dutton***, 585 F.2d 1289, 1295-96 (5th Cir.1978) (D had burden of proving accidental death to collect on insurance policy).

§2.3 Multiple parties. When several parties have separate claims or defenses, the order of their arguments rests within the sound discretion of the court. *E.g.*, ***Martin v. Chesebrough-Pond's, Inc.***, 614 F.2d 498, 501 (5th Cir. 1980) (no abuse of discretion in barring rebuttal argument between Ds).

§3. MOTION TO OPEN & CLOSE

In most cases, the plaintiff will open and close the argument and the evidence. If the defendant believes it is entitled to open and close, it should move to do so before trial.

§3.1 Motion. The motion should state that the defendant should be permitted to open and close the argument and the evidence because it is the party with the burden of proof on the case as a whole. *See* ***Moylan v. Meadow***

Club, Inc., 979 F.2d 1246, 1251 (7th Cir.1992); ***Montwood Corp. v. Hot Springs Theme Park Corp.***, 766 F.2d 359, 364 (8th Cir.1985). The motion should state why the defendant has the burden—for example, the defendant admitted the plaintiff's claim in its pleadings but alleged an affirmative defense or counterclaim.

§3.2 Deadline. Once the trial begins, the defendant can no longer request the right to open and close. *E.g.*, ***Dortch v. New York Life Ins.***, 268 F.2d 149, 158 (8th Cir.1959) (D's request to open and close argument after testimony completed was untimely).

§3.3 Response. The plaintiff should file a response stating that it, and not the defendant, has the burden of proof on the issues to be submitted to the jury.

§3.4 Ruling. The court has the discretion to decide which party opens and closes. ***Fernandez v. Corporacion Insular de Seguros***, 79 F.3d 207, 209 (1st Cir.1996); ***Montwood Corp. v. Hot Springs Theme Park Corp.***, 766 F.2d 359, 364 (8th Cir.1985).

§4. NATURE OF OPENING STATEMENT

§4.1 Time limit. Generally, the court can set a time limit on the opening statement. *See, e.g.*, ***Glenn v. Cessna Aircraft Co.***, 32 F.3d 1462, 1464-65 (10th Cir.1994) (under plain-error review, 10 minutes for opening and 22 minutes for closing was not reversible error). The crucial question in reviewing time limits is whether the attorney was permitted to advocate effectively for the client. ***U.S. v. Gray***, 105 F.3d 956, 963 (5th Cir.1997).

§4.2 Brief statement of case. The party that is permitted to open should briefly tell the jury the nature of its claim or defense, what it expects to prove, and the relief sought. After the initial opening statement, the other parties may make similar statements.

§4.3 Improper opening. In an opening statement, the attorney cannot (1) discuss inadmissible or nonexistent evidence, (2) make personal attacks on the witnesses, the other party, or opposing counsel, (3) appeal to the prejudice of the jury, or (4) make legal arguments. *See, e.g.*, ***Testa v. Village of Mundelein***, 89 F.3d 443, 446 (7th Cir.1996) (statement about inadmissible evidence was improper); ***Cox v. Treadway***, 75 F.3d 230, 237 (6th Cir.1996) (court stopped attorney from making legal arguments); ***Coursey v. Broadhurst***, 888 F.2d 338, 343 (5th Cir.1989) (statement about D's felony conviction was improper). Legal arguments are prohibited because it is the judge's role to explain the law to the jury. ***Schwartz v. System Software Assocs.***, 32 F.3d 284, 288 (7th Cir.1994).

§5. OBJECTING TO OPENING STATEMENT & PRESERVING ERROR

§5.1 Specific & timely objection. An objection to the opening statement must be specific and timely (i.e., made at the earliest practical moment). *See* ***Glenn v. Cessna Aircraft Co.***, 32 F.3d 1462, 1464 (10th Cir.1994) (objection must be contemporaneous).

§5.2 Pursue adverse ruling. If the court sustains the objection, the objecting party must pursue the objection to an adverse ruling to preserve error. See "Instruction to Disregard & Motion for Mistrial," ch. 8-D, §8, p. 705.

1. Request instruction. If the improper comment is prejudicial, the objecting party must ask the court to instruct the jury to disregard it. *See* ***Bright v. Coastal Lumber Co.***, 962 F.2d 365, 370-71 (4th Cir.1992).

2. Move for mistrial. If the effect of the improper comment is so prejudicial that an instruction to disregard it will not remove the prejudice, the objecting party must move for a mistrial. *See* ***Moses v. Union Pac. R.R.***, 64 F.3d 413, 417-18 (8th Cir.1995); ***Martin v. Cavalier Hotel Corp.***, 48 F.3d 1343, 1358 (4th Cir.1995). In most cases, however, the harm can be cured by an instruction. ***Cavalier Hotel***, 48 F.3d at 1358.

§6. APPELLATE REVIEW

§6.1 Objection – abuse of discretion. If the appellant objected to the court's ruling on the opening statement, the appellate court will review the ruling for abuse of discretion. *See* ***U.S. v. Burns***, 298 F.3d 523, 543 (6th Cir.2002).

§6.2 No objection – plain error. If the appellant did not make a timely objection, the appellate court will review the conduct of opening statements only for plain error. ***Glenn v. Cessna Aircraft Co.***, 32 F.3d 1462, 1464 (10th Cir.1994). The "plain error" exception in civil cases is limited to errors that seriously affect the fairness, integrity, or public reputation of judicial proceedings. *Id.*

§6.3 Choice of party to open. The court's choice of which party will open and close cannot be the basis for an appeal. ***Commercial Iron & Metal Co. v. Bache Halsey Stuart, Inc.***, 581 F.2d 246, 250 (10th Cir.1978); ***U.S. v. 2,353.28 Acres of Land***, 414 F.2d 965, 972 (5th Cir.1969). The court's allocation of the right to open and close does not go to the merits of the controversy and is not considered a ground for error. ***Moylan v. Meadow Club, Inc.***, 979 F.2d 1246, 1251 (7th Cir.1992); ***Montwood Corp. v. Hot Springs Theme Park Corp.***, 766 F.2d 359, 364 (8th Cir. 1985).

C. INTRODUCING EVIDENCE

§1. GENERAL

§1.1 Rules. FRE 103, 402, 403, 701-705, 1008; see also FRCP 43(a).

§1.2 Purpose. The parties prove their case for the jury (or the judge in a bench trial) by introducing evidence. The fact-finder resolves the fact issues by appraising the testimony of the witnesses, the documentary evidence introduced as exhibits, and the stipulated facts. The decision to admit evidence—as opposed to the task of evaluating it—is within the exclusive authority of the judge.

§1.3 Forms. *O'Connor's Federal Civil Forms* (2012), FORMS 8C.

§1.4 Other references. 9A Wright & Miller, *Federal Practice & Procedure 3d* §§2401-2417, 2431-2437 (2008 & Supp.2012); 22A Wright & Graham, *Federal Practice & Procedure* §§5261-5269 (2012 & Supp.2012); 29 Wright & Gold, *Federal Practice & Procedure* §6234 (1997 & Supp.2012); 31 Wright & Gold, *Federal Practice & Procedure* §8004 (2000 & Supp.2012); 8 *Moore's Federal Practice 3d* ch. 43 (2012); Joseph, *A Simplified Approach to Computer-Generated Evidence & Animations*, 156 F.R.D. 327 (1994); Harvey, Comment, *The United States & the Hague Convention Abolishing the Requirement of Legalisation for Foreign Public Documents*, 11 Harv. Int'l L.J. 476 (1970); Annotation, *Jurors Questioning Witnesses in Federal Court*, 80 ALR Fed. 892 (1986 & Supp.2012-13); Berry & Kiernan, *Authenticating Web Pages as Evidence*, Law Technology News (2010), www.law.com/jsp/lawtechnologynews/index.jsp (referred to as Berry & Kiernan, *Authenticating Web Pages as Evidence*); Kerr, *Computer Records & the Federal Rules of Evidence*, 49 U.S. Attorneys' USA Bull., No. 2 (Dept. of Justice, Mar.2001), http://content.hccfl.edu/pollock/aunix2/KerrComputerRecords.pdf.

§2. RIGHT TO OPEN EVIDENCE

The conduct of the trial, the order of introducing evidence, and the time when evidence is to be introduced are matters vested in the court's discretion. *See* ***U.S. v. Burns***, 298 F.3d 523, 543 (6th Cir.2002); ***Sims v. ANR Freight Sys.***, 77 F.3d 846, 849 (5th Cir.1996). Generally, the party with the burden of proof on the entire case has the right to present its evidence first. Usually the opening party is the plaintiff, not because the plaintiff filed the suit, but because the plaintiff is the party seeking relief. However, determining which party opens and closes is within the court's discretion. ***Green Constr. Co. v. Kansas Power & Light Co.***, 1 F.3d 1005, 1011 (10th Cir.1993); ***Moreau v. Oppenheim***, 663 F.2d 1300, 1311 (5th Cir.1981). See "Opportunity to Open & Close," ch. 8-B, §2, p. 686.

§3. SCOPE OF EXAMINATION

§3.1 Direct examination. The scope of direct examination is limited to relevant evidence under the pleadings. If evidence has no bearing on the probability of a fact that is of consequence in determining the case, it is not relevant and should be excluded. *See* FRE 401, 402; ***Black v. Ryder/P.I.E. Nationwide, Inc.***, 15 F.3d 573, 587 (6th Cir. 1994). To be relevant, evidence must have a tendency to make a fact that is of consequence more or less probable than it would be without the evidence. ***U.S. v. Leonard***, 439 F.3d 648, 651 (10th Cir.2006); ***Conway v. Icahn & Co.***,

16 F.3d 504, 511 (2d Cir.1994). If evidence is relevant but its prejudicial effect outweighs its probative value, it should not be admitted. *See* FRE 403. Generally, the court should admit all relevant evidence unless some rule or principle requires its exclusion. *See* FRE 402.

§3.2 Cross-examination. The scope of cross-examination is limited to the matters covered by direct examination. FRE 611(b). If the court is concerned about harassment, prejudice, confusion of the issues, the witness's safety, or interrogation that is repetitive or only marginally relevant, it may impose reasonable limits on cross-examination. ***Delaware v. Van Arsdall***, 475 U.S. 673, 679 (1986); ***U.S. v. Hernandez***, 84 F.3d 931, 934 (7th Cir.1996); *see, e.g.*, ***U.S. v. Lin***, 101 F.3d 760, 767-78 (D.C.Cir.1996) (court properly limited cross-examination of witness because questions about alleged illegal activities would be highly prejudicial and the only source for allegations was D).

§3.3 Rebuttal. A party is generally expected to present all of its evidence in its case-in-chief. On rebuttal, a party is limited to introducing evidence to rebut new facts brought out in the opponent's case-in-chief. *See* ***Tramonte v. Fibreboard Corp.***, 947 F.2d 762, 764 (5th Cir.1991). Generally, rebuttal testimony is not permitted when the party had access to the evidence during its case-in-chief and the testimony it seeks to rebut was not unexpected. *See* ***Pandit v. American Honda Motor Co.***, 82 F.3d 376, 383 (10th Cir.1996); ***Lubanski v. Coleco Indus.***, 929 F.2d 42, 47 (1st Cir.1991). Whether a court permits a party to present additional evidence on rebuttal depends on the circumstances of the case and rests in the court's discretion. *See* ***Amarel v. Connell***, 102 F.3d 1494, 1515 (9th Cir.1996); ***FDIC v. Suna Assocs.***, 80 F.3d 681, 687-88 (2d Cir.1996). If a party challenges the court's decision to admit rebuttal testimony, it must prove that (1) it was surprised by the testimony, (2) it did not have an opportunity to address the evidence admitted, and (3) admission of the testimony was detrimental because of the order in which the evidence was introduced. ***U.S. v. Luschen***, 614 F.2d 1164, 1170 (8th Cir.1980); *see, e.g.*, ***Mercado v. Ahmed***, 974 F.2d 863, 872 (7th Cir.1992) (because surprise was caused by P's own failure to prepare for testimony, court did not abuse discretion in barring testimony).

§3.4 Questions from jurors. The court has discretion under FRE 611(a) to permit jurors to submit questions to witnesses. *See* ***U.S. v. Bascope-Zurita***, 68 F.3d 1057, 1064 (8th Cir.1995); 29 Wright & Gold §6235 & nn.55-62; Annotation, *Jurors Questioning Witnesses in Federal Court*, 80 ALR Fed. at 893. Questions from jurors can lessen jurors' uncertainties, clear up confusion, or alert attorneys to issues that need further attention. ***U.S. v. Smith***, 569 F.3d 1209, 1214 (10th Cir.2009). But because of the potential for harm, such questioning is usually restricted to extraordinary circumstances. *See* ***Smith***, 569 F.3d at 1214; ***U.S. v. Thompson***, 76 F.3d 442, 448 (2d Cir.1996); 29 Wright & Gold §6235 & n.62. When the procedure is used, it must be accompanied by certain safeguards, including a screening process by which the juror poses the question but the court asks it. *See* ***Smith***, 569 F.3d at 1214; ***U.S. v. Collins***, 226 F.3d 457, 461-65 (6th Cir.2000).

§4. INTRODUCING EVIDENCE

§4.1 Types of testimony. The court may receive testimony from witnesses (1) in open court or (2) by contemporaneous electronic transmission from another location for good cause, in compelling circumstances, and with appropriate safeguards. FRCP 43(a); *see* 1996 Notes to FRCP 43 at ¶¶3-10, p. 1207, this book; *see, e.g.*, ***Parkhurst v. Belt***, 567 F.3d 995, 1003 (8th Cir.2009) (need to protect abused child's welfare was compelling circumstance to allow testimony by closed-circuit television). The court may receive testimony from a witness orally, by sign language, or in writing. 1996 Notes to FRCP 43 at ¶2, p. 1207, this book.

§4.2 Discovery products. See "Using Deposition in Court Proceedings," ch. 6-F, §4, p. 551; "Using Interrogatories," ch. 6-G, §6, p. 563; "Using Admissions," ch. 6-H, §8, p. 568; "Introducing Documents," §7, p. 694.

§4.3 Subpoenaed witness. Subpoenas to compel trial witnesses can be issued under FRCP 45 or a federal statute. *See* FRCP 45(b)(2), (b)(3); *see, e.g.*, 28 U.S.C. §1785 (subpoenas in multiparty, multiforum cases).

1. Subpoenas under FRCP 45. A party seeking to invoke the court's ability to compel a witness to attend a trial usually issues a subpoena for the witness under FRCP 45. See "Subpoenas Under FRCP 45," ch. 1-H, p. 47.

2. Subpoenas under federal statute. In some cases, a party seeking to invoke the court's ability to compel a witness to attend a trial can subpoena the witness under a specific federal statute authorizing issuance.

E.g., 26 U.S.C. §7428(d) (hearing and trial subpoenas in taxpayer suits challenging IRS determination on tax-exempt status); 28 U.S.C. §1785 (hearing and trial subpoenas in multiparty, multiforum cases under 28 U.S.C. §1369); 31 U.S.C. §3731(a) (hearing and trial subpoenas in False Claims Act qui tam actions); *see* FRCP 45(b)(2)(D). Unlike FRCP 45, federal statutes usually authorize subpoenas to be served anywhere within the United States. *E.g.*, 28 U.S.C. §1785 (subpoenas in multiparty, multiforum cases).

§4.4 Expert testimony. A witness who is qualified as an expert may testify in the form of an opinion "or otherwise." FRE 702; *see* ***Kumho Tire Co. v. Carmichael***, 526 U.S. 137, 147 (1999); ***Daubert v. Merrell Dow Pharms.***, 509 U.S. 579, 589-90 (1993). For expert testimony to be admitted, the party offering the expert's opinion must establish that (1) the expert's scientific, technical, or other specialized knowledge will help the fact-finder in understanding the evidence or deciding a fact issue, (2) the testimony is based on sufficient facts or data, (3) the testimony is the product of reliable principles and methods, and (4) the expert reliably applied those principles and methods to the facts of the case. FRE 702; *see* ***Crowe v. Marchand***, 506 F.3d 13, 17 (1st Cir.2007); ***Westberry v. Gislaved Gummi AB***, 178 F.3d 257, 260 (4th Cir.1999). If the expert relied on inadmissible evidence, that evidence can be disclosed only if its probative value substantially outweighs its prejudicial effect. FRE 703. See "Motion to Exclude Expert Witness," ch. 5-N, p. 376.

§4.5 Learned treatise, periodical, or pamphlet. For a party to use a "learned treatise" (usually a scholarly work), periodical, or pamphlet on direct examination, (1) the statement from the learned treatise, periodical, or pamphlet must be relied on by the expert, and (2) the publication must be established as a reliable authority by the expert's admission or testimony, by another expert's testimony, or by judicial notice. FRE 803(18). For a party to use a learned treatise, periodical, or pamphlet on cross-examination, (1) the statement from the learned treatise, periodical, or pamphlet must be called to the expert's attention, and (2) the publication must be established as a reliable authority by the expert's admission or testimony, by another expert's testimony, or by judicial notice. *Id.*; *see* ***Twin City Fire Ins. v. Country Mut. Ins.***, 23 F.3d 1175, 1184 (7th Cir.1994) (author of article must be shown to be authority before article can be used in cross-examination); ***Meschino v. North Am. Drager, Inc.***, 841 F.2d 429, 433-34 (1st Cir.1988) (article is not reliable authority merely because reputable editor sees fit to publish it); *see, e.g.*, ***Carroll v. Morgan***, 17 F.3d 787, 790 (5th Cir.1994) (when another expert recognized materials as authoritative, P should have been allowed to cross-examine D's expert who refused to recognize same materials as authoritative); *see also* ***In re Welding Fume Prods. Liab. Litig.***, 534 F.Supp.2d 761, 765-66 (N.D.Ohio 2008) (article's reliability may be challenged on cross-examination for author bias). If the statement from the learned treatise, periodical, or pamphlet is admitted, that statement can be read into evidence, but it cannot be received as an exhibit. FRE 803(18); ***Finchum v. Ford Motor Co.***, 57 F.3d 526, 532 (7th Cir.1995); *see* ***Dartez v. Fibreboard Corp.***, 765 F.2d 456, 465 (5th Cir.1985) (learned treatises must be read, not given, to jury); *see, e.g.*, ***Graham v. Wyeth Labs.***, 906 F.2d 1399, 1413-14 (10th Cir.1990) (court abused discretion by submitting redacted portions of treatise to jury).

§4.6 Opinion testimony from lay witness. If a lay witness's testimony in the form of an opinion would be helpful to the determination of a fact issue, the offering party must prove that (1) the witness's testimony is based on her personal observation and recollection of concrete facts and (2) the opinion helps clarify the witness's testimony or a fact in issue. *See* FRE 701; ***Hirst v. Inverness Hotel Corp.***, 544 F.3d 221, 225-26 (3d Cir.2008); ***U.S. v. Durham***, 464 F.3d 976, 982 (9th Cir.2006); ***Agro Air Assocs. v. Houston Cas. Co.***, 128 F.3d 1452, 1455-56 (11th Cir. 1997); ***Wactor v. Spartan Transp.***, 27 F.3d 347, 350 (8th Cir.1994); *see, e.g.*, ***Gossett v. Oklahoma***, 245 F.3d 1172, 1179-80 (10th Cir.2001) (affidavit describing pattern of discrimination at nursing school was admissible as lay opinion testimony when it was based on affiant's firsthand observation of school's practices as instructor and admissions committee member).

NOTE

As part of the restyling of FRE 701, the reference to "inference" was deleted. 2011 Notes to FRE 701 at ¶1, p. 1258, this book. See "Caution," ch. 1-A, §1.1.2, p. 3. The deletion of that term was made (1) to make the rule flow better and easier to read and (2) because any "inference" is cov-

ered by the broader term "opinion." 2011 Notes to FRE 701 at ¶1, p. 1258, this book. The deletion is not intended to change current practice under FRE 701. 2011 Notes to FRE 701 at ¶1, p. 1258, this book.

1. Lay vs. expert testimony. The distinction between lay and expert testimony is that lay testimony results from a process of reasoning familiar in everyday life, while expert testimony results from a process of reasoning that can be mastered only by specialists in a particular field. ***U.S. v. Christian***, 673 F.3d 702, 709 (7th Cir.2012); ***Donlin v. Philips Lighting N. Am. Corp.***, 564 F.3d 207, 214-15 (3d Cir.2009); 2000 Notes to FRE 701 at ¶5, p. 1259, this book; *see, e.g.*, ***U.S. v. Colon Osorio***, 360 F.3d 48, 53 (1st Cir.2004) (opinion based on personal experience qualified as lay opinion). Testimony based on scientific, technical, or other specialized knowledge is expressly excluded from the scope of lay testimony. FRE 701(c); ***DIJO, Inc. v. Hilton Hotels Corp.***, 351 F.3d 679, 685 (5th Cir.2003); *see* ***U.S. v. Peoples***, 250 F.3d 630, 641 (8th Cir.2001); *see, e.g.*, ***Donlin***, 564 F.3d at 217 (although Ps in employment-discrimination suits can generally testify about projected earnings, P's testimony about front pay "crossed the line" to expert testimony when testimony required forward-looking speculation and P did not have relevant specialized training or extensive experience with company); ***Compania Administradora de Recuperacion de Activos Administradora v. Titan Int'l***, 533 F.3d 555, 560-61 (7th Cir.2008) (although business owners generally can testify to valuation of business as lay witnesses, affidavit from D's CEO was properly excluded as expert testimony when he testified to valuation based on his specialized knowledge and not his personal knowledge of goods at issue); *see also* ***U.S. v. LeCroy***, 441 F.3d 914, 927 (11th Cir.2006) (although witness's position and experience could have qualified her as an expert, witness's testimony is not automatically considered "expert testimony").

2. Examples of lay testimony. Some common examples of the types of evidence allowed under FRE 701 include the appearance of persons or things, the identity of a person, the manner of conduct, the competency of a person, degrees of light or darkness, sound, size, weight, and distance. 2000 Notes to FRE 701 at ¶3, p. 1259, this book; *see* ***Asplundh Mfg. Div. v. Benton Harbor Eng'g***, 57 F.3d 1190, 1196 (3d Cir.1995); *see, e.g.*, ***Range Road Music, Inc. v. East Coast Foods, Inc.***, 668 F.3d 1148, 1153 (9th Cir.2012) (identifying popular songs is proper lay testimony).

3. Testimony on ultimate issue. Lay testimony is not inadmissible merely because it bears on an ultimate issue. ***Lightfoot v. Union Carbide Corp.***, 110 F.3d 898, 911 (2d Cir.1997).

§4.7 Prior or subsequent bad acts. To introduce the witness's prior or subsequent bad acts, the party should prove the following: (1) the witness's prior or subsequent bad acts are being introduced to prove motive, opportunity, intent, preparation, plan, knowledge, identity, absence of mistake, or lack of accident under FRE 404(b)(2) and not as character evidence under FRE 608 or 609, (2) the evidence is relevant under FRE 401, and (3) the evidence's probative value outweighs its prejudicial effect under FRE 403. *See* ***Huddleston v. U.S.***, 485 U.S. 681, 691-92 (1988); ***Batiste-Davis v. Lincare, Inc.***, 526 F.3d 377, 380 (8th Cir.2008); ***U.S. v. Mares***, 441 F.3d 1152, 1156 (10th Cir.2006); ***U.S. v. Vo***, 413 F.3d 1010, 1018-19 (9th Cir.2005). The bad acts must also be similar to and sufficiently close in time to the charged act. ***Batiste-Davis***, 526 F.3d at 380; ***Mares***, 441 F.3d at 1157-58; *see, e.g.*, ***Vo***, 413 F.3d at 1018-19 (conviction from 13 years earlier was not too remote to be admitted under FRE 404(b)). The party must ask the court to charge the jury to consider the evidence only for the limited purpose for which it is being admitted. ***Huddleston***, 485 U.S. at 691-92; ***Orjias v. Stevenson***, 31 F.3d 995, 1000 (10th Cir.1994); *see* ***U.S. v. Perry***, 438 F.3d 642, 648-49 (6th Cir.2006); ***J&R Ice Cream Corp. v. California Smoothie Licensing Corp.***, 31 F.3d 1259, 1268 (3d Cir.1994).

§4.8 Dying declaration. To introduce a dying declaration, the party should prove the following: (1) the declarant made an out-of-court statement, (2) the declarant believed that her death was imminent, and (3) the statement was made about the cause or circumstances of the declarant's imminent death. FRE 804(b)(2); *see* ***Shepard v. U.S.***, 290 U.S. 96, 100-01 (1933); ***Webb v. Lane***, 922 F.2d 390, 395 (7th Cir.1991). Although the declarant must believe that her death is imminent when she makes the statement, the declarant's expression of imminent death does not have to coincide with the out-of-court statement. ***Webb***, 922 F.2d at 395-96. For the dying-declaration exception to the hearsay rule to apply, the witness must be unable to testify. FRE 804(b)(2).

§4.9 Audio or video recording. If a recording fairly represents a transaction, conversation, or occurrence, it is admissible. To introduce a recording, the party should prove the following: (1) the recording machine can accurately record and reproduce sounds or images, (2) the operator was competent to operate the recording machine, (3) the recording is authentic and correct, (4) no changes, additions, or deletions were made to the recording, (5) the recording was properly preserved, (6) the witness recognizes and can identify the voices (or the locations and persons seen) on the recording, and (7) if the subject of the recording is a conversation, the testimony elicited was voluntarily made without any kind of inducement. ***McAlinney v. Marion Merrell Dow, Inc.***, 992 F.2d 839, 842 (8th Cir.1993); *see* ***U.S. v. Branch***, 970 F.2d 1368, 1371-72 (4th Cir.1992) (presentation of all factors not required in every case; factors merely provide guidance when court considers authentication).

§4.10 Demonstrative evidence. Charts and other demonstrative exhibits are admissible if they are fairly accurate and helpful in understanding the matters at issue, and if any deficiencies are identified for the fact-finder. Joseph, *A Simplified Approach to Computer-Generated Evidence & Animations*, 156 F.R.D. 327, 327-28 (1994); *see* ***U.S. v. Martinez***, 588 F.3d 301, 311 (6th Cir.2009); ***U.S. v. Williams***, 657 F.2d 199, 203 (8th Cir.1981). To introduce demonstrative evidence designed to re-create an accident, the party must prove that the experiment re-creating the accident was conducted under conditions substantially similar to those of the accident. ***Burchfield v. CSX Transp.***, 636 F.3d 1330, 1336-37 (11th Cir.2011); ***Hinkle v. City of Clarksburg***, 81 F.3d 416, 425 (4th Cir.1996); ***Fusco v. General Motors Corp.***, 11 F.3d 259, 264 (1st Cir.1993). If an experiment is offered to demonstrate general principles used in forming an expert's opinion, the party must show that the experiment is being offered as an illustration of the expert's testimonial theory of the accident—an illustration of scientific principles—and not as a reenactment of the accident. ***Hinkle***, 81 F.3d at 425; ***Montag v. Honda Motor Co.***, 75 F.3d 1414, 1420 (10th Cir.1996); ***Crossley v. General Motors Corp.***, 33 F.3d 818, 822 (7th Cir.1994); *see* ***Burchfield***, 636 F.3d at 1334. Because of the dramatic power of computer-animated videotapes, courts are encouraged to review video outside the jury's presence and to carefully examine it for proper foundation, relevance, and potential for undue prejudice. ***Hinkle***, 81 F.3d at 425; ***Robinson v. Missouri Pac. R.R.***, 16 F.3d 1083, 1088 (10th Cir.1994).

§5. IMPEACHING WITNESSES

The FREs do not provide rules covering all methods of impeaching witnesses (i.e., challenging their credibility). *See* ***U.S. v. Cerno***, 529 F.3d 926, 933-34 (10th Cir.2008). The court should permit a party to impeach a witness, subject to the balancing of probative value and prejudicial effect set out in FRE 403, if the method of impeachment is not barred by the U.S. Constitution, statutes, or other rules and if impeachment is relevant to the credibility of the witness. *See* ***U.S. v. Smith***, 77 F.3d 511, 516 (D.C.Cir.1996) (mental-health records may be material as impeachment evidence because they can cast doubt on accuracy of witness's testimony); ***U.S. v. Sasso***, 59 F.3d 341, 347 (2d Cir.1995) (evidence of witness's psychological history may be admissible when it relates to issue of credibility); ***East v. Scott***, 55 F.3d 996, 1003 (5th Cir.1995) (mental-health records may be material as impeachment evidence relating to accuracy of witness's testimony); *see, e.g.*, ***U.S. v. Royal***, 972 F.2d 643, 646 (5th Cir.1992) (evidence about witness's bias was admissible); ***U.S. v. Kaplan***, 832 F.2d 676, 685 (1st Cir.1987) (evidence impeaching witness's ability to observe and remember should have been permitted). Any party, including the party that called the witness, may attack the witness's credibility. FRE 607.

§5.1 Impeaching by reputation. The only proper questions to ask a witness about the reputation of another witness are the following: (1) Does the witness know the general reputation for truthfulness that the witness to be impeached has in the community? And, if so, (2) what is the reputation of the witness to be impeached? *See* FRE 405, 608; ***U.S. v. Kaufman***, 429 F.2d 240, 247 (2d Cir.1970). The court then may allow an inquiry into the witness's specific acts that are probative of truthfulness or untruthfulness. FRE 608(b). Acts that are generally probative of untruthfulness under FRE 608(b) include forgery, perjury, and fraud. ***Ad-Vantage Tel. Directory Consultants, Inc. v. GTE Directories Corp.***, 37 F.3d 1460, 1464 (11th Cir.1994). For example, testimony that a witness filed a false workers' compensation claim could be probative of untruthfulness. ***Hynes v. Coughlin***, 79 F.3d 285, 293-94 (2d Cir. 1996). After the court determines that the impeaching witness is qualified to testify about the general reputation of the other witness, the party opposing the impeachment may ask to take the impeaching witness on voir dire to test her competence and the means of her knowledge before she testifies. *See* FRE 405, 608.

§5.2 Impeaching by prior inconsistent statement. A witness's credibility can be impeached by an earlier statement (oral or written) that is inconsistent with her trial statement. The earlier statement can be admitted only to demonstrate self-contradiction by the witness and not to prove any material fact, and the judge must instruct the jury on the statement's limited purpose. ***Firemen's Fund Ins. v. Thien***, 8 F.3d 1307, 1312 (8th Cir.1993). When introducing a prior inconsistent statement, the attorney must (1) show that the statement is inconsistent with the witness's current testimony, (2) show that the statement relates to a matter of sufficient relevance and not just a collateral issue, (3) give the witness an opportunity to explain or deny the earlier statement, and (4) give the opposing party an opportunity to examine the witness. FRE 613; ***U.S. v. Strother***, 49 F.3d 869, 874 (2d Cir.1995); ***Thien***, 8 F.3d at 1312; *see* ***U.S. v. Kelly***, 436 F.3d 992, 996 (8th Cir.2006) (requirement that witness be given opportunity to explain or deny prior inconsistent statement does not mean witness must actually do so); ***U.S. v. Cody***, 114 F.3d 772, 776 (8th Cir.1997) (requirement that prior statement be inconsistent with current testimony does not mean statements must be diametrically opposed). The attorney does not need to disclose the specific contents of the earlier statement to the witness, but the attorney must disclose the contents to the opposing party's attorney on request. FRE 613(a). If the witness unequivocally admits having made the earlier statement, extrinsic evidence of the statement should be excluded. ***BankAtlantic v. Blythe Eastman Paine Webber, Inc.***, 955 F.2d 1467, 1476 (11th Cir.1992); *see* FRE 613(b). Extrinsic evidence of the earlier statement can be admitted only if the witness denies making it. *See* FRE 613(b); ***U.S. v. Mitchell***, 113 F.3d 1528, 1532 (10th Cir.1997); ***McAlinney v. Marion Merrell Dow, Inc.***, 992 F.2d 839, 842-43 (8th Cir.1993). If the earlier statement is an opposing party's statement under FRE 801(d)(2), extrinsic evidence of the statement can be admitted without giving the opposing party an opportunity to explain or deny the statement. FRE 613(b).

NOTE

A testifying witness's own prior inconsistent statement may be admissible for the purpose of impeaching that witness. See FRE 801(d)(1)(A). However, a party cannot introduce a contradictory account given by another source to impeach the credibility of the witness. ***Bemis v. Edwards***, *45 F.3d 1369, 1372 (9th Cir.1995); see FRE 801(d)(1).*

---

§5.3 Impeaching by bias. Although the FREs do not provide for it, a witness can be impeached on the ground of bias. ***U.S. v. Abel***, 469 U.S. 45, 49-51 (1984); ***Bachenski v. Malnati***, 11 F.3d 1371, 1375 (7th Cir.1993). When impeaching based on bias or interest on the part of the witness, the attorney must give the witness an opportunity to explain or deny the circumstances or statement that created the alleged bias. *See* ***U.S. v. Betts***, 16 F.3d 748, 764 (7th Cir.1994), *abrogated on other grounds*, ***U.S. v. Mills***, 122 F.3d 346 (7th Cir.1997); *cf.* FRE 613(b) (impeaching by prior inconsistent statement). To impeach by bias, an attorney should follow the same steps used for impeaching based on a prior inconsistent statement. See "Impeaching by prior inconsistent statement," §5.2, this page.

§5.4 Impeaching by conviction. A witness's character for truthfulness can be attacked on the ground that the witness was convicted of a crime if (1) the crime was punishable by death or by imprisonment for more than one year, and the court determines that the probative value of admitting the evidence outweighs its prejudicial effect, or (2) the elements of the crime required proving—or the witness's admitting—a dishonest act or false statement. FRE 403, 609(a); *see* ***U.S. v. Lamarr***, 75 F.3d 964, 970 (4th Cir.1996) (former FRE 609; credibility of witness); ***Wilson v. Groaning***, 25 F.3d 581, 586 (7th Cir.1994) (same); *see also* ***U.S. v. Valentine***, 401 F.3d 609, 615 (5th Cir.2005) (in 5th Circuit, deferred adjudication is not conviction under FRE 609). No other conviction can be used, even if the witness exhibited dishonesty or made a false statement during the commission of the crime. 2006 Notes to FRE 609 at ¶1, p. 1258, this book. To impeach based on a criminal conviction, the party should prove the following: (1) the witness was convicted of a crime under FRE 609(a)(1) or (a)(2), (2) the conviction or release of the witness is not more than ten years old (or longer in certain circumstances), (3) the witness has not been pardoned, had the conviction annulled, or had a certificate of rehabilitation issued, and (4) the conviction was not the result of a juvenile adjudication. FRE 609(a)-(d); *see* ***U.S. v. Estrada***, 430 F.3d 606, 615-16 (2d Cir.2005) (impeachment evidence includes essential facts, e.g., statutory name of offense, date of conviction, sentence imposed). A conviction more than

ten years old is admissible only if its probative value substantially outweighs its prejudicial effect and the offering party gives the adverse party written notice of the intent to use the conviction. FRE 609(b); *see **U.S. v. Hamilton***, 48 F.3d 149, 154 (5th Cir.1995). A party intending to impeach by conviction should be prepared to prove the conviction with evidence—generally, a self-authenticating, attested copy of the judgment of conviction.

§6. REHABILITATING WITNESSES

§6.1 Proving character or reputation for truthfulness. Supporting evidence of a witness's good character is not usually admissible in a civil case. *See **Deary v. City of Gloucester***, 9 F.3d 191, 196 (1st Cir.1993). However, evidence of a witness's truthful character is admissible after the witness's character for truthfulness has been attacked. FRE 608(a); ***Deary***, 9 F.3d at 196. Because the court may limit rehabilitation testimony to the same type as the opponent's evidence, a party must determine whether it needs to present reputation testimony or opinion testimony.

1. Reputation testimony. If offering reputation testimony, a party should prove the following through the testimony of another witness: (1) the rebuttal witness is a member of the same community as the person who was attacked and has knowledge of the person's character (the party should establish facts showing how the witness knows of the person's character), (2) the person has a reputation for truthfulness, and (3) the rebuttal witness knows the person's reputation for truthfulness. *See* FRE 405(a); 22A Wright & Graham §5264; *see also **Blackburn v. United Parcel Serv.***, 179 F.3d 81, 101 (3d Cir.1999) (witness must demonstrate true familiarity with community in which reputation has been formed, and that basis of reputation is likely to be reliable).

2. Opinion testimony. If offering opinion testimony, a party should prove the following through the testimony of another witness: (1) the rebuttal witness personally knows the person who was attacked, (2) the rebuttal witness knows the person well enough to have formed an opinion of the person's truthfulness, (3) the rebuttal witness has an opinion of the person's truthfulness, and (4) the rebuttal witness has the opinion that the person is truthful. *See* FRE 405(a); 22A Wright & Graham §5265; *see also **U.S. v. Polsinelli***, 649 F.2d 793, 795 (10th Cir.1981) (knowledge of person's reputation in community not required for opinion testimony).

§6.2 Rebutting charge of recent fabrication or improper influence. To introduce a prior consistent statement to rebut a charge of recent fabrication or improper influence, a party must prove through the testimony of another witness that (1) before testifying, the witness made out-of-court statements consistent with her testimony, and (2) the statements were made before the witness had reason to fabricate. *See* FRE 801(d)(1)(B); ***Tome v. U.S.***, 513 U.S. 150, 156-59 (1995); ***U.S. v. Frederick***, 78 F.3d 1370, 1377 (9th Cir.1996).

§7. INTRODUCING DOCUMENTS

§7.1 Original required. Generally, the original writing, recording, or photograph is required to prove its contents. FRE 1002. However, the original is not required when (1) the original is lost or destroyed, (2) the original cannot be obtained, (3) the opposing party had control of the original but did not produce it, or (4) the writing, recording, or photograph is not closely related to a controlling issue in the case. FRE 1004; ***U.S. v. George Washington Univ.***, 522 F.Supp.2d 135, 145 (D.D.C.2007).

§7.2 Authentication. Documentary evidence introduced in federal court must be authenticated under FRE 901 or 902. ***Amoco Prod. v. U.S.***, 619 F.2d 1383, 1391 (10th Cir.1980). Specifically, the proponent must produce evidence showing that the document in question is what the proponent claims it is. *Id.*; *see **U.S. v. Lebowitz***, 676 F.3d 1000, 1009 (11th Cir.2012), *cert. filed*, ___ S.Ct. ___ (2012) (No. 12-429; 10-8-12). The document may be authenticated using circumstantial evidence. ***In re McLain***, 516 F.3d 301, 308 (5th Cir.2008); ***U.S. v. Smith***, 918 F.2d 1501, 1510 (11th Cir.1990); *see, e.g.*, ***Jones v. National Am. Univ.***, 608 F.3d 1039, 1044-45 (8th Cir.2010) (in employment-discrimination suit, job posting was sufficiently authenticated by testimony of two university employees who had seen posting on two different bulletin boards on campus; authentication was sufficient even though posting differed in format from other positions and no university employee could identify posting's author).

1. Documents that require authentication.

(1) Signed document. To introduce a signed document, a party should do one of the following: (1) call the signing party (if necessary, as an adverse witness) to acknowledge the signature, (2) call a witness who saw the party sign the document, (3) call a witness who is familiar with the party's signature and can identify it, or (4) call a handwriting expert who can testify that, based on handwriting comparisons, the signature was made by the party. *See* FRE 901(b)(1)-(b)(3); *see also* ***Hall v. United Ins.***, 367 F.3d 1255, 1259 (11th Cir.2004) (handwriting testimony must satisfy specific requirements of FRE 901(b)(2) and general requirements of FRE 701).

(2) Copy of document. To introduce a copy of a document, a party should show that (1) the original was lost, was destroyed, or cannot be obtained, the opposing party had control of the original but did not produce it, or the document is not closely related to a controlling issue in the case, (2) a copy of the original was made, and (3) the offered document or record is a true and accurate copy of the original. *See* FRE 1001(e), 1003, 1004; *see, e.g.*, ***U.S. v. Stockton***, 968 F.2d 715, 719 (8th Cir.1992) (photographs of documents properly introduced as duplicates under FRE 1003); ***Amoco Prod.***, 619 F.2d at 1391 (court properly excluded "file copy" of deed that was not complete reproduction of original). A duplicate is admissible as an original unless (1) a question is raised about the original's authenticity or (2) the circumstances make it unfair to admit the duplicate. FRE 1003; *see* ***U.S. v. Childs***, 5 F.3d 1328, 1335 (9th Cir.1993); ***Tyson v. Jones & Laughlin Steel Corp.***, 958 F.2d 756, 761 (7th Cir.1992); 31 Wright & Gold §8004.

(3) Photograph. To introduce a photograph, a party should prove the following: (1) the witness recognizes the subject of the photograph, (2) the witness identifies the photograph as a representation of the subject seen at or near the time of the event in issue, and (3) the witness testifies that the photograph is a true and accurate representation of the subject as it appeared at the relevant time. *See* ***U.S. v. Clayton***, 643 F.2d 1071, 1074 (5th Cir.1981); ***Hendricks v. Swenson***, 456 F.2d 503, 506 (8th Cir.1972). If a verbal description of an item is admissible, a photograph depicting it is also admissible. The term "photograph" means a photographic image or its equivalent stored in any form. FRE 1001(c). Generally, to prove the content of a photograph, an original is required; an "original" of a photograph includes the negative or any print made from it. FRE 1001(d), 1002.

(4) Summary, chart, or calculation. To introduce a summary, chart, or calculation to prove the content of voluminous writings, recordings, or photographs, a party should prove the following: (1) the summary, chart, or calculation is a summary of other records, (2) the other records are voluminous writings, recordings, or photographs that are admissible, (3) the other records cannot be conveniently examined in court, (4) the other records were made available to the other parties for examination and copying at a reasonable time and place, and (5) if ordered by the court, the other records can be presented in the courtroom. *See* FRE 1006; *see also* ***Bristol Steel & Iron Works, Inc. v. Bethlehem Steel Corp.***, 41 F.3d 182, 189-90 (4th Cir.1994) (when summaries are introduced as evidence, underlying records cannot be shown to jury); ***Vasey v. Martin Marietta Corp.***, 29 F.3d 1460, 1468 (10th Cir.1994) (summaries must accurately reflect contents of underlying records).

(5) Business record. To introduce a business record, a party has two options—it can introduce the record through a witness or through an affidavit.

(a) Witness. To introduce a business record through a witness, a party should prove the following: (1) the record was made at or near the time of the act by, or from information transmitted by, someone with knowledge of the facts, (2) the record was kept in the course of regularly conducted activity of a business, an organization, an occupation, or a calling (whether or not for profit), (3) the record was made as part of the regular practice of that activity, (4) the witness is the custodian of the record or another qualified witness, and (5) neither the source of information nor the method or circumstances of preparation indicate a lack of trustworthiness. FRE 803(6); *see, e.g.*, ***Phoenix Assocs. III v. Stone***, 60 F.3d 95, 101 (2d Cir.1995) (wire-transfer record admissible); ***Monotype Corp. v. International Typeface Corp.***, 43 F.3d 443, 449-50 (9th Cir.1994) (comparative report inadmissible because not made in regular course of business); ***Resolution Trust Corp. v. Eason***, 17 F.3d 1126, 1131-32 (8th Cir. 1994) (loan "workpapers" admissible); *see also* 28 U.S.C. §1732 (description of business records). If the other requirements of FRE 803(6) are met, the custodian or other qualified witness does not need to have personal knowledge about the creation of the offered document, have personally participated in its creation, or even know who actually recorded the information. ***Eason***, 17 F.3d at 1132.

(b) Affidavit, declaration, or other certification. To introduce a business record through an affidavit, declaration, or other certification, a party must prepare an affidavit, declaration, or other certification by the custodian or another qualified person certifying that the record (1) was made at or near the time of the act, event, condition, opinion, or diagnosis by, or from information transmitted by, someone with knowledge of the facts, (2) the record was kept in the course of regularly conducted activity of a business, an organization, an occupation, or a calling (whether or not for profit), and (3) the record was made as part of the regular practice of that activity. *See* FRE 803(6)(A)-(6)(C), 902(11), (12). A declaration that satisfies 28 U.S.C. §1746 is sufficient, as well as any comparable certification under oath. 2000 Notes to FRE 902 at ¶2, p. 1265, this book. To allow the adverse party a fair opportunity to challenge the business record, the offering party must (1) provide written notice to the adverse party of the intent to offer a record and (2) make the record and certification available for inspection. FRE 902(11), (12).

(6) Electronically stored information. To introduce paper records of electronically stored information (ESI), a party should prove (1) that the paper records accurately reflect the ESI, (2) that the system or process that generated the ESI is reliable, and (3) the identity of the person who created the ESI. *See* ***Lorraine v. Markel Am. Ins.***, 241 F.R.D. 534, 542-43 (D.Md.2007); Kerr, *Computer Records & the Federal Rules of Evidence*, 49 U.S. Attorneys' USA Bull., No. 2, http://content.hccfl.edu/pollock/aunix2/KerrComputerRecords.pdf. Establishing the reliability of a system or process does not require the testimony of an expert. *See* ***U.S. v. Salgado***, 250 F.3d 438, 453 (6th Cir.2001); ***U.S. v. Whitaker***, 127 F.3d 595, 601 (7th Cir.1997); ***U.S. v. Miller***, 771 F.2d 1219, 1237 (9th Cir.1985). Without specific evidence of alteration or manipulation, questions about the accuracy of ESI go to its weight rather than its admissibility. ***U.S. v. Meienberg***, 263 F.3d 1177, 1181 (10th Cir.2001); ***U.S. v. Tank***, 200 F.3d 627, 630-31 (9th Cir.2000).

NOTE

The foundational requirements for ESI may be more difficult to establish than the requirements for non-ESI. See ***Lorraine****, 241 F.R.D. at 542-43. The degree of foundation required for ESI depends on the quality and completeness of the data input, the complexity of the computer processing, the routineness of the computer operation, and the ability to test and verify results of the computer processing. Id. at 544. For an in-depth discussion of authenticating various forms of ESI, see* ***Lorraine v. Markel Am. Ins.****, 241 F.R.D. 534 (D.Md.2007).*

(a) Original required. Generally, to prove the content of ESI, an original is required. FRE 1002. An "original" of ESI means any printout or other output readable by sight if it accurately reflects the information. FRE 1001(d).

(b) Method of authentication. ESI can be authenticated by a witness with personal knowledge under FRE 901(b)(1); at a minimum, the witness must provide factual specificity about the process by which the ESI was created, acquired, maintained, and preserved without alteration. ***Lorraine***, 241 F.R.D. at 545; *see* ***U.S. v. Bansal***, 663 F.3d 634, 667-68 (3d Cir.2011). ESI can also be authenticated through distinctive characteristics under FRE 901(b)(4). ***Lorraine***, 241 F.R.D. at 546-47.

(c) Examples. The following are examples of ESI used as evidence:

[1] Records of business and financial transactions. ***Meienberg***, 263 F.3d at 1181; ***Whitaker***, 127 F.3d at 601 & n.3; ***U.S. v. Moore***, 923 F.2d 910, 915 (1st Cir.1991); *see* ***Lorraine***, 241 F.R.D. at 556-57 (computer-stored records and data).

[2] Phone records. ***Salgado***, 250 F.3d at 451-53; ***U.S. v. Briscoe***, 896 F.2d 1476, 1494 (7th Cir.1990); ***Miller***, 771 F.2d at 1237.

[3] E-mail. ***U.S. v. Siddiqui***, 235 F.3d 1318, 1322 (11th Cir.2000); ***Lorraine***, 241 F.R.D. at 554-55; ***U.S. v. Ferber***, 966 F.Supp. 90, 98 (D.Mass.1997).

[4] Web pages. *See* ***Bansal***, 663 F.3d at 667-68; ***Boim v. Holy Land Found. for Relief & Dev.***, 549 F.3d 685, 703-05 (7th Cir.2008); ***Lorraine***, 241 F.R.D. at 555-56; *see, e.g.*, ***Jones***, 608 F.3d at 1045-46 (in employment-discrimination case, testimony was sufficient to authenticate D-university's online job posting when

D's president testified that he was familiar with university's website section for postings and exhibit was in same format as posting on website); ***Trade Media Holdings Ltd. v. Huang & Assocs.***, 123 F.Supp.2d 233, 240 & n.3 (D. N.J.2000) (in trademark case, evidence presented that infringing website automatically linked to trademark holder's site); *see also* ***Victaulic Co. v. Tieman***, 499 F.3d 227, 236 (3d Cir.2007) (court cannot take judicial notice of website without some other means of authentication); ***ACTONet, Ltd. v. Allou Health & Beauty Care***, 219 F.3d 836, 848 (8th Cir.2000) (HTML code treated as photographs).

PRACTICE TIP

To authenticate a screenshot of a web page, the party producing the screenshot can obtain requests for admissions or deposition or affidavit testimony from the person who took the screenshot or the website's webmaster to show that the image accurately reflects (1) the content of the website and (2) the image of the website on the computer at which the screenshot was made. Berry & Kiernan, Authenticating Web Pages as Evidence; see ***Lorraine****, 241 F.R.D. at 555-56; see, e.g.,* ***Bansal****, 663 F.3d at 667-68 (to authenticate screenshots of D's website that P received from company that catalogues all websites on Internet, P's witness testified about how company works and the reliability of its database and compared screenshots with previously authenticated and admitted screenshots of D's website). If the party is seeking to authenticate a screenshot from the opposing party's website, the offering party should try to authenticate the screenshot through a deposition or requests for admissions. Berry & Kiernan, Authenticating Web Pages as Evidence.*

[5] Chat-room content and text messages. ***Lorraine***, 241 F.R.D. at 556; *see* ***U.S. v. Lundy***, 676 F.3d 444, 454 (5th Cir.2012); ***Tank***, 200 F.3d at 630-31; ***U.S. v. Simpson***, 152 F.3d 1241, 1249-50 (10th Cir.1998).

2. Documents that are self-authenticating under FRE 902. If a document is admissible under FRE 902, the document is self-authenticating—that is, it does not need to be supported by separate evidence.

(1) Domestic public records that are sealed & signed. To introduce a public record that is sealed and signed, a party must show the following: (1) the document bears a seal of the United States, a state, or any other political subdivision listed in FRE 902(1)(A), and (2) the document bears a signature purporting to be an attestation or execution. FRE 902(1); ***AMFAC Distrib. v. Harrelson***, 842 F.2d 304, 306-07 (11th Cir.1988); *see* FRE 1005; ***Hughes v. U.S.***, 953 F.2d 531, 540 (9th Cir.1992).

(2) Domestic public records that are not sealed. To introduce a public record that is not sealed, a party must show the following: (1) the document bears the signature of an officer or employee of an entity listed in FRE 902(1)(A), and (2) another public officer who has a seal and official duties within that same entity certifies under seal, or its equivalent, that the signer has the official capacity and that the signature is genuine. FRE 902(2); *see* FRE 1005; ***Hunt v. Liberty Lobby***, 720 F.2d 631, 651 (11th Cir.1983).

(3) Foreign public documents. To introduce a foreign public document, a party must show the following: (1) the document purports to be signed or attested by a person authorized to do so by the foreign country's law, and (2) the document is accompanied by a final certification that certifies the genuineness from an authorized governmental official listed in FRE 902(3). FRE 902(3); *see* FRE 1005; ***Raphaely Int'l v. Waterman S.S. Corp.***, 972 F.2d 498, 502 (2d Cir.1992). If all parties have been given a reasonable opportunity to investigate the document's authenticity and accuracy, the court may, for good cause, (1) order that the document be treated as presumptively authentic without final certification or (2) allow the document to be introduced by an attested summary with or without final certification. FRE 902(3); *see* ***Fox & Assocs. v. M/V Hanjin Yokohama***, 977 F.Supp. 1022, 1029 (C.D.Cal. 1997). In immigration cases, a foreign public document may be authenticated by any recognized method of authentication. *See* ***Yan v. Gonzales***, 438 F.3d 1249, 1256 n.7 (10th Cir.2006); ***Liu v. Ashcroft***, 372 F.3d 529, 532-33 (3d Cir.2004); *see, e.g.,* ***Vatyan v. Mukasey***, 508 F.3d 1179, 1183, 1185-86 (9th Cir.2007) (in asylum case, P's testimony was proper method to authenticate foreign public documents).

(4) Certified copies of public records. To introduce a certified copy of a public record, a party must show the following: (1) the document is a copy of an official record or a copy of a document that was recorded or filed in a public office as authorized by law, and (2) the document was certified as correct by the custodian or another person authorized to make the certification or by a certificate that complies with FRE 902(1), (2), or (3), a federal statute, or a rule prescribed by the Supreme Court. FRE 902(4); *see* FRE 1005; ***U.S. v. Pent-R-Books, Inc.***, 538 F.2d 519, 527-28 (2d Cir.1976).

(5) Official publications. To introduce an official publication, a party must show that the document is a book, pamphlet, or other publication purporting to be issued by a public authority. FRE 902(5); *see, e.g.*, ***Williams v. Long***, 585 F.Supp.2d 679, 689 (D.Md.2008) (page from Maryland Judiciary Case Search website); ***Conjour v. Whitehall Township***, 850 F.Supp. 309, 312 n.1 (E.D.Pa.1994) (local ordinances and regulations); ***Biggers v. Southern Ry.***, 820 F.Supp. 1409, 1415 (N.D.Ga.1993) (map issued by Georgia Department of Transportation); ***California Ass'n of Bioanalysts v. Rank***, 577 F.Supp. 1342, 1355 n.23 (C.D.Cal.1983) (report published under seal of U.S. Department of Health and Human Services).

(6) Newspapers & periodicals. To introduce a newspaper or periodical, a party must show that the document is printed material purporting to be a newspaper or periodical. FRE 902(6); *see, e.g.*, ***Price v. Rochford***, 947 F.2d 829, 833 (7th Cir.1991) (newspapers); ***Snyder v. Whittaker Corp.***, 839 F.2d 1085, 1089 (5th Cir.1988) (magazine article).

(7) Trade inscriptions. To introduce a trade inscription, a party must show that the inscription, sign, tag, or label (1) purports to have been affixed in the course of business and (2) indicates origin, ownership, or control. FRE 902(7); *e.g.*, ***Whitted v. General Motors Corp.***, 58 F.3d 1200, 1204 (7th Cir.1995) (car owner's manual not trade inscription); ***U.S. v. Alvarez***, 972 F.2d 1000, 1004 (9th Cir.1992) (inscription used to show national origin of firearm); ***U.S. v. Chan***, 680 F.Supp. 521, 526 (E.D.N.Y.1988) (hotel records had printed and embossed trade inscriptions indicating origin).

(8) Acknowledged documents. To introduce an acknowledged document, a party must show the following: (1) the document is accompanied by a certificate of acknowledgment, and (2) the certificate was lawfully executed by a notary public or other authorized officer. FRE 902(8); *e.g.*, ***Howard-Ahmad v. Chicago Sch. Reform Bd. of Trs.***, 161 F.Supp.2d 857, 861 (N.D.Ill.2001) (unsigned and unnotarized affidavit was not admissible under FRE 902(8)).

(9) Commercial paper. To introduce a commercial paper, a party must show that the document is either commercial paper (e.g., a promissory note or check) or a document relating to commercial paper. *See* FRE 902(9); ***U.S. v. Varner***, 13 F.3d 1503, 1510 (11th Cir.1994).

3. Documents that are self-authenticating under statute. A signature, document, or anything else may be declared presumptively authentic by a federal statute. FRE 902(10). In such a case, the party must cite the statute. *See, e.g.*, 15 U.S.C. §77f(a) (signature on SEC registration presumed genuine); 26 U.S.C. §6064 (signature on tax return presumed genuine).

4. Domestic & foreign official records. FRCP 44(a) provides a method for authenticating official records. Before a party can introduce domestic or foreign official records, it must substantially comply with FRCP 44(a). *See* ***AMFAC Distrib.***, 842 F.2d at 306.

(1) Domestic authentication. Under FRCP 44(a)(1), a party may authenticate an official record that is kept within the United States, or any state, district, commonwealth, or territory subject to the administrative or judicial jurisdiction of the United States, by introducing either of the following:

(a) An official publication of the record. FRCP 44(a)(1)(A).

(b) A copy of the record attested to by the officer with legal custody of the record or by the officer's deputy. FRCP 44(a)(1)(B); ***AMFAC Distrib.***, 842 F.2d at 306; *see* ***Espinoza v. INS***, 45 F.3d 308, 310 (9th Cir. 1995); ***First Nat'l Life Ins. v. California Pac. Life Ins.***, 876 F.2d 877, 881 (11th Cir.1989). A certificate that the at-

testing officer has legal custody must accompany the copy of the record. FRCP 44(a)(1)(B); ***Espinoza***, 45 F.3d at 310; ***AMFAC Distrib.***, 842 F.2d at 306. This certificate must be made under seal by one of the following officials:

[1] A judge of a court in the district or political subdivision where the record is kept. FRCP 44(a)(1)(B)(i); ***First Nat'l Life Ins.***, 876 F.2d at 881.

[2] Any public officer with a seal of office and official duties in the district or political subdivision where the record is kept. FRCP 44(a)(1)(B)(ii).

PRACTICE TIP

Make sure that the attestation and certificate are stapled to the back of the copy of the official record and that both documents expressly refer to the copy of the official record. See ***AMFAC Distrib.****, 842 F.2d at 306. If there is any problem in linking the attestation and certificate to the official record, the court may not admit the copy into evidence.*

---

(2) Foreign authentication. To authenticate a foreign official record, a party should do the following:

(a) Prove document by official publication. The party may provide an official publication of a foreign country in the same manner as a domestic record. *See* FRCP 44(a)(2)(A)(i); 9A Wright & Miller §2435.

(b) Attach attestation & certificate to record. The party may provide a copy of the official publication. FRCP 44(a)(2)(A)(ii). The copy of the record must be attested to by a person authorized to make the attestation. *Id.* A final certificate supporting the genuineness of the signature and official position of the attester, or a chain of certificates leading to the person authorized to make the attestation, must be attached to the copy of the foreign record. FRCP 44(a)(2)(B). The certification may be made by any of the following: a secretary of a U.S. embassy or legation; a consul general, vice-consul, or consular agent of the United States; or a diplomatic or consular official of the foreign country assigned or accredited to the United States. *Id.*

(c) Show good cause to admit into evidence. On a showing of good cause, and if reasonable opportunity has been given to all parties to investigate the authenticity and accuracy of the documents, the court may either admit an attested copy without final certification or permit the foreign official record to be evidenced by an attested summary with or without final certification. FRCP 44(a)(2)(C).

(d) Follow requirements of treaty or convention. If the United States and the foreign country where the record is located are parties to a treaty or convention that abolishes the requirement of a final certificate, the treaty or convention must be followed. 1991 Notes to FRCP 44 at ¶2, p. 1207, this book; *see* FRCP 44(a)(2)(A)(ii). For example, signatories to the Hague Public Documents Convention have established a system for authenticating foreign documents. *See* 1991 Notes to FRCP 44 at ¶3, p. 1207, this book. *See generally* Harvey, Comment, *The United States & the Hague Convention Abolishing the Requirement of Legalisation for Foreign Public Documents*, 11 Harv. Int'l L.J. 476, 481-82 (1970) (suggesting that while Hague Convention abolishes legalization requirement, it replaces old process with new requirements).

(3) Lack of record. A written statement that a diligent search of designated records revealed no specific record or entry is admissible as evidence that the records contain no such record or entry. FRCP 44(b). This statement must be authenticated under FRCP 44(a)(1) for domestic records, or it must comply with the requirements of FRCP 44(a)(2)(C)(ii) for foreign records. FRCP 44(b).

(4) Other proof. Any other method authorized by law may be used to prove a record. FRCP 44(c); 9A Wright & Miller §2437.

§8. APPELLATE REVIEW

The district court's evidentiary rulings are reviewed for abuse of discretion. ***Sprint/United Mgmt. v. Mendelsohn***, 552 U.S. 379, 384 (2008); ***General Elec. Co. v. Joiner***, 522 U.S. 136, 144 (1997); ***U.S. v. Abel***, 469 U.S. 45, 53-54

(1984); *see* ***Compaq Computer Corp. v. Ergonome Inc.***, 387 F.3d 403, 408 (5th Cir.2004) (admission or exclusion of evidence); ***U.S. v. Stelmokas***, 100 F.3d 302, 312 (3d Cir.1996) (authentication ruling). If there was no objection when the ruling was made, however, the ruling is reviewed for plain error. *See* FRE 103(e).

D. OBJECTING TO EVIDENCE

§1. GENERAL

§1.1 Rules. FRE 103, 403.

§1.2 Purpose. The main reason to object to evidence is to prevent it from being introduced in the trial and heard by the jury. Another reason is to preserve the issue for appellate review. *See* FRE 103(a).

§1.3 Forms. ***O'Connor's Federal Civil Forms*** (2012), FORMS 8D.

§1.4 Other references. 21 Wright & Graham, *Federal Practice & Procedure 2d* §§5036-5043 (2005 & Supp.2012); 9 *Moore's Federal Practice 3d* ch. 46 (2012).

§2. TIMING & SPECIFICITY OF OBJECTIONS

§2.1 Objections before trial. The first time a party may object to evidence is before trial—in a motion to exclude evidence or a motion in limine. *See* FRCP 16(c)(2)(C), (c)(2)(D), (c)(2)(L). A motion in limine without an additional objection at trial generally does not preserve error. ***Gill v. Thomas***, 83 F.3d 537, 540 (1st Cir.1996); ***Huff v. Heckendorn Mfg. Co.***, 991 F.2d 464, 466 (8th Cir.1993). See "Motion in Limine," ch. 5-H, p. 341; "Motion to Exclude Expert Witness," ch. 5-N, p. 376.

§2.2 Trial objections. When objectionable evidence is offered at trial, the party that believes it is not admissible must object to it and have the court rule on the objection. ***Bartleson v. U.S.***, 96 F.3d 1270, 1277-78 (9th Cir. 1996); ***Jetcraft Corp. v. Flight Safety Int'l***, 16 F.3d 362, 366 (10th Cir.1993). If a party does not object, the party waives all error in the admission of the evidence except plain error. FRE 103(a)(1), (e); ***Marbled Murrelet v. Babbitt***, 83 F.3d 1060, 1066 (9th Cir.1996); ***McKeel v. City of Pine Bluff***, 73 F.3d 207, 211 (8th Cir.1996); ***Peaches Entm't Corp. v. Entertainment Repertoire Assocs.***, 62 F.3d 690, 694 (5th Cir.1995); *see* ***Judd v. Rodman***, 105 F.3d 1339, 1342 (11th Cir.1997) (objection on specific grounds does not preserve error for purposes of appeal on other grounds). To preserve error, the party must state the specific grounds for the objection on the record. FRE 103(a)(1)(B). But if the defect in the evidence is apparent from the context of the objection, the objection alone will preserve error. *Id.*

§2.3 Timing. An objection must be made as soon as the reason for it becomes apparent. ***McKnight v. Johnson Controls, Inc.***, 36 F.3d 1396, 1407-08 (8th Cir.1994); ***Government of the V.I. v. Archibald***, 987 F.2d 180, 184 (3d Cir.1993); *see* FRE 103(a)(1)(A).

1. Too early. If an objection is premature, it does not preserve error. For example, an objection made in a motion in limine that is not definitively ruled on before trial and is not repeated at trial usually does not preserve error. *See* ***U.S. v. Gajo***, 290 F.3d 922, 927 (7th Cir.2002). However, if the ruling on the motion in limine is clearly definitive, error may be preserved. *See id.*; ***Zachar v. Lee***, 363 F.3d 70, 75 (1st Cir.2004); ***U.S. v. Malik***, 345 F.3d 999, 1001 (8th Cir.2003); 2000 Notes to FRE 103 at ¶¶1, 2, p. 1240, this book.

2. On time. In most cases, the objection must be made at the same time as the introduction of the evidence. *See* ***San Antonio Cmty. Hosp. v. Southern Cal. Dist. Council of Carpenters***, 125 F.3d 1230, 1238 (9th Cir.1997); ***McEwen v. City of Norman***, 926 F.2d 1539, 1547 (10th Cir.1991).

(1) Testimonial evidence. For testimonial evidence, the objection should be made after the question is asked but before the witness answers. ***Hutchinson v. Groskin***, 927 F.2d 722, 725 (2d Cir.1991). An objection made after the witness answers is timely in some situations, such as when the witness makes an objectionable answer to a proper question, answers an objectionable question too quickly for the objection to be made, or volunteers an objectionable statement. *See* ***Archibald***, 987 F.2d at 184; ***U.S. v. Pujana-Mena***, 949 F.2d 24, 32-33 (2d Cir.1991).

(2) Depositions & documentary evidence. For depositions or documentary evidence, a party must object within 14 days after the other party disclosed its list of evidence. FRCP 26(a)(3)(B). If a party does not timely object, it waives all objections, except for those made under FRE 402 and 403 or unless the objection is excused by the court for good cause. FRCP 26(a)(3)(B).

3. Too late. An objection is not timely if it is not made the first time the evidence is offered or if it comes after several questions have been asked on the same subject. *See* ***McAlinney v. Marion Merrell Dow, Inc.***, 992 F.2d 839, 844 (8th Cir.1993). However, if the ground for the objection does not become apparent until several questions have been asked, the attorney may properly object at that time. ***Pujana-Mena***, 949 F.2d at 32-33. A motion to strike the testimony after the witness finishes testifying does not preserve error. *See* ***Terrell v. Poland***, 744 F.2d 637, 638-39 (8th Cir.1984).

NOTE

A party is not required to object in the presence of the jury when the court asks the witness a question. See FRE 614(c). If the objection is not made at the time of the question, an objection made at the next occasion when the jury is not present is timely. Id.; see ***U.S. v. Van De Walker***, *141 F.3d 1451, 1452 n.4 (11th Cir.1998).*

§2.4 Specificity. An objection must be specific. FRE 103(a)(1)(B); ***Miksis v. Howard***, 106 F.3d 754, 761 (7th Cir.1997); ***Angelo v. Armstrong World Indus.***, 11 F.3d 957, 960-61 (10th Cir.1993); *see* ***Microfinancial, Inc. v. Premier Holidays Int'l***, 385 F.3d 72, 81 (1st Cir.2004) (unless ground is obvious, objection must be specific). The party must make its objection clear; the judge should not have to imagine all the possible grounds for an objection. ***Angelo***, 11 F.3d at 960-61. There are at least three reasons why the courts require a specific objection: (1) to enable the judge to understand the challenge, (2) to permit the judge to make an intelligent ruling, and (3) to permit the party offering the evidence the opportunity to remedy the defect and reoffer it in admissible form. A specific objection must identify two things:

1. The exact part of the question or evidence that is objectionable. *See* ***U.S. v. Adamson***, 665 F.2d 649, 660 (5th Cir.1982) (objection inadequate when not made with particularity), *reinstated in relevant part*, 700 F.2d 953 (5th Cir.1983).

2. The specific legal principle the court will violate by admitting the evidence, if it is not apparent from the context. FRE 103(a)(1)(B); *see, e.g.,* ***U.S. v. Nnanyererugo***, 39 F.3d 1205, 1208-09 (D.C.Cir.1994) (hearsay objection did not preserve objection based on lack of personal knowledge); ***Prymer v. Ogden***, 29 F.3d 1208, 1213-14 (7th Cir.1994) (objections based on relevance and prejudice did not preserve objection that elements of collateral estoppel were not met); ***Merrick v. Farmers Ins.***, 892 F.2d 1434, 1440 (9th Cir.1990) (objection to photograph on grounds of relevance and lack of foundation did not preserve objection based on authentication).

§2.5 No general objections. A general objection is one that merely challenges the admissibility of the evidence or objects to evidence for vague reasons. *See* ***U.S. v. Berry***, 977 F.2d 915, 918 (5th Cir.1992) (objection must provide basis to identify and correct the problem). A loosely formulated and imprecise objection will not preserve error on appeal. ***U.S. v. Waldrip***, 981 F.2d 799, 804 (5th Cir.1993); *see, e.g.,* ***Owen v. Patton***, 925 F.2d 1111, 1114 (8th Cir.1991) ("I'm going to object to that" is not adequate objection); ***U.S. v. Akitoye***, 923 F.2d 221, 223-24 (1st Cir.1991) ("I object" and "objection" are not adequate objections); ***U.S. v. Sandini***, 803 F.2d 123, 126 (3d Cir.1986) (that evidence is "irrelevant" is not adequate objection). However, if the nature of the objection is obvious from its context, the lack of specificity does not waive the objection. FRE 103(a)(1)(B); *see* ***Microfinancial, Inc. v. Premier Holidays Int'l***, 385 F.3d 72, 81 (1st Cir.2004).

§3. OBJECTION TO WITNESS

§3.1 Taking witness on voir dire. A party may take a witness on voir dire to test that person's qualifications as a witness, to challenge the existence of a privilege, or to challenge the admissibility of evidence. *See* FRE 104(a);

U.S. Football League v. National Football League, 842 F.2d 1335, 1375 (2d Cir.1988). For example, if a party believes a witness is not able to testify because of lack of knowledge, the party should object; if the objection is overruled, the party should ask to take the witness on voir dire. *See **U.S. v. Mares***, 940 F.2d 455, 463 (9th Cir.1991). The procedure is a limited cross-examination on the issue of knowledge, and it occurs during the proponent's direct examination of the witness.

1. Scope of examination. The purpose of the voir dire examination is to test the competence of the witness or the admissibility of evidence. *See, e.g.*, ***U.S. v. Robinson***, 922 F.2d 1531, 1533 (11th Cir.1991) (to challenge introduction of photographs, D took witness on voir dire to show that witness had no recollection of location identified in pictures).

2. Time for voir dire. A party should ask to take a witness on voir dire before the witness testifies about the objectionable matter.

3. No right to voir dire. The court has the discretion to deny a request to take a witness on voir dire. When allowing a party to conduct voir dire, the court can require that it be done in front of the jury.

4. Repeat objection after voir dire. After taking a witness on voir dire to inquire into the witness's knowledge, the party should repeat its objection to the qualification of the witness or the admissibility of the proposed evidence. *See, e.g.*, ***Loudermill v. Dow Chem. Co.***, 863 F.2d 566, 568 (8th Cir.1988) (after eliciting testimony from expert on voir dire, D used expert's statement to object to his qualifications).

§3.2 Objection to expert testimony. For a discussion of objecting to an expert witness, see "Motion to Exclude Expert Witness," ch. 5-N, p. 376.

§3.3 Objection to witness who violated sequestration order. To exclude witnesses from the courtroom during the trial, a party must request that the court sequester the witnesses before testimony begins. FRE 615. This procedure is commonly known as "invoking the rule." FRE 615 requires the court, at a party's request, to remove the witnesses from the courtroom so they cannot hear other witnesses' testimony. ***Hollman v. Dale Elec., Inc.***, 752 F.2d 311, 313 (8th Cir.1985); *see also* ***U.S. v. Greschner***, 802 F.2d 373, 375-76 (10th Cir.1986) (FRE 615 requires court to exclude prospective witnesses from courtroom and prohibit them from discussing case with other witnesses). The court can invoke the rule on its own initiative. FRE 615.

PRACTICE TIP

FRE 615 does not apply to the examination of witnesses at depositions. FRCP 30(c)(1). To exclude other deponents from the deposition of a witness, a party should seek a protective order under FRCP 26(c)(1)(E).

1. Exemption. The following witnesses are exempt from exclusion under FRE 615: (1) a party who is a natural person, (2) an officer or employee of a party that is not a natural person, after being designated as the party's representative by its attorney, (3) a person whose presence is shown to be essential to a party's case, or (4) a person authorized by statute to be present. FRE 615. Expert witnesses are frequently exempted from sequestration orders because their presence is shown to be essential. *See* ***Opus 3 Ltd. v. Heritage Park, Inc.***, 91 F.3d 625, 629 (4th Cir.1996) (declining to adopt per se rule exempting experts); ***Morvant v. Construction Aggregates Corp.***, 570 F.2d 626, 629-30 (6th Cir.1978) (decision to exempt expert is within court's discretion); *see, e.g.*, ***U.S. v. Olofson***, 563 F.3d 652, 660-61 (7th Cir.2009) (when D did not explain why expert's presence was essential, D's expert was properly excluded; D's expert did not need to be present for government expert's testimony because D's expert already had most of relevant information from government expert's report).

2. Violation. If the rule is invoked but a witness violates the exclusion order, the court must determine whether to permit the witness to testify. ***U.S. v. Washington***, 653 F.3d 1251, 1268 (10th Cir.2011); *see* ***U.S. v. Hobbs***, 31 F.3d 918, 921 (9th Cir.1994) (court may hold witness in contempt, allow cross-examination regarding violation, or prohibit testimony). A significant consideration for the court is whether a party knowingly or intentionally violated

the exclusion order. ***Washington***, 653 F.3d at 1269. After considering all the circumstances, the court can bar the testimony. *See* ***Jerry Parks Equip. Co. v. Southeast Equip. Co.***, 817 F.2d 340, 342-43 (5th Cir.1987).

§3.4 Objection to undisclosed witness. The parties must disclose the names of potential witnesses before trial. FRCP 26(a)(1)(A)(i). Generally, a party is not allowed to call an undisclosed witness to testify at trial. FRCP 37(c)(1). The exclusion is self-executing unless the party proves that concealing the witness was substantially justified or that the nondisclosure is harmless to the other party. *See id.*; ***Salgado v. General Motors Corp.***, 150 F.3d 735, 742 (7th Cir.1998); 1993 Notes to FRCP 37 at ¶9, p. 1206, this book. See "Sanctions for refusing to disclose," ch. 6-A, §15.5.2, p. 451. Although a motion is not required, the challenging party should (1) object to the testimony of an undisclosed witness either when the witness is offered or in a pretrial motion to exclude, and (2) argue either that the fact witness was not disclosed under FRCP 26(a)(1)(A)(i) or that the expert witness was not disclosed under FRCP 26(a)(2)(A). The challenging party should also assert that the nondisclosure prejudiced its ability to prepare for and conduct its case at trial. *See, e.g.*, ***Rowland v. American Gen. Fin., Inc.***, 340 F.3d 187, 195-96 (4th Cir. 2003) (failure to comply with FRCP 26(a)(3) requirement of pretrial disclosures was excused because no harm was shown).

§4. OBJECTION TO QUESTION

If an improper question is asked, a party should object and ask for an instruction to disregard. If the error cannot be cured by an instruction, the party should also ask for a mistrial. But an improper question that is not answered by the witness usually does not constitute reversible error.

§5. OBJECTION TO EVIDENCE

§5.1 Multiple parties. In a multiparty case, when one party objects and thus brings an issue to the court's attention, further objections by coparties are unnecessary. ***U.S. v. Church***, 970 F.2d 401, 409 (7th Cir.1992); ***Loose v. Offshore Nav., Inc.***, 670 F.2d 493, 496-97 (5th Cir.1982). A coparty may raise the point on appeal. ***Loose***, 670 F.2d at 496. This rule does not apply when the objection was clearly not made on behalf of all coparties. ***Fortier v. Dona Anna Plaza Partners***, 747 F.2d 1324, 1331 (10th Cir.1984).

§5.2 Repeating the objection. A party is not required to renew an objection each time inadmissible evidence is offered as long as (1) the party has satisfied the objection requirements of FRE 103(a)(1) for that evidence and (2) the court, either before or at trial, has made a definitive ruling on the record admitting the evidence. FRE 103(b); 2000 Notes to FRE 103 at ¶2, p. 1240, this book; *see* ***U.S. v. Harrison***, 296 F.3d 994, 1002 (10th Cir.2002) (party does not need to renew objection once court makes definitive ruling); *see also* ***Fuesting v. Zimmer, Inc.***, 448 F.3d 936, 940 (7th Cir.2006) (party does not need to renew objection through postverdict motion). FRE 103(a) applies to all of the court's rulings on evidence, including in limine rulings. 2000 Notes to FRE 103 at ¶1, p. 1240, this book. See "Motion in Limine," ch. 5-H, p. 341. However, the party may need to renew its objection in the following instances:

1. Court's ruling was provisional. If the court has reserved its ruling or indicated that the ruling is provisional, the party must object every time evidence subject to the ruling is sought to be introduced. 2000 Notes to FRE 103 at ¶2, p. 1240, this book. For example, if the court decides before trial that certain evidence is admissible subject to the introduction of a foundation, the party must object to the introduction of the evidence if that foundation is never provided, or else it waives error on appeal. *Id.* at ¶5, p. 1240, this book.

2. Attorney did not seek clarification. An attorney must seek a clarification from the court that its ruling on admissibility is "definitive." 2000 Notes to FRE 103 at ¶3, p. 1241, this book. Whether a ruling is definitive is determined by the facts and circumstances before the court at the time of the ruling. *Id.* at ¶5, p. 1241, this book. If the attorney does not seek the clarification and there is some doubt about whether the court's ruling is definitive, to preserve error for appeal, the attorney must object every time evidence subject to the ruling is introduced. *See id.*; *see, e.g.*, ***Walden v. Georgia-Pac. Corp.***, 126 F.3d 506, 520 (3d Cir.1997) (attorney never requested clarification of court's directive not to reargue every ruling).

3. Changed circumstances. If the relevant facts and circumstances supporting the initial objection have materially changed after the ruling has been made, to preserve error for appeal, the party must make a renewed and timely objection that allows the court to revisit its earlier ruling. ***Harrison***, 296 F.3d at 1002-03; 2000 Notes to FRE 103 at ¶5, p. 1241, this book.

4. Opposing party violates ruling. If the opposing party violates the ruling and seeks to introduce the excluded evidence, the party must object to preserve error for appeal. 2000 Notes to FRE 103 at ¶4, p. 1241, this book; *see* ***U.S. Aviation Underwriters, Inc. v. Olympia Wings, Inc.***, 896 F.2d 949, 956 (5th Cir.1990).

5. Court changes ruling. If the court changes its ruling, the party must object when evidence is offered to preserve error for appeal. 2000 Notes to FRE 103 at ¶4, p. 1241, this book; *see* ***U.S. Aviation***, 896 F.2d at 956.

CAUTION

FRE 103(a) does not resolve the issue of whether a party waives its right to appeal when (1) it objects to evidence that the court finds admissible in a definitive ruling and (2) it then offers the evidence to "remove the sting" of its anticipated prejudicial effect. 2000 Notes to FRE 103 at ¶8, p. 1241, this book. However, the Supreme Court has held that a party who preemptively introduces evidence on direct examination cannot claim on appeal that the admission of the evidence was error. ***Ohler v. U.S.****, 529 U.S. 753, 758-60 (2000); see* ***U.S. v. Delgado****, 401 F.3d 290, 301 (5th Cir.2005);* ***U.S. v. Saunders****, 359 F.3d 874, 877-78 (7th Cir.2004).*

§5.3 Running objection. A party is not required to make a running objection (i.e., renew an objection each time inadmissible evidence is offered) as long as (1) the party has satisfied the objection requirements of FRE 103(a)(1) for that evidence and (2) the court, either before or at trial, has made a definitive ruling on the record admitting the evidence. FRE 103(b); 2000 Notes to FRE 103 at ¶2, p. 1240, this book. See "Repeating the objection," §5.2, p. 703.

§5.4 Different forms of same evidence. To preserve an objection to evidence, a party must object to all forms of the same evidence. If any evidence that proves the same point is admitted, even in a different form, the objection is waived.

PRACTICE TIP

FRE 1002, often referred to as the "best-evidence rule," is not necessarily a good objection to prevent a witness from discussing or reading from a document that has already been introduced into evidence. The best-evidence rule comes into play only when a witness is asked to prove the contents of a disputed document without the introduction of the original or a copy. See ***U.S. v. Smith****, 566 F.3d 410, 413-14 (4th Cir.2009);* ***U.S. v. Bennett****, 363 F.3d 947, 953 (9th Cir.2004).*

§6. RULING ON OBJECTION

§6.1 Ruling.

1. Sustained. If the court sustains the objection, it will not admit the evidence. The offering party can ask the court to admit the evidence for a limited purpose or for a particular party.

2. Overruled. If the court overrules the objection, it will admit the evidence. The objecting party can ask the court to restrict the jury's consideration of the evidence to a limited purpose or to a particular party.

3. Request for limited admissibility. The court may instruct the jury to consider the evidence only for limited purposes. FRE 105; *see* ***Sprynczynatyk v. General Motors Corp.***, 771 F.2d 1112, 1117 (8th Cir.1985). Failure to request a limiting instruction waives error on appeal. *See* ***U.S. v. Cudlitz***, 72 F.3d 992, 1002 (1st Cir.1996) (stressing importance of request for contemporaneous instruction); ***Engebretsen v. Fairchild Aircraft Corp.***, 21 F.3d 721, 730-31 (6th Cir.1994) (party opposing admission of statement forfeits right to exclude if specific request

not made). If a timely request has been made, the court preferably should give the limiting instruction to the jury both at the time the evidence is conditionally admitted and at the close of the evidence. ***U.S. v. Holley***, 23 F.3d 902, 912 (5th Cir.1994); *see* ***U.S. v. Misle Bus & Equip. Co.***, 967 F.2d 1227, 1233-34 (8th Cir.1992). But the timing of the instruction is not reversible error if an adequate instruction was given at some point. *See* ***Holley***, 23 F.3d at 912; ***Misle Bus***, 967 F.2d at 1234.

§6.2 Nonruling. If the court does not rule, or if no ruling appears on the record, the error is waived. *See* FRE 103(a); 2000 Notes to FRE 103 at ¶2, p. 1240, this book. To preserve error, an objection must actually be overruled.

1. Equivocal ruling. If the court says it will rule on an objection later, the statement is not a ruling and does not preserve error. If the court invites the party to reurge the objection later, it is not a ruling.

2. Refusal to rule. If the court refuses to rule, the party must make sure its request for a ruling and the refusal appear on the record.

§7. PRESERVING ERROR WHEN EVIDENCE IS EXCLUDED

If any of its evidence is excluded, a party generally must make an offer of proof to preserve the evidence so the appellate court can determine whether the exclusion was harmful. *See* FRE 103(a)(2). See "Offer of Proof," ch. 8-E, p. 707.

§8. INSTRUCTION TO DISREGARD & MOTION FOR MISTRIAL

Sometimes evidence is presented to a jury before the party can object, such as when a witness blurts out an answer or gives a nonresponsive answer. To preserve error when the jury hears inadmissible evidence (or improper comments by the attorneys in opening statements or closing arguments), a party should follow the steps illustrated in chart 8-1 and explained below.

8-1. PURSUING AN ADVERSE RULING

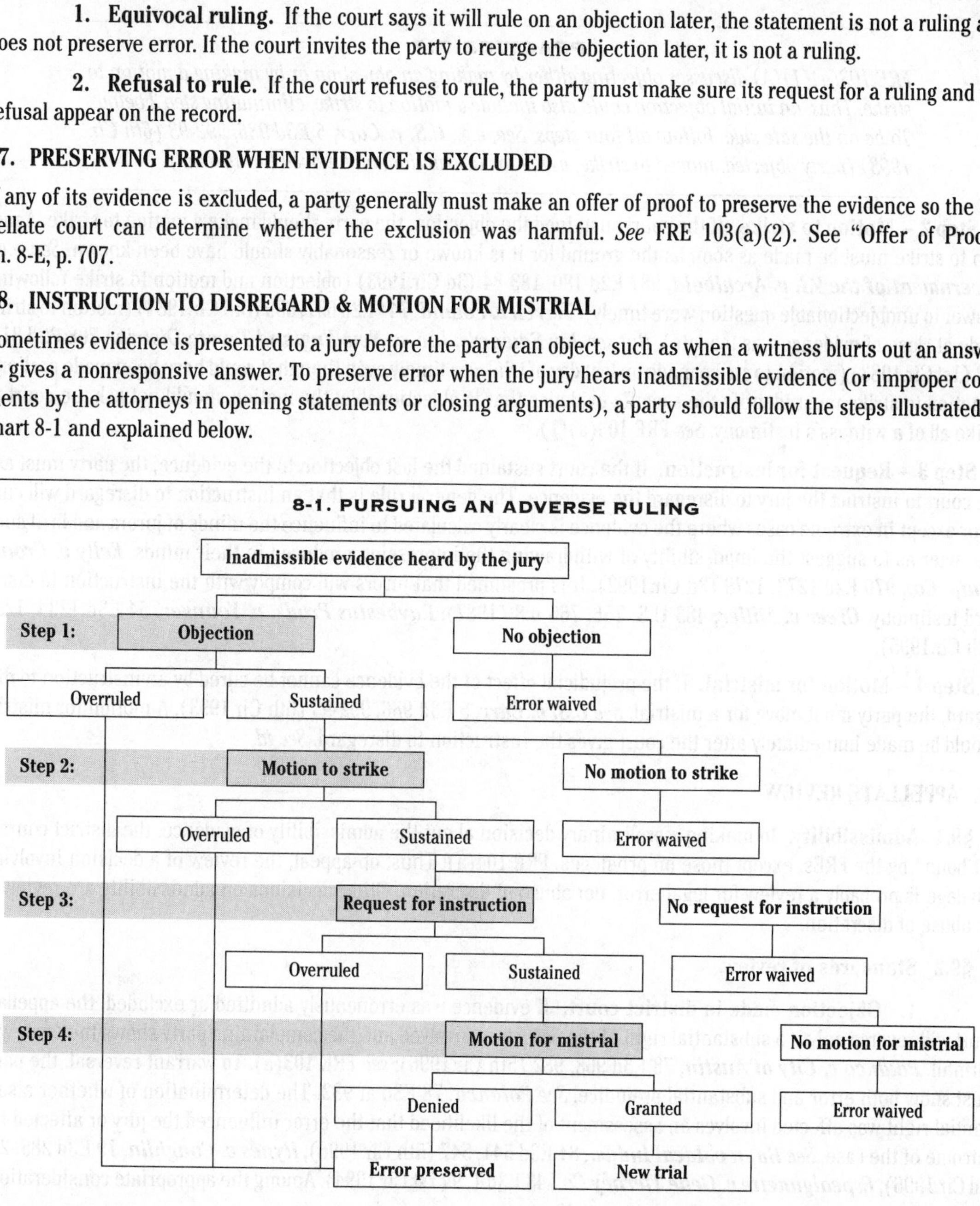

Inadmissible evidence heard by the jury

Step 1: **Objection** → Overruled / Sustained | **No objection** → Error waived

Step 2: **Motion to strike** → Overruled / Sustained | **No motion to strike** → Error waived

Step 3: **Request for instruction** → Overruled / Sustained | **No request for instruction** → Error waived

Step 4: **Motion for mistrial** → Denied / Granted | **No motion for mistrial** → Error waived

Error preserved (Overruled at Step 1, 2 or 3; Denied at Step 4)

New trial (Granted at Step 4)

Step 1 – Objection. The party should make a timely and specific objection. Whether additional steps are necessary depends on the court's ruling on the objection.

- **Objection overruled – error preserved.** If the court overrules the objection, error is preserved.
- **Objection sustained – pursue adverse ruling.** If the court sustains the objection to the evidence, the party must continue to object by taking steps 2 through 4 below. This is called "pursuing an adverse ruling." Only when the court denies one of the requests (generally the request for a mistrial) is error preserved. If the party stops objecting before receiving an adverse ruling, error is not preserved.

PRACTICE TIP

FRE 103(a)(1)(A) discusses objecting either by making an objection or by making a motion to strike. Thus, an initial objection could also include a motion to strike, eliminating step 2 below. To be on the safe side, follow all four steps. See, e.g., ***U.S. v. Carr****, 5 F.3d 986, 992-93 (6th Cir. 1993) (party objected, moved to strike, asked for instruction, and moved for mistrial).*

Step 2 – Motion to strike. If the court sustained the objection, the party should make a motion to strike. A motion to strike must be made as soon as the ground for it is known or reasonably should have been known. *See, e.g.*, ***Government of the V.I. v. Archibald***, 987 F.2d 180, 183-84 (3d Cir.1993) (objection and motion to strike following answer to unobjectionable question were timely); ***Terrell v. Poland***, 744 F.2d 637, 639 (8th Cir.1984) (motion to strike made at close of evidence was too late). *But see* ***Jay Edwards, Inc. v. New England Toyota Distrib.***, 708 F.2d 814, 822 (1st Cir.1983) (motion to strike made on last day of trial was timely even though it could have been made earlier). A motion to strike must identify the specific evidence that is objectionable; the motion should not ask the court to strike all of a witness's testimony. *See* FRE 103(a)(1).

Step 3 – Request for instruction. If the court sustained the last objection to the evidence, the party must ask the court to instruct the jury to disregard the evidence. The general rule is that an instruction to disregard will cure error except in extreme cases where the evidence is clearly calculated to influence the minds of jurors and is of such character as to suggest the impossibility of withdrawing the impression produced in their minds. ***Kelly v. Crown Equip. Co.***, 970 F.2d 1273, 1279 (3d Cir.1992). It is presumed that jurors will comply with the instruction to disregard testimony. ***Greer v. Miller***, 483 U.S. 756, 766 n.8 (1987); ***Raybestos Prods. v. Younger***, 54 F.3d 1234, 1239 (7th Cir.1995).

Step 4 – Motion for mistrial. If the prejudicial effect of the evidence cannot be cured by an instruction to disregard, the party must move for a mistrial. *See* ***U.S. v. Carr***, 5 F.3d 986, 992-93 (6th Cir.1993). A motion for mistrial should be made immediately after the court gives the instruction to disregard. *See id.*

§9. APPELLATE REVIEW

§9.1 Admissibility. In making a preliminary decision about the admissibility of evidence, the district court is not bound by the FREs, except those on privileges. FRE 104(a). Thus, on appeal, the review of a decision involving privilege is probably a review for legal error, not abuse of discretion. Other decisions on admissibility are reviewed for abuse of discretion.

§9.2 Standards of review.

1. Objection made in district court. If evidence was erroneously admitted or excluded, the appellate court will reverse only if a substantial right of the party was involved and the complaining party shows the error was harmful. ***Polanco v. City of Austin***, 78 F.3d 968, 982 (5th Cir.1996); *see* FRE 103(a). To warrant reversal, the party must show both error and substantial prejudice. *See* ***Polanco***, 78 F.3d at 982. The determination of whether a substantial right was affected involves an assessment of the likelihood that the error influenced the jury or affected the outcome of the case. *See* ***Haun v. Ideal Indus.***, 81 F.3d 541, 547 (5th Cir.1996); ***Hynes v. Coughlin***, 79 F.3d 285, 291 (2d Cir.1996); ***Espeaignnette v. Gene Tierney Co.***, 43 F.3d 1, 9 (1st Cir.1994). Among the appropriate considerations

are the number of errors, the closeness of the factual disputes, the prejudicial effect of the evidence, the instructions given, and whether the attorney intentionally elicited the evidence and focused on it during the trial. ***Ad-Vantage Tel. Directory Consultants, Inc. v. GTE Directories Corp.***, 37 F.3d 1460, 1465 (11th Cir.1994); *see also* ***Hynes***, 79 F.3d at 291 (error is harmless if court concludes testimony was unimportant in relation to everything considered by jury on issue in question).

2. Objection raised on appeal. If a party did not preserve error in the district court, the court's ruling admitting or excluding evidence will not be reversed on appeal unless the objecting party shows plain error. ***Foradori v. Harris***, 523 F.3d 477, 508 (5th Cir.2008); ***U.S. v. Seymour***, 468 F.3d 378, 387 (6th Cir.2006); ***McKeel v. City of Pine Bluff***, 73 F.3d 207, 211 (8th Cir.1996). Plain error is error so obvious and substantial that failure to notice and correct it would affect the fairness, integrity, or public reputation of the judicial proceeding. ***Douglass v. United Servs. Auto. Ass'n***, 79 F.3d 1415, 1424 (5th Cir.1996).

E. OFFER OF PROOF

§1. GENERAL

§1.1 Rule. FRE 103.

§1.2 Purpose. An offer of proof serves two purposes: (1) it allows the district court to make an informed evidentiary ruling, and (2) it creates a record that an appellate court can review to determine whether the exclusion of evidence amounts to reversible error. ***Polys v. Trans-Colo. Airlines, Inc.***, 941 F.2d 1404, 1406-07 (10th Cir.1991); *see* ***Fusco v. General Motors Corp.***, 11 F.3d 259, 263 n.3 (1st Cir.1993); ***U.S. v. Sheffield***, 992 F.2d 1164, 1169 (11th Cir.1993). An appellate court cannot review whether evidence was erroneously excluded unless the proponent of the evidence makes a proper offer of proof. *See* FRE 103(a)(2); ***Smith v. Hy-Vee, Inc.***, 622 F.3d 904, 908 (8th Cir.2010); ***U.S. v. Akpan***, 407 F.3d 360, 374 (5th Cir.2005); ***Snyder v. Ag Trucking, Inc.***, 57 F.3d 484, 492 (6th Cir.1995).

§1.3 Forms. *O'Connor's Federal Civil Forms* (2012), FORMS 8E.

§1.4 Other references. 21 Wright & Graham, *Federal Practice & Procedure 2d* §5040 (2005 & Supp.2012); 9 *Moore's Federal Practice 3d* §§46.02, 46.03 (2012).

§2. TIMING OF OFFER

§2.1 General rule. If the court rules that certain evidence is inadmissible, the party offering the evidence should make an offer of proof at the same time as the court's ruling. *See* ***Polys v. Trans-Colo. Airlines, Inc.***, 941 F.2d 1404, 1409 (10th Cir.1991); 2000 Notes to FRE 103 at ¶2, p. 1240, this book; *see, e.g.*, ***Germano v. International Profit Ass'n***, 544 F.3d 798, 801 (7th Cir.2008) (P's offer of proof included in response to D's MSJ was sufficient to preserve error when P had no other opportunity to litigate whether evidence should have been excluded); ***Pedigo v. Unum Life Ins.***, 145 F.3d 804, 808 (6th Cir.1998) (district court properly denied request to submit offer of proof made 2½ months after trial); ***Murphy v. City of Flagler Beach***, 761 F.2d 622, 626 (11th Cir.1985) (offer of proof was timely when made at conference on evidentiary questions held after P's attempt to elicit objectionable evidence during trial). If the court has reserved its ruling or indicated that the ruling is provisional, the party should offer the evidence during trial; if, at that time, the court definitively rules that the evidence is inadmissible, the party should then make an offer of proof. *See* ***Smith v. Hy-Vee, Inc.***, 622 F.3d 904, 908 (8th Cir.2010); ***Fusco v. General Motors Corp.***, 11 F.3d 259, 262 (1st Cir.1993); 2000 Notes to FRE 103 at ¶2, p. 1240, this book. If, after a reserved or provisional ruling, the party does not offer the evidence during trial, the party waives any error on appeal regarding the court's ruling. *See* ***Fusco***, 11 F.3d at 262; 2000 Notes to FRE 103 at ¶2, p. 1240, this book.

§2.2 Exceptions. The party seeking to introduce evidence is not always required to make an offer of proof to preserve an argument that the evidence was wrongly excluded. Some exceptions to the requirement of making an offer of proof include the following:

1. Apparent from context. If the substance of the evidence sought to be admitted is apparent from the context in which the questions were asked, the party does not need to make the substance of the excluded testimony known by an offer of proof. FRE 103(a)(2); ***Beech Aircraft Corp. v. Rainey***, 488 U.S. 153, 174 (1988).

2. After definitive ruling excluding evidence. A party is not required to make an offer of proof when the evidence is excluded as long as (1) the party makes clear what evidence the party wants admitted and why it is admissible and (2) the court, either before or at trial, has made a definitive ruling on the record excluding the evidence. 2000 Notes to FRE 103 at ¶2, p. 1240, this book; *see* FRE 103(b); ***Walden v. Georgia-Pac. Corp.***, 126 F.3d 506, 520 (3d Cir.1997); ***Unit Drilling Co. v. Enron Oil & Gas Co.***, 108 F.3d 1186, 1193 n.10 (10th Cir.1997); ***Fusco v. General Motors Corp.***, 11 F.3d 259, 262-63 & n.3 (1st Cir.1993); *see, e.g.*, ***Heyne v. Caruso***, 69 F.3d 1475, 1481-82 (9th Cir.1995) (once court excluded all testimony about other incidents of sexual harassment, party was not required to make offer of proof on exact purpose and substance of each witness's testimony). An attorney must seek a clarification from the court that its ruling on admissibility is definitive. 2000 Notes to FRE 103 at ¶3, p. 1241, this book. Whether a ruling is definitive is determined by the facts and circumstances before the court at the time of the ruling. *Id.* at ¶5, p. 1241, this book. FRE 103(a) applies to all of the court's rulings on evidence, including in limine rulings. 2000 Notes to FRE 103 at ¶1, p. 1240, this book. See "Motion in Limine," ch. 5-H, p. 341. However, the party may still need to make a formal offer of proof after a definitive ruling in the following instances:

(1) Attorney did not seek clarification. If the attorney does not seek the clarification and there is some doubt about whether the court's ruling is definitive, the attorney must make a formal offer of proof or motion to strike. *See* 2000 Notes to FRE 103 at ¶¶3, 5, p. 1241, this book.

(2) Changed circumstances. If the relevant facts and circumstances supporting the exclusion have materially changed after the ruling has been made, to preserve error for appeal, the party must make a renewed and timely offer of proof to allow the court to revisit its earlier ruling. ***U.S. v. Harrison***, 296 F.3d 994, 1002-03 (10th Cir. 2002); 2000 Notes to FRE 103 at ¶5, p. 1241, this book. Some examples of changed circumstances include a new basis for admissibility becoming apparent and the court's initial reason for exclusion becoming moot. *See* ***Fusco***, 11 F.3d at 263 n.3.

(3) Court invites reconsideration. If the court invites the party to renew its challenge to the ruling that excluded its evidence, the party must follow up on the invitation by renewing its offer of proof, or else it will waive error on appeal. ***Favala v. Cumberland Eng'g***, 17 F.3d 987, 991 (7th Cir.1994).

§3. OFFER OF PROOF

An offer of proof is not just a statement of the proposed evidence. It is a record of evidence that was excluded from the trial and a statement of the reasons why the evidence is admissible. *See* ***Perkins v. Silver Mountain Sports Club & Spa, LLC***, 557 F.3d 1141, 1147 (10th Cir.2009). There are three steps for making an offer of proof.

§3.1 Attempt to introduce. The proponent must offer the evidence at trial, and the court must exclude it. *See* ***Pau v. Yosemite Park & Curry Co.***, 928 F.2d 880, 887 (9th Cir.1991).

§3.2 Make an objection. Once the court refuses to admit the evidence, the proponent must object to its exclusion. *See* FRE 103(a)(2). The party objects to a ruling to inform the court of the grounds for the objection and the action the party wants the court to take. FRCP 46; ***Beech Aircraft Corp. v. Rainey***, 488 U.S. 153, 174 (1988). The proponent must show the following:

1. Admissibility. The proponent must explain why the evidence is admissible. ***Church of God in Christ, Inc. v. Graham***, 54 F.3d 522, 528 (8th Cir.1995); ***Polys v. Trans-Colo. Airlines, Inc.***, 941 F.2d 1404, 1407 (10th Cir. 1991); ***Evanston Bank v. Brink's, Inc.***, 853 F.2d 512, 516 & n.6 (7th Cir.1988).

2. Purpose. The proponent must explain the purpose of the evidence. ***Beech Aircraft***, 488 U.S. at 174; ***Heyne v. Caruso***, 69 F.3d 1475, 1481 (9th Cir.1995); ***Polys***, 941 F.2d at 1407; ***Evanston Bank***, 853 F.2d at 516 & n.6.

§3.3 Offer the evidence. The proponent must inform the court what evidence it wants to produce. ***Porter-Cooper v. Dalkon Shield Claimants Trust***, 49 F.3d 1285, 1287 (8th Cir.1995); ***Polys v. Trans-Colo. Airlines, Inc.***, 941 F.2d 1404, 1407 (10th Cir.1991). In the offer, the proponent must make the court aware of the substance of the evidence that the proponent wants to introduce before the jury. ***Paschal v. Flagstar Bank***, 295 F.3d 565, 581 (6th

Cir.2002); ***Okai v. Verfuth***, 275 F.3d 606, 611-12 (7th Cir.2001); ***Inselman v. S&J Oper. Co.***, 44 F.3d 894, 896 (10th Cir.1995); *see **U.S. v. Akpan***, 407 F.3d 360, 374 (5th Cir.2005) (appellate court will not review challenge to excluded evidence unless party made offer of proof at trial).

1. Nonjury presentation. To make a record of the evidence that the court ruled inadmissible, the party must offer the evidence on the record in the presence of the judge, the opposing counsel, and the court reporter. The offer of proof is conducted outside the jury's presence to prevent the jury from hearing evidence that the court has ruled inadmissible. *See* FRE 103(d).

2. Form of evidence. The attorney may make a record of testimonial evidence either by interrogating a witness under oath or by precisely stating the substance of the excluded evidence in a statement to the court. ***Porter-Cooper***, 49 F.3d at 1287. The court can order that a summary of the evidence be made in question-and-answer form. FRE 103(c). To make an offer of excluded documentary evidence, the attorney should identify the document on the record by an exhibit number and formally present it to be filed as the offer of proof. *See, e.g.*, ***Bommarito v. Penrod Drilling Corp.***, 929 F.2d 186, 191 (5th Cir.1991) (court's exclusion of report upheld when report was not offered to court).

§4. RESPONSE

An offer of proof follows the court's ruling excluding evidence. *See* FRE 103(a)(2). The opponent of the evidence will likely have already stated why it believes the evidence is inadmissible and will not need to respond to an offer of proof. But if the opponent has not made its position clear on the record, or if there are additional reasons for objection, the opponent may want to object after the offer of proof.

§5. RULING

The proponent of the evidence should make sure to secure a ruling on the offer of proof on the record. After the offer of proof, the court may make any statement about the character or form of the evidence, the objection made, and the ruling. FRE 103(c).

§6. APPELLATE REVIEW

§6.1 Record.

§6.1 Record. Testimonial and documentary evidence offered as part of an offer of proof must be included in the record. *See* ***Jetcraft Corp. v. Flight Safety Int'l***, 16 F.3d 362, 366 (10th Cir.1993); ***Bommarito v. Penrod Drilling Corp.***, 929 F.2d 186, 191 (5th Cir.1991).

§6.2 Standard of review.

1. Abuse of discretion. If the party made a proper offer of proof, the court's ruling excluding evidence is reversible only if the court abused its broad discretion and the court's decision affected a substantial right of that party. ***Polanco v. City of Austin***, 78 F.3d 968, 982 (5th Cir.1996); ***Heyne v. Caruso***, 69 F.3d 1475, 1478 (9th Cir.1995); ***Polys v. Trans-Colo. Airlines, Inc.***, 941 F.2d 1404, 1407-08 (10th Cir.1991); *see* FRE 103(a).

2. Plain error. If the party did not make a proper offer of proof, the court's ruling excluding evidence is reversible only if there is plain error that affected a substantial right of that party. *See* FRE 103(e); ***Klein v. Grynberg***, 44 F.3d 1497, 1505 n.6 (10th Cir.1995). To establish plain error, the complaining party must show that the error was so obvious and substantial that it seriously affected the fairness, integrity, or public reputation of the judicial proceeding. ***Douglass v. United Servs. Auto. Ass'n***, 79 F.3d 1415, 1424 (5th Cir.1996); ***Polys***, 941 F.2d at 1408.

F. MOTION TO AMEND PLEADINGS—TRIAL & POST-TRIAL

§1. GENERAL

§1.1 Rule. FRCP 15.

§1.2 Purpose. The issue of trial and post-trial amendment of the pleadings is most often raised when one party objects that either the other party's evidence or a jury instruction is not supported by the pleadings. When this issue is raised, the party with the deficient pleadings should move to amend on the ground that the matter was tried by express or implied consent.

§1.3 Forms. ***O'Connor's Federal Civil Forms*** (2012), FORMS 8F.

§1.4 Other references. 6, 6A Wright, Miller & Kane, *Federal Practice & Procedure 3d* §§1471-1490, 1493, 1494, 1496, 1497 (2010 & Supp.2012); 3 *Moore's Federal Practice 3d* §§15.01-15.20 (2012); 1 Childress & Davis, *Federal Standards of Review 4th* §4.20 (2010 & Supp.2011).

NOTE

The rules for amending pleadings vary significantly depending on when the amendment occurs. This subchapter only discusses motions to amend the pleadings during and after trial. For a discussion of motions to amend the pleadings before trial, see "Motion to Amend or Supplement Pleadings—Pretrial," ch. 5-I, p. 345.

---

§2. MOTION TO AMEND

§2.1 Form. For the general requirements for the form of a motion, see "Drafting motions," ch. 1-B, §3.1, p. 14.

§2.2 Motion. The motion should request leave to amend the pleadings *and* the pretrial order. *See* ***Rockwell Int'l v. U.S.***, 549 U.S. 457, 474 (2007); ***Kirkland v. District of Columbia***, 70 F.3d 629, 634 (D.C.Cir.1995); ***Roland M. v. Concord Sch. Cmte.***, 910 F.2d 983, 998-99 (1st Cir.1990); *see also* ***Wilson v. Muckala***, 303 F.3d 1207, 1215 (10th Cir.2002) (inclusion of claim in amended pretrial order is deemed to amend any previous pleading that did not include claim). The pretrial order, not the pleadings, controls the issues to be tried. *See* FRCP 16(d). Therefore, a matter included in the pretrial order is subject to trial even if it was not included in the pleadings. See "Pretrial order," ch. 5-A, §4.5, p. 293. Most courts are reluctant to permit a trial amendment if the issue was not included in the final pretrial order. *See* ***Rios v. Bigler***, 67 F.3d 1543, 1549 (10th Cir.1995); ***Roland M.***, 910 F.2d at 998-99. The motion should do the following:

1. Explain why the issue was not contained in the operative pleadings or in the court's final pretrial order. *See* ***Roland M.***, 910 F.2d at 999.

2. State whether the issue was tried by express or implied consent and explain how it was tried by consent.

3. State that the party was not guilty of undue delay, bad faith, or dilatory motive in requesting the amendment. ***Foman v. Davis***, 371 U.S. 178, 182 (1962).

4. State that the party has cured all pleading deficiencies. *Id.*

5. Explain why the opposing party would not be unduly prejudiced or surprised by the amendment. ***Davey v. Lockheed Martin Corp.***, 301 F.3d 1204, 1210-11 (10th Cir.2002); *see* FRCP 15(b)(1); ***Foman***, 371 U.S. at 182; ***In re Cumberland Farms, Inc.***, 284 F.3d 216, 226 (1st Cir.2002).

6. Explain why the amendment would not be futile. ***Foman***, 371 U.S. at 182.

7. Explain how the amendment will aid in presenting the merits. FRCP 15(b)(1).

8. Explain how the amendment will serve the interests of justice. ***Moody v. FMC Corp.***, 995 F.2d 63, 66 (5th Cir.1993); ***Hillburn v. Maher***, 795 F.2d 252, 264 (2d Cir.1986).

§2.3 Trial by express or implied consent. An issue that is tried by express or implied consent is treated the same as if it had been raised in the pleadings. FRCP 15(b)(2); *see* ***Net MoneyIN, Inc. v. VeriSign, Inc.***, 545 F.3d 1359, 1372 (Fed.Cir.2008) (although court has broad discretion in deciding motion to amend, amendment is mandatory when issue is tried by express or implied consent).

1. Express consent. The parties can expressly consent to try the issues in the pleadings and the pretrial order.

2. Implied consent. If the party moving to amend the pleadings alleges that the issue was tried by implied consent, that party must identify some action or inaction during the course of the lawsuit from which the court can determine that the other party recognized the issue was involved in the case and consented to the trial of the issue. ***Smith v. EMC Corp.***, 393 F.3d 590, 596 (5th Cir.2004); ***Kirkland v. District of Columbia***, 70 F.3d 629, 633 (D.C.Cir.1995); *see* ***In re Cumberland Farms, Inc.***, 284 F.3d 216, 225-26 (1st Cir.2002); 6A Wright, Miller & Kane §1493; *see also* ***Filipowicz v. American Stores Benefit Plans Cmte.***, 56 F.3d 807, 812 (7th Cir.1995) (appellate court deemed pleading was amended when it appeared that issue was actually tried by implied consent). The party should also identify any evidence supporting the issue that was introduced at trial without objection and state that a finding of implied consent would not prejudice the opposing party. *See* ***National Bus. Forms & Printing, Inc. v. Ford Motor Co.***, 671 F.3d 526, 538 (5th Cir.2012).

(1) Tried by implied consent. The following have been found sufficient to show implied consent to try an unpleaded issue: • Not objecting to evidence that raised the issue. ***Antilles Cement Corp. v. Fortuño***, 670 F.3d 310, 319 (1st Cir.2012); ***LeFever v. Commissioner***, 100 F.3d 778, 785 (10th Cir.1996); ***Winger v. Winger***, 82 F.3d 140, 144 (7th Cir.1996); ***Kirkland***, 70 F.3d at 633. • Presenting controverting evidence on the unpleaded issue. ***Kirkland***, 70 F.3d at 633; ***Farmland Indus. v. Morrison-Quirk Grain Corp.***, 54 F.3d 478, 481 (8th Cir.1995); ***Conjugal Prtshp. Comprised by Jones & Jones v. Conjugal Prtshp. Comprised of Pineda & Pineda***, 22 F.3d 391, 401 (1st Cir.1994); ***Fejta v. GAF Cos.***, 800 F.2d 1395, 1396 (5th Cir.1986). • Filing a brief that addressed the issue. ***Antilles Cement Corp.***, 670 F.3d at 319; ***Dell v. Heard***, 532 F.2d 1330, 1332 (10th Cir.1976). • Submitting jury instructions on the issue. ***Conjugal Prtshp. Comprised by Jones & Jones***, 22 F.3d at 401; ***Snell v. Suffolk Cty.***, 782 F.2d 1094, 1102 (2d Cir.1986). • Not objecting to jury instructions or special-verdict questions on the issue. ***Winger***, 82 F.3d at 144. • Not objecting when the court made a statement on the record that the issue was involved in the case. ***Galindo v. Stoody Co.***, 793 F.2d 1502, 1513 (9th Cir.1986); ***Snell***, 782 F.2d at 1102; *see* ***Fisher v. Vassar Coll.***, 70 F.3d 1420, 1449 (2d Cir.1995). • Addressing the issue in closing argument. ***Gamma-10 Plastics, Inc. v. American President Lines, Ltd.***, 32 F.3d 1244, 1256 (8th Cir.1994); ***Galindo***, 793 F.2d at 1513. • Receiving notice from the other party about the issue in the other party's pretrial submissions. ***Winger***, 82 F.3d at 144; ***Gamma-10***, 32 F.3d at 1256. • Not responding to a motion on the issue. ***U.S. v. Banks***, 115 F.3d 916, 918 n.4 (11th Cir.1997). • Addressing the issue in an amended complaint. ***Barrett v. Fields***, 941 F.Supp. 980, 982 n.1 (D.Kan.1996).

(2) Not tried by implied consent. The following have been found insufficient to show implied consent to try an unpleaded issue: • Contesting the introduction of evidence on the unpleaded issue by objecting that the evidence was not within the issues raised by the pleadings or the pretrial order. *See* ***Rios v. Bigler***, 67 F.3d 1543, 1549 (10th Cir.1995); ***DCPB, Inc. v. City of Lebanon***, 957 F.2d 913, 917 (1st Cir.1992). • Objecting to the submission of a jury question on the unpleaded issue on the ground that the issue was not raised by the pleadings or the pretrial order. *See* ***Douglas v. Owens***, 50 F.3d 1226, 1235-36 (3d Cir.1995); ***DCPB, Inc.***, 957 F.2d at 917. • Raising the issue for the first time in a post-trial brief. ***Grand Light & Sup. Co. v. Honeywell, Inc.***, 771 F.2d 672, 679-80 (2d Cir.1985). • Not contesting the introduction of evidence because the party did not recognize the significance of the evidence. ***Domar Ocean Transp. v. Independent Ref. Co.***, 783 F.2d 1185, 1188 (5th Cir.1986). • Introducing evidence relevant to both a pleaded and an unpleaded matter. ***U.S. v. Ideal Elec. Sec. Co.***, 81 F.3d 240, 247 (D.C.Cir. 1996); ***Douglas***, 50 F.3d at 1235-36; ***DCPB, Inc.***, 957 F.2d at 917.

§2.4 Amended pleading. The movant should attach the amended pleading to the motion to amend. See "Proposed amended pleading," ch. 5-I, §5.5, p. 351.

§2.5 Deadline.

1. As soon as possible. The motion to amend the pleadings and the pretrial order should be made as soon as the party realizes the amendment is necessary. *See, e.g.*, ***Shanahan v. City of Chi.***, 82 F.3d 776, 781 (7th Cir.1996) (amendment proposed over a year after discovery ended was untimely); ***Hom v. Squires***, 81 F.3d 969, 973 (10th Cir.1996) (two years after deadline and only two months before trial was too late). Delay in seeking leave to amend, by itself, is not grounds for denial of amendment. ***Security Ins. v. Kevin Tucker & Assocs.***, 64 F.3d 1001, 1009 (6th Cir.1995); ***Johnson v. Trueblood***, 629 F.2d 287, 294 (3d Cir.1980). But when delay combines with other factors that result in actual prejudice, denial is appropriate. ***Johnson***, 629 F.2d at 294. The longer the period of an unexplained delay, the less prejudice the nonmovant is required to show. ***Block v. First Blood Assocs.***, 988 F.2d 344, 350 (2d Cir.1993); *see* ***Minter v. Prime Equip. Co.***, 451 F.3d 1196, 1205 (10th Cir.2006).

2. After judgment. A motion to conform the pleadings to the evidence may be made after judgment. FRCP 15(b)(2); ***Domar Ocean Transp. v. Independent Ref. Co.***, 783 F.2d 1185, 1188 (5th Cir.1986); *see* ***First Nat'l Bank v. Continental Ill. Nat'l Bank***, 933 F.2d 466, 468 (7th Cir.1991).

§3. RESPONSE

§3.1 Response. Some of the objections the nonmovant can make to a motion to amend during or after trial include the following:

1. The motion for leave to amend is too late. ***Foman v. Davis***, 371 U.S. 178, 182 (1962); ***American Fed. Grp. v. Rothenberg***, 136 F.3d 897, 905 (2d Cir.1998); ***Orix Credit Alliance, Inc. v. Taylor Mach. Works, Inc.***, 125 F.3d 468, 480-81 (7th Cir.1997); ***Consolidated Data Terminals v. Applied Digital Data Sys.***, 708 F.2d 385, 396-97 (9th Cir.1983); *see, e.g.*, ***Johnson v. Trueblood***, 629 F.2d 287, 294-95 (3d Cir.1980) (court denied amendment sought on 43rd day of trial because it would force Ds to prepare defense on new issue).

2. The movant did not include the issue in its draft of the pretrial order, did not raise the issue at the pretrial conference, and did not object to the court's final pretrial order. *See* FRCP 16; ***Roland M. v. Concord Sch. Cmte.***, 910 F.2d 983, 998-99 (1st Cir.1990).

3. The issue was not tried by consent because the evidence the movant claims in support of the unpleaded issue was introduced in support of another issue that was included in the pleadings. ***U.S. v. Ideal Elec. Sec. Co.***, 81 F.3d 240, 247 (D.C.Cir.1996); ***Douglas v. Owens***, 50 F.3d 1226, 1236 (3d Cir.1995). The nonmovant objected to evidence that was introduced in support of the unpleaded issue on the ground that the issue was not contained in the pleadings. *See* ***Rios v. Bigler***, 67 F.3d 1543, 1549 (10th Cir.1995); ***DCPB, Inc. v. City of Lebanon***, 957 F.2d 913, 917 (1st Cir.1992).

4. The amendment will cause the nonmovant substantial prejudice because the nonmovant will not have the opportunity to introduce evidence on that issue. ***Fisher v. Vassar Coll.***, 70 F.3d 1420, 1449 (2d Cir.1995); ***Douglas***, 50 F.3d at 1236. Prejudice by a late amendment is often inevitable if the other party does not have a fair opportunity to defend against the issue. *See* ***Douglas***, 50 F.3d at 1236.

5. No discovery was conducted on the unpleaded issue. If the court grants leave to amend, it will disrupt the trial because the nonmovant will move for a continuance to secure evidence to respond to the new issue. *See* ***Prudhomme v. Tenneco Oil Co.***, 955 F.2d 390, 391 (5th Cir.1992); ***Trinity Carton Co. v. Falstaff Brewing Corp.***, 767 F.2d 184, 194 (5th Cir.1985). The amendment will require the nonmovant to secure additional discovery, locate additional witnesses and physical evidence, amend the witness and exhibit lists, and file new pretrial stipulations. ***Prudhomme***, 955 F.2d at 391. The nonmovant should support the allegations with facts and not make bare allegations. *See id.* at 394.

6. The amendment will cause substantial prejudice to the nonmovant's ability to prosecute the suit because the amendment changes the theory and tactics of the suit. ***Deakyne v. Commissioners of Lewes***, 416 F.2d 290, 300 (3d Cir.1969). A party is substantially prejudiced if an added claim would require it to reopen discovery and prepare a defense for a claim different from the one that was before the court. ***Smith v. EMC Corp.***, 393 F.3d 590, 596 (5th Cir.2004).

7. The movant did not first move to have the judgment set aside (when the motion to amend is made after trial). ***Sparrow v. Heller***, 116 F.3d 204, 205 (7th Cir.1997).

8. The movant delayed in making the motion when it had an opportunity to present the amendment earlier. ***Diersen v. Chicago Car Exch.***, 110 F.3d 481, 489 (7th Cir.1997).

9. The amendment adds an element of surprise. *E.g.*, ***Orix Credit Alliance***, 125 F.3d at 480-81 (new counts added prospect of punitive damages, which might have caused D to take different measures to protect himself from additional liability).

10. The movant is guilty of bad faith or dilatory motive in requesting the amendment, or has not cured pleading deficiencies. ***Foman***, 371 U.S. at 182.

11. The amendment would be futile. *Id.* An amendment is futile when, if granted, it would not withstand a motion to dismiss. *See* ***Walton v. Mental Health Ass'n***, 168 F.3d 661, 665 (3d Cir.1999); ***Advanced Magnetics, Inc. v. Bayfront Partners***, 106 F.3d 11, 18-19 (2d Cir.1997).

§3.2 Request continuance. If the court grants the motion to amend, the nonmovant should consider filing a motion for continuance. *See* FRCP 15(b)(1). The nonmovant is entitled to adequate time to address any new issue interjected by trial amendment, and its only trial remedy is to seek a continuance to prepare its defense. *See* ***Consolidated Data Terminals v. Applied Digital Data Sys.***, 708 F.2d 385, 396-97 (9th Cir.1983) (late amendment plus denial of continuance was reversible error); *see also* ***Black v. J.I. Case Co.***, 22 F.3d 568, 573 (5th Cir.1994) (continuance more appropriate than exclusion of evidence). If the nonmovant does not request a continuance, the appellate court may consider it a factor showing that the nonmovant was not prejudiced by the amendment. *See* ***Conjugal Prtshp. Comprised by Jones & Jones v. Conjugal Prtshp. Comprised of Pineda & Pineda***, 22 F.3d 391, 401 (1st Cir.1994). See "Motion for Continuance," ch. 5-G, p. 337.

§3.3 Motion for additional discovery. If the court grants the motion to amend, the nonmovant should consider filing a motion for additional discovery on the unpleaded issue.

§3.4 Affidavit. If the response contains facts outside the record, it should be verified by an affidavit.

§4. RULING

FRCP 15 embodies a strong policy in favor of liberal amendments to the pleadings. *See* ***Gamma-10 Plastics, Inc. v. American President Lines, Ltd.***, 32 F.3d 1244, 1255 (8th Cir.1994); *see also* ***In re Prescott***, 805 F.2d 719, 725 (7th Cir.1986) (intent of FRCP 15(b) is to provide opportunity for each claim to be decided on merits rather than procedural technicalities). Courts routinely grant amendments to conform the pleadings to the evidence received during trial. ***Gamma-10***, 32 F.3d at 1256; *see* ***U.S. v. Ideal Elec. Sec. Co.***, 81 F.3d 240, 245 (D.C.Cir.1996); ***Vermont Plastics, Inc. v. Brine, Inc.***, 79 F.3d 272, 279 (2d Cir.1996); *cf.* ***In re Rauh***, 119 F.3d 46, 52 (1st Cir.1997) (motions to amend under Fed. R. Bankr. P. are liberally allowed). However, courts are reluctant to grant leave to amend after judgment. ***Morse v. McWhorter***, 290 F.3d 795, 800 (6th Cir.2002); ***Rodriguez v. U.S.***, 286 F.3d 972, 980 (7th Cir. 2002); ***Vielma v. Eureka Co.***, 218 F.3d 458, 468 (5th Cir.2000); *see* 6 Wright, Miller & Kane §1489. As a general rule, a court should permit a party to amend its pleadings unless the court finds that (1) the party is guilty of undue delay, bad faith, or dilatory motive, (2) the party has repeatedly failed to cure pleading deficiencies by amendments, (3) the opposing party would be unduly prejudiced by the amendment, or (4) the amendment would be futile. *E.g.*, ***Foman v. Davis***, 371 U.S. 178, 182 (1962) (reversed because district court should have permitted P to amend after case dismissed on pleading deficiency); *see, e.g.*, ***Maldonado v. Dominguez***, 137 F.3d 1, 11 (1st Cir.1998) (revision of complaint would be futile). If the court decides an issue was tried by consent, the court must treat the issue as if it had been pleaded. ***Winger v. Winger***, 82 F.3d 140, 144 (7th Cir.1996).

CIRCUIT SPLIT

The courts of appeals are split on whether the liberal standard for amendments under FRCP 15 is affected by the heightened pleading standard in the Private Securities Litigation Reform Act of 1995 (PSLRA). Compare ***ACA Fin. Guar. Corp. v. Advest, Inc.****, 512 F.3d 46, 56 (1st Cir.2008) (PSLRA does not affect liberal standard of FRCP 15),* ***Belizan v. Hershon****, 434 F.3d 579, 583-84 (D.C.Cir.2006) (same), and* ***Eminence Capital, LLC v. Aspeon, Inc.****, 316 F.3d 1048, 1052-53 (9th Cir.2003) (same), with* ***Miller v. Champion Enters.****, 346 F.3d 660, 692 (6th Cir.2003) (PSLRA's heightened pleading standard would be frustrated if amendment allowed).*

§5. APPELLATE REVIEW

The decision whether to allow amendment of a pleading during or after trial is a matter of discretion for the district court. ***Wilson v. Morgan***, 477 F.3d 326, 344 (6th Cir.2007); ***Vermont Plastics, Inc. v. Brine, Inc.***, 79 F.3d 272, 279 (2d Cir.1996); *see* ***LeFever v. Commissioner***, 100 F.3d 778, 785 (10th Cir.1996) (determination of whether issue was tried by consent is within sound discretion of district court). If the nonmovant does not have a chance to introduce evidence in response to the amendment, the court abuses its discretion in permitting the amendment. *See* ***Douglas v. Owens***, 50 F.3d 1226, 1236-37 (3d Cir.1995). The appellate court will reverse the district court's ruling on a motion to amend pleadings only if the district court abused its discretion. ***Smith v. EMC Corp.***, 393 F.3d 590, 595 (5th Cir.2004); ***Orix Credit Alliance, Inc. v. Taylor Mach. Works, Inc.***, 125 F.3d 468, 480 (7th Cir.1997); ***Kim v. Nash Finch Co.***, 123 F.3d 1046, 1064 (8th Cir.1997); ***Atchinson v. District of Columbia***, 73 F.3d 418, 426 (D.C.Cir.1996); ***Security Ins. v. Kevin Tucker & Assocs.***, 64 F.3d 1001, 1008 (6th Cir.1995).

G. MOTION FOR JUDGMENT AS A MATTER OF LAW

§1. GENERAL

§1.1 Rule. FRCP 50(a).

§1.2 Purpose. A motion for judgment as a matter of law (JMOL), formerly called a motion for directed verdict, allows the court to remove cases or issues from the jury's consideration when the facts make it sufficiently clear that the law requires a particular result. ***Weisgram v. Marley Co.***, 528 U.S. 440, 447-48 (2000); *see* FRCP 50(a). There are two types of motions for JMOL: one made during the trial and one made after the jury returns a verdict. This subchapter discusses motions for JMOL made during trial. For a discussion of motions for JMOL made after the jury returns a verdict, see "Renewed Motion for Judgment as a Matter of Law," ch. 10-B, p. 775.

§1.3 Forms. *O'Connor's Federal Civil Forms* (2012), FORMS 8G.

§1.4 Other references. 9B Wright & Miller, *Federal Practice & Procedure 3d* §§2521-2536 (2008 & Supp.2012); 9 *Moore's Federal Practice 3d* ch. 50 (2012); Childress, *Judicial Review & Diversity Jurisdiction: Solving an Irrepressible Erie Mystery?*, 47 SMU L.Rev. 271 (1994).

§2. DIVERSITY CASES & MOTION FOR JMOL

The Supreme Court has never decided whether the amount of evidence needed to avoid a JMOL in a diversity case is controlled by state or federal law. *See* ***Dick v. New York Life Ins.***, 359 U.S. 437, 444-45 (1959) (recognizing but not resolving issue). The circuits do not agree on whether to apply state or federal law when deciding whether to grant a JMOL in a diversity case. *See generally* Childress, *Judicial Review & Diversity Jurisdiction: Solving an Irrepressible Erie Mystery?*, 47 SMU L.Rev. at 295-308 (contrasting different standards applied by circuits). Some circuits hold that deciding whether to grant a JMOL is a procedural issue that must be determined by federal law. *See* ***Ellis v. Weasler Eng'g***, 258 F.3d 326, 336-37 (5th Cir.2001), *amended*, 274 F.3d 881 (5th Cir.2001); ***Conoco Inc. v. ONEOK, Inc.***, 91 F.3d 1405, 1407 (10th Cir.1996); ***Brendle's Stores v. OTR***, 978 F.2d 150, 157 (4th Cir.1992); 9B Wright & Miller §2525. Other circuits hold that deciding whether to grant a JMOL is a substantive issue that must be determined by state law. *See* ***American & Foreign Ins. v. General Elec. Co.***, 45 F.3d 135, 139 (6th Cir.1995); 9B Wright & Miller

§2525. Some circuits have even issued conflicting panel opinions on this point. *Compare* ***Groom v. Days Inn***, 62 F.3d 204, 207 (7th Cir.1995) (procedural issue determined by federal law), *with* ***Winger v. Winger***, 82 F.3d 140, 143 (7th Cir.1996) (substantive issue determined by state law).

§3. TIME TO MAKE MOTION

§3.1 After presenting evidence. A party can move for JMOL only after the opposing party has been "fully heard" on an issue. FRCP 50(a)(1); ***Francis v. Clark Equip. Co.***, 993 F.2d 545, 554-55 (6th Cir.1993); *see* ***Echeverria v. Chevron USA Inc.***, 391 F.3d 607, 610-11 (5th Cir.2004) ("fully heard" means party has rested its case before jury); ***Teneyck v. Omni Shoreham Hotel***, 365 F.3d 1139, 1149 (D.C.Cir.2004) (party has not been fully heard until it has submitted all evidence and closed case); *see, e.g.*, ***Summers v. Delta Air Lines, Inc.***, 508 F.3d 923, 928 (9th Cir. 2007) (under FRCP 50(a)(1), P was not fully heard when court required witness testimony be given through offer of proof rather than by live testimony). A court can enter a JMOL anytime after it becomes apparent during the trial that a party cannot carry its burden of proof on an issue essential to the case. 1991 Notes to FRCP 50 at ¶5, p. 1215, this book; *see* FRCP 50(a); ***American & Foreign Ins. v. General Elec. Co.***, 45 F.3d 135, 139-40 (6th Cir.1995); *see, e.g.*, ***Greene v. Potter***, 557 F.3d 765, 768 (7th Cir.2009) (district court properly granted JMOL before P finished her case-in-chief when P's admitted evidence and evidence that she planned to submit defeated her claim; completion of case-in-chief would have been futile). A JMOL may even be granted after opening statements, although this is appropriate only in extremely rare circumstances. ***Brown v. United Mo. Bank***, 78 F.3d 382, 387 (8th Cir.1996); *see* ***Riverwoods Chappaqua Corp. v. Marine Midland Bank***, 30 F.3d 339, 343 (2d Cir.1994) (JMOL proper only if opening statement clearly demonstrates P has no claim). In no event can the court enter judgment against a party who has not been made aware of the dispositive issues and been given an opportunity to present any available evidence on those issues. ***Echeverria***, 391 F.3d at 611-12; ***Teneyck***, 365 F.3d at 1149; ***Jackson v. Quanex Corp.***, 191 F.3d 647, 657 (6th Cir.1999); ***Francis***, 993 F.2d at 555; 1991 Notes to FRCP 50 at ¶5, p. 1215, this book. An appellate court cannot review the sufficiency of the evidence underlying the jury verdict when a party does not move for JMOL at any phase of the litigation. ***Advanced Display Sys. v. Kent State Univ.***, 212 F.3d 1272, 1281 (Fed.Cir.2000); *see* 9B Wright & Miller §2536 & n.l.

§3.2 After opportunity to cure. Once a party makes a motion for JMOL, the nonmovant must be given an opportunity to cure any deficiency in its proof. ***Echeverria v. Chevron USA Inc.***, 391 F.3d 607, 611 (5th Cir.2004); ***Teneyck v. Omni Shoreham Hotel***, 365 F.3d 1139, 1149 (D.C.Cir.2004); ***Waters v. Young***, 100 F.3d 1437, 1440-41 (9th Cir.1996); *see* ***Farley Transp. v. Santa Fe Trail Transp.***, 786 F.2d 1342, 1346 (9th Cir.1985); 1991 Notes to FRCP 50 at ¶5, p. 1215, this book; *see, e.g.*, ***Francis v. Clark Equip. Co.***, 993 F.2d 545, 555 (6th Cir.1993) (P should have been given opportunity to use another expert). The purpose of requiring that a motion for JMOL be made before submission of the case to the jury is to give the responding party a chance to cure any deficiency in its proof. ***Piesco v. Koch***, 12 F.3d 332, 340 (2d Cir.1993). See "Motion to Reopen for Additional Evidence," ch. 8-H, p. 718. Once the nonmovant has had the opportunity to introduce additional evidence, the movant may reurge its motion for JMOL.

§4. MOTION

§4.1 Oral or written. The motion for JMOL should be in writing if possible. *See* FRCP 7(b)(1)(A). Although a party may make an oral motion for JMOL on the record, oral motions are sometimes not stated with the specificity required by FRCP 50. *See, e.g.*, ***Piesco v. Koch***, 12 F.3d 332, 341 (2d Cir.1993) (oral statement that "Defendants move for directed verdict" was not sufficient); ***McGee v. Bauer***, 956 F.2d 730, 733-34 (7th Cir.1992) (mere oral statement that party renews its earlier motion was not sufficient). The adequacy of an oral motion depends largely on the context in which the motion is made. *E.g.*, ***Orion IP, LLC v. Hyundai Motor Am.***, 605 F.3d 967, 973-74 (Fed.Cir.2010) (D's oral statement requesting "partial judgment as a matter of law," which standing alone was cursory and insufficient, was sufficient because statement was made after lengthy discussion about objected-to jury instructions).

§4.2 Grounds.

1. Specific. In a motion for JMOL, the movant must specify the judgment sought and set out the specific law and facts that entitle it to judgment. FRCP 50(a)(2); ***Gordon v. County of Rockland***, 110 F.3d 886, 887 n.2 (2d Cir.1997); ***Whelan v. Abell***, 48 F.3d 1247, 1251 (D.C.Cir.1995); *see* ***Galdieri-Ambrosini v. National Rlty. & Dev.***

Corp., 136 F.3d 276, 286 (2d Cir.1998) (at minimum, D must identify specific element it contends is insufficiently supported); *see, e.g.*, ***Smith v. Northwest Fin. Acceptance, Inc.***, 129 F.3d 1408, 1415 (10th Cir.1997) (Ds did not specifically object to or identify challenged issue in motion for JMOL or in renewed motion for JMOL). Technical precision is not required as long as the motion makes the court aware of the movant's position. ***Kusens v. Pascal Co.***, 448 F.3d 349, 361 (6th Cir.2006); ***Aguinaga v. United Food & Commercial Workers Int'l Un.***, 993 F.2d 1463, 1470 (10th Cir.1993). The movant cannot rely solely on conclusory theories or abstract principles; the motion must explain precisely why the evidence is insufficient. ***Perdoni Bros. v. Concrete Sys.***, 35 F.3d 1, 3 (1st Cir.1994). The requirement that the motion be specific gives the opposing party an opportunity to correct the deficiencies in its case. ***Galdieri-Ambrosini***, 136 F.3d at 286; ***Lightning Lube, Inc. v. Witco Corp.***, 4 F.3d 1153, 1173 (3d Cir.1993).

2. Insufficient evidence. The motion should state that a reasonable jury would not have a legally sufficient evidentiary basis to find for the opposing party on the particular issue. FRCP 50(a). Generally, a JMOL is granted in two types of situations:

(1) When there is a complete absence of pleading or proof on an issue material to the claim or defense. *See* ***Singer v. Dungan***, 45 F.3d 823, 827 (4th Cir.1995); ***Baker v. Delo***, 38 F.3d 1024, 1027 (8th Cir.1994). A mere scintilla of evidence is not sufficient to present a question for the jury. ***Hunter v. Knoll Rig & Equip. Mfg. Co.***, 70 F.3d 803, 808 (5th Cir.1995); *see* ***Gardner v. Buerger***, 82 F.3d 248, 254 (8th Cir.1996); ***Smith v. F.W. Morse & Co.***, 76 F.3d 413, 425-26 (1st Cir.1996).

NOTE

In Weisgram v. Marley Co., 528 U.S. 440, 457 (2000), the Supreme Court held that the court of appeals' authority to direct the entry of judgment as a matter of law extends to cases in which, after it excludes the erroneously admitted testimony, there remains insufficient evidence to support the jury's verdict.

(2) When there are no controverted issues of fact on which reasonable persons could differ. ***Powers v. Bayliner Mar. Corp.***, 83 F.3d 789, 796 (6th Cir.1996).

§4.3 Burden on movant. The party moving for JMOL has a difficult burden of persuasion because the court must view all the evidence in the light most favorable to the nonmovant and indulge all reasonable inferences in favor of the nonmovant. ***Jarvis v. Ford Motor Co.***, 283 F.3d 33, 43 (2d Cir.2002); ***Russell v. McKinney Hosp. Venture***, 235 F.3d 219, 222 (5th Cir.2000); ***Huffman v. County of L.A.***, 147 F.3d 1054, 1057 (9th Cir.1998); ***Cowan v. Strafford R-VI Sch. Dist.***, 140 F.3d 1153, 1157 (8th Cir.1998); ***Smith v. F.W. Morse & Co.***, 76 F.3d 413, 425 (1st Cir. 1996). The court should grant the JMOL only if, after viewing the evidence, (1) there is a complete absence of proof on the issues or (2) reasonable persons could not differ on issues of fact. ***Powers v. Bayliner Mar. Corp.***, 83 F.3d 789, 796 (6th Cir.1996).

§5. RESPONSE

§5.1 Form. If the movant files a written motion for JMOL, the nonmovant should probably respond in writing; if the movant makes an oral motion on the record, the nonmovant may respond orally on the record.

§5.2 Grounds. The nonmovant should point out why the court should deny the motion. The following are some possible grounds:

1. The nonmovant's pleadings and proof support issues material to the claim or defense.

2. There are controverted issues of fact on which reasonable persons could differ and that must be resolved by the jury. Because reasonable people could differ on the conclusions to be drawn from the conflicting evidence, the motion should be denied. ***Mitchell v. Maynard***, 80 F.3d 1433, 1443 (10th Cir.1996); ***Pierce v. Multnomah Cty.***, 76 F.3d 1032, 1037 (9th Cir.1996).

3. The motion argues the weight of conflicting evidence, which is not appropriate for a JMOL. ***Samuels v. Air Transp.***, 992 F.2d 12, 15 (2d Cir.1993). The court cannot make credibility determinations or weigh the evidence when ruling on a JMOL. ***Reeves v. Sanderson Plumbing Prods.***, 530 U.S. 133, 150 (2000); ***Russell v. McKinney Hosp. Venture***, 235 F.3d 219, 222 (5th Cir.2000).

4. The motion for JMOL considers the evidence in the light most favorable to the movant, which is the wrong standard. The evidence must be considered in the light most favorable to the nonmovant. ***Russell***, 235 F.3d at 222; ***Haynes v. Bee-Line Trucking Co.***, 80 F.3d 1235, 1238 (8th Cir.1996); ***Zamalloa v. Hart***, 31 F.3d 911, 913 (9th Cir.1994). All reasonable inferences must be drawn in favor of the nonmovant. ***Reeves***, 530 U.S. at 150.

§5.3 Additional evidence. The nonmovant must be given an opportunity to cure any deficiency in its proof by introducing additional evidence. ***Francis v. Clark Equip. Co.***, 993 F.2d 545, 555 (6th Cir.1993); 1991 Notes to FRCP 50 at ¶5, p. 1215, this book. See "Motion to Reopen for Additional Evidence," ch. 8-H, p. 718.

§6. RENEWING MOTION

Before FRCP 50 was amended in 2006, a party was required to renew the motion for JMOL at the close of all the evidence if the court had denied the party's motion for JMOL during the trial and then additional evidence was introduced. *See* ***McKenzie v. Lee***, 259 F.3d 372, 374 (5th Cir.2001); ***Duckworth v. Ford***, 83 F.3d 999, 1001 (8th Cir. 1996); ***Fineman v. Armstrong World Indus.***, 980 F.2d 171, 183-84 (3d Cir.1992). This preverdict renewal was eliminated by the 2006 amendments to FRCP 50 in favor of a more functional approach that only requires the party to renew the motion after a verdict has been reached—that is, no later than 28 days after the entry of judgment. *See* FRCP 50(b); 2006 Notes to FRCP 50 at ¶¶2, 3, p. 1214, this book. See "Renewed Motion for Judgment as a Matter of Law," ch. 10-B, p. 775.

PRACTICE TIP

Many judges invite motions for JMOL at the close of all the evidence. Although it is no longer required, a party should still renew the motion for JMOL at the close of all the evidence if the original motion was made at the close of the plaintiff's evidence. See 2006 Notes to FRCP 50 at ¶4, p. 1214, this book.

§7. RULING

§7.1 Standard. The court should grant a motion for JMOL when there is no "legally sufficient evidentiary basis" for a reasonable jury to find for the party on an issue on which that party has been fully heard. FRCP 50(a)(1); ***Reeves v. Sanderson Plumbing Prods.***, 530 U.S. 133, 149 (2000); ***Wilson v. Morgan***, 477 F.3d 326, 333 (6th Cir. 2007); ***Anthony v. Chevron USA, Inc.***, 284 F.3d 578, 582-83 (5th Cir.2002). The court may consider only the grounds specified in the motion. ***Summers v. Delta Air Lines, Inc.***, 508 F.3d 923, 927-28 (9th Cir.2007). When considering a motion for JMOL, the court should review all the evidence in the record. ***Reeves***, 530 U.S. at 150. In doing so, however, the court must (1) draw all reasonable inferences in favor of the nonmovant, (2) give credence to evidence supporting the movant that is uncontradicted and unimpeached, and (3) refrain from making credibility determinations or weighing the evidence. *Id.* at 150-51; ***Evans v. Ford Motor Co.***, 484 F.3d 329, 334 (5th Cir.2007). The ruling on a motion for JMOL must take into account the movant's burden of proof. ***Harsco Corp. v. Kerkam, Stowell, Kondracki & Clarke***, 965 F.Supp. 580, 584 (M.D.Pa.1997).

1. **Grant motion.** The court should grant the motion if there is no conflict in the evidence. If there is only a "mere scintilla" of evidence, the court should not submit the issue to the jury. ***Jones v. Bessemer Carraway Med. Ctr.***, 137 F.3d 1306, 1310 (11th Cir.1998), *modified on other grounds*, 151 F.3d 1321 (11th Cir.1998); *see* ***Anthony***, 284 F.3d at 583. The court may enter a partial JMOL if there is no legally sufficient basis for a jury to find for a particular party on a particular issue. FRCP 50(a)(1); *see* 1991 Notes to FRCP 50 at ¶5, p. 1215, this book.

2. **Deny motion.** The court should deny the motion and submit the case to the jury only if there is a conflict in "substantial evidence." ***Anthony***, 284 F.3d at 583; ***Jones***, 137 F.3d at 1310.

§7.2 Written judgment. Whenever the court grants a motion for JMOL, the court should enter a formal judgment disposing of the issue. ***Ag-Chem Equip. Co. v. Hahn, Inc.***, 480 F.2d 482, 492-93 (8th Cir.1973). It is not necessary for the court to enter a written order overruling a motion for JMOL made during the trial.

§8. MOTION FOR JUDGMENT IN NONJURY CASE

A motion for JMOL is proper only for matters tried by a jury and not those in which the court acts as the fact-finder. ***Geddes v. Northwest Mo. State Univ.***, 49 F.3d 426, 429 n.7 (8th Cir.1995). Thus, a motion for JMOL in a nonjury trial is actually a motion for judgment on partial findings. *See* FRCP 52(c); ***Geddes***, 49 F.3d at 429 n.7.

§8.1 Standard. After a party has been fully heard on an issue during a nonjury trial, if the court finds that the party cannot prevail on the issue and the party's claim or defense cannot be maintained or defeated without a favorable finding on the issue, the court can enter judgment on partial findings against that party on that issue. FRCP 52(c); *see* ***Geddes v. Northwest Mo. State Univ.***, 49 F.3d 426, 429 n.7 (8th Cir.1995); ***Carter v. Ball***, 33 F.3d 450, 457 (4th Cir.1994). In ruling on an FRCP 52(c) motion, the court does not need to consider the evidence in a light favorable to the nonmovant but may render judgment for the movant if it believes the nonmovant's evidence is insufficient to support its claim or defense. ***Geddes***, 49 F.3d at 429 n.7; *see* ***EBC, Inc. v. Clark Bldg. Sys.***, 618 F.3d 253, 271-72 (3d Cir.2010).

§8.2 Findings of fact & conclusions of law. The court must support its judgment with findings of fact and conclusions of law. FRCP 52(a)(1); ***EBC, Inc. v. Clark Bldg. Sys.***, 618 F.3d 253, 273 (3d Cir.2010). A finding made under FRCP 52(c) is reversible only if it is clearly erroneous. ***Schoedinger v. United Healthcare***, 557 F.3d 872, 878 (8th Cir.2009); ***Price v. U.S. Navy***, 39 F.3d 1011, 1021 (9th Cir.1994); ***Carter v. Ball***, 33 F.3d 450, 457 (4th Cir.1994); 1991 Notes to FRCP 52 at ¶4, p. 1218, this book.

§9. APPELLATE REVIEW

The appellate court reviews the district court's ruling on a motion for JMOL de novo, applying the same standard as the district court. ***Wilson v. Morgan***, 477 F.3d 326, 333 (6th Cir.2007); ***Anthony v. Chevron USA, Inc.***, 284 F.3d 578, 583 (5th Cir.2002); ***Jarvis v. Ford Motor Co.***, 283 F.3d 33, 43 (2d Cir.2002); ***Brennan v. GTE Gov't Sys.***, 150 F.3d 21, 25 (1st Cir.1998); ***Nobelpharma AB v. Implant Innovations, Inc.***, 141 F.3d 1059, 1064 (Fed.Cir.1998); ***SEC v. Adler***, 137 F.3d 1325, 1340 (11th Cir.1998); ***Winger v. Winger***, 82 F.3d 140, 143 (7th Cir.1996); ***Starceski v. Westinghouse Elec. Corp.***, 54 F.3d 1089, 1095 (3d Cir.1995). The decision to grant a motion for JMOL is not a matter of discretion; rather, it is a conclusion of law based on a finding that there is insufficient evidence to create a fact question for the jury. ***Conkling v. Turner***, 18 F.3d 1285, 1300-01 (5th Cir.1994); ***Houston v. Reich***, 932 F.2d 883, 888 (10th Cir.1991).

H. MOTION TO REOPEN FOR ADDITIONAL EVIDENCE

§1. GENERAL

§1.1 Rule. None.

§1.2 Purpose. A motion to reopen the evidence gives the party an opportunity to include additional evidence in the record. Reopening is particularly important when the other party makes a motion for judgment as a matter of law (JMOL) for lack of evidence. See "Motion for Judgment as a Matter of Law," ch. 8-G, p. 714.

§1.3 Forms. *O'Connor's Federal Civil Forms* (2012), FORMS 8H.

§1.4 Other references. 28 Wright & Gold, *Federal Practice & Procedure 2d* §6164 (2012); 12 *Moore's Federal Practice 3d* §59.13[3][c] (2012).

§2. MOTION

§2.1 Form. Motions to reopen are generally made orally in open court when the party realizes it should have offered additional evidence. An oral motion to reopen is sufficient, but if the party has the opportunity, it should file a written one.

§2.2 Grounds. When asking the court to reopen, the party should present and prove the following:

1. The nature of the evidence to be introduced. *See, e.g.*, ***Johnson v. Busby***, 953 F.2d 349, 351 (8th Cir. 1991) (denial of motion was proper when movant did not identify any noncumulative proof sought from additional testimony); ***Air et Chaleur v. Janeway***, 757 F.2d 489, 495 (2d Cir.1985) (movant offered no proof about nature of additional evidence).

2. The gathering of evidence will not cause undue delay. ***Blinzler v. Marriott Int'l***, 81 F.3d 1148, 1160 (1st Cir.1996). When the missing evidence can be added without undue delay, the court should usually reopen the evidence. ***Capital Mar. Sup. v. M/V Roland Thomas, II***, 719 F.2d 104, 107 (5th Cir.1983).

3. The introduction of additional evidence will not cause an injustice or undue prejudice to the opposing party. ***Blinzler***, 81 F.3d at 1160.

4. The party was diligent in producing its evidence but was reasonably and genuinely surprised by the need for additional evidence. *See* ***Rivera-Flores v. Puerto Rico Tel. Co.***, 64 F.3d 742, 747 (1st Cir.1995); ***Air et Chaleur***, 757 F.2d at 495; ***Playboy Enters. v. Dumas***, 960 F.Supp. 710, 723 (S.D.N.Y.1997), *aff'd*, 159 F.3d 1347 (2d Cir.1998) (table case).

5. The evidence is relevant, admissible, technically adequate, and helpful to the jury. ***U.S. v. Parker***, 73 F.3d 48, 53 (5th Cir.1996), *reh'g granted*, 80 F.3d 1042 (5th Cir.1996), *reinstated in relevant part*, 104 F.3d 72 (5th Cir.1997). This factor is also described as assessing the probative value of the proposed evidence. ***Garcia v. Woman's Hosp. of Tex.***, 97 F.3d 810, 814 (5th Cir.1996); ***Blinzler***, 81 F.3d at 1160.

6. The evidence is not cumulative. *See* ***Johnson***, 953 F.2d at 351; ***Playboy Enters.***, 960 F.Supp. at 723.

§2.3 Court's initiative. The court may reopen the case on its own initiative. Sua sponte reopening is unusual, but it is within the court's discretion. ***Lussier v. Runyon***, 50 F.3d 1103, 1113 (1st Cir.1995); ***Calage v. University of Tenn.***, 544 F.2d 297, 302 (6th Cir.1976); ***Arthur Murray, Inc. v. Oliver***, 364 F.2d 28, 34 (8th Cir.1966). The court should reopen to add evidence on its own initiative only to prevent injustice and only if the evidence is readily available. ***Calage***, 544 F.2d at 302.

§3. RESPONSE

A party must object to the other party's motion to reopen, or else it waives error involving the reopening. *See* FRCP 46.

§4. RULING

§4.1 Factors. In ruling on a motion to reopen, the court should consider when the motion was made, the nature of the additional evidence, and the prejudice in granting or denying the motion. ***Garcia v. Woman's Hosp. of Tex.***, 97 F.3d 810, 814 (5th Cir.1996); ***Blinzler v. Marriott Int'l***, 81 F.3d 1148, 1160 (1st Cir.1996); ***Joseph v. Terminix Int'l Co.***, 17 F.3d 1282, 1285 (10th Cir.1994); *see* 12 *Moore's Federal Practice 3d* §59.13[3][c]. The test is whether the new evidence is sufficiently probative to offset the procedural disruption caused by reopening. ***Garcia***, 97 F.3d at 814; ***Rivera-Flores v. Puerto Rico Tel. Co.***, 64 F.3d 742, 746 (1st Cir.1995).

§4.2 Jury trial. In a jury trial, when the defendant moves for JMOL at the end of the evidence, the court should permit the plaintiff to reopen to cure any deficiency in its proof. *See* ***Piesco v. Koch***, 12 F.3d 332, 340 (2d Cir.1993); ***Francis v. Clark Equip. Co.***, 993 F.2d 545, 555 (6th Cir.1993); ***Farley Transp. v. Santa Fe Trail Transp.***, 786 F.2d 1342, 1346 (9th Cir.1985); 1991 Notes to FRCP 50 at ¶5, p. 1215, this book.

§4.3 Nonjury trial. In a nonjury trial, the court should permit the plaintiff to reopen when the defendant moves to dismiss. ***Capital Mar. Sup. v. M/V Roland Thomas, II***, 719 F.2d 104, 107 (5th Cir.1983).

§5. DEADLINE

The motion to reopen should be made as soon as the need for additional evidence becomes evident. The court can reopen anytime before the entry of judgment.

§6. APPELLATE REVIEW

The district court's decision on a motion to reopen is reviewed for abuse of discretion. ***Zenith Radio Corp. v. Hazeltine Research, Inc.***, 401 U.S. 321, 331 (1971); ***Blanke v. Alexander***, 152 F.3d 1224, 1238 (10th Cir.1998); ***Rivera-Flores v. Puerto Rico Tel. Co.***, 64 F.3d 742, 746 (1st Cir.1995); ***Doe v. Johnson***, 52 F.3d 1448, 1462 (7th Cir.1995); ***Hibiscus Assocs. v. Board of Trs.***, 50 F.3d 908, 917-18 (11th Cir.1995); *see* ***Level 3 Comms. v. City of St. Louis***, 540 F.3d 794, 796 (8th Cir.2008) (gross abuse of discretion).

I. JURY CHARGE

§1. GENERAL

§1.1 Rules. FRCP 48, 49, 51.

§1.2 Purpose. The jury charge is the collection of instructions, definitions, and questions that the court submits to the jury to resolve the factual disputes in the case.

§1.3 Forms. ***O'Connor's Federal Civil Forms*** (2012), FORM 8I:1. There are many sources of pattern jury instructions. The most authoritative source is the book published by the district judges in the circuit where the case is tried. *See, e.g., Manual of Model Civil Jury Instructions for the District Courts of the Eighth Circuit* (2012), http://juryinstructions.ca8.uscourts.gov/civil_instructions.htm. There are also pattern instructions for specific areas of law and specific topics. For example, state bar associations often publish pattern jury instructions on state substantive law, the Litigation Section of the American Bar Association publishes a book of model jury instructions for employment cases, and the Judicial Conference Committee on Court Administration and Case Management periodically proposes model jury instructions.

§1.4 Other references. 9C Wright & Miller, *Federal Practice & Procedure 3d* §§2551-2558 (2008 & Supp.2012); 9, 12 *Moore's Federal Practice 3d* ch. 51, §59.13[2][b][i][B] (2012); 1 Childress & Davis, *Federal Standards of Review 4th* §§4.23, 4.24 (2010 & Supp.2011); 1 O'Malley et al., *Federal Jury Practice & Instructions* §§7:1-7:6 (6th ed.2006 & Supp.2012); Thornburg, *The Power & the Process: Instructions & the Civil Jury*, 66 Fordham L.Rev. 1837 (1998).

§2. TYPES OF VERDICTS

The charge may be prepared to solicit two types of verdicts: special or general. Special verdicts are favored over general verdicts. ***Bristol Steel & Iron Works, Inc. v. Bethlehem Steel Corp.***, 41 F.3d 182, 190 (4th Cir.1994); *see* ***Petes v. Hayes***, 664 F.2d 523, 525 n.2 (5th Cir.1981). Even so, the court has broad discretion in choosing the type of verdict form to be submitted to the jury. *See* ***Reyes-Mata v. IBP, Inc.***, 299 F.3d 504, 506 (5th Cir.2002); ***Workman v. Frito-Lay, Inc.***, 165 F.3d 460, 465 (6th Cir.1999); ***Hoechst Celanese Corp. v. BP Chems. Ltd.***, 78 F.3d 1575, 1581 (Fed. Cir.1996); ***Mangold v. California Pub. Utils. Comm'n***, 67 F.3d 1470, 1475 (9th Cir.1995); ***Bills v. Aseltine***, 52 F.3d 596, 605 (6th Cir.1995). A court can combine the two verdict forms, submitting some issues on a general-verdict form and others on a special-verdict form. ***Putnam Res. v. Pateman***, 958 F.2d 448, 456 (1st Cir.1992).

§2.1 Special verdict. A special verdict permits the jury to answer specific fact questions without deciding who wins. *See* FRCP 49(a)(1); ***Simms v. Village of Albion***, 115 F.3d 1098, 1105 (2d Cir.1997); ***Lattimore v. Polaroid Corp.***, 99 F.3d 456, 468 (1st Cir.1996); ***Bills v. Aseltine***, 52 F.3d 596, 605 (6th Cir.1995); ***Quaker City Gear Works, Inc. v. Skil Corp.***, 747 F.2d 1446, 1453 (Fed.Cir.1984). To decide who wins, the court applies the law to the facts found by the jury. ***Bills***, 52 F.3d at 605; ***Quaker City***, 747 F.2d at 1453; *cf.* ***Simms***, 115 F.3d at 1107 (district court did not commit reversible error by instructing jury on legal implications of its factual determinations). In a special-verdict form, the court submits to the jury written questions that elicit brief answers. FRCP 49(a)(1)(A); *see* ***Floyd v. Laws***, 929 F.2d 1390, 1395 (9th Cir.1991). The court must include any instructions and explanations necessary to enable the jury to make its findings on each submitted issue. FRCP 49(a)(2). A special verdict identifies the basis for the jury's verdict and thus helps avoid confusion, appellate uncertainty, and the need for additional proceedings. ***Simms***, 115 F.3d at 1105; ***Bristol Steel & Iron Works, Inc. v. Bethlehem Steel Corp.***, 41 F.3d 182, 190 (4th Cir.1994). The use of special verdicts rests within the court's discretion. ***Broadcast Satellite Int'l v. National Digital TV Ctr., Inc.***,

323 F.3d 339, 342 (5th Cir.2003); ***Transamerica Premier Ins. v. Ober***, 107 F.3d 925, 933 (1st Cir.1997); ***Hoechst Celanese Corp. v. BP Chems. Ltd.***, 78 F.3d 1575, 1581 (Fed.Cir.1996); ***Mangold v. California Pub. Utils. Comm'n***, 67 F.3d 1470, 1475 (9th Cir.1995); ***Bills***, 52 F.3d at 605.

1. Omitted issue. A party waives the right to a jury trial on any fact issue raised by the pleadings or evidence but not submitted to the jury, unless the party objects before the jury retires. FRCP 49(a)(3). If the party does not object, the court can make a finding on the issue. *Id.* But the court can neither reform issues decided by the jury nor make findings contrary to the jury verdict. ***Gaia Techs. v. Recycled Prods.***, 175 F.3d 365, 370-71 (5th Cir.1999). If the court does not make an explicit finding on the omitted issue, it is considered to have made a finding consistent with the special verdict. FRCP 49(a)(3).

2. Incomplete verdict. If the jury does not reach a verdict on every question, the court may accept the answered questions if they support a partial verdict. ***Simms***, 115 F.3d at 1105; ***Baxter Healthcare Corp. v. Spectramed, Inc.***, 49 F.3d 1575, 1580-81 (Fed.Cir.1995); ***Bridges v. Chemrex Specialty Coatings, Inc.***, 704 F.2d 175, 180 (5th Cir.1983). The court may also reject an incomplete verdict and resubmit the case to the jury. ***Baxter Healthcare***, 49 F.3d at 1580-81; *see* ***Hauser v. Kubalak***, 929 F.2d 1305, 1308 (8th Cir.1991).

§2.2 General verdict. A general verdict permits the jury to decide who wins. *See* FRCP 49(b)(1). The court may submit a general-verdict form alone or accompanied by written questions on one or more issues of fact that must be decided before a verdict may be rendered. *Id.*; *see* ***Bills v. Aseltine***, 52 F.3d 596, 605 (6th Cir.1995). The court must give any instructions and explanations necessary to enable the jury both to answer the specific questions and to render a general verdict. FRCP 49(b)(1).

§3. PREPARING PROPOSED INSTRUCTIONS

§3.1 Deadline.

1. Timely – at or before close of evidence. The parties should submit their requests for instructions to the court and to each party at the close of the evidence or at any earlier reasonable time that the court orders. FRCP 51(a)(1).

(1) By court order. A party can file in the court and furnish to the other parties its requests for instructions at a time ordered by the court. FRCP 51(a)(1). The deadline for filing and furnishing requests for instructions may be set in the pretrial order. *See* FRCP 16(b)(3). However, the court should not insist on a pretrial deadline for requests in all cases because trial evidence may raise new issues or reshape issues the parties thought they had understood. 2003 Notes to FRCP 51 at ¶5, p. 1216, this book. If the deadline is set in the pretrial order, a party may still file requests after the deadline to address issues that could not have been reasonably anticipated. FRCP 51(a)(2)(A); 2003 Notes to FRCP 51 at ¶5, p. 1216, this book.

(2) At close of evidence. A party can file in the court and furnish to the other parties its requests for instructions at the close of the evidence. FRCP 51(a)(1). This deadline arises after all intended evidence on an identified phase of the trial is completed and before the case is submitted to the jury. *See* 2003 Notes to FRCP 51 at ¶4, p. 1216, this book.

2. Untimely – after close of evidence. A party can file requests for instructions after the close of the evidence only in the following circumstances:

(1) With court's permission. A party can file untimely requests for instructions on any issue with the court's permission. FRCP 51(a)(2)(B). The party should file the request before final instructions and final jury arguments. 2003 Notes to FRCP 51 at ¶6, p. 1216, this book. In deciding whether the untimely instruction should be given, the court should consider the importance of the issue to the case and the party's reason for not making a timely submission. *Id.*

(2) Without court's permission. A party can file untimely requests for instructions without the court's permission only on issues that could not have been reasonably anticipated by the deadline the court set for the requests. FRCP 51(a)(2)(A).

§3.2 Draft of charge.

1. In writing. Requests for instructions must be in writing. FRCP 51(a)(1). Each request should be submitted on a separate page, or as required by local rules. If a party does not present a specific written instruction to the court, the party cannot argue on appeal that the instruction was not given. ***Kanida v. Gulf Coast Med. Pers. LP***, 363 F.3d 568, 580 (5th Cir.2004).

2. All material issues. Each material legal issue should be addressed in a separate instruction.

3. Correct wording. Each request should be worded correctly. If a request is not a correct statement of the law, the court is not required to submit it. ***Campbell v. Vinjamuri***, 19 F.3d 1274, 1278 (8th Cir.1994). However, if an incorrectly worded request clearly raises an important legal issue in the case, the court has the duty to frame the instruction correctly and submit it to the jury. ***Katch v. Speidel, Div. of Textron, Inc.***, 746 F.2d 1136, 1139 (6th Cir. 1984); *see* ***Walker v. AT&T Techs.***, 995 F.2d 846, 849 (8th Cir.1993); ***Jones v. Miles***, 656 F.2d 103, 107 n.6 (5th Cir. 1981). Even if the wording is correct, the court is not required to submit an instruction in the exact language submitted by the parties. ***Rolscreen Co. v. Pella Prods.***, 64 F.3d 1202, 1211 (8th Cir.1995); ***Hardin v. Ski Venture, Inc.***, 50 F.3d 1291, 1294 (4th Cir.1995).

4. Clear statement of law. The proposed instructions should relate the law to the evidence in the case. ***Choy v. Bouchelle***, 436 F.2d 319, 325 (3d Cir.1970); *see* ***Perry v. Ethan Allen, Inc.***, 115 F.3d 143, 153 (2d Cir.1997) (party not entitled to jury instruction for which there was no evidentiary predicate at trial). Abstract discussions of the law do not help the jury apply the law to the facts. *See* ***Perry***, 115 F.3d at 153; ***FDIC v. Henderson***, 61 F.3d 421, 429 (5th Cir.1995). If a case is controlled by a statute, the charge should use the statutory language. ***Monahan v. Flannery***, 755 F.2d 678, 681 (8th Cir.1985). Unless the meaning of the statute is clear without any explanation, the charge should include definitions. *E.g.*, ***Phillips v. Cameron Tool Corp.***, 950 F.2d 488, 490 (7th Cir.1991) (because court refused to define term, jury could have erroneously interpreted law); *cf.* ***Cook v. Rhode Island, Dept. of Mental Health, Retardation, & Hosps.***, 10 F.3d 17, 25 (1st Cir.1993) (unless there is objection, court may charge in language of statute without further definition).

5. Authority. After the text of the proposed instruction, the party should include a citation to authority that supports the submission of the instruction. The citation can be to statutes, case law, or pattern jury instructions.

§4. CHARGE CONFERENCE

The court must inform the parties of its proposed instructions and its proposed action on the parties' requests before the jury is charged and before final argument. FRCP 51(b)(1); *see* ***DeCaro v. Hasbro, Inc.***, 580 F.3d 55, 65 (1st Cir.2009) (court is not required to provide parties with final written instructions before delivery to jury; parties are sufficiently informed if they know intended instructions). Most courts schedule a charge conference at the end of the evidence and meet with the attorneys in chambers to discuss the charge. At the conference, the court decides on the instructions to be submitted to the jury from the proposed instructions submitted by the parties. The parties usually voice their initial objections to the instructions. *See* ***Booker v. Massachusetts Dept. of Pub. Health***, 612 F.3d 34, 41 (1st Cir.2010).

§5. OBJECTIONS

§5.1 Opportunity to object. The court must give the parties an opportunity to object to the charge on the record and out of the jury's hearing before the charge is given and arguments are delivered. FRCP 51(b)(2); *see* ***Booker v. Massachusetts Dept. of Pub. Health***, 612 F.3d 34, 40-41 (1st Cir.2010).

§5.2 Multiple parties. In a multiparty case, one party's objection to the charge is not sufficient for all parties; each party must object to preserve error. ***Kenney v. Lewis Revels Rare Coins, Inc.***, 741 F.2d 378, 382 (11th Cir.1984); *see* FRCP 51(d)(1). *But see* ***U.S. v. Amerigroup Ill., Inc.***, 488 F.Supp.2d 719, 735 (N.D.Ill.2007) (one party's objection to the charge was sufficient when further objections by coparties would be fruitless).

§5.3 Form of objection. The objecting party must make specific challenges on the record that distinctly identify the matter objected to and the grounds for the objection. FRCP 51(c)(1); ***Jimenez v. Wood Cty.***, 660 F.3d 841, 844-45 (5th Cir.2011); ***DeCaro v. Hasbro, Inc.***, 580 F.3d 55, 60 (1st Cir.2009); ***Bostic v. Smyrna Sch. Dist.***, 418 F.3d 355, 359 (3d Cir.2005). The objection must be sufficiently clear for the court to take appropriate action if it is valid. ***Navigant Consulting, Inc. v. Wilkinson***, 508 F.3d 277, 294 (5th Cir.2007); *see* ***Dupre v. Fru-Con Eng'g***, 112 F.3d 329, 333-34 (8th Cir.1997); ***Unit Drilling Co. v. Enron Oil & Gas Co.***, 108 F.3d 1186, 1190 (10th Cir.1997); *see, e.g.*, ***Colón-Millín v. Sears Roebuck***, 455 F.3d 30, 40 (1st Cir.2006) (error was not preserved under FRCP 51 when P only listed objections by referring to number designated for each instruction).

§5.4 Timing of objection. The timing of the objection determines whether error is preserved. To make a timely objection, the party must object as follows:

1. Party informed of instruction or action. If a party is informed of an instruction or court action before the jury is instructed and final arguments are made, the party must object to the instruction or action at the opportunity given by the court as required by FRCP 51(b)(2). FRCP 51(c)(2); *see* ***Jimenez v. Wood Cty.***, 660 F.3d 841, 845 (5th Cir.2011); ***Moore v. American Family Mut. Ins.***, 576 F.3d 781, 786 (8th Cir.2009); *see, e.g.*, ***Booker v. Massachusetts Dept. of Pub. Health***, 612 F.3d 34, 41-42 (1st Cir.2010) (when court modified instruction to accommodate P's objection and P did not object to modified instruction, error was not preserved).

2. Party not informed of instruction or action. If a party is not informed of an instruction or court action until after the jury is instructed and final arguments are made, the party must promptly object after learning that the instruction or request will be, or has been, given or refused. FRCP 51(c)(2)(B).

§5.5 Preserving error.

1. Instruction given. An objection made to an instruction actually given preserves error if the party properly objected. FRCP 51(d)(1)(A).

2. Instruction omitted. An objection made to an omitted instruction preserves error if the objecting party made a proper request (see "Preparing Proposed Instructions," §3, p. 721) and one of the following occurred:

(1) The court made a definitive ruling on the record rejecting the request. FRCP 51(d)(1)(B).

(2) The objecting party made a proper objection. *Id.* See "Form of objection," §5.3, this page.

3. Plain error. The court may consider a plain error in the instructions that affects a party's substantial rights even if the party did not object or waived its objection under FRCP 51(d)(1). *See* FRCP 51(d)(2); ***Jimenez v. Wood Cty.***, 660 F.3d 841, 845 (5th Cir.2011); ***Booker v. Massachusetts Dept. of Pub. Health***, 612 F.3d 34, 42-43 (1st Cir.2010); ***Moore v. American Family Mut. Ins.***, 576 F.3d 781, 786 (8th Cir.2009); *see also* 2003 Notes to FRCP 51 at ¶12, p. 1217, this book (plain-error language of FRCP 51(d)(2) is derived from Fed. R. Crim. P. 52). See "Error not preserved," §9.2.2, p. 726.

§6. FINAL CHARGE

§6.1 Responsibility for charge. The proper submission of the charge is the court's duty. ***Banc One Capital Partners v. Kneipper***, 67 F.3d 1187, 1192 (5th Cir.1995). The court should ensure that the jury is correctly apprised of the law to be applied to the facts of the case. *See, e.g.*, ***Chuman v. Wright***, 76 F.3d 292, 294-95 (9th Cir.1996) (instruction that broadened legal standard was not harmless error; jury could have found liability on improper ground). The court must submit to the jury all material issues raised by the pleadings and the evidence. ***Broadcast Satellite Int'l v. National Digital TV Ctr., Inc.***, 323 F.3d 339, 342 (5th Cir.2003).

§6.2 Comment on evidence. To assist the jury, the court may comment on the evidence. ***Quercia v. U.S.***, 289 U.S. 466, 469 (1933). The court may summarize the evidence and comment on the facts and the evidence as long as the court makes it clear that the jury is the sole judge of the facts. ***Turlington v. Phillips Pet. Co.***, 795 F.2d 434, 443 (5th Cir.1986). The court is not required to comment on the evidence. ***Hardin v. Ski Venture, Inc.***, 50 F.3d 1291, 1294-95 (4th Cir.1995).

§6.3 Timing of charge. The court may instruct the jury at any time after trial begins and before the jury is discharged. FRCP 51(b)(3). The advantage of instructing the jury before the attorneys make their final arguments is that the attorneys know the exact language of the charge and can explain the instructions to the jury, argue their application to the facts, and give the jury the maximum assistance in determining the issues and arriving at a good verdict on the law and the evidence. *See* 1987 Notes to FRCP 51 at ¶1, p. 1217, this book; *see also* ***Trawick v. Manhattan Life Ins.***, 484 F.2d 535, 538 (5th Cir.1973) (under certain circumstances, if court changes instructions after parties argue, it should permit parties to reargue changed issue).

§7. VERDICT-URGING INSTRUCTIONS

When a jury notifies the court that it is unable to reach a verdict, the court may instruct the jury to resume its deliberations and attempt to reach a verdict. ***Carter v. Burch***, 34 F.3d 257, 264-65 (4th Cir.1994); ***Mason v. Texaco, Inc.***, 948 F.2d 1546, 1557 (10th Cir.1991); ***Brooks v. Bay State Abrasive Prods.***, 516 F.2d 1003, 1004 (5th Cir.1975); *see* 9C Wright & Miller §2556 & nn.30-33. In general, the court should reveal the existence and contents of any jury notes to both sides and allow the attorneys to suggest an appropriate response. ***U.S. v. Henry***, 325 F.3d 93, 105 (2d Cir. 2003).

§7.1 Origin of *Allen* charge. The supplemental charge that instructs the jury to attempt to reach a verdict is sometimes called an "*Allen* charge," after ***Allen v. U.S.***, 164 U.S. 492 (1896), or a "dynamite charge," because it is used to "blast" a jury out of deadlock to reach a verdict. ***U.S. v. Zabriskie***, 415 F.3d 1139, 1147-48 & n.13 (10th Cir. 2005). The ***Allen*** charge originated in a criminal case and has been the subject of controversy on the criminal side of the docket. *See* ***U.S. v. Rey***, 811 F.2d 1453, 1458-60 (11th Cir.1987); ***U.S. v. Fioravanti***, 412 F.2d 407, 415-20 (3d Cir.1969). The controversy about the ***Allen*** charge has not extended to the civil side of the docket. 9C Wright & Miller §2556 & nn.30-32. As used in this section, "***Allen*** charge" does not mean the charge given in the ***Allen*** case, but refers to any supplemental jury instruction urging the jury to attempt to reach a verdict.

§7.2 Propriety of charge. The key to a permissible *Allen* charge in civil cases (as well as criminal cases) is that the charge not be coercive. *See* ***Lowenfield v. Phelps***, 484 U.S. 231, 237 (1988); ***U.S. v. Zabriskie***, 415 F.3d 1139, 1148 (10th Cir.2005); ***U.S. v. McClatchy***, 249 F.3d 348, 359 (5th Cir.2001). An ***Allen*** charge is not coercive if it makes clear to the jury that (1) a juror is duty-bound to adhere to honest opinion and (2) a juror is doing nothing improper by maintaining a good-faith opinion even though a mistrial may result. ***Blair v. Eagle-Picher Indus.***, 962 F.2d 1492, 1501 (10th Cir.1992); ***Brooks v. Bay State Abrasive Prods.***, 516 F.2d 1003, 1004 (5th Cir.1975).

§7.3 Factors determining coercive effect. Courts must determine the coercive effect of an ***Allen*** charge on a case-by-case basis. ***Mason v. Texaco, Inc.***, 948 F.2d 1546, 1557 (10th Cir.1991). Courts must consider the totality of the circumstances in which the supplemental charge is given. ***Bristol Steel & Iron Works, Inc. v. Bethlehem Steel Corp.***, 41 F.3d 182, 191 (4th Cir.1994). To determine if an ***Allen*** charge was impermissibly coercive, the court must consider (1) the content of the instruction, (2) the length of deliberation after the ***Allen*** charge, (3) the total length of deliberation, and (4) any indication in the record of coercion or pressure on the jury. ***Williams v. Fermenta Animal Health Co.***, 984 F.2d 261, 266 (8th Cir.1993).

1. No coercion. The following tend to show that the ***Allen*** charge was not coercive: • The district court used an ***Allen*** charge approved in that circuit, either by case law or by local rules. *See, e.g.*, ***Carter v. Burch***, 34 F.3d 257, 264-65 & n.3 (4th Cir.1994) (approved ***Allen*** charge set out in footnote 3); *Manual of Model Civil Jury Instructions for the District Courts of the Eighth Circuit* 3.07, http://juryinstructions.ca8.uscourts.gov/civil_instructions.htm (***Allen*** charge approved by 8th Circuit). *But see* ***U.S. v. Clinton***, 338 F.3d 483, 490-91 (6th Cir.2003) (failure to use circuit-approved pattern jury instruction not reversible error). • The ***Allen*** charge did not inform the jury that it was required to reach a verdict. ***Lowenfield v. Phelps***, 484 U.S. 231, 239-41 (1988). • The district court placed no limit on the time the jury could deliberate after the ***Allen*** charge. ***Bristol Steel***, 41 F.3d at 191. • The jury deliberated for an extended period after the court gave the ***Allen*** charge. ***Williams***, 984 F.2d at 266-67; ***Mason***, 948 F.2d at 1557. • The court did not ask the identity of the holdout jurors. ***U.S. v. Ajiboye***, 961 F.2d 892, 893-94 (9th Cir.1992). • The charge encouraged both the majority and minority to give consideration to each other's views. ***U.S. v. Burgos***, 55 F.3d 933, 937 (4th Cir.1995).

2. Coercion. The following tend to show that the *Allen* charge was coercive: • The *Allen* charge was given only to dissenting jurors and only in private. ***U.S. v. Zabriskie***, 415 F.3d 1139, 1148 (10th Cir.2005). • The language of the *Allen* charge focused on the obligation of holdout jurors to conform to the majority view. *See* ***Burgos***, 55 F.3d at 936. • The court knew the numerical division of the panel and the identity of the holdout jurors. *See* ***U.S. v. Sae-Chua***, 725 F.2d 530, 531-32 (9th Cir.1984) (great risk of coercion when dissenting juror knows that judge knows his identity). • The court suggested the jurors surrender their conscientious convictions. ***Burgos***, 55 F.3d at 939-40.

PRACTICE TIP

If the court plans to poll the jurors to determine if additional time would help them reach a verdict, suggest that the court ask the jury "how many jurors feel that further deliberations will help them arrive at a verdict." ***Lowenfield****, 484 U.S. at 240-41. The court should not inquire into how the votes are split or who the holdouts are. See id. at 239-40.*

§7.4 Objecting to *Allen* charge. To preserve error, the party should object to the supplemental charge, identify each statement that is coercive or otherwise objectionable and state why, and submit proposed language, if applicable. *See* FRCP 51(c)(1). The court should allow the attorneys an opportunity to suggest appropriate responses to any note from the jury. ***U.S. v. Henry***, 325 F.3d 93, 105 (2d Cir.2003).

§8. REQUEST TO POLL JURY

A court must on a party's request, or may on its own, poll jurors individually after a verdict is returned but before the jury is discharged. FRCP 48(c). The court should read the general verdict or the questions and answers, call the name of each juror, and ask if that is the verdict of that juror. If the poll shows that the verdict was not unanimous or that the number of jurors stipulated by the parties have not agreed to the verdict, the court may order the jury to deliberate further or may order a new trial. FRCP 48(c); *see* ***Castleberry v. NRM Corp.***, 470 F.2d 1113, 1117 (10th Cir.1972).

§9. APPELLATE REVIEW

§9.1 Standard of review. The standard of review for an error in a jury instruction depends on the nature of the error—whether the error is in the formulation of the jury instruction or a misstatement of the elements of the claim at issue. ***Medtronic, Inc. v. White***, 526 F.3d 487, 493 (9th Cir.2008); *see* ***DeCaro v. Hasbro, Inc.***, 580 F.3d 55, 61 (1st Cir.2009). An incorrect instruction is reversible if, considering all the instructions, the evidence, and the arguments, the appellate court believes that the jury was misled or did not have a sufficient understanding of the issues and its duty to determine them. ***Gruca v. Alpha Therapeutic Corp.***, 51 F.3d 638, 644 (7th Cir.1995); *see* ***Burks v. Oklahoma Publ'g***, 81 F.3d 975, 978 (10th Cir.1996); ***Circa, Ltd. v. City of Miami***, 79 F.3d 1057, 1064 (11th Cir. 1996); *see also* ***C.P. Interests, Inc. v. California Pools, Inc.***, 238 F.3d 690, 700 (5th Cir.2001) (reversal is appropriate only when charge as whole creates substantial doubt about whether jury was properly guided in its deliberations).

1. Formulation of instruction. When a party alleges an error in the formulation of the jury instructions, the appellate court considers the instructions as a whole and applies the abuse-of-discretion standard to determine if they are misleading or inadequate. ***Phillips v. IRS***, 73 F.3d 939, 941 (9th Cir.1996); *see* ***DeCaro***, 580 F.3d at 61; ***U.S. Surgical Corp. v. Ethicon, Inc.***, 103 F.3d 1554, 1564 (Fed.Cir.1997); *see, e.g.,* ***Kanida v. Gulf Coast Med. Pers. LP***, 363 F.3d 568, 578 (5th Cir.2004) (district court's refusal to provide requested jury instruction reviewed for abuse of discretion); *see also* ***Greenleaf v. Garlock, Inc.***, 174 F.3d 352, 361 (3d Cir.1999) (plenary review to determine whether there was misstatement; if no misstatement, decisions regarding jury instructions reviewed for abuse of discretion).

2. Misstatement of law. When a party alleges that the charge misstated the elements that must be proved, the appellate court reviews the issue de novo. ***DeCaro***, 580 F.3d at 61; ***Medtronic, Inc.***, 526 F.3d at 493; ***Perry v. Ethan Allen, Inc.***, 115 F.3d 143, 153 (2d Cir.1997); *see* ***Rice v. Office of Servicemembers' Grp. Life Ins.***, 260 F.3d 1240, 1247 (10th Cir.2001) (legal objections reviewed de novo). The district court will be reversed only if the instructions as a whole do not fairly and adequately state the applicable law. *See* ***Kanida***, 363 F.3d at 580; ***Garcia v. Wal-Mart Stores***, 209 F.3d 1170, 1173 (10th Cir.2000); ***Luciano v. Olsten Corp.***, 110 F.3d 210, 218 (2d Cir.1997); ***Soller v. Moore***, 84 F.3d 964, 969 (7th Cir.1996).

3. *Allen* charge. The district court's verdict-urging instruction will be upheld on appeal unless it is clear from the record that the charge was impermissibly coercive. *See **Bristol Steel & Iron Works, Inc. v. Bethlehem Steel Corp.***, 41 F.3d 182, 190-91 (4th Cir.1994); ***Williams v. Fermenta Animal Health Co.***, 984 F.2d 261, 266-67 (8th Cir.1993); ***Mason v. Texaco, Inc.***, 948 F.2d 1546, 1557 (10th Cir.1991). See "Verdict-Urging Instructions," §7, p. 724. The district court has broad discretion to decide whether an ***Allen*** charge will coerce the jury. ***U.S. v. McClatchy***, 249 F.3d 348, 359 (5th Cir.2001).

4. Findings under FRCP 49(a)(3). FRCP 49(a)(3) allows the district court to make its own findings on issues not submitted to the jury when the failure to submit is not objected to by a party. Whether the district court was entitled to make additional findings is reviewed de novo. ***Gaia Techs. v. Recycled Prods.***, 175 F.3d 365, 370 (5th Cir.1999).

§9.2 Preservation of error. Whether the party made an adequate and timely objection determines the standard of appellate review applied to the charge.

1. Error preserved. When the objection was properly preserved, the appellate court applies the abuse-of-discretion standard to determine whether the charge was misleading or inadequate. *See **Phillips v. IRS***, 73 F.3d 939, 941 (9th Cir.1996).

2. Error not preserved. When the objection was not properly preserved as required by FRCP 51(d)(1), the appellate court can only consider a plain error in the instructions that affects substantial rights. FRCP 51(d)(2); ***Jimenez v. Wood Cty.***, 660 F.3d 841, 845 (5th Cir.2011); ***Slidell, Inc. v. Millennium Inorganic Chems., Inc.***, 460 F.3d 1047, 1054 (8th Cir.2006); *see **Colón-Millín v. Sears Roebuck***, 455 F.3d 30, 41 (1st Cir.2006). The Supreme Court has held that the criminal rule that FRCP 51(d)(2) is based on also requires that the error seriously affect the fairness, integrity, or public reputation of judicial proceedings. ***Johnson v. U.S.***, 520 U.S. 461, 467 (1997); *see* 2003 Notes to FRCP 51 at ¶12, p. 1217, this book (language of FRCP 51(d)(2) is borrowed from Fed. R. Crim. P. 52).

§9.3 Harmful error. If the charge was erroneous, the party must still show that the error was harmful before the appellate court will reverse. *See **Martin's Herend Imps., Inc. v. Diamond & Gem Trading U.S.***, 195 F.3d 765, 774 (5th Cir.1999) (even though instruction may erroneously state applicable law or provide insufficient guidance, court will not reverse judgment unless error affected outcome of trial). The issue is whether the jury was misled by the error. *See **Cross v. Cleaver***, 142 F.3d 1059, 1067 (8th Cir.1998); *see, e.g.*, ***Dinco v. Dylex Ltd.***, 111 F.3d 964, 969 (1st Cir.1997) (partnership instruction could not be justified and may well have misled jury when there was no evidence of partnership); ***Thornley v. Penton Publ'g***, 104 F.3d 26, 30 (2d Cir.1997) (charge in age-discrimination suit that permitted jury to infer discrimination based on reasonableness of employer's standards was harmful error). Some courts have stated that if it is uncertain whether the jury was actually misled, the erroneous instruction cannot be considered harmless. ***Busby v. City of Orlando***, 931 F.2d 764, 777 (11th Cir.1991); ***Miller v. Universal City Studios, Inc.***, 650 F.2d 1365, 1372 (5th Cir.1981); *cf.* ***Unit Drilling Co. v. Enron Oil & Gas Co.***, 108 F.3d 1186, 1190-91 (10th Cir.1997) (instruction may have misled jury, but on the whole instructions correctly stated law; thus, imperfections were not plain error). Generally, an erroneous instruction will be grounds for reversal if it causes "substantial and ineradicable doubt" about whether the jury was properly guided in its deliberations. ***Reyes-Mata v. IBP, Inc.***, 299 F.3d 504, 506 (5th Cir.2002); ***Bateman v. Mnemonics, Inc.***, 79 F.3d 1532, 1543 (11th Cir.1996); *see also* ***Burks v. Oklahoma Publ'g***, 81 F.3d 975, 978 (10th Cir.1996) (court used less drastic test of "substantial doubt").

J. CLOSING ARGUMENT

§1. GENERAL

§1.1 Rule. None.

§1.2 Purpose. After all the evidence is introduced, the attorneys summarize their case and argue the effect of the evidence.

§1.3 Forms. *O'Connor's Federal Civil Forms* (2012), FORMS 8B.

§1.4 Other references. 9B Wright & Miller, *Federal Practice & Procedure 3d* §2509 (2008 & Supp.2012); 16AA Wright, Miller, Cooper & Struve, *Federal Practice & Procedure 4th* §3980 (2008 & Supp.2012); 35B C.J.S. *Federal Civil Procedure* §943 (2003 & Supp.2012); Larrabee & Drucker, *Adieu Voir Dire: The Jury Questionnaire*, 21 Litig. 37 (Fall 1994).

§2. MANAGEMENT OF ARGUMENT

§2.1 Federal law. The propriety of closing argument is a procedural question governed by federal law. ***Boardman v. National Med. Enters.***, 106 F.3d 840, 844 (8th Cir.1997).

§2.2 Court's supervisory responsibility. The court is required to regulate closing argument and to remedy the effect of an erroneous argument by sustaining any proper objection. *See **Jonas v. City of Atlanta***, 647 F.2d 580, 586 (5th Cir.1981), *overruled on other grounds, **Hudson v. Palmer***, 468 U.S. 517 (1984).

§2.3 Order of argument. The plaintiff usually opens and closes the argument. When the defendant has the burden of proving the issues in the charge, the court may allow the defendant to argue first and last. ***Moylan v. Meadow Club, Inc.***, 979 F.2d 1246, 1251 (7th Cir.1992). The order of closing arguments is a matter within the court's discretion. *Id.* See "Opportunity to Open & Close," ch. 8-B, §2, p. 686.

§2.4 Nonjury trial. In a nonjury trial, the court has broad discretion to decide whether to hear oral arguments; the refusal to hear arguments is not grounds for reversal. ***Defenders of Wildlife, Inc. v. Endangered Species Sci. Auth.***, 659 F.2d 168, 182 (D.C.Cir.1981).

§2.5 Time limit. Generally, the court can set a time limit on the closing argument. *See, e.g.,* ***Glenn v. Cessna Aircraft Co.***, 32 F.3d 1462, 1464-65 (10th Cir.1994) (under plain-error review, 10 minutes for opening and 22 minutes for closing was not reversible error). The crucial question in reviewing time limits on closing arguments is whether the attorney was permitted to advocate effectively for the client. ***U.S. v. Gray***, 105 F.3d 956, 963 (5th Cir. 1997). One factor the reviewing court considers is whether the time limits hamper the jury's ability to understand the information and issues at trial. *Id.*

§3. LIMITS OF ARGUMENT

Although attorneys have great latitude to indulge in flights of oratory, there are limits. ***Schleunes v. American Cas. Co.***, 528 F.2d 634, 638 (5th Cir.1976). An argument should never encourage a jury to depart from neutrality and decide the case on bias rather than evidence. *See id.; see, e.g.,* ***Pappas v. Middle Earth Condo. Ass'n***, 963 F.2d 534, 539-40 (2d Cir.1992) (attorney appealed to prejudices against out-of-state tourists).

§3.1 Permitted argument.

1. Questions of fact. Attorneys should summarize the facts and discuss the evidence and its probative effect. *See* ***Harris v. Steelweld Equip. Co.***, 869 F.2d 396, 405 (8th Cir.1989) (argument describing opponent's case as false and fraudulent is proper if facts supporting that conclusion were introduced at trial).

2. Inferences from facts. Attorneys may argue reasonable deductions and inferences from the facts. ***Ratliff v. Schiber Truck Co.***, 150 F.3d 949, 957 (8th Cir.1998); ***Lentomyynti Oy v. Medivac, Inc.***, 997 F.2d 364, 374 (7th Cir.1993).

3. Missing witness. Attorneys may make a "missing witness" argument about a witness under the control of the other party who was not called to testify but who would have been called if her testimony had been favorable to the other party. *See* ***Kostelec v. State Farm Fire & Cas. Co.***, 64 F.3d 1220, 1228-29 (8th Cir.1995); ***McQuaig v. McCoy***, 806 F.2d 1298, 1303 (5th Cir.1987); ***Auto Owners Ins. v. Bass***, 684 F.2d 764, 769 (11th Cir.1982). The inference from this argument is that the other party did not call the witness because that witness's testimony would have been unfavorable. ***Littlefield v. McGuffey***, 954 F.2d 1337, 1346-47 (7th Cir.1992); ***McQuaig***, 806 F.2d at 1303. An attorney cannot make this argument if the witness was equally available to both parties. ***Littlefield***, 954 F.2d at 1346-47; ***McQuaig***, 806 F.2d at 1303. *But see* ***Kostelec***, 64 F.3d at 1228-29 (permissible to comment on failure to call equally available witness whose testimony the party would naturally be expected to produce if favorable). The question of whether to permit a missing-witness argument is within the court's discretion. ***Littlefield***, 954 F.2d at 1347.

4. Inadmissible evidence admitted without objection. If inadmissible evidence is introduced without objection, the evidence may be argued to the jury. *E.g.*, ***U.S. Aviation Underwriters, Inc. v. Olympia Wings, Inc.***, 896 F.2d 949, 956 (5th Cir.1990) (because party did not object to testimony about settlement negotiations, other party could refer to it in closing argument).

5. Legal effect of answer. When a general verdict is submitted under FRCP 49(b), the jury can be informed of the effect of its answers. *See* 9B Wright & Miller §2509. Courts of appeals are divided on whether the jury may be told the effect of its answers when special-verdict questions are submitted. *Compare* ***Beul v. ASSE Int'l***, 233 F.3d 441, 450 (7th Cir.2000) (no rule against telling jury effect of its answers), ***Vinieris v. Byzantine Maritime Corp.***, 731 F.2d 1061, 1065 (2d Cir.1984) (jury should have been told effect of its answers), *and* ***Perricone v. Kansas City S. Ry.***, 704 F.2d 1376, 1378 (5th Cir.1983) (proper to tell jury effect of its answers), *with* ***Carvalho v. Raybestos-Manhattan, Inc.***, 794 F.2d 454, 457 n.2 (9th Cir.1986) (refusing to inform jury of consequences of its answers not abuse of discretion), *and* ***Gullett v. St. Paul Fire & Mar. Ins.***, 446 F.2d 1100, 1105 (7th Cir.1971) (comments on legal effects of answers could, in certain cases, have prejudicial effect).

6. Matters invited by improper argument. When an attorney raises improper topics during summation, the other side may discuss the same matters. There are, however, limits to what can be argued in response to improper argument. *See* ***Reed v. Philadelphia Bethlehem & New England R.R.***, 939 F.2d 128, 133 (3d Cir.1991) (party cannot respond to improper argument by discussing evidence outside the record).

§3.2 Prohibited argument.

1. Questions of law. Attorneys cannot argue questions of law to the jury. *Cf.* ***Schwartz v. System Software Assocs.***, 32 F.3d 284, 288 (7th Cir.1994) (opening statement). The attorneys must address arguments on questions of law to the court.

2. Outside the record. Attorneys cannot discuss matters that were not introduced as evidence during the trial. ***Trytko v. Hubbell, Inc.***, 28 F.3d 715, 727 (7th Cir.1994); ***Reed v. Philadelphia Bethlehem & New England R.R.***, 939 F.2d 128, 133 (3d Cir.1991); ***Pearce v. Cornerstone Clinic for Women***, 938 F.2d 855, 859 (8th Cir. 1991); *see, e.g.*, ***Jonas v. City of Atlanta***, 647 F.2d 580, 586 (5th Cir.1981) (attorney argued details of marijuana transactions that were not in evidence).

3. Matters calculated to cause prejudice. Attorneys cannot make arguments that are calculated to cause jury prejudice. The following are some examples:

(1) Personal attack on opposing counsel. Attorneys cannot make personal attacks on the character of opposing counsel or make abusive references about them. ***Bufford v. Rowan Cos.***, 994 F.2d 155, 157-59 (5th Cir.1993); *see* ***Hofer v. Mack Trucks, Inc.***, 981 F.2d 377, 385 (8th Cir.1992); ***Fineman v. Armstrong World Indus.***, 980 F.2d 171, 209 (3d Cir.1992); *see, e.g.*, ***Davis v. General Acc. Ins.***, 153 F.Supp.2d 598, 603 (E.D.Pa.2001) (statements made by defense counsel apologizing for length of trial were merely introductory banter and had no bearing on jury's evaluation of evidence, and thus were not considered improper personal attacks).

(2) Golden rule. Because it encourages the jury to depart from neutrality and decide the case on bias rather than evidence, attorneys cannot ask jurors to put themselves in the shoes of one of the parties. ***Loose v.***

Offshore Nav., Inc., 670 F.2d 493, 496-97 (5th Cir.1982). The so-called "golden rule" argument is universally condemned by the courts. ***Joan W. v. City of Chi.***, 771 F.2d 1020, 1022 (7th Cir.1985); *see also* ***McNely v. Ocala Star-Banner Corp.***, 99 F.3d 1068, 1071 n.3 (11th Cir.1996) (party makes impermissible "golden rule" argument when jury is exhorted to place itself in party's position with respect to damages but not when argument relates only to reasonableness of party's actions).

(3) Jurors' personal finances. Defense attorneys cannot suggest that the jurors themselves will suffer financially should they decide in favor of the plaintiff. ***Allstate Ins. v. James***, 845 F.2d 315, 319 (11th Cir.1988).

(4) Insurance or indemnity. If insurance or other indemnity is not an issue, the attorneys cannot mention it in their arguments. *See, e.g.*, ***Moses v. Union Pac. R.R.***, 64 F.3d 413, 417 (8th Cir.1995) (improper to appeal to prejudice against insurance companies and to invite jury to find D not liable because P would be compensated for his loss by insurance); ***Fruge v. Penrod Drilling Co.***, 918 F.2d 1163, 1167-69 (5th Cir.1990) (reference in tort case to workers' compensation benefits could affect jury deliberation or violate collateral-source doctrine); ***Polansky v. CNA Ins.***, 852 F.2d 626, 630 (1st Cir.1988) (improper to argue that if jury found against P-arsonist, victims of his arson would not get insurance recovery).

(5) Wealth or poverty of party. If the wealth or poverty of the party is not at issue, the attorneys should not discuss it in their closing arguments. ***Adams Labs. v. Jacobs Eng'g Co.***, 761 F.2d 1218, 1226 (7th Cir. 1985); *see, e.g.*, ***Greenleaf v. Garlock, Inc.***, 174 F.3d 352, 364 n.9 (3d Cir.1999) (improper to appeal to financial disparity between parties); ***Gonzalez v. Volvo of Am. Corp.***, 752 F.2d 295, 298 (7th Cir.1985) (argument contrasted D's wealth against P's poverty).

(6) Personal opinions. An attorney should not inject her personal opinions into jury argument. ***Polansky***, 852 F.2d at 628; ***Canada Dry Corp. v. Nehi Bev. Co.***, 723 F.2d 512, 526-27 (7th Cir.1983). During closing argument, the attorney cannot vouch for the credibility of the witnesses, assert personal opinions about the justness of the cause, or attest to the culpability of a civil litigant. *See, e.g.*, ***Trademark Research Corp. v. Maxwell Online, Inc.***, 995 F.2d 326, 340 (2d Cir.1993) (attorney vouched for credibility of expert); ***Fineman***, 980 F.2d at 206-07 (attorney essentially testified to his own truthfulness, supplied facts outside record about credibility of witnesses, and accused witnesses of being liars); ***Polansky***, 852 F.2d at 627-28 (attorney repeatedly said he did not believe witness); ***Canada Dry***, 723 F.2d at 526-27 (attorney vouched for honesty and credibility of witness).

(7) Regional bias. Attorneys cannot ask the jury to serve as the conscience of the community or otherwise appeal to regional bias. ***Pappas v. Middle Earth Condo. Ass'n***, 963 F.2d 534, 539 (2d Cir.1992); ***Westbrook v. General Tire & Rubber Co.***, 754 F.2d 1233, 1238-39 (5th Cir.1985). This type of argument distracts the jurors from their duty to base the verdict on evidence, not prejudice. ***Pappas***, 963 F.2d at 539.

(8) Irrelevant, erroneous, or prejudicial matters. Attorneys cannot argue matters that are not supported by relevant, admissible evidence. *See, e.g.*, ***Gruca v. Alpha Therapeutic Corp.***, 51 F.3d 638, 645 (7th Cir. 1995) (argument that Ds could have sued FDA was improper, unwarranted, and misstatement of law); ***Polansky***, 852 F.2d at 629-30 (in suit to recover for property damage, argument about death claims of nonparties was irrelevant and prejudicial).

§4. OBJECTING TO IMPROPER ARGUMENT

To preserve error on an improper argument, the party should do the following:

§4.1 Make proper objection. A party should always object to improper jury argument. *See, e.g.*, ***Guides, Ltd. v. Yarmouth Grp. Prop. Mgmt.***, 295 F.3d 1065, 1075 (10th Cir.2002) (attorney did not object to improper statements during closing argument, so issue not addressed on appeal); ***Ramirez v. New York City Off-Track Betting Corp.***, 112 F.3d 38, 40 (2d Cir.1997) (attorney's suggestion to jury of amount it should award party did not rise to level of prejudicial error, especially because no objection was made); ***Greenway v. Buffalo Hilton Hotel***, 951 F.Supp. 1039, 1053 (W.D.N.Y.1997) (objection to improper argument waived when not made at trial), *aff'd as modified*, 143 F.3d 47 (2d Cir.1998). A party who does not object to statements made during closing argument waives any objection. ***Guides,***

Ltd., 295 F.3d at 1075; ***Billingsley v. City of Omaha***, 277 F.3d 990, 997 (8th Cir.2002). To make a proper objection to closing argument, the attorney must identify the objectionable comment and inform the court why the comment is objectionable. In some cases, objecting to every objectionable remark is not necessary. *E.g.*, ***Fineman v. Armstrong World Indus.***, 980 F.2d 171, 207 n.26 (3d Cir.1992) (objecting to each and every remark would create unnecessary prejudice against D in eyes of jury).

§4.2 Make timely objection. To make a timely objection to improper argument, the attorney must object as soon as the other attorney makes the objectionable statement. *See* ***Fleming v. Harris***, 39 F.3d 905, 908 (8th Cir.1994); ***Johnson v. National Sea Prods.***, 35 F.3d 626, 631 (1st Cir.1994). Although some courts permit attorneys to wait until the end of the closing argument to make an objection rather than call more attention to the impropriety by objecting at once, they do not permit waiting until the jury begins deliberating. ***Walden v. Illinois Cent. Gulf R.R.***, 975 F.2d 361, 366 (7th Cir.1992); *see also* ***Doe v. Johnson***, 52 F.3d 1448, 1465 (7th Cir.1995) (temerity or trial tactics do not excuse failure to object).

§4.3 Secure ruling. The party should ensure that the court rules on the objection by either sustaining or overruling it.

1. Objection overruled. If the court overrules an objection to improper jury argument, no additional action is required, and the complaint is preserved. If the court overrules a proper objection and refuses to instruct the jury, its actions suggest approval of the jury argument. ***Allstate Ins. v. James***, 845 F.2d 315, 319 (11th Cir.1988). If the court improperly overrules an objection, the relevant inquiry on appeal is whether the court's response, or lack of response, was a prejudicial abuse of discretion. ***Moses v. Union Pac. R.R.***, 64 F.3d 413, 417 (8th Cir.1995); ***Gorlikowski v. Tolbert***, 52 F.3d 1439, 1446 (7th Cir.1995); *see* ***Slathar v. Sather Trucking Corp.***, 78 F.3d 415, 420 (8th Cir.1996).

2. Objection sustained. If the court sustains an objection to improper jury argument, the attorney should do the following:

(1) Ask for instruction. The party should ask the court to instruct the jury to disregard the improper argument. In most cases, the court can cure potential prejudice with a prompt instruction that the attorney's statements are not evidence in the case. *See* ***Slathar***, 78 F.3d at 420; ***Martin v. Cavalier Hotel Corp.***, 48 F.3d 1343, 1358 (4th Cir.1995). If the court refuses to limit the impact of improper argument by an instruction, it heightens the possibility that the jury will be persuaded by an improper tone or suggestion within the improper argument. ***Allstate Ins.***, 845 F.2d at 319.

(2) Move for mistrial. If the argument was truly egregious and the harm is not curable, the party should also ask the court for a mistrial. *See* ***Fineman v. Armstrong World Indus.***, 980 F.2d 171, 207 n.26 (3d Cir. 1992). This is called "pursuing an adverse ruling." See "Instruction to Disregard & Motion for Mistrial," ch. 8-D, §8, p. 705.

§4.4 Repeat objection. If opposing counsel continues to make the same objectionable jury argument, the party should continue to object. To avoid drawing attention to the improper remarks, the attorney may want to make a running objection outside the presence of the jury. In the eyes of the jury, multiple objections may create more prejudice than the objectionable evidence itself. ***Fineman v. Armstrong World Indus.***, 980 F.2d 171, 207 n.26 (3d Cir. 1992).

§5. ERROR IN ARGUMENT

There are two types of error in jury argument: curable and incurable.

§5.1 Curable. Most improper jury arguments can be cured of their harmful effects by an objection, an instruction to the jury to disregard, and if necessary, an admonition to the attorney to refrain from further improper comments. *See, e.g.*, ***Moulton v. Rival Co.***, 116 F.3d 22, 27 (1st Cir.1997) (immediate curative instruction given). The errors in the following arguments were considered curable by an instruction, and objection was necessary to preserve the issue for appeal: • Misstating the evidence. ***Thomure v. Truck Ins. Exch.***, 781 F.2d 141, 143 (8th Cir.

1986). • A reference to insurance or other indemnity. *See, e.g.*, ***Griffin v. Hilke***, 804 F.2d 1052, 1057-58 (8th Cir.1986) (Ds objected to argument that government, not Ds, would pay the judgment). • The "golden rule" argument. *See, e.g.*, ***Fleming v. Harris***, 39 F.3d 905, 908 (8th Cir.1994) (failure to object to "golden rule" argument waived error). The "golden rule" argument is not considered incurable argument even though it is universally condemned by the courts. ***Joan W. v. City of Chi.***, 771 F.2d 1020, 1022 (7th Cir.1985). See "Golden rule," §3.2.3(2), p. 728. • The "conscience of the community" argument. ***Reese v. Mercury Mar. Div. of Brunswick Corp.***, 793 F.2d 1416, 1429 (5th Cir.1986). See "Regional bias," §3.2.3(7), p. 729. • An improper interpretation of a contract. ***Golden Rule Ins. v. Atallah***, 45 F.3d 512, 519 n.12 (1st Cir.1995).

§5.2 Incurable. Incurable arguments are so prejudicial or inflammatory that an instruction to the jury to disregard them cannot eliminate their harm. The errors in the following arguments were considered so egregious that no objection was necessary to preserve them: • Appealing to religious beliefs by telling the jury that a finding that the decedent committed suicide would condemn him to eternal damnation. ***Schleunes v. American Cas. Co.***, 528 F.2d 634, 638 (5th Cir.1976). • An argument that contesting the amount of damages was a tacit admission of liability by the defendant. ***San Antonio v. Timko***, 368 F.2d 983, 986 & n.4 (2d Cir.1966).

§6. APPELLATE REVIEW

§6.1 Record. The party objecting to the final argument must provide the appellate court with a transcript of the argument and the district court's final ruling on the argument. *See* FRAP 10(a), (b)(1); ***Sylla-Sawdon v. Uniroyal Goodrich Tire Co.***, 47 F.3d 277, 286 (8th Cir.1995).

§6.2 Standard of review.

1. Abuse of discretion. If error was preserved, the district court's ruling on closing arguments will not be disturbed unless the court abused its discretion. ***Billingsley v. City of Omaha***, 277 F.3d 990, 997 (8th Cir.2002); ***Waldorf v. Shuta***, 142 F.3d 601, 627-28 (3d Cir.1998); ***Miksis v. Howard***, 106 F.3d 754, 764 (7th Cir.1997); ***Johnson v. National Sea Prods.***, 35 F.3d 626, 631 (1st Cir.1994). The following are some of the considerations for determining whether improper remarks during closing argument warrant reversal of the judgment:

(1) Substantial prejudice. Improper remarks during closing argument warrant reversal only if they influenced the jury in such a way that substantial prejudice resulted to the opposing party. ***Groom v. Days Inn***, 62 F.3d 204, 208 (7th Cir.1995); *see also* ***Greenleaf v. Garlock, Inc.***, 174 F.3d 352, 363 (3d Cir.1999) (new trial may be granted only if improper statements made it "reasonably probable" that verdict was influenced by prejudicial statements).

(2) Unwarranted & injurious. To constitute reversible error, statements made in closing arguments must be plainly unwarranted and clearly injurious. ***Slathar v. Sather Trucking Corp.***, 78 F.3d 415, 420 (8th Cir.1996); ***Gruca v. Alpha Therapeutic Corp.***, 51 F.3d 638, 644 (7th Cir.1995).

(3) Entire argument. The appellate court looks at the entire argument within the context of the district court's rulings on objections, its corrective measures, and the jury charge to determine whether the argument affected the jury's consideration of the case. ***Guaranty Serv. v. American Employers' Ins.***, 893 F.2d 725, 729 (5th Cir.1990), *modified on other grounds*, 898 F.2d 453 (5th Cir.1990); *see also* ***Official Airline Guides, Inc. v. Goss***, 6 F.3d 1385, 1396 (9th Cir.1993) (court instructed jury to disregard attorney's swearing to witness's testimony).

(4) Other factors. When considering the argument as a whole, the court will sometimes consider the length of the jury's deliberations and the fact that only a few paragraphs of a lengthy closing included any improper comments. ***Smith v. National R.R. Passenger Corp.***, 856 F.2d 467, 472 (2d Cir.1988); *see* ***Benedi v. McNeil-P.P.C., Inc.***, 66 F.3d 1378, 1389 (4th Cir.1995).

2. Plain error. If error in closing argument was not preserved by objection, review is for plain error. ***Ratliff v. Schiber Truck Co.***, 150 F.3d 949, 957 (8th Cir.1998); ***Oxford Furniture Cos. v. Drexel Heritage Furnishings, Inc.***, 984 F.2d 1118, 1128 (11th Cir.1993). However, few cases are reversed based on claims of unobjected-to plain error. *See* ***Hemmings v. Tidyman's Inc.***, 285 F.3d 1174, 1193 (9th Cir.2002); ***Smith v. Kmart Corp.***, 177 F.3d

19, 26 (1st Cir.1999); ***Oxford Furniture***, 984 F.2d at 1128. In many cases, parties challenge error in argument as "incurable" simply because they did not object to the argument at trial. *See* ***Doe v. Johnson***, 52 F.3d 1448, 1465 (7th Cir.1995). Appellate courts will consider a forfeited objection if all the following elements are met:

(1) An error was committed. ***Hemmings***, 285 F.3d at 1193; ***Kmart Corp.***, 177 F.3d at 26.

(2) The error was "plain"—obvious and clear under current law. ***Hemmings***, 285 F.3d at 1193; ***Kmart Corp.***, 177 F.3d at 26.

(3) The error was prejudicial in that it affected substantive rights. ***Hemmings***, 285 F.3d at 1193; ***Kmart Corp.***, 177 F.3d at 26.

(4) Review is necessary to prevent a miscarriage of justice. ***Hemmings***, 285 F.3d at 1193; ***Kmart Corp.***, 177 F.3d at 26; *see* ***Oxford Furniture***, 984 F.2d at 1128 (when interests of substantial justice are at stake, new trial may be ordered).

COMMENTARIES

CHAPTER 9. THE JUDGMENT
TABLE OF CONTENTS

A. ENTRY OF JUDGMENT 735

§1. GENERAL 735
§2. REQUIREMENTS FOR FINAL JUDGMENT 735
§2.1 In writing 735
§2.2 Separate document 735
§2.3 Form 736
§2.4 Preparation 736
§2.5 Entered on docket 737
§3. APPEALABLE JUDGMENTS & ORDERS 737
§3.1 Final judgments 737
§3.2 Judgments covering fewer than all claims or parties 738
§3.3 Appealable orders 739
§4. NOTICE OF JUDGMENT 741
§4.1 Clerk's duty to give notice 741
§4.2 Time periods run from entry of judgment 742
§5. POWER TO CHANGE JUDGMENT 742
§5.1 Changing substance 742
§5.2 Correcting clerical mistakes 742
§6. ACCEPTING JUDGMENT 743
§6.1 Plaintiff 743
§6.2 Defendant 743

B. MOTION FOR ENTRY OF JUDGMENT 743

§1. GENERAL 743
§2. MOTION 743
§2.1 Separate-document requirement 743
§2.2 Requesting entry of judgment 744
§2.3 Form 745
§2.4 Grounds 745
§3. MOTION FOR SEVERANCE 745
§4. HEARING 745

C. MOTION FOR ATTORNEY FEES 745

§1. GENERAL 745
§2. DETERMINING NATURE OF ATTORNEY FEES 745
§2.1 Costs vs. damages 746
§2.2 Fees as costs 746
§2.3 Fees as damages 746
§3. ENTITLEMENT TO FEES 747
§4. MOTION 747
§4.1 Deadline 747
§4.2 Grounds 749
§4.3 Amount 753
§4.4 Terms of agreement 753
§4.5 Certificate of conference 753
§4.6 Affidavit 754
§4.7 Request hearing 754
§5. DETERMINING REASONABLE ATTORNEY FEES 754
§5.1 Lodestar method 754
§5.2 Common-fund cases 758
§5.3 Substantial-benefit cases 759
§5.4 Public-interest litigation 759
§5.5 Nontaxable expenses 759
§6. RESPONSE 759
§7. HEARING 759
§7.1 Necessity of hearing 759
§7.2 Order of proof 760
§8. RULING 760
§8.1 No separate document 760
§8.2 Findings 760
§9. APPELLATE REVIEW 760
§9.1 Extending time to file notice of appeal 760
§9.2 Standard of review 761

D. TAXABLE COSTS 761

§1. GENERAL 761
§2. TAXABLE COSTS 761
§2.1 Taxable costs under 28 U.S.C. §1920 761
§2.2 Other recoverable costs 764
§2.3 Costs that are not recoverable 764
§3. JUDGMENT FOR COSTS 765
§3.1 Prevailing party 765
§3.2 Who pays costs 765
§3.3 Form of judgment 766
§4. BILL OF COSTS 766
§4.1 Contents of bill 766
§4.2 Deadlines to file bill 766
§4.3 Objections to bill 767
§5. CLERK TO TAX COSTS 767
§5.1 Clerk taxes 767
§5.2 No delay of judgment 767
§5.3 Finality 767
§6. MOTION TO RETAX COSTS 767
§6.1 Deadline 767
§6.2 Grounds 767
§6.3 Certificate of conference 769
§6.4 Affidavit 769
§7. RESPONSE 769
§7.1 Deadline 769
§7.2 Grounds 769
§7.3 Affidavit 769
§8. DISTRICT COURT'S REVIEW 769
§9. APPELLATE REVIEW 769
§9.1 Standard of review 769
§9.2 Error in award of costs 770

CHAPTER 9

COMMENTARIES
CHAPTER 9. THE JUDGMENT

9. THE JUDGMENT

A. ENTRY OF JUDGMENT

§1. GENERAL

§1.1 Rules. FRCP 54-63, 77, 79. See also 28 U.S.C. §§1291, 1292; FRAP 4.

§1.2 Purpose. The judgment reflects the final disposition of a dispute. ***Remington Prods. v. North Am. Philips Corp.***, 763 F.Supp. 683, 688 (D.Conn.1991). A judgment is final when it terminates the litigation on the merits and leaves the court with nothing more to do but execute it. ***McClendon v. City of Albuquerque***, 630 F.3d 1288, 1292 (10th Cir.2011); ***Zinc v. U.S.***, 929 F.2d 1015, 1020 (5th Cir.1991).

§1.3 Timetable & forms. Timetable, Appeal of Civil Trial, p. 1591; ***O'Connor's Federal Civil Forms*** (2012), FORMS 9A.

§1.4 Other references. 16A Wright, Miller, Cooper & Struve, *Federal Practice & Procedure 4th* §§3949-3950 (2008 & Supp.2012); 11 Wright, Miller & Kane, *Federal Practice & Procedure 2d* §§2781-2787 (1995 & Supp.2012); 12 *Moore's Federal Practice 3d* §§58.03-58.05 (2012).

§2. REQUIREMENTS FOR FINAL JUDGMENT

Whether a judgment is final has important implications for both parties. Only a final judgment can be appealed, unless the judgment falls within a specific class of interlocutory orders made appealable by statute or case law. ***Lauro Lines S.R.L. v. Chasser***, 490 U.S. 495, 497-98 (1989); ***In re Grand Jury Proceedings***, 43 F.3d 966, 969 (5th Cir.1994); *see* 28 U.S.C. §§1291, 1292. See "Appealable Judgments & Orders," §3, p. 737. The appellate deadlines are calculated from the entry of the final judgment (or appealable order) on the docket. FRAP 4(a)(1), (a)(7); ***Jenkins v. Burtzloff***, 69 F.3d 460, 461 (10th Cir.1995); *see* ***Otis v. City of Chi.***, 29 F.3d 1159, 1167 (7th Cir.1994). If the winner is entitled to a monetary award, postjudgment interest begins to accrue on the date the judgment is entered. ***Kaiser Aluminum & Chem. Corp. v. Bonjorno***, 494 U.S. 827, 835 (1990); ***Wilson v. Union Pac. R.R.***, 56 F.3d 1226, 1233 (10th Cir.1995). Only a final judgment is given preclusive effect in later suits. Most importantly, only a final judgment can be enforced.

§2.1 In writing. A final judgment must be in writing. *See* FRCP 58(a).

§2.2 Separate document.

1. Generally. To be final and appealable, most judgments (as well as appealable interlocutory orders) must be set out in a separate document. FRCP 58(a); ***Bankers Trust Co. v. Mallis***, 435 U.S. 381, 383-84 (1978); ***Taylor Brands, LLC v. GB II Corp.***, 627 F.3d 874, 877 (Fed.Cir.2010); ***Webb v. Ada Cty.***, 285 F.3d 829, 836 (9th Cir.2002); *see, e.g.*, ***Perry v. Sheet Metal Workers' Local No. 73 Pension Fund***, 585 F.3d 358, 361 (7th Cir.2009) (memorandum opinion granting summary judgment and resolving all claims did not satisfy separate-document requirement); ***Nocula v. UGS Corp.***, 520 F.3d 719, 724 (7th Cir.2008) (minute order terminating case satisfied separate-document requirement); *see also* ***Barber v. Shinseki***, 660 F.3d 877, 878 (5th Cir.2011) (judgment must be in separate document, but that document may be electronic). The separate-document requirement must be "mechanically applied" when determining whether an appeal is timely. ***Bankers Trust***, 435 U.S. at 386; ***Mullane v. Chambers***, 333 F.3d 322, 336 (1st Cir.2003).

(1) Effect of compliance with separate-document requirement. When the court complies with the separate-document requirement, the judgment set out in the separate document (1) indicates that the case has ended and the appellate deadlines have started and (2) provides a statement of the terms on which the case ended. *See* ***Perry***, 585 F.3d at 362; 2002 Notes to FRCP 58 at ¶¶1-3, p. 1228, this book; *see also* ***Casey v. Albertson's Inc.***, 362 F.3d 1254, 1258 (9th Cir.2004) (separate document is required so parties know exactly when judgment has been entered and can begin preparing postverdict motions or appeal).

(2) **Effect of noncompliance with separate-document requirement.** When the court does not comply with the separate-document requirement, the finality of the judgment is not affected; the lack of a separate document merely extends the time to file a notice of appeal. ***Constien v. U.S.***, 628 F.3d 1207, 1210 (10th Cir.2010); *see* FRAP 4(a)(7)(B). When a separate document is required but the court does not provide one, the party wanting to appeal can do one of the following:

(a) File a motion for entry of judgment. See "Motion for Entry of Judgment," ch. 9-B, p. 743.

(b) Wait 150 days, at which time the judgment is considered entered, and file the notice of appeal within 30 days (60 days if the United States is a party) after that 150-day period. *See* FRAP 4(a)(1), (a)(7)(A)(ii); ***Constien***, 628 F.3d at 1211.

(c) Waive the separate-document requirement and file the notice of appeal before the end of the 150-day period under FRAP 4(a)(7)(A)(ii). ***Constien***, 628 F.3d at 1212. The separate-document requirement may be waived when the court clearly indicates its intent to enter a final judgment in the issued document (e.g., dismissal order, memorandum opinion) and the parties do not object. *See* ***Bankers Trust***, 435 U.S. at 387-88; ***Constien***, 628 F.3d at 1211-12; ***Long v. County of L.A.***, 442 F.3d 1178, 1184 n.3 (9th Cir.2006); *see also* ***Pramco, LLC v. San Juan Bay Marina, Inc.***, 435 F.3d 51, 54 (1st Cir.2006) (remand not required merely for technical entry of separate document).

2. **Exceptions.** Certain orders are exempt from the separate-document requirement. For a list of those orders, see "When not to file motion," ch. 9-B, §2.2.2, p. 744.

§2.3 Form. The judgment should be a self-contained document stating who has won and what relief has been awarded but omitting the reasons for the disposition, which should appear only in the court's opinion. ***Otis v. City of Chi.***, 29 F.3d 1159, 1163 (7th Cir.1994); *see* ***Whitaker v. City of Houston***, 963 F.2d 831, 833 (5th Cir.1992) (statement tacked on at end of opinion is not separate document); *see, e.g.*, ***In re Metropolitan Gov't of Nashville & Davidson Cty.***, 606 F.3d 855, 860 (6th Cir.2010) (post-trial order, which was not titled "entry of judgment," did not use term "judgment" at all, and reserved claims for court to decide, was not entry of judgment); ***Clough v. Rush***, 959 F.2d 182, 185 (10th Cir.1992) (15-page document containing detailed legal analysis and reasoning was not separate judgment); *see also* ***In re Cendant Corp. Secs. Litig.***, 454 F.3d 235, 241 (3d Cir.2006) (order's label as "order" rather than "judgment" does not mean it fails separate-document requirement). For an example of a separate document that recites the terms of the judgment without offering additional explanation or citation to authority, see FRCP Forms 70, 71, p. 999, this book. A judgment is not self-contained if it refers to other proceedings or documents. *See, e.g.*, ***Massey Ferguson Div. of Varity Corp. v. Gurley***, 51 F.3d 102, 104 (7th Cir.1995) (document that referred to opinion for essential terms of judgment was not self-contained).

§2.4 Preparation.

1. **Judgment prepared & entered by clerk.** Some judgments are prepared and entered by the clerk without court approval. *See* FRCP 58(b)(1). Unless the court orders otherwise, the clerk must prepare, sign, and enter the following judgments without direction from the court: (1) a general verdict of the jury, (2) a decision by the court that a party will recover only a fixed award or costs, and (3) a decision by the court that all relief will be denied. FRCP 58(b)(1); *see* ***Butler v. Stover Bros. Trucking Co.***, 546 F.2d 544, 547-48 (7th Cir.1977); ***Milton v. U.S.***, 120 F.2d 794, 795-96 (5th Cir.1941).

2. **Judgment approved by court before clerk's entry.** Other judgments are prepared by the clerk but require the court's approval before entry. *See* FRCP 58(b)(2). These include (1) judgments in which the court grants relief not listed in FRCP 58(b) and (2) judgments on special verdicts or on general verdicts with answers to written questions. FRCP 58(b)(2). For example, when a judgment involves multiple parties seeking various kinds of relief, the court should participate in drafting the judgment. ***American Interinsurance Exch. v. Occidental Fire & Cas. Co.***, 835 F.2d 157, 160 (7th Cir.1987). Once the court approves the judgment, the clerk must promptly enter it. FRCP 58(b)(2); *see* ***Burnley v. City of San Antonio***, 470 F.3d 189, 196-97 (5th Cir.2006) (even when court does not promptly approve form of separate judgment, clerk still has independent authority and duty to make entry in civil docket under FRCP 79(a)).

§2.5 Entered on docket. A judgment is not effective until the clerk enters it on the civil docket. *See* FRCP 79(a); ***Spurlock v. FBI***, 69 F.3d 1010, 1014-15 (9th Cir.1995); ***Gross v. Burggraf Constr. Co.***, 53 F.3d 1531, 1536 (10th Cir. 1995); ***Willhauck v. Halpin***, 919 F.2d 788, 793 (1st Cir.1990). Entering the judgment is a ministerial duty of the clerk. ***Diaz-Reyes v. Fuentes-Ortiz***, 471 F.3d 299, 301 (1st Cir.2006). If the clerk enters a judgment that the judge did not intend to be a final judgment, the entry is void. *See id.*

1. Time of entry. When a judgment is considered entered depends on whether a separate document is required.

(1) Separate document required. If FRCP 58(a) requires a separate document, a judgment is considered entered after the following occur:

(a) the judgment is entered on the civil docket under FRCP 79(a); and

(b) either the judgment is set out in a separate document or 150 days have run from the entry of the judgment on the civil docket, whichever comes first. FRCP 58(c)(2).

(2) No separate document required. If FRCP 58(a) does not require a separate document, a judgment is considered entered when it is entered on the civil docket under FRCP 79(a). FRCP 58(c)(1).

2. Appellate deadlines. The deadline for an appeal begins to run from the entry of the judgment (or appealable order) on the docket. FRAP 4(a)(1), (a)(7); ***Jenkins v. Burtzloff***, 69 F.3d 460, 461-62 (10th Cir.1995); *see* ***Axel Johnson Inc. v. Arthur Andersen & Co.***, 6 F.3d 78, 84 (2d Cir.1993). Certain motions listed in FRAP 4(a)(4)(A) delay the deadline to file an appeal. See "Postjudgment Motions," chart 10-1, p. 775.

§3. APPEALABLE JUDGMENTS & ORDERS

An appeal can originate from a final judgment under 28 U.S.C. §1291, a judgment covering fewer than all claims or parties that is certified by the district court under FRCP 54(b), or an order that is made appealable by statute or a case-law exception.

§3.1 Final judgments. A final judgment may be appealed. *See* 28 U.S.C. §1291. A final judgment conclusively determines the rights of the parties, leaving nothing for the court to do but execute the judgment. ***Coopers & Lybrand v. Livesay***, 437 U.S. 463, 467 (1978); ***Meadowbriar Home for Children, Inc. v. Gunn***, 81 F.3d 521, 528 (5th Cir.1996); *see* ***Bagdasarian Prods. v. Twentieth Century Fox Film Corp.***, 673 F.3d 1267, 1270 (9th Cir.2012); ***Kerr-McGee Chem. Corp. v. Lefton Iron & Metal Co.***, 570 F.3d 856, 857-58 (7th Cir.2009); *see, e.g.,* ***iLOR, LLC v. Google, Inc.***, 550 F.3d 1067, 1071-72 (Fed.Cir.2008) (judgment was not final when district court disposed of all of P's claims but did not dispose of or mention D's counterclaims); *see also* ***Casey v. Albertson's Inc.***, 362 F.3d 1254, 1258 (9th Cir.2004) (ruling is final under 28 U.S.C. §1291 if it is a full adjudication of issues and clearly evidences judge's intention that ruling is court's final act). The judgment or order of the court, not extraneous comments by the judge, determines the finality of the ruling. *E.g.,* ***Murdaugh Volkswagen, Inc. v. First Nat'l Bank***, 741 F.2d 41, 44 (4th Cir.1984) (language of order that judgment was not final prevailed over judge's intent). *But see* ***Fiataruolo v. U.S.***, 8 F.3d 930, 937 (2d Cir.1993) (court looked at circumstances surrounding judgment, including timing, to determine finality of judgment).

CIRCUIT SPLIT

The circuits disagree on the finality of a judgment when the court dismisses or disposes of some claims (e.g., for failure to state a claim, on summary judgment) and the remaining claims are voluntarily dismissed without prejudice. See ***Robinson-Reeder v. American Council on Educ.***, *571 F.3d 1333, 1338-39 (D.C.Cir.2009); 15A Wright, Miller & Cooper, Federal Practice & Procedure 2d §3914.8 nn.7-8 (1992 & Supp.2012). Compare* ***Rabbi Jacob Joseph Sch. v. Province of Mendoza***, *425 F.3d 207, 210 (2d Cir.2005) (judgment is not final and appealable when unresolved claims are voluntarily dismissed),* ***Marshall v. Kansas City S. Ry.***, *378 F.3d 495, 499-500 (5th Cir.2004) (party cannot use voluntary dismissal without prejudice to get around*

final-judgment rule), and ***Heimann v. Snead****, 133 F.3d 767, 769 (10th Cir.1998) (party must obtain FRCP 54(b) certification when there is no final adjudication of all claims), with* ***Doe v. U.S.****, 513 F.3d 1348, 1352-53 (Fed.Cir.2008) (no bright-line rule that judgments must always be treated as nonfinal whenever unresolved claims are voluntarily dismissed without prejudice), and* ***James v. Price Stern Sloan, Inc.****, 283 F.3d 1064, 1070 (9th Cir.2002) (judgment can be final and appealable when court approves voluntary dismissal of remaining claims without prejudice and there is no evidence of intent to manipulate appellate jurisdiction).*

§3.2 Judgments covering fewer than all claims or parties.

1. Most cases. Under FRCP 54(b), a judgment entered for fewer than all of the claims or parties may be appealable if the court certifies that it is final. ***Brown v. Columbia Sussex Corp.***, 664 F.3d 182, 186 (7th Cir.2011); ***Edwards v. Prime, Inc.***, 602 F.3d 1276, 1288 (11th Cir.2010); *see* ***Lava Trading, Inc. v. Sonic Trading Mgmt.***, 445 F.3d 1348, 1350-51 (Fed.Cir.2006) (FRCP 54(b) allows court to act as "dispatcher" and determine when each decision in a suit involving multiple claims is ready for appeal). The appeal is limited to the claims or parties identified in the court's certification. *E.g.*, ***Edwards***, 602 F.3d at 1288-89 (when court dismissed four claims in their entirety and partially dismissed seven other claims in one order, appeal was limited to four claims that court expressly certified for final judgment). To certify a judgment as final, the court must do all of the following:

(1) Determine that the decision is final for those particular claims or parties. ***Curtiss-Wright Corp. v. General Elec. Co.***, 446 U.S. 1, 7 (1980); *see* FRCP 54(b); ***N.W. Enters. v. City of Houston***, 352 F.3d 162, 179 (5th Cir.2003), *vacated in part on other grounds*, 372 F.3d 333 (5th Cir.2004). The decision must be final to an entire claim, not to only certain issues within a claim. ***Weigel v. Broad***, 544 F.3d 1143, 1151 n.3 (10th Cir.2008); *see, e.g.*, ***Lloyd Noland Found. v. Tenet Health Care Corp.***, 483 F.3d 773, 781-82 (11th Cir.2007) (summary-judgment ruling was not final because ruling did not resolve entire substantive claim). The court's decision on the finality of a judgment under FRCP 54(b) is subject to de novo review. ***Ultra-Precision Mfg. v. Ford Motor Co.***, 338 F.3d 1353, 1356 (Fed. Cir.2003).

(2) Determine that there is no just reason for delay. ***Curtiss-Wright***, 446 U.S. at 8; *see* FRCP 54(b) (express determination required); ***Eldredge v. Martin Marietta Corp.***, 207 F.3d 737, 740 (5th Cir.2000) (express certification usually required). The court should consider judicial administrative interests, the equities involved, and the resulting hardship or injustice if there is not an immediate appeal. *See* ***Curtiss-Wright***, 446 U.S. at 8; ***Taco John's v. Bix Produce Co.***, 569 F.3d 401, 402 (8th Cir.2009); ***Ergo Sci., Inc. v. Martin***, 73 F.3d 595, 597-98 (5th Cir.1996). The court's determination that there is no just reason for delay is reviewed for abuse of discretion. ***Ultra-Precision Mfg.***, 338 F.3d at 1356; *see, e.g.*, ***National Ass'n of Home Builders v. Norton***, 340 F.3d 835, 840 (9th Cir.2003) (appellate court gave deference to district court's determination that FRCP 54(b) certification was appropriate); *see also* ***Huggins v. FedEx Ground Package Sys.***, 566 F.3d 771, 774 (8th Cir.2009) (when district court does not evaluate factors or show familiarity with case or reasons for delay, appellate court will carefully scrutinize decision).

(3) Direct the entry of judgment. FRCP 54(b). The court should not merely repeat the language of FRCP 54(b) but should instead provide a reasoned—even if brief—explanation for its conclusion. ***Novick v. AXA Network, LLC***, 642 F.3d 304, 310 (2d Cir.2011); *see* ***Akers v. Alvey***, 338 F.3d 491, 495 (6th Cir.2003); *see, e.g.*, ***iLOR, LLC v. Google, Inc.***, 550 F.3d 1067, 1072-73 (Fed.Cir.2008) (judgment was not certified because order did not cite FRCP 54(b) and did not identify any circumstances justifying immediate appeal). The court can consider any of the following factors when making its determination: (1) the relationship between the adjudicated and nonadjudicated claims, (2) the possibility that future developments in the court will affect the need for review in the present case, (3) the possibility that the reviewing court will need to consider the same issue in the future, (4) the existence or absence of counterclaims that could set off the judgment, and (5) miscellaneous considerations such as delay, expense, solvency of the parties, shortening the time of trial, and frivolity of competing claims. ***Corrosioneering, Inc. v. Thyssen Env'tl Sys.***, 807 F.2d 1279, 1283 (6th Cir.1986); ***Allis-Chalmers Corp. v. Philadelphia Elec. Co.***, 521 F.2d 360, 364 (3d Cir.1975).

2. Consolidated cases. When the court consolidates cases and later resolves one of them by judgment, the circuits are divided on whether to allow the resolved case to be appealed without an FRCP 54(b) certification. The following are the different lines of authority on this issue:

(1) Certification never required. The First and Sixth Circuits hold that an FRCP 54(b) certification is not required for judgments disposing of fewer than all claims in a consolidated case. *See* ***Beil v. Lakewood Eng'g & Mfg.***, 15 F.3d 546, 551 (6th Cir.1994); ***Albert v. Maine Cent. R.R.***, 898 F.2d 5, 6-7 (1st Cir.1990). These circuits reason that the cases retain their separate identities despite consolidation, and no FRCP 54(b) certification is required to seek review of the disposition of an individual case. ***Spraytex, Inc. v. DJS&T***, 96 F.3d 1377, 1380 (Fed. Cir.1996).

(2) Certification always required. The Ninth, Tenth, and Federal Circuits hold that an FRCP 54(b) certification is required for every judgment disposing of fewer than all claims in a consolidated case. *See* ***Schnabel v. Lui***, 302 F.3d 1023, 1036 (9th Cir.2002); ***Spraytex***, 96 F.3d at 1382; ***Trinity Broad. Corp. v. Eller***, 827 F.2d 673, 675 (10th Cir.1987). These circuits reason that the cases merge and are similar to a single case with several claims and counterclaims, and FRCP 54(b) certification is required for a separate appeal. ***Spraytex***, 96 F.3d at 1380.

(3) Certification presumed required. The Second Circuit holds that when a judgment in a consolidated case does not dispose of all claims, there is a strong presumption that the judgment is not final and appealable. ***Hageman v. City Investing Co.***, 851 F.2d 69, 71 (2d Cir.1988); *see* ***New York v. Amro Rlty. Corp.***, 936 F.2d 1420, 1425-26 (2d Cir.1991). Thus, a judgment disposing of some but not all claims in a consolidated case is not appealable without an FRCP 54(b) certification.

(4) Necessity depends on reasons for consolidation. The remaining circuits determine appealability of a consolidated case on a case-by-case basis, looking at the reasons for consolidation. ***Spraytex***, 96 F.3d at 1380-81.

(a) Consolidation for all purposes. When cases have been consolidated for all purposes, a judgment in one of the cases is not final and appealable without an FRCP 54(b) certification. *See* ***Tri-State Hotels, Inc. v. FDIC***, 79 F.3d 707, 711 (8th Cir.1996); ***In re Unisys Sav. Plan Litig.***, 74 F.3d 420, 432-33 n.9 (3d Cir.1996); ***EEOC v. Harris Chernin, Inc.***, 10 F.3d 1286, 1289 (7th Cir.1993); ***Phillips v. Heine***, 984 F.2d 489, 490 (D.C.Cir.1993); ***Road Sprinkler Fitters Local Un. v. Continental Sprinkler Co.***, 967 F.2d 145, 149-50 (5th Cir.1992).

(b) Limited consolidation. When cases have been consolidated only for limited purposes, such as discovery or other pretrial proceedings, a judgment in one of the cases is final and appealable without an FRCP 54(b) certification. *See* ***Tri-State***, 79 F.3d at 711; ***Harris Chernin***, 10 F.3d at 1289; ***Road Sprinkler***, 967 F.2d at 149-51; ***Lewis Charters, Inc. v. Huckins Yacht Corp.***, 871 F.2d 1046, 1049 (11th Cir.1989); ***Bergman v. City of Atl. City***, 860 F.2d 560, 566-67 (3d Cir.1988).

(c) Nature of consolidation uncertain. If the court's consolidation order is unclear about whether the consolidation is limited or unlimited, the court will decide whether the parties and issues in the resolved case are distinct from the remaining issues. *See* ***Sandwiches, Inc. v. Wendy's Int'l***, 822 F.2d 707, 709-10 (7th Cir. 1987). If the parties and issues are distinct, the judgment in the resolved case is final and appealable without an FRCP 54(b) certification. ***Sandwiches, Inc.***, 822 F.2d at 710.

§3.3 Appealable orders. To be appealable, an order must fall within (1) a specific class of interlocutory orders made appealable by statute or (2) an exception created by case law. ***In re Grand Jury Proceedings***, 43 F.3d 966, 969 (5th Cir.1994); *see* 28 U.S.C. §1292.

1. Statutory provisions. A party can appeal an order that is not final under either of the following statutes:

(1) 28 U.S.C. §1292(a). Courts of appeals have jurisdiction to hear appeals from a limited number of interlocutory orders under 28 U.S.C. §1292(a). These orders include the following:

(a) Interlocutory orders that grant, continue, modify, refuse, dissolve, or refuse to modify or dissolve injunctions. 28 U.S.C. §1292(a)(1); ***Edwards v. Prime, Inc.***, 602 F.3d 1276, 1289 (11th Cir.2010); ***Doeblers' Pa. Hybrids, Inc. v. Doebler***, 442 F.3d 812, 819 (3d Cir.2006); ***Credit Suisse First Boston Corp. v. Grunwald***, 400 F.3d 1119, 1123 (9th Cir.2005); ***Cavalier Tel., LLC v. Virginia Elec. & Power Co.***, 303 F.3d 316, 320 (4th Cir.2002). To obtain review, the litigant should show that the interlocutory order may have a serious and perhaps irreparable consequence and that the order can be effectively challenged only by immediate appeal. ***Edwards***, 602 F.3d at 1290; ***In re M.T.G., Inc.***, 403 F.3d 410, 413 (6th Cir.2005). Certain interlocutory orders relating to injunctions can be appealed directly to the Supreme Court. *E.g.*, 28 U.S.C. §1253 (injunctions in civil suits that are required to be heard by three-judge district court).

(b) Interlocutory orders that appoint receivers or refuse orders to wind up receivership. 28 U.S.C. §1292(a)(2).

(c) Interlocutory orders that determine the rights and liabilities of parties in admiralty cases in which appeals from final decrees are allowed. *Id.* §1292(a)(3); ***In re Complaint of PMD Enters.***, 301 F.3d 147, 149 (3d Cir.2002); ***Underwriters at Interest on Cover Note JHB92M10582079 v. Nautronix, Ltd.***, 79 F.3d 480, 483-84 (5th Cir.1996).

(2) 28 U.S.C. §1292(b).

(a) Discretionary jurisdiction allowed. Appellate courts have discretionary jurisdiction to hear an appeal from an interlocutory order if the district court certifies the following:

[1] The case involves a controlling question of law about which there is a substantial ground for difference of opinion. 28 U.S.C. §1292(b); ***Linton v. Shell Oil Co.***, 563 F.3d 556, 557-58 (5th Cir.2009); ***Union Cty. v. Piper Jaffray & Co.***, 525 F.3d 643, 646 (8th Cir.2008); ***Spinelli v. Goss***, 446 F.3d 159, 160 (D.C.Cir. 2006); *see, e.g.*, ***In re Text Messaging Antitrust Litig.***, 630 F.3d 622, 626-27 (7th Cir.2010) (in antitrust case, interlocutory appeal allowed on question of law about adequacy of amended complaint under ***Twombly*** standard). To determine if there is a substantial ground for difference of opinion, the district court must examine to what extent the controlling law is unclear. ***Couch v. Telescope Inc.***, 611 F.3d 629, 633 (9th Cir.2010). During that examination, the district court can consider the following:

[a] Whether the courts of appeals are in dispute on the question. *Id.*

[b] Whether the court of appeals for that district court has addressed the question. *Id.*

[c] Whether complicated questions arise under foreign law. *Id.*

[d] Whether novel and difficult questions of first impression are present. *Id.*

[2] An immediate appeal from the order may materially advance the ultimate termination of the litigation. 28 U.S.C. §1292(b); ***Linton***, 563 F.3d at 557-58; ***Union Cty.***, 525 F.3d at 646; ***Spinelli***, 446 F.3d at 160.

(b) Discretion for district & appellate courts. This form of appellate jurisdiction is discretionary on two levels: (1) the district court has discretion to decide whether to issue a §1292(b) certification, and (2) the appellate court has discretion to decide whether to accept a §1292(b) certification. ***In re Text Messaging Antitrust Litig.***, 630 F.3d at 624; *see also* **Camacho v. Puerto Rico Ports Auth.**, 369 F.3d 570, 573 (1st Cir.2004) (§1292(b) is meant to be used sparingly). The appellate court is not limited to the specific issues the district court has designated; it may address any issue "fairly included" within the certified order. ***Rivera v. NIBCO, Inc.***, 364 F.3d 1057, 1063 (9th Cir.2004); ***Colonial Life & Acc. Ins. v. Hartford Fire Ins.***, 358 F.3d 1306, 1307 n.1 (11th Cir.2004); *see* ***EEOC v. Seafarers Int'l Un.***, 394 F.3d 197, 200 (4th Cir.2005) (court certifying interlocutory appeal under §1292(b) assumes jurisdiction over entire certified order); *see also* **Ferrostaal, Inc. v. M/V Sea Phoenix**, 447 F.3d 212, 216 (3d Cir.2006) (jurisdiction extends to all questions in summary-judgment order, not just particular issue certified).

2. Case-law exceptions.

(1) Collateral orders. Some prejudgment orders are deemed to be final and appealable judgments under §1291 even though they do not end the litigation because they are "collateral to" the merits and are too important to be denied immediate review. ***Mohawk Indus. v. Carpenter***, ___ U.S. ___, 130 S.Ct. 599, 603 (2009); ***Cohen v. Beneficial Indus. Loan Corp.***, 337 U.S. 541, 545-46 (1949); *e.g.*, ***Behrens v. Pelletier***, 516 U.S. 299, 311 (1996) (order denying governmental officers' claims of qualified immunity was appealable); *see* ***W.R. Huff Asset Mgmt. Co. v. Kohlberg, Kravis, Roberts & Co.***, 566 F.3d 979, 984 (11th Cir.2009); ***Falcon v. Transportes Aeros de Coahuila, S.A.***, 169 F.3d 309, 311 (5th Cir.1999). The class of orders that are collaterally appealable is narrow. ***Mohawk Indus.***, ___ U.S. at ___, 130 S.Ct. at 609; *see also* ***Gillespie v. U.S. Steel Corp.***, 379 U.S. 148, 152 (1964) (whether order is final for purpose of appeal is often a difficult question to resolve). An order is collaterally appealable if the following occur:

(a) Conclusiveness. The order conclusively determines the disputed question. ***Mohawk Indus.***, ___ U.S. at ___, 130 S.Ct. at 605; ***Lauro Lines S.R.L. v. Chasser***, 490 U.S. 495, 498 (1989).

(b) Separateness. The order resolves an important issue separate from and collateral to the merits. ***Mohawk Indus.***, ___ U.S. at ___, 130 S.Ct. at 605; ***Lauro Lines***, 490 U.S. at 498.

(c) Effective unreviewability. The order is effectively unreviewable on appeal from a final judgment. ***Mohawk Indus.***, ___ U.S. at ___, 130 S.Ct. at 605; ***Lauro Lines***, 490 U.S. at 498. An order is effectively unreviewable if it protects a right that would be destroyed if not vindicated before trial. ***Lauro Lines***, 490 U.S. at 498-99; *see* ***Mohawk Indus.***, ___ U.S. at ___, 130 S.Ct. at 605 (question is whether deferring review until final judgment would imperil a substantial public interest or other substantial right); *see, e.g.*, ***W.R. Huff Asset Mgmt.***, 566 F.3d at 987 (interlocutory orders in federal district court were not effectively unreviewable because they could be reviewed on remand to state court by state appellate court after final judgment). The focus of effective unreviewability should be on the entire category to which a claim belongs; whether an order is effectively unreviewable should not be an individualized jurisdictional inquiry. *E.g.*, ***Mohawk Indus.***, ___ U.S. at ___, 130 S.Ct. at 605-06 (disclosure orders adverse to attorney-client privilege do not qualify for immediate appeal because postjudgment review sufficiently protects privilege).

(2) Inextricably intertwined orders. Some prejudgment orders can be reviewed on interlocutory appeal if they are inextricably intertwined with an independently appealable order. ***Turi v. Main St. Adoption Servs.***, 633 F.3d 496, 502 (6th Cir.2011); ***Research Automation, Inc. v. Schrader-Bridgeport Int'l***, 626 F.3d 973, 976-77 (7th Cir.2010). The inextricably-intertwined requirement is satisfied if the normally nonappealable claim is subsumed by the independently appealable issue—that is, the appealable issue "necessarily and unavoidably" decides the nonappealable issue. ***Turi***, 633 F.3d at 503.

(3) No authority to act. When the district court does not have the authority to act, the order is final and appealable. ***In re Saffady***, 524 F.3d 799, 802 (6th Cir.2008); *e.g.*, ***Stradley v. Cortez***, 518 F.2d 488, 491-92 (3d Cir.1975) (court did not have authority to grant motion for new trial four years after judgment; order was immediately appealable).

§4. NOTICE OF JUDGMENT

§4.1 Clerk's duty to give notice. The clerk must give the parties or their attorneys immediate notice of the entry of a judgment in the manner provided by FRCP 5(b). FRCP 77(d)(1). See "Notice of Ruling," ch. 1-G, §6, p. 46. The clerk must make a note on the docket of the date it sent the notice of the judgment to the parties. The clerk's docket entry is proof that notice was given. ***Howard v. Local 74***, 208 F.2d 930, 934 (7th Cir.1953); *see* ***Nunley v. City of L.A.***, 52 F.3d 792, 796 (9th Cir.1995). If the clerk does not send the notice or the parties do not receive it, the lack of notice does not affect the time to appeal. FRCP 77(d)(2); *e.g.*, ***In re City of Memphis***, 293 F.3d 345, 349 (6th Cir. 2002) (party did not receive notice); ***Bortugno v. Metro-N. Commuter R.R.***, 905 F.2d 674, 676 (2d Cir.1990) (clerk did not send notice). FRCP 77(d) is intended to preserve the finality of judgments. ***In re City of Memphis***, 293 F.3d

at 349; ***Expeditions Unlimited Aquatic Enters. v. Smithsonian Inst.***, 500 F.2d 808, 809 (D.C.Cir.1974). However, two FRAP provisions and one FRCP provision allow a party to file a late notice of appeal when notice of the judgment is late.

1. FRAP 4(a)(5). The district court may extend the time to file a notice of appeal on a party's motion filed no later than 30 days after the notice of appeal was due if excusable neglect or good cause is shown. FRAP 4(a)(5)(A)(ii). Relief under FRAP 4(a)(5) is severely limited. See "Motion to Extend Time to File Notice of Appeal," ch. 10-G, p. 817.

2. FRAP 4(a)(6). The district court may reopen the time to file a notice of appeal if (1) a party filed a motion within either 180 days after the judgment was entered or 14 days after the party received notice of the judgment, whichever was earlier, and (2) no party would be prejudiced. FRAP 4(a)(6); *see* ***Benavides v. Bureau of Prisons***, 79 F.3d 1211, 1214 (D.C.Cir.1996) (applying former seven-day deadline); ***Zimmer St. Louis, Inc. v. Zimmer Co.***, 32 F.3d 357, 360 (8th Cir.1994) (same); ***Avolio v. County of Suffolk***, 29 F.3d 50, 52 (2d Cir.1994) (same). Most courts have held that a party cannot seek relief from late notice of the judgment beyond 180 days, even under FRCP 60(b). ***Vencor Hosps., Inc. v. Standard Life & Acc. Ins.***, 279 F.3d 1306, 1310-11 (11th Cir.2002); ***Clark v. Lavallie***, 204 F.3d 1038, 1041 (10th Cir.2000); ***In re Stein***, 197 F.3d 421, 425 (9th Cir.1999); ***Benavides***, 79 F.3d at 1214; ***Zimmer St. Louis***, 32 F.3d at 360-61; *see also* 16A Wright, Miller, Cooper & Struve §3950.6 & n.16 (once 180-day period has expired, district court cannot vacate and reenter judgment to create new appeal period). If a party received notice of the judgment under FRCP 77(d) from either the clerk or another party, the receiving party cannot move to reopen the time for appeal. FRAP 4(a)(6)(A); *see* FRCP 77(d); 2005 Notes to FRAP 4 at ¶¶4, 6, 7, p. 1267, this book. See "Motion to Reopen Time for Appeal," ch. 10-H, p. 821.

3. FRCP 60(b). Before the 1991 addition of FRAP 4(a)(6), courts held that a judgment could be vacated and reentered under FRCP 60(b) when (1) neither party had actual notice of the entry of judgment, (2) the winning party was not prejudiced by the appeal, (3) the losing party moved to vacate within a reasonable time after learning of entry of judgment, and (4) the attorney proved due diligence, or the reasons for lack of due diligence, in attempting to be informed of the date of decision. ***DeRango v. U.S.***, 864 F.2d 520, 523 (7th Cir.1988); *see* ***Wilson v. Atwood Grp.***, 702 F.2d 77, 79-80 (5th Cir.1983). FRAP 4(a)(6) seemingly makes these cases obsolete. *See* ***Nowak v. INS***, 94 F.3d 390, 391-92 (7th Cir.1996).

§4.2 Time periods run from entry of judgment. If the parties receive notice of the judgment within 21 days after the judgment was entered, the clerk's entry date is the date from which the parties calculate the time periods for filing postjudgment motions and the notice of appeal. *See* FRAP 4(a)(6)(A); FRCP 50(b), 52(b), 54(d)(2)(B), 58, 59, 60(b).

§5. POWER TO CHANGE JUDGMENT

For a summary of the motions that can be filed to modify the judgment, see "Postjudgment Motions," chart 10-1, p. 775.

§5.1 Changing substance. The court may change the substance of its judgment during the times and according to the terms stated in FRCP 59(a), (b), (d), and (e) and 60(b). *See* ***Nowicki v. U.S.***, 536 F.2d 1171, 1174-75 (7th Cir.1976).

§5.2 Correcting clerical mistakes. The court may correct a clerical mistake in a judgment, order, or other part of the record at any time (except when an appeal is pending), on motion or on its own, with or without notice. FRCP 60(a). While a case is pending on appeal, the district court is divested of jurisdiction to correct mistakes or omissions in the judgment unless the appellate court grants leave. *Id.*; ***In re Modern Textile, Inc.***, 900 F.2d 1184, 1193 (8th Cir.1990); ***Petrol Stops Nw. v. Continental Oil Co.***, 647 F.2d 1005, 1010 (9th Cir.1981). If a judgment pending appeal is not final or appealable, the district court may amend the judgment without leave of the appellate court because the notice of appeal did not divest the district court of jurisdiction. *E.g.*, ***Burger King Corp. v. Horn & Hardart Co.***, 893 F.2d 525, 527 (2d Cir.1990) (court amended judgment during appeal to dispose of complaint and to make judgment final); *see* ***In re U.S. Abatement Corp.***, 39 F.3d 563, 568 (5th Cir.1994). See "Motion to Correct Clerical Error in Judgment," ch. 10-I, p. 825.

§6. ACCEPTING JUDGMENT

§6.1 Plaintiff. The general rule for a plaintiff (the judgment creditor) is that if it accepts the benefits of a judgment, it is estopped from challenging the judgment by appeal. ***Cherokee Nation v. U.S.***, 355 F.2d 945, 949 (Ct.Cl. 1966); ***Spanel v. Berkman***, 171 F.2d 513, 515 (7th Cir.1948). However, the acceptance of payment of an unsatisfactory judgment does not by itself amount to an accord and satisfaction of the entire claim and does not prevent an appeal. ***U.S. v. Hougham***, 364 U.S. 310, 312 (1960); ***Gloria v. Valley Grain Prods.***, 72 F.3d 497, 498 (5th Cir.1996); ***Klein v. Grynberg***, 44 F.3d 1497, 1502 (10th Cir.1995); ***Commercial Un. Ins. v. Walbrook Ins. Co.***, 41 F.3d 764, 769 (1st Cir.1994). The plaintiff may still appeal the sufficiency of damages. ***Hougham***, 364 U.S. at 312. To act as a waiver of appeal, the judgment creditor's acceptance must be voluntary and intended as final satisfaction of the judgment. ***Klein***, 44 F.3d at 1502; *see* ***Gloria***, 72 F.3d at 499. Some of the exceptions to the general rule that acceptance of the judgment waives the appeal include the following:

1. **Separate & independent part of judgment.** A plaintiff who accepts payment of part of the judgment is not estopped from appealing a separate and independent part of the judgment. ***Embry v. Palmer***, 107 U.S. 3, 8 (1883); ***Luther v. U.S.***, 225 F.2d 495, 497 (10th Cir.1954); ***Spanel***, 171 F.2d at 514-15.

2. **Sum absolutely due or uncontested.** A plaintiff who accepts payment of part of the judgment is not estopped from appealing when the accepted sum is absolutely due or uncontested. ***Fifth Ave. Bank v. Hammond Rlty. Co.***, 130 F.2d 993, 994 (7th Cir.1942); ***Armstrong v. Lone Star Ref. Co.***, 20 F.2d 625, 626 (8th Cir.1927); *e.g.*, ***Commercial Un. Ins.***, 41 F.3d at 769 (P collected undisputed amount and appealed disputed issue).

3. **No effect of reversal.** A plaintiff who accepts payment of part of the judgment is not estopped from appealing when that part of the judgment will not be affected by a reversal. ***Embry***, 107 U.S. at 8; ***Luther***, 225 F.2d at 497; ***Carson Lumber Co. v. St. Louis & S.F. R.R.***, 209 F. 191, 193-94 (8th Cir.1913).

4. **Involuntary acceptance.** A plaintiff who does not voluntarily accept an award is not estopped from appealing. *E.g.*, ***Klein***, 44 F.3d at 1502 (P protested district court's order to accept $4 for breach of fiduciary duty).

§6.2 Defendant. In most cases, when the defendant (the judgment debtor) pays the judgment, the defendant waives its right to appeal and the case is dismissed. ***American Book Co. v. Kansas***, 193 U.S. 49, 52 (1904). However, the payment of a judgment does not by itself prevent an appeal unless the judgment debtor intended to abandon its right to appeal. *E.g.*, ***Tungseth v. Mutual of Omaha Ins.***, 43 F.3d 406, 409 (8th Cir.1994) (D did not intend to abandon appeal by paying judgment); *see also* ***Little v. Bowers***, 134 U.S. 547, 552-53 (1890) (D paid taxes but argued it was involuntary); ***Barnes v. Bosley***, 828 F.2d 1253, 1257 n.4 (8th Cir.1987) (payment of judgment to stop accrual of interest did not make issue of award moot); ***Ferrell v. Trailmobile, Inc.***, 223 F.2d 697, 698 (5th Cir.1955) (payment of judgment to prevent foreclosure did not make appeal moot).

B. MOTION FOR ENTRY OF JUDGMENT

§1. GENERAL

§1.1 Rules. FRCP 54-63, 77, 79.

§1.2 Purpose. The purpose of a motion for entry of judgment is either to ask the court to issue the judgment or to require the clerk to enter the judgment on the docket. *See* ***Perry v. Sheet Metal Workers' Local No. 73 Pension Fund***, 585 F.3d 358, 362 (7th Cir.2009).

§1.3 Timetable & forms. Timetable, Appeal of Civil Trial, p. 1591; ***O'Connor's Federal Civil Forms*** (2012), FORMS 9B.

§1.4 Other references. 11 Wright, Miller & Kane, *Federal Practice & Procedure 2d* §§2781-2787 (1995 & Supp.2012); 12 *Moore's Federal Practice 3d* ch. 58 (2012).

§2. MOTION

§2.1 Separate-document requirement. Most judgments must be set out in a separate document. FRCP 58(a). See "Separate document," ch. 9-A, §2.2, p. 735. When there is no separate document, the judgment will be considered entered 150 days after the judgment is entered on the civil docket. FRCP 58(c)(2); ***Constien v. U.S.***, 628 F.3d

1207, 1211 (10th Cir.2010); ***Perry v. Sheet Metal Workers' Local No. 73 Pension Fund***, 585 F.3d 358, 362 (7th Cir. 2009); *see* 2002 Notes to FRCP 58 at ¶4, p. 1228, this book. However, when a party wants to have a separate judgment entered earlier, it can move for entry of judgment. ***Perry***, 585 F.3d at 362.

§2.2 Requesting entry of judgment.

1. When to file motion.

(1) When clerk must prepare judgment. The clerk must promptly prepare, sign, and enter a judgment in a separate document when (1) the jury returns a general verdict, (2) the court awards only costs or a sum certain, or (3) the court denies all relief. FRCP 58(b)(1); *see* ***Bouboulis v. Transport Workers Un.***, 442 F.3d 55, 60 (2d Cir.2006) (judgment should be entered when court dismisses case); ***Marshall v. Perez-Arzuaga***, 866 F.2d 521, 523-24 (1st Cir.1989) (judgment should be entered without delay after jury verdict). Thus, a party ordinarily does not need to file a motion requesting entry of judgment. *See* ***Otis v. City of Chi.***, 29 F.3d 1159, 1163 (7th Cir.1994) (burden of preparing judgment is on clerk). However, if the clerk does not promptly prepare and enter the judgment, a motion for entry of judgment on a separate document may be necessary. *See* FRCP 58(d); 2002 Notes to FRCP 58 at ¶7, p. 1229, this book. For example, the winning party may be interested in the rapid entry of a separate judgment to limit the losing party's time to consider an appeal and to begin the accrual of postjudgment interest. *See* ***Kaiser Aluminum & Chem. Corp. v. Bonjorno***, 494 U.S. 827, 839-40 (1990) (postjudgment interest does not accrue until entry of judgment); ***Wilson v. Union Pac. R.R.***, 56 F.3d 1226, 1233 (10th Cir.1995) (same).

(2) When court must approve form of judgment. When the jury returns a special verdict or a general verdict with answers to written questions, or when the court grants other relief not described in FRCP 58(b), the court must promptly approve the form of the judgment and the clerk must promptly enter the judgment. FRCP 58(b)(2); *see* ***Casey v. Long Island R.R.***, 406 F.3d 142, 144 (2d Cir.2005). If the court has not requested assistance from the attorneys in drafting the judgment and does not promptly approve the form of the judgment, a motion for entry of judgment in a separate document may be necessary. *See* FRCP 58(d); 2002 Notes to FRCP 58 at ¶7, p. 1229, this book; *see, e.g.*, ***Gold v. U.S.***, 552 F.Supp. 66, 72-73 (D.Colo.1982) (court directed attorneys to submit proposed judgment because case involved complex calculations).

2. When not to file motion. It is not necessary to file a motion for entry of judgment in a separate document after an order disposing of the following motions has been entered:

(1) Motion for JMOL under FRCP 50(b). FRCP 58(a)(1).

(2) Motion to amend or make additional findings of fact under FRCP 52(b). FRCP 58(a)(2).

(3) Motion for attorney fees under FRCP 54. FRCP 58(a)(3).

(4) Motion for new trial under FRCP 59. FRCP 58(a)(4).

(5) Motion to alter or amend the judgment under FRCP 59. FRCP 58(a)(4).

NOTE

The Seventh Circuit has held that the exception to the separate-document requirement for motions to alter or amend the judgment under FRCP 59(e) applies only to orders denying the motion; orders ***granting*** *the motion should still be set out in a separate document. See, e.g.,* ***Kunz v. DeFelice****, 538 F.3d 667, 673-74 (7th Cir.2008) ("disposing" in FRCP 58(a) should be read as "denying"; order granting motion to amend should have been set out in separate document); see also 2002 Notes to FRCP 58 at ¶3, p. 1228, this book (if disposition of motion results in amended judgment, amended judgment must be set out in separate document).*

(6) Motion to correct a clerical error in the judgment under FRCP 60(a). FRCP 58(a)(5).

(7) Motion for relief from the judgment under FRCP 60(b). FRCP 58(a)(5).

§2.3 Form. For the general requirements for the form of a motion, see "Drafting motions," ch. 1-B, §3.1, p. 14.

§2.4 Grounds. The party moving for entry of judgment should include all of the following in its motion:

1. A statement that one of the conditions under FRCP 58(b), which permits the entry of judgment, has been met.
2. A statement that (1) the clerk has not promptly prepared and entered judgment, (2) the court has not promptly approved the form of the judgment, or (3) the court has approved the form of the judgment but the clerk has not promptly entered it.
3. A statement that judgment on a separate document is required by FRCP 58(a).
4. A request that judgment on a separate document be promptly entered. FRCP 58(d).

§3. MOTION FOR SEVERANCE

If the court is entering judgment on only part of the lawsuit, the parties may file a motion to sever, making that part of the lawsuit final and appealable. See "Motion for Severance or Separate Trials," ch. 5-L, p. 366.

§4. HEARING

The court does not need to hold a hearing on the motion for entry of judgment. If a party wants a hearing, it should request one in writing.

C. MOTION FOR ATTORNEY FEES

§1. GENERAL

§1.1 Rules. 28 U.S.C. §2412; FRCP 54(d)(2).

§1.2 Purpose. Under what is called the "American rule," federal courts are generally prohibited from requiring the losing party to pay attorney fees to the party who prevails on the merits. ***Buckhannon Bd. & Care Home, Inc. v. West Va. Dept. of H&HR***, 532 U.S. 598, 602 (2001). However, a party may be entitled to attorney fees that are specifically provided for by contract, statute, or equity. ***Summit Valley Indus. v. Local 112, United Bhd. of Carpenters & Joiners***, 456 U.S. 717, 721 (1982); ***Payne v. Milwaukee Cty.***, 288 F.3d 1021, 1026 (7th Cir.2002); *see* Hirsch & Sheehey, *Awarding Attorneys' Fees & Managing Fee Litigation*, at 1-2 (2d ed.2005), Federal Judicial Center, www.fjc.gov. FRCP 54(d) establishes a procedure for presenting claims for attorney fees as costs of the litigation. It does not apply to attorney fees recoverable as an element of the plaintiff's damages (e.g., fees provided for by contract) or to attorney fees awarded as sanctions under the FRCPs or 28 U.S.C. §1927. *See* FRCP 54(d)(2)(A), (d)(2)(E). See "Fees as damages," §2.3, p. 746.

§1.3 Timetable & forms. Timetable, Appeal of Civil Trial, p. 1591; ***O'Connor's Federal Civil Forms*** (2012), FORMS 9C.

§1.4 Other references. 10 Wright, Miller & Kane, *Federal Practice & Procedure 3d* §§2675-2675.2, 2679, 2680 (1998 & Supp.2012); 10 *Moore's Federal Practice 3d* §§54.150-54.174 (2012); 1 Childress & Davis, *Federal Standards of Review 4th* §4.15 (2010 & Supp.2011); Hirsch & Sheehey, *Awarding Attorneys' Fees & Managing Fee Litigation* (2d ed.2005), Federal Judicial Center, www.fjc.gov; Annotation, *Right of Defendant in Civil Rights Case to Receive Award of Attorney's Fees Under Civil Rights Attorney's Fees Awards Act of 1976*, 104 ALR Fed. 14 (1991 & Supp.2012-13); Report of the Third Circuit Task Force, Oct. 8, 1985, *Court Awarded Attorney Fees*, 108 F.R.D. 237 (1986).

§2. DETERMINING NATURE OF ATTORNEY FEES

Determining whether a motion requesting attorney fees must be filed requires a party to determine if it is seeking attorney fees as costs, damages, or sanctions. A party must file a motion for attorney fees within 14 days after entry of the judgment, unless the fees are (1) to be proved at trial as an element of damages or (2) sanctions for a violation under the FRCPs or 28 U.S.C. §1927. *See* FRCP 54(d)(2)(A), (d)(2)(B), (d)(2)(E). Most of the confusion in this

area involves the distinction between fees as damages and fees as costs; there is usually no disagreement about whether a party is seeking attorney fees as sanctions under the FRCPs or §1927. See "Motion for Sanctions," ch. 5-O, p. 384.

§2.1 Costs vs. damages. Most claims for attorney fees are as costs, not damages. *See* ***Budinich v. Becton Dickinson & Co.***, 486 U.S. 196, 200 (1988). A party seeking attorney fees as costs is usually seeking fees for work done during the case. *See* ***Rissman v. Rissman***, 229 F.3d 586, 588 (7th Cir.2000). A party seeking attorney fees as damages is usually seeking fees that were incurred before the litigation began. *Id.* To determine whether attorney fees are costs or damages, the party should consider the nature of the plaintiff's claim and the source of its entitlement to attorney fees. *See* FRCP 54(d)(2)(B)(ii); ***Simplot v. Chevron Pipeline Co.***, 563 F.3d 1102, 1115-16 (10th Cir. 2009). The following questions are helpful in distinguishing between the two types of fees:

1. Are the attorney fees part of the harm to the plaintiff and thus an element of the claim that must be submitted to the trier of fact? If so, the fees are damages. *See, e.g.*, ***McGuire v. Russell Miller, Inc.***, 1 F.3d 1306, 1313 (2d Cir.1993) (jury must determine whether party can recover attorney fees under indemnity provision in contract); ***Borunda v. Richmond***, 885 F.2d 1384, 1389-90 (9th Cir.1988) (fees incurred in defending earlier improper criminal charge can be recovered as element of damages if proved in later civil-rights suit). For example, in a suit against an insurer for not defending an underlying claim as required by an insurance policy, the plaintiff's costs and fees in defending the underlying claim are considered part of its damages. ***Justine Rlty. Co. v. American Nat'l Can Co.***, 945 F.2d 1044, 1048 (8th Cir.1991).

2. Does a statute specifically provide for attorney fees as costs of suit? When a statute defines "costs" to include attorney fees, the fees are not damages. ***Marek v. Chesny***, 473 U.S. 1, 9 (1985); ***Mellon v. World Publ'g***, 20 F.2d 613, 618 (8th Cir.1927).

§2.2 Fees as costs. If attorney fees are recoverable as costs of suit, the party must file a motion under FRCP 54(d)(2) requesting them. FRCP 54(d)(2)(A); ***United Indus. v. Simon-Hartley, Ltd.***, 91 F.3d 762, 765-66 (5th Cir. 1996). When attorney fees are recoverable as costs, the party usually does not have to include a demand for them in the complaint. FRCP 54(d)(2)(A); ***Riordan v. State Farm Mut. Auto. Ins.***, 589 F.3d 999, 1005 (9th Cir.2009); ***United Indus.***, 91 F.3d at 765-66; ***Mellon v. World Publ'g***, 20 F.2d 613, 618-19 (8th Cir.1927). However, in some cases, it may be necessary to plead for attorney fees as costs in the complaint or request them in the pretrial order to avoid waiving the right to the fees after the trial. *See, e.g.*, ***Atlantic Purchasers, Inc. v. Aircraft Sales, Inc.***, 705 F.2d 712, 716 n.4 (4th Cir.1983) (P's state-law claim for fees was barred because P did not specifically plead for fees under state statute or prove condition precedent to recovery); ***Wilson v. William Hall Chevrolet, Inc.***, 871 F.Supp. 279, 282-83 (S.D.Miss.1994) (request for attorney fees under state deceptive-trade-practices act was waived because right to fees was not inherent under amended version of statute and P did not request fees in pleadings or before jury's verdict), *rev'd in part on other grounds sub nom.* ***Wilson v. Nelson Hall Chevrolet, Inc.***, 77 F.3d 479 (5th Cir.1996) (table case).

§2.3 Fees as damages. If attorney fees are recoverable as damages, the party does not have to file a motion under FRCP 54(d)(2) requesting them. *See* FRCP 54(d)(2)(A); ***United Indus. v. Simon-Hartley, Ltd.***, 91 F.3d 762, 766 n.7 (5th Cir.1996). Instead, the party must specifically plead for them. ***United Indus.***, 91 F.3d at 766 n.7; *see* ***Simplot v. Chevron Pipeline Co.***, 563 F.3d 1102, 1115-16 (10th Cir.2009); *see, e.g.*, ***Maidmore Rlty. Co. v. Maidmore Rlty. Co.***, 474 F.2d 840, 843 (3d Cir.1973) (request for fees waived; P did not specifically plead provisions in mortgage obligating D to pay all costs of collection including attorney fees); *see also* ***Rissman v. Rissman***, 229 F.3d 586, 588 (7th Cir.2000) (party seeking attorney fees as damages must raise its claim before trial, not after).

1. **Amending pleadings.** If the pleadings do not contain a request for attorney fees, a court may permit the party to add the request by amendment. ***Crosby v. Old Republic Ins.***, 978 F.2d 210, 211 n.1 (5th Cir.1992). See "Motion to Amend or Supplement Pleadings—Pretrial," ch. 5-I, p. 345; "Motion to Amend Pleadings—Trial & Posttrial," ch. 8-F, p. 710.

2. **Waiving request.** Generally, a party waives the right to recover attorney fees as damages if it does not plead for the fees. ***United Indus.***, 91 F.3d at 764; ***Rural Water Dist. v. City of Wilson***, 184 F.R.D. 632, 633

(D.Kan.1998). In breach-of-contract cases in which the underlying contract provides for the award of attorney fees to the prevailing party, some courts permit requests for attorney fees to be raised for the first time after trial if the movant's entitlement to the fees is not in dispute and the late request would not prejudice the opposing party. *See* ***Engel v. Teleprompter Corp.***, 732 F.2d 1238, 1241-42 (5th Cir.1984) (relying on FRCP 54(c)); ***Paliaga v. Luckenbach S.S. Co.***, 301 F.2d 403, 410 (2d Cir.1962) (same); *see, e.g.*, ***Eastern Trading Co. v. Refco, Inc.***, 229 F.3d 617, 626-27 (7th Cir.2000) (although issue of attorney fees was not in pretrial order, there was no issue of entitlement to fees to submit to jury; right to fees was issue to be resolved after trial); *see also* ***City of Wilson***, 184 F.R.D. at 633 n.2 (substantial increase in party's potential ultimate liability is prejudice that can bar additional relief under FRCP 54(c)).

3. Application still required. Although the party requesting attorney fees as damages does not have to file a motion under FRCP 54(d)(2), it must still make an application for an award of fees. ***Engel***, 732 F.2d at 1242. The application should state the amount sought or a fair estimate of it and be supported by documentation. *See, e.g., id.* (D submitted application for fees and most of supporting documentation). There is no deadline for filing the application, but it should be filed within a reasonable time after the entitlement to fees becomes certain. *See, e.g.*, ***Capital Asset Research Corp. v. Finnegan***, 216 F.3d 1268, 1272-73 (11th Cir.2000) (D timely filed application after entitlement to attorney fees became certain following appeal); ***Engel***, 732 F.2d at 1242 (same).

§3. ENTITLEMENT TO FEES

The party, not the party's attorney, is entitled to attorney fees. ***Astrue v. Ratliff***, ___ U.S. ___, 130 S.Ct. 2521, 2529 (2010); ***U.S. v. $186,416 in U.S. Currency***, 642 F.3d 753, 756 (9th Cir.2011); *e.g.*, ***Venegas v. Mitchell***, 495 U.S. 82, 87 (1990) (attorney fees under Civil Rights Act, 42 U.S.C. §1988); ***Mathur v. Board of Trs. of S. Ill. Univ.***, 317 F.3d 738, 741 (7th Cir.2003) (attorney fees under Title VII, 42 U.S.C. §2000e-5(k)). Thus, the party, not the attorney, must apply for the fees. *See* ***Manning v. Astrue***, 510 F.3d 1246, 1251 (10th Cir.2007); *see also* ***Mathur***, 317 F.3d at 741 (whether motion for fees is in name of party or attorney is "technicality"); ***Willard v. City of L.A.***, 803 F.2d 526, 527 (9th Cir.1986) (attorney does not have standing to pursue attorney fees on her own behalf). Once the party applies and is awarded attorney fees, the attorney has a vested right to collect the fees. *See* ***Gonter v. Hunt Valve Co.***, 510 F.3d 610, 614 (6th Cir.2007); *see also* ***Astrue***, ___ U.S. at ___, 130 S.Ct. at 2529 (practical reality is that attorneys are beneficiaries of statutory fees awarded to prevailing party). The courts are split on whether the attorney has standing to appeal an attorney-fee award. *Compare* ***Gonter***, 510 F.3d at 615-16 (attorneys had standing to bring appeal), *and* ***Mathur***, 317 F.3d at 741 (same), *with* ***Willis v. Government Accountability Office***, 448 F.3d 1341, 1349 (Fed. Cir.2006) (attorney did not have standing to bring appeal).

PRACTICE TIP

An attorney may be able to establish standing to pursue attorney fees independently by showing that the client agreed to pay the attorney any statutory attorney fees awarded. See ***Samuels v. American Motors Sales Corp.***, *969 F.2d 573, 577 (7th Cir.1992). But see* ***Manning***, *510 F.3d at 1252 (party cannot assign right to seek attorney fees).*

§4. MOTION

§4.1 Deadline.

1. Fees as costs.

(1) Calculating deadline.

(a) Generally. When attorney fees are sought under FRCP 54, the motion for attorney fees and related nontaxable expenses must be filed within 14 days after the judgment is entered. FRCP 54(d)(2)(B)(i); *see also* 2002 Notes to FRCP 54 at ¶2, p. 1223, this book (although FRCP 54(d) does not require that motion for attorney fees be both filed and served, service of motion continues to be required under FRCP 5(a)). The term "judgment" in FRCP 54 includes only final judgments and appealable interlocutory orders. ***Sakon v. Andreo***, 119 F.3d 109, 113 (2d

Cir.1997); *see* FRCP 54(a); *see also* ***Hutchinson v. Patrick***, 636 F.3d 1, 12 (1st Cir.2011) (after court-approved settlement agreement, Ps moved for attorney fees; although there was no final judgment, case was closed as practical matter and fee award was proper).

NOTE

Some courts toll the deadline for the motion for attorney fees until after all timely filed post-judgment motions are resolved. ***Bailey v. County of Riverside****, 414 F.3d 1023, 1025 (9th Cir. 2005); see* ***Members First Fed. Credit Un. v. Members First Credit Un. of Fla.****, 244 F.3d 806, 807 (11th Cir.2001). But the 2009 amendments to the FRCPs extended the deadline for filing postjudgment motions from 10 to 28 days after the entry of judgment; thus, the 14-day deadline for a motion for attorney fees will often expire before a postjudgment motion is filed. See "Post-judgment Motions," ch. 10, p. 771. Because it would be inefficient for a prevailing party to have to file a motion for attorney fees both before the filing of a postjudgment motion and after the ruling on the postjudgment motion, at least one court has held that a motion for attorney fees is timely when it is filed within 14 days after the resolution of a postjudgment motion that was filed between 15 and 28 days after the entry of judgment. See* ***Drumgold v. Callahan****, 806 F.Supp.2d 428, 435 (D.Mass.2011).*

(b) Exceptions. The 14-day deadline can be modified by court order or statute. FRCP 54(d)(2)(B); *see* FRCP 6(b)(2) (motion for attorney fees is not included in list of motions with deadlines that cannot be extended); *see, e.g.*, ***Crue v. Aiken***, 370 F.3d 668, 680-81 (7th Cir.2004) (based on excusable neglect, court allowed motion for attorney fees that was one day late).

[1] Local rules. Local rules may provide additional time to file a motion for attorney fees. *E.g.*, Local Rules Ill. (N.D.), Rule 54.3(b) (91 days after entry of judgment or settlement agreement); Local Rules Minn., Rule 54.3(b)(1) (30 days after entry of judgment); *see, e.g.*, ***Port of Stockton v. Western Bulk Carrier KS***, 371 F.3d 1119, 1121 n.1 (9th Cir.2004) (local rule provided 30 days after entry of judgment). The time period set out by a local rule is considered an order of the court. ***Green v. Administrators of the Tulane Educ. Fund***, 284 F.3d 642, 664 (5th Cir.2002); ***Tire Kingdom, Inc. v. Morgan Tire & Auto, Inc.***, 253 F.3d 1332, 1335 (11th Cir.2001); *see* FRCP 54(d)(2)(B).

[2] Deadline for interim fee awards. Interim attorney fees are attorney fees awarded before the entry of judgment. District courts have discretion to award interim attorney fees when necessary for a party to continue pursuing the lawsuit after the party achieves enough success to make it a prevailing party, regardless of the stage of the litigation. *See* ***Hanrahan v. Hampton***, 446 U.S. 754, 757-58 (1980) (in civil-rights case, court may award interim attorney fees when party prevails on merits of some of its claims); ***Dupuy v. Samuels***, 423 F.3d 714, 719 (7th Cir.2005) (in civil-rights case, court may award interim attorney fees when party obtains substantive relief not affected by further proceedings); *see, e.g.*, ***Bradley v. School Bd. of Richmond***, 416 U.S. 696, 722-23 (1974) (P received partial summary judgment establishing liability on one issue). The deadline for seeking interim fee awards is set by the FRCPs, statutes, local rules, or case law.

[3] Deadline under 28 U.S.C. §2412. When a party seeks attorney fees from the federal government under the Equal Access to Justice Act, the party seeking fees must file the motion within 30 days after the final judgment. 28 U.S.C. §2412(d)(1)(B). The 30-day period begins to run on the date that the time to appeal expires, not the date the judgment is entered. ***Shalala v. Schaefer***, 509 U.S. 292, 303 (1993).

(2) Effect of missing deadline. If a party does not file a motion for attorney fees before the deadline, it waives its right to them. ***Sol Salins, Inc. v. W.M. Ercanbrack Co.***, 155 F.R.D. 4, 5 (D.D.C.1994); *see* ***Port of Stockton***, 371 F.3d at 1121-22.

(3) Effect on appellate deadlines. See "Extending time to file notice of appeal," §9.1, p. 760.

2. Fees as damages. When attorney fees are sought as an element of damages, the party must plead for them in the complaint. ***Riordan v. State Farm Mut. Auto. Ins.***, 589 F.3d 999, 1005 (9th Cir.2009).

3. Fees as sanctions. When attorney fees are sought as sanctions under the FRCPs or 28 U.S.C. §1927, FRCP 54(d)(2) does not apply. FRCP 54(d)(2)(E). Thus, the deadline for filing a fee motion when attorney fees are sanctions is set by the applicable FRCPs, statutes, local rules, or case law. *See* FRCP 11(c)(2) (motion for sanctions must provide opposing party a 21-day "safe harbor" period to withdraw or correct challenged papers); FRCP 23(h)(1) (motion for attorney fees in class action must be made at time set by court); ***1st Source Bank v. First Res. Fed. Credit Un.***, 167 F.R.D. 61, 64 (N.D.Ind.1996) (deadline for moving for sanctions under FRCP 37(c)(1) is deadline for filing motion in limine); *see, e.g.*, ***Levine v. FDIC***, 2 F.3d 476, 479 (2d Cir.1993) (local rule provided that motions for attorney fees or sanctions must be filed and served within 30 days after entry of judgment; because no judgment had been entered, FRCP 11 motion for sanctions was timely); ***Kaplan v. Zenner***, 956 F.2d 149, 151 (7th Cir.1992) (latest deadline for filing FRCP 11 motion for sanctions was either 30 or 90 days after entry of judgment, depending on whether party sought costs or attorney fees). See "Deadline to serve & file," ch. 5-O, §5.1.3, p. 392.

§4.2 Grounds. The motion must specify the judgment and the statute, rule, contract, or equitable ground that entitles the movant to the award of fees and related nontaxable expenses. FRCP 54(d)(2)(B)(ii); *see* ***Combs v. Shelter Mut. Ins.***, 551 F.3d 991, 1001 (10th Cir.2008).

1. Statutory grounds. Many statutes permit the district court to award attorney fees. *See* ***Perdue v. Kenny A.***, ___ U.S. ___, 130 S.Ct. 1662, 1671 n.3 (2010); *see, e.g.*, 15 U.S.C. §1117(a) (Trademark Act); 17 U.S.C. §505 (Copyright Act); 28 U.S.C. §1447(c) (wrongful removal); 29 U.S.C. §1132(g)(1) (ERISA); 42 U.S.C. §2000e-5(k) (Civil Rights Act); 49 U.S.C. §11704(d)(3) (Interstate Commerce Act). To be eligible for a fee award under most federal statutes, the party must be considered a prevailing party. *See* ***Lefemine v. Wideman***, ___ U.S. ___, ___ S.Ct. ___ (2012) (No. 12-168; 11-5-12); ***Hutchinson v. Patrick***, 636 F.3d 1, 8 (1st Cir.2011); ***Klamath Siskiyou Wildlands Ctr. v. U.S. Bureau of Land Mgmt.***, 589 F.3d 1027, 1030 (9th Cir.2009); *see, e.g.*, ***Grissom v. Mills Corp.***, 549 F.3d 313, 318-19 (4th Cir.2008) (although whistleblower claim under 18 U.S.C. §1514A (Sarbanes-Oxley Act) does not use phrase "prevailing party," statutory language of "employee prevailing" was treated same as prevailing party); *see also* ***Hardt v. Reliance Std. Life Ins.***, ___ U.S. ___, 130 S.Ct. 2149, 2156 (2010) (fee claimant under 29 U.S.C. §1132(g)(1) (ERISA) does not need to be prevailing party; rather, either party can be awarded fees at court's discretion).

NOTE

Some statutes state that the court "shall" award attorney fees to the prevailing party, while others state that the court "may" award them. Compare 28 U.S.C. §2412(d)(1)(A) (under Equal Access to Justice Act, court "shall" award attorney fees to prevailing party in litigation against United States) with 42 U.S.C. §2000e-5(k) (in suit for unlawful employment practices, court "may" allow prevailing party reasonable attorney fees). For statutes stating that the court "may" award attorney fees to the prevailing party, the award is discretionary. ***Fogerty v. Fantasy, Inc.***, *510 U.S. 517, 534 (1994). However, the Supreme Court has stated that if a statute provides for an award of attorney fees, an award should be given unless "special circumstances" render it unjust.* ***Blanchard v. Bergeron***, *489 U.S. 87, 89 n.1 (1989);* ***Hensley v. Eckerhart***, *461 U.S. 424, 429 (1983); see, e.g.,* ***San Francisco NAACP v. San Francisco Unified Sch. Dist.***, *284 F.3d 1163, 1168-69 (9th Cir.2002) (special circumstances barred award of fees to prevailing party in original suit under 42 U.S.C. §1988 when, in later proceeding, party sought fees for unsuccessfully defending its consent decree from collateral attack by third party);* ***Doe v. Board of Educ. of Baltimore Cty.***, *165 F.3d 260, 264-65 (4th Cir.1998) (special circumstances barred award of fees for attorney-parent who represented his child in suit under Individuals with Disabilities Education Act). Courts of appeals have followed this lead, upholding most statutory attorney-fee awards. See* ***St. John's Organic Farm v. Gem Cty. Mosquito Abatement Dist.***, *574 F.3d 1054, 1062-63 (9th Cir.2009);* ***Cooper v. Utah***, *894 F.2d 1169, 1171 (10th Cir.1990).*

(1) Prevailing party. A prevailing party is generally a party who succeeds on any significant issue in the litigation and that success provides some benefit that had been sought by the party. ***Hensley***, 461 U.S. at 433; ***Myers v. Central Fla. Invs.***, 592 F.3d 1201, 1225 (11th Cir.2010); ***Thoroughbred Software Int'l v. Dice Corp.***, 488 F.3d 352, 362 (6th Cir.2007); ***Davidson v. Veneman***, 317 F.3d 503, 506 (5th Cir.2003); *see also* ***Klamath Siskiyou Wildlands Ctr.***, 589 F.3d at 1031 (prevailing-party status involves enforceable, judicially sanctioned award of much of relief sought by P). The Supreme Court has listed two judicial outcomes under which a party may be considered "prevailing" for the purpose of awarding attorney fees: (1) an enforceable judgment on the merits or (2) a settlement agreement enforceable through a court-ordered consent decree. ***Buckhannon Bd. & Care Home, Inc. v. West Va. Dept. of H&HR***, 532 U.S. 598, 604 (2001); *see* ***Biodiversity Conserv. Alliance v. Stem***, 519 F.3d 1226, 1230 (10th Cir.2008) (P is prevailing party only if she can obtain court order to enforce judgment on merits of claim); *see also* ***Dearmore v. City of Garland***, 519 F.3d 517, 521 (5th Cir.2008) (two outcomes in ***Buckhannon*** are not exclusive). In certain circumstances, a private settlement agreement can support an award of attorney fees; for a settlement agreement to support an award, the court must either incorporate the terms of the settlement into the final order or expressly retain jurisdiction to enforce the settlement. ***American Disability Ass'n v. Chmielarz***, 289 F.3d 1315, 1320 (11th Cir.2002); *see* ***Buckhannon***, 532 U.S. at 604; ***Hutchinson***, 636 F.3d at 9-10; ***Roberson v. Giuliani***, 346 F.3d 75, 84 (2d Cir.2003); *see, e.g.*, ***Bill M. v. Nebraska Dept. of H&HS Fin. & Support***, 570 F.3d 1001, 1003-04 (8th Cir.2009) (Ps were not prevailing parties when court did not determine fairness of settlement agreement, did not incorporate agreement into dismissal order, and did not retain jurisdiction to enforce agreement).

NOTE

Even if a party is the prevailing party, the court can deny attorney fees under its inherent power. See, e.g., ***Sahyers v. Prugh, Holliday & Karatinos, P.L.***, *560 F.3d 1241, 1245-46 & n.9 (11th Cir.2009) (although P was prevailing party under Fair Labor Standards Act, court used its inherent power to deny P attorney fees when (1) P's attorney provided no notice of suit to Ds and did not meaningfully attempt to resolve dispute and (2) such conduct rose to level of bad faith).* *See "Bad-faith litigation," §4.2.4(3), p. 753.*

(a) Prevailing plaintiff.

[1] Plaintiff obtained preliminary injunction. A plaintiff who obtained a preliminary injunction may be considered a prevailing party when the injunction provides the final relief the plaintiff sought. *See* ***Lefemine***, ___ U.S. at ___, ___ S.Ct. at ___; ***Kansas Judicial Watch v. Stout***, 653 F.3d 1230, 1238 (10th Cir. 2011); *see, e.g.*, ***Sole v. Wyner***, 551 U.S. 74, 84-86 (2007) (P was not prevailing party when granting of P's preliminary injunction was based on argument that court later rejected and P's request for permanent injunction was denied). A plaintiff who is prevented from seeking final relief may still be a prevailing party if the preliminary injunction was obtained based on an unambiguous indication of the plaintiff's probable success on the merits but events that are outside the plaintiff's control make the case moot before trial. ***Kansas Judicial Watch***, 653 F.3d at 1238; *see, e.g.*, ***Dearmore***, 519 F.3d at 523-24 (after P obtained preliminary injunction, D amended offending city-ordinance provision, making P's claim moot; P was prevailing party); *see also* ***Singer Mgmt. Consultants, Inc. v. Milgram***, 650 F.3d 223, 229 (3d Cir.2011) (Ps who obtain preliminary injunction will usually not be considered prevailing parties because preliminary injunctions only require likelihood of success on merits).

[2] Plaintiff awarded damages. A plaintiff who was awarded damages is generally considered a prevailing party. *See* ***Buckhannon***, 532 U.S. at 603.

[a] Nominal damages. A plaintiff who was awarded only nominal damages may be considered a prevailing party. *See* ***Gray v. Bostic***, 613 F.3d 1035, 1040 (11th Cir.2010); ***Jama v. Esmor Corr. Servs.***, 577 F.3d 169, 175-76 (3d Cir.2009); *see, e.g.*, ***Farrar v. Hobby***, 506 U.S. 103, 112 (1992) (in civil-rights case, P was awarded nominal damages and was considered prevailing party). To obtain an award of attorney fees, the plaintiff awarded nominal damages must make an additional showing of how the litigation succeeded. ***Benton v. Oregon***

Student Assistance Comm'n, 421 F.3d 901, 905 (9th Cir.2005); *see* ***Gray***, 613 F.3d at 1040. This requirement can be satisfied by showing a change in policy, a finding of fact with collateral-estoppel effects, or another benefit to the public at large or to the plaintiff individually. *See* ***Gray***, 613 F.3d at 1040; ***Benton***, 421 F.3d at 905-06.

NOTE

When a suit involves federal and state-law claims and there is only nominal success on the federal claim, success on the state-law claim can be a consideration for awarding attorney fees under the federal claim if the claims involve a common core of facts or are based on related legal theories. See ***Jama***, *577 F.3d at 179-80.*

---

[b] Punitive damages. A plaintiff who was awarded only punitive damages may be considered a prevailing party. *See, e.g.*, ***De Jesús Nazario v. Morris Rodríguez***, 554 F.3d 196, 202 (1st Cir.2009) (in civil-rights case, P was awarded only punitive damages that were not challenged by D; P was considered prevailing party).

[3] Pro se plaintiff. A pro se litigant, even if an attorney, is not entitled to attorney fees. *See, e.g.*, ***Kay v. Ehrler***, 499 U.S. 432, 438 (1991) (attorney pro se P); ***White v. Armontrout***, 29 F.3d 357, 361-62 (8th Cir.1994) (nonattorney pro se P).

(b) Prevailing defendant. A defendant can be a prevailing party if the court finds that the plaintiff's claim was frivolous or was brought in bad faith or for harassment. *See* 10 Wright, Miller & Kane §2675.2 n.16; *see, e.g.*, 15 U.S.C. §1692k(a)(3) (under Fair Debt Collection Act, D may be awarded attorney fees for action brought in bad faith or for purpose of harassment); 31 U.S.C. §3730(d)(4) (in some False Claims Act cases, D may be awarded attorney fees when action was clearly frivolous, clearly vexatious, or brought to harass); ***Christiansburg Garment Co. v. EEOC***, 434 U.S. 412, 421 (1978) (in civil-rights case, fees allowed if P's suit was frivolous, unreasonable, or without foundation); ***Myers v. City of W. Monroe***, 211 F.3d 289, 292 (5th Cir.2000) (same). When considering whether a suit is frivolous, courts have looked at factors such as whether the plaintiff established a prima facie case, whether a dispositive motion was denied, whether the defendant offered to settle, and whether the court held a full trial. ***E.E.O.C. v. Great Steaks, Inc.***, 667 F.3d 510, 517-18 (4th Cir.2012) (civil-rights case); ***Bonner v. Mobile Energy Servs. Co.***, 246 F.3d 1303, 1304 (11th Cir.2001) (same); ***Myers***, 211 F.3d at 292 (same); *see also* Annotation, *Right of Defendant in Civil Rights Case to Receive Award of Attorney's Fees*, 104 ALR Fed. at 32 (court will not assume case is frivolous merely because P did not prevail).

NOTE

In 2011, the Supreme Court held that a prevailing defendant in a civil-rights case under 42 U.S.C. §1983 can recover attorney fees even if some of the plaintiff's claims are nonfrivolous. ***Fox v. Vice***, *___ U.S. ___, 131 S.Ct. 2205, 2211 (2011). In holding that a district court can grant reasonable fees to the defendant when the plaintiff asserts both frivolous and nonfrivolous claims, the Court limited the fees to those that the defendant would not have incurred but for the frivolous claims. Id. at ___, 131 S.Ct. at 2211. That is, if the defendant would have incurred the fees to defend against the nonfrivolous claims anyway, the district court cannot shift those fees to the plaintiff. Id. at ___, 131 S.Ct. at 2215. It remains unclear how this holding will apply to other causes of action that allow for fee-shifting to a prevailing defendant.*

(c) Prevailing intervenor. An intervenor can be a prevailing party if the court finds that the intervenor contributed importantly or played a significant role in producing the outcome. ***Wilder v. Bernstein***, 965 F.2d 1196, 1204 (2d Cir.1992); *see* ***Donnell v. U.S.***, 682 F.2d 240, 248-49 (D.C.Cir.1982) (intervenor should be awarded attorney fees only if it contributed substantially to success of litigation); *see, e.g.*, ***Sierra Club v. Hamilton Cty. Bd.***

of Cty. Comm'rs, 504 F.3d 634, 644-45 (6th Cir.2007) (intervenors considered prevailing party because participation in lawsuit resulted in more comprehensive consent decree); ***King v. Illinois State Bd. of Elections***, 410 F.3d 404, 420-21 (7th Cir.2005) (intervenors considered prevailing party because intervenors' efforts were not duplicative of named D's efforts).

(2) Theories of recovery.

(a) Material alteration. A party is the prevailing party when the resolution of the dispute between the plaintiff and the defendant results in a material alteration in the legal relationship between the two. ***Lefemine***, ___ U.S. at ___, ___ S.Ct. at ___; ***Buckhannon***, 532 U.S. at 604; ***Farrar***, 506 U.S. at 111-12; *see also* ***Central Fla. Invs.***, 592 F.3d at 1225 (material alteration occurs when D is required to modify its behavior in way that directly benefits P). The material alteration must provide the actual relief sought; a mere legal determination is not sufficient. ***Klamath Siskiyou Wildlands Ctr.***, 589 F.3d at 1030. The form of the relief awarded to a prevailing party is not important as long as the relief is that sought by the prevailing party. *Id.*

NOTE

Voluntary or involuntary dismissals without prejudice or dismissals based on forum non conveniens do not create a material alteration of the legal relationship between the parties because the plaintiff can refile the suit; thus, there is no prevailing party in these situations. E.g., ***Oscar v. Alaska Dept. of Educ. & Early Dev.****, 541 F.3d 978, 981-82 (9th Cir.2008) (involuntary dismissal without prejudice);* ***Dattner v. Conagra Foods, Inc.****, 458 F.3d 98, 103 (2d Cir.2006) (dismissal based on forum non conveniens);* ***Szabo Food Serv. v. Canteen Corp.****, 823 F.2d 1073, 1076-77 (7th Cir.1987) (voluntary dismissal without prejudice); see, e.g.,* ***Sequa Corp. v. Cooper****, 245 F.3d 1036, 1037-38 (8th Cir.2001) (although court upheld costs award, D was not prevailing party when P voluntarily dismissed its complaint without prejudice). But see* ***Cantrell v. International Bhd. of Elec. Workers****, 69 F.3d 456, 458 (10th Cir.1995) (court has discretion to award costs to D as prevailing party when P voluntarily dismisses suit with or without prejudice).*

(b) Catalyst theory. Under the "catalyst theory," a plaintiff could claim prevailing-party status if its suit was a substantial factor or a significant catalyst in obtaining the relief sought. ***Center for Biological Diversity v. Norton***, 262 F.3d 1077, 1080-81 (10th Cir.2001). The Supreme Court, however, has repudiated the catalyst theory for conferring prevailing-party status on a party seeking attorney fees. ***Buckhannon***, 532 U.S. at 605-06; *see* ***Hamilton Cty.***, 504 F.3d at 643; ***American Disability Ass'n***, 289 F.3d at 1318. *But see* ***Davis v. U.S. Dept. of Justice***, 610 F.3d 750, 752 (D.C.Cir.2010) (Freedom of Information Act amended to specifically provide that "prevailing party" includes party who obtained relief by voluntary or unilateral change in position by government agency). At least three circuits have limited ***Buckhannon*** to statutes that contain an express prevailing-party requirement; these circuits continue to apply the catalyst theory to fee requests brought under statutes that do not contain the requirement. *See* ***Sierra Club v. EPA***, 322 F.3d 718, 725-26 (D.C.Cir.2003); ***Loggerhead Turtle v. County Council***, 307 F.3d 1318, 1327 (11th Cir.2002); ***Norton***, 262 F.3d at 1080 n.2.

2. FRCP grounds. An award of attorney fees may be authorized by rule. *See, e.g.*, FRCP 23(h) (court may award reasonable attorney fees and nontaxable costs in certified class action).

3. Contractual grounds. An award of attorney fees may be authorized by a contract providing for attorney fees. *See* ***Travelers Cas. & Sur. Co. v. Pacific Gas & Elec. Co.***, 549 U.S. 443, 448 (2007); ***Frankenmuth Mut. Ins. v. Escambia Cty.***, 289 F.3d 723, 733 (11th Cir.2002).

4. Equitable grounds. An award of attorney fees may be authorized on equitable grounds.

(1) Common-fund doctrine. The court may award attorney fees under the common-fund doctrine, which authorizes an award of attorney fees from a common fund when a suit (most often a class action or interpleader) produces a recovery for persons other than the principal litigant. ***Victor v. Argent Classic Convertible Arbitrage Fund L.P.***, 623 F.3d 82, 86 (2d Cir.2010); *see* ***Alyeska Pipeline Serv. v. Wilderness Soc'y***, 421 U.S. 240, 257-58

(1975); ***Rosenbaum v. MacAllister***, 64 F.3d 1439, 1444 (10th Cir.1995). The common-fund doctrine also applies to suits that directly affect a fund, such as creating, discovering, increasing, preserving, or providing access to a fund. *See* ***Sprague v. Ticonic Nat'l Bank***, 307 U.S. 161, 166-67 (1939); ***Vincent v. Hughes Air W., Inc.***, 557 F.2d 759, 769 (9th Cir.1977); ***Abbott, Puller & Myers v. Peyser***, 124 F.2d 524, 525 (D.C.Cir.1941).

(2) Substantial-benefit doctrine. The court may award attorney fees under the substantial-benefit doctrine, which authorizes an award of attorney fees to a successful plaintiff who, although suing on her own behalf rather than as a representative of a class, either (1) established the right of others to recover out of specific assets of the same defendant through the operation of stare decisis or (2) corrected or prevented an abuse that would be prejudicial to the rights and interests of others. ***Hall v. Cole***, 412 U.S. 1, 5 n.7 (1973); ***Mills v. Electric Auto-Lite Co.***, 396 U.S. 375, 393-94 (1970); *see* Hirsch & Sheehey, *Awarding Attorneys' Fees & Managing Fee Litigation*, at 83-84. This doctrine applies only when the litigation has created a "substantial benefit" for a class of beneficiaries and the court has personal jurisdiction over an entity, such as a corporation or labor union, that is composed of the class of beneficiaries to the suit. *See* ***Mills***, 396 U.S. at 393-94. The substantial-benefit doctrine is most commonly applied to shareholder derivative suits and to suits against unions. 10 *Moore's Federal Practice 3d* §54.171[2][b][iv].

(3) Bad-faith litigation. The court may award attorney fees under its inherent powers when a party has acted in bad faith, vexatiously, wantonly, or oppressively. ***Chambers v. NASCO, Inc.***, 501 U.S. 32, 45-46 (1991); ***F.D. Rich Co. v. U.S.***, 417 U.S. 116, 129-30 (1974). "Bad faith" is defined as conduct without at least a colorable basis in law. ***Glick v. Koenig***, 766 F.2d 265, 270 (7th Cir.1985). For example, filing a frivolous lawsuit demonstrates bad faith when the suit is so completely without hope of succeeding that the court can infer that the plaintiff brought the suit to harass the defendants rather than to obtain a favorable judgment. *Id.* Simply because the court could have awarded attorney fees as sanctions under other statutes or the FRCPs does not prevent the court from assessing fees under its inherent power. ***Chambers***, 501 U.S. at 50. See "Bad-faith conduct," ch. 5-O, §3.9, p. 389.

(4) Interpleader. The court may award attorney fees in interpleader actions. ***Sun Life Assur. Co. v. Sampson***, 556 F.3d 6, 8 (1st Cir.2009); ***Schirmer Stevedoring Co. v. Seaboard Stevedoring Corp.***, 306 F.2d 188, 193 (9th Cir.1962). See "Costs & attorney fees," ch. 2-C, §8.3.2, p. 92.

§4.3 Amount. The motion should state the amount of attorney fees and related nontaxable expenses sought or a fair estimate of the fees. FRCP 54(d)(2)(B)(iii). The amount for work done by attorneys is often determined by the "lodestar" method. See "Lodestar method," §5.1, p. 754. The amount may include the following:

1. Fees for paralegals & other contributing individuals. Fees for paralegals, database managers, support staff, attorneys who are not yet licensed, and other individuals who contribute to the attorney's work product can be included. *See* ***Richlin Sec. Serv. v. Chertoff***, 553 U.S. 571, 581 (2008); *see, e.g.*, ***Winterrowd v. American Gen. Annuity Ins.***, 556 F.3d 815, 823-24 (9th Cir.2009) (fees were recoverable for work contributed by attorney who was not member of state bar because his conduct did not rise to level of "appearance" in district court when he did not physically appear in court, did not sign pleadings, had minimal contact with Ps, and was not solely responsible to Ps).

2. Expenses for electronic legal research. Expenses for electronic legal research can be included. ***Arbor Hill Concerned Citizens Neighborhood Ass'n v. County of Albany***, 369 F.3d 91, 97-98 (2d Cir.2004); ***Haroco, Inc. v. American Nat'l Bank & Trust Co.***, 38 F.3d 1429, 1440-41 (7th Cir.1994); *see, e.g.*, ***Role Models Am., Inc. v. Brownlee***, 353 F.3d 962, 975 (D.C.Cir.2004) (court awarded as expenses the actual billed amount for Westlaw and Lexis).

§4.4 Terms of agreement. If ordered by the court, the motion must disclose the terms of any agreement about fees for the services for which the claim is made. FRCP 54(d)(2)(B)(iv).

§4.5 Certificate of conference. Many local rules require motions to contain a statement that the movant's attorney has conferred with the other party's attorney and they cannot agree about the disposition of the motion. *E.g.*, Local Rules Tex. (S.D.), Rule 7.1.D.

§4.6 Affidavit.

1. From attorney in case. The motion should be supported by an affidavit from each attorney involved in the case that includes a detailed list of the time spent and type of work performed so the court can identify allowable fees. *See* ***Hensley v. Eckerhart***, 461 U.S. 424, 433 (1983); ***Berry v. Stevinson Chevrolet***, 74 F.3d 980, 989 (10th Cir.1996). See "Amount," §4.3, p. 753.

2. From disinterested attorney. The motion should be supported by the affidavit of a disinterested attorney specifically stating the prevailing local rate for the type of work for which the movant seeks an award. *See* ***Blum v. Stenson***, 465 U.S. 886, 895-96 n.11 (1984); ***Schwarz v. Secretary of H&HS***, 73 F.3d 895, 908 (9th Cir.1995); ***Wheeler v. MHMR Auth.***, 752 F.2d 1063, 1073 (5th Cir.1985). The affidavit should state the factual basis for the affiant's opinion.

§4.7 Request hearing. If the motion presents contested fact issues, the movant should request a hearing. The movant should comply with any requirements of the local rules for securing a hearing on the motion. See "Hearing," §7, p. 759.

§5. DETERMINING REASONABLE ATTORNEY FEES

To calculate reasonable attorney fees, the court in most cases should use the "lodestar" method outlined in ***Pennsylvania v. Delaware Valley Citizens' Council for Clean Air***, 478 U.S. 546, 563-66 (1986).

§5.1 Lodestar method. The lodestar method is commonly used when attorney fees are authorized by a fee-shifting statute. ***Ferland v. Conrad Credit Corp.***, 244 F.3d 1145, 1149 n.4 (9th Cir.2001); ***Adcock-Ladd v. Secretary of Treasury***, 227 F.3d 343, 349 (6th Cir.2000); ***Luciano v. Olsten Corp.***, 109 F.3d 111, 115 (2d Cir.1997); *see* ***Gonter v. Hunt Valve Co.***, 510 F.3d 610, 616 (6th Cir.2007) (lodestar method is starting point for determining reasonable fees). *But see* ***Wells v. Sullivan***, 907 F.2d 367, 370 (2d Cir.1990) (adopting "contingent fee" method). A "reasonable" fee is one that is sufficient to induce a capable attorney to take on a case, and there is a strong presumption that the lodestar method results in a reasonable fee. ***Perdue v. Kenny A.***, ___ U.S. ___, 130 S.Ct. 1662, 1672-73 (2010); ***Pennsylvania v. Delaware Valley Citizens' Council for Clean Air***, 478 U.S. 546, 565 (1986); ***Ferland***, 244 F.3d at 1149 n.4; ***Board of Trs. of the Hotel & Rest. Empls. v. JPR, Inc.***, 136 F.3d 794, 801 (D.C.Cir.1998).

1. Determining lodestar amount. The court should determine the base, or lodestar, amount by multiplying the number of hours the attorney reasonably spent on the case by a reasonable hourly rate. ***Delaware Valley***, 478 U.S. at 565; ***Hensley v. Eckerhart***, 461 U.S. 424, 433 (1983); ***Interfaith Cmty. Org. v. Honeywell Int'l***, 426 F.3d 694, 703 n.5 (3d Cir.2005); ***Green v. Administrators of the Tulane Educ. Fund***, 284 F.3d 642, 661 (5th Cir.2002); ***Emery v. Hunt***, 272 F.3d 1042, 1046 (8th Cir.2001); ***Ferland***, 244 F.3d at 1149 n.4. The fee claimant has the burden of substantiating the hours worked and the rate claimed. ***Strange v. Monogram Credit Card Bank***, 129 F.3d 943, 946 (7th Cir.1997).

(1) Hours reasonably spent. To determine the reasonable number of hours, the court should subtract the hours that were duplicative, unproductive, excessive, or otherwise unnecessary from the number of hours actually spent. ***Van Gerwen v. Guarantee Mut. Life Co.***, 214 F.3d 1041, 1045 (9th Cir.2000); ***Public Interest Research Grp. v. Windall***, 51 F.3d 1179, 1188 (3d Cir.1995); ***Watkins v. Fordice***, 7 F.3d 453, 457 (5th Cir.1993); *see* Hirsch & Sheehey, *Awarding Attorneys' Fees & Managing Fee Litigation*, at 26-27. The court may reduce the lodestar amount because of redundant staffing. *See* ***Hensley***, 461 U.S. at 434 (excessive, redundant, or otherwise unnecessary fees should be excluded); *see, e.g.*, ***Halderman v. Pennhurst State Sch. & Hosp.***, 49 F.3d 939, 944 (3d Cir.1995) (fees for additional attorneys reviewing findings of fact could not be included); ***West Va. Univ. Hosps., Inc. v. Casey***, 898 F.2d 357, 365 (3d Cir.1990) (fees for more than two attorneys at oral argument could not be included). The test is whether, at the time the work was performed, a reasonable attorney would have spent the same amount of time. ***Grant v. Martinez***, 973 F.2d 96, 99 (2d Cir.1992). The attorney's hours usually must be supported by time records.

CAUTION

In certain circumstances, billing records of the nonprevailing party may be helpful in determining whether the amount of time and labor expended by the prevailing party was reasonable. E.g., ***Serricchio v. Wachovia Secs., LLC****, 258 F.R.D. 43, 46-47 (D.Conn.2009) (court allowed prevailing party to discover opposing counsel's billing records when opposing counsel claimed that time spent by prevailing party's counsel was grossly excessive; opposing counsel's own time could be useful measure of reasonableness of prevailing party's time); see* ***Shaw v. AAA Eng'g & Drafting, Inc.****, 213 F.3d 538, 543 (10th Cir.2000). Any comparison, however, must take into account that the nonprevailing party does not necessarily have the same responsibilities as the prevailing party and that the parties may not be similarly situated. See* ***Ferland****, 244 F.3d at 1151.*

(a) Contemporaneous time records. Contemporaneous time records of hours worked are preferred over reconstructed time records. ***Webb v. Board of Educ. of Dyer Cty.***, 471 U.S. 234, 238 n.6 (1985). Several circuits require contemporaneous time records and will substantially reduce or even deny a fee award without them. *See* ***In re Olson***, 884 F.2d 1415, 1428-29 (D.C.Cir.1989); ***Lightfoot v. Walker***, 826 F.2d 516, 522 n.7 (7th Cir. 1987); ***Grendel's Den, Inc. v. Larkin***, 749 F.2d 945, 952 (1st Cir.1984); ***Ramos v. Lamm***, 713 F.2d 546, 553 (10th Cir.1983); ***McCann v. Coughlin***, 698 F.2d 112, 131 (2d Cir.1983). *But see* ***Jean v. Nelson***, 863 F.2d 759, 772 (11th Cir.1988) (fee application can be granted even without contemporaneous records), *aff'd sub nom.* ***Commissioner, INS v. Jean***, 496 U.S. 154 (1990).

(b) Reconstructed time records. Reconstructed time records—time records compiled after the fact—may suffice to prove the reasonableness of the time spent if they are supported by other evidence such as testimony or secondary documentation. ***Frank Music Corp. v. Metro-Goldwyn-Mayer, Inc.***, 886 F.2d 1545, 1557 (9th Cir.1989); ***Jean***, 863 F.2d at 772. The Eighth Circuit has said that "whether reconstructed records accurately document the time attorneys have spent is best left to the discretion of the [trial] court." ***MacDissi v. Valmont Indus.***, 856 F.2d 1054, 1061 (8th Cir.1988).

(2) Reasonable hourly rate. The reasonable hourly rate is the prevailing hourly rate in the community for similar work. ***Perdue***, ___ U.S. at ___, 130 S.Ct. at 1672; ***Adcock-Ladd***, 227 F.3d at 350; ***Windall***, 51 F.3d at 1185; ***Louisiana Power & Light Co. v. Kellstrom***, 50 F.3d 319, 328 (5th Cir.1995).

(a) Prevailing hourly rate. The prevailing hourly rate is generally shown by evidence, usually in the form of affidavits from other attorneys, that the charged rate is in line with the market rate in the community. *See* ***Blum v. Stenson***, 465 U.S. 886, 895 & n.11 (1984); ***Lucero v. City of Trinidad***, 815 F.2d 1384, 1385 (10th Cir.1987); *see, e.g.*, ***Barjon v. Dalton***, 132 F.3d 496, 502 (9th Cir.1997) (court applied prevailing rate for similarly qualified local attorney); *see also* ***Gonter***, 510 F.3d at 618 (prevailing rate is the market rate in the community sufficient to encourage competent representation). Some courts, however, have stated that a court may rely on its own knowledge of the market. *See* ***Ingram v. Oroudjian***, 647 F.3d 925, 928 (9th Cir.2011); ***Norman v. Housing Auth. of Montgomery***, 836 F.2d 1292, 1303 (11th Cir.1988).

(b) Community. The community is most commonly considered to be the place where the district court sits. *See* ***Bywaters v. U.S.***, 670 F.3d 1221, 1232-33 (Fed.Cir.2012); ***Simmons v. New York City Transit Auth.***, 575 F.3d 170, 174 (2d Cir.2009); ***Interfaith Cmty. Org.***, 426 F.3d at 705; ***Schwarz v. Secretary of H&HS***, 73 F.3d 895, 907 (9th Cir.1995).

NOTE

When a nonlocal attorney is hired to represent a party, the court can consider the prevailing rate in that attorney's community (i.e., the out-of-district rate). ***Simmons****, 575 F.3d at 175;* ***Interfaith Cmty. Org.****, 426 F.3d at 705. The in-district rate is presumed, but that presumption can be overcome if a reasonable client would have selected an out-of-district attorney because doing so would likely—not just possibly—produce a substantially better result.* ***Simmons****, 575*

F.3d at 175. To overcome the presumption, the party requesting the out-of-district rate can show that the out-of-district attorney has expertise in litigating the particular type of case, that an experienced in-district attorney was unwilling or unable to take the case, or that there were no in-district attorneys who had the special expertise necessary to litigate the case. ***Simmons****, 575 F.3d at 175-76; see, e.g.,* ***Bywaters****, 670 F.3d at 1233-34 (in case filed in Texas, higher rate charged by attorney based in Washington, D.C., was inappropriate when P's only evidence that he could not find another attorney was his conclusory declaration);* ***Adcock-Ladd****, 227 F.3d at 351 (in case filed in Tennessee, higher rate was appropriate for out-of-district attorney when P was required to depose Washington D.C. bureaucrat in D.C. and deposition was helpful to favorable settlement for P).*

(c) Reasonableness of hourly rate. When deciding the reasonableness of the hourly rate, the court may consider factors that bear on the market rate and the hours reasonably spent. *See* ***Hensley***, 461 U.S. at 433-34. Some of these factors include the level of skill necessary, the time limitations, the amount at stake in the litigation, the attorney's reputation, and the undesirability of the case. ***Copeland v. Marshall***, 641 F.2d 880, 892 (D.C.Cir.1980). An attorney's success is generally the most significant factor for a court to consider in deciding what is a reasonable fee. ***Hensley***, 461 U.S. at 435-36; ***Adcock-Ladd***, 227 F.3d at 349.

2. Adjusting lodestar amount. After determining the lodestar amount, the court may enhance or reduce it in light of a number of factors (generally referred to as the ***Johnson*** factors) that account for the specific facts of the case. *See* ***Blanchard v. Bergeron***, 489 U.S. 87, 94 (1989); ***Jimenez v. Wood Cty.***, 621 F.3d 372, 380 (5th Cir.2010); ***Phelps v. Hamilton***, 120 F.3d 1126, 1131 (10th Cir.1997); *see also* ***Nilsen v. York Cty.***, 400 F.Supp.2d 266, 273-74 (D.Me.2005) (specific factors vary by circuit). See "*Johnson* factors," §5.1.2(2), p. 757. The party who asks for the fees to be adjusted has the burden of proving that an adjustment is necessary. ***Blum***, 465 U.S. at 898; ***Gonter***, 510 F.3d at 621; *see* ***Perdue***, ___ U.S. at ___, 130 S.Ct. at 1673.

(1) Adjustment. Although a court can enhance or reduce the lodestar amount, there is a strong presumption that the lodestar amount is a reasonable fee award; thus, adjustments are made only in rare and exceptional cases. *See* ***Perdue***, ___ U.S. at ___, 130 S.Ct. at 1673; ***Delaware Valley***, 478 U.S. at 565; ***Bywaters***, 670 F.3d at 1229-30; *see, e.g.,* ***Blum***, 465 U.S. at 897-98 (upward adjustment reversed). Once the lodestar amount is determined, a court is not required to consider the ***Johnson*** factors for enhancement or reduction. *See* ***Anchondo v. Anderson, Crenshaw, & Assocs.***, 616 F.3d 1098, 1103-04 (10th Cir.2010); ***Ladd v. Pickering***, 783 F.Supp.2d 1079, 1091 n.5 (E.D.Mo.2011). Many of the ***Johnson*** factors will already have been considered as part of the initial lodestar calculation. ***Hensley***, 461 U.S. at 434 n.9; *see* ***Perdue***, ___ U.S. at ___, 130 S.Ct. at 1673. If the court makes an adjustment, it must provide a clear and concise explanation of its reasons for adjusting the fee award. ***Perdue***, ___ U.S. at ___, 130 S.Ct. at 1676; ***Pickett v. Sheridan Health Care Ctr.***, 664 F.3d 632, 651 (7th Cir.2011); ***Gonter***, 510 F.3d at 616.

(a) Enhancement. An enhancement is an upward adjustment of a fee award. Because the lodestar amount may include most (if not all) of the relevant factors that constitute a reasonable attorney fee, an enhancement may not be awarded on a factor that was already considered as a part of the lodestar amount. ***Perdue***, ___ U.S. at ___, 130 S.Ct. at 1673; ***Delaware Valley***, 478 U.S. at 566. See §5.1.2(2)(b), (d), (h), (i), below. For example, if an attorney's superior performance was adequately considered during the calculation of the lodestar amount, that performance cannot then be a consideration for enhancement. *See* ***Perdue***, ___ U.S. at ___, 130 S.Ct. at 1674. But if the attorney's superior performance was not adequately considered, it can be a consideration for enhancement if, for example, (1) the method used in determining the hourly rate does not adequately measure the attorney's true market value (e.g., the method considers only the years since the attorney's admission to the bar), (2) there was an extraordinary outlay of expenses by the attorney and the litigation is exceptionally prolonged, or (3) there is an exceptional delay in payment of fees. ***Perdue***, ___ U.S. at ___, 130 S.Ct. at 1674-75; *see* ***Gray v. Bostic***, 613 F.3d 1035, 1044-45 (11th Cir.2010).

(b) Reduction. A reduction is a downward adjustment of a fee award. The lodestar amount can be reduced to reflect results that are far below expectations. *See* ***Bankston v. Illinois***, 60 F.3d 1249, 1256 (7th Cir. 1995); *see, e.g.*, ***Lohman v. Duryea Borough***, 574 F.3d 163, 167-69 (3d Cir.2009) (court reduced fee award when P rejected $75,000 settlement offer during trial but recovered only $12,205 from jury). If the actual recovery is less than what was claimed, the court cannot, however, mechanically reduce the lodestar amount by the percentage difference between the amount recovered and the amount claimed. ***Cole v. Wodziak***, 169 F.3d 486, 487 (7th Cir.1999). For example, if the plaintiff demanded $50,000 but received only $45,000, the court could not automatically reduce the lodestar amount by 10%. *Id.* If the actual recovery is a nominal amount (e.g., $1), the court can abandon the lodestar method and choose an appropriate fee using other means. *See* ***Farrar v. Hobby***, 506 U.S. 103, 114-15 (1992); ***Hensley***, 461 U.S. at 436-37. If abandoning the lodestar method, the court should consider the following factors: (1) the difference between the actual recovery and the recovery sought, (2) the significance of the legal issues on which the plaintiff prevailed, and (3) the public purpose served by the litigation. *See* ***Cartwright v. Stamper***, 7 F.3d 106, 109 (7th Cir.1993). If those factors indicate the victory is purely technical, a low fee or no fee should be awarded. *Id.*; *see* ***Farrar***, 506 U.S. at 117-18 (O'Connor, J., concurring).

NOTE

The proportionality of damages to attorney fees, and any reduction of a fee award based on proportionality, involves multiple concepts. See ***Anderson v. AB Painting & Sandblasting Inc.***, *578 F.3d 542, 544-45 (7th Cir.2009). On one hand, if a plaintiff brings a relatively small claim, recovers the small amount of damages that were claimed, and then seeks a disproportionate amount of attorney fees, the fee amount should not be calculated proportionally to the damages recovered—in these circumstances, measuring the fees against the damages recovered does not help to determine whether the fees are reasonable. See id. at 545-46. That is, reducing a fee amount to make it proportional to the small amount of damages claimed and recovered is not appropriate. See id. But on the other hand, if the plaintiff brings a claim, recovers only a small percentage of the damages claimed, and then seeks a disproportionate amount of attorney fees, the fee amount may be reduced to reflect results that are far below expectations. See* ***Cole***, *169 F.3d at 489. But see* ***Anderson***, *578 F.3d at 545 (reduction of a fee award based on P recovering only small percentage of claimed damages is "losing favor").*

(2) *Johnson* factors. When considering whether to enhance or reduce the lodestar amount, the court generally considers the following 12 ***Johnson*** factors.

(a) The time and labor required. ***Kerr v. Screen Extras Guild, Inc.***, 526 F.2d 67, 70 (9th Cir. 1975); ***Johnson v. Georgia Highway Express, Inc.***, 488 F.2d 714, 717 (5th Cir.1974).

(b) The novelty and difficulty of the issues. ***Kerr***, 526 F.2d at 70; ***Johnson***, 488 F.2d at 718. But this factor generally cannot be used to increase the lodestar amount because it is presumed to be reflected in the number of billable hours recorded by the attorney. ***Blum***, 465 U.S. at 898; *see* ***Delaware Valley***, 478 U.S. at 565; ***Van Gerwen***, 214 F.3d at 1045 n.2.

(c) The skill required to perform the legal service properly. ***Kerr***, 526 F.2d at 70; ***Johnson***, 488 F.2d at 718.

(d) The loss of other employment in taking the case. ***Kerr***, 526 F.2d at 70; ***Johnson***, 488 F.2d at 718. But this factor generally cannot be used to increase the lodestar amount because it is presumed to be reflected in the attorney's reasonable hourly rate. *See* ***Heidtman v. County of El Paso***, 171 F.3d 1038, 1043 (5th Cir.1999).

(e) The customary fee. ***Kerr***, 526 F.2d at 70; ***Johnson***, 488 F.2d at 718. An attorney's customary fee usually reflects a variety of expenses, such as fees for support staff, travel and meal expenses, and other overhead. *See* ***Calderon v. Witvoet***, 112 F.3d 275, 276 (7th Cir.1997) (meal and travel expenses reimbursable as part of attor-

ney's bill for professional services); ***Herold v. Hajoca Corp.***, 864 F.2d 317, 322 (4th Cir.1988) (paralegal and law-clerk time is included within term "attorney fee"); *see, e.g.*, ***LULAC v. Roscoe ISD***, 119 F.3d 1228, 1234-35 (5th Cir. 1997) (for community at issue, attorney's fee reflected paralegal and law-clerk fees).

(f) Whether the fee is fixed or contingent. ***Kerr***, 526 F.2d at 70; ***Johnson***, 488 F.2d at 718. However, this factor is likely no longer a valid consideration for enhancement or reduction. *See* ***City of Burlington v. Dague***, 505 U.S. 557, 567 (1992) (contingent fee cannot be used as risk factor to increase attorney fees under fee-shifting statute); ***Bywaters***, 670 F.3d at 1232 & n.7 (contingent fee cannot be used to reduce attorney fees under fee-shifting statute); ***Pickett***, 664 F.3d at 645 (same); ***Van Gerwen***, 214 F.3d at 1045 n.2 (under ***Burlington***, contingent fee cannot be considered as factor for adjusting amount of attorney fees). Fees under a contingency-fee agreement and a fee-shifting statute are distinct; thus, a contingent fee cannot influence the determination of a reasonable hourly rate. *See* ***Pickett***, 664 F.3d at 642; *see also* ***Venegas v. Mitchell***, 495 U.S. 82, 90 (1990) (fee-shifting statute controls what losing party must pay prevailing party, but it does not control what prevailing P must pay her attorney).

(g) The time limits imposed by the client or the circumstances. ***Kerr***, 526 F.2d at 70; ***Johnson***, 488 F.2d at 718.

(h) The amount of money involved in the litigation and the result obtained. ***Kerr***, 526 F.2d at 70; ***Johnson***, 488 F.2d at 718. But this factor generally cannot be used to increase the lodestar amount because it is presumed to be reflected in the attorney's reasonable hourly rate. ***Blum***, 465 U.S. at 900; *see* ***Delaware Valley***, 478 U.S. at 565; ***Bywaters***, 670 F.3d at 1230-31; ***Van Gerwen***, 214 F.3d at 1045 n.2.

(i) The attorney's experience, reputation, and ability. ***Kerr***, 526 F.2d at 70; ***Johnson***, 488 F.2d at 718-19. But this factor generally cannot be used to increase the lodestar amount because it is presumed to be reflected in the attorney's reasonable hourly rate. ***Blum***, 465 U.S. at 899; *see* ***Delaware Valley***, 478 U.S. at 565; ***Van Gerwen***, 214 F.3d at 1045 n.2.

(j) The undesirability of the case. ***Kerr***, 526 F.2d at 70; ***Johnson***, 488 F.2d at 719.

(k) The nature and length of the attorney's professional relationship with the client. ***Kerr***, 526 F.2d at 70; ***Johnson***, 488 F.2d at 719.

(*l*) Fee awards in similar cases. ***Kerr***, 526 F.2d at 70; ***Johnson***, 488 F.2d at 719; *see* ***Thorne v. Welk Inv.***, 197 F.3d 1205, 1213 (8th Cir.1999) (court must consider awards in comparable cases if requested fees are significantly higher than normal).

3. Multiple-defendant cases. After determining the lodestar amount and any adjustments, the court may need to consider apportionment of the fees. In cases in which the plaintiffs have prevailed over more than one defendant, the court must determine whether the fees should be run jointly and severally against the defendants or, if not, what portion of the award each defendant should bear. ***Torres-Rivera v. O'Neill-Cancel***, 524 F.3d 331, 337 (1st Cir.2008). If the fees are apportioned by the court, the fees may be divided equally, divided relative to liability, or divided based on time reasonably expended against each defendant. *Id.*; *see* ***Nash v. Chandler***, 848 F.2d 567, 573 (5th Cir.1988).

§5.2 Common-fund cases. In common-fund cases—when the attorney fees and the client's award come from the same source—the fees are generally based on a percentage of the client's award rather than the lodestar method. ***Gunter v. Ridgewood Energy Corp.***, 223 F.3d 190, 195 n.1 (3d Cir.2000); *see* ***Powers v. Eichen***, 229 F.3d 1249, 1256 (9th Cir.2000) (court has discretion to use either lodestar method or percentage-of-the-fund method in common-fund cases); ***Goldberger v. Integrated Res.***, 209 F.3d 43, 50 (2d Cir.2000) (same); ***Petrovic v. Amoco Oil Co.***, 200 F.3d 1140, 1157 (8th Cir.1999) (same); ***U.S. v. 8.0 Acres of Land***, 197 F.3d 24, 33 (1st Cir.1999) (same); ***Gottlieb v. Barry***, 43 F.3d 474, 482-83 (10th Cir.1994) (same); ***Camden I Condo. Ass'n v. Dunkle***, 946 F.2d 768, 774 (11th Cir. 1991) (percentage-of-the-fund method should be used in common-fund cases). *See generally* ***Shaw v. Toshiba Am. Info. Sys.***, 91 F.Supp.2d 942, 963-64 (E.D.Tex.2000) (trend among federal courts is toward percentage-of-the-fund method); Report of the Third Circuit Task Force, Oct. 8, 1985, *Court Awarded Attorney Fees*, 108 F.R.D. at 255-58 (describing lodestar method as "cumbersome, enervating and often surrealistic process of preparing and evaluating fee

petitions"). The Seventh Circuit has taken the approach that courts in common-fund cases should award attorneys the market rate for legal services, considering the risk of nonpayment and the normal rate of compensation in the market at the time. ***In re Synthroid Mktg. Litig.***, 264 F.3d 712, 718 (7th Cir.2001).

1. Setting fee award. If a court opts for the percentage method, it must find an appropriate percentage of the fund to be awarded as fees. *See, e.g.*, ***Petrovic***, 200 F.3d at 1157 (24% was reasonable); ***8.0 Acres of Land***, 197 F.3d at 33 (23% was reasonable). The Ninth Circuit has indicated that 25% is an appropriate "benchmark" award. ***Six Mexican Workers v. Arizona Citrus Growers***, 904 F.2d 1301, 1311 (9th Cir.1990). *But see* ***Goldberger***, 209 F.3d at 51-53 (expressing concern over use of "benchmarks" in common-fund cases and upholding district court's award). When setting the fee award, the district court should consider the following factors: (1) the size of the fund created and the number of persons benefited, (2) the presence or absence of substantial objections by members of the class to the settlement terms or fees requested, (3) the skill and efficiency of the attorneys involved, (4) the complexity and duration of the litigation, (5) the risk of nonpayment, (6) the amount of time devoted to the case by the plaintiffs' attorney, and (7) the awards in similar cases. ***Gunter***, 223 F.3d at 195 n.1; ***Goldberger***, 209 F.3d at 50.

2. Checking fee award. A number of circuits encourage the district court to check the percentage award by comparing it to a fee calculated using the lodestar method. ***In re Rite Aid Corp. Secs. Litig.***, 396 F.3d 294, 300 (3d Cir.2005); ***Goldberger***, 209 F.3d at 50; *e.g.*, ***Petrovic***, 200 F.3d at 1157.

§5.3 Substantial-benefit cases. In shareholder derivative suits, called "substantial benefit" cases, the lodestar method is the appropriate method for calculating attorney-fee awards. *See* ***Rosenbaum v. MacAllister***, 64 F.3d 1439, 1447 (10th Cir.1995); ***Edelman v. PSI Assocs. II, Inc.***, 147 F.R.D. 217, 221 n.7 (C.D.Cal.1993).

§5.4 Public-interest litigation. Attorney fees in public-interest litigation are calculated like other attorney fees.

1. Public-interest lawyers. Fee awards to public-interest lawyers or those in private practice who donate their services to a public-interest organization are calculated the same way as fee awards to lawyers in private practice. ***Ramos v. Lamm***, 713 F.2d 546, 551 (10th Cir.1983); *see* ***Board of Trs. of the Hotel & Rest. Empls. v. JPR, Inc.***, 136 F.3d 794, 808 (D.C.Cir.1998) (attorney who charges discounted rate for public-spirited reasons may still receive award of fees at market rates).

2. Payment from public funds. Fee awards from public funds should not be reduced simply because they are to be paid from taxes. ***Ramos***, 713 F.2d at 552.

§5.5 Nontaxable expenses. A claim for attorney fees may include related expenses that are not taxable as costs, as long as those expenses are recoverable under the governing law. FRCP 54(d)(2)(A); *see* 1993 Notes to FRCP 54 at ¶3, p. 1223, this book; *see also* FRCP 23(h) (recovery of nontaxable costs in class actions). See "Amount," §4.3, p. 753.

§6. RESPONSE

Subject to FRCP 23(h), the court, on request, must allow an opportunity for adversary submissions on a motion for attorney fees in accordance with FRCP 43(c) or 78. FRCP 54(d)(2)(C); *see* FRCP 23(h)(2) (class member or party from whom payment is sought may object to motion). The response allows a party opposing a motion for attorney fees to present issues evaluating the legal services that are the basis for the fees. ***New Windsor Volunteer Ambulance Corps, Inc. v. Meyers***, 442 F.3d 101, 116 (2d Cir.2006); 1993 Notes to FRCP 54 at ¶10, p. 1224, this book. If the party opposing the motion attempts to rebut the request for attorney fees, it should attach an affidavit to its response that is as precise as the affidavit attached to the motion. ***National Ass'n of Concerned Veterans v. Secretary of Def.***, 675 F.2d 1319, 1326 (D.C.Cir.1982).

§7. HEARING

§7.1 Necessity of hearing. Generally, the court is not required to conduct a hearing on attorney fees. *See* ***DeJesus v. Banco Popular***, 951 F.2d 3, 7 (1st Cir.1991); ***Carey v. Crescenzi***, 923 F.2d 18, 22 (2d Cir.1991); ***Norman***

v. Housing Auth. of Montgomery, 836 F.2d 1292, 1304 (11th Cir.1988); *see, e.g.*, FRCP 23(h)(3) (court may hold hearing on motion for attorney fees in class action). *But see* ***Wulf v. City of Wichita***, 883 F.2d 842, 875-76 (10th Cir. 1989) (appellate court remanded to district court to conduct evidentiary hearing to determine appropriate amount of attorney fees). But when there are factual disputes (e.g., whether the plaintiff is a prevailing party) or when the court raises issues based on its independent review of the record, an evidentiary hearing may be necessary. *See* ***Pickett v. Sheridan Health Care Ctr.***, 664 F.3d 632, 652 (7th Cir.2011); ***Herrera v. Valentine***, 653 F.2d 1220, 1233 (8th Cir.1981); ***Henson v. Columbus Bank & Trust Co.***, 651 F.2d 320, 329-30 (5th Cir.1981). An evidentiary hearing may also be necessary in a common-fund case. ***In re Fine Paper Antitrust Litig.***, 751 F.2d 562, 584 (3d Cir.1984).

1. Local rules. The court may establish special procedures to resolve fee-related issues without extensive evidentiary hearings. FRCP 54(d)(2)(D); *see* Hirsch & Sheehey, *Awarding Attorneys' Fees & Managing Fee Litigation*, at 105-16 (methods for dealing with fee applications and hearings).

2. Referral to magistrate. The court may refer a motion for attorney fees to a magistrate judge under FRCP 72(b) as if it were a dispositive pretrial matter. FRCP 54(d)(2)(D); *see also* FRCP 23(h)(4) (court may refer issue of attorney fees in class action to magistrate).

3. Referral to special master. The court may refer issues relating to the value of services to a special master under FRCP 53 without regard to the limitations of FRCP 53(a)(1). FRCP 54(d)(2)(D); *see also* FRCP 23(h)(4) (court may refer issue of attorney fees in class action to special master).

§7.2 Order of proof. The court may determine issues of liability for fees before receiving evidence on the value of the services for which liability is imposed by the court. FRCP 54(d)(2)(C).

§8. RULING

§8.1 No separate document. A separate document is not required for an order imposing attorney fees. FRCP 58(a)(3); 2002 Notes to FRCP 54 at ¶1, p. 1223, this book.

§8.2 Findings. The court must make findings of fact and conclusions of law. FRCP 54(d)(2)(C); *see* FRCP 52(a). The court should provide a reasonably specific explanation for all aspects of a fee determination. ***Perdue v. Kenny A.***, ___ U.S. ___, 130 S.Ct. 1662, 1676 (2010); ***Pickett v. Sheridan Health Care Ctr.***, 664 F.3d 632, 651 (7th Cir. 2011); ***Adcock-Ladd v. Secretary of Treasury***, 227 F.3d 343, 349 (6th Cir.2000); *see* ***Van Gerwen v. Guarantee Mut. Life Co.***, 214 F.3d 1041, 1045 (9th Cir.2000) (any adjustment should be supported by specific evidence on record and detailed findings by court); *see also* FRCP 23(h)(3) (court must find facts and state legal conclusions on motion for attorney fees in class action). A fee award may be vacated and remanded for reassessment if the district court's explanation for granting the fees is inadequate. ***Ferland v. Conrad Credit Corp.***, 244 F.3d 1145, 1151 (9th Cir.2001).

1. Enhancement. The court should provide a reasonably specific explanation if it orders an enhanced award. ***Perdue***, ___ U.S. at ___, 130 S.Ct. at 1676; *see, e.g.*, ***Pennsylvania v. Delaware Valley Citizens' Council for Clean Air***, 478 U.S. 546, 568 (1986) (because district court enhanced lodestar amount without findings of fact, Supreme Court reversed statutory attorney fees).

2. Reduction. The court should provide a reasonably specific explanation if it orders an award lower than what was proposed and documented by the party awarded attorney fees. *See* ***Norman v. Housing Auth. of Montgomery***, 836 F.2d 1292, 1304 (11th Cir.1988); *see, e.g.*, ***Ferland***, 244 F.3d at 1149 (court discounted hourly rate but did not explain why it allowed particular excessive hours). The court may be able to reduce the number of hours by a lump sum, rather than evaluating every entry, as a "practical means of trimming fat" from an inadequately documented petition. ***Tomazzoli v. Sheedy***, 804 F.2d 93, 98 (7th Cir.1986); *see also* ***Ferland***, 244 F.3d at 1149 ("meat-axe approach" is appropriate in some circumstances).

§9. APPELLATE REVIEW

§9.1 Extending time to file notice of appeal. A timely motion for attorney fees under FRCP 54(d)(2) does not automatically extend the time to file a notice of appeal. *See* FRCP 58(e); FRAP 4(a)(4)(A)(iii); *see also* ***Shales v.***

General Chauffeurs, Sales Drivers & Helpers Local Un., 557 F.3d 746, 748 (7th Cir.2009) (tolling of appellate deadline is determined by filing of motion, not by decision that motion has merit). If, however, the motion for attorney fees is timely filed and no notice of appeal has been filed and become effective, the court may order that the motion for attorney fees has the same effect as a timely motion under FRCP 59 and may extend the time to file an appeal under FRAP 4(a)(4). FRCP 58(e); *see* FRAP 4(a)(4)(A)(iii); *see, e.g.*, ***Yost v. Stout***, 607 F.3d 1239, 1242-43 (10th Cir. 2010) (when P filed motion challenging denial of attorney fees under FRCP 59(e), appellate deadline was not tolled even though court construed motion under FRCP 54(d) because court had not exercised discretion to extend time to file notice of appeal under FRCP 58).

§9.2 Standard of review. A district court's ultimate decision to award attorney fees is reviewed for abuse of discretion. ***Pickett v. Sheridan Health Care Ctr.***, 664 F.3d 632, 639 (7th Cir.2011); ***In re Nortel Networks Corp. Secs. Litig.***, 539 F.3d 129, 134 (2d Cir.2008); ***Bailey v. Mississippi***, 407 F.3d 684, 686 (5th Cir.2005); ***Gettings v. Building Laborers Local 310 Fringe Benefits Fund***, 349 F.3d 300, 309 (6th Cir.2003). However, any statutory interpretation or other legal conclusion that provides a basis for the award is reviewed de novo. ***Center for Biological Diversity v. Norton***, 262 F.3d 1077, 1080 (10th Cir.2001); ***Ferland v. Conrad Credit Corp.***, 244 F.3d 1145, 1147-48 (9th Cir.2001); ***Ellis v. University of Kan. Med. Ctr.***, 163 F.3d 1186, 1193 (10th Cir.1998); *see* ***Dearmore v. City of Garland***, 519 F.3d 517, 520 (5th Cir.2008) (prevailing-party status under fee-shifting statutes is reviewed de novo).

D. TAXABLE COSTS

§1. GENERAL

§1.1 Rules. 28 U.S.C. §§1920-1931; FRCP 54(d)(1), 58(e).

§1.2 Purpose. Taxable costs—that is, costs other than attorney fees—are awarded to the prevailing party as a matter of course, unless a federal statute, the FRCPs, or the court provides otherwise. FRCP 54(d)(1); *see* ***Pacheco v. Mineta***, 448 F.3d 783, 793 (5th Cir.2006). The procedure to secure an award of costs involves the following steps: (1) the court awards an unspecified amount of costs in the judgment, (2) the prevailing party files a bill of costs with the clerk, about which there may or may not be disagreement, (3) the clerk taxes costs, and (4) if necessary, the parties ask the court to retax costs.

§1.3 Timetable & forms. Timetable, Appeal of Civil Trial, p. 1591; *O'Connor's Federal Civil Forms* (2012), FORMS 9D.

§1.4 Other references. 10 Wright, Miller & Kane, *Federal Practice & Procedure 3d* §§2667, 2679 (1998 & Supp.2012); 10 *Moore's Federal Practice 3d* §§54.100-54.105 (2012); 1 Childress & Davis, *Federal Standards of Review 4th* §4.15 (2010 & Supp.2011); 10 Miller, *Cyclopedia of Federal Procedure 3d* §38.54 (1991 & Supp.1996); Annotation, *Taxation of Costs Associated with Videotaped Depositions Under 28 U.S.C.A. §1920 & Rule 54(d) of Federal Rules of Civil Procedure*, 156 ALR Fed. 311 (1999 & Supp.2012-13).

§2. TAXABLE COSTS

§2.1 Taxable costs under 28 U.S.C. §1920. 28 U.S.C. §1920 lists the taxable costs that can be awarded to a prevailing party. If the parties agree to share taxable costs, the cost-sharing agreement is controlling over §1920. *See, e.g.*, ***In re Ricoh Co., Ltd. Patent Litig.***, 661 F.3d 1361, 1365-67 (Fed.Cir.2011) (database that was used as means for document production was taxable under §1920(4), but parties' agreement to share costs of database was controlling). The following items are designated as taxable costs under §1920:

1. Clerk & marshal fees. Taxable costs include fees of the clerk and marshal. 28 U.S.C. §1920(1); *see* 28 U.S.C. §1921 (listing marshal's fees that are taxable as costs); ***Rangolan v. County of Nassau***, 370 F.3d 239, 250 (2d Cir.2004) (not all marshal's fees are taxable as costs; only those expressly listed in §1921 can be taxed as costs); *see also* ***Craftsmen Limousine, Inc. v. Ford Motor Co.***, 579 F.3d 894, 898 (8th Cir.2009) (some courts have allowed pro hac vice costs as fees of clerk).

2. Recorded-transcript fees. Taxable costs include fees for a printed or electronically recorded transcript "necessarily obtained" for use in the case, including both trial and deposition transcripts. 28 U.S.C. §1920(2); ***Manildra Milling Corp. v. Ogilvie Mills, Inc.***, 76 F.3d 1178, 1184 (Fed.Cir.1996); ***Coats v. Penrod Drilling Corp.***, 5 F.3d 877, 891 (5th Cir.1993), *reh'g granted*, 20 F.3d 614 (5th Cir.1994), *reinstated in relevant part*, 61 F.3d 1113 (5th Cir.1995); *see also* ***U.S. v. Kolesar***, 313 F.2d 835, 837-38 (5th Cir.1963) (costs incurred in obtaining copies of deposition transcripts recoverable). The costs of the original deposition and one copy are recoverable. *See* ***Fogleman v. ARAMCO***, 920 F.2d 278, 285 (5th Cir.1991). It is not necessary that the deposition transcript be used at trial; it is enough if the party thought the transcript was reasonably necessary when the deposition was taken. ***Manildra***, 76 F.3d at 1184; ***Coats***, 5 F.3d at 891; *see, e.g.*, ***In re Baby Food Antitrust Litig.***, 166 F.3d 112, 138 (3d Cir.1999) (court permitted taxation of costs for depositions used in deciding summary-judgment motions); *see also* ***Sea Coast Foods, Inc. v. Lu-Mar Lobster & Shrimp, Inc.***, 260 F.3d 1054, 1061 (9th Cir.2001) (deposition costs recoverable even if not used at trial). Section 1920(2) does not include the cost of summarizing depositions. ***Zuill v. Shanahan***, 80 F.3d 1366, 1371 (9th Cir.1996).

3. Fees for videotaped depositions. Taxable costs include fees for a videotaped deposition, including the printed or electronically recorded transcripts, if both the videotaped deposition and the transcript were necessarily obtained for use in the litigation. ***In re Ricoh Co., Ltd. Patent Litig.***, 661 F.3d at 1370; ***Craftsmen Limousine***, 579 F.3d at 897-98; ***Little v. Mitsubishi Motors N. Am., Inc.***, 514 F.3d 699, 701-02 (7th Cir.2008); ***Cherry v. Champion Int'l***, 186 F.3d 442, 449 (4th Cir.1999); ***Tilton v. Capital Cities/ABC, Inc.***, 115 F.3d 1471, 1477-78 (10th Cir.1997); ***Morrison v. Reichhold Chems., Inc.***, 97 F.3d 460, 464-65 (11th Cir.1996); ***Eolas Techs. v. Adobe Sys.***, No. 6:09-CV-446 (E.D.Tex.2012) (slip op.; 7-19-12); *see* 28 U.S.C. §1920(2); FRCP 30(b)(3); *see also* Annotation, *Taxation of Costs Associated with Videotaped Depositions*, 156 ALR Fed. at 323 (some courts allow costs associated with videotaped depositions to be taxed under 28 U.S.C. §1920 and FRCP 54(d)). *But see* ***Mota v. University of Tex. Houston Health Sci. Ctr.***, 261 F.3d 512, 529-30 (5th Cir.2001) (no provision in §1920 allows recovery of costs for videotaped deposition; applying pre-2008 version of §1920).

NOTE

In 2008, 28 U.S.C. §1920(2) was amended to allow fees "for printed or electronically recorded transcripts." This phrase replaced the allowance for fees "of the court reporter for … the stenographic transcript." It is unclear whether the amendment was intended to allow for the recovery of costs for only a stenographic transcription or a videotaping or for the recovery of both. Compare ***Chism v. New Holland N. Am., Inc.***, *No. 2:07CV00150 (E.D.Ark.2010) (slip op.; 5-13-10) (phrase "electronically recorded transcripts" includes videotaped depositions, and based on addition of "or" to statutory language, costs can be recovered for either stenographic transcription or videotaping, but not both), and* ***Thomas v. Newton***, *No. 4:07CV556 (E.D.Mo. 2009) (slip op.; 6-26-09) (same), with* ***In re Ricoh Co., Ltd. Patent Litig.***, *661 F.3d at 1370 (no indication in text or history of amendment that it was intended to disallow recovery of both), and* ***Eolas Techs.***, *No. 6:09-CV-446 (slip op.) (without "either" before "printed or electronically recorded," phrase allows costs for printed and electronically recorded transcripts).*

4. Printing fees. Taxable costs include fees and disbursements for printing. 28 U.S.C. §1920(3); *see* ***Shannon v. U.S. Dept. of HUD***, 433 F.Supp. 249, 252 (E.D.Pa.1977).

5. Witness fees. Taxable costs include fees and disbursements for witnesses. 28 U.S.C. §1920(3); ***NLFC, Inc. v. Devcom Mid-Am., Inc.***, 916 F.Supp. 751, 764 (N.D.Ill.1996). The itemized fees for the witnesses should include the name, address, days in attendance, subsistence, mileage, and total cost for each witness. Expert-witness fees exceeding the standard witness fees cannot be taxed unless expressly authorized by statute. ***Tyler v. Union Oil Co.***, 304 F.3d 379, 404 & n.16 (5th Cir.2002); *see* ***Arlington Cent. Sch. Dist. Bd. of Educ. v. Murphy***, 548 U.S. 291, 300-01 (2006); ***L&W Sup. v. Acuity***, 475 F.3d 737, 739-40 (6th Cir.2007). See "Paying the Expert," ch. 6-D, §8, p. 530.

(1) Restrictions by local rule. By adopting local rules, courts can impose restrictions on the payment of fees to witnesses. For example, under some local rules, a fee cannot be paid unless the witness testifies. *See, e.g.*, Local Rules N.Y. (E.D. & S.D.), Rule 54.1(c)(3).

(2) Exclusion of party. Generally, a party to the case cannot collect a witness fee. ***Haroco, Inc. v. American Nat'l Bank & Trust Co.***, 38 F.3d 1429, 1442 (7th Cir.1994). *But see* ***NLFC, Inc.***, 916 F.Supp. at 764 (corporate representative who testified was entitled to witness fee). If the witness is not a named party but is a real party in interest, courts sometimes permit witness fees. *E.g.*, ***Barber v. Ruth***, 7 F.3d 636, 646 (7th Cir.1993) (witness fee granted); ***Morrison v. Alleluia Cushion Co.***, 73 F.R.D. 70, 71-72 (N.D.Miss.1976) (witness fee denied).

6. Fees for exemplification & making copies. Taxable costs include fees for exemplification and the costs of making copies of any materials when the copies are necessarily obtained for use in the case. 28 U.S.C. §1920(4); ***Rundus v. City of Dallas***, 634 F.3d 309, 316 (5th Cir.2011); *see, e.g.*, ***Crandall v. City & Cty. of Denver, Colo.***, 594 F.Supp.2d 1245, 1251-52 (D.Colo.2009) (costs for computerized presentation of exhibit were not necessary and reasonable because presentation was redundant with paper form and could have been made by less expensive means). The party seeking costs must demonstrate some connection between the costs and the litigation. *See* ***Fogleman***, 920 F.2d at 286; ***Business Sys. Eng'g v. International Bus. Machs. Corp.***, 249 F.R.D. 313, 315-16 (N.D. Ill.2008).

(1) Exemplification. An exemplification is defined as an official transcript of public record, authenticated as a true copy for use as evidence. *See Black's Law Dictionary* 653 (9th ed. 2009). But courts disagree on the actual meaning and breadth of the term "exemplification." *See* ***Race Tires Am., Inc. v. Hoosier Racing Tire Corp.***, 674 F.3d 158, 166 (3d Cir.2012). *Compare* ***Summit Tech. v. Nidek Co.***, 435 F.3d 1371, 1376-77 (Fed.Cir.2006) (fees denied for costs of computer animations, videos, PowerPoint presentations, and graphic illustrations), ***Coats***, 5 F.3d at 891 (fees denied for "blow-ups" used at trial), *and* ***Romero v. City of Pomona***, 883 F.2d 1418, 1427-28 (9th Cir. 1989) (fees denied for expert's research expenses incurred in preparing exhibits), *with* ***Cefalu v. Village of Elk Grove***, 211 F.3d 416, 427-28 (7th Cir.2000) (under appropriate circumstances, fees may be allowed for multimedia presentations).

(2) Making copies. Copying costs for discovery, documents filed in the court, and exhibits used at trial are generally recoverable; however, costs for multiple copies, attorney correspondence, and other similar items are not recoverable. *See* ***Fogleman***, 920 F.2d at 286; *see, e.g.*, ***Francisco v. Verizon S., Inc.***, 272 F.R.D. 436, 445 (E.D. Va.2011) (D could recover costs for only one set of copies when D did not explain why it needed two sets); *see also* ***Haroco***, 38 F.3d at 1441 (extra copies for attorney's convenience are not compensable); ***NLFC, Inc.***, 916 F.Supp. at 763 (same).

(a) Types of copies.

[1] Paper copies. The term "copies," which is often used to refer to photocopies or xerox copies, has been interpreted to allow for the recovery of photocopying costs under §1920(4). ***Race Tires Am.***, 674 F.3d at 166. But the party seeking copying costs does not need to identify every xerox copy used during the legal proceedings. ***Fogleman***, 920 F.2d at 286.

[2] Electronic copies. The term "materials" in §1920(4) signifies that copying costs are not limited to paper copying. ***Race Tires Am.***, 674 F.3d at 166; ***Eolas Techs.***, No. 6:09-CV-446 (slip op.). For example, costs for scanning and converting native files to an agreed-on format have been allowed as costs for making copies. ***Race Tires Am.***, 674 F.3d at 167.

NOTE

Courts disagree on the extent to which §1920(4) covers costs incurred for e-discovery vendors who assist in the collection, processing, and production of ESI. Compare ***Race Tires Am.***, *674 F.3d at 167-69 (fees for e-discovery vendor limited to scanning of documents, conversion of native files to TIFF, and transfer of VHS tapes to DVD; vendor services for locating, collecting,*

and reviewing ESI are not taxable), and ***Eolas Techs.****, No. 6:09-CV-446 (slip op.) (statute is not so broad as to cover general electronic-discovery costs that come before copying or scanning materials), with* ***In re Ricoh Co., Ltd. Patent Litig.****, 661 F.3d at 1365-67 (fees for electronic-document database that was used as means for document production would have been recoverable under §1920(4) but for parties' agreement to share costs of database).*

(b) Itemizing copying costs. When itemizing copying costs, a party should identify what was copied and why the copying was necessary for the case; otherwise, the court can reduce or deny the costs. *See* 28 U.S.C. §1920; *see, e.g.*, ***U.S. v. Merritt Meridian Constr. Corp.***, 95 F.3d 153, 173 (2d Cir.1996) (costs for photocopying were reduced when P did not itemize costs or explain why they were necessary); ***Eolas Techs.***, No. 6:09-CV-446 (slip op.) (some costs for photocopying were reduced by 50% when D provided only limited details about costs); *see also* ***Northbrook Excess & Surplus Ins. v. Procter & Gamble Co.***, 924 F.2d 633, 643 (7th Cir.1991) (costs of $50,000 for photocopying were allowed even though P did not itemize costs because P's documentation established that copies were made for case and billed in normal course of business).

7. Docket fees. Taxable costs include docket fees under 28 U.S.C. §1923. 28 U.S.C. §1920(5).

8. Compensation of experts & interpreters. Taxable costs include compensation of court-appointed experts and interpreters, as well as salaries, fees, expenses, and costs associated with special interpretation services under 28 U.S.C. §1828. 28 U.S.C. §1920(6). Fees for mediators are not included. ***Cook Children's Med. Ctr. v. New England PPO Plan of Gen. Consol. Mgmt.***, 491 F.3d 266, 277 (5th Cir.2007); ***Brisco-Wade v. Carnahan***, 297 F.3d 781, 782 (8th Cir.2002); ***Sea Coast Foods***, 260 F.3d at 1061.

NOTE

In 2012, the Supreme Court resolved a disagreement over whether "interpreters" in §1920(6) included translators (i.e., people who translate documents but not live speech). ***Taniguchi v. Kan Pac. Saipan, Ltd.****, ___ U.S. ___, 132 S.Ct. 1997, 2000-01 (2012). The Court held that because "interpreter" means a person who translates orally, §1920(6) is limited to the cost of oral translation and does not include document translation.* ***Taniguchi****, ___ U.S. at ___, 132 S.Ct. at 2000.*

§2.2 Other recoverable costs. The items listed in 28 U.S.C. §1920 are not the only items that can qualify as taxable costs. Additional costs may be recoverable under case law and rules, including the following:

1. Ad litem fees. Ad litem fees may be awarded as costs if they do not include fees for work that the ad litem performed as an attorney. ***Gaddis v. U.S.***, 381 F.3d 444, 459 (5th Cir.2004); ***Hull v. U.S.***, 53 F.3d 1125, 1128 (10th Cir.1995); ***Kollsman v. Cohen***, 996 F.2d 702, 706 (4th Cir.1993).

2. Fees under state statutes. Additional items of recoverable costs authorized by state statutes may be awarded if they do not conflict with FRCP 54(d)(1). *See* ***Garcia v. Wal-Mart Stores***, 209 F.3d 1170, 1176-77 (10th Cir.2000) (state statute that shifts actual costs applies to the extent that it does not conflict with FRCP 54(d)(1) or any federal statute authorizing costs); ***Abrams v. Lightolier, Inc.***, 50 F.3d 1204, 1223 (3d Cir.1995) (same).

3. Fees to empanel jury. The costs to empanel a jury can be assessed against an attorney who does not inform the court that the parties have settled. ***Sally Beauty Co. v. Beautyco, Inc.***, 372 F.3d 1186, 1190 (10th Cir. 2004). This assessment is not a sanction and thus does not require proof of the attorney's "bad faith." *Id.* at 1189.

4. Travel expenses for out-of-district counsel. The travel expenses and costs of counsel outside the forum may be recovered if a party is unable to obtain counsel within a forum (i.e., a local attorney refused to represent the party). *See* ***Hahnemann Univ. Hosp. v. All Shore, Inc.***, 514 F.3d 300, 312 (3d Cir.2008).

§2.3 Costs that are not recoverable.

1. Litigation expenses. Litigants sometimes assume that taxable costs include all litigation-related expenses (e.g., expenses for retaining experts). But general expenses of litigation are not taxable as costs unless they

are listed in 28 U.S.C. §1920. *See* ***Sea Coast Foods, Inc. v. Lu-Mar Lobster & Shrimp, Inc.***, 260 F.3d 1054, 1060-61 (9th Cir.2001); *see also* ***In re Williams Secs. Litig.-WCG Subclass***, 558 F.3d 1144, 1147-48 (10th Cir.2009) (costs for materials that are merely for attorney's convenience are not taxable).

2. Expenses for electronic legal research. Expenses for electronic legal research are categorized as attorney fees and are not taxable as costs. *See, e.g.*, ***Haroco, Inc. v. American Nat'l Bank & Trust Co.***, 38 F.3d 1429, 1440-41 (7th Cir.1994) (district court awarded costs for computerized-legal-research fees but no attorney fees; circuit court reduced costs because fees for computerized legal research are considered attorney fees and not costs). See "Amount," ch. 9-C, §4.3, p. 753.

§3. JUDGMENT FOR COSTS

§3.1 Prevailing party. Under FRCP 54(d)(1), a prevailing party must be awarded costs, unless a federal statute, the FRCPs, or the court provides otherwise. ***Byers v. Dallas Morning News, Inc.***, 209 F.3d 419, 430 (5th Cir. 2000); ***Smith v. Southeastern Pa. Transp. Auth.***, 47 F.3d 97, 99 (3d Cir.1995); *see, e.g.*, ***Sequa Corp. v. Cooper***, 245 F.3d 1036, 1037-38 (8th Cir.2001) (even though D was not considered prevailing party, court awarded costs based on "court orders otherwise" language when P voluntarily dismissed suit without prejudice); *see also* ***Quan v. Computer Sci. Corp.***, 623 F.3d 870, 888 (9th Cir.2010) (to "provide otherwise" under FRCP 54(d)(1), statute or rule would have to bar award of costs to prevailing party).

1. Determining prevailing party. The court must determine who qualifies as the prevailing party before awarding costs. ***Shum v. Intel Corp.***, 629 F.3d 1360, 1366 (Fed.Cir.2010); *see* ***Taniguchi v. Kan Pac. Saipan, Ltd.***, ___ U.S. ___, 132 S.Ct. 1997, 2001 (2012); *see also* ***Milton v. Des Moines***, 47 F.3d 944, 947 (8th Cir.1995) (prevailing D is one who defeats liability); 10 Wright, Miller & Kane §2667 & n.14 (if suit is dismissed, D is generally considered prevailing party). There can be only one prevailing party; FRCP 54 does not allow every party that won on some claims to be deemed a prevailing party. ***Shum***, 629 F.3d at 1367. But the prevailing party does not have to prevail on all claims. *Id.* at 1367-68; *see* ***Klein v. Grynberg***, 44 F.3d 1497, 1506-07 (10th Cir.1995). Some local rules define the prevailing party. *E.g.*, Local Rules Cal. (C.D.), Rule 54-2.1 (P is prevailing party when it recovers on entire complaint).

NOTE

Generally, the prevailing party for the purpose of attorney fees is also the prevailing party for the purpose of costs. ***Dattner v. Conagra Foods, Inc.****, 458 F.3d 98, 101 (2d Cir.2006);* ***Barber v. T.D. Williamson, Inc.****, 254 F.3d 1223, 1234 (10th Cir.2001); 10 Moore's Federal Practice 3d §54.101[3].* *See "Prevailing party," ch. 9-C, §4.2.1(1), p. 750.*

---

2. Presumption. There is a presumption that a prevailing party is entitled to an award of costs. ***Quan***, 623 F.3d at 888; ***Reger v. Nemours Found.***, 599 F.3d 285, 288 (3d Cir.2010); ***Pacheco v. Mineta***, 448 F.3d 783, 793 (5th Cir.2006); *see* ***Rangolan v. County of Nassau***, 370 F.3d 239, 254 (2d Cir.2004) (costs cannot be taxed against prevailing party).

§3.2 Who pays costs.

1. Costs against party. Generally, the court imposes costs against the party, not the attorney. ***In re Cardizem CD Antitrust Litig.***, 481 F.3d 355, 359 (6th Cir.2007).

2. Costs against attorney. An attorney who "unreasonably and vexatiously" multiplies the proceedings can be personally required to pay the excess costs, expenses, and attorney fees as sanctions. 28 U.S.C. §1927. See "Multiplying proceedings unreasonably," ch. 5-O, §3.8, p. 388.

3. Costs against United States. The court can award costs against the United States, its officers, and its agencies only to the extent permitted by law. 28 U.S.C. §2412; FRCP 54(d)(1). Whether there is a presumption in favor of costs to the prevailing party in cases involving the United States depends on the statute involved. *See, e.g.*, ***In re Turner***, 14 F.3d 637, 641 (D.C.Cir.1994) (Equal Access to Justice Act does not prevent award of costs).

4. Costs in multiparty & multidistrict suits. In multiparty or multidistrict suits, apportionment or joint-and-several liability of costs may be appropriate so that the prevailing party does not obtain double recovery for the same costs. *See* ***Ortho-McNeil Pharm. v. Mylan Labs.***, 569 F.3d 1353, 1357-58 (Fed.Cir.2009); *see, e.g.*, ***Marmo v. Tyson Fresh Meats, Inc.***, 457 F.3d 748, 764 (8th Cir.2006) (in case that had been consolidated for discovery and pretrial proceedings but proceeded to trial separately, costs were divided among 13 cases; first P to proceed to trial could not be awarded costs incurred by other Ps). For a multiparty suit before a single judge, the court has discretion to apportion payment of costs among the losing parties or to award costs jointly and severally against the losing parties. ***Ortho-McNeil Pharm.***, 569 F.3d at 1357.

§3.3 Form of judgment.

1. Blank for costs. The court awards costs in the judgment even if the amount of costs has not yet been determined by the time the judgment is entered. Sometimes, the judgment awards costs by simply stating that they are "taxed at ________," leaving a blank for the amount. *See* 10 Miller, *Cyclopedia of Federal Procedure* §38.54.

2. Silent on costs. If the judgment is silent on costs and the court has not made a contrary ruling elsewhere, there is a presumption that the prevailing party is entitled to costs. *See, e.g.*, ***Matei v. Cessna Aircraft Co.***, 35 F.3d 1142, 1148 (7th Cir.1994) (appellate court did not presume award of costs to prevailing party because district court announced on record that no costs would be awarded).

3. Denial or reduction of costs. If the court denies or reduces costs to the prevailing party, it must provide a valid reason for its decision in writing. ***Pacheco v. Mineta***, 448 F.3d 783, 794 (5th Cir.2006); ***Cantrell v. International Bhd. of Elec. Workers***, 69 F.3d 456, 459 (10th Cir.1995). See "Motion to Retax Costs," §6, p. 767.

§4. BILL OF COSTS

§4.1 Contents of bill.

After the case is resolved, the prevailing party should file a bill of costs with the clerk.

1. Form of bill. District clerks have a standard form for a bill of costs, but a party can prepare its own. *See, e.g.*, Local Rules Cal. (C.D.), Rule 54-3. See ***O'Connor's Federal Forms***, FORM 9D:2.

2. Itemized costs. The bill should contain an itemized list of allowable costs. *See* 28 U.S.C. §1920.

3. Proof of service. The bill of costs should be served on all other parties. *See* Local Rules N.Y. (E.D. & S.D.), Rule 54.1(a).

4. Affidavit. The bill of costs must be verified by an affidavit from the party, the attorney, or the party's agent. 28 U.S.C. §1924; *see* Local Rules Fla. (S.D.), Rule 7.3(a)(7); Local Rules N.Y. (E.D. & S.D.), Rule 54.1(a). The affidavit should state that (1) the costs claimed are allowed by law, are correctly stated, and were necessarily incurred in the case, and (2) the services for which fees have been charged were actually and necessarily performed. *See* 28 U.S.C. §1924; Local Rules N.Y. (E.D. & S.D.), Rule 54.1(a).

5. Exhibits. Some local rules require that the bill of costs include proof as exhibits (e.g., canceled checks or invoices for costs claimed). *E.g.*, Local Rules N.Y. (E.D. & S.D.), Rule 54.1(a).

6. Certificate of conference. Some local rules require that the bill of costs include a certificate stating that the parties have met and conferred in an effort to submit an agreed bill of costs. *E.g.*, Local Rules Tex. (E.D.), Rule CV-54(b)(2). If the parties disagree, the bill of costs should indicate the areas of agreement and disagreement. *Id.*

§4.2 Deadlines to file bill.

1. Local rules. The deadline to file a bill of costs is governed by local rules. ***S.A. Healy Co. v. Milwaukee Metro Sewerage Dist.***, 60 F.3d 305, 307 (7th Cir.1995). Most local rules require that the bill of costs be filed and served within 30 days after the entry of judgment allowing costs. *E.g.*, Local Rules Fla. (S.D.), Rule 7.3(c); Local Rules Ill. (N.D.), Rule 54.1(a); Local Rules N.Y. (E.D. & S.D.), Rule 54.1(a); *see* ***Matei v. Cessna Aircraft Co.***, 35 F.3d 1142, 1147 n.4 (7th Cir.1994). Some local rules provide for a shorter time period. *See, e.g.*, Local Rules Conn., Rule 54(a)(1)

(within 14 days after judgment becomes final due to expiration of appeal period); Local Rules Tex. (S.D.), Rule 54.2 (within 14 days after entry of judgment). Some local rules permit an extension of time. *E.g.*, Local Rules Ill. (N.D.), Rule 54.1(a).

2. Waiver. Most local rules provide that if a party does not file a bill of costs on time, it waives the recovery of costs. *See, e.g.*, Local Rules Ill. (N.D.), Rule 54.1(a) (waiver of §1920 costs); Local Rules N.Y. (E.D. & S.D.), Rule 54.1(a) (party waives costs if it does not file bill within 30 days unless good cause shown).

§4.3 Objections to bill.

1. In writing. A party's objections to the opposing party's bill of costs must be in writing. Local Rules Cal. (C.D.), Rule 54-7; *see* Local Rules N.Y. (E.D. & S.D.), Rule 54.1(b).

2. Deadline. Some local rules provide a specific deadline to file objections, while others merely state that objections must be filed before the time for taxation of costs. *See, e.g.*, Local Rules Conn., Rule 54(b) (clerk must award costs if objections are not made within 14 days after filing bill of costs); Local Rules N.Y. (E.D. & S.D.), Rule 54.1(b) (objections must be served before or at date and time scheduled for taxation); Local Rules Tex. (S.D.), Rule 54.2 (objections must be filed within seven days after filing bill of costs).

PRACTICE TIP

Once written objections have been filed, the easiest way for the parties to resolve the dispute about costs is to have a conference with the clerk before the clerk taxes the costs.

§5. CLERK TO TAX COSTS

§5.1 Clerk taxes. The clerk may tax costs after giving 14 days' notice to the parties. FRCP 54(d)(1); *see also* 2009 Notes to FRCP 54 at ¶1, p. 1222, this book (former period for clerk to tax costs on one day's notice was unrealistically short, and amended 14-day notice provides sufficient time).

§5.2 No delay of judgment. A delay in taxing costs under FRCP 54(d)(1) does not delay the entry of judgment or extend the time for appeal. FRCP 58(e). By comparison, a delay in awarding attorney fees under FRCP 54(d)(2) may extend the time to appeal if the district court enters the appropriate order. *See* FRCP 58(e). See "Extending time to file notice of appeal," ch. 9-C, §9.1, p. 760.

§5.3 Finality. If the court does not modify the clerk's determination of costs, the clerk's determination is final. A final order taxing costs can be appealed. ***LoSacco v. City of Middletown***, 71 F.3d 88, 91 (2d Cir.1995).

§6. MOTION TO RETAX COSTS

Either the prevailing party or the losing party may ask the district court to review and change costs that were awarded by the clerk. *See* FRCP 54(d)(1).

§6.1 Deadline. The deadline to challenge the clerk's assessment of costs is seven days after the clerk taxes costs. FRCP 54(d)(1). The deadline for filing and serving a motion to retax costs may be extended by the court. *See* FRCP 6(b); *see also* ***In re Paoli R.R. Yard PCB Litig.***, 221 F.3d 449, 459 (3d Cir.2000) (court may review untimely challenges because deadline for challenging costs is not jurisdictional; applying former five-day deadline).

§6.2 Grounds.

1. Prevailing party. A motion to retax costs filed by the prevailing party will generally allege that (1) the assessment of costs was too low or (2) the party was not awarded costs and believes it is entitled to an award. The prevailing party must state the specific amount of the costs to be adjusted and that (1) the adjusted costs are allowed by law, are correctly stated, and were necessarily incurred in the case and (2) the services for which fees have been charged were actually and necessarily performed. *See* 28 U.S.C. §1924.

2. Losing party. A motion to retax costs filed by the losing party will generally allege that (1) the assessment of costs was too high or the items were not properly taxable as costs or (2) based on equity, the party should not be required to pay any costs. The losing party must state the specific amount of the costs to be adjusted. The court must provide in writing a valid reason for reducing or denying costs to the prevailing party. *See* ***Cantrell v. International Bhd. of Elec. Workers***, 69 F.3d 456, 459 (10th Cir.1995).

(1) Incorrect costs. The losing party can allege that (1) the costs are not correctly stated or were not necessarily incurred in the case or (2) the services for which fees were charged were not actually and necessarily performed. *See* 28 U.S.C. §1924.

(2) Inequitable costs. To overcome the presumption that the prevailing party is entitled to costs, the losing party can allege that an award of costs is inequitable under the circumstances. ***In re Paoli R.R. Yard PCB Litig.***, 221 F.3d 449, 462-63 (3d Cir.2000); *see* ***Quan v. Computer Sci. Corp.***, 623 F.3d 870, 888 (9th Cir.2010); ***AXA Versicherung AG v. New Hampshire Ins.***, 769 F.Supp.2d 623, 625-26 (S.D.N.Y.2011).

(a) Nominal damages. An award of costs can be reduced or denied because either the prevailing party obtained only a nominal victory or the taxable costs of the litigation were disproportionate to the result achieved. ***Cantrell***, 69 F.3d at 459; *e.g.*, ***Richmond v. Southwire Co.***, 980 F.2d 518, 520 (8th Cir.1992) ($1 recovery; cost of 24 depositions denied); *see* ***Lichter Found. v. Welch***, 269 F.2d 142, 146 (6th Cir.1959) (prevailing party is prima facie entitled to costs unless judgment recovered was insignificant compared to award sought and effectively amounted to victory for losing party).

(b) Unclean hands. An award of costs can be reduced or denied because the prevailing party was obstructive, acted in bad faith during the litigation, or incurred unnecessary or unreasonably high costs. ***In re Paoli R.R. Yard PCB Litig.***, 221 F.3d at 463; ***Cantrell***, 69 F.3d at 459. The denial of costs to the prevailing party acts as a penalty for some misconduct during the course of the litigation. ***Association of Mexican-Am. Educators v. California***, 231 F.3d 572, 592 (9th Cir.2000); ***Smith v. Southeastern Pa. Transp. Auth.***, 47 F.3d 97, 99 (3d Cir.1995); ***ADM Corp. v. Speedmaster Packaging Corp.***, 525 F.2d 662, 665 (3d Cir.1975).

(c) Inability to pay. An award of costs can be reduced or denied based on the losing party's inability to pay the full amount of costs. ***Rodriguez v. Whiting Farms, Inc.***, 360 F.3d 1180, 1190 (10th Cir.2004); ***In re Paoli R.R. Yard PCB Litig.***, 221 F.3d at 463; *see* ***Rivera v. City of Chi.***, 469 F.3d 631, 635 (7th Cir.2006); *see, e.g.*, ***Cherry v. Champion Int'l***, 186 F.3d 442, 447 (4th Cir.1999) (evaluating whether nonindigent losing party had ability to satisfy bill of costs or was of such modest means that it would be unjust or inequitable to enforce award). However, a losing party's indigency or inability to pay costs does not automatically mean that an award of costs against that party is inequitable. ***In re Paoli R.R. Yard PCB Litig.***, 221 F.3d at 463; *see* ***Weaver v. Toombs***, 948 F.2d 1004, 1008 (6th Cir.1991).

3. Improper grounds. The following are generally improper grounds for a motion to retax costs:

(1) Disparity between parties' financial resources. An award of costs cannot be reduced or denied based on the disparity between the parties' financial resources (i.e., the relative wealth of the parties) if the losing party is able to pay costs. ***Reger v. Nemours Found.***, 599 F.3d 285, 289 (3d Cir.2010); ***Pion v. Liberty Dairy Co.***, 922 F.Supp. 48, 51-52 (W.D.Mich.1996); *see, e.g.*, ***In re Paoli R.R. Yard PCB Litig.***, 221 F.3d at 468 (court could not rely on comparison of wealth between Ps, many of whom were poor and living on fixed incomes, and Ds, who were multibillion-dollar corporations); *see also* ***McDonald v. Petree***, 409 F.3d 724, 732 (6th Cir.2005) (courts should ignore size of prevailing party's recovery and ability to pay its own costs).

(2) Prisoner. An award of costs cannot be reduced or denied because the losing party is an indigent prisoner. 28 U.S.C. §1915(f)(2)(A); *see* ***In re Prison Litig. Reform Act***, 105 F.3d 1131, 1138 (6th Cir.1997) (prisoner's ability to pay costs is no longer an issue; prisoner must pay fully or in accordance with payment process under statute).

(3) Good faith. An award of costs cannot be reduced or denied solely because the losing party acted in good faith. ***Pacheco v. Mineta***, 448 F.3d 783, 795 (5th Cir.2006); ***Cherry***, 186 F.3d at 446.

(4) Complexity, closeness, or delay. An award of costs cannot be reduced or denied based on the complexity, closeness, or delay of the litigation. *See* ***In re Paoli R.R. Yard PCB Litig.***, 221 F.3d at 467; ***Klein v. Grynberg***, 44 F.3d 1497, 1506-07 (10th Cir.1995). *But see* ***White & White, Inc. v. American Hosp. Sup.***, 786 F.2d 728, 730 (6th Cir.1986) (denial of costs is proper exercise of discretion in cases that are "close and difficult").

NOTE

Although the grounds of the losing party's good faith or the complexity, closeness, or delay of the litigation alone are generally improper for a motion to retax costs, they may be considered in conjunction with other grounds. See, e.g., ***Teague v. Bakker****, 35 F.3d 978, 996-97 (4th Cir. 1994) (in large class action, costs were denied when Ps had proceeded in good faith, case was close and difficult, and, considering that Ps had been defrauded by D1, taxing Ps for costs incurred by other Ds would be inequitable);* ***Moody Nat'l Bank v. GE Life & Annuity Assur. Co.****, 423 F.Supp.2d 651, 652 (S.D.Tex.2003) (costs were denied when P presented close questions of law in good faith and D's discovery tactics unnecessarily delayed case).*

§6.3 Certificate of conference. Some local rules require the motion to include a certificate of conference stating (1) that the attorney conferred with opposing counsel in good faith to resolve the issues by agreement, (2) what resulted from their conference, and (3) whether a hearing is requested. *See, e.g.*, Local Rules Fla. (S.D.), Rule 7.3(b).

§6.4 Affidavit. A motion that presents facts outside the record should be supported by an affidavit. Some local rules specifically require that an affidavit be attached to the motion. *E.g.*, Local Rules N.Y. (E.D. & S.D.), Rule 54.1(a).

§7. RESPONSE

§7.1 Deadline. There is no deadline to file a response to a motion to retax costs, but it should be filed and served as soon as possible after the motion is received.

§7.2 Grounds. The response should negate the statements in the motion as necessary.

§7.3 Affidavit. If the response relies on facts outside the record, it should be supported by an affidavit.

§8. DISTRICT COURT'S REVIEW

The district court's review of the clerk's determination of costs is reviewed de novo. ***Reger v. Nemours Found.***, 599 F.3d 285, 288 (3d Cir.2010). If a party does not challenge the clerk's assessment of costs in the district court, the party waives its right to challenge costs on appeal. *See* ***Ahlberg v. Chrysler Corp.***, 481 F.3d 630, 638 (8th Cir.2007); ***Bloomer v. United Parcel Serv.***, 337 F.3d 1220, 1220-21 (10th Cir.2003); ***Cooper v. Eagle River Mem'l Hosp., Inc.***, 270 F.3d 456, 464 (7th Cir.2001). If the district court denies or reduces an award of costs, it must make findings that explain its ruling. ***Reger***, 599 F.3d at 288; *see* ***Quan v. Computer Sci. Corp.***, 623 F.3d 870, 888 (9th Cir.2010).

§9. APPELLATE REVIEW

§9.1 Standard of review.

1. Abuse of discretion. The standard of review for the district court's award or denial of costs under FRCP 54(d)(1) is abuse of discretion. ***Cheatham v. Allstate Ins.***, 465 F.3d 578, 586 (5th Cir.2006); ***BDT Prods. v. Lexmark Int'l***, 405 F.3d 415, 417 (6th Cir.2005), *overruled on other grounds*, ***Taniguchi v. Kan Pac. Saipan, Ltd.***, ___ U.S. ___, 132 S.Ct. 1997 (2012); ***Allison v. Bank One–Denver***, 289 F.3d 1223, 1248 (10th Cir.2002); ***In re Baby Food Antitrust Litig.***, 166 F.3d 112, 138 (3d Cir.1999); ***Denzler v. Questech, Inc.***, 80 F.3d 97, 103 (4th Cir.1996); ***Milton v. Des Moines***, 47 F.3d 944, 947 (8th Cir.1995). The district court's determination of whether costs were reasonably necessary is given great deference. ***Rundus v. City of Dallas***, 634 F.3d 309, 316 (5th Cir.2011).

2. De novo. The standard of review for whether the court exceeded its statutory authority by allowing a particular item to be taxed as costs is de novo. ***SK Hand Tool Corp. v. Dresser Indus.***, 852 F.2d 936, 948 (7th Cir. 1988); *see, e.g.*, ***L&W Sup. v. Acuity***, 475 F.3d 737, 738 (6th Cir.2007) (expert fees taxed as costs).

§9.2 Error in award of costs. If the judgment does not accurately reflect the district court's decision on costs, the party objecting to the error must challenge the costs in a motion to alter or amend the judgment under FRCP 59(e). *E.g.*, ***Matei v. Cessna Aircraft Co.***, 35 F.3d 1142, 1148 (7th Cir.1994) (when judgment was silent on costs, party needed to file timely motion to alter or amend judgment instead of presuming that costs were awarded to prevailing party). This motion must be filed within 28 days after the entry of judgment. FRCP 59(e). See "Motion to Alter or Amend Judgment," ch. 10-D, p. 793.

COMMENTARIES
CHAPTER 10. POSTJUDGMENT MOTIONS
TABLE OF CONTENTS

A. GENERAL 775
B. RENEWED MOTION FOR JUDGMENT AS A MATTER OF LAW 775
§1. GENERAL 775
§2. PROCEDURAL PREREQUISITES 776
§2.1 Motion before case submitted to jury 776
§2.2 No motion before case submitted to jury 776
§2.3 No renewed motion for JMOL after judgment 776
§3. DEADLINE 776
§3.1 28-day deadline 776
§3.2 No extension 777
§3.3 Premature motion 777
§4. MOTION 778
§4.1 Form 778
§4.2 By either party 778
§4.3 In writing 778
§4.4 Grounds 778
§4.5 Request new trial 779
§4.6 Request hearing 779
§5. RESPONSE 779
§5.1 Objections 779
§5.2 Deadline 779
§6. HEARING 779
§7. RULING 779
§7.1 Written order 779
§7.2 Standard 779
§7.3 Relief 780
§8. POST-JMOL MOTION FOR NEW TRIAL 781
§9. APPELLATE REVIEW 781
§9.1 Deadline 781
§9.2 Standard of review 781
§9.3 Review under alternative motion for new trial 782
C. MOTION FOR NEW TRIAL 783
§1. GENERAL 783
§2. DEADLINE 783
§2.1 28-day deadline 783
§2.2 No extension 783
§2.3 Premature motion 784
§2.4 Amended motion 784
§3. MOTION 784
§3.1 Form 784
§3.2 In writing 784
§3.3 When required to preserve error 784
§3.4 Grounds 784
§3.5 Affidavits 785
§3.6 Request hearing 785
§4. RESPONSE 786
§4.1 Objections 786
§4.2 Deadline 786
§4.3 Affidavits 786
§5. HEARING 786
§5.1 Generally 786
§5.2 Exception 786
§6. RULING 786
§6.1 Standard 786
§6.2 Written order 786
§6.3 No deadline for order 786
§6.4 On court's initiative 787
§6.5 On party's motion 787
§6.6 Court's reasons 788
§7. STANDARD APPLIED BY DISTRICT COURT 788
§7.1 Verdict against weight of evidence 788
§7.2 Damages inadequate or excessive 788
§7.3 Trial errors 789
§7.4 Newly discovered evidence 791
§7.5 Unfair surprise 791
§8. APPELLATE REVIEW 791
§8.1 Appealability 791
§8.2 Deadline 792
§8.3 Standard of review 792
D. MOTION TO ALTER OR AMEND JUDGMENT 793
§1. GENERAL 793
§2. DEADLINE 793
§2.1 28-day deadline 793
§2.2 No extension 794
§2.3 Premature motion 794
§3. MOTION 795
§3.1 Form 795
§3.2 Grounds 795
§3.3 Affidavits 796
§3.4 Request hearing 796
§3.5 Misnomer of motions under FRCP 59(e) 796
§4. RESPONSE 796
§4.1 Objections 796
§4.2 Deadline 797
§4.3 Affidavits 797
§5. HEARING 797
§6. RULING 797
§6.1 By court 797
§6.2 Written order 797
§7. APPELLATE REVIEW 797
§7.1 Deadline 797
§7.2 Standard of review 798
E. MOTION TO ADD OR AMEND FINDINGS OF FACT 799
§1. GENERAL 799
§2. COURT'S FINDINGS 799
§2.1 Findings necessary 799
§2.2 Findings unnecessary 799
§2.3 No request for initial findings 799
§2.4 When findings should be filed 800
§2.5 Purpose of court's findings 800
§3. DEADLINE 800
§3.1 28-day deadline 800
§3.2 No extension 800
§3.3 Premature motion 801
§4. MOTION 801
§4.1 Form 801
§4.2 In writing 801
§4.3 Grounds 801
§4.4 Affidavits 802
§4.5 Request hearing 802
§4.6 With motion for new trial 802
§5. RESPONSE 802
§5.1 Objections 802
§5.2 Deadline 802
§5.3 Affidavits 802
§6. HEARING 802
§7. RULING 802
§7.1 No clear standard 802
§7.2 Written order 802
§7.3 Court should grant 802

COMMENTARIES

CHAPTER 10. POSTJUDGMENT MOTIONS

TABLE OF CONTENTS

§8. APPELLATE REVIEW 803
§8.1 Deadline 803
§8.2 Appellate procedure when findings inadequate 803
§8.3 Standard of review 803

F. MOTION FOR RELIEF FROM JUDGMENT 804

§1. GENERAL 804
§2. DEADLINE 804
§2.1 For motion 804
§2.2 To toll time for appeal 806
§3. MOTION 806
§3.1 Form 806
§3.2 In writing 806
§3.3 Sua sponte 806
§3.4 Grounds 806
§3.5 Party or representative 810
§3.6 Affidavits 811
§3.7 Request hearing 811
§3.8 Request indicative ruling 811
§4. RESPONSE 811
§4.1 Objections 811
§4.2 Deadline 811
§4.3 Affidavits 811
§5. HEARING 812
§6. RULING 812
§6.1 Written order 812
§6.2 Not without notice 812
§6.3 Court's discretion 812
§6.4 Filed during appeal 812
§7. OTHER RELIEF 812
§7.1 Clerical error 812
§7.2 Substantive error 812
§8. INDICATIVE RULING 813
§8.1 Timely motion for relief from judgment 813
§8.2 District court's ruling 814
§8.3 Notice to appellate court of indicative ruling 814
§8.4 Appellate court's ruling 815
§8.5 District court's ruling after remand 815
§8.6 Notice to appellate court of district court's ruling 815
§9. APPELLATE REVIEW 815
§9.1 Deadline 815
§9.2 Standard of review 816

G. MOTION TO EXTEND TIME TO FILE NOTICE OF APPEAL 817

§1. GENERAL 817
§2. NOTICE OF JUDGMENT 817
§3. DEADLINE TO FILE NOTICE OF APPEAL 817
§3.1 Generally 817
§3.2 Premature notice 818
§4. DEADLINE TO FILE MOTION TO EXTEND TIME 818
§4.1 Deadline for ex parte motion 818
§4.2 Deadline for motion 818
§5. MOTION 818
§5.1 Form 818
§5.2 In writing 818
§5.3 Grounds 818
§5.4 Period of delay 819
§5.5 Affidavits 819
§5.6 Request hearing 819
§5.7 File in district court 819
§5.8 Certificate of service 819
§5.9 Notice of appeal 819
§6. RESPONSE 820
§6.1 Objections 820
§6.2 Deadline 820
§6.3 Affidavits 820
§7. HEARING 820
§7.1 Need for hearing 820
§7.2 Burden 820
§8. RULING 820
§8.1 Written order 820
§8.2 Extension of time 820
§9. FILING NOTICE OF APPEAL 820
§10. APPELLATE REVIEW 820
§10.1 Standard of review 820
§10.2 Court grants motion 821
§10.3 Court denies motion 821

H. MOTION TO REOPEN TIME FOR APPEAL 821

§1. GENERAL 821
§2. NOTICE OF JUDGMENT 821
§2.1 Who must give notice 821
§2.2 Written notice 821
§2.3 Service of notice 821
§2.4 Receipt of notice 821
§3. DEADLINE 822
§3.1 Window opens 822
§3.2 Window closes 822
§3.3 Period reopens 822
§3.4 No extension 822
§4. MOTION 823
§4.1 Form 823
§4.2 In writing 823
§4.3 Grounds 823
§4.4 Affidavits 823
§4.5 Request hearing 823
§5. RESPONSE 823
§5.1 Objections 823
§5.2 Deadline 824
§5.3 Affidavits 824
§6. HEARING 824
§6.1 Hearing unnecessary 824
§6.2 Burden 824
§6.3 Presumption that notice was received 824
§7. RULING 824
§7.1 Written order 824
§7.2 Standard 824
§7.3 Court grants motion 825
§7.4 Findings 825
§8. APPELLATE REVIEW 825
§8.1 Standard of review 825
§8.2 Court grants motion 825
§8.3 Court denies motion 825

I. MOTION TO CORRECT CLERICAL ERROR IN JUDGMENT 825

§1. GENERAL 825
§2. NO DEADLINE 826
§3. CLERICAL VS. SUBSTANTIVE ERRORS 826
§3.1 Error is clerical 826
§3.2 Error is not clerical 827
§4. MOTION 827
§4.1 Form 827
§4.2 In writing or on court's initiative 827
§4.3 Grounds 827
§4.4 Affidavits 828
§4.5 Request hearing 828

COMMENTARIES

CHAPTER 10. POSTJUDGMENT MOTIONS

TABLE OF CONTENTS

§5. RESPONSE 828
§5.1 Objections 828
§5.2 Deadline 828
§5.3 Affidavits 828
§6. HEARING 828
§7. RULING 828
§7.1 Written order 828
§7.2 Clerical errors only 828
§8. APPELLATE REVIEW 828
§8.1 Deadline 828
§8.2 Standard of review 829

10. POSTJUDGMENT MOTIONS

A. GENERAL

The FRCPs recognize at least ten different postjudgment motions that a party can consider filing in district court. These motions are listed in chart 10-1, below. After checking the deadlines and requirements in the FRCPs, parties should also check the local rules on motion practice for any additional requirements.

10-1. POSTJUDGMENT MOTIONS

	Type of motion	Rule	Deadline	Purpose	Delays appeal?	Discussed at
1	Motion for attorney fees	FRCP 54(d)(2)	14 days after judgment	Award attorney fees as costs of litigation	Yes, if court signs order	ch. 9-C, p. 745
2	Motion to retax costs	FRCP 54(d)(1)	7 days after clerk taxes costs	Change award of costs	No	ch. 9-D, p. 761
3	Renewed motion for JMOL	FRCP 50(b)	28 days after judgment or jury discharge, if no verdict	Rendition of judgment contrary to verdict	Yes	ch. 10-B, this page
4	Motion for new trial	FRCP 59(a), (b), (d)	28 days after judgment	New trial	Yes	ch. 10-C, p. 783
5	Motion to alter or amend judgment	FRCP 59(e)	28 days after judgment	Amend judgment	Yes	ch. 10-D, p. 793
6	Motion to add or amend findings of fact	FRCP 52(b)	28 days after judgment	Add or amend findings	Yes	ch. 10-E, p. 799
7	Motion for relief from judgment	FRCP 60(b), (c)	Variable—see ch. 10-F, §2, p. 804	Set aside judgment	Only if filed within 28 days after judgment	ch. 10-F, p. 804
8	Motion to extend time to file notice of appeal	FRAP 4(a)(5)	30 days after notice of appeal due	Extend time to file notice of appeal	Yes, for notice of appeal	ch. 10-G, p. 817
9	Motion to reopen time for appeal	FRAP 4(a)(6)	Variable—see ch. 10-H, §3, p. 822	Restart appellate deadlines	Yes	ch. 10-H, p. 821
10	Motion to correct clerical error in judgment	FRCP 60(a)	No time limit	Correct clerical error in judgment	Only if filed within 28 days after judgment	ch. 10-I, p. 825

B. RENEWED MOTION FOR JUDGMENT AS A MATTER OF LAW

§1. GENERAL

§1.1 Rule. FRCP 50(b).

§1.2 Purpose. A renewed motion for judgment as a matter of law (JMOL), formerly called a motion for judgment notwithstanding the verdict (JNOV), asks the district court to disregard the jury findings and enter judgment for the movant even though the jury returned a verdict for the nonmovant. *See* ***Ortiz v. Jordan***, ___ U.S. ___, 131 S.Ct. 884, 891-92 (2011). There are two motions for JMOL: one made during the trial under FRCP 50(a), and one made after the jury returns a verdict under FRCP 50(b). This subchapter discusses renewed motions for JMOL made after the jury returns a verdict. For a discussion of motions for JMOL made during the trial, see "Motion for Judgment as a Matter of Law," ch. 8-G, p. 714.

§1.3 Timetable & forms. Timetable, Appeal of Civil Trial, p. 1591; ***O'Connor's Federal Civil Forms*** (2012), FORMS 10B.

§1.4 Other references. 9B Wright & Miller, *Federal Practice & Procedure 3d* §§2521-2540 (2008 & Supp.2012); 9 *Moore's Federal Practice 3d* ch. 50 (2012); 1 Childress & Davis, *Federal Standards of Review 4th* ch. 3 (2010 & Supp.2011).

§2. PROCEDURAL PREREQUISITES

The district court can consider a renewed motion for JMOL only if the moving party made a motion for JMOL before the case was submitted to the jury. *See* FRCP 50(b).

§2.1 Motion before case submitted to jury. By making a motion for JMOL before the case is submitted to the jury, the party lays the foundation for making a renewed motion for JMOL after the entry of judgment. *See* FRCP 50(a)(2), (b); ***Delta-X Corp. v. Baker Hughes Prod. Tools, Inc.***, 984 F.2d 410, 412 (Fed.Cir.1993). The first purpose of the preverdict motion is to preserve an appellate complaint of insufficiency of the evidence. ***Freund v. Nycomed Amersham***, 347 F.3d 752, 761 (9th Cir.2003). To preserve the error, the party must file both a preverdict motion and a postverdict motion. *See* ***Unitherm Food Sys. v. Swift-Eckrich, Inc.***, 546 U.S. 394, 399-401 (2006); ***Tortu v. Las Vegas Metro. Police Dept.***, 556 F.3d 1075, 1081-82 (9th Cir.2009). The second purpose of the preverdict motion is to give the nonmovant an opportunity to repair gaps in its proof. ***Laborers' Pension Fund v. A&C Env'tl, Inc.***, 301 F.3d 768, 775 (7th Cir.2002); ***Barber v. Nabors Drilling U.S.A., Inc.***, 130 F.3d 702, 710 (5th Cir.1997); ***Hoechst Celanese Corp. v. BP Chems. Ltd.***, 78 F.3d 1575, 1582 (Fed.Cir.1996); *see* ***Marshall v. Columbia Lea Reg'l Hosp.***, 474 F.3d 733, 739 (10th Cir.2007) (one purpose is to give party enough notice to cure alleged error before resting). See "After opportunity to cure," ch. 8-G, §3.2, p. 715.

§2.2 No motion before case submitted to jury. If a party did not move for JMOL before the case was submitted to the jury, the party did not preserve error. The consequences of not making a timely motion for JMOL are as follows:

1. The party is not entitled to challenge the sufficiency of the evidence in a renewed motion for JMOL after the entry of judgment. *See* ***Tortu v. Las Vegas Metro. Police Dept.***, 556 F.3d 1075, 1083 (9th Cir.2009).

2. The party is not entitled to challenge the sufficiency of the evidence on appeal. *See* ***Greenleaf v. Garlock, Inc.***, 174 F.3d 352, 364 (3d Cir.1999); ***Polanco v. City of Austin***, 78 F.3d 968, 974 (5th Cir.1996). Instead, appellate review is limited to a determination of whether there was any evidence to support the jury's verdict. ***Polanco***, 78 F.3d at 974. See "Party did not move for JMOL before case submitted to jury," §9.2.2, p. 781.

§2.3 No renewed motion for JMOL after judgment. If the party made a preverdict motion but did not make a renewed motion for JMOL after the judgment, neither the district court nor the appellate court can direct entry of judgment in favor of that party. ***Unitherm Food Sys. v. Swift-Eckrich, Inc.***, 546 U.S. 394, 400-01 (2006); ***Nitco Holding Corp. v. Boujikian***, 491 F.3d 1086, 1089-90 (9th Cir.2007); *e.g.*, ***Johnson v. New York, New Haven & Hartford R.R.***, 344 U.S. 48, 54 (1952) (because D did not move for JNOV, now JMOL, D was entitled only to new trial, not rendition). A party who does not renew the motion for JMOL after the verdict waives any complaint of insufficiency of the evidence on appeal. *See* ***Unitherm Food***, 546 U.S. at 404; ***Belk, Inc. v. Meyer Corp.***, 679 F.3d 146, 155 (4th Cir.2012).

§3. DEADLINE

§3.1 28-day deadline.

1. After entry of judgment. A renewed motion for JMOL must be filed with the clerk no later than 28 days after the entry of judgment. FRCP 50(b). The judgment is considered entered when it is placed in a separate document and entered on the docket in compliance with FRCP 58. See "Requirements for Final Judgment," ch. 9-A, §2, p. 735. The motion must be received by—not just mailed to—the clerk by the deadline. When calculating the

28-day time period, the date the judgment is entered is the trigger event and is excluded; counting begins the day after the entry of judgment. FRCP 6(a)(1)(A); *see also* ***Laborers' Pension Fund v. A&C Env'tl, Inc.***, 301 F.3d 768, 775 n.5 (7th Cir.2002) (entry date of judgment on docket—not date judgment is signed—triggers time period; applying former ten-day deadline). See "Identify trigger event," ch. 1-C, §6.1.1(1), p. 24.

2. After jury discharged. If a renewed motion for JMOL addresses a jury issue that was not decided by a verdict, the motion must be filed no later than 28 days after the jury is discharged. FRCP 50(b); *see* 2006 Notes to FRCP 50 at ¶5, p. 1214, this book (discussing former ten-day deadline). When calculating the 28-day time period, the date the district court dismisses the jury is the trigger event and is excluded; counting begins the day after the jury is dismissed. *See* ***Art Attacks Ink, LLC v. MGA Entm't Inc.***, 581 F.3d 1138, 1142 (9th Cir.2009) (applying former ten-day deadline). See "Identify trigger event," ch. 1-C, §6.1.1(1), p. 24.

§3.2 No extension. The deadline for filing a renewed motion for JMOL cannot be extended by the court or the parties. *See* FRCP 6(b)(2); ***U.S. Leather, Inc. v. H&W Prtshp.***, 60 F.3d 222, 225 (5th Cir.1995); ***Rodick v. City of Schenectady***, 1 F.3d 1341, 1346 (2d Cir.1993). Some circuits have held that the deadline is jurisdictional; thus, in those circuits, a late motion is ineffective even if the other party does not object. *See* ***Rodick***, 1 F.3d at 1346. Although the deadline cannot be extended, other circuits have held that FRCP 6(b)(2) and 50(b) are nonjurisdictional claim-processing rules; thus, in those circuits, objections to the timeliness of the motion can be waived. *See, e.g.*, ***Blue v. International Bhd. of Elec. Workers Local Un.***, 676 F.3d 579, 584-85 (7th Cir.2012); ***Advanced Bodycare Solutions, LLC v. Thione Int'l***, 615 F.3d 1352, 1359 n.14 (11th Cir.2010); ***Art Attacks Ink, LLC v. MGA Entm't Inc.***, 581 F.3d 1138, 1143 (9th Cir.2009); ***Dill v. General Am. Life Ins.***, 525 F.3d 612, 618 (8th Cir.2008). That is, if the movant does not file its renewed motion for JMOL within the 28-day deadline but the nonmovant does not object to the untimeliness, the objection is waived and the district court has jurisdiction over the motion. *See* ***Art Attacks Ink***, 581 F.3d at 1143.

CAUTION

Even if the district court has jurisdiction over an untimely motion, the circuits disagree on whether that motion tolls the deadline to file a notice of appeal under FRAP 4(a)(4)(A). Compare ***Blue***, *676 F.3d at 582-83 (untimely motion listed under FRAP 4(a)(4)(A) does not toll time for filing appeal), and* ***Advanced Bodycare Solutions***, *615 F.3d at 1359 n.14 (because FRAP 4(a)(4) is jurisdictional, untimely motion listed under FRAP 4(a)(4)(A) does not toll time for filing appeal), with* ***Obaydullah v. Obama***, *___ F.3d ___ (D.C.Cir.2012) (No. 11-5123; 8-10-12) (because FRAP 4(a)(4) is nonjurisdictional claim-processing rule, untimely motion listed under FRAP 4(a)(4)(A) can toll time for filing appeal; objections to timeliness for tolling purposes can be waived), and* ***National Ecological Found. v. Alexander***, *496 F.3d 466, 476 (6th Cir. 2007) (untimely motion listed under FRAP 4(a)(4)(A) tolls time for filing appeal). If the appellate deadline is not tolled, an appeal after the ruling on the untimely motion is limited to that ruling and would not include appellate review of the underlying judgment. See* ***Advanced Bodycare Solutions***, *615 F.3d at 1359 n.14. See "Deadline," §9.1, p. 781. Thus, check the law of your circuit to determine whether untimeliness objections under FRCP 50(b) or for tolling purposes can be waived.*

---

§3.3 Premature motion. A renewed motion for JMOL should be filed after the judgment is entered or the jury is discharged, not before. FRCP 50(b). But if it is filed before the judgment is entered or the jury is discharged, it is still timely because FRCP 50(b) sets only the outer filing limits. *See* ***Dunn v. Truck World, Inc.***, 929 F.2d 311, 312-13 (7th Cir.1991) (motions for new trial and JNOV—now JMOL). If the motion is filed early, the movant should ask the court to sign a written order ruling on the motion without prejudice to filing another renewed motion for JMOL after the judgment is entered.

CIRCUIT SPLIT

The circuits disagree on whether a postjudgment motion filed before the entry of final judgment is implicitly overruled when the final judgment is entered. This issue is significant for determining when the 30-day period for filing a notice of appeal under FRAP 4 begins. Some circuits hold that the motion is implicitly overruled and the 30-day period is triggered on the date the judgment is entered. E.g., ***Dunn****, 929 F.2d at 313;* ***Mosier v. Federal Reserve Bank****, 132 F.2d 710, 712 (2d Cir.1942). The Fourth Circuit holds that the motion must be explicitly overruled and the 30-day period is not triggered until the motion is overruled.* ***Havird Oil Co. v. Marathon Oil Co.****, 149 F.3d 283, 289 (4th Cir.1998); see also* ***Simmons v. Reliance Std. Life Ins.****, 310 F.3d 865, 868 (5th Cir.2002) (notice of appeal not effective until last postjudgment motion disposed of). Other circuits look at the record to determine whether the court intended the judgment to overrule the motion and then calculate the deadline from either the date the judgment was entered or the date the motion was explicitly overruled. E.g.,* ***Calculators Haw., Inc. v. Brandt, Inc.****, 724 F.2d 1332, 1335 (9th Cir.1983) (record reflected that district court did not intend final judgment to overrule motion to amend findings; deadline to file notice of appeal ran from date order denying motion to amend findings was entered);* ***Director of Revenue v. U.S.****, 392 F.2d 307, 309 (10th Cir.1968) (motion for new trial was not implicitly denied by entry of judgment when district court formally ruled on motion after entry of judgment; deadline to file notice of appeal ran from date order denying motion for new trial was entered);* ***Partridge v. Presley****, 189 F.2d 645, 646-47 (D.C.Cir.1951) (record reflected that district judge had not consciously disposed of prematurely filed motion for new trial when he entered judgment; deadline to file notice of appeal ran from date order denying motion for new trial was entered).*

§4. MOTION

§4.1 Form. For the general requirements for the form of a motion, see "Drafting motions," ch. 1-B, §3.1, p. 14.

§4.2 By either party. Either party can make a renewed motion for JMOL, and a JMOL can be entered against either party. 1993 Notes to FRCP 50 at ¶1, p. 1214, this book.

§4.3 In writing. A renewed motion for JMOL should be in writing. *See* FRCP 7(b)(1)(A); *see also* ***Belk, Inc. v. Meyer Corp.***, 679 F.3d 146, 156-57 (4th Cir.2012) (in limited circumstances, party may satisfy requirements of FRCP 50(b) motion orally, but party must still make adequate record).

§4.4 Grounds. A renewed motion for JMOL is proper if a motion for JMOL would have been proper. A motion for JMOL must specify the judgment sought and the law and facts that entitle the movant to the judgment. FRCP 50(a)(2); ***Whelan v. Abell***, 48 F.3d 1247, 1251 (D.C.Cir.1995).

1. Same grounds asserted earlier. Because a renewed motion for JMOL is a renewal of the preverdict motion, it can assert only the grounds raised in the earlier motion. ***EEOC v. Go Daddy Software, Inc.***, 581 F.3d 951, 961 (9th Cir.2009); ***Marshall v. Columbia Lea Reg'l Hosp.***, 474 F.3d 733, 738-39 (10th Cir.2007); ***Arsement v. Spinnaker Expl. Co.***, 400 F.3d 238, 247 (5th Cir.2005); ***Conseco Fin. Servicing Corp. v. North Am. Mortg. Co.***, 381 F.3d 811, 821 (8th Cir.2004); 2006 Notes to FRCP 50 at ¶2, p. 1214, this book.

2. Entitlement to JMOL. The renewed motion for JMOL must assert that the movant is entitled to a JMOL. The renewed motion is similar to a motion for summary judgment because both challenge the existence of a genuine dispute of fact and both seek a final judgment. ***Urti v. Transport Commercial Corp.***, 479 F.2d 766, 768 (5th Cir.1973).

3. Types of challenges.

(1) Legal sufficiency. Renewed motions for JMOL are most often used to challenge the legal sufficiency of the evidence supporting a verdict. *See* ***Fox v. T-H Cont'l L.P.***, 78 F.3d 409, 413 (8th Cir.1996); ***Texas Farm***

Bur. v. U.S., 53 F.3d 120, 123 (5th Cir.1995). A JMOL can be granted when a reasonable jury would not have a legally sufficient evidentiary basis to find against the movant. *See* FRCP 50(a)(1). See "Insufficient evidence," ch. 8-G, §4.2.2, p. 716.

(2) General verdict inconsistent with written answers. A party can make a renewed motion for JMOL when the jury's general verdict is inconsistent with the jury's answers to written questions. *See* FRCP 49(b)(3), (b)(4); *see, e.g.*, ***Porter v. Eckert***, 465 F.2d 1307, 1310 (5th Cir.1972) (JNOV, now JMOL, affirmed when answers to interrogatories were not consistent with general verdict). See "Types of Verdicts," ch. 8-I, §2, p. 720.

(3) Legal bar to recovery. A party can make a renewed motion for JMOL to assert a legal bar to the jury's verdict, such as res judicata, collateral estoppel, or the statute of limitations. *See* ***Coons v. Industrial Knife Co.***, 620 F.3d 38, 41 (1st Cir.2010); *see, e.g.*, ***Mozingo v. Correct Mfg.***, 752 F.2d 168, 172 (5th Cir.1985) (court erred in granting JNOV, now JMOL, on ground of collateral estoppel because party did not raise issue in motion for directed verdict).

§4.5 Request new trial. A party can either request a new trial or join the renewed motion for JMOL with a motion for new trial under FRCP 59. FRCP 50(b). See "Motion for New Trial," ch. 10-C, p. 783.

§4.6 Request hearing. If oral argument will help the court resolve the motion, the movant should request a hearing. The movant should comply with any requirements of local rules for securing a hearing on the motion. *Cf.* ***Kendall v. Hoover Co.***, 751 F.2d 171, 172-73 (6th Cir.1984) (motion for summary judgment).

§5. RESPONSE

§5.1 Objections. The nonmovant should file a response to the renewed motion for JMOL and explain why the court should overrule the motion. For example, the nonmovant can assert the following:

1. **Motion untimely.** The movant did not file the motion within the 28-day deadline. *See* FRCP 50(b).

2. **No preverdict motion.** The movant did not make a preverdict motion for JMOL and thus cannot challenge the sufficiency of the evidence. See "No motion before case submitted to jury," §2.2.1, p. 776.

3. **Different grounds.** The grounds in the renewed motion for JMOL were not included in the original motion; thus, the movant waived those grounds and cannot assert them in the renewed motion for JMOL. ***Chainey v. Street***, 523 F.3d 200, 218 (3d Cir.2008); ***Marshall v. Columbia Lea Reg'l Hosp.***, 474 F.3d 733, 738-39 (10th Cir. 2007); ***Arsement v. Spinnaker Expl. Co.***, 400 F.3d 238, 247 (5th Cir.2005). If the nonmovant does not raise the issue of waiver in response to the renewed motion for JMOL, it cannot argue waiver on appeal. ***Howard v. Walgreen Co.***, 605 F.3d 1239, 1243-44 (11th Cir.2010); ***Chainey***, 523 F.3d at 218; ***Marshall***, 474 F.3d at 739; ***Arsement***, 400 F.3d at 247.

4. **Fact issues.** There were fact issues that could be resolved only by the jury, and they were not established as a matter of law. *See* ***Parfait v. Central Towing, Inc.***, 667 F.2d 1189, 1190 (5th Cir.1982).

§5.2 Deadline. FRCP 50 does not specify a deadline for the response, but it should be filed within any limits set by local rules for responses.

§6. HEARING

A hearing may be held for parties to make legal arguments on the renewed motion for JMOL. Because no facts are in dispute, a court reporter is not necessary.

§7. RULING

§7.1 Written order. The court should sign a written order granting or denying the motion. The order does not need to be set out in a separate document. FRCP 58(a)(1). See "Orders," ch. 1-G, §4.2, p. 45.

§7.2 Standard. The court can grant a motion for JMOL if a reasonable jury would not have a legally sufficient evidentiary basis to find for the nonmovant on the issue in question. FRCP 50(a)(1); *see* ***Rivera v. Union Pac. R.R.***, 378 F.3d 502, 505 (5th Cir.2004); ***Snyder v. Ag Trucking, Inc.***, 57 F.3d 484, 490 (6th Cir.1995). The standard for granting a renewed motion for JMOL is the same as the standard for granting a preverdict motion for JMOL. ***Geldermann,***

Inc. v. Financial Mgmt. Consultants, Inc., 27 F.3d 307, 310 n.4 (7th Cir.1994); ***City of Omaha Empls. Betterment Ass'n v. City of Omaha***, 883 F.2d 650, 651 (8th Cir.1989). The motion can be granted only if the nonmovant did not present "substantial evidence ... of such quality and weight that reasonable and fair-minded [people] in the exercise of impartial judgment might reach different conclusions." ***Boeing Co. v. Shipman***, 411 F.2d 365, 374 (5th Cir. 1969), *overruled on other grounds*, ***Gautreaux v. Scurlock Mar., Inc.***, 107 F.3d 331 (5th Cir.1997). The court can grant a renewed motion for JMOL only if the evidence is such that, without weighing or evaluating the evidence or considering questions of credibility, the court can reach only one reasonable conclusion about the verdict. ***Butler v. French***, 83 F.3d 942, 943 (8th Cir.1996); ***Wardlaw v. Inland Container Corp.***, 76 F.3d 1372, 1375 (5th Cir.1996). The court must view the evidence and all reasonable inferences in the light most favorable to the nonmovant. ***Stevenson v. E.I. DuPont De Nemours & Co.***, 327 F.3d 400, 405 (5th Cir.2003); ***Glenn Distribs. v. Carlisle Plastics, Inc.***, 297 F.3d 294, 299 (3d Cir.2002); ***Ryther v. KARE 11***, 108 F.3d 832, 836 (8th Cir.1997); ***Mathis v. Pacific Gas & Elec. Co.***, 75 F.3d 498, 501 (9th Cir.1996). The standard for granting a motion for JMOL is more stringent than the standard for granting a motion for new trial. ***Winter v. Brenner Tank, Inc.***, 926 F.2d 468, 473 (5th Cir.1991); ***Katara v. D.E. Jones Commodities, Inc.***, 835 F.2d 966, 970 (2d Cir.1987).

§7.3 Relief.

1. Relief for JMOL. If the court grants the renewed motion for JMOL, it can either render judgment for the movant or grant a new trial, depending on the timing of the motion. ***Cone v. West Va. Pulp & Paper Co.***, 330 U.S. 212, 217-18 (1947); *see, e.g.*, ***Fleet Nat'l Bank v. Anchor Media TV, Inc.***, 45 F.3d 546, 551-52 (1st Cir.1995) (instead of rendering judgment, court ordered new trial because it could not determine from general verdict whether jury relied on legally defective allegations).

(1) If the movant made a motion for JMOL before the case was submitted to the jury, the court can render judgment. *See* FRCP 50(b).

(2) If the movant did not make a motion for JMOL before the case was submitted to the jury, the court can only grant a new trial and cannot render judgment. *See* ***U.S. v. Reisz***, 718 F.2d 1004, 1007 (11th Cir.1983) (discussing former FRCP 50(b)).

2. Relief under alternative motion for new trial. If a party files a renewed motion for JMOL along with a motion for new trial, the court's ruling on the motion for new trial will depend on whether the renewed JMOL is granted or denied.

(1) JMOL granted. If the court grants the motion for JMOL, it must also conditionally rule on the motion for new trial. FRCP 50(c)(1); ***Montgomery Ward & Co. v. Duncan***, 311 U.S. 243, 253 (1940); ***Jennings v. Jones***, 499 F.3d 2, 21 (1st Cir.2007); ***Rhone Poulenc Rorer Pharms. v. Newman Glass Works***, 112 F.3d 695, 698 (3d Cir.1997). If the court does not conditionally rule on the motion for new trial, the movant should alert the court to the unruled-on motion and raise any arguments for the new trial on appeal. If the movant properly raised the issue at the appellate level, the court of appeals can then either remand for a ruling or make a ruling on its own motion. *E.g.*, ***Freund v. Nycomed Amersham***, 347 F.3d 752, 764-65 (9th Cir.2003) (appellate court remanded, electing not to interfere with district court's broad discretion in ruling on motion for new trial); ***Acosta v. City & Cty. of S.F.***, 83 F.3d 1143, 1149 (9th Cir.1996) (appellate court ruled on motion for new trial); *see also* ***Christopher v. Florida***, 449 F.3d 1360, 1364-65 & n.3 (11th Cir.2006) (when district court granted D1's conditional motion for new trial but D2 did not raise lack of conditional ruling on its motion until appeal, appellate court accepted that district court would have granted D2's motion for new trial because new-trial grounds applied equally to D1 and D2). If the movant does not seek a ruling from the district court or argue for the motion for new trial on appeal, the appellate court will usually remand the case for a ruling on the motion for new trial. *E.g.*, ***Rhone Poulenc***, 112 F.3d at 698-99 (district court erred when it dismissed motion for new trial as moot and parties did not file brief on merits; remanded for court to rule on motion); *see* 9B Wright & Miller §2539 & n.9 (appellate court must remand). Some courts have held, however, that if the movant did not raise the issue at either the district-court or the appellate level, the new-trial issue will be treated as abandoned. *See* ***Arenson v. Southern Univ. Law Ctr.***, 43 F.3d 194, 196 (5th Cir.1995); ***Edwards v. Board of Regents***, 2 F.3d 382, 384 n.6 (11th Cir.1993).

(2) JMOL denied. If the court denies the motion for JMOL, it is not required to conditionally rule on the motion for new trial. *Compare* FRCP 50(c)(1) (if motion for JMOL is granted, court must rule on motion for new trial) *with* FRCP 50(e) (if motion for JMOL is denied, court not required to rule on motion for new trial). The court of appeals can consider the motion for new trial for the first time on appeal if the denial of the JMOL is reversed. ***Neely v. Martin K. Eby Constr. Co.***, 386 U.S. 317, 324 (1967). FRCP 50(e) even recognizes that the "appellate court may prefer that the trial judge pass first upon the appellee's new trial suggestion." ***Neely***, 386 U.S. at 323-24 (FRCP 50(d), now FRCP 50(e), does not prohibit court of appeals from determining that appellee is entitled to new trial, or from directing district court to determine whether new trial should be granted).

§8. POST-JMOL MOTION FOR NEW TRIAL

If the court grants the renewed motion for JMOL and renders a judgment, the nonmovant can file a motion for new trial within 28 days after the entry of the JMOL. FRCP 50(d).

§9. APPELLATE REVIEW

§9.1 Deadline. The timely filing of a renewed motion for JMOL tolls the deadline to file a notice of appeal until an order disposing of the motion is entered. FRAP 4(a)(4)(A)(i); *see* ***Shales v. General Chauffeurs, Sales Drivers & Helpers Local Un.***, 557 F.3d 746, 748 (7th Cir.2009) (tolling of appellate deadline is determined by filing of motion, not by decision that motion has merit). An order is considered entered within the meaning of FRAP 4(a)(4) when it is entered on the civil docket under FRCP 79(a). FRAP 4(a)(7)(A)(i). The court does not need to render the order with the formality of a judgment, but it must clearly dispose of the post-trial motion. ***Ellison v. Conoco, Inc.***, 950 F.2d 1196, 1201 (5th Cir.1992). An appellant challenging either an order disposing of the renewed motion for JMOL or a judgment's alteration or amendment based on the renewed motion for JMOL must file the notice of appeal within 30 days (60 days if the United States is a party) after entry of the order, unless there are other outstanding motions that continue to toll the running of the appellate deadlines. *See* FRAP 4(a)(1)(A), (a)(1)(B), (a)(4)(B)(ii); 2009 Notes to FRAP 4 at ¶¶3, 4, p. 1266, this book.

§9.2 Standard of review. For a thorough discussion of how the standards of review for JMOL motions are applied, see 9B Wright & Miller, *Federal Practice & Procedure 3d* §2540 (2008 & Supp.2012), and 1 Childress & Davis, *Federal Standards of Review 4th* ch. 3 (2010 & Supp.2011).

1. Party moved for JMOL before case submitted to jury. If the party properly moved for JMOL before the case was submitted to the jury and made a renewed motion for JMOL, the standard of review on appeal is de novo, the same standard used by the district court. ***EEOC v. Go Daddy Software, Inc.***, 581 F.3d 951, 961 (9th Cir. 2009); ***Winger v. Winger***, 82 F.3d 140, 143 (7th Cir.1996); ***Heller Fin., Inc. v. Grammco Computer Sales, Inc.***, 71 F.3d 518, 523 (5th Cir.1996). In reviewing whether there was evidence sufficient to support a jury's verdict, the appellate court will review all the evidence in the record, drawing all reasonable inferences in favor of the nonmoving party without making determinations about the credibility of witnesses or the weight of the evidence. ***Reeves v. Sanderson Plumbing Prods.***, 530 U.S. 133, 150 (2000). The appellate court does not weigh the evidence, evaluate the credibility of the witnesses, or substitute its judgment for that of the jury. ***Harolds Stores v. Dillard Dept. Stores***, 82 F.3d 1533, 1546 (10th Cir.1996); *see* ***Go Daddy Software***, 581 F.3d at 961; ***Butler v. French***, 83 F.3d 942, 943 (8th Cir.1996).

2. Party did not move for JMOL before case submitted to jury. If the party did not move for JMOL before the case was submitted to the jury, the standard of review on appeal is plain error, which requires the court to decide whether there was any evidence to support the jury's verdict, regardless of its sufficiency. ***Polanco v. City of Austin***, 78 F.3d 968, 974 (5th Cir.1996). If the nonmovant presents any evidence, the appellate court will sustain the denial of the motion for JMOL. *Id.* Reversal for plain error is an extreme remedy and will occur only to avoid a miscarriage of justice. ***McKenzie v. Lee***, 259 F.3d 372, 374 (5th Cir.2001). If there is no evidence to support the verdict, the appellate court will order a new trial; it will not enter judgment for the movant. ***Polanco***, 78 F.3d at 974.

3. Party did not make renewed motion for JMOL. If the party did not make a renewed motion for JMOL after the judgment, the appellate court cannot render judgment for that party—the party's relief is limited to a remand and a new trial. *See **Unitherm Food Sys. v. Swift-Eckrich, Inc.***, 546 U.S. 394, 400-01 (2006); ***Cone v. West Va. Pulp & Paper Co.***, 330 U.S. 212, 217-18 (1947); ***Fuesting v. Zimmer, Inc.***, 448 F.3d 936, 939 (7th Cir.2006); ***Phillips v. Frey***, 20 F.3d 623, 627 (5th Cir.1994).

§9.3 Review under alternative motion for new trial. If the party made an alternative motion for new trial with its renewed motion for JMOL, the appealability of the orders depends on how the district court ruled on the motions.

1. Both motions denied. If the district court denied both the renewed motion for JMOL and the alternative motion for new trial, the appeal is from the final judgment. *See **Polanco v. City of Austin***, 78 F.3d 968, 971 (5th Cir.1996); 9B Wright & Miller §2540 & n.29. The party can appeal the district court's denial of both motions during the appeal of the final judgment.

2. JMOL denied, new trial granted. If the district court denied the renewed motion for JMOL and granted the alternative motion for new trial, the order is not appealable. An order granting a motion for new trial is interlocutory and cannot be appealed. *See **Hardin v. Hayes***, 52 F.3d 934, 937 & n.2 (11th Cir.1995); 9B Wright & Miller §2540 & n.4.

3. JMOL granted, new trial denied. If the district court granted the renewed motion for JMOL and conditionally denied the alternative motion for new trial, the appeal is from the final judgment. ***Montgomery Ward & Co. v. Duncan***, 311 U.S. 243, 254 (1940). If the motion for JMOL is reversed on appeal, the party who obtained the JMOL can complain about the denial of the new trial on appeal. FRCP 50(c)(2); 9B Wright & Miller §2540 & n.43; *see **Stone v. First Wyo. Bank***, 625 F.2d 332, 350 (10th Cir.1980) (denial of motion for new trial is not automatically abuse of discretion when JMOL is granted). If the district court made a conditional ruling on the motion for new trial and the appellate court reverses the JMOL, the appellate court can consider the grounds in the motion for new trial if the record is sufficient. *See, e.g.*, ***Olefins Trading, Inc. v. Han Yang Chem Corp.***, 9 F.3d 282, 290 (3d Cir.1993) (appellate court could not review because district court did not make complete conditional ruling on motion for new trial). If the district court did not make a conditional ruling on the motion for new trial and the appellate court reverses the JMOL, the appellate court will remand the motion for new trial to the district court for a ruling. *Id.* The district court's failure to make a conditional ruling on the motion for new trial is error, but it does not deprive the appellate court of jurisdiction over the appeal. ***Vollrath Co. v. Sammi Corp.***, 9 F.3d 1455, 1458 (9th Cir.1993).

4. Both motions granted. If the district court granted the renewed motion for JMOL and conditionally granted the alternative motion for new trial, the appeal is from the final judgment. FRCP 50(c)(2); *see **Williamson v. Consolidated Rail Corp.***, 926 F.2d 1344, 1347 (3d Cir.1991). When the district court grants both motions, the order granting the new trial is effective only if the JMOL is reversed on appeal. FRCP 50(c)(2); ***Persinger v. Norfolk & W. Ry.***, 920 F.2d 1185, 1189 (4th Cir.1990); 9B Wright & Miller §2540 & n.34. If the appellate court reverses the JMOL, it can also vacate the order granting the motion for new trial and reinstate the jury's verdict. ***Williamson***, 926 F.2d at 1352; *see* 9B Wright & Miller §2540 & n.40.

C. MOTION FOR NEW TRIAL

§1. GENERAL

§1.1 Rule. FRCP 59(a)-(d). See FRCP 50(b).

§1.2 Purpose. A motion for new trial asks the district court to correct an error by granting a new trial. There are several good reasons why an unsuccessful litigant should file a motion for new trial: (1) to force reconsideration of a trial error, (2) to challenge an error or unfairness in the proceeding that could not have been raised during trial, (3) to lay a foundation for challenging the sufficiency of the evidence on appeal, and (4) to extend the deadline for filing a notice of appeal.

§1.3 Timetable & forms. Timetable, Appeal of Civil Trial, p. 1591; ***O'Connor's Federal Civil Forms*** (2012), FORMS 10C.

§1.4 Other references. 11 Wright, Miller & Kane, *Federal Practice & Procedure 2d* §§2801-2821 (1995 & Supp.2012); 12 *Moore's Federal Practice 3d* ch. 59 (2012); 1 Childress & Davis, *Federal Standards of Review 4th* §§5.08-5.11 (2010 & Supp.2011).

§2. DEADLINE

§2.1 28-day deadline. A motion for new trial must be filed with the clerk no later than 28 days after the entry of judgment. FRCP 59(b); *see* FRCP 50(b). The judgment is considered entered when it is placed in a separate document and entered on the docket in compliance with FRCP 58. See "Requirements for Final Judgment," ch. 9-A, §2, p. 735. The motion must be received by—not just mailed to—the clerk by the deadline. When calculating the 28-day time period, the date the judgment is entered is the trigger event and is excluded; counting begins the day after the entry of judgment. FRCP 6(a)(1)(A); *cf.* ***Laborers' Pension Fund v. A&C Env'tl, Inc.***, 301 F.3d 768, 775 n.5 (7th Cir.2002) (for renewed motion for JMOL, entry date of judgment on docket—not date judgment is signed—triggers time period; applying former ten-day deadline). See "Identify trigger event," ch. 1-C, §6.1.1(1), p. 24.

§2.2 No extension. The deadline for filing a motion for new trial cannot be extended by the court or the parties. *See* FRCP 6(b)(2); ***U.S. Leather, Inc. v. H&W Prtshp.***, 60 F.3d 222, 225 (5th Cir.1995); ***Cavaliere v. Allstate Ins.***, 996 F.2d 1111, 1113 (11th Cir.1993); 2009 Notes to FRCP 59 at ¶1, p. 1229, this book. Some circuits have held that the deadline is jurisdictional; thus, in those circuits, a late motion is ineffective even if the other party does not object. *See* ***Rodick v. City of Schenectady***, 1 F.3d 1341, 1346 (2d Cir.1993). Although the deadline cannot be extended, other circuits have held that FRCP 6(b)(2) and 59(b) are nonjurisdictional claim-processing rules; thus, in those circuits, objections to the timeliness of the postjudgment motion can be waived. *See, e.g.*, ***Blue v. International Bhd. of Elec. Workers Local Un.***, 676 F.3d 579, 584-85 (7th Cir.2012); ***Advanced Bodycare Solutions, LLC v. Thione Int'l***, 615 F.3d 1352, 1359 n.14 (11th Cir.2010). That is, if the movant does not file its motion for new trial within the 28-day deadline but the nonmovant does not object to the untimeliness, the objection is waived and the court has jurisdiction over the motion. *See* ***Advanced Bodycare Solutions***, 615 F.3d at 1359 n.14.

CAUTION

*Even if the district court has jurisdiction over an untimely motion, the circuits disagree on whether that motion tolls the deadline to file a notice of appeal under FRAP 4(a)(4)(A). Compare **Blue**, 676 F.3d at 582-83 (untimely motion listed under FRAP 4(a)(4)(A) does not toll time for filing appeal), and **Advanced Bodycare Solutions**, 615 F.3d at 1359 n.14 (because FRAP 4(a)(4) is jurisdictional, untimely motion listed under FRAP 4(a)(4)(A) does not toll time for filing appeal), with **Obaydullah v. Obama**, ___ F.3d ___ (D.C.Cir.2012) (No. 11-5123; 8-10-12) (because FRAP 4(a)(4) is nonjurisdictional claim-processing rule, untimely motion listed under FRAP 4(a)(4)(A) can toll time for filing appeal; objections to timeliness for tolling purposes can be waived), and **National Ecological Found. v. Alexander**, 496 F.3d 466, 476 (6th Cir.*

*2007) (untimely motion listed under FRAP 4(a)(4)(A) tolls time for filing appeal). If the appellate deadline is not tolled, an appeal after the ruling on the untimely motion is limited to that ruling and would not include appellate review of the underlying judgment. See **Advanced Bodycare Solutions**, 615 F.3d at 1359 n.14. See "Deadline," §8.2, p. 792. Thus, check the law of your circuit to determine whether untimeliness objections under FRCP 59(b) or for tolling purposes can be waived.*

§2.3 Premature motion. A motion for new trial should be filed after the judgment is entered, not before. *See* FRCP 59(b). But if it is filed before the judgment is entered, it is still timely because FRCP 59(b) sets only the outer filing limits. *See* ***Dunn v. Truck World, Inc.***, 929 F.2d 311, 313 (7th Cir.1991); ***Greater Houston Chapter of the ACLU v. Eckels***, 755 F.2d 426, 427 (5th Cir.1985). If the motion is filed early, the movant should ask the court to sign a written order ruling on the motion without prejudice to filing another motion for new trial after the judgment is entered.

CIRCUIT SPLIT

The circuits disagree on whether a postjudgment motion filed before the entry of final judgment is implicitly overruled when the final judgment is entered. This issue is significant for determining when the 30-day period for filing a notice of appeal under FRAP 4 begins. See "Premature motion," ch. 10-B, §3.3, p. 777.

§2.4 Amended motion. A party can amend its motion for new trial before the 28-day deadline. But the circuits disagree on whether a party can amend its motion for new trial to add new grounds after the deadline has passed. *Compare* ***Dresdner Bank AG v. M/V Olympia Voyager***, 465 F.3d 1267, 1271 (11th Cir.2006) (district court can permit amendment after deadline; applying former ten-day deadline), ***Abbott v. Equity Grp.***, 2 F.3d 613, 628 (5th Cir. 1993) (same), *and* ***Pogue v. International Indus.***, 524 F.2d 342, 344 (6th Cir.1975) (same), *with* ***Arkwright Mut. Ins. v. Philadelphia Elec. Co.***, 427 F.2d 1273, 1275 (3d Cir.1970) (district court cannot permit amendment after deadline; applying former ten-day deadline), *and* ***Fine v. Paramount Pictures, Inc.***, 181 F.2d 300, 303 (7th Cir.1950) (same).

§3. MOTION

§3.1 Form. For the general requirements for the form of a motion, see "Drafting motions," ch. 1-B, §3.1, p. 14.

§3.2 In writing. A motion for new trial should be in writing. *See* FRCP 59(a)(1); *see also* ***Fine v. Paramount Pictures, Inc.***, 181 F.2d 300, 303 (7th Cir.1950) (FRCP 59 seems to require written motion). However, it can be oral if it is made during a hearing or trial. FRCP 7(b)(1)(A). An oral motion for new trial is not recommended.

§3.3 When required to preserve error. A motion for new trial is not required to preserve error for appeal if the error was objected to during trial and ruled on by the district court. ***Floyd v. Laws***, 929 F.2d 1390, 1400-01 (9th Cir.1991); *e.g.*, ***Haley v. Wyrick***, 740 F.2d 12, 13 (8th Cir.1984) (error waived because P did not include his argument about inadequacy of damages in motion for new trial or otherwise present argument to court); ***Sherrill v. Royal Indus.***, 526 F.2d 507, 509 n.2 (8th Cir.1975) (error preserved and no motion for new trial necessary because objections were made and overruled at trial); *see* ***In re Pan Am. World Airways, Inc.***, 905 F.2d 1457, 1461-62 (11th Cir. 1990). Thus, a motion for new trial is necessary to preserve error only when a party must object to an error that could not have been challenged at trial (e.g., the jury verdict is against the weight of the evidence or there is newly discovered evidence). *See* 12 *Moore's Federal Practice 3d* §59.55.

§3.4 Grounds. The movant must state the grounds for the motion "with particularity"—that is, with enough specificity to inform the district court and the opposing party of the reasons for the request for a new trial. *See* FRCP 7(b)(1)(B); ***Cambridge Plating Co. v. Napco, Inc.***, 85 F.3d 752, 760 (1st Cir.1996). This requirement gives the nonmovant notice and an opportunity to respond. ***Cambridge Plating***, 85 F.3d at 760; ***Registration Control Sys. v. Compusystems, Inc.***, 922 F.2d 805, 807-08 (Fed.Cir.1990). A brief filed with the motion can fulfill the particularity requirement. ***Lac Du Flambeau Band of Chippewa Indians v. Wisconsin***, 957 F.2d 515, 516-17 (7th Cir.1992).

1. Jury trials. The court has the power to grant a new trial based on its appraisal of the fairness of the initial trial and the reliability of the jury's verdict. ***Gray v. Bicknell***, 86 F.3d 1472, 1480 (8th Cir.1996); ***Smith v. Transworld Drilling Co.***, 773 F.2d 610, 612-13 (5th Cir.1985); *see* FRCP 59(a), (d). Commonly asserted grounds for a new trial in cases tried to a jury include the following:

(1) The verdict was against the great weight of the evidence. ***Cates v. Creamer***, 431 F.3d 456, 460 (5th Cir.2005); ***Winger v. Winger***, 82 F.3d 140, 143 (7th Cir.1996).

(2) The damages awarded were inadequate or excessive. *See* ***Gasperini v. Center for Humanities, Inc.***, 518 U.S. 415, 437 n.22 (1996); ***Winger***, 82 F.3d at 143.

(3) The court made erroneous evidentiary rulings that affected the jury's verdict. ***Ruvalcaba v. City of L.A.***, 64 F.3d 1323, 1328 (9th Cir.1995); *see, e.g.*, ***CERAbio LLC v. Wright Med. Tech.***, 410 F.3d 981, 997 (7th Cir. 2005) (blanket exclusion of evidence on fundamental piece of D's case likely affected jury's conclusion; D entitled to new trial).

(4) The court erroneously charged the jury. ***Goodgame v. American Cast Iron Pipe Co.***, 75 F.3d 1516, 1521 (11th Cir.1996); *see* ***Minks v. Polaris Indus.***, 546 F.3d 1364, 1375-76 (Fed.Cir.2008).

(5) Opposing counsel made improper or inflammatory arguments in front of the jury. ***Benedi v. McNeil-P.P.C., Inc.***, 66 F.3d 1378, 1388-89 (4th Cir.1995); ***Johnson v. Ford Motor Co.***, 988 F.2d 573, 582 (5th Cir. 1993); *see* ***Whiting v. Westray***, 294 F.3d 943, 944 (7th Cir.2002) (new trial on grounds of attorney misconduct requires showing that misconduct occurred and prejudiced party's case).

(6) The jury, or one of its members, engaged in misconduct. ***Mayhue v. St. Francis Hosp.***, 969 F.2d 919, 922 (10th Cir.1992); ***Yarbrough v. Sturm, Ruger & Co.***, 964 F.2d 376, 380 (5th Cir.1992).

(7) The jury was coerced into reaching a verdict. ***Witco Chem. Corp. v. Peachtree Doors, Inc.***, 787 F.2d 1545, 1548-49 (Fed.Cir.1986).

(8) Newly discovered evidence would probably change the outcome of the trial. ***Compass Tech. v. Tseng Labs.***, 71 F.3d 1125, 1131 (3d Cir.1995); ***Diaz v. Methodist Hosp.***, 46 F.3d 492, 495 (5th Cir.1995). The same factors apply for newly discovered evidence in a motion for new trial under FRCP 59 or a motion for relief from the judgment under FRCP 60(b)(2). See "Newly discovered evidence," ch. 10-F, §3.4.2, p. 808.

(9) The complaining party was unfairly surprised by something that occurred at trial. ***Genmoora Corp. v. Moore Bus. Forms, Inc.***, 939 F.2d 1149, 1156 (5th Cir.1991).

(10) The trial was not fair to the moving party for any other reason. ***Winger***, 82 F.3d at 143; *e.g.*, ***Santa Maria v. Metro-N. Commuter R.R.***, 81 F.3d 265, 273 (2d Cir.1996) (court's biased treatment of attorney and display of antipathy toward merits warranted new trial).

2. Nonjury trials. In nonjury trials, courts have recognized three grounds for a new trial: (1) manifest error of law, (2) manifest error of fact, and (3) newly discovered evidence. ***Brown v. Wright***, 588 F.2d 708, 710 (9th Cir.1978); ***Wilcher v. City of Wilmington***, 924 F.Supp. 613, 616 (D.Del.1996), *vacated in part on other grounds*, 139 F.3d 366 (3d Cir.1998). For the factors for newly discovered evidence, see "Newly discovered evidence," ch. 10-F, §3.4.2, p. 808.

§3.5 Affidavits. If the party moving for a new trial wants to present new facts not already in the record, it must file affidavits with its motion. FRCP 59(c); *see* ***Kleinschmidt v. U.S.***, 146 F.Supp. 253, 256-57 (D.Mass.1956) (newly discovered evidence). If the nonmovant files responsive affidavits, the movant can ask the court for permission to file affidavits in reply. *See* FRCP 59(c).

§3.6 Request hearing. If a motion for new trial presents contested fact issues, or if oral argument will help the court resolve the motion, the movant should request a hearing. The movant should comply with any requirements of the local rules for securing a hearing on the motion. *See* ***Kendall v. Hoover Co.***, 751 F.2d 171, 172-73 (6th Cir. 1984).

§4. RESPONSE

§4.1 Objections. If the nonmovant opposes the motion for new trial, it should file a response objecting to the grounds in the motion.

1. Substantive. The response should negate whatever substantive grounds are asserted in the motion. For example, the nonmovant can assert the following:

(1) Through due diligence, the movant could have discovered the newly discovered evidence in time to introduce it at trial.

(2) There was no jury misconduct or other type of misconduct.

(3) The evidence supports the jury's verdict or the court's findings.

2. Procedural. The response should identify any procedural reasons why the motion should be denied (e.g., the motion was filed after the 28-day deadline passed). *See* FRCP 59(b).

§4.2 Deadline. FRCP 59 does not specify a deadline for the response, but it should be filed within any limits set by local rules for responses. FRCP 59(c) does, however, contain a deadline for filing opposing affidavits.

§4.3 Affidavits. If the response contains facts outside the record, it should be supported by affidavits. Generally, if the movant attached affidavits to its motion for new trial, the nonmovant should attach affidavits to its response.

1. Deadline. The opposing affidavits must be filed within 14 days after service of the motion. FRCP 59(c).

2. Additional time. If the nonmovant needs additional time to secure affidavits, the court can extend the time for serving the affidavits under FRCP 6(b)(1). *See* 2009 Notes to FRCP 59 at ¶2, p. 1229, this book. See "Motion to Extend Time," ch. 5-F, p. 332. Also, if local rules provide a deadline for the response that is longer than the 14-day deadline for the affidavits, the nonmovant can ask the court to extend the affidavit deadline to match the response deadline. *See* FRCP 6(b)(1).

§5. HEARING

§5.1 Generally. Most motions for new trial do not require an evidentiary hearing. If a hearing is held, it is usually to allow the parties to make legal arguments.

§5.2 Exception. Some motions for new trial, such as motions based on newly discovered evidence or jury misconduct, may require evidentiary hearings. *See* ***Robinson v. Monsanto Co.***, 758 F.2d 331, 334 (8th Cir.1985) (court must conduct evidentiary hearing on jury misconduct if movant establishes prima facie case that right to peremptory challenge was prejudicially impaired); *see, e.g.*, ***Branca v. Security Benefit Life Ins.***, 789 F.2d 1511, 1513 (11th Cir.1986) (newly discovered report by foreign government entitled P to hearing on whether court should issue letters rogatory). If a motion is based on jury misconduct, the trial judge generally determines whether an evidentiary hearing is necessary. ***Yannacopoulos v. General Dynamics Corp.***, 75 F.3d 1298, 1305 (8th Cir.1996); ***Morgan v. Woessner***, 997 F.2d 1244, 1261-62 (9th Cir.1993).

§6. RULING

§6.1 Standard. The court has broad discretion in granting new trials. ***Allied Chem. Corp. v. Daiflon, Inc.***, 449 U.S. 33, 36 (1980); *see* ***Consolo v. George***, 58 F.3d 791, 795 (1st Cir.1995) (court can grant new trial to prevent miscarriage of justice). See "Standard Applied by District Court," §7, p. 788.

§6.2 Written order. The court should sign a written order granting or denying the motion. However, the order does not need to be set out in a separate document. FRCP 58(a)(4). See "Orders," ch. 1-G, §4.2, p. 45.

§6.3 No deadline for order. If the motion for new trial is filed before the 28-day deadline, the finality of the judgment is suspended, and the court can rule on the motion after the 28-day deadline has passed. *See* 11 Wright, Miller & Kane §2812 & nn.13-14 (applying former ten-day deadline).

§6.4 On court's initiative. The court can grant a new trial on its own initiative for any reason for which it could have granted a new trial on the motion of a party. FRCP 59(d); ***Central Microfilm Serv. v. Basic/Four Corp.***, 688 F.2d 1206, 1211 (8th Cir.1982). When the court grants a new trial on its own initiative, it must enter an order that specifies the reasons for the new trial within 28 days after the entry of judgment. FRCP 59(d). When a motion for new trial is pending, the court acts on its own initiative if it grants a new trial on a ground not mentioned in the motion. ***Central Microfilm***, 688 F.2d at 1211. When the court grants a new trial on a ground not mentioned in a pending motion, it can enter the order for new trial more than 28 days after the entry of judgment if it gives the parties notice and an opportunity to be heard. FRCP 59(d); 11 Wright, Miller & Kane §2813 & n.15; *see* ***Central Microfilm***, 688 F.2d at 1211 (applying former ten-day deadline).

§6.5 On party's motion.

1. Court denies new trial. An order denying a motion for new trial is generally not appealable. But because the denial of a motion for new trial usually follows a final, appealable judgment, the movant should prepare for an appeal. See "New trial denied," §8.1.1, p. 791.

2. Court grants new trial. If the court grants the motion for new trial, the parties should begin preparing for the retrial. See "New trial granted," §8.1.2, p. 792. But the district court can set aside the order at any time if it decides the order was erroneous. *See* ***Hardin v. Hayes***, 52 F.3d 934, 938 (11th Cir.1995); ***Gallimore v. Missouri Pac. R.R.***, 635 F.2d 1165, 1171 (5th Cir.1981). If the court grants a new trial, it can enter an order for any of the following:

(1) Complete new trial. The court can order a new trial on all the issues. FRCP 59(a)(1).

(2) Partial new trial. The court can order a partial new trial if "the issue to be retried is so distinct and separable from the others that a trial of it alone may be had without injustice." ***Gasoline Prods. Co. v. Champlin Ref. Co.***, 283 U.S. 494, 500 (1931); ***Brooks v. Brattleboro Mem'l Hosp.***, 958 F.2d 525, 530 (2d Cir.1992); ***Shessel v. Murphy***, 920 F.2d 784, 787 (11th Cir.1991); *see* FRCP 59(a)(1) (new trial can be granted on some issues); ***Rice v. Community Health Ass'n***, 203 F.3d 283, 290 (4th Cir.2000) (partial new trials are usually confined to damages); *see also* ***Poullard v. Turner***, 298 F.3d 421, 424 (5th Cir.2002) (new trial granted on compensatory damages must also be granted on punitive damages).

(3) Remittitur.

(a) Generally. The court can grant a new trial conditioned on a remittitur if it determines that the damages awarded by the jury are excessive. ***Thomas v. iStar Fin., Inc.***, 652 F.3d 141, 146 (2d Cir.2010); ***Thorne v. Welk Inv.***, 197 F.3d 1205, 1212 (8th Cir.1999); ***Eiland v. Westinghouse Elec. Corp.***, 58 F.3d 176, 183 (5th Cir. 1995); *see* ***Rodriguez v. Farm Stores Grocery, Inc.***, 518 F.3d 1259, 1266 (11th Cir.2008) (remittitur reduces excessive damages award to amount established by evidence). A new trial conditioned on a remittitur forces the plaintiff to choose between a nonappealable reduced damages award and a new trial. ***Eiland***, 58 F.3d at 183; *see* ***Donovan v. Penn Shipping Co.***, 429 U.S. 648, 649 (1977) (P who accepts reduced award cannot appeal that award); *see also* ***Sulzer Carbomedics, Inc. v. Oregon Cardio-Devices, Inc.***, 257 F.3d 449, 460 (5th Cir.2001) (acceptance of remittitur on one claim does not bar appeal of adverse judgment on claim that is separate and distinct). Remittitur cannot be ordered without the plaintiff's consent. ***Hetzel v. Prince William Cty.***, 523 U.S. 208, 211 (1998); ***Thorne***, 197 F.3d at 1212; *see* ***Thomas***, 652 F.3d at 146. However, if an award is based on a legal error, the court may be able to reduce the award without offering the option of a new trial. *See, e.g.*, ***New York, Lake Erie & W. R.R. v. Estill***, 147 U.S. 591, 621-23 (1893) (court reduced award without option of new trial after jury awarded interest on compensatory damages, which was not allowed under state law); ***Minks v. Polaris Indus.***, 546 F.3d 1364, 1371-72 (Fed.Cir. 2008) (court could not reduce compensatory-damages award without option of new trial because court engaged in independent review of evidence and error in damages was not one of law); *see also* ***Johansen v. Combustion Eng'g***, 170 F.3d 1320, 1331 (11th Cir.1999) (court reduced punitive-damages award without option of new trial when award was unconstitutionally excessive; reducing unconstitutionally excessive verdict is mandatory and is not considered remittitur). If the jury awarded punitive damages out of passion and prejudice, remittitur is not appropriate because a new trial is usually required. ***Thorne***, 197 F.3d at 1210; 11 Wright, Miller & Kane §2815 & n.14.

(b) No additur. The court cannot grant a new trial conditioned on an additur (i.e., forcing the defendant to choose between an increased damages award and a new trial) if it determines that the damages awarded by the jury are inadequate. ***Dimick v. Schiedt***, 293 U.S. 474, 486-87 (1935). *But see* ***Liriano v. Hobart Corp.***, 170 F.3d 264, 272-73 (2d Cir.1999) (courts can adjust jury award upward if discrete amount should have been part of damages calculations and that amount is not in dispute).

(4) Other relief – nonjury trial. When a motion for new trial is filed in a nonjury case, the court can do the following: (1) open the judgment if one has been entered, (2) take additional testimony, (3) amend findings of fact and conclusions of law or make new ones, and (4) direct the entry of a new judgment. FRCP 59(a)(2).

§6.6 Court's reasons. If the court grants a new trial because the verdict is against the great weight of the evidence, it must state the reasons for its decision. ***Shaffer v. Wilkes***, 65 F.3d 115, 118 (8th Cir.1995). But if the court denies a motion for new trial, it does not need to write a comprehensive opinion or give any explanation. ***Dunn v. Truck World, Inc.***, 929 F.2d 311, 313 (7th Cir.1991).

§7. STANDARD APPLIED BY DISTRICT COURT

The standard applied by the district court depends on the grounds for relief asserted in the motion for new trial. 1 Childress & Davis §5.08.

§7.1 Verdict against weight of evidence. When a motion for new trial is based on insufficiency of the evidence, a stringent standard applies, and the motion should be granted only if the verdict "is against the great weight of the evidence, or it is quite clear that the jury has reached a seriously erroneous result." ***Hemmings v. Tidyman's Inc.***, 285 F.3d 1174, 1189 (9th Cir.2002); ***Holmes v. City of Massillon***, 78 F.3d 1041, 1047 (6th Cir.1996); ***Fredette v. Allied Van Lines, Inc.***, 66 F.3d 369, 375 (1st Cir.1995); *see* ***Raedle v. Credit Agricole Indosuez***, 670 F.3d 411, 418-19 (2d Cir.2012); ***International Ins. v. RSR Corp.***, 426 F.3d 281, 300 (5th Cir.2005). The court cannot grant a new trial merely because it would have decided the case differently. ***Jennings v. Jones***, 587 F.3d 430, 436 (1st Cir.2009); ***Coastal Fuels v. Caribbean Pet. Corp.***, 79 F.3d 182, 201 (1st Cir.1996). The court can, however, weigh all of the evidence. ***Jennings***, 587 F.3d at 436; ***Dennis v. Columbia Colleton Med. Ctr., Inc.***, 290 F.3d 639, 650 (4th Cir.2002); *see* ***Smith v. Transworld Drilling Co.***, 773 F.2d 610, 613 (5th Cir.1985). In determining whether the verdict is against the great weight of the evidence, the court does not need to view the evidence in the light most favorable to the nonmovant. ***Smith***, 773 F.2d at 613.

§7.2 Damages inadequate or excessive. The standard for granting a new trial based on the amount of damages depends on the type and amount of damages.

1. Compensatory damages. When a party complains that the amount of compensatory damages is inadequate or excessive, the court has the discretion to weigh the evidence. The question from the court's perspective is whether the award is so inadequate, excessive, or lacking a rational connection to the evidence that it offends the conscience of the court and warrants a new trial. *See* ***Palmer v. City of Monticello***, 31 F.3d 1499, 1508 (10th Cir. 1994); ***Holmes v. Elgin, Joliet & E. Ry.***, 18 F.3d 1393, 1395-96 (7th Cir.1994). The fact that the court would have made a smaller award is not sufficient to render the verdict excessive. *See, e.g.*, ***Dunn v. HOVIC***, 1 F.3d 1362, 1367 (3d Cir.1993) ($500,000 compensatory award was generous, but did not shock judicial conscience). Nor does the fact that the court would have made a larger award render the damages inadequate. ***General Mills, Inc. v. Calumet Harbor Terminals, Inc.***, 47 F.R.D. 189, 190-91 (N.D.Ill.1969).

2. Punitive damages. When a party complains that the amount of punitive damages is excessive, the court must determine whether the jury's verdict is within the confines of state and federal law and whether a new trial or a remittitur should be ordered. *See* ***Cooper Indus. v. Leatherman Tool Grp.***, 532 U.S. 424, 433 (2001); ***Browning-Ferris Indus. v. Kelco Disposal, Inc.***, 492 U.S. 257, 279 (1989). For example, a defendant can complain that the amount of punitive damages is so excessive that it violates its due-process rights. ***State Farm Mut. Auto. Ins. v. Campbell***, 538 U.S. 408, 417-18 (2003); *see* ***Cooper Indus.***, 532 U.S. at 434. In evaluating a punitive-damages award for a violation of due-process rights, the court should consider the following "guideposts": (1) the degree of

reprehensibility of the defendant's misconduct, (2) the disparity between the harm (or potential harm) suffered by the plaintiff and the punitive-damages award, and (3) the difference between the punitive damages awarded by the jury and the civil penalties authorized or imposed in comparable cases. ***Campbell***, 538 U.S. at 418; ***BMW of N. Am., Inc. v. Gore***, 517 U.S. 559, 574-75 (1996); *see also* ***Tingley Sys. v. Norse Sys.***, 49 F.3d 93, 96 (2d Cir.1995) (punitive damages cannot be so excessive that they "shock" judicial conscience). While a jury can consider evidence of harm to nonparties to determine the level of reprehensibility, it cannot use a punitive-damages award to punish the defendant for harm suffered by nonparties. ***Philip Morris USA v. Williams***, 549 U.S. 346, 356-57 (2007).

NOTE

*In **Campbell**, the Supreme Court reversed and remanded a punitive-damages award of $145 million when the compensatory damages were only $1 million. Applying the **Gore** due-process guideposts to the facts, the Court stated that an appropriate punitive-damages award would be "at or near the amount of compensatory damages." **Campbell**, 538 U.S. at 429; see also **Willow Inn, Inc. v. Public Serv. Mut. Ins.**, 399 F.3d 224, 236-37 (3d Cir.2005) (attorney fees and costs could be included with compensatory award to determine whether punitive-damages award was constitutionally permissible). In discussing the second guidepost, the ratio of harm (or potential harm) suffered to the amount of punitive damages, the Court indicated that few awards exceeding a single-digit ratio would satisfy due process. **Campbell**, 538 U.S. at 425; see **Mathias v. Accor Econ. Lodging, Inc.**, 347 F.3d 672, 676-78 (7th Cir.2003) (appellate court affirmed award exceeding ratio in **Campbell** and stated that judicial function is "to police a range, not a point"); see, e.g., **CGB Occupational Therapy, Inc. v. RHA Health Servs.**, 499 F.3d 184, 192-93 (3d Cir.2007) (18:1 ratio reduced to 7:1); see also **Exxon Shipping Co. v. Baker**, 554 U.S. 471, 494 (2008) (heavier punitive-damages awards may be justified when wrongdoing is hard to detect or value of injury and compensatory award are small). After the punitive-damages award was reduced to just over $9 million on remand, State Farm again petitioned for certiorari, which the Supreme Court denied, allowing the award to stand. **Campbell v. State Farm Mut. Auto Ins.**, 98 P.3d 409, 418 (Utah 2004), cert. denied, 543 U.S. 874 (2004). While the reduced award is within the single-digit ratio laid out by the Court, it is arguably higher than the amount that the Court considered justifiable in its original opinion.*

§7.3 Trial errors. The standard for granting a new trial based on errors committed during the trial is whether the district court made an erroneous ruling that substantially prejudiced the movant. ***Ruvalcaba v. City of L.A.***, 64 F.3d 1323, 1328 (9th Cir.1995). The appellate courts give the district court "great latitude" in determining whether to grant a new trial based on trial error because the district court is in the best position to estimate the prejudicial impact of the error on the jury. ***Cruthirds v. RCI, Inc.***, 624 F.2d 632, 635 (5th Cir.1980). The party moving for new trial must be prepared to demonstrate that it preserved the right to complain about the trial error. *See* 11 Wright, Miller & Kane §2805 & nn. 12-13.

1. Erroneous admission of evidence. When a party complains about the erroneous admission of evidence, the court can properly deny the motion if the movant did not object to the evidence when it was actually admitted. *See* ***Hose v. Chicago Nw. Transp.***, 70 F.3d 968, 972-73 (8th Cir.1995); ***Johnson v. Michelin Tire Corp.***, 812 F.2d 200, 210 n.8 (5th Cir.1987). If the movant offered similar evidence during its case-in-chief, it waived its objection to any error in the admission of the evidence. *See* ***Johnson v. Bowers***, 884 F.2d 1053, 1056 n.2 (8th Cir.1989). If the movant preserved the complaint and the jury considered the inadmissible and prejudicial evidence, the court can grant a new trial. ***Jackson v. Pleasant Grove Health Care Ctr.***, 980 F.2d 692, 696 n.4 (11th Cir.1993); ***Carson v. Polley***, 689 F.2d 562, 570 (5th Cir.1982).

2. Erroneous jury instruction. When moving for a new trial on the grounds that the jury was improperly instructed on the law, the movant must demonstrate the following:

(1) There was error in the jury charge. ***Advanced Display Sys. v. Kent State Univ.***, 212 F.3d 1272, 1281 (Fed.Cir.2000). The instructions, taken as a whole, must have given the jury a misleading impression or inadequate understanding of the law and the issues to be resolved. ***Kavorkian v. CSX Transp.***, 117 F.3d 953, 956 (6th Cir.1997); ***BAII Banking Corp. v. UPG, Inc.***, 985 F.2d 685, 696 (2d Cir.1993).

(2) The movant made a timely and proper objection to the erroneous charge. ***Advanced Display***, 212 F.3d at 1281; *see* ***Crist v. Dickson Welding, Inc.***, 957 F.2d 1281, 1286 (5th Cir.1992) (after the charge and before the jury retires). If the movant did not object to the charge during the trial, it must show, on appeal, that the error rose to the level of a plain error or resulted in a miscarriage of justice. *See* ***Bening v. Muegler***, 67 F.3d 691, 696 (8th Cir. 1995); ***Wagner v. Fair Acres Geriatric Ctr.***, 49 F.3d 1002, 1018 n.17 (3d Cir.1995); ***Fruge v. Penrod Drilling Co.***, 918 F.2d 1163, 1169 (5th Cir.1990).

(3) The error had a prejudicial effect. ***Advanced Display***, 212 F.3d at 1281.

(4) The party requested alternative instructions that would have remedied the error. *Id.*

3. Jury misconduct. When a party complains about jury misconduct, the court has broad discretion in determining which methods will be used to gather sufficient evidence to decide the issue. ***Carson***, 689 F.2d at 580; *see* ***Hard v. Burlington N. R.R.***, 812 F.2d 482, 485 (9th Cir.1987). However, because of the limitations on proving misconduct, obtaining a new trial based on jury misconduct is difficult. *See* FRE 606(b); 11 Wright, Miller & Kane §2810; *see also* ***Big John, B.V. v. Indian Head Grain Co.***, 718 F.2d 143, 150 (5th Cir.1983) (before juror can be questioned, there must be showing of specific instances of misconduct).

(1) Misconduct during voir dire. A party seeking a new trial based on a juror's inaccurate answers during voir dire must demonstrate that the juror answered a material question dishonestly and that a proper response would have provided a valid basis for a challenge for cause. ***McDonough Power Equip., Inc. v. Greenwood***, 464 U.S. 548, 556 (1984); ***Crowley v. L.L. Bean, Inc.***, 303 F.3d 387, 407 (1st Cir.2002). To obtain a new trial because of nondisclosure by a juror during voir dire, a party must do more than raise speculative allegations that the juror's possible bias may have influenced the outcome of the trial; the party must show actual juror bias. ***Crowley***, 303 F.3d at 407-08.

(2) Misconduct during deliberations. A party seeking a new trial based on a juror's misconduct during deliberations must demonstrate that exposure of extraneous prejudicial evidence to the jury was harmful to the losing party. ***Porous Media Corp. v. Pall Corp.***, 110 F.3d 1329, 1340 (8th Cir.1997); *see* 11 Wright, Miller & Kane §2810 & n.13. A juror can testify about (1) whether extraneous prejudicial information was improperly brought to the jury's attention, (2) whether an outside influence was improperly brought to bear on any juror, or (3) whether a mistake was made in entering the verdict on the verdict form. FRE 606(b)(2); ***U.S. v. Wintermute***, 443 F.3d 993, 1002 (8th Cir.2006) (elements 1 and 2); ***U.S. v. Lloyd***, 269 F.3d 228, 237 (3d Cir.2001) (same); ***U.S. v. Henley***, 238 F.3d 1111, 1117 (9th Cir.2001) (same); *see, e.g.*, ***White v. Cooper***, 919 F.Supp. 1022, 1025-26 (E.D.Tex.1996) (jurors testified about whether another juror brought dictionary into jury room to define legal terms and whether it influenced jurors' decisions), *aff'd*, 129 F.3d 609 (5th Cir.1997) (table case). A juror cannot testify about (1) any statement made or incident that occurred during the jury's deliberations, (2) the effect of anything on that juror's or another juror's vote, or (3) any juror's mental processes about the verdict or indictment. FRE 606(b)(1); ***U.S. v. Logan***, 250 F.3d 350, 379 (6th Cir.2001); ***Haugh v. Jones & Laughlin Steel Corp.***, 949 F.2d 914, 917 (7th Cir.1991); ***Carson***, 689 F.2d at 580-81.

NOTE

Although a juror cannot testify about the jury's deliberations unless one of the three explicit exceptions under FRE 606(b)(2) applies, some courts have recognized an implicit exception that allows evidence of racial bias that occurred during voir dire or deliberations. See ***U.S. v. Villar****, 586 F.3d 76, 87 (1st Cir.2009) (FRE 606(b) does not bar juror testimony in rare cases in which racial bias during deliberations offends party's right to due process and impartial jury);*

*Henley, 238 F.3d at 1121 (FRE 606(b) does not bar juror testimony that another juror was untruthful when he denied racial bias during voir dire but exhibited racial bias during trial). But see **U.S. v. Benally**, 546 F.3d 1230, 1236, 1238-39 (10th Cir.2008) (allowing juror testimony through use of voir dire challenge would risk undercutting FRE 606(b); rule does not contain implicit exception that allows juror testimony on racially biased statements made during deliberations).*

§7.4 Newly discovered evidence. To be entitled to a new trial on the ground of newly discovered evidence, the movant should show the following factors.

NOTE

*The same factors apply for newly discovered evidence in a motion for new trial under FRCP 59 or a motion for relief from the judgment under FRCP 60(b)(2). See **WMS Gaming, Inc. v. International Game Tech.**, 184 F.3d 1339, 1361 n.11 (Fed.Cir.1999); 11 Wright, Miller & Kane §2808 & n.3. See "Motion for Relief from Judgment," ch. 10-F, p. 804.*

1. The evidence existed at the time of trial. *Cf.* ***Government Fin. Servs. One L.P. v. Peyton Place, Inc.***, 62 F.3d 767, 771 (5th Cir.1995) (FRCP 60(b)(2) motion).

2. The evidence was discovered after trial. ***Joseph v. Terminix Int'l Co.***, 17 F.3d 1282, 1285 (10th Cir. 1994).

3. The movant exercised due diligence to discover the evidence. ***Diaz v. Methodist Hosp.***, 46 F.3d 492, 495 (5th Cir.1995); ***Joseph***, 17 F.3d at 1285.

4. The evidence is admissible. *Cf.* ***Provident Life & Acc. Ins. v. Goel***, 274 F.3d 984, 1000 (5th Cir.2001) (FRCP 60(b)(2) motion).

5. The evidence is credible. *Cf.* ***Goel***, 274 F.3d at 1000 (FRCP 60(b)(2) motion).

6. The evidence is material. ***Joseph***, 17 F.3d at 1285; *cf.* ***Peyton Place***, 62 F.3d at 771 (under FRCP 60(b)(2) motion, evidence is material and controlling).

7. The evidence is not merely cumulative or impeaching. ***Diaz***, 46 F.3d at 495; ***Joseph***, 17 F.3d at 1285.

8. The evidence probably would have caused a different result. ***Diaz***, 46 F.3d at 495; ***Joseph***, 17 F.3d at 1285.

§7.5 Unfair surprise. The ground of unfair surprise is limited to situations in which a party unfairly introduced surprise testimony that prejudiced the other party. *See* ***Conway v. Chemical Leaman Tank Lines, Inc.***, 687 F.2d 108, 111-12 (5th Cir.1982). To warrant a new trial, the unfair surprise must be inconsistent with substantial justice. *E.g.*, ***Erskine v. Consolidated Rail Corp.***, 814 F.2d 266, 272 (6th Cir.1987) (documents produced at trial had not been produced in discovery); ***Conway***, 687 F.2d at 111-12 (witness who was not identified in discovery testified about new theory). A party faced with unfair surprise should ask for a continuance. *See, e.g.*, ***U.S. v. Midwest Suspension & Brake***, 49 F.3d 1197, 1205-06 (6th Cir.1995) (court did not abuse its discretion when it denied D's motion for new trial based on unfair surprise and D did not move for continuance during trial).

§8. APPELLATE REVIEW

§8.1 Appealability.

1. New trial denied.

(1) Order not appealable. An order denying a motion for new trial is generally not appealable. ***Wright v. Harris Cty.***, 536 F.3d 436, 438 (5th Cir.2008); ***McGowne v. Challenge-Cook Bros.***, 672 F.2d 652, 659 (8th Cir.1982). *But see* ***Fiore v. Washington Cty. Cmty. Mental Health Ctr.***, 960 F.2d 229, 233 n.8 (1st Cir.1992) (denials of motion for new trial and other postjudgment motions are final orders, appealable separately from underlying

judgment). However, because the motion is usually made after a final, appealable judgment, the order may be reviewable on appeal from the final judgment. ***Railroad Dynamics, Inc. v. A. Stucki Co.***, 727 F.2d 1506, 1512 (Fed. Cir.1984); 11 Wright, Miller & Kane §2818 & n.9. Even if an appellant incorrectly appeals from an order denying a motion for new trial rather than a final judgment, the appellate court may treat the appeal as if it had been taken from the final judgment. ***McGowne***, 672 F.2d at 659; 11 Wright, Miller & Kane §2818 & n.11.

(2) Order appealable. Under exceptional circumstances, an order denying a motion for new trial may be appealable. ***Clark v. Heidrick***, 150 F.3d 912, 916 (8th Cir.1998). The order may be appealable when new matters arise after the entry of judgment. ***John E. Smith's Sons Co. v. Lattimer Foundry & Mach. Co.***, 239 F.2d 815, 816 (3d Cir.1956); *see* ***Wright***, 536 F.3d at 438.

2. New trial granted. An order granting a motion for new trial is usually not reviewable until after the case is resolved by a final judgment. *See* ***Allied Chem. Corp. v. Daiflon, Inc.***, 449 U.S. 33, 36 (1980); ***Gilliland v. Lyons***, 278 F.2d 56, 58 (9th Cir.1960). An order granting a motion for new trial is interlocutory and is not a final, appealable order because it leaves the case unresolved and the parties before the court. *See* ***Allied Chem.***, 449 U.S. at 34. However, if the district court lacked jurisdiction to grant a new trial (e.g., a new trial was granted after the deadline passed), the order is considered final and appealable. ***Gilliland***, 278 F.2d at 58; *see* 11 Wright, Miller & Kane §2818 & n.4.

3. Mandamus. An order on a motion for new trial is rarely, if ever, reviewable by mandamus. *See* ***Allied Chem.***, 449 U.S. at 36.

§8.2 Deadline. The timely filing of a motion for new trial tolls the deadline to file a notice of appeal until an order disposing of the motion is entered. FRAP 4(a)(4)(A)(v); *see* ***Shales v. General Chauffeurs, Sales Drivers & Helpers Local Un.***, 557 F.3d 746, 748 (7th Cir.2009) (tolling of appellate deadline is determined by filing of motion, not by decision that motion has merit). An order is considered entered within the meaning of FRAP 4(a)(4) when it is entered on the civil docket under FRCP 79(a). FRAP 4(a)(7)(A)(i). The court does not need to render the order with the formality of a judgment, but it must clearly dispose of the post-trial motion. ***Ellison v. Conoco, Inc.***, 950 F.2d 1196, 1201 (5th Cir.1992). An appellant challenging either an order disposing of the motion for new trial or a judgment's alteration or amendment based on the motion for new trial must file the notice of appeal within 30 days (60 days if the United States is a party) after entry of the order, unless there are other outstanding motions that continue to toll the running of the appellate deadlines. *See* FRAP 4(a)(1)(A), (a)(1)(B), (a)(4)(B)(ii); 2009 Notes to FRAP 4 at ¶¶3, 4, p. 1266, this book.

§8.3 Standard of review.

1. Question of fact. The district court's ruling on questions of fact in a motion for new trial is reviewed for abuse of discretion. *See* ***Jennings v. Jones***, 587 F.3d 430, 436-37 & n.7 (1st Cir.2009); ***U.S. v. Hinkson***, 585 F.3d 1247, 1261 (9th Cir.2009); ***Cates v. Creamer***, 431 F.3d 456, 460 (5th Cir.2005); ***Whiting v. Westray***, 294 F.3d 943, 944 (7th Cir.2002); ***Medforms, Inc. v. Healthcare Mgmt. Solutions, Inc.***, 290 F.3d 98, 106 (2d Cir.2002). In reviewing the district court's decision, the appellate court does not view the evidence in the light most favorable to the nonmoving party. ***Jennings***, 587 F.3d at 438-39; *see* ***Moss v. Feldmeyer***, 979 F.2d 1454, 1462 (10th Cir.1992). *Contra* ***Medforms***, 290 F.3d at 106.

(1) New trial denied. When the district court denies a motion for new trial, the scope of the appellate court's review is narrow because the district court's decision accords with the jury verdict. ***Langevine v. District of Columbia***, 106 F.3d 1018, 1023 (D.C.Cir.1997).

(2) New trial granted. When the district court grants a motion for new trial, the scope of the appellate court's review is broader because there is a concern that the district court's granting of the motion infringes on the jury's fact-finding responsibility. *See* ***Langevine***, 106 F.3d at 1023; *see also* ***Davis v. Wisconsin Dept. of Corr.***, 445 F.3d 971, 979 (7th Cir.2006) (new trial should be granted only when record shows verdict resulted in miscarriage of justice, "cries out to be overturned," or "shocks" court's conscience). But the appellate court's degree of scrutiny

can differ depending on the district court's reasons for granting a motion for new trial. ***Wilburn v. Maritrans GP Inc.***, 139 F.3d 350, 363 (3d Cir.1998). For example, if the district court grants a motion for new trial because it believes the jury verdict is against the weight of the evidence, the appellate court may apply a close degree of scrutiny. *Id.*; ***Langevine***, 106 F.3d at 1023; *see* ***Kode v. Carlson***, 596 F.3d 608, 612-13 (9th Cir.2010); ***Cates***, 431 F.3d at 460-61. See "Standard Applied by District Court," §7, p. 788.

2. Question of law. When the grounds asserted in a motion for new trial depend only on the resolution of a legal question, the appellate courts are less deferential to the district court's judgment than they are when reviewing the evidence. *See* ***Advanced Display Sys. v. Kent State Univ.***, 212 F.3d 1272, 1282 (Fed.Cir.2000) (error in charge); ***County of Maricopa v. Maberry***, 555 F.2d 207, 223 (9th Cir.1977) (same). Thus, if the disposition of the motion for new trial is based on the application of legal principles, appellate review is de novo. ***Hook v. Ernst & Young***, 28 F.3d 366, 370 (3d Cir.1994); *see, e.g.*, ***Cooper Indus. v. Leatherman Tool Grp.***, 532 U.S. 424, 435-36 (2001) (appellate court's review of district court's determination of whether award of punitive damages is constitutionally excessive is reviewed de novo); ***Kode***, 596 F.3d at 611 (appellate court's review of district court's determination of whether P had waived objection to jury is reviewed de novo).

D. MOTION TO ALTER OR AMEND JUDGMENT

§1. GENERAL

§1.1 Rule. FRCP 59(e).

§1.2 Purpose. A motion to alter or amend the judgment asks the district court to substantively change—or even vacate—the judgment. *See* ***Foman v. Davis***, 371 U.S. 178, 180-81 (1962); ***Yost v. Stout***, 607 F.3d 1239, 1243 (10th Cir.2010); ***Borrero v. City of Chi.***, 456 F.3d 698, 699 (7th Cir.2006); ***Ford v. Elsbury***, 32 F.3d 931, 937 (5th Cir.1994); *see also* ***Simmons v. Reliance Std. Life Ins.***, 310 F.3d 865, 868 n.1 (5th Cir.2002) (FRCP 59 motion also referred to as motion for rehearing or motion for reconsideration). For a discussion of how to correct clerical errors in the judgment, see "Motion to Correct Clerical Error in Judgment," ch. 10-I, p. 825.

§1.3 Timetable & forms. Timetable, Appeal of Civil Trial, p. 1591; ***O'Connor's Federal Civil Forms*** (2012), FORMS 10D:1-3.

§1.4 Other references. 11 Wright, Miller & Kane, *Federal Practice & Procedure 2d* §§2810.1, 2817 (1995 & Supp.2012); 12 *Moore's Federal Practice 3d* §§59.30-59.54 (2012); 1 Childress & Davis, *Federal Standards of Review 4th* §5.13 (2010 & Supp.2011).

§2. DEADLINE

§2.1 28-day deadline. A motion to alter or amend the judgment must be filed with the clerk within 28 days after the entry of judgment. FRCP 59(e); ***Wells Fargo Bank v. WMR e-Pin, LLC***, 653 F.3d 702, 714 (8th Cir.2011). The judgment is considered entered when it is placed in a separate document and entered on the docket in compliance with FRCP 58. See "Requirements for Final Judgment," ch. 9-A, §2, p. 735. The motion must be received by—not just mailed to—the clerk by the deadline. When calculating the 28-day time period, the date the judgment is entered is the trigger event and is excluded; counting begins the day after the entry of judgment. FRCP 6(a)(1)(A); *cf.* ***Laborers' Pension Fund v. A&C Env'tl, Inc.***, 301 F.3d 768, 775 n.5 (7th Cir.2002) (for renewed motion for JMOL, entry date of judgment on docket—not date judgment is signed—triggers time period; applying former ten-day deadline). See "Identify trigger event," ch. 1-C, §6.1.1(1), p. 24.

NOTE

Do not confuse a motion to alter or amend the judgment under FRCP 59(e) with a motion for relief from the judgment under FRCP 60(b). Although both motions can be used to correct similar errors, a motion filed within 28 days after the judgment is generally considered a motion under FRCP 59(e); an untimely FRCP 59(e) motion is generally treated as an FRCP 60(b) motion.

*See **Justice v. Town of Cicero**, 682 F.3d 662, 665 (7th Cir.2012) (applying current 28-day deadline); **Robinson v. Wix Filtration Corp.**, 599 F.3d 403, 411-12 (4th Cir.2010) (applying former ten-day deadline); **Price v. Philpot**, 420 F.3d 1158, 1167 n.9 (10th Cir.2005) (same); **Lavespere v. Niagara Mach. & Tool Works, Inc.**, 910 F.2d 167, 173 (5th Cir.1990) (same). But see **Obriecht v. Raemisch**, 517 F.3d 489, 493 (7th Cir.2008) (characterization of motion depends on substance of motion, not timing or label). See "Misnomer of motions under FRCP 59(e)," §3.5, p. 796. Motions under FRCP 60(b), however, have stricter substantive requirements than motions under FRCP 59(e). See **Lavespere**, 910 F.2d at 173-74 (applying former ten-day deadline). See "Motion for Relief from Judgment," ch. 10-F, p. 804.*

§2.2 No extension. The deadline for filing a motion to alter or amend the judgment cannot be extended by the court or the parties. *See* FRCP 6(b)(2); ***U.S. Leather, Inc. v. H&W Prtshp.***, 60 F.3d 222, 225 (5th Cir.1995); ***Hope v. U.S.***, 43 F.3d 1140, 1143 (7th Cir.1994); 2009 Notes to FRCP 59 at ¶1, p. 1229, this book. Some circuits have held that the deadline is jurisdictional; thus, in those circuits, a late motion is ineffective even if the other party does not object. *See* ***U.S. Leather***, 60 F.3d at 225; *see also* ***Fisher v. Kadant, Inc.***, 589 F.3d 505, 511 (1st Cir.2009) (untimely motion under FRCP 59(e) is a nullity). Although the deadline cannot be extended, other circuits have held that FRCP 6(b)(2) and 59(e) are nonjurisdictional claim-processing rules; thus, in those circuits, objections to the timeliness of the motion can be waived. *See, e.g.*, ***Lizardo v. U.S.***, 619 F.3d 273, 277-78 (3d Cir.2010); ***National Ecological Found. v. Alexander***, 496 F.3d 466, 475-76 (6th Cir.2007); ***In re OneCast Media, Inc.***, 439 F.3d 558, 562-63 (9th Cir.2006). That is, if the movant does not file its motion to alter or amend the judgment within the 28-day deadline but the nonmovant does not object to the untimeliness, the objection is waived and the court has jurisdiction over the motion. *See* ***Lizardo v. U.S.***, 619 F.3d 273, 278 (3d Cir.2010).

CAUTION

*Even if the district court has jurisdiction over an untimely motion, the circuits disagree on whether that motion tolls the deadline to file a notice of appeal under FRAP 4(a)(4)(A). Compare **Blue v. International Bhd. of Elec. Workers Local Un.**, 676 F.3d 579, 582-83 (7th Cir. 2012) (untimely motion listed under FRAP 4(a)(4)(A) does not toll time for filing appeal), and **Advanced Bodycare Solutions, LLC v. Thione Int'l**, 615 F.3d 1352, 1359 n.14 (11th Cir.2010) (because FRAP 4(a)(4) is jurisdictional, untimely motion listed under FRAP 4(a)(4)(A) does not toll time for filing appeal), with **Obaydullah v. Obama**, ___ F.3d ___ (D.C.Cir.2012) (No. 11-5123; 8-10-12) (because FRAP 4(a)(4) is nonjurisdictional claim-processing rule, untimely motion listed under FRAP 4(a)(4)(A) can toll time for filing appeal; objections to timeliness for tolling purposes can be waived), and **National Ecological Found.**, 496 F.3d at 476 (untimely motion listed under FRAP 4(a)(4)(A) tolls time for filing appeal). If the appellate deadline is not tolled, an appeal after the ruling on the untimely motion is limited to that ruling and would not include appellate review of the underlying judgment. See **Advanced Bodycare Solutions**, 615 F.3d at 1359 n.14. See "Deadline," §7.1, p. 797. Thus, check the law of your circuit to determine whether untimeliness objections under FRCP 59(e) or for tolling purposes can be waived.*

§2.3 Premature motion. A motion to alter or amend the judgment should be filed after the judgment is entered, not before. *See* FRCP 59(e). But if it is filed before the judgment is entered, it is still timely because FRCP 59(e) specifies only the outer filing limits. *See* ***Jurgens v. McKasy***, 905 F.2d 382, 386 (Fed.Cir.1990); *cf.* ***Dunn v. Truck World, Inc.***, 929 F.2d 311, 312-13 (7th Cir.1991) (motions for JNOV—now JMOL, new trial, or remittitur). If the motion is filed early, the movant should ask the court to sign a written order ruling on the motion without prejudice to filing another motion to alter or amend the judgment after the judgment is entered.

CIRCUIT SPLIT

The circuits disagree on whether a postjudgment motion filed before the entry of final judgment is implicitly overruled when the final judgment is entered. This issue is significant for determining when the 30-day period for filing a notice of appeal under FRAP 4 begins. See "Premature motion," ch. 10-B, §3.3, p. 777.

§3. MOTION

§3.1 Form. For the general requirements for the form of a motion, see "Drafting motions," ch. 1-B, §3.1, p. 14.

§3.2 Grounds. There are three grounds on which a judgment can be altered or amended: (1) to accommodate an intervening change in controlling law, (2) to account for new evidence not available at trial, and (3) to correct a clear error or prevent manifest injustice. ***U.S. v. Westinghouse Savannah River Co.***, 305 F.3d 284, 290 (4th Cir. 2002); ***Servants of the Paraclete v. Does***, 204 F.3d 1005, 1012 (10th Cir.2000); ***Firestone v. Firestone***, 76 F.3d 1205, 1208 (D.C.Cir.1996).

NOTE

Although there are no specific grounds listed in FRCP 59(e), courts generally recognize only the three grounds discussed below for motions to alter or amend the judgment. ***Zinkand v. Brown***, *478 F.3d 634, 637 (4th Cir.2007). But in unusual circumstances, courts may allow a motion that is outside of those grounds. See* ***Allstate Ins. v. Herron***, *634 F.3d 1101, 1111 (9th Cir.2011) (motion under FRCP 59(e) may be appropriate to request amendment that is a basic, clerical task of incorporating undisputed facts into judgment).*

1. Intervening change in law. A party can file a motion to alter or amend the judgment if the law changes after the judgment is entered. ***Allstate Ins.***, 634 F.3d at 1111; ***U.S. v. All Assets & Equip. of W. Side Bldg. Corp.***, 58 F.3d 1181, 1191-92 (7th Cir.1995); 11 Wright, Miller & Kane §2810.1 & n.19; *see, e.g.*, ***Knish v. Stine***, 347 F.Supp.2d 682, 686 (D.Minn.2004) (8th Circuit opinion finding jurisdiction under 28 U.S.C. §2241 was intervening change in law requiring amendment of judgment dismissing for lack of jurisdiction).

2. New evidence. A party can file a motion to alter or amend the judgment on the basis of newly discovered evidence. ***Allstate Ins.***, 634 F.3d at 1111; *see* ***Lavespere v. Niagara Mach. & Tool Works, Inc.***, 910 F.2d 167, 174 (5th Cir.1990). In deciding whether to consider late-filed evidence, the court must strike a balance between two competing interests: the need to bring litigation to an end and the need to render just decisions on all the facts. ***Lavespere***, 910 F.2d at 174. The court should consider the following:

(1) The reasons for the movant's delay in submitting the evidence. ***Leisure Caviar, LLC v. U.S. Fish & Wildlife Serv.***, 616 F.3d 612, 616 (6th Cir.2010); ***Hale v. Townley***, 45 F.3d 914, 921 (5th Cir.1995); *see* ***Garner v. Arvin Indus.***, 77 F.3d 255, 258 (8th Cir.1996) (party must explain why evidence that could and should have been presented was not); ***Retired Chi. Police Ass'n v. City of Chi.***, 76 F.3d 856, 867 (7th Cir.1996) (same).

(2) The importance of the evidence to the movant's case. ***Hale***, 45 F.3d at 921.

(3) Whether the evidence was available to the movant. *Id.*; *see* ***Leisure Caviar***, 616 F.3d at 617. Depending on the circuit, the movant may need to show that (1) the evidence was newly discovered after the judgment or (2) the evidence was available before the judgment but was not discovered earlier despite the movant's diligence. *Compare* ***Williams v. Hobbs***, 658 F.3d 842, 854 (8th Cir.2011) (movant must show it exercised diligence to obtain evidence before entry of judgment), ***Bell v. Board of Cty. Comm'rs***, 451 F.3d 1097, 1102 (10th Cir.2006) (movant must show diligence or that evidence is newly discovered), *and* ***Dixon v. Wallowa Cty.***, 336 F.3d 1013, 1022 (9th Cir.2003) (movant must show that evidence could not have been discovered earlier through due diligence), *with* ***Ford v. Elsbury***, 32 F.3d 931, 937 (5th Cir.1994) (not necessary for movant to show that it could not have, with greater diligence, obtained evidence earlier).

(4) The likelihood that the nonmovant will suffer unfair prejudice if the case is reopened. ***Hale***, 45 F.3d at 921.

3. Clear error or manifest injustice. A party can file a motion to alter or amend the judgment on the basis of a clear error or to prevent manifest injustice. ***Allstate Ins.***, 634 F.3d at 1111; *see* ***Duran v. Town of Cicero***, 653 F.3d 632, 642 (7th Cir.2011) (error of law or fact); ***SFH, Inc. v. Millard Refrigerated Servs.***, 339 F.3d 738, 746 (8th Cir.2003) (same); ***Collison v. International Chem. Workers Un.***, 34 F.3d 233, 236 (4th Cir.1994) (error of law); *see, e.g.*, ***Robinson v. Wix Filtration Corp.***, 599 F.3d 403, 407-08 (4th Cir.2010) (no manifest injustice; court denied P's motion to alter or amend Ds' MSJ when P's attorney had experienced computer problems and thus did not receive notice of or file response to Ds' MSJ but deliberately chose not to inform Ds or court of computer problems); *see also* ***Coons v. Industrial Knife Co.***, 620 F.3d 38, 41 (1st Cir.2010) (motion to alter or amend to correct manifest error of law is proper motion—but not necessarily typical motion—to raise statute-of-limitations defense that was rejected by jury); ***Winslow v. Federal Energy Regulatory Comm'n***, 587 F.3d 1133, 1135 (D.C.Cir.2009) (motion to alter or amend judgment is proper motion to challenge court's omission of discretionary or mandatory prejudgment interest).

§3.3 Affidavits. If a motion to alter or amend the judgment contains facts outside the record, it should be supported by affidavits. *Cf.* FRCP 59(c) (affidavit for motion for new trial).

§3.4 Request hearing. If a motion to alter or amend the judgment presents contested fact issues, or if oral argument will help the court resolve the motion, the movant should request a hearing. The movant should comply with any requirements of local rules for securing a hearing on the motion. *See* ***Kendall v. Hoover Co.***, 751 F.2d 171, 172-73 (6th Cir.1984).

§3.5 Misnomer of motions under FRCP 59(e). A variety of differently named motions are considered motions to alter or amend the judgment under FRCP 59(e) (e.g., motion to reurge, motion for reconsideration). *See* ***Ford v. Elsbury***, 32 F.3d 931, 937 & n.7 (5th Cir.1994); *see also* ***GSS Grp. v. National Port Auth.***, 680 F.3d 805, 812 (D.C. Cir.2012) (FRCP 59(e) motions are aimed at reconsideration, not initial consideration). Some courts hold that a motion that is filed within 28 days after the entry of judgment and questions the correctness of the judgment will be treated as an FRCP 59(e) motion, regardless of its label. *See* ***Robinson v. Wix Filtration Corp.***, 599 F.3d 403, 412 (4th Cir.2010) (applying former ten-day deadline); ***Norman v. Arkansas Dept. of Educ.***, 79 F.3d 748, 750 (8th Cir. 1996) (same); ***Ford***, 32 F.3d at 937 & n.7 (same). Other courts hold that the substance—and not the timing or label—of a motion determines whether it is a motion to alter or amend the judgment under FRCP 59(e) or a motion for relief from the judgment under FRCP 60(b). *See* ***Obriecht v. Raemisch***, 517 F.3d 489, 493 (7th Cir.2008); *see, e.g.*, ***Harrington v. City of Chi.***, 433 F.3d 542, 545-46 (7th Cir.2006) (motion filed within ten days was treated as FRCP 60(b) motion because it was vague and relief requested could only be granted under FRCP 60(b)'s excusable-neglect standard; applying former ten-day deadline). If the motion under FRCP 59(e) is filed more than 28 days after the entry of judgment but includes allegations that fit under FRCP 60(b), it may be treated as an FRCP 60(b) motion. *See* ***Computer Prof'ls for Soc. Responsibility v. U.S. Secret Serv.***, 72 F.3d 897, 902-03 (D.C.Cir.1996) (applying former ten-day deadline); ***In re Stangel***, 68 F.3d 857, 859 (5th Cir.1995) (same); *see also* ***Benson v. St. Joseph Reg'l Health Ctr.***, 575 F.3d 542, 547 (5th Cir.2009) (after denial of first FRCP 59(e) motion, party improperly filed second FRCP 59(e) motion; court treated second motion as FRCP 60(b) motion). See "Motion for Relief from Judgment," ch. 10-F, p. 804.

§4. RESPONSE

§4.1 Objections. If the nonmovant opposes the motion to alter or amend the judgment, it should file a response objecting to the grounds in the motion. The following are some examples:

1. No intervening change in law. There has not been an intervening change in the law. *See* ***North River Ins. v. CIGNA Reinsurance Co.***, 52 F.3d 1194, 1219 (3d Cir.1995).

2. No new evidence. There is no new evidence. Or, if there is new evidence, the nonmovant should object to it by arguing that the balance of interests between the late-filed evidence and the finality of judgment requires the court to deny the motion. *See* ***Lavespere v. Niagara Mach. & Tool Works, Inc.***, 910 F.2d 167, 174 (5th Cir.1990).

In circuits that do not permit new evidence in an FRCP 59(e) motion, the nonmovant should argue that the new evidence could and should have been submitted before judgment.

3. No clear error of law or manifest injustice. The motion does not present a clear error of law or demonstrate a manifest injustice. *See* ***Bogosian v. Woloohojian Rlty. Corp.***, 323 F.3d 55, 72 (1st Cir.2003).

4. Already overruled. The motion raises issues that have already been overruled. FRCP 59(e) should not be used to reargue matters that were already presented to the court and overruled. *See* ***Diebitz v. Arreola***, 834 F.Supp. 298, 302 (E.D.Wis.1993); *see, e.g.*, ***Atkins v. Marathon LeTourneau Co.***, 130 F.R.D. 625, 626 (S.D.Miss.1990) (rearguing motion for summary judgment was unwarranted).

5. No new legal theory. The motion is an attempt to raise a legal argument that should have been raised before the judgment. An FRCP 59(e) motion cannot be used to raise a legal theory for the first time. ***Jorge Rivera Surillo & Co. v. Falconer Glass Indus.***, 37 F.3d 25, 29 (1st Cir.1994); ***Concordia Coll. Corp. v. W.R. Grace & Co.***, 999 F.2d 326, 330 (8th Cir.1993); *see* ***U.S. v. Resnick***, 594 F.3d 562, 568 (7th Cir.2010). *But see* ***New York Life Ins. v. Brown***, 84 F.3d 137, 141 n.4 (5th Cir.1996) (legal issues may be raised for first time in postjudgment motion).

6. Procedural reasons. The response should identify any procedural reasons why the motion should be denied (e.g., the motion was filed after the 28-day deadline passed). *See* FRCP 59(e).

§4.2 Deadline. FRCP 59(e) does not specify a deadline for the response, but it should be filed within any limits set by local rules for responses.

§4.3 Affidavits. If the response contains facts outside the record, it should be verified by affidavit. Generally, if the movant attached affidavits to its motion, the nonmovant should attach affidavits to its response.

§5. HEARING

If the facts are in dispute, the court can hold a hearing on the motion or consider affidavits attached to the motion. Even if the facts are not in dispute, a hearing may be helpful to argue the application of legal principles.

§6. RULING

§6.1 By court. The court may be able to alter or amend the judgment on its own initiative. *See* ***Burnam v. Amoco Container Co.***, 738 F.2d 1230, 1232 (11th Cir.1984) (applying former ten-day deadline); ***Bryant v. New Jersey DOT***, 998 F.Supp. 438, 442 (D.N.J.1998) (same). If the court does so, it must enter an order within 28 days after the entry of judgment. *See* FRCP 59(e); *cf.* FRCP 59(d) (court, on its own, can order new trial within 28 days after entry of judgment).

§6.2 Written order. The court should sign a written order granting or denying the motion. However, the order does not need to be set out in a separate document. FRCP 58(a)(4). See "Orders," ch. 1-G, §4.2, p. 45.

§7. APPELLATE REVIEW

§7.1 Deadline. The timely filing of a motion to alter or amend the judgment tolls the deadline to file a notice of appeal until an order disposing of the motion is entered. FRAP 4(a)(4)(A)(iv); ***Colón-Santiago v. Rosario***, 438 F.3d 101, 107 (1st Cir.2006); ***Intera Corp. v. Henderson***, 428 F.3d 605, 611 (6th Cir.2005); ***Simmons v. Reliance Std. Life Ins.***, 310 F.3d 865, 868 (5th Cir.2002); ***Jones v. UNUM Life Ins.***, 223 F.3d 130, 136 (2d Cir.2000); *see* ***Shales v. General Chauffeurs, Sales Drivers & Helpers Local Un.***, 557 F.3d 746, 748 (7th Cir.2009) (tolling of appellate deadline is determined by filing of motion, not by decision that motion has merit). An order is considered entered within the meaning of FRAP 4(a)(4) when it is entered on the civil docket under FRCP 79(a). FRAP 4(a)(7)(A)(i). The court does not need to render the order with the formality of a judgment, but it must clearly dispose of the post-trial motion. ***Ellison v. Conoco, Inc.***, 950 F.2d 1196, 1201 (5th Cir.1992). An appellant challenging either an order disposing of the motion to alter or amend the judgment or a judgment's alteration or amendment based on the motion to alter or amend must file the notice of appeal within 30 days (60 days if the United States is a party) after entry of the order, unless there are other outstanding motions that continue to toll the running of the appellate deadlines. *See* FRAP 4(a)(1)(A), (a)(1)(B), (a)(4)(B)(ii); 2009 Notes to FRAP 4 at ¶¶3, 4, p. 1266, this book.

CAUTION

Do not withdraw a motion to alter or amend the judgment after the untolled deadline for a notice of appeal for the underlying judgment or order has passed because the notice of appeal may be untimely. See "Deadline," §7.1, p. 797. The withdrawal of the motion—without a district-court order at least acknowledging the withdrawal—leaves the record as if the motion had never been filed, and the deadline for the notice of appeal may run from the entry of the judgment or order, not the date of withdrawal. E.g., ***Vanderwerf v. SmithKline Beecham Corp.****, 603 F.3d 842, 845-46 (10th Cir.2010) (when Ps withdrew unruled-on motion to alter or amend seven months after denial of MSJ and then filed notice of appeal, notice of appeal was untimely because deadline had passed six months earlier, i.e., 30 days after denial of MSJ); see* ***De Leon v. Marcos****, 659 F.3d 1276, 1281-82 (10th Cir.2011). But see* ***U.S. v. Rodriguez****, 892 F.2d 233, 236 (2d Cir.1989) (appellate deadline tolled at least until date when motion is withdrawn, and probably until district court takes some official action to acknowledge the withdrawal). Instead of withdrawing a postjudgment motion that tolls the appellate deadlines, a party can (1) file a motion requesting a ruling, (2) seek a writ of mandamus compelling the court to rule, (3) file a motion to extend time to file a notice of appeal, (4) file a premature notice of appeal that would ripen into a timely notice of appeal when the court rules on the motion to alter or amend, or (5) move to withdraw the motion to alter or amend to encourage the court to rule on the motion to withdrawal, thus triggering the 30-day period to file the notice of appeal.* ***Vanderwerf****, 603 F.3d at 848; see, e.g.,* ***De Leon****, 659 F.3d at 1281-82 (after P filed motion asking court to acknowledge withdrawal of P's motion to vacate, court granted motion and ordered that motion to vacate was deemed withdrawn and rendered moot; order sufficiently disposed of motion to vacate to toll appellate deadline).*

§7.2 Standard of review.

1. Motion.

(1) Abuse of discretion. Generally, the courts will review the district court's ruling on an FRCP 59(e) motion for abuse of discretion. ***U.S. v. Resnick***, 594 F.3d 562, 568 (7th Cir.2010); ***In re Syncor ERISA Litig.***, 516 F.3d 1095, 1100 (9th Cir.2008); ***Arthur v. King***, 500 F.3d 1335, 1343 (11th Cir.2007); ***Flynn v. Dick Corp.***, 481 F.3d 824, 829 (D.C.Cir.2007); ***Palmer v. Champion Mortg.***, 465 F.3d 24, 30 (1st Cir.2006); ***U.S. v. Westinghouse Savannah River Co.***, 305 F.3d 284, 290 (4th Cir.2002); ***Tyler v. Union Oil Co.***, 304 F.3d 379, 405 (5th Cir.2002); ***Phelps v. Hamilton***, 122 F.3d 1309, 1324 (10th Cir.1997). *But see* ***In re Sun Pipe Line Co.***, 831 F.2d 22, 25 (1st Cir.1987) (applying more deferential standard of "manifest abuse of discretion"). Under the abuse-of-discretion standard, the district court's decision and decision-making process need only to be reasonable. ***Midland W. Corp. v. FDIC***, 911 F.2d 1141, 1145 (5th Cir.1990). A district court does not have discretion to deny a party the right to file a motion under FRCP 59. *See* ***Collins v. Morgan Stanley Dean Witter***, 224 F.3d 496, 502 (5th Cir.2000).

(2) De novo. When the district court's ruling on an FRCP 59(e) motion is based on the application of law, the courts will review the ruling de novo. ***National Ecological Found. v. Alexander***, 496 F.3d 466, 476 (6th Cir.2007); ***Smith v. Pacific Props. & Dev. Corp.***, 358 F.3d 1097, 1100 (9th Cir.2004); ***Pioneer Nat'l Res. USA, Inc. v. Paper, Allied Indus., Chem. & Energy Workers Int'l Un.***, 328 F.3d 818, 820 (5th Cir.2003), *modified on other grounds*, 338 F.3d 440 (5th Cir.2003); ***Perez v. Volvo Car Corp.***, 247 F.3d 303, 318-19 (1st Cir.2001).

2. Entire judgment. If an FRCP 59(e) motion is timely, thus tolling the deadline to file a notice of appeal for the underlying judgment or order, the appellate jurisdiction from a timely notice of appeal after the ruling on the FRCP 59(e) motion will cover the entire judgment (i.e., the underlying judgment or order and the decision on the FRCP 59(e) motion). *See* ***Lora v. O'Heaney***, 602 F.3d 106, 110 (2d Cir.2010); ***Martinez v. Johnson***, 104 F.3d 769, 771 (5th Cir.1997); ***Federal Kemper Ins. v. Rauscher***, 807 F.2d 345, 348 (3d Cir.1986). But if the FRCP 59(e) motion is untimely and a notice of appeal was not timely filed directly from the underlying judgment or order, the ap-

pellate court does not have jurisdiction over the underlying judgment, only the ruling on the FRCP 59(e) motion. *See* ***Lora***, 602 F.3d at 110. Although the standard of review for a denial of an FRCP 59(e) motion is usually abuse of discretion, the standard may be de novo if the entire judgment is brought up on appeal and the underlying judgment or order involves a question of law. *See, e.g.*, ***Federal Kemper Ins.***, 807 F.2d at 348-49 (issue in underlying judgment was legal question of whether Ps had standing, resulting in de novo review rather than review for abuse of discretion).

E. MOTION TO ADD OR AMEND FINDINGS OF FACT

§1. GENERAL

§1.1 Rule. FRCP 52(b).

§1.2 Purpose. In a bench trial, if the district court made findings of fact and conclusions of law that are deficient in some respect, a party can file a motion asking the court to make additional findings or to amend the original findings. The main purpose of FRCP 52 is to provide the appellate court with a correct understanding of the findings of fact that served as the basis for the district court's conclusions of law and its judgment. 9C Wright & Miller, *Federal Practice & Procedure 3d* §2582 & n.4 (2008 & Supp.2012).

§1.3 Timetable & forms. Timetable, Appeal of Civil Trial, p. 1591; ***O'Connor's Federal Civil Forms*** (2012), FORMS 10E.

§1.4 Other references. 9C Wright & Miller, *Federal Practice & Procedure 3d* §2582 (2008 & Supp.2012); 9 *Moore's Federal Practice 3d* §§52.60-52.62 (2012); 1 Childress & Davis, *Federal Standards of Review 4th* §§2.01-2.12 (2010 & Supp.2011).

§2. COURT'S FINDINGS

§2.1 Findings necessary. The court must enter findings of fact in the following:

1. Nonjury trials. FRCP 52(a)(1); ***Adams Cty. Reg'l Water Dist. v. Village of Manchester***, 226 F.3d 513, 517 (6th Cir.2000); *see* FRCP 52(c) (judgment on partial findings entered as a matter of law).

2. Suits tried to an advisory jury. FRCP 52(a)(1); ***Adams Cty.***, 226 F.3d at 517.

3. When granting or refusing interlocutory injunctions. FRCP 52(a)(2); ***Prayze FM v. FCC***, 214 F.3d 245, 248 n.1 (2d Cir.2000); *see also* ***Prairie Band of Potawatomi Indians v. Pierce***, 253 F.3d 1234, 1245 (10th Cir.2001) (when entering preliminary injunction).

4. When adopting the findings of a master. FRCP 52(a)(4); *see* FRCP 53(e), 72(b)(1). The findings of a master, to the extent that the court adopts them, are considered the findings of the court. FRCP 52(a)(4). See "District court's consideration of recommendations & proposed findings," ch. 5-B, §2.2.9, p. 301.

5. When a party received late notice of the entry of judgment. *See* FRAP 4(a)(6).

§2.2 Findings unnecessary. The court does not need to enter findings of fact in the following:

1. Jury trials. *See* FRCP 52(a)(1).

2. Judgments as a matter of law. *See id.*

3. Defenses and objections under FRCP 12. FRCP 52(a)(3).

4. Summary judgments under FRCP 56. FRCP 52(a)(3).

5. Any other motion, unless the FRCPs provide otherwise. FRCP 52(a)(3).

§2.3 No request for initial findings. A party does not need to request that the court make findings of fact and conclusions of law for the purpose of appellate review. *See* FRCP 52(a)(1).

§2.4 When findings should be filed. The court should file findings before the entry of judgment. ***In re Texas Extrusion Corp.***, 836 F.2d 217, 220 (5th Cir.1988). The court cannot include findings in the judgment. *See* FRCP 58(a). The court can state its findings orally on the record in open court or include them in an opinion or memorandum of the court. FRCP 52(a)(1). The findings should be stated separately from the conclusions of law. *See id.*

§2.5 Purpose of court's findings. The purpose of the court's findings of fact and conclusions of law is to (1) aid the court in its adjudication process, (2) promote the doctrines of res judicata and estoppel by judgment, and (3) aid the appellate courts in their review. ***Chandler v. City of Dallas***, 958 F.2d 85, 88 (5th Cir.1992); ***In re Texas Extrusion Corp.***, 836 F.2d 217, 220 (5th Cir.1988). The findings and conclusions provide the appellate courts with a clear understanding of the grounds for the decision. *See* ***Henry v. Champlain Enters.***, 445 F.3d 610, 622 (2d Cir.2006); ***Reich v. Newspapers of New England, Inc.***, 44 F.3d 1060, 1078-79 (1st Cir.1995).

§3. DEADLINE

§3.1 28-day deadline. A motion to add or amend findings must be filed with the clerk no later than 28 days after the entry of judgment. FRCP 52(b). The judgment is considered entered when it is placed in a separate document and entered on the docket in compliance with FRCP 58. See "Requirements for Final Judgment," ch. 9-A, §2, p. 735. The motion must be received by—not just mailed to—the clerk by the deadline. When calculating the 28-day time period, the date the judgment is entered is the trigger event and is excluded; counting begins the day after the entry of judgment. FRCP 6(a)(1)(A); *cf.* ***Laborers' Pension Fund v. A&C Env'tl, Inc.***, 301 F.3d 768, 775 n.5 (7th Cir.2002) (for renewed motion for JMOL, entry date of judgment on docket—not date judgment is signed—triggers time period; applying former ten-day deadline). See "Identify trigger event," ch. 1-C, §6.1.1(1), p. 24.

§3.2 No extension. The deadline for filing a motion to add or amend findings is jurisdictional and cannot be extended by the court or the parties. *See* FRCP 6(b)(2); ***In re Texas Extrusion Corp.***, 836 F.2d 217, 220 (5th Cir. 1988); 9C Wright & Miller §2582 & n.17; 2009 Notes to FRCP 52 at ¶1, p. 1217, this book; *see also* ***U.S. Leather, Inc. v. H&W Prtshp.***, 60 F.3d 222, 225 (5th Cir.1995) (parties cannot extend deadline in post-trial motions). Thus, a late motion is ineffective even if the other party does not object. *See* ***In re Texas Extrusion Corp.***, 836 F.2d at 220; *cf.* ***Rodick v. City of Schenectady***, 1 F.3d 1341, 1346 (2d Cir.1993) (renewed motion for JMOL). But if a motion to add or amend findings is filed after the deadline and it states an appropriate ground for relief, such as a mistake of fact, the court can treat it as a motion for relief from the judgment. *See* ***Nisson v. Lundy***, 975 F.2d 802, 806 (11th Cir.1992) (applying former ten-day deadline).

CAUTION

Although the deadline for a motion to add or amend findings cannot be extended, some circuits have held that FRCP 6(b)(2) and certain other rules governing deadlines for postjudgment motions are nonjurisdictional claim-processing rules and that objections to the timeliness of the postjudgment motion can be waived. Cf. ***Lizardo v. U.S.****, 619 F.3d 273, 277-78 (3d Cir.2010) (FRCP 59(e));* ***Advanced Bodycare Solutions****, 615 F.3d at 1359 n.14 (FRCP 50(b), 59(b), (e));* ***Art Attacks Ink, LLC v. MGA Entm't Inc.****, 581 F.3d 1138, 1143 (9th Cir.2009) (FRCP 50(b)). That is, if the movant does not file its motion to add or amend findings of fact within the 28-day deadline but the nonmovant does not object to the untimeliness, the objection is waived and the court has jurisdiction over the motion.* *See "No extension," ch. 10-B, §3.2, p. 777; "No extension," ch. 10-C, §2.2, p. 783; "No extension," ch. 10-D, §2.2, p. 794.* *Even if the district court has jurisdiction over an untimely motion, the circuits disagree on whether that motion tolls the deadline to file a notice of appeal under FRAP 4(a)(4)(A). Compare* ***Blue v. International Bhd. of Elec. Workers Local Un.****, 676 F.3d 579, 582-83 (7th Cir.2012) (untimely motion listed under FRAP 4(a)(4)(A) does not toll time for filing appeal), and* ***Advanced Bodycare Solutions****, 615 F.3d at 1359 n.14 (because FRAP 4(a)(4) is jurisdictional, untimely motion listed under FRAP 4(a)(4)(A) does not toll time for filing appeal), with* ***Obaydullah v. Obama****, ___ F.3d ___ (D.C.Cir.2012) (No. 11-5123; 8-10-12) (because FRAP 4(a)(4) is nonjurisdictional*

claim-processing rule, untimely motion listed under FRAP 4(a)(4)(A) can toll time for filing appeal; objections to timeliness for tolling purposes can be waived), and ***National Ecological Found. v. Alexander****, 496 F.3d 466, 476 (6th Cir.2007) (untimely motion listed under FRAP 4(a)(4)(A) tolls time for filing appeal). If the appellate deadline is not tolled, an appeal after the ruling on the untimely motion is limited to that ruling and would not include appellate review of the underlying judgment. See* ***Advanced Bodycare Solutions****, 615 F.3d at 1359 n.14. See "Deadline," §8.1, p. 803. Thus, check the law of your circuit to determine whether untimeliness objections under FRCP 52(b) or for tolling purposes can be waived.*

§3.3 Premature motion. A motion to add or amend findings should be filed after the judgment is entered, not before. FRCP 52(b). But if it is filed before the judgment is entered, it is still timely because FRCP 52(b) specifies only the outer filing limits. *See* ***Calculators Haw., Inc. v. Brandt, Inc.***, 724 F.2d 1332, 1335 (9th Cir.1983). If the motion is filed early, the nonmovant should ask the court to sign a written order disposing of the premature motion without prejudice to filing another motion to amend findings after the judgment is entered.

CIRCUIT SPLIT

The circuits disagree on whether a postjudgment motion filed before the entry of final judgment is implicitly overruled when the final judgment is entered. This issue is significant for determining when the 30-day period for filing a notice of appeal begins. See "Premature motion," ch. 10-B, §3.3, p. 777.

§4. MOTION

§4.1 Form. For the general requirements for the form of a motion, see "Drafting motions," ch. 1-B, §3.1, p. 14.

§4.2 In writing. A motion to add or amend findings should be in writing. *See* FRCP 7(b)(1)(A).

§4.3 Grounds. The movant must state the grounds for the motion "with particularity"—that is, with enough specificity to put the court and the opposing party on notice of the reasons to add or amend the findings. *See* FRCP 7(b)(1)(B); *see, e.g.*, ***Riley v. Northwestern Bell Tel. Co.***, 1 F.3d 725, 727 (8th Cir.1993) (bare-bones motion did not toll appellate deadlines); ***Martinez v. Trainor***, 556 F.2d 818, 819-20 (7th Cir.1977) (D failed to meet minimum standard of "reasonable specification").

1. Findings incomplete. If the court makes incomplete or erroneous findings, the party should file a motion asking the court to make additional or alternate findings. ***Glaverbel Societe Anonyme v. Northlake Mktg. & Sup.***, 45 F.3d 1550, 1555-56 (Fed.Cir.1995); ***U.S. v. Tosca***, 18 F.3d 1352, 1355 (6th Cir.1994). Some courts hold that if the party does not ask for additional or alternate findings under FRCP 52(b), it can challenge any erroneous findings but cannot complain that certain findings are not specific enough. ***Glaverbel***, 45 F.3d at 1555; ***Evans v. Suntreat Growers & Shippers, Inc.***, 531 F.2d 568, 570 (Temp.Emer.Ct.App.1976). If the court allows a party to supplement the findings, it is error for the court to omit the supplemental findings. ***Rossini v. Ogilvy & Mather, Inc.***, 798 F.2d 590, 606 (2d Cir.1986). A party's failure to supplement may suggest that the court's findings were not deficient, but it does not necessarily constitute a waiver. *See* ***Lynch Corp. v. MII Liquidating Co.***, 717 F.2d 1184, 1187 (8th Cir.1993).

2. Manifest error. A motion to add or amend findings can be used to correct manifest errors of law or fact. ***National Metal Finishing Co. v. BarclaysAmerican/Commercial, Inc.***, 899 F.2d 119, 123 (1st Cir.1990); ***Fontenot v. Mesa Pet. Co.***, 791 F.2d 1207, 1219 (5th Cir.1986).

3. Newly discovered evidence. In some limited situations, a motion to add or amend findings can be used to present newly discovered evidence. ***Fontenot***, 791 F.2d at 1219; ***In re Braithwaite***, 197 B.R. 834, 835 (Bankr.N.D.Ohio 1996). But motions to add or amend findings should not be used to relitigate issues, advance new theories, secure a rehearing on the merits, or introduce evidence that was available at trial. ***Fontenot***, 791 F.2d at 1219; ***In re Braithwaite***, 197 B.R. at 835.

§4.4 Affidavits. If a motion to add or amend findings relies on facts outside the record, the party should attach affidavits to the motion.

§4.5 Request hearing. If a motion to add or amend findings presents contested fact issues, or if oral argument will help the court resolve the motion, the movant should request a hearing. The movant should comply with any requirements of local rules for securing a hearing on the motion. *See* ***Kendall v. Hoover Co.***, 751 F.2d 171, 172-73 (6th Cir.1984).

§4.6 With motion for new trial. A motion to add or amend findings can be made along with a motion for new trial under FRCP 59. FRCP 52(b); *see* FRCP 59(a)(2). See "Motion for New Trial," ch. 10-C, p. 783.

§5. RESPONSE

§5.1 Objections. If the nonmovant opposes additional or amended findings, it should file a response objecting to the grounds in the motion. The following are some examples:

1. **Findings not incomplete.** The motion should be denied because the findings are not incomplete or erroneous, and additional findings are not necessary.

2. **No manifest error.** The motion should be denied because there is no manifest error, and even if there is some error, it is not a manifest error of law or fact.

3. **No newly discovered evidence.** The motion should be denied because the movant did not meet the test of newly discovered evidence and thus is not entitled to introduce additional evidence. The movant is attempting to relitigate issues, advance new theories, secure a rehearing on the merits, or introduce evidence that was available at trial. ***Fontenot v. Mesa Pet. Co.***, 791 F.2d 1207, 1219 (5th Cir.1986).

4. **Procedural reasons.** The motion should be denied for procedural reasons (e.g., the motion was filed after the 28-day deadline passed). *See* FRCP 52(b).

§5.2 Deadline. FRCP 52 does not specify a deadline for the response, but it should be filed within any limits set by local rules for the responses.

§5.3 Affidavits. If the response relies on facts outside the record, the party should attach affidavits to the motion. Generally, if the movant attached affidavits to the motion, the nonmovant should attach affidavits to the response.

§6. HEARING

The court can hold a hearing on the motion regardless of whether facts in the motion are in dispute. If the facts are in dispute, the court can hold a hearing on the motion or consider affidavits attached to the motion. Even if the facts are not in dispute, a hearing may be helpful to argue the application of legal principles.

§7. RULING

§7.1 No clear standard. There is no clear standard governing the granting of motions to add or amend findings.

§7.2 Written order. The court should sign a written order granting or denying the motion. However, the order does not need to be set out in a separate document. FRCP 58(a)(2). See "Orders," ch. 1-G, §4.2, p. 45.

§7.3 Court should grant. Because FRCP 52(a)(1) imposes a duty on the court to make findings of fact and conclusions of law, the court should grant a motion to add or amend findings in the following instances:

1. If the original findings did not include an essential finding. *See* ***Armstrong v. Collier***, 536 F.2d 72, 77 (5th Cir.1976).

2. If the motion demonstrates a manifest error of law or fact or makes a compelling case that newly discovered evidence would change the outcome. ***Fontenot v. Mesa Pet. Co.***, 791 F.2d 1207, 1219 (5th Cir.1986). The court can grant the motion even if doing so would reverse the existing judgment. ***National Metal Finishing Co. v. BarclaysAmerican/Commercial, Inc.***, 899 F.2d 119, 123 (1st Cir.1990); ***Diebitz v. Arreola***, 834 F.Supp. 298, 302 (E.D.Wis.1993).

§8. APPELLATE REVIEW

§8.1 Deadline. The timely filing of a motion to add or amend findings tolls the deadline to file a notice of appeal until an order disposing of the motion is entered. FRAP 4(a)(4)(A)(ii); *see* ***Shales v. General Chauffeurs, Sales Drivers & Helpers Local Un.***, 557 F.3d 746, 748 (7th Cir.2009) (tolling of appellate deadline is determined by filing of motion, not by decision that motion has merit). An order is considered entered within the meaning of FRAP 4(a)(4) when it is entered on the civil docket under FRCP 79(a). FRAP 4(a)(7)(A)(i). The court does not need to render the order with the formality of a judgment, but it must clearly dispose of the post-trial motion. ***Ellison v. Conoco, Inc.***, 950 F.2d 1196, 1201 (5th Cir.1992). An appellant challenging either an order disposing of the motion to add or amend findings or a judgment's alteration or amendment based on the motion to add or amend must file the notice of appeal within 30 days (60 days if the United States is a party) after entry of the order, unless there are other outstanding motions that continue to toll the running of the appellate deadlines. *See* FRAP 4(a)(1)(A), (a)(1)(B), (a)(4)(B)(ii); 2009 Notes to FRAP 4 at ¶¶3, 4, p. 1266, this book. See "Computing Deadlines," ch. 1-C, §6, p. 23.

§8.2 Appellate procedure when findings inadequate. If the district court did not make specific findings, the appellate court can vacate the judgment and remand the case for appropriate findings. *See* ***Olcott v. Delaware Flood Co.***, 76 F.3d 1538, 1549 (10th Cir.1996); ***Brice v. Virginia Beach Corr. Ctr.***, 58 F.3d 101, 106 (4th Cir.1995).

1. Record sufficiently complete. An appellate court can review a case without remanding for findings if (1) the record is exceptionally clear and (2) remand would serve no useful purpose. *See* ***In re Marchiando***, 13 F.3d 1111, 1114 (7th Cir.1994) (when record permits only one finding, appellate court can make the finding itself); *see, e.g.*, ***Landmark Land Co. v. Office of Thrift Supervision***, 990 F.2d 807, 811-12 (5th Cir.1993) (remanded for findings). If the appellate court can understand the issues without the aid of findings, the case does not need to be remanded. ***EEOC v. Hendrix Coll.***, 53 F.3d 209, 211-12 (8th Cir.1995); *see* ***Williams v. U.S.***, 50 F.3d 299, 303-04 (4th Cir.1995).

2. Record incomplete. If the record does not provide sufficient information for a clear understanding of the district court's decision, the appellate court will remand the case for additional findings. *See* ***Joseph A. v. New Mexico Dept. of Human Servs.***, 69 F.3d 1081, 1088-89 (10th Cir.1995); ***Liddell v. Board of Educ.***, 20 F.3d 324, 326 (8th Cir.1994); ***Landmark Land***, 990 F.2d at 811-12.

§8.3 Standard of review. Findings of fact, whether based on testimony or documentary evidence, cannot be set aside unless they are clearly erroneous. FRCP 52(a)(6); ***Pullman-Std. v. Swint***, 456 U.S. 273, 287 (1982); ***Bonds v. District of Columbia***, 93 F.3d 801, 808 (D.C.Cir.1996); *see* ***Bituminous Cas. Corp. v. Vacuum Tanks, Inc.***, 75 F.3d 1048, 1051 (5th Cir.1996); 1 Childress & Davis §§2.01, 2.04. A finding is "clearly erroneous" when, even though there is some evidence to support it, the appellate court is left with the definite belief that a mistake has been made. ***U.S. v. U.S. Gypsum Co.***, 333 U.S. 364, 395 (1948); ***Ellis v. Grant Thornton LLP***, 530 F.3d 280, 287 (4th Cir.2008); ***Spinden v. GS Roofing Prods. Co.***, 94 F.3d 421, 426 (8th Cir.1996). When, however, the evidence will support a conclusion either way, the district court's choice between the two views is not clearly erroneous. ***U.S. v. Yellow Cab Co.***, 338 U.S. 338, 342 (1949); ***Granite State Ins. v. Smart Modular Techs.***, 76 F.3d 1023, 1028 (9th Cir.1996); ***SEC v. Lorin***, 76 F.3d 458, 460 (2d Cir.1996). The appellate court must give due regard to the district court's opportunity to judge the witnesses' credibility. FRCP 52(a)(6).

F. MOTION FOR RELIEF FROM JUDGMENT

§1. GENERAL

§1.1 Rule. FRCP 60(b).

§1.2 Purpose. FRCP 60(b) allows the parties to seek relief from a final judgment, order, or proceeding, by asking the court to set aside the judgment, order, or proceeding and reopen the case. *See* ***United Student Aid Funds, Inc. v. Espinosa***, ___ U.S. ___, 130 S.Ct. 1367, 1376 (2010); ***Gelder v. Coxcom, Inc.***, ___ F.3d ___ (10th Cir.2012) (No. 12-706; 8-8-12). This exception to finality is allowed only under a limited set of circumstances, including newly discovered evidence, fraud, and mistake, and it should not be used as a substitute for an appeal. *See* ***United Student Aid Funds***, ___ U.S. at ___, 130 S.Ct. at ___at 1376-77; ***Russell v. Delco Remy Div. of Gen. Motors Corp.***, 51 F.3d 746, 749 (7th Cir.1995). The rule does not limit a court's power to entertain an independent suit to relieve a party from a judgment. FRCP 60(d)(1).

> **NOTE**
>
> *Although FRCP 60(b) allows a party to seek relief not only from a final judgment but also from a final order or proceeding, we use the phrase "relief from the judgment" in this subchapter to cover relief from a final judgment, order, or proceeding.*

§1.3 Timetable & forms. Timetable, Appeal of Civil Trial, p. 1591; *O'Connor's Federal Civil Forms* (2012), FORMS 10F.

§1.4 Other references. 10A Wright, Miller & Kane, *Federal Practice & Procedure 3d* §2698 (1998 & Supp.2012); 11 Wright, Miller & Kane, *Federal Practice & Procedure 2d* §§2808, 2851-2853, 2857-2866 (1995 & Supp.2012); 12 *Moore's Federal Practice 3d* ch. 60 (2012); 1 Childress & Davis, *Federal Standards of Review 4th* §5.12 (2010 & Supp.2011); Annotation, *Who Is "Legal Representative" Within Provision of Rule 60(b) of Federal Rules of Civil Procedure Permitting Court to Relieve "Party or His Legal Representative" from Final Judgment or Order*, 136 ALR Fed. 651 (1997 & Supp.2012-13).

§2. DEADLINE

§2.1 For motion. The deadline to file a motion for relief from the judgment depends on whether the grounds asserted in the motion are under FRCP 60(b)(1)-(b)(3) or FRCP 60(b)(4)-(b)(6).

> **NOTE**
>
> *Do not confuse a motion to alter or amend the judgment under FRCP 59(e) with a motion for relief from the judgment under FRCP 60(b). Although both motions can be used to correct similar errors, a motion filed within 28 days after the judgment is generally considered a motion under FRCP 59(e); an untimely FRCP 59(e) motion is generally treated as an FRCP 60(b) motion. See* ***Justice v. Town of Cicero****, 682 F.3d 662, 665 (7th Cir.2012) (applying current 28-day deadline);* ***Robinson v. Wix Filtration Corp.****, 599 F.3d 403, 411-12 (4th Cir.2010) (applying former ten-day deadline);* ***Price v. Philpot****, 420 F.3d 1158, 1167 n.9 (10th Cir.2005) (same);* ***Lavespere v. Niagara Mach. & Tool Works, Inc.****, 910 F.2d 167, 173 (5th Cir.1990) (same). But see* ***Obriecht v. Raemisch****, 517 F.3d 489, 493 (7th Cir.2008) (characterization of motion depends on substance of motion, not timing or label). See "Motion to Alter or Amend Judgment," ch. 10-D, p. 793. Motions under FRCP 60(b), however, have stricter substantive requirements than motions under FRCP 59(e). See* ***Lavespere****, 910 F.2d at 173-74 (applying former ten-day deadline). See "Grounds," §3.4, p. 806.*

1. Deadline under FRCP 60(b)(1)-(b)(3). A party must file a motion for relief from the judgment based on the grounds under FRCP 60(b)(1)-(b)(3) within a reasonable time but no more than one year after the entry of the judgment or order or the date of the proceeding. FRCP 60(c)(1). For a discussion of how to compute deadlines stated in years, see "Computing Deadlines," ch. 1-C, §6, p. 23.

(1) Grounds. The one-year deadline for filing a motion for relief from the judgment under FRCP 60(b)(1)-(b)(3) applies when it is based on the following grounds:

(a) Mistake, inadvertence, surprise, or excusable neglect. FRCP 60(b)(1); ***Truskoski v. ESPN, Inc.***, 60 F.3d 74, 76 (2d Cir.1995); ***Robinson v. Armontrout***, 8 F.3d 6, 7 (8th Cir.1993); ***Cotto v. U.S.***, 993 F.2d 274, 278 n.4 (1st Cir.1993).

(b) Newly discovered evidence. FRCP 60(b)(2); ***Central States, Se. & Sw. Areas Pension Fund v. Central Cartage Co.***, 69 F.3d 1312, 1314 (7th Cir.1995).

(c) Fraud (intrinsic or extrinsic), misrepresentation, or misconduct by an adverse party. FRCP 60(b)(3); ***In re International Nutronics, Inc.***, 28 F.3d 965, 969 (9th Cir.1994). The one-year time period under FRCP 60(b)(3) does not apply to an independent action to relieve a party from a judgment procured by fraud. ***Robinson v. Volkswagenwerk AG***, 56 F.3d 1268, 1273-74 (10th Cir.1995). See "Substantive error," §7.2, p. 812.

(2) No extension. The one-year deadline for filing a motion for relief from the judgment under FRCP 60(b)(1)-(b)(3) is jurisdictional and cannot be extended by the court or the parties. *See* FRCP 6(b)(2); ***Arrieta v. Battaglia***, 461 F.3d 861, 864 (7th Cir.2006). Thus, a late motion is ineffective even if the other party does not object. *See* ***Arrieta***, 461 F.3d at 864; *cf.* ***Rodick v. City of Schenectady***, 1 F.3d 1341, 1346 (2d Cir.1993) (renewed motion for JMOL).

CAUTION

Although the deadline for a motion for relief from the judgment cannot be extended, some circuits have held that FRCP 6(b)(2) and certain other rules governing deadlines for postjudgment motions are nonjurisdictional claim-processing rules and that objections to the timeliness of the postjudgment motion can be waived. Cf. ***Lizardo v. U.S.***, *619 F.3d 273, 277-78 (3d Cir.2010) (FRCP 59(e));* ***Advanced Bodycare Solutions, LLC v. Thione Int'l***, *615 F.3d 1352, 1359 n.14 (11th Cir.2010) (FRCP 50(b), 59(b), (e));* ***Art Attacks Ink, LLC v. MGA Entm't Inc.***, *581 F.3d 1138, 1143 (9th Cir.2009) (FRCP 50(b)). That is, if the movant does not file its motion for relief from the judgment within the one-year deadline but the nonmovant does not object to the untimeliness, the objection is waived and the court has jurisdiction over the motion.* *See "No extension," ch. 10-B, §3.2, p. 777; "No extension," ch. 10-C, §2.2, p. 783; "No extension," ch. 10-D, §2.2, p. 794.* *Thus, check the law of your circuit to determine whether untimeliness objections under FRCP 60(b)(1)-(b)(3) can be waived.*

2. Deadline under FRCP 60(b)(4)-(b)(6). A party must file a motion for relief from the judgment based on the grounds listed below within a reasonable time after the entry of the judgment or order or the date of the proceeding. FRCP 60(c)(1). "Reasonable time" is interpreted according to the particular facts of each case, including the length of and reasons for the delay, the prejudice of the delay to the opposing party, and the circumstances compelling equitable relief. ***Thompson v. Bell***, 580 F.3d 423, 443 (6th Cir.2009); *see* ***BUC Int'l v. International Yacht Council Ltd.***, 517 F.3d 1271, 1275 (11th Cir.2008); ***Travelers Ins. v. Liljeberg Enters.***, 38 F.3d 1404, 1410 (5th Cir. 1994). A reasonable time may be longer than one year. *See, e.g.*, ***Associated Builders & Contractors v. Michigan Dept. of Labor & Econ. Growth***, 543 F.3d 275, 278-79 (6th Cir.2008) (motion filed 14 years after injunction was timely because of intervening change in law); ***Harris v. Union Elec. Co.***, 846 F.2d 482, 484-85 (8th Cir.1988) (motion filed 23 months after judgment and exhaustion of appeal process was timely). The reasonable-time deadline for filing a motion for relief from the judgment under FRCP 60(b)(4)-(b)(6) applies when it is based on the following grounds:

(1) The judgment is void. FRCP 60(b)(4); ***Jackson v. FIE Corp.***, 302 F.3d 515, 523-24 (5th Cir.2002). A void judgment can be challenged at any time. ***Philos Techs. v. Philos & D, Inc.***, 645 F.3d 851, 857 (7th Cir.2011); *see* ***New York Life Ins. v. Brown***, 84 F.3d 137, 142-43 (5th Cir.1996); 10A Wright, Miller & Kane §2698 & n.2.

(2) The judgment has been satisfied, released, or discharged; the judgment is based on an earlier judgment that has been reversed or vacated; or applying the judgment prospectively is no longer equitable. FRCP 60(b)(5); ***Federal Land Bank v. Cupples Bros.***, 889 F.2d 764, 766 n.4 (8th Cir.1989); *e.g.*, ***Association for Retarded Citizens, Inc. v. Thorne***, 68 F.3d 547, 553 (2d Cir.1995) (motion made less than one month after judgment was reasonable); ***NOW v. Operation Rescue***, 47 F.3d 667, 669 (4th Cir.1995) (motion made less than one year after judgment was not reasonable).

(3) Any other reason that justifies relief. FRCP 60(b)(6); *see, e.g.*, ***Thompson***, 580 F.3d at 443-44 (motion to reopen habeas petition made more than four years after change to state supreme court's procedure was reasonable); ***Rivera v. Puerto Rico Tel. Co.***, 921 F.2d 393, 394-95 (1st Cir.1990) (motion to clarify ruling on notice of appeal made within 23 days was reasonable); *cf.* ***Travelers Ins.***, 38 F.3d at 1410-11 (motion to disqualify judge made more than two months after learning basis for motion was not reasonable); ***McLawhorn v. John W. Daniel & Co.***, 924 F.2d 535, 538 (4th Cir.1991) (motion challenging summary judgment made 3½ months after judgment was entered was not reasonable).

§2.2 To toll time for appeal. The deadline to file a motion for relief from the judgment that tolls the time for appeal is 28 days after entry of judgment. FRAP 4(a)(4)(A)(vi). See "Motion filed within 28 days after judgment," §9.1.1, p. 815.

§3. MOTION

§3.1 Form. For the general requirements for the form of a motion, see "Drafting motions," ch. 1-B, §3.1, p. 14.

§3.2 In writing. A motion for relief from the judgment should be in writing. *See* FRCP 7(b)(1)(A).

§3.3 Sua sponte. The circuits disagree on whether a district court has the authority to grant relief under FRCP 60(b) on its own initiative. ***Pierson v. Dormire***, 484 F.3d 486, 491 (8th Cir.2007), *vacated in part on other grounds*, No. 06-2545 (8th Cir.2008) (no pub.; 5-6-08); ***U.S. v. Pauley***, 321 F.3d 578, 581 n.1 (6th Cir.2003). The Second, Fourth, Fifth, Eighth, and Ninth Circuits have held that a district court has the power to vacate its judgment sua sponte under FRCP 60(b). *See* ***Baum v. Blue Moon Ventures, LLC***, 513 F.3d 181, 190 (5th Cir.2008); ***Pierson***, 484 F.3d at 491-92; ***Fort Knox Music Inc. v. Baptiste***, 257 F.3d 108, 110-11 (2d Cir.2001); ***Kingvision Pay-Per-View Ltd. v. Lake Alice Bar***, 168 F.3d 347, 351-52 (9th Cir.1999); ***U.S. v. Jacobs***, 298 F.2d 469, 472 (4th Cir.1961). The Sixth and Tenth Circuits have held that a district court cannot grant relief sua sponte under FRCP 60(b). *See* ***Pauley***, 321 F.3d at 581 (FRCP 60(b) explicitly requires relief to occur "on motion"); ***Dow v. Baird***, 389 F.2d 882, 884-85 (10th Cir.1968) (grounds listed in FRCP 60(b) can be corrected only "on motion"). The Seventh Circuit has noted the circuit split but declined to decide the issue. ***Judson Atkinson Candies, Inc. v. Latini-Hohberger Dhimantec***, 529 F.3d 371, 385-86 (7th Cir.2008). If a court allows sua sponte relief under FRCP 60(b), it must give the parties notice before granting the relief. ***Kingvision***, 168 F.3d at 352; *see* ***Dr. José S. Belaval, Inc. v. Peréz-Perdomo***, 465 F.3d 33, 37 (1st Cir.2006) (dicta); ***Fort Knox Music***, 257 F.3d at 111. *But see* ***Pierson***, 484 F.3d at 491-92 (during proceedings, parties addressed statute of limitations and had opportunity to brief issue; lack of notice was harmless error).

§3.4 Grounds. The movant can ask the court to relieve a party from a judgment on one of the six grounds identified in FRCP 60(b).

NOTE

Most of the cases in which the courts actually grant relief under FRCP 60(b) involve default judgments. See, e.g., ***Information Sys. & Networks Corp. v. U.S.****, 994 F.2d 792, 795 (Fed.Cir. 1993);* ***Azzopardi v. Ocean Drilling & Expl. Co.****, 742 F.2d 890, 895 (5th Cir.1984). If the case involves a default judgment,* *see "Motion to Vacate Default Judgment Under FRCP 60(b)," ch. 7-A, §8, p. 598.*

1. Mistake, inadvertence, surprise, or excusable neglect. A party can seek relief from a judgment when there has been mistake, inadvertence, surprise, or excusable neglect. FRCP 60(b)(1). But it is difficult to obtain relief on these grounds. *See* ***Jones v. Phipps***, 39 F.3d 158, 162 (7th Cir.1994) (standard is "nearly insurmountable hurdle").

(1) Mistake. A mistake in the judgment affecting the substantive rights of the parties should be challenged under FRCP 60(b)(1). *See* ***Olle v. Henry & Wright Corp.***, 910 F.2d 357, 363-64 (6th Cir.1990); *see, e.g.*, ***Jones v. Anderson-Tully Co.***, 722 F.2d 211, 212-13 (5th Cir.1984) (mistake in description of real property). However, an error of law by an attorney will not ordinarily constitute a mistake justifying relief under FRCP 60(b)(1). ***Russell v. Delco Remy Div. of Gen. Motors Corp.***, 51 F.3d 746, 749 (7th Cir.1995); *see* ***McMillan v. MBank Fort Worth***, 4 F.3d 362, 367 (5th Cir.1993) (dicta); *see, e.g.*, ***Eskridge v. Cook Cty.***, 577 F.3d 806, 809 (7th Cir.2009) (P's mistake of law did not justify relief under FRCP 60(b)(1); P voluntarily dismissed second suit in federal court without recognizing that D would have defense in third suit in state court).

CIRCUIT SPLIT

The circuits are split on whether an error by the court, including an error of law, can be remedied under FRCP 60(b)(1). See 12 Moore's Federal Practice 3d §60.41[4][a]-[b]. Compare ***Benson v. St. Joseph Reg'l Health Ctr.***, *575 F.3d 542, 547 (5th Cir.2009) (obvious error of law can be "mistake" under FRCP 60(b)(1) if motion is filed within time to file notice of appeal), and* ***U.S. v. Reyes***, *307 F.3d 451, 455 (6th Cir.2002) (substantive error of law or fact by court can be "mistake" under FRCP 60(b)(1)), with* ***Fisher v. Kadant, Inc.***, *589 F.3d 505, 513 n.5 (1st Cir.2009) (error of law cannot be "mistake" under FRCP 60(b)(1)), and* ***McKnight v. U.S. Steel Corp.***, *726 F.2d 333, 338 (7th Cir.1984) (error of law cannot be corrected under FRCP 60(b)(1); appropriate remedy is to timely appeal).*

(2) Inadvertence. When an error is made in the judgment through no one's fault, the error can be corrected under FRCP 60(b)(1). *See* ***Oklahoma Radio Assocs. v. FDIC***, 987 F.2d 685, 696-97 (10th Cir.1993); ***Murray v. Ford Motor Co.***, 770 F.2d 461, 464-65 (5th Cir.1985).

(3) Surprise. A party can seek relief from a judgment on the ground of unfair surprise. FRCP 60(b)(1); *see, e.g.*, ***Jones v. U.S.***, 255 F.3d 507, 511 (8th Cir.2001) (finding of surprise could not be made on ground that government belatedly raised sovereign-immunity defense because defense can be raised anytime).

(4) Excusable neglect. To be entitled to relief from the judgment because of "excusable neglect" under FRCP 60(b)(1), a party must show the following:

(a) Neglect. The party or its attorney was partly to blame for the neglect. *See* ***Pioneer Inv. Servs. v. Brunswick Assocs.***, 507 U.S. 380, 392 (1993); ***Eskridge***, 577 F.3d at 809. "Neglect" under FRCP 60(b)(1) means negligence. ***Pioneer Inv.***, 507 U.S. at 394; ***Briones v. Riviera Hotel & Casino***, 116 F.3d 379, 381 (9th Cir.1997); *see, e.g.*, ***Robb v. Norfolk & W. Ry.***, 122 F.3d 354, 359-60 (7th Cir.1997) (failing to inform or seek approval of court after litigants had agreed to extension to file was neglect); ***Cheney v. Anchor Glass Container Corp.***, 71 F.3d 848, 850 (11th Cir.1996) (failure to file was due to negligence, not deliberate disregard for local rules).

(b) Excusable. The neglect is excusable under the four ***Pioneer*** factors: (1) the danger of prejudice to the opposing party, (2) the length of delay and its potential impact on the proceedings, (3) the reason for the delay, including whether it was reasonably within the movant's control, and (4) whether the movant acted in good faith. ***Briones***, 116 F.3d at 381; ***Cheney***, 71 F.3d at 850. Although these factors are not exclusive, each of the ***Pioneer*** factors should be addressed. *See* ***Pioneer Inv.***, 507 U.S. at 395 (because Congress provided no guidelines for determining what categories of neglect are excusable, court must conduct equitable inquiry "taking account of all relevant circumstances surrounding the party's omission"); ***Ahanchian v. Xenon Pictures, Inc.***, 624 F.3d 1253, 1261-62 (9th Cir.2010) (district court abuses its discretion by not addressing each of four ***Pioneer*** factors and by adopting per se rules for application of ***Pioneer*** factors); *see also* ***Lemoge v. U.S.***, 587 F.3d 1188, 1195-96 (9th Cir.2009) (prejudice to movant can be additional factor).

The following are examples of excusable neglect: • Complaint and summons not timely served because of attorney's injury and later complications. ***Lemoge***, 587 F.3d at 1195-96. • Answer not filed because of legal department's recording error. ***Union Pac. R.R. v. Progress Rail Servs.***, 256 F.3d 781, 782-83 (8th Cir.2001). • Answer not filed because

of exigent personal circumstances. ***TCI Grp. Life Ins. Plan v. Knoebber***, 244 F.3d 691, 699 (9th Cir.2001). • Response to motion for summary judgment not filed because of negligence and carelessness after attorney's family emergency. ***Bateman v. U.S. Postal Serv.***, 231 F.3d 1220, 1224-25 (9th Cir.2000). • Jury demand filed late because of miscommunication between associate and lead attorney. ***Cheney***, 71 F.3d at 850. • Party's inaction due to circumstances beyond its control. *See* ***Pioneer Inv.***, 507 U.S. at 394; ***Klapprott v. U.S.***, 335 U.S. 601, 613-14 (1949), *amended*, 336 U.S. 942 (1949); ***Briones***, 116 F.3d at 382 n.1.

The following are examples of inexcusable neglect: • Mere legal blunders. ***Cash v. Illinois Div. of Mental Health***, 209 F.3d 695, 697-98 (7th Cir.2000). • Mere carelessness. ***In re Woods***, 173 F.3d 770, 779 (10th Cir.1999). • Ignorance of the rules or mistakes construing the rules. *See* ***Pioneer Inv.***, 507 U.S. at 392 (noting that this circumstance does not usually constitute excusable neglect, but recognizing that it could); ***Briones***, 116 F.3d at 382 (same). • Failure of party's attorney to plead correct jurisdictional amount. ***Sparrow v. Heller***, 116 F.3d 204, 206-07 (7th Cir.1997).

2. Newly discovered evidence. A party can seek relief from a judgment on the grounds of newly discovered evidence. FRCP 60(b)(2). Motions for relief on this basis are viewed with disfavor. ***Mitchell v. Shalala***, 48 F.3d 1039, 1041 (8th Cir.1995). The following are the prerequisites for granting such a motion.

NOTE

The same factors apply for newly discovered evidence in a motion for new trial under FRCP 59 or a motion for relief from the judgment under FRCP 60(b)(2). See ***Williams v. Hobbs****, 658 F.3d 842, 853-54 (8th Cir.2011);* ***WMS Gaming, Inc. v. International Game Tech.****, 184 F.3d 1339, 1361 n.11 (Fed.Cir.1999); 11 Wright, Miller & Kane §2808 & n.3. See "Motion for New Trial," ch. 10-C, p. 783.*

(1) The evidence existed at the time of trial. ***Government Fin. Servs. One L.P. v. Peyton Place, Inc.***, 62 F.3d 767, 771 (5th Cir.1995).

(2) The evidence was discovered after trial. ***In re Chicago, Milwaukee, St. Paul & Pac. R.R.***, 78 F.3d 285, 293 (7th Cir.1996); ***Callanan v. Runyun***, 75 F.3d 1293, 1297 (8th Cir.1996). If the evidence was known before trial, it cannot be the subject of a motion under FRCP 60(b)(2). ***United Mine Workers of Am. 1974 Pension v. Pittston Co.***, 984 F.2d 469, 476 (D.C.Cir.1993); *see, e.g.*, ***Medical Mut. of Ohio v. k. Amalia Enters.***, 548 F.3d 383, 394 & n.8 (6th Cir.2008) (evidence from depositions taken after summary-judgment briefing was not considered new for FRCP 60(b)(2) motion when party was seeking reconsideration of denial of summary-judgment motion; party should have sought FRCP 56(f) extension instead).

(3) The movant exercised due diligence to discover the evidence. ***Dronsejko v. Thornton***, 632 F.3d 658, 672 (10th Cir.2011); ***In re Chicago***, 78 F.3d at 293; ***Peyton Place***, 62 F.3d at 771. Even if the party can show all the other factors, it is not entitled to a new trial on the ground of newly discovered evidence unless it also shows diligence. *See* ***U.S. v. McGaughey***, 977 F.2d 1067, 1075-76 (7th Cir.1992).

(4) The evidence is admissible. ***Provident Life & Acc. Ins. v. Goel***, 274 F.3d 984, 1000 (5th Cir.2001); ***McGaughey***, 977 F.2d at 1075.

(5) The evidence is credible. ***Goel***, 274 F.3d at 1000; ***McGaughey***, 977 F.2d at 1075.

(6) The evidence is material and controlling. ***Peyton Place***, 62 F.3d at 771; ***Hoult v. Hoult***, 57 F.3d 1, 6 (1st Cir.1995).

(7) The evidence is not merely cumulative or impeaching. ***Mitchell***, 48 F.3d at 1041.

(8) The evidence clearly or probably would have caused a different result. ***In re Chicago***, 78 F.3d at 293-94; ***Peyton Place***, 62 F.3d at 771.

3. Misconduct by adverse party. A party can seek relief from a judgment when there has been fraud (intrinsic or extrinsic), misrepresentation, or misconduct by an adverse party. FRCP 60(b)(3). The purpose of a motion under FRCP 60(b)(3) is to provide relief from a judgment that was unfairly obtained, not one that may be factu-

ally incorrect. ***Peyton Place***, 62 F.3d at 772. To obtain relief from a judgment under FRCP 60(b)(3), the movant must show (1) it had a meritorious claim at trial and (2) it was prevented from fully and fairly presenting its case at trial because of the adverse party's fraud, misrepresentation, or misconduct. ***Walsh v. McCain Foods Ltd.***, 81 F.3d 722, 726 (7th Cir.1996). Relief under FRCP 60(b)(3) requires proof of fraud, misrepresentation, or misconduct by clear and convincing evidence. ***Cox Nuclear Pharm. v. CTI, Inc.***, 478 F.3d 1303, 1314 (11th Cir.2007); ***Muñiz v. Rovira-Martinó***, 453 F.3d 10, 12 (1st Cir.2006); ***Peyton Place***, 62 F.3d at 772; *see also* ***Ty Inc. v. Softbelly's, Inc.***, 353 F.3d 528, 537 (7th Cir.2003) (questioning whether standard for fraud under FRCP 60(b)(3) should be clear and convincing evidence when most federal fraud laws require proof only by preponderance of evidence).

4. Void judgment. A party can seek relief from a void judgment. FRCP 60(b)(4); ***United Student Aid Funds, Inc. v. Espinosa***, ___ U.S. ___, 130 S.Ct. 1367, 1376 (2010); ***Fafel v. DiPaola***, 399 F.3d 403, 409 (1st Cir. 2005). A motion based on FRCP 60(b)(4) can be granted only in narrow circumstances. ***United Student Aid Funds***, ___ U.S. at ___, 130 S.Ct. at 1376. In the interest of the finality of judgments, the concept of void judgments is narrowly construed. ***Wendt v. Leonard***, 431 F.3d 410, 412 (4th Cir.2005); ***Hoult***, 57 F.3d at 6. FRCP 60(b)(4) relieves a party of a void judgment not because the judgment is wrong, but rather because the judgment is based either on a certain type of jurisdictional defect or on a violation of due process. ***United Student Aid Funds***, ___ U.S. at ___, 130 S.Ct. at 1377; ***Northridge Ch. v. Charter Township of Plymouth***, 647 F.3d 606, 611 (6th Cir.2011).

(1) Jurisdictional defect. A judgment is void if the court that rendered it lacked subject-matter or personal jurisdiction. ***Eberhardt v. Integrated Design & Constr., Inc.***, 167 F.3d 861, 871 (4th Cir.1999); ***New York Life Ins. v. Brown***, 84 F.3d 137, 143 (5th Cir.1996); *see* ***United Student Aid Funds***, ___ U.S. at ___, 130 S.Ct. at 1377; ***Philos Techs. v. Philos & D, Inc.***, 645 F.3d 851, 855 (7th Cir.2011). The jurisdictional defect is generally limited to exceptional cases in which the court that rendered judgment did not have even an "arguable basis" for jurisdiction. ***United Student Aid Funds***, ___ U.S. at ___, 130 S.Ct. at 1377.

(2) Violation of due process. A judgment is void if there is a violation of due process that deprives a party of notice or the opportunity to be heard. ***United Student Aid Funds***, ___ U.S. at ___, 130 S.Ct. at 1377; *see* ***New York Life***, 84 F.3d at 143; ***Antoine v. Atlas Turner, Inc.***, 66 F.3d 105, 108 (6th Cir.1995); *see also* ***Marshall v. Board of Educ.***, 575 F.2d 417, 422 (3d Cir.1978) (judgment is void when court had no legal authority to grant decree).

5. Intervening event. A party can seek relief from a judgment when there is an intervening event. *See* FRCP 60(b)(5). Under FRCP 60(b)(5), the court can grant a motion for relief from the judgment based on the following events:

(1) The judgment was satisfied, released, or discharged. FRCP 60(b)(5); *e.g.*, ***AIG Baker Sterling Heights, LLC v. American Multi-Cinema, Inc.***, 579 F.3d 1268, 1272-73 (11th Cir.2009) (partial relief from arbitration award that required D to pay property taxes to P was proper when D presented conclusive evidence it had already paid some of the taxes directly to taxing authority).

(2) An earlier judgment, on which the judgment at issue was based, was reversed or vacated. FRCP 60(b)(5). The judgment from which the movant seeks relief must be based on (in the sense of res judicata or collateral estoppel) the earlier judgment that was reversed. ***Manzanares v. City of Albuquerque***, 628 F.3d 1237, 1240 (10th Cir.2010); *see* ***In re Racing Servs.***, 571 F.3d 729, 732 (8th Cir.2009); ***Comfort v. Lynn Sch. Cmte.***, 560 F.3d 22, 27 (1st Cir.2009); *see also* ***Lowry Dev., L.L.C. v. Groves & Assocs. Ins.***, 690 F.3d 382, 386 (5th Cir.2012) ("earlier" is not limited to earlier in time; earlier judgment can be contemporaneous judgment). It is insufficient if the earlier case provides only a precedent for the later one. ***Manzanares***, 628 F.3d at 1240; ***In re Racing Servs.***, 571 F.3d at 732; ***Comfort***, 560 F.3d at 27.

(3) Applying the judgment prospectively is no longer equitable. FRCP 60(b)(5). For example, it is appropriate to grant an FRCP 60(b)(5) motion when the party seeking relief from an injunction or consent decree can show that a significant change in either the facts or the law renders the continued enforcement of an injunction or consent decree detrimental to the public interest. ***Horne v. Flores***, 557 U.S. 433, 447 (2009); *see* ***Rufo v. Inmates of Suffolk Cty. Jail***, 502 U.S. 367, 383-84 (1992); ***Northridge Ch.***, 647 F.3d at 613-14; *see, e.g.*, ***Agostini v. Felton***,

521 U.S. 203, 237 (1997) (based on significant changes in Establishment Clause law since entry of original injunction, petitioners were entitled to relief under FRCP 60(b)(5)); ***In re Racing Servs.***, 571 F.3d at 733-34 (after debtor's criminal convictions were reversed, bankruptcy court under FRCP 60(b)(5) properly vacated subordination order, which had allowed debtor's claim for rent but had subordinated it to all other claims, because criminal convictions had been critical to subordination order).

6. Catchall provision. If none of the other specifically named grounds is available, a party can assert a motion for relief from the judgment under the catchall provision in FRCP 60(b)(6). *See* ***Aikens v. Ingram***, 652 F.3d 496, 500 (4th Cir.2011); *see also* ***In re Woods***, 173 F.3d at 780 (FRCP 60(b)(6) has been described as a "grand reservoir of equitable power to do justice in a particular case"). Because FRCP 60(b)(6) is a catchall provision, bright-line rules for FRCP 60(b)(6) relief generally are not appropriate. *E.g.*, ***Ungar v. Palestine Liberation Org.***, 599 F.3d 79, 84 (1st Cir.2010) (no absolute bar to relief for party that willfully defaults and later seeks relief under FRCP 60(b)(6)); *see also* ***In re Sealed Case (Bowles)***, 624 F.3d 482, 486-87 (D.C.Cir.2010) (catchall provision cannot be used as equitable exception to circumvent jurisdictional deadline for filing notice of appeal). Relief under this section is seldom granted. To obtain relief under FRCP 60(b)(6), the party must show that it is not entitled to relief under FRCP 60(b)(1)-(b)(5) and that there are exceptional circumstances.

NOTE

Some circuits require the party to also show that it has a meritorious claim or defense and that the opposing party will not be unfairly prejudiced if the judgment is set aside. E.g., ***Aikens****, 652 F.3d at 501; see* ***Carter v. Fenner****, 136 F.3d 1000, 1005 (5th Cir.1998).*

(1) No relief under other provisions of FRCP 60(b). The party must show that it was not entitled to relief under subsections (1)-(5) of FRCP 60(b). ***Liljeberg v. Health Servs. Acquisition Corp.***, 486 U.S. 847, 863 (1988); ***Aikens***, 652 F.3d at 500. FRCP 60(b)(6) and FRCP 60(b)(1)-(b)(5) are mutually exclusive. ***Pioneer Inv.***, 507 U.S. at 393; *see* ***Liljeberg***, 486 U.S. at 863; ***Peyton Place***, 62 F.3d at 773-74.

(2) Exceptional circumstances. The party must show exceptional circumstances. ***Bakery Mach. & Fabrication, Inc. v. Traditional Baking, Inc.***, 570 F.3d 845, 848 (7th Cir.2009); ***U.S. v. Orleans Parish Sch. Bd.***, 397 F.3d 334, 337 (5th Cir.2005); *e.g.*, ***In re Gledhill***, 76 F.3d 1070, 1080-81 (10th Cir.1996) (in bankruptcy case, conversion of case from chapter 11 to chapter 7, increase in property value, and likelihood that estate might be distributed to more creditors were exceptional circumstances); ***Computer Prof'ls for Soc. Responsibility v. U.S. Secret Serv.***, 72 F.3d 897, 903 (D.C.Cir.1996) (party disclosing previously undisclosed evidence that was central to litigation and would have affected outcome of case was exceptional circumstance); *see* ***United Airlines, Inc. v. Brien***, 588 F.3d 158, 175-76 (2d Cir.2009) (potential hardship resulting from inconsistent judgments can constitute exceptional circumstances); *see also* ***Middle Rio Grande Conservancy Dist. v. Norton***, 294 F.3d 1220, 1225 (10th Cir. 2002) (court should grant relief under FRCP 60(b)(6) only when it offends justice to deny such relief).

NOTE

Exceptional circumstances may exist when a judicial action is taken in violation of 28 U.S.C. §455(a), which is a recusal statute. See ***Liljeberg****, 486 U.S. at 864. A court considering whether a judgment should be vacated because of this type of violation should evaluate (1) the risk of injustice to the parties in the particular case, (2) the risk that the denial of relief will produce injustice in other cases, and (3) the risk of undermining the public's confidence in the judicial process. Id.;* ***U.S. v. Cerceda****, 172 F.3d 806, 812 (11th Cir.1999).*

§3.5 Party or representative. A party or its legal representative can seek relief from the judgment. FRCP 60(b). A "legal representative" is defined as a person who stands in the place of another. ***U.S. v. 8136 S. Dobson Street***, 125 F.3d 1076, 1082 (7th Cir.1997); ***In re El Paso Ref., LP***, 37 F.3d 230, 234 (5th Cir.1994); *see* ***Western Steel Erec-***

tion Co. v. U.S., 424 F.2d 737, 739 (10th Cir.1970) (legal representative is person who, by operation of law, is tantamount to party for matter involved); Annotation, *Who Is "Legal Representative" Within Provision of Rule 60(b) ... Permitting Court to Relieve "Party or His Legal Representative" from Final Judgment or Order*, 136 ALR Fed. at 660-61 (same).

§3.6 Affidavits. If a motion for relief from the judgment contains facts outside the record, it should be supported by affidavits.

§3.7 Request hearing. If a motion for relief from the judgment presents contested fact issues, or if oral argument will help the court resolve the motion, the movant should request a hearing. The movant should comply with any requirements of local rules for securing a hearing on the motion. *See* ***Kendall v. Hoover Co.***, 751 F.2d 171, 172-73 (6th Cir.1984).

§3.8 Request indicative ruling. If the district court can entertain but cannot grant the motion for relief from the judgment because of an appeal that is docketed and pending, the movant should request an indicative ruling. See "Indicative Ruling," §8, p. 813.

§4. RESPONSE

§4.1 Objections. If the nonmovant opposes the motion for relief from the judgment, it should file a response objecting to the grounds in the motion.

1. Substantive. The response should negate whatever grounds are asserted in the motion. The following are some examples:

(1) There was no mistake, inadvertence, surprise, or excusable neglect. FRCP 60(b)(1).

(2) The movant could have discovered the newly discovered evidence by using due diligence in time to move for a new trial under FRCP 59(b). FRCP 60(b)(2).

(3) There was no fraud, misrepresentation, or misconduct by the nonmovant. FRCP 60(b)(3).

(4) The judgment is not void. FRCP 60(b)(4).

(5) There was no intervening event. *See* FRCP 60(b)(5).

(a) The judgment was not satisfied, released, or discharged. *Id.*

(b) The earlier judgment, on which the judgment at issue is based, was not reversed or vacated. *Id.*

(c) Applying the judgment prospectively is equitable. *Id.*

(6) Any other reason that justifies overruling the motion. FRCP 60(b)(6); *see* ***In re Woods***, 173 F.3d 770, 780 (10th Cir.1999) (because FRCP 60(b) is inherently equitable, granting of relief can be challenged on equitable grounds).

2. Procedural. The response should identify any procedural reasons why the motion should be denied. The following are some examples:

(1) The motion was not timely because it was not made within a reasonable time. FRCP 60(c)(1).

(2) The motion was not timely because it was made outside the one-year time limit. *Id.*

(3) The same ground was presented in a motion under FRCP 59(e), which was denied.

§4.2 Deadline. FRCP 60(b) does not specify a deadline for the response, but it should be filed within any limits set by local rules for responses.

§4.3 Affidavits. If the response contains facts outside the record, it should be supported by affidavits. Generally, if the movant attached affidavits to the motion, the nonmovant should attach affidavits to the response.

§5. HEARING

If the facts are in dispute, the court should hold a hearing on the motion. *See, e.g.*, ***Sheng v. Starkey Labs.***, 53 F.3d 192, 194-95 (8th Cir.1995) (court reversed denial of FRCP 60(b) motion and remanded with instructions to conduct hearing). However, even when the facts are in dispute, the court may consider affidavits attached to the motion. If the facts are not in dispute, a hearing may be helpful to argue the application of legal principles. *See, e.g.*, ***Buck v. U.S. Dept. of Agric.***, 960 F.2d 603, 609 (6th Cir.1992) (court's record sufficient to support ruling and hearing not necessary).

§6. RULING

§6.1 Written order. The court should sign a written order granting or denying the motion. However, the order does not need to be set out in a separate document. FRCP 58(a)(5). See "Orders," ch. 1-G, §4.2, p. 45.

§6.2 Not without notice. FRCP 60(b) allows the court to act only on a motion. If the court decides to change the judgment on its own initiative, the court must notify the parties in writing. *See* ***In re Timely Secretarial Serv.***, 987 F.2d 1167, 1171 (5th Cir.1993). See "Sua sponte," §3.3, p. 806.

§6.3 Court's discretion. The need for order and predictability in the judicial process requires the courts to exercise caution before reopening a case. *Cf.* ***Edward H. Bohlin Co. v. Banning Co.***, 6 F.3d 350, 356-57 (5th Cir.1993) (denial of motion to dismiss not abuse of discretion when party's justification is "inadvertent mistake"). FRCP 60(b) attempts to strike a balance between two conflicting interests: the finality of judgments and the need to do justice. ***Stipelcovich v. Sand Dollar Mar., Inc.***, 805 F.2d 599, 604 (5th Cir.1986); *e.g.*, ***Cano v. Baker***, 435 F.3d 1337, 1339-40 (11th Cir.2006) (prevailing P in abortion case sought FRCP 60(b) relief 32 years later because her views changed; finality of judgments outweighed her circumstances); *see* ***United Student Aid Funds, Inc. v. Espinosa***, ___ U.S. ___, 130 S.Ct. 1367, 1380 (2010). FRCP 60(b) should be liberally construed to do substantial justice. *See* ***In re Roxford Foods, Inc.***, 12 F.3d 875, 879 (9th Cir.1993) (because of remedial nature of FRCP 60(b), it must be liberally applied).

§6.4 Filed during appeal. If a motion for relief from the judgment is filed while the case is on appeal, FRCP 62.1 and FRAP 12.1 provide procedures that allow an appellate court to remand the case so the district court can resolve the motion while the appeal is pending. See "Indicative Ruling," §8, p. 813.

§7. OTHER RELIEF

If a party misses the one-year deadline to assert complaints about errors in the judgment that are listed in FRCP 60(b)(1)-(b)(3), only limited avenues of relief remain.

§7.1 Clerical error. If the party can convince the district court that the error in the judgment is clerical, not substantive, the court can amend the judgment at any time, unless an appeal is docketed and pending. FRCP 60(a). See "Motion to Correct Clerical Error in Judgment," ch. 10-I, p. 825.

§7.2 Substantive error. If the error in the judgment is substantive, a party can challenge the error under FRCP 60(d). FRCP 60(d) does not limit the power of a court to entertain an independent action, but the relief is available only under unusual and exceptional circumstances. *See* ***U.S. v. Beggerly***, 524 U.S. 38, 47 (1998); ***Superior Seafoods, Inc. v. Tyson Foods, Inc.***, 620 F.3d 873, 878 (8th Cir.2010); 11 Wright, Miller & Kane §2868 & nn.6-6.2.

1. Independent action. A party can challenge a substantive error by filing an independent action for relief from the judgment. FRCP 60(d)(1). An independent action can be based on fraud, accident, or mistake. ***Mitchell v. Rees***, 651 F.3d 593, 595 (6th Cir.2011); ***Southmark Props. v. Charles House Corp.***, 742 F.2d 862, 872 & n.14 (5th Cir.1984); 11 Wright, Miller & Kane §2868 & nn.10-15; *see* ***Geo. P. Reintjes Co. v. Riley Stoker Corp.***, 71 F.3d 44, 47-48 (1st Cir.1995). To pursue an independent action, the party must satisfy the following requirements:

(1) There is a judgment that, based on equity and good conscience, should not be enforced. ***Turner v. Pleasant***, 663 F.3d 770, 776 (5th Cir.2011); ***Mitchell***, 651 F.3d at 595.

(2) There is a meritorious claim or defense in the underlying case. ***Turner***, 663 F.3d at 776; ***Mitchell***, 651 F.3d at 595.

(3) The party was prevented from obtaining the benefit of the claim or defense because of fraud, accident, or mistake. ***Turner***, 663 F.3d at 776; ***Mitchell***, 651 F.3d at 595.

(4) The party is not at fault or negligent. ***Turner***, 663 F.3d at 776; ***Mitchell***, 651 F.3d at 595.

(5) There is no other adequate remedy of law. ***Turner***, 663 F.3d at 776; ***Mitchell***, 651 F.3d at 595.

2. Relief under 28 U.S.C. §1655. A party can challenge a substantive error by asking for relief under 28 U.S.C. §1655 for a defendant who was not personally notified of the action. FRCP 60(d)(2); *see* 11 Wright, Miller & Kane §2869.

3. Fraud on the court. A party can challenge a substantive error by asking the court to set aside the judgment for fraud on the court. FRCP 60(d)(3). The fraud must consist of acts that "defile the court"—that is, acts that seriously affect the integrity of the judicial system. ***In re Golf 255, Inc.***, 652 F.3d 806, 809 (7th Cir.2011); ***Hadges v. Yonkers Racing Corp.***, 48 F.3d 1320, 1325 (2d Cir.1995). Examples of fraud on the court include (1) bribery of a judge, (2) jury tampering, and (3) fraudulent submissions by an attorney of documents or testimony that she knows are forged or perjured. ***In re Golf 255***, 652 F.3d at 809; *see* ***Robinson v. Volkswagenwerk AG***, 56 F.3d 1268, 1274 n.6 (10th Cir.1995).

§8. INDICATIVE RULING

FRCP 62.1 and FRAP 12.1 standardize the procedure known as an "indicative ruling," which allows a party to request a remand to resolve a motion for relief from the judgment while a case is pending on appeal. *See* 2009 Notes to FRCP 62.1 at ¶1, p. 1230, this book; 2009 Notes to FRAP 12.1 at ¶1, p. 1276, this book. Most circuits had previously allowed indicative rulings based on case law or local rules. Struve, *Power, Protocol, & Practicality: Communications from the District Court During an Appeal*, 84 Notre Dame L.Rev. 2053, 2098-99 (2009); *see* ***Dominguez v. Gulf Coast Mar. & Assocs.***, 607 F.3d 1066, 1073-74 & n.5 (5th Cir.2010); ***Crateo, Inc. v. Intermark, Inc.***, 536 F.2d 862, 869 (9th Cir. 1976). Typically, a district court cannot grant a motion for relief from the judgment once an appeal has been docketed and is pending. *See* 2009 Notes to FRCP 62.1 at ¶¶1, 2, p. 1230, this book; 2009 Notes to FRAP 12.1 at ¶1, p. 1276, this book. But the district court can (1) defer the consideration of the motion, (2) deny the motion, or (3) state either that it would grant the motion if the appellate court remands or that the motion raises a substantial issue. FRCP 62.1(a); 2009 Notes to FRCP 62.1 at ¶1, p. 1230, this book. If the district court states that it would grant the motion or that the motion raises a substantial issue, a party filing the motion for relief from the judgment can request that the appellate court order a remand to allow the district court to grant or further consider the motion. *See* FRCP 62.1(b), (c); FRAP 12.1; 2009 Notes to FRCP 62.1 at ¶3, p. 1230, this book; 2009 Notes to FRAP 12.1 at ¶5, p. 1276, this book.

NOTE

FRCP 62.1 and FRAP 12.1 apply only when the district court does not have authority to grant relief without the appellate court's permission. 2009 Notes to FRCP 62.1 at ¶2, p. 1230, this book; 2009 Notes to FRAP 12.1 at ¶3, p. 1276, this book. For example, if a party has filed one of the six motions listed in FRAP 4(a)(4) that suspend the time for filing a notice of appeal until the last such motion is disposed of, the district court has authority to grant that motion and does not need to resort to the indicative-ruling procedure. 2009 Notes to FRCP 62.1 at ¶1, p. 1230, this book; 2009 Notes to FRAP 12.1 at ¶1, p. 1276, this book.

§8.1 Timely motion for relief from judgment. A party must have filed a timely motion for relief from the judgment that the court cannot grant because of an appeal that is docketed and pending. *See* FRCP 62.1(a); ***Dominguez v. Gulf Coast Mar. & Assocs.***, 607 F.3d 1066, 1073-74 (5th Cir.2010). When a party files a motion for relief from the judgment after the expiration of the 28-day deadline in FRAP 4(a)(4) that suspends the time for fil-

ing a notice of appeal or after a notice of appeal has been docketed, the party should include a request for an indicative ruling in its motion for relief from the judgment.

EXAMPLE

The following is an example of a timely motion for relief from the judgment that the district court can entertain but cannot grant without a remand. If a party loses on a jury verdict, files a timely notice of appeal within 30 days after the judgment, but discovers new evidence two months after the judgment, the party can timely file a motion for relief from the judgment based on the new evidence within one year after the judgment is entered. See FRCP 60(b)(2), (c)(1); Struve, 84 Notre Dame L.Rev. at 2097. In this scenario, the motion for relief from the judgment under FRCP 60(b)(2) is timely because it was filed within one year after the judgment; however, the district court cannot grant the motion because it lost jurisdiction after the notice of appeal was filed.

§8.2 District court's ruling. If a timely motion for relief from the judgment is made but cannot be granted because of a pending appeal, the district court can do one of the following:

1. Defer motion. The district court can defer considering the motion. FRCP 62.1(a)(1).

2. Deny motion. The district court can deny the motion. FRCP 62.1(a)(2).

3. Make indicative ruling. The district court can state that (1) it would grant the motion if the appellate court remands for that purpose or (2) the motion raises a substantial issue. FRCP 62.1(a)(3).

(1) Court would grant motion. If the district court would grant the motion for relief from the judgment as long as the appellate court remands for that purpose, the district court should indicate that it would in fact grant the motion. *See* 2009 Notes to FRCP 62.1 at ¶4, p. 1230, this book.

(2) Motion raises substantial issue. If the district court determines the motion for relief from the judgment presents complex issues that require extensive litigation and that may be either made moot or presented in a different context by the appellate decision, the district court should (1) indicate that the motion raises a substantial issue and (2) state the reasons why it prefers to decide the motion only if the appellate court agrees that it would be useful for the district court to decide the motion before the issues pending on appeal are decided. 2009 Notes to FRCP 62.1 at ¶4, p. 1230, this book.

EXAMPLE

The following is an example of when a substantial issue may arise. After a district court has granted summary judgment dismissing a case and while an appeal is pending, the plaintiff files a motion for relief from the judgment claiming newly discovered evidence and fraud by the defendant during discovery. 2009 Notes to FRAP 12.1 at ¶4, p. 1276, this book. If the district court reviews the motion and states that it raises a substantial issue, the appellate court may remand for the district court's determination rather than decide the case on appeal. Id.

§8.3 Notice to appellate court of indicative ruling. If the district court states that it would grant the motion or that the motion raises a substantial issue, the party who filed the motion for relief from the judgment must promptly notify the circuit clerk of the district court's indicative ruling. FRCP 62.1(b); FRAP 12.1(a); 2009 Notes to FRCP 62.1 at ¶3, p. 1230, this book; 2009 Notes to FRAP 12.1 at ¶4, p. 1276, this book. That party should then ask the appellate court to order a remand so the district court can make its final ruling on the motion. 2009 Notes to FRAP 12.1 at ¶5, p. 1276, this book. The notification ensures that the proceedings in the district court and the appellate court are properly coordinated. 2009 Notes to FRCP 62.1 at ¶3, p. 1230, this book; 2009 Notes to FRAP 12.1 at ¶4, p. 1276, this book. Local appellate rules may provide the format and requirements for the notice. 2009 Notes to FRAP 12.1 at ¶5, p. 1276, this book; *see, e.g.*, Local Rules 11th Cir., Rule 12.1-1.

§8.4 Appellate court's ruling. After notification, the appellate court can remand for further proceedings. FRAP 12.1(b); *see* 2009 Notes to FRAP 12.1 at ¶6, p. 1276, this book (remand is in appellate court's discretion). The appellate court can grant either a limited remand or an unlimited remand. *See* 2009 Notes to FRAP 12.1 at ¶¶6, 7, pp. 1276, 1277, this book.

1. Limited remand. In a limited remand, the appellate court remands only for a ruling on the motion for relief from the judgment; thus, the appellate court retains jurisdiction to proceed with the appeal after the district court rules on the motion, assuming the appeal is not moot and the parties want to proceed. *See* ***Ohio Willow Wood Co. v. Thermo-Ply, Inc.***, 629 F.3d 1374, 1375 (Fed.Cir.2011); 2009 Notes to FRAP 12.1 at ¶7, p. 1277, this book. The appellate court may want to hear the appeal even after the district court has granted the relief on remand; that is, even when the district court indicates that it would grant relief, the appellate court can choose a limited remand rather than an unlimited remand. 2009 Notes to FRAP 12.1 at ¶7, p. 1277, this book.

2. Unlimited remand. In an unlimited remand, the appellate court remands the entire proceeding. *See* 2009 Notes to FRAP 12.1 at ¶6, p. 1276, this book. By expressly terminating the appeal, the appellate court loses jurisdiction over the case. *See* FRAP 12.1(b); 2009 Notes to FRAP 12.1 at ¶6, p. 1276, this book. The appellate court should ordinarily follow this procedure only when the appellant has clearly stated an intention to abandon the appeal. 2009 Notes to FRAP 12.1 at ¶6, p. 1276, this book. Otherwise, if the district court denies the requested relief after the appeal is terminated, the appellant may be limited to appealing the denial of the postjudgment motion rather than challenging issues that could have been raised on appeal from the underlying judgment. *Id.*

§8.5 District court's ruling after remand. The district court may decide the motion for relief from the judgment if the appellate court remands for that purpose. FRCP 62.1(c). The district court does not have to grant the motion after stating that it raises a substantial issue; proceedings on remand may indicate that the motion should not be granted. 2009 Notes to FRCP 62.1 at ¶4, p. 1230, this book.

PRACTICE TIP

To challenge the district court's disposition of the motion for relief from the judgment on remand, a party should file a new or amended notice of appeal. See 2009 Notes to FRAP 12.1 at ¶9, p. 1277, this book; see, e.g., ***TAAG Linhas Aereas de Angola v. Transamerica Airlines, Inc.****, 915 F.2d 1351, 1354 (9th Cir.1990) (to appeal issues from motion for relief on limited remand, party must file new notice of appeal).*

§8.6 Notice to appellate court of district court's ruling. If the appellate court remands but retains jurisdiction, any party—not just the party who filed the motion for relief from the judgment—must promptly notify the circuit clerk when the district court has decided the motion on remand. FRAP 12.1(b); *see* ***Ohio Willow Wood Co. v. Thermo-Ply, Inc.***, 629 F.3d 1374, 1375 (Fed.Cir.2011) (parties must promptly notify appellate court of district court's ruling and propose how appeal should proceed based on district court's ruling); 2009 Notes to FRAP 12.1 at ¶8 (any party involved in motion in district court can provide notice to appellate court), p. 1277, this book.

§9. APPELLATE REVIEW

§9.1 Deadline. Whether a motion for relief from the judgment extends the deadline to appeal depends on when the motion is filed and whether the court makes a material alteration of the judgment.

1. Motion filed within 28 days after judgment. A motion for relief from the judgment filed within 28 days after entry of judgment tolls the deadline to file a notice of appeal until an order disposing of the motion is entered. FRAP 4(a)(4)(A)(vi); *see* ***Shales v. General Chauffeurs, Sales Drivers & Helpers Local Un.***, 557 F.3d 746, 748 (7th Cir.2009) (tolling of appellate deadline is determined by filing of motion, not by decision that motion has merit). According to FRAP 4(a), an order is considered entered when it is entered on the civil docket under FRCP 79(a). FRAP 4(a)(7)(A)(i). The court does not need to render the order with the formality of a judgment, but it must

clearly dispose of the post-trial motion. ***Ellison v. Conoco, Inc.***, 950 F.2d 1196, 1201 (5th Cir.1992). An appellant challenging either an order disposing of the motion for relief from the judgment or a judgment's alteration or amendment based on the motion for relief must file the notice of appeal within 30 days (60 days if the United States is a party) after entry of the order, unless there are other outstanding motions that continue to toll the running of the appellate deadlines. *See* FRAP 4(a)(1)(A), (a)(1)(B), (a)(4)(B)(ii); 2009 Notes to FRAP 4 at ¶¶3, 4, p. 1266, this book.

CAUTION

The circuits disagree on whether the 28-day deadline that tolls the time to file a notice of appeal is a nonjurisdictional claim-processing rule such that objections to the timeliness of an FRCP 60(b) motion for tolling purposes can be waived. Compare ***Blue v. International Bhd. of Elec. Workers Local Un.****, 676 F.3d 579, 582-83 (7th Cir.2012) (untimely motion listed under FRAP 4(a)(4)(A) does not toll time for filing appeal), and* ***Advanced Bodycare Solutions, LLC v. Thione Int'l****, 615 F.3d 1352, 1359 n.14 (11th Cir.2010) (because FRAP 4(a)(4) is jurisdictional, untimely motion listed under FRAP 4(a)(4)(A) does not toll time for filing appeal), with* ***Obaydullah v. Obama****, ___ F.3d ___ (D.C.Cir.2012) (No. 11-5123; 8-10-12) (because FRAP 4(a)(4) is nonjurisdictional claim-processing rule, untimely motion listed under FRAP 4(a)(4)(A) can toll time for filing appeal; objections to timeliness for tolling purposes can be waived), and* ***National Ecological Found. v. Alexander****, 496 F.3d 466, 476 (6th Cir.2007) (untimely motion listed under FRAP 4(a)(4)(A) tolls time for filing appeal).*

2. Motion filed more than 28 days after judgment. When a motion for relief from the judgment is filed more than 28 days after the judgment, the appellate timetable is restarted only for any material alteration of the judgment that the court made in response to the motion. *See* ***American Fed'n of Grain Millers v. Cargill Inc.***, 15 F.3d 726, 728 (7th Cir.1994); *see also* ***FTC v. Minneapolis-Honeywell Regulator Co.***, 344 U.S. 206, 211-12 (1952) (appellate deadlines should be restarted only when lower court changes matters of substance or resolves genuine ambiguity in previously rendered judgment). The entry of a corrected judgment does not permit a late appeal of issues that are not affected by the correction. *See* ***Buggs v. Elgin, Joliet & E. Ry.***, 852 F.2d 318, 323 (7th Cir.1988).

§9.2 Standard of review.

1. Abuse of discretion. A motion for relief from the judgment is generally reviewed for an abuse of discretion. ***Johnson v. Arden***, 614 F.3d 785, 799 (8th Cir.2010); ***Ungar v. Palestine Liberation Org.***, 599 F.3d 79, 83 (1st Cir.2010); ***In re Syncor ERISA Litig.***, 516 F.3d 1095, 1099 (9th Cir.2008); ***Charter Township of Muskegon v. City of Muskegon***, 303 F.3d 755, 759 (6th Cir.2002); ***Middle Rio Grande Conservancy Dist. v. Norton***, 294 F.3d 1220, 1225 (10th Cir.2002); ***Cash v. Illinois Div. of Mental Health***, 209 F.3d 695, 697 (7th Cir.2000); ***Reform Party of Allegheny Cty. v. Allegheny Cty. Dept. of Elections***, 174 F.3d 305, 311 (3d Cir.1999). However, a motion asserting that the judgment is void is reviewed de novo. ***Johnson***, 614 F.3d at 799; ***Jackson v. FIE Corp.***, 302 F.3d 515, 521-22 (5th Cir.2002); ***General Star Nat'l Ins. v. Administratia Asigurarilor de Stat***, 289 F.3d 434, 437 (6th Cir. 2002). A district court does not have discretion to deny a party the right to file a motion for reconsideration under FRCP 60. ***Collins v. Morgan Stanley Dean Witter***, 224 F.3d 496, 502 (5th Cir.2000).

(1) Liberal view of relief. Many circuits have held that motions for relief from the judgment should be liberally construed. ***In re Roxford Foods, Inc.***, 12 F.3d 875, 879 (9th Cir.1993); ***Cavaliere v. Allstate Ins.***, 996 F.2d 1111, 1115 (11th Cir.1993); *see also* ***In re Woods***, 173 F.3d 770, 780 (10th Cir.1999) (decision under FRCP 60(b)(6) will be reversed "only if we find a complete absence of a reasonable basis and are certain that the … decision is wrong"). Despite the requirement of liberal construction, a litigant's actual chance of relief is poor. *See* ***Swaim v. Moltan Co.***, 73 F.3d 711, 722 (7th Cir.1996); ***Cavaliere***, 996 F.2d at 1115.

(2) Motion filed within 30 days. If a motion for relief from the judgment is filed within the period for an appeal on the ground that the court has overlooked some controlling principle of law, the court abuses its discretion by denying the motion, even in the absence of a motion for new trial or appeal. ***Harrison v. Byrd***, 765 F.2d 501, 503 (5th Cir.1985).

2. No review of merits. In reviewing a district court's decision to deny a motion for relief from the judgment, the court generally cannot review the merits of the underlying judgment. ***Johnson***, 614 F.3d at 799; ***Lora v. O'Heaney***, 602 F.3d 106, 111 (2d Cir.2010); ***U.S. v. Reyes***, 307 F.3d 451, 456 (6th Cir.2002). If the motion for relief from the judgment is filed within 28 days, however, the court can review the merits of the underlying judgment. *See **Reyes***, 307 F.3d at 456. But a motion for relief filed within 28 days will generally be construed as an FRCP 59(e) motion. *See **Lora***, 602 F.3d at 110-11 (applying former ten-day deadline); ***Hawkins v. Evans***, 64 F.3d 543, 546 (10th Cir.1995) (same). See "Note," §2.1, p. 804; "Standard of review," ch. 10-D, §7.2, p. 798.

G. MOTION TO EXTEND TIME TO FILE NOTICE OF APPEAL

§1. GENERAL

§1.1 Rule. FRAP 4(a)(5). See also 28 U.S.C. §2107(c).

§1.2 Timetable & forms. Timetable, Appeal of Civil Trial, p. 1591; ***O'Connor's Federal Civil Forms*** **(2012)**, FORMS 10G.

§1.3 Purpose. Under FRAP 4(a)(5), a party can ask the district court to extend the time to file a notice of appeal.

§1.4 Other references. 16A Wright, Miller, Cooper & Struve, *Federal Practice & Procedure 4th* §§3950-3950.7 (2008 & Supp.2012); 19 *Moore's Federal Practice 3d* §205.04[3][c]-[e] (2012); Knibb, *Federal Court of Appeals Manual* ch. 12 (5th ed.2007 & Supp.2012).

CAUTION

Do not confuse a motion to extend the time to file a notice of appeal under FRAP 4(a)(5) with a motion to reopen the time for appeal under FRAP 4(a)(6). The relief under FRAP 4(a)(5) is limited to additional time to file a notice of appeal, while the relief under FRAP 4(a)(6) gives the movant additional time to file postjudgment motions as well. See "Motion to Reopen Time for Appeal," ch. 10-H, p. 821.

§2. NOTICE OF JUDGMENT

The clerk has a duty to serve the parties or their attorneys with immediate notice, in accordance with FRCP 5(b), of the entry of a judgment or order, and to note the service on the docket. FRCP 77(d)(1). See "Notice of Judgment," ch. 9-A, §4, p. 741. The parties should therefore find out about the judgment and the orders overruling any post-trial motions in time to file a notice of appeal.

§3. DEADLINE TO FILE NOTICE OF APPEAL

§3.1 Generally. A party must file a notice of appeal with the clerk of the district court within 30 days (60 days if the United States is a party) after entry of the order sought to be appealed. FRAP 4(a)(1)(A), (a)(1)(B); *see **Bowles v. Russell***, 551 U.S. 205, 208 (2007); ***Kinsley v. Lakeview Reg'l Med. Ctr. LLC***, 570 F.3d 586, 588 (5th Cir.2009); ***Pincay v. Andrews***, 389 F.3d 853, 854-55 (9th Cir.2004). If the party files any of the motions listed in FRAP 4(a)(4)(A), the time to appeal is tolled until the last motion is overruled by the court. FRAP 4(a)(4)(A).

CAUTION

*FRCP 6(d) and FRAP 26(c), which add three days to a response period after service by any method other than hand delivery, do not extend the period to file a notice of appeal. **Ultimate Appliance CC v. Kirby Co.**, 601 F.3d 414, 416 (6th Cir.2010). Even though the notice of the entry of judgment must be served, the deadline for a notice of appeal is triggered by entry of judgment on the docket, not service of the notice of the entry of judgment. Id. See "Notice of Judgment," ch. 9-A, §4, p. 741.*

§3.2 Premature notice. If the party files a notice of appeal after the court announces a decision or order, but before it enters the judgment or disposes of any motion listed in FRAP 4(a)(4)(A), the notice may be treated as filed on the date of the entry of the judgment or order. FRAP 4(a)(2); *see* FRAP 4(a)(4)(B)(i).

1. Notice relates forward. A premature notice of appeal from a nonfinal decision will relate forward and serve as an effective notice for a later-entered final judgment if the decision would be final and appealable if immediately followed by the entry of judgment. ***FirsTier Mortg. Co. v. Investors Mortg. Ins.***, 498 U.S. 269, 276 (1991); *e.g.*, ***Bonner v. Perry***, 564 F.3d 424, 428-29 (6th Cir.2009) (P's premature notice of appeal from decision to grant summary judgment dismissing D1—but not D2—served as notice of appeal from final judgment after D2 was later dismissed, but appeal covered only D1's dismissal); *see* ***Fields v. Oklahoma State Penitentiary***, 511 F.3d 1109, 1111 (10th Cir.2007) (decision leading to premature notice of appeal must have some "indicia of finality" and remain unchanged until entry of judgment). If the case involves multiple parties or claims, a premature notice of appeal from a nonfinal dismissal of a party or claim can relate forward and serve as an effective notice if the district court later enters an FRCP 54(b) certification. ***Brown v. Columbia Sussex Corp.***, 664 F.3d 182, 189 (7th Cir.2011); ***National Ass'n of Bds. of Pharm. v. Board of Regents***, 633 F.3d 1297, 1306 (11th Cir.2011).

2. Notice does not relate forward. A premature notice of appeal from a clearly interlocutory decision (e.g., a discovery order, an FRCP 11 sanction) will not relate forward and serve as a notice of appeal for a later-entered final judgment; the party must file a new or amended notice of appeal from the final judgment. *See* ***FirsTier Mortg.***, 498 U.S. at 276; *cf.* ***U.S. v. Cooper***, 135 F.3d 960, 962-63 (5th Cir.1998) (in criminal case, D's premature notice of appeal filed after magistrate judge's decision but before district court's final judgment adopting that decision did not relate forward because magistrate judge's decision could never be final judgment and did not dispose of any of D's claims).

§4. DEADLINE TO FILE MOTION TO EXTEND TIME

§4.1 Deadline for ex parte motion. A party can file an ex parte motion to extend the time to file a notice of appeal if it files the motion before the deadline for filing the notice of appeal. FRAP 4(a)(5)(B); ***Malone v. Avenenti***, 850 F.2d 569, 571 (9th Cir.1988). In most cases, if a party can still file a notice of appeal, it will not file a motion to extend time but will instead simply file the notice itself. If the party wants to file a motion to extend time instead of a notice of appeal and the original 30 days have not passed, the party can move for the extension ex parte by showing either good cause or excusable neglect. Knibb, *Federal Court of Appeals Manual* §12:1; *see* FRAP 4(a)(5)(A), (a)(5)(B); ***Gibbons v. U.S.***, 317 F.3d 852, 853 (8th Cir.2003).

§4.2 Deadline for motion. After the time to file the notice of appeal expires, a party who wants additional time must file a motion within 30 days after the original deadline, show good cause or excusable neglect, and serve the other party with a copy of the motion. 28 U.S.C. §2107(c); FRAP 4(a)(5)(A), (a)(5)(B); ***Malone v. Avenenti***, 850 F.2d 569, 571-72 (9th Cir.1988). See "Computing Deadlines," ch. 1-C, §6, p. 23. Therefore, because a party has 30 days to file the notice of appeal (60 days if the United States is a party), it has a total of 60 days (90 days if the United States is a party) from the date the judgment was entered to file the motion to extend time. *E.g.*, ***Ultimate Appliance CC v. Kirby Co.***, 601 F.3d 414, 415 (6th Cir.2010). See "Generally," §3.1, p. 817. If the movant does not serve the motion on the other party by the deadline, the district court has no jurisdiction to grant the extension. ***Oda v. Transcon Lines Corp.***, 650 F.2d 231, 233 (10th Cir.1981); *see* ***Ultimate Appliance CC***, 601 F.3d at 415-16.

§5. MOTION

§5.1 Form. For the general requirements for the form of a motion, see "Drafting motions," ch. 1-B, §3.1, p. 14.

§5.2 In writing. A motion to extend the time to file a notice of appeal must be in writing. *See* FRCP 7(b)(1)(A). An ex parte request for an extension must also be made by written motion. *See* ***Nunley v. City of L.A.***, 52 F.3d 792, 795 (9th Cir.1995); 1979 Notes to FRAP 4 at ¶9, p. 1275, this book.

§5.3 Grounds. A motion to extend the time to file a notice of appeal should contain the following:

1. Explanation for delay. The movant should explain why the notice of appeal will not be or was not timely filed. Depending on the movant's burden, additional facts may need to be shown to justify the delay.

2. **Burden.** The movant must show either good cause or excusable neglect, depending on whether the movant is at fault for causing the delay. FRAP 4(a)(5)(A)(ii); 2002 Notes to FRAP 4 at ¶10, p. 1269, this book.

(1) **Good cause.** If the movant is not at fault for causing the delay, the movant must show good cause for the delay. *See* FRAP 4(a)(5)(A)(ii); 2002 Notes to FRAP 4 at ¶¶10-11, p. 1269, this book.

(2) **Excusable neglect.** If the movant is at fault for causing the delay, the movant must show that the delay was the result of excusable neglect. *See* FRAP 4(a)(5)(A)(ii); 2002 Notes to FRAP 4 at ¶¶10-11, p. 1269, this book. When deciding whether the movant's conduct satisfies the excusable-neglect standard, the district court should consider the factors the Supreme Court outlined in ***Pioneer Inv. Servs. v. Brunswick Assocs.***, 507 U.S. 380 (1993). These factors include (1) the danger of prejudice to the opposing party, (2) the length of delay and its potential impact on the proceedings, (3) the reason for the delay, including whether it was reasonably within the movant's control, and (4) whether the movant acted in good faith. ***Pioneer Inv.***, 507 U.S. at 395; ***Zipperer v. School Bd. of Seminole Cty.***, 111 F.3d 847, 849 (11th Cir.1997); *see* ***Abuelyaman v. Illinois State Univ.***, 667 F.3d 800, 808 (7th Cir.2011) (most important factors are prejudice to opposing party and movant's good faith). These factors are not exclusive, and all relevant circumstances should be considered. *See* ***Pioneer Inv.***, 507 U.S. at 395; ***Ragguette v. Premier Wine & Spirits***, 691 F.3d 315, 331 (3d Cir.2012); ***Abuelyaman***, 667 F.3d at 808; ***Pincay v. Andrews***, 389 F.3d 853, 856 (9th Cir.2004). See "Excusable neglect," ch. 10-F, §3.4.1(4), p. 807.

NOTE

Check the law of your circuit to determine what constitutes excusable neglect. See ***Pincay***, *389 F.3d at 857 (circuits are in disarray in interpreting* ***Pioneer*** *factors). The circuits differ even when faced with similar facts. Compare* ***Mendez v. Knowles***, *556 F.3d 757, 764-65 (9th Cir. 2009) (extension granted when notice was filed on Wednesday (one day late) even though D mailed notice on Saturday before Tuesday deadline and Monday was legal holiday; reliance on normal mail delivery constituted excusable neglect), and* ***Zipperer***, *111 F.3d at 850 (extension granted when Ps mailed notice six days before deadline even though notice was filed one day late; reliance on normal mail delivery constituted excusable neglect), with* ***Thompson v. E.I. DuPont de Nemours & Co.***, *76 F.3d 530, 534-35 (4th Cir.1996) (extension not granted when P mailed notice at least three days before the deadline; reliance on normal mail delivery did not constitute excusable neglect).*

§5.4 Period of delay. The movant should identify how many days after the judgment was entered that the motion to extend time is being filed.

§5.5 Affidavits. Because a motion to extend the time to file a notice of appeal will contain facts outside the record, it should be supported by affidavits. The movant should attach the affidavit of any person who should have learned about the judgment but did not—usually the attorney.

§5.6 Request hearing. If a motion to extend the time to file a notice of appeal presents contested fact issues, or if oral argument will help the court resolve the motion, the movant should request a hearing. The movant should comply with any requirements of the local rules for securing a hearing on the motion. *See* ***Kendall v. Hoover Co.***, 751 F.2d 171, 172-73 (6th Cir.1984).

§5.7 File in district court. A motion to extend the time to file a notice of appeal must be filed in the district court, not in the court of appeals. ***Merritt v. Broglin***, 841 F.2d 184, 185 (7th Cir.1988).

§5.8 Certificate of service. A motion to extend the time to file a notice of appeal must be served on the other party unless it can be heard ex parte. FRCP 5(a)(1)(D). Even when making the motion ex parte, the movant should send a copy of the motion to the other parties. *See* FRCP 5(a)(1); FRAP 4(a)(5)(B).

§5.9 Notice of appeal. The movant should file the notice of appeal at the same time as the motion. If the motion is granted, the notice will be filed as of the date of the court's order. *See* Knibb, *Federal Court of Appeals Manual* §12:1.

§6. RESPONSE

§6.1 Objections. If the nonmovant opposes the motion to extend time, it should file a response objecting to the grounds in the motion.

1. Substantive. The response should negate whatever grounds are asserted in the motion. In particular, the nonmovant should allege that the movant did not show good cause or excusable neglect for the delay. *See* FRAP 4(a)(5)(A)(ii).

2. Procedural. The response should identify any procedural reasons why the motion should be denied (e.g., the motion was filed after the deadline passed). *See* FRAP 4(a)(5)(A)(i).

§6.2 Deadline. FRAP 4(a)(5) does not specify a deadline for the response, but it should be filed within any limits set by local rules for responses.

§6.3 Affidavits. If the response contains facts outside the record, it should be supported by affidavits. Generally, if the movant attached affidavits to the motion, the nonmovant should attach affidavits to the response.

§7. HEARING

§7.1 Need for hearing. If the facts are in dispute, the court can hold a hearing on the motion or consider affidavits attached to the motion. Even if the facts are not in dispute, a hearing may be helpful to argue the application of legal principles.

§7.2 Burden. At the hearing, it is the movant's burden to prove the allegations in the motion.

§8. RULING

§8.1 Written order. The court should sign a written order granting or denying the motion. See "Orders," ch. 1-G, §4.2, p. 45.

§8.2 Extension of time. If the court grants the motion, it cannot extend the time to file the notice of appeal more than 30 days beyond the date it was due or more than 14 days after the motion is granted, whichever is later. FRAP 4(a)(5)(C).

NOTE

The D.C. Circuit has held that FRAP 4(a)(5)(C) is a nonjurisdictional claim-processing rule; thus, in that circuit, objections to the timeliness of an FRAP 4(a)(5)(C) extension can be waived. E.g., ***Youkelsone v. FDIC****, 660 F.3d 473, 475 (D.C.Cir.2011) (although district court erroneously granted P a 31-day extension under FRAP 4(a)(5)(C), D did not object; thus, D waived its untimeliness objection and appellate court had jurisdiction over appeal). Other deadlines under FRAP 4(a), however, have been held to be jurisdictional and cannot be waived. See, e.g.,* ***Advanced Bodycare Solutions, LLC v. Thione Int'l****, 615 F.3d 1352, 1359 n.14 (11th Cir.2010) (FRAP 4(a)(4) is jurisdictional).*

§9. FILING NOTICE OF APPEAL

If the court grants the motion, the movant must file the notice of appeal within the time permitted by the court's order. The notice of appeal should be filed at the same time as the motion to extend time, subject to the court's ruling on the motion. *See* Knibb, *Federal Court of Appeals Manual* §12:1. The movant should check with the clerk about the filing fee for the notice of appeal.

§10. APPELLATE REVIEW

§10.1 Standard of review. The district court's ruling on a motion to extend the time to file a notice of appeal under FRAP 4(a)(5) is reviewed for abuse of discretion. ***U.S. v. Carson***, 52 F.3d 1173, 1180 (2d Cir.1995); *see* ***Thompson v. E.I. DuPont de Nemours & Co.***, 76 F.3d 530, 532 (4th Cir.1996); ***Prizevoits v. Indiana Bell Tel. Co.***, 76 F.3d 132, 134 (7th Cir.1996).

§10.2 Court grants motion. If the district court grants the motion and extends the time to file the notice of appeal, the nonmovant can challenge the ruling on appeal. *See **U.S. v. Carson***, 52 F.3d 1173, 1180 (2d Cir.1995).

§10.3 Court denies motion. If the district court denies the motion, the movant can appeal the order as a final judgment under 28 U.S.C. §1291. ***In re Diet Drugs Prods. Liab. Litig.***, 401 F.3d 143, 153 (3d Cir.2005); *see **Bishop v. Corsentino***, 371 F.3d 1203, 1206 (10th Cir.2004).

H. MOTION TO REOPEN TIME FOR APPEAL

§1. GENERAL

§1.1 Rule. FRAP 4(a)(6). See also 28 U.S.C. §2107(c).

§1.2 Purpose. FRAP 4(a)(6) allows for an extension of time when a party would be unfairly deprived of an appeal because it did not receive notice of the judgment. ***Benavides v. Bureau of Prisons***, 79 F.3d 1211, 1214 (D.C. Cir.1996); ***Marcangelo v. Boardwalk Regency***, 47 F.3d 88, 90 (3d Cir.1995); ***Zimmer St. Louis, Inc. v. Zimmer Co.***, 32 F.3d 357, 360 (8th Cir.1994).

§1.3 Timetable & forms. Timetable, Appeal of Civil Trial, p. 1591; *O'Connor's Federal Civil Forms* (2012), FORMS 10H.

§1.4 Other references. 16A Wright, Miller, Cooper & Struve, *Federal Practice & Procedure 4th* §3950.6 (2008 & Supp.2012); 20 *Moore's Federal Practice 3d* §304.14 (2012).

CAUTION

Do not confuse a motion to extend the time to file a notice of appeal under FRAP 4(a)(5) with a motion to reopen the time for appeal under FRAP 4(a)(6). The relief under FRAP 4(a)(5) is limited to additional time to file a notice of appeal, while the relief under FRAP 4(a)(6) gives the movant additional time to file postjudgment motions as well. See "Motion to Extend Time to File Notice of Appeal," ch. 10-G, p. 817.

---

§2. NOTICE OF JUDGMENT

If the party adversely affected by the judgment does not receive notice within 21 days after the entry of judgment, that party can file a motion under FRAP 4(a)(6) to reopen the time for appeal. FRAP 4(a)(6)(A). Simply filing a late notice of appeal is not the equivalent of a motion under FRAP 4(a)(6). ***Jenkins v. Burtzloff***, 69 F.3d 460, 462-63 (10th Cir.1995).

§2.1 Who must give notice. Notice of the entry of judgment must be given directly by either the clerk or any party; notice from another source is not sufficient. *See* FRAP 4(a)(6)(A); FRCP 77(d)(1); ***Benavides v. Bureau of Prisons***, 79 F.3d 1211, 1214 (D.C.Cir.1996). See "FRAP 4(a)(6)," ch. 9-A, §4.1.2, p. 742.

§2.2 Written notice. Notice of the entry of judgment must be written. *See* FRCP 77(d); FRAP 4(a)(6); 2005 Notes to FRAP 4 at ¶7, p. 1267, this book; 16A Wright, Miller, Cooper & Struve §3950.6.

§2.3 Service of notice. Notice of the entry of judgment must be served according to FRCP 77(d). FRAP 4(a)(6)(B). FRCP 77(d)(1) requires that service on parties be made in the manner provided for under FRCP 5(b). See "Methods of service," ch. 1-D, §4.1, p. 30.

§2.4 Receipt of notice.

1. Who must receive notice. When a party is represented by an attorney, notice of the entry of judgment must be received by the attorney. ***Ryan v. First Unum Life Ins.***, 174 F.3d 302, 305 (2d Cir.1999). If a party is represented by two attorneys, timely notice to either one prevents a motion under FRAP 4(a)(6). *E.g.*, ***Marcangelo v. Boardwalk Regency***, 47 F.3d 88, 90 (3d Cir.1995) (motion denied when notice was received by in-state attorney but not out-of-state attorney who primarily handled case).

2. When notice is received. Notice of the entry of judgment is received when it is delivered to the proper address. *E.g.*, ***Lim v. Courtcall Inc.***, 683 F.3d 378, 380-81 (7th Cir.2012) (P received notice when it was delivered by mail to his house, not when he actually opened his mail).

§3. DEADLINE

The motion to reopen the time for appeal must be filed within 14 days after receipt of notice or within 180 days after the entry of judgment, whichever is earlier. 28 U.S.C. §2107(c); FRAP 4(a)(6)(B). The phrase "window of opportunity" is a useful description for the time limits of a motion to reopen the time for appeal under FRAP 4(a)(6). The window for filing the motion opens on the 22nd day after the judgment is entered and closes on the 180th day after the judgment is entered. The motion must be received by—not just mailed to—the clerk by the deadline. *See* ***U.S. v. Heller***, 957 F.2d 26, 30 (1st Cir.1992). For the rule applicable to pro se prisoners in this context, see ***Benavides v. Bureau of Prisons***, 79 F.3d 1211, 1213 (D.C.Cir.1996).

§3.1 Window opens. The first chance to file a motion to reopen the time for appeal is when a party receives notice of the judgment from the clerk or the other party more than 21 days after the judgment is entered (i.e., on the 22nd day after judgment or later). Although a party who receives notice on the 22nd day (or up until the 30th day—i.e., when the notice of appeal is due) after the entry of judgment can still file a notice of appeal or seek an extension of time under FRAP 4(a)(5), the use of FRAP 4(a)(6) is also possible under the literal terms of the rule. See "Generally," ch. 10-G, §3.1, p. 817.

§3.2 Window closes. The window closes on the earlier of the following two dates:

1. 14 days after notice. If a party receives notice of the judgment more than 21 days after it is entered, the party must file the motion within 14 days after receiving the notice. 28 U.S.C. §2107(c); FRAP 4(a)(6)(A), (a)(6)(B); *see* ***Martinez v. Hoke***, 38 F.3d 655, 656 (2d Cir.1994) (applying former seven-day deadline).

2. 180 days after judgment is entered. The last day to file a motion to reopen the time for appeal is 180 days after the judgment is entered. 28 U.S.C. §2107(c); FRAP 4(a)(6)(B); ***Benavides v. Bureau of Prisons***, 79 F.3d 1211, 1214 (D.C.Cir.1996); ***Zimmer St. Louis, Inc. v. Zimmer Co.***, 32 F.3d 357, 359 (8th Cir.1994). A party cannot file a motion to reopen under FRAP 4(a)(6) beyond the 180-day deadline. *E.g.*, ***Garner v. Klein***, 882 F.Supp. 66, 67 (S.D.N.Y.1995) (motion filed seven months after entry of judgment was too late).

§3.3 Period reopens. If the motion to reopen is filed within the "window of opportunity," the district court can reopen the time to file an appeal for 14 days after the order to reopen is entered. *See* 28 U.S.C. §2107(c); FRAP 4(a)(6).

§3.4 No extension. The district court cannot extend the time periods under FRAP 4(a)(6). *See, e.g.*, ***Bowles v. Russell***, 551 U.S. 205, 207-08 (2007) (no extension for 14-day deadline under FRAP 4(a)(6) to file notice of appeal after period had been reopened); ***Baker v. U.S.***, 670 F.3d 448, 451 n.4, 456 (3d Cir.2012) (no extension to earlier of 180-day or 14-day deadline to file motion to reopen under FRAP 4(a)(6)(B); applying former 7-day deadline). The time limits in FRAP 4(a)(6) and 28 U.S.C. §2107(c) are mandatory and jurisdictional and cannot be waived by the parties. *See* ***Bowles***, 551 U.S. at 213-14; ***Baker***, 670 F.3d at 456. FRCP 60(b) cannot be used to extend the time limit in FRAP 4(a)(6). *See* ***Vencor Hosps., Inc. v. Standard Life & Acc. Ins.***, 279 F.3d 1306, 1311 (11th Cir.2002) (FRAP 4(a)(6) trumps FRCP 60(b)); ***Clark v. Lavallie***, 204 F.3d 1038, 1040-41 (10th Cir.2000) (same); ***In re Stein***, 197 F.3d 421, 425 (9th Cir.1999) (same); *see also* ***In re Sealed Case (Bowles)***, 624 F.3d 482, 486-87 (D.C.Cir.2010) (FRCP 60(b)(6) cannot be used to circumvent 180-day deadline under FRAP 4(a)(6)).

NOTE

Before the Supreme Court's decision in ***Bowles***, *courts had recognized a limited exception to the strict jurisdictional requirements for the timely filing of appeals, known as the "unique circumstances" doctrine. Under this doctrine, an otherwise untimely appeal was deemed timely when (1) a party had performed an act that, if properly done, would postpone the deadline for*

filing its appeal, and (2) the party had received specific assurance by a judicial officer that this act had been properly done. ***Osterneck v. Ernst & Whinney****, 489 U.S. 169, 179 (1989). In a 5-4 decision in* ***Bowles****, the Supreme Court overturned this doctrine and held that the timely filing of a notice of appeal is jurisdictional under FRAP 4(a)(6) and not subject to equitable exceptions.* ***Bowles****, 551 U.S. at 213-14; see* ***In re Sealed Case (Bowles)****, 624 F.3d at 486-87.*

§4. MOTION

§4.1 Form. For the general requirements for the form of a motion, see "Drafting motions," ch. 1-B, §3.1, p. 14.

§4.2 In writing. A motion to reopen the time for appeal must be in writing. *See* FRCP 7(b)(1)(A).

§4.3 Grounds. A motion to reopen the time for appeal should contain the following information:

1. The movant or the movant's attorney received notice of the judgment on a certain date, and that date was more than 21 days after the judgment was entered. FRAP 4(a)(6)(A); *see* ***Baker v. U.S.***, 670 F.3d 448, 454 (3d Cir.2012).

2. A description of how the movant or the attorney received notice of the judgment. The motion should state why the notice was late and other details known by the party.

3. The motion is being filed within 14 days after notice of the judgment was received or within 180 days after the entry of judgment, whichever is earlier. FRAP 4(a)(6)(B); *see* ***Baker***, 670 F.3d at 454.

4. No party will be prejudiced by reopening the time for appeal. FRAP 4(a)(6)(C); *see* ***Baker***, 670 F.3d at 454.

§4.4 Affidavits. In most cases, all the movant can do to prove nonreceipt is submit affidavits. ***Nunley v. City of L.A.***, 52 F.3d 792, 796 (9th Cir.1995). The movant should attach the affidavit of any person who should have learned about the judgment but did not—usually the attorney.

1. **Attorney.** The attorney should swear that she did not receive timely notice of the judgment and state the exact date that notice was eventually received. The attorney should probably describe the office procedure for processing notices from the court and state that a review of the process revealed that no notice was received. *See* ***Nunley***, 52 F.3d at 796.

2. **Pro se party.** The pro se party should swear that she did not receive timely notice of the judgment and state the exact date that notice was eventually received. *See* ***Benavides v. Bureau of Prisons***, 79 F.3d 1211, 1213-14 (D.C.Cir.1996).

§4.5 Request hearing. If a motion to reopen the time for appeal presents contested fact issues, or if oral argument will help the court resolve the motion, the movant should request a hearing. The movant should comply with any requirements of the local rules for securing a hearing on the motion. *See* ***Kendall v. Hoover Co.***, 751 F.2d 171, 172-73 (6th Cir.1984).

§5. RESPONSE

§5.1 Objections. If the nonmovant opposes the motion, it should file a response objecting to the grounds in the motion. The response should also negate whatever grounds are asserted in the motion. For example, the nonmovant can assert the following:

1. The movant or its attorney received notice of the judgment within 21 days after the judgment was entered. FRAP 4(a)(6)(A); *see* ***Lim v. Courtcall Inc.***, 683 F.3d 378, 380-81 (7th Cir.2012); *see, e.g.*, ***American Boat Co. v. Unknown Sunken Barge***, 567 F.3d 348, 352-53 (8th Cir.2009) (P's motion to reopen was denied because P could not satisfy lack-of-notice requirement when D's computer expert testified he was 95% certain that P received Notice of Electronic Filing of order denying motion to amend judgment).

2. The movant filed the motion more than 180 days after the judgment was entered. FRAP 4(a)(6)(B).

3. The movant filed the motion more than 14 days after receiving notice of the entry of judgment. *Id.*
4. The nonmovant would be prejudiced by reopening the time for appeal. FRAP 4(a)(6)(C).

§5.2 Deadline. FRAP 4(a)(6) does not specify a deadline for the response, but it should be filed within any limits set by local rules for responses.

§5.3 Affidavits. If the response contains facts outside the record, it should be supported by affidavits. Generally, if the movant attached affidavits to the motion, the nonmovant should attach affidavits to the response.

§6. HEARING

§6.1 Hearing unnecessary. If the facts are in dispute, the court can hold a hearing on the motion or consider affidavits attached to the motion. Even if the facts are not in dispute, a hearing may be helpful to argue the application of legal principles.

§6.2 Burden. If a hearing is held, the movant should prove the following: (1) it filed and served the motion within 14 days after receiving notice or within 180 days after the entry of judgment, whichever was earlier, (2) it received notice within the 22-to-180-day window, and (3) the nonmovant would not be prejudiced by reopening the time for appeal. *See* FRAP 4(a)(6).

§6.3 Presumption that notice was received. When the record shows that the clerk sent the notice, it establishes a rebuttable presumption that the notice was received by the addressee. ***Nunley v. City of L.A.***, 52 F.3d 792, 796 (9th Cir.1995). The burden of proving nonreceipt of the notice is on the party seeking to reopen the time for appeal. ***McDaniel v. Moore***, 292 F.3d 1304, 1307 (11th Cir.2002). Once the movant presents evidence that it did not receive the notice, the presumption disappears. ***Nunley***, 52 F.3d at 796; *see* FRE 301.

NOTE

Because many judgments are now served electronically, parties may have to address the issue of electronic receipt of a Notice of Electronic Filing (NEF) through the court's Case Management/Electronic Case Files (CM/ECF) system. See, e.g., ***American Boat Co. v. Unknown Sunken Barge****, 567 F.3d 348, 353 (8th Cir.2009) (P's motion to reopen was denied when P did not rebut presumption of receipt of court's NEF of order denying motion to amend judgment). The presumption of receipt applies to e-mails served through the CM/ECF system. Id. at 350.*

§7. RULING

§7.1 Written order. The court should sign a written order granting or denying the motion. See "Orders," ch. 1-G, §4.2, p. 45.

§7.2 Standard. The standard the district court uses to consider a motion to reopen the time for appeal under FRAP 4(a)(6) is less onerous than either good cause or excusable neglect, which are the standards for a motion to extend the time to file a notice of appeal under FRAP 4(a)(5). ***Benavides v. Bureau of Prisons***, 79 F.3d 1211, 1213-14 (D.C.Cir.1996); *see* ***Nunley v. City of L.A.***, 52 F.3d 792, 797-98 (9th Cir.1995) (denial of extension under FRAP 4(a)(6) cannot be based on inexcusable neglect); ***Avolio v. County of Suffolk***, 29 F.3d 50, 53-54 (2d Cir.1994) (same). See "Burden," ch. 10-G, §5.3.2, p. 819. Even when the requirements of FRAP 4(a)(6) have been met, the court has discretion to deny the motion. ***Arai v. Leff***, 316 F.3d 1066, 1069 (9th Cir.2003).

NOTE

If the movant contributed to the lack of notice of the judgment—such as by not notifying the clerk of a change of address or not registering with the CM/ECF system to receive court orders—the court has discretion to deny the motion. ***Benavides****, 79 F.3d at 1214; see, e.g.,* ***Kuhn v. Sulzer Orthopedics, Inc.****, 498 F.3d 365, 372 (6th Cir.2007) (court denied motion to reopen when attorney did not register with CM/ECF system and did not monitor electronic docket).*

§7.3 Court grants motion. If the court finds that the movant met the requirements of FRAP 4(a)(6), the court can reopen the time for appeal for a period of 14 days after the order to reopen is entered.

§7.4 Findings. If the court grants the motion, it must make findings that the requirements of FRAP 4(a)(6) were met. ***In re Marchiando***, 13 F.3d 1111, 1114 (7th Cir.1994). The omission of findings is not fatal, however. *E.g.*, *id.* (affidavit was uncontradicted). The court should find the following:

1. The movant was a party entitled to notice of the entry of judgment. *See* FRCP 77(d); FRAP 4(a)(6)(A).

2. The movant's attorney did not receive notice of the entry of judgment from the clerk or another party within 21 days after entry. FRAP 4(a)(6)(A).

3. The date the movant's attorney received notice and the date the movant filed the motion. *See* FRAP 4(a)(6)(B).

4. The movant filed the motion either within 180 days after the entry of judgment or within 14 days after the receipt of notice, whichever came first. *See id.*

5. No party will be prejudiced by the extension. FRAP 4(a)(6)(C). The appellate court will treat the finding of prejudice as a factual finding, which will not be reversed unless clearly wrong. *See* ***TBG, Inc. v. Bendis***, 36 F.3d 916, 920 (10th Cir.1994). If the nonmovant does not contest the movant's assertions about lack of prejudice, opposition to the motion is deemed waived. ***Benavides v. Bureau of Prisons***, 79 F.3d 1211, 1215 (D.C.Cir.1996).

§8. APPELLATE REVIEW

§8.1 Standard of review. The district court's order on a motion to reopen the time for appeal under FRAP 4(a)(6) is reviewed for abuse of discretion. ***American Boat Co. v. Unknown Sunken Barge***, 567 F.3d 348, 352 (8th Cir.2009); ***Nguyen v. Southwest Leasing & Rental Inc.***, 282 F.3d 1061, 1064 (9th Cir.2002); ***Ogden v. San Juan Cty.***, 32 F.3d 452, 455 (10th Cir.1994). The court's findings are reviewed using the clearly-erroneous standard that applies to findings of fact. ***American Boat***, 567 F.3d at 352; *see* ***TBG, Inc. v. Bendis***, 36 F.3d 916, 920 (10th Cir.1994).

§8.2 Court grants motion. If the district court grants the motion and reopens the time for appeal, the nonmovant can challenge the ruling on appeal. *See* ***Nguyen v. Southwest Leasing & Rental Inc.***, 282 F.3d 1061, 1063-64 (9th Cir.2002).

§8.3 Court denies motion. If the district court denies the motion, the movant can appeal the order as a final judgment under 28 U.S.C. §1291. *See* ***Kuhn v. Sulzer Orthopedics, Inc.***, 498 F.3d 365, 368 (6th Cir.2007); ***U.S. v. Rinaldi***, 447 F.3d 192, 195 (3d Cir.2006); ***Eltayib v. U.S.***, 294 F.3d 397, 399 (2d Cir.2002).

I. MOTION TO CORRECT CLERICAL ERROR IN JUDGMENT

§1. GENERAL

§1.1 Rule. FRCP 60(a).

§1.2 Purpose. Under FRCP 60(a), a party can ask the district court to correct clerical errors in the judgment caused by mistake, oversight, or omission. ***In re West Tex. Mktg. Corp.***, 12 F.3d 497, 503 (5th Cir.1994); *see* ***American Fed'n of Grain Millers v. Cargill Inc.***, 15 F.3d 726, 728 (7th Cir.1994); *see also* ***LeBeau v. Taco Bell, Inc.***, 892 F.2d 605, 609 n.3 (7th Cir.1989) (FRCP 60(a) replaced use of nunc pro tunc orders to correct ministerial errors).

§1.3 Timetable & forms. Timetable, Appeal of Civil Trial, p. 1591; ***O'Connor's Federal Civil Forms*** (2012), FORMS 10I.

§1.4 Other references. 11 Wright, Miller & Kane, *Federal Practice & Procedure 2d* §§2854-2856 (1995 & Supp.2012); 12 *Moore's Federal Practice 3d* §§60.10-60.13 (2012); 1 Childress & Davis, *Federal Standards of Review 4th* §5.12 (2010 & Supp.2011).

§2. NO DEADLINE

Although a motion to correct a clerical error in the judgment should be filed as soon as the party realizes there is an error, the corrections can be made at any time. *See* ***Truskoski v. ESPN, Inc.***, 60 F.3d 74, 77 (2d Cir.1995); ***In re West Tex. Mktg. Corp.***, 12 F.3d 497, 503 (5th Cir.1994). Clerical errors can be corrected before, during, or after an appeal. To correct clerical errors during an appeal, the district court must secure the appellate court's permission. FRCP 60(a); *see also* ***Local 1545, United Mine Workers v. Inland Steel Coal Co.***, 876 F.2d 1288, 1291 n.4 (7th Cir.1989) (court of appeals requested correction).

§3. CLERICAL VS. SUBSTANTIVE ERRORS

Only clerical errors can be corrected under FRCP 60(a). Errors affecting substantive rights cannot be corrected under this rule. ***Rivera v. PNS Stores***, 647 F.3d 188, 198-99 (5th Cir.2011). Thus, the scope of relief permitted under FRCP 60(a) is extremely specific and limited. ***In re Transtexas Gas Corp.***, 303 F.3d 571, 581 (5th Cir.2002).

§3.1 Error is clerical. A clerical error is a mistake, oversight, or omission in the recitation of the judgment that causes the judgment to inaccurately reflect what was intended by the court. ***Rivera v. PNS Stores***, 647 F.3d 188, 193-94 (5th Cir.2011); ***Truskoski v. ESPN, Inc.***, 60 F.3d 74, 77 (2d Cir.1995); ***American Fed'n of Grain Millers v. Cargill Inc.***, 15 F.3d 726, 728 (7th Cir.1994); *see also* ***In re Walter***, 282 F.3d 434, 440 (6th Cir.2002) (basic purpose of rule is to authorize court to correct mechanical errors that arise from oversight or omission). A clerical error correctable under FRCP 60(a) can be made by the clerk, the judge, or even the parties. ***In re West Tex. Mktg. Corp.***, 12 F.3d 497, 503-04 (5th Cir.1994). Under FRCP 60(a), the district court can correct the judgment to reflect the court's actual intention. ***In re West Tex. Mktg.***, 12 F.3d at 503 n.4; ***Robi v. Five Platters, Inc.***, 918 F.2d 1439, 1445 (9th Cir. 1990).

1. To correct damages. The court can enter an order to correct the following errors in a damages award:

(1) Add postjudgment interest. The court can correct a judgment to reflect postjudgment interest. ***Paddington Partners v. Bouchard***, 34 F.3d 1132, 1141-42 (2d Cir.1994).

(2) Correct mathematical error. The court can correct a judgment if there is a mathematical error in the damages award, whether made by the jury or by the court. *See, e.g.*, ***In re West Tex. Mktg.***, 12 F.3d at 504-05 (remanded to determine intention of parties and to correct any mathematical error).

(3) Add stipulated damages. The court can correct a judgment if it inadvertently omitted some of the stipulated damages (e.g., attorney fees). ***Dura-Wood Treating Co. v. Century Forest Indus.***, 694 F.2d 112, 114 (5th Cir.1982).

(4) Add liquidated damages. The court can correct a judgment if liquidated damages were inadvertently omitted. ***Chavez v. Balesh***, 704 F.2d 774, 776-77 (5th Cir.1983).

(5) Add date of prejudgment interest. The court can correct a judgment if it awarded prejudgment interest but omitted the date from which the interest was to run. ***Kosnoski v. Howley***, 33 F.3d 376, 380 (4th Cir.1994); ***McNickle v. Bankers Life & Cas. Co.***, 888 F.2d 678, 681-82 (10th Cir.1989).

2. To correct interpretation of order. The court can correct a judgment that incorrectly interprets a previously issued court order. ***American Fed'n***, 15 F.3d at 728.

3. To add omitted part of decision. The court can correct a judgment that omits part of the court's decision. *See, e.g.*, ***Truskoski***, 60 F.3d at 77 (because court did not intend to award certain benefits, omission from judgment was not clerical error); ***Hasbrouck v. Texaco, Inc.***, 879 F.2d 632, 636 (9th Cir.1989) (when court inadvertently omitted issues of costs and interest it had decided, omissions were clerical error).

4. To correct order based on error in docket. The court can correct an error in an order that is the result of the clerk's docketing error. *E.g.*, ***In re American Precision Vibrator Co.***, 863 F.2d 428, 431 (5th Cir.1989) (court corrected order of dismissal that resulted when clerk did not docket opposition to motion to dismiss).

5. To revise dismissal order. The court can amend a dismissal order if it inadvertently dismisses the plaintiff's lawsuit. *E.g.*, ***Jones & Guerrero Co. v. Sealift Pac.***, 650 F.2d 1072, 1074 (9th Cir.1981) (court inadvertently dismissed P's suit instead of petition).

6. To add party to summary judgment. The court can amend a judgment to include a defendant in whose favor a summary judgment was entered. ***Local 1545, United Mine Workers v. Inland Steel Coal Co.***, 876 F.2d 1288, 1291 n.4 (7th Cir.1989).

7. To clarify intention of judgment. The court can amend its judgment to clarify its intention. *See, e.g.*, ***Robi***, 918 F.2d at 1445 (court amended judgment to clarify its intention to cancel all trademarks and service marks held by D).

§3.2 Error is not clerical. If the error affects the substantive rights of the parties or if the error is in a judgment that accurately reflects the decisions rendered by the court or jury, it is not clerical and therefore not correctable under FRCP 60(a). ***Paddington Partners v. Bouchard***, 34 F.3d 1132, 1140 (2d Cir.1994); ***In re West Tex. Mktg. Corp.***, 12 F.3d 497, 504-05 (5th Cir.1994).

1. To correct certain errors in damages. The court cannot correct the following errors in a damages award:

(1) Add or change prejudgment interest. The court cannot add prejudgment interest under FRCP 60(a). ***Paddington Partners***, 34 F.3d at 1140-41. The court also cannot change the percentage of the prejudgment interest under FRCP 60(a). ***Warner v. City of Bay St. Louis***, 526 F.2d 1211, 1212 (5th Cir.1976).

(2) Add postjudgment damages. The court cannot add damages to a judgment to compensate the plaintiff for a depreciation in the value of the damages award that occurred while the appeal was pending. ***Trahan v. First Nat'l Bank***, 720 F.2d 832, 833-34 (5th Cir.1983).

2. To correct description of real estate. The court cannot correct a description of real estate under FRCP 60(a). *E.g.*, ***Jones v. Anderson-Tully Co.***, 722 F.2d 211, 212-13 (5th Cir.1984) (judgment unintentionally gave 18 acres to wrong party).

3. To add legal reasoning. The court cannot add legal reasoning or authority to a judgment or order under FRCP 60(a). *See, e.g.*, ***In re Galiardi***, 745 F.2d 335, 337 (5th Cir.1984) (court did not have jurisdiction to correct transfer order two years after entry to add reason for transfer to another district).

4. To add claims to judgment. The court cannot broaden a summary-judgment order to include a dismissal of all the plaintiff's claims. ***Britt v. Whitmire***, 956 F.2d 509, 515 (5th Cir.1992).

§4. MOTION

§4.1 Form. For the general requirements for the form of a motion, see "Drafting motions," ch. 1-B, §3.1, p. 14.

§4.2 In writing or on court's initiative. The motion must be in writing. *See* FRCP 7(b)(1)(A). The court can correct clerical errors in the judgment on its own initiative. ***In re West Tex. Mktg. Corp.***, 12 F.3d 497, 503 n.4. (5th Cir.1994). If the court decides to change the judgment on its own initiative under FRCP 60(a), the court must still notify the parties. *Cf.* ***In re Timely Secretarial Serv.***, 987 F.2d 1167, 1171 (5th Cir.1993) (relief under FRCP 60(b)).

§4.3 Grounds. A motion for relief from the judgment can be granted under FRCP 60(a) only when the error in the judgment is clerical in nature. See "Clerical vs. Substantive Errors," §3, p. 826. A motion to correct a clerical error in the judgment should contain the following:

1. A description of the error.
2. A statement that the error was clerical.
3. A statement that the motion to correct the error is not subject to any time limit because the error was clerical. *See* FRCP 60(a).

§4.4 Affidavits. If the motion contains facts outside the record, it should be supported by affidavits.

§4.5 Request hearing. If the motion presents contested fact issues, or if oral argument will help the court resolve the motion, the movant should request a hearing. The movant should comply with any requirements of the local rules for securing a hearing on the motion. *See* ***Kendall v. Hoover Co.***, 751 F.2d 171, 172-73 (6th Cir.1984).

§5. RESPONSE

§5.1 Objections. If the nonmovant objects to the allegations in the motion to correct a clerical error in the judgment, it should file a response challenging the motion. The following are some examples:

1. There is no error in the judgment; the court intended to include the statement in (or omit it from) the judgment.
2. If there is error, it is not a clerical error because it affects the substantive rights of the parties.
3. If there is error, it should have been challenged within 28 days after the entry of judgment under some other post-trial motion. *See* FRCP 59(b), (e).
4. The court has the discretion to deny the motion.

§5.2 Deadline. FRCP 60(a) does not specify a deadline for the response, but it should be filed within any limits set by local rules for responses.

§5.3 Affidavits. If the response contains facts outside the record, it should be supported by affidavits. Generally, if the movant attached affidavits to the motion, the nonmovant should attach affidavits to the response.

§6. HEARING

If the facts are in dispute, the court can hold a hearing on the motion or consider affidavits attached to the motion. Even if the facts are not in dispute, a hearing may be helpful to argue the application of legal principles.

§7. RULING

§7.1 Written order. The court should sign a written order granting or denying the motion. However, the order does not need to be set out in a separate document. FRCP 58(a)(5). See "Orders," ch. 1-G, §4.2, p. 45.

§7.2 Clerical errors only. The court can correct only clerical errors in the judgment. FRCP 60(a). The court cannot make substantive changes affecting parties' rights. *See* FRCP 60(a); *see also* ***Mamedov v. Ashcroft***, 387 F.3d 918, 920 (7th Cir.2004) (although court can correct clerical error at any time, it cannot alter judgment after notice of appeal is filed); ***King v. Ionization Int'l***, 825 F.2d 1180, 1188 (7th Cir.1987) (purpose of nunc pro tunc orders is not to make substantive changes).

§8. APPELLATE REVIEW

§8.1 Deadline. Whether a motion to correct a clerical error in the judgment extends the deadline to appeal depends on when it is filed and what correction the court makes in response to it.

1. Motion filed within 28 days after judgment. A motion to correct a clerical error in the judgment that is filed within 28 days after entry of judgment tolls the deadline to file a notice of appeal until an order disposing of the motion is entered. FRAP 4(a)(4)(A)(vi); *see* ***Catz v. Chalker***, 566 F.3d 839, 841-42 (9th Cir.2009) (applying former ten-day deadline). An order is considered entered when it is entered on the civil docket under FRCP 79(a). FRAP 4(a)(7)(A)(i). The court does not need to render the order with the formality of a judgment, but it must clearly dispose of the post-trial motion. ***Ellison v. Conoco, Inc.***, 950 F.2d 1196, 1201 (5th Cir.1992). An appellant challenging either an order disposing of the motion to correct a clerical error in the judgment or a judgment's alteration or amendment based on the motion to correct must file the notice of appeal within 30 days (60 days if the United States is a party) after entry of the order, unless there are other outstanding motions that continue to toll the running of the appellate deadlines. *See* FRAP 4(a)(1)(A), (a)(1)(B), (a)(4)(B)(ii); 2009 Notes to FRAP 4 at ¶¶3, 4, p. 1266, this book.

NOTE

To extend the time to file a notice of appeal under former FRAP 4(a)(4)(A)(vi), a party had to file a motion to correct a clerical error in the judgment within ten days after the entry of judgment. The ten-day deadline was expanded to 28 days to match the amendments in the FRCPs. 2009 Notes to FRAP 4 at ¶1, p. 1266, this book.

2. **Motion filed more than 28 days after judgment.** If the FRCP 60(a) motion is not filed within 28 days after the entry of judgment, the deadline to appeal is extended only for corrections by the court that raise a new issue that could not have been challenged by an earlier appeal. *See, e.g.*, ***Robi v. Five Platters, Inc.***, 918 F.2d 1439, 1445 (9th Cir.1990) (appellant appealed from amended order that identified three trademarks canceled by judgment); *cf.* ***Buggs v. Elgin, Joliet & E. Ry.***, 852 F.2d 318, 323 (7th Cir.1988) (order granting FRCP 60(b) relief did not entitle party to appeal entire judgment).

§8.2 Standard of review. The district court's ruling on a FRCP 60(a) motion is reviewed for abuse of discretion. ***Paddington Partners v. Bouchard***, 34 F.3d 1132, 1140 (2d Cir.1994); ***Robi v. Five Platters, Inc.***, 918 F.2d 1439, 1445 (9th Cir.1990); ***Kelly v. Matlack, Inc.***, 903 F.2d 978, 981 (3d Cir.1990).

Federal Rules of Civil Procedure

Table of Contents

Title I. Scope of Rules; Form of Action

FRCP 1 Scope & purpose 833
FRCP 2 One form of action 833

Title II. Commencing an Action; Service of Process, Pleadings, Motions, & Orders

FRCP 3 Commencing an action 833
FRCP 4 Summons 833
FRCP 4.1 Serving other process 840
FRCP 5 Serving & filing pleadings & other papers 841
FRCP 5.1 Constitutional challenge to a statute—notice, certification, & intervention 842
FRCP 5.2 Privacy protection for filings made with the court 843
FRCP 6 Computing & extending time; time for motion papers 844

Title III. Pleadings & Motions

FRCP 7 Pleadings allowed; form of motions & other papers 846
FRCP 7.1 Disclosure statement 847
FRCP 8 General rules of pleading 847
FRCP 9 Pleading special matters 850
FRCP 10 Form of pleadings 851
FRCP 11 Signing pleadings, motions, & other papers; representations to the court; sanctions 852
FRCP 12 Defenses & objections: when & how presented; motion for judgment on the pleadings; consolidating motions; waiving defenses; pretrial hearing 855
FRCP 13 Counterclaim & crossclaim 860
FRCP 14 Third-party practice 862
FRCP 15 Amended & supplemental pleadings 863
FRCP 16 Pretrial conferences; scheduling; management 867

Title IV. Parties

FRCP 17 Plaintiff & defendant; capacity; public officers 870
FRCP 18 Joinder of claims 872
FRCP 19 Required joinder of parties 873
FRCP 20 Permissive joinder of parties 875
FRCP 21 Misjoinder & nonjoinder of parties 876
FRCP 22 Interpleader 877
FRCP 23 Class actions 877
FRCP 23.1 Derivative actions 886
FRCP 23.2 Actions relating to unincorporated associations 887
FRCP 24 Intervention 887
FRCP 25 Substitution of parties 890

Title V. Disclosures & Discovery

FRCP 26 Duty to disclose; general provisions governing discovery 892
FRCP 27 Depositions to perpetuate testimony 901
FRCP 28 Persons before whom depositions may be taken 902
FRCP 29 Stipulations about discovery procedure 903
FRCP 30 Depositions by oral examination 903
FRCP 31 Depositions by written questions 907
FRCP 32 Using depositions in court proceedings 908
FRCP 33 Interrogatories to parties 910
FRCP 34 Producing documents, electronically stored information, & tangible things, or entering onto land, for inspection & other purposes 911
FRCP 35 Physical & mental examinations 912
FRCP 36 Requests for admission 913
FRCP 37 Failure to make disclosures or to cooperate in discovery; sanctions 915

Title VI. Trials

FRCP 38 Right to a jury trial; demand 919
FRCP 39 Trial by jury or by the court 921
FRCP 40 Scheduling cases for trial 922
FRCP 41 Dismissal of actions 922
FRCP 42 Consolidation; separate trials 925
FRCP 43 Taking testimony 926
FRCP 44 Proving an official record 927
FRCP 44.1 Determining foreign law 928
FRCP 45 Subpoena 929
FRCP 46 Objecting to a ruling or order 933
FRCP 47 Selecting jurors 933
FRCP 48 Number of jurors; verdict; polling 934
FRCP 49 Special verdict; general verdict & questions 934
FRCP 50 Judgment as a matter of law in a jury trial; related motion for a new trial; conditional ruling 936
FRCP 51 Instructions to the jury; objections; preserving a claim of error 938
FRCP 52 Findings & conclusions by the court; judgment on partial findings 940
FRCP 53 Masters 941

Title VII. Judgment

FRCP 54 Judgment; costs 943
FRCP 55 Default; default judgment 948
FRCP 56 Summary judgment 950
FRCP 57 Declaratory judgment 954
FRCP 58 Entering judgment 955
FRCP 59 New trial; altering or amending a judgment 956
FRCP 60 Relief from a judgment or order 958
FRCP 61 Harmless error 965
FRCP 62 Stay of proceedings to enforce a judgment 965
FRCP 62.1 Indicative ruling on a motion for relief that is barred by a pending appeal 967
FRCP 63 Judge's inability to proceed 967

Title VIII. Provisional & Final Remedies

FRCP 64 Seizing a person or property 968
FRCP 65 Injunctions & restraining orders 968
FRCP 65.1 Proceedings against a surety 972
FRCP 66 Receivers 973
FRCP 67 Deposit into court 973
FRCP 68 Offer of judgment 974
FRCP 69 Execution 976
FRCP 70 Enforcing a judgment for a specific act 977
FRCP 71 Enforcing relief for or against a nonparty 978

FEDERAL RULES OF CIVIL PROCEDURE

TABLE OF CONTENTS

FRCP

TITLE IX. SPECIAL PROCEEDINGS

FRCP 71.1 Condemning real or personal property....978
FRCP 72 Magistrate judges: pretrial order....982
FRCP 73 Magistrate judges: trial by consent; appeal....983

TITLE X. DISTRICT COURTS & CLERKS: CONDUCTING BUSINESS; ISSUING ORDERS

FRCP 77 Conducting business; clerk's authority; notice of an order or judgment....984
FRCP 78 Hearing motions; submission on briefs....985
FRCP 79 Records kept by the clerk....985
FRCP 80 Stenographic transcript as evidence....986

TITLE XI. GENERAL PROVISIONS

FRCP 81 Applicability of the rules in general; removed actions....987
FRCP 82 Jurisdiction & venue unaffected....988
FRCP 83 Rules by district courts; judge's directives....989
FRCP 84 Forms....989
FRCP 85 Title....990
FRCP 86 Effective dates....990

Appendix of Forms

Form 1 Caption....991
Form 2 Date, signature, address, e-mail address, & telephone number....991
Form 3 Summons....991
Form 4 Summons on a third-party complaint....991
Form 5 Notice of a lawsuit & request to waive service of a summons....991
Form 6 Waiver of the service of summons....992
Form 7 Statement of jurisdiction....992
Form 8 Statement of reasons for omitting a party....993
Form 9 Statement noting a party's death....993
Form 10 Complaint to recover a sum certain....993
Form 11 Complaint for negligence....993
Form 12 Complaint for negligence when the plaintiff does not know who is responsible....993
Form 13 Complaint for negligence under the Federal Employers' Liability Act....994
Form 14 Complaint for damages under the Merchant Marine Act....994
Form 15 Complaint for the conversion of property....994
Form 16 Third-party complaint....994
Form 17 Complaint for specific performance of a contract to convey land....994
Form 18 Complaint for patent infringement....995
Form 19 Complaint for copyright infringement & unfair competition....995
Form 20 Complaint for interpleader & declaratory relief....995
Form 21 Complaint on a claim for a debt & to set aside a fraudulent conveyance under Rule 18(b)....996
Form 30 Answer presenting defenses under Rule 12(b)....996
Form 31 Answer to a complaint for money had & received with a counterclaim for interpleader....997
Form 40 Motion to dismiss under Rule 12(b) for lack of jurisdiction, improper venue, insufficient service of process, or failure to state a claim....997
Form 41 Motion to bring in a third-party defendant....997
Form 42 Motion to intervene as a defendant under Rule 24....997
Form 50 Request to produce documents & tangible things, or to enter onto land under Rule 34....997
Form 51 Request for admissions under Rule 36....998
Form 52 Report of the parties' planning meeting....998
Form 60 Notice of condemnation....998
Form 61 Complaint for condemnation....999
Form 70 Judgment on a jury verdict....999
Form 71 Judgment by the court without a jury....999
Form 80 Notice of a magistrate judge's availability....1000
Form 81 Consent to an assignment to a magistrate judge....1000
Form 82 Order of assignment to a magistrate judge....1000

Supplemental Rules for Admiralty or Maritime Claims & Asset Forfeiture Actions....1001

TITLE I. SCOPE OF RULES; FORM OF ACTION

FRCP 1. SCOPE & PURPOSE

These rules govern the procedure in all civil actions and proceedings in the United States district courts, except as stated in Rule 81. They should be construed and administered to secure the just, speedy, and inexpensive determination of every action and proceeding.

See selected Notes of Advisory Committee to FRCP 1, p. 1137.

History of FRCP 1: Adopted Dec. 20, 1937, eff. Sept. 16, 1938. Amended Dec. 29, 1948, eff. Oct. 20, 1949; Feb. 28, 1966, eff. July 1, 1966; Apr. 22, 1993, eff. Dec. 1, 1993; Apr. 30, 2007, eff. Dec. 1, 2007.

See *Commentaries*, "Introduction to Federal Rules," ch. 1-A, p. 3.

See also 28 U.S.C. §119 (district court for District of Puerto Rico governed by the rules), §2072 (power of Supreme Court to prescribe rules of procedure and evidence); 48 U.S.C. §1614 (district court for District of Virgin Islands governed by the rules).

ANNOTATIONS

Jones v. Bock, 549 U.S. 199, 212-13 (2007). "[W]e have explained that courts should generally not depart from the usual practice under the [FRCPs] on the basis of perceived policy concerns. [A revision of the FRCPs] 'must be obtained by the process of amending the [FRCPs], and not by judicial interpretation.'"

Celotex Corp. v. Catrett, 477 U.S. 317, 327 (1986). The FRCPs are designed "'to secure the just, speedy and inexpensive determination of every action.'" *See also **In re Phenylpropanolamine (PPA) Prods. Liab. Litig.***, 460 F.3d 1217, 1227 (9th Cir.2006).

U.S. v. Orr Water Ditch Co., 391 F.3d 1077, 1082 (9th Cir.2004), *amended*, 400 F.3d 1117 (9th Cir.2005). "The [FRCPs] 'govern the procedure in the U.S. district courts in all suits of a civil nature.' Thus, '[w]hen a situation is covered by one of the [FRCPs], ... the [district court must] apply the [FRCP], and can refuse to do so only if ... the Rule in question transgresses[] the terms of the [Rules] Enabling Act [or the Constitution].'"

FRCP 2. ONE FORM OF ACTION

There is one form of action—the civil action.

History of FRCP 2: Adopted Dec. 20, 1937, eff. Sept. 16, 1938. Amended Apr. 30, 2007, eff. Dec. 1, 2007.

See *Commentaries*, "Pleading Practice," ch. 1-B, §2, p. 7; *O'Connor's Federal Civil Forms* (2012), FORMS 1B.

ANNOTATIONS

United Mine Workers v. Gibbs, 383 U.S. 715, 724 (1966). "Under the [FRCPs], the impulse is toward entertaining the broadest possible scope of action consistent with fairness to the parties; joinder of claims, parties and remedies is strongly encouraged."

TITLE II. COMMENCING AN ACTION; SERVICE OF PROCESS, PLEADINGS, MOTIONS, & ORDERS

FRCP 3. COMMENCING AN ACTION

A civil action is commenced by filing a complaint with the court.

History of FRCP 3: Adopted Dec. 20, 1937, eff. Sept. 16, 1938. Amended Apr. 30, 2007, eff. Dec. 1, 2007.

See *Commentaries*, "Serving the Defendant with Process," ch. 2-H, p. 149; *O'Connor's Federal Civil Forms* (2012), FORMS 2H.

ANNOTATIONS

Walker v. Armco Steel Corp., 446 U.S. 740, 751 (1980). "[I]n diversity actions, Rule 3 governs the date from which various timing requirements of the [FRCPs] begin to run, but does not affect state statutes of limitations." *See also* ***West v. Conrail***, 481 U.S. 35, 39 (1987) (when cause of action is based on federal law with no express statute of limitations, action is not barred when commenced in compliance with FRCP 3 within borrowed statute of limitations); ***McAtee v. Capital One***, 479 F.3d 1143, 1146 (9th Cir.2007) (federal definition of "commence" applies for action based on federal law; state-law definition of "commence" applies for action based on state law).

McIntosh v. Antonino, 71 F.3d 29, 36 (1st Cir. 1995). FRCP 3 "makes it transpicuously clear that an action is commenced when the papers are filed. ... When papers are mailed to the clerk's office, filing is complete only upon the clerk's receipt of them. *At 37:* [T]he general rule is that merely placing a complaint in the mail does not constitute filing sufficient to mark the commencement of an action in a federal court."

FRCP 4. SUMMONS

(a) Contents; Amendments.

(1) ***Contents.*** A summons must:

(A) name the court and the parties;

(B) be directed to the defendant;

(C) state the name and address of the plaintiff's attorney or—if unrepresented—of the plaintiff;

(D) state the time within which the defendant must appear and defend;

(E) notify the defendant that a failure to appear and defend will result in a default judgment against the defendant for the relief demanded in the complaint;

(F) be signed by the clerk; and

(G) bear the court's seal.

(2) *Amendments.* The court may permit a summons to be amended.

(b) **Issuance.** On or after filing the complaint, the plaintiff may present a summons to the clerk for signature and seal. If the summons is properly completed, the clerk must sign, seal, and issue it to the plaintiff for service on the defendant. A summons—or a copy of a summons that is addressed to multiple defendants—must be issued for each defendant to be served.

(c) **Service.**

(1) *In General.* A summons must be served with a copy of the complaint. The plaintiff is responsible for having the summons and complaint served within the time allowed by Rule 4(m) and must furnish the necessary copies to the person who makes service.

(2) *By Whom.* Any person who is at least 18 years old and not a party may serve a summons and complaint.

(3) *By a Marshal or Someone Specially Appointed.* At the plaintiff's request, the court may order that service be made by a United States marshal or deputy marshal or by a person specially appointed by the court. The court must so order if the plaintiff is authorized to proceed in forma pauperis under 28 U.S.C. §1915 or as a seaman under 28 U.S.C. §1916.

(d) **Waiving Service.**

(1) *Requesting a Waiver.* An individual, corporation, or association that is subject to service under Rule 4(e), (f), or (h) has a duty to avoid unnecessary expenses of serving the summons. The plaintiff may notify such a defendant that an action has been commenced and request that the defendant waive service of a summons. The notice and request must:

(A) be in writing and be addressed:

(i) to the individual defendant; or

(ii) for a defendant subject to service under Rule 4(h), to an officer, a managing or general agent, or any other agent authorized by appointment or by law to receive service of process;

(B) name the court where the complaint was filed;

(C) be accompanied by a copy of the complaint, 2 copies of a waiver form, and a prepaid means for returning the form;

(D) inform the defendant, using text prescribed in Form 5, of the consequences of waiving and not waiving service;

(E) state the date when the request is sent;

(F) give the defendant a reasonable time of at least 30 days after the request was sent—or at least 60 days if sent to the defendant outside any judicial district of the United States—to return the waiver; and

(G) be sent by first-class mail or other reliable means.

(2) *Failure to Waive.* If a defendant located within the United States fails, without good cause, to sign and return a waiver requested by a plaintiff located within the United States, the court must impose on the defendant:

(A) the expenses later incurred in making service; and

(B) the reasonable expenses, including attorney's fees, of any motion required to collect those service expenses.

(3) *Time to Answer After a Waiver.* A defendant who, before being served with process, timely returns a waiver need not serve an answer to the complaint until 60 days after the request was sent—or until 90 days after it was sent to the defendant outside any judicial district of the United States.

(4) *Results of Filing a Waiver.* When the plaintiff files a waiver, proof of service is not required and these rules apply as if a summons and complaint had been served at the time of filing the waiver.

(5) *Jurisdiction and Venue Not Waived.* Waiving service of a summons does not waive any objection to personal jurisdiction or to venue.

(e) **Serving an Individual Within a Judicial District of the United States.** Unless federal law provides otherwise, an individual—other than a minor, an incompetent person, or a person whose waiver has been filed—may be served in a judicial district of the United States by:

(1) following state law for serving a summons in an action brought in courts of general jurisdiction

in the state where the district court is located or where service is made; or

(2) doing any of the following:

(A) delivering a copy of the summons and of the complaint to the individual personally;

(B) leaving a copy of each at the individual's dwelling or usual place of abode with someone of suitable age and discretion who resides there; or

(C) delivering a copy of each to an agent authorized by appointment or by law to receive service of process.

(f) **Serving an Individual in a Foreign Country.** Unless federal law provides otherwise, an individual—other than a minor, an incompetent person, or a person whose waiver has been filed—may be served at a place not within any judicial district of the United States:

(1) by any internationally agreed means of service that is reasonably calculated to give notice, such as those authorized by the Hague Convention on the Service Abroad of Judicial and Extrajudicial Documents;

(2) if there is no internationally agreed means, or if an international agreement allows but does not specify other means, by a method that is reasonably calculated to give notice:

(A) as prescribed by the foreign country's law for service in that country in an action in its courts of general jurisdiction;

(B) as the foreign authority directs in response to a letter rogatory or letter of request; or

(C) unless prohibited by the foreign country's law, by:

(i) delivering a copy of the summons and of the complaint to the individual personally; or

(ii) using any form of mail that the clerk addresses and sends to the individual and that requires a signed receipt; or

(3) by other means not prohibited by international agreement, as the court orders.

(g) **Serving a Minor or an Incompetent Person.** A minor or an incompetent person in a judicial district of the United States must be served by following state law for serving a summons or like process on such a defendant in an action brought in the courts of general jurisdiction of the state where service is made. A minor or an incompetent person who is not within any judicial district of the United States must be served in the manner prescribed by Rule 4(f)(2)(A), (f)(2)(B), or (f)(3).

(h) **Serving a Corporation, Partnership, or Association.** Unless federal law provides otherwise or the defendant's waiver has been filed, a domestic or foreign corporation, or a partnership or other unincorporated association that is subject to suit under a common name, must be served:

(1) in a judicial district of the United States:

(A) in the manner prescribed by Rule 4(e)(1) for serving an individual; or

(B) by delivering a copy of the summons and of the complaint to an officer, a managing or general agent, or any other agent authorized by appointment or by law to receive service of process and—if the agent is one authorized by statute and the statute so requires—by also mailing a copy of each to the defendant; or

(2) at a place not within any judicial district of the United States, in any manner prescribed by Rule 4(f) for serving an individual, except personal delivery under (f)(2)(C)(i).

(i) **Serving the United States and Its Agencies, Corporations, Officers, or Employees.**

(1) *United States.* To serve the United States, a party must:

(A)(i) deliver a copy of the summons and of the complaint to the United States attorney for the district where the action is brought—or to an assistant United States attorney or clerical employee whom the United States attorney designates in a writing filed with the court clerk—or

(ii) send a copy of each by registered or certified mail to the civil-process clerk at the United States attorney's office;

(B) send a copy of each by registered or certified mail to the Attorney General of the United States at Washington, D.C.; and

(C) if the action challenges an order of a nonparty agency or officer of the United States, send a copy of each by registered or certified mail to the agency or officer.

(2) ***Agency; Corporation; Officer or Employee Sued in an Official Capacity.*** To serve a United States agency or corporation, or a United States officer or employee sued only in an official capacity, a party must serve the United States and also send a copy of the summons and of the complaint by registered or certified mail to the agency, corporation, officer, or employee.

(3) ***Officer or Employee Sued Individually.*** To serve a United States officer or employee sued in an individual capacity for an act or omission occurring in connection with duties performed on the United States' behalf (whether or not the officer or employee is also sued in an official capacity), a party must serve the United States and also serve the officer or employee under Rule 4(e), (f), or (g).

(4) ***Extending Time.*** The court must allow a party a reasonable time to cure its failure to:

(A) serve a person required to be served under Rule 4(i)(2), if the party has served either the United States attorney or the Attorney General of the United States; or

(B) serve the United States under Rule 4(i)(3), if the party has served the United States officer or employee.

(j) Serving a Foreign, State, or Local Government.

(1) ***Foreign State.*** A foreign state or its political subdivision, agency, or instrumentality must be served in accordance with 28 U.S.C. §1608.

(2) ***State or Local Government.*** A state, a municipal corporation, or any other state-created governmental organization that is subject to suit must be served by:

(A) delivering a copy of the summons and of the complaint to its chief executive officer; or

(B) serving a copy of each in the manner prescribed by that state's law for serving a summons or like process on such a defendant.

(k) Territorial Limits of Effective Service.

(1) ***In General.*** Serving a summons or filing a waiver of service establishes personal jurisdiction over a defendant:

(A) who is subject to the jurisdiction of a court of general jurisdiction in the state where the district court is located;

(B) who is a party joined under Rule 14 or 19 and is served within a judicial district of the United States and not more than 100 miles from where the summons was issued; or

(C) when authorized by a federal statute.

(2) ***Federal Claim Outside State-Court Jurisdiction.*** For a claim that arises under federal law, serving a summons or filing a waiver of service establishes personal jurisdiction over a defendant if:

(A) the defendant is not subject to jurisdiction in any state's courts of general jurisdiction; and

(B) exercising jurisdiction is consistent with the United States Constitution and laws.

(*l*) Proving Service.

(1) ***Affidavit Required.*** Unless service is waived, proof of service must be made to the court. Except for service by a United States marshal or deputy marshal, proof must be by the server's affidavit.

(2) ***Service Outside the United States.*** Service not within any judicial district of the United States must be proved as follows:

(A) if made under Rule 4(f)(1), as provided in the applicable treaty or convention; or

(B) if made under Rule 4(f)(2) or (f)(3), by a receipt signed by the addressee, or by other evidence satisfying the court that the summons and complaint were delivered to the addressee.

(3) ***Validity of Service; Amending Proof.*** Failure to prove service does not affect the validity of service. The court may permit proof of service to be amended.

(m) Time Limit for Service. If a defendant is not served within 120 days after the complaint is filed, the court—on motion or on its own after notice to the plaintiff—must dismiss the action without prejudice against that defendant or order that service be made within a specified time. But if the plaintiff shows good cause for the failure, the court must extend the time for service for an ap-

propriate period. This subdivision (m) does not apply to service in a foreign country under Rule 4(f) or 4(j)(1).

(n) Asserting Jurisdiction over Property or Assets.

(1) ***Federal Law.*** The court may assert jurisdiction over property if authorized by a federal statute. Notice to claimants of the property must be given as provided in the statute or by serving a summons under this rule.

(2) ***State Law.*** On a showing that personal jurisdiction over a defendant cannot be obtained in the district where the action is brought by reasonable efforts to serve a summons under this rule, the court may assert jurisdiction over the defendant's assets found in the district. Jurisdiction is acquired by seizing the assets under the circumstances and in the manner provided by state law in that district.

See selected Notes of Advisory Committee to FRCP 4, p. 1138.

History of FRCP 4: Adopted Dec. 20, 1937, eff. Sept. 16, 1938. Amended Jan. 21, 1963, eff. July 1, 1963; Feb. 28, 1966, eff. July 1, 1966; Apr. 29, 1980, eff. Aug. 1, 1980; Jan. 12, 1983, P.L. 97-462, §2, 96 Stat. 2527; Mar. 2, 1987, eff. Aug. 1, 1987; Apr. 22, 1993, eff. Dec. 1, 1993; Apr. 17, 2000, eff. Dec. 1, 2000; Apr. 30, 2007, eff. Dec. 1, 2007.

See ***Commentaries***, "Serving the Defendant with Process," ch. 2-H, p. 149; ***O'Connor's Federal Civil Forms*** (2012), FORMS 2H.

See also 28 U.S.C. §§1691-1697 (process generally); Hague Convention on Service Abroad of Judicial & Extrajudicial Documents (foreign process), p. 1563, this book.

ANNOTATIONS

Generally

Murphy Bros. v. Michetti Pipe Stringing, Inc., 526 U.S. 344, 347-48 (1999). "[A] named defendant's time to remove is triggered by simultaneous service of the summons and complaint, or receipt of the complaint, 'through service or otherwise,' after and apart from service of the summons, but not by mere receipt of the complaint unattended by any formal service."

Volkswagenwerk A.G. v. Schlunk, 486 U.S. 694, 700 (1988). "[T]he term 'service of process' ... refers to a formal delivery of documents that is legally sufficient to charge the defendant with notice of a pending action. *At 707:* [T]he Due Process Clause requires every method of service to provide 'notice reasonably calculated ... to apprise interested parties of the pendency of the action and afford them an opportunity to present their objections.'"

Omni Capital Int'l v. Rudolf Wolff & Co., 484 U.S. 97, 104 (1987). "Before a federal court may exercise personal jurisdiction over a defendant, the procedural requirement of service of summons must be satisfied. [B]efore a court may exercise personal jurisdiction over a defendant, there ... must be a basis for the defendant's amenability to service of summons."

Kurzberg v. Ashcroft, 619 F.3d 176, 185 (2d Cir. 2010). "[Ps] contend that absent ... a determination by the district court [that service on the U.S. was defective], there was nothing to cure. [¶] We disagree. Nothing in the language of Rule 4(i)(3)(A) suggests that a defect in the service of process can be identified for purposes of permitting the plaintiff to cure the defect only by the court. The Advisory Committee described the cure provision as requiring that '[a] reasonable time to effect service on the U.S. must be allowed after the failure is pointed out.' Had the Committee meant to require that the error be pointed out *by the court*, it could easily, and surely would, have said so. [¶] Other circuits ... have concluded that notification to the plaintiff by the defendant, rather than by the court, of a defect in the service of process is sufficient to start the clock on the reasonable amount of time afforded to the plaintiff to cure the defect. [¶] There is nothing we perceive to be inherently wrong with requiring [Ps] to adhere to a rule of procedure when their failure to do so has been correctly pointed out by an adversary."

Employee Painters' Trust v. Ethan Enters., 480 F.3d 993, 999 (9th Cir.2007). "Although the parties and the district court assumed ... that [FRCP] 4 governed service of the amended complaint, that is not so. Instead, it is [FRCP] 5 that was applicable. ... The amended complaint in this case qualifies as a 'pleading subsequent to the original complaint,' thus allowing it to be served in any manner prescribed in Rule 5(b). [¶] An amended complaint need only be served in the manner provided by Rule 4 when (1) a party is 'in default for failure to appear' *and* (2) the 'pleadings assert[] new or additional claims for relief.'" *See also* ***Johnson v. Crown Enters.***, 398 F.3d 339, 344 (5th Cir. 2005).

McMasters v. U.S., 260 F.3d 814, 817 (7th Cir. 2001). "While a court must give a plaintiff reasonable time to cure a defect in service under Rule 4(i)(3) [now Rule 4(i)(4)] or grant an appropriate extension of time for service under Rule 4(m), nothing in the

[FRCPs] allows a judge to excuse service altogether. Actual notice to the defendant is insufficient; the plaintiff must comply with the directives of Rule 4."

FRCP 4(c)

Constien v. U.S., 628 F.3d 1207, 1213-14 (10th Cir. 2010). See annotation under *FRCP 4(i) – Service on United States*, this page.

FRCP 4(d) – Waiver of Service

Estate of Darulis v. Garate, 401 F.3d 1060, 1063 (9th Cir.2005). "[P] contends that because [Ds] failed to waive service of process, he is entitled to an award of the costs he incurred in effecting service on [Ds]. [¶] [Ds] do not contest [P's] assertion that they did not respond to his waiver requests, nor do they suggest [P's] requests did not satisfy the requirements of [FRCP] 4(d)(2) or that they had good cause for failing to respond. Rather, they argue—and the district court held—that because they are the prevailing party, they are entitled to costs pursuant to [FRCP] 54(d)(1), including any costs they would otherwise have to pay [P] pursuant to Rule 4(d)(2). [¶] We disagree with the district court's interpretation of the interplay between Rules 4(d)(2) and 54(d)(1). *At 1064:* In light of the express language of Rules 4(d)(2) and 54(d)(1), as well as the indications of the Advisory Committee's intent, we hold the district court abused its discretion in denying [P] an award of costs for service of process. Rule 4(d)(2) provides for an award of such costs regardless of which party can recover other costs pursuant to Rule 54(d)(1)."

FRCP 4(e) – Service on Individuals Within United States

Travelers Cas. & Sur. Co. v. Brenneke, 551 F.3d 1132, 1136 (9th Cir.2009). "Sufficient service may be found where there is a good faith effort to comply with the requirements of Rule 4(e)(2) which has resulted in placement of the summons and complaint within the defendant's immediate proximity and further compliance with Rule 4(e)(2) is only prevented by the defendant's knowing and intentional actions to evade service. '[W]here a defendant attempts to avoid service *e.g.* by refusing to take the papers, it is sufficient if the server is in close proximity to the defendant, clearly communicates intent to serve court documents, and makes reasonable efforts to leave the papers with the defendant.'"

Homer v. Jones-Bey, 415 F.3d 748, 754 (7th Cir. 2005). "[A]ll methods of service specifically described by the [FRCPs] involve in-hand delivery. Here, however, the alleged service was executed by certified mail, a state-law method not specifically enumerated in Rule 4(e). Accordingly, the validity of service here turns not on the specifications of the [FRCPs] themselves but on the relevant provisions of [state] law."

FRCP 4(f) – Service on Individuals Outside United States

Lozano v. Bosdet, ___ F.3d ___ (5th Cir.2012) (No. 11-60736; 8-31-12). "The final sentence [of FRCP 4(m)] makes clear that the 120-day requirement does not apply to service of individuals abroad such as under the Hague Convention, or service of a foreign state under [FRCP 4(j)(1)]. As a result, [the Ninth Circuit] has indicated that when the defendants are foreign, an unlimited window-of-opportunity for service under [FRCP] 4(f) exists. [¶] Rather differently, the Second Circuit only allows plaintiffs to avoid the 120-day period if they attempt to serve the defendant in the foreign country within that time. We decline to require [the Second Circuit] approach for two reasons. First, to do so would effect a rewrite of [FRCP] 4. The rule states that subdivision (m) does not apply to service in a foreign country, not that a litigant has 120 days in which to initiate foreign service. [¶] Second, that interpretation would make it difficult for plaintiffs to use the less costly and potentially more efficient methods of serving foreign defendants. [¶] Our conclusion that the rules do not require immediate resort to the Hague Convention or other international methods does not, however, lead us to agree with the Ninth Circuit that unlimited time exists. Most courts faced with a challenge to the timeliness of foreign service have applied a 'flexible due diligence' standard to determine whether the delay should be excused. This view has been endorsed by the Seventh Circuit, by the First Circuit … as well as by many district courts. Judging it the most sound interpretation, we expressly adopt it." (Internal quotes omitted.)

FRCP 4(i) – Service on United States

Constien v. U.S., 628 F.3d 1207, 1213-14 (10th Cir. 2010). "Rule 4(i) states the requirements for serving the U.S., its agencies, and its officers and employees. [¶] [FRCP] 4(c) … limits who can be used to serve process. … Even when service is effected by use of the mail, only a nonparty can place the summons and com-

plaint in the mail. Although one could question the wisdom of this requirement, ... the rule contains no mailing exception to the nonparty requirement for service. [¶] [The] language [of FRCP 4]—which distinguishes between the 'plaintiff' and the 'person making service,' and includes the mailing to the Attorney General as a component of how [service must be made]—strongly implies that the mailing must be by the person effecting service. *At 1215 n.7:* [T]he present language of Rule 4(i) could be read to permit a party herself to mail process to the Attorney General. ... But that language was introduced in the 2007 style revision to the [FRCPs], and the language change was not intended to produce a substantive change but 'to be stylistic only.' [W]e read the language in present Rule 4(i) that 'a party must send a copy ... to the Attorney General' as implicitly incorporating the requirement that the party act through a proper process server."

FRCP 4(k)(1) – Territorial Limits

Bellum v. PCE Constructors, Inc., 407 F.3d 734, 740 n.7 (5th Cir.2005). "[M]easuring 'as the crow flies' is the proper method for measuring the 100-mile distance for service of process under [FRCP] 4(k)(1)(B). [W]e specifically [reject] the use of road miles because that standard lacks uniformity and simplicity."

FRCP 4(k)(2) – Nationwide Jurisdiction

Getz v. Boeing Co., 654 F.3d 852, 858 (9th Cir. 2011). "Rule [4(k)(2)], which is commonly known as the federal long-arm statute, permits federal courts to exercise personal jurisdiction over a defendant that lacks contacts with any single state if the complaint alleges federal claims and the defendant maintains sufficient contacts with the U.S. as a whole. *At 859:* However, '[t]his narrow extension of the federal reach applies only if a claim is made against the defendant under federal law. It does not establish personal jurisdiction if the *only claims are those arising under state law* or the law of another country, even though there might be diversity or alienage subject matter jurisdiction as to such claims.' Thus, ... Rule 4(k)(2) is available only to plaintiffs who allege a 'federally created cause of action.'"

Touchcom, Inc. v. Bereskin & Parr, 574 F.3d 1403, 1413 (Fed.Cir.2009). "The second requirement of Rule 4(k)(2), that the defendant is not subject to the jurisdiction of any state's courts of general jurisdiction, poses practical difficulties ... because the requirement either places a burden on the plaintiff of proving a negative many times over, *viz.*, that defendant is *not* subject to jurisdiction in any of the 50 states, or requires that the defendant concede its potential amenability to suit in federal court (by denying its amenability to suit in any state court) or submitting to jurisdiction in a particular state, an uninviting choice. *At 1414:* [T]he Fifth, Seventh, Ninth, Eleventh, and DC Circuits have adopted an approach that places the burden on the defendant. Under that approach, a court is entitled to use Rule 4(k)(2) to determine whether it possesses personal jurisdiction over the defendant unless the defendant names a state in which the suit can proceed. *At 1415:* We conclude that ... the purposes of Rule 4(k)(2) are best achieved when the defendant is afforded the opportunity to avoid the application of the rule only when it designates a suitable forum in which the plaintiff could have brought suit." *See also* ***Porina v. Marward Shipping Co.***, 521 F.3d 122, 127 (2d Cir. 2008). *But see* ***U.S. v. Swiss Am. Bank, Ltd.***, this page.

Saudi v. Northrop Grumman Corp., 427 F.3d 271, 275 (4th Cir.2005). "[W]hile Rule 4(k)(2) is designed to facilitate obtaining jurisdiction over foreign defendants, it does not operate to relax the requirement that the defendant's contacts with the forum be constitutionally sufficient."

Mwani v. Bin Laden, 417 F.3d 1, 11 (D.C.Cir.2005). "'A defendant who wants to preclude use of Rule 4(k)(2) has only to name some other state in which the suit could proceed. Naming a more appropriate state would amount to a consent to personal jurisdiction there (personal jurisdiction, unlike federal subject-matter jurisdiction, is waivable). If, however, the defendant contends that he cannot be sued in the forum state and refuses to identify any other where suit is possible, then the federal court is entitled to use Rule 4(k)(2).'" *See also* ***Adams v. Unione Mediterranea di Sicurta***, 364 F.3d 646, 651 (5th Cir.2004); ***ISI Int'l v. Borden Ladner Gervais LLP***, 256 F.3d 548, 552 (7th Cir.2001).

U.S. v. Swiss Am. Bank, Ltd., 191 F.3d 30, 41 (1st Cir.1999). "[A] plaintiff who seeks to invoke Rule 4(k)(2) must make a prima facie case for the applicability of the rule. This includes a tripartite showing (1) that the claim asserted arises under federal law, (2) that personal jurisdiction is not available under any situation-specific federal statute, and (3) that the putative defendant's contacts with the nation as a whole suffice to satisfy the applicable constitutional requirements. The plaintiff, moreover, must certify that, based

on the information that is readily available to the plaintiff and his counsel, the defendant is not subject to suit in the courts of general jurisdiction of any state. If the plaintiff makes out his prima facie case, the burden shifts to the defendant to produce evidence which, if credited, would show either that one or more specific states exist in which it would be subject to suit or that its contacts with the U.S. are constitutionally insufficient." *But see* ***Touchcom, Inc. v. Bereskin & Parr***, p. 839.

FRCP 4(m) – Dismissal

Cruz v. Louisiana, 528 F.3d 375, 379 (5th Cir.2008). "In federal court, a dismissal under Rule 4(m) constitutes an abandonment of a claim, meaning that the claim is treated as having never been filed and thus fails to interrupt the running of a prescription period."

Bowling v. Hasbro, Inc., 403 F.3d 1373, 1376 (Fed. Cir.2005). "[P] argues that because the order to show cause only referred to [FRCP] 4(m), under which dismissal without prejudice is required, the district court's order to show cause was not sufficient notice prior to the imposition of a dismissal with prejudice. *At 1377:* [W]e believe the Ninth Circuit would likely agree with the Fifth Circuit that failure to heed a warning based on Rule 4(m) is not sufficient to justify dismissal with prejudice without more egregious conduct on the part of the plaintiff. [¶] The district court found, as part of its consideration of less drastic alternatives, that [P] was on notice of the potential for dismissal pursuant to [FRCP] 41(b). This finding was clearly erroneous. The mere pendency of a court order is insufficient to constitute notice of impending dismissal with prejudice. ... Because the district court's initial order in this case only warned of dismissal pursuant to Rule 4(m)—a dismissal *without* prejudice—we are compelled to conclude that [P] was not on notice of the threat of dismissal *with* prejudice. Thus, the less drastic alternatives factor weighs against dismissal with prejudice."

FRCP 4(m) – Time Limits

Horenkamp v. Van Winkle & Co., 402 F.3d 1129, 1132 (11th Cir.2005). FRCP 4(m) "grants discretion to the district court to extend the time for service of process even in the absence of a showing of good cause." *See also* ***Efaw v. Williams***, 473 F.3d 1038, 1041 (9th Cir. 2007) (court may consider factors such as statute-of-limitations bar, prejudice to D, actual notice of suit, and eventual service).

Nylok Corp. v. Fastener World Inc., 396 F.3d 805, 807 (7th Cir.2005). "The explicit language of [FRCP 4(m)] makes it very clear that the 120-day limit is inapplicable in cases involving service in a foreign country. This rule seems to recognize that the timeliness of foreign service is often out of the plaintiff's control. [P] offers proof that service of process in Taiwan generally takes between 6 and 12 months and in Korea it can exceed 4 months. [¶] Because district courts need to be able to control their dockets, we have stated that the amount of time allowed for foreign service is not unlimited. If, for example, a plaintiff made no attempt to begin the process of foreign service within 120 days, it might be proper for a court to dismiss the claim. [¶] [P] took all of the necessary affirmative steps, [but] it could not control the timing of service. [¶] [P is thus] entitled to litigate its trademark infringement case in federal court, and dismissal of its claim was improper."

FRCP 4.1. SERVING OTHER PROCESS

(a) In General. Process—other than a summons under Rule 4 or a subpoena under Rule 45—must be served by a United States marshal or deputy marshal or by a person specially appointed for that purpose. It may be served anywhere within the territorial limits of the state where the district court is located and, if authorized by a federal statute, beyond those limits. Proof of service must be made under Rule 4(*l*).

(b) Enforcing Orders: Committing for Civil Contempt. An order committing a person for civil contempt of a decree or injunction issued to enforce federal law may be served and enforced in any district. Any other order in a civil-contempt proceeding may be served only in the state where the issuing court is located or elsewhere in the United States within 100 miles from where the order was issued.

History of FRCP 4.1: Adopted Apr. 22, 1993, eff. Dec. 1, 1993. Amended Apr. 30, 2007, eff. Dec. 1, 2007.

ANNOTATIONS

Schneider v. National R.R. Passenger Corp., 72 F.3d 17, 19-20 (2d Cir.1995). FRCP 4, now FRCP 4.1, "trumps state law to the extent that it determines *who* can levy on a writ of execution issued by a federal court. ... Rule 4.1(a)[] does not give blanket authority for service of process by state sheriffs. ... 'Process' under this provision includes writs of execution. Because

[sheriff] was not specially appointed, his execution of the writ and levy on [D's] property violated [FRCP 4.1(a)] and was thus defective."

FRCP 5. SERVING & FILING PLEADINGS & OTHER PAPERS

(a) Service: When Required.

(1) ***In General.*** Unless these rules provide otherwise, each of the following papers must be served on every party:

(A) an order stating that service is required;

(B) a pleading filed after the original complaint, unless the court orders otherwise under Rule 5(c) because there are numerous defendants;

(C) a discovery paper required to be served on a party, unless the court orders otherwise;

(D) a written motion, except one that may be heard ex parte; and

(E) a written notice, appearance, demand, or offer of judgment, or any similar paper.

(2) ***If a Party Fails to Appear.*** No service is required on a party who is in default for failing to appear. But a pleading that asserts a new claim for relief against such a party must be served on that party under Rule 4.

(3) ***Seizing Property.*** If an action is begun by seizing property and no person is or need be named as a defendant, any service required before the filing of an appearance, answer, or claim must be made on the person who had custody or possession of the property when it was seized.

(b) Service: How Made.

(1) ***Serving an Attorney.*** If a party is represented by an attorney, service under this rule must be made on the attorney unless the court orders service on the party.

(2) ***Service in General.*** A paper is served under this rule by:

(A) handing it to the person;

(B) leaving it:

(i) at the person's office with a clerk or other person in charge or, if no one is in charge, in a conspicuous place in the office; or

(ii) if the person has no office or the office is closed, at the person's dwelling or usual place of abode with someone of suitable age and discretion who resides there;

(C) mailing it to the person's last known address—in which event service is complete upon mailing;

(D) leaving it with the court clerk if the person has no known address;

(E) sending it by electronic means if the person consented in writing—in which event service is complete upon transmission, but is not effective if the serving party learns that it did not reach the person to be served; or

(F) delivering it by any other means that the person consented to in writing—in which event service is complete when the person making service delivers it to the agency designated to make delivery.

(3) ***Using Court Facilities.*** If a local rule so authorizes, a party may use the court's transmission facilities to make service under Rule 5(b)(2)(E).

(c) Serving Numerous Defendants.

(1) ***In General.*** If an action involves an unusually large number of defendants, the court may, on motion or on its own, order that:

(A) defendants' pleadings and replies to them need not be served on other defendants;

(B) any crossclaim, counterclaim, avoidance, or affirmative defense in those pleadings and replies to them will be treated as denied or avoided by all other parties; and

(C) filing any such pleading and serving it on the plaintiff constitutes notice of the pleading to all parties.

(2) ***Notifying Parties.*** A copy of every such order must be served on the parties as the court directs.

(d) Filing.

(1) ***Required Filings; Certificate of Service.*** Any paper after the complaint that is required to be served—together with a certificate of service—must be filed within a reasonable time after service. But disclosures under Rule 26(a)(1) or (2) and the following discovery requests and responses must not be filed until they are used in the proceeding or the court or-

ders filing: depositions, interrogatories, requests for documents or tangible things or to permit entry onto land, and requests for admission.

(2) ***How Filing Is Made—In General.*** A paper is filed by delivering it:

(A) to the clerk; or

(B) to a judge who agrees to accept it for filing, and who must then note the filing date on the paper and promptly send it to the clerk.

(3) ***Electronic Filing, Signing, or Verification.*** A court may, by local rule, allow papers to be filed, signed, or verified by electronic means that are consistent with any technical standards established by the Judicial Conference of the United States. A local rule may require electronic filing only if reasonable exceptions are allowed. A paper filed electronically in compliance with a local rule is a written paper for purposes of these rules.

(4) ***Acceptance by the Clerk.*** The clerk must not refuse to file a paper solely because it is not in the form prescribed by these rules or by a local rule or practice.

See selected Notes of Advisory Committee to FRCP 5, p. 1145.

History of FRCP 5: Adopted Dec. 20, 1937, eff. Sept. 16, 1938. Amended Jan. 21, 1963, eff. July 1, 1963; Mar. 30, 1970, eff. July 1, 1970; Apr. 29, 1980, eff. Aug. 1, 1980; Mar. 2, 1987, eff. Aug. 1, 1987; Apr. 30, 1991, eff. Dec. 1, 1991; Apr. 22, 1993, eff. Dec. 1, 1993; Apr. 23, 1996, eff. Dec. 1, 1996; Apr. 17, 2000, eff. Dec. 1, 2000; Apr. 23, 2001, eff. Dec. 1, 2001; Apr. 12, 2006, eff. Dec. 1, 2006; Apr. 30, 2007, eff. Dec. 1, 2007.

See ***Commentaries***, "Filing Documents," ch. 1-C, p. 17; ***O'Connor's Federal Civil Forms*** (2012), FORMS 1D.

ANNOTATIONS

Employee Painters' Trust v. Ethan Enters., 480 F.3d 993, 999 (9th Cir.2007). See annotation under FRCP 4, p. 837.

Farzana K. v. Indiana Dept. of Educ., 473 F.3d 703, 707-08 (7th Cir.2007). "Clerks … must take in whatever is tendered to them; a document may be rejected later if a judicial officer finds a problem, but the initial filing ensures that the process of vetting papers for compliance with the rules does not prevent satisfaction of time limits. An e-filing system likewise must accept every document tendered for filing; it cannot reject any paper that the clerk must accept."

Raymond v. Ameritech Corp., 442 F.3d 600, 604-05 (7th Cir.2006). "The posting of papers addressed to the clerk's office does not constitute 'filing' under Rule 5(e) [now Rule 5(d)]. Unlike some state court rules the [FRCPs] do not authorize filing to be accomplished by deposit of papers in the mail." *See also* ***Castleberry v. Goldome Credit Corp.***, 408 F.3d 773, 784 (11th Cir. 2005) (cross-claim).

Robinson v. Doe, 272 F.3d 921, 923 (7th Cir.2001). "[T]he practice of returning complaints that don't comply with local rules [has been disapproved], but in any event that practice cannot defeat a right, which in this case is a right to arrest the running of the statute of limitations by filing a complaint in the district court, that is conferred by the national rules." *See also* ***Hooker v. Sivley***, 187 F.3d 680, 682 (5th Cir.1999) (only judge, not clerk, can reject pleading for lack of conformity).

Greene v. WCI Holdings Corp., 136 F.3d 313, 315 (2d Cir.1998). "[T]here is nothing in Rule 5(b) or our case law to indicate that the date of postmark, or the date of receipt, rather than the date of placing it in the mail controls."

Magnuson v. Video Yesteryear, 85 F.3d 1424, 1430 (9th Cir.1996). "Both [FRCPs 4 and 5] contain provisions for service by mail. However, Rule 4, unlike Rule 5, allows a litigant to opt for state law procedures in serving a complaint instead of the federal procedure. *At 1431:* [W]e hold that Federal Express does not satisfy the requirements of Rule 5(b)."

FRCP 5.1. CONSTITUTIONAL CHALLENGE TO A STATUTE—NOTICE, CERTIFICATION, & INTERVENTION

(a) Notice by a Party. A party that files a pleading, written motion, or other paper drawing into question the constitutionality of a federal or state statute must promptly:

(1) file a notice of constitutional question stating the question and identifying the paper that raises it, if:

(A) a federal statute is questioned and the parties do not include the United States, one of its agencies, or one of its officers or employees in an official capacity; or

(B) a state statute is questioned and the parties do not include the state, one of its agencies, or one of its officers or employees in an official capacity; and

(2) serve the notice and paper on the Attorney General of the United States if a federal statute is questioned—or on the state attorney gen-

eral if a state statute is questioned—either by certified or registered mail or by sending it to an electronic address designated by the attorney general for this purpose.

(b) Certification by the Court. The court must, under 28 U.S.C. §2403, certify to the appropriate attorney general that a statute has been questioned.

(c) Intervention; Final Decision on the Merits. Unless the court sets a later time, the attorney general may intervene within 60 days after the notice is filed or after the court certifies the challenge, whichever is earlier. Before the time to intervene expires, the court may reject the constitutional challenge, but may not enter a final judgment holding the statute unconstitutional.

(d) No Forfeiture. A party's failure to file and serve the notice, or the court's failure to certify, does not forfeit a constitutional claim or defense that is otherwise timely asserted.

See selected Notes of Advisory Committee to FRCP 5.1, p. 1147.

History of FRCP 5.1: Adopted Apr. 12, 2006, eff. Dec. 1, 2006. Amended Apr. 30, 2007, eff. Dec. 1, 2007.

See *Commentaries*, "Notice of constitutional question," ch. 1-B, §2.1.11, p. 12; *O'Connor's Federal Civil Forms* (2012), FORM 1B:8.

ANNOTATIONS

Oklahoma v. Pope, 516 F.3d 1214, 1216 (10th Cir. 2008). "When the parties and the court statutorily charged with notifying the Attorney General of a constitutional challenge to a federal statute fail to do so, the appellate court has discretion to respond in different ways, depending on the nature of the arguments and the progress of the litigation. It often may suffice to notify the Attorney General and allow him to intervene on appeal. [¶] In this case, ... we find it appropriate to remand to the district court."

FRCP 5.2. PRIVACY PROTECTION FOR FILINGS MADE WITH THE COURT

(a) Redacted Filings. Unless the court orders otherwise, in an electronic or paper filing with the court that contains an individual's social-security number, taxpayer-identification number, or birth date, the name of an individual known to be a minor, or a financial-account number, a party or nonparty making the filing may include only:

(1) the last four digits of the social-security number and taxpayer-identification number;

(2) the year of the individual's birth;

(3) the minor's initials; and

(4) the last four digits of the financial-account number.

(b) Exemptions from the Redaction Requirement. The redaction requirement does not apply to the following:

(1) a financial-account number that identifies the property allegedly subject to forfeiture in a forfeiture proceeding;

(2) the record of an administrative or agency proceeding;

(3) the official record of a state-court proceeding;

(4) the record of a court or tribunal, if that record was not subject to the redaction requirement when originally filed;

(5) a filing covered by Rule 5.2(c) or (d); and

(6) a pro se filing in an action brought under 28 U.S.C. §§2241, 2254, or 2255.

(c) Limitations on Remote Access to Electronic Files; Social-Security Appeals and Immigration Cases. Unless the court orders otherwise, in an action for benefits under the Social Security Act, and in an action or proceeding relating to an order of removal, to relief from removal, or to immigration benefits or detention, access to an electronic file is authorized as follows:

(1) the parties and their attorneys may have remote electronic access to any part of the case file, including the administrative record;

(2) any other person may have electronic access to the full record at the courthouse, but may have remote electronic access only to:

(A) the docket maintained by the court; and

(B) an opinion, order, judgment, or other disposition of the court, but not any other part of the case file or the administrative record.

(d) Filings Made Under Seal. The court may order that a filing be made under seal without redaction. The court may later unseal the filing or order the person who made the filing to file a redacted version for the public record.

(e) Protective Orders. For good cause, the court may by order in a case:

(1) require redaction of additional information; or

(2) limit or prohibit a nonparty's remote electronic access to a document filed with the court.

FRCP 5.2

(f) Option for Additional Unredacted Filing Under Seal. A person making a redacted filing may also file an unredacted copy under seal. The court must retain the unredacted copy as part of the record.

(g) Option for Filing a Reference List. A filing that contains redacted information may be filed together with a reference list that identifies each item of redacted information and specifies an appropriate identifier that uniquely corresponds to each item listed. The list must be filed under seal and may be amended as of right. Any reference in the case to a listed identifier will be construed to refer to the corresponding item of information.

(h) Waiver of Protection of Identifiers. A person waives the protection of Rule 5.2(a) as to the person's own information by filing it without redaction and not under seal.

See selected Notes of Advisory Committee to FRCP 5.2, p. 1148.
History of FRCP 5.2: Adopted Apr. 30, 2007, eff. Dec. 1, 2007.
See *Commentaries*, "Redacted filing," ch. 1-C, §2.1, p. 17; *O'Connor's Federal Civil Forms* (2012), FORMS 5Q.

FRCP 6. COMPUTING & EXTENDING TIME; TIME FOR MOTION PAPERS

(a) Computing Time. The following rules apply in computing any time period specified in these rules, in any local rule or court order, or in any statute that does not specify a method of computing time.

(1) ***Period Stated in Days or a Longer Unit.*** When the period is stated in days or a longer unit of time:

(A) exclude the day of the event that triggers the period;

(B) count every day, including intermediate Saturdays, Sundays, and legal holidays; and

(C) include the last day of the period, but if the last day is a Saturday, Sunday, or legal holiday, the period continues to run until the end of the next day that is not a Saturday, Sunday, or legal holiday.

(2) ***Period Stated in Hours.*** When the period is stated in hours:

(A) begin counting immediately on the occurrence of the event that triggers the period;

(B) count every hour, including hours during intermediate Saturdays, Sundays, and legal holidays; and

(C) if the period would end on a Saturday, Sunday, or legal holiday, the period continues to run until the same time on the next day that is not a Saturday, Sunday, or legal holiday.

(3) ***Inaccessibility of the Clerk's Office.*** Unless the court orders otherwise, if the clerk's office is inaccessible:

(A) on the last day for filing under Rule 6(a)(1), then the time for filing is extended to the first accessible day that is not a Saturday, Sunday, or legal holiday; or

(B) during the last hour for filing under Rule 6(a)(2), then the time for filing is extended to the same time on the first accessible day that is not a Saturday, Sunday, or legal holiday.

(4) ***"Last Day" Defined.*** Unless a different time is set by a statute, local rule, or court order, the last day ends:

(A) for electronic filing, at midnight in the court's time zone; and

(B) for filing by other means, when the clerk's office is scheduled to close.

(5) ***"Next Day" Defined.*** The "next day" is determined by continuing to count forward when the period is measured after an event and backward when measured before an event.

(6) ***"Legal Holiday" Defined.*** "Legal holiday" means:

(A) the day set aside by statute for observing New Year's Day, Martin Luther King Jr.'s Birthday, Washington's Birthday, Memorial Day, Independence Day, Labor Day, Columbus Day, Veterans' Day, Thanksgiving Day, or Christmas Day;

(B) any day declared a holiday by the President or Congress; and

(C) for periods that are measured after an event, any other day declared a holiday by the state where the district court is located.

(b) Extending Time.

(1) ***In General.*** When an act may or must be done within a specified time, the court may, for good cause, extend the time:

(A) with or without motion or notice if the court acts, or if a request is made, before the original time or its extension expires; or

(B) on motion made after the time has expired if the party failed to act because of excusable neglect.

(2) ***Exceptions.*** A court must not extend the time to act under Rules 50(b) and (d), 52(b), 59(b), (d), and (e), and 60(b).

(c) Motions, Notices of Hearing, and Affidavits.

(1) ***In General.*** A written motion and notice of the hearing must be served at least 14 days before the time specified for the hearing, with the following exceptions:

(A) when the motion may be heard ex parte;

(B) when these rules set a different time; or

(C) when a court order—which a party may, for good cause, apply for ex parte—sets a different time.

(2) ***Supporting Affidavit.*** Any affidavit supporting a motion must be served with the motion. Except as Rule 59(c) provides otherwise, any opposing affidavit must be served at least 7 days before the hearing, unless the court permits service at another time.

(d) Additional Time After Certain Kinds of Service. When a party may or must act within a specified time after service and service is made under Rule 5(b)(2)(C), (D), (E), or (F), 3 days are added after the period would otherwise expire under Rule 6(a).

See selected Notes of Advisory Committee to FRCP 6, p. 1149.

History of FRCP 6: Adopted Dec. 20, 1937, eff. Sept. 16, 1938. Amended Dec. 27, 1946, eff. Mar. 19, 1948; Jan. 21, 1963, eff. July 1, 1963; Feb. 28, 1966, eff. July 1, 1966; Dec. 4, 1967, eff. July 1, 1968; Mar. 1, 1971, eff. July 1, 1971; Apr. 28, 1983, eff. Aug. 1, 1983; Apr. 29, 1985, eff. Aug. 1, 1985; Mar. 2, 1987, eff. Aug. 1, 1987; Apr. 29, 1999, eff. Dec. 1, 1999; Apr. 23, 2001, eff. Dec. 1, 2001; Apr. 25, 2005, eff. Dec. 1, 2005; Apr. 30, 2007, eff. Dec. 1, 2007; Mar. 26, 2009, eff. Dec. 1, 2009.

See ***Commentaries***, "Computing Deadlines," ch. 1-C, §6, p. 23; "Computing Response Deadlines," ch. 1-D, §6, p. 33; "Motion to Extend Time," ch. 5-F, p. 332; ***O'Connor's Federal Civil Forms*** (2012), FORMS 5F.

ANNOTATIONS

Windland v. Quarterman, 578 F.3d 314, 317 (5th Cir.2009). "'Rule 6(a) is a general statutory rule, which may be supplanted when the statute at issue provides more specific direction.' Thus, before relying on the default provisions in Rule 6(a) [to compute the deadline of a limitations period], we must first look to the plain language of the provision at issue to determine whether Congress has provided … 'more specific direction.'"

Lewis v. School Dist. #70, 523 F.3d 730, 739-40 (7th Cir.2008). "Rule 6(e) [now Rule 6(d)] grants a party an extension of time to respond only 'after the service of a notice or other paper *upon* the party' by a method other than personal service. This extension does not appear to apply to actions taken by a party after the service of a notice or other paper *by* that party. [A] facial reading of the [FRCPs] makes clear that [Ds] were not entitled to an additional three days under Rule 6(e).… [¶] A finding of excusable neglect 'is not limited to situations where the failure to timely file is due to circumstances beyond the control of the filer,' … but extends to some cases in which the delay is 'caused by inadvertence, mistake, or carelessness.' [¶] Here … we have a plausible misinterpretation of a procedural rule—a misinterpretation based on a reading so plausible that both the magistrate judge and the district judge made the same misinterpretation." Held: There was excusable neglect for the untimely filed answer.

Violette v. P.A. Days, Inc., 427 F.3d 1015, 1017-18 (6th Cir.2005). "By its plain language, [FRCP 6(a)] applies to the relatively common situation in which litigants are required to file papers within a given number of days following a particular event or order. … The language of Rule 6(a) does not address situations where litigants are required to file papers on a particular, stated, calendar date. *At 1019:* [R]equiring that date-certain deadlines be extended under the computational algorithm of … Rule 6(a) would inhibit the discretion of judges and parties to establish deadlines for performance of trial-related activities; there is no indication that those who adopted [FRCP 6(a)] considered or desired such a policy."

Hart v. Sheahan, 396 F.3d 887, 890 (7th Cir.2005). "[Ds] argue that because Executive Order 13320, on which [Ps] rely for the proposition that December 26 of 2003 was a legal holiday, does not *say* that the President has declared December 26 to be a holiday, [Ps' FRCP] 59(e) motion was untimely. [¶] [T]he fact that the executive order expressly incorporated provisions governing compensation of federal employees on legal holidays was a sufficient indication that the President had declared December 26 a holiday. *At 891:* The clincher is the superior simplicity of a rule that says that when the President closes the government for celebratory or commemorative reasons …, rather than because of a budgetary crisis …, or for a snow emergency, terrorist act, or some other *force majeure*, the presumption is

that he has declared a legal holiday. The presumption has not been rebutted."

In re PaineWebber LPs Litig., 147 F.3d 132, 135 (2d Cir.1998). "The determination whether a party's conduct constitutes 'excusable neglect' is an equitable one that requires a court to consider all relevant circumstances. For that reason the notion is an 'elastic concept.' Excusable neglect may be found where the relevant circumstances reveal inadvertent delays, mistakes, or carelessness. Hence, it clearly is broad enough to encompass even those omissions caused by circumstances within the movant's control. To establish excusable neglect, however, a movant must show good faith and a reasonable basis for noncompliance." *See also* ***Bennett v. City of Holyoke***, 362 F.3d 1, 5 (1st Cir. 2004).

Lerro v. Quaker Oats Co., 84 F.3d 239, 242 (7th Cir. 1996). "Neither Rule 6 nor the committee note explaining its rationale discusses whether to apply Rule 6(a) before or after Rule 6(e) [now Rule 6(d)]. [¶] Rule 6(e) is designed to give a litigant approximately the same *effective* time to respond whether papers are served by hand or by mail.... The only way to carry out Rule 6(e)'s function of adding time to compensate for delays in mail delivery is to employ Rule 6(a) first."

TITLE III. PLEADINGS & MOTIONS

FRCP 7. PLEADINGS ALLOWED; FORM OF MOTIONS & OTHER PAPERS

(a) Pleadings. Only these pleadings are allowed:

(1) a complaint;

(2) an answer to a complaint;

(3) an answer to a counterclaim designated as a counterclaim;

(4) an answer to a crossclaim;

(5) a third-party complaint;

(6) an answer to a third-party complaint; and

(7) if the court orders one, a reply to an answer.

(b) Motions and Other Papers.

(1) ***In General.*** A request for a court order must be made by motion. The motion must:

(A) be in writing unless made during a hearing or trial;

(B) state with particularity the grounds for seeking the order; and

(C) state the relief sought.

(2) ***Form.*** The rules governing captions and other matters of form in pleadings apply to motions and other papers.

See selected Notes of Advisory Committee to FRCP 7, p. 1151.

History of FRCP 7: Adopted Dec. 20, 1937, eff. Sept. 16, 1938. Amended Dec. 27, 1946, eff. Mar. 19, 1948; Jan. 21, 1963, eff. July 1, 1963; Apr. 28, 1983, eff. Aug. 1, 1983; Apr. 30, 2007, eff. Dec. 1, 2007.

See *Commentaries*, "Pleading Practice," ch. 1-B, §2, p. 7; *O'Connor's Federal Civil Forms* (2012), FORMS 2B; FORMS 3L.

ANNOTATIONS

A. Bauer Mech., Inc. v. Joint Arbitration Bd. of the Plumbing Contractors' Ass'n & Chi. Journeymen Plumbers' Local Un., 562 F.3d 784, 790 (7th Cir. 2009). "Nowhere in the [FRCPs] is there a prohibition on a court's recognition of a pleading attached to a motion.... Rules 7(a) and (b) do not limit the methods by which a pleading may be filed. [¶] The practice of accepting pleadings attached to motions for leave to file *instanter* is one of judicial economy and is with a district court's discretion."

CRST Van Expedited, Inc. v. Werner Enters., 479 F.3d 1099, 1104 n.3 (9th Cir.2007). An FRCP 12(b)(6) "motion to dismiss is not ... a responsive pleading...." *See also* ***Haven v. Polska***, 215 F.3d 727, 732 (7th Cir. 2000).

Intera Corp. v. Henderson, 428 F.3d 605, 612 (6th Cir.2005). "'[P]articularity' has been interpreted to mean 'reasonable specification.' [¶] [T]he particularity requirement of Rule 7(b)(1) may be supplemented by local district court rules that require a party to file written motions with concomitant briefs that contain legal argument."

Casey v. Long Island R.R., 406 F.3d 142, 148 (2d Cir.2005). "For purposes of [FRCP] 7, [a] motion made immediately upon the pronouncement of the verdict is made during the trial. [¶] In the present case, immediately after the jury's verdict, defense counsel renew[ed] [D's] earlier motion[s] for judgment as a matter of law.... *At 149:* That oral motion in open court following the return of the jury's verdict was plainly within the time limit imposed by [FRCP] 59(b)." (Internal quotes omitted.)

Swanson v. U.S. Forest Serv., 87 F.3d 339, 345 (9th Cir.1996). FRCP 7(b)(2) "holds only that the rules that apply to the *form* of pleadings shall apply to 'other papers.' Thus, the reach of the [FRCP] 10(c) provision permitting the adoption by reference of material from pleadings cannot be extended by [FRCP] 7(b)(2) to include the adoption of *substantive material* in 'other pa-

pers.' Accordingly, the incorporation of substantive material by reference is not sanctioned by the federal rules…."

Cambridge Plating Co. v. Napco, Inc., 85 F.3d 752, 760 (1st Cir.1996). "When a motion is challenged for lack of particularity the question is whether any party is prejudiced by a lack of particularity or whether the court can comprehend the basis for the motion and deal with it fairly." (Internal quotes omitted.)

FRCP 7.1. DISCLOSURE STATEMENT

(a) Who Must File; Contents. A nongovernmental corporate party must file 2 copies of a disclosure statement that:

(1) identifies any parent corporation and any publicly held corporation owning 10% or more of its stock; or

(2) states that there is no such corporation.

(b) Time to File; Supplemental Filing. A party must:

(1) file the disclosure statement with its first appearance, pleading, petition, motion, response, or other request addressed to the court; and

(2) promptly file a supplemental statement if any required information changes.

See selected Notes of Advisory Committee to FRCP 7.1, p. 1152.

History of FRCP 7.1: Adopted Apr. 29, 2002, eff. Dec. 1, 2002. Amended Apr. 30, 2007, eff. Dec. 1, 2007.

See *Commentaries*, "Disclosure statement," ch. 2-B, §16.3, p. 86; "Disclosure Statement," ch. 3-L, §6, p. 237; *O'Connor's Federal Civil Forms* (2012), FORM 1B:9.

FRCP 8. GENERAL RULES OF PLEADING

(a) Claim for Relief. A pleading that states a claim for relief must contain:

(1) a short and plain statement of the grounds for the court's jurisdiction, unless the court already has jurisdiction and the claim needs no new jurisdictional support;

(2) a short and plain statement of the claim showing that the pleader is entitled to relief; and

(3) a demand for the relief sought, which may include relief in the alternative or different types of relief.

(b) Defenses; Admissions and Denials.

(1) ***In General.*** In responding to a pleading, a party must:

(A) state in short and plain terms its defenses to each claim asserted against it; and

(B) admit or deny the allegations asserted against it by an opposing party.

(2) ***Denials—Responding to the Substance.*** A denial must fairly respond to the substance of the allegation.

(3) ***General and Specific Denials.*** A party that intends in good faith to deny all the allegations of a pleading—including the jurisdictional grounds—may do so by a general denial. A party that does not intend to deny all the allegations must either specifically deny designated allegations or generally deny all except those specifically admitted.

(4) ***Denying Part of an Allegation.*** A party that intends in good faith to deny only part of an allegation must admit the part that is true and deny the rest.

(5) ***Lacking Knowledge or Information.*** A party that lacks knowledge or information sufficient to form a belief about the truth of an allegation must so state, and the statement has the effect of a denial.

(6) ***Effect of Failing to Deny.*** An allegation—other than one relating to the amount of damages—is admitted if a responsive pleading is required and the allegation is not denied. If a responsive pleading is not required, an allegation is considered denied or avoided.

(c) Affirmative Defenses.

(1) ***In General.*** In responding to a pleading, a party must affirmatively state any avoidance or affirmative defense, including:

- accord and satisfaction;
- arbitration and award;
- assumption of risk;
- contributory negligence;
- duress;
- estoppel;
- failure of consideration;
- fraud;
- illegality;
- injury by fellow servant;
- laches;
- license;
- payment;
- release;

- res judicata;
- statute of frauds;
- statute of limitations; and
- waiver.

(2) ***Mistaken Designation.*** If a party mistakenly designates a defense as a counterclaim, or a counterclaim as a defense, the court must, if justice requires, treat the pleading as though it were correctly designated, and may impose terms for doing so.

(d) Pleading to Be Concise and Direct; Alternative Statements; Inconsistency.

(1) ***In General.*** Each allegation must be simple, concise, and direct. No technical form is required.

(2) ***Alternative Statements of a Claim or Defense.*** A party may set out 2 or more statements of a claim or defense alternatively or hypothetically, either in a single count or defense or in separate ones. If a party makes alternative statements, the pleading is sufficient if any one of them is sufficient.

(3) ***Inconsistent Claims or Defenses.*** A party may state as many separate claims or defenses as it has, regardless of consistency.

(e) Construing Pleadings. Pleadings must be construed so as to do justice.

See selected Notes of Advisory Committee to FRCP 8, p. 1152.

History of FRCP 8: Adopted Dec. 20, 1937, eff. Sept. 16, 1938. Amended Feb. 28, 1966, eff. July 1, 1966; Mar. 2, 1987, eff. Aug. 1, 1987; Apr. 30, 2007, eff. Dec. 1, 2007; Apr. 28, 2010, eff. Dec. 1, 2010.

See ***Commentaries***, "Pleading Practice," ch. 1-B, §2, p. 7; "Statement of Claim," ch. 2-B, §5, p. 80; "Motion to Dismiss for Failure to State a Claim—FRCP 12(b)(6)," ch. 3-F, p. 204; ***O'Connor's Federal Civil Forms*** (2012), FORMS 2B; FORMS 3F; FORMS 3J; FORMS 3L.

ANNOTATIONS

Pleading Standard

Ashcroft v. Iqbal, 556 U.S. 662, 678-79 (2009). "[T]he pleading standard Rule 8 announces does not require detailed factual allegations, but it demands more than an unadorned, the-defendant-unlawfully-harmed-me accusation. [A] complaint [does not] suffice if it tenders naked assertions devoid of further factual enhancement. [¶] To survive a motion to dismiss, a complaint must contain sufficient factual matter, accepted as true, to state a claim to relief that is plausible on its face. A claim has facial plausibility when the plaintiff pleads factual content that allows the court to draw the reasonable inference that the defendant is liable for the misconduct alleged. The plausibility standard is not akin to a probability requirement, but it asks for more than a sheer possibility that a defendant has acted unlawfully. [¶] Two working principles underlie our decision in ***Twombly***. First, the tenet that a court must accept as true all of the allegations contained in a complaint is inapplicable to legal conclusions. Threadbare recitals of the elements of a cause of action, supported by mere conclusory statements, do not suffice. ... Second, only a complaint that states a plausible claim for relief survives a motion to dismiss. Determining whether a complaint states a plausible claim for relief will ... be a context-specific task that requires the reviewing court to draw on its judicial experience and common sense. But where the well-pleaded facts do not permit the court to infer more than the mere possibility of misconduct, the complaint has alleged—but it has not shown—that the pleader is entitled to relief. [¶] [A] court considering a motion to dismiss can choose to begin by identifying pleadings that, because they are no more than conclusions, are not entitled to the assumption of truth. While legal conclusions can provide the framework of a complaint, they must be supported by factual allegations. When there are well-pleaded factual allegations, a court should assume their veracity and then determine whether they plausibly give rise to an entitlement to relief. [¶] Our decision in ***Twombly*** illustrates the two-pronged approach." (Internal quotes omitted.)

Bell Atlantic Corp. v. Twombly, 550 U.S. 544, 555 (2007). "While a complaint ... does not need detailed factual allegations ..., a plaintiff's obligation to provide the 'grounds' of his 'entitle[ment] to relief' requires more than labels and conclusions, and a formulaic recitation of the elements of a cause of action will not do.... Factual allegations must be enough to raise a right to relief above the speculative level ..., on the assumption that all the allegations in the complaint are true (even if doubtful in fact)...." *See also* ***Erickson v. Pardus***, 551 U.S. 89, 93-94 (2007); ***Jones v. Bock***, 549 U.S. 199, 212 (2007).

Atkins v. City of Chi., 631 F.3d 823, 831-32 (7th Cir. 2011). "The Court explained in ***Iqbal*** that the plausibility standard is not akin to a 'probability requirement,' but it asks for more than a sheer possibility that a defendant has acted unlawfully. This is a little unclear because plausibility, probability, and possibility overlap. ... But one sees more or less what the Court was driving at: the fact that the allegations undergirding a [plaintiff's] claim could be true is no longer enough to save it. [T]he complaint taken as a whole must establish a nonnegligible probability that the claim is valid, though it need not be so great a probability as such terms as 'preponderance of the evidence' connote. [¶] After *Twombly* and *Iqbal* a plaintiff to survive dismissal must plead some facts that suggest a right to relief that is beyond the 'speculative level.' ... So suppose some of the [plaintiff's] factual allegations are unrealistic or nonsensical and others not, some contradict others, and some are speculative in the sense of implausible and ungrounded. The district court has to consider all these features of a complaint en route to deciding whether it has enough substance to warrant putting the defendant to the expense of discovery...." (Internal quotes omitted.)

West Penn Allegheny Health Sys. v. UPMC, 627 F.3d 85, 98 (3d Cir.2010). "[J]udging the sufficiency of a pleading is a context-dependent exercise. Some claims require more factual explication than others to state a plausible claim for relief. For example, it generally takes fewer factual allegations to state a claim for simple battery than to state a claim for antitrust conspiracy. But, contrary to the able District Court's suggestion, this does not mean that *Twombly*'s plausibility standard functions more like a probability requirement in complex cases. [¶] We conclude that it is inappropriate to apply *Twombly*'s plausibility standard with extra bite in ... complex cases."

Chao v. Rivendell Woods, Inc., 415 F.3d 342, 349 (4th Cir.2005). "[A] complaint need not 'make a case' against a defendant or '*forecast evidence* sufficient to *prove* an element' of the claim. It need only '*allege facts* sufficient to *state* elements' of the claim. Thus, the sufficiency of a complaint does not depend on whether it provides enough information to enable the defendant 'to prepare a defense,' but merely 'whether the document's allegations are detailed and informative enough to enable the defendant to respond.'" *See also* ***U.S. v. Melrose-Wakefield Hosp.***, 360 F.3d 220, 240 (1st Cir. 2004); ***McManus v. Fleetwood Enters.***, 320 F.3d 545, 551 (5th Cir.2003).

Affirmative Defenses

Best v. City of Portland, 554 F.3d 698, 700 (7th Cir. 2009). "[A] district court can raise an affirmative defense sua sponte when 'a valid affirmative defense is so plain from the face of the complaint that the suit can be regarded as frivolous.'"

First Un. Nat'l Bank v. Pictet Overseas Trust Corp., 477 F.3d 616, 622 (8th Cir.2007). "Generally, failure to plead an affirmative defense results in a waiver of that defense. ... We have ... eschewed a literal interpretation of [FRCP 8(c)] that places form over substance, ... and instead have held that when an affirmative defense is raised in the trial court in a manner that does not result in unfair surprise, technical failure to comply with Rule 8(c) is not fatal." (Internal quotes omitted.) *See also* ***Pasco v. Knoblauch***, 566 F.3d 572, 577 (5th Cir.2009).

Davignon v. Clemmey, 322 F.3d 1, 15 (1st Cir. 2003). "Rule 8(c) is designed to provide plaintiffs with adequate notice of a defendant's intention to litigate an affirmative defense, thereby affording an opportunity to develop any evidence and offer responsive arguments relating to the defense. There are certain exceptions to the Rule 8(c) bar which might be invoked ... either where (i) the defendant asserts it without undue delay and the plaintiff is not unfairly prejudiced by any delay; or (ii) the circumstances necessary to establish entitlement to the affirmative defense did not obtain at the time the answer was filed...." *See also* ***In re Sterten***, 546 F.3d 278, 285 (3d Cir.2008); ***Mickowski v. Visi-Trak Worldwide, LLC***, 415 F.3d 501, 506 (6th Cir. 2005).

Roskam Baking Co. v. Lanham Mach. Co., 288 F.3d 895, 901 (6th Cir.2002). In a diversity action, "the district court was correct ... to look to ... state law to determine whether or not the [state-law statute of repose] is an affirmative defense for the purposes of Rule 8(c)."

Inconsistent Claims or Defenses

Independent Enters. v. Pittsburgh Water & Sewer Auth., 103 F.3d 1165, 1175 (3d Cir.1997). FRCP 8(e)(2), now FRCP 8(d)(2) and (3), "permits inconsistency in both legal and factual allegations, and has been interpreted to mean that a court 'may not construe [a plaintiff's] first claim as an admission against another alternative or inconsistent claim.'"

Motion to Dismiss or Strike

Davis v. Ruby Foods, Inc., 269 F.3d 818, 820-21 (7th Cir.2001). "[W]hen the complaint adequately performs the notice function prescribed for complaints by the civil rules, the presence of extraneous matter does

FRCP 8

not warrant dismissal. [¶] [D]efense counsel [is advised] against moving to strike extraneous matter unless its presence in the complaint is actually prejudicial to the defense."

Simmons v. Abruzzo, 49 F.3d 83, 86-87 (2d Cir. 1995). "When a complaint fails to comply with [the] requirements [of FRCP 8], the district court has the power, on motion or *sua sponte*, to dismiss the complaint or to strike such parts as are redundant or immaterial. [I]f the court dismisses the complaint for failure to comply with Rule 8, it should generally give the plaintiff leave to amend."

FRCP 9. PLEADING SPECIAL MATTERS

(a) Capacity or Authority to Sue; Legal Existence.

(1) ***In General.*** Except when required to show that the court has jurisdiction, a pleading need not allege:

(A) a party's capacity to sue or be sued;

(B) a party's authority to sue or be sued in a representative capacity; or

(C) the legal existence of an organized association of persons that is made a party.

(2) ***Raising Those Issues.*** To raise any of those issues, a party must do so by a specific denial, which must state any supporting facts that are peculiarly within the party's knowledge.

(b) Fraud or Mistake; Conditions of Mind. In alleging fraud or mistake, a party must state with particularity the circumstances constituting fraud or mistake. Malice, intent, knowledge, and other conditions of a person's mind may be alleged generally.

(c) Conditions Precedent. In pleading conditions precedent, it suffices to allege generally that all conditions precedent have occurred or been performed. But when denying that a condition precedent has occurred or been performed, a party must do so with particularity.

(d) Official Document or Act. In pleading an official document or official act, it suffices to allege that the document was legally issued or the act legally done.

(e) Judgment. In pleading a judgment or decision of a domestic or foreign court, a judicial or quasi-judicial tribunal, or a board or officer, it suffices to plead the judgment or decision without showing jurisdiction to render it.

(f) Time and Place. An allegation of time or place is material when testing the sufficiency of a pleading.

(g) Special Damages. If an item of special damage is claimed, it must be specifically stated.

(h) Admiralty or Maritime Claim.

(1) ***How Designated.*** If a claim for relief is within the admiralty or maritime jurisdiction and also within the court's subject-matter jurisdiction on some other ground, the pleading may designate the claim as an admiralty or maritime claim for purposes of Rules 14(c), 38(e), and 82 and the Supplemental Rules for Admiralty or Maritime Claims and Asset Forfeiture Actions. A claim cognizable only in the admiralty or maritime jurisdiction is an admiralty or maritime claim for those purposes, whether or not so designated.

(2) ***Designation for Appeal.*** A case that includes an admiralty or maritime claim within this subdivision (h) is an admiralty case within 28 U.S.C. §1292(a)(3).

See selected Notes of Advisory Committee to FRCP 9, p. 1152.

History of FRCP 9: Adopted Dec. 20, 1937, eff. Sept. 16, 1938. Amended Feb. 28, 1966, eff. July 1, 1966; Dec. 4, 1967, eff. July 1, 1968; Mar. 30, 1970, eff. July 1, 1970; Mar. 2, 1987, eff. Aug. 1, 1987; Apr. 11, 1997, eff. Dec. 1, 1997; Apr. 30, 2007, eff. Dec. 1, 2007.

See ***Commentaries***, "Plaintiff's Complaint," ch. 2-B, p. 75; ***O'Connor's Federal Civil Forms*** (2012), FORMS 2B; FORMS 3J.

ANNOTATIONS

Rotella v. Wood, 528 U.S. 549, 560 (2000). "[P] argues that unless a pattern discovery rule is recognized [for civil RICO claims,] a RICO plaintiff will sometimes be barred from suit by [FRCP] 9(b), which provides that fraud must be pleaded with particularity. [P] has presented no case in which Rule 9(b) has effectively barred a claim like his, and he ignores the flexibility provided by [FRCP] 11(b)(3), allowing pleadings based on evidence reasonably anticipated after further investigation or discovery."

Myers v. Central Fla. Invs., 592 F.3d 1201, 1224 (11th Cir.2010). "Should a defendant [deny that a condition precedent has occurred or been performed under FRCP 9], '[t]he plaintiff then bears the burden of proving that the conditions precedent … have been satisfied.' Should a defendant 'not deny the satisfaction of the conditions precedent specifically and with particularity, however, the allegations are assumed admitted and cannot later be attacked.'"

Kearns v. Ford Motor Co., 567 F.3d 1120, 1125 (9th Cir.2009). "Rule 9(b) serves three purposes: (1) to provide defendants with adequate notice to allow them to defend the charge and deter plaintiffs from the filing of complaints 'as a pretext for the discovery of unknown wrongs'; (2) to protect those whose reputation would be harmed as a result of being subject to fraud charges; and (3) to 'prohibit[ ] plaintiff[s] from unilaterally imposing upon the court, the parties and society enormous social and economic costs absent some factual basis.'"

St. Paul Fire & Mar. Ins. v. Lago Canyon, Inc., 561 F.3d 1181, 1184 (11th Cir.2009). "Rule 9(h) ... allows plaintiffs to elect admiralty jurisdiction over 'some other ground' of federal jurisdiction. In other words, if there are two grounds for jurisdiction in the same case—such as admiralty and diversity jurisdiction—Rule 9(h) provides that the plaintiff may elect to proceed in admiralty." *See also* ***Luera v. M/V Alberta***, 635 F.3d 181, 187 (5th Cir.2011) (P can change FRCP 9(h) election by amending complaint as long as there is not prejudice to court or Ds).

Borsellino v. Goldman Sachs Grp., 477 F.3d 502, 507 (7th Cir.2007). "Rule 9(b) applies to 'averments of fraud,' not claims of fraud, so whether the rule applies will depend on the plaintiff's factual allegations. A claim that 'sounds in fraud'—in other words, one that is premised upon a course of fraudulent conduct—can implicate Rule 9(b)'s heightened pleading requirements."

Southland Secs. Corp. v. INSpire Ins. Solutions Inc., 365 F.3d 353, 362 (5th Cir.2004). FRCP 9(b) "requires the plaintiffs in securities fraud causes to plead with particularity the circumstances constituting the alleged fraud. To satisfy Rule 9(b)'s pleading requirements, the plaintiffs must 'specify the statements contended to be fraudulent, identify the speaker, state when and where the statements were made, and explain why the statements were fraudulent.'" *See also* ***U.S. v. Melrose-Wakefield Hosp.***, 360 F.3d 220, 226 (1st Cir.2004); ***Schaller Tel. Co. v. Golden Sky Sys.***, 298 F.3d 736, 746 (8th Cir.2002).

In re Burlington Coat Factory Sec. Litig., 114 F.3d 1410, 1418 (3d Cir.1997). "[T]he normally rigorous particularity rule has been relaxed somewhat where the factual information is peculiarly within the defendant's knowledge or control. But even under a relaxed application of Rule 9(b), boilerplate and conclusory allegations will not suffice. [¶] While state of mind may be averred generally, plaintiffs must still allege facts that show the court their basis for inferring that the defendants acted with 'scienter.'"

Avitia v. Metropolitan Club, 49 F.3d 1219, 1226 (7th Cir.1995). "A plaintiff is not required to itemize his damages claims in his complaint. [T]here is an exception: [FRCP] 9(g) requires that the complaint plead 'special damage.' These are damages that are unusual for the type of claim in question—that are not the natural damages associated with such a claim." *See also* ***United Indus. v. Simon-Hartley, Ltd.***, 91 F.3d 762, 764 (5th Cir.1996) (attorney fees are special damages).

FRCP 10. FORM OF PLEADINGS

(a) Caption; Names of Parties. Every pleading must have a caption with the court's name, a title, a file number, and a Rule 7(a) designation. The title of the complaint must name all the parties; the title of other pleadings, after naming the first party on each side, may refer generally to other parties.

(b) Paragraphs; Separate Statements. A party must state its claims or defenses in numbered paragraphs, each limited as far as practicable to a single set of circumstances. A later pleading may refer by number to a paragraph in an earlier pleading. If doing so would promote clarity, each claim founded on a separate transaction or occurrence—and each defense other than a denial—must be stated in a separate count or defense.

(c) Adoption by Reference; Exhibits. A statement in a pleading may be adopted by reference elsewhere in the same pleading or in any other pleading or motion. A copy of a written instrument that is an exhibit to a pleading is a part of the pleading for all purposes.

History of FRCP 10: Adopted Dec. 20, 1937, eff. Sept. 16, 1938. Amended Apr. 30, 2007, eff. Dec. 1, 2007.

See ***Commentaries***, "Pleading Practice," ch. 1-B, §2, p. 7; ***O'Connor's Federal Civil Forms*** (2012), FORMS 1B; FORMS 2B; FORMS 3L.

ANNOTATIONS

Doe v. Megless, 654 F.3d 404, 408-09 (3d Cir.2011). "While not expressly permitted under [FRCP] 10(a), in exceptional cases courts have allowed a party to proceed anonymously. That a plaintiff may suffer embarrassment or economic harm is not enough. Instead, a plaintiff must show 'both (1) a fear of severe harm, and (2) that the fear of severe harm is reasonable.' Examples of areas where courts have allowed pseudonyms

include cases involving 'abortion, birth control, transexuality, mental illness, welfare rights of illegitimate children, AIDS, and homosexuality.' [¶] When a litigant sufficiently alleges that ... she has a reasonable fear of severe harm from litigating without a pseudonym, courts of appeals are in agreement that district courts should balance a plaintiff's interest and fear against the public's strong interest in an open litigation process. [E]ach court has agreed that [its] list of factors is not exhaustive. Further, each court agrees that the purpose of the balancing test is to allow a district court to determine whether a litigant has a reasonable fear of severe harm that outweighs the public's interest in open litigation."

Phillips v. Girdich, 408 F.3d 124, 125 (2d Cir.2005). "Although [FRCP 10(b)] contains important guidelines for the form of pleadings in federal court, we hold that harmless violations of [FRCP 10(b)] should be excused so that claims may be resolved on their merits."

Rosenblum v. Travelbyus.com Ltd., 299 F.3d 657, 661 (7th Cir.2002). "[D]ocuments [under FRCP 10(c)] attached to a motion to dismiss are considered part of the pleadings if they are referred to in the plaintiff's complaint and are central to his claim. Such documents may be considered by a district court in ruling on the motion to dismiss. This exception is aimed at cases interpreting, for example, a contract. The court is not bound to accept the pleader's allegations as to the effect of the exhibit, but can independently examine the document and form its own conclusions as to the proper construction and meaning to be given the material." (Internal quotes omitted.) *See also* ***Ferrer v. Chevron Corp.***, 484 F.3d 776, 780 (5th Cir.2007).

ALA, Inc. v. CCAIR, Inc., 29 F.3d 855, 859 n.8 (3d Cir.1994). "Where there is a disparity between a written instrument annexed to a pleading and an allegation in the pleading based thereon, the written instrument will control."

FRCP 11. SIGNING PLEADINGS, MOTIONS, & OTHER PAPERS; REPRESENTATIONS TO THE COURT; SANCTIONS

(a) Signature. Every pleading, written motion, and other paper must be signed by at least one attorney of record in the attorney's name—or by a party personally if the party is unrepresented. The paper must state the signer's address, e-mail address, and telephone number. Unless a rule or statute specifically states otherwise, a pleading need not be verified or accompanied by an affidavit. The court must strike an unsigned paper unless the omission is promptly corrected after being called to the attorney's or party's attention.

(b) Representations to the Court. By presenting to the court a pleading, written motion, or other paper—whether by signing, filing, submitting, or later advocating it—an attorney or unrepresented party certifies that to the best of the person's knowledge, information, and belief, formed after an inquiry reasonable under the circumstances:

(1) it is not being presented for any improper purpose, such as to harass, cause unnecessary delay, or needlessly increase the cost of litigation;

(2) the claims, defenses, and other legal contentions are warranted by existing law or by a nonfrivolous argument for extending, modifying, or reversing existing law or for establishing new law;

(3) the factual contentions have evidentiary support or, if specifically so identified, will likely have evidentiary support after a reasonable opportunity for further investigation or discovery; and

(4) the denials of factual contentions are warranted on the evidence or, if specifically so identified, are reasonably based on belief or a lack of information.

(c) Sanctions.

(1) ***In General.*** If, after notice and a reasonable opportunity to respond, the court determines that Rule 11(b) has been violated, the court may impose an appropriate sanction on any attorney, law firm, or party that violated the rule or is responsible for the violation. Absent exceptional circumstances, a law firm must be held jointly responsible for a violation committed by its partner, associate, or employee.

(2) ***Motion for Sanctions.*** A motion for sanctions must be made separately from any other motion and must describe the specific conduct that allegedly violates Rule 11(b). The motion must be served under Rule 5, but it must not be filed or be presented to the court if the challenged paper, claim, defense, contention, or denial is withdrawn or appropriately corrected within 21 days after service or within another time the court sets. If warranted, the court may award to the prevailing party the reasonable expenses, including attorney's fees, incurred for the motion.

(3) ***On the Court's Initiative.*** On its own, the court may order an attorney, law firm, or party to show cause why conduct specifically described in the order has not violated Rule 11(b).

(4) ***Nature of a Sanction.*** A sanction imposed under this rule must be limited to what suffices to deter repetition of the conduct or comparable conduct by others similarly situated. The sanction may include nonmonetary directives; an order to pay a penalty into court; or, if imposed on motion and warranted for effective deterrence, an order directing payment to the movant of part or all of the reasonable attorney's fees and other expenses directly resulting from the violation.

(5) ***Limitations on Monetary Sanctions.*** The court must not impose a monetary sanction:

(A) against a represented party for violating Rule 11(b)(2); or

(B) on its own, unless it issued the show-cause order under Rule 11(c)(3) before voluntary dismissal or settlement of the claims made by or against the party that is, or whose attorneys are, to be sanctioned.

(6) ***Requirements for an Order.*** An order imposing a sanction must describe the sanctioned conduct and explain the basis for the sanction.

(d) Inapplicability to Discovery. This rule does not apply to disclosures and discovery requests, responses, objections, and motions under Rules 26 through 37.

See selected Notes of Advisory Committee to FRCP 11, p. 1152.

History of FRCP 11: Adopted Dec. 20, 1937, eff. Sept. 16, 1938. Amended Apr. 28, 1983, eff. Aug. 1, 1983; Mar. 2, 1987, eff. Aug. 1, 1987; Apr. 22, 1993, eff. Dec. 1, 1993; Apr. 30, 2007, eff. Dec. 1, 2007.

See ***Commentaries***, "Motion for Sanctions," ch. 5-O, p. 384; ***O'Connor's Federal Civil Forms*** (2012), FORMS 5O.

See also 5 U.S.C. §2903 (notary public and other persons authorized to administer oaths).

ANNOTATIONS

Generally

Cooter & Gell v. Hartmarx Corp., 496 U.S. 384, 399 (1990). "Determining whether an attorney has violated Rule 11 involves a consideration of three types of issues. The court must consider factual questions regarding the nature of the attorney's prefiling inquiry and the factual basis of the pleading or other paper. Legal issues are raised in considering whether a pleading is 'warranted by existing law or a good faith argument' for changing the law and whether the attorney's conduct violated Rule 11. Finally, the district court must exercise its discretion to tailor an 'appropriate sanction.'"

In re Bees, 562 F.3d 284, 289 (4th Cir.2009). "Rule 11 … severely limits a court's ability to sanction counsel for oral statements. … Rule 11 'applies only to assertions contained in papers filed with or submitted to the court.' The rule 'does not cover matters arising for the first time during oral presentations to the court, when counsel may make statements that would not have been made if there had been more time for study and reflection.' [A]n oral statement may form a basis for Rule 11 sanctions *only* if it advocates a contention previously contained within a written submission." *See also* ***O'Brien v. Alexander***, 101 F.3d 1479, 1490 (2d Cir. 1996).

FRCP 11(a) – Signature

Becker v. Montgomery, 532 U.S. 757, 764 (2001). "[W]e are not disposed to extend the meaning of the word 'signed,' as that word appears in [FRCP] 11(a), to permit typed names. As Rule 11(a) is now framed, we read the requirement of a signature to indicate, as a signature requirement commonly does, and as it did in John Hancock's day, a name handwritten (or a mark handplaced)." *See also* ***Edelman v. Lynchburg Coll.***, 535 U.S. 106, 115-16 (2002).

Kovilic Constr. Co. v. Missbrenner, 106 F.3d 768, 772 (7th Cir.1997). "Rule 11(a) provides only that the court may strike the unsigned document. We have held that documents should be struck only where the failure to sign severely prejudiced the opposing party."

Garr v. U.S. Healthcare, Inc., 22 F.3d 1274, 1278 (3d Cir.1994). "[T]he signer has a 'personal, nondelegable responsibility' to comply with the requirements of Rule 11 before signing the document. [¶] A signer's obligation … does not preclude the signer from any reliance on information from other persons. For example, … it would [not] be unreasonable for an attorney to rely on witnesses to an accident before bringing a personal injury action."

FRCP 11(b) – Representations to Court

Lucas v. Duncan, 574 F.3d 772, 776 (D.C.Cir.2009). The magistrate judge "imposed sanctions [based on] his finding that many of the 11 statements that [attorney] drafted were 'classic examples of inferences dis-

FRCP 11

guised as statements of fact.' *At 777:* There is no basis in the text of Rule 11(b)(3) for the legal proposition that an attorney must separately identify 'fact' and 'inference.' [FRCP 11(b)(3)] merely requires an attorney to certify that the factual contentions in a paper he presents to the court 'have evidentiary support.'"

Jenkins v. Methodist Hosps., 478 F.3d 255, 265 (5th Cir.2007). "Under certain circumstances, ... an isolated factual misrepresentation may serve as the basis for [FRCP 11 sanctions]."

Roger Edwards, LLC v. Fiddes & Son Ltd., 437 F.3d 140, 142 (1st Cir.2006). "To support a finding of frivolousness [under FRCP 11(b)(2)], some degree of fault is required, but the fault need not be a wicked or subjectively reckless state of mind; rather, an individual 'must, at the very least, be culpably careless to commit a violation.'"

Harper v. AutoAlliance Int'l, 392 F.3d 195, 201-02 (6th Cir.2004). "To remove a civil action from state court to federal court, ... the defendant or defendants must file in the district court a notice of removal signed pursuant to [FRCP] 11.... [¶] [P] argues that the statement of [D1's] concurrence in [D2's] notice of removal did not comply with the rule of unanimity because 28 U.S.C. §1446(a) states that a notice of removal must be signed pursuant to Rule 11 ..., but that Rule 11 'does not authorize any one party to make representations or file pleadings on behalf of another party.' We disagree. Rule 11 merely requires any pleading to be signed 'by at least one attorney of record' and states that by presenting such pleading the attorney is certifying that, *inter alia*, 'the allegations and other factual contentions have evidentiary support.' Thus, the attorney for [other Ds] was bound by Rule 11 when she represented to the district court that [D1] consented to the removal. Nothing in Rule 11, however, required [D1] or his attorney to submit a pleading, written motion, or other paper directly expressing that concurrence or prohibited counsel for the other [Ds] from making such a representation on [D1's] behalf."

Macken v. Jensen, 333 F.3d 797, 800 (7th Cir. 2003). FRCP 11(b)(3) "requires the plaintiff (personally or through counsel) to establish evidentiary support, or at least a likelihood of obtaining that support, *before* filing suit in federal court." *See also* **Morris v. Wachovia Secs., Inc.**, 448 F.3d 268, 277 (4th Cir.2006).

Whitehead v. Food Max of Miss., Inc., 332 F.3d 796, 805 (5th Cir.2003). "It is true that, generally, district courts do not sanction attorneys who make nonfrivolous representations. [¶] [Under FRCP 11(b)(1), a] district court may sanction an attorney for presenting a paper to the court for '*any* improper purpose, *such as to harass*....' Although a district court is not to read an ulterior motive into a document 'well grounded in fact and law,' it may do so in exceptional cases, such as this, where the improper purpose is objectively ascertainable. *At 808:* District courts have an independent duty to maintain the integrity of the judicial process and may impose Rule 11 sanctions where necessary, regardless of whether state bar discipline is concurrent."

Byrne v. Nezhat, 261 F.3d 1075, 1117-18 (11th Cir. 2001). "A client may be sanctioned under Rule 11 even if the client did not sign the frivolous pleadings. Rule 11 does not permit sanctioning a client, however, when the basis for the sanction is that the pleading was legally frivolous. Typically, sanctions are levied against a client when he misrepresents facts in the pleadings."

Primus Auto. Fin. Servs. v. Batarse, 115 F.3d 644, 648 (9th Cir.1997). "Rule 11 imposes a duty on attorneys to certify that all pleadings are legally tenable and well-grounded in fact; it governs only papers filed with the court." *See also* **Legault v. Zambarano**, 105 F.3d 24, 27 (1st Cir.1997) (courts reluctant to characterize letters generally as "other paper" in weighing FRCP 11 sanctions); **Griffen v. City of Okla. City**, 3 F.3d 336, 339 (10th Cir.1993) (federal court cannot impose FRCP 11 sanctions against signer of paper filed in state court based solely on that paper's frivolousness).

FRCP 11(c) – Sanctions

Star Mark Mgmt. v. Koon Chun Hing Kee Soy & Sauce Factory, Ltd., 682 F.3d 170, 175 (2d Cir.2012). "The safe-harbor provision [of FRCP 11(c)] is a strict procedural requirement. An informal warning in the form of a letter without service of a separate Rule 11 motion is not sufficient to trigger the 21-day safe harbor period. *At 176:* [But] Rule 11(c)(2) requires only the service of '[a] motion' or '[t]he motion.' It does not require the service of a memorandum of law or affidavits, nor does it use the words 'formal fully supported motion.'"

PAE Gov't Servs. v. MPRI, Inc., 514 F.3d 856, 859 (9th Cir.2007). "The district court has no free-standing authority to strike pleadings simply because it believes that a party has taken inconsistent positions in the litigation. *At 860:* Unless there is a showing that the party acted in bad faith—a showing that can only be made after the party is given an opportunity to respond under

the procedures of Rule 11—inconsistent allegations are simply not a basis for striking the pleading."

Budget Rent-A-Car Sys. v. Consolidated Equity LLC, 428 F.3d 717, 718 (7th Cir.2005). "When an award of fees is permissive, denial is an appropriate sanction for requesting an award that is not merely excessive, but so exorbitant as to constitute an abuse of the process of the court asked to make the award."

In re Pennie & Edmonds LLP, 323 F.3d 86, 90 (2d Cir.2003). "The mental state applicable to liability for Rule 11 sanctions initiated by motion is objective unreasonableness, *i.e.*, liability may be imposed if the lawyer's claim to have evidentiary support is not objectively reasonable. That standard is appropriate in circumstances where the lawyer whose submission is challenged by motion has the opportunity, afforded by the 'safe harbor' provision, to correct or withdraw the challenged submission. [Appellant] contends that, because the 'safe harbor' protection does not exist when a lawyer's submission is challenged in a show cause proceeding initiated by a trial judge, the more rigorous standard of bad faith should apply. That position draws support from the Advisory Committee's expectation that court-initiated sanction proceedings will ordinarily be used only in situations that are 'akin to a contempt of court.'" *See also* ***Young v. City of Providence***, 404 F.3d 33, 39-40 (1st Cir.2005); ***United Nat'l Ins. v. R&D Latex Corp.***, 242 F.3d 1102, 1115-16 (9th Cir.2001).

Divane v. Krull Elec. Co., 319 F.3d 307, 314 (7th Cir.2003). "[I]f the court determines that an award of attorney's fees will serve the deterrent purpose of Rule 11, it has an obligation to award only those fees which directly resulted from the sanctionable conduct. This ensures that the proponent of a sanctionable position ultimately pays the cost resulting from it, serving a dual purpose of deterrence and restitution, while avoiding blanket fee-shifting, which would have the tendency to overcompensate the opponent and penalize the proponent."

FRCP 12. DEFENSES & OBJECTIONS: WHEN & HOW PRESENTED; MOTION FOR JUDGMENT ON THE PLEADINGS; CONSOLIDATING MOTIONS; WAIVING DEFENSES; PRETRIAL HEARING

(a) Time to Serve a Responsive Pleading.

(1) ***In General.*** Unless another time is specified by this rule or a federal statute, the time for serving a responsive pleading is as follows:

(A) A defendant must serve an answer:

(i) within 21 days after being served with the summons and complaint; or

(ii) if it has timely waived service under Rule 4(d), within 60 days after the request for a waiver was sent, or within 90 days after it was sent to the defendant outside any judicial district of the United States.

(B) A party must serve an answer to a counterclaim or crossclaim within 21 days after being served with the pleading that states the counterclaim or crossclaim.

(C) A party must serve a reply to an answer within 21 days after being served with an order to reply, unless the order specifies a different time.

(2) ***United States and Its Agencies, Officers, or Employees Sued in an Official Capacity.*** The United States, a United States agency, or a United States officer or employee sued only in an official capacity must serve an answer to a complaint, counterclaim, or crossclaim within 60 days after service on the United States attorney.

(3) ***United States Officers or Employees Sued in an Individual Capacity.*** A United States officer or employee sued in an individual capacity for an act or omission occurring in connection with duties performed on the United States' behalf must serve an answer to a complaint, counterclaim, or crossclaim within 60 days after service on the officer or employee or service on the United States attorney, whichever is later.

(4) ***Effect of a Motion.*** Unless the court sets a different time, serving a motion under this rule alters these periods as follows:

(A) if the court denies the motion or postpones its disposition until trial, the responsive pleading must be served within 14 days after notice of the court's action; or

(B) if the court grants a motion for a more definite statement, the responsive pleading must be served within 14 days after the more definite statement is served.

(b) How to Present Defenses. Every defense to a claim for relief in any pleading must be asserted in

the responsive pleading if one is required. But a party may assert the following defenses by motion:

(1) lack of subject-matter jurisdiction;
(2) lack of personal jurisdiction;
(3) improper venue;
(4) insufficient process;
(5) insufficient service of process;
(6) failure to state a claim upon which relief can be granted; and
(7) failure to join a party under Rule 19.

A motion asserting any of these defenses must be made before pleading if a responsive pleading is allowed. If a pleading sets out a claim for relief that does not require a responsive pleading, an opposing party may assert at trial any defense to that claim. No defense or objection is waived by joining it with one or more other defenses or objections in a responsive pleading or in a motion.

(c) Motion for Judgment on the Pleadings. After the pleadings are closed—but early enough not to delay trial—a party may move for judgment on the pleadings.

(d) Result of Presenting Matters Outside the Pleadings. If, on a motion under Rule 12(b)(6) or 12(c), matters outside the pleadings are presented to and not excluded by the court, the motion must be treated as one for summary judgment under Rule 56. All parties must be given a reasonable opportunity to present all the material that is pertinent to the motion.

(e) Motion for a More Definite Statement. A party may move for a more definite statement of a pleading to which a responsive pleading is allowed but which is so vague or ambiguous that the party cannot reasonably prepare a response. The motion must be made before filing a responsive pleading and must point out the defects complained of and the details desired. If the court orders a more definite statement and the order is not obeyed within 14 days after notice of the order or within the time the court sets, the court may strike the pleading or issue any other appropriate order.

(f) Motion to Strike. The court may strike from a pleading an insufficient defense or any redundant, immaterial, impertinent, or scandalous matter. The court may act:

(1) on its own; or
(2) on motion made by a party either before responding to the pleading or, if a response is not allowed, within 21 days after being served with the pleading.

(g) Joining Motions.

(1) ***Right to Join.*** A motion under this rule may be joined with any other motion allowed by this rule.

(2) ***Limitation on Further Motions.*** Except as provided in Rule 12(h)(2) or (3), a party that makes a motion under this rule must not make another motion under this rule raising a defense or objection that was available to the party but omitted from its earlier motion.

(h) Waiving and Preserving Certain Defenses.

(1) ***When Some Are Waived.*** A party waives any defense listed in Rule 12(b)(2)-(5) by:

(A) omitting it from a motion in the circumstances described in Rule 12(g)(2); or
(B) failing to either:
(i) make it by motion under this rule; or
(ii) include it in a responsive pleading or in an amendment allowed by Rule 15(a)(1) as a matter of course.

(2) ***When to Raise Others.*** Failure to state a claim upon which relief can be granted, to join a person required by Rule 19(b), or to state a legal defense to a claim may be raised:

(A) in any pleading allowed or ordered under Rule 7(a);
(B) by a motion under Rule 12(c); or
(C) at trial.

(3) ***Lack of Subject-Matter Jurisdiction.*** If the court determines at any time that it lacks subject-matter jurisdiction, the court must dismiss the action.

(i) Hearing Before Trial. If a party so moves, any defense listed in Rule 12(b)(1)-(7)—whether made in a pleading or by motion—and a motion under Rule 12(c) must be heard and decided before trial unless the court orders a deferral until trial.

See selected Notes of Advisory Committee to FRCP 12, p. 1156.

History of FRCP 12: Adopted Dec. 20, 1937, eff. Sept. 16, 1938. Amended Dec. 27, 1946, eff. Mar. 19, 1948; Jan. 21, 1963, eff. July 1, 1963; Feb. 28, 1966, eff. July 1, 1966; Mar. 2, 1987, eff. Aug. 1, 1987; Apr. 22, 1993, eff. Dec. 1, 1993; Apr. 17, 2000, eff. Dec. 1, 2000; Apr. 30, 2007, eff. Dec. 1, 2007; Mar. 26, 2009, eff. Dec. 1, 2009.

See ***Commentaries***, "Defendant's Responses & Pleadings," ch. 3, p. 167; ***O'Connor's Federal Civil Forms*** (2012), FORMS 3B-3D; 3F-3I; 3L.

See also 28 U.S.C. §1406 (curing and waiving venue defects).

ANNOTATIONS

Answer

Beller & Keller v. Tyler, 120 F.3d 21, 25-26 (2d Cir. 1997). "[A] defendant [must] file an answer [after receipt of the summons and within the specified time of FRCP 12(a)] unless a federal statute provides otherwise. This is so even if, as permitted by [FRCP] 4(e), the defendant is served pursuant to a state law method of service and the state law provides a longer time in which to answer."

FRCP 12(b) Defenses

Hemispherx Biopharma, Inc. v. Johannesburg Consol. Invs., 553 F.3d 1351, 1360 (11th Cir.2008). "The question [is] did [D's] objection to personal jurisdiction properly raise a challenge to the sufficiency of service of process? [We] hold that objecting to personal jurisdiction is not sufficient to raise an objection to service of process under Rule 12. [¶] Lack of personal jurisdiction, Rule 12(b)(2), and insufficiency of service of process, Rule 12(b)(5), are listed as separate defenses under Rule 12. [A] litigant must cite each separate Rule 12(b) defense in the pre-answer motion or if no pre-answer motion is filed, then in the responsive pleading. Citing one Rule 12(b) defense in the hope that it will sufficiently raise another defense is not permissible."

Schnabel v. Lui, 302 F.3d 1023, 1034 (9th Cir.2002). "[W]hen any motion is brought under Rule 12, all Rule 12 defenses must be raised in the motion, unless exempt from waiver under Rule 12(h)(2). [¶] Despite the policy concerns underlying the waiver provisions of Rule 12, nothing in the rule requires codefendants represented by the same counsel to raise or waive all their defenses together."

FRCP 12(b)(1)

Caterpillar Inc. v. Lewis, 519 U.S. 61, 76-77 (1996). "Despite a federal trial court's threshold denial of a motion to remand, if, at the end of the day and case, a *jurisdictional* defect remains uncured, the judgment must be vacated."

Holloway v. Pagan River Dockside Seafood, Inc., 669 F.3d 448, 452 (4th Cir.2012). An FRCP "12(b)(1) motion addresses whether [P] has a right to be in the district court at all and whether the court has the power to hear and dispose of his claim, and [an FRCP] 12(b)(6) motion addresses whether [P] has stated a cognizable claim, a challenge to the sufficiency of the complaint. [¶] [T]he subject matter jurisdiction of a federal court is not generally resolved by concluding that the plaintiff has failed to allege an element of a federal cause of action or that the plaintiff might not be able to prove an element of a federal cause of action. Rather, a court must look more fundamentally at whether the plaintiff's claim is determined by application of a federal law over which Congress has given the federal courts jurisdiction. If it is, his complaint should not be dismissed for a lack of subject matter jurisdiction.... [¶] Deficiencies in the statement of a federal cause of action should normally be addressed by a motion under rules challenging the sufficiency of the complaint or the evidence pleaded to support the complaint, such as authorized by [FRCPs] 12(b)(6), 12(c), or 56."

Michigan S. R.R. v. Branch & St. Joseph Cty. Rail Users Ass'n, 287 F.3d 568, 573 (6th Cir.2002). "Lack of subject-matter jurisdiction is an affirmative defense that a defendant may assert in a motion to dismiss. Where subject-matter jurisdiction is challenged pursuant to [FRCP] 12(b)(1), the plaintiff has the burden of proving jurisdiction in order to survive the motion. Specifically, the plaintiff must show that the complaint alleges a claim under federal law, and that the claim is 'substantial.' The plaintiff will survive the motion to dismiss by showing any arguable basis in law for the claims set forth in the complaint." (Internal quotes omitted.)

Nowak v. Ironworkers Local 6 Pension Fund, 81 F.3d 1182, 1188 (2d Cir.1996). "[T]here are two important characteristics of a dismissal based on lack of subject-matter jurisdiction that can have a great impact on the disposition of a case. First, because a dismissal pursuant to Rule 12(b)(1) is not on the merits, it can have no *res judicata* effect. Second, ... a dismissal pursuant to Rule 12(b)(1) precludes a district court from exercising supplemental jurisdiction over related state claims."

FRCP 12(b)(2)

Conn v. Zakharov, 667 F.3d 705, 711 (6th Cir. 2012). "[W]here ... the defendant has moved to dismiss the case under Rule 12(b)(2) for lack of personal jurisdiction and the district court rules on the motion without an evidentiary hearing, the plaintiff need only make a 'prima facie' case that the court has personal jurisdiction. [But] where ... 'the plaintiff has received all of the discovery it sought with respect to personal ju-

risdiction and there does not appear to be any real dispute over the facts relating to jurisdiction,' the prima facie 'proposition loses some of its significance.'" *See also* ***Felch v. Transportes Lar-Mex SA de CV***, 92 F.3d 320, 326 (5th Cir.1996).

McGinnis v. Ingram Equip. Co., 918 F.2d 1491, 1494 (11th Cir.1990). "Where the 'defendant's challenge to the court's jurisdiction is also a challenge to the existence of a federal cause of action, the proper course of action for the district court ... is to find that jurisdiction exists and deal with the objection as a direct attack on the merits of the plaintiff's case.'"

FRCP 12(b)(3)

Hillis v. Heineman, 626 F.3d 1014, 1017 (9th Cir. 2010). "[Ps] contend that [Ds] waived any 12(b)(3) defense of improper venue by filing counterclaims and a third-party complaint. But there is nothing in the language of these rules to support such a position. Only the most compelling of reasons will persuade us to imply an exception where the statutory text does not supply one. *At 1018:* We hold that the filing of a counterclaim, permissive or otherwise, [or a third-party complaint,] does not constitute a waiver of a defense of improper venue asserted in an answer."

FRCP 12(b)(4)

Chan v. Society Expeditions, Inc., 39 F.3d 1398, 1404 (9th Cir.1994). FRCP 4 "is a flexible rule that should be liberally construed to uphold service so long as a party receives sufficient notice of the complaint. Technical defects in a summons do not justify dismissal unless a party is able to demonstrate actual prejudice."

FRCP 12(b)(6)

Ashcroft v. Iqbal, 556 U.S. 662, 678-79 (2009). See annotation under FRCP 8, p. 848.

Jones v. Bock, 549 U.S. 199, 215 (2007). "If the allegations ... show that relief is barred by the applicable statute of limitations, the complaint is subject to dismissal for failure to state a claim; that does not make the statute of limitations any less an affirmative defense.... Whether a particular ground for opposing a claim may be the basis for dismissal for failure to state a claim depends on whether the allegations in the complaint suffice to establish that ground, not on the nature of the ground in the abstract."

Arbaugh v. Y&H Corp., 546 U.S. 500, 507 (2006). "[T]he objection that a complaint 'fail[s] to state a claim upon which relief can be granted' ... may not be asserted post trial."

Richards v. Mitcheff, ___ F.3d ___ (7th Cir.2012) (No. 11-3227; 8-9-12). See annotation under *FRCP 12(c)*, p. 859.

Holloway v. Pagan River Dockside Seafood, Inc., 669 F.3d 448, 452 (4th Cir.2012). See annotation under *FRCP 12(b)(1)*, p. 857.

ClearOne Comms. v. Biamp Sys., 653 F.3d 1163, 1171 (10th Cir.2011). "We have not previously addressed whether a defendant may appeal the denial of a motion to dismiss for failure to state a claim after the plaintiff has successfully prevailed at trial on the claim at issue. *At 1172:* [T]he Fifth Circuit ... has held that a defendant may not [make such an appeal]. [T]he Fifth Circuit concluded that '[w]hen a plaintiff has prevailed after a full trial on the merits, a district court's denial of a [motion to dismiss] becomes moot.' This is because ... '[a]fter a trial on the merits, the sufficiency of the allegations in the complaint is irrelevant': the plaintiff 'has proved, not merely alleged, facts sufficient to support relief.' [¶] We are persuaded by the Fifth Circuit's reasoning and hold that, as a general rule, a defendant may not, after a plaintiff has prevailed at trial, appeal from the pretrial denial of a Rule 12(b)(6) motion to dismiss, but must instead challenge the legal sufficiency of the plaintiff's claim through a motion for judgment as a matter of law."

Travelers Indem. Co. v. Dammann & Co., 594 F.3d 238, 256 n.14 (3d Cir.2010). "'[I]f a complaint is vulnerable to [an FRCP] 12(b)(6) dismissal, a district court must permit a curative amendment, unless an amendment would be inequitable or futile.' That rule applies 'even if the plaintiff does not seek leave to amend.'"

Thompson v. Drug Enforcement Admin., 492 F.3d 428, 438 (D.C.Cir.2007). "Courts frequently treat failure to exhaust as an affirmative defense.... But if a particular statute requires the plaintiff to plead exhaustion and the plaintiff fails to do so, the court may dismiss the complaint on a Rule 12(b)(6) motion. Further, even when failure to exhaust is treated as an affirmative defense, it may be invoked in a Rule 12(b)(6) motion if the complaint somehow reveals the exhaustion defense on its face." *See also* ***Cottone v. Jenne***, 326 F.3d 1352, 1357 (11th Cir.2003).

American United Life Ins. v. Martinez, 480 F.3d 1043, 1057 (11th Cir.2007). "[T]his Court has prohibited *sua sponte* dismissals under [FRCP] 12(b)(6) where: (1) the defendant had not filed an answer and

the plaintiff still had a right to amend his complaint pursuant to [FRCP] 15(a); (2) the plaintiff brought his claim in good faith; and (3) the district court failed to provide the plaintiff with notice of its intent to dismiss or an opportunity to respond." *See also* ***Phelps v. U.S. Bur. of Prisons***, 62 F.3d 1020, 1022 (8th Cir.1995) (court should dismiss sua sponte only after service of process).

Mercado v. Ritz-Carlton San Juan Hotel, Spa & Casino, 410 F.3d 41, 48 n.9 (1st Cir.2005). "Although a court's consideration of materials outside the pleadings typically converts a motion to dismiss into one for summary judgment, … an affirmative defense may be adjudicated on a motion to dismiss for failure to state a claim in an appropriate case…." (Internal quotes omitted.)

Elvig v. Calvin Presbyterian Ch., 375 F.3d 951, 954 (9th Cir.2004). "A Rule 12(b)(6) motion must be made *before* the responsive pleading. [Ds] filed their motion to dismiss *after* filing their answer. Thus, the motion should have been treated as a motion for judgment on the pleadings, pursuant to Rule 12(c) or 12(h)(2)." *See also* ***Jacobsen v. Deseret Book Co.***, 287 F.3d 936, 941 n.2 (10th Cir.2002).

Memphis, Tenn. Area Local, Am. Postal Workers Un. v. City of Memphis, 361 F.3d 898, 904 (6th Cir. 2004). "A complaint need not anticipate every defense and accordingly need not plead every response to a potential defense."

U.S. v. Lockheed Martin Eng'g & Sci. Servs., 336 F.3d 346, 350 (5th Cir.2003). "'[T]he questions of subject-matter jurisdiction and the merits will normally be considered intertwined where the statute provides both the basis of federal court subject-matter jurisdiction and the cause of action[, and those challenges should be resolved under FRCP 12(b)(6) or 56].'" *See also* ***U.S. v. Consumer Ins.***, 318 F.3d 1199, 1203 (10th Cir.2003).

Official Cmte. of the Unsecured Creditors of Color Tile, Inc. v. Coopers & Lybrand, L.L.P., 322 F.3d 147, 158 (2d Cir.2003). "A court's task in ruling on a Rule 12(b)(6) motion is merely to assess the legal feasibility of the complaint, not to assay the weight of the evidence which might be offered in support thereof." (Internal quotes omitted.)

FRCP 12(b)(7)

University of Pittsburgh v. Varian Med. Sys., 569 F.3d 1328, 1332 (Fed.Cir.2009). "[D]ismissal for failure to join a party is not an adjudication on the merits, and thus, should not have preclusive effect—i.e. such a dismissal should be without prejudice."

FRCP 12(c)

Richards v. Mitcheff, ___ F.3d ___ (7th Cir.2012) (No. 11-3227; 8-9-12). "[B]ecause complaints need not anticipate defenses, [FRCP] 12(b)(6) is not designed for motions under [FRCP] 8(c)(1). [¶] A plaintiff whose allegations show that there is an airtight defense has pleaded himself out of court, and the judge may dismiss the suit on the pleadings under Rule 12(c). This comes to the same thing as a dismissal under Rule 12(b)(6), and opinions … often use the two interchangeably. But in principle a complaint that alleges an impenetrable defense to what would otherwise be a good claim should be dismissed … under Rule 12(c), not Rule 12(b)(6). After all, the defendants may waive or forfeit their defense, and then the case should proceed."

Grajales v. Puerto Rico Ports Auth., 682 F.3d 40, 45-46 (1st Cir.2012). "Under ordinary circumstances, a court may measure the plausibility of a complaint by means of a motion for judgment on the pleadings. [But an] obvious anomaly arises [when the plausibility standard is applied after substantial discovery has taken place] because a court attempting to determine whether a complaint should be dismissed for implausibility must decide, on the basis of the complaint alone, if the complaint lacks enough factual content to allow a 'reasonable inference that the defendant is liable for the misconduct alleged.' This is, by its nature, a threshold inquiry, and logic strongly suggests that it occur prior to discovery. Ignoring the entire panoply of facts developed during discovery makes little sense. [¶] An artificial evaluation of this sort seems especially awkward because one of the main goals of the plausibility standard is the avoidance of unnecessary discovery. [Thus,] once the parties have invested substantial resources in discovery, a district court should hesitate to entertain a Rule 12(c) motion that asserts a complaint's failure to satisfy the plausibility requirement."

Ackerson v. Bean Dredging LLC, 589 F.3d 196, 209 (5th Cir.2009). "'A motion for judgment on the pleadings under Rule 12(c) is subject to the same standard as a motion to dismiss under Rule 12(b)(6).' Thus, the 'inquiry focuses on the allegations in the pleadings' and not on whether the 'plaintiff actually has sufficient evidence to succeed on the merits.'" *See also* ***HDC, LLC v. City of Ann Arbor***, 675 F.3d 608, 611 (6th Cir.2012)

(pleading requirements under ***Twombly*** and ***Iqbal*** apply to FRCP 12(c) motions).

SEC v. Wolfson, 539 F.3d 1249, 1264 (10th Cir. 2008). "Although a motion for judgment of the pleadings can be filed at any time before trial, nothing in the language of [FRCP 12(c)] implies that the motion must be disposed of prior to other pending motions, including a motion for summary judgment. Moreover, when a motion for judgment on the pleadings is filed and 'matters outside the pleadings are presented to and not excluded by the court, the motion *must* be treated as one for summary judgment and disposed of as provided in [FRCP] 56.'"

FRCP 12(d)

Harper v. Lawrence Cty., 592 F.3d 1227, 1232 (11th Cir.2010). "A judge need not convert a motion to dismiss into a motion for summary judgment as long as ... she does not consider matters outside the pleadings. According to case law, 'not considering' such matters is the functional equivalent of 'excluding' them—there is no more formal step required."

Sahu v. Union Carbide Corp., 548 F.3d 59, 67 (2d Cir.2008). "When a district court converts a motion to dismiss into one for summary judgment, '[a]ll parties must be given a reasonable opportunity to present all the material that is pertinent to the motion.' Ordinarily, this means that a district court 'must give notice to the parties *before* converting a motion to dismiss pursuant to Rule 12(b)(6) into one for summary judgment and considering matters outside the pleading.'"

FRCP 12(e)

Casanova v. Ulibarri, 595 F.3d 1120, 1125 (10th Cir.2010). "It may be tempting to dismiss a complaint that fails to provide specific dates when their inclusion could show that the complaint should be dismissed.... But inclusion of a specific date may not be necessary to state a claim if the complaint alleges sufficient detail about an event to identify it. [¶] [T]he preferable procedure when a specific date could support a dispositive defense motion is to require the plaintiff to provide a more definite statement under [FRCP] 12(e)."

Thomas v. Independence Township, 463 F.3d 285, 301 (3d Cir.2006). "When presented with an appropriate Rule 12(e) motion for a more definite statement, the district court shall grant the motion and demand more specific factual allegations from the plaintiff concerning the conduct underlying the claims for relief. Even when a defendant has not formally expressed the need for a definite statement, the district court has the discretion to order a more definite statement...."

FRCP 12(h)

Arbaugh v. Y&H Corp., 546 U.S. 500, 506 (2006). "The objection that a federal court lacks subject-matter jurisdiction ... may be raised by a party, or by a court on its own initiative, at any stage in litigation, even after trial and the entry of judgment."

Friends of the Earth, Inc. v. Gaston Copper Recycling Corp., 629 F.3d 387, 400 (4th Cir.2011). The issue "is whether [D] raised its defense 'at trial.' [¶] [W]hile authority is sparse as to what constitutes presenting a defense 'at' the trial, it would appear that the defense must be presented so that the court may consider whether there has been a failure to state a claim before disposition on the merits. [¶] [A]lthough [D's] challenge ... was raised about two years after the district court had concluded hearing evidence in the case, [D] nevertheless made [the] argument before the district court disposed of the merits of [Ps'] complaint. Therefore, [D] adequately preserved [the defense] under the requirement of Rule 12(h)(2) that challenges to the legal sufficiency of a claim must be raised 'at trial,' if not before." (Internal quotes omitted.)

FRCP 13. COUNTERCLAIM & CROSSCLAIM

(a) Compulsory Counterclaim.

(1) ***In General.*** A pleading must state as a counterclaim any claim that—at the time of its service—the pleader has against an opposing party if the claim:

(A) arises out of the transaction or occurrence that is the subject matter of the opposing party's claim; and

(B) does not require adding another party over whom the court cannot acquire jurisdiction.

(2) ***Exceptions.*** The pleader need not state the claim if:

(A) when the action was commenced, the claim was the subject of another pending action; or

(B) the opposing party sued on its claim by attachment or other process that did not establish personal jurisdiction over the pleader on that claim, and the pleader does not assert any counterclaim under this rule.

(b) Permissive Counterclaim. A pleading may state as a counterclaim against an opposing party any claim that is not compulsory.

(c) Relief Sought in a Counterclaim. A counterclaim need not diminish or defeat the recovery sought by the opposing party. It may request relief that exceeds in amount or differs in kind from the relief sought by the opposing party.

(d) Counterclaim Against the United States. These rules do not expand the right to assert a counterclaim—or to claim a credit—against the United States or a United States officer or agency.

(e) Counterclaim Maturing or Acquired After Pleading. The court may permit a party to file a supplemental pleading asserting a counterclaim that matured or was acquired by the party after serving an earlier pleading.

(f) [Abrogated.]

(g) Crossclaim Against a Coparty. A pleading may state as a crossclaim any claim by one party against a coparty if the claim arises out of the transaction or occurrence that is the subject matter of the original action or of a counterclaim, or if the claim relates to any property that is the subject matter of the original action. The crossclaim may include a claim that the coparty is or may be liable to the crossclaimant for all or part of a claim asserted in the action against the crossclaimant.

(h) Joining Additional Parties. Rules 19 and 20 govern the addition of a person as a party to a counterclaim or crossclaim.

(i) Separate Trials; Separate Judgments. If the court orders separate trials under Rule 42(b), it may enter judgment on a counterclaim or crossclaim under Rule 54(b) when it has jurisdiction to do so, even if the opposing party's claims have been dismissed or otherwise resolved.

See selected Notes of Advisory Committee to FRCP 13, p. 1156.

History of FRCP 13: Adopted Dec. 20, 1937, eff. Sept. 16, 1938. Amended Dec. 27, 1946, eff. Mar. 19, 1948; Jan. 21, 1963, eff. July 1, 1963; Feb. 28, 1966, eff. July 1, 1966; Mar. 2, 1987, eff. Aug. 1, 1987; Apr. 30, 2007, eff. Dec. 1, 2007; Mar. 26, 2009, eff. Dec. 1, 2009.

See ***Commentaries***, "Defendant's Claims," ch. 3-L, §5, p. 235; ***O'Connor's Federal Civil Forms*** (2012), FORMS 3L.

ANNOTATIONS

Southern Constr. Co. v. Pickard, 371 U.S. 57, 60 (1962). FRCP 13(a) "was designed to prevent multiplicity of actions and to achieve resolution in a single lawsuit of all disputes arising out of common matters. The Rule was particularly directed against [a party] who failed to assert a counterclaim in one action and then instituted a second action in which that counterclaim became the basis of the complaint." *See also* ***Handy v. Shaw, Bransford, Veilleux & Roth***, 325 F.3d 346, 350 (D.C.Cir.2003).

Nasalok Coating Corp. v. Nylok Corp., 522 F.3d 1320, 1325-26 (Fed.Cir.2008). Courts have "utilized three tests to determine whether the 'transaction or occurrence' test of Rule 13(a) is met: (1) whether the legal and factual issues raised by the claim and counterclaim are largely the same; (2) whether substantially the same evidence supports or refutes both the claim and the counterclaim; and (3) whether there is a logical relationship between the claim and the counterclaim. In each of the three tests for what constitutes the same 'transaction or occurrence,' the question is the extent of factual overlap between what the plaintiff *must* establish to prove its claim and what the defendant *must* establish to prove its counterclaim. The mere possibility that, as a result of affirmative defenses, the first suit might involve additional issues does not obligate the defendant to assert those affirmative defenses as a counterclaim." *See also* ***Driver Music Co. v. Commercial Un. Ins.***, 94 F.3d 1428, 1435 (10th Cir.1996).

Allan Block Corp. v. County Materials Corp., 512 F.3d 912, 915 (7th Cir.2008). "Failing to file a compulsory counterclaim does normally preclude its being made the subject of another lawsuit. The doctrine of res judicata bars a person from splitting his claim between two suits.... *At 916:* But there is an exception to res judicata for cases in which the only relief sought in the first suit is a declaratory judgment. *At 917:* To invoke Rule 13(a) as a bar to basing a suit on a claim that might be thought a compulsory counterclaim in a declaratory judgment action would bring about what refusing to apply res judicata to defendants in such actions is designed to prevent: forcing the defendant's claims to be litigated as counterclaims in such an action."

Valley Disposal Inc. v. Central Vt. Solid Waste Mgmt. Dist., 113 F.3d 357, 364 (2d Cir.1997). "The provision in [FRCP 13(a)] for '[c]ompulsory' counterclaims does not mean that a defendant is compelled to assert the claim and cannot waive it. It means merely

that if the claim is one that is within the scope of Rule 13(a) and is not asserted as a counterclaim, its assertion in a later action will be vulnerable to a defense of estoppel."

FRCP 14. THIRD-PARTY PRACTICE

(a) When a Defending Party May Bring in a Third Party.

(1) ***Timing of the Summons and Complaint.*** A defending party may, as third-party plaintiff, serve a summons and complaint on a nonparty who is or may be liable to it for all or part of the claim against it. But the third-party plaintiff must, by motion, obtain the court's leave if it files the third-party complaint more than 14 days after serving its original answer.

(2) ***Third-Party Defendant's Claims and Defenses.*** The person served with the summons and third-party complaint—the "third-party defendant":

(A) must assert any defense against the third-party plaintiff's claim under Rule 12;

(B) must assert any counterclaim against the third-party plaintiff under Rule 13(a), and may assert any counterclaim against the third-party plaintiff under Rule 13(b) or any crossclaim against another third-party defendant under Rule 13(g);

(C) may assert against the plaintiff any defense that the third-party plaintiff has to the plaintiff's claim; and

(D) may also assert against the plaintiff any claim arising out of the transaction or occurrence that is the subject matter of the plaintiff's claim against the third-party plaintiff.

(3) ***Plaintiff's Claims Against a Third-Party Defendant.*** The plaintiff may assert against the third-party defendant any claim arising out of the transaction or occurrence that is the subject matter of the plaintiff's claim against the third-party plaintiff. The third-party defendant must then assert any defense under Rule 12 and any counterclaim under Rule 13(a), and may assert any counterclaim under Rule 13(b) or any crossclaim under Rule 13(g).

(4) ***Motion to Strike, Sever, or Try Separately.*** Any party may move to strike the third-party claim, to sever it, or to try it separately.

(5) ***Third-Party Defendant's Claim Against a Nonparty.*** A third-party defendant may proceed under this rule against a nonparty who is or may be liable to the third-party defendant for all or part of any claim against it.

(6) ***Third-Party Complaint In Rem.*** If it is within the admiralty or maritime jurisdiction, a third-party complaint may be in rem. In that event, a reference in this rule to the "summons" includes the warrant of arrest, and a reference to the defendant or third-party plaintiff includes, when appropriate, a person who asserts a right under Supplemental Rule C(6)(a)(i) in the property arrested.

(b) When a Plaintiff May Bring in a Third Party. When a claim is asserted against a plaintiff, the plaintiff may bring in a third party if this rule would allow a defendant to do so.

(c) Admiralty or Maritime Claim.

(1) ***Scope of Impleader.*** If a plaintiff asserts an admiralty or maritime claim under Rule 9(h), the defendant or a person who asserts a right under Supplemental Rule C(6)(a)(i) may, as a third-party plaintiff, bring in a third-party defendant who may be wholly or partly liable—either to the plaintiff or to the third-party plaintiff—for remedy over, contribution, or otherwise on account of the same transaction, occurrence, or series of transactions or occurrences.

(2) ***Defending Against a Demand for Judgment for the Plaintiff.*** The third-party plaintiff may demand judgment in the plaintiff's favor against the third-party defendant. In that event, the third-party defendant must defend under Rule 12 against the plaintiff's claim as well as the third-party plaintiff's claim; and the action proceeds as if the plaintiff had sued both the third-party defendant and the third-party plaintiff.

See selected Notes of Advisory Committee to FRCP 14, p. 1156.

History of FRCP 14: Adopted Dec. 20, 1937, eff. Sept. 16, 1938. Amended Dec. 27, 1946, eff. Mar. 19, 1948; Jan. 21, 1963, eff. July 1, 1963; Feb. 28, 1966, eff. July 1, 1966; Mar. 2, 1987, eff. Aug. 1, 1987; Apr. 17, 2000, eff. Dec. 1, 2000; Apr. 30, 2007, eff. Dec. 1, 2007; Mar. 26, 2009, eff. Dec. 1, 2009.

See ***Commentaries***, "Defendant's Claims," ch. 3-L, §5, p. 235; ***O'Connor's Federal Civil Forms*** (2012), FORMS 3L.

ANNOTATIONS

Discovery Grp. v. Chapel Dev., LLC, 574 F.3d 986, 989 n.* (8th Cir.2009). Third-party Ps' cause of action "was not premature, even though it had not yet accrued when their third-party complaint was filed. [FRCP] 14 allows a defendant to implead another party 'who is or may be liable' to the defendant for all or part of the plaintiff's claim. The words 'may be liable' mean that defendant is permitted to join someone against whom a cause of action has not yet accrued, provided that the claim is contingent upon the success of plaintiff's action and will accrue when defendant's liability is determined or plaintiff's claim is satisfied." (Internal quotes omitted.)

Frank's Casing Crew & Rental Tools, Inc. v. PMR Techs., 292 F.3d 1363, 1372 (Fed.Cir.2002). "[D] urges that the defense of lack of personal jurisdiction is not waived when a party brings a third party into an existing lawsuit. [But] that principle is limited to situations in which the [FRCPs] authorize the joining of an additional claim, for example, where there is a compulsory counterclaim arising out of the same transaction or occurrence; where an unrelated claim is brought as a permissive counterclaim against the plaintiff; or where a third-party complaint arising out of the same transaction or occurrence is brought against a third-party. Where, as here, a defendant seeks to bring into the action new claims against new parties, not arising out of the same transaction or occurrence, such action is not authorized by the joinder rules, and we think that such an attempted joinder constitutes a waiver as to [defenses] then pending in the action against the party seeking to add the additional claims." *See also* ***FDIC v. Bathgate***, 27 F.3d 850, 873 (3d Cir.1994); ***King Fisher Mar. Serv. v. 21st Phoenix Corp.***, 893 F.2d 1155, 1158 n.1 (10th Cir.1990).

Thomas v. Barton Lodge II, Ltd., 174 F.3d 636, 652 (5th Cir.1999). "Under rule 14(a), third party defendants can join additional parties to the lawsuit to resolve claims related to the claim made against them. It therefore seems strange to conclude that they cannot bring those claims against parties already involved in the suit. The practical effect of adhering to [D's] reasoning would be to hold that when a third party defendant wishes to allege a claim against an original defendant, he must file a separate complaint against the original defendant and then move for joinder of the two actions. We will not require third party defendants to jump through these additional hoops. [U]nder Rule 14(a), a third party defendant may file a cross-claim against an original defendant even if it would be inappropriate to characterize the third party defendant as a co-defendant of the original defendant."

Fernandez v. Corporacion Insular de Seguros, 79 F.3d 207, 210 (1st Cir.1996). "[T]hough [FRCP] 14(a) *permits* defendants to implead a joint tortfeasor, ... Rule 14 is not mandatory. [Ps] do not cite, nor have we found, any authority for the proposition that a jury must be permitted to draw an adverse inference from a defendant's decision to forego a Rule 14 impleader."

Kansas Pub. Empls. Ret. Sys. v. Reimer & Koger Assocs., 4 F.3d 614, 619-20 (8th Cir.1993). "Under ... the [FRCPs], a 'third-party defendant may assert against the plaintiff any defenses which the third-party plaintiff has to the plaintiff's claim.' Because a third-party defendant cannot relitigate the question of a third-party plaintiff's liability to the original plaintiff, this provision protects the third-party defendant against any prejudice that might result from the third-party plaintiff's failure to assert a particular defense against the original plaintiff."

FRCP 15. AMENDED & SUPPLEMENTAL PLEADINGS

(a) Amendments Before Trial.

(1) ***Amending as a Matter of Course.*** A party may amend its pleading once as a matter of course within:

(A) 21 days after serving it, or

(B) if the pleading is one to which a responsive pleading is required, 21 days after service of a responsive pleading or 21 days after service of a motion under Rule 12(b), (e), or (f), whichever is earlier.

(2) ***Other Amendments.*** In all other cases, a party may amend its pleading only with the opposing party's written consent or the court's leave. The court should freely give leave when justice so requires.

(3) ***Time to Respond.*** Unless the court orders otherwise, any required response to an amended pleading must be made within the time remaining to respond to the original pleading or within 14 days after service of the amended pleading, whichever is later.

(b) Amendments During and After Trial.

(1) ***Based on an Objection at Trial.*** If, at trial, a party objects that evidence is not within the issues raised in the pleadings, the court may permit the pleadings to be amended. The court should freely permit an amendment when doing so will aid in presenting the merits and the objecting party fails to satisfy the court that the evidence would prejudice that party's action or defense on the merits. The court may grant a continuance to enable the objecting party to meet the evidence.

(2) ***For Issues Tried by Consent.*** When an issue not raised by the pleadings is tried by the parties' express or implied consent, it must be treated in all respects as if raised in the pleadings. A party may move—at any time, even after judgment—to amend the pleadings to conform them to the evidence and to raise an unpleaded issue. But failure to amend does not affect the result of the trial of that issue.

(c) Relation Back of Amendments.

(1) ***When an Amendment Relates Back.*** An amendment to a pleading relates back to the date of the original pleading when:

(A) the law that provides the applicable statute of limitations allows relation back;

(B) the amendment asserts a claim or defense that arose out of the conduct, transaction, or occurrence set out—or attempted to be set out—in the original pleading; or

(C) the amendment changes the party or the naming of the party against whom a claim is asserted, if Rule 15(c)(1)(B) is satisfied and if, within the period provided by Rule 4(m) for serving the summons and complaint, the party to be brought in by amendment:

(i) received such notice of the action that it will not be prejudiced in defending on the merits; and

(ii) knew or should have known that the action would have been brought against it, but for a mistake concerning the proper party's identity.

(2) ***Notice to the United States.*** When the United States or a United States officer or agency is added as a defendant by amendment, the notice requirements of Rule 15(c)(1)(C)(i) and (ii) are satisfied if, during the stated period, process was delivered or mailed to the United States attorney or the United States attorney's designee, to the Attorney General of the United States, or to the officer or agency.

(d) Supplemental Pleadings. On motion and reasonable notice, the court may, on just terms, permit a party to serve a supplemental pleading setting out any transaction, occurrence, or event that happened after the date of the pleading to be supplemented. The court may permit supplementation even though the original pleading is defective in stating a claim or defense. The court may order that the opposing party plead to the supplemental pleading within a specified time.

See selected Notes of Advisory Committee to FRCP 15, p. 1157.

History of FRCP 15: Adopted Dec. 20, 1937, eff. Sept. 16, 1938. Amended Jan. 21, 1963, eff. July 1, 1963; Feb. 28, 1966, eff. July 1, 1966; Mar. 2, 1987, eff. Aug. 1, 1987; Apr. 30, 1991, eff. Dec. 1, 1991; Dec. 9, 1991, P.L. 102-198, §11(a), 105 Stat. 1626; Apr. 22, 1993, eff. Dec. 1, 1993; Apr. 30, 2007, eff. Dec. 1, 2007; Mar. 26, 2009, eff. Dec. 1, 2009.

See ***Commentaries***, "Amending & supplementing pleadings," ch. 1-B, §2.2, p. 12; "Motion to Amend or Supplement Pleadings—Pretrial," ch. 5-I, p. 345; "Motion to Amend Pleadings—Trial & Post-trial," ch. 8-F, p. 710; ***O'Connor's Federal Civil Forms*** (2012), FORMS 5I; FORMS 8F.

See also 28 U.S.C. §1653 (amending to cure jurisdictional defects).

ANNOTATIONS

FRCP 15(a)

Foman v. Davis, 371 U.S. 178, 182 (1962). "If the underlying facts or circumstances relied upon by a plaintiff may be a proper subject of relief, he ought to be afforded an opportunity to test his claim on the merits. [Unless there is a] reason—such as undue delay, bad faith or dilatory motive on the part of the movant, repeated failure to cure deficiencies by amendments previously allowed, undue prejudice to the opposing party by virtue of allowance of the amendment, futility of amendment, etc.—the leave sought should, as the rules require, be 'freely given.' Of course, the grant or denial of an opportunity to amend is within the discretion of the District Court, but outright refusal to grant the leave without any justifying reason … is not an exercise of discretion; it is merely abuse of that discretion and inconsistent with the spirit of the [FRCPs]." *See also* ***Zucco Partners v. Digimarc Corp.***, 552 F.3d 981, 1007 (9th Cir.2009) (court has particularly broad discretion to deny leave to amend if P has previously been granted leave and failed to add required particularity to its claim); ***Bediako v. Stein Mart, Inc.***, 354 F.3d 835,

841 (8th Cir.2004) (there must be more than delay alone to deny motion to amend; there must also be prejudice to nonmovant).

Leisure Caviar, LLC v. U.S. Fish & Wildlife Serv., 616 F.3d 612, 615-16 (6th Cir.2010). "[T]his is not a traditional motion to amend the complaint. [FRCP] 15 requests to amend the complaint are ..., generally speaking, 'freely' allowed. But when a Rule 15 motion comes *after* a judgment against the plaintiff, that is a different story. Courts in that setting must 'consider[] the competing interest of protecting the finality of judgments and the expeditious termination of litigation.' [¶] When a party seeks to amend a complaint after an adverse judgment, it ... must shoulder a heavier burden. Instead of meeting only the modest requirements of Rule 15, the claimant must meet the requirements for reopening a case established by [FRCP] 59 or 60. In post-judgment motions to amend, ... 'the Rule 15 and Rule 59 inquiries turn on the same factors.' A court acts within its discretion in denying a Rule 15 and a Rule 59 motion on account of 'undue delay'—including delay resulting from a failure to incorporate 'previously [ ]available' evidence[—]and ought to pay particular attention to 'the movant's explanation for failing to seek leave to amend prior to the entry of judgment.' [¶] A plaintiff cannot use a Rule 59 motion (or for that matter a post-judgment Rule 15 motion) 'to raise arguments which could, and should, have been made before judgment issued.'" *See also* ***Tool Box, Inc. v. Ogden City Corp.***, 419 F.3d 1084, 1087 (10th Cir.2005); ***Ahmed v. Dragovich***, 297 F.3d 201, 207-08 (3d Cir.2002).

Bailey v. Bayer CropScience L.P., 563 F.3d 302, 309 (8th Cir.2009). "The district court, when faced with an amended pleading naming a new nondiverse defendant in a removed case, should scrutinize that amendment more closely than an ordinary amendment. [FRCP] 15(a) ... provides that leave to amend should be freely given when justice so requires, and [FRCP] 20 permits joinder of proper parties. In this situation, justice requires that the district court consider a number of factors to balance the defendant's interests in maintaining the federal forum with the competing interests of not having parallel lawsuits. The Court is required to consider (1) the extent to which the joinder of the nondiverse party is sought to defeat federal jurisdiction, (2) whether the plaintiff has been dilatory in asking for amendment, and (3) whether the plaintiff will be significantly injured if amendment is not allowed." (Internal quotes omitted.)

Bjorgung v. Whitetail Resort, LP, 550 F.3d 263, 266 (3d Cir.2008). "Delay becomes 'undue,' and thereby creates grounds for the district court to refuse leave, when it places an unwarranted burden on the court or when the plaintiff has had previous opportunities to amend. [T]he question of undue delay ... will 'focus on the movant's reasons for not amending sooner,' ... and we will balance these reasons against the burden of delay on the District Court."

Laber v. Harvey, 438 F.3d 404, 426-27 (4th Cir. 2006). "We have interpreted Rule 15(a) to provide that 'leave to amend a pleading should be denied only when the amendment would be prejudicial to the opposing party, there has been bad faith on the part of the moving party, or the amendment would have been futile.' Whether an amendment is prejudicial will often be determined by the nature of the amendment and its timing. A common example of a prejudicial amendment is one that 'raises a new legal theory that would require the gathering and analysis of facts not already considered by [the defendant and] is offered shortly before or during trial.' An amendment is not prejudicial, by contrast, if it merely adds an additional theory of recovery to the facts already pled and is offered before any discovery has occurred." *See also* ***In re Rauh***, 119 F.3d 46, 52 (1st Cir.1997).

U.S. v. Humana Health Plan of Tex. Inc., 336 F.3d 375, 387 (5th Cir.2003). "Rule 15(a) applies where plaintiffs 'expressly requested' to amend even though their request 'was not contained in a properly captioned motion paper.' A formal motion is not always required, so long as the requesting party has set forth with particularity the grounds for the amendment and the relief sought. '[A] bare request in an opposition to a motion to dismiss—without any indication of the particular grounds on which the amendment is sought[—]does not constitute a motion within the contemplation of Rule 15(a).'" *See also* ***Fidel v. Farley***, 392 F.3d 220, 236 (6th Cir.2004).

Snyder v. Pascack Valley Hosp., 303 F.3d 271, 276 (3d Cir.2002). "[A] defendant is required to answer the amended complaint even if the new version does not change the charges against him."

Campania Mgmt. v. Rooks, Pitts & Poust, 290 F.3d 843, 849 (7th Cir.2002). "A trial court may deny leave to amend when the amendment would cause the opposing party to bear additional discovery costs litigating a new issue and the moving party does not offer to

reimburse the nonmoving party for its expenses. *At 850:* A court may determine that a proposed amendment is futile if it sets forth facts or legal theories that are redundant, immaterial, or unresponsive to the allegations in the complaint. *At 851 n.5:* [T]he availability of an alternative forum is a factor to consider when ruling on a motion to amend a complaint and assert new causes of action." *See also* ***Sound of Music Co. v. Minnesota Mining & Mfg.***, 477 F.3d 910, 922-23 (7th Cir. 2007) (if amended claim would not survive motion for summary judgment, amendment is futile).

Harrison v. Rubin, 174 F.3d 249, 253 (D.C.Cir. 1999). "Although this Circuit has recognized undue delay as a basis for denying a motion to amend, we have done so only where plaintiffs sought to add new factual allegations. Where an amendment would do no more than clarify legal theories or make technical corrections, we have consistently held that delay, without a showing of prejudice, is not a sufficient ground for denying the motion." *See also* ***BCS Fin. Corp. v. U.S.***, 118 F.3d 522, 524 (7th Cir.1997).

Moore v. Indiana, 999 F.2d 1125, 1131 (7th Cir. 1993). "In addressing the sufficiency of a motion for leave to amend, courts may require the submission of a copy of the proposed amended complaint, … although the motion itself may be acceptable so long as it puts the opposing party on notice of the content of the amendment. [T]he submission of a motion for leave to amend, properly accompanied by the proposed amended complaint that provides notice of the substance of those amendments, tolls the statute of limitations, even though technically the amended complaint will not be filed until the court rules on the motion." *See also* ***Fletcher-Harlee Corp. v. Pote Concrete Contractors, Inc.***, 482 F.3d 247, 252 (3d Cir.2007) (P must submit draft of amended complaint so court can determine whether amendment is futile).

FRCP 15(b)

Banks v. Dretke, 540 U.S. 668, 704-05 (2004). "We see no reason why an evidentiary hearing should not qualify [for purposes of FRCP 15(b),] so long as the respondent gave 'any sort of consent' and had a full and fair 'opportunity to present evidence bearing on th[e] claim's resolution.'"

Farfaras v. Citizens Bank & Trust, 433 F.3d 558, 568 (7th Cir.2006). "The intent of rule 15(b) is 'to provide the maximum opportunity for each claim to be decided on its merits rather than on procedural niceties.' [¶] The key factor in determining whether the pleadings have been amended is whether the issue has been tried with the express or implied consent of the parties. The test for such consent is 'whether the opposing party had a fair opportunity to defend and whether he could have presented additional evidence had he known sooner the substance of the amendment.' One sign of implied consent is that issues not raised by the pleadings are presented and argued without proper objection by opposing counsel."

Cruz v. Coach Stores, 202 F.3d 560, 569 (2d Cir. 2000). "Under [FRCP] 15(b), a district court may consider claims outside those raised in the pleadings so long as doing so does not cause prejudice. In opposing a Rule 15(b) amendment, 'a party cannot normally show that it suffered prejudice simply because of a change in its opponent's legal theory. Instead, a party's failure to plead an issue it later presented must have disadvantaged its opponent in presenting its case.'"

Gilbane Bldg. Co. v. Federal Reserve Bank, 80 F.3d 895, 901 (4th Cir.1996). FRCP 15(b) "is designed to allow amendment of a pleading when the facts proven at trial differ from those alleged in the complaint, and thus support a cause of action that the claimant did not plead. Because notice to the defendant of the allegations to be proven is essential to sustaining a cause of action, Rule 15(b) applies only when the defendant has consented to trial of the non-pled factual issues and will not be prejudiced by amendment of the pleadings to include them."

FRCP 15(c)

Krupski v. Costa Crociere S.p.A., ___ U.S. ___, 130 S.Ct. 2485, 2493-94 (2010). FRCP 15(c)(1)(C)(ii) "asks what the prospective *defendant* knew or should have known during the [FRCP] 4(m) period, not what the *plaintiff* knew or should have known at the time of filing her original complaint. [¶] Information in the plaintiff's possession is relevant only if it bears on the defendant's understanding of whether the plaintiff made a mistake regarding the proper party's identity. For purposes of that inquiry, it would be error to conflate knowledge of a party's existence with the absence of mistake. *At 2496:* [FRCP 15(c)] plainly sets forth an exclusive list of requirements for relation back, and the amending party's diligence is not among them. [FRCP 15(c)] mandates relation back once [FRCP 15(c)'s] requirements are satisfied; it does not leave the decision whether to grant relation back to the district court's eq-

uitable discretion. [¶] The mandatory nature of the inquiry for relation back under Rule 15(c) is particularly striking in contrast to the inquiry under Rule 15(a), which [b]y its terms, ... gives discretion to the district court in deciding whether to grant a motion to amend a pleading to add a party or a claim. [T]he speed with which a plaintiff moves to amend her complaint or files an amended complaint after obtaining leave to do so has no bearing on whether the amended complaint relates back."

Nelson v. Adams USA, Inc., 529 U.S. 460, 467 (2000). "[A] prospective party cannot fairly be required to answer an amended pleading not yet permitted, framed, and served. *At 467 n.1:* Even when an amendment relates back to the original date of pleading under Rule 15(c) ..., the relation back cannot, consistently with due process, deny a party all opportunity to be heard in response to the amendment."

Hall v. Spencer Cty., 583 F.3d 930, 934 (6th Cir. 2009). "Rule 15(c) is based on the notion that once litigation involving particular conduct or a given transaction or occurrence has been instituted, the parties are not entitled to the protection of the statute of limitations against the later assertion by amendment of defenses or claims that arise out of the same 'conduct, transaction, or occurrence.' In short, a court will permit a party to add even a new legal theory in an amended pleading as long as it arises out of the same transaction or occurrence. Rule 15(c)(2) does not define the scope of the terms 'conduct, transaction, or occurrence.' When applying this standard to the facts of a given case, we give meaning to those terms not by generic or ideal notions of what constitutes a 'conduct, transaction, or occurrence,' but instead by asking whether the party asserting the statute of limitations defense had been placed on notice that he could be called to answer for the allegations in the amended pleading. [FRCP 15(c)] also must be interpreted in light of the fundamental tenor of the [FRCPs], which is one of liberality rather than technicality." (Internal quotes omitted.)

Morel v. DaimlerChrysler AG, 565 F.3d 20, 23 (1st Cir.2009). "[T]he question reduces to whether the amended complaint relates back to the time of filing the initial complaint. [¶] [T]he answer ... hinges on whether federal or state law furnishes the controlling relation-back rule. [¶] [Ds argue that] if relation back under a federal standard would require a party to defend a claim that would otherwise be barred by operation of a substantive state rule, then the state rule must take precedence. *At 25:* [E]ven though Rule 15(c) is 'intimately connected with the policy of the statute of limitations,' [FRCP 15(c)] does not actually alter state limitations periods. Under Rule 15(c), the original complaint still must be filed within that state-supplied limitations period. So viewed, '[t]he state's underlying interest ... in protecting persons against stale claims is adequately protected by the practical notice requirements built into Rule 15(c).' [¶] The conclusion [is] that Rule 15(c) applies in a diversity case notwithstanding the incidence of a more restrictive state rule...."

Farris v. U.S., 333 F.3d 1211, 1215 (11th Cir.2003). "Congress intended Rule 15(c) to be used for a relatively narrow purpose; it did not inten[d] for the rule to be so broad to allow an amended pleading to add an entirely new claim based on a different set of facts. ... The untimely claim must have arisen from the 'same set of facts' as the timely filed claim, not from separate conduct or a separate occurrence in 'both time and type.'"

Young v. Lepone, 305 F.3d 1, 14 (1st Cir.2002). "Although the text of Rule 15(c)(3) [now Rule 15(c)(1)(C)] seems to contemplate changes in the identity of *defendants*, we have recognized that [FRCP 15(c)(1)(C)] can be applied to amendments that change the identity of plaintiffs. [¶] [W]e have laid down three separate requirements applicable to plaintiffs who seek succor under Rule 15(c)(3): '[T]he amended complaint must arise out of the conduct, transaction, or occurrence set forth or attempted to be set forth in the original pleading; there must be a sufficient identity of interest between the new plaintiff, the old plaintiff, and their respective claims so that the defendants can be said to have been given fair notice of the latecomer's claim against them; and undue prejudice must be absent.' *At 15:* [W]e repudiate the conceit that an action filed by one plaintiff gives a defendant notice of the impending joinder of any or all similarly situated plaintiffs." *See also* ***Intown Props. Mgmt. v. Wheaton Van Lines, Inc.***, 271 F.3d 164, 170 (4th Cir. 2001) (D must have fair notice of claims); ***SMS Fin., L.L.C. v. ABCO Homes, Inc.***, 167 F.3d 235, 244-45 (5th Cir.1999) (same as annotation).

FRCP 16. PRETRIAL CONFERENCES; SCHEDULING; MANAGEMENT

(a) Purposes of a Pretrial Conference. In any action, the court may order the attorneys and any un-

represented parties to appear for one or more pretrial conferences for such purposes as:

(1) expediting disposition of the action;

(2) establishing early and continuing control so that the case will not be protracted because of lack of management;

(3) discouraging wasteful pretrial activities;

(4) improving the quality of the trial through more thorough preparation; and

(5) facilitating settlement.

(b) Scheduling.

(1) ***Scheduling Order.*** Except in categories of actions exempted by local rule, the district judge—or a magistrate judge when authorized by local rule—must issue a scheduling order:

(A) after receiving the parties' report under Rule 26(f); or

(B) after consulting with the parties' attorneys and any unrepresented parties at a scheduling conference or by telephone, mail, or other means.

(2) ***Time to Issue.*** The judge must issue the scheduling order as soon as practicable, but in any event within the earlier of 120 days after any defendant has been served with the complaint or 90 days after any defendant has appeared.

(3) ***Contents of the Order.***

(A) *Required Contents.* The scheduling order must limit the time to join other parties, amend the pleadings, complete discovery, and file motions.

(B) *Permitted Contents.* The scheduling order may:

(i) modify the timing of disclosures under Rules 26(a) and 26(e)(1);

(ii) modify the extent of discovery;

(iii) provide for disclosure or discovery of electronically stored information;

(iv) include any agreements the parties reach for asserting claims of privilege or of protection as trial-preparation material after information is produced;

(v) set dates for pretrial conferences and for trial; and

(vi) include other appropriate matters.

(4) ***Modifying a Schedule.*** A schedule may be modified only for good cause and with the judge's consent.

(c) Attendance and Matters for Consideration at a Pretrial Conference.

(1) ***Attendance.*** A represented party must authorize at least one of its attorneys to make stipulations and admissions about all matters that can reasonably be anticipated for discussion at a pretrial conference. If appropriate, the court may require that a party or its representative be present or reasonably available by other means to consider possible settlement.

(2) ***Matters for Consideration.*** At any pretrial conference, the court may consider and take appropriate action on the following matters:

(A) formulating and simplifying the issues, and eliminating frivolous claims or defenses;

(B) amending the pleadings if necessary or desirable;

(C) obtaining admissions and stipulations about facts and documents to avoid unnecessary proof, and ruling in advance on the admissibility of evidence;

(D) avoiding unnecessary proof and cumulative evidence, and limiting the use of testimony under Federal Rule of Evidence 702;

(E) determining the appropriateness and timing of summary adjudication under Rule 56;

(F) controlling and scheduling discovery, including orders affecting disclosures and discovery under Rule 26 and Rules 29 through 37;

(G) identifying witnesses and documents, scheduling the filing and exchange of any pretrial briefs, and setting dates for further conferences and for trial;

(H) referring matters to a magistrate judge or a master;

(I) settling the case and using special procedures to assist in resolving the dispute when authorized by statute or local rule;

(J) determining the form and content of the pretrial order;

(K) disposing of pending motions;

(L) adopting special procedures for managing potentially difficult or protracted actions

that may involve complex issues, multiple parties, difficult legal questions, or unusual proof problems;

(M) ordering a separate trial under Rule 42(b) of a claim, counterclaim, crossclaim, third-party claim, or particular issue;

(N) ordering the presentation of evidence early in the trial on a manageable issue that might, on the evidence, be the basis for a judgment as a matter of law under Rule 50(a) or a judgment on partial findings under Rule 52(c);

(O) establishing a reasonable limit on the time allowed to present evidence; and

(P) facilitating in other ways the just, speedy, and inexpensive disposition of the action.

(d) Pretrial Orders. After any conference under this rule, the court should issue an order reciting the action taken. This order controls the course of the action unless the court modifies it.

(e) Final Pretrial Conference and Orders. The court may hold a final pretrial conference to formulate a trial plan, including a plan to facilitate the admission of evidence. The conference must be held as close to the start of trial as is reasonable, and must be attended by at least one attorney who will conduct the trial for each party and by any unrepresented party. The court may modify the order issued after a final pretrial conference only to prevent manifest injustice.

(f) Sanctions.

(1) ***In General.*** On motion or on its own, the court may issue any just orders, including those authorized by Rule 37(b)(2)(A)(ii)-(vii), if a party or its attorney:

(A) fails to appear at a scheduling or other pretrial conference;

(B) is substantially unprepared to participate—or does not participate in good faith—in the conference; or

(C) fails to obey a scheduling or other pretrial order.

(2) ***Imposing Fees and Costs.*** Instead of or in addition to any other sanction, the court must order the party, its attorney, or both to pay the reasonable expenses—including attorney's fees—incurred because of any noncompliance with this rule, unless the noncompliance was substantially justified or other circumstances make an award of expenses unjust.

See selected Notes of Advisory Committee to FRCP 16, p. 1158.

History of FRCP 16: Adopted Dec. 20, 1937, eff. Sept. 16, 1938. Amended Apr. 28, 1983, eff. Aug. 1, 1983; Mar. 2, 1987, eff. Aug. 1, 1987; Apr. 22, 1993, eff. Dec. 1, 1993; Apr. 12, 2006, eff. Dec. 1, 2006; Apr. 30, 2007, eff. Dec. 1, 2007.

See *Commentaries*, "Scheduling Order & Pretrial Conference," ch. 5-A, p. 289; *O'Connor's Federal Civil Forms* (2012), FORMS 5A.

ANNOTATIONS

Tracinda Corp. v. DaimlerChrysler AG, 502 F.3d 212, 242 (3d Cir.2007). "[T]he standard ... relevant in defining 'unjust' is the contrast between the nature of the violation of Rule 16 and the impact on the parties caused by the delay. Therefore, the fact that the party with the obligation to produce documents may have been negligent is a fact to consider. Nevertheless, even if the failure to produce has been inadvertent, sanctions may be called for under Rule 16(f) if the impact is severe on the party who was due the discovery."

S&W Enters. v. SouthTrust Bank, 315 F.3d 533, 536 (5th Cir.2003). "Rule 16(b) governs amendment of pleadings after a scheduling order deadline has expired. [¶] [In determining whether the district court's refusal to grant an untimely motion to amend pleadings was an abuse of discretion, the court will] consider (1) the explanation for the failure to timely move for leave to amend; (2) the importance of the amendment; (3) potential prejudice in allowing the amendment; and (4) the availability of a continuance to cure such prejudice." (Internal quotes omitted.)

In re Atlantic Pipe Corp., 304 F.3d 135, 140 (1st Cir.2002). "There are four potential sources of judicial authority for ordering mandatory non-binding mediation of pending cases, namely, (a) the court's local rules, (b) an applicable statute, (c) the [FRCPs], and (d) the court's inherent powers. *At 142:* [T]he words 'when authorized by statute or local rule' [in FRCP 16(c)(9), now FRCP 16(c)(2)(I),] are a frank limitation on the district courts' authority to order mediation [under that rule], and we must adhere to that [limitation]. *At 145:* [I]t is within a district court's inherent power to order non-consensual mediation in those cases in which that step seems reasonably likely to serve the interests of justice." *See also* ***FTC v. Freecom Comms.***, 401 F.3d 1192, 1208 n.9 (10th Cir.2005) (court can require parties to engage in good-faith settlement negotiations, and if party refuses, court can impose sanctions after notice and hearing).

Wilson v. Muckala, 303 F.3d 1207, 1216 (10th Cir. 2002). "Should a new claim or defense appear for the first time in the pretrial order, it is incumbent upon opposing counsel to meticulously examine the order, taking exception, if necessary, to the additions, and recording their objection in the pretrial order. Meanwhile, the party seeking to add a claim or defense should do so with specificity and clarity so as to minimize the ill effects of that practice. Specificity and clarity provide the trial court with a fair opportunity to consider whether to approve or deny what is obviously an attempt to amend the pleadings at a rather late date."

Tower Ventures, Inc. v. City of Westfield, 296 F.3d 43, 45-46 (1st Cir.2002). "A 'litigant who ignores case-management deadlines does so at his peril.' Consequently, when noncompliance occurs, the court may choose from a broad universe of possible sanctions. [T]he choice of an appropriate sanction must be handled on a case-by-case basis. [¶] From a plaintiff's standpoint, the most dreaded sanction is dismissal with prejudice. ... Although dismissal ordinarily should be employed only when a plaintiff's misconduct is extreme, ... disobedience of court orders, in and of itself, constitutes extreme misconduct (and, thus, warrants dismissal).... [¶] This principle applies with undiminished force to scheduling orders. [¶] [However, a] violation of a scheduling order may be excused if good cause exists for the offender's failure to comply." *See also* ***Spain v. Board of Educ.***, 214 F.3d 925, 929-30 (7th Cir.2000) (court must give due warning to party's counsel before dismissing case when party fails to attend pretrial conference).

Inge v. Rock Fin. Corp., 281 F.3d 613, 625 (6th Cir. 2002). "Pursuant to Rule 16(b), a scheduling order establishing deadlines for matters such as joinder and amendments to pleadings shall not be modified except upon a showing of good cause and by leave of the district judge. The primary measure of Rule 16's 'good cause' standard is the moving party's diligence in attempting to meet the case management order's requirements. Another relevant consideration is possible prejudice to the party opposing the modification." (Internal quotes omitted.) *See also* ***Slip Track Sys. v. Metal-Lite, Inc.***, 304 F.3d 1256, 1270 (Fed.Cir.2002).

Elvis Presley Enters. v. Capece, 141 F.3d 188, 206 (5th Cir.1998). "Once the pretrial order is entered, it controls the course and scope of the proceedings ..., and if a claim or issue is omitted from the order, it is waived, even if it appeared in the complaint." *See also* ***Friedman & Friedman, Ltd. v. Tim McCandless, Inc.***, 606 F.3d 494, 498 (8th Cir.2010); ***McLean Contracting Co. v. Waterman S.S. Corp.***, 277 F.3d 477, 480 (4th Cir.2002).

Trierweiler v. Croxton & Trench Holding Corp., 90 F.3d 1523, 1543 (10th Cir.1996). "The pretrial order controls the subsequent course of action in a case unless it is modified by a later order, and it is modified only to prevent manifest injustice. We interpret the assertion of an issue not listed in the pretrial order as the equivalent of a formal motion to amend the order, and review the denial of such motions under an abuse of discretion standard."

Robson v. Hallenbeck, 81 F.3d 1, 2 (1st Cir.1996). "[A] district court has broad authority to enforce pretrial discipline and to dismiss a case for failure to obey pre-trial orders. [¶] [Before dismissing a case, the court should consider the] severity of the violation, the legitimacy of the party's excuse, repetition of violations, the deliberateness *vel non* of the misconduct, mitigating excuses, prejudice to the other side and to the operations of the court, and the adequacy of lesser sanctions. *At 3:* [C]ounsel's disregard of a prior warning from the court exacerbates the offense, and the lack of warning sometimes mitigates it. Ordinarily, the plaintiff is given an opportunity to explain the default or argue for a lesser penalty; but again there is no mechanical rule. The presence or absence of an explanation by the district court may also be a factor."

In re Maurice, 21 F.3d 767, 773 (7th Cir.1994). "Two purposes for requiring the parties to comply with a pre-hearing (or pretrial) order include identifying witnesses and resolving evidentiary disputes in advance of trial, thus narrowing the issues and expediting the trial. When one party fails to comply with a court's pre-hearing order without justifiable excuse, thus frustrating the purposes of the pre-hearing order, the court is certainly within its authority to prohibit that party from introducing witnesses or evidence as a sanction."

TITLE IV. PARTIES

FRCP 17. PLAINTIFF & DEFENDANT; CAPACITY; PUBLIC OFFICERS

(a) Real Party in Interest.

(1) ***Designation in General.*** An action must be prosecuted in the name of the real party in interest. The following may sue in their own

names without joining the person for whose benefit the action is brought:

(A) an executor;

(B) an administrator;

(C) a guardian;

(D) a bailee;

(E) a trustee of an express trust;

(F) a party with whom or in whose name a contract has been made for another's benefit; and

(G) a party authorized by statute.

(2) ***Action in the Name of the United States for Another's Use or Benefit.*** When a federal statute so provides, an action for another's use or benefit must be brought in the name of the United States.

(3) ***Joinder of the Real Party in Interest.*** The court may not dismiss an action for failure to prosecute in the name of the real party in interest until, after an objection, a reasonable time has been allowed for the real party in interest to ratify, join, or be substituted into the action. After ratification, joinder, or substitution, the action proceeds as if it had been originally commenced by the real party in interest.

(b) Capacity to Sue or Be Sued. Capacity to sue or be sued is determined as follows:

(1) for an individual who is not acting in a representative capacity, by the law of the individual's domicile;

(2) for a corporation, by the law under which it was organized; and

(3) for all other parties, by the law of the state where the court is located, except that:

(A) a partnership or other unincorporated association with no such capacity under that state's law may sue or be sued in its common name to enforce a substantive right existing under the United States Constitution or laws; and

(B) 28 U.S.C. §§754 and 959(a) govern the capacity of a receiver appointed by a United States court to sue or be sued in a United States court.

(c) Minor or Incompetent Person.

(1) ***With a Representative.*** The following representatives may sue or defend on behalf of a minor or an incompetent person:

(A) a general guardian;

(B) a committee;

(C) a conservator; or

(D) a like fiduciary.

(2) ***Without a Representative.*** A minor or an incompetent person who does not have a duly appointed representative may sue by a next friend or by a guardian ad litem. The court must appoint a guardian ad litem—or issue another appropriate order—to protect a minor or incompetent person who is unrepresented in an action.

(d) Public Officer's Title and Name. A public officer who sues or is sued in an official capacity may be designated by official title rather than by name, but the court may order that the officer's name be added.

See selected Notes of Advisory Committee to FRCP 17, p. 1164.

History of FRCP 17: Adopted Dec. 20, 1937, eff. Sept. 16, 1938. Amended Dec. 27, 1946, eff. Mar. 19, 1948; Dec. 29, 1948, eff. Oct. 20, 1949; Feb. 28, 1966, eff. July 1, 1966; Mar. 2, 1987, eff. Aug. 1, 1987; Apr. 25, 1988, eff. Aug. 1, 1988; Nov. 18, 1988, P.L. 100-690, §7049, 102 Stat. 4401; Apr. 30, 2007, eff. Dec. 1, 2007.

See *Commentaries*, "Parties," ch. 2-B, §2, p. 75; ***O'Connor's Federal Civil Forms*** (2012), FORMS 2B.

ANNOTATIONS

U.S. v. City of N.Y., 556 U.S. 928, 934-35 (2009). "The phrase, 'real party in interest,' is a term of art utilized in federal law to refer to an actor with a substantive right whose interests may be represented in litigation by another."

Kuelbs v. Hill, 615 F.3d 1037, 1042 (8th Cir.2010). See annotation under FRCP 25, p. 891.

Sam M. v. Carcieri, 608 F.3d 77, 85 (1st Cir.2010). "Rule 17(c) … governs a minor or incompetent's access to federal court. It directs that a minor or incompetent may sue in federal court through a duly appointed representative which includes a general guardian, committee, conservator, or like fiduciary. If a minor lacks a general guardian or a duly appointed representative, Rule 17(c)(2) directs the court either appoint a legal guardian or Next Friend, or issue an order to protect a minor or incompetent who is unrepresented in the federal suit. [¶] The appointment of a Next Friend or guardian ad litem is not mandatory. Thus, where a minor or incompetent is represented by a general

guardian or a duly appointed representative, a Next Friend need not be appointed. However, Rule 17(c) 'gives a federal court power to authorize someone other than a lawful representative to sue on behalf of an infant or incompetent person where that representative is unable, unwilling or refuses to act or has interests which conflict with those of the infant or incompetent.'" *See also* ***Fonner v. Fairfax Cty.***, 415 F.3d 325, 330 (4th Cir.2005); ***Burke v. Smith***, 252 F.3d 1260, 1264 (11th Cir.2001).

In re Signal Int'l, 579 F.3d 478, 487-88 (5th Cir. 2009). FRCP 17(a)(3) "requires the defendant to object in time to allow the opportunity for joinder of the ostensible real party in interest, and the defense may be waived if the defendant does not timely object. The defendant timely objects so long as joinder of the real party in interest remains 'practical and convenient.' Objection is typically practical in the early stages of litigation—disputes regarding the real party in interest are likely to be evident to a defendant at the onset of suit, because he almost always knows whether he has been sued by the party who 'owns' the claim. The earlier the defense is raised, the more likely that the high cost of trial preparation for both parties can be avoided if a real party in interest question is determined adversely to a plaintiff. [¶] The relevant factors for [determining practicality and convenience] are when the defendant knew or should have known about the facts giving rise to the plaintiff's disputed status as a real party in interest; whether the objection was raised in time to allow the plaintiff a meaningful opportunity to prove its status; whether it was raised in time to allow the real party in interest a reasonable opportunity to join the action if the objection proved successful; and other case-specific considerations of judicial efficiency or fairness to the parties." (Internal quotes omitted.) *See also* ***RK Co. v. See***, 622 F.3d 846, 850 (7th Cir.2010).

United HealthCare Corp. v. American Trade Ins., 88 F.3d 563, 569 (8th Cir.1996). FRCP 17(a) "requires that the party who brings an action actually possess, under the substantive law, the right sought to be enforced. Such a requirement is in place 'to protect the defendant against a subsequent action by the party actually entitled to recover, and to insure generally that the judgment will have its proper effect as res judicata.'" *See also* ***Marina Mgmt. Servs. v. Vessel My Girls***, 202 F.3d 315, 318 (D.C.Cir.2000).

Jaramillo v. Burkhart, 999 F.2d 1241, 1246 (8th Cir.1993). "If an objection to a plaintiff's right to institute an action is sustained, [FRCP] 17 allows the joinder of the real party in interest in order to avoid injustice." *See also* ***Lunney v. U.S.***, 319 F.3d 550, 557 (2d Cir. 2003) (purpose of FRCP 17(a) is to protect against forfeiture and injustice).

Mutuelles Unies v. Kroll & Linstrom, 957 F.2d 707, 712 (9th Cir.1992). "A proper ratification pursuant to Rule 17(a) requires the ratifying party to: (1) authorize continuation of the action; and (2) agree to be bound by the lawsuit's result."

FRCP 18. JOINDER OF CLAIMS

(a) In General. A party asserting a claim, counterclaim, crossclaim, or third-party claim may join, as independent or alternative claims, as many claims as it has against an opposing party.

(b) Joinder of Contingent Claims. A party may join two claims even though one of them is contingent on the disposition of the other; but the court may grant relief only in accordance with the parties' relative substantive rights. In particular, a plaintiff may state a claim for money and a claim to set aside a conveyance that is fraudulent as to that plaintiff, without first obtaining a judgment for the money.

See selected Notes of Advisory Committee to FRCP 18, p. 1164.

History of FRCP 18: Adopted Dec. 20, 1937, eff. Sept. 16, 1938. Amended Feb. 28, 1966, eff. July 1, 1966; Mar. 2, 1987, eff. Aug. 1, 1987; Apr. 30, 2007, eff. Dec. 1, 2007.

See *Commentaries*, "Interpleader," ch. 2-C, p. 87; "Motion to Dismiss for Failure to Join a Party Under FRCP 19—FRCP 12(b)(7)," ch. 3-I, p. 214; "Defendant's Claims," ch. 3-L, §5, p. 235; "Motion to Intervene," ch. 5-J, p. 356; *O'Connor's Federal Civil Forms* (2012), FORMS 2C; FORMS 5J.

ANNOTATIONS

King Fisher Mar. Serv. v. 21st Phoenix Corp., 893 F.2d 1155, 1158 n.2 (10th Cir.1990). "[A] court may decide claims joined under rule 18(a) only if independent jurisdiction and venue requirements are satisfied. *At 1159:* '[I]n determining whether jurisdiction over a nonfederal claim exists, the *context* in which the nonfederal claim is asserted is *crucial*.'"

Friedman v. Hartmann, 787 F.Supp. 411, 422 (S.D. N.Y.1992). "'[O]nce a party has asserted a proper impleader claim, he qualifies under Rule 18(a) to assert any and all additional claims—regardless of whether transactionally related to the impleader claims—he may have against the third-party defendant.'"

FRCP 19. REQUIRED JOINDER OF PARTIES

(a) Persons Required to Be Joined if Feasible.

(1) ***Required Party.*** A person who is subject to service of process and whose joinder will not deprive the court of subject-matter jurisdiction must be joined as a party if:

(A) in that person's absence, the court cannot accord complete relief among existing parties; or

(B) that person claims an interest relating to the subject of the action and is so situated that disposing of the action in the person's absence may:

(i) as a practical matter impair or impede the person's ability to protect the interest; or

(ii) leave an existing party subject to a substantial risk of incurring double, multiple, or otherwise inconsistent obligations because of the interest.

(2) ***Joinder by Court Order.*** If a person has not been joined as required, the court must order that the person be made a party. A person who refuses to join as a plaintiff may be made either a defendant or, in a proper case, an involuntary plaintiff.

(3) ***Venue.*** If a joined party objects to venue and the joinder would make venue improper, the court must dismiss that party.

(b) When Joinder Is Not Feasible. If a person who is required to be joined if feasible cannot be joined, the court must determine whether, in equity and good conscience, the action should proceed among the existing parties or should be dismissed. The factors for the court to consider include:

(1) the extent to which a judgment rendered in the person's absence might prejudice that person or the existing parties;

(2) the extent to which any prejudice could be lessened or avoided by:

(A) protective provisions in the judgment;

(B) shaping the relief; or

(C) other measures;

(3) whether a judgment rendered in the person's absence would be adequate; and

(4) whether the plaintiff would have an adequate remedy if the action were dismissed for nonjoinder.

(c) Pleading the Reasons for Nonjoinder. When asserting a claim for relief, a party must state:

(1) the name, if known, of any person who is required to be joined if feasible but is not joined; and

(2) the reasons for not joining that person.

(d) Exception for Class Actions. This rule is subject to Rule 23.

See selected Notes of Advisory Committee to FRCP 19, p. 1164.

History of FRCP 19: Adopted Dec. 20, 1937, eff. Sept. 16, 1938. Amended Feb. 28, 1966, eff. July 1, 1966; Mar. 2, 1987, eff. Aug. 1, 1987; Apr. 30, 2007, eff. Dec. 1, 2007.

See *Commentaries*, "Interpleader," ch. 2-C, p. 87; "Motion to Dismiss for Failure to Join a Party Under FRCP 19—FRCP 12(b)(7)," ch. 3-I, p. 214; "Motion to Intervene," ch. 5-J, p. 356; *O'Connor's Federal Civil Forms* (2012), FORMS 2C; FORMS 3I; FORMS 5J.

ANNOTATIONS

Republic of the Phil. v. Pimentel, 553 U.S. 851, 862-63 (2008). FRCP 19(a) "states the principles that determine when persons or entities must be joined in a suit. [FRCP 19] instructs that nonjoinder even of a required person does not always result in dismissal. Subdivision (a) opens by noting that it addresses joinder 'if Feasible.' Where joinder is not feasible, the question whether the action should proceed turns on the factors outlined in subdivision (b). The considerations set forth in subdivision (b) are nonexclusive.... The design of [FRCP 19], then, indicates that the determination whether to proceed will turn upon factors that are case specific.... [¶] Under the earlier [FRCPs] the term 'indispensable party' might have implied a certain rigidity that would be in tension with this case-specific approach. The word 'indispensable' had an unforgiving connotation that did not fit easily with a system that permits actions to proceed even when some persons who otherwise should be parties to the action cannot be joined. [T]he use of 'indispensable' in Rule 19 created the 'verbal anomaly' of an 'indispensable person who turns out to be dispensable after all.' Though the text has changed, [FRCP 19, as amended in 2007,] has the same design and, to some extent, the same tension. Required persons may turn out not to be required for the action to proceed after all. [¶] In all events it is clear that multiple factors must bear on the decision whether to proceed without a required person. This decision 'must be based on factors varying with the different cases, some such factors being substantive, some pro-

cedural, some compelling by themselves, and some subject to balancing against opposing interests.'"

Lincoln Prop. Co. v. Roche, 546 U.S. 81, 90 (2005). "Neither [FRCP] 17(a) ... nor [FRCP] 19 ... requires plaintiffs or defendants to name and join any additional parties to this action. Both Rules ... address party joinder, not federal-court subject-matter jurisdiction."

Orff v. U.S., 545 U.S. 596, 602-03 (2005). "Before 1966, the term 'necessary' described the class of parties now called 'Persons to be Joined if Feasible' under [FRCP] 19(a). [¶] Though [FRCP 19(a)] no longer describes such parties as 'necessary,' 'necessary party' is a term of art whose meaning parallels Rule 19(a)'s requirements."

Provident Tradesmens Bank & Trust Co. v. Patterson, 390 U.S. 102, 109-10 (1968). "Rule 19(b) suggests four 'interests' that must be examined in each case to determine whether, in equity and good conscience, the court should proceed without a party whose absence from the litigation is compelled. ... First, the plaintiff has an interest in having a forum. ... Second, the defendant may properly wish to avoid multiple litigation, or inconsistent relief, or sole responsibility for a liability he shares with another. [¶] Third, there is the interest of the outsider whom it would have been desirable to join. *At 111:* Fourth ... the interest of the courts and the public in complete, consistent, and efficient settlement of controversies." *See also **Zambelli Fireworks Mfg. Co. v. Wood***, 592 F.3d 412, 421 (3d Cir.2010).

Salt River Project Agric. Imprv. & Power Dist. v. Lee, 672 F.3d 1176, 1180 (9th Cir.2012). "An absent party with an interest in the action is not a necessary party under Rule 19(a) 'if the absent party is adequately represented in the suit.' '[I]f a legally protected interest exists, the court must further determine whether that interest will be *impaired or impeded* by the suit. Impairment may be minimized if the absent party is adequately represented in the suit.' [¶] We consider three factors in determining whether an existing party adequately represents the interests of an absent party: (1) 'whether the interests of a present party to the suit are such that it will undoubtedly make all of the absent party's arguments'; (2) 'whether the party is capable of and willing to make such arguments'; and (3) 'whether the absent party would offer any necessary element to the proceedings that the present parties would neglect.'" *See also **MasterCard Int'l v. Visa Int'l Serv. Ass'n***, 471 F.3d 377, 387-88 (2d Cir.2006).

Askew v. Sheriff of Cook Cty., 568 F.3d 632, 634 (7th Cir.2009). "The purpose of Rule 19 is to 'permit joinder of all materially interested parties to a single lawsuit so as to protect interested parties and avoid waste of judicial resources.' Dismissal, however, is not the preferred outcome under the Rules. *At 635:* Once such a party has been identified [as required], [FRCP 19] prescribes what the court must do. [A]s part of the ... inquiry [of whether a person is required], the court has already considered whether the absentee is a person who is subject to service of process and whose joinder will not deprive the court of subject-matter jurisdiction. For the set of absentees who meet those criteria, it is Rule 19(a)(2) that specifies the correct response by the court, not Rule 19(b). [¶] Only if the court determines that a party meets the criteria of Rule 19(a)(1)(A) and (B), but the party cannot be joined (usually because joinder would destroy complete diversity or the court lacks personal jurisdiction over it) must the court turn to Rule 19(b) and decide what to do about the problem. Even then, dismissal is not automatic. Instead, the court must 'determine whether, in equity and good conscience, the action should proceed among the existing parties or should be dismissed.' Rule 19(b) spells out factors for the court to consider in making that judgment, with an emphasis on practical measures that will allow either the entire suit or part of it to go forward."

Huber v. Taylor, 532 F.3d 237, 248 (3d Cir.2008). "Under Rule 19(a)(1) [now Rule 19(a)(1)(A)], the Court must consider whether—in the absence of an un-joined party—complete relief can be granted to the persons already parties to the lawsuit. The effect that a decision may have on an absent party is immaterial. In contrast, under Rule 19(a)(2)(i) [now Rule 19(a)(1)(B)(i)], the Court must consider the effect, if any, that resolution of the dispute among the named parties will have on an absent party."

Hooper v. Wolfe, 396 F.3d 744, 749 n.4 (6th Cir. 2005). "In this diversity case, the question of whether a party is necessary or indispensable is a question of federal law. State law provides guidance in determining whether the parties have an interest in the litigation, as defined by Rule 19, but state law is not determinative of the question of whether a party is necessary or indispensable for purposes of Rule 19."

Diagnostic Unit Inmate Council v. Films Inc., 88 F.3d 651, 654 (8th Cir.1996). "[A]n involuntary plaintiff may be joined to cure the original plaintiff's inability to press a claim if the original plaintiff and the involuntary plaintiff have 'such a relationship that the absent party must allow the use of his name as plaintiff.'"

FRCP 20. PERMISSIVE JOINDER OF PARTIES

(a) Persons Who May Join or Be Joined.

(1) ***Plaintiffs.*** Persons may join in one action as plaintiffs if:

(A) they assert any right to relief jointly, severally, or in the alternative with respect to or arising out of the same transaction, occurrence, or series of transactions or occurrences; and

(B) any question of law or fact common to all plaintiffs will arise in the action.

(2) ***Defendants.*** Persons—as well as a vessel, cargo, or other property subject to admiralty process in rem—may be joined in one action as defendants if:

(A) any right to relief is asserted against them jointly, severally, or in the alternative with respect to or arising out of the same transaction, occurrence, or series of transactions or occurrences; and

(B) any question of law or fact common to all defendants will arise in the action.

(3) ***Extent of Relief.*** Neither a plaintiff nor a defendant need be interested in obtaining or defending against all the relief demanded. The court may grant judgment to one or more plaintiffs according to their rights, and against one or more defendants according to their liabilities.

(b) Protective Measures. The court may issue orders—including an order for separate trials—to protect a party against embarrassment, delay, expense, or other prejudice that arises from including a person against whom the party asserts no claim and who asserts no claim against the party.

History of FRCP 20: Adopted Dec. 20, 1937, eff. Sept. 16, 1938. Amended Feb. 28, 1966, eff. July 1, 1966; Mar. 2, 1987, eff. Aug. 1, 1987; Apr. 30, 2007, eff. Dec. 1, 2007.

See ***Commentaries***, "Motion for Severance or Separate Trials," ch. 5-L, p. 366; ***O'Connor's Federal Civil Forms*** (2012), FORMS 5L.

See also 28 U.S.C. §1359 (collusive and improper joinder of parties).

ANNOTATIONS

Snyder v. Harris, 394 U.S. 332, 337 (1969). "[W]here two or more plaintiffs join their claims under the joinder provisions of Rule 20, each and every joined plaintiff is bound by the judgment."

In re EMC Corp., 677 F.3d 1351, 1356 (Fed.Cir. 2012). "[W]here defendants are alleged to be jointly liable, they may be joined under Rule 20 because the transaction-or-occurrence test is always satisfied. But the language of Rule 20 makes clear that joinder is not limited to such situations. Defendants may be joined if 'any right to relief is asserted against them jointly, *severally, or in the alternative*,' … so an allegation of joint liability is not required. [¶] The cases make equally clear that the fact that the defendants are independent actors does not preclude joinder as long as their actions are part of the 'same transaction, occurrence, or series of transactions or occurrences.' *At 1358:* [I]ndependent defendants satisfy the transaction-or-occurrence test of Rule 20 when there is a logical relationship between the separate causes of action. The logical relationship test is satisfied if there is substantial evidentiary overlap in the facts giving rise to the cause of action against each defendant."

Lee v. Cook Cty., 635 F.3d 969, 971 (7th Cir.2011). Under FRCP 20(a), "[m]ultiple plaintiffs are free to join their claims in a single suit when '*any* question of law or fact common to all plaintiffs will arise in the action.' The common question need not predominate; that's a requirement for class actions, not for permissive joinder. [¶] If other issues predominate over the common question, the district judge is entitled to sever the suit or order separate trials. When a federal civil action is severed, it is not dismissed. Instead, the clerk of court creates multiple docket numbers for the action already on file, and the severed claims proceed as if suits had been filed separately."

Alexander v. Fulton Cty., 207 F.3d 1303, 1323 (11th Cir.2000). "In determining what constitutes a transaction or occurrence for the purposes of [FRCP] 20(a), courts have looked for meaning to [FRCP] 13(a) governing compulsory counterclaims. For the purposes of Rule 13(a), 'transaction' is a word of flexible meaning. It may comprehend a series of many occurrences, depending not so much upon the immediateness of their connection as upon their logical relationship. Accordingly, all 'logically related' events entitling a person to institute a legal action against another generally are

regarded as comprising a transaction or occurrence." (Internal quotes omitted.)

Tapscott v. MS Dealer Serv., 77 F.3d 1353, 1360 (11th Cir.1996), *overruled on other grounds*, ***Cohen v. Office Depot, Inc.***, 204 F.3d 1069 (11th Cir.2000). "Joinder of defendants under Rule 20 requires: (1) a claim for relief asserting joint, several, or alternative liability and arising from the same transaction, occurrence, or series of transactions or occurrences, and (2) a common question of law or fact."

FRCP 21. MISJOINDER & NONJOINDER OF PARTIES

Misjoinder of parties is not a ground for dismissing an action. On motion or on its own, the court may at any time, on just terms, add or drop a party. The court may also sever any claim against a party.

History of FRCP 21: Adopted Dec. 20, 1937, eff. Sept. 16, 1938. Amended Apr. 30, 2007, eff. Dec. 1, 2007.

See ***Commentaries***, "Motion for Severance or Separate Trials," ch. 5-L, p. 366; ***O'Connor's Federal Civil Forms*** (2012), FORMS 5L.

See also 28 U.S.C. §1359 (collusive and improper joinder of parties), §1447 (procedure after removal generally).

ANNOTATIONS

Newman-Green, Inc. v. Alfonzo-Larrain, 490 U.S. 826, 832-33 (1989). "The narrow question before us … is whether a court of appeals may do what a district court can do and dismiss a dispensable nondiverse party itself, or whether a court of appeals must remand the case to the district court, leaving it to the district court's discretion to dismiss the party? *At 837-38:* [W]e hold that the courts of appeals have the authority to dismiss a dispensable nondiverse party, [but] we emphasize that such authority should be exercised sparingly. In each case, the appellate court should carefully consider whether the dismissal of a nondiverse party will prejudice any of the parties in the litigation."

Dexia Crédit Local v. Rogan, 629 F.3d 612, 621 (7th Cir.2010). "Rule 21 dismissals are retroactive, … and the complaint is read as if the dismissed party had never been included…. Retroactive applications of Rule 21 have permitted appellate courts to affirm decisions of district courts on the merits despite the fact that the change in the parties did not occur until much later in the litigation, thereby avoiding the 'waste of time and resources [that] would be engendered by remanding to the District Court or by forcing the[] parties to begin anew.'"

Perry v. Blum, 629 F.3d 1, 16-17 (1st Cir.2010). "Although [FRCP 21] permits joinder at any stage of the proceedings, joinder in a particular case must comport with the strictures of due process. These strictures include notice and an opportunity to be heard at a meaningful time and in a meaningful manner. [¶] For obvious reasons, joinder of a defendant after trial is disfavored. In such a situation, concerns about possible prejudice to the late-joined party loom large."

DirecTV, Inc. v. Leto, 467 F.3d 842, 844 (3d Cir. 2006). "Misjoinder … occurs when there is no common question of law or fact or when … the events that give rise to the plaintiff's claims against defendants do not stem from the same transaction. *At 845:* To remedy misjoinder, … a court may not simply dismiss a suit altogether. Instead, the court has two remedial options: (1) misjoined parties may be dropped 'on such terms as are just'; or (2) any claims against misjoined parties 'may be severed and proceeded with separately.' [¶] Because a district court's decision to remedy misjoinder by dropping and dismissing a party, rather than severing the relevant claim, may have important and potentially adverse statute-of-limitations consequences, the discretion delegated to the trial judge to dismiss under Rule 21 is restricted to what is 'just.'"

Gaffney v. Riverboat Servs., 451 F.3d 424, 442 (7th Cir.2006). "'A separate trial order under [FRCP] 42(b) is interlocutory and non-appealable.' By contrast, '[s]everance under [FRCP] 21 creates two separate actions or suits where previously there was but one. Where a single claim is severed out of a suit, it proceeds as a discrete, independent action, and a court may render a final, appealable judgment in either one of the resulting two actions notwithstanding the continued existence of unresolved claims in the other.'" *See also* ***Chrysler Credit Corp. v. Country Chrysler, Inc.***, 928 F.2d 1509, 1519 n.8 (10th Cir.1991).

Balgowan v. New Jersey, 115 F.3d 214, 217 (3d Cir. 1997). "Resort to Rule 21 is appropriate where 'requiring dismissal after years of litigation would impose unnecessary and wasteful burdens on the parties, judges, and other litigants waiting for judicial attention.'"

Safeco Ins. v. City of White House, 36 F.3d 540, 545 (6th Cir.1994). FRCP 21 "permits a district court to retain diversity jurisdiction over a case by dropping a nondiverse party if that party's presence in the action is not required under [FRCP] 19, that is, the party to be dropped must not be a necessary party. '[I]t is well settled that Rule 21 invests district courts with author-

ity to allow a dispensable nondiverse party to be dropped at any time, even after judgment has been rendered.'"

FRCP 22. INTERPLEADER

(a) Grounds.

(1) ***By a Plaintiff.*** Persons with claims that may expose a plaintiff to double or multiple liability may be joined as defendants and required to interplead. Joinder for interpleader is proper even though:

(A) the claims of the several claimants, or the titles on which their claims depend, lack a common origin or are adverse and independent rather than identical; or

(B) the plaintiff denies liability in whole or in part to any or all of the claimants.

(2) ***By a Defendant.*** A defendant exposed to similar liability may seek interpleader through a crossclaim or counterclaim.

(b) Relation to Other Rules and Statutes. This rule supplements—and does not limit—the joinder of parties allowed by Rule 20. The remedy this rule provides is in addition to—and does not supersede or limit—the remedy provided by 28 U.S.C. §§1335, 1397, and 2361. An action under those statutes must be conducted under these rules.

History of FRCP 22: Adopted Dec. 20, 1937, eff. Sept. 16, 1938. Amended Dec. 29, 1948, eff. Oct. 20, 1949; Mar. 2, 1987, eff. Aug. 1, 1987; Apr. 30, 2007, eff. Dec. 1, 2007.

See ***Commentaries***, "Interpleader," ch. 2-C, p. 87; ***O'Connor's Federal Civil Forms*** (2012), FORMS 2C.

ANNOTATIONS

State Farm Fire & Cas. Co. v. Tashire, 386 U.S. 523, 528 n.3 (1967). "Whereas statutory interpleader may be brought in the district where any claimant resides, Rule interpleader based upon diversity of citizenship may be brought only in the district where all plaintiffs or all defendants reside. And whereas statutory interpleader enables a plaintiff to employ nationwide service of process, service of process under [FRCP] 22 is confined to that provided in [FRCP] 4."

Bradley v. Kochenash, 44 F.3d 166, 168 (2d Cir. 1995). "The requirement that the claims as to which interpleader is sought be adverse to each other is not met when … the stakeholder may be liable to both claimants. Thus, the protection against double or multiple liability provided by Rule 22 is protection only against double or multiple liability that is unjustifiable because the plaintiff has but a single obligation. *At 169:* Interpleader is designed to prevent multiple recoveries only where there are not multiple obligations; it is not intended to telescope multiple obligations into one." (Internal quotes omitted.)

Commercial Un. Ins. v. U.S., 999 F.2d 581, 583 (D.C.Cir.1993). "Interpleader may be brought in federal court under either the Federal Interpleader Act … or under [FRCP] 22…. *At 584:* The central distinction between statutory interpleader and rule interpleader is the basis for a federal court's subject matter jurisdiction under each. The Act requires that two or more of the adverse claimants to a contested fund be 'of diverse citizenship as defined in [28 U.S.C.] §1332….' Rule 22 … 'is merely a procedural device; it confers no jurisdiction on the federal courts.' Thus, an interpleader brought under Rule 22 must fall within one of the general statutory grants of federal jurisdiction." *See also* ***Correspondent Servs. v. First Equities Corp.***, 338 F.3d 119, 124 (2d Cir.2003) (rule interpleader does not provide independent basis for jurisdiction); ***Metropolitan Life Ins. v. Marsh***, 119 F.3d 415, 418 (6th Cir. 1997) (same); ***Angst v. Royal Maccabees Life Ins.***, 77 F.3d 701, 703-04 (3d Cir.1996) (diversity between stakeholder and claimants is sufficient to confer federal jurisdiction).

FRCP 23. CLASS ACTIONS

(a) Prerequisites. One or more members of a class may sue or be sued as representative parties on behalf of all members only if:

(1) the class is so numerous that joinder of all members is impracticable;

(2) there are questions of law or fact common to the class;

(3) the claims or defenses of the representative parties are typical of the claims or defenses of the class; and

(4) the representative parties will fairly and adequately protect the interests of the class.

(b) Types of Class Actions. A class action may be maintained if Rule 23(a) is satisfied and if:

(1) prosecuting separate actions by or against individual class members would create a risk of:

(A) inconsistent or varying adjudications with respect to individual class members that

would establish incompatible standards of conduct for the party opposing the class; or

(B) adjudications with respect to individual class members that, as a practical matter, would be dispositive of the interests of the other members not parties to the individual adjudications or would substantially impair or impede their ability to protect their interests;

(2) the party opposing the class has acted or refused to act on grounds that apply generally to the class, so that final injunctive relief or corresponding declaratory relief is appropriate respecting the class as a whole; or

(3) the court finds that the questions of law or fact common to class members predominate over any questions affecting only individual members, and that a class action is superior to other available methods for fairly and efficiently adjudicating the controversy. The matters pertinent to these findings include:

(A) the class members' interests in individually controlling the prosecution or defense of separate actions;

(B) the extent and nature of any litigation concerning the controversy already begun by or against class members;

(C) the desirability or undesirability of concentrating the litigation of the claims in the particular forum; and

(D) the likely difficulties in managing a class action.

(c) Certification Order; Notice to Class Members; Judgment; Issues Classes; Subclasses.

(1) ***Certification Order.***

(A) *Time to Issue.* At an early practicable time after a person sues or is sued as a class representative, the court must determine by order whether to certify the action as a class action.

(B) *Defining the Class; Appointing Class Counsel.* An order that certifies a class action must define the class and the class claims, issues, or defenses, and must appoint class counsel under Rule 23(g).

(C) *Altering or Amending the Order.* An order that grants or denies class certification may be altered or amended before final judgment.

(2) ***Notice.***

(A) *For (b)(1) or (b)(2) Classes.* For any class certified under Rule 23(b)(1) or (b)(2), the court may direct appropriate notice to the class.

(B) *For (b)(3) Classes.* For any class certified under Rule 23(b)(3), the court must direct to class members the best notice that is practicable under the circumstances, including individual notice to all members who can be identified through reasonable effort. The notice must clearly and concisely state in plain, easily understood language:

(i) the nature of the action;

(ii) the definition of the class certified;

(iii) the class claims, issues, or defenses;

(iv) that a class member may enter an appearance through an attorney if the member so desires;

(v) that the court will exclude from the class any member who requests exclusion;

(vi) the time and manner for requesting exclusion; and

(vii) the binding effect of a class judgment on members under Rule 23(c)(3).

(3) ***Judgment.*** Whether or not favorable to the class, the judgment in a class action must:

(A) for any class certified under Rule 23(b)(1) or (b)(2), include and describe those whom the court finds to be class members; and

(B) for any class certified under Rule 23(b)(3), include and specify or describe those to whom the Rule 23(c)(2) notice was directed, who have not requested exclusion, and whom the court finds to be class members.

(4) ***Particular Issues.*** When appropriate, an action may be brought or maintained as a class action with respect to particular issues.

(5) ***Subclasses.*** When appropriate, a class may be divided into subclasses that are each treated as a class under this rule.

(d) Conducting the Action.

(1) ***In General.*** In conducting an action under this rule, the court may issue orders that:

(A) determine the course of proceedings or prescribe measures to prevent undue repetition or complication in presenting evidence or argument;

(B) require—to protect class members and fairly conduct the action—giving appropriate notice to some or all class members of:

(i) any step in the action;

(ii) the proposed extent of the judgment; or

(iii) the members' opportunity to signify whether they consider the representation fair and adequate, to intervene and present claims or defenses, or to otherwise come into the action;

(C) impose conditions on the representative parties or on intervenors;

(D) require that the pleadings be amended to eliminate allegations about representation of absent persons and that the action proceed accordingly; or

(E) deal with similar procedural matters.

(2) ***Combining and Amending Orders.*** An order under Rule 23(d)(1) may be altered or amended from time to time and may be combined with an order under Rule 16.

(e) Settlement, Voluntary Dismissal, or Compromise. The claims, issues, or defenses of a certified class may be settled, voluntarily dismissed, or compromised only with the court's approval. The following procedures apply to a proposed settlement, voluntary dismissal, or compromise:

(1) The court must direct notice in a reasonable manner to all class members who would be bound by the proposal.

(2) If the proposal would bind class members, the court may approve it only after a hearing and on finding that it is fair, reasonable, and adequate.

(3) The parties seeking approval must file a statement identifying any agreement made in connection with the proposal.

(4) If the class action was previously certified under Rule 23(b)(3), the court may refuse to approve a settlement unless it affords a new opportunity to request exclusion to individual class members who had an earlier opportunity to request exclusion but did not do so.

(5) Any class member may object to the proposal if it requires court approval under this subdivision (e); the objection may be withdrawn only with the court's approval.

(f) Appeals. A court of appeals may permit an appeal from an order granting or denying class-action certification under this rule if a petition for permission to appeal is filed with the circuit clerk within 14 days after the order is entered. An appeal does not stay proceedings in the district court unless the district judge or the court of appeals so orders.

(g) Class Counsel.

(1) ***Appointing Class Counsel.*** Unless a statute provides otherwise, a court that certifies a class must appoint class counsel. In appointing class counsel, the court:

(A) must consider:

(i) the work counsel has done in identifying or investigating potential claims in the action;

(ii) counsel's experience in handling class actions, other complex litigation, and the types of claims asserted in the action;

(iii) counsel's knowledge of the applicable law; and

(iv) the resources that counsel will commit to representing the class;

(B) may consider any other matter pertinent to counsel's ability to fairly and adequately represent the interests of the class;

(C) may order potential class counsel to provide information on any subject pertinent to the appointment and to propose terms for attorney's fees and nontaxable costs;

(D) may include in the appointing order provisions about the award of attorney's fees or nontaxable costs under Rule 23(h); and

(E) may make further orders in connection with the appointment.

(2) ***Standard for Appointing Class Counsel.*** When one applicant seeks appointment as class counsel, the court may appoint that applicant only if the applicant is adequate under

Rule 23(g)(1) and (4). If more than one adequate applicant seeks appointment, the court must appoint the applicant best able to represent the interests of the class.

(3) ***Interim Counsel.*** The court may designate interim counsel to act on behalf of a putative class before determining whether to certify the action as a class action.

(4) ***Duty of Class Counsel.*** Class counsel must fairly and adequately represent the interests of the class.

(h) Attorney's Fees and Nontaxable Costs. In a certified class action, the court may award reasonable attorney's fees and nontaxable costs that are authorized by law or by the parties' agreement. The following procedures apply:

(1) A claim for an award must be made by motion under Rule 54(d)(2), subject to the provisions of this subdivision (h), at a time the court sets. Notice of the motion must be served on all parties and, for motions by class counsel, directed to class members in a reasonable manner.

(2) A class member, or a party from whom payment is sought, may object to the motion.

(3) The court may hold a hearing and must find the facts and state its legal conclusions under Rule 52(a).

(4) The court may refer issues related to the amount of the award to a special master or a magistrate judge, as provided in Rule 54(d)(2)(D).

See selected Notes of Advisory Committee to FRCP 23, p. 1164.

History of FRCP 23: Adopted Dec. 20, 1937, eff. Sept. 16, 1938. Amended Feb. 28, 1966, eff. July 1, 1966; Mar. 2, 1987, eff. Aug. 1, 1987; Apr. 24, 1998, eff. Dec. 1, 1998; Mar. 27, 2003, eff. Dec. 1, 2003; Apr. 30, 2007, eff. Dec. 1, 2007; Mar. 26, 2009, eff. Dec. 1, 2009.

See ***Commentaries***, "Motion for Class Certification," ch. 5-P, p. 398; ***O'Connor's Federal Civil Forms*** (2012), FORMS 5P.

See also 28 U.S.C. §1401 (venue in stockholder's derivative action), §1695 (process on corporations in stockholder's derivative action).

ANNOTATIONS

Generally

Shady Grove Orthopedic Assocs. v. Allstate Ins., ___ U.S. ___, 130 S.Ct. 1431, 1437 (2010) (plurality op.). "The question in dispute is whether [P's] suit[, which seeks to recover statutory interest as a class action but is prohibited under New York law,] may proceed as a class action [in federal court based on diversity jurisdiction]. Rule 23 provides an answer. It states that '[a] class action may be maintained' if two conditions are met: The suit must satisfy the criteria set forth in subdivision (a) ..., and it also must fit into one of the three categories described in subdivision (b). By its terms this creates a categorical rule entitling a plaintiff whose suit meets the specified criteria to pursue his claim as a class action. (The Federal Rules regularly use 'may' to confer categorical permission, ... as do federal statutes that establish procedural entitlements....) Thus, Rule 23 provides a one-size-fits-all formula for deciding the class-action question. *At S.Ct. 1438:* There is no reason ... to read Rule 23 as addressing only whether claims made eligible for class treatment by some *other* law should be certified as class actions. [D] asserts that Rule 23 neither explicitly nor implicitly empowers a federal court 'to certify a class in each and every case' where the Rule's criteria are met. But that is *exactly* what Rule 23 does: It says that if the prescribed preconditions are satisfied '[a] class action *may be maintained*' ... [,] not '*a class action may be permitted.*' Courts do not maintain actions; litigants do. The discretion suggested by Rule 23's 'may' is discretion residing in the plaintiff: He may bring his claim in a class action if he wishes. And like the rest of the [FRCPs], Rule 23 *automatically* applies 'in all civil actions and proceedings in the U.S. district courts'...."

Gulf Oil Co. v. Bernard, 452 U.S. 89, 101-02 (1981). "[A]n order limiting communications between parties and potential class members should be based on a clear record and specific findings that reflect a weighing of the need for a limitation and the potential interference with the rights of the parties. Only such a determination can ensure that the court is furthering, rather than hindering, the policies embodied in the [FRCPs], especially Rule 23. In addition, such a weighing—identifying the potential abuses being addressed—should result in a carefully drawn order that limits speech as little as possible, consistent with the rights of the parties under the circumstances."

Loeb Indus. v. Sumitomo Corp., 306 F.3d 469, 496 (7th Cir.2002). "[Ds] argue that [Ps'] claims were abandoned when [Ps] attempted to certify a class for the federal antitrust claims but not for the state claims. But no inference of abandonment should flow from a limited request for a class action.... It would be entirely consistent ... to seek certification on issues governed by federal law, while declining to do so for more particularized state law issues."

In re Visa Check/Mastermoney Antitrust Litig., 280 F.3d 124, 141 (2d Cir.2001), *overruled on other grounds*, ***In re Initial Pub. Offerings Secs. Litig.***, 471 F.3d 24 (2d Cir.2006). "There are a number of management tools available to a district court to address any individualized damages issues that might arise in a class action, including: (1) bifurcating liability and damage trials with the same or different juries; (2) appointing a magistrate judge or special master to preside over individual damages proceedings; (3) decertifying the class after the liability trial and providing notice to class members concerning how they may proceed to prove damages; (4) creating subclasses; or (5) altering or amending the class."

FRCP 23(a) Prerequisites

Wal-Mart Stores v. Dukes, ___ U.S. ___, 131 S.Ct. 2541, 2550-51 (2011). "[T]he rule requiring a plaintiff to show that there are questions of law or fact common to the class … is easy to misread, since any competently crafted class complaint literally raises common questions. … Commonality requires the plaintiff to demonstrate that the class members have suffered the same injury…. This does not mean merely that they have all suffered a violation of the same provision of law. [The] claims must depend upon a common contention [and that] common contention … must be of such a nature that it is capable of classwide resolution—which means that determination of its truth or falsity will resolve an issue that is central to the validity of each one of the claims in one stroke. *At 2556:* [F]or purposes of Rule 23(a)(2) even a single common question will do…. We consider dissimilarities [between putative class members] not … to determine (as Rule 23(b)(3) requires) whether common questions *predominate*, but … to determine (as Rule 23(a)(2) requires) whether there *is* even a single common question." (Internal quotes omitted.)

Pigford v. Veneman, 292 F.3d 918, 926 (D.C.Cir. 2002). "The Rule 23(a)(4) finding of class counsel adequacy may partially substitute for the free choice found in conventional non-class litigation. Like most presumptions, however, this one is rebuttable. And in litigation involving a class—defined from the outset by its numerosity—where counsel is not in fact freely chosen by class members, it is logical that the presumption should be more easily overcome than if the clients had in fact freely chosen their attorneys."

Piazza v. EBSCO Indus., 273 F.3d 1341, 1346 (11th Cir.2001). "Typicality, along with the related requirement of commonality, focuses on whether a sufficient nexus exists between the legal claims of the named class representatives and those of individual class members to warrant class certification. Traditionally, commonality refers to the group characteristics of the class as a whole, while typicality refers to the individual characteristics of the named plaintiff in relation to the class. Typicality also encompasses the question of the named plaintiff's standing, for '[w]ithout individual standing to raise a legal claim, a named representative does not have the requisite typicality to raise the same claim on behalf of a class.' 'Adequacy of representation' means that the class representative has common interests with unnamed class members and will vigorously prosecute the interests of the class through qualified counsel."

Twelve John Does v. District of Columbia, 117 F.3d 571, 575 (D.C.Cir.1997). "Among the many factors governing the district court's decision that [Ps] are adequately represented are the quality of class counsel, any disparity in interest between class representatives and members of a would-be subclass, communication between class counsel and the class, and the overall context of the litigation." *See also* ***Robinson v. Metro-N. Commuter R.R.***, 267 F.3d 147, 170 (2d Cir. 2001) (absence of conflict and assurance of vigorous prosecution are two factors to determine if Ps are adequately represented).

In re Brand Name Prescription Drugs Antitrust Litig., 115 F.3d 456, 457-58 (7th Cir.1997). "If the certified class representative does not adequately represent the interests of some of the class members, those class members can opt out of the class action, can seek the creation of a separately represented subclass, can ask for the replacement of the class representative, or can intervene of right and become named plaintiffs themselves, or even class representatives, represented by their own lawyer." *See also* ***Taylor v. United Parcel Serv.***, 554 F.3d 510, 517 (5th Cir.2008) (class representative's responsibility is to protect interests of all class members; class members should not have to monitor litigation to ensure their interests are being protected); ***Maywalt v. Parker & Parsley Pet. Co.***, 67 F.3d 1072, 1078 (2d Cir.1995) (class representatives and counsel must report any conflicts of interest).

FRCP 23

FRCP 23(b)(1) Actions

McReynolds v. Richards-Cantave, 588 F.3d 790, 800 (2d Cir.2009). See annotation under *FRCP 23(b)(2) Actions*, this page.

FRCP 23(b)(2) Actions

Wal-Mart Stores v. Dukes, ___ U.S. ___, 131 S.Ct. 2541, 2557 (2011). "[C]laims for monetary relief ... may not [be certified under FRCP 23(b)(2)], at least where ... the monetary relief is not incidental to the injunctive or declaratory relief. [¶] One possible reading of [Rule 23(b)(2)] is that it applies *only* to requests for such injunctive or declaratory relief and does not authorize the class certification of monetary claims at all. We need not reach that broader question in this case, because we think that, at a minimum, claims for *individualized* relief ... do not satisfy the Rule. ... Rule 23(b)(2) applies only when a single injunction or declaratory judgment would provide relief to each member of the class. It does not authorize class certification when each individual class member would be entitled to a *different* injunction or declaratory judgment against the defendant. Similarly, it does not authorize class certification when each class member would be entitled to an individualized award of monetary damages. *At 2558-59:* Given [the] structure [of Rule 23(b)], we think it clear that individualized monetary claims belong in Rule 23(b)(3). The procedural protections attending the (b)(3) class—predominance, superiority, mandatory notice, and the right to opt out—are missing from (b)(2) not because the Rule considers them unnecessary, but because it considers them unnecessary *to a (b)(2) class*. When a class seeks an indivisible injunction benefitting all its members at once, there is no reason to undertake a case-specific inquiry into whether class issues predominate or whether class action is a superior method of adjudicating the dispute. Predominance and superiority are self-evident. But with respect to each class member's individualized claim for money, that is not so—which is precisely why (b)(3) requires the judge to make findings about predominance and superiority before allowing the class. Similarly, (b)(2) does not require that class members be given notice and opt-out rights, presumably because it is thought (rightly or wrongly) that notice has no purpose when the class is mandatory, and that depriving people of their right to sue in this manner complies with the Due Process Clause."

McReynolds v. Richards-Cantave, 588 F.3d 790, 800 (2d Cir.2009). "The right of a class member to opt-out in Rule 23(b)(1) and (b)(2) actions is not obvious on the face of the rule; however, 'the language of Rule 23 is sufficiently flexible to afford district courts discretion to grant opt-out rights in (b)(1) and (b)(2) class actions.' Where ... the right to opt out in a Rule 23(b)(2) class action is permitted by the court, we have noted that class members may exercise that right by '[a]ny reasonable indication of a desire to opt out [of the class action lawsuit].' In this regard, however, a mere objection to a proposed settlement cannot necessarily be deemed a 'reasonable indication of a desire to opt out' of the class action. Rule 23(e)(5) provides a separate right of class members to object to a settlement proposal, and there is no authority for the questionable proposition that an automatic 'opt-out' occurs by filing or raising an objection." *But see* ***McManus v. Fleetwood Enters.***, this page.

McManus v. Fleetwood Enters., 320 F.3d 545, 553 (5th Cir.2003). "Unlike Rule 23(b)(3), class members are not permitted to opt-out of a Rule 23(b)(2) class to pursue their claims individually. '[B]ecause of the group nature of the harm alleged and the broad character of the relief sought, the (b)(2) class is, by its very nature, assumed to be a homogeneous and cohesive group with few conflicting interests among its members.'" *But see* ***McReynolds v. Richards-Cantave***, this page.

FRCP 23(b)(3) Actions

Wal-Mart Stores v. Dukes, ___ U.S. ___, 131 S.Ct. 2541, 2558-59 (2011). See annotation under *FRCP 23(b)(2) Actions*, this page.

Smilow v. Southwestern Bell Mobile Sys., 323 F.3d 32, 39-40 (1st Cir.2003). "[W]here common issues otherwise predominated, courts have usually certified Rule 23(b)(3) classes even though individual issues were present in one or more affirmative defenses. After all, Rule 23(b)(3) requires merely that common issues predominate, not that all issues be common to the class. If ... evidence later shows that an affirmative defense is likely to bar claims against at least some class members, then a court has available adequate procedural mechanisms."

Ruling

Wal-Mart Stores v. Dukes, ___ U.S. ___, 131 S.Ct. 2541, 2551-52 (2011). "[C]ertification is proper only if the trial court is satisfied, after a rigorous analysis, that

the prerequisites of Rule 23(a) have been satisfied.... Frequently that rigorous analysis will entail some overlap with the merits of the plaintiff's underlying claim. That cannot be helped. The class determination generally involves considerations that are enmeshed in the factual and legal issues comprising the plaintiff's cause of action. Nor is there anything unusual about that consequence: The necessity of touching aspects of the merits ... to resolve preliminary matters, *e.g.*, jurisdiction and venue, is a familiar feature of litigation." (Internal quotes omitted.)

In re Pharmaceutical Indus. Average Wholesale Price Litig., 588 F.3d 24, 39 (1st Cir.2009). "Rule 23(c)(1)(B) explains the contents of a certification order: the order must clarify and detail the identity of a class and the class claims, issues, or defenses in a class action. ... The federal rules contemplate district courts issuing an order certifying a class and detailing the class composition and the case's issues and claims, an order the court can amend before final judgment. [¶] Rule 23(c)(1)(B)'s text appears to apply to any order certifying a class, including orders certifying an amended class. The rule governs '[a]n order that certifies a class action.' The text uses 'an' rather than 'the,' which suggests the drafters did not mean to restrict 23(c)(1)(B) to a single certification order in a case. [¶] The text of Rule 23(c)(1) does not specify how courts can accomplish the rule's aims, but the rule is meant to serve certain functions. The depth of explanation courts should provide in amended certification orders depends on the circumstances. Courts can amend certification orders to reflect major changes or minor adjustments to the class. District courts should ensure that, after the new order, the class's composition and claims remain well defined. *At 40:* Overall, better comprehension and explanation of the class and the class claims helps district courts, appellate courts, attorneys, and parties all proceed with more information and mutual understanding."

Miami Univ. Wrestling Club v. Miami Univ., 302 F.3d 608, 616 (6th Cir.2002). "[A] district court is not required to rule on a motion for class certification before ruling on the merits of the case. Accordingly, we hold that the district court did not abuse its discretion in ruling first on the merits of [Ps'] claims before addressing [Ps'] motion for class certification." *But see* ***Wiesmueller v. Kosobucki***, 513 F.3d 784, 787 (7th Cir. 2008) (exceptional case to decide motion for summary judgment before motion for class certification).

In re American Med. Sys., 75 F.3d 1069, 1086 (6th Cir.1996). "The court should defer decision on certification pending discovery if the existing record is inadequate for resolving the relevant issues."

Interlocutory Appeals

Gene & Gene, L.L.C. v. BioPay, L.L.C., 624 F.3d 698, 703 (5th Cir.2010). "While [FRCP 23(c)(1)(C)] vests significant discretion in the district court [to alter or amend the certification order before final judgment], 'the district court's discretion in managing trials [after an FRCP 23(f) appeal] extends [only to] areas not covered by the higher court's mandate.' [¶] To be certain, in some scenarios, a district court may properly alter or amend a certification order after remand from this court on a Rule 23(f) appeal; a Rule 23(f) decision does not operate to automatically divest the district court of its powers under Rule 23(c)(1)(C). For example, if a district court certifies a class after preliminary discovery and the court of appeals affirms pursuant to Rule 23(f), and then during subsequent discovery it becomes clear that the district court needs to alter, amend, or even decertify the class, the district court can and should do so under Rule 23(c)(1)(C)."

In re DC Water & Sewer Auth., 561 F.3d 494, 495-97 (D.C.Cir.2009). "The ... deadline to file a petition for permission to appeal is 'strict and mandatory.' Other circuits have drawn a 'narrow exception to the rigid ... time limit,' providing that 'a timely-filed motion to reconsider the grant or denial of class certification tolls the ... time limit within which to file a petition for permission to appeal under Rule 23(f)'—or, more precisely, 'postpones' or 'resets' the ... period, which 'begins anew when the district court rules on the motion to reconsider'.... [¶] The ... order denying [D's] motion to clarify did not restart the Rule 23(f) clock because it was not 'an order granting or denying class-action certification' as the plain language of [FRCP 23(f)] requires.... To hold otherwise would leave Rule 23(f)'s deadline toothless, for any party could then cause the clock to restart at any time simply by filing a pleading styled as a 'motion to clarify.'"

In re New Motor Vehicles Canadian Exp. Antitrust Litig., 522 F.3d 6, 8 (1st Cir.2008). "Interlocutory appeals from class certification under Rule 23(f) are especially appropriate where the plaintiffs' theory is novel or where a doubtful class certification results in

financial exposure to defendants so great as to provide substantial incentives for defendants to settle non-meritorious cases in an effort to avoid both risk of liability and litigation expense. [¶] By the same token, an erroneous failure to certify a class where individual claims are small may deprive plaintiffs of the only realistic mechanism to vindicate meritorious claims."

Prado-Steiman v. Bush, 221 F.3d 1266, 1274 (11th Cir.2000). "[T]he following guideposts may be utilized in determining whether to grant an interlocutory appeal under Rule 23(f). [¶] First, and most important, the court should examine whether the district court's ruling is likely dispositive of the litigation by creating a 'death knell' for either plaintiff or defendant. [¶] Second, a court should consider whether the petitioner has shown a *substantial* weakness in the class certification decision, such that the decision likely constitutes an abuse of discretion. *At 1275:* Third, a court should consider whether the appeal will permit the resolution of an unsettled legal issue that is 'important to the particular litigation as well as important in itself.' *At 1276:* Fourth, a court should consider the nature and status of the litigation before the district court. [¶] Finally, a court should consider the likelihood that future events may make immediate appellate review more or less appropriate. [¶] We reiterate, however, that interlocutory appeals are inherently 'disruptive, time-consuming, and expensive,' and consequently are generally disfavored." *See also* ***Vallario v. Vandehey***, 554 F.3d 1259, 1263 (10th Cir.2009).

Notice to Class Members

Larson v. AT&T Mobility LLC, 687 F.3d 109, 124 (3d Cir.2012). "[I]ndividual notice must be delivered to class members who can be reasonably identified, and ... the costs required to actually deliver notice should not easily cause a court to permit the less satisfactory substitute of notice by publication. *At 126:* We have been ... stringent in enforcing the individual notice requirement. [W]here names and addresses of members of the class are easily ascertainable, due process ... dictate[s] that the best notice practicable under the circumstances would be individual notice. [I]t [is] the ultimate responsibility of the district court to ensure that the parties [comply] with notice requirements because the district court is the guardian of the rights of the absentees." (Internal quotes omitted.) *See also* ***Juris v. Inamed Corp.***, 685 F.3d 1294, 1317-19 (11th Cir. 2012).

Settlement Agreements

Devlin v. Scardelletti, 536 U.S. 1, 14 (2002). "[N]onnamed class members like petitioner who have objected in a timely manner to approval of the settlement at the fairness hearing have the power to bring an appeal without first intervening."

Evans v. Jeff D., 475 U.S. 717, 726-27 (1986). "Although changed circumstances may justify a court-ordered modification of a consent decree [in a class-action suit] over the objections of a party after the decree has been entered, ... Rule 23(e) does not give the court the power ... to modify a proposed consent decree and order its acceptance over either party's objection. The options available to the District Court were essentially the same as those available to respondents: it could have accepted the proposed settlement; it could have rejected the proposal and postponed the trial to see if a different settlement could be achieved; or it could have decided to try the case." *See also* ***Ehrheart v. Verizon Wireless***, 609 F.3d 590, 592 (3d Cir.2010).

Poplar Creek Dev. Co. v. Chesapeake Appalachia, L.L.C., 636 F.3d 235, 244 (6th Cir.2011). "To determine whether a settlement agreement satisfies Rule 23's standard, courts in this circuit are required to consider: '(1) the risk of fraud or collusion; (2) the complexity, expense and likely duration of the litigation; (3) the amount of discovery engaged in by the parties; (4) the likelihood of success on the merits; (5) the opinions of class counsel and class representatives; (6) the reaction of absent class members; and (7) the public interest.' *At 245:* 'The most important of the factors ... is the probability of success on the merits. The likelihood of success, in turn, provides a gauge from which the benefits of the settlement must be measured.' 'Even the denial of all relief ... might be justified if careful scrutiny indicated that the class had no realistic prospect of sufficient success to enable an actual distribution to the class members.'" *See also* ***Sullivan v. DB Invs.***, 667 F.3d 273, 319-20 (3d Cir.2011); ***In re Bluetooth Headset Prods. Liab. Litig.***, 654 F.3d 935, 946-47 (9th Cir.2011).

McReynolds v. Richards-Cantave, 588 F.3d 790, 800 (2d Cir.2009). See annotation under *FRCP 23(b)(1) Actions*, p. 882.

In re Insurance Brokerage Antitrust Litig., 579 F.3d 241, 257 (3d Cir.2009). "In order to approve a class settlement agreement, a district court must determine that the requirements for class certification under

[FRCP] 23(a) and (b) are met and must determine that the settlement is fair to the class under [FRCP] 23(e). … '[I]f a fairness inquiry under Rule 23(e) controlled certification, eclipsing Rule 23(a) and (b), and permitting class designation despite the impossibility of litigation, both class counsel and court would be disarmed.' Thus, it is important to 'apply[] the class certification requirements of Rules 23(a) and (b) separately from [the] fairness determination under Rule 23(e).' *At 258:* '[W]here settlement negotiations precede class certification, and approval for settlement and certification are sought simultaneously, we require district courts to be even more scrupulous than usual when examining the fairness of the proposed settlement.'"

Wal-Mart Stores v. Visa U.S.A., Inc., 396 F.3d 96, 114 (2d Cir.2005). "There are no rigid rules to determine whether a settlement notice to the class satisfies constitutional or Rule 23(e) requirements; the settlement notice must 'fairly apprise the prospective members of the class of the terms of the proposed settlement and of the options that are open to them in connection with the proceedings.' *At 115-16:* [T]he district court [held] that the law merely requires a class notice to describe effectively the scope of a release. Since the release was quoted in its entirety, the court concluded that 'the expansive reach of the release[] could not have been clearer. This is all that was required.' We agree … and do 'not believe that due process requires further explanation of the effects of the release provision in addition to the clear meaning of the words of the release.'" *See also* ***Rodriguez v. West Publ'g***, 563 F.3d 948, 962-63 (9th Cir.2009) (class notice communicated essentials of settlement in sufficiently balanced, accurate, and informative way to satisfy due-process concerns); ***White v. Alabama***, 74 F.3d 1058, 1066 n.27 (11th Cir.1996) (class notice must be understandable, and notice printed in very small type and filled with dense legalese was not).

Tennessee Ass'n of HMOs, Inc. v. Grier, 262 F.3d 559, 565-66 (6th Cir.2001). "[T]he procedure which courts must follow in order to approve a class action settlement [is]: (1) the court must preliminarily approve the proposed settlement, i.e., the court should determine whether the compromise embodied in the decree is illegal or tainted with collusion; (2) members of the class must be given notice of the proposed settlement; and (3) a hearing must be held to determine whether the decree is fair to those affected, adequate and reasonable." *See also* ***In re Vitamins Antitrust Class Actions***, 215 F.3d 26, 30 (D.C.Cir.2000).

Settlement Classes

Ortiz v. Fibreboard Corp., 527 U.S. 815, 821 (1999). "This case turns on the conditions for certifying a mandatory settlement class on a limited fund theory under [FRCP] 23(b)(1)(B). We hold that applicants for contested certification on this rationale must show that the fund is limited by more than the agreement of the parties, and has been allocated to claimants belonging within the class by a process addressing any conflicting interests of class members."

Amchem Prods. v. Windsor, 521 U.S. 591, 620 (1997). "Confronted with a request for settlement-only class certification, a district court need not inquire whether the case, if tried, would present intractable management problems, for the proposal is that there be no trial. But other specifications of [FRCP 23]—those designed to protect absentees by blocking unwarranted or overbroad class definitions—demand undiluted, even heightened, attention in the settlement context. Such attention is of vital importance, for a court asked to certify a settlement class will lack the opportunity, present when a case is litigated, to adjust the class, informed by the proceedings as they unfold."

Attorney Fees

In re Bluetooth Headset Prods. Liab. Litig., 654 F.3d 935, 941 (9th Cir.2011). "While attorneys' fees and costs may be awarded in a certified class action where so authorized by law or the parties' agreement, … courts have an independent obligation to ensure that the award, like the settlement itself, is reasonable, even if the parties have already agreed to an amount. The reasonableness of any fee award must be considered against the backdrop of the 'American Rule,' which provides that courts generally are without discretion to award attorneys' fees to a prevailing plaintiff unless (1) fee-shifting is expressly authorized by the governing statute; (2) the opponents acted in bad faith or willfully violated a court order; or (3) 'the successful litigants have created a common fund for recovery or extended a substantial benefit to a class.'"

In re Mercury Interactive Corp. Secs. Litig., 618 F.3d 988, 993-94 (9th Cir.2010). "We hold that the district court abused its discretion when it erred as a matter of law by misapplying Rule 23(h) in setting the objection deadline for class members on a date before the

FRCP 23

deadline for lead counsel to file their fee motion. [T]he practice borders on a denial of due process because it deprives objecting class members of a full and fair opportunity to contest class counsel's fee motion. [¶] The plain text of the rule requires a district court to set the deadline for objections to counsel's fee request on a date *after* the motion and documents supporting it have been filed. [T]he rule requires that any class member be allowed an opportunity to object to the fee 'motion' itself, not merely to the preliminary notice that such a motion will be filed. *At 995:* We do not adopt a bright-line rule of a time period that would meet Rule 23(h)'s requirement that the class have an adequate opportunity to oppose class counsel's fee motion. Obviously, that period will vary from case to case, and the district court is better positioned to make that decision after consideration of all of the circumstances in the case. But a schedule that requires objections to be filed before the fee motion itself is filed denies the class the full and fair opportunity to examine and oppose the motion that Rule 23(h) contemplates."

FRCP 23.1. DERIVATIVE ACTIONS

(a) Prerequisites. This rule applies when one or more shareholders or members of a corporation or an unincorporated association bring a derivative action to enforce a right that the corporation or association may properly assert but has failed to enforce. The derivative action may not be maintained if it appears that the plaintiff does not fairly and adequately represent the interests of shareholders or members who are similarly situated in enforcing the right of the corporation or association.

(b) Pleading Requirements. The complaint must be verified and must:

(1) allege that the plaintiff was a shareholder or member at the time of the transaction complained of, or that the plaintiff's share or membership later devolved on it by operation of law;

(2) allege that the action is not a collusive one to confer jurisdiction that the court would otherwise lack; and

(3) state with particularity:

(A) any effort by the plaintiff to obtain the desired action from the directors or comparable authority and, if necessary, from the shareholders or members; and

(B) the reasons for not obtaining the action or not making the effort.

(c) Settlement, Dismissal, and Compromise. A derivative action may be settled, voluntarily dismissed, or compromised only with the court's approval. Notice of a proposed settlement, voluntary dismissal, or compromise must be given to shareholders or members in the manner that the court orders.

History of FRCP 23.1: Adopted Feb. 28, 1966, eff. July 1, 1966. Amended Mar. 2, 1987, eff. Aug. 1, 1987; Apr. 30, 2007, eff. Dec. 1, 2007.

See ***Commentaries***, "Verification & affidavits," ch. 1-B, §2.1.10(2), p. 11; "Verification & Affidavits," ch. 2-B, §14, p. 86; *O'Connor's Federal Civil Forms* (2012), FORMS 1B.

ANNOTATIONS

Kamen v. Kemper Fin. Servs., 500 U.S. 90, 96 (1991). "[A]lthough Rule 23.1 clearly *contemplates* both the demand requirement and the possibility that demand may be excused, it does not *create* a demand requirement of any particular dimension. ... The purpose of the demand requirement is to afford the directors an opportunity to exercise their reasonable business judgment and waive a legal right vested in the corporation in the belief that its best interests will be promoted by not insisting on such right." (Internal quotes omitted.)

Halebian v. Berv, 590 F.3d 195, 204 (2d Cir.2009). "Rule 23.1 is a rule of pleading that creates a federal standard as to the specificity of facts alleged with regard to efforts made to urge a corporation's directors to bring the action in question. It does not abridge, enlarge or modify any substantive right. The underlying demand requirement, by contrast, in delimiting the respective powers of the individual shareholder and of the directors to control corporate litigation, clearly is a matter of 'substance,' not 'procedure.' It is therefore governed by state law." (Internal quotes omitted.)

Potter v. Hughes, 546 F.3d 1051, 1056 (9th Cir. 2008). A plaintiff "must 'allege with particularity the efforts, if any, made by the plaintiff to obtain the action the plaintiff desires from the directors' (the 'demand requirement'). *At 1057-58:* The identity of the shareholder is also an important practical element of a demand. The identity of the complaining shareholder may shed light on the veracity or significance of the facts alleged in the demand letter, and the Board might properly take a different course of action depending on the shareholder's identity. Before a demand letter can properly invoke a duty of a corporate board to take action to correct alleged wrongdoing, the board is entitled to know with specificity the identity of the person making

the demand. [¶] '[T]he demand requirement is designed to promote the basic principle of corporate governance that the board of directors, and not individual shareholders, manages the affairs of the corporation.'"

In re Bank of N.Y. Derivative Litig., 320 F.3d 291, 298 (2d Cir.2003). "[I]n order to invoke derivative standing pursuant to [FRCP] 23.1 …, a plaintiff must have owned stock in the corporation *throughout* the course of the activities that constitute the *primary basis* of the complaint." *See also* ***Quinn v. Anvil Corp.***, 620 F.3d 1005, 1012 (9th Cir.2010).

Stepak v. Addison, 20 F.3d 398, 402 (11th Cir. 1994). "The heightened pleading standard [of FRCP 23.1] further reinforces the notion that a shareholder derivative suit is an extraordinary procedural device, 'to be used only when it is clear that the corporation will not act to redress the alleged injury to itself.'"

Gottlieb v. Wiles, 11 F.3d 1004, 1011 (10th Cir. 1993), *overruled on other grounds*, ***Devlin v. Scardelletti***, 536 U.S. 1 (2002). "Unlike class actions under [FRCP] 23, in shareholder derivative suits under [FRCP] 23.1, a preliminary affirmative determination that the named plaintiffs will fairly and adequately represent the interests of the other class members is not a prerequisite to the maintenance of the action. … In addition, there is no opt-out provision in shareholder derivative suits. Thus, all shareholders are bound by the outcome regardless of their objections."

FRCP 23.2. ACTIONS RELATING TO UNINCORPORATED ASSOCIATIONS

This rule applies to an action brought by or against the members of an unincorporated association as a class by naming certain members as representative parties. The action may be maintained only if it appears that those parties will fairly and adequately protect the interests of the association and its members. In conducting the action, the court may issue any appropriate orders corresponding with those in Rule 23(d), and the procedure for settlement, voluntary dismissal, or compromise must correspond with the procedure in Rule 23(e).

History of FRCP 23.2: Adopted Feb. 28, 1966, eff. July 1, 1966. Amended Apr. 30, 2007, eff. Dec. 1, 2007.

See also FRCP 23 (class actions).

ANNOTATIONS

Aetna Cas. & Sur. Co. v. Iso-Tex, Inc., 75 F.3d 216, 218 (5th Cir.1996). Under FRCP 23.2, "the position of the members of [an unincorporated association] for jurisdictional purposes is analogous to that of unnamed class members: their citizenship is disregarded."

Resolution Trust Corp. v. Deloitte & Touche, 822 F.Supp. 1512, 1515 (D.Colo.1993). "The requirement of 'fair and adequate representation' is satisfied when: (1) the named representatives have common interests with the other class members; and (2) the class representatives will vigorously prosecute the interests of the class through qualified counsel. [¶] [I]t is not necessary to satisfy the other prerequisites of [FRCP] 23 if the requirements of [FRCP] 23.2 are met." *See also* ***Curley v. Brignoli, Curley & Roberts Assocs.***, 915 F.2d 81, 85 (2d Cir.1990).

FRCP 24. INTERVENTION

(a) Intervention of Right. On timely motion, the court must permit anyone to intervene who:

(1) is given an unconditional right to intervene by a federal statute; or

(2) claims an interest relating to the property or transaction that is the subject of the action, and is so situated that disposing of the action may as a practical matter impair or impede the movant's ability to protect its interest, unless existing parties adequately represent that interest.

(b) Permissive Intervention.

(1) ***In General.*** On timely motion, the court may permit anyone to intervene who:

(A) is given a conditional right to intervene by a federal statute; or

(B) has a claim or defense that shares with the main action a common question of law or fact.

(2) ***By a Government Officer or Agency.*** On timely motion, the court may permit a federal or state governmental officer or agency to intervene if a party's claim or defense is based on:

(A) a statute or executive order administered by the officer or agency; or

(B) any regulation, order, requirement, or agreement issued or made under the statute or executive order.

(3) ***Delay or Prejudice.*** In exercising its discretion, the court must consider whether the intervention will unduly delay or prejudice the adjudication of the original parties' rights.

(c) **Notice and Pleading Required.** A motion to intervene must be served on the parties as provided in Rule 5. The motion must state the grounds for intervention and be accompanied by a pleading that sets out the claim or defense for which intervention is sought.

See selected Notes of Advisory Committee to FRCP 24, p. 1171.

History of FRCP 24: Adopted Dec. 20, 1937, eff. Sept. 16, 1938. Amended Dec. 27, 1946, eff. Mar. 19, 1948; Dec. 29, 1948, eff. Oct. 20, 1949; Jan. 21, 1963, eff. July 1, 1963; Feb. 28, 1966, eff. July 1, 1966; Mar. 2, 1987, eff. Aug. 1, 1987; Apr. 30, 1991, eff. Dec. 1, 1991; Apr. 30, 2007, eff. Dec. 1, 2007.

See ***Commentaries***, "Motion to Intervene," ch. 5-J, p. 356; ***O'Connor's Federal Civil Forms*** (2012), FORMS 5J.

ANNOTATIONS

Generally

Disability Advocates, Inc. v. New York Coalition for Quality Assisted Living, Inc., 675 F.3d 149, 160 (2d Cir.2012). "[I]f jurisdiction is lacking at the commencement of a suit, it cannot be aided by the intervention of a plaintiff with a sufficient claim. [¶] That is, Rule 24 does not itself provide a basis for jurisdiction. *At 161:* [But a district court has] discretion to treat the pleading of an intervenor as a separate action … to adjudicate the claims raised by the intervenor even if the underlying claim [is] jurisdictionally deficient [as long as] the intervention [has] occurred before any action by the defendants [has] been taken. [¶] [H]owever, [permitting] interven[tion] *after the trial had concluded* … would allow the … exception (that curative interventions be construed as separate actions when they are effected at the beginning of the proceedings) to swallow the clearly-established constitutional rule that intervention cannot cure any jurisdictional defect that would have barred the federal court from hearing the original action. [¶] The relevant question … is not whether the curative intervenor is prepared to take the case 'as he finds it' for the sake of judicial economy, but rather, whether he entered sufficiently early in the litigation to ensure that parties invoking the court's jurisdiction have alleged such a personal stake in the outcome of the controversy as to assure that concrete adverseness which sharpens the presentation of issues upon which the court so largely depends for illumination of difficult questions." (Internal quotes omitted.)

In re Bayshore Ford Trucks Sales, Inc., 471 F.3d 1233, 1246 (11th Cir.2006). "Once a court grants intervention, whether of right or by permission, the 'intervenor is treated as if [it] were an original party and has equal standing with the original parties.' Toward that end, both Rule 24(a) and Rule 24(b) require the prospective intervenor to anchor its request in the dispute giving rise to the pending lawsuit. The prospective intervenor must demonstrate 'an interest relating to the property or transaction which is *the subject of the action*' if relying on Rule 24(a), or it must show that its 'claim or defense and *the main action* have a question of law or fact in common' if relying on Rule 24(b). In either case, the plain language of Rule 24 requires the intervenor's interest to be based on the action pending before the court."

Canatella v. California, 404 F.3d 1106, 1112 (9th Cir.2005). Intervenor "contends that the district court erred as a matter of law in denying intervention solely on the basis of ***Younger*** [***v. Harris***, 401 U.S. 37 (1971),] abstention. [¶] Although the district court did not explicitly acknowledge the issue, its disposition necessarily implies the holding that ***Younger*** abstention trumps intervention as of right. *At 1113:* ***Younger*** abstention is essentially a jurisdictional doctrine, whereas intervention is essentially a procedural matter. Although ***Younger*** neither provides a basis for nor destroys federal jurisdiction, ***Younger*** does determine when the federal courts must 'refrain from exercising jurisdiction.' Intervention as of right is merely a procedural means for entering an existing federal action. … The procedural mechanism of Rule 24 may facilitate the invocation of ancillary jurisdiction; however, Rule 24 does not itself provide the jurisdictional hook. … Because Rule 24 cannot extend federal jurisdiction and ***Younger*** abstention imposes mandatory limits on the federal courts' ability to exercise jurisdiction, we hold that intervention as of right cannot be used to circumvent ***Younger*** abstention."

Intervention of Right

Trbovich v. United Mine Workers, 404 U.S. 528, 538 n.10 (1972). FRCP 24(a) "is satisfied if the applicant shows that representation of his interest 'may be' inadequate; and the burden of making that showing should be treated as minimal."

WildEarth Guardians v. National Park Serv., 604 F.3d 1192, 1198 (10th Cir.2010). "We follow 'a somewhat liberal line in allowing intervention.' The factors of Rule 24(a)(2) are intended to 'capture the circumstances in which the practical effect on the prospective intervenor justifies its participation in the litigation,' and '[t]hose factors are not rigid, technical requirements.' [¶] The *interest* element is 'a practical guide to

disposing of lawsuits by involving as many apparently concerned persons as is compatible with efficiency and due process.' The movant's claimed interest is measured in terms of its relationship to the property or transaction that is the subject of the action, not in terms of the particular issue before the district court. *At 1199:* The second element—*impairment*—presents a minimal burden. '[A] would-be intervenor must show only that impairment of its substantial legal interest is possible if intervention is denied.' … 'We may consider any significant legal effect in the applicant's interest and we are not restricted to a rigid *res judicata* test.' *At 1200:* Finally, the *inadequate representation* element of Rule 24(a)(2) also presents a minimal burden. The movant must show only the possibility that representation may be inadequate. 'The possibility that the interests of the applicant and the parties may diverge need not be great in order to satisfy this minimal burden.'"

San Juan Cty. v. U.S., 503 F.3d 1163, 1199 (10th Cir.2007). "Rule 24(a)(2) … is not a mechanical rule. It requires courts to exercise judgment based on the specific circumstances of the case. … The applicant must have an interest that could be adversely affected by the litigation. But practical judgment must be applied in determining whether the strength of the interest and the potential risk of injury to that interest justify intervention. *At 1203:* 'Strictly to require that the movant in intervention have a *direct* interest in the outcome of the lawsuit strikes us as being too narrow a construction of Rule 24(a)(2).' We agree with the Eighth Circuit: 'Although the intervenor cannot rely on an interest that is wholly remote and speculative, the intervention may be based on an interest that is contingent upon the outcome of the litigation.'"

California v. U.S., 450 F.3d 436, 441 (9th Cir.2006). "An applicant has a significant protectable interest in an action if (1) it asserts an interest that is protected under some law, and (2) there is a relationship between its legally protected interest and the plaintiff's claims." (Internal quotes omitted.) *See also* ***Medical Liab. Mut. Ins. v. Alan Curtis LLC***, 485 F.3d 1006, 1008 (8th Cir.2007) (economic interest in outcome of litigation and interest contingent on occurrence of sequence of events are insufficient to allow intervention); ***Mountain Top Condo. Ass'n v. Dave Stabbert Master Builder, Inc.***, 72 F.3d 361, 366 (3d Cir.1995) (mere economic interest is insufficient to allow intervention, but interest in specific fund is sufficient).

Liberty Mut. Ins. v. Treesdale, Inc., 419 F.3d 216, 230 (3d Cir.2005). "There is … a difference between [FRCP] 19 and [FRCP] 24. Although both Rules speak of the applicant's ability to protect an interest, Rule 24 contains an additional element, i.e., the adequacy of representation. … Rule 19 does not invite inquiry into the adequacy of representation. It is therefore illogical to conclude that a party who meets the joinder requirements of Rule 19(a)(2)(I)[, now Rule 19(a)(1)(B)(i),] automatically qualifies to intervene as of right under Rule 24(a)(2). That interpretation would read the 'adequacy of representation' requirement out of Rule 24(a)(2) by creating a backdoor into the litigation through the less restrictive inquiry of Rule 19(a)(2)(I)."

Armstrong v. Capshaw, Goss & Bowers, LLP, 404 F.3d 933, 936-37 (5th Cir.2005). "We agree with [intervenor's] assertion that his intervention in the Texas state court action was procedurally correct. [I]n Texas state court, anyone is permitted to intervene unless another party objects and the court agrees with that objection. Because no party objected in the state court here, [intervenor] was designated as an intervenor and then allowed to remove the case to federal court. [¶] Once [intervenor] removed the lawsuit from state court, however, the action was governed by federal, rather than state, procedural rules. [Intervenor] was therefore required to meet federal intervention standards to remain as an intervenor in the removed case. Accordingly, the district court did not err in reviewing the propriety of [intervenor's] status … under the federal requirements for intervention."

In re Bank of N.Y. Derivative Litig., 320 F.3d 291, 300 (2d Cir.2003). "'In order to intervene as a matter of right under [FRCP] 24(a)(2), an applicant must (1) timely file an application, (2) show an interest in the action, (3) demonstrate that the interest may be impaired by the disposition of the action, and (4) show that the interest is not protected adequately by the parties to the action.' 'Failure to satisfy *any one* of these requirements is a sufficient ground to deny the application.'" *See also* ***Ligas v. Maram***, 478 F.3d 771, 773 (7th Cir.2007); ***Northeast Ohio Coalition for the Homeless v. Blackwell***, 467 F.3d 999, 1007 (6th Cir.2006).

Clark v. Putnam Cty., 168 F.3d 458, 461 (11th Cir. 1999). "We presume adequate representation when an existing party seeks the same objectives as the would-be interveners. But the presumption is weak; in

effect, it merely imposes upon the proposed interveners the burden of coming forward with some evidence to the contrary. Once the would-be interveners have carried their burden, the court returns to the general rule that adequate representation exists 'if no collusion is shown between the representative and an opposing party, if the representative does not have or represent an interest adverse to the proposed interven[e]r, and if the representative does not fail in fulfillment of his duty.'" *See also* ***South Dakota v. U.S. Dept. of Interior***, 317 F.3d 783, 785 (8th Cir.2003) (applicant for intervention bears heavier burden to prove inadequate representation when party already in suit has obligation to represent applicant's interests); ***Jenkins v. Missouri***, 78 F.3d 1270, 1275 (8th Cir.1996) (difference of opinion concerning litigation strategy or individual aspects of remedy does not overcome presumption of adequate representation).

Permissive Intervention

Nebraska v. Wyoming, 515 U.S. 1, 21-22 (1995). "A state is presumed to speak in the best interests of those citizens, and requests to intervene by individual contractees may be treated under the general rule that an individual's motion for leave to intervene in this court will be denied absent a 'showing [of] some compelling interest in his own right, apart from his interest in a class with all other citizens and creatures of the state, which interest is not properly represented by the state.'"

Arizona v. California, 460 U.S. 605, 615 (1983). "[P]ermission to intervene does not carry with it the right to relitigate matters already determined in the case…."

Timing of Intervention

NAACP v. New York, 413 U.S. 345, 365-66 (1973). "Whether intervention be claimed of right or as permissive, it is … apparent, from the initial words of both Rule 24(a) and Rule 24(b), that the application must be 'timely.' If it is untimely, intervention must be denied. … Although the point to which the suit has progressed is one factor … it is not solely dispositive. Timeliness is to be determined from all the circumstances."

Trans Chem. Ltd. v. China Nat'l Mach. Imp. & Exp. Corp., 332 F.3d 815, 822 (5th Cir.2003). "Timeliness of intervention [under FRCP 24(a)] depends on a review of all the circumstances, and the Fifth Circuit has identified four factors to consider: (1) the length of time the intervenor knew or should have known of his interest in the case; (2) prejudice to the existing parties resulting from the intervenor's failure to apply for intervention sooner; (3) prejudice to the intervenor if his application for intervention is denied; and (4) the existence of unusual circumstances." *See also* ***Geiger v. Foley Hoag LLP Ret. Plan***, 521 F.3d 60, 65 (1st Cir. 2008); ***Roeder v. Islamic Republic of Iran***, 333 F.3d 228, 233 (D.C.Cir.2003).

FRCP 25. SUBSTITUTION OF PARTIES

(a) Death.

(1) ***Substitution if the Claim Is Not Extinguished.*** If a party dies and the claim is not extinguished, the court may order substitution of the proper party. A motion for substitution may be made by any party or by the decedent's successor or representative. If the motion is not made within 90 days after service of a statement noting the death, the action by or against the decedent must be dismissed.

(2) ***Continuation Among the Remaining Parties.*** After a party's death, if the right sought to be enforced survives only to or against the remaining parties, the action does not abate, but proceeds in favor of or against the remaining parties. The death should be noted on the record.

(3) ***Service.*** A motion to substitute, together with a notice of hearing, must be served on the parties as provided in Rule 5 and on nonparties as provided in Rule 4. A statement noting death must be served in the same manner. Service may be made in any judicial district.

(b) Incompetency. If a party becomes incompetent, the court may, on motion, permit the action to be continued by or against the party's representative. The motion must be served as provided in Rule 25(a)(3).

(c) Transfer of Interest. If an interest is transferred, the action may be continued by or against the original party unless the court, on motion, orders the transferee to be substituted in the action or joined with the original party. The motion must be served as provided in Rule 25(a)(3).

(d) Public Officers; Death or Separation from Office. An action does not abate when a public officer who is a party in an official capacity dies, re-

signs, or otherwise ceases to hold office while the action is pending. The officer's successor is automatically substituted as a party. Later proceedings should be in the substituted party's name, but any misnomer not affecting the parties' substantial rights must be disregarded. The court may order substitution at any time, but the absence of such an order does not affect the substitution.

See selected Notes of Advisory Committee to FRCP 25, p. 1171.

History of FRCP 25: Adopted Dec. 20, 1937, eff. Sept. 16, 1938. Amended Dec. 29, 1948, eff. Oct. 20, 1949; Apr. 17, 1961, eff. July 19, 1961; Jan. 21, 1963, eff. July 1, 1963; Mar. 2, 1987, eff. Aug. 1, 1987; Apr. 30, 2007, eff. Dec. 1, 2007.

See *Commentaries*, "Substituted defendant," ch. 2-F, §3.2.2(4), p. 122; "Extending Deadlines," ch. 5-F, §2, p. 332; "Substituting parties," ch. 6-F, §4.2.4, p. 552.

ANNOTATIONS

In re Baycol Prods. Litig., 616 F.3d 778, 785 (8th Cir.2010). FRCP 25(a)(1) "'does not provide for the survival of rights or liabilities but merely provides the method by which the original action may proceed if the right of action survives.' [I]n a diversity case, we look to state substantive law to determine whether the cause of action survives. [¶] Rule 25(a) is a procedural rule setting forth the proper method for the substitution of parties, and federal courts must apply federal rules, rather than state law, in determining the proper procedure for substitution following a party's death. This is true even if the court must apply state substantive law ..., or where the state procedural rules are inconsistent with federal law.... While it is often said that Rule 25 is strictly procedural, ... some courts and commentators have recognized, in many instances, state law governs *who* can be a 'representative' or 'successor,' and therefore, who can qualify as a proper party for substitution under Rule 25(a)(1)."

Kuelbs v. Hill, 615 F.3d 1037, 1042 (8th Cir.2010). FRCP 25 "sets forth the substitution procedure to be followed when a party becomes incompetent while an action is pending. [¶] [W]hen a party becomes incompetent, a motion for substitution is required before a court may order substitution. [W]hen reading Rule 25(b) in conjunction with [FRCP] 17(a)'s requirement that an action *must* be prosecuted by the real party in interest, the court has no power to permit such an action to continue without the real party in interest unless a motion for substitution is brought under Rule 25(b). [¶] In contrast, if a party transfers an interest while a case is pending, 'the action may be continued by or against the original party[.]' While the court, upon motion, may order 'the transferee to be substituted in the action or joined with the original party,' ... a substitution motion is not required for the action to continue. [¶] In sum, in an action in which a party becomes incompetent while the action is pending, a motion for substitution must be brought under Rule 25(b) for the action to continue."

Negrón-Almeda v. Santiago, 579 F.3d 45, 52-53 (1st Cir.2009). "Rule 25(c) governs substitution where a party to a lawsuit transfers an interest during the pendency of the lawsuit or after judgment has been rendered. [T]he rule is a discretionary 'procedural vehicle' in which 'the transferee is brought into court solely because it has come to own the property in issue.' The rule applies to a wide variety of transfers in interest. [F]or example, ... Rule 25(c) has been 'invoked to substitute a successor in interest who ... obtained the assets of the corporation against whom judgment had been rendered.'"

Atkins v. City of Chi., 547 F.3d 869, 873 (7th Cir. 2008). FRCP 25(a) "does not say which nonparties must be served.... But nonparties with a significant financial interest in the case, namely the decedent's successors ... or personal representative ... should certainly be served."

Sinito v. U.S. Dept. of Justice, 176 F.3d 512, 516 (D.C.Cir.1999). "Although it is generally accepted that the proper party for substitution must be a 'legal representative' of the deceased, ... the word 'successor' ... means that a proper party need not necessarily be the appointed executor or administrator of the deceased party's estate. Thus, we have held not only that an executor or administrator of a decedent's estate is a proper party for substitution, but also that the distributee of a decedent's estate may be a 'successor' of an estate that has been distributed and thus can be a proper party."

Andrews v. Lakeshore Rehab. Hosp., 140 F.3d 1405, 1407 (11th Cir.1998). "Rule 25(c) applies only to transfers of interest occurring during the pendency of litigation and not to those occurring before the litigation begins."

Barlow v. Ground, 39 F.3d 231, 233 (9th Cir.1994). FRCP 25 "requires two affirmative steps in order to trigger the running of the 90 day period. First, a party must formally suggest the death of the party.... Second, the suggesting party must serve other parties and nonparty successors or representatives of the deceased with a suggestion of death in the same manner as required for service of the motion to substitute. Thus, a

FRCP 25

party may be served the suggestion of death by service on his or her attorney while non-party successors or representatives of the deceased party must be served ... in the manner provided by [FRCP] 4 for the service of a summons." *See also* ***McKenna v. Pacific Rail Serv.***, 32 F.3d 820, 836 (3d Cir.1994) (FRCP 25 does not say that suggestion of death must be made or provide time frame for doing so).

Continental Bank v. Meyer, 10 F.3d 1293, 1297 (7th Cir.1993). "While couched in mandatory terms, the Advisory Committee Notes to Rule 25 indicate that the 90-day requirement [to dismiss] may be extended...."

TITLE V. DISCLOSURES & DISCOVERY

FRCP 26. DUTY TO DISCLOSE; GENERAL PROVISIONS GOVERNING DISCOVERY

(a) Required Disclosures.

(1) ***Initial Disclosure.***

(A) *In General.* Except as exempted by Rule 26(a)(1)(B) or as otherwise stipulated or ordered by the court, a party must, without awaiting a discovery request, provide to the other parties:

(i) the name and, if known, the address and telephone number of each individual likely to have discoverable information—along with the subjects of that information—that the disclosing party may use to support its claims or defenses, unless the use would be solely for impeachment;

(ii) a copy—or a description by category and location—of all documents, electronically stored information, and tangible things that the disclosing party has in its possession, custody, or control and may use to support its claims or defenses, unless the use would be solely for impeachment;

(iii) a computation of each category of damages claimed by the disclosing party—who must also make available for inspection and copying as under Rule 34 the documents or other evidentiary material, unless privileged or protected from disclosure, on which each computation is based, including materials bearing on the nature and extent of injuries suffered; and

(iv) for inspection and copying as under Rule 34, any insurance agreement under which an insurance business may be liable to satisfy all or part of a possible judgment in the action or to indemnify or reimburse for payments made to satisfy the judgment.

(B) *Proceedings Exempt from Initial Disclosure.* The following proceedings are exempt from initial disclosure:

(i) an action for review on an administrative record;

(ii) a forfeiture action in rem arising from a federal statute;

(iii) a petition for habeas corpus or any other proceeding to challenge a criminal conviction or sentence;

(iv) an action brought without an attorney by a person in the custody of the United States, a state, or a state subdivision;

(v) an action to enforce or quash an administrative summons or subpoena;

(vi) an action by the United States to recover benefit payments;

(vii) an action by the United States to collect on a student loan guaranteed by the United States;

(viii) a proceeding ancillary to a proceeding in another court; and

(ix) an action to enforce an arbitration award.

(C) *Time for Initial Disclosures—In General.* A party must make the initial disclosures at or within 14 days after the parties' Rule 26(f) conference unless a different time is set by stipulation or court order, or unless a party objects during the conference that initial disclosures are not appropriate in this action and states the objection in the proposed discovery plan. In ruling on the objection, the court must determine what disclosures, if any, are to be made and must set the time for disclosure.

(D) *Time for Initial Disclosures—For Parties Served or Joined Later.* A party that is first served or otherwise joined after the Rule

26(f) conference must make the initial disclosures within 30 days after being served or joined, unless a different time is set by stipulation or court order.

(E) *Basis for Initial Disclosure; Unacceptable Excuses.* A party must make its initial disclosures based on the information then reasonably available to it. A party is not excused from making its disclosures because it has not fully investigated the case or because it challenges the sufficiency of another party's disclosures or because another party has not made its disclosures.

(2) ***Disclosure of Expert Testimony.***

(A) *In General.* In addition to the disclosures required by Rule 26(a)(1), a party must disclose to the other parties the identity of any witness it may use at trial to present evidence under Federal Rule of Evidence 702, 703, or 705.

(B) *Witnesses Who Must Provide a Written Report.* Unless otherwise stipulated or ordered by the court, this disclosure must be accompanied by a written report—prepared and signed by the witness—if the witness is one retained or specially employed to provide expert testimony in the case or one whose duties as the party's employee regularly involve giving expert testimony. The report must contain:

(i) a complete statement of all opinions the witness will express and the basis and reasons for them;

(ii) the facts or data considered by the witness in forming them;

(iii) any exhibits that will be used to summarize or support them;

(iv) the witness's qualifications, including a list of all publications authored in the previous 10 years;

(v) a list of all other cases in which, during the previous 4 years, the witness testified as an expert at trial or by deposition; and

(vi) a statement of the compensation to be paid for the study and testimony in the case.

(C) *Witnesses Who Do Not Provide a Written Report.* Unless otherwise stipulated or ordered by the court, if the witness is not required to provide a written report, this disclosure must state:

(i) the subject matter on which the witness is expected to present evidence under Federal Rule of Evidence 702, 703, or 705; and

(ii) a summary of the facts and opinions to which the witness is expected to testify.

(D) *Time to Disclose Expert Testimony.* A party must make these disclosures at the times and in the sequence that the court orders. Absent a stipulation or a court order, the disclosures must be made:

(i) at least 90 days before the date set for trial or for the case to be ready for trial; or

(ii) if the evidence is intended solely to contradict or rebut evidence on the same subject matter identified by another party under Rule 26(a)(2)(B) or (C), within 30 days after the other party's disclosure.

(E) *Supplementing the Disclosure.* The parties must supplement these disclosures when required under Rule 26(e).

(3) ***Pretrial Disclosures.***

(A) *In General.* In addition to the disclosures required by Rule 26(a)(1) and (2), a party must provide to the other parties and promptly file the following information about the evidence that it may present at trial other than solely for impeachment:

(i) the name and, if not previously provided, the address and telephone number of each witness—separately identifying those the party expects to present and those it may call if the need arises;

(ii) the designation of those witnesses whose testimony the party expects to present by deposition and, if not taken stenographically, a transcript of the pertinent parts of the deposition; and

(iii) an identification of each document or other exhibit, including summaries of

other evidence—separately identifying those items the party expects to offer and those it may offer if the need arises.

(B) *Time for Pretrial Disclosures; Objections.* Unless the court orders otherwise, these disclosures must be made at least 30 days before trial. Within 14 days after they are made, unless the court sets a different time, a party may serve and promptly file a list of the following objections: any objections to the use under Rule 32(a) of a deposition designated by another party under Rule 26(a)(3)(A)(ii); and any objection, together with the grounds for it, that may be made to the admissibility of materials identified under Rule 26(a)(3)(A)(iii). An objection not so made—except for one under Federal Rule of Evidence 402 or 403—is waived unless excused by the court for good cause.

(4) ***Form of Disclosures.*** Unless the court orders otherwise, all disclosures under Rule 26(a) must be in writing, signed, and served.

(b) Discovery Scope and Limits.

(1) ***Scope in General.*** Unless otherwise limited by court order, the scope of discovery is as follows: Parties may obtain discovery regarding any nonprivileged matter that is relevant to any party's claim or defense—including the existence, description, nature, custody, condition, and location of any documents or other tangible things and the identity and location of persons who know of any discoverable matter. For good cause, the court may order discovery of any matter relevant to the subject matter involved in the action. Relevant information need not be admissible at the trial if the discovery appears reasonably calculated to lead to the discovery of admissible evidence. All discovery is subject to the limitations imposed by Rule 26(b)(2)(C).

(2) ***Limitations on Frequency and Extent.***

(A) *When Permitted.* By order, the court may alter the limits in these rules on the number of depositions and interrogatories or on the length of depositions under Rule 30. By order or local rule, the court may also limit the number of requests under Rule 36.

(B) *Specific Limitations on Electronically Stored Information.* A party need not provide discovery of electronically stored information from sources that the party identifies as not reasonably accessible because of undue burden or cost. On motion to compel discovery or for a protective order, the party from whom discovery is sought must show that the information is not reasonably accessible because of undue burden or cost. If that showing is made, the court may nonetheless order discovery from such sources if the requesting party shows good cause, considering the limitations of Rule 26(b)(2)(C). The court may specify conditions for the discovery.

(C) *When Required.* On motion or on its own, the court must limit the frequency or extent of discovery otherwise allowed by these rules or by local rule if it determines that:

(i) the discovery sought is unreasonably cumulative or duplicative, or can be obtained from some other source that is more convenient, less burdensome, or less expensive;

(ii) the party seeking discovery has had ample opportunity to obtain the information by discovery in the action; or

(iii) the burden or expense of the proposed discovery outweighs its likely benefit, considering the needs of the case, the amount in controversy, the parties' resources, the importance of the issues at stake in the action, and the importance of the discovery in resolving the issues.

(3) ***Trial Preparation: Materials.***

(A) *Documents and Tangible Things.* Ordinarily, a party may not discover documents and tangible things that are prepared in anticipation of litigation or for trial by or for another party or its representative (including the other party's attorney, consultant, surety, indemnitor, insurer, or agent). But, subject to Rule 26(b)(4), those materials may be discovered if:

(i) they are otherwise discoverable under Rule 26(b)(1); and

(ii) the party shows that it has substantial need for the materials to prepare its case and cannot, without undue hardship, obtain their substantial equivalent by other means.

(B) *Protection Against Disclosure.* If the court orders discovery of those materials, it must protect against disclosure of the mental impressions, conclusions, opinions, or legal theories of a party's attorney or other representative concerning the litigation.

(C) *Previous Statement.* Any party or other person may, on request and without the required showing, obtain the person's own previous statement about the action or its subject matter. If the request is refused, the person may move for a court order, and Rule 37(a)(5) applies to the award of expenses. A previous statement is either:

(i) a written statement that the person has signed or otherwise adopted or approved; or

(ii) a contemporaneous stenographic, mechanical, electrical, or other recording—or a transcription of it—that recites substantially verbatim the person's oral statement.

(4) ***Trial Preparation: Experts.***

(A) *Deposition of an Expert Who May Testify.* A party may depose any person who has been identified as an expert whose opinions may be presented at trial. If Rule 26(a)(2)(B) requires a report from the expert, the deposition may be conducted only after the report is provided.

(B) *Trial-Preparation Protection for Draft Reports or Disclosures.* Rules 26(b)(3)(A) and (B) protect drafts of any report or disclosure required under Rule 26(a)(2), regardless of the form in which the draft is recorded.

(C) *Trial-Preparation Protection for Communications Between a Party's Attorney and Expert Witnesses.* Rules 26(b)(3)(A) and (B) protect communications between the party's attorney and any witness required to provide a report under Rule 26(a)(2)(B), regardless of the form of the communications, except to the extent that the communications:

(i) relate to compensation for the expert's study or testimony;

(ii) identify facts or data that the party's attorney provided and that the expert considered in forming the opinions to be expressed; or

(iii) identify assumptions that the party's attorney provided and that the expert relied on in forming the opinions to be expressed.

(D) *Expert Employed Only for Trial Preparation.* Ordinarily, a party may not, by interrogatories or deposition, discover facts known or opinions held by an expert who has been retained or specially employed by another party in anticipation of litigation or to prepare for trial and who is not expected to be called as a witness at trial. But a party may do so only:

(i) as provided in Rule 35(b); or

(ii) on showing exceptional circumstances under which it is impracticable for the party to obtain facts or opinions on the same subject by other means.

(E) *Payment.* Unless manifest injustice would result, the court must require that the party seeking discovery:

(i) pay the expert a reasonable fee for time spent in responding to discovery under Rule 26(b)(4)(A) or (D); and

(ii) for discovery under (D), also pay the other party a fair portion of the fees and expenses it reasonably incurred in obtaining the expert's facts and opinions.

(5) ***Claiming Privilege or Protecting Trial-Preparation Materials.***

(A) *Information Withheld.* When a party withholds information otherwise discoverable by claiming that the information is privileged or subject to protection as trial-preparation material, the party must:

(i) expressly make the claim; and

(ii) describe the nature of the documents, communications, or tangible things not produced or disclosed—and do so in a manner that, without revealing information itself privileged or protected, will enable other parties to assess the claim.

(B) *Information Produced.* If information produced in discovery is subject to a claim of privilege or of protection as trial-preparation material, the party making the claim may notify any party that received the information of the claim and the basis for it. After being notified, a party must promptly return, sequester, or destroy the specified information and any copies it has; must not use or disclose the information until the claim is resolved; must take reasonable steps to retrieve the information if the party disclosed it before being notified; and may promptly present the information to the court under seal for a determination of the claim. The producing party must preserve the information until the claim is resolved.

(c) Protective Orders.

(1) ***In General.*** A party or any person from whom discovery is sought may move for a protective order in the court where the action is pending—or as an alternative on matters relating to a deposition, in the court for the district where the deposition will be taken. The motion must include a certification that the movant has in good faith conferred or attempted to confer with other affected parties in an effort to resolve the dispute without court action. The court may, for good cause, issue an order to protect a party or person from annoyance, embarrassment, oppression, or undue burden or expense, including one or more of the following:

(A) forbidding the disclosure or discovery;

(B) specifying terms, including time and place, for the disclosure or discovery;

(C) prescribing a discovery method other than the one selected by the party seeking discovery;

(D) forbidding inquiry into certain matters, or limiting the scope of disclosure or discovery to certain matters;

(E) designating the persons who may be present while the discovery is conducted;

(F) requiring that a deposition be sealed and opened only on court order;

(G) requiring that a trade secret or other confidential research, development, or commercial information not be revealed or be revealed only in a specified way; and

(H) requiring that the parties simultaneously file specified documents or information in sealed envelopes, to be opened as the court directs.

(2) ***Ordering Discovery.*** If a motion for a protective order is wholly or partly denied, the court may, on just terms, order that any party or person provide or permit discovery.

(3) ***Awarding Expenses.*** Rule 37(a)(5) applies to the award of expenses.

(d) Timing and Sequence of Discovery.

(1) ***Timing.*** A party may not seek discovery from any source before the parties have conferred as required by Rule 26(f), except in a proceeding exempted from initial disclosure under Rule 26(a)(1)(B), or when authorized by these rules, by stipulation, or by court order.

(2) ***Sequence.*** Unless, on motion, the court orders otherwise for the parties' and witnesses' convenience and in the interests of justice:

(A) methods of discovery may be used in any sequence; and

(B) discovery by one party does not require any other party to delay its discovery.

(e) Supplementing Disclosures and Responses.

(1) ***In General.*** A party who has made a disclosure under Rule 26(a)—or who has responded to an interrogatory, request for production, or request for admission—must supplement or correct its disclosure or response:

(A) in a timely manner if the party learns that in some material respect the disclosure or response is incomplete or incorrect, and if the additional or corrective information has not

otherwise been made known to the other parties during the discovery process or in writing; or

(B) as ordered by the court.

(2) ***Expert Witness.*** For an expert whose report must be disclosed under Rule 26(a)(2)(B), the party's duty to supplement extends both to information included in the report and to information given during the expert's deposition. Any additions or changes to this information must be disclosed by the time the party's pretrial disclosures under Rule 26(a)(3) are due.

(f) Conference of the Parties; Planning for Discovery.

(1) ***Conference Timing.*** Except in a proceeding exempted from initial disclosure under Rule 26(a)(1)(B) or when the court orders otherwise, the parties must confer as soon as practicable—and in any event at least 21 days before a scheduling conference is to be held or a scheduling order is due under Rule 16(b).

(2) ***Conference Content; Parties' Responsibilities.*** In conferring, the parties must consider the nature and basis of their claims and defenses and the possibilities for promptly settling or resolving the case; make or arrange for the disclosures required by Rule 26(a)(1); discuss any issues about preserving discoverable information; and develop a proposed discovery plan. The attorneys of record and all unrepresented parties that have appeared in the case are jointly responsible for arranging the conference, for attempting in good faith to agree on the proposed discovery plan, and for submitting to the court within 14 days after the conference a written report outlining the plan. The court may order the parties or attorneys to attend the conference in person.

(3) ***Discovery Plan.*** A discovery plan must state the parties' views and proposals on:

(A) what changes should be made in the timing, form, or requirement for disclosures under Rule 26(a), including a statement of when initial disclosures were made or will be made;

(B) the subjects on which discovery may be needed, when discovery should be completed, and whether discovery should be conducted in phases or be limited to or focused on particular issues;

(C) any issues about disclosure or discovery of electronically stored information, including the form or forms in which it should be produced;

(D) any issues about claims of privilege or of protection as trial-preparation materials, including—if the parties agree on a procedure to assert these claims after production—whether to ask the court to include their agreement in an order;

(E) what changes should be made in the limitations on discovery imposed under these rules or by local rule, and what other limitations should be imposed; and

(F) any other orders that the court should issue under Rule 26(c) or under Rule 16(b) and (c).

(4) ***Expedited Schedule.*** If necessary to comply with its expedited schedule for Rule 16(b) conferences, a court may by local rule:

(A) require the parties' conference to occur less than 21 days before the scheduling conference is held or a scheduling order is due under Rule 16(b); and

(B) require the written report outlining the discovery plan to be filed less than 14 days after the parties' conference, or excuse the parties from submitting a written report and permit them to report orally on their discovery plan at the Rule 16(b) conference.

(g) Signing Disclosures and Discovery Requests, Responses, and Objections.

(1) ***Signature Required; Effect of Signature.*** Every disclosure under Rule 26(a)(1) or (a)(3) and every discovery request, response, or objection must be signed by at least one attorney of record in the attorney's own name—or by the party personally, if unrepresented—and must state the signer's address, e-mail address, and telephone number. By signing, an attorney or party certifies that to the best of the person's knowledge, information, and belief formed after a reasonable inquiry:

(A) with respect to a disclosure, it is complete and correct as of the time it is made; and

(B) with respect to a discovery request, response, or objection, it is:

(i) consistent with these rules and warranted by existing law or by a nonfrivolous argument for extending, modifying, or reversing existing law, or for establishing new law;

(ii) not interposed for any improper purpose, such as to harass, cause unnecessary delay, or needlessly increase the cost of litigation; and

(iii) neither unreasonable nor unduly burdensome or expensive, considering the needs of the case, prior discovery in the case, the amount in controversy, and the importance of the issues at stake in the action.

(2) ***Failure to Sign.*** Other parties have no duty to act on an unsigned disclosure, request, response, or objection until it is signed, and the court must strike it unless a signature is promptly supplied after the omission is called to the attorney's or party's attention.

(3) ***Sanction for Improper Certification.*** If a certification violates this rule without substantial justification, the court, on motion or on its own, must impose an appropriate sanction on the signer, the party on whose behalf the signer was acting, or both. The sanction may include an order to pay the reasonable expenses, including attorney's fees, caused by the violation.

See selected Notes of Advisory Committee to FRCP 26, p. 1172.

History of FRCP 26: Adopted Dec. 20, 1937, eff. Sept. 16, 1938. Amended Dec. 27, 1946, eff. Mar. 19, 1948; Jan. 21, 1963, eff. July 1, 1963; Feb. 28, 1966, eff. July 1, 1966; Mar. 30, 1970, eff. July 1, 1970; Apr. 29, 1980, eff. Aug. 1, 1980; Apr. 28, 1983, eff. Aug. 1, 1983; Mar. 2, 1987, eff. Aug. 1, 1987; Apr. 22, 1993, eff. Dec. 1, 1993; Apr. 17, 2000, eff. Dec. 1, 2000; Apr. 12, 2006, eff. Dec. 1, 2006; Apr. 30, 2007, eff. Dec. 1, 2007; Apr. 28, 2010, eff. Dec. 1, 2010.

See ***Commentaries***, "Discovery," ch. 6, p. 409; ***O'Connor's Federal Civil Forms*** (2012), FORM 2A:4; FORMS 6.

ANNOTATIONS

Asserting Privileges

Burlington N. & Santa Fe Ry. v. U.S. Dist. Ct. for the Dist. of Mont., 408 F.3d 1142, 1147 (9th Cir.2005). "[D] argues that the district court erred as a matter of law by reading into [FRCP] 34 a *per se* rule that failure to produce a privilege log in a timely manner triggers waiver of privileges. *At 1149:* We hold that boilerplate objections or blanket refusals inserted into a response to a Rule 34 request for production of documents are insufficient to assert a privilege. However, we also reject a *per se* waiver rule that deems a privilege waived if a privilege log is not produced within Rule 34's 30-day time limit. Instead, using the 30-day period as a default guideline, a district court should make a case-by-case determination, taking into account the following factors: [(1)] the degree to which the objection or assertion of privilege enables the litigant seeking discovery and the court to evaluate whether each of the withheld documents is privileged (where providing particulars typically contained in a privilege log is presumptively sufficient and boilerplate objections are presumptively insufficient); [(2)] the timeliness of the objection and accompanying information about the withheld documents (where service within 30 days, as a default guideline, is sufficient); [(3)] the magnitude of the document production; and [(4)] other particular circumstances of the litigation that make responding to discovery unusually easy (such as … the fact that many of the same documents were the subject of discovery in an earlier action) or unusually hard." *See also* ***U.S. v. Construction Prods. Research, Inc.***, 73 F.3d 464, 473 (2d Cir.1996) (court may require adequately detailed privilege log to fill in factual gaps in evidentiary submissions).

Discovery Obligations

Wegener v. Johnson, 527 F.3d 687, 690-91 (8th Cir. 2008). "Rule 26 does not require the disclosure of evidence used solely for impeachment purposes. … To attack the credibility of witnesses by the presentation of evidence showing that facts asserted or relied upon in their testimony are false is to impeach by contradiction. It does not impeach, however, to show that an expert's opinion about the meaning of facts merely differs from that of other experts. It is often difficult to distinguish between foundational facts and expert opinion, and so to distinguish between impeachment and substantive evidence, … but Rule 26(a)(2)(C)(ii) resolves the dilemma in favor of disclosure by requiring parties to disclose expert testimony offered to contradict the expert testimony of the opposing party."

Disclosures

Tribble v. Evangelides, 670 F.3d 753, 759-60 (7th Cir.2012). FRCP 26(a)(1) "requires … the disclosure of the names and addresses of fact witnesses. Rule 26(a)(2) requires that expert witnesses be disclosed. That duty to disclose a witness as *an expert* is *not* ex-

cused when a witness who will testify as a fact witness *and* as an expert witness is disclosed as a fact witness. ... Without proper disclosures, a party may miss its opportunity to disqualify the expert, retain rebuttal experts, or hold depositions for an expert not required to provide a report. Because of these and other ways a party may be prejudiced by an improperly disclosed expert, the sanction is severe. Under [FRCP] 37(c)(1) 'exclusion of non-disclosed evidence is automatic and mandatory ... unless non-disclosure was justified or harmless.'"

Expert Fees

Gwin v. American River Transp., 482 F.3d 969, 975 (7th Cir.2007). "The mandatory language of [FRCP 26(b)(4)(C)] is tempered by two limitations: (1) the costs may not be imposed if doing so would result in manifest injustice, and (2) the expert's fees must be reasonable. In other words, before refusing to order a deposing party to pay the other party's expert, the district court must explicitly find either manifest injustice or that the fee was unreasonable."

Ellis v. United Airlines, Inc., 73 F.3d 999, 1011 (10th Cir.1996), *overruled on other grounds*, ***Pippin v. Burlington Res. Oil & Gas Co.***, 440 F.3d 1186 (10th Cir.2006). "Rule 26(b)(4)(C) itself does not specify whether or when a party must demand payment of fees to its expert. However, the advisory committee notes ... provide that '[t]he court may issue the latter order [to pay fees and expenses that a party incurs in obtaining information from an expert] as a condition of discovery, or it may delay the order until after discovery is completed.' [Thus,] courts have awarded fees under Rule 26(b)(4)(C) after trial."

Expert Reports

Metavante Corp. v. Emigrant Sav. Bank, 619 F.3d 748, 762 (7th Cir.2010). "'The purpose of ... [expert] reports is not to replicate every word that the expert might say on the stand. It is instead to convey the substance of the expert's opinion ... so that the opponent will be ready to rebut, to cross-examine, and to offer a competing expert if necessary.' They allow attorneys, not experts in the fields at issue, to prepare intelligently for trial and to solicit the views of other experts."

Muldrow v. Re-Direct, Inc., 493 F.3d 160, 167 (D.C.Cir.2007). "The purpose of [the expert report under FRCP 26(a)(2)(B)] is to eliminate 'unfair surprise to the opposing party.' But it 'does not limit an expert's testimony simply to reading his report.... The rule contemplates that the expert will supplement, elaborate upon, [and] explain ... his report' in his oral testimony."

Protective Orders

In re Roman Catholic Archbishop of Portland, 661 F.3d 417, 424 (9th Cir.2011). "Under Rule 26, [t]he party opposing disclosure has the burden of proving 'good cause,' which requires a showing that specific prejudice or harm will result if the protective order is not granted. [¶] While courts generally make a finding of good cause before issuing a protective order, a court need not do so where ... the parties stipulate to such an order. When the protective order was a stipulated order and no party has made a 'good cause' showing, then the burden of proof remains with the party seeking protection. If a party takes steps to release documents subject to a stipulated order, the party opposing disclosure has the burden of establishing that there is good cause to continue the protection of the discovery material." (Internal quotes omitted.) *See also* ***Foltz v. State Farm Mut. Auto. Ins.***, 331 F.3d 1122, 1130 (9th Cir.2003).

Gill v. Gulfstream Park Racing Ass'n, 399 F.3d 391, 400 (1st Cir.2005). "Under Rule 26, the trial court is required to balance the burden of proposed discovery against the likely benefit. *At 401:* As we read the district court's order, it ruled that once it had decided there was no informant's privilege, it had no need to engage in any balancing of any other interests on the part of [the interested party]. *At 402:* That there is no informant's privilege [under state law] does not mean there are no interests of the public or other persons involved in the balance. [¶] Evidentiary privileges formally recognized by state law are not the only relevant factors in the Rule 26 balancing act. 'Rule 26(c) is highly flexible, having been designed to accommodate all relevant interests as they arise.... [T]he good cause standard in [FRCP 26(c)] is a flexible one that requires an individualized balancing of the many interests that may be present in a particular case.'"

Phillips v. General Motors Corp., 307 F.3d 1206, 1210 (9th Cir.2002). "Generally, the public can gain access to litigation documents and information produced during discovery unless the party opposing disclosure shows good cause why a protective order is necessary. [¶] For good cause to exist, the party seeking protection bears the burden of showing specific prejudice or harm will result if no protective order is granted. If a court finds particularized harm will result from disclo-

sure of information to the public, then it balances the public and private interests to decide whether a protective order is necessary. *At 1212:* If … the court finds good cause exists to protect [the] information, then it must determine whether the [intervenor] has a right to [the information] under the common law right of access, a separate and independent basis for obtaining this information. *At 1213:* [But] the federal common law right of access does not apply to documents filed under seal. … When a court grants a protective order for information produced during discovery, it already has determined that good cause exists to protect this information from being disclosed to the public by balancing the needs for discovery against the need for confidentiality. [¶] [W]hen a party attaches a sealed discovery document to a nondispositive motion, the usual presumption of the public's right of access is rebutted, so that the party seeking disclosure must present sufficiently compelling reasons why the sealed discovery document should be released." (Internal quotes omitted.)

Sanctions

David v. Caterpillar, Inc., 324 F.3d 851, 857 (7th Cir.2003). "This court has stated that 'the sanction of exclusion is automatic and mandatory unless the sanctioned party can show that its violation of Rule 26(a) was either justified or harmless.' However, we also have stated that '[t]he determination of whether a Rule 26(a) violation is justified or harmless is entrusted to the broad discretion of the district court.'" *See also* ***Westefer v. Snyder***, 422 F.3d 570, 584 n.21 (7th Cir.2005).

Thibeault v. Square D Co., 960 F.2d 239, 245 (1st Cir.1992). FRCP 26(e) does not require "that a court order must be in effect, and then violated, as a prerequisite for the imposition of sanctions…. The rule itself furnishes fair warning."

Scope of Discovery

Surles v. Greyhound Lines, Inc., 474 F.3d 288, 305 (6th Cir.2007). "[D]istrict courts have discretion to limit the scope of discovery where the information sought is overly broad or would prove unduly burdensome to produce. … Although a plaintiff should not be denied access to information necessary to establish her claim, neither may a plaintiff be permitted to go fishing…." (Internal quotes omitted.)

Abrahamsen v. Trans-State Express, Inc., 92 F.3d 425, 428 (6th Cir.1996). "The rules of discovery … do not permit parties to withhold material simply because the opponent could discover it on his or her own."

Supplementing Discovery

Colón-Millín v. Sears Roebuck, 455 F.3d 30, 37 (1st Cir.2006). "Under [FRCP] 26(e), a party must 'supplement its answers to interrogatories if the party learns that the response is in some material respect incomplete or incorrect and the other party is unaware of the new or corrective information…. This supplementation requirement increases the quality and fairness of the trial by narrowing the issues and eliminating surprise.'" *See also* ***Reed v. Iowa Mar. & Repair Corp.***, 16 F.3d 82, 84-85 (5th Cir.1994).

Schreiber Foods, Inc. v. Beatrice Cheese, Inc., 402 F.3d 1198, 1205 (Fed.Cir.2005). "Once counsel became aware that highly material false statements had been made by a witness, in pleadings submitted to the court and in response to discovery requests, and that highly material documents had not been produced as required, [P] and its counsel were under an obligation to promptly correct the record."

Miller v. Pfizer, Inc., 356 F.3d 1326, 1332 (10th Cir. 2004). "[A]n expert's initial Rule 26 report cannot always anticipate every possible challenge to the report. Accordingly, on occasion it may be appropriate to permit the party using the expert to submit supplements to the report in response to assertions by opposing experts that there are gaps in the expert's chain of reasoning. A court's failure to permit such supplementation could even constitute an abuse of discretion in some circumstances."

Work Product

Hickman v. Taylor, 329 U.S. 495, 511 (1947). "Where relevant and non-privileged facts remain hidden in an attorney's file and where production of those facts is essential to the preparation of one's case, discovery may properly be had. *At 512:* [T]he general policy against invading the privacy of an attorney's course of preparation is so well recognized and so essential to an orderly working of our system of legal procedure that a burden rests on the one who would invade that privacy to establish adequate reasons to justify production through a subpoena or court order." *See also* ***U.S. v. Nobles***, 422 U.S. 225, 238 (1975).

U.S. v. Deloitte LLP, 610 F.3d 129, 136 (D.C.Cir. 2010). "The government mistakenly assumes that Rule 26(b)(3) provides an exhaustive definition of what constitutes work product. On the contrary, Rule 26(b)(3) only partially codifies the work-product doctrine announced in ***Hickman***. Rule 26(b)(3) addresses only 'documents and tangible things,' but ***Hickman***'s definition of work product extends to 'intangible' things. Moreover, in ***Hickman***, the Court explained that the attorney's 'mental impressions' were protected from discovery, so that he could not be forced to 'repeat or write out' that information in discovery. Thus ***Hickman*** provides work-product protection for intangible work product independent of Rule 26(b)(3)."

In re Sealed Case, 107 F.3d 46, 51 (D.C.Cir.1997). "With respect to work product immunity, the crime-fraud exception calls for a somewhat different inquiry than with the attorney-client privilege. The focus is not on the client's intent regarding a particular communication, but on the client's intent in consulting the lawyer or in using the materials the lawyer prepared. The question is: Did the client consult the lawyer or use the material for the purpose of committing a crime or fraud? [¶] [T]he crime-fraud exception for work product immunity cannot apply if the attorney prepared the material after his client's wrongdoing ended."

FRCP 27. DEPOSITIONS TO PERPETUATE TESTIMONY

(a) Before an Action Is Filed.

(1) ***Petition.*** A person who wants to perpetuate testimony about any matter cognizable in a United States court may file a verified petition in the district court for the district where any expected adverse party resides. The petition must ask for an order authorizing the petitioner to depose the named persons in order to perpetuate their testimony. The petition must be titled in the petitioner's name and must show:

(A) that the petitioner expects to be a party to an action cognizable in a United States court but cannot presently bring it or cause it to be brought;

(B) the subject matter of the expected action and the petitioner's interest;

(C) the facts that the petitioner wants to establish by the proposed testimony and the reasons to perpetuate it;

(D) the names or a description of the persons whom the petitioner expects to be adverse parties and their addresses, so far as known; and

(E) the name, address, and expected substance of the testimony of each deponent.

(2) ***Notice and Service.*** At least 21 days before the hearing date, the petitioner must serve each expected adverse party with a copy of the petition and a notice stating the time and place of the hearing. The notice may be served either inside or outside the district or state in the manner provided in Rule 4. If that service cannot be made with reasonable diligence on an expected adverse party, the court may order service by publication or otherwise. The court must appoint an attorney to represent persons not served in the manner provided in Rule 4 and to cross-examine the deponent if an unserved person is not otherwise represented. If any expected adverse party is a minor or is incompetent, Rule 17(c) applies.

(3) ***Order and Examination.*** If satisfied that perpetuating the testimony may prevent a failure or delay of justice, the court must issue an order that designates or describes the persons whose depositions may be taken, specifies the subject matter of the examinations, and states whether the depositions will be taken orally or by written interrogatories. The depositions may then be taken under these rules, and the court may issue orders like those authorized by Rules 34 and 35. A reference in these rules to the court where an action is pending means, for purposes of this rule, the court where the petition for the deposition was filed.

(4) ***Using the Deposition.*** A deposition to perpetuate testimony may be used under Rule 32(a) in any later-filed district-court action involving the same subject matter if the deposition either was taken under these rules or, although not so taken, would be admissible in evidence in the courts of the state where it was taken.

(b) Pending Appeal.

(1) ***In General.*** The court where a judgment has been rendered may, if an appeal has been taken or may still be taken, permit a party to de-

FRCP 27

pose witnesses to perpetuate their testimony for use in the event of further proceedings in that court.

(2) ***Motion.*** The party who wants to perpetuate testimony may move for leave to take the depositions, on the same notice and service as if the action were pending in the district court. The motion must show:

(A) the name, address, and expected substance of the testimony of each deponent; and

(B) the reasons for perpetuating the testimony.

(3) ***Court Order.*** If the court finds that perpetuating the testimony may prevent a failure or delay of justice, the court may permit the depositions to be taken and may issue orders like those authorized by Rules 34 and 35. The depositions may be taken and used as any other deposition taken in a pending district-court action.

(c) Perpetuation by an Action. This rule does not limit a court's power to entertain an action to perpetuate testimony.

See selected Notes of Advisory Committee to FRCP 27, p. 1195.

History of FRCP 27: Adopted Dec. 20, 1937, eff. Sept. 16, 1938. Amended Dec. 27, 1946, eff. Mar. 19, 1948; Dec. 29, 1948, eff. Oct. 20, 1949; Mar. 1, 1971, eff. July 1, 1971; Mar. 2, 1987, eff. Aug. 1, 1987; Apr. 25, 2005, eff. Dec. 1, 2005; Apr. 30, 2007, eff. Dec. 1, 2007; Mar. 26, 2009, eff. Dec. 1, 2009.

See ***Commentaries***, "Deposition to Perpetuate Testimony," ch. 6-F, §6, p. 555; ***O'Connor's Federal Civil Forms*** (2012), FORMS 6F.

ANNOTATIONS

In re Deiulemar Compagnia Di Navigazione S.p.A., 198 F.3d 473, 486-87 (4th Cir.1999). "To show that Rule 27 perpetuation of testimony may prevent a failure or delay of justice, a petitioner must demonstrate a need for the testimony or evidence that cannot easily be accommodated by other potential witnesses. The testimony to be perpetuated must be relevant, not simply cumulative, and likely to provide material distinctly useful to a finder of fact. Evidence that throws a different, greater, or additional light on a key issue might well prevent a failure or delay of justice." (Internal quotes omitted.) *See also* ***In re City of El Paso***, 887 F.2d 1103, 1105 (D.C.Cir.1989).

In re Bay Cty. Middlegrounds Landfill Site, 171 F.3d 1044, 1046 (6th Cir.1999). "[N]othing in [FRCP 27] indicates that the requirement that petitioner 'show' certain matters means the 'showing' must include material proffered in a form admissible at trial. We hold that the judge's discretion encompasses the nature and quality of evidence required to make or rebut the required showing in Rule 27(a)(1). *At 1047:* Under the standard of 'prevent the failure or delay of justice,' we hold that the best interpretation of [FRCP 27(a)(1)] is that the testimony to be perpetuated must be relevant, not simply cumulative, and likely to provide material distinctly useful to a finder of fact. A determination that the evidence is absolutely unique is not necessary."

Penn Mut. Life Ins. v. U.S., 68 F.3d 1371, 1373 (D.C.Cir.1995). "Unlike other discovery rules, Rule 27(a) allows a party to take depositions *prior* to litigation if it demonstrates an expectation of future litigation, explains the substance of the testimony it expects to elicit and the reasons the testimony is important, and establishes a risk that testimony will be lost if not preserved. *At 1374:* [A] party need not demonstrate that litigation is an absolute certainty…."

FRCP 28. PERSONS BEFORE WHOM DEPOSITIONS MAY BE TAKEN

(a) Within the United States.

(1) ***In General.*** Within the United States or a territory or insular possession subject to United States jurisdiction, a deposition must be taken before:

(A) an officer authorized to administer oaths either by federal law or by the law in the place of examination; or

(B) a person appointed by the court where the action is pending to administer oaths and take testimony.

(2) ***Definition of "Officer."*** The term "officer" in Rules 30, 31, and 32 includes a person appointed by the court under this rule or designated by the parties under Rule 29(a).

(b) In a Foreign Country.

(1) ***In General.*** A deposition may be taken in a foreign country:

(A) under an applicable treaty or convention;

(B) under a letter of request, whether or not captioned a "letter rogatory";

(C) on notice, before a person authorized to administer oaths either by federal law or by the law in the place of examination; or

(D) before a person commissioned by the court to administer any necessary oath and take testimony.

(2) ***Issuing a Letter of Request or a Commission.*** A letter of request, a commission, or both may be issued:

(A) on appropriate terms after an application and notice of it; and

(B) without a showing that taking the deposition in another manner is impracticable or inconvenient.

(3) ***Form of a Request, Notice, or Commission.*** When a letter of request or any other device is used according to a treaty or convention, it must be captioned in the form prescribed by that treaty or convention. A letter of request may be addressed "To the Appropriate Authority in [name of country]." A deposition notice or a commission must designate by name or descriptive title the person before whom the deposition is to be taken.

(4) ***Letter of Request—Admitting Evidence.*** Evidence obtained in response to a letter of request need not be excluded merely because it is not a verbatim transcript, because the testimony was not taken under oath, or because of any similar departure from the requirements for depositions taken within the United States.

(c) **Disqualification.** A deposition must not be taken before a person who is any party's relative, employee, or attorney; who is related to or employed by any party's attorney; or who is financially interested in the action.

History of FRCP 28: Adopted Dec. 20, 1937, eff. Sept. 16, 1938. Amended Dec. 27, 1946, eff. Mar. 19, 1948; Jan. 21, 1963, eff. July 1, 1963; Apr. 29, 1980, eff. Aug. 1, 1980; Mar. 2, 1987, eff. Aug. 1, 1987; Apr. 22, 1993, eff. Dec. 1, 1993; Apr. 30, 2007, eff. Dec. 1, 2007.

See *Commentaries*, "Taking deposition before authorized officer," ch. 6-F, §3.3, p. 544.

See also 28 U.S.C. §1781 (transmittal of letters rogatory), §1821 (compensation of person being deposed); Hague Convention on the Taking of Evidence Abroad in Civil or Commercial Matters (foreign discovery), p. 1566, this book.

ANNOTATIONS

U.S. v. Salim, 855 F.2d 944, 951 (2d Cir.1988). "[I]t is not always possible to take a deposition in a foreign country in the manner that we might prefer, or even that we might require for a deposition taken domestically. Yet, that does not mean that depositions taken according to foreign law are inferior to those taken under U.S. law. *At 952:* [E]xamination by a foreign judicial officer was specifically anticipated by the Advisory Committee…. [T]he French judicial system, while different from our own, is neither less impartial nor less interested in obtaining accurate testimony from witnesses."

FRCP 29. STIPULATIONS ABOUT DISCOVERY PROCEDURE

Unless the court orders otherwise, the parties may stipulate that:

(a) a deposition may be taken before any person, at any time or place, on any notice, and in the manner specified—in which event it may be used in the same way as any other deposition; and

(b) other procedures governing or limiting discovery be modified—but a stipulation extending the time for any form of discovery must have court approval if it would interfere with the time set for completing discovery, for hearing a motion, or for trial.

See selected Notes of Advisory Committee to FRCP 29, p. 1196.

History of FRCP 29: Adopted Dec. 20, 1937, eff. Sept. 16, 1938. Amended Mar. 30, 1970, eff. July 1, 1970; Apr. 22, 1993, eff. Dec. 1, 1993; Apr. 30, 2007, eff. Dec. 1, 2007.

See *Commentaries*, "By stipulation," ch. 6-A, §7.2.4, p. 421; *O'Connor's Federal Civil Forms* (2012), FORMS 6A.

ANNOTATIONS

Angell v. Shawmut Bank Conn. Nat'l Ass'n, 153 F.R.D. 585, 590 (M.D.N.C.1994). "Private agreements save time and expense for the parties and valuable court time as well. Therefore, it is in the interest of justice … to enforce such agreements…."

FRCP 30. DEPOSITIONS BY ORAL EXAMINATION

(a) **When a Deposition May Be Taken.**

(1) ***Without Leave.*** A party may, by oral questions, depose any person, including a party, without leave of court except as provided in Rule 30(a)(2). The deponent's attendance may be compelled by subpoena under Rule 45.

(2) ***With Leave.*** A party must obtain leave of court, and the court must grant leave to the extent consistent with Rule 26(b)(2):

(A) if the parties have not stipulated to the deposition and:

(i) the deposition would result in more than 10 depositions being taken under this rule or Rule 31 by the plaintiffs, or by the defendants, or by the third-party defendants;

(ii) the deponent has already been deposed in the case; or

(iii) the party seeks to take the deposition before the time specified in Rule 26(d), unless the party certifies in the notice, with supporting facts, that the deponent is expected to leave the United States and be unavailable for examination in this country after that time; or

(B) if the deponent is confined in prison.

(b) Notice of the Deposition; Other Formal Requirements.

(1) ***Notice in General.*** A party who wants to depose a person by oral questions must give reasonable written notice to every other party. The notice must state the time and place of the deposition and, if known, the deponent's name and address. If the name is unknown, the notice must provide a general description sufficient to identify the person or the particular class or group to which the person belongs.

(2) ***Producing Documents.*** If a subpoena duces tecum is to be served on the deponent, the materials designated for production, as set out in the subpoena, must be listed in the notice or in an attachment. The notice to a party deponent may be accompanied by a request under Rule 34 to produce documents and tangible things at the deposition.

(3) ***Method of Recording.***

(A) *Method Stated in the Notice.* The party who notices the deposition must state in the notice the method for recording the testimony. Unless the court orders otherwise, testimony may be recorded by audio, audiovisual, or stenographic means. The noticing party bears the recording costs. Any party may arrange to transcribe a deposition.

(B) *Additional Method.* With prior notice to the deponent and other parties, any party may designate another method for recording the testimony in addition to that specified in the original notice. That party bears the expense of the additional record or transcript unless the court orders otherwise.

(4) ***By Remote Means.*** The parties may stipulate—or the court may on motion order—that a deposition be taken by telephone or other remote means. For the purpose of this rule and Rules 28(a), 37(a)(2), and 37(b)(1), the deposition takes place where the deponent answers the questions.

(5) ***Officer's Duties.***

(A) *Before the Deposition.* Unless the parties stipulate otherwise, a deposition must be conducted before an officer appointed or designated under Rule 28. The officer must begin the deposition with an on-the-record statement that includes:

(i) the officer's name and business address;

(ii) the date, time, and place of the deposition;

(iii) the deponent's name;

(iv) the officer's administration of the oath or affirmation to the deponent; and

(v) the identity of all persons present.

(B) *Conducting the Deposition; Avoiding Distortion.* If the deposition is recorded nonstenographically, the officer must repeat the items in Rule 30(b)(5)(A)(i)-(iii) at the beginning of each unit of the recording medium. The deponent's and attorneys' appearance or demeanor must not be distorted through recording techniques.

(C) *After the Deposition.* At the end of a deposition, the officer must state on the record that the deposition is complete and must set out any stipulations made by the attorneys about custody of the transcript or recording and of the exhibits, or about any other pertinent matters.

(6) ***Notice or Subpoena Directed to an Organization.*** In its notice or subpoena, a party may name as the deponent a public or private corporation, a partnership, an association, a governmental agency, or other entity and must describe with reasonable particularity the matters for examination. The named organization must then designate one or more officers, directors, or managing agents, or designate other persons who consent to testify on its behalf; and it may set out the matters on which each person designated will testify. A subpoena must advise a nonparty organization of its duty to make this designation. The persons desig-

nated must testify about information known or reasonably available to the organization. This paragraph (6) does not preclude a deposition by any other procedure allowed by these rules.

(c) Examination and Cross-Examination; Record of the Examination; Objections; Written Questions.

(1) *Examination and Cross-Examination.* The examination and cross-examination of a deponent proceed as they would at trial under the Federal Rules of Evidence, except Rules 103 and 615. After putting the deponent under oath or affirmation, the officer must record the testimony by the method designated under Rule 30(b)(3)(A). The testimony must be recorded by the officer personally or by a person acting in the presence and under the direction of the officer.

(2) *Objections.* An objection at the time of the examination—whether to evidence, to a party's conduct, to the officer's qualifications, to the manner of taking the deposition, or to any other aspect of the deposition—must be noted on the record, but the examination still proceeds; the testimony is taken subject to any objection. An objection must be stated concisely in a nonargumentative and nonsuggestive manner. A person may instruct a deponent not to answer only when necessary to preserve a privilege, to enforce a limitation ordered by the court, or to present a motion under Rule 30(d)(3).

(3) *Participating Through Written Questions.* Instead of participating in the oral examination, a party may serve written questions in a sealed envelope on the party noticing the deposition, who must deliver them to the officer. The officer must ask the deponent those questions and record the answers verbatim.

(d) Duration; Sanction; Motion to Terminate or Limit.

(1) *Duration.* Unless otherwise stipulated or ordered by the court, a deposition is limited to 1 day of 7 hours. The court must allow additional time consistent with Rule 26(b)(2) if needed to fairly examine the deponent or if the deponent, another person, or any other circumstance impedes or delays the examination.

(2) *Sanction.* The court may impose an appropriate sanction—including the reasonable expenses and attorney's fees incurred by any party—on a person who impedes, delays, or frustrates the fair examination of the deponent.

(3) *Motion to Terminate or Limit.*

(A) *Grounds.* At any time during a deposition, the deponent or a party may move to terminate or limit it on the ground that it is being conducted in bad faith or in a manner that unreasonably annoys, embarrasses, or oppresses the deponent or party. The motion may be filed in the court where the action is pending or the deposition is being taken. If the objecting deponent or party so demands, the deposition must be suspended for the time necessary to obtain an order.

(B) *Order.* The court may order that the deposition be terminated or may limit its scope and manner as provided in Rule 26(c). If terminated, the deposition may be resumed only by order of the court where the action is pending.

(C) *Award of Expenses.* Rule 37(a)(5) applies to the award of expenses.

(e) Review by the Witness; Changes.

(1) *Review; Statement of Changes.* On request by the deponent or a party before the deposition is completed, the deponent must be allowed 30 days after being notified by the officer that the transcript or recording is available in which:

(A) to review the transcript or recording; and

(B) if there are changes in form or substance, to sign a statement listing the changes and the reasons for making them.

(2) *Changes Indicated in the Officer's Certificate.* The officer must note in the certificate prescribed by Rule 30(f)(1) whether a review was requested and, if so, must attach any changes the deponent makes during the 30-day period.

(f) Certification and Delivery; Exhibits; Copies of the Transcript or Recording; Filing.

(1) *Certification and Delivery.* The officer must certify in writing that the witness was duly

FRCP 30

sworn and that the deposition accurately records the witness's testimony. The certificate must accompany the record of the deposition. Unless the court orders otherwise, the officer must seal the deposition in an envelope or package bearing the title of the action and marked "Deposition of [witness's name]" and must promptly send it to the attorney who arranged for the transcript or recording. The attorney must store it under conditions that will protect it against loss, destruction, tampering, or deterioration.

(2) ***Documents and Tangible Things.***

(A) *Originals and Copies.* Documents and tangible things produced for inspection during a deposition must, on a party's request, be marked for identification and attached to the deposition. Any party may inspect and copy them. But if the person who produced them wants to keep the originals, the person may:

(i) offer copies to be marked, attached to the deposition, and then used as originals—after giving all parties a fair opportunity to verify the copies by comparing them with the originals; or

(ii) give all parties a fair opportunity to inspect and copy the originals after they are marked—in which event the originals may be used as if attached to the deposition.

(B) *Order Regarding the Originals.* Any party may move for an order that the originals be attached to the deposition pending final disposition of the case.

(3) ***Copies of the Transcript or Recording.*** Unless otherwise stipulated or ordered by the court, the officer must retain the stenographic notes of a deposition taken stenographically or a copy of the recording of a deposition taken by another method. When paid reasonable charges, the officer must furnish a copy of the transcript or recording to any party or the deponent.

(4) ***Notice of Filing.*** A party who files the deposition must promptly notify all other parties of the filing.

(g) Failure to Attend a Deposition or Serve a Subpoena; Expenses. A party who, expecting a deposition to be taken, attends in person or by an attorney may recover reasonable expenses for attending, including attorney's fees, if the noticing party failed to:

(1) attend and proceed with the deposition; or

(2) serve a subpoena on a nonparty deponent, who consequently did not attend.

See selected Notes of Advisory Committee to FRCP 30, p. 1196.

History of FRCP 30: Adopted Dec. 20, 1937, eff. Sept. 16, 1938. Amended Jan. 21, 1963, eff. July 1, 1963; Mar. 30, 1970, eff. July 1, 1970; Mar. 1, 1971, eff. July 1, 1971; Nov. 20, 1972, eff. July 1, 1975; Apr. 29, 1980, eff. Aug. 1, 1980; Mar. 2, 1987, eff. Aug. 1, 1987; Apr. 22, 1993, eff. Dec. 1, 1993; Apr. 17, 2000, eff. Dec. 1, 2000; Apr. 30, 2007, eff. Dec. 1, 2007.

See ***Commentaries***, "Depositions," ch. 6-F, p. 538; ***O'Connor's Federal Civil Forms*** (2012), FORMS 6F.

See also 5 U.S.C. §2903 (notary public and other persons authorized to administer oaths); 28 U.S.C. §636 (power of U.S. magistrate judges to administer oaths and take depositions).

ANNOTATIONS

Brazos River Auth. v. GE Ionics, Inc., 469 F.3d 416, 432-34 (5th Cir.2006). "Rule 30(b)(6) is designed to avoid the possibility that several officers and managing agents might be deposed in turn, with each disclaiming personal knowledge of facts that are clearly known to persons within the organization and thus to the organization itself. Therefore, the deponent must make a conscientious good-faith endeavor to designate the persons having knowledge of the matters sought by the party noticing the deposition and to *prepare* those persons in order that they can answer fully, completely, unevasively, the questions posed as to the relevant subject matters. The duty to present and prepare a Rule 30(b)(6) designee goes beyond matters personally known to that designee or to matters in which that designee was personally involved. The deponent must prepare the designee to the extent matters are reasonably available, whether from documents, past employees, or other sources. [¶] [A] rule 30(b)(6) designee does not give his personal opinions, but presents the corporation's position on the topic. When a corporation produces an employee pursuant to a rule 30(b)(6) notice, it represents that the employee has the authority to speak on behalf of the corporation with respect to the areas within the notice of deposition. This extends not only to facts, but also to subjective beliefs and opinions. If it becomes obvious that the deposition representative designated by the corporation is deficient, the corporation is obligated to provide a substitute. [¶] If the designated agent is not knowledgeable about relevant

facts, and the principal has failed to designate an available, knowledgeable, and readily identifiable witness, then the appearance is, for all practical purposes, no appearance at all." (Internal quotes omitted.) *See also* ***Reilly v. NatWest Mkts. Grp.***, 181 F.3d 253, 268 (2d Cir.1999) (when party does not comply, court may impose various sanctions, including preclusion of evidence).

In re Terra Int'l, 134 F.3d 302, 306 (5th Cir.1998). FRCP 30(c)'s "exclusion of depositions from the strictures of [FRE] 615 was intended to establish a general rule that 'other witnesses are not automatically excluded from a deposition simply by the request of a party.' Rather, exclusion of other witnesses requires that the court grant a protective order pursuant to [FRCP 26(c)(5), now FRCP 26(c)(1)(E)]."

FRCP 31. DEPOSITIONS BY WRITTEN QUESTIONS

(a) When a Deposition May Be Taken.

(1) ***Without Leave.*** A party may, by written questions, depose any person, including a party, without leave of court except as provided in Rule 31(a)(2). The deponent's attendance may be compelled by subpoena under Rule 45.

(2) ***With Leave.*** A party must obtain leave of court, and the court must grant leave to the extent consistent with Rule 26(b)(2):

(A) if the parties have not stipulated to the deposition and:

(i) the deposition would result in more than 10 depositions being taken under this rule or Rule 30 by the plaintiffs, or by the defendants, or by the third-party defendants;

(ii) the deponent has already been deposed in the case; or

(iii) the party seeks to take a deposition before the time specified in Rule 26(d); or

(B) if the deponent is confined in prison.

(3) ***Service; Required Notice.*** A party who wants to depose a person by written questions must serve them on every other party, with a notice stating, if known, the deponent's name and address. If the name is unknown, the notice must provide a general description sufficient to identify the person or the particular class or group to which the person belongs. The notice must also state the name or descriptive title and the address of the officer before whom the deposition will be taken.

(4) ***Questions Directed to an Organization.*** A public or private corporation, a partnership, an association, or a governmental agency may be deposed by written questions in accordance with Rule 30(b)(6).

(5) ***Questions from Other Parties.*** Any questions to the deponent from other parties must be served on all parties as follows: cross-questions, within 14 days after being served with the notice and direct questions; redirect questions, within 7 days after being served with cross-questions; and recross-questions, within 7 days after being served with redirect questions. The court may, for good cause, extend or shorten these times.

(b) Delivery to the Officer; Officer's Duties. The party who noticed the deposition must deliver to the officer a copy of all the questions served and of the notice. The officer must promptly proceed in the manner provided in Rule 30(c), (e), and (f) to:

(1) take the deponent's testimony in response to the questions;

(2) prepare and certify the deposition; and

(3) send it to the party, attaching a copy of the questions and of the notice.

(c) Notice of Completion or Filing.

(1) ***Completion.*** The party who noticed the deposition must notify all other parties when it is completed.

(2) ***Filing.*** A party who files the deposition must promptly notify all other parties of the filing.

See selected Notes of Advisory Committee to FRCP 31, p. 1199.

History of FRCP 31: Adopted Dec. 20, 1937, eff. Sept. 16, 1938. Amended Mar. 30, 1970, eff. July 1, 1970; Mar. 2, 1987, eff. Aug. 1, 1987; Apr. 22, 1993, eff. Dec. 1, 1993; Apr. 30, 2007, eff. Dec. 1, 2007.

See *Commentaries*, "Deposition by Written Questions," ch. 6-F, §5, p. 554; *O'Connor's Federal Civil Forms* (2012), FORMS 6F.

ANNOTATIONS

National Life Ins. v. Hartford Acc. & Indem. Co., 615 F.2d 595, 599-600 (3d Cir.1980). FRCP 31 "gives the party, not the witness, the option of conducting a deposition by written questions. We see no policy justification for allowing the witness the option of reviewing written questions prior to the deposition."

Peterson v. Nadler, 452 F.2d 754, 756-57 (8th Cir. 1971), *overruled on other grounds*, ***Mallard v. U.S. Dist. Ct. for the S. Dist. of Iowa***, 490 U.S. 296 (1989). "Rule 31 … expressly provides the right of any party to discover and perpetuate evidence from nonparty witnesses by deposition upon written questions."

FRCP 32. USING DEPOSITIONS IN COURT PROCEEDINGS

(a) Using Depositions.

(1) ***In General.*** At a hearing or trial, all or part of a deposition may be used against a party on these conditions:

(A) the party was present or represented at the taking of the deposition or had reasonable notice of it;

(B) it is used to the extent it would be admissible under the Federal Rules of Evidence if the deponent were present and testifying; and

(C) the use is allowed by Rule 32(a)(2) through (8).

(2) ***Impeachment and Other Uses.*** Any party may use a deposition to contradict or impeach the testimony given by the deponent as a witness, or for any other purpose allowed by the Federal Rules of Evidence.

(3) ***Deposition of Party, Agent, or Designee.*** An adverse party may use for any purpose the deposition of a party or anyone who, when deposed, was the party's officer, director, managing agent, or designee under Rule 30(b)(6) or 31(a)(4).

(4) ***Unavailable Witness.*** A party may use for any purpose the deposition of a witness, whether or not a party, if the court finds:

(A) that the witness is dead;

(B) that the witness is more than 100 miles from the place of hearing or trial or is outside the United States, unless it appears that the witness's absence was procured by the party offering the deposition;

(C) that the witness cannot attend or testify because of age, illness, infirmity, or imprisonment;

(D) that the party offering the deposition could not procure the witness's attendance by subpoena; or

(E) on motion and notice, that exceptional circumstances make it desirable—in the interest of justice and with due regard to the importance of live testimony in open court—to permit the deposition to be used.

(5) ***Limitations on Use.***

(A) *Deposition Taken on Short Notice.* A deposition must not be used against a party who, having received less than 14 days' notice of the deposition, promptly moved for a protective order under Rule 26(c)(1)(B) requesting that it not be taken or be taken at a different time or place—and this motion was still pending when the deposition was taken.

(B) *Unavailable Deponent; Party Could Not Obtain an Attorney.* A deposition taken without leave of court under the unavailability provision of Rule 30(a)(2)(A)(iii) must not be used against a party who shows that, when served with the notice, it could not, despite diligent efforts, obtain an attorney to represent it at the deposition.

(6) ***Using Part of a Deposition.*** If a party offers in evidence only part of a deposition, an adverse party may require the offeror to introduce other parts that in fairness should be considered with the part introduced, and any party may itself introduce any other parts.

(7) ***Substituting a Party.*** Substituting a party under Rule 25 does not affect the right to use a deposition previously taken.

(8) ***Deposition Taken in an Earlier Action.*** A deposition lawfully taken and, if required, filed in any federal- or state-court action may be used in a later action involving the same subject matter between the same parties, or their representatives or successors in interest, to the same extent as if taken in the later action. A deposition previously taken may also be used as allowed by the Federal Rules of Evidence.

(b) Objections to Admissibility. Subject to Rules 28(b) and 32(d)(3), an objection may be made at a hearing or trial to the admission of any deposition testimony that would be inadmissible if the witness were present and testifying.

(c) Form of Presentation. Unless the court orders otherwise, a party must provide a transcript of any

deposition testimony the party offers, but may provide the court with the testimony in nontranscript form as well. On any party's request, deposition testimony offered in a jury trial for any purpose other than impeachment must be presented in nontranscript form, if available, unless the court for good cause orders otherwise.

(d) Waiver of Objections.

(1) ***To the Notice.*** An objection to an error or irregularity in a deposition notice is waived unless promptly served in writing on the party giving the notice.

(2) ***To the Officer's Qualification.*** An objection based on disqualification of the officer before whom a deposition is to be taken is waived if not made:

(A) before the deposition begins; or

(B) promptly after the basis for disqualification becomes known or, with reasonable diligence, could have been known.

(3) ***To the Taking of the Deposition.***

(A) *Objection to Competence, Relevance, or Materiality.* An objection to a deponent's competence—or to the competence, relevance, or materiality of testimony—is not waived by a failure to make the objection before or during the deposition, unless the ground for it might have been corrected at that time.

(B) *Objection to an Error or Irregularity.* An objection to an error or irregularity at an oral examination is waived if:

(i) it relates to the manner of taking the deposition, the form of a question or answer, the oath or affirmation, a party's conduct, or other matters that might have been corrected at that time; and

(ii) it is not timely made during the deposition.

(C) *Objection to a Written Question.* An objection to the form of a written question under Rule 31 is waived if not served in writing on the party submitting the question within the time for serving responsive questions or, if the question is a recross-question, within 7 days after being served with it.

(4) ***To Completing and Returning the Deposition.*** An objection to how the officer transcribed the testimony—or prepared, signed, certified, sealed, endorsed, sent, or otherwise dealt with the deposition—is waived unless a motion to suppress is made promptly after the error or irregularity becomes known or, with reasonable diligence, could have been known.

See selected Notes of Advisory Committee to FRCP 32, p. 1199.

History of FRCP 32: Adopted Dec. 20, 1937, eff. Sept. 16, 1938. Amended Mar. 30, 1970, eff. July 1, 1970; Nov. 20, 1972, eff. July 1, 1975; Apr. 29, 1980, eff. Aug. 1, 1980; Mar. 2, 1987, eff. Aug. 1, 1987; Apr. 22, 1993, eff. Dec. 1, 1993; Apr. 30, 2007, eff. Dec. 1, 2007; Mar. 26, 2009, eff. Dec. 1, 2009.

See *Commentaries*, "Using Deposition in Court Proceedings," ch. 6-F, §4, p. 551.

FRCP 32

ANNOTATIONS

Delgado v. Pawtucket Police Dept., 668 F.3d 42, 49 (1st Cir.2012). "Rule 32(a)(4)(C) ... requires as a prerequisite to the admission of deposition testimony that the court find 'that the witness cannot attend or testify *because of*' one of the enumerated conditions. By its terms, then, the rule does not permit the use of deposition testimony where the age, illness, infirmity, or imprisonment of a witness provides no basis to conclude that the witness is unable to provide live testimony. ... It would be startling to suggest that deposition testimony should be substituted, based on nothing more than merely citing a witness's age or asserting that a witness was ill, without establishing why age or illness presented a genuine barrier to live testimony."

Thomas v. Cook Cty. Sheriff's Dept., 604 F.3d 293, 308 (7th Cir.2010). "Implicit in [FRCP 32(a)(4)(D)] is an obligation to use reasonable diligence to secure the witness's presence, and the district court has broad discretion to determine whether the proponent has satisfied this requirement." *See also* ***Griman v. Makousky***, 76 F.3d 151, 154 (7th Cir.1996).

Garcia-Martinez v. City & Cty. of Denver, 392 F.3d 1187, 1190 (10th Cir.2004). P argues "that the district court should have admitted his deposition testimony under [FRCP] 32 and [FRE] 804 because he was 'unavailable' at the time of trial. [¶] Prior to trial ..., [P's] attorney designated and submitted portions of [P's] deposition testimony to the district court. [P's] attorney claimed this testimony should be admitted at trial under the [FRCPs] and the [FREs] because [P] was out of the country and therefore unavailable for trial. In response, [Ds] submitted ... a motion in limine opposing the admission of the deposition testimony, arguing that [P] was not 'unavailable' ... because he had procured his own absence by voluntarily leaving the country. [¶] The judge concluded that the

deposition was inadmissible because [P] procured his own unavailability. The court rejected counsel's argument that [P] faced the Catch 22 of choosing between staying in the U.S. for trial and risking imprisonment or leaving the U.S. and losing the opportunity to testify at trial. *At 1191:* We conclude that the district court did not abuse its discretion in applying [FRCP] 32 and [FRE] 804 to these facts."

Ueland v. U.S., 291 F.3d 993, 996 (7th Cir.2002). FRCP 32(a), "as a freestanding exception to the hearsay rule, is one of the 'other rules' to which [FRE] 802 refers. Evidence authorized by Rule 32(a) cannot be excluded as hearsay, unless it would be inadmissible even if delivered in court." *See also* ***Creative Consumer Concepts, Inc. v. Kreisler***, 563 F.3d 1070, 1080 (10th Cir.2009).

Daigle v. Maine Med. Ctr., Inc., 14 F.3d 684, 692 n.11 (1st Cir.1994). FRCP 32's "'general principle is to require defects in the taking of depositions to be pointed out promptly [so as] to prevent waste of time and money by a subsequent claim that a deposition must be suppressed because of some technical error long ago.'"

FRCP 33. INTERROGATORIES TO PARTIES

(a) In General.

(1) ***Number.*** Unless otherwise stipulated or ordered by the court, a party may serve on any other party no more than 25 written interrogatories, including all discrete subparts. Leave to serve additional interrogatories may be granted to the extent consistent with Rule 26(b)(2).

(2) ***Scope.*** An interrogatory may relate to any matter that may be inquired into under Rule 26(b). An interrogatory is not objectionable merely because it asks for an opinion or contention that relates to fact or the application of law to fact, but the court may order that the interrogatory need not be answered until designated discovery is complete, or until a pretrial conference or some other time.

(b) Answers and Objections.

(1) ***Responding Party.*** The interrogatories must be answered:

(A) by the party to whom they are directed; or

(B) if that party is a public or private corporation, a partnership, an association, or a governmental agency, by any officer or agent, who must furnish the information available to the party.

(2) ***Time to Respond.*** The responding party must serve its answers and any objections within 30 days after being served with the interrogatories. A shorter or longer time may be stipulated to under Rule 29 or be ordered by the court.

(3) ***Answering Each Interrogatory.*** Each interrogatory must, to the extent it is not objected to, be answered separately and fully in writing under oath.

(4) ***Objections.*** The grounds for objecting to an interrogatory must be stated with specificity. Any ground not stated in a timely objection is waived unless the court, for good cause, excuses the failure.

(5) ***Signature.*** The person who makes the answers must sign them, and the attorney who objects must sign any objections.

(c) Use. An answer to an interrogatory may be used to the extent allowed by the Federal Rules of Evidence.

(d) Option to Produce Business Records. If the answer to an interrogatory may be determined by examining, auditing, compiling, abstracting, or summarizing a party's business records (including electronically stored information), and if the burden of deriving or ascertaining the answer will be substantially the same for either party, the responding party may answer by:

(1) specifying the records that must be reviewed, in sufficient detail to enable the interrogating party to locate and identify them as readily as the responding party could; and

(2) giving the interrogating party a reasonable opportunity to examine and audit the records and to make copies, compilations, abstracts, or summaries.

See selected Notes of Advisory Committee to FRCP 33, p. 1199.

History of FRCP 33: Adopted Dec. 20, 1937, eff. Sept. 16, 1938. Amended Dec. 27, 1946, eff. Mar. 19, 1948; Mar. 30, 1970, eff. July 1, 1970; Apr. 29, 1980, eff. Aug. 1, 1980; Apr. 22, 1993, eff. Dec. 1, 1993; Apr. 12, 2006, eff. Dec. 1, 2006; Apr. 30, 2007, eff. Dec. 1, 2007.

See ***Commentaries***, "Interrogatories," ch. 6-G, p. 557; ***O'Connor's Federal Civil Forms*** (2012), FORMS 6G.

ANNOTATIONS

Oppenheimer Fund, Inc. v. Sanders, 437 U.S. 340, 357 (1978). "[W]hen one party directs an interrogatory to another party which can be answered by examination of the responding party's business records, 'it is a sufficient answer to such interrogatory to specify the records from which the answer may be derived or ascertained and to afford to the party serving the interrogatory reasonable opportunity to' examine and copy the records, if the burden of deriving the answer would be 'substantially the same' for either party."

University of Tex. v. Vratil, 96 F.3d 1337, 1340 (10th Cir.1996). "The district court erred in characterizing the unserved, nonparty petitioners as 'real parties in interest' for discovery purposes, and acted without jurisdiction in ordering them to respond to interrogatories propounded under [FRCP] 33. [¶] The [FRCPs] provide a clear-cut procedure for obtaining responses to interrogatories from an [unincorporated] association.... Under [FRCP] 33(a), interrogatories may only be directed to a party to an action. Where that party is an association, Rule 33(a) [now Rule 33(b)(1)(B)] allows it to select an officer or agent to respond on its behalf. In the event the officer or agent fails to respond, enforcement of the court's orders regarding discovery is obtained under [FRCP] 37, which, notably, contains no procedure for requiring responses from unserved, nonparty members of the association."

Venezia v. Robinson, 16 F.3d 209, 212 (7th Cir. 1994). "Interrogatories and requests to produce are authorized ... only after the defendant has been served with process."

FRCP 34. PRODUCING DOCUMENTS, ELECTRONICALLY STORED INFORMATION, & TANGIBLE THINGS, OR ENTERING ONTO LAND, FOR INSPECTION & OTHER PURPOSES

(a) **In General.** A party may serve on any other party a request within the scope of Rule 26(b):

(1) to produce and permit the requesting party or its representative to inspect, copy, test, or sample the following items in the responding party's possession, custody, or control:

(A) any designated documents or electronically stored information—including writings, drawings, graphs, charts, photographs, sound recordings, images, and other data or data compilations—stored in any medium from which information can be obtained either directly or, if necessary, after translation by the responding party into a reasonably usable form; or

(B) any designated tangible things; or

(2) to permit entry onto designated land or other property possessed or controlled by the responding party, so that the requesting party may inspect, measure, survey, photograph, test, or sample the property or any designated object or operation on it.

(b) **Procedure.**

(1) ***Contents of the Request.*** The request:

(A) must describe with reasonable particularity each item or category of items to be inspected;

(B) must specify a reasonable time, place, and manner for the inspection and for performing the related acts; and

(C) may specify the form or forms in which electronically stored information is to be produced.

(2) ***Responses and Objections.***

(A) *Time to Respond.* The party to whom the request is directed must respond in writing within 30 days after being served. A shorter or longer time may be stipulated to under Rule 29 or be ordered by the court.

(B) *Responding to Each Item.* For each item or category, the response must either state that inspection and related activities will be permitted as requested or state an objection to the request, including the reasons.

(C) *Objections.* An objection to part of a request must specify the part and permit inspection of the rest.

(D) *Responding to a Request for Production of Electronically Stored Information.* The response may state an objection to a requested form for producing electronically stored information. If the responding party objects to a requested form—or if no form was specified in the request—the party must state the form or forms it intends to use.

(E) *Producing the Documents or Electronically Stored Information.* Unless otherwise stipulated or ordered by the court, these procedures apply to producing documents or electronically stored information:

(i) A party must produce documents as they are kept in the usual course of business or must organize and label them to correspond to the categories in the request;

(ii) If a request does not specify a form for producing electronically stored information, a party must produce it in a form or forms in which it is ordinarily maintained or in a reasonably usable form or forms; and

(iii) A party need not produce the same electronically stored information in more than one form.

(c) Nonparties. As provided in Rule 45, a nonparty may be compelled to produce documents and tangible things or to permit an inspection.

See selected Notes of Advisory Committee to FRCP 34, p. 1202.

History of FRCP 34: Adopted Dec. 20, 1937, eff. Sept. 16, 1938. Amended Dec. 27, 1946, eff. Mar. 19, 1948; Mar. 30, 1970, eff. July 1, 1970; Apr. 29, 1980, eff. Aug. 1, 1980; Mar. 2, 1987, eff. Aug. 1, 1987; Apr. 30, 1991, eff. Dec. 1, 1991; Apr. 22, 1993, eff. Dec. 1, 1993; Apr. 12, 2006, eff. Dec. 1, 2006; Apr. 30, 2007, eff. Dec. 1, 2007.

See *Commentaries*, "Requests for Production," ch. 6-I, p. 569; "Request for Entry on Land," ch. 6-K, p. 579; *O'Connor's Federal Civil Forms* (2012), FORMS 6I; FORMS 6K.

ANNOTATIONS

Burlington N. & Santa Fe Ry. v. U.S. Dist. Ct. for the Dist. of Mont., 408 F.3d 1142, 1147 (9th Cir.2005). See annotation under FRCP 26, *Asserting Privileges*, p. 898.

Wiwa v. Royal Dutch Pet. Co., 392 F.3d 812, 821 (5th Cir.2004). "[T]he subpoena requests all documents to which [nonparty] has 'access.' [Nonparty] contends that the term 'access' is overbroad because [FRCP] 34 requires only the production of documents in the 'possession, custody, or control' of the person to whom the subpoena is directed. [Nonparty] argues that the term 'access' encompasses documents that he does not have under his 'possession, custody, or control.' We agree. The phrase 'to which he has access' is overbroad; it would require the retrieval of documents … not under [nonparty's] custody, control, or possession, but to which he could conceivably have access by virtue of his prior position with [D]. We therefore limit the document request in the subpoena to documents within [nonparty's] custody, control, or possession."

Resolution Trust Corp. v. North Bridge Assocs., 22 F.3d 1198, 1205 (1st Cir.1994). FRCP 34(b) gives "the discovering party, not the discovery target, the option of specifying the time, place, and manner of production and inspection. Absent a court order or an agreement among the litigants, a party from whom discovery is sought cannot unilaterally alter these directives to suit its fancy [especially] where … the discovering party's notice [provided] an entirely reasonable time/place/manner format for document production."

FRCP 35. PHYSICAL & MENTAL EXAMINATIONS

(a) Order for an Examination.

(1) ***In General.*** The court where the action is pending may order a party whose mental or physical condition—including blood group—is in controversy to submit to a physical or mental examination by a suitably licensed or certified examiner. The court has the same authority to order a party to produce for examination a person who is in its custody or under its legal control.

(2) ***Motion and Notice; Contents of the Order.*** The order:

(A) may be made only on motion for good cause and on notice to all parties and the person to be examined; and

(B) must specify the time, place, manner, conditions, and scope of the examination, as well as the person or persons who will perform it.

(b) Examiner's Report.

(1) ***Request by the Party or Person Examined.*** The party who moved for the examination must, on request, deliver to the requester a copy of the examiner's report, together with like reports of all earlier examinations of the same condition. The request may be made by the party against whom the examination order was issued or by the person examined.

(2) ***Contents.*** The examiner's report must be in writing and must set out in detail the examiner's findings, including diagnoses, conclusions, and the results of any tests.

(3) ***Request by the Moving Party.*** After delivering the reports, the party who moved for the exami-

nation may request—and is entitled to receive—from the party against whom the examination order was issued like reports of all earlier or later examinations of the same condition. But those reports need not be delivered by the party with custody or control of the person examined if the party shows that it could not obtain them.

(4) ***Waiver of Privilege.*** By requesting and obtaining the examiner's report, or by deposing the examiner, the party examined waives any privilege it may have—in that action or any other action involving the same controversy—concerning testimony about all examinations of the same condition.

(5) ***Failure to Deliver a Report.*** The court on motion may order—on just terms—that a party deliver the report of an examination. If the report is not provided, the court may exclude the examiner's testimony at trial.

(6) ***Scope.*** This subdivision (b) applies also to an examination made by the parties' agreement, unless the agreement states otherwise. This subdivision does not preclude obtaining an examiner's report or deposing an examiner under other rules.

History of FRCP 35: Adopted Dec. 20, 1937, eff. Sept. 16, 1938. Amended Mar. 30, 1970, eff. July 1, 1970; Mar. 2, 1987, eff. Aug. 1, 1987; Nov. 18, 1988, P.L. 100-690, §7047(b), 102 Stat. 4401; Apr. 30, 1991, eff. Dec. 1, 1991; Apr. 30, 2007, eff. Dec. 1, 2007.

See *Commentaries*, "Physical & Mental Examinations of Persons," ch. 6-J, p. 574; *O'Connor's Federal Civil Forms* (2012), FORMS 6J.

ANNOTATIONS

Schlagenhauf v. Holder, 379 U.S. 104, 121 (1964). "The 'good cause' and 'in controversy' requirements of Rule 35 make it very apparent that sweeping examinations of a party who has not affirmatively put into issue his own mental or physical condition are not to be automatically ordered merely because the person has been involved in an accident—or, as in this case, two accidents—and a general charge of negligence is lodged."

Herrera v. Lufkin Indus., 474 F.3d 675, 689 (10th Cir.2007). "Unlike other discovery mechanisms, such as interrogatories or depositions, which a party can invoke on his own, Rule 35 requires the party seeking to conduct a medical examination first to obtain the district court's permission. … Notwithstanding Rule 35's requirements, however, 'physical and mental examinations are usually arranged by stipulation of the attorneys, with the rule standing as a compulsory sanction that helps to produce stipulations.' And '[p]laintiffs who voluntarily submit to an examination by a physician selected by defendant waive their right to insist upon a [Rule 35] motion for an order of examination.'"

FRCP 36. REQUESTS FOR ADMISSION

(a) Scope and Procedure.

(1) ***Scope.*** A party may serve on any other party a written request to admit, for purposes of the pending action only, the truth of any matters within the scope of Rule 26(b)(1) relating to:

(A) facts, the application of law to fact, or opinions about either; and

(B) the genuineness of any described documents.

(2) ***Form; Copy of a Document.*** Each matter must be separately stated. A request to admit the genuineness of a document must be accompanied by a copy of the document unless it is, or has been, otherwise furnished or made available for inspection and copying.

(3) ***Time to Respond; Effect of Not Responding.*** A matter is admitted unless, within 30 days after being served, the party to whom the request is directed serves on the requesting party a written answer or objection addressed to the matter and signed by the party or its attorney. A shorter or longer time for responding may be stipulated to under Rule 29 or be ordered by the court.

(4) ***Answer.*** If a matter is not admitted, the answer must specifically deny it or state in detail why the answering party cannot truthfully admit or deny it. A denial must fairly respond to the substance of the matter; and when good faith requires that a party qualify an answer or deny only a part of a matter, the answer must specify the part admitted and qualify or deny the rest. The answering party may assert lack of knowledge or information as a reason for failing to admit or deny only if the party states that it has made reasonable inquiry and that the information it knows or can readily obtain is insufficient to enable it to admit or deny.

(5) ***Objections.*** The grounds for objecting to a request must be stated. A party must not object

solely on the ground that the request presents a genuine issue for trial.

(6) ***Motion Regarding the Sufficiency of an Answer or Objection.*** The requesting party may move to determine the sufficiency of an answer or objection. Unless the court finds an objection justified, it must order that an answer be served. On finding that an answer does not comply with this rule, the court may order either that the matter is admitted or that an amended answer be served. The court may defer its final decision until a pretrial conference or a specified time before trial. Rule 37(a)(5) applies to an award of expenses.

(b) Effect of an Admission; Withdrawing or Amending It. A matter admitted under this rule is conclusively established unless the court, on motion, permits the admission to be withdrawn or amended. Subject to Rule 16(e), the court may permit withdrawal or amendment if it would promote the presentation of the merits of the action and if the court is not persuaded that it would prejudice the requesting party in maintaining or defending the action on the merits. An admission under this rule is not an admission for any other purpose and cannot be used against the party in any other proceeding.

See selected Notes of Advisory Committee to FRCP 36, p. 1204.

History of FRCP 36: Adopted Dec. 20, 1937, eff. Sept. 16, 1938. Amended Dec. 27, 1946, eff. Mar. 19, 1948; Mar. 30, 1970, eff. July 1, 1970; Mar. 2, 1987, eff. Aug. 1, 1987; Apr. 22, 1993, eff. Dec. 1, 1993; Apr. 30, 2007, eff. Dec. 1, 2007.

See *Commentaries*, "Requests for Admissions," ch. 6-H, p. 563; *O'Connor's Federal Civil Forms* (2012), FORMS 6H.

ANNOTATIONS

Conlon v. U.S., 474 F.3d 616, 621 (9th Cir.2007). "Rule 36(b) is permissive, not mandatory, with respect to the withdrawal of admissions. *At 625:* [I]n deciding whether to exercise its discretion when the moving party has met the two-pronged test of Rule 36(b), the district court may consider other factors, including whether the moving party can show good cause for the delay and whether the moving party appears to have a strong case on the merits."

Raiser v. Utah Cty., 409 F.3d 1243, 1246 (10th Cir. 2005). The first prong of the FRCP 36(b) "'test emphasizes the importance of having the action resolved on the merits, and is satisfied when upholding the admissions would practically eliminate any presentation of the merits of the case.' Here, the admissions at issue conceded the core elements of [P's] case. Indeed, the district court's grant of summary judgment was based on the admissions. Thus, allowing the admissions to be withdrawn would subserve the presentation of the merits of the action."

Johnson v. Royal Coal Co., 326 F.3d 421, 427 (4th Cir.2003). "[A]n opposing party's introduction of evidence on a matter admitted does not constitute either a waiver by the party possessing the admissions, or as a constructive motion for withdrawal or amendment of admissions. Nor does a party's introduction of evidence on issues overlapping matters admitted by the opposing party constitute a waiver of their right to rely on the admissions."

Perez v. Miami-Dade Cty., 297 F.3d 1255, 1268-69 (11th Cir.2002). "[I]t is inappropriate ... for a plaintiff to serve a request for admissions along with the complaint. It is simply too early for the defendant, having not yet received the allegations, to perceive what facts should or should not be contested."

Sonoda v. Cabrera, 255 F.3d 1035, 1039 (9th Cir. 2001). "The prejudice contemplated by [FRCP] 36(b) is not simply that the party who obtained the admission will now have to convince the factfinder of the truth; rather, it relates to the difficulty a party may face in proving its case, for example by the unavailability of key witnesses in light of the delay." *See also* ***Conlon v. U.S.***, 474 F.3d 616, 623 (9th Cir.2007) (court should focus on prejudice nonmoving party would suffer at trial).

Walsh v. McCain Foods Ltd., 81 F.3d 722, 726 (7th Cir.1996). "A party who fails to respond to requests for admissions within 30 days is deemed to have admitted those requests. However, those admissions are still subject to the limitation on hearsay evidence and must fit within an exception to the rule to be properly admitted...."

Kohler v. Leslie Hindman, Inc., 80 F.3d 1181, 1185 (7th Cir.1996). "[A] statement made in one lawsuit cannot be a judicial admission in another. It can be *evidence* in the other lawsuit, but no more."

Asea, Inc. v. Southern Pac. Transp., 669 F.2d 1242, 1247 (9th Cir.1981). "A party requesting an admission may, if he feels [the FRCP 36(a)] requirements have not been met, move to determine the sufficiency of the answer, to compel a proper response, or to have the matter ordered admitted. Although the district court should ordinarily first order an amended answer, and deem the matter admitted only if a sufficient an-

swer is not timely filed, this determination … is left to the sound discretion of the district judge."

FRCP 37. FAILURE TO MAKE DISCLOSURES OR TO COOPERATE IN DISCOVERY; SANCTIONS

Editor's note: The Committee on Rules of Practice and Procedure of the Judicial Conference of the United States has proposed amendments to FRCP 37, to be effective December 1, 2013. For the proposed amendments, see www.uscourts.gov/RulesAndPolicies/rules/pending-rules.aspx.

(a) Motion for an Order Compelling Disclosure or Discovery.

(1) ***In General.*** On notice to other parties and all affected persons, a party may move for an order compelling disclosure or discovery. The motion must include a certification that the movant has in good faith conferred or attempted to confer with the person or party failing to make disclosure or discovery in an effort to obtain it without court action.

(2) ***Appropriate Court.*** A motion for an order to a party must be made in the court where the action is pending. A motion for an order to a nonparty must be made in the court where the discovery is or will be taken.

(3) ***Specific Motions.***

(A) *To Compel Disclosure.* If a party fails to make a disclosure required by Rule 26(a), any other party may move to compel disclosure and for appropriate sanctions.

(B) *To Compel a Discovery Response.* A party seeking discovery may move for an order compelling an answer, designation, production, or inspection. This motion may be made if:

(i) a deponent fails to answer a question asked under Rule 30 or 31;

(ii) a corporation or other entity fails to make a designation under Rule 30(b)(6) or 31(a)(4);

(iii) a party fails to answer an interrogatory submitted under Rule 33; or

(iv) a party fails to respond that inspection will be permitted—or fails to permit inspection—as requested under Rule 34.

(C) *Related to a Deposition.* When taking an oral deposition, the party asking a question may complete or adjourn the examination before moving for an order.

(4) ***Evasive or Incomplete Disclosure, Answer, or Response.*** For purposes of this subdivision (a), an evasive or incomplete disclosure, answer, or response must be treated as a failure to disclose, answer, or respond.

(5) ***Payment of Expenses; Protective Orders.***

(A) *If the Motion Is Granted (or Disclosure or Discovery Is Provided After Filing).* If the motion is granted—or if the disclosure or requested discovery is provided after the motion was filed—the court must, after giving an opportunity to be heard, require the party or deponent whose conduct necessitated the motion, the party or attorney advising that conduct, or both to pay the movant's reasonable expenses incurred in making the motion, including attorney's fees. But the court must not order this payment if:

(i) the movant filed the motion before attempting in good faith to obtain the disclosure or discovery without court action;

(ii) the opposing party's nondisclosure, response, or objection was substantially justified; or

(iii) other circumstances make an award of expenses unjust.

(B) *If the Motion Is Denied.* If the motion is denied, the court may issue any protective order authorized under Rule 26(c) and must, after giving an opportunity to be heard, require the movant, the attorney filing the motion, or both to pay the party or deponent who opposed the motion its reasonable expenses incurred in opposing the motion, including attorney's fees. But the court must not order this payment if the motion was substantially justified or other circumstances make an award of expenses unjust.

(C) *If the Motion Is Granted in Part and Denied in Part.* If the motion is granted in part and denied in part, the court may issue any protective order authorized under Rule 26(c) and may, after giving an opportunity to be heard, apportion the reasonable expenses for the motion.

(b) Failure to Comply with a Court Order.

(1) ***Sanctions in the District Where the Deposition Is Taken.*** If the court where the discovery is taken orders a deponent to be sworn or to answer a question and the deponent fails to obey, the failure may be treated as contempt of court.

(2) ***Sanctions in the District Where the Action Is Pending.***

(A) *For Not Obeying a Discovery Order.* If a party or a party's officer, director, or managing agent—or a witness designated under Rule 30(b)(6) or 31(a)(4)—fails to obey an order to provide or permit discovery, including an order under Rule 26(f), 35, or 37(a), the court where the action is pending may issue further just orders. They may include the following:

(i) directing that the matters embraced in the order or other designated facts be taken as established for purposes of the action, as the prevailing party claims;

(ii) prohibiting the disobedient party from supporting or opposing designated claims or defenses, or from introducing designated matters in evidence;

(iii) striking pleadings in whole or in part;

(iv) staying further proceedings until the order is obeyed;

(v) dismissing the action or proceeding in whole or in part;

(vi) rendering a default judgment against the disobedient party; or

(vii) treating as contempt of court the failure to obey any order except an order to submit to a physical or mental examination.

(B) *For Not Producing a Person for Examination.* If a party fails to comply with an order under Rule 35(a) requiring it to produce another person for examination, the court may issue any of the orders listed in Rule 37(b)(2)(A)(i)-(vi), unless the disobedient party shows that it cannot produce the other person.

(C) *Payment of Expenses.* Instead of or in addition to the orders above, the court must order the disobedient party, the attorney advising that party, or both to pay the reasonable expenses, including attorney's fees, caused by the failure, unless the failure was substantially justified or other circumstances make an award of expenses unjust.

(c) Failure to Disclose, to Supplement an Earlier Response, or to Admit.

(1) ***Failure to Disclose or Supplement.*** If a party fails to provide information or identify a witness as required by Rule 26(a) or (e), the party is not allowed to use that information or witness to supply evidence on a motion, at a hearing, or at a trial, unless the failure was substantially justified or is harmless. In addition to or instead of this sanction, the court, on motion and after giving an opportunity to be heard:

(A) may order payment of the reasonable expenses, including attorney's fees, caused by the failure;

(B) may inform the jury of the party's failure; and

(C) may impose other appropriate sanctions, including any of the orders listed in Rule 37(b)(2)(A)(i)-(vi).

(2) ***Failure to Admit.*** If a party fails to admit what is requested under Rule 36 and if the requesting party later proves a document to be genuine or the matter true, the requesting party may move that the party who failed to admit pay the reasonable expenses, including attorney's fees, incurred in making that proof. The court must so order unless:

(A) the request was held objectionable under Rule 36(a);

(B) the admission sought was of no substantial importance;

(C) the party failing to admit had a reasonable ground to believe that it might prevail on the matter; or

(D) there was other good reason for the failure to admit.

(d) Party's Failure to Attend Its Own Deposition, Serve Answers to Interrogatories, or Respond to a Request for Inspection.

(1) ***In General.***

(A) *Motion; Grounds for Sanctions.* The court where the action is pending may, on motion, order sanctions if:

(i) a party or a party's officer, director, or managing agent—or a person designated under Rule 30(b)(6) or 31(a)(4)—fails, after being served with proper notice, to appear for that person's deposition; or

(ii) a party, after being properly served with interrogatories under Rule 33 or a request for inspection under Rule 34, fails to serve its answers, objections, or written response.

(B) *Certification.* A motion for sanctions for failing to answer or respond must include a certification that the movant has in good faith conferred or attempted to confer with the party failing to act in an effort to obtain the answer or response without court action.

(2) ***Unacceptable Excuse for Failing to Act.*** A failure described in Rule 37(d)(1)(A) is not excused on the ground that the discovery sought was objectionable, unless the party failing to act has a pending motion for a protective order under Rule 26(c).

(3) ***Types of Sanctions.*** Sanctions may include any of the orders listed in Rule 37(b)(2)(A)(i)-(vi). Instead of or in addition to these sanctions, the court must require the party failing to act, the attorney advising that party, or both to pay the reasonable expenses, including attorney's fees, caused by the failure, unless the failure was substantially justified or other circumstances make an award of expenses unjust.

(e) **Failure to Provide Electronically Stored Information.** Absent exceptional circumstances, a court may not impose sanctions under these rules on a party for failing to provide electronically stored information lost as a result of the routine, good-faith operation of an electronic information system.

(f) **Failure to Participate in Framing a Discovery Plan.** If a party or its attorney fails to participate in good faith in developing and submitting a proposed discovery plan as required by Rule 26(f), the court may, after giving an opportunity to be heard, require that party or attorney to pay to any other party the reasonable expenses, including attorney's fees, caused by the failure.

See selected Notes of Advisory Committee to FRCP 37, p. 1204.

History of FRCP 37: Adopted Dec. 20, 1937, eff. Sept. 16, 1938. Amended Dec. 29, 1948, eff. Oct. 20, 1949; Mar. 30, 1970, eff. July 1, 1970; Apr. 29, 1980, eff. Aug. 1, 1980; Oct. 21, 1980, P.L. 96-481, §205(a), 94 Stat. 2330; Mar. 2, 1987, eff. Aug. 1, 1987; Apr. 22, 1993, eff. Dec. 1, 1993; Apr. 17, 2000, eff. Dec. 1, 2000; Apr. 12, 2006, eff. Dec. 1, 2006; Apr. 30, 2007, eff. Dec. 1, 2007.

See ***Commentaries***, "Motion to Compel Discovery," ch. 6-A, §14, p. 444; "Sanctions for Lost ESI," ch. 6-C, §12, p. 513; *O'Connor's Federal Civil Forms* (2012), FORMS 6A.

ANNOTATIONS

Cunningham v. Hamilton Cty., 527 U.S. 198, 204 (1999). An FRCP 37(a) sanction against an attorney "neither ended the litigation nor left the court only to execute its judgment. Thus, it ordinarily would not be considered a final decision under [28 U.S.C.] §1291. However, we have interpreted the term 'final decision' in §1291 to permit jurisdiction over appeals from a small category of orders that do not terminate the litigation. 'That small category includes only decisions that are conclusive, that resolve important questions separate from the merits, and that are effectively unreviewable on appeal from the final judgment in the underlying action.' *At 205:* We do not think, however, that appellate review of a sanctions order can remain completely separate from the merits. *At 208-09:* To permit an immediate appeal from [an order for sanctions against an attorney under FRCP 37(a)] would undermine the very purposes of Rule 37(a), which was designed to protect courts and opposing parties from delaying or harassing tactics during the discovery process. Immediate appeals of such orders would undermine trial judges' discretion to structure a sanction in the most effective manner."

Pierce v. Underwood, 487 U.S. 552, 565 (1988). "[T]he test for avoiding the imposition of attorney's fees for resisting discovery in district court is whether the resistance was 'substantially justified....' [This means] there is a 'genuine dispute,' ... or [that] 'reasonable people could differ as to [the appropriateness of the contested action].'" *See also* ***Maddow v. Procter & Gamble Co.***, 107 F.3d 846, 853 (11th Cir.1997).

Hutto v. Finney, 437 U.S. 678, 695 n.24 (1978). "[L]ike the power to award attorney's fees for litigating in bad faith, the power to assess costs is an important and well-recognized tool used to restrain the behavior of parties during litigation."

National Hockey League v. Metropolitan Hockey Club, Inc., 427 U.S. 639, 643 (1976). "[T]he most severe in the spectrum of sanctions provided by statute or rule must be available to the district court in appropriate cases, not merely to penalize those whose conduct may be deemed to warrant such a sanction, but to deter those who might be tempted to such conduct in the absence of such a deterrent."

Tribble v. Evangelides, 670 F.3d 753, 759-60 (7th Cir.2012). See annotation under FRCP 26, *Disclosures*, p. 898.

Brown v. Columbia Sussex Corp., 664 F.3d 182, 190-91 (7th Cir.2011). "The standards for dismissal under [FRCP] 41(b) and [FRCP] 37(b) overlap, but there are differences.... Under Rule 41(b), a case should only be dismissed when 'there is a clear record of delay or contumacious conduct, or when other less drastic sanctions have proven unavailing.' Rule 37, on the other hand, requires a finding of willfulness, bad faith or fault on the part of the defaulting party. The difference between these two standards has caused some confusion, but we have made clear that the Rule 41(b) standard is actually a stricter standard than the Rule 37(b) standard, ... and we have intimated that a finding of willfulness, bad faith or fault is only necessary if Rule 41(b)'s 'clear record' of delay is not present. *At 192:* [Ps] assert that [the court must adequately warn parties before] a Rule 37 dismissal.... [Ps] are correct that we encourage district courts to provide an explicit warning before a Rule 37 or Rule 41 dismissal is ordered. More recent case law, however, has clarified that an explicit warning is not absolutely necessary.... Further, a warning of dismissal need not come from the judge. [F]or example, the fact that the defendant requested dismissal if the plaintiff continued to violate discovery orders was deemed to contribute to the plaintiff's warning that dismissal was a possibility."

Dreith v. Nu Image, Inc., 648 F.3d 779, 787 (9th Cir.2011). FRCP 37(b) "sanctions ... may be issued if a party fails to obey an order to provide or permit discovery, including an order under [FRCP] 26(f), 35, or 37(a). The definition of 'order' in Rule 37(b) has been read broadly. Sanctions may be imposed even for violation of a court's oral order, as long as a party has unequivocal notice that a court has asked that certain documents be produced. ... As Rule 37(b) states, an order stemming from a noticed motion to compel is but one example of an order which may, upon violation thereof, result in sanctions." (Internal quotes omitted.) *See also* ***McMullen v. Bay Ship Mgmt.***, 335 F.3d 215, 217 (3d Cir.2003).

Connecticut Gen. Life Ins. v. New Images, 482 F.3d 1091, 1096 (9th Cir.2007). "A terminating sanction, whether default judgment against a defendant or dismissal of a plaintiff's action, is very severe. ... Only 'willfulness, bad faith, and fault' justify terminating sanctions. [¶] We have constructed a five-part test, with three subparts to the fifth part, to determine whether a case-dispositive sanction under Rule 37(b)(2) is just: '(1) the public's interest in expeditious resolution of litigation; (2) the court's need to manage its dockets; (3) the risk of prejudice to the party seeking sanctions; (4) the public policy favoring disposition of cases on their merits; and (5) the availability of less drastic sanctions.' The sub-parts of the fifth factor are whether the court has considered lesser sanctions, whether it tried them, and whether it warned the recalcitrant party about the possibility of case-dispositive sanctions. This 'test' is not mechanical. It provides the district court with a way to think about what to do, not a set of conditions precedent for sanctions or a script that the district court must follow.... *At 1097:* The most critical factor to be considered ... is whether 'a party's discovery violations make it impossible for a court to be confident that the parties will ever have access to the true facts.' ... 'It is appropriate to reject lesser sanctions where the court anticipates continued deceptive misconduct.'" *See also* ***Bonds v. District of Columbia***, 93 F.3d 801, 808 (D.C. Cir.1996).

Cotton v. Massachusetts Mut. Life Ins., 402 F.3d 1267, 1292 (11th Cir.2005). "When a district court imposes sanctions under [FRCP] 37(b), 'the propriety of [the sanctions] depends in large part on the propriety of the earlier compel order.' Thus, '[i]n evaluating whether a district court abuses its discretion when it imposes severe sanctions upon a party that violates an order, we believe that an important factor is whether the entry of that order was itself an abuse of discretion.' This is not to say, however, that sanctions based on erroneous discovery orders will never be upheld. 'Because we expect litigants to obey all orders, even those they believe were improvidently entered, sanctions will very often be sustained, particularly when the infirmity

of the violated order is not clear and the sanctions imposed are moderate.'"

Roberts v. Galen of Va., Inc., 325 F.3d 776, 782 (6th Cir.2003). FRCP 37(c)(1) "requires absolute compliance with [FRCP] 26(a), that is, it 'mandates that a trial court punish a party for discovery violations in connection with Rule 26 unless the violation was harmless or is substantially justified.' *At 783-84:* Rule 37(c)(1), however, provides several remedies to a district judge who is faced with violations of the mandatory-disclosure provisions of Rule 26. ... Rule 37(c)(1) does not compel the district judge to exclude testimony in its entirety."

Residential Funding Corp. v. DeGeorge Fin. Corp., 306 F.3d 99, 113 (2d Cir.2002). "[W]here ... the nature of the alleged breach of a discovery obligation is the non-production of evidence, a District Court has broad discretion in fashioning an appropriate sanction, including the discretion to delay the start of a trial (at the expense of the party that breached its obligation), to declare a mistrial if trial has already commenced, or to proceed with a trial with an adverse inference instruction[.] [¶] [D]iscovery sanctions, including an adverse inference instruction, may be imposed upon a party that has breached a discovery obligation not only through bad faith or gross negligence, but also through ordinary negligence[.] [¶] [A] judge's finding that a party acted with gross negligence or in bad faith with respect to discovery obligations is ordinarily sufficient to support a finding that the missing or destroyed evidence would have been harmful to that party, even if the destruction or unavailability of the evidence was not caused by the acts constituting bad faith or gross negligence...." *See also* ***Aramburu v. Boeing Co.***, 112 F.3d 1398, 1407 (10th Cir.1997) (adverse inference must be based on bad faith; mere negligence insufficient).

Smith v. Kmart Corp., 177 F.3d 19, 29 (1st Cir. 1999). "Rule 37(b)(2)(A) [now Rule 37(b)(2)(A)(i)] authorizes the district court to enter an order stating that the matters that were the subject of the discovery order that was violated shall be taken to be established. ... When [D] violated the court's order by failing to produce [witness] for deposition, it was proper for the district court to sanction [D] by instructing the jury to accept the unfavorable proposition that [Ps] hoped to prove during [witness's] testimony: that unsafe merchandise display practices had caused similar accidents and injuries in the relevant [D-store]. Therefore, the giving of this particular sanction instruction does not warrant a new trial."

R.W. Int'l v. Welch Foods, Inc., 937 F.2d 11, 15 (1st Cir.1991). "When [P] refused to answer the questions ..., no Rule 37(a) order to compel answers to those questions was extant. Instead of ... adjourning the deposition and seeking an order to compel [P] to respond to the questions and to pay the expenses ..., [D's] counsel elected to bypass Rule 37(a) and seek immediate dismissal of the suit. ... Under such circumstances, the district court's premature resort to Rule 37(b)(2) cannot be upheld." *But see* ***Sierra Club v. Cedar Point Oil Co.***, 73 F.3d 546, 572 (5th Cir.1996) (FRCP 37 does not require that party file motion to compel before moving for sanctions).

TITLE VI. TRIALS

FRCP 38. RIGHT TO A JURY TRIAL; DEMAND

(a) Right Preserved. The right of trial by jury as declared by the Seventh Amendment to the Constitution—or as provided by a federal statute—is preserved to the parties inviolate.

(b) Demand. On any issue triable of right by a jury, a party may demand a jury trial by:

- **(1)** serving the other parties with a written demand—which may be included in a pleading—no later than 14 days after the last pleading directed to the issue is served; and
- **(2)** filing the demand in accordance with Rule 5(d).

(c) Specifying Issues. In its demand, a party may specify the issues that it wishes to have tried by a jury; otherwise, it is considered to have demanded a jury trial on all the issues so triable. If the party has demanded a jury trial on only some issues, any other party may—within 14 days after being served with the demand or within a shorter time ordered by the court—serve a demand for a jury trial on any other or all factual issues triable by jury.

(d) Waiver; Withdrawal. A party waives a jury trial unless its demand is properly served and filed. A proper demand may be withdrawn only if the parties consent.

(e) Admiralty and Maritime Claims. These rules do not create a right to a jury trial on issues in a claim that is an admiralty or maritime claim under Rule 9(h).

See selected Notes of Advisory Committee to FRCP 38, p. 1206.

History of FRCP 38: Adopted Dec. 20, 1937, eff. Sept. 16, 1938. Amended Feb. 28, 1966, eff. July 1, 1966; Mar. 2, 1987, eff. Aug. 1, 1987; Apr. 22, 1993, eff. Dec. 1, 1993; Apr. 30, 2007, eff. Dec. 1, 2007; Mar. 26, 2009, eff. Dec. 1, 2009.

See *Commentaries*, "Demand for Jury Trial," ch. 5-C, p. 309; *O'Connor's Federal Civil Forms* (2012), FORMS 5C.

ANNOTATIONS

Chauffeurs, Teamsters & Helpers v. Terry, 494 U.S. 558, 564 (1990). "The right to a jury trial includes more than the common-law forms of action recognized in 1791; the phrase 'Suits at common law' refers to 'suits in which *legal* rights [are] to be ascertained and determined, in contradistinction to those where equitable rights alone [are] recognized, and equitable remedies [are] administered.'"

Granfinanciera, S.A. v. Nordberg, 492 U.S. 33, 42 n.4 (1989). "[W]e do not declare that the Seventh Amendment provides a right to a jury trial on all legal rather than equitable claims. If a claim that is legal in nature asserts a 'public right,' ... then the Seventh Amendment does not entitle the parties to a jury trial if Congress assigns its adjudication to an administrative agency or specialized court of equity."

Tull v. U.S., 481 U.S. 412, 417-18 (1987). "The Court has construed [the Seventh Amendment] to require a jury trial on the merits in those actions that are analogous to 'Suits at common law.' Prior to the Amendment's adoption, a jury trial was customary in suits brought in the English *law* courts. [¶] To determine whether a statutory action is more similar to cases that were tried in courts of law than to suits tried in courts of equity or admiralty, the Court must examine both the nature of the action and of the remedy sought. First, we compare the statutory action to 18th-century actions brought in the courts of England prior to the merger of the courts of law and equity. Second, we examine the remedy sought and determine whether it is legal or equitable in nature."

Ross v. Bernhard, 396 U.S. 531, 542 (1970). "Given the availability in a derivative action of both legal and equitable remedies, we think the Seventh Amendment preserves to the parties in a stockholder's suit the same right to a jury trial that historically belonged to the corporation and to those against whom the corporation pressed its legal claims."

Solis v. County of L.A., 514 F.3d 946, 955 (9th Cir. 2008). "[P] did not stipulate, either orally or in writing, to consent to a bench trial. Thus, it is clear that, under [FRCPs] 38 and 39, [P] never withdrew his jury trial demand. [¶] Nevertheless, ... 'knowing participation in a bench trial without objection is sufficient to constitute a jury waiver,' the literal requirements of Rule 39(a) notwithstanding. [T]his narrow exception to the formal requirements of Rules 38 and 39 applies only when the party claiming the jury trial right is attempting to act strategically—participating in the bench trial in the hopes of achieving a favorable outcome, then asserting lack of consent to the bench trial when the result turns out to be unfavorable to him. *At 956:* Not every participation in a bench trial constitutes consent to the waiver of a jury trial, however. When a party participates in the bench trial ordered by the trial court while continuing to demand a jury trial, his 'continuing objection' is 'sufficient to preserve his right to appeal the denial of his request for a jury.' ... Reluctant participation in a bench trial does not waive one's Seventh Amendment right to a jury trial...."

IFC Credit Corp. v. United Bus. & Indus. Fed. Credit Un., 512 F.3d 989, 994 (7th Cir.2008). "Agreement to a bench trial cannot logically be treated less favorably than agreement to confess judgment, or arbitrate, or litigate in a forum that will not use a jury. Many courts accordingly hold that an agreement to resolve a dispute in a bench trial is no less valid than the rest of the contract in which the clause appears." Held: Bench-trial clause was valid and enforceable.

Lutz v. Glendale Un. High Sch., 403 F.3d 1061, 1065 (9th Cir.2005). FRCP 38 "provides that a party may 'demand a trial by jury *of any issue* triable of right by a jury.' But it does not require that a party itemize every issue it wants presented to a jury. Instead, '[i]n the demand a party may specify the issues which the party wishes so tried; otherwise the party shall be deemed to have demanded trial by jury for all the issues so triable.' A party seeking a jury trial thus has a choice: either list specific issues for the jury to consider, or make a general demand, which will be deemed to cover all issues triable to a jury. As the word 'otherwise' indicates, though, a jury demand will be deemed to cover all issues only if it doesn't specify particular issues. Any other construction would render the first clause of Rule 38(c) a nullity. [P] did specify particular issues: She requested that a jury determine back pay and certain

compensatory damages. As a result, we cannot deem her requests 'to have demanded trial by jury for all of the issues … triable' to a jury pursuant to Rule 38(c)."

Wright v. Lewis, 76 F.3d 57, 59 (2d Cir.1996). "While acknowledging that a *timely served* civil cover sheet on which the 'Jury Demand' box is checked can, without more, constitute a proper jury trial demand, … we held that failure to serve the cover sheet deprives the other party of the notice mandated by Rule 38(b)." (Internal quotes omitted.)

Bennett v. Pippin, 74 F.3d 578, 586-87 (5th Cir. 1996). "The complaint included a demand for a jury trial. Under [FRCP] 38(d), [D] could rely on that demand, and [P] could not withdraw it without the consent of all parties …, including [D]. When the district court reinstated [D] on the morning of trial, [D] returned to the case with its right to a jury trial." *See also* ***Fuller v. City of Oakland***, 47 F.3d 1522, 1531 (9th Cir. 1995) (once one party files demand, other parties are entitled to rely on it).

FRCP 39. TRIAL BY JURY OR BY THE COURT

(a) When a Demand Is Made. When a jury trial has been demanded under Rule 38, the action must be designated on the docket as a jury action. The trial on all issues so demanded must be by jury unless:

(1) the parties or their attorneys file a stipulation to a nonjury trial or so stipulate on the record; or

(2) the court, on motion or on its own, finds that on some or all of those issues there is no federal right to a jury trial.

(b) When No Demand Is Made. Issues on which a jury trial is not properly demanded are to be tried by the court. But the court may, on motion, order a jury trial on any issue for which a jury might have been demanded.

(c) Advisory Jury; Jury Trial by Consent. In an action not triable of right by a jury, the court, on motion or on its own:

(1) may try any issue with an advisory jury; or

(2) may, with the parties' consent, try any issue by a jury whose verdict has the same effect as if a jury trial had been a matter of right, unless the action is against the United States and a federal statute provides for a nonjury trial.

History of FRCP 39: Adopted Dec. 20, 1937, eff. Sept. 16, 1938. Amended Apr. 30, 2007, eff. Dec. 1, 2007.

See *Commentaries*, "Demand for Jury Trial," ch. 5-C, p. 309; *O'Connor's Federal Civil Forms* (2012), FORMS 5C.

See also 28 U.S.C. §959 (right to jury trial in actions against trustees and receivers), §§1861-1878 (juries generally), §1872 (jury trial in original actions at law in Supreme Court), §1873 (jury trial on fact issues in admiralty and maritime cases), §1874 (jury assessment of amount due in recovery of forfeitures in actions on bonds and specialties), §2402 (jury trial denied in actions against U.S.).

ANNOTATIONS

Tracinda Corp. v. DaimlerChrysler AG, 502 F.3d 212, 226-27 (3d Cir.2007). "Parties 'have a great deal of latitude on the timing of motions to strike a jury demand.' Since 'a court has the power to act sua sponte at any time' under Rule 39, 'it follows that a court has the discretion to permit a motion to strike a jury demand at any time, even on the eve of trial.' [¶] [W]e conclude that [Ds] did not commit inexcusable delay by filing its motion to strike after the close of discovery."

DeFelice v. American Int'l Life Assur. Co., 112 F.3d 61, 65 (2d Cir.1997). "[T]he longstanding tradition in common law courts is that a trial court may consult with an advisory jury during a bench trial so long as the court retains the ultimate responsibility for findings of fact and conclusions."

Goodgame v. American Cast Iron Pipe Co., 75 F.3d 1516, 1520 (11th Cir.1996). "Rule 39(c) plainly does not apply to claims … that are triable by jury as a matter of right. It is axiomatic in such cases that a trial court cannot disregard a jury's verdict and substitute its own findings in deciding claims…. When an advisory jury is empaneled under Rule 39(c), '[i]ts findings of fact are not binding on the trial court.' Just the opposite must be true when a jury is demanded as a matter of right by a party."

Fuller v. City of Oakland, 47 F.3d 1522, 1531 (9th Cir.1995). "Once a demand has been made, it may only be withdrawn through an oral or written stipulation by all parties. [¶] On its face, Rule 39(a) makes no distinction between parties who have offered express waivers and those who have stood silent."

Merex A.G. v. Fairchild Weston Sys., 29 F.3d 821, 827 (2d Cir.1994). "[W]hen both parties consent, Rule 39(c) invests the trial court with the discretion—but not the duty—to submit an equitable claim to the jury for a binding verdict."

Reboy v. Cozzi Iron & Metal, Inc., 9 F.3d 1303, 1306 (7th Cir.1993). "[A] party's conduct at trial may effectively waive its right to a jury trial. [¶] A party's conduct must clearly and explicitly signal such a waiver for this Court to give it effect. The right to a jury trial is

important and this Court will not find a waiver without clear, unequivocal evidence that the party intended to waive its right." *See also* ***Tray-Wrap, Inc. v. Six L's Packing Co.***, 984 F.2d 65, 68 (2d Cir.1993).

Thompson v. Parkes, 963 F.2d 885, 889 (6th Cir. 1992). "The term 'with an advisory jury' implies a jury known to the parties to be merely advisory at the time of trial (and, for the sake of efficiency, sufficiently in advance of trial that counsel may prepare a case appropriate to the trier of fact)."

Graefenhain v. Pabst Brewing Co., 870 F.2d 1198, 1206 (7th Cir.1989). A stipulation to let the court resolve damages issues "is binding unless relief from the stipulation is necessary to prevent a 'manifest injustice' or the stipulation was entered into through inadvertence or based on an erroneous view of the facts or law."

FRCP 40. SCHEDULING CASES FOR TRIAL

Each court must provide by rule for scheduling trials. The court must give priority to actions entitled to priority by a federal statute.

See selected Notes of Advisory Committee to FRCP 40, p. 1206.

History of FRCP 40: Adopted Dec. 20, 1937, eff. Sept. 16, 1938. Amended Apr. 30, 2007, eff. Dec. 1, 2007.

See *Commentaries*, "Scheduling Conference & Order," ch. 5-A, §3, p. 289.

FRCP 41. DISMISSAL OF ACTIONS

(a) Voluntary Dismissal.

(1) *By the Plaintiff.*

(A) *Without a Court Order.* Subject to Rules 23(e), 23.1(c), 23.2, and 66 and any applicable federal statute, the plaintiff may dismiss an action without a court order by filing:

(i) a notice of dismissal before the opposing party serves either an answer or a motion for summary judgment; or

(ii) a stipulation of dismissal signed by all parties who have appeared.

(B) *Effect.* Unless the notice or stipulation states otherwise, the dismissal is without prejudice. But if the plaintiff previously dismissed any federal- or state-court action based on or including the same claim, a notice of dismissal operates as an adjudication on the merits.

(2) *By Court Order; Effect.* Except as provided in Rule 41(a)(1), an action may be dismissed at the plaintiff's request only by court order, on terms that the court considers proper. If a defendant has pleaded a counterclaim before being served with the plaintiff's motion to dismiss, the action may be dismissed over the defendant's objection only if the counterclaim can remain pending for independent adjudication. Unless the order states otherwise, a dismissal under this paragraph (2) is without prejudice.

(b) Involuntary Dismissal; Effect. If the plaintiff fails to prosecute or to comply with these rules or a court order, a defendant may move to dismiss the action or any claim against it. Unless the dismissal order states otherwise, a dismissal under this subdivision (b) and any dismissal not under this rule—except one for lack of jurisdiction, improper venue, or failure to join a party under Rule 19—operates as an adjudication on the merits.

(c) Dismissing a Counterclaim, Crossclaim, or Third-Party Claim. This rule applies to a dismissal of any counterclaim, crossclaim, or third-party claim. A claimant's voluntary dismissal under Rule 41(a)(1)(A)(i) must be made:

(1) before a responsive pleading is served; or

(2) if there is no responsive pleading, before evidence is introduced at a hearing or trial.

(d) Costs of a Previously Dismissed Action. If a plaintiff who previously dismissed an action in any court files an action based on or including the same claim against the same defendant, the court:

(1) may order the plaintiff to pay all or part of the costs of that previous action; and

(2) may stay the proceedings until the plaintiff has complied.

See selected Notes of Advisory Committee to FRCP 41, p. 1206.

History of FRCP 41: Adopted Dec. 20, 1937, eff. Sept. 16, 1938. Amended Dec. 27, 1946, eff. Mar. 19, 1948; Jan. 21, 1963, eff. July 1, 1963; Feb. 28, 1966, eff. July 1, 1966; Dec. 4, 1967, eff. July 1, 1968; Mar. 2, 1987, eff. Aug. 1, 1987; Apr. 30, 1991, eff. Dec. 1, 1991; Apr. 30, 2007, eff. Dec. 1, 2007.

See *Commentaries*, "Voluntary Dismissal," ch. 7-C, p. 629; "Involuntary Dismissal," ch. 7-D, p. 642; ***O'Connor's Federal Civil Forms*** (2012), FORMS 7C; FORMS 7D.

See also 8 U.S.C. §1329 (discontinuance of civil actions arising under immigration laws); 28 U.S.C. §1920 (taxation of costs); 31 U.S.C. §3730 (dismissal of civil actions for false claims against U.S.).

ANNOTATIONS

Voluntary Dismissal

Nelson v. Napolitano, 657 F.3d 586, 588 (7th Cir. 2011). "The district court was uncertain whether it retained jurisdiction to consider the [FRCP] 60(b) mo-

tion following a voluntary dismissal under [FRCP] 41(a)(1)(A)(i). Although it is true that a suit that has been voluntarily dismissed under Rule 41(a)(1)(A)(i) generally is treated as if it had never been filed, the Supreme Court and this court have recognized the limits of that characterization. For example, the Supreme Court held that 'a federal court may consider collateral issues after an action is no longer pending.' Thus, after a voluntary dismissal under Rule 41(a)(1)(A)(i), a court may still impose sanctions under [FRCP] 11, or adjudicate a criminal contempt charge even after the action in which the contempt arose has been terminated. *At 589:* A voluntary dismissal pursuant to Rule 41(a)(1)(A)(i), therefore, does not deprive a district court of jurisdiction for all purposes. [T]here may be instances where a district court may grant relief under Rule 60(b) to a plaintiff who has voluntarily dismissed the action."

Michigan Surgery Inv. v. Arman, 627 F.3d 572, 576 (6th Cir.2010). "The requirement of 'notice of the court's intention to dismiss with prejudice' ... means that the district court must inform the plaintiff that the court intends to grant a Rule 41(a)(2) motion with prejudice. It is not enough that the plaintiff is aware that dismissal with prejudice is possible under Rule 41(a)(2), or even that the defendant has requested that any grant of a Rule 41(a)(2) motion be with prejudice. The language of Rule 41(a)(2), providing that the district court may grant a voluntary dismissal 'on terms that the court considers proper,' ... permits the court to 'condition' the grant of a Rule 41(a)(2) motion on dismissal with prejudice. Because dismissal with prejudice is a 'term' or 'condition' of voluntary dismissal, it must be presented to the plaintiff as such. Otherwise, the plaintiff has to gamble on what the court will do. Forcing plaintiffs to forecast the terms on which a district court intends to condition a voluntary dismissal would discourage plaintiffs from filing Rule 41(a)(2) motions in the first place."

SmallBizPros, Inc. v. MacDonald, 618 F.3d 458, 462-63 (5th Cir.2010). "Under Rule 41(a)(1)(A)(ii), it is clear that the parties to a case may enter into a settlement agreement, sign and file a stipulation of dismissal with the district court, and the dismissal will be effective upon filing notwithstanding any other action by the district court. Under ***Kokkonen*** [***v. Guardian Life Ins.***, 511 U.S. 375 (1994),] and ***Hospitality House***[, ***Inc. v. Gilbert***, 298 F.3d 424 (5th Cir.2002)], it is also clear that a district court may incorporate or embody the terms of a settlement agreement in a dismissal order or expressly retain jurisdiction over a settlement agreement by clearly indicating such intent in a dismissal order. [¶] Because filing a voluntary stipulation of dismissal under Rule 41(a)(1)(A)(ii) is effective immediately, any action by the district court after the filing of such a stipulation can have no force or effect because the matter has already been dismissed by the parties themselves without any court action. Any dismissal order entered by a district court after the filing of a voluntary dismissal is 'superfluous.' Therefore, to ensure that jurisdiction is retained so a district court has the power to enforce the terms of a settlement agreement, either (i) all of the requirements for retaining jurisdiction must be met at the time of filing, or (ii) the filing's effectiveness must be contingent upon a future act (such as the district court issuing an order retaining jurisdiction)."

Garber v. Chicago Mercantile Exch., 570 F.3d 1361, 1365 (Fed.Cir.2009). FRCP 41(a)(1)(A) "permits dismissal by a plaintiff acting alone if a notice of the dismissal is filed before the defendant has entered either an answer or a motion for summary judgment [and] dismissal at any time during the proceedings if all parties sign a stipulation of dismissal. In contrast, Rule 41(a)(2) contemplates dismissal of the action by the plaintiff at a latter stage of the proceedings without agreement from all parties involved. Such a dismissal is permitted only 'on terms the court considers proper.' 'If an answer or a motion for summary judgment has been served, the plaintiff no longer has the right to dismiss and, unless all of the parties stipulate to dismissal, both Rule 41(a)(2) and a myriad of cases demand that a plaintiff who wishes to dismiss must obtain an order of the district court.' The stipulation entered in this case is more properly viewed as having been brought pursuant to Rule 41(a)(1) precisely because it was a stipulation agreed to by all parties. Rule 41(a)(2) is properly reserved for those cases in which the parties have not formally entered into an agreement regarding dismissal." *See also* ***RFR Indus. v. Century Steps, Inc.***, 477 F.3d 1348, 1351 (Fed.Cir.2007) (adverse party must actually serve P with answer or motion for summary judgment to prevent P from dismissing under Rule 41(a)(1)(A)(i); mere filing is not enough).

Schmier v. McDonald's LLC, 569 F.3d 1240, 1243 (10th Cir.2009). "Here ... a plaintiff is seeking to set aside his own voluntary dismissal. We know of no rea-

FRCP 41

son to deny jurisdiction to a district court to consider granting a dismissing plaintiff relief under [FRCP] 60(b). [A] plaintiff who has dismissed his claim by filing notice under [FRCP] 41(a)(1)(A)(i) 'may move before the district court to vacate the notice on any of the grounds specified in Rule 60(b).'"

Walter Kidde Portable Equip., Inc. v. Universal Sec. Instrs., Inc., 479 F.3d 1330, 1336 (Fed.Cir.2007). "[T]he court may not dismiss [a defendant's counterclaims] on a plaintiff's Rule 41 motion if the defendant filed them before the dismissal motion was filed. *At 1339:* [R]ule 41(a)(2) … expressly prohibits a district court from dismissing a defendant's counterclaims, unless those counterclaims 'can remain pending for independent adjudication by the court.' [I]n order for that prohibition to apply, 'the counterclaim must have been properly filed—that is, the district court must have properly had subject matter jurisdiction over the claim.'"

GF Gaming Corp. v. City of Black Hawk, 405 F.3d 876, 888 (10th Cir.2005). "When a party seeking to voluntarily dismiss a claim pursuant to Rule 41(a)(2) is silent as to whether the dismissal should be with or without prejudice, the district judge is required to interpret the motion one way or the other. … The district court in interpreting [Ps'] voluntary dismissal here relied on the procedural history of the case, including [Ps'] apparent concession that the dismissal was with prejudice and failure to present any arguments to the contrary. [Ps] present no explanation on appeal as to how the court abused its discretion in making this determination. This court therefore declines to reverse the district court on this ground."

Hells Canyon Pres. Council v. U.S. Forest Serv., 403 F.3d 683, 687-88 (9th Cir.2005). "As its title, Dismissal of Actions, suggests, [FRCP] 41, or at least Rule 41(a), governs dismissals of *entire actions*, not of individual claims. [¶] In the specific context of Rule 41(a)(1), we have held that the Rule does not allow for piecemeal dismissals. Instead, withdrawals of individual claims against a given defendant are governed by [FRCP] 15, which addresses amendments to pleadings. [A] plaintiff may not use Rule 41(a)(1)(i) to dismiss, unilaterally, a single claim from a multi-claim complaint. Instead [FRCP] 15(a) is the appropriate mechanism where a plaintiff desires to eliminate an issue, or one or more but less than all of several claims, but without dismissing as to any of the defendants. [¶] [W]e have not had an opportunity to consider whether the same logic extends to the other method of voluntary dismissal under Rule 41—voluntary dismissal with judicial consent, under Rule 41(a)(2). Other courts to consider this issue, however, have not suggested any meaningful distinction between Rules 41(a)(1) and 41(a)(2) in this context. [¶] We agree that there is no reason to make such a distinction here. *At 689:* We therefore disagree with [P] that we should construe its withdrawal of its … claim … as a voluntary dismissal under Rule 41(a)(2), and therefore as a dismissal without prejudice." (Internal quotes omitted.)

Role v. Eureka Lodge, 402 F.3d 314, 318-19 (2d Cir. 2005). "'[A]n oral stipulation in open court can effect dismissal.' [A] voluntary, clear, explicit, and unqualified stipulation of dismissal entered into by the parties in court and on the record is enforceable even if the agreement is never reduced to writing, signed, or filed, as contemplated by [FRCP] 41(a). The record of the … proceedings before [the] Magistrate Judge … discloses such an agreement. We therefore find no procedural defect in the agreement and stipulation of dismissal."

Involuntary Dismissal

Semtek Int'l v. Lockheed Martin Corp., 531 U.S. 497, 503 (2001). "[I]t is no longer true that a judgment 'on the merits' is necessarily a judgment entitled to claim-preclusive effect; and there are a number of reasons for believing that the phrase 'adjudication upon the merits' does not bear that meaning in Rule 41(b). *At 505:* We think the key to a more reasonable interpretation of the meaning of 'operates as an adjudication upon the merits' in Rule 41(b) is to be found in Rule 41(a), which … makes clear that an 'adjudication upon the merits' is the opposite of a 'dismissal without prejudice.'"

Link v. Wabash R.R., 370 U.S. 626, 630-31 (1962). "Neither the permissive language of [FRCP 41(b)]—which merely authorizes a motion by the defendant—nor its policy requires us to conclude that it was the purpose of the Rule to abrogate the power of the courts, acting on their own initiative, to clear their calendars of cases that have remained dormant because of the inaction or dilatoriness of the parties seeking relief." Held: Court may enter an involuntary dismissal on its own motion.

Brown v. Columbia Sussex Corp., 664 F.3d 182, 190-91 (7th Cir.2011). See annotation under FRCP 37, p. 918.

Omstead v. Dell, Inc., 594 F.3d 1081, 1084 (9th Cir. 2010). "A Rule 41(b) dismissal 'must be supported by a showing of unreasonable delay.' In addition, the district court must weigh the following factors in determining whether a Rule 41(b) dismissal is warranted: '(1) the public's interest in expeditious resolution of litigation; (2) the court's need to manage its docket; (3) the risk of prejudice to the defendants; (4) the public policy favoring disposition of cases on their merits and (5) the availability of less drastic sanctions.'" *See also* ***Olsen v. Mapes***, 333 F.3d 1199, 1204 (10th Cir.2003).

Lewis v. Rawson, 564 F.3d 569, 580 (2d Cir.2009). "'[A] district court may dismiss a case under Rule 41(b) when the plaintiff refuses to go forward with a properly scheduled trial.' [¶] [W]here a district court is confronted with a 'plaintiff's unwillingness to proceed on the date scheduled for trial, as opposed to the more typical failure to comply with her discovery obligations on time, or to meet some other pre-trial deadline,' it is 'not unreasonable' to consider treating such unwillingness 'more severely.' *At 581:* [W]here a plaintiff refuses to proceed with trial following a district court's unfavorable ruling on a request for continuance or *in limine* motion, we have noted that a district court 'ha[s] no real choice but to dismiss the case.' [¶] [W]here a party fails to appear or refuses to proceed with trial '*after* the jury ha[s] been drawn,' dismissal with prejudice may be particularly appropriate. *At 583:* To summarize, [t]he challenged judgment of dismissal for failure to prosecute pursuant to [FRCP] 41(b), entered after the jury was sworn, is properly reviewed by considering (a) the district court's refusal to grant an adjournment and transfer of the case; and (b) the district court's decision to dismiss the case with prejudice when plaintiff, upon failing to secure the requested adjournment and transfer, refused to testify at trial."

Betty K Agencies, Ltd. v. M/V Monada, 432 F.3d 1333, 1337-38 (11th Cir.2005). "[A] dismissal *with prejudice*, whether on motion or *sua sponte*, is an extreme sanction that may be properly imposed *only* when: '(1) a party engages in a clear pattern of delay or willful contempt (contumacious conduct); and (2) the district court specifically finds that lesser sanctions would not suffice.' [T]he harsh sanction of dismissal with prejudice is thought to be more appropriate in a case where a party, as distinct from counsel, is culpable." *See also* ***Smith v. Gold Dust Casino***, 526 F.3d 402, 404-05 (8th Cir.2008); ***Grun v. Pneumo Abex Corp.***, 163 F.3d 411, 425 (7th Cir.1998).

Intera Corp. v. Henderson, 428 F.3d 605, 620 (6th Cir.2005). "[I]n declaring that a dismissal for lack of jurisdiction does not 'operate[] as an adjudication upon the merits,' Rule 41(b) does not distinguish between subject matter and personal jurisdiction. Within the subject matter jurisdiction context, we have interpreted Rule 41(b) to mean that 'a dismissal for lack of subject matter jurisdiction does not operate as an adjudication on the merits for preclusive purposes.' *At 621:* [O]ur rationale … applies with equal force to the personal jurisdiction context." *See also* ***Hernandez v. Conriv Rlty. Assocs.***, 182 F.3d 121, 123 (2d Cir.1999).

Catz v. Chalker, 142 F.3d 279, 286 (6th Cir.1998), *amended*, 243 F.3d 234 (6th Cir.2001). "As demanded by general concepts of fairness, … a district court's notice of its intent to dismiss *sua sponte* should be unmistakable (whether oral or written), and should specify a date by which the parties must respond to the court's motion, giving them reasonable time under the circumstances to do so." *See also* ***GCIU Empl. Ret. Fund v. Chicago Tribune Co.***, 8 F.3d 1195, 1199 (7th Cir.1993).

FRCP 42. CONSOLIDATION; SEPARATE TRIALS

(a) Consolidation. If actions before the court involve a common question of law or fact, the court may:

(1) join for hearing or trial any or all matters at issue in the actions;

(2) consolidate the actions; or

(3) issue any other orders to avoid unnecessary cost or delay.

(b) Separate Trials. For convenience, to avoid prejudice, or to expedite and economize, the court may order a separate trial of one or more separate issues, claims, crossclaims, counterclaims, or third-party claims. When ordering a separate trial, the court must preserve any federal right to a jury trial.

History of FRCP 42: Adopted Dec. 20, 1937, eff. Sept. 16, 1938. Amended Feb. 28, 1966, eff. July 1, 1966; Apr. 30, 2007, eff. Dec. 1, 2007.

See ***Commentaries***, "Motion to Consolidate," ch. 5-K, p. 362; ***O'Connor's Federal Civil Forms*** (2012), FORMS 5K.

ANNOTATIONS

Johnson v. Manhattan Ry., 289 U.S. 479, 496-97 (1933). "[C]onsolidation is permitted as a matter of convenience and economy in administration, but does

not merge the suits into a single cause, or change the rights of the parties, or make those who are parties in one suit parties in another."

Gaffney v. Riverboat Servs., 451 F.3d 424, 442 (7th Cir.2006). See annotation under FRCP 21, p. 876.

Krocka v. City of Chi., 203 F.3d 507, 516 (7th Cir. 2000). "The district court may bifurcate a trial provided that this ruling (1) serves the interests of judicial economy or is done to prevent prejudice to a party; (2) does not unfairly prejudice the non-moving party; and (3) does not violate the Seventh Amendment." *See also* ***Martin v. Heideman***, 106 F.3d 1308, 1311 (6th Cir. 1997) (court must consider potential prejudice to parties, possible jury confusion, and resulting convenience); ***O'Dell v. Hercules Inc.***, 904 F.2d 1194, 1201-02 (8th Cir.1990) (court should consider preservation of constitutional rights, clarity, judicial economy, likelihood of inconsistent results, and jury confusion).

In re Repetitive Stress Injury Litig., 11 F.3d 368, 374 (2d Cir.1993). "The burden is on the party seeking aggregation of discovery or other proceedings to show common factual or legal issues warranting it. A party may not use aggregation as a method of increasing the costs of its adversaries … by forcing them to participate in discovery or other proceedings that are irrelevant to their case."

McDaniel v. Anheuser-Busch, Inc., 987 F.2d 298, 304 n.19 (5th Cir.1993). "The procedure authorized by [FRCP] 42(b) should be distinguished from severance under [FRCP] 21. Separate trials will usually result in one judgment, but severed claims become entirely independent actions to be tried, and judgment entered thereon, independently. *At 305:* 'There is an important limitation on ordering a separate trial of issues under Rule 42(b): the issue to be tried must be so distinct and separate from the others that a trial of it alone may be had without injustice.' … This rule has an additional, pragmatic basis—if two juries were allowed to pass on an issue involving the same factual and legal elements, the verdicts rendered by those juries could be inconsistent, producing intolerably anomalous results."

FRCP 43. TAKING TESTIMONY

(a) In Open Court. At trial, the witnesses' testimony must be taken in open court unless a federal statute, the Federal Rules of Evidence, these rules, or other rules adopted by the Supreme Court provide otherwise. For good cause in compelling circumstances and with appropriate safeguards, the court may permit testimony in open court by contemporaneous transmission from a different location.

(b) Affirmation Instead of an Oath. When these rules require an oath, a solemn affirmation suffices.

(c) Evidence on a Motion. When a motion relies on facts outside the record, the court may hear the matter on affidavits or may hear it wholly or partly on oral testimony or on depositions.

(d) Interpreter. The court may appoint an interpreter of its choosing; fix reasonable compensation to be paid from funds provided by law or by one or more parties; and tax the compensation as costs.

See selected Notes of Advisory Committee to FRCP 43, p. 1207.

History of FRCP 43: Adopted Dec. 20, 1937, eff. Sept. 16, 1938. Amended Feb. 28, 1966, eff. July 1, 1966; Nov. 20, 1972 and Dec. 18, 1972, eff. July 1, 1975; Mar. 2, 1987, eff. Aug. 1, 1987; Apr. 23, 1996, eff. Dec. 1, 1996; Apr. 30, 2007, eff. Dec. 1, 2007.

See *Commentaries*, "Introducing Evidence," ch. 8-C, p. 688.

See also 28 U.S.C. §§1731-1746 (documentary evidence generally), §1732 (record made in regular course of business), §1783 (person in foreign country to appear as witness), §§1821-1828 (witnesses generally), §1822 (competency of interested persons).

ANNOTATIONS

Parkhurst v. Belt, 567 F.3d 995, 1003 (8th Cir. 2009). Rule 43(a) "plainly permits a district court '[f]or good cause in compelling circumstances and with appropriate safeguards' to permit a child to testify by closed circuit television. [D's] offer to leave the courtroom prior to [child's] testimony is only one factor that the district court could consider in making its decision. [¶] The district court also ensured that appropriate safeguards were instituted. [T]he jury could listen to [child] and observe her demeanor, [D's] attorney was able to cross examine [child], and the transmission was instantaneous."

Boit v. Gar-Tec Prods., 967 F.2d 671, 676 (1st Cir. 1992). "If issues of credibility are presented and must be resolved to determine an issue of fact material to the court's disposition of the motion to dismiss, it may be an abuse of discretion not to allow an opportunity for cross-examination of an affiant if requested. Even in such circumstances, however, a court may take most of the evidence at the pretrial evidentiary hearing by affidavits, authenticated documents, answers to interrogatories or requests for admissions, and depositions."

In re Adair, 965 F.2d 777, 780 (9th Cir.1992). "The primary purposes of Rule 43(a) are to ensure that the accuracy of witness statements may be tested by cross-

examination and to allow the trier of fact to observe the appearance and demeanor of the witnesses."

United Commercial Ins. Serv. v. Paymaster Corp., 962 F.2d 853, 858 (9th Cir.1992). "Under [FRCP 43(e), now FRCP 43(c)], which normally governs motions, the trial court has wide discretion in deciding whether to admit or deny oral testimony. [¶] Where factual questions not readily ascertainable from the declarations of witnesses or questions of credibility predominate, the district court should hear oral testimony." *See also* ***Stewart v. M.D.F., Inc.***, 83 F.3d 247, 251 (8th Cir.1996).

Stewart v. RCA Corp., 790 F.2d 624, 628 (7th Cir. 1986). "Although [FRCP 43(e), now FRCP 43(c),] does not say expressly that the judge may take evidence in open court in order to pass on a motion for summary judgment, and although [FRCP] 56(c) suggests that the decision should be made on affidavits and documentary evidence, several courts have held that because Rule 43(e) mentions 'motions' in general it covers motions for summary judgment in particular. *At 629:* Yet oral testimony … could waste a lot of … time. [Therefore,] Rule 43(e) hearings on motions for summary judgment … should be rare."

FRCP 44. PROVING AN OFFICIAL RECORD

(a) Means of Proving.

(1) ***Domestic Record.*** Each of the following evidences an official record—or an entry in it—that is otherwise admissible and is kept within the United States, any state, district, or commonwealth, or any territory subject to the administrative or judicial jurisdiction of the United States:

(A) an official publication of the record; or

(B) a copy attested by the officer with legal custody of the record—or by the officer's deputy—and accompanied by a certificate that the officer has custody. The certificate must be made under seal:

(i) by a judge of a court of record in the district or political subdivision where the record is kept; or

(ii) by any public officer with a seal of office and with official duties in the district or political subdivision where the record is kept.

(2) ***Foreign Record.***

(A) *In General.* Each of the following evidences a foreign official record—or an entry in it—that is otherwise admissible:

(i) an official publication of the record; or

(ii) the record—or a copy—that is attested by an authorized person and is accompanied either by a final certification of genuineness or by a certification under a treaty or convention to which the United States and the country where the record is located are parties.

(B) *Final Certification of Genuineness.* A final certification must certify the genuineness of the signature and official position of the attester or of any foreign official whose certificate of genuineness relates to the attestation or is in a chain of certificates of genuineness relating to the attestation. A final certification may be made by a secretary of a United States embassy or legation; by a consul general, vice consul, or consular agent of the United States; or by a diplomatic or consular official of the foreign country assigned or accredited to the United States.

(C) *Other Means of Proof.* If all parties have had a reasonable opportunity to investigate a foreign record's authenticity and accuracy, the court may, for good cause, either:

(i) admit an attested copy without final certification; or

(ii) permit the record to be evidenced by an attested summary with or without a final certification.

(b) Lack of a Record. A written statement that a diligent search of designated records revealed no record or entry of a specified tenor is admissible as evidence that the records contain no such record or entry. For domestic records, the statement must be authenticated under Rule 44(a)(1). For foreign records, the statement must comply with (a)(2)(C)(ii).

(c) Other Proof. A party may prove an official record—or an entry or lack of an entry in it—by any other method authorized by law.

See selected Notes of Advisory Committee to FRCP 44, p. 1207.

History of FRCP 44: Adopted Dec. 20, 1937, eff. Sept. 16, 1938. Amended Feb. 28, 1966, eff. July 1, 1966; Mar. 2, 1987, eff. Aug. 1, 1987; Apr. 30, 1991, eff. Dec. 1, 1991; Apr. 30, 2007, eff. Dec. 1, 2007.

See ***Commentaries***, "Domestic & foreign official records," ch. 8-C, §7.2.4, p. 698; ***O'Connor's Federal Civil Forms*** (2012), FORMS 8C:3-5.

See also 44 U.S.C. §2116 (authenticated and certified copy of government record by archivist admissible in evidence).

ANNOTATIONS

Espinoza v. INS, 45 F.3d 308, 309-10 (9th Cir.1995). "Authentication serves to establish a chain of custody for government records. The Ninth Circuit requires only that immigration forms be authenticated through some recognized procedure, such as those required by [government] regulations or by the [FRCPs]."

AMFAC Distrib. v. Harrelson, 842 F.2d 304, 306-07 (11th Cir.1988). "Under [FRCP] 44(a)(1), two things are required to authenticate a copy of a state court judgment. First, the copy must be attested to by the officer having the legal custody of the judgment or by his deputy. Second, there must be a certificate that the attesting officer has legal custody; this certificate is to be made by a judge of a court of record of the district or political subdivision in which the judgment is kept and must be authenticated by the seal of the court. [¶] [If P] did not substantially comply with Rule 44(a), … the Texas judgment is admissible under the [FREs]. [FRE] 902 provides for authentication by certificate when a copy of the judgment bears a seal purporting to be that of a state court and a signature purporting to be an attestation of the custodian of the original judgment."

FRCP 44.1. DETERMINING FOREIGN LAW

A party who intends to raise an issue about a foreign country's law must give notice by a pleading or other writing. In determining foreign law, the court may consider any relevant material or source, including testimony, whether or not submitted by a party or admissible under the Federal Rules of Evidence. The court's determination must be treated as a ruling on a question of law.

See selected Notes of Advisory Committee to FRCP 44.1, p. 1208.

History of FRCP 44.1: Adopted Feb. 28, 1966, eff. July 1, 1966. Amended Nov. 20, 1972, eff. July 1, 1975; Mar. 2, 1987, eff. Aug. 1, 1987; Apr. 30, 2007, eff. Dec. 1, 2007.

See ***Commentaries***, "Motion for Judicial Notice," ch. 5-M, p. 370; ***O'Connor's Federal Civil Forms*** (2012), FORMS 5M.

See also FRE 201 (judicial notice).

ANNOTATIONS

In re Griffin Trading Co., 683 F.3d 819, 822 (7th Cir.2012). "Although it is true that Rule 44.1 requires any party who intends to present evidence of foreign law to 'give notice by a pleading or other writing,' the language of the rule itself reveals that no particular formality is required. Any 'other writing' will do, as long as it suffices to give proper notice of an intent to rely on foreign law. *At 823:* 'If notice is given by one party it need not be repeated by any other and serves as a basis for presentation of material on the foreign law by all parties.'"

Northrop Grumman Ship Sys. v. Ministry of Def. of the Republic of Venez., 575 F.3d 491, 496-97 (5th Cir.2009). FRCP 44.1 "is intended to 'avoid unfair surprise,' not to 'set any definite limit on the party's time for giving the notice of an issue of foreign law….' When the applicability of foreign law is not obvious, notice is sufficient if it allows the opposing party time to research the foreign rules. Some of the factors that should be considered in determining whether notice is reasonable include '[t]he stage which the case had reached at the time of the notice, the reason proffered by the party for his failure to give earlier notice, and the importance to the case as a whole of the issue of foreign law sought to be raised….'" *See also* ***APL Co. Pte. Ltd. v. UK Aerosols Ltd.***, 582 F.3d 947, 955-56 (9th Cir. 2009).

Mutual Serv. Ins. v. Frit Indus., 358 F.3d 1312, 1321 (11th Cir.2004). "The district court is not required to conduct its own research into the content of foreign law if the party urging its application declines to do so." *See also* ***Grand Entm't Grp. v. Star Media Sales, Inc.***, 988 F.2d 476, 488 (3d Cir.1993) (court may conduct its own supplemental research).

DP Aviation v. Smiths Indus. Aerospace & Def. Sys., 268 F.3d 829, 848 (9th Cir.2001). "Absent extenuating circumstances, notice of issues of foreign law that reasonably would be expected to be part of the proceedings should be provided in the pretrial conference and contentions about applicability of foreign law should be incorporated in the pretrial order. This gives parties ample opportunity to marshal resources pertinent to foreign law, which normally will not be as well known as domestic law to parties and courts."

Republic of Turk. v. OKS Partners, 146 F.R.D. 24, 27 (D.Mass.1993). "'Statutes, administrative material, and judicial decisions can be established most easily by introducing an official or authenticated copy of the applicable provisions or court reports supported by expert testimony as to their meaning…[.] In addition … a litigant may present any other information concerning

foreign law he believes will further his cause, including secondary sources such as texts, learned journals, and a wide variety of unauthenticated documents relating to foreign law.'"

FRCP 45. SUBPOENA

Editor's note: *The Committee on Rules of Practice and Procedure of the Judicial Conference of the United States has proposed amendments to FRCP 45, to be effective December 1, 2013. For the proposed amendments, see www.uscourts.gov/RulesAndPolicies/rules/pending-rules.aspx.*

(a) In General.

(1) ***Form and Contents.***

(A) *Requirements—In General.* Every subpoena must:

(i) state the court from which it issued;

(ii) state the title of the action, the court in which it is pending, and its civil-action number;

(iii) command each person to whom it is directed to do the following at a specified time and place: attend and testify; produce designated documents, electronically stored information, or tangible things in that person's possession, custody, or control; or permit the inspection of premises; and

(iv) set out the text of Rule 45(c) and (d).

(B) *Command to Attend a Deposition—Notice of the Recording Method.* A subpoena commanding attendance at a deposition must state the method for recording the testimony.

(C) *Combining or Separating a Command to Produce or to Permit Inspection; Specifying the Form for Electronically Stored Information.* A command to produce documents, electronically stored information, or tangible things or to permit the inspection of premises may be included in a subpoena commanding attendance at a deposition, hearing, or trial, or may be set out in a separate subpoena. A subpoena may specify the form or forms in which electronically stored information is to be produced.

(D) *Command to Produce; Included Obligations.* A command in a subpoena to produce documents, electronically stored information, or tangible things requires the responding party to permit inspection, copying, testing, or sampling of the materials.

(2) ***Issued from Which Court.*** A subpoena must issue as follows:

(A) for attendance at a hearing or trial, from the court for the district where the hearing or trial is to be held;

(B) for attendance at a deposition, from the court for the district where the deposition is to be taken; and

(C) for production or inspection, if separate from a subpoena commanding a person's attendance, from the court for the district where the production or inspection is to be made.

(3) ***Issued by Whom.*** The clerk must issue a subpoena, signed but otherwise in blank, to a party who requests it. That party must complete it before service. An attorney also may issue and sign a subpoena as an officer of:

(A) a court in which the attorney is authorized to practice; or

(B) a court for a district where a deposition is to be taken or production is to be made, if the attorney is authorized to practice in the court where the action is pending.

(b) Service.

(1) ***By Whom; Tendering Fees; Serving a Copy of Certain Subpoenas.*** Any person who is at least 18 years old and not a party may serve a subpoena. Serving a subpoena requires delivering a copy to the named person and, if the subpoena requires that person's attendance, tendering the fees for 1 day's attendance and the mileage allowed by law. Fees and mileage need not be tendered when the subpoena issues on behalf of the United States or any of its officers or agencies. If the subpoena commands the production of documents, electronically stored information, or tangible things or the inspection of premises before trial, then before it is served, a notice must be served on each party.

(2) ***Service in the United States.*** Subject to Rule 45(c)(3)(A)(ii), a subpoena may be served at any place:

FRCP 45

(A) within the district of the issuing court;

(B) outside that district but within 100 miles of the place specified for the deposition, hearing, trial, production, or inspection;

(C) within the state of the issuing court if a state statute or court rule allows service at that place of a subpoena issued by a state court of general jurisdiction sitting in the place specified for the deposition, hearing, trial, production, or inspection; or

(D) that the court authorizes on motion and for good cause, if a federal statute so provides.

(3) ***Service in a Foreign Country.*** 28 U.S.C. §1783 governs issuing and serving a subpoena directed to a United States national or resident who is in a foreign country.

(4) ***Proof of Service.*** Proving service, when necessary, requires filing with the issuing court a statement showing the date and manner of service and the names of the persons served. The statement must be certified by the server.

(c) Protecting a Person Subject to a Subpoena.

(1) ***Avoiding Undue Burden or Expense; Sanctions.*** A party or attorney responsible for issuing and serving a subpoena must take reasonable steps to avoid imposing undue burden or expense on a person subject to the subpoena. The issuing court must enforce this duty and impose an appropriate sanction—which may include lost earnings and reasonable attorney's fees—on a party or attorney who fails to comply.

(2) ***Command to Produce Materials or Permit Inspection.***

(A) *Appearance Not Required.* A person commanded to produce documents, electronically stored information, or tangible things, or to permit the inspection of premises, need not appear in person at the place of production or inspection unless also commanded to appear for a deposition, hearing, or trial.

(B) *Objections.* A person commanded to produce documents or tangible things or to permit inspection may serve on the party or attorney designated in the subpoena a written objection to inspecting, copying, testing or sampling any or all of the materials or to inspecting the premises—or to producing electronically stored information in the form or forms requested. The objection must be served before the earlier of the time specified for compliance or 14 days after the subpoena is served. If an objection is made, the following rules apply:

(i) At any time, on notice to the commanded person, the serving party may move the issuing court for an order compelling production or inspection.

(ii) These acts may be required only as directed in the order, and the order must protect a person who is neither a party nor a party's officer from significant expense resulting from compliance.

(3) ***Quashing or Modifying a Subpoena.***

(A) *When Required.* On timely motion, the issuing court must quash or modify a subpoena that:

(i) fails to allow a reasonable time to comply;

(ii) requires a person who is neither a party nor a party's officer to travel more than 100 miles from where that person resides, is employed, or regularly transacts business in person—except that, subject to Rule 45(c)(3)(B)(iii), the person may be commanded to attend a trial by traveling from any such place within the state where the trial is held;

(iii) requires disclosure of privileged or other protected matter, if no exception or waiver applies; or

(iv) subjects a person to undue burden.

(B) *When Permitted.* To protect a person subject to or affected by a subpoena, the issuing court may, on motion, quash or modify the subpoena if it requires:

(i) disclosing a trade secret or other confidential research, development, or commercial information;

(ii) disclosing an unretained expert's opinion or information that does not describe specific occurrences in dispute and results from the expert's study that was not requested by a party; or

(iii) a person who is neither a party nor a party's officer to incur substantial expense to travel more than 100 miles to attend trial.

(C) *Specifying Conditions as an Alternative.* In the circumstances described in Rule 45(c)(3)(B), the court may, instead of quashing or modifying a subpoena, order appearance or production under specified conditions if the serving party:

(i) shows a substantial need for the testimony or material that cannot be otherwise met without undue hardship; and

(ii) ensures that the subpoenaed person will be reasonably compensated.

(d) Duties in Responding to a Subpoena.

(1) ***Producing Documents or Electronically Stored Information.*** These procedures apply to producing documents or electronically stored information:

(A) *Documents.* A person responding to a subpoena to produce documents must produce them as they are kept in the ordinary course of business or must organize and label them to correspond to the categories in the demand.

(B) *Form for Producing Electronically Stored Information Not Specified.* If a subpoena does not specify a form for producing electronically stored information, the person responding must produce it in a form or forms in which it is ordinarily maintained or in a reasonably usable form or forms.

(C) *Electronically Stored Information Produced in Only One Form.* The person responding need not produce the same electronically stored information in more than one form.

(D) *Inaccessible Electronically Stored Information.* The person responding need not provide discovery of electronically stored information from sources that the person identifies as not reasonably accessible because of undue burden or cost. On motion to compel discovery or for a protective order, the person responding must show that the information is not reasonably accessible because of undue burden or cost. If that showing is made, the court may nonetheless order discovery from such sources if the requesting party shows good cause, considering the limitations of Rule 26(b)(2)(C). The court may specify conditions for the discovery.

(2) ***Claiming Privilege or Protection.***

(A) *Information Withheld.* A person withholding subpoenaed information under a claim that it is privileged or subject to protection as trial-preparation material must:

(i) expressly make the claim; and

(ii) describe the nature of the withheld documents, communications, or tangible things in a manner that, without revealing information itself privileged or protected, will enable the parties to assess the claim.

(B) *Information Produced.* If information produced in response to a subpoena is subject to a claim of privilege or of protection as trial-preparation material, the person making the claim may notify any party that received the information of the claim and the basis for it. After being notified, a party must promptly return, sequester, or destroy the specified information and any copies it has; must not use or disclose the information until the claim is resolved; must take reasonable steps to retrieve the information if the party disclosed it before being notified; and may promptly present the information to the court under seal for a determination of the claim. The person who produced the information must preserve the information until the claim is resolved.

(e) Contempt. The issuing court may hold in contempt a person who, having been served, fails without adequate excuse to obey the subpoena. A nonparty's failure to obey must be excused if the subpoena purports to require the nonparty to attend or produce at a place outside the limits of Rule 45(c)(3)(A)(ii).

See selected Notes of Advisory Committee to FRCP 45, p. 1209.

History of FRCP 45: Adopted Dec. 20, 1937, eff. Sept. 16, 1938. Amended Dec. 27, 1946, eff. Mar. 19, 1948; Dec. 29, 1948, eff. Oct. 20, 1949; Mar. 30, 1970, eff. July 1, 1970; Apr. 29, 1980, eff. Aug. 1, 1980; Apr. 29, 1985, eff. Aug. 1, 1985; Mar. 2, 1987, eff. Aug. 1, 1987; Apr. 30, 1991, eff. Dec. 1, 1991; Apr. 25, 2005, eff. Dec. 1, 2005; Apr. 30, 2007, eff. Dec. 1, 2007.

See *Commentaries*, "Subpoenas Under FRCP 45," ch. 1-H, p. 47; *O'Connor's Federal Civil Forms* (2012), FORMS 1H.

See also 15 U.S.C. §23 (subpoenas in civil cases brought by U.S. under antitrust laws).

ANNOTATIONS

SEC v. Hyatt, 621 F.3d 687, 693-94 (7th Cir.2010). "The contempt provision in [FRCP 45(e)] does not distinguish between subpoenas issued with some court involvement—those issued in blank by the court clerk and completed by the party who requests it—and those issued without any court involvement at all by an attorney as an officer of the court. Instead, subsection (e) ... broadly refers to the contempt power of the 'issuing court,' which implies that all discovery subpoenas are contempt-sanctionable orders of the court whether issued in blank by the clerk or by an attorney as an officer of the court. [¶] Nothing in Rule 45 or the accompanying commentary purports to limit the contempt power to subpoenas issued with more direct district court involvement or to require an intervening court order when the subpoena is issued by an attorney. [¶] [W]e reject [nonparty-contemnor's] argument that a subpoena issued under Rule 45(a)(3) by an attorney as an officer of the court is not itself a court order subject to contempt sanctions if disobeyed. [¶] It does not follow, however, that a contempt motion for disobedience of a non-party subpoena should be treated in exactly the same way as a contempt motion for violation of another kind of court order. ... Rule 45 ... contains important provisions to protect the recipient of a subpoena from undue burden or expense, invasion of a privilege, or disclosure of protected material. ... These provisions suggest at a minimum that contempt motions for noncompliance with a discovery subpoena should be entertained with special attention to the procedural and substantive rights of the nonparty witness."

Dynegy Midstream Servs. v. Trammochem, 451 F.3d 89, 95 (2d Cir.2006). "Not only is service of process geographically limited by Rule 45, but enforcement proceedings are too. Rule 45(e) ... provides that failure to comply with a properly issued subpoena 'may be deemed a contempt of the court from which the subpoena issued.' Ordinarily, in the case of a subpoena for the production of documents alone, that court would be 'the court for the district where the production or inspection is to be made.'"

In re Subpoena Duces Tecum Issued to Commodity Futures Trading Comm'n WD Energy Servs., 439 F.3d 740, 751 (D.C.Cir.2006). "Although [FRCP] 45(d)(2) does not speak directly to the burden on third parties raising claims of privilege under the ***Perlman*** [***v. U.S.***, 247 U.S. 7 (1918),] doctrine, the applicability of a similar burden is natural. Rule 45(d)(2) is generally satisfied by the submission of a privilege log detailing each document withheld and the reason. ... Rule 45(d)(2) serves two purposes, both of which are relevant in ancillary actions under ***Perlman*** and acquire special moment when a court is faced with the challenge of applying ***Jaffee*** [***v. Redmond***, 518 U.S. 1 (1996),] to assertions of historically novel privileges. First, it prevents courts from addressing often difficult questions in the abstract. Second, timely and detailed explanation of the grounds of the privilege protects the subpoenaing party's right to contest the claims of privilege."

Wiwa v. Royal Dutch Pet. Co., 392 F.3d 812, 818 (5th Cir.2004). "Whether a burdensome subpoena is reasonable must be determined according to the facts of the case, such as the party's need for the documents and the nature and importance of the litigation. To determine whether the subpoena presents an undue burden, we consider the following factors: (1) relevance of the information requested; (2) the need of the party for the documents; (3) the breadth of the document request; (4) the time period covered by the request; (5) the particularity with which the party describes the requested documents; and (6) the burden imposed. Further, if the person to whom the document request is made is a non-party, the court may also consider the expense and inconvenience to the non-party. A court may find that a subpoena presents an undue burden when the subpoena is facially overbroad." (Internal quotes omitted.)

In re Dennis, 330 F.3d 696, 704 (5th Cir.2003). "The conjunctive form of [FRCP 45(b)(1)] indicates that proper service requires not only personal delivery of the subpoena, but also tendering of the witness fee and a reasonable mileage allowance. '[T]he plain meaning of Rule 45[(b)(1)] requires simultaneous tendering of witness fees and the reasonably estimated mileage allowed by law with service of a subpoena.'"

Linder v. Calero-Portocarrero, 251 F.3d 178, 182 (D.C.Cir.2001). "[T]he questions before the district court are whether the subpoena imposes expenses on the non-party, and whether those expenses are 'significant.' If they are, the court must protect the non-party by requiring the party seeking discovery to bear at least enough of the expense to render the remainder 'non-significant.'"

Food Lion, Inc. v. United Food & Commercial Workers Int'l Un., 103 F.3d 1007, 1016 (D.C.Cir.1997). "[A] party moving to hold another party in contempt must demonstrate by clear and convincing evidence that the alleged contemnor *violated the court's prior order*. [A] finding of bad faith on the part of the contemnor is *not* required. *At 1017-18:* Although a party's good faith may be a factor in determining whether substantial compliance occurred, and may be considered in mitigation of damages, good faith alone is not sufficient to excuse contempt."

Daval Steel Prods. v. M/V Fakredine, 951 F.2d 1357, 1364 (2d Cir.1991). "Undeniably, a valid subpoena is a legal instrument, non-compliance with which can constitute contempt of court. Nonetheless, '[a] subpoena, obtainable as of course from the Clerk of the Court, is not of the same order as one issued by a judicial officer in the resolution of a specific dispute.'"

McGill v. Duckworth, 944 F.2d 344, 353-54 (7th Cir.1991). FRCP 45(a) "provides a simple procedure: a litigant asks the clerk of the district court (*not* the district judge) to command someone to attend trial and give testimony. The judge has the power to enforce the subpoena if the witness opposes the demand to appear. … The way to test whether a witness is beyond a federal court's power to hale him into court is to issue a subpoena under Rule 45(a). … It is no abuse of discretion to refuse to compel the attendance of a witness when the party requesting the order not only disdains proper procedures but also fails to explain why the testimony is needed."

Micro Motion, Inc. v. Kane Steel Co., 894 F.2d 1318, 1322-23 (Fed.Cir.1990). "Under [FRCP] 45(d), a nonparty subpoenaed for testimony and production of documents may move for a protective order under [FRCP] 26(c)…. A nonparty also may merely object to production of documents and things. By merely objecting, such discovery is foreclosed except pursuant to an order of the court."

Mohamed v. Mazda Motor Corp., 90 F.Supp.2d 757, 778 (E.D.Tex.2000). "[L]itigants in this Court often make the argument that witnesses outside the Eastern District of Texas and over 100 miles from the Marshall courthouse are beyond its subpoena range. Well that's just wrong. [FRCP 45] underwent a complete revision in 1991. [O]ne of the purposes of this provision was to 'enable the court to compel a witness found within the state in which the court sits to attend trial.'"

FRCP 46. OBJECTING TO A RULING OR ORDER

A formal exception to a ruling or order is unnecessary. When the ruling or order is requested or made, a party need only state the action that it wants the court to take or objects to, along with the grounds for the request or objection. Failing to object does not prejudice a party who had no opportunity to do so when the ruling or order was made.

History of FRCP 46: Adopted Dec. 20, 1937, eff. Sept. 16, 1938. Amended Mar. 2, 1987, eff. Aug. 1, 1987; Apr. 30, 2007, eff. Dec. 1, 2007.

See ***Commentaries***, "Making Objections & Preserving Error," ch. 1-F, p. 41; "Objecting to Evidence," ch. 8-D, p. 700.

ANNOTATIONS

Nelson v. Adams USA, Inc., 529 U.S. 460, 469 (2000). "It is indeed the general rule that issues must be raised in lower courts in order to be preserved as potential grounds of decision in higher courts. But this principle does not demand the incantation of particular words; rather, it requires that the lower court be fairly put on notice as to the substance of the issue."

Beech Aircraft Corp. v. Rainey, 488 U.S. 153, 174 (1988). FRCP 46 "requires that a party seeking to preserve an objection to the court's ruling must 'mak[e] known to the court the action which the party desires the court to take or the party's objection to the action of the court and the grounds therefor.' Although … counsel did not explain the evidentiary basis of his argument as thoroughly as might ideally be desired, we are satisfied that he substantially satisfied the requirement of putting the court on notice as to his concern."

Hartford Lloyd's Ins. v. Teachworth, 898 F.2d 1058, 1060-61 (5th Cir.1990). "The purpose of [FRCP 46] is that the district court should be given notice of an alleged defect so the court has an opportunity to cure it. '[This] purpose can be adequately served only by the making of an objection on the record, but if the court and the other litigants know what action a party desires the court to take, the purpose of the rule is served.' In such circumstances, a formal objection is not required…."

FRCP 47. SELECTING JURORS

(a) Examining Jurors. The court may permit the parties or their attorneys to examine prospective jurors or may itself do so. If the court examines the

FRCP 47

jurors, it must permit the parties or their attorneys to make any further inquiry it considers proper, or must itself ask any of their additional questions it considers proper.

(b) Peremptory Challenges. The court must allow the number of peremptory challenges provided by 28 U.S.C. §1870.

(c) Excusing a Juror. During trial or deliberation, the court may excuse a juror for good cause.

History of FRCP 47: Adopted Dec. 20, 1937, eff. Sept. 16, 1938. Amended Feb. 28, 1966, eff. July 1, 1966; Apr. 30, 1991, eff. Dec. 1, 1991; Apr. 30, 2007, eff. Dec. 1, 2007.

See ***Commentaries***, "Jury Selection," ch. 8-A, p. 673; ***O'Connor's Federal Civil Forms*** (2012), FORMS 8A.

See also 28 U.S.C. §§1861-1878 (juries generally).

ANNOTATIONS

Jones v. Wellham, 104 F.3d 620, 630 (4th Cir.1997). "The form of *voir dire* questions to be submitted under [FRCP] 47(a) ... is committed to the discretion of the district courts and there is of course no compulsion to ask every question requested by counsel. Abuse of discretion in declining to ask a particular question occurs only if the failure hinders a party's ability to make reasonable use of its challenges."

Murray v. Laborers Un., 55 F.3d 1445, 1451-52 (9th Cir.1995). "While Rule 47(c) ... allows a judge to excuse a juror from service during deliberation for good cause, '[i]t is not grounds for the dismissal of a juror that the juror refuses to join with fellow jurors in reaching a unanimous verdict.' [¶] [T]he removal of [juror] due to his scheduling conflict meets the 'good cause' standard. Although '[s]ickness, family emergency or juror misconduct that might occasion a mistrial are examples of appropriate grounds' for excusing a juror, the judge's discretion is not limited to those scenarios."

Montiel v. City of L.A., 2 F.3d 335, 340-41 (9th Cir. 1993). "In our view, this case presents a good reason why, in certain situations, district courts should exercise their discretion under [FRCP 47(a)] to expand the amount of time permitted parties to voir dire jury panels. Providing parties with an opportunity to question more fully prospective jurors often flushes-out parties' true motivations in exercising their peremptory challenges. At the very least, it provides the trial judge with a more complete picture when ***Batson*** objections are presented."

FRCP 48. NUMBER OF JURORS; VERDICT; POLLING

(a) Number of Jurors. A jury must begin with at least 6 and no more than 12 members, and each juror must participate in the verdict unless excused under Rule 47(c).

(b) Verdict. Unless the parties stipulate otherwise, the verdict must be unanimous and must be returned by a jury of at least 6 members.

(c) Polling. After a verdict is returned but before the jury is discharged, the court must on a party's request, or may on its own, poll the jurors individually. If the poll reveals a lack of unanimity or lack of assent by the number of jurors that the parties stipulated to, the court may direct the jury to deliberate further or may order a new trial.

See selected Notes of Advisory Committee to FRCP 48, p. 1213.

History of FRCP 48: Adopted Dec. 20, 1937, eff. Sept. 16, 1938. Amended Apr. 30, 1991, eff. Dec. 1, 1991; Apr. 30, 2007, eff. Dec. 1, 2007; Mar. 26, 2009, eff. Dec. 1, 2009.

See ***Commentaries***, "Jury Selection," ch. 8-A, p. 673; ***O'Connor's Federal Civil Forms*** (2012), FORMS 8A.

See also U.S. Const. amend. 7 (right to jury trial); 28 U.S.C. §§1861-1878 (juries generally).

ANNOTATIONS

Montiel v. City of L.A., 2 F.3d 335, 338 (9th Cir. 1993). "[P] first contends the district court's decision to seat 12 jurors, instead of a lower number, violated the 'spirit and intent' of [FRCP] 48. [¶] The rule clearly states that a district court may empanel between 6 and 12 jurors. Nothing in the Committee Notes to the rule or the case law interpreting the rule suggests that a court opting for a 12-member jury violates the rule."

FRCP 49. SPECIAL VERDICT; GENERAL VERDICT & QUESTIONS

(a) Special Verdict.

(1) *In General.* The court may require a jury to return only a special verdict in the form of a special written finding on each issue of fact. The court may do so by:

(A) submitting written questions susceptible of a categorical or other brief answer;

(B) submitting written forms of the special findings that might properly be made under the pleadings and evidence; or

(C) using any other method that the court considers appropriate.

(2) ***Instructions.*** The court must give the instructions and explanations necessary to enable the jury to make its findings on each submitted issue.

(3) ***Issues Not Submitted.*** A party waives the right to a jury trial on any issue of fact raised by the pleadings or evidence but not submitted to the jury unless, before the jury retires, the party demands its submission to the jury. If the party does not demand submission, the court may make a finding on the issue. If the court makes no finding, it is considered to have made a finding consistent with its judgment on the special verdict.

(b) General Verdict with Answers to Written Questions.

(1) ***In General.*** The court may submit to the jury forms for a general verdict, together with written questions on one or more issues of fact that the jury must decide. The court must give the instructions and explanations necessary to enable the jury to render a general verdict and answer the questions in writing, and must direct the jury to do both.

(2) ***Verdict and Answers Consistent.*** When the general verdict and the answers are consistent, the court must approve, for entry under Rule 58, an appropriate judgment on the verdict and answers.

(3) ***Answers Inconsistent with the Verdict.*** When the answers are consistent with each other but one or more is inconsistent with the general verdict, the court may:

(A) approve, for entry under Rule 58, an appropriate judgment according to the answers, notwithstanding the general verdict;

(B) direct the jury to further consider its answers and verdict; or

(C) order a new trial.

(4) ***Answers Inconsistent with Each Other and the Verdict.*** When the answers are inconsistent with each other and one or more is also inconsistent with the general verdict, judgment must not be entered; instead, the court must direct the jury to further consider its answers and verdict, or must order a new trial.

History of FRCP 49: Adopted Dec. 20, 1937, eff. Sept. 16, 1938. Amended Jan. 21, 1963, eff. July 1, 1963; Mar. 2, 1987, eff. Aug. 1, 1987; Apr. 30, 2007, eff. Dec. 1, 2007.

See *Commentaries*, "Jury Charge," ch. 8-I, p. 720; *O'Connor's Federal Civil Forms* (2012), FORMS 8I.

ANNOTATIONS

Radvansky v. City of Olmsted Falls, 496 F.3d 609, 618 (6th Cir.2007). "[A] party must make its Rule 49(b) objection prior to the district court discharging the jury. … 'It is well-settled that if, after answers to special interrogatories are read, a party does not object to the discharge of the jury or raise any issue with respect to the jury's responses, that party should be deemed to have waived any objection as to inconsistency, ambiguity, or lack of clarity in the answers.'"

Johnson v. ABLT Trucking Co., 412 F.3d 1138, 1140 (10th Cir.2005). "This Court has interpreted Rule 49 … to require a contemporaneous objection if a party believes a general verdict with special interrogatories is internally inconsistent, but has not required such an objection in the case of a special verdict. In this case, [Ds] seek a new trial on the basis of an alleged inconsistency in the jury's verdict to which they did not object. The case thus raises two difficult questions: whether the jury's verdict was a special verdict or a general verdict with answers to interrogatories, and, if the former, whether the jury's verdict was irreconcilably inconsistent. *At 1143:* Because the verdict was special, [D's] failure to object was not a waiver of its right to seek a new trial on the basis of the supposed inconsistency in the verdict. We must therefore determine whether the jury's verdict was inconsistent. *At 1144:* To be irreconcilably inconsistent, the jury's answers must be 'logically incompatible, thereby indicating that the jury was confused or abused its power.' … A verdict is irreconcilably inconsistent only when 'the essential controlling findings are in conflict, the jury has failed utterly to perform its function of determining the facts, and its verdict is a nullity.'"

JGR, Inc. v. Thomasville Furniture Indus., 370 F.3d 519, 527 (6th Cir.2004). FRCP 49(b) "permits a trial court to submit interrogatories to a jury on issues of fact that are necessary for a verdict, but the rule does not require the court to do so."

Duk v. MGM Grand Hotel, Inc., 320 F.3d 1052, 1056 (9th Cir.2003). "The practice of resubmitting an inconsistent verdict to the jury for clarification is well-accepted. [FRCP] 49(b) provides that general verdict sheets may be 'return[ed] to the jury for further consideration of its answers and verdict' when the answers to interrogatories are inconsistent with each other or

with the general verdict. Although Rule 49(a), dealing with special verdicts such as this one, does not explicitly provide for resubmission in case of an inconsistency, we have held that, because the rule does not prohibit it, special verdicts are also subject to the practice."

Gaia Techs. v. Recycled Prods., 175 F.3d 365, 370-71 (5th Cir.1999). "Nothing in the text of Rule 49(a) authorizes a district court to reform a jury's decision on issues submitted to the jury. Rule 49(a) allows the district court to make its own findings only as to issues not submitted to the jury. … Rule 49(a) does not permit a district court to make findings contrary to the jury verdict."

In re Air Crash Disaster, 86 F.3d 498, 533-34 (6th Cir.1996). "We do not believe that hiding the legal consequences of a decision from a jury is the best or only means of coping with the danger of prejudice in a case…. If we think the jury unable to grasp the importance of maintaining a legal distinction between two liability tests, the answer … is … to educate their discretion. If a jury is told of the reasons behind a certain legal distinction, … there is no reason … to think that they will not uphold the law."

Bradway v. Gonzales, 26 F.3d 313, 316-17 (2d Cir. 1994). FRCP 49 "provides for two different verdict forms. … 'The distinction between the two provisions is that under Rule 49(a) the jury answers primarily factual questions for the benefit of the trial court…. Under Rule 49(b), the jury after being fully instructed answers the interrogatories, renders a general verdict and the trial court enters judgment on the jury's verdict.' [¶] [F]ailure to challenge the omission of an issue from a Rule 49(a) verdict form before the jury retires to deliberate constitutes a waiver of the right to a trial by jury on that issue."

Abou-Khadra v. Mahshie, 4 F.3d 1071, 1083 (2d Cir.1993). FRCP 49(b) allows "the trial judge to enter a judgment based on the answers to specific interrogatories where those answers find facts that compel a result as a matter of law that is inconsistent with the general verdict. The theory is that the jury, having found such facts, must have reached the general verdict by erroneous legal reasoning that the judge is entitled to correct." *See also* ***McGuire v. Russell Miller, Inc.***, 1 F.3d 1306, 1310 (2d Cir.1993).

FRCP 50. JUDGMENT AS A MATTER OF LAW IN A JURY TRIAL; RELATED MOTION FOR A NEW TRIAL; CONDITIONAL RULING

(a) Judgment as a Matter of Law.

(1) ***In General.*** If a party has been fully heard on an issue during a jury trial and the court finds that a reasonable jury would not have a legally sufficient evidentiary basis to find for the party on that issue, the court may:

(A) resolve the issue against the party; and

(B) grant a motion for judgment as a matter of law against the party on a claim or defense that, under the controlling law, can be maintained or defeated only with a favorable finding on that issue.

(2) ***Motion.*** A motion for judgment as a matter of law may be made at any time before the case is submitted to the jury. The motion must specify the judgment sought and the law and facts that entitle the movant to the judgment.

(b) Renewing the Motion After Trial; Alternative Motion for a New Trial. If the court does not grant a motion for judgment as a matter of law made under Rule 50(a), the court is considered to have submitted the action to the jury subject to the court's later deciding the legal questions raised by the motion. No later than 28 days after the entry of judgment—or if the motion addresses a jury issue not decided by a verdict, no later than 28 days after the jury was discharged—the movant may file a renewed motion for judgment as a matter of law and may include an alternative or joint request for a new trial under Rule 59. In ruling on the renewed motion, the court may:

(1) allow judgment on the verdict, if the jury returned a verdict;

(2) order a new trial; or

(3) direct the entry of judgment as a matter of law.

(c) Granting the Renewed Motion; Conditional Ruling on a Motion for a New Trial.

(1) ***In General.*** If the court grants a renewed motion for judgment as a matter of law, it must also conditionally rule on any motion for a new trial by determining whether a new trial should be granted if the judgment is later vacated or reversed. The court must state the grounds for conditionally granting or denying the motion for a new trial.

(2) ***Effect of a Conditional Ruling.*** Conditionally granting the motion for a new trial does not affect the judgment's finality; if the judgment is reversed, the new trial must proceed unless the appellate court orders otherwise. If the motion for a new trial is conditionally denied, the appellee may assert error in that denial; if the judgment is reversed, the case must proceed as the appellate court orders.

(d) **Time for a Losing Party's New-Trial Motion.** Any motion for a new trial under Rule 59 by a party against whom judgment as a matter of law is rendered must be filed no later than 28 days after the entry of the judgment.

(e) **Denying the Motion for Judgment as a Matter of Law; Reversal on Appeal.** If the court denies the motion for judgment as a matter of law, the prevailing party may, as appellee, assert grounds entitling it to a new trial should the appellate court conclude that the trial court erred in denying the motion. If the appellate court reverses the judgment, it may order a new trial, direct the trial court to determine whether a new trial should be granted, or direct the entry of judgment.

See selected Notes of Advisory Committee to FRCP 50, p. 1213.

History of FRCP 50: Adopted Dec. 20, 1937, eff. Sept. 16, 1938. Amended Jan. 21, 1963, eff. July 1, 1963; Mar. 2, 1987, eff. Aug. 1, 1987; Apr. 30, 1991, eff. Dec. 1, 1991; Apr. 22, 1993, eff. Dec. 1, 1993; Apr. 27, 1995, eff. Dec. 1, 1995; Apr. 12, 2006, eff. Dec. 1, 2006; Apr. 30, 2007, eff. Dec. 1, 2007; Mar. 26, 2009, eff. Dec. 1, 2009.

See ***Commentaries***, "Motion for Judgment as a Matter of Law," ch. 8-G, p. 714; "Renewed Motion for Judgment as a Matter of Law," ch. 10-B, p. 775; *O'Connor's Federal Civil Forms* (2012), FORMS 8G; FORMS 10B.

ANNOTATIONS

Unitherm Food Sys. v. Swift-Eckrich, Inc., 546 U.S. 394, 404 (2006). "[T]he precise subject matter of a party's Rule 50(a) motion—namely, its entitlement to judgment as a matter of law—cannot be appealed unless that motion is renewed pursuant to Rule 50(b). [D] does not seek to pursue on appeal ... its entitlement to judgment as a matter of law. Rather, [D] seeks a *new trial* based on the legal insufficiency of the evidence. [If] a litigant that has failed to file a Rule 50(b) motion is foreclosed from seeking the relief it sought in its Rule 50(a) motion[,] then surely [D] is foreclosed from seeking a new trial...."

Reeves v. Sanderson Plumbing Prods., 530 U.S. 133, 150-51 (2000). "[I]n entertaining a motion for judgment as a matter of law, the court should review all of the evidence in the record. [¶] [H]owever, the court must draw all reasonable inferences in favor of the nonmoving party, and it may not make credibility determinations or weigh the evidence. [A]lthough the court should review the record as a whole, it must disregard all evidence favorable to the moving party that the jury is not required to believe. That is, the court should give credence to the evidence favoring the nonmovant as well as that 'evidence supporting the moving party that is uncontradicted and unimpeached, at least to the extent that that evidence comes from disinterested witnesses.'" *See also* ***Ritchie v. U.S.***, 451 F.3d 1019, 1022-23 (9th Cir.2006).

Weisgram v. Marley Co., 528 U.S. 440, 448 (2000). FRCP 50 "allows the trial court to remove cases or issues from the jury's consideration 'when the facts are sufficiently clear that the law requires a particular result.'"

St. Mary's Honor Ctr. v. Hicks, 509 U.S. 502, 509 (1993). "At the close of the defendant's case, the court is asked to decide whether an issue of fact remains for the trier of fact to determine. None does if, on the evidence presented, (1) any rational person would have to find the existence of facts constituting a prima facie case, and (2) the defendant has failed to meet its burden of production.... In that event, the court must award judgment to the plaintiff as a matter of law under [FRCP] 50(a)(1) (in the case of jury trials) or [FRCP] 52(c) (in the case of bench trials)."

Neely v. Martin K. Eby Constr. Co., 386 U.S. 317, 322-23 (1967). "Rule 50(c)(1) contemplates that the appellate court will review on appeal both the grant of judgment n.o.v. and, if necessary, the trial court's conditional disposition of the motion for new trial." *See also* ***Tuttle v. Metropolitan Gov't of Nashville***, 474 F.3d 307, 323 (6th Cir.2007).

Smart Mktg. Grp. v. Publications Int'l, 624 F.3d 824, 832 (7th Cir.2010). See annotation under FRCP 59, p. 957.

Howard v. Walgreen Co., 605 F.3d 1239, 1243 (11th Cir.2010). "'This Court repeatedly has made clear that any renewal of a motion for judgment as a matter of law under Rule 50(b) must be based upon the same grounds as the original request for judgment as a matter of law made under Rule 50(a)....' [T]he purpose of requiring the grounds asserted in a Rule 50(b) motion to align with those asserted in a Rule 50(a) motion 'is to avoid making a trap of the motion for judgment notwithstanding the verdict, either at the trial stage or on

appeal. When a claimed deficiency in the evidence is called to the attention of the trial judge and of counsel before the jury has commenced deliberations, counsel still may do whatever can be done to mend the case.' ... Strict identity of issues, however, is not required. So long as they are 'closely related,' such that opposing counsel and the trial court may be deemed to have notice of the deficiencies asserted by the moving party, the purposes of the rule will be satisfied. If 'the new and old grounds vary greatly,' we may not rely upon the new grounds to reverse a district court's denial of a Rule 50(b) motion." *See also* ***EEOC v. Go Daddy Software, Inc.***, 581 F.3d 951, 961 (9th Cir.2009); ***Kusens v. Pascal Co.***, 448 F.3d 349, 361 (6th Cir.2006).

Chaney v. City of Orlando, 483 F.3d 1221, 1228 (11th Cir.2007). "The fact that Rule 50(b) uses the word 'renew[ed]' makes clear that a Rule 50(b) motion should be decided in the same way it would have been decided prior to the jury's verdict, and that the jury's particular findings are not germane to the legal analysis. The jury's findings should be excluded from the decision-making calculus on a Rule 50(b) motion, other than to ask whether there was sufficient evidence, as a legal matter, from which a reasonable jury could find for the party who prevailed at trial."

Federal Ins. v. HPSC, Inc., 480 F.3d 26, 32 (1st Cir. 2007). See annotation under FRCP 52, p. 941.

EEOC v. Kohler Co., 335 F.3d 766, 772 (8th Cir. 2003). "[J]udges must be extremely guarded in granting judgments as a matter of law after a jury verdict. As this court has often repeated, the standard to be applied is as follows: '[T]he district court must (1) consider the evidence in the light most favorable to the prevailing party, (2) assume that all conflicts in the evidence were resolved in favor of the prevailing party, (3) assume as proved all facts that the prevailing party's evidence tended to prove, and (4) give the prevailing party the benefit of all favorable inferences that may reasonably be drawn from the facts proved. [T]he court must then deny the motion if reasonable persons could differ as to the conclusions to be drawn from the evidence.'"

Rhone Poulenc Rorer Pharms. v. Newman Glass Works, 112 F.3d 695, 698 (3d Cir.1997). "When granting a motion for judgment as a matter of law, the district court ... is required to rule conditionally on any motion for a new trial. The court must determine whether the motion for a new trial should be granted or denied if the judgment is thereafter vacated or reversed. ... The district court's dismissal of the new trial motion as moot does not satisfy the rule's conditional ruling requirement." Held: Remanded to district court for ruling on undecided motion for new trial. *See also* ***Jennings v. Jones***, 499 F.3d 2, 20-21 (1st Cir.2007). *But see* ***Arenson v. Southern Univ. Law Ctr.***, 43 F.3d 194, 196-97 (5th Cir.1995) (when movant does not seek ruling from district court or argue on appeal for motion for new trial, motion is considered abandoned).

Palmer v. Fox Software, Inc., 107 F.3d 415, 418 (6th Cir.1997). "[A] federal court sitting in diversity reviews *de novo* legal determinations raised by a Rule 50 motion, and must apply the forum state's standard of review 'only when a Rule 50 challenge is mounted to the sufficiency of the evidence supporting a jury's findings. No deference is appropriate in diversity cases to the trial court's resolutions of legal questions.' Importantly, 'it is clear that we need show no deference to the *trial court's* assessment of the sufficiency of the evidence before a jury, even if state law so requires.'"

American & Foreign Ins. v. Bolt, 106 F.3d 155, 159 (6th Cir.1997). "While it is accepted that a judge may *sua sponte* grant a directed verdict pursuant to [FRCP] 50(a), ... allowing a judge to *sua sponte* raise a new issue post-verdict, and proceed to overturn a jury verdict on that basis contravenes the dictates of Rule 50(b). *At 160:* [R]ule 50(b) is applicable to post-verdict motions whether brought by the parties or by the trial judge." *See also* **Doe v. Celebrity Cruises, Inc.**, 394 F.3d 891, 903 (11th Cir.2004).

FRCP 51. INSTRUCTIONS TO THE JURY; OBJECTIONS; PRESERVING A CLAIM OF ERROR

(a) Requests.

(1) ***Before or at the Close of the Evidence.*** At the close of the evidence or at any earlier reasonable time that the court orders, a party may file and furnish to every other party written requests for the jury instructions it wants the court to give.

(2) ***After the Close of the Evidence.*** After the close of the evidence, a party may:

(A) file requests for instructions on issues that could not reasonably have been anticipated by an earlier time that the court set for requests; and

(B) with the court's permission, file untimely requests for instructions on any issue.

(b) Instructions. The court:

(1) must inform the parties of its proposed instructions and proposed action on the requests before instructing the jury and before final jury arguments;

(2) must give the parties an opportunity to object on the record and out of the jury's hearing before the instructions and arguments are delivered; and

(3) may instruct the jury at any time before the jury is discharged.

(c) Objections.

(1) ***How to Make.*** A party who objects to an instruction or the failure to give an instruction must do so on the record, stating distinctly the matter objected to and the grounds for the objection.

(2) ***When to Make.*** An objection is timely if:

(A) a party objects at the opportunity provided under Rule 51(b)(2); or

(B) a party was not informed of an instruction or action on a request before that opportunity to object, and the party objects promptly after learning that the instruction or request will be, or has been, given or refused.

(d) Assigning Error; Plain Error.

(1) ***Assigning Error.*** A party may assign as error:

(A) an error in an instruction actually given, if that party properly objected; or

(B) a failure to give an instruction, if that party properly requested it and—unless the court rejected the request in a definitive ruling on the record—also properly objected.

(2) ***Plain Error.*** A court may consider a plain error in the instructions that has not been preserved as required by Rule 51(d)(1) if the error affects substantial rights.

See selected Notes of Advisory Committee to FRCP 51, p. 1216.

History of FRCP 51: Adopted Dec. 20, 1937, eff. Sept. 16, 1938. Amended Mar. 2, 1987, eff. Aug. 1, 1987; Mar. 27, 2003, eff. Dec. 1, 2003; Apr. 30, 2007, eff. Dec. 1, 2007.

See *Commentaries*, "Jury Charge," ch. 8-I, p. 720; *O'Connor's Federal Civil Forms* (2012), FORMS 8I.

ANNOTATIONS

Long v. Howard Univ., 550 F.3d 21, 25-26 (D.C.Cir. 2008). "To prevail on a plain-error argument, the objecting party must establish four elements: (1) there must be an error; (2) the error must be plain; (3) the error must affect substantial rights; and (4) the error must seriously affect the fairness, integrity, or public reputation of judicial proceedings. [P]lain error review under Rule 51 is suited to correcting *obvious* instances of injustice or misapplied law. … Reversal under the plain error standard is thus reserved only for exceptional circumstances." (Internal quotes omitted.) *See also* ***Production Specialties Grp. v. Minsor Sys.***, 513 F.3d 695, 700 (7th Cir.2008).

Baron v. Suffolk Cty. Sheriff's Dept., 402 F.3d 225, 235-36 (1st Cir.2005). "A petitioner's failure to object when the court issued the jury instruction constitutes a forfeiture of her right to object on appeal. Under [FRCP] 51(c)(2)(A), a timely objection to jury instructions must be raised before the instructions are delivered. Our interpretation of Rule 51 is quite strict. There is a good reason for this strictness. We enforce our object-or-forfeit rule to compel litigants to afford the trial court an opportunity to cure a defective instruction and to prevent the litigants from ensuring a new trial in the event of an adverse verdict by covertly relying on the error. Accordingly, we review [D's] forfeited claim only for plain error." (Internal quotes omitted.)

Positive Black Talk, Inc. v. Cash Money Records, Inc., 394 F.3d 357, 368-69 (5th Cir.2004), *overruled on other grounds*, ***Reed Elsevier, Inc. v. Muchnick***, ___ U.S. ___, 130 S.Ct. 1237 (2010). "[P's] off-the-record objections, regardless of how specific, cannot satisfy Rule 51's requirements. Thus, [P] did not preserve the error, and we review the jury instructions for plain error."

Foley v. Commonwealth Elec. Co., 312 F.3d 517, 521 (1st Cir.2002). "Rule 51 is quite strict. Even if the initial request for instruction is made in detail, the requesting party must object again after the instructions are given but before the jury retires for deliberation. '[I]t is not enough for counsel in renewing an objection merely to refer back generically to objections made before the charge.'"

Schobert v. Illinois DOT, 304 F.3d 725, 729-30 (7th Cir.2002). "Rule 51 provides in relevant part that any party wishing to contest a jury instruction must distinctly state the matter objected to and the ground of the objection. The objection must be specific enough that the nature of the error is brought into focus. The party must also explain what is wrong with the proposed instruction; it is not enough simply to submit an alternative instruction. There are no formal require-

ments, but pragmatically speaking the district court must be made aware of the error prior to instructing the jury, so that the judge can fix the problem before the case goes to the jury. Consistency is required as well; to preserve the objection, the party must state the same grounds when objecting to the jury instruction as it does in its motion for a new trial or on appeal." *See also Niemiec v. Union Pac. R.R.*, 449 F.3d 854, 857 (8th Cir. 2006).

Parker v. City of Nashua, 76 F.3d 9, 12 (1st Cir. 1996). "[T]o satisfy Rule 51 'the judge must be told *precisely* what the problem is, and as importantly, what the attorney would consider a satisfactory cure.' And the lawyer must propose a lawful instruction or correction, and not one that substantially overstates the law in that party's favor."

FRCP 52. FINDINGS & CONCLUSIONS BY THE COURT; JUDGMENT ON PARTIAL FINDINGS

(a) Findings and Conclusions.

(1) ***In General.*** In an action tried on the facts without a jury or with an advisory jury, the court must find the facts specially and state its conclusions of law separately. The findings and conclusions may be stated on the record after the close of the evidence or may appear in an opinion or a memorandum of decision filed by the court. Judgment must be entered under Rule 58.

(2) ***For an Interlocutory Injunction.*** In granting or refusing an interlocutory injunction, the court must similarly state the findings and conclusions that support its action.

(3) ***For a Motion.*** The court is not required to state findings or conclusions when ruling on a motion under Rule 12 or 56 or, unless these rules provide otherwise, on any other motion.

(4) ***Effect of a Master's Findings.*** A master's findings, to the extent adopted by the court, must be considered the court's findings.

(5) ***Questioning the Evidentiary Support.*** A party may later question the sufficiency of the evidence supporting the findings, whether or not the party requested findings, objected to them, moved to amend them, or moved for partial findings.

(6) ***Setting Aside the Findings.*** Findings of fact, whether based on oral or other evidence, must not be set aside unless clearly erroneous, and the reviewing court must give due regard to the trial court's opportunity to judge the witnesses' credibility.

(b) Amended or Additional Findings. On a party's motion filed no later than 28 days after the entry of judgment, the court may amend its findings—or make additional findings—and may amend the judgment accordingly. The motion may accompany a motion for a new trial under Rule 59.

(c) Judgment on Partial Findings. If a party has been fully heard on an issue during a nonjury trial and the court finds against the party on that issue, the court may enter judgment against the party on a claim or defense that, under the controlling law, can be maintained or defeated only with a favorable finding on that issue. The court may, however, decline to render any judgment until the close of the evidence. A judgment on partial findings must be supported by findings of fact and conclusions of law as required by Rule 52(a).

See selected Notes of Advisory Committee to FRCP 52, p. 1217.

History of FRCP 52: Adopted Dec. 20, 1937, eff. Sept. 16, 1938. Amended Dec. 27, 1946, eff. Mar. 19, 1948; Jan. 21, 1963, eff. July 1, 1963; Apr. 28, 1983, eff. Aug. 1, 1983; Apr. 29, 1985, eff. Aug. 1, 1985; Apr. 30, 1991, eff. Dec. 1, 1991; Apr. 22, 1993, eff. Dec. 1, 1993; Apr. 27, 1995, eff. Dec. 1, 1995; Apr. 30, 2007, eff. Dec. 1, 2007; Mar. 26, 2009, eff. Dec. 1, 2009.

See *Commentaries*, "Motion to Add or Amend Findings of Fact," ch. 10-E, p. 799; *O'Connor's Federal Civil Forms* (2012), FORMS 10E.

ANNOTATIONS

Anderson v. City of Bessemer City, 470 U.S. 564, 573 (1985). "[A] finding is 'clearly erroneous' when although there is evidence to support it, the reviewing court on the entire evidence is left with the definite and firm conviction that a mistake has been committed. *At 574:* Where there are two permissible views of the evidence, the factfinder's choice between them cannot be clearly erroneous. *At 575:* When findings are based on determinations regarding the credibility of witnesses, Rule 52(a) demands even greater deference to the trial court's findings; for only the trial judge can be aware of the variations in demeanor and tone of voice that bear so heavily on the listener's understanding of and belief in what is said." (Internal quotes omitted.)

Bose Corp. v. Consumers Un., 466 U.S. 485, 500 (1984). "The requirement that special deference be given to a trial judge's credibility determinations is ... a recognition of the broader proposition that the presumption of correctness that attaches to factual findings is stronger in some cases than in others. The same

'clearly erroneous' standard applies to findings based on documentary evidence as to those based entirely on oral testimony, ... but the presumption has lesser force in the former situation than in the latter. *At 501:* Rule 52(a) applies to findings of fact, including those described as 'ultimate facts' because they may determine the outcome of litigation."

Federal Ins. v. HPSC, Inc., 480 F.3d 26, 32 (1st Cir. 2007). "The strictures of [FRCP] 50 ... do not apply in non-jury trials. Rather, we treat motions for judgment as a matter of law made during bench trials as motions for judgment on partial findings under [FRCP] 52(c). [P] made such a motion at the close of [D's] case, but then proceeded to put on evidence, thus waiving its right to appeal the denial of that motion. Consequently, we treat the arguments [P] makes on appeal under the heading of 'motion for judgment as a matter of law' simply as challenges to the factual and legal sufficiency of the district court's determinations based on all the evidence...." (Internal quotes omitted.)

OCI Wyo., L.P. v. PacifiCorp, 479 F.3d 1199, 1203-04 (10th Cir.2007). "The district court's findings of fact [under FRCP 52(a)] 'should be sufficient to indicate the factual basis for the court's general conclusion as to ultimate facts[,] ... should indicate the legal standards against which the evidence was measured[,] ... [and] should be broad enough to cover all material issues.' 'If a district court fails to meet this standard—i.e. making only general, conclusory or inexact findings—we must vacate the judgment and remand the case for proper findings.' [¶] Rule 52(a) does not require the district court to set out its findings and conclusions in excruciating detail. '[T]he judge need only make brief, definite, pertinent findings and conclusions upon the contested matters; there is no necessity for overelaboration of detail or particularization of facts.'" *See also* ***Leonard v. Dorsey & Whitney LLP***, 553 F.3d 609, 613 (8th Cir.2009); ***Supermercados Econo, Inc. v. Integrand Assur. Co.***, 375 F.3d 1, 3 (1st Cir.2004).

Zack v. Commissioner, 291 F.3d 407, 412 (6th Cir. 2002). "When evaluating whether the requirements of Rule 52(a) have been satisfied, we do not insist that trial courts make factual findings directly addressing each issue that a litigant raises. We instead adhere to 'a liberal standard for reviewing the adequacy of the [trial court's] findings.' As a result, 'findings are to be liberally construed in support of a judgment, even if the findings are not as explicit or detailed as might be desired.' [¶] Despite this liberal approach, the trial court's findings must support the ultimate legal conclusions reached. The findings are necessary not only to reveal the logic behind the trial court's decision, but also to enable an appellate court to conduct a meaningful review of the trial court's order. Nevertheless, in accordance with a liberal review of the facts supporting the trial court's decision, this court has explained that '[i]f, from the facts found, other facts may be inferred which will support the judgment, such inferences should be deemed to have been drawn by the District Court.'" *See also* ***Henry v. Champlain Enters.***, 445 F.3d 610, 622 (2d Cir.2006).

FRCP 53

Six Clinics Holding Corp., II v. Cafcomp Sys., 119 F.3d 393, 400 (6th Cir.1997). "The purpose of [FRCP 52] is to provide an appellate court with a clear understanding of the district court's decision. [However, findings of fact] are not an unwaivable jurisdictional requirement to appeal. '[T]he failure of [a] District Court to comply with Rule 52(a) in respect of findings of fact does not demand reversal of the correct judgment of the District Court, if a full understanding of the issues could be reached without the aid of findings even though such findings would have been helpful.'" *See also* ***Reich v. Newspapers of New England, Inc.***, 44 F.3d 1060, 1079 (1st Cir.1995).

Granite State Ins. v. Smart Modular Techs., 76 F.3d 1023, 1031 (9th Cir.1996). "Rule 52(c) provides the court may enter judgment after a party has been 'fully heard.' [¶] We conclude the offer of proof was an appropriate means for the court to receive and consider [P's] proffered evidence. The court was not required to receive live testimony."

Transmatic, Inc. v. Gulton Indus., 53 F.3d 1270, 1275-76 (Fed.Cir.1995). "When [a] trial is held before the district court with an advisory jury, the court must find the facts specially just as it would when conducting a bench trial without an advisory jury. The requirement that the district court make factual findings permits meaningful review on appeal because this court may not engage in fact-finding on its own."

FRCP 53. MASTERS

(a) Appointment.

(1) ***Scope.*** Unless a statute provides otherwise, a court may appoint a master only to:

(A) perform duties consented to by the parties;

(B) hold trial proceedings and make or recommend findings of fact on issues to be decided without a jury if appointment is warranted by:

(i) some exceptional condition; or

(ii) the need to perform an accounting or resolve a difficult computation of damages; or

(C) address pretrial and posttrial matters that cannot be effectively and timely addressed by an available district judge or magistrate judge of the district.

(2) ***Disqualification.*** A master must not have a relationship to the parties, attorneys, action, or court that would require disqualification of a judge under 28 U.S.C. §455, unless the parties, with the court's approval, consent to the appointment after the master discloses any potential grounds for disqualification.

(3) ***Possible Expense or Delay.*** In appointing a master, the court must consider the fairness of imposing the likely expenses on the parties and must protect against unreasonable expense or delay.

(b) Order Appointing a Master.

(1) ***Notice.*** Before appointing a master, the court must give the parties notice and an opportunity to be heard. Any party may suggest candidates for appointment.

(2) ***Contents.*** The appointing order must direct the master to proceed with all reasonable diligence and must state:

(A) the master's duties, including any investigation or enforcement duties, and any limits on the master's authority under Rule 53(c);

(B) the circumstances, if any, in which the master may communicate ex parte with the court or a party;

(C) the nature of the materials to be preserved and filed as the record of the master's activities;

(D) the time limits, method of filing the record, other procedures, and standards for reviewing the master's orders, findings, and recommendations; and

(E) the basis, terms, and procedure for fixing the master's compensation under Rule 53(g).

(3) ***Issuing.*** The court may issue the order only after:

(A) the master files an affidavit disclosing whether there is any ground for disqualification under 28 U.S.C. §455; and

(B) if a ground is disclosed, the parties, with the court's approval, waive the disqualification.

(4) ***Amending.*** The order may be amended at any time after notice to the parties and an opportunity to be heard.

(c) Master's Authority.

(1) ***In General.*** Unless the appointing order directs otherwise, a master may:

(A) regulate all proceedings;

(B) take all appropriate measures to perform the assigned duties fairly and efficiently; and

(C) if conducting an evidentiary hearing, exercise the appointing court's power to compel, take, and record evidence.

(2) ***Sanctions.*** The master may by order impose on a party any noncontempt sanction provided by Rule 37 or 45, and may recommend a contempt sanction against a party and sanctions against a nonparty.

(d) Master's Orders. A master who issues an order must file it and promptly serve a copy on each party. The clerk must enter the order on the docket.

(e) Master's Reports. A master must report to the court as required by the appointing order. The master must file the report and promptly serve a copy on each party, unless the court orders otherwise.

(f) Action on the Master's Order, Report, or Recommendations.

(1) ***Opportunity for a Hearing; Action in General.*** In acting on a master's order, report, or recommendations, the court must give the parties notice and an opportunity to be heard; may receive evidence; and may adopt or affirm, modify, wholly or partly reject or reverse, or resubmit to the master with instructions.

(2) *Time to Object or Move to Adopt or Modify.* A party may file objections to—or a motion to adopt or modify—the master's order, report, or recommendations no later than 21 days after a copy is served, unless the court sets a different time.

(3) ***Reviewing Factual Findings.*** The court must decide de novo all objections to findings of fact made or recommended by a master, unless the parties, with the court's approval, stipulate that:

(A) the findings will be reviewed for clear error; or

(B) the findings of a master appointed under Rule 53(a)(1)(A) or (C) will be final.

(4) ***Reviewing Legal Conclusions.*** The court must decide de novo all objections to conclusions of law made or recommended by a master.

(5) ***Reviewing Procedural Matters.*** Unless the appointing order establishes a different standard of review, the court may set aside a master's ruling on a procedural matter only for an abuse of discretion.

(g) Compensation.

(1) *Fixing Compensation.* Before or after judgment, the court must fix the master's compensation on the basis and terms stated in the appointing order, but the court may set a new basis and terms after giving notice and an opportunity to be heard.

(2) *Payment.* The compensation must be paid either:

(A) by a party or parties; or

(B) from a fund or subject matter of the action within the court's control.

(3) *Allocating Payment.* The court must allocate payment among the parties after considering the nature and amount of the controversy, the parties' means, and the extent to which any party is more responsible than other parties for the reference to a master. An interim allocation may be amended to reflect a decision on the merits.

(h) Appointing a Magistrate Judge. A magistrate judge is subject to this rule only when the order referring a matter to the magistrate judge states that the reference is made under this rule.

See selected Notes of Advisory Committee to FRCP 53, p. 1218.

History of FRCP 53: Adopted Dec. 20, 1937, eff. Sept. 16, 1938. Amended Feb. 28, 1966, eff. July 1, 1966; Apr. 28, 1983, eff. Aug. 1, 1983; Mar. 2, 1987, eff. Aug. 1, 1987; Apr. 30, 1991, eff. Dec. 1, 1991; Apr. 22, 1993, eff. Dec. 1, 1993; Mar. 27, 2003, eff. Dec. 1, 2003; Apr. 30, 2007, eff. Dec. 1, 2007; Mar. 26, 2009, eff. Dec. 1, 2009.

See ***Commentaries***, "Appointment of Special Master," ch. 5-B, §4, p. 302; ***O'Connor's Federal Civil Forms*** (2012), FORMS 5B.

See also 28 U.S.C. §2284 (no appointment of master by single judge in three-judge court); FRCP 52 (adoption of master's findings by court), FRCP 55 (in default judgment, court can make referral to conduct an accounting, determine amount of damages, evaluate evidence, or investigate other matters).

ANNOTATIONS

La Buy v. Howes Leather Co., 352 U.S. 249, 256 (1957). "The use of masters is 'to aid judges in the performance of specific judicial duties, as they may arise in the progress of a cause,' ... and not to displace the court. *At 259:* [C]ongestion in itself is not such an exceptional circumstance as to warrant a reference to a master. If such were the test, present congestion would make references the rule rather than the exception."

Sierra Club v. Clifford, 257 F.3d 444, 446 (5th Cir. 2001). "[T]he Supreme Court [has] expressly held that a congested docket, the complexity of issues, and the extensive amount of time required for a trial do not, either individually or as a whole, constitute an exceptional condition justifying a Rule 53 reference to a special master…. *At 447:* The fact that a case has been pending for two years is not so exceptional as to require the reference of dispositive matters such as summary judgment motions to a special master. The same applies to voluminous filings containing highly technical documents and declarations…."

Aird v. Ford Motor Co., 86 F.3d 216, 221 (D.C.Cir. 1996). "[T]he district court enjoys broad discretion to allocate the master's fees…. [¶] While in some cases the costs might best be divided among the parties, or charged at least to some extent against the party that created the need for … the master, the district court has the authority in appropriate cases to tax the master's fees as costs against the losing party."

In re Bituminous Coal Operators' Ass'n, 949 F.2d 1165, 1168 (D.C.Cir.1991). "Rule 53 … authorizes the appointment of special masters to *assist*, not to replace, the adjudicator, whether judge or jury, constitutionally indicated for federal court litigation."

TITLE VII. JUDGMENT

FRCP 54. JUDGMENT; COSTS

(a) Definition; Form. "Judgment" as used in these rules includes a decree and any order from which

an appeal lies. A judgment should not include recitals of pleadings, a master's report, or a record of prior proceedings.

(b) Judgment on Multiple Claims or Involving Multiple Parties. When an action presents more than one claim for relief—whether as a claim, counterclaim, crossclaim, or third-party claim—or when multiple parties are involved, the court may direct entry of a final judgment as to one or more, but fewer than all, claims or parties only if the court expressly determines that there is no just reason for delay. Otherwise, any order or other decision, however designated, that adjudicates fewer than all the claims or the rights and liabilities of fewer than all the parties does not end the action as to any of the claims or parties and may be revised at any time before the entry of a judgment adjudicating all the claims and all the parties' rights and liabilities.

(c) Demand for Judgment; Relief to Be Granted. A default judgment must not differ in kind from, or exceed in amount, what is demanded in the pleadings. Every other final judgment should grant the relief to which each party is entitled, even if the party has not demanded that relief in its pleadings.

(d) Costs; Attorney's Fees.

(1) ***Costs Other Than Attorney's Fees.*** Unless a federal statute, these rules, or a court order provides otherwise, costs—other than attorney's fees—should be allowed to the prevailing party. But costs against the United States, its officers, and its agencies may be imposed only to the extent allowed by law. The clerk may tax costs on 14 days' notice. On motion served within the next 7 days, the court may review the clerk's action.

(2) ***Attorney's Fees.***

(A) *Claim to Be by Motion.* A claim for attorney's fees and related nontaxable expenses must be made by motion unless the substantive law requires those fees to be proved at trial as an element of damages.

(B) *Timing and Contents of the Motion.* Unless a statute or a court order provides otherwise, the motion must:

(i) be filed no later than 14 days after the entry of judgment;

(ii) specify the judgment and the statute, rule, or other grounds entitling the movant to the award;

(iii) state the amount sought or provide a fair estimate of it; and

(iv) disclose, if the court so orders, the terms of any agreement about fees for the services for which the claim is made.

(C) *Proceedings.* Subject to Rule 23(h), the court must, on a party's request, give an opportunity for adversary submissions on the motion in accordance with Rule 43(c) or 78. The court may decide issues of liability for fees before receiving submissions on the value of services. The court must find the facts and state its conclusions of law as provided in Rule 52(a).

(D) *Special Procedures by Local Rule; Reference to a Master or a Magistrate Judge.* By local rule, the court may establish special procedures to resolve fee-related issues without extensive evidentiary hearings. Also, the court may refer issues concerning the value of services to a special master under Rule 53 without regard to the limitations of Rule 53(a)(1), and may refer a motion for attorney's fees to a magistrate judge under Rule 72(b) as if it were a dispositive pretrial matter.

(E) *Exceptions.* Subparagraphs (A)-(D) do not apply to claims for fees and expenses as sanctions for violating these rules or as sanctions under 28 U.S.C. §1927.

See selected Notes of Advisory Committee to FRCP 54, p. 1222.

History of FRCP 54: Adopted Dec. 20, 1937, eff. Sept. 16, 1938. Amended Dec. 27, 1946, eff. Mar. 19, 1948; Apr. 17, 1961, eff. July 19, 1961; Mar. 2, 1987, eff. Aug. 1, 1987; Apr. 22, 1993, eff. Dec. 1, 1993; Apr. 29, 2002, eff. Dec. 1, 2002; Mar. 27, 2003, eff. Dec. 1, 2003; Apr. 30, 2007, eff. Dec. 1, 2007; Mar. 26, 2009, eff. Dec. 1, 2009.

See ***Commentaries***, "The Judgment," ch. 9, p. 733; ***O'Connor's Federal Civil Forms*** (2012), FORMS 9.

See also 28 U.S.C. §1915 (forma pauperis proceeding), §1916 (seamen's suits), §1920 (taxation of costs), §§1920, 1922 (witness fees), §§1920, 1923 (docket fees), §1921 (U.S. Marshal's fees), §1923 (printing costs of briefs in admiralty appeals), §1924 (verification of bill of costs), §1925 (taxation of admiralty and maritime cases), §1927 (counsel's liability for excessive costs), §§1961, 2411 (interest on judgment), §1962 (certain judgments to constitute lien), §1963 (registration of judgment), §§2001-2007 (execution and sales under judgment), §§2201, 2202 (declaratory judgment), §2405 (garnishment in suit by U.S. against corporation), §2407 (motion for judgment in action by U.S. against delinquents for public money), §2408 (security not required of U.S.).

ANNOTATIONS

FRCP 54(b)

Reiter v. Cooper, 507 U.S. 258, 265 (1993). FRCP 54(b) "permits a district court to enter separate final judgment on any claim or counterclaim, after making 'an express determination that there is no just reason for delay.'" *See also* ***O'Bert v. Vargo***, 331 F.3d 29, 40 (2d Cir.2003).

Elliott v. Archdiocese of N.Y., 682 F.3d 213, 224 (3d Cir.2012). "If [a court] fails to [state expressly that it determined that there is no just reason for delay], that judgment is not a final judgment under Rule 54(b), and we do not have jurisdiction over an appeal from that judgment. We note that although we part ways with … the Fifth Circuit on this issue, our decision in this case aligns us with the positions of … the Second, Ninth, Tenth, and District of Columbia Circuits. *At 225:* We also are persuaded, however, that Rule 54(b) does not require that a district court use the talismanic phrase 'there is no just reason for delay.' The district court may state that it has determined expressly that 'there is no just reason for delay' using those precise words, or it may paraphrase or use language 'of an indisputably similar effect,' … so long as the district court's order clearly contains the 'express' determination Rule 54(b) requires."

Cambridge Holdings Grp. v. Federal Ins., 489 F.3d 1356, 1360-61 (D.C.Cir.2007). "[A] district court order disposing of all claims against all properly served defendants satisfies the requirements of Rule 54(b), even if claims against those not properly served remain unresolved. [¶] [W]hen a district court dismisses a suit as to all served defendants and only an unserved defendant remains, there is generally no reason to anticipate additional proceedings before the district court. Indeed, unless the procedural requirements of effective service of process have been satisfied, the court lacks personal jurisdiction to act with respect to that defendant at all."

U.S. v. Columbia/HCA Healthcare Corp., 318 F.3d 214, 216 (D.C.Cir.2003). "Some circuits hold that consolidated cases remain separate actions and no Rule 54(b) certification is needed to appeal the dismissal of any one of them. Others treat consolidated cases as a single action…. Still other circuits apply no hard and fast rule, but focus on the reasons for the consolidation to determine whether the actions are one or separate. [¶] We have held that when a district court consolidates cases and treats them as such 'for all purposes,' an order deciding fewer than all the claims of all the parties cannot be appealed without a Rule 54(b) certification." *See also* ***Spraytex, Inc. v. DJS&T***, 96 F.3d 1377, 1382 (Fed.Cir.1996).

Downie v. City of Middleburg Heights, 301 F.3d 688, 692-93 (6th Cir.2002). "Under Rule 54(b), a party may appeal a district court order prior to the ultimate disposition of a case, but the district court is first required to certify that the order is appealable. To certify an order for immediate appeal, a district court must: (1) 'expressly direct the entry of final judgment as to one or more but fewer than all the claims or parties in a case'; and (2) 'express[ly] determin[e] that there is no just reason to delay appellate review.' [¶] '[T]he first step in certification, entry of partial final judgment, is satisfied where *some decision* made by the district court ultimately disposes of one or more but fewer than all of the claims or parties in a multi-claim/multi-party action.' The district court need not *enter* the partial final judgment in its certification of an immediate appeal pursuant to Rule 54(b); it simply must *recognize* that such a partial final judgment has been entered." *See also* ***MCI Constructors, LLC v. City of Greensboro***, 610 F.3d 849, 855 (4th Cir.2010); ***Lloyd Noland Found. v. Tenet Health Care Corp.***, 483 F.3d 773, 777-78 (11th Cir.2007).

Tubos de Acero v. American Int'l Inv. Corp., 292 F.3d 471, 485 (5th Cir.2002). "The Rule 54(b) requirement that the district court must have disposed of 'one or more … claims' in order to enter a final judgment is jurisdictional. [¶] When some of the same facts form the basis for several claims, the existence of separate claims for purposes of Rule 54(b) depends on an analysis of their distinctness. … This Court has not expressly adopted a method for determining what constitutes a distinct 'claim for relief' under Rule 54(b). We have recognized, however, that various courts have looked to the possibility of separate recoveries, have concentrated on the underlying facts, and have invoked claim-preclusion rules."

Waldorf v. Shuta, 142 F.3d 601, 608 (3d Cir.1998). "[T]o certify an order pursuant to Rule 54(b), the judgment must be final and there must be no just reason for delay in entering the final judgment. *At 609:* [To determine] whether there was any just reason for delay … courts should consider the following factors: '(1) the presence or absence of a claim or counterclaim which

could result in a set-off against the judgment sought to be made final; (2) the relationship between the adjudicated and unadjudicated claims; (3) the possibility that the need for review might or might not be mooted by future developments in the district court; (4) the possibility that the reviewing court might be obliged to consider the same issue a second time; and (5) miscellaneous factors such as delay, economic and solvency considerations, shortening the time of trial, frivolity of competing claims, expense, and the like.' *At 610-11:* We consistently have required district courts to provide a reasoned opinion as a prerequisite for appellate review of a judgment certified as final. Because the district court did not provide a written opinion outlining its reasons for its first certification of the judgment, we dismissed the appeal for want of jurisdiction." *See also* ***iLOR, LLC v. Google, Inc.***, 550 F.3d 1067, 1072 (Fed. Cir.2008) (bare recitation of "no just reason for delay" standard is not sufficient by itself to certify order under FRCP 54(b)).

Lawyers Title Ins. v. Dearborn Title Corp., 118 F.3d 1157, 1162 (7th Cir.1997). "The test for separate claims under [FRCP 54(b)] is whether the claim that is contended to be separate so overlaps the claim or claims that have been retained for trial that if the latter were to give rise to a separate appeal at the end of the case the court would have to go over the same ground that it had covered in the first appeal."

FRCP 54(c)

USX Corp. v. Barnhart, 395 F.3d 161, 165 (3d Cir. 2004). FRCP 54(c) "'requires that a court ascertain whether the plaintiffs are entitled to any remedy. As long as the plaintiffs have stated a claim for relief, it is the court's obligation to grant the relief to which the prevailing party is entitled whether it has been specifically demanded or not.' [¶] [FRCP 54(c)] was meant to protect a plaintiff from clumsy pleading, which, through technical oversight, might deprive it of a deserved recovery. '[FRCP 54(c)'s] most common usage is when the amount of the award varies from the demand for relief.' [FRCP 54(c)] has also been used to allow for the award of attorney's fees and costs even though none was demanded, or for recovering interest on a claim as damages."

Powell v. National Bd. of Med. Exam'rs, 364 F.3d 79, 86 (2d Cir.2004). "Under Rule 54(c) …, a court can grant any relief to which a prevailing party is entitled, whether or not that relief was expressly sought in the complaint. The sole exception to this rule is when a court grants relief not requested and of which the opposing party has no notice, thereby prejudicing that party." *See also* ***Knight v. Alabama***, 476 F.3d 1219, 1229 n.19 (11th Cir.2007); ***Gilbane Bldg. Co. v. Federal Reserve Bank***, 80 F.3d 895, 901 (4th Cir.1996).

FRCP 54(d)

Taniguchi v. Kan Pac. Saipan, Ltd., ___ U.S. ___, 132 S.Ct. 1997, 2006 (2012). "Although 'costs' has an everyday meaning synonymous with 'expenses,' the concept of taxable costs under [FRCP] 54(d) is more limited and represents those expenses, including, for example, court fees, that a court will assess against a litigant. Taxable costs are limited to relatively minor, incidental expenses as is evident from [28 U.S.C.] §1920…. Indeed, the assessment of costs most often is merely a clerical matter that can be done by the court clerk. Taxable costs are a fraction of the nontaxable expenses borne by litigants for attorneys, experts, consultants, and investigators. It comes as little surprise, therefore, that costs almost always amount to less than the successful litigant's total expenses in connection with a lawsuit." (Internal quotes omitted.)

Budinich v. Becton Dickinson & Co., 486 U.S. 196, 202 (1988). "[A]n unresolved issue of attorney's fees for the litigation in question does not prevent judgment on the merits from being final."

Crawford Fitting Co. v. J.T. Gibbons, Inc., 482 U.S. 437, 439 (1987). "[W]hen a prevailing party seeks reimbursement for fees paid to its own expert witnesses, a federal court is bound by the limit of [28 U.S.C.] §1821(b), absent contract or explicit statutory authority to the contrary. *At 442:* We think that the inescapable effect of [28 U.S.C. §§1821 and 1920] is that a federal court may tax expert witness fees in excess of the [dollar]-per-day limit set out in §1821(b) only when the witness is court-appointed. The discretion granted by [FRCP] 54(d) is not a power to evade this specific congressional command. Rather, it is solely a power to decline to tax, as costs, the items enumerated in §1920."

Gay v. Chandra, 682 F.3d 590, 593-94 (7th Cir. 2012). "[B]efore requiring a bond to cover costs under Rule 54(d), a court must consider a party's ability to pay. A court abuses its discretion when it requires a cost bond that it knows the party cannot afford. By contrast, courts can bar *future* suits as a sanction to punish a refusal to pay past court costs and sanctions even if

the litigant is indigent. [¶] The district court correctly reasoned that its authority to award costs to a prevailing party implies a power to require the posting of a bond reasonably calculated to cover those costs, even though no statute or rule expressly authorizes such an order. A court may require a bond where 'there is reason to believe that the prevailing party will find it difficult to collect its costs' when the litigation ends. [¶] A cost bond is not a sanction. It is meant 'to insure that whatever assets a party *does* possess will not have been dissipated or otherwise have become unreachable by the time such costs actually are awarded.'"

Shum v. Intel Corp., 629 F.3d 1360, 1367 (Fed.Cir. 2010). "[J]ust because a party can be said to have 'prevailed' on a claim does not necessarily make him a 'prevailing party' as the term is used in Rule 54. [¶] [T]he plain language of Rule 54 unambiguously limits the number of prevailing parties in a given case to one because the operative term, 'prevailing party,' is singular. [¶] Thus, even in mixed judgment cases, punting is not an option; Rule 54 does not allow every party that won on some claims to be deemed a 'prevailing party.' ... A court must choose one, and only one, 'prevailing party' to receive any costs award."

Republic Tobacco Co. v. North Atl. Trading Co., 481 F.3d 442, 446 (7th Cir.2007). Prevailing party means "'the party in whose favor judgment has been entered.' '[A] determination of who is the prevailing party for purposes of awarding costs should not depend on the position of the parties at each stage of the litigation but should be made when the controversy is finally decided.' *At 447:* [P] prevailed, notwithstanding [D's] successful post-trial motion, because the district court entered ... judgment in [P's] favor." *See also* ***Miles v. California***, 320 F.3d 986, 988 (9th Cir.2003) (if underlying claim is dismissed for lack of subject-matter jurisdiction, the dismissed party is not a prevailing party); ***Testa v. Village of Mundelein***, 89 F.3d 443, 447 (7th Cir.1996) (prevailing party is party who prevails as to substantial part of the litigation).

In re Cardizem CD Antitrust Litig., 481 F.3d 355, 359 (6th Cir.2007). "The costs that courts may tax under [FRCP] 54(d)(1) are confined to the costs itemized in 28 U.S.C. §1920. [T]he discretion that Rule 54(d)(1) gives courts ... is discretion to decline requests for costs, not discretion to award costs that §1920 fails to enumerate. [¶] [R]ule 54(d) and §1920 do not permit district courts to impose costs on attorneys, as opposed to the parties they represent."

Andretti v. Borla Performance Indus., 426 F.3d 824, 835 (6th Cir.2005). "In the context of fee-shifting statutes, the Supreme Court has held that a plaintiff is a 'prevailing party' when he receives 'at least some relief on the merits of his claim,' even nominal damages. [F]or a party to be 'prevailing' there must be a 'judicially sanctioned change in the legal relationship of the parties.'" *See also* ***San Diego Police Officers' Ass'n v. San Diego City Employees' Ret. Sys.***, 568 F.3d 725, 742 (9th Cir.2009).

Carolina Power & Light Co. v. Dynegy Mktg. & Trade, 415 F.3d 354, 358 (4th Cir.2005). FRCP 54 "creates a division in the handling of attorneys fees claims between claims that are not part of the underlying substantive claim, which must be made by motion, and claims that are an element of damages, which presumably must be made by complaint." *See also* ***Riordan v. State Farm Mut. Auto. Ins.***, 589 F.3d 999, 1005 (9th Cir.2009).

Miltimore Sales, Inc. v. International Rectifier, Inc., 412 F.3d 685, 687-88 (6th Cir.2005). FRCP 54 "addresses petitions for attorney fees and the time within which a motion for fees must be filed. [¶] The first step in ascertaining whether a fee application is timely is determining when to start the clock. [P says] if a timely filed [FRCP] 59(e) motion prevents an appeal of the underlying judgment until the Rule 59(e) motion is disposed of, then logically, the judgment cannot be 'an order from which an appeal lies' until the disposition of the Rule 59(e) motion. We agree. *At 691:* [B]ecause a timely filed Rule 59(e) motion destroys the finality of judgment, a motion for attorney fees filed pursuant to [FRCP] 54(d)(2)(B) is timely if filed within 14 days of the order disposing of the Rule 59(e) motion."

BDT Prods. v. Lexmark Int'l, 405 F.3d 415, 417 (6th Cir.2005), *overruled on other grounds*, ***Taniguchi v. Kan Pac. Saipan, Ltd.***, ___ U.S. ___, 132 S.Ct. 1997 (2012). FRCP 54(d) "establishes that the prevailing party shall be allowed to recover its costs unless the court directs otherwise. Costs that may be taxed are specified in 28 U.S.C. §1920. The usual procedure is for the clerk to fix the costs, after which a motion may be made for judicial review of the clerk's decision.... 'The function of the court in the process of taxing costs is merely to review the determination of the clerk.' *At 418-19:* [D] argues that the language of Rule 54 is permis-

sive and that … §1920 expressly provides that either a 'judge or clerk' may tax costs. [D] urges the court to hold that 'Rule 54(d) … does not operate to divest the district court of its statutory and inherent authority to award costs without action by the clerk.' [¶] [T]here is no controlling case authority on this issue. We … hold that the district court has the inherent and statutory authority to act on motions related to costs prior to any action by the clerk based on the permissive language of Rule 54, the language of §1920, and the fact that any decision by the clerk would have been subject to *de novo* review by the district court."

Estate of Darulis v. Garate, 401 F.3d 1060, 1063 (9th Cir.2005). "[P] contends that because [Ds] failed to waive service of process, he is entitled to an award of the costs he incurred in effecting service on [Ds]. [¶] [Ds] do not contest [P's] assertion that they did not respond to his waiver requests, nor do they suggest [P's] requests did not satisfy the requirements of [FRCP] 4(d)(2) or that they had good cause for failing to respond. Rather, they argue—and the district court held—that because they are the prevailing party, they are entitled to costs pursuant to [FRCP] 54(d)(1), including any costs they would otherwise have to pay [P] pursuant to Rule 4(d)(2). [¶] We disagree with the district court's interpretation of the interplay between Rules 4(d)(2) and 54(d)(1). *At 1064:* In light of the express language of Rules 4(d)(2) and 54(d)(1), as well as the indications of the Advisory Committee's intent, we hold the district court abused its discretion in denying [P] an award of costs for service of process. Rule 4(d)(2) provides for an award of such costs regardless of which party can recover other costs pursuant to Rule 54(d)(1)."

Cherry v. Champion Int'l, 186 F.3d 442, 446 (4th Cir.1999). FRCP 54(d)(1) "creates the presumption that costs are to be awarded to the prevailing party. To overcome the presumption, a district court must justify its decision to deny costs by articulating some good reason for doing so. Costs may be denied to the prevailing party only when there would be an element of injustice in a presumptive cost award. [¶] [O]nly misconduct by the prevailing party worthy of a penalty or the losing party's inability to pay will suffice to justify denying costs. We have recognized additional factors to justify denying an award of costs, such as their excessiveness in a particular case, the limited value of the prevailing party's victory, or the closeness and difficulty of the issues decided. [T]he losing party's … good faith, standing alone, is an insufficient basis for refusing to assess costs against that party." (Internal quotes omitted.) *See also **McDonald v. Petree***, 409 F.3d 724, 732 (6th Cir. 2005) (court should ignore size of prevailing party's recovery and its ability to pay its own costs); ***In re Paoli R.R. Yard PCB Litig.***, 221 F.3d 449, 463 (3d Cir.2000) (court may consider losing party's indigence in determining costs).

Johnson v. Lafayette Fire Fighters Ass'n, 51 F.3d 726, 729 (7th Cir.1995). "[T]he Supreme Court and Congress have frequently used the [FRCPs] to adopt default rules of procedure that are modifiable by the districts through the adoption of local rules. We believe that the 14-day filing period contained in [FRCP] 54(d)(2)(B) is one such default rule and that the districts are free to modify the filing period through local rules."

FRCP 55. DEFAULT; DEFAULT JUDGMENT

(a) Entering a Default. When a party against whom a judgment for affirmative relief is sought has failed to plead or otherwise defend, and that failure is shown by affidavit or otherwise, the clerk must enter the party's default.

(b) Entering a Default Judgment.

(1) ***By the Clerk.*** If the plaintiff's claim is for a sum certain or a sum that can be made certain by computation, the clerk—on the plaintiff's request, with an affidavit showing the amount due—must enter judgment for that amount and costs against a defendant who has been defaulted for not appearing and who is neither a minor nor an incompetent person.

(2) ***By the Court.*** In all other cases, the party must apply to the court for a default judgment. A default judgment may be entered against a minor or incompetent person only if represented by a general guardian, conservator, or other like fiduciary who has appeared. If the party against whom a default judgment is sought has appeared personally or by a representative, that party or its representative must be served with written notice of the application at least 7 days before the hearing. The court may conduct hearings or make referrals—preserving any federal statutory right to a jury trial—when, to enter or effectuate judgment, it needs to:

(A) conduct an accounting;
(B) determine the amount of damages;
(C) establish the truth of any allegation by evidence; or
(D) investigate any other matter.

(c) **Setting Aside a Default or a Default Judgment.** The court may set aside an entry of default for good cause, and it may set aside a default judgment under Rule 60(b).

(d) **Judgment Against the United States.** A default judgment may be entered against the United States, its officers, or its agencies only if the claimant establishes a claim or right to relief by evidence that satisfies the court.

See selected Notes of Advisory Committee to FRCP 55, p. 1224.

History of FRCP 55: Adopted Dec. 20, 1937, eff. Sept. 16, 1938. Amended Mar. 2, 1987, eff. Aug. 1, 1987; Apr. 30, 2007, eff. Dec. 1, 2007; Mar. 26, 2009, eff. Dec. 1, 2009.

See *Commentaries*, "Default Judgment," ch. 7-A, p. 583; *O'Connor's Federal Civil Forms* (2012), FORMS 7A.

ANNOTATIONS

U.S. v. $23,000 in U.S. Currency, 356 F.3d 157, 164 (1st Cir.2004). FRCP 55(c) "applies different standards for setting aside an entry of default under Rule 55(a) and a judgment by default under Rule 55(b). A court may set aside an entry of default 'for good cause.' [T]he relevant factors are 'whether (1) the default was willful, (2) a set-aside would prejudice plaintiff, and (3) the alleged defense was meritorious.' By contrast, the court can set aside a final judgment by default only 'in accordance with [FRCP] 60(b).'"

Olcott v. Delaware Flood Co., 327 F.3d 1115, 1119 n.3 (10th Cir.2003). "Although the court termed the anticipated proceeding a 'trial,' the proceeding described is not a trial on the merits but a hearing to determine the amount of damages. Entry of default [under FRCP 55(b)(2)] precludes a trial on the merits. *At 1124:* Following the entry of default, [FRCP] 55(b)(2) authorizes the district court to conduct an evidentiary hearing to determine the amount of damages. [FRCP 55(b)(2)] does not contain an inherent jury requirement, but preserves the right to a jury 'when and as required by any statute of the U.S.'"

Rogers v. Hartford Life & Acc. Ins., 167 F.3d 933, 938 (5th Cir.1999). "Like formal service of process, a waiver of service of process marks the point in a lawsuit after which the defendant must answer or risk default. Waiver of service of process does not in any way indicate that a defendant intends to defend. Thus, like accepting formal service of process, executing a waiver of service of process does not constitute an appearance for purposes of Rule 55(b)(2)."

New York Life Ins. v. Brown, 84 F.3d 137, 141 (5th Cir.1996). "A *default* occurs when a defendant has failed to plead or otherwise respond to the complaint within the time required by the [FRCPs]. An *entry of default* is what the clerk enters when the default is established by affidavit or otherwise. After defendant's default has been entered, plaintiff may apply for a judgment based on such default. This is a *default judgment*."

Key Bank v. Tablecloth Textile Co., 74 F.3d 349, 353 (1st Cir.1996). "[A] defaulting party 'has appeared' for Rule 55 purposes if it has 'indicated to the moving party a clear purpose to defend the suit.' *At 354:* [O]nce [Ds] 'appeared' for Rule 55 purposes they were entitled to notice of the application for default judgment under Rule 55(b)(2)." *See also* ***New York v. Green***, 420 F.3d 99, 105 (2d Cir.2005).

Commercial Bank of Kuwait v. Rafidain Bank, 15 F.3d 238, 242 (2d Cir.1994). "Congress promulgated [28 U.S.C.] §1608(e) to provide foreign sovereigns with the same protections from default judgments that the federal government enjoys under [FRCP 55(e), now FRCP 55(d)]. However, ... the sovereign [is not relieved] from the duty to defend cases and to obey court orders. [¶] Thus, when the U.S. or a foreign sovereign defaults, the district court must determine whether the plaintiff's allegations are supported by evidence."

U.S. v. Timbers Preserve, 999 F.2d 452, 454 (10th Cir.1993). "Under [FRCP] 60(b), which standards [FRCP] 55(c) invokes when a party is seeking relief from a default judgment, a court may set aside a final judgment '[o]n motion and upon such terms as are just.' [¶] Courts have established three requirements which must be met when setting aside a default judgment under Rule 60(b): (1) the moving party's culpable conduct did not cause the default; (2) the moving party has a meritorious defense; and (3) the non-moving party will not be prejudiced by setting aside the judgment.... Generally a party's conduct will be considered culpable only if the party defaulted willfully or has no excuse for the default." *See also* ***Katzir's Floor & Home Design, Inc. v. M-MLS.com***, 394 F.3d 1143, 1148 n.1 (9th Cir.2004) (once default judgment has been entered, party must proceed under FRCP 60(b) to have judgment set aside).

Eitel v. McCool, 782 F.2d 1470, 1471-72 (9th Cir. 1986). Factors to consider when determining whether to grant a default judgment include: "(1) the possibility of prejudice to the plaintiff, (2) the merits of plaintiff's substantive claim, (3) the sufficiency of the complaint, (4) the sum of money at stake in the action, (5) the possibility of a dispute concerning material facts, (6) whether default was due to excusable neglect, and (7) the strong policy underlying the [FRCPs] favoring decisions on the merits."

FRCP 56. SUMMARY JUDGMENT

(a) Motion for Summary Judgment or Partial Summary Judgment. A party may move for summary judgment, identifying each claim or defense—or the part of each claim or defense—on which summary judgment is sought. The court shall grant summary judgment if the movant shows that there is no genuine dispute as to any material fact and the movant is entitled to judgment as a matter of law. The court should state on the record the reasons for granting or denying the motion.

(b) Time to File a Motion. Unless a different time is set by local rule or the court orders otherwise, a party may file a motion for summary judgment at any time until 30 days after the close of all discovery.

(c) Procedures.

(1) *Supporting Factual Positions.* A party asserting that a fact cannot be or is genuinely disputed must support the assertion by:

(A) citing to particular parts of materials in the record, including depositions, documents, electronically stored information, affidavits or declarations, stipulations (including those made for purposes of the motion only), admissions, interrogatory answers, or other materials; or

(B) showing that the materials cited do not establish the absence or presence of a genuine dispute, or that an adverse party cannot produce admissible evidence to support the fact.

(2) *Objection That a Fact Is Not Supported by Admissible Evidence.* A party may object that the material cited to support or dispute a fact cannot be presented in a form that would be admissible in evidence.

(3) *Materials Not Cited.* The court need consider only the cited materials, but it may consider other materials in the record.

(4) *Affidavits or Declarations.* An affidavit or declaration used to support or oppose a motion must be made on personal knowledge, set out facts that would be admissible in evidence, and show that the affiant or declarant is competent to testify on the matters stated.

(d) When Facts Are Unavailable to the Nonmovant. If a nonmovant shows by affidavit or declaration that, for specified reasons, it cannot present facts essential to justify its opposition, the court may:

(1) defer considering the motion or deny it;

(2) allow time to obtain affidavits or declarations or to take discovery; or

(3) issue any other appropriate order.

(e) Failing to Properly Support or Address a Fact. If a party fails to properly support an assertion of fact or fails to properly address another party's assertion of fact as required by Rule 56(c), the court may:

(1) give an opportunity to properly support or address the fact;

(2) consider the fact undisputed for purposes of the motion;

(3) grant summary judgment if the motion and supporting materials—including the facts considered undisputed—show that the movant is entitled to it; or

(4) issue any other appropriate order.

(f) Judgment Independent of the Motion. After giving notice and a reasonable time to respond, the court may:

(1) grant summary judgment for a nonmovant;

(2) grant the motion on grounds not raised by a party; or

(3) consider summary judgment on its own after identifying for the parties material facts that may not be genuinely in dispute.

(g) Failing to Grant All the Requested Relief. If the court does not grant all the relief requested by the motion, it may enter an order stating any material fact—including an item of damages or other relief—that is not genuinely in dispute and treating the fact as established in the case.

(h) Affidavit or Declaration Submitted in Bad Faith. If satisfied that an affidavit or declaration under this rule is submitted in bad faith or solely for delay, the court—after notice and a reasonable time to respond—may order the submitting party to pay the other party the reasonable expenses, including attorney's fees, it incurred as a result. An offending party or attorney may also be held in contempt or subjected to other appropriate sanctions.

See selected Notes of Advisory Committee to FRCP 56, p. 1224.

History of FRCP 56: Adopted Dec. 20, 1937, eff. Sept. 16, 1938. Amended Dec. 27, 1946, eff. Mar. 19, 1948; Jan. 21, 1963, eff. July 1, 1963; Mar. 2, 1987, eff. Aug. 1, 1987; Apr. 30, 2007, eff. Dec. 1, 2007; Mar. 26, 2009, eff. Dec. 1, 2009; Apr. 28, 2010, eff. Dec. 1, 2010.

See *Commentaries*, "Summary Judgment," ch. 7-B, p. 603; *O'Connor's Federal Civil Forms* (2012), FORMS 7B.

ANNOTATIONS

Generally

Wells Real Estate Inv. Trust II, Inc. v. Chardon/Hato Rey Prtshp., S.E., 615 F.3d 45, 51 (1st Cir.2010). "Cross-motions for summary judgment do not alter the summary judgment standard, but instead simply 'require us to determine whether either of the parties deserves judgment as a matter of law on the facts that are not disputed.' Although it is well-settled that the court must decide each motion for summary judgment on its own merits, this does not mean that 'each motion must be considered in a vacuum. Where … cross-motions for summary judgment are filed simultaneously, or nearly so, the district court ordinarily should consider the two motions at the same time,' applying the same standards to each motion."

Hoffman v. Tonnemacher, 593 F.3d 908, 911 (9th Cir.2010). FRCP 56 "does not limit the number of motions that may be filed. … Rule 56 … does not bar successive motions. [¶] [W]e have held that, in effect, the possibility of summary judgment remains on the table even after a district court has denied a summary judgment motion because that order is 'subject to reconsideration by the court at any time.' [A]llowing a party to file a second motion for summary judgment is logical, and it fosters the 'just, speedy, and inexpensive' resolution of suits. Nevertheless, we are conscious of the potential for abuse of the procedure and reiterate here that district courts retain discretion to 'weed out frivolous or simply repetitive motions.' [¶] In holding that district courts have discretion to permit successive motions for summary judgment, we join at least five of our sister circuits."

Carter v. Ford Motor Co., 561 F.3d 562, 565 (6th Cir.2009). "The issue in a challenge to the sufficiency of a pleading is notice. *At 567:* Had the challenge to the sufficiency of [P's] pleading arisen in the context of a [FRCP] 12(b)(6) motion, the district court would have applied the 'extremely modest standard' of notice pleading, which 'direct[s] courts to construe plead-ing[s] liberally.' But there is a 'crucial' 'difference in timing' when the sufficiency of a complaint arises at the summary judgment stage after 'a plaintiff has had an opportunity for discovery.' *At 568:* 'Once a case has progressed to the summary judgment stage … the liberal pleading standards … are inapplicable.'"

Timmerman v. U.S. Bank, 483 F.3d 1106, 1112 (10th Cir.2007). "[O]ne value implicit in [FRCP] 56 is that each party to a summary judgment motion, both moving and non-moving, be given an adequate opportunity to present argument and evidence supporting its respective position. We can imagine a case where a page limitation … would be an abuse of discretion, and so district courts should remain flexible in the application of such a limitation. Nonetheless, [P] has not demonstrated that the district court's 20-page limitation [is] an abuse of discretion."

SJ Burden—Movant

Celotex Corp. v. Catrett, 477 U.S. 317, 322 (1986). FRCP 56 "mandates the entry of summary judgment, after adequate time for discovery and upon motion, against a party who fails to make a showing sufficient to establish the existence of an element essential to that party's case, and on which that party will bear the burden of proof at trial. *At 324:* [T]he nonmoving party [must] go beyond the pleadings and by her own affidavits, or by the 'depositions, answers to interrogatories, and admissions on file,' designate 'specific facts showing that there is a genuine issue for trial.' *At 327:* Rule 56 must be construed with due regard not only for the rights of persons asserting claims and defenses … to have those claims and defenses tried to a jury, but also for the rights of persons opposing such claims and defenses to demonstrate … prior to trial, that the claims and defenses have no factual basis."

Adickes v. S.H. Kress & Co., 398 U.S. 144, 157 (1970). To support a motion for summary judgment, "the moving party [has] the burden of showing the absence of a genuine issue as to any material fact, and for these purposes the material it lodged must be viewed in the light most favorable to the opposing party."

SJ Burden—Nonmovant

Scott v. Harris, 550 U.S. 372, 380-81 (2007). "[W]hen the moving party has carried its [summary-judgment] burden ..., its opponent must do more than simply show that there is some metaphysical doubt as to the material facts. Where the record taken as a whole could not lead a rational trier of fact to find for the nonmoving party, there is no genuine issue for trial. The mere existence of *some* alleged factual dispute between the parties will not defeat an otherwise properly supported motion for summary judgment; the requirement is that there be no *genuine* issue of *material* fact. When opposing parties tell two different stories, one of which is blatantly contradicted by the record, so that no reasonable jury could believe it, a court should not adopt that version of the facts for purposes of ruling on a motion for summary judgment. [¶] [P's] version of events is so utterly discredited by [the videotape in] the record that no reasonable jury could have believed him. [The lower court] should have viewed the facts in the light depicted by the videotape." (Internal quotes omitted.) *See also* ***Matsushita Elec. Indus. Co. v. Zenith Radio Corp.***, 475 U.S. 574, 586-87 (1986); ***Holcomb v. Powell***, 433 F.3d 889, 895 (D.C.Cir.2006).

Payne v. Pauley, 337 F.3d 767, 771 (7th Cir.2003). "We have routinely found that a nonmoving party's own affidavit can constitute affirmative evidence to defeat a summary judgment motion. *At 773:* [A] self-serving affidavit is an acceptable method for a non-moving party to present evidence of disputed material facts."

SJ Evidence

Beard v. Banks, 548 U.S. 521, 529-30 (2006). "We recognize that at [the summary-judgment] stage we must draw 'all justifiable inferences' in [P's] 'favor.' In doing so, however, we must distinguish between evidence of disputed facts and disputed matters of professional judgment."

Lujan v. National Wildlife Fed'n, 497 U.S. 871, 888 (1990). "The object of [FRCP 56] is not to replace conclusory allegations of the complaint or answer with conclusory allegations of an affidavit."

In re Family Dollar FLSA Litig., 637 F.3d 508, 512-13 (4th Cir.2011). A movant "cannot create a dispute about a fact that is contained in deposition testimony by referring to a subsequent affidavit of the deponent contradicting the deponent's prior testimony, for 'it is well established that a genuine issue of fact is not created where the only issue of fact is to determine which of the two conflicting versions of a party's testimony is correct.' ... 'If a party who has been examined at length on deposition could raise an issue of fact simply by submitting an affidavit contradicting his own prior testimony, this would greatly diminish the utility of summary judgment as a procedure for screening out sham issues of fact.'"

Johnson v. Weld Cty., 594 F.3d 1202, 1210 (10th Cir.2010). FRCP 56 "permits parties at summary judgment to produce their evidence by means of affidavit, a *form* of evidence that is usually inadmissible at trial given our adversarial system's preference for live testimony. Yet, ... Rule 56 does not suggest we enjoy a license to relax the *content* or *substance* of the [FREs] when viewing a summary judgment affidavit: [FRCP 56] does nothing to intimate 'hearsay testimony that would be inadmissible at trial' somehow becomes admissible simply by being 'included in an affidavit to defeat summary judgment.' To the contrary, Rule 56 expressly prescribes that a summary judgment affidavit must 'be made on personal knowledge, set forth facts that would be admissible in evidence, and show that the affiant is competent to testify on the matters stated.' [¶] So it is that, although evidence presented in the form of an affidavit at summary judgment can be 'converted' in form into live testimony at trial, the content or substance of the affidavit must be otherwise admissible, and any hearsay contained in a summary judgment affidavit remains hearsay, beyond the bounds of the court's consideration." *See also* ***Juarez v. Menard, Inc.***, 366 F.3d 479, 484 n.4 (7th Cir.2004); ***Bailey v. Floyd Cty. Bd. of Educ.***, 106 F.3d 135, 145 (6th Cir. 1997).

Velázquez-García v. Horizon Lines, 473 F.3d 11, 17 (1st Cir.2007). "[T]he distinction in Rule 56 between 'specific facts' and 'mere allegations' is important. *At 18:* [W]hether a nonmovant's deposition testimony or affidavits might be self-serving is not dispositive. It is true that testimony and affidavits that 'merely reiterate allegations made in the complaint, without providing specific factual information made on the basis of personal knowledge' are insufficient. However, a 'party's own affidavit, containing relevant information of which he has first-hand knowledge, may be self-serving, but it is nonetheless competent to support or defeat summary judgment.'"

Club Italia Soccer & Sports Org. v. Charter Township of Shelby, Mich., 470 F.3d 286, 295 (6th Cir. 2006). "[A] plaintiff need not supply an affidavit setting forth facts unless those facts are actually contested."

Payne v. Pauley, 337 F.3d 767, 772 (7th Cir.2003). "[A]lthough personal knowledge may include reasonable inferences, those inferences must be 'grounded in observation or other first-hand personal experience. They must not be flights of fancy, speculations, hunches, intuitions, or rumors about matters remote from that experience.'" *See also* ***Cadle Co. v. Hayes***, 116 F.3d 957, 961 (1st Cir.1997) (statements must be based on personal knowledge, not on information and belief).

TFWS, Inc. v. Schaefer, 325 F.3d 234, 241 (4th Cir. 2003). "'The fact that both parties simultaneously are arguing [under FRCP 56] that there is no genuine issue of fact does not establish that a trial is unnecessary thereby empowering the court to enter judgment as it sees fit.' In other words, '[a] district court may not resolve conflicts in the evidence on summary judgment motions.'"

Rodgers v. Monumental Life Ins., 289 F.3d 442, 448 (6th Cir.2002). "An issue of fact is 'genuine' if the evidence is such that a reasonable trier of fact could return a verdict for the nonmovant. The substantive law identifies facts that are 'material.' Facts are 'material' only if establishment thereof might affect the outcome of the lawsuit under governing substantive law. A complete failure of proof concerning an essential element necessarily renders all other facts immaterial." *See also* ***SEC v. Ficken***, 546 F.3d 45, 51 (1st Cir.2008).

Amnesty Am. v. Town of W. Hartford, 288 F.3d 467, 470-71 (2d Cir.2002). FRCP 56 "does not impose an obligation on a district court to perform an independent review of the record to find proof of a factual dispute. [D]istrict courts are entitled to order litigants to provide specific record citations. [¶] [I]n the absence of a local rule, a district court may not grant summary judgment on the ground that the nonmovant's papers failed to cite to the record unless the parties are given actual notice of the requirement. [¶] [A]ctual notice or the existence of a local rule providing notice is a precondition to the imposition of a sanction for failing to comply with a citation requirement."

Schoonejongen v. Curtiss-Wright Corp., 143 F.3d 120, 130 (3d Cir.1998). "[C]ertain scenarios may arise where a material fact cannot be resolved without weighing the credibility of a particular witness or individual—such as when the defendant's liability turns on an individual's state of mind and the plaintiff has presented circumstantial evidence probative of intent. In such a case, ... summary judgment is inappropriate because there is a sufficient quantum of evidence on either side for reasonable minds to differ and therefore the issue is 'genuine.' [I]ssues of credibility only defeat summary judgment '[w]here an issue of material fact *cannot be resolved* without observation of the demeanor of witnesses in order to evaluate their credibility.'"

Colon v. Coughlin, 58 F.3d 865, 872 (2d Cir.1995). "A verified complaint is to be treated as an affidavit for summary judgment purposes...."

Motion for Continuance

Nader v. Blair, 549 F.3d 953, 961 (4th Cir.2008). "[A] party generally must comply with [FRCP] 56(f) [now FRCP 56(d)], which requires that it set out the reasons for discovery in an affidavit [or declaration], and it cannot withstand a motion for summary judgment by merely asserting in its brief that discovery was necessary. Nevertheless, strict compliance with Rule 56(f) [now Rule 56(d)] ... may not be necessary where the circumstances are such that 'the nonmoving party, through no fault of its own, has had little or no opportunity to conduct discovery, and when fact-intensive issues, such as intent, are involved,' provided that 'the nonmoving party has adequately informed the district court that the motion is premature and that more discovery is necessary.'" *See also* ***Stults v. Conoco, Inc.***, 76 F.3d 651, 657-58 (5th Cir.1996) (party must indicate by some statement, in writing but not necessarily by affidavit, why additional discovery is necessary and how it will create a genuine issue of material fact). *But see* ***Hackworth v. Progressive Cas. Ins.***, this page.

Hackworth v. Progressive Cas. Ins., 468 F.3d 722, 732-33 (10th Cir.2006). "The crux of Rule 56(f) [now Rule 56(d)] is that 'summary judgment [should] be refused where the nonmoving party has not had the opportunity to discover information that is essential to his opposition.' The nonmoving party, however, ... must satisfy certain requirements. [S]pecifically, the nonmovant must submit an affidavit [or declaration] 'identifying the probable facts not available and what steps

have been taken to obtain these facts' and must 'explain how additional time will enable him to rebut movant's allegations of no genuine issue of fact.' [¶] A nonmoving party wishing to invoke ... Rule 56(f) [now Rule 56(d)] must attempt to do so by submitting an affidavit [or declaration] in direct response to a motion for summary judgment, not following the district court's disposition of that motion. [T]he district court ... does not [have] the power to vacate a prior grant of summary judgment so that additional discovery can be conducted." *See also* ***Davis v. G.N. Mortg. Corp.***, 396 F.3d 869, 885-86 (7th Cir.2005). *But see* ***Nader v. Blair***, p. 953.

Employers Teamsters Local Nos. 175 & 505 Pension Trust Fund v. Clorox Co., 353 F.3d 1125, 1129-30 (9th Cir.2004). "To prevail under [FRCP 56(f), now FRCP 56(d)], parties opposing a motion for summary judgment must make '(a) a timely application which (b) specifically identifies (c) relevant information, (d) where there is some basis for believing that the information sought actually exists.' 'The burden is on the party seeking additional discovery to proffer sufficient facts to show that the evidence sought exists, and that it would prevent summary judgment.' 'The district court does not abuse its discretion by denying further discovery if the movant has failed diligently to pursue discovery in the past, or if the movant fails to show how the information sought would preclude summary judgment.'"

Allen v. CSX Transp., 325 F.3d 768, 775 (6th Cir. 2003). "A party who opposes a motion for summary judgment by seeking additional discovery ... 'has no absolute right to additional time for discovery.... The nonmoving party must show how postponement of a ruling on the motion will enable him to rebut the motion for summary judgment.'" *See also* ***Thomas v. Pacificorp***, 324 F.3d 1176, 1179 (10th Cir.2003).

Ruling

Anderson v. Liberty Lobby, Inc., 477 U.S. 242, 252 (1986). "[A] judge must ask himself not whether he thinks the evidence unmistakably favors one side or the other but whether a fair-minded jury could return a verdict for [nonmovant] on the evidence presented. The mere existence of a scintilla of evidence in support of [nonmovant's] position will be insufficient; there must be evidence on which the jury could reasonably find for [nonmovant]."

Johnson v. Diversicare Afton Oaks, LLC, 597 F.3d 673, 676 (5th Cir.2010). "In a non-jury case, ... 'a district court has somewhat greater discretion to consider what weight it will accord the evidence.' When deciding a motion for summary judgment prior to a bench trial, the district court 'has the limited discretion to decide that the same evidence, presented to him or her as a trier of fact in a plenary trial, could not possibly lead to a different result.'"

Appeal

Michalik v. Hermann, 422 F.3d 252, 257 (5th Cir. 2005). "The denial of a motion for summary judgment is generally not a final, appealable order over which we have jurisdiction. Under the collateral order doctrine, however, a small class of interlocutory orders that (1) conclusively determine, (2) important issues, which are separate from the merits of the action, and (3) which would be effectively unreviewable on appeal from a final judgment, are deemed 'final' for the purposes of appeal." (Internal quotes omitted.)

FRCP 57. DECLARATORY JUDGMENT

These rules govern the procedure for obtaining a declaratory judgment under 28 U.S.C. §2201. Rules 38 and 39 govern a demand for a jury trial. The existence of another adequate remedy does not preclude a declaratory judgment that is otherwise appropriate. The court may order a speedy hearing of a declaratory-judgment action.

History of FRCP 57: Adopted Dec. 20, 1937, eff. Sept. 16, 1938. Amended Dec. 29, 1948, eff. Oct. 20, 1949; Apr. 30, 2007, eff. Dec. 1, 2007.

See ***Commentaries***, "Declaratory Judgment," ch. 2-E, p. 107; ***O'Connor's Federal Civil Forms*** (2012), FORMS 2E.

See also 28 U.S.C. §§2201, 2202 (creation of remedy in declaratory judgment actions).

ANNOTATIONS

Wilton v. Seven Falls Co., 515 U.S. 277, 288 (1995). "By the Declaratory Judgment Act, Congress sought to place a remedial arrow in the district court's quiver; it created an opportunity, rather than a duty, to grant a new form of relief to qualifying litigants. Consistent with the nonobligatory nature of the remedy, a district court is authorized, in the sound exercise of its discretion, to stay or to dismiss an action seeking a declaratory judgment before trial or after all arguments have drawn to a close. In the declaratory judgment context, the normal principle that federal courts should adjudicate claims within their jurisdiction yields to considerations of practicality and wise judicial administration."

Golden v. Zwickler, 394 U.S. 103, 108 (1969). "The difference between an abstract question and a 'controversy' contemplated by the Declaratory Judgment Act is necessarily one of degree, and it would be difficult … to fashion a precise test for determining in every case whether there is such a controversy. Basically, the question in each case is whether the facts alleged, under all the circumstances, show that there is a substantial controversy, between parties having adverse legal interests, of sufficient immediacy and reality to warrant the issuance of a declaratory judgment." (Internal quotes omitted.)

Beacon Theatres, Inc. v. Westover, 359 U.S. 500, 504 (1959). "[I]f [D] would have been entitled to a jury trial in a treble damages suit against [P] it cannot be deprived of that right merely because [P] took advantage of the availability of declaratory relief to sue … first."

FRCP 58. ENTERING JUDGMENT

(a) Separate Document. Every judgment and amended judgment must be set out in a separate document, but a separate document is not required for an order disposing of a motion:

(1) for judgment under Rule 50(b);

(2) to amend or make additional findings under Rule 52(b);

(3) for attorney's fees under Rule 54;

(4) for a new trial, or to alter or amend the judgment, under Rule 59; or

(5) for relief under Rule 60.

(b) Entering Judgment.

(1) ***Without the Court's Direction.*** Subject to Rule 54(b) and unless the court orders otherwise, the clerk must, without awaiting the court's direction, promptly prepare, sign, and enter the judgment when:

(A) the jury returns a general verdict;

(B) the court awards only costs or a sum certain; or

(C) the court denies all relief.

(2) ***Court's Approval Required.*** Subject to Rule 54(b), the court must promptly approve the form of the judgment, which the clerk must promptly enter, when:

(A) the jury returns a special verdict or a general verdict with answers to written questions; or

(B) the court grants other relief not described in this subdivision (b).

(c) Time of Entry. For purposes of these rules, judgment is entered at the following times:

(1) if a separate document is not required, when the judgment is entered in the civil docket under Rule 79(a); or

(2) if a separate document is required, when the judgment is entered in the civil docket under Rule 79(a) and the earlier of these events occurs:

(A) it is set out in a separate document; or

(B) 150 days have run from the entry in the civil docket.

(d) Request for Entry. A party may request that judgment be set out in a separate document as required by Rule 58(a).

(e) Cost or Fee Awards. Ordinarily, the entry of judgment may not be delayed, nor the time for appeal extended, in order to tax costs or award fees. But if a timely motion for attorney's fees is made under Rule 54(d)(2), the court may act before a notice of appeal has been filed and become effective to order that the motion have the same effect under Federal Rule of Appellate Procedure 4(a)(4) as a timely motion under Rule 59.

See selected Notes of Advisory Committee to FRCP 58, p. 1228.

History of FRCP 58: Adopted Dec. 20, 1937, eff. Sept. 16, 1938. Amended Dec. 27, 1946, eff. Mar. 19, 1948; Jan. 21, 1963, eff. July 1, 1963; Apr. 22, 1993, eff. Dec. 1, 1993; Apr. 29, 2002, eff. Dec. 1, 2002; Apr. 30, 2007, eff. Dec. 1, 2007.

See ***Commentaries***, "Entry of Judgment," ch. 9-A, p. 735; ***O'Connor's Federal Civil Forms*** (2012), FORMS 9B.

ANNOTATIONS

Bankers Trust Co. v. Mallis, 435 U.S. 381, 386 (1978). FRCP 58(a)'s "separate-document rule must be 'mechanically applied' in determining whether an appeal is timely. Technical application of the separate-judgment requirement is necessary in that context to avoid the uncertainties that once plagued the determination of when an appeal must be brought. The need for certainty as to the timeliness of an appeal, however, should not prevent the parties from waiving the separate-judgment requirement where one has accidentally not been entered. '[FRCP 58(a)] is designed to simplify and make certain the matter of appealability. It is not designed as a trap for the inexperienced. [FRCP 58(a)] should be interpreted to prevent loss of the right of appeal, not to facilitate loss.'" *See also* ***Peng v. Peng Hu***,

335 F.3d 970, 975 n.4 (9th Cir.2003) (decision to waive entry of separate judgment belongs to appellant).

Stephanie-Cardona LLC v. Smith's Food & Drug Ctrs., Inc., 476 F.3d 701, 703 (9th Cir.2007). FRAP 4 and FRCP 58 "set forth the framework for determining when the time to appeal begins to run. Subject to some exceptions, [FRAP 4] requires a notice of appeal to be filed within 30 days 'after the ... order appealed from is entered.' In turn, [FRAP 4(a)(7)(A) and FRCP 58(b), now FRCP 58(c),] define what it means for a final order or judgment to be entered. Although ... every judgment [must] be set forth on a separate document, judgment may be deemed entered even if the district court fails to comply with that requirement. ... Thus, even if the district court does not set forth the judgment on a separate document, an appealable final order is considered entered when 150 days have run from the time the final order is docketed. Under [FRAP] 4(a)(1)(A), an appellant must then file a notice of appeal within 30 days after the end of that 150-day period."

Long v. County of L.A., 442 F.3d 1178, 1184 n.3 (9th Cir.2006). "[W]here the district court's order is a full adjudication of the issues and clearly evidences the judge's intention that it be the court's final act in the matter, the filing of an appeal, in conjunction with the parties proceeding before the appellate court as if a separate judgment had been entered, indicates an acknowledgment by the parties that a final judgment has been entered. A mechanical application of Rule 58 is not required when the parties and the judge all have indicated that they treat a district court entry as a final, separate judgment."

Alinsky v. U.S., 415 F.3d 639, 643 (7th Cir.2005). "The question then becomes when did the district court 'enter' a final judgment in the ... case. [T]he district court issued its Memorandum Opinion and Order ..., and that order was docketed.... However, [t]he district court had also prepared a Rule 58 judgment, ... but that form was mistakenly stapled to the end of the Memorandum Opinion and Order and not separately docketed at that time. Because the judgment form was not a separate document, ... we conclude that judgment ... was not 'entered'...."

Houston v. Greiner, 174 F.3d 287, 288-89 (2d Cir. 1999). "The time for filing a notice of appeal from a final judgment or order runs from the date the judgment or order 'is entered.' 'Entry of judgment,' which is required by [FRCP] 58, is the act of recording in a docket maintained by the clerk of a court the fact that a judgment has been rendered. The 'entry' date is not necessarily the same date that the judgment is dated, *i.e.*, signed by the judge or court clerk, nor the same date that it is filed, *i.e.*, date- and time-stamped as officially received by the clerk's office, thereby then formally becoming part of the clerk's office file. [¶] Every docket entry shows, in the left-hand column of the docket sheet, the date that the document being entered on the docket was *filed*. The docket entry then states the general nature of the document being entered, including, in the case of a judgment, the 'substance' of the judgment. Some, *but not all*, docket entries include a notation that explicitly shows the date the document was *entered*. [¶] We are informed that the computer program used in district courts for making docket entries in *civil* cases is designed to show an explicit notation of an entry date *only when the entry date is later than the filing date*. [¶] This absence of an explicit entry date arguably violates [FRCP] 79...." *See also* ***U.S. v. Fiorelli***, 337 F.3d 282, 287 (3d Cir.2003).

National Distrib. Agency v. Nationwide Mut. Ins., 117 F.3d 432, 434 (9th Cir.1997). "A district court ruling is not final if the court reserves the option of further modifying its ruling. This rule is easily complied with and avoids confusion as to the time for appeal."

Otis v. City of Chi., 29 F.3d 1159, 1163 (7th Cir. 1994). "Rule 58 is designed to produce a distinct indication that the case is at an end, coupled with a precise statement of the terms on which it has ended. It should be a self-contained document, saying who has won and what relief has been awarded, but omitting the reasons for this disposition, which should appear in the court's opinion. [¶] Rule 58 puts the onus of preparing a judgment squarely on the shoulders of the clerk of the district court."

FRCP 59. NEW TRIAL; ALTERING OR AMENDING A JUDGMENT

(a) In General.

(1) ***Grounds for New Trial.*** The court may, on motion, grant a new trial on all or some of the issues—and to any party—as follows:

(A) after a jury trial, for any reason for which a new trial has heretofore been granted in an action at law in federal court; or

(B) after a nonjury trial, for any reason for which a rehearing has heretofore been granted in a suit in equity in federal court.

(2) *Further Action After a Nonjury Trial.* After a nonjury trial, the court may, on motion for a new trial, open the judgment if one has been entered, take additional testimony, amend findings of fact and conclusions of law or make new ones, and direct the entry of a new judgment.

(b) Time to File a Motion for a New Trial. A motion for a new trial must be filed no later than 28 days after the entry of judgment.

(c) Time to Serve Affidavits. When a motion for a new trial is based on affidavits, they must be filed with the motion. The opposing party has 14 days after being served to file opposing affidavits. The court may permit reply affidavits.

(d) New Trial on the Court's Initiative or for Reasons Not in the Motion. No later than 28 days after the entry of judgment, the court, on its own, may order a new trial for any reason that would justify granting one on a party's motion. After giving the parties notice and an opportunity to be heard, the court may grant a timely motion for a new trial for a reason not stated in the motion. In either event, the court must specify the reasons in its order.

(e) Motion to Alter or Amend a Judgment. A motion to alter or amend a judgment must be filed no later than 28 days after the entry of the judgment.

See selected Notes of Advisory Committee to FRCP 59, p. 1229.

History of FRCP 59: Adopted Dec. 20, 1937, eff. Sept. 16, 1938. Amended Dec. 27, 1946, eff. Mar. 19, 1948; Feb. 28, 1966, eff. July 1, 1966; Apr. 27, 1995, eff. Dec. 1995; Apr. 30, 2007, eff. Dec. 1, 2007; Mar. 26, 2009, eff. Dec. 1, 2009.

See ***Commentaries***, "Motion for New Trial," ch. 10-C, p. 783; "Motion to Alter or Amend Judgment," ch. 10-D, p. 793; ***O'Connor's Federal Civil Forms*** (2012), FORMS 10C; FORMS 10D.

ANNOTATIONS

Gasperini v. Center for Humanities, Inc., 518 U.S. 415, 433 (1996). "'The trial judge in the federal system' ... 'has ... discretion to grant a new trial if the verdict appears ... to be against the weight of the evidence.' This discretion includes overturning verdicts for excessiveness and ordering a new trial without qualification, or conditioned on the verdict winner's refusal to agree to a reduction (remittitur). *At 437 n.22:* It is ... 'Hornbook' law that a most usual ground for a Rule 59 motion is that 'the damages are excessive.'"

Osterneck v. Ernst & Whinney, 489 U.S. 169, 175 (1989). "[A] postjudgment motion for discretionary prejudgment interest constitutes a motion to alter or amend the judgment under Rule 59(e)." *See also* ***Redondo Constr. Corp. v. Puerto Rico Hwy. & Transp. Auth.***, 678 F.3d 115, 122 (1st Cir.2012) (grant or denial of prejudgment interest can be raised for first time in FRCP 59(e) motion).

Smart Mktg. Grp. v. Publications Int'l, 624 F.3d 824, 832 (7th Cir.2010). "A district court is entitled to find that an award is unsupported by the evidence and thus that a motion for a new trial under [FRCP] 59 should be granted, even if there was enough evidence in the record to justify sending the issue to the jury in the first instance (a finding that would require denial of a motion for judgment as a matter of law under [FRCP] 50)."

Leisure Caviar, LLC v. U.S. Fish & Wildlife Serv., 616 F.3d 612, 615-16 (6th Cir.2010). See annotation under FRCP 15, *FRCP 15(a)*, p. 865.

Zinkand v. Brown, 478 F.3d 634, 637 (4th Cir. 2007). "Rule 59(e), in essence, gives the district court a chance to correct its own mistake if it believes one has been made. [T]he court ... has some discretion to determine whether additional evidence should be considered or further argument heard. If the court elects to look at additional evidence represented as having been unavailable at the prior hearing, the court must satisfy itself as to the unavailability of the evidence and likewise examine the justification for its omission."

Borrero v. City of Chi., 456 F.3d 698, 699-700 (7th Cir.2006). "[W]e and most other courts do not cavil if ... the [FRCP 59(e)] motion is filed *before* the [FRCP] 58 judgment order has been docketed or even before there *is* a Rule 58 judgment, provided that a final judgment has been rendered. Rule 58 prescribes a formality, a useful one but not one that is prerequisite to appealing. The losing party can appeal a judgment ... before the entry of the Rule 58 judgment order if[,] though not embodied in the separate document that Rule 58 requires[,] the judgment really is final within the meaning of 28 U.S.C. §1291. And that just means: if the district judge is finished with the case. By the same token, the party should be allowed to file a motion to alter or amend the judgment within the time permitted for such motions even if the Rule 58 judgment order has not yet been made or docketed." *See also* ***Jones v. UNUM Life Ins.***, 223 F.3d 130, 136 (2d Cir.2000).

Harrington v. City of Chi., 433 F.3d 542, 546 (7th Cir.2006). "Altering or amending a judgment under [FRCP] 59(e) is permissible when there is newly dis-

covered evidence or there has been a manifest error of law or fact. Vacating a judgment under [FRCP] 60(b) is permissible for a variety of reasons including mistake, excusable neglect, newly discovered evidence, and fraud. While the two rules have similarities, Rule 60(b) relief is an extraordinary remedy and is granted only in exceptional circumstances. Rule 59(e), by contrast, requires that the movant clearly establish one of the … grounds for relief. [¶] [Although Ps' attorney] filed the motion within [the time limit of] Rule 59(e)[, the] motion [is] a Rule 60(b) motion because the only arguable basis for relief presented in the motion is Rule 60(b)'s excusable neglect. … Rule 59(e) does not provide a vehicle for a party to undo its own procedural failures, which is precisely what [Ps' attorney] attempts in the motion here. [T]he motion in this case not only did not mention Rule 59(e); it was not captioned a motion to alter or amend judgment, which is the language of that rule, and indeed used the word 'vacate,' which is the language of Rule 60(b). … If a litigant wants the benefit of whatever lower threshold of proof Rule 59(e) may offer, it behooves him to indicate that his motion is under Rule 59(e)." (Internal quotes omitted.) *See also* ***Rosenzweig v. Azurix Corp.***, 332 F.3d 854, 863-64 (5th Cir.2003); ***Zukowski v. St. Lukes Home Care Program***, 326 F.3d 278, 282 n.3 (1st Cir.2003).

Credit Suisse First Boston Corp. v. Grunwald, 400 F.3d 1119, 1123 n.6 (9th Cir.2005). FRCP 59(e) "applies to '[a]ny motion to alter or amend a judgment,' and under [FRCP] 54(a), a *judgment* is defined to include 'any order from which an appeal lies.' Because 28 U.S.C. §1292(a)(1) establishes appellate jurisdiction over an appeal from a preliminary injunction, a preliminary injunction order is a 'judgment' and is therefore subject to Rule 59(e)…."

Anderson v. Siemens Corp., 335 F.3d 466, 475-76 (5th Cir.2003). "[P]artial new trials should not be resorted to unless it appears that the issue to be retried is so distinct and separable from the others that a trial of it alone may be had without injustice. Thus, in cases where the issues subject to retrial are so interwoven with other issues in the case that they cannot be submitted to the jury independently without confusion and uncertainty, which would amount to a denial of a fair trial, then it is proper to grant a new trial on all of the issues raised." (Internal quotes omitted.) *See also* ***Rice v. Community Health Ass'n***, 203 F.3d 283, 290 (4th Cir.2000).

Schobert v. Illinois DOT, 304 F.3d 725, 729 (7th Cir.2002). "When a motion for a new trial under [FRCP] 59 is based on a challenge to jury instructions, we consider a trial court's jury instructions with deference, analyzing them as a whole to determine if they accurately stated the law and did not confuse the jury."

Farm Credit Bank v. Guidry, 110 F.3d 1147, 1154 (5th Cir.1997). "Under [FRCP] 59, a new trial may be granted on the basis of newly discovered evidence if '(1) the facts discovered are of such a nature that they would probably change the outcome; (2) the facts alleged are actually newly discovered and could not have been discovered earlier by proper diligence; and (3) the facts are not merely cumulative or impeaching.' [The court joins other] circuits that have recognized the rule that facts known to a party before trial, even though they were not disclosed to his attorney until after trial, need not be regarded as 'newly discovered' facts for purposes of Rule 59."

FRCP 60. RELIEF FROM A JUDGMENT OR ORDER

(a) Corrections Based on Clerical Mistakes; Oversights and Omissions. The court may correct a clerical mistake or a mistake arising from oversight or omission whenever one is found in a judgment, order, or other part of the record. The court may do so on motion or on its own, with or without notice. But after an appeal has been docketed in the appellate court and while it is pending, such a mistake may be corrected only with the appellate court's leave.

(b) Grounds for Relief from a Final Judgment, Order, or Proceeding. On motion and just terms, the court may relieve a party or its legal representative from a final judgment, order, or proceeding for the following reasons:

(1) mistake, inadvertence, surprise, or excusable neglect;

(2) newly discovered evidence that, with reasonable diligence, could not have been discovered in time to move for a new trial under Rule 59(b);

(3) fraud (whether previously called intrinsic or extrinsic), misrepresentation, or misconduct by an opposing party;

(4) the judgment is void;

(5) the judgment has been satisfied, released, or discharged; it is based on an earlier judgment

that has been reversed or vacated; or applying it prospectively is no longer equitable; or

(6) any other reason that justifies relief.

(c) **Timing and Effect of the Motion.**

(1) *Timing.* A motion under Rule 60(b) must be made within a reasonable time—and for reasons (1), (2), and (3) no more than a year after the entry of the judgment or order or the date of the proceeding.

(2) *Effect on Finality.* The motion does not affect the judgment's finality or suspend its operation.

(d) **Other Powers to Grant Relief.** This rule does not limit a court's power to:

(1) entertain an independent action to relieve a party from a judgment, order, or proceeding;

(2) grant relief under 28 U.S.C. §1655 to a defendant who was not personally notified of the action; or

(3) set aside a judgment for fraud on the court.

(e) **Bills and Writs Abolished.** The following are abolished: bills of review, bills in the nature of bills of review, and writs of coram nobis, coram vobis, and audita querela.

See selected Notes of Advisory Committee to FRCP 60, p. 1229.

History of FRCP 60: Adopted Dec. 20, 1937, eff. Sept. 16, 1938. Amended Dec. 27, 1946, eff. Mar. 19, 1948; Dec. 29, 1948, eff. Oct. 20, 1949; Mar. 2, 1987, eff. Aug. 1, 1987; Apr. 30, 2007, eff. Dec. 1, 2007.

See ***Commentaries***, "Motion for Relief from Judgment," ch. 10-F, p. 804; "Motion to Correct Clerical Error in Judgment," ch. 10-I, p. 825; ***O'Connor's Federal Civil Forms*** (2012), FORMS 10F; FORMS 10I.

ANNOTATIONS

Generally

F.A.C., Inc. v. Cooperativa de Seguros de Vida, 449 F.3d 185, 191 (1st Cir.2006). "The judge's authority to amend the judgment is perhaps clearest where the judgment as entered merely failed to express the court's intention. Here, within a few months of the original … judgment, both the judge and parties acted *as if* the court had originally intended to reserve authority to superintend enforcement. The inference that this was the judge's *original* intention is not especially strong, but it is at least colorable. [¶] That is all that matters. The district judge had subject matter jurisdiction to determine *whether* to find that the circumstances permitted and warranted amendment. … If his decision to amend was mistaken, it was up to the party objecting to amendment to file a timely appeal from the amended judgment, which [D] failed to do."

FRCP 60(a)

Rivera v. PNS Stores, 647 F.3d 188, 193-94 (5th Cir. 2011). "Because the court can exercise its authority under [FRCP] 60(a) at any time, it may do so only to provide a specific and very limited type of relief, relief that is different in kind from an alteration or amendment of the judgment under [FRCP] 59(e) or relief due to mistake or inadvertence under Rule 60(b)(1). [¶] To be correctable under Rule 60(a), the mistake must not be one of judgment or even of misidentification, but merely of recitation, of the sort that a clerk or amanuensis might commit, mechanical in nature. Clerical mistakes, inaccuracies of transcription, inadvertent omissions, and errors in mathematical calculation are within Rule 60(a)'s scope; missteps involving substantive legal reasoning are not. … In short, [a] Rule 60(a) motion can only be used to make the judgment or record speak the truth and cannot be used to make it say something other than what originally was pronounced. *At 195-96:* Rule 60(a) does not provide for the correction of the deliberate choice of the district judge, even where that deliberate choice is based on a mistake of law. Rather, Rule 60(a) finds application where the record makes apparent that the court intended one thing but by merely clerical mistake or oversight did another." (Internal quotes omitted.) *See also* ***Garamendi v. Hénin***, 683 F.3d 1069, 1079-81 (9th Cir.2012).

Catz v. Chalker, 566 F.3d 839, 841 (9th Cir.2009). "[FRAP] 4(a)(4)(A)(vi) tolls the time for the filing of an appeal if a party has moved 'for relief under [FRCP] 60.' [¶] The language of [FRAP] 4—'for relief under Rule 60'—is thus susceptible to two interpretations. [FRAP 4] could pertain only to Rule 60(b) motions because [FRAP 4] uses the words 'for relief' and only a Rule 60(b) motion 'relieve[s] a party.' Alternatively, because [FRAP 4] refers to motions under 'Rule 60,' and not 'Rule 60(b),' the tolling provision could apply to both 60(a) and 60(b) motions. In the former interpretation, the words 'for relief' would serve as a qualifier; in the latter, the words would serve as a descriptor. [¶] The two courts that have addressed the issue both held that a 60(a) motion does toll the time for appeal. [¶] We agree and join those decisions in holding that a motion under Rule 60(a) tolls the time for filing a notice of appeal."

Pfizer Inc. v. Uprichard, 422 F.3d 124, 130 (3d Cir. 2005). "[W]here a party seeks to alter a judgment to reflect the District Court's grant of pre-judgment interest,

Rule 60(a) is the proper avenue for making such a request." *See also* ***Robert Lewis Rosen Assocs. v. Webb***, 473 F.3d 498, 504-05 & n.11 (2d Cir.2007).

Hodge v. Hodge, 269 F.3d 155, 158 (2d Cir.2001). "A motion under Rule 60(a) is available only to correct a judgment 'for the purpose of reflecting accurately a decision that the court actually made.' [¶] [W]hen a judgment is corrected under [FRCP] 60(a), the time for filing postjudgment motions runs from the date of entry of the first judgment, not the second."

In re West Tex. Mktg. Corp., 12 F.3d 497, 503 (5th Cir.1994). "[T]he power of a court to reform a judgment under Rule 60(a) [for clerical mistakes] is not limited by the one year constraint of Rule 60(b). [¶] 'Rule 60(a) [applies] where the record makes apparent that the court intended one thing but by merely clerical mistake or oversight did another.'"

FRCP 60(b)

Dominguez v. Gulf Coast Mar. & Assocs., 607 F.3d 1066, 1074-75 (5th Cir.2010). See annotation under FRCP 62.1, p. 967.

e360 Insight v. Spamhaus Project, 500 F.3d 594, 601 (7th Cir.2007). "[A]lthough a party is not required to file a [FRCP] 60(b) motion in the district court to raise challenges to the entry of a default judgment, this court has recognized that when a party does so, the failure to raise certain defenses specifically may waive those defenses for purposes of appeal of the underlying judgment. Although our cases applying this rule have dealt with issues of personal jurisdiction, service to bring a party into the action[,] and capacity to be sued, ... the logic employed in those cases applies with equal force to the particular defense of failure of notice under [FRCP] 55(b)."

Townsend v. Social Sec. Admin., 486 F.3d 127, 134 (6th Cir.2007). "[I]n some situations, a district court may grant a [FRCP] 60(b) motion 'to revive a lost right of appeal.' [S]uch a decision is proper only where a number of elements are met: the failure to appeal timely must result from one of Rule 60(b)'s enumerated reasons; there must be a lack of prejudice to the respondent; the moving party must file the motion promptly after discovering the failure to appeal timely; and counsel must exercise due diligence in attempting to comply with the time limitations of [FRAP] 4(a)."

Pierson v. Dormire, 484 F.3d 486, 491-92 (8th Cir. 2007), *vacated in part on other grounds*, No. 06-2545 (8th Cir.2008) (no pub.; 5-6-08). The circuits are split on the issue of "[w]hether a district court has the authority to grant a party relief pursuant to Rule 60(b) *sua sponte*.... [¶] We agree with the reasoning of the Second, Fourth, Fifth, and Ninth Circuits, and hold that a district court can grant relief from a judgment pursuant to Rule 60(b) *sua sponte*. [T]he holdings of these cases are premised on the fact that the parties had notice of the district courts' actions before the courts issued new orders. We agree that providing notice and an opportunity for the parties to be heard is the preferable means of action in such a case." *See also* ***Judson Atkinson Candies, Inc. v. Latini-Hohberger Dhimantec***, 529 F.3d 371, 385 (7th Cir.2008). *But see* ***Mahone v. Ray***, this page.

Harrington v. City of Chi., 433 F.3d 542, 546 (7th Cir.2006). See annotation under FRCP 59, p. 957.

Mahone v. Ray, 326 F.3d 1176, 1180 (11th Cir. 2003). "'Where a party seeks to make a motion under [FRCP] 60(b) to vacate the judgment of a district court, after notice of appeal has been filed, the proper procedure is for that party to file the motion in the district court. If the district judge believes there should be relief from the judgment, the district court is to indicate that it would grant the motion. The appellant should then make a motion in this court for a remand of the case so that the district court can grant relief.'" *See also* ***Davis v. Yageo Corp.***, 481 F.3d 661, 685 (9th Cir.2007); ***U.S. v. Pauley***, 321 F.3d 578, 581 (6th Cir.2003). *But see* ***Pierson v. Dormire***, this page.

Ahmed v. Dragovich, 297 F.3d 201, 209 (3d Cir. 2002). "When a party requests post-judgment amendment of a pleading, a court will normally conjoin the [FRCP] 60(b) and [FRCP] 15(a) motions to decide them simultaneously, as it 'would be a needless formality for the court to grant the motion to reopen the judgment only to deny the motion for leave to amend.' Therefore, 'the fact that the amended pleading offered by the movant will not cure the defects in the original pleading that resulted in the judgment of dismissal may be a valid reason both for denying a motion to amend under Rule 15(a) and for refusing to reopen the judgment under Rule 60(b).'"

FRCP 60(b)(1)

Pioneer Inv. Servs. v. Brunswick Assocs., 507 U.S. 380, 392 (1993). "Although inadvertence, ignorance of the rules, or mistakes construing the rules do not usually constitute 'excusable' neglect, it is clear that 'excusable neglect' under [FRCP] 6(b) is a somewhat 'elastic concept' and is not limited strictly to omis-

sions caused by circumstances beyond the control of the movant. *At 395:* Because Congress has provided no other guideposts for determining what sorts of neglect will be considered 'excusable,' we conclude that the determination is at bottom an equitable one, taking account of all relevant circumstances surrounding the party's omission. These include, as the Court of Appeals found, the danger of prejudice to the [opposing party], the length of the delay and its potential impact on judicial proceedings, the reason for the delay, including whether it was within the reasonable control of the movant, and whether the movant acted in good faith." *See also* ***Stonkus v. City of Brockton Sch. Dept.***, 322 F.3d 97, 101 (1st Cir.2003) (attorney's confusion about filing deadlines and belated opposition to summary judgment not excusable neglect); ***Sparrow v. Heller***, 116 F.3d 204, 206 (7th Cir.1997) (attorney's inexcusable neglect not grounds for relief under either FRCP 60(b)(1) or 60(b)(6)).

Yeschick v. Mineta, 675 F.3d 622, 628-29 (6th Cir. 2012). "In determining whether relief is appropriate under Rule 60(b)(1), courts consider three factors: (1) culpability—that is, whether the neglect was excusable; (2) any prejudice to the opposing party; and (3) whether the party holds a meritorious underlying claim or defense. A party seeking relief must first demonstrate a lack of culpability before the court examines the remaining two factors. Clients are held accountable for their attorneys' acts and omissions. Thus, in assessing a claim of excusable neglect, the proper focus is upon whether the neglect of the parties *and their counsel* was excusable." (Internal quotes omitted.)

United Airlines, Inc. v. Brien, 588 F.3d 158, 175 (2d Cir.2009). See annotation under *FRCP 60(b)(6)*, p. 964.

McCurry v. Adventist Health Sys./Sunbelt, Inc., 298 F.3d 586, 595 (6th Cir.2002). FRCP 60(b)(1) "does not permit litigants and their counsel to evade the consequences of their legal positions and litigation strategies, even though these might prove unsuccessful, ill-advised, or even flatly erroneous. *At 596:* To the extent that [Ps] cite strategic misjudgments and flawed legal analysis by their counsel as bases for relief, these are most aptly termed 'mistakes'—but not of a sort that would warrant relief under [FRCP 60(b)(1)]." *See also* ***Eskridge v. Cook Cty.***, 577 F.3d 806, 809-10 (7th Cir. 2009) (strategic choice to dismiss lawsuit did not compel FRCP 60(b) relief, but some legal errors, such as those based on pitfalls of parallel federal and state lawsuits, may justify FRCP 60(b) relief).

Union Pac. R.R. v. Progress Rail Servs., 256 F.3d 781, 782 (8th Cir.2001). "The term 'excusable neglect' in [FRCP 60(b)(1)] 'is understood to encompass situations in which the failure to comply with a filing deadline is attributable to negligence.' [¶] In deciding whether to set aside a default judgment for 'excusable neglect,' a district court ought not to focus narrowly on the negligent act that caused the default and ask whether the act was itself in some sense excusable. Instead, the court should take account of 'all relevant circumstances surrounding the party's omission.'"

FRCP 60(b)(2)

U.S. Xpress Enters. v. J.B. Hunt Transp., 320 F.3d 809, 815 (8th Cir.2003). "Motions under Rule 60(b)(2) on the ground of newly discovered evidence are viewed with disfavor. [¶] 'In order to prevail under Rule 60(b)(2), the movant must show that (1) the evidence was discovered after trial; (2) due diligence was exercised to discover the evidence; (3) the evidence is material and not merely cumulative or impeaching; and (4) the evidence is such that a new trial would probably produce a different result.'" *See also* ***Thermacor Process, L.P. v. BASF Corp.***, 567 F.3d 736, 744 (5th Cir. 2009); ***Feature Rlty., Inc. v. City of Spokane***, 331 F.3d 1082, 1093 (9th Cir.2003).

FRCP 60(b)(3)

Wickens v. Shell Oil Co., 620 F.3d 747, 758-59 (7th Cir.2010). "To obtain relief under Rule 60(b)(3), a party must show that she has a meritorious claim that she was prevented from 'fully and fairly presenting' at trial as a result of the adverse party's fraud, misrepresentation, or misconduct. ... Rule 60(b)(3) does not, however, displace a judge's power to set aside a judgment for fraud on the court [under FRCP 60(d)(3)]. Fraud on the court is actionable only if it prejudices the adverse party. A party seeking to set aside a judgment under Rule 60(b)(3) or the court's inherent power must prove fraud by clear and convincing evidence." *See also* ***Thomas v. Parker***, 609 F.3d 1114, 1119-20 (10th Cir. 2010) (fraud under FRCP 60(b)(3) can be a claim of fraud on court); ***Tiller v. Baghdady***, 294 F.3d 277, 282 n.6 (1st Cir.2002) (fraud under FRCP 60(b)(3) does not need to rise to level of fraud on court, which is required for independent action under FRCP 60(b), now FRCP 60(d)(3)).

Roger Edwards, LLC v. Fiddes & Son Ltd., 427 F.3d 129, 134 (1st Cir.2005). "In parsing Rule 60(b)(3), an initial, and important, distinction to grasp is between fraud or misstatements that are committed during the course of a commercial transaction ..., and fraud or misstatements perpetrated in the course of litigation.... The former is the subject-matter of litigation, meant to be investigated through the discovery process and resolved by the evidence at trial. [¶] By contrast, fraud perpetrated in the course of litigation interferes with the process of adjudication, and it is this kind of litigation-related fraud that principally concerns Rule 60(b)(3)'s fraud provision. Once such fraud is proved, the judgment may be set aside merely upon the movant's showing that the fraud substantially interfered with the movant's ability fully and fairly to prepare for, and proceed at, trial. This is a far less demanding burden than showing that a different result would probably have ensued. [¶] The case law under Rule 60(b)(3) does not often articulate this distinction between 'out of court' conduct and trial-related conduct. But the vast bulk of reported fraud cases under Rule 60(b), whether under subsection (3) or (6), involve fraud or misstatements perpetrated in the course of litigation or other misconduct aimed directly at the trial process; those few litigants who seek to utilize Rule 60(b) fraud motions to redress non-litigation conduct are typically rebuffed at the threshold." (Internal quotes omitted.)

Government Fin. Servs. One L.P. v. Peyton Place, Inc., 62 F.3d 767, 772-73 (5th Cir.1995). "[A] party may engage in rule 60(b)(3) misconduct if he fails to disclose evidence he knows about and the production of such evidence was clearly called for by any fair reading of the discovery order." (Internal quotes omitted.)

FRCP 60(b)(4)

United Student Aid Funds, Inc. v. Espinosa, ___ U.S. ___, 130 S.Ct. 1367, 1377 (2010). "A void judgment is a legal nullity. Although the term 'void' describes a result, rather than the conditions that render a judgment unenforceable, it suffices to say that a void judgment is one so affected by a fundamental infirmity that the infirmity may be raised even after the judgment becomes final. The list of such infirmities is exceedingly short; otherwise, Rule 60(b)(4)'s exception to finality would swallow the rule. [¶] 'A judgment is not void,' for example, 'simply because it is or may have been erroneous.' Similarly, a motion under Rule 60(b)(4) is not a substitute for a timely appeal. Instead, Rule 60(b)(4) applies only in the rare instance where a judgment is premised either on a certain type of jurisdictional error or on a violation of due process that deprives a party of notice or the opportunity to be heard. [¶] Federal courts considering Rule 60(b)(4) motions that assert a judgment is void because of a jurisdictional defect generally have reserved relief only for the exceptional case in which the court that rendered judgment lacked even an 'arguable basis' for jurisdiction." *See also* ***Wendt v. Leonard***, 431 F.3d 410, 412-13 (4th Cir.2005).

Philos Techs. v. Philos & D, Inc., 645 F.3d 851, 854-55 (7th Cir.2011). "We review the denial of most motions for relief under Rule 60(b) only for an abuse of discretion. The standard of review for denial of a Rule 60(b)(4) motion is less deferential, however. [D]istrict courts have 'little leeway' under Rule 60(b)(4): 'Once a district court decides that the underlying judgment is void, the trial judge has no discretion and must grant the appropriate Rule 60(b) relief,' and it is 'a *per se* abuse of discretion to deny a Rule 60(b)(4) motion when the trial court has no jurisdiction over the action.' A judgment entered against a defendant over whom the court had no jurisdiction is void, and no court has the discretion to refuse to vacate that judgment once it recognizes its lack of jurisdiction."

Budget Blinds, Inc. v. White, 536 F.3d 244, 259 (3d Cir.2008). "[W]e do not think a registering court seriously threatens the interest in comity when it vacates a rendering court's default judgment under Rule 60(b)(4) for lack of personal jurisdiction."

FRCP 60(b)(5)

Horne v. Flores, 557 U.S. 433, 453 (2009). An FRCP 60(b)(5) "inquiry makes no reference to the presence or absence of a timely appeal. It takes the original judgment as a given and asks only whether 'a significant change either in factual conditions or in law' renders continued enforcement of the judgment 'detrimental to the public interest.' *At 454:* Rule 60(b)(5) permits relief from a judgment where '(i) the judgment has been satisfied, released or discharged; (ii) it is based on an earlier judgment that has been reversed or vacated; *or* (iii) applying it prospectively is no longer equitable.' Use of the disjunctive 'or' makes it clear that each of the provision's three grounds for relief is independently sufficient and therefore that relief may be warranted even if petitioners have not 'satisfied' the original or-

der. [A party seeking relief under Rule 60(b)(5)] may obtain relief if prospective enforcement of that order 'is no longer equitable.'"

Agostini v. Felton, 521 U.S. 203, 215 (1997). "[I]t is appropriate to grant a Rule 60(b)(5) motion when the party seeking relief from an injunction or consent decree can show 'a significant change either in factual conditions or in law.' A court may recognize subsequent changes in either statutory or decisional law. A court errs when it refuses to modify an injunction or consent decree in light of such changes." *See also* ***Frazar v. Ladd***, 457 F.3d 432, 436 (5th Cir.2006).

Lowry Dev., L.L.C. v. Groves & Assocs. Ins., 690 F.3d 382, 386 (5th Cir.2012). "The second clause of Rule 60(b)(5) ... permits a court to set aside a final judgment that is based on an earlier judgment that has been reversed or vacated.... *At 387:* The question ... is whether the word 'earlier' in Rule 60(b)(5) cognizes ... logical relations between simultaneous judgments. [W]hen one judgment rests upon a contemporaneous judgment which has been reversed or otherwise vacated, Rule 60(b)(5) should nevertheless apply if all the other conditions are met. We think the word 'prior' in Rule 60(b)(5) refers not only to prior in time but also to prior as a matter of legal significance. [This] reasoning prevents a needlessly cramped interpretation of the word 'earlier,' and we adopt it here." (Internal quotes omitted.)

Manzanares v. City of Albuquerque, 628 F.3d 1237, 1240 (10th Cir.2010). "For a judgment to be based on an earlier judgment it is not enough that the earlier judgment was relied on as precedent; rather it is necessary that the present judgment be based on the prior judgment in the sense of res judicata or collateral estoppel. ... Claims once tried, decided on the merits, appealed, and closed should—with only a few exceptions—be considered forever settled as between parties. This imperative would consist of nothing more than empty rhetoric were courts compelled to re-litigate past cases whenever they glimpsed a material change in decisional law. Cases in which one judgment is 'based' on another are not that frequent or obvious." (Internal quotes omitted.) *See also* ***In re Racing Servs.***, 571 F.3d 729, 732-34 (8th Cir.2009).

Arkansas Blue Cross & Blue Shield v. Little Rock Cardiology Clinic, P.A., 551 F.3d 812, 820 (8th Cir. 2009). "The term 'prospectively,' as it is used in Rule 60(b)(5), limits the types of judgments from which courts may provide relief. For example, since money judgments do not apply prospectively, we have held that 'relief from a final money judgment is ... not available under the equitable leg of Rule 60(b)(5).' Injunctions, by contrast, are 'executory,' and therefore eligible for relief under Rule 60(b)(5), because they characteristically require 'the supervision of changing conduct or conditions.'" *See also* ***Kalamazoo River Study Grp. v. Rockwell Int'l***, 355 F.3d 574, 587 (6th Cir.2004) (permanent or temporary injunctions, some declaratory judgments, and consent decrees are prospective judgments).

Parton v. White, 203 F.3d 552, 555 (8th Cir.2000). "Modification may be appropriate when changed factual conditions make compliance with the decree substantially more onerous, a decree proves to be unworkable because of unforeseen obstacles, or enforcement of the decree without modification would be detrimental to the public interest. ... To be 'suitably tailored to the changed circumstance,' the modification 'must not create or perpetuate a constitutional violation,' or 'strive to rewrite a consent decree so that it conforms to the constitutional floor.'"

FRCP 60(b)(6)

Aikens v. Ingram, 652 F.3d 496, 501 (4th Cir.2011). "To give Rule 60(b)(6) broad application would undermine numerous other rules that favor the finality of judgments.... [¶] We have thus required—in addition to the explicitly stated requirements that the motion under Rule 60(b)(6) be filed on 'just terms' and within 'a reasonable time'—that the party filing the motion have a meritorious claim or defense and that the opposing party not be unfairly prejudiced by having the judgment set aside. And if the reason asserted for the Rule 60(b)(6) motion could have been addressed on appeal from the judgment, we have denied the motion as merely an inappropriate substitute for an appeal. *At 503:* Stated simply, 'extraordinary circumstances' do not arise due to limitations that otherwise apply, and a plaintiff cannot use Rule 60(b)(6) to evade such time limitations." (Internal quotes omitted.) *See also* ***Blanchard v. Cortés-Molina***, 453 F.3d 40, 44 (1st Cir.2006) (FRCP 60(b)(6) relief is not available to party who is partly to blame for delay); ***McCurry v. Adventist Health Sys./Sunbelt, Inc.***, 298 F.3d 586, 596 (6th Cir. 2002) (FRCP 60(b)(6) relief is not available for straightforward claims of attorney error and strategic miscalculation).

Ungar v. Palestine Liberation Org., 599 F.3d 79, 83-84 (1st Cir.2010). "[I]n addition to the usual medley of factors that influence the resolution of Rule 60(b) motions, granting or withholding relief from a default judgment entails balancing the importance of finality in litigation against the desirability of deciding cases on the merits. [¶] A variety of factors can help an inquiring court to strike the requisite balance. Such factors include the timing of the request for relief, the extent of any prejudice to the opposing party, the existence or non-existence of meritorious claims of defense, and the presence or absence of exceptional circumstances. This compendium is neither exclusive nor rigidly applied. [¶] Because Rule 60(b)(6) is a catch-all provision, its contours are peculiarly malleable. Thus, hard-and-fast rules generally are not compatible with Rule 60(b)(6) determinations."

United Airlines, Inc. v. Brien, 588 F.3d 158, 175 (2d Cir.2009). "Courts of Appeals do not appear to have addressed the precise situation presented here: the district court's issuance of conflicting decisions in two separate lawsuits with substantial overlap in parties and substantial similarity in subject matter. [T]he Fifth Circuit has suggested that inconsistency claims, where meritorious, are properly brought under Rule 60(b)(6). *At 176:* We find that the motion was timely filed under Rule 60(b)(6) to the extent that it was based on the potential hardship resulting from inconsistent judgments. Such a claim is not easily categorized as 'mistake' or 'inadvertence' under Rule 60(b)(1), and it should therefore be allowed to proceed under Rule 60(b)(6)."

Stokes v. Williams, 475 F.3d 732, 735 (6th Cir. 2007). "Even stricter standards are routinely applied to motions under [FRCP 60(b)(6)] than to motions made under other provisions of [FRCP 60(b)]. [R]elief may be granted under Rule 60(b)(6) only in exceptional or extraordinary circumstances which are not addressed by the first five numbered clauses of [FRCP 60(b)]. Courts must apply subsection (b)(6) only as a means to achieve substantial justice when something more than one of the grounds contained in Rule 60(b)'s first five clauses in present. The 'something more' must include unusual and extreme situations where principles of equity *mandate* relief. [¶] [F]ederal courts have consistently held that a change in decisional law is usually not, by itself, an extraordinary circumstance meriting Rule 60(b)(6) relief." (Internal quotes omitted.)

FRCP 60(c)

Associated Builders & Contractors v. Michigan Dept. of Labor & Econ. Growth, 543 F.3d 275, 278 (6th Cir.2008). "A party bringing a Rule 60(b)(5) motion must do so 'within a reasonable time,'... a requirement that turns on the length of the delay, the explanations for the delay, the prejudice to the opposing party caused by the delay and the circumstances warranting relief. Also relevant is the nature of the dispute and whether it involves a purely private disagreement or a matter of public interest." *See also* ***Ingram v. Merrill Lynch, Pierce, Fenner & Smith, Inc.***, 371 F.3d 950, 952 (7th Cir.2004) (FRCP 60(b)(6) motion).

"R" Best Produce, Inc. v. DiSapio, 540 F.3d 115, 123-24 (2d Cir.2008). "Although Rule 60(b) [now Rule 60(c)(1)] provides that most motions for relief, including a motion under Rule 60(b)(4), must be made 'within a reasonable time,' ... this Court has been exceedingly lenient in defining the term 'reasonable time,' with respect to voidness challenges. [I]t has been oft-stated that ... a motion to vacate a default judgment as void 'may be made at any time.'"

Jones v. Swanson, 512 F.3d 1045, 1048 (8th Cir. 2008). "'[A] new, one-year period under Rule 60(b) [now Rule 60(c)(1)] might be triggered if [a] subsequent appellate ruling substantially alters the district court's judgment in a manner that disturbs or revises the previous, plainly settled legal rights and obligations of the parties.' *At 1049:* [T]he amended judgment in no way altered, disturbed, or revised the previous, plainly settled legal rights and obligations of the parties with respect to liability. Because [D's] Rule 60(b)(2) motion only focuses on the issue of liability, we hold the one-year limitations period for bringing the motion began to run when the [original] judgment was entered...."

FRCP 60(d)

U.S. v. Beggerly, 524 U.S. 38, 46 (1998). "Independent actions must ... be reserved for those cases of 'injustices which, in certain instances, are deemed sufficiently gross to demand a departure' from rigid adherence to the doctrine of res judicata." *See also* ***Superior Seafoods, Inc. v. Tyson Foods, Inc.***, 620 F.3d 873, 878 (8th Cir.2010) (relief under FRCP 60(d)(3) only available when "manifestly unconscionable" to allow judgment to stand).

In re Golf 255, Inc., 652 F.3d 806, 809 (7th Cir. 2011). "The term 'fraud on the court' is not defined in Rule 60 or elsewhere in the federal rules, and the defi-

nition most often offered by the courts[—]that it consists of acts that 'defile the court'[—]though vivid, doesn't advance the ball very far. [¶] The problem of definition arises from the fact that a motion to set aside a judgment on the ground of fraud on the court has no deadline. It must therefore be defined narrowly lest it 'become an open sesame to collateral attacks, unlimited as to the time within which they can be made by virtue of the express provision in Rule 60(b) [now 60(d)] on this matter, on civil judgments.' [W]e need to consider what kind of fraud ought to be a ground for setting aside a judgment perhaps many years after it was entered. The answer is the kind of fraud that ordinarily couldn't be discovered, despite diligent inquiry, within a year, and in some cases within many years—cases in which there are no grounds for suspicion and the fraud comes to light serendipitously. Examples are bribery of a judge or exertion of other undue influence on him, jury tampering, and fraudulent submissions by a lawyer for one of the parties in a judicial proceeding, such as tendering documents he knows to be forged or testimony he knows to be perjured." *See also* ***Turner v. Pleasant***, 663 F.3d 770, 777-78 (5th Cir.2011); ***Pumphrey v. K.W. Thompson Tool Co.***, 62 F.3d 1128, 1130 (9th Cir.1995).

FRCP 61. HARMLESS ERROR

Unless justice requires otherwise, no error in admitting or excluding evidence—or any other error by the court or a party—is ground for granting a new trial, for setting aside a verdict, or for vacating, modifying, or otherwise disturbing a judgment or order. At every stage of the proceeding, the court must disregard all errors and defects that do not affect any party's substantial rights.

History of FRCP 61: Adopted Dec. 20, 1937, eff. Sept. 16, 1938. Amended Apr. 30, 2007, eff. Dec. 1, 2007.

See also 28 U.S.C. §2106 (power of appellate courts to affirm, modify, reverse, and remand case), §2111 (harmless error on appeal or certiorari); FRCP 46 (formal exceptions unnecessary).

ANNOTATIONS

Liu v. Price Waterhouse LLP, 302 F.3d 749, 756 (7th Cir.2002). "[W]e recognize that an error is harmless if it did not contribute to the verdict in a meaningful manner."

Environ Prods. v. Furon Co., 215 F.3d 1261, 1265 (Fed.Cir.2000). "If an asserted error did not prejudice any substantial interest of a party, that error is deemed harmless and the jury verdict is not disturbed."

Sasaki v. Class, 92 F.3d 232, 237 (4th Cir.1996). "In awarding a significantly larger amount of damages ..., the jury almost undoubtedly adjusted its award to account for the federal cap. Although the basis for the jury's decision can ... never be known to a certainty, when a jury's damages award itself indicates so strongly that the error substantially influenced the jury's verdict, the error cannot be dismissed as harmless under Rule 61.... [¶] The district court's admonition to the jury that statements and arguments 'of counsel are not evidence,' did not 'cure' the error resulting from counsel's improper mention of the cap."

In re Air Crash Disaster, 86 F.3d 498, 535 (6th Cir. 1996). "We generally will not reverse even an erroneous evidentiary ruling if it merely resulted in the submission of redundant information to the jury."

Peterson v. Willie, 81 F.3d 1033, 1036 (11th Cir. 1996). "'Errors in evidentiary rulings are not grounds for reversal unless substantial prejudice results.' Statements made in oral arguments must be plainly unwarranted and clearly injurious to constitute reversible error." *See also* ***Costantino v. David M. Herzog, M.D., P.C.***, 203 F.3d 164, 174 (2d Cir.2000).

Douglass v. United Servs. Auto. Ass'n, 79 F.3d 1415, 1424 (5th Cir.1996). "Although the [FRCPs] do not contain a plain error rule, our court has applied the plain error standard of [FRCrP] 52(b) in civil cases. [FRCP] 61 supports that approach. ... Rule 61 describes both the conditions for which an error should be disregarded and those for which it should not.... [¶] Thus, ... Rule 61 combines in a single rule the harmless and plain error rules stated in [FRCrP] 52(a) and (b)."

FRCP 62. STAY OF PROCEEDINGS TO ENFORCE A JUDGMENT

(a) Automatic Stay; Exceptions for Injunctions, Receiverships, and Patent Accountings. Except as stated in this rule, no execution may issue on a judgment, nor may proceedings be taken to enforce it, until 14 days have passed after its entry. But unless the court orders otherwise, the following are not stayed after being entered, even if an appeal is taken:

(1) an interlocutory or final judgment in an action for an injunction or a receivership; or

(2) a judgment or order that directs an accounting in an action for patent infringement.

(b) Stay Pending the Disposition of a Motion. On appropriate terms for the opposing party's security, the court may stay the execution of a judgment—or any proceedings to enforce it—pending disposition of any of the following motions:

(1) under Rule 50, for judgment as a matter of law;

(2) under Rule 52(b), to amend the findings or for additional findings;

(3) under Rule 59, for a new trial or to alter or amend a judgment; or

(4) under Rule 60, for relief from a judgment or order.

(c) Injunction Pending an Appeal. While an appeal is pending from an interlocutory order or final judgment that grants, dissolves, or denies an injunction, the court may suspend, modify, restore, or grant an injunction on terms for bond or other terms that secure the opposing party's rights. If the judgment appealed from is rendered by a statutory three-judge district court, the order must be made either:

(1) by that court sitting in open session; or

(2) by the assent of all its judges, as evidenced by their signatures.

(d) Stay with Bond on Appeal. If an appeal is taken, the appellant may obtain a stay by supersedeas bond, except in an action described in Rule 62(a)(1) or (2). The bond may be given upon or after filing the notice of appeal or after obtaining the order allowing the appeal. The stay takes effect when the court approves the bond.

(e) Stay Without Bond on an Appeal by the United States, Its Officers, or Its Agencies. The court must not require a bond, obligation, or other security from the appellant when granting a stay on an appeal by the United States, its officers, or its agencies or on an appeal directed by a department of the federal government.

(f) Stay in Favor of a Judgment Debtor Under State Law. If a judgment is a lien on the judgment debtor's property under the law of the state where the court is located, the judgment debtor is entitled to the same stay of execution the state court would give.

(g) Appellate Court's Power Not Limited. This rule does not limit the power of the appellate court or one of its judges or justices:

(1) to stay proceedings—or suspend, modify, restore, or grant an injunction—while an appeal is pending; or

(2) to issue an order to preserve the status quo or the effectiveness of the judgment to be entered.

(h) Stay with Multiple Claims or Parties. A court may stay the enforcement of a final judgment entered under Rule 54(b) until it enters a later judgment or judgments, and may prescribe terms necessary to secure the benefit of the stayed judgment for the party in whose favor it was entered.

See selected Notes of Advisory Committee to FRCP 62, p. 1229.

History of FRCP 62: Adopted Dec. 20, 1937, eff. Sept. 16, 1938. Amended Dec. 27, 1946, eff. Mar. 19, 1948; Dec. 29, 1948, eff. Oct. 20, 1949; Apr. 17, 1961, eff. July 19, 1961; Mar. 2, 1987, eff. Aug. 1, 1987; Apr. 30, 2007, eff. Dec. 1, 2007; Mar. 26, 2009, eff. Dec. 1, 2009.

See *Commentaries*, "Appellate Review," ch. 10-F, §9, p. 815.

See also 28 U.S.C. §2408 (security not required of U.S.); 31 U.S.C. §9303 (deposit of bonds or notes of U.S. in lieu of surety).

ANNOTATIONS

Peacock v. Thomas, 516 U.S. 349, 359 n.8 (1996). "The district court may only stay execution of the judgment pending the disposition of certain post-trial motions or appeal if the court provides for the security of the judgment creditor."

Hilton v. Braunskill, 481 U.S. 770, 776 (1987). Under FRCP 62(c), "the factors regulating the issuance of a stay are … (1) whether the stay applicant has made a strong showing that he is likely to succeed on the merits; (2) whether the applicant will be irreparably injured absent a stay; (3) whether issuance of the stay will substantially injure the other parties interested in the proceeding; and (4) where the public interest lies."

Olcott v. Delaware Flood Co., 76 F.3d 1538, 1559-60 (10th Cir.1996). "The purpose of requiring a supersedeas bond pending appeal 'is to secure the judgment … against the possibility of the judgment debtor's insolvency.' Typically, the amount of the bond matches the full amount of the judgment. We have recognized, '[d]istrict courts, however, have inherent discretionary authority in setting supersedeas bonds.'"

Sierra Club v. Cedar Point Oil Co., 73 F.3d 546, 579 (5th Cir.1996). "[A] court should only modify an injunction to achieve the original purposes of the injunction, if those purposes have not been fully achieved."

Fish Mkt. Nominee Corp. v. Pelofsky, 72 F.3d 4, 6 (1st Cir.1995). FRCP 62 "primarily serves to give one against whom a money judgment is entered time to

post a supersedeas bond to stay enforcement of that judgment pending appeal. [¶] Rule 62(a) does not purport to make a judgment ineffective [during the time period before the judgment is enforced]; on the contrary, the judgment retains full force and effect for other purposes—*e.g., res judicata*. ... Rule 62(a) merely stays proceedings to *enforce* the judgment, for example, discovery to determine the location of a judgment debtor's property available to satisfy the judgment."

FRCP 62.1. INDICATIVE RULING ON A MOTION FOR RELIEF THAT IS BARRED BY A PENDING APPEAL

(a) **Relief Pending Appeal.** If a timely motion is made for relief that the court lacks authority to grant because of an appeal that has been docketed and is pending, the court may:

(1) defer considering the motion;

(2) deny the motion; or

(3) state either that it would grant the motion if the court of appeals remands for that purpose or that the motion raises a substantial issue.

(b) **Notice to the Court of Appeals.** The movant must promptly notify the circuit clerk under Federal Rule of Appellate Procedure 12.1 if the district court states that it would grant the motion or that the motion raises a substantial issue.

(c) **Remand.** The district court may decide the motion if the court of appeals remands for that purpose.

See selected Notes of Advisory Committee to FRCP 62.1, p. 1230.

History of FRCP 62.1: Adopted Mar. 26, 2009, eff. Dec. 1, 2009.

See *Commentaries*, "Indicative Ruling," ch. 10-F, §8, p. 813; *O'Connor's Federal Civil Forms* (2012), FORMS 10F:4-6.

ANNOTATIONS

Dominguez v. Gulf Coast Mar. & Assocs., 607 F.3d 1066, 1074-75 (5th Cir.2010). "Although an effective notice of appeal strips district courts of jurisdiction to *grant* a [FRCP] 60(b) motion, it does not prevent litigants from filing them in the district court while an appeal is pending. Instead, the district court retains jurisdiction to consider and deny Rule 60(b) motions, and if it indicates that it will grant the motion, [under FRCP 62.1] the appellant may then make a motion in the Court of Appeals for a remand of the case in order that the district court may grant such motion. [Ps] have not heeded this guidance—they seek a remand but have not already filed a Rule 60(b) motion [in the district court]. [¶] [Ps] should have filed a Rule 60(b) motion ..., but we have previously explained that the procedures for filing post-appeal Rule 60(b) motions are not a judicial tightrope to be walked at peril. Instead, where the litigant has timely initiated procedure for relief, he should not be penalized for choice of the 'wrong' procedure." (Internal quotes omitted.)

FRCP 63. JUDGE'S INABILITY TO PROCEED

If a judge conducting a hearing or trial is unable to proceed, any other judge may proceed upon certifying familiarity with the record and determining that the case may be completed without prejudice to the parties. In a hearing or a nonjury trial, the successor judge must, at a party's request, recall any witness whose testimony is material and disputed and who is available to testify again without undue burden. The successor judge may also recall any other witness.

History of FRCP 63: Adopted Dec. 20, 1937, eff. Sept. 16, 1938. Amended Mar. 2, 1987, eff. Aug. 1, 1987; Apr. 30, 1991, eff. Dec. 1, 1991; Apr. 30, 2007, eff. Dec. 1, 2007.

ANNOTATIONS

Jackson v. Alabama State Tenure Comm'n, 405 F.3d 1276, 1286-87 (11th Cir.2005). "Although [original judge] had orally granted [D's FRCP] 50 motion for judgment as a matter of law ... after the close of the evidence in the second trial, he died before he made any written findings of fact and conclusions of law or entered final judgment. Without recalling any witnesses or entering written findings of fact or conclusions of law of his own, [successor judge] entered a formal judgment in favor of [D] based on [original judge's] oral grant of [D's] Rule 50 motion for judgment as a matter of law. [¶] [P] argues that before entering judgment [successor judge] was obligated by [FRCP] 63 to recall witnesses and hear for himself the testimony that had been presented at the second trial. [P] asserts that ... under Rule 63, any time a judge in a civil case becomes disabled or dies before issuing findings of fact and conclusions of law, the successor judge must retry the case. [P] is wrong. [¶] Rule 63 treats bench trials and jury trials differently. The rule gives the parties the right to insist that a witness be recalled in a bench trial. The rule does not give that right where a jury trial is involved. What we have here is a jury trial, not a bench trial. [¶] [Successor judge certified] that he was familiar with the record and he determined that the proceedings in the case could be completed without prejudice to the parties; Rule 63 required no more."

Patelco Credit Un. v. Sahni, 262 F.3d 897, 906 (9th Cir.2001). "[A]s an alternative to stepping into the shoes of the unavailable district judge under Rule 63, the successor judge may examine the trial transcript as if it were supporting affidavits for summary judgment purposes and enter summary judgment if no credibility determinations are required. … Thus, Rule 63 is not violated when no material facts are in dispute and the successor judge rules as a matter of law." (Internal quotes omitted.)

Mergentime Corp. v. Washington Metro. Area Transit Auth., 166 F.3d 1257, 1265 (D.C.Cir.1999). "[Ps] argue that the successor judge violated Rule 63 because he never expressly certified his familiarity with the record before resolving the outstanding issues. [¶] First, successor judges need only certify their familiarity with those portions of the record that relate to the issues before them. Second, the extent of the certification obligation depends upon the nature of the successor judge's role in a given case. A successor judge who inherits a jury trial before the close of evidence must become familiar with the *entire* record in order to have the context necessary to rule on evidentiary objections based on relevance. By comparison, a successor judge who inherits a case after the entry of verdict or judgment and who must consider only a narrow post-trial motion—such as one challenging the sufficiency of the evidence regarding a single factual finding—need only review the portion of the record relevant to that particular issue." *See also* ***Canseco v. U.S.***, 97 F.3d 1224, 1226 (9th Cir.1996).

Chicago Prof'l Sports Ltd. v. National Basketball Ass'n, 95 F.3d 593, 601 (7th Cir.1996). "Although the judge who presided at the trial died earlier this year, [on reversal and remand to district court] the parties may be willing to agree that an assessment of credibility is unnecessary, so that a new judge could resolve the dispute after reviewing the transcript, exhibits, and stipulations, and entertaining argument."

TITLE VIII. PROVISIONAL & FINAL REMEDIES

FRCP 64. SEIZING A PERSON OR PROPERTY

(a) Remedies Under State Law—In General. At the commencement of and throughout an action, every remedy is available that, under the law of the state where the court is located, provides for seizing a person or property to secure satisfaction of the potential judgment. But a federal statute governs to the extent it applies.

(b) Specific Kinds of Remedies. The remedies available under this rule include the following—however designated and regardless of whether state procedure requires an independent action:

- arrest;
- attachment;
- garnishment;
- replevin;
- sequestration; and
- other corresponding or equivalent remedies.

See selected Notes of Advisory Committee to FRCP 64, p. 1230.

History of FRCP 64: Adopted Dec. 20, 1937, eff. Sept. 16, 1938. Amended Apr. 30, 2007, eff. Dec. 1, 2007.

See also FRCP 69 (execution).

ANNOTATIONS

Mitsubishi Int'l v. Cardinal Textile Sales, Inc., 14 F.3d 1507, 1521 (11th Cir.1994). "Attachment is an ancillary remedy by which a plaintiff acquires a lien upon the property of a defendant in order to obtain satisfaction of a judgment that the plaintiff may ultimately obtain at the conclusion of the litigation."

HMG Prop. Investors, Inc. v. Parque Indus. Rio Canas, Inc., 847 F.2d 908, 913 (1st Cir.1988). "Rule 64 … sets out a quadrat of requirements: the provisional remedy must (1) involve a seizure, (2) be entered for the purpose of 'securing satisfaction of the judgment ultimately to be rendered in the action,' (3) be permitted under the law of the forum state, and (4) be issued in a manner compatible with state law."

FRCP 65. INJUNCTIONS & RESTRAINING ORDERS

(a) Preliminary Injunction.

(1) ***Notice.*** The court may issue a preliminary injunction only on notice to the adverse party.

(2) ***Consolidating the Hearing with the Trial on the Merits.*** Before or after beginning the hearing on a motion for a preliminary injunction, the court may advance the trial on the merits and consolidate it with the hearing. Even when consolidation is not ordered, evidence that is received on the motion and that would be admissible at trial becomes part of the trial record and need not be repeated at trial. But the court must preserve any party's right to a jury trial.

(b) Temporary Restraining Order.

(1) ***Issuing Without Notice.*** The court may issue a temporary restraining order without written or oral notice to the adverse party or its attorney only if:

(A) specific facts in an affidavit or a verified complaint clearly show that immediate and irreparable injury, loss, or damage will result to the movant before the adverse party can be heard in opposition; and

(B) the movant's attorney certifies in writing any efforts made to give notice and the reasons why it should not be required.

(2) ***Contents; Expiration.*** Every temporary restraining order issued without notice must state the date and hour it was issued; describe the injury and state why it is irreparable; state why the order was issued without notice; and be promptly filed in the clerk's office and entered in the record. The order expires at the time after entry—not to exceed 14 days—that the court sets, unless before that time the court, for good cause, extends it for a like period or the adverse party consents to a longer extension. The reasons for an extension must be entered in the record.

(3) ***Expediting the Preliminary-Injunction Hearing.*** If the order is issued without notice, the motion for a preliminary injunction must be set for hearing at the earliest possible time, taking precedence over all other matters except hearings on older matters of the same character. At the hearing, the party who obtained the order must proceed with the motion; if the party does not, the court must dissolve the order.

(4) ***Motion to Dissolve.*** On 2 days' notice to the party who obtained the order without notice—or on shorter notice set by the court—the adverse party may appear and move to dissolve or modify the order. The court must then hear and decide the motion as promptly as justice requires.

(c) Security. The court may issue a preliminary injunction or a temporary restraining order only if the movant gives security in an amount that the court considers proper to pay the costs and damages sustained by any party found to have been wrongfully enjoined or restrained. The United States, its officers, and its agencies are not required to give security.

(d) Contents and Scope of Every Injunction and Restraining Order.

(1) ***Contents.*** Every order granting an injunction and every restraining order must:

(A) state the reasons why it issued;

(B) state its terms specifically; and

(C) describe in reasonable detail—and not by referring to the complaint or other document—the act or acts restrained or required.

(2) ***Persons Bound.*** The order binds only the following who receive actual notice of it by personal service or otherwise:

(A) the parties;

(B) the parties' officers, agents, servants, employees, and attorneys; and

(C) other persons who are in active concert or participation with anyone described in Rule 65(d)(2)(A) or (B).

(e) Other Laws Not Modified. These rules do not modify the following:

(1) any federal statute relating to temporary restraining orders or preliminary injunctions in actions affecting employer and employee;

(2) 28 U.S.C. §2361, which relates to preliminary injunctions in actions of interpleader or in the nature of interpleader; or

(3) 28 U.S.C. §2284, which relates to actions that must be heard and decided by a three-judge district court.

(f) Copyright Impoundment. This rule applies to copyright-impoundment proceedings.

See selected Notes of Advisory Committee to FRCP 65, p. 1230.

History of FRCP 65: Adopted Dec. 20, 1937, eff. Sept. 16, 1938. Amended Dec. 27, 1946, eff. Mar. 19, 1948; Dec. 29, 1948, eff. Oct. 20, 1949; Feb. 28, 1966, eff. July 1, 1966; Mar. 2, 1987, eff. Aug. 1, 1987; Apr. 23, 2001, eff. Dec. 1, 2001; Apr. 30, 2007, eff. Dec. 1, 2007; Mar. 26, 2009, eff. Dec. 1, 2009.

See ***Commentaries***, "Injunctive Relief," ch. 2-D, p. 93; ***O'Connor's Federal Civil Forms*** (2012), FORMS 2D.

See also 15 U.S.C. §4 (restraining violations of antitrust laws), §§25, 26 (restraining violations of Clayton Act), §77t (restraining violations of Securities Act), §78u-3 (restraining violations of Securities Exchange Act), §1116 (injunction against infringement of trademarks and trade names); 17 U.S.C. §502 (injunction against infringement of copyrights); 26 U.S.C. §7421 (prohibition of suits to restrain assessment or collection); 28 U.S.C. §1292 (appellate jurisdiction over interlocutory injunctive orders); 29 U.S.C. §160 (restraining unfair labor practices), §178 (petition by Attorney General to enjoin strike or lockout), §217 (restraining violations of Fair Labor Standards Act); 35 U.S.C. §283 (injunction as remedy for patent infringement).

ANNOTATIONS

Notice

Lamex Foods, Inc. v. Audeliz Lebrón Corp., 646 F.3d 100, 106-07 (1st Cir.2011). "Although [FRCP 65(a)(2)] facilitates the generally admirable objective of saving time and duplication of effort [by advancing the trial on the merits and consolidating it with the preliminary injunction hearing], there are hazards inherent in fully disposing of cases in such an expedited fashion—among them incomplete coverage of relevant issues and failure to present all relevant evidence. Such risks are especially acute in cases that turn on credibility determinations, as a truncated hearing will often limit the parties' opportunity to present and thoroughly examine witnesses. For this reason, our law demands that a trial court provide 'indisputably clear notice' to the parties before approving consolidation. [¶] Failure to provide indisputably clear notice of consolidation can constitute reversible error even if the right to a jury trial is not at issue. The stakes are even higher where … the surprise consolidation would result in the deprivation of a party's right to prosecute or defend the remaining legal claims before a jury. In these situations, we indulge every reasonable presumption against construing the parties' participation in the consolidated hearing as waiver." (Internal quotes omitted.)

Ciena Corp. v. Jarrard, 203 F.3d 312, 319 (4th Cir. 2000). "Although [FRCP 65] does not specify how much notice must be given to an adverse party before a court can enter a preliminary injunction, the Supreme Court has held that same-day notice is not enough. [¶] The interplay between Rule 65(a) (governing preliminary injunctions) and Rule 65(b) (governing TROs) is fluid, requiring greater procedural formality and notice for preliminary injunctions that remain operative for an unlimited time period. Thus, Rule 65(b), which authorizes a … TRO *without notice* to the defendant, nevertheless includes a requirement that whatever notice is practical be given. … Because a preliminary injunction is unlimited in duration, its entry always requires notice to the opposing party sufficient to give that party an opportunity to prepare an opposition to entry of an injunction. But broad discretion is given to the district court to manage the timing and process for entry of all interlocutory injunctions—both TROs and preliminary injunctions—so long as the opposing party is given a reasonable opportunity, commensurate with the scarcity of time under the circumstances, to prepare a defense and advance reasons why the injunction should not issue." *See also* ***U.S. v. Microsoft Corp.***, 147 F.3d 935, 944 (D.C.Cir.1998).

Hearing

Certified Restoration Dry Cleaning Network, L.L.C. v. Tenke Corp., 511 F.3d 535, 552 (6th Cir.2007). FRCP 65(a)(1)'s notice requirement implies "'a hearing in which the defendant is given a fair opportunity to oppose the application and to prepare for such opposition.' *At 553:* '[W]here the resolution of the questions to be considered in issuing a preliminary injunction turns on legal rather than factual conclusions, the taking or oral testimony by both sides is not a prerequisite to a fair hearing.' '[W]here facts are bitterly contested and credibility determinations must be made to decide whether injunctive relief should issue, an evidentiary hearing must be held. [However,] where material facts are not in dispute, or where facts in dispute are not material to the preliminary injunction sought, district courts generally need not hold an evidentiary hearing.'" *See also* ***PCI Transp. v. Fort Worth & W. R.R.***, 418 F.3d 535, 546 (5th Cir.2005).

Grounds

Cobell v. Norton, 391 F.3d 251, 258 (D.C.Cir.2004). "A preliminary injunction is an extraordinary remedy that should be granted only when the party seeking the relief, by a clear showing, carries the burden of persuasion. To prevail, the moving party must demonstrate (1) a substantial likelihood of success on the merits, (2) that it would suffer irreparable harm without injunctive relief, (3) that an injunction would not substantially harm other interested parties, and (4) that issuance of the injunction is in the public interest. *At 260-61:* Furthermore, the district court seemed to be insisting on compliance with [FRCP] 56(e) …, which expressly requires affidavits to be based on personal knowledge. But that rule applies to a motion for summary judgment. Here the district court treated the matter as a preliminary injunction proceeding. Nothing in the rules specifies what sort of affidavits are required at the preliminary injunction stage. This court has never decided that the Rule 56(e) standard should apply to such proceedings and there is good reason to believe it should not." *See also* ***Westar Energy, Inc. v. Lake***, 552 F.3d 1215, 1224 (10th Cir.2009).

U.S. v. Laerdal Mfg., 73 F.3d 852, 854-55 (9th Cir. 1995). "A district court cannot issue an injunction un-

less 'there exists some cognizable danger of recurrent violation.' ... Factors that a district court may consider in making this finding include 'the degree of scienter involved; the isolated or recurrent nature of the infraction; the defendant's recognition of the wrongful nature of his conduct; the extent to which the defendant's professional and personal characteristics might enable or tempt him to commit future violations; and the sincerity of any assurances against future violations.'"

Duration

U.S. Philips Corp. v. KBC Bank N.V., 590 F.3d 1091, 1093-94 (9th Cir.2010). "We restate the controlling rule governing the lifespan of a preliminary injunction: A preliminary injunction imposed according to the procedures outlined in [FRCP] 65 dissolves *ipso facto* when a final judgment is entered in the cause. This principle stems from the very purpose of a preliminary injunction, which is to preserve the status quo and the rights of the parties until a final judgment issues in the cause."

Levine v. Comcoa Ltd., 70 F.3d 1191, 1193 (11th Cir.1995). "The Supreme Court has said a TRO that is continued beyond the time permissible under Rule 65 should be treated as a preliminary injunction. This treatment is especially appropriate where ... there has been notice to the parties, a full hearing on a preliminary injunction, and then a stated and clear decision from the bench to extend the terms of the restraining order indefinitely...." *See also* ***In re Criminal Contempt Proceedings Against Crawford***, 329 F.3d 131, 137 (2d Cir.2003).

TRO or Injunction

Madsen v. Women's Health Ctr., Inc., 512 U.S. 753, 762 (1994). "An injunction, by its very nature, applies only to a particular group (or individuals) and regulates the activities, and perhaps the speech, of that group. It does so, however, because of the group's past actions in the context of a specific dispute between real parties."

City of N.Y. v. Mickalis Pawn Shop, LLC, 645 F.3d 114, 144 (2d Cir.2011). "Rule 65(d) is satisfied only if the enjoined party can ascertain from the four corners of the order precisely what acts are forbidden or required. [¶] Rule 65(d) is said to serve two general purposes: to prevent uncertainty and confusion on the part of those to whom the injunction is directed, and to ensure that the appellate court knows precisely what it is reviewing. [¶] In addition to complying with Rule 65(d)'s specificity requirements, district courts must take care to ensure that injunctive relief is not overbroad.... We have instructed that injunctive relief should be narrowly tailored to fit specific legal violations, ... and that the court must mould each decree to the necessities of the particular case.... An injunction may not enjoin all possible breaches of the law." (Internal quotes omitted.) *See also* ***U.S. v. Pentrack***, 428 F.3d 986, 990 (10th Cir.2005).

Bond

Nokia Corp. v. InterDigital, Inc., 645 F.3d 553, 556-57 (2d Cir.2011). "We ... consider the question of whether a wrongfully enjoined party is entitled to a presumption in favor of recovery against a bond posted pursuant to Rule 65(c).... [¶] We conclude that a presumption in favor of recovery is warranted for several reasons. Rule 65(c)'s bond requirement serves a number of functions. It assures the enjoined party that it may readily collect damages from the funds posted in the event that it was wrongfully enjoined, and that it may do so without further litigation and without regard to the possible insolvency of the plaintiff. In addition, the bond provides the plaintiff with notice of the maximum extent of its potential liability. *At 558:* The existence of such a presumption is strongly implied by the text of Rule 65(c).... The drafters' choice of words indicates that where a bond is posted, it serves as security for the 'costs and damages' incurred by the wrongfully restrained party. If they intended that district courts would have unfettered discretion as to how to handle costs associated with a wrongfully obtained injunction, certainly Rule 65(c) would have been worded differently. [¶] Other circuits that have explicitly addressed the question of whether a presumption in favor of recovery applies have answered it in the affirmative. *At 559:* Applying this presumption, the district court must have a 'good reason' to deny recovery against the bond. The burden of demonstrating that recovery should be denied is on the party opposing recovery. Good reasons to deny recovery of all or a portion of the alleged damages would be that the damages sought were unreasonable in amount or that a party failed to mitigate them." *See also* ***Global NAPs, Inc. v. Verizon New England, Inc.***, 489 F.3d 13, 23 (1st Cir.2007).

Zambelli Fireworks Mfg. Co. v. Wood, 592 F.3d 412, 426 (3d Cir.2010). "[W]e have recognized exceptions [for requiring a bond] only where 'the balance of [the] equities weighs overwhelmingly in favor of the party seeking the injunction' and when the District

Court 'make[s] specific findings.' [¶] Rule 65(c) constrains a district court's authority to enter a preliminary injunction, making it contingent upon the posting of a bond. It does not impose any obligation on the parties to seek a bond. [¶] We therefore hold that a district court lacks discretion under Rule 65(c) to waive a bond requirement except in the exceptionally narrow circumstance where the nature of the action necessarily precludes any monetary harm to the defendant, and that such bond shall be issued irrespective of any request by the parties." *See also* ***Johnson v. Couturier***, 572 F.3d 1067, 1086 (9th Cir.2009) (despite seemingly mandatory language, courts have discretion as to amount of bond, if any). *But see* ***Hoechst Diafoil Co. v. Nan Ya Plastics Corp.***, this page.

Connecticut Gen. Life Ins. v. New Images, 321 F.3d 878, 883 (9th Cir.2003). "We recognize that some other circuits have held that a motion to set bond is not required to preserve the issue for appeal. We do not, however, believe that the language of Rule 65(c) absolves the party affected by the injunction from its obligation of presenting evidence that a bond is needed, so that the district court is afforded an opportunity to exercise its discretion in setting the amount of the bond. Without such evidence before it, the district court did not abuse its discretion by not reaching the bond issue."

Hoechst Diafoil Co. v. Nan Ya Plastics Corp., 174 F.3d 411, 421 (4th Cir.1999). "A district court must fix a bond whenever it grants a preliminary injunction or restraining order.... This rule is mandatory and unambiguous. Although the district court has discretion to set the bond amount 'in such sum as the court deems proper,' it is not free to disregard the bond requirement altogether. In view of the clear language of Rule 65(c), failure to require a bond upon issuing injunctive relief is reversible error." *But see* ***Zambelli Fireworks Mfg. Co. v. Wood***, p. 971.

Persons Bound

Blockowicz v. Williams, 630 F.3d 563, 567 (7th Cir. 2010). "[W]e have explained that a person is in 'active concert or participation' with an enjoined party, and thus bound by the injunction, if 'he aids or abets an enjoined party in violating [the] injunction,' or if he is in privity with an enjoined party. *At 568:* Actions that aid and abet in violating the injunction must occur after the injunction is imposed for the purposes of Rule 65(d)(2)(C), and certainly after the wrongdoing that led to the injunction occurred. This requirement is apparent from Rule 65(d)(2)'s text, which requires that nonparties have 'actual notice' of the injunction. A nonparty who engages in conduct before an injunction is imposed cannot have 'actual notice' of the injunction at the time of their relevant conduct." *See also* ***Eli Lilly & Co. v. Gottstein***, 617 F.3d 186, 195 (2d Cir.2010); ***Independent Fed'n of Flight Attendants v. Cooper***, 134 F.3d 917, 920 (8th Cir.1998).

National Spiritual Assembly of the Bahá'ís of the U.S. of Am. Under the Hereditary Guardianship, Inc. v. National Spiritual Assembly of the Bahá'ís of the U.S. of Am., Inc., 628 F.3d 837, 848-49 (7th Cir. 2010). "Broadly speaking, [FRCP 65(d)] and the common-law doctrine [that an injunction binds the parties and those in privity with the parties] contemplate two categories of nonparties potentially bound by an injunction. [¶] [One] category is captured under the general rubric of 'privity.' It is generally accepted that an injunction may be enforced against a nonparty in 'privity' with an enjoined party. This concept can be hard to pin down.... [¶] The concept ..., however[,] is ultimately bounded by due process.... [¶] When privity is invoked as a basis for binding a nonparty to an injunction, it is 'restricted to persons so identified in interest with those named in the decree that it would be reasonable to conclude that their rights and interests have been represented and adjudicated in the original injunction proceeding.'"

Comedy Club, Inc. v. Improv W. Assocs., 553 F.3d 1277, 1287 (9th Cir.2009). "[A]n injunction may bind not only parties to the action but also 'their officers, agents, servants, employees, and attorneys, and [upon] those persons in active concert or participation with them.' [The contract at issue] reaches beyond persons with an agency or assignee relationship with [P's] partners, and literally purports to bind [P's] ex-wife and his ex-wife's cousins, nephews, uncles, and aunts. The text of Rule 65(d) is exclusive [and] does not list collateral relatives of former spouses, or even grandparents, as potential non-parties who may be bound by a contract.... *At 1288:* Such nonparties can only be restrained to the extent permitted by Rule 65(d)."

FRCP 65.1. PROCEEDINGS AGAINST A SURETY

Whenever these rules (including the Supplemental Rules for Admiralty or Maritime Claims and Asset Forfeiture Actions) require or allow a party to give security,

and security is given through a bond or other undertaking with one or more sureties, each surety submits to the court's jurisdiction and irrevocably appoints the court clerk as its agent for receiving service of any papers that affect its liability on the bond or undertaking. The surety's liability may be enforced on motion without an independent action. The motion and any notice that the court orders may be served on the court clerk, who must promptly mail a copy of each to every surety whose address is known.

See selected Notes of Advisory Committee to FRCP 65.1, p. 1231.

History of FRCP 65.1: Adopted Feb. 28, 1966, eff. July 1, 1966. Amended Mar. 2, 1987, eff. Aug. 1, 1987; Apr. 30, 2007, eff. Dec. 1, 2007.

ANNOTATIONS

Celotex Corp. v. Edwards, 514 U.S. 300, 312 (1995). FRCP 65.1 "outlines a streamlined *procedure* for executing on bonds. It assures judgment creditors ... that they do not have to bring a separate action against sureties, and instead allows them to collect on the supersedeas bond by merely filing a motion. Just because [FRCP 65.1] provides a simplified procedure for collecting on a bond, however, does not mean that such a procedure, like a more complicated procedure of a full-fledged lawsuit, cannot be stayed by a lawfully entered injunction." *See also U.S. v. Lacey*, 982 F.2d 410, 412 n.2 (10th Cir.1992).

Global NAPs, Inc. v. Verizon New England, Inc., 489 F.3d 13, 20 (1st Cir.2007). Enforcement of liability against a surety "may be done on motion, without the need for filing an independent action. Although the terms of Rule 65.1 apply only to sureties, courts have applied that rule's procedures when imposing liability on a principal as well."

FRCP 66. RECEIVERS

These rules govern an action in which the appointment of a receiver is sought or a receiver sues or is sued. But the practice in administering an estate by a receiver or a similar court-appointed officer must accord with the historical practice in federal courts or with a local rule. An action in which a receiver has been appointed may be dismissed only by court order.

History of FRCP 66: Adopted Dec. 20, 1937, eff. Sept. 16, 1938. Amended Dec. 27, 1946, eff. Mar. 19, 1948; Dec. 29, 1948, eff. Oct. 20, 1949; Apr. 30, 2007, eff. Dec. 1, 2007.

See also 28 U.S.C. §959 (receiver suable without leave of court).

ANNOTATIONS

Canada Life Assur. Co. v. LaPeter, 563 F.3d 837, 842 (9th Cir.2009). "We have never squarely addressed the issue of whether federal or state law governs the appointment of a receiver by a district court where federal jurisdiction is based on diversity. Those circuits that have considered the issue have held that federal law governs. *At 843:* '[T]o the extent Rule 66 dictates what principles should be applied to federal receiverships, courts must comply with the Rule even in the face of differing state law.' [¶] [R]egardless of whether state law provides a vehicle by which to appoint a receiver, the federal courts are free to provide that remedy solely by virtue of their equitable powers. [W]e join the Eleventh and Eighth Circuits in holding that federal law governs the issue of whether to appoint a receiver in a diversity action."

Aviation Sup. v. R.S.B.I. Aerospace, Inc., 999 F.2d 314, 316-17 (8th Cir.1993). "The appointment of a receiver in a diversity case is a procedural matter governed by federal law and federal equitable principles. A receiver is an extraordinary equitable remedy that is only justified in extreme situations. Although there is no precise formula for determining when a receiver may be appointed, factors typically warranting appointment are a valid claim by the party seeking the appointment; the probability that fraudulent conduct has occurred or will occur to frustrate that claim; imminent danger that property will be concealed, lost, or diminished in value; inadequacy of legal remedies; lack of a less drastic equitable remedy; and likelihood that appointing the receiver will do more good than harm." *See also* ***Brill & Harrington Invs. v. Vernon S&L Ass'n***, 787 F.Supp. 250, 253-54 (D.D.C.1992).

FRCP 67. DEPOSIT INTO COURT

(a) Depositing Property. If any part of the relief sought is a money judgment or the disposition of a sum of money or some other deliverable thing, a party—on notice to every other party and by leave of court—may deposit with the court all or part of the money or thing, whether or not that party claims any of it. The depositing party must deliver to the clerk a copy of the order permitting deposit.

(b) Investing and Withdrawing Funds. Money paid into court under this rule must be deposited and withdrawn in accordance with 28 U.S.C. §§2041 and 2042[1] and any like statute. The money must be deposited in an interest-bearing account or invested in a court-approved, interest-bearing instrument.

1. **Editor's note:** References in text: Act of June 26, 1934, c. 756, §23, as amended (48 Stat. 1236, 58 Stat. 845), 31 U.S.C. §725v, referred to in text, was repealed by P.L. 97-258, §5(b), Sept. 13, 1982, 96 Stat. 1074, the first section of

which enacted Title 31, Money and Finance. Insofar it was not superseded by 28 U.S.C. §§2041 and 2042, Judiciary and Judicial Procedure, the Act of June 26, 1934, §23, as amended (31 U.S.C. §725v) was reenacted as 28 U.S.C. §§572a and 2043 by P.L. 97-258, §2(g)(3), (4).

History of FRCP 67: Adopted Dec. 20, 1937, eff. Sept. 16, 1938. Amended Dec. 29, 1948, eff. Oct. 20, 1949; Apr. 28, 1983, eff. Aug. 1, 1983; Apr. 30, 2007, eff. Dec. 1, 2007.

ANNOTATIONS

In re Craig's Stores, 402 F.3d 522, 530-31 (5th Cir. 2005) (Dennis, J., concurring). "Under [FRCP] 67, the disbursement of funds is governed by 28 U.S.C. §§2041 and 2042; these statutory provisions assign the power and duty of approving disbursements exclusively to the depositary court; and §§2041 [and] 2042 require that the depositary court disburse the funds only to persons judicially determined to be rightful owners. The purpose of a deposit under Rule 67 is to relieve the depositor of responsibility for the money or thing in dispute while the parties litigate their differences with respect to the res. [¶] Once the deposit is made, the funds can be withdrawn only by order of the depositary court. Rule 67 specifically states that … §§2041 and 2042 provide the rules that must be followed by the court and the parties with respect to orders of withdrawal or disbursement. … Funds deposited in court are held only for those persons judicially found by the court to be entitled to them as rightful owners. The burden is on the claimant to establish his right to withdraw money deposited with the court. The right to recover from a fund deposited in court must be based on the strength of the title of the claimant and not on the weakness of the title or another claimant. Rule 67 providing for deposit in court, generally, continues in effect similar special provisions contained in statutes and rules pertaining to bills of interpleader, bills in the nature of interpleader, and admiralty. Proceedings for disbursement of funds deposited in court are equitable in nature and in the nature of interpleader." *See also* ***Alstom Caribe, Inc. v. Geo. P. Reintjes, Co.***, 484 F.3d 106, 113-14 (1st Cir. 2007).

LTV Corp. v. Gulf States Steel, Inc., 969 F.2d 1050, 1063 (D.C.Cir.1992). "The decision whether to allow a Rule 67 deposit generally lies within the discretion of the district court. [¶] It is well-settled that Rule 67 … 'shall not abridge, enlarge or modify any substantive right.' 'The Rule 67 procedure provides a place of safekeeping for disputed funds pending the resolution of a legal dispute, but it cannot be used as a means of altering the contractual relationships and legal duties of the parties.'"

Cordero v. De Jesus-Mendez, 922 F.2d 11, 18 (1st Cir.1990). "Responsibility for placing money deposited with a court in an interest-bearing account rests with the clerk of the court. … The requirement that an order of deposit be served on the court clerk 'is simply to assure that the clerk knows what is being deposited and what his responsibilities are with respect to the deposit.'"

Ziaee v. Vest, 916 F.2d 1204, 1209 (7th Cir.1990). "Registry funds 'shall be deposited in an interest-bearing account or invested in an interest-bearing instrument approved by the court.' Interest earned on these funds will be credited against the judgment. … The court's 'approval' is required under Rule 67 only when funds are to be invested in an interest-bearing 'instrument'; in all other cases the clerk should put the money in an interest-bearing 'account' without ado."

FRCP 68. OFFER OF JUDGMENT

(a) Making an Offer; Judgment on an Accepted Offer. At least 14 days before the date set for trial, a party defending against a claim may serve on an opposing party an offer to allow judgment on specified terms, with the costs then accrued. If, within 14 days after being served, the opposing party serves written notice accepting the offer, either party may then file the offer and notice of acceptance, plus proof of service. The clerk must then enter judgment.

(b) Unaccepted Offer. An unaccepted offer is considered withdrawn, but it does not preclude a later offer. Evidence of an unaccepted offer is not admissible except in a proceeding to determine costs.

(c) Offer After Liability Is Determined. When one party's liability to another has been determined but the extent of liability remains to be determined by further proceedings, the party held liable may make an offer of judgment. It must be served within a reasonable time—but at least 14 days—before the date set for a hearing to determine the extent of liability.

(d) Paying Costs After an Unaccepted Offer. If the judgment that the offeree finally obtains is not more favorable than the unaccepted offer, the offeree must pay the costs incurred after the offer was made.

See selected Notes of Advisory Committee to FRCP 68, p. 1231.

History of FRCP 68: Adopted Dec. 20, 1937, eff. Sept. 16, 1938. Amended Dec. 27, 1946, eff. Mar. 19, 1948; Feb. 28, 1966, eff. July 1, 1966; Mar. 2, 1987, eff. Aug. 1, 1987; Apr. 30, 2007, eff. Dec. 1, 2007; Mar. 26, 2009, eff. Dec. 1, 2009.

See *Commentaries*, "Offer of Judgment," ch. 5-D, p. 317; *O'Connor's Federal Civil Forms* (2012), FORMS 5D.

ANNOTATIONS

Marek v. Chesny, 473 U.S. 1, 6 (1985). FRCP 68 does not "require that a defendant's offer itemize the respective amounts being tendered for settlement of the underlying substantive claim and for costs. [¶] If an offer recites that costs are included or specifies an amount for costs, and the plaintiff accepts the offer, the judgment will necessarily include costs; if the offer does not state that costs are included and an amount for costs is not specified, the court will be obliged ... to include in its judgment an additional amount ... to cover the costs. In either case, however, the offer has *allowed* judgment to be entered against the defendant both for damages caused by the challenged conduct and for costs."

Lucero v. Bureau of Collection Recovery, Inc., 639 F.3d 1239, 1243 (10th Cir.2011). "As Rule 68 operates, if an offer is made for a plaintiff[']s maximum recovery, his action may be rendered moot. [O]ther circuits have concluded that if a defendant makes an offer of judgment in complete satisfaction of a plaintiff[']s claims *in a non-class action*, the plaintiff[']s claims are rendered moot because he lacks a remaining interest in the outcome of the case. We must query, however, whether a Rule 68 offer made to the representative of a proposed class before the district court could reasonably be expected to rule on class certification moots the case. [¶] Rule 68 has been applied inconsistently in proposed class actions prior to class certification. While the Supreme Court has provided guidance on the effect of offers of judgment made *once a decision has been rendered on a motion to certify a class*, uncertainty prevails among the lower courts regarding the jurisdictional effect of offers of judgment made prior to class certification. Some courts conclude that an offer of judgment renders the claim moot, while others conclude it does not. At least one court has distinguished the non-moot case from the moot based upon the period of time elapsed prior to the offer of judgment. In a similar vein, some courts have decided the question of mootness based on whether the motion for class certification was filed during the pendency of the offer of judgment. *At 1244:* [T]he operation of Rule 68 in the class action context has been criticized for its tendency to force plaintiffs to move for class certification on an inadequate record. *At 1250:* In sum, we hold that a named plaintiff in a proposed class action for monetary relief may proceed to seek timely class certification where an unaccepted offer of judgment is tendered in satisfaction of the plaintiff[']s individual claim before the court can reasonably be expected to rule on the class certification motion."

Fafel v. DiPaola, 399 F.3d 403, 413-14 (1st Cir. 2005). "In order to trigger entry of judgment under [FRCP] 68, one party must first 'file the offer and notice of acceptance together with proof of service thereof.' Upon filing, the clerk of court 'shall enter judgment.' In the event that an offeree rejects an offer of judgment made in compliance with Rule 68, the court may be called upon to enforce the rule's cost-shifting provision, thus imbuing the decision to reject a fair offer of judgment with meaningful consequences. In order to enforce the cost-shifting provision, ... a court necessarily must evaluate the terms of the rejected offer in order to compare it against the value of any 'judgment finally obtained by the offeree' and thereby determine whether the offeree is liable for 'costs incurred after making of the offer.' [¶] If an offer of judgment is accepted and judgment entered, a court may still be called upon ... to decide a motion brought under [FRCP] 60(b) to vacate the Rule 68 judgment. Again, in doing so, a court may have to interpret the terms of the underlying offer of judgment in order to determine whether relief from judgment is warranted. [¶] Finally, when a district court is called upon to enforce a Rule 68 judgment, it may examine the parties' intent regarding the effect of that judgment, as manifested by the offer and acceptance of judgment filed with the court."

Pouillon v. Little, 326 F.3d 713, 718-19 (6th Cir. 2003). "Nothing in the language of Rule 68 suggests that a Rule 68 offer that is not [timely] accepted ... ever loses its cost-shifting effect in the life of a case. Rule 68, by its own language, requires that an offer made pursuant to the rule be compared to the judgment 'finally obtained.' There is no requirement that a Rule 68 offer must be renewed after an appeal and remand to continue its effectiveness."

Utility Automation 2000, Inc. v. Choctawhatchee Elec. Coop., 298 F.3d 1238, 1243 (11th Cir. 2002). "[W]here an offer is ambiguous with respect to whether it includes fees, that ambiguity will be construed against the drafter. [¶] An offer that does unambiguously include attorneys' fees, on the other hand, will bar the [party] who accepts it from seeking addi-

FRCP 68

tional attorneys' fees under the relevant statute (or as 'costs then accrued')."

Payne v. Milwaukee Cty., 288 F.3d 1021, 1024 (7th Cir.2002). "Rule 68 is designed to change the incentive structure of a plaintiff faced with a reasonable offer. The twin aims of the rule, in its *ex post* application, are to compensate the defense for costs it ought not to have incurred, and to deter future plaintiffs from lightly disregarding reasonable settlement offers made with the formalities prescribed by the rule. [¶] [P] claims that [D's] failure to renew its Rule 68 offer after the result in the original trial was partially set aside by this court means that there was no operative Rule 68 offer at all to bar his right to full fees and costs. That is simply wrong."

Amati v. City of Woodstock, 176 F.3d 952, 958 (7th Cir.1999). "We cannot find anything in [FRCP 68], or the case law, to support the view that the condition which [Ds] imposed—all [Ps] must accept the offer of judgment for it to be effective—is invalid, or if it is that the offer is therefore enforceable. [S]ince the purpose of an offer of judgment is to settle the case in advance of trial, conditioning it on acceptance by all plaintiffs may be necessary to head off the trial."

Cole v. Wodziak, 169 F.3d 486, 487 (7th Cir.1999). "The legal problem is that the judge gave oral negotiations the same effect as a written offer of judgment under [FRCP] 68. A spurned Rule 68 offer, followed by a lower recovery at trial, precludes an award of costs (including attorneys' fees, when a statute defines them as part of costs) incurred after the offer's rejection. But to obtain the benefits of Rule 68 a defendant must follow its requirements, which [D] did not." *See also* ***Berkla v. Corel Corp.***, 302 F.3d 909, 922 (9th Cir.2002).

Adsani v. Miller, 139 F.3d 67, 72 (2d Cir.1998). "[T]he most reasonable inference is that the term 'costs' in Rule 68 was intended to refer to all costs properly awardable under the relevant substantive statute or other authority. [A]ll costs properly awardable in an action are to be considered within the scope of Rule 68 'costs.' Thus, absent congressional expressions to the contrary, where the underlying statute defines 'costs' to include attorney's fees, we are satisfied such fees are to be included as costs for purposes of Rule 68." *See also* ***Sharpe v. Cureton***, 319 F.3d 259, 274 (6th Cir.2003) (in 42 U.S.C. §1983, FRCP 68 costs include P's attorney fees).

Jordan v. Time, Inc., 111 F.3d 102, 105 (11th Cir. 1997). "We believe that the mandatory language of [FRCP 68] leaves no room for district court discretion. When a proper Rule 68 offer is made and the other requirements of the rule are met, the district court must award costs measured from the time the offer was served. As such, the proper interpretation of Rule 68 is a legal question which we review de novo. However, any disputed facts concerning the events surrounding a Rule 68 offer are reviewed for clear error."

Goos v. National Ass'n of Realtors, 68 F.3d 1380, 1382 n.1 (D.C.Cir.1995). "[W]here an offer has been made pursuant to Rule 68, the district court must first determine the proper pre-settlement offer fees and then add them to the damages awarded. Only if that sum exceeds the offer should the district court proceed to determine the post-settlement fees."

Haworth v. Nevada, 56 F.3d 1048, 1052-53 (9th Cir. 1995). "When a plaintiff rejects a Rule 68 offer, the reasonableness of an attorney fee award ... will depend, at least in part, on the district court's consideration of the results the plaintiff obtained by going to trial compared to the Rule 68 offer. [¶] In determining what fee is reasonable in this circumstance, the district court must take into consideration the amount of the Rule 68 offer, the stage of the litigation at which the offer was made, what services were rendered thereafter, the amount obtained by judgment, and whether it was reasonable to continue litigating the case after the Rule 68 offer was made."

Lang v. Gates, 36 F.3d 73, 75 (9th Cir.1994). "[T]o require that plaintiffs be allowed to accept or to reject joint offers individually 'might encourage multiple plaintiffs to hedge their bets by collusively having at least one party accept the offer and at least one other decline. That way they could both benefit if the judgment is greater than the offer, and could both avoid incurring costs and [losing] attorney's fees if it is less.' Because joint offers will most often be made where plaintiffs have a common interest, the risk of collusion is great."

FRCP 69. EXECUTION

(a) In General.

(1) ***Money Judgment; Applicable Procedure.*** A money judgment is enforced by a writ of execution, unless the court directs otherwise. The procedure on execution—and in proceedings supplementary to and in aid of judgment or ex-

ecution—must accord with the procedure of the state where the court is located, but a federal statute governs to the extent it applies.

(2) *Obtaining Discovery.* In aid of the judgment or execution, the judgment creditor or a successor in interest whose interest appears of record may obtain discovery from any person—including the judgment debtor—as provided in these rules or by the procedure of the state where the court is located.

(b) Against Certain Public Officers. When a judgment has been entered against a revenue officer in the circumstances stated in 28 U.S.C. §2006, or against an officer of Congress in the circumstances stated in 2 U.S.C. §118, the judgment must be satisfied as those statutes provide.

See selected Notes of Advisory Committee to FRCP 69, p. 1231.

History of FRCP 69: Adopted Dec. 20, 1937, eff. Sept. 16, 1938. Amended Dec. 29, 1948, eff. Oct. 20, 1949; Mar. 30, 1970, eff. July 1, 1970; Mar. 2, 1987, eff. Aug. 1, 1987; Apr. 30, 2007, eff. Dec. 1, 2007.

See also 28 U.S.C. §1651 (power to issue writ of execution), §§2001-2007 (executions and judicial sales), §2006 (execution against revenue officers), §2413 (executions in favor of the U.S.).

ANNOTATIONS

EM Ltd. v. Republic of Arg., ___ F.3d ___ (2d Cir. 2012) (No. 11-4065-cv(L); 8-20-12). "Post-judgment discovery is governed by [FRCP] 69.... The scope of discovery under Rule 69(a)(2) is constrained principally in that it must be calculated to assist in collecting on a judgment. [¶] It is not uncommon to seek asset discovery from third parties, including banks, that possess information pertaining to the judgment debtor's assets. [¶] Nor is it unusual for the judgment creditor to seek disclosure related to assets held outside the jurisdiction of the court where the discovery request is made."

In re Clerici, 481 F.3d 1324, 1336 (11th Cir.2007). FRCP 69(a) "provides the process by which a judgment creditor can enforce a money judgment and authorizes post-judgment discovery in aid of execution of that judgment. Rule 69(a) itself does not prescribe a practice and procedure for gathering evidence, but gives the judgment creditor the choice of federal or state discovery rules. Rule 69(a) simply authorizes a setting, post-judgment execution, in which discovery may take place, not the specific manner or procedures in which testimony should be taken or documents should be produced." *See also* ***Star Ins. v. Risk Mktg. Grp.***, 561 F.3d 656, 661 (7th Cir.2009); ***Natural Gas Pipeline Co. v. Energy Gathering, Inc.***, 2 F.3d 1397, 1405 (5th Cir. 1993).

Andrews v. Roadway Express Inc., 473 F.3d 565, 568-69 (5th Cir.2006). Based on the language of FRCP 69(a), Ps "contend that state law does not apply ... because the [court's order] 'directed otherwise.' [¶] [W]e have not found[] any authority supporting [Ps'] assertion that the district court's retention of continuing jurisdiction to enforce its judgment is tantamount to electing a process of enforcement other than execution according to state law. [W]e hesitate to interpret the [o]rder's language so broadly as to override Rule 69(a)'s standard writ of enforcement procedures, especially since Rule 69(a)'s 'otherwise' clause is to be construed narrowly. [T]he district court's mere retention of continued limited jurisdiction to enforce a final judgment does not trigger the 'otherwise' clause of Rule 69(a)."

Schneider v. National R.R. Passenger Corp., 72 F.3d 17, 19 (2d Cir.1995). FRCP 69(a) "adopts state procedures for execution only to the extent that they do not conflict with any applicable 'statute of the U.S.' This term includes the [FRCPs]. [¶] Rule 69(a) is thereby made subject to [FRCP] 4(c)[, which] trumps state law to the extent that it determines *who* can levy on a writ of execution issued by a federal court." *See also* ***Aetna Cas. & Sur. Co. v. Markarian***, 114 F.3d 346, 349 (1st Cir.1997); ***Leroy v. City of Houston***, 906 F.2d 1068, 1085 (5th Cir.1990).

Citizens Elec. Corp. v. Bituminous Fire & Mar. Ins., 68 F.3d 1016, 1020 (7th Cir.1995). "In federal practice, garnishment to collect a judgment is not—at least, need not be—an independent suit. It is part of the main action, prosecuted under [FRCP] 69 by virtue of the supplemental jurisdiction."

FRCP 70. ENFORCING A JUDGMENT FOR A SPECIFIC ACT

(a) Party's Failure to Act; Ordering Another to Act. If a judgment requires a party to convey land, to deliver a deed or other document, or to perform any other specific act and the party fails to comply within the time specified, the court may order the act to be done—at the disobedient party's expense—by another person appointed by the court. When done, the act has the same effect as if done by the party.

(b) Vesting Title. If the real or personal property is within the district, the court—instead of ordering a conveyance—may enter a judgment divesting any party's title and vesting it in others. That judgment has the effect of a legally executed conveyance.

(c) Obtaining a Writ of Attachment or Sequestration. On application by a party entitled to performance of an act, the clerk must issue a writ of attachment or sequestration against the disobedient party's property to compel obedience.

(d) Obtaining a Writ of Execution or Assistance. On application by a party who obtains a judgment or order for possession, the clerk must issue a writ of execution or assistance.

(e) Holding in Contempt. The court may also hold the disobedient party in contempt.

History of FRCP 70: Adopted Dec. 20, 1937, eff. Sept. 16, 1938. Amended Apr. 30, 2007, eff. Dec. 1, 2007.

See also 18 U.S.C. §401 (power of court to punish or hold in contempt); 28 U.S.C. §1651 (power to issue writs).

ANNOTATIONS

Maness v. Meyers, 419 U.S. 449, 458 (1975). "We begin with the basic proposition that all orders and judgments of courts must be complied with promptly. If a person to whom a court directs an order believes that order is incorrect the remedy is to appeal, but, absent a stay, he must comply promptly with the order pending appeal."

Analytical Eng'g v. Baldwin Filters, Inc., 425 F.3d 443, 451 (7th Cir.2005). "The express language of Rule 70 establishes the extent of the district court's limited post-judgment authority.... We recognize that a district court's purview under Rule 70 is limited to effectuating its final-judgment orders, and that in granting relief under Rule 70, a district court cannot grant new rights or extinguish previous rights held by either party. Under Rule 70, therefore, a district court may direct a party to complete a specific act where the district court previously directed the same party to perform the same act in its final judgment and that party has failed to comply."

Westlake N. Prop. Owners Ass'n v. City of Thousand Oaks, 915 F.2d 1301, 1304 (9th Cir.1990). "According to its plain language, [FRCP 70] applies only to parties who have failed to perform specific acts pursuant to a judgment. ... Consequently, rule 70 cannot apply [to the attorneys representing the parties]."

Leroy v. City of Houston, 906 F.2d 1068, 1085-86 (5th Cir.1990). "[W]e have held that under Rule 70 a federal court may enforce a money judgment against a state or local government by ordering the defendant to pay it."

Arnold v. BLaST Intermediate Unit 17, 843 F.2d 122, 128 n.11 (3d Cir.1988). "Rule 70's equitable remedies are ordinarily not applied to the enforcement of a monetary judgment. However, a district court may order payment under Rule 70 in unusual circumstances, as where state intransigence precludes the enforcement of the judgment through normal procedures."

FRCP 71. ENFORCING RELIEF FOR OR AGAINST A NONPARTY

When an order grants relief for a nonparty or may be enforced against a nonparty, the procedure for enforcing the order is the same as for a party.

History of FRCP 71: Adopted Dec. 20, 1937, eff. Sept. 16, 1938. Amended Mar. 2, 1987, eff. Aug. 1, 1987; Apr. 30, 2007, eff. Dec. 1, 2007.

See also 28 U.S.C. §1651 (power to issue writs); FRCP 4, 4.1 (process generally), FRCP 64 (writs of attachment, sequestration, and equivalent remedies).

ANNOTATIONS

Westlake N. Prop. Owners Ass'n v. City of Thousand Oaks, 915 F.2d 1301, 1304 (9th Cir.1990). "Rule 71 was designed to memorialize the common sense rule that courts can enforce their orders against both parties and non-parties. It therefore cannot provide an *independent* basis upon which to impose sanctions against attorneys."

Washington Hosp. v. White, 889 F.2d 1294, 1299 (3d Cir.1989). FRCP 71 "allows a non-party to enforce a court order in its favor just as a party could."

TITLE IX. SPECIAL PROCEEDINGS

FRCP 71.1. CONDEMNING REAL OR PERSONAL PROPERTY

(a) Applicability of Other Rules. These rules govern proceedings to condemn real and personal property by eminent domain, except as this rule provides otherwise.

(b) Joinder of Properties. The plaintiff may join separate pieces of property in a single action, no matter whether they are owned by the same persons or sought for the same use.

(c) Complaint.

(1) ***Caption.*** The complaint must contain a caption as provided in Rule 10(a). The plaintiff

must, however, name as defendants both the property—designated generally by kind, quantity, and location—and at least one owner of some part of or interest in the property.

(2) *Contents.* The complaint must contain a short and plain statement of the following:

(A) the authority for the taking;

(B) the uses for which the property is to be taken;

(C) a description sufficient to identify the property;

(D) the interests to be acquired; and

(E) for each piece of property, a designation of each defendant who has been joined as an owner or owner of an interest in it.

(3) ***Parties.*** When the action commences, the plaintiff need join as defendants only those persons who have or claim an interest in the property and whose names are then known. But before any hearing on compensation, the plaintiff must add as defendants all those persons who have or claim an interest and whose names have become known or can be found by a reasonably diligent search of the records, considering both the property's character and value and the interests to be acquired. All others may be made defendants under the designation "Unknown Owners."

(4) ***Procedure.*** Notice must be served on all defendants as provided in Rule 71.1(d), whether they were named as defendants when the action commenced or were added later. A defendant may answer as provided in Rule 71.1(e). The court, meanwhile, may order any distribution of a deposit that the facts warrant.

(5) ***Filing; Additional Copies.*** In addition to filing the complaint, the plaintiff must give the clerk at least one copy for the defendants' use and additional copies at the request of the clerk or a defendant.

(d) Process.

(1) ***Delivering Notice to the Clerk.*** On filing a complaint, the plaintiff must promptly deliver to the clerk joint or several notices directed to the named defendants. When adding defendants, the plaintiff must deliver to the clerk additional notices directed to the new defendants.

(2) ***Contents of the Notice.***

(A) *Main Contents.* Each notice must name the court, the title of the action, and the defendant to whom it is directed. It must describe the property sufficiently to identify it, but need not describe any property other than that to be taken from the named defendant. The notice must also state:

(i) that the action is to condemn property;

(ii) the interest to be taken;

(iii) the authority for the taking;

(iv) the uses for which the property is to be taken;

(v) that the defendant may serve an answer on the plaintiff's attorney within 21 days after being served with the notice;

(vi) that the failure to so serve an answer constitutes consent to the taking and to the court's authority to proceed with the action and fix the compensation; and

(vii) that a defendant who does not serve an answer may file a notice of appearance.

(B) *Conclusion.* The notice must conclude with the name, telephone number, and e-mail address of the plaintiff's attorney and an address within the district in which the action is brought where the attorney may be served.

(3) ***Serving the Notice.***

(A) *Personal Service.* When a defendant whose address is known resides within the United States or a territory subject to the administrative or judicial jurisdiction of the United States, personal service of the notice (without a copy of the complaint) must be made in accordance with Rule 4.

(B) *Service by Publication.*

(i) A defendant may be served by publication only when the plaintiff's attorney files a certificate stating that the attorney believes the defendant cannot be personally served, because after diligent inquiry within the state where the complaint is filed, the defendant's place of residence is still unknown or, if known, that it is beyond the territorial limits of

personal service. Service is then made by publishing the notice—once a week for at least 3 successive weeks—in a newspaper published in the county where the property is located or, if there is no such newspaper, in a newspaper with general circulation where the property is located. Before the last publication, a copy of the notice must also be mailed to every defendant who cannot be personally served but whose place of residence is then known. Unknown owners may be served by publication in the same manner by a notice addressed to "Unknown Owners."

(ii) Service by publication is complete on the date of the last publication. The plaintiff's attorney must prove publication and mailing by a certificate, attach a printed copy of the published notice, and mark on the copy the newspaper's name and the dates of publication.

(4) ***Effect of Delivery and Service.*** Delivering the notice to the clerk and serving it have the same effect as serving a summons under Rule 4.

(5) ***Amending the Notice; Proof of Service and Amending the Proof.*** Rule 4(a)(2) governs amending the notice. Rule 4(*l*) governs proof of service and amending it.

(e) Appearance or Answer.

(1) ***Notice of Appearance.*** A defendant that has no objection or defense to the taking of its property may serve a notice of appearance designating the property in which it claims an interest. The defendant must then be given notice of all later proceedings affecting the defendant.

(2) ***Answer.*** A defendant that has an objection or defense to the taking must serve an answer within 21 days after being served with the notice. The answer must:

(A) identify the property in which the defendant claims an interest;

(B) state the nature and extent of the interest; and

(C) state all the defendant's objections and defenses to the taking.

(3) ***Waiver of Other Objections and Defenses; Evidence on Compensation.*** A defendant waives all objections and defenses not stated in its answer. No other pleading or motion asserting an additional objection or defense is allowed. But at the trial on compensation, a defendant—whether or not it has previously appeared or answered—may present evidence on the amount of compensation to be paid and may share in the award.

(f) Amending Pleadings. Without leave of court, the plaintiff may—as often as it wants—amend the complaint at any time before the trial on compensation. But no amendment may be made if it would result in a dismissal inconsistent with Rule 71.1(i)(1) or (2). The plaintiff need not serve a copy of an amendment, but must serve notice of the filing, as provided in Rule 5(b), on every affected party who has appeared and, as provided in Rule 71.1(d), on every affected party who has not appeared. In addition, the plaintiff must give the clerk at least one copy of each amendment for the defendants' use, and additional copies at the request of the clerk or a defendant. A defendant may appear or answer in the time and manner and with the same effect as provided in Rule 71.1(e).

(g) Substituting Parties. If a defendant dies, becomes incompetent, or transfers an interest after being joined, the court may, on motion and notice of hearing, order that the proper party be substituted. Service of the motion and notice on a nonparty must be made as provided in Rule 71.1(d)(3).

(h) Trial of the Issues.

(1) ***Issues Other Than Compensation; Compensation.*** In an action involving eminent domain under federal law, the court tries all issues, including compensation, except when compensation must be determined:

(A) by any tribunal specially constituted by a federal statute to determine compensation; or

(B) if there is no such tribunal, by a jury when a party demands one within the time to answer or within any additional time the court sets, unless the court appoints a commission.

(2) ***Appointing a Commission; Commission's Powers and Report.***

(A) *Reasons for Appointing.* If a party has demanded a jury, the court may instead appoint a three-person commission to determine compensation because of the character, location, or quantity of the property to be condemned or for other just reasons.

(B) *Alternate Commissioners.* The court may appoint up to two additional persons to serve as alternate commissioners to hear the case and replace commissioners who, before a decision is filed, the court finds unable or disqualified to perform their duties. Once the commission renders its final decision, the court must discharge any alternate who has not replaced a commissioner.

(C) *Examining the Prospective Commissioners.* Before making its appointments, the court must advise the parties of the identity and qualifications of each prospective commissioner and alternate, and may permit the parties to examine them. The parties may not suggest appointees, but for good cause may object to a prospective commissioner or alternate.

(D) *Commission's Powers and Report.* A commission has the powers of a master under Rule 53(c). Its action and report are determined by a majority. Rule 53(d), (e), and (f) apply to its action and report.

(i) Dismissal of the Action or a Defendant.

(1) ***Dismissing the Action.***

(A) *By the Plaintiff.* If no compensation hearing on a piece of property has begun, and if the plaintiff has not acquired title or a lesser interest or taken possession, the plaintiff may, without a court order, dismiss the action as to that property by filing a notice of dismissal briefly describing the property.

(B) *By Stipulation.* Before a judgment is entered vesting the plaintiff with title or a lesser interest in or possession of property, the plaintiff and affected defendants may, without a court order, dismiss the action in whole or in part by filing a stipulation of dismissal. And if the parties so stipulate, the court may vacate a judgment already entered.

(C) *By Court Order.* At any time before compensation has been determined and paid, the court may, after a motion and hearing, dismiss the action as to a piece of property. But if the plaintiff has already taken title, a lesser interest, or possession as to any part of it, the court must award compensation for the title, lesser interest, or possession taken.

(2) ***Dismissing a Defendant.*** The court may at any time dismiss a defendant who was unnecessarily or improperly joined.

(3) ***Effect.*** A dismissal is without prejudice unless otherwise stated in the notice, stipulation, or court order.

(j) Deposit and Its Distribution.

(1) ***Deposit.*** The plaintiff must deposit with the court any money required by law as a condition to the exercise of eminent domain and may make a deposit when allowed by statute.

(2) ***Distribution; Adjusting Distribution.*** After a deposit, the court and attorneys must expedite the proceedings so as to distribute the deposit and to determine and pay compensation. If the compensation finally awarded to a defendant exceeds the amount distributed to that defendant, the court must enter judgment against the plaintiff for the deficiency. If the compensation awarded to a defendant is less than the amount distributed to that defendant, the court must enter judgment against that defendant for the overpayment.

(k) Condemnation Under a State's Power of Eminent Domain. This rule governs an action involving eminent domain under state law. But if state law provides for trying an issue by jury—or for trying the issue of compensation by jury or commission or both—that law governs.

(*l*) Costs. Costs are not subject to Rule 54(d).

See selected Notes of Advisory Committee to FRCP 71.1, p. 1231.

History of FRCP 71.1: Adopted Apr. 30, 1951, eff. Aug. 1, 1951. Amended Jan. 21, 1963, eff. July 1, 1963; Apr. 29, 1985, eff. Aug. 1, 1985; Mar. 2, 1987, eff. Aug. 1, 1987; Apr. 25, 1988, eff. Aug. 1, 1988; Nov. 18, 1988, P.L. 100-690, §7050, 102 Stat. 4401; Apr. 22, 1993, eff. Dec. 1, 1993; Mar. 27, 2003, eff. Dec. 1, 2003; Apr. 30, 2007, eff. Dec. 1, 2007; Mar. 26, 2009, eff. Dec. 1, 2009.

See also 16 U.S.C. §831x (TVA procedure in condemnation proceedings); 28 U.S.C. §§1358, 1403 (jurisdiction and venue in condemnation proceedings); 43 U.S.C. §945b (public lands, reclamation projects, compensation for rights-of-way).

ANNOTATIONS

U.S. v. Reynolds, 397 U.S. 14, 19 (1970). "[E]xcept for the single issue of just compensation, the trial judge is to decide all issues, legal and factual, that may be presented."

U.S. v. 14.02 Acres of Land, 547 F.3d 943, 954-55 (9th Cir.2008). "Applying [FRCP] 71.1(e)(1), ... the government was not required [under FRCP 5] to serve non-objecting defendants who did not file a notice of appearance with its motion for judgment on the pleadings."

Guardian Pipeline, L.L.C. v. 950.80 Acres of Land, 525 F.3d 554, 556 (7th Cir.2008). "[C]ircuits have disagreed about the application of [28 U.S.C.] §455 to special masters and land commissioners. To resolve this conflict, the Supreme Court amended [FRCP] 53(a)(2) in 2003 to subject special masters to the requirements of §455—but it left [FRCP] 71.1 alone. It says that commissioners are covered by particular subsections of Rule 53. Those subsections are (c), (d), (e), and (f), which have nothing to do with §455. The subsection of Rule 53 that incorporates §455 for masters is not among those to which Rule 71.1 points. [¶] Rule 71.1 treats commissioners more like jurors than like judicial officers. Parties may 'examine' commissioners ... and ask the judge to excuse them for cause. ... Since 2003, ... no court has held that §455 supplies the standards for members of commissions in condemnation proceedings."

U.S. v. Hardage, 58 F.3d 569, 576 (10th Cir.1995). "[T]he right to a jury trial is provided in condemnation proceedings.... [T]he rule explicitly provides for a jury upon demand unless federal law governing the case creates another 'tribunal' for that purpose. Any party to a condemnation proceeding is ordinarily entitled to a jury trial to fix the value of the property taken where demand is made as provided in Rule 71A(h) [now Rule 71.1(h)]."

City of Arlington v. Golddust Twins Rlty. Corp., 41 F.3d 960, 964 n.2 (5th Cir.1994). "Both state and federal procedure require that a condemning authority state the purpose for which it intends to condemn a property interest. [E]xcept for the issue of whether a jury may hear the case, a federal court hearing a condemnation case under a state's power of eminent domain must follow the procedures in Rule 71A [now FRCP 71.1]."

KLK, Inc. v. U.S. Dept. of Interior, 35 F.3d 454, 457 (9th Cir.1994). FRCP 71A, now FRCP 71.1, "provides procedures for traditional condemnation proceedings, initiated by the government under 40 U.S.C. §257, not for inverse condemnation actions. [¶] [T]he existence of [FRCP 71.1] does not undercut the rule that the right to a jury trial must be clearly expressed in the relevant legislation."

FRCP 72. MAGISTRATE JUDGES: PRETRIAL ORDER

(a) Nondispositive Matters. When a pretrial matter not dispositive of a party's claim or defense is referred to a magistrate judge to hear and decide, the magistrate judge must promptly conduct the required proceedings and, when appropriate, issue a written order stating the decision. A party may serve and file objections to the order within 14 days after being served with a copy. A party may not assign as error a defect in the order not timely objected to. The district judge in the case must consider timely objections and modify or set aside any part of the order that is clearly erroneous or is contrary to law.

(b) Dispositive Motions and Prisoner Petitions.

(1) ***Findings and Recommendations.*** A magistrate judge must promptly conduct the required proceedings when assigned, without the parties' consent, to hear a pretrial matter dispositive of a claim or defense or a prisoner petition challenging the conditions of confinement. A record must be made of all evidentiary proceedings and may, at the magistrate judge's discretion, be made of any other proceedings. The magistrate judge must enter a recommended disposition, including, if appropriate, proposed findings of fact. The clerk must promptly mail a copy to each party.

(2) ***Objections.*** Within 14 days after being served with a copy of the recommended disposition, a party may serve and file specific written objections to the proposed findings and recommendations. A party may respond to another party's objections within 14 days after being served with a copy. Unless the district judge orders otherwise, the objecting party must promptly

arrange for transcribing the record, or whatever portions of it the parties agree to or the magistrate judge considers sufficient.

(3) ***Resolving Objections.*** The district judge must determine de novo any part of the magistrate judge's disposition that has been properly objected to. The district judge may accept, reject, or modify the recommended disposition; receive further evidence; or return the matter to the magistrate judge with instructions.

See selected Notes of Advisory Committee to FRCP 72, p. 1231.

History of FRCP 72: Adopted Apr. 28, 1983, eff. Aug. 1, 1983. Amended Apr. 30, 1991, eff. Dec. 1, 1991; Apr. 22, 1993, eff. Dec. 1, 1993; Apr. 30, 2007, eff. Dec. 1, 2007; Mar. 26, 2009, eff. Dec. 1, 2009.

See ***Commentaries***, "Magistrate Judges & Special Masters," ch. 5-B, p. 297; ***O'Connor's Federal Civil Forms*** (2012), FORMS 5B.

ANNOTATIONS

Thomas v. Arn, 474 U.S. 140, 154 (1985). "The district judge has jurisdiction over the case at all times. He retains full authority to decide whether to refer a case to the magistrate, to review the magistrate's report, and to enter judgment. [W]hile the statute does not require the judge to review an issue *de novo* if no objections are filed, it does not preclude further review by the district judge, *sua sponte* or at the request of a party, under a *de novo* or any other standard."

Fielding v. Tollaksen, 510 F.3d 175, 179 (2d Cir. 2007). "[W]hen a district judge enters an order disposing of a case without expressly ruling on a pending objection filed pursuant to [FRCP] 72(a), the judgment entered pursuant to that order functions as a final order overruling the objection."

Farrow v. West, 320 F.3d 1235, 1248 n.21 (11th Cir. 2003). "A party failing to appeal a magistrate judge's order in a nondispositive matter to the district court may not raise an objection to it on appeal to a circuit court."

Phinney v. Wentworth Douglas Hosp., 199 F.3d 1, 4 (1st Cir.1999). "[A]n objection to a magistrate judge's order must apprise the district court of all the objector's claims of error, and new claims of error on the part of the magistrate judge cannot thereafter be raised in [the circuit court]. *At 5-6:* [T]he terms dispositive and nondispositive as used in [FRCP] 72 must be construed in harmony with the classifications limned in [28 U.S.C.] §636(b)(1). This does not mean, of course, that dispositive motions are those excepted motions specifically enumerated in §636(b)(1)(A), and no others. Rather, that enumeration informs the classification of other motions as dispositive or nondispositive. Motions for sanctions premised on alleged discovery violations are not specifically excepted under 28 U.S.C. §636(b)(1)(A) and, in general, they are not of the same genre as the enumerated motions. We hold, therefore, that such motions ordinarily should be classified as nondispositive."

Johnson v. Zema Sys., 170 F.3d 734, 741 (7th Cir. 1999). "Our interpretation of specific as used in Rule 72(b) understands the term to require a party only to specify each issue for which review is sought and not the factual or legal basis of the objection. This interpretation is supported by the section of the Magistrates Act which defines the powers and jurisdiction of the magistrate judges. [W]e understand Rule 72(b)'s requirement of specific, written objection to require a litigant to specify each issue for which review is sought and not the factual or legal basis of the objection."

Douglass v. United Servs. Auto. Ass'n, 79 F.3d 1415, 1419 (5th Cir.1996). "[T]here is a … split between the circuits as to the consequences for a failure to … object [under the appellate waiver rule]. *At 1420:* '[F]ailure to make timely objection to the magistrate's report prior to its adoption by the district judge may constitute a waiver of appellate review of the district judge's order.' [¶] [The Supreme Court has condoned] the denial of appellate review not only of factual findings, *but also* of legal conclusions. *At 1422:* Our court … has limited its rule to accepted unobjected-to proposed factual findings…."

FRCP 73. MAGISTRATE JUDGES: TRIAL BY CONSENT; APPEAL

(a) Trial by Consent. When authorized under 28 U.S.C. §636(c), a magistrate judge may, if all parties consent, conduct a civil action or proceeding, including a jury or nonjury trial. A record must be made in accordance with 28 U.S.C. §636(c)(5).

(b) Consent Procedure.

(1) ***In General.*** When a magistrate judge has been designated to conduct civil actions or proceedings, the clerk must give the parties written notice of their opportunity to consent under 28 U.S.C. §636(c). To signify their consent, the parties must jointly or separately file a statement consenting to the referral. A district judge or magistrate judge may be informed of a par-

FRCP 73

ty's response to the clerk's notice only if all parties have consented to the referral.

(2) ***Reminding the Parties About Consenting.*** A district judge, magistrate judge, or other court official may remind the parties of the magistrate judge's availability, but must also advise them that they are free to withhold consent without adverse substantive consequences.

(3) ***Vacating a Referral.*** On its own for good cause—or when a party shows extraordinary circumstances—the district judge may vacate a referral to a magistrate judge under this rule.

(c) **Appealing a Judgment.** In accordance with 28 U.S.C. §636(c)(3), an appeal from a judgment entered at a magistrate judge's direction may be taken to the court of appeals as would any other appeal from a district-court judgment.

See selected Notes of Advisory Committee to FRCP 73, p. 1232.

History of FRCP 73: Adopted Apr. 28, 1983, eff. Aug. 1, 1983. Amended Mar. 2, 1987, eff. Aug. 1, 1987; Apr. 22, 1993, eff. Dec. 1, 1993; Apr. 11, 1997, eff. Dec. 1, 1997; Apr. 30, 2007, eff. Dec. 1, 2007.

See ***Commentaries***, "Magistrate Judges & Special Masters," ch. 5-B, p. 297; ***O'Connor's Federal Civil Forms*** (2012), FORMS 5B.

ANNOTATIONS

Beazer E., Inc. v. Mead Corp., 412 F.3d 429, 437 (3d Cir.2005). "The District Court did not rely on any specific provision of the Magistrates Act in its order of referral or its order rejecting [D's] objections to the referral, but it is clear from the context that the court considered the equitable allocation issue a 'pretrial matter' under [28 U.S.C.] §636(b)(1). *At 437 n.10:* We agree with the Fifth Circuit that '[g]ood practice would indicate that court orders of designation or reference state plainly under what statutory provision the court is proceeding.'"

Gomez v. Vernon, 255 F.3d 1118, 1126 (9th Cir. 2001). "A magistrate judge may conduct civil proceedings and order the entry of judgment only if the magistrate judge has been 'specially designated to exercise such jurisdiction by the district court,' ... and all parties clearly and unambiguously consent. [¶] [W]ritten consent authorizes a magistrate judge to enter judgment. Absent such consent, ... the magistrate judge lacks jurisdiction, and any judgment entered is a nullity, which [an appellate court has] no jurisdiction to review." *See also* ***Hall v. Sharpe***, 812 F.2d 644, 647 (11th Cir.1987).

Rembert v. Apfel, 213 F.3d 1331, 1334 (11th Cir. 2000). The FRCPs "provide that if the parties agree to allow a magistrate judge to finally dispose of their case, they shall execute and file a joint form of consent or separate forms of consent setting forth such election. [¶] The consent must be express and on the record. It cannot be inferred by conduct of the parties. Failure to object is not equal to consent." (Internal quotes omitted.)

FRCP 74. [ABROGATED]

See selected Notes of Advisory Committee to FRCP 74, p. 1233.

FRCP 75. [ABROGATED]

See selected Notes of Advisory Committee to FRCP 75, p. 1233.

FRCP 76. [ABROGATED]

See selected Notes of Advisory Committee to FRCP 76, p. 1233.

TITLE X. DISTRICT COURTS & CLERKS: CONDUCTING BUSINESS; ISSUING ORDERS

FRCP 77. CONDUCTING BUSINESS; CLERK'S AUTHORITY; NOTICE OF AN ORDER OR JUDGMENT

(a) **When Court Is Open.** Every district court is considered always open for filing any paper, issuing and returning process, making a motion, or entering an order.

(b) **Place for Trial and Other Proceedings.** Every trial on the merits must be conducted in open court and, so far as convenient, in a regular courtroom. Any other act or proceeding may be done or conducted by a judge in chambers, without the attendance of the clerk or other court official, and anywhere inside or outside the district. But no hearing—other than one ex parte—may be conducted outside the district unless all the affected parties consent.

(c) **Clerk's Office Hours; Clerk's Orders.**

(1) ***Hours.*** The clerk's office—with a clerk or deputy on duty—must be open during business hours every day except Saturdays, Sundays, and legal holidays. But a court may, by local rule or order, require that the office be open for specified hours on Saturday or a particular legal holiday other than one listed in Rule 6(a)(4)(A).

(2) ***Orders.*** Subject to the court's power to suspend, alter, or rescind the clerk's action for good cause, the clerk may:

(A) issue process;

(B) enter a default;

(C) enter a default judgment under Rule 55(b)(1); and

(D) act on any other matter that does not require the court's action.

(d) Serving Notice of an Order or Judgment.

(1) ***Service.*** Immediately after entering an order or judgment, the clerk must serve notice of the entry, as provided in Rule 5(b), on each party who is not in default for failing to appear. The clerk must record the service on the docket. A party also may serve notice of the entry as provided in Rule 5(b).

(2) ***Time to Appeal Not Affected by Lack of Notice.*** Lack of notice of the entry does not affect the time for appeal or relieve—or authorize the court to relieve—a party for failing to appeal within the time allowed, except as allowed by Federal Rule of Appellate Procedure (4)(a).

See selected Notes of Advisory Committee to FRCP 77, p. 1233.

History of FRCP 77: Adopted Dec. 20, 1937, eff. Sept. 16, 1938. Amended Dec. 27, 1946, eff. Mar. 19, 1948; Jan. 21, 1963, eff. July 1, 1963; Dec. 4, 1967, eff. July 1, 1968; Mar. 1, 1971, eff. July 1, 1971; Mar. 2, 1987, eff. Aug. 1, 1987; Apr. 30, 1991, eff. Dec. 1, 1991; Apr. 23, 2001, eff. Dec. 1, 2001; Apr. 30, 2007, eff. Dec. 1, 2007.

See *Commentaries*, "Where to File," ch. 1-C, §3, p. 18; "Entry of Judgment," ch. 9-A, p. 735.

See also 28 U.S.C. §452 (courts always open).

ANNOTATIONS

Nunley v. City of L.A., 52 F.3d 792, 795 (9th Cir. 1995). "Rule 77(d) allows prevailing parties 'to send their own notice [of the entry of final judgment to the opposition] in order to lessen the chance that a [district] judge will accept a claim of non-receipt in the face of evidence that notices were sent by both the clerk and the winning party.'"

B.H. v. McDonald, 49 F.3d 294, 297 (7th Cir.1995). FRCP 77(b) "allows district judges the discretion to conduct proceedings in chambers, as long as the trial upon the merits is held in open court. *At 298:* Rule 77(b) simply articulates the traditional authority of a judge to speak privately with the parties to a suit, whether in bench conferences or in chambers."

Avolio v. County of Suffolk, 29 F.3d 50, 53 (2d Cir. 1994). "Since [Ps] were ... represented by counsel, the notice of entry [of judgment] had to be received by counsel, not the party. [T]he notice contemplated by this rule is written notice; an oral communication simply is not sufficient to trigger the relevant time periods."

Witty v. Dukakis, 3 F.3d 517, 520 (1st Cir.1993). "[P]arties to an ongoing case have an independent obligation to monitor all developments in the case and cannot rely on the clerk's office to do their homework for them."

FRCP 78. HEARING MOTIONS; SUBMISSION ON BRIEFS

(a) Providing a Regular Schedule for Oral Hearings. A court may establish regular times and places for oral hearings on motions.

(b) Providing for Submission on Briefs. By rule or order, the court may provide for submitting and determining motions on briefs, without oral hearings.

See selected Notes of Advisory Committee to FRCP 78, p. 1233.

History of FRCP 78: Adopted Dec. 20, 1937, eff. Sept. 16, 1938. Amended Mar. 2, 1987, eff. Aug. 1, 1987; Apr. 30, 2007, eff. Dec. 1, 2007.

See *Commentaries*, "Hearings," ch. 1-E, p. 38.

See also FRCP 6 (service of affidavits in support of and in opposition to motions and time for noticing motions), FRCP 7 (motions and other papers), FRCP 43 (use of affidavits on motions), FRCP 83 (local rules not to be inconsistent with these rules).

ANNOTATIONS

Willis v. Pacific Maritime Ass'n, 244 F.3d 675, 684 n.2 (9th Cir.2001). "A district court judge has the discretion, when considering a motion for summary judgment, to determine whether or not to hold an oral hearing."

Riddle v. Mondragon, 83 F.3d 1197, 1208 (10th Cir. 1996). "[T]he district judge [did not abuse] his discretion in deciding the motions to dismiss without a hearing and in excluding from his consideration the evidentiary materials plaintiffs had submitted. ... The district courts are authorized by [FRCP] 78 to provide by local rule for disposition of most motions without oral argument, and such a local rule is in force in [this district]." *See also* ***Hill v. Porter Mem'l Hosp.***, 90 F.3d 220, 224 (7th Cir.1996).

FRCP 79. RECORDS KEPT BY THE CLERK

(a) Civil Docket.

(1) ***In General.*** The clerk must keep a record known as the "civil docket" in the form and manner prescribed by the Director of the Administrative Office of the United States Courts with the approval of the Judicial Conference of

FRCP 79

the United States. The clerk must enter each civil action in the docket. Actions must be assigned consecutive file numbers, which must be noted in the docket where the first entry of the action is made.

(2) ***Items to be Entered.*** The following items must be marked with the file number and entered chronologically in the docket:

(A) papers filed with the clerk;

(B) process issued, and proofs of service or other returns showing execution; and

(C) appearances, orders, verdicts, and judgments.

(3) ***Contents of Entries; Jury Trial Demanded.*** Each entry must briefly show the nature of the paper filed or writ issued, the substance of each proof of service or other return, and the substance and date of entry of each order and judgment. When a jury trial has been properly demanded or ordered, the clerk must enter the word "jury" in the docket.

(b) Civil Judgments and Orders. The clerk must keep a copy of every final judgment and appealable order; of every order affecting title to or a lien on real or personal property; and of any other order that the court directs to be kept. The clerk must keep these in the form and manner prescribed by the Director of the Administrative Office of the United States Courts with the approval of the Judicial Conference of the United States.

(c) Indexes; Calendars. Under the court's direction, the clerk must:

(1) keep indexes of the docket and of the judgments and orders described in Rule 79(b); and

(2) prepare calendars of all actions ready for trial, distinguishing jury trials from nonjury trials.

(d) Other Records. The clerk must keep any other records required by the Director of the Administrative Office of the United States Courts with the approval of the Judicial Conference of the United States.

History of FRCP 79: Adopted Dec. 20, 1937, eff. Sept. 16, 1938. Amended Dec. 27, 1946, eff. Mar. 19, 1948; Dec. 29, 1948, eff. Oct. 20, 1949; Jan. 21, 1963, eff. July 1, 1963; Apr. 30, 2007, eff. Dec. 1, 2007.

See *Commentaries*, "Filing Documents," ch. 1-C, p. 17.

See also 28 U.S.C. §331 (survey and recommendation of Judicial Conference of the U.S.), §457 (obsolete papers disposed of in accordance with rules of Judicial Conference of the U.S.), §604 (examination of court dockets by Director of Administrative Office of U.S. Courts), §1962 (lien of judgment), §1963 (registration of judgments for money or property in other districts).

ANNOTATIONS

Silivanch v. Celebrity Cruises, Inc., 333 F.3d 355, 364-65 (2d Cir.2003). FRCP 79(a) calls "for the entry of all 'orders, verdicts, and judgments' in the docket, but the reason for the requirement is the docket's 'public record keeping function.' The rule is directed to the clerk, not to the parties or the court."

Atlantic Richfield Co. v. Monarch Leasing Co., 84 F.3d 204, 207 (6th Cir.1996). "[U]nder federal procedural law, a federal court judgment is 'rendered' only when it is set forth in writing on a separate, discrete document and entered on the civil docket."

Zimmer St. Louis, Inc. v. Zimmer Co., 32 F.3d 357, 361 (8th Cir.1994). It is undisputed that the "order was correctly entered on the official 'civil docket'.... That ... leads us to conclude that if [D's] lawyers had asked to see that official civil docket instead of relying on the case file, they would have learned of the order. Indeed, we believe that one of the purposes of [FRCP] 79(a) is to establish an 'official' record that may be relied on by lawyers, litigants, and others interested in the proceedings of the courts."

Axel Johnson Inc. v. Arthur Andersen & Co., 6 F.3d 78, 84 (2d Cir.1993). "Rule 79(a) requires the clerk of the court to record a judgment or order in the civil docket sheet. [¶] In compliance with Rule 79(a), the clerk of the court made an entry in the docket sheet indicating that the case had been dismissed. However, the clerk did not file a separate document denominated as a judgment. ... Thus, the judgment was not constitutionally 'final.'"

FRCP 80. STENOGRAPHIC TRANSCRIPT AS EVIDENCE

If stenographically reported testimony at a hearing or trial is admissible in evidence at a later trial, the testimony may be proved by a transcript certified by the person who reported it.

History of FRCP 80: Adopted Dec. 20, 1937, eff. Sept. 16, 1938. Amended Dec. 27, 1946, eff. Mar. 19, 1948; Apr. 30, 2007, eff. Dec. 1, 2007.

See *Commentaries*, "Request for court reporter," ch. 1-E, §3.5, p. 40.

See also 28 U.S.C. §753 (appointment and compensation of court reporters and fees for transcripts), §§753(f), 1915 (payment by U.S. for fees for transcripts on appeal furnished to persons proceeding in forma pauperis), §1920 (fees of court reporter for stenographic transcript taxable as costs).

TITLE XI. GENERAL PROVISIONS

FRCP 81. APPLICABILITY OF THE RULES IN GENERAL; REMOVED ACTIONS

(a) Applicability to Particular Proceedings.

(1) ***Prize Proceedings.*** These rules do not apply to prize proceedings in admiralty governed by 10 U.S.C. §§7651-7681.

(2) ***Bankruptcy.*** These rules apply to bankruptcy proceedings to the extent provided by the Federal Rules of Bankruptcy Procedure.

(3) ***Citizenship.*** These rules apply to proceedings for admission to citizenship to the extent that the practice in those proceedings is not specified in federal statutes and has previously conformed to the practice in civil actions. The provisions of 8 U.S.C. §1451 for service by publication and for answer apply in proceedings to cancel citizenship certificates.

(4) ***Special Writs.*** These rules apply to proceedings for habeas corpus and for quo warranto to the extent that the practice in those proceedings:

(A) is not specified in a federal statute, the Rules Governing Section 2254 Cases, or the Rules Governing Section 2255 Cases; and

(B) has previously conformed to the practice in civil actions.

(5) ***Proceedings Involving a Subpoena.*** These rules apply to proceedings to compel testimony or the production of documents through a subpoena issued by a United States officer or agency under a federal statute, except as otherwise provided by statute, by local rule, or by court order in the proceedings.

(6) ***Other Proceedings.*** These rules, to the extent applicable, govern proceedings under the following laws, except as these laws provide other procedures:

(A) 7 U.S.C. §§292, 499g(c), for reviewing an order of the Secretary of Agriculture;

(B) 9 U.S.C., relating to arbitration;

(C) 15 U.S.C. §522, for reviewing an order of the Secretary of the Interior;

(D) 15 U.S.C. §715d(c), for reviewing an order denying a certificate of clearance;

(E) 29 U.S.C. §§159, 160, for enforcing an order of the National Labor Relations Board;

(F) 33 U.S.C. §§918, 921, for enforcing or reviewing a compensation order under the Longshore and Harbor Workers' Compensation Act; and

(G) 45 U.S.C. §159, for reviewing an arbitration award in a railway-labor dispute.

(b) Scire Facias and Mandamus. The writs of scire facias and mandamus are abolished. Relief previously available through them may be obtained by appropriate action or motion under these rules.

(c) Removed Actions.

(1) ***Applicability.*** These rules apply to a civil action after it is removed from a state court.

(2) ***Further Pleading.*** After removal, repleading is unnecessary unless the court orders it. A defendant who did not answer before removal must answer or present other defenses or objections under these rules within the longest of these periods:

(A) 21 days after receiving—through service or otherwise—a copy of the initial pleading stating the claim for relief;

(B) 21 days after being served with the summons for an initial pleading on file at the time of service; or

(C) 7 days after the notice of removal is filed.

(3) ***Demand for a Jury Trial.***

(A) *As Affected by State Law.* A party who, before removal, expressly demanded a jury trial in accordance with state law need not renew the demand after removal. If the state law did not require an express demand for a jury trial, a party need not make one after removal unless the court orders the parties to do so within a specified time. The court must so order at a party's request and may so order on its own. A party who fails to make a demand when so ordered waives a jury trial.

(B) *Under Rule 38.* If all necessary pleadings have been served at the time of removal, a party entitled to a jury trial under Rule 38 must be given one if the party serves a demand within 14 days after:

(i) it files a notice of removal; or

(ii) it is served with a notice of removal filed by another party.

(d) **Law Applicable.**

(1) **"State Law" Defined.** When these rules refer to state law, the term "law" includes the state's statutes and the state's judicial decisions.

(2) **"State" Defined.** The term "state" includes, where appropriate, the District of Columbia and any United States commonwealth or territory.

(3) **"Federal Statute" Defined in the District of Columbia.** In the United States District Court for the District of Columbia, the term "federal statute" includes any Act of Congress that applies locally to the District.

See selected Notes of Advisory Committee to FRCP 81, p. 1233.

History of FRCP 81: Adopted Dec. 20, 1937, eff. Sept. 16, 1938. Amended Dec. 28, 1939, eff. Apr. 3, 1941; Dec. 27, 1946, eff. Mar. 19, 1948; Dec. 29, 1948, eff. Oct. 20, 1949; Apr. 30, 1951, eff. Aug. 1, 1951; Jan. 21, 1963, eff. July 1, 1963; Feb. 28, 1966, eff. July 1, 1966; Dec. 4, 1967, eff. July 1, 1968; Mar. 1, 1971, eff. July 1, 1971; Mar. 2, 1987, eff. Aug. 1, 1987; Apr. 23, 2001, eff. Dec. 1, 2001; Apr. 29, 2002, eff. Dec. 1, 2002; Apr. 30, 2007, eff. Dec. 1, 2007; Mar. 26, 2009, eff. Dec. 1, 2009.

See ***Commentaries***, "Removal & Remand," ch. 4, p. 239; ***O'Connor's Federal Civil Forms*** (2012), FORMS 4.

See also 48 U.S.C. §1614 (applicability of rules to district court for Virgin Islands).

ANNOTATIONS

Donaldson v. U.S., 400 U.S. 517, 528-29 (1971). The FRCPs "do have an application to a summons proceeding. Rule 81(a)(3) [now Rule 81(a)(5)] expressly so provides. But the [FRCPs] are not inflexible in this application. [A] district court, by local rule or by order, may limit the application of the rules in a summons proceeding." *See also* ***U.S. v. McCoy***, 954 F.2d 1000, 1004 (5th Cir.1992).

Preferred Sites, LLC v. Troup Cty., 296 F.3d 1210, 1220-21 (11th Cir.2002). "Although the writ of mandamus was abolished by [FRCP] 81(b), federal courts 'may issue all writs necessary or appropriate in aid of their respective jurisdictions and agreeable to the usages and principles of law.' [¶] Pursuant to their powers under 28 U.S.C. §1651, federal courts continue to grant equitable relief, which sometimes are referred to as 'writs of mandamus.' As a result, a 'writ of mandamus' frequently grants the same relief to a party as a mandatory injunction, which orders a party to 'take action.'"

In re Deiulemar Compagnia Di Navigazione S.p.A., 198 F.3d 473, 483 (4th Cir.1999). FRCP 81(a)(3), now FRCP 81(a)(6)(B), "does not affirmatively authorize application of the federal rules to matters that are incident to an arbitrable dispute because Rule 81 does not apply to an underlying arbitration proceeding. Rather, it applies only to allow or prohibit use of the federal rules in Title 9 proceedings. Consequently, a district court could … use federal discovery rules to determine whether a dispute is arbitrable. The district court could not, however, invoke Rule 81 to authorize discovery in aid of arbitration because Rule 81 simply does not apply with respect to the arbitration proceeding itself."

Silva v. City of Madison, 69 F.3d 1368, 1375 (7th Cir.1995). "Because receipt of the complaint triggers the removal period under [28 U.S.C.] §1446(b) and also triggers the time period within which a responsive pleading must be filed under [FRCP] 81(c), a defendant could be required both to remove an action to federal court and to file a responsive pleading before proper service is effected. *At 1376:* [W]e perceive nothing in the statute, the rule or their respective legislative histories that would justify our concluding that the drafters … intended to abrogate … service of process. *At 1377:* [U]nder … Rule 81(c), [D] was not required to file a responsive pleading because it had not been served with a summons."

Kuehl v. FDIC, 8 F.3d 905, 907 (1st Cir.1993). "[A]n action that is removed from state to federal court need not be repled 'unless the court so orders.' *At 908:* [R]epleading ordered under [FRCP] 81(c) does not automatically deprive the plaintiff of the one-time option to amend granted by [FRCP] 15(a)."

FRCP 82. JURISDICTION & VENUE UNAFFECTED

These rules do not extend or limit the jurisdiction of the district courts or the venue of actions in those courts. An admiralty or maritime claim under Rule 9(h) is not a civil action for purposes of 28 U.S.C. §§1391-1392.[1]

1. **Editor's note:** The Federal Courts Jurisdiction and Venue Clarification Act of 2011, P.L. 112-63, §§203, 205, Dec. 7, 2011, 125 Stat. 764, repealed 28 U.S.C. §1392.

See selected Notes of Advisory Committee to FRCP 82, p. 1234.

History of FRCP 82: Adopted Dec. 20, 1937, eff. Sept. 16, 1938. Amended Dec. 29, 1948, eff. Oct. 20, 1949; Feb. 28, 1966, eff. July 1, 1966; Apr. 23, 2001, eff. Dec. 1, 2001; Apr. 30, 2007, eff. Dec. 1, 2007.

See ***Commentaries***, "Introduction to Federal Rules," ch. 1-A, p. 3.

ANNOTATIONS

Cresswell v. Sullivan & Cromwell, 922 F.2d 60, 70 (2d Cir.1990). "The [FRCPs] do not provide an independent ground for subject matter jurisdiction over an action for which there is no other basis for jurisdiction. [¶] An independent action for relief from the judgment ... must be supported by its own jurisdictional grounds."

FRCP 83. RULES BY DISTRICT COURTS; JUDGE'S DIRECTIVES

(a) Local Rules.

(1) *In General.* After giving public notice and an opportunity for comment, a district court, acting by a majority of its district judges, may adopt and amend rules governing its practice. A local rule must be consistent with—but not duplicate—federal statutes and rules adopted under 28 U.S.C. §§2072 and 2075, and must conform to any uniform numbering system prescribed by the Judicial Conference of the United States. A local rule takes effect on the date specified by the district court and remains in effect unless amended by the court or abrogated by the judicial council of the circuit. Copies of rules and amendments must, on their adoption, be furnished to the judicial council and the Administrative Office of the United States Courts and be made available to the public.

(2) *Requirement of Form.* A local rule imposing a requirement of form must not be enforced in a way that causes a party to lose any right because of a nonwillful failure to comply.

(b) Procedure When There Is No Controlling Law. A judge may regulate practice in any manner consistent with federal law, rules adopted under 28 U.S.C. §§2072 and 2075, and the district's local rules. No sanction or other disadvantage may be imposed for noncompliance with any requirement not in federal law, federal rules, or the local rules unless the alleged violator has been furnished in the particular case with actual notice of the requirement.

See selected Notes of Advisory Committee to FRCP 83, p. 1234.

History of FRCP 83: Adopted Dec. 20, 1937, eff. Sept. 16, 1938. Amended Apr. 29, 1985, eff. Aug. 1, 1985; Apr. 27, 1995, eff. Dec. 1, 1995; Apr. 30, 2007, eff. Dec. 1, 2007. Change of name: Reference to U.S. magistrate or to magistrate deemed to refer to U.S. magistrate judge pursuant to §321 of P.L. 101-650, set out as a note under 28 U.S.C. §631.

See *Commentaries*, "Local Rules," ch. 1-A, §2, p. 5.

See also 28 U.S.C. §2071 (rule-making power generally).

ANNOTATIONS

Weibrecht v. Southern Ill. Transfer, Inc., 241 F.3d 875, 879 (7th Cir.2001). "Federal district courts are authorized to promulgate local rules under [FRCP] 83.... [L]ocal rules must be 'consistent with Acts of Congress.' To the extent a local rule conflicts with a federal statute, this requirement is violated, and so the local rule must be held invalid."

Carroll v. Jaques Admiralty Law Firm, P.C., 110 F.3d 290, 293 (5th Cir.1997). "Rule 83(b) ensures that litigants are not unfairly sanctioned for failure to comply with a local rule of the court or internal operating procedures or the like of which they are unaware. Rule 83(b) does not eliminate a court's inherent power to sanction, and it does not prevent sanction for failure to respond to deposition questions and intentional disruption of the discovery process—misconduct that is recognized in the [FRCPs], in common sense, and in respect for the court's processes."

Brown v. Crawford Cty., 960 F.2d 1002, 1008 n.8 (11th Cir.1992). FRCP 83 "provides that local rules result from action by a majority of the judges of the specific district 'after giving appropriate public notice and an opportunity to comment....' [T]he name given to local procedures is irrelevant. If the *purpose* of such local procedures, practices or policies is to control practice in a district court in this circuit, such procedures effectively are local rules and must be created in accordance with Rule 83."

FRCP 84. FORMS

The forms in the Appendix suffice under these rules and illustrate the simplicity and brevity that these rules contemplate.

History of FRCP 84: Adopted Dec. 20, 1937, eff. Sept. 16, 1938. Amended Dec. 27, 1946, eff. Mar. 19, 1948; Apr. 30, 2007, eff. Dec. 1, 2007.

ANNOTATIONS

In re Bill of Lading Transmission & Processing Sys. Patent Litig., 681 F.3d 1323, 1334 (Fed.Cir.2012). "Rule 84 and the Advisory Committee Notes make 'clear that a pleading, motion, or other paper that follows one of the Official Forms cannot be successfully attacked.' [A]ny changes to the [FRCPs] 'must be obtained by the process of amending the Federal Rules, and not by judicial interpretation.' [T]o the extent ... parties argue

that *Twombly* and its progeny conflict with the Forms and create differing pleadings requirements, the Forms control."

Bartholet v. Reishauer A.G., 953 F.2d 1073, 1078 (7th Cir.1992). "None of the forms in the appendix spells out a legal theory."

Perkin Elmer v. Trans Mediterranean Airways, S.A.L., 107 F.R.D. 55, 58-59 (E.D.N.Y.1985). "Although the forms provided in the Appendix of Forms of the [FRCPs] 'are sufficient under the rules,' ... it is clear that they need not be used in haec verba."

FRCP 85. TITLE

These rules may be cited as the Federal Rules of Civil Procedure.

History of FRCP 85: Adopted Dec. 20, 1937, eff. Sept. 16, 1938. Amended Apr. 30, 2007, eff. Dec. 1, 2007.

FRCP 86. EFFECTIVE DATES

(a) In General. These rules and any amendments take effect at the time specified by the Supreme Court, subject to 28 U.S.C. §2074. They govern:

- **(1)** proceedings in an action commenced after their effective date; and
- **(2)** proceedings after that date in an action then pending unless:
  - **(A)** the Supreme Court specifies otherwise; or
  - **(B)** the court determines that applying them in a particular action would be infeasible or work an injustice.

(b) December 1, 2007 Amendments. If any provision in Rules 1-5.1, 6-73, or 77-86 conflicts with another law, priority in time for the purpose of 28 U.S.C. §2072(b) is not affected by the amendments taking effect on December 1, 2007.

See selected Notes of Advisory Committee to FRCP 86, p. 1234.

History of FRCP 86: Adopted Dec. 20, 1937, eff. Sept. 16, 1938. Amended Dec. 27, 1946, eff. Mar. 19, 1948; Dec. 29, 1948, eff. Oct. 20, 1949; Apr. 17, 1961, eff. July 19, 1961; Jan. 21, 1963 and Mar. 18, 1963, eff. July 1, 1963; Apr. 30, 2007, eff. Dec. 1, 2007.

See also 28 U.S.C. §2072 (all laws in conflict with these rules to be of no further force and effect).

FORM 1. CAPTION

(Use on every summons, complaint, answer, motion, or other document.)

UNITED STATES DISTRICT COURT FOR THE
_______ DISTRICT OF _______

A B, Plaintiff	§	
v.	§	Civil Action No. ___
C D, Defendant	§	
v.	§	
E F, Third-Party	§	
Defendant	§	
(Use if needed.)	§	

(Name of Document)

History of FRCP Form 1: Adopted Apr. 30, 2007, eff. Dec. 1, 2007.

FORM 2. DATE, SIGNATURE, ADDRESS, E-MAIL ADDRESS, & TELEPHONE NUMBER

(Use at the conclusion of pleadings and other papers that require a signature.)

Date __________

____
(Signature of the attorney or unrepresented party)

____
(Printed name)

____
(Address)

____
(E-mail address)

____
(Telephone number)

History of FRCP Form 2: Adopted Apr. 30, 2007, eff. Dec. 1, 2007.

FORM 3. SUMMONS

(Caption—See Form 1.)

To *name the defendant*:

A lawsuit has been filed against you.

Within 21 days after service of this summons on you (not counting the day you received it), you must serve on the plaintiff an answer to the attached complaint or a motion under Rule 12 of the Federal Rules of Civil Procedure. The answer or motion must be served on the plaintiff's attorney, _____, whose address is _____. If you fail to do so, judgment by default will be entered against you for the relief demanded in the complaint. You also must file your answer or motion with the court.

Date __________

____
Clerk of Court

(Court Seal)

(Use 60 days if the defendant is the United States or a United States agency, or is an officer or employee of the United States allowed 60 days by Rule 12(a)(3).)

History of FRCP Form 3: Adopted Apr. 30, 2007, eff. Dec. 1, 2007. Amended Mar. 26, 2009, eff. Dec. 1, 2009.

FORM 4. SUMMONS ON A THIRD-PARTY COMPLAINT

(Caption—See Form 1.)

To *name the third-party defendant*:

A lawsuit has been filed against defendant _____, who as third-party plaintiff is making this claim against you to pay part or all of what [he] may owe to the plaintiff _____.

Within 21 days after service of this summons on you (not counting the day you received it), you must serve on the plaintiff and on the defendant an answer to the attached third-party complaint or a motion under Rule 12 of the Federal Rules of Civil Procedure. The answer or motion must be served on the defendant's attorney, _____, whose address is, _____, and also on the plaintiff's attorney, _____, whose address is, _____. If you fail to do so, judgment by default will be entered against you for the relief demanded in the third-party complaint. You also must file the answer or motion with the court and serve it on any other parties.

A copy of the plaintiff's complaint is also attached. You may—but are not required to—respond to it.

Date __________

____
Clerk of Court

(Court Seal)

History of FRCP Form 4: Adopted Apr. 30, 2007, eff. Dec. 1, 2007. Amended Mar. 26, 2009, eff. Dec. 1, 2009.

FORM 5. NOTICE OF A LAWSUIT & REQUEST TO WAIVE SERVICE OF A SUMMONS

(Caption—See Form 1.)

To (*name the defendant—or if the defendant is a corporation, partnership, or association name an officer or agent authorized to receive service*):

Why are you getting this?

A lawsuit has been filed against you, or the entity you represent, in this court under the number shown above. A copy of the complaint is attached.

This is not a summons, or an official notice from the court. It is a request that, to avoid expenses, you waive formal service of a summons by signing and returning the enclosed waiver. To avoid these expenses, you must return the signed waiver within (*give at least 30 days or at least 60 days if the defendant is outside any judicial district of the United States*) from the date shown below, which is the date this notice was sent. Two copies of the waiver form are enclosed, along with a stamped, self-addressed envelope or other prepaid means for returning one copy. You may keep the other copy.

What happens next?

If you return the signed waiver, I will file it with the court. The action will then proceed as if you had been served on the date the waiver is filed, but no summons will be served on you and you will have 60 days from the date this notice is sent (see the date below) to answer the complaint (or 90 days if this notice is sent to you outside any judicial district of the United States).

If you do not return the signed waiver within the time indicated, I will arrange to have the summons and complaint served on you. And I will ask the court to require you, or the entity you represent, to pay the expenses of making service.

Please read the enclosed statement about the duty to avoid unnecessary expenses.

I certify that this request is being sent to you on the date below.

(Date and sign—See Form 2.)

History of FRCP Form 5: Adopted Apr. 30, 2007, eff. Dec. 1, 2007.

FORM 6. WAIVER OF THE SERVICE OF SUMMONS

(Caption—See Form 1.)

To *name the plaintiff's attorney or the unrepresented plaintiff*:

I have received your request to waive service of a summons in this action along with a copy of the complaint, two copies of this waiver form, and a prepaid means of returning one signed copy of the form to you.

I, or the entity I represent, agree to save the expense of serving a summons and complaint in this case.

I understand that I, or the entity I represent, will keep all defenses or objections to the lawsuit, the court's jurisdiction, and the venue of the action, but that I waive any objections to the absence of a summons or of service.

I also understand that I, or the entity I represent, must file and serve an answer or a motion under Rule 12 within 60 days from _____, the date when this request was sent (or 90 days if it was sent outside the United States). If I fail to do so, a default judgment will be entered against me or the entity I represent.

(Date and sign—See Form 2.)

(*Attach the following to Form 6.*)

Duty to Avoid Unnecessary Expenses of Serving a Summons

Rule 4 of the Federal Rules of Civil Procedure requires certain defendants to cooperate in saving unnecessary expenses of serving a summons and complaint. A defendant who is located in the United States and who fails to return a signed waiver of service requested by a plaintiff located in the United States will be required to pay the expenses of service, unless the defendant shows good cause for the failure.

"Good cause" does *not* include a belief that the lawsuit is groundless, or that it has been brought in an improper venue, or that the court has no jurisdiction over this matter or over the defendant or the defendant's property.

If the waiver is signed and returned, you can still make these and all other defenses and objections, but you cannot object to the absence of a summons or of service.

If you waive service, then you must, within the time specified on the waiver form, serve an answer or a motion under Rule 12 on the plaintiff and file a copy with the court. By signing and returning the waiver form, you are allowed more time to respond than if a summons had been served.

History of FRCP Form 6: Adopted Apr. 30, 2007, eff. Dec. 1, 2007.

FORM 7. STATEMENT OF JURISDICTION

a. (*For diversity-of-citizenship jurisdiction.*) The plaintiff is [a citizen of *Michigan*] [a corporation incorporated under the laws of *Michigan* with its principal place of business in *Michigan*]. The defendant is [a citizen of *New York*] [a corporation incorporated under the laws of *New York* with its principal place of business in *New York*]. The amount in controversy, without interest and costs, exceeds the sum or value specified by 28 U.S.C. §1332.

b. (*For federal-question jurisdiction.*) This action arises under [the United States Constitution, *specify the article or amendment and the section*] [a United States treaty, *specify*] [a federal statute, _____ U.S.C. §_____].

c. (*For a claim in the admiralty or maritime jurisdiction.*) This is a case of admiralty or maritime jurisdiction. (*To invoke admiralty status under Rule 9(h) use the following*: This is an admiralty or maritime claim within the meaning of Rule 9(h).)

History of FRCP Form 7: Adopted Apr. 30, 2007, eff. Dec. 1, 2007.

FORM 8. STATEMENT OF REASONS FOR OMITTING A PARTY

(*If a person who ought to be made a party under Rule 19(a) is not named, include this statement in accordance with Rule 19(c).*)

This complaint does not join as a party *name* who [is not subject to this court's personal jurisdiction] [cannot be made a party without depriving this court of subject-matter jurisdiction] because *state the reason*.

History of FRCP Form 8: Adopted Apr. 30, 2007, eff. Dec. 1, 2007.

FORM 9. STATEMENT NOTING A PARTY'S DEATH

(Caption—See Form 1.)

In accordance with Rule 25(a) *name the person*, who is [a party to this action] [a representative of or successor to the deceased party] notes the death during the pendency of this action of *name*, [*describe as party* in this action].

(Date and sign—See Form 2.)

History of FRCP Form 9: Adopted Apr. 30, 2007, eff. Dec. 1, 2007.

FORM 10. COMPLAINT TO RECOVER A SUM CERTAIN

(Caption—See Form 1.)

1. (Statement of Jurisdiction—See Form 7.)

(*Use one or more of the following as appropriate and include a demand for judgment.*)

(a) On a Promissory Note

2. On *date*, the defendant executed and delivered a note promising to pay the plaintiff on *date* the sum of $_____ with interest at the rate of _____ percent. A copy of the note [is attached as Exhibit A] [is summarized as follows: _____.]

3. The defendant has not paid the amount owed.

(b) On an Account

2. The defendant owes the plaintiff $_____ according to the account set out in Exhibit A.

(c) For Goods Sold and Delivered

2. The defendant owes the plaintiff $_____ for goods sold and delivered by the plaintiff to the defendant from *date* to *date*.

(d) For Money Lent

2. The defendant owes the plaintiff $_____ for money lent by the plaintiff to the defendant on *date*.

(e) For Money Paid by Mistake

2. The defendant owes the plaintiff $_____ for money paid by mistake to the defendant on *date* under these circumstances: *describe with particularity in accordance with Rule 9(b)*.

(f) For Money Had and Received

2. The defendant owes the plaintiff $_____ for money that was received from *name* on *date* to be paid by the defendant to the plaintiff.

Demand for Judgment

Therefore, the plaintiff demands judgment against the defendant for $_____, plus interest and costs.

(Date and sign—See Form 2.)

History of FRCP Form 10: Adopted Apr. 30, 2007, eff. Dec. 1, 2007.

FORM 11. COMPLAINT FOR NEGLIGENCE

(Caption—See Form 1.)

1. (Statement of Jurisdiction—See Form 7.)

2. On *date*, at *place*, the defendant negligently drove a motor vehicle against the plaintiff.

3. As a result, the plaintiff was physically injured, lost wages or income, suffered physical and mental pain, and incurred medical expenses of $_____.

Therefore, the plaintiff demands judgment against the defendant for $_____, plus costs.

(Date and sign—See Form 2.)

History of FRCP Form 11: Adopted Apr. 30, 2007, eff. Dec. 1, 2007.

FORM 12. COMPLAINT FOR NEGLIGENCE WHEN THE PLAINTIFF DOES NOT KNOW WHO IS RESPONSIBLE

(Caption—See Form 1.)

1. (Statement of Jurisdiction—See Form 7.)

2. On *date*, at *place*, defendant *name* or defendant *name* or both of them willfully or recklessly or negligently drove, or caused to be driven, a motor vehicle against the plaintiff.

3. As a result, the plaintiff was physically injured, lost wages or income, suffered mental and physical pain, and incurred medical expenses of $_____.

Therefore, the plaintiff demands judgment against one or both defendants for $ _____, plus costs.

(Date and sign—See Form 2.)

History of FRCP Form 12: Adopted Apr. 30, 2007, eff. Dec. 1, 2007.

FORM 13. COMPLAINT FOR NEGLIGENCE UNDER THE FEDERAL EMPLOYERS' LIABILITY ACT

(Caption—See Form 1.)

1. (Statement of Jurisdiction—See Form 7.)

2. At the times below, the defendant owned and operated in interstate commerce a railroad line that passed through a tunnel located at _____.

3. On *date*, the plaintiff was working to repair and enlarge the tunnel to make it convenient and safe for use in interstate commerce.

4. During this work, the defendant, as the employer, negligently put the plaintiff to work in a section of the tunnel that the defendant had left unprotected and unsupported.

5. The defendant's negligence caused the plaintiff to be injured by a rock that fell from an unsupported portion of the tunnel.

6. As a result, the plaintiff was physically injured, lost wages or income, suffered mental and physical pain, and incurred medical expenses of $ _____.

Therefore, the plaintiff demands judgment against the defendant for $ _____, and costs.

(Date and sign—See Form 2.)

History of FRCP Form 13: Adopted Apr. 30, 2007, eff. Dec. 1, 2007.

FORM 14. COMPLAINT FOR DAMAGES UNDER THE MERCHANT MARINE ACT

(Caption—See Form 1.)

1. (Statement of Jurisdiction—See Form 7.)

2. At the times below, the defendant owned and operated the vessel *name* and used it to transport cargo for hire by water in interstate and foreign commerce.

3. On *date*, at *place*, the defendant hired the plaintiff under seamen's articles of customary form for a voyage from _____ to _____ and return at a wage of $ _____ a month and found, which is equal to a shore worker's wage of $ _____ a month.

4. On *date*, the vessel was at sea on the return voyage. (*Describe the weather and the condition of the vessel.*)

5. (*Describe as in Form 11 the defendant's negligent conduct.*)

6. As a result of the defendant's negligent conduct and the unseaworthiness of the vessel, the plaintiff was physically injured, has been incapable of any gainful activity, suffered mental and physical pain, and has incurred medical expenses of $ _____.

Therefore, the plaintiff demands judgment against the defendant for $ _____, plus costs.

(Date and sign—See Form 2.)

History of FRCP Form 14: Adopted Apr. 30, 2007, eff. Dec. 1, 2007.

FORM 15. COMPLAINT FOR THE CONVERSION OF PROPERTY

(Caption—See Form 1.)

1. (Statement of Jurisdiction—See Form 7.)

2. On *date*, at *place*, the defendant converted to the defendant's own use property owned by the plaintiff. The property converted consists of *describe*.

3. The property is worth $ _____.

Therefore, the plaintiff demands judgment against the defendant for $ _____, plus costs.

(Date and sign—See Form 2.)

History of FRCP Form 15: Adopted Apr. 30, 2007, eff. Dec. 1, 2007.

FORM 16. THIRD-PARTY COMPLAINT

(Caption—See Form 1.)

1. Plaintiff *name* has filed against defendant *name* a complaint, a copy of which is attached.

2. (*State grounds entitling defendant's name to recover from third-party defendant's name for (all or an identified share) of any judgment for plaintiff's name against defendant's name.*)

Therefore, the defendant demands judgment against third-party defendant's name for all or an identified share of sums that may be adjudged against the defendant in the plaintiff's favor.

(Date and sign—See Form 2.)

History of FRCP Form 16: Adopted Apr. 30, 2007, eff. Dec. 1, 2007.

FORM 17. COMPLAINT FOR SPECIFIC PERFORMANCE OF A CONTRACT TO CONVEY LAND

(Caption—See Form 1.)

1. (Statement of Jurisdiction—See Form 7.)

2. On *date*, the parties agreed to the contract [attached as Exhibit A] [summarize the contract].

3. As agreed, the plaintiff tendered the purchase price and requested a conveyance of the land, but the defendant refused to accept the money or make a conveyance.

FRCP FORMS

4. The plaintiff now offers to pay the purchase price.

Therefore, the plaintiff demands that:

(a) the defendant be required to specifically perform the agreement and pay damages of $_____, plus interest and costs, or

(b) if specific performance is not ordered, the defendant be required to pay damages of $_____, plus interest and costs.

(Date and sign—See Form 2.)

History of FRCP Form 17: Adopted Apr. 30, 2007, eff. Dec. 1, 2007.

FORM 18. COMPLAINT FOR PATENT INFRINGEMENT

(Caption—See Form 1.)

1. (Statement of Jurisdiction—See Form 7.)

2. On date, United States Letters Patent No. _____ were issued to the plaintiff for an invention in an electric motor. The plaintiff owned the patent throughout the period of the defendant's infringing acts and still owns the patent.

3. The defendant has infringed and is still infringing the Letters Patent by making, selling, and using electric motors that embody the patented invention, and the defendant will continue to do so unless enjoined by this court.

4. The plaintiff has complied with the statutory requirement of placing a notice of the Letters Patent on all electric motors it manufactures and sells and has given the defendant written notice of the infringement.

Therefore, the plaintiff demands:

(a) a preliminary and final injunction against the continuing infringement;

(b) an accounting for damages; and

(c) interest and costs.

(Date and sign—See Form 2.)

History of FRCP Form 18: Adopted Apr. 30, 2007, eff. Dec. 1, 2007.

FORM 19. COMPLAINT FOR COPYRIGHT INFRINGEMENT & UNFAIR COMPETITION

(Caption—See Form 1.)

1. (Statement of Jurisdiction—See Form 7.)

2. Before *date*, the plaintiff, a United States citizen, wrote a book entitled _____.

3. The book is an original work that may be copyrighted under United States law. A copy of the book is attached as Exhibit A.

4. Between *date* and *date*, the plaintiff applied to the copyright office and received a certificate of registration dated _____ and identified as *date, class, number*.

5. Since *date*, the plaintiff has either published or licensed for publication all copies of the book in compliance with the copyright laws and has remained the sole owner of the copyright.

6. After the copyright was issued, the defendant infringed the copyright by publishing and selling a book entitled _____, which was copied largely from the plaintiff's book. A copy of the defendant's book is attached as Exhibit B.

7. The plaintiff has notified the defendant in writing of the infringement.

8. The defendant continues to infringe the copyright by continuing to publish and sell the infringing book in violation of the copyright, and further has engaged in unfair trade practices and unfair competition in connection with its publication and sale of the infringing book, thus causing irreparable damage.

Therefore, the plaintiff demands that:

(a) until this case is decided the defendant and the defendant's agents be enjoined from disposing of any copies of the defendant's book by sale or otherwise;

(b) the defendant account for and pay as damages to the plaintiff all profits and advantages gained from unfair trade practices and unfair competition in selling the defendant's book, and all profits and advantages gained from infringing the plaintiff's copyright (but no less than the statutory minimum);

(c) the defendant deliver for impoundment all copies of the book in the defendant's possession or control and deliver for destruction all infringing copies and all plates, molds, and other materials for making infringing copies;

(d) the defendant pay the plaintiff interest, costs, and reasonable attorney's fees; and

(e) the plaintiff be awarded any other just relief.

(Date and sign—See Form 2.)

History of FRCP Form 19: Adopted Apr. 30, 2007, eff. Dec. 1, 2007.

FORM 20. COMPLAINT FOR INTERPLEADER & DECLARATORY RELIEF

(Caption—See Form 1.)

1. (Statement of Jurisdiction—See Form 7.)

2. On *date*, the plaintiff issued a life insurance policy on the life of *name* with *name* as the named beneficiary.

FRCP FORMS

3. As a condition for keeping the policy in force, the policy required payment of a premium during the first year and then annually.

4. The premium due on _date_ was never paid, and the policy lapsed after that date.

5. On _date_, after the policy had lapsed, both the insured and the named beneficiary died in an automobile collision.

6. Defendant _name_ claims to be the beneficiary in place of _name_ and has filed a claim to be paid the policy's full amount.

7. The other two defendants are representatives of the deceased persons' estates. Each defendant has filed a claim on behalf of each estate to receive payment of the policy's full amount.

8. If the policy was in force at the time of death, the plaintiff is in doubt about who should be paid.

Therefore, the plaintiff demands that:

(a) each defendant be restrained from commencing any action against the plaintiff on the policy;

(b) a judgment be entered that no defendant is entitled to the proceeds of the policy or any part of it, but if the court determines that the policy was in effect at the time of the insured's death, that the defendants be required to interplead and settle among themselves their rights to the proceeds, and that the plaintiff be discharged from all liability except to the defendant determined to be entitled to the proceeds; and

(c) the plaintiff recover its costs.

(Date and sign—See Form 2.)

History of FRCP Form 20: Adopted Apr. 30, 2007, eff. Dec. 1, 2007.

FORM 21. COMPLAINT ON A CLAIM FOR A DEBT & TO SET ASIDE A FRAUDULENT CONVEYANCE UNDER RULE 18(b)

(Caption—See Form 1.)

1. (Statement of Jurisdiction—See Form 7.)

2. On _date_, defendant _name_ signed a note promising to pay to the plaintiff on _date_ the sum of $ _____ with interest at the rate of _____ percent. [The pleader may, but need not, attach a copy or plead the note verbatim.]

3. Defendant _name_ owes the plaintiff the amount of the note and interest.

4. On _date_, defendant _name_ conveyed all defendant's real and personal property _if less than all, describe it fully_ to defendant _name_ for the purpose of defrauding the plaintiff and hindering or delaying the collection of the debt.

Therefore, the plaintiff demands that:

(a) judgment for $ _____, plus costs, be entered against defendant(s) _name(s)_; and

(b) the conveyance to defendant _name_ be declared void and any judgment granted be made a lien on the property.

(Date and sign—See Form 2.)

History of FRCP Form 21: Adopted Apr. 30, 2007, eff. Dec. 1, 2007.

FORM 30. ANSWER PRESENTING DEFENSES UNDER RULE 12(b)

(Caption—See Form 1.)

Responding to Allegations in the Complaint

1. Defendant admits the allegations in paragraphs _____.

2. Defendant lacks knowledge or information sufficient to form a belief about the truth of the allegations in paragraphs _____.

3. Defendant admits _identify part of the allegation_ in paragraph _____ and denies or lacks knowledge or information sufficient to form a belief about the truth of the rest of the paragraph.

Failure to State a Claim

4. The complaint fails to state a claim upon which relief can be granted.

Failure to Join a Required Party

5. If there is a debt, it is owed jointly by the defendant and _name_ who is a citizen of _____. This person can be made a party without depriving this court of jurisdiction over the existing parties.

Affirmative Defense—Statute of Limitations

6. The plaintiff's claim is barred by the statute of limitations because it arose more than _____ years before this action was commenced.

Counterclaim

7. (_Set forth any counterclaim in the same way a claim is pleaded in a complaint. Include a further statement of jurisdiction if needed._)

Crossclaim

8. (_Set forth a crossclaim against a coparty in the same way a claim is pleaded in a complaint. Include a further statement of jurisdiction if needed._)

(Date and sign—See Form 2.)

History of FRCP Form 30: Adopted Apr. 30, 2007, eff. Dec. 1, 2007.

FORM 31. ANSWER TO A COMPLAINT FOR MONEY HAD & RECEIVED WITH A COUNTERCLAIM FOR INTERPLEADER

(Caption—See Form 1.)

Response to the Allegations in the Complaint

(See Form 30.)

Counterclaim for Interpleader

1. The defendant received from name a deposit of $_____.

2. The plaintiff demands payment of the deposit because of a purported assignment from name, who has notified the defendant that the assignment is not valid and who continues to hold the defendant responsible for the deposit.

Therefore, the defendant demands that:

(a) name be made a party to this action;

(b) the plaintiff and name be required to interplead their respective claims;

(c) the court decide whether the plaintiff or name or either of them is entitled to the deposit and discharge the defendant of any liability except to the person entitled to the deposit; and

(d) the defendant recover costs and attorney's fees.

(Date and sign—See Form 2.)

History of FRCP Form 31: Adopted Apr. 30, 2007, eff. Dec. 1, 2007.

FORM 40. MOTION TO DISMISS UNDER RULE 12(b) FOR LACK OF JURISDICTION, IMPROPER VENUE, INSUFFICIENT SERVICE OF PROCESS, OR FAILURE TO STATE A CLAIM

(Caption—See Form 1.)

The defendant moves to dismiss the action because:

1. the amount in controversy is less than the sum or value specified by 28 U.S.C. §1332;

2. the defendant is not subject to the personal jurisdiction of this court;

3. venue is improper (this defendant does not reside in this district and no part of the events or omissions giving rise to the claim occurred in the district);

4. the defendant has not been properly served, as shown by the attached affidavits of _____; or

5. the complaint fails to state a claim upon which relief can be granted.

(Date and sign—See Form 2.)

History of FRCP Form 40: Adopted Apr. 30, 2007, eff. Dec. 1, 2007.

FORM 41. MOTION TO BRING IN A THIRD-PARTY DEFENDANT

(Caption—See Form 1.)

The defendant, as third-party plaintiff, moves for leave to serve on name a summons and third-party complaint, copies of which are attached.

(Date and sign—See Form 2.)

History of FRCP Form 41: Adopted Apr. 30, 2007, eff. Dec. 1, 2007.

FORM 42. MOTION TO INTERVENE AS A DEFENDANT UNDER RULE 24

(Caption—See Form 1.)

1. [Name] moves for leave to intervene as a defendant in this action and to file the attached answer.

(State grounds under Rule 24(a) or (b).)

2. The plaintiff alleges patent infringement. We manufacture and sell to the defendant the articles involved, and we have a defense to the plaintiff's claim.

3. Our defense presents questions of law and fact that are common to this action.

(Date and sign—See Form 2.)

[An Intervener's Answer must be attached. See Form 30.]

History of FRCP Form 42: Adopted Apr. 30, 2007, eff. Dec. 1, 2007.

FORM 50. REQUEST TO PRODUCE DOCUMENTS & TANGIBLE THINGS, OR TO ENTER ONTO LAND UNDER RULE 34

(Caption—See Form 1.)

The plaintiff name requests that the defendant name respond within _____ days to the following requests:

1. To produce and permit the plaintiff to inspect and copy and to test or sample the following documents, including electronically stored information:

(Describe each document and the electronically stored information, either individually or by category.)

(State the time, place, and manner of the inspection and any related acts.)

2. To produce and permit the plaintiff to inspect and copy—and to test or sample—the following tangible things:

(Describe each thing, either individually or by category.)

(State the time, place, and manner of the inspection and any related acts.)

3. To permit the plaintiff to enter onto the following land to inspect, photograph, test, or sample the property or an object or operation on the property.

FRCP FORMS

(Describe the property and each object or operation.)

(State the time and manner of the inspection and any related acts.)

(Date and sign—See Form 2.)

History of FRCP Form 50: Adopted Apr. 30, 2007, eff. Dec. 1, 2007.

FORM 51. REQUEST FOR ADMISSIONS UNDER RULE 36

(Caption—See Form 1.)

The plaintiff <u>*name*</u> asks the defendant <u>*name*</u> to respond within 30 days to these requests by admitting, for purposes of this action only and subject to objections to admissibility at trial:

1. The genuineness of the following documents, copies of which [are attached] [are or have been furnished or made available for inspection and copying].

(List each document.)

2. The truth of each of the following statements:

(List each statement.)

(Date and sign—See Form 2.)

History of FRCP Form 51: Adopted Apr. 30, 2007, eff. Dec. 1, 2007.

FORM 52. REPORT OF THE PARTIES' PLANNING MEETING

(Caption—See Form 1.)

1. The following persons participated in a Rule 26(f) conference on <u>*date*</u> by <u>*state the method of conferring*</u>:

<u>Name</u>, representing the <u>*plaintiff*</u>
<u>Name</u>, representing the <u>*defendant*</u>

2. Initial Disclosures. The parties [have completed] [will complete by <u>*date*</u>] the initial disclosures required by Rule 26(a)(1).

3. Discovery Plan. The parties propose this discovery plan:

(Use separate paragraphs or subparagraphs if the parties disagree.)

(a) Discovery will be needed on these subjects: *(describe.)*

(b) Disclosure or discovery of electronically stored information should be handled as follows: *(briefly describe the parties' proposals, including the form or forms for production.)*

(c) The parties have agreed to an order regarding claims of privilege or of protection as trial-preparation material asserted after production, as follows: *(briefly describe the provisions of the proposed order.)*

(d) (Dates for commencing and completing discovery, including discovery to be commenced or completed before other discovery.)

(e) (Maximum number of interrogatories by each party to another party, along with the dates the answers are due.)

(f) (Maximum number of requests for admission, along with the dates responses are due.)

(g) (Maximum number of depositions by each party.)

(h) (Limits on the length of depositions, in hours.)

(i) (Dates for exchanging reports of expert witnesses.)

(j) (Dates for supplementations under Rule 26(e).)

4. Other Items:

(a) (A date if the parties ask to meet with the court before a scheduling order.)

(b) (Requested dates for pretrial conferences.)

(c) (Final dates for the plaintiff to amend pleadings or to join parties.)

(d) (Final dates for the defendant to amend pleadings or to join parties.)

(e) (Final dates to file dispositive motions.)

(f) (State the prospects for settlement.)

(g) (Identify any alternative dispute resolution procedure that may enhance settlement prospects.)

(h) (Final dates for submitting Rule 26(a)(3) witness lists, designations of witnesses whose testimony will be presented by deposition, and exhibit lists.)

(i) (Final dates to file objections under Rule 26(a)(3).)

(j) (Suggested trial date and estimate of trial length.)

(k) (Other matters.)

(Date and sign—see Form 2.)

History of FRCP Form 52: Adopted Apr. 30, 2007, eff. Dec. 1, 2007. Amended Apr. 28, 2010, eff. Dec. 1, 2010.

FORM 60. NOTICE OF CONDEMNATION

(Caption—See Form 1.)

To <u>*name the defendant*</u>.

1. A complaint in condemnation has been filed in the United States District Court for the ______ District of ______, to take property to use for <u>*purpose*</u>. The interest to be taken is <u>*describe*</u>. The court is located in the United States courthouse at this address: ______.

2. The property to be taken is described below. You have or claim an interest in it.

(*Describe the property.*)

3. The authority for taking this property is *cite*.

4. If you want to object or present any defense to the taking you must serve an answer on the plaintiff's attorney within 21 days [after being served with this notice] [from (*insert the date of the last publication of notice*)]. Send your answer to this address: _____.

5. Your answer must identify the property in which you claim an interest, state the nature and extent of that interest, and state all your objections and defenses to the taking. Objections and defenses not presented are waived.

6. If you fail to answer you consent to the taking and the court will enter a judgment that takes your described property interest.

7. Instead of answering, you may serve on the plaintiff's attorney a notice of appearance that designates the property in which you claim an interest. After you do that, you will receive a notice of any proceedings that affect you. Whether or not you have previously appeared or answered, you may present evidence at a trial to determine compensation for the property and share in the overall award.

(Date and sign—See Form 2.)

History of FRCP Form 60: Adopted Apr. 30, 2007, eff. Dec. 1, 2007. Amended Mar. 26, 2009, eff. Dec. 1, 2009.

FORM 61. COMPLAINT FOR CONDEMNATION

(Caption—See Form 1; name as defendants the property and at least one owner.)

1. (Statement of Jurisdiction—See Form 7.)

2. This is an action to take property under the power of eminent domain and to determine just compensation to be paid to the owners and parties in interest.

3. The authority for the taking is _____.

4. The property is to be used for _____.

5. The property to be taken is (*describe in enough detail for identification—or attach the description and state "is described in Exhibit A, attached."*)

6. The interest to be acquired is _____.

7. The persons known to the plaintiff to have or claim an interest in the property are: _____. (*For each person include the interest claimed.*)

8. There may be other persons who have or claim an interest in the property and whose names could not be found after a reasonably diligent search. They are made parties under the designation "Unknown Owners."

Therefore, the plaintiff demands judgment:

(a) condemning the property;

(b) determining and awarding just compensation; and

(c) granting any other lawful and proper relief.

(Date and sign—See Form 2.)

History of FRCP Form 61: Adopted Apr. 30, 2007, eff. Dec. 1, 2007.

FORM 70. JUDGMENT ON A JURY VERDICT

(Caption—See Form 1.)

This action was tried by a jury with Judge _____ presiding, and the jury has rendered a verdict.

It is ordered that:

[the plaintiff *name* recover from the defendant *name* the amount of $_____ with interest at the rate of _____%, along with costs.]

[the plaintiff recover nothing, the action be dismissed on the merits, and the defendant *name* recover costs from the plaintiff *name*.]

Date __________ __________________

Clerk of Court

History of FRCP Form 70: Adopted Apr. 30, 2007, eff. Dec. 1, 2007.

FORM 71. JUDGMENT BY THE COURT WITHOUT A JURY

(Caption—See Form 1.)

This action was tried by Judge _____ without a jury and the following decision was reached:

It is ordered that [the plaintiff *name* recover from the defendant *name* the amount of $_____, with prejudgment interest at the rate of _____%, postjudgment interest at the rate of _____%, along with costs.] [the plaintiff recover nothing, the action be dismissed on the merits, and the defendant *name* recover costs from the plaintiff *name*.]

Date __________ __________________

Clerk of Court

History of FRCP Form 71: Adopted Apr. 30, 2007, eff. Dec. 1, 2007.

FRCP FORMS

FORM 80. NOTICE OF A MAGISTRATE JUDGE'S AVAILABILITY

1. A magistrate judge is available under title 28 U.S.C. §636(c) to conduct the proceedings in this case, including a jury or nonjury trial and the entry of final judgment. But a magistrate judge can be assigned only if all parties voluntarily consent.

2. You may withhold your consent without adverse substantive consequences. The identity of any party consenting or withholding consent will not be disclosed to the judge to whom the case is assigned or to any magistrate judge.

3. If a magistrate judge does hear your case, you may appeal directly to a United States court of appeals as you would if a district judge heard it.

A form called *Consent to an Assignment to a United States Magistrate Judge* is available from the court clerk's office.

History of FRCP Form 80: Adopted Apr. 30, 2007, eff. Dec. 1, 2007.

FORM 81. CONSENT TO AN ASSIGNMENT TO A MAGISTRATE JUDGE

(Caption—See Form 1.)

I voluntarily consent to have a United States magistrate judge conduct all further proceedings in this case, including a trial, and order the entry of final judgment. (Return this form to the court clerk—not to a judge or magistrate judge.)

Date ___________ ____________________
Signature of the Party

History of FRCP Form 81: Adopted Apr. 30, 2007, eff. Dec. 1, 2007.

FORM 82. ORDER OF ASSIGNMENT TO A MAGISTRATE JUDGE

(Caption—See Form 1.)

With the parties' consent it is ordered that this case be assigned to United States Magistrate Judge ______ of this district to conduct all proceedings and enter final judgment in accordance with 28 U.S.C. §636(c).

Date ___________ ____________________
United States District Judge

History of FRCP Form 82: Adopted Apr. 30, 2007, eff. Dec. 1, 2007.

SUPPLEMENTAL RULES FOR ADMIRALTY OR MARITIME CLAIMS & ASSET FORFEITURE ACTIONS

RULE A. SCOPE OF RULES

(1) These Supplemental Rules apply to:

(A) the procedure in admiralty and maritime claims within the meaning of Rule 9(h) with respect to the following remedies:

(i) maritime attachment and garnishment,

(ii) actions in rem,

(iii) possessory, petitory, and partition actions, and

(iv) actions for exoneration from or limitation of liability;

(B) forfeiture actions in rem arising from a federal statute; and

(C) the procedure in statutory condemnation proceedings analogous to maritime actions in rem, whether within the admiralty and maritime jurisdiction or not. Except as otherwise provided, references in these Supplemental Rules to actions in rem include such analogous statutory condemnation proceedings.

(2) The Federal Rules of Civil Procedure also apply to the foregoing proceedings except to the extent that they are inconsistent with these Supplemental Rules.

History of Rule A: Adopted Feb. 28, 1966, eff. July 1, 1966. Amended Apr. 12, 2006, eff. Dec. 1, 2006.

RULE B. IN PERSONAM ACTIONS: ATTACHMENT & GARNISHMENT

(1) When Available; Complaint, Affidavit, Judicial Authorization, and Process. In an in personam action:

(a) If a defendant is not found within the district when a verified complaint praying for attachment and the affidavit required by Rule B(1)(b) are filed, a verified complaint may contain a prayer for process to attach the defendant's tangible or intangible personal property—up to the amount sued for—in the hands of garnishees named in the process.

(b) The plaintiff or the plaintiff's attorney must sign and file with the complaint an affidavit stating that, to the affiant's knowledge, or on information and belief, the defendant cannot be found within the district. The court must review the complaint and affidavit and, if the conditions of this Rule B appear to exist, enter an order so stating and authorizing process of attachment and garnishment. The clerk may issue supplemental process enforcing the court's order upon application without further court order.

(c) If the plaintiff or the plaintiff's attorney certifies that exigent circumstances make court review impracticable, the clerk must issue the summons and process of attachment and garnishment. The plaintiff has the burden in any post-attachment hearing under Rule E(4)(f) to show that exigent circumstances existed.

(d)(i) If the property is a vessel or tangible property on board a vessel, the summons, process, and any supplemental process must be delivered to the marshal for service.

(ii) If the property is other tangible or intangible property, the summons, process, and any supplemental process must be delivered to a person or organization authorized to serve it, who may be (A) a marshal; (B) someone under contract with the United States; (C) someone specially appointed by the court for that purpose; or, (D) in an action brought by the United States, any officer or employee of the United States.

(e) The plaintiff may invoke state-law remedies under Rule 64 for seizure of person or property for the purpose of securing satisfaction of the judgment.

(2) Notice to Defendant. No default judgment may be entered except upon proof—which may be by affidavit—that:

(a) the complaint, summons, and process of attachment or garnishment have been served on the defendant in a manner authorized by Rule 4;

(b) the plaintiff or the garnishee has mailed to the defendant the complaint, summons, and process of attachment or garnishment, using any form of mail requiring a return receipt; or

(c) the plaintiff or the garnishee has tried diligently to give notice of the action to the defendant but could not do so.

(3) Answer.

(a) *By Garnishee.* The garnishee shall serve an answer, together with answers to any interrogatories served with the complaint, within 21 days after service of process upon the garnishee. Interrogatories to the garnishee may be served with the complaint without leave of court. If the garnishee refuses or neglects to answer on oath as to the debts, credits, or effects of the defendant in the garnishee's hands, or any interrogatories concerning such debts, credits, and effects that may be propounded by the plaintiff, the court may award compulsory process against the garnishee. If the garnishee admits any debts, credits, or effects, they

shall be held in the garnishee's hands or paid into the registry of the court, and shall be held in either case subject to the further order of the court.

(b) *By Defendant.* The defendant shall serve an answer within 30 days after process has been executed, whether by attachment of property or service on the garnishee.

See selected Notes of Advisory Committee to Rule B, p. 1235.

History of Rule B: Adopted Feb. 28, 1966, eff. July 1, 1966. Amended Apr. 29, 1985, eff. Aug. 1, 1985; Mar. 2, 1987, eff. Aug. 1, 1987; Apr. 17, 2000, eff. Dec. 1, 2000; Mar. 26, 2009, eff. Dec. 1, 2009.

RULE C. IN REM ACTIONS: SPECIAL PROVISIONS

(1) When Available. An action in rem may be brought:

(a) To enforce any maritime lien;

(b) Whenever a statute of the United States provides for a maritime action in rem or a proceeding analogous thereto.

Except as otherwise provided by law a party who may proceed in rem may also, or in the alternative, proceed in personam against any person who may be liable.

Statutory provisions exempting vessels or other property owned or possessed by or operated by or for the United States from arrest or seizure are not affected by this rule. When a statute so provides, an action against the United States or an instrumentality thereof may proceed on in rem principles.

(2) Complaint. In an action in rem the complaint must:

(a) be verified;

(b) describe with reasonable particularity the property that is the subject of the action; and

(c) state that the property is within the district or will be within the district while the action is pending.

(3) Judicial Authorization and Process.

(a) *Arrest Warrant.*

(i) The court must review the complaint and any supporting papers. If the conditions for an in rem action appear to exist, the court must issue an order directing the clerk to issue a warrant for the arrest of the vessel or other property that is the subject of the action.

(ii) If the plaintiff or the plaintiff's attorney certifies that exigent circumstances make court review impracticable, the clerk must promptly issue a summons and a warrant for the arrest of the vessel or other property that is the subject of the action. The plaintiff has the burden in any post-arrest hearing under Rule E(4)(f) to show that exigent circumstances existed.

(b) *Service.*

(i) If the property that is the subject of the action is a vessel or tangible property on board a vessel, the warrant and any supplemental process must be delivered to the marshal for service.

(ii) If the property that is the subject of the action is other property, tangible or intangible, the warrant and any supplemental process must be delivered to a person or organization authorized to enforce it, who may be: (A) a marshal; (B) someone under contract with the United States; (C) someone specially appointed by the court for that purpose; or, (D) in an action brought by the United States, any officer or employee of the United States.

(c) *Deposit in Court.* If the property that is the subject of the action consists in whole or in part of freight, the proceeds of property sold, or other intangible property, the clerk must issue—in addition to the warrant—a summons directing any person controlling the property to show cause why it should not be deposited in court to abide the judgment.

(d) *Supplemental Process.* The clerk may upon application issue supplemental process to enforce the court's order without further court order.

(4) Notice. No notice other than execution of process is required when the property that is the subject of the action has been released under Rule E(5). If the property is not released within 14 days after execution, the plaintiff must promptly—or within the time that the court allows—give public notice of the action and arrest in a newspaper designated by court order and having general circulation in the district, but publication may be terminated if the property is released before publication is completed. The notice must specify the time under Rule C(6) to file a statement of interest in or right against the seized property and to answer. This rule does not affect the notice requirements in an action to foreclose a preferred ship mortgage under 46 U.S.C. §§31301 et seq., as amended.

(5) Ancillary Process. In any action in rem in which process has been served as provided by this rule, if any part of the property that is the subject of the action has not been brought within the control of the court because it has been removed or sold, or because it is intangible property in the hands of a person who has not been served with process, the court may, on motion,

order any person having possession or control of such property or its proceeds to show cause why it should not be delivered into the custody of the marshal or other person or organization having a warrant for the arrest of the property, or paid into court to abide the judgment; and, after hearing, the court may enter such judgment as law and justice may require.

(6) Responsive Pleading; Interrogatories.

(a) *Statement of Interest; Answer.* In an action in rem:

(i) a person who asserts a right of possession or any ownership interest in the property that is the subject of the action must file a verified statement of right or interest:

(A) within 14 days after the execution of process, or

(B) within the time that the court allows;

(ii) the statement of right or interest must describe the interest in the property that supports the person's demand for its restitution or right to defend the action;

(iii) an agent, bailee, or attorney must state the authority to file a statement of right or interest on behalf of another; and

(iv) a person who asserts a right of possession or any ownership interest must serve an answer within 21 days after filing the statement of interest or right.

(b) *Interrogatories.* Interrogatories may be served with the complaint in an in rem action without leave of court. Answers to the interrogatories must be served with the answer to the complaint.

See selected Notes of Advisory Committee to Rule C, p. 1235.

History of Rule C: Adopted Feb. 28, 1966, eff. July 1, 1966. Amended Apr. 29, 1985, eff. Aug. 1, 1985; Mar. 2, 1987, eff. Aug. 1, 1987; Apr. 30, 1991, eff. Dec. 1, 1991; Apr. 17, 2000, eff. Dec. 1, 2000; Apr. 29, 2002, eff. Dec. 1, 2002; Apr. 12, 2006, eff. Dec. 1, 2006; Apr. 23, 2008, eff. Dec. 1, 2008; Mar. 26, 2009, eff. Dec. 1, 2009.

RULE D. POSSESSORY, PETITORY, & PARTITION ACTIONS

In all actions for possession, partition, and to try title maintainable according to the course of the admiralty practice with respect to a vessel, in all actions so maintainable with respect to the possession of cargo or other maritime property, and in all actions by one or more part owners against the others to obtain security for the return of the vessel from any voyage undertaken without their consent, or by one or more part owners against the others to obtain possession of the vessel for any voyage on giving security for its safe return, the process shall be by a warrant of arrest of the vessel, cargo, or other property, and by notice in the manner provided by Rule B(2) to the adverse party or parties.

History of Rule D: Adopted Feb. 28, 1966, eff. July 1, 1966.

RULE E. ACTIONS IN REM & QUASI IN REM: GENERAL PROVISIONS

(1) Applicability. Except as otherwise provided, this rule applies to actions in personam with process of maritime attachment and garnishment, actions in rem, and petitory, possessory, and partition actions, supplementing Rules B, C, and D.

(2) Complaint; Security.

(a) *Complaint.* In actions to which this rule is applicable the complaint shall state the circumstances from which the claim arises with such particularity that the defendant or claimant will be able, without moving for a more definite statement, to commence an investigation of the facts and to frame a responsive pleading.

(b) *Security for Costs.* Subject to the provisions of Rule 54(d) and of relevant statutes, the court may, on the filing of the complaint or on the appearance of any defendant, claimant, or any other party, or at any later time, require the plaintiff, defendant, claimant, or other party to give security, or additional security, in such sum as the court shall direct to pay all costs and expenses that shall be awarded against the party by any interlocutory order or by the final judgment, or on appeal by any appellate court.

(3) Process.

(a) In admiralty and maritime proceedings process in rem or of maritime attachment and garnishment may be served only within the district.

(b) *Issuance and Delivery.* Issuance and delivery of process in rem, or of maritime attachment and garnishment, shall be held in abeyance if the plaintiff so requests.

(4) Execution of Process; Marshal's Return; Custody of Property; Procedures for Release.

(a) *In General.* Upon issuance and delivery of the process, or, in the case of summons with process of attachment and garnishment, when it appears that the defendant cannot be found within the district, the marshal or other person or organization having a warrant shall forthwith execute the process in accordance with this subdivision (4), making due and prompt return.

(b) *Tangible Property.* If tangible property is to be attached or arrested, the marshal or other person or or-

ganization having the warrant shall take it into the marshal's possession for safe custody. If the character or situation of the property is such that the taking of actual possession is impracticable, the marshal or other person executing the process shall affix a copy thereof to the property in a conspicuous place and leave a copy of the complaint and process with the person having possession or the person's agent. In furtherance of the marshal's custody of any vessel the marshal is authorized to make a written request to the collector of customs not to grant clearance to such vessel until notified by the marshal or deputy marshal or by the clerk that the vessel has been released in accordance with these rules.

(c) *Intangible Property.* If intangible property is to be attached or arrested the marshal or other person or organization having the warrant shall execute the process by leaving with the garnishee or other obligor a copy of the complaint and process requiring the garnishee or other obligor to answer as provided in Rules B(3)(a) and C(6); or the marshal may accept for payment into the registry of the court the amount owed to the extent of the amount claimed by the plaintiff with interest and costs, in which event the garnishee or other obligor shall not be required to answer unless alias process shall be served.

(d) *Directions With Respect to Property in Custody.* The marshal or other person or organization having the warrant may at any time apply to the court for directions with respect to property that has been attached or arrested, and shall give notice of such application to any or all of the parties as the court may direct.

(e) *Expenses of Seizing and Keeping Property; Deposit.* These rules do not alter the provisions of Title 28, U.S.C., §1921, as amended, relative to the expenses of seizing and keeping property attached or arrested and to the requirement of deposits to cover such expenses.

(f) *Procedure for Release From Arrest or Attachment.* Whenever property is arrested or attached, any person claiming an interest in it shall be entitled to a prompt hearing at which the plaintiff shall be required to show why the arrest or attachment should not be vacated or other relief granted consistent with these rules. This subdivision shall have no application to suits for seamen's wages when process is issued upon a certification of sufficient cause filed pursuant to Title 46, U.S.C. §§603 and 604[1] or to actions by the United States for forfeitures for violation of any statute of the United States.

(5) Release of Property.

(a) *Special Bond.* Whenever process of maritime attachment and garnishment or process in rem is issued the execution of such process shall be stayed, or the property released, on the giving of security, to be approved by the court or clerk, or by stipulation of the parties, conditioned to answer the judgment of the court or of any appellate court. The parties may stipulate the amount and nature of such security. In the event of the inability or refusal of the parties to stipulate the court shall fix the principal sum of the bond or stipulation at an amount sufficient to cover the amount of the plaintiff's claim fairly stated with accrued interest and costs; but the principal sum shall in no event exceed (i) twice the amount of the plaintiff's claim or (ii) the value of the property on due appraisement, whichever is smaller. The bond or stipulation shall be conditioned for the payment of the principal sum and interest thereon at 6 per cent per annum.

(b) *General Bond.* The owner of any vessel may file a general bond or stipulation, with sufficient surety, to be approved by the court, conditioned to answer the judgment of such court in all or any actions that may be brought thereafter in such court in which the vessel is attached or arrested. Thereupon the execution of all such process against such vessel shall be stayed so long as the amount secured by such bond or stipulation is at least double the aggregate amount claimed by plaintiffs in all actions begun and pending in which such vessel has been attached or arrested. Judgments and remedies may be had on such bond or stipulation as if a special bond or stipulation had been filed in each of such actions. The district court may make necessary orders to carry this rule into effect, particularly as to the giving of proper notice of any action against or attachment of a vessel for which a general bond has been filed. Such bond or stipulation shall be indorsed by the clerk with a minute of the actions wherein process is so stayed. Further security may be required by the court at any time.

If a special bond or stipulation is given in a particular case, the liability on the general bond or stipulation shall cease as to that case.

(c) *Release by Consent or Stipulation; Order of Court or Clerk; Costs.* Any vessel, cargo, or other property in the custody of the marshal or other person or or-

ganization having the warrant may be released forthwith upon the marshal's acceptance and approval of a stipulation, bond, or other security, signed by the party on whose behalf the property is detained or the party's attorney and expressly authorizing such release, if all costs and charges of the court and its officers shall have first been paid. Otherwise no property in the custody of the marshal, other person or organization having the warrant, or other officer of the court shall be released without an order of the court; but such order may be entered as of course by the clerk, upon the giving of approved security as provided by law and these rules, or upon the dismissal or discontinuance of the action; but the marshal or other person or organization having the warrant shall not deliver any property so released until the costs and charges of the officers of the court shall first have been paid.

(d) *Possessory, Petitory, and Partition Actions.* The foregoing provisions of this subdivision (5) do not apply to petitory, possessory, and partition actions. In such cases the property arrested shall be released only by order of the court, on such terms and conditions and on the giving of such security as the court may require.

(6) Reduction or Impairment of Security. Whenever security is taken the court may, on motion and hearing, for good cause shown, reduce the amount of security given; and if the surety shall be or become insufficient, new or additional sureties may be required on motion and hearing.

(7) Security on Counterclaim.

(a) When a person who has given security for damages in the original action asserts a counterclaim that arises from the transaction or occurrence that is the subject of the original action, a plaintiff for whose benefit the security has been given must give security for damages demanded in the counterclaim unless the court, for cause shown, directs otherwise. Proceedings on the original claim must be stayed until this security is given, unless the court directs otherwise.

(b) The plaintiff is required to give security under Rule E(7)(a) when the United States or its corporate instrumentality counterclaims and would have been required to give security to respond in damages if a private party but is relieved by law from giving security.

(8) Restricted Appearance. An appearance to defend against an admiralty and maritime claim with respect to which there has issued process in rem, or process of attachment and garnishment, may be expressly restricted to the defense of such claim, and in that event is not an appearance for the purposes of any other claim with respect to which such process is not available or has not been served.

(9) Disposition of Property; Sales.

(a) *Interlocutory Sales; Delivery.*

(i) On application of a party, the marshal, or other person having custody of the property, the court may order all or part of the property sold—with the sales proceeds, or as much of them as will satisfy the judgment, paid into court to await further orders of the court—if:

(A) the attached or arrested property is perishable, or liable to deterioration, decay, or injury by being detained in custody pending the action;

(B) the expense of keeping the property is excessive or disproportionate; or

(C) there is an unreasonable delay in securing release of the property.

(ii) In the circumstances described in Rule E(9)(a)(i), the court, on motion by a defendant or a person filing a statement of interest or right under Rule C(6), may order that the property, rather than being sold, be delivered to the movant upon giving security under these rules.

(b) *Sales, Proceeds.* All sales of property shall be made by the marshal or a deputy marshal, or by other person or organization having the warrant, or by any other person assigned by the court where the marshal or other person or organization having the warrant is a party in interest; and the proceeds of sale shall be forthwith paid into the registry of the court to be disposed of according to law.

(10) Preservation of Property. When the owner or another person remains in possession of property attached or arrested under the provisions of Rule E(4)(b) that permit execution of process without taking actual possession, the court, on a party's motion or on its own, may enter any order necessary to preserve the property and to prevent its removal.

1. **Editor's note:** Sections 603 and 604 of Title 46 were repealed by P.L. 98-89, §4(b), Aug. 26, 1983, 97 Stat. 600, §1 of which enacted Title 46, Shipping.

History of Rule E: Adopted Feb. 28, 1966, eff. July 1, 1966. Amended Apr. 29, 1985, eff. Aug. 1, 1985; Mar. 2, 1987, eff. Aug. 1, 1987; Apr. 30, 1991, eff. Dec. 1, 1991; Apr. 17, 2000, eff. Dec. 1, 2000; Apr. 12, 2006, eff. Dec. 1, 2006.

RULE F. LIMITATION OF LIABILITY

(1) Time for Filing Complaint; Security. Not later than six months after receipt of a claim in writing, any vessel owner may file a complaint in the appropri-

ate district court, as provided in subdivision (9) of this rule, for limitation of liability pursuant to statute. The owner (a) shall deposit with the court, for the benefit of claimants, a sum equal to the amount or value of the owner's interest in the vessel and pending freight, or approved security therefor, and in addition such sums, or approved security therefor, as the court may from time to time fix as necessary to carry out the provisions of the statutes as amended; or (b) at the owner's option shall transfer to a trustee to be appointed by the court, for the benefit of claimants, the owner's interest in the vessel and pending freight, together with such sums, or approved security therefor, as the court may from time to time fix as necessary to carry out the provisions of the statutes as amended. The plaintiff shall also give security for costs and, if the plaintiff elects to give security, for interest at the rate of 6 percent per annum from the date of the security.

(2) Complaint. The complaint shall set forth the facts on the basis of which the right to limit liability is asserted and all facts necessary to enable the court to determine the amount to which the owner's liability shall be limited. The complaint may demand exoneration from as well as limitation of liability. It shall state the voyage if any, on which the demands sought to be limited arose, with the date and place of its termination; the amount of all demands including all unsatisfied liens or claims of lien, in contract or in tort or otherwise, arising on that voyage, so far as known to the plaintiff, and what actions and proceedings, if any, are pending thereon; whether the vessel was damaged, lost, or abandoned, and, if so, when and where; the value of the vessel at the close of the voyage or, in case of wreck, the value of her wreckage, strippings, or proceeds, if any, and where and in whose possession they are; and the amount of any pending freight recovered or recoverable. If the plaintiff elects to transfer the plaintiff's interest in the vessel to a trustee, the complaint must further show any prior paramount liens thereon, and what voyages or trips, if any, she has made since the voyage or trip on which the claims sought to be limited arose, and any existing liens arising upon any such subsequent voyage or trip, with the amounts and causes thereof, and the names and addresses of the lienors, so far as known; and whether the vessel sustained any injury upon or by reason of such subsequent voyage or trip.

(3) Claims Against Owner; Injunction. Upon compliance by the owner with the requirements of subdivision (1) of this rule all claims and proceedings against the owner or the owner's property with respect to the matter in question shall cease. On application of the plaintiff the court shall enjoin the further prosecution of any action or proceeding against the plaintiff or the plaintiff's property with respect to any claim subject to limitation in the action.

(4) Notice to Claimants. Upon the owner's compliance with subdivision (1) of this rule the court shall issue a notice to all persons asserting claims with respect to which the complaint seeks limitation, admonishing them to file their respective claims with the clerk of the court and to serve on the attorneys for the plaintiff a copy thereof on or before a date to be named in the notice. The date so fixed shall not be less than 30 days after issuance of the notice. For cause shown, the court may enlarge the time within which claims may be filed. The notice shall be published in such newspaper or newspapers as the court may direct once a week for four successive weeks prior to the date fixed for the filing of claims. The plaintiff not later than the day of second publication shall also mail a copy of the notice to every person known to have made any claim against the vessel or the plaintiff arising out of the voyage or trip on which the claims sought to be limited arose. In cases involving death a copy of such notice shall be mailed to the decedent at the decedent's last known address, and also to any person who shall be known to have made any claim on account of such death.

(5) Claims and Answer. Claims shall be filed and served on or before the date specified in the notice provided for in subdivision (4) of this rule. Each claim shall specify the facts upon which the claimant relies in support of the claim, the items thereof, and the dates on which the same accrued. If a claimant desires to contest either the right to exoneration from or the right to limitation of liability the claimant shall file and serve an answer to the complaint unless the claim has included an answer.

(6) Information to Be Given Claimants. Within 30 days after the date specified in the notice for filing claims, or within such time as the court thereafter may allow, the plaintiff shall mail to the attorney for each claimant (or if the claimant has no attorney to the claimant) a list setting forth (a) the name of each claimant, (b) the name and address of the claimant's

attorney (if the claimant is known to have one), (c) the nature of the claim, i.e., whether property loss, property damage, death, personal injury etc., and (d) the amount thereof.

(7) Insufficiency of Fund or Security. Any claimant may by motion demand that the funds deposited in court or the security given by the plaintiff be increased on the ground that they are less than the value of the plaintiff's interest in the vessel and pending freight. Thereupon the court shall cause due appraisement to be made of the value of the plaintiff's interest in the vessel and pending freight; and if the court finds that the deposit or security is either insufficient or excessive it shall order its increase or reduction. In like manner any claimant may demand that the deposit or security be increased on the ground that it is insufficient to carry out the provisions of the statutes relating to claims in respect of loss of life or bodily injury; and, after notice and hearing, the court may similarly order that the deposit or security be increased or reduced.

(8) Objections to Claims: Distribution of Fund. Any interested party may question or controvert any claim without filing an objection thereto. Upon determination of liability the fund deposited or secured, or the proceeds of the vessel and pending freight, shall be divided pro rata, subject to all relevant provisions of law, among the several claimants in proportion to the amounts of their respective claims, duly proved, saving, however, to all parties any priority to which they may be legally entitled.

(9) Venue; Transfer. The complaint shall be filed in any district in which the vessel has been attached or arrested to answer for any claim with respect to which the plaintiff seeks to limit liability; or, if the vessel has not been attached or arrested, then in any district in which the owner has been sued with respect to any such claim. When the vessel has not been attached or arrested to answer the matters aforesaid, and suit has not been commenced against the owner, the proceedings may be had in the district in which the vessel may be, but if the vessel is not within any district and no suit has been commenced in any district, then the complaint may be filed in any district. For the convenience of parties and witnesses, in the interest of justice, the court may transfer the action to any district; if venue is wrongly laid the court shall dismiss or, if it be in the interest of justice, transfer the action to any district in which it could have been brought. If the vessel shall have been sold, the proceeds shall represent the vessel for the purposes of these rules.

History of Rule F: Adopted Feb. 28, 1966, eff. July 1, 1966. Amended Mar. 2, 1987, eff. Aug. 1, 1987.

RULE G. FORFEITURE ACTIONS IN REM

(1) Scope. This rule governs a forfeiture action in rem arising from a federal statute. To the extent that this rule does not address an issue, Supplemental Rules C and E and the Federal Rules of Civil Procedure also apply.

(2) Complaint. The complaint must:

(a) be verified;

(b) state the grounds for subject-matter jurisdiction, in rem jurisdiction over the defendant property, and venue;

(c) describe the property with reasonable particularity;

(d) if the property is tangible, state its location when any seizure occurred and—if different—its location when the action is filed;

(e) identify the statute under which the forfeiture action is brought; and

(f) state sufficiently detailed facts to support a reasonable belief that the government will be able to meet its burden of proof at trial.

(3) Judicial Authorization and Process.

(a) *Real Property.* If the defendant is real property, the government must proceed under 18 U.S.C. §985.

(b) *Other Property; Arrest Warrant.* If the defendant is not real property:

(i) the clerk must issue a warrant to arrest the property if it is in the government's possession, custody, or control;

(ii) the court—on finding probable cause—must issue a warrant to arrest the property if it is not in the government's possession, custody, or control and is not subject to a judicial restraining order; and

(iii) a warrant is not necessary if the property is subject to a judicial restraining order.

(c) *Execution of Process.*

(i) The warrant and any supplemental process must be delivered to a person or organization authorized to execute it, who may be: (A) a marshal or any other United States officer or employee; (B) someone under contact[1] with the United States; or (C) someone specially appointed by the court for that purpose.

ADM. RULE G

(ii) The authorized person or organization must execute the warrant and any supplemental process on property in the United States as soon as practicable unless:

(A) the property is in the government's possession, custody, or control; or

(B) the court orders a different time when the complaint is under seal, the action is stayed before the warrant and supplemental process are executed, or the court finds other good cause.

(iii) The warrant and any supplemental process may be executed within the district or, when authorized by statute, outside the district.

(iv) If executing a warrant on property outside the United States is required, the warrant may be transmitted to an appropriate authority for serving process where the property is located.

(4) Notice.

(a) *Notice by Publication.*

(i) *When Publication Is Required.* A judgment of forfeiture may be entered only if the government has published notice of the action within a reasonable time after filing the complaint or at a time the court orders. But notice need not be published if:

(A) the defendant property is worth less than $1,000 and direct notice is sent under Rule G(4)(b) to every person the government can reasonably identify as a potential claimant; or

(B) the court finds that the cost of publication exceeds the property's value and that other means of notice would satisfy due process.

(ii) *Content of the Notice.* Unless the court orders otherwise, the notice must:

(A) describe the property with reasonable particularity;

(B) state the times under Rule G(5) to file a claim and to answer; and

(C) name the government attorney to be served with the claim and answer.

(iii) *Frequency of Publication.* Published notice must appear:

(A) once a week for three consecutive weeks; or

(B) only once if, before the action was filed, notice of nonjudicial forfeiture of the same property was published on an official internet government forfeiture site for at least 30 consecutive days, or in a newspaper of general circulation for three consecutive weeks in a district where publication is authorized under Rule G(4)(a)(iv).

(iv) *Means of Publication.* The government should select from the following options a means of publication reasonably calculated to notify potential claimants of the action:

(A) if the property is in the United States, publication in a newspaper generally circulated in the district where the action is filed, where the property was seized, or where property that was not seized is located;

(B) if the property is outside the United States, publication in a newspaper generally circulated in a district where the action is filed, in a newspaper generally circulated in the country where the property is located, or in legal notices published and generally circulated in the country where the property is located; or

(C) instead of (A) or (B), posting a notice on an official internet government forfeiture site for at least 30 consecutive days.

(b) *Notice to Known Potential Claimants.*

(i) *Direct Notice Required.* The government must send notice of the action and a copy of the complaint to any person who reasonably appears to be a potential claimant on the facts known to the government before the end of the time for filing a claim under Rule G(5)(a)(ii)(B).

(ii) *Content of the Notice.* The notice must state:

(A) the date when the notice is sent;

(B) a deadline for filing a claim, at least 35 days after the notice is sent;

(C) that an answer or a motion under Rule 12 must be filed no later than 21 days after filing the claim; and

(D) the name of the government attorney to be served with the claim and answer.

(iii) *Sending Notice.*

(A) The notice must be sent by means reasonably calculated to reach the potential claimant.

(B) Notice may be sent to the potential claimant or to the attorney representing the potential claimant with respect to the seizure of the property or in a related investigation, administrative forfeiture proceeding, or criminal case.

(C) Notice sent to a potential claimant who is incarcerated must be sent to the place of incarceration.

(D) Notice to a person arrested in connection with an offense giving rise to the forfeiture who is not incar-

cerated when notice is sent may be sent to the address that person last gave to the agency that arrested or released the person.

(E) Notice to a person from whom the property was seized who is not incarcerated when notice is sent may be sent to the last address that person gave to the agency that seized the property.

(iv) *When Notice Is Sent.* Notice by the following means is sent on the date when it is placed in the mail, delivered to a commercial carrier, or sent by electronic mail.

(v) *Actual Notice.* A potential claimant who had actual notice of a forfeiture action may not oppose or seek relief from forfeiture because of the government's failure to send the required notice.

(5) Responsive Pleadings.

(a) *Filing a Claim.*

(i) A person who asserts an interest in the defendant property may contest the forfeiture by filing a claim in the court where the action is pending. The claim must:

(A) identify the specific property claimed;

(B) identify the claimant and state the claimant's interest in the property;

(C) be signed by the claimant under penalty of perjury; and

(D) be served on the government attorney designated under Rule G(4)(a)(ii)(C) or (b)(ii)(D).

(ii) Unless the court for good cause sets a different time, the claim must be filed:

(A) by the time stated in a direct notice sent under Rule G(4)(b);

(B) if notice was published but direct notice was not sent to the claimant or the claimant's attorney, no later than 30 days after final publication of newspaper notice or legal notice under Rule G(4)(a) or no later than 60 days after the first day of publication on an official internet government forfeiture site; or

(C) if notice was not published and direct notice was not sent to the claimant or the claimant's attorney:

(1) if the property was in the government's possession, custody, or control when the complaint was filed, no later than 60 days after the filing, not counting any time when the complaint was under seal or when the action was stayed before execution of a warrant issued under Rule G(3)(b); or

(2) if the property was not in the government's possession, custody, or control when the complaint was filed, no later than 60 days after the government complied with 18 U.S.C. §985(c) as to real property, or 60 days after process was executed on the property under Rule G(3).

(iii) A claim filed by a person asserting an interest as a bailee must identify the bailor, and if filed on the bailor's behalf must state the authority to do so.

(b) *Answer.* A claimant must serve and file an answer to the complaint or a motion under Rule 12 within 21 days after filing the claim. A claimant waives an objection to in rem jurisdiction or to venue if the objection is not made by motion or stated in the answer.

(6) Special Interrogatories.

(a) *Time and Scope.* The government may serve special interrogatories limited to the claimant's identity and relationship to the defendant property without the court's leave at any time after the claim is filed and before discovery is closed. But if the claimant serves a motion to dismiss the action, the government must serve the interrogatories within 21 days after the motion is served.

(b) *Answers or Objections.* Answers or objections to these interrogatories must be served within 21 days after the interrogatories are served.

(c) *Government's Response Deferred.* The government need not respond to a claimant's motion to dismiss the action under Rule G(8)(b) until 21 days after the claimant has answered these interrogatories.

(7) Preserving, Preventing Criminal Use, and Disposing of Property; Sales.

(a) *Preserving and Preventing Criminal Use of Property.* When the government does not have actual possession of the defendant property the court, on motion or on its own, may enter any order necessary to preserve the property, to prevent its removal or encumbrance, or to prevent its use in a criminal offense.

(b) *Interlocutory Sale or Delivery.*

(i) *Order to Sell.* On motion by a party or a person having custody of the property, the court may order all or part of the property sold if:

(A) the property is perishable or at risk of deterioration, decay, or injury by being detained in custody pending the action;

(B) the expense of keeping the property is excessive or is disproportionate to its fair market value;

(C) the property is subject to a mortgage or to taxes on which the owner is in default; or

(D) the court finds other good cause.

(ii) *Who Makes the Sale.* A sale must be made by a United States agency that has authority to sell the property, by the agency's contractor, or by any person the court designates.

(iii) *Sale Procedures.* The sale is governed by 28 U.S.C. §§2001, 2002, and 2004, unless all parties, with the court's approval, agree to the sale, aspects of the sale, or different procedures.

(iv) *Sale Proceeds.* Sale proceeds are a substitute res subject to forfeiture in place of the property that was sold. The proceeds must be held in an interest-bearing account maintained by the United States pending the conclusion of the forfeiture action.

(v) *Delivery on a Claimant's Motion.* The court may order that the property be delivered to the claimant pending the conclusion of the action if the claimant shows circumstances that would permit sale under Rule G(7)(b)(i) and gives security under these rules.

(c) *Disposing of Forfeited Property.* Upon entry of a forfeiture judgment, the property or proceeds from selling the property must be disposed of as provided by law.

(8) Motions.

(a) *Motion To Suppress Use of the Property as Evidence.* If the defendant property was seized, a party with standing to contest the lawfulness of the seizure may move to suppress use of the property as evidence. Suppression does not affect forfeiture of the property based on independently derived evidence.

(b) *Motion To Dismiss the Action.*

(i) A claimant who establishes standing to contest forfeiture may move to dismiss the action under Rule 12(b).

(ii) In an action governed by 18 U.S.C. §983(a)(3)(D) the complaint may not be dismissed on the ground that the government did not have adequate evidence at the time the complaint was filed to establish the forfeitability of the property. The sufficiency of the complaint is governed by Rule G(2).

(c) *Motion To Strike a Claim or Answer.*

(i) At any time before trial, the government may move to strike a claim or answer:

(A) for failing to comply with Rule G(5) or (6), or

(B) because the claimant lacks standing.

(ii) The motion:

(A) must be decided before any motion by the claimant to dismiss the action; and

(B) may be presented as a motion for judgment on the pleadings or as a motion to determine after a hearing or by summary judgment whether the claimant can carry the burden of establishing standing by a preponderance of the evidence.

(d) *Petition To Release Property.*

(i) If a United States agency or an agency's contractor holds property for judicial or nonjudicial forfeiture under a statute governed by 18 U.S.C. §983(f), a person who has filed a claim to the property may petition for its release under §983(f).

(ii) If a petition for release is filed before a judicial forfeiture action is filed against the property, the petition may be filed either in the district where the property was seized or in the district where a warrant to seize the property issued. If a judicial forfeiture action against the property is later filed in another district—or if the government shows that the action will be filed in another district—the petition may be transferred to that district under 28 U.S.C. §1404.

(e) *Excessive Fines.* A claimant may seek to mitigate a forfeiture under the Excessive Fines Clause of the Eighth Amendment by motion for summary judgment or by motion made after entry of a forfeiture judgment if:

(i) the claimant has pleaded the defense under Rule 8; and

(ii) the parties have had the opportunity to conduct civil discovery on the defense.

(9) Trial. Trial is to the court unless any party demands trial by jury under Rule 38.

1. **Editor's note:** So in original. Probably should be "contract."

See selected Notes of Advisory Committee to Rule G, p. 1235.

History of Rule G: Adopted Apr. 12, 2006, eff. Dec. 1, 2006. Amended Mar. 26, 2009, eff. Dec. 1, 2009.

RULES OF PROCEDURE OF THE UNITED STATES JUDICIAL PANEL ON MULTIDISTRICT LITIGATION (EFFECTIVE OCTOBER 4, 2010, AMENDED JULY 6, 2011)

I. Rules for Multidistrict Litigation Under 28 U.S.C. §1407
Rule 1.1 Definitions....1011
Rule 2.1 Rules & Practice....1012
Rule 3.1 Electronic Records & Files; Copy Fees....1012
Rule 3.2 ECF Users: Filing Requirements....1012
Rule 3.3 Non-ECF Users: Filing Requirements....1013
Rule 4.1 Service of Pleadings....1013
Rule 5.1 Corporate Disclosure Statement....1014
Rule 6.1 Motion Practice....1014
Rule 6.2 Motions to Transfer for Coordinated or Consolidated Pretrial Proceedings....1015
Rule 6.3 Motions for Miscellaneous Relief....1015
Rule 7.1 Conditional Transfer Orders (CTO) for Tag-Along Actions....1015
Rule 7.2 Miscellaneous Provisions Concerning Tag-Along Actions....1016
Rule 8.1 Show Cause Orders....1016
Rule 9.1 Transfer of Files; Notification Requirements....1016
Rule 10.1 Termination & Remand....1017
Rule 10.2 Conditional Remand Orders (CRO)....1017
Rule 10.3 Motion to Remand....1017
Rule 10.4 Transfer of Files on Remand....1018
Rule 11.1 Hearing Sessions & Oral Argument....1018
II. Rules for Multicircuit Petitions for Review Under 28 U.S.C. §2112(a)(3)
Rule 25.1 Definitions....1019
Rule 25.2 Filing of Notices....1019
Rule 25.3 Service of Notices....1019
Rule 25.4 Form of Notices; Place of Filing....1019
Rule 25.5 Random Selection....1019
Rule 25.6 Service of Panel Consolidation Order....1020

***Editor's note:** The Multidistrict Litigation Rules can be amended at any time; therefore, you should check the website of the United States Judicial Panel on Multidistrict Litigation (www.jpml.uscourts.gov/rules-procedures) for modifications to the Rules. These Rules are effective as of this book's publication date.*

I. RULES FOR MULTIDISTRICT LITIGATION UNDER 28 U.S.C. §1407

The United States Judicial Panel on Multidistrict Litigation promulgates these Rules pursuant to its authority under 28 U.S.C. §1407(f).

RULE 1.1. DEFINITIONS

(a) "Panel" means the members of the United States Judicial Panel on Multidistrict Litigation appointed by the Chief Justice of the United States pursuant to 28 U.S.C. §1407.

(b) "Chair" means the Chair of the Panel appointed by the Chief Justice of the United States pursuant to Section 1407, or the member of the Panel properly designated to act as Chair.

(c) "Clerk of the Panel" means the official that the Panel appoints to that position. The Clerk of the Panel shall perform such duties that the Panel or the Panel Executive delegates.

(d) "Electronic Case Filing (ECF)" refers to the Panel's automated system that receives and stores documents filed in electronic form. All attorneys filing pleadings with the Panel must do so using ECF. All pro se individuals are non-ECF users, unless the Panel orders otherwise.

(e) "MDL" means a multidistrict litigation docket which the Panel is either considering or has created by transferring cases to a transferee district for coordinated or consolidated pretrial proceedings pursuant to Section 1407.

(f) "Panel Executive" means the official appointed to act as the Panel's Chief Executive and Legal Officer. The Panel Executive may appoint, with the approval of the Panel, necessary deputies, clerical assistants and other employees to perform or assist in the performance of the duties of the Panel Executive. The Panel Executive, with the approval of the Panel, may make such delegations of authority as are necessary for the Panel's efficient operation.

(g) "Pleadings" means all papers, motions, responses, or replies of any kind filed with the Panel, including exhibits attached thereto, as well as all orders and notices that the Panel issues.

(h) "Tag-along action" refers to a civil action pending in a district court which involves common questions of fact with either (1) actions on a pending motion to transfer to create an MDL or (2) actions previously transferred to an existing MDL, and which the Panel would consider transferring under Section 1407.

(i) "Transferee district" is the federal district court to which the Panel transfers an action pursuant to Section 1407, for inclusion in an MDL.

(j) "Transferor district" is the federal district court where an action was pending prior to its transfer pursuant to Section 1407, for inclusion in an MDL, and where the Panel may remand that action at or before the conclusion of pretrial proceedings.

RULE 2.1. RULES & PRACTICE

(a) Customary Practice. The Panel's customary practice shall govern, unless otherwise fixed by statute or these Rules.

(b) Failure to Comply with Rules. When a pleading does not comply with these Rules, the Clerk of the Panel may advise counsel of the deficiencies and set a date for full compliance. If counsel does not fully comply within the established time, the Clerk of the Panel shall file the non-complying pleading, but the Chair may thereafter order it stricken.

(c) Admission to Practice before the Panel. Every member in good standing of the Bar of any district court of the United States is entitled to practice before the Panel, provided, however, that he or she has established and maintains a CM/ECF account with any United States federal court. Any attorney of record in any action transferred under Section 1407 may continue to represent his or her client in any district court of the United States to which such action is transferred. Parties are not required to obtain local counsel.

(d) Pendency of Motion or Conditional Order. The pendency of a motion, order to show cause, conditional transfer order or conditional remand order before the Panel pursuant to 28 U.S.C. §1407 does not affect or suspend orders and pretrial proceedings in any pending federal district court action and does not limit the pretrial jurisdiction of that court. An order to transfer or remand pursuant to 28 U.S.C. §1407 shall be effective only upon its filing with the clerk of the transferee district court.

(e) Reassignment. If for any reason the transferee judge is unable to continue those responsibilities, the Panel shall make the reassignment of a new transferee judge.

RULE 3.1. ELECTRONIC RECORDS & FILES; COPY FEES

(a) Electronic Record. Effective October 4, 2010, the official Panel record shall be the electronic file maintained on the Panel's servers. This record includes, but is not limited to, Panel pleadings, documents filed in paper and then scanned and made part of the electronic record, and Panel orders and notices filed. The official record also includes any documents or exhibits that may be impractical to scan. These documents and exhibits shall be kept in the Panel offices.

(b) Maintaining Records. Records and files generated prior to October 4, 2010, may be (i) maintained at the Panel offices, (ii) temporarily or permanently removed to such places at such times as the Clerk of the Panel or the Chair shall direct, or (iii) transferred whenever appropriate to the Federal Records Center.

(c) Fees. The Clerk of the Panel may charge fees for duplicating records and files, as prescribed by the Judicial Conference of the United States.

RULE 3.2. ECF USERS: FILING REQUIREMENTS

(a) Form of Pleadings. This Rule applies to pleadings that ECF users file with the Panel.

(i) Each pleading shall bear the heading "Before the United States Judicial Panel on Multidistrict Litigation," the identification "MDL No. ____" and the descriptive title designated by the Panel. If the Panel has not yet designated a title, counsel shall use an appropriate description.

(ii) The final page of each pleading shall contain the name, address, telephone number, fax number and email address of the attorney or party designated to receive service of pleadings in the case, and the name of each party represented.

(iii) Each brief submitted with a motion and any response to it shall not exceed 20 pages, exclusive of exhibits. Each reply shall not exceed 10 pages and shall address arguments raised in the response(s). Absent exceptional circumstances and those set forth in Rule 6.1(d), the Panel will not grant motions to exceed page limits.

(iv) Each pleading shall be typed in size 12 point font (for both text and footnotes), double spaced (text only), in a letter size document (8½ x 11 inch) with sequentially numbered pages.

(v) Each exhibit shall be separately numbered and clearly identified.

(vi) Proposed Panel orders shall not be submitted.

(b) Place of Filing. Counsel shall sign and verify all pleadings electronically in accordance with these Rules and the Panel's Administrative Policies and Procedures for Electronic Case Filing found at www.jpml.uscourts.gov. A pleading filed electronically constitutes a written document for the purpose of these Rules and the Federal Rules of Civil Procedure and is deemed the electronically signed original thereof. All pleadings, except by pro se litigants, shall conform with this Rule beginning on October 4, 2010.

(i) Pleadings shall not be transmitted directly to any Panel member.

(c) Attorney Registration. Only attorneys identified, or to be identified, pursuant to Rule 4.1, shall file pleadings. Each of these attorneys must register as a Panel CM/ECF user through www.jpml.uscourts.gov. Registration/possession of a CM/ECF account with any United States federal court shall be deemed consent to receive electronic service of all Panel orders and notices as well as electronic service of pleadings from other parties before the Panel.

(d) Courtesy Copy of Specified Pleadings. Counsel shall serve the Clerk of the Panel, for delivery within 1 business day of filing, with a courtesy paper copy of any of the following pleadings: (i) a motion to transfer and its supporting brief; (ii) a response to a show cause order; (iii) a motion to vacate a conditional transfer order or a conditional remand order; (iv) any response, reply, supplemental information or interested party response related to the pleadings listed in (i), (ii) and (iii); and (v) a corporate disclosure statement. No courtesy copies of any other pleadings are required. Courtesy copies of pleadings totaling 10 pages or less (including any attachments) may be faxed to the Panel. The courtesy copy shall include all exhibits, shall be clearly marked "Courtesy Copy-Do Not File," shall contain the CM/ECF pleading number (if known), and shall be mailed or delivered to:

Clerk of the Panel

United States Judicial Panel on Multidistrict Litigation

Thurgood Marshall Federal Judiciary Building

One Columbus Circle, NE, Room G-255, North Lobby

Washington, DC 20002-8041

(e) Privacy Protections. The privacy protections contained in Rule 5.2 of the Federal Rules of Civil Procedure shall apply to all Panel filings.

RULE 3.3. NON-ECF USERS: FILING REQUIREMENTS

(a) Definition of Non-ECF Users. Non-ECF users are all pro se individuals, unless the Panel orders otherwise. This Rule shall apply to all motions, responses and replies that non-ECF users file with the Panel.

(b) Form of Pleadings. Unless otherwise set forth in this Rule, the provisions of Rule 3.2 shall apply to non-ECF users.

(i) Each pleading shall be flat and unfolded; plainly written or typed in size 12 point font (for both text and footnotes), double spaced (text only), and printed single-sided on letter size (8½ x 11 inch) white paper with sequentially numbered pages; and fastened at the top-left corner without side binding or front or back covers.

(ii) Each exhibit shall be separately numbered and clearly identified. Any exhibits exceeding a cumulative total of 50 pages shall be bound separately.

(c) Place of Filing. File an original and one copy of all pleadings with the Clerk of the Panel by mailing or delivering to:

Clerk of the Panel

United States Judicial Panel on Multidistrict Litigation

Thurgood Marshall Federal Judiciary Building

One Columbus Circle, NE, Room G-255, North Lobby

Washington, DC 20002-8041

(i) Pleadings not exceeding a total of 10 pages, including exhibits, may be faxed to the Panel office.

(ii) The Clerk of the Panel shall endorse the date for filing on all pleadings submitted for filing.

RULE 4.1. SERVICE OF PLEADINGS

(a) Proof of Service. The Panel's notice of electronic filing shall constitute service of pleadings. Registration/possession by counsel of a CM/ECF account with any United States federal court shall be deemed consent to receive electronic service of all pleadings. All pleadings shall contain a proof of service on all other parties in all involved actions. The proof of service shall indicate the name and manner of service. If a party is not represented by counsel, the proof of service shall indicate the name of the party and the party's last known address. The proof of service shall indicate why any person named as a party in a constituent complaint was not served with the Section 1407 pleading.

(b) Service Upon Transferor Court. The proof of service pertaining to motions for a transfer or remand pursuant to 28 U.S.C. §1407 shall certify that counsel has transmitted a copy of the motion for filing to the clerk of each district court where an affected action is pending.

(c) Notice of Appearance. Within 14 days after the issuance of a (i) notice of filing of a motion to initiate transfer under Rule 6.2, (ii) notice of filed opposition to a CTO under Rule 7.1, (iii) a show cause order

under Rules 8.1, (iv) notice of filed opposition to a CRO under Rule 10.2, or (v) notice of filing of a motion to remand under Rule 10.3, each party or designated attorney as required hereinafter shall file a Notice of Appearance notifying the Clerk of the Panel of the name, address and email address of the attorney designated to file and receive service of all pleadings. Each party shall designate only one attorney. Any party not represented by counsel shall be served by mailing such pleadings to the party's last known address. Except in extraordinary circumstances, the Panel will not grant requests for an extension of time to file the Notice of Appearance.

(d) Liaison Counsel. If the transferee district court appoints liaison counsel, this Rule shall be satisfied by serving each party in each affected action and all liaison counsel. Liaison counsel shall receive copies of all Panel orders concerning their particular litigation and shall be responsible for distribution to the parties for whom he or she serves as liaison counsel.

RULE 5.1. CORPORATE DISCLOSURE STATEMENT

(a) Requirements. A nongovernmental corporate party must file a disclosure statement that: (1) identifies any parent corporation and any publicly held corporation owning 10% or more of its stock; or (2) states that there is no such corporation.

(b) Deadline. A party shall file the corporate disclosure statement within 14 days after issuance of a notice of the filing of a motion to transfer or remand, an order to show cause, or a motion to vacate a conditional transfer order or a conditional remand order.

(c) Updating. Each party must update its corporate disclosure statement to reflect any change in the information therein (i) until the matter before the Panel is decided, and (ii) within 14 days after issuance of a notice of the filing of any subsequent motion to transfer or remand, order to show cause, or motion to vacate a conditional transfer order or a conditional remand order in that docket.

RULE 6.1. MOTION PRACTICE

(a) Application. This Rule governs all motions requesting Panel action generally. More specific provisions may apply to motions to transfer (Rule 6.2), miscellaneous motions (Rule 6.3), conditional transfer orders (Rule 7.1), show cause orders (Rule 8.1), conditional remand orders (Rule 10.2) and motions to remand (Rule 10.3).

(b) Form of Motions. All motions shall briefly describe the action or relief sought and shall include:

(i) a brief which concisely states the background of the litigation and movant's factual and legal contentions;

(ii) a numbered schedule providing

(A) the complete name of each action involved, listing the full name of each party included as such on the district court's docket sheet, not shortened by the use of references such as "et al." or "etc.";

(B) the district court and division where each action is pending;

(C) the civil action number of each action; and

(D) the name of the judge assigned each action, if known;

(iii) a proof of service providing

(A) a service list listing the full name of each party included on the district court's docket sheet and the complaint, including opt-in plaintiffs not listed on the docket sheet; and

(B) in actions where there are 25 or more plaintiffs listed on the docket sheet, list the first named plaintiff with the reference "et al." if all the plaintiffs are represented by the same attorney(s);

(iv) a copy of all complaints and docket sheets for all actions listed on the Schedule; and

(v) exhibits, if any, identified by number or letter and a descriptive title.

(c) Responses and Joinders. Any other party may file a response within 21 days after filing of a motion. Failure to respond to a motion shall be treated as that party's acquiescence to it. A joinder in a motion shall not add any action to that motion.

(d) Replies. The movant may file a reply within 7 days after the lapse of the time period for filing a response. Where a movant is replying to more than one response in opposition, the movant may file a consolidated reply with a limit of 20 pages.

(e) Alteration of Time Periods. The Clerk of the Panel has the discretion to shorten or enlarge the time periods set forth in this Rule as necessary.

(f) Notification of Developments. Counsel shall promptly notify the Clerk of the Panel of any development that would partially or completely moot any Panel matter.

RULE 6.2. MOTIONS TO TRANSFER FOR COORDINATED OR CONSOLIDATED PRETRIAL PROCEEDINGS

(a) Initiation of Transfer. A party to an action may initiate proceedings to transfer under Section 1407 by filing a motion in accordance with these Rules. A copy of the motion shall be filed in each district court where the motion affects a pending action.

(b) Notice of Filing of Motion to Transfer. Upon receipt of a motion, the Clerk of the Panel shall issue a "Notice of Filing of Motion to Transfer" to the service list recipients. The Notice shall contain the following: the filing date of the motion, caption, MDL docket number, briefing schedule and pertinent Panel policies. After a motion is filed, the Clerk of the Panel shall consider any other pleading to be a response unless the pleading adds an action. The Clerk of the Panel may designate such a pleading as a motion, and distribute a briefing schedule applicable to all or some of the parties, as appropriate.

(c) Notice of Appearance. Within 14 days of issuance of a "Notice of the Filing of a Motion to Transfer," each party or designated attorney shall file a Notice of Appearance in accordance with Rule 4.1(c).

(d) Notice of Potential Tag-along Actions. Any party or counsel in a new group of actions under consideration for transfer under Section 1407 shall promptly notify the Clerk of the Panel of any potential tag-along actions in which that party is also named or in which that counsel appears.

(e) Interested Party Responses. Any party or counsel in one or more potential tag-along actions as well as amicus curiae may file a response to a pending motion to transfer. Such a pleading shall be deemed an Interested Party Response.

(f) Amendment to a Motion. Before amending a motion to transfer, a party shall first contact the Clerk of the Panel to ascertain whether such amendment is feasible and permissible considering the Panel's hearing schedule. Any such amendment shall be entitled "Amendment to Motion for Transfer," and shall clearly and specifically identify and describe the nature of the amendment.

(i) Where the amended motion includes new civil actions, the amending party shall file a "Schedule of Additional Actions" and a revised Proof of Service.

(ii) The Proof of Service shall state (A) that all new counsel have been served with a copy of the amendment and all previously-filed motion papers, and (B) that all counsel previously served with the original motion have been served with a copy of the amendment.

(iii) The Clerk of the Panel may designate the amendment with a different denomination (*e.g.*, a notice of potential tag-along action(s)) and treatment.

(h)[1] Oral Argument. The Panel shall schedule oral arguments as needed and as set forth in Rule 11.1.

1. **Editor's note:** So in original. Probably should be (g).

RULE 6.3. MOTIONS FOR MISCELLANEOUS RELIEF

(a) Definition. Motions for miscellaneous relief include, but are not limited to, requests for extensions of time, exemption from ECF requirements, page limit extensions, or expedited consideration of any motion.

(b) Panel Action. The Panel, through the Clerk, may act upon any motion for miscellaneous relief, at any time, without waiting for a response. A motion for extension of time to file a pleading or perform an act under these Rules must state specifically the revised date sought and must be filed before the deadline for filing the pleading or performing the act. Any party aggrieved by the Clerk of the Panel's action may file objections for consideration. Absent exceptional circumstances, the Panel will not grant any extensions of time to file a notice of opposition to either a conditional transfer order or a conditional remand order.

RULE 7.1. CONDITIONAL TRANSFER ORDERS (CTO) FOR TAG-ALONG ACTIONS

(a) Notice of Potential Tag-along Actions. Any party or counsel in actions previously transferred under Section 1407 shall promptly notify the Clerk of the Panel of any potential tag-along actions in which that party is also named or in which that counsel appears. The Panel has several options: (i) filing a CTO under Rule 7.1, (ii) filing a show cause order under Rule 8.1, or (iii) declining to act (Rule 7.1(b)(i)).

(b) Initiation of CTO. Upon learning of the pendency of a potential tag-along action, the Clerk of the Panel may enter a conditional order transferring that action to the previously designated transferee district court for the reasons expressed in the Panel's previous opinions and orders. The Clerk of the Panel shall serve

MDL RULE 7.1

this order on each party to the litigation but shall not send the order to the clerk of the transferee district court until 7 days after its entry.

(i) If the Clerk of the Panel determines that a potential tag-along action is not appropriate for inclusion in an MDL proceeding and does not enter a CTO, an involved party may move for its transfer pursuant to Rule 6.1.

(c) Notice of Opposition to CTO. Any party opposing the transfer shall file a notice of opposition with the Clerk of the Panel within the 7-day period. In such event, the Clerk of the Panel shall not transmit the transfer order to the clerk of the transferee district court, but shall notify the parties of the briefing schedule.

(d) Failure to Respond. Failure to respond to a CTO shall be treated as that party's acquiescence to it.

(e) Notice of Appearance. Within 14 days after the issuance of a "Notice of Filed Opposition" to a CTO, each opposing party or designated attorney shall file a Notice of Appearance in accordance with Rule 4.1(c).

(f) Motion to Vacate CTO. Within 14 days of the filing of its notice of opposition, the party opposing transfer shall file a motion to vacate the CTO and brief in support thereof. The Clerk of the Panel shall set the motion for the next appropriate hearing session. Failure to file and serve a motion and brief shall be treated as withdrawal of the opposition and the Clerk of the Panel shall forthwith transmit the order to the clerk of the transferee district court.

(g) Notification of Developments. Parties to an action subject to a CTO shall notify the Clerk of the Panel if that action is no longer pending in its transferor district court.

(h) Effective Date of CTO. CTOs are effective when filed with the clerk of the transferee district court.

RULE 7.2. MISCELLANEOUS PROVISIONS CONCERNING TAG-ALONG ACTIONS

(a) Potential Tag-alongs in Transferee Court. Potential tag-along actions filed in the transferee district do not require Panel action. A party should request assignment of such actions to the Section 1407 transferee judge in accordance with applicable local rules.

(b) Failure to Serve. Failure to serve one or more of the defendants in a potential tag-along action with the complaint and summons as required by Rule 4 of the Federal Rules of Civil Procedure does not preclude transfer of such action under Section 1407. Such failure, however, may constitute grounds for denying the proposed transfer where prejudice can be shown. The failure of the Clerk of the Panel to serve a CTO on all plaintiffs or defendants or their counsel may constitute grounds for the Clerk to reinstate the CTO or for the aggrieved party to seek §1407(c) remand.

RULE 8.1. SHOW CAUSE ORDERS

(a) Entry of Show Cause Order. When transfer of multidistrict litigation is being considered on the initiative of the Panel pursuant to 28 U.S.C. §1407(c)(i), the Clerk of the Panel may enter an order directing the parties to show cause why a certain civil action or actions should not be transferred for coordinated or consolidated pretrial proceedings. Any party shall also promptly notify the Clerk of the Panel whenever they learn of any other federal district court actions which are similar to those which the show cause order encompasses.

(b) Notice of Appearance. Within 14 days of the issuance of an order to show cause, each party or designated attorney shall file a Notice of Appearance in accordance with Rule 4.1(c).

(c) Responses. Unless otherwise provided by order, any party may file a response within 21 days of the filing of the show cause order. Failure to respond to a show cause order shall be treated as that party's acquiescence to the Panel action.

(d) Replies. Within 7 days after the lapse of the time period for filing a response, any party may file a reply.

(e) Notification of Developments. Counsel shall promptly notify the Clerk of the Panel of any development that would partially or completely moot any matter subject to a show cause order.

RULE 9.1. TRANSFER OF FILES; NOTIFICATION REQUIREMENTS

(a) Notice to Transferee Court Clerk. The Clerk of the Panel, via a notice of electronic filing, will notify the clerk of the transferee district whenever a Panel transfer order should be filed in the transferee district court. Upon receipt of an electronically certified copy of a Panel transfer order from the clerk of the transferee district, the clerk of the transferor district shall transmit the record of each transferred action to the trans-

feree district and then, unless Rule 9.1(b) applies, close the transferred action in the transferor district.

(b) Retention of Claims. If the transfer order provides for the separation and simultaneous remand of any claim, cross-claim, counterclaim, or third-party claim, the clerk of the transferor district shall retain jurisdiction over any such claim and shall not close the action.

(c) Notice to Clerk of Panel. The clerk of the transferee district shall promptly provide the Clerk of the Panel with the civil action numbers assigned to all transferred actions and the identity of liaison counsel, if or when designated. The clerk of the transferee district shall also promptly notify the Clerk of the Panel of any dispositive ruling that terminates a transferred action.

RULE 10.1. TERMINATION & REMAND

(a) Termination. Where the transferee district court terminates an action by valid order, including but not limited to summary judgment, judgment of dismissal and judgment upon stipulation, the transferee district court clerk shall transmit a copy of that order to the Clerk of the Panel. The terminated action shall not be remanded to the transferor court and the transferee court shall retain the original files and records unless the transferee judge or the Panel directs otherwise.

(b) Initiation of Remand. Typically, the transferee judge recommends remand of an action, or a part of it, to the transferor court at any time by filing a suggestion of remand with the Panel. However, the Panel may remand an action or any separable claim, cross-claim, counterclaim or third-party claim within it, upon

(i) the transferee court's suggestion of remand,

(ii) the Panel's own initiative by entry of an order to show cause, a conditional remand order or other appropriate order, or

(iii) motion of any party.

RULE 10.2. CONDITIONAL REMAND ORDERS (CRO)

(a) Entering a CRO. Upon the suggestion of the transferee judge or the Panel's own initiative, the Clerk of the Panel shall enter a conditional order remanding the action or actions to the transferor district court. The Clerk of the Panel shall serve this order on each party to the litigation but shall not send the order to the clerk of the transferee district court for 7 days from the entry thereof.

(i) The Panel may, on its own initiative, also enter an order that the parties show cause why a matter should not be remanded. Rule 8.1 applies to responses and replies with respect to such a show cause order.

(b) Notice of Opposition. Any party opposing the CRO shall file a notice of opposition with the Clerk of the Panel within the 7-day period. In such event, the Clerk of the Panel shall not transmit the remand order to the clerk of the transferee district court and shall notify the parties of the briefing schedule.

(c) Failure to Respond. Failure to respond to a CRO shall be treated as that party's acquiescence to it.

(d) Notice of Appearance. Within 14 days after the issuance of a "Notice of Filed Opposition" to a CRO, each opposing party or designated attorney shall file a Notice of Appearance in accordance with Rule 4.1(c).

(e) Motion to Vacate CRO. Within 14 days of the filing of its notice of opposition, the party opposing remand shall file a motion to vacate the CRO and brief in support thereof. The Clerk of the Panel shall set the motion for the next appropriate Panel hearing session. Failure to file and serve a motion and brief shall be treated as a withdrawal of the opposition and the Clerk of the Panel shall forthwith transmit the order to the clerk of the transferee district court.

(f) Effective Date of CRO. CROs are not effective until filed with the clerk of the transferee district court.

RULE 10.3. MOTION TO REMAND

(a) Requirements of the Motion. If the Clerk of the Panel does not enter a CRO, a party may file a motion to remand to the transferor court pursuant to these Rules. Because the Panel is reluctant to order a remand absent the suggestion of the transferee judge, the motion must include:

(i) An affidavit reciting whether the movant has requested a suggestion of remand and the judge's response, whether the parties have completed common discovery and other pretrial proceedings, and whether the parties have complied with all transferee court orders.

(ii) A copy of the transferee district court's final pretrial order, if entered.

(b) Filing Copy of Motion. Counsel shall file a copy of the motion to remand in the affected transferee district court.

(c) Notice of Appearance. Within 14 days of the issuance of a "Notice of Filing" of a motion to remand, each party or designated attorney shall file a Notice of Appearance in accordance with Rule 4.1(c).

RULE 10.4. TRANSFER OF FILES ON REMAND

(a) Designating the Record. Upon receipt of an order to remand from the Clerk of the Panel, the parties shall furnish forthwith to the transferee district clerk a stipulation or designation of the contents of the record or part thereof to be remanded.

(b) Transfer of Files. Upon receipt of an order to remand from the Clerk of the Panel, the transferee district shall transmit to the clerk of the transferor district the following concerning each remanded action:

(i) a copy of the individual docket sheet for each action remanded;

(ii) a copy of the master docket sheet, if applicable;

(iii) the entire file for each action remanded, as originally received from the transferor district and augmented as set out in this Rule;

(iv) a copy of the final pretrial order, if applicable; and

(v) a "record on remand" as designated by the parties in accordance with 10.4(a).

RULE 11.1. HEARING SESSIONS & ORAL ARGUMENT

(a) Schedule. The Panel shall schedule sessions for oral argument and consideration of other matters as desirable or necessary. The Chair shall determine the time, place and agenda for each hearing session. The Clerk of the Panel shall give appropriate notice to counsel for all parties. The Panel may continue its consideration of any scheduled matters.

(b) Oral Argument Statement. Any party affected by a motion may file a separate statement setting forth reasons why oral argument should, or need not, be heard. Such statements shall be captioned "Reasons Why Oral Argument Should [Need Not] Be Heard" and shall be limited to 2 pages.

(i) The parties affected by a motion to transfer may agree to waive oral argument. The Panel will take this into consideration in determining the need for oral argument.

(c) Hearing Session. The Panel shall not consider transfer or remand of any action pending in a federal district court when any party timely opposes such transfer or remand without first holding a hearing session for the presentation of oral argument. The Panel may dispense with oral argument if it determines that:

(i) the dispositive issue(s) have been authoritatively decided; or

(ii) the facts and legal arguments are adequately presented and oral argument would not significantly aid the decisional process.

Unless otherwise ordered, the Panel shall consider all other matters, such as a motion for reconsideration, upon the basis of the pleadings.

(d) Notification of Oral Argument. The Panel shall promptly notify counsel of those matters in which oral argument is scheduled, as well as those matters that the Panel will consider on the pleadings. The Clerk of the Panel shall require counsel to file and serve notice of their intent to either make or waive oral argument. Failure to do so shall be deemed a waiver of oral argument. If counsel does not attend oral argument, the matter shall not be rescheduled and that party's position shall be treated as submitted for decision on the basis of the pleadings filed.

(i) Absent Panel approval and for good cause shown, only those parties to actions who have filed a motion or written response to a motion or order shall be permitted to present oral argument.

(ii) The Panel will not receive oral testimony except upon notice, motion and an order expressly providing for it.

(e) Duty to Confer. Counsel in an action set for oral argument shall confer separately prior to that argument for the purpose of organizing their arguments and selecting representatives to present all views without duplication. Oral argument is a means for counsel to emphasize the key points of their arguments, and to update the Panel on any events since the conclusion of briefing.

(f) Time Limit for Oral Argument. Barring exceptional circumstances, the Panel shall allot a maximum of 20 minutes for oral argument in each matter. The time shall be divided among those with varying viewpoints. Counsel for the moving party or parties shall generally be heard first.

Rules 12-15: [Reserved]

II. RULES FOR MULTICIRCUIT PETITIONS FOR REVIEW UNDER 28 U.S.C. §2112(a)(3)

RULE 25.1. DEFINITIONS

The Panel promulgates these Rules pursuant to its authority under 28 U.S.C. §2112(a)(3) to provide a means for the random selection of one circuit court of appeals to hear consolidated petitions for review of agency decisions.

An "Agency" means an agency, board, commission or officer of the United States government, that has received two or more petitions for review in a circuit court of appeals to enjoin, set aside, suspend, modify or otherwise review or enforce an action.

RULE 25.2. FILING OF NOTICES

(a) Submitting Notice. An affected agency shall submit a notice of multicircuit petitions for review pursuant to 28 U.S.C. §2112(a)(3) to the Clerk of the Panel by electronic means in the manner these Rules require and in accordance with the Panel's Administrative Policies and Procedures for Electronic Case Filing, except that the portion of Rule 3.2(d) requiring a courtesy copy is suspended in its entirety.

(b) Accompaniments to Notices. All notices of multicircuit petitions for review shall include:

(i) a copy of each involved petition for review as the petition for review is defined in 28 U.S.C. §2112(a)(2);

(ii) a schedule giving

(A) the date of the relevant agency order;

(B) the case name of each petition for review involved;

(C) the circuit court of appeals in which each petition for review is pending;

(D) the appellate docket number of each petition for review;

(E) the date of filing by the court of appeals of each petition for review; and

(F) the date of receipt by the agency of each petition for review; and

(iii) proof of service (*see* Rule 25.3).

(c) Scope of Notice. All notices of multicircuit petitions for review shall embrace exclusively petitions for review filed in the courts of appeals within 10 days after issuance of an agency order and received by the affected agency from the petitioners within that 10-day period.

(d) Filing at the Panel. The Clerk of the Panel shall file the notice of multicircuit petitions for review and endorse thereon the date of filing.

(e) Filing with Each Circuit Clerk. The affected agency shall file copies of notices of multicircuit petitions for review with the clerk of each circuit court of appeals in which a petition for review is pending.

RULE 25.3. SERVICE OF NOTICES

(a) Proof of Service. Notices of multicircuit petitions for review shall include proof of service on all other parties in the petitions for review included in the notice. Rule 25 of the Federal Rules of Appellate Procedure governs service and proof of service. The proof of service shall state the name, address and email address of each person served and shall indicate the party represented by each and the manner in which service was accomplished on each party. If a party is not represented by counsel, the proof of service shall indicate the name of the party and his or her last known address. The affected party shall submit proof of service for filing with the Clerk of the Panel and shall send copies thereof to each person included within the proof of service.

(b) Service on Clerk of Circuit. The proof of service pertaining to notices of multicircuit petitions for review shall certify the affected party has mailed or delivered copies of the notices to the clerk of each circuit court of appeals in which a petition for review is pending that is included in the notice. The Clerk shall file the notice with the circuit court.

RULE 25.4. FORM OF NOTICES; PLACE OF FILING

(a) Unless otherwise provided here, Rule 3.2 governs the form of a notice of multicircuit petitions for review. Each notice shall bear the heading ["]Notice to the United States Judicial Panel on Multidistrict Litigation of Multicircuit Petitions for Review," followed by a brief caption identifying the involved agency, the relevant agency order, and the date of the order.

(b) Rule 3.2(b) and (c) govern the manner of filing a notice of multicircuit petitions for review.

RULE 25.5. RANDOM SELECTION

(a) Selection Process. Upon filing a notice of multicircuit petitions for review, the Clerk of the Panel shall randomly select a circuit court of appeals from a drum containing an entry for each circuit wherein a constituent petition for review is pending. Multiple pe-

titions for review pending in a single circuit shall be allotted only a single entry in the drum. A designated deputy other than the random selector shall witness the random selection. Thereafter, an order on behalf of the Panel shall be issued, signed by the random selector and the witness,

(i) consolidating the petitions for review in the court of appeals for the circuit that was randomly selected; and

(ii) designating that circuit as the one in which the record is to be filed pursuant to Rules 16 and 17 of the Federal Rules of Appellate Procedure.

(b) Effective Date. A consolidation of petitions for review shall be effective when the Clerk of the Panel enters the consolidation order.

RULE 25.6. SERVICE OF PANEL CONSOLIDATION ORDER

(a) The Clerk of the Panel shall serve the Panel's consolidation order on the affected agency through the individual or individuals, as identified in Rule 25.2(a), who submitted the notice of multicircuit petitions for review on behalf of the agency.

(b) That individual or individuals, or anyone else designated by the agency, shall promptly serve the Panel's consolidation order on all other parties in all petitions for review included in the Panel's consolidation order, and shall promptly submit a proof of that service to the Clerk of the Panel. Rule 25.3 governs service.

(c) The Clerk of the Panel shall serve the Panel's consolidation order on the clerks of all circuit courts of appeals that were among the candidates for the Panel's random selection.

III. CONVERSION TABLE – OCTOBER 2010

NEW TO OLD:	
New Rule	**Previous Rule**
1.1	1.1
2.1	1.2, 1.3, 1.4, 1.5
3.1	5.1
3.2	5.1.1, 5.1.2, 7.1
3.3	5.1.1, 5.1.2, 7.1
4.1	5.2
5.1	5.3
6.1	7.2
6.2	7.2
6.3	6.2
7.1	7.4
7.2	7.5
8.1	7.3
9.1	1.6
10.1	7.6
10.2	7.6
10.3	7.6
10.4	1.6
11.1	16.1
25.1	25.1
25.2	25.1, 25.2
25.3	25.3
25.4	25.1, 25.4
25.5	17.1
25.6	25.5

OLD TO NEW:	
Previous Rule	**New Rule**
1.1	1.1
1.2	2.1
1.3	2.1
1.4	2.1
1.5	2.1
1.6	10.4
5.1	3.1
5.1.1	3.2, 3.3
5.1.2	3.2, 3.3
5.1.3	–
5.2	4.1
5.3	5.1
6.2	6.3
7.1	3.2, 3.3
7.2	6.1
7.3	8.1
7.4	7.1
7.5	7.2
7.6	10.1
16.1	11.1
17.1	25.5
25.1	25.1, 25.2, 25.4
25.2	25.2
25.3	25.3
25.4	25.4
25.5	25.6

FEDERAL RULES OF EVIDENCE

TABLE OF CONTENTS

ARTICLE I. GENERAL PROVISIONS

FRE 101 Scope; definitions 1028
FRE 102 Purpose 1028
FRE 103 Rulings on evidence 1028
FRE 104 Preliminary questions 1030
FRE 105 Limiting evidence that is not admissible against other parties or for other purposes 1030
FRE 106 Remainder of or related writings or recorded statements 1031

ARTICLE II. JUDICIAL NOTICE

FRE 201 Judicial notice of adjudicative facts 1031

ARTICLE III. PRESUMPTIONS IN CIVIL CASES

FRE 301 Presumptions in civil cases generally 1032
FRE 302 Applying state law to presumptions in civil cases 1033

ARTICLE IV. RELEVANCE & ITS LIMITS

FRE 401 Test for relevant evidence 1033
FRE 402 General admissibility of relevant evidence 1033
FRE 403 Excluding relevant evidence for prejudice, confusion, waste of time, or other reasons 1034
FRE 404 Character evidence; crimes or other acts 1035
FRE 405 Methods of proving character 1036
FRE 406 Habit; routine practice 1037
FRE 407 Subsequent remedial measures 1037
FRE 408 Compromise offers & negotiations 1038
FRE 409 Offers to pay medical & similar expenses 1039
FRE 410 Pleas, plea discussions, & related statements 1040
FRE 411 Liability insurance 1040
FRE 412 Sex-offense cases: the victim's sexual behavior or predisposition 1040
FRE 413 Similar crimes in sexual-assault cases 1042
FRE 414 Similar crimes in child-molestation cases 1043
FRE 415 Similar acts in civil cases involving sexual assault or child molestation 1043

ARTICLE V. PRIVILEGES

FRE 501 Privilege in general 1044
FRE 502 Attorney-client privilege & work product; limitations on waiver 1046

ARTICLE VI. WITNESSES

FRE 601 Competency to testify in general 1047
FRE 602 Need for personal knowledge 1047
FRE 603 Oath or affirmation to testify truthfully 1048
FRE 604 Interpreter 1048
FRE 605 Judge's competency as a witness 1048
FRE 606 Juror's competency as a witness 1049
FRE 607 Who may impeach a witness 1051
FRE 608 A witness's character for truthfulness or untruthfulness 1051
FRE 609 Impeachment by evidence of a criminal conviction 1052
FRE 610 Religious beliefs or opinions 1054
FRE 611 Mode & order of examining witnesses & presenting evidence 1054
FRE 612 Writing used to refresh a witness's memory 1055
FRE 613 Witness's prior statement 1056
FRE 614 Court's calling or examining a witness 1056
FRE 615 Excluding witnesses 1057

ARTICLE VII. OPINIONS & EXPERT TESTIMONY

FRE 701 Opinion testimony by lay witnesses 1058
FRE 702 Testimony by expert witnesses 1059
FRE 703 Bases of an expert's opinion testimony 1061
FRE 704 Opinion on an ultimate issue 1061
FRE 705 Disclosing the facts or data underlying an expert's opinion 1062
FRE 706 Court-appointed expert witnesses 1063

ARTICLE VIII. HEARSAY

FRE 801 Definitions that apply to this article; exclusions from hearsay 1064
FRE 802 The rule against hearsay 1067
FRE 803 Exceptions to the rule against hearsay—regardless of whether the declarant is available as a witness 1067
FRE 804 Exceptions to the rule against hearsay—when the declarant is unavailable as a witness 1075
FRE 805 Hearsay within hearsay 1077
FRE 806 Attacking & supporting the declarant's credibility 1077
FRE 807 Residual exception 1077

ARTICLE IX. AUTHENTICATION & IDENTIFICATION

FRE 901 Authenticating or identifying evidence 1078
FRE 902 Evidence that is self-authenticating 1081
FRE 903 Subscribing witness's testimony 1082

ARTICLE X. CONTENTS OF WRITINGS, RECORDINGS, & PHOTOGRAPHS

FRE 1001 Definitions that apply to this article 1082
FRE 1002 Requirement of the original 1083
FRE 1003 Admissibility of duplicates 1084
FRE 1004 Admissibility of other evidence of content 1084
FRE 1005 Copies of public records to prove content 1084
FRE 1006 Summaries to prove content 1085
FRE 1007 Testimony or statement of a party to prove content 1086
FRE 1008 Functions of the court & jury 1086

ARTICLE XI. MISCELLANEOUS RULES

FRE 1101 Applicability of the rules 1086
FRE 1102 Amendments 1087
FRE 1103 Title 1087

FRE COMPARISON TABLE – FORMER & CURRENT RULES

On December 1, 2011, the restyling revisions to the FREs went into effect.

The purpose of the restyling is to make the FREs more easily understood and to make the style and language consistent throughout the FREs. 2011 Notes to FRE 101 at ¶1, p. 1239, this book. Each revision is intended to be stylistic only, and there is no intent to change any result in any ruling on evidence admissibility. *Id.*

The restyling resulted in the following:

(1) Formatting changes. The restyled FREs are reformatted to achieve clearer presentations. Specifically, the rules are broken down, and they use progressively indented subparagraphs. 2011 Notes to FRE 101 at ¶5, p. 1239, this book. See FRE 103, 404(b), 606(b), or 612 as examples.

(2) Language changes. The restyled FREs made the following language changes:

- The use of inconsistent terms that mean the same thing was lessened. 2011 Notes to FRE 101 at ¶6, p. 1239, this book. In addition, the use of ambiguous terms was reduced; for example, the word "shall" was changed to "must," "may," or "should," depending on the context and established interpretation of the rule. *Id.* at ¶7, p. 1240, this book.
- The use of redundant "intensifiers" was reduced. *Id.* at ¶8, p. 1240, this book. These intensifiers are expressions that attempt to add emphasis but instead state the obvious and create negative implications for other rules. *Id.*
- Outdated or redundant words and concepts were removed. *Id.* at ¶9, p. 1240, this book.

(3) Numbering changes. The restyled FREs kept the same numbers to minimize the effect on research. 2011 Notes to FRE 101 at ¶10, p. 1240, this book. But some subdivisions have been rearranged to achieve greater clarity and simplicity. *Id.* To determine if a particular subdivision has been rearranged, see FRE Comparison Chart, below.

(4) No substantive changes. The restyled FREs did not include any purported style improvements that might result in a substantive change. 2011 Notes to FRE 101 at ¶11, p. 1240, this book. A change was considered substantive if the change (1) could lead to a different result on a question of admissibility, (2) could lead to a change in the procedure by which an admissibility decision is made, (3) could lead to altering the approach that courts and litigants have used to think about, and argue about, questions of admissibility, or (4) would change a "sacred phrase" (e.g., "unfair prejudice" or "truth of the matter asserted"). *Id.*

The chart below shows the rearranging of the subdivisions based on the restyling. This chart also footnotes significant language changes, including omissions and additions.

Former FRE	Current FRE
101	101(a)
	101(b)(1)-(6)[1]
102	102
103(a)	103(a)(1)(A), (B), (2), (b)
103(b)	103(c)
103(c)	103(d)
103(d)	103(e)
104(a)	104(a)

Former FRE	Current FRE
104(b)	104(b)
104(c)	104(c)(1)-(3)
104(d)	104(d)
104(e)	104(e)
105	105
106	106
201(a)	201(a)
201(b)	201(b)(1), (2)
201(c), (d)	201(c)(1), (2)

Former FRE	Current FRE
201(e)	201(e)
201(f)	201(d)
201(g)	201(f)
301	301
302	302
401	401(a), (b)
402	402
403	403
404(a)	404(a)(1)

1. FRE 101(b) is a new subsection, which added definitions for the FREs. 2011 Notes to FRE 101 at ¶1, p. 1239, this book. The reference to "electronically stored information" is intended to track the language of FRCP 34. 2011 Notes to FRE 101 at ¶2, p. 1239, this book.

FRE COMPARISON TABLE – FORMER & CURRENT RULES

Former FRE	Current FRE
404(a)(1)	404(a)(2)(A), (B)(ii)
404(a)(2)	404(a)(2)(B)(i), (C)
404(a)(3)	404(a)(3)
404(b)	404(b)(1), (2)(A), (B)
405(a)	405(a)
405(b)	405(b)
406	406
407	407[2]
408(a)(1), (2)	408(a)(1), (2)[3]
408(b)	408(b)[4]
409	409
410	410(a)(1)-(4), (b)(1), (2)
411	411[5]
412(a)(1), (2)	412(a)(1), (2)
412(b)(1)(A)-(C)	412(b)(1)(A)-(C)
412(b)(2)	412(b)(2)
412(c)(1)(A)	412(c)(1)(A), (B)
412(c)(1)(B)	412(c)(1)(C), (D)
412(c)(2)	412(c)(2)
	412(d)[6]
413(a)	413(a)
413(b)	413(b)
413(c)	413(c)
413(d)(1)-(5)	413(d)(1)-(5)
414(a)	414(a)
414(b)	414(b)

Former FRE	Current FRE
414(c)	414(c)
414(d)	414(d)(1), (2)
414(d)(1)	414(d)(2)(A)
414(d)(2)	414(d)(2)(B)
414(d)(3)	414(d)(2)(C)
414(d)(4)	414(d)(2)(D)
414(d)(5)	414(d)(2)(E)
414(d)(6)	414(d)(2)(F)
415(a)	415(a)
415(b)	415(b)
415(c)	415(c)
501	501
502	502
502(a)(1)-(3)	502(a)(1)-(3)
502(b)(1)-(3)	502(b)(1)-(3)
502(c)(1), (2)	502(c)(1), (2)
502(d)	502(d)
502(e)	502(e)
502(f)	502(f)
502(g)(1), (2)	502(g)(1), (2)
601	601
602	602
603	603
604	604
605	605
606(a)	606(a)
606(b)	606(b)(1), (2)(A)-(C)
607	607

Former FRE	Current FRE
608(a)	608(a)
608(b)	608(b)(1), (2)
609(a)	609(a)
609(a)(1)	609(a)(1)(A), (B)
609(a)(2)	609(a)(2)
609(b)	609(b)(1), (2)
609(c)	609(c)(1), (2)
609(d)	609(d)(1)-(4)
609(e)	609(e)
610	610
611(a)	611(a)(1)-(3)
611(b)	611(b)
611(c)	611(c)(1), (2)
612	612(a)(1), (2), (b), (c)
613(a)	613(a)
613(b)	613(b)
614(a)	614(a)
614(b)	614(b)
614(c)	614(c)
615	615(a)-(d)
701	701(a)-(c)[7]
702	702(a)-(d)
703	703[8]
704(a)	704(a)[9]
704(b)	704(b)[9]
705	705[10]
706(a)	706(a), (b)(1)-(4)
706(b)	706(c)(1), (2)

2. Former FRE 407 provided that the "rule does not require the exclusion of evidence" of subsequent remedial measures "when offered for another purpose"; FRE 407 now provides that the "court may admit [subsequent-remedial-measures] evidence for another purpose…." Despite the language change, there is no intent to change the process for admitting evidence covered by FRE 407. 2011 Notes to FRE 407 at ¶1, p. 1246, this book.

3. The reference to "liability" was omitted from current FRE 408(a) for readability and because "liability" is covered by the broader term "validity." 2011 Notes to FRE 408 at ¶2, p. 1247, this book.

4. Former FRE 408(b) provided that the rule "does not require exclusion" of compromise or offers to compromise for permitted uses; FRE 408(b) now provides that the "court may admit … evidence [of compromise offers or negotiations] for another purpose." Despite the language change, there is no intent to change the process for admitting evidence covered by FRE 408(b). 2011 Notes to FRE 408 at ¶1, p. 1247, this book.

5. Former FRE 411 provided that the rule "does not require the exclusion" of evidence that a person was or was not insured; FRE 411 now provides that the "court may admit … evidence [of liability insurance] for another purpose." 2011 Notes to FRE 411 at ¶1, p. 1248, this book. Despite the language change, there is no intent to change the process for admitting evidence covered by FRE 411. 2011 Notes to FRE 411 at ¶1, p. 1248, this book.

6. FRE 412(d) is a new subsection. In former FRE 412, the term "alleged victim" appeared in the title.

FRE COMPARISON TABLE – FORMER & CURRENT RULES

Former FRE	Current FRE
706(c)	706(d)
706(d)	706(e)
801(a)	801(a)
801(b)	801(b)
801(c)	801(c)(1), (2)
801(d)(1)	801(d)(1)(A)-(C)
801(d)(2)	801(d)(2)(A)-(E)[11]
802	802
803(1)	803(1)
803(2)	803(2)
803(3)	803(3)
803(4)	803(4)(A), (B)
803(5)	803(5)(A)-(C)
803(6)	803(6)(A)-(E)
803(7)	803(7)(A)-(C)
803(8)	803(8)(A)(i)-(iii), (B)
803(9)	803(9)
803(10)	803(10)(A), (B)
803(11)	803(11)
803(12)	803(12)(A)-(C)
803(13)	803(13)
803(14)	803(14)(A)-(C)
803(15)	803(15)
803(16)	803(16)

Former FRE	Current FRE
803(17)	803(17)
803(18)	803(18)(A), (B)[12]
803(19)	803(19)
803(20)	803(20)
803(21)	803(21)
803(22)	803(22)(A)-(D)
803(23)	803(23)(A), (B)
803(24)	803(24)
804(a)(1)	804(a)(1)
804(a)(2)	804(a)(2)
804(a)(3)	804(a)(3)
804(a)(4)	804(a)(4)
804(a)(5)	804(a)(5)(A), (B)
804(b)	804(b)
804(b)(1)	804(b)(1)(A), (B)
804(b)(2)	804(b)(2)
804(b)(3)(A), (B)	804(b)(3)(A), (B)
804(b)(4)	804(b)(4)(A), (B)
804(b)(5)	804(b)(5)
804(b)(6)	804(b)(6)
805	805
806	806
807	807(a)(1)-(4), (b)
901(a)	901(a)
901(b)	901(b)

Former FRE	Current FRE
901(b)(1)	901(b)(1)
901(b)(2)	901(b)(2)
901(b)(3)	901(b)(3)
901(b)(4)	901(b)(4)
901(b)(5)	901(b)(5)
901(b)(6)	901(b)(6)(A), (B)
901(b)(7)	901(b)(7)(A), (B)
901(b)(8)	901(b)(8)(A)-(C)
901(b)(9)	901(b)(9)
901(b)(10)	901(b)(10)
902	902
902(1)	902(1)(A), (B)
902(2)	902(2)(A), (B)
902(3)	902(3)(A), (B)
902(4)	902(4)(A), (B)
902(5)	902(5)
902(6)	902(6)
902(7)	902(7)
902(8)	902(8)
902(9)	902(9)
902(10)	902(10)
902(11)(A)-(C)	902(11)
902(12)(A)-(C)	902(12)
903	903
1001(1)	1001(a), (b)

COMPARISON TABLE

7. The references to "inferences" were omitted from current FRE 701 because the omissions made the rule easier to read and because "inference" is covered by the broader term "opinion." 2011 Notes to FRE 701 at ¶1, p. 1258, this book.

8. The references to "inferences" were omitted from current FRE 703 because the omissions made the rule easier to read and because "inference" is covered by the broader term "opinion." 2011 Notes to FRE 703 at ¶1, p. 1263, this book.

9. The references to "inferences" were omitted from current FRE 704 because the omissions made the rule easier to read and because "inference" is covered by the broader term "opinion." 2011 Notes to FRE 704 at ¶1, p. 1264, this book.

10. The reference to "inference" was omitted from current FRE 705 because the omission made the rule easier to read and because "inference" is covered by the broader term "opinion." 2011 Notes to FRE 705 at ¶1, p. 1264, this book.

11. The reference to an "admission" as an exclusion from hearsay was omitted from the title of FRE 801(d)(2). The term was confusing (1) because a statement can be within the exclusion even if it "admitted" nothing and was not against the party's interest when made and (2) in comparison with the FRE 804(b)(3) hearsay exception for declarations against interest. 2011 Notes to FRE 801 at ¶1, p. 1264, this book.

12. Former FRE 803(18) provided that the "statements contained in published treatises, periodicals, or pamphlets on a subject of history, medicine, or other science or art" could be hearsay exceptions; FRE 803(18) now provides simply that "[a] statement contained in a treatise, periodical, or pamphlet" can be an exception to the rule against hearsay, thus deleting the list of possible subjects of the treatise, periodical, or pamphlet.

FRE COMPARISON TABLE – FORMER & CURRENT RULES

Former FRE	Current FRE
1001(2)	1001(c)
1001(3)	1001(d)
1001(4)	1001(e)
1002	1002
1003	1003
1004	1004
1004(1)	1004(a)
1004(2)	1004(b)
1004(3)	1004(c)
1004(4)	1004(d)
1005	1005
1006	1006
1007	1007
1008	1008(a)-(c)
1101(a)	1101(a)
1101(b)	1101(b)
1101(c)	1101(c)
1101(d)(1)-(3)	1101(d)(1)-(3)
1101(e)	1101(e)
1102	1102
1103	1103

ARTICLE I. GENERAL PROVISIONS

FRE 101. SCOPE; DEFINITIONS

(a) Scope. These rules apply to proceedings in United States courts. The specific courts and proceedings to which the rules apply, along with exceptions, are set out in Rule 1101.

(b) Definitions. In these rules:

(1) "civil case" means a civil action or proceeding;

(2) "criminal case" includes a criminal proceeding;

(3) "public office" includes a public agency;

(4) "record" includes a memorandum, report, or data compilation;

(5) a "rule prescribed by the Supreme Court" means a rule adopted by the Supreme Court under statutory authority; and

(6) a reference to any kind of written material or any other medium includes electronically stored information.

See selected Notes of Advisory Committee to FRE 101, p. 1239.

History of FRE 101: Adopted Jan. 2, 1975, P.L. 93-595, §1, 88 Stat. 1926, eff. July 1, 1975. Amended Mar. 2, 1987, eff. Oct. 1, 1987; Apr. 25, 1988, eff. Nov. 1, 1988; Apr. 22, 1993, eff. Dec. 1, 1993; Apr. 26, 2011, eff. Dec. 1, 2011.

See *Commentaries*, "Introduction to Federal Rules," ch. 1-A, p. 3.

See also 28 U.S.C. §2072 (power of Supreme Court to prescribe rules of procedure and evidence).

ANNOTATIONS

Sims v. Great Am. Life Ins., 469 F.3d 870, 883 (10th Cir.2006). "The [FREs] are an act of Congress and, thus, subject neither to the dictates of the ***Erie*** doctrine nor to the Rules Enabling Act or Rules of Decision Act. Yet, we are mindful that ***Erie*** 'recognized that the scheme of our Constitution envisions an allocation of law-making functions between state and federal legislative processes which is undercut if the federal judiciary can make substantive law affecting state affairs beyond the bounds of congressional legislative powers.' [¶] But we also recognize that Congress may 'prescribe housekeeping rules for federal courts even though some of those rules will inevitably differ from comparable state rules.'"

In re Nautilus Motor Tanker Co., 85 F.3d 105, 111 (3d Cir.1996). The FREs "were enacted by Congress and must be regarded … as any other federal statute. *At 112:* Accordingly, [administrative regulations cannot] limit the authority of Congress to prescribe and enforce rules for the admissibility of evidence in the federal courts."

FRE 102. PURPOSE

These rules should be construed so as to administer every proceeding fairly, eliminate unjustifiable expense and delay, and promote the development of evidence law, to the end of ascertaining the truth and securing a just determination.

History of FRE 102: Adopted Jan. 2, 1975, P.L. 93-595, §1, 88 Stat. 1926, eff. July 1, 1975. Amended Apr. 26, 2011, eff. Dec. 1, 2011.

See *Commentaries*, "Introduction to Federal Rules," ch. 1-A, p. 3.

ANNOTATIONS

New York v. Operation Rescue Nat'l, 80 F.3d 64, 72 (2d Cir.1996). "[T]he mandate of [FRCP 1] that those rules be construed 'to secure the just, speedy, and inexpensive determination of every action,' the dictate of [FRE 102] that those rules be construed to eliminate 'unjustifiable expense and delay,' and the allowance in [FRE 1006] for complex evidence to be presented in summary form should be read to preclude an absolute right of a litigant to command that a videotape be shown in full, or every word of a document be read, in open court."

Gentile v. County of Suffolk, 129 F.R.D. 435, 458 (E.D.N.Y.1990), *aff'd*, 926 F.2d 142 (2d Cir.1991). "The trial court is given broad discretion to control the trial by the [FREs]. In controlling the trial the court will necessarily consider (1) whether the jury is in a position to properly evaluate the evidence before it without further help and (2) the amount of time the evidence will require as compared to alternate forms of proof. These general administrative considerations for the judicial officer presiding at the trial are designed to carry out the direction and policy of [FRE] 102. They are related to, but much broader in scope, than the special factors set out in [FRE] 403."

FRE 103. RULINGS ON EVIDENCE

(a) Preserving a Claim of Error. A party may claim error in a ruling to admit or exclude evidence only if the error affects a substantial right of the party and:

(1) if the ruling admits evidence, a party, on the record:

(A) timely objects or moves to strike; and

(B) states the specific ground, unless it was apparent from the context; or

(2) if the ruling excludes evidence, a party informs the court of its substance by an offer of proof, unless the substance was apparent from the context.

(b) Not Needing to Renew an Objection or Offer of Proof. Once the court rules definitively on the record—either before or at trial—a party need not renew an objection or offer of proof to preserve a claim of error for appeal.

(c) Court's Statement About the Ruling; Directing an Offer of Proof. The court may make any statement about the character or form of the evidence, the objection made, and the ruling. The court may direct that an offer of proof be made in question-and-answer form.

(d) Preventing the Jury from Hearing Inadmissible Evidence. To the extent practicable, the court must conduct a jury trial so that inadmissible evidence is not suggested to the jury by any means.

(e) Taking Notice of Plain Error. A court may take notice of a plain error affecting a substantial right, even if the claim of error was not properly preserved.

See selected Notes of Advisory Committee to FRE 103, p. 1240.

History of FRE 103: Adopted Jan. 2, 1975, P.L. 93-595, §1, 88 Stat. 1926, eff. July 1, 1975. Amended Apr. 17, 2000, eff. Dec. 1, 2000; Apr. 26, 2011, eff. Dec. 1, 2011.

See *Commentaries*, "Making Objections & Preserving Error," ch. 1-F, p. 41; "Objecting to Evidence," ch. 8-D, p. 700.

ANNOTATIONS

Ohler v. U.S., 529 U.S. 753, 755-56 (2000). "Generally, a party introducing evidence cannot complain on appeal that the evidence was erroneously admitted. [D] seeks to avoid the consequences of this … principle by invoking Rule[ ] 103…. Rule 103 sets forth the unremarkable propositions that a party must make a timely objection to a ruling admitting evidence and that a party cannot challenge an evidentiary ruling unless it affects a substantial right. The Rule does not purport to determine when a party waives a prior objection, and it is silent with respect to the effect of introducing evidence on direct examination, and later assigning its admission as error on appeal. *At 760:* [W]e conclude that a defendant who preemptively introduces evidence of a prior conviction on direct examination may not on appeal claim that the admission of such evidence was error." *See also* ***U.S. v. Delgado***, 401 F.3d 290, 301 (5th Cir.2005).

U.S. v. Vargas, 471 F.3d 255, 262 (1st Cir.2006). FRE 103(a)(1) "requires that an objection to the admission or exclusion of evidence be timely and specific in order to preserve the issue for appeal. This mandate for specificity requires the objecting party to object with the degree of detail that will adequately apprise the trial court of the basis of the objection, unless the specific ground is apparent from the context." *See also* ***U.S. v. Seale***, 600 F.3d 473, 486 (5th Cir.2010).

Fuesting v. Zimmer, Inc., 448 F.3d 936, 940 (7th Cir.2006). "[A] party is not required to renew an objection to an evidentiary motion in order to preserve its right to appeal. … Though … Rule 103 is primarily focused on renewal at trial, it follows that renewal through postverdict motions is unnecessary if the rule dictates that a claim of error for appeal is preserved by the original objection or motion *in limine*." *See also* ***Dream Games v. PC Onsite***, 561 F.3d 983, 988 n.3 (9th Cir.2009).

U.S. v. Moore, 425 F.3d 1061, 1068 (7th Cir.2005). FRE 103(a)(2) "requires a defendant to present his evidentiary arguments to the trial court in order to preserve the issue for appeal. Although this circuit does not require litigants to make formal offers of proof when evidence is excluded, 'the record must show the equivalent: grounds for admissibility, the proponent must inform the court and opposing counsel what he expects to prove by the excluded evidence, and he must demonstrate the significance of the excluded testimony.'"

U.S. v. Polishan, 336 F.3d 234, 241 n.6 (3d Cir. 2003). "We may reverse a district court for a plain error [under former FRE 103(d), now FRE 103(e),] only if we conclude (1) an error was committed, (2) it was plain (clear and obvious), and (3) it affected the outcome of the district court proceedings. If we conclude that the error is both obvious and prejudicial, we may order its correction, but are not required to do so. We correct only if the error 'seriously affects the fairness, integrity, or public reputation of judicial proceedings.'"

Ahern v. Scholz, 85 F.3d 774, 786 (1st Cir.1996). "In determining whether an error affected a party's substantial right, the central question is whether this court can say with fair assurance that the judgment was not substantially swayed by the error. Factors we must consider in determining whether substantial rights are implicated include both the centrality of the evidence and the prejudicial effect of its exclusion or inclusion. We weigh these factors in the context of the case as gleaned from the record as a whole. [N]o substantial right of the party is affected where the evidence omitted was cumulative as to other admitted evidence." (In-

FRE 103

Effective December 1, 2011, FREs 101-1103 were restyled. For a discussion of the changes and a chart comparing the former and current rules, see p. 1024.

ternal quotes omitted.) *See also* ***U.S. v. Garcia***, 413 F.3d 201, 210 (2d Cir.2005).

FRE 104. PRELIMINARY QUESTIONS

(a) In General. The court must decide any preliminary question about whether a witness is qualified, a privilege exists, or evidence is admissible. In so deciding, the court is not bound by evidence rules, except those on privilege.

(b) Relevance That Depends on a Fact. When the relevance of evidence depends on whether a fact exists, proof must be introduced sufficient to support a finding that the fact does exist. The court may admit the proposed evidence on the condition that the proof be introduced later.

(c) Conducting a Hearing So That the Jury Cannot Hear It. The court must conduct any hearing on a preliminary question so that the jury cannot hear it if:

(1) the hearing involves the admissibility of a confession;

(2) a defendant in a criminal case is a witness and so requests; or

(3) justice so requires.

(d) Cross-Examining a Defendant in a Criminal Case. By testifying on a preliminary question, a defendant in a criminal case does not become subject to cross-examination on other issues in the case.

(e) Evidence Relevant to Weight and Credibility. This rule does not limit a party's right to introduce before the jury evidence that is relevant to the weight or credibility of other evidence.

History of FRE 104: Adopted Jan. 2, 1975, P.L. 93-595, §1, 88 Stat. 1926, eff. July 1, 1975. Amended Mar. 2, 1987, eff. Oct. 1, 1987; Apr. 26, 2011, eff. Dec. 1, 2011.

See ***Commentaries***, "Making Objections & Preserving Error," ch. 1-F, p. 41; "Motion to Exclude Expert Witness," ch. 5-N, p. 376; "Objecting to Evidence," ch. 8-D, p. 700; ***O'Connor's Federal Civil Forms*** (2012), FORMS 5N, 8D.

ANNOTATIONS

U.S. v. Zolin, 491 U.S. 554, 572 (1989). "Before engaging in *in camera* review to determine the applicability of the ... exception [to a privilege], 'the judge should require a showing of a factual basis adequate to support a good faith belief by a reasonable person,' ... that *in camera* review of the materials may reveal evidence to establish the claim that the ... exception applies. [¶] Once that showing is made, the decision whether to engage in *in camera* review rests in the sound discretion of the district court."

Huddleston v. U.S., 485 U.S. 681, 690 n.7 (1988). "When an item of evidence is conditionally relevant, it is often not possible for the offeror to prove the fact upon which relevance is conditioned at the time the evidence is offered. In such cases, it is customary to permit him to introduce the evidence and connect it up later. Rule 104(b) continues this practice, specifically authorizing the judge to admit the evidence subject to proof of the preliminary fact. It is, of course, not the responsibility of the judge sua sponte to insure that the foundation evidence is offered; the objector must move to strike the evidence if at the close of the trial the offeror has failed to satisfy the condition." (Internal quotes omitted.)

Bourjaily v. U.S., 483 U.S. 171, 175 (1987). "We have traditionally required that these matters [under FRE 104(a)] be established by a preponderance of proof."

Blake v. Pellegrino, 329 F.3d 43, 48 (1st Cir.2003). FRE 104(a) "enables a trial judge to decide whether foundational facts have been established (and, thus, whether particular pieces of evidence are eligible for admission). The trial court 'act[s] as a gatekeeper' when such issues arise."

FRE 105. LIMITING EVIDENCE THAT IS NOT ADMISSIBLE AGAINST OTHER PARTIES OR FOR OTHER PURPOSES

If the court admits evidence that is admissible against a party or for a purpose—but not against another party or for another purpose—the court, on timely request, must restrict the evidence to its proper scope and instruct the jury accordingly.

History of FRE 105: Adopted Jan. 2, 1975, P.L. 93-595, §1, 88 Stat. 1926, eff. July 1, 1975. Amended Apr. 26, 2011, eff. Dec. 1, 2011.

See ***Commentaries***, "Request for limited admissibility," ch. 8-D, §6.1.3, p. 704.

ANNOTATIONS

U.S. v. Smith, 459 F.3d 1276, 1297 (11th Cir.2006). "[B]ecause [FRE] 105, which provides for limiting instructions in appropriate circumstances, only operates 'upon request,' ... '[t]he failure to give a limiting instruction is error only when such an instruction is requested.'"

Rush v. Illinois Cent. R.R., 399 F.3d 705, 721 (6th Cir.2005). "The text of [FRE 105] 'does not clearly require the trial court to give the instruction at the same

FRE 103

time the jury is exposed to the evidence.'" *See also* ***U.S. v. Beasley***, 495 F.3d 142, 150 (4th Cir.2007) (timing of instruction is within district court's discretion).

FRE 106. REMAINDER OF OR RELATED WRITINGS OR RECORDED STATEMENTS

If a party introduces all or part of a writing or recorded statement, an adverse party may require the introduction, at that time, of any other part—or any other writing or recorded statement—that in fairness ought to be considered at the same time.

History of FRE 106: Adopted Jan. 2, 1975, P.L. 93-595, §1, 88 Stat. 1926, eff. July 1, 1975. Amended Mar. 2, 1987, eff. Oct. 1, 1987; Apr. 26, 2011, eff. Dec. 1, 2011.

ANNOTATIONS

Beech Aircraft Corp. v. Rainey, 488 U.S. 153, 172 (1988). "[W]hen one party has made use of a portion of a document, such that misunderstanding or distortion can be averted only through presentation of another portion, the material required for completeness is *ipso facto* relevant and therefore admissible…." *See also* ***U.S. v. Phillips***, 543 F.3d 1197, 1203 (10th Cir.2008).

McCoy v. Augusta Fiberglass Coatings, Inc., 593 F.3d 737, 747 (8th Cir.2010). "Rule 106 applies only to writings or recorded statements, not to acts or conversations. It has no application where the party does not introduce the document into evidence or inquire into it. [¶] To sustain a Rule 106 objection, the party urging admission of an excluded conversation must specify the portion of the testimony that is relevant to the issue at trial and that qualifies or explains portions already admitted." (Internal quotes omitted.) *See also* ***U.S. v. Garcia***, 530 F.3d 348, 353 (5th Cir.2008) (FRE 106 does not apply to witness's testimony at trial).

U.S. v. Holden, 557 F.3d 698, 705-06 (6th Cir.2009). "Whether a party waives their right of completeness [by failing to invoke FRE 106 when the evidence is introduced] is an open question in this circuit, but we now reject the waiver rule…. [T]he rule does not restrict admission of completeness evidence to the time the misleading evidence is introduced: 'The rule does not in any way circumscribe the right of the adversary to develop the matter on cross-examination or as part of his own case.' [T]he purpose of the rule of completeness is to ensure fairness in the presentation of evidence at trial; in delaying completion or denying it altogether a strict waiver rule frustrates this purpose without serving any corresponding value. If a party fails to invoke the rule at the time the misleading evidence is introduced, the chance to do so is lost independent of the effect of a waiver rule, and allowing parties to invoke the rule of completeness after the misleading evidence is introduced does not limit the district judge's discretion to determine whether and when the curative evidence should be admitted."

U.S. v. Hoffecker, 530 F.3d 137, 192 (3d Cir.2008). "[A]dditional portions of a recording may be played 'if it is necessary to (1) explain the admitted portion, (2) place the admitted portion in context, (3) avoid misleading the trier of fact, or (4) insure a fair and impartial understanding.' '[FRE 106] does not require introduction of portions of a statement that are neither explanatory of nor relevant to the passages that have been admitted.'" *See also* ***U.S. v. Lopez-Medina***, 596 F.3d 716, 735 (10th Cir.2010); ***U.S. v. Kopp***, 562 F.3d 141, 144 (2d Cir.2009).

ARTICLE II. JUDICIAL NOTICE

FRE 201. JUDICIAL NOTICE OF ADJUDICATIVE FACTS

(a) **Scope.** This rule governs judicial notice of an adjudicative fact only, not a legislative fact.

(b) **Kinds of Facts That May Be Judicially Noticed.** The court may judicially notice a fact that is not subject to reasonable dispute because it:

(1) is generally known within the trial court's territorial jurisdiction; or

(2) can be accurately and readily determined from sources whose accuracy cannot reasonably be questioned.

(c) **Taking Notice.** The court:

(1) may take judicial notice on its own; or

(2) must take judicial notice if a party requests it and the court is supplied with the necessary information.

(d) **Timing.** The court may take judicial notice at any stage of the proceeding.

(e) **Opportunity to Be Heard.** On timely request, a party is entitled to be heard on the propriety of taking judicial notice and the nature of the fact to be noticed. If the court takes judicial notice before notifying a party, the party, on request, is still entitled to be heard.

(f) **Instructing the Jury.** In a civil case, the court must instruct the jury to accept the noticed fact as

FRE 201

Effective December 1, 2011, FREs 101-1103 were restyled. For a discussion of the changes and a chart comparing the former and current rules, see p. 1024.

conclusive. In a criminal case, the court must instruct the jury that it may or may not accept the noticed fact as conclusive.

See selected Notes of Advisory Committee to FRE 201, p. 1242.

History of FRE 201: Adopted Jan. 2, 1975, P.L. 93-595, §1, 88 Stat. 1926, eff. July 1, 1975. Amended Apr. 26, 2011, eff. Dec. 1, 2011.

See ***Commentaries***, "Motion for Judicial Notice," ch. 5-M, p. 370; ***O'Connor's Federal Civil Forms*** (2012), FORMS 5M.

See also FRCP 44.1 (determining foreign law).

ANNOTATIONS

U.S. v. Bari, 599 F.3d 176, 179 n.4 (2d Cir.2010). See annotation under FRE 605, p. 1048.

von Saher v. Norton Simon Museum of Art, 592 F.3d 954, 960 (9th Cir.2010). "Courts may take judicial notice of publications introduced to 'indicate what was in the public realm at the time, not whether the contents of those articles were in fact true.'"

Group One Ltd. v. Hallmark Cards, Inc., 407 F.3d 1297, 1306 (Fed.Cir.2005). "Despite the breadth of [FRE 201], there are circumstances under which it is improper for the district court to take judicial notice after the verdict, such as where unfairness results."

Rivera v. Philip Morris, Inc., 395 F.3d 1142, 1151 (9th Cir.2005). "'[A] high degree of indisputability is the essential prerequisite' to taking judicial notice of adjudicative facts and ... 'the tradition [of taking judicial notice] has been one of caution in requiring that the matter be beyond reasonable controversy.' 'Because the effect of judicial notice is to deprive a party of an opportunity to use rebuttal evidence, cross-examination, and argument to attack contrary evidence, caution must be used in determining that a fact is beyond controversy under Rule 201(b).'" *See also* ***Doss v. Clearwater Title Co.***, 551 F.3d 634, 640 (7th Cir.2008).

Qualley v. Clo-Tex Int'l, 212 F.3d 1123, 1128 (8th Cir.2000). "Adjudicative facts are 'facts that normally go to the jury in a jury case. They relate to the parties, their activities, their properties, their businesses.' By contrast, '[l]egislative facts do not relate specifically to the activities or characteristics of the litigants. A court generally relies upon legislative facts when it purports to develop a particular law or policy and thus considers material wholly unrelated to the activities of the parties.'" *See also* ***O'Toole v. Northrop Grumman Corp.***, 499 F.3d 1218, 1224 (10th Cir.2007).

ARTICLE III. PRESUMPTIONS IN CIVIL CASES

FRE 301. PRESUMPTIONS IN CIVIL CASES GENERALLY

In a civil case, unless a federal statute or these rules provide otherwise, the party against whom a presumption is directed has the burden of producing evidence to rebut the presumption. But this rule does not shift the burden of persuasion, which remains on the party who had it originally.

History of FRE 301: Adopted Jan. 2, 1975, P.L. 93-595, §1, 88 Stat. 1926, eff. July 1, 1975. Amended Apr. 26, 2011, eff. Dec. 1, 2011.

ANNOTATIONS

St. Mary's Honor Ctr. v. Hicks, 509 U.S. 502, 506-07 (1993). "To establish a 'presumption' is to say that a finding of the predicate fact (here, the prima facie case) produces 'a required conclusion in the absence of explanation' (here, the finding of unlawful discrimination). Thus, the ... presumption places upon the defendant the burden of producing an explanation to rebut the prima facie case.... [¶] 'If the defendant carries this burden of production, the presumption raised by the prima facie case is rebutted,' ... and 'drops from the case....'" *See also* ***ITC Ltd. v. Punchgini, Inc.***, 482 F.3d 135, 148 (2d Cir.2007); ***McCann v. Newman Irrevocable Trust***, 458 F.3d 281, 287-88 (3d Cir.2006).

Cappuccio v. Prime Capital Funding LLC, 649 F.3d 180, 189 (3d Cir.2011). "[U]nless Congress or the [FREs] provide otherwise, a presumption in a civil case imposes the burden of production on the party against whom it is directed, but does not shift the burden of persuasion. Under this theory, called the Thayer-Wigmore 'bursting bubble' theory of presumptions, the introduction of evidence to rebut a presumption destroys that presumption, leaving only that evidence and its inferences to be judged against the competing evidence and its inferences to determine the ultimate question at issue. This view of Rule 301 is widely accepted." (Internal quotes omitted.)

Nunley v. City of L.A., 52 F.3d 792, 796 (9th Cir. 1995). "Under the common law mailbox rule, proper and timely mailing of a document raises a rebuttable presumption that it is received by the addressee. [¶] Under the so-called 'bursting bubble' approach to presumptions, a presumption disappears where rebuttal evidence is presented. [¶] Regardless of the quantum of evidence necessary to rebut the presumption, the

movant still bears the burden of proving non-receipt. Even after the 'bubble' of presumption has 'burst,' the factual question of receipt remains and may be decided in favor of receipt by a fact finder who may choose to draw inferences of receipt from the evidence of mailing, in spite of contrary evidence."

Allseas Maritime, S.A. v. M/V MIMOSA, 812 F.2d 243, 248 (5th Cir.1987). "An exception to [the bursting-bubble view of presumptions under] Rule 301 occurs when 'the facts with regard to an issue lie peculiarly in the knowledge of one party,' and it would therefore be 'particularly onerous' to require the other party to bear the burden of persuasion on the issue."

FRE 302. APPLYING STATE LAW TO PRESUMPTIONS IN CIVIL CASES

In a civil case, state law governs the effect of a presumption regarding a claim or defense for which state law supplies the rule of decision.

History of FRE 302: Adopted Jan. 2, 1975, P.L. 93-595, §1, 88 Stat. 1926, eff. July 1, 1975. Amended Apr. 26, 2011, eff. Dec. 1, 2011.

ANNOTATIONS

Herbert v. Wal-Mart Stores, 911 F.2d 1044, 1047 (5th Cir.1990). FRE 302 "does not require that we apply state law. Rule 302 applies only to presumptions. While often labelled as such, there is no dispute that the uncalled-witness rule does not create a true 'presumption,' but merely permits an inference. As such, it falls outside the scope of Rule 302."

ARTICLE IV. RELEVANCE & ITS LIMITS

FRE 401. TEST FOR RELEVANT EVIDENCE

Evidence is relevant if:

(a) it has any tendency to make a fact more or less probable than it would be without the evidence; and

(b) the fact is of consequence in determining the action.

History of FRE 401: Adopted Jan. 2, 1975, P.L. 93-595, §1, 88 Stat. 1926, eff. July 1, 1975. Amended Apr. 26, 2011, eff. Dec. 1, 2011.

See *Commentaries*, "Introducing Evidence," ch. 8-C, p. 688.

ANNOTATIONS

Sprint/United Mgmt. v. Mendelsohn, 552 U.S. 379, 387 (2008). "Relevance and prejudice under [FREs] 401 and 403 are determined in the context of the facts and arguments in a particular case, and thus are generally not amenable to broad *per se* rules [that would exclude the evidence]."

Old Chief v. U.S., 519 U.S. 172, 179 (1997). "If … relevant evidence is inadmissible in the presence of other evidence related to it, its exclusion must rest not on the ground that the other evidence has rendered it 'irrelevant,' but on its character as unfairly prejudicial, cumulative or the like…."

Daubert v. Merrell Dow Pharms., 509 U.S. 579, 587 (1993). FRE 401's "basic standard of relevance … is a liberal one." *See also* ***Dortch v. Fowler***, 588 F.3d 396, 400 (6th Cir.2009) (standard is extremely liberal).

U.S. v. Parkes, 668 F.3d 295, 304 (6th Cir.2012). "The *purpose* of an item of evidence cannot be determined solely by reference to its *content*. That's because '[r]elevancy is not an inherent characteristic of any item of evidence but exists only as a relation between an item of evidence and a matter properly provable in the case.' And frequently evidence will be logically relevant in more than one way."

Thompson v. City of Chi., 472 F.3d 444, 453 (7th Cir.2006). "To be relevant, evidence need not conclusively decide the ultimate issue in a case, nor make the proposition appear more probable, but it must in some degree advance the inquiry." (Internal quotes omitted.) *See also* ***U.S. v. Oldbear***, 568 F.3d 814, 820 (10th Cir. 2009); ***U.S. v. Fountain***, 2 F.3d 656, 667 n.6 (6th Cir. 1993).

U.S. v. Turner, 198 F.3d 425, 429 n.2 (4th Cir.1999). "The partiality of a witness is always relevant as discrediting the witness and affecting the weight of his testimony."

Spain v. Gallegos, 26 F.3d 439, 452 (3d Cir.1994). FRE 401, "'while giving judges great freedom to admit evidence, diminishes substantially their authority to exclude evidence as irrelevant.'" *See also* ***Gomez v. Martin Marietta Corp.***, 50 F.3d 1511, 1518 (10th Cir. 1995).

FRE 402. GENERAL ADMISSIBILITY OF RELEVANT EVIDENCE

Relevant evidence is admissible unless any of the following provides otherwise:

- the United States Constitution;
- a federal statute;
- these rules; or
- other rules prescribed by the Supreme Court.

Irrelevant evidence is not admissible.

History of FRE 402: Adopted Jan. 2, 1975, P.L. 93-595, §1, 88 Stat. 1926, eff. July 1, 1975. Amended Apr. 26, 2011, eff. Dec. 1, 2011.

See *Commentaries*, "Introducing Evidence," ch. 8-C, p. 688.

ANNOTATIONS

U.S. v. Lowery, 166 F.3d 1119, 1125 (11th Cir.1999). FRE 402 "is an exclusive list of the sources of authority for exclusion of evidence in federal court. State rules of professional conduct are not included in the list. [¶] Local rules of federal courts are not listed in Rule 402, either."

FRE 403. EXCLUDING RELEVANT EVIDENCE FOR PREJUDICE, CONFUSION, WASTE OF TIME, OR OTHER REASONS

The court may exclude relevant evidence if its probative value is substantially outweighed by a danger of one or more of the following: unfair prejudice, confusing the issues, misleading the jury, undue delay, wasting time, or needlessly presenting cumulative evidence.

History of FRE 403: Adopted Jan. 2, 1975, P.L. 93-595, §1, 88 Stat. 1926, eff. July 1, 1975. Amended Apr. 26, 2011, eff. Dec. 1, 2011.

See *Commentaries*, "Introducing Evidence," ch. 8-C, p. 688.

ANNOTATIONS

Sprint/United Mgmt. v. Mendelsohn, 552 U.S. 379, 387 (2008). See annotation under FRE 401, p. 1033.

Old Chief v. U.S., 519 U.S. 172, 184-85 (1997). "[W]hen Rule 403 confers discretion by providing that evidence 'may' be excluded, the [court's] discretionary judgment may be informed not only by assessing an evidentiary item's twin tendencies[, i.e., its probative value compared to the danger of undue prejudice,] but by placing the result of that assessment alongside similar assessments of evidentiary alternatives [to the proffered evidence]." *See also* ***U.S. v. Higuera-Llamos***, 574 F.3d 1206, 1209 (9th Cir.2009).

U.S. v. Fields, 483 F.3d 313, 354 (5th Cir.2007). "One purpose of Rule 403 is to prevent evidence from 'inducing decision on a purely emotional basis.' However, to warrant exclusion, the danger of unfair prejudice ... must *substantially* outweigh the probative value of the evidence. Accordingly, we have recognized that Rule 403's scope is narrow. '[T]he application of Rule 403 must be cautious and sparing. Its major function is limited to excluding matter of scant or cumulative probative force, dragged in by the heels for the sake of its prejudicial effect.' [¶] Although reviewing courts use a great variety of verbal formulae ..., all agree that we must afford an especially high level of deference to district courts in such circumstances. Thus, a district court's decision on Rule 403 grounds is disturbed 'rarely' and only when there has been 'a clear abuse of discretion.'" *See also* ***In re Paoli R.R. Yard PCB Litig.***, 113 F.3d 444, 453 (3d Cir.1997).

Adams v. Ameritech Servs., 231 F.3d 414, 428 (7th Cir.2000). "[W]hile it is not unheard of to exclude evidence under Rule 403 at the summary judgment stage, ... normally the balancing process contemplated by that rule is best undertaken at the trial itself." *See also* ***Ramírez Rodríguez v. Boehringer Ingelheim Pharms.***, 425 F.3d 67, 77 n.10 (1st Cir.2005).

U.S. v. Smithers, 212 F.3d 306, 316 (6th Cir.2000). "Not all delay authorizes the exclusion of relevant evidence—only 'undue delay.' Moreover, the term 'delay' does not connote delay in the submission of motions or proffers; rather, it encompasses the prolonging of the length of the trial, and can be read properly in conjunction with the other exclusionary factors: 'waste of time, or needless presentation of cumulative evidence.' [¶] 'Delay' is a consideration of efficiency and is not readily distinguishable from 'waste of time.' 'Delay' in Rule 403 does not mean 'filed late'...."

In re Air Crash Disaster, 86 F.3d 498, 538 (6th Cir. 1996). "Rule 403 does not exclude evidence because it is strongly persuasive or compellingly relevant—the rule only applies when it is likely that the jury will be moved by a piece of evidence in a manner that is somehow unfair or inappropriate. The truth may hurt, but Rule 403 does not make it inadmissible on that account." *See also* ***U.S. v. Farrington***, 499 F.3d 854, 859 (8th Cir.2007); ***Brazos River Auth. v. GE Ionics, Inc.***, 469 F.3d 416, 427 (5th Cir.2006).

U.S. v. Blackstone, 56 F.3d 1143, 1146 (9th Cir. 1995). "'Unfair prejudice' in the context of balancing evidence means 'an undue tendency to suggest decision on an improper basis, commonly, though not necessarily, an emotional one.' Evidence is prejudicial if it 'appeals to the jury's sympathies, arouses its sense of horror, provokes its instincts to punish, or triggers other mainsprings of human action....' It is particularly prejudicial when ... 'the proffered evidence connects a party with a highly charged public issue....'" *See also* ***U.S. v. Basham***, 561 F.3d 302, 327 (4th Cir.2009) (unfair prejudice occurs when evidence lures "'the factfinder into declaring guilt on a ground different from proof specific to the offense charged'"); ***U.S. v. O'Shea***,

426 F.3d 475, 485 (1st Cir.2005) (virtually all evidence is prejudicial, but it is only unfair prejudice that the law protects against).

FRE 404. CHARACTER EVIDENCE; CRIMES OR OTHER ACTS

(a) Character Evidence.

(1) ***Prohibited Uses.*** Evidence of a person's character or character trait is not admissible to prove that on a particular occasion the person acted in accordance with the character or trait.

(2) ***Exceptions for a Defendant or Victim in a Criminal Case.*** The following exceptions apply in a criminal case:

(A) a defendant may offer evidence of the defendant's pertinent trait, and if the evidence is admitted, the prosecutor may offer evidence to rebut it;

(B) subject to the limitations in Rule 412, a defendant may offer evidence of an alleged victim's pertinent trait, and if the evidence is admitted, the prosecutor may:

(i) offer evidence to rebut it; and

(ii) offer evidence of the defendant's same trait; and

(C) in a homicide case, the prosecutor may offer evidence of the alleged victim's trait of peacefulness to rebut evidence that the victim was the first aggressor.

(3) ***Exceptions for a Witness.*** Evidence of a witness's character may be admitted under Rules 607, 608, and 609.

(b) Crimes, Wrongs, or Other Acts.

(1) ***Prohibited Uses.*** Evidence of a crime, wrong, or other act is not admissible to prove a person's character in order to show that on a particular occasion the person acted in accordance with the character.

(2) ***Permitted Uses; Notice in a Criminal Case.*** This evidence may be admissible for another purpose, such as proving motive, opportunity, intent, preparation, plan, knowledge, identity, absence of mistake, or lack of accident. On request by a defendant in a criminal case, the prosecutor must:

(A) provide reasonable notice of the general nature of any such evidence that the prosecutor intends to offer at trial; and

(B) do so before trial—or during trial if the court, for good cause, excuses lack of pretrial notice.

See selected Notes of Advisory Committee to FRE 404, p. 1245.

History of FRE 404: Adopted Jan. 2, 1975, P.L. 93-595, §1, 88 Stat. 1926, eff. July 1, 1975. Amended Mar. 2, 1987, eff. Oct. 1, 1987; Apr. 30, 1991, eff. Dec. 1, 1991; Apr. 17, 2000, eff. Dec. 1, 2000; Apr. 12, 2006, eff. Dec. 1, 2006; Apr. 26, 2011, eff. Dec. 1, 2011.

See *Commentaries*, "Introducing Evidence," ch. 8-C, p. 688.

ANNOTATIONS

FRE 404(a)

Halvorsen v. Baird, 146 F.3d 680, 686 (9th Cir. 1998). In a civil suit for wrongful detention, "[P] claimed at all times that he was not drunk…. He argues that alcoholism was a 'trait of character' inadmissible under [FRE] 404(a). The judge let expert opinion in that [P] was an alcoholic, and that one typical characteristic of alcoholics is denial that they have been drinking when they plainly have. The judge said that this had a bearing on whether [P's] testimony that he was not drunk could be subjectively truthful, yet false. Alcoholism testimony has sometimes been regarded as inadmissible evidence of character, as [P] argues. But the judge was within his discretion in admitting it in this instance, as evidence of a disease which, if the jury believed the expert testimony, would cause [P] to be mistaken in his claim of sobriety on the night at issue."

U.S. v. Candoli, 870 F.2d 496, 506 (9th Cir.1989). "Pursuant to [FREs] 404(a)(3) and 608(a), evidence of [witness's] reputation should have been limited to evidence of [his] reputation for *truthfulness*. Moreover, such reputation evidence would have been admissible only if [witness's] character for truthfulness had been attacked." Held: One expert witness could not testify about favorable professional reputation of another expert witness.

FRE 404(b)

Huddleston v. U.S., 485 U.S. 681, 691-92 (1988). The protection against the introduction of unduly prejudicial evidence under FRE 404(b) "emanates not from a requirement of a preliminary finding by the trial court, but rather from four other sources: first, from the requirement of Rule 404(b) that the evidence be offered for a proper purpose; second, from the relevancy requirement of [FRE] 402—as enforced through [FRE] 104(b); third, from the assessment the trial court must make under [FRE] 403 to determine whether the probative value of the similar acts evidence is substantially outweighed by its potential for

FRE 404

Effective December 1, 2011, FREs 101-1103 were restyled. For a discussion of the changes and a chart comparing the former and current rules, see p. 1024.

unfair prejudice, ... and fourth, from [FRE] 105, which provides that the trial court shall, upon request, instruct the jury that the similar acts evidence is to be considered only for the proper purpose for which it was admitted."

U.S. v. Davis, 636 F.3d 1281, 1298 (10th Cir.2011). "Evidence admitted under Rule 404(b) may relate to conduct occurring either *before or after* the charged offense." *See also* ***U.S. v. Bergrin***, 682 F.3d 261, 281 n.25 (3d Cir.2012).

U.S. v. Thomas, 593 F.3d 752, 758 (8th Cir.2010). "'There is no absolute rule regarding the number of years that can separate offenses' admitted under Rule 404(b). ... Where the extrinsic act is extremely similar to the crime at issue, evidence of the act will usually be rendered irrelevant only by 'an enormous lapse of time.' *At 759:* We have approved the admission of evidence of similar crimes that occurred a decade before the charged crime. ... Considering the similarities between the crimes charged and the subsequent-acts evidence, we cannot say the mere passage of four years' time renders the evidence irrelevant to show knowledge or intent."

Brazos River Auth. v. GE Ionics, Inc., 469 F.3d 416, 423 (5th Cir.2006). FRE 404(b) "is applied most frequently in the criminal law context, ... and we have limited its application to civil actions 'where the focus is on essentially criminal aspects....' An example is a civil action for trade secret misappropriation in which the plaintiff seeks to introduce evidence of the defendant's having taken proprietary trade secrets before from a prior employer (because this would prove 'propensity' to commit misappropriation)."

Agushi v. Duerr, 196 F.3d 754, 760 (7th Cir.1999). "Rule 404(b) speaks not of the parties to a case, but of a 'person.' ... Neither the plain language of Rule 404(b) ..., nor any other consideration, suggests that a court should distinguish between the criminal and civil contexts when determining the admissibility of [Rule 404(b)] evidence."

FRE 404(b) Procedure

U.S. v. Everett, 270 F.3d 986, 991-92 (6th Cir.2001). "When admitting evidence under Rule 404(b), the court 'must carefully identify, in its instructions to the jury, the specific factor named in the rule that is relied upon to justify admission of the other-acts evidence, explain why that factor is material, and warn the jurors against using the evidence to draw the inferences expressly forbidden [by] Rule 404(b).'"

U.S. v. Merriweather, 78 F.3d 1070, 1076-77 (6th Cir.1996). "After requiring the proponent to identify the specific purpose for which the [FRE 404(b)] evidence is offered, the district court must [then] determine whether the identified purpose, whether to prove motive or intent or identity [or] some other purpose, is 'material'; that is, whether it is 'in issue' in the case. If the court finds it is, the court must then determine ... whether the probative value of the evidence is substantially outweighed by the danger of unfair prejudice under [FRE] 403. If the evidence satisfies Rule 403, then, after receiving the evidence, the district court must 'clearly, simply, and correctly' instruct the jury as to the *specific* purpose for which they may consider the evidence."

FRE 405. METHODS OF PROVING CHARACTER

(a) By Reputation or Opinion. When evidence of a person's character or character trait is admissible, it may be proved by testimony about the person's reputation or by testimony in the form of an opinion. On cross-examination of the character witness, the court may allow an inquiry into relevant specific instances of the person's conduct.

(b) By Specific Instances of Conduct. When a person's character or character trait is an essential element of a charge, claim, or defense, the character or trait may also be proved by relevant specific instances of the person's conduct.

History of FRE 405: Adopted Jan. 2, 1975, P.L. 93-595, §1, 88 Stat. 1926, eff. July 1, 1975. Amended Mar. 2, 1987, eff. Oct. 1, 1987; Apr. 26, 2011, eff. Dec. 1, 2011.

See *Commentaries*, "Introducing Evidence," ch. 8-C, p. 688.

ANNOTATIONS

U.S. v. Coumaris, 399 F.3d 343, 348 (D.C.Cir.2005). "[W]hen a defendant offers witnesses to testify regarding his character, on cross-examination 'inquiry is allowable into relevant specific instances of conduct, ... including prior convictions or arrests of the accused....' [S]uch inquiry is limited to instances that are relevant to the traits of character about which the witnesses have testified." *See also* ***SEC v. Peters***, 978 F.2d 1162, 1169 (10th Cir.1992).

U.S. v. Keiser, 57 F.3d 847, 856 (9th Cir.1995). "The relevant question [under FRE 405] should be: would proof, or failure of proof, of the character trait by itself

actually satisfy an element of the charge, claim, or defense? If not, then character is not essential and evidence should be limited to opinion or reputation."

U.S. v. Piche, 981 F.2d 706, 713 (4th Cir.1992). "Evidence of specific instances of conduct is the most convincing of Rule 405's three methods of proving character, but it also 'possesses the greatest capacity to arouse prejudice, to confuse, to surprise, and to consume time.'"

FRE 406. HABIT; ROUTINE PRACTICE

Evidence of a person's habit or an organization's routine practice may be admitted to prove that on a particular occasion the person or organization acted in accordance with the habit or routine practice. The court may admit this evidence regardless of whether it is corroborated or whether there was an eyewitness.

History of FRE 406: Adopted Jan. 2, 1975, P.L. 93-595, §1, 88 Stat. 1926, eff. July 1, 1975. Amended Apr. 26, 2011, eff. Dec. 1, 2011.

ANNOTATIONS

Goldsmith v. Bagby Elevator Co., 513 F.3d 1261, 1285 (11th Cir.2008). "We have not announced a precise formula for determining when a practice of an organization is so consistent that it becomes routine or habitual, but we have determined that adequacy of sampling and uniformity of response are controlling considerations in making such a determination. [W]e emphasize[] that conduct admitted as evidence of habit must reflect a systematic response to specific situations to avoid the danger of unfair prejudice that ordinarily accompanies the admission of propensity evidence…." (Internal quotes omitted.) *See also* ***U.S. v. Newman***, 982 F.2d 665, 668 (1st Cir.1992).

U.S. v. Angwin, 271 F.3d 786, 799 (9th Cir.2001), *overruled on other grounds*, ***U.S. v. Lopez***, 484 F.3d 1186 (9th Cir.2007). "In deciding whether certain conduct constitutes habit, courts consider three factors: (1) the degree to which the conduct is reflexive or semi-automatic as opposed to volitional; (2) the specificity or particularity of the conduct; and (3) the regularity or numerosity of the examples of the conduct." *See also* ***U.S. v. Oldbear***, 568 F.3d 814, 822 (10th Cir. 2009); ***Thompson v. Boggs***, 33 F.3d 847, 854 (7th Cir. 1994).

Mobil Expl. & Prod'g U.S., Inc. v. Cajun Constr. Servs., 45 F.3d 96, 99-100 (5th Cir.1995). "Habit evidence is relevant to prove that a business acted in a certain way. [¶] To obtain a Rule 406 inference of the routine practice of a business, a plaintiff must show a sufficient number of specific instances of conduct to support that inference. Evidence of the defendant's actions on only a few occasions or only in relation to the plaintiff are not enough; the plaintiff must show regularity over substantially all occasions or with substantially all other parties with whom the defendant has had similar business transactions." *See also* ***U.S. v. Warner***, 498 F.3d 666, 692 (7th Cir.2007).

FRE 407. SUBSEQUENT REMEDIAL MEASURES

When measures are taken that would have made an earlier injury or harm less likely to occur, evidence of the subsequent measures is not admissible to prove:

- negligence;
- culpable conduct;
- a defect in a product or its design; or
- a need for a warning or instruction.

But the court may admit this evidence for another purpose, such as impeachment or—if disputed—proving ownership, control, or the feasibility of precautionary measures.

See selected Notes of Advisory Committee to FRE 407, p. 1246.

History of FRE 407: Adopted Jan. 2, 1975, P.L. 93-595, §1, 88 Stat. 1926, eff. July 1, 1975. Amended Apr. 11, 1997, eff. Dec. 1, 1997; Apr. 26, 2011, eff. Dec. 1, 2011.

See ***Commentaries***, "Motion in Limine," ch. 5-H, p. 341; ***O'Connor's Federal Civil Forms*** (2012), FORMS 5H.

ANNOTATIONS

Pastor v. State Farm Mut. Auto. Ins., 487 F.3d 1042, 1045 (7th Cir.2007). "[T]o use at a trial a revision in a contract to argue the meaning of the original version would violate Rule 407 … by discouraging efforts to clarify contractual obligations, thus perpetuating any confusion caused by unclarified language in the contract. [P] wants to use the evidence that [D], to avert future liability to persons in the position of [P], changed the policy, to establish [D's] 'culpable conduct.' That is one of the grounds that evidence of subsequent corrective action may *not* be used to establish."

Minter v. Prime Equip. Co., 451 F.3d 1196, 1212-13 (10th Cir.2006). "The impeachment exception … must be read narrowly, lest it swallow the rule. Applied loosely, 'any evidence of subsequent remedial measures might be thought to contradict and so in a sense impeach [a party's] testimony.' [¶] Consequently, the impeachment exception has been confined to evidence of subsequent remedial measures that is 'necessary to

Effective December 1, 2011, FREs 101-1103 were restyled. For a discussion of the changes and a chart comparing the former and current rules, see p. 1024.

prevent the jury from being misled.'" *See also* ***In re Consolidation Coal Co.***, 123 F.3d 126, 136 (3d Cir. 1997) (evidence offered for impeachment must contradict witness's testimony directly).

In re Air Crash Disaster, 86 F.3d 498, 529 (6th Cir. 1996). "There is nothing in the text of Rule 407 that limits its application to measures by a 'responsible' party—i.e., measures by a party against whom the evidence is offered. *At 531:* Rule 407 bars the admission of evidence of remedial measures taken after an event that would have made the event less likely to occur. Here, however, the evidence was of measures taken *after* the design of a product but *before* the accident. Inasmuch as the exhibits related to pre-accident changes …, they fell outside the reach of Rule 407." *See also* ***Moulton v. Rival Co.***, 116 F.3d 22, 26 n.4 (1st Cir. 1997).

TLT-Babcock, Inc. v. Emerson Elec. Co., 33 F.3d 397, 400 (4th Cir.1994). "Rule 407 is based on the policy of encouraging potential defendants to remedy hazardous conditions without fear that their actions will be used as evidence against them. A nondefendant, however, will not be inhibited from taking remedial measures if such actions are allowed into evidence against a defendant. The courts of appeals, therefore, have held that evidence of subsequent repairs may be admitted where those repairs have been performed by someone other than the defendant." *See also* ***Millennium Partners v. Colmar Storage, LLC***, 494 F.3d 1293, 1302-03 (11th Cir.2007); ***Mehojah v. Drummond***, 56 F.3d 1213, 1215 (10th Cir.1995).

FRE 407

FRE 408. COMPROMISE OFFERS & NEGOTIATIONS

(a) Prohibited Uses. Evidence of the following is not admissible—on behalf of any party—either to prove or disprove the validity or amount of a disputed claim or to impeach by a prior inconsistent statement or a contradiction:

(1) furnishing, promising, or offering—or accepting, promising to accept, or offering to accept—a valuable consideration in compromising or attempting to compromise the claim; and

(2) conduct or a statement made during compromise negotiations about the claim—except when offered in a criminal case and when the negotiations related to a claim by a public office in the exercise of its regulatory, investigative, or enforcement authority.

(b) Exceptions. The court may admit this evidence for another purpose, such as proving a witness's bias or prejudice, negating a contention of undue delay, or proving an effort to obstruct a criminal investigation or prosecution.

See selected Notes of Advisory Committee to FRE 408, p. 1247.

History of FRE 408: Adopted Jan. 2, 1975, P.L. 93-595, §1, 88 Stat. 1926, eff. July 1, 1975. Amended Apr. 12, 2006, eff. Dec. 1, 2006; Apr. 26, 2011, eff. Dec. 1, 2011.

See *Commentaries*, "Motion in Limine," ch. 5-H, p. 341; *O'Connor's Federal Civil Forms* (2012), FORMS 5H.

ANNOTATIONS

In re MSTG, Inc., 675 F.3d 1337, 1345-46 (Fed.Cir. 2012). "Rule 408 … contemplates a host of scenarios under which documents related to settlement negotiations would be admissible for purposes other than 'prov[ing] or disprov[ing] the validity or amount of a disputed claim or … impeach[ing] by a prior inconsistent statement or a contradiction.' For example, settlement negotiation evidence would be admissible where the settlement itself or its interpretation is at issue or where evidence of the ingredients of the settlement might be relevant to an issue of double recovery. Documents related to settlement negotiations would typically be relevant and discoverable to the extent that such evidence would be admissible under Rule 408."

Portugues-Santana v. Rekomdiv Int'l, 657 F.3d 56, 63 (1st Cir.2011). The prohibition under FRE 408 "applies equally to settlement agreements between a defendant and a third party and between a plaintiff and a third party. This is so because '[t]he admission of such evidence would discourage settlements in either case.'"

Lyondell Chem. Co. v. Occidental Chem. Corp., 608 F.3d 284, 296-98 (5th Cir.2010). "Courts vary widely in their understanding of the term ['claim'], and thus in their understanding of when evidence is introduced to prove liability for, invalidity of, or the amount of *the claim* subject to compromise. Most do agree that 'claim' does not mean 'legal claim' and that, as a result, '[t]he dispute being settled need not be the one being tried in the case where the settlement is being offered in order for Rule 408 to bar its admission.' [¶] Caselaw … can be organized around a loose 'transactional' test. Four circuits—including this one—have applied Rule 408 to distinct legal claims arising out of a common event. Other circuits have gone further, applying the rule to distinct legal claims arising, for example, out of the same failed business relationship…. On the other

hand, settlement evidence is not inadmissible merely because it relates to circumstances that are 'similar' to those being litigated. [¶] The Seventh Circuit eschews any strict 'transaction' test, but looks to 'the spirit and purpose of the rule and decide[s] whether the need for the settlement evidence outweighs the potentially chilling effect on future settlement negotiations.' That balance is said to more likely 'tip in favor of admitting evidence when the settlement communications at issue arise out of a dispute distinct from the one for which the evidence is being offered.' [¶] We too decline to adopt any rigid definition of 'claim.' Our application of Rule 408 has been and remains fact-specific, and tethered to the rationales underlying the rule." *See also* ***Weems v. Tyson Foods, Inc.***, 665 F.3d 958, 965 (8th Cir.2011) (dispute is considered within scope of FRE 408 when there is actual dispute or difference of opinion about party's liability for or amount of claim); ***Affiliated Mfrs. v. Aluminum Co.***, 56 F.3d 521, 528 (3d Cir.1995) (compromise is considered within scope of FRE 408 when it occurs during litigation or at less formal stages of dispute); ***Pierce v. F.R. Tripler & Co.***, 955 F.2d 820, 827 (2d Cir.1992) (compromise is considered within scope of FRE 408 when party is represented by counsel, threatens litigation, and has initiated administrative steps in that litigation).

U.S. v. Davis, 596 F.3d 852, 859 (D.C.Cir.2010). "Offers to settle are excluded even if no settlement negotiations follow. [FRE 408] is meant to promote settlements. If one party attempts to initiate negotiations with a settlement offer, the offer is excluded from evidence even if the counterparty responds: 'I'm not negotiating with you.' It makes no sense to force the party who initiates negotiations to do so at his peril."

Lohman v. Duryea Borough, 574 F.3d 163, 167-68 (3d Cir.2009). "Rule 408 does not bar a court's consideration of settlement negotiations in its analysis of what constitutes a reasonable fee award in a particular case. [¶] While evidence of settlement negotiations is inadmissible to prove the merit or lack of merit of a claim, the use of such evidence as bearing on the issue of what relief was sought by a plaintiff does not offend the clear terms of Rule 408. Such evidence can be relevant when comparing what a plaintiff 'requested' to what the plaintiff was ultimately 'awarded.' … While evidence of settlement negotiations is only one indicator of the measure of success, it is a permissible indicator that is not precluded by Rule 408."

EEOC v. UMB Bank Fin. Corp., 558 F.3d 784, 791 (8th Cir.2009). "The spirit of [FRE 408] supports the exclusion of certain work product, internal memos, and other materials created specifically for the purpose of conciliation, even if not communicated to the other party. [W]e agree that it is appropriate to view Rule 408 as being sufficiently broad to encompass certain material in addition to actual offers of settlement."

Stockman v. Oakcrest Dental Ctr., P.C., 480 F.3d 791, 798 (6th Cir.2007). FRE 408 "exceptions have been used only to admit the occurrence of settlement talks or the settlement agreement itself for 'another purpose.' We have also viewed 'another purpose' as including the use of settlement agreements to prove facts unrelated to the subject matter of the negotiations or where the claim was based upon some wrong that was committed in the course of the settlement discussions; e.g., libel, assault, breach of contract, unfair labor practice, and the like." (Internal quotes omitted.)

Uforma/Shelby Bus. Forms, Inc. v. NLRB, 111 F.3d 1284, 1294 (6th Cir.1997). "Evidence of the compromise of a claim different than the claim currently in dispute … is admissible unless 'the compromise evidence require[s] an inference as to the offeror's belief concerning the validity or invalidity of the compromised claim.' [¶] [W]e hold that Rule 408 does not exclude evidence of alleged threats to retaliate for protected activity when the statements occurred during negotiations focused on the protected activity and the evidence serves to prove liability either for making, or later acting upon, the threats." *See also* ***Towerridge, Inc. v. T.A.O., Inc.***, 111 F.3d 758, 770 (10th Cir.1997) (evidence of settlement negotiations from separate suit not precluded when offered to prove D acted in bad faith); ***Coakley & Williams Constr., Inc. v. Structural Concrete Equip., Inc.***, 973 F.2d 349, 353-54 (4th Cir.1992) (evidence of settlement negotiations from previous suit not precluded when offered to prove party's intent regarding release).

FRE 409. OFFERS TO PAY MEDICAL & SIMILAR EXPENSES

Evidence of furnishing, promising to pay, or offering to pay medical, hospital, or similar expenses resulting from an injury is not admissible to prove liability for the injury.

History of FRE 409: Adopted Jan. 2, 1975, P.L. 93-595, §1, 88 Stat. 1926, eff. July 1, 1975. Amended Apr. 26, 2011, eff. Dec. 1, 2011.

See *Commentaries*, "Motion in Limine," ch. 5-H, p. 341; *O'Connor's Federal Civil Forms* (2012), FORMS 5H.

Effective December 1, 2011, FREs 101-1103 were restyled. For a discussion of the changes and a chart comparing the former and current rules, see p. 1024.

FRE 410. PLEAS, PLEA DISCUSSIONS, & RELATED STATEMENTS

(a) **Prohibited Uses.** In a civil or criminal case, evidence of the following is not admissible against the defendant who made the plea or participated in the plea discussions:

(1) a guilty plea that was later withdrawn;

(2) a nolo contendere plea;

(3) a statement made during a proceeding on either of those pleas under Federal Rule of Criminal Procedure 11 or a comparable state procedure; or

(4) a statement made during plea discussions with an attorney for the prosecuting authority if the discussions did not result in a guilty plea or they resulted in a later-withdrawn guilty plea.

(b) **Exceptions.** The court may admit a statement described in Rule 410(a)(3) or (4):

(1) in any proceeding in which another statement made during the same plea or plea discussions has been introduced, if in fairness the statements ought to be considered together; or

(2) in a criminal proceeding for perjury or false statement, if the defendant made the statement under oath, on the record, and with counsel present.

History of FRE 410: Adopted Jan. 2, 1975, P.L. 93-595, §1, 88 Stat. 1926, eff. July 1, 1975. Amended Dec. 12, 1975, P.L. 94-149, §1(9), 89 Stat. 805; Apr. 30, 1979, eff. Dec. 1, 1980; Apr. 26, 2011, eff. Dec. 1, 2011.

See *Commentaries*, "Motion in Limine," ch. 5-H, p. 341; *O'Connor's Federal Civil Forms* (2012), FORMS 5H.

ANNOTATIONS

U.S. v. Mitchell, 633 F.3d 997, 1003 (10th Cir.2011). "Rule 410 grew out of longstanding case law excluding [withdrawn guilty pleas]. As far back as [1927], the Supreme Court has held withdrawn guilty pleas could not be entered into evidence in a subsequent trial for the same offense. Rejecting the common law argument that a withdrawn guilty plea was more or less a form of prior testimony, the Court reasoned a plea 'shown to have been unfairly obtained or given through ignorance, fear or inadvertence' should not be admissible. When a court allows a defendant to withdraw a guilty plea, it makes the implicit determination the plea should 'be held for naught,' and thus admitting the withdrawn plea into evidence would be 'in direct conflict with that determination.'"

U.S. v. Barrow, 400 F.3d 109, 116 (2d Cir.2005). "The underlying purpose of Rule 410 is to promote plea negotiations by permitting defendants to talk to prosecutors without sacrificing their ability to defend themselves if no disposition agreement is reached. Statements made by defendants in proffer sessions are covered by Rule 410. [¶] Because Rule 410 is an exception to the general principle that all relevant evidence is admissible at trial …, its limitations are 'not to be read broadly….' Moreover, its protections are waivable. *At 119:* A waiver agreement between the parties does not divest a district court of its considerable discretion to exclude relevant evidence that may inject 'unfair prejudice' or 'confusion' into the jury's resolution of the issues in dispute."

FRE 411. LIABILITY INSURANCE

Evidence that a person was or was not insured against liability is not admissible to prove whether the person acted negligently or otherwise wrongfully. But the court may admit this evidence for another purpose, such as proving a witness's bias or prejudice or proving agency, ownership, or control.

See selected Notes of Advisory Committee to FRE 411, p. 1248.

History of FRE 411: Adopted Jan. 2, 1975, P.L. 93-595, §1, 88 Stat. 1926, eff. July 1, 1975. Amended Mar. 2, 1987, eff. Oct. 1, 1987; Apr. 26, 2011, eff. Dec. 1, 2011.

See *Commentaries*, "Motion in Limine," ch. 5-H, p. 341; *O'Connor's Federal Civil Forms* (2012), FORMS 5H.

ANNOTATIONS

Conde v. Starlight I, Inc., 103 F.3d 210, 214 (1st Cir.1997). "Rule 411 does permit mention of insurance coverage, not to prove negligence, but collaterally to show the possible 'bias or prejudice of a witness.'"

FRE 412. SEX-OFFENSE CASES: THE VICTIM'S SEXUAL BEHAVIOR OR PREDISPOSITION

(a) **Prohibited Uses.** The following evidence is not admissible in a civil or criminal proceeding involving alleged sexual misconduct:

(1) evidence offered to prove that a victim engaged in other sexual behavior; or

(2) evidence offered to prove a victim's sexual predisposition.

(b) **Exceptions.**

(1) ***Criminal Cases.*** The court may admit the following evidence in a criminal case:

(A) evidence of specific instances of a victim's sexual behavior, if offered to prove that

FRE 410

someone other than the defendant was the source of semen, injury, or other physical evidence;

(B) evidence of specific instances of a victim's sexual behavior with respect to the person accused of the sexual misconduct, if offered by the defendant to prove consent or if offered by the prosecutor; and

(C) evidence whose exclusion would violate the defendant's constitutional rights.

(2) ***Civil Cases.*** In a civil case, the court may admit evidence offered to prove a victim's sexual behavior or sexual predisposition if its probative value substantially outweighs the danger of harm to any victim and of unfair prejudice to any party. The court may admit evidence of a victim's reputation only if the victim has placed it in controversy.

(c) Procedure to Determine Admissibility.

(1) ***Motion.*** If a party intends to offer evidence under Rule 412(b), the party must:

(A) file a motion that specifically describes the evidence and states the purpose for which it is to be offered;

(B) do so at least 14 days before trial unless the court, for good cause, sets a different time;

(C) serve the motion on all parties; and

(D) notify the victim or, when appropriate, the victim's guardian or representative.

(2) ***Hearing.*** Before admitting evidence under this rule, the court must conduct an in camera hearing and give the victim and parties a right to attend and be heard. Unless the court orders otherwise, the motion, related materials, and the record of the hearing must be and remain sealed.

(d) Definition of "Victim." In this rule, "victim" includes an alleged victim.

See selected Notes of Advisory Committee to FRE 412, p. 1248.

History of FRE 412: Adopted Oct. 28, 1978, P.L. 95-540, §2(a), 92 Stat. 2046. Amended Nov. 18, 1988, P.L. 100-690, §7046(a), 102 Stat. 4400; Apr. 29, 1994, eff. Dec. 1, 1994; Sept. 13, 1994, P.L. 103-322, §40141(b), 108 Stat. 1919, eff. Dec. 1, 1994; Apr. 26, 2011, eff. Dec. 1, 2011.

ANNOTATIONS

U.S. v. Courtright, 632 F.3d 363, 368-69 (7th Cir. 2011). See annotation under FRE 413, p. 1042.

U.S. v. Papakee, 573 F.3d 569, 573 (8th Cir.2009). "[A] sexual proposition is 'other sexual behavior' within the meaning of Rule 412(a)(1). The ordinary meaning of 'behavior' extends to the manner in which a person conducts herself, … and when a person undertakes conduct aimed at engaging in sexual activity, that conduct is naturally understood to be 'sexual behavior.' There is no reason to believe that the rule is limited to sexual intercourse or sexual contact. To the contrary, … the word 'behavior' should be construed to include 'activities of the mind,' such as fantasies or dreams. If a person's unexpressed desire to engage in sexual activity is inadmissible, then surely her expression of that desire to another person also comes within the scope of the rule."

B.K.B. v. Maui Police Dept., 276 F.3d 1091, 1104 (9th Cir.2002). "[I]n a sexual harassment lawsuit as in any civil case, evidence offered to prove a victim's sexual behavior or sexual predisposition is admissible (if it is otherwise admissible) only if 'its probative value substantially outweighs the danger of harm to any victim and of unfair prejudice to any party.' With respect to [FRE 412(b)(2)], the Advisory Committee Notes clarify that the balancing test to be employed in assessing whether to admit proposed evidence is 'more stringent' than that governing [FRE] 403…." *See also* ***Rodriguez-Hernandez v. Miranda-Velez***, 132 F.3d 848, 856 (1st Cir.1998).

Wolak v. Spucci, 217 F.3d 157, 159-60 (2d Cir. 2000). "Rule 412 … states that evidence of an alleged victim's 'sexual behavior' or 'sexual predisposition' is inadmissible, with limited exceptions, in all 'civil or criminal proceeding[s] involving alleged sexual misconduct.' The Rule's expanded protection 'aims to safeguard the alleged victim against the invasion of privacy, potential embarrassment and sexual stereotyping that is associated with public disclosure of intimate sexual details and the infusion of sexual innuendo into the factfinding process.' In a civil case, 'otherwise admissible' evidence may only be introduced if the proponent can show that 'its probative value substantially outweighs the danger of harm to any victim and of unfair prejudice to any party.' [¶] We hold that Rule 412, which explicitly includes civil cases involving sexual misconduct, encompasses sexual harassment lawsuits. Thus, we find that the district court erred in concluding that Rule 412 did not govern the admissibility of evidence of [P's] sexual behavior."

FRE 412

Effective December 1, 2011, FREs 101-1103 were restyled. For a discussion of the changes and a chart comparing the former and current rules, see p. 1024.

FRE 413. SIMILAR CRIMES IN SEXUAL-ASSAULT CASES

(a) **Permitted Uses.** In a criminal case in which a defendant is accused of a sexual assault, the court may admit evidence that the defendant committed any other sexual assault. The evidence may be considered on any matter to which it is relevant.

(b) **Disclosure to the Defendant.** If the prosecutor intends to offer this evidence, the prosecutor must disclose it to the defendant, including witnesses' statements or a summary of the expected testimony. The prosecutor must do so at least 15 days before trial or at a later time that the court allows for good cause.

(c) **Effect on Other Rules.** This rule does not limit the admission or consideration of evidence under any other rule.

(d) **Definition of "Sexual Assault."** In this rule and Rule 415, "sexual assault" means a crime under federal law or under state law (as "state" is defined in 18 U.S.C. §513) involving:

(1) any conduct prohibited by 18 U.S.C. chapter 109A;

(2) contact, without consent, between any part of the defendant's body—or an object—and another person's genitals or anus;

(3) contact, without consent, between the defendant's genitals or anus and any part of another person's body;

(4) deriving sexual pleasure or gratification from inflicting death, bodily injury, or physical pain on another person; or

(5) an attempt or conspiracy to engage in conduct described in subparagraphs (1)-(4).

See selected Congressional Discussion to FRE 413, p. 1251.

History of FRE 413: Adopted Sept. 13, 1994, P.L. 103-322, §320935(a), 108 Stat. 2135, eff. July 9, 1995. Amended Apr. 26, 2011, eff. Dec. 1, 2011.

ANNOTATIONS

U.S. v. O'Connor, 650 F.3d 839, 853 (2d Cir.2011). "Courts confronted with remote-in-time evidence offered under [FRE] 413 or [FRE] 414 should conduct a fact-specific and case-specific analysis[.] 'Exclusion of proof of other acts that are too remote in time caters principally to the dual concerns for relevance and reliability. The evaluation of the proffered evidence in light of these concerns must be made on a case-by-case basis to determine whether the significance of the prior acts has become too attenuated and whether the memories of the witnesses has likely become too frail. Neither [FRE] 403 nor any analogous Rule provides any bright-line rule as to how old is too old.' [W]e [have previously] found no abuse of discretion in the admission of testimony about acts that occurred 16 to 20 years before the trial where '[t]he similarity of the events clearly demonstrated the ... testimony's relevance.'" *See also* ***U.S. v. Horn***, 523 F.3d 882, 888-89 (8th Cir.2008).

U.S. v. Courtright, 632 F.3d 363, 368-69 (7th Cir. 2011). "[T]he district court interpreted the word 'accused' broadly, holding that [FRE] 413 is triggered when a defendant has been verbally accused of sexual assault during the course of an investigation into a separate offense. [¶] We do not agree with the district court's reading of Rule 413. [A]t the time Rule 413 was drafted (and today), the word 'accused' was often used in a technical sense to describe someone who was charged with a crime. [¶] We find additional support for this reading of Rule 413 in nearby [FRE] 412. Rule 412 permits the admission of a victim's sexual behavior by the accused in certain limited circumstances. The committee notes to Rule 412 specify that, for this Rule, 'accused' is meant in a broader, 'non-technical sense,' and that there is 'no requirement that there be a criminal charge pending against the person or even that the misconduct would constitute a criminal offense' before evidence of a victim's sexual behavior can be admitted. Rule 413 provides no similar clarification for the use of the word 'accused,' nor do the rest of the rules. [¶] We therefore conclude that Rule 413 uses the term 'accused' in the more narrow, technical sense generally invoked throughout the federal rules."

Seeley v. Chase, 443 F.3d 1290, 1294-95 (10th Cir. 2006). "Evidence of prior sexual assaults may be admitted under [FRE] 413 if (1) the defendant is on trial for a sexual assault offense, (2) the evidence proffered is of another sexual assault, and (3) the court finds the evidence is relevant. To be relevant, 'the evidence must show both that the defendant has particular propensity, and that the propensity it demonstrates has a bearing on the charged crime.' Finally, the trial court 'must make a reasoned, *recorded* finding that the prejudicial value of the evidence does not substantially outweigh its probative value' under [FRE] 403. The court must give 'careful attention to both the significant probative value and the strong prejudicial qualities inherent in all

evidence submitted under 413.'" *See also **U.S. v. McHorse***, 179 F.3d 889, 897-98 (10th Cir.1999).

U.S. v. Sumner, 119 F.3d 658, 661 (8th Cir.1997). FREs 413, 414, and 415 "were enacted as companion rules by Congress as part of the Violent Crime Control and Law Enforcement Act of 1994.... *At 662:* 'The practical effect of the new rules is to put evidence of uncharged offenses in sexual assault and child molestation cases on the same footing as other types of relevant evidence that are not subject to a special exclusionary rule. The presumption is in favor of admission. The underlying legislative judgment is that the evidence admissible pursuant to the proposed rules is typically relevant and probative, and that its probative value is normally not outweighed by any risk of prejudice or other adverse effects.'"

FRE 414. SIMILAR CRIMES IN CHILD-MOLESTATION CASES

(a) Permitted Uses. In a criminal case in which a defendant is accused of child molestation, the court may admit evidence that the defendant committed any other child molestation. The evidence may be considered on any matter to which it is relevant.

(b) Disclosure to the Defendant. If the prosecutor intends to offer this evidence, the prosecutor must disclose it to the defendant, including witnesses' statements or a summary of the expected testimony. The prosecutor must do so at least 15 days before trial or at a later time that the court allows for good cause.

(c) Effect on Other Rules. This rule does not limit the admission or consideration of evidence under any other rule.

(d) Definition of "Child" and "Child Molestation." In this rule and Rule 415:

(1) "child" means a person below the age of 14; and

(2) "child molestation" means a crime under federal law or under state law (as "state" is defined in 18 U.S.C. §513) involving:

(A) any conduct prohibited by 18 U.S.C. chapter 109A and committed with a child;

(B) any conduct prohibited by 18 U.S.C. chapter 110;

(C) contact between any part of the defendant's body—or an object—and a child's genitals or anus;

(D) contact between the defendant's genitals or anus and any part of a child's body;

(E) deriving sexual pleasure or gratification from inflicting death, bodily injury, or physical pain on a child; or

(F) an attempt or conspiracy to engage in conduct described in subparagraphs (A)-(E).

See selected Congressional Discussion to FRE 414, p. 1251.

History of FRE 414: Adopted Sept. 13, 1994, P.L. 103-322, §320935(a), 108 Stat. 2135, eff. July 9, 1995. Amended Apr. 26, 2011, eff. Dec. 1, 2011.

ANNOTATIONS

U.S. v. O'Connor, 650 F.3d 839, 853 (2d Cir.2011). See annotation under FRE 413, p. 1042.

U.S. v. Kelly, 510 F.3d 433, 437 (4th Cir.2007). "[E]ven if a prior conviction qualifies for admission under [FRE] 414, evidence of that conviction may nonetheless [be excluded under FRE 403]. In applying the Rule 403 balancing test to prior offenses admissible under Rule 414, a district court should consider a number of factors, including (i) the similarity between the previous offense and the charged crime, (ii) the temporal proximity between the two crimes, (iii) the frequency of the prior acts, (iv) the presence or absence of any intervening acts, and (v) the reliability of the evidence of the past offense." *See also **U.S. v. Summage***, 575 F.3d 864, 877 (8th Cir.2009).

U.S. v. Sumner, 119 F.3d 658, 661 (8th Cir.1997). See annotation under FRE 413, this page.

FRE 415. SIMILAR ACTS IN CIVIL CASES INVOLVING SEXUAL ASSAULT OR CHILD MOLESTATION

(a) Permitted Uses. In a civil case involving a claim for relief based on a party's alleged sexual assault or child molestation, the court may admit evidence that the party committed any other sexual assault or child molestation. The evidence may be considered as provided in Rules 413 and 414.

(b) Disclosure to the Opponent. If a party intends to offer this evidence, the party must disclose it to the party against whom it will be offered, including witnesses' statements or a summary of the expected testimony. The party must do so at least 15 days before trial or at a later time that the court allows for good cause.

(c) Effect on Other Rules. This rule does not limit the admission or consideration of evidence under any other rule.

Effective December 1, 2011, FREs 101-1103 were restyled. For a discussion of the changes and a chart comparing the former and current rules, see p. 1024.

See selected Congressional Discussion to FRE 415, p. 1251.

History of FRE 415: Adopted Sept. 13, 1994, P.L. 103-322, §320935(a), 108 Stat. 2135, eff. July 9, 1995. Amended Apr. 26, 2011, eff. Dec. 1, 2011.

ANNOTATIONS

Martinez v. Cui, 608 F.3d 54, 60-61 (1st Cir.2010). "After [FREs] 413-415 were enacted, the question arose whether evidence admissible under these rules was subject to [FRE] 403's balancing test…. [¶] Some appellate courts have imposed external, judicially crafted rules as to district judges' consideration of evidence under Rule 415. [¶] [But we] have no reason to adopt special rules constraining district courts' usual exercise of discretion under Rule 403 when considering evidence under Rule 415…. [¶] Of course district courts must apply Rule 403 with awareness that Rule 415 reflects a congressional judgment to remove the propensity bar to admissibility of certain evidence. That awareness includes the fact that the Rule 403 analysis also applies. Nothing in the text of Rules 413-415 suggests these rules somehow change Rule 403."

Seeley v. Chase, 443 F.3d 1290, 1294 (10th Cir. 2006). "This court has not addressed at length the requirements for admitting prior sexual assault testimony under [FRE] 415. We have, however, discussed these requirements in the context of [FRE] 413, which covers admission of prior sexual assaults in the context of a criminal trial. *At 1295:* Although we have not specifically stated that a district court must follow these procedures when applying Rule 415, we have stated that [a court] must 'make a reasoned, recorded statement of its [FRE] 403 decision when it admits evidence under [FREs] 413-415.' Moreover, we have noted that Rule 413 and Rule 415 are 'companion' rules. As such, … a district court must follow the same procedure for determining whether evidence is admissible under Rule 415 as it would when admitting evidence under Rule 413." *See also* annotation under FRE 413, p. 1042; ***Johnson v. Elk Lake Sch. Dist.***, 283 F.3d 138, 143-44 (3d Cir.2002).

ARTICLE V. PRIVILEGES

FRE 501. PRIVILEGE IN GENERAL

The common law—as interpreted by United States courts in the light of reason and experience—governs a claim of privilege unless any of the following provides otherwise:

- the United States Constitution;
- a federal statute; or
- rules prescribed by the Supreme Court.

But in a civil case, state law governs privilege regarding a claim or defense for which state law supplies the rule of decision.

See selected Notes of Committee on the Judiciary to FRE 501, p. 1252.

History of FRE 501: Adopted Jan. 2, 1975, P.L. 93-595, §1, 88 Stat. 1926, eff. July 1, 1975. Amended Apr. 26, 2011, eff. Dec. 1, 2011.

See *Commentaries*, "What Is Not Discoverable?," ch. 6-B, §3, p. 460.

ANNOTATIONS

Generally

University of Pa. v. EEOC, 493 U.S. 182, 189 (1990). "We do not create and apply an evidentiary privilege unless it 'promotes sufficiently important interests to outweigh the need for probative evidence….' [¶] [A]lthough Rule 501 manifests a congressional desire 'not to freeze the law of privilege' but rather to provide the courts with flexibility to develop rules of privilege on a case-by-case basis, … we are disinclined to exercise this authority expansively. We are especially reluctant to recognize a privilege in an area where it appears that Congress has considered the relevant competing concerns but has not provided the privilege itself. The balancing of conflicting interests of this type is particularly a legislative function."

Carman v. McDonnell Douglas Corp., 114 F.3d 790, 794 (8th Cir.1997). "To justify the creation of a privilege, [the proponent of the privilege] must first establish that society benefits in some significant way from the particular brand of confidentiality that the privilege affords. Only then can a court decide whether the advantages of the proposed privilege overcome the strong presumption in favor of disclosure of all relevant information."

Hancock v. Hobbs, 967 F.2d 462, 466-67 (11th Cir. 1992). "Rule 501 is not clear as to which rule of decision should be followed when the federal and state laws of privilege are in conflict. … We therefore hold that the federal law of privilege provides the rule of decision in a civil proceeding where the court's jurisdiction is premised upon a federal question, even if the witness-testimony is relevant to a pendent state law count which may be controlled by a contrary state law of privilege." *See also* ***Agster v. Maricopa Cty.***, 422 F.3d 836, 839 (9th Cir.2005); ***EEOC v. Illinois Dept. of Empl. Sec.***, 995 F.2d 106, 107 (7th Cir.1993).

Attorney-Client Privilege

Swidler & Berlin v. U.S., 524 U.S. 399, 407 (1998). "Knowing that communications will remain confidential even after death encourages the client to communicate fully and frankly with counsel. While the fear of disclosure, and the consequent withholding of information from counsel, may be reduced if disclosure is limited to posthumous disclosure in a criminal context, it seems unreasonable to assume that it vanishes altogether. ... Posthumous disclosure of such communications may be as feared as disclosure during the client's lifetime."

U.S. v. Zolin, 491 U.S. 554, 562 (1989). "We have recognized the attorney-client privilege under federal law, as 'the oldest of the privileges for confidential communications known to the common law.' [The privilege's] central concern [is] 'to encourage full and frank communication between attorneys and their clients and thereby promote broader public interests in the observance of law and administration of justice.' That purpose ... requires that clients be free to 'make full disclosure to their attorneys' of past wrongdoings ... in order that the client may obtain 'the aid of persons having knowledge of the law and skilled in its practice....' *At 563:* It is the purpose of the crime-fraud exception to the attorney-client privilege to assure that the 'seal of secrecy[ ]' ... between lawyer and client does not extend to communications 'made for the purpose of getting advice for the commission of a fraud' or crime."

Journalist's Privilege

McKevitt v. Pallasch, 339 F.3d 530, 532 (7th Cir. 2003). "A large number of cases conclude ... that there is a reporter's privilege, though they do not agree on its scope. A few cases refuse to recognize the privilege.... Our court has not taken sides."

Shoen v. Shoen, 5 F.3d 1289, 1292 (9th Cir.1993). "[T]he journalist's privilege [is] a 'partial First Amendment shield' that protects journalists against compelled disclosure in all judicial proceedings, civil and criminal alike. *At 1293:* Before we weigh the competing interests ..., we must first decide two threshold legal questions ...: whether ... an investigative book author[ ] has standing to invoke the journalist's privilege, and whether the privilege operates to shield information provided by a source without an expectation of confidentiality." Held: Privilege applied.

von Bulow v. von Bulow, 811 F.2d 136, 144 (2d Cir. 1987). "We hold that the individual claiming the [journalist's] privilege must demonstrate, through competent evidence, the intent to use material—sought, gathered or received—to disseminate information to the public and that such intent existed at the inception of the newsgathering process. This requires an intent-based factual inquiry to be made by the district court. [¶] The intended manner of dissemination may be by newspaper, magazine, book, public or private broadcast medium, handbill or the like...."

Marital-Communications Privilege

Trammel v. U.S., 445 U.S. 40, 50-51 (1980). "Testimonial exclusionary rules and privileges contravene the fundamental principle that the public has a right to every man's evidence. As such, they must be strictly construed and accepted only to the very limited extent that permitting a refusal to testify or excluding relevant evidence has a public good transcending the normally predominant principle of utilizing all rational means for ascertaining truth. Here we must decide whether the privilege against adverse spousal testimony promotes sufficiently important interests to outweigh the need for probative evidence in the administration of criminal justice. *At 53:* [W]e conclude that the existing rule should be modified so that the witness-spouse alone has a privilege to refuse to testify adversely; the witness may be neither compelled to testify nor foreclosed from testifying." (Internal quotes omitted.) *See also* ***U.S. v. Acker***, 52 F.3d 509, 514 (4th Cir.1995).

U.S. v. Singleton, 260 F.3d 1295, 1300 (11th Cir. 2001). The marital-communications "privilege is not available when the parties are permanently separated; that is, living separately with no reasonable expectation of reconciliation."

Psychotherapist-Patient Privilege

Jaffee v. Redmond, 518 U.S. 1, 8-9 (1996). FRE 501 "did not freeze the law governing the privileges of witnesses in federal trials at a particular point in our history, but rather directed federal courts to 'continue the evolutionary development of testimonial privileges.' *At 15:* [W]e hold that confidential communications between a licensed psychotherapist and her patients in the course of diagnosis or treatment are protected from compelled disclosure under Rule 501.... [¶] [T]he federal privilege should also extend to confidential communications made to licensed social workers in the course of psychotherapy."

Effective December 1, 2011, FREs 101-1103 were restyled. For a discussion of the changes and a chart comparing the former and current rules, see p. 1024.

Miscellaneous Privileges

U.S. v. Weber Aircraft Corp., 465 U.S. 792, 796 (1984). "Confidential statements made to air crash safety investigators [are] privileged with respect to pretrial discovery [under the ***Machin v. Zukert***, 316 F.2d 336 (D.C.Cir.1963), privilege]. *At 803 n.25:* Congressional refusal to codify the ***Machin*** privilege [does not limit] the power of courts to recognize the privilege under Rule 501. Indeed, Rule 501 was adopted precisely because Congress wished to leave privilege questions to the courts rather than attempt to codify them."

Virmani v. Novant Health Inc., 259 F.3d 284, 293 (4th Cir.2001). "We hold that the interest in obtaining probative evidence in an action for discrimination outweighs the interest that would be furthered by recognition of a privilege for medical peer review materials. Therefore, we decline to recognize such a privilege." *See also* ***Memorial Hosp. v. Shadur***, 664 F.2d 1058, 1063 (7th Cir.1981).

FRE 502. ATTORNEY-CLIENT PRIVILEGE & WORK PRODUCT; LIMITATIONS ON WAIVER

The following provisions apply, in the circumstances set out, to disclosure of a communication or information covered by the attorney-client privilege or work-product protection.

(a) Disclosure Made in a Federal Proceeding or to a Federal Office or Agency; Scope of a Waiver. When the disclosure is made in a federal proceeding or to a federal office or agency and waives the attorney-client privilege or work-product protection, the waiver extends to an undisclosed communication or information in a federal or state proceeding only if:

(1) the waiver is intentional;

(2) the disclosed and undisclosed communications or information concern the same subject matter; and

(3) they ought in fairness to be considered together.

(b) Inadvertent Disclosure. When made in a federal proceeding or to a federal office or agency, the disclosure does not operate as a waiver in a federal or state proceeding if:

(1) the disclosure is inadvertent;

(2) the holder of the privilege or protection took reasonable steps to prevent disclosure; and

(3) the holder promptly took reasonable steps to rectify the error, including (if applicable) following Federal Rule of Civil Procedure 26(b)(5)(B).

(c) Disclosure Made in a State Proceeding. When the disclosure is made in a state proceeding and is not the subject of a state-court order concerning waiver, the disclosure does not operate as a waiver in a federal proceeding if the disclosure:

(1) would not be a waiver under this rule if it had been made in a federal proceeding; or

(2) is not a waiver under the law of the state where the disclosure occurred.

(d) Controlling Effect of a Court Order. A federal court may order that the privilege or protection is not waived by disclosure connected with the litigation pending before the court—in which event the disclosure is also not a waiver in any other federal or state proceeding.

(e) Controlling Effect of a Party Agreement. An agreement on the effect of disclosure in a federal proceeding is binding only on the parties to the agreement, unless it is incorporated into a court order.

(f) Controlling Effect of this Rule. Notwithstanding Rules 101 and 1101, this rule applies to state proceedings and to federal court-annexed and federal court-mandated arbitration proceedings, in the circumstances set out in the rule. And notwithstanding Rule 501, this rule applies even if state law provides the rule of decision.

(g) Definitions. In this rule:

(1) "attorney-client privilege" means the protection that applicable law provides for confidential attorney-client communications; and

(2) "work-product protection" means the protection that applicable law provides for tangible material (or its intangible equivalent) prepared in anticipation of litigation or for trial.

See selected Notes of Advisory Committee, Explanatory Note, and Statement of Congressional Intent to FRE 502, p. 1253.

History of FRE 502: Adopted Sept. 19, 2008, P.L. 110-322, §1, 122 Stat. 3537. Effective date: The amendments made by this Act shall apply in all proceedings commenced after the date of enactment of this Act and, insofar as is just and practicable, in all proceedings pending on such date of enactment. Amended Apr. 26, 2011, eff. Dec. 1, 2011.

FRE 501

See *Commentaries*, "Asserting claims of privilege & protection," ch. 6-A, §4.4.5(4), p. 417; "Disclosure of privileged or protected information – attorney-related privileges," ch. 6-A, §9.3.2, p. 432; *O'Connor's Federal Civil Forms* (2012), FORMS 6A:5, 20-22.

ARTICLE VI. WITNESSES

FRE 601. COMPETENCY TO TESTIFY IN GENERAL

Every person is competent to be a witness unless these rules provide otherwise. But in a civil case, state law governs the witness's competency regarding a claim or defense for which state law supplies the rule of decision.

History of FRE 601: Adopted Jan. 2, 1975, P.L. 93-595, §1, 88 Stat. 1926, eff. July 1, 1975. Amended Apr. 26, 2011, eff. Dec. 1, 2011.

ANNOTATIONS

Estate of Suskovich v. Anthem Health Plans, 553 F.3d 559, 570 (7th Cir.2009). "[W]here state law provides a federal court with the grounds for its decisions, that court should ... apply state law restrictions on the competency of witnesses. The evidentiary standard in a case ... where both federal and state law claims are involved[ ] is less certain. District courts in this circuit ... have ... held that [FRE] 601, which creates a broad presumption of competency, applies to cases alleging both federal and state law claims. '[I]f the rule ... results in two conflicting bodies of privilege law applying to the same piece of evidence in the same case, ... the rule favoring reception of the evidence should be applied.' Accordingly, [we apply] Rule 601 ... to the competency of witnesses, at least insofar as the evidence relates to any of the federal claims." *See also* ***Rosenfeld v. Basquiat***, 78 F.3d 84, 88 (2d Cir.1996) (applying state competency law in diversity case).

U.S. v. Bedonie, 913 F.2d 782, 799 (10th Cir.1990). "'A witness wholly without capacity is difficult to imagine. The question is one particularly suited to the jury as one of weight and credibility, subject to judicial authority to review the sufficiency of the evidence.' *At 800:* 'There is no rule which excludes an insane person as such, or a child of any specified age, from testifying, but in each case the traditional test is whether the witness has intelligence enough to make it worthwhile to hear him at all and whether he feels a duty to tell the truth....'"

U.S. v. Moreno, 899 F.2d 465, 469 (6th Cir.1990). "What ... is often confused, is that 'competency' is a matter of status not ability. Thus, the only two groups of persons specifically rendered incompetent as witnesses by the [FREs] are judges ([FRE] 605) and jurors ([FRE] 606)." (Internal quotes omitted.)

U.S. v. Roman, 884 F.Supp. 126, 127 (S.D.N.Y.1995). "Whether a witness is competent to testify depends on the individual's ability to observe, to remember, to communicate, and to understand that the oath imposes a duty to tell the truth. Competency is usually an issue for the trier of fact."

FRE 602. NEED FOR PERSONAL KNOWLEDGE

A witness may testify to a matter only if evidence is introduced sufficient to support a finding that the witness has personal knowledge of the matter. Evidence to prove personal knowledge may consist of the witness's own testimony. This rule does not apply to a witness's expert testimony under Rule 703.

History of FRE 602: Adopted Jan. 2, 1975, P.L. 93-595, §1, 88 Stat. 1926, eff. July 1, 1975. Amended Mar. 2, 1987, eff. Oct. 1, 1987; Apr. 25, 1988, eff. Nov. 1, 1988; Apr. 26, 2011, eff. Dec. 1, 2011.

ANNOTATIONS

U.S. v. Franklin, 415 F.3d 537, 549 (6th Cir.2005). "The threshold for admitting testimony under Rule 602 is 'low.' 'Testimony should not be excluded for lack of personal knowledge unless no reasonable juror could believe that the witness had the ability and opportunity to perceive the event that he testifies about.'"

Payne v. Pauley, 337 F.3d 767, 772 (7th Cir.2003). "[A]lthough personal knowledge may include reasonable inferences, those inferences must be 'grounded in observation or other first-hand personal experience. They must not be flights of fancy, speculations, hunches, intuitions, or rumors about matters remote from that experience.'"

U.S. v. Sinclair, 109 F.3d 1527, 1536 (10th Cir. 1997). "Although Rule 602 provides that a witness's testimony must be based on personal knowledge, it 'does not require that the witness' knowledge be positive or rise to the level of absolute certainty. Evidence is inadmissible ... only if in the proper exercise of the trial court's discretion it finds that the witness could not have actually perceived or observed that which he testifies to.'" *See also* ***U.S. v. Brown***, 669 F.3d 10, 22 (1st Cir. 2012).

SEC v. Singer, 786 F.Supp. 1158, 1167 (S.D.N.Y. 1992). "Testimony is admissible even though the witness is not positive about what he perceived, provided the witness had an opportunity to observe and obtained some impressions based on his observations. [¶] Tes-

FRE 602

timony can be admissible under Rule 602 even if the witness has only a broad general recollection of the subject matter. [¶] [A] witness' *conclusion based on personal observations over time* may constitute personal knowledge despite the witness' inability to recall the specific incidents upon which he based his conclusions."

FRE 603. OATH OR AFFIRMATION TO TESTIFY TRUTHFULLY

Before testifying, a witness must give an oath or affirmation to testify truthfully. It must be in a form designed to impress that duty on the witness's conscience.

History of FRE 603: Adopted Jan. 2, 1975, P.L. 93-595, §1, 88 Stat. 1926, eff. July 1, 1975. Amended Mar. 2, 1987, eff. Oct. 1, 1987; Apr. 26, 2011, eff. Dec. 1, 2011.

ANNOTATIONS

U.S. v. Solorio, 669 F.3d 943, 950 (9th Cir.2012). See annotation under FRE 604, this page.

U.S. v. Frazier, 469 F.3d 85, 92 (3d Cir.2006). "Oaths are administered to witnesses as a reminder to them of their obligation to testify *truthfully*. They are not intended to guarantee *accuracy*. The fact that a witness is under oath has no bearing on the quality of a witness' memory (such that one is more or less likely to make a mistake under oath)." *See also* ***U.S. v. Zizzo***, 120 F.3d 1338, 1348 (7th Cir.1997) (idea of oath is to make witness amenable to perjury prosecution if he lies).

U.S. v. Ward, 989 F.2d 1015, 1019 (9th Cir.1992). FRE 603 "'is designed to afford the flexibility required in dealing with religious adults, atheists, conscientious objectors, mental defectives, and children. Affirmation is simply a solemn undertaking to tell the truth; no special verbal formula is required.'" *See also* ***Doe v. Phillips***, 81 F.3d 1204, 1211 (2d Cir.1996); ***U.S. v. Saget***, 991 F.2d 702, 710 (11th Cir.1993).

FRE 604. INTERPRETER

An interpreter must be qualified and must give an oath or affirmation to make a true translation.

History of FRE 604: Adopted Jan. 2, 1975, P.L. 93-595, §1, 88 Stat. 1926, eff. July 1, 1975. Amended Mar. 2, 1987, eff. Oct. 1, 1987; Apr. 26, 2011, eff. Dec. 1, 2011.

ANNOTATIONS

U.S. v. Solorio, 669 F.3d 943, 950 (9th Cir.2012). "[FRE] 604 does not … indicate whether … an oath must be administered in any particular manner or at any specified time, including whether the oath must be administered for each trial. … Although some courts administer oaths to interpreters each day, or once for an entire case, others 'administer the oath to staff and contract interpreters once, and keep it on file.' [¶] We agree with the courts that proceed in the latter fashion that there is no requirement that the oath be administered during each trial. Most telling in that regard is the absence of any such requirement—or any indication as to how or when interpreters are to be qualified and their oaths administered—in Rule 604. In contrast, [FRE] 603, applicable to witnesses, specifies that the oath must be administered '[b]efore testifying,' suggesting a temporal nexus to the actual appearance of each witness at a particular trial. Unlike witnesses, an interpreter's role is not limited to a specific trial, and there is no apparent reason the oath need be either. *At 951:* That Rule 604, which is specifically directed at interpreters, exists *in addition* to Rule 603 indicates that the two rules impose independent requirements that must *both* be met."

FRE 605. JUDGE'S COMPETENCY AS A WITNESS

The presiding judge may not testify as a witness at the trial. A party need not object to preserve the issue.

History of FRE 605: Adopted Jan. 2, 1975, P.L. 93-595, §1, 88 Stat. 1926, eff. July 1, 1975. Amended Apr. 26, 2011, eff. Dec. 1, 2011.

ANNOTATIONS

U.S. v. Bari, 599 F.3d 176, 179 n.4 (2d Cir.2010). FRE 605 "prohibits the judge presiding at the trial from testifying in that trial as a witness. [FRE] 201 permits a judge to take judicial notice of certain types of facts. Logically, then, if a fact is of a kind that a judge may properly take judicial notice of it, then he is not improperly 'testifying' at trial by noting that fact. Any other conclusion would lead to Rule 605 effectively subsuming Rule 201. If, after all, a judge was improperly testifying at trial each time he took judicial notice of a fact, it would be effectively impermissible to take judicial notice of any fact. Accordingly, we must first consider whether the judge was taking permissible judicial notice of a fact, pursuant to Rule 201. If he could not have taken judicial notice of that fact within the bounds of Rule 201—because, for example, it was not a 'matter[] of common knowledge'—then we consider whether the judge violated Rule 605."

U.S. v. Blanchard, 542 F.3d 1133, 1148-49 (7th Cir. 2008). "Although a district court judge may facilitate the jury's understanding of the case by questioning witnesses and explaining, summarizing, and commenting on the evidence, ... it is improper for the judge to add to the evidence by assuming the role of a witness.... Where a trial judge's comments are based upon his own personal knowledge of matters external to the trial, those comments may constitute impermissible judicial testimony."

U.S. v. Berber-Tinoco, 510 F.3d 1083, 1091 (9th Cir. 2007). "[T]he judge violated Rule 605 when he interjected his own observations regarding the location of the stop signs ... and the narrowness of the road.... At the time the judge first stated these facts, they were not in the record nor were they reasonable inferences from the record. [¶] A trial judge is not a competent witness to such factual issues. Nor can the judge take judicial notice of such issues. A trial judge is prohibited from relying on his personal experience to support the taking of judicial notice. It is therefore plainly accepted that the judge is not to use from the bench, under the guise of judicial knowledge, that which he knows *only as an individual* observer outside of court. ... While a resident judge's background knowledge of an area may inform the judge's assessment of the historical facts, ... the judge may not actually testify in the proceeding or interject facts (excluding facts for which proper judicial notice is taken). Therefore, the judge erred in making his observations about such issues." (Internal quotes omitted.)

U.S. v. Nickl, 427 F.3d 1286, 1293 (10th Cir.2005). "Rule 605's prohibition on judicial testimony eliminates difficult questions 'which arise when the judge abandons the bench for the witness stand. Who rules on objections? Who compels him to answer? Can he rule impartially on the weight and admissibility of his own testimony? Can he be impeached or cross-examined effectively?' Adherence to Rule 605 also prevents prejudice which may arise from a judge's testimony because of the judge's influential position with the jury."

FRE 606. JUROR'S COMPETENCY AS A WITNESS

(a) At the Trial. A juror may not testify as a witness before the other jurors at the trial. If a juror is called to testify, the court must give a party an opportunity to object outside the jury's presence.

(b) During an Inquiry into the Validity of a Verdict or Indictment.

(1) ***Prohibited Testimony or Other Evidence.*** During an inquiry into the validity of a verdict or indictment, a juror may not testify about any statement made or incident that occurred during the jury's deliberations; the effect of anything on that juror's or another juror's vote; or any juror's mental processes concerning the verdict or indictment. The court may not receive a juror's affidavit or evidence of a juror's statement on these matters.

(2) ***Exceptions.*** A juror may testify about whether:

(A) extraneous prejudicial information was improperly brought to the jury's attention;

(B) an outside influence was improperly brought to bear on any juror; or

(C) a mistake was made in entering the verdict on the verdict form.

See selected Notes of Advisory Committee to FRE 606, p. 1256.

History of FRE 606: Adopted Jan. 2, 1975, P.L. 93-595, §1, 88 Stat. 1926, eff. July 1, 1975. Amended Dec. 12, 1975, P.L. 94-149, §1(10), 89 Stat. 805; Mar. 2, 1987, eff. Oct. 1, 1987; Apr. 12, 2006, eff. Dec. 1, 2006; Apr. 26, 2011, eff. Dec. 1, 2011.

ANNOTATIONS

U.S. v. Jadlowe, 628 F.3d 1, 20-21 (1st Cir.2010). "Inquiries into jury deliberations are ... narrowly restricted by [FRE] 606(b).... The relevant inquiry ... is not into the nature of the formal deliberations that occurred once the presentation of evidence concluded, but the nature of any juror discussion about the case prior to the formal deliberations. Probing such premature discussions is neither impermissible nor impossible. Indeed, courts routinely examine allegations of juror misconduct involving improper external influences and communications among jurors.... The threshold question would be whether any premature discussion took place. If so, was it among all jurors or just a few? Did discussion occur regularly through the proceedings, or only once—and at what point? What was the content of the discussion?"

U.S. v. Villar, 586 F.3d 76, 83 (1st Cir.2009). "Rule 606(b)[, now Rule 606(b)(2),] contains three exceptions, two of which—'extraneous prejudicial information' and 'outside influence'—are relevant to our analysis. [¶] The 'external/internal distinction' ... is not a 'locational distinction' but rather is 'based on the nature of the allegation.' Juror testimony about a matter characterized as 'external' to the jury is admissible

Effective December 1, 2011, FREs 101-1103 were restyled. For a discussion of the changes and a chart comparing the former and current rules, see p. 1024.

under Rule 606(b), while testimony about 'internal' matters is barred by the Rule."

U.S. v. Benally, 546 F.3d 1230, 1235-36 (10th Cir. 2008). "It is true that juror testimony can be used to show dishonesty during voir dire, for purposes of contempt proceedings against the dishonest juror. Thus, if the purpose of the post-verdict proceeding were to charge the jury foreman or the other juror with contempt of court, Rule 606(b) would not apply. However, it does not follow that juror testimony that shows a failure to answer honestly during voir dire can be used to overturn the verdict. [¶] There is a split in the Circuits on this point. The Ninth Circuit has held that statements which tend to show deceit during voir dire are not barred by Rule 606(b), even when the improper voir dire is the basis of a motion for a new trial. [¶] The Third Circuit, by contrast, has held that such an interpretation would be plainly too broad, and that Rule 606(b) categorically bars juror testimony as to any matter or statement occurring during the course of the jury's deliberations even if the testimony is not offered to explore the jury's decision-making process in reaching the verdict. [¶] The Third Circuit's approach best comports with Rule 606(b).... A broad question during voir dire could ... justify the admission of any number of jury statements that would ... be re-characterized as challenges to voir dire rather than challenges to the verdict. [W]e cannot read [FRE 606(b)] to justify [such a large] loophole...." (Internal quotes omitted.)

U.S. v. Honken, 541 F.3d 1146, 1168 (8th Cir.2008). "The circuits disagree whether Rule 606(b) prohibits a juror from testifying as to whether extraneous information or an outside influence affected the juror's ability to be impartial. [Some circuits] have concluded such questioning is improper. [¶] [However,] the Sixth Circuit found a district court abused its discretion by *not* asking jurors about whether their exposure to outside influences affected their ability to be impartial. The Ninth Circuit appears to agree with the Sixth. [¶] We now hold Rule 606(b) prohibits a juror from testifying at a post-verdict hearing as to whether extraneous information or an outside influence affected that juror's ability to be impartial."

Craig Outdoor Adver., Inc. v. Viacom Outdoor, Inc., 528 F.3d 1001, 1022 (8th Cir.2008). "A district court is generally prohibited from receiving testimony from jurors after the jury has returned a verdict and has been discharged. A district court may, however, consider juror testimony that because of some oversight or mistake, the verdict announced at trial was not the verdict on which the jurors had agreed. In other words, the admission of a juror's testimony is proper to indicate the possibility of a clerical error in the verdict, but not the validity of the verdict. ... Here, [Ps'] charges of mistake or ambiguity in the verdict form cannot be characterized as clerical error. Instead, the affidavits obtained by [Ps] purport to explain what the jury meant by its verdict and how the jury determined what numbers to transcribe onto the verdict forms. The District Court did not err in refusing to consider the juror affidavits." (Internal quotes omitted.)

U.S. v. Burns, 495 F.3d 873, 875 (8th Cir.2007). FRE 606(b) "generally prohibits a juror from testifying about her or other jurors' mental processes during jury deliberations. [T]he principle behind this prohibition extends to testimony about what those mental processes would have been had the evidence at trial been different."

U.S. v. Lakhani, 480 F.3d 171, 184-85 (3d Cir.2007). Policies that FRE 606(b) fosters are "(1) discouraging harassment of jurors by losing parties eager to have the verdict set aside; (2) encouraging free and open discussion among jurors; (3) reducing incentives for jury tampering; (4) promoting verdict finality; and (5) maintaining the viability of the jury as a judicial decision-making body. Therefore, evidence of discussions among jurors, intimidation or harassment of one juror by another, and other intra-jury influences on the verdict is within the rule, rather than the exception, and is not competent to impeach a verdict. At the same time, we also identified several circumstances that would fall under the rule's exception for extraneous prejudicial information, including (1) exposure of the jury to news items about the matter pending before the jury; (2) consideration by the jury of extra-record facts about the case; (3) communications between third parties and jurors that are relevant to the case under consideration; and (4) pressures or partiality on the part of the court. [¶] Though we hope that jury deliberations proceed in a manner respectful of every juror's opinion, ... testimony concerning intimidation or harassment of one juror by another falls squarely within the core prohibition of the Rule. [¶] If intra-jury comments carried the coercive force of threats or bribery, only then would we be justified in treating them, factually, as extrane-

ous influences." (Internal quotes omitted.) *See also* ***U.S. v. Wintermute***, 443 F.3d 993, 1002 (8th Cir.2006).

FRE 607. WHO MAY IMPEACH A WITNESS

Any party, including the party that called the witness, may attack the witness's credibility.

History of FRE 607: Adopted Jan. 2, 1975, P.L. 93-595, §1, 88 Stat. 1926, eff. July 1, 1975. Amended Mar. 2, 1987, eff. Oct. 1, 1987; Apr. 26, 2011, eff. Dec. 1, 2011.

See *Commentaries*, "Impeaching Witnesses," ch. 8-C, §5, p. 692.

ANNOTATIONS

U.S. v. Abel, 469 U.S. 45, 49 (1984). The FREs "do not by their terms deal with impeachment for 'bias….' *At 51:* We think … that it is permissible to impeach a witness by showing his bias under the [FREs]. *At 52:* Bias is a term used in the 'common law of evidence' to describe the relationship between a party and a witness which might lead the witness to slant, unconsciously or otherwise, his testimony in favor of or against a party. Bias may be induced by a witness' like, dislike, or fear of a party, or by the witness' self-interest. Proof of bias is almost always relevant because the jury, as finder of fact and weigher of credibility, has historically been entitled to assess all evidence which might bear on the accuracy and truth of a witness' testimony. [¶] A witness' and a party's common membership in an organization, even without proof that the witness or party has personally adopted its tenets, is certainly probative of bias."

U.S. v. Gilmore, 553 F.3d 266, 271 (3d Cir.2009). "Impeachment by contradiction is a means of policing the defendant's obligation to speak the truth in response to proper questions. Accordingly, where a defendant testifies on direct examination regarding a specific fact, the prosecution may prove on cross-examination that the defendant lied as to that fact. [FRE] 607 … authorizes impeachment by contradiction, and [FRE] 403 governs its application. *At 272:* [FRE] 609 controls the use of prior felony convictions to impeach a witness' general character for truthfulness, but impeachment by contradiction concerns the use of evidence to impeach a witness' specific testimony. Accordingly, prior felony convictions more than ten years old may be used to impeach by contradiction even if they do not satisfy Rule 609's balancing and notice conditions. *At 273:* Notwithstanding Rule 609's inapplicability, a prior conviction's age may still bear on the Rule 403 analysis required for impeachment by contradiction. For example, a conviction's age may affect its probative value. A witness' broad denial of ever selling drugs makes any drug sale conviction probative, regardless of its age. A more limited denial like 'I don't sell drugs,' however, may make the probative value of a prior drug sale conviction dependent on its age; the more recent the conviction, the more probative it will be. Additionally, the age of a conviction may influence its potential for unfair prejudice. … Accordingly, a district judge faced with the proffer of past criminal conduct to impeach a witness' testimony by contradiction may properly consider the age of that conviction using standard Rule 403 analysis, though without resort to Rule 609." (Internal quotes omitted.)

U.S. v. Ienco, 92 F.3d 564, 568 (7th Cir.1996). "Rule 607 … allows the credibility of a witness to be impeached by any party, including the party calling the witness, and the asking of leading questions is a standard technique of impeachment. … Rule 607 abolishes the voucher rule and its corollaries, such as having to declare your witness adverse before cross-examining him or to show that his testimony surprised you."

U.S. v. Gilbert, 57 F.3d 709, 711 (9th Cir.1995). "Impeachment is improper when employed as a guise to present substantive evidence to the jury that would be otherwise inadmissible."

U.S. v. Ince, 21 F.3d 576, 579 (4th Cir.1994). "One method of attacking the credibility of (*i.e.*, impeaching) a witness is to show that he has previously made a statement that is inconsistent with his present testimony. Even if that prior inconsistent statement would otherwise be inadmissible as hearsay, it may be admissible for the limited purpose of impeaching the witness."

FRE 608. A WITNESS'S CHARACTER FOR TRUTHFULNESS OR UNTRUTHFULNESS

(a) Reputation or Opinion Evidence. A witness's credibility may be attacked or supported by testimony about the witness's reputation for having a character for truthfulness or untruthfulness, or by testimony in the form of an opinion about that character. But evidence of truthful character is admissible only after the witness's character for truthfulness has been attacked.

(b) Specific Instances of Conduct. Except for a criminal conviction under Rule 609, extrinsic evidence is not admissible to prove specific instances of a witness's conduct in order to attack or support

Effective December 1, 2011, FREs 101-1103 were restyled. For a discussion of the changes and a chart comparing the former and current rules, see p. 1024.

the witness's character for truthfulness. But the court may, on cross-examination, allow them to be inquired into if they are probative of the character for truthfulness or untruthfulness of:

(1) the witness; or

(2) another witness whose character the witness being cross-examined has testified about.

By testifying on another matter, a witness does not waive any privilege against self-incrimination for testimony that relates only to the witness's character for truthfulness.

See selected Notes of Advisory Committee to FRE 608, p. 1257.

History of FRE 608: Adopted Jan. 2, 1975, P.L. 93-595, §1, 88 Stat. 1926, eff. July 1, 1975. Amended Mar. 2, 1987, eff. Oct. 1, 1987; Apr. 25, 1988, eff. Nov. 1, 1988; Mar. 27, 2003, eff. Dec. 1, 2003; Apr. 26, 2011, eff. Dec. 1, 2011.

See *Commentaries*, "Impeaching Witnesses," ch. 8-C, §5, p. 692.

ANNOTATIONS

U.S. v. Abel, 469 U.S. 45, 55 (1984). FRE 608(b) "allows a cross-examiner to impeach a witness by asking him about specific instances of past conduct, other than crimes covered by [FRE] 609, which are probative of his veracity or 'character for truthfulness or untruthfulness.' [FRE 608(b)] limits the inquiry to cross-examination of the witness, however, and prohibits the cross-examiner from introducing extrinsic evidence of the witness' past conduct." *See also* ***U.S. v. Andujar***, 49 F.3d 16, 26 (1st Cir.1995).

U.S. v. Schmitz, 634 F.3d 1247, 1268-69 (11th Cir. 2011). "We hold that it is improper to ask a testifying defendant whether another witness is lying. [¶] [T]he [FREs] do not permit such questions. While Rule 608(a) permits a witness to testify, in the form of opinion or reputation evidence, that another witness has a general character for truthfulness or untruthfulness, that rule does not permit a witness to testify that another witness was truthful or not on a specific occasion. Moreover, the were-they-lying questions have little or no probative value because they seek an answer beyond the personal knowledge of the witness. The were-they-lying questions are also not relevant because one witness's opinion that another person has or has not lied does not make it more or less likely that the person actually lied. And, the were-they-lying questions distract the jury from the central task of determining what version of events is accurate in order to determine a defendant's guilt or innocence."

U.S. v. Skelton, 514 F.3d 433, 445 (5th Cir.2008). FRE 608(b) "permits 'did you know' or 'have you heard' questions regarding specific instances of conduct of the principal witness probative of truthfulness or untruthfulness to impeach the credibility of a rebuttal character witness, subject to [FRE] 403."

U.S. v. Montelongo, 420 F.3d 1169, 1175 (10th Cir. 2005). FRE 608(b) "only applies to specific instances of conduct used to attack or support the witness' character for truthfulness. [H]owever, [Ds] did not seek to cross-examine [witness] on the prior incident in order to 'attack' his 'character for truthfulness,' but rather to negate [Ds'] guilt of the crime charged against them.... As such, Rule 608(b) does not bar [Ds'] cross-examination of [witness]."

U.S. v. Drury, 396 F.3d 1303, 1316 (11th Cir.2005). FRE 608 "permits rehabilitative evidence only when a witness's reputation for truthfulness has actually been attacked. [T]he prosecution's questioning the veracity of the accused's testimony and calling attention to inconsistencies therein does not constitute an attack on the accused's reputation for truthfulness permitting rehabilitative testimony."

U.S. v. Geston, 299 F.3d 1130, 1137 n.2 (9th Cir. 2002). FRE 403 "modifies [FRE 608(b)] by providing that otherwise admissible and relevant evidence may be excluded if the court determines that its probative value is substantially outweighed by the danger of unfair prejudice."

U.S. v. Shay, 57 F.3d 126, 131 (1st Cir.1995). FRE 608(a), "governing the admissibility of opinion testimony concerning a witness's character, contemplates that truthful or untruthful character may be proved by expert testimony."

FRE 609. IMPEACHMENT BY EVIDENCE OF A CRIMINAL CONVICTION

(a) In General. The following rules apply to attacking a witness's character for truthfulness by evidence of a criminal conviction:

(1) for a crime that, in the convicting jurisdiction, was punishable by death or by imprisonment for more than one year, the evidence:

(A) must be admitted, subject to Rule 403, in a civil case or in a criminal case in which the witness is not a defendant; and

(B) must be admitted in a criminal case in which the witness is a defendant, if the probative value of the evidence outweighs its prejudicial effect to that defendant; and

FRE 608

(2) for any crime regardless of the punishment, the evidence must be admitted if the court can readily determine that establishing the elements of the crime required proving—or the witness's admitting—a dishonest act or false statement.

(b) Limit on Using the Evidence After 10 Years. This subdivision (b) applies if more than 10 years have passed since the witness's conviction or release from confinement for it, whichever is later. Evidence of the conviction is admissible only if:

(1) its probative value, supported by specific facts and circumstances, substantially outweighs its prejudicial effect; and

(2) the proponent gives an adverse party reasonable written notice of the intent to use it so that the party has a fair opportunity to contest its use.

(c) Effect of a Pardon, Annulment, or Certificate of Rehabilitation. Evidence of a conviction is not admissible if:

(1) the conviction has been the subject of a pardon, annulment, certificate of rehabilitation, or other equivalent procedure based on a finding that the person has been rehabilitated, and the person has not been convicted of a later crime punishable by death or by imprisonment for more than one year; or

(2) the conviction has been the subject of a pardon, annulment, or other equivalent procedure based on a finding of innocence.

(d) Juvenile Adjudications. Evidence of a juvenile adjudication is admissible under this rule only if:

(1) it is offered in a criminal case;

(2) the adjudication was of a witness other than the defendant;

(3) an adult's conviction for that offense would be admissible to attack the adult's credibility; and

(4) admitting the evidence is necessary to fairly determine guilt or innocence.

(e) Pendency of an Appeal. A conviction that satisfies this rule is admissible even if an appeal is pending. Evidence of the pendency is also admissible.

See selected Notes of Advisory Committee to FRE 609, p. 1258.

History of FRE 609: Adopted Jan. 2, 1975, P.L. 93-595, §1, 88 Stat. 1926, eff. July 1, 1975. Amended Mar. 2, 1987, eff. Oct. 1, 1987; Jan. 26, 1990, eff. Dec. 1, 1990; Apr. 12, 2006, eff. Dec. 1, 2006; Apr. 26, 2011, eff. Dec. 1, 2011.

See ***Commentaries***, "Impeaching by conviction," ch. 8-C, §5.4, p. 693.

ANNOTATIONS

Ohler v. U.S., 529 U.S. 753, 755-56 (2000). See annotation under FRE 103, p. 1029.

Schmude v. Tricam Indus., 556 F.3d 624, 627-28 (7th Cir.2009). "The rationale for … allowing a prior crime to be used to undermine testimony is that a person who has committed a serious crime is more likely than a law-abiding person to lie on the stand even if the case in which he is testifying has nothing to do with that crime. The rationale is underinclusive, since many people who have committed a felony have not been caught or if caught have not been convicted, because of the prosecution's heavy burden of proof. Moreover, every judge is aware that many people who do not have a criminal record will lie in a trial when it is to their advantage."

U.S. v. Gilmore, 553 F.3d 266, 271 (3d Cir.2009). See annotation under FRE 607, p. 1051.

U.S. v. Rogers, 542 F.3d 197, 201 (7th Cir.2008). "[W]e have now defined both the starting and ending points for the calculation of Rule 609(b)'s ten-year time limit. The clock starts at the witness's release from any physical confinement, or in the absence of confinement, the date of the conviction. [T]he end date of the time limit for impeaching convictions is the start of the trial at which the witness is testifying." *See also **U.S. v. Stoltz***, 683 F.3d 934, 939 (8th Cir.2012) (clock starts when witness is released from physical confinement; confinement does not include probation).

U.S. v. Estrada, 430 F.3d 606, 615-16 (2d Cir.2005). "The presumption under Rule 609(a)(2)—as recognized by the district court—is that the 'essential facts' of a witness's convictions, including the statutory name of each offense, the date of conviction, and the sentence imposed, are included within the 'evidence' that is to be admitted for impeachment purposes. We see no reason why the presumption should be different under Rule 609(a)(1). … We see nothing … that would justify the conclusion that the 'evidence' of a witness's convictions contemplated by Rule 609(a)(1) is automatically more circumscribed than the evidence that is automatically admissible under Rule 609(a)(2)."

U.S. v. Valentine, 401 F.3d 609, 615 (5th Cir.2005). "[A] deferred adjudication does not subject a witness to impeachment with the use of a prior 'conviction.'"

FRE 609

Effective December 1, 2011, FREs 101-1103 were restyled. For a discussion of the changes and a chart comparing the former and current rules, see p. 1024.

Gill v. Thomas, 83 F.3d 537, 540 (1st Cir.1996). "[P] maintains that but for the magistrate judge having indicated that he would permit [D] to raise them on cross-examination, [P] never would have revealed his misdemeanor convictions on direct examination. *At 541:* At trial, rather than waiting for [D] to introduce the misdemeanors, objecting, and allowing the magistrate judge to reconsider his in limine ruling, [P] opted to introduce the misdemeanors preemptively to 'remove the sting' from [D's] anticipated impeachment. [A]s a consequence, [P] 'opened the door' to [D's] cross-examination on the misdemeanors and thereby eliminated any potential evidentiary error. [¶] To preserve his in limine objection ..., [P] should have refrained from offering the evidence himself, waited to see if [D] introduced [his misdemeanor convictions] on cross-examination, and if so, objected then."

FRE 610. RELIGIOUS BELIEFS OR OPINIONS

Evidence of a witness's religious beliefs or opinions is not admissible to attack or support the witness's credibility.

History of FRE 610: Adopted Jan. 2, 1975, P.L. 93-595, §1, 88 Stat. 1926, eff. July 1, 1975. Amended Mar. 2, 1987, eff. Oct. 1, 1987; Apr. 26, 2011, eff. Dec. 1, 2011.

ANNOTATIONS

Malek v. Federal Ins., 994 F.2d 49, 54-55 (2d Cir. 1993). "Because it is apparent from these questions that defense counsel attempted to show that [witness's] character for truthfulness was affected by his religious beliefs and that such questioning may have prejudiced [Ps], the district court erred in permitting the defendants to pursue this line of questioning. We are particularly troubled about this line of questioning, especially where the impeached witness' religious affiliation is the same as that of [Ps]."

Government of V.I. v. Petersen, 553 F.2d 324, 328 (3d Cir.1977). "The colloquy at side bar clearly reveals that counsel sought to put before the jury the religious affiliation and beliefs of [alibi witness]. [FRE 610] clearly prohibits such testimony when it is used to enhance the witness' credibility and no other purpose for its admission has been suggested."

FRE 611. MODE & ORDER OF EXAMINING WITNESSES & PRESENTING EVIDENCE

(a) **Control by the Court; Purposes.** The court should exercise reasonable control over the mode and order of examining witnesses and presenting evidence so as to:

(1) make those procedures effective for determining the truth;

(2) avoid wasting time; and

(3) protect witnesses from harassment or undue embarrassment.

(b) **Scope of Cross-Examination.** Cross-examination should not go beyond the subject matter of the direct examination and matters affecting the witness's credibility. The court may allow inquiry into additional matters as if on direct examination.

(c) **Leading Questions.** Leading questions should not be used on direct examination except as necessary to develop the witness's testimony. Ordinarily, the court should allow leading questions:

(1) on cross-examination; and

(2) when a party calls a hostile witness, an adverse party, or a witness identified with an adverse party.

History of FRE 611: Adopted Jan. 2, 1975, P.L. 93-595, §1, 88 Stat. 1926, eff. July 1, 1975. Amended Mar. 2, 1987, eff. Oct. 1, 1987; Apr. 26, 2011, eff. Dec. 1, 2011.

See *Commentaries*, "Right to Open Evidence," ch. 8-C, §2, p. 688.

ANNOTATIONS

U.S. v. Hill, 643 F.3d 807, 845-46 (11th Cir.2011). "'The discharge of [the court's] responsibility [under FRE 611(a)] necessarily entails the exercise of discretion.' And that discretion is broad. [¶] In conducting a trial, the judge 'may comment on the evidence, may question witnesses and elicit facts not yet adduced or clarify those previously presented, and may maintain the pace of the trial by interrupting or cutting off counsel as a matter of discretion.' The trial court abuses its discretion '[o]nly when the judge's conduct strays from neutrality,' ... and even then only when its remarks demonstrate 'pervasive bias and unfairness' that actually prejudice a party...."

McCabe v. Parker, 608 F.3d 1068, 1076 (8th Cir. 2010). "[U]nder [FRE] 611(c) '[t]he standard, acceptable, and preferred procedure is to permit counsel to lead an adverse or hostile witness on direct examination' but ... the Rule 'is permissive and must be read in context with the trial court's general authority and discretion to control the conduct of the trial.'" *See also* *Sanders v. New York City Human Res. Admin.*, 361 F.3d 749, 757 (2d Cir.2004).

U.S. v. McElroy, 587 F.3d 73, 81-82 (1st Cir.2009). See annotation under FRE 1006, p. 1085.

In re Gergely, 110 F.3d 1448, 1452 (9th Cir.1997). "Requiring evidence to be presented by declaration is 'an accepted and encouraged technique for shortening bench trials' that is consistent with Rule 611(a)(2). And requiring evidence responding to an opposing witness's declaration to be submitted prior to trial is also consistent with the need to ascertain the truth. The opposing witness can still be cross-examined regarding the contradictory evidence, and the court can assess his demeanor during that cross-examination. If the testimony is false, that falsity will be revealed by the reply evidence and related cross-examination."

MDU Res. v. W.R. Grace & Co., 14 F.3d 1274, 1282 (8th Cir.1994). "[T]he scope of cross-examination ... should not be allowed to get out of hand. When cross-examination goes beyond the scope of direct ... and is designed ... to establish an affirmative defense, ... the examiner must be required to ask questions of non-hostile witnesses as if on direct." *See also* ***U.S. v. Tomblin***, 46 F.3d 1369, 1386 (5th Cir.1995) (district court can permit cross-examination that exceeds scope of direct).

FRE 612. WRITING USED TO REFRESH A WITNESS'S MEMORY

(a) Scope. This rule gives an adverse party certain options when a witness uses a writing to refresh memory:

(1) while testifying; or

(2) before testifying, if the court decides that justice requires the party to have those options.

(b) Adverse Party's Options; Deleting Unrelated Matter. Unless 18 U.S.C. §3500 provides otherwise in a criminal case, an adverse party is entitled to have the writing produced at the hearing, to inspect it, to cross-examine the witness about it, and to introduce in evidence any portion that relates to the witness's testimony. If the producing party claims that the writing includes unrelated matter, the court must examine the writing in camera, delete any unrelated portion, and order that the rest be delivered to the adverse party. Any portion deleted over objection must be preserved for the record.

(c) Failure to Produce or Deliver the Writing. If a writing is not produced or is not delivered as ordered, the court may issue any appropriate order. But if the prosecution does not comply in a criminal case, the court must strike the witness's testimony or—if justice so requires—declare a mistrial.

History of FRE 612: Adopted Jan. 2, 1975, P.L. 93-595, §1, 88 Stat. 1926, eff. July 1, 1975. Amended Mar. 2, 1987, eff. Oct. 1, 1987; Apr. 26, 2011, eff. Dec. 1, 2011.

ANNOTATIONS

U.S. v. Marrero, 651 F.3d 453, 471-72 (6th Cir. 2011). "By its terms, Rule 612 does not limit the type of writings that might be used as refreshers...."

U.S. v. Holden, 557 F.3d 698, 703-04 (6th Cir.2009). "Rule 612 is not an independent source of admissibility, but rather a means to refresh a witness's memory on an admissible subject of testimony: 'Rule 612 does not apply where a witness refers to documents for purposes other than refreshing recollection. In such a case, Rule 612 is inapplicable and the question becomes whether the writing is admissible under laws regulating the admissibility of documentary evidence.'"

Rush v. Illinois Cent. R.R., 399 F.3d 705, 716 (6th Cir.2005). "The propriety of permitting a witness to refresh his memory from a writing prepared by another largely lies within the sound discretion of the trial court. [¶] 'Proper foundation requires that the witness's recollection ... be exhausted, and that the time, place and person to whom the statement was given be identified. When the court is satisfied that the memorandum on its face reflects the witness's statement or one the witness acknowledges, and in his discretion the court is further satisfied that it may be of help in refreshing the person's memory, the witness should be allowed to refer to the document.' [¶] Upon establishing the proper foundation, 'counsel will typically offer the witness the writing to inspect, and will show a copy of the writing to the opposing parties.' 'The best practice is for the trial court to have the witness silently read the writing and then to state whether the writing has refreshed his or her recollection.'"

U.S. v. Darden, 70 F.3d 1507, 1540-41 (8th Cir. 1995). "Rule 612 requires only 'disclosure of the passage actually used by the witness, and other portions relating to the same subject matter.' Access is limited to those writings that arguably have an impact upon the testimony of the witness. In this case the court permitted [Ds] to access the entirety of the ... reports through a witness of their own; the court simply limited

FRE 612

Effective December 1, 2011, FREs 101-1103 were restyled. For a discussion of the changes and a chart comparing the former and current rules, see p. 1024.

cross examination to those portions of the reports that the witness was able to recall."

U.S. v. Sheffield, 55 F.3d 341, 343 (8th Cir.1995). "[E]ven if a writing has been used to refresh memory of a witness before testifying, the court may require furnishing the statement only if in its discretion it determines it is necessary in the interest of justice. ... Rule 612 is not a vehicle for a plenary search for contradictory or rebutting evidence that may be in a file but rather is a means to reawaken recollection of the witness to the witness's past perception about a writing. The contents of such a writing may not even be read into evidence."

FRE 613. WITNESS'S PRIOR STATEMENT

(a) Showing or Disclosing the Statement During Examination. When examining a witness about the witness's prior statement, a party need not show it or disclose its contents to the witness. But the party must, on request, show it or disclose its contents to an adverse party's attorney.

(b) Extrinsic Evidence of a Prior Inconsistent Statement. Extrinsic evidence of a witness's prior inconsistent statement is admissible only if the witness is given an opportunity to explain or deny the statement and an adverse party is given an opportunity to examine the witness about it, or if justice so requires. This subdivision (b) does not apply to an opposing party's statement under Rule 801(d)(2).

History of FRE 613: Adopted Jan. 2, 1975, P.L. 93-595, §1, 88 Stat. 1926, eff. July 1, 1975. Amended Mar. 2, 1987, eff. Oct. 1, 1987; Apr. 25, 1988, eff. Nov. 1, 1988; Apr. 26, 2011, eff. Dec. 1, 2011.

See ***Commentaries***, "Impeaching by prior inconsistent statement," ch. 8-C, §5.2, p. 693.

ANNOTATIONS

U.S. v. Kelly, 436 F.3d 992, 996 (8th Cir.2006). FRE 613(b) "only states that a witness be afforded the *opportunity* to explain; Rule 613(b) does not require a witness to actually explain or deny the prior inconsistent statements." *See also* ***U.S. v. Della Rose***, 403 F.3d 891, 903 (7th Cir.2005).

U.S. v. Larry Reed & Sons Prtshp., 280 F.3d 1212, 1215 (8th Cir.2002). "To introduce a witness's own earlier statement for impeachment, (1) the statements must be inconsistent, (2) the inconsistency must be relevant, (3) the inconsistent statement must, on request, be disclosed to opposing counsel, the witness allowed to explain the inconsistency, and opposing counsel allowed to question the witness, and (4) the district court should instruct the jury about the limited purpose of the earlier statement. In [D's] situation, the first three prongs of the impeachment standard were satisfied, but the fourth prong was not: the district court did not give the jury a limiting instruction. When neither party requests a limiting instruction at trial, however, we review the trial court's failure to issue such an instruction for plain error."

U.S. v. Hudson, 970 F.2d 948, 955 (1st Cir.1992). "[T]he Fifth, Ninth, and Tenth Circuits have upheld the refusal to admit proof through extrinsic evidence of prior inconsistent statements unless the witness has first been afforded the opportunity to deny or explain those statements. The Eighth Circuit has followed suit, at least in circumstances in which there are considerable logistical difficulties in arranging for the recall of inmate witnesses sought to be impeached through extrinsic evidence of prior inconsistent statements. We decline the invitation. ... '[T]he traditional insistence that the attention of the witness be directed to the statement on cross examination is relaxed in favor of simply providing the witness an opportunity to explain and the opposite party an opportunity to examine the statement, with no specification of any particular time or sequence,' and is supported by the great weight of authority."

FRE 614. COURT'S CALLING OR EXAMINING A WITNESS

(a) Calling. The court may call a witness on its own or at a party's request. Each party is entitled to cross-examine the witness.

(b) Examining. The court may examine a witness regardless of who calls the witness.

(c) Objections. A party may object to the court's calling or examining a witness either at that time or at the next opportunity when the jury is not present.

History of FRE 614: Adopted Jan. 2, 1975, P.L. 93-595, §1, 88 Stat. 1926, eff. July 1, 1975. Amended Apr. 26, 2011, eff. Dec. 1, 2011.

ANNOTATIONS

U.S. v. Smith, 452 F.3d 323, 332 (4th Cir.2006). "[I]t is settled beyond doubt that in a federal court the judge has the right, and often the obligation, to interrupt the presentations of counsel in order to clarify misunderstandings. ... This obligation is not, of course, without its limits. Trial judges are not backstop counsel, entitled to step in whenever a point may be more eloquently de-

FRE 612

livered or a tactical misstep avoided. But it remains their prerogative to make certain that matters are clearly presented to the jury." (Internal quotes omitted.) *See also* ***U.S. v. Saenz***, 134 F.3d 697, 701-02 (5th Cir.1998) (district court's "effort to move case along may not come at the cost of strict impartiality").

U.S. v. Washington, 417 F.3d 780, 784 (7th Cir. 2005). "A district judge is free to interject during a direct or cross-examination to clarify an issue, to require an attorney to lay a foundation, or to encourage an examining attorney to get to the point. The judge may also choose to play a more passive role when the case calls for it. But in exercising his discretion regarding when to intercede and when to cede the floor to the attorneys, the judge must refrain from 'assum[ing] the role of an advocate for either side.' If a party claims that a trial judge crossed the line and displayed partiality towards the other side, we analyze the issue pursuant to a two-step inquiry. First, we inquire whether the judge in fact conveyed a bias regarding the defendant's honesty or guilt. If so, we consider whether the complaining party has shown serious prejudice resulting from the district court's comments or questions." *See also* ***U.S. v. Almeida-Perez***, 549 F.3d 1162, 1174 (8th Cir.2008).

FRE 615. EXCLUDING WITNESSES

At a party's request, the court must order witnesses excluded so that they cannot hear other witnesses' testimony. Or the court may do so on its own. But this rule does not authorize excluding:

(a) a party who is a natural person;

(b) an officer or employee of a party that is not a natural person, after being designated as the party's representative by its attorney;

(c) a person whose presence a party shows to be essential to presenting the party's claim or defense; or

(d) a person authorized by statute to be present.

See selected Notes of Advisory Committee to FRE 615, p. 1258.

History of FRE 615: Adopted Jan. 2, 1975, P.L. 93-595, §1, 88 Stat. 1926, eff. July 1, 1975. Amended Mar. 2, 1987, eff. Oct. 1, 1987; Apr. 25, 1988, eff. Nov. 1, 1988; Nov. 18, 1988, P.L. 100-690, §7075(a), 102 Stat. 4405; Apr. 24, 1998, eff. Dec. 1, 1998; Apr. 26, 2011, eff. Dec. 1, 2011.

See ***Commentaries***, "Objection to witness who violated sequestration order," ch. 8-D, §3.3, p. 702.

ANNOTATIONS

Holder v. U.S., 150 U.S. 91, 92 (1893). "If a witness disobeys [a sequestration] order ..., while he may be proceeded against for contempt, and his testimony is open to comment to the jury by reason of his conduct, he is not thereby disqualified, and the weight of authority is that he cannot be excluded on that ground, merely, although the right to exclude under particular circumstances may be supported as within the sound discretion of the trial court." *See also* ***U.S. v. Washington***, 653 F.3d 1251, 1268 (10th Cir.2011); ***U.S. v. Green***, 305 F.3d 422, 428 (6th Cir.2002).

U.S. v. Olofson, 563 F.3d 652, 660 (7th Cir.2009). "[M]erely because [FRE] 703 contemplates that an expert may render an opinion based on facts or data made known at trial does not necessarily mean that an expert witness is exempt from [an FRE] 615 sequestration order. The text of Rule 615 plainly does not provide for such a per se exception; rather, [former Rule 615(3), now Rule 615(c),] confers discretion upon district courts to determine whether a given witness (of whatever stripe) is essential. We agree ... that Rule 703 is not an automatic exemption for expert witnesses from Rule 615 sequestration." *See also* ***Opus 3 Ltd. v. Heritage Park, Inc.***, 91 F.3d 625, 629 (4th Cir.1996).

U.S. v. Magana, 127 F.3d 1, 5 (1st Cir.1997). "Apart from ... Rule 615, the court retains discretion to add other restrictions or not, as it judges appropriate. The regulation of witness conduct outside the courtroom is ... left to the district judge's discretion. The court may, for example, order that witnesses not converse with each other about the case. Further, the court has the discretion to prohibit counsel from conferring with a witness during the witness's testimony, including during any recesses in the trial." *See also* ***U.S. v. Samuels***, 493 F.3d 1187, 1190 (10th Cir.2007) (when witnesses are excluded from courtroom, they are also prohibited from discussing case with other witnesses).

U.S. v. Jackson, 60 F.3d 128, 133 (2d Cir.1995). "Rule 615 codified a well-established common law tradition of sequestering witnesses as a means of discouraging and exposing fabrication, inaccuracy, and collusion. [T]his practice ... serves two purposes: it exercises a restraint on witnesses 'tailoring' their testimony to that of earlier witnesses; and it aids in detecting testimony that is less than candid." (Internal quotes omitted.) *See also* ***U.S. v. Charles***, 456 F.3d 249, 258 (1st Cir.2006).

U.S. v. Hobbs, 31 F.3d 918, 921 (9th Cir.1994). "[T]he Supreme Court has recognized three sanctions for the violation of a sequestration order: (1) holding the offending witness in contempt; (2) permitting cross-examination concerning the violation; and (3) precluding the witness from testifying."

FRE 615

Effective December 1, 2011, FREs 101-1103 were restyled. For a discussion of the changes and a chart comparing the former and current rules, see p. 1024.

ARTICLE VII. OPINIONS & EXPERT TESTIMONY

FRE 701. OPINION TESTIMONY BY LAY WITNESSES

If a witness is not testifying as an expert, testimony in the form of an opinion is limited to one that is:

(a) rationally based on the witness's perception;

(b) helpful to clearly understanding the witness's testimony or to determining a fact in issue; and

(c) not based on scientific, technical, or other specialized knowledge within the scope of Rule 702.

See selected Notes of Advisory Committee to FRE 701, p. 1259.

History of FRE 701: Adopted Jan. 2, 1975, P.L. 93-595, §1, 88 Stat. 1926, eff. July 1, 1975. Amended Mar. 2, 1987, eff. Oct. 1, 1987; Apr. 17, 2000, eff. Dec. 1, 2000; Apr. 26, 2011, eff. Dec. 1, 2011.

See *Commentaries*, "Opinion testimony from lay witness," ch. 8-C, §4.6, p. 690.

ANNOTATIONS

U.S. v. Locke, 643 F.3d 235, 239-40 (7th Cir.2011). "The [FREs] limit—but do not bar—lay witnesses' ability to testify as to their opinions and inferences, even about ultimate issues in the case. In some situations, even 'lay opinion testimony as to the mental state of another is indeed competent,' … and it is within the discretion of the trial judge to determine whether such testimony is helpful under [FRE] 701 and appropriate under [FRE] 403's balancing test…. [W]e look to Rule 701's helpfulness requirement [and] ask whether the district court rightfully could have determined, in its broad discretion, that these lay witnesses' testimonies were helpful to the jury and not meaningless assertions."

Harris v. J.B. Robinson Jewelers, 627 F.3d 235, 240 (6th Cir.2010). "In distinguishing proper lay testimony from expert testimony, this court has specified that 'lay testimony results from a process of reasoning familiar in everyday life, whereas an expert's testimony results from a process of reasoning which can be mastered only by specialists in the field.' Thus, a lay witness may testify, for example, that 'a footprint in snow looked like someone had slipped, or that a substance appeared to be blood[,]' but cannot testify that 'skull trauma caused the bruises on a victim's face.' '[T]he modern trend among courts favors the admission of opinion testimony, provided that it is well founded on personal knowledge and susceptible to specific cross-examination.' *At 241:* 'The prototypical example of the type of evidence contemplated by the adoption of Rule 701 relates to the appearance of persons or things, identity, the manner of conduct, competency of a person, degrees of light or darkness, sound, size, weight, distance, and an endless number of items that cannot be described factually in words apart from inferences.' This court has previously acknowledged a lay witness's ability to identify objects based upon personal observation. … In addition, our sister circuits have recognized that lay witnesses may testify regarding matters open to the senses." *See also* ***Donlin v. Philips Lighting N. Am. Corp.***, 564 F.3d 207, 214-15 (3d Cir.2009).

U.S. v. Stadtmauer, 620 F.3d 238, 262-63 (3d Cir. 2010). FRE 701 is "designed to exclude lay opinion testimony that amounts to little more than choosing up sides, … or that merely tells the jury what result to reach…. Lay testimony in the form of an opinion about what a defendant did or did not know often comes dangerously close to doing just this. Though we have never held that lay opinion evidence concerning the knowledge of a third party is *per se* inadmissible, we have explained that this kind of evidence is difficult to admit under either prong of Rule 701[.] If the witness fails to describe the opinion's basis, in the form of descriptions of specific incidents, the opinion testimony should be rejected on the ground that it is not based on the witness's perceptions. To the extent the witness describes the basis of his or her opinion, that testimony should be rejected on the ground that it is not helpful because the fact finder is able to reach his or her own conclusion, making the opinion testimony irrelevant." (Internal quotes omitted.)

U.S. v. Rigas, 490 F.3d 208, 224 (2d Cir.2007). "A witness's specialized knowledge, or the fact that he was chosen to carry out an investigation because of this knowledge, does not render his testimony 'expert' as long as it was based on his 'investigation and reflected his investigatory findings and conclusions, and was not rooted exclusively in his expertise….' If, however, the witness's testimony was 'not a product of his investigation, but rather reflected [his] specialized knowledge,' then it was impermissible expert testimony. In particular, [FRE] 701(c), which prohibits testimony from a lay witness that is 'based on scientific, technical, or other specialized knowledge,' is intended 'to eliminate the risk that the reliability requirements set forth in [FRE] 702 will be evaded through the simple expedient of proffering an expert in lay witness clothing.'" *See also* ***Compania Administradora de Recuperacion de Activos Administradora v. Titan Int'l***, 533 F.3d 555, 561

(7th Cir.2008) (witness's valuation attempt was based on special experience in tire industry, not on personal knowledge of goods in question; testimony inadmissible under FRE 701).

U.S. v. Perkins, 470 F.3d 150, 155-56 (4th Cir.2006). See annotation under FRE 702, p. 1060.

U.S. v. Polishan, 336 F.3d 234, 242 (3d Cir.2003). "A witness testifying [under FRE 701] about business operations may testify about 'inferences that he could draw from his perception' of a business's records, or 'facts or data perceived' by him in his corporate capacity. Lay opinion testimony may be based on the witness's own perceptions and 'knowledge and participation in the day-to-day affairs of [the] business.'" *See also* ***Allied Sys. v. Teamsters Auto. Transp. Chaffeurs***, 304 F.3d 785, 792 (8th Cir.2002).

U.S. v. Parris, 243 F.3d 286, 288 (6th Cir.2001). Under FRE 701, "'opinions phrased in terms of inadequately explored legal criteria' [should be excluded]. Similarly, we expressed strong disfavor for this sort of testimony when it consists of a legal conclusion, realizing the danger of 'conveying the witness's unexpressed, and perhaps erroneous, legal standards to the jury[ ]'…."

FRE 702. TESTIMONY BY EXPERT WITNESSES

A witness who is qualified as an expert by knowledge, skill, experience, training, or education may testify in the form of an opinion or otherwise if:

(a) the expert's scientific, technical, or other specialized knowledge will help the trier of fact to understand the evidence or to determine a fact in issue;

(b) the testimony is based on sufficient facts or data;

(c) the testimony is the product of reliable principles and methods; and

(d) the expert has reliably applied the principles and methods to the facts of the case.

See selected Notes of Advisory Committee to FRE 702, p. 1259.

History of FRE 702: Adopted Jan. 2, 1975, P.L. 93-595, §1, 88 Stat. 1926, eff. July 1, 1975. Amended Apr. 17, 2000, eff. Dec. 1, 2000; Apr. 26, 2011, eff. Dec. 1, 2011.

See ***Commentaries***, "Motion to Exclude Expert Witness," ch. 5-N, p. 376; "Introducing Evidence," ch. 8-C, §4, p. 689.

ANNOTATIONS

Kumho Tire Co. v. Carmichael, 526 U.S. 137, 141 (1999). "***Daubert***'s general holding—setting forth the trial judge's general 'gatekeeping' obligation—applies not only to testimony based on 'scientific' knowledge, but also to testimony based on 'technical' and 'other specialized' knowledge. [A] trial court *may* consider one or more of the more specific factors that ***Daubert*** mentioned when doing so will help determine that testimony's reliability. But, … the test of reliability is 'flexible,' and ***Daubert***'s list of specific factors neither necessarily nor exclusively applies to all experts or in every case."

Daubert v. Merrell Dow Pharms., 509 U.S. 579, 592-93 (1993). "Faced with a proffer of expert scientific testimony, … the trial judge must determine at the outset … whether the expert is proposing to testify to (1) scientific knowledge that (2) will assist the trier of fact to understand or determine a fact in issue. This entails a preliminary assessment of whether the reasoning or methodology underlying the testimony is scientifically valid and of whether that reasoning or methodology properly can be applied to the facts in issue. [¶] Ordinarily, a key question to be answered in determining whether a theory or technique is scientific knowledge that will assist the trier of fact will be whether it can be (and has been) tested. [¶] Another pertinent consideration is whether the theory or technique has been subjected to peer review and publication. *At 594:* Additionally, [the court] should consider the known or potential rate of error … and the existence and maintenance of standards controlling the technique's operation. [¶] Widespread acceptance can be an important factor in ruling particular evidence admissible, and 'a known technique that has been able to attract only minimal support within the community' may properly be viewed with skepticism."

U.S. v. Offill, 666 F.3d 168, 175 (4th Cir.2011). "The touchstone of [FRE 702] is whether the testimony will assist the jury. [W]e have held that it does not help the jury for an expert to give testimony that 'states a legal standard or draws a legal conclusion by applying law to the facts,' … because it 'supplies the jury with no information other than the witness's view of how the verdict should read[ ]'…. Determining when legal conclusions would be helpful to the jury must also take into account the role that the judge has in instructing the jury on the law. We have noted, for example, that when a witness gives an opinion about the meaning of a specialized legal term, the witness is giving a legal conclusion that is better handled by the judge and, coming from the witness, will be of little assistance to the jury. [¶] Nonetheless, we have also noted that when the legal regime

FRE 702

Effective December 1, 2011, FREs 101-1103 were restyled. For a discussion of the changes and a chart comparing the former and current rules, see p. 1024.

is complex and the judge determines that the witness' testimony would be helpful in explaining it to the jury, the testimony may be admitted. Indeed, courts and commentators have consistently concluded that expert testimony that ordinarily might be excluded on the ground that it gives legal conclusions may nonetheless be admitted in cases that involve highly technical legal issues."

U.S. v. Nacchio, 555 F.3d 1234, 1241 (10th Cir. 2009). "Reliability questions may concern the expert's data, method, or his application of the method to the data. The party offering the expert 'must show that the method employed by the expert ... is scientifically sound and that the opinion is based on facts which satisfy Rule 702's reliability requirements.' 'Under ***Daubert***, any step that renders the expert's analysis unreliable ... renders the expert's testimony inadmissible. This is true whether the step completely changes a reliable methodology or merely misapplies that methodology.' In making a reliability determination, '[g]enerally, the district court should focus on an expert's methodology rather than the conclusions it generates.'"

U.S. v. Mejia, 545 F.3d 179, 188-89 (2d Cir.2008). "The broad phrasing of the description 'scientific, technical, or other specialized knowledge' brings within the scope of [FRE 702] both experts in the strict sense of the word, such as scientists, and the large group sometimes called 'skilled' witnesses, such as bankers or landowners testifying to land values. On the question of when expert testimony is appropriate, ... expert testimony is called for when the untrained layman would be unable intelligently to determine the particular issue in the absence of guidance from an expert." (Internal quotes omitted.)

U.S. v. Two Elk, 536 F.3d 890, 903 (8th Cir.2008). "'A district court ... enjoys broad latitude when it decides *how* to determine reliability, and [t]here is no requirement that the [d]istrict [c]ourt always hold a ***Daubert*** hearing prior to qualifying an expert witness.' Accordingly, so long as the court is satisfied with the expert's knowledge, skill, experience, training, or education, 'and the expert's testimony is reasonably based' on that expertise, 'the court does not abuse its discretion by admitting the testimony without a preliminary hearing.'"

Pineda v. Ford Motor Co., 520 F.3d 237, 244 (3d Cir.2008). "Qualification requires 'that the witness possess specialized expertise.' We have interpreted Rule 702's qualification requirement liberally. We have held that a 'broad range of knowledge, skills, and training qualify an expert.' [¶] This liberal policy of admissibility extends to the substantive as well as the formal qualifications of experts. '[I]t is an abuse of discretion to exclude testimony simply because the trial court does not deem the proposed expert to be the best qualified or because the proposed expert does not have the specialization that the court considers most appropriate.'" *See also* ***Huss v. Gayden***, 571 F.3d 442, 452 (5th Cir.2009); ***U.S. v. Parra***, 402 F.3d 752, 758 (7th Cir. 2005).

Stilwell v. Smith & Nephew, Inc., 482 F.3d 1187, 1192 (9th Cir.2007). "The court ... mingled the analysis required by [FRE] 702 for the admissibility of expert testimony and [FRCP] 56 for summary judgment. Though summary judgment enquires whether there *is* a 'genuine issue of material fact,' ... Rule 702's analysis is ordinarily prospective. Expert testimony is helpful if it '*will* assist the trier of fact.' Thus a district court may not exclude expert testimony simply because the court can, at the time of summary judgment, determine that the testimony does not result in a triable issue of fact. Rather the court must determine whether there is 'a link between the expert's testimony and the matter to be proved.' The chain necessary to prevail on a claim may be weakened by the absence of other evidence or testimony, but that does not undermine the admissibility of Rule 702 evidence." *See also* ***Thomas v. City of Chattanooga***, 398 F.3d 426, 432 (6th Cir.2005).

U.S. v. Perkins, 470 F.3d 150, 155-56 (4th Cir.2006). "While we have noted that '[a] critical distinction between [FRE] 701 and [FRE] 702 testimony is that an expert witness must possess some specialized knowledge or skill or education that is not in possession of the jurors,' ... we also have acknowledged that the 'subject matter of Rule 702 testimony need not be arcane or even especially difficult to comprehend....' The interpretive waters are muddier still: while lay opinion testimony *must* be based on personal knowledge, ... 'expert opinions may [also] be based on firsthand observation and experience.' At bottom, then, Rule 701 forbids the admission of expert testimony dressed in lay witness clothing, but it 'does not interdict all inference drawing by lay witnesses.'" *See also* ***U.S. v. White***,

492 F.3d 380, 403 (6th Cir.2007); ***U.S. v. Caballero***, 277 F.3d 1235, 1247 (10th Cir.2002).

U.S. v. Mornan, 413 F.3d 372, 380 (3d Cir.2005). "[H]andwriting analysis in general is sufficiently technical in nature to be the subject of expert testimony under Rule 702 and the standard articulated by the Supreme Court in ***Daubert***…."

Norris v. Baxter Healthcare Corp., 397 F.3d 878, 886 (10th Cir.2005). "'Although it is not always a straightforward exercise to disaggregate method and conclusion, when the conclusion simply does not follow from the data, a district court is free to determine that an impermissible analytical gap exists between premises and conclusion.' Although '[t]rained experts commonly extrapolate from existing data,' neither ***Daubert*** nor the [FREs] 'require[] a district court to admit opinion evidence which is connected to existing data only by the *ipse dixit* of the expert. A court may conclude that there is simply too great an analytical gap between the data and the opinion proffered.'" *See also* ***U.S. v. Mamah***, 332 F.3d 475, 478 (7th Cir.2003).

FRE 703. BASES OF AN EXPERT'S OPINION TESTIMONY

An expert may base an opinion on facts or data in the case that the expert has been made aware of or personally observed. If experts in the particular field would reasonably rely on those kinds of facts or data in forming an opinion on the subject, they need not be admissible for the opinion to be admitted. But if the facts or data would otherwise be inadmissible, the proponent of the opinion may disclose them to the jury only if their probative value in helping the jury evaluate the opinion substantially outweighs their prejudicial effect.

See selected Notes of Advisory Committee to FRE 703, p. 1263.

History of FRE 703: Adopted Jan. 2, 1975, P.L. 93-595, §1, 88 Stat. 1926, eff. July 1, 1975. Amended Mar. 2, 1987, eff. Oct. 1, 1987; Apr. 17, 2000, eff. Dec. 1, 2000; Apr. 26, 2011, eff. Dec. 1, 2011.

See ***Commentaries***, "Introducing Evidence," ch. 8-C, §4, p. 689.

ANNOTATIONS

Williams v. Illinois, ___ U.S. ___, 132 S.Ct. 2221, 2239-40 (2012) (plurality op.). Under Rule 703, "'basis evidence' that is not admissible for its truth may be disclosed … in a jury trial under appropriate circumstances. The purpose for allowing this disclosure is that it may 'assis[t] the jury to evaluate the expert's opinion.' The Rule 703 approach, which was controversial when adopted, is based on the idea that the disclosure of basis evidence can help the factfinder understand the expert's thought process and determine what weight to give to the expert's opinion. For example, if the factfinder were to suspect that the expert relied on factual premises with no support in the record, or that the expert drew an unwarranted inference from the premises on which the expert relied, then the probativeness or credibility of the expert's opinion would be seriously undermined. The purpose of disclosing the facts on which the expert relied is to allay these fears—to show that the expert's reasoning was not illogical, and that the weight of the expert's opinion does not depend on factual premises unsupported by other evidence in the record—not to prove the truth of the underlying facts."

U.S. v. Mejia, 545 F.3d 179, 197 (2d Cir.2008). "Under Rule 703, experts can testify to opinions based on inadmissible evidence, including hearsay, if 'experts in the field reasonably rely on such evidence in forming their opinions.' [¶] The expert may not, however, simply transmit that hearsay to the jury. Instead, the expert must form his own opinions by 'applying his extensive experience and a reliable methodology' to the inadmissible materials. Otherwise, the expert is simply 'repeating hearsay evidence without applying any expertise whatsoever,' [which allows circumvention of] 'the rules prohibiting hearsay.'" *See also* ***U.S. v. Dixon***, 413 F.3d 520, 524-25 (5th Cir.2005), *aff'd*, 548 U.S. 1 (2006).

In re Paoli R.R. Yard PCB Litig., 35 F.3d 717, 747 (3d Cir.1994). "While [FRE] 702 focuses on an expert's methodology, [FRE] 703 focuses on the data underlying the expert's opinion. [¶] We have held that the district judge must make a factual finding as to what data experts find reliable … and that if an expert avers that his testimony is based on a type of data on which experts reasonably rely, that is generally enough to survive the Rule 703 inquiry." *See also* ***U.S. v. Grace***, 504 F.3d 745, 759 (9th Cir.2007).

FRE 704. OPINION ON AN ULTIMATE ISSUE

(a) In General—Not Automatically Objectionable. An opinion is not objectionable just because it embraces an ultimate issue.

(b) Exception. In a criminal case, an expert witness must not state an opinion about whether the defendant did or did not have a mental state or condition that constitutes an element of the crime charged or of a defense. Those matters are for the trier of fact alone.

See selected Notes of Advisory Committee to FRE 704, p. 1264.

Effective December 1, 2011, FREs 101-1103 were restyled. For a discussion of the changes and a chart comparing the former and current rules, see p. 1024.

History of FRE 704: Adopted Jan. 2, 1975, P.L. 93-595, §1, 88 Stat. 1926, eff. July 1, 1975. Amended Oct. 12, 1984, P.L. 98-473, §406, 98 Stat. 2067; Apr. 26, 2011, eff. Dec. 1, 2011.

ANNOTATIONS

U.S. v. Offill, 666 F.3d 168, 177 (4th Cir.2011). "It is well established that experts may offer opinions based on hypothetical questions proposed by the attorneys questioning them. Such testimony would be admissible even though the hypothetical question[] mirrored the defendant's conduct, subject of course to the limitations that the witness not testify as to the defendant's 'intent,' as precluded by Rule 704(b)."

U.S. v. Goodman, 633 F.3d 963, 968-69 (10th Cir. 2011). "[T]here is no theoretical prohibition against allowing lay witnesses to give their opinions as to the mental states of others. [¶] Indeed, Rule 704(a) specifically allows testimony in the form of an opinion that embraces an ultimate issue.... Lay opinion of a witness as to a person's sanity is admissible if the witness is sufficiently acquainted with the person involved and has observed his conduct and has personal knowledge regarding the person's unusual, abnormal or bizarre conduct. [¶] We would have a quite different result if the question were the scope of expert opinion testimony. Rule 704(b) provides an exception to Rule 704(a) and expressly forbids *experts* from offering opinions as to the state of mind of a criminal defendant if that mental state is an element of the crime of which they are accused.... Such ultimate issues are matters for the trier of fact alone. Rule 704(b) does not, however, forbid lay witnesses from offering opinion testimony. Indeed, the rule's plain text limits its application to experts only. We recognize that Rule 704(b)'s last sentence ... could be understood to bar both lay and expert witness opinions, but the sentence cannot be read without referring to the one preceding it, which is clearly directed only at expert witnesses. Moreover, the legislative history of subdivision (b), which was added in 1984, indicates that the drafters and Congress focused only on problems with regard to expert witnesses, not lay witnesses." (Internal quotes omitted.)

U.S. v. Perkins, 470 F.3d 150, 157-58 (4th Cir.2006). "Although [FRE 704] officially abolished the so-called 'ultimate issue' rule, ... it did not lower the bar so as to admit all opinions. Testimony on ultimate issues still must be otherwise admissible under the [FREs]. ... The touchstone of admissibility of testimony that goes to the ultimate issue, then, is helpfulness to the jury. Thus, the district court's task is to distinguish helpful opinion testimony that embraces an ultimate fact from unhelpful opinion testimony that states a legal conclusion.... [¶] We have stated that the best way to determine whether opinion testimony is unhelpful because it merely states legal conclusions, is to determine whether the terms used by the witness have a separate, distinct and specialized meaning in the law different from that present in the vernacular. The district court should first consider whether the question tracks the language of the legal principle at issue or of the applicable statute; then, the court should consider whether any terms employed have a specialized legal meaning." (Internal quotes omitted.)

Berckeley Inv. Grp. v. Colkitt, 455 F.3d 195, 217 (3d Cir.2006). "Although [FRE] 704 permits an expert witness to give expert testimony that 'embraces an ultimate issue ...,' an expert witness is prohibited from rendering a legal opinion. Such testimony is prohibited because it would usurp the District Court's pivotal role in explaining the law to the jury." *See also* ***Anderson v. Suiters***, 499 F.3d 1228, 1237 (10th Cir.2007); ***U.S. v. Moran***, 493 F.3d 1002, 1008 (9th Cir.2007).

U.S. v. Hayward, 359 F.3d 631, 636 (3d Cir.2004). "[U]nder Rule 704(b), 'expert testimony is admissible if it merely supports an inference or conclusion that the defendant did or did not have the requisite mens rea, so long as the expert does not draw the ultimate inference or conclusion for the jury and the ultimate inference or conclusion does not necessarily follow from the testimony.'" *See also* ***U.S. v. Morris***, 576 F.3d 661, 674-75 (7th Cir.2009).

U.S. v. Two Eagle, 318 F.3d 785, 792 (8th Cir.2003). "[T]estimony is not defective merely because it utilized the words of the legal standard. Commonly used words and their plain meaning often match their legal meaning."

FRE 705. DISCLOSING THE FACTS OR DATA UNDERLYING AN EXPERT'S OPINION

Unless the court orders otherwise, an expert may state an opinion—and give the reasons for it—without first testifying to the underlying facts or data. But the expert may be required to disclose those facts or data on cross-examination.

See selected Notes of Advisory Committee to FRE 705, p. 1264.

History of FRE 705: Adopted Jan. 2, 1975, P.L. 93-595, §1, 88 Stat. 1926, eff. July 1, 1975. Amended Mar. 2, 1987, eff. Oct. 1, 1987; Apr. 22, 1993, eff. Dec. 1, 1993; Apr. 26, 2011, eff. Dec. 1, 2011.

FRE 704

ANNOTATIONS

B.F. Goodrich v. Betkoski, 99 F.3d 505, 525 (2d Cir. 1996). "An expert's testimony, in order to be admissible under Rule 705, need not detail all the facts and data underlying his opinion in order to present that opinion."

University of R.I. v. A.W. Chesterton Co., 2 F.3d 1200, 1218 (1st Cir.1993). FREs 703 and 705 "normally relieve the proponent of expert testimony from engaging in the awkward art of hypothetical questioning, which involves the ... process of laying a full factual foundation *prior* to asking the expert to state an opinion. In the interests of efficiency, the [FREs] deliberately shift the burden to the cross-examiner to ferret out whatever empirical deficiencies may lurk in the expert opinion. Nevertheless, Rules 703 and 705 do not afford automatic entitlements to proponents of expert testimony. [U]nder the broad exception to Rule 705 ..., the trial court is given considerable latitude over the order in which evidence will be presented to the jury."

FRE 706. COURT-APPOINTED EXPERT WITNESSES

(a) Appointment Process. On a party's motion or on its own, the court may order the parties to show cause why expert witnesses should not be appointed and may ask the parties to submit nominations. The court may appoint any expert that the parties agree on and any of its own choosing. But the court may only appoint someone who consents to act.

(b) Expert's Role. The court must inform the expert of the expert's duties. The court may do so in writing and have a copy filed with the clerk or may do so orally at a conference in which the parties have an opportunity to participate. The expert:

- **(1)** must advise the parties of any findings the expert makes;
- **(2)** may be deposed by any party;
- **(3)** may be called to testify by the court or any party; and
- **(4)** may be cross-examined by any party, including the party that called the expert.

(c) Compensation. The expert is entitled to a reasonable compensation, as set by the court. The compensation is payable as follows:

- **(1)** in a criminal case or in a civil case involving just compensation under the Fifth Amendment, from any funds that are provided by law; and
- **(2)** in any other civil case, by the parties in the proportion and at the time that the court directs—and the compensation is then charged like other costs.

(d) Disclosing the Appointment to the Jury. The court may authorize disclosure to the jury that the court appointed the expert.

(e) Parties' Choice of Their Own Experts. This rule does not limit a party in calling its own experts.

History of FRE 706: Adopted Jan. 2, 1975, P.L. 93-595, §1, 88 Stat. 1926, eff. July 1, 1975. Amended Mar. 2, 1987, eff. Oct. 1, 1987; Apr. 26, 2011, eff. Dec. 1, 2011.

ANNOTATIONS

Daubert v. Merrell Dow Pharms., 509 U.S. 579, 595 (1993). "Rule 706 allows the court at its discretion to procure the assistance of an expert of its own choosing."

Quiet Tech. DC-8, Inc. v. Hurel-DuBois UK Ltd., 326 F.3d 1333, 1348-49 (11th Cir.2003). "[W]e are unfamiliar with any set of circumstances under which a district court bears an affirmative obligation to appoint an independent expert [under FRE 706(a)]. Quite the contrary, as long as the district court thoroughly considers a request for the appointment of such an expert and reasonably explains its ultimate decision thereon, that decision is vested in the sound discretion of the trial court." *See also* ***Gaviria v. Reynolds***, 476 F.3d 940, 945 (D.C.Cir.2007); ***Walker v. American Home Shield Long Term Disability Plan***, 180 F.3d 1065, 1071 (9th Cir.1999).

Techsearch L.L.C. v. Intel Corp., 286 F.3d 1360, 1378 (Fed.Cir.2002). "A district court's appointment of a technical advisor, outside of the purview of Rule 706 ..., falls within the district court's inherent authority, and the Ninth Circuit has held that district courts may use technical advisors when desirable and necessary. It also implicitly recognized that district courts should use this inherent authority sparingly and then only in exceptionally technically complicated cases. *At 1379:* [I]n appointing a technical advisor[, the court] must: use a 'fair and open procedure for appointing a neutral technical advisor ... addressing any allegations of bias, partiality or lack of qualifications' in the candidates; clearly define and limit the technical

FRE 706

advisor's duties, presumably in a writing disclosed to all parties; guard against extra-record information; and make explicit, perhaps through a report or record, the nature and content of the technical advisor's tutelage concerning the technology. The fact that the use of a technical advisor is permissible under such guidelines does not mean that it is invariably desirable or that safeguards are not required. As a practical matter, there is a risk that some of the judicial decision-making function will be delegated to the technical advisor. District court judges need to be extremely sensitive to this risk and minimize the potential for its occurrence." *See also* ***In re Joint E.&S. Dist. Asbestos Litig.***, 830 F.Supp. 686, 693 (E.D.N.Y.1993) (work of appointed experts is especially critical in dealing with complex mass-tort problems).

Ledford v. Sullivan, 105 F.3d 354, 361 (7th Cir. 1997). "In this case, when the district court stated that no funds existed to pay for the appointment of an expert, it failed to recognize that it had the discretion [under former Rule 706(b), now Rule 706(c),] to apportion all the costs to one side. We caution against reading [former Rule 706(b), now Rule 706(c),] in such a narrow fashion that the rule would allow for court-appointed experts only when *both* sides are able to pay their respective shares. Read in such a restrictive way, [former Rule 706(b), now Rule 706(c),] would hinder a district court from appointing an expert witness whenever one of the parties is indigent, even when that expert's testimony would substantially aid the court."

ARTICLE VIII. HEARSAY

FRE 801. DEFINITIONS THAT APPLY TO THIS ARTICLE; EXCLUSIONS FROM HEARSAY

(a) Statement. "Statement" means a person's oral assertion, written assertion, or nonverbal conduct, if the person intended it as an assertion.

(b) Declarant. "Declarant" means the person who made the statement.

(c) Hearsay. "Hearsay" means a statement that:

(1) the declarant does not make while testifying at the current trial or hearing; and

(2) a party offers in evidence to prove the truth of the matter asserted in the statement.

(d) Statements That Are Not Hearsay. A statement that meets the following conditions is not hearsay:

(1) ***A Declarant-Witness's Prior Statement.*** The declarant testifies and is subject to cross-examination about a prior statement, and the statement:

(A) is inconsistent with the declarant's testimony and was given under penalty of perjury at a trial, hearing, or other proceeding or in a deposition;

(B) is consistent with the declarant's testimony and is offered to rebut an express or implied charge that the declarant recently fabricated it or acted from a recent improper influence or motive in so testifying; or

(C) identifies a person as someone the declarant perceived earlier.

(2) ***An Opposing Party's Statement.*** The statement is offered against an opposing party and:

(A) was made by the party in an individual or representative capacity;

(B) is one the party manifested that it adopted or believed to be true;

(C) was made by a person whom the party authorized to make a statement on the subject;

(D) was made by the party's agent or employee on a matter within the scope of that relationship and while it existed; or

(E) was made by the party's coconspirator during and in furtherance of the conspiracy.

The statement must be considered but does not by itself establish the declarant's authority under (C); the existence or scope of the relationship under (D); or the existence of the conspiracy or participation in it under (E).

See selected Notes of Advisory Committee to FRE 801, p. 1264.

History of FRE 801: Adopted Jan. 2, 1975, P.L. 93-595, §1, 88 Stat. 1926, eff. July 1, 1975. Amended Oct. 16, 1975, P.L. 94-113, §1, 89 Stat. 576, eff. Oct. 31, 1975; Mar. 2, 1987, eff. Oct. 1, 1987; Apr. 11, 1997, eff. Dec. 1, 1997; Apr. 26, 2011, eff. Dec. 1, 2011.

ANNOTATIONS

Generally

U.S. v. Benitez-Avila, 570 F.3d 364, 367-68 (1st Cir. 2009). "The principal vice of hearsay is the inability of the opponent of the evidence to cross-examine the person who made the out-of-court statement (the 'declarant'). The opponent of the evidence is thus unable to get the declarant's testimony as to whether in fact the declarant said what has been attributed to him, what he meant by it, whether he had a reliable basis for the as-

sertion, and whether he might have been influenced by a bias which undermines his reliability."

Definition – Statement

U.S. v. Waters, 627 F.3d 345, 358 (9th Cir.2010). "'Tell the truth' is an imperative and not an assertion of fact. It therefore does not fall within the meaning of 'statement' in Rule 801(a) and cannot be hearsay, because a nonassertion cannot have been offered to prove the truth of the matter asserted." *See also **Katzenmeier v. Blackpowder Prods.***, 628 F.3d 948, 951 (8th Cir. 2010) (instruction to someone to do something is not hearsay).

U.S. v. Pang, 362 F.3d 1187, 1192 (9th Cir.2004). "[O]ut-of-court statements that are offered as evidence of legally operative verbal conduct are not hearsay. They are considered 'verbal acts.' Checks [written on a bank account] fall squarely in this category of legally-operative verbal acts that are not barred by the hearsay rule."

Exclusion – Prior Statements

Tome v. U.S., 513 U.S. 150, 157-58 (1995). FRE 801 "defines prior consistent statements as nonhearsay only if they are offered to rebut a charge of 'recent fabrication or improper influence or motive.' [¶] The [FREs] do not accord this weighty, nonhearsay status to all prior consistent statements. ... Prior consistent statements may not be admitted to counter all forms of impeachment or to bolster the witness merely because she has been discredited. ... The Rule speaks of a party rebutting an alleged motive, not bolstering the veracity of the story told."

U.S. v. Caracappa, 614 F.3d 30, 39 (2d Cir.2010). "To come within Rule 801(d)(1)(B), the prior consistent statement need not be proffered through the testimony of the declarant but may be proffered through any witness who has first-hand knowledge of the statement. Further, where the declarant has already testified and the prior consistent statement is proffered through the testimony of another witness, the Rule's 'subject to cross-examination' requirement is satisfied if the opposing party is not denied the opportunity to recall the declarant to the stand for cross-examination concerning the statement."

U.S. v. Liu, 538 F.3d 1078, 1086 (9th Cir.2008). "[T]o admit statements under Rule 801(d)(1)(B), the party that seeks to admit the statements must satisfy four elements: '(1) the declarant must testify at trial and be subject to cross-examination; (2) there must be an express or implied charge of recent fabrication or improper influence or motive of the declarant's testimony; (3) the proponent must offer a prior consistent statement that is consistent with the declarant's challenged in-court testimony; and, (4) the prior consistent statement must be made prior to the time that the supposed motive to falsify arose.'" *See also **U.S. v. Anderson***, 303 F.3d 847, 858-59 (7th Cir.2002).

U.S. v. Frazier, 469 F.3d 85, 88-89 (3d Cir.2006). To trigger FRE 801(d)(1)(B), "'there need be only a suggestion that the witness consciously altered his testimony in order to permit the use of earlier statements that are generally consistent with the testimony at trial.' [¶] The statement ... that 'there need be only a suggestion' leaves substantial discretion to the District Court to allow prior consistent statements to be admitted as evidence under Rule 801(d)(1)(B). However, ... the suggestion of a *conscious alteration* by the opposing counsel, whether it be in an opening statement or on cross-examination[, is still mandated]. In this respect, ... 'Rule 801(d)(1)(B) cannot be construed to allow the admission of what would otherwise be hearsay every time a [witness's] credibility or memory is challenged; otherwise, cross-examination would always transform [the prior consistent statement] into admissible evidence.' The line between challenging credibility or memory and alleging conscious alteration can be drawn when a district court determines whether the cross-examiner's questions reasonably imply intent on the part of the witness to fabricate."

U.S. v. Mornan, 413 F.3d 372, 379 (3d Cir.2005). "[A] witness's lack of memory regarding a prior statement is not diametrically opposed to the substance of that statement. However, inconsistency under Rule 801(d)(1)(A) is not limited to diametrically opposed statements. Although this Court [has] noted ... that a prior statement should not be admitted if the witness's current memory loss regarding that statement is genuine, we join several other circuits in holding that a prior statement may be admitted under Rule 801(d)(1)(A) *where the witness's memory loss is not genuine*." *See also **U.S. v. Matlock***, 109 F.3d 1313, 1319 (8th Cir. 1997).

Exclusion – Opposing Party's Statement – Generally

U.S. v. McDaniel, 398 F.3d 540, 545 (6th Cir.2005). "Rule 801(d)(2) ... does not extend to a party's attempt to introduce his or her *own* statements through the testimony of other witnesses. Indeed, if such statements

Effective December 1, 2011, FREs 101-1103 were restyled. For a discussion of the changes and a chart comparing the former and current rules, see p. 1024.

were deemed admissible under Rule 801(d)(2), parties could effectuate an end-run around the adversarial process by, in effect, testifying without swearing an oath, facing cross-examination, or being subjected to first-hand scrutiny by the jury." *See also* ***Fischer v. Forestwood Co.***, 525 F.3d 972, 984-85 (10th Cir.2008).

Exclusion – Adoptive Statements

U.S. v. Miller, 478 F.3d 48, 51 (1st Cir.2007). "The law of evidence long has recognized 'adoptive admissions.' This doctrine provides that, in certain circumstances, a party's agreement with a fact stated by another may be inferred from (or 'adopted' by) silence. Such an inference may arise when (i) a statement is made in a party's presence, (ii) the nature of the statement is such that it normally would induce the party to respond, and (iii) the party nonetheless fails to take exception. In such an instance, the statement may be considered 'adopted' by virtue of the party's failure to respond." *See also* ***U.S. v. Ward***, 377 F.3d 671, 675 (7th Cir.2004).

Exclusion – Agent/Employee Statements

McDonough v. City of Quincy, 452 F.3d 8, 21 (1st Cir.2006). "For a statement to be an admission under [FRE] 801(d)(2)(D), it must be made by a party, a party's agent, or a servant within the scope of an agency or employment. The employee's station within the organization is not relevant to the Rule 801(d)(2) analysis. The relevant inquiry is whether the employee's statement was made within the scope of employment." *See also* ***Marra v. Philadelphia Hous. Auth.***, 497 F.3d 286, 297-98 (3d Cir.2007).

Marcic v. Reinauer Transp., 397 F.3d 120, 128-29 (2d Cir.2005). "In order to introduce evidence of an out-of-court statement as nonhearsay under Rule 801(d)(2)(D), a party must lay a sufficient foundation by establishing '(1) the existence of the agency relationship, (2) that the statement was made during the course of the relationship, and (3) that it relates to a matter within the scope of the agency.'" *See also* ***Ahlberg v. Chrysler Corp.***, 481 F.3d 630, 636 (8th Cir. 2007).

Exclusion – Coconspirator Statements

Bourjaily v. U.S., 483 U.S. 171, 181 (1987). "[A] court, in making a preliminary factual determination under Rule 801(d)(2)(E), may examine the hearsay statements sought to be admitted."

U.S. v. Rivera-Donate, 682 F.3d 120, 131 (1st Cir. 2012). "'A district court faced with a challenge to the admission of a co-conspirator's statement must provisionally admit the statement and then wait until the end of the trial to consider whether, in light of all the evidence, [the elements of FRE 801(d)(2)(E)] are satisfied by a preponderance of the evidence.' The preponderance of the evidence required in this context 'must necessarily comprise more than the weight of the statement itself,' requiring some corroborating extrinsic evidence." *See also* ***U.S. v. Mitchell***, 596 F.3d 18, 23 (1st Cir.2010).

U.S. v. El-Mezain, 664 F.3d 467, 502 (5th Cir.2011). "Although the rule speaks of statements made in furtherance of a conspiracy, we have recognized that admissibility under Rule 801(d)(2)(E) does not turn on the criminal nature of the endeavor. Instead, a statement may be admissible under Rule 801(d)(2)(E) if it is made in furtherance of a lawful joint undertaking. One can qualify as a joint venturer for the purposes of Rule 801(d)(2)(E) merely by engaging in a joint plan—distinct from the criminal conspiracy charged—that was non-criminal in nature. Pursuant to this joint venture theory, a statement is not hearsay if it was made during the course and in furtherance of a common plan or endeavor with a party, regardless of the non-criminal nature of that endeavor. *At 503:* [W]e are not alone in our construction of Rule 801(d)(2)(E), as our sister circuits have also held that statements made in furtherance of a lawful common enterprise are admissible. [¶] [C]onspiracy as an evidentiary rule differs from conspiracy as a crime. The crime of conspiracy comprehends much more than just a joint venture or concerted action, whereas the evidentiary rule of conspiracy is founded on concepts of agency law. Just as coconspirators are generally considered partners in crime and therefore agents of each other, joint venturers may be considered partners in the joint undertaking." (Internal quotes omitted.) *See also* ***Smith v. Bray***, 681 F.3d 888, 904 (7th Cir.2012); ***U.S. v. Gewin***, 471 F.3d 197, 201 (D.C.Cir.2006).

U.S. v. Bobb, 471 F.3d 491, 498 (3d Cir.2006). "Before any ... statement [under FRE 801(d)(2)(E)] may be admitted ..., the proponent must establish by a preponderance of the evidence that (1) the conspiracy existed; (2) both the defendant and the declarant were members of the conspiracy; and (3) the statement was made in the course of the conspiracy and in furtherance of the conspiracy. In determining whether the statement is admissible as a statement of a co-con-

spirator, the court may consider the statement itself. While a casual conversation between co-conspirators does not meet the 'in furtherance' requirement, 'statements between co-conspirators which provide reassurance, serve to maintain trust and cohesiveness among them, or inform each other of the current status of the conspiracy further the ends of the conspiracy and are admissible so long as the other requirements of Rule 801(d)(2)(E) are met.'"

U.S. v. Franklin, 415 F.3d 537, 552 (6th Cir.2005). "Statements that are designed to facilitate the concealment of a conspiracy's criminal accomplishments are admissible under Rule 801(d)(2)(E). ... Statements that identify participants and their roles in the conspiracy also qualify as statements made in furtherance of the conspiracy. Similarly, statements that keep a conspirator abreast of a co-conspirator's activities are admissible." (Internal quotes omitted.)

FRE 802. THE RULE AGAINST HEARSAY

Hearsay is not admissible unless any of the following provides otherwise:

- a federal statute;
- these rules; or
- other rules prescribed by the Supreme Court.

History of FRE 802: Adopted Jan. 2, 1975, P.L. 93-595, §1, 88 Stat. 1926, eff. July 1, 1975. Amended Apr. 26, 2011, eff. Dec. 1, 2011.

See also 10 U.S.C. §7730 (admissibility of affidavit, statement, or testimony of unavailable witness in action that is for damages caused by vessel in naval service, or towage or salvage of same, and that is delayed or stayed for security reasons); 38 U.S.C. §8506 (affidavit as proof of posting notice of sale of unclaimed property by Veterans Administration).

ANNOTATIONS

Williamson v. U.S., 512 U.S. 594, 598 (1994). FRE 802 "is premised on the theory that out-of-court statements are subject to particular hazards. The declarant might be lying; he might have misperceived the events which he relates; he might have faulty memory; his words might be misunderstood or taken out of context by the listener. And the ways in which these dangers are minimized for in-court statements—the oath, the witness' awareness of the gravity of the proceedings, the jury's ability to observe the witness' demeanor, and, most importantly, the right of the opponent to cross-examine—are generally absent for things said out of court."

U.S. v. Williams, 358 F.3d 956, 963 (D.C.Cir.2004). "As a general matter, [FREs 801 and 802] prohibit the admission of an out-of-court statement offered in evidence to prove the truth of the matter asserted. Such a statement may be admitted to serve a non-hearsay purpose, however, such as elucidating a speaker's or a listener's state of mind ... or providing background information...."

U.S. v. Cardascia, 951 F.2d 474, 486-87 (2d Cir. 1991). "Generally [hearsay] is not admissible ... because traditional conditions of admissibility, including that the witness be present at the trial, testify under oath, and be subject to cross-examination, [which] permit a jury to evaluate the ... trustworthiness of a statement, are not present. [T]he purpose for which the statement is being introduced must be examined and the trial judge must determine whether—if that purpose is to prove the truth of its assertion—the proffered statement fits within any of the categories excepted from the rule's prohibition. [¶] '[I]f the significance of an offered statement lies solely in the fact that it was made, no issue is raised as to the truth of anything asserted, [then] the statement is not hearsay.' Statements not considered hearsay are typically verbal acts that give rise to legal consequences."

FRE 803. EXCEPTIONS TO THE RULE AGAINST HEARSAY—REGARDLESS OF WHETHER THE DECLARANT IS AVAILABLE AS A WITNESS

Editor's note: *The Committee on Rules of Practice and Procedure of the Judicial Conference of the United States has proposed amendments to FRE 803, to be effective December 1, 2013. For the proposed amendments, see www.uscourts.gov/RulesAndPolicies/rules/pending-rules.aspx.*

The following are not excluded by the rule against hearsay, regardless of whether the declarant is available as a witness:

(1) ***Present Sense Impression.*** A statement describing or explaining an event or condition, made while or immediately after the declarant perceived it.

(2) ***Excited Utterance.*** A statement relating to a startling event or condition, made while the declarant was under the stress of excitement that it caused.

(3) ***Then-Existing Mental, Emotional, or Physical Condition.*** A statement of the declarant's then-existing state of mind (such as motive,

Effective December 1, 2011, FREs 101-1103 were restyled. For a discussion of the changes and a chart comparing the former and current rules, see p. 1024.

intent, or plan) or emotional, sensory, or physical condition (such as mental feeling, pain, or bodily health), but not including a statement of memory or belief to prove the fact remembered or believed unless it relates to the validity or terms of the declarant's will.

(4) ***Statement Made for Medical Diagnosis or Treatment.*** A statement that:

(A) is made for—and is reasonably pertinent to—medical diagnosis or treatment; and

(B) describes medical history; past or present symptoms or sensations; their inception; or their general cause.

(5) ***Recorded Recollection.*** A record that:

(A) is on a matter the witness once knew about but now cannot recall well enough to testify fully and accurately;

(B) was made or adopted by the witness when the matter was fresh in the witness's memory; and

(C) accurately reflects the witness's knowledge.

If admitted, the record may be read into evidence but may be received as an exhibit only if offered by an adverse party.

(6) ***Records of a Regularly Conducted Activity.*** A record of an act, event, condition, opinion, or diagnosis if:

(A) the record was made at or near the time by—or from information transmitted by—someone with knowledge;

(B) the record was kept in the course of a regularly conducted activity of a business, organization, occupation, or calling, whether or not for profit;

(C) making the record was a regular practice of that activity;

(D) all these conditions are shown by the testimony of the custodian or another qualified witness, or by a certification that complies with Rule 902(11) or (12) or with a statute permitting certification; and

(E) neither the source of information nor the method or circumstances of preparation indicate a lack of trustworthiness.

(7) ***Absence of a Record of a Regularly Conducted Activity.*** Evidence that a matter is not included in a record described in paragraph (6) if:

(A) the evidence is admitted to prove that the matter did not occur or exist;

(B) a record was regularly kept for a matter of that kind; and

(C) neither the possible source of the information nor other circumstances indicate a lack of trustworthiness.

(8) ***Public Records.*** A record or statement of a public office if:

(A) it sets out:

(i) the office's activities;

(ii) a matter observed while under a legal duty to report, but not including, in a criminal case, a matter observed by law-enforcement personnel; or

(iii) in a civil case or against the government in a criminal case, factual findings from a legally authorized investigation; and

(B) neither the source of information nor other circumstances indicate a lack of trustworthiness.

(9) ***Public Records of Vital Statistics.*** A record of a birth, death, or marriage, if reported to a public office in accordance with a legal duty.

(10) ***Absence of a Public Record.*** Testimony—or a certification under Rule 902—that a diligent search failed to disclose a public record or statement if the testimony or certification is admitted to prove that:

(A) the record or statement does not exist; or

(B) a matter did not occur or exist, if a public office regularly kept a record or statement for a matter of that kind.

(11) ***Records of Religious Organizations Concerning Personal or Family History.*** A statement of birth, legitimacy, ancestry, marriage, divorce, death, relationship by blood or marriage, or similar facts of personal or family history, contained in a regularly kept record of a religious organization.

(12) ***Certificates of Marriage, Baptism, and Similar Ceremonies.*** A statement of fact contained in a certificate:

(A) made by a person who is authorized by a religious organization or by law to perform the act certified;

(B) attesting that the person performed a marriage or similar ceremony or administered a sacrament; and

(C) purporting to have been issued at the time of the act or within a reasonable time after it.

(13) ***Family Records.*** A statement of fact about personal or family history contained in a family record, such as a Bible, genealogy, chart, engraving on a ring, inscription on a portrait, or engraving on an urn or burial marker.

(14) ***Records of Documents That Affect an Interest in Property.*** The record of a document that purports to establish or affect an interest in property if:

(A) the record is admitted to prove the content of the original recorded document, along with its signing and its delivery by each person who purports to have signed it;

(B) the record is kept in a public office; and

(C) a statute authorizes recording documents of that kind in that office.

(15) ***Statements in Documents That Affect an Interest in Property.*** A statement contained in a document that purports to establish or affect an interest in property if the matter stated was relevant to the document's purpose—unless later dealings with the property are inconsistent with the truth of the statement or the purport of the document.

(16) ***Statements in Ancient Documents.*** A statement in a document that is at least 20 years old and whose authenticity is established.

(17) ***Market Reports and Similar Commercial Publications.*** Market quotations, lists, directories, or other compilations that are generally relied on by the public or by persons in particular occupations.

(18) ***Statements in Learned Treatises, Periodicals, or Pamphlets.*** A statement contained in a treatise, periodical, or pamphlet if:

(A) the statement is called to the attention of an expert witness on cross-examination or relied on by the expert on direct examination; and

(B) the publication is established as a reliable authority by the expert's admission or testimony, by another expert's testimony, or by judicial notice.

If admitted, the statement may be read into evidence but not received as an exhibit.

(19) ***Reputation Concerning Personal or Family History.*** A reputation among a person's family by blood, adoption, or marriage—or among a person's associates or in the community—concerning the person's birth, adoption, legitimacy, ancestry, marriage, divorce, death, relationship by blood, adoption, or marriage, or similar facts of personal or family history.

(20) ***Reputation Concerning Boundaries or General History.*** A reputation in a community—arising before the controversy—concerning boundaries of land in the community or customs that affect the land, or concerning general historical events important to that community, state, or nation.

(21) ***Reputation Concerning Character.*** A reputation among a person's associates or in the community concerning the person's character.

(22) ***Judgment of a Previous Conviction.*** Evidence of a final judgment of conviction if:

(A) the judgment was entered after a trial or guilty plea, but not a nolo contendere plea;

(B) the conviction was for a crime punishable by death or by imprisonment for more than a year;

(C) the evidence is admitted to prove any fact essential to the judgment; and

(D) when offered by the prosecutor in a criminal case for a purpose other than impeachment, the judgment was against the defendant.

The pendency of an appeal may be shown but does not affect admissibility.

(23) ***Judgments Involving Personal, Family, or General History, or a Boundary.*** A judgment that is admitted to prove a matter of personal, family, or general history, or boundaries, if the matter:

(A) was essential to the judgment; and

(B) could be proved by evidence of reputation.

(24) [***Other Exceptions.***] [Transferred to Rule 807.]

See selected Notes of Advisory Committee to FRE 803, p. 1264.

History of FRE 803: Adopted Jan. 2, 1975, P.L. 93-595, §1, 88 Stat. 1926, eff. July 1, 1975. Amended Dec. 12, 1975, P.L. 94-149, §1(11), 89 Stat. 805; Mar. 2, 1987, eff. Oct. 1, 1987; Apr. 11, 1997, eff. Dec. 1, 1997; Apr. 17, 2000, eff. Dec. 1, 2000; Apr. 26, 2011, eff. Dec. 1, 2011.

Effective December 1, 2011, FREs 101-1103 were restyled. For a discussion of the changes and a chart comparing the former and current rules, see p. 1024.

ANNOTATIONS

FRE 803(1)

U.S. v. McElroy, 587 F.3d 73, 85 (1st Cir.2009). "Notably, [the present-sense-impression] exception does not include, explicitly, a requirement for corroboration. [T]he lack of such a requirement is justified because the 'underlying rationale offers sufficient assurances of reliability.' In most settings, the 'limitation of the exception in terms of time and subject matter … insure[s] that the witness who reports the making of the statement will have perceived the event or at least observed circumstances strongly suggesting it.' The declarant and the reporting witness are present at the event or condition and both experience, at least to some degree, the event or condition sought to be admitted into evidence. Therefore, the testimony of the witness describing the circumstances in which the hearsay utterance was made corroborate, to a significant degree, the trustworthiness of the statement."

U.S. v. Green, 556 F.3d 151, 155-56 (3d Cir.2009). "The fundamental premise behind [FRE 803(1)] 'is that substantial contemporaneity of event and statement minimizes unreliability due to [the declarant's] defective recollection or conscious fabrication.' 'The idea of immediacy lies at the heart of the exception,' thus, the time requirement underlying the exception 'is strict because it is *the* factor that assures trustworthiness.' Put differently, the temporality requirement must be rigorous because the passage of time—or the lack thereof—is the effective proxy for the reliability of the substance of the declaration; hence the greater the passage of time, the less truthworthy the statement is presumed to be, and the more the scales should tip toward inadmissibility. Nevertheless, some brief temporal lapse is permissible so as to accommodate 'the human realities that the condition or event may happen so fast that the words do not quite keep pace.'"

Schindler v. Seiler, 474 F.3d 1008, 1011 (7th Cir. 2007). "There are three criteria for the admission of statements under Rule 803(1): '(1) the statement must describe an event or condition without calculated narration; (2) the speaker must have personally perceived the event or condition described; and (3) the statement must have been made while the speaker was perceiving the event or condition, or immediately thereafter.' 'A declarant who deliberates about what to say or provides statements for a particular reason creates the possibility that the statements are not contemporaneous, and, more likely, are calculated interpretations of events rather than near simultaneous perceptions.'" *See also* ***Dávila v. Corporación de P.R. Para la Difusión Pública***, 498 F.3d 9, 18 (1st Cir.2007).

FRE 803(2)

U.S. v. Pursley, 577 F.3d 1204, 1220 (10th Cir.2009). "The excited-utterance exception has three requirements: (1) a startling event; (2) the statement was made while the declarant was under the stress of the event's excitement; and (3) a nexus between the content of the statement and the event. [¶] Courts consider a range of factors in determining whether a declarant made a statement while under the stress of a particular event. Among the more relevant factors are: the amount of time between the event and the statement; the nature of the event; the subject matter of the statement; the age and condition of the declarant; the presence or absence of self-interest; and whether the statement was volunteered or in response to questioning." *See also* ***Brunsting v. Lutsen Mountains Corp.***, 601 F.3d 813, 817-18 (8th Cir.2010).

U.S. v. Alexander, 331 F.3d 116, 122-23 (D.C.Cir. 2003). "The rationale underlying the 'excited utterance' exception is that 'excitement suspends the declarant's powers of reflection and fabrication, consequently minimizing the possibility that the utterance will be influenced by self interest and therefore rendered unreliable.' Thus, to qualify as an excited utterance, 'the declarant's state of mind at the time that the statement was made [must] preclude conscious reflection on the subject of the statement.' [¶] [U]nlike the hearsay exception for present sense impressions [under FRE 803(1)], '[a]n excited utterance need not be contemporaneous with the startling event to be admissible….' 'Rather, the utterance must be contemporaneous with the excitement engendered by the startling event.' [¶] Although the lapse of time between the startling event and the declarant's statement is relevant to whether the declarant made the statement while under the stress of excitement, the temporal gap between the event and the utterance is not itself dispositive." *See also* ***Biegas v. Quickway Carriers, Inc.***, 573 F.3d 365, 379 (6th Cir.2009).

Miller v. Keating, 754 F.2d 507, 510 (3d Cir.1985). "The next question is whether the excited utterance exception may ever authorize the admission of a statement by an anonymous declarant. [¶] We do not con-

clude ... that statements by unidentified declarants are ipso facto inadmissible under [FRE] 803(2). Such statements are admissible if they otherwise meet the criteria of [FRE] 803(2). But unlike unavailability, which is immaterial to admission under Rule 803, the unidentifiability of the declarant is germane to the admissibility determination. A party seeking to introduce such a statement carries a burden heavier than where the declarant is identified to demonstrate the statement's circumstantial trustworthiness."

FRE 803(3)

U.S. v. Ledford, 443 F.3d 702, 709 (10th Cir.2005). The FREs "contemplate an exception to the exception: a statement that would otherwise be admissible under the state-of-mind exception is inadmissible if it is a statement of memory or belief offered to prove the fact remembered or believed. [¶] [A] witness may testify to a declarant saying 'I am scared,' but not 'I am scared because the defendant threatened me.' The first statement indicates an actual state of mind or condition, while the second statement expresses belief about why the declarant is frightened. The phrase 'because the defendant threatened me' is expressly outside the state-of-mind exception because the explanation for the fear expresses a *belief* different from the *state of mind* of being afraid." *See also* ***Stelwagon Mfg. v. Tarmac Roofing Sys.***, 63 F.3d 1267, 1274 (3d Cir.1995).

Colasanto v. Life Ins. Co. of N. Am., 100 F.3d 203, 212 (1st Cir.1996). "Rule 803(3) removes from the hearsay prohibition statements that exhibit a declarant's 'then-existing state of mind.' But, this exception is not to be construed as a sweeping endorsement of all state-of-mind evidence. To be admissible under this exception, a declaration, among other things, must 'mirror a state of mind, which, in light of all the circumstances, including proximity in time, is reasonably likely to have been the same condition existing at the material time.' Because disputes over whether particular statements come within the state-of-mind exception are fact-sensitive, the trial court is in the best position to resolve them."

FRE 803(4)

U.S. v. Bercier, 506 F.3d 625, 632 (8th Cir.2007). "Statements to a medical professional concerning the cause of an injury—'I was assaulted'—are usually admissible under Rule 803(4). But statements identifying the assailant are 'seldom, if ever,' sufficiently related to diagnosis or treatment to be admissible. Such statements may be admissible if the identity of the abuser is relevant to treating the victim's emotional or psychological injuries. But the government must demonstrate that (i) the physician made clear to the victim that inquiry into the abuser's identity was essential to diagnosis and treatment, and (ii) 'the victim manifest[ed] such an understanding.'"

U.S. v. Kappell, 418 F.3d 550, 556 (6th Cir.2005). "We hold that Rule 803(4) covers statements made to a psychotherapist for purposes of medical diagnosis or treatment, even though the therapist is not a physician or nurse."

Willingham v. Crooke, 412 F.3d 553, 562 (4th Cir. 2005). FRE 803(4) "is premised on the notion that a declarant seeking treatment 'has a selfish motive to be truthful' because 'the effectiveness of medical treatment depends upon the accuracy of the information provided.' Admissibility of a statement pursuant to Rule 803(4) is governed by a two-part test: '(1) the declarant's motive in making the statement must be consistent with the purposes of promoting treatment; and, (2) the content of the statement must be such as is reasonably relied on by a physician in treatment or diagnosis.' With respect to the second prong, we note that '[i]n general, a patient's statement describing how an injury occurred is pertinent to a physician's diagnosis and treatment.'" *See also* ***U.S. v. Tome***, 61 F.3d 1446, 1449 (10th Cir.1995).

Bucci v. Essex Ins., 393 F.3d 285, 298 (1st Cir. 2005). "There is no requirement, either in the text of [FRE 803(4)], or the case law, that the speaker be the patient himself. In general, under Rule 803(4), 'the declarant's motive to promote treatment or diagnosis is the factor crucial to reliability.' [¶] Sometimes, when the declarant of an out-of-court statement is unknown, there is less certainty that the statement was made for the purpose of treating or diagnosing the patient, and the statement itself may not bear the indicia of that purpose."

FRE 803(5)

U.S. v. Jones, 601 F.3d 1247, 1262 (11th Cir.2010). FRE 803(5) "requires the proponent to demonstrate that the witness-declarant's memory has faded so that he is no longer able 'to testify fully and accurately.' [¶] Rule 803(5) also requires that the witness verify the contents of the past statement. 'The witness must be able now to assert that the record accurately represented his knowledge and recollection at the time. The

Effective December 1, 2011, FREs 101-1103 were restyled. For a discussion of the changes and a chart comparing the former and current rules, see p. 1024.

usual phrase requires the witness to affirm that he knew it to be true at the time.'"

U.S. v. Mornan, 413 F.3d 372, 377-78 (3d Cir.2005). Former FRE 803(5), now FRE 803(5)(B), "requires the witness to have either made the record herself, or to have reviewed and adopted the statement, at a time when the matter it concerned was fresh in her memory. Where ... the statement was recorded by someone other than the declarant, accuracy may be established through the testimony of the person who recorded the statement."

U.S. v. Hernandez, 333 F.3d 1168, 1178 (10th Cir. 2003). "The most logical reading of the phrase 'by the witness' [in former FRE 803(5), now FRE 803(5)(B),] is that that phrase modifies both of the preceding verbs 'made' and 'adopted.'"

FRE 803(6)

U.S. v. Blechman, 657 F.3d 1052, 1065-66 (10th Cir. 2011). "Double hearsay in the context of a business record exists when the record is prepared by an employee with information supplied by another person. If the person who provides the information is an outsider to the business who is not under a business duty to provide accurate information, then the reliability rationale that underlies the business records exception ordinarily does not apply. Accordingly, the general rule is that any information provided by an outsider to the business preparing the record must itself fall within a hearsay exception to be admissible. [¶] This Court, however, has recognized one exception to the general rule: information provided by an outsider that is included in a business record may come in under the business records exception if the business entity has adequate verification or other assurance of accuracy of the information provided by the outside person. In the context of identity information provided by an outsider, we have identified two ways to demonstrate this guarantee of trustworthiness: (1) proof that the business has a policy of verifying the accuracy of information provided by someone outside the business; or (2) proof that the business possesses a sufficient self-interest in the accuracy of the record to justify an inference of trustworthiness." (Internal quotes omitted.) *See also* ***U.S. v. Gurr***, 471 F.3d 144, 151-52 (D.C.Cir.2006); ***Wilson v. Zapata Off-Shore Co.***, FRE 805, p. 1077.

U-Haul Int'l v. Lumbermens Mut. Cas. Co., 576 F.3d 1040, 1043 (9th Cir.2009). "[F]or the purposes of Rule 803(6), it is immaterial that the business record is maintained in a computer rather than in company books. A logical extension on that principle is that evidence that has been compiled from a computer database is also admissible as a business record, provided it meets the criteria of Rule 803(6)." (Internal quotes omitted.) *See also* ***U.S. v. Jackson***, 208 F.3d 633, 638 (7th Cir.2000).

Thanongsinh v. Board of Educ., 462 F.3d 762, 777 (7th Cir.2006). Former FRE 803(6), now FRE 803(6)(D), "permits the authentication of a business record by the 'custodian' of the record or [another] 'qualified witness.' Ordinarily, the custodian or other qualified witness will testify in court that it was the 'regular practice' of the business to make and keep the business record. Alternatively, the plaintiff can certify the document under [FRE] 902(11) or 902(12).... [¶] In both situations, the custodian need not be the individual who 'personally gather[ed] ... a business record. The custodian of the records need not be in control of or have individual knowledge of the particular corporate records, but need only be familiar with the company's recordkeeping practices.'" *See also* ***U.S. Commodity Futures Trading Comm'n v. Dizona***, 594 F.3d 408, 415-16 (5th Cir.2010); ***Brawner v. Allstate Indem. Co.***, 591 F.3d 984, 987 (8th Cir.2010).

Conoco Inc. v. Department of Energy, 99 F.3d 387, 392 (Fed.Cir.1996). "[T]he sufficiency of the foundation evidence must be assessed in light of the nature of the documents at issue; documents that are standard records of the type regularly maintained by firms in a particular industry may require less by way of foundation testimony than less conventional documents proffered for admission as business records."

FRE 803(7)

U.S. v. Muñoz-Franco, 487 F.3d 25, 39 (1st Cir. 2007). "We think [the] repetition [in FRE 803(6)(E) and FRE 803(7)(C)] indicates that even if a business record is deemed sufficiently trustworthy to be admissible for its contents under Rule 803(6), other circumstances might render omissions in that record untrustworthy to show that the events omitted did not occur."

Kaiser Aluminum & Chem. Corp. v. Illinois Cent. Gulf R.R., 615 F.2d 470, 476 (8th Cir.1980). "Although [P] introduced testimony that its normal business practice was to inspect and clean its cars and to retain a record of this information, no such records were intro-

FRE 803

duced into evidence. [T]he nonoccurrence or nonexistence of any cleaning or inspection of these cars may be presumed under Rule 803(7)…."

FRE 803(8)

Beech Aircraft Corp. v. Rainey, 488 U.S. 153, 167 (1988). The "trustworthiness inquiry [under former FRE 803(8)(C), now FRE 803(8)(B),] applies to all elements of the report. Thus, a trial judge has the discretion, and indeed the obligation, to exclude an entire report or portions thereof … that she determines to be untrustworthy. *At 167 n.11:* The Advisory Committee proposed a nonexclusive list of four factors it thought would be helpful in passing on this question: (1) the timeliness of the investigation; (2) the investigator's skill or experience; (3) whether a hearing was held; and (4) possible bias when reports are prepared with a view to possible litigation."

U.S. v. Lang, 672 F.3d 17, 23-24 (1st Cir.2012). "Two principal justifications for [FRE 803(8)] are 'the presumed trustworthiness of public documents prepared in the discharge of official functions, and the necessity of using such documents, due to the likelihood that a public official would have no independent memory of a particular action or entry where his duties require the constant repetition of routine tasks.'"

Sullivan v. Dollar Tree Stores, 623 F.3d 770, 777 (9th Cir.2010). "Does [former Rule 803(8)(C), now Rule 803(8)(A)(iii),] cover an investigative report's *legal conclusions* as well as its *factual findings*? [¶] Only one circuit court has addressed that open question at any length. [T]he Eleventh Circuit held that [former Rule 803(8)(C), now Rule 803(8)(A)(iii),] does not provide for the admissibility of the legal conclusions contained within an otherwise admissible public report. Legal conclusions are inadmissible because the jury would have no way of knowing whether the preparer of the report was cognizant of the requirements underlying the legal conclusion and, if not, whether the preparer might have a higher or lower standard than the law requires. That court cautioned, however, that the amorphous line between 'factual' and 'legal' conclusions may obscure a practical analysis under this rubric. The Fourth Circuit has agreed, albeit without analysis. [¶] We agree with the Eleventh and Fourth Circuits. Pure legal conclusions are not admissible as factual findings." (Internal quotes omitted.)

In re Nautilus Motor Tanker Co., 85 F.3d 105, 112-13 (3d Cir.1996). FRE 803(8) does "not preclude the introduction of opinions and conclusions in [public] reports so long as two criteria [are] met. First, all statements in such a report must be based on factual investigation. Second, any portion of the report that is admitted must be sufficiently trustworthy. [P]ublic reports are presumed admissible in the first instance and the party opposing their introduction bears the burden of coming forward with enough 'negative factors' to persuade a court that a report should not be admitted." *See also* ***English v. District of Columbia***, 651 F.3d 1, 7-8 (D.C.Cir.2011).

FRE 803(9)

Oglesby v. Williams, 484 F.Supp. 865, 867 (M.D.Fla. 1980). "Birth certificates are widely accepted and relied upon in any context in which date and place of birth, or parentage, is a material concern. Indeed, Rule 803(9) … specifically provides that such records are admissible in evidence as an exception to the hearsay rule."

FRE 803(10)

Hunt v. Liberty Lobby, 720 F.2d 631, 651 (11th Cir. 1983). "[D] complains of the admission into evidence of the affidavits of certain CIA officials. The affiant in each document stated that he was the custodian of particular records at the CIA and that, after diligent search of the appropriate files, he was unable to locate any evidence of CIA memoranda…. [¶] The affidavits were properly admitted. They fell within an exception to the hearsay rule [under FRE 803(10)], and were self-authenticating [under FRE 902(2)]."

FRE 803(11)

Hall v. Commissioner, 729 F.2d 632, 635 (9th Cir. 1984). "[T]he evidence did not fall under the religious records exception to the hearsay rule. … Statements of contributions to a church do not constitute such personal information. Thus, the contribution statement was properly excluded."

FRE 803(14)

Greycas, Inc. v. Proud, 826 F.2d 1560, 1567 (7th Cir.1987). "[A] judgment, insofar as it fixes property rights, should be admissible as the official record of such rights, just like other documents of title…."

FRE 803(16)

Threadgill v. Armstrong World Indus., 928 F.2d 1366, 1375 (3d Cir.1991). "Once a document qualifies as an ancient document, it is automatically excepted from the hearsay rule under [FRE] 803(16)."

FRE 803

Effective December 1, 2011, FREs 101-1103 were restyled. For a discussion of the changes and a chart comparing the former and current rules, see p. 1024.

Dartez v. Fibreboard Corp., 765 F.2d 456, 464 (5th Cir.1985). "The authentication requirement [in FRE 803(16)] is governed by the standards set forth in [FRE] 901(a). ... Ancient documents are most frequently authenticated under the provisions of Rule 901(b)(8)...."

FRE 803(17)

Conoco Inc. v. Department of Energy, 99 F.3d 387, 393 (Fed.Cir.1996). "Unlike market reports, telephone directories, weather reports, mortality tables, or like documents that come within the ambit of Rule 803(17), the purchase summaries at issue in this case were not prepared with the view that they would be in general use by an industry or members of the public having a general need to rely on information of that type. And unlike the publishers of the types of commercial documents that are typically admissible under Rule 803(17), the purchasers who prepared the summaries did not, by transmitting them to [P], stake their business or public reputations on the accuracy of the summaries. The summaries therefore do not have the same indicia of reliability as commercial publications that are admissible under Rule 803(17)."

Ellis v. International Playtex, Inc., 745 F.2d 292, 303 n.10 (4th Cir.1984). "[D] contends that because the statistical findings were based on interviews they constituted multiple hearsay. We do not believe this a proper ground upon which to deny admission. Survey and poll data have repeatedly been admitted under an exception to the rule against hearsay."

FRE 803(18)

U.S. v. Martinez, 588 F.3d 301, 311-12 (6th Cir. 2009). "[T]he video [in this case] may ... be admissible if it fits under one of the hearsay exceptions. The most relevant exception [is] the 'learned treatise' exception.... The Second Circuit [held] that [a 15-minute training video from the audiovisual library of the American College of Obstetricians and Gynecologists] was a contemporary variant of a published treatise, and the video's use as a training resource—written primarily and impartially for professionals, subject to scrutiny and exposure for accuracy, with the reputation of its producers and sponsors at stake—is clearly an important index of its authoritativeness. [¶] Learned treatises usually have sufficient assurances of trustworthiness. *Authors of treatises have no bias in any particular case* and are acutely aware that their material will be read and evaluated by others in their field, and accordingly feel a strong pressure to be accurate. Because the ... video [in this case] does not have the necessary qualities of reliability, we do not need to decide whether a video *could* satisfy the 'learned treatise' exception...." (Internal quotes omitted.)

Twin City Fire Ins. v. Country Mut. Ins., 23 F.3d 1175, 1184 (7th Cir.1994). "[N]o proper foundation was laid for the use of the article in cross-examination. It is not enough that the journal in which it appeared was reputable; the author of the particular article had to be shown to be an authority before the article could be used consistently with [FRE] 803(18)."

FRE 803(19)

Blackburn v. United Parcel Serv., 179 F.3d 81, 99-100 (3d Cir.1999). "[W]e believe that Rule 803(19), in referring to 'reputation ... among a person's associates, or in the community,' encompasses one's reputation at a place of work. ... In the context of reputation evidence of a person's character, 'courts have readily extended the concept of community to include the community in which one works, as well as where one lives.' [¶] As for the basis of the reputation evidence regarding relationships within a workplace, we find little guidance in the sparse case law surrounding Rule 803(19). We believe, however, that the principle behind admitting such evidence despite its hearsay origin—i.e., 'that general reputation about facts of interest to the community is probably trustworthy,'—requires that a proponent of Rule 803(19) evidence establish that the reputation testimony arises from sufficient inquiry and discussion among persons with personal knowledge of the matter to constitute a trustworthy 'reputation.' Rumors and speculation are clearly insufficient in this regard."

Government of V.I. v. Joseph, 765 F.2d 394, 397 n.5 (3d Cir.1985). "[D] argues that [complainant's] testimony as to her own age was inadmissible as relating information obtained through hearsay. This contention is without merit for two reasons. First, courts have uniformly accepted testimony regarding one's own age despite its hearsay nature because, practically speaking, 'a person's belief on this point has a satisfactory basis.' Second, the date of one's birth can be considered reputation concerning personal or family history, for which an exception has been made to the hearsay rule under the [FREs]."

FRE 803(20)

Ute Indian Tribe v. Utah, 521 F.Supp. 1072, 1149 (D.Utah 1981), *rev'd in part on other grounds*, 773 F.2d 1087 (10th Cir.1985). "While a long-standing reputation may serve as important evidence of the status of a boundary of immediate personal importance, e.g., a private property line among neighbors, or of more universal importance, such as a national or state boundary, reputation in a non-Indian community as to Indian boundaries, rights, etc., is indeed a treacherous ground for decision. [¶] To have significant probative value, the matter in question 'must be one of general interest, so that it can accurately be said that there is a high probability that the matter underwent general scrutiny as the community reputation was formed.'"

FRE 803(21)

Trade Waste Mgmt. v. Hughey, 780 F.2d 221, 239 n.8 (3d Cir.1985). "While evidence of character is usually not admissible for the purpose of proving that a person acted in conformance with that character in a given instance, it is generally admitted for other purposes. Thus, although it is often the case that a bad reputation is undeserved, it is reasonable for the New Jersey Legislature to consider reputation in the context of a licensing scheme."

FRE 803(22)

Hancock v. Dodson, 958 F.2d 1367, 1371 (6th Cir. 1992). "A guilty plea to a misdemeanor charge made by a non-party is hearsay, and is not made an exception to the general rule barring admissibility of hearsay evidence by application of FRE 803(22). ... However, where a guilty plea to a misdemeanor charge is made by a party, such an out of court statement is not hearsay by virtue of FRE 801(d)(2)(A) which excludes admissions by parties opponent from the definition of hearsay."

New York v. Hendrickson Bros., 840 F.2d 1065, 1081 (2d Cir.1988). "A prior judgment of conviction may be used as prima facie evidence in a subsequent civil suit only with respect to matters of fact or law 'necessarily decided by the conviction and the verdict on which it was based.' ... What issues were decided in the criminal case is a question of law that 'must be determined by the trial judge hearing the treble-damage suit, upon an examination of the record, including the pleadings, the evidence submitted, the instructions under which the jury arrived at its verdict, and any opinions of the courts.'"

FRE 803(23)

McKinney v. Galvin, 701 F.2d 584, 586 n.5 (6th Cir. 1983). "'[P]rior civil judgments are inadmissible, except to the limited extent provided by Rule 803(23), or as given effect by the substantive doctrine of res judicata which lies outside the scope of rules of evidence. Civil judgments are not given evidential effect because the lower applicable burden of proof makes them less reliable than criminal judgments.'"

FRE 804. EXCEPTIONS TO THE RULE AGAINST HEARSAY—WHEN THE DECLARANT IS UNAVAILABLE AS A WITNESS

(a) Criteria for Being Unavailable. A declarant is considered to be unavailable as a witness if the declarant:

(1) is exempted from testifying about the subject matter of the declarant's statement because the court rules that a privilege applies;

(2) refuses to testify about the subject matter despite a court order to do so;

(3) testifies to not remembering the subject matter;

(4) cannot be present or testify at the trial or hearing because of death or a then-existing infirmity, physical illness, or mental illness; or

(5) is absent from the trial or hearing and the statement's proponent has not been able, by process or other reasonable means, to procure:

(A) the declarant's attendance, in the case of a hearsay exception under Rule 804(b)(1) or (6); or

(B) the declarant's attendance or testimony, in the case of a hearsay exception under Rule 804(b)(2), (3), or (4).

But this subdivision (a) does not apply if the statement's proponent procured or wrongfully caused the declarant's unavailability as a witness in order to prevent the declarant from attending or testifying.

(b) The Exceptions. The following are not excluded by the rule against hearsay if the declarant is unavailable as a witness:

(1) ***Former Testimony.*** Testimony that:

(A) was given as a witness at a trial, hearing, or lawful deposition, whether given during the current proceeding or a different one; and

Effective December 1, 2011, FREs 101-1103 were restyled. For a discussion of the changes and a chart comparing the former and current rules, see p. 1024.

(B) is now offered against a party who had—or, in a civil case, whose predecessor in interest had—an opportunity and similar motive to develop it by direct, cross-, or redirect examination.

(2) ***Statement Under the Belief of Imminent Death.*** In a prosecution for homicide or in a civil case, a statement that the declarant, while believing the declarant's death to be imminent, made about its cause or circumstances.

(3) ***Statement Against Interest.*** A statement that:

(A) a reasonable person in the declarant's position would have made only if the person believed it to be true because, when made, it was so contrary to the declarant's proprietary or pecuniary interest or had so great a tendency to invalidate the declarant's claim against someone else or to expose the declarant to civil or criminal liability; and

(B) is supported by corroborating circumstances that clearly indicate its trustworthiness, if it is offered in a criminal case as one that tends to expose the declarant to criminal liability.

(4) ***Statement of Personal or Family History.*** A statement about:

(A) the declarant's own birth, adoption, legitimacy, ancestry, marriage, divorce, relationship by blood, adoption, or marriage, or similar facts of personal or family history, even though the declarant had no way of acquiring personal knowledge about that fact; or

(B) another person concerning any of these facts, as well as death, if the declarant was related to the person by blood, adoption, or marriage or was so intimately associated with the person's family that the declarant's information is likely to be accurate.

(5) [***Other Exceptions.***] [Transferred to Rule 807.]

(6) ***Statement Offered Against a Party That Wrongfully Caused the Declarant's Unavailability.*** A statement offered against a party that wrongfully caused—or acquiesced in wrongfully causing—the declarant's unavailability as a witness, and did so intending that result.

See selected Notes of Advisory Committee to FRE 804, p. 1265.

History of FRE 804: Adopted Jan. 2, 1975, P.L. 93-595, §1, 88 Stat. 1926, eff. July 1, 1975. Amended Dec. 12, 1975, P.L. 94-149, §1(12), (13), 89 Stat. 806; Mar. 2, 1987, eff. Oct. 1, 1987; Nov. 18, 1988, P.L. 100-690, §7075(b), 102 Stat. 4405; Apr. 11, 1997, eff. Dec. 1, 1997; Apr. 28, 2010, eff. Dec. 1, 2010; Apr. 26, 2011, eff. Dec. 1, 2011.

ANNOTATIONS

Giles v. California, 554 U.S. 353, 367 (2008). FRE 804(b)(6) "'codifies the forfeiture doctrine.' [T]he requirement of intent 'means that the exception applies only if the defendant has in mind the particular purpose of making the witness unavailable.'"

Williamson v. U.S., 512 U.S. 594, 600-01 (1994). "In our view, the most faithful reading of Rule 804(b)(3) is that it does not allow admission of non-self-inculpatory statements, even if they are made within a broader narrative that is generally self-inculpatory. The district court may not just assume for purposes of Rule 804(b)(3) that a statement is self-inculpatory because it is part of a fuller confession, and this is especially true when the statement implicates someone else."

Pierce v. County of Orange, 526 F.3d 1190, 1201-02 (9th Cir.2008). "[Ps] assert that the district court abused its discretion when it ruled that they could not submit deposition testimony of class members who were incarcerated in prisons more than 100 miles from the courthouse. ... The district court judge refused to admit the proposed testimony under Rule 804[(a)(5)] because he concluded that [Ps] had not made an adequate attempt to procure the witnesses' attendance. He noted that the parties had been warned about the 'necessary administrative steps' to subpoena the prisoners, and found that [Ps] had waited too long to seek the subpoenas. [T]he district court judge's determination was not an abuse of discretion." *See also* ***Elnashar v. Speedway SuperAmerica, LLC***, 484 F.3d 1046, 1057 (8th Cir.2007).

U.S. v. Rivera, 412 F.3d 562, 567 (4th Cir.2005). "Acquiescence consists of 'the act or condition of acquiescing or giving tacit assent; agreement or consent by silence or without objection.' [¶] [T]he plain language of Rule 804(b)(6) allows the admissibility of hearsay against a defendant by virtue of his having acquiesced in the acts taken to procure the declarant's unavailability."

U.S. v. Gray, 405 F.3d 227, 241 (4th Cir.2005). FRE 804(b)(6) "codifies the common-law doctrine of forfeiture by wrongdoing as an exception to the general rule barring admission of hearsay evidence. [T]o apply the forfeiture-by-wrongdoing exception, the district court must find, by the preponderance of the evidence, … that (1) the defendant engaged or acquiesced in wrongdoing (2) that was intended to render the declarant unavailable as a witness and (3) that did, in fact, render the declarant unavailable as a witness. The district court need not hold an independent evidentiary hearing if the requisite findings may be made based upon evidence presented in the course of the trial. [¶] The text of Rule 804(b)(6) requires only that the defendant intend to render the declarant unavailable 'as a witness.' The text does not require that the declarant would otherwise be a witness at any *particular* trial, nor does it limit the subject matter of admissible statements to events distinct from the events at issue in the trial in which the statements are offered." *See also* ***U.S. v. Johnson***, 495 F.3d 951, 970 (8th Cir.2007); ***U.S. v. Stewart***, 485 F.3d 666, 670-71 (2d Cir.2007).

FRE 805. HEARSAY WITHIN HEARSAY

Hearsay within hearsay is not excluded by the rule against hearsay if each part of the combined statements conforms with an exception to the rule.

History of FRE 805: Adopted Jan. 2, 1975, P.L. 93-595, §1, 88 Stat. 1926, eff. July 1, 1975. Amended Apr. 26, 2011, eff. Dec. 1, 2011.

ANNOTATIONS

Hoselton v. Metz Baking Co., 48 F.3d 1056, 1061 (8th Cir.1995). "When evidence contains multiple levels of out-of-court statements, courts must examine each level to determine whether the statements are in fact hearsay and, if so, whether each level meets the requirements of some exception to the hearsay rule. The [FREs] do not require each level of hearsay to meet the requirements of the same exception."

Wilson v. Zapata Off-Shore Co., 939 F.2d 260, 271 (5th Cir.1991). "Double hearsay in the context of a business record exists when the record is prepared by an employee with information supplied by another person. If both the source and the recorder of the information, as well as every other participant in the chain producing the record, are acting in the regular course of business, the multiple hearsay is excused by [FRE] 803(6). However, if the source of the information is an outsider, [t]he outsider's statement must fall within another hearsay exception to be admissible…. [FRE] 805 requires that all levels of hearsay satisfy exception hearsay requirements before the statement is admissible."

FRE 806. ATTACKING & SUPPORTING THE DECLARANT'S CREDIBILITY

When a hearsay statement—or a statement described in Rule 801(d)(2)(C), (D), or (E)—has been admitted in evidence, the declarant's credibility may be attacked, and then supported, by any evidence that would be admissible for those purposes if the declarant had testified as a witness. The court may admit evidence of the declarant's inconsistent statement or conduct, regardless of when it occurred or whether the declarant had an opportunity to explain or deny it. If the party against whom the statement was admitted calls the declarant as a witness, the party may examine the declarant on the statement as if on cross-examination.

History of FRE 806: Adopted Jan. 2, 1975, P.L. 93-595, §1, 88 Stat. 1926, eff. July 1, 1975. Amended Mar. 2, 1987, eff. Oct. 1, 1987; Apr. 11, 1997, eff. Dec. 1, 1997; Apr. 26, 2011, eff. Dec. 1, 2011.

ANNOTATIONS

U.S. v. Saada, 212 F.3d 210, 221-22 (3d Cir.2000). FRE 806 "makes no allowance for the unavailability of a hearsay declarant in the context of impeachment by specific instances of misconduct, but makes such an allowance in the context of impeachment by prior inconsistent statements. … The fact that Rule 806 does not provide a comparable allowance for the unavailability of a hearsay declarant in the context of [FRE] 608(b)'s ban on extrinsic evidence indicates that the latter's ban on extrinsic evidence applies with equal force in the context of hearsay declarants."

Vaughn v. Willis, 853 F.2d 1372, 1379 (7th Cir. 1988). "A deposition, as a statement not made by the declarant while testifying at trial, is hearsay. Accordingly, the letter is admissible as impeachment of the deposition only if it would have been admissible had [declarant] testified. Had [declarant] testified, the letter would have been admissible only if (1) it was relevant as impeachment of the deposition, … and (2) its probative value as impeachment was not substantially outweighed by unfair prejudice…."

FRE 807. RESIDUAL EXCEPTION

(a) **In General.** Under the following circumstances, a hearsay statement is not excluded by the rule

FRE 807

Effective December 1, 2011, FREs 101-1103 were restyled. For a discussion of the changes and a chart comparing the former and current rules, see p. 1024.

against hearsay even if the statement is not specifically covered by a hearsay exception in Rule 803 or 804:

(1) the statement has equivalent circumstantial guarantees of trustworthiness;

(2) it is offered as evidence of a material fact;

(3) it is more probative on the point for which it is offered than any other evidence that the proponent can obtain through reasonable efforts; and

(4) admitting it will best serve the purposes of these rules and the interests of justice.

(b) Notice. The statement is admissible only if, before the trial or hearing, the proponent gives an adverse party reasonable notice of the intent to offer the statement and its particulars, including the declarant's name and address, so that the party has a fair opportunity to meet it.

History of FRE 807: Adopted Apr. 11, 1997, eff. Dec. 1, 1997. Amended Apr. 26, 2011, eff. Dec. 1, 2011.

ANNOTATIONS

U.S. v. Bonds, 608 F.3d 495, 501 (9th Cir.2010). "[W]here a statement 'almost fit[s]' into other hearsay exceptions, the circumstance cuts in favor of admissibility under the [FRE 807] residual exception. We [do] not, however, hold the factor [to be] determinative…."

U.S. v. Laster, 258 F.3d 525, 530 (6th Cir.2001). "[T]his court interprets [FRE] 807, along with the majority of circuits, to mean that if a statement is admissible under one of the hearsay exceptions, that exception should be relied on instead of the residual exception. We endorse the reasoning … that the phrase 'specifically covered' by a hearsay exception means only that if a statement is *admissible* under one of the [FRE] 803 exceptions, such subsection should be relied upon instead of the residual exception. Therefore, the analysis of a hearsay statement should not end when a statement fails to qualify as a prior inconsistent statement, but should be evaluated under the residual hearsay exception." (Internal quotes omitted.)

Conoco Inc. v. Department of Energy, 99 F.3d 387, 392 (Fed.Cir.1996). "The two residual hearsay exceptions[, FREs] 803(24) and 804(b)(5) [now consolidated under FRE 807], were meant to be reserved for exceptional cases. They were not intended to confer 'a broad license' on trial judges 'to admit hearsay statements that do not fall within one of the other exceptions contained in rules 803 and 804(b).'"

Harolds Stores v. Dillard Dept. Stores, 82 F.3d 1533, 1544 (10th Cir.1996). "We allow the admission of survey evidence 'as an exception to the hearsay rule [under FRE 803(24), now FRE 807,] if the survey is material, more probative on the issue than other evidence and if it has guarantees of trustworthiness.' 'A survey is trustworthy if it is shown to have been conducted according to generally accepted survey principles.' [¶] The district court should exclude the survey 'when the sample is clearly not representative of the universe it is intended to reflect.' Technical and methodological deficiencies in the survey, including the sufficiency of the universe sampled, bear on the weight of the evidence, not the survey's admissibility."

ARTICLE IX. AUTHENTICATION & IDENTIFICATION

FRE 901. AUTHENTICATING OR IDENTIFYING EVIDENCE

(a) In General. To satisfy the requirement of authenticating or identifying an item of evidence, the proponent must produce evidence sufficient to support a finding that the item is what the proponent claims it is.

(b) Examples. The following are examples only—not a complete list—of evidence that satisfies the requirement:

(1) ***Testimony of a Witness with Knowledge.*** Testimony that an item is what it is claimed to be.

(2) ***Nonexpert Opinion About Handwriting.*** A nonexpert's opinion that handwriting is genuine, based on a familiarity with it that was not acquired for the current litigation.

(3) ***Comparison by an Expert Witness or the Trier of Fact.*** A comparison with an authenticated specimen by an expert witness or the trier of fact.

(4) ***Distinctive Characteristics and the Like.*** The appearance, contents, substance, internal patterns, or other distinctive characteristics of the item, taken together with all the circumstances.

(5) ***Opinion About a Voice.*** An opinion identifying a person's voice—whether heard firsthand or through mechanical or electronic transmis-

sion or recording—based on hearing the voice at any time under circumstances that connect it with the alleged speaker.

(6) ***Evidence About a Telephone Conversation.*** For a telephone conversation, evidence that a call was made to the number assigned at the time to:

(A) a particular person, if circumstances, including self-identification, show that the person answering was the one called; or

(B) a particular business, if the call was made to a business and the call related to business reasonably transacted over the telephone.

(7) ***Evidence About Public Records.*** Evidence that:

(A) a document was recorded or filed in a public office as authorized by law; or

(B) a purported public record or statement is from the office where items of this kind are kept.

(8) ***Evidence About Ancient Documents or Data Compilations.*** For a document or data compilation, evidence that it:

(A) is in a condition that creates no suspicion about its authenticity;

(B) was in a place where, if authentic, it would likely be; and

(C) is at least 20 years old when offered.

(9) ***Evidence About a Process or System.*** Evidence describing a process or system and showing that it produces an accurate result.

(10) ***Methods Provided by a Statute or Rule.*** Any method of authentication or identification allowed by a federal statute or a rule prescribed by the Supreme Court.

History of FRE 901: Adopted Jan. 2, 1975, P.L. 93-595, §1, 88 Stat. 1926, eff. July 1, 1975. Amended Apr. 26, 2011, eff. Dec. 1, 2011.

See *Commentaries*, "Introducing Documents," ch. 8-C, §7, p. 694.

ANNOTATIONS

Las Vegas Sands, LLC v. Nehme, 632 F.3d 526, 533 (9th Cir.2011). "A document *authenticated through personal knowledge* must be attached to an affidavit, and the affiant must be a competent witness who wrote the document, signed it, used it, or saw others do so. But the requirement that documents be authenticated through personal knowledge when submitted in a summary judgment motion is limited to situations where exhibits are introduced by being attached to an affidavit of a person whose personal knowledge is essential to establish the document is what it purports to be—that it is authentic. Where documents are otherwise submitted to the court, and where personal knowledge is *not* relied upon to authenticate the document, the district court must consider alternative means of authentication under [FRE] 901(b)(4). Under Rule 901(b)(4), documents could be authenticated by review of their contents if they appear to be sufficiently genuine." (Internal quotes omitted.)

U.S. v. Rawlins, 606 F.3d 73, 82-83 (3d Cir.2010). "Physical evidence must be authenticated before it is admitted. Authenticity is elemental to relevance, for 'evidence cannot have a tendency to make the existence of a disputed fact more or less likely if the evidence is not that which its proponent claims[.]' ... 'Establishing a chain of custody is one form of proof sufficient to support a finding that the matter in question is what its proponent claims.' [¶] To establish a chain of custody sufficient to make evidence admissible, the proponent 'need only prove a rational basis from which to conclude' that the evidence is what the party claims it to be. ... This 'burden is not a heavy one.' [¶] We have long rejected the proposition that evidence may only be admitted if a 'complete and exclusive' chain of custody is established. '[S]erious' gaps may render a chain of custody so deficient that exclusion is required, ... but in the ordinary case gaps in the chain go to the weight of the evidence, not its admissibility...." *See also **U.S. v. Vidacak***, 553 F.3d 344, 349-50 (4th Cir.2009) (burden of authentication is not demanding; burden can be satisfied by offering circumstantial evidence that documents in question are what they purport to be).

U-Haul Int'l v. Lumbermens Mut. Cas. Co., 576 F.3d 1040, 1045 (9th Cir.2009). "[E]vidence describing a process or system used to produce a result and showing that the process or system produces an accurate result is an example of a method of authenticating a process or system. [¶] [I]t is not necessary that the computer programmer testify in order to authenticate computer-generated records. A computer printout may be authenticated by one who has knowledge of the particular record system. Similarly, a party need not produce expert testimony as to the mechanical accuracy of a computer where it presented evidence that the com-

Effective December 1, 2011, FREs 101-1103 were restyled. For a discussion of the changes and a chart comparing the former and current rules, see p. 1024.

puter was sufficiently accurate so that the company relied upon it in conducting its business." (Internal quotes omitted.)

U.S. v. Kalymon, 541 F.3d 624, 632 (6th Cir.2008). "[E]xpert opinion on handwriting is not necessary for authentication under [FRE] 901. [T]he trier of fact can authenticate a signature by identifying and comparing it with a signature already authenticated." *See also* ***U.S. v. Binzel***, 907 F.2d 746, 749 (7th Cir.1990).

U.S. v. Washington, 498 F.3d 225, 231 (4th Cir. 2007). "[T]he raw data generated by ... machines do not constitute 'statements,' and the machines are not 'declarants.' [¶] When information provided by machines is mainly a product of 'mechanical measurement or manipulation of data by well-accepted scientific or mathematical techniques,' ... reliability concerns are addressed by requiring the proponent to show that the machine and its functions are reliable, that it was correctly adjusted or calibrated, and that the data ... put into the machine was accurate.... In other words, a foundation must be established for the information through authentication, which [FRE] 901(b)(9) allows such proof to be authenticated by evidence 'describing [the] process or system used to produce [the] result' and showing it 'produces an accurate result.'"

U.S. v. Firishchak, 468 F.3d 1015, 1022 (7th Cir. 2006). "[D] particularly questions the authentication of those documents that lacked specific dates. While it is true that several of the documents bear no specific date, their age can be proven by other means. For example, the appearance of the proffered evidence or even the contents of the material itself together with the surrounding circumstances can be used to determine a document's age."

U.S. v. García, 452 F.3d 36, 40 (1st Cir.2006). "There is no single way ... to authenticate evidence. '[T]he direct testimony of a custodian or a percipient witness is not a *sine qua non* to the authentication of a writing. Thus, a document's appearance, contents, substance, internal patterns, or other distinctive characteristics, taken in conjunction with circumstances, can, in cumulation, even without direct testimony, provide sufficient indicia of reliability to permit a finding that it is authentic.'" *See also* ***U.S. v. Al-Moayad***, 545 F.3d 139, 172-73 (2d Cir.2008) (proof of authentication may be direct or circumstantial; standard is whether reasonable juror could find in favor of authenticity); ***In re McLain***, 516 F.3d 301, 308 (5th Cir.2008) (document may be authenticated with circumstantial evidence, including document's own characteristics).

U.S. v. Bush, 405 F.3d 909, 918-19 (10th Cir.2005). "[V]oice identification testimony is permissible under Rule 901 where there exists 'any basis for identifying the voice,' '[leaving] all questions of weight and credibility for the jury.' [¶] Such voice identification need only rise to the level of minimal familiarity. Once minimal familiarity is satisfied, it is for the jury to assess any issues regarding the extent of the witness' familiarity with the voice." *See also* ***U.S. v. Jones***, 600 F.3d 847, 858 (7th Cir.2010).

Stringel v. Methodist Hosp., 89 F.3d 415, 420 (7th Cir.1996). "When offered into evidence, a tape recording must normally be accompanied by proof that the recording is what it is purported to be. ... ***U.S. v. McKeever***, 169 F.Supp. 426, 430 (S.D.N.Y.1958), *rev'd on other grounds*, 271 F.2d 669 (2d Cir.1959), sets out a rather formal, seven-step checklist for the authentication of tape recordings, and we have looked to some of the factors included in that list, including the competency of the operator, the fidelity of the recording equipment, the absence of material alterations in the relevant portions of the recording, and the identity of the speakers. We have also emphasized the district court's obligation to ascertain that the recording itself is sufficiently audible to constitute reliable evidence of the conversation recorded. But, consistent with [FREs] 901(a) and 1003, we have eschewed any formalistic approach to the admission of tape recordings or copies thereof." (Internal quotes omitted.) *See also* ***U.S. v. Hamilton***, 334 F.3d 170, 186-87 (2d Cir.2003) (once tape recording has been authenticated, any question about veracity of recorded statements and credibility of speakers goes to evidence's weight, not admissibility).

Threadgill v. Armstrong World Indus., 928 F.2d 1366, 1376 (3d Cir.1991). "[T]he point of a Rule 901(b)(8) inquiry is to determine whether the documents in question are, in fact, what they appear to be. ... Questions as to the documents' content and completeness bear upon the weight to be accorded the evidence and do not affect the threshold question of authenticity. The determination that a set of [ancient] documents are, indeed, *prima facie* authentic in no way precludes counsel from challenging the content of the documents or from arguing that missing documents subject the contents to a different interpretation."

FRE 902. EVIDENCE THAT IS SELF-AUTHENTICATING

The following items of evidence are self-authenticating; they require no extrinsic evidence of authenticity in order to be admitted:

(1) ***Domestic Public Documents That Are Sealed and Signed.*** A document that bears:

(A) a seal purporting to be that of the United States; any state, district, commonwealth, territory, or insular possession of the United States; the former Panama Canal Zone; the Trust Territory of the Pacific Islands; a political subdivision of any of these entities; or a department, agency, or officer of any entity named above; and

(B) a signature purporting to be an execution or attestation.

(2) ***Domestic Public Documents That Are Not Sealed but Are Signed and Certified.*** A document that bears no seal if:

(A) it bears the signature of an officer or employee of an entity named in Rule 902(1)(A); and

(B) another public officer who has a seal and official duties within that same entity certifies under seal—or its equivalent—that the signer has the official capacity and that the signature is genuine.

(3) ***Foreign Public Documents.*** A document that purports to be signed or attested by a person who is authorized by a foreign country's law to do so. The document must be accompanied by a final certification that certifies the genuineness of the signature and official position of the signer or attester—or of any foreign official whose certificate of genuineness relates to the signature or attestation or is in a chain of certificates of genuineness relating to the signature or attestation. The certification may be made by a secretary of a United States embassy or legation; by a consul general, vice consul, or consular agent of the United States; or by a diplomatic or consular official of the foreign country assigned or accredited to the United States. If all parties have been given a reasonable opportunity to investigate the document's authenticity and accuracy, the court may, for good cause, either:

(A) order that it be treated as presumptively authentic without final certification; or

(B) allow it to be evidenced by an attested summary with or without final certification.

(4) ***Certified Copies of Public Records.*** A copy of an official record—or a copy of a document that was recorded or filed in a public office as authorized by law—if the copy is certified as correct by:

(A) the custodian or another person authorized to make the certification; or

(B) a certificate that complies with Rule 902(1), (2), or (3), a federal statute, or a rule prescribed by the Supreme Court.

(5) ***Official Publications.*** A book, pamphlet, or other publication purporting to be issued by a public authority.

(6) ***Newspapers and Periodicals.*** Printed material purporting to be a newspaper or periodical.

(7) ***Trade Inscriptions and the Like.*** An inscription, sign, tag, or label purporting to have been affixed in the course of business and indicating origin, ownership, or control.

(8) ***Acknowledged Documents.*** A document accompanied by a certificate of acknowledgment that is lawfully executed by a notary public or another officer who is authorized to take acknowledgments.

(9) ***Commercial Paper and Related Documents.*** Commercial paper, a signature on it, and related documents, to the extent allowed by general commercial law.

(10) ***Presumptions Under a Federal Statute.*** A signature, document, or anything else that a federal statute declares to be presumptively or prima facie genuine or authentic.

(11) ***Certified Domestic Records of a Regularly Conducted Activity.*** The original or a copy of a domestic record that meets the requirements of Rule 803(6)(A)-(C), as shown by a certification of the custodian or another qualified person that complies with a federal statute or a rule prescribed by the Supreme Court. Before the trial or hearing, the proponent must give an adverse party reasonable written notice of the intent to offer the record—and must make the record and certi-

FRE 902

Effective December 1, 2011, FREs 101-1103 were restyled. For a discussion of the changes and a chart comparing the former and current rules, see p. 1024.

fication available for inspection—so that the party has a fair opportunity to challenge them.

(12) ***Certified Foreign Records of a Regularly Conducted Activity.*** In a civil case, the original or a copy of a foreign record that meets the requirements of Rule 902(11), modified as follows: the certification, rather than complying with a federal statute or Supreme Court rule, must be signed in a manner that, if falsely made, would subject the maker to a criminal penalty in the country where the certification is signed. The proponent must also meet the notice requirements of Rule 902(11).

See selected Notes of Advisory Committee to FRE 902, p. 1265.

History of FRE 902: Adopted Jan. 2, 1975, P.L. 93-595, §1, 88 Stat. 1926, eff. July 1, 1975. Amended Mar. 2, 1987, eff. Oct. 1, 1987; Apr. 25, 1988, eff. Nov. 1, 1988; Apr. 17, 2000, eff. Dec. 1, 2000; Apr. 26, 2011, eff. Dec. 1, 2011.

See *Commentaries*, "Introducing Documents," ch. 8-C, §7, p. 694.

ANNOTATIONS

U.S. v. Green, 648 F.3d 569, 579 (7th Cir.2011). "Rule 902(11) streamlines the admission of certain inherently reliable documents by allowing a party to introduce a record of regularly conducted activity without live testimony from a records custodian so long as the record is accompanied by a proper written certification from a custodian or otherwise qualified person. *At 580:* Rule 902(11) is a powerful and efficient short-cut, but it includes important built-in safeguards that cannot be taken lightly. Those safeguards include providing opposing counsel with advance notice of any Rule 902(11) certifications to give that party 'a fair opportunity to challenge' the certifications…. [T]he Rule does not give a party license to dump business records into evidence without giving an adverse party an opportunity to question the certificate's signer where such questioning may be warranted." *See also* ***U.S. v. Olguin***, 643 F.3d 384, 390 (5th Cir.2011); ***U.S. v. Brown***, 553 F.3d 768, 793 (5th Cir.2008).

U.S. v. Deverso, 518 F.3d 1250, 1255 (11th Cir. 2008). "There is no requirement in Rule 902(3) that the document itself be signed. *At 1256:* There are[, however,] two requirements for the authentication of a foreign document. 'First, there must be some indication that the *document* is what [it] purports to be. Thus, the proffered document must be executed by a proper official in his official capacity, or the genuineness of the document must be attested to by a proper official in his official capacity.' 'Second, there must be some indication that the *official* vouching for the document is who he purports to be.'" *See also* ***Tu v. Mutual Life Ins.***, 136 F.3d 77, 81 n.2 (1st Cir.1998).

Thanongsinh v. Board of Educ., 462 F.3d 762, 777 (7th Cir.2006). See annotation under FRE 803, *FRE 803(6)*, p. 1072.

Acosta-Mestre v. Hilton Int'l, 156 F.3d 49, 57 (1st Cir.1998). "[A] notarized document does not constitute '[a] copy of an official record or report or entry therein, or of a document authorized by law to be recorded or filed and actually recorded or filed in a public office….' Moreover, Rule 902 addresses only the requirement of authentication. 'Self-authenticating' documents are not necessarily admissible."

Whitted v. General Motors Corp., 58 F.3d 1200, 1204 (7th Cir.1995). FRE 902(7) "provides that trade inscriptions affixed in the course of business, indicating ownership or control, need not be supported by extrinsic evidence to establish genuineness of commercial labels. The owner's manual is not a trade inscription and admitting the manual because it had a trade inscription on its cover does not comport with the rule."

FRE 903. SUBSCRIBING WITNESS'S TESTIMONY

A subscribing witness's testimony is necessary to authenticate a writing only if required by the law of the jurisdiction that governs its validity.

History of FRE 903: Adopted Jan. 2, 1975, P.L. 93-595, §1, 88 Stat. 1926, eff. July 1, 1975. Amended Apr. 26, 2011, eff. Dec. 1, 2011.

See *Commentaries*, "Introducing Documents," ch. 8-C, §7, p. 694.

ANNOTATIONS

U.S. v. Paulino, 13 F.3d 20, 23 (1st Cir.1994). "Under the [FREs], authentication can be accomplished without the direct testimony of either a custodian or a percipient witness."

ARTICLE X. CONTENTS OF WRITINGS, RECORDINGS, & PHOTOGRAPHS

FRE 1001. DEFINITIONS THAT APPLY TO THIS ARTICLE

In this article:

(a) A "writing" consists of letters, words, numbers, or their equivalent set down in any form.

(b) A "recording" consists of letters, words, numbers, or their equivalent recorded in any manner.

(c) A "photograph" means a photographic image or its equivalent stored in any form.

FRE 902

(d) An "original" of a writing or recording means the writing or recording itself or any counterpart intended to have the same effect by the person who executed or issued it. For electronically stored information, "original" means any printout—or other output readable by sight—if it accurately reflects the information. An "original" of a photograph includes the negative or a print from it.

(e) A "duplicate" means a counterpart produced by a mechanical, photographic, chemical, electronic, or other equivalent process or technique that accurately reproduces the original.

History of FRE 1001: Adopted Jan. 2, 1975, P.L. 93-595, §1, 88 Stat. 1926, eff. July 1, 1975. Amended Apr. 26, 2011, eff. Dec. 1, 2011.

See *Commentaries*, "Introducing Documents," ch. 8-C, §7, p. 694.

ANNOTATIONS

Asociación de Periodistas de P.R. v. Mueller, 680 F.3d 70, 80 (1st Cir.2012). "[A] copy of a video recording is a 'duplicate' admissible 'to the same extent as the original[]'...."

U.S. v. Haddock, 956 F.2d 1534, 1545 (10th Cir. 1992), *modified on other grounds*, 961 F.2d 933 (10th Cir.1992). "Under [former Rule 1001(4), now Rule 1001(e)], photocopies are considered duplicates."

FRE 1002. REQUIREMENT OF THE ORIGINAL

An original writing, recording, or photograph is required in order to prove its content unless these rules or a federal statute provides otherwise.

History of FRE 1002: Adopted Jan. 2, 1975, P.L. 93-595, §1, 88 Stat. 1926, eff. July 1, 1975. Amended Apr. 26, 2011, eff. Dec. 1, 2011.

See *Commentaries*, "Introducing Documents," ch. 8-C, §7, p. 694.

ANNOTATIONS

U.S. v. Diaz-Lopez, 625 F.3d 1198, 1200-01 (9th Cir. 2010). "We must decide if testimony that a search of a computer database revealed no record of a matter violates the best evidence rule when it is offered without the production of an 'original' printout showing the search results. We hold that it does not. *At 1202-03:* [T]he advisory committee's note to Rule 1002 states that the best evidence rule does not apply to 'testimony that books or records have been examined and found not to contain any reference to a designated matter.' [¶] [D] asserts that, although the Rule applies to computer databases, the advisory committee note's limitation on the Rule applies only to searches of 'physical' records. We decline to adopt such a position. First, we do not see any meaningful difference between a search of a physical file and a search of a database. Databases contain 'physical' records, too, even if those records are not printed on paper. Second, the best evidence rule ... survives in the 21st century. It is common sense, and not mere symmetry, to say that because the rule applies to computer databases, the rule's limitations must also apply to such databases. It is reasonable to apply the best evidence rule to new circumstances as technology evolves, but when the rule is extended, courts will necessarily be required to decide if the limits on the rule extend as well. When, by virtue of new technology, the best evidence rule can be applied to testimony about databases, the traditional limits on the rule should be properly extended as well."

U.S. v. Smith, 566 F.3d 410, 413 (4th Cir.2009). FRE 1002 "exists to afford guarantees against inaccuracies and fraud by requiring that *the original* of the document be offered, subject to exceptions in [FRE] 1003 (allowing the use of duplicates) and [FRE] 1004 (providing exceptions to the requirement of an original). Thus it is more accurate to refer to Rule 1002 as the 'original document rule,' not the 'best evidence rule.'" *See also* ***U.S. v. Mayans***, 17 F.3d 1174, 1185 (9th Cir. 1994); ***U.S. v. Stockton***, 968 F.2d 715, 719 (8th Cir. 1992).

Railroad Mgmt. Co. v. CFS La. Midstream Co., 428 F.3d 214, 217 (5th Cir.2005). "Difficulty applying [FRE 1002] commonly arises in situations ... where the party proffering the affidavit or testimony contends that it is not intended to 'prove the content' of the document it discusses, but merely its 'existence.' The [FREs] do not define the difference, but in practice '[t]estimony about a document cannot go very far without referring to its terms.'"

U.S. v. Holton, 116 F.3d 1536, 1545 (D.C.Cir.1997). "'The elementary wisdom of the best evidence rule rests on the fact that the [recording itself] is a more reliable, complete and accurate source of information as to its contents and meaning than anyone's description [of it].' ... When the original tape is available and presented to the jury and the accuracy of the transcript has been stipulated or is made an issue for the jury to decide, concerns addressed by the best evidence rule are not at issue."

U.S. v. Workinger, 90 F.3d 1409, 1415 (9th Cir. 1996). "[A] tape recording cannot be said to be the best evidence of a conversation when a party seeks to call a

FRE 1002

Effective December 1, 2011, FREs 101-1103 were restyled. For a discussion of the changes and a chart comparing the former and current rules, see p. 1024.

participant in or observer of the conversation to testify to it. In that instance, the best evidence rule has no application at all."

FRE 1003. ADMISSIBILITY OF DUPLICATES

A duplicate is admissible to the same extent as the original unless a genuine question is raised about the original's authenticity or the circumstances make it unfair to admit the duplicate.

History of FRE 1003: Adopted Jan. 2, 1975, P.L. 93-595, §1, 88 Stat. 1926, eff. July 1, 1975. Amended Apr. 26, 2011, eff. Dec. 1, 2011.

See *Commentaries*, "Introducing Documents," ch. 8-C, §7, p. 694.

ANNOTATIONS

Buziashvili v. Inman, 106 F.3d 709, 717 (6th Cir. 1997). "Photocopies are allowed into evidence as if they were originals."

U.S. v. Haddock, 956 F.2d 1534, 1545 (10th Cir. 1992), *modified on other grounds*, 961 F.2d 933 (10th Cir.1992). "Rule 1003 is part of a broadened set of evidentiary rules that reflect the fact that, due to modern and accurate reproduction techniques, duplicates and originals should normally be treated interchangeably. However, despite our age of technology, a trial court must still be wary of admitting duplicates 'where the circumstances surrounding the execution of the writing present a substantial possibility of fraud.'"

U.S. v. Carroll, 860 F.2d 500, 507 (1st Cir.1988). "[W]hen a print of a microfilm copy of bank checks, kept by the bank in the regular course of business, is properly identified by a custodian of records as a complete and accurate reproduction thereof … such prints are 'duplicates' under the [FREs] and the microfilm itself need not be produced." *See also* ***U.S. v. Mulinelli-Navas***, 111 F.3d 983, 989-90 (1st Cir.1997).

FRE 1004. ADMISSIBILITY OF OTHER EVIDENCE OF CONTENT

An original is not required and other evidence of the content of a writing, recording, or photograph is admissible if:

(a) all the originals are lost or destroyed, and not by the proponent acting in bad faith;

(b) an original cannot be obtained by any available judicial process;

(c) the party against whom the original would be offered had control of the original; was at that time put on notice, by pleadings or otherwise, that the original would be a subject of proof at the trial or hearing; and fails to produce it at the trial or hearing; or

(d) the writing, recording, or photograph is not closely related to a controlling issue.

History of FRE 1004: Adopted Jan. 2, 1975, P.L. 93-595, §1, 88 Stat. 1926, eff. July 1, 1975. Amended Mar. 2, 1987, eff. Oct. 1, 1987; Apr. 26, 2011, eff. Dec. 1, 2011.

See *Commentaries*, "Introducing Documents," ch. 8-C, §7, p. 694.

ANNOTATIONS

U.S. v. Ross, 33 F.3d 1507, 1513 (11th Cir.1994). "[W]here the original of a recording has been lost or destroyed, the original is not required and other evidence of its content is admissible, unless the proponent lost or destroyed the original in bad faith. Once the terms of Rule 1004 are satisfied, the party seeking to prove the contents of the recording … may do so by any kind of secondary evidence."

Servants of the Paraclete, Inc. v. Great Am. Ins., 857 F.Supp. 822, 828 (D.N.M.1994), *amended*, 866 F.Supp. 1560 (D.N.M.1994). "[T]o be permitted to introduce [secondary] evidence, [movant] must make a threshold showing of (1) the loss or destruction of the original policy and (2) the absence of bad faith. Loss or destruction of the original is most commonly shown through circumstantial evidence of a 'diligent but unsuccessful search and inquiry for the missing document.'"

FRE 1005. COPIES OF PUBLIC RECORDS TO PROVE CONTENT

The proponent may use a copy to prove the content of an official record—or of a document that was recorded or filed in a public office as authorized by law—if these conditions are met: the record or document is otherwise admissible; and the copy is certified as correct in accordance with Rule 902(4) or is testified to be correct by a witness who has compared it with the original. If no such copy can be obtained by reasonable diligence, then the proponent may use other evidence to prove the content.

History of FRE 1005: Adopted Jan. 2, 1975, P.L. 93-595, §1, 88 Stat. 1926, eff. July 1, 1975. Amended Apr. 26, 2011, eff. Dec. 1, 2011.

See *Commentaries*, "Introducing Documents," ch. 8-C, §7, p. 694.

ANNOTATIONS

U.S. v. Childs, 5 F.3d 1328, 1335 (9th Cir.1993). FRE 1005 "is designed to insure the reliability of public records while making it easier to prove their content. [¶] While the term 'record' should be read to embrace

FRE 1002

every kind of official document ..., the reasons underlying Rule 1005 suggest that the provision ought not to extend to a copy of such material made from an original in the hands of an outsider, and that any such copy should be received, if at all, only under [FRE] 1003." (Internal quotes omitted.)

FRE 1006. SUMMARIES TO PROVE CONTENT

The proponent may use a summary, chart, or calculation to prove the content of voluminous writings, recordings, or photographs that cannot be conveniently examined in court. The proponent must make the originals or duplicates available for examination or copying, or both, by other parties at a reasonable time and place. And the court may order the proponent to produce them in court.

History of FRE 1006: Adopted Jan. 2, 1975, P.L. 93-595, §1, 88 Stat. 1926, eff. July 1, 1975. Amended Apr. 26, 2011, eff. Dec. 1, 2011.

See *Commentaries*, "Introducing Documents," ch. 8-C, §7, p. 694.

ANNOTATIONS

U.S. v. Irvin, 682 F.3d 1254, 1261 (10th Cir.2012). "Although the materials upon which a Rule 1006 summary is based need not themselves be admitted into evidence, they must at least be *admissible. At 1262:* The materials summarized by Rule 1006 evidence must themselves be admissible because a contrary rule 'would inappropriately provide litigants with a means of avoiding rules governing the admission of evidence such as hearsay.' Accordingly, just as the proponent of hearsay evidence bears the burden of establishing the applicability of a hearsay exception, ... so too must the proponent of a Rule 1006 summary based on hearsay evidence establish that the materials summarized are admissible." *See also* **Eichorn v. AT&T Corp.**, 484 F.3d 644, 650 (3d Cir.2007).

U.S. v. Rizk, 660 F.3d 1125, 1130 (9th Cir.2011). "A proponent of summary evidence must establish that the underlying materials upon which the summary is based ... were made available to the opposing party for inspection. ... The availability requirement ensures that the opposing party has 'an opportunity to verify the reliability and accuracy of the summary prior to trial.'"

U.S. v. Spires, 628 F.3d 1049, 1053 (8th Cir.2011). "'Summary evidence is properly admitted when (1) the charts fairly summarize voluminous trial evidence; (2) they assist the jury in understanding the testimony already introduced; and (3) the witness who prepared the charts is subject to cross-examination with all documents used to prepare the summary.' Also, summaries may include assumptions and conclusions so long as they are 'based upon evidence in the record.'"

U.S. v. Morin, 627 F.3d 985, 997 (5th Cir.2010). FRE 1006 "'does not specifically address summary witnesses,' but '[n]evertheless, for complex cases, this court has allowed summary witnesses in a limited capacity.'"

U.S. v. McElroy, 587 F.3d 73, 81-82 (1st Cir.2009). "Our case law permits the use of summary tools to clarify complex testimony and evidence. ... '[I]n most cases a [FRE] 1006 chart will be the *only* evidence the fact finder will examine concerning a voluminous set of documents.' In some instances, however, a Rule 1006 chart may itself be admitted into evidence or summary witness testimony may be permitted pursuant to [FRE] 611(a). Rule 611(a) testimony and exhibits 'typically are used as pedagogical devices to clarify and simplify complex testimony or other information and evidence or to assist counsel in the presentation of argument to the court or jury.' In some cases, 'such pedagogical devices may be sufficiently accurate and reliable that they, too, are admissible in evidence, even though they do not meet the specific requirements of Rule 1006.'" *See also* ***U.S. v. Irvin***, 682 F.3d 1254, 1263 (10th Cir. 2012) (summary tools used as pedagogical devices must be linked to previously admitted evidence); ***U.S. v. Buck***, 324 F.3d 786, 790-91 (5th Cir.2003) (same).

U.S. v. Modena, 302 F.3d 626, 633 (6th Cir.2002). "This court has interpreted Rule 1006 as imposing five requirements for the admission of an evidentiary summary: (1) the underlying documents must be so voluminous that they cannot be conveniently examined in court, (2) the proponent of the summary must have made the documents available for examination or copying at a reasonable time and place, (3) the underlying documents must be admissible in evidence, (4) the summary must be accurate and nonprejudicial, and (5) the summary must be properly introduced through the testimony of a witness who supervised its preparation. [¶] Rule 1006 'operates independently of the discovery rules....' The government, therefore, had a duty to 'state when and where' the documents underlying its summaries could be viewed, without regard to whether [D] made a request for these records."

Daniel v. Ben E. Keith Co., 97 F.3d 1329, 1335 (10th Cir.1996). "'Summaries must be accurate and nonprejudicial. Summaries not offered as evidence

Effective December 1, 2011, FREs 101-1103 were restyled. For a discussion of the changes and a chart comparing the former and current rules, see p. 1024.

should be used only with a limiting instruction stating that the summary itself is not evidence.'"

Air Safety, Inc. v. Roman Catholic Archbishop of Boston, 94 F.3d 1, 8 (1st Cir.1996). "[T]he failure to request or obtain the documents during discovery does not negate a party's 'absolute right to subsequent production of material under Rule 1006, should that material become incorporated in a chart, summary, or calculation.' Common sense dictates that this guaranteed access, designed to give the opponent the ability to check the summary's accuracy and prepare for cross-examination …, must include unequivocal notice of the other party's intent to invoke Rule 1006." *See also* ***Amarel v. Connell***, 102 F.3d 1494, 1516 (9th Cir.1996).

FRE 1007. TESTIMONY OR STATEMENT OF A PARTY TO PROVE CONTENT

The proponent may prove the content of a writing, recording, or photograph by the testimony, deposition, or written statement of the party against whom the evidence is offered. The proponent need not account for the original.

History of FRE 1007: Adopted Jan. 2, 1975, P.L. 93-595, §1, 88 Stat. 1926, eff. July 1, 1975. Amended Mar. 2, 1987, eff. Oct. 1, 1987; Apr. 26, 2011, eff. Dec. 1, 2011.

See *Commentaries*, "Introducing Documents," ch. 8-C, §7, p. 694.

FRE 1008. FUNCTIONS OF THE COURT & JURY

Ordinarily, the court determines whether the proponent has fulfilled the factual conditions for admitting other evidence of the content of a writing, recording, or photograph under Rule 1004 or 1005. But in a jury trial, the jury determines—in accordance with Rule 104(b)—any issue about whether:

(a) an asserted writing, recording, or photograph ever existed;

(b) another one produced at the trial or hearing is the original; or

(c) other evidence of content accurately reflects the content.

History of FRE 1008: Adopted Jan. 2, 1975, P.L. 93-595, §1, 88 Stat. 1926, eff. July 1, 1975. Amended Apr. 26, 2011, eff. Dec. 1, 2011.

ANNOTATIONS

Seiler v. Lucasfilm, Ltd., 613 F.Supp. 1253, 1260 (N.D.Cal.1984), *aff'd*, 808 F.2d 1316 (9th Cir.1986). FRE 1008 "states that the determination of whether a condition has been fulfilled is ordinarily for the court to decide. Therefore, [FRE] 1004 read in conjunction with Rule 1008 makes the determination of whether the proponent of the evidence has established that all the originals were lost or destroyed without bad faith a question for the court. Rule 1008 provides further that the trier of fact is to determine the question of whether the originals ever existed."

ARTICLE XI. MISCELLANEOUS RULES

FRE 1101. APPLICABILITY OF THE RULES

(a) To Courts and Judges. These rules apply to proceedings before:

- United States district courts;
- United States bankruptcy and magistrate judges;
- United States courts of appeals;
- the United States Court of Federal Claims; and
- the district courts of Guam, the Virgin Islands, and the Northern Mariana Islands.

(b) To Cases and Proceedings. These rules apply in:

- civil cases and proceedings, including bankruptcy, admiralty, and maritime cases;
- criminal cases and proceedings; and
- contempt proceedings, except those in which the court may act summarily.

(c) Rules on Privilege. The rules on privilege apply to all stages of a case or proceeding.

(d) Exceptions. These rules—except for those on privilege—do not apply to the following:

(1) the court's determination, under Rule 104(a), on a preliminary question of fact governing admissibility;

(2) grand-jury proceedings; and

(3) miscellaneous proceedings such as:

- extradition or rendition;
- issuing an arrest warrant, criminal summons, or search warrant;
- a preliminary examination in a criminal case;
- sentencing;
- granting or revoking probation or supervised release; and
- considering whether to release on bail or otherwise.

(e) Other Statutes and Rules. A federal statute or a rule prescribed by the Supreme Court may provide for admitting or excluding evidence independently from these rules.

History of FRE 1101: Adopted Jan. 2, 1975, P.L. 93-595, §1, 88 Stat. 1926, eff. July 1, 1975. Amended Dec. 12, 1975, P.L. 94-149, §1(14), 89 Stat. 806; Nov. 6, 1978, P.L. 95-598, §§251, 252, 92 Stat. 2673, eff. Oct. 1, 1979; Apr. 2, 1982, P.L. 97-164, §142, 96 Stat. 45, eff. Oct. 1, 1982; Mar. 2, 1987, eff. Oct. 1, 1987; Apr. 25, 1988, eff. Nov. 1, 1988; Nov. 18, 1988, P.L. 100-690, §7075(c), 102 Stat. 4405; Apr. 22, 1993, eff. Dec. 1, 1993; Apr. 26, 2011, eff. Dec. 1, 2011.

See *Commentaries*, "Introduction to Federal Rules," ch. 1-A, p. 3.

ANNOTATIONS

U.S. v. Dexter Corp., 132 F.R.D. 8, 9 (D.Conn.1990). "Since privileges enumerated in the [FREs] apply to 'all stages of all actions, cases and proceedings[,]' the [FREs] determine which matters and communications are shielded from discovery."

FRE 1102. AMENDMENTS

These rules may be amended as provided in 28 U.S.C. §2072.

History of FRE 1102: Adopted Jan. 2, 1975, P.L. 93-595, §1, 88 Stat. 1926, eff. July 1, 1975. Amended Apr. 30, 1991, eff. Dec. 1, 1991; Apr. 26, 2011, eff. Dec. 1, 2011.

See *Commentaries*, "Introduction to Federal Rules," ch. 1-A, p. 3.

FRE 1103. TITLE

These rules may be cited as the Federal Rules of Evidence.

History of FRE 1103: Adopted Jan. 2, 1975, P.L. 93-595, §1, 88 Stat. 1926, eff. July 1, 1975. Amended Apr. 26, 2011, eff. Dec. 1, 2011.

See *Commentaries*, "Introduction to Federal Rules," ch. 1-A, p. 3.

Effective December 1, 2011, FREs 101-1103 were restyled. For a discussion of the changes and a chart comparing the former and current rules, see p. 1024.

FEDERAL RULES OF APPELLATE PROCEDURE

TABLE OF CONTENTS

TITLE I. APPLICABILITY OF RULES

FRAP 1 Scope of rules; definition; title ... 1090
FRAP 2 Suspension of rules ... 1090

TITLE II. APPEAL FROM A JUDGMENT OR ORDER OF A DISTRICT COURT

FRAP 3 Appeal as of right—how taken ... 1090
FRAP 4 Appeal as of right—when taken ... 1091
FRAP 5 Appeal by permission ... 1094
FRAP 6 Appeal in a bankruptcy case from a final judgment, order, or decree of a district court or bankruptcy appellate panel ... 1095
FRAP 7 Bond for costs on appeal in a civil case ... 1096
FRAP 8 Stay or injunction pending appeal ... 1096
FRAP 9 Release in a criminal case ... 1097
FRAP 10 The record on appeal ... 1097
FRAP 11 Forwarding the record ... 1098
FRAP 12 Docketing the appeal; filing a representation statement; filing the record ... 1099
FRAP 12.1 Remand after an indicative ruling by the district court on a motion for relief that is barred by a pending appeal ... 1100

TITLE III. REVIEW OF A DECISION OF THE UNITED STATES TAX COURT

FRAP 13 Review of a decision of the Tax Court ... 1100
FRAP 14 Applicability of other rules to the review of a Tax Court decision ... 1101

TITLE IV. REVIEW OR ENFORCEMENT OF AN ORDER OF AN ADMINISTRATIVE AGENCY, BOARD, COMMISSION, OR OFFICER

FRAP 15 Review or enforcement of an agency order—how obtained; intervention ... 1101
FRAP 15.1 Briefs & oral argument in a National Labor Relations Board proceeding ... 1102
FRAP 16 The record on review or enforcement ... 1102
FRAP 17 Filing the record ... 1102
FRAP 18 Stay pending review ... 1102
FRAP 19 Settlement of a judgment enforcing an agency order in part ... 1103
FRAP 20 Applicability of rules to the review or enforcement of an agency order ... 1103

TITLE V. EXTRAORDINARY WRITS

FRAP 21 Writs of mandamus & prohibition, & other extraordinary writs ... 1103

TITLE VI. HABEAS CORPUS; PROCEEDINGS IN FORMA PAUPERIS

FRAP 22 Habeas corpus & section 2255 proceedings ... 1104
FRAP 23 Custody or release of a prisoner in a habeas corpus proceeding ... 1104
FRAP 24 Proceeding in forma pauperis ... 1105

TITLE VII. GENERAL PROVISIONS

FRAP 25 Filing & service ... 1105
FRAP 26 Computing & extending time ... 1107
FRAP 26.1 Corporate disclosure statement ... 1108
FRAP 27 Motions ... 1108
FRAP 28 Briefs ... 1109
FRAP 28.1 Cross-appeals ... 1111
FRAP 29 Brief of an amicus curiae ... 1112
FRAP 30 Appendix to the briefs ... 1113
FRAP 31 Serving & filing briefs ... 1114
FRAP 32 Form of briefs, appendices, & other papers ... 1115
FRAP 32.1 Citing judicial dispositions ... 1116
FRAP 33 Appeal conferences ... 1116
FRAP 34 Oral argument ... 1116
FRAP 35 En banc determination ... 1117
FRAP 36 Entry of judgment; notice ... 1118
FRAP 37 Interest on judgment ... 1118
FRAP 38 Frivolous appeal—damages & costs ... 1118
FRAP 39 Costs ... 1118
FRAP 40 Petition for panel rehearing ... 1119
FRAP 41 Mandate: contents; issuance & effective date; stay ... 1119
FRAP 42 Voluntary dismissal ... 1120
FRAP 43 Substitution of parties ... 1120
FRAP 44 Case involving a constitutional question when the United States or the relevant state is not a party ... 1121
FRAP 45 Clerk's duties ... 1121
FRAP 46 Attorneys ... 1122
FRAP 47 Local rules by courts of appeals ... 1122
FRAP 48 Masters ... 1123

Appendix of Forms

Form 1 Notice of appeal to a court of appeals from a judgment or order of a district court ... 1125
Form 2 Notice of appeal to a court of appeals from a decision of the United States Tax Court ... 1125
Form 3 Petition for review of order of an agency, board, commission or officer ... 1126
Form 4 Affidavit accompanying motion for permission to appeal in forma pauperis ... 1126
Form 5 Notice of appeal to a court of appeals from a judgment or order of a district court or a bankruptcy appellate panel ... 1131
Form 6 Certificate of compliance with Rule 32(a) ... 1132

TITLE I. APPLICABILITY OF RULES

FRAP 1. SCOPE OF RULES; DEFINITION; TITLE

(a) Scope of Rules.

(1) These rules govern procedure in the United States courts of appeals.

(2) When these rules provide for filing a motion or other document in the district court, the procedure must comply with the practice of the district court.

(b) Definition. In these rules, 'state' includes the District of Columbia and any United States commonwealth or territory.

(c) Title. These rules are to be known as the Federal Rules of Appellate Procedure.

See selected Notes of Advisory Committee to FRAP 1, p. 1265.

History of FRAP 1: Adopted Dec. 4, 1967, eff. July 1, 1968. Amended Apr. 30, 1979, eff. Aug. 1, 1979; Apr. 25, 1989, eff. Dec. 1, 1989; Apr. 24, 1998, eff. Dec. 1, 1998. Former FRAP 48 as renumbered 1(c), Apr. 29, 1994, eff. Dec. 1, 1994. Amended Apr. 29, 2002, eff. Dec. 1, 2002; Apr. 28, 2010, eff. Dec. 1, 2010.

See also U.S. Const. art. 3, §1 (authority to create courts inferior to Supreme Court); 18 U.S.C. §505 (penalties of forging or counterfeiting seals of courts); 28 U.S.C. §41 (number and composition of circuits), §43 (creation and composition of courts), §451 ("Courts of the United States" as including courts of appeals), §1691 (writs and process issued by court to be under seal), §2072 (power of Supreme Court to prescribe rules of procedure and evidence).

FRAP 2. SUSPENSION OF RULES

On its own or a party's motion, a court of appeals may—to expedite its decision or for other good cause—suspend any provision of these rules in a particular case and order proceedings as it directs, except as otherwise provided in Rule 26(b).

History of FRAP 2: Adopted Dec. 4, 1967, eff. July 1, 1968. Amended Apr. 24, 1998, eff. Dec. 1, 1998.

TITLE II. APPEAL FROM A JUDGMENT OR ORDER OF A DISTRICT COURT

FRAP 3. APPEAL AS OF RIGHT—HOW TAKEN

(a) Filing the Notice of Appeal.

(1) An appeal permitted by law as of right from a district court to a court of appeals may be taken only by filing a notice of appeal with the district clerk within the time allowed by Rule 4. At the time of filing, the appellant must furnish the clerk with enough copies of the notice to enable the clerk to comply with Rule 3(d).

(2) An appellant's failure to take any step other than the timely filing of a notice of appeal does not affect the validity of the appeal, but is ground only for the court of appeals to act as it considers appropriate, including dismissing the appeal.

(3) An appeal from a judgment by a magistrate judge in a civil case is taken in the same way as an appeal from any other district court judgment.

(4) An appeal by permission under 28 U.S.C. §1292(b) or an appeal in a bankruptcy case may be taken only in the manner prescribed by Rules 5 and 6, respectively.

(b) Joint or Consolidated Appeals.

(1) When two or more parties are entitled to appeal from a district-court judgment or order, and their interests make joinder practicable, they may file a joint notice of appeal. They may then proceed on appeal as a single appellant.

(2) When the parties have filed separate timely notices of appeal, the appeals may be joined or consolidated by the court of appeals.

(c) Contents of the Notice of Appeal.

(1) The notice of appeal must:

(A) specify the party or parties taking the appeal by naming each one in the caption or body of the notice, but an attorney representing more than one party may describe those parties with such terms as "all plaintiffs," "the defendants," "the plaintiffs A, B, et al.," or "all defendants except X";

(B) designate the judgment, order, or part thereof being appealed; and

(C) name the court to which the appeal is taken.

(2) A pro se notice of appeal is considered filed on behalf of the signer and the signer's spouse and minor children (if they are parties), unless the notice clearly indicates otherwise.

(3) In a class action, whether or not the class has been certified, the notice of appeal is sufficient if it names one person qualified to bring the appeal as representative of the class.

(4) An appeal must not be dismissed for informality of form or title of the notice of appeal, or for failure to name a party whose intent to appeal is otherwise clear from the notice.

(5) Form 1 in the Appendix of Forms is a suggested form of a notice of appeal.

(d) Serving the Notice of Appeal.

(1) The district clerk must serve notice of the filing of a notice of appeal by mailing a copy to each party's counsel of record—excluding the appellant's—or, if a party is proceeding pro se, to the party's last known address. When a defendant in a criminal case appeals, the clerk must also serve a copy of the notice of appeal on the defendant, either by personal service or by mail addressed to the defendant. The clerk must promptly send a copy of the notice of appeal and of the docket entries—and any later docket entries—to the clerk of the court of appeals named in the notice. The district clerk must note, on each copy, the date when the notice of appeal was filed.

(2) If an inmate confined in an institution files a notice of appeal in the manner provided by Rule 4(c), the district clerk must also note the date when the clerk docketed the notice.

(3) The district clerk's failure to serve notice does not affect the validity of the appeal. The clerk must note on the docket the names of the parties to whom the clerk mails copies, with the date of mailing. Service is sufficient despite the death of a party or the party's counsel.

(e) Payment of Fees. Upon filing a notice of appeal, the appellant must pay the district clerk all required fees. The district clerk receives the appellate docket fee on behalf of the court of appeals.

History of FRAP 3: Adopted Dec. 4, 1967, eff. July 1, 1968. Amended Apr. 30, 1979, eff. Aug. 1, 1979; Mar. 10, 1986, eff. July 1, 1986; Apr. 25, 1989, eff. Dec. 1, 1989; Apr. 22, 1993, eff. Dec. 1, 1993; Apr. 29, 1994, eff. Dec. 1, 1994; Apr. 24, 1998, eff. Dec. 1, 1998.

See also 28 U.S.C. §1291 (final decisions of district court appealable to court of appeals), §1292 (interlocutory decisions of district court appealable to court of appeals), §1294 (circuits in which decisions reviewable).

FRAP 3.1. ABROGATED

Abrogated by order of Apr. 24, 1998, eff. Dec. 1, 1998.

FRAP 4. APPEAL AS OF RIGHT—WHEN TAKEN

(a) Appeal in a Civil Case.

(1) Time for Filing a Notice of Appeal.

(A) In a civil case, except as provided in Rules 4(a)(1)(B), 4(a)(4), and 4(c), the notice of appeal required by Rule 3 must be filed with the district clerk within 30 days after entry of the judgment or order appealed from.

(B) The notice of appeal may be filed by any party within 60 days after entry of the judgment or order appealed from if one of the parties is:

(i) the United States;

(ii) a United States agency;

(iii) a United States officer or employee sued in an official capacity; or

(iv) a current or former United States officer or employee sued in an individual capacity for an act or omission occurring in connection with duties performed on the United States' behalf—including all instances in which the United States represents that person when the judgment or order is entered or files the appeal for that person.

(C) An appeal from an order granting or denying an application for a writ of error *coram nobis* is an appeal in a civil case for purposes of Rule 4(a).

(2) Filing Before Entry of Judgment. A notice of appeal filed after the court announces a decision or order—but before the entry of the judgment or order—is treated as filed on the date of and after the entry.

(3) Multiple Appeals. If one party timely files a notice of appeal, any other party may file a notice of appeal within 14 days after the date when the first notice was filed, or within the time otherwise prescribed by this Rule 4(a), whichever period ends later.

(4) Effect of a Motion on a Notice of Appeal.

(A) If a party timely files in the district court any of the following motions under the Federal Rules of Civil Procedure, the time to file an appeal runs for all parties from the entry of the order disposing of the last such remaining motion:

(i) for judgment under Rule 50(b);

(ii) to amend or make additional factual findings under Rule 52(b), whether or not granting the motion would alter the judgment;

(iii) for attorney's fees under Rule 54 if the district court extends the time to appeal under Rule 58;

(iv) to alter or amend the judgment under Rule 59;

(v) for a new trial under Rule 59; or

(vi) for relief under Rule 60 if the motion is filed no later than 28 days after the judgment is entered.

(B)(i) If a party files a notice of appeal after the court announces or enters a judgment—but before it disposes of any motion listed in Rule 4(a)(4)(A)—the notice becomes effective to appeal a judgment or order, in whole or in part, when the order disposing of the last such remaining motion is entered.

(ii) A party intending to challenge an order disposing of any motion listed in Rule 4(a)(4)(A), or a judgment's alteration or amendment upon such a motion, must file a notice of appeal, or an amended notice of appeal—in compliance with Rule 3(c)—within the time prescribed by this Rule measured from the entry of the order disposing of the last such remaining motion.

(iii) No additional fee is required to file an amended notice.

(5) Motion for Extension of Time.

(A) The district court may extend the time to file a notice of appeal if:

(i) a party so moves no later than 30 days after the time prescribed by this Rule 4(a) expires; and

(ii) regardless of whether its motion is filed before or during the 30 days after the time prescribed by this Rule 4(a) expires, that party shows excusable neglect or good cause.

(B) A motion filed before the expiration of the time prescribed in Rule 4(a)(1) or (3) may be ex parte unless the court requires otherwise. If the motion is filed after the expiration of the prescribed time, notice must be given to the other parties in accordance with local rules.

(C) No extension under this Rule 4(a)(5) may exceed 30 days after the prescribed time or 14 days after the date when the order granting the motion is entered, whichever is later.

(6) Reopening the Time to File an Appeal. The district court may reopen the time to file an appeal for a period of 14 days after the date when its order to reopen is entered, but only if all the following conditions are satisfied:

(A) the court finds that the moving party did not receive notice under Federal Rule of Civil Procedure 77(d) of the entry of the judgment or order sought to be appealed within 21 days after entry;

(B) the motion is filed within 180 days after the judgment or order is entered or within 14 days after the moving party receives notice under Federal Rule of Civil Procedure 77(d) of the entry, whichever is earlier; and

(C) the court finds that no party would be prejudiced.

(7) Entry Defined.

(A) A judgment or order is entered for purposes of this Rule 4(a):

(i) if Federal Rule of Civil Procedure 58(a) does not require a separate document, when the judgment or order is entered in the civil docket under Federal Rule of Civil Procedure 79(a); or

(ii) if Federal Rule of Civil Procedure 58(a) requires a separate document, when the judgment or order is entered in the civil docket under Federal Rule of Civil Procedure 79(a) and when the earlier of these events occurs:

- the judgment or order is set forth on a separate document, or
- 150 days have run from entry of the judgment or order in the civil docket under Federal Rule of Civil Procedure 79(a).

(B) A failure to set forth a judgment or order on a separate document when required by Federal Rule of Civil Procedure 58(a) does not affect the validity of an appeal from that judgment or order.

(b) Appeal in a Criminal Case.

(1) Time for Filing a Notice of Appeal.

(A) In a criminal case, a defendant's notice of appeal must be filed in the district court within 14 days after the later of:

(i) the entry of either the judgment or the order being appealed; or

(ii) the filing of the government's notice of appeal.

(B) When the government is entitled to appeal, its notice of appeal must be filed in the district court within 30 days after the later of:

(i) the entry of the judgment or order being appealed; or

(ii) the filing of a notice of appeal by any defendant.

(2) Filing Before Entry of Judgment. A notice of appeal filed after the court announces a decision, sentence, or order—but before the entry of the judgment or order—is treated as filed on the date of and after the entry.

(3) Effect of a Motion on a Notice of Appeal.

(A) If a defendant timely makes any of the following motions under the Federal Rules of Criminal Procedure, the notice of appeal from a judgment of conviction must be filed within 14 days after the entry of the order disposing of the last such remaining motion, or within 14 days after the entry of the judgment of conviction, whichever period ends later. This provision applies to a timely motion:

(i) for judgment of acquittal under Rule 29;

(ii) for a new trial under Rule 33, but if based on newly discovered evidence, only if the motion is made no later than 14 days after the entry of the judgment; or

(iii) for arrest of judgment under Rule 34.

(B) A notice of appeal filed after the court announces a decision, sentence, or order—but before it disposes of any of the motions referred to in Rule 4(b)(3)(A)—becomes effective upon the later of the following:

(i) the entry of the order disposing of the last such remaining motion; or

(ii) the entry of the judgment of conviction.

(C) A valid notice of appeal is effective—without amendment—to appeal from an order disposing of any of the motions referred to in Rule 4(b)(3)(A).

(4) Motion for Extension of Time. Upon a finding of excusable neglect or good cause, the district court may—before or after the time has expired, with or without motion and notice—extend the time to file a notice of appeal for a period not to exceed 30 days from the expiration of the time otherwise prescribed by this Rule 4(b).

(5) Jurisdiction. The filing of a notice of appeal under this Rule 4(b) does not divest a district court of jurisdiction to correct a sentence under Federal Rule of Criminal Procedure 35(a), nor does the filing of a motion under 35(a) affect the validity of a notice of appeal filed before entry of the order disposing of the motion. The filing of a motion under Federal Rule of Criminal Procedure 35(a) does not suspend the time for filing a notice of appeal from a judgment of conviction.

(6) Entry Defined. A judgment or order is entered for purposes of this Rule 4(b) when it is entered on the criminal docket.

(c) Appeal by an Inmate Confined in an Institution.

(1) If an inmate confined in an institution files a notice of appeal in either a civil or a criminal case, the notice is timely if it is deposited in the institution's internal mail system on or before the last day for filing. If an institution has a system designed for legal mail, the inmate must use that system to receive the benefit of this rule. Timely filing may be shown by a declaration in compliance with 28 U.S.C. §1746 or by a notarized statement, either of which must set forth the date of deposit and state that first-class postage has been prepaid.

(2) If an inmate files the first notice of appeal in a civil case under this Rule 4(c), the 14-day period provided in Rule 4(a)(3) for another party to file a notice of appeal runs from the date when the district court dockets the first notice.

(3) When a defendant in a criminal case files a notice of appeal under this Rule 4(c), the 30-day

period for the government to file its notice of appeal runs from the entry of the judgment or order appealed from or from the district court's docketing of the defendant's notice of appeal, whichever is later.

(d) Mistaken Filing in the Court of Appeals. If a notice of appeal in either a civil or a criminal case is mistakenly filed in the court of appeals, the clerk of that court must note on the notice the date when it was received and send it to the district clerk. The notice is then considered filed in the district court on the date so noted.

See selected Notes of Advisory Committee to FRAP 4, p. 1266.

History of FRAP 4: Adopted Dec. 4, 1967, eff. July 1, 1968. Amended Apr. 30, 1979, eff. Aug. 1, 1979; Nov. 18, 1988, P.L. 100-690, §7111, 102 Stat. 4419; Apr. 30, 1991, eff. Dec. 1, 1991; Apr. 22, 1993, eff. Dec. 1, 1993; Apr. 27, 1995, eff. Dec. 1, 1995; Apr. 24, 1998, eff. Dec. 1, 1998; Apr. 29, 2002, eff. Dec. 1, 2002; Apr. 25, 2005, eff. Dec. 1, 2005; Mar. 26, 2009, eff. Dec. 1, 2009; Apr. 28, 2010, eff. Dec. 1, 2010; Apr. 26, 2011, eff. Dec. 1, 2011.

See ***Commentaries***, "Motion to Extend Time to File Notice of Appeal," ch. 10-G, p. 817; "Motion to Reopen Time for Appeal," ch. 10-H, p. 821; ***O'Connor's Federal Civil Forms*** (2012), FORMS 10G; FORMS 10H.

See also 28 U.S.C. §1291 (final decisions of district courts reviewable by courts of appeals), §1294 (circuits in which decisions reviewable generally), §2071 (rulemaking power generally), §2105 (review of matters in abatement), §2106 (determination of appeal generally), §2107 (time for appeal to court of appeals), §2108 (amount or value in controversy affecting right to review).

FRAP 5. APPEAL BY PERMISSION

(a) Petition for Permission to Appeal.

(1) To request permission to appeal when an appeal is within the court of appeals' discretion, a party must file a petition for permission to appeal. The petition must be filed with the circuit clerk with proof of service on all other parties to the district-court action.

(2) The petition must be filed within the time specified by the statute or rule authorizing the appeal or, if no such time is specified, within the time provided by Rule 4(a) for filing a notice of appeal.

(3) If a party cannot petition for appeal unless the district court first enters an order granting permission to do so or stating that the necessary conditions are met, the district court may amend its order, either on its own or in response to a party's motion, to include the required permission or statement. In that event, the time to petition runs from entry of the amended order.

(b) Contents of the Petition; Answer or Cross-Petition; Oral Argument.

(1) The petition must include the following:

(A) the facts necessary to understand the question presented;

(B) the question itself;

(C) the relief sought;

(D) the reasons why the appeal should be allowed and is authorized by a statute or rule; and

(E) an attached copy of:

(i) the order, decree, or judgment complained of and any related opinion or memorandum, and

(ii) any order stating the district court's permission to appeal or finding that the necessary conditions are met.

(2) A party may file an answer in opposition or a cross-petition within 10 days after the petition is served.

(3) The petition and answer will be submitted without oral argument unless the court of appeals orders otherwise.

(c) Form of Papers; Number of Copies. All papers must conform to Rule 32(c)(2). Except by the court's permission, a paper must not exceed 20 pages, exclusive of the disclosure statement, the proof of service, and the accompanying documents required by Rule 5(b)(1)(E). An original and 3 copies must be filed unless the court requires a different number by local rule or by order in a particular case.

(d) Grant of Permission; Fees; Cost Bond; Filing the Record.

(1) Within 14 days after the entry of the order granting permission to appeal, the appellant must:

(A) pay the district clerk all required fees; and

(B) file a cost bond if required under Rule 7.

(2) A notice of appeal need not be filed. The date when the order granting permission to appeal is entered serves as the date of the notice of appeal for calculating time under these rules.

(3) The district clerk must notify the circuit clerk once the petitioner has paid the fees. Upon receiving this notice, the circuit clerk must enter

FRAP 4

the appeal on the docket. The record must be forwarded and filed in accordance with Rules 11 and 12(c).

See selected Notes of Advisory Committee to FRAP 5, p. 1275.

History of FRAP 5: Adopted Dec. 4, 1967, eff. July 1, 1968. Amended Apr. 30, 1979, eff. Aug. 1, 1979; Apr. 29, 1994, eff. Dec. 1, 1994; Apr. 24, 1998, eff. Dec. 1, 1998; Apr. 29, 2002, eff. Dec. 1, 2002; Mar. 26, 2009, eff. Dec. 1, 2009.

See also 28 U.S.C. §1294 (circuits in which decisions reviewable generally).

FRAP 5.1. ABROGATED

Abrogated by order of Apr. 24, 1998, eff. Dec. 1, 1998.

FRAP 6. APPEAL IN A BANKRUPTCY CASE FROM A FINAL JUDGMENT, ORDER, OR DECREE OF A DISTRICT COURT OR BANKRUPTCY APPELLATE PANEL

(a) Appeal From a Judgment, Order, or Decree of a District Court Exercising Original Jurisdiction in a Bankruptcy Case. An appeal to a court of appeals from a final judgment, order, or decree of a district court exercising jurisdiction under 28 U.S.C. §1334 is taken as any other civil appeal under these rules.

(b) Appeal From a Judgment, Order, or Decree of a District Court or Bankruptcy Appellate Panel Exercising Appellate Jurisdiction in a Bankruptcy Case.

(1) Applicability of Other Rules. These rules apply to an appeal to a court of appeals under 28 U.S.C. §158(d) from a final judgment, order, or decree of a district court or bankruptcy appellate panel exercising appellate jurisdiction under 28 U.S.C. §158(a) or (b). But there are 3 exceptions:

(A) Rules 4(a)(4), 4(b), 9, 10, 11, 12(b), 13-20, 22-23, and 24(b) do not apply;

(B) the reference in Rule 3(c) to "Form 1 in the Appendix of Forms" must be read as a reference to Form 5; and

(C) when the appeal is from a bankruptcy appellate panel, the term "district court," as used in any applicable rule, means "appellate panel."

(2) Additional Rules. In addition to the rules made applicable by Rule 6(b)(1), the following rules apply:

(A) Motion for rehearing.

(i) If a timely motion for rehearing under Bankruptcy Rule 8015 is filed, the time to appeal for all parties runs from the entry of the order disposing of the motion. A notice of appeal filed after the district court or bankruptcy appellate panel announces or enters a judgment, order, or decree—but before disposition of the motion for rehearing—becomes effective when the order disposing of the motion for rehearing is entered.

(ii) Appellate review of the order disposing of the motion requires the party, in compliance with Rules 3(c) and 6(b)(1)(B), to amend a previously filed notice of appeal. A party intending to challenge an altered or amended judgment, order, or decree must file a notice of appeal or amended notice of appeal within the time prescribed by Rule 4—excluding Rules 4(a)(4) and 4(b)—measured from the entry of the order disposing of the motion.

(iii) No additional fee is required to file an amended notice.

(B) The record on appeal.

(i) Within 14 days after filing the notice of appeal, the appellant must file with the clerk possessing the record assembled in accordance with Bankruptcy Rule 8006—and serve on the appellee—a statement of the issues to be presented on appeal and a designation of the record to be certified and sent to the circuit clerk.

(ii) An appellee who believes that other parts of the record are necessary must, within 14 days after being served with the appellant's designation, file with the clerk and serve on the appellant a designation of additional parts to be included.

(iii) The record on appeal consists of:

- the redesignated record as provided above;
- the proceedings in the district court or bankruptcy appellate panel; and
- a certified copy of the docket entries prepared by the clerk under Rule 3(d).

FRAP 6

(C) Forwarding the record.

(i) When the record is complete, the district clerk or bankruptcy appellate panel clerk must number the documents constituting the record and send them promptly to the circuit clerk together with a list of the documents correspondingly numbered and reasonably identified. Unless directed to do so by a party or the circuit clerk, the clerk will not send to the court of appeals documents of unusual bulk or weight, physical exhibits other than documents, or other parts of the record designated for omission by local rule of the court of appeals. If the exhibits are unusually bulky or heavy, a party must arrange with the clerks in advance for their transportation and receipt.

(ii) All parties must do whatever else is necessary to enable the clerk to assemble and forward the record. The court of appeals may provide by rule or order that a certified copy of the docket entries be sent in place of the redesignated record, but any party may request at any time during the pendency of the appeal that the redesignated record be sent.

(D) Filing the record. Upon receiving the record—or a certified copy of the docket entries sent in place of the redesignated record—the circuit clerk must file it and immediately notify all parties of the filing date.

See selected Notes of Advisory Committee to FRAP 6, p. 1276.

History of FRAP 6: Adopted Dec. 4, 1967, eff. July 1, 1968. Amended Apr. 30, 1979, eff. Aug. 1, 1979; Apr. 25, 1989, eff. Dec. 1, 1989; Apr. 30, 1991, eff. Dec. 1, 1991; Apr. 22, 1993, eff. Dec. 1, 1993; Apr. 24, 1998, eff. Dec. 1, 1998; Mar. 26, 2009, eff. Dec. 1, 2009.

See also 28 U.S.C. §1291 (final decisions of district court appealable to courts of appeals), §1292 (interlocutory decisions of district court appealable to courts of appeals).

FRAP 7. BOND FOR COSTS ON APPEAL IN A CIVIL CASE

In a civil case, the district court may require an appellant to file a bond or provide other security in any form and amount necessary to ensure payment of costs on appeal. Rule 8(b) applies to a surety on a bond given under this rule.

History of FRAP 7: Adopted Dec. 4, 1967, eff. July 1, 1968. Amended Apr. 30, 1979, eff. Aug. 1, 1979; Apr. 24, 1998, eff. Dec. 1, 1998.

See also 28 U.S.C. §2408 (security for damages or costs not required of U.S.); 31 U.S.C. §9303 (deposit of bonds or notes of U.S. in lieu of surety).

FRAP 8. STAY OR INJUNCTION PENDING APPEAL

(a) Motion for Stay.

(1) Initial Motion in the District Court. A party must ordinarily move first in the district court for the following relief:

(A) a stay of the judgment or order of a district court pending appeal;

(B) approval of a supersedeas bond; or

(C) an order suspending, modifying, restoring, or granting an injunction while an appeal is pending.

(2) Motion in the Court of Appeals; Conditions on Relief. A motion for the relief mentioned in Rule 8(a)(1) may be made to the court of appeals or to one of its judges.

(A) The motion must:

(i) show that moving first in the district court would be impracticable; or

(ii) state that, a motion having been made, the district court denied the motion or failed to afford the relief requested and state any reasons given by the district court for its action.

(B) The motion must also include:

(i) the reasons for granting the relief requested and the facts relied on;

(ii) originals or copies of affidavits or other sworn statements supporting facts subject to dispute; and

(iii) relevant parts of the record.

(C) The moving party must give reasonable notice of the motion to all parties.

(D) A motion under this Rule 8(a)(2) must be filed with the circuit clerk and normally will be considered by a panel of the court. But in an exceptional case in which time requirements make that procedure impracticable, the motion may be made to and considered by a single judge.

(E) The court may condition relief on a party's filing a bond or other appropriate security in the district court.

(b) Proceeding Against a Surety. If a party gives security in the form of a bond or stipulation or other

undertaking with one or more sureties, each surety submits to the jurisdiction of the district court and irrevocably appoints the district clerk as the surety's agent on whom any papers affecting the surety's liability on the bond or undertaking may be served. On motion, a surety's liability may be enforced in the district court without the necessity of an independent action. The motion and any notice that the district court prescribes may be served on the district clerk, who must promptly mail a copy to each surety whose address is known.

(c) Stay in a Criminal Case. Rule 38 of the Federal Rules of Criminal Procedure governs a stay in a criminal case.

History of FRAP 8: Adopted Dec. 4, 1967, eff. July 1, 1968. Amended Mar. 10, 1986, eff. July 1, 1986; Apr. 24, 1998, eff. Dec. 1, 1998.

See also 28 U.S.C. §2408 (security for damages or costs not required of U.S.); 31 U.S.C. §9303 (deposit of bonds or notes of U.S. in lieu of surety).

FRAP 9. RELEASE IN A CRIMINAL CASE

(a) Release Before Judgment of Conviction.

(1) The district court must state in writing, or orally on the record, the reasons for an order regarding the release or detention of a defendant in a criminal case. A party appealing from the order must file with the court of appeals a copy of the district court's order and the court's statement of reasons as soon as practicable after filing the notice of appeal. An appellant who questions the factual basis for the district court's order must file a transcript of the release proceedings or an explanation of why a transcript was not obtained.

(2) After reasonable notice to the appellee, the court of appeals must promptly determine the appeal on the basis of the papers, affidavits, and parts of the record that the parties present or the court requires. Unless the court so orders, briefs need not be filed.

(3) The court of appeals or one of its judges may order the defendant's release pending the disposition of the appeal.

(b) Release After Judgment of Conviction. A party entitled to do so may obtain review of a district-court order regarding release after a judgment of conviction by filing a notice of appeal from that order in the district court, or by filing a motion in the court of appeals if the party has already filed a notice of appeal from the judgment of conviction. Both the order and the review are subject to Rule 9(a). The papers filed by the party seeking review must include a copy of the judgment of conviction.

(c) Criteria for Release. The court must make its decision regarding release in accordance with the applicable provisions of 18 U.S.C. §§3142, 3143, and 3145(c).

History of FRAP 9: Adopted Dec. 4, 1967, eff. July 1, 1968. Amended Apr. 24, 1972, eff. Oct. 1, 1972; Oct. 12, 1984, P.L. 98-473, §210, 98 Stat. 1987; Apr. 29, 1994, eff. Dec. 1, 1994; Apr. 24, 1998, eff. Dec. 1, 1998.

See also 18 U.S.C. §§3141-3156 (release and detention pending judicial proceedings).

FRAP 10. THE RECORD ON APPEAL

(a) Composition of the Record on Appeal. The following items constitute the record on appeal:

(1) the original papers and exhibits filed in the district court;

(2) the transcript of proceedings, if any; and

(3) a certified copy of the docket entries prepared by the district clerk.

(b) The Transcript of Proceedings.

(1) **Appellant's Duty to Order.** Within 14 days after filing the notice of appeal or entry of an order disposing of the last timely remaining motion of a type specified in Rule 4(a)(4)(A), whichever is later, the appellant must do either of the following:

(A) order from the reporter a transcript of such parts of the proceedings not already on file as the appellant considers necessary, subject to a local rule of the court of appeals and with the following qualifications:

(i) the order must be in writing;

(ii) if the cost of the transcript is to be paid by the United States under the Criminal Justice Act, the order must so state; and

(iii) the appellant must, within the same period, file a copy of the order with the district clerk; or

(B) file a certificate stating that no transcript will be ordered.

(2) **Unsupported Finding or Conclusion.** If the appellant intends to urge on appeal that a finding or conclusion is unsupported by the evidence or is contrary to the evidence, the appellant must include in the record a transcript of all evidence relevant to that finding or conclusion.

(3) Partial Transcript. Unless the entire transcript is ordered:

(A) the appellant must—within the 14 days provided in Rule 10(b)(1)—file a statement of the issues that the appellant intends to present on the appeal and must serve on the appellee a copy of both the order or certificate and the statement;

(B) if the appellee considers it necessary to have a transcript of other parts of the proceedings, the appellee must, within 14 days after the service of the order or certificate and the statement of the issues, file and serve on the appellant a designation of additional parts to be ordered; and

(C) unless within 14 days after service of that designation the appellant has ordered all such parts, and has so notified the appellee, the appellee may within the following 14 days either order the parts or move in the district court for an order requiring the appellant to do so.

(4) Payment. At the time of ordering, a party must make satisfactory arrangements with the reporter for paying the cost of the transcript.

(c) Statement of the Evidence When the Proceedings Were Not Recorded or When a Transcript Is Unavailable. If the transcript of a hearing or trial is unavailable, the appellant may prepare a statement of the evidence or proceedings from the best available means, including the appellant's recollection. The statement must be served on the appellee, who may serve objections or proposed amendments within 14 days after being served. The statement and any objections or proposed amendments must then be submitted to the district court for settlement and approval. As settled and approved, the statement must be included by the district clerk in the record on appeal.

(d) Agreed Statement as the Record on Appeal. In place of the record on appeal as defined in Rule 10(a), the parties may prepare, sign, and submit to the district court a statement of the case showing how the issues presented by the appeal arose and were decided in the district court. The statement must set forth only those facts averred and proved or sought to be proved that are essential to the court's resolution of the issues. If the statement is truthful, it—together with any additions that the district court may consider necessary to a full presentation of the issues on appeal—must be approved by the district court and must then be certified to the court of appeals as the record on appeal. The district clerk must then send it to the circuit clerk within the time provided by Rule 11. A copy of the agreed statement may be filed in place of the appendix required by Rule 30.

(e) Correction or Modification of the Record.

(1) If any difference arises about whether the record truly discloses what occurred in the district court, the difference must be submitted to and settled by that court and the record conformed accordingly.

(2) If anything material to either party is omitted from or misstated in the record by error or accident, the omission or misstatement may be corrected and a supplemental record may be certified and forwarded:

(A) on stipulation of the parties;

(B) by the district court before or after the record has been forwarded; or

(C) by the court of appeals.

(3) All other questions as to the form and content of the record must be presented to the court of appeals.

See selected Notes of Advisory Committee to FRAP 10, p. 1276.

History of FRAP 10: Adopted Dec. 4, 1967, eff. July 1, 1968. Amended Apr. 30, 1979, eff. Aug. 1, 1979; Mar. 10, 1986, eff. July 1, 1986; Apr. 30, 1991, eff. Dec. 1, 1991; Apr. 22, 1993, eff. Dec. 1, 1993; Apr. 27, 1995, eff. Dec. 1, 1995; Apr. 24, 1998, eff. Dec. 1, 1998; Mar. 26, 2009, eff. Dec. 1, 2009.

See also 28 U.S.C. §457 (records, obsolete papers), §753 (reporters' transcript of proceedings).

FRAP 11. FORWARDING THE RECORD

(a) Appellant's Duty. An appellant filing a notice of appeal must comply with Rule 10(b) and must do whatever else is necessary to enable the clerk to assemble and forward the record. If there are multiple appeals from a judgment or order, the clerk must forward a single record.

(b) Duties of Reporter and District Clerk.

(1) Reporter's Duty to Prepare and File a Transcript. The reporter must prepare and file a transcript as follows:

(A) Upon receiving an order for a transcript, the reporter must enter at the foot of the

order the date of its receipt and the expected completion date and send a copy, so endorsed, to the circuit clerk.

(B) If the transcript cannot be completed within 30 days of the reporter's receipt of the order, the reporter may request the circuit clerk to grant additional time to complete it. The clerk must note on the docket the action taken and notify the parties.

(C) When a transcript is complete, the reporter must file it with the district clerk and notify the circuit clerk of the filing.

(D) If the reporter fails to file the transcript on time, the circuit clerk must notify the district judge and do whatever else the court of appeals directs.

(2) **District Clerk's Duty to Forward.** When the record is complete, the district clerk must number the documents constituting the record and send them promptly to the circuit clerk together with a list of the documents correspondingly numbered and reasonably identified. Unless directed to do so by a party or the circuit clerk, the district clerk will not send to the court of appeals documents of unusual bulk or weight, physical exhibits other than documents, or other parts of the record designated for omission by local rule of the court of appeals. If the exhibits are unusually bulky or heavy, a party must arrange with the clerks in advance for their transportation and receipt.

(c) **Retaining the Record Temporarily in the District Court for Use in Preparing the Appeal.** The parties may stipulate, or the district court on motion may order, that the district clerk retain the record temporarily for the parties to use in preparing the papers on appeal. In that event the district clerk must certify to the circuit clerk that the record on appeal is complete. Upon receipt of the appellee's brief, or earlier if the court orders or the parties agree, the appellant must request the district clerk to forward the record.

(d) [Abrogated.]

(e) **Retaining the Record by Court Order.**

(1) The court of appeals may, by order or local rule, provide that a certified copy of the docket entries be forwarded instead of the entire record. But a party may at any time during the appeal request that designated parts of the record be forwarded.

(2) The district court may order the record or some part of it retained if the court needs it while the appeal is pending, subject, however, to call by the court of appeals.

(3) If part or all of the record is ordered retained, the district clerk must send to the court of appeals a copy of the order and the docket entries together with the parts of the original record allowed by the district court and copies of any parts of the record designated by the parties.

(f) **Retaining Parts of the Record in the District Court by Stipulation of the Parties.** The parties may agree by written stipulation filed in the district court that designated parts of the record be retained in the district court subject to call by the court of appeals or request by a party. The parts of the record so designated remain a part of the record on appeal.

(g) **Record for a Preliminary Motion in the Court of Appeals.** If, before the record is forwarded, a party makes any of the following motions in the court of appeals:

- for dismissal;
- for release;
- for a stay pending appeal;
- for additional security on the bond on appeal or on a supersedeas bond; or
- for any other intermediate order—

the district clerk must send the court of appeals any parts of the record designated by any party.

History of FRAP 11: Adopted Dec. 4, 1967, eff. July 1, 1968. Amended Apr. 30, 1979, eff. Aug. 1, 1979; Mar. 10, 1986, eff. July 1, 1986; Apr. 24, 1998, eff. Dec. 1, 1998.

See also 28 U.S.C. §457 (records, obsolete papers), §753 (reporters' transcript of proceedings).

FRAP 12. DOCKETING THE APPEAL; FILING A REPRESENTATION STATEMENT; FILING THE RECORD

(a) **Docketing the Appeal.** Upon receiving the copy of the notice of appeal and the docket entries from the district clerk under Rule 3(d), the circuit clerk must docket the appeal under the title of the district-court action and must identify the appellant, adding the appellant's name if necessary.

(b) Filing a Representation Statement. Unless the court of appeals designates another time, the attorney who filed the notice of appeal must, within 14 days after filing the notice, file a statement with the circuit clerk naming the parties that the attorney represents on appeal.

(c) Filing the Record, Partial Record, or Certificate. Upon receiving the record, partial record, or district clerk's certificate as provided in Rule 11, the circuit clerk must file it and immediately notify all parties of the filing date.

See selected Notes of Advisory Committee to FRAP 12, p. 1276.

History of FRAP 12: Adopted Dec. 4, 1967, eff. July 1, 1968. Amended Apr. 30, 1979, eff. Aug. 1, 1979; Mar. 10, 1986, eff. July 1, 1986; Apr. 22, 1993, eff. Dec. 1, 1993; Apr. 24, 1998, eff. Dec. 1, 1998; Mar. 26, 2009, eff. Dec. 1, 2009.

See also 28 U.S.C. §1651 (power of courts to issue writs), §1691 (seal and teste of process), §2071 (rulemaking power generally).

FRAP 12.1. REMAND AFTER AN INDICATIVE RULING BY THE DISTRICT COURT ON A MOTION FOR RELIEF THAT IS BARRED BY A PENDING APPEAL

(a) Notice to the Court of Appeals. If a timely motion is made in the district court for relief that it lacks authority to grant because of an appeal that has been docketed and is pending, the movant must promptly notify the circuit clerk if the district court states either that it would grant the motion or that the motion raises a substantial issue.

(b) Remand After an Indicative Ruling. If the district court states that it would grant the motion or that the motion raises a substantial issue, the court of appeals may remand for further proceedings but retains jurisdiction unless it expressly dismisses the appeal. If the court of appeals remands but retains jurisdiction, the parties must promptly notify the circuit clerk when the district court has decided the motion on remand.

See selected Notes of Advisory Committee to FRAP 12.1, p. 1276.

History of FRAP 12.1: Adopted Mar. 26, 2009, eff. Dec. 1, 2009.

See *Commentaries*, "Indicative Ruling," ch. 10-F, §8, p. 813; *O'Connor's Federal Civil Forms* (2012), FORMS 10F:4-6.

FRAP 12

TITLE III. REVIEW OF A DECISION OF THE UNITED STATES TAX COURT

FRAP 13. REVIEW OF A DECISION OF THE TAX COURT

Editor's note: *The Committee on Rules of Practice and Procedure of the Judicial Conference of the United States has proposed amendments to FRAP 13, to be effective December 1, 2013. For the proposed amendments, see www.uscourts.gov/RulesAndPolicies/rules/pending-rules.aspx.*

(a) How Obtained; Time for Filing Notice of Appeal.

(1) Review of a decision of the United States Tax Court is commenced by filing a notice of appeal with the Tax Court clerk within 90 days after the entry of the Tax Court's decision. At the time of filing, the appellant must furnish the clerk with enough copies of the notice to enable the clerk to comply with Rule 3(d). If one party files a timely notice of appeal, any other party may file a notice of appeal within 120 days after the Tax Court's decision is entered.

(2) If, under Tax Court rules, a party makes a timely motion to vacate or revise the Tax Court's decision, the time to file a notice of appeal runs from the entry of the order disposing of the motion or from the entry of a new decision, whichever is later.

(b) Notice of Appeal; How Filed. The notice of appeal may be filed either at the Tax Court clerk's office in the District of Columbia or by mail addressed to the clerk. If sent by mail the notice is considered filed on the postmark date, subject to §7502 of the Internal Revenue Code, as amended, and the applicable regulations.

(c) Contents of the Notice of Appeal; Service; Effect of Filing and Service. Rule 3 prescribes the contents of a notice of appeal, the manner of service, and the effect of its filing and service. Form 2 in the Appendix of Forms is a suggested form of a notice of appeal.

(d) The Record on Appeal; Forwarding; Filing.

(1) An appeal from the Tax Court is governed by the parts of Rules 10, 11, and 12 regarding the record on appeal from a district court, the time and manner of forwarding and filing, and the docketing in the court of appeals. References in those rules and in Rule 3 to the district court and district clerk are to be read as referring to the Tax Court and its clerk.

(2) If an appeal from a Tax Court decision is taken to more than one court of appeals, the original record must be sent to the court named in the first notice of appeal filed. In an appeal to any

other court of appeals, the appellant must apply to that other court to make provision for the record.

History of FRAP 13: Adopted Dec. 4, 1967, eff. July 1, 1968. Amended Apr. 30, 1979, eff. Aug. 1, 1979; Apr. 29, 1994, eff. Dec. 1, 1994; Apr. 24, 1998, eff. Dec. 1, 1998.

See also 26 U.S.C. §7481(a)(3)(B) (finality of decision on mandate of court of appeals), §7482 (jurisdiction and venue for courts of review), §7483 (notice of appeal).

FRAP 14. APPLICABILITY OF OTHER RULES TO THE REVIEW OF A TAX COURT DECISION

Editor's note: *The Committee on Rules of Practice and Procedure of the Judicial Conference of the United States has proposed amendments to FRAP 14, to be effective December 1, 2013. For the proposed amendments, see www.uscourts.gov/RulesAndPolicies/rules/pending-rules.aspx.*

All provisions of these rules, except Rules 4-9, 15-20, and 22-23, apply to the review of a Tax Court decision.

History of FRAP 14: Adopted Dec. 4, 1967, eff. July 1, 1968. Amended Apr. 24, 1998, eff. Dec. 1, 1998.

See also 26 U.S.C. §§7453-7465 (rules of practice before U.S. Tax Court), §7481(a)(3)(B) (finality of decision on mandate of court of appeals), §7482 (jurisdiction and venue for courts of review), §7483 (notice of appeal).

TITLE IV. REVIEW OR ENFORCEMENT OF AN ORDER OF AN ADMINISTRATIVE AGENCY, BOARD, COMMISSION, OR OFFICER

FRAP 15. REVIEW OR ENFORCEMENT OF AN AGENCY ORDER—HOW OBTAINED; INTERVENTION

(a) Petition for Review; Joint Petition.

(1) Review of an agency order is commenced by filing, within the time prescribed by law, a petition for review with the clerk of a court of appeals authorized to review the agency order. If their interests make joinder practicable, two or more persons may join in a petition to the same court to review the same order.

(2) The petition must:

(A) name each party seeking review either in the caption or the body of the petition—using such terms as "et al.," "petitioners," or "respondents" does not effectively name the parties;

(B) name the agency as a respondent (even though not named in the petition, the United States is a respondent if required by statute); and

(C) specify the order or part thereof to be reviewed.

(3) Form 3 in the Appendix of Forms is a suggested form of a petition for review.

(4) In this rule "agency" includes an agency, board, commission, or officer; "petition for review" includes a petition to enjoin, suspend, modify, or otherwise review, or a notice of appeal, whichever form is indicated by the applicable statute.

(b) Application or Cross-Application to Enforce an Order; Answer; Default.

(1) An application to enforce an agency order must be filed with the clerk of a court of appeals authorized to enforce the order. If a petition is filed to review an agency order that the court may enforce, a party opposing the petition may file a cross-application for enforcement.

(2) Within 21 days after the application for enforcement is filed, the respondent must serve on the applicant an answer to the application and file it with the clerk. If the respondent fails to answer in time, the court will enter judgment for the relief requested.

(3) The application must contain a concise statement of the proceedings in which the order was entered, the facts upon which venue is based, and the relief requested.

(c) Service of the Petition or Application. The circuit clerk must serve a copy of the petition for review, or an application or cross-application to enforce an agency order, on each respondent as prescribed by Rule 3(d), unless a different manner of service is prescribed by statute. At the time of filing, the petitioner must:

(1) serve, or have served, a copy on each party admitted to participate in the agency proceedings, except for the respondents;

(2) file with the clerk a list of those so served; and

(3) give the clerk enough copies of the petition or application to serve each respondent.

(d) Intervention. Unless a statute provides another method, a person who wants to intervene in a proceeding under this rule must file a motion for leave to intervene with the circuit clerk and serve a copy on all parties. The motion—or other notice of intervention authorized by statute—must be filed

within 30 days after the petition for review is filed and must contain a concise statement of the interest of the moving party and the grounds for intervention.

(e) **Payment of Fees.** When filing any separate or joint petition for review in a court of appeals, the petitioner must pay the circuit clerk all required fees.

See selected Notes of Advisory Committee to FRAP 15, p. 1277.

History of FRAP 15: Adopted Dec. 4, 1967, eff. July 1, 1968. Amended Apr. 22, 1993, eff. Dec. 1, 1993; Apr. 24, 1998, eff. Dec. 1, 1998; Mar. 26, 2009, eff. Dec. 1, 2009.

See also 5 U.S.C. §§551-559 (administrative procedure generally), §§701-706 (review of orders of federal agencies generally); 15 U.S.C. §21 (review of orders of Federal Communications Commission, Board of Governors of Federal Reserve System, and Secretary of Transportation), §45 (review of orders of Federal Trade Commission); 16 U.S.C. §825l (review of orders of Federal Power Act); 28 U.S.C. §§2321-2323 (review of orders of Surface Transportation Board), §§2341-2351 (review of orders of federal agencies generally).

FRAP 15.1. BRIEFS & ORAL ARGUMENT IN A NATIONAL LABOR RELATIONS BOARD PROCEEDING

In either an enforcement or a review proceeding, a party adverse to the National Labor Relations Board proceeds first on briefing and at oral argument, unless the court orders otherwise.

History of FRAP 15.1: Adopted Mar. 10, 1986, eff. July 1, 1986. Amended Apr. 24, 1998, eff. Dec. 1, 1998.

FRAP 16. THE RECORD ON REVIEW OR ENFORCEMENT

(a) **Composition of the Record.** The record on review or enforcement of an agency order consists of:

(1) the order involved;

(2) any findings or report on which it is based; and

(3) the pleadings, evidence, and other parts of the proceedings before the agency.

(b) **Omissions From or Misstatements in the Record.** The parties may at any time, by stipulation, supply any omission from the record or correct a misstatement, or the court may so direct. If necessary, the court may direct that a supplemental record be prepared and filed.

History of FRAP 16: Adopted Dec. 4, 1967, eff. July 1, 1968. Amended Apr. 24, 1998, eff. Dec. 1, 1998.

FRAP 17. FILING THE RECORD

(a) **Agency to File; Time for Filing; Notice of Filing.** The agency must file the record with the circuit clerk within 40 days after being served with a petition for review, unless the statute authorizing review provides otherwise, or within 40 days after it files an application for enforcement unless the respondent fails to answer or the court orders otherwise. The court may shorten or extend the time to file the record. The clerk must notify all parties of the date when the record is filed.

(b) **Filing—What Constitutes.**

(1) The agency must file:

(A) the original or a certified copy of the entire record or parts designated by the parties; or

(B) a certified list adequately describing all documents, transcripts of testimony, exhibits, and other material constituting the record, or describing those parts designated by the parties.

(2) The parties may stipulate in writing that no record or certified list be filed. The date when the stipulation is filed with the circuit clerk is treated as the date when the record is filed.

(3) The agency must retain any portion of the record not filed with the clerk. All parts of the record retained by the agency are a part of the record on review for all purposes and, if the court or a party so requests, must be sent to the court regardless of any prior stipulation.

History of FRAP 17: Adopted Dec. 4, 1967, eff. July 1, 1968. Amended Apr. 24, 1998, eff. Dec. 1, 1998.

FRAP 18. STAY PENDING REVIEW

(a) **Motion for a Stay.**

(1) **Initial Motion Before the Agency.** A petitioner must ordinarily move first before the agency for a stay pending review of its decision or order.

(2) **Motion in the Court of Appeals.** A motion for a stay may be made to the court of appeals or one of its judges.

(A) The motion must:

(i) show that moving first before the agency would be impracticable; or

(ii) state that, a motion having been made, the agency denied the motion or failed to afford the relief requested and state any reasons given by the agency for its action.

(B) The motion must also include:

(i) the reasons for granting the relief requested and the facts relied on;

(ii) originals or copies of affidavits or other sworn statements supporting facts subject to dispute; and

FRAP 15

(iii) relevant parts of the record.

(C) The moving party must give reasonable notice of the motion to all parties.

(D) The motion must be filed with the circuit clerk and normally will be considered by a panel of the court. But in an exceptional case in which time requirements make that procedure impracticable, the motion may be made to and considered by a single judge.

(b) Bond. The court may condition relief on the filing of a bond or other appropriate security.

History of FRAP 18: Adopted Dec. 4, 1967, eff. July 1, 1968. Amended Apr. 24, 1998, eff. Dec. 1, 1998.

FRAP 19. SETTLEMENT OF A JUDGMENT ENFORCING AN AGENCY ORDER IN PART

When the court files an opinion directing entry of judgment enforcing the agency's order in part, the agency must within 14 days file with the clerk and serve on each other party a proposed judgment conforming to the opinion. A party who disagrees with the agency's proposed judgment must within 10 days file with the clerk and serve the agency with a proposed judgment that the party believes conforms to the opinion. The court will settle the judgment and direct entry without further hearing or argument.

See selected Notes of Advisory Committee to FRAP 19, p. 1277.

History of FRAP 19: Adopted Dec. 4, 1967, eff. July 1, 1968. Amended Mar. 10, 1986, eff. July 1, 1986; Apr. 24, 1998, eff. Dec. 1, 1998; Mar. 26, 2009, eff. Dec. 1, 2009.

FRAP 20. APPLICABILITY OF RULES TO THE REVIEW OR ENFORCEMENT OF AN AGENCY ORDER

All provisions of these rules, except Rules 3-14 and 22-23, apply to the review or enforcement of an agency order. In these rules, "appellant" includes a petitioner or applicant, and "appellee" includes a respondent.

History of FRAP 20: Adopted Dec. 4, 1967, eff. July 1, 1968. Amended Apr. 24, 1998, eff. Dec. 1, 1998.

TITLE V. EXTRAORDINARY WRITS

FRAP 21. WRITS OF MANDAMUS & PROHIBITION, & OTHER EXTRAORDINARY WRITS

(a) Mandamus or Prohibition to a Court: Petition, Filing, Service, and Docketing.

(1) A party petitioning for a writ of mandamus or prohibition directed to a court must file a petition with the circuit clerk with proof of service on all parties to the proceeding in the trial court. The party must also provide a copy to the trial-court judge. All parties to the proceeding in the trial court other than the petitioner are respondents for all purposes.

(2)(A) The petition must be titled "In re [name of petitioner]."

(B) The petition must state:

(i) the relief sought;

(ii) the issues presented;

(iii) the facts necessary to understand the issue presented by the petition; and

(iv) the reasons why the writ should issue.

(C) The petition must include a copy of any order or opinion or parts of the record that may be essential to understand the matters set forth in the petition.

(3) Upon receiving the prescribed docket fee, the clerk must docket the petition and submit it to the court.

(b) Denial; Order Directing Answer; Briefs; Precedence.

(1) The court may deny the petition without an answer. Otherwise, it must order the respondent, if any, to answer within a fixed time.

(2) The clerk must serve the order to respond on all persons directed to respond.

(3) Two or more respondents may answer jointly.

(4) The court of appeals may invite or order the trial-court judge to address the petition or may invite an amicus curiae to do so. The trial-court judge may request permission to address the petition but may not do so unless invited or ordered to do so by the court of appeals.

(5) If briefing or oral argument is required, the clerk must advise the parties, and when appropriate, the trial-court judge or amicus curiae.

(6) The proceeding must be given preference over ordinary civil cases.

(7) The circuit clerk must send a copy of the final disposition to the trial-court judge.

(c) Other Extraordinary Writs. An application for an extraordinary writ other than one provided for in Rule 21(a) must be made by filing a petition with the circuit clerk with proof of service on the respondents. Proceedings on the application must con-

form, so far as is practicable, to the procedures prescribed in Rule 21(a) and (b).

(d) Form of Papers; Number of Copies. All papers must conform to Rule 32(c)(2). Except by the court's permission, a paper must not exceed 30 pages, exclusive of the disclosure statement, the proof of service, and the accompanying documents required by Rule 21(a)(2)(C). An original and 3 copies must be filed unless the court requires the filing of a different number by local rule or by order in a particular case.

See selected Notes of Advisory Committee to FRAP 21, p. 1277.

History of FRAP 21: Adopted Dec. 4, 1967, eff. July 1, 1968. Amended Apr. 29, 1994, eff. Dec. 1, 1994; Apr. 23, 1996, eff. Dec. 1, 1996; Apr. 24, 1998, eff. Dec. 1, 1998; Apr. 29, 2002, eff. Dec. 1, 2002.

See also 28 U.S.C. §1651 (All Writs Act).

TITLE VI. HABEAS CORPUS; PROCEEDINGS IN FORMA PAUPERIS

FRAP 22. HABEAS CORPUS & SECTION 2255 PROCEEDINGS

(a) Application for the Original Writ. An application for a writ of habeas corpus must be made to the appropriate district court. If made to a circuit judge, the application must be transferred to the appropriate district court. If a district court denies an application made or transferred to it, renewal of the application before a circuit judge is not permitted. The applicant may, under 28 U.S.C. §2253, appeal to the court of appeals from the district court's order denying the application.

(b) Certificate of Appealability.

(1) In a habeas corpus proceeding in which the detention complained of arises from process issued by a state court, or in a 28 U.S.C. §2255 proceeding, the applicant cannot take an appeal unless a circuit justice or a circuit or district judge issues a certificate of appealability under 28 U.S.C. §2253(c). If an applicant files a notice of appeal, the district clerk must send to the court of appeals the certificate (if any) and the statement described in Rule 11(a) of the Rules Governing Proceedings Under 28 U.S.C. §2254 or §2255 (if any), along with the notice of appeal and the file of the district-court proceedings. If the district judge has denied the certificate, the applicant may request a circuit judge to issue it.

(2) A request addressed to the court of appeals may be considered by a circuit judge or judges, as the court prescribes. If no express request for a certificate is filed, the notice of appeal constitutes a request addressed to the judges of the court of appeals.

(3) A certificate of appealability is not required when a state or its representative or the United States or its representative appeals.

See selected Notes of Advisory Committee to FRAP 22, p. 1277.

History of FRAP 22: Adopted Dec. 4, 1967, eff. July 1, 1968. Amended Apr. 24, 1996, P.L. 104-132, §103, 110 Stat. 1218; Apr. 24, 1998, eff. Dec. 1, 1998; Mar. 26, 2009, eff. Dec. 1, 2009.

See also U.S. Const. art. 1, §9, cl. 2 (suspension of habeas corpus); 28 U.S.C. §§2241-2255 (habeas corpus generally).

FRAP 23. CUSTODY OR RELEASE OF A PRISONER IN A HABEAS CORPUS PROCEEDING

(a) Transfer of Custody Pending Review. Pending review of a decision in a habeas corpus proceeding commenced before a court, justice, or judge of the United States for the release of a prisoner, the person having custody of the prisoner must not transfer custody to another unless a transfer is directed in accordance with this rule. When, upon application, a custodian shows the need for a transfer, the court, justice, or judge rendering the decision under review may authorize the transfer and substitute the successor custodian as a party.

(b) Detention or Release Pending Review of Decision Not to Release. While a decision not to release a prisoner is under review, the court or judge rendering the decision, or the court of appeals, or the Supreme Court, or a judge or justice of either court, may order that the prisoner be:

(1) detained in the custody from which release is sought;

(2) detained in other appropriate custody; or

(3) released on personal recognizance, with or without surety.

(c) Release Pending Review of Decision Ordering Release. While a decision ordering the release of a prisoner is under review, the prisoner must—unless the court or judge rendering the decision, or the court of appeals, or the Supreme Court, or a judge or justice of either court orders otherwise—be released on personal recognizance, with or without surety.

(d) Modification of the Initial Order on Custody. An initial order governing the prisoner's custody or release, including any recognizance or surety, continues in effect pending review unless for special

reasons shown to the court of appeals or the Supreme Court, or to a judge or justice of either court, the order is modified or an independent order regarding custody, release, or surety is issued.

History of FRAP 23: Adopted Dec. 4, 1967, eff. July 1, 1968. Amended Mar. 10, 1986, eff. July 1, 1986; Apr. 24, 1998, eff. Dec. 1, 1998.

See also U.S. Const. art. 1, §9, cl. 2 (suspension of habeas corpus); 28 U.S.C. §§2241-2255 (habeas corpus generally).

FRAP 24. PROCEEDING IN FORMA PAUPERIS

***Editor's note:** The Committee on Rules of Practice and Procedure of the Judicial Conference of the United States has proposed amendments to FRAP 24, to be effective December 1, 2013. For the proposed amendments, see www.uscourts.gov/RulesAndPolicies/rules/pending-rules.aspx.*

(a) Leave to Proceed in Forma Pauperis.

(1) Motion in the District Court. Except as stated in Rule 24(a)(3), a party to a district-court action who desires to appeal in forma pauperis must file a motion in the district court. The party must attach an affidavit that:

(A) shows in the detail prescribed by Form 4 of the Appendix of Forms the party's inability to pay or to give security for fees and costs;

(B) claims an entitlement to redress; and

(C) states the issues that the party intends to present on appeal.

(2) Action on the Motion. If the district court grants the motion, the party may proceed on appeal without prepaying or giving security for fees and costs, unless a statute provides otherwise. If the district court denies the motion, it must state its reasons in writing.

(3) Prior Approval. A party who was permitted to proceed in forma pauperis in the district-court action, or who was determined to be financially unable to obtain an adequate defense in a criminal case, may proceed on appeal in forma pauperis without further authorization, unless:

(A) the district court—before or after the notice of appeal is filed—certifies that the appeal is not taken in good faith or finds that the party is not otherwise entitled to proceed in forma pauperis and states in writing its reasons for the certification or finding; or

(B) a statute provides otherwise.

(4) Notice of District Court's Denial. The district clerk must immediately notify the parties and the court of appeals when the district court does any of the following:

(A) denies a motion to proceed on appeal in forma pauperis;

(B) certifies that the appeal is not taken in good faith; or

(C) finds that the party is not otherwise entitled to proceed in forma pauperis.

(5) Motion in the Court of Appeals. A party may file a motion to proceed on appeal in forma pauperis in the court of appeals within 30 days after service of the notice prescribed in Rule 24(a)(4). The motion must include a copy of the affidavit filed in the district court and the district court's statement of reasons for its action. If no affidavit was filed in the district court, the party must include the affidavit prescribed by Rule 24(a)(1).

(b) Leave to Proceed in Forma Pauperis on Appeal or Review of an Administrative-Agency Proceeding. When an appeal or review of a proceeding before an administrative agency, board, commission, or officer (including for the purpose of this rule the United States Tax Court) proceeds directly in a court of appeals, a party may file in the court of appeals a motion for leave to proceed on appeal in forma pauperis with an affidavit prescribed by Rule 24(a)(1).

(c) Leave to Use Original Record. A party allowed to proceed on appeal in forma pauperis may request that the appeal be heard on the original record without reproducing any part.

See selected Notes of Advisory Committee to FRAP 24, p. 1277.

History of FRAP 24: Adopted Dec. 4, 1967, eff. July 1, 1968. Amended Apr. 30, 1979, eff. Aug. 1, 1979; Mar. 10, 1986, eff. July 1, 1986; Apr. 24, 1998, eff. Dec. 1, 1998; Apr. 29, 2002, eff. Dec. 1, 2002.

See also 18 U.S.C. §3191 (witnesses for indigent fugitives), §3495 (affidavit of inability to pay fees and expenses of consuls, counsel, interpreters, and witnesses); 28 U.S.C. §753(f) (fees for transcripts in criminal or habeas corpus proceedings to persons allowed to sue, defend, or appeal in forma pauperis; payment by U.S.), §2250 (indigent petitioner entitled to documents without cost in habeas corpus proceeding).

TITLE VII. GENERAL PROVISIONS

FRAP 25. FILING & SERVICE

(a) Filing.

(1) Filing with the Clerk. A paper required or permitted to be filed in a court of appeals must be filed with the clerk.

(2) Filing: Method and Timeliness.

(A) In general. Filing may be accomplished by mail addressed to the clerk, but filing is not timely unless the clerk receives the papers within the time fixed for filing.

(B) A brief or appendix. A brief or appendix is timely filed, however, if on or before the last day for filing, it is:

(i) mailed to the clerk by First-Class Mail, or other class of mail that is at least as expeditious, postage prepaid; or

(ii) dispatched to a third-party commercial carrier for delivery to the clerk within 3 days.

(C) Inmate filing. A paper filed by an inmate confined in an institution is timely if deposited in the institution's internal mailing system on or before the last day for filing. If an institution has a system designed for legal mail, the inmate must use that system to receive the benefit of this rule. Timely filing may be shown by a declaration in compliance with 28 U.S.C. §1746 or by a notarized statement, either of which must set forth the date of deposit and state that first-class postage has been prepaid.

(D) Electronic filing. A court of appeals may by local rule permit or require papers to be filed, signed, or verified by electronic means that are consistent with technical standards, if any, that the Judicial Conference of the United States establishes. A local rule may require filing by electronic means only if reasonable exceptions are allowed. A paper filed by electronic means in compliance with a local rule constitutes a written paper for the purpose of applying these rules.

(3) Filing a Motion with a Judge. If a motion requests relief that may be granted by a single judge, the judge may permit the motion to be filed with the judge; the judge must note the filing date on the motion and give it to the clerk.

(4) Clerk's Refusal of Documents. The clerk must not refuse to accept for filing any paper presented for that purpose solely because it is not presented in proper form as required by these rules or by any local rule or practice.

(5) Privacy Protection. An appeal in a case whose privacy protection was governed by Federal Rule of Bankruptcy Procedure 9037, Federal Rule of Civil Procedure 5.2, or Federal Rule of Criminal Procedure 49.1 is governed by the same rule on appeal. In all other proceedings, privacy protection is governed by Federal Rule of Civil Procedure 5.2, except that Federal Rule of Criminal Procedure 49.1 governs when an extraordinary writ is sought in a criminal case.

(b) Service of All Papers Required. Unless a rule requires service by the clerk, a party must, at or before the time of filing a paper, serve a copy on the other parties to the appeal or review. Service on a party represented by counsel must be made on the party's counsel.

(c) Manner of Service.

(1) Service may be any of the following:

(A) personal, including delivery to a responsible person at the office of counsel;

(B) by mail;

(C) by third-party commercial carrier for delivery within 3 days; or

(D) by electronic means, if the party being served consents in writing.

(2) If authorized by local rule, a party may use the court's transmission equipment to make electronic service under Rule 25(c)(1)(D).

(3) When reasonable considering such factors as the immediacy of the relief sought, distance, and cost, service on a party must be by a manner at least as expeditious as the manner used to file the paper with the court.

(4) Service by mail or by commercial carrier is complete on mailing or delivery to the carrier. Service by electronic means is complete on transmission, unless the party making service is notified that the paper was not received by the party served.

(d) Proof of Service.

(1) A paper presented for filing must contain either of the following:

(A) an acknowledgment of service by the person served; or

(B) proof of service consisting of a statement by the person who made service certifying:

(i) the date and manner of service;

(ii) the names of the persons served; and

(iii) their mail or electronic addresses, facsimile numbers, or the addresses of the places of delivery, as appropriate for the manner of service.

(2) When a brief or appendix is filed by mailing or dispatch in accordance with Rule 25(a)(2)(B), the proof of service must also state the date and manner by which the document was mailed or dispatched to the clerk.

(3) Proof of service may appear on or be affixed to the papers filed.

(e) **Number of Copies.** When these rules require the filing or furnishing of a number of copies, a court may require a different number by local rule or by order in a particular case.

See selected Notes of Advisory Committee to FRAP 25, p. 1278.

History of FRAP 25: Adopted Dec. 4, 1967, eff. July 1, 1968. Amended Mar. 10, 1986, eff. July 1, 1986; Apr. 30, 1991, eff. Dec. 1, 1991; Apr. 22, 1993, eff. Dec. 1, 1993; Apr. 29, 1994, eff. Dec. 1, 1994; Apr. 23, 1996, eff. Dec. 1, 1996; Apr. 24, 1998, eff. Dec. 1, 1998; Apr. 29, 2002, eff. Dec. 1, 2002; Apr. 12, 2006, eff. Dec. 1, 2006; Apr. 30, 2007, eff. Dec. 1, 2007; Mar. 26, 2009, eff. Dec. 1, 2009.

FRAP 26. COMPUTING & EXTENDING TIME

(a) **Computing Time.** The following rules apply in computing any time period specified in these rules, in any local rule or court order, or in any statute that does not specify a method of computing time.

(1) **Period Stated in Days or a Longer Unit.** When the period is stated in days or a longer unit of time:

(A) exclude the day of the event that triggers the period;

(B) count every day, including intermediate Saturdays, Sundays, and legal holidays; and

(C) include the last day of the period, but if the last day is a Saturday, Sunday, or legal holiday, the period continues to run until the end of the next day that is not a Saturday, Sunday, or legal holiday.

(2) **Period Stated in Hours.** When the period is stated in hours:

(A) begin counting immediately on the occurrence of the event that triggers the period;

(B) count every hour, including hours during intermediate Saturdays, Sundays, and legal holidays; and

(C) if the period would end on a Saturday, Sunday, or legal holiday, the period continues to run until the same time on the next day that is not a Saturday, Sunday, or legal holiday.

(3) **Inaccessibility of the Clerk's Office.** Unless the court orders otherwise, if the clerk's office is inaccessible:

(A) on the last day for filing under Rule 26(a)(1), then the time for filing is extended to the first accessible day that is not a Saturday, Sunday, or legal holiday; or

(B) during the last hour for filing under Rule 26(a)(2), then the time for filing is extended to the same time on the first accessible day that is not a Saturday, Sunday, or legal holiday.

(4) **"Last Day" Defined.** Unless a different time is set by a statute, local rule, or court order, the last day ends:

(A) for electronic filing in the district court, at midnight in the court's time zone;

(B) for electronic filing in the court of appeals, at midnight in the time zone of the circuit clerk's principal office;

(C) for filing under Rules 4(c)(1), 25(a)(2)(B), and 25(a)(2)(C)—and filing by mail under Rule 13(b)—at the latest time for the method chosen for delivery to the post office, third-party commercial carrier, or prison mailing system; and

(D) for filing by other means, when the clerk's office is scheduled to close.

(5) **"Next Day" Defined.** The "next day" is determined by continuing to count forward when the period is measured after an event and backward when measured before an event.

(6) **"Legal Holiday" Defined.** "Legal holiday" means:

(A) the day set aside by statute for observing New Year's Day, Martin Luther King Jr.'s Birthday, Washington's Birthday, Memorial Day, Independence Day, Labor Day, Columbus Day, Veterans' Day, Thanksgiving Day, or Christmas Day;

(B) any day declared a holiday by the President or Congress; and

(C) for periods that are measured after an event, any other day declared a holiday by

the state where either of the following is located: the district court that rendered the challenged judgment or order, or the circuit clerk's principal office.

(b) Extending Time. For good cause, the court may extend the time prescribed by these rules or by its order to perform any act, or may permit an act to be done after that time expires. But the court may not extend the time to file:

(1) a notice of appeal (except as authorized in Rule 4) or a petition for permission to appeal; or

(2) a notice of appeal from or a petition to enjoin, set aside, suspend, modify, enforce, or otherwise review an order of an administrative agency, board, commission, or officer of the United States, unless specifically authorized by law.

(c) Additional Time after Service. When a party may or must act within a specified time after service, 3 days are added after the period would otherwise expire under Rule 26(a), unless the paper is delivered on the date of service stated in the proof of service. For purposes of this Rule 26(c), a paper that is served electronically is not treated as delivered on the date of service stated in the proof of service.

See selected Notes of Advisory Committee to FRAP 26, p. 1279.

History of FRAP 26: Adopted Dec. 4, 1967, eff. July 1, 1968. Amended Mar. 1, 1971, eff. July 1, 1971; Mar. 10, 1986, eff. July 1, 1986; Apr. 25, 1989, eff. Dec. 1, 1989; Apr. 30, 1991, eff. Dec. 1, 1991; Apr. 23, 1996, eff. Dec. 1, 1996; Apr. 24, 1998, eff. Dec. 1, 1998; Apr. 29, 2002, eff. Dec. 1, 2002; Apr. 25, 2005, eff. Dec. 1, 2005; Mar. 26, 2009, eff. Dec. 1, 2009.

See also 28 U.S.C. §2107 (time to appeal to court of appeals).

FRAP 26.1. CORPORATE DISCLOSURE STATEMENT

(a) Who Must File. Any nongovernmental corporate party to a proceeding in a court of appeals must file a statement that identifies any parent corporation and any publicly held corporation that owns 10% or more of its stock or states that there is no such corporation.

(b) Time for Filing; Supplemental Filing. A party must file the Rule 26.1(a) statement with the principal brief or upon filing a motion, response, petition, or answer in the court of appeals, whichever occurs first, unless a local rule requires earlier filing. Even if the statement has already been filed, the party's principal brief must include the statement before the table of contents. A party must supplement its statement whenever the information that must be disclosed under Rule 26.1(a) changes.

(c) Number of Copies. If the Rule 26.1(a) statement is filed before the principal brief, or if a supplemental statement is filed, the party must file an original and 3 copies unless the court requires a different number by local rule or by order in a particular case.

See selected Notes of Advisory Committee to FRAP 26.1, p. 1282.

History of FRAP 26.1: Adopted Apr. 25, 1989, eff. Dec. 1, 1989. Amended Apr. 30, 1991, eff. Dec. 1, 1991; Apr. 29, 1994, eff. Dec. 1, 1994; Apr. 24, 1998, eff. Dec. 1, 1998; Apr. 29, 2002, eff. Dec. 1, 2002.

FRAP 27. MOTIONS

(a) In General.

(1) Application for Relief. An application for an order or other relief is made by motion unless these rules prescribe another form. A motion must be in writing unless the court permits otherwise.

(2) Contents of a Motion.

(A) Grounds and relief sought. A motion must state with particularity the grounds for the motion, the relief sought, and the legal argument necessary to support it.

(B) Accompanying documents.

(i) Any affidavit or other paper necessary to support a motion must be served and filed with the motion.

(ii) An affidavit must contain only factual information, not legal argument.

(iii) A motion seeking substantive relief must include a copy of the trial court's opinion or agency's decision as a separate exhibit.

(C) Documents barred or not required.

(i) A separate brief supporting or responding to a motion must not be filed.

(ii) A notice of motion is not required.

(iii) A proposed order is not required.

(3) Response.

(A) Time to file. Any party may file a response to a motion; Rule 27(a)(2) governs its contents. The response must be filed within 10 days after service of the motion unless the court shortens or extends the time. A motion authorized by Rules 8, 9, 18, or 41 may

be granted before the 10-day period runs only if the court gives reasonable notice to the parties that it intends to act sooner.

(B) Request for affirmative relief. A response may include a motion for affirmative relief. The time to respond to the new motion, and to reply to that response, are governed by Rule 27(a)(3)(A) and (a)(4). The title of the response must alert the court to the request for relief.

(4) Reply to Response. Any reply to a response must be filed within 7 days after service of the response. A reply must not present matters that do not relate to the response.

(b) Disposition of a Motion for a Procedural Order. The court may act on a motion for a procedural order—including a motion under Rule 26(b)—at any time without awaiting a response, and may, by rule or by order in a particular case, authorize its clerk to act on specified types of procedural motions. A party adversely affected by the court's, or the clerk's, action may file a motion to reconsider, vacate, or modify that action. Timely opposition filed after the motion is granted in whole or in part does not constitute a request to reconsider, vacate, or modify the disposition; a motion requesting that relief must be filed.

(c) Power of a Single Judge to Entertain a Motion. A circuit judge may act alone on any motion, but may not dismiss or otherwise determine an appeal or other proceeding. A court of appeals may provide by rule or by order in a particular case that only the court may act on any motion or class of motions. The court may review the action of a single judge.

(d) Form of Papers; Page Limits; and Number of Copies.

(1) Format.

(A) Reproduction. A motion, response, or reply may be reproduced by any process that yields a clear black image on light paper. The paper must be opaque and unglazed. Only one side of the paper may be used.

(B) Cover. A cover is not required, but there must be a caption that includes the case number, the name of the court, the title of the case, and a brief descriptive title indicating the purpose of the motion and identifying the party or parties for whom it is filed. If a cover is used, it must be white.

(C) Binding. The document must be bound in any manner that is secure, does not obscure the text, and permits the document to lie reasonably flat when open.

(D) Paper size, line spacing, and margins. The document must be on 8½ by 11 inch paper. The text must be double-spaced, but quotations more than two lines long may be indented and single-spaced. Headings and footnotes may be single-spaced. Margins must be at least one inch on all four sides. Page numbers may be placed in the margins, but no text may appear there.

(E) Typeface and type styles. The document must comply with the typeface requirements of Rule 32(a)(5) and the type-style requirements of Rule 32(a)(6).

(2) Page Limits. A motion or a response to a motion must not exceed 20 pages, exclusive of the corporate disclosure statement and accompanying documents authorized by Rule 27(a)(2)(B), unless the court permits or directs otherwise. A reply to a response must not exceed 10 pages.

(3) Number of Copies. An original and 3 copies must be filed unless the court requires a different number by local rule or by order in a particular case.

(e) Oral Argument. A motion will be decided without oral argument unless the court orders otherwise.

See selected Notes of Advisory Committee to FRAP 27, p. 1282.

History of FRAP 27: Adopted Dec. 4, 1967, eff. July 1, 1968. Amended Apr. 30, 1979, eff. Aug. 1, 1979; Apr. 25, 1989, eff. Dec. 1, 1989; Apr. 29, 1994, eff. Dec. 1, 1994; Apr. 24, 1998, eff. Dec. 1, 1998; Apr. 29, 2002, eff. Dec. 1, 2002; Apr. 25, 2005, eff. Dec. 1, 2005; Mar. 26, 2009, eff. Dec. 1, 2009.

FRAP 28. BRIEFS

***Editor's note:** The Committee on Rules of Practice and Procedure of the Judicial Conference of the United States has proposed amendments to FRAP 28, to be effective December 1, 2013. For the proposed amendments, see www.uscourts.gov/RulesAndPolicies/rules/pending-rules.aspx.*

(a) Appellant's Brief. The appellant's brief must contain, under appropriate headings and in the order indicated:

(1) a corporate disclosure statement if required by Rule 26.1;

(2) a table of contents, with page references;

(3) a table of authorities—cases (alphabetically arranged), statutes, and other authorities—with references to the pages of the brief where they are cited;

(4) a jurisdictional statement, including:

(A) the basis for the district court's or agency's subject-matter jurisdiction, with citations to applicable statutory provisions and stating relevant facts establishing jurisdiction;

(B) the basis for the court of appeals' jurisdiction, with citations to applicable statutory provisions and stating relevant facts establishing jurisdiction;

(C) the filing dates establishing the timeliness of the appeal or petition for review; and

(D) an assertion that the appeal is from a final order or judgment that disposes of all parties' claims, or information establishing the court of appeals' jurisdiction on some other basis;

(5) a statement of the issues presented for review;

(6) a statement of the case briefly indicating the nature of the case, the course of proceedings, and the disposition below;

(7) a statement of facts relevant to the issues submitted for review with appropriate references to the record (see Rule 28(e));

(8) a summary of the argument, which must contain a succinct, clear, and accurate statement of the arguments made in the body of the brief, and which must not merely repeat the argument headings;

(9) the argument, which must contain:

(A) appellant's contentions and the reasons for them, with citations to the authorities and parts of the record on which the appellant relies; and

(B) for each issue, a concise statement of the applicable standard of review (which may appear in the discussion of the issue or under a separate heading placed before the discussion of the issues);

(10) a short conclusion stating the precise relief sought; and

(11) the certificate of compliance, if required by Rule 32(a)(7).

(b) **Appellee's Brief.** The appellee's brief must conform to the requirements of Rule 28(a)(1)-(9) and (11), except that none of the following need appear unless the appellee is dissatisfied with the appellant's statement:

(1) the jurisdictional statement;

(2) the statement of the issues;

(3) the statement of the case;

(4) the statement of the facts; and

(5) the statement of the standard of review.

(c) **Reply Brief.** The appellant may file a brief in reply to the appellee's brief. Unless the court permits, no further briefs may be filed. A reply brief must contain a table of contents, with page references, and a table of authorities—cases (alphabetically arranged), statutes, and other authorities—with references to the pages of the reply brief where they are cited.

(d) **References to Parties.** In briefs and at oral argument, counsel should minimize use of the terms "appellant" and "appellee." To make briefs clear, counsel should use the parties' actual names or the designations used in the lower court or agency proceeding, or such descriptive terms as "the employee," "the injured person," "the taxpayer," "the ship," "the stevedore."

(e) **References to the Record.** References to the parts of the record contained in the appendix filed with the appellant's brief must be to the pages of the appendix. If the appendix is prepared after the briefs are filed, a party referring to the record must follow one of the methods detailed in Rule 30(c). If the original record is used under Rule 30(f) and is not consecutively paginated, or if the brief refers to an unreproduced part of the record, any reference must be to the page of the original document. For example:

- Answer .... p. 7;
- Motion for Judgment .... p. 2;
- Transcript .... p. 231.

Only clear abbreviations may be used. A party referring to evidence whose admissibility is in controversy must cite the pages of the appendix or of the transcript at which the evidence was identified, offered, and received or rejected.

FRAP 28

(f) Reproduction of Statutes, Rules, Regulations, etc. If the court's determination of the issues presented requires the study of statutes, rules, regulations, etc., the relevant parts must be set out in the brief or in an addendum at the end, or may be supplied to the court in pamphlet form.

(g) [Reserved]

(h) [Reserved]

(i) Briefs in a Case Involving Multiple Appellants or Appellees. In a case involving more than one appellant or appellee, including consolidated cases, any number of appellants or appellees may join in a brief, and any party may adopt by reference a part of another's brief. Parties may also join in reply briefs.

(j) Citation of Supplemental Authorities. If pertinent and significant authorities come to a party's attention after the party's brief has been filed—or after oral argument but before decision—a party may promptly advise the circuit clerk by letter, with a copy to all other parties, setting forth the citations. The letter must state the reasons for the supplemental citations, referring either to the page of the brief or to a point argued orally. The body of the letter must not exceed 350 words. Any response must be made promptly and must be similarly limited.

See selected Notes of Advisory Committee to FRAP 28, p. 1283.

History of FRAP 28: Adopted Dec. 4, 1967, eff. July 1, 1968. Amended Apr. 30, 1979, eff. Aug. 1, 1979; Mar. 10, 1986, eff. July 1, 1986; Apr. 25, 1989, eff. Dec. 1, 1989; Apr. 30, 1991, eff. Dec. 1, 1991; Apr. 22, 1993, eff. Dec. 1, 1993; Apr. 29, 1994, eff. Dec. 1, 1994; Apr. 24, 1998, eff. Dec. 1, 1998; Apr. 29, 2002, eff. Dec. 1, 2002; Apr. 25, 2005, eff. Dec. 1. 2005.

See also 28 U.S.C. §2111 (harmless error).

FRAP 28.1. CROSS-APPEALS

Editor's note: *The Committee on Rules of Practice and Procedure of the Judicial Conference of the United States has proposed amendments to FRAP 28.1, to be effective December 1, 2013. For the proposed amendments, see www.uscourts.gov/RulesAndPolicies/rules/pending-rules.aspx.*

(a) Applicability. This rule applies to a case in which a cross-appeal is filed. Rules 28(a)-(c), 31(a)(1), 32(a)(2), and 32(a)(7)(A)-(B) do not apply to such a case, except as otherwise provided in this rule.

(b) Designation of Appellant. The party who files a notice of appeal first is the appellant for the purposes of this rule and Rules 30 and 34. If notices are filed on the same day, the plaintiff in the proceeding below is the appellant. These designations may be modified by the parties' agreement or by court order.

(c) Briefs. In a case involving a cross-appeal:

(1) Appellant's Principal Brief. The appellant must file a principal brief in the appeal. That brief must comply with Rule 28(a).

(2) Appellee's Principal and Response Brief. The appellee must file a principal brief in the cross-appeal and must, in the same brief, respond to the principal brief in the appeal. That appellee's brief must comply with Rule 28(a), except that the brief need not include a statement of the case or a statement of the facts unless the appellee is dissatisfied with the appellant's statement.

(3) Appellant's Response and Reply Brief. The appellant must file a brief that responds to the principal brief in the cross-appeal and may, in the same brief, reply to the response in the appeal. That brief must comply with Rule 28(a)(2)-(9) and (11), except that none of the following need appear unless the appellant is dissatisfied with the appellee's statement in the cross-appeal:

(A) the jurisdictional statement;

(B) the statement of the issues;

(C) the statement of the case;

(D) the statement of the facts; and

(E) the statement of the standard of review.

(4) Appellee's Reply Brief. The appellee may file a brief in reply to the response in the cross-appeal. That brief must comply with Rule 28(a)(2)-(3) and (11) and must be limited to the issues presented by the cross-appeal.

(5) No Further Briefs. Unless the court permits, no further briefs may be filed in a case involving a cross appeal.

(d) Cover. Except for filings by unrepresented parties, the cover of the appellant's principal brief must be blue; the appellee's principal and response brief, red; the appellant's response and reply brief, yellow; the appellee's reply brief, gray; and[1] intervenor's or amicus curiae's brief, green; and any supplemental brief, tan. The front cover of a brief

must contain the information required by Rule 32(a)(2).

(e) Length.

(1) Page Limitation. Unless it complies with Rule 28.1(e)(2) and (3), the appellant's principal brief must not exceed 30 pages; the appellee's principal and response brief, 35 pages; the appellant's response and reply brief, 30 pages; and the appellee's reply brief, 15 pages.

(2) Type-Volume Limitation.

(A) The appellant's principal brief or the appellant's response and reply brief is acceptable if:

(i) it contains no more than 14,000 words; or

(ii) it uses a monospaced face and contains no more than 1,300 lines of text.

(B) The appellee's principal and response brief is acceptable if:

(i) it contains no more than 16,500 words; or

(ii) it uses a monospaced face and contains no more than 1,500 lines of text.

(C) The appellee's reply brief is acceptable if it contains no more than half of the type volume specified in Rule 28.1(e)(2)(A).

(3) Certificate of Compliance. A brief submitted under Rule 28.1(e)(2) must comply with Rule 32(a)(7)(C).

(f) Time to Serve and File a Brief. Briefs must be served and filed as follows:

(1) the appellant's principal brief, within 40 days after the record is filed;

(2) the appellee's principal and response brief, within 30 days after the appellant's principal brief is served;

(3) the appellant's response and reply brief, within 30 days after the appellee's principal and response brief is served; and

(4) the appellee's reply brief, within 14 days after the appellant's response and reply brief is served, but at least 7 days before argument unless the court, for good cause, allows a later filing.

1. **Editor's note:** So in original. Probably should be "an."

See selected Notes of Advisory Committee to FRAP 28.1, p. 1284.

History of FRAP 28.1: Adopted Apr. 25, 2005, eff. Dec. 1. 2005; Mar. 26, 2009, eff. Dec. 1, 2009.

FRAP 29. BRIEF OF AN AMICUS CURIAE

(a) When Permitted. The United States or its officer or agency or a state may file an amicus-curiae brief without the consent of the parties or leave of court. Any other amicus curiae may file a brief only by leave of court or if the brief states that all parties have consented to its filing.

(b) Motion for Leave to File. The motion must be accompanied by the proposed brief and state:

(1) the movant's interest; and

(2) the reason why an amicus brief is desirable and why the matters asserted are relevant to the disposition of the case.

(c) Contents and Form. An amicus brief must comply with Rule 32. In addition to the requirements of Rule 32, the cover must identify the party or parties supported and indicate whether the brief supports affirmance or reversal. An amicus brief need not comply with Rule 28, but must include the following:

(1) if the amicus curiae is a corporation, a disclosure statement like that required of parties by Rule 26.1;

(2) a table of contents, with page references;

(3) a table of authorities—cases (alphabetically arranged), statutes, and other authorities—with references to the pages of the brief where they are cited;

(4) a concise statement of the identity of the amicus curiae, its interest in the case, and the source of its authority to file;

(5) unless the amicus curiae is one listed in the first sentence of Rule 29(a), a statement that indicates whether:

(A) a party's counsel authored the brief in whole or in part;

(B) a party or a party's counsel contributed money that was intended to fund preparing or submitting the brief; and

(C) a person—other than the amicus curiae, its members, or its counsel—contributed money that was intended to fund preparing or submitting the brief and, if so, identifies each such person;

(6) an argument, which may be preceded by a summary and which need not include a statement of the applicable standard of review; and

FRAP 28.1

(7) a certificate of compliance, if required by Rule 32(a)(7).

(d) Length. Except by the court's permission, an amicus brief may be no more than one-half the maximum length authorized by these rules for a party's principal brief. If the court grants a party permission to file a longer brief, that extension does not affect the length of an amicus brief.

(e) Time for Filing. An amicus curiae must file its brief, accompanied by a motion for filing when necessary, no later than 7 days after the principal brief of the party being supported is filed. An amicus curiae that does not support either party must file its brief no later than 7 days after the appellant's or petitioner's principal brief is filed. A court may grant leave for later filing, specifying the time within which an opposing party may answer.

(f) Reply Brief. Except by the court's permission, an amicus curiae may not file a reply brief.

(g) Oral Argument. An amicus curiae may participate in oral argument only with the court's permission.

See selected Notes of Advisory Committee to FRAP 29, p. 1285.

History of FRAP 29: Adopted Dec. 4, 1967, eff. July 1, 1968. Amended Apr. 24, 1998, eff. Dec. 1, 1998; Apr. 28, 2010, eff. Dec. 1, 2010.

See also 28 U.S.C. §2071 (rulemaking power generally).

FRAP 30. APPENDIX TO THE BRIEFS

(a) Appellant's Responsibility.

(1) Contents of the Appendix. The appellant must prepare and file an appendix to the briefs containing:

(A) the relevant docket entries in the proceeding below;

(B) the relevant portions of the pleadings, charge, findings, or opinion;

(C) the judgment, order, or decision in question; and

(D) other parts of the record to which the parties wish to direct the court's attention.

(2) Excluded Material. Memoranda of law in the district court should not be included in the appendix unless they have independent relevance. Parts of the record may be relied on by the court or the parties even though not included in the appendix.

(3) Time to File; Number of Copies. Unless filing is deferred under Rule 30(c), the appellant must file 10 copies of the appendix with the brief and must serve one copy on counsel for each party separately represented. An unrepresented party proceeding in forma pauperis must file 4 legible copies with the clerk, and one copy must be served on counsel for each separately represented party. The court may by local rule or by order in a particular case require the filing or service of a different number.

(b) All Parties' Responsibilities.

(1) Determining the Contents of the Appendix. The parties are encouraged to agree on the contents of the appendix. In the absence of an agreement, the appellant must, within 14 days after the record is filed, serve on the appellee a designation of the parts of the record the appellant intends to include in the appendix and a statement of the issues the appellant intends to present for review. The appellee may, within 14 days after receiving the designation, serve on the appellant a designation of additional parts to which it wishes to direct the court's attention. The appellant must include the designated parts in the appendix. The parties must not engage in unnecessary designation of parts of the record, because the entire record is available to the court. This paragraph applies also to a cross-appellant and a cross-appellee.

(2) Costs of Appendix. Unless the parties agree otherwise, the appellant must pay the cost of the appendix. If the appellant considers parts of the record designated by the appellee to be unnecessary, the appellant may advise the appellee, who must then advance the cost of including those parts. The cost of the appendix is a taxable cost. But if any party causes unnecessary parts of the record to be included in the appendix, the court may impose the cost of those parts on that party. Each circuit must, by local rule, provide for sanctions against attorneys who unreasonably and vexatiously increase litigation costs by including unnecessary material in the appendix.

(c) Deferred Appendix.

(1) Deferral Until After Briefs Are Filed. The court may provide by rule for classes of cases or by order in a particular case that preparation of the appendix may be deferred until after the briefs have been filed and that the appendix

may be filed 21 days after the appellee's brief is served. Even though the filing of the appendix may be deferred, Rule 30(b) applies; except that a party must designate the parts of the record it wants included in the appendix when it serves its brief, and need not include a statement of the issues presented.

(2) References to the Record.

(A) If the deferred appendix is used, the parties may cite in their briefs the pertinent pages of the record. When the appendix is prepared, the record pages cited in the briefs must be indicated by inserting record page numbers, in brackets, at places in the appendix where those pages of the record appear.

(B) A party who wants to refer directly to pages of the appendix may serve and file copies of the brief within the time required by Rule 31(a), containing appropriate references to pertinent pages of the record. In that event, within 14 days after the appendix is filed, the party must serve and file copies of the brief, containing references to the pages of the appendix in place of or in addition to the references to the pertinent pages of the record. Except for the correction of typographical errors, no other changes may be made to the brief.

(d) Format of the Appendix. The appendix must begin with a table of contents identifying the page at which each part begins. The relevant docket entries must follow the table of contents. Other parts of the record must follow chronologically. When pages from the transcript of proceedings are placed in the appendix, the transcript page numbers must be shown in brackets immediately before the included pages. Omissions in the text of papers or of the transcript must be indicated by asterisks. Immaterial formal matters (captions, subscriptions, acknowledgments, etc.) should be omitted.

(e) Reproduction of Exhibits. Exhibits designated for inclusion in the appendix may be reproduced in a separate volume, or volumes, suitably indexed. Four copies must be filed with the appendix, and one copy must be served on counsel for each separately represented party. If a transcript of a proceeding before an administrative agency, board, commission, or officer was used in a district-court action and has been designated for inclusion in the appendix, the transcript must be placed in the appendix as an exhibit.

(f) Appeal on the Original Record Without an Appendix. The court may, either by rule for all cases or classes of cases or by order in a particular case, dispense with the appendix and permit an appeal to proceed on the original record with any copies of the record, or relevant parts, that the court may order the parties to file.

See selected Notes of Advisory Committee to FRAP 30, p. 1285.

History of FRAP 30: Adopted Dec. 4, 1967, eff. July 1, 1968. Amended Mar. 30, 1970, eff. July 1, 1970; Mar. 10, 1986, eff. July 1, 1986; Apr. 30, 1991, eff. Dec. 1, 1991; Apr. 29, 1994, eff. Dec. 1, 1994; Apr. 24, 1998, eff. Dec. 1, 1998; Mar. 26, 2009, eff. Dec. 1, 2009.

FRAP 31. SERVING & FILING BRIEFS

(a) Time to Serve and File a Brief.

(1) The appellant must serve and file a brief within 40 days after the record is filed. The appellee must serve and file a brief within 30 days after the appellant's brief is served. The appellant may serve and file a reply brief within 14 days after service of the appellee's brief but a reply brief must be filed at least 7 days before argument, unless the court, for good cause, allows a later filing.

(2) A court of appeals that routinely considers cases on the merits promptly after the briefs are filed may shorten the time to serve and file briefs, either by local rule or by order in a particular case.

(b) Number of Copies. Twenty-five copies of each brief must be filed with the clerk and 2 copies must be served on each unrepresented party and on counsel for each separately represented party. An unrepresented party proceeding in forma pauperis must file 4 legible copies with the clerk, and one copy must be served on each unrepresented party and on counsel for each separately represented party. The court may by local rule or by order in a particular case require the filing or service of a different number.

(c) Consequence of Failure to File. If an appellant fails to file a brief within the time provided by this rule, or within an extended time, an appellee may move to dismiss the appeal. An appellee who fails

FRAP 30

to file a brief will not be heard at oral argument unless the court grants permission.

See selected Notes of Advisory Committee to FRAP 31, p. 1285.

History of FRAP 31: Adopted Dec. 4, 1967, eff. July 1, 1968. Amended Mar. 30, 1970, eff. July 1, 1970; Mar. 10, 1986, eff. July 1, 1986; Apr. 29, 1994, eff. Dec. 1, 1994; Apr. 24, 1998, eff. Dec. 1, 1998; Apr. 29, 2002, eff. Dec. 1, 2002; Mar. 26, 2009, eff. Dec. 1, 2009.

FRAP 32. FORM OF BRIEFS, APPENDICES, & OTHER PAPERS

(a) Form of a Brief.

(1) Reproduction.

(A) A brief may be reproduced by any process that yields a clear black image on light paper. The paper must be opaque and unglazed. Only one side of the paper may be used.

(B) Text must be reproduced with a clarity that equals or exceeds the output of a laser printer.

(C) Photographs, illustrations, and tables may be reproduced by any method that results in a good copy of the original; a glossy finish is acceptable if the original is glossy.

(2) Cover. Except for filings by unrepresented parties, the cover of the appellant's brief must be blue; the appellee's, red; an intervenor's or amicus curiae's, green; any reply brief, gray and any supplemental brief, tan. The front cover of a brief must contain:

(A) the number of the case centered at the top;

(B) the name of the court;

(C) the title of the case (see Rule 12(a));

(D) the nature of the proceeding (e.g., Appeal, Petition for Review) and the name of the court, agency, or board below;

(E) the title of the brief, identifying the party or parties for whom the brief is filed; and

(F) the name, office address, and telephone number of counsel representing the party for whom the brief is filed.

(3) Binding. The brief must be bound in any manner that is secure, does not obscure the text, and permits the brief to lie reasonably flat when open.

(4) Paper Size, Line Spacing, and Margins. The brief must be on 8½ by 11 inch paper. The text must be double-spaced, but quotations more than two lines long may be indented and single-spaced. Headings and footnotes may be single-spaced. Margins must be at least one inch on all four sides. Page numbers may be placed in the margins, but no text may appear there.

(5) Typeface. Either a proportionally spaced or a monospaced face may be used.

(A) A proportionally spaced face must include serifs, but sans-serif type may be used in headings and captions. A proportionally spaced face must be 14-point or larger.

(B) A monospaced face may not contain more than 10½ characters per inch.

(6) Type Styles. A brief must be set in a plain, roman style, although italics or boldface may be used for emphasis. Case names must be italicized or underlined.

(7) Length.

(A) Page limitation. A principal brief may not exceed 30 pages, or a reply brief 15 pages, unless it complies with Rule 32(a)(7)(B) and (C).

(B) Type-volume limitation.

(i) A principal brief is acceptable if:

- it contains no more than 14,000 words; or
- it uses a monospaced face and contains no more than 1,300 lines of text

(ii) A reply brief is acceptable if it contains no more than half of the type volume specified in Rule 32(a)(7)(B)(i).

(iii) Headings, footnotes, and quotations count toward the word and line limitations. The corporate disclosure statement, table of contents, table of citations, statement with respect to oral argument, any addendum containing statutes, rules or regulations, and any certificates of counsel do not count toward the limitation.

(C) Certificate of compliance.

(i) A brief submitted under Rules 28.1(e)(2) or 32(a)(7)(B) must include a certificate by the attorney, or an unrepresented party, that the brief complies with the type-volume limitation. The person preparing the certificate

FRAP 32

may rely on the word or line count of the word-processing system used to prepare the brief. The certificate must state either:

- the number of words in the brief; or
- the number of lines of monospaced type in the brief.

(ii) Form 6 in the Appendix of Forms is a suggested form of a certificate of compliance. Use of Form 6 must be regarded as sufficient to meet the requirements of Rules 28.1(e)(3) and 32(a)(7)(C)(i).

(b) Form of an Appendix. An appendix must comply with Rule 32(a)(1), (2), (3), and (4), with the following exceptions:

(1) The cover of a separately bound appendix must be white.

(2) An appendix may include a legible photocopy of any document found in the record or of a printed judicial or agency decision.

(3) When necessary to facilitate inclusion of odd-sized documents such as technical drawings, an appendix may be a size other than 8½ by 11 inches, and need not lie reasonably flat when opened.

(c) Form of Other Papers.

(1) Motion. The form of a motion is governed by Rule 27(d).

(2) Other Papers. Any other paper, including a petition for panel rehearing and a petition for hearing or rehearing en banc, and any response to such a petition, must be reproduced in the manner prescribed by Rule 32(a), with the following exceptions:

(A) A cover is not necessary if the caption and signature page of the paper together contain the information required by Rule 32(a)(2). If a cover is used, it must be white.

(B) Rule 32(a)(7) does not apply.

(d) Signature. Every brief, motion, or other paper filed with the court must be signed by the party filing the paper or, if the party is represented, by one of the party's attorneys.

(e) Local Variation. Every court of appeals must accept documents that comply with the form requirements of this rule. By local rule or order in a particular case a court of appeals may accept documents that do not meet all of the form requirements of this rule.

See selected Notes of Advisory Committee to FRAP 32, p. 1286.

History of FRAP 32: Adopted Dec. 4, 1967, eff. July 1, 1968. Amended Apr. 24, 1998, eff. Dec. 1, 1998; Apr. 29, 2002, eff. Dec. 1, 2002; Apr. 25, 2005, eff. Dec. 1, 2005.

FRAP 32.1. CITING JUDICIAL DISPOSITIONS

(a) Citation Permitted. A court may not prohibit or restrict the citation of federal judicial opinions, orders, judgments, or other written dispositions that have been:

(i) designated as "unpublished," "not for publication," "non-precedential," "not precedent," or the like; and

(ii) issued on or after January 1, 2007.

(b) Copies Required. If a party cites a federal judicial opinion, order, judgment, or other written disposition that is not available in a publicly accessible electronic database, the party must file and serve a copy of that opinion, order, judgment, or disposition with the brief or other paper in which it is cited.

See selected Notes of Advisory Committee to FRAP 32.1, p. 1286.

History of FRAP 32.1: Adopted Apr. 12, 2006, eff. Dec. 1, 2006.

FRAP 33. APPEAL CONFERENCES

The court may direct the attorneys—and, when appropriate, the parties—to participate in one or more conferences to address any matter that may aid in disposing of the proceedings, including simplifying the issues and discussing settlement. A judge or other person designated by the court may preside over the conference, which may be conducted in person or by telephone. Before a settlement conference, the attorneys must consult with their clients and obtain as much authority as feasible to settle the case. The court may, as a result of the conference, enter an order controlling the course of the proceedings or implementing any settlement agreement.

History of FRAP 33: Adopted Dec. 4, 1967, eff. July 1, 1968. Amended Apr. 29, 1994, eff. Dec. 1, 1994; Apr. 24, 1998, eff. Dec. 1, 1998.

FRAP 34. ORAL ARGUMENT

(a) In General.

(1) Party's Statement. Any party may file, or a court may require by local rule, a statement explaining why oral argument should, or need not, be permitted.

(2) **Standards.** Oral argument must be allowed in every case unless a panel of three judges who have examined the briefs and record unanimously agrees that oral argument is unnecessary for any of the following reasons:

(A) the appeal is frivolous;

(B) the dispositive issue or issues have been authoritatively decided; or

(C) the facts and legal arguments are adequately presented in the briefs and record, and the decisional process would not be significantly aided by oral argument.

(b) **Notice of Argument; Postponement.** The clerk must advise all parties whether oral argument will be scheduled, and, if so, the date, time, and place for it, and the time allowed for each side. A motion to postpone the argument or to allow longer argument must be filed reasonably in advance of the hearing date.

(c) **Order and Contents of Argument.** The appellant opens and concludes the argument. Counsel must not read at length from briefs, records, or authorities.

(d) **Cross-Appeals and Separate Appeals.** If there is a cross-appeal, Rule 28.1(b) determines which party is the appellant and which is the appellee for purposes of oral argument. Unless the court directs otherwise, a cross-appeal or separate appeal must be argued when the initial appeal is argued. Separate parties should avoid duplicative argument.

(e) **Nonappearance of a Party.** If the appellee fails to appear for argument, the court must hear appellant's argument. If the appellant fails to appear for argument, the court may hear the appellee's argument. If neither party appears, the case will be decided on the briefs, unless the court orders otherwise.

(f) **Submission on Briefs.** The parties may agree to submit a case for decision on the briefs, but the court may direct that the case be argued.

(g) **Use of Physical Exhibits at Argument; Removal.** Counsel intending to use physical exhibits other than documents at the argument must arrange to place them in the courtroom on the day of the argument before the court convenes. After the argument, counsel must remove the exhibits from the courtroom, unless the court directs otherwise. The clerk may destroy or dispose of the exhibits if counsel does not reclaim them within a reasonable time after the clerk gives notice to remove them.

See selected Notes of Advisory Committee to FRAP 34, p. 1287.

History of FRAP 34: Adopted Dec. 4, 1967, eff. July 1, 1968. Amended Apr. 30, 1979, eff. Aug. 1, 1979; Mar. 10, 1986, eff. July 1, 1986; Apr. 30, 1991, eff. Dec. 1, 1991; Apr. 22, 1993, eff. Dec. 1, 1993; Apr. 24, 1998, eff. Dec. 1, 1998; Apr. 25, 2005, eff. Dec. 1, 2005.

FRAP 35. EN BANC DETERMINATION

(a) **When Hearing or Rehearing En Banc May Be Ordered.** A majority of the circuit judges who are in regular active service and who are not disqualified may order that an appeal or other proceeding be heard or reheard by the court of appeals en banc. An en banc hearing or rehearing is not favored and ordinarily will not be ordered unless:

(1) en banc consideration is necessary to secure or maintain uniformity of the court's decisions; or

(2) the proceeding involves a question of exceptional importance.

(b) **Petition for Hearing or Rehearing En Banc.** A party may petition for a hearing or rehearing en banc.

(1) The petition must begin with a statement that either:

(A) the panel decision conflicts with a decision of the United States Supreme Court or of the court to which the petition is addressed (with citation to the conflicting case or cases) and consideration by the full court is therefore necessary to secure and maintain uniformity of the court's decisions; or

(B) the proceeding involves one or more questions of exceptional importance, each of which must be concisely stated; for example, a petition may assert that a proceeding presents a question of exceptional importance if it involves an issue on which the panel decision conflicts with the authoritative decisions of other United States Courts of Appeals that have addressed the issue.

(2) Except by the court's permission, a petition for an en banc hearing or rehearing must not exceed 15 pages, excluding material not counted under Rule 32.

(3) For purposes of the page limit in Rule 35(b)(2), if a party files both a petition for

panel rehearing and a petition for rehearing en banc, they are considered a single document even if they are filed separately, unless separate filing is required by local rule.

(c) Time for Petition for Hearing or Rehearing En Banc. A petition that an appeal be heard initially en banc must be filed by the date when the appellee's brief is due. A petition for a rehearing en banc must be filed within the time prescribed by Rule 40 for filing a petition for rehearing.

(d) Number of Copies. The number of copies to be filed must be prescribed by local rule and may be altered by order in a particular case.

(e) Response. No response may be filed to a petition for an en banc consideration unless the court orders a response.

(f) Call for a Vote. A vote need not be taken to determine whether the case will be heard or reheard en banc unless a judge calls for a vote.

See selected Notes of Advisory Committee to FRAP 35, p. 1287.

History of FRAP 35: Adopted Dec. 4, 1967, eff. July 1, 1968. Amended Apr. 30, 1979, eff. Aug. 1, 1979; Apr. 29, 1994, eff. Dec. 1, 1994; Apr. 24, 1998, eff. Dec. 1, 1998; Apr. 25, 2005, eff. Dec. 1, 2005.

See also 28 U.S.C. §46 (composition of court sitting in banc).

FRAP 36. ENTRY OF JUDGMENT; NOTICE

(a) Entry. A judgment is entered when it is noted on the docket. The clerk must prepare, sign, and enter the judgment:

(1) after receiving the court's opinion—but if settlement of the judgment's form is required, after final settlement; or

(2) if a judgment is rendered without an opinion, as the court instructs.

(b) Notice. On the date when judgment is entered, the clerk must serve on all parties a copy of the opinion—or the judgment, if no opinion was written—and a notice of the date when the judgment was entered.

See selected Notes of Advisory Committee to FRAP 36, p. 1288.

History of FRAP 36: Adopted Dec. 4, 1967, eff. July 1, 1968. Amended Apr. 24, 1998, eff. Dec. 1, 1998; Apr. 29, 2002, eff. Dec. 1, 2002.

FRAP 37. INTEREST ON JUDGMENT

(a) When the Court Affirms. Unless the law provides otherwise, if a money judgment in a civil case is affirmed, whatever interest is allowed by law is payable from the date when the district court's judgment was entered.

(b) When the Court Reverses. If the court modifies or reverses a judgment with a direction that a money judgment be entered in the district court, the mandate must contain instructions about the allowance of interest.

History of FRAP 37: Adopted Dec. 4, 1967, eff. July 1, 1968. Amended Apr. 24, 1998, eff. Dec. 1, 1998.

See also 28 U.S.C. §1912 (damages and costs on affirmance).

FRAP 38. FRIVOLOUS APPEAL—DAMAGES & COSTS

If a court of appeals determines that an appeal is frivolous, it may, after a separately filed motion or notice from the court and reasonable opportunity to respond, award just damages and single or double costs to the appellee.

History of FRAP 38: Adopted Dec. 4, 1967, eff. July 1, 1968. Amended Apr. 29, 1994, eff. Dec. 1, 1994; Apr. 24, 1998, eff. Dec. 1, 1998.

See also 28 U.S.C. §1912 (damages and costs on affirmance).

FRAP 39. COSTS

(a) Against Whom Assessed. The following rules apply unless the law provides or the court orders otherwise:

(1) if an appeal is dismissed, costs are taxed against the appellant, unless the parties agree otherwise;

(2) if a judgment is affirmed, costs are taxed against the appellant;

(3) if a judgment is reversed, costs are taxed against the appellee;

(4) if a judgment is affirmed in part, reversed in part, modified, or vacated, costs are taxed only as the court orders.

(b) Costs For and Against the United States. Costs for or against the United States, its agency, or officer will be assessed under Rule 39(a) only if authorized by law.

(c) Costs of Copies. Each court of appeals must, by local rule, fix the maximum rate for taxing the cost of producing necessary copies of a brief or appendix, or copies of records authorized by Rule 30(f). The rate must not exceed that generally charged for such work in the area where the clerk's office is located and should encourage economical methods of copying.

(d) Bill of Costs: Objections; Insertion in Mandate.

(1) A party who wants costs taxed must—within 14 days after entry of judgment—file with the cir-

FRAP 35

cuit clerk, with proof of service, an itemized and verified bill of costs.

(2) Objections must be filed within 14 days after service of the bill of costs, unless the court extends the time.

(3) The clerk must prepare and certify an itemized statement of costs for insertion in the mandate, but issuance of the mandate must not be delayed for taxing costs. If the mandate issues before costs are finally determined, the district clerk must—upon the circuit clerk's request—add the statement of costs, or any amendment of it, to the mandate.

(e) **Costs on Appeal Taxable in the District Court.** The following costs on appeal are taxable in the district court for the benefit of the party entitled to costs under this rule:

(1) the preparation and transmission of the record;

(2) the reporter's transcript, if needed to determine the appeal;

(3) premiums paid for a supersedeas bond or other bond to preserve rights pending appeal; and

(4) the fee for filing the notice of appeal.

See selected Notes of Advisory Committee to FRAP 39, p. 1288.

History of FRAP 39: Adopted Dec. 4, 1967, eff. July 1, 1968. Amended Apr. 30, 1979, eff. Aug. 1, 1979; Mar. 10, 1986, eff. July 1, 1986; Apr. 24, 1998, eff. Dec. 1, 1998; Mar. 26, 2009, eff. Dec. 1, 2009.

See also 28 U.S.C. §711 (payment by clerk into Treasury of all costs, fees, and other money collected), §1912 (damages and costs on affirmance), §1913 (Judicial Conference of U.S. to prescribe charges), §2412 (liability of U.S. for costs).

FRAP 40. PETITION FOR PANEL REHEARING

(a) **Time to File; Contents; Answer; Action by the Court if Granted.**

(1) **Time.** Unless the time is shortened or extended by order or local rule, a petition for panel rehearing may be filed within 14 days after entry of judgment. But in a civil case, unless an order shortens or extends the time, the petition may be filed by any party within 45 days after entry of judgment if one of the parties is:

(A) the United States;

(B) a United States agency;

(C) a United States officer or employee sued in an official capacity; or

(D) a current or former United States officer or employee sued in an individual capacity for an act or omission occurring in connection with duties performed on the United States' behalf—including all instances in which the United States represents that person when the court of appeals' judgment is entered or files the petition for that person.

(2) **Contents.** The petition must state with particularity each point of law or fact that the petitioner believes the court has overlooked or misapprehended and must argue in support of the petition. Oral argument is not permitted.

(3) **Answer.** Unless the court requests, no answer to a petition for panel rehearing is permitted. But ordinarily rehearing will not be granted in the absence of such a request.

(4) **Action by the Court.** If a petition for panel rehearing is granted, the court may do any of the following:

(A) make a final disposition of the case without reargument;

(B) restore the case to the calendar for reargument or resubmission; or

(C) issue any other appropriate order.

(b) **Form of Petition; Length.** The petition must comply in form with Rule 32. Copies must be served and filed as Rule 31 prescribes. Unless the court permits or a local rule provides otherwise, a petition for panel rehearing must not exceed 15 pages.

See selected Notes of Advisory Committee to FRAP 40, p. 1288.

History of FRAP 40: Adopted Dec. 4, 1967, eff. July 1, 1968. Amended Apr. 30, 1979, eff. Aug. 1, 1979; Apr. 29, 1994, eff. Dec. 1, 1994; Apr. 24, 1998, eff. Dec. 1, 1998; Apr. 26, 2011, eff. Dec. 1, 2011.

FRAP 41. MANDATE: CONTENTS; ISSUANCE & EFFECTIVE DATE; STAY

(a) **Contents.** Unless the court directs that a formal mandate issue, the mandate consists of a certified copy of the judgment, a copy of the court's opinion, if any, and any direction about costs.

(b) **When Issued.** The court's mandate must issue 7 days after the time to file a petition for rehearing expires, or 7 days after entry of an order denying a timely petition for panel rehearing, petition for rehearing en banc, or motion for stay of mandate, whichever is later. The court may shorten or extend the time.

(c) **Effective Date.** The mandate is effective when issued.

(d) Staying the Mandate.

(1) On Petition for Rehearing or Motion. The timely filing of a petition for panel rehearing, petition for rehearing en banc, or motion for stay of mandate, stays the mandate until disposition of the petition or motion, unless the court orders otherwise.

(2) Pending Petition for Certiorari.

(A) A party may move to stay the mandate pending the filing of a petition for a writ of certiorari in the Supreme Court. The motion must be served on all parties and must show that the certiorari petition would present a substantial question and that there is good cause for a stay.

(B) The stay must not exceed 90 days, unless the period is extended for good cause or unless the party who obtained the stay files a petition for the writ and so notifies the circuit clerk in writing within the period of the stay. In that case, the stay continues until the Supreme Court's final disposition.

(C) The court may require a bond or other security as a condition to granting or continuing a stay of the mandate.

(D) The court of appeals must issue the mandate immediately when a copy of a Supreme Court order denying the petition for writ of certiorari is filed.

See selected Notes of Advisory Committee to FRAP 41, p. 1288.

History of FRAP 41: Adopted Dec. 4, 1967, eff. July 1, 1968. Amended Apr. 29, 1994, eff. Dec. 1, 1994; Apr. 24, 1998, eff. Dec. 1, 1998; Apr. 29, 2002, eff. Dec. 1, 2002; Mar. 26, 2009, eff. Dec. 1, 2009.

See also 28 U.S.C. §§1254, 2101 (certiorari to Supreme Court); FRAP 40 (petition for rehearing).

FRAP 42. VOLUNTARY DISMISSAL

(a) Dismissal in the District Court. Before an appeal has been docketed by the circuit clerk, the district court may dismiss the appeal on the filing of a stipulation signed by all parties or on the appellant's motion with notice to all parties.

(b) Dismissal in the Court of Appeals. The circuit clerk may dismiss a docketed appeal if the parties file a signed dismissal agreement specifying how costs are to be paid and pay any fees that are due. But no mandate or other process may issue without a court order. An appeal may be dismissed on the appellant's motion on terms agreed to by the parties or fixed by the court.

History of FRAP 42: Adopted Dec. 4, 1967, eff. July 1, 1968. Amended Apr. 24, 1998, eff. Dec. 1, 1998.

FRAP 43. SUBSTITUTION OF PARTIES

(a) Death of a Party.

(1) After Notice of Appeal Is Filed. If a party dies after a notice of appeal has been filed or while a proceeding is pending in the court of appeals, the decedent's personal representative may be substituted as a party on motion filed with the circuit clerk by the representative or by any party. A party's motion must be served on the representative in accordance with Rule 25. If the decedent has no representative, any party may suggest the death on the record, and the court of appeals may then direct appropriate proceedings.

(2) Before Notice of Appeal Is Filed—Potential Appellant. If a party entitled to appeal dies before filing a notice of appeal, the decedent's personal representative—or, if there is no personal representative, the decedent's attorney of record—may file a notice of appeal within the time prescribed by these rules. After the notice of appeal is filed, substitution must be in accordance with Rule 43(a)(1).

(3) Before Notice of Appeal Is Filed—Potential Appellee. If a party against whom an appeal may be taken dies after entry of a judgment or order in the district court, but before a notice of appeal is filed, an appellant may proceed as if the death had not occurred. After the notice of appeal is filed, substitution must be in accordance with Rule 43(a)(1).

(b) Substitution for a Reason Other Than Death. If a party needs to be substituted for any reason other than death, the procedure prescribed in Rule 43(a) applies.

(c) Public Officer: Identification; Substitution.

(1) Identification of Party. A public officer who is a party to an appeal or other proceeding in an official capacity may be described as a party by the public officer's official title rather than by name. But the court may require the public officer's name to be added.

(2) Automatic Substitution of Officeholder. When a public officer who is a party to an appeal or other proceeding in an official capacity

FRAP 41

dies, resigns, or otherwise ceases to hold office, the action does not abate. The public officer's successor is automatically substituted as a party. Proceedings following the substitution are to be in the name of the substituted party, but any misnomer that does not affect the substantial rights of the parties may be disregarded. An order of substitution may be entered at any time, but failure to enter an order does not affect the substitution.

History of FRAP 43: Adopted Dec. 4, 1967, eff. July 1, 1968. Amended Mar. 10, 1986, eff. July 1, 1986; Apr. 24, 1998, eff. Dec. 1, 1998.

FRAP 44. CASE INVOLVING A CONSTITUTIONAL QUESTION WHEN THE UNITED STATES OR THE RELEVANT STATE IS NOT A PARTY

(a) Constitutional Challenge to Federal Statute. If a party questions the constitutionality of an Act of Congress in a proceeding in which the United States or its agency, officer, or employee is not a party in an official capacity, the questioning party must give written notice to the circuit clerk immediately upon the filing of the record or as soon as the question is raised in the court of appeals. The clerk must then certify that fact to the Attorney General.

(b) Constitutional Challenge to State Statute. If a party questions the constitutionality of a statute of a State in a proceeding in which that State or its agency, officer, or employee is not a party in an official capacity, the questioning party must give written notice to the circuit clerk immediately upon the filing of the record or as soon as the question is raised in the court of appeals. The clerk must then certify that fact to the attorney general of the State.

See selected Notes of Advisory Committee to FRAP 44, p. 1289.

History of FRAP 44: Adopted Dec. 4, 1967, eff. July 1, 1968. Amended Apr. 24, 1998, eff. Dec. 1, 1998; Apr. 29, 2002, eff. Dec. 1, 2002.

See also 28 U.S.C. §2403 (intervention by U.S.).

FRAP 45. CLERK'S DUTIES

(a) General Provisions.

(1) Qualifications. The circuit clerk must take the oath and post any bond required by law. Neither the clerk nor any deputy clerk may practice as an attorney or counselor in any court while in office.

(2) When Court Is Open. The court of appeals is always open for filing any paper, issuing and returning process, making a motion, and entering an order. The clerk's office with the clerk or a deputy in attendance must be open during business hours on all days except Saturdays, Sundays, and legal holidays. A court may provide by local rule or by order that the clerk's office be open for specified hours on Saturdays or on legal holidays other than New Year's Day, Martin Luther King, Jr.'s Birthday, Washington's Birthday, Memorial Day, Independence Day, Labor Day, Columbus Day, Veterans' Day, Thanksgiving Day, and Christmas Day.

(b) Records.

(1) The Docket. The circuit clerk must maintain a docket and an index of all docketed cases in the manner prescribed by the Director of the Administrative Office of the United States Courts. The clerk must record all papers filed with the clerk and all process, orders, and judgments.

(2) Calendar. Under the court's direction, the clerk must prepare a calendar of cases awaiting argument. In placing cases on the calendar for argument, the clerk must give preference to appeals in criminal cases and to other proceedings and appeals entitled to preference by law.

(3) Other Records. The clerk must keep other books and records required by the Director of the Administrative Office of the United States Courts, with the approval of the Judicial Conference of the United States, or by the court.

(c) Notice of an Order or Judgment. Upon the entry of an order or judgment, the circuit clerk must immediately serve a notice of entry on each party, with a copy of any opinion, and must note the date of service on the docket. Service on a party represented by counsel must be made on counsel.

(d) Custody of Records and Papers. The circuit clerk has custody of the court's records and papers. Unless the court orders or instructs otherwise, the clerk must not permit an original record or paper to be taken from the clerk's office. Upon disposition of the case, original papers constituting the record on appeal or review must be returned to the court or agency from which they were received. The clerk must preserve a copy of any brief, appendix, or other paper that has been filed.

See selected Notes of Advisory Committee to FRAP 45, p. 1289.

History of FRAP 45: Adopted Dec. 4, 1967, eff. July 1, 1968. Amended Mar. 1, 1971, eff. July 1, 1971; Mar. 10, 1986, eff. July 1, 1986; Apr. 24, 1998, eff. Dec. 1, 1998; Apr. 29, 2002, eff. Dec. 1, 2002; Apr. 25, 2005 eff. Dec. 1, 2005.

See also 28 U.S.C. §711 (appointment and removal of clerk and employees; payment by clerk into Treasury of all costs, fees, and other money collected), §951 (oath of office of clerks), §955 (practice of law restricted).

FRAP 46. ATTORNEYS

(a) Admission to the Bar.

(1) Eligibility. An attorney is eligible for admission to the bar of a court of appeals if that attorney is of good moral and professional character and is admitted to practice before the Supreme Court of the United States, the highest court of a state, another United States court of appeals, or a United States district court (including the district courts for Guam, the Northern Mariana Islands, and the Virgin Islands).

(2) Application. An applicant must file an application for admission, on a form approved by the court that contains the applicant's personal statement showing eligibility for membership. The applicant must subscribe to the following oath or affirmation:

"I, _____, do solemnly swear [or affirm] that I will conduct myself as an attorney and counselor of this court, uprightly and according to law; and that I will support the Constitution of the United States."

(3) Admission Procedures. On written or oral motion of a member of the court's bar, the court will act on the application. An applicant may be admitted by oral motion in open court. But, unless the court orders otherwise, an applicant need not appear before the court to be admitted. Upon admission, an applicant must pay the clerk the fee prescribed by local rule or court order.

(b) Suspension or Disbarment.

(1) Standard. A member of the court's bar is subject to suspension or disbarment by the court if the member:

(A) has been suspended or disbarred from practice in any other court; or

(B) is guilty of conduct unbecoming a member of the court's bar.

(2) Procedure. The member must be given an opportunity to show good cause, within the time prescribed by the court, why the member should not be suspended or disbarred.

(3) Order. The court must enter an appropriate order after the member responds and a hearing is held, if requested, or after the time prescribed for a response expires, if no response is made.

(c) Discipline. A court of appeals may discipline an attorney who practices before it for conduct unbecoming a member of the bar or for failure to comply with any court rule. First, however, the court must afford the attorney reasonable notice, an opportunity to show cause to the contrary, and, if requested, a hearing.

History of FRAP 46: Adopted Dec. 4, 1967, eff. July 1, 1968. Amended Mar. 10, 1986, eff. July 1, 1986; Apr. 24, 1998, eff. Dec. 1, 1998.

See also 28 U.S.C. §568 (U.S. marshal or deputy marshal prohibited from practicing law), §955 (clerk prohibited from practicing law).

FRAP 47. LOCAL RULES BY COURTS OF APPEALS

(a) Local Rules.

(1) Each court of appeals acting by a majority of its judges in regular active service may, after giving appropriate public notice and opportunity for comment, make and amend rules governing its practice. A generally applicable direction to parties or lawyers regarding practice before a court must be in a local rule rather than an internal operating procedure or standing order. A local rule must be consistent with—but not duplicative of—Acts of Congress and rules adopted under 28 U.S.C. §2072 and must conform to any uniform numbering system prescribed by the Judicial Conference of the United States. Each circuit clerk must send the Administrative Office of the United States Courts a copy of each local rule and internal operating procedure when it is promulgated or amended.

(2) A local rule imposing a requirement of form must not be enforced in a manner that causes a party to lose rights because of a nonwillful failure to comply with the requirement.

(b) Procedure When There Is No Controlling Law. A court of appeals may regulate practice in a particular case in any manner consistent with federal law, these rules, and local rules of the circuit. No sanction or other disadvantage may be imposed for noncompliance with any requirement not in fed-

eral law, federal rules, or the local circuit rules unless the alleged violator has been furnished in the particular case with actual notice of the requirement.

History of FRAP 47: Adopted Dec. 4, 1967, eff. July 1, 1968. Amended Apr. 27, 1995, eff. Dec. 1, 1995; Apr. 24, 1998, eff. Dec. 1, 1998.

FRAP 48. MASTERS

(a) Appointment; Powers. A court of appeals may appoint a special master to hold hearings, if necessary, and to recommend factual findings and disposition in matters ancillary to proceedings in the court. Unless the order referring a matter to a master specifies or limits the master's powers, those powers include, but are not limited to, the following:

(1) regulating all aspects of a hearing;

(2) taking all appropriate action for the efficient performance of the master's duties under the order;

(3) requiring the production of evidence on all matters embraced in the reference; and

(4) administering oaths and examining witnesses and parties.

(b) Compensation. If the master is not a judge or court employee, the court must determine the master's compensation and whether the cost is to be charged to any party.

History of FRAP 48: Adopted Dec. 4, 1967, eff. July 1, 1968. Amended Apr. 29, 1994, eff. Dec. 1, 1994; Apr. 24, 1998, eff. Dec. 1, 1998.

FORM 1. NOTICE OF APPEAL TO A COURT OF APPEALS FROM A JUDGMENT OR ORDER OF A DISTRICT COURT

UNITED STATES DISTRICT COURT FOR
THE ____ DISTRICT OF ______

FILE NUMBER ____

A.B., Plaintiff	§	
v.	§	Notice of Appeal
C.D., Defendant	§	

Notice is hereby given that (*here name all parties taking the appeal*), (*plaintiffs*) (*defendants*) in the above named case,[1] hereby appeal to the United States Court of Appeals for the ___ Circuit (*from the final judgment*) (*from an order (describing it)*) entered in this action on the ____ day of _________, 20__.

(s) ______________________
Attorney for ______________
Address: ________________

1. For permissible ways of identifying appellants, see FRAP 3(c).

History of FRAP Form 1: Amended Apr. 22, 1993, eff. Dec. 1, 1993; Mar. 27, 2003, eff. Dec. 1, 2003.

FORM 2. NOTICE OF APPEAL TO A COURT OF APPEALS FROM A DECISION OF THE UNITED STATES TAX COURT

UNITED STATES TAX COURT
WASHINGTON, D.C.

A.B., Petitioner	§	
v.	§	Docket No. ____
Commissioner of Internal Revenue,	§	
Respondent	§	

NOTICE OF APPEAL

Notice is hereby given that (*here name all parties taking the appeal*)[1] hereby appeal to the United States Court of Appeals for the ____ Circuit from (*that part of*) the decision of this court entered in the above captioned proceeding on the _____ day of __________, 20__ (*relating to* ______).

(s) ______________________
Counsel for ______________
Address: ________________

1. For permissible ways of identifying appellants, see FRAP 3(c).

History of FRAP Form 2: Adopted Dec. 4, 1967, eff. July 1, 1968. Amended Apr. 22, 1993, eff. Dec. 1, 1993; Mar. 27, 2003, eff. Dec. 1, 2003.

FORM 3. PETITION FOR REVIEW OF ORDER OF AN AGENCY, BOARD, COMMISSION OR OFFICER

UNITED STATES COURT OF APPEALS FOR
THE ____ CIRCUIT

A.B., Petitioner	§	
v.	§	Petition for Review
XYZ Commission, Respondent	§	

________________ (*here name all parties bringing the petition*)[1] hereby petition the court for review of the Order of the XYZ Commission (*describe the order*) entered on ________, 20__.

(s) ____________________
Attorney for Petitioners
Address: ________________

1. See FRAP 15.

History of FRAP Form 3: Adopted Dec. 4, 1967, eff. July 1, 1968. Amended Apr. 22, 1993, eff. Dec. 1, 1993; Mar. 27, 2003, eff. Dec. 1, 2003.

FORM 4. AFFIDAVIT ACCOMPANYING MOTION FOR PERMISSION TO APPEAL IN FORMA PAUPERIS

Editor's note: *The Committee on Rules of Practice and Procedure of the Judicial Conference of the United States has proposed amendments to FRAP Form 4, to be effective December 1, 2013. For the proposed amendments, see www .uscourts.gov/RulesAndPolicies/rules/pending-rules.aspx.*

UNITED STATES DISTRICT COURT
FOR THE ________ DISTRICT OF ________

A.B., Plaintiff	§	
v.	§	Case No.________
C.D., Defendant	§	

AFFIDAVIT IN SUPPORT OF MOTION

I swear or affirm under penalty of perjury that, because of my poverty, I cannot prepay the docket fees of my appeal or post a bond for them. I believe I am entitled to redress. I swear or affirm under penalty of perjury under United States laws that my answers on this form are true and correct. (28 U.S.C. §1746; 18 U.S.C §1621.)

INSTRUCTIONS

Complete all questions in this application and then sign it. Do not leave any blanks: if the answer to a question is "0," "none," or "not applicable (N/A)," write in that response. If you need more space to answer a question or to explain your answer, attach a separate sheet of paper identified with your name, your case's docket number, and the question number.

Signed: ________________ Date: ________________

My issues on appeal are:

____

____

____

1. For both you and your spouse estimate the average amount of money received from each of the following sources during the past 12 months. Adjust any amount that was received weekly, biweekly, quarterly, semiannually, or annually to show the monthly rate. Use gross amounts, that is, amounts before any deductions for taxes or otherwise.

INCOME SOURCE	AVERAGE MONTHLY AMOUNT DURING THE PAST 12 MONTHS		AMOUNT EXPECTED NEXT MONTH	
	YOU	SPOUSE	YOU	SPOUSE
Employment	$______	$______	$______	$______
Self-employment	$______	$______	$______	$______
Income from real property (such as rental income)	$______	$______	$______	$______
Interest and dividends	$______	$______	$______	$______
Gifts	$______	$______	$______	$______
Alimony	$______	$______	$______	$______
Child support	$______	$______	$______	$______
Retirement (such as social security, pensions, annuities, insurance)	$______	$______	$______	$______
Disability (such as social security, insurance payments)	$______	$______	$______	$______
Unemployment payments	$______	$______	$______	$______
Public-assistance (such as welfare)	$______	$______	$______	$______
Other (specify): ______________	$______	$______	$______	$______
TOTAL MONTHLY INCOME:	$______	$______	$______	$______

2. List your employment history, most recent employer first. (Gross monthly pay is before taxes or other deductions.)

Employer	Address	Dates of employment	Gross monthly pay
______________	______________________	__________	__________
______________	______________________	__________	__________
______________	______________________	__________	__________

3. List your spouse's employment history, most recent employer first. (Gross monthly pay is before taxes or other deductions.)

Employer	Address	Dates of employment	Gross monthly pay
______________	______________________	__________	__________
______________	______________________	__________	__________
______________	______________________	__________	__________

4. *How much cash do you and your spouse have?* $________

Below, state any money you or your spouse have in bank accounts or in any other financial institution.

Financial institution	Type of account	Amount you have	Amount your spouse has
		$	$
		$	$
		$	$

If you are a prisoner, you must attach a statement certified by the appropriate institutional officer showing all receipts, expenditures, and balances during the last six months in your institutional accounts. If you have multiple accounts, perhaps because you have been in multiple institutions, attach one certified statement of each account.

5. *List the assets, and their values, which you own or your spouse owns. Do not list clothing and ordinary household furnishings.*

Home	(Value)	Other real estate	(Value)	Motor vehicle #1	(Value)
				Make & year:	
				Model:	
				Registration #:	

Motor vehicle #2	(Value)	Other assets	(Value)	Other assets	(Value)
Make & year:					
Model:					
Registration #:					

6. *State every person, business, or organization owing you or your spouse money, and the amount owed.*

Person owing you or your spouse money	Amount owed to you	Amount owed to your spouse

7. *State the persons who rely on you or your spouse for support.*

Name [or, if under 18, initials only]	Relationship	Age

8. Estimate the average monthly expenses of you and your family. Show separately the amounts paid by your spouse. Adjust any payments that are made weekly, biweekly, quarterly, semiannually, or annually to show the monthly rate.

	YOU	YOUR SPOUSE
Rent or home-mortgage payment (include lot rented for mobile home) Are real-estate taxes included? ☐Yes ☐No Is property insurance included? ☐Yes ☐No	$______	$______
Utilities (electricity, heating fuel, water, sewer, and telephone)	$______	$______
Home maintenance (repairs and upkeep)	$______	$______
Food	$______	$______
Clothing	$______	$______
Laundry and dry-cleaning	$______	$______
Medical and dental expenses	$______	$______
Transportation (not including motor vehicle payments)	$______	$______
Recreation, entertainment, newspapers, magazines, etc.	$______	$______
Insurance (not deducted from wages or included in mortgage payments) Homeowner's or renter's Life Health Motor Vehicle Other: ____________	$______	$______
Taxes (not deducted from wages or included in mortgage payments) (specify): ____________	$______	$______
Installment payments Motor Vehicle Credit card (name): ____________ Department store (name): ____________ Other: ____________	$______	$______
Alimony, maintenance, and support paid to others	$______	$______
Regular expenses for operation of business, profession, or farm (attach detailed statement)	$______	$______
Other (specify): ____________	$______	$______
TOTAL MONTHLY EXPENSES:	$______	$______

9. Do you expect any major changes to your monthly income or expenses or in your assets or liabilities during the next 12 months?

☐Yes ☐No If yes, describe on an attached sheet.

10. *Have you paid—or will you be paying—an attorney any money for services in connection with this case, including the completion of this form?*

☐ Yes ☐ No

If yes, how much? $__________

If yes, state the attorney's name, address, and telephone number:

____

____

____

11. *Have you paid—or will you be paying—anyone other than an attorney (such as a paralegal or a typist) any money for services in connection with this case, including the completion of this form?*

☐ Yes ☐ No

If yes, how much? $__________

If yes, state the person's name, address, and telephone number:

____

____

____

12. *Provide any other information that will help explain why you cannot pay the docket fees for your appeal.*

____

____

13. *State the city and state of your legal residence.*

____

____

Your daytime phone number: (____) __________________

Your age: __________ Your years of schooling: __________

Last four digits of your social-security number: __________

History of FRAP Form 4: Adopted Dec. 4, 1967, eff. July 1, 1968. Amended Apr. 24, 1998, eff. Dec. 1, 1998; Apr. 28, 2010, eff. Dec. 1, 2010.

FORM 5. NOTICE OF APPEAL TO A COURT OF APPEALS FROM A JUDGMENT OR ORDER OF A DISTRICT COURT OR A BANKRUPTCY APPELLATE PANEL

UNITED STATES DISTRICT COURT FOR
THE ___ DISTRICT OF

In re ____________,	§	
Debtor	§	
____________,	§	
Plaintiff	§	File No.________
v.	§	
____________,	§	
Defendant	§	

NOTICE OF APPEAL TO UNITED STATES COURT
OF APPEALS FOR THE ______ CIRCUIT

__________, the plaintiff (*or defendant or other party*) appeals to the United States Court of Appeals for the ________ Circuit from the final judgment (*or order or decree*) of the district court for the district of ________ (*or bankruptcy appellate panel of the* ________ *circuit*), entered in this case on ________, 20__ (*here describe the judgment, order, or decree*) ________.

The parties to the judgment (*or order or decree*) appealed from and the names and addresses of their respective attorneys are as follows:

Dated ____________________________
Signed ___________________________
Attorney for Appellant
Address: _________________________

History of FRAP Form 5: Adopted Apr. 25, 1989, eff. Dec. 1, 1989. Amended Mar. 27, 2003, eff. Dec. 1, 2003.

FORM 6. CERTIFICATE OF COMPLIANCE WITH RULE 32(a)

CERTIFICATE OF COMPLIANCE WITH TYPE-VOLUME LIMITATION, TYPEFACE REQUIREMENTS, AND TYPE STYLE REQUIREMENTS

1. This brief complies with the type-volume limitation of Fed. R. App. P. 32(a)(7)(B) because:

   ☐ this brief contains (*state the number of*) words, excluding the parts of the brief exempted by Fed. R. App. P. 32(a)(7)(B)(iii), *or*

   ☐ this brief uses a monospaced typeface and contains (*state the number of*) lines of text, excluding the parts of the brief exempted by Fed. R. App. P. 32(a)(7)(B)(iii).

2. This brief complies with the typeface requirements of Fed. R. App. P. 32(a)(5) and the type style requirements of Fed. R. App. P. 32(a)(6) because:

   ☐ this brief has been prepared in a proportionally spaced typeface using (*state name and version of word processing program*) in (*state font size and name of type style*), *or*

   ☐ this brief has been prepared in a monospaced typeface using (*state name and version of word processing program*) with (*state number of characters per inch and name of type style*).

(s) ______________________
Attorney for ______________________
Dated: ______________________

History of FRAP Form 6: Adopted Apr. 29, 2002, eff. Dec. 1, 2002.

FRAP FORM 6

Advisory Committee Notes

Table of Contents

FRCP NOTES

FRCP 1
2007 Notes of Advisory Committee 1137
FRCP 4
2007 Notes of Advisory Committee 1138
2000 Notes of Advisory Committee 1138
1993 Notes of Advisory Committee 1139
FRCP 5
2007 Notes of Advisory Committee 1145
2006 Notes of Advisory Committee 1145
2001 Notes of Advisory Committee 1145
2000 Notes of Advisory Committee 1146
1996 Notes of Advisory Committee 1146
1991 Notes of Advisory Committee 1147
1970 Notes of Advisory Committee 1147
FRCP 5.1
2006 Notes of Advisory Committee 1147
FRCP 5.2
2007 Notes of Advisory Committee 1148
FRCP 6
2009 Notes of Advisory Committee 1149
2005 Notes of Advisory Committee 1151
2001 Notes of Advisory Committee 1151
FRCP 7
2007 Notes of Advisory Committee 1151
FRCP 7.1
2002 Notes of Advisory Committee 1152
FRCP 8
2010 Notes of Advisory Committee 1152
2007 Notes of Advisory Committee 1152
FRCP 9
2007 Notes of Advisory Committee 1152
2006 Notes of Advisory Committee 1152
FRCP 11
2007 Notes of Advisory Committee 1152
1993 Notes of Advisory Committee 1152
FRCP 12
2009 Notes of Advisory Committee 1156
2007 Notes of Advisory Committee 1156
2000 Notes of Advisory Committee 1156
FRCP 13
2009 Notes of Advisory Committee 1156
2007 Notes of Advisory Committee 1156
FRCP 14
2009 Notes of Advisory Committee 1156
2007 Notes of Advisory Committee 1157
2006 Notes of Advisory Committee 1157
2000 Notes of Advisory Committee 1157
FRCP 15
2009 Notes of Advisory Committee 1157
2007 Notes of Advisory Committee 1157
1963 Notes of Advisory Committee 1157
FRCP 16
2007 Notes of Advisory Committee 1158
2006 Notes of Advisory Committee 1158
1993 Notes of Advisory Committee 1158
1983 Notes of Advisory Committee 1160
FRCP 17
2007 Notes of Advisory Committee 1164
FRCP 18
2007 Notes of Advisory Committee 1164
FRCP 19
2007 Notes of Advisory Committee 1164
FRCP 23
2009 Notes of Advisory Committee 1164
2007 Notes of Advisory Committee 1164
2003 Notes of Advisory Committee 1164
1998 Notes of Advisory Committee 1170
FRCP 24
2007 Notes of Advisory Committee 1171
2006 Notes of Advisory Committee 1171
FRCP 25
2007 Notes of Advisory Committee 1171
1963 Notes of Advisory Committee 1171
FRCP 26
2010 Notes of Advisory Committee 1172
2007 Notes of Advisory Committee 1173
2006 Notes of Advisory Committee 1174
2000 Notes of Advisory Committee 1178
1993 Notes of Advisory Committee 1182
1970 Notes of Advisory Committee 1188
FRCP 27
2009 Notes of Advisory Committee 1195
2005 Notes of Advisory Committee 1196
FRCP 29
1993 Notes of Advisory Committee 1196
FRCP 30
2007 Notes of Advisory Committee 1196
2000 Notes of Advisory Committee 1196
1993 Notes of Advisory Committee 1197
FRCP 31
2007 Notes of Advisory Committee 1199
FRCP 32
2009 Notes of Advisory Committee 1199
2007 Notes of Advisory Committee 1199
FRCP 33
2007 Notes of Advisory Committee 1199
2006 Notes of Advisory Committee 1199
1993 Notes of Advisory Committee 1200
1970 Notes of Advisory Committee 1200
FRCP 34
2007 Notes of Advisory Committee 1202
2006 Notes of Advisory Committee 1203
FRCP 36
2007 Notes of Advisory Committee 1204

Advisory Committee Notes

Table of Contents

FRCP 37
2006 Notes of Advisory Committee....1204
2000 Notes of Advisory Committee....1205
1993 Notes of Advisory Committee....1205
FRCP 38
2009 Notes of Advisory Committee....1206
FRCP 40
2007 Notes of Advisory Committee....1206
FRCP 41
2007 Notes of Advisory Committee....1206
FRCP 43
1996 Notes of Advisory Committee....1207
FRCP 44
1991 Notes of Advisory Committee....1207
FRCP 44.1
1966 Notes of Advisory Committee....1208
FRCP 45
2007 Notes of Advisory Committee....1209
2006 Notes of Advisory Committee....1209
2005 Notes of Advisory Committee....1210
1991 Notes of Advisory Committee....1210
FRCP 48
2009 Notes of Advisory Committee....1213
1991 Notes of Advisory Committee....1213
FRCP 50
2009 Notes of Advisory Committee....1213
2007 Notes of Advisory Committee....1213
2006 Notes of Advisory Committee....1214
1995 Notes of Advisory Committee....1214
1993 Notes of Advisory Committee....1214
1991 Notes of Advisory Committee....1214
FRCP 51
2003 Notes of Advisory Committee....1216
1987 Notes of Advisory Committee....1217
FRCP 52
2009 Notes of Advisory Committee....1217
2007 Notes of Advisory Committee....1217
1995 Notes of Advisory Committee....1218
1991 Notes of Advisory Committee....1218
FRCP 53
2009 Notes of Advisory Committee....1218
2003 Notes of Advisory Committee....1218
FRCP 54
2009 Notes of Advisory Committee....1222
2007 Notes of Advisory Committee....1222
2002 Notes of Advisory Committee....1223
1993 Notes of Advisory Committee....1223
FRCP 55
2009 Notes of Advisory Committee....1224
2007 Notes of Advisory Committee....1224
FRCP 56
2010 Notes of Advisory Committee....1224
2009 Notes of Advisory Committee....1227
2007 Notes of Advisory Committee....1227
1946 Notes of Advisory Committee....1227
FRCP 58
2002 Notes of Advisory Committee....1228
FRCP 59
2009 Notes of Advisory Committee....1229
1995 Notes of Advisory Committee....1229
FRCP 60
2007 Notes of Advisory Committee....1229
FRCP 62
2009 Notes of Advisory Committee....1229
2007 Notes of Advisory Committee....1230
FRCP 62.1
2009 Notes of Advisory Committee....1230
FRCP 64
2007 Notes of Advisory Committee....1230
FRCP 65
2009 Notes of Advisory Committee....1230
2007 Notes of Advisory Committee....1230
2001 Notes of Advisory Committee....1230
FRCP 65.1
2006 Notes of Advisory Committee....1231
FRCP 68
2009 Notes of Advisory Committee....1231
FRCP 69
2007 Notes of Advisory Committee....1231
FRCP 71.1
2009 Notes of Advisory Committee....1231
2007 Notes of Advisory Committee....1231
FRCP 72
2009 Notes of Advisory Committee....1231
1983 Notes of Advisory Committee....1231
FRCP 73
1997 Notes of Advisory Committee....1232
1983 Notes of Advisory Committee....1232
FRCP 74
2007 Notes of Advisory Committee....1233
FRCP 75
2007 Notes of Advisory Committee....1233
FRCP 76
2007 Notes of Advisory Committee....1233
FRCP 77
2001 Notes of Advisory Committee....1233
FRCP 78
2007 Notes of Advisory Committee....1233
FRCP 81
2009 Notes of Advisory Committee....1233
2007 Notes of Advisory Committee....1233
2002 Notes of Advisory Committee....1233
2001 Notes of Advisory Committee....1234
FRCP 82
2001 Notes of Advisory Committee....1234

Advisory Committee Notes

Table of Contents

FRCP 83
1995 Notes of Advisory Committee....1234

FRCP 86
2007 Notes of Advisory Committee....1234

SUPPLEMENTAL RULES NOTES

Supplemental Rule B
2009 Notes of Advisory Committee....1235

Supplemental Rule C
2009 Notes of Advisory Committee....1235
2008 Notes of Advisory Committee....1235

Supplemental Rule G
2009 Notes of Advisory Committee....1235
2006 Notes of Advisory Committee....1235

FRE NOTES

FRE 101
2011 Notes of Advisory Committee....1239

FRE 103
2000 Notes of Advisory Committee....1240

FRE 201
1972 Notes of Advisory Committee....1242

FRE 404
2006 Notes of Advisory Committee....1245
2000 Notes of Advisory Committee....1245

FRE 407
2011 Notes of Advisory Committee....1246
1997 Notes of Advisory Committee....1246

FRE 408
2011 Notes of Advisory Committee....1247
2006 Notes of Advisory Committee....1247

FRE 411
2011 Notes of Advisory Committee....1248

FRE 412
1994 Notes of Advisory Committee....1248

FRE 413-415
1995 Congressional Discussion....1251

FRE 501
Notes of Committee on the Judiciary, House Report No. 93-650....1252

FRE 502
2011 Notes of Advisory Committee....1253
2008 Explanatory Note on FRE 502 Prepared by the Judicial Conference Advisory Committee on Evidence Rules....1253
2008 Statement of Congressional Intent Regarding FRE 502....1255

FRE 606
2006 Notes of Advisory Committee....1256

FRE 608
2011 Notes of Advisory Committee....1257
2003 Notes of Advisory Committee....1257

FRE 609
2006 Notes of Advisory Committee....1258

FRE 615
1998 Notes of Advisory Committee....1258

FRE 701
2011 Notes of Advisory Committee....1258
2000 Notes of Advisory Committee....1259

FRE 702
2000 Notes of Advisory Committee....1259

FRE 703
2011 Notes of Advisory Committee....1263
2000 Notes of Advisory Committee....1263

FRE 704
2011 Notes of Advisory Committee....1264

FRE 705
2011 Notes of Advisory Committee....1264

FRE 801
2011 Notes of Advisory Committee....1264
1997 Notes of Advisory Committee....1264

FRE 803
2000 Notes of Advisory Committee....1264

FRE 804
2011 Notes of Advisory Committee....1265
2010 Notes of Advisory Committee....1265
1997 Notes of Advisory Committee....1265

FRE 902
2000 Notes of Advisory Committee....1265

FRAP NOTES

FRAP 1
2010 Notes of Advisory Committee....1265
2002 Notes of Advisory Committee....1265

FRAP 4
2011 Notes of Advisory Committee....1266
2010 Notes of Advisory Committee....1266
2009 Notes of Advisory Committee....1266
2005 Notes of Advisory Committee....1267
2002 Notes of Advisory Committee....1268
1998 Notes of Advisory Committee....1271
1995 Notes of Advisory Committee....1272
1993 Notes of Advisory Committee....1272
1991 Notes of Advisory Committee....1274
1979 Notes of Advisory Committee....1274

FRAP 5
2009 Notes of Advisory Committee....1275
2002 Notes of Advisory Committee....1276

FRAP 6
2009 Notes of Advisory Committee....1276

FRAP 10
2009 Notes of Advisory Committee....1276

FRAP 12
2009 Notes of Advisory Committee....1276

FRAP 12.1
2009 Notes of Advisory Committee....1276

Advisory Committee Notes

Table of Contents

FRAP 15
2009 Notes of Advisory Committee....1277
FRAP 19
2009 Notes of Advisory Committee....1277
FRAP 21
2002 Notes of Advisory Committee....1277
FRAP 22
2009 Notes of Advisory Committee....1277
FRAP 24
2002 Notes of Advisory Committee....1277
FRAP 25
2009 Notes of Advisory Committee....1278
2007 Notes of Advisory Committee....1278
2006 Notes of Advisory Committee....1278
2002 Notes of Advisory Committee....1278
FRAP 26
2009 Notes of Advisory Committee....1279
2005 Notes of Advisory Committee....1282
2002 Notes of Advisory Committee....1282
FRAP 26.1
2002 Notes of Advisory Committee....1282
FRAP 27
2009 Notes of Advisory Committee....1282
2005 Notes of Advisory Committee....1283
2002 Notes of Advisory Committee....1283
FRAP 28
2005 Notes of Advisory Committee....1283
2002 Notes of Advisory Committee....1283
FRAP 28.1
2009 Notes of Advisory Committee....1284
2005 Notes of Advisory Committee....1284
FRAP 29
2010 Notes of Advisory Committee....1285
FRAP 30
2009 Notes of Advisory Committee....1285
FRAP 31
2009 Notes of Advisory Committee....1285
2002 Notes of Advisory Committee....1285
FRAP 32
2005 Notes of Advisory Committee....1286
2002 Notes of Advisory Committee....1286
FRAP 32.1
2006 Notes of Advisory Committee....1286
FRAP 34
2005 Notes of Advisory Committee....1287
FRAP 35
2005 Notes of Advisory Committee....1287
FRAP 36
2002 Notes of Advisory Committee....1288
FRAP 39
2009 Notes of Advisory Committee....1288
FRAP 40
2011 Notes of Advisory Committee....1288
FRAP 41
2009 Notes of Advisory Committee....1288
2002 Notes of Advisory Committee....1289
FRAP 44
2002 Notes of Advisory Committee....1289
FRAP 45
2005 Notes of Advisory Committee....1289
2002 Notes of Advisory Committee....1289

***Editor's note:** Included below are selections from the Advisory Committee Notes to the Federal Rules of Civil Procedure, Federal Rules of Evidence, and Federal Rules of Appellate Procedure. We have made these selections because the full set of Advisory Committee Notes is voluminous, and the omitted notes are no longer relevant or are redundant. The notes are numbered by rule in reverse chronological order for easy reference.*

FRCP NOTES

FRCP 1 – 2007 NOTES OF ADVISORY COMMITTEE

[¶1] The language of Rule 1 has been amended as part of the general restyling of the Civil Rules to make them more easily understood and to make style and terminology consistent throughout the rules. These changes are intended to be stylistic only.[1]

[¶2] The merger of law, equity, and admiralty practice is complete. There is no need to carry forward the phrases that initially accomplished the merger.

[¶3] The former reference to "suits of a civil nature" is changed to the more modern "civil actions and proceedings." This change does not affect such questions as whether the Civil Rules apply to summary proceedings created by statute. *See SEC v. McCarthy*, 322 F.3d 650 (9th Cir.2003); *see also New Hampshire Fire Ins. Co. v. Scanlon*, 362 U.S. 404 (1960).

[¶4] *The Style Project.* The Civil Rules are the third set of the rules to be restyled. The restyled Rules of Appellate Procedure took effect in 1998. The restyled Rules of Criminal Procedure took effect in 2002. The restyled Rules of Civil Procedure apply the same general drafting guidelines and principles used in restyling the Appellate and Criminal Rules.

[¶5] *General Guidelines.* Guidance in drafting, usage, and style was provided by Bryan Garner, *Guidelines for Drafting and Editing Court Rules*, Administrative Office of the United States Courts (1996) and Bryan Garner, *Dictionary of Modern Legal Usage* (2d ed. 1995). *See also* Joseph Kimble, *Guiding Principles for Restyling the Civil Rules*, in *Preliminary Draft of Proposed Style Revision of the Federal Rules of Civil Procedure,* at x (Feb. 2005) [(www.uscourts.gov/uscourts/RulesAndPolicies/rules/Prelim_draft_proposed_pt1.pdf)].

[¶6] *Formatting Changes.* Many of the changes in the restyled Civil Rules result from using format to achieve clearer presentation. The rules are broken down into constituent parts, using progressively indented subparagraphs with headings and substituting vertical for horizontal lists. "Hanging indents" are used throughout. These formatting changes make the structure of the rules graphic and make the restyled rules easier to read and understand even when the words are not changed. Rule 14(a) illustrates the benefits of formatting changes.

[¶7] *Changes to Reduce Inconsistent, Ambiguous, Redundant, Repetitive, or Archaic Words.* The restyled rules reduce the use of inconsistent terms that say the same thing in different ways. Because different words are presumed to have different meanings, such inconsistencies can result in confusion. The restyled rules reduce inconsistencies by using the same words to express the same meaning. For example, consistent expression is achieved without affecting meaning by the changes from "infant" in many rules to "minor" in all rules; from "upon motion or on its own initiative" in Rule 4(m) and variations in many other rules to "on motion or on its own"; and from "deemed" to "considered" in Rules 5(c), 12(e), and elsewhere. Some variations of expression have been carried forward when the context made that appropriate. As an example, "stipulate," "agree," and "consent" appear throughout the rules, and "written" qualifies these words in some places but not others. The number of variations has been reduced, but at times the former words were carried forward. None of the changes, when made, alters the rule's meaning.

[¶8] The restyled rules minimize the use of inherently ambiguous words. For example, the word "shall" can mean "must," "may," or something else, depending on context. The potential for confusion is exacerbated by the fact that "shall" is no longer generally used in spoken or clearly written English. The restyled rules replace "shall" with "must," "may," or "should," depending on which one the context and established interpretation make correct in each rule.

[¶9] The restyled rules minimize the use of redundant "intensifiers." These are expressions that attempt to add emphasis, but instead state the obvious and create negative implications for other rules. "The court in its discretion may" becomes "the court may"; "unless the order expressly directs otherwise" becomes "unless the court orders otherwise." The absence of intensifiers in the restyled rules does not change their substantive meaning. For example, the absence of the word "reasonable" to describe the written notice of foreign law required in Rule 44.1 does not mean that "unreasonable" notice is permitted.

[¶10] The restyled rules also remove words and concepts that are outdated or redundant. The reference to "at law or in equity" in Rule 1 has become redundant with the merger of law and equity. Outdated words and concepts include the reference to "demurrers, pleas, and exceptions" in Rule 7(c); the reference to "mesne" process in Rule 77(c); and the reference in Rule 81(f) to a now-abolished official position.

[¶11] The restyled rules remove a number of redundant cross-references. For example, Rule 8(b) states that a general denial is subject to the obligations of Rule 11, but all pleadings are subject to Rule 11. Removing such cross-references does not defeat application of the formerly cross-referenced rule.

[¶12] *Rule Numbers.* The restyled rules keep the same rule numbers to minimize the effect on research. Subdivisions have been rearranged within some rules to achieve greater clarity and simplicity. The only change that moves one part of a rule to another is the transfer of former Rule 25(d)(2) to Rule 17(d). The restyled rules include a comparison chart to make it easy to identify transfers of provisions between subdivisions and redesignations of some subdivisions.

[¶13] *Other Changes.* The style changes to the rules are intended to make no changes in substantive meaning. A very small number of minor technical amendments that arguably do change meaning were approved separately from the restyled rules, but become effective at the same time. An example is adding "e-mail address" to the information that must be included in pleadings. These minor changes occur in Rules 4(k), 9(h), 11(a), 14(b), 16(c)(1), 26(g)(1), 30(b), 31, 40, 71.1, and 78.

1. **Editor's note:** The Advisory Committee Note in ¶1 was repeated for every FRCP. Because this note was redundant, we have omitted it from FRCPs 2-86.

FRCP 4 – 2007 NOTES OF ADVISORY COMMITTEE

[¶1] Rule 4(d)(1)(C) corrects an inadvertent error in former Rule 4(d)(2)(G). The defendant needs two copies of the waiver form, not an extra copy of the notice and request.

[¶2] Rule 4(g) changes "infant" to "minor." "Infant" in the present rule means "minor." Modern word usage suggests that "minor" will better maintain the intended meaning. The same change from "infant" to "minor" is made throughout the rules. In addition, subdivision (f)(3) is added to the description of methods of service that the court may order; the addition ensures the evident intent that the court not order service by means prohibited by international agreement.

[¶3] Rule 4(i)(4) corrects a misleading reference to "the plaintiff" in former Rule 4(i)(3). A party other than a plaintiff may need a reasonable time to effect service. Rule 4(i)(4) properly covers any party.

[¶4] Former Rule 4(j)(2) refers to service upon an "other governmental organization subject to suit." This is changed to "any other state-created governmental organization that is subject to suit." The change entrenches the meaning indicated by the caption ("Serving a Foreign, State, or Local Government"), and the invocation of state law. It excludes any risk that this rule might be read to govern service on a federal agency, or other entities not created by state law.

[¶5] The former provision describing service on interpleader claimants is deleted as redundant in light of the general provision in (k)(1)(C) recognizing personal jurisdiction authorized by a federal statute.

FRCP 4 – 2000 NOTES OF ADVISORY COMMITTEE

[¶1] Paragraph (2)(B) is added to Rule 4(i) to require service on the United States when a United States officer or employee is sued in an individual capacity for acts or omissions occurring in connection with duties performed on behalf of the United States. Decided cases provide uncertain guidance on the question whether the United States must be served in such actions. *See Vaccaro v. Dobre*, 81 F.3d 854, 856-857 (9th Cir.1996); *Armstrong v. Sears*, 33 F.3d 182, 185-187 (2d Cir.1994); *Ecclesiastical Order of the Ism of Am v. Chasin*, 845 F.2d 113, 116 (6th Cir.1988); *Light v. Wolf*, 816 F.2d 746 (D.C. Cir.1987); *see also Simpkins v. District of Columbia*, 108 F.3d 366, 368-369 (D.C. Cir.1997). Service on the United States will help to protect the interest of the individual defendant in securing representation by the United States, and will expedite the process of determining whether the United States will provide representation. It has been understood that the individual defendant must be served as an individual defendant, a requirement that is made explicit. Invocation of the individual service provisions of subdivisions (e), (f), and (g) invokes also the waiver-of-service provisions of subdivision (d).

[¶2] Paragraph 2(B) reaches service when an officer or employee of the United States is sued in an individual capacity "for acts or omissions occurring in connection with the performance of duties on behalf of the United States." This phrase has been chosen as a functional phrase that can be applied without the occasionally distracting associations of such phrases as "scope of employment," "color of office," or "arising out of the employment." Many actions are brought against individual federal officers or employees of the United States for acts or omissions that have no connection whatever to their governmental roles. There is no reason to require service on the United States in these actions. The connection to federal employment that requires service on the United States must be determined as a practical matter, considering whether the individual defendant has reasonable grounds to look to the United States for assistance and whether the United States has reasonable grounds for demanding formal notice of the action.

[¶3] An action against a former officer or employee of the United States is covered by paragraph (2)(B) in the same way as an action against a present officer or employee. Termination of the relationship between the individual defendant and the United States does not reduce the need to serve the United States.

[¶4] Paragraph (3) is amended to ensure that failure to serve the United States in an action governed by paragraph 2(B) does not defeat an action. This protection is adopted because there will be cases in which the plaintiff reasonably fails to appreciate the need to serve the United States. There is no requirement, however, that the plaintiff show that the failure to serve the United States was reasonable. A reasonable time to effect service on the United States must be allowed after the failure is pointed out. An additional change ensures that if the United States or United States attorney is served in an action governed by paragraph 2(A), additional time is to be allowed even though no officer, employee, agency, or corporation of the United States was served.

FRCP 4 – 1993 NOTES OF ADVISORY COMMITTEE

[¶1] Purposes of Revision. The general purpose of this revision is to facilitate the service of the summons and complaint. The revised rule explicitly authorizes a means for service of the summons and complaint on any defendant. While the methods of service so authorized always provide appropriate notice to persons against whom claims are made, effective service under this rule does not assure that personal jurisdiction has been established over the defendant served.

[¶2] First, the revised rule authorizes the use of any means of service provided by the law not only of the forum state, but also of the state in which a defendant is served, unless the defendant is a minor or incompetent.

[¶3] Second, the revised rule clarifies and enhances the cost-saving practice of securing the assent of the defendant to dispense with actual service of the summons and complaint. This practice was introduced to the rule in 1983 by an act of Congress authorizing "service-by-mail," a procedure that effects economic service with cooperation of the defendant. Defendants that magnify costs of service by requiring expensive service not necessary to achieve full notice of an action brought against them are required to bear the wasteful costs. This provision is made available in actions against defendants who cannot be served in the districts in which the actions are brought.

[¶4] Third, the revision reduces the hazard of commencing an action against the United States or its officers, agencies, and corporations. A party failing to effect service on all the offices of the United States as required by the rule is assured adequate time to cure defects in service.

[¶5] Fourth, the revision calls attention to the important effect of the Hague Convention and other treaties bearing on service of documents in foreign countries and favors the use of internationally agreed means of service. In some respects, these treaties have facilitated service in foreign countries but are not fully known to the bar.

[¶6] Finally, the revised rule extends the reach of federal courts to impose jurisdiction over the person of all defendants against whom federal law claims are made and who can be constitutionally subjected to the jurisdiction of the courts of the United States. The present territorial limits on the effectiveness of service to subject a defendant to the jurisdiction of the court over the defendant's person are retained for all actions in which there is a state in which personal jurisdiction can be asserted consistently with state law and the Fourteenth Amendment. A new provision enables district courts to exercise jurisdiction, if permissible under the Constitution and not precluded by statute, when a federal claim is made against a defendant not subject to the jurisdiction of any single state.

[¶7] The revised rule is reorganized to make its provisions more accessible to those not familiar with all of them. Additional subdivisions in this rule allow for more captions; several overlaps among subdivisions are eliminated; and several disconnected provisions are removed, to be relocated in a new Rule 4.1.

[¶8] The Caption of the Rule. Prior to this revision, Rule 4 was entitled "Process" and applied to the service of not only the summons but also other process as well, although these are not covered by the revised rule. Service of process in eminent domain proceedings is governed by Rule 71A. Service of a subpoena is governed by Rule 45, and service of papers such as orders, motions, notices, pleadings, and other documents is governed by Rule 5.

[¶9] The revised rule is entitled "Summons" and applies only to that form of legal process. Unless service of the summons is waived, a summons must be served whenever a person is joined as a party against whom a claim is made. Those few provisions of the former rule which relate specifically to service of process other than a summons are relocated in Rule 4.1 in order to simplify the text of this rule.

[¶10] Subdivision (a). Revised subdivision (a) contains most of the language of the former subdivision (b). The second sentence of the former subdivision (b) has been stricken, so that the federal court summons will be the same in all cases. Few states now employ distinctive requirements of form for a summons and the applicability of such a requirement in federal court can only serve as a trap for an unwary party or attorney. A sentence is added to this subdivision authorizing an amendment of a summons. This sentence replaces the rarely used former subdivision 4(h). See 4A Wright & Miller, Federal Practice and Procedure §1131 (2d ed. 1987).

[¶11] Subdivision (b). Revised subdivision (b) replaces the former subdivision (a). The revised text makes clear that the responsibility for filling in the summons falls on the plaintiff, not the clerk of the court. If there are multiple defendants, the plaintiff may secure issuance of a summons for each defendant, or may serve copies of a single original bearing the names of multiple defendants if the addressee of the summons is effectively identified.

[¶12] Subdivision (c). Paragraph (1) of revised subdivision (c) retains language from the former subdivision (d)(1). Paragraph (2) retains language from the former subdivision (a), and adds an appropriate caution regarding the time limit for service set forth in subdivision (m).

[¶13] The 1983 revision of Rule 4 relieved the marshals' offices of much of the burden of serving the summons. Subdivision (c) eliminates the requirement for service by the marshal's office in actions in which the party seeking service is the United States. The United States, like other civil litigants, is now permitted to designate any person who is 18 years of age and not a party to serve its summons.

[¶14] The court remains obligated to appoint a marshal, a deputy, or some other person to effect service of a summons in two classes of cases specified by statute: actions brought in forma pauperis or by a seaman. 28 U.S.C. §§1915, 1916. The

court also retains discretion to appoint a process server on motion of a party. If a law enforcement presence appears to be necessary or advisable to keep the peace, the court should appoint a marshal or deputy or other official person to make the service. The Department of Justice may also call upon the Marshals Service to perform services in actions brought by the United States. 28 U.S.C. §651.

[¶15] Subdivision (d). This text is new, but is substantially derived from the former subdivisions (c)(2)(C) and (D), added to the rule by Congress in 1983. The aims of the provision are to eliminate the costs of service of a summons on many parties and to foster cooperation among adversaries and counsel. The rule operates to impose upon the defendant those costs that could have been avoided if the defendant had cooperated reasonably in the manner prescribed. This device is useful in dealing with defendants who are furtive, who reside in places not easily reached by process servers, or who are outside the United States and can be served only at substantial and unnecessary expense. Illustratively, there is no useful purpose achieved by requiring a plaintiff to comply with all the formalities of service in a foreign country, including costs of translation, when suing a defendant manufacturer, fluent in English, whose products are widely distributed in the United States. *See Bankston v. Toyota Motor Corp.*, 889 F.2d 172 (8th Cir.1989).

[¶16] The former text described this process as service-by-mail. This language misled some plaintiffs into thinking that service could be effected by mail without the affirmative cooperation of the defendant. *E.g., Gulley v. Mayo Foundation*, 886 F.2d 161 (8th Cir.1989). It is more accurate to describe the communication sent to the defendant as a request for a waiver of formal service.

[¶17] The request for waiver of service may be sent only to defendants subject to service under subdivision (e), (f), or (h). The United States is not expected to waive service for the reason that its mail receiving facilities are inadequate to assure that the notice is actually received by the correct person in the Department of Justice. The same principle is applied to agencies, corporations, and officers of the United States and to other governments and entities subject to service under subdivision (j). Moreover, there are policy reasons why governmental entities should not be confronted with the potential for bearing costs of service in cases in which they ultimately prevail. Infants or incompetent persons likewise are not called upon to waive service because, due to their presumed inability to understand the request and its consequences, they must generally be served through fiduciaries.

[¶18] It was unclear whether the former rule authorized mailing of a request for "acknowledgment of service" to defendants outside the forum state. See 1 R. Casad, Jurisdiction in Civil Actions (2d Ed.) 5-29, 30 (1991) and cases cited. But, as Professor Casad observed, there was no reason not to employ this device in an effort to obtain service outside the state, and there are many instances in which it was in fact so used, with respect both to defendants within the United States and to defendants in other countries.

[¶19] The opportunity for waiver has distinct advantages to a foreign defendant. By waiving service, the defendant can reduce the costs that may ultimately be taxed against it if unsuccessful in the lawsuit, including the sometimes substantial expense of translation that may be wholly unnecessary for defendants fluent in English. Moreover, a defendant that waives service is afforded substantially more time to defend against the action than if it had been formally served: under Rule 12, a defendant ordinarily has only 20 days after service in which to file its answer or raise objections by motion, but by signing a waiver it is allowed 90 days after the date the request for waiver was mailed in which to submit its defenses. Because of the additional time needed for mailing and the unreliability of some foreign mail services, a period of 60 days (rather than the 30 days required for domestic transmissions) is provided for a return of a waiver sent to a foreign country.

[¶20] It is hoped that, since transmission of the notice and waiver forms is a private nonjudicial act, does not purport to effect service, and is not accompanied by any summons or directive from a court, use of the procedure will not offend foreign sovereignties, even those that have withheld their assent to formal service by mail or have objected to the "service-by-mail" provisions of the former rule. Unless the addressee consents, receipt of the request under the revised rule does not give rise to any obligation to answer the lawsuit, does not provide a basis for default judgment, and does not suspend the statute of limitations in those states where the period continues to run until service. Nor are there any adverse consequences to a foreign defendant, since the provisions for shifting the expense of service to a defendant that declines to waive service apply only if the plaintiff and defendant are both located in the United States.

[¶21] With respect to a defendant located in a foreign country like the United Kingdom, which accepts documents in English, whose Central Authority acts promptly in effecting service, and whose policies discourage its residents from waiving formal service, there will be little reason for a plaintiff to send the notice and request under subdivision (d) rather than use convention methods. On the other hand, the procedure offers significant potential benefits to a plaintiff when suing a defendant that, though fluent in English, is located in a country where, as a condition to formal service under a convention, documents must be translated into another language or where formal service will be otherwise costly or time-consuming.

[¶22] Paragraph (1) is explicit that a timely waiver of service of a summons does not prejudice the right of a defendant to object by means of a motion authorized by Rule 12(b)(2) to the absence of jurisdiction over the defendant's person, or to assert other defenses that may be available. The

only issues eliminated are those involving the sufficiency of the summons or the sufficiency of the method by which it is served.

[¶23] Paragraph (2) states what the present rule implies: the defendant has a duty to avoid costs associated with the service of a summons not needed to inform the defendant regarding the commencement of an action. The text of the rule also sets forth the requirements for a Notice and Request for Waiver sufficient to put the cost-shifting provision in place. These requirements are illustrated in Forms 1A and 1B, which replace the former Form 18-A.

[¶24] Paragraph (2)(A) is explicit that a request for waiver of service by a corporate defendant must be addressed to a person qualified to receive service. The general mail rooms of large organizations cannot be required to identify the appropriate individual recipient for an institutional summons.

[¶25] Paragraph (2)(B) permits the use of alternatives to the United States mails in sending the Notice and Request. While private messenger services or electronic communications may be more expensive than the mail, they may be equally reliable and on occasion more convenient to the parties. Especially with respect to transmissions to foreign countries, alternative means may be desirable, for in some countries facsimile transmission is the most efficient and economical means of communication. If electronic means such as facsimile transmission are employed, the sender should maintain a record of the transmission to assure proof of transmission if receipt is denied, but a party receiving such a transmission has a duty to cooperate and cannot avoid liability for the resulting cost of formal service if the transmission is prevented at the point of receipt.

[¶26] A defendant failing to comply with a request for waiver shall be given an opportunity to show good cause for the failure, but sufficient cause should be rare. It is not a good cause for failure to waive service that the claim is unjust or that the court lacks jurisdiction. Sufficient cause not to shift the cost of service would exist, however, if the defendant did not receive the request or was insufficiently literate in English to understand it. It should be noted that the provisions for shifting the cost of service apply only if the plaintiff and the defendant are both located in the United States, and accordingly a foreign defendant need not show "good cause" for its failure to waive service.

[¶27] Paragraph (3) extends the time for answer if, before being served with process, the defendant waives formal service. The extension is intended to serve as an inducement to waive service and to assure that a defendant will not gain any delay by declining to waive service and thereby causing the additional time needed to effect service. By waiving service, a defendant is not called upon to respond to the complaint until 60 days from the date the notice was sent to it—90 days if the notice was sent to a foreign country—rather than within the 20 day period from date of service specified in Rule 12.

[¶28] Paragraph (4) clarifies the effective date of service when service is waived; the provision is needed to resolve an issue arising when applicable law requires service of process to toll the statute of limitations. *E.g., Morse v. Elmira Country Club*, 752 F.2d 35 (2d Cir.1984). *Cf. Walker v. Armco Steel Corp.*, 446 U.S. 740 (1980).

[¶29] The provisions in former subdivision (c)(2)(C)(ii) of this rule may have been misleading to some parties. Some plaintiffs, not reading the rule carefully, supposed that receipt by the defendant of the mailed complaint had the effect both of establishing the jurisdiction of the court over the defendant's person and of tolling the statute of limitations in actions in which service of the summons is required to toll the limitations period. The revised rule is clear that, if the waiver is not returned and filed, the limitations period under such a law is not tolled and the action will not otherwise proceed until formal service of process is effected.

[¶30] Some state limitations laws may toll an otherwise applicable statute at the time when the defendant receives notice of the action. Nevertheless, the device of requested waiver of service is not suitable if a limitations period which is about to expire is not tolled by filing the action. Unless there is ample time, the plaintiff should proceed directly to the formal methods for service identified in subdivisions (e), (f), or (h).

[¶31] The procedure of requesting waiver of service should also not be used if the time for service under subdivision (m) will expire before the date on which the waiver must be returned. While a plaintiff has been allowed additional time for service in that situation, *e.g., Prather v. Raymond Constr. Co.*, 570 F.Supp. 278 (N.D. Ga. 1983), the court could refuse a request for additional time unless the defendant appears to have evaded service pursuant to subdivision (e) or (h). It may be noted that the presumptive time limit for service under subdivision (m) does not apply to service in a foreign country.

[¶32] Paragraph (5) is a cost-shifting provision retained from the former rule. The costs that may be imposed on the defendant could include, for example, the cost of the time of a process server required to make contact with a defendant residing in a guarded apartment house or residential development. The paragraph is explicit that the costs of enforcing the cost-shifting provision are themselves recoverable from a defendant who fails to return the waiver. In the absence of such a provision, the purpose of the rule would be frustrated by the cost of its enforcement, which is likely to be high in relation to the small benefit secured by the plaintiff.

[¶33] Some plaintiffs may send a notice and request for waiver and, without waiting for return of the waiver, also proceed with efforts to effect formal service on the defendant. To discourage this practice, the cost-shifting provisions in paragraphs (2) and (5) are limited to costs of effecting service incurred after the time expires for the defendant to return the waiver. Moreover, by returning the waiver within the time allowed and before being served with process, a defendant receives the benefit of the longer period for responding to the complaint afforded for waivers under paragraph (3).

[¶34] **Subdivision (e).** This subdivision replaces former subdivisions (c)(2)(C)(i) and (d)(1). It provides a means for service of summons on individuals within a judicial district of the United States. Together with subdivision (f), it provides for service on persons anywhere, subject to constitutional and statutory constraints.

[¶35] Service of the summons under this subdivision does not conclusively establish the jurisdiction of the court over the person of the defendant. A defendant may assert the territorial limits of the court's reach set forth in subdivision (k), including the constitutional limitations that may be imposed by the Due Process Clause of the Fifth Amendment.

[¶36] Paragraph (1) authorizes service in any judicial district in conformity with state law. This paragraph sets forth the language of former subdivision (c)(2)(C)(i), which authorized the use of the law of the state in which the district court sits, but adds as an alternative the use of the law of the state in which the service is effected.

[¶37] Paragraph (2) retains the text of the former subdivision (d)(1) and authorizes the use of the familiar methods of personal or abode service or service on an authorized agent in any judicial district.

[¶38] To conform to these provisions, the former subdivision (e) bearing on proceedings against parties not found within the state is stricken. Likewise stricken is the first sentence of the former subdivision (f), which had restricted the authority of the federal process server to the state in which the district court sits.

[¶39] **Subdivision (f).** This subdivision provides for service on individuals who are in a foreign country, replacing the former subdivision (i) that was added to Rule 4 in 1963. Reflecting the pattern of Rule 4 in incorporating state law limitations on the exercise of jurisdiction over persons, the former subdivision (i) limited service outside the United States to cases in which extraterritorial service was authorized by state or federal law. The new rule eliminates the requirement of explicit authorization. On occasion, service in a foreign country was held to be improper for lack of statutory authority. *E.g.*, *Martens v. Winder*, 341 F.2d 197 (9th Cir.), cert. denied, 382 U.S. 937 (1965). This authority, however, was found to exist by implication. *E.g.*, *SEC v. VTR, Inc.*, 39 F.R.D. 19 (S.D. N.Y.1966). Given the substantial increase in the number of international transactions and events that are the subject of litigation in federal courts, it is appropriate to infer a general legislative authority to effect service on defendants in a foreign country.

[¶40] A secondary effect of this provision for foreign service of a federal summons is to facilitate the use of federal long-arm law in actions brought to enforce the federal law against defendants who cannot be served under any state law but who can be constitutionally subjected to the jurisdiction of the federal court. Such a provision is set forth in paragraph (2) of subdivision (k) of this rule, applicable only to persons not subject to the territorial jurisdiction of any particular state.

[¶41] Paragraph (1) gives effect to the Hague Convention on the Service Abroad of Judicial and Extrajudicial Documents, which entered into force for the United States on February 10, 1969. See 28 U.S.C.A., FRCP 4 (Supp.1986). This Convention is an important means of dealing with problems of service in a foreign country. See generally 1 B. Ristau, International Judicial Assistance §§4-1-1 to 4-5-2 (1990). Use of the Convention procedures, when available, is mandatory if documents must be transmitted abroad to effect service. *See Volkswagenwerk Aktiengesellschaft v. Schlunk*, 486 U.S. 694 (1988) (noting that voluntary use of these procedures may be desirable even when service could constitutionally be effected in another manner); J. Weis, The Federal Rules and the Hague Conventions: Concerns of Conformity and Comity, 50 U. Pitt. L. Rev. 903 (1989). Therefore, this paragraph provides that, when service is to be effected outside a judicial district of the United States, the methods of service appropriate under an applicable treaty shall be employed if available and if the treaty so requires.

[¶42] The Hague Convention furnishes safeguards against the abridgment of rights of parties through inadequate notice. Article 15 provides for verification of actual notice or a demonstration that process was served by a method prescribed by the internal laws of the foreign state before a default judgment may be entered. Article 16 of the Convention also enables the judge to extend the time for appeal after judgment if the defendant shows a lack of adequate notice either to defend or to appeal the judgment, or has disclosed a prima facie case on the merits.

[¶43] The Hague Convention does not specify a time within which a foreign country's Central Authority must effect service, but Article 15 does provide that alternate methods may be used if a Central Authority does not respond within six months. Generally, a Central Authority can be expected to respond much more quickly than that limit might permit, but there have been occasions when the signatory state was dilatory or refused to cooperate for substantive reasons. In such cases, resort may be had to the provision set forth in subdivision (f)(3).

[¶44] Two minor changes in the text reflect the Hague Convention. First, the term "letter of request" has been added. Although these words are synonymous with "letter rogatory," "letter of request" is preferred in modern usage. The provision should not be interpreted to authorize use of a letter of request when there is in fact no treaty obligation on the receiving country to honor such a request from this country or when the United States does not extend diplomatic recognition to the foreign nation. Second, the passage formerly found in subdivision (i)(1)(B), "when service in either case is reasonably calculated to give actual notice," has been relocated.

[¶45] Paragraph (2) provides alternative methods for use when internationally agreed methods are not intended to be exclusive, or where there is no international agreement applicable. It contains most of the language formerly set forth in subdivision (i) of the rule. Service by methods that would violate foreign law is not generally authorized. Subparagraphs (A) and (B) prescribe the more appropriate methods for conforming to local practice or using a local authority. Subparagraph (C) prescribes other methods authorized by the former rule.

[¶46] Paragraph (3) authorizes the court to approve other methods of service not prohibited by international agreements. The Hague Convention, for example, authorizes special forms of service in cases of urgency if convention methods will not permit service within the time required by the circumstances. Other circumstances that might justify the use of additional methods include the failure of the foreign country's Central Authority to effect service within the six-month period provided by the Convention, or the refusal of the Central Authority to serve a complaint seeking punitive damages or to enforce the antitrust laws of the United States. In such cases, the court may direct a special method of service not explicitly authorized by international agreement if not prohibited by the agreement. Inasmuch as our Constitution requires that reasonable notice be given, an earnest effort should be made to devise a method of communication that is consistent with due process and minimizes offense to foreign law. A court may in some instances specially authorize use of ordinary mail. *Cf. Levin v. Ruby Trading Corp.*, 248 F.Supp. 537 (S.D. N.Y.1965).

[¶47] Subdivision (g). This subdivision retains the text of former subdivision (d)(2). Provision is made for service upon an infant or incompetent person in a foreign country.

[¶48] Subdivision (h). This subdivision retains the text of former subdivision (d)(3), with changes reflecting those made in subdivision (e). It also contains the provisions for service on a corporation or association in a foreign country, as formerly found in subdivision (i).

[¶49] Frequent use should be made of the Notice and Request procedure set forth in subdivision (d) in actions against corporations. Care must be taken, however, to address the request to an individual officer or authorized agent of the corporation. It is not effective use of the Notice and Request procedure if the mail is sent undirected to the mail room of the organization.

[¶50] Subdivision (i). This subdivision retains much of the text of former subdivisions (d)(4) and (d)(5). Paragraph (1) provides for service of a summons on the United States; it amends former subdivision (d)(4) to permit the United States attorney to be served by registered or certified mail. The rule does not authorize the use of the Notice and Request procedure of revised subdivision (d) when the United States is the defendant. To assure proper handling of mail in the United States attorney's office, the authorized mail service must be specifically addressed to the civil process clerk of the office of the United States attorney.

[¶51] Paragraph (2) replaces former subdivision (d)(5). Paragraph (3) saves the plaintiff from the hazard of losing a substantive right because of failure to comply with the complex requirements of multiple service under this subdivision. That risk has proved to be more than nominal. *E.g., Whale v. United States*, 792 F.2d 951 (9th Cir.1986). This provision should be read in connection with the provisions of subdivision (c) of Rule 15 to preclude the loss of substantive rights against the United States or its agencies, corporations, or officers resulting from a plaintiff's failure to correctly identify and serve all the persons who should be named or served.

[¶52] Subdivision (j). This subdivision retains the text of former subdivision (d)(6) without material change. The waiver-of-service provision is also inapplicable to actions against governments subject to service pursuant to this subdivision.

[¶53] The revision adds a new paragraph (1) referring to the statute governing service of a summons on a foreign state and its political subdivisions, agencies, and instrumentalities, the Foreign Sovereign Immunities Act of 1976, 28 U.S.C. §1608. The caption of the subdivision reflects that change.

[¶54] Subdivision (k). This subdivision replaces the former subdivision (f), with no change in the title. Paragraph (1) retains the substance of the former rule in explicitly authorizing the exercise of personal jurisdiction over persons who can be reached under state long-arm law, the "100-mile bulge" provision added in 1963, or the federal interpleader act. Paragraph (1)(D) is new, but merely calls attention to federal legislation that may provide for nationwide or even world-wide service of process in cases arising under particular federal laws. Congress has provided for nationwide service of process and full exercise of territorial jurisdiction by all district courts with respect to specified federal actions. See 1 R. Casad, Jurisdiction in Civil Actions (2d Ed.) chap. 5 (1991).

[¶55] Paragraph (2) is new. It authorizes the exercise of territorial jurisdiction over the person of any defendant against whom is made a claim arising under any federal law if that person is subject to personal jurisdiction in no state. This addition is a companion to the amendments made in revised subdivisions (e) and (f).

[¶56] This paragraph corrects a gap in the enforcement of federal law. Under the former rule, a problem was presented when the defendant was a non-resident of the United States having contacts with the United States sufficient to justify the application of United States law and to satisfy federal standards of forum selection, but having insufficient contact with any single state to support jurisdiction under state long-arm legislation or meet the requirements of the Fourteenth Amendment limitation on state court territorial jurisdiction. In such cases, the defendant was shielded from the enforcement of federal law by the fortuity of a favorable limitation on the power of state courts, which was incorporated into the federal practice by the former rule. In this respect, the revision responds to the suggestion of the Supreme Court made in *Omni Capital Int'l v. Rudolf Wolff & Co., Ltd.*, 484 U.S. 97, 111 (1987).

[¶57] There remain constitutional limitations on the exercise of territorial jurisdiction by federal courts over persons outside the United States. These restrictions arise from the Fifth Amendment rather than from the Fourteenth Amendment, which limits state-court reach and which was incorporated into federal practice by the reference to state law in the text of the former subdivision (e) that is deleted by this revision. The Fifth Amendment requires that any defendant have affiliating contacts with the United States sufficient to justify the exercise of personal jurisdiction over that party. *Cf. Wells Fargo & Co. v. Wells Fargo Express Co.*, 556 F.2d 406, 418 (9th Cir.1977). There also may be a further Fifth Amendment constraint in that a plaintiff's forum selection might be so inconvenient to a defendant that it would be a denial of "fair play and substantial justice" required by the due process clause, even though the defendant had significant affiliating contacts with the United States. *See DeJames v. Magnificent Carriers*, 654 F.2d 280, 286 n.3 (3rd Cir.), cert. denied, 454 U.S. 1085 (1981). *Compare World-Wide Volkswagen Corp. v. Woodson*, 444 U.S. 286, 293-294 (1980); *Insurance Corp. of Ireland v. Compagnie des Bauxites de Guinee*, 456 U.S. 694, 702-03 (1982); *Burger King Corp. v. Rudzewicz*, 471 U.S. 462, 476-78 (1985); *Asahi Metal Indus. v. Superior Court of Cal., Solano County*, 480 U.S. 102, 108-13 (1987). *See generally* R. Lusardi, Nationwide Service of Process: Due Process Limitations on the Power of the Sovereign, 33 Vill. L. Rev. 1 (1988).

[¶58] This provision does not affect the operation of federal venue legislation. *See generally* 28 U.S.C. §1391. Nor does it affect the operation of federal law providing for the change of venue. 28 U.S.C. §§1404, 1406. The availability of transfer for fairness and convenience under §1404 should preclude most conflicts between the full exercise of territorial jurisdiction permitted by this rule and the Fifth Amendment requirement of "fair play and substantial justice."

[¶59] The district court should be especially scrupulous to protect aliens who reside in a foreign country from forum selections so onerous that injustice could result. "[G]reat care and reserve should be exercised when extending our notions of personal jurisdiction into the international field." *Asahi Metal Indus. v. Superior Court of Cal., Solano County*, 480 U.S. 102, 115 (1987), quoting *United States v. First Nat'l City Bank*, 379 U.S. 378, 404 (1965) (Harlan, J., dissenting).

[¶60] This narrow extension of the federal reach applies only if a claim is made against the defendant under federal law. It does not establish personal jurisdiction if the only claims are those arising under state law or the law of another country, even though there might be diversity or alienage subject matter jurisdiction as to such claims. If, however, personal jurisdiction is established under this paragraph with respect to a federal claim, then 28 U.S.C. §1367(a) provides supplemental jurisdiction over related claims against that defendant, subject to the court's discretion to decline exercise of that jurisdiction under 28 U.S.C. §1367(c).

[¶61] Subdivision (*l*). This subdivision assembles in one place all the provisions of the present rule bearing on proof of service. No material change in the rule is effected. The provision that proof of service can be amended by leave of court is retained from the former subdivision (h). See generally 4A Wright & Miller, Federal Practice and Procedure §1132 (2d ed. 1987).

[¶62] Subdivision (m). This subdivision retains much of the language of the present subdivision (j).

[¶63] The new subdivision explicitly provides that the court shall allow additional time if there is good cause for the plaintiff's failure to effect service in the prescribed 120 days, and authorizes the court to relieve a plaintiff of the consequences of an application of this subdivision even if there is no good cause shown. Such relief formerly was afforded in some cases, partly in reliance on Rule 6(b). Relief may be justified, for example, if the applicable statute of limitations would bar the refiled action, or if the defendant is evading service or conceals a defect in attempted service. *E.g., Ditkof v. Owens-Illinois, Inc.*, 114 F.R.D. 104 (E.D. Mich.1987). A specific instance of good cause is set forth in paragraph (3) of this rule, which provides for extensions if necessary to correct oversights in compliance with the requirements of multiple service in actions against the United States or its officers, agencies, and corporations. The district court should also take care to protect pro se plaintiffs from consequences of confusion or delay attending the resolution of an *in forma pauperis* petition. *Robinson v. America's Best Contacts & Eyeglasses*, 876 F.2d 596 (7th Cir.1989).

[¶64] The 1983 revision of this subdivision referred to the "party on whose behalf such service was required," rather than to the "plaintiff," a term used generically elsewhere in this rule to refer to any party initiating a claim against a person who is not a party to the action. To simplify the text, the revision returns to the usual practice in the rule of referring simply to the plaintiff even though its principles apply with equal force to defendants who may assert claims against nonparties under Rules 13(h), 14, 19, 20, or 21.

[¶65] Subdivision (n). This subdivision provides for in rem and quasi-in-rem jurisdiction. Paragraph (1) incorporates any requirements of 28 U.S.C. §1655 or similar provisions bearing on seizures or liens.

[¶66] Paragraph (2) provides for other uses of quasi-in-rem jurisdiction but limits its use to exigent circumstances. Provisional remedies may be employed as a means to secure jurisdiction over the property of a defendant whose person is not within reach of the court, but occasions for the use of this provision should be rare, as where the defendant is a fugitive or assets are in imminent danger of disappearing. Until 1963, it was not possible under Rule 4 to assert jurisdiction in a federal court over the property of a defendant not personally served. The 1963 amendment to subdivision (e) authorized the use of state law procedures authorizing seizures of assets as a basis for jurisdiction. Given the liberal availability of long-arm jurisdiction, the exercise of power quasi-in-rem has become almost an anachronism. Circumstances too spare to affiliate the defendant to the forum state sufficiently to support long-arm jurisdiction over the defendant's person are also inadequate to support seizure of the defendant's assets fortuitously found within the state. *Shaffer v. Heitner*, 433 U.S. 186 (1977).

FRCP 5 – 2007 NOTES OF ADVISORY COMMITTEE

[¶1] Rule 5(a)(1)(E) omits the former reference to a designation of record on appeal. Appellate Rule 10 is a self-contained provision for the record on appeal, and provides for service.

[¶2] Former Rule 5(b)(2)(D) literally provided that a local rule may authorize use of the court's transmission facilities to make service by non-electronic means agreed to by the parties. That was not intended. Rule 5(b)(3) restores the intended meaning—court transmission facilities can be used only for service by electronic means.

[¶3] Rule 5(d)(2)(B) provides that "a" judge may accept a paper for filing, replacing the reference in former Rule 5(e) to "the" judge. Some courts do not assign a designated judge to each case, and it may be important to have another judge accept a paper for filing even when a case is on the individual docket of a particular judge. The ministerial acts of accepting the paper, noting the time, and transmitting the paper to the court clerk do not interfere with the assigned judge's authority over the action.

FRCP 5 – 2006 NOTES OF ADVISORY COMMITTEE

[¶1] Amended Rule 5(e) acknowledges that many courts have required electronic filing by means of a standing order, procedures manual, or local rule. These local practices reflect the advantages that courts and most litigants realize from electronic filing. Courts that mandate electronic filing recognize the need to make exceptions when requiring electronic filing imposes a hardship on a party. Under amended Rule 5(e), a local rule that requires electronic filing must include reasonable exceptions, but Rule 5(e) does not define the scope of those exceptions. Experience with the local rules that have been adopted and that will emerge will aid in drafting new local rules and will facilitate gradual convergence on uniform exceptions, whether in local rules or in an amended Rule 5(e).

FRCP 5 – 2001 NOTES OF ADVISORY COMMITTEE

[¶1] Rule 5(b) is restyled.

[¶2] Rule 5(b)(1) makes it clear that the provision for service on a party's attorney applies only to service made under Rules 5(a) and 77(d). Service under Rules 4, 4.1, 45(b), and 71A(d)(3)—as well as rules that invoke those rules—must be made as provided in those rules.

[¶3] Subparagraphs (A), (B), and (C) of Rule 5(b)(2) carry forward the method-of-service provisions of former Rule 5(b).

[¶4] Subparagraph (D) of Rule 5(b)(2) is new. It authorizes service by electronic means or any other means, but only if consent is obtained from the person served. The consent must be express, and cannot be implied from conduct. Early experience with electronic filing as authorized by Rule 5(d) is positive, supporting service by electronic means as well. Consent is required, however, because it is not yet possible to assume universal entry into the world of electronic communication. Subparagraph (D) also authorizes service by nonelectronic means. The Rule 5(b)(2)(B) provision making mail service complete on mailing is extended in subparagraph (D) to make service by electronic means complete on transmission; transmission is effected when the sender does the last act that must be performed by the sender. Service by other agencies is complete on delivery to the designated agency.

[¶5] Finally, subparagraph (D) authorizes adoption of local rules providing for service through the court. Electronic case filing systems will come to include the capacity to make service by using the court's facilities to transmit all documents filed in the case. It may prove most efficient to establish an environment in which a party can file with the court, making use of the court's transmission facilities to serve the filed paper on all other parties. Transmission might be by such means as direct transmission of the paper, or by transmission of a notice of filing that includes an electronic link for direct access to the paper. Because service is under subparagraph (D), consent must be obtained from the persons served.

[¶6] Consent to service under Rule 5(b)(2)(D) must be in writing, which can be provided by electronic means. Parties are encouraged to specify the scope and duration of the consent. The specification should include at least the persons to whom service should be made, the appropriate address or location for such service—such as the e-mail address or facsimile machine number, and the format to be used for attachments. A district court may establish a registry or other facility that allows advance consent to service by specified means for future actions.

[¶7] Rule 6(e) is amended to allow additional time to respond when service is made under Rule 5(b)(2)(D). The additional time does not relieve a party who consents to service under Rule 5(b)(2)(D) of the responsibilities to monitor the facility designated for receiving service and to provide prompt notice of any address change.

[¶8] Paragraph (3) addresses a question that may arise from a literal reading of the provision that service by electronic means is complete on transmission. Electronic communication is rapidly improving, but lawyers report continuing failures of transmission, particularly with respect to attachments. Ordinarily the risk of non-receipt falls on the person being served, who has consented to this form of service. But the risk should not extend to situations in which the person attempting service learns that the attempted service in fact did not reach the person to be served. Given actual knowledge that the attempt failed, service is not effected. The person attempting service must either try again or show circumstances that justify dispensing with service.

[¶9] Paragraph (3) does not address the similar questions that may arise when a person attempting service learns that service by means other than electronic means in fact did not reach the person to be served. Case law provides few illustrations of circumstances in which a person attempting service actually knows that the attempt failed but seeks to act as if service had been made. This negative history suggests there is no need to address these problems in Rule 5(b)(3). This silence does not imply any view on these issues, nor on the circumstances that justify various forms of judicial action even though service has not been made.

FRCP 5 – 2000 NOTES OF ADVISORY COMMITTEE

[¶1] **Subdivision (d).** Rule 5(d) is amended to provide that disclosures under Rule 26(a)(1) and (2), and discovery requests and responses under Rules 30, 31, 33, 34, and 36 must not be filed until they are used in the action. "Discovery requests" includes deposition notices and "discovery responses" includes objections. The rule supersedes and invalidates local rules that forbid, permit, or require filing of these materials before they are used in the action. The former Rule 26(a)(4) requirement that disclosures under Rule 26(a)(1) and (2) be filed has been removed. Disclosures under Rule 26(a)(3), however, must be promptly filed as provided in Rule 26(a)(3). Filings in connection with Rule 35 examinations, which involve a motion proceeding when the parties do not agree, are unaffected by these amendments.

[¶2] Recognizing the costs imposed on parties and courts by required filing of discovery materials that are never used in an action, Rule 5(d) was amended in 1980 to authorize court orders that excuse filing. Since then, many districts have adopted local rules that excuse or forbid filing. In 1989 the Judicial Conference Local Rules Project concluded that these local rules were inconsistent with Rule 5(d), but urged the Advisory Committee to consider amending the rule. *Local Rules Project* at 92 (1989). The Judicial Conference of the Ninth Circuit gave the Committee similar advice in 1997. The reality of nonfiling reflected in these local rules has even been assumed in drafting the national rules. In 1993, Rule 30(f)(1) was amended to direct that the officer presiding at a deposition file it with the court or send it to the attorney who arranged for the transcript or recording. The Committee Note explained that this alternative to filing was designed for "courts which direct that depositions not be automatically filed." Rule 30(f)(1) has been amended to conform to this change in Rule 5(d).

[¶3] Although this amendment is based on widespread experience with local rules, and confirms the results directed by these local rules, it is designed to supersede and invalidate local rules. There is no apparent reason to have different filing rules in different districts. Even if districts vary in present capacities to store filed materials that are not used in an action, there is little reason to continue expending court resources for this purpose. These costs and burdens would likely change as parties make increased use of audio- and videotaped depositions. Equipment to facilitate review and reproduction of such discovery materials may prove costly to acquire, maintain, and operate.

[¶4] The amended rule provides that discovery materials and disclosures under Rule 26(a)(1) and (a)(2) must not be filed until they are "used in the proceeding." This phrase is meant to refer to proceedings in court. This filing requirement is not triggered by "use" of discovery materials in other discovery activities, such as depositions. In connection with proceedings in court, however, the rule is to be interpreted broadly; any use of discovery materials in court in connection with a motion, a pretrial conference under Rule 16, or otherwise, should be interpreted as use in the proceeding.

[¶5] Once discovery or disclosure materials are used in the proceeding, the filing requirements of Rule 5(d) should apply to them. But because the filing requirement applies only with regard to materials that are used, only those parts of voluminous materials that are actually used need be filed. Any party would be free to file other pertinent portions of materials that are so used. *See* Fed. R. Evid. 106; *cf.* Rule 32(a)(4). If the parties are unduly sparing in their submissions, the court may order further filings. By local rule, a court could provide appropriate direction regarding the filing of discovery materials, such as depositions, that are used in proceedings.

[¶6] "Shall" is replaced by "must" under the program to conform amended rules to current style conventions when there is no ambiguity.

FRCP 5 – 1996 NOTES OF ADVISORY COMMITTEE

[¶1] The present Rule 5(e) has authorized filing by facsimile or other electronic means on two conditions. The filing must be authorized by local rule. Use of this means of filing must be authorized by the Judicial Conference of the United

States and must be consistent with standards established by the Judicial Conference. Attempts to develop Judicial Conference standards have demonstrated the value of several adjustments in the rule.

[¶2] The most significant change discards the requirement that the Judicial Conference authorize local electronic filing rules. As before, each district may decide for itself whether it has the equipment and personnel required to establish electronic filing, but a district that wishes to establish electronic filing need no longer await Judicial Conference action.

[¶3] The role of Judicial Conference standards is clarified by specifying that the standards are to govern technical matters. Technical standards can provide nationwide uniformity, enabling ready use of electronic filing without pausing to adjust for the otherwise inevitable variations among local rules. Judicial Conference adoption of technical standards should prove superior to specification in these rules. Electronic technology has advanced with great speed. The process of adopting Judicial Conference standards should prove speedier and more flexible in determining the time for the first uniform standards, in adjusting standards at appropriate intervals, and in sparing the Supreme Court and Congress the need to consider technological details. Until Judicial Conference standards are adopted, however, uniformity will occur only to the extent that local rules deliberately seek to copy other local rules.

[¶4] It is anticipated that Judicial Conference standards will govern such technical specifications as data formatting, speed of transmission, means to transmit copies of supporting documents, and security of communication. Perhaps more important, standards must be established to assure proper maintenance and integrity of the record and to provide appropriate access and retrieval mechanisms. Local rules must address these issues until Judicial Conference standards are adopted.

[¶5] The amended rule also makes clear the equality of filing by electronic means with written filings. An electronic filing that complies with the local rule satisfies all requirements for filing on paper, signature, or verification. An electronic filing that otherwise satisfies the requirements of 28 U.S.C. §1746 need not be separately made in writing. Public access to electronic filings is governed by the same rules as govern written filings.

[¶6] The separate reference to filing by facsimile transmission is deleted. Facsimile transmission continues to be included as an electronic means.

FRCP 5 – 1991 NOTES OF ADVISORY COMMITTEE

[¶1] **Subdivision (d).** This subdivision is amended to require that the person making service under the rule certify that service has been effected. Such a requirement has generally been imposed by local rule.

[¶2] Having such information on file may be useful for many purposes, including proof of service if an issue arises concerning the effectiveness of the service. The certificate will generally specify the date as well as the manner of service, but parties employing private delivery services may sometimes be unable to specify the date of delivery. In the latter circumstance, a specification of the date of transmission of the paper to the delivery service may be sufficient for the purposes of this rule.

[¶3] **Subdivision (e).** The words "pleading and other" are stricken as unnecessary. Pleadings are papers within the meaning of the rule. The revision also accommodates the development of the use of facsimile transmission for filing.

[¶4] Several local district rules have directed the office of the clerk to refuse to accept for filing papers not conforming to certain requirements of form imposed by local rules or practice. This is not a suitable role for the office of the clerk, and the practice exposes litigants to the hazards of time bars; for these reasons, such rules are proscribed by this revision. The enforcement of these rules and of the local rules is a role for a judicial officer. A clerk may of course advise a party or counsel that a particular instrument is not in proper form, and may be directed to so inform the court.

FRCP 5 – 1970 NOTES OF ADVISORY COMMITTEE

[¶1] The amendment makes clear that all papers relating to discovery which are required to be served on any party must be served on all parties, unless the court orders otherwise. The present language expressly includes notices and demands, but it is not explicit as to answers or responses as provided in Rules 33, 34, and 36. Discovery papers may be voluminous or the parties numerous, and the court is empowered to vary the requirement if in a given case it proves needlessly onerous.

[¶2] In actions begun by seizure of property, service will at times have to be made before the absent owner of the property has filed an appearance. For example, a prompt deposition may be needed in a maritime action in rem. See Rules 30(a) and 30(b)(2) and the related notes. A provision is added authorizing service on the person having custody or possession of the property at the time of its seizure.

FRCP 5.1 – 2006 NOTES OF ADVISORY COMMITTEE

[¶1] Rule 5.1 implements 28 U.S.C. §2403, replacing the final three sentences of Rule 24(c). New Rule 5.1 requires a party that files a pleading, written motion, or other paper drawing in question the constitutionality of a federal or state statute to file a notice of constitutional question and serve it on the United States Attorney General or state attorney general. The party must promptly file and serve the notice of constitutional question. This notice requirement supplements the court's duty to certify a constitutional challenge to the United States Attorney General or state attorney general. The notice of constitutional question will ensure that the attorney general is notified of constitutional challenges and has an opportunity to exercise the statutory right to intervene at the earliest possible point in the litigation. The court's certification obligation remains, and is the only notice when the constitutionality of a federal or state statute is drawn in question by means other than a party's pleading, written motion, or other paper.

[¶2] Moving the notice and certification provisions from Rule 24(c) to a new rule is designed to attract the parties' attention to these provisions by locating them in the vicinity of the rules that require notice by service and pleading.

[¶3] Rule 5.1 goes beyond the requirements of §2403 and the former Rule 24(c) provisions by requiring notice and certification of a constitutional challenge to any federal or state statute, not only those "affecting the public interest." It is better to assure, through notice, that the attorney general is able to determine whether to seek intervention on the ground that the act or statute affects a public interest. Rule 5.1 refers to a "federal statute," rather than the §2403 reference to an "Act of Congress," to maintain consistency in the Civil Rules vocabulary. In Rule 5.1 "statute" means any congressional enactment that would qualify as an "Act of Congress."

[¶4] Unless the court sets a later time, the 60-day period for intervention runs from the time a party files a notice of constitutional question or from the time the court certifies a constitutional challenge, whichever is earlier. Rule 5.1(a) directs that a party promptly serve the notice of constitutional question. The court may extend the 60-period[1] on its own or on motion. One occasion for extension may arise if the court certifies a challenge under §2403 after a party files a notice of constitutional question. Pretrial activities may continue without interruption during the intervention period, and the court retains authority to grant interlocutory relief. The court may reject a constitutional challenge to a statute at any time. But the court may not enter a final judgment holding a statute unconstitutional before the attorney general has responded or the intervention period has expired without response. This rule does not displace any of the statutory or rule procedures that permit dismissal of all or part of an action—including a constitutional challenge—at any time, even before service of process.

1. **Editor's note:** So in original. Probably should be "60-day period."

FRCP 5.2 – 2007 NOTES OF ADVISORY COMMITTEE

[¶1] The rule is adopted in compliance with section 205(c)(3) of the E-Government Act of 2002, Public Law 107-347. Section 205(c)(3) requires the Supreme Court to prescribe rules "to protect privacy and security concerns relating to electronic filing of documents and the public availability … of documents filed electronically." The rule goes further than the E-Government Act in regulating paper filings even when they are not converted to electronic form. But the number of filings that remain in paper form is certain to diminish over time. Most districts scan paper filings into the electronic case file, where they become available to the public in the same way as documents initially filed in electronic form. It is electronic availability, not the form of the initial filing, that raises the privacy and security concerns addressed in the E-Government Act.

[¶2] The rule is derived from and implements the policy adopted by the Judicial Conference in September 2001 to address the privacy concerns resulting from public access to electronic case files. *See* www.privacy.uscourts.gov/Policy.htm. The Judicial Conference policy is that documents in case files generally should be made available electronically to the same extent they are available at the courthouse, provided that certain "personal data identifiers" are not included in the public file.

[¶3] While providing for the public filing of some information, such as the last four digits of an account number, the rule does not intend to establish a presumption that this information never could or should be protected. For example, it may well be necessary in individual cases to prevent remote access by nonparties to any part of an account number or social security number. It may also be necessary to protect information not covered by the redaction requirement—such as driver's license numbers and alien registration numbers—in a particular case. In such cases, protection may be sought under subdivision (d) or (e). Moreover, the Rule does not affect the protection available under other rules, such as Civil Rules 16 and 26(c), or under other sources of protective authority.

[¶4] Parties must remember that any personal information not otherwise protected by sealing or redaction will be made available over the internet. Counsel should notify clients of this fact so that an informed decision may be made on what information is to be included in a document filed with the court.

[¶5] The clerk is not required to review documents filed with the court for compliance with this rule. The responsibility to redact filings rests with counsel and the party or nonparty making the filing.

[¶6] Subdivision (c) provides for limited public access in Social Security cases and immigration cases. Those actions are entitled to special treatment due to the prevalence of sensitive information and the volume of filings. Remote electronic access by nonparties is limited to the docket and the written dispositions of the court unless the court orders otherwise. The rule contemplates, however, that nonparties can obtain full access to the case file at the courthouse, including access through the court's public computer terminal.

[¶7] Subdivision (d) reflects the interplay between redaction and filing under seal. It does not limit or expand the judicially developed rules that govern sealing. But it does reflect the possibility that redaction may provide an alternative to sealing.

[¶8] Subdivision (e) provides that the court can by order in a particular case for good cause require more extensive redaction than otherwise required by the Rule. Nothing in this subdivision is intended to affect the limitations on sealing that are otherwise applicable to the court.

[¶9] Subdivision (f) allows a person who makes a redacted filing to file an unredacted document under seal. This provision is derived from section 205(c)(3)(iv) of the E-Government Act.

[¶10] Subdivision (g) allows the option to file a register of redacted information. This provision is derived from section 205(c)(3)(v) of the E-Government Act, as amended in 2004. In accordance with the E-Government Act, subdivision (g) refers to "redacted" information. The term "redacted" is intended to govern a filing that is prepared with abbreviated identifiers in the first instance, as well as a filing in which a personal identifier is edited after its preparation.

[¶11] Subdivision (h) allows a person to waive the protections of the rule as to that person's own personal information by filing it unsealed and in unredacted form. One may wish to waive the protection if it is determined that the costs of redaction outweigh the benefits to privacy. If a person files an unredacted identifier by mistake, that person may seek relief from the court.

[¶12] Trial exhibits are subject to the redaction requirements of Rule 5.2 to the extent they are filed with the court. Trial exhibits that are not initially filed with the court must be redacted in accordance with the rule if and when they are filed as part of an appeal or for other reasons.

FRCP 6 – 2009 NOTES OF ADVISORY COMMITTEE

[¶1] **Subdivision (a).** Subdivision (a) has been amended to simplify and clarify the provisions that describe how deadlines are computed. Subdivision (a) governs the computation of any time period found in these rules, in any local rule or court order, or in any statute that does not specify a method of computing time. In accordance with Rule 83(a)(1), a local rule may not direct that a deadline be computed in a manner inconsistent with subdivision (a).

[¶2] The time-computation provisions of subdivision (a) apply only when a time period must be computed. They do not apply when a fixed time to act is set. The amendments thus carry forward the approach taken in *Violette v. P.A. Days, Inc.*, 427 F.3d 1015, 1016 (6th Cir. 2005) (holding that Civil Rule 6(a) "does not apply to situations where the court has established a specific calendar day as a deadline"), and reject the contrary holding of *In re American Healthcare Management, Inc.*, 900 F.2d 827, 832 (5th Cir. 1990) (holding that Bankruptcy Rule 9006(a) governs treatment of date-certain deadline set by court order). If, for example, the date for filing is "no later than November 1, 2007," subdivision (a) does not govern. But if a filing is required to be made "within 10 days" or "within 72 hours," subdivision (a) describes how that deadline is computed.

[¶3] Subdivision (a) does not apply when computing a time period set by a statute if the statute specifies a method of computing time. *See, e.g.*, 2 U.S.C. §394 (specifying method for computing time periods prescribed by certain statutory provisions relating to contested elections to the House of Representatives).

[¶4] **Subdivision (a)(1).** New subdivision (a)(1) addresses the computation of time periods that are stated in days. It also applies to time periods that are stated in weeks, months, or years. *See, e.g.*, Rule 60(c)(1). Subdivision (a)(1)(B)'s directive to "count every day" is relevant only if the period is stated in days (not weeks, months or years).

[¶5] Under former Rule 6(a), a period of 11 days or more was computed differently than a period of less than 11 days. Intermediate Saturdays, Sundays, and legal holidays were included in computing the longer periods, but excluded in computing the shorter periods. Former Rule 6(a) thus made computing deadlines unnecessarily complicated and led to counterintuitive results. For example, a 10-day period and a 14-day period that started on the same day usually ended on the same day—and the 10-day period not infrequently ended later than the 14-day period. *See Miltimore Sales, Inc. v. Int'l Rectifier, Inc.*, 412 F.3d 685, 686 (6th Cir. 2005).

[¶6] Under new subdivision (a)(1), all deadlines stated in days (no matter the length) are computed in the same way. The day of the event that triggers the deadline is not counted. All other days—including intermediate Saturdays, Sundays, and legal holidays—are counted, with only one exception: If the period ends on a Saturday, Sunday, or legal holiday, then the deadline falls on the next day that is not a Saturday, Sunday, or legal holiday. An illustration is provided below in the discussion of subdivision (a)(5). Subdivision (a)(3) addresses filing deadlines that expire on a day when the clerk's office is inaccessible.

[¶7] Where subdivision (a) formerly referred to the "act, event, or default" that triggers the deadline, new subdivision (a) refers simply to the "event" that triggers the deadline; this change in terminology is adopted for brevity and simplicity, and is not intended to change meaning.

[¶8] Periods previously expressed as less than 11 days will be shortened as a practical matter by the decision to count intermediate Saturdays, Sundays, and legal holidays in computing all periods. Many of those periods have been lengthened to compensate for the change. *See, e.g.*, Rule 14(a)(1).

[¶9] Most of the 10-day periods were adjusted to meet the change in computation method by setting 14 days as the new period. A 14-day period corresponds to the most frequent result of a 10-day period under the former computation method—two Saturdays and two Sundays were excluded, giving 14 days in all. A 14-day period has an additional advantage. The final day falls on the same day of the week as the event that triggered the period—the 14th day after a Monday,

for example, is a Monday. This advantage of using week-long periods led to adopting 7-day periods to replace some of the periods set at less than 10 days, and 21-day periods to replace 20-day periods. Thirty-day and longer periods, however, were generally retained without change.

[¶10] Subdivision (a)(2). New subdivision (a)(2) addresses the computation of time periods that are stated in hours. No such deadline currently appears in the Federal Rules of Civil Procedure. But some statutes contain deadlines stated in hours, as do some court orders issued in expedited proceedings.

[¶11] Under subdivision (a)(2), a deadline stated in hours starts to run immediately on the occurrence of the event that triggers the deadline. The deadline generally ends when the time expires. If, however, the time period expires at a specific time (say, 2:17 p.m.) on a Saturday, Sunday, or legal holiday, then the deadline is extended to the same time (2:17 p.m.) on the next day that is not a Saturday, Sunday, or legal holiday. Periods stated in hours are not to be "rounded up" to the next whole hour. Subdivision (a)(3) addresses situations when the clerk's office is inaccessible during the last hour before a filing deadline expires.

[¶12] Subdivision (a)(2)(B) directs that every hour be counted. Thus, for example, a 72-hour period that commences at 10:23 a.m. on Friday, November 2, 2007, will run until 9:23 a.m. on Monday, November 5; the discrepancy in start and end times in this example results from the intervening shift from daylight saving time to standard time.

[¶13] Subdivision (a)(3). When determining the last day of a filing period stated in days or a longer unit of time, a day on which the clerk's office is not accessible because of the weather or another reason is treated like a Saturday, Sunday, or legal holiday. When determining the end of a filing period stated in hours, if the clerk's office is inaccessible during the last hour of the filing period computed under subdivision (a)(2) then the period is extended to the same time on the next day that is not a weekend, holiday, or day when the clerk's office is inaccessible.

[¶14] Subdivision (a)(3)'s extensions apply "[u]nless the court orders otherwise." In some circumstances, the court might not wish a period of inaccessibility to trigger a full 24-hour extension; in those instances, the court can specify a briefer extension.

[¶15] The text of the rule no longer refers to "weather or other conditions" as the reason for the inaccessibility of the clerk's office. The reference to "weather" was deleted from the text to underscore that inaccessibility can occur for reasons unrelated to weather, such as an outage of the electronic filing system. Weather can still be a reason for inaccessibility of the clerk's office. The rule does not attempt to define inaccessibility. Rather, the concept will continue to develop through caselaw, *see, e.g.*, William G. Phelps, *When Is Office of Clerk of Court Inaccessible Due to Weather or Other Conditions for Purpose of Computing Time Period for Filing Papers under Rule 6(a) of Federal Rules of Civil Procedure*, 135 A.L.R. Fed. 259 (1996) (collecting cases). In addition, many local provisions address inaccessibility for purposes of electronic filing, *see, e.g.*, D. Kan. Rule 5.4.11 ("A Filing User whose filing is made untimely as the result of a technical failure may seek appropriate relief from the court.").

[¶16] Subdivision (a)(4). New subdivision (a)(4) defines the end of the last day of a period for purposes of subdivision (a)(1). Subdivision (a)(4) does not apply in computing periods stated in hours under subdivision (a)(2), and does not apply if a different time is set by a statute, local rule, or order in the case. A local rule may, for example, address the problems that might arise if a single district has clerk's offices in different time zones, or provide that papers filed in a drop box after the normal hours of the clerk's office are filed as of the day that is date-stamped on the papers by a device in the drop box.

[¶17] 28 U.S.C. §452 provides that "[a]ll courts of the United States shall be deemed always open for the purpose of filing proper papers, issuing and returning process, and making motions and orders." A corresponding provision exists in Rule 77(a). Some courts have held that these provisions permit an after-hours filing by handing the papers to an appropriate official. *See, e.g.*, *Casalduc v. Diaz*, 117 F.2d 915, 917 (1st Cir. 1941). Subdivision (a)(4) does not address the effect of the statute on the question of after-hours filing; instead, the rule is designed to deal with filings in the ordinary course without regard to Section 452.

[¶18] Subdivision (a)(5). New subdivision (a)(5) defines the "next" day for purposes of subdivisions (a)(1)(C) and (a)(2)(C). The Federal Rules of Civil Procedure contain both forward-looking time periods and backward-looking time periods. A forward-looking time period requires something to be done within a period of time *after* an event. *See, e.g.*, Rule 59(b) (motion for new trial "must be filed no later than 28 days after entry of the judgment"). A backward-looking time period requires something to be done within a period of time *before* an event. *See, e.g.*, Rule 26(f) (parties must hold Rule 26(f) conference "as soon as practicable and in any event at least 21 days before a scheduling conference is held or a scheduling order is due under Rule 16(b)"). In determining what is the "next" day for purposes of subdivisions (a)(1)(C) and (a)(2)(C), one should continue counting in the same direction—that is, forward when computing a forward-looking period and backward when computing a backward-looking period. If, for example, a filing is due within 30 days *after* an event, and the thirtieth day falls on Saturday, September 1, 2007, then the filing is due on Tuesday, September 4, 2007 (Monday, September 3, is Labor Day). But if a filing is due 21 days *before* an event, and the twenty-first day falls on Saturday, September 1, then the filing is due on Friday, August 31. If the clerk's office is inaccessible on August 31, then subdivision (a)(3) extends the filing deadline forward to the next accessible day that is not a Saturday, Sunday, or legal holiday—no later than Tuesday, September 4.

[¶19] Subdivision (a)(6). New subdivision (a)(6) defines "legal holiday" for purposes of the Federal Rules of Civil Procedure, including the time-computation provisions of subdivision (a). Subdivision (a)(6) continues to include within the definition of "legal holiday" days that are declared a holiday by the President or Congress.

[¶20] For forward-counted periods—*i.e.*, periods that are measured after an event—subdivision (a)(6)(C) includes certain state holidays within the definition of legal holidays. However, state legal holidays are not recognized in computing backward-counted periods. For both forward- and backward-counted periods, the rule thus protects those who may be unsure of the effect of state holidays. For forward-counted deadlines, treating state holidays the same as federal holidays extends the deadline. Thus, someone who thought that the federal courts might be closed on a state holiday would be safeguarded against an inadvertent late filing. In contrast, for backward-counted deadlines, not giving state holidays the treatment of federal holidays allows filing on the state holiday itself rather than the day before. Take, for example, Monday, April 21, 2008 (Patriot's Day, a legal holiday in the relevant state). If a filing is due 14 days after an event, and the fourteenth day is April 21, then the filing is due on Tuesday, April 22 because Monday, April 21 counts as a legal holiday. But if a filing is due 14 days before an event, and the fourteenth day is April 21, the filing is due on Monday, April 21; the fact that April 21 is a state holiday does not make April 21 a legal holiday for purposes of computing this backward-counted deadline. But note that if the clerk's office is inaccessible on Monday, April 21, then subdivision (a)(3) extends the April 21 filing deadline forward to the next accessible day that is not a Saturday, Sunday or legal holiday—no earlier than Tuesday, April 22.

[¶21] The times set in the former rule at 1 or 5 days have been revised to 7 or 14 days. See the Note to Rule 6.[1]

1. **Editor's note:** The cross-reference to "Note to Rule 6" refers to ¶¶1-20 above.

FRCP 6 – 2005 NOTES OF ADVISORY COMMITTEE

[¶1] Rule 6(e) is amended to remove any doubt as to the method for extending the time to respond after service by mail, leaving with the clerk of court, electronic means, or other means consented to by the party served. Three days are added after the prescribed period otherwise expires under Rule 6(a). Intermediate Saturdays, Sundays, and legal holidays are included in counting these added three days. If the third day is a Saturday, Sunday, or legal holiday, the last day to act is the next day that is not a Saturday, Sunday, or legal holiday. The effect of invoking the day when the prescribed period would otherwise expire under Rule 6(a) can be illustrated by assuming that the thirtieth day of a thirty-day period is a Saturday. Under Rule 6(a) the period expires on the next day that is not a Sunday or legal holiday. If the following Monday is a legal holiday, under Rule 6(a) the period expires on Tuesday. Three days are then added—Wednesday, Thursday, and Friday as the third and final day to act. If the period prescribed expires on a Friday, the three added days are Saturday, Sunday, and Monday, which is the third and final day to act unless it is a legal holiday. If Monday is a legal holiday, the next day that is not a legal holiday is the third and final day to act.

[¶2] Application of Rule 6(e) to a period that is less than eleven days can be illustrated by a paper that is served by mailing on a Friday. If ten days are allowed to respond, intermediate Saturdays, Sundays, and legal holidays are excluded in determining when the period expires under Rule 6(a). If there is no legal holiday, the period expires on the Friday two weeks after the paper was mailed. The three added Rule 6(e) days are Saturday, Sunday, and Monday, which is the third and final day to act unless it is a legal holiday. If Monday is a legal holiday, the next day that is not a legal holiday is the final day to act.

FRCP 6 – 2001 NOTES OF ADVISORY COMMITTEE

[¶1] The additional three days provided by Rule 6(e) is extended to the means of service authorized by the new paragraph (D) added to Rule 5(b), including—with the consent of the person served—service by electronic or other means. The three-day addition is provided as well for service on a person with no known address by leaving a copy with the clerk of the court.

FRCP 7 – 2007 NOTES OF ADVISORY COMMITTEE

[¶1] Former Rule 7(a) stated that "there shall be * * * an answer to a cross-claim, if the answer contains a cross-claim * * *." Former Rule 12(a)(2) provided more generally that "[a] party served with a pleading stating a cross-claim against that party shall serve an answer thereto * * *." New Rule 7(a) corrects this inconsistency by providing for an answer to a crossclaim.

[¶2] For the first time, Rule 7(a)(7) expressly authorizes the court to order a reply to a counterclaim answer. A reply may be as useful in this setting as a reply to an answer, a third-party answer, or a crossclaim answer.

[¶3] Former Rule 7(b)(1) stated that the writing requirement is fulfilled if the motion is stated in a written notice of hearing. This statement was deleted as redundant because a single written document can satisfy the writing requirements both for a motion and for a Rule 6(c)(1) notice.

[¶4] The cross-reference to Rule 11 in former Rule 7(b)(3) is deleted as redundant. Rule 11 applies by its own terms. The force and application of Rule 11 are not diminished by the deletion.

[¶5] Former Rule 7(c) is deleted because it has done its work. If a motion or pleading is described as a demurrer, plea, or exception for insufficiency, the court will treat the paper as if properly captioned.

FRCP 7.1 – 2002 NOTES OF ADVISORY COMMITTEE

[¶1] Rule 7.1 is drawn from Rule 26.1 of the Federal Rules of Appellate Procedure, with changes to adapt to the circumstances of district courts that dictate different provisions for the time of filing, number of copies, and the like. The information required by Rule 7.1(a) reflects the "financial interest" standard of Canon 3C(1)(c) of the Code of Conduct for United States Judges. This information will support properly informed disqualification decisions in situations that call for automatic disqualification under Canon 3C(1)(c). It does not cover all of the circumstances that may call for disqualification under the financial interest standard, and does not deal at all with other circumstances that may call for disqualification.

[¶2] Although the disclosures required by Rule 7.1(a) may seem limited, they are calculated to reach a majority of the circumstances that are likely to call for disqualification on the basis of financial information that a judge may not know or recollect. Framing a rule that calls for more detailed disclosure will be difficult. Unnecessary disclosure requirements place a burden on the parties and on courts. Unnecessary disclosure of volumes of information may create a risk that a judge will overlook the one bit of information that might require disqualification, and also may create a risk that unnecessary disqualifications will be made rather than attempt to unravel a potentially difficult question. It has not been feasible to dictate more detailed disclosure requirements in Rule 7.1(a).

[¶3] Rule 7.1 does not prohibit local rules that require disclosures in addition to those required by Rule 7.1. Developing experience with local disclosure practices and advances in electronic technology may provide a foundation for adopting more detailed disclosure requirements by future amendments of Rule 7.1.

FRCP 8 – 2010 NOTES OF ADVISORY COMMITTEE

[¶1] Subdivision (c)(1). "[D]ischarge in bankruptcy" is deleted from the list of affirmative defenses. Under 11 U.S.C. §524(a)(1) and (2) a discharge voids a judgment to the extent that it determines a personal liability of the debtor with respect to a discharged debt. The discharge also operates as an injunction against commencement or continuation of an action to collect, recover, or offset a discharged debt. For these reasons it is confusing to describe discharge as an affirmative defense. But §524(a) applies only to a claim that was actually discharged. Several categories of debt set out in 11 U.S.C. §523(a) are excepted from discharge. The issue whether a claim was excepted from discharge may be determined either in the court that entered the discharge or—in most instances—in another court with jurisdiction over the creditor's claim.

FRCP 8 – 2007 NOTES OF ADVISORY COMMITTEE

[¶1] The former Rule 8(b) and 8(e) cross-references to Rule 11 are deleted as redundant. Rule 11 applies by its own terms. The force and application of Rule 11 are not diminished by the deletion.

[¶2] Former Rule 8(b) required a pleader denying part of an averment to "specify so much of it as is true and material and * * * deny only the remainder." "[A]nd material" is deleted to avoid the implication that it is proper to deny something that the pleader believes to be true but not material.

[¶3] Deletion of former Rule 8(e)(2)'s "whether based on legal, equitable, or maritime grounds" reflects the parallel deletions in Rule 1 and elsewhere. Merger is now successfully accomplished.

FRCP 9 – 2007 NOTES OF ADVISORY COMMITTEE

[¶1] Rule 15 governs pleading amendments of its own force. The former redundant statement that Rule 15 governs an amendment that adds or withdraws a Rule 9(h) designation as an admiralty or maritime claim is deleted. The elimination of paragraph (2) means that "(3)" will be redesignated as "(2)" in Style Rule 9(h).

FRCP 9 – 2006 NOTES OF ADVISORY COMMITTEE

[¶1] Rule 9(h) is amended to conform to the changed title of the Supplemental Rules.

FRCP 11 – 2007 NOTES OF ADVISORY COMMITTEE

[¶1] Providing an e-mail address is useful, but does not of itself signify consent to filing or service by e-mail.

FRCP 11 – 1993 NOTES OF ADVISORY COMMITTEE

[¶1] Purpose of revision. This revision is intended to remedy problems that have arisen in the interpretation and application of the 1983 revision of the rule. For empirical examination of experience under the 1983 rule, *see, e.g.*, New York State Bar Committee on Federal Courts, Sanctions and Attorneys' Fees (1987); T. Willging, The Rule 11 Sanctioning Process (1989); American Judicature Society, Report of the Third Circuit Task Force on Federal Rule of Civil Procedure 11 (S. Burbank ed., 1989); E. Wiggins, T. Willging, and D. Stienstra, Report on Rule 11 (Federal Judicial Center 1991). For book-length analyses of the case law, see G. Joseph, Sanctions: The Federal Law of Litigation Abuse (1989); J. Solovy, The Federal Law of Sanctions (1991); G. Vairo, Rule 11 Sanctions: Case Law Perspectives and Preventive Measures (1991).

[¶2] The rule retains the principle that attorneys and pro se litigants have an obligation to the court to refrain from conduct that frustrates the aims of Rule 1. The revision broadens the scope of this obligation, but places greater constraints on the imposition of sanctions and should reduce the number of motions for sanctions presented to the court. New subdivision (d) removes from the ambit of this rule all discovery requests, responses, objections, and motions subject to the provisions of Rule 26 through 37.

[¶3] **Subdivision (a).** Retained in this subdivision are the provisions requiring signatures on pleadings, written motions, and other papers. Unsigned papers are to be received by the Clerk, but then are to be stricken if the omission of the signature is not corrected promptly after being called to the attention of the attorney or pro se litigant. Correction can be made by signing the paper on file or by submitting a duplicate that contains the signature. A court may require by local rule that papers contain additional identifying information regarding the parties or attorneys, such as telephone numbers to facilitate facsimile transmissions, though, as for omission of a signature, the paper should not be rejected for failure to provide such information.

[¶4] The sentence in the former rule relating to the effect of answers under oath is no longer needed and has been eliminated. The provision in the former rule that signing a paper constitutes a certificate that it has been read by the signer also has been eliminated as unnecessary. The obligations imposed under subdivision (b) obviously require that a pleading, written motion, or other paper be read before it is filed or submitted to the court.

[¶5] **Subdivisions (b) and (c).** These subdivisions restate the provisions requiring attorneys and pro se litigants to conduct a reasonable inquiry into the law and facts before signing pleadings, written motions, and other documents, and prescribing sanctions for violation of these obligations. The revision in part expands the responsibilities of litigants to the court, while providing greater constraints and flexibility in dealing with infractions of the rule. The rule continues to require litigants to "stop-and-think" before initially making legal or factual contentions. It also, however, emphasizes the duty of candor by subjecting litigants to potential sanctions for insisting upon a position after it is no longer tenable and by generally providing protection against sanctions if they withdraw or correct contentions after a potential violation is called to their attention.

[¶6] The rule applies only to assertions contained in papers filed with or submitted to the court. It does not cover matters arising for the first time during oral presentations to the court, when counsel may make statements that would not have been made if there had been more time for study and reflection. However, a litigant's obligations with respect to the contents of these papers are not measured solely as of the time they are filed with or submitted to the court, but include reaffirming to the court and advocating positions contained in those pleadings and motions after learning that they cease to have any merit. For example, an attorney who during a pretrial conference insists on a claim or defense should be viewed as "presenting to the court" that contention and would be subject to the obligations of subdivision (b) measured as of that time. Similarly, if after a notice of removal is filed, a party urges in federal court the allegations of a pleading filed in state court (whether as claims, defenses, or in disputes regarding removal or remand), it would be viewed as "presenting"—and hence certifying to the district court under Rule 11—those allegations.

[¶7] The certification with respect to allegations and other factual contentions is revised in recognition that sometimes a litigant may have good reason to believe that a fact is true or false but may need discovery, formal or informal, from opposing parties or third persons to gather and confirm the evidentiary basis for the allegation. Tolerance of factual contentions in initial pleadings by plaintiffs or defendants when specifically identified as made on information and belief does not relieve litigants from the obligation to conduct an appropriate investigation into the facts that is reasonable under the circumstances; it is not a license to join parties, make claims, or present defenses without any factual basis or justification. Moreover, if evidentiary support is not obtained after a reasonable opportunity for further investigation or discovery, the party has a duty under the rule not to persist with that contention. Subdivision (b) does not require a formal amendment to pleadings for which evidentiary support is not obtained, but rather calls upon a litigant not thereafter to advocate such claims or defenses.

[¶8] The certification is that there is (or likely will be) "evidentiary support" for the allegation, not that the party will prevail with respect to its contention regarding the fact. That summary judgment is rendered against a party does not necessarily mean, for purposes of this certification, that it had no evidentiary support for its position. On the other hand, if a party has evidence with respect to a contention that would suffice to defeat a motion for summary judgment based thereon, it would have sufficient "evidentiary support" for purposes of Rule 11.

[¶9] Denials of factual contentions involve somewhat different considerations. Often, of course, a denial is premised upon the existence of evidence contradicting the alleged fact. At other times a denial is permissible because, after an appropriate investigation, a party has no information concerning the matter or, indeed, has a reasonable basis for doubting the credibility of the only evidence relevant to the matter. A party should not deny an allegation it knows to be true; but it is not required, simply because it lacks contradictory evidence, to admit an allegation that it believes is not true.

[¶10] The changes in subdivisions (b)(3) and (b)(4) will serve to equalize the burden of the rule upon plaintiffs and defendants, who under Rule 8(b) are in effect allowed to deny allegations by stating that from their initial investigation they lack sufficient information to form a belief as to the truth of the allegation. If, after further investigation or discovery, a denial is no longer warranted, the defendant should not

continue to insist on that denial. While sometimes helpful, formal amendment of the pleadings to withdraw an allegation or denial is not required by subdivision (b).

[¶11] Arguments for extensions, modifications, or reversals of existing law or for creation of new law do not violate subdivision (b)(2) provided they are "nonfrivolous." This establishes an objective standard, intended to eliminate any "empty-head pure-heart" justification for patently frivolous arguments. However, the extent to which a litigant has researched the issues and found some support for its theories even in minority opinions, in law review articles, or through consultation with other attorneys should certainly be taken into account in determining whether paragraph (2) has been violated. Although arguments for a change of law are not required to be specifically so identified, a contention that is so identified should be viewed with greater tolerance under the rule.

[¶12] The court has available a variety of possible sanctions to impose for violations, such as striking the offending paper; issuing an admonition, reprimand, or censure; requiring participation in seminars or other educational programs; ordering a fine payable to the court; referring the matter to disciplinary authorities (or, in the case of government attorneys, to the Attorney General, Inspector General, or agency head), etc. See Manual for Complex Litigation, Second, §42.3. The rule does not attempt to enumerate the factors a court should consider in deciding whether to impose a sanction or what sanctions would be appropriate in the circumstances; but, for emphasis, it does specifically note that a sanction may be nonmonetary as well as monetary. Whether the improper conduct was willful, or negligent; whether it was part of a pattern of activity, or an isolated event; whether it infected the entire pleading, or only one particular count or defense; whether the person has engaged in similar conduct in other litigation; whether it was intended to injure; what effect it had on the litigation process in time or expense; whether the responsible person is trained in the law; what amount, given the financial resources of the responsible person, is needed to deter that person from repetition in the same case; what amount is needed to deter similar activity by other litigants: all of these may in a particular case be proper considerations. The court has significant discretion in determining what sanctions, if any, should be imposed for a violation, subject to the principle that the sanctions should not be more severe than reasonably necessary to deter repetition of the conduct by the offending person or comparable conduct by similarly situated persons.

[¶13] Since the purpose of Rule 11 sanctions is to deter rather than to compensate, the rule provides that, if a monetary sanction is imposed, it should ordinarily be paid into court as a penalty. However, under unusual circumstances, particularly for [subdivision] (b)(1) violations, deterrence may be ineffective unless the sanction not only requires the person violating the rule to make a monetary payment, but also directs that some or all of this payment be made to those injured by the violation. Accordingly, the rule authorizes the court, if requested in a motion and if so warranted, to award attorney's fees to another party. Any such award to another party, however, should not exceed the expenses and attorneys' fees for the services directly and unavoidably caused by the violation of the certification requirement. If, for example, a wholly unsupportable count were included in a multi-count complaint or counterclaim for the purpose of needlessly increasing the cost of litigation to an impecunious adversary, any award of expenses should be limited to those directly caused by inclusion of the improper count, and not those resulting from the filing of the complaint or answer itself. The award should not provide compensation for services that could have been avoided by an earlier disclosure of evidence or an earlier challenge to the groundless claims or defenses. Moreover, partial reimbursement of fees may constitute a sufficient deterrent with respect to violations by persons having modest financial resources. In cases brought under statutes providing for fees to be awarded to prevailing parties, the court should not employ cost-shifting under this rule in a manner that would be inconsistent with the standards that govern the statutory award of fees, such as stated in *Christiansburg Garment Co. v. EEOC*, 434 U.S. 412 (1978).

[¶14] The sanction should be imposed on the persons—whether attorneys, law firms, or parties—who have violated the rule or who may be determined to be responsible for the violation. The person signing, filing, submitting, or advocating a document has a nondelegable responsibility to the court, and in most situations should be sanctioned for a violation. Absent exceptional circumstances, a law firm is to be held also responsible when, as a result of a motion under subdivision (c)(1)(A), one of its partners, associates, or employees is determined to have violated the rule. Since such a motion may be filed only if the offending paper is not withdrawn or corrected within 21 days after service of the motion, it is appropriate that the law firm ordinarily be viewed as jointly responsible under established principles of agency. This provision is designed to remove the restrictions of the former rule. *Cf. Pavelic & LeFlore v. Marvel Entertainment Group*, 493 U.S. 120 (1989) (1983 version of Rule 11 does not permit sanctions against law firm of attorney signing groundless complaint).

[¶15] The revision permits the court to consider whether other attorneys in the firm, co-counsel, other law firms, or the party itself should be held accountable for their part in causing a violation. When appropriate, the court can make an additional inquiry in order to determine whether the sanction should be imposed on such persons, firms, or parties either in addition to or, in unusual circumstances, instead of the person actually making the presentation to the court. For example, such an inquiry may be appropriate in cases involving governmental agencies or other institutional parties that frequently impose substantial restrictions on the discretion of individual attorneys employed by it.

[¶16] Sanctions that involve monetary awards (such as a fine or an award of attorney's fees) may not be imposed on a represented party for violations of subdivision (b)(2), involving frivolous contentions of law. Monetary responsibility for such violations is more properly placed solely on the party's attorneys. With this limitation, the rule should not be subject to attack under the Rules Enabling Act. *See Willy v. Coastal Corp.*, [503 U.S. 131, 112 S.Ct. 1076] (1992); *Business Guides, Inc. v. Chromatic Communications Enter. Inc.*, [498 U.S. 533, 111 S.Ct. 922] (1991). This restriction does not limit the court's power to impose sanctions or remedial orders that may have collateral financial consequences upon a party, such as dismissal of a claim, preclusion of a defense, or preparation of amended pleadings.

[¶17] Explicit provision is made for litigants to be provided notice of the alleged violation and an opportunity to respond before sanctions are imposed. Whether the matter should be decided solely on the basis of written submissions or should be scheduled for oral argument (or, indeed, for evidentiary presentation) will depend on the circumstances. If the court imposes a sanction, it must, unless waived, indicate its reasons in a written order or on the record; the court should not ordinarily have to explain its denial of a motion for sanctions. Whether a violation has occurred and what sanctions, if any, to impose for a violation are matters committed to the discretion of the trial court; accordingly, as under current law, the standard for appellate review of these decisions will be for abuse of discretion. *See Cooter & Gell v. Hartmarx Corp.*, 496 U.S. 384 (1990) (noting, however, that an abuse would be established if the court based its ruling on an erroneous view of the law or on a clearly erroneous assessment of the evidence).

[¶18] The revision leaves for resolution on a case-by-case basis, considering the particular circumstances involved, the question as to when a motion for violation of Rule 11 should be served and when, if filed, it should be decided. Ordinarily the motion should be served promptly after the inappropriate paper is filed, and, if delayed too long, may be viewed as untimely. In other circumstances, it should not be served until the other party has had a reasonable opportunity for discovery. Given the "safe harbor" provisions discussed below, a party cannot delay serving its Rule 11 motion until conclusion of the case (or judicial rejection of the offending contention).

[¶19] Rule 11 motions should not be made or threatened for minor, inconsequential violations of the standards prescribed by subdivision (b). They should not be employed as a discovery device or to test the legal sufficiency or efficacy of allegations in the pleadings; other motions are available for those purposes. Nor should Rule 11 motions be prepared to emphasize the merits of a party's position, to exact an unjust settlement, to intimidate an adversary into withdrawing contentions that are fairly debatable, to increase the costs of litigation, to create a conflict of interest between attorney and client, or to seek disclosure of matters otherwise protected by the attorney-client privilege or the work-product doctrine. As under the prior rule, the court may defer its ruling (or its decision as to the identity of the persons to be sanctioned) until final resolution of the case in order to avoid immediate conflicts of interest and to reduce the disruption created if a disclosure of attorney-client communications is needed to determine whether a violation occurred or to identify the person responsible for the violation.

[¶20] The rule provides that requests for sanctions must be made as a separate motion, *i.e.*, not simply included as an additional prayer for relief contained in another motion. The motion for sanctions is not, however, to be filed until at least 21 days (or such other period as the court may set) after being served. If, during this period, the alleged violation is corrected, as by withdrawing (whether formally or informally) some allegation or contention, the motion should not be filed with the court. These provisions are intended to provide a type of "safe harbor" against motions under Rule 11 in that a party will not be subject to sanctions on the basis of another party's motion unless, after receiving the motion, it refuses to withdraw that position or to acknowledge candidly that it does not currently have evidence to support a specified allegation. Under the former rule, parties were sometimes reluctant to abandon a questionable contention lest that be viewed as evidence of a violation of Rule 11; under the revision, the timely withdrawal of a contention will protect a party against a motion for sanctions.

[¶21] To stress the seriousness of a motion for sanctions and to define precisely the conduct claimed to violate the rule, the revision provides that the "safe harbor" period begins to run only upon service of the motion. In most cases, however, counsel should be expected to give informal notice to the other party, whether in person or by a telephone call or letter, of a potential violation before proceeding to prepare and serve a Rule 11 motion.

[¶22] As under former Rule 11, the filing of a motion for sanctions is itself subject to the requirements of the rule and can lead to sanctions. However, service of a cross motion under Rule 11 should rarely be needed since under the revision the court may award to the person who prevails on a motion under Rule 11—whether the movant or the target of the motion—reasonable expenses, including attorney's fees, incurred in presenting or opposing the motion.

[¶23] The power of the court to act on its own initiative is retained, but with the condition that this be done through a show cause order. This procedure provides the person with notice and an opportunity to respond. The revision provides that a monetary sanction imposed after a court-initiated show cause order be limited to a penalty payable to the court and that it be imposed only if the show cause order is issued before any voluntary dismissal or an agreement of the parties to settle the claims made by or against the litigant. Parties settling a case should not be subsequently faced with an unex-

pected order from the court leading to monetary sanctions that might have affected their willingness to settle or voluntarily dismiss a case. Since show cause orders will ordinarily be issued only in situations that are akin to a contempt of court, the rule does not provide a "safe harbor" to a litigant for withdrawing a claim, defense, etc., after a show cause order has been issued on the court's own initiative. Such corrective action, however, should be taken into account in deciding what sanction to impose if, after consideration of the litigant's response, the court concludes that a violation has occurred.

[¶24] Subdivision (d). Rules 26(g) and 37 establish certification standards and sanctions that apply to discovery disclosures, requests, responses, objections, and motions. It is appropriate that Rules 26 through 37, which are specially designed for the discovery process, govern such documents and conduct rather than the more general provisions of Rule 11. Subdivision (d) has been added to accomplish this result.

[¶25] Rule 11 is not the exclusive source for control of improper presentations of claims, defenses, or contentions. It does not supplant statutes permitting awards of attorney's fees to prevailing parties or alter the principles governing such awards. It does not inhibit the court in punishing for contempt, in exercising its inherent powers, or in imposing sanctions, awarding expenses, or directing remedial action authorized under other rules or under 28 U.S.C. §1927. *See Chambers v. NASCO*, [501 U.S. 32, 111 S.Ct. 2123] (1991). Chambers cautions, however, against reliance upon inherent powers if appropriate sanctions can be imposed under provisions such as Rule 11, and the procedures specified in Rule 11—notice, opportunity to respond, and findings—should ordinarily be employed when imposing a sanction under the court's inherent powers. Finally, it should be noted that Rule 11 does not preclude a party from initiating an independent action for malicious prosecution or abuse of process.

FRCP 12 – 2009 NOTES OF ADVISORY COMMITTEE

[¶1] The times set in the former rule at 10 or 20 days have been revised to 14 or 21 days. See the Note to Rule 6.[1]

1. **Editor's note:** The cross-reference to "Note to Rule 6" refers to 2009 Notes to FRCP 6 at ¶¶1-20, p. 1149, this book.

FRCP 12 – 2007 NOTES OF ADVISORY COMMITTEE

[¶1] Former Rule 12(a)(4)(A) referred to an order that postpones disposition of a motion "until the trial on the merits." Rule 12(a)(4) now refers to postponing disposition "until trial." The new expression avoids the ambiguity that inheres in "trial on the merits," which may become confusing when there is a separate trial of a single issue or another event different from a single all-encompassing trial.

FRCP 12 – 2000 NOTES OF ADVISORY COMMITTEE

[¶1] Rule 12(a)(3)(B) is added to complement the addition of Rule 4(i)(2)(B). The purposes that underlie the requirement that service be made on the United States in an action that asserts individual liability of a United States officer or employee for acts occurring in connection with the performance of duties on behalf of the United States also require that the time to answer be extended to 60 days. Time is needed for the United States to determine whether to provide representation to the defendant officer or employee. If the United States provides representation, the need for an extended answer period is the same as in actions against the United States, a United States agency, or a United States officer sued in an official capacity.

[¶2] An action against a former officer or employee of the United States is covered by subparagraph (3)(B) in the same way as an action against a present officer or employee. Termination of the relationship between the individual defendant and the United States does not reduce the need for additional time to answer.

FRCP 13 – 2009 NOTES OF ADVISORY COMMITTEE

[¶1] Rule 13(f) is deleted as largely redundant and potentially misleading. An amendment to add a counterclaim will be governed by Rule 15. Rule 15(a)(1) permits some amendments to be made as a matter of course or with the opposing party's written consent. When the court's leave is required, the reasons described in Rule 13(f) for permitting amendment of a pleading to add an omitted counterclaim sound different from the general amendment standard in Rule 15(a)(2), but seem to be administered—as they should be—according to the same standard directing that leave should be freely given when justice so requires. The independent existence of Rule 13(f) has, however, created some uncertainty as to the availability of relation back of the amendment under Rule 15(c). *See 6 C. Wright, A. Miller & M. Kane, Federal Practice & Procedure: Civil 2d, §1430 (1990)*. Deletion of Rule 13(f) ensures that relation back is governed by the tests that apply to all other pleading amendments.

FRCP 13 – 2007 NOTES OF ADVISORY COMMITTEE

[¶1] The meaning of former Rule 13(b) is better expressed by deleting "not arising out of the transaction or occurrence that is the subject matter of the opposing party's claim." Both as a matter of intended meaning and current practice, a party may state as a permissive counterclaim a claim that does grow out of the same transaction or occurrence as an opposing party's claim even though one of the exceptions in Rule 13(a) means the claim is not a compulsory counterclaim.

FRCP 14 – 2009 NOTES OF ADVISORY COMMITTEE

[¶1] The time set in the former rule at 10 days has been revised to 14 days. See the Note to Rule 6.[1]

1. **Editor's note:** The cross-reference to "Note to Rule 6" refers to 2009 Notes to FRCP 6 at ¶¶1-20, p. 1149, this book.

FRCP 14 – 2007 NOTES OF ADVISORY COMMITTEE

[¶1] Former Rule 14 twice refers to counterclaims under Rule 13. In each case, the operation of Rule 13(a) depends on the state of the action at the time the pleading is filed. If plaintiff and third-party defendant have become opposing parties because one has made a claim for relief against the other, Rule 13(a) requires assertion of any counterclaim that grows out of the transaction or occurrence that is the subject matter of that claim. Rules 14(a)(2)(B) and (a)(3) reflect the distinction between compulsory and permissive counterclaims.

[¶2] A plaintiff should be on equal footing with the defendant in making third-party claims, whether the claim against the plaintiff is asserted as a counterclaim or as another form of claim. The limit imposed by the former reference to "counterclaim" is deleted.

FRCP 14 – 2006 NOTES OF ADVISORY COMMITTEE

[¶1] Rule 14 is amended to conform to changes in designating the paragraphs of Supplemental Rule C(6).

FRCP 14 – 2000 NOTES OF ADVISORY COMMITTEE

[¶1] Subdivisions (a) and (c) are amended to reflect revisions in Supplemental Rule C(6).

FRCP 15 – 2009 NOTES OF ADVISORY COMMITTEE

[¶1] Rule 15(a)(1) is amended to make three changes in the time allowed to make one amendment as a matter of course.

[¶2] Former Rule 15(a) addressed amendment of a pleading to which a responsive pleading is required by distinguishing between the means used to challenge the pleading. Serving a responsive pleading terminated the right to amend. Serving a motion attacking the pleading did not terminate the right to amend, because a motion is not a "pleading" as defined in Rule 7. The right to amend survived beyond decision of the motion unless the decision expressly cut off the right to amend.

[¶3] The distinction drawn in former Rule 15(a) is changed in two ways. First, the right to amend once as a matter of course terminates 21 days after service of a motion under Rule 12(b), (e), or (f). This provision will force the pleader to consider carefully and promptly the wisdom of amending to meet the arguments in the motion. A responsive amendment may avoid the need to decide the motion or reduce the number of issues to be decided, and will expedite determination of issues that otherwise might be raised seriatim. It also should advance other pretrial proceedings.

[¶4] Second, the right to amend once as a matter of course is no longer terminated by service of a responsive pleading. The responsive pleading may point out issues that the original pleader had not considered and persuade the pleader that amendment is wise. Just as amendment was permitted by former Rule 15(a) in response to a motion, so the amended rule permits one amendment as a matter of course in response to a responsive pleading. The right is subject to the same 21-day limit as the right to amend in response to a motion.

[¶5] The 21-day periods to amend once as a matter of course after service of a responsive pleading or after service of a designated motion are not cumulative. If a responsive pleading is served after one of the designated motions is served, for example, there is no new 21-day period.

[¶6] Finally, amended Rule 15(a)(1) extends from 20 to 21 days the period to amend a pleading to which no responsive pleading is allowed and omits the provision that cuts off the right if the action is on the trial calendar. Rule 40 no longer refers to a trial calendar, and many courts have abandoned formal trial calendars. It is more effective to rely on scheduling orders or other pretrial directions to establish time limits for amendment in the few situations that otherwise might allow one amendment as a matter of course at a time that would disrupt trial preparations. Leave to amend still can be sought under Rule 15(a)(2), or at and after trial under Rule 15(b). Amended Rule 15(a)(3) extends from 10 to 14 days the period to respond to an amended pleading.

[¶7] Abrogation of Rule 13(f) establishes Rule 15 as the sole rule governing amendment of a pleading to add a counterclaim.

[¶8] The times set in the former rule at 10 or 20 days have been revised to 14 or 21 days. See the Note to Rule 6.[1]

1. **Editor's note:** The cross-reference to "Note to Rule 6" refers to 2009 Notes to FRCP 6 at ¶¶1-20, p. 1149, this book.

FRCP 15 – 2007 NOTES OF ADVISORY COMMITTEE

[¶1] Former Rule 15(c)(3)(A) called for notice of the "institution" of the action. Rule 15(c)(1)(C)(i) omits the reference to "institution" as potentially confusing. What counts is that the party to be brought in have notice of the existence of the action, whether or not the notice includes details as to its "institution."

FRCP 15 – 1963 NOTES OF ADVISORY COMMITTEE

[¶1] Rule 15(d) is intended to give the court broad discretion in allowing a supplemental pleading. However, some cases, opposed by other cases and criticized by the commentators, have taken the rigid and formalistic view that where the original complaint fails to state a claim upon which relief can be granted, leave to serve a supplemental complaint must be denied. *See Bonner v. Elizabeth Arden, Inc.*, 177 F.2d 703 (2d Cir.1949); *Bowles v. Senderowitz*, 65 F.Supp. 548 (E.D.Pa.), *rev'd on other grounds*, 158 F.2d 435 (3d Cir.1946), *cert. denied*, *Senderowitz v. Fleming*, 330 U.S. 848, 67 S.Ct. 1091, 91 L.Ed. 1292 (1947); *cf. LaSalle Nat. Bank v. 222 East*

Chestnut St. Corp., 267 F.2d 247 (7th Cir.), *cert. denied*, 361 U.S. 836, 80 S.Ct. 88, 4 L.Ed.2d 77 (1959). *But see Camilla Cotton Oil Co. v. Spencer Kellogg & Sons*, 257 F.2d 162 (5th Cir.1958); *Genuth v. National Biscuit Co.*, 81 F.Supp. 213 (S.D. N.Y.1948), *app. dism.*, 177 F.2d 962 (2d Cir.1949); 3 Moore's Federal Practice §15.01 [5] (Supp. 1960); 1A Barron & Holtzoff, Federal Practice & Procedure 820-21 (Wright ed. 1960). Thus plaintiffs have sometimes been needlessly remitted to the difficulties of commencing a new action even though events occurring after the commencement of the original action have made clear the right to relief.

[¶2] Under the amendment the court has discretion to permit a supplemental pleading despite the fact that the original pleading is defective. As in other situations where a supplemental pleading is offered, the court is to determine in the light of the particular circumstances whether filing should be permitted, and if so, upon what terms. The amendment does not attempt to deal with such questions as the relation of the statute of limitations to supplemental pleadings, the operation of the doctrine of laches, or the availability of other defenses. All these questions are for decision in accordance with the principles applicable to supplemental pleadings generally. *Cf. Blau v. Lamb*, 191 F.Supp. 906 (S.D. N.Y.1961); *Lendonsol Amusement Corp. v. B. & Q. Assoc., Inc.*, 23 F.R.Serv. 15d. 3, Case 1 (D. Mass.1957).

FRCP 16 – 2007 NOTES OF ADVISORY COMMITTEE

[¶1] When a party or its representative is not present, it is enough to be reasonably available by any suitable means, whether telephone or other communication device.

FRCP 16 – 2006 NOTES OF ADVISORY COMMITTEE

[¶1] The amendment to Rule 16(b) is designed to alert the court to the possible need to address the handling of discovery of electronically stored information early in the litigation if such discovery is expected to occur. Rule 26(f) is amended to direct the parties to discuss discovery of electronically stored information if such discovery is contemplated in the action. Form 35 is amended to call for a report to the court about the results of this discussion. In many instances, the court's involvement early in the litigation will help avoid difficulties that might otherwise arise.

[¶2] Rule 16(b) is also amended to include among the topics that may be addressed in the scheduling order any agreements that the parties reach to facilitate discovery by minimizing the risk of waiver of privilege or work-product protection. Rule 26(f) is amended to add to the discovery plan the parties' proposal for the court to enter a case-management or other order adopting such an agreement. The parties may agree to various arrangements. For example, they may agree to initial provision of requested materials without waiver of privilege or protection to enable the party seeking production to designate the materials desired or protection for actual production, with the privilege review of only those materials to follow. Alternatively, they may agree that if privileged or protected information is inadvertently produced, the producing party may by timely notice assert the privilege or protection and obtain return of the materials without waiver. Other arrangements are possible. In most circumstances, a party who receives information under such an arrangement cannot assert that production of the information waived a claim of privilege or of protection as trial-preparation material.

[¶3] An order that includes the parties' agreement may be helpful in avoiding delay and excessive cost in discovery. *See Manual for Complex Litigation* (4th) §11.446. Rule 16(b)(6) recognizes the propriety of including such agreements in the court's order. The rule does not provide the court with authority to enter such a case-management or other order without party agreement, or limit the court's authority to act on motion.

FRCP 16 – 1993 NOTES OF ADVISORY COMMITTEE

[¶1] Subdivision (b). One purpose of this amendment is to provide a more appropriate deadline for the initial scheduling order required by the rule. The former rule directed that the order be entered within 120 days from the filing of the complaint. This requirement has created problems because Rule 4(m) allows 120 days for service and ordinarily at least one defendant should be available to participate in the process of formulating the scheduling order. The revision provides that the order is to be entered within 90 days after the date a defendant first appears (whether by answer or by a motion under Rule 12) or, if earlier (as may occur in some actions against the United States or if service is waived under Rule 4), within 120 days after service of the complaint on a defendant. The longer time provided by the revision is not intended to encourage unnecessary delays in entering the scheduling order. Indeed, in most cases the order can and should be entered at a much earlier date. Rather, the additional time is intended to alleviate problems in multi-defendant cases and should ordinarily be adequate to enable participation by all defendants initially named in the action.

[¶2] In many cases the scheduling order can and should be entered before this deadline. However, when setting a scheduling conference, the court should take into account the effect this setting will have in establishing deadlines for the parties to meet under revised Rule 26(f) and to exchange information under revised Rule 26(a)(1). While the parties are expected to stipulate to additional time for making their disclosures when warranted by the circumstances, a scheduling conference held before defendants have had time to learn much about the case may result in diminishing the value of the Rule 26(f) meeting, the parties' proposed discovery plan, and indeed the conference itself.

[¶3] New paragraph (4) has been added to highlight that it will frequently be desirable for the scheduling order to include provisions relating to the timing of disclosures under Rule 26(a). While the initial disclosures required by Rule 26(a)(1) will ordinarily have been made before entry of the scheduling order, the timing and sequence for disclosure of expert testimony and of the witnesses and exhibits to be used at trial should be tailored to the circumstances of the case and is a matter that should be considered at the initial scheduling conference. Similarly, the scheduling order might contain provisions modifying the extent of discovery (*e.g.*, number and length of depositions) otherwise permitted under these rules or by a local rule.

[¶4] The report from the attorneys concerning their meeting and proposed discovery plan, as required by revised Rule 26(f), should be submitted to the court before the scheduling order is entered. Their proposals, particularly regarding matters on which they agree, should be of substantial value to the court in setting the timing and limitations on discovery and should reduce the time of the court needed to conduct a meaningful conference under Rule 16(b). As under the prior rule, while a scheduling order is mandated, a scheduling conference is not. However, in view of the benefits to be derived from the litigants and a judicial officer meeting in person, a Rule 16(b) conference should, to the extent practicable, be held in all cases that will involve discovery.

[¶5] This subdivision, as well as subdivision (c)(8), also is revised to reflect the new title of United States Magistrate Judges pursuant to the Judicial Improvements Act of 1990.

[¶6] Subdivision (c). The primary purposes of the changes in subdivision (c) are to call attention to the opportunities for structuring of trial under Rules 42, 50, and 52 and to eliminate questions that have occasionally been raised regarding the authority of the court to make appropriate orders designed either to facilitate settlement or to provide for an efficient and economical trial. The prefatory language of this subdivision is revised to clarify the court's power to enter appropriate orders at a conference notwithstanding the objection of a party. Of course settlement is dependent upon agreement by the parties and, indeed, a conference is most effective and productive when the parties participate in a spirit of cooperation and mindful of their responsibilities under Rule 1.

[¶7] Paragraph (4) is revised to clarify that in advance of trial the court may address the need for, and possible limitations on, the use of expert testimony under Rule 702 of the Federal Rules of Evidence. Even when proposed expert testimony might be admissible under the standards of Rules 403 and 702 of the evidence rules, the court may preclude or limit such testimony if the cost to the litigants—which may include the cost to adversaries of securing testimony on the same subjects by other experts—would be unduly expensive given the needs of the case and the other evidence available at trial.

[¶8] Paragraph (5) is added (and the remaining paragraphs renumbered) in recognition that use of Rule 56 to avoid or reduce the scope of trial is a topic that can, and often should, be considered at a pretrial conference. Renumbered paragraph (11) enables the court to rule on pending motions for summary adjudication that are ripe for decision at the time of the conference. Often, however, the potential use of Rule 56 is a matter that arises from discussions during a conference. The court may then call for motions to be filed.

[¶9] Paragraph (6) is added to emphasize that a major objective of pretrial conferences should be to consider appropriate controls on the extent and timing of discovery. In many cases the court should also specify the times and sequence for disclosure of written reports from experts under revised Rule 26(a)(2)(B) and perhaps direct changes in the types of experts from whom written reports are required. Consideration should also be given to possible changes in the timing or form of the disclosure of trial witnesses and documents under Rule 26(a)(3).

[¶10] Paragraph (9) is revised to describe more accurately the various procedures that, in addition to traditional settlement conferences, may be helpful in settling litigation. Even if a case cannot immediately be settled, the judge and attorneys can explore possible use of alternative procedures such as mini-trials, summary jury trials, mediation, neutral evaluation, and nonbinding arbitration that can lead to consensual resolution of the dispute without a full trial on the merits. The rule acknowledges the presence of statutes and local rules or plans that may authorize use of some of these procedures even when not agreed to by the parties. See 28 U.S.C. §§473(a)(6), 473(b)(4), 651-58; Section 104(b)(2), Pub.L. 101-650. The rule does not attempt to resolve questions as to the extent a court would be authorized to require such proceedings as an exercise of its inherent powers.

[¶11] The amendment of paragraph (9) should be read in conjunction with the sentence added to the end of subdivision (c), authorizing the court to direct that, in appropriate cases, a responsible representative of the parties be present or available by telephone during a conference in order to discuss possible settlement of the case. The sentence refers to participation by a party or its representative. Whether this would be the individual party, an officer of a corporate party, a representative from an insurance carrier, or someone else would depend on the circumstances. Particularly in litigation in which governmental agencies or large amounts of money are involved, there may be no one with on-the-spot settlement authority, and the most that should be expected is access to a person who would have a major role in submitting a recommendation to the body or board with ultimate decision-making responsibility. The selection of the appropriate representative should ordinarily be left to the party and its counsel. Finally, it should be noted that the unwillingness of a party to be available, even by telephone, for a settlement conference may be a clear signal that the time and expense involved in

pursuing settlement is likely to be unproductive and that personal participation by the parties should not be required.

[¶12] The explicit authorization in the rule to require personal participation in the manner stated is not intended to limit the reasonable exercise of the court's inherent powers, *e.g.*, *G. Heileman Brewing Co. v. Joseph Oat Corp.*, 871 F.2d 648 (7th Cir. 1989), or its power to require party participation under the Civil Justice Reform Act of 1990. See 28 U.S.C. §473(b)(5) (civil justice expense and delay reduction plans adopted by district courts may include requirement that representatives "with authority to bind [parties] in settlement discussions" be available during settlement conferences).

[¶13] New paragraphs (13) and (14) are added to call attention to the opportunities for structuring of trial under Rule 42 and under revised Rules 50 and 52.

[¶14] Paragraph (15) is also new. It supplements the power of the court to limit the extent of evidence under Rules 403 and 611(a) of the Federal Rules of Evidence, which typically would be invoked as a result of developments during trial. Limits on the length of trial established at a conference in advance of trial can provide the parties with a better opportunity to determine priorities and exercise selectivity in presenting evidence than when limits are imposed during trial. Any such limits must be reasonable under the circumstances, and ordinarily the court should impose them only after receiving appropriate submissions from the parties outlining the nature of the testimony expected to be presented through various witnesses, and the expected duration of direct and cross-examination.

FRCP 16 – 1983 NOTES OF ADVISORY COMMITTEE

[¶1] INTRODUCTION

[¶2] Rule 16 has not been amended since the Federal Rules were promulgated in 1938. In many respects, the rule has been a success. For example, there is evidence that pretrial conferences may improve the quality of justice rendered in the federal courts by sharpening the preparation and presentation of cases, tending to eliminate trial surprise, and improving, as well as facilitating, the settlement process. See 6 Wright & Miller, Federal Practice and Procedure: Civil §1522 (1971). However, in other respects particularly with regard to case management, the rule has not always been as helpful as it might have been. Thus there has been a widespread feeling that amendment is necessary to encourage pretrial management that meets the needs of modern litigation. See Report of the National Commission for the Review of Antitrust Laws and Procedures (1979).

[¶3] Major criticism of Rule 16 has centered on the fact that its application can result in over-regulation of some cases and under-regulation of others. In simple, run-of-the-mill cases, attorneys have found pretrial requirements burdensome. It is claimed that over-administration leads to a series of mini-trials that result in a waste of an attorney's time and needless expense to a client. Pollack, Pretrial Procedures More Effectively Handled, 65 F.R.D. 475 (1974). This is especially likely to be true when pretrial proceedings occur long before trial. At the other end of the spectrum, the discretionary character of Rule 16 and its orientation toward a single conference late in the pretrial process has led to under-administration of complex or protracted cases. Without judicial guidance beginning shortly after institution, these cases often become mired in discovery.

[¶4] Four sources of criticism of pretrial have been identified. First, conferences often are seen as a mere exchange of legalistic contentions without any real analysis of the particular case. Second, the result frequently is nothing but a formal agreement on minutiae. Third, the conferences are seen as unnecessary and time-consuming in cases that will be settled before trial. Fourth, the meetings can be ceremonial and ritualistic, having little effect on the trial and being of minimal value, particularly when the attorneys attending the sessions are not the ones who will try the case or lack authority to enter into binding stipulations. *See generally McCargo v. Hedrick*, 545 F.2d 393 (4th Cir. 1976); Pollack, Pretrial Procedures More Effectively Handled, 65 F.R.D. 475 (1974); Rosenberg, The Pretrial Conference and Effective Justice 45 (1964).

[¶5] There also have been difficulties with the pretrial orders that issue following Rule 16 conferences. When an order is entered far in advance of trial, some issues may not be properly formulated. Counsel naturally are cautious and often try to preserve as many options as possible. If the judge who tries the case did not conduct the conference, he could find it difficult to determine exactly what was agreed to at the conference. But any insistence on a detailed order may be too burdensome, depending on the nature or posture of the case.

[¶6] Given the significant changes in federal civil litigation since 1938 that are not reflected in Rule 16, it has been extensively rewritten and expanded to meet the challenges of modern litigation. Empirical studies reveal that when a trial judge intervenes personally at an early stage to assume judicial control over a case and to schedule dates for completion by the parties of the principal pretrial steps, the case is disposed of by settlement or trial more efficiently and with less cost and delay than when the parties are left to their own devices. Flanders, Case Management and Court Management in United States District Courts 17, Federal Judicial Center (1977). Thus, the rule mandates a pretrial scheduling order. However, although scheduling and pretrial conferences are encouraged in appropriate cases, they are not mandated.

[¶7] DISCUSSION

[¶8] **Subdivision (a); Pretrial Conferences; Objectives.** The amended rule makes scheduling and case management an express goal of pretrial procedure. This is done in Rule 16(a) by shifting the emphasis away from a conference focused solely on the trial and toward a process of judicial management that embraces the entire pretrial phase, especially motions and discovery. In addition, the amendment explicitly recognizes some of the objectives of pretrial conferences and the powers that many courts already have assumed. Rule 16 thus will be a more accurate reflection of actual practice.

[¶9] Subdivision (b); Scheduling and Planning. The most significant change in Rule 16 is the mandatory scheduling order described in Rule 16(b), which is based in part on Wisconsin Civil Procedure Rule 802.10. The idea of scheduling orders is not new. It has been used by many federal courts. *See, e.g.*, Southern District of Indiana, Local Rule 19.

[¶10] Although a mandatory scheduling order encourages the court to become involved in case management early in the litigation, it represents a degree of judicial involvement that is not warranted in many cases. Thus, subdivision (b) permits each district court to promulgate a local rule under Rule 83 exempting certain categories of cases in which the burdens of scheduling orders exceed the administrative efficiencies that would be gained. See Eastern District of Virginia, Local Rule 12(1). Logical candidates for this treatment include social security disability matters, habeas corpus petitions, forfeitures, and reviews of certain administrative actions.

[¶11] A scheduling conference may be requested either by the judge, a magistrate when authorized by district court rule, or a party within 120 days after the summons and complaint are filed. If a scheduling conference is not arranged within that time and the case is not exempted by local rule, a scheduling order must be issued under Rule 16(b), after some communication with the parties, which may be by telephone or mail rather than in person. The use of the term "judge" in subdivision (b) reflects the Advisory Committee's judgment that it is preferable that this task should be handled by a district judge rather than a magistrate, except when the magistrate is acting under 28 U.S.C. §636(c). While personal supervision by the trial judge is preferred, the rule, in recognition of the impracticality or difficulty of complying with such a requirement in some districts, authorizes a district by local rule to delegate the duties to a magistrate. In order to formulate a practicable scheduling order, the judge, or a magistrate when authorized by district court rule, and attorneys are required to develop a timetable for the matters listed in Rule 16(b)(1)-(3). As indicated in Rule 16(b)(4)-(5), the order may also deal with a wide range of other matters. The rule is phrased permissively as to clauses (4) and (5), however, because scheduling these items at an early point may not be feasible or appropriate. Even though subdivision (b) relates only to scheduling, there is no reason why some of the procedural matters listed in Rule 16(c) cannot be addressed at the same time, at least when a scheduling conference is held.

[¶12] Item (1) assures that at some point both the parties and the pleadings will be fixed, by setting a time within which joinder of parties shall be completed and the pleadings amended.

[¶13] Item (2) requires setting time limits for interposing various motions that otherwise might be used as stalling techniques.

[¶14] Item (3) deals with the problem of procrastination and delay by attorneys in a context in which scheduling is especially important—discovery. Scheduling the completion of discovery can serve some of the same functions as the conference described in Rule 26(f).

[¶15] Item (4) refers to setting dates for conferences and for trial. Scheduling multiple pretrial conferences may well be desirable if the case is complex and the court believes that a more elaborate pretrial structure, such as that described in the Manual for Complex Litigation, should be employed. On the other hand, only one pretrial conference may be necessary in an uncomplicated case.

[¶16] As long as the case is not exempted by local rule, the court must issue a written scheduling order even if no scheduling conference is called. The order, like pretrial orders under the former rule and those under new Rule 16(c), normally will "control the subsequent course of the action." See Rule 16(e). After consultation with the attorneys for the parties and any unrepresented parties—a formal motion is not necessary—the court may modify the schedule on a showing of good cause if it cannot reasonably be met despite the diligence of the party seeking the extension. Since the scheduling order is entered early in the litigation, this standard seems more appropriate than a "manifest injustice" or "substantial hardship" test. Otherwise, a fear that extensions will not be granted may encourage counsel to request the longest possible periods for completing pleading, joinder, and discovery. Moreover, changes in the court's calendar sometimes will oblige the judge or magistrate when authorized by district court rule to modify the scheduling order.

[¶17] The district courts undoubtedly will develop several prototype scheduling orders for different types of cases. In addition, when no formal conference is held, the court may obtain scheduling information by telephone, mail, or otherwise. In many instances this will result in a scheduling order better suited to the individual case than a standard order, without taking the time that would be required by a formal conference.

[¶18] Rule 16(b) assures that the judge will take some early control over the litigation, even when its character does not warrant holding a scheduling conference. Despite the fact that the process of preparing a scheduling order does not always bring the attorneys and judge together, the fixing of time limits serves "to stimulate litigants to narrow the areas of inquiry and advocacy to those they believe are truly relevant and material. Time limits not only compress the amount of time for litigation, they should also reduce the amount of resources invested in litigation. Litigants are forced to establish discovery priorities and thus to do the most important work first." Report of the National Commission for the Review of Antitrust Laws and Procedures 28 (1979).

[¶19] Thus, except in exempted cases, the judge or a magistrate when authorized by district court rule will have taken some action in every case within 120 days after the complaint is filed that notifies the attorneys that the case will be moving toward trial. Subdivision (b) is reenforced by subdivision (f), which makes it clear that the sanctions for violating a scheduling order are the same as those for violating a pretrial order.

[¶20] Subdivision (c); Subjects to be Discussed at Pretrial Conferences. This subdivision expands upon the list of things that may be discussed at a pretrial conference that appeared in original Rule 16. The intention is to encourage better planning and management of litigation. Increased judicial control during the pretrial process accelerates the processing and termination of cases. Flanders, Case Management and Court Management in United States District Courts, Federal Judicial Center (1977). See also Report of the National Commission for the Review of Antitrust Laws and Procedures (1979).

[¶21] The reference in Rule 16(c)(1) to "formulation" is intended to clarify and confirm the court's power to identify the litigable issues. It has been added in the hope of promoting efficiency and conserving judicial resources by identifying the real issues prior to trial, thereby saving time and expense for everyone. *See generally Meadow Gold Prods. Co. v. Wright*, 278 F.2d 867 (D.C. Cir.1960). The notion is emphasized by expressly authorizing the elimination of frivolous claims or defenses at a pretrial conference. There is no reason to require that this await a formal motion for summary judgment. Nor is there any reason for the court to wait for the parties to initiate the process called for in Rule 16(c)(1).

[¶22] The timing of any attempt at issue formulation is a matter of judicial discretion. In relatively simple cases it may not be necessary or may take the form of a stipulation between counsel or a request by the court that counsel work together to draft a proposed order.

[¶23] Counsel bear a substantial responsibility for assisting the court in identifying the factual issues worthy of trial. If counsel fail to identify an issue for the court, the right to have the issue tried is waived. Although an order specifying the issues is intended to be binding, it may be amended at trial to avoid manifest injustice. See Rule 16(e). However, the rule's effectiveness depends on the court employing its discretion sparingly.

[¶24] Clause (6) acknowledges the widespread availability and use of magistrates. The corresponding provision in the original rule referred only to masters and limited the function of the reference to the making of "findings to be used as evidence" in a case to be tried to a jury. The new text is not limited and broadens the potential use of a magistrate to that permitted by the Magistrate's Act.

[¶25] Clause (7) explicitly recognizes that it has become commonplace to discuss settlement at pretrial conferences. Since it obviously eases crowded court dockets and results in savings to the litigants and the judicial system, settlement should be facilitated at as early a stage of the litigation as possible. Although it is not the purpose of Rule 16(b)(7) to impose settlement negotiations on unwilling litigants, it is believed that providing a neutral forum for discussing the subject might foster it. See Moore's Federal Practice §16.17; 6 Wright & Miller, Federal Practice and Procedure: Civil §1522 (1971). For instance, a judge to whom a case has been assigned may arrange, on his own motion or a at a party's request, to have settlement conferences handled by another member of the court or by a magistrate. The rule does not make settlement conferences mandatory because they would be a waste of time in many cases. See Flanders, Case Management and Court Management in the United States District Courts, 39, Federal Judicial Center (1977). Requests for a conference from a party indicating a willingness to talk settlement normally should be honored, unless thought to be frivolous or dilatory.

[¶26] A settlement conference is appropriate at any time. It may be held in conjunction with a pretrial or discovery conference, although various objectives of pretrial management, such as moving the case toward trial, may not always be compatible with settlement negotiations, and thus a separate settlement conference may be desirable. See 6 Wright & Miller, Federal Practice and Procedure: Civil §1522, at p. 751 (1971).

[¶27] In addition to settlement, Rule 16(c)(7) refers to exploring the use of procedures other than litigation to resolve the dispute. This includes urging the litigants to employ adjudicatory techniques outside the courthouse. See, for example, the experiment described in Green, Marks & Olson, Settling Large Case Litigation: An Alternative Approach, 11 Loyola of L.A. L.Rev. 493 (1978).

[¶28] Rule 16(c)(10) authorizes the use of special pretrial procedures to expedite the adjudication of potentially difficult or protracted cases. Some district courts obviously have done so for many years. See Rubin, *The Managed Calendar: Some Pragmatic Suggestions About Achieving the Just, Speedy and Inexpensive Determination of Civil Cases in Federal Courts*, 4 Just. Sys. J. 135 (1976). Clause 10 provides an explicit authorization for such procedures and encourages their use. No particular techniques have been described; the Committee felt that flexibility and experience are the keys to efficient management of complex cases. Extensive guidance is offered in such documents as the *Manual for Complex Litigation*.

[¶29] The rule simply identifies characteristics that make a case a strong candidate for special treatment. The four mentioned are illustrative, not exhaustive, and overlap to some degree. But experience has shown that one or more of them will be present in every protracted or difficult case and it seems desirable to set them out. See Kendig, Procedures for Management of Non-Routine Cases, 3 Hofstra L.Rev. 701 (1975).

[¶30] The last sentence of subdivision (c) is new. See Wisconsin Civil Procedure Rule 802.11(2). It has been added to meet one of the criticisms of the present practice described earlier and insure proper preconference preparation so that the meeting is more than a ceremonial or ritualistic event. The reference to "authority" is not intended to insist upon the ability to settle the litigation. Nor should the rule be read to encourage the judge conducting the conference to compel attorneys to enter into stipulations or to make admissions that they consider to be unreasonable, that touch on matters that could not normally have been anticipated to arise at the conference, or on subjects of a dimension that normally require prior consultation with and approval from the client.

[¶31] Subdivision (d); Final Pretrial Conference. This provision has been added to make it clear that the time between any final pretrial conference (which in a simple case may be the only pretrial conference) and trial should be as short as possible to be certain that the litigants make substantial progress with the case and avoid the inefficiency of having that preparation repeated when there is a delay between the last pretrial conference and trial. An optimum time of 10 days to two weeks has been suggested by one federal judge. Rubin, The Managed Calendar: Some Pragmatic Suggestions About Achieving the Just, Speedy and Inexpensive Determination of Civil Cases in Federal Courts, 4 Just. Sys. J. 135, 141 (1976). The Committee, however, concluded that it would be inappropriate to fix a precise time in the rule, given the numerous variables that could bear on the matter. Thus the timing has been left to the court's discretion.

[¶32] At least one of the attorneys who will conduct the trial for each party must be present at the final pretrial conference. At this late date there should be no doubt as to which attorney or attorneys this will be. Since the agreements and stipulations made at this final conference will control the trial, the presence of lawyers who will be involved in it is especially useful to assist the judge in structuring the case, and to lead to a more effective trial.

[¶33] Subdivision (e); Pretrial Orders. Rule 16(e) does not substantially change the portion of the original rule dealing with pretrial orders. The purpose of an order is to guide the course of the litigation and the language of the original rule making that clear has been retained. No compelling reason has been found for major revision, especially since this portion of the rule has been interpreted and clarified by over forty years of judicial decisions with comparatively little difficulty. See 6 Wright & Miller, Federal Practice and Procedure: Civil §§1521-30 (1971). Changes in language therefore have been kept to a minimum to avoid confusion.

[¶34] Since the amended rule encourages more extensive pretrial management than did the original, two or more conferences may be held in many cases. The language of Rule 16(e) recognizes this possibility and the corresponding need to issue more than one pretrial order in a single case.

[¶35] Once formulated, pretrial orders should not be changed lightly; but total inflexibility is undesirable. *See, e.g.*, *Clark v. Pennsylvania R.R. Co.*, 328 F.2d 591 (2d Cir.1964). The exact words used to describe the standard for amending the pretrial order probably are less important than the meaning given them in practice. By not imposing any limitation on the ability to modify a pretrial order, the rule reflects the reality that in any process of continuous management what is done at one conference may have to be altered at the next. In the case of the final pretrial order, however, a more stringent standard is called for and the words "to prevent manifest injustice," which appeared in the original rule, have been retained. They have the virtue of familiarity and adequately describe the restraint the trial judge should exercise.

[¶36] Many local rules make the plaintiff's attorney responsible for drafting a proposed pretrial order, either before or after the conference. Others allow the court to appoint any of the attorneys to perform the task, and others leave it to the court. See Note, Pretrial Conference: A Critical Examination of Local Rules Adopted by Federal District Courts, 64 Va.L.Rev. 467 (1978). Rule 16 has never addressed this matter. Since there is no consensus about which method of drafting the order works best and there is no reason to believe that nationwide uniformity is needed, the rule has been left silent on the point. See Handbook for Effective Pretrial Procedure, 37 F.R.D. 225 (1964).

[¶37] Subdivision (f); Sanctions. Original Rule 16 did not mention the sanctions that might be imposed for failing to comply with the rule. However, courts have not hesitated to enforce it by appropriate measures. *See, e.g.*, *Link v. Wabash R. Co.*, 370 U.S. 628 (1962) (district court's dismissal under Rule 41(b) after plaintiff's attorney failed to appear at a pretrial conference upheld); *Admiral Theatre Corp. v. Douglas Theatre*, 585 F.2d 877 (8th Cir.1978) (district court has discretion to exclude exhibits or refuse to permit the testimony of a witness not listed prior to trial in contravention of its pretrial order).

[¶38] To reflect that existing practice, and to obviate dependence upon Rule 41(b) or the court's inherent power to regulate litigation, *cf. Societe Internationale Pour Participations Industrielles et Commerciales, S.A. v. Rogers*, 357 U.S. 197 (1958), Rule 16(f) expressly provides for imposing sanctions on disobedient or recalcitrant parties, their attorneys, or both in four types of situations. Rodes, Ripple & Mooney, Sanctions Imposable for Violations of the Federal Rules of Civil Procedure 65-67, 80-84, Federal Judicial Center (1981). Furthermore, explicit reference to sanctions reenforces the rule's intention to encourage forceful judicial management.

[¶39] Rule 16(f) incorporates portions of Rule 37(b)(2), which prescribes sanctions for failing to make discovery. This should facilitate application of Rule 16(f), since courts and lawyers already are familiar with the Rule 37 standards. Among the sanctions authorized by the new subdivision are: preclusion order, striking a pleading, staying the proceeding,

default judgment, contempt, and charging a party, his attorney, or both with the expenses, including attorney's fees, caused by noncompliance. The contempt sanction, however, is only available for a violation of a court order. The references in Rule 16(f) are not exhaustive.

[¶40] As is true under Rule 37(b)(2), the imposition of sanctions may be sought by either the court or a party. In addition, the court has discretion to impose whichever sanction it feels is appropriate under the circumstances. Its action is reviewable under the abuse-of-discretion standard. *See National Hockey League v. Metropolitan Hockey Club, Inc.*, 427 U.S. 639 (1976).

FRCP 17 – 2007 NOTES OF ADVISORY COMMITTEE

[¶1] Rule 17(d) incorporates the provisions of former Rule 25(d)(2), which fit better with Rule 17.

FRCP 18 – 2007 NOTES OF ADVISORY COMMITTEE

[¶1] Modification of the obscure former reference to a claim "heretofore cognizable only after another claim has been prosecuted to a conclusion" avoids any uncertainty whether Rule 18(b)'s meaning is fixed by retrospective inquiry from some particular date.

FRCP 19 – 2007 NOTES OF ADVISORY COMMITTEE

[¶1] Former Rule 19(b) described the conclusion that an action should be dismissed for inability to join a Rule 19(a) party by carrying forward traditional terminology: "the absent person being thus regarded as indispensable." "Indispensable" was used only to express a conclusion reached by applying the tests of Rule 19(b). It has been discarded as redundant.

FRCP 23 – 2009 NOTES OF ADVISORY COMMITTEE

[¶1] The time set in the former rule at 10 days has been revised to 14 days. See the Note to Rule 6.[1]

1. **Editor's note:** The cross-reference to "Note to Rule 6" refers to 2009 Notes to FRCP 6 at ¶¶1-20, p. 1149, this book.

FRCP 23 – 2007 NOTES OF ADVISORY COMMITTEE

[¶1] Amended Rule 23(d)(2) carries forward the provisions of former Rule 23(d) that recognize two separate propositions. First, a Rule 23(d) order may be combined with a pretrial order under Rule 16. Second, the standard for amending the Rule 23(d) order continues to be the more open-ended standard for amending Rule 23(d) orders, not the more exacting standard for amending Rule 16 orders.

[¶2] As part of the general restyling, intensifiers that provide emphasis but add no meaning are consistently deleted. Amended Rule 23(f) omits as redundant the explicit reference to court of appeals discretion in deciding whether to permit an interlocutory appeal. The omission does not in any way limit the unfettered discretion established by the original rule.

FRCP 23 – 2003 NOTES OF ADVISORY COMMITTEE

[¶1] Subdivision (c). Subdivision (c) is amended in several respects. The requirement that the court determine whether to certify a class "as soon as practicable after commencement of an action" is replaced by requiring determination "at an early practicable time." The notice provisions are substantially revised.

[¶2] Paragraph (1). Subdivision (c)(1)(A) is changed to require that the determination whether to certify a class be made "at an early practicable time." The "as soon as practicable" exaction neither reflects prevailing practice nor captures the many valid reasons that may justify deferring the initial certification decision. See Willging, Hooper & Niemic, *Empirical Study of Class Actions in Four Federal District Courts: Final Report to the Advisory Committee on Civil Rules 26-36* (Federal Judicial Center 1996).

[¶3] Time may be needed to gather information necessary to make the certification decision. Although an evaluation of the probable outcome on the merits is not properly part of the certification decision, discovery in aid of the certification decision often includes information required to identify the nature of the issues that actually will be presented at trial. In this sense it is appropriate to conduct controlled discovery into the "merits," limited to those aspects relevant to making the certification decision on an informed basis. Active judicial supervision may be required to achieve the most effective balance that expedites an informed certification determination without forcing an artificial and ultimately wasteful division between "certification discovery" and "merits discovery." A critical need is to determine how the case will be tried. An increasing number of courts require a party requesting class certification to present a "trial plan" that describes the issues likely to be presented at trial and tests whether they are susceptible of class-wide proof. See Manual For Complex Litigation Third, §21.213, p. 44; §30.11, p. 214; §30.12, p. 215.

[¶4] Other considerations may affect the timing of the certification decision. The party opposing the class may prefer to win dismissal or summary judgment as to the individual plaintiffs without certification and without binding the class that might have been certified. Time may be needed to explore designation of class counsel under Rule 23(g), recognizing that in many cases the need to progress toward the certification determination may require designation of interim counsel under Rule 23(g)(2)(A).

[¶5] Although many circumstances may justify deferring the certification decision, active management may be necessary to ensure that the certification decision is not unjustifiably delayed.

[¶6] Subdivision (c)(1)(C) reflects two amendments. The provision that a class certification "may be conditional" is deleted. A court that is not satisfied that the requirements of Rule 23 have been met should refuse certification until they have been met. The provision that permits alteration or amendment of an order granting or denying class certification is amended to set the cut-off point at final judgment rather than "the decision on the merits." This change avoids the possible ambiguity in referring to "the decision on the merits." Following a determination of liability, for example, proceedings to define the remedy may demonstrate the need to amend the class definition or subdivide the class. In this setting the final judgment concept is pragmatic. It is not the same as the concept used for appeal purposes, but it should be flexible, particularly in protracted litigation.

[¶7] The authority to amend an order under Rule 23(c)(1) before final judgment does not restore the practice of "one-way intervention" that was rejected by the 1966 revision of Rule 23. A determination of liability after certification, however, may show a need to amend the class definition. Decertification may be warranted after further proceedings.

[¶8] If the definition of a class certified under Rule 23(b)(3) is altered to include members who have not been afforded notice and an opportunity to request exclusion, notice—including an opportunity to request exclusion—must be directed to the new class members under Rule 23(c)(2)(B).

[¶9] Paragraph (2). The first change made in Rule 23(c)(2) is to call attention to the court's authority—already established in part by Rule 23(d)(2)—to direct notice of certification to a Rule 23(b)(1) or (b)(2) class. The present rule expressly requires notice only in actions certified under Rule 23(b)(3). Members of classes certified under Rules 23(b)(1) or (b)(2) have interests that may deserve protection by notice.

[¶10] The authority to direct notice to class members in a (b)(1) or (b)(2) class action should be exercised with care. For several reasons, there may be less need for notice than in a (b)(3) class action. There is no right to request exclusion from a (b)(1) or (b)(2) class. The characteristics of the class may reduce the need for formal notice. The cost of providing notice, moreover, could easily cripple actions that do not seek damages. The court may decide not to direct notice after balancing the risk that notice costs may deter the pursuit of class relief against the benefits of notice.

[¶11] When the court does direct certification notice in a (b)(1) or (b)(2) class action, the discretion and flexibility established by subdivision (c)(2)(A) extend to the method of giving notice. Notice facilitates the opportunity to participate. Notice calculated to reach a significant number of class members often will protect the interests of all. Informal methods may prove effective. A simple posting in a place visited by many class members, directing attention to a source of more detailed information, may suffice. The court should consider the costs of notice in relation to the probable reach of inexpensive methods.

[¶12] If a Rule 23(b)(3) class is certified in conjunction with a (b)(2) class, the (c)(2)(B) notice requirements must be satisfied as to the (b)(3) class.

[¶13] The direction that class-certification notice be couched in plain, easily understood language is a reminder of the need to work unremittingly at the difficult task of communicating with class members. It is difficult to provide information about most class actions that is both accurate and easily understood by class members who are not themselves lawyers. Factual uncertainty, legal complexity, and the complication of class-action procedure raise the barriers high. The Federal Judicial Center has created illustrative clear-notice forms that provide a helpful starting point for actions similar to those described in the forms.

[¶14] Subdivision (e). Subdivision (e) is amended to strengthen the process of reviewing proposed class-action settlements. Settlement may be a desirable means of resolving a class action. But court review and approval are essential to assure adequate representation of class members who have not participated in shaping the settlement.

[¶15] Paragraph (1). Subdivision (e)(1)(A) expressly recognizes the power of a class representative to settle class claims, issues, or defenses.

[¶16] Rule 23(e)(1)(A) resolves the ambiguity in former Rule 23(e)'s reference to dismissal or compromise of "a class action." That language could be—and at times was—read to require court approval of settlements with putative class representatives that resolved only individual claims. See Manual for Complex Litigation Third, §30.41. The new rule requires approval only if the claims, issues, or defenses of a certified class are resolved by a settlement, voluntary dismissal, or compromise.

[¶17] Subdivision (e)(1)(B) carries forward the notice requirement of present Rule 23(e) when the settlement binds the class through claim or issue preclusion; notice is not required when the settlement binds only the individual class representatives. Notice of a settlement binding on the class is required either when the settlement follows class certification or when the decisions on certification and settlement proceed simultaneously.

[¶18] Reasonable settlement notice may require individual notice in the manner required by Rule 23(c)(2)(B) for certification notice to a Rule 23(b)(3) class. Individual notice is appropriate, for example, if class members are required to take action—such as filing claims—to participate in the judgment, or if the court orders a settlement opt-out opportunity under Rule 23(e)(3).

[¶19] Subdivision (e)(1)(C) confirms and mandates the already common practice of holding hearings as part of the process of approving settlement, voluntary dismissal, or compromise that would bind members of a class.

[¶20] Subdivision (e)(1)(C) states the standard for approving a proposed settlement that would bind class mem-

bers. The settlement must be fair, reasonable, and adequate. A helpful review of many factors that may deserve consideration is provided by *In re: Prudential Ins. Co. America Sales Practice Litigation Agent Actions*, 148 F.3d 283, 316-324 (3d Cir.1998). Further guidance can be found in the Manual for Complex Litigation.

[¶21] The court must make findings that support the conclusion that the settlement is fair, reasonable, and adequate. The findings must be set out in sufficient detail to explain to class members and the appellate court the factors that bear on applying the standard.

[¶22] Settlement review also may provide an occasion to review the cogency of the initial class definition. The terms of the settlement themselves, or objections, may reveal divergent interests of class members and demonstrate the need to redefine the class or to designate subclasses. Redefinition of a class certified under Rule 23(b)(3) may require notice to new class members under Rule 23(c)(2)(B). See Rule 23(c)(1)(C).

[¶23] Paragraph (2). Subdivision (e)(2) requires parties seeking approval of a settlement, voluntary dismissal, or compromise under Rule 23(e)(1) to file a statement identifying any agreement made in connection with the settlement. This provision does not change the basic requirement that the parties disclose all terms of the settlement or compromise that the court must approve under Rule 23(e)(1). It aims instead at related undertakings that, although seemingly separate, may have influenced the terms of the settlement by trading away possible advantages for the class in return for advantages for others. Doubts should be resolved in favor of identification.

[¶24] Further inquiry into the agreements identified by the parties should not become the occasion for discovery by the parties or objectors. The court may direct the parties to provide to the court or other parties a summary or copy of the full terms of any agreement identified by the parties. The court also may direct the parties to provide a summary or copy of any agreement not identified by the parties that the court considers relevant to its review of a proposed settlement. In exercising discretion under this rule, the court may act in steps, calling first for a summary of any agreement that may have affected the settlement and then for a complete version if the summary does not provide an adequate basis for review. A direction to disclose a summary or copy of an agreement may raise concerns of confidentiality. Some agreements may include information that merits protection against general disclosure. And the court must provide an opportunity to claim work-product or other protections.

[¶25] Paragraph (3). Subdivision (e)(3) authorizes the court to refuse to approve a settlement unless the settlement affords class members a new opportunity to request exclusion from a class certified under Rule 23(b)(3) after settlement terms are known. An agreement by the parties themselves to permit class members to elect exclusion at this point by the settlement agreement may be one factor supporting approval of the settlement. Often there is an opportunity to opt out at this point because the class is certified and settlement is reached in circumstances that lead to simultaneous notice of certification and notice of settlement. In these cases, the basic opportunity to elect exclusion applies without further complication. In some cases, particularly if settlement appears imminent at the time of certification, it may be possible to achieve equivalent protection by deferring notice and the opportunity to elect exclusion until actual settlement terms are known. This approach avoids the cost and potential confusion of providing two notices and makes the single notice more meaningful. But notice should not be delayed unduly after certification in the hope of settlement.

[¶26] Rule 23(e)(3) authorizes the court to refuse to approve a settlement unless the settlement affords a new opportunity to elect exclusion in a case that settles after a certification decision if the earlier opportunity to elect exclusion provided with the certification notice has expired by the time of the settlement notice. A decision to remain in the class is likely to be more carefully considered and is better informed when settlement terms are known.

[¶27] The opportunity to request exclusion from a proposed settlement is limited to members of a (b)(3) class. Exclusion may be requested only by individual class members; no class member may purport to opt out other class members by way of another class action.

[¶28] The decision whether to approve a settlement that does not allow a new opportunity to elect exclusion is confided to the court's discretion. The court may make this decision before directing notice to the class under Rule 23(e)(1)(B) or after the Rule 23(e)(1)(C) hearing. Many factors may influence the court's decision. Among these are changes in the information available to class members since expiration of the first opportunity to request exclusion, and the nature of the individual class members' claims.

[¶29] The terms set for permitting a new opportunity to elect exclusion from the proposed settlement of a Rule 23(b)(3) class action may address concerns of potential misuse. The court might direct, for example, that class members who elect exclusion are bound by rulings on the merits made before the settlement was proposed for approval. Still other terms or conditions may be appropriate.

[¶30] Paragraph (4). Subdivision (e)(4) confirms the right of class members to object to a proposed settlement, voluntary dismissal, or compromise. The right is defined in relation to a disposition that, because it would bind the class, requires court approval under subdivision (e)(1)(C).

[¶31] Subdivision (e)(4)(B) requires court approval for withdrawal of objections made under subdivision (e)(4)(A). Review follows automatically if the objections are withdrawn on terms that lead to modification of the settlement with the class. Review also is required if the objector formally withdraws the objections. If the objector simply abandons pursuit of the objection, the court may inquire into the circumstances.

[¶32] Approval under paragraph (4)(B) may be given or denied with little need for further inquiry if the objection and the disposition go only to a protest that the individual treatment afforded the objector under the proposed settlement is unfair because of factors that distinguish the objector from other class members. Different considerations may apply if the objector has protested that the proposed settlement is not fair, reasonable, or adequate on grounds that apply generally to a class or subclass. Such objections, which purport to represent class-wide interests, may augment the opportunity for obstruction or delay. If such objections are surrendered on terms that do not affect the class settlement or the objector's participation in the class settlement, the court often can approve withdrawal of the objections without elaborate inquiry.

[¶33] Once an objector appeals, control of the proceeding lies in the court of appeals. The court of appeals may undertake review and approval of a settlement with the objector, perhaps as part of appeal settlement procedures, or may remand to the district court to take advantage of the district court's familiarity with the action and settlement.

[¶34] Subdivision (g). Subdivision (g) is new. It responds to the reality that the selection and activity of class counsel are often critically important to the successful handling of a class action. Until now, courts have scrutinized proposed class counsel as well as the class representative under Rule 23(a)(4). This experience has recognized the importance of judicial evaluation of the proposed lawyer for the class, and this new subdivision builds on that experience rather than introducing an entirely new element into the class certification process. Rule 23(a)(4) will continue to call for scrutiny of the proposed class representative, while this subdivision will guide the court in assessing proposed class counsel as part of the certification decision. This subdivision recognizes the importance of class counsel, states the obligation to represent the interests of the class, and provides a framework for selection of class counsel. The procedure and standards for appointment vary depending on whether there are multiple applicants to be class counsel. The new subdivision also provides a method by which the court may make directions from the outset about the potential fee award to class counsel in the event the action is successful.

[¶35] Paragraph (1) sets out the basic requirement that class counsel be appointed if a class is certified and articulates the obligation of class counsel to represent the interests of the class, as opposed to the potentially conflicting interests of individual class members. It also sets out the factors the court should consider in assessing proposed class counsel.

[¶36] Paragraph (1)(A) requires that the court appoint class counsel to represent the class. Class counsel must be appointed for all classes, including each subclass that the court certifies to represent divergent interests.

[¶37] Paragraph (1)(A) does not apply if "a statute provides otherwise." This recognizes that provisions of the Private Securities Litigation Reform Act of 1995, Pub.L. No. 104-67, 109 Stat. 737 (1995) (codified in various sections of 15 U.S.C.), contain directives that bear on selection of a lead plaintiff and the retention of counsel. This subdivision does not purport to supersede or to affect the interpretation of those provisions, or any similar provisions of other legislation.

[¶38] Paragraph 1(B) recognizes that the primary responsibility of class counsel, resulting from appointment as class counsel, is to represent the best interests of the class. The rule thus establishes the obligation of class counsel, an obligation that may be different from the customary obligations of counsel to individual clients. Appointment as class counsel means that the primary obligation of counsel is to the class rather than to any individual members of it. The class representatives do not have an unfettered right to "fire" class counsel. In the same vein, the class representatives cannot command class counsel to accept or reject a settlement proposal. To the contrary, class counsel must determine whether seeking the court's approval of a settlement would be in the best interests of the class as a whole.

[¶39] Paragraph (1)(C) articulates the basic responsibility of the court to appoint class counsel who will provide the adequate representation called for by paragraph (1)(B). It identifies criteria that must be considered and invites the court to consider any other pertinent matters. Although couched in terms of the court's duty, the listing also informs counsel seeking appointment about the topics that should be addressed in an application for appointment or in the motion for class certification.

[¶40] The court may direct potential class counsel to provide additional information about the topics mentioned in paragraph (1)(C) or about any other relevant topic. For example, the court may direct applicants to inform the court concerning any agreements about a prospective award of attorney fees or nontaxable costs, as such agreements may sometimes be significant in the selection of class counsel. The court might also direct that potential class counsel indicate how parallel litigation might be coordinated or consolidated with the action before the court.

[¶41] The court may also direct counsel to propose terms for a potential award of attorney fees and nontaxable costs. Attorney fee awards are an important feature of class action practice, and attention to this subject from the outset may often be a productive technique. Paragraph (2)(C) therefore authorizes the court to provide directions about attorney fees and costs when appointing class counsel. Because there will be numerous class actions in which this information is not likely to be useful, the court need not consider it in all class actions.

[¶42] Some information relevant to class counsel appointment may involve matters that include adversary preparation in a way that should be shielded from disclosure to other parties. An appropriate protective order may be necessary to preserve confidentiality.

[¶43] In evaluating prospective class counsel, the court should weigh all pertinent factors. No single factor should necessarily be determinative in a given case. For example, the resources counsel will commit to the case must be appropriate to its needs, but the court should be careful not to limit consideration to lawyers with the greatest resources.

[¶44] If, after review of all applicants, the court concludes that none would be satisfactory class counsel, it may deny class certification, reject all applications, recommend that an application be modified, invite new applications, or make any other appropriate order regarding selection and appointment of class counsel.

[¶45] Paragraph (2). This paragraph sets out the procedure that should be followed in appointing class counsel. Although it affords substantial flexibility, it provides the framework for appointment of class counsel in all class actions. For counsel who filed the action, the materials submitted in support of the motion for class certification may suffice to justify appointment so long as the information described in paragraph (g)(1)(C) is included. If there are other applicants, they ordinarily would file a formal application detailing their suitability for the position.

[¶46] In a plaintiff class action the court usually would appoint as class counsel only an attorney or attorneys who have sought appointment. Different considerations may apply in defendant class actions.

[¶47] The rule states that the court should appoint "class counsel." In many instances, the applicant will be an individual attorney. In other cases, however, an entire firm, or perhaps numerous attorneys who are not otherwise affiliated but are collaborating on the action will apply. No rule of thumb exists to determine when such arrangements are appropriate; the court should be alert to the need for adequate staffing of the case, but also to the risk of overstaffing or an ungainly counsel structure.

[¶48] Paragraph (2)(A) authorizes the court to designate interim counsel during the pre-certification period if necessary to protect the interests of the putative class. Rule 23(c)(1)(B) directs that the order certifying the class include appointment of class counsel. Before class certification, however, it will usually be important for an attorney to take action to prepare for the certification decision. The amendment to Rule 23(c)(1) recognizes that some discovery is often necessary for that determination. It also may be important to make or respond to motions before certification. Settlement may be discussed before certification. Ordinarily, such work is handled by the lawyer who filed the action. In some cases, however, there may be rivalry or uncertainty that makes formal designation of interim counsel appropriate. Rule 23(g)(2)(A) authorizes the court to designate interim counsel to act on behalf of the putative class before the certification decision is made. Failure to make the formal designation does not prevent the attorney who filed the action from proceeding in it. Whether or not formally designated interim counsel, an attorney who acts on behalf of the class before certification must act in the best interests of the class as a whole. For example, an attorney who negotiates a pre-certification settlement must seek a settlement that is fair, reasonable, and adequate for the class.

[¶49] Rule 23(c)(1) provides that the court should decide whether to certify the class "at an early practicable time," and directs that class counsel should be appointed in the order certifying the class. In some cases, it may be appropriate for the court to allow a reasonable period after commencement of the action for filing applications to serve as class counsel. The primary ground for deferring appointment would be that there is reason to anticipate competing applications to serve as class counsel. Examples might include instances in which more than one class action has been filed, or in which other attorneys have filed individual actions on behalf of putative class members. The purpose of facilitating competing applications in such a case is to afford the best possible representation for the class. Another possible reason for deferring appointment would be that the initial applicant was found inadequate, but it seems appropriate to permit additional applications rather than deny class certification.

[¶50] Paragraph (2)(B) states the basic standard the court should use in deciding whether to certify the class and appoint class counsel in the single applicant situation—that the applicant be able to provide the representation called for by paragraph (1)(B) in light of the factors identified in paragraph (1)(C).

[¶51] If there are multiple adequate applicants, paragraph (2)(B) directs the court to select the class counsel best able to represent the interests of the class. This decision should also be made using the factors outlined in paragraph (1)(C), but in the multiple applicant situation the court is to go beyond scrutinizing the adequacy of counsel and make a comparison of the strengths of the various applicants. As with the decision whether to appoint the sole applicant for the position, no single factor should be dispositive in selecting class counsel in cases in which there are multiple applicants. The fact that a given attorney filed the instant action, for example, might not weigh heavily in the decision if that lawyer had not done significant work identifying or investigating claims. Depending on the nature of the case, one important consideration might be the applicant's existing attorney-client relationship with the proposed class representative.

[¶52] Paragraph (2)(C) builds on the appointment process by authorizing the court to include provisions regarding attorney fees in the order appointing class counsel. Courts may find it desirable to adopt guidelines for fees or nontaxable costs, or to direct class counsel to report to the court at regular intervals on the efforts undertaken in the action, to facilitate the court's later determination of a reasonable attorney fee.

[¶53] Subdivision (h). Subdivision (h) is new. Fee awards are a powerful influence on the way attorneys initiate, develop, and conclude class actions. Class action attorney fee awards have heretofore been handled, along with all other attorney fee awards, under Rule 54(d)(2), but that rule is not addressed to the particular concerns of class actions. This subdivision is designed to work in tandem with new subdivision (g) on appointment of class counsel, which may afford an opportunity for the court to provide an early framework for an eventual fee award, or for monitoring the work of class counsel during the pendency of the action.

[¶54] Subdivision (h) applies to "an action certified as a class action." This includes cases in which there is a simultaneous proposal for class certification and settlement even though technically the class may not be certified unless the court approves the settlement pursuant to review under Rule 23(e). When a settlement is proposed for Rule 23(e) approval, either after certification or with a request for certification, notice to class members about class counsel's fee motion would ordinarily accompany the notice to the class about the settlement proposal itself.

[¶55] This subdivision does not undertake to create new grounds for an award of attorney fees or nontaxable costs. Instead, it applies when such awards are authorized by law or by agreement of the parties. Against that background, it provides a format for all awards of attorney fees and nontaxable costs in connection with a class action, not only the award to class counsel. In some situations, there may be a basis for making an award to other counsel whose work produced a beneficial result for the class, such as attorneys who acted for the class before certification but were not appointed class counsel, or attorneys who represented objectors to a proposed settlement under Rule 23(e) or to the fee motion of class counsel. Other situations in which fee awards are authorized by law or by agreement of the parties may exist.

[¶56] This subdivision authorizes an award of "reasonable" attorney fees and nontaxable costs. This is the customary term for measurement of fee awards in cases in which counsel may obtain an award of fees under the "common fund" theory that applies in many class actions, and is used in many fee-shifting statutes. Depending on the circumstances, courts have approached the determination of what is reasonable in different ways. In particular, there is some variation among courts about whether in "common fund" cases the court should use the lodestar or a percentage method of determining what fee is reasonable. The rule does not attempt to resolve the question whether the lodestar or percentage approach should be viewed as preferable.

[¶57] Active judicial involvement in measuring fee awards is singularly important to the proper operation of the class-action process. Continued reliance on caselaw development of fee-award measures does not diminish the court's responsibility. In a class action, the district court must ensure that the amount and mode of payment of attorney fees are fair and proper whether the fees come from a common fund or are otherwise paid. Even in the absence of objections, the court bears this responsibility.

[¶58] Courts discharging this responsibility have looked to a variety of factors. One fundamental focus is the result actually achieved for class members, a basic consideration in any case in which fees are sought on the basis of a benefit achieved for class members. The Private Securities Litigation Reform Act of 1995 explicitly makes this factor a cap for a fee award in actions to which it applies. See 15 U.S.C. §§77z-1(a)(6); 78u-4(a)(6) (fee award should not exceed a "reasonable percentage of the amount of any damages and prejudgment interest actually paid to the class"). For a percentage approach to fee measurement, results achieved is the basic starting point.

[¶59] In many instances, the court may need to proceed with care in assessing the value conferred on class members. Settlement regimes that provide for future payments, for example, may not result in significant actual payments to class members. In this connection, the court may need to scrutinize the manner and operation of any applicable claims procedure. In some cases, it may be appropriate to defer some portion of the fee award until actual payouts to class members are known. Settlements involving nonmonetary provisions for class members also deserve careful scrutiny to ensure that these provisions have actual value to the class. On occasion the court's Rule 23(e) review will provide a solid basis for this sort of evaluation, but in any event it is also important to assessing the fee award for the class.

[¶60] At the same time, it is important to recognize that in some class actions the monetary relief obtained is not the sole determinant of an appropriate attorney fees award. *Cf. Blanchard v. Bergeron*, 489 U.S. 87, 95 (1989) (cautioning in an individual case against an "undesirable emphasis" on "the importance of the recovery of damages in civil rights litigation" that might "shortchange efforts to seek effective injunctive or declaratory relief").

[¶61] Any directions or orders made by the court in connection with appointing class counsel under Rule 23(g) should weigh heavily in making a fee award under this subdivision.

[¶62] Courts have also given weight to agreements among the parties regarding the fee motion, and to agreements between class counsel and others about the fees claimed by the motion. Rule 54(d)(2)(B) provides: "If directed by the court, the motion shall also disclose the terms of any agreement with respect to fees to be paid for the services for which claim is made." The agreement by a settling party not to oppose a fee application up to a certain amount, for example, is worthy of consideration, but the court remains responsible to determine a reasonable fee. "Side agreements" regarding fees provide at least perspective pertinent to an appropriate fee award.

[¶63] In addition, courts may take account of the fees charged by class counsel or other attorneys for representing individual claimants or objectors in the case. In determining a fee for class counsel, the court's objective is to ensure an overall fee that is fair for counsel and equitable within the class. In some circumstances individual fee agreements between class counsel and class members might have provisions inconsistent with those goals, and the court might determine that adjustments in the class fee award were necessary as a result.

[¶64] Finally, it is important to scrutinize separately the application for an award covering nontaxable costs. If costs were addressed in the order appointing class counsel, those directives should be a presumptive starting point in determining what is an appropriate award.

[¶65] Paragraph (1). Any claim for an award of attorney fees must be sought by motion under Rule 54(d)(2), which invokes the provisions for timing of appeal in Rule 58 and Appellate Rule 4. Owing to the distinctive features of class action fee motions, however, the provisions of this subdivision control disposition of fee motions in class actions, while Rule 54(d)(2) applies to matters not addressed in this subdivision.

[¶66] The court should direct when the fee motion must be filed. For motions by class counsel in cases subject to court review of a proposed settlement under Rule 23(e), it would be important to require the filing of at least the initial motion in time for inclusion of information about the motion in the notice to the class about the proposed settlement that is required by Rule 23(e). In cases litigated to judgment, the court might also order class counsel's motion to be filed promptly so that notice to the class under this subdivision (h) can be given.

[¶67] Besides service of the motion on all parties, notice of class counsel's motion for attorney fees must be "directed to the class in a reasonable manner." Because members of the class have an interest in the arrangements for payment of class counsel whether that payment comes from the class fund or is made directly by another party, notice is required in all instances. In cases in which settlement approval is contemplated under Rule 23(e), notice of class counsel's fee motion should be combined with notice of the proposed settlement, and the provision regarding notice to the class is parallel to the requirements for notice under Rule 23(e). In adjudicated class actions, the court may calibrate the notice to avoid undue expense.

[¶68] Paragraph (2). A class member and any party from whom payment is sought may object to the fee motion. Other parties—for example, nonsettling defendants—may not object because they lack a sufficient interest in the amount the court awards. The rule does not specify a time limit for making an objection. In setting the date objections are due, the court should provide sufficient time after the full fee motion is on file to enable potential objectors to examine the motion.

[¶69] The court may allow an objector discovery relevant to the objections. In determining whether to allow discovery, the court should weigh the need for the information against the cost and delay that would attend discovery. See Rule 26(b)(2). One factor in determining whether to authorize discovery is the completeness of the material submitted in support of the fee motion, which depends in part on the fee measurement standard applicable to the case. If the motion provides thorough information, the burden should be on the objector to justify discovery to obtain further information.

[¶70] Paragraph (3). Whether or not there are formal objections, the court must determine whether a fee award is justified and, if so, set a reasonable fee. The rule does not require a formal hearing in all cases. The form and extent of a hearing depend on the circumstances of the case. The rule does require findings and conclusions under Rule 52(a).

[¶71] Paragraph (4). By incorporating Rule 54(d)(2), this provision gives the court broad authority to obtain assistance in determining the appropriate amount to award. In deciding whether to direct submission of such questions to a special master or magistrate judge, the court should give appropriate consideration to the cost and delay that such a process might entail.

FRCP 23 – 1998 NOTES OF ADVISORY COMMITTEE

[¶1] Subdivision (f). This permissive interlocutory appeal provision is adopted under the power conferred by 28 U.S.C. §1292(e). Appeal from an order granting or denying class certification is permitted in the sole discretion of the court of appeals. No other type of Rule 23 order is covered by this provision. The court of appeals is given unfettered discretion whether to permit the appeal, akin to the discretion exercised by the Supreme Court in acting on a petition for certiorari. This discretion suggests an analogy to the provision in 28 U.S.C. §1292(b) for permissive appeal on certification by a district court. Subdivision (f), however, departs from the §1292(b) model in two significant ways. It does not require that the district court certify the certification ruling for appeal, although the district court often can assist the parties and court of appeals by offering advice on the desirability of appeal. And it does not include the potentially limiting requirements of §1292(b) that the district court order "involve[ ] a controlling question of law as to which there is substantial ground for difference of opinion and that an immediate appeal from the order may materially advance the ultimate termination of the litigation."

[¶2] The courts of appeals will develop standards for granting review that reflect the changing areas of uncertainty in class litigation. The Federal Judicial Center study supports the view that many suits with class-action allegations present familiar and almost routine issues that are no more worthy of immediate appeal than many other interlocutory rulings. Yet several concerns justify expansion of present opportunities to appeal. An order denying certification may confront the plaintiff with a situation in which the only sure path to appellate review is by proceeding to final judgment on the merits of an individual claim that, standing alone, is far smaller than the costs of litigation. An order granting certification, on the other hand, may force a defendant to settle rather than incur the costs of defending a class action and run the risk of potentially ruinous liability. These concerns can be met at low cost by establishing in the court of appeals a discretionary power to grant interlocutory review in cases that show appeal-worthy certification issues.

[¶3] Permission to appeal may be granted or denied on the basis of any consideration that the court of appeals finds persuasive. Permission is most likely to be granted when the certification decision turns on a novel or unsettled question of law, or when, as a practical matter, the decision on certification is likely dispositive of the litigation.

[¶4] The district court, having worked through the certification decision, often will be able to provide cogent advice on the factors that bear on the decision whether to permit appeal. This advice can be particularly valuable if the certification decision is tentative. Even as to a firm certification decision, a statement of reasons bearing on the probable benefits and costs of immediate appeal can help focus the court of appeals decision, and may persuade the disappointed party that an attempt to appeal would be fruitless.

[¶5] The 10-day period for seeking permission to appeal is designed to reduce the risk that attempted appeals will disrupt continuing proceedings. It is expected that the courts of appeals will act quickly in making the preliminary determination whether to permit appeal. Permission to appeal does not stay trial court proceedings. A stay should be sought first from the trial court. If the trial court refuses a stay, its action and any explanation of its views should weigh heavily with the court of appeals.

[¶6] Appellate Rule 5 has been modified to establish the procedure for petitioning for leave to appeal under subdivision (f).

FRCP 24 – 2007 NOTES OF ADVISORY COMMITTEE

[¶1] The former rule stated that the same procedure is followed when a United States statute gives a right to intervene. This statement is deleted because it added nothing.

FRCP 24 – 2006 NOTES OF ADVISORY COMMITTEE

[¶1] New Rule 5.1 replaces the final three sentences of Rule 24(c), implementing the provisions of 28 U.S.C. §2403. Section 2403 requires notification to the Attorney General of the United States when the constitutionality of an Act of Congress is called in question, and to the state attorney general when the constitutionality of a state statute is drawn into question.

FRCP 25 – 2007 NOTES OF ADVISORY COMMITTEE

[¶1] Former Rule 25(d)(2) is transferred to become Rule 17(d) because it deals with designation of a public officer, not substitution.

FRCP 25 – 1963 NOTES OF ADVISORY COMMITTEE

[¶1] Present Rule 25(a)(1), together with present Rule 6(b), results in an inflexible requirement that an action be dismissed as to a deceased party if substitution is not carried out within a fixed period measured from the time of the death. The hardships and inequities of this unyielding requirement plainly appear from the cases. *See, e.g., Anderson v. Yungkau*, 329 U.S. 482, 67 S.Ct. 428, 91 L.Ed. 436 (1947); *Iovino v. Waterson*, 274 F.2d 41 (1959), *cert. denied, Carlin v. Sovino*, 362 U.S. 949, 80 S.Ct. 860, 4 L.Ed.2d 867 (1960); *Perry v. Allen*, 239 F.2d 107 (5th Cir.1956); *Starnes v. Pennsylvania R.R.*, 26 F.R.D. 625 (E.D. N.Y.), *aff'd per curiam*, 295 F.2d 704 (2d Cir.1961), *cert. denied*, 369 U.S. 813, 82 S.Ct. 688, 7 L.Ed.2d 612 (1962); *Zdanok v. Glidden Co.*, 28 F.R.D. 346 (S.D. N.Y.1961). See also 4 Moore's Federal Practice §25.01[9] (Supp.1960); 2 Barron & Holtzoff, Federal Practice & Procedure §621, at 420-21 (Wright ed. 1961).

[¶2] The amended rule establishes a time limit for the motion to substitute based not upon the time of the death, but rather upon the time information of the death is provided by means of a suggestion of death upon the record, i.e. service of a statement of the fact of the death. *Cf.* Ill.Ann.Stat., c. 110, §54(2) (Smith-Hurd 1956). The motion may not be made later than 90 days after the service of the statement unless the period is extended pursuant to Rule 6(b), as amended. See the Advisory Committee's Note to amended Rule 6(b). See also the new Official Form 30.

[¶3] A motion to substitute may be made by any party or by the representative of the deceased party without awaiting the suggestion of death. Indeed, the motion will usually be so made. If a party or the representative of the deceased party desires to limit the time within which another may make the motion, he may do so by suggesting the death upon the record.

[¶4] A motion to substitute made within the prescribed time will ordinarily be granted, but under the permissive language of the first sentence of the amended rule ("the court may order") it may be denied by the court in the exercise of a sound discretion if made long after the death—as can occur if the suggestion of death is not made or is delayed—and circumstances have arisen rendering it unfair to allow substitution. *Cf. Anderson v. Yungkau*, supra, 329 U.S. at 485, 486, 67 S.Ct. at 430, 431, 91 L.Ed. 436, where it was noted under the present rule that settlement and distribution of the estate of a deceased defendant might be so far advanced as to warrant denial of a motion for substitution even though made within the time limit prescribed by that rule. Accordingly, a party interested in securing substitution under the amended rule should not assume that he can rest indefinitely awaiting the suggestion of death before he makes his motion to substitute.

FRCP 26 – 2010 NOTES OF ADVISORY COMMITTEE

[¶1] Rule 26. Rules 26(a)(2) and (b)(4) are amended to address concerns about expert discovery. The amendments to Rule 26(a)(2) require disclosure regarding expected expert testimony of those expert witnesses not required to provide expert reports and limit the expert report to facts or data (rather than "data or other information," as in the current rule) considered by the witness. Rule 26(b)(4) is amended to provide work-product protection against discovery regarding draft expert disclosures or reports and—with three specific exceptions—communications between expert witnesses and counsel.

[¶2] In 1993, Rule 26(b)(4)(A) was revised to authorize expert depositions and Rule 26(a)(2) was added to provide disclosure, including—for many experts—an extensive report. Many courts read the disclosure provision to authorize discovery of all communications between counsel and expert witnesses and all draft reports. The Committee has been told repeatedly that routine discovery into attorney-expert communications and draft reports has had undesirable effects. Costs have risen. Attorneys may employ two sets of experts—one for purposes of consultation and another to testify at trial—because disclosure of their collaborative interactions with expert consultants would reveal their most sensitive and confidential case analyses. At the same time, attorneys often feel compelled to adopt a guarded attitude toward their interaction with testifying experts that impedes effective communication, and experts adopt strategies that protect against discovery but also interfere with their work.

[¶3] Subdivision (a)(2)(B). Rule 26(a)(2)(B)(ii) is amended to provide that disclosure include all "facts or data considered by the witness in forming" the opinions to be offered, rather than the "data or other information" disclosure prescribed in 1993. This amendment is intended to alter the outcome in cases that have relied on the 1993 formulation in requiring disclosure of all attorney-expert communications and draft reports. The amendments to Rule 26(b)(4) make this change explicit by providing work-product protection against discovery regarding draft reports and disclosures or attorney-expert communications.

[¶4] The refocus of disclosure on "facts or data" is meant to limit disclosure to material of a factual nature by excluding theories or mental impressions of counsel. At the same time, the intention is that "facts or data" be interpreted broadly to require disclosure of any material considered by the expert, from whatever source, that contains factual ingredients. The disclosure obligation extends to any facts or data "considered" by the expert in forming the opinions to be expressed, not only those relied upon by the expert.

[¶5] Subdivision (a)(2)(C). Rule 26(a)(2)(C) is added to mandate summary disclosures of the opinions to be offered by expert witnesses who are not required to provide reports under Rule 26(a)(2)(B) and of the facts supporting those opinions. This disclosure is considerably less extensive than the report required by Rule 26(a)(2)(B). Courts must take care against requiring undue detail, keeping in mind that these witnesses have not been specially retained and may not be as responsive to counsel as those who have.

[¶6] This amendment resolves a tension that has sometimes prompted courts to require reports under Rule 26(a)(2)(B) even from witnesses exempted from the report requirement. An (a)(2)(B) report is required only from an expert described in (a)(2)(B).

[¶7] A witness who is not required to provide a report under Rule 26(a)(2)(B) may both testify as a fact witness and also provide expert testimony under Evidence Rule 702, 703, or 705. Frequent examples include physicians or other health care professionals and employees of a party who do not regularly provide expert testimony. Parties must identify such witnesses under Rule 26(a)(2)(A) and provide the disclosure required under Rule 26(a)(2)(C). The (a)(2)(C) disclosure obligation does not include facts unrelated to the expert opinions the witness will present.

[¶8] Subdivision (a)(2)(D). This provision (formerly Rule 26(a)(2)(C)) is amended slightly to specify that the time limits for disclosure of contradictory or rebuttal evidence apply with regard to disclosures under new Rule 26(a)(2)(C), just as they do with regard to reports under Rule 26(a)(2)(B).

[¶9] Subdivision (b)(4). Rule 26(b)(4)(B) is added to provide work-product protection under Rule 26(b)(3)(A) and (B) for drafts of expert reports or disclosures. This protection applies to all witnesses identified under Rule 26(a)(2)(A), whether they are required to provide reports under Rule 26(a)(2)(B) or are the subject of disclosure under Rule 26(a)(2)(C). It applies regardless of the form in which the draft is recorded, whether written, electronic, or otherwise. It also applies to drafts of any supplementation under Rule 26(e); *see* Rule 26(a)(2)(E).

[¶10] Rule 26(b)(4)(C) is added to provide work-product protection for attorney-expert communications regardless of the form of the communications, whether oral, written, electronic, or otherwise. The addition of Rule 26(b)(4)(C) is designed to protect counsel's work product and ensure that lawyers may interact with retained experts without fear of exposing those communications to searching discovery. The protection is limited to communications between an expert witness required to provide a report under Rule 26(a)(2)(B) and the attorney for the party on whose behalf the witness will be testifying, including any "preliminary" expert opinions. Protected "communications" include those between the party's attorney and assistants of the expert witness. The rule does not itself protect communications between counsel and other expert witnesses, such as those for whom disclosure is required under Rule 26(a)(2)(C). The rule does not exclude protection under other doctrines, such as privilege or independent development of the work-product doctrine.

[¶11] The most frequent method for discovering the work of expert witnesses is by deposition, but Rules 26(b)(4)(B) and (C) apply to all forms of discovery.

[¶12] Rules 26(b)(4)(B) and (C) do not impede discovery about the opinions to be offered by the expert or the development, foundation, or basis of those opinions. For example, the expert's testing of material involved in litigation, and notes of any such testing, would not be exempted from discovery by this rule. Similarly, inquiry about communications the expert had with anyone other than the party's counsel about the opinions expressed is unaffected by the rule. Counsel are also free to question expert witnesses about alternative analyses, testing methods, or approaches to the issues on which they are testifying, whether or not the expert considered them in forming the opinions expressed. These discovery changes therefore do not affect the gatekeeping functions called for by *Daubert v. Merrell Dow Pharmaceuticals, Inc.*, 509 U.S. 579 (1993), and related cases.

[¶13] The protection for communications between the retained expert and "the party's attorney" should be applied in a realistic manner, and often would not be limited to communications with a single lawyer or a single law firm. For example, a party may be involved in a number of suits about a given product or service, and may retain a particular expert witness to testify on that party's behalf in several of the cases. In such a situation, the protection applies to communications between the expert witness and the attorneys representing the party in any of those cases. Similarly, communications with in-house counsel for the party would often be regarded as protected even if the in-house attorney is not counsel of record in the action. Other situations may also justify a pragmatic application of the "party's attorney" concept.

[¶14] Although attorney-expert communications are generally protected by Rule 26(b)(4)(C), the protection does not apply to the extent the lawyer and the expert communicate about matters that fall within three exceptions. But the discovery authorized by the exceptions does not extend beyond those specific topics. Lawyer-expert communications may cover many topics and, even when the excepted topics are included among those involved in a given communication, the protection applies to all other aspects of the communication beyond the excepted topics.

[¶15] First, under Rule 26(b)(4)(C)(i) attorney-expert communications regarding compensation for the expert's study or testimony may be the subject of discovery. In some cases, this discovery may go beyond the disclosure requirement in Rule 26(a)(2)(B)(vi). It is not limited to compensation for work forming the opinions to be expressed, but extends to all compensation for the study and testimony provided in relation to the action. Any communications about additional benefits to the expert, such as further work in the event of a successful result in the present case, would be included. This exception includes compensation for work done by a person or organization associated with the expert. The objective is to permit full inquiry into such potential sources of bias.

[¶16] Second, under Rule 26(b)(4)(C)(ii) discovery is permitted to identify facts or data the party's attorney provided to the expert and that the expert considered in forming the opinions to be expressed. The exception applies only to communications "identifying" the facts or data provided by counsel; further communications about the potential relevance of the facts or data are protected.

[¶17] Third, under Rule 26(b)(4)(C)(iii) discovery regarding attorney-expert communications is permitted to identify any assumptions that counsel provided to the expert and that the expert relied upon in forming the opinions to be expressed. For example, the party's attorney may tell the expert to assume the truth of certain testimony or evidence, or the correctness of another expert's conclusions. This exception is limited to those assumptions that the expert actually did rely on in forming the opinions to be expressed. More general attorney-expert discussions about hypotheticals, or exploring possibilities based on hypothetical facts, are outside this exception.

[¶18] Under the amended rule, discovery regarding attorney-expert communications on subjects outside the three exceptions in Rule 26(b)(4)(C), or regarding draft expert reports or disclosures, is permitted only in limited circumstances and by court order. A party seeking such discovery must make the showing specified in Rule 26(b)(3)(A)(ii)—that the party has a substantial need for the discovery and cannot obtain the substantial equivalent without undue hardship. It will be rare for a party to be able to make such a showing given the broad disclosure and discovery otherwise allowed regarding the expert's testimony. A party's failure to provide required disclosure or discovery does not show the need and hardship required by Rule 26(b)(3)(A); remedies are provided by Rule 37.

[¶19] In the rare case in which a party does make this showing, the court must protect against disclosure of the attorney's mental impressions, conclusions, opinions, or legal theories under Rule 26(b)(3)(B). But this protection does not extend to the expert's own development of the opinions to be presented; those are subject to probing in deposition or at trial.

[¶20] Former Rules 26(b)(4)(B) and (C) have been renumbered (D) and (E), and a slight revision has been made in (E) to take account of the renumbering of former (B).

FRCP 26 – 2007 NOTES OF ADVISORY COMMITTEE

[¶1] Former Rule 26(a)(5) served as an index of the discovery methods provided by later rules. It was deleted as redundant. Deletion does not affect the right to pursue discovery in addition to disclosure.

[¶2] Former Rule 26(b)(1) began with a general statement of the scope of discovery that appeared to function as a preface to each of the five numbered paragraphs that followed. This preface has been shifted to the text of paragraph (1) because it does not accurately reflect the limits embodied in paragraphs (2), (3), or (4), and because paragraph (5) does not address the scope of discovery.

[¶3] The reference to discovery of "books" in former Rule 26(b)(1) was deleted to achieve consistent expression throughout the discovery rules. Books remain a proper subject of discovery.

[¶4] Amended Rule 26(b)(3) states that a party may obtain a copy of the party's own previous statement "on request." Former Rule 26(b)(3) expressly made the request procedure available to a nonparty witness, but did not describe the procedure to be used by a party. This apparent gap is closed by adopting the request procedure, which ensures that a party need not invoke Rule 34 to obtain a copy of the party's own statement.

[¶5] Rule 26(e) stated the duty to supplement or correct a disclosure or discovery response "to include information thereafter acquired." This apparent limit is not reflected in practice; parties recognize the duty to supplement or correct by providing information that was not originally provided although it was available at the time of the initial disclosure or response. These words are deleted to reflect the actual meaning of the present rule.

[¶6] Former Rule 26(e) used different phrases to describe the time to supplement or correct a disclosure or discovery response. Disclosures were to be supplemented "at appropriate intervals." A prior discovery response must be "seasonably * * * amend[ed]." The fine distinction between these phrases has not been observed in practice. Amended Rule 26(e)(1)(A) uses the same phrase for disclosures and discovery responses. The party must supplement or correct "in a timely manner."

[¶7] Former Rule 26(g)(1) did not call for striking an unsigned disclosure. The omission was an obvious drafting oversight. Amended Rule 26(g)(2) includes disclosures in the list of matters that the court must strike unless a signature is provided "promptly * * * after being called to the attorney's or party's attention."

[¶8] Former Rule 26(b)(2)(A) referred to a "good faith" argument to extend existing law. Amended Rule 26(b)(1)(B)(i) changes this reference to a "nonfrivolous" argument to achieve consistency with Rule 11(b)(2).

[¶9] As with the Rule 11 signature on a pleading, written motion, or other paper, disclosure and discovery signatures should include not only a postal address but also a telephone number and electronic-mail address. A signer who lacks one or more of those addresses need not supply a nonexistent item.

[¶10] Rule 11(b)(2) recognizes that it is legitimate to argue for establishing new law. An argument to establish new law is equally legitimate in conducting discovery.

FRCP 26 – 2006 NOTES OF ADVISORY COMMITTEE

[¶1] **Subdivision (a).** Rule 26(a)(1)(B) is amended to parallel Rule 34(a) by recognizing that a party must disclose electronically stored information as well as documents that it may use to support its claims or defenses. The term "electronically stored information" has the same broad meaning in Rule 26(a)(1) as in Rule 34(a). This amendment is consistent with the 1993 addition of Rule 26(a)(1)(B). The term "data compilations" is deleted as unnecessary because it is a subset of both documents and electronically stored information.

[¶2] Civil forfeiture actions are added to the list of exemptions from Rule 26(a)(1) disclosure requirements. These actions are governed by new Supplemental Rule G. Disclosure is not likely to be useful.

[¶3] **Subdivision (b)(2).** The amendment to Rule 26(b)(2) is designed to address issues raised by difficulties in locating, retrieving, and providing discovery of some electronically stored information. Electronic storage systems often make it easier to locate and retrieve information. These advantages are properly taken into account in determining the reasonable scope of discovery in a particular case. But some sources of electronically stored information can be accessed only with substantial burden and cost. In a particular case, these burdens and costs may make the information on such sources not reasonably accessible.

[¶4] It is not possible to define in a rule the different types of technological features that may affect the burdens and costs of accessing electronically stored information. Information systems are designed to provide ready access to information used in regular ongoing activities. They also may be designed so as to provide ready access to information that is not regularly used. But a system may retain information on sources that are accessible only by incurring substantial burdens or costs. Subparagraph (B) is added to regulate discovery from such sources.

[¶5] Under this rule, a responding party should produce electronically stored information that is relevant, not privileged, and reasonably accessible, subject to the (b)(2)(C) limitations that apply to all discovery. The responding party must also identify, by category or type, the sources containing potentially responsive information that it is neither searching nor producing. The identification should, to the extent possible, provide enough detail to enable the requesting party to evaluate the burdens and costs of providing the discovery and the likelihood of finding responsive information on the identified sources.

[¶6] A party's identification of sources of electronically stored information as not reasonably accessible does not relieve the party of its common-law or statutory duties to preserve evidence. Whether a responding party is required to preserve unsearched sources of potentially responsive information that it believes are not reasonably accessible depends on the circumstances of each case. It is often useful for the parties to discuss this issue early in discovery.

[¶7] The volume of—and the ability to search—much electronically stored information means that in many cases the responding party will be able to produce information from reasonably accessible sources that will fully satisfy the parties' discovery needs. In many circumstances the requesting party should obtain and evaluate the information from such sources before insisting that the responding party search and produce information contained on sources that are not reasonably accessible. If the requesting party continues to seek discovery of information from sources identified as not reasonably accessible, the parties should discuss the burdens and costs of accessing and retrieving the information, the needs that may establish good cause for requiring all or part of the requested discovery even if the information sought is not reasonably accessible, and conditions on obtaining and producing the information that may be appropriate.

[¶8] If the parties cannot agree whether, or on what terms, sources identified as not reasonably accessible should be searched and discoverable information produced, the issue may be raised either by a motion to compel discovery or by a motion for a protective order. The parties must confer before bringing either motion. If the parties do not resolve the issue and the court must decide, the responding party must show that the identified sources of information are not reasonably accessible because of undue burden or cost. The requesting party may need discovery to test this assertion. Such discovery might take the form of requiring the responding party to conduct a sampling of information contained on the sources identified as not reasonably accessible; allowing some form of inspection of such sources; or taking depositions of witnesses knowledgeable about the responding party's information systems.

[¶9] Once it is shown that a source of electronically stored information is not reasonably accessible, the requesting party may still obtain discovery by showing good cause, considering the limitations of Rule 26(b)(2)(C) that balance the costs and potential benefits of discovery. The decision whether to require a responding party to search for and produce information that is not reasonably accessible depends not only on the burdens and costs of doing so, but also on whether those burdens and costs can be justified in the circumstances of the case. Appropriate considerations may include: (1) the specificity of the discovery request; (2) the quantity of information available from other and more easily accessed sources; (3) the failure to produce relevant information that seems likely to have existed but is no longer available on more easily accessed sources; (4) the likelihood of finding relevant, responsive information that cannot be obtained from other, more easily accessed sources; (5) predictions as to the importance and usefulness of the further information; (6) the importance of the issues at stake in the litigation; and (7) the parties' resources.

[¶10] The responding party has the burden as to one aspect of the inquiry—whether the identified sources are not reasonably accessible in light of the burdens and costs required to search for, retrieve, and produce whatever responsive information may be found. The requesting party has the burden of showing that its need for the discovery outweighs the burdens and costs of locating, retrieving, and producing the information. In some cases, the court will be able to determine whether the identified sources are not reasonably accessible and whether the requesting party has shown good cause for some or all of the discovery, consistent with the limitations of Rule 26(b)(2)(C), through a single proceeding or presentation. The good-cause determination, however, may be complicated because the court and parties may know little about what information the sources identified as not reasonably accessible might contain, whether it is relevant, or how valuable it may be to the litigation. In such cases, the parties may need some focused discovery, which may include sampling of the sources, to learn more about what burdens and costs are involved in accessing the information, what the information consists of, and how valuable it is for the litigation in light of information that can be obtained by exhausting other opportunities for discovery.

[¶11] The good-cause inquiry and consideration of the Rule 26(b)(2)(C) limitations are coupled with the authority to set conditions for discovery. The conditions may take the form of limits on the amount, type, or sources of information required to be accessed and produced. The conditions may also include payment by the requesting party of part or all of the reasonable costs of obtaining information from sources that are not reasonably accessible. A requesting party's willingness to share or bear the access costs may be weighed by the court in determining whether there is good cause. But the producing party's burdens in reviewing the information for relevance and privilege may weigh against permitting the requested discovery.

[¶12] The limitations of Rule 26(b)(2)(C) continue to apply to all discovery of electronically stored information, including that stored on reasonably accessible electronic sources.

[¶13] Subdivision (b)(5). The Committee has repeatedly been advised that the risk of privilege waiver, and the work necessary to avoid it, add to the costs and delay of discovery. When the review is of electronically stored information, the risk of waiver, and the time and effort required to avoid it, can increase substantially because of the volume of electronically stored information and the difficulty in ensuring that all information to be produced has in fact been reviewed. Rule 26(b)(5)(A) provides a procedure for a party that has withheld information on the basis of privilege or protection as trial-preparation material to make the claim so that the requesting party can decide whether to contest the claim and the court can resolve the dispute. Rule 26(b)(5)(B) is added to provide a procedure for a party to assert a claim of privilege or trial-preparation material protection after information is produced in discovery in the action and, if the claim is contested, permit any party that received the information to present the matter to the court for resolution.

[¶14] Rule 26(b)(5)(B) does not address whether the privilege or protection that is asserted after production was waived by the production. The courts have developed principles to determine whether, and under what circumstances, waiver results from inadvertent production of privileged or protected information. Rule 26(b)(5)(B) provides a procedure for presenting and addressing these issues. Rule 26(b)(5)(B) works in tandem with Rule 26(f), which is amended to direct the parties to discuss privilege issues in preparing their discovery plan, and which, with amended Rule 16(b), allows the parties to ask the court to include in an order any agreements the parties reach regarding issues of privilege or trial-preparation material protection. Agreements reached under Rule 26(f)(4) and orders including such agreements entered under Rule 16(b)(6) may be considered when a court determines whether a waiver has occurred. Such agreements and orders ordinarily control if they adopt procedures different from those in Rule 26(b)(5)(B).

[¶15] A party asserting a claim of privilege or protection after production must give notice to the receiving party. That notice should be in writing unless the circumstances preclude it. Such circumstances could include the assertion of the claim during a deposition. The notice should be as specific as possible in identifying the information and stating the basis for the claim. Because the receiving party must decide whether to challenge the claim and may sequester the information and submit it to the court for a ruling on whether the claimed privilege or protection applies and whether it has been waived, the notice should be sufficiently detailed so as to enable the receiving party and the court to understand the basis for the claim and to determine whether waiver has occurred. Courts will continue to examine whether a claim of privilege or protection was made at a reasonable time when delay is part of the waiver determination under the governing law.

[¶16] After receiving notice, each party that received the information must promptly return, sequester, or destroy the information and any copies it has. The option of sequestering or destroying the information is included in part because the receiving party may have incorporated the information in protected trial-preparation materials. No receiving party may use or disclose the information pending resolution of the privilege claim. The receiving party may present to the court the questions whether the information is privileged or protected as trial-preparation material, and whether the privilege or protection has been waived. If it does so, it must provide the court with the grounds for the privilege or protection specified in the producing party's notice, and serve all parties. In presenting the question, the party may use the content of the information only to the extent permitted by the applicable law of privilege, protection for trial-preparation material, and professional responsibility.

[¶17] If a party disclosed the information to nonparties before receiving notice of a claim of privilege or protection as trial-preparation material, it must take reasonable steps to retrieve the information and to return it, sequester it until the claim is resolved, or destroy it.

[¶18] Whether the information is returned or not, the producing party must preserve the information pending the court's ruling on whether the claim of privilege or of protection is properly asserted and whether it was waived. As with claims made under Rule 26(b)(5)(A), there may be no ruling if the other parties do not contest the claim.

[¶19] Subdivision (f). Rule 26(f) is amended to direct the parties to discuss discovery of electronically stored information during their discovery-planning conference. The rule focuses on "issues relating to disclosure or discovery of electronically stored information"; the discussion is not required in cases not involving electronic discovery, and the amendment imposes no additional requirements in those cases. When the parties do anticipate disclosure or discovery of electronically stored information, discussion at the outset may avoid later difficulties or ease their resolution.

[¶20] When a case involves discovery of electronically stored information, the issues to be addressed during the Rule 26(f) conference depend on the nature and extent of the contemplated discovery and of the parties' information systems. It may be important for the parties to discuss those systems, and accordingly important for counsel to become familiar with those systems before the conference. With that information, the parties can develop a discovery plan that takes into account the capabilities of their computer systems. In appropriate cases identification of, and early discovery from, individuals with special knowledge of a party's computer systems may be helpful.

[¶21] The particular issues regarding electronically stored information that deserve attention during the discovery planning stage depend on the specifics of the given case. *See Manual for Complex Litigation* (4th) §40.25(2) (listing topics for discussion in a proposed order regarding meet-and-confer sessions). For example, the parties may specify the topics for such discovery and the time period for which discovery will be sought. They may identify the various sources of such information within a party's control that should be searched for electronically stored information. They may discuss whether the information is reasonably accessible to the party that has it, including the burden or cost of retrieving and reviewing the information. *See* Rule 26(b)(2)(B). Rule 26(f)(3) explicitly directs the parties to discuss the form or forms in which electronically stored information might be produced. The parties may be able to reach agreement on the forms of production, making discovery more efficient. Rule 34(b) is amended to permit a requesting party to specify the form or forms in which it wants electronically stored information produced. If the requesting party does not specify a form, Rule 34(b) directs the responding party to state the forms it intends to use in the production. Early discussion of the forms of production may facilitate the application of Rule 34(b) by allowing the parties to determine what forms of production will meet both parties' needs. Early identification of disputes over the forms of production may help avoid the expense and delay of searches or productions using inappropriate forms.

[¶22] Rule 26(f) is also amended to direct the parties to discuss any issues regarding preservation of discoverable information during their conference as they develop a discovery plan. This provision applies to all sorts of discoverable information, but can be particularly important with regard to electronically stored information. The volume and dynamic nature of electronically stored information may complicate preservation obligations. The ordinary operation of computers involves both the automatic creation and the automatic deletion or overwriting of certain information. Failure to address preservation issues early in the litigation increases uncertainty and raises a risk of disputes.

[¶23] The parties' discussion should pay particular attention to the balance between the competing needs to preserve relevant evidence and to continue routine operations critical to ongoing activities. Complete or broad cessation of a party's routine computer operations could paralyze the party's activities. *Cf. Manual for Complex Litigation* (4th) §11.422 ("A blanket preservation order may be prohibitively expensive and unduly burdensome for parties dependent on computer systems for their day-to-day operations."). The parties should take account of these considerations in their discussions, with the goal of agreeing on reasonable preservation steps.

[¶24] The requirement that the parties discuss preservation does not imply that courts should routinely enter preservation orders. A preservation order entered over objections should be narrowly tailored. Ex parte preservation orders should issue only in exceptional circumstances.

[¶25] Rule 26(f) is also amended to provide that the parties should discuss any issues relating to assertions of privilege or of protection as trial-preparation materials, including whether the parties can facilitate discovery by agreeing on procedures for asserting claims of privilege or protection after production and whether to ask the court to enter an order that includes any agreement the parties reach. The Committee has repeatedly been advised about the discovery difficulties that can result from efforts to guard against waiver of privilege and work-product protection. Frequently parties find it necessary to spend large amounts of time reviewing materials requested through discovery to avoid waiving privilege. These efforts are necessary because materials subject to a claim of privilege or protection are often difficult to identify. A failure to withhold even one such item may result in an argument that there has been a waiver of privilege as to all other privileged materials on that subject matter. Efforts to avoid the risk of waiver can impose substantial costs on the party producing the material and the time required for the privilege review can substantially delay access for the party seeking discovery.

[¶26] These problems often become more acute when discovery of electronically stored information is sought. The volume of such data, and the informality that attends use of e-mail and some other types of electronically stored information, may make privilege determinations more difficult, and privilege review correspondingly more expensive and time consuming. Other aspects of electronically stored information pose particular difficulties for privilege review. For example, production may be sought of information automatically included in electronic files but not apparent to the creator or to readers. Computer programs may retain draft language, editorial comments, and other deleted matter (sometimes referred to as "embedded data" or "embedded edits") in an electronic file but not make them apparent to the reader. Information describing the history, tracking, or management of an electronic file (sometimes called "metadata") is usually not apparent to the reader viewing a hard copy or a screen image. Whether this information should be produced may be among the topics discussed in the Rule 26(f) conference. If it is, it may need to be reviewed to ensure that no privileged information is included, further complicating the task of privilege review.

[¶27] Parties may attempt to minimize these costs and delays by agreeing to protocols that minimize the risk of waiver. They may agree that the responding party will provide certain requested materials for initial examination without waiving any privilege or protection—sometimes known as a "quick peek." The requesting party then designates the documents it wishes to have actually produced. This designation is the Rule 34 request. The responding party then responds in the usual course, screening only those documents actually requested for formal production and asserting privilege claims as provided in Rule 26(b)(5)(A). On other occasions, parties enter agreements—sometimes called "clawback agreements"—that production without intent to waive privilege or protection should not be a waiver so long as the responding party identifies the documents mistakenly produced, and that the documents should be returned under those circumstances. Other voluntary arrangements may be appropriate depending on the circumstances of each litigation. In most circumstances, a party who receives information under such an arrangement cannot assert that production of the information waived a claim of privilege or of protection as trial-preparation material.

[¶28] Although these agreements may not be appropriate for all cases, in certain cases they can facilitate prompt and economical discovery by reducing delay before the discovering party obtains access to documents, and by reducing the cost and burden of review by the producing party. A case-management or other order including such agreements may further facilitate the discovery process. Form 35 is amended to include a report to the court about any agreement regarding protections against inadvertent forfeiture or waiver of privilege or protection that the parties have reached, and Rule 16(b) is amended to recognize that the court may include such an agreement in a case-management or other order. If the parties agree to entry of such an order, their proposal should be included in the report to the court.

[¶29] Rule 26(b)(5)(B) is added to establish a parallel procedure to assert privilege or protection as trial-preparation material after production, leaving the question of waiver to later determination by the court.

FRCP 26 – 2000 NOTES OF ADVISORY COMMITTEE

[¶1] Purposes of amendments. The Rule 26(a)(1) initial disclosure provisions are amended to establish a nationally uniform practice. The scope of the disclosure obligation is narrowed to cover only information that the disclosing party may use to support its position. In addition, the rule exempts specified categories of proceedings from initial disclosure, and permits a party who contends that disclosure is not appropriate in the circumstances of the case to present its objections to the court, which must then determine whether disclosure should be made. Related changes are made in Rules 26(d) and (f).

[¶2] The initial disclosure requirements added by the 1993 amendments permitted local rules directing that disclosure would not be required or altering its operation. The inclusion of the "opt out" provision reflected the strong opposition to initial disclosure felt in some districts, and permitted experimentation with differing disclosure rules in those districts that were favorable to disclosure. The local option also recognized that—partly in response to the first publication in 1991 of a proposed disclosure rule—many districts had adopted a variety of disclosure programs under the aegis of the Civil Justice Reform Act. It was hoped that developing experience under a variety of disclosure systems would support eventual refinement of a uniform national disclosure practice. In addition, there was hope that local experience could identify categories of actions in which disclosure is not useful.

[¶3] A striking array of local regimes in fact emerged for disclosure and related features introduced in 1993. *See* D. Stienstra, *Implementation of Disclosure in United States District Courts, With Specific Attention to Courts' Responses to Selected Amendments to Federal Rule of Civil Procedure 26* (Federal Judicial Center, March 30, 1998) (describing and categorizing local regimes). In its final report to Congress on the CJRA experience, the Judicial Conference recommended reexamination of the need for national uniformity, particularly in regard to initial disclosure. Judicial Conference, *Alternative Proposals for Reduction of Cost and Delay: Assessment of Principles, Guidelines and Techniques*, 175 F.R.D. 62, 98 (1997).

[¶4] At the Committee's request, the Federal Judicial Center undertook a survey in 1997 to develop information on current disclosure and discovery practices. *See* T. Willging, J. Shapard, D. Stienstra & D. Miletich, *Discovery and Disclosure Practice, Problems, and Proposals for Change* (Federal Judicial Center, 1997). In addition, the Committee convened two conferences on discovery involving lawyers from around the country and received reports and recommendations on possible discovery amendments from a number of bar groups. Papers and other proceedings from the second conference are published in 39 Boston Col. L. Rev. 517-840 (1998).

[¶5] The Committee has discerned widespread support for national uniformity. Many lawyers have experienced difficulty in coping with divergent disclosure and other practices as they move from one district to another. Lawyers surveyed by the Federal Judicial Center ranked adoption of a uniform national disclosure rule second among proposed rule changes (behind increased availability of judges to resolve discovery disputes) as a means to reduce litigation expenses without interfering with fair outcomes. *Discovery and Disclosure Practice, supra*, at 44-45. National uniformity is also a central purpose of the Rules Enabling Act of 1934, as amended, 28 U.S.C. §§2072-2077.

[¶6] These amendments restore national uniformity to disclosure practice. Uniformity is also restored to other aspects of discovery by deleting most of the provisions authorizing local rules that vary the number of permitted discovery events or the length of depositions. Local rule options are also deleted from Rules 26(d) and (f).

[¶7] Subdivision (a)(1). The amendments remove the authority to alter or opt out of the national disclosure requirements by local rule, invalidating not only formal local rules but also informal "standing" orders of an individual judge or court that purport to create exemptions from—or limit or expand—the disclosure provided under the national rule. *See* Rule 83. Case-specific orders remain proper, however, and are expressly required if a party objects that initial disclosure is not appropriate in the circumstances of the action. Specified categories of proceedings are excluded from initial disclosure under subdivision (a)(1)(E). In addition, the parties can stipulate to forgo disclosure, as was true before. But even in a case excluded by subdivision (a)(1)(E) or in which the parties stipulate to bypass disclosure, the court can order exchange of similar information in managing the action under Rule 16.

[¶8] The initial disclosure obligation of subdivisions (a)(1)(A) and (B) has been narrowed to identification of witnesses and documents that the disclosing party may use to support its claims or defenses. "Use" includes any use at a pretrial conference, to support a motion, or at trial. The disclosure obligation is also triggered by intended use in discovery, apart from use to respond to a discovery request; use of a document to question a witness during a deposition is a common example. The disclosure obligation attaches both to witnesses and documents a party intends to use and also to witnesses and to documents the party intends to use if—in the language of Rule 26(a)(3)—"the need arises."

[¶9] A party is no longer obligated to disclose witnesses or documents, whether favorable or unfavorable, that it does not intend to use. The obligation to disclose information the party may use connects directly to the exclusion sanction of Rule 37(c)(1). Because the disclosure obligation is limited to material that the party may use, it is no longer tied to particularized allegations in the pleadings. Subdivision (e)(1), which is unchanged, requires supplementation if information later acquired would have been subject to the disclosure requirement. As case preparation continues, a party must supplement its disclosures when it determines that it may use a witness or document that it did not previously intend to use.

[¶10] The disclosure obligation applies to "claims and defenses," and therefore requires a party to disclose information it may use to support its denial or rebuttal of the allegations, claim, or defense of another party. It thereby bolsters the requirements of Rule 11(b)(4), which authorizes denials "warranted on the evidence," and disclosure should include the identity of any witness or document that the disclosing party may use to support such denials.

[¶11] Subdivision (a)(3) presently excuses pretrial disclosure of information solely for impeachment. Impeachment information is similarly excluded from the initial disclosure requirement.

[¶12] Subdivisions (a)(1)(C) and (D) are not changed. Should a case be exempted from initial disclosure by Rule 26(a)(1)(E) or by agreement or order, the insurance information described by subparagraph (D) should be subject to discovery, as it would have been under the principles of former Rule 26(b)(2), which was added in 1970 and deleted in 1993 as redundant in light of the new initial disclosure obligation.

[¶13] New subdivision (a)(1)(E) excludes eight specified categories of proceedings from initial disclosure. The objective of this listing is to identify cases in which there is likely to be little or no discovery, or in which initial disclosure appears unlikely to contribute to the effective development of the case. The list was developed after a review of the categories excluded by local rules in various districts from the operation of Rule 16(b) and the conference requirements of subdivision (f). Subdivision (a)(1)(E) refers to categories of "proceedings" rather than categories of "actions" because some might not properly be labeled "actions." Case designations made by the parties or the clerk's office at the time of filing do not control application of the exemptions. The descriptions in the rule are generic and are intended to be administered by the parties—and, when needed, the courts—with the flexibility needed to adapt to gradual evolution in the types of proceedings that fall within these general categories. The exclusion of an action for review on an administrative record, for example, is intended to reach a proceeding that is framed as an "appeal" based solely on an administrative record. The exclusion should not apply to a proceeding in a form that commonly permits admission of new evidence to supplement the record. Item (vii), excluding a proceeding ancillary to proceedings in other courts, does not refer to bankruptcy proceedings; application of the Civil Rules to bankruptcy proceedings is determined by the Bankruptcy Rules.

[¶14] Subdivision (a)(1)(E) is likely to exempt a substantial proportion of the cases in most districts from the initial disclosure requirement. Based on 1996 and 1997 case filing statistics, Federal Judicial Center staff estimate that, nationwide, these categories total approximately one-third of all civil filings.

[¶15] The categories of proceedings listed in subdivision (a)(1)(E) are also exempted from the subdivision (f) conference requirement and from the subdivision (d) moratorium on discovery. Although there is no restriction on commencement of discovery in these cases, it is not expected that this opportunity will often lead to abuse since there is likely to be little or no discovery in most such cases. Should a defendant need more time to respond to discovery requests filed at the beginning of an exempted action, it can seek relief by motion under Rule 26(c) if the plaintiff is unwilling to defer the due date by agreement.

[¶16] Subdivision (a)(1)(E)'s enumeration of exempt categories is exclusive. Although a case-specific order can alter or excuse initial disclosure, local rules or "standing" orders that purport to create general exemptions are invalid. *See* Rule 83.

[¶17] The time for initial disclosure is extended to 14 days after the subdivision (f) conference unless the court orders otherwise. This change is integrated with corresponding changes requiring that the subdivision (f) conference be held 21 days before the Rule 16(b) scheduling conference or scheduling order, and that the report on the subdivision (f) conference be submitted to the court 14 days after the meeting. These changes provide a more orderly opportunity for the parties to review the disclosures, and for the court to consider the report. In many instances, the subdivision (f) conference and the effective preparation of the case would benefit from disclosure before the conference, and earlier disclosure is encouraged.

[¶18] The presumptive disclosure date does not apply if a party objects to initial disclosure during the subdivision (f) conference and states its objection in the subdivision (f) discovery plan. The right to object to initial disclosure is not intended to afford parties an opportunity to "opt out" of disclosure unilaterally. It does provide an opportunity for an objecting party to present to the court its position that disclosure would be "inappropriate in the circumstances of the action." Making the objection permits the objecting party to present the question to the judge before any party is required to make disclosure. The court must then rule on the objection and determine what disclosures—if any—should be made. Ordinarily, this determination would be included in the Rule 16(b) scheduling order, but the court could handle the matter in a different fashion. Even when circumstances warrant suspending some disclosure obligations, others—such as the damages and insurance information called for by subdivisions (a)(1)(C) and (D)—may continue to be appropriate.

[¶19] The presumptive disclosure date is also inapplicable to a party who is "first served or otherwise joined" after the subdivision (f) conference. This phrase refers to the date of service of a claim on a party in a defensive posture (such as a defendant or third-party defendant), and the date of joinder of a party added as a claimant or an intervenor. Absent court order or stipulation, a new party has 30 days in which to make its initial disclosures. But it is expected that later-added parties will ordinarily be treated the same as the original parties when the original parties have stipulated to forgo initial disclosure, or the court has ordered disclosure in a modified form.

[¶20] Subdivision (a)(3). The amendment to Rule 5(d) forbids filing disclosures under subdivisions (a)(1) and (a)(2) until they are used in the proceeding, and this change is reflected in an amendment to subdivision (a)(4). Disclosures under subdivision (a)(3), however, may be important to the court in connection with the final pretrial conference or otherwise in preparing for trial. The requirement that objections to certain matters be filed points up the court's need to be provided with these materials. Accordingly, the requirement that subdivision (a)(3) materials be filed has been moved from subdivision (a)(4) to subdivision (a)(3), and it has also been made clear that they—and any objections—should be filed "promptly."

[¶21] Subdivision (a)(4). The filing requirement has been removed from this subdivision. Rule 5(d) has been amended to provide that disclosures under subdivisions (a)(1) and (a)(2) must not be filed until used in the proceeding. Subdivision (a)(3) has been amended to require that the disclosures it directs, and objections to them, be filed promptly. Subdivision (a)(4) continues to require that all disclosures under subdivisions (a)(1), (a)(2), and (a)(3) be in writing, signed, and served.

[¶22] "Shall" is replaced by "must" under the program to conform amended rules to current style conventions when there is no ambiguity.

[¶23] Subdivision (b)(1). In 1978, the Committee published for comment a proposed amendment, suggested by the Section of Litigation of the American Bar Association, to refine the scope of discovery by deleting the "subject matter" language. This proposal was withdrawn, and the Committee has since then made other changes in the discovery rules to address concerns about overbroad discovery. Concerns about costs and delay of discovery have persisted nonetheless, and other bar groups have repeatedly renewed similar proposals for amendment to this subdivision to delete the "subject matter" language. Nearly one-third of the lawyers surveyed in 1997 by the Federal Judicial Center endorsed narrowing the scope of discovery as a means of reducing litigation expense without interfering with fair case resolutions. *Discovery and Disclosure Practice*, *supra*, at 44-45 (1997). The Committee has heard that in some instances, particularly cases involving large quantities of discovery, parties seek to justify discovery requests that sweep far beyond the claims and defenses of the parties on the ground that they nevertheless have a bearing on the "subject matter" involved in the action.

[¶24] The amendments proposed for subdivision (b)(1) include one element of these earlier proposals but also differ from these proposals in significant ways. The similarity is that the amendments describe the scope of party-controlled discovery in terms of matter relevant to the claim or defense of any party. The court, however, retains authority to order discovery of any matter relevant to the subject matter involved in the action for good cause. The amendment is designed to involve the court more actively in regulating the breadth of sweeping or contentious discovery. The Committee has been informed repeatedly by lawyers that involvement of the court in managing discovery is an important method of controlling problems of inappropriately broad discovery. Increasing the availability of judicial officers to resolve discovery disputes and increasing court management of discovery were both strongly endorsed by the attorneys surveyed by the Federal Judicial Center. *See Discovery and Disclosure Practice*, *supra*, at 44. Under the amended provisions, if there is an objection that discovery goes beyond material relevant to the parties' claims or defenses, the court would become involved to determine whether the discovery is relevant to the claims or defenses and, if not, whether good cause exists for authorizing it so long as it is relevant to the subject matter of the action. The good-cause standard warranting broader discovery is meant to be flexible.

[¶25] The Committee intends that the parties and the court focus on the actual claims and defenses involved in the action. The dividing line between information relevant to the claims and defenses and that relevant only to the subject matter of the action cannot be defined with precision. A variety of types of information not directly pertinent to the incident in suit could be relevant to the claims or defenses raised in a given action. For example, other incidents of the same type, or involving the same product, could be properly discoverable under the revised standard. Information about organizational arrangements or filing systems of a party could be discoverable if likely to yield or lead to the discovery of admissible information. Similarly, information that could be used to impeach a likely witness, although not otherwise relevant to the claims or defenses, might be properly discoverable. In each instance, the determination whether such information is discoverable because it is relevant to the claims or defenses depends on the circumstances of the pending action.

[¶26] The rule change signals to the court that it has the authority to confine discovery to the claims and defenses asserted in the pleadings, and signals to the parties that they have no entitlement to discovery to develop new claims or defenses that are not already identified in the pleadings. In general, it is hoped that reasonable lawyers can cooperate to manage discovery without the need for judicial intervention. When judicial intervention is invoked, the actual scope of discovery should be determined according to the reasonable needs of the action. The court may permit broader discovery in a particular case depending on the circumstances of the case, the nature of the claims and defenses, and the scope of the discovery requested.

[¶27] The amendments also modify the provision regarding discovery of information not admissible in evidence. As added in 1946, this sentence was designed to make clear that otherwise relevant material could not be withheld because it was hearsay or otherwise inadmissible. The Committee was concerned that the "reasonably calculated to lead to the discovery of admissible evidence" standard set forth in this sentence might swallow any other limitation on the scope of discovery. Accordingly, this sentence has been amended to clarify that information must be relevant to be discoverable, even though inadmissible, and that discovery of such material is permitted if reasonably calculated to lead to the discovery of admissible evidence. As used here, "relevant" means within the scope of discovery as defined in this subdivision, and it would include information relevant to the subject matter involved in the action if the court has ordered discovery to that limit based on a showing of good cause.

[¶28] Finally, a sentence has been added calling attention to the limitations of subdivision (b)(2)(i), (ii), and (iii). These limitations apply to discovery that is otherwise within the scope of subdivision (b)(1). The Committee has been told repeatedly that courts have not implemented these limitations with the vigor that was contemplated. *See* 8 *Federal Practice & Procedure* §2008.1 at 121. This otherwise redundant cross-reference has been added to emphasize the need for active judicial use of subdivision (b)(2) to control excessive discovery. *Cf. Crawford-El v. Britton*, 118 S. Ct. 1584, 1597 (1998) (quoting Rule 26(b)(2)(iii) and stating that "Rule 26 vests the trial judge with broad discretion to tailor discovery narrowly").

[¶29] **Subdivision (b)(2).** Rules 30, 31, and 33 establish presumptive national limits on the numbers of depositions and interrogatories. New Rule 30(d)(2) establishes a presumptive limit on the length of depositions. Subdivision (b)(2) is amended to remove the previous permission for local rules that establish different presumptive limits on these discovery activities. There is no reason to believe that unique circumstances justify varying these nationally-applicable presumptive limits in certain districts. The limits can be modified by court order or agreement in an individual action, but "standing" orders imposing different presumptive limits are not authorized. Because there is no national rule limiting the number of Rule 36 requests for admissions, the rule continues to authorize local rules that impose numerical limits on them. This change is not intended to interfere with differentiated case management in districts that use this technique by case-specific order as part of their Rule 16 process.

[¶30] **Subdivision (d).** The amendments remove the prior authority to exempt cases by local rule from the moratorium on discovery before the subdivision (f) conference, but the categories of proceedings exempted from initial disclosure under subdivision (a)(1)(E) are excluded from subdivision (d). The parties may agree to disregard the moratorium where it applies, and the court may so order in a case, but "standing" orders altering the moratorium are not authorized.

[¶31] **Subdivision (f).** As in subdivision (d), the amendments remove the prior authority to exempt cases by local rule from the conference requirement. The Committee has been informed that the addition of the conference was one of the most successful changes made in the 1993 amendments, and it therefore has determined to apply the conference requirement nationwide. The categories of proceedings exempted from initial disclosure under subdivision (a)(1)(E) are exempted from the conference requirement for the reasons that warrant exclusion from initial disclosure. The court may order that the conference need not occur in a case where otherwise required, or that it occur in a case otherwise exempted by subdivision (a)(1)(E). "Standing" orders altering the conference requirement for categories of cases are not authorized.

[¶32] The rule is amended to require only a "conference" of the parties, rather than a "meeting." There are important benefits to face-to-face discussion of the topics to be covered in the conference, and those benefits may be lost if other means of conferring were routinely used when face-to-face meetings would not impose burdens. Nevertheless, geographic conditions in some districts may exact costs far out of proportion to these benefits. The amendment allows the court by case-specific order to require a face-to-face meeting, but "standing" orders so requiring are not authorized.

[¶33] As noted concerning the amendments to subdivision (a)(1), the time for the conference has been changed to at least 21 days before the Rule 16 scheduling conference, and the time for the report is changed to no more than 14 days after the Rule 26(f) conference. This should ensure that the court will have the report well in advance of the scheduling conference or the entry of the scheduling order.

[¶34] Since Rule 16 was amended in 1983 to mandate some case management activities in all courts, it has included deadlines for completing these tasks to ensure that all courts do so within a reasonable time. Rule 26(f) was fit into this scheme when it was adopted in 1993. It was never intended, however, that the national requirements that certain activities be completed by a certain time should delay case management in districts that move much faster than the national rules direct, and the rule is therefore amended to permit such a court to adopt a local rule that shortens the period specified for the completion of these tasks.

[¶35] "Shall" is replaced by "must," "does," or an active verb under the program to conform amended rules to current style conventions when there is no ambiguity.

FRCP 26 – 1993 NOTES OF ADVISORY COMMITTEE

[¶1] Subdivision (a). Through the addition of paragraphs (1)-(4), this subdivision imposes on parties a duty to disclose, without awaiting formal discovery requests, certain basic information that is needed in most cases to prepare for trial or make an informed decision about settlement. The rule requires all parties (1) early in the case to exchange information regarding potential witnesses, documentary evidence, damages, and insurance, (2) at an appropriate time during the discovery period to identify expert witnesses and provide a detailed written statement of the testimony that may be offered at trial through specially retained experts, and (3) as the trial date approaches to identify the particular evidence that may be offered at trial. The enumeration in Rule 26(a) of items to be disclosed does not prevent a court from requiring by order or local rule that the parties disclose additional information without a discovery request. Nor are parties precluded from using traditional discovery methods to obtain further information regarding these matters, as for example asking an expert during a deposition about testimony given in other litigation beyond the four-year period specified in Rule 26(a)(2)(B).

[¶2] A major purpose of the revision is to accelerate the exchange of basic information about the case and to eliminate the paper work involved in requesting such information, and the rule should be applied in a manner to achieve those objectives. The concepts of imposing a duty of disclosure were set forth in Brazil, The Adversary Character of Civil Discovery: A Critique and Proposals for Change, 31 Vand. L. Rev. 1348 (1978), and Schwarzer, The Federal Rules, the Adversary Process, and Discovery Reform, 50 U. Pitt. L. Rev. 703, 721-23 (1989).

[¶3] The rule is based upon the experience of district courts that have required disclosure of some of this information through local rules, court-approved standard interrogatories, and standing orders. Most have required pretrial disclosure of the kind of information described in Rule 26(a)(3). Many have required written reports from experts containing information like that specified in Rule 26(a)(2)(B). While far more limited, the experience of the few state and federal courts that have required pre-discovery exchange of core information such as is contemplated in Rule 26(a)(1) indicates that savings in time and expense can be achieved, particularly if the litigants meet and discuss the issues in the case as a predicate for this exchange and if a judge supports the process, as by using the results to guide further proceedings in the case. Courts in Canada and the United Kingdom have for many years required disclosure of certain information without awaiting a request from an adversary.

[¶4] Paragraph (1). As the functional equivalent of court-ordered interrogatories, this paragraph requires early disclosure, without need for any request, of four types of information that have been customarily secured early in litigation through formal discovery. The introductory clause permits the court, by local rule, to exempt all or particular types of cases from these disclosure requirement[s] or to modify the nature of the information to be disclosed. It is expected that courts would, for example, exempt cases like Social Security reviews and government collection cases in which discovery would not be appropriate or would be unlikely. By order the court may eliminate or modify the disclosure requirements in a particular case, and similarly the parties, unless precluded by order or local rule, can stipulate to elimination or modification of the requirements for that case. The disclosure obligations specified in paragraph (1) will not be appropriate for all cases, and it is expected that changes in these obligations will be made by the court or parties when the circumstances warrant.

[¶5] Authorization of these local variations is, in large measure, included in order to accommodate the Civil Justice Reform Act of 1990, which implicitly directs districts to experiment during the study period with differing procedures to reduce the time and expense of civil litigation. The civil justice delay and expense reduction plans adopted by the courts under the Act differ as to the type, form, and timing of disclosures required. Section 105(c)(1) of the Act calls for a report by the Judicial Conference to Congress by December 31, 1995, comparing experience in twenty of these courts; and section 105(c)(2)(B) contemplates that some changes in the Rules may then be needed. While these studies may indicate the desirability of further changes in Rule 26(a)(1), these changes probably could not become effective before December 1998 at the earliest. In the meantime, the present revision puts in place a series of disclosure obligations that, unless a court acts affirmatively to impose other requirements or indeed to reject all such requirements for the present, are designed to eliminate certain discovery, help focus the discovery that is needed, and facilitate preparation for trial or settlement.

[¶6] Subparagraph (A) requires identification of all persons who, based on the investigation conducted thus far, are likely to have discoverable information relevant to the factual disputes between the parties. All persons with such information should be disclosed, whether or not their testimony will be supportive of the position of the disclosing party. As officers of the court, counsel are expected to disclose the identity of those persons who may be used by them as witnesses or who, if their potential testimony were known, might reasonably be expected to be deposed or called as a witness by any of the other parties. Indicating briefly the general topics on which such persons have information should not be burdensome, and will assist other parties in deciding which depositions will actually be needed.

[¶7] Subparagraph (B) is included as a substitute for the inquiries routinely made about the existence and location of documents and other tangible things in the possession, custody, or control of the disclosing party. Although, unlike subdivision (a)(3)(C), an itemized listing of each exhibit is not required, the disclosure should describe and categorize, to the extent identified during the initial investigation, the nature and location of potentially relevant documents and records, including computerized data and other electronically-recorded information, sufficiently to enable opposing parties (1) to make an informed decision concerning which documents might need to be examined, at least initially, and (2) to frame their document requests in a manner likely to avoid squabbles resulting from the wording of the requests. As with potential witnesses, the requirement for disclosure of documents applies to all potentially relevant items then known to the party, whether or not supportive of its contentions in the case.

[¶8] Unlike subparagraphs (C) and (D), subparagraph (B) does not require production of any documents. Of course, in cases involving few documents a disclosing party may prefer to provide copies of the documents rather than describe them, and the rule is written to afford this option to the disclosing party. If, as will be more typical, only the description is provided, the other parties are expected to obtain the documents desired by proceeding under Rule 34 or through informal requests. The disclosing party does not, by describing documents under subparagraph (B), waive its right to object to production on the basis of privilege or work product protection, or to assert that the documents are not sufficiently relevant to justify the burden or expense of production.

[¶9] The initial disclosure requirements of subparagraphs (A) and (B) are limited to identification of potential evidence "relevant to disputed facts alleged with particularity in the pleadings." There is no need for a party to identify potential evidence with respect to allegations that are admitted. Broad, vague, and conclusory allegations sometimes tolerated in notice pleading—for example, the assertion that a product with many component parts is defective in some unspecified manner—should not impose upon responding parties the obligation at that point to search for and identify all persons possibly involved in, or all documents affecting, the design, manufacture, and assembly of the product. The greater the specificity and clarity of the allegations in the pleadings, the more complete should be the listing of potential witnesses and types of documentary evidence. Although paragraphs (1)(A) and (1)(B) by their terms refer to the factual disputes defined in the pleadings, the rule contemplates that these issues would be informally refined and clarified during the meeting of the parties under subdivision (f) and that the disclosure obligations would be adjusted in the light of these discussions. The disclosure requirements should, in short, be applied with common sense in light of the principles of Rule 1, keeping in mind the salutary purposes that the rule is intended to accomplish. The litigants should not indulge in gamesmanship with respect to the disclosure obligations.

[¶10] Subparagraph (C) imposes a burden of disclosure that includes the functional equivalent of a standing Request for Production under Rule 34. A party claiming damages or other monetary relief must, in addition to disclosing the calculation of such damages, make available the supporting documents for inspection and copying as if a request for such materials had been made under Rule 34. This obligation applies only with respect to documents then reasonably available to it and not privileged or protected as work product. Likewise, a party would not be expected to provide a calculation of damages which, as in many patent infringement actions, depends on information in the possession of another party or person.

[¶11] Subparagraph (D) replaces subdivision (b)(2) of Rule 26, and provides that liability insurance policies be made available for inspection and copying. The last two sentences of that subdivision have been omitted as unnecessary, not to signify any change of law. The disclosure of insurance information does not thereby render such information admissible in evidence. See Rule 411, Federal Rules of Evidence. Nor does subparagraph (D) require disclosure of applications for insurance, though in particular cases such information may be discoverable in accordance with revised subdivision (a)(5).

[¶12] Unless the court directs a different time, the disclosures required by subdivision (a)(1) are to be made at or within 10 days after the meeting of the parties under subdivision (f). One of the purposes of this meeting is to refine the factual disputes with respect to which disclosures should be made under paragraphs (1)(A) and (1)(B), particularly if an answer has not been filed by a defendant, or, indeed, to afford the parties an opportunity to modify by stipulation the timing or scope of these obligations. The time of this meeting is generally left to the parties provided it is held at least 14 days before a scheduling conference is held or before a scheduling order is due under Rule 16(b). In cases in which no scheduling conference is held, this will mean that the meeting must ordinarily be held within 75 days after a defendant has first appeared in the case and hence that the initial disclosures would be due no later than 85 days after the first appearance of a defendant.

[¶13] Before making its disclosures, a party has the obligation under subdivision (g)(1) to make a reasonable inquiry into the facts of the case. The rule does not demand an exhaustive investigation at this stage of the case, but one that is reasonable under the circumstances, focusing on the facts that are alleged with particularity in the pleadings. The type of investigation that can be expected at this point will vary based upon such factors as the number and complexity of the issues; the location, nature, number, and availability of potentially relevant witnesses and documents; the extent of past working relationships between the attorney and the client, particularly in handling related or similar litigation; and of course how long the party has to conduct an investigation, either before or after filing of the case. As provided in the last sentence of subdivision (a)(1), a party is not excused from the duty of disclosure merely because its investigation is incomplete. The party should make its initial disclosures based on the pleadings and the information then reasonably available to it. As its investigation continues and as the issues in the pleadings are clarified, it should supplement its disclosures as required by subdivision (e)(1). A party is not relieved from its obligation of disclosure merely because another party has not made its disclosures or has made an inadequate disclosure.

[¶14] It will often be desirable, particularly if the claims made in the complaint are broadly stated, for the parties to have their Rule 26(f) meeting early in the case, perhaps before a defendant has answered the complaint or had time to conduct other than a cursory investigation. In such circumstances, in order to facilitate more meaningful and useful initial disclosures, they can and should stipulate to a period of more than 10 days after the meeting in which to make these disclosures, at least for defendants who had no advance notice of the potential litigation. A stipulation at an early meeting affording such a defendant at least 60 days after receiving the complaint in which to make its disclosures under subdivision (a)(1)—a period that is two weeks longer than the time formerly specified for responding to interrogatories served with a complaint—should be adequate and appropriate in most cases.

[¶15] Paragraph (2). This paragraph imposes an additional duty to disclose information regarding expert testimony sufficiently in advance of trial that opposing parties have a reasonable opportunity to prepare for effective cross examination and perhaps arrange for expert testimony from other witnesses. Normally the court should prescribe a time for these disclosures in a scheduling order under Rule 16(b), and in most cases the party with the burden of proof on an issue should disclose its expert testimony on that issue before other parties are required to make their disclosures with respect to that issue. In the absence of such a direction, the disclosures are to be made by all parties at least 90 days before the trial date or the date by which the case is to be ready for trial, except that an additional 30 days is allowed (unless the court specifies another time) for disclosure of expert testimony to be used solely to contradict or rebut the testimony that may be presented by another party's expert. For a discussion of procedures that have been used to enhance the reliability of expert testimony, see M. Graham, Expert Witness Testimony and the Federal Rules of Evidence: Insuring Adequate Assurance of Trustworthiness, 1986 U. Ill. L. Rev. 90.

[¶16] Paragraph (2)(B) requires that persons retained or specially employed to provide expert testimony, or whose duties as an employee of the party regularly involve the giving of expert testimony, must prepare a detailed and complete written report, stating the testimony the witness is expected to present during direct examination, together with the reasons therefor. The information disclosed under the former rule in answering interrogatories about the "substance" of expert testimony was frequently so sketchy and vague that it rarely dispensed with the need to depose the expert and often was even of little help in preparing for a deposition of the witness. Revised Rule 37(c)(1) provides an incentive for full disclosure; namely, that a party will not ordinarily be permitted to use on direct examination any expert testimony not so disclosed. Rule 26(a)(2)(B) does not preclude counsel from providing assistance to experts in preparing the reports, and indeed, with experts such as automobile mechanics, this assistance may be needed. Nevertheless, the report, which is intended to set forth the substance of the direct examination, should be written in a manner that reflects the testimony to be given by the witness and it must be signed by the witness.

[¶17] The report is to disclose the data and other information considered by the expert and any exhibits or charts that summarize or support the expert's opinions. Given this obligation of disclosure, litigants should no longer be able to argue that materials furnished to their experts to be used in forming their opinions—whether or not ultimately relied upon by the expert—are privileged or otherwise protected from disclosure when such persons are testifying or being deposed.

[¶18] Revised subdivision (b)(4)(A) authorizes the deposition of expert witnesses. Since depositions of experts required to prepare a written report may be taken only after the report has been served, the length of the deposition of such experts should be reduced, and in many cases the report may eliminate the need for a deposition. Revised subdivision (e)(1) requires disclosure of any material changes made in the opinions of an expert from whom a report is required, whether the changes are in the written report or in testimony given at a deposition.

[¶19] For convenience, this rule and revised Rule 30 continue to use the term "expert" to refer to those persons who will testify under Rule 702 of the Federal Rules of Evidence with respect to scientific, technical, and other specialized matters. The requirement of a written report in paragraph (2)(B), however, applies only to those experts who are retained or specially employed to provide such testimony in the case or whose duties as an employee of a party regularly involve the giving of such testimony. A treating physician, for example, can be deposed or called to testify at trial without any requirement for a written report. By local rule, order, or written stipulation, the requirement of a written report may be waived for particular experts or imposed upon additional persons who will provide opinions under Rule 702.

[¶20] Paragraph (3). This paragraph imposes an additional duty to disclose, without any request, information customarily needed in final preparation for trial. These disclosures are to be made in accordance with schedules adopted by the court under Rule 16(b) or by special order. If no such schedule is directed by the court, the disclosures are to be made at least 30 days before commencement of the trial. By its terms, rule 26(a)(3) does not require disclosure of evidence to be used solely for impeachment purposes; however, disclosure of such evidence—as well as other items relating to conduct of trial—may be required by local rule or a pretrial order.

[¶21] Subparagraph (A) requires the parties to designate the persons whose testimony they may present as substantive evidence at trial, whether in person or by deposition. Those who will probably be called as witnesses should be listed separately from those who are not likely to be called but who are being listed in order to preserve the right to do so if needed because of developments during trial. Revised Rule 37(c)(1) provides that only persons so listed may be used at trial to present substantive evidence. This restriction does not apply unless the omission was "without substantial justification" and hence would not bar an unlisted witness if the need for such testimony is based upon developments during trial that could not reasonably have been anticipated—*e.g.*, a change of testimony.

[¶22] Listing a witness does not obligate the party to secure the attendance of the person at trial, but should preclude the party from objecting if the person is called to testify by another party who did not list the person as a witness.

[¶23] Subparagraph (B) requires the party to indicate which of these potential witnesses will be presented by deposition at trial. A party expecting to use at trial a deposition not recorded by stenographic means is required by revised Rule 32 to provide the court with a transcript of the pertinent portions of such depositions. This rule requires that copies of the transcript of a nonstenographic deposition be provided to other parties in advance of trial for verification, an obvious concern since counsel often utilize their own personnel to prepare transcripts from audio or video tapes. By order or local rule, the court may require that parties designate the particular portions of stenographic depositions to be used at trial.

[¶24] Subparagraph (C) requires disclosure of exhibits, including summaries (whether to be offered in lieu of other documentary evidence or to be used as an aid in understanding such evidence), that may be offered as substantive evidence. The rule requires a separate listing of each such exhibit, though it should permit voluminous items of a similar or standardized character to be described by meaningful categories. For example, unless the court has otherwise directed, a series of vouchers might be shown collectively as a single exhibit with their starting and ending dates. As with witnesses, the exhibits that will probably be offered are to be listed separately from those which are unlikely to be offered but which are listed in order to preserve the right to do so if needed because of developments during trial. Under revised Rule 37(c)(1) the court can permit use of unlisted documents the need for which could not reasonably have been anticipated in advance of trial.

[¶25] Upon receipt of these final pretrial disclosures, other parties have 14 days (unless a different time is specified by the court) to disclose any objections they wish to preserve to the usability of the deposition testimony or to the admissibility of the documentary evidence (other than under Rules 402 and 403 of the Federal Rules of Evidence). Similar provisions have become commonplace either in pretrial orders or by local rules, and significantly expedite the presentation of evidence at trial, as well as eliminate the need to have available witnesses to provide "foundation" testimony for most items of documentary evidence. The listing of a potential objection does not constitute the making of that objection or require the court to rule on the objection; rather, it preserves the right of the party to make the objection when and as appropriate during trial. The court may, however, elect to treat the listing as a motion "in limine" and rule upon the objections in advance of trial to the extent appropriate.

[¶26] The time specified in the rule for the final pretrial disclosures is relatively close to the trial date. The objective is to eliminate the time and expense in making these disclosures of evidence and objections in those cases that settle shortly before trial, while affording a reasonable time for final preparation for trial in those cases that do not settle. In many cases, it will be desirable for the court in a scheduling or pretrial order to set an earlier time for disclosures of evidence and provide more time for disclosing potential objections.

[¶27] Paragraph (4). This paragraph prescribes the form of disclosures. A signed written statement is required, reminding the parties and counsel of the solemnity of the obligations imposed; and the signature on the initial or pretrial disclosure is a certification under subdivision (g)(1) that it is complete and correct as of the time when made. Consistent with Rule 5(d), these disclosures are to be filed with the court unless otherwise directed. It is anticipated that many courts will direct that expert reports required under paragraph (2)(B) not be filed until needed in connection with a motion or for trial.

[¶28] Paragraph (5). This paragraph is revised to take note of the availability of revised Rule 45 for inspection from non-parties of documents and premises without the need for a deposition.

[¶29] Subdivision (b). This subdivision is revised in several respects. First, former paragraph (1) is subdivided into two paragraphs for ease of reference and to avoid renumbering of paragraphs (3) and (4). Textual changes are then made in new paragraph (2) to enable the court to keep tighter rein on the extent of discovery. The information explosion of recent decades has greatly increased both the potential cost of wide-ranging discovery and the potential for discovery to be used as an instrument for delay or oppression. Amendments to Rules 30, 31, and 33 place presumptive limits on the number of depositions and interrogatories, subject to leave of court to pursue additional discovery. The revisions in Rule 26(b)(2) are intended to provide the court with broader discretion to impose additional restrictions on the scope and extent of discovery and to authorize courts that develop case tracking systems based on the complexity of cases to increase or decrease by local rule the presumptive number of depositions and interrogatories allowed in particular types or classifications of cases. The revision also dispels any doubt as to the power of the court to impose limitations on the length of depositions under Rule 30 or on the number of requests for admission under Rule 36.

[¶30] Second, former paragraph (2), relating to insurance, has been relocated as part of the required initial disclosures under subdivision (a)(1)(D), and revised to provide for disclosure of the policy itself.

[¶31] Third, paragraph (4)(A) is revised to provide that experts who are expected to be witnesses will be subject to deposition prior to trial, conforming the norm stated in the rule to the actual practice followed in most courts, in which depositions of experts have become standard. Concerns regarding the expense of such depositions should be mitigated by the fact that the expert's fees for the deposition will ordinarily be borne by the party taking the deposition. The requirement under subdivision (a)(2)(B) of a complete and detailed report of the expected testimony of certain forensic experts may, moreover, eliminate the need for some such depositions or at least reduce the length of the depositions. Accordingly, the deposition of an expert required by subdivision (a)(2)(B) to provide a written report may be taken only after the report has been served.

[¶32] Paragraph (4)(C), bearing on compensation of experts, is revised to take account of the changes in paragraph (4)(A).

[¶33] Paragraph (5) is a new provision. A party must notify other parties if it is withholding materials otherwise subject to disclosure under the rule or pursuant to a discovery request because it is asserting a claim of privilege or work product protection. To withhold materials without such notice is contrary to the rule, subjects the party to sanctions under Rule 37(b)(2), and may be viewed as a waiver of the privilege or protection.

[¶34] The party must also provide sufficient information to enable other parties to evaluate the applicability of the claimed privilege or protection. Although the person from whom the discovery is sought decides whether to claim a privilege or protection, the court ultimately decides whether, if this claim is challenged, the privilege or protection applies. Providing information pertinent to the applicability of the privilege or protection should reduce the need for in camera examination of the documents.

[¶35] The rule does not attempt to define for each case what information must be provided when a party asserts a claim of privilege or work product protection. Details concerning time, persons, general subject matter, etc., may be appropriate if only a few items are withheld, but may be unduly burdensome when voluminous documents are claimed to be privileged or protected, particularly if the items can be described by categories. A party can seek relief through a protective order under subdivision (c) if compliance with the requirement for providing this information would be an unreasonable burden. In rare circumstances some of the pertinent information affecting applicability of the claim, such as the identity of the client, may itself be privileged; the rule provides that such information need not be disclosed.

[¶36] The obligation to provide pertinent information concerning withheld privileged materials applies only to items "otherwise discoverable." If a broad discovery request is made—for example, for all documents of a particular type during a twenty year period—and the responding party believes in good faith that production of documents for more than the past three years would be unduly burdensome, it should make its objection to the breadth of the request and, with respect to the documents generated in that three year period, produce the unprivileged documents and describe those withheld under the claim of privilege. If the court later rules that documents for a seven year period are properly discoverable, the documents for the additional four years should then be either produced (if not privileged) or described (if claimed to be privileged).

[¶37] Subdivision (c). The revision requires that before filing a motion for a protective order the movant must confer—either in person or by telephone—with the other affected parties in a good faith effort to resolve the discovery dispute without the need for court intervention. If the movant is unable to get opposing parties even to discuss the matter, the efforts in attempting to arrange such a conference should be indicated in the certificate.

[¶38] Subdivision (d). This subdivision is revised to provide that formal discovery—as distinguished from interviews of potential witnesses and other informal discovery—not commence until the parties have met and conferred as required by subdivision (f). Discovery can begin earlier if authorized under Rule 30(a)(2)(C) (deposition of person about to leave the country) or by local rule, order, or stipulation. This will be appropriate in some cases, such as those involving requests for a preliminary injunction or motions challenging personal jurisdiction. If a local rule exempts any types of cases in which discovery may be needed from the requirement of a meeting under Rule 26(f), it should specify when discovery may commence in those cases.

[¶39] The meeting of counsel is to take place as soon as practicable and in any event at least 14 days before the date of the scheduling conference under Rule 16(b) or the date a scheduling order is due under Rule 16(b). The court can assure that discovery is not unduly delayed either by entering a special order or by setting the case for a scheduling conference.

[¶40] Subdivision (e). This subdivision is revised to provide that the requirement for supplementation applies to all disclosures required by subdivisions (a)(1)-(3). Like the former rule, the duty, while imposed on a "party," applies whether the corrective information is learned by the client or by the attorney. Supplementations need not be made as each new item of information is learned but should be made at appropriate intervals during the discovery period, and with special promptness as the trial date approaches. It may be useful for the scheduling order to specify the time or times when supplementations should be made.

[¶41] The revision also clarifies that the obligation to supplement responses to formal discovery requests applies to interrogatories, requests for production, and requests for admissions, but not ordinarily to deposition testimony. However, with respect to experts from whom a written report is required under subdivision (a)(2)(B), changes in the opinions expressed by the expert whether in the report or at a subsequent deposition are subject to a duty of supplemental disclosure under subdivision (e)(1).

[¶42] The obligation to supplement disclosures and discovery responses applies whenever a party learns that its prior disclosures or responses are in some material respect incomplete or incorrect. There is, however, no obligation to provide supplemental or corrective information that has been otherwise made known to the parties in writing or during the discovery process, as when a witness not previously disclosed is identified during the taking of a deposition or when an expert during a deposition corrects information contained in an earlier report.

[¶43] Subdivision (f). This subdivision was added in 1980 to provide a party threatened with abusive discovery with a special means for obtaining judicial intervention other than through discrete motions under Rules 26(c) and 37(a). The amendment envisioned a two-step process: first, the parties would attempt to frame a mutually agreeable plan; second, the court would hold a "discovery conference" and then enter an order establishing a schedule and limitations for the conduct of discovery. It was contemplated that the procedure, an elective one triggered on request of a party, would be used in special cases rather than as a routine matter. As expected, the device has been used only sparingly in most courts, and judicial controls over the discovery process have ordinarily been imposed through scheduling orders under Rule 16(b) or through rulings on discovery motions.

[¶44] The provisions relating to a conference with the court are removed from subdivision (f). This change does not signal any lessening of the importance of judicial supervision. Indeed, there is a greater need for early judicial involvement to consider the scope and timing of the disclosure requirements of Rule 26(a) and the presumptive limits on discovery imposed under these rules or by local rules. Rather, the change is made because the provisions addressing the use of conferences with the court to control discovery are more properly included in Rule 16, which is being revised to highlight the court's powers regarding the discovery process.

[¶45] The desirability of some judicial control of discovery can hardly be doubted. Rule 16, as revised, requires that the court set a time for completion of discovery and authorizes various other orders affecting the scope, timing, and extent of discovery and disclosures. Before entering such orders, the court should consider the views of the parties, preferably by means of a conference, but at the least through written submissions. Moreover, it is desirable that the parties' proposals regarding discovery be developed through a process where they meet in person, informally explore the nature and basis of the issues, and discuss how discovery can be conducted most efficiently and economically.

[¶46] As noted above, former subdivision (f) envisioned the development of proposed discovery plans as an optional procedure to be used in relatively few cases. The revised rule directs that in all cases not exempted by local rule or special order the litigants must meet in person and plan for discovery. Following this meeting, the parties submit to the court their proposals for a discovery plan and can begin formal discovery. Their report will assist the court in seeing that the timing and scope of disclosures under revised Rule 26(a) and the limitations on the extent of discovery under these rules and local rules are tailored to the circumstances of the particular case.

[¶47] To assure that the court has the litigants' proposals before deciding on a scheduling order and that the commencement of discovery is not delayed unduly, the rule provides that the meeting of the parties take place as soon as practicable and in any event at least 14 days before a scheduling conference is held or before a scheduling order is due under Rule 16(b). (Rule 16(b) requires that a scheduling order be entered within 90 days after the first appearance of a defendant or, if earlier, within 120 days after the complaint has been served on any defendant.) The obligation to participate in the planning process is imposed on all parties that have appeared in the case, including defendants who, because of a pending Rule 12 motion, may not have yet filed an answer in the case. Each such party should attend the meeting, either through one of its attorneys or in person if unrepresented. If more parties are joined or appear after the initial meeting, an additional meeting may be desirable.

[¶48] Subdivision (f) describes certain matters that should be accomplished at the meeting and included in the proposed discovery plan. This listing does not exclude consideration of other subjects, such as the time when any dispositive motions should be filed and when the case should be ready for trial.

[¶49] The parties are directed under subdivision (a)(1) to make the disclosures required by that subdivision at or within 10 days after this meeting. In many cases the parties

should use the meeting to exchange, discuss, and clarify their respective disclosures. In other cases, it may be more useful if the disclosures are delayed until after the parties have discussed at the meeting the claims and defenses in order to define the issues with respect to which the initial disclosures should be made. As discussed in the Notes to subdivision (a)(1), the parties may also need to consider whether a stipulation extending this 10-day period would be appropriate, as when a defendant would otherwise have less than 60 days after being served in which to make its initial disclosure. The parties should also discuss at the meeting what additional information, although not subject to the disclosure requirements, can be made available informally without the necessity for formal discovery requests.

[¶50] The report is to be submitted to the court within 10 days after the meeting and should not be difficult to prepare. In most cases counsel should be able to agree that one of them will be responsible for its preparation and submission to the court. Form 35 has been added in the Appendix to the Rules, both to illustrate the type of report that is contemplated and to serve as a checklist for the meeting.

[¶51] The litigants are expected to attempt in good faith to agree on the contents of the proposed discovery plan. If they cannot agree on all aspects of the plan, their report to the court should indicate the competing proposals of the parties on those items, as well as the matters on which they agree. Unfortunately, there may be cases in which, because of disagreements about time or place or for other reasons, the meeting is not attended by all parties or, indeed, no meeting takes place. In such situations, the report—or reports—should describe the circumstances and the court may need to consider sanctions under Rule 37(g).

[¶52] By local rule or special order, the court can exempt particular cases or types of cases from the meet-and-confer requirement of subdivision (f). In general this should include any types of cases which are exempted by local rule from the requirement for a scheduling order under Rule 16(b), such as cases in which there will be no discovery (*e.g.*, bankruptcy appeals and reviews of social security determinations). In addition, the court may want to exempt cases in which discovery is rarely needed (*e.g.*, government collection cases and proceedings to enforce administrative summonses) or in which a meeting of the parties might be impracticable (*e.g.*, actions by unrepresented prisoners). Note that if a court exempts from the requirements for a meeting any types of cases in which discovery may be needed, it should indicate when discovery may commence in those cases.

[¶53] Subdivision (g). Paragraph (1) is added to require signatures on disclosures, a requirement that parallels the provisions of paragraph (2) with respect to discovery requests, responses, and objections. The provisions of paragraph (3) have been modified to be consistent with Rules 37(a)(4) and 37(c)(1); in combination, these rules establish sanctions for violation of the rules regarding disclosures and discovery matters. Amended Rule 11 no longer applies to such violations.

FRCP 26 – 1970 NOTES OF ADVISORY COMMITTEE

[¶1] A limited rearrangement of the discovery rules is made, whereby certain rule provisions are transferred, as follows: Existing Rule 26(a) is transferred to Rules 30(a) and 31(a). Existing Rule 26(c) is transferred to Rule 30(c). Existing Rules 26(d), (e), and (f) are transferred to Rule 32. Revisions of the transferred provisions, if any, are discussed in the notes appended to Rules 30, 31, and 32. In addition, Rule 30(b) is transferred to Rule 26(c). The purpose of this rearrangement is to establish Rule 26 as a rule governing discovery in general. (The reasons are set out in the Advisory Committee's explanatory statement.)

[¶2] Subdivision (a)—Discovery Devices. This is a new subdivision listing all of the discovery devices provided in the discovery rules and establishing the relationship between the general provisions of Rule 26 and the specific rules for particular discovery devices. The provision that the frequency of use of these methods is not limited confirms existing law. It incorporates in general form a provision now found in Rule 33.

[¶3] Subdivision (b)—Scope of Discovery. This subdivision is recast to cover the scope of discovery generally. It regulates the discovery obtainable through any of the discovery devices listed in Rule 26(a).

[¶4] All provisions as to scope of discovery are subject to the initial qualification that the court may limit discovery in accordance with these rules. Rule 26(c) (transferred from 30(b)) confers broad powers on the courts to regulate or prevent discovery even though the materials sought are within the scope of 26(b), and these powers have always been freely exercised. For example, a party's income tax return is generally held not privileged, 2A Barron & Holtzoff, Federal Practice and Procedure, §65.2 (Wright ed. 1961), and yet courts have recognized that interests in privacy may call for a measure of extra protection. *E.g.*, *Wiesenberger v. W. E. Hutton & Co.*, 35 F.R.D. 556 (S.D. N.Y.1964). Similarly, the courts have in appropriate circumstances protected materials that are primarily of an impeaching character. These two types of materials merely illustrate the many situations, not capable of governance by precise rule, in which courts must exercise judgment. The new subsections in Rule 26(d) do not change existing law with respect to such situations.

[¶5] Subdivision (b)(1)—In General. The language is changed to provide for the scope of discovery in general terms. The existing subdivision, although in terms applicable only to depositions, is incorporated by reference in existing Rules 33 and 34. Since decisions as to relevance to the subject matter of the action are made for discovery purposes well in advance of trial, a flexible treatment of relevance is required and the making of discovery, whether voluntary or under court order, is not a concession or determination of relevance for purposes of trial. *Cf.* 4 Moore's Federal Practice §26-16[1] (2d ed. 1966).

[¶6] Subdivision (b)(2)—Insurance Policies. Both cases and commentators are sharply in conflict on the question whether defendant's liability insurance coverage is subject to discovery in the usual situation when the insurance coverage is not itself admissible and does not bear on another issue on the case. Examples of Federal cases requiring disclosure and supporting comments: *Cook v. Welty*, 253 F.Supp. 875 (D. D.C.1966) (cases cited); *Johanek v. Aberle*, 27 F.R.D. 272 (D. Mont.1961); Williams, Discovery of Dollar Limits in Liability Policies in Automobile Tort Cases, 10 Ala.L.Rev. 355 (1958); Thode, Some Reflections on the 1957 Amendments to the Texas Rules, 37 Tex.L.Rev. 33, 40-42 (1958). Examples of Federal cases refusing disclosure and supporting comments: *Bisserier v. Manning*, 207 F.Supp. 476 (D. N.J.1962); *Cooper v. Stender*, 30 F.R.D. 389 (E.D. Tenn. 1962); Frank, Discovery and Insurance Coverage, 1959 Ins.L.J. 281; Fournier, Pre-Trial Discovery of Insurance Coverage and Limits, 28 Ford L.Rev. 215 (1959).

[¶7] The division in reported cases is close. State decisions based on provisions similar to the federal rules are similarly divided. See cases collected in 2A Barron & Holtzoff, Federal Practice and Procedure §647.1, nn. 45.5, 45.6 (Wright ed. 1961). It appears to be difficult if not impossible to obtain appellate review of the issue. Resolution by rule amendment is indicated. The question is essentially procedural in that it bears upon preparation for trial and settlement before trial, and courts confronting the question, however, they have decided it, have generally treated it as procedural and governed by the rules.

[¶8] The amendment resolves this issue in favor of disclosure. Most of the decisions denying discovery, some explicitly, reason from the text of Rule 26(b) that it permits discovery only of matters which will be admissible in evidence or appear reasonably calculated to lead to such evidence; they avoid considerations of policy, regarding them as foreclosed. *See Bisserier v. Manning*, supra. Some note also that facts about a defendant's financial status are not discoverable as such, prior to judgment with execution unsatisfied, and fear that, if courts hold insurance coverage discoverable, they must extend the principle to other aspects of the defendant's financial status. The cases favoring disclosure rely heavily on the practical significance of insurance in the decisions lawyers make about settlement and trial preparation. In *Clauss v. Danker*, 264 F.Supp. 246 (S.D. N.Y.1967), the court held that the rules forbid disclosure but called for an amendment to permit it.

[¶9] Disclosure of insurance coverage will enable counsel for both sides to make the same realistic appraisal of the case, so that settlement and litigation strategy are based on knowledge and not speculation. It will conduce to settlement and avoid protracted litigation in some cases, though in others it may have an opposite effect. The amendment is limited to insurance coverage, which should be distinguished from any other facts concerning defendant's financial status (1) because insurance is an asset created specifically to satisfy the claim; (2) because the insurance company ordinarily controls the litigation; (3) because information about coverage is available only from defendant or his insurer; and (4) because disclosure does not involve a significant invasion of privacy.

[¶10] Disclosure is required when the insurer "may be liable" on part or all of the judgment. Thus, an insurance company must disclose even when it contests liability under the policy, and such disclosure does not constitute a waiver of its claim. It is immaterial whether the liability is to satisfy the judgment directly or merely to indemnify or reimburse another after he pays the judgment.

[¶11] The provision applies only to persons "carrying on an insurance business" and thus covers insurance companies and not the ordinary business concern that enters into a contract of indemnification. *Cf.* N.Y.Ins. Law §41. Thus, the provision makes no change in existing law on discovery of indemnity agreements other than insurance agreements by persons carrying on an insurance business. Similarly, the provision does not cover the business concern that creates a reserve fund for purposes of self-insurance.

[¶12] For some purposes other than discovery, an application for insurance is treated as a part of the insurance agreement. The provision makes clear that, for discovery purposes, the application is not to be so treated. The insurance application may contain personal and financial information concerning the insured, discovery of which is beyond the purpose of this provision.

[¶13] In no instance does disclosure make the facts concerning insurance coverage admissible in evidence.

[¶14] Subdivision (b)(3)—Trial Preparation: Materials. Some of the most controversial and vexing problems to emerge from the discovery rules have arisen out of requests for the production of documents or things prepared in anticipation of litigation or for trial. The existing rules make no explicit provision for such materials. Yet, two verbally distinct doctrines have developed, each conferring a qualified immunity on these materials—the "good cause" requirement in Rule 34 (now generally held applicable to discovery of documents via deposition under Rule 45 and interrogatories under Rule 33) and the work-product doctrine of *Hickman v. Taylor*, 329 U.S. 495 (1947). Both demand a showing of justification before production can be had, the one of "good cause" and the other variously described in the *Hickman* case: "necessity or justification," "denial * * * would unduly prejudice the preparation of petitioner's case," or "cause hardship or injustice" 329 U.S. at 509-510.

[¶15] In deciding the *Hickman* case, the Supreme Court appears to have expressed a preference in 1947 for an ap-

proach to the problem of trial preparation materials by judicial decision rather than by rule. Sufficient experience has accumulated, however, with lower court applications of the *Hickman* decision to warrant a reappraisal.

[¶16] The major difficulties visible in the existing case law are (1) confusion and disagreement as to whether "good cause" is made out by a showing of relevance and lack of privilege, or requires an additional showing of necessity, (2) confusion and disagreement as to the scope of the *Hickman* work-product doctrine, particularly whether it extends beyond work actually performed by lawyers, and (3) the resulting difficulty of relating the "good cause" required by Rule 34 and the "necessity or justification" of the work-product doctrine, so that their respective roles and the distinctions between them are understood.

[¶17] Basic Standard. Since Rule 34 in terms requires a showing of "good cause" for the production of all documents and things, whether or not trial preparation is involved, courts have felt that a single formula is called for and have differed over whether a showing of relevance and lack of privilege is enough or whether more must be shown. When the facts of the cases are studied, however, a distinction emerges based upon the type of materials. With respect to documents not obtained or prepared with an eye to litigation, the decisions, while not uniform, reflect a strong and increasing tendency to relate "good cause" to a showing that the documents are relevant to the subject matter of the action. *E.g., Connecticut Mutual Life Ins. Co. v. Shields*, 17 F.R.D. 273 (S.D. N.Y.1959), with cases cited; *Houdry Process Corp. v. Commonwealth Oil Refining Co.*, 24 F.R.D. 58 (S.D. N.Y.1955); *see Bell v. Commercial Ins. Co.*, 280 F.2d 514, 517 (3d Cir. 1960). When the party whose documents are sought shows that the request for production is unduly burdensome or oppressive, courts have denied discovery for lack of "good cause", although they might just as easily have based their decision on the protective provisions of existing Rule 30(b) (new Rule 26(c)). *E.g., Lauer v. Tankrederi*, 39 F.R.D. 334 (E.D. Pa.1966).

[¶18] As to trial-preparation materials, however, the courts are increasingly interpreting "good cause" as requiring more than relevance. When lawyers have prepared or obtained the materials for trial, all courts require more than relevance; so much is clearly commanded by *Hickman*. But even as to the preparatory work of nonlawyers, while some courts ignore work-product and equate "good cause" with relevance, *e.g., Brown v. New York*, N.H. & H. RR., 17 F.R.D. 324 (S.D. N.Y.1955), the more recent trend is to read "good cause" as requiring inquiry into the importance of and need for the materials as well as into alternative sources for securing the same information. In *Guilford Nat'l Bank v. Southern Ry.*, 297 F.2d 921 (4th Cir.1962), statements of witnesses obtained by claim agents were held not discoverable because both parties had had equal access to the witnesses at about the same time, shortly after the collision in question. The decision was based solely on Rule 34 and "good cause"; the court declined to rule on whether the statements were work-product. The court's treatment of "good cause" is quoted at length and with approval in *Schlagenhauf v. Holder*, 379 U.S. 104, 117-118 (1964). *See also Mitchell v. Bass*, 252 F.2d 513 (8th Cir.1958); *Hauger v. Chicago*, R.I. & Pac. RR., 216 F.2d 501 (7th Cir.1954); *Burke v. United States*, 32 F.R.D. 213 (E.D. N.Y.1963). While the opinions dealing with "good cause" do not often draw an explicit distinction between trial preparation materials and other materials, in fact an overwhelming proportion of the cases in which special showing is required are cases involving trial preparation materials.

[¶19] The rules are amended by eliminating the general requirement of "good cause" from Rule 34 but retaining a requirement of a special showing for trial preparation materials in this subdivision. The required showing is expressed, not in terms of "good cause" whose generality has tended to encourage confusion and controversy, but in terms of the elements of the special showing to be made: substantial need of the materials in the preparation of the case and inability without undue hardship to obtain the substantial equivalent of the materials by other means.

[¶20] These changes conform to the holdings of the cases, when viewed in light of their facts. Apart from trial preparation, the fact that the materials sought are documentary does not in and of itself require a special showing beyond relevance and absence of privilege. The protective provisions are of course available, and if the party from whom production is sought raises a special issue of privacy (as with respect to income tax returns or grand jury minutes) or points to evidence primarily impeaching, or can show serious burden or expense, the court will exercise its traditional power to decide whether to issue a protective order. On the other hand, the requirement of a special showing for discovery of trial preparation materials reflects the view that each side's informal evaluation of its case should be protected, that each side should be encouraged to prepare independently, and that one side should not automatically have the benefit of the detailed preparatory work of the other side. See Field and McKusick, Maine Civil Practice 264 (1959).

[¶21] Elimination of a "good cause" requirement from Rule 34 and the establishment of a requirement of a special showing in this subdivision will eliminate the confusion caused by having two verbally distinct requirements of justification that the courts have been unable to distinguish clearly. Moreover, the language of the subdivision suggests the factors which the courts should consider in determining whether the requisite showing has been made. The importance of the materials sought to the party seeking them in preparation of his case and the difficulty he will have obtaining them by other means are factors noted in the *Hickman* case. The courts should also consider the likelihood that the party, even if he obtains the information by independent means, will not have the substantial equivalent of the documents the production of which he seeks.

[¶22] Consideration of these factors may well lead the court to distinguish between witness statements taken by an investigator, on the one hand, and other parts of the investigative file, on the other. The court in *Southern Ry. v. Lanham*, 403 F.2d 119 (5th Cir.1968), while it naturally addressed itself to the "good cause" requirements of Rule 34, set forth as controlling considerations the factors contained in the language of this subdivision. The analysis of the court suggests circumstances under which witness statements will be discoverable. The witness may have given a fresh and contemporaneous account in a written statement while he is available to the party seeking discovery only a substantial time thereafter. *Lanham*, supra at 127-128; Guilford, supra at 926. Or he may be reluctant or hostile. *Lanham*, supra at 128-129; *Brookshire v. Pennsylvania RR.*, 14 F.R.D. 154 (N.D. Ohio 1953); *Diamond v. Mohawk Rubber Co.*, 33 F.R.D. 264 (D. Colo.1963). Or he may have a lapse of memory. *Tannenbaum v. Walker*, 16 F.R.D. 570 (E.D. Pa.1954). Or he may probably be deviating from his prior statement. *Cf. Hauger v. Chicago, R.I. & Pac. RR.*, 216 F.2d 501 (7th Cir.1954). On the other hand, a much stronger showing is needed to obtain evaluative materials in an investigator's reports. *Lanham*, supra at 131-133; *Pickett v. L. R. Ryan, Inc.*, 237 F.Supp. 198 (E.D. S.C.1965).

[¶23] Materials assembled in the ordinary course of business, or pursuant to public requirements unrelated to litigation, or for other nonlitigation purposes are not under the qualified immunity provided by this subdivision. *Goosman v. A. Duie Pyle, Inc.*, 320 F.2d 45 (4th Cir.1963); *cf. United States v. New York Foreign Trade Zone Operators, Inc.*, 304 F.2d 792 (2d Cir.1962). No change is made in the existing doctrine, noted in the *Hickman* case, that one party may discover relevant facts known or available to the other party, even though such facts are contained in a document which is not itself discoverable.

[¶24] Treatment of Lawyers; Special Protection of Mental Impressions, Conclusions, Opinions, and Legal Theories Concerning the Litigation. The courts are divided as to whether the work-product doctrine extends to the preparatory work only of lawyers. The *Hickman* case left this issue open since the statements in that case were taken by a lawyer. As to courts of appeals, *compare Alltmont v. United States*, 177 F.2d 971, 976 (3d Cir. 1949), *cert. denied*, 339 U.S. 967 (1950) (*Hickman* applied to statements obtained by FBI agents on theory it should apply to "all statements of prospective witnesses which a party has obtained for his trial counsel's use"), *with Southern Ry. v. Campbell*, 309 F.2d 569 (5th Cir.1962) (statements taken by claim agents not work-product), *and Guilford Nat'l Bank v. Southern Ry.*, 297 F.2d 921 (4th Cir.1962) (avoiding issue of work-product as to claim agents, deciding case instead under Rule 34 "good cause"). Similarly, the district courts are divided on statements obtained by claim agents, *compare, e.g., Brown v. New York, N.H. & H. RR.*, 17 F.R.D. 324 (S.D. N.Y.1955) *with Hanke v. Milwaukee Electric Ry. & Transp. Co.*, 7 F.R.D. 540 (E.D. Wis.1947); investigators, *compare Burke v. United States*, 32 F.R.D. 213 (E.D. N.Y.1963) *with Snyder v. United States*, 20 F.R.D. 7 (E.D. N.Y.1956); and insurers, *compare Gottlieb v. Bresler*, 24 F.R.D. 371 (D. D.C.1959) *with Burns v. Mulder*, 20 F.R.D. 605 (E.D. Pa.1957). See 4 Moore's Federal Practice §26.23[8.1] (2d ed. 1966); 2A Barron & Holtzoff, Federal Practice and Procedure §652.2 (Wright ed. 1961).

[¶25] A complication is introduced by the use made by courts of the "good cause" requirement of Rule 34, as described above. A court may conclude that trial preparation materials are not work-product because not the result of lawyer's work and yet hold that they are not producible because "good cause" has not been shown. *Cf. Guilford Nat'l Bank v. Southern Ry.*, 297 F.2d 921 (4th Cir.1962), cited and described above. When the decisions on "good cause" are taken into account, the weight of authority affords protection of the preparatory work of both lawyers and nonlawyers (though not necessarily to the same extent) by requiring more than a showing of relevance to secure production.

[¶26] Subdivision (b)(3) reflects the trend of the cases by requiring a special showing, not merely as to materials prepared by an attorney, but also as to materials prepared in anticipation of litigation or preparation for trial by or for a party or any representative acting on his behalf. The subdivision then goes on to protect against disclosure the mental impressions, conclusions, opinions, or legal theories concerning the litigation of an attorney or other representative of a party. The *Hickman* opinion drew special attention to the need for protecting an attorney against discovery of memoranda prepared from recollection of oral interviews. The courts have steadfastly safeguarded against disclosure of lawyers' mental impressions and legal theories, as well as mental impressions and subjective evaluations of investigators and claim-agents. In enforcing this provision of the subdivision, the courts will sometimes find it necessary to order disclosure of a document but with portions deleted.

[¶27] Rules 33 and 36 have been revised in order to permit discovery calling for opinions, contentions, and admissions relating not only to fact but also to the application of law to fact. Under those rules, a party and his attorney or other representative may be required to disclose, to some extent, mental impressions, opinions, or conclusions. But documents or parts of documents containing these matters are protected against discovery by this subdivision. Even though a party may ultimately have to disclose in response to interrogatories or requests to admit, he is entitled to keep confidential documents containing such matters prepared for internal use.

[¶28] Party's Right to Own Statement. An exception to the requirement of this subdivision enables a party to secure production of his own statement without any special showing. The cases are divided. *Compare, e.g., Safeway Stores, Inc. v. Reynolds*, 176 F.2d 476 (D.C. Cir.1949); *Shupe v. Pennsylvania RR.*, 19 F.R.D. 144 (W.D. Pa.1956); *with e.g.*,

New York Central RR. v. Carr, 251 F.2d 433 (4th Cir.1957); *Belback v. Wilson Freight Forwarding Co.*, 40 F.R.D. 16 (W.D. Pa.1966).

[¶29] Courts which treat a party's statement as though it were that of any witness overlook the fact that the party's statement is, without more, admissible in evidence. Ordinarily, a party gives a statement without insisting on a copy because he does not yet have a lawyer and does not understand the legal consequences of his actions. Thus, the statement is given at a time when he functions at a disadvantage. Discrepancies between his trial testimony and earlier statement may result from lapse of memory or ordinary inaccuracy; a written statement produced for the first time at trial may give such discrepancies a prominence which they do not deserve. In appropriate cases the court may order a party to be deposed before his statement is produced. *E.g.*, *Smith v. Central Linen Service Co.*, 39 F.R.D. 15 (D. Md.1966); *McCoy v. General Motors Corp.*, 33 F.R.D. 354 (W.D. Pa.1963).

[¶30] Commentators strongly support the view that a party be able to secure his statement without a showing. 4 Moore's Federal Practice 26.23 (8.4) (2d ed. 1966); 2A Barron & Holtzoff, Federal Practice and Procedure §652.3 (Wright ed. 1961); see also Note, Developments in the Law – Discovery, 74 Harv.L.Rev. 940, 1039 (1961). The following states have by statute or rule taken the same position: Statutes: Fla. Stat.Ann. §92.33; Ga.Code Ann. §38-2109(b); La.Stat.Ann.R.S. 13:3732; Mass.Gen.Laws Ann. c. 271, §44; Minn.Stat.Ann. §602.01; N.Y.C.P.L.R. §3101(e). Rules: Mo.R.C.P. 56.01(a); N.Dak.R.C.P. 34(b); Wyo.R.C.P. 34(b); cf. Mich.G.C.R. 306.2.

[¶31] In order to clarify and tighten the provision on statements by a party, the term "statement" is defined. The definition is adapted from 18 U.S.C. §3500(e) (Jencks Act). The statement of a party may of course be that of plaintiff or defendant, and it may be that of an individual or of a corporation or other organization.

[¶32] Witness' Right to Own Statement. A second exception to the requirement of this subdivision permits a nonparty witness to obtain a copy of his own statement without any special showing. Many, though not all, of the considerations supporting a party's right to obtain his statement apply also to the non-party witness. Insurance companies are increasingly recognizing that a witness is entitled to a copy of his statement and are modifying their regular practice accordingly.

[¶33] Subdivision (b)(4)—Trial Preparation: Experts. This is a new provision dealing with discovery of information (including facts and opinions) obtained by a party from an expert retained by that party in relation to litigation or obtained by the expert and not yet transmitted to the party. The subdivision deals separately with those experts whom the party expects to call as trial witnesses and with those experts who have been retained or specially employed by the party but who are not expected to be witnesses. It should be noted that the subdivision does not address itself to the expert whose information was not acquired in preparation for trial but rather because he was an actor or viewer with respect to transactions or occurrences that are part of the subject matter of the lawsuit. Such an expert should be treated as an ordinary witness.

[¶34] Subsection (b)(4)(A) deals with discovery of information obtained by or through experts who will be called as witnesses at trial. The provision is responsive to problems suggested by a relatively recent line of authorities. Many of these cases present intricate and difficult issues as to which expert testimony is likely to be determinative. Prominent among them are food and drug, patent, and condemnation cases. *See, e.g.*, *United States v. Nysco Laboratories, Inc.*, 26 F.R.D. 159, 162 (E.D. N.Y.1960) (food and drug); *E. I. du Pont de Nemours & Co. v. Phillips Petroleum Co.*, 24 F.R.D. 416, 421 (D. Del.1959) (patent); *Cold Metal Process Co. v. Aluminum Co. of America*, 7 F.R.D. 425 (N.D. Ohio 1947), *aff'd*, *Sachs v. Aluminum Co. of America*, 167 F.2d 570 (6th Cir.1948) (same); *United States v. 50.34 Acres of Land*, 13 F.R.D. 19 (E.D. N.Y.1952) (condemnation).

[¶35] In cases of this character, a prohibition against discovery of information held by expert witnesses produces in acute form the very evils that discovery has been created to prevent. Effective cross-examination of an expert witness requires advance preparation. The lawyer even with the help of his own experts frequently cannot anticipate the particular approach his adversary's expert will take or the data on which he will base his judgment on the stand. McGlothlin, Some Practical Problems in Proof of Economic, Scientific, and Technical Facts, 23 F.R.D. 467, 478 (1958). A California study of discovery and pretrial in condemnation cases notes that the only substitute for discovery of experts' valuation materials is "lengthy—and often fruitless—cross-examination during trial," and recommends pretrial exchange of such material. Calif.Law Rev.Comm'n, Discovery in Eminent Domain Proceedings 707-710 (Jan.1963). Similarly, effective rebuttal requires advance knowledge of the line of testimony of the other side. If the latter is foreclosed by a rule against discovery, then the narrowing of issues and elimination of surprise which discovery normally produces are frustrated.

[¶36] These considerations appear to account for the broadening of discovery against experts in the cases cited where expert testimony was central to the case. In some instances, the opinions are explicit in relating expanded discovery to improved cross-examination and rebuttal at trial. *Franks v. National Dairy Products Corp.*, 41 F.R.D. 234 (W.D. Tex.1966); *United States v. 23.76 Acres*, 32 F.R.D. 593 (D. Md.1963); see also an unpublished opinion of Judge Hincks, quoted in *United States v. 48 Jars, etc.*, 23 F.R.D. 192, 198 (D. D.C.1958). On the other hand, the need for a new provision is shown by the many cases in which discovery of expert trial witnesses is needed for effective cross-examination and rebuttal, and yet courts apply the traditional doctrine and refuse disclosure. *E.g.*, *United States v. Certain Parcels of*

Land, 25 F.R.D. 192 (N.D. Cal.1959); *United States v. Certain Acres*, 18 F.R.D. 98 (M.D. Ga.1955).

[¶37] Although the trial problems flowing from lack of discovery of expert witnesses are most acute and noteworthy when the case turns largely on experts, the same problems are encountered when a single expert testifies. Thus, subdivision (b)(4)(A) draws no line between complex and simple cases, or between cases with many experts and those with but one. It establishes by rule substantially the procedure adopted by decision of the court in *Knighton v. Villian & Fassio*, 39 F.R.D. 11 (D. Md.1965). For a full analysis of the problem and strong recommendations to the same effect, see Friedenthal, Discovery and Use of an Adverse Party's Expert Information, 14 Stan.L.Rev. 455, 485-488 (1962); Long, Discovery and Experts under the Federal Rules of Civil Procedure, 38 F.R.D. 111 (1965).

[¶38] Past judicial restrictions on discovery of an adversary's expert, particularly as to his opinions, reflect the fear that one side will benefit unduly from the other's better preparation. The procedure established in subsection (b)(4)(A) holds the risk to a minimum. Discovery is limited to trial witnesses, and may be obtained only at a time when the parties know who their expert witnesses will be. A party must as a practical matter prepare his own case in advance of that time, for he can hardly hope to build his case out of his opponent's experts.

[¶39] Subdivision (b)(4)(A) provides for discovery of an expert who is to testify at the trial. A party can require one who intends to use the expert to state the substance of the testimony that the expert is expected to give. The court may order further discovery, and it has ample power to regulate its timing and scope and to prevent abuse. Ordinarily, the order for further discovery shall compensate the expert for his time, and may compensate the party who intends to use the expert for past expenses reasonably incurred in obtaining facts or opinions from the expert. Those provisions are likely to discourage abusive practices.

[¶40] Subdivision (b)(4)(B) deals with an expert who has been retained or specially employed by the party in anticipation of litigation or preparation for trial (thus excluding an expert who is simply a general employee of the party not specially employed on the case), but who is not expected to be called as a witness. Under its provisions, a party may discover facts known or opinions held by such an expert only on a showing of exceptional circumstances under which it is impracticable for the party seeking discovery to obtain facts or opinions on the same subject by other means.

[¶41] Subdivision (b)(4)(B) is concerned only with experts retained or specially consulted in relation to trial preparation. Thus the subdivision precludes discovery against experts who were informally consulted in preparation for trial, but not retained or specially employed. As an ancillary procedure, a party may on a proper showing require the other party to name experts retained or specially employed, but not those informally consulted.

[¶42] These new provisions of subdivision (b)(4) repudiate the few decisions that have held an expert's information privileged simply because of his status as an expert, *e.g.*, *American Oil Co. v. Pennsylvania Petroleum Products Co.*, 23 F.R.D. 680, 685-686 (D. R.I.1959). See Louisell, Modern California Discovery 315-316 (1963). They also reject as ill-considered the decisions which have sought to bring expert information within the work-product doctrine. *See United States v. McKay*, 372 F.2d 174, 176-177 (5th Cir.1967). The provisions adopt a form of the more recently developed doctrine of "unfairness". *See, e.g.*, *United States v. 23.76 Acres of Land*, 32 F.R.D. 593, 597 (D. Md.1963); Louisell, supra, at 317-318; 4 Moore's Federal Practice §26.24 (2d ed. 1966).

[¶43] Under subdivision (b)(4)(C), the court is directed or authorized to issue protective orders, including an order that the expert be paid a reasonable fee for time spent in responding to discovery, and that the party whose expert is made subject to discovery be paid a fair portion of the fees and expenses that the party incurred in obtaining information from the expert. The court may issue the latter order as a condition of discovery, or it may delay the order until after discovery is completed. These provisions for fees and expenses meet the objection that it is unfair to permit one side to obtain without cost the benefit of an expert's work for which the other side has paid, often a substantial sum. *E.g.*, *Lewis v. United Air Lines Transp. Corp.*, 32 F.Supp. 21 (W.D. Pa.1940); *Walsh v. Reynolds Metal Co.*, 15 F.R.D. 376 (D. N.J.1954). On the other hand, a party may not obtain discovery simply by offering to pay fees and expenses. *Cf. Boynton v. R. J. Reynolds Tobacco Co.*, 36 F.Supp. 593 (D. Mass.1941).

[¶44] In instances of discovery under subdivision (b)(4)(B), the court is directed to award fees and expenses to the other party, since the information is of direct value to the discovering party's preparation of his case. In ordering discovery under (b)(4)(A)(ii), the court has discretion whether to award fees and expenses to the other party; its decision should depend upon whether the discovering party is simply learning about the other party's case or is going beyond this to develop his own case. Even in cases where the court is directed to issue a protective order, it may decline to do so if it finds that manifest injustice would result. Thus, the court can protect, when necessary and appropriate, the interests of an indigent party.

[¶45] Subdivision (c)—Protective Orders. The provisions of existing Rule 30(b) are transferred to this subdivision (c), as part of the rearrangement of Rule 26. The language has been changed to give it application to discovery generally. The subdivision recognizes the power of the court in the district where a deposition is being taken to make protective orders. Such power is needed when the deposition is being taken far from the court where the action is pending.

The court in the district where the deposition is being taken may, and frequently will, remit the deponent or party to the court where the action is pending.

[¶46] In addition, drafting changes are made to carry out and clarify the sense of the rule. Insertions are made to avoid any possible implication that a protective order does not extend to "time" as well as to "place" or may not safeguard against "undue burden or expense."

[¶47] The new reference to trade secrets and other confidential commercial information reflects existing law. The courts have not given trade secrets automatic and complete immunity against disclosure, but have in each case weighed their claim to privacy against the need for disclosure. Frequently, they have been afforded a limited protection. *See, e.g., Covey Oil Co. v. Continental Oil Co.*, 340 F.2d 993 (10th Cir.1965); *Julius M. Ames Co. v. Bostitch, Inc.*, 235 F.Supp. 856 (S.D. N.Y.1964).

[¶48] The subdivision contains new matter relating to sanctions. When a motion for a protective order is made and the court is disposed to deny it, the court may go a step further and issue an order to provide or permit discovery. This will bring the sanctions of Rule 37(b) directly into play. Since the court has heard the contentions of all interested persons, an affirmative order is justified. See Rosenberg, Sanctions to Effectuate Pretrial Discovery, 58 Col.L.Rev. 480, 492-493 (1958). In addition, the court may require the payment of expenses incurred in relation to the motion.

[¶49] Subdivision (d)—Sequence and Priority. This new provision is concerned with the sequence in which parties may proceed with discovery and with related problems of timing. The principal effects of the new provision are first, to eliminate any fixed priority in the sequence of discovery, and second, to make clear and explicit the court's power to establish priority by an order issued in a particular case.

[¶50] A priority rule developed by some courts, which confers priority on the party who first serves notice of taking a deposition, is unsatisfactory in several important respects:

[¶51] First, this priority rule permits a party to establish a priority running to all depositions as to which he has given earlier notice. Since he can on a given day serve notice of taking many depositions he is in a position to delay his adversary's taking of depositions for an inordinate time. Some courts have ruled that deposition priority also permits a party to delay his answers to interrogatories and production of documents. *E.g., E. I. du Pont de Nemours & Co. v. Phillips Petroleum Co.*, 23 F.R.D. 237 (D. Del.1959); *but cf. Sturdevant v. Sears, Roebuck & Co.*, 32 F.R.D. 426 (W.D. Mo.1963).

[¶52] Second, since notice is the key to priority, if both parties wish to take depositions first a race results. *See Caldwell-Clements, Inc. v. McGraw-Hill Pub. Co.*, 11 F.R.D. 156 (S.D. N.Y.1951) (description of tactics used by parties). But the existing rules on notice of deposition create a race with runners starting from different positions. The plaintiff may not give notice without leave of court until 20 days after commencement of the action, whereas the defendant may serve notice at any time after commencement. Thus, a careful and prompt defendant can almost always secure priority. This advantage of defendants is fortuitous, because the purpose of requiring plaintiff to wait 20 days is to afford defendant an opportunity to obtain counsel, not to confer priority.

[¶53] Third, although courts have ordered a change in the normal sequence of discovery on a number of occasions, *e.g., Kaeppler v. James H. Matthews & Co.*, 200 F.Supp. 229 (E.D. Pa.1961); *Park & Tilford Distillers Corp. v. Distillers Co.*, 19 F.R.D. 169 (S.D. N.Y.1956), and have at all times avowed discretion to vary the usual priority, most commentators are agreed that courts in fact grant relief only for "the most obviously compelling reasons." 2A Barron & Holtzoff, Federal Practice and Procedure 447-47 (Wright ed. 1961); see also Younger, Priority of Pretrial Examination in the Federal Courts – A Comment, 34 N.Y.U.L.Rev. 1271 (1959); Freund, The Pleading and Pretrial of an Antitrust Claim, 46 Corn.L.Q. 555, 564 (1964). Discontent with the fairness of actual practice has been evinced by other observers. Comments, 59 Yale L.J. 117, 134-136 (1949); Yudkin, Some Refinements in Federal Discovery Procedure, 11 Fed.B.J. 289, 296-297 (1951); Developments in the Law – Discovery, 74 Harv.L. Rev. 940, 954-958 (1961).

[¶54] Despite these difficulties, some courts have adhered to the priority rule, presumably because it provides a test which is easily understood and applied by the parties without much court intervention. It thus permits deposition discovery to function extrajudicially, which the rules provide for and the courts desire. For these same reasons, courts are reluctant to make numerous exceptions to the rule.

[¶55] The Columbia Survey makes clear that the problem of priority does not affect litigants generally. It found that most litigants do not move quickly to obtain discovery. In over half of the cases, both parties waited at least 50 days. During the first 20 days after commencement of the action—the period when defendant might assure his priority by noticing depositions—16 percent of the defendants acted to obtain discovery. A race could not have occurred in more than 16 percent of the cases and it undoubtedly occurred in fewer. On the other hand, five times as many defendants as plaintiffs served notice of deposition during the first 19 days. To the same effect, see Comment, Tactical Use and Abuse of Depositions Under the Federal Rules, 59 Yale L.J. 117, 134 (1949).

[¶56] These findings do not mean, however, that the priority rule is satisfactory or that a problem of priority does not exist. The court decisions show that parties do bottle[1] on this issue and carry their disputes to court. The statistics show that these court cases are not typical. By the same token, they reveal that more extensive exercise of judicial discretion to vary the priority will not bring a flood of litigation, and that a change in the priority rule will in fact affect only a small fraction of the cases.

[¶57] It is contended by some that there is no need to alter the existing priority practice. In support, it is urged that there is no evidence that injustices in fact result from present practice and that, in any event, the courts can and do promulgate local rules, as in New York, to deal with local situations and issue orders to avoid possible injustice in particular cases.

[¶58] Subdivision (d) is based on the contrary view that the rule of priority based on notice is unsatisfactory and unfair in its operation. Subdivision (d) follows an approach adapted from Civil Rule 4 of the District Court for the Southern District of New York. That rule provides that starting 40 days after commencement of the action, unless otherwise ordered by the court, the fact that one part[2] is taking a deposition shall not prevent another party from doing so "concurrently." In practice, the depositions are not usually taken simultaneously; rather, the parties work out arrangements for alternation in the taking of depositions. One party may take a complete deposition and then the other, or, if the depositions are extensive, one party deposes for a set time, and then the other. *See Caldwell-Clements, Inc. v. McGraw-Hill Pub. Co.*, 11 F.R.D. 156 (S.D. N.Y.1951).

[¶59] In principle, one party's initiation of discovery should not wait upon the other's completion, unless delay is dictated by special considerations. Clearly the principle is feasible with respect to all methods of discovery other than depositions. And the experience of the Southern District of New York shows that the principle can be applied to depositions as well. The courts have not had an increase in motion business on this matter. Once it is clear to lawyers that they bargain on an equal footing, they are usually able to arrange for an orderly succession of depositions without judicial intervention. Professor Moore has called attention to Civil Rule 4 and suggested that it may usefully be extended to other areas. 4 Moore's Federal Practice 1154 (2d ed. 1966).

[¶60] The court may upon motion and by order grant priority in a particular case. But a local court rule purporting to confer priority in certain classes of cases would be inconsistent with this subdivision and thus void.

[¶61] Subdivision (e)—Supplementation of Responses. The rules do not now state whether interrogatories (and questions at deposition as well as requests for inspection and admissions) impose a "continuing burden" on the responding party to supplement his answers if he obtains new information. The issue is acute when new information renders substantially incomplete or inaccurate an answer which was complete and accurate when made. It is essential that the rules provide an answer to this question. The parties can adjust to a rule either way, once they know what it is. See 4 Moore's Federal Practice §33.25[4] (2d ed. 1966).

[¶62] Arguments can be made both ways. Imposition of a continuing burden reduces the proliferation of additional sets of interrogatories. Some courts have adopted local rules establishing such a burden. *E.g.*, E.D.Pa.R. 20(f), quoted in *Taggart v. Vermont Transp. Co.*, 32 F.R.D. 587 (E.D. Pa.1963); D.Me.R.15(c). Others have imposed the burden by decision. *E.g.*, *Chenault v. Nebraska Farm Products, Inc.*, 9 F.R.D. 529, 533 (D. Nebr.1949). On the other hand, there are serious objections to the burden, especially in protracted cases. Although the party signs the answers, it is his lawyer who understands their significance and bears the responsibility to bring answers up to date. In a complex case all sorts of information reaches the party, who little understands its bearing on answers previously given to interrogatories. In practice, therefore, the lawyer under a continuing burden must periodically recheck all interrogatories and canvass all new information. But a full set of new answers may no longer be needed by the interrogating party. Some issues will have been dropped from the case, some questions are now seen as unimportant, and other questions must in any event be reformulated. *See Novick v. Pennsylvania RR.*, 18 F.R.D. 296, 298 (W.D. Pa.1955).

[¶63] Subdivision (e) provides that a party is not under a continuing burden except as expressly provided. *Cf.* Note, 68 Harv.L.Rev. 673, 677 (1955). An exception is made as to the identity of persons having knowledge of discoverable matters, because of the obvious importance to each side of knowing all witnesses and because information about witnesses routinely comes to each lawyer's attention. Many of the decisions on the issue of a continuing burden have in fact concerned the identity of witnesses. An exception is also made as to expert trial witnesses in order to carry out the provisions of Rule 26(b)(4). *See Diversified Products Corp. v. Sports Center Co.*, 42 F.R.D. 3 (D. Md.1967).

[¶64] Another exception is made for the situation in which a party, or more frequently his lawyer, obtains actual knowledge that a prior response is incorrect. This exception does not impose a duty to check the accuracy of prior responses, but it prevents knowing concealment by a party or attorney. Finally, a duty to supplement may be imposed by order of the court in a particular case (including an order resulting from a pretrial conference) or by agreement of the parties. A party may of course make a new discovery request which requires supplementation of prior responses.

[¶65] The duty will normally be enforced, in those limited instances where it is imposed, through sanctions imposed by the trial court, including exclusion of evidence, continuance, or other action, as the court may deem appropriate.

1. **Editor's note:** So in original. Probably should be "battle."
2. **Editor's note:** So in original. Probably should be "party."

FRCP 27 – 2009 NOTES OF ADVISORY COMMITTEE

[¶1] The time set in the former rule at 20 days has been revised to 21 days. See the Note to Rule 6.[1]

1. **Editor's note:** The cross-reference to "Note to Rule 6" refers to 2009 Notes to FRCP 6 at ¶¶1-20, p. 1149, this book.

FRCP 27 – 2005 NOTES OF ADVISORY COMMITTEE

[¶1] The outdated cross-reference to former Rule 4(d) is corrected to incorporate all Rule 4 methods of service. Former Rule 4(d) has been allocated to many different subdivisions of Rule 4. Former Rule 4(d) did not cover all categories of defendants or modes of service, and present Rule 4 reaches further than all of former Rule 4. But there is no reason to distinguish between the different categories of defendants and modes of service encompassed by Rule 4. Rule 4 service provides effective notice. Notice by such means should be provided to any expected adverse party that comes within Rule 4.

[¶2] Other changes are made to conform Rule 27(a)(2) to current style conventions.

FRCP 29 – 1993 NOTES OF ADVISORY COMMITTEE

[¶1] This rule is revised to give greater opportunity for litigants to agree upon modifications to the procedures governing discovery or to limitations upon discovery. Counsel are encouraged to agree on less expensive and time-consuming methods to obtain information, as through voluntary exchange of documents, use of interviews in lieu of depositions, etc. Likewise, when more depositions or interrogatories are needed than allowed under these rules or when more time is needed to complete a deposition than allowed under a local rule, they can, by agreeing to the additional discovery, eliminate the need for a special motion addressed to the court.

[¶2] Under the revised rule, the litigants ordinarily are not required to obtain the court's approval of these stipulations. By order or local rule, the court can, however, direct that its approval be obtained for particular types of stipulations; and, in any event, approval must be obtained if a stipulation to extend the 30-day period for responding to interrogatories, requests for production, or requests for admissions would interfere with dates set by the court for completing discovery, for hearing of a motion, or for trial.

FRCP 30 – 2007 NOTES OF ADVISORY COMMITTEE

[¶1] The right to arrange a deposition transcription should be open to any party, regardless of the means of recording and regardless of who noticed the deposition.

[¶2] "[O]ther entity" is added to the list of organizations that may be named as deponent. The purpose is to ensure that the deposition process can be used to reach information known or reasonably available to an organization no matter what abstract fictive concept is used to describe the organization. Nothing is gained by wrangling over the place to fit into current rule language such entities as limited liability companies, limited partnerships, business trusts, more exotic common-law creations, or forms developed in other countries.

FRCP 30 – 2000 NOTES OF ADVISORY COMMITTEE

[¶1] **Subdivision (d).** Paragraph (1) has been amended to clarify the terms regarding behavior during depositions. The references to objections "to evidence" and limitations "on evidence" have been removed to avoid disputes about what is "evidence" and whether an objection is to, or a limitation is on, discovery instead. It is intended that the rule apply to any objection to a question or other issue arising during a deposition, and to any limitation imposed by the court in connection with a deposition, which might relate to duration or other matters.

[¶2] The current rule places limitations on instructions that a witness not answer only when the instruction is made by a "party." Similar limitations should apply with regard to anyone who might purport to instruct a witness not to answer a question. Accordingly, the rule is amended to apply the limitation to instructions by any person. The amendment is not intended to confer new authority on nonparties to instruct witnesses to refuse to answer deposition questions. The amendment makes it clear that, whatever the legitimacy of giving such instructions, the nonparty is subject to the same limitations as parties.

[¶3] Paragraph (2) imposes a presumptive durational limitation of one day of seven hours for any deposition. The Committee has been informed that overlong depositions can result in undue costs and delays in some circumstances. This limitation contemplates that there will be reasonable breaks during the day for lunch and other reasons, and that the only time to be counted is the time occupied by the actual deposition. For purposes of this durational limit, the deposition of each person designated under Rule 30(b)(6) should be considered a separate deposition. The presumptive duration may be extended, or otherwise altered, by agreement. Absent agreement, a court order is needed. The party seeking a court order to extend the examination, or otherwise alter the limitations, is expected to show good cause to justify such an order.

[¶4] Parties considering extending the time for a deposition—and courts asked to order an extension—might consider a variety of factors. For example, if the witness needs an interpreter, that may prolong the examination. If the examination will cover events occurring over a long period of time, that may justify allowing additional time. In cases in which the witness will be questioned about numerous or lengthy documents, it is often desirable for the interrogating party to send copies of the documents to the witness sufficiently in advance of the deposition so that the witness can become familiar with them. Should the witness nevertheless not read the documents in advance, thereby prolonging the deposition, a court could consider that a reason for extending the time limit. If the examination reveals that documents have been requested but not produced, that may justify further examination once production has occurred. In multi-party cases, the need for each party to examine the witness may warrant additional time, although duplicative questioning should be avoided and parties with similar interests should strive to designate one lawyer to question about areas of common interest. Similarly, should the lawyer for the witness want to examine the witness, that may require additional time. Finally, with regard to expert witnesses, there may more often be a need for additional time—even after the submission of the report required by Rule 26(a)(2)—for full exploration of the theories upon which the witness relies.

[¶5] It is expected that in most instances the parties and the witness will make reasonable accommodations to avoid the need for resort to the court. The limitation is phrased in terms of a single day on the assumption that ordinarily a single day would be preferable to a deposition extending over multiple days; if alternative arrangements would better suit the parties, they may agree to them. It is also assumed that there will be reasonable breaks during the day. Preoccupation with timing is to be avoided.

[¶6] The rule directs the court to allow additional time where consistent with Rule 26(b)(2) if needed for a fair examination of the deponent. In addition, if the deponent or another person impedes or delays the examination, the court must authorize extra time. The amendment makes clear that additional time should also be allowed where the examination is impeded by an "other circumstance," which might include a power outage, a health emergency, or other event.

[¶7] In keeping with the amendment to Rule 26(b)(2), the provision added in 1993 granting authority to adopt a local rule limiting the time permitted for depositions has been removed. The court may enter a case-specific order directing shorter depositions for all depositions in a case or with regard to a specific witness. The court may also order that a deposition be taken for limited periods on several days.

[¶8] Paragraph (3) includes sanctions provisions formerly included in paragraph (2). It authorizes the court to impose an appropriate sanction on any person responsible for an impediment that frustrated the fair examination of the deponent. This could include the deponent, any party, or any other person involved in the deposition. If the impediment or delay results from an "other circumstance" under paragraph (2), ordinarily no sanction would be appropriate.

[¶9] Former paragraph (3) has been renumbered (4) but is otherwise unchanged.

[¶10] Subdivision (f)(1). This subdivision is amended because Rule 5(d) has been amended to direct that discovery materials, including depositions, ordinarily should not be filed. The rule already has provisions directing that the lawyer who arranged for the transcript or recording preserve the deposition. Rule 5(d) provides that, once the deposition is used in the proceeding, the attorney must file it with the court.

[¶11] "Shall" is replaced by "must" or "may" under the program to conform amended rules to current style conventions when there is no ambiguity.

FRCP 30 – 1993 NOTES OF ADVISORY COMMITTEE

[¶1] Subdivision (a). Paragraph (1) retains the first and third sentences from the former subdivision (a) without significant modification. The second and fourth sentences are relocated.

[¶2] Paragraph (2) collects all provisions bearing on requirements of leave of court to take a deposition.

[¶3] Paragraph (2)(A) is new. It provides a limit on the number of depositions the parties may take, absent leave of court or stipulation with the other parties. One aim of this revision is to assure judicial review under the standards stated in Rule 26(b)(2) before any side will be allowed to take more than ten depositions in a case without agreement of the other parties. A second objective is to emphasize that counsel have a professional obligation to develop a mutual cost-effective plan for discovery in the case. Leave to take additional depositions should be granted when consistent with the principles of Rule 26(b)(2), and in some cases the ten-per-side limit should be reduced in accordance with those same principles. Consideration should ordinarily be given at the planning meeting of the parties under Rule 26(f) and at the time of a scheduling conference under Rule 16(b) as to enlargements or reductions in the number of depositions, eliminating the need for special motions.

[¶4] A deposition under Rule 30(b)(6) should, for purposes of this limit, be treated as a single deposition even though more than one person may be designated to testify.

[¶5] In multi-party cases, the parties on any side are expected to confer and agree as to which depositions are most needed, given the presumptive limit on the number of depositions they can take without leave of court. If these disputes cannot be amicably resolved, the court can be requested to resolve the dispute or permit additional depositions.

[¶6] Paragraph (2)(B) is new. It requires leave of court if any witness is to be deposed in the action more than once. This requirement does not apply when a deposition is temporarily recessed for convenience of counsel or the deponent or to enable additional materials to be gathered before resuming the deposition. If significant travel costs would be incurred to resume the deposition, the parties should consider the feasibility of conducting the balance of the examination by telephonic means.

[¶7] Paragraph (2)(C) revises the second sentence of the former subdivision (a) as to when depositions may be taken. Consistent with the changes made in Rule 26(d), providing that formal discovery ordinarily not commence until after the litigants have met and conferred as directed in revised Rule 26(f), the rule requires leave of court or agreement of

the parties if a deposition is to be taken before that time (except when a witness is about to leave the country).

[¶8] Subdivision (b). The primary change in subdivision (b) is that parties will be authorized to record deposition testimony by nonstenographic means without first having to obtain permission of the court or agreement from other counsel.

[¶9] Former subdivision (b)(2) is partly relocated in subdivision (a)(2)(C) of this rule. The latter two sentences of the first paragraph are deleted, in part because they are redundant to Rule 26(g) and in part because Rule 11 no longer applies to discovery requests. The second paragraph of the former subdivision (b)(2), relating to use of depositions at trial where a party was unable to obtain counsel in time for an accelerated deposition, is relocated in Rule 32.

[¶10] New paragraph (2) confers on the party taking the deposition the choice of the method of recording, without the need to obtain prior court approval for one taken other than stenographically. A party choosing to record a deposition only by videotape or audiotape should understand that a transcript will be required by Rule 26(a)(3)(B) and Rule 32(c) if the deposition is later to be offered as evidence at trial or on a dispositive motion under Rule 56. Objections to the nonstenographic recording of a deposition, when warranted by the circumstances, can be presented to the court under Rule 26(c).

[¶11] Paragraph (3) provides that other parties may arrange, at their own expense, for the recording of a deposition by a means (stenographic, visual, or sound) in addition to the method designated by the person noticing the deposition. The former provisions of this paragraph, relating to the court's power to change the date of a deposition, have been eliminated as redundant in view of Rule 26(c)(2).

[¶12] Revised paragraph (4) requires that all depositions be recorded by an officer designated or appointed under Rule 28 and contains special provisions designed to provide basic safeguards to assure the utility and integrity of recordings taken other than stenographically.

[¶13] Paragraph (7) is revised to authorize the taking of a deposition not only by telephone but also by other remote electronic means, such as satellite television, when agreed to by the parties or authorized by the court.

[¶14] Subdivision (c). Minor changes are made in this subdivision to reflect those made in subdivision (b) and to complement the new provisions of subdivision (d)(1), aimed at reducing the number of interruptions during depositions.

[¶15] In addition, the revision addresses a recurring problem as to whether other potential deponents can attend a deposition. Courts have disagreed, some holding that witnesses should be excluded through invocation of Rule 615 of the evidence rules, and others holding that witnesses may attend unless excluded by an order under Rule 26(c)(5). The revision provides that other witnesses are not automatically excluded from a deposition simply by the request of a party. Exclusion, however, can be ordered under Rule 26(c)(5) when appropriate; and, if exclusion is ordered, consideration should be given as to whether the excluded witnesses likewise should be precluded from reading, or being otherwise informed about, the testimony given in the earlier depositions. The revision addresses only the matter of attendance by potential deponents, and does not attempt to resolve issues concerning attendance by others, such as members of the public or press.

[¶16] Subdivision (d). The first sentence of new paragraph (1) provides that any objections during a deposition must be made concisely and in a non-argumentative and non-suggestive manner. Depositions frequently have been unduly prolonged, if not unfairly frustrated, by lengthy objections and colloquy, often suggesting how the deponent should respond. While objections may, under the revised rule, be made during a deposition, they ordinarily should be limited to those that under Rule 32(d)(3) might be waived if not made at that time, *i.e.*, objections on grounds that might be immediately obviated, removed, or cured, such as to the form of a question or the responsiveness of an answer. Under Rule 32(b), other objections can, even without the so-called "usual stipulation" preserving objections, be raised for the first time at trial and therefore should be kept to a minimum during a deposition.

[¶17] Directions to a deponent not to answer a question can be even more disruptive than objections. The second sentence of new paragraph (1) prohibits such directions except in the three circumstances indicated: to claim a privilege or protection against disclosure (*e.g.*, as work product), to enforce a court directive limiting the scope or length of permissible discovery, or to suspend a deposition to enable presentation of a motion under paragraph (3).

[¶18] Paragraph (2) is added to this subdivision to dispel any doubts regarding the power of the court by order or local rule to establish limits on the length of depositions. The rule also explicitly authorizes the court to impose the cost resulting from obstructive tactics that unreasonably prolong a deposition on the person engaged in such obstruction. This sanction may be imposed on a non-party witness as well as a party or attorney, but is otherwise congruent with Rule 26(g).

[¶19] It is anticipated that limits on the length of depositions prescribed by local rules would be presumptive only, subject to modification by the court or by agreement of the parties. Such modifications typically should be discussed by the parties in their meeting under Rule 26(f) and included in the scheduling order required by Rule 16(b). Additional time, moreover, should be allowed under the revised rule when justified under the principles stated in Rule 26(b)(2). To reduce the number of special motions, local rules should ordinarily permit—and indeed encourage—the parties to agree to additional time, as when, during the taking of a deposition, it becomes clear that some additional examination is needed.

ADVISORY CMTE. NOTES

[¶20] Paragraph (3) authorizes appropriate sanctions not only when a deposition is unreasonably prolonged, but also when an attorney engages in other practices that improperly frustrate the fair examination of the deponent, such as making improper objections or giving directions not to answer prohibited by paragraph (1). In general, counsel should not engage in any conduct during a deposition that would not be allowed in the presence of a judicial officer. The making of an excessive number of unnecessary objections may itself constitute sanctionable conduct, as may the refusal of an attorney to agree with other counsel on a fair apportionment of the time allowed for examination of a deponent or a refusal to agree to a reasonable request for some additional time to complete a deposition, when that is permitted by the local rule or order.

[¶21] Subdivision (e). Various changes are made in this subdivision to reduce problems sometimes encountered when depositions are taken stenographically. Reporters frequently have difficulties obtaining signatures—and the return of depositions—from deponents. Under the revision prefiling review by the deponent is required only if requested before the deposition is completed. If review is requested, the deponent will be allowed 30 days to review the transcript or recording and to indicate any changes in form or substance. Signature of the deponent will be required only if review is requested and changes are made.

[¶22] Subdivision (f). Minor changes are made in this subdivision to reflect those made in subdivision (b). In courts which direct that depositions not be automatically filed, the reporter can transmit the transcript or recording to the attorney taking the deposition (or ordering the transcript or record), who then becomes custodian for the court of the original record of the deposition. Pursuant to subdivision (f)(2), as under the prior rule, any other party is entitled to secure a copy of the deposition from the officer designated to take the deposition; accordingly, unless ordered or agreed, the officer must retain a copy of the recording or the stenographic notes.

FRCP 31 – 2007 NOTES OF ADVISORY COMMITTEE

[¶1] The party who noticed a deposition on written questions must notify all other parties when the deposition is completed, so that they may make use of the deposition. A deposition is completed when it is recorded and the deponent has either waived or exercised the right of review under Rule 30(e)(1).

FRCP 32 – 2009 NOTES OF ADVISORY COMMITTEE

[¶1] The times set in the former rule at less than 11 days and within 5 days have been revised to 14 days and 7 days. See the Note to Rule 6.[1]

1. **Editor's note:** The cross-reference to "Note to Rule 6" refers to 2009 Notes to FRCP 6 at ¶¶1-20, p. 1149, this book.

FRCP 32 – 2007 NOTES OF ADVISORY COMMITTEE

[¶1] Former Rule 32(a) applied "[a]t the trial or upon the hearing of a motion or an interlocutory proceeding." The amended rule describes the same events as "a hearing or trial."

[¶2] The final paragraph of former Rule 32(a) allowed use in a later action of a deposition "lawfully taken and duly filed in the former action." Because of the 2000 amendment of Rule 5(d), many depositions are not filed. Amended Rule 32(a)(8) reflects this change by excluding use of an unfiled deposition only if filing was required in the former action.

FRCP 33 – 2007 NOTES OF ADVISORY COMMITTEE

[¶1] The final sentence of former Rule 33(a) was a redundant cross-reference to the discovery moratorium provisions of Rule 26(d). Rule 26(d) is now familiar, obviating any need to carry forward the redundant cross-reference.

[¶2] Former Rule 33(b)(5) was a redundant reminder of Rule 37(a) procedure and is omitted as no longer useful.

[¶3] Former Rule 33(c) stated that an interrogatory "is not necessarily objectionable merely because an answer * * * involves an opinion or contention * * *." "[I]s not necessarily" seemed to imply that the interrogatory might be objectionable merely for this reason. This implication has been ignored in practice. Opinion and contention interrogatories are used routinely. Amended Rule 33(a)(2) embodies the current meaning of Rule 33 by omitting "necessarily."

FRCP 33 – 2006 NOTES OF ADVISORY COMMITTEE

[¶1] Rule 33(d) is amended to parallel Rule 34(a) by recognizing the importance of electronically stored information. The term "electronically stored information" has the same broad meaning in Rule 33(d) as in Rule 34(a). Much business information is stored only in electronic form; the Rule 33(d) option should be available with respect to such records as well.

[¶2] Special difficulties may arise in using electronically stored information, either due to its form or because it is dependent on a particular computer system. Rule 33(d) allows a responding party to substitute access to documents or electronically stored information for an answer only if the burden of deriving the answer will be substantially the same for either party. Rule 33(d) states that a party electing to respond to an interrogatory by providing electronically stored information must ensure that the interrogating party can locate and identify it "as readily as can the party served," and that the responding party must give the interrogating party a "reasonable opportunity to examine, audit, or inspect" the information. Depending on the circumstances, satisfying these provisions with regard to electronically stored information may require the responding party to provide some combination of technical support, information on application software, or

other assistance. The key question is whether such support enables the interrogating party to derive or ascertain the answer from the electronically stored information as readily as the responding party. A party that wishes to invoke Rule 33(d) by specifying electronically stored information may be required to provide direct access to its electronic information system, but only if that is necessary to afford the requesting party an adequate opportunity to derive or ascertain the answer to the interrogatory. In that situation, the responding party's need to protect sensitive interests of confidentiality or privacy may mean that it must derive or ascertain and provide the answer itself rather than invoke Rule 33(d).

FRCP 33 – 1993 NOTES OF ADVISORY COMMITTEE

[¶1] ***Purpose of revision.*** The purpose of this revision is to reduce the frequency and increase the efficiency of interrogatory practice. The revision is based on experience with local rules. For ease of reference, subdivision (a) is divided into two subdivisions and the remaining subdivisions renumbered.

[¶2] *Note to Subdivision (a).* Revision of this subdivision limits interrogatory practice. Because Rule 26(a)(1)-(3) requires disclosure of much of the information previously obtained by this form of discovery, there should be less occasion to use it. Experience in over half of the district courts has confirmed that limitations on the number of interrogatories are useful and manageable. Moreover, because the device can be costly and may be used as a means of harassment, it is desirable to subject its use to the control of the court consistent with the principles stated in Rule 26(b)(2), particularly in multi-party cases where it has not been unusual for the same interrogatory to be propounded to a party by more than one of its adversaries.

[¶3] Each party is allowed to serve 25 interrogatories upon any other party, but must secure leave of court (or a stipulation from the opposing party) to serve a larger number. Parties cannot evade this presumptive limitation through the device of joining as "subparts" questions that seek information about discrete separate subjects. However, a question asking about communications of a particular type should be treated as a single interrogatory even though it requests that the time, place, persons present, and contents be stated separately for each such communication.

[¶4] As with the number of depositions authorized by Rule 30, leave to serve additional interrogatories is to be allowed when consistent with Rule 26(b)(2). The aim is not to prevent needed discovery, but to provide judicial scrutiny before parties make potentially excessive use of this discovery device. In many cases it will be appropriate for the court to permit a larger number of interrogatories in the scheduling order entered under Rule 16(b).

[¶5] Unless leave of court is obtained, interrogatories may not be served prior to the meeting of the parties under Rule 26(f).

[¶6] When a case with outstanding interrogatories exceeding the number permitted by this rule is removed to federal court, the interrogating party must seek leave allowing the additional interrogatories, specify which twenty-five are to be answered, or resubmit interrogatories that comply with the rule. Moreover, under Rule 26(d), the time for response would be measured from the date of the parties' meeting under Rule 26(f). See Rule 81(c), providing that these rules govern procedures after removal.

[¶7] *Note to Subdivision (b).* A separate subdivision is made of the former second paragraph of subdivision (a). Language is added to paragraph (1) of this subdivision to emphasize the duty of the responding party to provide full answers to the extent not objectionable. If, for example, an interrogatory seeking information about numerous facilities or products is deemed objectionable, but an interrogatory seeking information about a lesser number of facilities or products would not have been objectionable, the interrogatory should be answered with respect to the latter even though an objection is raised as to the balance of the facilities or products. Similarly, the fact that additional time may be needed to respond to some questions (or to some aspects of questions) should not justify a delay in responding to those questions (or other aspects of questions) that can be answered within the prescribed time.

[¶8] Paragraph (4) is added to make clear that objections must be specifically justified, and that unstated or untimely grounds for objection ordinarily are waived. Note also the provisions of revised Rule 26(b)(5), which require a responding party to indicate when it is withholding information under a claim of privilege or as trial preparation materials.

[¶9] These provisions should be read in light of Rule 26(g), authorizing the court to impose sanctions on a party and attorney making an unfounded objection to an interrogatory.

[¶10] *Note to Subdivisions (c) and (d).* The provisions of former subdivisions (b) and (c) are renumbered.

FRCP 33 – 1970 NOTES OF ADVISORY COMMITTEE

[¶1] Subdivision (a). The mechanics of the operation of Rule 33 are substantially revised by the proposed amendment, with a view to reducing court intervention. There is general agreement that interrogatories spawn a greater percentage of objections and motions than any other discovery device. The Columbia Survey shows that, although half of the litigants resorted to depositions and about one-third used interrogatories, about 65 percent of the objections were made with respect to interrogatories and 26 percent related to depositions. See also Speck, the Use of Discovery in the United States District Courts, 60 Yale L.J. 1132, 1144, 1151 (1951); Note, 36 Minn L Rev 364, 379 (1952).

[¶2] The procedures now provided in Rule 33 seem calculated to encourage objections and court motions. The time periods now allowed for responding to interrogatories—15 days for answers and 10 days for objections—are too short. The Columbia Survey shows that tardy response to interrogatories is common, virtually expected. The same was reported in Speck, supra, 60 Yale L.J. 1132, 1144. The time pressures tend to encourage objections as a means of gaining time to answer.

[¶3] The time for objections is even shorter than for answers, and the party runs the risk that if he fails to object in time he may have waived his objections. *E.g., Cleminshaw v. Beech Aircraft Corp.*, 21 FRD 300 (D Del 1957); see 4 Moore's Federal Practice, para. 33.27 (2d ed 1966); 2A Barron & Holtzoff, Federal Practice and Procedure 372-373 (Wright ed. 1961). It often seems easier to object than to seek an extension of time. Unlike Rules 30(d) and 37(a), Rule 33 imposes no sanction of expenses on a party whose objections are clearly unjustified.

[¶4] Rule 33 assures that the objections will lead directly to court, through its requirement that they be served with a notice of hearing. Although this procedure does not preclude an out-of-court resolution of the dispute, the procedure tends to discourage informal negotiations. If answers are served and they are thought inadequate, the interrogating party may move under Rule 37(a) for an order compelling adequate answers. There is no assurance that the hearing on objections and that on inadequate answers will be heard together.

[¶5] The amendment improves the procedure of Rule 33 in the following respects:

[¶6] (1) The time allowed for response is increased to 30 days and this time period applies to both answers and objections, but a defendant need not respond in less than 45 days after service of the summons and complaint upon him. As is true under existing law, the responding party who believes that some parts or all of the interrogatories are objectionable may choose to seek a protective order under new Rule 26(c) or may serve objections under this rule. Unless he applies for a protective order, he is required to serve answers or objections in response to the interrogatories, subject to the sanctions provided in Rule 37(d). Answers and objections are served together, so that a response to each interrogatory is encouraged, and any failure to respond is easily noted.

[¶7] (2) In view of the enlarged time permitted for response, it is no longer necessary to require leave of court for service of interrogatories. The purpose of this requirement—that defendant have time to obtain counsel before a response must be made—is adequately fulfilled by the requirement that interrogatories be served upon a party with or after service of the summons and complaint upon him.

[¶8] Some would urge that the plaintiff nevertheless not be permitted to serve interrogatories with the complaint. They fear that a routine practice might be invited, whereby form interrogatories would accompany most complaints. More fundamentally, they feel that, since very general complaints are permitted in present-day pleading, it is fair that the defendant have a right to take the lead in serving interrogatories. (These views apply also to Rule 36.) The amendment of Rule 33 rejects these views, in favor of allowing both parties to go forward with discovery, each free to obtain the information he needs respecting the case.

[¶9] (3) If objections are made, the burden is on the interrogating party to move under Rule 37(a) for a court order compelling answers, in the course of which the court will pass on the objections. The change in the burden of going forward does not alter the existing obligation of an objecting party to justify his objections. *E.g., Pressley v. Boehlke*, 33 FRD 316 (WD NC 1963). If the discovering party asserts that an answer is incomplete or evasive, again he may look to Rule 37(a) for relief, and he should add this assertion to his motion to overrule objections. There is no requirement that the parties consult informally concerning their differences, but the new procedure should encourage consultation, and the court may by local rule require it.

[¶10] The proposed changes are similar in approach to those adopted by California in 1961. See Calif Code Civ Proc §2030(a). The experience of the Los Angeles Superior Court is informally reported as showing that the California amendment resulted in a significant reduction in court motions concerning interrogatories. Rhode Island takes a similar approach. See R 33, RIR Civ Proc Official Draft, p. 74 (Boston Law Book Co.).

[¶11] A change is made in subdivision (a) which is not related to the sequence of procedures. The restriction to "adverse" parties is eliminated. The courts have generally construed this restriction as precluding interrogatories unless an issue between the parties is disclosed by the pleadings—even though the parties may have conflicting interests. *E.g., Mozeika v. Kaufman Construction Co.*, 25 FRD 233 (ED Pa 1960) (plaintiff and third-party defendant); *Biddle v. Hutchinson*, 24 FRD 256 (MD Pa 1959) (co-defendants). The resulting distinctions have often been highly technical. In *Schlagenhauf v. Holder*, 379 US 104 (1964), the Supreme Court rejected a contention that examination under Rule 35 could be had only against an "opposing" party, as not in keeping "with the aims of a liberal, nontechnical application of the Federal Rules." 379 US at 116. Eliminating the requirement of "adverse" parties from Rule 33 brings it into line with all other discovery rules.

[¶12] A second change in subdivision (a) is the addition of the term "governmental agency" to the listing of organizations whose answers are to be made by any officer or agent of the organization. This does not involve any change in existing law. Compare the similar listing in Rule 30(b)(6).

[¶13] The duty of a party to supplement his answers to interrogatories is governed by a new provision in Rule 26(e).

[¶14] Subdivision (b). There are numerous and conflicting decisions on the question whether and to what extent interrogatories are limited to matters "of fact," or may elicit opinions, contentions, and legal conclusions. *Compare, e.g.*, *Payer, Hewitt & Co. v. Bellanca Corp.*, 26 FRD 219 (D Del 1960) (opinions bad); *Zinsky v. New York Central R.R.*, 36 FRD 680 (ND Ohio 1964) (factual opinion or contention good, but legal theory bad); *United States v. Carter Products, Inc.*, 28 FRD 373 (SD NY 1961) (factual contentions and legal theories bad) *with Taylor v. Sound Steamship Lines, Inc.*, 100 F Supp 388 (D Conn 1951) (opinions good); *Bynum v. United States*, 36 FRD 14 (ED La 1964) (contentions as to facts constituting negligence good). For lists of the many conflicting authorities, see 4 Moore's Federal Practice para. 33.17 (2d ed 1966); 2A Barron & Holtzoff, Federal Practice and Procedure §768 (Wright ed. 1961).

[¶15] Rule 33 is amended to provide that an interrogatory is not objectionable merely because it calls for an opinion or contention that relates to fact or the application of law to fact. Efforts to draw sharp lines between facts and opinions have invariably been unsuccessful, and the clear trend of the cases is to permit "factual" opinions. As to requests for opinions or contentions that call for the application of law to fact, they can be most useful in narrowing and sharpening the issues, which is a major purpose of discovery. *See Diversified Products Corp. v. Sports Center Co.*, 42 FRD 3 (D Md 1967); Moore, supra; Field & McKusick, Maine Civil Practice §26.18 (1959). On the other hand, under the new language interrogatories may not extend to issues of "pure law," *i.e.*, legal issues unrelated to the facts of the case. *Cf. United States v. Maryland & Va. Milk Producers Assn., Inc.*, 22 FRD 300 (D DC 1958).

[¶16] Since interrogatories involving mixed questions of law and fact may create disputes between the parties which are best resolved after much or all of the other discovery has been completed, the court is expressly authorized to defer an answer. Likewise, the court may delay determination until pretrial conference, if it believes that the dispute is best resolved in the presence of the judge.

[¶17] The principal question raised with respect to the cases permitting such interrogatories is whether they reintroduce undesirable aspects of the prior pleading practice, whereby parties were chained to misconceived contentions or theories, and ultimate determination on the merits was frustrated. See James, The Revival of Bills of Particulars under the Federal Rules, 71 Harv L Rev 1473 (1958). But there are few if any instances in the recorded cases demonstrating that such frustration has occurred. The general rule governing the use of answers to interrogatories is that under ordinary circumstances they do not limit proof. *See, e.g., McElroy v. United Air Lines, Inc.*, 21 FRD 100 (WD Mo 1967); *Pressley v. Boehlke*, 33 FRD 316, 317 (WD NC 1963). Although in exceptional circumstances reliance on an answer may cause such prejudice that the court will hold the answering party bound to his answer, *e.g., Zielinski v. Philadelphia Piers, Inc.*, 139 F Supp 408 (ED Pa 1956), the interrogating party will ordinarily not be entitled to rely on the unchanging character of the answers he receives and cannot base prejudice on such reliance. The rule does not affect the power of a court to permit withdrawal or amendment of answers to interrogatories.

[¶18] The use of answers to interrogatories at trial is made subject to the rules of evidence. The provisions governing use of depositions, to which Rule 33 presently refers, are not entirely apposite to answers to interrogatories, since deposition practice contemplates that all parties will ordinarily participate through cross-examination. See 4 Moore's Federal Practice para. 33.29[1] (2d ed. 1966).

[¶19] Certain provisions are deleted from subdivision (b) because they are fully covered by new Rule 26(c) providing for protective orders and Rules 26(a) and 26(d). The language of the subdivision is thus simplified without any change of substance.

[¶20] Subdivision (c). This is a new subdivision, adapted from Calif Code Civ Proc §2030(c), relating especially to interrogatories which require a party to engage in burdensome or expensive research into his own business records in order to give an answer. The subdivision gives the party an option to make the records available and place the burden of research on the party who seeks the information. "This provision, without undermining the liberal scope of interrogatory discovery, places the burden of discovery upon its potential benefitee," Louisell, Modern California Discovery, 124-125 (1963), and alleviates a problem which in the past has troubled Federal courts. See Speck, The Use of Discovery in United States District Courts, 60 Yale L.J. 1132, 1142-1144 (1951). The interrogating party is protected against abusive use of this provision through the requirement that the burden of ascertaining the answer be substantially the same for both sides. A respondent may not impose on an interrogating party a mass of records as to which research is feasible only for one familiar with the records. At the same time, the respondent unable to invoke this subdivision does not on that account lose the protection available to him under new Rule 26(c) against oppressive or unduly burdensome or expensive interrogatories. And even when the respondent successfully invokes the subdivision, the court is not deprived of its usual power, in appropriate cases, to require that the interrogating party reimburse the respondent for the expense of assembling his records and making them intelligible.

FRCP 34 – 2007 NOTES OF ADVISORY COMMITTEE

[¶1] The final sentence in the first paragraph of former Rule 34(b) was a redundant cross-reference to the discovery moratorium provisions of Rule 26(d). Rule 26(d) is now familiar, obviating any need to carry forward the redundant cross-reference.

[¶2] The redundant reminder of Rule 37(a) procedure in the second paragraph of former Rule 34(b) is omitted as no longer useful.

FRCP 34 – 2006 NOTES OF ADVISORY COMMITTEE

[¶1] Subdivision (a). As originally adopted, Rule 34 focused on discovery of "documents" and "things." In 1970, Rule 34(a) was amended to include discovery of data compilations, anticipating that the use of computerized information would increase. Since then, the growth in electronically stored information and in the variety of systems for creating and storing such information has been dramatic. Lawyers and judges interpreted the term "documents" to include electronically stored information because it was obviously improper to allow a party to evade discovery obligations on the basis that the label had not kept pace with changes in information technology. But it has become increasingly difficult to say that all forms of electronically stored information, many dynamic in nature, fit within the traditional concept of a "document." Electronically stored information may exist in dynamic databases and other forms far different from fixed expression on paper. Rule 34(a) is amended to confirm that discovery of electronically stored information stands on equal footing with discovery of paper documents. The change clarifies that Rule 34 applies to information that is fixed in a tangible form and to information that is stored in a medium from which it can be retrieved and examined. At the same time, a Rule 34 request for production of "documents" should be understood to encompass, and the response should include, electronically stored information unless discovery in the action has clearly distinguished between electronically stored information and "documents."

[¶2] Discoverable information often exists in both paper and electronic form, and the same or similar information might exist in both. The items listed in Rule 34(a) show different ways in which information may be recorded or stored. Images, for example, might be hard-copy documents or electronically stored information. The wide variety of computer systems currently in use, and the rapidity of technological change, counsel against a limiting or precise definition of electronically stored information. Rule 34(a)(1) is expansive and includes any type of information that is stored electronically. A common example often sought in discovery is electronic communications, such as e-mail. The rule covers—either as documents or as electronically stored information—information "stored in any medium," to encompass future developments in computer technology. Rule 34(a)(1) is intended to be broad enough to cover all current types of computer-based information, and flexible enough to encompass future changes and developments.

[¶3] References elsewhere in the rules to "electronically stored information" should be understood to invoke this expansive approach. A companion change is made to Rule 33(d), making it explicit that parties choosing to respond to an interrogatory by permitting access to responsive records may do so by providing access to electronically stored information. More generally, the term used in Rule 34(a)(1) appears in a number of other amendments, such as those to Rules 26(a)(1), 26(b)(2), 26(b)(5)(B), 26(f), 34(b), 37(f), and 45. In each of these rules, electronically stored information has the same broad meaning it has under Rule 34(a)(1). References to "documents" appear in discovery rules that are not amended, including Rules 30(f), 36(a), and 37(c)(2). These references should be interpreted to include electronically stored information as circumstances warrant.

[¶4] The term "electronically stored information" is broad, but whether material that falls within this term should be produced, and in what form, are separate questions that must be addressed under Rules 26(b), 26(c), and 34(b).

[¶5] The Rule 34(a) requirement that, if necessary, a party producing electronically stored information translate it into reasonably usable form does not address the issue of translating from one human language to another. *See In re Puerto Rico Elect. Power Auth.*, 687 F.2d 501, 504-510 (1st Cir.1989).

[¶6] Rule 34(a)(1) is also amended to make clear that parties may request an opportunity to test or sample materials sought under the rule in addition to inspecting and copying them. That opportunity may be important for both electronically stored information and hard-copy materials. The current rule is not clear that such testing or sampling is authorized; the amendment expressly permits it. As with any other form of discovery, issues of burden and intrusiveness raised by requests to test or sample can be addressed under Rules 26(b)(2) and 26(c). Inspection or testing of certain types of electronically stored information or of a responding party's electronic information system may raise issues of confidentiality or privacy. The addition of testing and sampling to Rule 34(a) with regard to documents and electronically stored information is not meant to create a routine right of direct access to a party's electronic information system, although such access might be justified in some circumstances. Courts should guard against undue intrusiveness resulting from inspecting or testing such systems.

[¶7] Rule 34(a)(1) is further amended to make clear that tangible things must—like documents and land sought to be examined—be designated in the request.

[¶8] Subdivision (b). Rule 34(b) provides that a party must produce documents as they are kept in the usual course of business or must organize and label them to correspond with the categories in the discovery request. The production of electronically stored information should be subject to comparable requirements to protect against deliberate or inadvertent production in ways that raise unnecessary obstacles for the requesting party. Rule 34(b) is amended to ensure similar protection for electronically stored information.

[¶9] The amendment to Rule 34(b) permits the requesting party to designate the form or forms in which it wants electronically stored information produced. The form of production is more important to the exchange of electronically stored information than of hard-copy materials, al-

though a party might specify hard copy as the requested form. Specification of the desired form or forms may facilitate the orderly, efficient, and cost-effective discovery of electronically stored information. The rule recognizes that different forms of production may be appropriate for different types of electronically stored information. Using current technology, for example, a party might be called upon to produce word processing documents, e-mail messages, electronic spreadsheets, different image or sound files, and material from databases. Requiring that such diverse types of electronically stored information all be produced in the same form could prove impossible, and even if possible could increase the cost and burdens of producing and using the information. The rule therefore provides that the requesting party may ask for different forms of production for different types of electronically stored information.

[¶10] The rule does not require that the requesting party choose a form or forms of production. The requesting party may not have a preference. In some cases, the requesting party may not know what form the producing party uses to maintain its electronically stored information, although Rule 26(f)(3) is amended to call for discussion of the form of production in the parties' prediscovery conference.

[¶11] The responding party also is involved in determining the form of production. In the written response to the production request that Rule 34 requires, the responding party must state the form it intends to use for producing electronically stored information if the requesting party does not specify a form or if the responding party objects to a form that the requesting party specifies. Stating the intended form before the production occurs may permit the parties to identify and seek to resolve disputes before the expense and work of the production occurs. A party that responds to a discovery request by simply producing electronically stored information in a form of its choice, without identifying that form in advance of the production in the response required by Rule 34(b), runs a risk that the requesting party can show that the produced form is not reasonably usable and that it is entitled to production of some or all of the information in an additional form. Additional time might be required to permit a responding party to assess the appropriate form or forms of production.

[¶12] If the requesting party is not satisfied with the form stated by the responding party, or if the responding party has objected to the form specified by the requesting party, the parties must meet and confer under Rule 37(a)(2)(B) in an effort to resolve the matter before the requesting party can file a motion to compel. If they cannot agree and the court resolves the dispute, the court is not limited to the forms initially chosen by the requesting party, stated by the responding party, or specified in this rule for situations in which there is no court order or party agreement.

[¶13] If the form of production is not specified by party agreement or court order, the responding party must produce electronically stored information either in a form or forms in which it is ordinarily maintained or in a form or forms that are reasonably usable. Rule 34(a) requires that, if necessary, a responding party "translate" information it produces into a "reasonably usable" form. Under some circumstances, the responding party may need to provide some reasonable amount of technical support, information on application software, or other reasonable assistance to enable the requesting party to use the information. The rule does not require a party to produce electronically stored information in the form in which it is ordinarily maintained, as long as it is produced in a reasonably usable form. But the option to produce in a reasonably usable form does not mean that a responding party is free to convert electronically stored information from the form in which it is ordinarily maintained to a different form that makes it more difficult or burdensome for the requesting party to use the information efficiently in the litigation. If the responding party ordinarily maintains the information it is producing in a way that makes it searchable by electronic means, the information should not be produced in a form that removes or significantly degrades this feature.

[¶14] Some electronically stored information may be ordinarily maintained in a form that is not reasonably usable by any party. One example is "legacy" data that can be used only by superseded systems. The questions whether a producing party should be required to convert such information to a more usable form, or should be required to produce it at all, should be addressed under Rule 26(b)(2)(B).

[¶15] Whether or not the requesting party specified the form of production, Rule 34(b) provides that the same electronically stored information ordinarily need be produced in only one form.

FRCP 36 – 2007 NOTES OF ADVISORY COMMITTEE

[¶1] The final sentence of the first paragraph of former Rule 36(a) was a redundant cross-reference to the discovery moratorium provisions of Rule 26(d). Rule 26(d) is now familiar, obviating any need to carry forward the redundant cross-reference. The redundant reminder of Rule 37(c) in the second paragraph was likewise omitted.

FRCP 37 – 2006 NOTES OF ADVISORY COMMITTEE

[¶1] Subdivision (f). Subdivision (f) is new. It focuses on a distinctive feature of computer operations, the routine alteration and deletion of information that attends ordinary use. Many steps essential to computer operation may alter or destroy information, for reasons that have nothing to do with how that information might relate to litigation. As a result, the ordinary operation of computer systems creates a risk that a party may lose potentially discoverable information without culpable conduct on its part. Under Rule 37(f), absent exceptional circumstances, sanctions cannot be imposed for loss of electronically stored information resulting from the routine, good-faith operation of an electronic information system.

[¶2] Rule 37(f) applies only to information lost due to the "routine operation of an electronic information system"—the ways in which such systems are generally designed, programmed, and implemented to meet the party's technical and business needs. The "routine operation" of computer systems includes the alteration and overwriting of information, often without the operator's specific direction or awareness, a feature with no direct counterpart in hard-copy documents. Such features are essential to the operation of electronic information systems.

[¶3] Rule 37(f) applies to information lost due to the routine operation of an information system only if the operation was in good faith. Good faith in the routine operation of an information system may involve a party's intervention to modify or suspend certain features of that routine operation to prevent the loss of information, if that information is subject to a preservation obligation. A preservation obligation may arise from many sources, including common law, statutes, regulations, or a court order in the case. The good faith requirement of Rule 37(f) means that a party is not permitted to exploit the routine operation of an information system to thwart discovery obligations by allowing that operation to continue in order to destroy specific stored information that it is required to preserve. When a party is under a duty to preserve information because of pending or reasonably anticipated litigation, intervention in the routine operation of an information system is one aspect of what is often called a "litigation hold." Among the factors that bear on a party's good faith in the routine operation of an information system are the steps the party took to comply with a court order in the case or party agreement requiring preservation of specific electronically stored information.

[¶4] Whether good faith would call for steps to prevent the loss of information on sources that the party believes are not reasonably accessible under Rule 26(b)(2) depends on the circumstances of each case. One factor is whether the party reasonably believes that the information on such sources is likely to be discoverable and not available from reasonably accessible sources.

[¶5] The protection provided by Rule 37(f) applies only to sanctions "under these rules." It does not affect other sources of authority to impose sanctions or rules of professional responsibility.

[¶6] This rule restricts the imposition of "sanctions." It does not prevent a court from making the kinds of adjustments frequently used in managing discovery if a party is unable to provide relevant responsive information. For example, a court could order the responding party to produce an additional witness for deposition, respond to additional interrogatories, or make similar attempts to provide substitutes or alternatives for some or all of the lost information.

FRCP 37 – 2000 NOTES OF ADVISORY COMMITTEE

[¶1] Subdivision (c)(1). When this subdivision was added in 1993 to direct exclusion of materials not disclosed as required, the duty to supplement discovery responses pursuant to Rule 26(e)(2) was omitted. In the face of this omission, courts may rely on inherent power to sanction for failure to supplement as required by Rule 26(e)(2), *see* 8 *Federal Practice & Procedure* §2050 at 607-09, but that is an uncertain and unregulated ground for imposing sanctions. There is no obvious occasion for a Rule 37(a) motion in connection with failure to supplement, and ordinarily only Rule 37(c)(1) exists as rule-based authority for sanctions if this supplementation obligation is violated.

[¶2] The amendment explicitly adds failure to comply with Rule 26(e)(2) as a ground for sanctions under Rule 37(c)(1), including exclusion of withheld materials. The rule provides that this sanction power only applies when the failure to supplement was "without substantial justification." Even if the failure was not substantially justified, a party should be allowed to use the material that was not disclosed if the lack of earlier notice was harmless.

[¶3] "Shall" is replaced by "is" under the program to conform amended rules to current style conventions when there is no ambiguity.

FRCP 37 – 1993 NOTES OF ADVISORY COMMITTEE

[¶1] Subdivision (a). This subdivision is revised to reflect the revision of Rule 26(a), requiring disclosure of matters without a discovery request.

[¶2] Pursuant to new subdivision (a)(2)(A), a party dissatisfied with the disclosure made by an opposing party may under this rule move for an order to compel disclosure. In providing for such a motion, the revised rule parallels the provisions of the former rule dealing with failures to answer particular interrogatories. Such a motion may be needed when the information to be disclosed might be helpful to the party seeking the disclosure but not to the party required to make the disclosure. If the party required to make the disclosure would need the material to support its own contentions, the more effective enforcement of the disclosure requirement will be to exclude the evidence not disclosed, as provided in subdivision (c)(1) of this revised rule.

[¶3] Language is included in the new paragraph and added to the subparagraph (B) that requires litigants to seek to resolve discovery disputes by informal means before filing a motion with the court. This requirement is based on successful experience with similar local rules of court promulgated pursuant to Rule 83.

[¶4] The last sentence of paragraph (2) is moved into paragraph (4).

[¶5] Under revised paragraph (3), evasive or incomplete disclosures and responses to interrogatories and production requests are treated as failures to disclose or respond. Interrogatories and requests for production should not be read or interpreted in an artificially restrictive or hypertechnical manner to avoid disclosure of information fairly covered by the discovery request, and to do so is subject to appropriate sanctions under subdivision (a).

[¶6] Revised paragraph (4) is divided into three subparagraphs for ease of reference, and in each the phrase "after opportunity for hearing" is changed to "after affording an opportunity to be heard" to make clear that the court can consider such questions on written submissions as well as on oral hearings.

[¶7] Subparagraph (A) is revised to cover the situation where information that should have been produced without a motion to compel is produced after the motion is filed but before it is brought on for hearing. The rule also is revised to provide that a party should not be awarded its expenses for filing a motion that could have been avoided by conferring with opposing counsel.

[¶8] Subparagraph (C) is revised to include the provision that formerly was contained in subdivision (a)(2) and to include the same requirement of an opportunity to be heard that is specified in subparagraphs (A) and (B).

[¶9] Subdivision (c). The revision provides a self-executing sanction for failure to make a disclosure required by Rule 26(a), without need for a motion under subdivision (a)(2)(A).

[¶10] Paragraph (1) prevents a party from using as evidence any witnesses or information that, without substantial justification, has not been disclosed as required by Rules 26(a) and 26(e)(1). This automatic sanction provides a strong inducement for disclosure of material that the disclosing party would expect to use as evidence, whether at a trial, at a hearing, or on a motion, such as one under Rule 56. As disclosure of evidence offered solely for impeachment purposes is not required under those rules, this preclusion sanction likewise does not apply to that evidence.

[¶11] Limiting the automatic sanction to violations "without substantial justification," coupled with the exception for violations that are "harmless," is needed to avoid unduly harsh penalties in a variety of situations: *e.g.*, the inadvertent omission from a Rule 26(a)(1)(A) disclosure of the name of a potential witness known to all parties; the failure to list as a trial witness a person so listed by another party; or the lack of knowledge of a pro se litigant of the requirement to make disclosures. In the latter situation, however, exclusion would be proper if the requirement for disclosure had been called to the litigant's attention by either the court or another party.

[¶12] Preclusion of evidence is not an effective incentive to compel disclosure of information that, being supportive of the position of the opposing party, might advantageously be concealed by the disclosing party. However, the rule provides the court with a wide range of other sanctions—such as declaring specified facts to be established, preventing contradictory evidence, or, like spoliation of evidence, allowing the jury to be informed of the fact of nondisclosure—that, though not self-executing, can be imposed when found to be warranted after a hearing. The failure to identify a witness or document in a disclosure statement would be admissible under the Federal Rules of Evidence under the same principles that allow a party's interrogatory answers to be offered against it.

[¶13] Subdivision (d). This subdivision is revised to require that, where a party fails to file any response to interrogatories or a Rule 34 request, the discovering party should informally seek to obtain such responses before filing a motion for sanctions.

[¶14] The last sentence of this subdivision is revised to clarify that it is the pendency of a motion for protective order that may be urged as an excuse for a violation of subdivision (d). If a party's motion has been denied, the party cannot argue that its subsequent failure to comply would be justified. In this connection, it should be noted that the filing of a motion under Rule 26(c) is not self-executing—the relief authorized under that rule depends on obtaining the court's order to that effect.

[¶15] Subdivision (g). This subdivision is modified to conform to the revision of Rule 26(f).

FRCP 38 – 2009 NOTES OF ADVISORY COMMITTEE

[¶1] The times set in the former rule at 10 days have been revised to 14 days. See the Note to Rule 6.[1]

1. **Editor's note:** The cross-reference to "Note to Rule 6" refers to 2009 Notes to FRCP 6 at ¶¶1-20, p. 1149, this book.

FRCP 40 – 2007 NOTES OF ADVISORY COMMITTEE

[¶1] The best methods for scheduling trials depend on local conditions. It is useful to ensure that each district adopts an explicit rule for scheduling trials. It is not useful to limit or dictate the provisions of local rules.

FRCP 41 – 2007 NOTES OF ADVISORY COMMITTEE

[¶1] When Rule 23 was amended in 1966, Rules 23.1 and 23.2 were separated from Rule 23. Rule 41(a)(1) was not then amended to reflect the Rule 23 changes. In 1968 Rule 41(a)(1) was amended to correct the cross-reference to what had become Rule 23(e), but Rules 23.1 and 23.2 were inadvertently overlooked. Rules 23.1 and 23.2 are now added to the list of exceptions in Rule 41(a)(1)(A). This change does not affect established meaning. Rule 23.2 explicitly incorporates Rule 23(e), and thus was already absorbed directly into the exceptions in Rule 41(a)(1). Rule 23.1 requires court approval of a compromise or dismissal in language parallel to Rule 23(e) and thus supersedes the apparent right to dismiss by notice of dismissal.

FRCP 43 – 1996 NOTES OF ADVISORY COMMITTEE

[¶1] Rule 43(a) is revised to conform to the style conventions adopted for simplifying the present Civil Rules. The only intended changes of meaning are described below.

[¶2] The requirement that testimony be taken "orally" is deleted. The deletion makes it clear that testimony of a witness may be given in open court by other means if the witness is not able to communicate orally. Writing or sign language are common examples. The development of advanced technology may enable testimony to be given by other means. A witness unable to sign or write by hand may be able to communicate through a computer or similar device.

[¶3] Contemporaneous transmission of testimony from a different location is permitted only on showing good cause in compelling circumstances. The importance of presenting live testimony in court cannot be forgotten. The very ceremony of trial and the presence of the factfinder may exert a powerful force for truthtelling. The opportunity to judge the demeanor of a witness face-to-face is accorded great value in our tradition. Transmission cannot be justified merely by showing that it is inconvenient for the witness to attend the trial.

[¶4] The most persuasive showings of good cause and compelling circumstances are likely to arise when a witness is unable to attend trial for unexpected reasons, such as accident or illness, but remains able to testify from a different place. Contemporaneous transmission may be better than an attempt to reschedule the trial, particularly if there is a risk that other—and perhaps more important—witnesses might not be available at a later time.

[¶5] Other possible justifications for remote transmission must be approached cautiously. Ordinarily depositions, including video depositions, provide a superior means of securing the testimony of a witness who is beyond the reach of a trial subpoena, or of resolving difficulties in scheduling a trial that can be attended by all witnesses. Deposition procedures ensure the opportunity of all parties to be represented while the witness is testifying. An unforeseen need for the testimony of a remote witness that arises during trial, however, may establish good cause and compelling circumstances. Justification is particularly likely if the need arises from the interjection of new issues during trial or from the unexpected inability to present testimony as planned from a different witness.

[¶6] Good cause and compelling circumstances may be established with relative ease if all parties agree that testimony should be presented by transmission. The court is not bound by a stipulation, however, and can insist on live testimony. Rejection of the parties' agreement will be influenced, among other factors, by the apparent importance of the testimony in the full context of the trial.

[¶7] A party who could reasonably foresee the circumstances offered to justify transmission of testimony will have special difficulty in showing good cause and the compelling nature of the circumstances. Notice of a desire to transmit testimony from a different location should be given as soon as the reasons are known, to enable other parties to arrange a deposition, or to secure an advance ruling on transmission so as to know whether to prepare to be present with the witness while testifying.

[¶8] No attempt is made to specify the means of transmission that may be used. Audio transmission without video images may be sufficient in some circumstances, particularly as to less important testimony. Video transmission ordinarily should be preferred when the cost is reasonable in relation to the matters in dispute, the means of the parties, and the circumstances that justify transmission. Transmission that merely produces the equivalent of a written statement ordinarily should not be used.

[¶9] Safeguards must be adopted that ensure accurate identification of the witness and that protect against influence by persons present with the witness. Accurate transmission likewise must be assured.

[¶10] Other safeguards should be employed to ensure that advance notice is given to all parties of foreseeable circumstances that may lead the proponent to offer testimony by transmission. Advance notice is important to protect the opportunity to argue for attendance of the witness at trial. Advance notice also ensures an opportunity to depose the witness, perhaps by video record, as a means of supplementing transmitted testimony.

FRCP 44 – 1991 NOTES OF ADVISORY COMMITTEE

[¶1] The amendment to paragraph (a)(1) strikes the references to specific territories, two of which are no longer subject to the jurisdiction of the United States, and adds a generic term to describe governments having a relationship with the United States such that their official records should be treated as domestic records.

[¶2] The amendment to paragraph (a)(2) adds a sentence to dispense with the final certification by diplomatic officers when the United States and the foreign country where the record is located are parties to a treaty or convention that abolishes or displaces the requirement. In that event the treaty or convention is to be followed. This changes the former procedure for authenticating foreign official records only with respect to records from countries that are parties to the Hague Convention Abolishing the Requirement of Legalization for Foreign Public Documents. Moreover, it does not affect the former practice of attesting the records, but only changes the method of certifying the attestation.

[¶3] The Hague Public Documents Convention provides that the requirement of a final certification is abolished and replaced with a model apostille, which is to be issued by officials of the country where the records are located. See Hague Public Documents Convention, Arts. 2-4. The apostille certifies the signature, official position, and seal of the attesting officer. The authority who issues the apostille must maintain a register or card index showing the serial number of the apostille and other relevant information recorded on it. A foreign court can then check the serial number and information on the apostille with the issuing authority in order to guard against the use of fraudulent apostilles. This system provides a reliable method for maintaining the integrity of the authentication process, and the apostille can be accorded greater weight than the normal authentication procedure because foreign officials are more likely to know the precise capacity under their law of the attesting officer than would an American official. See generally Comment, The United States and the Hague Convention Abolishing the Requirement of Legalization for Foreign Public Documents, 11 Harv. Int'l L.J. 476, 482, 488 (1970).

FRCP 44.1 – 1966 NOTES OF ADVISORY COMMITTEE

[¶1] Rule 44.1 is added by amendment to furnish Federal courts with a uniform and effective procedure for raising and determining an issue concerning the law of a foreign country.

[¶2] To avoid unfair surprise, the first sentence of the new rule requires that a party who intends to raise an issue of foreign law shall give notice thereof. The uncertainty under Rule 8(a) about whether foreign law must be pleaded—*compare Siegelman v. Cunard White Star, Ltd.*, 221 F.2d 189 (2d Cir.1955), *and Pedersen v. United States*, 191 F.Supp. 95 (D. Guam 1961), *with Harrison v. United Fruit Co.*, 143 F.Supp. 598 (S.D. N.Y. 1956)—is eliminated by the provision that the notice shall be "written" and "reasonable." It may, but need not be, incorporated in the pleadings. In some situations the pertinence of foreign law is apparent from the outset; accordingly the necessary investigation of that law will have been accomplished by the party at the pleading stage, and the notice can be given conveniently in the pleadings. In other situations the pertinence of foreign law may remain doubtful until the case is further developed. A requirement that notice of foreign law be given only through the medium of the pleadings would tend in the latter instances to force the party to engage in a peculiarly burdensome type of investigation which might turn out to be unnecessary; and correspondingly the adversary would be forced into a possible wasteful investigation. The liberal provisions for amendment of the pleadings afford help if the pleadings are used as the medium of giving notice of the foreign law; but it seems best to permit a written notice to be given outside of and later than the pleadings, provided the notice is reasonable.

[¶3] The new rule does not attempt to set any definite limit on the party's time for giving the notice of an issue of foreign law; in some cases the issue may not become apparent until the trial and notice then given may still be reasonable. The stage which the case has reached at the time of the notice, the reason proffered by the party for his failure to give earlier notice, and the importance to the case as a whole of the issue of foreign law sought to be raised, are among the factors which the court should consider in deciding a question of the reasonableness of a notice. If notice is given by one party it need not be repeated by any other and serves as a basis for presentation of material on the foreign law by all parties.

[¶4] The second sentence of the new rule describes the materials to which the court may resort in determining an issue of foreign law. Heretofore the district courts, applying Rule 43(a), have looked in certain cases to State law to find the rules of evidence by which the content of foreign-country law is to be established. The State laws vary; some embody procedures which are inefficient, time consuming and expensive. See, generally, Nussbaum, Proving the Law of Foreign Countries, 3 Am.J.Comp.L. 60 (1954). In all events the ordinary rules of evidence are often inapposite to the problem of determining foreign law and have in the past prevented examination of material which could have provided a proper basis for the determination. The new rule permits consideration by the court of any relevant material, including testimony, without regard to its admissibility under Rule 43. *Cf.* N.Y.Civ.Prac.Law & Rules, R. 4511 (effective Sept. 1, 1963); 2 Va.Code Ann. tit. 8, §8-273; 2 W.Va.Code Ann. §5711.

[¶5] In further recognition of the peculiar nature of the issue of foreign law, the new rule provides that in determining this law the court is not limited by material presented by the parties; it may engage in its own research and consider any relevant material thus found. The court may have at its disposal better foreign law materials than counsel have presented, or may wish to reexamine and amplify material that has been presented by counsel in partisan fashion or in insufficient detail. On the other hand, the court is free to insist on a complete presentation by counsel.

[¶6] There is no requirement that the court give formal notice to the parties of its intention to engage in its own research on an issue of foreign law which has been raised by them, or of its intention to raise and determine independently an issue not raised by them. Ordinarily the court should inform the parties of material it has found diverging substantially from the material which they have presented; and in general the court should give the parties an opportunity to analyze and counter new points upon which it proposes to rely. See Schlesinger, Comparative Law 142 (2d ed. 1959); Wyzanski, A Trial Judge's Freedom and Responsibility, 65 Harv.L.Rev. 1281, 1296 (1952); *cf. Siegelman v. Cunard White Star, Ltd.*, supra, 221 F.2d at 197. To require, however, that the court give formal notice from time to time as it proceeds with its study of the foreign law would add an element of undesirable rigidity to the procedure for determining issues of foreign law.

[¶7] The new rule refrains from imposing an obligation on the court to take "judicial notice" of foreign law because this would put an extreme burden on the court in many cases;

and it avoids use of the concept of "judicial notice" in any form because of the uncertain meaning of that concept as applied to foreign law. *See, e.g.*, Stern, Foreign Law in the Courts: Judicial Notice and Proof, 45 Calif.L.Rev. 23, 43 (1957). Rather the rule provides flexible procedures for presenting and utilizing material on issues of foreign law by which a sound result can be achieved with fairness to the parties.

[¶8] Under the third sentence, the court's determination of an issue of foreign law is to be treated as a ruling on a question of "law," not "fact," so that appellate review will not be narrowly confined by the "clearly erroneous" standard of Rule 52(a). *Cf.* Uniform Judicial Notice of Foreign Law Act §3; Note, 72 Harv.L. Rev. 318 (1958).

[¶9] The new rule parallels Article IV of the Uniform Interstate and International Procedure Act, approved by the Commissioners on Uniform State Laws in 1962, except that section 4.03 of Article IV states that "(t)he court, not the jury" shall determine foreign law. The new rule does not address itself to this problem, since the Rules refrain from allocating functions as between the court and the jury. See Rule 38(a). It has long been thought, however, that the jury is not the appropriate body to determine issues of foreign law. *See, e.g.*, Story, Conflict of Laws, §638 (1st ed. 1834, 8th ed. 1883); 1 Greenleaf, Evidence, §486 (1st ed. 1842, 16th ed. 1899); 4 Wigmore, Evidence §2558 (1st ed. 1905); 9 id. §2558 (3d ed. 1940). The majority of the States have committed such issues to determination by the court. See Article 5 of the Uniform Judicial Notice of Foreign Law Act, adopted by twenty-six states, 9A U.L.A. 318 (1957) (Suppl. 1961, at 134); N.Y.Civ.Prac.Law & Rules, R. 4511 (effective Sept. 1, 1963); Wigmore, loc. cit. And Federal courts that have considered the problem in recent years have reached the same conclusion without reliance on statute. *See Jansson v. Swedish American Line*, 185 F.2d 212, 216 (1st Cir.1950); *Bank of Nova Scotia v. San Miguel*, 196 F.2d 950, 957, n. 6 (1st Cir.1952); *Liechti v. Roche*, 198 F.2d 174 (5th Cir.1952); *Daniel Lumber Co. v. Empresas Hondurenas, S.A.*, 215 F.2d 465 (5th Cir.1954).

FRCP 45 – 2007 NOTES OF ADVISORY COMMITTEE

[¶1] The reference to discovery of "books" in former Rule 45(a)(1)(C) was deleted to achieve consistent expression throughout the discovery rules. Books remain a proper subject of discovery.

[¶2] Former Rule 45(b)(1) required "prior notice" to each party of any commanded production of documents and things or inspection of premises. Courts have agreed that notice must be given "prior" to the return date, and have tended to converge on an interpretation that requires notice to the parties before the subpoena is served on the person commanded to produce or permit inspection. That interpretation is adopted in amended Rule 45(b)(1) to give clear notice of general present practice.

[¶3] The language of former Rule 45(d)(2) addressing the manner of asserting privilege is replaced by adopting the wording of Rule 26(b)(5). The same meaning is better expressed in the same words.

FRCP 45 – 2006 NOTES OF ADVISORY COMMITTEE

[¶1] Rule 45 is amended to conform the provisions for subpoenas to changes in other discovery rules, largely related to discovery of electronically stored information. Rule 34 is amended to provide in greater detail for the production of electronically stored information. Rule 45(a)(1)(C) is amended to recognize that electronically stored information, as defined in Rule 34(a), can also be sought by subpoena. Like Rule 34(b), Rule 45(a)(1) is amended to provide that the subpoena can designate a form or forms for production of electronic data. Rule 45(c)(2) is amended, like Rule 34(b), to authorize the person served with a subpoena to object to the requested form or forms. In addition, as under Rule 34(b), Rule 45(d)(1)(B) is amended to provide that if the subpoena does not specify the form or forms for electronically stored information, the person served with the subpoena must produce electronically stored information in a form or forms in which it is usually maintained or in a form or forms that are reasonably usable. Rule 45(d)(1)(C) is added to provide that the person producing electronically stored information should not have to produce the same information in more than one form unless so ordered by the court for good cause.

[¶2] As with discovery of electronically stored information from parties, complying with a subpoena for such information may impose burdens on the responding person. Rule 45(c) provides protection against undue impositions on nonparties. For example, Rule 45(c)(1) directs that a party serving a subpoena "shall take reasonable steps to avoid imposing undue burden or expense on a person subject to the subpoena," and Rule 45(c)(2)(B) permits the person served with the subpoena to object to it and directs that an order requiring compliance "shall protect a person who is neither a party nor a party's officer from significant expense resulting from" compliance. Rule 45(d)(1)(D) is added to provide that the responding person need not provide discovery of electronically stored information from sources the party identifies as not reasonably accessible, unless the court orders such discovery for good cause, considering the limitations of Rule 26(b)(2)(C), on terms that protect a nonparty against significant expense. A parallel provision is added to Rule 26(b)(2).

[¶3] Rule 45(a)(1)(B) is also amended, as is Rule 34(a), to provide that a subpoena is available to permit testing and sampling as well as inspection and copying. As in Rule 34, this change recognizes that on occasion the opportunity to perform testing or sampling may be important, both for documents and for electronically stored information. Because testing or sampling may present particular issues of burden or intrusion for the person served with the subpoena, however, the protective provisions of Rule 45(c) should be enforced with vigilance when such demands are made. Inspection or testing of certain types of electronically stored information or of a person's electronic information system may raise issues of confidentiality or privacy. The addition of sampling and testing to Rule 45(a) with regard to documents and electronically stored information is not meant to create a routine right of direct access to a person's electronic information system, although such access might be justified in some circumstances. Courts should guard against undue intrusiveness resulting from inspecting or testing such systems.

[¶4] Rule 45(d)(2) is amended, as is Rule 26(b)(5), to add a procedure for assertion of privilege or of protection as trial-preparation materials after production. The receiving party may submit the information to the court for resolution of the privilege claim, as under Rule 26(b)(5)(B).

[¶5] Other minor amendments are made to conform the rule to the changes described above.

FRCP 45 – 2005 NOTES OF ADVISORY COMMITTEE

[¶1] This amendment closes a small gap in regard to notifying witnesses of the manner for recording a deposition. A deposition subpoena must state the method for recording the testimony.

[¶2] Rule 30(b)(2) directs that the party noticing a deposition state in the notice the manner for recording the testimony, but the notice need not be served on the deponent. The deponent learns of the recording method only if the deponent is a party or is informed by a party. Rule 30(b)(3) permits another party to designate an additional method of recording with prior notice to the deponent and the other parties. The deponent thus has notice of the recording method when an additional method is designated. This amendment completes the notice provisions to ensure that a nonparty deponent has notice of the recording method when the recording method is described only in the deposition notice.

[¶3] A subpoenaed witness does not have a right to refuse to proceed with a deposition due to objections to the manner of recording. But under rare circumstances, a nonparty witness might have a ground for seeking a protective order under Rule 26(c) with regard to the manner of recording or the use of the deposition if recorded in a certain manner. Should such a witness not learn of the manner of recording until the deposition begins, undesirable delay or complication might result. Advance notice of the recording method affords an opportunity to raise such protective issues.

[¶4] Other changes are made to conform Rule 45(a)(2) to current style conventions.

FRCP 45 – 1991 NOTES OF ADVISORY COMMITTEE

[¶1] Purposes of Revision. The purposes of this revision are (1) to clarify and enlarge the protections afforded persons who are required to assist the court by giving information or evidence; (2) to facilitate access outside the deposition procedure provided by Rule 30 to documents and other information in the possession of persons who are not parties; (3) to facilitate service of subpoenas for depositions or productions of evidence at places distant from the district in which an action is proceeding; (4) to enable the court to compel a witness found within the state in which the court sits to attend trial; (5) to clarify the organization of the text of the rule.

[¶2] Subdivision (a). This subdivision is amended in seven significant respects.

[¶3] First, Paragraph (a)(3) modifies the requirement that a subpoena be issued by the clerk of court. Provision is made for the issuance of subpoenas by attorneys as officers of the court. This revision perhaps culminates an evolution. Subpoenas were long issued by specific order of the court. As this became a burden to the court, general orders were made authorizing clerks to issue subpoenas on request. Since 1948, they have been issued in blank by the clerk of any federal court to any lawyer, the clerk serving as stationer to the bar. In allowing counsel to issue the subpoena, the rule is merely a recognition of present reality.

[¶4] Although the subpoena is in a sense the command of the attorney who completes the form, defiance of a subpoena is nevertheless an act in defiance of a court order and exposes the defiant witness to contempt sanctions. In *ICC v. Brimson*, 154 U.S. 447 (1894), the Court upheld a statute directing federal courts to issue subpoenas to compel testimony before the ICC. In *CAB v. Hermann*, 353 U.S. 322 (1957), the Court approved as established practice the issuance of administrative subpoenas as a matter of absolute agency right. And in *NLRB v. Warren Co.*, 350 U.S. 107 (1955), the Court held that the lower court had no discretion to withhold sanctions against a contemnor who violated such subpoenas. The 1948 revision of Rule 45 put the attorney in a position similar to that of the administrative agency, as a public officer entitled to use the court's contempt power to investigate facts in dispute. Two courts of appeals have touched on the issue and have described lawyer-issued subpoenas as mandates of the court. *Waste Conversion, Inc. v. Rollins Environmental Services (NJ), Inc.*, 893 F.2d 605 (3d Cir.1990); *Fisher v. Marubent Cotton Corp.*, 526 F.2d 1338, 1340 (8th Cir.1975). *Cf. Young v. United States ex rel Vuitton et Fils S.A.*, 481 U.S. 787, 821 (1987) (Scalia, J., concurring). This revision makes the rule explicit that the attorney acts as an officer of the court in issuing and signing subpoenas.

[¶5] Necessarily accompanying the evolution of this power of the lawyer as officer of the court is the development of increased responsibility and liability for the misuse of this power. The latter development is reflected in the provisions of subdivision (c) of this rule, and also in the requirement imposed by paragraph (3) of this subdivision that the attorney issuing a subpoena must sign it.

[¶6] Second, Paragraph (a)(3) authorizes attorneys in distant districts to serve as officers authorized to issue commands in the name of the court. Any attorney permitted to represent a client in a federal court, even one admitted pro hac vice, has the same authority as a clerk to issue a subpoena from any federal court for the district in which the subpoena is served and enforced. In authorizing attorneys to issue subpoenas from distant courts, the amended rule effectively authorizes service of a subpoena anywhere in the United States by an attorney representing any party. This change is intended to ease the administrative burdens of inter-district law practice. The former rule resulted in delay and expense caused by the need to secure forms from clerks' offices some distance from the place at which the action proceeds. This change does not enlarge the burden on the witness.

[¶7] Pursuant to Paragraph (a)(2), a subpoena for a deposition must still issue from the court in which the deposition or production would be compelled. Accordingly, a motion to quash such a subpoena if it overbears the limits of the subpoena power must, as under the previous rule, be presented to the court for the district in which the deposition would occur. Likewise, the court in whose name the subpoena is issued is responsible for its enforcement.

[¶8] Third, in order to relieve attorneys of the need to secure an appropriate seal to affix to a subpoena issued as an officer of a distant court, the requirement that a subpoena be under seal is abolished by the provisions of Paragraph (a)(1).

[¶9] Fourth, Paragraph (a)(1) authorizes the issuance of a subpoena to compel a non-party to produce evidence independent of any deposition. This revision spares the necessity of a deposition of the custodian of evidentiary material required to be produced. A party seeking additional production from a person subject to such a subpoena may serve an additional subpoena requiring additional production at the same time and place.

[¶10] Fifth, Paragraph (a)(2) makes clear that the person subject to the subpoena is required to produce materials in that person's control whether or not the materials are located within the district or within the territory within which the subpoena can be served. The non-party witness is subject to the same scope of discovery under this rule as that person would be as a party to whom a request is addressed pursuant to Rule 34.

[¶11] Sixth, Paragraph (a)(1) requires that the subpoena include a statement of the rights and duties of witnesses by setting forth in full the text of the new subdivisions (c) and (d).

[¶12] Seventh, the revised rule authorizes the issuance of a subpoena to compel the inspection of premises in the possession of a non-party. Rule 34 has authorized such inspections of premises in the possession of a party as discovery compelled under Rule 37, but prior practice required an independent proceeding to secure such relief ancillary to the federal proceeding when the premises were not in the possession of a party. Practice in some states has long authorized such use of a subpoena for this purpose without apparent adverse consequence.

[¶13] **Subdivision (b).** Paragraph (b)(1) retains the text of the former subdivision (c) with minor changes.

[¶14] The reference to the United States marshal and deputy marshal is deleted because of the infrequency of the use of these officers for this purpose. Inasmuch as these officers meet the age requirement, they may still be used if available.

[¶15] A provision requiring service of prior notice pursuant to Rule 5 of compulsory pretrial production or inspection has been added to paragraph (b)(1). The purpose of such notice is to afford other parties an opportunity to object to the production or inspection, or to serve a demand for additional documents or things. Such additional notice is not needed with respect to a deposition because of the requirement of notice imposed by Rule 30 or 31. But when production or inspection is sought independently of a deposition, other parties may need notice in order to monitor the discovery and in order to pursue access to any information that may or should be produced.

[¶16] Paragraph (b)(2) retains language formerly set forth in subdivision (e) and extends its application to subpoenas for depositions or production.

[¶17] Paragraph (b)(3) retains language formerly set forth in paragraph (d)(1) and extends its applications to subpoenas for trial or hearing or production.

[¶18] **Subdivision (c).** This provision is new and states the rights of witnesses. It is not intended to diminish rights conferred by Rules 26-37 or any other authority.

[¶19] Paragraph (c)(1) gives specific application to the principle stated in Rule 26(g) and specifies liability for earnings lost by a non-party witness as a result of a misuse of the subpoena. No change in existing law is thereby effected. Abuse of a subpoena is an actionable tort, *Board of Ed. v. Farmingdale Classroom Teach. Ass'n*, 38 N.Y.2d 397, 380 N.Y.S.2d 635, 343 N.E.2d 278 (1975), and the duty of the attorney to the non-party is also embodied in Model Rule of Professional Conduct 4.4. The liability of the attorney is correlative to the expanded power of the attorney to issue subpoenas. The liability may include the cost of fees to collect attorneys' fees owed as a result of a breach of this duty.

[¶20] Paragraph (c)(2) retains language from the former subdivision (b) and paragraph (d)(1). The 10-day period for response to a subpoena is extended to 14 days to avoid the complex calculations associated with short time periods under Rule 6 and to allow a bit more time for such objections to be made.

[¶21] A non-party required to produce documents or materials is protected against significant expense resulting from involuntary assistance to the court. This provision applies, for example, to a non-party required to provide a list of class members. The court is not required to fix the costs in advance of production, although this will often be the most satisfactory accommodation to protect the party seeking discovery from excessive costs. In some instances, it may be preferable to leave uncertain costs to be determined after the materials have been produced, provided that the risk of uncertainty is fully disclosed to the discovering party. *See, e.g., United States v. Columbia Broadcasting Systems, Inc.*, 666 F.2d 364 (9th Cir.1982).

[¶22] Paragraph (c)(3) explicitly authorizes the quashing of a subpoena as a means of protecting a witness from misuse of the subpoena power. It replaces and enlarges on the former subdivision (b) of this rule and tracks the provisions of Rule 26(c). While largely repetitious, this rule is addressed to the witness who may read it on the subpoena, where it is required to be printed by the revised paragraph (a)(1) of this rule.

[¶23] Subparagraph (c)(3)(A) identifies those circumstances in which a subpoena must be quashed or modified. It restates the former provisions with respect to the limits of mandatory travel that are set forth in the former paragraphs (d)(2) and (e)(1), with one important change. Under the revised rule, a federal court can compel a witness to come from any place in the state to attend trial, whether or not the local state law so provides. This extension is subject to the qualification provided in the next paragraph, which authorizes the court to condition enforcement of a subpoena compelling a non-party witness to bear substantial expense to attend trial. The traveling non-party witness may be entitled to reasonable compensation for the time and effort entailed.

[¶24] Clause (c)(3)(A)(iv) requires the court to protect all persons from undue burden imposed by the use of the subpoena power. Illustratively, it might be unduly burdensome to compel an adversary to attend trial as a witness if the adversary is known to have no personal knowledge of matters in dispute, especially so if the adversary would be required to incur substantial travel burdens.

[¶25] Subparagraph (c)(3)(B) identifies circumstances in which a subpoena should be quashed unless the party serving the subpoena shows a substantial need and the court can devise an appropriate accommodation to protect the interests of the witness. An additional circumstance in which such action is required is a request for costly production of documents; that situation is expressly governed by subparagraph (b)(2)(B).[1]

[¶26] Clause (c)(3)(B)(i) authorizes the court to quash, modify, or condition a subpoena to protect the person subject to or affected by the subpoena from unnecessary or unduly harmful disclosures of confidential information. It corresponds to Rule 26(c)(7).

[¶27] Clause (c)(3)(B)(ii) provides appropriate protection for the intellectual property of the non-party witness; it does not apply to the expert retained by a party, whose information is subject to the provisions of Rule 26(b)(4). A growing problem has been the use of subpoenas to compel the giving of evidence and information by unretained experts. Experts are not exempt from the duty to give evidence, even if they cannot be compelled to prepare themselves to give effective testimony, *e.g., Carter-Wallace, Inc. v. Otte*, 474 F.2d 529 (2d Cir.1972), but compulsion to give evidence may threaten the intellectual property of experts denied the opportunity to bargain for the value of their services. See generally Maurer, Compelling the Expert Witness: Fairness and Utility Under the Federal Rules of Civil Procedure, 19 GA.L.REV. 71 (1984); Note, Discovery and Testimony of Unretained Experts, 1987 DUKE L.J. 140. Arguably the compulsion to testify can be regarded as a "taking" of intellectual property. The rule establishes the right of such persons to withhold their expertise, at least unless the party seeking it makes the kind of showing required for a conditional denial of a motion to quash as provided in the final sentence of subparagraph (c)(3)(B); that requirement is the same as that necessary to secure work product under Rule 26(b)(3) and gives assurance of reasonable compensation. The Rule thus approves the accommodation of competing interests exemplified in *United States v. Columbia Broadcasting Systems Inc.*, 666 F.2d 364 (9th Cir.1982). *See also Wright v. Jeep Corporation*, 547 F.Supp. 871 (E.D. Mich.1982).

[¶28] As stated in *Kaufman v. Edelstein*, 539 F.2d 811, 822 (2d Cir.1976), the district court's discretion in these matters should be informed by "the degree to which the expert is being called because of his knowledge of facts relevant to the case rather than in order to give opinion testimony; the difference between testifying to a previously formed or expressed opinion and forming a new one; the possibility that, for other reasons, the witness is a unique expert; the extent to which the calling party is able to show the unlikelihood that any comparable witness will willingly testify; and the degree to which the witness is able to show that he has been oppressed by having continually to testify...."

[¶29] Clause (c)(3)(B)(iii) protects non-party witnesses who may be burdened to perform the duty to travel in order to provide testimony at trial. The provision requires the court to condition a subpoena requiring travel of more than 100 miles on reasonable compensation.

[¶30] Subdivision (d). This provision is new. Paragraph (d)(1) extends to non-parties the duty imposed on parties by the last paragraph of Rule 34(b), which was added in 1980.

[¶31] Paragraph (d)(2) is new and corresponds to the new Rule 26(b)(5). Its purpose is to provide a party whose discovery is constrained by a claim of privilege or work product protection with information sufficient to evaluate such a claim and to resist if it seems unjustified. The person claiming a privilege or protection cannot decide the limits of that party's own entitlement.

[¶32] A party receiving a discovery request who asserts a privilege or protection but fails to disclose that claim is at risk of waiving the privilege or protection. A person claiming a privilege or protection who fails to provide adequate information about the privilege or protection claim to the party seeking the information is subject to an order to show cause why the person should not be held in contempt under subdivision (e). Motions for such orders and responses to motions are subject to the sanctions provisions of Rules 7 and 11.

[¶33] A person served a subpoena that is too broad may be faced with a burdensome task to provide full information regarding all that person's claims to privilege or work product protection. Such a person is entitled to protection that may be secured through an objection made pursuant to paragraph (c)(2).

[¶34] **Subdivision (e).** This provision retains most of the language of the former subdivision (f).

[¶35] "Adequate cause" for a failure to obey a subpoena remains undefined. In at least some circumstances, a non-party might be guilty of contempt for refusing to obey a subpoena even though the subpoena manifestly overreaches the appropriate limits of the subpoena power. *E.g., Walker v. City of Birmingham*, 388 U.S. 307 (1967). But, because the command of the subpoena is not in fact one uttered by a judicial officer, contempt should be very sparingly applied when the non-party witness has been overborne by a party or attorney. The language added to subdivision (f) is intended to assure that result where a non-party has been commanded, on the signature of an attorney, to travel greater distances than can be compelled pursuant to this rule.

1. **Editor's note:** So in original. Probably should be "subparagraph (c)(2)(B)."

FRCP 48 – 2009 NOTES OF ADVISORY COMMITTEE

[¶1] Jury polling is added as new subdivision (c), which is drawn from Criminal Rule 31(d) with minor revisions to reflect Civil Rules Style and the parties' opportunity to stipulate to a nonunanimous verdict.

FRCP 48 – 1991 NOTES OF ADVISORY COMMITTEE

[¶1] The former rule was rendered obsolete by the adoption in many districts of local rules establishing six as the standard size for a civil jury.

[¶2] It appears that the minimum size of a jury consistent with the Seventh Amendment is six. *Cf. Ballew v. Georgia*, 435 U.S. 223 (1978) (holding that a conviction based on a jury of less than six is a denial of due process of law). If the parties agree to trial before a smaller jury, a verdict can be taken, but the parties should not other than in exceptional circumstances be encouraged to waive the right to a jury of six, not only because of the constitutional stature of the right, but also because smaller juries are more erratic and less effective in serving to distribute responsibility for the exercise of judicial power.

[¶3] Because the institution of the alternate juror has been abolished by the proposed revision of Rule 47, it will ordinarily be prudent and necessary, in order to provide for sickness or disability among jurors, to seat more than six jurors. The use of jurors in excess of six increases the representativeness of the jury and harms no interest of a party. *Ray v. Parkside Surgery Center*, 13 F.R. Serv. 585 (6th Cir.1989).

[¶4] If the court takes the precaution of seating a jury larger than six, an illness occurring during the deliberation period will not result in a mistrial, as it did formerly, because all seated jurors will participate in the verdict and a sufficient number will remain to render a unanimous verdict of six or more.

[¶5] In exceptional circumstances, as where a jury suffers depletions during trial and deliberation that are greater than can reasonably be expected, the parties may agree to be bound by a verdict rendered by fewer than six jurors. The court should not, however, rely upon the availability of such an agreement, for the use of juries smaller than six is problematic for reasons fully explained in *Ballew v. Georgia*, supra.

FRCP 50 – 2009 NOTES OF ADVISORY COMMITTEE

[¶1] Former Rules 50, 52, and 59 adopted 10-day periods for their respective post-judgment motions. Rule 6(b) prohibits any expansion of those periods. Experience has proved that in many cases it is not possible to prepare a satisfactory post-judgment motion in 10 days, even under the former rule that excluded intermediate Saturdays, Sundays, and legal holidays. These time periods are particularly sensitive because Appellate Rule 4 integrates the time to appeal with a timely motion under these rules. Rather than introduce the prospect of uncertainty in appeal time by amending Rule 6(b) to permit additional time, the former 10-day periods are expanded to 28 days. Rule 6(b) continues to prohibit expansion of the 28-day period.

FRCP 50 – 2007 NOTES OF ADVISORY COMMITTEE

[¶1] Former Rule 50(b) stated that the court reserves ruling on a motion for judgment as a matter of law made at the close of all the evidence "[i]f, for any reason, the court does not grant" the motion. The words "for any reason" reflected the proposition that the reservation is automatic and inescapable. The ruling is reserved even if the court explicitly denies the motion. The same result follows under the amended rule. If the motion is not granted, the ruling is reserved.

[¶2] Amended Rule 50(e) identifies the appellate court's authority to direct the entry of judgment. This authority was not described in former Rule 50(d), but was recognized in *Weisgram v. Marley Co.*, 528 U.S. 440 (2000), and in *Neely v. Martin K. Eby Construction Company*, 386 U.S. 317 (1967). When Rule 50(d) was drafted in 1963, the Committee

Note stated that "[s]ubdivision (d) does not attempt a regulation of all aspects of the procedure where the motion for judgment n.o.v. and any accompanying motion for a new trial are denied * * *." Express recognition of the authority to direct entry of judgment does not otherwise supersede this caution.

FRCP 50 – 2006 NOTES OF ADVISORY COMMITTEE

[¶1] The language of Rule 50(a) has been amended as part of the general restyling of the Civil Rules to make them more easily understood and to make style and terminology consistent throughout the rules. These changes are intended to be stylistic only.

[¶2] Rule 50(b) is amended to permit renewal of any Rule 50(a) motion for judgment as a matter of law, deleting the requirement that a motion be made at the close of all the evidence. Because the Rule 50(b) motion is only a renewal of the preverdict motion, it can be granted only on grounds advanced in the preverdict motion. The earlier motion informs the opposing party of the challenge to the sufficiency of the evidence and affords a clear opportunity to provide additional evidence that may be available. The earlier motion also alerts the court to the opportunity to simplify the trial by resolving some issues, or even all issues, without submission to the jury. This fulfillment of the functional needs that underlie present Rule 50(b) also satisfies the Seventh Amendment. Automatic reservation of the legal questions raised by the motion conforms to the decision in *Baltimore & Carolina Line v. Redman*, 297 U.S. 654 (1935).

[¶3] This change responds to many decisions that have begun to move away from requiring a motion for judgment as a matter of law at the literal close of all the evidence. Although the requirement has been clearly established for several decades, lawyers continue to overlook it. The courts are slowly working away from the formal requirement. The amendment establishes the functional approach that courts have been unable to reach under the present rule and makes practice more consistent and predictable.

[¶4] Many judges expressly invite motions at the close of all the evidence. The amendment is not intended to discourage this useful practice.

[¶5] Finally, an explicit time limit is added for making a posttrial motion when the trial ends without a verdict or with a verdict that does not dispose of all issues suitable for resolution by verdict. The motion must be made no later than 10 days after the jury was discharged.

FRCP 50 – 1995 NOTES OF ADVISORY COMMITTEE

[¶1] The only change, other than stylistic, intended by this revision is to prescribe a uniform explicit time for filing of post-judgment motions under this rule—no later than 10 days after entry of the judgment. Previously, there was an inconsistency in the wording of Rules 50, 52, and 59 with respect to whether certain post-judgment motions had to be filed, or merely served, during that period. This inconsistency caused special problems when motions for a new trial were joined with other post-judgment motions. These motions affect the finality of the judgment, a matter often of importance to third persons as well as the parties and the court. The Committee believes that each of these rules should be revised to require filing before end of the 10-day period. Filing is an event that can be determined with certainty from court records. The phrase "no later than" is used—rather than "within"—to include post-judgment motions that sometimes are filed before actual entry of the judgment by the clerk. It should be noted that under Rule 6(a) Saturdays, Sundays, and legal holidays are excluded in measuring the 10-day period, and that under Rule 5 the motions when filed are to contain a certificate of service on other parties.

FRCP 50 – 1993 NOTES OF ADVISORY COMMITTEE

[¶1] This technical amendment corrects an ambiguity in the text of the 1991 revision of the rule, which, as indicated in the Notes, was not intended to change the existing standards under which "directed verdicts" could be granted. This amendment makes clear that judgments as a matter of law in jury trials may be entered against both plaintiffs and defendants and with respect to issues or defenses that may not be wholly dispositive of a claim or defense.

FRCP 50 – 1991 NOTES OF ADVISORY COMMITTEE

[¶1] Subdivision (a). The revision of this subdivision aims to facilitate the exercise by the court of its responsibility to assure the fidelity of its judgment to the controlling law, a responsibility imposed by the Due Process Clause of the Fifth Amendment. *Cf. Galloway v. United States*, 319 U.S. 372 (1943).

[¶2] The revision abandons the familiar terminology of direction of verdict for several reasons. The term is misleading as a description of the relationship between judge and jury. It is also freighted with anachronisms some of which are the subject of the text of former subdivision (a) of this rule that is deleted in this revision. Thus, it should not be necessary to state in the text of this rule that a motion made pursuant to it is not a waiver of the right to jury trial, and only the antiquities of directed verdict practice suggest that it might have been. The term "judgment as a matter of law" is an almost equally familiar term and appears in the text of Rule 56; its use in Rule 50 calls attention to the relationship between the two rules. Finally, the change enables the rule to refer to preverdict and post-verdict motions with a terminology that does not conceal the common identity of two motions made at different times in the proceeding.

[¶3] If a motion is denominated a motion for directed verdict or for judgment notwithstanding the verdict, the par-

ty's error is merely formal. Such a motion should be treated as a motion for judgment as a matter of law in accordance with this rule.

[¶4] Paragraph (a)(1) articulates the standard for the granting of a motion for judgment as a matter of law. It effects no change in the existing standard. That existing standard was not expressed in the former rule, but was articulated in long-standing case law. See generally Cooper, Directions for Directed Verdicts: A Compass for Federal Courts, 55 MINN. L. REV. 903 (1971). The expressed standard makes clear that action taken under the rule is a performance of the court's duty to assure enforcement of the controlling law and is not an intrusion on any responsibility for factual determinations conferred on the jury by the Seventh Amendment or any other provision of federal law. Because this standard is also used as a reference point for entry of summary judgment under 56(a), it serves to link the two related provisions.

[¶5] The revision authorizes the court to perform its duty to enter judgment as a matter of law at any time during the trial, as soon as it is apparent that either party is unable to carry a burden of proof that is essential to that party's case. Thus, the second sentence of paragraph (a)(1) authorizes the court to consider a motion for judgment as a matter of law as soon as a party has completed a presentation on a fact essential to that party's case. Such early action is appropriate when economy and expedition will be served. In no event, however, should the court enter judgment against a party who has not been apprised of the materiality of the dispositive fact and been afforded an opportunity to present any available evidence bearing on that fact. In order further to facilitate the exercise of the authority provided by this rule, Rule 16 is also revised to encourage the court to schedule an order of trial that proceeds first with a presentation on an issue that is likely to be dispositive, if such an issue is identified in the course of pretrial. Such scheduling can be appropriate where the court is uncertain whether favorable action should be taken under Rule 56. Thus, the revision affords the court the alternative of denying a motion for summary judgment while scheduling a separate trial of the issue under Rule 42(b) or scheduling the trial to begin with a presentation on that essential fact which the opposing party seems unlikely to be able to maintain.

[¶6] Paragraph (a)(2) retains the requirement that a motion for judgment be made prior to the close of the trial, subject to renewal after a jury verdict has been rendered. The purpose of this requirement is to assure the responding party an opportunity to cure any deficiency in that party's proof that may have been overlooked until called to the party's attention by a late motion for judgment. *Cf. Farley Transp. Co. v. Santa Fe Trail Transp. Co.*, 786 F.2d 1342 (9th Cir.1986) ("If the moving party is then permitted to make a later attack on the evidence through a motion for judgment notwithstanding the verdict or an appeal, the opposing party may be prejudiced by having lost the opportunity to present additional evidence before the case was submitted to the jury"); *Benson v. Allphin*, 786 F.2d 268 (7th Cir.1986) ("the motion for directed verdict at the close of all the evidence provides the nonmovant an opportunity to do what he can to remedy the deficiencies in his case..."); *McLaughlin v. The Fellows Gear Shaper Co.*, 4 F.R.Serv. 3d 607 (3d Cir.1986) (per Adams, J., dissenting: "This Rule serves important practical purposes in ensuring that neither party is precluded from presenting the most persuasive case possible and in preventing unfair surprise after a matter has been submitted to the jury"). At one time, this requirement was held to be of constitutional stature, being compelled by the Seventh Amendment. *Cf. Slocum v. New York Insurance Co.*, 228 U.S. 364 (1913). *But cf. Baltimore & Carolina Line v. Redman*, 295 U.S. 654 (1935).

[¶7] The second sentence of paragraph (a)(2) does impose a requirement that the moving party articulate the basis on which a judgment as a matter of law might be rendered. The articulation is necessary to achieve the purpose of the requirement that the motion be made before the case is submitted to the jury, so that the responding party may seek to correct any overlooked deficiencies in the proof. The revision thus alters the result in cases in which courts have used various techniques to avoid the requirement that a motion for a directed verdict be made as a predicate to a motion for judgment notwithstanding the verdict. *E.g., Benson v. Allphin*, 788 F.2d 268 (7th Cir.1986) ("this circuit has allowed something less than a formal motion for directed verdict to preserve a party's right to move for judgment notwithstanding the verdict"). See generally 9 Wright & Miller, Federal Practice & Procedure §2537 (1971 and Supp.). The information required with the motion may be supplied by explicit reference to materials and argument previously supplied to the court.

[¶8] This subdivision deals only with the entry of judgment and not with the resolution of particular factual issues as a matter of law. The court may, as before, properly refuse to instruct a jury to decide an issue if a reasonable jury could on the evidence presented decide that issue in only one way.

[¶9] Subdivision (b). This provision retains the concept of the former rule that the post-verdict motion is a renewal of an earlier motion made at the close of the evidence. One purpose of this concept was to avoid any question arising under the Seventh Amendment. *Montgomery Ward & Co. v. Duncan*, 311 U.S. 243 (1940). It remains useful as a means of defining the appropriate issue posed by the post-verdict motion. A post-trial motion for judgment can be granted only on grounds advanced in the pre-verdict motion. *E.g., Kutner Buick, Inc. v. American Motors Corp.*, 848 F.2d 614 (3d Cir.1989).

[¶10] Often it appears to the court or to the moving party that a motion for judgment as a matter of law made at the close of the evidence should be reserved for a post-verdict decision. This is so because a jury verdict for the moving party moots the issue and because a pre-verdict ruling gambles that a reversal may result in a new trial that might have been avoided. For these reasons, the court may often wisely decline to rule on a motion for judgment as a matter of law made at the close of the evidence, and it is not inappropriate for the moving party to suggest such a postponement of the ruling until after the verdict has been rendered.

[¶11] In ruling on such a motion, the court should disregard any jury determination for which there is no legally sufficient evidentiary basis enabling a reasonable jury to make it. The court may then decide such issues as a matter of law and enter judgment if all other material issues have been decided by the jury on the basis of legally sufficient evidence, or by the court as a matter of law.

[¶12] The revised rule is intended for use in this manner with Rule 49. Thus, the court may combine facts established as a matter of law either before trial under Rule 56 or at trial on the basis of the evidence presented with other facts determined by the jury under instructions provided under Rule 49 to support a proper judgment under this rule.

[¶13] This provision also retains the former requirement that a post-trial motion under the rule must be made within 10 days after entry of a contrary judgment. The renewed motion must be served and filed as provided by Rule 5. A purpose of this requirement is to meet the requirements of FRAP 4(a)(4).

[¶14] Subdivision (c). Revision of this subdivision conforms the language to the change in diction set forth in subdivision (a) of this revised rule.

[¶15] Subdivision (d). Revision of this subdivision conforms the language to that of the previous subdivisions.

FRCP 51 – 2003 NOTES OF ADVISORY COMMITTEE

[¶1] Rule 51 is revised to capture many of the interpretations that have emerged in practice. The revisions in text will make uniform the conclusions reached by a majority of decisions on each point. Additions also are made to cover some practices that cannot now be anchored in the text of Rule 51.

[¶2] *Scope.* Rule 51 governs instructions to the trial jury on the law that governs the verdict. A variety of other instructions cannot practicably be brought within Rule 51. Among these instructions are preliminary instructions to a venire, and cautionary or limiting instructions delivered in immediate response to events at trial.

[¶3] *Requests.* Subdivision (a) governs requests. Apart from the plain error doctrine recognized in subdivision (d)(2), a court is not obliged to instruct the jury on issues raised by the evidence unless a party requests an instruction. The revised rule recognizes the court's authority to direct that requests be submitted before trial.

[¶4] The close-of-the-evidence deadline may come before trial is completed on all potential issues. Trial may be formally bifurcated or may be sequenced in some less formal manner. The close of the evidence is measured by the occurrence of two events: completion of all intended evidence on an identified phase of the trial and impending submission to the jury with instructions.

[¶5] The risk in directing a pretrial request deadline is that trial evidence may raise new issues or reshape issues the parties thought they had understood. Courts need not insist on pretrial requests in all cases. Even if the request time is set before trial or early in the trial, subdivision (a)(2)(A) permits requests after the close of the evidence to address issues that could not reasonably have been anticipated at the earlier time for requests set by the court.

[¶6] Subdivision (a)(2)(B) expressly recognizes the court's discretion to act on an untimely request. The most important consideration in exercising the discretion confirmed by subdivision (a)(2)(B) is the importance of the issue to the case—the closer the issue lies to the "plain error" that would be recognized under subdivision (d)(2), the better the reason to give an instruction. The cogency of the reason for failing to make a timely request also should be considered. To be considered under subdivision (a)(2)(B) a request should be made before final instructions and before final jury arguments. What is a "final" instruction and argument depends on the sequence of submitting the case to the jury. If separate portions of the case are submitted to the jury in sequence, the final arguments and final instructions are those made on submitting to the jury the portion of the case addressed by the arguments and instructions.

[¶7] *Instructions.* Subdivision (b)(1) requires the court to inform the parties, before instructing the jury and before final jury arguments related to the instruction, of the proposed instructions as well as the proposed action on instruction requests. The time limit is addressed to final jury arguments to reflect the practice that allows interim arguments during trial in complex cases; it may not be feasible to develop final instructions before such interim arguments. It is enough that counsel know of the intended instructions before making final arguments addressed to the issue. If the trial is sequenced or bifurcated, the final arguments addressed to an issue may occur before the close of the entire trial.

[¶8] Subdivision (b)(2) complements subdivision (b)(1) by carrying forward the opportunity to object established by present Rule 51. It makes explicit the opportunity to object on the record, ensuring a clear memorial of the objection.

[¶9] Subdivision (b)(3) reflects common practice by authorizing instructions at any time after trial begins and before the jury is discharged.

[¶10] *Objections.* Subdivision (c) states the right to object to an instruction or the failure to give an instruction. It carries forward the formula of present Rule 51 requiring that the objection state distinctly the matter objected to and the grounds of the objection, and makes explicit the requirement that the objection be made on the record. The provisions on the time to object make clear that it is timely to object promptly after learning of an instruction or action on a request when the court has not provided advance information as required by subdivision (b)(1). The need to repeat a request by way of objection is continued by new subdivision (d)(1)(B) except where the court made a definitive ruling on the record.

[¶11] *Preserving a claim of error and plain error.* Many cases hold that a proper request for a jury instruction is not alone enough to preserve the right to appeal failure to give the instruction. The request must be renewed by objection. This doctrine is appropriate when the court may not have sufficiently focused on the request, or may believe that the request has been granted in substance although in different words. But this doctrine may also prove a trap for the unwary who fail to add an objection after the court has made it clear that the request has been considered and rejected on the merits. Subdivision (d)(1)(B) establishes authority to review the failure to grant a timely request, despite a failure to add an objection, when the court has made a definitive ruling on the record rejecting the request.

[¶12] Many circuits have recognized that an error not preserved under Rule 51 may be reviewed in exceptional circumstances. The language adopted to capture these decisions in subdivision (d)(2) is borrowed from Criminal Rule 52. Although the language is the same, the context of civil litigation often differs from the context of criminal prosecution; actual application of the plain-error standard takes account of the differences. The Supreme Court has summarized application of Criminal Rule 52 as involving four elements: (1) there must be an error; (2) the error must be plain; (3) the error must affect substantial rights; and (4) the error must seriously affect the fairness, integrity, or public reputation of judicial proceedings. *Johnson v. U.S.*, 520 U.S. 461, 466-467, 469-470 (1997). (The Johnson case quoted the fourth element from its decision in a civil action, *U.S. v. Atkinson*, 297 U.S. 157, 160 (1936): "In exceptional circumstances, especially in criminal cases, appellate courts, in the public interest, may, of their own motion, notice errors to which no exception has been taken, if the errors are obvious, or if they otherwise substantially affect the fairness, integrity, or public reputation of judicial proceedings.")

[¶13] The court's duty to give correct jury instructions in a civil action is shaped by at least four factors.

[¶14] The factor most directly implied by a "plain" error rule is the obviousness of the mistake. The importance of the error is a second major factor. The costs of correcting an error reflect a third factor that is affected by a variety of circumstances. In a case that seems close to the fundamental error line, account also may be taken of the impact a verdict may have on nonparties.

FRCP 51 – 1987 NOTES OF ADVISORY COMMITTEE

[¶1] Although Rule 51 in its present form specifies that the court shall instruct the jury only after the arguments of the parties are completed, in some districts (typically those in states where the practice is otherwise) it is common for the parties to stipulate to instruction before the arguments. The purpose of the amendment is to give the court discretion to instruct the jury either before or after argument. Thus, the rule as revised will permit resort to the long-standing federal practice or to an alternative procedure, which has been praised because it gives counsel the opportunity to explain the instructions, argue their application to the facts and thereby give the jury the maximum assistance in determining the issues and arriving at a good verdict on the law and the evidence. As an ancillary benefit, this approach aids counsel by supplying a natural outline so that arguments may be directed to the essential fact issues which the jury must decide. See generally Raymond, Merits and Demerits of the Missouri System of Instructing Juries, 5 St. Louis U.L.J. 317 (1959). Moreover, if the court instructs before an argument, counsel then know the precise words the court has chosen and need not speculate as to the words the court will later use in its instructions. Finally, by instructing ahead of argument the court has the attention of the jurors when they are fresh and can given[1] their full attention to the court's instructions. It is more difficult to hold the attention of jurors after lengthy arguments.

1. **Editor's note:** So in original. Probably should be "give."

FRCP 52 – 2009 NOTES OF ADVISORY COMMITTEE

[¶1] Former Rules 50, 52, and 59 adopted 10-day periods for their respective post-judgment motions. Rule 6(b) prohibits any expansion of those periods. Experience has proved that in many cases it is not possible to prepare a satisfactory post-judgment motion in 10 days, even under the former rule that excluded intermediate Saturdays, Sundays, and legal holidays. These time periods are particularly sensitive because Appellate Rule 4 integrates the time to appeal with a timely motion under these rules. Rather than introduce the prospect of uncertainty in appeal time by amending Rule 6(b) to permit additional time, the former 10-day periods are expanded to 28 days. Rule 6(b) continues to prohibit expansion of the 28-day period.

FRCP 52 – 2007 NOTES OF ADVISORY COMMITTEE

[¶1] Former Rule 52(a) said that findings are unnecessary on decisions of motions "except as provided in subdivision (c) of this rule." Amended Rule 52(a)(3) says that findings are unnecessary "unless these rules provide otherwise." This change reflects provisions in other rules that require Rule 52 findings on deciding motions. Rules 23(e), 23(h), and 54(d)(2)(C) are examples.

[¶2] Amended Rule 52(a)(5) includes provisions that appeared in former Rule 52(a) and 52(b). Rule 52(a) provided that requests for findings are not necessary for purposes of review. It applied both in an action tried on the facts without a jury and also in granting or refusing an interlocutory injunction. Rule 52(b), applicable to findings "made in actions tried without a jury," provided that the sufficiency of the evidence might be "later questioned whether or not in the district court the party raising the question objected to the findings, moved to amend them, or moved for partial findings." Former Rule 52(b) did not explicitly apply to decisions granting or refusing an interlocutory injunction. Amended Rule 52(a)(5) makes explicit the application of this part of former Rule 52(b) to interlocutory injunction decisions.

[¶3] Former Rule 52(c) provided for judgment on partial findings, and referred to it as "judgment as a matter of law." Amended Rule 52(c) refers only to "judgment," to avoid any confusion with a Rule 50 judgment as a matter of law in a jury case. The standards that govern judgment as a matter of law in a jury case have no bearing on a decision under Rule 52(c).

FRCP 52 – 1995 NOTES OF ADVISORY COMMITTEE

[¶1] The only change, other than stylistic, intended by this revision is to require that any motion to amend or add findings after a nonjury trial must be filed no later than 10 days after entry of the judgment. Previously, there was an inconsistency in the wording of Rules 50, 52, and 59 with respect to whether certain post-judgment motions had to be filed, or merely served, during that period. This inconsistency caused special problems when motions for a new trial were joined with other post-judgment motions. These motions affect the finality of the judgment, a matter often of importance to third persons as well as the parties and the court. The Committee believes that each of these rules should be revised to require filing before end of the 10-day period. Filing is an event that can be determined with certainty from court records. The phrase "no later than" is used—rather than "within"—to include post-judgment motions that sometimes are filed before actual entry of the judgment by the clerk. It should be noted that under Rule 6(a) Saturdays, Sundays, and legal holidays are excluded in measuring the 10-day period, and that under Rule 5 the motions when filed are to contain a certificate of service on other parties.

FRCP 52 – 1991 NOTES OF ADVISORY COMMITTEE

[¶1] Subdivision (c) is added. It parallels the revised Rule 50(a), but is applicable to non-jury trials. It authorizes the court to enter judgment at any time that it can appropriately make a dispositive finding of fact on the evidence.

[¶2] The new subdivision replaces part of Rule 41(b), which formerly authorized a dismissal at the close of the plaintiff's case if the plaintiff had failed to carry an essential burden of proof. Accordingly, the reference to Rule 41 formerly made in subdivision (a) of this rule is deleted.

[¶3] As under the former Rule 41(b), the court retains discretion to enter no judgment prior to the close of the evidence.

[¶4] Judgment entered under this rule differs from a summary judgment under Rule 56 in the nature of the evaluation made by the court. A judgment on partial findings is made after the court has heard all the evidence bearing on the crucial issue of fact, and the finding is reversible only if the appellate court finds it to be "clearly erroneous." A summary judgment, in contrast, is made on the basis of facts established on account of the absence of contrary evidence or presumptions; such establishments of fact are rulings on questions of law as provided in Rule 56(a) and are not shielded by the "clear error" standard of review.

FRCP 53 – 2009 NOTES OF ADVISORY COMMITTEE

[¶1] The time set in the former rule at 20 days has been revised to 21 days. See the Note to Rule 6.[1]

1. **Editor's note:** The cross-reference to "Note to Rule 6" refers to 2009 Notes to FRCP 6 at ¶¶1-20, p. 1149, this book.

FRCP 53 – 2003 NOTES OF ADVISORY COMMITTEE

[¶1] Rule 53 is revised extensively to reflect changing practices in using masters. From the beginning in 1938, Rule 53 focused primarily on special masters who perform trial functions. Since then, however, courts have gained experience with masters appointed to perform a variety of pretrial and post-trial functions. See Willging, Hooper, Leary, Miletich, Reagan, & Shapard, *Special Masters' Incidence and Activity* (Federal Judicial Center 2000). This revised Rule 53 recognizes that in appropriate circumstances masters may properly be appointed to perform these functions and regulates such appointments. Rule 53 continues to address trial masters as well, but permits appointment of a trial master in an action to be tried to a jury only if the parties consent. The new rule clarifies the provisions that govern the appointment and function of masters for all purposes. Rule 53(g) also changes the standard of review for findings of fact made or recommended by a master. The core of the original Rule 53 remains, including its prescription that appointment of a master must be the exception and not the rule.

[¶2] Special masters are appointed in many circumstances outside the Civil Rules. Rule 53 applies only to proceedings that Rule 1 brings within its reach.

[¶3] Subdivision (a)(1). District judges bear primary responsibility for the work of their courts. A master should be appointed only in limited circumstances. Subdivision (a)(1) describes three different standards, relating to appointments by consent of the parties, appointments for trial duties, and appointments for pretrial or post-trial duties.

[¶4] Consent Masters. Subparagraph (a)(1)(A) authorizes appointment of a master with the parties' consent. Party consent does not require that the court make the appointment; the court retains unfettered discretion to refuse appointment.

[¶5] Trial Masters. Use of masters for the core functions of trial has been progressively limited. These limits are reflected in the provisions of subparagraph (a)(1)(B) that restrict appointments to exercise trial functions. The Supreme Court gave clear direction to this trend in *La Buy v. Howes Leather Co.*, 352 U.S. 249 (1957); earlier roots are sketched in *Los Angeles Brush Mfg. Corp. v. James*, 272 U.S. 701 (1927). As to nonjury trials, this trend has developed through elaboration of the "exceptional condition" requirement in present Rule 53(b). This phrase is retained, and will continue to have the same force as it has developed. Although the provision that a reference "shall be the exception and not the rule" is deleted, its meaning is embraced for this setting by the exceptional condition requirement.

[¶6] Subparagraph (a)(1)(B)(ii) carries forward the approach of present Rule 53(b), which exempts from the "exceptional condition" requirement "matters of account and of difficult computation of damages." This approach is justified only as to essentially ministerial determinations that require mastery of much detailed information but that do not require extensive determinations of credibility. Evaluations of witness credibility should only be assigned to a trial master when justified by an exceptional condition.

[¶7] The use of a trial master without party consent is abolished as to matters to be decided by a jury unless a statute provides for this practice.

[¶8] Abolition of the direct power to appoint a trial master as to issues to be decided by a jury leaves the way free to appoint a trial master with the consent of all parties. A trial master should be appointed in a jury case, with consent of the parties and concurrence of the court, only if the parties waive jury trial with respect to the issues submitted to the master or if the master's findings are to be submitted to the jury as evidence in the manner provided by former Rule 53(e)(3). In no circumstance may a master be appointed to preside at a jury trial.

[¶9] The central function of a trial master is to preside over an evidentiary hearing on the merits of the claims or defenses in the action. This function distinguishes the trial master from most functions of pretrial and post-trial masters. If any master is to be used for such matters as a preliminary injunction hearing or a determination of complex damages issues, for example, the master should be a trial master. The line, however, is not distinct. A pretrial master might well conduct an evidentiary hearing on a discovery dispute, and a post-trial master might conduct evidentiary hearings on questions of compliance.

[¶10] Rule 53 has long provided authority to report the evidence without recommendations in nonjury trials. This authority is omitted from Rule 53(a)(1)(B). In some circumstances a master may be appointed under Rule 53(a)(1)(A) or (C) to take evidence and report without recommendations.

[¶11] For nonjury cases, a master also may be appointed to assist the court in discharging trial duties other than conducting an evidentiary hearing.

[¶12] Pretrial and Post-Trial Masters. Subparagraph (a)(1)(C) authorizes appointment of a master to address pretrial or post-trial matters. Appointment is limited to matters that cannot be addressed effectively and in a timely fashion by an available district judge or magistrate judge of the district. A master's pretrial or post-trial duties may include matters that could be addressed by a judge, such as reviewing discovery documents for privilege, or duties that might not be suitable for a judge. Some forms of settlement negotiations, investigations, or administration of an organization are familiar examples of duties that a judge might not feel free to undertake.

[¶13] *Magistrate Judges.* Particular attention should be paid to the prospect that a magistrate judge may be available for special assignments. United States magistrate judges are authorized by statute to perform many pretrial functions in civil actions. 28 U.S.C. §636(b)(1). Ordinarily a district judge who delegates these functions should refer them to a magistrate judge acting as magistrate judge.

[¶14] There is statutory authority to appoint a magistrate judge as special master. 28 U.S.C. §636(b)(2). In special circumstances, or when expressly authorized by a statute other than §636(b)(2), it may be appropriate to appoint a magistrate judge as a master when needed to perform functions outside those listed in §636(b)(1). There is no apparent reason to appoint a magistrate judge to perform as master duties that could be performed in the role of magistrate judge. Party consent is required for trial before a magistrate judge, moreover, and this requirement should not be undercut by resort to Rule 53 unless specifically authorized by statute; see 42 U.S.C. §2000e-5(f)(5).

[¶15] *Pretrial Masters.* The appointment of masters to participate in pretrial proceedings has developed extensively over the last two decades as some district courts have felt the need for additional help in managing complex litigation. This practice is not well regulated by present Rule 53, which focuses on masters as trial participants. Rule 53 is amended to confirm the authority to appoint—and to regulate the use of—pretrial masters.

[¶16] A pretrial master should be appointed only when the need is clear. Direct judicial performance of judicial functions may be particularly important in cases that involve important public issues or many parties. At the extreme, a broad delegation of pretrial responsibility as well as a delegation of trial responsibilities can run afoul of Article III.

[¶17] A master also may be appointed to address matters that blur the divide between pretrial and trial functions. The court's responsibility to interpret patent claims as a matter of law, for example, may be greatly assisted by appointing a master who has expert knowledge of the field in which the patent operates. Review of the master's findings will be de novo under Rule 53(g)(4), but the advantages of initial determination by a master may make the process more effective and timely than disposition by the judge acting alone. Deter-

mination of foreign law may present comparable difficulties. The decision whether to appoint a master to address such matters is governed by subdivision (a)(1)(C), not the trial-master provisions of subdivision (a)(1)(B).

[¶18] *Post-Trial Masters.* Courts have come to rely on masters to assist in framing and enforcing complex decrees. Present Rule 53 does not directly address this practice. Amended Rule 53 authorizes appointment of post-trial masters for these and similar purposes. The constraint of subdivision (a)(1)(C) limits this practice to cases in which the master's duties cannot be performed effectively and in a timely fashion by an available district judge or magistrate judge of the district.

[¶19] Reliance on a master is appropriate when a complex decree requires complex policing, particularly when a party has proved resistant or intransigent. This practice has been recognized by the Supreme Court, see *Local 28, Sheet Metal Workers' Internat. Assn. v. EEOC*, 478 U.S. 421, 481-482 (1986). The master's role in enforcement may extend to investigation in ways that are quite unlike the traditional role of judicial officers in an adversary system.

[¶20] Expert Witness Overlap. This rule does not address the difficulties that arise when a single person is appointed to perform overlapping roles as master and as court-appointed expert witness under Evidence Rule 706. Whatever combination of functions is involved, the Rule 53(a)(1)(B) limit that confines trial masters to issues to be decided by the court does not apply to a person who also is appointed as an expert witness under Evidence Rule 706.

[¶21] Subdivision (a)(2) and (3). Masters are subject to the Code of Conduct for United States Judges, with exceptions spelled out in the Code. Special care must be taken to ensure that there is no actual or apparent conflict of interest involving a master. The standard of disqualification is established by 28 U.S.C. §455. The affidavit required by Rule 53(b)(3) provides an important source of information about possible grounds for disqualification, but careful inquiry should be made at the time of making the initial appointment. The disqualification standards established by §455 are strict. Because a master is not a public judicial officer, it may be appropriate to permit the parties to consent to appointment of a particular person as master in circumstances that would require disqualification of a judge. The judge must be careful to ensure that no party feels any pressure to consent, but with such assurances—and with the judge's own determination that there is no troubling conflict of interests or disquieting appearance of impropriety—consent may justify an otherwise barred appointment.

[¶22] One potential disqualification issue is peculiar to the master's role. It may happen that a master who is an attorney represents a client whose litigation is assigned to the judge who appointed the attorney as master. Other parties to the litigation may fear that the attorney-master will gain special respect from the judge. A flat prohibition on appearance before the appointing judge during the time of service as master, however, might in some circumstances unduly limit the opportunity to make a desirable appointment. These matters may be regulated to some extent by state rules of professional responsibility. The question of present conflicts, and the possibility of future conflicts, can be considered at the time of appointment. Depending on the circumstances, the judge may consider it appropriate to impose a non-appearance condition on the lawyer master, and perhaps on the master's firm as well.

[¶23] Subdivision (b). The order appointing a pretrial master is vitally important in informing the master and the parties about the nature and extent of the master's duties and authority. Care must be taken to make the order as precise as possible. The parties must be given notice and opportunity to be heard on the question whether a master should be appointed and on the terms of the appointment. To the extent possible, the notice should describe the master's proposed duties, time to complete the duties, standards of review, and compensation. Often it will be useful to engage the parties in the process of identifying the master, inviting nominations, and reviewing potential candidates. Party involvement may be particularly useful if a pretrial master is expected to promote settlement.

[¶24] The hearing requirement of Rule 53(b)(1) can be satisfied by an opportunity to make written submissions unless the circumstances require live testimony.

[¶25] Rule 53(b)(2) requires precise designation of the master's duties and authority. Clear identification of any investigating or enforcement duties is particularly important. Clear delineation of topics for any reports or recommendations is also an important part of this process. And it is important to protect against delay by establishing a time schedule for performing the assigned duties. Early designation of the procedure for fixing the master's compensation also may provide useful guidance to the parties.

[¶26] Ex parte communications between a master and the court present troubling questions. Ordinarily the order should prohibit such communications, assuring that the parties know where authority is lodged at each step of the proceedings. Prohibiting ex parte communications between master and court also can enhance the role of a settlement master by assuring the parties that settlement can be fostered by confidential revelations that will not be shared with the court. Yet there may be circumstances in which the master's role is enhanced by the opportunity for ex parte communications with the court. A master assigned to help coordinate multiple proceedings, for example, may benefit from off-the-record exchanges with the court about logistical matters. The rule does not directly regulate these matters. It requires only that the court exercise its discretion and address the topic in the order of appointment.

[¶27] Similarly difficult questions surround ex parte communications between a master and the parties. Ex parte communications may be essential in seeking to advance settlement. Ex parte communications also may prove useful in other settings, as with in camera review of documents to resolve privilege questions. In most settings, however, ex parte communications with the parties should be discouraged or prohibited. The rule requires that the court address the topic in the order of appointment.

[¶28] Subdivision (b)(2)(C) provides that the appointment order must state the nature of the materials to be preserved and filed as the record of the master's activities, and (b)(2)(D) requires that the order state the method of filing the record. It is not feasible to prescribe the nature of the record without regard to the nature of the master's duties. The records appropriate to discovery duties may be different from those appropriate to encouraging settlement, investigating possible violations of a complex decree, or making recommendations for trial findings. A basic requirement, however, is that the master must make and file a complete record of the evidence considered in making or recommending findings of fact on the basis of evidence. The order of appointment should routinely include this requirement unless the nature of the appointment precludes any prospect that the master will make or recommend evidence-based findings of fact. In some circumstances it may be appropriate for a party to file materials directly with the court as provided by Rule 5(e), but in many circumstances filing with the court may be inappropriate. Confidentiality is important with respect to many materials that may properly be considered by a master. Materials in the record can be transmitted to the court, and filed, in connection with review of a master's order, report, or recommendations under subdivisions (f) and (g). Independently of review proceedings, the court may direct filing of any materials that it wishes to make part of the public record.

[¶29] The provision in subdivision (b)(2)(D) that the order must state the standards for reviewing the master's orders, findings, or recommendations is a reminder of the provisions of subdivision (g)(3) that recognize stipulations for review less searching than the presumptive requirement of de novo decision by the court. Subdivision (b)(2)(D) does not authorize the court to supersede the limits of subdivision (g)(3).

[¶30] In setting the procedure for fixing the master's compensation, it is useful at the outset to establish specific guidelines to control total expense. The court has power under subdivision (h) to change the basis and terms for determining compensation after notice to the parties.

[¶31] Subdivision (b)(3) permits entry of the order appointing a master only after the master has filed an affidavit disclosing whether there is any ground for disqualification under 28 U.S.C. §455. If the affidavit discloses a possible ground for disqualification, the order can enter only if the court determines that there is no ground for disqualification or if the parties, knowing of the ground for disqualification, consent with the court's approval to waive the disqualification.

[¶32] The provision in Rule 53(b)(4) for amending the order of appointment is as important as the provisions for the initial order. Anything that could be done in the initial order can be done by amendment. The hearing requirement can be satisfied by an opportunity to make written submissions unless the circumstances require live testimony.

[¶33] Subdivision (c). Subdivision (c) is a simplification of the provisions scattered throughout present Rule 53. It is intended to provide the broad and flexible authority necessary to discharge the master's responsibilities. The most important delineation of a master's authority and duties is provided by the Rule 53(b) appointing order.

[¶34] Subdivision (d). The subdivision (d) provisions for evidentiary hearings are reduced from the extensive provisions in current Rule 53. This simplification of the rule is not intended to diminish the authority that may be delegated to a master. Reliance is placed on the broad and general terms of subdivision (c).

[¶35] Subdivision (e). Subdivision (e) provides that a master's order must be filed and entered on the docket. It must be promptly served on the parties, a task ordinarily accomplished by mailing or other means as permitted by Rule 5(b). In some circumstances it may be appropriate to have the clerk's office assist the master in mailing the order to the parties.

[¶36] Subdivision (f). Subdivision (f) restates some of the provisions of present Rule 53(e)(1). The report is the master's primary means of communication with the court. The materials to be provided to support review of the report will depend on the nature of the report. The master should provide all portions of the record preserved under Rule 53(b)(2)(C) that the master deems relevant to the report. The parties may designate additional materials from the record, and may seek permission to supplement the record with evidence. The court may direct that additional materials from the record be provided and filed. Given the wide array of tasks that may be assigned to a pretrial master, there may be circumstances that justify sealing a report or review record against public access—a report on continuing or failed settlement efforts is the most likely example. A post-trial master may be assigned duties in formulating a decree that deserve similar protection. Such circumstances may even justify denying access to the report or review materials by the parties, although this step should be taken only for the most compelling reasons. Sealing is much less likely to be appropriate with respect to a trial master's report.

[¶37] Before formally making an order, report, or recommendations, a master may find it helpful to circulate a draft to the parties for review and comment. The usefulness of this practice depends on the nature of the master's proposed action.

[¶38] Subdivision (g). The provisions of subdivision (g)(1), describing the court's powers to afford a hearing, take evidence, and act on a master's order, report, or recommendations are drawn from present Rule 53(e)(2), but are not limited, as present Rule 53(e)(2) is limited, to the report of a trial master in a nonjury action. The requirement that the court must afford an opportunity to be heard can be satisfied by taking written submissions when the court acts on the report without taking live testimony.

[¶39] The subdivision (g)(2) time limits for objecting to—or seeking adoption or modification of—a master's order, report, or recommendations, are important. They are not jurisdictional. Although a court may properly refuse to entertain untimely review proceedings, the court may excuse the failure to seek timely review. The basic time period is lengthened to 20 days because the present 10-day period may be too short to permit thorough study and response to a complex report dealing with complex litigation. If no party asks the court to act on a master's report, the court is free to adopt the master's action or to disregard it at any relevant point in the proceedings.

[¶40] Subdivision (g)(3) establishes the standards of review for a master's findings of fact or recommended findings of fact. The court must decide de novo all objections to findings of fact made or recommended by the master unless the parties stipulate, with the court's consent, that the findings will be reviewed for clear error or—with respect to a master appointed on the parties' consent or appointed to address pretrial or post-trial matters—that the findings will be final. Clear-error review is more likely to be appropriate with respect to findings that do not go to the merits of the underlying claims or defenses, such as findings of fact bearing on a privilege objection to a discovery request. Even if no objection is made, the court is free to decide the facts de novo; to review for clear error if an earlier approved stipulation provided clear-error review; or to withdraw its consent to a stipulation for clear-error review or finality, and then to decide de novo. If the court withdraws its consent to a stipulation for finality or clear-error review, it may reopen the opportunity to object.

[¶41] Under Rule 53(g)(4), the court must decide de novo all objections to conclusions of law made or recommended by a master. As with findings of fact, the court also may decide conclusions of law de novo when no objection is made.

[¶42] Apart from factual and legal questions, masters often make determinations that, when made by a trial court, would be treated as matters of procedural discretion. The court may set a standard for review of such matters in the order of appointment, and may amend the order to establish the standard. If no standard is set by the original or amended order appointing the master, review of procedural matters is for abuse of discretion. The subordinate role of the master means that the trial court's review for abuse of discretion may be more searching than the review that an appellate court makes of a trial court.

[¶43] If a master makes a recommendation on any matter that does not fall within Rule 53(g)(3), (4), or (5), the court may act on the recommendation under Rule 53(g)(1).

[¶44] Subdivision (h). The need to pay compensation is a substantial reason for care in appointing private persons as masters.

[¶45] Payment of the master's fees must be allocated among the parties and any property or subject-matter within the court's control. The amount in controversy and the means of the parties may provide some guidance in making the allocation. The nature of the dispute also may be important—parties pursuing matters of public interest, for example, may deserve special protection. A party whose unreasonable behavior has occasioned the need to appoint a master, on the other hand, may properly be charged all or a major portion of the master's fees. It may be proper to revise an interim allocation after decision on the merits. The revision need not await a decision that is final for purposes of appeal, but may be made to reflect disposition of a substantial portion of the case.

[¶46] The basis and terms for fixing compensation should be stated in the order of appointment. The court retains power to alter the initial basis and terms, after notice and an opportunity to be heard, but should protect the parties against unfair surprise.

[¶47] The provision of former Rule 53(a) that the "provision for compensation shall not apply when a United States Magistrate Judge is designated to serve as a master" is deleted as unnecessary. Other provisions of law preclude compensation.

[¶48] Subdivision (i). Rule 53(i) carries forward unchanged former Rule 53(f).

FRCP 54 – 2009 NOTES OF ADVISORY COMMITTEE

[¶1] Former Rule 54(d)(1) provided that the clerk may tax costs on 1 day's notice. That period was unrealistically short. The new 14-day period provides a better opportunity to prepare and present a response. The former 5-day period to serve a motion to review the clerk's action is extended to 7 days to reflect the change in the Rule 6(a) method for computing periods of less than 11 days.

FRCP 54 – 2007 NOTES OF ADVISORY COMMITTEE

[¶1] The words "or class member" have been removed from Rule 54(d)(2)(C) because Rule 23(h)(2) now addresses objections by class members to attorney-fee motions. Rule 54(d)(2)(C) is amended to recognize that Rule 23(h) now controls those aspects of attorney-fee motions in class actions to which it is addressed.

FRCP 54 – 2002 NOTES OF ADVISORY COMMITTEE

[¶1] Subdivision (d)(2)(C) is amended to delete the requirement that judgment on a motion for attorney fees be set forth in a separate document. This change complements the amendment of Rule 58(a)(1), which deletes the separate document requirement for an order disposing of a motion for attorney fees under Rule 54. These changes are made to support amendment of Rule 4 of the Federal Rules of Appellate Procedure. It continues to be important that a district court make clear its meaning when it intends an order to be the final disposition of a motion for attorney fees.

[¶2] The requirement in subdivision (d)(2)(B) that a motion for attorney fees be not only filed but also served no later than 14 days after entry of judgment is changed to require filing only, to establish a parallel with Rules 50, 52, and 59. Service continues to be required under Rule 5(a).

FRCP 54 – 1993 NOTES OF ADVISORY COMMITTEE

[¶1] Subdivision (d). This revision adds paragraph (2) to this subdivision to provide for a frequently recurring form of litigation not initially contemplated by the rules—disputes over the amount of attorneys' fees to be awarded in the large number of actions in which prevailing parties may be entitled to such awards or in which the court must determine the fees to be paid from a common fund. This revision seeks to harmonize and clarify procedures that have been developed through case law and local rules.

[¶2] Paragraph (1). Former subdivision (d), providing for taxation of costs by the clerk, is renumbered as paragraph (1) and revised to exclude applications for attorneys' fees.

[¶3] Paragraph (2). This new paragraph establishes a procedure for presenting claims for attorneys' fees, whether or not denominated as "costs." It applies also to requests for reimbursement of expenses, not taxable as costs, when recoverable under governing law incident to the award of fees. *Cf. West Virginia Univ. Hosp. v. Casey*, U.S. (1991), holding, prior to the Civil Rights Act of 1991, that expert witness fees were not recoverable under 42 U.S.C. §1988. As noted in subparagraph (A), it does not, however, apply to fees recoverable as an element of damages, as when sought under the terms of a contract; such damages typically are to be claimed in a pleading and may involve issues to be resolved by a jury. Nor, as provided in subparagraph (E), does it apply to awards of fees as sanctions authorized or mandated under these rules or under 28 U.S.C. §1927.

[¶4] Subparagraph (B) provides a deadline for motions for attorneys' fees—14 days after final judgment unless the court or a statute specifies some other time. One purpose of this provision is to assure that the opposing party is informed of the claim before the time for appeal has elapsed. Prior law did not prescribe any specific time limit on claims for attorneys' fees. *White v. New Hampshire Dep't of Employment Sec.*, 455 U.S. 445 (1982). In many nonjury cases the court will want to consider attorneys' fee issues immediately after rendering its judgment on the merits of the case. Note that the time for making claims is specifically stated in some legislation, such as the Equal Access to Justice Act, 28 U.S.C. §2412 (d)(1)(B) (30-day filing period).

[¶5] Prompt filing affords an opportunity for the court to resolve fee disputes shortly after trial, while the services performed are freshly in mind. It also enables the court in appropriate circumstances to make its ruling on a fee request in time for any appellate review of a dispute over fees to proceed at the same time as review on the merits of the case.

[¶6] Filing a motion for fees under this subdivision does not affect the finality or the appealability of a judgment, though revised Rule 58 provides a mechanism by which prior to appeal the court can suspend the finality to resolve a motion for fees. If an appeal on the merits of the case is taken, the court may rule on the claim for fees, may defer its ruling on the motion, or may deny the motion without prejudice, directing under subdivision (d)(2)(B) a new period for filing after the appeal has been resolved. A notice of appeal does not extend the time for filing a fee claim based on the initial judgment, but the court under subdivision (d)(2)(B) may effectively extend the period by permitting claims to be filed after resolution of the appeal. A new period for filing will automatically begin if a new judgment is entered following a reversal or remand by the appellate court or the granting of a motion under Rule 59.

[¶7] The rule does not require that the motion be supported at the time of filing with the evidentiary material bearing on the fees. This material must of course be submitted in due course, according to such schedule as the court may direct in light of the circumstances of the case. What is required is the filing of a motion sufficient to alert the adversary and the court that there is a claim for fees and the amount of such fees (or a fair estimate).

[¶8] If directed by the court, the moving party is also required to disclose any fee agreement, including those between attorney and client, between attorneys sharing a fee to be awarded, and between adversaries made in partial settlement of a dispute where the settlement must be implemented by court action as may be required by Rules 23(e) and 23.1 or other like provisions. With respect to the fee arrangements requiring court approval, the court may also by local rule require disclosure immediately after such arrangements are agreed to. *E.g.*, Rule 5 of United States District Court for the Eastern District of New York; *cf. In re "Agent Orange" Product Liability Litigation* (MDL 381), 611 F.Supp. 1452, 1464 (E.D.N.Y. 1985).

[¶9] In the settlement of class actions resulting in a common fund from which fees will be sought, courts frequently have required that claims for fees be presented in advance of hearings to consider approval of the proposed settlement. The rule does not affect this practice, as it permits the court to require submissions of fee claims in advance of entry of judgment.

[¶10] Subparagraph (C) assures the parties of an opportunity to make an appropriate presentation with respect to issues involving the evaluation of legal services. In some cases, an evidentiary hearing may be needed, but this is not required in every case. The amount of time to be allowed for the preparation of submissions both in support of and in opposition to awards should be tailored to the particular case.

[¶11] The court is explicitly authorized to make a determination of the liability for fees before receiving submissions by the parties bearing on the amount of an award. This option may be appropriate in actions in which the liability issue is doubtful and the evaluation issues are numerous and complex.

[¶12] The court may order disclosure of additional information, such as that bearing on prevailing local rates or on the appropriateness of particular services for which compensation is sought.

[¶13] On rare occasion, the court may determine that discovery under Rules 26-37 would be useful to the parties. Compare Rules Governing Section 2254 Cases in the U.S. District Courts, Rule 6. See Note, Determining the Reasonableness of Attorneys' Fees—the Discoverability of Billing Records, 64 B.U.L. Rev. 241 (1984). In complex fee disputes, the court may use case management techniques to limit the scope of the dispute or to facilitate the settlement of fee award disputes.

[¶14] Fee awards should be made in the form of a separate judgment under Rule 58 since such awards are subject to review in the court of appeals. To facilitate review, the paragraph provides that the court set forth its findings and conclusions as under Rule 52(a), though in most cases this explanation could be quite brief.

[¶15] Subparagraph (D) explicitly authorizes the court to establish procedures facilitating the efficient and fair resolution of fee claims. A local rule, for example, might call for matters to be presented through affidavits, or might provide for issuance of proposed findings by the court, which would be treated as accepted by the parties unless objected to within a specified time. A court might also consider establishing a schedule reflecting customary fees or factors affecting fees within the community, as implicitly suggested by Justice O'Connor in *Pennsylvania v. Delaware Valley Citizens' Council*, 483 U.S. 711, 733 (1987) (O'Connor, J., concurring) (how particular markets compensate for contingency). *Cf. Thompson v. Kennickell*, 710 F. Supp.1 (D.D.C. 1989) (use of findings in other cases to promote consistency). The parties, of course, should be permitted to show that in the circumstances of the case such a schedule should not be applied or that different hourly rates would be appropriate.

[¶16] The rule also explicitly permits, without need for a local rule, the court to refer issues regarding the amount of a fee award in a particular case to a master under Rule 53. The district judge may designate a magistrate judge to act as a master for this purpose or may refer a motion for attorneys' fees to a magistrate judge for proposed findings and recommendations under Rule 72(b). This authorization eliminates any controversy as to whether such references are permitted under Rule 53(b) as "matters of account and of difficult computation of damages" and whether motions for attorneys' fees can be treated as the equivalent of a dispositive pretrial matter that can be referred to a magistrate judge. For consistency and efficiency, all such matters might be referred to the same magistrate judge.

[¶17] Subparagraph (E) excludes from this rule the award of fees as sanctions under these rules or under 28 U.S.C. §1927.

FRCP 55 – 2009 NOTES OF ADVISORY COMMITTEE

[¶1] The time set in the former rule at 3 days has been revised to 7 days. See the Note to Rule 6.[1]

1. **Editor's note:** The cross-reference to "Note to Rule 6" refers to 2009 Notes to FRCP 6 at ¶¶1-20, p. 1149, this book.

FRCP 55 – 2007 NOTES OF ADVISORY COMMITTEE

[¶1] Former Rule 55(a) directed the clerk to enter a default when a party failed to plead or otherwise defend "as provided by these rules." The implication from the reference to defending "as provided by these rules" seemed to be that the clerk should enter a default even if a party did something showing an intent to defend, but that act was not specifically described by the rules. Courts in fact have rejected that implication. Acts that show an intent to defend have frequently prevented a default even though not connected to any particular rule. "[A]s provided by these rules" is deleted to reflect Rule 55(a)'s actual meaning.

[¶2] Amended Rule 55 omits former Rule 55(d), which included two provisions. The first recognized that Rule 55 applies to described claimants. The list was incomplete and unnecessary. Rule 55(a) applies Rule 55 to any party against whom a judgment for affirmative relief is requested. The second provision was a redundant reminder that Rule 54(c) limits the relief available by default judgment.

FRCP 56 – 2010 NOTES OF ADVISORY COMMITTEE

[¶1] Rule 56 is revised to improve the procedures for presenting and deciding summary-judgment motions and to make the procedures more consistent with those already used in many courts. The standard for granting summary judgment remains unchanged. The language of subdivision (a) continues to require that there be no genuine dispute as to any material fact and that the movant be entitled to judgment as a matter of law. The amendments will not affect continuing development of the decisional law construing and applying these phrases.

[¶2] Subdivision (a). Subdivision (a) carries forward the summary-judgment standard expressed in former subdivision (c), changing only one word—genuine "issue" becomes genuine "dispute." "Dispute" better reflects the focus of a summary-judgment determination. As explained below, "shall" also is restored to the place it held from 1938 to 2007.

[¶3] The first sentence is added to make clear at the beginning that summary judgment may be requested not only as to an entire case but also as to a claim, defense, or part of a claim or defense. The subdivision caption adopts the common phrase "partial summary judgment" to describe disposition of less than the whole action, whether or not the order grants all the relief requested by the motion.

[¶4] "Shall" is restored to express the direction to grant summary judgment. The word "shall" in Rule 56 acquired significance over many decades of use. Rule 56 was amended in 2007 to replace "shall" with "should" as part of the Style Project, acting under a convention that prohibited any use of "shall." Comments on proposals to amend Rule 56, as published in 2008, have shown that neither of the choices available under the Style Project conventions—"must" or "should"—is suitable in light of the case law on whether a district court has discretion to deny summary judgment when there appears to be no genuine dispute as to any material fact. Compare *Anderson v. Liberty Lobby, Inc.*, 477 U.S. 242, 255 (1986) ("Neither do we suggest that the trial courts should act other than with caution in granting summary judgment or that the trial court may not deny summary judgment in a case in which there is reason to believe that the better course would be to proceed to a full trial. *Kennedy v. Silas Mason Co.*, 334 U.S. 249 * * * (1948))," with *Celotex Corp. v. Catrett*, 477 U.S. 317, 322 (1986) ("In our view, the plain language of Rule 56(c) mandates the entry of summary judgment, after adequate time for discovery and upon motion, against a party who fails to make a showing sufficient to establish the existence of an element essential to that party's case, and on which that party will bear the burden of proof at trial."). Eliminating "shall" created an unacceptable risk of changing the summary-judgment standard. Restoring "shall" avoids the unintended consequences of any other word.

[¶5] Subdivision (a) also adds a new direction that the court should state on the record the reasons for granting or denying the motion. Most courts recognize this practice. Among other advantages, a statement of reasons can facilitate an appeal or subsequent trial-court proceedings. It is particularly important to state the reasons for granting summary judgment. The form and detail of the statement of reasons are left to the court's discretion.

[¶6] The statement on denying summary judgment need not address every available reason. But identification of central issues may help the parties to focus further proceedings.

[¶7] Subdivision (b). The timing provisions in former subdivisions (a) and (c) are superseded. Although the rule allows a motion for summary judgment to be filed at the commencement of an action, in many cases the motion will be premature until the nonmovant has had time to file a responsive pleading or other pretrial proceedings have been had. Scheduling orders or other pretrial orders can regulate timing to fit the needs of the case.

[¶8] Subdivision (c). Subdivision (c) is new. It establishes a common procedure for several aspects of summary-judgment motions synthesized from similar elements developed in the cases or found in many local rules.

[¶9] Subdivision (c)(1) addresses the ways to support an assertion that a fact can or cannot be genuinely disputed. It does not address the form for providing the required support. Different courts and judges have adopted different forms including, for example, directions that the support be included in the motion, made part of a separate statement of facts, interpolated in the body of a brief or memorandum, or provided in a separate statement of facts included in a brief or memorandum.

[¶10] Subdivision (c)(1)(A) describes the familiar record materials commonly relied upon and requires that the movant cite the particular parts of the materials that support its fact positions. Materials that are not yet in the record—including materials referred to in an affidavit or declaration—must be placed in the record. Once materials are in the record, the court may, by order in the case, direct that the materials be gathered in an appendix, a party may voluntarily submit an appendix, or the parties may submit a joint appendix. The appendix procedure also may be established by local rule. Pointing to a specific location in an appendix satisfies the citation requirement. So too it may be convenient to direct that a party assist the court in locating materials buried in a voluminous record.

[¶11] Subdivision (c)(1)(B) recognizes that a party need not always point to specific record materials. One party, without citing any other materials, may respond or reply that materials cited to dispute or support a fact do not establish the absence or presence of a genuine dispute. And a party who does not have the trial burden of production may rely on a showing that a party who does have the trial burden cannot produce admissible evidence to carry its burden as to the fact.

[¶12] Subdivision (c)(2) provides that a party may object that material cited to support or dispute a fact cannot be presented in a form that would be admissible in evidence. The objection functions much as an objection at trial, adjusted for the pretrial setting. The burden is on the proponent to show that the material is admissible as presented or to explain the admissible form that is anticipated. There is no need to make a separate motion to strike. If the case goes to trial, failure to challenge admissibility at the summary-judgment stage does not forfeit the right to challenge admissibility at trial.

[¶13] Subdivision (c)(3) reflects judicial opinions and local rules provisions stating that the court may decide a motion for summary judgment without undertaking an independent search of the record. Nonetheless, the rule also recognizes that a court may consider record materials not called to its attention by the parties.

[¶14] Subdivision (c)(4) carries forward some of the provisions of former subdivision (e)(1). Other provisions are relocated or omitted. The requirement that a sworn or certified copy of a paper referred to in an affidavit or declaration be attached to the affidavit or declaration is omitted as unnecessary given the requirement in subdivision (c)(1)(A) that a statement or dispute of fact be supported by materials in the record.

[¶15] A formal affidavit is no longer required. 28 U.S.C. §1746 allows a written unsworn declaration, certificate, verification, or statement subscribed in proper form as true under penalty of perjury to substitute for an affidavit.

[¶16] Subdivision (d). Subdivision (d) carries forward without substantial change the provisions of former subdivision (f).

[¶17] A party who seeks relief under subdivision (d) may seek an order deferring the time to respond to the summary-judgment motion.

[¶18] Subdivision (e). Subdivision (e) addresses questions that arise when a party fails to support an assertion of fact or fails to properly address another party's assertion of fact as required by Rule 56(c). As explained below, summary judgment cannot be granted by default even if there is a complete failure to respond to the motion, much less when an attempted response fails to comply with Rule 56(c) requirements. Nor should it be denied by default even if the movant completely fails to reply to a nonmovant's response. Before deciding on other possible action, subdivision (e)(1) recognizes that the court may afford an opportunity to properly support or address the fact. In many circumstances this opportunity will be the court's preferred first step.

[¶19] Subdivision (e)(2) authorizes the court to consider a fact as undisputed for purposes of the motion when response or reply requirements are not satisfied. This approach reflects the "deemed admitted" provisions in many local rules. The fact is considered undisputed only for purposes of the motion; if summary judgment is denied, a party who failed to make a proper Rule 56 response or reply remains free to contest the fact in further proceedings. And the court may choose not to consider the fact as undisputed, particularly if the court knows of record materials that show grounds for genuine dispute.

[¶20] Subdivision (e)(3) recognizes that the court may grant summary judgment only if the motion and supporting materials—including the facts considered undisputed under subdivision (e)(2)—show that the movant is entitled to it. Considering some facts undisputed does not of itself allow summary judgment. If there is a proper response or reply as to some facts, the court cannot grant summary judgment without determining whether those facts can be genuinely disputed. Once the court has determined the set of facts—both those it has chosen to consider undisputed for want of a proper response or reply and any that cannot be genuinely disputed despite a procedurally proper response or reply—it must determine the legal consequences of these facts and permissible inferences from them.

[¶21] Subdivision (e)(4) recognizes that still other orders may be appropriate. The choice among possible orders should be designed to encourage proper presentation of the record. Many courts take extra care with pro se litigants, advising them of the need to respond and the risk of losing by summary judgment if an adequate response is not filed. And the court may seek to reassure itself by some examination of the record before granting summary judgment against a pro se litigant.

[¶22] Subdivision (f). Subdivision (f) brings into Rule 56 text a number of related procedures that have grown up in practice. After giving notice and a reasonable time to respond the court may grant summary judgment for the nonmoving party; grant a motion on legal or factual grounds not raised by the parties; or consider summary judgment on its own. In many cases it may prove useful first to invite a motion; the invited motion will automatically trigger the regular procedure of subdivision (c).

[¶23] Subdivision (g). Subdivision (g) applies when the court does not grant all the relief requested by a motion for summary judgment. It becomes relevant only after the court has applied the summary-judgment standard carried forward in subdivision (a) to each claim, defense, or part of a claim or defense, identified by the motion. Once that duty is discharged, the court may decide whether to apply the summary-judgment standard to dispose of a material fact that is not genuinely in dispute. The court must take care that this determination does not interfere with a party's ability to accept a fact for purposes of the motion only. A nonmovant, for example, may feel confident that a genuine dispute as to one or a few facts will defeat the motion, and prefer to avoid the cost of detailed response to all facts stated by the movant. This position should be available without running the risk that the fact will be taken as established under subdivision (g) or otherwise found to have been accepted for other purposes.

[¶24] If it is readily apparent that the court cannot grant all the relief requested by the motion, it may properly decide that the cost of determining whether some potential fact disputes may be eliminated by summary disposition is greater than the cost of resolving those disputes by other means, including trial. Even if the court believes that a fact is not genuinely in dispute it may refrain from ordering that the fact be treated as established. The court may conclude that it is better to leave open for trial facts and issues that may be better illuminated by the trial of related facts that must be tried in any event.

[¶25] Subdivision (h). Subdivision (h) carries forward former subdivision (g) with three changes. Sanctions are made discretionary, not mandatory, reflecting the experience that courts seldom invoke the independent Rule 56 authority to impose sanctions. *See* Cecil & Cort, Federal Judicial Center Memorandum on Federal Rule of Civil Procedure 56(g) Motions for Sanctions (April 2, 2007). In addition, the rule text is expanded to recognize the need to provide notice and a reasonable time to respond. Finally, authority to impose other appropriate sanctions also is recognized.

FRCP 56 – 2009 NOTES OF ADVISORY COMMITTEE

[¶1] The timing provisions for summary judgment are outmoded. They are consolidated and substantially revised in new subdivision (c)(1). The new rule allows a party to move for summary judgment at any time, even as early as the commencement of the action. If the motion seems premature both subdivision (c)(1) and Rule 6(b) allow the court to extend the time to respond. The rule does set a presumptive deadline at 30 days after the close of all discovery.

[¶2] The presumptive timing rules are default provisions that may be altered by an order in the case or by local rule. Scheduling orders are likely to supersede the rule provisions in most cases, deferring summary-judgment motions until a stated time or establishing different deadlines. Scheduling orders tailored to the needs of the specific case, perhaps adjusted as it progresses, are likely to work better than default rules. A scheduling order may be adjusted to adopt the parties' agreement on timing, or may require that discovery and motions occur in stages—including separation of expert-witness discovery from other discovery.

[¶3] Local rules may prove useful when local docket conditions or practices are incompatible with the general Rule 56 timing provisions.

[¶4] If a motion for summary judgment is filed before a responsive pleading is due from a party affected by the motion, the time for responding to the motion is 21 days after the responsive pleading is due.

FRCP 56 – 2007 NOTES OF ADVISORY COMMITTEE

[¶1] Former Rule 56(a) and (b) referred to summary-judgment motions on or against a claim, counterclaim, or crossclaim, or to obtain a declaratory judgment. The list was incomplete. Rule 56 applies to third-party claimants, intervenors, claimants in interpleader, and others. Amended Rule 56(a) and (b) carry forward the present meaning by referring to a party claiming relief and a party against whom relief is sought.

[¶2] Former Rule 56(c), (d), and (e) stated circumstances in which summary judgment "shall be rendered," the court "shall if practicable" ascertain facts existing without substantial controversy, and "if appropriate, shall" enter summary judgment. In each place "shall" is changed to "should." It is established that although there is no discretion to enter summary judgment when there is a genuine issue as to any material fact, there is discretion to deny summary judgment when it appears that there is no genuine issue as to any material fact. *Kennedy v. Silas Mason Co.*, 334 U.S. 249, 256-257 (1948). Many lower court decisions are gathered in 10A Wright, Miller & Kane, Federal Practice & Procedure: Civil 3d, §2728. "Should" in amended Rule 56(c) recognizes that courts will seldom exercise the discretion to deny summary judgment when there is no genuine issue as to any material fact. Similarly sparing exercise of this discretion is appropriate under Rule 56(e)(2). Rule 56(d)(1), on the other hand, reflects the more open-ended discretion to decide whether it is practicable to determine what material facts are not genuinely at issue.

[¶3] Former Rule 56(d) used a variety of different phrases to express the Rule 56(c) standard for summary judgment—that there is no genuine issue as to any material fact. Amended Rule 56(d) adopts terms directly parallel to Rule 56(c).

FRCP 56 – 1946 NOTES OF ADVISORY COMMITTEE

[¶1] Subdivision (a). The amendment allows a claimant to move for a summary judgment at any time after the expiration of 20 days from the commencement of the action or after service of a motion for summary judgment by the adverse party. This will normally operate to permit an earlier motion by the claimant than under the original rule, where the phrase "at any time after the pleading in answer thereto has been served" operates to prevent a claimant from moving for summary judgment, even in a case clearly proper for its exercise, until a formal answer has been filed. Thus in *Peoples Bank v. Federal Reserve Bank of San Francisco*, N.D.Cal.1944, 58 F.Supp. 25, the plaintiff's countermotion for a summary judgment was stricken as premature, because the defendant had not filed an answer. Since Rule 12(a) allows at least 20 days for an answer, that time plus the 10 days required in Rule 56(c) means that under original Rule 56(a) a minimum period of 30 days necessarily has to elapse in every case before the claimant can be heard on his right to a summary judgment. An extension of time by the court or the service of preliminary motions of any kind will prolong that period even further. In many cases this merely represents unnecessary delay. *See United States v. Adler's Creamery, Inc.*, C.C.A.2, 1939, 107 F.2d 987. The changes are in the interest of more expeditious litigation. The 20-day period, as provided, gives the defendant an opportunity to secure counsel and determine a course of action. But in a case where the defendant himself makes a motion for summary judgment within that time, there is no reason to restrict the plaintiff and the amended rule so provides.

[¶2] Subdivision (c). The amendment of Rule 56(c), by the addition of the final sentence, resolves a doubt expressed in *Sartor v. Arkansas Natural Gas Corp.*, 1944, 64 S.Ct.

724, 321 U.S. 620, 88 L.Ed. 967. See also Commentary, Summary Judgment as to Damages, 1944, 7 Fed.Rules Serv. 974; *Madeirense Do Brasil S/A v. Stulman-Emrick Lumber Co.*, C.C.A.2d, 1945, 147 F.2d 399, cert. den. (1945), 65 S.Ct. 1201, 325 U.S. 861, 89 L.Ed. 1982. It makes clear that although the question of recovery depends on the amount of damages, the summary judgment rule is applicable and summary judgment may be granted in a proper case. If the case is not fully adjudicated it may be dealt with as provided in subdivision (d) of Rule 56, and the right to summary recovery determined by a preliminary order, interlocutory in character, and the precise amount of recovery left for trial.

[¶3] Subdivision (d). Rule 54(a) defines "judgment" as including a decree and "any order from which an appeal lies." Subdivision (d) of Rule 56 indicates clearly, however, that a partial summary "judgment" is not a final judgment, and, therefore, that it is not appealable, unless in the particular case some statute allows an appeal from the interlocutory order involved. The partial summary judgment is merely a pretrial adjudication that certain issues shall be deemed established for the trial of the case. This adjudication is more nearly akin to the preliminary order under Rule 16, and likewise serves the purpose of speeding up litigation by eliminating before trial matters wherein there is no genuine issue of fact. *See Leonard v. Socony-Vacuum Oil Co.*, C.C.A.7, 1942, 130 F.2d 535; *Biggins v. Oltmer Iron Works*, C.C.A.7, 1946, 154 F.2d 214; 3 Moore's Federal Practice, 1938, 3190-3192. Since interlocutory appeals are not allowed, except where specifically provided by statute, see 3 Moore, op. cit. supra, 3155-3156, this interpretation is in line with that policy, *Leonard v. Socony-Vacuum Oil Co.*, supra. *See also Audi Vision Inc. v. RCA Mfg. Co.*, C.C.A.2, 1943, 136 F.2d 621; *Toomey v. Toomey*, 1945, 149 F.2d 19, 80 U.S.App.D.C. 77; *Biggins v. Oltmer Iron Works*, supra; *Catlin v. United States*, 1945, 65 S.Ct. 631, 324 U.S. 229, 89 L.Ed. 911.

FRCP 58 – 2002 NOTES OF ADVISORY COMMITTEE

[¶1] Rule 58 has provided that a judgment is effective only when set forth on a separate document and entered as provided in Rule 79(a). This simple separate document requirement has been ignored in many cases. The result of failure to enter judgment on a separate document is that the time for making motions under Rules 50, 52, 54(d)(2)(B), 59, and some motions under Rule 60, never begins to run. The time to appeal under Appellate Rule 4(a) also does not begin to run. There have been few visible problems with respect to Rule 50, 52, 54(d)(2)(B), 59, or 60 motions, but there have been many and horridly confused problems under Appellate Rule 4(a). These amendments are designed to work in conjunction with Appellate Rule 4(a) to ensure that appeal time does not linger on indefinitely, and to maintain the integration of the time periods set for Rules 50, 52, 54(d)(2)(B), 59, and 60 with Appellate Rule 4(a).

[¶2] Rule 58(a) preserves the core of the present separate document requirement, both for the initial judgment and for any amended judgment. No attempt is made to sort through the confusion that some courts have found in addressing the elements of a separate document. It is easy to prepare a separate document that recites the terms of the judgment without offering additional explanation or citation of authority. Forms 31 and 32 provide examples.

[¶3] Rule 58 is amended, however, to address a problem that arises under Appellate Rule 4(a). Some courts treat such orders as those that deny a motion for new trial as a "judgment," so that appeal time does not start to run until the order is entered on a separate document. Without attempting to address the question whether such orders are appealable, and thus judgments as defined by Rule 54(a), the amendment provides that entry on a separate document is not required for an order disposing of the motions listed in Appellate Rule 4(a). The enumeration of motions drawn from the Appellate Rule 4(a) list is generalized by omitting details that are important for appeal time purposes but that would unnecessarily complicate the separate document requirement. As one example, it is not required that any of the enumerated motions be timely. Many of the enumerated motions are frequently made before judgment is entered. The exemption of the order disposing of the motion does not excuse the obligation to set forth the judgment itself on a separate document. And if disposition of the motion results in an amended judgment, the amended judgment must be set forth on a separate document.

[¶4] Rule 58(b) discards the attempt to define the time when a judgment becomes "effective." Taken in conjunction with the Rule 54(a) definition of a judgment to include "any order from which an appeal lies," the former Rule 58 definition of effectiveness could cause strange difficulties in implementing pretrial orders that are appealable under interlocutory appeal provisions or under expansive theories of finality. Rule 58(b) replaces the definition of effectiveness with a new provision that defines the time when judgment is entered. If judgment is promptly set forth on a separate document, as should be done when required by Rule 58(a)(1), the new provision will not change the effect of Rule 58. But in the cases in which court and clerk fail to comply with this simple requirement, the motion time periods set by Rules 50, 52, 54, 59, and 60 begin to run after expiration of 150 days from entry of the judgment in the civil docket as required by Rule 79(a).

[¶5] A companion amendment of Appellate Rule 4(a)(7) integrates these changes with the time to appeal.

[¶6] The new all-purpose definition of the entry of judgment must be applied with common sense to other questions that may turn on the time when judgment is entered. If the 150-day provision in Rule 58(b)(2)(B)—designed to integrate the time for post-judgment motions with appeal time—serves no purpose, or would defeat the purpose of another rule, it should be disregarded. In theory, for example, the separate document requirement continues to apply to an interlocutory order that is appealable as a final decision under collateral-order doctrine. Appealability under collateral-order doctrine should not be complicated by failure to enter the order as a judgment on a separate document—there is little reason to force trial judges to speculate about the potential appealability of every order, and there is no means to ensure that the trial judge will always reach the same conclusion as the court of appeals. Appeal time should start to run when the collateral order is entered without regard to creation of a separate document and without awaiting expiration of the 150 days provided by Rule 58(b)(2). Drastic surgery on Rules 54(a) and 58 would be required to address this and related issues, however, and it is better to leave this conundrum to the pragmatic disregard that seems its present fate. The present amendments do not seem to make matters worse, apart from one false appearance. If a pretrial order is set forth on a separate document that meets the requirements of Rule 58(b), the time to move for reconsideration seems to begin to run, perhaps years before final judgment. And even if there is no separate document, the time to move for reconsideration seems to begin 150 days after entry in the civil docket. This apparent problem is resolved by Rule 54(b), which expressly permits revision of all orders not made final under Rule 54(b) "at any time before the entry of judgment adjudicating all the claims and the rights and liabilities of all the parties."

[¶7] New Rule 58(d) replaces the provision that attorneys shall not submit forms of judgment except on direction of the court. This provision was added to Rule 58 to avoid the delays that were frequently encountered by the former practice of directing the attorneys for the prevailing party to prepare a form of judgment, and also to avoid the occasionally inept drafting that resulted from attorney-prepared judgments. See *11 Wright, Miller & Kane, Federal Practice & Procedure: Civil 2d, §2786*. The express direction in Rule 58(a)(2) for prompt action by the clerk, and by the court if court action is required, addresses this concern. The new provision allowing any party to move for entry of judgment on a separate document will protect all needs for prompt commencement of the periods for motions, appeals, and execution or other enforcement.

FRCP 59 – 2009 NOTES OF ADVISORY COMMITTEE

[¶1] Former Rules 50, 52, and 59 adopted 10-day periods for their respective post-judgment motions. Rule 6(b) prohibits any expansion of those periods. Experience has proved that in many cases it is not possible to prepare a satisfactory post-judgment motion in 10 days, even under the former rule that excluded intermediate Saturdays, Sundays, and legal holidays. These time periods are particularly sensitive because Appellate Rule 4 integrates the time to appeal with a timely motion under these rules. Rather than introduce the prospect of uncertainty in appeal time by amending Rule 6(b) to permit additional time, the former 10-day periods are expanded to 28 days. Rule 6(b) continues to prohibit expansion of the 28-day period.

[¶2] Former Rule 59(c) set a 10-day period after being served with a motion for new trial to file opposing affidavits. It also provided that the period could be extended for up to 20 days for good cause or by stipulation. The apparent 20-day limit on extending the time to file opposing affidavits seemed to conflict with the Rule 6(b) authority to extend time without any specific limit. This tension between the two rules may have been inadvertent. It is resolved by deleting the former Rule 59(c) limit. Rule 6(b) governs. The underlying 10-day period was extended to 14 days to reflect the change in the Rule 6(a) method for computing periods of less than 11 days.

FRCP 59 – 1995 NOTES OF ADVISORY COMMITTEE

[¶1] The only change, other than stylistic, intended by this revision is to add explicit time limits for filing motions for a new trial, motions to alter or amend a judgment, and affidavits opposing a new trial motion. Previously, there was an inconsistency in the wording of Rules 50, 52, and 59 with respect to whether certain post-judgment motions had to be filed, or merely served, during the prescribed period. This inconsistency caused special problems when motions for a new trial were joined with other post-judgment motions. These motions affect the finality of the judgment, a matter often of importance to third persons as well as the parties and the court. The Committee believes that each of these rules should be revised to require filing before end of the 10-day period. Filing is an event that can be determined with certainty from court records. The phrase "no later than" is used—rather than "within"—to include post-judgment motions that sometimes are filed before actual entry of the judgment by the clerk. It should be noted that under Rule 5 the motions when filed are to contain a certificate of service on other parties. It also should be noted that under Rule 6(a) Saturdays, Sundays, and legal holidays are excluded in measuring the 10-day period, but that Bankruptcy Rule 9006(a) excludes intermediate Saturdays, Sundays, and legal holidays only in computing periods less than 8 days.

FRCP 60 – 2007 NOTES OF ADVISORY COMMITTEE

[¶1] The final sentence of former Rule 60(b) said that the procedure for obtaining any relief from a judgment was by motion as prescribed in the Civil Rules or by an independent action. That provision is deleted as unnecessary. Relief continues to be available only as provided in the Civil Rules or by independent action.

FRCP 62 – 2009 NOTES OF ADVISORY COMMITTEE

[¶1] The time set in the former rule at 10 days has been revised to 14 days. See the Note to Rule 6.[1]

1. **Editor's note:** The cross-reference to "Note to Rule 6" refers to 2009 Notes to FRCP 6 at ¶¶1-20, p. 1149, this book.

ADVISORY CMTE. NOTES

FRCP 62 – 2007 NOTES OF ADVISORY COMMITTEE

[¶1] The final sentence of former Rule 62(a) referred to Rule 62(c). It is deleted as an unnecessary. Rule 62(c) governs of its own force.

FRCP 62.1 – 2009 NOTES OF ADVISORY COMMITTEE

[¶1] This new rule adopts for any motion that the district court cannot grant because of a pending appeal the practice that most courts follow when a party makes a Rule 60(b) motion to vacate a judgment that is pending on appeal. After an appeal has been docketed and while it remains pending, the district court cannot grant a Rule 60(b) motion without a remand. But it can entertain the motion and deny it, defer consideration, or state that it would grant the motion if the the[1] court of appeals remands for that purpose or state that the motion raises a substantial issue. Experienced lawyers often refer to the suggestion for remand as an "indicative ruling." (Appellate Rule 4(a)(4) lists six motions that, if filed within the relevant time limit, suspend the effect of a notice of appeal filed before or after the motion is filed until the last such motion is disposed of. The district court has authority to grant the motion without resorting to the indicative ruling procedure.)

[¶2] This clear procedure is helpful whenever relief is sought from an order that the court cannot reconsider because the order is the subject of a pending appeal. Rule 62.1 does not attempt to define the circumstances in which an appeal limits or defeats the district court's authority to act in the face of a pending appeal. The rules that govern the relationship between trial courts and appellate courts may be complex, depending in part on the nature of the order and the source of appeal jurisdiction. Rule 62.1 applies only when those rules deprive the district court of authority to grant relief without appellate permission. If the district court concludes that it has authority to grant relief without appellate permission, it can act without falling back on the indicative ruling procedure.

[¶3] To ensure proper coordination of proceedings in the district court and in the appellate court, the movant must notify the circuit clerk under Federal Rule of Appellate Procedure 12.1 if the district court states that it would grant the motion or that the motion raises a substantial issue. Remand is in the court of appeals' discretion under Appellate Rule 12.1.

[¶4] Often it will be wise for the district court to determine whether it in fact would grant the motion if the court of appeals remands for that purpose. But a motion may present complex issues that require extensive litigation and that may either be mooted or be presented in a different context by decision of the issues raised on appeal. In such circumstances the district court may prefer to state that the motion raises a substantial issue, and to state the reasons why it prefers to decide only if the court of appeals agrees that it would be useful to decide the motion before decision of the pending appeal. The district court is not bound to grant the motion after stating that the motion raises a substantial issue; further proceedings on remand may show that the motion ought not be granted.

1. **Editor's note:** So in original. The second "the" probably should not appear.

FRCP 64 – 2007 NOTES OF ADVISORY COMMITTEE

[¶1] Former Rule 64 stated that the Civil Rules govern an action in which any remedy available under Rule 64(a) is used. The Rules were said to govern from the time the action is commenced if filed in federal court, and from the time of removal if removed from state court. These provisions are deleted as redundant. Rule 1 establishes that the Civil Rules apply to all actions in a district court, and Rule 81(c)(1) adds reassurance that the Civil Rules apply to a removed action "after it is removed."

FRCP 65 – 2009 NOTES OF ADVISORY COMMITTEE

[¶1] The time set in the former rule at 10 days has been revised to 14 days. See the Note to Rule 6.[1]

1. **Editor's note:** The cross-reference to "Note to Rule 6" refers to 2009 Notes to FRCP 6 at ¶¶1-20, p. 1149, this book.

FRCP 65 – 2007 NOTES OF ADVISORY COMMITTEE

[¶1] The final sentence of former Rule 65(c) referred to Rule 65.1. It is deleted as unnecessary. Rule 65.1 governs of its own force.

[¶2] Rule 65(d)(2) clarifies two ambiguities in former Rule 65(d). The former rule was adapted from former 28 U.S.C. §363, but omitted a comma that made clear the common doctrine that a party must have actual notice of an injunction in order to be bound by it. Amended Rule 65(d) restores the meaning of the earlier statute, and also makes clear the proposition that an injunction can be enforced against a person who acts in concert with a party's officer, agent, servant, employee, or attorney.

FRCP 65 – 2001 NOTES OF ADVISORY COMMITTEE

[¶1] New subdivision (f) is added in conjunction with abrogation of the antiquated Copyright Rules of Practice adopted for proceedings under the 1909 Copyright Act. Courts have naturally turned to Rule 65 in response to the apparent inconsistency of the former Copyright Rules with the discretionary impoundment procedure adopted in 1976, 17 U.S.C. §503(a). Rule 65 procedures also have assuaged well-founded doubts whether the Copyright Rules satisfy more contemporary requirements of due process. *See, e.g.*, *Religious Technology Center v. Netcom On-Line Communications Servs., Inc.*, 923 F.Supp. 1231, 1260-1265 (N.D.Cal.1995); *Paramount Pictures Corp. v. Doe*, 821 F.Supp. 82 (E.D.N.Y.1993); *WPOW, Inc. v. MRLJ Enterprises*, 584 F.Supp. 132 (D.D.C.1984).

[¶2] A common question has arisen from the experience that notice of a proposed impoundment may enable an infringer to defeat the court's capacity to grant effective relief. Impoundment may be ordered on an ex parte basis under subdivision (b) if the applicant makes a strong showing of the reasons why notice is likely to defeat effective relief. Such no-notice procedures are authorized in trademark infringement proceedings, see 15 U.S.C. §1116(d), and courts have provided clear illustrations of the kinds of showings that support ex parte relief. *See Matter of Vuitton et Fils S.A.*, 606 F.2d 1 (2d Cir.1979); *Vuitton v. White*, 945 F.2d 569 (3d Cir.1991). In applying the tests for no-notice relief, the court should ask whether impoundment is necessary, or whether adequate protection can be had by a less intrusive form of no-notice relief shaped as a temporary restraining order.

[¶3] This new subdivision (f) does not limit use of trademark procedures in cases that combine trademark and copyright claims. Some observers believe that trademark procedures should be adopted for all copyright cases, a proposal better considered by Congressional processes than by rulemaking processes.

FRCP 65.1 – 2006 NOTES OF ADVISORY COMMITTEE

[¶1] Rule 65.1 is amended to conform to the changed title of the Supplemental Rules.

FRCP 68 – 2009 NOTES OF ADVISORY COMMITTEE

[¶1] Former Rule 68 allowed service of an offer of judgment more than 10 days before the trial begins, or—if liability has been determined—at least 10 days before a hearing to determine the extent of liability. It may be difficult to know in advance when trial will begin or when a hearing will be held. The time is now measured from the date set for trial or hearing; resetting the date establishes a new time for serving the offer.

[¶2] The former 10-day periods are extended to 14 days to reflect the change in the Rule 6(a) method for computing periods less than 11 days.

FRCP 69 – 2007 NOTES OF ADVISORY COMMITTEE

[¶1] Amended Rule 69(b) incorporates directly the provisions of 2 U.S.C. §118 and 28 U.S.C. §2006, deleting the incomplete statement in former Rule 69(b) of the circumstances in which execution does not issue against an officer.

FRCP 71.1 – 2009 NOTES OF ADVISORY COMMITTEE

[¶1] The times set in the former rule at 20 days have been revised to 21 days. See the Note to Rule 6.[1]

1. **Editor's note:** The cross-reference to "Note to Rule 6" refers to 2009 Notes to FRCP 6 at ¶¶1-20, p. 1149, this book.

FRCP 71.1 – 2007 NOTES OF ADVISORY COMMITTEE

[¶1] Former Rule 71A has been redesignated as Rule 71.1 to conform to the designations used for all other rules added within the original numbering system.

[¶2] Rule 71.1(e) allows a defendant to appear without answering. Former form 28 (now form 60) includes information about this right in the Rule 71.1(d)(2) notice. It is useful to confirm this practice in the rule.

[¶3] The information that identifies the attorney is changed to include telephone number and electronic-mail address, in line with similar amendments to Rules 11(a) and 26(g)(1).

FRCP 72 – 2009 NOTES OF ADVISORY COMMITTEE

[¶1] The times set in the former rule at 10 days have been revised to 14 days. See the Note to Rule 6.[1]

1. **Editor's note:** The cross-reference to "Note to Rule 6" refers to 2009 Notes to FRCP 6 at ¶¶1-20, p. 1149, this book.

FRCP 72 – 1983 NOTES OF ADVISORY COMMITTEE

[¶1] **Subdivision (a).** This subdivision addresses court-ordered referrals of nondispositive matters under 28 U.S.C. §636(b)(1)(A). The rule calls for a written order of the magistrate's disposition to preserve the record and facilitate review. An oral order read into the record by the magistrate will satisfy this requirement.

[¶2] No specific procedures or timetables for raising objections to the magistrate's rulings on nondispositive matters are set forth in the Magistrates Act. The rule fixes a 10-day period in order to avoid uncertainty and provide uniformity that will eliminate the confusion that might arise if different periods were prescribed by local rule in different districts. It also is contemplated that a party who is successful before the magistrate will be afforded an opportunity to respond to objections raised to the magistrate's ruling.

[¶3] The last sentence of subdivision (a) specifies that reconsideration of a magistrate's order, as provided for in the Magistrates Act, shall be by the district judge to whom the case is assigned. This rule does not restrict experimentation by the district courts under 28 U.S.C. §636(b)(3) involving references of matters other than pretrial matters, such as appointment of counsel, taking of default judgments, and acceptance of jury verdicts when the judge is unavailable.

[¶4] **Subdivision (b).** This subdivision governs court-ordered referrals of dispositive pretrial matters and prisoner petitions challenging conditions of confinement, pursuant to statutory authorization in 28 U.S.C. §636(b)(1)(B). This rule does not extend to habeas corpus petitions, which are covered by the specific rules relating to proceedings under Sections 2254 and 2255 of Title 28.

[¶5] This rule implements the statutory procedures for making objections to the magistrate's proposed findings and recommendations. The 10-day period, as specified in the statute, is subject to Rule 6(e) which provides for an additional 3-day period when service is made by mail. Although no specific provision appears in the Magistrates Act, the rule specifies a 10-day period for a party to respond to objections to the magistrate's recommendation.

[¶6] Implementing the statutory requirements, the rule requires the district judge to whom the case is assigned to make a de novo determination of those portions of the report, findings, or recommendations to which timely objection is made. The term "de novo" signifies that the magistrate's findings are not protected by the clearly erroneous doctrine, but does not indicate that a second evidentiary hearing is required. *See United States v. Raddatz*, 417 [447] U.S. 667 (1980). *See also* Silberman, Masters and Magistrates Part II: The American Analogue, 50 N.Y.U. L.Rev. 1297, 1367 (1975). When no timely objection is filed, the court need only satisfy itself that there is no clear error on the face of the record in order to accept the recommendation. *See Campbell v. United States Dist. Court*, 501 F.2d 196, 206 (9th Cir.1974), cert. denied, 419 U.S. 879, quoted in House Report No. 94-1609, 94th Cong. 2d Sess. (1976) at 3. *Compare Park Motor Mart, Inc. v. Ford Motor Co.*, 616 F.2d 603 (1st Cir.1980). Failure to make timely objection to the magistrate's report prior to its adoption by the district judge may constitute a waiver of appellate review of the district judge's order. *See United States v. Walters*, 638 F.2d 947 (6th Cir.1981).

FRCP 73 – 1997 NOTES OF ADVISORY COMMITTEE

[¶1] The Federal Courts Improvement Act of 1996 repealed the former provisions of 28 U.S.C. §636(c)(4) and (5) that enabled parties that had agreed to trial before a magistrate judge to agree also that appeal should be taken to the district court. Rule 73 is amended to conform to this change. Rules 74, 75, and 76 are abrogated for the same reason. The portions of Form 33 and Form 34 that referred to appeals to the district court also are deleted.

FRCP 73 – 1983 NOTES OF ADVISORY COMMITTEE

[¶1] **Subdivision (a).** This subdivision implements the broad authority of the 1979 amendments to the Magistrates Act, 28 U.S.C. §636(c), which permit a magistrate to sit in lieu of a district judge and exercise civil jurisdiction over a case, when the parties consent. See McCabe, The Federal Magistrate Act of 1979, 16 Harv. J. Legis. 343, 364-79 (1979). In order to exercise this jurisdiction, a magistrate must be specially designated under 28 U.S.C. §636(c)(1) by the district court or courts he serves. The only exception to a magistrate's exercise of civil jurisdiction, which includes the power to conduct jury and nonjury trials and decide dispositive motions, is the contempt power. A hearing on contempt is to be conducted by the district judge upon certification of the facts and an order to show cause by the magistrate. See 28 U.S.C. §639(e). In view of 28 U.S.C. §636(c)(1) and this rule, it is unnecessary to amend Rule 58 to provide that the decision of a magistrate is a "decision by the court" for the purposes of that rule and a "final decision of the district court" for purposes of 28 U.S.C. §1291 governing appeals.

[¶2] **Subdivision (b).** This subdivision implements the blind consent provision of 28 U.S.C. §636(c)(2) and is designed to ensure that neither the judge nor the magistrate attempts to induce a party to consent to reference of a civil matter under this rule to a magistrate. See House Rep. No. 96-444, 96th Cong. 1st Sess. 8 (1979).

[¶3] The rule opts for a uniform approach in implementing the consent provision by directing the clerk to notify the parties of their opportunity to elect to proceed before a magistrate and by requiring the execution and filing of a consent form or forms setting forth the election. However, flexibility at the local level is preserved in that local rules will determine how notice shall be communicated to the parties, and local rules will specify the time period within which an election must be made.

[¶4] The last paragraph of subdivision (b) reiterates the provision in 28 U.S.C. §636(c)(6) for vacating a reference to the magistrate.

[¶5] **Subdivision (c).** Under 28 U.S.C. §636(c)(3), the normal route of appeal from the judgment of a magistrate—the only route that will be available unless the parties otherwise agree in advance—is an appeal by the aggrieved party "directly to the appropriate United States court of appeals from the judgment of the magistrate in the same manner as an appeal from any other judgment of a district court." The quoted statutory language indicates Congress' intent that the same procedures and standards of appealability that govern appeals from district court judgments govern appeals from magistrates' judgments.

[¶6] **Subdivision (d).** 28 U.S.C. §636(c)(4) offers parties who consent to the exercise of civil jurisdiction by a magistrate an alternative appeal route to that provided in subdivision (c) of this rule. This optional appellate route was provided by Congress in recognition of the fact that not all civil cases warrant the same appellate treatment. In cases where the amount in controversy is not great and there are no difficult questions of law to be resolved, the parties may desire to avoid the expense and delay of appeal to the court of appeals by electing an appeal to the district judge. See McCabe, The Federal Magistrate Act of 1979, 16 Harv. J. Legis. 343, 388 (1979). This subdivision provides that the parties may elect the optional appeal route at the time of reference to a magistrate. To this end, the notice by the clerk under subdivision (b) of this rule shall explain the appeal option and the corollary restriction on review by the court of appeals. This approach will avoid later claims of lack of consent to the avenue of appeal. The choice of

the alternative appeal route to the judge of the district court should be made by the parties in their forms of consent. Special appellate rules to govern appeals from a magistrate to a district judge appear in new Rules 74 through 76.

FRCP 74 – 2007 NOTES OF ADVISORY COMMITTEE

[¶1] Rule 74 was abrogated in 1997 to reflect repeal of the statute providing for appeal from a magistrate judge's judgment to the district court. The rule number is reserved for possible future use.

FRCP 75 – 2007 NOTES OF ADVISORY COMMITTEE

[¶1] Rule 75 was abrogated in 1997 to reflect repeal of the statute providing for appeal from a magistrate judge's judgment to the district court. The rule number is reserved for possible future use.

FRCP 76 – 2007 NOTES OF ADVISORY COMMITTEE

[¶1] Rule 76 was abrogated in 1997 to reflect repeal of the statute providing for appeal from a magistrate judge's judgment to the district court. The rule number is reserved for possible future use.

FRCP 77 – 2001 NOTES OF ADVISORY COMMITTEE

[¶1] Rule 77(d) is amended to reflect changes in Rule 5(b). A few courts have experimented with serving Rule 77(d) notices by electronic means on parties who consent to this procedure. The success of these experiments warrants express authorization. Because service is made in the manner provided in Rule 5(b), party consent is required for service by electronic or other means described in Rule 5(b)(2)(D). The same provision is made for a party who wishes to ensure actual communication of the Rule 77(d) notice by also serving notice.

FRCP 78 – 2007 NOTES OF ADVISORY COMMITTEE

[¶1] Rule 16 has superseded any need for the provision in former Rule 78 for orders for the advancement, conduct, and hearing of actions.

FRCP 81 – 2009 NOTES OF ADVISORY COMMITTEE

[¶1] Several Rules incorporate local state practice. Rule 81(d) now provides that "the term 'state' includes, where appropriate, the District of Columbia." The definition is expanded to include any commonwealth or territory of the United States. As before, these entities are included only "where appropriate." They are included for the reasons that counsel incorporation of state practice. For example, state holidays are recognized in computing time under Rule 6(a). Other, quite different, examples are Rules 64(a), invoking state law for prejudgment remedies, and 69(a)(1), relying on state law for the procedure on execution. Including commonwealths and territories in these and other rules avoids the gaps that otherwise would result when the federal rule relies on local practice rather than provide a uniform federal approach. Including them also establishes uniformity between federal courts and local courts in areas that may involve strong local interests, little need for uniformity among federal courts, or difficulty in defining a uniform federal practice that integrates effectively with local practice.

[¶2] Adherence to a local practice may be refused as not "appropriate" when the local practice would impair a significant federal interest.

[¶3] The times set in the former rule at 5, 10, and 20 days have been revised to 7, 14, and 21 days, respectively. See the Note to Rule 6.[1]

1. **Editor's note:** The cross-reference to "Note to Rule 6" refers to 2009 Notes to FRCP 6 at ¶¶1-20, p. 1149, this book.

FRCP 81 – 2007 NOTES OF ADVISORY COMMITTEE

[¶1] Rule 81(c) has been revised to reflect the amendment of 28 U.S.C. §1446(a) that changed the procedure for removal from a petition for removal to a notice of removal.

[¶2] Former Rule 81(e), drafted before the decision in *Erie R.R. v. Tompkins*, 304 U.S. 64 (1938), defined state law to include "the statutes of that state and the state judicial decisions construing them." The *Erie* decision reinterpreted the Rules of Decision Act, now 28 U.S.C. §1652, recognizing that the "laws" of the states include the common law established by judicial decisions. Long-established practice reflects this understanding, looking to state common law as well as statutes and court rules when a Civil Rule directs use of state law. Amended Rule 81(d)(1) adheres to this practice, including all state judicial decisions, not only those that construe state statutes.

[¶3] Former Rule 81(f) is deleted. The office of district director of internal revenue was abolished by restructuring under the Internal Revenue Service Restructuring and Reform Act of 1998, Pub.L. 105-206, July 22, 1998, 26 U.S.C. §1 Note.

FRCP 81 – 2002 NOTES OF ADVISORY COMMITTEE

[¶1] This amendment brings Rule 81(a)(2) into accord with the Rules Governing §2254 and §2255 proceedings. In its present form, Rule 81(a)(2) includes return-time provisions that are inconsistent with the provisions in the Rules Governing §§2254 and 2255. The inconsistency should be eliminated, and it is better that the time provisions continue to be set out in the other rules without duplication in Rule 81. Rule 81 also directs that the writ be directed to the person having custody of the person detained. Similar directions exist in the §2254 and §2255 rules, providing additional detail for applicants subject to future custody. There is no need for partial duplication in Rule 81.

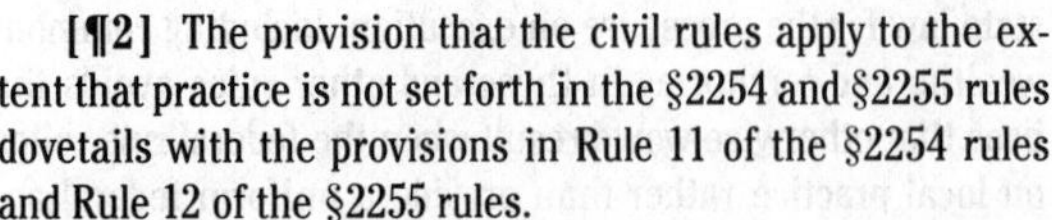

[¶2] The provision that the civil rules apply to the extent that practice is not set forth in the §2254 and §2255 rules dovetails with the provisions in Rule 11 of the §2254 rules and Rule 12 of the §2255 rules.

FRCP 81 – 2001 NOTES OF ADVISORY COMMITTEE

[¶1] Former Copyright Rule 1 made the Civil Rules applicable to copyright proceedings except to the extent the Civil Rules were inconsistent with Copyright Rules. Abrogation of the Copyright Rules leaves the Civil Rules fully applicable to copyright proceedings. Rule 81(a)(1) is amended to reflect this change.

[¶2] The District of Columbia Court Reform and Criminal Procedure Act of 1970, Pub.L. 91-358, 84 Stat. 473, transferred mental health proceedings formerly held in the United States District Court for the District of Columbia to local District of Columbia courts. The provision that the Civil Rules do not apply to these proceedings is deleted as superfluous.

[¶3] The reference to incorporation of the Civil Rules in the Federal Rules of Bankruptcy Procedure has been restyled.

FRCP 82 – 2001 NOTES OF ADVISORY COMMITTEE

[¶1] The final sentence of Rule 82 is amended to delete the reference to 28 U.S.C. §1393, which has been repealed.

FRCP 83 – 1995 NOTES OF ADVISORY COMMITTEE

[¶1] **Subdivision (a).** This rule is amended to reflect the requirement that local rules be consistent not only with the national rules but also with Acts of Congress. The amendment also states that local rules should not repeat Acts of Congress or local rules.

[¶2] The amendment also requires that the numbering of local rules conform with any uniform numbering system that may be prescribed by the Judicial Conference. Lack of uniform numbering might create unnecessary traps for counsel and litigants. A uniform numbering system would make it easier for an increasingly national bar and for litigants to locate a local rule that applies to a particular procedural issue.

[¶3] Paragraph (2) is new. Its aim is to protect against loss of rights in the enforcement of local rules relating to matters of form. For example, a party should not be deprived of a right to a jury trial because its attorney, unaware of—or forgetting—a local rule directing that jury demands be noted in the caption of the case, includes a jury demand only in the body of the pleading. The proscription of paragraph (2) is narrowly drawn—covering only violations attributable to nonwillful failure to comply and only those involving local rules directed to matters of form. It does not limit the court's power to impose substantive penalties upon a party if it or its attorney contumaciously or willfully violates a local rule, even one involving merely a matter of form. Nor does it affect the court's power to enforce local rules that involve more than mere matters of form—for example, a local rule requiring parties to identify evidentiary matters relied upon to support or oppose motions for summary judgment.

[¶4] **Subdivision (b).** This rule provides flexibility to the court in regulating practice when there is no controlling law. Specifically, it permits the court to regulate practice in any manner consistent with Acts of Congress, with rules adopted under 28 U.S.C. §§2072 and 2075, and with the district local rules.

[¶5] This rule recognizes that courts rely on multiple directives to control practice. Some courts regulate practice through the published Federal Rules and the local rules of the court. Some courts also have used internal operating procedures, standing orders, and other internal directives. Although such directives continue to be authorized, they can lead to problems. Counsel or litigants may be unaware of various directives. In addition, the sheer volume of directives may impose an unreasonable barrier. For example, it may be difficult to obtain copies of the directives. Finally, counsel or litigants may be unfairly sanctioned for failing to comply with a directive. For these reasons, the amendment to this rule disapproves imposing any sanction or other disadvantage on a person for noncompliance with such an internal directive, unless the alleged violator has been furnished actual notice of the requirement in a particular case.

[¶6] There should be no adverse consequence to a party or attorney for violating special requirements relating to practice before a particular court unless the party or attorney has actual notice of those requirements. Furnishing litigants with a copy outlining the judge's practices—or attaching instructions to a notice setting a case for conference or trial—would suffice to give actual notice, as would an order in a case specifically adopting by reference a judge's standing order and indicating how copies can be obtained.

FRCP 86 – 2007 NOTES OF ADVISORY COMMITTEE

[¶1] The subdivisions that provided a list of the effective dates of the original Civil Rules and amendments made up to 1963 are deleted as no longer useful.

[¶2] Rule 86(b) is added to clarify the relationship of amendments taking effect on December 1, 2007, to other laws for the purpose of applying the "supersession" clause in 28 U.S.C. §2072(b). Section 2072(b) provides that a law in conflict with an Enabling Act Rule "shall be of no further force or effect after such rule[ ] ha[s] taken effect." The amendments that take effect on December 1, 2007, result from the general restyling of the Civil Rules and from a small number of technical revisions adopted on a parallel track. None of these amendments is intended to affect resolution of any conflict that might arise between a rule and another law. Rule 86(b) makes this intent explicit. Any conflict that arises should be resolved by looking to the date the specific conflicting rule provision first became effective.

SUPPLEMENTAL RULES NOTES

RULE B – 2009 NOTES OF ADVISORY COMMITTEE

[¶1] The time set in the former rule at 20 days has been revised to 21 days. See the Note to Rule 6.[1]

1. **Editor's note:** The cross-reference to "Note to Rule 6" refers to 2009 Notes to FRCP 6 at ¶¶1-20, p. 1149, this book.

RULE C – 2009 NOTES OF ADVISORY COMMITTEE

[¶1] The times set in former rule at 10 or 20 days have been revised to 14 or 21 days. See the Note to Rule 6.[1]

1. **Editor's note:** The cross-reference to "Note to Rule 6" refers to 2009 Notes to FRCP 6 at ¶¶1-20, p. 1149, this book.

RULE C – 2008 NOTES OF ADVISORY COMMITTEE

[¶1] Supplemental Rule C(6)(a)(i) is amended to correct an inadvertent omission in the 2006 amendment to Rule C. The amendment is technical and stylistic in nature. No substantive change is intended.

RULE G – 2009 NOTES OF ADVISORY COMMITTEE

[¶1] The times set in the former rule at 20 days have been revised to 21 days. See the Note to Rule 6.[1]

1. **Editor's note:** The cross-reference to "Note to Rule 6" refers to 2009 Notes to FRCP 6 at ¶¶1-20, p. 1149, this book.

RULE G – 2006 NOTES OF ADVISORY COMMITTEE

[¶1] Rule G is added to bring together the central procedures that govern civil forfeiture actions. Civil forfeiture actions are in rem proceedings, as are many admiralty proceedings. As the number of civil forfeiture actions has increased, however, reasons have appeared to create sharper distinctions within the framework of the Supplemental Rules. Civil forfeiture practice will benefit from distinctive provisions that express and focus developments in statutory, constitutional, and decisional law. Admiralty practice will be freed from the pressures that arise when the needs of civil forfeiture proceedings counsel interpretations of common rules that may not be suitable for admiralty proceedings.

[¶2] Rule G generally applies to actions governed by the Civil Asset Forfeiture Reform Act of 2000 (CAFRA) and also to actions excluded from it. The rule refers to some specific CAFRA provisions; if these statutes are amended, the rule should be adapted to the new provisions during the period required to amend the rule.

[¶3] Rule G is not completely self-contained. Subdivision (1) recognizes the need to rely at times on other Supplemental Rules and the place of the Supplemental Rules within the basic framework of the Civil Rules.

[¶4] Supplemental Rules A, C, and E are amended to reflect the adoption of Rule G.

Subdivision (1)

[¶5] Rule G is designed to include the distinctive procedures that govern a civil forfeiture action. Some details, however, are better supplied by relying on Rules C and E. Subdivision (1) incorporates those rules for issues not addressed by Rule G. This general incorporation is at times made explicit—subdivision (7)(b)(v), for example, invokes the security provisions of Rule E. But Rules C and E are not to be invoked to create conflicts with Rule G. They are to be used only when Rule G, fairly construed, does not address the issue.

[¶6] The Civil Rules continue to provide the procedural framework within which Rule G and the other Supplemental Rules operate. Both Rule G(1) and Rule A state this basic proposition. Rule G, for example, does not address pleadings amendments. Civil Rule 15 applies, in light of the circumstances of a forfeiture action.

Subdivision (2)

[¶7] Rule E(2)(a) requires that the complaint in an admiralty action "state the circumstances from which the claim arises with such particularity that the defendant or claimant will be able, without moving for a more definite statement, to commence an investigation of the facts and to frame a responsive pleading." Application of this standard to civil forfeiture actions has evolved to the standard stated in subdivision (2)(f). The complaint must state sufficiently detailed facts to support a reasonable belief that the government will be able to meet its burden of proof at trial. *See U.S. v. Mondragon*, 313 F.3d 862 (4th Cir.2002). Subdivision (2)(f) carries this forfeiture case law forward without change.

Subdivision (3)

[¶8] Subdivision (3) governs in rem process in a civil forfeiture action.

[¶9] Paragraph (a). Paragraph (a) reflects the provisions of 18 U.S.C. §985.

[¶10] Paragraph (b). Paragraph (b) addresses arrest warrants when the defendant is not real property. Subparagraph (i) directs the clerk to issue a warrant if the property is in the government's possession, custody, or control. If the property is not in the government's possession, custody, or control and is not subject to a restraining order, subparagraph (ii) provides that a warrant issues only if the court finds probable cause to arrest the property. This provision departs from former Rule C(3)(a)(i), which authorized issuance of summons and warrant by the clerk without a probable-cause finding. The probable-cause finding better protects the interests of persons interested in the property. Subparagraph (iii) recognizes that a warrant is not necessary if the property is subject to a judicial restraining order. The government remains free, however, to seek a warrant if it anticipates that the restraining order may be modified or vacated.

[¶11] Paragraph (c). Subparagraph (ii) requires that the warrant and any supplemental process be served as soon as practicable unless the property is already in the government's possession, custody, or control. But it authorizes the court to order a different time. The authority to order a different time recognizes that the government may have secured orders sealing the complaint in a civil forfeiture action or have won a stay after filing. The seal or stay may be ordered for reasons, such as protection of an ongoing criminal investigation, that would be defeated by prompt service of the warrant. Subparagraph (ii) does not reflect any independent ground for ordering a seal or stay, but merely reflects the consequences for execution when sealing or a stay is ordered. A court also may order a different time for service if good cause is shown for reasons unrelated to a seal or stay. Subparagraph (iv) reflects the uncertainty surrounding service of an arrest warrant on property not in the United States. It is not possible to identify in the rule the appropriate authority for serving process in all other countries. Transmission of the warrant to an appropriate authority, moreover, does not ensure that the warrant will be executed. The rule requires only that the warrant be transmitted to an appropriate authority.

Subdivision (4)

[¶12] Paragraph (a). Paragraph (a) reflects the traditional practice of publishing notice of an in rem action.

[¶13] Subparagraph (i) recognizes two exceptions to the general publication requirement. Publication is not required if the defendant property is worth less than $1,000 and direct notice is sent to all reasonably identifiable potential claimants as required by subdivision (4)(b). Publication also is not required if the cost would exceed the property's value and the court finds that other means of notice would satisfy due process. Publication on a government-established internet forfeiture site, as contemplated by subparagraph (iv), would be at a low marginal publication cost, which would likely be the cost to compare to the property value.

[¶14] Subparagraph (iv) states the basic criterion for selecting the means and method of publication. The purpose is to adopt a means reasonably calculated to reach potential claimants. The government should choose from among these means a method that is reasonably likely to reach potential claimants at a cost reasonable in the circumstances.

[¶15] If the property is in the United States and newspaper notice is chosen, publication may be where the action is filed, where the property was seized, or—if the property was not seized—where the property is located. Choice among these places is influenced by the probable location of potential claimants.

[¶16] If the property is not in the United States, account must be taken of the sensitivities that surround publication of legal notices in other countries. A foreign country may forbid local publication. If potential claimants are likely to be in the United States, publication in the district where the action is filed may be the best choice. If potential claimants are likely to be located abroad, the better choice may be publication by means generally circulated in the country where the property is located.

[¶17] Newspaper publication is not a particularly effective means of notice for most potential claimants. Its traditional use is best defended by want of affordable alternatives. Paragraph (iv)(C) contemplates a government-created internet forfeiture site that would provide a single easily identified means of notice. Such a site could allow much more direct access to notice as to any specific property than publication provides.

[¶18] Paragraph (b). Paragraph (b) is entirely new. For the first time, Rule G expressly recognizes the due process obligation to send notice to any person who reasonably appears to be a potential claimant.

[¶19] Subparagraph (i) states the obligation to send notice. Many potential claimants will be known to the government because they have filed claims during the administrative forfeiture stage. Notice must be sent, however, no matter what source of information makes it reasonably appear that a person is a potential claimant. The duty to send notice terminates when the time for filing a claim expires.

[¶20] Notice of the action does not require formal service of summons in the manner required by Rule 4 to initiate a personal action. The process that begins an in rem forfeiture action is addressed by subdivision (3). This process commonly gives notice to potential claimants. Publication of notice is required in addition to this process. Due process requirements have moved beyond these traditional means of notice, but are satisfied by practical means that are reasonably calculated to accomplish actual notice.

[¶21] Subparagraph (ii)(B) directs that the notice state a deadline for filing a claim that is at least 35 days after the notice is sent. This provision applies both in actions that fall within 18 U.S.C. §983(a)(4)(A) and in other actions. Section 983(a)(4)(A) states that a claim should be filed no later than 30 days after service of the complaint. The variation introduced by subparagraph (ii)(B) reflects the procedure of §983(a)(2)(B) for nonjudicial forfeiture proceedings. The nonjudicial procedure requires that a claim be filed "not later than the deadline set forth in a personal notice letter (which may be not earlier than 35 days after the date the letter is sent) * * *." This procedure is as suitable in a civil forfeiture action as in a nonjudicial forfeiture proceeding. Thirty-five days after notice is sent ordinarily will extend the claim time by no more than a brief period; a claimant anxious to expedite proceedings can file the claim before the deadline; and the government has flexibility to set a still longer period when circumstances make that desirable.

[¶22] Subparagraph (iii) begins by stating the basic requirement that notice must be sent by means reasonably calculated to reach the potential claimant. No attempt is made to list the various means that may be reasonable in different circumstances. It may be reasonable, for example, to rely on means that have already been established for communication with a particular potential claimant. The government's interest in choosing a means likely to accomplish actual notice is bolstered by its desire to avoid post-forfeiture challenges based on arguments that a different method would have been more likely to accomplish actual notice. Flexible rule language accommodates the rapid evolution of communications technology.

[¶23] Notice may be directed to a potential claimant through counsel, but only to counsel already representing the claimant with respect to the seizure of the property, or in a related investigation, administrative forfeiture proceeding, or criminal case.

[¶24] Subparagraph (iii)(C) reflects the basic proposition that notice to a potential claimant who is incarcerated must be sent to the place of incarceration. Notice directed to some other place, such as a preincarceration residence, is less likely to reach the potential claimant. This provision does not address due process questions that may arise if a particular prison has deficient procedures for delivering notice to prisoners. *See Dusenbery v. U.S.*, 534 U.S. 161 (2002).

[¶25] Items (D) and (E) of subparagraph (iii) authorize the government to rely on an address given by a person who is not incarcerated. The address may have been given to the agency that arrested or released the person, or to the agency that seized the property. The government is not obliged to undertake an independent investigation to verify the address.

[¶26] Subparagraph (iv) identifies the date on which notice is considered to be sent for some common means, without addressing the circumstances for choosing among the identified means or other means. The date of sending should be determined by analogy for means not listed. Facsimile transmission, for example, is sent upon transmission. Notice by personal delivery is sent on delivery.

[¶27] Subparagraph (v), finally, reflects the purpose to effect actual notice by providing that a potential claimant who had actual notice of a forfeiture proceeding cannot oppose or seek relief from forfeiture because the government failed to comply with subdivision (4)(b).

Subdivision (5)

[¶28] Paragraph (a). Paragraph (a) establishes that the first step of contesting a civil forfeiture action is to file a claim. A claim is required by 18 U.S.C. §983(a)(4)(A) for actions covered by §983. Paragraph (a) applies this procedure as well to actions not covered by §983. "Claim" is used to describe this first pleading because of the statutory references to claim and claimant. It functions in the same way as the statement of interest prescribed for an admiralty proceeding by Rule C(6), and is not related to the distinctive meaning of "claim" in admiralty practice.

[¶29] If the claimant states its interest in the property to be as bailee, the bailor must be identified. A bailee who files a claim on behalf of a bailor must state the bailee's authority to do so.

[¶30] The claim must be signed under penalty of perjury by the person making it. An artificial body that can act only through an agent may authorize an agent to sign for it. Excusable inability of counsel to obtain an appropriate signature may be grounds for an extension of time to file the claim.

[¶31] Paragraph (a)(ii) sets the time for filing a claim. Item (C) applies in the relatively rare circumstance in which notice is not published and the government did not send direct notice to the claimant because it did not know of the claimant or did not have an address for the claimant.

[¶32] Paragraph (b). Under 18 U.S.C. §983(a)(4)(B), which governs many forfeiture proceedings, a person who asserts an interest by filing a claim "shall file an answer to the Government's complaint for forfeiture not later than 20 days after the date of the filing of the claim." Paragraph (b) recognizes that this statute works within the general procedures established by Civil Rule 12. Rule 12(a)(4) suspends the time to answer when a Rule 12 motion is served within the time allowed to answer. Continued application of this rule to proceedings governed by §983(a)(4)(B) serves all of the purposes advanced by Rule 12(a)(4), *see U.S. v. $8,221,877.16*, 330 F.3d 141 (3d Cir.2003); permits a uniform procedure for all civil forfeiture actions; and recognizes that a motion under Rule 12 can be made only after a claim is filed that provides background for the motion.

[¶33] Failure to present an objection to in rem jurisdiction or to venue by timely motion or answer waives the objection. Waiver of such objections is familiar. An answer may be amended to assert an objection initially omitted. But Civil Rule 15 should be applied to an amendment that for the first time raises an objection to in rem jurisdiction by analogy to the personal jurisdiction objection provision in Civil Rule 12(h)(1)(B). The amendment should be permitted only if it is permitted as a matter of course under Rule 15(a).

[¶34] A claimant's motion to dismiss the action is further governed by subdivisions (6)(c), (8)(b), and (8)(c).

Subdivision (6)

[¶35] Subdivision (6) illustrates the adaptation of an admiralty procedure to the different needs of civil forfeiture. Rule C(6) permits interrogatories to be served with the complaint in an in rem action without limiting the subjects of inquiry. Civil forfeiture practice does not require such an extensive departure from ordinary civil practice. It remains useful, however, to permit the government to file limited interrogatories at any time after a claim is filed to gather information that bears on the claimant's standing. Subdivisions (8)(b) and (c) allow a claimant to move to dismiss only if the claimant has standing, and recognize the government's right to move to dismiss a claim for lack of standing. Subdivision (6) interrogatories are integrated with these provisions in that the interrogatories are limited to the claimant's identity and relationship to the defendant property. If the claimant asserts a relationship to the property as bailee, the interrogatories can inquire into the bailor's interest in the property and the bailee's relationship to the bailor. The claimant can accelerate the time to serve subdivision (6) interrogatories by serving a motion to dismiss—the interrogatories must be served within 20 days after the motion is served. Integration is further accomplished by deferring the government's obligation to respond to a motion to dismiss until 20 days after the claimant moving to dismiss has answered the interrogatories.

[¶36] Special interrogatories served under Rule G(6) do not count against the presumptive 25-interrogatory limit established by Rule 33(a). Rule 33 procedure otherwise applies to these interrogatories.

[¶37] Subdivision (6) supersedes the discovery "moratorium" of Rule 26(d) and the broader interrogatories permitted for admiralty proceedings by Rule C(6).

Subdivision (7)

[¶38] Paragraph (a). Paragraph (a) is adapted from Rule E(9)(b). It provides for preservation orders when the government does not have actual possession of the defendant property. It also goes beyond Rule E(9) by recognizing the need to prevent use of the defendant property in ongoing criminal offenses.

[¶39] Paragraph (b). Paragraph (b)(i)(C) recognizes the authority, already exercised in some cases, to order sale of property subject to a defaulted mortgage or to defaulted taxes. The authority is narrowly confined to mortgages and tax liens; other lien interests may be addressed, if at all, only through the general good-cause provision. The court must carefully weigh the competing interests in each case.

[¶40] Paragraph (b)(i)(D) establishes authority to order sale for good cause. Good cause may be shown when the property is subject to diminution in value. Care should be taken before ordering sale to avoid diminished value.

[¶41] Paragraph (b)(iii) recognizes that if the court approves, the interests of all parties may be served by their agreement to sale, aspects of the sale, or sale procedures that depart from governing statutory procedures.

[¶42] Paragraph (c) draws from Rule E(9)(a), (b), and (c). Disposition of the proceeds as provided by law may require resolution of disputed issues. A mortgagee's claim to the property or sale proceeds, for example, may be disputed on the ground that the mortgage is not genuine. An undisputed lien claim, on the other hand, may be recognized by payment after an interlocutory sale.

Subdivision (8)

[¶43] Subdivision (8) addresses a number of issues that are unique to civil forfeiture actions.

[¶44] Paragraph (a). Standing to suppress use of seized property as evidence is governed by principles distinct from the principles that govern claim standing. A claimant with standing to contest forfeiture may not have standing to seek suppression. Rule G does not of itself create a basis of suppression standing that does not otherwise exist.

[¶45] Paragraph (b). Paragraph (b)(i) is one element of the system that integrates the procedures for determining a claimant's standing to claim and for deciding a claimant's motion to dismiss the action. Under paragraph (c)(ii), a motion to dismiss the action cannot be addressed until the court has decided any government motion to strike the claim or answer. This procedure is reflected in the (b)(i) reminder that a motion to dismiss the forfeiture action may be made only by a claimant who establishes claim standing. The government, moreover, need not respond to a claimant's motion to dismiss until 20 days after the claimant has answered any subdivision (6) interrogatories.

[¶46] Paragraph (b)(ii) mirrors 18 U.S.C. §983(a)(3)(D). It applies only to an action independently governed by §983(a)(3)(D), implying nothing as to actions outside §983(a)(3)(D). The adequacy of the complaint is measured against the pleading requirements of subdivision (2), not against the quality of the evidence available to the government when the complaint was filed.

[¶47] Paragraph (c). As noted with paragraph (b), paragraph (c) governs the procedure for determining whether a claimant has standing. It does not address the principles that govern claim standing.

[¶48] Paragraph (c)(i)(A) provides that the government may move to strike a claim or answer for failure to comply with the pleading requirements of subdivision (5) or to answer subdivision (6) interrogatories. As with other pleadings, the court should strike a claim or answer only if satisfied that an opportunity should not be afforded to cure the defects under Rule 15. Not every failure to respond to subdivision (6) interrogatories warrants an order striking the claim. But the special role that subdivision (6) plays in the scheme for determining claim standing may justify a somewhat more demanding approach than the general approach to discovery sanctions under Rule 37.

[¶49] Paragraph (c)(ii) directs that a motion to strike a claim or answer be decided before any motion by the claimant to dismiss the action. A claimant who lacks standing is not entitled to challenge the forfeiture on the merits.

[¶50] Paragraph (c)(ii) further identifies three procedures for addressing claim standing. If a claim fails on its face to show facts that support claim standing, the claim can be dismissed by judgment on the pleadings. If the claim shows facts that would support claim standing, those facts can be tested by a motion for summary judgment. If material facts are disputed, precluding a grant of summary judgment, the court may hold an evidentiary hearing. The evidentiary hearing is held by the court without a jury. The claimant has the burden to establish claim standing at a hearing; procedure on a government summary judgment motion reflects this allocation of the burden.

[¶51] Paragraph (d). The hardship release provisions of 18 U.S.C. §983(f) do not apply to a civil forfeiture action exempted from §983 by §983(i).

[¶52] Paragraph (d)(ii) reflects the venue provisions of 18 U.S.C. §983(f)(3)(A) as a guide to practitioners. In addition, it makes clear the status of a civil forfeiture action as a "civil action" eligible for transfer under 28 U.S.C. §1404. A transfer decision must be made on the circumstances of the particular proceeding. The district where the forfeiture action is filed has the advantage of bringing all related proceedings together, avoiding the waste that flows from consideration of different parts of the same forfeiture proceeding in the court where the warrant issued or the court where the property was seized. Transfer to that court would serve consolidation, the purpose that underlies nationwide enforcement of a seizure warrant. But there may be offsetting advantages in retaining the petition where it was filed. The claimant may not be able to litigate, effectively or at all, in a distant court. Issues relevant to the petition may be better litigated where the property was seized or where the warrant issued. One element, for example, is whether the claimant has sufficient ties to the community to provide assurance that the property will be available at the time of trial. Another is whether continued government possession would prevent the claimant from working. Determining whether seizure of the claimant's automobile prevents work may turn on assessing the realities of local public transit facilities.

[¶53] Paragraph (e). The Excessive Fines Clause of the Eighth Amendment forbids an excessive forfeiture. *U.S. v. Bajakajian*, 524 U.S. 321 (1998). 18 U.S.C. §983(g) provides a "petition" "to determine whether the forfeiture was constitutionally excessive" based on finding "that the forfeiture is grossly disproportional to the offense." Paragraph (e) describes the procedure for §983(g) mitigation petitions and adopts the same procedure for forfeiture actions that fall outside §983(g). The procedure is by motion, either for summary judgment or for mitigation after a forfeiture judgment is entered. The claimant must give notice of this defense by pleading, but failure to raise the defense in the initial answer may be cured by amendment under Rule 15. The issues that bear on mitigation often are separate from the issues that determine forfeiture. For that reason it may be convenient to resolve the issue by summary judgment before trial on the forfeiture issues. Often, however, it will be more convenient to determine first whether the property is to be forfeited. Whichever time is chosen to address mitigation, the parties must have had the opportunity to conduct civil discovery on the defense. The extent and timing of discovery are governed by the ordinary rules.

Subdivision (9)

[¶54] Subdivision (9) serves as a reminder of the need to demand jury trial under Rule 38. It does not expand the right to jury trial. *See U.S. v. One Parcel of Property Located at 32 Medley Lane*, 2005 WL 465241 (D.Conn.2005), ruling that the court, not the jury, determines whether a forfeiture is constitutionally excessive.

FRE NOTES

FRE 101 – 2011 NOTES OF ADVISORY COMMITTEE

[¶1] The language of Rule 101 has been amended, and definitions have been added, as part of the general restyling of the Evidence Rules to make them more easily understood and to make style and terminology consistent throughout the rules. These changes are intended to be stylistic only. There is no intent to change any result in any ruling on evidence admissibility.[1]

[¶2] The reference to electronically stored information is intended to track the language of Fed. R. Civ. P. 34.

[¶3] *The Style Project.* The Evidence Rules are the fourth set of national procedural rules to be restyled. The restyled Rules of Appellate Procedure took effect in 1998. The restyled Rules of Criminal Procedure took effect in 2002. The restyled Rules of Civil Procedure took effect in 2007. The restyled Rules of Evidence apply the same general drafting guidelines and principles used in restyling the Appellate, Criminal, and Civil Rules.

[¶4] *General Guidelines.* Guidance in drafting, usage, and style was provided by Bryan Garner, *Guidelines for Drafting and Editing Court Rules*, Administrative Office of the United States Courts (1969) and Bryan Garner, *Dictionary of Modern Legal Usage* (2d ed. 1995). *See also* Joseph Kimble, *Guiding Principles for Restyling the Civil Rules*, in *Preliminary Draft of Proposed Style Revision of the Federal Rules of Civil Procedure*, at page x (Feb. 2005) (available at http://www.uscourts.gov/uscourts/RulesAndPolicies/rules/Prelim_draft_proposed_pt1.pdf); Joseph Kimble, *Lessons in Drafting from the New Federal Rules of Civil Procedure*, 12 Scribes J. Legal Writing 25 (2008-2009). For specific commentary on the Evidence restyling project, see Joseph Kimble, *Drafting Examples from the Proposed New Federal Rules of Evidence*, 88 Mich. B.J. 52 (Aug. 2009); 88 Mich. B.J. 46 (Sept. 2009); 88 Mich. B.J. 54 (Oct. 2009); 88 Mich. B.J. 50 (Nov. 2009).

[¶5] *Formatting Changes.* Many of the changes in the restyled Evidence Rules result from using format to achieve clearer presentations. The rules are broken down into constituent parts, using progressively indented subparagraphs with headings and substituting vertical for horizontal lists. "Hanging indents" are used throughout. These formatting changes make the structure of the rules graphic and make the restyled rules easier to read and understand even when the words are not changed. Rules 103, 404(b), 606(b), and 612 illustrate the benefits of formatting changes.

[¶6] *Changes to Reduce Inconsistent, Ambiguous, Redundant, Repetitive, or Archaic Words.* The restyled rules reduce the use of inconsistent terms that say the same thing in different ways. Because different words are presumed to have different meanings, such inconsistencies can result in confusion. The restyled rules reduce inconsistencies by using the same words to express the same meaning. For example, consistent expression is achieved by not switching between "accused" and "defendant" or between "party opponent" and "opposing party" or between the various formulations of civil and criminal action/case/proceeding.

[¶7] The restyled rules minimize the use of inherently ambiguous words. For example, the word "shall" can mean "must," "may," or something else, depending on context. The potential for confusion is exacerbated by the fact the word "shall" is no longer generally used in spoken or clearly written English. The restyled rules replace "shall" with "must," "may," or "should," depending on which one the context and established interpretation make correct in each rule.

[¶8] The restyled rules minimize the use of redundant "intensifiers." These are expressions that attempt to add emphasis, but instead state the obvious and create negative implications for other rules. The absence of intensifiers in the restyled rules does not change their substantive meaning. *See, e.g.*, Rule 104(c) (omitting "in all cases"); Rule 602 (omitting "but need not"); Rule 611(b) (omitting "in the exercise of discretion").

[¶9] The restyled rules also remove words and concepts that are outdated or redundant.

[¶10] *Rule Numbers.* The restyled rules keep the same numbers to minimize the effect on research. Subdivisions have been rearranged within some rules to achieve greater clarity and simplicity.

[¶11] *No Substantive Change.* The Committee made special efforts to reject any purported style improvement that might result in a substantive change in the application of a rule. The Committee considered a change to be "substantive" if any of the following conditions were met:

a. Under the existing practice in any circuit, the change could lead to a different result on a question of admissibility (e.g., a change that requires a court to provide either a less or more stringent standard in evaluating the admissibility of particular evidence);

b. Under the existing practice in any circuit, it could lead to a change in the procedure by which an admissibility decision is made (e.g., a change in the time in which an objection must be made, or a change in whether a court must hold a hearing on an admissibility question);

c. The change would restructure a rule in a way that would alter the approach that courts and litigants have used to think about, and argue about, questions of admissibility (e.g., merging Rules 104(a) and 104(b) into a single subdivision); or

d. The amendment would change a "sacred phrase"—one that has become so familiar in practice that to alter it would be unduly disruptive to practice and expectations. Examples in the Evidence Rules include "unfair prejudice" and "truth of the matter asserted."

1. **Editor's note:** The Advisory Committee Note in ¶1 was repeated for every FRE. Because this note was redundant, we have omitted it from FREs 102-1103.

FRE 103 – 2000 NOTES OF ADVISORY COMMITTEE

[¶1] The amendment applies to all rulings on evidence whether they occur at or before trial, including so-called "*in limine*" rulings. One of the most difficult questions arising from *in limine* and other evidentiary rulings is whether a losing party must renew an objection or offer of proof when the evidence is or would be offered at trial, in order to preserve a claim of error on appeal. Courts have taken differing approaches to this question. Some courts have held that a renewal at the time the evidence is to be offered at trial is always required. *See, e.g., Collins v. Wayne Corp.*, 621 F.2d 777 (5th Cir.1980). Some courts have taken a more flexible approach, holding that renewal is not required if the issue decided is one that (1) was fairly presented to the trial court for an initial ruling, (2) may be decided as a final matter before the evidence is actually offered, and (3) was ruled on definitively by the trial judge. *See, e.g., Rosenfeld v. Basquiat*, 78 F.3d 84 (2d Cir.1996) (admissibility of former testimony under the Dead Man's Statute; renewal not required). Other courts have distinguished between objections to evidence, which must be renewed when evidence is offered, and offers of proof, which need not be renewed after a definitive determination is made that the evidence is inadmissible. *See, e.g., Fusco v. General Motors Corp.*, 11 F.3d 259 (1st Cir.1993). Another court, aware of this Committee's proposed amendment, has adopted its approach. *Wilson v. Williams*, 182 F.3d 562 (7th Cir.1999) (en banc). Differing views on this question create uncertainty for litigants and unnecessary work for the appellate courts.

[¶2] The amendment provides that a claim of error with respect to a definitive ruling is preserved for review when the party has otherwise satisfied the objection or offer of proof requirements of Rule 103(a). When the ruling is definitive, a renewed objection or offer of proof at the time the evidence is to be offered is more a formalism than a necessity. *See* Fed.R.Civ.P. 46 (formal exceptions unnecessary); Fed.R.Cr.P. 51 (same); *United States v. Mejia-Alarcon*, 995 F.2d 982, 986 (10th Cir.1993) ("Requiring a party to renew an objection when the district court has issued a definitive ruling on a matter that can be fairly decided before trial would be in the nature of a formal exception and therefore unnecessary."). On the other hand, when the trial court appears to have reserved its ruling or to have indicated that the ruling is provisional, it makes sense to require the party to bring the issue to the court's attention subsequently. *See, e.g., United States v. Vest*, 116 F.3d 1179, 1188 (7th Cir.1997) (where the trial court ruled *in limine* that testimony from defense witnesses could not be admitted, but allowed the defendant to seek leave at trial to call the witnesses should their testimony turn out to be relevant, the defendant's failure to seek such leave at trial meant that it was "too late to reopen the issue now on appeal"); *United States v. Valenti*, 60 F.3d 941 (2d Cir.1995) (failure to proffer evidence at trial waives any claim of error where the trial judge had stated that he would reserve judgment on the *in limine* motion until he had heard the trial evidence).

[¶3] The amendment imposes the obligation on counsel to clarify whether an *in limine* or other evidentiary ruling is definitive when there is doubt on that point. *See, e.g., Walden v. Georgia-Pacific Corp.*, 126 F.3d 506, 520 (3d Cir.1997) (although "the district court told plaintiffs' counsel not to reargue every ruling, it did not countermand its clear opening statement that all of its rulings were tentative, and counsel never requested clarification, as he might have done.").

[¶4] Even where the court's ruling is definitive, nothing in the amendment prohibits the court from revisiting its decision when the evidence is to be offered. If the court changes its initial ruling, or if the opposing party violates the terms of the initial ruling, objection must be made when the evidence is offered to preserve the claim of error for appeal. The error, if any, in such a situation occurs only when the evidence is offered and admitted. *United States Aviation Underwriters, Inc. v. Olympia Wings, Inc.*, 896 F.2d 949, 956 (5th Cir.1990) ("objection is required to preserve error when an opponent, or the court itself, violates a motion *in limine* that was granted"); *United States v. Roenigk*, 810 F.2d 809 (8th Cir.1987) (claim of error was not preserved where the defendant failed to object at trial to secure the benefit of a favorable advance ruling).

[¶5] A definitive advance ruling is reviewed in light of the facts and circumstances before the trial court at the time of the ruling. If the relevant facts and circumstances change materially after the advance ruling has been made, those facts and circumstances cannot be relied upon on appeal unless they have been brought to the attention of the trial court by way of a renewed, and timely, objection, offer of proof, or motion to strike. *See Old Chief v. United States*, 519 U.S. 172, 182, n.6 (1997) ("It is important that a reviewing court evaluate the trial court's decision from its perspective when it had to rule and not indulge in review by hindsight."). Similarly, if the court decides in an advance ruling that proffered evidence is admissible subject to the eventual introduction by the proponent of a foundation for the evidence, and that foundation is never provided, the opponent cannot claim error based on the failure to establish the foundation unless the opponent calls that failure to the court's attention by a timely motion to strike or other suitable motion. *See Huddleston v. United States*, 485 U.S. 681, 690, n.7 (1988) ("It is, of course, not the responsibility of the judge *sua sponte* to ensure that the foundation evidence is offered; the objector must move to strike the evidence if at the close of the trial the offeror has failed to satisfy the condition.").

[¶6] Nothing in the amendment is intended to affect the provisions of Fed.R.Civ.P. 72(a) or 28 U.S.C. §636(b)(1) pertaining to nondispositive pretrial rulings by magistrate judges in proceedings that are not before a magistrate judge by consent of the parties. Fed.R.Civ.P. 72(a) provides that a party who fails to file a written objection to a magistrate judge's nondispositive order within ten days of receiving a copy "may not thereafter assign as error a defect" in the order. 28 U.S.C. §636(b)(1) provides that any party "may serve and file written objections to such proposed findings and recommendations as provided by rules of court" within ten days of receiving a copy of the order. Several courts have held that a party must comply with this statutory provision in order to preserve a claim of error. *See, e.g., Wells v. Shriners Hospital*, 109 F.3d 198, 200 (4th Cir.1997) ("[i]n this circuit, as in others, a party 'may' file objections within ten days or he may not, as he chooses, but he 'shall' do so if he wishes further consideration."). When Fed.R.Civ.P. 72(a) or 28 U.S.C. §636(b)(1) is operative, its requirement must be satisfied in order for a party to preserve a claim of error on appeal, even where Evidence Rule 103(a) would not require a subsequent objection or offer of proof.

[¶7] Nothing in the amendment is intended to affect the rule set forth in *Luce v. United States*, 469 U.S. 38 (1984), and its progeny. The amendment provides that an objection or offer of proof need not be renewed to preserve a claim of error with respect to a definitive pretrial ruling. Luce answers affirmatively a separate question: whether a criminal defendant must testify at trial in order to preserve a claim of error predicated upon a trial court's decision to admit the defendant's prior convictions for impeachment. The Luce principle has been extended by many lower courts to other situations. *See United States v. DiMatteo*, 759 F.2d 831 (11th Cir.1985) (applying Luce where the defendant's witness would be impeached with evidence offered under Rule 608). *See also United States v. Goldman*, 41 F.3d 785, 788 (1st Cir.1994) ("Although Luce involved impeachment by conviction under Rule 609, the reasons given by the Supreme Court for requiring the defendant to testify apply with full force to the kind of Rule 403 and 404 objections that are advanced by Goldman in this case."); *Palmieri v. DeFaria*, 88 F.3d 136 (2d Cir.1996) (where the plaintiff decided to take an adverse judgment rather than challenge an advance ruling by putting on evidence at trial, the *in limine* ruling would not be reviewed on appeal); *United States v. Ortiz*, 857 F.2d 900 (2d Cir.1988) (where uncharged misconduct is ruled admissible if the defendant pursues a certain defense, the defendant must actually pursue that defense at trial in order to preserve a claim of error on appeal); *United States v. Bond*, 87 F.3d 695 (5th Cir.1996) (where the trial court rules *in limine* that the defendant would waive his fifth amendment privilege were he to testify, the defendant must take the stand and testify in order to challenge that ruling on appeal).

[¶8] The amendment does not purport to answer whether a party who objects to evidence that the court finds admissible in a definitive ruling, and who then offers the evidence to "remove the sting" of its anticipated prejudicial effect, thereby waives the right to appeal the trial court's ruling. *See, e.g., United States v. Fisher*, 106 F.3d 622 (5th Cir.1997) (where the trial judge ruled *in limine* that the government could use a prior conviction to impeach the defendant if he testified, the defendant did not waive his right to appeal by introducing the conviction on direct examination); *Judd v. Rodman*, 105 F.3d 1339 (11th Cir.1997) (an objection made *in limine* is sufficient to preserve a claim of error when the movant, as a matter of trial strategy, presents the objectionable evidence herself on direct examination to minimize its prejudicial effect); *Gill v. Thomas*, 83 F.3d 537, 540 (1st Cir. 1996) ("by offering the misdemeanor evidence himself, Gill waived his opportunity to object and thus did not preserve the issue for appeal"); *United States v. Williams*, 939 F.2d 721 (9th Cir.1991) (objection to impeachment evidence was waived where the defendant was impeached on direct examination).

FRE 201 – 1972 NOTES OF ADVISORY COMMITTEE

[¶1] Subdivision (a). This is the only evidence rule on the subject of judicial notice. It deals only with judicial notice of "adjudicative" facts. No rule deals with judicial notice of "legislative" facts. Judicial notice of matters of foreign law is treated in Rule 44.1 of the Federal Rules of Civil Procedure and Rule 26.1 of the Federal Rules of Criminal Procedure.

[¶2] The omission of any treatment of legislative facts results from fundamental differences between adjudicative facts and legislative facts. Adjudicative facts are simply the facts of the particular case. Legislative facts, on the other hand, are those which have relevance to legal reasoning and the lawmaking process, whether in the formulation of a legal principle or ruling by a judge or court or in the enactment of a legislative body. The terminology was coined by Professor Kenneth Davis in his article An Approach to Problems of Evidence in the Administrative Process, 55 Harv.L.Rev. 364, 404-407 (1942). The following discussion draws extensively upon his writings. In addition, see the same author's Judicial Notice, 55 Colum.L. Rev. 945 (1955); Administrative Law Treatise, ch. 15 (1958); A System of Judicial Notice Based on Fairness and Convenience, in Perspectives of Law 69 (1964).

[¶3] The usual method of establishing adjudicative facts in through the introduction of evidence, ordinarily consisting of the testimony of witnesses. If particular facts are outside of reasonable controversy, this process is dispensed with as unnecessary. A high degree of indisputability is the essential prerequisite.

[¶4] Legislative facts are quite different. As Professor Davis says:

[¶5] "My opinion is that judge-made law would stop growing if judges, in thinking about questions of law and policy, were forbidden to take into account the facts they believe, as distinguished from facts which are 'clearly * * * within the domain of the indisputable.' Facts most needed in thinking about difficult problems of law and policy have a way of being outside the domain of the clearly indisputable." A System of Judicial Notice Based on Fairness and Convenience, supra, at 82.

[¶6] An illustration is *Hawkins v. United States*, 358 U.S. 74, 79 S.Ct. 136, 3 L.Ed.2d 125 (1958), in which the Court refused to discard the common law rule that one spouse could not testify against the other, saying, "Adverse testimony given in criminal proceedings would, we think, be likely to destroy almost any marriage." This conclusion has a large intermixture of fact, but the factual aspect is scarcely "indisputable." *See* Hutchins and Slesinger, Some Observations on the Law of Evidence – Family Relations, 13 Minn.L.Rev. 675 (1929). If the destructive effect of the giving of adverse testimony by a spouse is not indisputable, should the Court have refrained from considering it in the absence of supporting evidence?

[¶7] "If the Model Code or the Uniform Rules had been applicable, the Court would have been barred from thinking about the essential factual ingredient of the problems before it, and such a result would be obviously intolerable. What the law needs as its growing points is more, not less, judicial thinking about the factual ingredients of problems of what the law ought to be, and the needed facts are seldom 'clearly' indisputable." Davis, supra, at 83.

[¶8] Professor Morgan gave the following description of the methodology of determining domestic law:

[¶9] "In determining the content or applicability of a rule of domestic law, the judge is unrestricted in his investigation and conclusion. He may reject the propositions of either party or of both parties. He may consult the sources of pertinent data to which they refer, or he may refuse to do so. He may make an independent search for persuasive data or rest content with what he has or what the parties present. * * * [T]he parties do no more than to assist; they control no part of the process." Morgan, Judicial Notice, 57 Harv.L.Rev. 269, 270-271 (1944).

[¶10] This is the view which should govern judicial access to legislative facts. It renders inappropriate any limitation in the form of indisputability, any formal requirements of notice other than those already inherent in affording opportunity to hear and be heard and exchanging briefs, and any requirement of formal findings at any level. It should, however, leave open the possibility of introducing evidence through regular channels in appropriate situations. *See Borden's Farm Products Co. v. Baldwin*, 293 U.S. 194, 55 S.Ct. 187, 79 L.Ed. 281 (1934), where the cause was remanded for the taking of evidence as to the economic conditions and trade practices underlying the New York Milk Control Law.

[¶11] Similar considerations govern the judicial use of nonadjudicative facts in ways other than formulating laws and rules. Thayer described them as a part of the judicial reasoning process.

[¶12] "In conducting a process of judicial reasoning, as of other reasoning, not a step can be taken without assuming something which has not been proved; and the capacity to do this with competent judgment and efficiency, is imputed to judges and juries as part of their necessary mental outfit." Thayer, Preliminary Treatise on Evidence 279-280 (1898).

[¶13] As Professor Davis points out, A System of Judicial Notice Based on Fairness and Convenience, in Perspectives of Law 69, 73 (1964), every case involves the use of hundreds or thousands of non-evidence facts. When a witness in an automobile accident case says "car," everyone, judge and jury included, furnishes, from non-evidence sources within himself, the supplementing information that the "car" is an automobile, not a railroad car, that it is self-propelled, probably by an internal combustion engine, that it may be assumed to have four wheels with pneumatic rubber tires, and so on. The judicial process cannot construct every case from scratch, like Descartes creating a world based on the postulate Cogito, ergo sum. These items could not possibly be introduced into evidence, and no one suggests that they be. Nor are they appropriate subjects for any formalized treatment of judicial notice of facts. See Levin and Levy, Persuading the Jury with Facts Not in Evidence: The Fiction-Science Spectrum, 105 U.Pa.L.Rev. 139 (1956).

[¶14] Another aspect of what Thayer had in mind is the use of non-evidence facts to appraise or assess the adjudicative facts of the case. Pairs of cases from two jurisdictions illustrate this use and also the difference between non-evidence facts thus used and adjudicative facts. In *People v. Strook*, 347 Ill. 460, 179 N.E. 821 (1932), venue in Cook County had been held not established by testimony that the crime was committed at 7956 South Chicago Avenue, since judicial notice would not be taken that the address was in Chicago. However, the same court subsequently ruled that venue in Cook County was established by testimony that a crime occurred at 8900 South Anthony Avenue, since notice would be taken of the common practice of omitting the name of the city when speaking of local addresses, and the witness was testifying in Chicago. *People v. Pride*, 16 Ill.2d 82, 156 N.E.2d 551 (1951). And in *Hughes v. Vestal*, 264 N.C. 500, 142 S.E.2d 361 (1965), the Supreme Court of North Carolina disapproved the trial judge's admission in evidence of a state-published table of automobile stopping distances on the basis of judicial notice, though the court itself had referred to the same table in an earlier case in a "rhetorical and illustrative" way in determining that the defendant could not have stopped her car in time to avoid striking a child who suddenly appeared in the highway and that a non-suit was properly granted. *Ennis v. Dupree*, 262 N.C. 224, 136 S.E.2d 702 (1964). *See also Brown v. Hale*, 263 N.C. 176, 139 S.E.2d 210 (1964); *Clayton v. Rimmer*, 262 N.C. 302, 136 S.E.2d 562 (1964). It is apparent that this use of non-evidence facts in evaluating the adjudicative facts of the case is not an appropriate subject for a formalized judicial notice treatment.

[¶15] In view of these considerations, the regulation of judicial notice of facts by the present rule extends only to adjudicative facts.

[¶16] What, then, are "adjudicative" facts? Davis refers to them as those "which relate to the parties," or more fully:

[¶17] "When a court or an agency finds facts concerning the immediate parties—who did what, where, when, how, and with what motive or intent—the court or agency is performing an adjudicative function, and the facts are conveniently called adjudicative facts. * * *

[¶18] "Stated in other terms, the adjudicative facts are those to which the law is applied in the process of adjudication. They are the facts that normally go to the jury in a jury case. They relate to the parties, their activities, their properties, their businesses." 2 Administrative Law Treatise 353.

[¶19] **Subdivision (b).** With respect to judicial notice of adjudicative facts, the tradition has been one of caution in requiring that the matter be beyond reasonable controversy. This tradition of circumspection appears to be soundly based, and no reason to depart from it is apparent. As Professor Davis says:

[¶20] "The reason we use trial-type procedure, I think, is that we make the practical judgement, on the basis of experience, that taking evidence, subject to cross-examination and rebuttal, is the best way to resolve controversies involving disputes of adjudicative facts, that is, facts pertaining to the parties. The reason we require a determination on the record is that we think fair procedure in resolving disputes of adjudicative facts calls for giving each party a chance to meet in the appropriate fashion the facts that come to the tribunal's attention, and the appropriate fashion for meeting disputed adjudicative facts includes rebuttal evidence, cross-examination, usually confrontation, and argument (either written or oral or both). The key to a fair trial is opportunity to use the appropriate weapons (rebuttal evidence, cross-examination, and argument) to meet adverse materials that come to the tribunal's attention." A System of Judicial Notice Based on Fairness and Convenience, in Perspectives of Law 69, 93 (1964).

[¶21] The rule proceeds upon the theory that these considerations call for dispensing with traditional methods of proof only in clear cases. Compare Professor Davis' conclusion that judicial notice should be a matter of convenience, subject to requirements of procedural fairness. *Id.*, 94.

[¶22] This rule is consistent with Uniform Rule 9(1) and (2) which limit judicial notice of facts to those "so universally known that they cannot reasonably be the subject of dispute," those "so generally known or of such common notoriety within the territorial jurisdiction of the court that they cannot reasonably be the subject of dispute," and those "capable of immediate and accurate determination by resort to easily accessible sources of indisputable accuracy." The traditional textbook treatment has included these general categories (matters of common knowledge, facts capable of verification), McCormick §§324, 325, and then has passed on into detailed treatment of such specific topics as facts relating to the personnel and records of the court, Id. §327, and other governmental facts, Id. §328. The California draftsmen, with a background of detailed statutory regulation of judicial notice, followed a somewhat similar pattern. California Evidence Code §§451, 452. The Uniform Rules, however, were drafted on the theory that these particular matters are included within the general categories and need no specific mention. This approach is followed in the present rule.

[¶23] The phrase "propositions of generalized knowledge," found in Uniform Rule 9(1) and (2) is not included in the present rule. It was, it is believed, originally included in Model Code Rules 801 and 802 primarily in order to afford some minimum recognition to the right of the judge in his "legislative" capacity (not acting as the trier of fact) to take judicial notice of very limited categories of generalized knowledge. The limitations thus imposed have been discarded herein as undesirable, unworkable, and contrary to existing practice. What is left, then, to be considered, is the status of a "proposition of generalized knowledge" as an "adjudicative" fact to be noticed judicially and communicated by the judge to the jury. Thus viewed, it is considered to be lacking practical significance. While judges use judicial notice of "propositions of generalized knowledge" in a variety of situations: determining the validity and meaning of statutes, formulating common law rules, deciding whether evidence should be admitted, assessing the sufficiency and effect of evidence, all are essentially nonadjudicative in nature. When judicial notice is seen as a significant vehicle for progress in the law, these are the areas involved, particularly in developing fields of scientific knowledge. See McCormick 712. It is not believed that judges now instruct juries as to "propositions of generalized knowledge" derived from encyclopedias or other sources, or that they are likely to do so, or, indeed, that it is desirable that they do so. There is a vast difference between ruling on the basis of judicial notice that radar evidence of speed is admissible and explaining to the jury its principles and degree of accuracy, or between using a table of stopping distances of automobiles at various speeds in a judicial evaluation of testimony and telling the jury its precise application in the case. For cases raising doubt as to the propriety of the use of medical texts by lay triers of fact in passing on disability claims in administrative proceedings, *see Sayers v. Gardner*, 380 F.2d 940 (6th Cir.1967); *Ross v. Gardner*, 365 F.2d 554 (6th Cir.1966); *Sosna v. Celebrezze*, 234 F.Supp. 289 (E.D. Pa.1964); *Glendenning v. Ribicoff*, 213 F.Supp. 301 (W.D. Mo.1962).

[¶24] Subdivisions (c) and (d). Under subdivision (c) the judge has a discretionary authority to take judicial notice, regardless of whether he is so requested by a party. The taking of judicial notice is mandatory, under subdivision (d), only when a party requests it and the necessary information is supplied. This scheme is believed to reflect existing practice. It is simple and workable. It avoids troublesome distinctions in the many situations in which the process of taking judicial notice is not recognized as such.

[¶25] Compare Uniform Rule 9 making judicial notice of facts universally known mandatory without request, and making judicial notice of facts generally known in the jurisdiction or capable of determination by resort to accurate sources discretionary in the absence of request but mandatory if request is made and the information furnished. But see Uniform Rule 10(3), which directs the judge to decline to take judicial notice if available information fails to convince him that the matter falls clearly within Uniform Rule 9 or is insufficient to enable him to notice it judicially. Substantially the same approach is found in California Evidence Code §§451-453 and in New Jersey Evidence Rule 9. In contrast, the present rule treats alike all adjudicative facts which are subject to judicial notice.

[¶26] Subdivision (e). Basic considerations of procedural fairness demand an opportunity to be heard on the propriety of taking judicial notice and the tenor of the matter noticed. The rule requires the granting of that opportunity upon request. No formal scheme of giving notice is provided. An adversely affected party may learn in advance that judicial notice is in contemplation, either by virtue of being served with a copy of a request by another party under subdivision (d) that judicial notice be taken, or through an advance indication by the judge. Or he may have no advance notice at all. The likelihood of the latter is enhanced by the frequent failure to recognize judicial notice as such. And in the absence of advance notice, a request made after the fact could not in fairness be considered untimely. See the provision for hearing on timely request in the Administrative Procedure Act, 5 U.S.C. §556(e). See also Revised Model State Administrative Procedure Act (1961), 9C U.L.A. §10(4) (Supp. 1967).

[¶27] Subdivision (f). In accord with the usual view, judicial notice may be taken at any stage of the proceedings, whether in the trial court or on appeal. Uniform Rule 12; California Evidence Code §459; Kansas Rules of Evidence §60-412; New Jersey Evidence Rule 12; McCormick §330, p. 712.

[¶28] Subdivision (g). Much of the controversy about judicial notice has centered upon the question whether evidence should be admitted in disproof of facts of which judicial notice is taken.

[¶29] The writers have been divided. Favoring admissibility are Thayer, Preliminary Treatise on Evidence 308 (1898); 9 Wigmore §2567; Davis, A System of Judicial Notice Based on Fairness and Convenience, in Perspectives of Law, 69, 76-77 (1964). Opposing admissibility are Keeffe, Landis and Shaad, Sense and Nonsense about Judicial Notice, 2 Stan.L.Rev. 664, 668 (1950); McNaughton, Judicial Notice – Excerpts Relating to the Morgan-Whitmore Controversy, 14 Vand.L.Rev. 779 (1961); Morgan, Judicial Notice, 57 Harv.L.Rev. 269, 279 (1944); McCormick 710-711. The Model Code and the Uniform Rules are predicated upon indisputability of judicially noticed facts.

[¶30] The proponents of admitting evidence in disproof have concentrated largely upon legislative facts. Since the present rule deals only with judicial notice of adjudicative facts, arguments directed to legislative facts lose their relevancy.

[¶31] Within its relatively narrow area of adjudicative facts, the rule contemplates there is to be no evidence before the jury in disproof. The judge instructs the jury to take judicially noticed facts as established. This position is justified by the undesirable effects of the opposite rule in limiting the rebutting party, though not his opponent, to admissible evidence, in defeating the reasons for judicial notice, and in affecting the substantive law to an extent and in ways largely unforeseeable. Ample protection and flexibility are afforded by the broad provision for opportunity to be heard on request, set forth in subdivision (e).

[¶32] Authority upon the propriety of taking judicial notice against an accused in a criminal case with respect to matters other than venue is relatively meager. Proceeding upon the theory that the right of jury trial does not extend to matters which are beyond reasonable dispute, the rule does not distinguish between criminal and civil cases. *People v. Mayes*, 113 Cal. 618, 45 P. 860 (1896); *Ross v. United States*, 374 F.2d 97 (8th Cir.1967). *Cf. State v. Main*, 94 R.I. 338, 180 A.2d 814 (1962); *State v. Lawrence*, 120 Utah 323, 234 P.2d 600 (1951).

[¶33] Note on Judicial Notice of Law. By rules effective July 1, 1966, the method of invoking the law of a foreign country is covered elsewhere. Rule 44.1 of the Federal Rules of Civil Procedure; Rule 26.1 of the Federal Rules of Criminal Procedure. These two new admirably designed rules are founded upon the assumption that the manner in which law is fed into the judicial process is never a proper concern of the rules of evidence but rather of the rules of procedure. The Advisory Committee on Evidence, believing that this assumption is entirely correct, proposes no evidence rule with respect to judicial notice of law, and suggests that those matters of law which, in addition to foreign-country law, have traditionally been treated as requiring pleading and proof and more recently as the subject of judicial notice be left to the Rules of Civil and Criminal Procedure.

FRE 404 – 2006 NOTES OF ADVISORY COMMITTEE

[¶1] The Rule has been amended to clarify that in a civil case evidence of a person's character is never admissible to prove that the person acted in conformity with the character trait. The amendment resolves the dispute in the case law over whether the exceptions in subdivisions (a)(1) and (2) permit the circumstantial use of character evidence in civil cases. *Compare Carson v. Polley*, 689 F.2d 562, 576 (5th Cir.1982) ("when a central issue in a case is close to one of a criminal nature, the exceptions to the Rule 404(a) ban on character evidence may be invoked"), *with SEC v. Towers Financial Corp.*, 966 F.Supp. 203 (S.D.N.Y.1997) (relying on the terms "accused" and "prosecution" in Rule 404(a) to conclude that the exceptions in subdivisions (a)(1) and (2) are inapplicable in civil cases). The amendment is consistent with the original intent of the Rule, which was to prohibit the circumstantial use of character evidence in civil cases, even where closely related to criminal charges. *See Ginter v. Northwestern Mut. Life Ins. Co.*, 576 F.Supp. 627, 629-30 (D.Ky. 1984) ("It seems beyond peradventure of doubt that the drafters of F.R.Evi. 404(a) explicitly intended that all character evidence, except where 'character is at issue' was to be excluded" in civil cases).

[¶2] The circumstantial use of character evidence is generally discouraged because it carries serious risks of prejudice, confusion and delay. *See Michelson v. United States*, 335 U.S. 469, 476 (1948) ("The overriding policy of excluding such evidence, despite its admitted probative value, is the practical experience that its disallowance tends to prevent confusion of issues, unfair surprise and undue prejudice."). In criminal cases, the so-called "mercy rule" permits a criminal defendant to introduce evidence of pertinent character traits of the defendant and the victim. But that is because the accused, whose liberty is at stake, may need "a counterweight against the strong investigative and prosecutorial resources of the government." C. Mueller & L. Kirkpatrick, *Evidence: Practice Under the Rules*, pp. 264-5 (2d ed. 1999). See also Richard Uviller, *Evidence of Character to Prove Conduct: Illusion, Illogic, and Injustice in the Courtroom*, 130 U.Pa.L.Rev. 845, 855 (1982) (the rule prohibiting circumstantial use of character evidence "was relaxed to allow the criminal defendant with so much at stake and so little available in the way of conventional proof to have special dispensation to tell the factfinder just what sort of person he really is"). Those concerns do not apply to parties in civil cases.

[¶3] The amendment also clarifies that evidence otherwise admissible under Rule 404(a)(2) may nonetheless be excluded in a criminal case involving sexual misconduct. In such a case, the admissibility of evidence of the victim's sexual behavior and predisposition is governed by the more stringent provisions of Rule 412.

[¶4] Nothing in the amendment is intended to affect the scope of Rule 404(b). While Rule 404(b) refers to the "accused," the "prosecution," and a "criminal case," it does so only in the context of a notice requirement. The admissibility standards of Rule 404(b) remain fully applicable to both civil and criminal cases.

FRE 404 – 2000 NOTES OF ADVISORY COMMITTEE

[¶1] Rule 404(a)(1) has been amended to provide that when the accused attacks the character of an alleged victim under subdivision (a)(2) of this Rule, the door is opened to an attack on the same character trait of the accused. Current law does not allow the government to introduce negative character evidence as to the accused unless the accused introduces evidence of good character. *See, e.g., United States v. Fountain*, 768 F.2d 790 (7th Cir.1985) (when the accused offers proof of self-defense, this permits proof of the alleged victim's character trait for peacefulness, but it does not permit proof of the accused's character trait for violence).

[¶2] The amendment makes clear that the accused cannot attack the alleged victim's character and yet remain shielded from the disclosure of equally relevant evidence concerning the same character trait of the accused. For example, in a murder case with a claim of self-defense, the accused, to bolster this defense, might offer evidence of the alleged victim's violent disposition. If the government has evidence that the accused has a violent character, but is not allowed to offer this evidence as part of its rebuttal, the jury has only part of the information it needs for an informed assessment of the probabilities as to who was the initial aggressor. This may be the case even if evidence of the accused's prior violent acts is admitted under Rule 404(b), because such evidence can be admitted only for limited purposes and not to show action in conformity with the accused's character on a specific occasion. Thus, the amendment is designed to permit a more balanced presentation of character evidence when an accused chooses to attack the character of the alleged victim.

[¶3] The amendment does not affect the admissibility of evidence of specific acts of uncharged misconduct offered for a purpose other than proving character under Rule 404(b). Nor does it affect the standards for proof of character by evidence of other sexual behavior or sexual offenses under Rules 412-415. By its placement in Rule 404(a)(1), the amendment covers only proof of character by way of reputation or opinion.

[¶4] The amendment does not permit proof of the accused's character if the accused merely uses character evidence for a purpose other than to prove the alleged victim's propensity to act in a certain way. *See United States v. Burks*, 470 F.2d 432, 434-5 (D.C. Cir.1972) (evidence of the alleged victim's violent character, when known by the accused, was admissible "on the issue of whether or not the defendant reasonably feared he was in danger of imminent great bodily harm"). Finally, the amendment does not permit proof of the accused's character when the accused attacks the alleged victim's character as a witness under Rule 608 or 609.

[¶5] The term "alleged" is inserted before each reference to "victim" in the Rule, in order to provide consistency with Evidence Rule 412.

[¶1] The amendment to Rule 407 makes two changes in the rule. First, the words "an injury or harm allegedly caused by" were added to clarify that the rule applies only to changes made after the occurrence that produced the damages giving rise to the action. Evidence of measures taken by the defendant prior to the "event" causing "injury or harm" do not fall within the exclusionary scope of Rule 407 even if they occurred after the manufacture or design of the product. *See Chase v. General Motors Corp.*, 856 F.2d 17, 21-22 (4th Cir.1988).

[¶2] Second, Rule 407 has been amended to provide that evidence of subsequent remedial measures may not be used to prove "a defect in a product or its design, or that a warning or instruction should have accompanied a product." This amendment adopts the view of a majority of the circuits that have interpreted Rule 407 to apply to products liability actions. *See Raymond v. Raymond Corp.*, 938 F.2d 1518, 1522 (1st Cir.1991); *In re Joint Eastern District and Southern District Asbestos Litigation v. Armstrong World Industries, Inc.*, 995 F.2d 343 (2d Cir.1993); *Cann v. Ford Motor Co.*, 658 F.2d 54, 60 (2d Cir.1981), *cert. denied*, 456 U.S. 960 (1982); *Kelly v. Crown Equipment Co.*, 970 F.2d 1273, 1275 (3d Cir.1992); *Werner v. Upjohn, Inc.*, 628 F.2d 848 (4th Cir.1980), *cert. denied*, 449 U.S. 1080 (1981); *Grenada Steel Industries, Inc. v. Alabama Oxygen Co., Inc.*, 695 F.2d 883 (5th Cir.1983); *Bauman v. Volkswagenwerk Aktiengesellschaft*, 621 F.2d 230, 232 (6th Cir.1980); *Flaminio v. Honda Motor Company, Ltd.*, 733 F.2d 463, 469 (7th Cir.1984); *Gauthier v. AMF, Inc.*, 788 F.2d 634, 636-37 (9th Cir.1986).

[¶3] Although this amendment adopts a uniform federal rule, it should be noted that evidence of subsequent remedial measures may be admissible pursuant to the second sentence of Rule 407. Evidence of subsequent measures that is not barred by Rule 407 may still be subject to exclusion on Rule 403 grounds when the dangers of prejudice or confusion substantially outweigh the probative value of the evidence.

FRE 407 – 2011 NOTES OF ADVISORY COMMITTEE

[¶1] Rule 407 previously provided that evidence was not excluded if offered for a purpose not explicitly prohibited by the Rule. To improve the language of the Rule, it now provides that the court may admit evidence if offered for a permissible purpose. There is no intent to change the process for admitting evidence covered by the Rule. It remains the case that if offered for an impermissible purpose, it must be excluded, and if offered for a purpose not barred by the Rule, its admissibility remains governed by the general principles of Rules 402, 403, 801, etc.

FRE 407 – 1997 NOTES OF ADVISORY COMMITTEE

[¶1] The amendment to Rule 407 makes two changes in the rule. First, the words "an injury or harm allegedly caused by" were added to clarify that the rule applies only to changes made after the occurrence that produced the damages giving rise to the action. Evidence of measures taken by the defendant prior to the "event" causing "injury or harm" do not fall within the exclusionary scope of Rule 407 even if they occurred after the manufacture or design of the product. *See Chase v. General Motors Corp.*, 856 F.2d 17, 21-22 (4th Cir.1988).

[¶2] Second, Rule 407 has been amended to provide that evidence of subsequent remedial measures may not be used to prove "a defect in a product or its design, or that a warning or instruction should have accompanied a product." This amendment adopts the view of a majority of the circuits

that have interpreted Rule 407 to apply to products liability actions. *See Raymond v. Raymond Corp.*, 938 F.2d 1518, 1522 (1st Cir.1991); *In re Joint Eastern District and Southern District Asbestos Litigation v. Armstrong World Industries, Inc.*, 995 F.2d 343 (2d Cir.1993); *Cann v. Ford Motor Co.*, 658 F.2d 54, 60 (2d Cir.1981), *cert. denied*, 456 U.S. 960 (1982); *Kelly v. Crown Equipment Co.*, 970 F.2d 1273, 1275 (3d Cir.1992); *Werner v. Upjohn, Inc.*, 628 F.2d 848 (4th Cir.1980), *cert. denied*, 449 U.S. 1080 (1981); *Grenada Steel Industries, Inc. v. Alabama Oxygen Co., Inc.*, 695 F.2d 883 (5th Cir.1983); *Bauman v. Volkswagenwerk Aktiengesellschaft*, 621 F.2d 230, 232 (6th Cir.1980); *Flaminio v. Honda Motor Company, Ltd.*, 733 F.2d 463, 469 (7th Cir.1984); *Gauthier v. AMF, Inc.*, 788 F.2d 634, 636-37 (9th Cir.1986).

[¶3] Although this amendment adopts a uniform federal rule, it should be noted that evidence of subsequent remedial measures may be admissible pursuant to the second sentence of Rule 407. Evidence of subsequent measures that is not barred by Rule 407 may still be subject to exclusion on Rule 403 grounds when the dangers of prejudice or confusion substantially outweigh the probative value of the evidence.

FRE 408 – 2011 NOTES OF ADVISORY COMMITTEE

[¶1] Rule 408 previously provided that evidence was not excluded if offered for a purpose not explicitly prohibited by the Rule. To improve the language of the Rule, it now provides that the court may admit evidence if offered for a permissible purpose. There is no intent to change the process for admitting evidence covered by the Rule. It remains the case that if offered for an impermissible purpose, it must be excluded, and if offered for a purpose not barred by the Rule, its admissibility remains governed by the general principles of Rules 402, 403, 801, etc.

[¶2] The Committee deleted the reference to "liability" on the ground that the deletion makes the Rule flow better and easier to read, and because "liability" is covered by the broader term "validity." Courts have not made substantive decisions on the basis of any distinction between validity and liability. No change in current practice or in the coverage of the Rule is intended.

FRE 408 – 2006 NOTES OF ADVISORY COMMITTEE

[¶1] Rule 408 has been amended to settle some questions in the courts about the scope of the Rule, and to make it easier to read. First, the amendment provides that Rule 408 does not prohibit the introduction in a criminal case of statements or conduct during compromise negotiations regarding a civil dispute by a government regulatory, investigative, or enforcement agency. *See, e.g., United States v. Prewitt*, 34 F.3d 436, 439 (7th Cir.1994) (admissions of fault made in compromise of a civil securities enforcement action were admissible against the accused in a subsequent criminal action for mail fraud). Where an individual makes a statement in the presence of government agents, its subsequent admission in a criminal case should not be unexpected. The individual can seek to protect against subsequent disclosure through negotiation and agreement with the civil regulator or an attorney for the government.

[¶2] Statements made in compromise negotiations of a claim by a government agency may be excluded in criminal cases where the circumstances so warrant under Rule 403. For example, if an individual was unrepresented at the time the statement was made in a civil enforcement proceeding, its probative value in a subsequent criminal case may be minimal. But there is no absolute exclusion imposed by Rule 408.

[¶3] In contrast, statements made during compromise negotiations of other disputed claims are not admissible in subsequent criminal litigation, when offered to prove liability for, invalidity of, or amount of those claims. When private parties enter into compromise negotiations they cannot protect against the subsequent use of statements in criminal cases by way of private ordering. The inability to guarantee protection against subsequent use could lead to parties refusing to admit fault, even if by doing so they could favorably settle the private matter. Such a chill on settlement negotiations would be contrary to the policy of Rule 408.

[¶4] The amendment distinguishes statements and conduct (such as a direct admission of fault) made in compromise negotiations of a civil claim by a government agency from an offer or acceptance of a compromise of such a claim. An offer or acceptance of a compromise of any civil claim is excluded under the Rule if offered against the defendant as an admission of fault. In that case, the predicate for the evidence would be that the defendant, by compromising with the government agency, has admitted the validity and amount of the civil claim, and that this admission has sufficient probative value to be considered as evidence of guilt. But unlike a direct statement of fault, an offer or acceptance of a compromise is not very probative of the defendant's guilt. Moreover, admitting such an offer or acceptance could deter a defendant from settling a civil regulatory action, for fear of evidentiary use in a subsequent criminal action. *See, e.g.*, Fishman, *Jones on Evidence, Civil and Criminal*, §22:16 at 199, n.83 (7th ed. 2000) ("A target of a potential criminal investigation may be unwilling to settle civil claims against him if by doing so he increases the risk of prosecution and conviction.").

[¶5] The amendment retains the language of the original rule that bars compromise evidence only when offered as evidence of the "validity," "invalidity," or "amount" of the disputed claim. The intent is to retain the extensive case law finding Rule 408 inapplicable when compromise evidence is offered for a purpose other than to prove the validity, invalidity, or amount of a disputed claim. *See, e.g., Athey v. Farmers Ins. Exchange*, 234 F.3d 357 (8th Cir.2000) (evidence of settlement offer by insurer was properly admitted to prove insurer's bad faith); *Coakley & Williams v. Structural Concrete Equip.*,

973 F.2d 349 (4th Cir.1992) (evidence of settlement is not precluded by Rule 408 where offered to prove a party's intent with respect to the scope of a release); *Cates v. Morgan Portable Bldg. Corp.*, 708 F.2d 683 (7th Cir.1985) (Rule 408 does not bar evidence of a settlement when offered to prove a breach of the settlement agreement, as the purpose of the evidence is to prove the fact of settlement as opposed to the validity or amount of the underlying claim); *Uforma/Shelby Bus. Forms, Inc. v. NLRB*, 111 F.3d 1284 (6th Cir.1997) (threats made in settlement negotiations were admissible; Rule 408 is inapplicable when the claim is based upon a wrong that is committed during the course of settlement negotiations). So for example, Rule 408 is inapplicable if offered to show that a party made fraudulent statements in order to settle a litigation.

[¶6] The amendment does not affect the case law providing that Rule 408 is inapplicable when evidence of the compromise is offered to prove notice. *See, e.g.*, *United States v. Austin*, 54 F.3d 394 (7th Cir.1995) (no error to admit evidence of the defendant's settlement with the FTC, because it was offered to prove that the defendant was on notice that subsequent similar conduct was wrongful); *Spell v. McDaniel*, 824 F.2d 1380 (4th Cir.1987) (in a civil rights action alleging that an officer used excessive force, a prior settlement by the City of another brutality claim was properly admitted to prove that the City was on notice of aggressive behavior by police officers).

[¶7] The amendment prohibits the use of statements made in settlement negotiations when offered to impeach by prior inconsistent statement or through contradiction. Such broad impeachment would tend to swallow the exclusionary rule and would impair the public policy of promoting settlements. *See McCormick on Evidence* at 186 (5th ed. 1999) ("Use of statements made in compromise negotiations to impeach the testimony of a party, which is not specifically treated in Rule 408, is fraught with danger of misuse of the statements to prove liability, threatens frank interchange of information during negotiations, and generally should not be permitted."). *See also EEOC v. Gear Petroleum, Inc.*, 948 F.2d 1542 (10th Cir.1991) (letter sent as part of settlement negotiation cannot be used to impeach defense witnesses by way of contradiction or prior inconsistent statement; such broad impeachment would undermine the policy of encouraging uninhibited settlement negotiations).

[¶8] The amendment makes clear that Rule 408 excludes compromise evidence even when a party seeks to admit its own settlement offer or statements made in settlement negotiations. If a party were to reveal its own statement or offer, this could itself reveal the fact that the adversary entered into settlement negotiations. The protections of Rule 408 cannot be waived unilaterally because the Rule, by definition, protects both parties from having the fact of negotiation disclosed to the jury. Moreover, proof of statements and offers made in settlement would often have to be made through the testimony of attorneys, leading to the risks and costs of disqualification. *See generally Pierce v. F.R. Tripler & Co.*, 955 F.2d 820, 828 (2d Cir.1992) (settlement offers are excluded under Rule 408 even if it is the offeror who seeks to admit them; noting that the "widespread admissibility of the substance of settlement offers could bring with it a rash of motions for disqualification of a party's chosen counsel who would likely become a witness at trial").

[¶9] The sentence of the Rule referring to evidence "otherwise discoverable" has been deleted as superfluous. *See, e.g.*, Advisory Committee Note to Maine Rule of Evidence 408 (refusing to include the sentence in the Maine version of Rule 408 and noting that the sentence "seems to state what the law would be if it were omitted"); Advisory Committee Note to Wyoming Rule of Evidence 408 (refusing to include the sentence in Wyoming Rule 408 on the ground that it was "superfluous"). The intent of the sentence was to prevent a party from trying to immunize admissible information, such as a pre-existing document, through the pretense of disclosing it during compromise negotiations. *See Ramada Development Co. v. Rauch*, 644 F.2d 1097 (5th Cir.1981). But even without the sentence, the Rule cannot be read to protect pre-existing information simply because it was presented to the adversary in compromise negotiations.

FRE 411 – 2011 NOTES OF ADVISORY COMMITTEE

[¶1] Rule 411 previously provided that evidence was not excluded if offered for a purpose not explicitly prohibited by the Rule. To improve the language of the Rule, it now provides that the court may admit evidence if offered for a permissible purpose. There is no intent to change the process for admitting evidence covered by the Rule. It remains the case that if offered for an impermissible purpose, it must be excluded, and if offered for a purpose not barred by the Rule, its admissibility remains governed by the general principles of Rules 402, 403, 801, etc.

FRE 412 – 1994 NOTES OF ADVISORY COMMITTEE

[¶1] Rule 412 has been revised to diminish some of the confusion engendered by the original rule and to expand the protection afforded alleged victims of sexual misconduct. Rule 412 applies to both civil and criminal proceedings. The rule aims to safeguard the alleged victim against the invasion of privacy, potential embarrassment and sexual stereotyping that is associated with public disclosure of intimate sexual details and the infusion of sexual innuendo into the factfinding process. By affording victims protection in most instances, the rule also encourages victims of sexual misconduct to institute and to participate in legal proceedings against alleged offenders.

[¶2] Rule 412 seeks to achieve these objectives by barring evidence relating to the alleged victim's sexual behavior or alleged sexual predisposition, whether offered as substantive evidence of for impeachment, except in designated circumstances in which the probative value of the evidence significantly outweighs possible harm to the victim.

[¶3] The revised rule applies in all cases involving sexual misconduct without regard to whether the alleged victim or person accused is a party to the litigation. Rule 412 extends to "pattern" witnesses in both criminal and civil cases whose testimony about other instances of sexual misconduct by the person accused is otherwise admissible. When the case does not involve alleged sexual misconduct, evidence relating to a third-party witness' alleged sexual activities is not within the ambit of Rule 412. The witness will, however, be protected by other rules such as Rules 404 and 608, as well as Rule 403.

[¶4] The terminology "alleged victim" is used because there will frequently be a factual dispute as to whether sexual misconduct occurred. It does not connote any requirement that the misconduct be alleged in the pleadings. Rule 412 does not, however, apply unless the person against whom the evidence is offered can reasonably be characterized as a "victim of alleged sexual misconduct." When this is not the case, as for instance in a defamation action involving statements concerning sexual misconduct in which the evidence is offered to show that the alleged defamatory statements were true or did not damage the plaintiff's reputation, neither Rule 404 nor this rule will operate to bar the evidence; Rule 401 and 403 will continue to control. Rule 412 will, however, apply in a Title VII action in which the plaintiff has alleged sexual harassment.

[¶5] The reference to a person "accused" is also used in a non-technical sense. There is no requirement that there be a criminal charge pending against the person or even that the misconduct would constitute a criminal offense. Evidence offered to prove allegedly false prior claims by the victim is not barred by Rule 412. However, this evidence is subject to the requirements of Rule 404.

[¶6] Subdivision (a). As amended, Rule 412 bars evidence offered to prove the victim's sexual behavior and alleged sexual predisposition. Evidence, which might otherwise be admissible under Rules 402, 404(b), 405, 607, 608, 609 or some other evidence rule, must be excluded if Rule 412 so requires. The word "other" is used to suggest some flexibility in admitting evidence "intrinsic" to the alleged sexual misconduct. *Cf.* Committee Note to 1991 amendment to Rule 404(b).

[¶7] Past sexual behavior connotes all activities that involve actual physical conduct, i.e. sexual intercourse and sexual contact, or that imply sexual intercourse or sexual contact. *See, e.g., United States v. Galloway*, 937 F.2d 542 (10th Cir.1991), cert. denied, 113 S.Ct. 418 (1992) (use of contraceptives inadmissible since use implies sexual activity); *United States v. One Feather*, 702 F.2d 736 (8th Cir.1983) (birth of an illegitimate child inadmissible); *State v. Carmichael*, 727 P.2d 918, 925 (Kan.1986) (evidence of venereal disease inadmissible). In addition, the word "behavior" should be construed to include activities of the mind, such as fantasies or dreams. See 23 C. Wright & K. Graham, Jr., Federal Practice and Procedure, §5384 at p. 548 (1980) ("While there may be some doubt under statutes that require 'conduct,' it would seem that the language of Rule 412 is broad enough to encompass the behavior of the mind.").

[¶8] The rule has been amended to also exclude all other evidence relating to an alleged victim of sexual misconduct that is offered to prove a sexual predisposition. This amendment is designed to exclude evidence that does not directly refer to sexual activities or thoughts but that the proponent believes may have a sexual connotation for the factfinder. Admission of such evidence would contravene Rule 412's objectives of shielding the alleged victim from potential embarrassment and safeguarding the victim against stereotypical thinking. Consequently, unless the (b)(2) exception is satisfied, evidence such as that relating to the alleged victim's mode of dress, speech, or life-style will not be admissible.

[¶9] The introductory phrase in subdivision (a) was deleted because it lacked clarity and contained no explicit reference to the other provisions of law that were intended to be overridden. The conditional clause, "except as provided in subdivisions (b) and (c)" is intended to make clear that evidence of the types described in subdivision (a) is admissible only under the strictures of those sections.

[¶10] The reason for extending the rule to all criminal cases is obvious. The strong social policy of protecting a victim's privacy and encouraging victims to come forward to report criminal acts is not confined to cases that involve a charge of sexual assault. The need to protect the victim is equally great when a defendant is charged with kidnapping, and evidence is offered, either to prove motive or as background, that the defendant sexually assaulted the victim.

[¶11] The reason for extending Rule 412 to civil cases is equally obvious. The need to protect alleged victims against invasions of privacy, potential embarrassment, and unwarranted sexual stereotyping, and the wish to encourage victims to come forward when they have been sexually molested do not disappear because the context has shifted from a criminal prosecution to a claim for damages or injunctive relief. There is a strong social policy in not only punishing those who engage in sexual misconduct, but in also providing relief to the victim. Thus, Rule 412 applies in any civil case in which a person claims to be the victim of sexual misconduct, such as actions for sexual battery or sexual harassment.

[¶12] Subdivision (b). Subdivision (b) spells out the specific circumstances in which some evidence may be admissible that would otherwise be barred by the general rule expressed in subdivision (a). As amended, Rule 412 will be virtually unchanged in criminal cases, but will provide protection to any person alleged to be a victim of sexual misconduct regardless of the charge actually brought against an accused. A new exception has been added for civil cases.

[¶13] In a criminal case, evidence may be admitted under subdivision (b)(1) pursuant to three possible exceptions, provided the evidence also satisfies other requirements for admissibility specified in the Federal Rules of Evidence, including Rule 403. Subdivisions (b)(1)(A) and (b)(1)(B) require proof in the form of specific instances of sexual behavior in recognition of the limited probative value and dubious reliability of evidence of reputation or evidence in the form of an opinion.

[¶14] Under subdivision (b)(1)(A), evidence of specific instances of sexual behavior with persons other than the person whose sexual misconduct is alleged may be admissible if it is offered to prove that another person was the source of semen, injury or other physical evidence. Where the prosecution has directly or indirectly asserted that the physical evidence originated with the accused, the defendant must be afforded an opportunity to prove that another person was responsible. *See United States v. Begay*, 937 F.2d 515, 523 n. 10 (10th Cir.1991). Evidence offered for the specific purpose identified in this subdivision may still be excluded if it does not satisfy Rules 401 or 403. *See, e.g., United States v. Azure*, 845 F.2d 1503, 1505-06 (8th Cir.1988) (10 year old victim's injuries indicated recent use of force; court excluded evidence of consensual sexual activities with witness who testified at in camera hearing that he had never hurt victim and failed to establish recent activities).

[¶15] Under the exception in subdivision (b)(1)(B), evidence of specific instances of sexual behavior with respect to the person whose sexual misconduct is alleged is admissible if offered to prove consent, or offered by the prosecution. Admissible pursuant to this exception might be evidence of prior instances of sexual activities between the alleged victim and the accused, as well as statements in which the alleged victim expressed an intent to engage in sexual intercourse with the accused, or voiced sexual fantasies involving the specific accused. In a prosecution for child sexual abuse, for example, evidence of uncharged sexual activity between the accused and the alleged victim offered by the prosecution may be admissible pursuant to Rule 404(b) to show a pattern of behavior. Evidence relating to the victim's alleged sexual predisposition is not admissible pursuant to this exception.

[¶16] Under subdivision (b)(1)(C), evidence of specific instances of conduct may not be excluded if the result would be to deny a criminal defendant the protections afforded by the Constitution. For example, statements in which the victim has expressed an intent to have sex with the first person encountered on a particular occasion might not be excluded without violating the due process right of a rape defendant seeking to prove consent. Recognition of this basic principle was expressed on subdivision (b)(1) of the original rule. The United States Supreme Court has recognized that in various circumstances a defendant may have a right to introduce evidence otherwise precluded by an evidence rule under the Confrontation Clause. *See, e.g., Olden v. Kentucky*, 488 U.S. 227 (1988) (defendant in rape cases had right to inquire into alleged victim's cohabitation with another man to show bias).

[¶17] Subdivision (b)(2) governs the admissibility of otherwise proscribed evidence in civil cases. It employs a balancing test rather than the specific exceptions stated in subdivision (b)(1) in recognition of the difficulty of foreseeing future developments in the law. Greater flexibility is needed to accommodate evolving causes of action such as claims for sexual harassment.

[¶18] The balancing test requires the proponent of the evidence, whether plaintiff or defendant, to convince the court that the probative value of the proffered evidence "substantially outweighs the danger of harm to any victim and of unfair prejudice of any party." This test for admitting evidence offered to prove sexual behavior or sexual propensity in civil cases differs in three respects from the general rule governing admissibility set forth in Rule 403. First, it reverses that usual procedure spelled out in Rule 403 by shifting the burden to the proponent to demonstrate admissibility rather than making the opponent justify exclusion of the evidence. Second, the standard expressed in subdivision (b)(2) is more stringent than in the original rule; it raises the threshold for admission by requiring that the probative value of the evidence substantially outweigh the specified dangers. Finally, the Rule 412 test puts "harm to the victim" on the scale in addition to prejudice to the parties.

[¶19] Evidence of reputation may be received in a civil case only if the alleged victim has put his or her reputation into controversy. The victim may do so without making a specific allegation in a pleading. *Cf.* Fed.R.Civ.P. 35(a).

[¶20] Subdivision (c). Amended subdivision (c) is more concise and understandable than the subdivision it replaces. The requirement of a motion before trial is continued in the amended rule, as is the provision that a late motion may be permitted for good cause shown. In deciding whether to permit late filing, the court may take into account the conditions previously included in the rule: namely whether the evidence is newly discovered and could not have been obtained earlier through the existence of due diligence, and whether the issue to which such evidence relates has newly arisen in the case. The rule recognizes that in some instances the circumstances that justify an application to introduce evidence otherwise barred by Rule 412 will not become apparent until trial.

[¶21] The amended rule provides that before admitting evidence that falls within the prohibition of Rule 412(a), the court must hold a hearing in camera at which the alleged victim and any party must be afforded the right to be present and an opportunity to be heard. All papers connected with the motion and any record of a hearing on the motion must be kept and remain under seal during the course of trial and appellate proceedings unless otherwise ordered. This is to assure that the privacy of the alleged victim is preserved in all cases in which the court rules that proffered evidence is not admissible, and in which the hearing refers to matters that are not received, or are received in another form.

[¶22] The procedures set forth in subdivision (c) do not apply to discovery of a victim's past sexual conduct or predisposition in civil cases, which will be continued to be governed by Fed. R. Civ. P. 26. In order not to undermine the rationale of Rule 412, however, courts should enter appropriate orders pursuant to Fed. R. Civ. P. 26(c) to protect the victim against unwarranted inquiries and to ensure confidentiality. Courts should presumptively issue protective orders barring discovery unless the party seeking discovery makes a showing that the evidence sought to be discovered would be relevant under the facts and theories of the particular case, and cannot be obtained except through discovery. In an action for sexual harassment, for instance, while some evidence of the alleged victim's sexual behavior and/or predisposition in the workplace may perhaps be relevant, non-work place conduct will usually be irrelevant. *Cf. Burns v. McGregor Electronic Industries, Inc.*, 989 F.2d 959, 962-63 (8th Cir.1993) (posing for a nude magazine outside work hours is irrelevant to issue of unwelcomeness of sexual advances at work). Confidentiality orders should be presumptively granted as well.

[¶23] One substantive change made in subdivision (c) is the elimination of the following sentence: "Notwithstanding subdivision (b) of Rule 104, if the relevancy of the evidence which the accused seeks to offer in the trial depends upon the fulfillment of a condition of fact, the court, at the hearing in chambers or at a subsequent hearing in chambers scheduled for such purpose, shall accept evidence on the issue of whether such condition of fact is fulfilled and shall determine such issue." On its face, this language would appear to authorize a trial judge to exclude evidence of past sexual conduct between an alleged victim and an accused or a defendant in a civil case based upon the judge's belief that such past acts did not occur. Such an authorization raises questions of invasion of the right to a jury trial under the Sixth and Seventh Amendments. See 1 S. Saltzburg & M. Martin, Federal Rules of Evidence Manual, 396-97 (5th ed. 1990).

[¶24] The Advisory Committee concluded that the amended rule provided adequate protection for all persons claiming to be the victims of sexual misconduct, and that it was inadvisable to continue to include a provision in the rule that has been confusing and that raises substantial constitutional issues.

[¶25] [The Supreme Court withheld that portion of the proposed amendment to FRE 412 transmitted to the Court by the Judicial Conference which would apply the Rule to civil cases. The proposed amendment was subsequently amended by Pub.L. 103-322, §40141(b). The Advisory Committee Note was adopted by Congressional Conference Report accompanying Pub.L. 103-322. H.R.Conf. Rep. No. 103-711, 103rd Cong., 2nd Sess., 383 (1994) ("The Conferees intend that the Advisory Committee Note on Rule 412, as transmitted by the Judicial Conference of the United States to the Supreme Court …, applies to Rule 412 as enacted….").]

FRE 413-415 – 1995 CONGRESSIONAL DISCUSSION

[¶1] Floor Statement of the Principal House Sponsor, Representative Susan Molinari, Concerning the Prior Crimes Evidence Rules for Sexual Assault and Child Molestation Cases (Cong.Rec. H8991-92, Aug. 21, 1994):

[¶2] Mr. Speaker, the revised conference bill contains a critical reform that I have long sought to protect the public from crimes of sexual violence—general rules of admissibility in sexual assault and child molestation cases for evidence that the defendant has committed offenses of the same type on other occasions. The enactment of this reform is first and foremost a triumph for the public—for the women who will not be raped and the children who will not be molested because we have strengthened the legal system's tools for bringing the perpetrators of these atrocious crimes to justice.

[¶3] Senator Dole and I initially proposed this reform in February of 1991 in the Women's Equal Opportunity Act bill, and we later re-introduced it in the Sexual Assault Prevention Act bills of the 102d and 103d Congresses. The proposal also enjoyed the strong support of the Administration in the 102d Congress, and was included in President Bush's violent crime bill of that Congress, S. 635. The Senate passed the proposed rules on Nov. 5, 1993, by a vote of 75 to 19, in a crime bill amendment offered by Senate Dole. This Chamber endorsed the same rules on June 29, 1994, by a vote of 348 to 62, through a motion to instruct conferees that I offered.

[¶4] The rules in the revised conference bill are substantially identical to our earlier proposals. We have agreed to a temporary deferral of the effective date of the new rules, pending a report by the Judicial Conference, in order to accommodate procedural objections raised by opponents of the reform. However, regardless of what the Judicial Conference may recommend, the new rules will take effect within at most 300 days of the enactment of this legislation, unless repealed or modified by subsequent legislation.

[¶5] The need for these rules, their precedential support, their interpretation, and the issues and policy questions they raise have been analyzed at length in the legislative history of this proposal. I would direct the Members' attention particularly to two earlier statements:

[¶6] The first is the portion of the section-by-section analysis accompanying these rules in section 801 of S. 635, which President Bush transmitted to Congress in 1991. That statement appears on pages S 3238 [to] S 3242 of the daily edition of the Congressional Record for March 13, 1991.

[¶7] The second is the prepared text of an address—entitled "Evidence of Propensity and Probability in Sex Offense Cases and Other Cases"—by Senior Counsel David J. Karp of the Office of Policy Development of the U.S. Department of Justice. Mr. Karp, who is the author of the new evidence

rules, presented this statement on behalf of the Justice Department to the Evidence Section of the Association of American Law Schools on January 9, 1993. The statement provided a detailed account of the views of the legislative sponsors and the Administration concerning the proposed reform, and should also be considered an authoritative part of its legislative history.

[¶8] These earlier statements address the issues raised by this reform in considerable detail. In my present remarks, I will simply emphasize the following essential points:

[¶9] The new rules will supersede in sex offense cases the restrictive aspects of Federal Rule of Evidence 404(b). In contrast to Rule 404(b)'s general prohibition of evidence of character or propensity, the new rules for sex offense cases authorize admission and consideration of evidence of an uncharged offense for its bearing "on any matter to which it is relevant." This includes the defendant's propensity to commit sexual assault or child molestation offenses, and assessment of the probability or improbability that the defendant has been falsely or mistakenly accused of such an offense.

[¶10] In other respects, the general standards of the rules of evidence will continue to apply, including the restrictions on hearsay evidence and the court's authority under Evidence Rule 403 to exclude evidence whose probative value is substantially outweighed by its prejudicial effect. Also, the government (or the plaintiff in a civil case) will generally have to disclose to the defendant any evidence that is to be offered under the new rules at least 15 days before trial.

[¶11] The proposed reform is critical to the protection of the public from rapists and child molesters, and is justified by the distinctive characteristics of the cases it will affect. In child molestation cases, for example, a history of similar acts tends to be exceptionally probative because it shows an unusual disposition of the defendant—a sexual or sadosexual interest in children—that simply does not exist in ordinary people. Moreover, such cases require reliance on child victims whose credibility can readily be attacked in the absence of substantial corroboration. In such cases, there is a compelling public interest in admitting all significant evidence that will illumine the credibility of the charge and any denial by the defense.

[¶12] Similarly, adult-victim sexual assault cases are distinctive, and often turn on difficult credibility determinations. Alleged consent by the victim is rarely an issue in prosecutions for other violent crimes—the accused mugger does not claim that the victim freely handed over [his] wallet as a gift—but the defendant in a rape case often contends that the victim engaged in consensual sex and then falsely accused him. Knowledge that the defendant has committed rapes on other occasions is frequently critical in assessing the relative plausibility of these claims and accurately deciding cases that would otherwise become unresolvable swearing matches.

[¶13] The practical effect of the new rules is to put evidence of uncharged offenses in sexual assault and child molestation cases on the same footing as other types of relevant evidence that are not subject to a special exclusionary rule. The presumption is in favor of admission. The underlying legislative judgment is that the evidence admissible pursuant to the proposed rules is typically relevant and probative, and that its probative value is normally not outweighed by any risk of prejudice or other adverse effects.

[¶14] In line with this judgment, the rules do not impose arbitrary or artificial restrictions on the admissibility of evidence. Evidence of offenses for which the defendant has not previously been prosecuted or convicted will be admissible, as well as evidence of prior convictions. No time limit is imposed on the uncharged offenses for which evidence may be admitted; as a practical matter, evidence of other sex offenses by the defendant is often probative and properly admitted, notwithstanding very substantial lapses of time in relation to the charged offense or offenses. *See, e.g., United States v. Hadley*, 918 F.2d 848, 850-51 (9th Cir.1990), *cert. dismissed*, 113 S.Ct. 486 (1992) (evidence of offenses occurring up to 15 years earlier admitted); *State v. Plymate*, 345 N.W.2d 327 (Neb.1984) (evidence of defendant's commission of other child molestations more than 20 years earlier admitted).

[¶15] Finally, the practical efficacy of these rules will depend on faithful execution by judges of the will of Congress in adopting this critical reform. To implement the legislative intent, the courts must liberally construe these rules to provide the basis for a fully informed decision of sexual assault and child molestation cases, including assessment of the defendant's propensities and questions of probability in light of the defendant's past conduct.

FRE 501 – NOTES OF COMMITTEE ON THE JUDICIARY, HOUSE REPORT NO. 93-650

[¶1] Article V as submitted to Congress contained thirteen Rules. Nine of those Rules defined specific non-constitutional privileges which the federal courts must recognize (i.e. required reports, lawyer-client, psychotherapist-patient, husband-wife, communications to clergymen, political vote, trade secrets, secrets of state and other official information, and identity of informer). Another Rule provided that only those privileges set forth in Article V or in some other Act of Congress could be recognized by the federal courts. The three remaining Rules addressed collateral problems as to waiver of privilege by voluntary disclosure, privileged matter disclosed under compulsion or without opportunity to claim privilege, comment upon or inference from a claim of privilege, and jury instruction with regard thereto.

[¶2] The Committee amended Article V to eliminate all of the Court's specific Rules on privileges. Instead, the Committee, through a single Rule, 501, left the law of privileges in its present state and further provided that privileges shall continue to be developed by the courts of the United States under a uniform standard applicable both in civil and criminal cases. That standard, derived from Rule 26 of the Federal

Rules of Criminal Procedure, mandates the application of the principles of the common law as interpreted by the Courts of the United States in the light of reason and experience. The words "person, government, State, or political subdivision thereof" were added by the Committee to the lone term "witness" used in Rule 26 to make clear that, as under present law, not only witnesses may have privileges. The Committee also included in its amendment a proviso modeled after Rule 302 and similar to language added by the Committee to Rule 601 relating to the competency of witnesses. The proviso is designed to require the application of State privilege law in civil actions and proceedings governed by *Erie R. Co. v. Tompkins*, 304 U.S. 64 (1938), a result in accord with current federal court decisions. *See Republic Gear Co. v. Borg-Warner Corp.*, 381 F.2d 551, 555-556 n.2 (2nd Cir.1967). The Committee deemed the proviso to be necessary in the light of the Advisory Committee's view (see its note to Court (proposed) Rule 501) that this result is not mandated under Erie.

[¶3] The rationale underlying the proviso is that federal law should not supersede that of the States in substantive areas such as privilege absent a compelling reason. The Committee believes that in civil cases in the federal courts where an element of a claim or defense is not grounded upon a federal question, there is no federal interest strong enough to justify departure from State policy. In addition, the Committee considered that the Court's proposed Article V would have promoted forum shopping in some civil actions, depending upon differences in the privilege law applied as among the State and federal courts. The Committee's proviso, on the other hand, under which the federal courts are bound to apply the State's privilege law in actions founded upon a State-created right or defense removes the incentive to "shop".

FRE 502 – 2011 NOTES OF ADVISORY COMMITTEE

[¶1] Rule 502 has been amended by changing the initial letter of a few words from uppercase to lowercase as part of the restyling of the Evidence Rules to make style and terminology consistent throughout the rules. There is no intent to change any result in any ruling on evidence admissibility.

FRE 502 – 2008 EXPLANATORY NOTE ON FRE 502 PREPARED BY THE JUDICIAL CONFERENCE ADVISORY COMMITTEE ON EVIDENCE RULES

[¶1] This new rule has two major purposes:

(1) It resolves some longstanding disputes in the courts about the effect of certain disclosures of communications or information protected by the attorney-client privilege or as work product—specifically those disputes involving inadvertent disclosure and subject matter waiver.

(2) It responds to the widespread complaint that litigation costs necessary to protect against waiver of attorney-client privilege or work product have become prohibitive due to the concern that any disclosure (however innocent or minimal) will operate as a subject matter waiver of all protected communications or information. This concern is especially troubling in cases involving electronic discovery. *See, e.g., Hopson v. City of Baltimore*, 232 F.R.D. 228, 244 (D.Md. 2005) (electronic discovery may encompass "millions of documents" and to insist upon "record-by-record pre-production privilege review, on pain of subject matter waiver, would impose upon parties costs of production that bear no proportionality to what is at stake in the litigation").

[¶2] The rule seeks to provide a predictable, uniform set of standards under which parties can determine the consequences of a disclosure of a communication or information covered by the attorney-client privilege or work-product protection. Parties to litigation need to know, for example, that if they exchange privileged information pursuant to a confidentiality order, the court's order will be enforceable. Moreover, if a federal court's confidentiality order is not enforceable in a state court then the burdensome costs of privilege review and retention are unlikely to be reduced.

[¶3] The rule makes no attempt to alter federal or state law on whether a communication or information is protected under the attorney-client privilege or work-product immunity as an initial matter. Moreover, while establishing some exceptions to waiver, the rule does not purport to supplant applicable waiver doctrine generally.

[¶4] The rule governs only certain waivers by disclosure. Other common-law waiver doctrines may result in a finding of waiver even where there is no disclosure of privileged information or work product. *See, e.g., Nguyen v. Excel Corp.*, 197 F.3d 200 (5th Cir. 1999) (reliance on an advice of counsel defense waives the privilege with respect to attorney-client communications pertinent to that defense); *Ryers v. Burleson*, 100 F.R.D. 436 (D.D.C. 1983) (allegation of lawyer malpractice constituted a waiver of confidential communications under the circumstances). The rule is not intended to displace or modify federal common law concerning waiver of privilege or work product where no disclosure has been made.

[¶5] **Subdivision (a).** The rule provides that a voluntary disclosure in a federal proceeding or to a federal office or agency, if a waiver, generally results in a waiver only of the communication or information disclosed; a subject matter waiver (of either privilege or work product) is reserved for those unusual situations in which fairness requires a further disclosure of related, protected information, in order to prevent a selective and misleading presentation of evidence to the disadvantage of the adversary. *See, e.g., In re United Mine Workers of America Employee Benefit Plans Litig.*, 159 F.R.D. 307, 312 (D.D.C. 1994) (waiver of work product limited to materials actually disclosed, because the party did not deliberately disclose documents in an attempt to gain a tactical advantage). Thus, subject matter waiver is limited to situations in which a party intentionally puts protected information into the litigation in a selective, misleading and unfair manner. It follows that an inadvertent disclosure of protected information can never result in a subject matter waiver. *See* Rule 502(b). The rule rejects the result in *In re Sealed Case*, 877 F.2d 976 (D.C.Cir. 1989), which held that inadvertent disclosure of documents during discovery automatically constituted a subject matter waiver.

[¶6] The language concerning subject matter waiver—"ought in fairness"—is taken from Rule 106, because the animating principle is the same. Under both Rules, a party that makes a selective, misleading presentation that is unfair to the adversary opens itself to a more complete and accurate presentation.

[¶7] To assure protection and predictability, the rule provides that if a disclosure is made at the federal level, the federal rule on subject matter waiver governs subsequent state court determinations on the scope of the waiver by that disclosure.

[¶8] Subdivision (b). Courts are in conflict over whether an inadvertent disclosure of a communication or information protected as privileged or work product constitutes a waiver. A few courts find that a disclosure must be intentional to be a waiver. Most courts find a waiver only if the disclosing party acted carelessly in disclosing the communication or information and failed to request its return in a timely manner. And a few courts hold that any inadvertent disclosure of a communication or information protected under the attorney-client privilege or as work product constitutes a waiver without regard to the protections taken to avoid such a disclosure. *See generally Hopson v. City of Baltimore*, 232 F.R.D. 228 (D.Md. 2005), for a discussion of this case law.

[¶9] The rule opts for the middle ground: inadvertent disclosure of protected communications or information in connection with a federal proceeding or to a federal office or agency does not constitute a waiver if the holder took reasonable steps to prevent disclosure and also promptly took reasonable steps to rectify the error. This position is in accord with the majority view on whether inadvertent disclosure is a waiver.

[¶10] Cases such as *Lois Sportswear, U.S.A., Inc. v. Levi Strauss & Co.*, 104 F.R.D. 103, 105 (S.D.N.Y. 1985) and *Hartford Fire Ins. Co. v. Garvey*, 109 F.R.D. 323, 332 (N.D.Cal. 1985), set out a multifactor test for determining whether inadvertent disclosure is a waiver. The stated factors (none of which is dispositive) are the reasonableness of precautions taken, the time taken to rectify the error, the scope of discovery, the extent of disclosure and the overriding issue of fairness. The rule does not explicitly codify that test, because it is really a set of non-determinative guidelines that vary from case to case. The rule is flexible enough to accommodate any of those listed factors. Other considerations bearing on the reasonableness of a producing party's efforts include the number of documents to be reviewed and the time constraints for production. Depending on the circumstances, a party that uses advanced analytical software applications and linguistic tools in screening for privilege and work product may be found to have taken "reasonable steps" to prevent inadvertent disclosure. The implementation of an efficient system of records management before litigation may also be relevant.

[¶11] The rule does not require the producing party to engage in a post-production review to determine whether any protected communication or information has been produced by mistake. But the rule does require the producing party to follow up on any obvious indications that a protected communication or information has been produced inadvertently.

[¶12] The rule applies to inadvertent disclosures made to a federal office or agency, including but not limited to an office or agency that is acting in the course of its regulatory, investigative or enforcement authority. The consequences of waiver, and the concomitant costs of pre-production privilege review, can be as great with respect to disclosures to offices and agencies as they are in litigation.

[¶13] Subdivision (c). Difficult questions can arise when 1) a disclosure of a communication or information protected by the attorney-client privilege or as work product is made in a state proceeding, 2) the communication or information is offered in a subsequent federal proceeding on the ground that the disclosure waived the privilege or protection, and 3) the state and federal laws are in conflict on the question of waiver. The Committee determined that the proper solution for the federal court is to apply the law that is most protective of privilege and work product. If the state law is more protective (such as where the state law is that an inadvertent disclosure can never be a waiver), the holder of the privilege or protection may well have relied on that law when making the disclosure in the state proceeding. Moreover, applying a more restrictive federal law of waiver could impair the state objective of preserving the privilege or work-product protection for disclosures made in state proceedings. On the other hand, if the federal law is more protective, applying the state law of waiver to determine admissibility in federal court is likely to undermine the federal objective of limiting the costs of production.

[¶14] The rule does not address the enforceability of a state court confidentiality order in a federal proceeding, as that question is covered both by statutory law and principles of federalism and comity. *See* 28 U.S.C. §1738 (providing that state judicial proceedings "shall have the same full faith and credit in every court within the United States ... as they have by law or usage in the courts of such State ... from which they are taken"). *See also Tucker v. Ohtsu Tire & Rubber Co.*, 191 F.R.D. 495, 499 (D.Md. 2000) (noting that a federal court considering the enforceability of a state confidentiality order is "constrained by principles of comity, courtesy, and ... federalism"). Thus, a state court order finding no waiver in connection with a disclosure made in a state court proceeding is enforceable under existing law in subsequent federal proceedings.

[¶15] Subdivision (d). Confidentiality orders are becoming increasingly important in limiting the costs of privilege review and retention, especially in cases involving electronic discovery. But the utility of a confidentiality order in reducing discovery costs is substantially diminished if it provides no protection outside the particular litigation in which the order is entered. Parties are unlikely to be able to reduce the costs of pre-production review for privilege and work product if the consequence of disclosure is that the communications or information could be used by non-parties to the litigation.

[¶16] There is some dispute on whether a confidentiality order entered in one case is enforceable in other proceedings. *See generally Hopson v. City of Baltimore*, 232 F.R.D. 228 (D.Md. 2005), for a discussion of this case law. The rule provides that when a confidentiality order governing the consequences of disclosure in that case is entered in a federal proceeding, its terms are enforceable against non-parties in any federal or state proceeding. For example, the court order may provide for return of documents without waiver irrespective of the care taken by the disclosing party; the rule contemplates enforcement of "claw-back" and "quick peek" arrangements as a way to avoid the excessive costs of pre-production review for privilege and work product. *See Zubulake v. UBS Warburg LLC*, 216 F.R.D. 280, 290 (S.D.N.Y. 2003) (noting that parties may enter into "so-called 'claw-back' agreements that allow the parties to forego privilege review altogether in favor of an agreement to return inadvertently produced privilege documents"). The rule provides a party with a predictable protection from a court order—predictability that is needed to allow the party to plan in advance to limit the prohibitive costs of privilege and work product review and retention.

[¶17] Under the rule, a confidentiality order is enforceable whether or not it memorializes an agreement among the parties to the litigation. Party agreement should not be a condition of enforceability of a federal court's order.

[¶18] Under subdivision (d), a federal court may order that disclosure of privileged or protected information "in connection with" a federal proceeding does not result in waiver. But subdivision (d) does not allow the federal court to enter an order determining the waiver effects of a separate disclosure of the same information in other proceedings, state or federal. If a disclosure has been made in a state proceeding (and is not the subject of a state-court order on waiver), then subdivision (d) is inapplicable. Subdivision (c) would govern the federal court's determination whether the state-court disclosure waived the privilege or protection in the federal proceeding.

[¶19] Subdivision (e). Subdivision (e) codifies the well-established proposition that parties can enter an agreement to limit the effect of waiver by disclosure between or among them. Of course such an agreement can bind only the parties to the agreement. The rule makes clear that if parties want protection against non-parties from a finding of waiver by disclosure, the agreement must be made part of a court order.

[¶20] Subdivision (f). The protections against waiver provided by Rule 502 must be applicable when protected communications or information disclosed in federal proceedings are subsequently offered in state proceedings. Otherwise the holders of protected communications and information, and their lawyers, could not rely on the protections provided by the Rule, and the goal of limiting costs in discovery would be substantially undermined. Rule 502(f) is intended to resolve any potential tension between the provisions of Rule 502 that apply to state proceedings and the possible limitations on the applicability of the Federal Rules of Evidence otherwise provided by Rules 101 and 1101.

[¶21] The rule is intended to apply in all federal court proceedings, including court-annexed and court-ordered arbitrations, without regard to any possible limitations of Rules 101 and 1101. This provision is not intended to raise an inference about the applicability of any other rule of evidence in arbitration proceedings more generally.

[¶22] The costs of discovery can be equally high for state and federal causes of action, and the rule seeks to limit those costs in all federal proceedings, regardless of whether the claim arises under state or federal law. Accordingly, the rule applies to state law causes of action brought in federal court.

[¶23] Subdivision (g). The rule's coverage is limited to attorney-client privilege and work product. The operation of waiver by disclosure, as applied to other evidentiary privileges, remains a question of federal common law. Nor does the rule purport to apply to the Fifth Amendment privilege against compelled self-incrimination.

[¶24] The definition of work product "materials" is intended to include both tangible and intangible information. *See In re Cendant Corp. Sec. Litig.*, 343 F.3d 658, 662 (3d Cir. 2003) ("work product protection extends to both tangible and intangible work product").

FRE 502 – 2008 STATEMENT OF CONGRESSIONAL INTENT REGARDING FRE 502

[¶1] During consideration of this rule in Congress, a number of questions were raised about the scope and contours of the effect of the proposed rule on current law regarding attorney-client privilege and work-product protection. These questions were ultimately answered satisfactorily, without need to revise the text of the rule as submitted to Congress by the Judicial Conference.

[¶2] In general, these questions are answered by keeping in mind the limited though important purpose and focus of the rule. The rule addresses only the effect of disclosure, under specified circumstances, of a communication that is otherwise protected by attorney-client privilege, or of information that is protected by work-product protection, on whether the disclosure itself operates as a waiver of the privilege or protection for purposes of admissibility of evidence in a federal or state judicial or administrative proceeding. The rule does not alter the substantive law regarding attorney-client privilege or work-product protection in any other respect, including the burden on the party invoking the privilege (or protection) to prove that the particular information (or communication) qualifies for it. And it is not intended to alter the rules and practices governing use of information outside this evidentiary context.

[¶3] Some of these questions are addressed more specifically below, in order to help further avoid uncertainty in the interpretation and application of the rule.

[¶4] Subdivision (a)—Disclosure vs. Use

[¶5] This subdivision does not alter the substantive law regarding when a party's strategic use in litigation of otherwise privileged information obliges that party to waive the privilege regarding other information concerning the same subject matter, so that the information being used can be fairly considered in context. One situation in which this issue arises, the assertion as a defense in patent-infringement litigation that a party was relying on advice of counsel, is discussed elsewhere in this Note. In this and similar situations, under subdivision (a)(1) the party using an attorney-client communication to its advantage in the litigation has, in so doing, intentionally waived the privilege as to other communications concerning the same subject matter, regardless of the circumstances in which the communication being so used was initially disclosed.

[¶6] Subdivision (b)—Fairness Considerations

[¶7] The standard set forth in this subdivision for determining whether a disclosure operates as a waiver of the privilege or protection is, as explained elsewhere in this Note, the majority rule in the federal courts. The majority rule has simply been distilled here into a standard designed to be predictable in its application. This distillation is not intended to foreclose notions of fairness from continuing to inform application of the standard in all aspects as appropriate in particular cases—for example, as to whether steps taken to rectify an erroneous inadvertent disclosure were sufficiently prompt under subdivision (b)(3) where the receiving party has relied on the information disclosed.

[¶8] Subdivisions (a) and (b)—Disclosures to Federal Office or Agency

[¶9] This rule, as a Federal Rule of Evidence, applies to admissibility of evidence. While subdivisions (a) and (b) are written broadly to apply as appropriate to disclosures of information to a federal office or agency, they do not apply to uses of information—such as routine use in government publications—that fall outside the evidentiary context. Nor do these subdivisions relieve the party seeking to protect the information as privileged from the burden of proving that the privilege applies in the first place.

[¶10] Subdivision (d)—Court Orders

[¶11] This subdivision authorizes a court to enter orders only in the context of litigation pending before the court. And it does not alter the law regarding waiver of privilege resulting from having acquiesced in the use of otherwise privileged information. Therefore, this subdivision does not provide a basis for a court to enable parties to agree to a selective waiver of the privilege, such as to a federal agency conducting an investigation, while preserving the privilege as against other parties seeking the information. This subdivision is designed to enable a court to enter an order, whether on motion of one or more parties or on its own motion, that will allow the parties to conduct and respond to discovery expeditiously, without the need for exhaustive pre-production privilege reviews, while still preserving each party's right to assert the privilege to preclude use in litigation of information disclosed in such discovery. While the benefits of a court order under this subdivision would be equally available in government enforcement actions as in private actions, acquiescence by the disclosing party in use by the federal agency of information disclosed pursuant to such an order would still be treated as under current law for purposes of determining whether the acquiescence in use of the information, as opposed to its mere disclosure, effects a waiver of the privilege. The same applies to acquiescence in use by another private party.

[¶12] Moreover, whether the order is entered on motion of one or more parties, or on the court's own motion, the court retains its authority to include the conditions it deems appropriate in the circumstances.

[¶13] Subdivision (e)—Party Agreements

[¶14] This subdivision simply makes clear that while parties to a case may agree among themselves regarding the effect of disclosures between each other in a federal proceeding, it is not binding on others unless it is incorporated into a court order. This subdivision does not confer any authority on a court to enter any order regarding the effect of disclosures. That authority must be found in subdivision (d), or elsewhere.

FRE 606 – 2006 NOTES OF ADVISORY COMMITTEE

[¶1] Rule 606(b) has been amended to provide that juror testimony may be used to prove that the verdict reported was the result of a mistake in entering the verdict on the verdict form. The amendment responds to a divergence between the text of the Rule and the case law that has established an exception for proof of clerical errors. *See, e.g., Plummer v. Springfield Term. Ry.*, 5 F.3d 1, 3 (1st Cir.1993) ("A number of circuits hold, and we agree, that juror testimony regarding an alleged clerical error, such as announcing a verdict different than that agreed upon, does not challenge the validity of the verdict or the deliberation of mental processes, and therefore is not subject to Rule 606(b)."); *Teevee Toons, Inc., v. MP3.Com, Inc.*, 148 F.Supp.2d 276, 278 (S.D.N.Y.2001) (noting that Rule 606(b) has been silent regarding inquiries designed to confirm the accuracy of a verdict).

[¶2] In adopting the exception for proof of mistakes in entering the verdict on the verdict form, the amendment specifically rejects the broader exception, adopted by some courts, permitting the use of juror testimony to prove that the jurors were operating under a misunderstanding about the consequences of the result that they agreed upon. *See, e.g., Attridge v. Cencorp Div. of Dover Techs. Int'l, Inc.*, 836 F.2d 113, 116 (2d Cir.1987); *Eastridge Development Co., v. Halpert Associates, Inc.*, 853 F.2d 772 (10th Cir.1988). The broader exception is rejected because an inquiry into whether the jury misunderstood or misapplied an instruction goes to the jurors' mental processes underlying the verdict, rather than the verdict's accuracy in capturing what the jurors had agreed upon. *See, e.g., Karl v. Burlington Northern R.R.*, 880 F.2d 68, 74 (8th Cir.1989) (error to receive juror testimony on whether verdict was the result of jurors' misunderstanding of instructions: "The jurors did not state that the figure written by the foreman was different from that which they agreed upon, but indicated that the figure the foreman wrote down was intended to be a net figure, not a gross figure. Receiving such statements violates Rule 606(b) because the testimony relates to how the jury interpreted the court's instructions, and concerns the jurors' 'mental processes,' which is forbidden by the rule."); *Robles v. Exxon Corp.*, 862 F.2d 1201, 1208 (5th Cir.1989) ("the alleged error here goes to the substance of what the jury was asked to decide, necessarily implicating the jury's mental processes insofar as it questions the jury's understanding of the court's instructions and application of those instructions to the facts of the case"). Thus, the exception established by the amendment is limited to cases such as "where the jury foreperson wrote down, in response to an interrogatory, a number different from that agreed upon by the jury, or mistakenly stated that the defendant was 'guilty' when the jury had actually agreed that the defendant was not guilty." *Id.*

[¶3] It should be noted that the possibility of errors in the verdict form will be reduced substantially by polling the jury. Rule 606(b) does not, of course, prevent this precaution. *See* 8 C. Wigmore, *Evidence*, §2350 at 691 (McNaughten ed. 1961) (noting that the reasons for the rule barring juror testimony, "namely, the dangers of uncertainty and of tampering with the jurors to procure testimony, disappear in large part if such investigation as may be desired is *made by the judge* and takes place *before the jurors' discharge* and separation") (emphasis in original). Errors that come to light after polling the jury "may be corrected on the spot, or the jury may be sent out to continue deliberations, or, if necessary, a new trial may be ordered." C. Mueller & L. Kirkpatrick, *Evidence Under the Rules* at 671 (2d ed. 1999) (citing *Sincox v. United States*, 571 F.2d 876, 878-79 (5th Cir.1978)).

FRE 608 – 2011 NOTES OF ADVISORY COMMITTEE

[¶1] The Committee is aware that the Rule's limitation of bad-act impeachment to "cross-examination" is trumped by Rule 607, which allows a party to impeach witnesses on direct examination. Courts have not relied on the term "on cross-examination" to limit impeachment that would otherwise be permissible under Rules 607 and 608. The Committee therefore concluded that no change to the language of the Rule was necessary in the context of a restyling project.

FRE 608 – 2003 NOTES OF ADVISORY COMMITTEE

[¶1] The Rule has been amended to clarify that the absolute prohibition on extrinsic evidence applies only when the sole reason for proffering that evidence is to attack or support the witness' character for truthfulness. *See United States v. Abel*, 469 U.S. 45 (1984); *United States v. Fusco*, 748 F.2d 996 (5th Cir. 1984) (Rule 608(b) limits the use of evidence "designed to show that the witness has done things, unrelated to the suit being tried, that make him more or less believable per se"); Ohio R.Evid. 608(b). On occasion the Rule's use of the overbroad term "credibility" has been read "to bar extrinsic evidence for bias, competency and contradiction impeachment since they too deal with credibility." American Bar Association Section of Litigation, *Emerging Problems Under the Federal Rules of Evidence* at 161 (3d ed. 1998). The amendment conforms the language of the Rule to its original intent, which was to impose an absolute bar on extrinsic evidence only if the sole purpose for offering the evidence was to prove the witness' character for veracity. *See* Advisory Committee Note to Rule 608(b) (stating that the Rule is "[i]n conformity with Rule 405, which forecloses use of evidence of specific incidents as proof in chief of character unless character is in issue in the case ...").

[¶2] By limiting the application of the Rule to proof of a witness' character for truthfulness, the amendment leaves the admissibility of extrinsic evidence offered for other grounds of impeachment (such as contradiction, prior inconsistent statement, bias and mental capacity) to Rules 402 and 403. *See, e.g., United States v. Winchenbach*, 197 F.3d 548 (1st Cir.1999) (admissibility of a prior inconsistent statement offered for impeachment is governed by Rules 402 and 403, not Rule 608(b)); *United States v. Tarantino*, 846 F.2d 1384 (D.C. Cir.1988) (admissibility of extrinsic evidence offered to contradict a witness is governed by Rules 402 and 403); *United States v. Lindemann*, 85 F.3d 1232 (7th Cir.1996) (admissibility of extrinsic evidence of bias is governed by Rules 402 and 403).

[¶3] It should be noted that the extrinsic evidence prohibition of Rule 608(b) bars any reference to the consequences that a witness might have suffered as a result of an alleged bad act. For example, Rule 608(b) prohibits counsel from mentioning that a witness was suspended or disciplined for the conduct that is the subject of impeachment, when that conduct is offered only to prove the character of the witness. *See United States v. Davis*, 183 F.3d 231, 257 n.12 (3d Cir.1999) (emphasizing that in attacking the defendant's character for truthfulness "the government cannot make reference to Davis's forty-four day suspension or that Internal Affairs found that he lied about" an incident because "[s]uch evi-

dence would not only be hearsay to the extent it contains assertion of fact, it would be inadmissible extrinsic evidence under Rule 608(b)"). *See also* Stephen A. Saltzburg, *Impeaching the Witness: Prior Bad Acts and Extrinsic Evidence*, 7 Crim. Just. 28, 31 (Winter 1993) ("counsel should not be permitted to circumvent the no-extrinsic-evidence provision by tucking a third person's opinion about prior acts into a question asked of the witness who has denied the act").

[¶4] For purposes of consistency the term "credibility" has been replaced by the term "character for truthfulness" in the last sentence of subdivision (b). The term "credibility" is also used in subdivision (a). But the Committee found it unnecessary to substitute "character for truthfulness" for "credibility" in Rule 608(a), because subdivision (a)(1) already serves to limit impeachment to proof of such character.

[¶5] Rules 609(a) and 610 also use the term "credibility" when the intent of those Rules is to regulate impeachment of a witness' character for truthfulness. No inference should be derived from the fact that the Committee proposed an amendment to Rule 608(b) but not to Rules 609 and 610.

FRE 609 – 2006 NOTES OF ADVISORY COMMITTEE

[¶1] The amendment provides that Rule 609(a)(2) mandates the admission of evidence of a conviction only when the conviction required the proof of (or in the case of a guilty plea, the admission of) an act of dishonesty or false statement. Evidence of all other convictions is inadmissible under this subsection, irrespective of whether the witness exhibited dishonesty or made a false statement in the process of the commission of the crime of conviction. Thus, evidence that a witness was convicted for a crime of violence, such as murder, is not admissible under Rule 609(a)(2), even if the witness acted deceitfully in the course of committing the crime.

[¶2] The amendment is meant to give effect to the legislative intent to limit the convictions that are to be automatically admitted under subdivision (a)(2). The Conference Committee provided that by "dishonesty and false statement" it meant "crimes such as perjury, subornation of perjury, false statement, criminal fraud, embezzlement, or false pretense, or any other offense in the nature of *crimen falsi*, the commission of which involves some element of deceit, untruthfulness, or falsification bearing on the [witness's] propensity to testify truthfully." Historically, offenses classified as *crimina falsi* have included only those crimes in which the ultimate criminal act was itself an act of deceit. *See* Green, *Deceit and the Classification of Crimes: Federal Rule of Evidence 609(a)(2) and the Origins of* Crimen Falsi, 90 J. Crim. L. & Criminology 1087 (2000).

[¶3] Evidence of crimes in the nature of *crimina falsi* must be admitted under Rule 609(a)(2), regardless of how such crimes are specifically charged. For example, evidence that a witness was convicted of making a false claim to a federal agent is admissible under this subdivision regardless of whether the crime was charged under a section that expressly references deceit (*e.g.*, 18 U.S.C. §1001, Material Misrepresentation to the Federal Government) or a section that does not (*e.g.*, 18 U.S.C. §1503, Obstruction of Justice).

[¶4] The amendment requires that the proponent have ready proof that the conviction required the factfinder to find, or the defendant to admit, an act of dishonesty or false statement. Ordinarily, the statutory elements of the crime will indicate whether it is one of dishonesty or false statement. Where the deceitful nature of the crime is not apparent from the statute and the face of the judgment—as, for example, where the conviction simply records a finding of guilt for a statutory offense that does not reference deceit expressly—a proponent may offer information such as an indictment, a statement of admitted facts, or jury instructions to show that the factfinder had to find, or the defendant had to admit, an act of dishonesty or false statement in order for the witness to have been convicted. *Cf. Taylor v. United States*, 495 U.S. 575, 602 (1990) (providing that a trial court may look to a charging instrument or jury instructions to ascertain the nature of a prior offense where the statute is insufficiently clear on its face); *Shepard v. United States*, 125 S.Ct. 1254 (2005) (the inquiry to determine whether a guilty plea to a crime defined by a nongeneric statute necessarily admitted elements of the generic offense was limited to the charging document's terms, the terms of a plea agreement or transcript of colloquy between judge and defendant in which the factual basis for the plea was confirmed by the defendant, or a comparable judicial record). But the amendment does not contemplate a "minitrial" in which the court plumbs the record of the previous proceeding to determine whether the crime was in the nature of *crimen falsi*.

[¶5] The amendment also substitutes the term "character for truthfulness" for the term "credibility" in the first sentence of the Rule. The limitations of Rule 609 are not applicable if a conviction is admitted for a purpose other than to prove the witness's character for untruthfulness. *See, e.g.*, *United States v. Lopez*, 979 F.2d 1024 (5th Cir.1992) (Rule 609 was not applicable where the conviction was offered for purposes of contradiction). The use of the term "credibility" in subdivision (d) is retained, however, as that subdivision is intended to govern the use of a juvenile adjudication for any type of impeachment.

FRE 615 – 1998 NOTES OF ADVISORY COMMITTEE

[¶1] The amendment is in response to: (1) the Victim's Rights and Restitution Act of 1990, 42 U.S.C. §10606, which guarantees, within certain limits, the right of a crime victim to attend the trial; and (2) the Victim Rights Clarification Act of 1997 (18 U.S.C. §3510).

FRE 701 – 2011 NOTES OF ADVISORY COMMITTEE

[¶1] The Committee deleted all reference to an "inference" on the grounds that the deletion made the Rule flow

better and easier to read, and because any "inference" is covered by the broader term "opinion." Courts have not made substantive decisions on the basis of any distinction between an opinion and an inference. No change in current practice is intended.

FRE 701 – 2000 NOTES OF ADVISORY COMMITTEE

[¶1] Rule 701 has been amended to eliminate the risk that the reliability requirements set forth in Rule 702 will be evaded through the simple expedient of proffering an expert in lay witness clothing. Under the amendment, a witness' testimony must be scrutinized under the rules regulating expert opinion to the extent that the witness is providing testimony based on scientific, technical, or other specialized knowledge within the scope of Rule 702. *See generally Asplundh Mfg. Div. v. Benton Harbor Eng'g*, 57 F.3d 1190 (3d Cir.1995). By channeling testimony that is actually expert testimony to Rule 702, the amendment also ensures that a party will not evade the expert witness disclosure requirements set forth in Fed.R.Civ.P. 26 and Fed.R.Crim.P. 16 by simply calling an expert witness in the guise of a layperson. *See* Joseph, *Emerging Expert Issues Under the 1993 Disclosure Amendments to the Federal Rules of Civil Procedure*, 164 F.R.D. 97, 108 (1996) (noting that "there is no good reason to allow what is essentially surprise expert testimony," and that "the Court should be vigilant to preclude manipulative conduct designed to thwart the expert disclosure and discovery process"). *See also United States v. Figueroa-Lopez*, 125 F.3d 1241, 1246 (9th Cir.1997) (law enforcement agents testifying that the defendant's conduct was consistent with that of a drug trafficker could not testify as lay witnesses; to permit such testimony under Rule 701 "subverts the requirements of Federal Rule of Criminal Procedure 16(a)(1)(E)").

[¶2] The amendment does not distinguish between expert and lay *witnesses*, but rather between expert and lay *testimony*. Certainly it is possible for the same witness to provide both lay and expert testimony in a single case. *See, e.g., United States v. Figueroa-Lopez*, 125 F.3d 1241, 1246 (9th Cir.1997) (law enforcement agents could testify that the defendant was acting suspiciously, without being qualified as experts; however, the rules on experts were applicable where the agents testified on the basis of extensive experience that the defendant was using code words to refer to drug quantities and prices). The amendment makes clear that any part of a witness' testimony that is based upon scientific, technical, or other specialized knowledge within the scope of Rule 702 is governed by the standards of Rule 702 and the corresponding disclosure requirements of the Civil and Criminal Rules.

[¶3] The amendment is not intended to affect the "prototypical example[s] of the type of evidence contemplated by the adoption of Rule 701 relat[ing] to the appearance of persons or things, identity, the manner of conduct, competency of a person, degrees of light or darkness, sound, size, weight, distance, and an endless number of items that cannot be described factually in words apart from inferences." *Asplundh Mfg. Div. v. Benton Harbor Eng'g*, 57 F.3d 1190, 1196 (3d Cir.1995).

[¶4] For example, most courts have permitted the owner or officer of a business to testify to the value or projected profits of the business, without the necessity of qualifying the witness as an accountant, appraiser, or similar expert. *See, e.g., Lightning Lube, Inc. v. Witco Corp.*, 4 F.3d 1153 (3d Cir.1993) (no abuse of discretion in permitting the plaintiff's owner to give lay opinion testimony as to damages, as it was based on his knowledge and participation in the day-to-day affairs of the business). Such opinion testimony is admitted not because of experience, training or specialized knowledge within the realm of an expert, but because of the particularized knowledge that the witness has by virtue of his or her position in the business. The amendment does not purport to change this analysis. Similarly, courts have permitted lay witnesses to testify that a substance appeared to be a narcotic, so long as a foundation of familiarity with the substance is established. *See, e.g., United States v. Westbrook*, 896 F.2d 330 (8th Cir.1990) (two lay witnesses who were heavy amphetamine users were properly permitted to testify that a substance was amphetamine; but it was error to permit another witness to make such an identification where she had no experience with amphetamines). Such testimony is not based on specialized knowledge within the scope of Rule 702, but rather is based upon a layperson's personal knowledge. If, however, that witness were to describe how a narcotic was manufactured, or to describe the intricate workings of a narcotic distribution network, then the witness would have to qualify as an expert under Rule 702. *United States v. Figueroa-Lopez, supra.*

[¶5] The amendment incorporates the distinctions set forth in *State v. Brown*, 836 S.W.2d 530, 549 (1992), a case involving former Tennessee Rule of Evidence 701, a rule that precluded lay witness testimony based on "special knowledge." In Brown, the court declared that the distinction between lay and expert witness testimony is that lay testimony "results from a process of reasoning familiar in everyday life," while expert testimony "results from a process of reasoning which can be mastered only by specialists in the field." The court in Brown noted that a lay witness with experience could testify that a substance appeared to be blood, but that a witness would have to qualify as an expert before he could testify that bruising around the eyes is indicative of skull trauma. That is the kind of distinction made by the amendment to this Rule.

FRE 702 – 2000 NOTES OF ADVISORY COMMITTEE

[¶1] Rule 702 has been amended in response to *Daubert v. Merrell Dow Pharmaceuticals, Inc.*, 509 U.S. 579 (1993), and to the many cases applying *Daubert*, including *Kumho Tire Co. v. Carmichael*, 119 S.Ct. 1167 (1999). In *Daubert* the Court charged trial judges with the responsibility of acting as gatekeepers to exclude unreliable expert testimony, and the Court in *Kumho* clarified that this gatekeeper function applies to all expert testimony, not just testimony based in science. *See also Kumho*, 119 S.Ct. at 1178 (citing the Committee Note to the proposed amendment to Rule 702, which had been released for public comment before the date of the *Kumho* decision). The amendment affirms the trial court's role as gatekeeper and provides some general standards that the trial court must use to assess the reliability and helpfulness of proffered expert testimony. Consistently with *Kumho*, the Rule as amended provides that all types of expert testimony present questions of admissibility for the trial court in deciding whether the evidence is reliable and helpful. Consequently, the admissibility of all expert testimony is governed by the principles of Rule 104(a). Under that Rule, the proponent has the burden of establishing that the pertinent admissibility requirements are met by a preponderance of the evidence. *See Bourjaily v. United States*, 483 U.S. 171 (1987).

[¶2] *Daubert* set forth a non-exclusive checklist for trial courts to use in assessing the reliability of scientific expert testimony. The specific factors explicated by the *Daubert* Court are (1) whether the expert's technique or theory can be or has been tested—that is, whether the expert's theory can be challenged in some objective sense, or whether it is instead simply a subjective, conclusory approach that cannot reasonably be assessed for reliability; (2) whether the technique or theory has been subject to peer review and publication; (3) the known or potential rate of error of the technique or theory when applied; (4) the existence and maintenance of standards and controls; and (5) whether the technique or theory has been generally accepted in the scientific community. The Court in *Kumho* held that these factors might also be applicable in assessing the reliability of nonscientific expert testimony, depending upon "the particular circumstances of the particular case at issue." 119 S.Ct. at 1175.

[¶3] No attempt has been made to "codify" these specific factors. Daubert itself emphasized that the factors were neither exclusive nor dispositive. Other cases have recognized that not all of the specific Daubert factors can apply to every type of expert testimony. In addition to *Kumho*, 119 S.Ct. at 1175, *see Tyus v. Urban Search Management*, 102 F.3d 256 (7th Cir.1996) (noting that the factors mentioned by the Court in Daubert do not neatly apply to expert testimony from a sociologist). *See also Kannankeril v. Terminix Int'l, Inc.*, 128 F.3d 802, 809 (3d Cir.1997) (holding that lack of peer review or publication was not dispositive where the expert's opinion was supported by "widely accepted scientific knowledge"). The standards set forth in the amendment are broad enough to require consideration of any or all of the specific Daubert factors where appropriate.

[¶4] Courts both before and after Daubert have found other factors relevant in determining whether expert testimony is sufficiently reliable to be considered by the trier of fact. These factors include:

(1) Whether experts are "proposing to testify about matters growing naturally and directly out of research they have conducted independent of the litigation, or whether they have developed their opinions expressly for purposes of testifying." *Daubert v. Merrell Dow Pharmaceuticals, Inc.*, 43 F.3d 1311, 1317 (9th Cir.1995).

(2) Whether the expert has unjustifiably extrapolated from an accepted premise to an unfounded conclusion. *See General Elec. Co. v. Joiner*, 522 U.S. 136, 146 (1997) (noting that in some cases a trial court "may conclude that there is simply too great an analytical gap between the data and the opinion proffered").

(3) Whether the expert has adequately accounted for obvious alternative explanations. *See Claar v. Burlington N.R.R.*, 29 F.3d 499 (9th Cir.1994) (testimony excluded where the expert failed to consider other obvious causes for the plaintiff's condition). *Compare Ambrosini v. Labarraque*, 101 F.3d 129 (D.C. Cir. 1996) (the possibility of some uneliminated causes presents a question of weight, so long as the most obvious causes have been considered and reasonably ruled out by the expert).

(4) Whether the expert "is being as careful as he would be in his regular professional work outside his paid litigation consulting." *Sheehan v. Daily Racing Form, Inc.*, 104 F.3d 940, 942 (7th Cir.1997). *See Kumho Tire Co. v. Carmichael*, 119 S.Ct. 1167, 1176 (1999) (*Daubert* requires the trial court to assure itself that the expert "employs in the courtroom the same level of intellectual rigor that characterizes the practice of an expert in the relevant field").

(5) Whether the field of expertise claimed by the expert is known to reach reliable results for the type of opinion the expert would give. *See Kumho Tire Co. v. Carmichael*, 119 S.Ct. 1167, 1175 (1999) (*Daubert's* general acceptance factor does not "help show that an expert's testimony is reliable where the discipline itself lacks reliability, as, for example, do theories grounded in any so-called generally accepted principles of astrology or necromancy."); *Moore v. Ashland Chemical, Inc.*, 151 F.3d 269 (5th Cir.1998) (en banc) (clinical doctor was properly precluded from testifying to the toxicological cause of the plaintiff's respiratory problem, where the opinion was not sufficiently grounded in scientific methodology); *Sterling v. Velsicol Chem. Corp.*, 855 F.2d 1188 (6th Cir.1988) (rejecting testimony based on "clinical ecology" as unfounded and unreliable).

[¶5] All of these factors remain relevant to the determination of the reliability of expert testimony under the Rule as amended. Other factors may also be relevant. *See Kumho*, 119 S.Ct. 1167, 1176 ("[W]e conclude that the trial judge must have considerable leeway in deciding in a particular case how to go about determining whether particular expert testimony is reliable."). Yet no single factor is necessarily dispositive of the reliability of a particular expert's testimony. *See, e.g., Heller v. Shaw Industries, Inc.*, 167 F.3d 146, 155 (3d Cir.1999) ("not only must each stage of the expert's testimony be reliable, but each stage must be evaluated practically and flexibly without bright-line exclusionary (or inclusionary) rules."); *Daubert v. Merrell Dow Pharmaceuticals, Inc.*, 43 F.3d 1311, 1317, n.5 (9th Cir.1995) (noting that some expert disciplines "have the courtroom as a principal theatre of operations" and as to these disciplines "the fact that the expert has developed an expertise principally for purposes of litigation will obviously not be a substantial consideration.").

[¶6] A review of the caselaw after *Daubert* shows that the rejection of expert testimony is the exception rather than the rule. *Daubert* did not work a "seachange over federal evidence law," and "the trial court's role as gatekeeper is not intended to serve as a replacement for the adversary system." *United States v. 14.38 Acres of Land Situated in Leflore County, Mississippi*, 80 F.3d 1074, 1078 (5th Cir.1996). As the Court in *Daubert* stated: "Vigorous cross-examination, presentation of contrary evidence, and careful instruction on the burden of proof are the traditional and appropriate means of attacking shaky but admissible evidence." 509 U.S. at 595. Likewise, this amendment is not intended to provide an excuse for an automatic challenge to the testimony of every expert. *See Kumho Tire Co. v. Carmichael*, 119 S.Ct. 1167, 1176 (1999) (noting that the trial judge has the discretion "both to avoid unnecessary 'reliability' proceedings in ordinary cases where the reliability of an expert's methods is properly taken for granted, and to require appropriate proceedings in the less usual or more complex cases where cause for questioning the expert's reliability arises.").

[¶7] When a trial court, applying this amendment, rules that an expert's testimony is reliable, this does not necessarily mean that contradictory expert testimony is unreliable. The amendment is broad enough to permit testimony that is the product of competing principles or methods in the same field of expertise. *See, e.g., Heller v. Shaw Industries, Inc.*, 167 F.3d 146, 160 (3d Cir.1999) (expert testimony cannot be excluded simply because the expert uses one test rather than another, when both tests are accepted in the field and both reach reliable results). As the court stated in *In re Paoli R.R. Yard PCB Litigation*, 35 F.3d 717, 744 (3d Cir.1994), proponents "do not have to demonstrate to the judge by a preponderance of the evidence that the assessments of their experts are correct, they only have to demonstrate by a preponderance of evidence that their opinions are reliable.... The evidentiary requirement of reliability is lower than the merits standard of correctness." *See also Daubert v. Merrell Dow Pharmaceuticals, Inc.*, 43 F.3d 1311, 1318 (9th Cir.1995) (scientific experts might be permitted to testify if they could show that the methods they used were also employed by "a recognized minority of scientists in their field."); *Ruiz-Troche v. Pepsi Cola*, 161 F.3d 77, 85 (1st Cir.1998) ("*Daubert* neither requires nor empowers trial courts to determine which of several competing scientific theories has the best provenance.").

[¶8] The Court in *Daubert* declared that the "focus, of course, must be solely on principles and methodology, not on the conclusions they generate." 509 U.S. at 595. Yet as the Court later recognized, "conclusions and methodology are not entirely distinct from one another." *General Elec. Co. v. Joiner*, 522 U.S. 136, 146 (1997). Under the amendment, as under *Daubert*, when an expert purports to apply principles and methods in accordance with professional standards, and yet reaches a conclusion that other experts in the field would not reach, the trial court may fairly suspect that the principles and methods have not been faithfully applied. *See Lust v. Merrell Dow Pharmaceuticals, Inc.*, 89 F.3d 594, 598 (9th Cir.1996). The amendment specifically provides that the trial court must scrutinize not only the principles and methods used by the expert, but also whether those principles and methods have been properly applied to the facts of the case. As the court noted in *In re Paoli R.R. Yard PCB Litig.*, 35 F.3d 717, 745 (3d Cir.1994), "*any* step that renders the analysis unreliable ... renders the expert's testimony inadmissible. *This is true whether the step completely changes a reliable methodology or merely misapplies that methodology*."

[¶9] If the expert purports to apply principles and methods to the facts of the case, it is important that this application be conducted reliably. Yet it might also be important in some cases for an expert to educate the factfinder about general principles, without ever attempting to apply these principles to the specific facts of the case. For example, experts might instruct the factfinder on the principles of thermodynamics, or bloodclotting, or on how financial markets respond to corporate reports, without ever knowing about or trying to tie their testimony into the facts of the case. The amendment does not alter the venerable practice of using expert testimony to educate the factfinder on general principles. For this kind of generalized testimony, Rule 702 simply requires that: (1) the expert be qualified; (2) the testimony address a subject matter on which the factfinder can be assisted by an expert; (3) the testimony be reliable; and (4) the testimony "fit" the facts of the case.

[¶10] As stated earlier, the amendment does not distinguish between scientific and other forms of expert testimony. The trial court's gatekeeping function applies to testimony by any expert. *See Kumho Tire Co. v. Carmichael*, 119 S.Ct. 1167, 1171 (1999) ("We conclude that Daubert's general holding—setting forth the trial judge's general 'gatekeeping' obligation—applies not only to testimony based on 'scientific' knowledge, but also to testimony based on 'technical' and 'other specialized' knowledge."). While the relevant factors for determining reliability will vary from expertise to expertise, the amendment rejects the premise that an expert's testimony should be treated more permissively simply because it is outside the realm of science. An opinion from an expert who is not a scientist should receive the same degree of scrutiny for reliability as an opinion from an expert who purports to be a scientist. *See Watkins v. Telsmith, Inc.*, 121 F.3d 984, 991 (5th Cir.1997) ("[I]t seems exactly backwards that experts who purport to rely on general engineering principles and practical experience might escape screening by the district court simply by stating that their conclusions were not reached by any particular method or technique."). Some types of expert testimony will be more objectively verifiable, and subject to the expectations of falsifiability, peer review, and publication, than others. Some types of expert testimony will not rely on anything like a scientific method, and so will have to be evaluated by reference to other standard principles attendant to the particular area of expertise. The trial judge in all cases of proffered expert testimony must find that it is properly grounded, well-reasoned, and not speculative before it can be admitted. The expert's testimony must be grounded in an accepted body of learning or experience in the expert's field, and the expert must explain how the conclusion is so grounded. *See, e.g.*, American College of Trial Lawyers, *Standards and Procedures for Determining the Admissibility of Expert Testimony after Daubert*, 157 F.R.D. 571, 579 (1994) ("[W]hether the testimony concerns economic principles, accounting standards, property valuation or other non-scientific subjects, it should be evaluated by reference to the 'knowledge and experience' of that particular field.").

[¶11] The amendment requires that the testimony must be the product of reliable principles and methods that are reliably applied to the facts of the case. While the terms "principles" and "methods" may convey a certain impression when applied to scientific knowledge, they remain relevant when applied to testimony based on technical or other specialized knowledge. For example, when a law enforcement agent testifies regarding the use of code words in a drug transaction, the principle used by the agent is that participants in such transactions regularly use code words to conceal the nature of their activities. The method used by the agent is the application of extensive experience to analyze the meaning of the conversations. So long as the principles and methods are reliable and applied reliably to the facts of the case, this type of testimony should be admitted.

[¶12] Nothing in this amendment is intended to suggest that experience alone—or experience in conjunction with other knowledge, skill, training or education—may not provide a sufficient foundation for expert testimony. To the contrary, the text of Rule 702 expressly contemplates that an expert may be qualified on the basis of experience. In certain fields, experience is the predominant, if not sole, basis for a great deal of reliable expert testimony. *See, e.g.*, *United States v. Jones*, 107 F.3d 1147 (6th Cir.1997) (no abuse of discretion in admitting the testimony of a handwriting examiner who had years of practical experience and extensive training, and who explained his methodology in detail); *Tassin v. Sears Roebuck*, 946 F.Supp. 1241, 1248 (M.D.La. 1996) (design engineer's testimony can be admissible when the expert's opinions "are based on facts, a reasonable investigation, and traditional technical/mechanical expertise, and he provides a reasonable link between the information and procedures he uses and the conclusions he reaches"). *See also Kumho Tire Co. v. Carmichael*, 119 S.Ct. 1167, 1178 (1999) (stating that "no one denies that an expert might draw a conclusion from a set of observations based on extensive and specialized experience.").

[¶13] If the witness is relying solely or primarily on experience, then the witness must explain how that experience leads to the conclusion reached, why that experience is a sufficient basis for the opinion, and how that experience is reliably applied to the facts. The trial court's gatekeeping function requires more than simply "taking the expert's word for it." *See Daubert v. Merrell Dow Pharmaceuticals, Inc.*, 43 F.3d 1311, 1319 (9th Cir.1995) ("We've been presented with only the experts' qualifications, their conclusions and their assurances of reliability. Under *Daubert*, that's not enough."). The more subjective and controversial the expert's inquiry, the more likely the testimony should be excluded as unreliable. *See O'Conner v. Commonwealth Edison Co.*, 13 F.3d 1090 (7th Cir.1994) (expert testimony based on a completely subjective methodology held properly excluded). *See also Kumho Tire Co. v. Carmichael*, 119 S.Ct. 1167, 1176 (1999) ("[I]t will at times be useful to ask even of a witness whose expertise is based purely on experience, say, a perfume tester able to distinguish among 140 odors at a sniff, whether his preparation is of a kind that others in the field would recognize as acceptable.").

[¶14] Subpart (1) of Rule 702 calls for a quantitative rather than qualitative analysis. The amendment requires that expert testimony be based on sufficient underlying "facts or data." The term "data" is intended to encompass the reliable opinions of other experts. See the original Advisory Committee Note to Rule 703. The language "facts or data" is broad enough to allow an expert to rely on hypothetical facts that are supported by the evidence. *Id.*

[¶15] When facts are in dispute, experts sometimes reach different conclusions based on competing versions of the facts. The emphasis in the amendment on "sufficient facts or data" is not intended to authorize a trial court to exclude an expert's testimony on the ground that the court believes one version of the facts and not the other.

[¶16] There has been some confusion over the relationship between Rules 702 and 703. The amendment makes clear that the sufficiency of the basis of an expert's testimony is to be decided under Rule 702. Rule 702 sets forth the overarching requirement of reliability, and an analysis of the sufficiency of the expert's basis cannot be divorced from the ultimate reliability of the expert's opinion. In contrast, the "reasonable reliance" requirement of Rule 703 is a relatively narrow inquiry. When an expert relies on inadmissible information, Rule 703 requires the trial court to determine whether that information is of a type reasonably relied on by other experts in the field. If so, the expert can rely on the information in reaching an opinion. However, the question whether the expert is relying on a *sufficient* basis of information—whether admissible information or not—is governed by the requirements of Rule 702.

[¶17] The amendment makes no attempt to set forth procedural requirements for exercising the trial court's gatekeeping function over expert testimony. *See* Daniel J. Capra, *The Daubert Puzzle*, 38 Ga.L.Rev. 699, 766 (1998) ("Trial courts should be allowed substantial discretion in dealing with Daubert questions; any attempt to codify procedures will likely give rise to unnecessary changes in practice and create difficult questions for appellate review."). Courts have shown considerable ingenuity and flexibility in considering challenges to expert testimony under Daubert, and it is contemplated that this will continue under the amended Rule. *See, e.g., Cortes-Irizarry v. Corporacion Insular*, 111 F.3d 184 (1st Cir.1997) (discussing the application of Daubert in ruling on a motion for summary judgment); *In re Paoli R.R. Yard PCB Litig.*, 35 F.3d 717, 736, 739 (3d Cir.1994) (discussing the use of *in limine* hearings); *Claar v. Burlington N.R.R.*, 29 F.3d 499, 502-05 (9th Cir.1994) (discussing the trial court's technique of ordering experts to submit serial affidavits explaining the reasoning and methods underlying their conclusions).

[¶18] The amendment continues the practice of the original Rule in referring to a qualified witness as an "expert." This was done to provide continuity and to minimize change. The use of the term "expert" in the Rule does not, however, mean that a jury should actually be informed that a qualified witness is testifying as an "expert." Indeed, there is much to be said for a practice that prohibits the use of the term "expert" by both the parties and the court at trial. Such a practice "ensures that trial courts do not inadvertently put their stamp of authority" on a witness's opinion, and protects against the jury's being "overwhelmed by the so-called 'experts'." Hon. Charles Richey, *Proposals to Eliminate the Prejudicial Effect of the Use of the Word "Expert" Under the Federal Rules of Evidence in Criminal and Civil Jury Trials*, 154 F.R.D. 537, 559 (1994) (setting forth limiting instructions and a standing order employed to prohibit the use of the term "expert" in jury trials).

FRE 703 – 2011 NOTES OF ADVISORY COMMITTEE

[¶1] The Committee deleted all reference to an "inference" on the grounds that the deletion made the Rule flow better and easier to read, and because any "inference" is covered by the broader term "opinion." Courts have not made substantive decisions on the basis of any distinction between an opinion and an inference. No change in current practice is intended.

FRE 703 – 2000 NOTES OF ADVISORY COMMITTEE

[¶1] Rule 703 has been amended to emphasize that when an expert reasonably relies on inadmissible information to form an opinion or inference, the underlying information is not admissible simply because the opinion or inference is admitted. Courts have reached different results on how to treat inadmissible information when it is reasonably relied upon by an expert in forming an opinion or drawing an inference. *Compare United States v. Rollins*, 862 F.2d 1282 (7th Cir.1988) (admitting, as part of the basis of an FBI agent's expert opinion on the meaning of code language, the hearsay statements of an informant), *with United States v. 0.59 Acres of Land*, 109 F.3d 1493 (9th Cir.1997) (error to admit hearsay offered as the basis of an expert opinion, without a limiting instruction). Commentators have also taken differing views. *See, e.g.*, Ronald Carlson, *Policing the Bases of Modern Expert Testimony*, 39 Vand.L.Rev. 577 (1986) (advocating limits on the jury's consideration of otherwise inadmissible evidence used as the basis for an expert opinion); Paul Rice, *Inadmissible Evidence as a Basis for Expert Testimony: A Response to Professor Carlson*, 40 Vand.L.Rev. 583 (1987) (advocating unrestricted use of information reasonably relied upon by an expert).

[¶2] When information is reasonably relied upon by an expert and yet is admissible only for the purpose of assisting the jury in evaluating an expert's opinion, a trial court applying this Rule must consider the information's probative value in assisting the jury to weigh the expert's opinion on the one hand, and the risk of prejudice resulting from the jury's potential misuse of the information for substantive purposes on the other. The information may be disclosed to the jury, upon objection, only if the trial court finds that the probative value of the information in assisting the jury to evaluate the expert's opinion substantially outweighs its prejudicial effect. If the otherwise inadmissible information is admitted under this balancing test, the trial judge must give a limiting instruction upon request, informing the jury that the underlying information must not be used for substantive purposes. *See* Rule 105. In determining the appropriate course, the trial court should consider the probable effectiveness or lack of effectiveness of a limiting instruction under the particular circumstances.

[¶3] The amendment governs only the disclosure to the jury of information that is reasonably relied on by an expert, when that information is not admissible for substantive purposes. It is not intended to affect the admissibility of an expert's testimony. Nor does the amendment prevent an expert from relying on information that is inadmissible for substantive purposes.

[¶4] Nothing in this Rule restricts the presentation of underlying expert facts or data when offered by an adverse party. *See* Rule 705. Of course, an adversary's attack on an expert's basis will often open the door to a proponent's rebuttal with information that was reasonably relied upon by the expert, even if that information would not have been discloseable initially under the balancing test provided by this amendment. Moreover, in some circumstances the proponent might wish to disclose information that is relied upon by the expert in order to "remove the sting" from the opponent's anticipated attack, and thereby prevent the jury from drawing an unfair negative inference. The trial court should take this consideration into account in applying the balancing test provided by this amendment.

[¶5] This amendment covers facts or data that cannot be admitted for any purpose other than to assist the jury to evaluate the expert's opinion. The balancing test provided in this amendment is not applicable to facts or data that are admissible for any other purpose but have not yet been offered for such a purpose at the time the expert testifies.

[¶6] The amendment provides a presumption against disclosure to the jury of information used as the basis of an expert's opinion and not admissible for any substantive purpose, when that information is offered by the proponent of the expert. In a multi-party case, where one party proffers an expert whose testimony is also beneficial to other parties, each such party should be deemed a "proponent" within the meaning of the amendment.

FRE 704 – 2011 NOTES OF ADVISORY COMMITTEE

[¶1] The Committee deleted all reference to an "inference" on the grounds that the deletion made the Rule flow better and easier to read, and because any "inference" is covered by the broader term "opinion." Courts have not made substantive decisions on the basis of any distinction between an opinion and an inference. No change in current practice is intended.

FRE 705 – 2011 NOTES OF ADVISORY COMMITTEE

[¶1] The Committee deleted all reference to an "inference" on the grounds that the deletion made the Rule flow better and easier to read, and because any "inference" is covered by the broader term "opinion." Courts have not made substantive decisions on the basis of any distinction between an opinion and an inference. No change in current practice is intended.

FRE 801 – 2011 NOTES OF ADVISORY COMMITTEE

[¶1] Statements falling under the hearsay exclusion provided by Rule 801(d)(2) are no longer referred to as "admissions" in the title to the subdivision. The term "admissions" is confusing because not all statements covered by the exclusion are admissions in the colloquial sense—a statement can be within the exclusion even if it "admitted" nothing and was not against the party's interest when made. The term "admissions" also raises confusion in comparison with the Rule 804(b)(3) exception for declarations against interest. No change in application of the exclusion is intended.

FRE 801 – 1997 NOTES OF ADVISORY COMMITTEE

[¶1] Rule 801(d)(2) has been amended in order to respond to three issues raised by *Bourjaily v. United States*, 483 U.S. 171 (1987). First, the amendment codifies the holding in Bourjaily by stating expressly that a court shall consider the contents of a coconspirator's statement in determining "the existence of the conspiracy and the participation therein of the declarant and the party against whom the statement is offered." According to Bourjaily, Rule 104(a) requires these preliminary questions to be established by a preponderance of the evidence.

[¶2] Second, the amendment resolves an issue on which the Court had reserved decision. It provides that the contents of the declarant's statement do not alone suffice to establish a conspiracy in which the declarant and the defendant participated. The court must consider in addition the circumstances surrounding the statement, such as the identity of the speaker, the context in which the statement was made, or evidence corroborating the contents of the statement in making its determination as to each preliminary question. This amendment is in accordance with existing practice. Every court of appeals that has resolved this issue requires some evidence in addition to the contents of the statement. *See, e.g., United States v. Beckham*, 968 F.2d 47, 51 (D.C. Cir.1992); *United States v. Sepulveda*, 15 F.3d 1161, 1181-82 (1st Cir.1993), *cert. denied*, 114 S. Ct. 2714 (1994); *United States v. Daly*, 842 F.2d 1380, 1386 (2d Cir.), *cert. denied*, 488 U.S. 821 (1988); *United States v. Clark*, 18 F.3d 1337, 1341-42 (6th Cir.), *cert. denied*, 115 S. Ct. 152 (1994); *United States v. Zambrana*, 841 F.2d 1320, 1344-45 (7th Cir.1988); *United States v. Silverman*, 861 F.2d 571, 577 (9th Cir.1988); *United States v. Gordon*, 844 F.2d 1397, 1402 (9th Cir.1988); *United States v. Hernandez*, 829 F.2d 988, 993 (10th Cir.1987), *cert. denied*, 485 U.S. 1013 (1988); *United States v. Byrom*, 910 F.2d 725, 736 (11th Cir.1990).

[¶3] Third, the amendment extends the reasoning of Bourjaily to statements offered under subdivisions (C) and (D) of Rule 801(d)(2). In Bourjaily, the Court rejected treating foundational facts pursuant to the law of agency in favor of an evidentiary approach governed by Rule 104(a). The Advisory Committee believes it appropriate to treat analogously preliminary questions relating to the declarant's authority under subdivision (C), and the agency or employment relationship and scope thereof under subdivision (D).

FRE 803 – 2000 NOTES OF ADVISORY COMMITTEE

[¶1] The amendment provides that the foundation requirements of Rule 803(6) can be satisfied under certain circumstances without the expense and inconvenience of producing time-consuming foundation witnesses. Under current law, courts have generally required foundation witnesses to testify. *See, e.g., Tongil Co., Ltd. v. Hyundai Merchant Marine Corp.*, 968 F.2d 999 (9th Cir.1992) (reversing a judgment based on business records where a qualified person filed an affidavit but did not testify). Protections are provided by the authentication requirements of Rule 902(11) for domestic records, Rule 902(12) for foreign records in civil cases, and 18 U.S.C. §3505 for foreign records in criminal cases.

FRE 804 – 2011 NOTES OF ADVISORY COMMITTEE

[¶1] No style changes were made to Rule 804(b)(3), because it was already restyled in conjunction with a substantive amendment, effective December 1, 2010.

FRE 804 – 2010 NOTES OF ADVISORY COMMITTEE

[¶1] Subdivision (b)(3). Rule 804(b)(3) has been amended to provide that the corroborating circumstances requirement applies to all declarations against penal interest offered in criminal cases. A number of courts have applied the corroborating circumstances requirement to declarations against penal interest offered by the prosecution, even though the text of the Rule did not so provide. *See, e.g., United States v. Alvarez*, 584 F.2d 694, 701 (5th Cir. 1978) ("by transplanting the language governing exculpatory statements onto the analysis for admitting inculpatory hearsay, a unitary standard is derived which offers the most workable basis for applying Rule 804(b)(3)"); *United States v. Shukri*, 207 F.3d 412 (7th Cir. 2000) (requiring corroborating circumstances for against-penal-interest statements offered by the government). A unitary approach to declarations against penal interest assures both the prosecution and the accused that the Rule will not be abused and that only reliable hearsay statements will be admitted under the exception.

[¶2] All other changes to the structure and wording of the Rule are intended to be stylistic only. There is no intent to change any other result in any ruling on evidence admissibility.

[¶3] The amendment does not address the use of the corroborating circumstances for declarations against penal interest offered in civil cases.

[¶4] In assessing whether corroborating circumstances exist, some courts have focused on the credibility of the witness who relates the hearsay statement in court. But the credibility of the witness who relates the statement is not a proper factor for the court to consider in assessing corroborating circumstances. To base admission or exclusion of a hearsay statement on the witness's credibility would usurp the jury's role of determining the credibility of testifying witnesses.

FRE 804 – 1997 NOTES OF ADVISORY COMMITTEE

[¶1] Subdivision (b)(5). The contents of Rule 803(24) and Rule 804(b)(5) have been combined and transferred to a new Rule 807. This was done to facilitate additions to Rules 803 and 804. No change in meaning is intended.

[¶2] Subdivision (b)(6). Rule 804(b)(6) has been added to provide that a party forfeits the right to object on hearsay grounds to the admission of a declarant's prior statement when the party's deliberate wrongdoing or acquiescence therein procured the unavailability of the declarant as a witness. This recognizes the need for a prophylactic rule to deal with abhorrent behavior "which strikes at the heart of the system of justice itself." *United States v. Mastrangelo*, 693 F.2d 269, 273 (2d Cir. 1982), cert. denied, 467 U.S. 1204 (1984). The wrongdoing need not consist of a criminal act. The rule applies to all parties, including the government.

[¶3] Every circuit that has resolved the question has recognized the principle of forfeiture by misconduct, although the tests for determining whether there is a forfeiture have varied. *See, e.g., United States v. Aguiar*, 975 F.2d 45, 47 (2d Cir.1992); *United States v. Potamitis*, 739 F.2d 784, 789 (2d Cir.), cert. denied, 469 U.S. 918 (1984); *Steele v. Taylor*, 684 F.2d 1193, 1199 (6th Cir.1982), *cert. denied*, 460 U.S. 1053 (1983); *United States v. Balano*, 618 F.2d 624, 629 (10th Cir.1979), *cert. denied*, 449 U.S. 840 (1980); *United States v. Carlson*, 547 F.2d 1346, 1358-59 (8th Cir.), cert. denied, 431 U.S. 914 (1977). The foregoing cases apply a preponderance of the evidence standard. *Contra, United States v. Thevis*, 665 F.2d 616, 631 (5th Cir.) (clear and convincing standard), cert. denied, 459 U.S. 825 (1982). The usual Rule 104(a) preponderance of the evidence standard has been adopted in light of the behavior the new Rule 804(b)(6) seeks to discourage.

FRE 902 – 2000 NOTES OF ADVISORY COMMITTEE

[¶1] The amendment adds two new paragraphs to the rule on self-authentication. It sets forth a procedure by which parties can authenticate certain records of regularly conducted activity, other than through the testimony of a foundation witness. See the amendment to Rule 803(6). 18 U.S.C. §3505 currently provides a means for certifying foreign records of regularly conducted activity in criminal cases, and this amendment is intended to establish a similar procedure for domestic records, and for foreign records offered in civil cases.

[¶2] A declaration that satisfies 28 U.S.C. §1746 would satisfy the declaration requirement of Rule 902(11), as would any comparable certification under oath.

[¶3] The notice requirement in Rules 902(11) and (12) is intended to give the opponent of the evidence a full opportunity to test the adequacy of the foundation set forth in the declaration.

FRAP NOTES

FRAP 1 – 2010 NOTES OF ADVISORY COMMITTEE

[¶1] Subdivision (b). New subdivision (b) defines the term "state" to include the District of Columbia and any commonwealth or territory of the United States. Thus, as used in these Rules, "state" includes the District of Columbia, Guam, American Samoa, the U.S. Virgin Islands, the Commonwealth of Puerto Rico, and the Commonwealth of the Northern Mariana Islands.

FRAP 1 – 2002 NOTES OF ADVISORY COMMITTEE

[¶1] Subdivision (b). Two recent enactments make it likely that, in the future, one or more of the Federal Rules of

Appellate Procedure ("FRAP") will extend or limit the jurisdiction of the courts of appeals. In 1990, Congress amended the Rules Enabling Act to give the Supreme Court authority to use the federal rules of practice and procedure to define when a ruling of a district court is final for purposes of 28 U.S.C. §1291. See 28 U.S.C. §2072(c). In 1992, Congress amended 28 U.S.C. §1292 to give the Supreme Court authority to use the federal rules of practice and procedure to provide for appeals of interlocutory decisions that are not already authorized by 28 U.S.C. §1292. See 28 U.S.C. §1292(e). Both §1291 and §1292 are unquestionably jurisdictional statutes, and thus, as soon as FRAP is amended to define finality for purposes of the former or to authorize interlocutory appeals not provided for by the latter, FRAP will "extend or limit the jurisdiction of the courts of appeals," and subdivision (b) will become obsolete. For that reason, subdivision (b) has been abrogated.

FRAP 4 – 2011 NOTES OF ADVISORY COMMITTEE

[¶1] Subdivision (a)(1)(B). Rule 4(a)(1)(B) has been amended to make clear that the 60-day appeal period applies in cases in which an officer or employee of the United States is sued in an individual capacity for acts or omissions occurring in connection with duties performed on behalf of the United States. (A concurrent amendment to Rule 40(a)(1) makes clear that the 45-day period to file a petition for panel rehearing also applies in such cases.)

[¶2] The amendment to Rule 4(a)(1)(B) is consistent with a 2000 amendment to Civil Rule 12(a)(3), which specified an extended 60-day period to respond to complaints when "[a] United States officer or employee [is] sued in an individual capacity for an act or omission occurring in connection with duties performed on the United States' behalf." The Committee Note to the 2000 amendment explained: "Time is needed for the United States to determine whether to provide representation to the defendant officer or employee. If the United States provides representation, the need for an extended answer period is the same as in actions against the United States, a United States agency, or a United States officer sued in an official capacity." The same reasons justify providing additional time to the Solicitor General to decide whether to file an appeal.

[¶3] However, because of the greater need for clarity of application when appeal rights are at stake, the amendment to Rule 4(a)(1)(B), and the corresponding legislative amendment to 28 U.S.C. §2107 that is simultaneously proposed, include safe harbor provisions that parties can readily apply and rely upon. Under new subdivision 4(a)(1)(B)(iv), a case automatically qualifies for the 60-day appeal period if (1) a legal officer of the United States has appeared in the case, in an official capacity, as counsel for the current or former officer or employee and has not withdrawn the appearance at the time of the entry of the judgment or order appealed from or (2) a legal officer of the United States appears on the notice of appeal as counsel, in an official capacity, for the current or former officer or employee. There will be cases that do not fall within either safe harbor but that qualify for the longer appeal period. An example would be a case in which a federal employee is sued in an individual capacity for an act occurring in connection with federal duties and the United States does not represent the employee either when the judgment is entered or when the appeal is filed but the United States pays for private counsel for the employee.

FRAP 4 – 2010 NOTES OF ADVISORY COMMITTEE

[¶1] Subdivision (a)(7). Subdivision (a)(7) is amended to reflect the renumbering of Civil Rule 58 as part of the 2007 restyling of the Civil Rules. References to Civil Rule "58(a)(1)" are revised to refer to Civil Rule "58(a)." No substantive change is intended.

FRAP 4 – 2009 NOTES OF ADVISORY COMMITTEE

[¶1] Subdivision (a)(4)(A)(vi). Subdivision (a)(4) provides that certain timely post-trial motions extend the time for filing an appeal. Lawyers sometimes move under Civil Rule 60 for relief that is still available under another rule such as Civil Rule 59. Subdivision (a)(4)(A)(vi) provides for such eventualities by extending the time for filing an appeal so long as the Rule 60 motion is filed within a limited time. Formerly, the time limit under subdivision (a)(4)(A)(vi) was 10 days, reflecting the 10-day limits for making motions under Civil Rules 50(b), 52(b), and 59. Subdivision (a)(4)(A)(vi) now contains a 28-day limit to match the revisions to the time limits in the Civil Rules.

[¶2] Subdivision (a)(4)(B)(ii). Subdivision (a)(4)(B)(ii) is amended to address problems that stemmed from the adoption—during the 1998 restyling project—of language referring to "a judgment altered or amended upon" a post-trial motion.

[¶3] Prior to the restyling, subdivision (a)(4) instructed that "[a]ppellate review of an order disposing of any of [the post-trial motions listed in subdivision (a)(4)] requires the party, in compliance with Appellate Rule 3(c), to amend a previously filed notice of appeal. A party intending to challenge an alteration or amendment of the judgment shall file a notice, or amended notice, of appeal within the time prescribed by this Rule 4 measured from the entry of the order disposing of the last such motion outstanding." After the restyling, subdivision (a)(4)(B)(ii) provided: "A party intending to challenge an order disposing of any motion listed in Rule 4(a)(4)(A), or a judgment altered or amended upon such a motion, must file a notice of appeal, or an amended notice of appeal—in compliance with Rule 3(c)—within the time prescribed by this Rule measured from the entry of the order disposing of the last such remaining motion."

[¶4] One court has explained that the 1998 amendment introduced ambiguity into the Rule: "The new formulation could be read to expand the obligation to file an amended notice to circumstances where the ruling on the post-trial motion alters the prior judgment in an insignificant manner or in a manner favorable to the appellant, even though the appeal is not directed against the alteration of the judgment." *Sorensen v. City of New York*, 413 F.3d 292, 296 n.2 (2d Cir. 2005). The current amendment removes that ambiguous reference to "a judgment altered or amended upon" a post-trial motion, and refers instead to "a judgment's alteration or amendment" upon such a motion. Thus, subdivision (a)(4)(B)(ii) requires a new or amended notice of appeal when an appellant wishes to challenge an order disposing of a motion listed in Rule 4(a)(4)(A) or a judgment's alteration or amendment upon such a motion.

[¶5] Subdivision (a)(5)(C). The time set in the former rule at 10 days has been revised to 14 days. See the Note to Rule 26.[1]

[¶6] Subdivision (a)(6)(B). The time set in the former rule at 7 days has been revised to 14 days. Under the time-computation approach set by former Rule 26(a), "7 days" always meant at least 9 days and could mean as many as 11 or even 13 days. Under current Rule 26(a), intermediate weekends and holidays are counted. Changing the period from 7 to 14 days offsets the change in computation approach. See the Note to Rule 26.[1]

[¶7] Subdivisions (b)(1)(A) and (b)(3)(A). The times set in the former rule at 10 days have been revised to 14 days. See the Note to Rule 26.[1]

1. **Editor's note:** The cross-reference to "Note to Rule 26" refers to 2009 Notes to FRAP 26 at ¶¶1-23, p. 1279, this book.

FRAP 4 – 2005 NOTES OF ADVISORY COMMITTEE

[¶1] Rule 4(a)(6) has permitted a district court to reopen the time to appeal a judgment or order upon finding that four conditions were satisfied. First, the district court had to find that the appellant did not receive notice of the entry of the judgment or order from the district court or any party within 21 days after the judgment or order was entered. Second, the district court had to find that the appellant moved to reopen the time to appeal within 7 days after the appellant received notice of the entry of the judgment or order. Third, the district court had to find that the appellant moved to reopen the time to appeal within 180 days after the judgment or order was entered. Finally, the district court had to find that no party would be prejudiced by the reopening of the time to appeal.

[¶2] Rule 4(a)(6) has been amended to specify more clearly what type of "notice" of the entry of a judgment or order precludes a party from later moving to reopen the time to appeal. In addition, Rule 4(a)(6) has been amended to address confusion about what type of "notice" triggers the 7-day period to bring a motion to reopen. Finally, Rule 4(a)(6) has been reorganized to set forth more logically the conditions that must be met before a district court may reopen the time to appeal.

[¶3] Subdivision (a)(6)(A). Former subdivision (a)(6)(B) has been redesignated as subdivision (a)(6)(A), and one substantive change has been made. As amended, the subdivision will preclude a party from moving to reopen the time to appeal a judgment or order only if the party receives (within 21 days) formal notice of the entry of that judgment or order under Civil Rule 77(d). No other type of notice will preclude a party.

[¶4] The reasons for this change take some explanation. Prior to 1998, former subdivision (a)(6)(B) permitted a district court to reopen the time to appeal if it found "that a party entitled to notice of the entry of a judgment or order did not receive such notice from the clerk or any party within 21 days of its entry." The rule was clear that the "notice" to which it referred was the notice required under Civil Rule 77(d), which must be served by the clerk pursuant to Civil Rule 5(b) and may also be served by a party pursuant to that same rule. In other words, prior to 1998, former subdivision (a)(6)(B) was clear that, if a party did not receive formal notice of the entry of a judgment or order under Civil Rule 77(d), that party could later move to reopen the time to appeal (assuming that the other requirements of subdivision (a)(6) were met).

[¶5] In 1998, former subdivision (a)(6)(B) was amended to change the description of the type of notice that would preclude a party from moving to reopen. As a result of the amendment, former subdivision (a)(6)(B) no longer referred to the failure of the moving party to receive "*such* notice"—that is, the notice required by Civil Rule 77(d)—but instead referred to the failure of the moving party to receive "*the* notice." And former subdivision (a)(6)(B) no longer referred to the failure of the moving party to receive notice from "the *clerk* or any party," both of whom are explicitly mentioned in Civil Rule 77(d). Rather, former subdivision (a)(6)(B) referred to the failure of the moving party to receive notice from "the *district court* or any party."

[¶6] The 1998 amendment meant, then, that the type of notice that precluded a party from moving to reopen the time to appeal was no longer limited to Civil Rule 77(d) notice. Under the 1998 amendment, *some* type of notice, in addition to Civil Rule 77(d) notice, precluded a party. But the text of the amended rule did not make clear what type of notice qualified. This was an invitation for litigation, confusion, and possible circuit splits.

[¶7] To avoid such problems, former subdivision (a)(6)(B)—new subdivision (a)(6)(A)—has been amended to restore its pre-1998 simplicity. Under new subdivision (a)(6)(A), if the court finds that the moving party was not notified under Civil Rule 77(d) of the entry of the judgment or order that the party seeks to appeal within 21 days after that judgment or order was entered, then the court is authorized to reopen the time to appeal (if all of the other requirements of subdivision (a)(6) are met). Because Civil Rule 77(d) requires that notice of the entry of a judgment or order be formally served under Civil Rule 5(b), any notice that is not so served will not operate to preclude the reopening of the time to appeal under new subdivision (a)(6)(A).

[¶8] Subdivision (a)(6)(B). Former subdivision (a)(6)(A) required a party to move to reopen the time to appeal "within 7 days after the moving party receives notice of the entry [of the judgment or order sought to be appealed]." Former subdivision (a)(6)(A) has been redesignated as subdivision (a)(6)(B), and one important substantive change has been made: The subdivision now makes clear that only formal notice of the entry of a judgment or order under Civil Rule 77(d) will trigger the 7-day period to move to reopen the time to appeal.

[¶9] The circuits have been split over what type of "notice" is sufficient to trigger the 7-day period. The majority of circuits that addressed the question held that only *written* notice was sufficient, although nothing in the text of the rule suggested such a limitation. *See, e.g., Bass v. United States Dep't of Agric.*, 211 F.3d 959, 963 (5th Cir.2000). By contrast, the Ninth Circuit held that while former subdivision (a)(6)(A) did not require written notice, "the quality of the communication [had to] rise to the functional equivalent of written notice." *Nguyen v. Southwest Leasing & Rental, Inc.*, 282 F.3d 1061, 1066 (9th Cir.2002). Other circuits suggested in dicta that former subdivision (a)(6)(A) required only "actual notice," which, presumably, could have included oral notice that was not "the functional equivalent of written notice." *See, e.g., Lowry v. McDonnell Douglas Corp.*, 211 F.3d 457, 464 (8th Cir.2000). And still other circuits read into former subdivision (a)(6)(A) restrictions that appeared only in former subdivision (a)(6)(B) (such as the requirement that notice be received "from the district court or any party," *see Benavides v. Bureau of Prisons*, 79 F.3d 1211, 1214 (D.C. Cir.1996)) or that appeared in neither former subdivision (a)(6)(A) nor former subdivision (a)(6)(B) (such as the requirement that notice be served in the manner prescribed by Civil Rule 5, *see Ryan v. First Unum Life Ins. Co.*, 174 F.3d 302, 304-05 (2d Cir.1999)).

[¶10] Former subdivision (a)(6)(A)—new subdivision (a)(6)(B)—has been amended to resolve this circuit split by providing that only formal notice of the entry of a judgment or order under Civil Rule 77(d) will trigger the 7-day period. Using Civil Rule 77(d) notice as the trigger has two advantages: First, because Civil Rule 77(d) is clear and familiar, circuit splits are unlikely to develop over its meaning. Second, because Civil Rule 77(d) notice must be served under Civil Rule 5(b), establishing whether and when such notice was provided should generally not be difficult.

[¶11] Using Civil Rule 77(d) notice to trigger the 7-day period will not unduly delay appellate proceedings. Rule 4(a)(6) applies to only a small number of cases—cases in which a party was not notified of a judgment or order by either the clerk or another party within 21 days after entry. Even with respect to those cases, an appeal cannot be brought more than 180 days after entry, no matter what the circumstances. In addition, Civil Rule 77(d) permits parties to serve notice of the entry of a judgment or order. The winning party can prevent Rule 4(a)(6) from even coming into play simply by serving notice of entry within 21 days. Failing that, the winning party can always trigger the 7-day deadline to move to reopen by serving belated notice.

FRAP 4 – 2002 NOTES OF ADVISORY COMMITTEE

[¶1] Subdivision (a)(1)(C). The federal courts of appeals have reached conflicting conclusions about whether an appeal from an order granting or denying an application for a writ of error coram nobis is governed by the time limitations of Rule 4(a) (which apply in civil cases) or by the time limitations of Rule 4(b) (which apply in criminal cases). *Compare United States v. Craig*, 907 F.2d 653, 655-57, *amended* 919 F.2d 57 (7th Cir.1990); *United States v. Cooper*, 876 F.2d 1192, 1193-94 (5th Cir.1989); and *United States v. Keogh*, 391 F.2d 138, 140 (2d Cir.1968) (applying the time limitations of Rule 4(a)); *with Yasui v. United States*, 772 F.2d 1496, 1498-99 (9th Cir.1985); and *United States v. Mills*, 430 F.2d 526, 527-28 (8th Cir.1970) (applying the time limitations of Rule 4(b)). A new part (C) has been added to Rule 4(a)(1) to resolve this conflict by providing that the time limitations of Rule 4(a) will apply.

[¶2] Subsequent to the enactment of Fed. R. Civ. P. 60(b) and 28 U.S.C. §2255, the Supreme Court has recognized the continued availability of a writ of error *coram nobis* in at least one narrow circumstance. In 1954, the Court permitted a litigant who had been convicted of a crime, served his full sentence, and been released from prison, but who was continuing to suffer a legal disability on account of the conviction, to seek a writ of error *coram nobis* to set aside the conviction. *United States v. Morgan*, 346 U.S. 502 (1954). As the Court recognized, in the *Morgan* situation an application for a writ of error *coram nobis* "is of the same general character as [a motion] under 28 U.S.C. §2255." *Id.* at 506 n.4. Thus, it seems appropriate that the time limitations of Rule 4(a), which apply when a district court grants or denies relief under 28 U.S.C. §2255, should also apply when a district court grants or denies a writ of error *coram nobis*. In addition, the strong public interest in the speedy resolution of criminal appeals that is reflected in the shortened deadlines of Rule 4(b) is not present in the *Morgan* situation, as the party seeking the writ of error *coram nobis* has already served his or her full sentence.

[¶3] Notwithstanding *Morgan*, it is not clear whether the Supreme Court continues to believe that the writ of error *coram nobis* is available in federal court. In civil cases, the writ has been expressly abolished by Fed. R. Civ. P. 60(b). In criminal cases, the Supreme Court has recently stated that it has become "'difficult to conceive of a situation'" in which the writ "'would be necessary or appropriate.'" *Carlisle v. United States*, 517 U.S. 416, 429 (1996) (quoting *United States* *v. Smith*, 331 U.S. 469, 475 n.4 (1947)). The amendment to Rule 4(a)(1) is not intended to express any view on this issue; rather, it is merely meant to specify time limitations for appeals.

[¶4] Rule 4(a)(1)(C) applies only to motions that are in substance, and not merely in form, applications for writs of error *coram nobis*. Litigants may bring and label as applications for a writ of error *coram nobis* what are in reality motions for a new trial under Fed. R. Crim. P. 33 or motions for correction or reduction of a sentence under Fed. R. Crim. P. 35. In such cases, the time limitations of Rule 4(b), and not those of Rule 4(a), should be enforced.

[¶5] Subdivision (a)(4)(A)(vi). Rule 4(a)(4)(A)(vi) has been amended to remove a parenthetical that directed that the 10-day deadline be "computed using Federal Rule of Civil Procedure 6(a)." That parenthetical has become superfluous because Rule 26(a)(2) has been amended to require that all deadlines under 11 days be calculated as they are under Fed. R. Civ. P. 6(a).

[¶6] Subdivision (a)(5)(A)(ii). Rule 4(a)(5)(A) permits the district court to extend the time to file a notice of appeal if two conditions are met. First, the party seeking the extension must file its motion no later than 30 days after the expiration of the time originally prescribed by Rule 4(a). Second, the party seeking the extension must show either excusable neglect or good cause. The text of Rule 4(a)(5)(A) does not distinguish between motions filed prior to the expiration of the original deadline and those filed after the expiration of the original deadline. Regardless of whether the motion is filed before or during the 30 days after the original deadline expires, the district court may grant an extension if a party shows either excusable neglect or good cause.

[¶7] Despite the text of Rule 4(a)(5)(A), most of the courts of appeals have held that the good cause standard applies only to motions brought prior to the expiration of the original deadline and that the excusable neglect standard applies only to motions brought during the 30 days following the expiration of the original deadline. *See Pontarelli v. Stone*, 930 F.2d 104, 109-10 (1st Cir.1991) (collecting cases from the Second, Fifth, Sixth, Seventh, Eighth, Ninth, and Eleventh Circuits). These courts have relied heavily upon the Advisory Committee Note to the 1979 amendment to Rule 4(a)(5). But the Advisory Committee Note refers to a draft of the 1979 amendment that was ultimately rejected. The rejected draft directed that the good cause standard apply only to motions filed prior to the expiration of the original deadline. Rule 4(a)(5), as actually amended, did not. *See* 16A Charles Alan Wright, et al., Federal Practice and Procedure §3950.3, at 148-49 (2d ed. 1996).

[¶8] The failure of the courts of appeals to apply Rule 4(a)(5)(A) as written has also created tension between that rule and Rule 4(b)(4). As amended in 1998, Rule 4(b)(4) permits the district court to extend the time for filing a notice of appeal in a *criminal* case for an additional 30 days upon a finding of excusable neglect or good cause. Both Rule 4(b)(4) and the Advisory Committee Note to the 1998 amendment make it clear that an extension can be granted for either excusable neglect or good cause, regardless of whether a motion for an extension is filed before or during the 30 days following the expiration of the original deadline.

[¶9] Rule 4(a)(5)(A)(ii) has been amended to correct this misunderstanding and to bring the rule in harmony in this respect with Rule 4(b)(4). A motion for an extension filed prior to the expiration of the original deadline may be granted if the movant shows either excusable neglect or good cause. Likewise, a motion for an extension filed during the 30 days following the expiration of the original deadline may be granted if the movant shows either excusable neglect or good cause.

[¶10] The good cause and excusable neglect standards have "different domains." *Lorenzen v. Employees Retirement Plan*, 896 F.2d 228, 232 (7th Cir.1990). They are not interchangeable, and one is not inclusive of the other. The excusable neglect standard applies in situations in which there is fault; in such situations, the need for an extension is usually occasioned by something within the control of the movant. The good cause standard applies in situations in which there is no fault—excusable or otherwise. In such situations, the need for an extension is usually occasioned by something that is not within the control of the movant.

[¶11] Thus, the good cause standard can apply to motions brought during the 30 days following the expiration of the original deadline. If, for example, the Postal Service fails to deliver a notice of appeal, a movant might have good cause to seek a post-expiration extension. It may be unfair to make such a movant prove that its "neglect" was excusable, given that the movant may not have been neglectful at all. Similarly, the excusable neglect standard can apply to motions brought prior to the expiration of the original deadline. For example, a movant may bring a pre-expiration motion for an extension of time when an error committed by the movant makes it unlikely that the movant will be able to meet the original deadline.

[¶12] Subdivision (a)(7). Several circuit splits have arisen out of uncertainties about how Rule 4(a)(7)'s definition of when a judgment or order is "entered" interacts with the requirement in Fed. R. Civ. P. 58 that, to be "effective," a judgment must be set forth on a separate document. Rule 4(a)(7) and Fed. R. Civ. P. 58 have been amended to resolve those splits.

[¶13] 1. The first circuit split addressed by the amendments to Rule 4(a)(7) and Fed. R. Civ. P. 58 concerns the extent to which orders that dispose of post-judgment motions must be set forth on separate documents. Under Rule 4(a)(4)(A), the filing of certain post-judgment motions tolls the time to appeal the underlying judgment until the "entry" of the order disposing of the last such remaining motion. Courts have disagreed about whether such an order must be

set forth on a separate document before it is treated as "entered." This disagreement reflects a broader dispute among courts about whether Rule 4(a)(7) independently imposes a separate document requirement (a requirement that is distinct from the separate document requirement that is imposed by the Federal Rules of Civil Procedure ("FRCP")) or whether Rule 4(a)(7) instead incorporates the separate document requirement as it exists in the FRCP. Further complicating the matter, courts in the former "camp" disagree among themselves about the scope of the separate document requirement that they interpret Rule 4(a)(7) as imposing, and courts in the latter "camp" disagree among themselves about the scope of the separate document requirement imposed by the FRCP.

[¶14] Rule 4(a)(7) has been amended to make clear that it simply incorporates the separate document requirement as it exists in Fed. R. Civ. P. 58. If Fed. R. Civ. P. 58 does not require that a judgment or order be set forth on a separate document, then neither does Rule 4(a)(7); the judgment or order will be deemed entered for purposes of Rule 4(a) when it is entered in the civil docket. If Fed. R. Civ. P. 58 requires that a judgment or order be set forth on a separate document, then so does Rule 4(a)(7); the judgment or order will not be deemed entered for purposes of Rule 4(a) until it is so set forth and entered in the civil docket (with one important exception, described below).

[¶15] In conjunction with the amendment to Rule 4(a)(7), Fed. R. Civ. P. 58 has been amended to provide that orders disposing of the post-judgment motions listed in new Fed. R. Civ. P. 58(a)(1) (which post-judgment motions include, but are not limited to, the post-judgment motions that can toll the time to appeal under Rule 4(a)(4)(A)) do not have to be set forth on separate documents. *See* Fed. R. Civ. P. 58(a)(1). Thus, such orders are entered for purposes of Rule 4(a) when they are entered in the civil docket pursuant to Fed. R. Civ. P. 79(a). *See* Rule 4(a)(7)(A)(1).

[¶16] 2. The second circuit split addressed by the amendments to Rule 4(a)(7) and Fed. R. Civ. P. 58 concerns the following question: When a judgment or order is required to be set forth on a separate document under Fed. R. Civ. P. 58 but is not, does the time to appeal the judgment or order—or the time to bring post-judgment motions, such as a motion for a new trial under Fed. R. Civ. P. 59—ever begin to run? According to every circuit except the First Circuit, the answer is "no." The First Circuit alone holds that parties will be deemed to have waived their right to have a judgment or order entered on a separate document three months after the judgment or order is entered in the civil docket. *See Fiore v. Washington County Community Mental Health Ctr.*, 960 F.2d 229, 236 (1st Cir.1992) (en banc). Other circuits have rejected this cap as contrary to the relevant rules. *See, e.g., United States v. Haynes*, 158 F.3d 1327, 1331 (D.C. Cir.1998); *Hammack v. Baroid Corp.*, 142 F.3d 266, 269-70 (5th Cir.1998); *Rubin v. Schottenstein, Zox & Dunn*, 110 F.3d 1247, 1253 n.4 (6th Cir.1997), *vacated on other grounds*, 143 F.3d 263 (6th Cir.1998) (en banc). However, no court has questioned the wisdom of imposing such a cap as a matter of policy.

[¶17] Both Rule 4(a)(7)(A) and Fed. R. Civ. P. 58 have been amended to impose such a cap. Under the amendments, a judgment or order is generally treated as entered when it is entered in the civil docket pursuant to Fed. R. Civ. P. 79(a). There is one exception: When Fed. R. Civ. P. 58(a)(1) requires the judgment or order to be set forth on a separate document, that judgment or order is not treated as entered until it is set forth on a separate document (in addition to being entered in the civil docket) or until the expiration of 150 days after its entry in the civil docket, whichever occurs first. This cap will ensure that parties will not be given forever to appeal (or to bring a post-judgment motion) when a court fails to set forth a judgment or order on a separate document in violation of Fed. R. Civ. P. 58(a)(1).

[¶18] 3. The third circuit split—this split addressed only by the amendment to Rule 4(a)(7)—concerns whether the appellant may waive the separate document requirement over the objection of the appellee. In *Bankers Trust Co. v. Mallis*, 435 U.S. 381, 387 (1978) (per curiam), the Supreme Court held that the "parties to an appeal may waive the separate-judgment requirement of Rule 58." Specifically, the Supreme Court held that when a district court enters an order and "clearly evidence[s] its intent that the ... order ... represent[s] the final decision in the case," the order is a "final decision" for purposes of 28 U.S.C. §1291, even if the order has not been set forth on a separate document for purposes of Fed. R. Civ. P. 58. *Id.* Thus, the parties can choose to appeal without waiting for the order to be set forth on a separate document.

[¶19] Courts have disagreed about whether the consent of all parties is necessary to waive the separate document requirement. Some circuits permit appellees to object to attempted *Mallis* waivers and to force appellants to return to the trial court, request that judgment be set forth on a separate document, and appeal a second time. *See, e.g., Selletti v. Carey*, 173 F.3d 104, 109-10 (2d Cir.1999); *Williams v. Borg*, 139 F.3d 737, 739-40 (9th Cir.1998); *Silver Star Enters., Inc. v. M/V Saramacca*, 19 F.3d 1008, 1013 (5th Cir.1994). Other courts disagree and permit *Mallis* waivers even if the appellee objects. *See, e.g., Haynes*, 158 F.3d at 1331; *Miller v. Artistic Cleaners*, 153 F.3d 781, 783-84 (7th Cir.1998); *Alvord-Polk, Inc. v. F. Schumacher & Co.*, 37 F.3d 996, 1006 n.8 (3d Cir.1994).

[¶20] New Rule 4(a)(7)(B) is intended both to codify the Supreme Court's holding in *Mallis* and to make clear that the decision whether to waive the requirement that the judgment or order be set forth on a separate document is the appellant's alone. It is, after all, the appellant who needs a clear signal as to when the time to file a notice of appeal has begun to run. If the appellant chooses to bring an appeal without waiting for the judgment or order to be set forth on a separate document, then there is no reason why the appellee should be able to object. All that would result from honoring the appellee's objection would be delay.

[¶21] 4. The final circuit split addressed by the amendment to Rule 4(a)(7) concerns the question whether an appellant who chooses to waive the separate document requirement must appeal within 30 days (60 days if the government is a party) from the entry in the civil docket of the judgment or order that should have been set forth on a separate document but was not. In *Townsend v. Lucas*, 745 F.2d 933 (5th Cir.1984), the district court dismissed a 28 U.S.C. §2254 action on May 6, 1983, but failed to set forth the judgment on a separate document. The plaintiff appealed on January 10, 1984. The Fifth Circuit dismissed the appeal, reasoning that, if the plaintiff waived the separate document requirement, then his appeal would be from the May 6 order, and if his appeal was from the May 6 order, then it was untimely under Rule 4(a)(1). The Fifth Circuit stressed that the plaintiff could return to the district court, move that the judgment be set forth on a separate document, and appeal from that judgment within 30 days. *Id.* at 934. Several other cases have embraced the *Townsend* approach. *See, e.g., Armstrong v. Ahitow*, 36 F.3d 574, 575 (7th Cir.1994) (per curiam); *Hughes v. Halifax County Sch. Bd.*, 823 F.2d 832, 835-36 (4th Cir.1987); *Harris v. McCarthy*, 790 F.2d 753, 756 n.1 (9th Cir.1986).

[¶22] Those cases are in the distinct minority. There are numerous cases in which courts have heard appeals that were not filed within 30 days (60 days if the government was a party) from the judgment or order that should have been set forth on a separate document but was not. *See, e.g., Haynes*, 158 F.3d at 1330-31; *Clough v. Rush*, 959 F.2d 182, 186 (10th Cir.1992); *McCalden v. California Library Ass'n*, 955 F.2d 1214, 1218-19 (9th Cir.1990). In the view of these courts, the remand in *Townsend* was "precisely the purposeless spinning of wheels abjured by the Court in the [*Mallis*] case." 15B Charles Alan Wright et al., Federal Practice and Procedure §3915, at 259 n.8 (3d ed. 1992).

[¶23] The Committee agrees with the majority of courts that have rejected the *Townsend* approach. In drafting new Rule 4(a)(7)(B), the Committee has been careful to avoid phrases such as "otherwise timely appeal" that might imply an endorsement of *Townsend*.

[¶24] Subdivision (b)(5). Federal Rule of Criminal Procedure 35(a) permits a district court, acting within 7 days after the imposition of sentence, to correct an erroneous sentence in a criminal case. Some courts have held that the filing of a motion for correction of a sentence suspends the time for filing a notice of appeal from the judgment of conviction. *See, e.g., United States v. Carmouche*, 138 F.3d 1014, 1016 (5th Cir.1998) (per curiam); *United States v. Morillo*, 8 F.3d 864, 869 (1st Cir.1993). Those courts establish conflicting timetables for appealing a judgment of conviction after the filing of a motion to correct a sentence. In the First Circuit, the time to appeal is suspended only for the period provided by Fed. R. Crim. P. 35(a) for the district court to correct a sentence; the time to appeal begins to run again once 7 days have passed after sentencing, even if the motion is still pending. By contrast, in the Fifth Circuit, the time to appeal does not begin to run again until the district court actually issues an order disposing of the motion.

[¶25] Rule 4(b)(5) has been amended to eliminate the inconsistency concerning the effect of a motion to correct a sentence on the time for filing a notice of appeal. The amended rule makes clear that the time to appeal continues to run, even if a motion to correct a sentence is filed. The amendment is consistent with Rule 4(b)(3)(A), which lists the motions that toll the time to appeal, and notably omits any mention of a Fed. R. Crim. P. 35(a) motion. The amendment also should promote certainty and minimize the likelihood of confusion concerning the time to appeal a judgment of conviction.

[¶26] If a district court corrects a sentence pursuant to Fed. R. Crim. P. 35(a), the time for filing a notice of appeal of the corrected sentence under Rule 4(b)(1) would begin to run when the court enters a new judgment reflecting the corrected sentence.

FRAP 4 – 1998 NOTES OF ADVISORY COMMITTEE

[¶1] The language and organization of the rule are amended to make the rule more easily understood. In addition to changes made to improve the understanding, the Advisory Committee has changed language to make style and terminology consistent throughout the appellate rules. These changes are intended to be stylistic only; in this rule, however, substantive changes are made in paragraphs (a)(6) and (b)(4), and in subdivision (c).

[¶2] Subdivision (a), paragraph (1). Although the Advisory Committee does not intend to make any substantive changes in this paragraph, cross-references to Rules 4(a)(1)(B) and 4(c) have been added to subparagraph (a)(1)(A).

[¶3] Subdivision (a), paragraph (4). Item (vi) in subparagraph (A) of Rule 4(a)(4) provides that filing a motion for relief under Fed. R. Civ. P. 60 will extend the time for filing a notice of appeal if the Rule 60 motion is filed no later than 10 days after judgment is entered. Again, the Advisory Committee does not intend to make any substantive change in this paragraph. But because Fed. R. Civ. P. 6(a) and Fed. R. App. P. 26(a) have different methods for computing time, one might be uncertain whether the 10-day period referred to in Rule 4(a)(4) is computed using Civil Rule 6(a) or Appellate Rule 26(a). Because the Rule 60 motion is filed in the district court, and because Fed. R. App. P. 1(a)(2) says that when the appellate rules provide for filing a motion in the district court, "the procedure must comply with the practice of the district court," the rule provides that the 10-day period is computed using Fed. R. Civ. P. 6(a).

[¶4] Subdivision (a), paragraph (6). Paragraph (6) permits a district court to reopen the time for appeal if a party has not received notice of the entry of judgment and no party would be prejudiced by the reopening. Before reopening the time for appeal, the existing rule requires the district court to find that the moving party was entitled to notice of the entry of judgment and did not receive it "from the clerk or any party within 21 days of its entry." The Advisory Committee makes a substantive change. The finding must be that the movant did not receive notice "from the district court or any party within 21 days after entry." This change broadens the type of notice that can preclude reopening the time for appeal. The existing rule provides that only notice from a party or from the clerk bars reopening. The new language precludes reopening if the movant has received notice from "the court."

[¶5] Subdivision (b). Two substantive changes are made in what will be paragraph (b)(4). The current rule permits an extension of time to file a notice of appeal if there is a "showing of excusable neglect." First, the rule is amended to permit a court to extend the time for "good cause" as well as for excusable neglect. Rule 4(a) permits extensions for both reasons in civil cases and the Advisory Committee believes that "good cause" should be sufficient in criminal cases as well. The amendment does not limit extensions for good cause to instances in which the motion for extension of time is filed before the original time has expired. The rule gives the district court discretion to grant extensions for good cause whenever the court believes it appropriate to do so provided that the extended period does not exceed 30 days after the expiration of the time otherwise prescribed by Rule 4(b). Second, paragraph (b)(4) is amended to require only a "finding" of excusable neglect or good cause and not a "showing" of them. Because the rule authorizes the court to provide an extension without a motion, a "showing" is obviously not required; a "finding" is sufficient.

[¶6] Subdivision (c). Substantive amendments are made in this subdivision. The current rule provides that if an inmate confined in an institution files a notice of appeal by depositing it in the institution's internal mail system, the notice is timely filed if deposited on or before the last day for filing. Some institutions have special internal mail systems for handling legal mail; such systems often record the date of deposit of mail by an inmate, the date of delivery of mail to an inmate, etc. The Advisory Committee amends the rule to require an inmate to use the system designed for legal mail, if there is one, in order to receive the benefit of this subdivision.

[¶7] When an inmate uses the filing method authorized by subdivision (c), the current rule provides that the time for other parties to appeal begins to run from the date the district court "receives" the inmate's notice of appeal. The rule is amended so that the time for other parties begins to run when the district court "dockets" the inmate's appeal. A court may "receive" a paper when its mail is delivered to it even if the mail is not processed for a day or two, making the date of receipt uncertain. "Docketing" is an easily identified event. The change eliminates uncertainty. Paragraph (c)(3) is further amended to make it clear that the time for the government to file its appeal runs from the later of the entry of the judgment or order appealed from or the district court's docketing of a defendant's notice filed under this paragraph (c).

FRAP 4 – 1995 NOTES OF ADVISORY COMMITTEE

[¶1] Subdivision (a). Fed. R. Civ. P. 50, 52, and 59 were previously inconsistent with respect to whether certain postjudgment motions had to be filed or merely served no later than 10 days after entry of judgment. As a consequence Rule 4(a)(4) spoke of making or serving such motions rather than filing them. Civil Rules 50, 52, and 59, are being revised to require filing before the end of the 10-day period. As a consequence, this rule is being amended to provide that "filing" must occur within the 10 day period in order to affect the finality of the judgment and extend the period for filing a notice of appeal.

[¶2] The Civil Rules require the filing of postjudgment motions "no later than 10 days after entry of judgment"—rather than "within" 10 days—to include postjudgment motions that are filed before actual entry of the judgment by the clerk. This rule is amended, therefore, to use the same terminology.

[¶3] The rule is further amended to clarify the fact that a party who wants to obtain review of an alteration or amendment of a judgment must file a notice of appeal or amend a previously filed notice to indicate intent to appeal from the altered judgment.

FRAP 4 – 1993 NOTES OF ADVISORY COMMITTEE

[¶1] Paragraph (a)(1). The amendment is intended to alert readers to the fact that paragraph (a)(4) extends the time for filing an appeal when certain posttrial motions are filed. The Committee hopes that awareness of the provisions of paragraph (a)(4) will prevent the filing of a notice of appeal when a posttrial tolling motion is pending.

[¶2] Paragraph (a)(2). The amendment treats a notice of appeal filed after the announcement of a decision or order, but before its formal entry, as if the notice had been filed after entry. The amendment deletes the language that made paragraph (a)(2) inapplicable to a notice of appeal filed after announcement of the disposition of a posttrial motion enumerated in paragraph (a)(4) but before the entry of the order, *see Acosta v. Louisiana Dep't of Health & Human Resources*, 478 U.S. 251 (1986) (per curiam); *Alerte v. McGinnis*, 898 F.2d 69 (7th Cir.1990). Because the amendment of paragraph (a)(4) recognizes all notices of appeal filed after announcement or entry of judgment—even those that are filed while the posttrial motions enumerated in paragraph (a)(4) are pending—the amendment of this paragraph is consistent with the amendment of paragraph (a)(4).

[¶3] Paragraph (a)(3). The amendment is technical in nature; no substantive change is intended.

[¶4] Paragraph (a)(4). The 1979 amendment of this paragraph created a trap for an unsuspecting litigant who files a notice of appeal before a posttrial motion, or while a posttrial motion is pending. The 1979 amendment requires a party to file a new notice of appeal after the motion's disposition. Unless a new notice is filed, the court of appeals lacks jurisdiction to hear the appeal. *Griggs v. Provident Consumer Discount Co.*, 459 U.S. 56 (1982). Many litigants, especially pro se litigants, fail to file the second notice of appeal, and several courts have expressed dissatisfaction with the rule. *See, e.g., Averhart v. Arrendondo*, 773 F.2d 919 (7th Cir.1985); *Harcon Barge Co. v. D & G Boat Rentals, Inc.*, 746 F.2d 278 (5th Cir.1984), *cert. denied*, 479 U.S. 930 (1986).

[¶5] The amendment provides that a notice of appeal filed before the disposition of a specified posttrial motion will become effective upon disposition of the motion. A notice filed before the filing of one of the specified motions or after the filing of a motion but before disposition of the motion is, in effect, suspended until the motion is disposed of, whereupon, the previously filed notice effectively places jurisdiction in the court of appeals.

[¶6] Because a notice of appeal will ripen into an effective appeal upon disposition of a posttrial motion, in some instances there will be an appeal from a judgment that has been altered substantially because the motion was granted in whole or in part. Many such appeals will be dismissed for want of prosecution when the appellant fails to meet the briefing schedule. But, the appellee may also move to strike the appeal. When responding to such a motion, the appellant would have an opportunity to state that, even though some relief sought in a posttrial motion was granted, the appellant still plans to pursue the appeal. Because the appellant's response would provide the appellee with sufficient notice of the appellant's intentions, the Committee does not believe that an additional notice of appeal is needed.

[¶7] The amendment provides that a notice of appeal filed before the disposition of a posttrial tolling motion is sufficient to bring the underlying case, as well as any orders specified in the original notice, to the court of appeals. If the judgment is altered upon disposition of a posttrial motion, however, and if a party wishes to appeal from the disposition of the motion, the party must amend the notice to so indicate. When a party files an amended notice, no additional fees are required because the notice is an amendment of the original and not a new notice of appeal.

[¶8] Paragraph (a)(4) is also amended to include, among motions that extend the time for filing a notice of appeal, a Rule 60 motion that is served within 10 days after entry of judgment. This eliminates the difficulty of determining whether a posttrial motion made within 10 days after entry of a judgment is a Rule 59(e) motion, which tolls the time for filing an appeal, or a Rule 60 motion, which historically has not tolled the time. The amendment comports with the practice in several circuits of treating all motions to alter or amend judgments that are made within 10 days after entry of judgment as Rule 59(e) motions for purposes of Rule 4(a)(4). *See, e.g., Finch v. City of Vernon*, 845 F.2d 256 (11th Cir.1988); *Rados v. Celotex Corp.*, 809 F.2d 170 (2d Cir.1986); *Skagerberg v. Oklahoma*, 797 F.2d 881 (10th Cir. 1986). To conform to a recent Supreme Court decision, however—*Budinich v. Becton Dickinson and Co.*, 486 U.S. 196 (1988)—the amendment excludes motions for attorney's fees from the class of motions that extend the filing time unless a district court, acting under Rule 58, enters an order extending the time for appeal. This amendment is to be read in conjunction with the amendment of Fed. R. Civ. P. 58.

[¶9] Subdivision (b). The amendment grammatically restructures the portion of this subdivision that lists the types of motions that toll the time for filing an appeal. This restructuring is intended to make the rule easier to read. No substantive change is intended other than to add a motion for judgment of acquittal under Criminal Rule 29 to the list of tolling motions. Such a motion is the equivalent of a Fed. R. Civ. P. 50(b) motion for judgment notwithstanding the verdict, which tolls the running of time for an appeal in a civil case.

[¶10] The proposed amendment also eliminates an ambiguity from the third sentence of this subdivision. Prior to this amendment, the third sentence provided that if one of the specified motions was filed, the time for filing an appeal would run from the entry of an order denying the motion. That sentence, like the parallel provision in Rule 4(a)(4), was intended to toll the running of time for appeal if one of the posttrial motions is timely filed. In a criminal case, however, the time for filing the motions runs not from entry of judgment (as it does in civil cases), but from the verdict or finding of guilt. Thus, in a criminal case, a posttrial motion may be disposed of more than 10 days before sentence is imposed, i.e. before the entry of judgment. *United States v. Hashagen*, 816 F.2d 899, 902 n.5 (3d Cir.1987). To make it clear that a notice of appeal need not be filed before entry of judgment, the amendment states that an appeal may be taken within 10 days after the entry of an order disposing of the motion, or within 10 days after the entry of judgment, whichever is later. The amendment also changes the language in the third sentence providing that an appeal may be taken within 10 days after the entry of an order denying the motion; the amendment says instead that an appeal may be taken within 10 days after the entry of an order disposing of the last such motion outstanding. (Emphasis added) The change recognizes that there may be multiple posttrial motions filed and that, although one or more motions may be granted in whole or in part, a defendant may still wish to pursue an appeal.

[¶11] The amendment also states that a notice of appeal filed before the disposition of any of the posttrial tolling motions becomes effective upon disposition of the motions. In most circuits this language simply restates the current practice. *See United States v. Cortes*, 895 F.2d 1245 (9th Cir.), cert. denied, 495 U.S. 939 (1990). Two circuits, however, have questioned that practice in light of the language of the rule, *see United States v. Gargano*, 826 F.2d 610 (7th Cir.1987), *and United States v. Jones*, 669 F.2d 559 (8th Cir.1982), and the Committee wishes to clarify the rule. The amendment is consistent with the proposed amendment of Rule 4(a)(4).

[¶12] Subdivision (b) is further amended in light of new Fed. R. Crim. P. 35(c), which authorizes a sentencing court to correct any arithmetical, technical, or other clear errors in sentencing within 7 days after imposing the sentence. The Committee believes that a sentencing court should be able to act under Criminal Rule 35(c) even if a notice of appeal has already been filed; and that a notice of appeal should not be affected by the filing of a Rule 35(c) motion or by correction of a sentence under Rule 35(c).

[¶13] Subdivision (c). In *Houston v. Lack*, 487 U.S. 266 (1988), the Supreme Court held that a pro se prisoner's notice of appeal is "filed" at the moment of delivery to prison authorities for forwarding to the district court. The amendment reflects that decision. The language of the amendment is similar to that in Supreme Court Rule 29.2.

[¶14] Permitting an inmate to file a notice of appeal by depositing it in an institutional mail system requires adjustment of the rules governing the filing of cross-appeals. In a civil case, the time for filing a cross-appeal ordinarily runs from the date when the first notice of appeal is filed. If an inmate's notice of appeal is filed by depositing it in an institution's mail system, it is possible that the notice of appeal will not arrive in the district court until several days after the "filing" date and perhaps even after the time for filing a cross-appeal has expired. To avoid that problem, subdivision (c) provides that in a civil case when an institutionalized person files a notice of appeal by depositing it in the institution's mail system, the time for filing a cross-appeal runs from the district court's receipt of the notice. The amendment makes a parallel change regarding the time for the government to appeal in a criminal case.

FRAP 4 – 1991 NOTES OF ADVISORY COMMITTEE

[¶1] The amendment provides a limited opportunity for relief in circumstances where the notice of entry of a judgment or order, required to be mailed by the clerk of the district court pursuant to Rule 77(d) of the Federal Rules of Civil Procedure, is either not received by a party or is received so late as to impair the opportunity to file a timely notice of appeal. The amendment adds a new subdivision (6) allowing a district court to reopen for a brief period the time for appeal upon a finding that notice of entry of a judgment or order was not received from the clerk or a party within 21 days of its entry and that no party would be prejudiced. By "prejudice" the Committee means some adverse consequence other than the cost of having to oppose the appeal and encounter the risk of reversal, consequences that are present in every appeal. Prejudice might arise, for example, if the appellee had taken some action in reliance on the expiration of the normal time period for filing a notice of appeal.

[¶2] Reopening may be ordered only upon a motion filed within 180 days of the entry of a judgment or order or within 7 days of receipt of notice of such entry, whichever is earlier. This provision establishes an outer time limit of 180 days for a party who fails to receive timely notice of entry of a judgment to seek additional time to appeal and enables any winning party to shorten the 180-day period by sending (and establishing proof of receipt of) its own notice of entry of a judgment, as authorized by Fed. R. Civ. P. 77(d). Winning parties are encouraged to send their own notice in order to lessen the chance that a judge will accept a claim of non-receipt in the face of evidence that notices were sent by both the clerk and the winning party. Receipt of a winning party's notice will shorten only the time for reopening the time for appeal under this subdivision, leaving the normal time periods for appeal unaffected.

[¶3] If the motion is granted, the district court may reopen the time for filing a notice of appeal only for a period of 14 days from the date of entry of the order reopening the time for appeal.

FRAP 4 – 1979 NOTES OF ADVISORY COMMITTEE

[¶1] Subdivision (a)(1). The words "(including a civil action which involves an admiralty or maritime claim and a proceeding in bankruptcy or a controversy arising therein)," which appear in the present rule are struck out as unnecessary and perhaps misleading in suggesting that there may be other categories that are not either civil or criminal within the meaning of Rule 4(a) and (b).

[¶2] The phrases "within 30 days of such entry" and "within 60 days of such entry" have been changed to read "after" instead of "or."[1] The change is for clarity only, since the word "of" in the present rule appears to be used to mean "after." Since the proposed amended rule deals directly with the premature filing of a notice of appeal, it was thought useful to emphasize the fact that except as provided, the period during which a notice of appeal may be filed is the 30 days, or 60 days as the case may be, following the entry of the judgment or order appealed from. See Notes to Rule 4(a)(2) and (4), below.

[¶3] Subdivision (a)(2). The proposed amendment to Rule 4(a)(2) would extend to civil cases the provisions of Rule 4(b), dealing with criminal cases, designed to avoid the loss of the right to appeal by filing the notice of appeal prematurely. Despite the absence of such a provision in Rule 4(a) the courts of appeals quite generally have held premature appeals effective. *See, e.g., Matter of Grand Jury Empanelled Jan. 21, 1975*, 541 F.2d 373 (3d Cir.1976); *Hodge v. Hodge*, 507 F.2d 87 (3d Cir. 1976); *Song Jook Suh v. Rosenberg*, 437 F.2d 1098

(9th Cir. 1971); *Ruby v. Secretary of the Navy*, 365 F.2d 385 (9th Cir. 1966); *Firchau v. Diamond Nat'l Corp.*, 345 F.2d 469 (9th Cir. 1965).

[¶4] The proposed amended rule would recognize this practice but make an exception in cases in which a post trial motion has destroyed the finality of the judgment. See Note to Rule 4(a)(4) below.

[¶5] Subdivision (a)(4). The proposed amendment would make it clear that after the filing of the specified post trial motions, a notice of appeal should await disposition of the motion. Since the proposed amendments to Rules 3, 10, and 12 contemplate that immediately upon the filing of the notice of appeal the fees will be paid and the case docketed in the court of appeals, and the steps toward its disposition set in motion, it would be undesirable to proceed with the appeal while the district court has before it a motion the granting of which would vacate or alter the judgment appealed from. *See, e.g., Kieth v. Newcourt*, 530 F.2d 826 (8th Cir.1976). Under the present rule, since docketing may not take place until the record is transmitted, premature filing is much less likely to involve waste effort. *See, e.g., Stokes v. Peyton's Inc.*, 508 F.2d 1287 (5th Cir.1975). Further, since a notice of appeal filed before the disposition of a post trial motion, even if it were treated as valid for purposes of jurisdiction, would not embrace objections to the denial of the motion, it is obviously preferable to postpone the notice of appeal until after the motion is disposed of.

[¶6] The present rule, since it provides for the "termination" of the "running" of the appeal time, is ambiguous in its application to a notice of appeal filed prior to a post trial motion filed within the 10 day limit. The amendment would make it clear that in such circumstances the appellant should not proceed with the appeal during pendency of the motion but should file a new notice of appeal after the motion is disposed of.

[¶7] Subdivision (a)(5). Under the present rule it is provided that upon a showing of excusable neglect the district court at any time may extend the time for the filing of a notice of appeal for a period not to exceed 30 days from the expiration of the time otherwise prescribed by the rule, but that if the application is made after the original time has run, the order may be made only on motion with such notice as the court deems appropriate.

[¶8] A literal reading of this provision would require that the extension be ordered and the notice of appeal filed within the 30 day period, but despite the surface clarity of the rule, it has produced considerable confusion. See the discussion by Judge Friendly in *In re Orbitek*, 520 F.2d 358 (2d Cir.1975). The proposed amendment would make it clear that a motion to extend the time must be filed no later than 30 days after the expiration of the original appeal time, and that if the motion is timely filed the district court may act upon the motion at a later date, and may extend the time not in excess of 10 days measured from the date on which the order granting the motion is entered.

[¶9] Under the present rule there is a possible implication that prior to the time the initial appeal time has run, the district court may extend the time on the basis of an informal application. The amendment would require that the application must be made by motion, though the motion may be made ex parte. After the expiration of the initial time a motion for the extension of the time must be made in compliance with the FRCP and local rules of the district court. See Note to proposed amended Rule 1, supra. And see Rules 6(d), 7(b) of the FRCPs.

[¶10] The proposed amended rule expands to some extent the standard for the grant of an extension of time. The present rule requires a "showing of excusable neglect." While this was an appropriate standard in cases in which the motion is made after the time for filing the notice of appeal has run, and remains so, it has never fit exactly the situation in which the appellant seeks an extension before the expiration of the initial time. In such a case "good cause," which is the standard that is applied in the granting of other extensions of time under Rule 26(b) seems to be more appropriate.

[¶11] Subdivision (a)(6). The proposed amendment would call attention to the requirement of Rule 58 of the FRCP that the judgment constitute a separate document. *See United States v. Indrelunas*, 411 U.S. 216 (1973). When a notice of appeal is filed, the clerk should ascertain whether any judgment designated therein has been entered in compliance with Rules 58 and 79(a) and if not, so advise all parties and the district judge. While the requirement of Rule 48 is not jurisdictional (see *Bankers Trust Co. v. Mallis*, 431 U.S. 928 (1977)), compliance is important since the time for the filing of a notice of appeal by other parties is measured by the time at which the judgment is properly entered.

1. **Editor's note:** So in original. Probably should be "of."

FRAP 5 – 2009 NOTES OF ADVISORY COMMITTEE

[¶1] Subdivision (b)(2). Subdivision (b)(2) is amended in the light of the change in Rule 26(a)'s time computation rules. Subdivision (b)(2) formerly required that an answer in opposition to a petition for permission to appeal, or a cross-petition for permission to appeal, be filed "within 7 days after the petition is served." Under former Rule 26(a), "7 days" always meant at least 9 days and could mean as many as 11 or even 13 days. Under current Rule 26(a), intermediate weekends and holidays are counted. Changing the period from 7 to 10 days offsets the change in computation approach. See the Note to Rule 26.[1]

[¶2] Subdivision (d)(1). The time set in the former rule at 10 days has been revised to 14 days. See the Note to Rule 26.[1]

1. **Editor's note:** The cross-reference to "Note to Rule 26" refers to 2009 Notes to FRAP 26 at ¶¶1-23, p. 1279, this book.

FRAP 5 – 2002 NOTES OF ADVISORY COMMITTEE

[¶1] Subdivision (c). A petition for permission to appeal, a cross-petition for permission to appeal, and an answer to a petition or cross-petition for permission to appeal are all "other papers" for purposes of Rule 32(c)(2), and all of the requirements of Rule 32(a) apply to those papers, except as provided in Rule 32(c)(2). During the 1998 restyling of the Federal Rules of Appellate Procedure, Rule 5(c) was inadvertently changed to suggest that only the requirements of Rule 32(a)(1) apply to such papers. Rule 5(c) has been amended to correct that error.

[¶2] Rule 5(c) has been further amended to limit the length of papers filed under Rule 5.

FRAP 6 – 2009 NOTES OF ADVISORY COMMITTEE

[¶1] Subdivision (b)(2)(B). The times set in the former rule at 10 days have been revised to 14 days. See the Note to Rule 26.[1]

1. **Editor's note:** The cross-reference to "Note to Rule 26" refers to 2009 Notes to FRAP 26 at ¶¶1-23, p. 1279, this book.

FRAP 10 – 2009 NOTES OF ADVISORY COMMITTEE

[¶1] Subdivisions (b)(1), (b)(3), and (c). The times set in the former rule at 10 days have been revised to 14 days. See the Note to Rule 26.[1]

1. **Editor's note:** The cross-reference to "Note to Rule 26" refers to 2009 Notes to FRAP 26 at ¶¶1-23, p. 1279, this book.

FRAP 12 – 2009 NOTES OF ADVISORY COMMITTEE

[¶1] Subdivision (b). The time set in the former rule at 10 days has been revised to 14 days. See the Note to Rule 26.[1]

1. **Editor's note:** The cross-reference to "Note to Rule 26" refers to 2009 Notes to FRAP 26 at ¶¶1-23, p. 1279, this book.

FRAP 12.1 – 2009 NOTES OF ADVISORY COMMITTEE

[¶1] This new rule corresponds to Federal Rule of Civil Procedure 62.1, which adopts for any motion that the district court cannot grant because of a pending appeal the practice that most courts follow when a party moves under Civil Rule 60(b) to vacate a judgment that is pending on appeal. After an appeal has been docketed and while it remains pending, the district court cannot grant relief under a rule such as Civil Rule 60(b) without a remand. But it can entertain the motion and deny it, defer consideration, state that it would grant the motion if the court of appeals remands for that purpose, or state that the motion raises a substantial issue. Experienced lawyers often refer to the suggestion for remand as an "indicative ruling." (Appellate Rule 4(a)(4) lists six motions that, if filed within the relevant time limit, suspend the effect of a notice of appeal filed before or after the motion is filed until the last such motion is disposed of. The district court has authority to grant the motion without resorting to the indicative ruling procedure.)

[¶2] The procedure formalized by Rule 12.1 is helpful when relief is sought from an order that the court cannot reconsider because the order is the subject of a pending appeal. In the criminal context, the Committee anticipates that Rule 12.1 will be used primarily if not exclusively for newly discovered evidence motions under Criminal Rule 33(b)(1) (*see United States v. Cronic*, 466 U.S. 648, 667 n.42 (1984)), reduced sentence motions under Criminal Rule 35(b), and motions under 18 U.S.C. §3582(c).

[¶3] Rule 12.1 does not attempt to define the circumstances in which an appeal limits or defeats the district court's authority to act in the face of a pending appeal. The rules that govern the relationship between trial courts and appellate courts may be complex, depending in part on the nature of the order and the source of appeal jurisdiction. Appellate Rule 12.1 applies only when those rules deprive the district court of authority to grant relief without appellate permission.

[¶4] To ensure proper coordination of proceedings in the district court and in the court of appeals, the movant must notify the circuit clerk if the district court states that it would grant the motion or that the motion raises a substantial issue. The "substantial issue" standard may be illustrated by the following hypothetical: The district court grants summary judgment dismissing a case. While the plaintiff's appeal is pending, the plaintiff moves for relief from the judgment, claiming newly discovered evidence and also possible fraud by the defendant during the discovery process. If the district court reviews the motion and indicates that the motion "raises a substantial issue," the court of appeals may well wish to remand rather than proceed to determine the appeal.

[¶5] If the district court states that it would grant the motion or that the motion raises a substantial issue, the movant may ask the court of appeals to remand so that the district court can make its final ruling on the motion. In accordance with Rule 47(a)(1), a local rule may prescribe the format for the litigants' notifications and the district court's statement.

[¶6] Remand is in the court of appeals' discretion. The court of appeals may remand all proceedings, terminating the initial appeal. In the context of postjudgment motions, however, that procedure should be followed only when the appellant has stated clearly its intention to abandon the appeal. The danger is that if the initial appeal is terminated and the district court then denies the requested relief, the time for appealing the initial judgment will have run out and a court might rule that the appellant is limited to appealing the denial of the postjudgment motion. The latter appeal may well not provide the appellant with the opportunity to raise all the challenges that could have been raised on appeal from the underlying judgment. *See, e.g., Browder v. Dir., Dep't of Corrections of Ill.*, 434 U.S. 257, 263 n.7 (1978) ("[A]n appeal from denial of Rule 60(b) relief does not bring up the underlying judgment for review."). The Committee does not endorse the notion that a court of appeals should decide that the initial appeal was abandoned—despite the absence of any clear statement of intent to abandon the appeal—merely because an unlimited remand occurred, but the possibility that a court might take that troubling view underscores the need for caution in delimiting the scope of the remand.

[¶7] The court of appeals may instead choose to remand for the sole purpose of ruling on the motion while retaining jurisdiction to proceed with the appeal after the district court rules on the motion (if the appeal is not moot at that point and if any party wishes to proceed). This will often be the preferred course in the light of the concerns expressed above. It is also possible that the court of appeals may wish to proceed to hear the appeal even after the district court has granted relief on remand; thus, even when the district court indicates that it would grant relief, the court of appeals may in appropriate circumstances choose a limited rather than unlimited remand.

[¶8] If the court of appeals remands but retains jurisdiction, subdivision (b) requires the parties to notify the circuit clerk when the district court has decided the motion on remand. This is a joint obligation that is discharged when the required notice is given by any litigant involved in the motion in the district court.

[¶9] When relief is sought in the district court during the pendency of an appeal, litigants should bear in mind the likelihood that a new or amended notice of appeal will be necessary in order to challenge the district court's disposition of the motion. *See, e.g., Jordan v. Bowen*, 808 F.2d 733, 736-37 (10th Cir. 1987) (viewing district court's response to appellant's motion for indicative ruling as a denial of appellant's request for relief under Rule 60(b), and refusing to review that denial because appellant had failed to take an appeal from the denial); *TAAG Linhas Aereas de Angola v. Transamerica Airlines, Inc.*, 915 F.2d 1351, 1354 (9th Cir. 1990) ("[W]here a 60(b) motion is filed subsequent to the notice of appeal and considered by the district court after a limited remand, an appeal specifically from the ruling on the motion must be taken if the issues raised in that motion are to be considered by the Court of Appeals.").

FRAP 15 – 2009 NOTES OF ADVISORY COMMITTEE

[¶1] Subdivision (b)(2). The time set in the former rule at 20 days has been revised to 21 days. See the Note to Rule 26.[1]

1. **Editor's note:** The cross-reference to "Note to Rule 26" refers to 2009 Notes to FRAP 26 at ¶¶1-23, p. 1279, this book.

FRAP 19 – 2009 NOTES OF ADVISORY COMMITTEE

[¶1] Rule 19 formerly required a party who disagreed with the agency's proposed judgment to file a proposed judgment "within 7 days." Under former Rule 26(a), "7 days" always meant at least 9 days and could mean as many as 11 or even 13 days. Under current Rule 26(a), intermediate weekends and holidays are counted. Changing the period from 7 to 10 days offsets the change in computation approach. See the Note to Rule 26.[1]

1. **Editor's note:** The cross-reference to "Note to Rule 26" refers to 2009 Notes to FRAP 26 at ¶¶1-23, p. 1279, this book.

FRAP 21 – 2002 NOTES OF ADVISORY COMMITTEE

[¶1] Subdivision (d). A petition for a writ of mandamus or prohibition, an application for another extraordinary writ, and an answer to such a petition or application are all "other papers" for purposes of Rule 32(c)(2), and all of the requirements of Rule 32(a) apply to those papers, except as provided in Rule 32(c)(2). During the 1998 restyling of the Federal Rules of Appellate Procedure, Rule 21(d) was inadvertently changed to suggest that only the requirements of Rule 32(a)(1) apply to such papers. Rule 21(d) has been amended to correct that error.

[¶2] Rule 21(d) has been further amended to limit the length of papers filed under Rule 21.

FRAP 22 – 2009 NOTES OF ADVISORY COMMITTEE

[¶1] Subdivision (b)(1). The requirement that the district judge who rendered the judgment either issue a certificate of appealability or state why a certificate should not issue has been deleted from subdivision (b)(1). Rule 11(a) of the Rules Governing Proceedings under 28 U.S.C. §2254 or §2255 now delineates the relevant requirement. When an applicant has filed a notice of appeal, the district clerk must transmit the record to the court of appeals; if the district judge has issued a certificate of appealability, the district clerk must include in this transmission the certificate and the statement of reasons for grant of the certificate.

FRAP 24 – 2002 NOTES OF ADVISORY COMMITTEE

[¶1] Subdivision (a)(2). Section 804 of the Prison Litigation Reform Act of 1995 ("PLRA") amended 28 U.S.C. §1915 to require that prisoners who bring civil actions or appeals from civil actions must "pay the full amount of a filing fee." 28 U.S.C. §1915(b)(1). Prisoners who are unable to pay the full amount of the filing fee at the time that their actions or appeals are filed are generally required to pay part of the fee and then to pay the remainder of the fee in installments. 28 U.S.C. §1915(b). By contrast, Rule 24(a)(2) has provided that, after the district court grants a litigant's motion to proceed on appeal in forma pauperis, the litigant may proceed "without prepaying or giving security for fees and costs." Thus, the PLRA and Rule 24(a)(2) appear to be in conflict.

[¶2] Rule 24(a)(2) has been amended to resolve this conflict. Recognizing that future legislation regarding prisoner litigation is likely, the Committee has not attempted to incorporate into Rule 24 all of the requirements of the current version of 28 U.S.C. §1915. Rather, the Committee has amended Rule 24(a)(2) to clarify that the rule is not meant to conflict with anything required by the PLRA or any other statute.

[¶3] Subdivision (a)(3). Rule 24(a)(3) has also been amended to eliminate an apparent conflict with the PLRA. Rule 24(a)(3) has provided that a party who was permitted to proceed in forma pauperis in the district court may continue to proceed in forma pauperis in the court of appeals without further authorization, subject to certain conditions. The PLRA, by contrast, provides that a prisoner who was permitted to proceed in forma pauperis in the district court and who wishes to continue to proceed in forma pauperis on appeal may not do so "automatically," but must seek permission. *See, e.g., Morgan v. Haro*, 112 F.3d 788, 789 (5th Cir.1997) ("A prisoner who seeks to proceed IFP on appeal must obtain leave to so proceed despite proceeding IFP in the district court.").

[¶4] Rule 24(a)(3) has been amended to resolve this conflict. Again, recognizing that future legislation regarding prisoner litigation is likely, the Committee has not attempted to incorporate into Rule 24 all of the requirements of the current version of 28 U.S.C. §1915. Rather, the Committee has amended Rule 24(a)(3) to clarify that the rule is not meant to conflict with anything required by the PLRA or any other statute.

FRAP 25 – 2009 NOTES OF ADVISORY COMMITTEE

[¶1] Under former Rule 26(a), short periods that span weekends or holidays were computed without counting those weekends or holidays. To specify that a period should be calculated by counting all intermediate days, including weekends or holidays, the Rules used the term "calendar days." Rule 26(a) now takes a "days-are-days" approach under which all intermediate days are counted, no matter how short the period. Accordingly, "3 calendar days" in subdivisions (a)(2)(B)(ii) and (c)(1)(C) is amended to read simply "3 days."

FRAP 25 – 2007 NOTES OF ADVISORY COMMITTEE

[¶1] Subdivision (a)(5). Section 205(c)(3)(A)(i) of the E-Government Act of 2002 (Public Law 107-347, as amended by Public Law 108-281) requires that the rules of practice and procedure be amended "to protect privacy and security concerns relating to electronic filing of documents and the public availability … of documents filed electronically." In response to that directive, the Federal Rules of Bankruptcy, Civil, and Criminal Procedure have been amended, not merely to address the privacy and security concerns raised by documents that are filed electronically, but also to address similar concerns raised by documents that are filed in paper form. See Fed. R. Bankr. P. 9037; Fed. R. Civ. P. 5.2; and Fed. R. Crim. P. 49.1.

[¶2] Appellate Rule 25(a)(5) requires that, in cases that arise on appeal from a district court, bankruptcy appellate panel, or bankruptcy court, the privacy rule that applied to the case below will continue to apply to the case on appeal. With one exception, all other cases—such as cases involving the review or enforcement of an agency order, the review of a decision of the tax court, or the consideration of a petition for an extraordinary writ—will be governed by Civil Rule 5.2. The only exception is when an extraordinary writ is sought in a criminal case—that is, a case in which the related trial-court proceeding is governed by Criminal Rule 49.1. In such a case, Criminal Rule 49.1 will govern in the court of appeals as well.

FRAP 25 – 2006 NOTES OF ADVISORY COMMITTEE

[¶1] Subdivision (a)(2)(D). Amended Rule 25(a)(2)(D) acknowledges that many courts have required electronic filing by means of a standing order, procedures manual, or local rule. These local practices reflect the advantages that courts and most litigants realize from electronic filing. Courts that mandate electronic filing recognize the need to make exceptions when requiring electronic filing imposes a hardship on a party. Under Rule 25(a)(2)(D), a local rule that requires electronic filing must include reasonable exceptions, but Rule 25(a)(2)(D) does not define the scope of those exceptions. Experience with the local rules that have been adopted and that will emerge will aid in drafting new local rules and will facilitate gradual convergence on uniform exceptions, whether in local rules or in an amended Rule 25(a)(2)(D).

[¶2] A local rule may require that both electronic and "hard" copies of a paper be filed. Nothing in the last sentence of Rule 25(a)(2)(D) is meant to imply otherwise.

FRAP 25 – 2002 NOTES OF ADVISORY COMMITTEE

[¶1] Rule 25(a)(2)(D) presently authorizes the courts of appeals to permit papers to be *filed* by electronic means. Rule 25 has been amended in several respects to permit papers also to be *served* electronically. In addition, Rule 25(c) has been reorganized and subdivided to make it easier to understand.

[¶2] Subdivision (c)(1)(D). New subdivision (c)(1)(D) has been added to permit service to be made electronically, such as by e-mail or fax. No party may be served electronically, either by the clerk or by another party, unless the party has consented in writing to such service.

[¶3] A court of appeals may not, by local rule, forbid the use of electronic service on a party that has consented to its use. At the same time, courts have considerable discretion to use local rules to regulate electronic service. Difficult and presently unforeseeable questions are likely to arise as electronic service becomes more common. Courts have the flexibility to use their local rules to address those questions. For example, courts may use local rules to set forth specific procedures that a party must follow before the party will be deemed to have given written consent to electronic service.

[¶4] Parties also have the flexibility to define the terms of their consent; a party's consent to electronic service does not have to be "all-or-nothing." For example, a party may consent to service by facsimile transmission, but not by electronic mail; or a party may consent to electronic service only if "courtesy" copies of all transmissions are mailed within 24 hours; or a party may consent to electronic service of only documents that were created with Corel WordPerfect.

[¶5] **Subdivision (c)(2).** The courts of appeals are authorized under Rule 25(a)(2)(D) to permit papers to be filed electronically. Technological advances may someday make it possible for a court to forward an electronically filed paper to all parties automatically or semi-automatically. When such court-facilitated service becomes possible, courts may decide to permit parties to use the courts' transmission facilities to serve electronically filed papers on other parties who have consented to such service. Court personnel would use the court's computer system to forward the papers, but the papers would be considered served by the filing parties, just as papers that are carried from one address to another by the United States Postal Service are considered served by the sending parties. New subdivision (c)(2) has been added so that the courts of appeals may use local rules to authorize such use of their transmission facilities, as well as to address the many questions that court-facilitated electronic service is likely to raise.

[¶6] **Subdivision (c)(4).** The second sentence of new subdivision (c)(4) has been added to provide that electronic service is complete upon transmission. Transmission occurs when the sender performs the last act that he or she must perform to transmit a paper electronically; typically, it occurs when the sender hits the "send" or "transmit" button on an electronic mail program. There is one exception to the rule that electronic service is complete upon transmission: If the sender is notified—by the sender's e-mail program or otherwise—that the paper was not received, service is not complete, and the sender must take additional steps to effect service. A paper has been "received" by the party on which it has been served as long as the party has the ability to retrieve it. A party cannot defeat service by choosing not to access electronic mail on its server.

[¶7] **Subdivision (d)(1)(B)(iii).** Subdivision (d)(1)(B)(iii) has been amended to require that, when a paper is served electronically, the proof of service of that paper must include the electronic address or facsimile number to which the paper was transmitted.

FRAP 26 – 2009 NOTES OF ADVISORY COMMITTEE

[¶1] **Subdivision (a).** Subdivision (a) has been amended to simplify and clarify the provisions that describe how deadlines are computed. Subdivision (a) governs the computation of any time period found in a statute that does not specify a method of computing time, a Federal Rule of Appellate Procedure, a local rule, or a court order. In accordance with Rule 47(a)(1), a local rule may not direct that a deadline be computed in a manner inconsistent with subdivision (a).

[¶2] The time-computation provisions of subdivision (a) apply only when a time period must be computed. They do not apply when a fixed time to act is set. The amendments thus carry forward the approach taken in *Violette v. P.A. Days, Inc.*, 427 F.3d 1015, 1016 (6th Cir. 2005) (holding that Civil Rule 6(a) "does not apply to situations where the court has established a specific calendar day as a deadline"), and reject the contrary holding of *In re American Healthcare Management, Inc.*, 900 F.2d 827, 832 (5th Cir. 1990) (holding that Bankruptcy Rule 9006(a) governs treatment of date-certain deadline set by court order). If, for example, the date for filing is "no later than November 1, 2007," subdivision (a) does not govern. But if a filing is required to be made "within 10 days" or "within 72 hours," subdivision (a) describes how that deadline is computed.

[¶3] Subdivision (a) does not apply when computing a time period set by a statute if the statute specifies a method of computing time. *See, e.g.*, 20 U.S.C. §7711(b)(1) (requiring certain petitions for review by a local educational agency or a state to be filed "within 30 working days (as determined by the local educational agency or State) after receiving notice of" federal agency decision).

[¶4] **Subdivision (a)(1).** New subdivision (a)(1) addresses the computation of time periods that are stated in days. It also applies to time periods that are stated in weeks, months, or years; though no such time period currently appears in the Federal Rules of Appellate Procedure, such periods may be set by other covered provisions such as a local rule. *See, e.g.*, Third Circuit Local Appellate Rule 46.3(c)(1). Subdivision (a)(1)(B)'s directive to "count every day" is relevant only if the period is stated in days (not weeks, months or years).

[¶5] Under former Rule 26(a), a period of 11 days or more was computed differently than a period of less than 11 days. Intermediate Saturdays, Sundays, and legal holidays were included in computing the longer periods, but excluded in computing the shorter periods. Former Rule 26(a) thus made computing deadlines unnecessarily complicated and led to counterintuitive results. For example, a 10-day period and a 14-day period that started on the same day usually ended on the same day—and the 10-day period not infrequently ended later than the 14-day period. *See Miltimore Sales, Inc. v. Int'l Rectifier, Inc.*, 412 F.3d 685, 686 (6th Cir. 2005).

[¶6] Under new subdivision (a)(1), all deadlines stated in days (no matter the length) are computed in the same way. The day of the event that triggers the deadline is not counted. All other days—including intermediate Saturdays, Sundays, and legal holidays—are counted, with only one exception: If the period ends on a Saturday, Sunday, or legal holiday, then the deadline falls on the next day that is not a Saturday, Sunday, or legal holiday. An illustration is provided below in the discussion of subdivision (a)(5). Subdivision (a)(3) addresses filing deadlines that expire on a day when the clerk's office is inaccessible.

[¶7] Where subdivision (a) formerly referred to the "act, event, or default" that triggers the deadline, new subdivision (a) refers simply to the "event" that triggers the deadline; this change in terminology is adopted for brevity and simplicity, and is not intended to change meaning.

[¶8] Periods previously expressed as less than 11 days will be shortened as a practical matter by the decision to count intermediate Saturdays, Sundays, and legal holidays in computing all periods. Many of those periods have been lengthened to compensate for the change. *See, e.g.*, Rules 5(b)(2), 5(d)(1), 28.1(f), & 31(a).

[¶9] Most of the 10-day periods were adjusted to meet the change in computation method by setting 14 days as the new period. A 14-day period corresponds to the most frequent result of a 10-day period under the former computation method—two Saturdays and two Sundays were excluded, giving 14 days in all. A 14-day period has an additional advantage. The final day falls on the same day of the week as the event that triggered the period—the 14th day after a Monday, for example, is a Monday. This advantage of using week-long periods led to adopting 7-day periods to replace some of the periods set at less than 10 days, and 21-day periods to replace 20-day periods. Thirty-day and longer periods, however, were retained without change.

[¶10] Subdivision (a)(2). New subdivision (a)(2) addresses the computation of time periods that are stated in hours. No such deadline currently appears in the Federal Rules of Appellate Procedure. But some statutes contain deadlines stated in hours, as do some court orders issued in expedited proceedings.

[¶11] Under subdivision (a)(2), a deadline stated in hours starts to run immediately on the occurrence of the event that triggers the deadline. The deadline generally ends when the time expires. If, however, the time period expires at a specific time (say, 2:17 p.m.) on a Saturday, Sunday, or legal holiday, then the deadline is extended to the same time (2:17 p.m.) on the next day that is not a Saturday, Sunday, or legal holiday. Periods stated in hours are not to be "rounded up" to the next whole hour. Subdivision (a)(3) addresses situations when the clerk's office is inaccessible during the last hour before a filing deadline expires.

[¶12] Subdivision (a)(2)(B) directs that every hour be counted. Thus, for example, a 72-hour period that commences at 10:00 a.m. on Friday, November 2, 2007, will run until 9:00 a.m. on Monday, November 5; the discrepancy in start and end times in this example results from the intervening shift from daylight saving time to standard time.

[¶13] Subdivision (a)(3). When determining the last day of a filing period stated in days or a longer unit of time, a day on which the clerk's office is not accessible because of the weather or another reason is treated like a Saturday, Sunday, or legal holiday. When determining the end of a filing period stated in hours, if the clerk's office is inaccessible during the last hour of the filing period computed under subdivision (a)(2) then the period is extended to the same time on the next day that is not a weekend, holiday or day when the clerk's office is inaccessible.

[¶14] Subdivision (a)(3)'s extensions apply "[u]nless the court orders otherwise." In some circumstances, the court might not wish a period of inaccessibility to trigger a full 24-hour extension; in those instances, the court can specify a briefer extension.

[¶15] The text of the rule no longer refers to "weather or other conditions" as the reason for the inaccessibility of the clerk's office. The reference to "weather" was deleted from the text to underscore that inaccessibility can occur for reasons unrelated to weather, such as an outage of the electronic filing system. Weather can still be a reason for inaccessibility of the clerk's office. The rule does not attempt to define inaccessibility. Rather, the concept will continue to develop through caselaw, *see, e.g.*, *Tchakmakjian v. Department of Defense*, 57 Fed. Appx. 438, 441 (Fed. Cir. 2003) (unpublished per curiam opinion) (inaccessibility "due to anthrax concerns"); *cf.* William G. Phelps, *When Is Office of Clerk of Court Inaccessible Due to Weather or Other Conditions for Purpose of Computing Time Period for Filing Papers under Rule 6(a) of Federal Rules of Civil Procedure*, 135 A.L.R. Fed. 259 (1996) (collecting cases). In addition, local provisions may address inaccessibility for purposes of electronic filing.

[¶16] Subdivision (a)(4). New subdivision (a)(4) defines the end of the last day of a period for purposes of subdivision (a)(1). Subdivision (a)(4) does not apply in computing periods stated in hours under subdivision (a)(2), and does not apply if a different time is set by a statute, local rule, or order in the case. A local rule may, for example, address the problems that might arise under subdivision (a)(4)(A) if a single district has clerk's offices in different time zones, or provide that papers filed in a drop box after the normal hours of the clerk's office are filed as of the day that is date-stamped on the papers by a device in the drop box.

[¶17] 28 U.S.C. §452 provides that "[a]ll courts of the United States shall be deemed always open for the purpose of filing proper papers, issuing and returning process, and making motions and orders." A corresponding provision exists in Rule 45(a)(2). Some courts have held that these provisions permit an after-hours filing by handing the papers to an appropriate official. *See, e.g.*, *Casalduc v. Diaz*, 117 F.2d 915, 917 (1st Cir. 1941). Subdivision (a)(4) does not address the effect of the statute on the question of after-hours filing; instead, the rule is designed to deal with filings in the ordinary course without regard to Section 452.

[¶18] Subdivision (a)(4)(A) addresses electronic filings in the district court. For example, subdivision (a)(4)(A) would apply to an electronically-filed notice of appeal. Subdivision (a)(4)(B) addresses electronic filings in the court of appeals.

[¶19] Subdivision (a)(4)(C) addresses filings by mail under Rules 25(a)(2)(B)(i) and 13(b), filings by third-party commercial carrier under Rule 25(a)(2)(B)(ii), and inmate filings under Rules 4(c)(1) and 25(a)(2)(C). For such filings, subdivision (a)(4)(C) provides that the "last day" ends at the latest time (prior to midnight in the filer's time zone) that the filer can properly submit the filing to the post office, third-party commercial carrier, or prison mail system (as applicable) using the filer's chosen method of submission. For example, if a correctional institution's legal mail system's rules of operation provide that items may only be placed in the mail system between 9:00 a.m. and 5:00 p.m., then the "last day" for filings under Rules 4(c)(1) and 25(a)(2)(C) by inmates in that institution ends at 5:00 p.m. As another example, if a filer uses a drop box maintained by a third-party commercial carrier, the "last day" ends at the time of that drop box's last scheduled pickup. Filings by mail under Rule 13(b) continue to be subject to §7502 of the Internal Revenue Code, as amended, and the applicable regulations.

[¶20] Subdivision (a)(4)(D) addresses all other nonelectronic filings; for such filings, the last day ends under (a)(4)(D) when the clerk's office in which the filing is made is scheduled to close.

[¶21] Subdivision (a)(5). New subdivision (a)(5) defines the "next" day for purposes of subdivisions (a)(1)(C) and (a)(2)(C). The Federal Rules of Appellate Procedure contain both forward-looking time periods and backward-looking time periods. A forward-looking time period requires something to be done within a period of time *after* an event. *See, e.g.*, Rule 4(a)(1)(A) (subject to certain exceptions, notice of appeal in a civil case must be filed "within 30 days after the judgment or order appealed from is entered"). A backward-looking time period requires something to be done within a period of time *before* an event. *See, e.g.*, Rule 31(a)(1) ("[A] reply brief must be filed at least 7 days before argument, unless the court, for good cause, allows a later filing."). In determining what is the "next" day for purposes of subdivisions (a)(1)(C) and (a)(2)(C), one should continue counting in the same direction—that is, forward when computing a forward-looking period and backward when computing a backward-looking period. If, for example, a filing is due within 10 days *after* an event, and the tenth day falls on Saturday, September 1, 2007, then the filing is due on Tuesday, September 4, 2007 (Monday, September 3, is Labor Day). But if a filing is due 10 days *before* an event, and the tenth day falls on Saturday, September 1, then the filing is due on Friday, August 31. If the clerk's office is inaccessible on August 31, then subdivision (a)(3) extends the filing deadline forward to the next accessible day that is not a Saturday, Sunday or legal holiday—no earlier than Tuesday, September 4.

[¶22] Subdivision (a)(6). New subdivision (a)(6) defines "legal holiday" for purposes of the Federal Rules of Appellate Procedure, including the time-computation provisions of subdivision (a). Subdivision (a)(6) continues to include within the definition of "legal holiday" days that are declared a holiday by the President or Congress.

[¶23] For forward-counted periods—i.e., periods that are measured after an event—subdivision (a)(6)(C) includes certain state holidays within the definition of legal holidays. However, state legal holidays are not recognized in computing backward-counted periods. For both forward- and backward-counted periods, the rule thus protects those who may be unsure of the effect of state holidays. For forward-counted deadlines, treating state holidays the same as federal holidays extends the deadline. Thus, someone who thought that the federal courts might be closed on a state holiday would be safeguarded against an inadvertent late filing. In contrast, for backward-counted deadlines, not giving state holidays the treatment of federal holidays allows filing on the state holiday itself rather than the day before. Take, for example, Monday, April 21, 2008 (Patriot's Day, a legal holiday in the relevant state). If a filing is due 14 days after an event, and the fourteenth day is April 21, then the filing is due on Tuesday, April 22 because Monday, April 21 counts as a legal holiday. But if a filing is due 14 days before an event, and the fourteenth day is April 21, the filing is due on Monday, April 21; the fact that April 21 is a state holiday does not make April 21 a legal holiday for purposes of computing this backward-counted deadline. But note that if the clerk's office is inaccessible on Monday, April 21, then subdivision (a)(3) extends the April 21 filing deadline forward to the next accessible day that is not a Saturday, Sunday or legal holiday—no earlier than Tuesday, April 22.

[¶24] Subdivision (c). To specify that a period should be calculated by counting all intermediate days, including weekends or holidays, the Rules formerly used the term "calendar days." Because new subdivision (a) takes a "days-are-days" approach under which all intermediate days are counted, no matter how short the period, "3 calendar days" in subdivision (c) is amended to read simply "3 days."

[¶25] Subdivision (c). Rule 26(c) has been amended to eliminate uncertainty about application of the 3-day rule. Civil Rule 6(e) was amended in 2004 to eliminate similar uncertainty in the Civil Rules.

[¶26] Under the amendment, a party that is required or permitted to act within a prescribed period should first calculate that period, without reference to the 3-day rule provided by Rule 26(c), but with reference to the other time computation provisions of the Appellate Rules. After the party has identified the date on which the prescribed period would expire but for the operation of Rule 26(c), the party should add 3 calendar days. The party must act by the third day of the extension, unless that day is a Saturday, Sunday, or legal holiday, in which case the party must act by the next day that is not a Saturday, Sunday, or legal holiday.

[¶27] To illustrate: A paper is served by mail on Thursday, November 1, 2007. The prescribed time to respond is 30 days. The prescribed period ends on Monday, December 3 (because the 30th day falls on a Saturday, the prescribed period extends to the following Monday). Under Rule 26(c), three calendar days are added—Tuesday, Wednesday, and Thursday—and thus the response is due on Thursday, December 6.

FRAP 26 – 2005 NOTES OF ADVISORY COMMITTEE

[¶1] Subdivision (a)(4). Rule 26(a)(4) has been amended to refer to the third Monday in February as "Washington's Birthday." A federal statute officially designates the holiday as "Washington's Birthday," reflecting the desire of Congress specially to honor the first president of the United States. *See* 5 U.S.C. §6103(a). During the 1998 restyling of the Federal Rules of Appellate Procedure, references to "Washington's Birthday" were mistakenly changed to "Presidents' Day." The amendment corrects that error.

FRAP 26 – 2002 NOTES OF ADVISORY COMMITTEE

[¶1] Subdivision (a)(2). The Federal Rules of Civil Procedure and the Federal Rules of Criminal Procedure compute time differently than the Federal Rules of Appellate Procedure. Fed. R. Civ. P. 6(a) and Fed. R. Crim. P. 45(a) provide that, in computing any period of time, "[w]hen the period of time prescribed or allowed is less than 11 days, intermediate Saturdays, Sundays, and legal holidays shall be excluded in the computation." By contrast, Rule 26(a)(2) provides that, in computing any period of time, a litigant should "[e]xclude intermediate Saturdays, Sundays, and legal holidays when the period is less than 7 days, unless stated in calendar days." Thus, deadlines of 7, 8, 9, and 10 days are calculated differently under the rules of civil and criminal procedure than they are under the rules of appellate procedure. This creates a trap for unwary litigants. No good reason for this discrepancy is apparent, and thus Rule 26(a)(2) has been amended so that, under all three sets of rules, intermediate Saturdays, Sundays, and legal holidays will be excluded when computing deadlines under 11 days but will be counted when computing deadlines of 11 days and over.

[¶2] Subdivision (c). Rule 26(c) has been amended to provide that when a paper is served on a party by electronic means, and that party is required or permitted to respond to that paper within a prescribed period, 3 calendar days are added to the prescribed period. Electronic service is usually instantaneous, but sometimes it is not, because of technical problems. Also, if a paper is electronically transmitted to a party on a Friday evening, the party may not realize that he or she has been served until two or three days later. Finally, extending the "3-day rule" to electronic service will encourage parties to consent to such service under Rule 25(c).

FRAP 26.1 – 2002 NOTES OF ADVISORY COMMITTEE

[¶1] Subdivision (a). Rule 26.1(a) requires nongovernmental corporate parties to file a "corporate disclosure statement." In that statement, a nongovernmental corporate party is required to identify all of its parent corporations and all publicly held corporations that own 10% or more of its stock. The corporate disclosure statement is intended to assist judges in determining whether they must recuse themselves by reason of "a financial interest in the subject matter in controversy." Code of Judicial Conduct, Canon 3C(1)(c) (1972).

[¶2] Rule 26.1(a) has been amended to require that nongovernmental corporate parties who have not been required to file a corporate disclosure statement—that is, nongovernmental corporate parties who do not have any parent corporations and at least 10% of whose stock is not owned by any publicly held corporation—inform the court of that fact. At present, when a corporate disclosure statement is not filed, courts do not know whether it has not been filed because there was nothing to report or because of ignorance of Rule 26.1.

[¶3] Subdivision (b). Rule 26.1(b) has been amended to require parties to file supplemental disclosure statements whenever there is a change in the information that Rule 26.1(a) requires the parties to disclose. For example, if a publicly held corporation acquires 10% or more of a party's stock after the party has filed its disclosure statement, the party should file a supplemental statement identifying that publicly held corporation.

[¶4] Subdivision (c). Rule 26.1(c) has been amended to provide that a party who is required to file a supplemental disclosure statement must file an original and 3 copies, unless a local rule or an order entered in a particular case provides otherwise.

FRAP 27 – 2009 NOTES OF ADVISORY COMMITTEE

[¶1] Subdivision (a)(3)(A). Subdivision (a)(3)(A) formerly required that a response to a motion be filed "within 8 days after service of the motion unless the court shortens or extends the time." Prior to the 2002 amendments to Rule 27, subdivision (a)(3)(A) set this period at 10 days rather than 8 days. The period was changed in 2002 to reflect the change from a time-computation approach that counted intermediate weekends and holidays to an approach that did not. (Prior to the 2002 amendments, intermediate weekends and holidays were excluded only if the period was less than 7 days; after those amendments, such days were excluded if the period was less than 11 days.) Under current Rule 26(a), intermediate weekends and holidays are counted for all periods. Accordingly, revised subdivision (a)(3)(A) once again sets the period at 10 days.

[¶2] Subdivision (a)(4). Subdivision (a)(4) formerly required that a reply to a response be filed "within 5 days af-

ter service of the response." Prior to the 2002 amendments, this period was set at 7 days; in 2002 it was shortened in the light of the 2002 change in time computation approach (discussed above). Under current Rule 26(a), intermediate weekends and holidays are counted for all periods, and revised subdivision (a)(4) once again sets the period at 7 days.

FRAP 27 – 2005 NOTES OF ADVISORY COMMITTEE

[¶1] **Subdivision (d)(1)(E).** A new subdivision (E) has been added to Rule 27(d)(1) to provide that a motion, a response to a motion, and a reply to a response to a motion must comply with the typeface requirements of Rule 32(a)(5) and the type-style requirements of Rule 32(a)(6). The purpose of the amendment is to promote uniformity in federal appellate practice and to prevent the abuses that might occur if no restrictions were placed on the size of typeface used in motion papers.

FRAP 27 – 2002 NOTES OF ADVISORY COMMITTEE

[¶1] **Subdivision (a)(3)(A).** Subdivision (a)(3)(A) presently requires that a response to a motion be filed within 10 days after service of the motion. Intermediate Saturdays, Sundays, and legal holidays are counted in computing that 10-day deadline, which means that, except when the 10-day deadline ends on a weekend or legal holiday, parties generally must respond to motions within 10 actual days.

[¶2] Fed. R. App. P. 26(a)(2) has been amended to provide that, in computing any period of time, a litigant should "[e]xclude intermediate Saturdays, Sundays, and legal holidays when the period is less than 11 days, unless stated in calendar days." This change in the method of computing deadlines means that 10-day deadlines (such as that in subdivision (a)(3)(A)) have been lengthened as a practical matter. Under the new computation method, parties would never have less than 14 actual days to respond to motions, and legal holidays could extend that period to as much as 18 days.

[¶3] Permitting parties to take two weeks or more to respond to motions would introduce significant and unwarranted delay into appellate proceedings. For that reason, the 10-day deadline in subdivision (a)(3)(A) has been reduced to 8 days. This change will, as a practical matter, ensure that every party will have at least 10 actual days—but, in the absence of a legal holiday, no more than 12 actual days—to respond to motions. The court continues to have discretion to shorten or extend that time in appropriate cases.

[¶4] **Subdivision (a)(4).** Subdivision (a)(4) presently requires that a reply to a response to a motion be filed within 7 days after service of the response. Intermediate Saturdays, Sundays, and legal holidays are counted in computing that 7-day deadline, which means that, except when the 7-day deadline ends on a weekend or legal holiday, parties generally must reply to responses to motions within one week.

[¶5] Fed. R. App. P. 26(a)(2) has been amended to provide that, in computing any period of time, a litigant should "[e]xclude intermediate Saturdays, Sundays, and legal holidays when the period is less than 11 days, unless stated in calendar days." This change in the method of computing deadlines means that 7-day deadlines (such as that in subdivision (a)(4)) have been lengthened as a practical matter. Under the new computation method, parties would never have less than 9 actual days to reply to responses to motions, and legal holidays could extend that period to as much as 13 days.

[¶6] Permitting parties to take 9 or more days to reply to a response to a motion would introduce significant and unwarranted delay into appellate proceedings. For that reason, the 7-day deadline in subdivision (a)(4) has been reduced to 5 days. This change will, as a practical matter, ensure that every party will have 7 actual days to file replies to responses to motions (in the absence of a legal holiday).

[¶7] **Subdivision (d)(1)(B).** A cover is not required on motions, responses to motions, or replies to responses to motions. However, Rule 27(d)(1)(B) has been amended to provide that if a cover is nevertheless used on such a paper, the cover must be white. The amendment is intended to promote uniformity in federal appellate practice.

FRAP 28 – 2005 NOTES OF ADVISORY COMMITTEE

[¶1] **Subdivision (c).** Subdivision (c) has been amended to delete a sentence that authorized an appellee who had cross-appealed to file a brief in reply to the appellant's response. All rules regarding briefing in cases involving cross-appeals have been consolidated into new Rule 28.1.

[¶2] **Subdivision (h).** Subdivision (h)—regarding briefing in cases involving cross-appeals—has been deleted. All rules regarding such briefing have been consolidated into new Rule 28.1.

FRAP 28 – 2002 NOTES OF ADVISORY COMMITTEE

[¶1] **Subdivision (j).** In the past, Rule 28(j) has required parties to describe supplemental authorities "without argument." Enforcement of this restriction has been lax, in part because of the difficulty of distinguishing "state[ment] ... [of] the reasons for the supplemental citations," which is required, from "argument" about the supplemental citations, which is forbidden.

[¶2] As amended, Rule 28(j) continues to require parties to state the reasons for supplemental citations, with reference to the part of a brief or oral argument to which the supplemental citations pertain. But Rule 28(j) no longer forbids "argument." Rather, Rule 28(j) permits parties to decide for themselves what they wish to say about supplemental authorities. The only restriction upon parties is that the body of a Rule 28(j) letter—that is, the part of the letter that begins with the first word after the salutation and ends with the last word before the complimentary close—cannot exceed 350 words. All words found in footnotes will count toward the 350-word limit.

FRAP 28.1 – 2009 NOTES OF ADVISORY COMMITTEE

[¶1] Subdivision (f)(4). Subdivision (f)(4) formerly required that the appellee's reply brief be served "at least 3 days before argument unless the court, for good cause, allows a later filing." Under former Rule 26(a), "3 days" could mean as many as 5 or even 6 days. See the Note to Rule 26.[1] Under revised Rule 26(a), intermediate weekends and holidays are counted. Changing "3 days" to "7 days" alters the period accordingly. Under revised Rule 26(a), when a period ends on a weekend or holiday, one must continue to count in the same direction until the next day that is not a weekend or holiday; the choice of the 7-day period for subdivision (f)(4) will minimize such occurrences.

1. **Editor's note:** The cross-reference to "Note to Rule 26" refers to 2009 Notes to FRAP 26 at ¶¶1-23, p. 1279, this book.

FRAP 28.1 – 2005 NOTES OF ADVISORY COMMITTEE

[¶1] The Federal Rules of Appellate Procedure have said very little about briefing in cases involving cross-appeals. This vacuum has frustrated judges, attorneys, and parties who have sought guidance in the rules. More importantly, this vacuum has been filled by conflicting local rules regarding such matters as the number and length of briefs, the colors of the covers of briefs, and the deadlines for serving and filing briefs. These local rules have created a hardship for attorneys who practice in more than one circuit.

[¶2] New Rule 28.1 provides a comprehensive set of rules governing briefing in cases involving cross-appeals. The few existing provisions regarding briefing in such cases have been moved into new Rule 28.1, and several new provisions have been added to fill the gaps in the existing rules. The new provisions reflect the practices of the large majority of circuits and, to a significant extent, the new provisions have been patterned after the requirements imposed by Rules 28, 31, and 32 on briefs filed in cases that do not involve cross-appeals.

[¶3] Subdivision (a). Subdivision (a) makes clear that, in a case involving a cross-appeal, briefing is governed by new Rule 28.1, and not by Rules 28(a), 28(b), 28(c), 31(a)(1), 32(a)(2), 32(a)(7)(A), and 32(a)(7)(B), except to the extent that Rule 28.1 specifically incorporates those rules by reference.

[¶4] Subdivision (b). Subdivision (b) defines who is the "appellant" and who is the "appellee" in a case involving a cross-appeal. Subdivision (b) is taken directly from former Rule 28(h), except that subdivision (b) refers to a party being designated as an appellant "for the purposes of this rule and Rules 30 and 34," whereas former Rule 28(h) also referred to Rule 31. Because the matter addressed by Rule 31(a)(1)—the time to serve and file briefs—is now addressed directly in new Rule 28.1(f), the cross-reference to Rule 31 is no longer necessary. In Rule 31 and in all rules other than Rules 28.1, 30, and 34, references to an "appellant" refer both to the appellant in an appeal and to the cross-appellant in a cross-appeal, and references to an "appellee" refer both to the appellee in an appeal and to the cross-appellee in a cross-appeal. *Cf.* Rule 31(c).

[¶5] Subdivision (c). Subdivision (c) provides for the filing of four briefs in a case involving a cross-appeal. This reflects the practice of every circuit except the Seventh. *See* 7th Cir.R. 28(d)(1)(a).

[¶6] The first brief is the "appellant's principal brief." That brief—like the appellant's principal brief in a case that does not involve a cross-appeal—must comply with Rule 28(a).

[¶7] The second brief is the "appellee's principal and response brief." Because this brief serves as the appellee's principal brief on the merits of the cross-appeal, as well as the appellee's response brief on the merits of the appeal, it must also comply with Rule 28(a), with the limited exceptions noted in the text of the rule.

[¶8] The third brief is the "appellant's response and reply brief." Like a response brief in a case that does not involve a cross-appeal—that is, a response brief that does not also serve as a principal brief on the merits of a cross-appeal—the appellant's response and reply brief must comply with Rule 28(a)(2)-(9) and (11), with the exceptions noted in the text of the rule. *See* Rule 28(b). The one difference between the appellant's response and reply brief, on the one hand, and a response brief filed in a case that does not involve a cross-appeal, on the other, is that the latter must include a corporate disclosure statement. *See* Rule 28(a)(1) and (b). An appellant filing a response and reply brief in a case involving a cross-appeal has already filed a corporate disclosure statement with its principal brief on the merits of the appeal.

[¶9] The fourth brief is the "appellee's reply brief." Like a reply brief in a case that does not involve a cross-appeal, it must comply with Rule 28(c), which essentially restates the requirements of Rule 28(a)(2)-(3) and (11). (Rather than restating the requirements of Rule 28(a)(2)-(3) and (11), as Rule 28(c) does, Rule 28.1(c)(4) includes a direct cross-reference.) The appellee's reply brief must also be limited to the issues presented by the cross-appeal.

[¶10] Subdivision (d). Subdivision (d) specifies the colors of the covers on briefs filed in a case involving a cross-appeal. It is patterned after Rule 32(a)(2), which does not specifically refer to cross-appeals.

[¶11] Subdivision (e). Subdivision (e) sets forth limits on the length of the briefs filed in a case involving a cross-appeal. It is patterned after Rule 32(a)(7), which does not specifically refer to cross-appeals. Subdivision (e) permits the appellee's principal and response brief to be longer than a typical principal brief on the merits because this brief serves not only as the principal brief on the merits of the cross-appeal, but also as the response brief on the merits of the appeal. Likewise, subdivision (e) permits the appellant's response and reply brief to be longer than a typical reply brief because this brief serves not only as the reply brief in the appeal, but also as the response brief in the cross-appeal. For purposes of determining the maximum length of an amicus curiae's brief filed in a case involving a cross-appeal, Rule 29(d)'s reference to "the maximum length authorized by these rules for a party's principal brief" should be understood to refer to subdivision (e)'s limitations on the length of an appellant's principal brief.

[¶12] Subdivision (f). Subdivision (f) provides deadlines for serving and filing briefs in a cross-appeal. It is patterned after Rule 31(a)(1), which does not specifically refer to cross-appeals.

FRAP 29 – 2010 NOTES OF ADVISORY COMMITTEE

[¶1] Subdivision (a). New Rule 1(b) defines the term "state" to include "the District of Columbia and any United States commonwealth or territory." That definition renders subdivision (a)'s reference to a "Territory, Commonwealth, or the District of Columbia" redundant. Accordingly, subdivision (a) is amended to refer simply to "[t]he United States or its officer or agency or a state."

[¶2] Subdivision (c). The subparts of subdivision (c) are renumbered due to the relocation of an existing provision in new subdivision (c)(1) and the addition of a new provision in new subdivision (c)(5). Existing subdivisions (c)(1) through (c)(5) are renumbered, respectively, (c)(2), (c)(3), (c)(4), (c)(6) and (c)(7). The new ordering of the subdivisions tracks the order in which the items should appear in the brief.

[¶3] Subdivision (c)(1). The requirement that corporate amici include a disclosure statement like that required of parties by Rule 26.1 was previously stated in the third sentence of subdivision (c). The requirement has been moved to new subdivision (c)(1) for ease of reference.

[¶4] Subdivision (c)(5). New subdivision (c)(5) sets certain disclosure requirements concerning authorship and funding. Subdivision (c)(5) exempts from the authorship and funding disclosure requirements entities entitled under subdivision (a) to file an amicus brief without the consent of the parties or leave of court. Subdivision (c)(5) requires amicus briefs to disclose whether counsel for a party authored the brief in whole or in part and whether a party or a party's counsel contributed money with the intention of funding the preparation or submission of the brief. A party's or counsel's payment of general membership dues to an amicus need not be disclosed. Subdivision (c)(5) also requires amicus briefs to state whether any other "person" (other than the amicus, its members, or its counsel) contributed money with the intention of funding the brief's preparation or submission, and, if so, to identify all such persons. "Person," as used in subdivision (c)(5), includes artificial persons as well as natural persons.

[¶5] The disclosure requirement, which is modeled on Supreme Court Rule 37.6, serves to deter counsel from using an amicus brief to circumvent page limits on the parties' briefs. *See Glassroth v. Moore*, 347 F.3d 916, 919 (11th Cir.2003) (noting the majority's suspicion "that amicus briefs are often used as a means of evading the page limitations on a party's briefs"). It also may help judges to assess whether the amicus itself considers the issue important enough to sustain the cost and effort of filing an amicus brief.

[¶6] It should be noted that coordination between the amicus and the party whose position the amicus supports is desirable, to the extent that it helps to avoid duplicative arguments. This was particularly true prior to the 1998 amendments, when deadlines for amici were the same as those for the party whose position they supported. Now that the filing deadlines are staggered, coordination may not always be essential in order to avoid duplication. In any event, mere coordination—in the sense of sharing drafts of briefs—need not be disclosed under subdivision (c)(5). *Cf.* Eugene Gressman et al., Supreme Court Practice 739 (9th ed. 2007) (Supreme Court Rule 37.6 does not "require disclosure of any coordination and discussion between party counsel and amici counsel regarding their respective arguments….").

FRAP 30 – 2009 NOTES OF ADVISORY COMMITTEE

[¶1] Subdivision (b)(1). The times set in the former rule at 10 days have been revised to 14 days. See the Note to Rule 26.[1]

1. **Editor's note:** The cross-reference to "Note to Rule 26" refers to 2009 Notes to FRAP 26 at ¶¶1-23, p. 1279, this book.

FRAP 31 – 2009 NOTES OF ADVISORY COMMITTEE

[¶1] Subdivision (a)(1). Subdivision (a)(1) formerly required that the appellant's reply brief be served "at least 3 days before argument, unless the court, for good cause, allows a later filing." Under former Rule 26(a), "3 days" could mean as many as 5 or even 6 days. See the Note to Rule 26.[1] Under revised Rule 26(a), intermediate weekends and holidays are counted. Changing "3 days" to "7 days" alters the period accordingly. Under revised Rule 26(a), when a period ends on a weekend or holiday, one must continue to count in the same direction until the next day that is not a weekend or holiday; the choice of the 7-day period for subdivision (a)(1) will minimize such occurrences.

1. **Editor's note:** The cross-reference to "Note to Rule 26" refers to 2009 Notes to FRAP 26 at ¶¶1-23, p. 1279, this book.

FRAP 31 – 2002 NOTES OF ADVISORY COMMITTEE

[¶1] Subdivision (b). In requiring that two copies of each brief "must be served on counsel for each separately represented party," Rule 31(b) may be read to imply that copies of briefs need not be served on unrepresented parties. The Rule has been amended to clarify that briefs must be served on all parties, including those who are not represented by counsel.

FRAP 32 – 2005 NOTES OF ADVISORY COMMITTEE

[¶1] Subdivision (a)(7)(C). Rule 32(a)(7)(C) has been amended to add cross-references to new Rule 28.1, which governs briefs filed in cases involving cross-appeals. Rule 28.1(e)(2) prescribes type-volume limitations that apply to such briefs, and Rule 28.1(e)(3) requires parties to certify compliance with those type-volume limitations under Rule 32(a)(7)(C).

FRAP 32 – 2002 NOTES OF ADVISORY COMMITTEE

[¶1] Subdivision (a)(2). On occasion, a court may permit or order the parties to file supplemental briefs addressing an issue that was not addressed—or adequately addressed—in the principal briefs. Rule 32(a)(2) has been amended to require that tan covers be used on such supplemental briefs. The amendment is intended to promote uniformity in federal appellate practice. At present, the local rules of the circuit courts conflict. *See, e.g.*, D.C. Cir.R. 28(g) (requiring yellow covers on supplemental briefs); 11th Cir.R. 32, I.O.P. 1 (requiring white covers on supplemental briefs).

[¶2] Subdivision (a)(7)(C). If the principal brief of a party exceeds 30 pages, or if the reply brief of a party exceeds 15 pages, Rule 32(a)(7)(C) provides that the party or the party's attorney must certify that the brief complies with the type-volume limitation of Rule 32(a)(7)(B). Rule 32(a)(7)(C) has been amended to refer to Form 6 (which has been added to the Appendix of Forms) and to provide that a party or attorney who uses Form 6 has complied with Rule 32(a)(7)(C). No court may provide to the contrary, in its local rules or otherwise.

[¶3] Form 6 requests not only the information mandated by Rule 32(a)(7)(C), but also information that will assist courts in enforcing the typeface requirements of Rule 32(a)(5) and the type style requirements of Rule 32(a)(6). Parties and attorneys are not required to use Form 6, but they are encouraged to do so.

[¶4] Subdivision (c)(2)(A). Under Rule 32(c)(2)(A), a cover is not required on a petition for panel rehearing, petition for hearing or rehearing en banc, answer to a petition for panel rehearing, response to a petition for hearing or rehearing en banc, or any other paper. Rule 32(d) makes it clear that no court can require that a cover be used on any of these papers. However, nothing prohibits a court from providing in its local rules that if a cover on one of these papers is "voluntarily" used, it must be a particular color. Several circuits have adopted such local rules. *See, e.g.*, Fed. Cir.R. 35(c) (requiring yellow covers on petitions for hearing or rehearing en banc and brown covers on responses to such petitions); Fed. Cir.R. 40(a) (requiring yellow covers on petitions for panel rehearing and brown covers on answers to such petitions); 7th Cir.R. 28 (requiring blue covers on petitions for rehearing filed by appellants or answers to such petitions, and requiring red covers on petitions for rehearing filed by appellees or answers to such petitions); 9th Cir.R. 40-1 (requiring blue covers on petitions for panel rehearing filed by appellants and red covers on answers to such petitions, and requiring red covers on petitions for panel rehearing filed by appellees and blue covers on answers to such petitions); 11th Cir.R. 35-6 (requiring white covers on petitions for hearing or rehearing en banc).

[¶5] These conflicting local rules create a hardship for counsel who practice in more than one circuit. For that reason, Rule 32(c)(2)(A) has been amended to provide that if a party chooses to use a cover on a paper that is not required to have one, that cover must be white. The amendment is intended to preempt all local rulemaking on the subject of cover colors and thereby promote uniformity in federal appellate practice.

[¶6] Subdivisions (d) and (e). Former subdivision (d) has been redesignated as subdivision (e), and a new subdivision (d) has been added. The new subdivision (d) requires that every brief, motion, or other paper filed with the court be signed by the attorney or unrepresented party who files it, much as Fed. R. Civ. P. 11(a) imposes a signature requirement on papers filed in district court. Only the original copy of every paper must be signed. An appendix filed with the court does not have to be signed at all.

[¶7] By requiring a signature, subdivision (d) ensures that a readily identifiable attorney or party takes responsibility for every paper. The courts of appeals already have authority to sanction attorneys and parties who file papers that contain misleading or frivolous assertions, *see, e.g.*, 28 U.S.C. §1912, Fed. R. App. P. 38 & 46(b)(1)(B), and thus subdivision (d) has not been amended to incorporate provisions similar to those found in Fed. R. Civ. P. 11(b) and 11(c).

FRAP 32.1 – 2006 NOTES OF ADVISORY COMMITTEE

[¶1] Rule 32.1 is a new rule addressing the citation of judicial opinions, orders, judgments, or other written dispositions that have been designated by a federal court as "unpublished," "not for publication," "non-precedential," "not precedent," or the like. This Committee Note will refer to these dispositions collectively as "unpublished" opinions.

[¶2] Rule 32.1 is extremely limited. It does not require any court to issue an unpublished opinion or forbid any court from doing so. It does not dictate the circumstances under which a court may choose to designate an opinion as "unpublished" or specify the procedure that a court must follow in making that determination. It says nothing about what effect a court must give to one of its unpublished opinions or to the unpublished opinions of another court. Rule 32.1 addresses only the *citation* of federal judicial dispositions that have been *designated* as "unpublished" or "non-precedential"—

whether or not those dispositions have been published in some way or are precedential in some sense.

[¶3] Subdivision (a). Every court of appeals has allowed unpublished opinions to be cited in some circumstances, such as to support a contention of issue preclusion or claim preclusion. But the circuits have differed dramatically with respect to the restrictions that they have placed on the citation of unpublished opinions for their persuasive value. Some circuits have freely permitted such citation, others have discouraged it but permitted it in limited circumstances, and still others have forbidden it altogether.

[¶4] Rule 32.1(a) is intended to replace these inconsistent standards with one uniform rule. Under Rule 32.1(a), a court of appeals may not prohibit a party from citing an unpublished opinion of a federal court for its persuasive value or for any other reason. In addition, under Rule 32.1(a), a court may not place any restriction on the citation of such opinions. For example, a court may not instruct parties that the citation of unpublished opinions is discouraged, nor may a court forbid parties to cite unpublished opinions when a published opinion addresses the same issue.

[¶5] Rule 32.1(a) applies only to unpublished opinions issued on or after January 1, 2007. The citation of unpublished opinions issued before January 1, 2007, will continue to be governed by the local rules of the circuits.

[¶6] Subdivision (b). Under Rule 32.1(b), a party who cites an opinion of a federal court must provide a copy of that opinion to the court of appeals and to the other parties, unless that opinion is available in a publicly accessible electronic database—such as a commercial database maintained by a legal research service or a database maintained by a court. A party who is required under Rule 32.1(b) to provide a copy of an opinion must file and serve the copy with the brief or other paper in which the opinion is cited. Rule 32.1(b) applies to all unpublished opinions, regardless of when they were issued.

FRAP 34 – 2005 NOTES OF ADVISORY COMMITTEE

[¶1] Subdivision (d). A cross-reference in subdivision (d) has been changed to reflect the fact that, as part of an effort to collect within one rule all provisions regarding briefing in cases involving cross-appeals, former Rule 28(h) has been abrogated and its contents moved to new Rule 28.1(b).

FRAP 35 – 2005 NOTES OF ADVISORY COMMITTEE

[¶1] Subdivision (a). Two national standards—28 U.S.C. §46(c) and Rule 35(a)—provide that a hearing or rehearing en banc may be ordered by "a majority of the circuit judges who are in regular active service." Although these standards apply to all of the courts of appeals, the circuits are deeply divided over the interpretation of this language when one or more active judges are disqualified.

[¶2] The Supreme Court has never addressed this issue. In *Shenker v. Baltimore & Ohio R.R. Co.*, 374 U.S. 1 (1963), the Court rejected a petitioner's claim that his rights under §46(c) had been violated when the Third Circuit refused to rehear his case en banc. The Third Circuit had 8 active judges at the time; 4 voted in favor of rehearing the case, 2 against, and 2 abstained. No judge was disqualified. The Supreme Court ruled against the petitioner, holding, in essence, that §46(c) did not provide a cause of action, but instead simply gave litigants "the right to know the administrative machinery that will be followed and the right to suggest that the *en banc* procedure be set in motion in his case." *Id.* at 5. *Shenker* did stress that a court of appeals has broad discretion in establishing internal procedures to handle requests for rehearings—or, as *Shenker* put it, "'to devise its own administrative machinery to provide the *means* whereby a majority may order such a hearing.'" *Id.* (quoting *Western Pac. R.R. Corp. v. Western Pac. R.R. Co.*, 345 U.S. 247, 250 (1953) (emphasis added)). But *Shenker* did not address what is meant by "a majority" in §46(c) (or Rule 35(a), which did not yet exist)—and *Shenker* certainly did not suggest that the phrase should have different meanings in different circuits.

[¶3] In interpreting that phrase, 7 of the courts of appeals follow the "absolute majority" approach. *See* Marie Leary, Defining the "Majority" Vote Requirement in Federal Rule of Appellate Procedure 35(a) for Rehearings En Banc in the United States Courts of Appeals 8 tbl.1 (Federal Judicial Center 2002). Under this approach, disqualified judges are counted in the base in calculating whether a majority of judges have voted to hear a case en banc. Thus, in a circuit with 12 active judges, 7 must vote to hear a case en banc. If 5 of the 12 active judges are disqualified, all 7 non-disqualified judges must vote to hear the case en banc. The votes of 6 of the 7 non-disqualified judges are not enough, as 6 is not a majority of 12.

[¶4] Six of the courts of appeals follow the "case majority" approach. *Id.* Under this approach, disqualified judges are not counted in the base in calculating whether a majority of judges have voted to hear a case en banc. Thus, in a case in which 5 of a circuit's 12 active judges are disqualified, only 4 judges (a majority of the 7 non-disqualified judges) must vote to hear a case en banc. (The First and Third Circuits explicitly qualify the case majority approach by providing that a case cannot be heard en banc unless a majority of all active judges—disqualified and non-disqualified—are eligible to participate.)

[¶5] Rule 35(a) has been amended to adopt the case majority approach as a uniform national interpretation of §46(c). The federal rules of practice and procedure exist to "maintain consistency," which Congress has equated with "promot[ing] the interest of justice." 28 U.S.C. §2073(b). The courts of appeals should not follow two inconsistent approaches in deciding whether sufficient votes exist to hear a case en banc, especially when there is a governing statute and governing rule that apply to all circuits and that use identical terms, and especially when there is nothing about the local conditions of each circuit that justifies conflicting approaches.

[¶6] The case majority approach represents the better interpretation of the phrase "the circuit judges ... in regular active service" in the first sentence of §46(c). The second sentence of §46(c)—which defines which judges are eligible to participate in a case being heard or reheard en banc—uses the similar expression "all circuit judges in regular active service." It is clear that "all circuit judges in regular active service" in the second sentence does not include disqualified judges, as disqualified judges clearly cannot participate in a case being heard or reheard en banc. Therefore, assuming that two nearly identical phrases appearing in adjacent sentences in a statute should be interpreted in the same way, the best reading of "the circuit judges ... in regular active service" in the first sentence of §46(c) is that it, too, does not include disqualified judges.

[¶7] This interpretation of §46(c) is bolstered by the fact that the case majority approach has at least two major advantages over the absolute majority approach:

[¶8] First, under the absolute majority approach, a disqualified judge is, as a practical matter, counted as voting against hearing a case en banc. This defeats the purpose of recusal. To the extent possible, the disqualification of a judge should not result in the equivalent of a vote for or against hearing a case en banc.

[¶9] Second, the absolute majority approach can leave the en banc court helpless to overturn a panel decision with which almost all of the circuit's active judges disagree. For example, in a case in which 5 of a circuit's 12 active judges are disqualified, the case cannot be heard en banc even if 6 of the 7 non-disqualified judges strongly disagree with the panel opinion. This permits one active judge—perhaps sitting on a panel with a visiting judge—effectively to control circuit precedent, even over the objection of all of his or her colleagues. *See Gulf Power Co. v. FCC*, 226 F.3d 1220, 1222-23 (11th Cir.2000) (Carnes, J., concerning the denial of reh'g en banc), *rev'd sub nom. National Cable & Telecomm. Ass'n, Inc. v. Gulf Power Co.*, 534 U.S. 327 (2002). Even though the en banc court may, in a future case, be able to correct an erroneous legal interpretation, the en banc court will never be able to correct the injustice inflicted by the panel on the parties to the case. Moreover, it may take many years before sufficient non-disqualified judges can be mustered to overturn the panel's erroneous legal interpretation. In the meantime, the lower courts of the circuit must apply—and the citizens of the circuit must conform their behavior to—an interpretation of the law that almost all of the circuit's active judges believe is incorrect.

[¶10] The amendment to Rule 35(a) is not meant to alter or affect the quorum requirement of 28 U.S.C. §46(d). In particular, the amendment is not intended to foreclose the possibility that §46(d) might be read to require that more than half of all circuit judges in regular active service be eligible to participate in order for the court to hear or rehear a case en banc.

FRAP 36 – 2002 NOTES OF ADVISORY COMMITTEE

[¶1] **Subdivision (b).** Subdivision (b) has been amended so that the clerk may use electronic means to serve a copy of the opinion or judgment or to serve notice of the date when judgment was entered upon parties who have consented to such service.

FRAP 39 – 2009 NOTES OF ADVISORY COMMITTEE

[¶1] **Subdivision (d)(2).** The time set in the former rule at 10 days has been revised to 14 days. See the Note to Rule 26.[1]

1. **Editor's note:** The cross-reference to "Note to Rule 26" refers to 2009 Notes to FRAP 26 at ¶¶1-23, p. 1279, this book.

FRAP 40 – 2011 NOTES OF ADVISORY COMMITTEE

[¶1] **Subdivision (a)(1).** Rule 40(a)(1) has been amended to make clear that the 45-day period to file a petition for panel rehearing applies in cases in which an officer or employee of the United States is sued in an individual capacity for acts or omissions occurring in connection with duties performed on behalf of the United States. (A concurrent amendment to Rule 4(a)(1)(B) makes clear that the 60-day period to file an appeal also applies in such cases.) In such cases, the Solicitor General needs adequate time to review the merits of the panel decision and decide whether to seek rehearing, just as the Solicitor General does when an appeal involves the United States, a United States agency, or a United States officer or employee sued in an official capacity.

[¶2] To promote clarity of application, the amendment to Rule 40(a)(1) includes safe harbor provisions that parties can readily apply and rely upon. Under new subdivision 40(a)(1)(D), a case automatically qualifies for the 45-day period if (1) a legal officer of the United States has appeared in the case, in an official capacity, as counsel for the current or former officer or employee and has not withdrawn the appearance at the time of the entry of the court of appeals' judgment that is the subject of the petition or (2) a legal officer of the United States appears on the petition as counsel, in an official capacity, for the current or former officer or employee. There will be cases that do not fall within either safe harbor but that qualify for the longer petition period. An example would be a case in which a federal employee is sued in an individual capacity for an act occurring in connection with federal duties and the United States does not represent the employee either when the court of appeals' judgment is entered or when the petition is filed but the United States pays for private counsel for the employee.

FRAP 41 – 2009 NOTES OF ADVISORY COMMITTEE

[¶1] Under former Rule 26(a), short periods that span weekends or holidays were computed without counting those weekends or holidays. To specify that a period should be cal-

culated by counting all intermediate days, including weekends or holidays, the Rules used the term "calendar days." Rule 26(a) now takes a "days-are-days" approach under which all intermediate days are counted, no matter how short the period. Accordingly, "7 calendar days" in subdivision (b) is amended to read simply "7 days."

FRAP 41 – 2002 NOTES OF ADVISORY COMMITTEE

[¶1] **Subdivision (b).** Subdivision (b) directs that the mandate of a court must issue 7 days after the time to file a petition for rehearing expires or 7 days after the court denies a timely petition for panel rehearing, petition for rehearing en banc, or motion for stay of mandate, whichever is later. Intermediate Saturdays, Sundays, and legal holidays are counted in computing that 7-day deadline, which means that, except when the 7-day deadline ends on a weekend or legal holiday, the mandate issues exactly one week after the triggering event.

[¶2] Fed. R. App. P. 26(a)(2) has been amended to provide that, in computing any period of time, one should "[e]xclude intermediate Saturdays, Sundays, and legal holidays when the period is less than 11 days, unless stated in calendar days." This change in the method of computing deadlines means that 7-day deadlines (such as that in subdivision (b)) have been lengthened as a practical matter. Under the new computation method, a mandate would never issue sooner than 9 actual days after a triggering event, and legal holidays could extend that period to as much as 13 days.

[¶3] Delaying mandates for 9 or more days would introduce significant and unwarranted delay into appellate proceedings. For that reason, subdivision (b) has been amended to require that mandates issue 7 *calendar* days after a triggering event.

FRAP 44 – 2002 NOTES OF ADVISORY COMMITTEE

[¶1] Rule 44 requires that a party who "questions the constitutionality of an Act of Congress" in a proceeding in which the United States is not a party must provide written notice of that challenge to the clerk. Rule 44 is designed to implement 28 U.S.C. §2403(a), which states that:

> [¶2] In any action, suit or proceeding in a court of the United States to which the United States or any agency, officer or employee thereof is not a party, wherein the constitutionality of any Act of Congress affecting the public interest is drawn in question, the court shall certify such fact to the Attorney General, and shall permit the United States to intervene ... for argument on the question of constitutionality.

[¶3] The subsequent section of the statute—§2403(b)—contains virtually identical language imposing upon the courts the duty to notify the attorney general of a *state* of a constitutional challenge to any statute of that state. But §2403(b), unlike §2403(a), was not implemented in Rule 44.

[¶4] Rule 44 has been amended to correct this omission. The text of former Rule 44 regarding constitutional challenges to federal statutes now appears as Rule 44(a), while new language regarding constitutional challenges to state statutes now appears as Rule 44(b).

FRAP 45 – 2005 NOTES OF ADVISORY COMMITTEE

[¶1] **Subdivision (a)(2).** Rule 45(a)(2) has been amended to refer to the third Monday in February as "Washington's Birthday." A federal statute officially designates the holiday as "Washington's Birthday," reflecting the desire of Congress specially to honor the first president of the United States. *See* 5 U.S.C. §6103(a). During the 1998 restyling of the Federal Rules of Appellate Procedure, references to "Washington's Birthday" were mistakenly changed to "Presidents' Day." The amendment corrects that error.

FRAP 45 – 2002 NOTES OF ADVISORY COMMITTEE

[¶1] **Subdivision (c).** Subdivision (c) has been amended so that the clerk may use electronic means to serve notice of entry of an order or judgment upon parties who have consented to such service.

TABLE OF CONTENTS

28 U.S.C.

Part I. Organization of Courts

Chapter 1. Supreme Court

§1 Number of justices; quorum 1301
§2 Terms of court 1301
§3 Vacancy in office of Chief Justice; disability 1301
§4 Precedence of associate justices 1301
§5 Salaries of justices 1301
§6 Records of former court of appeals 1301

Chapter 3. Courts of Appeals

§41 Number & composition of circuits 1301
§42 Allotment of Supreme Court justices to circuits 1301
§43 Creation & composition of courts 1301
§44 Appointment, tenure, residence & salary of circuit judges 1302
§45 Chief judges; precedence of judges 1302
§46 Assignment of judges; panels; hearings; quorum 1303
§47 Disqualification of trial judge to hear appeal 1303
§48 Terms of court 1303
§49 Assignment of judges to division to appoint independent counsels 1304

Chapter 5. District Courts

§81 Alabama 1304
§81A Alaska 1305
§82 Arizona 1305
§83 Arkansas 1305
§84 California 1305
§85 Colorado 1306
§86 Connecticut 1306
§87 Delaware 1306
§88 District of Columbia 1306
§89 Florida 1306
§90 Georgia 1306
§91 Hawaii 1307
§92 Idaho 1307
§93 Illinois 1307
§94 Indiana 1308
§95 Iowa 1308
§96 Kansas 1309
§97 Kentucky 1309
§98 Louisiana 1309
§99 Maine 1310
§100 Maryland 1310
§101 Massachusetts 1310
§102 Michigan 1310
§103 Minnesota 1310
§104 Mississippi 1311
§105 Missouri 1311
§106 Montana 1312
§107 Nebraska 1312
§108 Nevada 1312
§109 New Hampshire 1312
§110 New Jersey 1312
§111 New Mexico 1312
§112 New York 1312
§113 North Carolina 1312
§114 North Dakota 1313
§115 Ohio 1313
§116 Oklahoma 1313
§117 Oregon 1313
§118 Pennsylvania 1314
§119 Puerto Rico 1314
§120 Rhode Island 1314
§121 South Carolina 1314
§122 South Dakota 1314
§123 Tennessee 1315
§124 Texas 1315
§125 Utah 1317
§126 Vermont 1317
§127 Virginia 1317
§128 Washington 1317
§129 West Virginia 1318
§130 Wisconsin 1318
§131 Wyoming 1318
§132 Creation & composition of district courts 1318
§133 Appointment & number of district judges 1318
§134 Tenure & residence of district judges 1320
§135 Salaries of district judges 1320
§136 Chief judges; precedence of district judges 1320
§137 Division of business among district judges 1321
§138 Terms abolished 1321
§139 Times for holding regular sessions 1321
§140 Adjournment 1321
§141 Special sessions; places; notice 1321
§143 Vacant judgeship as affecting proceedings 1322
§144 Bias or prejudice of judge 1322

Chapter 6. Bankruptcy Judges

§151 Designation of bankruptcy courts 1322
§152 Appointment of bankruptcy judges 1322
§153 Salaries; character of service 1324
§154 Division of businesses; chief judge 1325
§155 Temporary transfer of bankruptcy judges 1325
§156 Staff; expenses 1325
§157 Procedures 1325
§158 Appeals 1326
§159 Bankruptcy statistics 1328

Chapter 7. United States Court of Federal Claims

§171 Appointment & number of judges; character of court; designation of chief judge 1328
§172 Tenure & salaries of judges 1328
§173 Times & places of holding court 1329
§174 Assignment of judges; decisions 1329
§175 Official duty station; residence 1329
§176 Removal from office 1329
§177 Disbarment of removed judges 1329
§178 Retirement of judges of the Court of Federal Claims 1329
§179 Personnel application & insurance programs 1332

TABLE OF CONTENTS

Chapter 11. Court of International Trade
§251 Appointment & number of judges; offices..........1332
§252 Tenure & salaries of judges..........1332
§253 Duties of chief judge..........1333
§254 Single-judge trials..........1333
§255 Three-judge trials..........1333
§256 Trials at ports other than New York..........1333
§257 Publication of decisions..........1333
§258 Chief judges; precedence of judges..........1333

Chapter 13. Assignment of Judges to Other Courts
§291 Circuit judges..........1334
§292 District judges..........1334
§293 Judges of the Court of International Trade..........1334
§294 Assignment of retired Justices or judges to active duty..........1334
§295 Conditions upon designation & assignment..........1335
§296 Powers upon designation & assignment..........1335
§297 Assignment of judges to courts of the freely associated compact states..........1335

Chapter 15. Conferences & Councils of Judges
§331 Judicial Conference of the United States..........1335
§332 Judicial councils of circuits..........1336
§333 Judicial conferences of circuits..........1338
§334 Institutes & joint councils on sentencing..........1338
§335 Judicial Conference of the Court of International Trade..........1339

Chapter 16. Complaints Against Judges & Judicial Discipline
§351 Complaints; judge defined..........1339
§352 Review of complaint by chief judge..........1339
§353 Special committees..........1340
§354 Action by judicial council..........1340
§355 Action by Judicial Conference..........1341
§356 Subpoena power..........1341
§357 Review of orders & actions..........1341
§358 Rules..........1341
§359 Restrictions..........1342
§360 Disclosure of information..........1342
§361 Reimbursement of expenses..........1342
§362 Other provisions & rules not affected..........1342
§363 Court of Federal Claims, Court of International Trade, Court of Appeals for the Federal Circuit..........1342
§364 Effect of felony conviction..........1342

Chapter 17. Resignation & Retirement of Justices & Judges
§371 Retirement on salary; retirement in senior status..........1343
§372 Retirement for disability; substitute judge on failure to retire..........1344
§373 Judges in territories & possessions..........1344
§374 Residence of retired judges; official station..........1345
§375 Recall of certain judges & magistrate judges..........1345
§376 Annuities for survivors of certain judicial officials of the United States..........1346
§377 Retirement of bankruptcy judges & magistrate judges..........1353

Chapter 19. Distribution of Reports & Digests
§411 Supreme Court reports; printing, binding, & distribution..........1357
§412 Sale of Supreme Court reports..........1357
§413 Publications; distribution to courts..........1357
§414 Transmittal of books to successors..........1357

Chapter 21. General Provisions Applicable to Courts & Judges
§451 Definitions..........1357
§452 Courts always open; powers unrestricted by expiration of sessions..........1358
§453 Oaths of justices & judges..........1358
§454 Practice of law by justices & judges..........1358
§455 Disqualification of justice, judge, or magistrate judge..........1358
§456 Traveling expenses of justices & judges; official duty stations..........1359
§457 Records; obsolete papers..........1359
§458 Relative of justice or judge ineligible to appointment..........1359
§459 Administration of oaths & acknowledgments..........1360
§460 Application to other courts..........1360
§461 Adjustments in certain salaries..........1360
§462 Court accommodations..........1360
§463 Expenses of litigation..........1360

Chapter 23. Civil Justice Expense & Delay Reduction Plans
§471 Requirement for a district court civil justice expense & delay reduction plan..........1361
§472 Development & implementation of a civil justice expense & delay reduction plan..........1361
§473 Content of civil justice expense & delay reduction plans..........1361
§474 Review of district court action..........1362
§475 Periodic district court assessment..........1362
§476 Enhancement of judicial information dissemination..........1363
§477 Model civil justice expense & delay reduction plan..........1363
§478 Advisory groups..........1363
§479 Information on litigation management & cost & delay reduction..........1363
§480 Training programs..........1364
§481 Automated case information..........1364
§482 Definitions..........1364

Part II. Department of Justice

Chapter 31. The Attorney General
§501 Executive department..........1364
§502 Seal..........1364
§503 Attorney General..........1364
§504 Deputy Attorney General..........1364
§504A Associate Attorney General..........1364
§505 Solicitor General..........1364
§506 Assistant Attorneys General..........1364
§507 Assistant Attorney General for Administration..........1365

TABLE OF CONTENTS

§507A Assistant Attorney General for National Security 1365
§508 Vacancies 1365
§509 Functions of the Attorney General 1365
§509A National Security Division 1365
§509B Section to enforce human rights laws 1365
§510 Delegation of authority 1366
§511 Attorney General to advise the President 1366
§512 Attorney General to advise heads of executive departments 1366
§513 Attorney General to advise Secretaries of military departments 1366
§514 Legal services on pending claims in departments & agencies 1366
§515 Authority for legal proceedings; commission, oath, & salary for special attorneys 1366
§516 Conduct of litigation reserved to Department of Justice 1366
§517 Interests of United States in pending suits 1366
§518 Conduct & argument of cases 1366
§519 Supervision of litigation 1367
§520 Transmission of petitions in United States Court of Federal Claims or in United States Court of Appeals for the Federal Circuit; statement furnished by departments 1367
§521 Publication & distribution of opinions 1367
§522 Report of business & statistics 1367
§523 Requisitions 1367
§524 Availability of appropriations 1368
§525 Procurement of law books, reference books, & periodicals; sale & exchange 1371
§526 Authority of Attorney General to investigate United States attorneys, marshals, trustees, clerks of court, & others 1371
§527 Establishment of working capital fund 1371
§528 Disqualification of officers & employees of the Department of Justice 1371
§529 Annual report of Attorney General 1372
§530 Payment of travel & transportation expenses of newly appointed special agents 1372
§530A Authorization of appropriations for travel & related expenses & for health care of personnel serving abroad 1373
§530B Ethical standards for attorneys for the Government 1373
§530C Authority to use available funds 1373
§530D Report on enforcement of laws 1375

Chapter 33. Federal Bureau of Investigation
§531 Federal Bureau of Investigation 1377
§532 Director of the Federal Bureau of Investigation 1377
§533 Investigative & other officials; appointment 1377
§534 Acquisition, preservation, & exchange of identification records & information; appointment of officials 1377
§535 Investigation of crimes involving Government officers & employees; limitations 1378
§536 Positions in excepted service 1378
§537 Expenses of unforeseen emergencies of a confidential character 1378
§538 Investigation of aircraft piracy & related violations 1379
§539 Counterintelligence official reception & representation expenses 1379
§540 Investigation of felonious killings of State or local law enforcement officers 1379
§540A Investigation of violent crimes against travelers 1379
§540B Investigation of serial killings 1379
§540C FBI police 1379

Chapter 35. United States Attorneys
§541 United States attorneys 1380
§542 Assistant United States attorneys 1380
§543 Special attorneys 1380
§544 Oath of office 1380
§545 Residence 1380
§546 Vacancies 1381
§547 Duties 1381
§548 Salaries 1381
§549 Expenses 1381
§550 Clerical assistants, messengers, & private process servers 1381

Chapter 37. United States Marshals Service
§561 United States Marshals Service 1381
§562 Vacancies 1382
§563 Oath of office 1382
§564 Powers as sheriff 1382
§565 Expenses of the Service 1382
§566 Powers & duties 1382
§567 Collection of fees; accounting 1383
§568 Practice of law prohibited 1383
§569 Reemployment rights 1383

Chapter 39. United States Trustees
§581 United States trustees 1384
§582 Assistant United States trustees 1384
§583 Oath of office 1384
§584 Official stations 1384
§585 Vacancies 1384
§586 Duties; supervision by Attorney General 1384
§587 Salaries 1387
§588 Expenses 1387
§589 Staff & other employees 1387
§589a United States Trustee System Fund 1387
§589b Bankruptcy data 1387

Chapter 40A. Bureau of Alcohol, Tobacco, Firearms, & Explosives
§599A Bureau of Alcohol, Tobacco, Firearms, & Explosives 1388
§599B Personnel Management Demonstration Project 1389

Part III. Court Officers & Employees

Chapter 41. Administrative Office of United States Courts
§601 Creation; Director & Deputy Director 1389
§602 Employees 1389

U.S.C.

TABLE OF CONTENTS

§603 Salaries ... 1389
§604 Duties of Director generally ... 1390
§605 Budget estimates ... 1392
§606 Duties of Deputy Director ... 1392
§607 Practice of law prohibited ... 1392
§608 Seal ... 1393
§609 Courts' appointive power unaffected ... 1393
§610 Courts defined ... 1393
§611 Retirement of Director ... 1393
§612 Judiciary Information Technology Fund ... 1393
§613 Disbursing & certifying officers ... 1395

Chapter 42. Federal Judicial Center
§620 Federal Judicial Center ... 1395
§621 Board; composition, tenure of members, compensation ... 1396
§622 Meetings; conduct of business ... 1396
§623 Duties of the Board ... 1396
§624 Powers of the Board ... 1397
§625 Director & staff ... 1397
§626 Compensation of the Director & Deputy Director ... 1397
§627 Retirement; employee benefits ... 1397
§628 Appropriations & accounting ... 1398
§629 Federal Judicial Center Foundation ... 1398

Chapter 43. United States Magistrate Judges
§631 Appointment & tenure ... 1399
§632 Character of service ... 1400
§633 Determination of number, locations, & salaries of magistrate judges ... 1400
§634 Compensation ... 1401
§635 Expenses ... 1402
§636 Jurisdiction, powers, & temporary assignment ... 1402
§637 Training ... 1404
§638 Dockets & forms; United States Code; seals ... 1404
§639 Definitions ... 1405

Chapter 44. Alternative Dispute Resolution
§651 Authorization of alternative dispute resolution ... 1405
§652 Jurisdiction ... 1405
§653 Neutrals ... 1406
§654 Arbitration ... 1406
§655 Arbitrators ... 1406
§656 Subpoenas ... 1406
§657 Arbitration award & judgment ... 1407
§658 Compensation of arbitrators & neutrals ... 1407

Chapter 45. Supreme Court
§671 Clerk ... 1407
§672 Marshal ... 1407
§673 Reporter ... 1408
§674 Librarian ... 1408
§675 Law clerks & secretaries ... 1408
§676 Printing & binding ... 1408
§677 Counselor to the Chief Justice ... 1408

Chapter 47. Courts of Appeals
§711 Clerks & employees ... 1409
§712 Law clerks & secretaries ... 1409
§713 Librarians ... 1409
§714 Criers & messengers ... 1409
§715 Staff attorneys & technical assistants ... 1409

Chapter 49. District Courts
§751 Clerks ... 1409
§752 Law clerks & secretaries ... 1410
§753 Reporters ... 1410
§754 Receivers of property in different districts ... 1411
§755 Criers & bailiffs ... 1411
§756 Power to appoint ... 1412

Chapter 51. United States Court of Federal Claims
§791 Clerk ... 1412
§794 Law clerks & secretaries ... 1412
§795 Bailiffs & messengers ... 1412
§796 Reporting of court proceedings ... 1412
§797 Recall of retired judges ... 1412
§798 Places of holding court; appointment of special masters ... 1413

Chapter 55. Court of International Trade
§871 Clerk, chief deputy clerk, assistant clerk, deputies, assistants, & other employees ... 1413
§872 Criers, bailiffs, & messengers ... 1413

Chapter 57. General Provisions Applicable to Court Officers & Employees
§951 Oath of office of clerks & deputies ... 1413
§953 Administration of oaths & acknowledgments ... 1413
§954 Vacancy in clerk position; absence of clerk ... 1413
§955 Practice of law restricted ... 1413
§956 Powers & duties of clerks & deputies ... 1413
§957 Clerks ineligible for certain offices ... 1414
§958 Persons ineligible as receivers ... 1414
§959 Trustees & receivers suable; management; State laws ... 1414
§960 Tax liability ... 1414
§961 Office expenses of clerks ... 1414
§963 Courts defined ... 1414

Chapter 58. United States Sentencing Commission
§991 United States Sentencing Commission; establishment & purposes ... 1414
§992 Terms of office; compensation ... 1415
§993 Powers & duties of Chair ... 1415
§994 Duties of the Commission ... 1415
§995 Powers of the Commission ... 1419
§996 Director & staff ... 1420
§997 Annual report ... 1420
§998 Definitions ... 1420

Part IV. Jurisdiction & Venue

Chapter 81. Supreme Court
§1251 Original jurisdiction ... 1421
§1253 Direct appeals from decisions of three-judge courts ... 1421

TABLE OF CONTENTS

§1254 Courts of appeals; certiorari; certified questions....1421
§1257 State courts; certiorari....1421
§1258 Supreme Court of Puerto Rico; certiorari....1421
§1259 Court of Appeals for the Armed Forces; certiorari....1421

Chapter 83. Courts of Appeals

§1291 Final decisions of district courts....1421
§1292 Interlocutory decisions....1422
§1294 Circuits in which decisions reviewable....1423
§1295 Jurisdiction of the United States Court of Appeals for the Federal Circuit....1423
§1296 Review of certain agency actions....1424

Chapter 85. District Courts; Jurisdiction

§1330 Actions against foreign states....1424
§1331 Federal question....1424
§1332 Diversity of citizenship; amount in controversy; costs....1424
§1333 Admiralty, maritime & prize cases....1426
§1334 Bankruptcy cases & proceedings....1426
§1335 Interpleader....1427
§1336 Surface Transportation Board's orders....1427
§1337 Commerce & antitrust regulations; amount in controversy, costs....1427
§1338 Patents, plant variety protection, copyrights, mask works, designs, trademarks, & unfair competition....1428
§1339 Postal matters....1428
§1340 Internal revenue; customs duties....1428
§1341 Taxes by States....1428
§1342 Rate orders of State agencies....1428
§1343 Civil rights & elective franchise....1428
§1344 Election disputes....1428
§1345 United States as plaintiff....1429
§1346 United States as defendant....1429
§1347 Partition action where United States is joint tenant....1429
§1348 Banking association as party....1430
§1349 Corporation organized under federal law as party....1430
§1350 Alien's action for tort....1430
§1351 Consuls, vice consuls, & members of a diplomatic mission as defendant....1430
§1352 Bonds executed under federal law....1430
§1353 Indian allotments....1430
§1354 Land grants from different states....1430
§1355 Fine, penalty or forfeiture....1430
§1356 Seizures not within admiralty & maritime jurisdiction....1431
§1357 Injuries under federal laws....1431
§1358 Eminent domain....1431
§1359 Parties collusively joined or made....1431
§1360 State civil jurisdiction in actions to which Indians are parties....1431
§1361 Action to compel an officer of the United States to perform his duty....1431
§1362 Indian tribes....1431
§1363 Jurors' employment rights....1431
§1364 Direct actions against insurers of members of diplomatic missions & their families....1431
§1365 Senate actions....1432
§1366 Construction of references to laws of the United States or Acts of Congress....1432
§1367 Supplemental jurisdiction....1432
§1368 Counterclaims in unfair practices in international trade....1433
§1369 Multiparty, multiforum jurisdiction....1433

Chapter 87. District Courts; Venue

§1390 Scope....1434
§1391 Venue generally....1434
§1394 Banking association's action against Comptroller of Currency....1435
§1395 Fine, penalty or forfeiture....1435
§1396 Internal revenue taxes....1435
§1397 Interpleader....1435
§1398 Interstate Commerce Commission's orders....1435
§1399 Partition action involving United States....1435
§1400 Patents & copyrights, mask works, & designs....1435
§1401 Stockholder's derivative action....1436
§1402 United States as defendant....1436
§1403 Eminent domain....1436
§1404 Change of venue....1436
§1405 Creation or alteration of district or division....1436
§1406 Cure or waiver of defects....1436
§1407 Multidistrict litigation....1437
§1408 Venue of cases under title 11....1438
§1409 Venue of proceedings arising under title 11 or arising in or related to cases under title 11....1438
§1410 Venue of cases ancillary to foreign proceedings....1438
§1411 Jury trials....1438
§1412 Change of venue....1438
§1413 Venue of cases under chapter 5 of title 3....1439

Chapter 89. District Courts; Removal of Cases from State Courts

§1441 Removal of civil actions....1439
§1442 Federal officers or agencies sued or prosecuted....1440
§1442a Members of armed forces sued or prosecuted....1440
§1443 Civil rights cases....1440
§1444 Foreclosure action against United States....1440
§1445 Nonremovable actions....1440
§1446 Procedure for removal of civil actions....1441
§1447 Procedure after removal generally....1442
§1448 Process after removal....1442
§1449 State court record supplied....1442
§1450 Attachment or sequestration; securities....1442
§1451 Definitions....1442
§1452 Removal of claims related to bankruptcy cases....1442
§1453 Removal of class actions....1443

U.S.C.

TABLE OF CONTENTS

§1454 Patent, plant variety protection, & copyright cases 1443
§1455 Procedure for removal of criminal prosecutions 1443

Chapter 91. United States Court of Federal Claims

§1491 Claims against United States generally; actions involving Tennessee Valley Authority....1444
§1492 Congressional reference cases 1445
§1494 Accounts of officers, agents or contractors 1445
§1495 Damages for unjust conviction & imprisonment; claim against United States 1445
§1496 Disbursing officers' claims....1445
§1497 Oyster growers' damages from dredging operations 1445
§1498 Patent & copyright cases 1445
§1499 Liquidated damages withheld from contractors under chapter 37 of title 40 1447
§1500 Pendency of claims in other courts....1447
§1501 Pensions....1447
§1502 Treaty cases 1447
§1503 Set-offs 1447
§1505 Indian claims 1447
§1507 Jurisdiction for certain declaratory judgments....1447
§1508 Jurisdiction for certain partnership proceedings....1447
§1509 No jurisdiction in cases involving refunds of tax shelter promoter & understatement penalties....1447

Chapter 95. Court of International Trade

§1581 Civil actions against the United States & agencies & officers thereof....1447
§1582 Civil actions commenced by the United States....1448
§1583 Counterclaims, cross-claims, & third-party actions....1449
§1584 Civil actions under the North American Free Trade Agreement or the United States-Canada Free-Trade Agreement....1449
§1585 Powers in law & equity....1449

Chapter 97. Jurisdictional Immunities of Foreign States

§1602 Findings & declaration of purpose....1449
§1603 Definitions....1449
§1604 Immunity of a foreign state from jurisdiction ...1449
§1605 General exceptions to the jurisdictional immunity of a foreign state 1449
§1605A Terrorism exception to the jurisdictional immunity of a foreign state 1451
§1606 Extent of liability 1452
§1607 Counterclaims 1453
§1608 Service; time to answer; default....1453
§1609 Immunity from attachment & execution of property of a foreign state 1454
§1610 Exceptions to the immunity from attachment or execution 1454
§1611 Certain types of property immune from execution....1455

Chapter 99. General Provisions

§1631 Transfer to cure want of jurisdiction 1456

Part V. Procedure

Chapter 111. General Provisions

§1651 Writs 1456
§1652 State laws as rules of decision 1456
§1653 Amendment of pleadings to show jurisdiction...1456
§1654 Appearance personally or by counsel....1456
§1655 Lien enforcement; absent defendants 1456
§1656 Creation of new district or division or transfer of territory; lien enforcement 1456
§1657 Priority of civil actions....1456
§1658 Time limitations on the commencement of civil actions arising under Acts of Congress....1457
§1659 Stay of certain actions pending disposition of related proceedings before the United States International Trade Commission....1457

Chapter 113. Process

§1691 Seal & teste of process....1457
§1692 Process & orders affecting property in different districts....1457
§1693 Place of arrest in civil action....1457
§1694 Patent infringement action 1457
§1695 Stockholder's derivative action 1457
§1696 Service in foreign & international litigation....1457
§1697 Service in multiparty, multiforum actions 1458

Chapter 114. Class Actions

§1711 Definitions....1458
§1712 Coupon settlements 1458
§1713 Protection against loss by class members....1458
§1714 Protection against discrimination based on geographic location....1459
§1715 Notifications to appropriate Federal & State officials....1459

Chapter 115. Evidence; Documentary

§1731 Handwriting....1460
§1732 Record made in regular course of business; photographic copies....1460
§1733 Government records & papers; copies....1460
§1734 Court record lost or destroyed, generally....1460
§1735 Court record lost or destroyed where United States interested 1460
§1736 Congressional Journals 1461
§1737 Copy of officer's bond....1461
§1738 State & Territorial statutes & judicial proceedings; full faith & credit 1461
§1738A Full faith & credit given to child custody determinations 1461
§1738B Full faith & credit for child support orders....1462
§1738C Certain acts, records, & proceedings & the effect thereof 1463

TABLE OF CONTENTS

§1739 State & Territorial nonjudicial records; full faith & credit 1464
§1740 Copies of consular papers 1464
§1741 Foreign official documents 1464
§1743 Demand on postmaster 1464
§1744 Copies of United States Patent & Trademark Office documents, generally 1464
§1745 Copies of foreign patent documents 1464
§1746 Unsworn declarations under penalty of perjury 1464

Chapter 117. Evidence; Depositions

§1781 Transmittal of letter rogatory or request 1465
§1782 Assistance to foreign & international tribunals & to litigants before such tribunals 1465
§1783 Subpoena of person in foreign country 1465
§1784 Contempt 1465
§1785 Subpoenas in multiparty, multiforum actions 1466

Chapter 119. Evidence; Witnesses

§1821 Per diem & mileage generally; subsistence 1466
§1822 Competency of interested persons; share of penalties payable 1467
§1824 Mileage fees under summons as both witness & juror 1467
§1825 Payment of fees 1467
§1826 Recalcitrant witnesses 1467
§1827 Interpreters in courts of the United States 1468
§1828 Special interpretation services 1470

Chapter 121. Juries; Trial by Jury

§1861 Declaration of policy 1470
§1862 Discrimination prohibited 1470
§1863 Plan for random jury selection 1470
§1864 Drawing of names from the master jury wheel; completion of juror qualification form 1472
§1865 Qualifications for jury service 1473
§1866 Selection & summoning of jury panels 1473
§1867 Challenging compliance with selection procedures 1474
§1868 Maintenance & inspection of records 1475
§1869 Definitions 1475
§1870 Challenges 1476
§1871 Fees 1476
§1872 Issues of fact in Supreme Court 1477
§1873 Admiralty & maritime cases 1477
§1874 Actions on bonds & specialties 1477
§1875 Protection of jurors' employment 1477
§1876 Trial by jury in the Court of International Trade 1478
§1877 Protection of jurors 1478
§1878 Optional use of a one-step summoning & qualification procedure 1478

Chapter 123. Fees & Costs

§1911 Supreme Court 1478
§1912 Damages & costs on affirmance 1478
§1913 Courts of appeals 1478
§1914 District court; filing & miscellaneous fees; rules of court 1478
§1915 Proceedings in forma pauperis 1479
§1915A Screening 1480
§1916 Seamen's suits 1480
§1917 District courts; fee on filing notice of or petition for appeal 1480
§1918 District courts; fines, forfeitures & criminal proceedings 1480
§1919 Dismissal for lack of jurisdiction 1480
§1920 Taxation of costs 1480
§1921 United States marshal's fees 1480
§1922 Witness fees before United States magistrate judges 1481
§1923 Docket fees & costs of briefs 1481
§1924 Verification of bill of costs 1482
§1925 Admiralty & maritime cases 1482
§1926 Court of Federal Claims 1482
§1927 Counsel's liability for excessive costs 1482
§1928 Patent infringement action; disclaimer not filed 1482
§1929 Extraordinary expenses not expressly authorized 1482
§1930 Bankruptcy fees 1482
§1931 Disposition of filing fees 1483
§1932[A*] Judicial Panel on Multidistrict Litigation 1484
§1932[B*] Revocation of earned release credit 1484

Chapter 125. Pending Actions & Judgments

§1961 Interest 1484
§1962 Lien 1484
§1963 Registration of judgments for enforcement in other districts 1484
§1964 Constructive notice of pending actions 1485

Chapter 127. Executions & Judicial Sales

§2001 Sale of realty generally 1485
§2002 Notice of sale of realty 1485
§2003 Marshal's incapacity after levy on or sale of realty 1485
§2004 Sale of personalty generally 1486
§2005 Appraisal of goods taken on execution 1486
§2006 Execution against revenue officer 1486
§2007 Imprisonment for debt 1486

Chapter 129. Moneys Paid into Court

§2041 Deposit of moneys in pending or adjudicated cases 1486
§2042 Withdrawal 1486
§2043 Deposit of other moneys 1486
§2044 Payment of fine with bond money 1486
§2045 Investment of court registry funds 1487

Chapter 131. Rules of Courts

§2071 Rule-making power generally 1487
§2072 Rules of procedure & evidence; power to prescribe 1487
§2073 Rules of procedure & evidence; method of prescribing 1487
§2074 Rules of procedure & evidence; submission to Congress; effective date 1488

U.S.C.

TABLE OF CONTENTS

§2075 Bankruptcy rules 1488
§2077 Publication of rules; advisory committees 1488

Chapter 133. Review—Miscellaneous Provisions

§2101 Supreme Court; time for appeal or certiorari; docketing; stay 1488
§2102 Priority of criminal case on appeal from State court 1489
§2104 Reviews of State court decisions 1489
§2105 Scope of review; abatement 1489
§2106 Determination 1489
§2107 Time for appeal to court of appeals 1489
§2108 Proof of amount in controversy 1490
§2109 Quorum of Supreme Court justices absent 1490
§2111 Harmless error 1490
§2112 Record on review & enforcement of agency orders 1490
§2113 Definition 1491

Part VI. Particular Proceedings

Chapter 151. Declaratory Judgments

§2201 Creation of remedy 1491
§2202 Further relief 1492

Chapter 153. Habeas Corpus

§2241 Power to grant writ 1492
§2242 Application 1492
§2243 Issuance of writ; return; hearing; decision 1492
§2244 Finality of determination 1493
§2245 Certificate of trial judge admissible in evidence 1494
§2246 Evidence; depositions; affidavits 1494
§2247 Documentary evidence 1494
§2248 Return or answer; conclusiveness 1494
§2249 Certified copies of indictment, plea & judgment; duty of respondent 1494
§2250 Indigent petitioner entitled to documents without cost 1494
§2251 Stay of State court proceedings 1494
§2252 Notice 1494
§2253 Appeal 1494
§2254 State custody; remedies in Federal courts 1495
§2255 Federal custody; remedies on motion attacking sentence 1496

Chapter 154. Special Habeas Corpus Procedures in Capital Cases

§2261 Prisoners in State custody subject to capital sentence; appointment of counsel; requirement of rule of court or statute; procedures for appointment 1496
§2262 Mandatory stay of execution; duration; limits on stays of execution; successive petitions 1497
§2263 Filing of habeas corpus application; time requirements; tolling rules 1497
§2264 Scope of Federal review; district court adjudications 1497
§2265 Certification & judicial review 1498
§2266 Limitation periods for determining applications & motions 1498

Chapter 155. Injunctions; Three-Judge Courts

§2283 Stay of State court proceedings 1499
§2284 Three-judge court; when required; composition; procedure 1499

Chapter 157. Surface Transportation Board Orders; Enforcement & Review

§2321 Judicial review of Board's orders & decisions; procedure generally; process 1500
§2322 United States as party 1500
§2323 Duties of Attorney General; intervenors 1500

Chapter 158. Orders of Federal Agencies; Review

§2341 Definitions 1500
§2342 Jurisdiction of court of appeals 1501
§2343 Venue 1501
§2344 Review of orders; time; notice; contents of petition; service 1501
§2345 Prehearing conference 1501
§2346 Certification of record on review 1501
§2347 Petitions to review; proceedings 1501
§2348 Representation in proceeding; intervention 1502
§2349 Jurisdiction of the proceeding 1502
§2350 Review in Supreme Court on certiorari or certification 1502
§2351 Enforcement of orders by district courts 1502

Chapter 159. Interpleader

§2361 Process & procedure 1502

Chapter 161. United States as Party Generally

§2401 Time for commencing action against United States 1503
§2402 Jury trial in actions against United States 1503
§2403 Intervention by United States or a State; constitutional question 1503
§2404 Death of defendant in damage action 1503
§2405 Garnishment 1503
§2406 Credits in actions by United States; prior disallowance 1504
§2407 Delinquents for public money; judgment at return term; continuance 1504
§2408 Security not required of United States 1504
§2409 Partition actions involving United States 1504
§2409a Real property quiet title actions 1504
§2410 Actions affecting property on which United States has lien 1505
§2411 Interest 1506
§2412 Costs & fees 1506
§2413 Executions in favor of United States 1508
§2414 Payment of judgments & compromise settlements 1508
§2415 Time for commencing actions brought by the United States 1508
§2416 Time for commencing actions brought by the United States—exclusions 1510

Chapter 163. Fines, Penalties & Forfeitures

§2461 Mode of recovery 1510
§2462 Time for commencing proceedings 1510

TABLE OF CONTENTS

§2463 Property taken under revenue law not repleviable....1510
§2464 Security; special bond....1510
§2465 Return of property to claimant; liability for wrongful seizure; attorney fees, costs & interest....1511
§2466 Fugitive disentitlement....1511
§2467 Enforcement of foreign judgment....1511

Chapter 165. United States Court of Federal Claims Procedure

§2501 Time for filing suit....1513
§2502 Aliens' privilege to sue....1513
§2503 Proceedings generally....1513
§2504 Plaintiff's testimony....1513
§2505 Trial before judges....1513
§2506 Interest of witness....1514
§2507 Calls & discovery....1514
§2508 Counterclaim or set-off; registration of judgment....1514
§2509 Congressional reference cases....1514
§2510 Referral of cases by Comptroller General....1515
§2511 Accounts of officers, agents or contractors....1515
§2512 Disbursing officers; relief....1515
§2513 Unjust conviction & imprisonment....1515
§2514 Forfeiture of fraudulent claims....1515
§2515 New trial; stay of judgment....1515
§2516 Interest on claims & judgments....1516
§2517 Payment of judgments....1516
§2519 Conclusiveness of judgment....1516
§2521 Subpoenas & incidental powers....1516
§2522 Notice of appeal....1516

Chapter 169. Court of International Trade Procedure

§2631 Persons entitled to commence a civil action....1516
§2632 Commencement of a civil action....1518
§2633 Procedure & fees....1518
§2634 Notice....1518
§2635 Filing of official documents....1518
§2636 Time for commencement of action....1519
§2637 Exhaustion of administrative remedies....1520
§2638 New grounds in support of a civil action....1520
§2639 Burden of proof; evidence of value....1520
§2640 Scope & standard of review....1520
§2641 Witnesses; inspection of documents....1521
§2642 Analysis of imported merchandise....1521
§2643 Relief....1521
§2644 Interest....1521
§2645 Decisions....1521
§2646 Retrial or rehearing....1522

Chapter 171. Tort Claims Procedure

§2671 Definitions....1522
§2672 Administrative adjustment of claims....1522
§2673 Reports to Congress....1523
§2674 Liability of United States....1523
§2675 Disposition by federal agency as prerequisite; evidence....1523
§2676 Judgment as bar....1523
§2677 Compromise....1523
§2678 Attorney fees; penalty....1523
§2679 Exclusiveness of remedy....1524
§2680 Exceptions....1525

Chapter 173. Attachment in Postal Suits

§2710 Right of attachment....1525
§2711 Application for warrant....1525
§2712 Issue of warrant....1526
§2713 Trial of ownership of property....1526
§2714 Investment of proceeds of attached property....1526
§2715 Publication....1526
§2716 Personal notice....1526
§2717 Discharge....1526
§2718 Interest on balances due department....1526

Chapter 176. Federal Debt Collection Procedure

Subchapter A. Definitions & General Provisions

§3001 Applicability of chapter....1526
§3002 Definitions....1527
§3003 Rules of construction....1527
§3004 Service of process; enforcement; notice....1528
§3005 Application of chapter to judgments....1528
§3006 Affidavit requirements....1528
§3007 Perishable personal property....1528
§3008 Proceedings before United States magistrate judges....1529
§3009 United States marshals' authority to designate keeper....1529
§3010 Co-owned property....1529
§3011 Assessment of surcharge on a debt....1529
§3012 Joinder of additional defendant....1529
§3013 Modification or protective order; supervision of enforcement....1529
§3014 Exempt property....1529
§3015 Discovery as to debtor's financial condition....1530

Subchapter B. Prejudgment Remedies

§3101 Prejudgment remedies....1530
§3102 Attachment....1531
§3103 Receivership....1533
§3104 Garnishment....1534
§3105 Sequestration....1534

Subchapter C. Postjudgment Remedies

§3201 Judgment liens....1535
§3202 Enforcement of judgments....1536
§3203 Execution....1537
§3204 Installment payment order....1539
§3205 Garnishment....1540
§3206 Discharge....1541

Subchapter D. Fraudulent Transfers Involving Debts

§3301 Definitions....1541
§3302 Insolvency....1542
§3303 Value for transfer or obligation....1542
§3304 Transfer fraudulent as to a debt to the United States....1543

§3305 When transfer is made or obligation is incurred....1543
§3306 Remedies of the United States....1544
§3307 Defenses, liability, & protection of transferee....1544
§3308 Supplementary provision....1544

Chapter 178. Professional & Amateur Sports Protection
§3701 Definitions....1544
§3702 Unlawful sports gambling....1545
§3703 Injunctions....1545
§3704 Applicability....1545

Chapter 179. Judicial Review of Certain Actions by Presidential Offices
§3901 Civil actions....1545
§3902 Judicial review of regulations....1545
§3903 Effect of failure to issue regulations....1546
§3904 Expedited review of certain appeals....1546
§3905 Attorney's fees & interest....1546
§3906 Payments....1546
§3907 Other judicial review prohibited....1546
§3908 Definitions....1546

Chapter 180. Assumption of Certain Contractual Obligations
§4001 Assumption of contractual obligations related to transfers of rights in motion pictures....1546

Chapter 181. Foreign Judgments
§4101 Definitions....1547
§4102 Recognition of foreign defamation judgments....1548
§4103 Removal....1548
§4104 Declaratory judgments....1549
§4105 Attorneys' fees....1549

42 U.S.C.

Chapter 21. Civil Rights
Subchapter I. Generally
§1981 Equal rights under the law....1549
§1982 Property rights of citizens....1549
§1983 Civil action for deprivation of rights....1549
§1988 Proceedings in vindication of civil rights....1549

50 U.S.C. APP.

Servicemembers Civil Relief Act
§521 Protection of servicemembers against default judgments....1550
§522 Stay of proceedings when servicemember has notice....1551

28 U.S.C.

PART I. ORGANIZATION OF COURTS

CHAPTER 1. SUPREME COURT

§1. NUMBER OF JUSTICES; QUORUM

The Supreme Court of the United States shall consist of a Chief Justice of the United States and eight associate justices, any six of whom shall constitute a quorum.

History of 28 U.S.C. §1: June 25, 1948, ch. 646, 62 Stat. 869.

§2. TERMS OF COURT

The Supreme Court shall hold at the seat of government a term of court commencing on the first Monday in October of each year and may hold such adjourned or special terms as may be necessary.

History of 28 U.S.C. §2: June 25, 1948, ch. 646, 62 Stat. 869.

§3. VACANCY IN OFFICE OF CHIEF JUSTICE; DISABILITY

Whenever the Chief Justice is unable to perform the duties of his office or the office is vacant, his powers and duties shall devolve upon the associate justice next in precedence who is able to act, until such disability is removed or another Chief Justice is appointed and duly qualified.

History of 28 U.S.C. §3: June 25, 1948, ch. 646, 62 Stat. 869.

§4. PRECEDENCE OF ASSOCIATE JUSTICES

Associate justices shall have precedence according to the seniority of their commissions. Justices whose commissions bear the same date shall have precedence according to seniority in age.

History of 28 U.S.C. §4: June 25, 1948, ch. 646, 62 Stat. 869.

§5. SALARIES OF JUSTICES

The Chief Justice and each associate justice shall each receive a salary at annual rates determined under section 225 of the Federal Salary Act of 1967 (2 U.S.C. 351-361), as adjusted by section 461 of this title.

History of 28 U.S.C. §5: June 25, 1948, ch. 646, 62 Stat. 870; Mar. 2, 1955, ch. 9, §1(a), 69 Stat. 9; Aug. 14, 1964, P.L. 88-426, §403(a), 78 Stat. 434; Aug. 9, 1975, P.L. 94-82, §205(b)(1), 89 Stat. 422.

§6. RECORDS OF FORMER COURT OF APPEALS

The records and proceedings of the court of appeals, appointed previous to the adoption of the Constitution, shall be kept until deposited with the National Archives of the United States in the office of the clerk of the Supreme Court, who shall furnish copies thereof to any person requiring and paying for them, in the manner provided by law for giving copies of the records and proceedings of the Supreme Court. Such copies shall have the same faith and credit as proceedings of the Supreme Court.

History of 28 U.S.C. §6: June 25, 1948, ch. 646, 62 Stat. 870; Oct. 25, 1951, ch. 562, §4(7), 65 Stat. 640.

CHAPTER 3. COURTS OF APPEALS

§41. NUMBER & COMPOSITION OF CIRCUITS

The thirteen judicial circuits of the United States are constituted as follows:

Circuits	*Composition*
District of Columbia	District of Columbia.
First	Maine, Massachusetts, New Hampshire, Puerto Rico, Rhode Island.
Second	Connecticut, New York, Vermont.
Third	Delaware, New Jersey, Pennsylvania, Virgin Islands.
Fourth	Maryland, North Carolina, South Carolina, Virginia, West Virginia.
Fifth	District of the Canal Zone, Louisiana, Mississippi, Texas.
Sixth	Kentucky, Michigan, Ohio, Tennessee.
Seventh	Illinois, Indiana, Wisconsin.
Eighth	Arkansas, Iowa, Minnesota, Missouri, Nebraska, North Dakota, South Dakota.
Ninth	Alaska, Arizona, California, Idaho, Montana, Nevada, Oregon, Washington, Guam, Hawaii.
Tenth	Colorado, Kansas, New Mexico, Oklahoma, Utah, Wyoming.
Eleventh	Alabama, Florida, Georgia.
Federal	All Federal judicial districts.

History of 28 U.S.C. §41: June 25, 1948, ch. 646, 62 Stat. 870; Oct. 31, 1951, ch. 655, §34, 65 Stat. 723; Oct. 14, 1980, P.L. 96-452, §2, 94 Stat. 1994; Apr. 2, 1982, P.L. 97-164, §101, 96 Stat. 25.

§42. ALLOTMENT OF SUPREME COURT JUSTICES TO CIRCUITS

The Chief Justice of the United States and the associate justices of the Supreme Court shall from time to time be allotted as circuit justices among the circuits by order of the Supreme Court. The Chief Justice may make such allotments in vacation.

A justice may be assigned to more than one circuit, and two or more justices may be assigned to the same circuit.

History of 28 U.S.C. §42: June 25, 1948, ch. 646, 62 Stat. 870.

§43. CREATION & COMPOSITION OF COURTS

(a) There shall be in each circuit a court of appeals, which shall be a court of record, known as the United States Court of Appeals for the circuit.

(b) Each court of appeals shall consist of the circuit judges of the circuit in regular active service. The circuit justice and justices or judges designated or assigned shall be competent to sit as judges of the court.

History of 28 U.S.C. §43: June 25, 1948, ch. 646, 62 Stat. 870; Nov. 13, 1963, P.L. 88-176, §1(a), 77 Stat. 331.

§44. APPOINTMENT, TENURE, RESIDENCE & SALARY OF CIRCUIT JUDGES

(a) The President shall appoint, by and with the advice and consent of the Senate, circuit judges for the several circuits as follows:

Circuits	*Number of Judges*
District of Columbia	11
First	6
Second	13
Third	14
Fourth	15
Fifth	17
Sixth	16
Seventh	11
Eighth	11
Ninth	29
Tenth	12
Eleventh	12
Federal	12

(b) Circuit judges shall hold office during good behavior.

(c) Except in the District of Columbia, each circuit judge shall be a resident of the circuit for which appointed at the time of his appointment and thereafter while in active service. While in active service, each circuit judge of the Federal judicial circuit appointed after the effective date of the Federal Courts Improvement Act of 1982, and the chief judge of the Federal judicial circuit, whenever appointed, shall reside within fifty miles of the District of Columbia. In each circuit (other than the Federal judicial circuit) there shall be at least one circuit judge in regular active service appointed from the residents of each state in that circuit.

(d) Each circuit judge shall receive a salary at an annual rate determined under section 225 of the Federal Salary Act of 1967 (2 U.S.C. 351-361), as adjusted by section 461 of this title.

History of 28 U.S.C. §44: June 25, 1948, ch. 646, 62 Stat. 871; Aug. 3, 1949, ch. 387, §1, 63 Stat. 493; Feb. 10, 1954, ch. 6, §1, 68 Stat. 8; Mar. 2, 1955, ch. 9, §1(b), 69 Stat. 10; May 19, 1961, P.L. 87-36, §1(b), 75 Stat. 80; Aug. 14, 1964, P.L. 88-426, §403(b), 78 Stat. 434; Mar. 18, 1966, P.L. 89-372, §1(b), 80 Stat. 75; June 18, 1968, P.L. 90-347, §3, 82 Stat. 184; Aug. 9, 1975, P.L. 94-82, §205(b)(2), 89 Stat. 422; Oct. 20, 1978, P.L. 95-486, §3(b), 92 Stat. 1632; Oct. 14, 1980, P.L. 96-452, §3, 94 Stat. 1994; Apr. 2, 1982, P.L. 97-164, §102, 96 Stat. 25; July 10, 1984, P.L. 98-353, §201(b), 98 Stat. 346; Dec. 1, 1990, P.L. 101-650, §202(b), 104 Stat. 5099; Dec. 9, 1991, P.L. 102-198, §10(c), 105 Stat. 1626; Nov. 26, 1997, P.L. 105-119, §307, 111 Stat. 2440; Jan. 7, 2008, P.L. 110-177, §509, 121 Stat. 2543.

§45. CHIEF JUDGES; PRECEDENCE OF JUDGES

(a)(1) The chief judge of the circuit shall be the circuit judge in regular active service who is senior in commission of those judges who—

(A) are sixty-four years of age or under;

(B) have served for one year or more as a circuit judge; and

(C) have not served previously as chief judge.

(2)(A) In any case in which no circuit judge meets the qualifications of paragraph (1), the youngest circuit judge in regular active service who is sixty-five years of age or over and who has served as circuit judge for one year or more shall act as the chief judge.

(B) In any case under subparagraph (A) in which there is no circuit judge in regular active service who has served as a circuit judge for one year or more, the circuit judge in regular active service who is senior in commission and who has not served previously as chief judge shall act as the chief judge.

(3)(A) Except as provided in subparagraph (C), the chief judge of the circuit appointed under paragraph (1) shall serve for a term of seven years and shall serve after expiration of such term until another judge is eligible under paragraph (1) to serve as chief judge of the circuit.

(B) Except as provided in subparagraph (C), a circuit judge acting as chief judge under subparagraph (A) or (B) of paragraph (2) shall serve until a judge has been appointed who meets the qualifications under paragraph (1).

(C) No circuit judge may serve or act as chief judge of the circuit after attaining the age of seventy years unless no other circuit judge is qualified to serve as chief judge of the circuit under paragraph (1) or is qualified to act as chief judge under paragraph (2).

(b) The chief judge shall have precedence and preside at any session of the court which he attends. Other circuit judges of the court in regular active service shall have precedence and preside according to the seniority of their commissions. Judges whose commissions bear the same date shall have precedence according to seniority in age. The circuit justice, however, shall have precedence over all the circuit judges and shall preside at any session which he attends.

(c) If the chief judge desires to be relieved of his duties as chief judge while retaining his active status as circuit judge, he may so certify to the Chief Justice of the United States, and thereafter the chief judge of the circuit shall be such other circuit judge who is qualified to serve or act as chief judge under subsection (a).

(d) If a chief judge is temporarily unable to perform his duties as such, they shall be performed by the circuit judge in

active service, present in the circuit and able and qualified to act, who is next in precedence.

History of 28 U.S.C. §45: June 25, 1948, ch. 646, 62 Stat. 871; Oct. 31, 1951, ch. 655, §35, 65 Stat. 723; Aug. 6, 1958, P.L. 85-593, §1, 72 Stat. 497; Apr. 2, 1982, P.L. 97-164, §§201, 204, 96 Stat. 51, 53.

§46. ASSIGNMENT OF JUDGES; PANELS; HEARINGS; QUORUM

(a) Circuit judges shall sit on the court and its panels in such order and at such times as the court directs.

(b) In each circuit the court may authorize the hearing and determination of cases and controversies by separate panels, each consisting of three judges, at least a majority of whom shall be judges of that court, unless such judges cannot sit because recused or disqualified, or unless the chief judge of that court certifies that there is an emergency including, but not limited to, the unavailability of a judge of the court because of illness. Such panels shall sit at the times and places and hear the cases and controversies assigned as the court directs. The United States Court of Appeals for the Federal Circuit shall determine by rule a procedure for the rotation of judges from panel to panel to ensure that all of the judges sit on a representative cross section of the cases heard and, notwithstanding the first sentence of this subsection, may determine by rule the number of judges, not less than three, who constitute a panel.

(c) Cases and controversies shall be heard and determined by a court or panel of not more than three judges (except that the United States Court of Appeals for the Federal Circuit may sit in panels of more than three judges if its rules so provide), unless a hearing or rehearing before the court in banc is ordered by a majority of the circuit judges of the circuit who are in regular active service. A court in banc shall consist of all circuit judges in regular active service, or such number of judges as may be prescribed in accordance with section 6 of Public Law 95-486 (92 Stat. 1633), except that any senior circuit judge of the circuit shall be eligible (1) to participate, at his election and upon designation and assignment pursuant to section 294(c) of this title and the rules of the circuit, as a member of an in banc court reviewing a decision of a panel of which such judge was a member, or (2) to continue to participate in the decision of a case or controversy that was heard or reheard by the court in banc at a time when such judge was in regular active service.

(d) A majority of the number of judges authorized to constitute a court or panel thereof, as provided in paragraph (c), shall constitute a quorum.

History of 28 U.S.C. §46: June 25, 1948, ch. 646, 62 Stat. 871; Nov. 13, 1963, P.L. 88-176, §1(b), 77 Stat. 331; Oct. 20, 1978, P.L. 95-486, §5(a), (b), 92 Stat. 1633; Apr. 2, 1982, P.L. 97-164, §§103, 205, 96 Stat. 25, 53; Aug. 6, 1996, P.L. 104-175, §1, 110 Stat. 1556.

§47. DISQUALIFICATION OF TRIAL JUDGE TO HEAR APPEAL

No judge shall hear or determine an appeal from the decision of a case or issue tried by him.

History of 28 U.S.C. §47: June 25, 1948, ch. 646, 62 Stat. 872.

§48. TERMS OF COURT

(a) The courts of appeals shall hold regular sessions at the places listed below, and at such other places within the respective circuit as each court may designate by rule.

Circuits	*Places*
District of Columbia	Washington.
First	Boston.
Second	New York.
Third	Philadelphia.
Fourth	Richmond, Asheville.
Fifth	New Orleans, Fort Worth, Jackson.
Sixth	Cincinnati.
Seventh	Chicago.
Eighth	St. Louis, Kansas City, Omaha, St. Paul.
Ninth	San Francisco, Los Angeles, Portland, Seattle.
Tenth	Denver, Wichita, Oklahoma City.
Eleventh	Atlanta, Jacksonville, Montgomery.
Federal	District of Columbia, and in any other place listed above as the court by rule directs.

(b) Each court of appeals may hold special sessions at any place within its circuit as the nature of the business may require, and upon such notice as the court orders. The court may transact any business at a special session which it might transact at a regular session.

(c) Any court of appeals may pretermit any regular session of court at any place for insufficient business or other good cause.

(d) The times and places of the sessions of the Court of Appeals for the Federal Circuit shall be prescribed with a view to securing reasonable opportunity to citizens to appear before the court with as little inconvenience and expense to citizens as is practicable.

(e) Each court of appeals may hold special sessions at any place within the United States outside the circuit as the nature of the business may require and upon such notice as the court orders, upon a finding by either the chief judge of the court of appeals (or, if the chief judge is unavailable, the most senior available active judge of the court of appeals) or the judicial council of the circuit that, because of emergency conditions, no location within the circuit is reasonably available where such special sessions could be held. The court may

transact any business at a special session outside the circuit which it might transact at a regular session.

(f) If a court of appeals issues an order exercising its authority under subsection (e), the court—

(1) through the Administrative Office of the United States Courts, shall—

(A) send notice of such order, including the reasons for the issuance of such order, to the Committee on the Judiciary of the Senate and the Committee on the Judiciary of the House of Representatives; and

(B) not later than 180 days after the expiration of such court order submit a brief report to the Committee on the Judiciary of the Senate and the Committee on the Judiciary of the House of Representatives describing the impact of such order, including—

(i) the reasons for the issuance of such order;

(ii) the duration of such order;

(iii) the impact of such order on litigants; and

(iv) the costs to the judiciary resulting from such order; and

(2) shall provide reasonable notice to the United States Marshals Service before the commencement of any special session held pursuant to such order.

History of 28 U.S.C. §48: June 25, 1948, ch. 646, 62 Stat. 872; Oct. 31, 1951, ch. 655, §36, 65 Stat. 723; Oct. 14, 1980, P.L. 96-452, §4, 94 Stat. 1994; Apr. 2, 1982, P.L. 97-164, §104, 96 Stat. 26; Oct. 29, 1992, P.L. 102-572, §501, 106 Stat. 4512; Sept. 9, 2005, P.L. 109-63, §2(a), 119 Stat. 1993.

§49. ASSIGNMENT OF JUDGES TO DIVISION TO APPOINT INDEPENDENT COUNSELS

(a) Beginning with the two-year period commencing on the date of the enactment of this section, three judges or justices shall be assigned for each successive two-year period to a division of the United States Court of Appeals for the District of Columbia to be the division of the court for the purpose of appointing independent counsels. The Clerk of the United States Court of Appeals for the District of Columbia Circuit shall serve as the clerk of such division of the court and shall provide such services as are needed by such division of the court.

(b) Except as provided under subsection (f) of this section, assignment to such division of the court shall not be a bar to other judicial assignments during the term of such division.

(c) In assigning judges or justices to sit on such division of the court, priority shall be given to senior circuit judges and retired justices.

(d) The Chief Justice of the United States shall designate and assign three circuit court judges or justices, one of whom shall be a judge of the United States Court of Appeals for the District of Columbia, to such division of the court. Not more than one judge or justice or senior or retired judge or justice may be named to such division from a particular court.

(e) Any vacancy in such division of the court shall be filled only for the remainder of the two-year period in which such vacancy occurs and in the same manner as initial assignments to such division were made.

(f) Except as otherwise provided in chapter 40 of this title, no member of such division of the court who participated in a function conferred on the division under chapter 40 of this title involving an independent counsel shall be eligible to participate in any judicial proceeding concerning a matter which involves such independent counsel while such independent counsel is serving in that office or which involves the exercise of such independent counsel's official duties, regardless of whether such independent counsel is still serving in that office.

History of 28 U.S.C. §49: Oct. 26, 1978, P.L. 95-521, §602(a), 92 Stat. 1873. Amended Jan. 3, 1983, P.L. 97-409, §2(b)(1), 96 Stat. 2039; Oct. 27, 1986, P.L. 99-554, §144(g)(3), 100 Stat. 3097; Dec. 15, 1987, P.L. 100-191, §§4, 5(a), 101 Stat. 1307.

CHAPTER 5. DISTRICT COURTS

§81. ALABAMA

Alabama is divided into three judicial districts to be known as the Northern, Middle, and Southern Districts of Alabama.

NORTHERN DISTRICT

(a) The Northern District comprises seven divisions.

(1) The Northwestern Division comprises the counties of Colbert, Franklin, and Lauderdale.

Court for the Northwestern Division shall be held at Florence.

(2) The Northeastern Division comprises the counties of Cullman, Jackson, Lawrence, Limestone, Madison, and Morgan.

Court for the Northeastern Division shall be held at Huntsville and Decatur.

(3) The Southern Division comprises the counties of Blount, Jefferson, and Shelby.

Court for the Southern Division shall be held at Birmingham.

(4) The Eastern Division comprises the counties of Calhoun, Clay, Cleburne, and Talladega.

Court for the Eastern Division shall be held at Anniston.

(5) The Western Division comprises the counties of Bibb, Greene, Pickens, Sumter, and Tuscaloosa.

Court for the Western Division shall be held at Tuscaloosa.

(6) The Middle Division comprises the counties of Cherokee, De Kalb, Etowah, Marshall, and Saint Clair.

Court for the Middle Division shall be held at Gadsden.

(7) The Jasper Division comprises the counties of Fayette, Lamar, Marion, Walker, and Winston.

Court for the Jasper Division shall be held at Jasper.

MIDDLE DISTRICT

(b) The Middle District comprises three divisions.

(1) The Northern Division comprises the counties of Autauga, Barbour, Bullock, Butler, Chilton, Coosa, Covington, Crenshaw, Elmore, Lowndes, Montgomery, and Pike.

Court for the Northern Division shall be held at Montgomery.

(2) The Southern Division comprises the counties of Coffee, Dale, Geneva, Henry, and Houston.

Court for the Southern Division shall be held at Dothan.

(3) The Eastern Division comprises the counties of Chambers, Lee, Macon, Randolph, Russell, and Tallapoosa.

Court for the Eastern Division shall be held at Opelika.

SOUTHERN DISTRICT

(c) The Southern District comprises two divisions.

(1) The Northern Division comprises the counties of Dallas, Hale, Marengo, Perry, and Wilcox.

Court for the Northern Division shall be held at Selma.

(2) The Southern Division comprises the counties of Baldwin, Choctaw, Clarke, Conecuh, Escambia, Mobile, Monroe, and Washington.

Court for the Southern Division shall be held at Mobile.

History of 28 U.S.C. §81: June 25, 1948, ch. 646, 62 Stat. 873; May 19, 1961, P.L. 87-36, §3(a), 75 Stat. 83.

§81A. ALASKA

Alaska constitutes one judicial district.

Court shall be held at Anchorage, Fairbanks, Juneau, Ketchikan, and Nome.

History of 28 U.S.C. §81A: July 7, 1958, P.L. 85-508, §12(b), 72 Stat. 348; June 25, 1959, P.L. 86-70, §23(b), 73 Stat. 147.

§82. ARIZONA

Arizona constitutes one judicial district.

Court shall be held at Globe, Phoenix, Prescott, and Tucson.

History of 28 U.S.C. §82: June 25, 1948, ch. 646, 62 Stat. 874.

§83. ARKANSAS

Arkansas is divided into two judicial districts to be known as the Eastern and Western Districts of Arkansas.

EASTERN DISTRICT

(a) The Eastern District comprises five divisions.

(1) The Eastern Division comprises the counties of Cross, Lee, Monroe, Phillips, Saint Francis, and Woodruff.

Court for the Eastern Division shall be held at Helena.

(2) The Western Division comprises the counties of Conway, Faulkner, Lonoke, Perry, Pope, Prairie, Pulaski, Saline, Van Buren, White, and Yell.

Court for the Western Division shall be held at Little Rock.

(3) The Pine Bluff Division comprises the counties of Arkansas, Chicot, Cleveland, Dallas, Desha, Drew, Grant, Jefferson, and Lincoln.

Court for the Pine Bluff Division shall be held at Pine Bluff.

(4) The Northern Division comprises the counties of Cleburne, Fulton, Independence, Izard, Jackson, Sharp, and Stone.

Court for the Northern Division shall be held at Batesville.

(5) The Jonesboro Division comprises the counties of Clay, Craighead, Crittenden, Greene, Lawrence, Mississippi, Poinsett, and Randolph.

Court for the Jonesboro Division shall be held at Jonesboro.

WESTERN DISTRICT

(b) The Western District comprises six divisions.

(1) The Texarkana Division comprises the counties of Hempstead, Howard, Lafayette, Little River, Miller, Nevada, and Sevier.

Court for the Texarkana Division shall be held at Texarkana, and may be held anywhere within the Federal courthouse in Texarkana that is located astride the State line between Texas and Arkansas.

(2) The El Dorado Division comprises the counties of Ashley, Bradley, Calhoun, Columbia, Ouachita, and Union.

Court for the El Dorado Division shall be held at El Dorado.

(3) The Fort Smith Division comprises the counties of Crawford, Franklin, Johnson, Logan, Polk, Scott, and Sebastian.

Court for the Fort Smith Division shall be held at Fort Smith.

(4) The Harrison Division comprises the counties of Baxter, Boone, Carroll, Marion, Newton, and Searcy.

Court for the Harrison Division shall be held at Harrison.

(5) The Fayetteville Division comprises the counties of Benton, Madison, and Washington.

Court for the Fayetteville Division shall be held at Fayetteville.

(6) The Hot Springs Division comprises the counties of Clark, Garland, Hot Springs, Montgomery, and Pike.

Court for the Hot Springs Division shall be held at Hot Springs.

History of 28 U.S.C. §83: June 25, 1948, ch. 646, 62 Stat. 874; May 19, 1961, P.L. 87-36, §5, 75 Stat. 84; Dec. 10, 2004, P.L. 108-455, §3, 118 Stat. 3628.

§84. CALIFORNIA

California is divided into four judicial districts to be known as the Northern, Eastern, Central, and Southern Districts of California.

NORTHERN DISTRICT

(a) The Northern District comprises the counties of Alameda, Contra Costa, Del Norte, Humboldt, Lake Marin, Mendocino, Monterey, Napa, San Benito, Santa Clara, Santa Cruz, San Francisco, San Mateo, and Sonoma.

Court for the Northern District shall be held at Eureka, Oakland, San Francisco, and San Jose.

EASTERN DISTRICT

(b) The Eastern District comprises the counties of Alpine, Amador, Butte, Calaveras, Colusa, El Dorado, Fresno, Glenn, Inyo, Kern, Kings, Lassen, Madera, Mariposa, Merced, Modoc, Mono, Nevada, Placer, Plumas, Sacramento, San Joaquin, Shasta, Sierra, Siskiyou, Solano, Stanislaus, Sutter, Tehama, Trinity, Tulare, Tuolumne, Yolo, and Yuba.

Court for the Eastern District shall be held at Fresno, Redding, and Sacramento.

CENTRAL DISTRICT

(c) The Central District comprises 3 divisions.

(1) The Eastern Division comprises the counties of Riverside and San Bernardino.

Court for the Eastern Division shall be held at a suitable site in the city of Riverside, the city of San Bernardino, or not more than 5 miles from the boundary of either such city.

(2) The Western Division comprises the counties of Los Angeles, San Luis Obispo, Santa Barbara, and Ventura.

Court for the Western Division shall be held at Los Angeles.

(3) The Southern Division comprises Orange County.

Court for the Southern Division shall be held at Santa Ana.

SOUTHERN DISTRICT

(d) The Southern District comprises the counties of Imperial and San Diego.

Court for the Southern District shall be held at San Diego.

History of 28 U.S.C. §84: June 25, 1948, ch. 646, 62 Stat. 875; Mar. 18, 1966, P.L. 89-372, §3(a), 80 Stat. 75; Oct. 15, 1980, P.L. 96-462, §2, 94 Stat. 2053; Aug. 26, 1992, P.L. 102-357, §2, 106 Stat. 958.

§85. COLORADO

Colorado constitutes one judicial district.

Court shall be held at Boulder, Colorado Springs, Denver, Durango, Grand Junction, Montrose, Pueblo, and Sterling.

History of 28 U.S.C. §85: June 25, 1948, ch. 646, 62 Stat. 875; Nov. 8, 1984, P.L. 98-620, §409, 98 Stat. 3362; Dec. 10, 2004, P.L. 108-455, §5, 118 Stat. 3629; Dec. 23, 2004, P.L. 108-482, §301, 118 Stat. 3918.

§86. CONNECTICUT

Connecticut constitutes one judicial district.

Court shall be held at Bridgeport, Hartford, New Haven, New London, and Waterbury.

History of 28 U.S.C. §86: June 25, 1948, ch. 646, 62 Stat. 875; May 19, 1961, P.L. 87-36, §3(b), 75 Stat. 83; Sept. 7, 1966, P.L. 89-558, 80 Stat. 705.

§87. DELAWARE

Delaware constitutes one judicial district.

Court shall be held at Wilmington.

History of 28 U.S.C. §87: June 25, 1948, ch. 646, 62 Stat. 875.

§88. DISTRICT OF COLUMBIA

The District of Columbia constitutes one judicial district.

Court shall be held at Washington.

History of 28 U.S.C. §88: June 25, 1948, ch. 646, 62 Stat. 875.

§89. FLORIDA

Florida is divided into three judicial districts to be known as the Northern, Middle, and Southern Districts of Florida.

NORTHERN DISTRICT

(a) The Northern District comprises the counties of Alachua, Bay, Calhoun, Dixie, Escambia, Franklin, Gadsden, Gilchrist, Gulf, Holmes, Jackson, Jefferson, Lafayette, Leon, Levy, Liberty, Madison, Okaloosa, Santa Rosa, Taylor, Wakulla, Walton, and Washington.

Court for the Northern District shall be held at Gainesville, Marianna, Panama City, Pensacola, and Tallahassee.

MIDDLE DISTRICT

(b) The Middle District comprises the counties of Baker, Bradford, Brevard, Charlotte, Citrus, Clay, Collier, Columbia, De Soto, Duval, Flagler, Glades, Hamilton, Hardee, Hendry, Hernando, Hillsborough, Lake, Lee, Manatee, Marion, Nassau, Orange, Osceola, Pasco, Pinellas, Polk, Putnam, St. Johns, Sarasota, Seminole, Sumter, Suwannee, Union, and Volusia.

Court for the Middle District shall be held at Fernandina, Fort Myers, Jacksonville, Live Oak, Ocala, Orlando, Saint Petersburg, and Tampa.

SOUTHERN DISTRICT

(c) The Southern District comprises the counties of Broward, Dade, Highlands, Indian River, Martin, Monroe, Okeechobee, Palm Beach, and Saint Lucie.

Court for the Southern District shall be held at Fort Lauderdale, Fort Pierce, Key West, Miami, and West Palm Beach.

History of 28 U.S.C. §89: June 25, 1948, ch. 646, 62 Stat. 876; July 17, 1952, ch. 929, 66 Stat. 757; May 19, 1961, P.L. 87-36, §3(f), 75 Stat. 83; July 30, 1962, P.L. 87-562, §1, 76 Stat. 247; June 2, 1970, P.L. 91-272, §10, 84 Stat. 298; Oct. 2, 1978, P.L. 95-408, §4(a), 92 Stat. 884; Nov. 19, 1988, P.L. 100-702, §1021(a), 102 Stat. 4672.

§90. GEORGIA

Georgia is divided into three judicial districts to be known as the Northern, Middle, and Southern Districts of Georgia.

NORTHERN DISTRICT

(a) The Northern District comprises four divisions.

(1) The Gainesville Division comprises the counties of Banks, Barrow, Dawson, Fannin, Forsyth, Gilmer, Habersham, Hall, Jackson, Lumpkin, Pickens, Rabun, Stephens, Towns, Union, and White.

Court for the Gainesville Division shall be held at Gainesville.

(2) The Atlanta Division comprises the counties of Cherokee, Clayton, Cobb, De Kalb, Douglas, Fulton, Gwinnett, Henry, Newton, and Rockdale.

Court for the Atlanta Division shall be held at Atlanta.

(3) The Rome Division comprises the counties of Bartow, Catoosa, Chattooga, Dade, Floyd, Gordon, Murray, Paulding, Polk, Walker, and Whitfield.

Court for the Rome Division shall be held at Rome.

(4) The Newnan Division comprises the counties of Carroll, Coweta, Fayette, Haralson, Heard, Meriwether, Pike, Spalding, and Troup.

Court for the Newnan Division shall be held at Newnan.

MIDDLE DISTRICT

(b) The Middle District comprises seven divisions.

(1) The Athens Division comprises the counties of Clarke, Elbert, Franklin, Greene, Hart, Madison, Morgan, Oconee, Oglethorpe, and Walton.

Court for the Athens Division shall be held at Athens.

(2) The Macon Division comprises the counties of Baldwin, Bibb, Bleckley, Butts, Crawford, Hancock, Houston, Jasper, Jones, Lamar, Monroe, Peach, Pulaski, Putnam, Twiggs, Upson, Washington, and Wilkinson.

Court for the Macon Division shall be held at Macon.

(3) The Columbus Division comprises the counties of Chattahoochee, Clay, Harris, Marion, Muscogee, Quitman, Randolph, Stewart, Talbot, and Taylor.

Court for the Columbus Division shall be held at Columbus.

(4) The Americus Division comprises the counties of Ben Hill, Crisp, Dooly, Lee, Macon, Schley, Sumter, Terrell, Webster, and Wilcox.

Court for the Americus Division shall be held at Americus.

(5) The Albany Division comprises the counties of Baker, Calhoun, Dougherty, Early, Miller, Mitchell, Turner, and Worth.

Court for the Albany Division shall be held at Albany.

(6) The Valdosta Division comprises the counties of Berrien, Clinch, Cook, Echols, Irwin, Lanier, Lowndes, and Tift.

Court for the Valdosta Division shall be held at Valdosta.

(7) The Thomasville Division comprises the counties of Brooks, Colquitt, Decatur, Grady, Seminole, and Thomas.

Court for the Thomasville Division shall be held at Thomasville.

SOUTHERN DISTRICT

(c) The Southern District comprises six divisions.

(1) The Augusta Division comprises the counties of Burke, Columbia, Glascock, Jefferson, Lincoln, McDuffie, Richmond, Taliaferro, Warren, and Wilkes.

Court for the Augusta Division shall be held at Augusta.

(2) The Dublin Division comprises the counties of Dodge, Johnson, Laurens, Montgomery, Telfair, Treutlen, and Wheeler.

Court for the Dublin Division shall be held at Dublin.

(3) The Savannah Division comprises the counties of Bryan, Chatham, Effingham, and Liberty.

Court for the Savannah Division shall be held at Savannah.

(4) The Waycross Division comprises the counties of Atkinson, Bacon, Brantley, Charlton, Coffee, Pierce, and Ware.

Court for the Waycross Division shall be held at Waycross.

(5) The Brunswick Division comprises the counties of Appling, Camden, Glynn, Jeff Davis, Long, McIntosh, and Wayne.

Court for the Brunswick Division shall be held at Brunswick.

(6) The Statesboro Division comprises the counties of Bulloch, Candler, Emanuel, Evans, Jenkins, Screven, Tattnall, and Toombs.

Court for the Statesboro Division shall be held at Statesboro.

History of 28 U.S.C. §90: June 25, 1948, ch. 646, 62 Stat. 876; Aug. 16, 1949, ch. 444, 63 Stat. 610; Oct. 31, 1951, ch. 655, §36a, 65 Stat. 723; Nov. 8, 1984, P.L. 98-620, §408(a)-(c), 98 Stat. 3362; Nov. 14, 1986, P.L. 99-657, §3, 100 Stat. 3670.

§91. HAWAII

Hawaii constitutes one judicial district which includes the Midway Islands, Wake Island, Johnston Island, Sand Island, Kingman Reef, Palmyra Island, Baker Island, Howland Island, Jarvis Island, Canton Island, and Enderbury Island: Provided, That the inclusion of Canton and Enderbury Islands in such judicial district shall in no way be construed to be prejudicial to the claims of the United Kingdom to said Islands in accordance with the agreement of April 6, 1939, between the Governments of the United States and of the United Kingdom to set up a regime for their use in common.

Court shall be held at Honolulu.

History of 28 U.S.C. §91: June 25, 1948, ch. 646, 62 Stat. 877; May 24, 1949, ch. 139, §64a, 63 Stat. 99; Mar. 18, 1959, P.L. 86-3, §14(i), 73 Stat. 11; July 12, 1960, P.L. 86-624, §19, 74 Stat. 416.

§92. IDAHO

Idaho, exclusive of Yellowstone National Park, constitutes one judicial district.

Court shall be held at Boise, Coeur d'Alene, Moscow, and Pocatello.

History of 28 U.S.C. §92: June 25, 1948, ch. 646, 62 Stat. 877; June 2, 1970, P.L. 91-272, §5, 84 Stat. 297.

§93. ILLINOIS

Illinois is divided into three judicial districts to be known as the Northern, Central, and Southern Districts of Illinois.

NORTHERN DISTRICT

(a) The Northern District comprises two divisions.

(1) The Eastern Division comprises the counties of Cook, Du Page, Grundy, Kane, Kendall, Lake, La Salle, and Will.

Court for the Eastern Division shall be held at Chicago and Wheaton.

(2) The Western Division comprises the counties of Boone, Carroll, De Kalb, Jo Daviess, Lee, McHenry, Ogle, Stephenson, Whiteside, and Winnebago.

Court for the Western Division shall be held at Freeport and Rockford.

CENTRAL DISTRICT

(b) The Central District comprises the counties of Adams, Brown, Bureau, Cass, Champaign, Christian, Coles, De Witt, Douglas, Edgar, Ford, Fulton, Greene, Hancock, Henderson, Henry, Iroquois, Kankakee, Knox, Livingston, Logan, McDonough, McLean, Macoupin, Macon, Marshall, Mason, Menard, Mercer, Montgomery, Morgan, Moultrie, Peoria, Piatt, Pike, Putnam, Rock Island, Sangamon, Schuyler, Scott, Shelby, Stark, Tazewell, Vermilion, Warren, and Woodford.

Court for the Central District shall be held at Champaign/Urbana, Danville, Peoria, Quincy, Rock Island, and Springfield.

SOUTHERN DISTRICT

(c) The Southern District comprises the counties of Alexander, Bond, Calhoun, Clark, Clay, Clinton, Crawford, Cumberland, Edwards, Effingham, Fayette, Franklin, Gallatin, Hamilton, Hardin, Jackson, Jasper, Jefferson, Jersey, Johnson, Lawrence, Madison, Marion, Massac, Monroe, Perry, Pope, Pulaski, Randolph, Richland, St. Clair, Saline, Union, Wabash, Washington, Wayne, White, and Williamson.

Court for the Southern District shall be held at Alton, Benton, Cairo, and East Saint Louis.

History of 28 U.S.C. §93: June 25, 1948, ch. 646, 62 Stat. 878; Aug. 10, 1950, ch. 675, §1, 64 Stat. 438; May 19, 1961, P.L. 87-36, §3(c), 75 Stat. 83; June 2, 1970, P.L. 91-272, §8, 84 Stat. 297; Oct. 2, 1978, P.L. 95-408, §4(b)(1), 92 Stat. 884; Nov. 2, 1978, P.L. 95-573, §1, 92 Stat. 2458; Nov. 8, 1984, P.L. 98-620, §406(a), (c), 98 Stat. 3361; Dec. 6, 1999, P.L. 106-130, §2, 113 Stat. 1677.

§94. INDIANA

Indiana is divided into two judicial districts to be known as the Northern and Southern Districts of Indiana.

NORTHERN DISTRICT

(a) The Northern District comprises three divisions.

(1) The Fort Wayne Division comprises the counties of Adams, Allen, Blackford, De Kalb, Grant, Huntington, Jay, Lagrange, Noble, Steuben, Wells, and Whitley.

Court for the Fort Wayne Division shall be held at Fort Wayne.

(2) The South Bend Division comprises the counties of Cass, Elkhart, Fulton, Kosciusko, La Porte, Marshall, Miami, Pulaski, St. Joseph, Starke, and Wabash.

Court for the South Bend Division shall be held at South Bend.

(3) The Hammond Division comprises the counties of Benton, Carroll, Jasper, Lake, Newton, Porter, Tippecanoe, Warren, and White.

Court for the Hammond Division shall be held at Hammond and Lafayette.

SOUTHERN DISTRICT

(b) The Southern District comprises four divisions.

(1) The Indianapolis Division comprises the counties of Bartholomew, Boone, Brown, Clinton, Decatur, Delaware, Fayette, Fountain, Franklin, Hamilton, Hancock, Hendricks, Henry, Howard, Johnson, Madison, Marion, Monroe, Montgomery, Morgan, Randolph, Rush, Shelby, Tipton, Union, and Wayne.

Court for the Indianapolis Division shall be held at Indianapolis and Richmond.

(2) The Terre Haute Division comprises the counties of Clay, Greene, Knox, Owen, Parke, Putnam, Sullivan, Vermilion, and Vigo.

Court for the Terre Haute Division shall be held at Terre Haute.

(3) The Evansville Division comprises the counties of Davies, Dubois, Gibson, Martin, Perry, Pike, Posey, Spencer, Vanderburgh, and Warrick.

Court for the Evansville Division shall be held at Evansville.

(4) The New Albany Division comprises the counties of Clark, Crawford, Dearborn, Floyd, Harrison, Jackson, Jefferson, Jennings, Lawrence, Ohio, Orange, Ripley, Scott, Switzerland, and Washington.

Court for the New Albany Division shall be held at New Albany.

History of 28 U.S.C. §94: June 25, 1948, ch. 646, 62 Stat. 878; Feb. 10, 1954, ch. 6, §2(b)(7), 68 Stat. 11; June 2, 1970, P.L. 91-272, §9, 84 Stat. 298.

§95. IOWA

Iowa is divided into two judicial districts to be known as the Northern and Southern Districts of Iowa.

NORTHERN DISTRICT

(a) The Northern District comprises four divisions.

(1) The Cedar Rapids Division comprises the counties of Benton, Cedar, Grundy, Hardin, Iowa, Jones, Linn, and Tama.

Court for the Cedar Rapids Division shall be held at Cedar Rapids.

(2) The Eastern Division comprises the counties of Allamakee, Black Hawk, Bremer, Buchanan, Chickasaw, Clayton, Delaware, Dubuque, Fayette, Floyd, Howard, Jackson, Mitchell, and Winneshiek.

Court for the Eastern Division shall be held at Dubuque and Waterloo.

(3) The Western Division comprises the counties of Buena Vista, Cherokee, Clay, Crawford, Dickinson, Ida, Lyon, Monona, O'Brien, Osceola, Plymouth, Sac, Sioux, and Woodbury.

Court for the Western Division shall be held at Sioux City.

(4) The Central Division comprises the counties of Butler, Calhoun, Carroll, Cerro Gordo, Emmet, Franklin, Hamilton, Hancock, Humboldt, Kossuth, Palo Alto, Pocahontas, Webster, Winnebago, Worth, and Wright.

Court for the Central Division shall be held at Fort Dodge and Mason City.

SOUTHERN DISTRICT

(b) The Southern District comprises six divisions.

(1) The Central Division comprises the counties of Boone, Dallas, Greene, Guthrie, Jasper, Madison, Marion, Marshall, Polk, Poweshiek, Story, and Warren.

Court for the Central Division shall be held at Des Moines.

(2) The Eastern Division comprises the counties of Des Moines, Henry, Lee, Louisa, and Van Buren.

Court for the Eastern Division shall be held at Keokuk.

(3) The Western Division comprises the counties of Audubon, Cass, Fremont, Harrison, Mills, Montgomery, Page, Pottawattamie, and Shelby.

Court for the Western Division shall be held at Council Bluffs.

(4) The Southern Division comprises the counties of Adair, Adams, Clarke, Decatur, Lucas, Ringgold, Taylor, Union, and Wayne.

Court for the Southern Division shall be held at Creston.

(5) The Davenport Division comprises the counties of Clinton, Johnson, Muscatine, Scott, and Washington.

Court for the Davenport Division shall be held at Davenport.

(6) The Ottumwa Division comprises the counties of Appanoose, Davis, Jefferson, Keokuk, Mahaska, Monroe, and Wapello.

Court for the Ottumwa Division shall be held at Ottumwa.

History of 28 U.S.C. §95: June 25, 1948, ch. 646, 62 Stat. 879; Oct. 15, 1980, P.L. 96-462, §3(a), 94 Stat. 2053.

§96. KANSAS

Kansas constitutes one judicial district.

Court shall be held at Kansas City, Lawrence, Leavenworth, Salina, Topeka, Hutchinson, Wichita, Dodge City, and Fort Scott.

History of 28 U.S.C. §96: June 25, 1948, ch. 646, 62 Stat. 880; Aug. 27, 1949, ch. 516, 63 Stat. 666; Oct. 27, 1986, P.L. 99-554, §141, 100 Stat. 3096.

§97. KENTUCKY

Kentucky is divided into two judicial districts to be known as the Eastern and Western Districts of Kentucky.

EASTERN DISTRICT

(a) The Eastern District comprises the counties of Anderson, Bath, Bell, Boone, Bourbon, Boyd, Boyle, Bracken, Breathitt, Campbell, Carroll, Carter, Clark, Clay, Elliott, Estill, Fayette, Fleming, Floyd, Franklin, Gallatin, Garrard, Grant, Greenup, Harlan, Harrison, Henry, Jackson, Jessamine, Johnson, Kenton, Knott, Knox, Laurel, Lawrence, Lee, Leslie, Letcher, Lewis, Lincoln, McCreary, Madison, Magoffin, Martin, Mason, Menifee, Mercer, Montgomery, Morgan, Nicholas, Owen, Owsley, Pendleton, Perry, Pike, Powell, Pulaski, Robertson, Rockcastle, Rowan, Scott, Shelby, Trimble, Wayne, Whitley, Wolfe, and Woodford.

Court for the Eastern District shall be held at Ashland, Catlettsburg, Covington, Frankfort, Jackson, Lexington, London, Pikeville, and Richmond.

WESTERN DISTRICT

(b) The Western District comprises the counties of Adair, Allen, Ballard, Barren, Breckenridge, Bullitt, Butler, Caldwell, Calloway, Carlisle, Casey, Christian, Clinton, Crittenden, Cumberland, Daviess, Edmonson, Fulton, Graves, Grayson, Green, Hancock, Hardin, Hart, Henderson, Hickman, Hopkins, Jefferson, Larue, Livingston, Logan, Lyon, McCracken, McLean, Marion, Marshall, Meade, Metcalfe, Monroe, Muhlenberg, Nelson, Ohio, Oldham, Russell, Simpson, Spencer, Taylor, Todd, Trigg, Union, Warren, Washington, and Webster.

Court for the Western District shall be held at Bowling Green, Louisville, Owensboro, and Paducah.

History of 28 U.S.C. §97: June 25, 1948, ch. 646, 62 Stat. 880; Oct. 2, 1978, P.L. 95-408, §2(a), 92 Stat. 883.

§98. LOUISIANA

Louisiana is divided into three judicial districts to be known as the Eastern, Middle, and Western Districts of Louisiana.

EASTERN DISTRICT

(a) The Eastern District comprises the parishes of Assumption, Jefferson, Lafourche, Orleans, Plaquemines, Saint Bernard, Saint Charles, Saint James, Saint John the Baptist, Saint Tammany, Tangipahoa, Terrebonne, and Washington.

Court for the Eastern District shall be held at New Orleans, and Houma.

MIDDLE DISTRICT

(b) The Middle District comprises the parishes of Ascension, East Baton Rouge, East Feliciana, Iberville, Livingston, Pointe Coupee, Saint Helena, West Baton Rouge, and West Feliciana.

Court for the Middle District shall be held at Baton Rouge.

WESTERN DISTRICT

(c) The Western District comprises the parishes of Acadia, Allen, Avoyelles, Beauregard, Bienville, Bossier, Caddo, Calcasieu, Caldwell, Cameron, Catahoula, Claiborne, Concordia, Jefferson Davis, De Soto, East Carroll, Evangeline, Franklin, Grant, Iberia, Jackson, Lafayette, La Salle, Lincoln, Madison, Morehouse, Natchitoches, Ouachita, Rapides, Red River, Richland, Sabine, Saint Landry, Saint Martin, Saint Mary, Tensas, Union, Vermilion, Vernon, Webster, West Carroll, and Winn.

Court for the Western District shall be held at Alexandria, Lafayette, Lake Charles, Monroe, Opelousas, and Shreveport.

History of 28 U.S.C. §98: June 25, 1948, ch. 646, 62 Stat. 881; May 19, 1961, P.L. 87-36, §4, 75 Stat. 83; Dec. 18, 1971, P.L. 92-208, §3(a), 85 Stat. 741; Oct. 2, 1978, P.L. 95-408, §3(a), 92 Stat. 883; July 10, 1984, P.L. 98-353, §203(b), 98 Stat. 350.

§99. MAINE

Maine constitutes one judicial district.

Court shall be held at Bangor and Portland.

History of 28 U.S.C. §99: June 25, 1948, ch. 646, 62 Stat. 881; Nov. 2, 1978, P.L. 95-573, §2, 92 Stat. 2458.

§100. MARYLAND

Maryland constitutes one judicial district comprising two divisions.

(1) The Northern Division comprises the counties of Allegany, Anne Arundel, Baltimore, Caroline, Carroll, Cecil, Dorchester, Frederick, Garrett, Harford, Howard, Kent, Queen Anne's, Somerset, Talbot, Washington, Wicomico, and Worcester, and the City of Baltimore.

Court for the Northern Division shall be held at Baltimore, Cumberland, and Denton.

(2) The Southern Division comprises the counties of Calvert, Charles, Montgomery, Prince George's, and St. Mary's.

Court for the Southern Division shall be held at a suitable site in Montgomery or Prince George's County not more than five miles from the boundary of Montgomery and Prince George's Counties.

History of 28 U.S.C. §100: June 25, 1948, ch. 646, 62 Stat. 882; Dec. 14, 1970, P.L. 91-546, §4, 84 Stat. 1412; Oct. 14, 1988, P.L. 100-487, §1, 102 Stat. 2431.

§101. MASSACHUSETTS

Massachusetts constitutes one judicial district.

Court shall be held at Boston, New Bedford, Springfield, and Worcester.

History of 28 U.S.C. §101: June 25, 1948, ch. 646, 62 Stat. 882.

§102. MICHIGAN

Michigan is divided into two judicial districts to be known as the Eastern and Western Districts of Michigan.

EASTERN DISTRICT

(a) The Eastern District comprises two divisions.

(1) The Southern Division comprises the counties of Genesee, Jackson, Lapeer, Lenawee, Livingston, Macomb, Monroe, Oakland, Saint Clair, Sanilac, Shiawassee, Washtenaw, and Wayne.

Court for the Southern Division shall be held at Ann Arbor, Detroit, Flint, and Port Huron.

(2) The Northern Division comprises the counties of Alcona, Alpena, Arenac, Bay, Cheboygan, Clare, Crawford, Gladwin, Gratiot, Huron, Iosco, Isabella, Midland, Montmorency, Ogemaw, Oscoda, Otsego, Presque Isle, Roscommon, Saginaw, and Tuscola.

Court for the Northern Division shall be held at Bay City.

WESTERN DISTRICT

(b) The Western District comprises two divisions.

(1) The Southern Division comprises the counties of Allegan, Antrim, Barry, Benzie, Berrien, Branch, Calhoun, Cass, Charlevoix, Clinton, Eaton, Emmet, Grand Traverse, Hillsdale, Ingham, Ionia, Kalamazoo, Kalkaska, Kent, Lake, Leelanau, Manistee, Mason, Mecosta, Missaukee, Montcalm, Muskegon, Newaygo, Oceana, Osceola, Ottawa, Saint Joseph, Van Buren, and Wexford.

Court for the Southern Division shall be held at Grand Rapids, Kalamazoo, Lansing, and Traverse City.

(2) The Northern Division comprises the counties of Alger, Baraga, Chippewa, Delta, Dickinson, Gogebic, Houghton, Iron, Keweenaw, Luce, Mackinac, Marquette, Menominee, Ontonagon, and Schoolcraft.

Court for the Northern Division shall be held at Marquette and Sault Sainte Marie.

History of 28 U.S.C. §102: June 25, 1948, ch. 646, 62 Stat. 882; Feb. 10, 1954, ch. 6, §2(b)(8), 68 Stat. 11; May 19, 1961, P.L. 87-36, §3(d), 75 Stat. 83; Oct. 6, 1964, P.L. 88-627, 78 Stat. 1003; June 2, 1970, P.L. 91-272, §11, 84 Stat. 298.

§103. MINNESOTA

Minnesota constitutes one judicial district comprising six divisions.

(1) The First Division comprises the counties of Dodge, Fillmore, Houston, Mower, Olmsted, Steele, Wabasha, and Winona.

Court for the First Division shall be held at Winona.

(2) The Second Division comprises the counties of Blue Earth, Brown, Cottonwood, Faribault, Freeborn, Jackson, Lac qui Parle, Le Sueur, Lincoln, Lyon, Martin, Murray, Nicollet, Nobles, Pipestone, Redwood, Rock, Sibley, Waseca, Watonwan, and Yellow Medicine.

Court for the Second Division shall be held at Mankato.

(3) The Third Division comprises the counties of Chisago, Dakota, Goodhue, Ramsey, Rice, Scott, and Washington.

Court for the Third Division shall be held at Saint Paul.

(4) The Fourth Division comprises the counties of Anoka, Carver, Chippewa, Hennepin, Isanti, Kandiyohi, McLeod, Meeker, Renville, Sherburne, Swift, and Wright.

Court for the Fourth Division shall be held at Minneapolis.

(5) The Fifth Division comprises the counties of Aitkin, Benton, Carlton, Cass, Cook, Crow Wing, Itasca, Kanabec, Koochiching, Lake, Mille Lacs, Morrison, Pine, and Saint Louis.

Court for the Fifth Division shall be held at Duluth.

(6) The Sixth Division comprises the counties of Becker, Beltrami, Big Stone, Clay, Clearwater, Douglas, Grant, Hubbard, Kittson, Lake of the Woods, Mahnomen, Marshall, Norman, Otter Tail, Pennington, Polk, Pope, Red Lake, Roseau, Stearns, Stevens, Todd, Traverse, Wadena, and Wilkin.

Court for the Sixth Division shall be held at Fergus Falls and Bemidji.

History of 28 U.S.C. §103: June 25, 1948, ch. 646, 62 Stat. 882; Oct. 13, 2008, P.L. 110-406, §18, 122 Stat. 4295.

A §104. MISSISSIPPI

Mississippi is divided into two judicial districts to be known as the northern and southern districts of Mississippi.

NORTHERN DISTRICT

(a) The northern district comprises three divisions.

(1) The Aberdeen Division comprises the counties of Alcorn, Chickasaw, Choctaw, Clay, Itawamba, Lee, Lowndes, Monroe, Oktibbeha, Prentiss, Tishomingo, Webster, and Winston.

Court for the Aberdeen Division shall be held at Aberdeen, Ackerman, and Corinth.

(2) The Oxford Division comprises the counties of Benton, Calhoun, DeSoto, Lafayette, Marshall, Panola, Pontotoc, Quitman, Tallahatchie, Tate, Tippah, Tunica, Union, and Yalobusha.

Court for the Oxford Division shall be held at Oxford.

(3) The Greenville Division comprises the counties of Attala, Bolivar, Carroll, Coahoma, Grenada, Humphreys, Leflore, Montgomery, Sunflower, and Washington.

Court for the Greenville Division shall be held at Clarksdale, Cleveland, and Greenville.

SOUTHERN DISTRICT

(b) The southern district comprises five divisions.

(1) The Jackson division comprises the counties of Amite, Copiah, Franklin, Hinds, Holmes, Leake, Lincoln, Madison, Pike, Rankin, Scott, Simpson, and Smith.

Court for the Jackson division shall be held at Jackson.

(2) The eastern division comprises the counties of Clarke, Jasper, Kemper, Lauderdale, Neshoba, Newton, Noxubee, and Wayne.

Court for the eastern division shall be held at Meridian.

(3) The western division comprises the counties of Adams, Claiborne, Issaquena, Jefferson, Sharkey, Warren, Wilkinson, and Yazoo.

Court for the western division shall be held at Natchez and Vicksburg.

(4) The southern division comprises the counties of George, Hancock, Harrison, Jackson, Pearl River, and Stone.

Court for the southern division shall be held at Biloxi and Gulfport.

(5) The Hattiesburg division comprises the counties of Covington, Forrest, Greene, Jefferson Davis, Jones, Lamar, Lawrence, Marion, Perry, and Walthall.

Court for the Hattiesburg division shall be held at Hattiesburg.

History of 28 U.S.C. §104: June 25, 1948, ch. 646, 62 Stat. 883; Aug. 7, 1950, ch. 601, 64 Stat. 415; Sept. 27, 1967, P.L. 90-92, 81 Stat. 229; Dec. 14, 1970, P.L. 91-546, §§2, 3, 84 Stat. 1412; Oct. 2, 1978, P.L. 95-408, §2(b), 92 Stat. 883; Dec. 6, 1999, P.L. 106-130, §1, 113 Stat. 1677; Dec. 10, 2004, P.L. 108-455, §2, 118 Stat. 3628; Oct. 5, 2012, P.L. 112-188, §3, 126 Stat. 1433.

A §105. MISSOURI

Missouri is divided into two judicial districts to be known as the Eastern and Western Districts of Missouri.

EASTERN DISTRICT

(a) The Eastern District comprises three divisions.

(1) The Eastern Division comprises the counties of Crawford, Dent, Franklin, Gasconade, Jefferson, Lincoln, Maries, Phelps, Saint Charles, Saint Francois, Saint Louis, Warren, and Washington, and the city of Saint Louis.

Court for the Eastern Division shall be held at Saint Louis.

(2) The Northern Division comprises the counties of Adair, Audrain, Chariton, Clark, Knox, Lewis, Linn, Macon, Marion, Monroe, Montgomery, Pike, Ralls, Randolph, Schuyler, Scotland, and Shelby.

Court for the Northern Division shall be held at Hannibal.

(3) The Southeastern Division comprises the counties of Bollinger, Butler, Cape Girardeau, Carter, Dunklin, Iron, Madison, Mississippi, New Madrid, Pemiscot, Perry, Reynolds, Ripley, Saint Genevieve, Scott, Shannon, Stoddard, and Wayne.

Court for the Southeastern Division shall be held at Cape Girardeau.

WESTERN DISTRICT

(b) The Western District comprises five divisions.

(1) The Western Division comprises the counties of Bates, Carroll, Cass, Clay, Henry, Jackson, Johnson, Lafayette, Ray, Saint Clair, and Saline.

Court for the Western Division shall be held at Kansas City.

(2) The Southwestern Division comprises the counties of Barton, Barry, Jasper, Lawrence, McDonald, Newton, Stone, and Vernon.

Court for the Southwestern Division shall be held at Joplin.

(3) The Saint Joseph Division comprises the counties of Andrew, Atchison, Buchanan, Caldwell, Clinton, Daviess, De Kalb, Gentry, Grundy, Harrison, Holt, Livingston, Mercer, Nodaway, Platte, Putnam, Sullivan, and Worth.

Court for the Saint Joseph Division shall be held at Saint Joseph.

(4) The Central Division comprises the counties of Benton, Boone, Callaway, Camden, Cole, Cooper, Hickory, Howard, Miller, Moniteau, Morgan, Osage, and Pettis.

Court for the Central Division shall be held at Jefferson City.

(5) The Southern Division comprises the counties of Cedar, Christian, Dade, Dallas, Douglas, Greene, Howell, Laclede, Oregon, Ozark, Polk, Pulaski, Taney, Texas, Webster, and Wright.

Court for the Southern Division shall be held at Springfield.

History of 28 U.S.C. §105: June 25, 1948, ch. 646, 62 Stat. 884; May 31, 1962, P.L. 87-461, 76 Stat. 85; Oct. 15, 1980, P.L. 96-462, §4(a), 94 Stat. 2053; Oct. 5, 2012, P.L. 112-188, §2, 126 Stat. 1433.

§106. MONTANA

Montana, exclusive of Yellowstone National Park, constitutes one judicial district.

Court shall be held at Billings, Butte, Glasgow, Great Falls, Havre, Helena, Kalispell, Lewistown, Livingston, Miles City, and Missoula.

History of 28 U.S.C. §106: June 25, 1948, ch. 646, 62 Stat. 884.

§107. NEBRASKA

Nebraska constitutes one judicial district.

Court shall be held at Lincoln, North Platte, and Omaha.

History of 28 U.S.C. §107: June 25, 1948, ch. 646, 62 Stat. 884; Aug. 9, 1955, ch. 627, §1, 69 Stat. 546.

§108. NEVADA

Nevada constitutes one judicial district.

Court shall be held at Carson City, Elko, Las Vegas, Reno, Ely, and Lovelock.

History of 28 U.S.C. §108: June 25, 1948, ch. 646, 62 Stat. 885; Dec. 1, 1990, P.L. 101-650, §324(a)(1), 104 Stat. 5120.

§109. NEW HAMPSHIRE

New Hampshire constitutes one judicial district.

Court shall be held at Concord and Littleton.

History of 28 U.S.C. §109: June 25, 1948, ch. 646, 62 Stat. 885.

§110. NEW JERSEY

New Jersey constitutes one judicial district.

Court shall be held at Camden, Newark and Trenton.

History of 28 U.S.C. §110: June 25, 1948, ch. 646, 62 Stat. 885.

§111. NEW MEXICO

New Mexico constitutes one judicial district.

Court shall be held at Albuquerque, Las Cruces, Las Vegas, Roswell, Santa Fe, and Silver City.

History of 28 U.S.C. §111: June 25, 1948, ch. 646, 62 Stat. 885.

§112. NEW YORK

New York is divided into four judicial districts to be known as the Northern, Southern, Eastern, and Western Districts of New York.

NORTHERN DISTRICT

(a) The Northern District comprises the counties of Albany, Broome, Cayuga, Chenango, Clinton, Columbia, Cortland, Delaware, Essex, Franklin, Fulton, Greene, Hamilton, Herkimer, Jefferson, Lewis, Madison, Montgomery, Oneida, Onondaga, Oswego, Otsego, Rensselaer, Saint Lawrence, Saratoga, Schenectady, Schoharie, Tioga, Tompkins, Ulster, Warren, and Washington.

Court for the Northern District shall be held at Albany, Auburn, Binghamton, Malone, Plattsburgh, Syracuse, Utica, and Watertown.[1]

SOUTHERN DISTRICT

(b) The Southern District comprises the counties of Bronx, Dutchess, New York, Orange, Putnam, Rockland, Sullivan, and Westchester and concurrently with the Eastern District, the waters within the Eastern District.

Court for the Southern District shall be held at New York, White Plains, and in the Middletown-Wallkill area of Orange County or such nearby location as may be deemed appropriate.

EASTERN DISTRICT

(c) The Eastern District comprises the counties of Kings, Nassau, Queens, Richmond, and Suffolk and concurrently with the Southern District, the waters within the counties of Bronx and New York.

Court for the Eastern District shall be held at Brooklyn, Hauppauge, Hempstead (including the village of Uniondale), and Central Islip.

WESTERN DISTRICT

(d) The Western District comprises the counties of Allegany, Cattaraugus, Chautauqua, Chemung, Erie, Genesee, Livingston, Monroe, Niagara, Ontario, Orleans, Schuyler, Seneca, Steuben, Wayne, Wyoming, and Yates.

Court for the Western District shall be held at Buffalo, Canandaigua, Elmira, Jamestown, and Rochester.

1. **Editor's note:** P.L. 108-455, §4 and 108-482, §302 both add Plattsburgh as a location to hold court in the Northern District, but 108-455, §4 adds "and Plattsburgh" to the end of the sentence.

History of 28 U.S.C. §112: June 25, 1948, ch. 646, 62 Stat. 885; Dec. 18, 1967, P.L. 90-217, 81 Stat. 662; Dec. 14, 1970, P.L. 91-546, §1, 84 Stat. 1412; Apr. 28, 1978, P.L. 95-271, §1, 92 Stat. 221; Oct. 2, 1978, P.L. 95-408, §4(c), 92 Stat. 885; Nov. 2, 1978, P.L. 95-573, §3, 92 Stat. 2458; Nov. 8, 1984, P.L. 98-620, §405, 98 Stat. 3361; Dec. 1, 1990, P.L. 101-650, §324(a)(2), 104 Stat. 5120; Oct. 19, 1996, P.L. 104-317, §609, 110 Stat. 3860; Nov. 29, 1999, P.L. 106-113-Appx. A, §306, 113 Stat. 1501A-37; Dec. 10, 2004, P.L. 108-455, §4, 118 Stat. 3628; Dec. 23, 2004, P.L. 108-482, §302, 118 Stat. 3918.

§113. NORTH CAROLINA

North Carolina is divided into three judicial districts to be known as the Eastern, Middle, and Western Districts of North Carolina.

EASTERN DISTRICT

(a) The Eastern District comprises the counties of Beaufort, Bertie, Bladen, Brunswick, Camden, Carteret, Chowan, Columbus, Craven, Cumberland, Currituck, Dare, Duplin, Edgecombe, Franklin, Gates, Granville, Greene, Halifax, Harnett, Hertford, Hyde, Johnston, Jones, Lenoir, Martin, Nash, New Hanover, Northampton, Onslow, Pamlico, Pasquotank, Pender, Perquimans, Pitt, Robeson, Sampson, Tyrrell, Vance, Wake, Warren, Washington, Wayne, and Wilson and that portion of Durham County encompassing the Federal Correctional Institution, Butner, North Carolina.

Court for the Eastern District shall be held at Elizabeth City, Fayetteville, Greenville, New Bern, Raleigh, Wilmington, and Wilson.

MIDDLE DISTRICT

(b) The Middle District comprises the counties of Alamance, Cabarrus, Caswell, Chatham, Davidson, Davie, Durham (excluding that portion of Durham County encompassing the Federal Correctional Institution, Butner, North Carolina), Forsythe, Guilford, Hoke, Lee, Montgomery, Moore, Orange, Person, Randolph, Richmond, Rockingham, Rowan, Scotland, Stanly, Stokes, Surry, and Yadkin.

Court for the Middle District shall be held at Durham, Greensboro, and Winston-Salem.

WESTERN DISTRICT

(c) The Western District comprises the counties of Alexander, Alleghany, Anson, Ashe, Avery, Buncombe, Burke, Caldwell, Catawba, Cherokee, Clay, Cleveland, Gaston, Graham, Haywood, Henderson, Iredell, Jackson, Lincoln, McDowell, Macon, Madison, Mecklenburg, Mitchell, Polk, Rutherford, Swain, Transylvania, Union, Watauga, Wilkes, and Yancey.

Court for the Western District shall be held at Asheville, Bryson City, Charlotte, Shelby, and Statesville.

History of 28 U.S.C. §113: June 25, 1948, ch. 646, 62 Stat. 886; Nov. 2, 1965, P.L. 89-319, 79 Stat. 1186; Oct. 15, 1980, P.L. 96-462, §5(a)-(c), 94 Stat. 2053, 2054; Apr. 21, 1992, P.L. 102-272, 106 Stat. 112.

§114. NORTH DAKOTA

North Dakota constitutes one judicial district.

Court shall be held at Bismarck, Fargo, Grand Forks, and Minot.

History of 28 U.S.C. §114: June 25, 1948, ch. 646, 62 Stat. 886; Oct. 2, 1978, P.L. 95-408, §3(b), 92 Stat. 883; May 27, 2010, P.L. 111-174, §3, 124 Stat. 1216.

§115. OHIO

Ohio is divided into two judicial districts to be known as the Northern and Southern Districts of Ohio.

NORTHERN DISTRICT

(a) The Northern District comprises two divisions.

(1) The Eastern Division comprises the counties of Ashland, Ashtabula, Carroll, Columbiana, Crawford, Cuyahoga, Geauga, Holmes, Lake, Lorain, Mahoning, Medina, Portage, Richland, Stark, Summit, Trumbull, Tuscarawas, and Wayne.

Court for the Eastern Division shall be held at Cleveland, Youngstown, and Akron.

(2) The Western Division comprises the counties of Allen, Auglaize, Defiance, Erie, Fulton, Hancock, Hardin, Henry, Huron, Lucas, Marion, Mercer, Ottawa, Paulding, Putnam, Sandusky, Seneca, Van Wert, Williams, Woods, and Wyandot.

Court for the Western Division shall be held at Lima and Toledo.

SOUTHERN DISTRICT

(b) The Southern District comprises two divisions.

(1) The Western Division comprises the counties of Adams, Brown, Butler, Champaign, Clark, Clermont, Clinton, Darke, Greene, Hamilton, Highland, Lawrence, Miami, Montgomery, Preble, Scioto, Shelby, and Warren.

Court for the Western Division shall be held at Cincinnati and Dayton.

(2) The Eastern Division comprises the counties of Athens, Belmont, Coshocton, Delaware, Fairfield, Fayette, Franklin, Gallia, Guernsey, Harrison, Hocking, Jackson, Jefferson, Knox, Licking, Logan, Madison, Meigs, Monroe, Morgan, Morrow, Muskingum, Noble, Perry, Pickaway, Pike, Ross, Union, Vinton, and Washington.

Court for the Eastern Division shall be held at Columbus[1] St. Clairsville, and Steubenville.

1. **Editor's note:** So in original. Probably should be followed by a comma.

History of 28 U.S.C. §115: June 25, 1948, ch. 646, 62 Stat. 887; Feb. 10, 1954, ch. 6, §2(b)(9), 68 Stat. 11; Nov. 2, 2002, P.L. 107-273, §11021, 116 Stat. 1829.

§116. OKLAHOMA

Oklahoma is divided into three judicial districts to be known as the Northern, Eastern, and Western Districts of Oklahoma.

NORTHERN DISTRICT

(a) The Northern District comprises the counties of Craig, Creek, Delaware, Mayes, Nowata, Osage, Ottawa, Pawnee, Rogers, Tulsa, and Washington.

Court for the Northern District shall be held at Bartlesville, Miami, Pawhuska, Tulsa, and Vinita.

EASTERN DISTRICT

(b) The Eastern District comprises the counties of Adair, Atoka, Bryan, Carter, Cherokee, Choctaw, Coal, Haskell, Hughes, Johnston, Latimer, Le Flore, Love, McCurtain, McIntosh, Marshall, Murray, Muskogee, Okfuskee, Okmulgee, Pittsburg, Pontotoc, Pushmataha, Seminole, Sequoyah, and Wagoner.

Court for the Eastern District shall be held at Ada, Ardmore, Durant, Hugo, Muskogee, Okmulgee, Poteau, and S. McAlester.

WESTERN DISTRICT

(c) The Western District comprises the counties of Alfalfa, Beaver, Beckham, Blaine, Caddo, Canadian, Cimarron, Cleveland, Comanche, Cotton, Custer, Dewey, Ellis, Garfield, Garvin, Grady, Grant, Greer, Harmon, Harper, Jackson, Jefferson, Kay, Kingfisher, Kiowa, Lincoln, Logan, McClain, Major, Noble, Oklahoma, Payne, Pottawatomie, Roger Mills, Stephens, Texas, Tillman, Washita, Woods, and Woodward.

Court for the Western District shall be held at Chickasha, Enid, Guthrie, Lawton, Mangum, Oklahoma City, Pauls Valley, Ponca City, Shawnee, and Woodward.

History of 28 U.S.C. §116: June 25, 1948, ch. 646, 62 Stat. 887; Aug. 4, 1966, P.L. 89-526, §1, 80 Stat. 335.

§117. OREGON

Oregon constitutes one judicial district.

Court shall be held at Coquille, Eugene or Springfield, Klamath Falls, Medford, Pendleton, and Portland.

History of 28 U.S.C. §117: June 25, 1948, ch. 646, 62 Stat. 888; Aug. 3, 1950, ch. 514, 64 Stat. 393; June 2, 1970, P.L. 91-272, §7, 84 Stat. 297; Nov. 13, 2000, P.L. 106-518, §502, 114 Stat. 2422.

§118. PENNSYLVANIA

Pennsylvania is divided into three judicial districts to be known as the Eastern, Middle, and Western Districts of Pennsylvania.

EASTERN DISTRICT

(a) The Eastern District comprises the counties of Berks, Bucks, Chester, Delaware, Lancaster, Lehigh, Montgomery, Northampton, and Philadelphia.

Court for the Eastern District shall be held at Allentown, Easton, Lancaster, Reading, and Philadelphia.

MIDDLE DISTRICT

(b) The Middle District comprises the counties of Adams, Bradford, Cameron, Carbon, Centre, Clinton, Columbia, Cumberland, Dauphin, Franklin, Fulton, Huntingdon, Juniata, Lackawanna, Lebanon, Luzerne, Lycoming, Mifflin, Monroe, Montour, Northumberland, Perry, Pike, Potter, Schuylkill, Snyder, Sullivan, Susquehanna, Tioga, Union, Wayne, Wyoming, and York.

Court for the Middle District shall be held at Harrisburg, Lewisburg, Scranton, Wilkes-Barre, and Williamsport.

WESTERN DISTRICT

(c) The Western District comprises the counties of Allegheny, Armstrong, Beaver, Bedford, Blair, Butler, Cambria, Clarion, Clearfield, Crawford, Elk, Erie, Fayette, Forest, Greene, Indiana, Jefferson, Lawrence, McKean, Mercer, Somerset, Venango, Warren, Washington, and Westmoreland.

Court for the Western District shall be held at Erie, Johnstown, and Pittsburgh.

History of 28 U.S.C. §118: June 25, 1948, ch. 646, 62 Stat. 888; June 2, 1970, P.L. 91-272, §6, 84 Stat. 297; Nov. 2, 1978, P.L. 95-573, §4, 92 Stat. 2458; Oct. 6, 1992, P.L. 102-396, §9161, 106 Stat. 1947; Oct. 21, 1998, P.L. 105-277, §101(b) [§624(a)], 112 Stat. 2681-116.

§119. PUERTO RICO

Puerto Rico constitutes one judicial district.

Court shall be held at Mayaguez, Ponce, and San Juan.

History of 28 U.S.C. §119: June 25, 1948, ch. 646, 62 Stat. 889.

§120. RHODE ISLAND

Rhode Island constitutes one judicial district.

Court shall be held at Providence.

History of 28 U.S.C. §120: June 25, 1948, ch. 646, 62 Stat. 889.

§121. SOUTH CAROLINA

South Carolina constitutes one judicial district comprising eleven divisions.

(1) The Charleston Division comprises the counties of Berkeley, Charleston, Clarendon, Colleton, Dorchester, and Georgetown.

Court for the Charleston Division shall be held at Charleston.

(2) The Columbia Division comprises the counties of Kershaw, Lee, Lexington, Richland, and Sumter.

Court for the Columbia Division shall be held at Columbia.

(3) The Florence Division comprises the counties of Chesterfield, Darlington, Dillon, Florence, Horry, Marion, Marlboro, and Williamsburg.

Court for the Florence Division shall be held at Florence.

(4) The Aiken Division comprises the counties of Aiken, Allendale, and Barnwell.

Court for the Aiken Division shall be held at Aiken.

(5) The Orangeburg Division comprises the counties of Bamberg, Calhoun, and Orangeburg.

Court for the Orangeburg Division shall be held at Orangeburg.

(6) The Greenville Division comprises the counties of Greenville and Laurens.

Court for the Greenville Division shall be held at Greenville.

(7) The Rock Hill Division comprises the counties of Chester, Fairfield, Lancaster, and York.

Court for the Rock Hill Division shall be held at Rock Hill.

(8) The Greenwood Division comprises the counties of Abbeville, Edgefield, Greenwood, McCormick, Newberry, and Saluda.

Court for the Greenwood Division shall be held at Greenwood.

(9) The Anderson Division comprises the counties of Anderson, Oconee, and Pickens.

Court for the Anderson Division shall be held at Anderson.

(10) The Spartanburg Division comprises the counties of Cherokee, Spartanburg, and Union.

Court for the Spartanburg Division shall be held at Spartanburg.

(11) The Beaufort Division comprises the counties of Beaufort, Hampton, and Jasper.

Court for the Beaufort Division shall be held at Beaufort.

History of 28 U.S.C. §121: June 25, 1948, ch. 646, 62 Stat. 889; Oct. 7, 1965, P.L. 89-242, §1(a), 79 Stat. 951; Nov. 14, 1986, P.L. 99-657, §2, 100 Stat. 3670; Oct. 28, 1991, P.L. 102-140, §304, 105 Stat. 810.

§122. SOUTH DAKOTA

South Dakota constitutes one judicial district comprising four divisions.

(1) The Northern Division comprises the counties of Brown, Campbell, Clark, Codington, Corson, Day, Deuel, Edmonds, Grant, Hamlin, McPherson, Marshall, Roberts, Spink, and Walworth.

Court for the Northern Division shall be held at Aberdeen.

(2) The Southern Division comprises the counties of Aurora, Beadle, Bon Homme, Brookings, Brule, Charles Mix, Clay, Davison, Douglas, Hanson, Hutchinson, Kingsbury,

Lake, Lincoln, McCook, Miner, Minnehaha, Moody, Sanborn, Turner, Union, and Yankton.

Court for the Southern Division shall be held at Sioux Falls.

(3) The central division comprises the counties of Buffalo, Dewey, Faulk, Gregory, Haakon, Hand, Hughes, Hyde, Jerauld, Jones, Lyman, Mellette, Potter, Stanley, Sully, Todd, Tripp, and Ziebach.

Court for the Central Division shall be held at Pierre.

(4) The Western Division comprises the counties of Bennett, Butte, Custer, Fall River, Harding, Jackson, Lawrence, Meade, Pennington, Perkins, and Shannon.

Court for the Western Division shall be held at Deadwood and Rapid City.

History of 28 U.S.C. §122: June 25, 1948, ch. 646, 62 Stat. 889; Oct. 10, 1966, P.L. 89-638, 80 Stat. 883; Aug. 10, 1972, P.L. 92-376, 86 Stat. 529; Dec. 1, 1990, P.L. 101-650, §324(b), 104 Stat. 5120.

§123. TENNESSEE

Tennessee is divided into three judicial districts to be known as the Eastern, Middle, and Western Districts of Tennessee.

EASTERN DISTRICT

(a) The Eastern District comprises four divisions.

(1) The Northern Division comprises the counties of Anderson, Blount, Campbell, Claiborne, Grainger, Jefferson, Knox, Loudon, Monroe, Morgan, Roane, Scott, Sevier, and Union.

Court for the Northern Division shall be held at Knoxville.

(2) The Northeastern Division comprises the counties of Carter, Cocke, Greene, Hamblen, Hancock, Hawkins, Johnson, Sullivan, Unicoi, and Washington.

Court for the Northeastern Division shall be held at Greenville.

(3) The Southern Division comprises the counties of Bledsoe, Bradley, Hamilton, McMinn, Marion, Meigs, Polk, Rhea, and Sequatchie.

Court for the Southern Division shall be held at Chattanooga.

(4) The Winchester Division comprises the counties of Bedford, Coffee, Franklin, Grundy, Lincoln, Moore, Van Buren, and Warren.

Court for the Winchester Division shall be held at Winchester.

MIDDLE DISTRICT

(b) The Middle District comprises three divisions.

(1) The Nashville Division comprises the counties of Cannon, Cheatham, Davidson, Dickson, Houston, Humphreys, Montgomery, Robertson, Rutherford, Stewart, Sumner, Trousdale, Williamson, and Wilson.

Court for the Nashville Division shall be held at Nashville.

(2) The Northeastern Division comprises the counties of Clay, Cumberland, De Kalb, Fentress, Jackson, Macon, Overton, Pickett, Putnam, Smith, and White.

Court for the Northeastern Division shall be held at Cookeville.

(3) The Columbia Division comprises the counties of Giles, Hickman, Lawrence, Lewis, Marshall, Maury, and Wayne.

Court for the Columbia Division shall be held at Columbia.

WESTERN DISTRICT

(c) The Western District comprises two divisions.

(1) The Eastern Division comprises the counties of Benton, Carroll, Chester, Crockett, Decatur, Dyer, Gibson, Hardeman, Hardin, Haywood, Henderson, Henry, Lake, McNairy, Madison, Obion, Perry, and Weakley.

The Eastern Division also includes the waters of Tennessee River to low-water mark on the eastern shore wherever such river forms the boundary between the western and middle districts from the north line of Alabama north to the point in Henry County, Tennessee, where the south boundary of Kentucky strikes the east bank of the river.

Court for the Eastern Division shall be held at Jackson and Dyersburg.

(2) The Western Division comprises the counties of Fayette, Lauderdale, Shelby, and Tipton.

Court for the Western Division shall be held at Memphis.

The district judge for the Eastern District in office on November 27, 1940, shall hold court in the Northern and Northeastern Divisions. The other judge of that district shall hold the terms of court in the Southern and Winchester Divisions. Each may appoint and remove all officers and employees of the court whose official headquarters are located in the divisions within which he holds court and whose appointments are vested by law in a district judge or chief judge of a district.

History of 28 U.S.C. §123: June 25, 1948, ch. 646, 62 Stat. 890; May 19, 1961, P.L. 87-36, §3(e), 75 Stat. 83; July 11, 1961, P.L. 87-86, 75 Stat. 203; June 2, 1970, P.L. 91-272, §12, 84 Stat. 298; Oct. 13, 2008, P.L. 110-406, §2(a), 122 Stat. 4291.

§124. TEXAS

Texas is divided into four judicial districts to be known as the Northern, Southern, Eastern, and Western Districts of Texas.

NORTHERN DISTRICT

(a) The Northern District comprises seven divisions.

(1) The Dallas Division comprises the counties of Dallas, Ellis, Hunt, Johnson, Kaufman, Navarro, and Rockwall.

Court for the Dallas Division shall be held at Dallas.

(2) The Fort Worth Division comprises the counties of Comanche, Erath, Hood, Jack, Palo Pinto, Parker, Tarrant, and Wise.

Court for the Fort Worth Division shall be held at Fort Worth.

(3) The Abilene Division comprises the counties of Callahan, Eastland, Fisher, Haskell, Howard, Jones, Mitchell, Nolan, Shackleford, Stephens, Stonewall, Taylor, and Throckmorton.

Court for the Abilene Division shall be held at Abilene.

(4) The San Angelo Division comprises the counties of Brown, Coke, Coleman, Concho, Crockett, Glasscock, Irion, Menard, Mills, Reagan, Runnels, Schleicher, Sterling, Sutton, and Tom Green.

Court for the San Angelo Division shall be held at San Angelo.

(5) The Amarillo Division comprises the counties of Armstrong, Brisco, Carson, Castro, Childress, Collingsworth, Dallam, Deaf Smith, Donley, Gray, Hall, Hansford, Hartley, Hemphill, Hutchinson, Lipscomb, Moore, Ochiltree, Oldham, Parmer, Potter, Randall, Roberts, Sherman, Swisher, and Wheeler.

Court for the Amarillo Division shall be held at Amarillo.

(6) The Wichita Falls Division comprises the counties of Archer, Baylor, Clay, Cottle, Foard, Hardeman, King, Knox, Montague, Wichita, Wilbarger, and Young.

Court for the Wichita Falls Division shall be held at Wichita Falls.

(7) The Lubbock Division comprises the counties of Bailey, Borden, Cochran, Crosby, Dawson, Dickens, Floyd, Gaines, Garza, Hale, Hockley, Kent, Lamb, Lubbock, Lynn, Motley, Scurry, Terry, and Yoakum.

Court for the Lubbock Division shall be held at Lubbock.

SOUTHERN DISTRICT

(b) The Southern District comprises seven divisions.

(1) The Galveston Division comprises the counties of Brazoria, Chambers, Galveston, and Matagorda.

Court for the Galveston Division shall be held at Galveston.

(2) The Houston Division comprises the counties of Austin, Brazos, Colorado, Fayette, Fort Bend, Grimes, Harris, Madison, Montgomery, San Jacinto, Walker, Waller, and Wharton.

Court for the Houston Division shall be held at Houston.

(3) The Laredo Division comprises the counties of Jim Hogg, La Salle, McMullen, Webb, and Zapata.

Court for the Laredo Division shall be held at Laredo.

(4) The Brownsville Division comprises the counties of Cameron and Willacy.

Court for the Brownsville Division shall be held at Brownsville.

(5) The Victoria Division comprises the counties of Calhoun, DeWitt, Goliad, Jackson, Lavaca, Refugio, and Victoria.

Court for the Victoria Division shall be held at Victoria.

(6) The Corpus Christi Division comprises the counties of Aransas, Bee, Brooks, Duval, Jim Wells, Kenedy, Kleberg, Live Oak, Nueces, and San Patricio.

Court for the Corpus Christi Division shall be held at Corpus Christi.

(7) The McAllen Division comprises the counties of Hidalgo and Starr.

Court for the McAllen Division shall be held at McAllen.

EASTERN DISTRICT

(c) The Eastern District comprises seven divisions.

(1) The Tyler Division comprises the counties of Anderson, Cherokee, Gregg, Henderson, Panola, Rains, Rusk, Smith, Van Zandt, and Wood.

Court for Tyler Division will be held at Tyler.

(2) The Beaumont Division comprises the counties of Hardin, Jasper, Jefferson, Liberty, Newton, and Orange.

Court for the Beaumont Division is to be held at Beaumont.

(3) The Sherman Division comprises the counties of Collin, Cook, Delta, Denton, Fannin, Grayson, Hopkins, and Lamar.

Court for the Sherman Division shall be held at Sherman and Plano.

(4) The Marshall Division comprises the counties of Camp, Cass, Harrison, Marion, Morris, and Upshur.

Court for the Marshall Division shall be held at Marshall.

(5) The Texarkana Division comprises the counties of Bowie, Franklin, Red River, and Titus.

Court for the Texarkana Division shall be held at Texarkana, and may be held anywhere within the Federal courthouse in Texarkana that is located astride the State line between Texas and Arkansas.

(6) The Lufkin Division comprises the counties of Angelina, Houston, Nacogdoches, Polk, Sabine, San Augustine, Shelby, Trinity, and Tyler.

Court for the Lufkin Division shall be held at Lufkin.

WESTERN DISTRICT

(d) The Western District comprises seven divisions.

(1) The Austin Division comprises the counties of Bastrop, Blanco, Burleson, Burnet, Caldwell, Gillespie, Hays, Kimble, Lampasas, Lee, Llano, Mason, McCulloch, San Saba, Travis, Washington, and Williamson.

Court for the Austin Division shall be held at Austin.

(2) The Waco Division comprises the counties of Bell, Bosque, Coryell, Falls, Freestone, Hamilton, Hill, Leon, Limestone, McLennan, Milam, Robertson, and Somervell.

Court for the Waco Division shall be held at Waco.

(3) The El Paso Division comprises the county of El Paso.

Court for the El Paso Division shall be held at El Paso.

(4) The San Antonio Division comprises the counties of Atascosa, Bandera, Bexar, Comal, Dimmit, Frio, Gonzales, Guadalupe, Karnes, Kendall, Kerr, Medina, Real, and Wilson.

Court for the San Antonio Division shall be held at San Antonio.

(5) The Del Rio Division comprises the counties of Edwards, Kinney, Maverick, Terrell, Uvalde, Val Verde, and Zavalla.

Court for the Del Rio Division shall be held at Del Rio.

(6) The Pecos Division comprises the counties of Brewster, Culberson, Jeff Davis, Hudspeth, Loving, Pecos, Presidio, Reeves, Ward, and Winkler.

Court for the Pecos Division shall be held at Pecos.

(7) The Midland-Odessa Division comprises the counties of Andrews, Crane, Ector, Martin, Midland, and Upton.

Court for the Midland-Odessa Division shall be held at Midland. Court may be held, in the discretion of the court, in Odessa, when courtroom facilities are made available at no expense to the Government.

History of 28 U.S.C. §124: June 25, 1948, ch. 646, 62 Stat. 891; Feb. 10, 1954, ch. 6, §2(b)(9)(a), (b), 68 Stat. 11; Sept. 4, 1957, P.L. 85-298, §§1, 2, 71 Stat. 618; Oct. 4, 1961, P.L. 87-352, 75 Stat. 772; Mar. 11, 1964, P.L. 88-282, 78 Stat. 163; Aug. 30, 1964, P.L. 88-512, 78 Stat. 695; Dec. 18, 1967, P.L. 90-216, 81 Stat. 661; Oct. 15, 1980, P.L. 96-462, §6, 94 Stat. 2054; Nov. 8, 1984, P.L. 98-620, §407(a), 98 Stat. 3362; Dec. 3, 2003, P.L. 108-157, §1, 117 Stat. 1947; Dec. 10, 2004, P.L. 108-455, §3, 118 Stat. 3628.

§125. UTAH

Utah constitutes one judicial district comprising two divisions.

(1) The Northern Division comprises the counties of Box Elder, Cache, Davis, Morgan, Rich, and Weber.

Court for the Northern Division shall be held at Salt Lake City and Ogden.

(2) The Central Division comprises the counties of Beaver, Carbon, Daggett, Duchesne, Emery, Garfield, Grand, Iron, Juab, Kane, Millard, Piute, Salt Lake, San Juan, Sanpete, Sevier, Summit, Tooele, Uintah, Utah, Wasatch, Washington, and Wayne.

Court for the Central Division shall be held at Salt Lake City, Provo, and St. George.

History of 28 U.S.C. §125: June 25, 1948, ch. 646, 62 Stat. 893; Oct. 19, 1996, P.L. 104-317, §606, 110 Stat. 3859.

§126. VERMONT

Vermont constitutes one judicial district.

Court shall be held at Bennington, Brattleboro, Burlington, Montpelier, Rutland, Saint Johnsbury, and Windsor.

History of 28 U.S.C. §126: June 25, 1948, ch. 646, 62 Stat. 893; May 28, 1964, P.L. 88-312, 78 Stat. 201; Nov. 8, 1984, P.L. 98-620, §410, 98 Stat. 3362.

§127. VIRGINIA

Virginia is divided into two judicial districts, to be known as the Eastern and Western districts of Virginia.

EASTERN DISTRICT

(a) The Eastern District comprises the counties of Accomac, Amelia, Arlington, Brunswick, Caroline, Charles City, Chesterfield, Dinwiddie, Elizabeth City, Essex, Fairfax, Fauquier, Gloucester, Goochland, Greensville, Hanover, Henrico, Isle of Wight, James City, King and Queen, King George, King William, Lancaster, Loudoun, Lunenburg, Mathews, Mecklenburg, Middlesex, Nansemond, New Kent, Norfolk, Northampton, Northumberland, Nottoway, Powhatan, Prince Edward, Prince George, Prince William, Princess Anne, Richmond, Southampton, Spotsylvania, Stafford, Surry, Sussex, Warwick, Westmoreland, and York.

Court for the Eastern District shall be held at Alexandria, Newport News, Norfolk, and Richmond.

WESTERN DISTRICT

(b) The Western District comprises the counties of Albemarle, Alleghany, Amherst, Appomattox, Augusta, Bath, Bedford, Bland, Botetourt, Buchanan, Buckingham, Campbell, Carroll, Charlotte, Clarke, Craig, Culpeper, Cumberland, Dickenson, Floyd, Fluvanna, Franklin, Frederick, Giles, Grayson, Greene, Halifax, Henry, Highland, Lee, Louisa, Madison, Montgomery, Nelson, Orange, Page, Patrick, Pittsylvania, Pulaski, Rappahannock, Roanoke, Rockbridge, Rockingham, Russell, Scott, Shenandoah, Smyth, Tazewell, Warren, Washington, Wise, and Wythe.

Court for the Western District shall be held at Abingdon, Big Stone Gap, Charlottesville, Danville, Harrisonburg, Lynchburg, and Roanoke.

(c) Cities and incorporated towns are included in that district in which are included the counties within the exterior boundaries of which such cities and incorporated towns are geographically located or out of the territory of which they have been incorporated.

History of 28 U.S.C. §127: June 25, 1948, ch. 646, 62 Stat. 893; July 5, 1968, P.L. 90-383, 82 Stat. 292; Dec. 10, 1991, P.L. 102-200, §1, 105 Stat. 1630.

§128. WASHINGTON

Washington is divided into two judicial districts to be known as the Eastern and Western Districts of Washington.

EASTERN DISTRICT

(a) The Eastern District comprises the counties of Adams, Asotin, Benton, Chelan, Columbia, Douglas, Ferry, Franklin, Garfield, Grant, Kittitas, Klickitat, Lincoln, Okanogan, Pend Oreille, Spokane, Stevens, Walla Walla, Whitman, and Yakima.

Court for the Eastern District shall be held at Spokane, Yakima, Walla Walla, and Richland.

WESTERN DISTRICT

(b) The Western District comprises the counties of Clallam, Clark, Cowlitz, Grays Harbor, Island, Jefferson, King, Kitsap, Lewis, Mason, Pacific, Pierce, San Juan, Skagit, Skamania, Snohomish, Thurston, Wahkiakum, and Whatcom.

Court for the Western District shall be held at Bellingham, Seattle, Tacoma, and Vancouver.

History of 28 U.S.C. §128: June 25, 1948, ch. 646, 62 Stat. 894; Sept. 25, 1962, P.L. 87-699, 76 Stat. 598; June 2, 1970, P.L. 91-272, §4, 84 Stat. 297; Dec. 26, 2007, P.L. 110-161, §308, 121 Stat. 1990.

§129. WEST VIRGINIA

West Virginia is divided into two judicial districts to be known as the Northern and Southern Districts of West Virginia.

NORTHERN DISTRICT

(a) The Northern District comprises the counties of Barbour, Berkeley, Braxton, Brooke, Calhoun, Doddridge, Gilmer, Grant, Hampshire, Hancock, Hardy, Harrison, Jefferson, Lewis, Marion, Marshall, Mineral, Monongalia, Morgan, Ohio, Pendleton, Pleasants, Pocahontas, Preston, Randolph, Ritchie, Taylor, Tucker, Tyler, Upshur, Webster, and Wetzel.

Court for the Northern District shall be held at Clarksburg, Elkins, Fairmont, Martinsburg, and Wheeling.

SOUTHERN DISTRICT

(b) The Southern District comprises the counties of Boone, Cabell, Clay, Fayette, Greenbrier, Jackson, Kanawha, Lincoln, Logan, McDowell, Mason, Mercer, Mingo, Monroe, Nicholas, Putnam, Raleigh, Roane, Summers, Wayne, Wirt, Wood, and Wyoming.

Court for the Southern District shall be held at Beckley, Bluefield, Charleston, Huntington, Lewisburg, and Parkersburg.

History of 28 U.S.C. §129: June 25, 1948, ch. 646, 62 Stat. 894; Jan. 14, 1983, P.L. 97-471, §1, 96 Stat. 2601.

§130. WISCONSIN

Wisconsin is divided into two judicial districts to be known as the Eastern and Western districts of Wisconsin.

EASTERN DISTRICT

(a) The Eastern District comprises the counties of Brown, Calumet, Dodge, Door, Florence, Fond du Lac, Forest, Green Lake, Kenosha, Kewaunee, Langlade, Manitowoc, Marinette, Marquette, Menominee, Milwaukee, Oconto, Outagamie, Ozaukee, Racine, Shawano, Sheboygan, Walworth, Washington, Waukesha, Waupaca, Waushara, and Winnebago.

Court for the Eastern District shall be held at Green Bay, Milwaukee, and Oshkosh.

WESTERN DISTRICT

(b) The Western District comprises the counties of Adams, Ashland, Barron, Bayfield, Buffalo, Burnett, Chippewa, Clark, Columbia, Crawford, Dane, Douglas, Dunn, Eau Claire, Grant, Green, Iowa, Iron, Jackson, Jefferson, Juneau, La Crosse, Lafayette, Lincoln, Marathon, Monroe, Oneida, Pepin, Pierce, Polk, Portage, Price, Richland, Rock, Rusk, Saint Croix, Sauk, Sawyer, Taylor, Trempealeau, Vernon, Vilas, Washburn, and Wood.

Court for the Western District shall be held at Eau Claire, La Crosse, Madison, Superior, and Wausau.

History of 28 U.S.C. §130: June 25, 1948, ch. 646, 62 Stat. 894; Aug. 6, 1962, P.L. 87-573, 76 Stat. 307.

§131. WYOMING

Wyoming and those portions of Yellowstone National Park situated in Montana and Idaho constitute one judicial district.

Court shall be held at Casper, Cheyenne, Evanston, Lander, Jackson, and Sheridan.

History of 28 U.S.C. §131: June 25, 1948, ch. 646, 62 Stat. 895; July 10, 1984, P.L. 98-353, §203(a), 98 Stat. 350.

§132. CREATION & COMPOSITION OF DISTRICT COURTS

(a) There shall be in each judicial district a district court which shall be a court of record known as the United States District Court for the district.

(b) Each district court shall consist of the district judge or judges for the district in regular active service. Justices or judges designated or assigned shall be competent to sit as judges of the court.

(c) Except as otherwise provided by law, or rule or order of court, the judicial power of a district court with respect to any action, suit or proceeding may be exercised by a single judge, who may preside alone and hold a regular or special session of court at the same time other sessions are held by other judges.

History of 28 U.S.C. §132: June 25, 1948, ch. 646, 62 Stat. 895; Nov. 13, 1963, P.L. 88-176, §2, 77 Stat. 331.

§133. APPOINTMENT & NUMBER OF DISTRICT JUDGES

(a) The President shall appoint, by and with the advice and consent of the Senate, district judges for the several judicial districts, as follows:

Districts	*Judges*
Alabama:	
Northern	7
Middle	3
Southern	3
Alaska	3
Arizona	12
Arkansas:	
Eastern	5
Western	3
California:	
Northern	14
Eastern	6
Central	27
Southern	13
Colorado	7
Connecticut	8
Delaware	4
District of Columbia	15

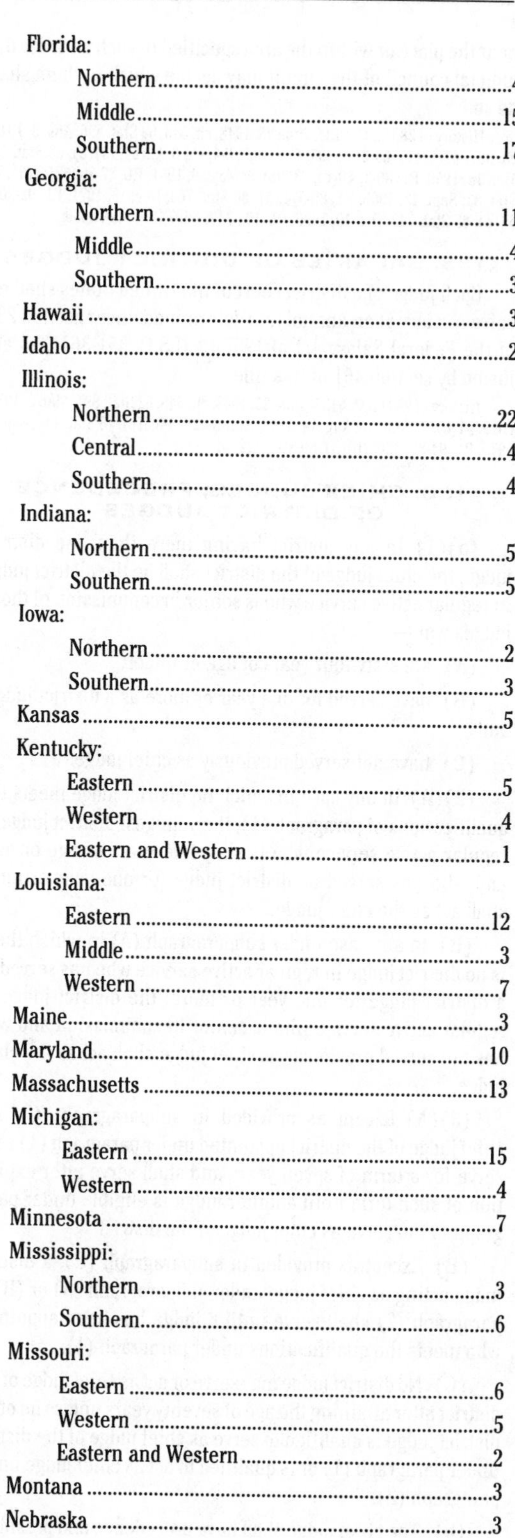

Florida:
- Northern 4
- Middle 15
- Southern 17

Georgia:
- Northern 11
- Middle 4
- Southern 3

Hawaii 3

Idaho 2

Illinois:
- Northern 22
- Central 4
- Southern 4

Indiana:
- Northern 5
- Southern 5

Iowa:
- Northern 2
- Southern 3

Kansas 5

Kentucky:
- Eastern 5
- Western 4
- Eastern and Western 1

Louisiana:
- Eastern 12
- Middle 3
- Western 7

Maine 3

Maryland 10

Massachusetts 13

Michigan:
- Eastern 15
- Western 4

Minnesota 7

Mississippi:
- Northern 3
- Southern 6

Missouri:
- Eastern 6
- Western 5
- Eastern and Western 2

Montana 3

Nebraska 3

Nevada 7

New Hampshire 3

New Jersey 17

New Mexico 6

New York:
- Northern 5
- Southern 28
- Eastern 15
- Western 4

North Carolina:
- Eastern 4
- Middle 4
- Western 4

North Dakota 2

Ohio:
- Northern 11
- Southern 8

Oklahoma:
- Northern 3
- Eastern 1
- Western 6
- Northern, Eastern, and Western 1

Oregon 6

Pennsylvania:
- Eastern 22
- Middle 6
- Western 10

Puerto Rico 7

Rhode Island 3

South Carolina 10

South Dakota 3

Tennessee:
- Eastern 5
- Middle 4
- Western 5

Texas:
- Northern 12
- Southern 19
- Eastern 7
- Western 13

Utah 5

Vermont 2

Virginia:
- Eastern 11
- Western 4

Washington:
- Eastern 4
- Western 7

West Virginia:

Northern ... 3

Southern ... 5

Wisconsin:

Eastern ... 5

Western ... 2

Wyoming ... 3

(b)(1) In any case in which a judge of the United States (other than a senior judge) assumes the duties of a full-time office of Federal judicial administration, the President shall appoint, by and with the advice and consent of the Senate, an additional judge for the court on which such judge serves. If the judge who assumes the duties of such full-time office leaves that office and resumes the duties as an active judge of the court, then the President shall not appoint a judge to fill the first vacancy which occurs thereafter in that court.

(2) For purposes of paragraph (1), the term "office of Federal judicial administration" means a position as Director of the Federal Judicial Center, Director of the Administrative Office of the United States Courts, or Counselor to the Chief Justice.

History of 28 U.S.C. §133: June 25, 1948, ch. 646, 62 Stat. 895; Aug. 3, 1949, ch. 387, §2(a), 63 Stat. 493; Aug. 14, 1950, ch. 708, 64 Stat. 443; Aug. 29, 1950, ch. 819, §1, 64 Stat. 562; Sept. 5, 1950, ch. 848, §1, 64 Stat. 578; Feb. 10, 1954, ch. 6, §2(a)(3), 68 Stat. 9; Sept. 7, 1957, P.L. 85-310, 71 Stat. 631; July 7, 1958, P.L. 85-508, §12(c), 72 Stat. 348; Mar. 18, 1959, P.L. 86-3, §9(b), 73 Stat. 8; May 19, 1961, P.L. 87-36, §2(d), 75 Stat. 81; July 30, 1962, P.L. 87-562, §3, 76 Stat. 248; Oct. 7, 1965, P.L. 89-242, §1(c), 79 Stat. 951; Mar. 18, 1966, P.L. 89-372, §4, 80 Stat. 77; June 2, 1970, P.L. 91-272, §1(d), 84 Stat. 295; Dec. 18, 1971, P.L. 92-208, §3(d), 85 Stat. 742; Oct. 2, 1978, P.L. 95-408, §4(b)(2), 92 Stat. 883; Oct. 20, 1978, P.L. 95-486, §1(c), 92 Stat. 1630; Jan. 14, 1983, P.L. 97-471, §3, 96 Stat. 2601; July 10, 1984, P.L. 98-353, §202(e), 98 Stat. 348; Dec. 1, 1990, P.L. 101-650, §§203(d), 303, 104 Stat. 5101, 5105; Oct. 6, 1997, P.L. 105-53, §4, 111 Stat. 1174; Nov. 29, 1999, P.L. 106-113-Appx. A, §309(b), 113 Stat. 1501A-37; Dec. 21, 2000, P.L. 106-553, §305(b), 114 Stat. 2762A-85; Nov. 2, 2002, P.L. 107-273, §312(a)(2), (b)(2), 116 Stat. 1786, 1787; Oct. 13, 2008, P.L. 110-402, §1(b)(1), 122 Stat. 4254.

§134. TENURE & RESIDENCE OF DISTRICT JUDGES

(a) The district judges shall hold office during good behavior.

(b) Each district judge, except in the District of Columbia, the Southern District of New York, and the Eastern District of New York, shall reside in the district or one of the districts for which he is appointed. Each district judge of the Southern District of New York and the Eastern District of New York may reside within 20 miles of the district to which he or she is appointed.

(c) If the public interest and the nature of the business of a district court require that a district judge should maintain his abode at or near a particular place for holding court in the district or within a particular part of the district the judicial council of the circuit may so declare and may make an appropriate order. If the district judges of such a district are unable to agree as to which of them shall maintain his abode at or near the place or within the area specified in such an order the judicial council of the circuit may decide which of them shall do so.

History of 28 U.S.C. §134: June 25, 1948, ch. 646, 62 Stat. 896; Aug. 3, 1949, ch. 387, §2(b)(1), 63 Stat. 495; Feb. 10, 1954, ch. 6, §2(b)(13)(a), 68 Stat. 12; Mar. 18, 1959, P.L. 86-3, §9(c), 73 Stat. 8; May 19, 1961, P.L. 87-36, §2(e)(3), 75 Stat. 83; Sept. 12, 1966, P.L. 89-571, §1, 80 Stat. 764; Dec. 18, 1971, P.L. 92-208, §3(e), 85 Stat. 742; Oct. 19, 1996, P.L. 104-317, §607, 110 Stat. 3860.

§135. SALARIES OF DISTRICT JUDGES

Each judge of a district court of the United States shall receive a salary at an annual rate determined under section 225 of the Federal Salary Act of 1967 (2 U.S.C. 351-361), as adjusted by section 461 of this title.

History of 28 U.S.C. §135: June 25, 1948, ch. 646, 62 Stat. 897; Mar. 2, 1955, ch. 9, §1(c), 69 Stat. 10; Aug. 14, 1964, P.L. 88-426, §403(c), 78 Stat. 434; Aug. 9, 1975, P.L. 94-82, §205(b)(3), 89 Stat. 422.

§136. CHIEF JUDGES; PRECEDENCE OF DISTRICT JUDGES

(a)(1) In any district having more than one district judge, the chief judge of the district shall be the district judge in regular active service who is senior in commission of those judges who—

(A) are sixty-four years of age or under;

(B) have served for one year or more as a district judge; and

(C) have not served previously as chief judge.

(2)(A) In any case in which no district judge meets the qualifications of paragraph (1), the youngest district judge in regular active service who is sixty-five years of age or over and who has served as district judge for one year or more shall act as the chief judge.

(B) In any case under subparagraph (A) in which there is no district judge in regular active service who has served as a district judge for one year or more, the district judge in regular active service who is senior in commission and who has not served previously as chief judge shall act as the chief judge.

(3)(A) Except as provided in subparagraph (C), the chief judge of the district appointed under paragraph (1) shall serve for a term of seven years and shall serve after expiration of such term until another judge is eligible under paragraph (1) to serve as chief judge of the district.

(B) Except as provided in subparagraph (C), a district judge acting as chief judge under subparagraph (A) or (B) of paragraph (2) shall serve until a judge has been appointed who meets the qualifications under paragraph (1).

(C) No district judge may serve or act as chief judge of the district after attaining the age of seventy years unless no other district judge is qualified to serve as chief judge of the district under paragraph (1) or is qualified to act as chief judge under paragraph (2).

(b) The chief judge shall have precedence and preside at any session which he attends.

Other district judges shall have precedence and preside according to the seniority of their commissions. Judges whose commissions bear the same date shall have precedence according to seniority in age.

(c) A judge whose commission extends over more than one district shall be junior to all district judges except in the district in which he resided at the time he entered upon the duties of his office.

(d) If the chief judge desires to be relieved of his duties as chief judge while retaining his active status as district judge, he may so certify to the Chief Justice of the United States, and thereafter, the chief judge of the district shall be such other district judge who is qualified to serve or act as chief judge under subsection (a).

(e) If a chief judge is temporarily unable to perform his duties as such, they shall be performed by the district judge in active service, present in the district and able and qualified to act, who is next in precedence.

History of 28 U.S.C. §136: June 25, 1948, ch. 646, 62 Stat. 897; Oct. 31, 1951, ch. 655, §37, 65 Stat. 723; Aug. 6, 1958, P.L. 85-593, §2, 72 Stat. 497; Apr. 2, 1982, P.L. 97-164, §202, 96 Stat. 52.

§137. DIVISION OF BUSINESS AMONG DISTRICT JUDGES

The business of a court having more than one judge shall be divided among the judges as provided by the rules and orders of the court.

The chief judge of the district court shall be responsible for the observance of such rules and orders, and shall divide the business and assign the cases so far as such rules and orders do not otherwise prescribe.

If the district judges in any district are unable to agree upon the adoption of rules or orders for that purpose the judicial council of the circuit shall make the necessary orders.

History of 28 U.S.C. §137: June 25, 1948, ch. 646, 62 Stat. 897.

§138. TERMS ABOLISHED

The district court shall not hold formal terms.

History of 28 U.S.C. §138: June 25, 1948, ch. 646, 62 Stat. 897; Oct. 16, 1963, P.L. 88-139, §1, 77 Stat. 248.

§139. TIMES FOR HOLDING REGULAR SESSIONS

The times for commencing regular sessions of the district court for transacting judicial business at the places fixed by this chapter shall be determined by the rules or orders of the court. Such rules or orders may provide that at one or more of such places the court shall be in continuous session for such purposes on all business days throughout the year. At other places a session of the court shall continue for such purposes until terminated by order of final adjournment or by commencement of the next regular session at the same place.

History of 28 U.S.C. §139: June 25, 1948, ch. 646, 62 Stat. 897; Oct. 16, 1963, P.L. 88-139, §1, 77 Stat. 248.

§140. ADJOURNMENT

(a) Any district court may, by order made anywhere within its district, adjourn or, with the consent of the judicial council of the circuit, pretermit any regular session of court for insufficient business or other good cause.

(b) If the judge of a district court is unable to attend and unable to make an order of adjournment, the clerk may adjourn the court to the next regular session or to any earlier day which he may determine.

History of 28 U.S.C. §140: June 25, 1948, ch. 646, 62 Stat. 897; Oct. 16, 1963, P.L. 88-139, §1, 77 Stat. 248.

§141. SPECIAL SESSIONS; PLACES; NOTICE

(a)(1) Special sessions of the district court may be held at such places in the district as the nature of the business may require, and upon such notice as the court orders.

(2) Any business may be transacted at a special session which might be transacted at a regular session.

(b)(1) Special sessions of the district court may be held at such places within the United States outside the district as the nature of the business may require and upon such notice as the court orders, upon a finding by either the chief judge of the district court (or, if the chief judge is unavailable, the most senior available active judge of the district court) or the judicial council of the circuit that, because of emergency conditions, no location within the district is reasonably available where such special sessions could be held.

(2) Pursuant to this subsection, any business which may be transacted at a regular session of a district court may be transacted at a special session conducted outside the district, except that a criminal trial may not be conducted at a special session outside the State in which the crime has been committed unless the defendant consents to such a criminal trial.

(3) Notwithstanding any other provision of law, in any case in which special sessions are conducted pursuant to this section, the district court may summon jurors—

(A) in civil proceedings, from any part of the district in which the court ordinarily conducts business or the district in which it is holding a special session; and

(B) in criminal trials, from any part of the district in which the crime has been committed and, if the defendant so consents, from any district in which the court is conducting business pursuant to this section.

(4) If a district court issues an order exercising its authority under paragraph (1), the court—

(A) through the Administrative Office of the United States Courts, shall—

(i) send notice of such order, including the reasons for the issuance of such order, to the Committee on the Judiciary of the Senate and the Committee on the Judiciary of the House of Representatives; and

(ii) not later than 180 days after the expiration of such court order submit a brief report to the Committee on the Ju-

diciary of the Senate and the Committee on the Judiciary of the House of Representatives describing the impact of such order, including—

(I) the reasons for the issuance of such order;

(II) the duration of such order;

(III) the impact of such order on litigants; and

(IV) the costs to the judiciary resulting from such order; and

(B) shall provide reasonable notice to the United States Marshals Service before the commencement of any special session held pursuant to such order.

(5) If a district court issues an order exercising its authority under paragraph (1), the court shall direct the United States marshal of the district where the court is meeting to furnish transportation and subsistence to the same extent as that provided in sections 4282 and 4285 of title 18.

History of 28 U.S.C. §141: June 25, 1948, ch. 646, 62 Stat. 897; Oct. 16, 1963, P.L. 88-139, §1, 77 Stat. 248; Sept. 9, 2005, P.L. 109-63, §2(b), 119 Stat. 1994; Jan. 5, 2006, P.L. 109-162, §1198(a), 119 Stat. 3132.

§142. REPEALED

Repealed Apr. 2, 1982, P.L. 97-164, §115(c)(3), 96 Stat. 32.

§143. VACANT JUDGESHIP AS AFFECTING PROCEEDINGS

When the office of a district judge becomes vacant, all pending process, pleadings and proceedings shall, when necessary, be continued by the clerk until a judge is appointed or designated to hold such court.

History of 28 U.S.C. §143: June 25, 1948, ch. 646, 62 Stat. 898.

§144. BIAS OR PREJUDICE OF JUDGE

Whenever a party to any proceeding in a district court makes and files a timely and sufficient affidavit that the judge before whom the matter is pending has a personal bias or prejudice either against him or in favor of any adverse party, such judge shall proceed no further therein, but another judge shall be assigned to hear such proceeding.

The affidavit shall state the facts and the reasons for the belief that bias or prejudice exists, and shall be filed not less than ten days before the beginning of the term at which the proceeding is to be heard, or good cause shall be shown for failure to file it within such time. A party may file only one such affidavit in any case. It shall be accompanied by a certificate of counsel of record stating that it is made in good faith.

History of 28 U.S.C. §144: June 25, 1948, ch. 646, 62 Stat. 898; May 24, 1949, ch. 139, §65, 63 Stat. 99.

See *Commentaries*, "Motion to Recuse," ch. 5-E, p. 321.

CHAPTER 6. BANKRUPTCY JUDGES

§151. DESIGNATION OF BANKRUPTCY COURTS

In each judicial district, the bankruptcy judges in regular active service shall constitute a unit of the district court to be known as the bankruptcy court for that district. Each bankruptcy judge, as a judicial officer of the district court, may exercise the authority conferred under this chapter with respect to any action, suit, or proceeding and may preside alone and hold a regular or special session of the court, except as otherwise provided by law or by rule or order of the district court.

History of 28 U.S.C. §151: July 10, 1984, P.L. 98-353, §104(a), 98 Stat. 336.

§152. APPOINTMENT OF BANKRUPTCY JUDGES

(a)(1) Each bankruptcy judge to be appointed for a judicial district, as provided in paragraph (2), shall be appointed by the court of appeals of the United States for the circuit in which such district is located. Such appointments shall be made after considering the recommendations of the Judicial Conference submitted pursuant to subsection (b). Each bankruptcy judge shall be appointed for a term of fourteen years, subject to the provisions of subsection (e). However, upon the expiration of the term, a bankruptcy judge may, with the approval of the judicial council of the circuit, continue to perform the duties of the office until the earlier of the date which is 180 days after the expiration of the term or the date of the appointment of a successor. Bankruptcy judges shall serve as judicial officers of the United States district court established under Article III of the Constitution.

(2) The bankruptcy judges appointed pursuant to this section shall be appointed for the several judicial districts as follows:

Districts	*Judges*
Alabama:	
Northern	5
Middle	2
Southern	2
Alaska	2
Arizona	7
Arkansas:	
Eastern and Western	3
California:	
Northern	9
Eastern	6
Central	21
Southern	4
Colorado	5
Connecticut	3
Delaware	1
District of Columbia	1
Florida:	
Northern	1
Middle	8
Southern	5
Georgia:	
Northern	8
Middle	3
Southern	2

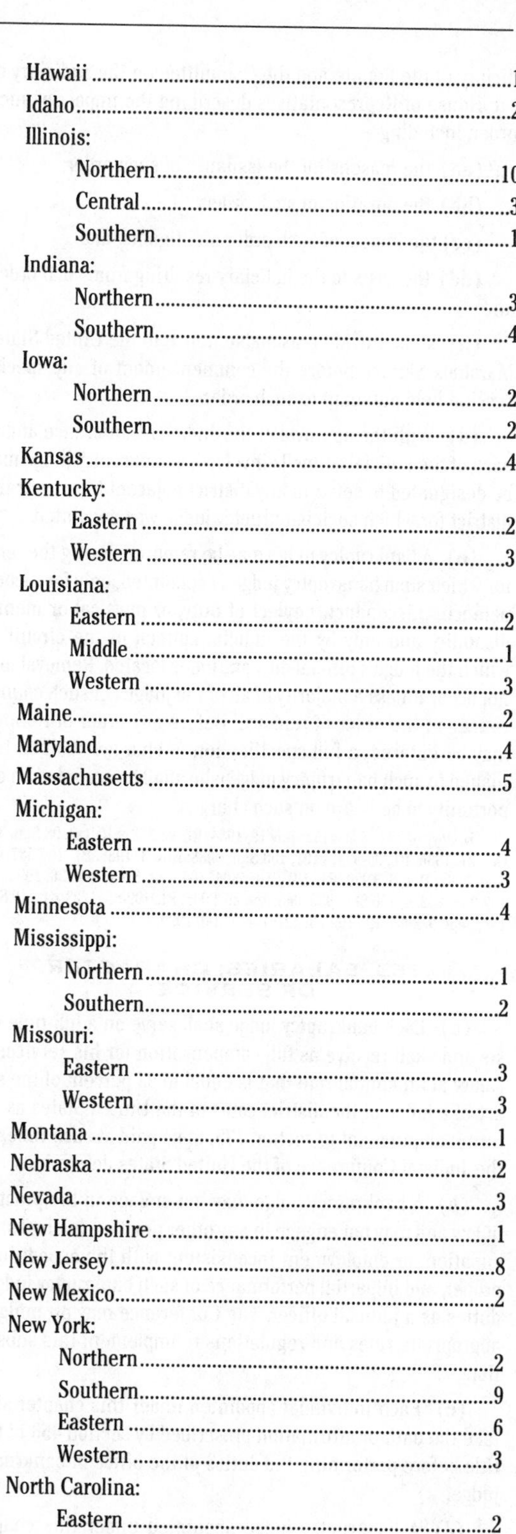

- Hawaii 1
- Idaho 2
- Illinois:
  - Northern 10
  - Central 3
  - Southern 1
- Indiana:
  - Northern 3
  - Southern 4
- Iowa:
  - Northern 2
  - Southern 2
- Kansas 4
- Kentucky:
  - Eastern 2
  - Western 3
- Louisiana:
  - Eastern 2
  - Middle 1
  - Western 3
- Maine 2
- Maryland 4
- Massachusetts 5
- Michigan:
  - Eastern 4
  - Western 3
- Minnesota 4
- Mississippi:
  - Northern 1
  - Southern 2
- Missouri:
  - Eastern 3
  - Western 3
- Montana 1
- Nebraska 2
- Nevada 3
- New Hampshire 1
- New Jersey 8
- New Mexico 2
- New York:
  - Northern 2
  - Southern 9
  - Eastern 6
  - Western 3
- North Carolina:
  - Eastern 2
  - Middle 2
  - Western 2
- North Dakota 1
- Ohio:
  - Northern 8
  - Southern 7
- Oklahoma:
  - Northern 2
  - Eastern 1
  - Western 3
- Oregon 5
- Pennsylvania:
  - Eastern 5
  - Middle 2
  - Western 4
- Puerto Rico 2
- Rhode Island 1
- South Carolina 2
- South Dakota 2
- Tennessee:
  - Eastern 3
  - Middle 3
  - Western 4
- Texas:
  - Northern 6
  - Eastern 2
  - Southern 6
  - Western 4
- Utah 3
- Vermont 1
- Virginia:
  - Eastern 5
  - Western 3
- Washington:
  - Eastern 2
  - Western 5
- West Virginia:
  - Northern 1
  - Southern 1
- Wisconsin:
  - Eastern 4
  - Western 2
- Wyoming 1

(3) Whenever a majority of the judges of any court of appeals cannot agree upon the appointment of a bankruptcy judge, the chief judge of such court shall make such appointment.

(4) The judges of the district courts for the territories shall serve as the bankruptcy judges for such courts. The

United States court of appeals for the circuit within which such a territorial district court is located may appoint bankruptcy judges under this chapter for such district if authorized to do so by the Congress of the United States under this section.

(b)(1) The Judicial Conference of the United States shall, from time to time, and after considering the recommendations submitted by the Director of the Administrative Office of the United States Courts after such Director has consulted with the judicial council of the circuit involved, determine the official duty stations of bankruptcy judges and places of holding court.

(2) The Judicial Conference shall, from time to time, submit recommendations to the Congress regarding the number of bankruptcy judges needed and the districts in which such judges are needed.

(3) Not later than December 31, 1994, and not later than the end of each 2-year period thereafter, the Judicial Conference of the United States shall conduct a comprehensive review of all judicial districts to assess the continuing need for the bankruptcy judges authorized by this section, and shall report to the Congress its findings and any recommendations for the elimination of any authorized position which can be eliminated when a vacancy exists by reason of resignation, retirement, removal, or death.

(c)(1) Each bankruptcy judge may hold court at such places within the judicial district, in addition to the official duty station of such judge, as the business of the court may require.

(2)(A) Bankruptcy judges may hold court at such places within the United States outside the judicial district as the nature of the business of the court may require, and upon such notice as the court orders, upon a finding by either the chief judge of the bankruptcy court (or, if the chief judge is unavailable, the most senior available bankruptcy judge) or by the judicial council of the circuit that, because of emergency conditions, no location within the district is reasonably available where the bankruptcy judges could hold court.

(B) Bankruptcy judges may transact any business at special sessions of court held outside the district pursuant to this paragraph that might be transacted at a regular session.

(C) If a bankruptcy court issues an order exercising its authority under subparagraph (A), the court—

(i) through the Administrative Office of the United States Courts, shall—

(I) send notice of such order, including the reasons for the issuance of such order, to the Committee on the Judiciary of the Senate and the Committee on the Judiciary of the House of Representatives; and

(II) not later than 180 days after the expiration of such court order submit a brief report to the Committee on the Judiciary of the Senate and the Committee on the Judiciary of the House of Representatives describing the impact of such order, including—

(aa) the reasons for the issuance of such order;

(bb) the duration of such order;

(cc) the impact of such order on litigants; and

(dd) the costs to the judiciary resulting from such order; and

(ii) shall provide reasonable notice to the United States Marshals Service before the commencement of any special session held pursuant to such order.

(d) With the approval of the Judicial Conference and of each of the judicial councils involved, a bankruptcy judge may be designated to serve in any district adjacent to or near the district for which such bankruptcy judge was appointed.

(e) A bankruptcy judge may be removed during the term for which such bankruptcy judge is appointed, only for incompetence, misconduct, neglect of duty, or physical or mental disability and only by the judicial council of the circuit in which the judge's official duty station is located. Removal may not occur unless a majority of all of the judges of such council concur in the order of removal. Before any order of removal may be entered, a full specification of charges shall be furnished to such bankruptcy judge who shall be accorded an opportunity to be heard on such charges.

History of 28 U.S.C. §152: July 10, 1984, P.L. 98-353, §104(a), 98 Stat. 336; Oct. 27, 1986, P.L. 99-554, §101, 100 Stat. 3088; Nov. 3, 1988, P.L. 100-587, 102 Stat. 2982; Dec. 1, 1990, P.L. 101-650, §304, 104 Stat. 5105; Aug. 26, 1992, P.L. 102-361, §§2, 4, 106 Stat. 965, 966; Apr. 20, 2005, P.L. 109-8, §1223(d), 119 Stat. 198; Sept. 9, 2005, P.L. 109-63, §2(c), 119 Stat. 1999.

§153. SALARIES; CHARACTER OF SERVICE

(a) Each bankruptcy judge shall serve on a full-time basis and shall receive as full compensation for his services, a salary at an annual rate that is equal to 92 percent of the salary of a judge of the district court of the United States as determined pursuant to section 135, to be paid at such times as the Judicial Conference of the United States determines.

(b) A bankruptcy judge may not engage in the practice of law and may not engage in any other practice, business, occupation, or employment inconsistent with the expeditious, proper, and impartial performance of such bankruptcy judge's duties as a judicial officer. The Conference may promulgate appropriate rules and regulations to implement this subsection.

(c) Each individual appointed under this chapter shall take the oath or affirmation prescribed by section 453 of this title before performing the duties of the office of bankruptcy judge.

(d) A bankruptcy judge appointed under this chapter shall be exempt from the provisions of subchapter I of chapter 63 of title 5.

History of 28 U.S.C. §153: July 10, 1984, P.L. 98-353, §104(a), 98 Stat. 338; Dec. 22, 1987, P.L. 100-202, §101(a) [§408(a)], 101 Stat. 1329-26; Nov. 19, 1988, P.L. 100-702, §1003(a)(1), 102 Stat. 4665; Sept. 9. 2005, P.L. 109-63, §2(c), 119 Stat. 1994.

§154. DIVISION OF BUSINESSES; CHIEF JUDGE

(a) Each bankruptcy court for a district having more than one bankruptcy judge shall by majority vote promulgate rules for the division of business among the bankruptcy judges to the extent that the division of business is not otherwise provided for by the rules of the district court.

(b) In each district court having more than one bankruptcy judge the district court shall designate one judge to serve as chief judge of such bankruptcy court. Whenever a majority of the judges of such district court cannot agree upon the designation as chief judge, the chief judge of such district court shall make such designation. The chief judge of the bankruptcy court shall ensure that the rules of the bankruptcy court and of the district court are observed and that the business of the bankruptcy court is handled effectively and expeditiously.

History of 28 U.S.C. §154: July 10, 1984, P.L. 98-353, §104(a), 98 Stat. 339.

§155. TEMPORARY TRANSFER OF BANKRUPTCY JUDGES

(a) A bankruptcy judge may be transferred to serve temporarily as a bankruptcy judge in any judicial district other than the judicial district for which such bankruptcy judge was appointed upon the approval of the judicial council of each of the circuits involved.

(b) A bankruptcy judge who has retired may, upon consent, be recalled to serve as a bankruptcy judge in any judicial district by the judicial council of the circuit within which such district is located. Upon recall, a bankruptcy judge may receive a salary for such service in accordance with regulations promulgated by the Judicial Conference of the United States, subject to the restrictions on the payment of an annuity in section 377 of this title or in subchapter III of chapter 83, and chapter 84, of title 5 which are applicable to such judge.

History of 28 U.S.C. §155: July 10, 1984, P.L. 98-353, §104(a), 98 Stat. 339; Nov. 14, 1986, P.L. 99-651, §202(a), 100 Stat. 3648; Nov. 15, 1988, P.L. 100-659, §4(a), 102 Stat. 3918.

§156. STAFF; EXPENSES

(a) Each bankruptcy judge may appoint a secretary, a law clerk, and such additional assistants as the Director of the Administrative Office of the United States Courts determines to be necessary. A law clerk appointed under this section shall be exempt from the provisions of subchapter I of chapter 63 of title 5, unless specifically included by the appointing judge or by local rule of court.

(b) Upon certification to the judicial council of the circuit involved and to the Director of the Administrative Office of the United States Courts that the number of cases and proceedings pending within the jurisdiction under section 1334 of this title within a judicial district so warrants, the bankruptcy judges for such district may appoint an individual to serve as clerk of such bankruptcy court. The clerk may appoint, with the approval of such bankruptcy judges, and in such number as may be approved by the Director, necessary deputies, and may remove such deputies with the approval of such bankruptcy judges.

(c) Any court may utilize facilities or services, either on or off the court's premises, which pertain to the provision of notices, dockets, calendars, and other administrative information to parties in cases filed under the provisions of title 11, United States Code, where the costs of such facilities or services are paid for out of the assets of the estate and are not charged to the United States. The utilization of such facilities or services shall be subject to such conditions and limitations as the pertinent circuit council may prescribe.

(d) No office of the bankruptcy clerk of court may be consolidated with the district clerk of court office without the prior approval of the Judicial Conference and the Congress.

(e) In a judicial district where a bankruptcy clerk has been appointed pursuant to subsection (b), the bankruptcy clerk shall be the official custodian of the records and dockets of the bankruptcy court.

(f) For purposes of financial accountability in a district where a bankruptcy clerk has been certified, such clerk shall be accountable for and pay into the Treasury all fees, costs, and other monies collected by such clerk except uncollected fees not required by an Act of Congress to be prepaid. Such clerk shall make returns thereof to the Director of the Administrative Office of the United States Courts and the Director of the Executive Office For United States Trustees, under regulations prescribed by such Directors.

History of 28 U.S.C. §156: July 10, 1984, P.L. 98-353, §104(a), 98 Stat. 339; Oct. 27, 1986, P.L. 99-554, §§103, 142, 144(a), 100 Stat. 3090, 3096; Nov. 19, 1988, P.L. 100-702, §1003(a)(3), 102 Stat. 4665.

§157. PROCEDURES

(a) Each district court may provide that any or all cases under title 11 and any or all proceedings arising under title 11 or arising in or related to a case under title 11 shall be referred to the bankruptcy judges for the district.

(b)(1) Bankruptcy judges may hear and determine all cases under title 11 and all core proceedings arising under title 11, or arising in a case under title 11, referred under subsection (a) of this section, and may enter appropriate orders and judgments, subject to review under section 158 of this title.

(2) Core proceedings include, but are not limited to—

(A) matters concerning the administration of the estate;

(B) allowance or disallowance of claims against the estate or exemptions from property of the estate, and estimation of claims or interests for the purposes of confirming a plan under chapter 11, 12, or 13 of title 11 but not the liquidation or estimation of contingent or unliquidated personal injury tort or

wrongful death claims against the estate for purposes of distribution in a case under title 11;

(C) counterclaims by the estate against persons filing claims against the estate;

(D) orders in respect to obtaining credit;

(E) orders to turn over property of the estate;

(F) proceedings to determine, avoid, or recover preferences;

(G) motions to terminate, annul, or modify the automatic stay;

(H) proceedings to determine, avoid, or recover fraudulent conveyances;

(I) determinations as to the dischargeability of particular debts;

(J) objections to discharges;

(K) determinations of the validity, extent, or priority of liens;

(L) confirmations of plans;

(M) orders approving the use or lease of property, including the use of cash collateral;

(N) orders approving the sale of property other than property resulting from claims brought by the estate against persons who have not filed claims against the estate;

(O) other proceedings affecting the liquidation of the assets of the estate or the adjustment of the debtor-creditor or the equity security holder relationship, except personal injury tort or wrongful death claims; and

(P) recognition of foreign proceedings and other matters under chapter 15 of title 11.

(3) The bankruptcy judge shall determine, on the judge's own motion or on timely motion of a party, whether a proceeding is a core proceeding under this subsection or is a proceeding that is otherwise related to a case under title 11. A determination that a proceeding is not a core proceeding shall not be made solely on the basis that its resolution may be affected by State law.

(4) Non-core proceedings under section 157(b)(2)(B) of title 28, United States Code, shall not be subject to the mandatory abstention provisions of section 1334(c)(2).

(5) The district court shall order that personal injury tort and wrongful death claims shall be tried in the district court in which the bankruptcy case is pending, or in the district court in the district in which the claim arose, as determined by the district court in which the bankruptcy case is pending.

(c)(1) A bankruptcy judge may hear a proceeding that is not a core proceeding but that is otherwise related to a case under title 11. In such proceeding, the bankruptcy judge shall submit proposed findings of fact and conclusions of law to the district court, and any final order or judgment shall be entered by the district judge after considering the bankruptcy judge's proposed findings and conclusions and after reviewing de novo those matters to which any party has timely and specifically objected.

(2) Notwithstanding the provisions of paragraph (1) of this subsection, the district court, with the consent of all the parties to the proceeding, may refer a proceeding related to a case under title 11 to a bankruptcy judge to hear and determine and to enter appropriate orders and judgments, subject to review under section 158 of this title.

(d) The district court may withdraw, in whole or in part, any case or proceeding referred under this section, on its own motion or on timely motion of any party, for cause shown. The district court shall, on timely motion of a party, so withdraw a proceeding if the court determines that resolution of the proceeding requires consideration of both title 11 and other laws of the United States regulating organizations or activities affecting interstate commerce.

(e) If the right to a jury trial applies in a proceeding that may be heard under this section by a bankruptcy judge, the bankruptcy judge may conduct the jury trial if specially designated to exercise such jurisdiction by the district court and with the express consent of all the parties.

History of 28 U.S.C. §157: July 10, 1984, P.L. 98-353, §104(a), 98 Stat. 340; Oct. 27, 1986, P.L. 99-554, §§143, 144(b), 100 Stat. 3096; Oct. 22, 1994, P.L. 103-394, §112, 108 Stat. 4117; Apr. 20, 2005, P.L. 109-8, §802(c)(1), 119 Stat. 145.

§158. APPEALS

(a) The district courts of the United States shall have jurisdiction to hear appeals

(1) from final judgments, orders, and decrees;

(2) from interlocutory orders and decrees issued under section 1121(d) of title 11 increasing or reducing the time periods referred to in section 1121 of such title; and

(3) with leave of the court, from other interlocutory orders and decrees;

and, with leave of the court, from interlocutory orders and decrees, of bankruptcy judges entered in cases and proceedings referred to the bankruptcy judges under section 157 of this title. An appeal under this subsection shall be taken only to the district court for the judicial district in which the bankruptcy judge is serving.

(b)(1) The judicial council of a circuit shall establish a bankruptcy appellate panel service composed of bankruptcy judges of the districts in the circuit who are appointed by the judicial council in accordance with paragraph (3), to hear and determine, with the consent of all the parties, appeals under subsection (a) unless the judicial council finds that—

(A) there are insufficient judicial resources available in the circuit; or

(B) establishment of such service would result in undue delay or increased cost to parties in cases under title 11.

Not later than 90 days after making the finding, the judicial council shall submit to the Judicial Conference of the United States a report containing the factual basis of such finding.

(2)(A) A judicial council may reconsider, at any time, the finding described in paragraph (1).

(B) On the request of a majority of the district judges in a circuit for which a bankruptcy appellate panel service is established under paragraph (1), made after the expiration of the 1-year period beginning on the date such service is established, the judicial council of the circuit shall determine whether a circumstance specified in subparagraph (A) or (B) of such paragraph exists.

(C) On its own motion, after the expiration of the 3-year period beginning on the date a bankruptcy appellate panel service is established under paragraph (1), the judicial council of the circuit may determine whether a circumstance specified in subparagraph (A) or (B) of such paragraph exists.

(D) If the judicial council finds that either of such circumstances exists, the judicial council may provide for the completion of the appeals then pending before such service and the orderly termination of such service.

(3) Bankruptcy judges appointed under paragraph (1) shall be appointed and may be reappointed under such paragraph.

(4) If authorized by the Judicial Conference of the United States, the judicial councils of 2 or more circuits may establish a joint bankruptcy appellate panel comprised of bankruptcy judges from the districts within the circuits for which such panel is established, to hear and determine, upon the consent of all the parties, appeals under subsection (a) of this section.

(5) An appeal to be heard under this subsection shall be heard by a panel of 3 members of the bankruptcy appellate panel service, except that a member of such service may not hear an appeal originating in the district for which such member is appointed or designated under section 152 of this title.

(6) Appeals may not be heard under this subsection by a panel of the bankruptcy appellate panel service unless the district judges for the district in which the appeals occur, by majority vote, have authorized such service to hear and determine appeals originating in such district.

(c)(1) Subject to subsections (b) and (d)(2), each appeal under subsection (a) shall be heard by a 3-judge panel of the bankruptcy appellate panel service established under subsection (b)(1) unless—

(A) the appellant elects at the time of filing the appeal; or

(B) any other party elects, not later than 30 days after service of notice of the appeal;

to have such appeal heard by the district court.

(2) An appeal under subsections (a) and (b) of this section shall be taken in the same manner as appeals in civil proceedings generally are taken to the courts of appeals from the district courts and in the time provided by Rule 8002 of the Bankruptcy Rules.

(d)(1) The courts of appeals shall have jurisdiction of appeals from all final decisions, judgments, orders, and decrees entered under subsections (a) and (b) of this section.

(2)(A) The appropriate court of appeals shall have jurisdiction of appeals described in the first sentence of subsection (a) if the bankruptcy court, the district court, or the bankruptcy appellate panel involved, acting on its own motion or on the request of a party to the judgment, order, or decree described in such first sentence, or all the appellants and appellees (if any) acting jointly, certify that—

(i) the judgment, order, or decree involves a question of law as to which there is no controlling decision of the court of appeals for the circuit or of the Supreme Court of the United States, or involves a matter of public importance;

(ii) the judgment, order, or decree involves a question of law requiring resolution of conflicting decisions; or

(iii) an immediate appeal from the judgment, order, or decree may materially advance the progress of the case or proceeding in which the appeal is taken;

and if the court of appeals authorizes the direct appeal of the judgment, order, or decree.

(B) If the bankruptcy court, the district court, or the bankruptcy appellate panel—

(i) on its own motion or on the request of a party, determines that a circumstance specified in clause (i), (ii), or (iii) of subparagraph (A) exists; or

(ii) receives a request made by a majority of the appellants and a majority of appellees (if any) to make the certification described in subparagraph (A);

then the bankruptcy court, the district court, or the bankruptcy appellate panel shall make the certification described in subparagraph (A).

(C) The parties may supplement the certification with a short statement of the basis for the certification.

(D) An appeal under this paragraph does not stay any proceeding of the bankruptcy court, the district court, or the bankruptcy appellate panel from which the appeal is taken, unless the respective bankruptcy court, district court, or bankruptcy appellate panel, or the court of appeals in which the appeal is pending, issues a stay of such proceeding pending the appeal.

(E) Any request under subparagraph (B) for certification shall be made not later than 60 days after the entry of the judgment, order, or decree.

History of 28 U.S.C. §158: July 10, 1984, P.L. 98-353, §104(a), 98 Stat. 341; Dec. 1, 1990, P.L. 101-650, §305, 104 Stat. 5105; Oct. 22, 1994, P.L. 103-394, §§102, 104(c), (d), 108 Stat. 4108, 4109; Apr. 20, 2005, P.L. 109-8, §1233(a), 119 Stat. 202; Dec. 22, 2010, P.L. 111-327, §2(c)(1), 124 Stat. 3563.

§159. BANKRUPTCY STATISTICS

(a) The clerk of the district court, or the clerk of the bankruptcy court if one is certified pursuant to section 156(b) of this title, shall collect statistics regarding debtors who are individuals with primarily consumer debts seeking relief under chapters 7, 11, and 13 of title 11. Those statistics shall be in a standardized format prescribed by the Director of the Administrative Office of the United States Courts (referred to in this section as the "Director").

(b) The Director shall—

(1) compile the statistics referred to in subsection (a);

(2) make the statistics available to the public; and

(3) not later than July 1, 2008, and annually thereafter, prepare, and submit to Congress a report concerning the information collected under subsection (a) that contains an analysis of the information.

(c) The compilation required under subsection (b) shall—

(1) be itemized, by chapter, with respect to title 11;

(2) be presented in the aggregate and for each district; and

(3) include information concerning—

(A) the total assets and total liabilities of the debtors described in subsection (a), and in each category of assets and liabilities, as reported in the schedules prescribed pursuant to section 2075 of this title and filed by debtors;

(B) the current monthly income, average income, and average expenses of debtors as reported on the schedules and statements that each such debtor files under sections 521 and 1322 of title 11;

(C) the aggregate amount of debt discharged in cases filed during the reporting period, determined as the difference between the total amount of debt and obligations of a debtor reported on the schedules and the amount of such debt reported in categories which are predominantly nondischargeable;

(D) the average period of time between the date of the filing of the petition and the closing of the case for cases closed during the reporting period;

(E) for cases closed during the reporting period—

(i) the number of cases in which a reaffirmation agreement was filed; and

(ii)(I) the total number of reaffirmation agreements filed;

(II) of those cases in which a reaffirmation agreement was filed, the number of cases in which the debtor was not represented by an attorney; and

(III) of those cases in which a reaffirmation agreement was filed, the number of cases in which the reaffirmation agreement was approved by the court;

(F) with respect to cases filed under chapter 13 of title 11, for the reporting period—

(i)(I) the number of cases in which a final order was entered determining the value of property securing a claim in an amount less than the amount of the claim; and

(II) the number of final orders entered determining the value of property securing a claim;

(ii) the number of cases dismissed, the number of cases dismissed for failure to make payments under the plan, the number of cases refiled after dismissal, and the number of cases in which the plan was completed, separately itemized with respect to the number of modifications made before completion of the plan, if any; and

(iii) the number of cases in which the debtor filed another case during the 6-year period preceding the filing;

(G) the number of cases in which creditors were fined for misconduct and any amount of punitive damages awarded by the court for creditor misconduct; and

(H) the number of cases in which sanctions under rule 9011 of the Federal Rules of Bankruptcy Procedure were imposed against the debtor's attorney or damages awarded under such Rule.

History of 28 U.S.C. §159: Apr. 20, 2005, P.L. 109-8, §601(a), 119 Stat. 119; Dec. 22, 2010, P.L. 111-327, §2(c)(2), 124 Stat. 3563.

CHAPTER 7. UNITED STATES COURT OF FEDERAL CLAIMS

§171. APPOINTMENT & NUMBER OF JUDGES; CHARACTER OF COURT; DESIGNATION OF CHIEF JUDGE

(a) The President shall appoint, by and with the advice and consent of the Senate, sixteen judges who shall constitute a court of record known as the United States Court of Federal Claims. The court is declared to be a court established under article I of the Constitution of the United States.

(b) The President shall designate one of the judges of the Court of Federal Claims who is less than seventy years of age to serve as chief judge. The chief judge may continue to serve as such until he reaches the age of seventy years or until another judge is designated as chief judge by the President. After the designation of another judge to serve as chief judge, the former chief judge may continue to serve as a judge of the court for the balance of the term to which appointed.

History of 28 U.S.C. §171: June 25, 1948, ch. 646, 62 Stat. 898; July 28, 1953, ch. 253, §1, 67 Stat. 226; Sept. 3, 1954, ch. 1263, §39(a), 68 Stat. 1240; May 11, 1966, P.L. 89-425, §1(b), 80 Stat. 140; Apr. 2, 1982, P.L. 97-164, §105(a), 96 Stat. 27; Oct. 29, 1992, P.L. 102-572, §902(a), 106 Stat. 4516.

§172. TENURE & SALARIES OF JUDGES

(a) Each judge of the United States Court of Federal Claims shall be appointed for a term of fifteen years.

(b) Each judge shall receive a salary at the rate of pay, and in the same manner, as judges of the district courts of the United States.

History of 28 U.S.C. §172: June 25, 1948, ch. 646, 62 Stat. 898; Apr. 2, 1982, P.L. 97-164, §105(a), 96 Stat. 27; Nov. 19, 1988, P.L. 100-702, §1023, 102 Stat. 4673; Oct. 29, 1992, P.L. 102-572, §902(a)(1), 106 Stat. 4516.

§173. TIMES & PLACES OF HOLDING COURT

The principal office of the United States Court of Federal Claims shall be in the District of Columbia, but the Court of Federal Claims may hold court at such times and in such places as it may fix by rule of court. The times and places of the sessions of the Court of Federal Claims shall be prescribed with a view to securing reasonable opportunity to citizens to appear before the Court of Federal Claims with as little inconvenience and expense to citizens as is practicable.

History of 28 U.S.C. §173: June 25, 1948, ch. 646, 62 Stat. 898; Mar. 2, 1955, ch. 9, §1(d), 69 Stat. 10; Aug. 14, 1964, P.L. 88-426, §403(d), 78 Stat. 434; Aug. 9, 1975, P.L. 94-82, §205(b)(4), 89 Stat. 422; Apr. 2, 1982, P.L. 97-164, §105(a), 96 Stat. 27; Oct. 29, 1992, P.L. 102-572, §902(a), 106 Stat. 4516.

§174. ASSIGNMENT OF JUDGES; DECISIONS

(a) The judicial power of the United States Court of Federal Claims with respect to any action, suit, or proceeding, except congressional reference cases, shall be exercised by a single judge, who may preside alone and hold a regular or special session of court at the same time other sessions are held by other judges.

(b) All decisions of the Court of Federal Claims shall be preserved and open to inspection.

History of 28 U.S.C. §174: June 25, 1948, ch. 646, 62 Stat. 898; Apr. 2, 1982, P.L. 97-164, §105(a), 96 Stat. 27; Oct. 29, 1992, P.L. 102-572, §902(a), 106 Stat. 4516.

§175. OFFICIAL DUTY STATION; RESIDENCE

(a) The official duty station of each judge of the United States Court of Federal Claims is the District of Columbia.

(b) After appointment and while in active service, each judge shall reside within fifty miles of the District of Columbia.

(c) Retired judges of the Court of Federal Claims are not subject to restrictions as to residence. The place where a retired judge maintains the actual abode in which such judge customarily lives shall be deemed to be the judge's official duty station for the purposes of section 456 of this title.

History of 28 U.S.C. §175: May 11, 1966, P.L. 89-425, §2, 80 Stat. 140; Apr. 2, 1982, P.L. 97-164, §105(a), 96 Stat. 27; Oct. 29, 1992, P.L. 102-572, §902(a)(1), 106 Stat. 4516; Nov. 13, 2000, P.L. 106-518, §307, 114 Stat. 2419.

§176. REMOVAL FROM OFFICE

(a) Removal of a judge of the United States Court of Federal Claims during the term for which he is appointed shall be only for incompetency, misconduct, neglect of duty, engaging in the practice of law, or physical or mental disability. Removal shall be by the United States Court of Appeals for the Federal Circuit, but removal may not occur unless a majority of all the judges of such court of appeals concur in the order of removal.

(b) Before any order of removal may be entered, a full specification of the charges shall be furnished to the judge involved, and such judge shall be accorded an opportunity to be heard on the charges.

(c) Any cause for removal of any judge of the United States Court of Federal Claims coming to the knowledge of the Director of the Administrative Office of the United States Courts shall be reported by him to the chief judge of the United States Court of Appeals for the Federal Circuit, and a copy of the report shall at the same time be transmitted to the judge.

History of 28 U.S.C. §176: Apr. 2, 1982, P.L. 97-164, §105(a), 96 Stat. 28; Oct. 29, 1992, P.L. 102-572, §902(a)(1), 106 Stat. 4516.

§177. DISBARMENT OF REMOVED JUDGES

A judge of the United States Court of Federal Claims removed from office in accordance with section 176 of this title shall not be permitted at any time to practice before the Court of Federal Claims.

History of 28 U.S.C. §177: Apr. 2, 1982, P.L. 97-164, §105(a), 96 Stat. 28; Oct. 29, 1992, P.L. 102-572, §902(a), 106 Stat. 4516.

§178. RETIREMENT OF JUDGES OF THE COURT OF FEDERAL CLAIMS

(a) A judge of the United States Court of Federal Claims who retires from office after attaining the age and meeting the service requirements, whether continuously or otherwise, of this subsection shall, subject to subsection (f), be entitled to receive, during the remainder of the judge's lifetime, an annuity equal to the salary payable to Court of Federal Claims judges in regular active service. The age and service requirements for retirement under this subsection are as follows:

Attained Age	*Years of Service*
65	15
66	14
67	13
68	12
69	11
70	10

(b) A judge of the Court of Federal Claims who is not reappointed following the expiration of the term of office of such judge, and who retires upon the completion of such term shall, subject to subsection (f), be entitled to receive, during the remainder of such judge's lifetime, an annuity equal to the salary payable to Court of Federal Claims judges in regular active service, if—

(1) such judge has served at least 1 full term as judge of the Court of Federal Claims, and

(2) not earlier than 9 months before the date on which the term of office of such judge expired, and not later than 6 months before such date, such judge advised the President in writing that such judge was willing to accept reappointment as a judge of the Court of Federal Claims.

(c) A judge of the Court of Federal Claims who has served at least 5 years, whether continuously or otherwise, as such a judge, and who retires or is removed from office upon the sole ground of mental or physical disability shall, subject to subsection (f), be entitled to receive, during the remainder of the judge's lifetime—

(1) an annuity equal to 50 percent of the salary payable to Court of Federal Claims judges in regular active service, if before retirement such judge served less than 10 years, or

(2) an annuity equal to the salary payable to Court of Federal Claims judges in regular active service, if before retirement such judge served at least 10 years.

(d) A judge who retires under subsection (a) or (b) may, at or after such retirement, be called upon by the chief judge of the Court of Federal Claims to perform such judicial duties with the Court of Federal Claims as may be requested of the retired judge for any period or periods specified by the chief judge, except that in the case of any such judge—

(1) the aggregate of such periods in any one calendar year shall not (without his or her consent) exceed 90 calendar days; and

(2) he or she shall be relieved of performing such duties during any period in which illness or disability precludes the performance of such duties.

Any act, or failure to act, by an individual performing judicial duties pursuant to this subsection shall have the same force and effect as if it were the act (or failure to act) of a Court of Federal Claims judge in regular active service. Any individual performing judicial duties pursuant to this subsection shall receive the allowances for official travel and other expenses of a judge in regular active service.

(e)(1) Any judge who retires under the provisions of subsection (a) or (b) of this section shall be designated "senior judge".

(2) Any judge who retires under this section shall not be counted as a judge of the Court of Federal Claims for purposes of the number of judgeships authorized by section 171 of this title.

(f)(1) A judge shall be entitled to an annuity under this section if the judge elects an annuity under this section by notifying the Director of the Administrative Office of the United States Courts in writing. Such an election—

(A) may be made only while an individual is a judge of the Court of Federal Claims (except that in the case of an individual who fails to be reappointed as judge at the expiration of a term of office, such election may be made at any time before the day after the day on which his or her successor takes office); and

(B) once made, shall, subject to subsection (k), be irrevocable.

(2) A judge who elects to receive an annuity under this section shall not be entitled to receive—

(A) any annuity to which such judge would otherwise have been entitled under subchapter III of chapter 83, or under chapter 84 (except for subchapters III and VII), of title 5, for service performed as a judge or otherwise;

(B) an annuity or salary in senior status or retirement under section 371 or 372 of this title;

(C) retired pay under section 7447 of the Internal Revenue Code of 1986; or

(D) retired pay under section 7296 of title 38.

(g) For purposes of calculating the years of service of an individual under subsections (a) and (c), only those years of service as a judge of the Court of Federal Claims or a commissioner of the United States Court of Claims shall be credited, and that portion of the aggregate number of years of such service that is a fractional part of 1 year shall not be credited if it is less than 6 months, and shall be credited if it is 6 months or more.

(h) An annuity under this section shall be payable at the times and in the same manner as the salary of a Court of Federal Claims judge in regular active service. Such annuity shall begin to accrue on the day following the day on which the annuitant's salary as a judge in regular active service ceases to accrue.

(i)(1) Payments under this section which would otherwise be made to a judge of the Court of Federal Claims based upon his or her service shall be paid (in whole or in part) by the Director of the Administrative Office of the United States Courts to another person if and to the extent expressly provided for in the terms of any court decree of divorce, annulment, or legal separation, or the terms of any court order or court-approved property settlement agreement incident to any court decree of divorce, annulment, or legal separation. Any payment under this paragraph to a person bars recovery by any other person.

(2) Paragraph (1) shall apply only to payments made by the Director of the Administrative Office of the United States Courts after the date of receipt by the Director of written notice of such decree, order, or agreement, and such additional information as the Director may prescribe.

(3) As used in this subsection, the term "court" means any court of any State, the District of Columbia, the Commonwealth of Puerto Rico, Guam, the Commonwealth of the Northern Mariana Islands, or the Virgin Islands, and any Indian tribal court or court of Indian offense.

(j)(1) Subject to paragraph (4), any judge of the Court of Federal Claims who retires under this section and who thereafter in the practice of law represents (or supervises or directs the representation of) a client in making any civil claim against the United States or any agency thereof shall forfeit all rights to an annuity under this section for all periods beginning on or after the first day on which he engages in any such activity.

(2) Subject to paragraph (4), if a judge of the Court of Federal Claims who retires under this section fails during any calendar year to perform judicial duties required of such judge by subsection (d), such judge shall forfeit all rights to an annuity under this section for the 1-year period which begins on the first day on which he or she so fails to perform such duties.

(3) If a judge of the Court of Federal Claims who retires under this section accepts compensation for civil office or employment under the Government of the United States (other than for the performance of judicial duties under subsection (d)), such judge shall forfeit all rights to an annuity under this section for the period for which such compensation is received.

(4)(A) If a judge makes an election under this paragraph—

(i) paragraphs (1) and (2) (and subsection (d)) shall not apply to such judge beginning on the date such election takes effect, and

(ii) the annuity payable under this section to such judge, for periods beginning on or after the date such election takes effect, shall be equal to the annuity to which such judge is entitled on the day before such effective date.

(B) An election under subparagraph (A)—

(i) may be made by a judge only if such judge meets the age and service requirements for retirement under subsection (a),

(ii) may be made only during the period during which such judge may make an election to receive an annuity under this section or while the judge is receiving an annuity under this section, and

(iii) shall be filed with the Director of the Administrative Office of the United States Courts.

Such an election, once it takes effect, shall be irrevocable.

(C) Any election under this paragraph shall take effect on the first day of the first month following the month in which the election is made.

(k)(1) Notwithstanding subsection (f)(1)(B), an individual who has filed an election under subsection (f) to receive an annuity may revoke such election at any time before the first day on which such annuity would (but for such revocation) begin to accrue with respect to such individual.

(2) Any revocation under this subsection shall be made by filing a notice thereof in writing with the Director of[1] Administrative Office of the United States Courts.

(3) In the case of any revocation under this subsection—

(A) for purposes of this section, the individual shall be treated as not having filed an election under subsection (f) to receive an annuity,

(B) for purposes of section 376 of this title—

(i) the individual shall be treated as not having filed an election under section 376(a)(1), and

(ii) section 376(g) shall not apply, and the amount credited to such individual's account (together with interest at 3 percent per annum, compounded on December 31 of each year to the date on which the revocation is filed) shall be returned to such individual,

(C) no credit shall be allowed for any service as a judge of the Court of Federal Claims or as a commissioner of the United States Court of Claims unless with respect to such service either there has been deducted and withheld the amount required by chapter 83 or 84 (as the case may be) of title 5 or there has been deposited in the Civil Service Retirement and Disability Fund an amount equal to the amount so required, with interest,

(D) the Court of Federal Claims shall deposit in the Civil Service Retirement and Disability Fund an amount equal to the additional amount it would have contributed to such Fund but for the election under subsection (f), and

(E) if subparagraph (D) is complied with, service on the Court of Federal Claims or as a commissioner of the United States Court of Claims shall be treated as service with respect to which deductions and contributions had been made during the period of service.

(*l*)(1) There is established in the Treasury a fund which shall be known as the "Court of Federal Claims Judges Retirement Fund". The Fund is appropriated for the payment of annuities and other payments under this section.

(2) The Secretary of the Treasury shall invest, in interest bearing securities of the United States, such currently available portions of the Court of Federal Claims Judges Retirement Fund as are not immediately required for payments from the Fund. The income derived from these investments constitutes a part of the Fund.

(3)(A) There are authorized to be appropriated to the Court of Federal Claims Judges Retirement Fund amounts required to reduce to zero the unfunded liability of the Fund.

(B) For purposes of subparagraph (A), the term "unfunded liability" means the estimated excess, determined on an annual basis in accordance with the provisions of section 9503 of title 31, of the present value of all benefits payable from the Court of Federal Claims Judges Retirement Fund, over the balance in the Fund as of the date the unfunded liability is determined. In making any determination under this subparagraph, the Comptroller General shall use the applicable information contained in the reports filed pursuant to section 9503 of title 31, with respect to the retirement annuities provided for in this section.

(C) There are authorized to be appropriated such sums as may be necessary to carry out this paragraph.

1. **Editor's note:** So in original. Probably should be "of the."

History of 28 U.S.C. §178: Dec. 1, 1990, P.L. 101-650, §306(a)(1), 104 Stat. 5105; May 7, 1991, P.L. 102-40, §402(d)(2), 105 Stat. 239; Dec. 9, 1991, P.L. 102-198, §7(a), 105 Stat. 1624; Oct. 29, 1992, P.L. 102-572, §902(a), 106 Stat. 4516.

§179. PERSONNEL APPLICATION & INSURANCE PROGRAMS

(a) For purposes of construing and applying title 5, a judge of the United States Court of Federal Claims shall be deemed to be an "officer" under section 2104(a) of such title.

(b)(1)(A) For purposes of construing and applying chapter 89 of title 5, a judge of the United States Court of Federal Claims who—

(i) is retired under subsection (b) of section 178 of this title, and

(ii) at the time of becoming such a retired judge—

(I) was enrolled in a health benefits plan under chapter 89 of title 5, but

(II) did not satisfy the requirements of section 8905(b)(1) of title 5 (relating to eligibility to continue enrollment as an annuitant),

shall be deemed to be an annuitant meeting the requirements of section 8905(b)(1) of title 5, in accordance with the succeeding provisions of this paragraph, if the judge gives timely written notification to the chief judge of the court that the judge is willing to be called upon to perform judicial duties under section 178(d) of this title during the period of continued eligibility for enrollment, as described in subparagraph (B)(ii) or (C)(ii) (whichever applies).

(B) Except as provided in subparagraph (C)—

(i) in order to be eligible for continued enrollment under this paragraph, notification under subparagraph (A) shall be made before the first day of the open enrollment period preceding the calendar year referred to in clause (ii)(II); and

(ii) if such notification is timely made, the retired judge shall be eligible for continued enrollment under this paragraph for the period—

(I) beginning on the date on which eligibility would otherwise cease, and

(II) ending on the last day of the calendar year next beginning after the end of the open enrollment period referred to in clause (i).

(C) For purposes of applying this paragraph for the first time in the case of any particular judge—

(i) subparagraph (B)(i) shall be applied by substituting "the expiration of the term of office of the judge" for the matter following "before"; and

(ii)(I) if the term of office of such judge expires before the first day of the open enrollment period referred to in subparagraph (B)(i), the period of continued eligibility for enrollment shall be as described in subparagraph (B)(ii); but

(II) if the term of office of such judge expires on or after the first day of the open enrollment period referred to in subparagraph (B)(i), the period of continued eligibility shall not end until the last day of the calendar year next beginning after the end of the next full open enrollment period beginning after the date on which the term expires.

(2) In the event that a retired judge remains enrolled under chapter 89 of title 5 for a period of 5 consecutive years by virtue of paragraph (1) (taking into account only periods of coverage as an active judge immediately before retirement and as a retired judge pursuant to paragraph (1)), then, effective as of the day following the last day of that 5-year period—

(A) the provisions of chapter 89 of title 5 shall be applied as if such judge had satisfied the requirements of section 8905(b)(1)[1] on the last day of such period; and

(B) the provisions of paragraph (1) shall cease to apply.

(3) For purposes of this subsection, the term "open enrollment period" refers to a period described in section 8905(g)(1) of title 5.

(c) For purposes of construing and applying chapter 87 of title 5, including any adjustment of insurance rates by regulation or otherwise, a judge of the United States Court of Federal Claims in regular active service or who is retired under section 178 of this title shall be deemed to be a judge of the United States described under section 8701(a)(5) of title 5.

1. **Editor's note:** So in original. Probably should be followed by "of title 5."

History of 28 U.S.C. §179: Nov. 13, 2000, P.L. 106-518, §309(a), 114 Stat. 2419.

§180. REPEALED

Repealed Oct. 30, 2000, P.L. 106-398, §654(b)(1), 114 Stat. 1654A-165.

CHAPTER 9. REPEALED

§§211 TO 216. REPEALED

Repealed Apr. 2, 1982, P.L. 97-164, §106, 96 Stat. 28.

CHAPTER 11. COURT OF INTERNATIONAL TRADE

§251. APPOINTMENT & NUMBER OF JUDGES; OFFICES

(a) The President shall appoint, by and with the advice and consent of the Senate, nine judges who shall constitute a court of record to be known as the United States Court of International Trade. Not more than five of such judges shall be from the same political party. The court is a court established under article III of the Constitution of the United States.

(b) The offices of the Court of International Trade shall be located in New York, New York.

History of 28 U.S.C. §251: June 25, 1948, ch. 646, 62 Stat. 899; July 14, 1956, ch. 589, §1, 70 Stat. 532; Oct. 10, 1980, P.L. 96-417, §101, 94 Stat. 1727; Oct. 19, 1996, P.L. 104-317, §501(b)(1), 110 Stat. 3856.

§252. TENURE & SALARIES OF JUDGES

Judges of the Court of International Trade shall hold office during good behavior. Each shall receive a salary at an annual

rate determined under section 225 of the Federal Salary Act of 1967 (2 U.S.C. 351-361), as adjusted by section 461 of this title.

History of 28 U.S.C. §252: June 25, 1948, ch. 646, 62 Stat. 899; Mar. 2, 1955, ch. 9, §1(f), 69 Stat. 10; Aug. 14, 1964, P.L. 88-426, §403(f), 78 Stat. 434; Aug. 9, 1975, P.L. 94-82, §205(b)(6), 89 Stat. 423; Oct. 10, 1980, P.L. 96-417, §502, 94 Stat. 1742.

§253. DUTIES OF CHIEF JUDGE

(a) The chief judge of the Court of International Trade, with the approval of the court, shall supervise the fiscal affairs and clerical force of the court;[1]

(b) The chief judge shall promulgate dockets.

(c) The chief judge, under rules of the court, may designate any judge or judges of the court to try any case and, when the circumstances so warrant, reassign the case to another judge or judges.

(d), (e) [Repealed Oct. 19, 1996, P.L. 104-317, §501(b)(2)(B), 110 Stat. 3856.]

1. **Editor's note:** So in original. The semicolon probably should be a period.

History of 28 U.S.C. §253: June 25, 1948, ch. 646, 62 Stat. 900; Sept. 9, 1959, P.L. 86-243, §3, 73 Stat. 474; June 2, 1970, P.L. 91-271, §105, 84 Stat. 276; Oct. 10, 1980, P.L. 96-417, §501(3), 94 Stat. 1742; Oct. 19, 1996, P.L. 104-317, §501(b)(2), 110 Stat. 3856.

§254. SINGLE-JUDGE TRIALS

Except as otherwise provided in section 255 of this title, the judicial power of the Court of International Trade with respect to any action, suit or proceeding shall be exercised by a single judge, who may preside alone and hold a regular or special session of court at the same time other sessions are held by other judges.

History of 28 U.S.C. §254: June 25, 1948, ch. 646, 62 Stat. 900; May 24, 1949, ch. 139, §66, 63 Stat. 99; June 2, 1970, P.L. 91-271, §106, 84 Stat. 277; Oct. 10, 1980, P.L. 96-417, §501(4), 94 Stat. 1742.

§255. THREE-JUDGE TRIALS

(a) Upon application of any party to a civil action, or upon his own initiative, the chief judge of the Court of International Trade shall designate any three judges of the court to hear and determine any civil action which the chief judge finds: (1) raises an issue of the constitutionality of an Act of Congress, a proclamation of the President or an Executive order; or (2) has broad or significant implications in the administration or interpretation of the customs laws.

(b) A majority of the three judges designated may hear and determine the civil action and all questions pending therein.

History of 28 U.S.C. §255: June 2, 1970, P.L. 91-271, §108, 84 Stat. 277; Oct. 10, 1980, P.L. 96-417, §501(5), 94 Stat. 1742.

§256. TRIALS AT PORTS OTHER THAN NEW YORK

(a) The chief judge may designate any judge or judges of the court to proceed, together with necessary assistants, to any port or to any place within the jurisdiction of the United States to preside at a trial or hearing at the port or place.

(b) Upon application of a party or upon his own initiative, and upon a showing that the interests of economy, efficiency, and justice will be served, the chief judge may issue an order authorizing a judge of the court to preside in an evidentiary hearing in a foreign country whose laws do not prohibit such a hearing: Provided, however, That an interlocutory appeal may be taken from such an order pursuant to the provisions of section 1292(d)(1) of this title, and the United States Court of Appeals for the Federal Circuit may, in its discretion, consider the appeal.

History of 28 U.S.C. §256: June 2, 1970, P.L. 91-271, §109, 84 Stat. 277; Apr. 2, 1982, P.L. 97-164, §107, 96 Stat. 28.

§257. PUBLICATION OF DECISIONS

All decisions of the Court of International Trade shall be preserved and open to inspection. The court shall forward copies of each decision to the Secretary of the Treasury or his designee and to the appropriate customs officer for the district in which the case arose. The Secretary shall publish weekly such decisions as he or the court may designate and abstracts of all other decisions.

History of 28 U.S.C. §257: June 25, 1948, ch. 646, 62 Stat. 900, §255. Renumbered as §257 and amended June 2, 1970, P.L. 91-271, §107, 84 Stat. 277. Oct. 10, 1980, P.L. 96-417, §501(6), 94 Stat. 1742.

§258. CHIEF JUDGES; PRECEDENCE OF JUDGES

(a)(1) The chief judge of the Court of International Trade shall be the judge of the court in regular active service who is senior in commission of those judges who—

(A) are 64 years of age or under;

(B) have served for 1 year or more as a judge of the court; and

(C) have not served previously as chief judge.

(2)(A) In any case in which no judge of the court meets the qualifications under paragraph (1), the youngest judge in regular active service who is 65 years of age or over and who has served as a judge of the court for 1 year or more shall act as the chief judge.

(B) In any case under subparagraph (A) in which there is no judge of the court in regular active service who has served as a judge of the court for 1 year or more, the judge of the court in regular active service who is senior in commission and who has not served previously as chief judge shall act as the chief judge.

(3)(A) Except as provided under subparagraph (C), the chief judge serving under paragraph (1) shall serve for a term of 7 years and shall serve after expiration of such term until another judge is eligible under paragraph (1) to serve as chief judge.

(B) Except as provided under subparagraph (C), a judge of the court acting as chief judge under subparagraph (A) or (B) of paragraph (2) shall serve until a judge meets the qualifications under paragraph (1).

(C) No judge of the court may serve or act as chief judge of the court after attaining the age of 70 years unless no other judge is qualified to serve as chief judge under paragraph (1) or is qualified to act as chief judge under paragraph (2).

(b) The chief judge shall have precedence and preside at any session of the court which such judge attends. Other judges of the court shall have precedence and preside according to the seniority of their commissions. Judges whose commissions bear the same date shall have precedence according to seniority in age.

(c) If the chief judge desires to be relieved of the duties as chief judge while retaining active status as a judge of the court, the chief judge may so certify to the Chief Justice of the United States, and thereafter the chief judge of the court shall be such other judge of the court who is qualified to serve or act as chief judge under subsection (a).

(d) If a chief judge is temporarily unable to perform the duties as such, such duties shall be performed by the judge of the court in active service, able and qualified to act, who is next in precedence.

History of 28 U.S.C. §258: Oct. 19, 1996, P.L. 104-317, §501(a), 110 Stat. 3855.

CHAPTER 13. ASSIGNMENT OF JUDGES TO OTHER COURTS

§291. CIRCUIT JUDGES

(a) The Chief Justice of the United States may, in the public interest, designate and assign temporarily any circuit judge to act as circuit judge in another circuit upon request by the chief judge or circuit justice of such circuit.

(b) The chief judge of a circuit or the circuit justice may, in the public interest, designate and assign temporarily any circuit judge within the circuit, including a judge designated and assigned to temporary duty therein, to hold a district court in any district within the circuit.

History of 28 U.S.C. §291: June 25, 1948, ch. 646, 62 Stat. 900; July 28, 1953, ch. 253, §2, 67 Stat. 226; Sept. 3, 1954, ch. 1263, §39(b), 68 Stat. 1240; July 9, 1956, ch. 517, §1(a), 70 Stat. 497; Aug. 25, 1958, P.L. 85-755, §2, 72 Stat. 848; Nov. 6, 1978, P.L. 95-598, §202, 92 Stat. 2660; Apr. 2, 1982, P.L. 97-164, §108, 96 Stat. 28; Oct. 29, 1992, P.L. 102-572, §104, 106 Stat. 4507.

§292. DISTRICT JUDGES

(a) The chief judge of a circuit may designate and assign one or more district judges within the circuit to sit upon the court of appeals or a division thereof whenever the business of that court so requires. Such designations or assignments shall be in conformity with the rules or orders of the court of appeals of the circuit.

(b) The chief judge of a circuit may, in the public interest, designate and assign temporarily any district judge of the circuit to hold a district court in any district within the circuit.

(c) The chief judge of the United States Court of Appeals for the District of Columbia Circuit may, upon presentation of a certificate of necessity by the chief judge of the Superior Court of the District of Columbia pursuant to section 11-908(c) of the District of Columbia Code, designate and assign temporarily any district judge of the circuit to serve as a judge of such Superior Court, if such assignment (1) is approved by the Attorney General of the United States following a determination by him to the effect that such assignment is necessary to meet the ends of justice, and (2) is approved by the chief judge of the United States District Court for the District of Columbia.

(d) The Chief Justice of the United States may designate and assign temporarily a district judge of one circuit for service in another circuit, either in a district court or court of appeals, upon presentation of a certificate of necessity by the chief judge or circuit justice of the circuit wherein the need arises.

(e) The Chief Justice of the United States may designate and assign temporarily any district judge to serve as a judge of the Court of International Trade upon presentation to him of a certificate of necessity by the chief judge of the court.

History of 28 U.S.C. §292: June 25, 1948, ch. 646, 62 Stat. 901; July 28, 1953, ch. 253, §3, 67 Stat. 226; Sept. 3, 1954, ch. 1263, §39(c), 68 Stat. 1240; July 9, 1956, ch. 517, §1(b), 70 Stat. 497; July 14, 1956, ch. 589, §2, 70 Stat. 532; Aug. 25, 1958, P.L. 85-755, §3, 72 Stat. 848; July 29, 1970, P.L. 91-358, §172(e), 84 Stat. 591; Nov. 6, 1978, P.L. 95-598, §§203, 204, 92 Stat. 2660; Oct. 10, 1980, P.L. 96-417, §501(7), 94 Stat. 1742; Apr. 2, 1982, P.L. 97-164, §109, 96 Stat. 28.

§293. JUDGES OF THE COURT OF INTERNATIONAL TRADE

(a)[1] The Chief Justice of the United States may designate and assign temporarily any judge of the Court of International Trade to perform judicial duties in any circuit, either in a court of appeals or district court, upon presentation of a certificate of necessity by the chief judge or circuit justice of the circuit in which the need arises.

1. **Editor's note:** No subsection (b) has been enacted.

History of 28 U.S.C. §293: June 25, 1948, ch. 646, 62 Stat. 901; July 14, 1956, ch. 589, §3(a), 70 Stat. 532; Aug. 25, 1958, P.L. 85-755, §4, 72 Stat. 848; Nov. 6, 1978, P.L. 95-598, §205, 92 Stat. 2660; Oct. 10, 1980, P.L. 96-417, §§102, 501(8), 94 Stat. 1727, 1742; Apr. 2, 1982, P.L. 97-164, §110(a), (b), 96 Stat. 29.

§294. ASSIGNMENT OF RETIRED JUSTICES OR JUDGES TO ACTIVE DUTY

(a) Any retired Chief Justice of the United States or Associate Justice of the Supreme Court may be designated and assigned by the Chief Justice of the United States to perform such judicial duties in any circuit, including those of a circuit justice, as he is willing to undertake.

(b) Any judge of the United States who has retired from regular active service under section 371(b) or 372(a) of this title shall be known and designated as a senior judge and may continue to perform such judicial duties as he is willing and able to undertake, when designated and assigned as provided in subsections (c) and (d).

(c) Any retired circuit or district judge may be designated and assigned by the chief judge or judicial council of his circuit to perform such judicial duties within the circuit as he is willing and able to undertake. Any other retired judge of the United States may be designated and assigned by the chief judge of his court to perform such judicial duties in such court as he is willing and able to undertake.

(d) The Chief Justice of the United States shall maintain a roster of retired judges of the United States who are

willing and able to undertake special judicial duties from time to time outside their own circuit, in the case of a retired circuit or district judge, or in a court other than their own, in the case of other retired judges, which roster shall be known as the roster of senior judges. Any such retired judge of the United States may be designated and assigned by the Chief Justice to perform such judicial duties as he is willing and able to undertake in a court outside his own circuit, in the case of a retired circuit or district judge, or in a court other than his own, in the case of any other retired judge of the United States. Such designation and assignment to a court of appeals or district court shall be made upon the presentation of a certificate of necessity by the chief judge or circuit justice of the circuit wherein the need arises and to any other court of the United States upon the presentation of a certificate of necessity by the chief judge of such court. No such designation or assignment shall be made to the Supreme Court.

(e) No retired Justice or judge shall perform judicial duties except when designated and assigned.

History of 28 U.S.C. §294: June 25, 1948, ch. 646, 62 Stat. 901; July 9, 1956, ch. 517, §1(c), 70 Stat. 497; Aug. 29, 1957, P.L. 85-219, 71 Stat. 495; Aug. 25, 1958, P.L. 85-755, §5, 72 Stat. 849; Nov. 6, 1978, P.L. 95-598, §206, 92 Stat. 2660.

§295. CONDITIONS UPON DESIGNATION & ASSIGNMENT

No designation and assignment of a circuit or district judge in active service shall be made without the consent of the chief judge or judicial council of the circuit from which the judge is to be designated and assigned. No designation and assignment of a judge of any other court of the United States in active service shall be made without the consent of the chief judge of such court.

All designations and assignments of justices and judges shall be filed with the clerks and entered on the minutes of the courts from and to which made.

The Chief Justice of the United States, a circuit justice or a chief judge of a circuit may make new designation and assignments in accordance with the provisions of this chapter and may revoke those previously made by him.

History of 28 U.S.C. §295: June 25, 1948, ch. 646, 62 Stat. 901; Sept. 3, 1954, ch. 1263, §39(d), 68 Stat. 1240; July 14, 1956, ch. 589, §3(b), 70 Stat. 532; Aug. 25, 1958, P.L. 85-755, §6, 72 Stat. 850; Nov. 6, 1978, P.L. 95-598, §207, 92 Stat. 2660.

§296. POWERS UPON DESIGNATION & ASSIGNMENT

A justice or judge shall discharge, during the period of his designation and assignment, all judicial duties for which he is designated and assigned. He may be required to perform any duty which might be required of a judge of the court or district or circuit to which he is designated and assigned.

Such justice or judge shall have all the powers of a judge of the court, circuit or district to which he is designated and assigned, except the power to appoint any person to a statutory position or to designate permanently a depository of funds or a newspaper for publication of legal notices. However, a district judge who has retired from regular active service under section 371(b) of this title, when designated and assigned to the court to which such judge was appointed, having performed in the preceding calendar year an amount of work equal to or greater than the amount of work an average judge in active service on that court would perform in 6 months, and having elected to exercise such powers, shall have the powers of a judge of that court to participate in appointment of court officers and magistrate judges, rulemaking, governance, and administrative matters.

A justice or judge who has sat by designation and assignment in another district or circuit may, notwithstanding his absence from such district or circuit or the expiration of the period of his designation and assignment, decide or join in the decision and final disposition of all matters submitted to him during such period and in the consideration and disposition of applications for rehearing or further proceedings in such matters.

History of 28 U.S.C. §296: June 25, 1948, ch. 646, 62 Stat. 901; Jan. 7, 2008, P.L. 110-177, §503, 121 Stat. 2542.

A §297. ASSIGNMENT OF JUDGES TO COURTS OF THE FREELY ASSOCIATED COMPACT STATES

(a) The Chief Justice or the chief judge of the United States Court of Appeals for the Ninth Circuit may assign any circuit, district, magistrate, or territorial judge of a court of the Ninth Circuit, with the consent of the judge so assigned, to serve temporarily as a judge of any duly constituted court of the freely associated compact states whenever an official duly authorized by the laws of the respective compact state requests such assignment and such assignment is necessary for the proper dispatch of the business of the respective court.

(b) The Congress consents to the acceptance and retention by any judge so authorized of reimbursement from the countries referred to in subsection (a) of all necessary travel expenses, including transportation, and of subsistence, or of a reasonable per diem allowance in lieu of subsistence. The judge shall report to the Administrative Office of the United States Courts any amount received pursuant to this subsection.

History of 28 U.S.C. §297: Nov. 19, 1988, P.L. 100-702, §1022(1), 102 Stat. 4672; July 26, 2012, P.L. 112-149, §3, 126 Stat. 1145.

CHAPTER 15. CONFERENCES & COUNCILS OF JUDGES

§331. JUDICIAL CONFERENCE OF THE UNITED STATES

The Chief Justice of the United States shall summon annually the chief judge of each judicial circuit, the chief judge of the Court of International Trade, and a district judge from each judicial circuit to a conference at such time and place in the United States as he may designate. He shall preside at such conference which shall be known as the Judicial Conference of the United States. Special sessions of the Conference may be called by the Chief Justice at such times and places as he may designate.

The district judge to be summoned from each judicial circuit shall be chosen by the circuit and district judges of the circuit and shall serve as a member of the Judicial Conference of the United States for a term of not less than 3 successive years nor more than 5 successive years, as established by majority vote of all circuit and district judges of the circuit. A district judge serving as a member of the Judicial Conference may be either a judge in regular active service or a judge retired from regular active service under section 371(b) of this title.

If the chief judge of any circuit, the chief judge of the Court of International Trade, or the district judge chosen by the judges of the circuit is unable to attend, the Chief Justice may summon any other circuit or district judge from such circuit or any other judge of the Court of International Trade, as the case may be. Every judge summoned shall attend and, unless excused by the Chief Justice, shall remain throughout the sessions of the conference and advise as to the needs of his circuit or court and as to any matters in respect of which the administration of justice in the courts of the United States may be improved.

The Conference shall make a comprehensive survey of the condition of business in the courts of the United States and prepare plans for assignment of judges to or from circuits or districts where necessary. It shall also submit suggestions and recommendations to the various courts to promote uniformity of management procedures and the expeditious conduct of court business. The Conference is authorized to exercise the authority provided in chapter 16 of this title as the Conference, or through a standing committee. If the Conference elects to establish a standing committee, it shall be appointed by the Chief Justice and all petitions for review shall be reviewed by that committee. The Conference or the standing committee may hold hearings, take sworn testimony, issue subpoenas and subpoenas duces tecum, and make necessary and appropriate orders in the exercise of its authority. Subpoenas and subpoenas duces tecum shall be issued by the clerk of the Supreme Court or by the clerk of any court of appeals, at the direction of the Chief Justice or his designee and under the seal of the court, and shall be served in the manner provided in rule 45(c) of the Federal Rules of Civil Procedure for subpoenas and subpoenas duces tecum issued on behalf of the United States or an officer or any agency thereof. The Conference may also prescribe and modify rules for the exercise of the authority provided in chapter 16 of this title. All judicial officers and employees of the United States shall promptly carry into effect all orders of the Judicial Conference or the standing committee established pursuant to this section.

The Conference shall also carry on a continuous study of the operation and effect of the general rules of practice and procedure now or hereafter in use as prescribed by the Supreme Court for the other courts of the United States pursuant to law. Such changes in and additions to those rules as the Conference may deem desirable to promote simplicity in procedure, fairness in administration, the just determination of litigation, and the elimination of unjustifiable expense and delay shall be recommended by the Conference from time to time to the Supreme Court for its consideration and adoption, modification or rejection, in accordance with law.

The Judicial Conference shall review rules prescribed under section 2071 of this title by the courts, other than the Supreme Court and the district courts, for consistency with Federal law. The Judicial Conference may modify or abrogate any such rule so reviewed found inconsistent in the course of such a review.

The Attorney General shall, upon request of the Chief Justice, report to such Conference on matters relating to the business of the several courts of the United States, with particular reference to cases to which the United States is a party.

The Chief Justice shall submit to Congress an annual report of the proceedings of the Judicial Conference and its recommendations for legislation.

The Judicial Conference shall consult with the Director of United States Marshals Service on a continuing basis regarding the security requirements for the judicial branch of the United States Government, to ensure that the views of the Judicial Conference regarding the security requirements for the judicial branch of the Federal Government are taken into account when determining staffing levels, setting priorities for programs regarding judicial security, and allocating judicial security resources. In this paragraph, the term "judicial security" includes the security of buildings housing the judiciary, the personal security of judicial officers, the assessment of threats made to judicial officers, and the protection of all other judicial personnel. The United States Marshals Service retains final authority regarding security requirements for the judicial branch of the Federal Government.

History of 28 U.S.C. §331: June 25, 1948, ch. 646, 62 Stat. 902; July 9, 1956, ch. 517, §1(d), 70 Stat. 497; Aug. 28, 1957, P.L. 85-202, 71 Stat. 476; July 11, 1958, P.L. 85-513, 72 Stat. 356; Sept. 19, 1961, P.L. 87-253, §§1, 2, 75 Stat. 521; Nov. 6, 1978, P.L. 95-598, §208, 92 Stat. 2660; Oct. 15, 1980, P.L. 96-458, §4, 94 Stat. 2040; Apr. 2, 1982, P.L. 97-164, §111, 96 Stat. 29; Oct. 14, 1986, P.L. 99-466, §1, 100 Stat. 1190; Nov. 19, 1988, P.L. 100-702, §402(b), 102 Stat. 4650; Oct. 19, 1996, P.L. 104-317, §601(a), 110 Stat. 3847; Nov. 2, 2002, P.L. 107-273, §11043(b), 116 Stat. 1855; Jan. 7, 2008, P.L. 110-177, §101(b), 121 Stat. 2534.

§332. JUDICIAL COUNCILS OF CIRCUITS

(a)(1) The chief judge of each judicial circuit shall call, at least twice in each year and at such places as he or she may designate, a meeting of the judicial council of the circuit, consisting of the chief judge of the circuit, who shall preside, and an equal number of circuit judges and district judges of the circuit, as such number is determined by majority vote of all such judges of the circuit in regular active service.

(2) Members of the council shall serve for terms established by a majority vote of all judges of the circuit in regular active service.

(3) Except for the chief judge of the circuit, either judges in regular active service or judges retired from regular active

service under section 371(b) of this title may serve as members of the council. Service as a member of a judicial council by a judge retired from regular active service under section 371(b) may not be considered for meeting the requirements of section 371(f)(1) (A), (B), or (C).

(4) No more than one district judge from any one district shall serve simultaneously on the council, unless at least one district judge from each district within the circuit is already serving as a member of the council.

(5) In the event of the death, resignation, retirement under section 371(a) or 372(a) of this title, or disability of a member of the council, a replacement member shall be designated to serve the remainder of the unexpired term by the chief judge of the circuit.

(6) Each member of the council shall attend each council meeting unless excused by the chief judge of the circuit.

(b) The council shall be known as the Judicial Council of the circuit.

(c) The chief judge shall submit to the council the semi-annual reports of the Director of the Administrative Office of the United States Courts. The council shall take such action thereon as may be necessary.

(d)(1) Each judicial council shall make all necessary and appropriate orders for the effective and expeditious administration of justice within its circuit. Any general order relating to practice and procedure shall be made or amended only after giving appropriate public notice and an opportunity for comment. Any such order so relating shall take effect upon the date specified by such judicial council. Copies of such orders so relating shall be furnished to the Judicial Conference and the Administrative Office of the United States Courts and be made available to the public. Each council is authorized to hold hearings, to take sworn testimony, and to issue subpoenas and subpoenas duces tecum. Subpoenas and subpoenas duces tecum shall be issued by the clerk of the court of appeals, at the direction of the chief judge of the circuit or his designee and under the seal of the court, and shall be served in the manner provided in rule 45(c) of the Federal Rules of Civil Procedure for subpoenas and subpoenas duces tecum issued on behalf of the United States or an officer or agency thereof.

(2) All judicial officers and employees of the circuit shall promptly carry into effect all orders of the judicial council. In the case of failure to comply with an order made under this subsection or a subpoena issued under chapter 16 of this title, a judicial council or a special committee appointed under section 353 of this title may institute a contempt proceeding in any district court in which the judicial officer or employee of the circuit who fails to comply with the order made under this subsection shall be ordered to show cause before the court why he or she should not be held in contempt of court.

(3) Unless an impediment to the administration of justice is involved, regular business of the courts need not be referred to the council.

(4) Each judicial council shall periodically review the rules which are prescribed under section 2071 of this title by district courts within its circuit for consistency with rules prescribed under section 2072 of this title. Each council may modify or abrogate any such rule found inconsistent in the course of such a review.

(e) The judicial council of each circuit may appoint a circuit executive. In appointing a circuit executive, the judicial council shall take into account experience in administrative and executive positions, familiarity with court procedures, and special training. The circuit executive shall exercise such administrative powers and perform such duties as may be delegated to him by the circuit council. The duties delegated to the circuit executive of each circuit may include but need not be limited to:

(1) Exercising administrative control of all nonjudicial activities of the court of appeals of the circuit in which he is appointed.

(2) Administering the personnel system of the court of appeals of the circuit.

(3) Administering the budget of the court of appeals of the circuit.

(4) Maintaining a modern accounting system.

(5) Establishing and maintaining property control records and undertaking a space management program.

(6) Conducting studies relating to the business and administration of the courts within the circuit and preparing appropriate recommendations and reports to the chief judge, the circuit council, and the Judicial Conference.

(7) Collecting, compiling, and analyzing statistical data with a view to the preparation and presentation of reports based on such data as may be directed by the chief judge, the circuit council, and the Administrative Office of the United States Courts.

(8) Representing the circuit as its liaison to the courts of the various States in which the circuit is located, the marshal's office, State and local bar associations, civic groups, news media, and other private and public groups having a reasonable interest in the administration of the circuit.

(9) Arranging and attending meetings of the judges of the circuit and of the circuit council, including preparing the agenda and serving as secretary in all such meetings.

(10) Preparing an annual report to the circuit and to the Administrative Office of the United States Courts for the preceding calendar year, including recommendations for more expeditious disposition of the business of the circuit.

All duties delegated to the circuit executive shall be subject to the general supervision of the chief judge of the circuit.

(f)(1) Each circuit executive shall be paid at a salary to be established by the Judicial Conference of the United States not to exceed the annual rate of level IV of the Executive Schedule pay rates under section 5315 of title 5.

(2) The circuit executive shall serve at the pleasure of the judicial council of the circuit.

(3) The circuit executive may appoint, with the approval of the council, necessary employees in such number as may be approved by the Director of the Administrative Office of the United States Courts.

(4) The circuit executive and his staff shall be deemed to be officers and employees of the judicial branch of the United States Government within the meaning of subchapter III of chapter 83 (relating to civil service retirement), chapter 87 (relating to Federal employees' life insurance program), and chapter 89 (relating to Federal employees' health benefits program) of title 5, United States Code.

(g) No later than January 31 of each year, each judicial council shall submit a report to the Administrative Office of the United States Courts on the number and nature of orders entered under this section during the preceding calendar year that relate to judicial misconduct or disability.

(h)(1) The United States Court of Appeals for the Federal Circuit may appoint a circuit executive, who shall serve at the pleasure of the court. In appointing a circuit executive, the court shall take into account experience in administrative and executive positions, familiarity with court procedures, and special training. The circuit executive shall exercise such administrative powers and perform such duties as may be delegated by the court. The duties delegated to the circuit executive may include the duties specified in subsection (e) of this section, insofar as such duties are applicable to the Court of Appeals for the Federal Circuit.

(2) The circuit executive shall be paid the salary for circuit executives established under subsection (f) of this section.

(3) The circuit executive may appoint, with the approval of the court, necessary employees in such number as may be approved by the Director of the Administrative Office of the United States Courts.

(4) The circuit executive and staff shall be deemed to be officers and employees of the United States within the meaning of the statutes specified in subsection (f)(4).

(5) The court may appoint either a circuit executive under this subsection or a clerk under section 711 of this title, but not both, or may appoint a combined circuit executive/clerk who shall be paid the salary of a circuit executive.

History of 28 U.S.C. §332: June 25, 1948, ch. 646, 62 Stat. 902; Nov. 13, 1963, P.L. 88-176, §3, 77 Stat. 331; Jan. 5, 1971, P.L. 91-647, 84 Stat. 1907; Nov. 6, 1978, P.L. 95-598, §209, 92 Stat. 2661; Oct. 15, 1980, P.L. 96-458, §2(a)-(d)(1), 94 Stat. 2035, 2036; Oct. 1, 1988, P.L. 100-459, §407, 102 Stat. 2213; Nov. 19, 1988, P.L. 100-702, §§403(a)(2), (b), 1018, 1020(a)(1), 102 Stat. 4651, 4670, 4671; Dec. 1, 1990, P.L. 101-650, §§323, 325(b)(1), 403, 104 Stat. 5120, 5121, 5124; Dec. 9, 1991, P.L. 102-198, §1, 105 Stat. 1623; Oct. 19, 1996, P.L. 104-317, §208, 110 Stat. 3851; Nov. 13, 2000, P.L. 106-518, §§205, 306, 114 Stat. 2414, 2418; Dec. 21, 2000, P.L. 106-553, §1(a)(2) [§306], 114 Stat. 2762A-85; Nov. 2, 2002, P.L. 107-273, §11043(b), 116 Stat. 1855.

§333. JUDICIAL CONFERENCES OF CIRCUITS

The chief judge of each circuit may summon biennially, and may summon annually, the circuit, district, magistrate, and bankruptcy judges of the circuit, in active service, to a conference at a time and place that he designates, for the purpose of considering the business of the courts and advising means of improving the administration of justice within such circuit. He may preside at such conference, which shall be known as the Judicial Conference of the circuit. The judges of the District Court of Guam, the District Court of the Virgin Islands, and the District Court of the Northern Mariana Islands may also be summoned biennially, and may be summoned annually, to the conferences of their respective circuits.

Every judge summoned may attend.

The court of appeals for each circuit shall provide by its rules for representation and active participation at such conference by members of the bar of such circuit.

History of 28 U.S.C. §333: June 25, 1948, ch. 646, 62 Stat. 903; Dec. 29, 1950, ch. 1185, 64 Stat. 1128; Oct. 31, 1951, ch. 655, §38, 65 Stat. 723; July 7, 1958, P.L. 85-508, §12(e), 72 Stat. 348; Nov. 6, 1978, P.L. 95-598, §210, 92 Stat. 2661; Dec. 1, 1990, P.L. 101-650, §320, 104 Stat. 5117; Apr. 26, 1996, P.L. 104-134, §101(a) [§305], 110 Stat. 1321-36; May 2, 1996, P.L. 104-140, §1(a), 110 Stat. 1327; Oct. 13, 2008, P.L. 110-406, §9, 122 Stat. 4293.

§334. INSTITUTES & JOINT COUNCILS ON SENTENCING

(a) In the interest of uniformity in sentencing procedures, there is hereby authorized to be established under the auspices of the Judicial Conference of the United States, institutes and joint councils on sentencing. The Attorney General and/or the chief judge of each circuit may at any time request, through the Director of the Administrative Office of the United States Courts, the Judicial Conference to convene such institutes and joint councils for the purpose of studying, discussing, and formulating the objectives, policies, standards, and criteria for sentencing those convicted of crimes and offenses in the courts of the United States. The agenda of the institutes and joint councils may include but shall not be limited to: (1) The development of standards for the content and utilization of presentence reports; (2) the establishment of factors to be used in selecting cases for special study and observation in prescribed diagnostic clinics; (3) the determination of the importance of psychiatric, emotional, sociological and physiological factors involved in crime and their bearing upon sentences; (4) the discussion of special sentencing problems in unusual cases such as treason, violation of public trust, subversion, or involving abnormal sex behavior, addiction to drugs or alcohol, and mental or physical handicaps; (5) the formulation of sentencing principles and criteria which will assist in promoting the equitable administration of the criminal laws of the United States.

(b) After the Judicial Conference has approved the time, place, participants, agenda, and other arrangements for such institutes and joint councils, the chief judge of each circuit is authorized to invite the attendance of district judges under

conditions which he thinks proper and which will not unduly delay the work of the courts.

(c) The Attorney General is authorized to select and direct the attendance at such institutes and meetings of United States attorneys and other officials of the Department of Justice and may invite the participation of other interested Federal officers. He may also invite specialists in sentencing methods, criminologists, psychiatrists, penologists, and others to participate in the proceedings.

(d) The expenses of attendance of judges shall be paid from applicable appropriations for the judiciary of the United States. The expenses connected with the preparation of the plans and agenda for the conference and for the travel and other expenses incident to the attendance of officials and other participants invited by the Attorney General shall be paid from applicable appropriations of the Department of Justice.

History of 28 U.S.C. §334: Aug. 25, 1958, P.L. 85-752, §1, 72 Stat. 845.

§335. JUDICIAL CONFERENCE OF THE COURT OF INTERNATIONAL TRADE

(a) The chief judge of the Court of International Trade is authorized to summon annually the judges of such court to a judicial conference, at a time and place that such chief judge designates, for the purpose of considering the business of such court and improvements in the administration of justice in such court.

(b) The Court of International Trade shall provide by its rules for representation and active participation at such conference by members of the bar.

History of 28 U.S.C. §335: Oct. 14, 1986, P.L. 99-466, §2(a), 100 Stat. 1190.

CHAPTER 16. COMPLAINTS AGAINST JUDGES & JUDICIAL DISCIPLINE

§351. COMPLAINTS; JUDGE DEFINED

(a) Filing of complaint by any person.—Any person alleging that a judge has engaged in conduct prejudicial to the effective and expeditious administration of the business of the courts, or alleging that such judge is unable to discharge all the duties of office by reason of mental or physical disability, may file with the clerk of the court of appeals for the circuit a written complaint containing a brief statement of the facts constituting such conduct.

(b) Identifying complaint by chief judge.—In the interests of the effective and expeditious administration of the business of the courts and on the basis of information available to the chief judge of the circuit, the chief judge may, by written order stating reasons therefor, identify a complaint for purposes of this chapter and thereby dispense with filing of a written complaint.

(c) Transmittal of complaint.—Upon receipt of a complaint filed under subsection (a), the clerk shall promptly transmit the complaint to the chief judge of the circuit, or, if the conduct complained of is that of the chief judge, to that circuit judge in regular active service next senior in date of commission (hereafter, for purposes of this chapter only, included in the term "chief judge"). The clerk shall simultaneously transmit a copy of the complaint to the judge whose conduct is the subject of the complaint. The clerk shall also transmit a copy of any complaint identified under subsection (b) to the judge whose conduct is the subject of the complaint.

(d) Definitions.—In this chapter—

(1) the term "judge" means a circuit judge, district judge, bankruptcy judge, or magistrate judge; and

(2) the term "complainant" means the person filing a complaint under subsection (a) of this section.

History of 28 U.S.C. §351: Nov. 2, 2002, P.L. 107-273, §11042(a), 116 Stat. 1848.

§352. REVIEW OF COMPLAINT BY CHIEF JUDGE

(a) Expeditious review; limited inquiry.—The chief judge shall expeditiously review any complaint received under section 351(a) or identified under section 351(b). In determining what action to take, the chief judge may conduct a limited inquiry for the purpose of determining—

(1) whether appropriate corrective action has been or can be taken without the necessity for a formal investigation; and

(2) whether the facts stated in the complaint are either plainly untrue or are incapable of being established through investigation.

For this purpose, the chief judge may request the judge whose conduct is complained of to file a written response to the complaint. Such response shall not be made available to the complainant unless authorized by the judge filing the response. The chief judge or his or her designee may also communicate orally or in writing with the complainant, the judge whose conduct is complained of, and any other person who may have knowledge of the matter, and may review any transcripts or other relevant documents. The chief judge shall not undertake to make findings of fact about any matter that is reasonably in dispute.

(b) Action by chief judge following review.—After expeditiously reviewing a complaint under subsection (a), the chief judge, by written order stating his or her reasons, may—

(1) dismiss the complaint—

(A) if the chief judge finds the complaint to be—

(i) not in conformity with section 351(a);

(ii) directly related to the merits of a decision or procedural ruling; or

(iii) frivolous, lacking sufficient evidence to raise an inference that misconduct has occurred, or containing allegations which are incapable of being established through investigation; or

(B) when a limited inquiry conducted under subsection (a) demonstrates that the allegations in the complaint lack any factual foundation or are conclusively refuted by objective evidence; or

(2) conclude the proceeding if the chief judge finds that appropriate corrective action has been taken or that action on the complaint is no longer necessary because of intervening events.

The chief judge shall transmit copies of the written order to the complainant and to the judge whose conduct is the subject of the complaint.

(c) Review of orders of chief judge.—A complainant or judge aggrieved by a final order of the chief judge under this section may petition the judicial council of the circuit for review thereof. The denial of a petition for review of the chief judge's order shall be final and conclusive and shall not be judicially reviewable on appeal or otherwise.

(d) Referral of petitions for review to panels of the judicial council.—Each judicial council may, pursuant to rules prescribed under section 358, refer a petition for review filed under subsection (c) to a panel of no fewer than 5 members of the council, at least 2 of whom shall be district judges.

History of 28 U.S.C. §352: Nov. 2, 2002, P.L. 107-273, §11042(a), 116 Stat. 1849.

§353. SPECIAL COMMITTEES

(a) Appointment.—If the chief judge does not enter an order under section 352(b), the chief judge shall promptly—

(1) appoint himself or herself and equal numbers of circuit and district judges of the circuit to a special committee to investigate the facts and allegations contained in the complaint;

(2) certify the complaint and any other documents pertaining thereto to each member of such committee; and

(3) provide written notice to the complainant and the judge whose conduct is the subject of the complaint of the action taken under this subsection.

(b) Change in status or death of judges.—A judge appointed to a special committee under subsection (a) may continue to serve on that committee after becoming a senior judge or, in the case of the chief judge of the circuit, after his or her term as chief judge terminates under subsection (a)(3) or (c) of section 45. If a judge appointed to a committee under subsection (a) dies, or retires from office under section 371(a), while serving on the committee, the chief judge of the circuit may appoint another circuit or district judge, as the case may be, to the committee.

(c) Investigation by special committee.—Each committee appointed under subsection (a) shall conduct an investigation as extensive as it considers necessary, and shall expeditiously file a comprehensive written report thereon with the judicial council of the circuit. Such report shall present both the findings of the investigation and the committee's recommendations for necessary and appropriate action by the judicial council of the circuit.

History of 28 U.S.C. §353: Nov. 2, 2002, P.L. 107-273, §11042(a), 116 Stat. 1850.

§354. ACTION BY JUDICIAL COUNCIL

(a) Actions upon receipt of report.—

(1) Actions.—The judicial council of a circuit, upon receipt of a report filed under section 353(c)—

(A) may conduct any additional investigation which it considers to be necessary;

(B) may dismiss the complaint; and

(C) if the complaint is not dismissed, shall take such action as is appropriate to assure the effective and expeditious administration of the business of the courts within the circuit.

(2) Description of possible actions if complaint not dismissed.—

(A) In general.—Action by the judicial council under paragraph (1)(C) may include—

(i) ordering that, on a temporary basis for a time certain, no further cases be assigned to the judge whose conduct is the subject of a complaint;

(ii) censuring or reprimanding such judge by means of private communication; and

(iii) censuring or reprimanding such judge by means of public announcement.

(B) For Article III judges.—If the conduct of a judge appointed to hold office during good behavior is the subject of the complaint, action by the judicial council under paragraph (1)(C) may include—

(i) certifying disability of the judge pursuant to the procedures and standards provided under section 372(b); and

(ii) requesting that the judge voluntarily retire, with the provision that the length of service requirements under section 371 of this title shall not apply.

(C) For magistrate judges.—If the conduct of a magistrate judge is the subject of the complaint, action by the judicial council under paragraph (1)(C) may include directing the chief judge of the district of the magistrate judge to take such action as the judicial council considers appropriate.

(3) Limitations on judicial council regarding removals.—

(A) Article III judges.—Under no circumstances may the judicial council order removal from office of any judge appointed to hold office during good behavior.

(B) Magistrate and bankruptcy judges.—Any removal of a magistrate judge under this subsection shall be in accordance with section 631 and any removal of a bankruptcy judge shall be in accordance with section 152.

(4) Notice of action to judge.—The judicial council shall immediately provide written notice to the complainant

and to the judge whose conduct is the subject of the complaint of the action taken under this subsection.

(b) Referral to Judicial Conference.—

(1) In general.—In addition to the authority granted under subsection (a), the judicial council may, in its discretion, refer any complaint under section 351, together with the record of any associated proceedings and its recommendations for appropriate action, to the Judicial Conference of the United States.

(2) Special circumstances.—In any case in which the judicial council determines, on the basis of a complaint and an investigation under this chapter, or on the basis of information otherwise available to the judicial council, that a judge appointed to hold office during good behavior may have engaged in conduct—

(A) which might constitute one or more grounds for impeachment under article II of the Constitution, or

(B) which, in the interest of justice, is not amenable to resolution by the judicial council,

the judicial council shall promptly certify such determination, together with any complaint and a record of any associated proceedings, to the Judicial Conference of the United States.

(3) Notice to complainant and judge.—A judicial council acting under authority of this subsection shall, unless contrary to the interests of justice, immediately submit written notice to the complainant and to the judge whose conduct is the subject of the action taken under this subsection.

History of 28 U.S.C. §354: Nov. 2, 2002, P.L. 107-273, §11042(a), 116 Stat. 1850.

§355. ACTION BY JUDICIAL CONFERENCE

(a) In general.—Upon referral or certification of any matter under section 354(b), the Judicial Conference, after consideration of the prior proceedings and such additional investigation as it considers appropriate, shall by majority vote take such action, as described in section 354(a)(1)(C) and (2), as it considers appropriate.

(b) If impeachment warranted.—

(1) In general.—If the Judicial Conference concurs in the determination of the judicial council, or makes its own determination, that consideration of impeachment may be warranted, it shall so certify and transmit the determination and the record of proceedings to the House of Representatives for whatever action the House of Representatives considers to be necessary. Upon receipt of the determination and record of proceedings in the House of Representatives, the Clerk of the House of Representatives shall make available to the public the determination and any reasons for the determination.

(2) In case of felony conviction.—If a judge has been convicted of a felony under State or Federal law and has exhausted all means of obtaining direct review of the conviction, or the time for seeking further direct review of the conviction has passed and no such review has been sought, the Judicial Conference may, by majority vote and without referral or certification under section 354(b), transmit to the House of Representatives a determination that consideration of impeachment may be warranted, together with appropriate court records, for whatever action the House of Representatives considers to be necessary.

History of 28 U.S.C. §355: Nov. 2, 2002, P.L. 107-273, §11042(a), 116 Stat. 1852.

§356. SUBPOENA POWER

(a) Judicial councils and special committees.—In conducting any investigation under this chapter, the judicial council, or a special committee appointed under section 353, shall have full subpoena powers as provided in section 332(d).

(b) Judicial Conference and standing committees.—In conducting any investigation under this chapter, the Judicial Conference, or a standing committee appointed by the Chief Justice under section 331, shall have full subpoena powers as provided in that section.

History of 28 U.S.C. §356: Nov. 2, 2002, P.L. 107-273, §11042(a), 116 Stat. 1852.

§357. REVIEW OF ORDERS & ACTIONS

(a) Review of action of judicial council.—A complainant or judge aggrieved by an action of the judicial council under section 354 may petition the Judicial Conference of the United States for review thereof.

(b) Action of Judicial Conference.—The Judicial Conference, or the standing committee established under section 331, may grant a petition filed by a complainant or judge under subsection (a).

(c) No judicial review.—Except as expressly provided in this section and section 352(c), all orders and determinations, including denials of petitions for review, shall be final and conclusive and shall not be judicially reviewable on appeal or otherwise.

History of 28 U.S.C. §357: Nov. 2, 2002, P.L. 107-273, §11042(a), 116 Stat. 1853.

§358. RULES

(a) In general.—Each judicial council and the Judicial Conference may prescribe such rules for the conduct of proceedings under this chapter, including the processing of petitions for review, as each considers to be appropriate.

(b) Required provisions.—Rules prescribed under subsection (a) shall contain provisions requiring that—

(1) adequate prior notice of any investigation be given in writing to the judge whose conduct is the subject of a complaint under this chapter;

(2) the judge whose conduct is the subject of a complaint under this chapter be afforded an opportunity to appear (in person or by counsel) at proceedings conducted by the investigating panel, to present oral and documentary evidence, to compel the attendance of witnesses or the production of documents, to cross-examine witnesses, and to present argument orally or in writing; and

(3) the complainant be afforded an opportunity to appear at proceedings conducted by the investigating panel, if the panel concludes that the complainant could offer substantial information.

(c) Procedures.—Any rule prescribed under this section shall be made or amended only after giving appropriate public notice and an opportunity for comment. Any such rule shall be a matter of public record, and any such rule promulgated by a judicial council may be modified by the Judicial Conference. No rule promulgated under this section may limit the period of time within which a person may file a complaint under this chapter.

History of 28 U.S.C. §358: Nov. 2, 2002, P.L. 107-273, §11042(a), 116 Stat. 1853.

§359. RESTRICTIONS

(a) Restriction on individuals who are subject of investigation.—No judge whose conduct is the subject of an investigation under this chapter shall serve upon a special committee appointed under section 353, upon a judicial council, upon the Judicial Conference, or upon the standing committee established under section 331, until all proceedings under this chapter relating to such investigation have been finally terminated.

(b) Amicus curiae.—No person shall be granted the right to intervene or to appear as amicus curiae in any proceeding before a judicial council or the Judicial Conference under this chapter.

History of 28 U.S.C. §359: Nov. 2, 2002, P.L. 107-273, §11042(a), 116 Stat. 1853.

§360. DISCLOSURE OF INFORMATION

(a) Confidentiality of proceedings.—Except as provided in section 355, all papers, documents, and records of proceedings related to investigations conducted under this chapter shall be confidential and shall not be disclosed by any person in any proceeding except to the extent that—

(1) the judicial council of the circuit in its discretion releases a copy of a report of a special committee under section 353(c) to the complainant whose complaint initiated the investigation by that special committee and to the judge whose conduct is the subject of the complaint;

(2) the judicial council of the circuit, the Judicial Conference of the United States, or the Senate or the House of Representatives by resolution, releases any such material which is believed necessary to an impeachment investigation or trial of a judge under article I of the Constitution; or

(3) such disclosure is authorized in writing by the judge who is the subject of the complaint and by the chief judge of the circuit, the Chief Justice, or the chairman of the standing committee established under section 331.

(b) Public availability of written orders.—Each written order to implement any action under section 354(a)(1)(C), which is issued by a judicial council, the Judicial Conference, or the standing committee established under section 331, shall be made available to the public through the appropriate clerk's office of the court of appeals for the circuit. Unless contrary to the interests of justice, each such order shall be accompanied by written reasons therefor.

History of 28 U.S.C. §360: Nov. 2, 2002, P.L. 107-273, §11042(a), 116 Stat. 1854.

§361. REIMBURSEMENT OF EXPENSES

Upon the request of a judge whose conduct is the subject of a complaint under this chapter, the judicial council may, if the complaint has been finally dismissed under section 354(a)(1)(B), recommend that the Director of the Administrative Office of the United States Courts award reimbursement, from funds appropriated to the Federal judiciary, for those reasonable expenses, including attorneys' fees, incurred by that judge during the investigation which would not have been incurred but for the requirements of this chapter.

History of 28 U.S.C. §361: Nov. 2, 2002, P.L. 107-273, §11042(a), 116 Stat. 1854.

§362. OTHER PROVISIONS & RULES NOT AFFECTED

Except as expressly provided in this chapter, nothing in this chapter shall be construed to affect any other provision of this title, the Federal Rules of Civil Procedure, the Federal Rules of Criminal Procedure, the Federal Rules of Appellate Procedure, or the Federal Rules of Evidence.

History of 28 U.S.C. §362: Nov. 2, 2002, P.L. 107-273, §11042(a), 116 Stat. 1854.

§363. COURT OF FEDERAL CLAIMS, COURT OF INTERNATIONAL TRADE, COURT OF APPEALS FOR THE FEDERAL CIRCUIT

The United States Court of Federal Claims, the Court of International Trade, and the Court of Appeals for the Federal Circuit shall each prescribe rules, consistent with the provisions of this chapter, establishing procedures for the filing of complaints with respect to the conduct of any judge of such court and for the investigation and resolution of such complaints. In investigating and taking action with respect to any such complaint, each such court shall have the powers granted to a judicial council under this chapter.

History of 28 U.S.C. §363: Nov. 2, 2002, P.L. 107-273, §11042(a), 116 Stat. 1854.

§364. EFFECT OF FELONY CONVICTION

In the case of any judge or judge of a court referred to in section 363 who is convicted of a felony under State or Federal law and has exhausted all means of obtaining direct review of the conviction, or the time for seeking further direct review of the conviction has passed and no such review has been sought, the following shall apply:

(1) The judge shall not hear or decide cases unless the judicial council of the circuit (or, in the case of a judge of a court referred to in section 363, that court) determines otherwise.

(2) Any service as such judge or judge of a court referred to in section 363, after the conviction is final and all time for filing appeals thereof has expired, shall not be included for purposes of determining years of service under section 371(c), 377, or 178 of this title or creditable service under subchapter III of chapter 83, or chapter 84, of title 5.

History of 28 U.S.C. §364: Nov. 2, 2002, P.L. 107-273, §11042(a), 116 Stat. 1855.

CHAPTER 17. RESIGNATION & RETIREMENT OF JUSTICES & JUDGES

§371. RETIREMENT ON SALARY; RETIREMENT IN SENIOR STATUS

(a) Any justice or judge of the United States appointed to hold office during good behavior may retire from the office after attaining the age and meeting the service requirements, whether continuous or otherwise, of subsection (c) and shall, during the remainder of his lifetime, receive an annuity equal to the salary he was receiving at the time he retired.

(b)(1) Any justice or judge of the United States appointed to hold office during good behavior may retain the office but retire from regular active service after attaining the age and meeting the service requirements, whether continuous or otherwise, of subsection (c) of this section and shall, during the remainder of his or her lifetime, continue to receive the salary of the office if he or she meets the requirements of subsection (e).

(2) In a case in which a justice or judge who retires under paragraph (1) does not meet the requirements of subsection (e), the justice or judge shall continue to receive the salary that he or she was receiving when he or she was last in active service or, if a certification under subsection (e) was made for such justice or judge, when such a certification was last in effect. The salary of such justice or judge shall be adjusted under section 461 of this title.

(c) The age and service requirements for retirement under this section are as follows:

Attained Age	*Years of Service*
65	15
66	14
67	13
68	12
69	11
70	10

(d) The President shall appoint, by and with the advice and consent of the Senate, a successor to a justice or judge who retires under this section.

(e)(1) In order to continue receiving the salary of the office under subsection (b), a justice must be certified in each calendar year by the Chief Justice, and a judge must be certified by the chief judge of the circuit in which the judge sits, as having met the requirements set forth in at least one of the following subparagraphs:

(A) The justice or judge must have carried in the preceding calendar year a caseload involving courtroom participation which is equal to or greater than the amount of work involving courtroom participation which an average judge in active service would perform in three months. In the instance of a justice or judge who has sat on both district courts and courts of appeals, the caseload of appellate work and trial work shall be determined separately and the results of those determinations added together for purposes of this paragraph.

(B) The justice or judge performed in the preceding calendar year substantial judicial duties not involving courtroom participation under subparagraph (A), including settlement efforts, motion decisions, writing opinions in cases that have not been orally argued, and administrative duties for the court to which the justice or judge is assigned. Any certification under this subparagraph shall include a statement describing in detail the nature and amount of work and certifying that the work done is equal to or greater than the work described in this subparagraph which an average judge in active service would perform in three months.

(C) The justice or judge has, in the preceding calendar year, performed work described in subparagraphs (A) and (B) in an amount which, when calculated in accordance with such subparagraphs, in the aggregate equals at least 3 months work.

(D) The justice or judge has, in the preceding calendar year, performed substantial administrative duties directly related to the operation of the courts, or has performed substantial duties for a Federal or State governmental entity. A certification under this subparagraph shall specify that the work done is equal to the full-time work of an employee of the judicial branch. In any year in which a justice or judge performs work described under this subparagraph for less than the full year, one-half of such work may be aggregated with work described under subparagraph (A), (B), or (C) of this paragraph for the purpose of the justice or judge satisfying the requirements of such subparagraph.

(E) The justice or judge was unable in the preceding calendar year to perform judicial or administrative work to the extent required by any of subparagraphs (A) through (D) because of a temporary or permanent disability. A certification under this subparagraph shall be made to a justice who certifies in writing his or her disability to the Chief Justice, and to a judge who certifies in writing his or her disability to the chief judge of the circuit in which the judge sits. A justice or judge who is certified under this subparagraph as having a permanent disability shall be deemed to have met the requirements of this subsection for each calendar year thereafter.

(2) Determinations of work performed under subparagraphs (A), (B), (C), and (D) of paragraph (1) shall be made pursuant to rules promulgated by the Judicial Conference of the United States. In promulgating such criteria, the Judicial Conference shall take into account existing standards promulgated by the Conference for allocation of space and staff for senior judges.

(3) If in any year a justice or judge who retires under subsection (b) does not receive a certification under this subsection (except as provided in paragraph (1)(E)), he or she may thereafter receive a certification for that year by satisfying the requirements of subparagraph (A), (B), (C), or (D) of paragraph (1) of this subsection in a subsequent year and attributing a sufficient part of the work performed in such subsequent year to the earlier year so that the work so attributed, when added to the work performed during such earlier year, satisfies the requirements for certification for that year. However, a justice or judge may not receive credit for the same work for purposes of certification for more than 1 year.

(4) In the case of any justice or judge who retires under subsection (b) during a calendar year, there shall be included in the determination under this subsection of work performed during that calendar year all work performed by that justice or judge (as described in subparagraphs (A), (B), (C), and (D) of paragraph (1)) during that calendar year before such retirement.

History of 28 U.S.C. §371: June 25, 1948, ch. 646, 62 Stat. 903; Oct. 31, 1951, ch. 655, §39, 65 Stat. 724; Feb. 10, 1954, ch. 6, §4(a), 68 Stat. 12; July 10, 1984, P.L. 98-353, §204(a), 98 Stat. 350; Nov. 19, 1988, P.L. 100-702, §1005(a), 102 Stat. 4666; Nov. 30, 1989, P.L. 101-194, §705(a), 103 Stat. 1770; Oct. 19, 1996, P.L. 104-317, §301, 110 Stat. 3851; Oct. 30, 2000, P.L. 106-398, §654(a), 114 Stat. 1654A-165; Nov. 13, 2000, P.L. 106-518, §303, 114 Stat. 2417.

§372. RETIREMENT FOR DISABILITY; SUBSTITUTE JUDGE ON FAILURE TO RETIRE

(a) Any justice or judge of the United States appointed to hold office during good behavior who becomes permanently disabled from performing his duties may retire from regular active service, and the President shall, by and with the advice and consent of the Senate, appoint a successor.

Any justice or judge of the United States desiring to retire under this section shall certify to the President his disability in writing.

Whenever an associate justice of the Supreme Court, a chief judge of a circuit or the chief judge of the Court of International Trade, desires to retire under this section, he shall furnish to the President a certificate of disability signed by the Chief Justice of the United States.

A circuit or district judge, desiring to retire under this section, shall furnish to the President a certificate of disability signed by the chief judge of his circuit.

A judge of the Court of International Trade desiring to retire under this section, shall furnish to the President a certificate of disability signed by the chief judge of his court.

Each justice or judge retiring under this section after serving ten years continuously or otherwise shall, during the remainder of his lifetime, receive the salary of the office. A justice or judge retiring under this section who has served less than ten years in all shall, during the remainder of his lifetime, receive one-half the salary of the office.

(b) Whenever any judge of the United States appointed to hold office during good behavior who is eligible to retire under this section does not do so and a certificate of his disability signed by a majority of the members of the Judicial Council of his circuit in the case of a circuit or district judge, or by the Chief Justice of the United States in the case of the Chief Judge of the Court of International Trade, or by the chief judge of his court in the case of a judge of the Court of International Trade, is presented to the President and the President finds that such judge is unable to discharge efficiently all the duties of his office by reason of permanent mental or physical disability and that the appointment of an additional judge is necessary for the efficient dispatch of business, the President may make such appointment by and with the advice and consent of the Senate. Whenever any such additional judge is appointed, the vacancy subsequently caused by the death, resignation, or retirement of the disabled judge shall not be filled. Any judge whose disability causes the appointment of an additional judge shall, for purpose of precedence, service as chief judge, or temporary performance of the duties of that office, be treated as junior in commission to the other judges of the circuit, district, or court.

History of 28 U.S.C. §372: June 25, 1948, ch. 646, 62 Stat. 903; May 24, 1949, ch. 139, §67, 63 Stat. 99; Feb. 10, 1954, ch. 6, §4(a), 68 Stat. 12; Sept. 2, 1957, P.L. 85-261, 71 Stat. 586; Oct. 10, 1980, P.L. 96-417, §501(9), 94 Stat. 1742; Oct. 15, 1980, P.L. 96-458, §3(a), (b), 94 Stat. 2036, 2040; Apr. 2, 1982, P.L. 97-164, §112, 96 Stat. 29; July 10, 1984, P.L. 98-353, §107, 98 Stat. 342; Nov. 19, 1988, P.L. 100-702, §403(c), 102 Stat. 4651; Dec. 1, 1990, P.L. 101-650, §402, 104 Stat. 5122; Oct. 29, 1992, P.L. 102-572, §902(b)(1), 106 Stat. 4516; Nov. 2, 2002, P.L. 107-273, §11043(a)(1), 116 Stat. 1855.

§373. JUDGES IN TERRITORIES & POSSESSIONS

(a) Any judge of the District Court of Guam, the District Court of the Northern Mariana Islands, or the District Court of the Virgin Islands who retires from office after attaining the age and meeting the service requirements whether continuous or otherwise, of subsection (b) shall, during the remainder of his lifetime, receive an annuity equal to the salary he is receiving at the time he retires.

(b) The age and service requirements for retirement under subsection (a) of this section are as follows:

Attained Age	*Years of Service*
65	15
66	14
67	13
68	12
69	11
70	10

(c)(1) Any judge or former judge who is receiving an annuity pursuant to this section may elect to become a senior judge of the court upon which he served before retiring.

(2) The chief judge of a judicial circuit may recall any such senior judge, with the judge's consent, to perform, for the court from which he retired, such judicial duties for such periods of time as the chief judge may specify.

(3) Any act or failure to act by a senior judge performing judicial duties pursuant to recall under paragraph (2) of this subsection shall have the same force and effect as if it were an act or failure to act of a judge on active duty; but such senior judge shall not be counted as a judge of the court on which he is serving as a recalled annuitant for purposes of the number of judgeships authorized for that court.

(4) Any senior judge performing judicial duties pursuant to recall under paragraph (2) of this subsection shall be paid, while performing such duties, the same compensation (in lieu of the annuity payable under subsection (a) of this section) and the same allowances for travel and other expenses as a judge on active duty with the court being served.

(5) Any senior judge performing judicial duties pursuant to recall under paragraph (2) of this subsection shall at all times be governed by the code of judicial conduct for United States judges approved by the Judicial Conference of the United States.

(d) Any judge who elects to become a senior judge under subsection (c) of this section and who thereafter—

(1) accepts civil office or employment under the Government of the United States (other than the performance of judicial duties pursuant to recall under subsection (c) of this section);

(2) engages in the practice of law; or

(3) materially violates the code of judicial conduct for United States judges,

shall cease to be a senior judge and to be eligible for recall pursuant to subsection (c) of this section.

(e) Any judge of the District Court of Guam, the District Court of the Northern Mariana Islands, or the District Court of the Virgin Islands who is removed by the President of the United States upon the sole ground of mental or physical disability, or who is not reappointed (as judge of such court), shall be entitled, upon attaining the age of sixty-five years or upon relinquishing office if he is then beyond the age of sixty-five years, (1) if his judicial service, continuous or otherwise, aggregates fifteen years or more, to receive during the remainder of his life an annuity equal to the salary he received when he left office, or (2) if his judicial service, continuous or otherwise, aggregated less than fifteen years but not less than ten years, to receive during the remainder of his life an annuity equal to that proportion of such salary which the aggregate number of his years of his judicial service bears to fifteen.

(f) Service at any time as a judge of the courts referred to in subsection (a) or of any other court of the United States, as defined by section 451 of this title, shall be included in the computation of aggregate years of judicial service for purposes of this section.

(g) Any retired judge who is entitled to receive an annuity under subsection (a) shall be entitled to a cost of living adjustment in the amount payable to him computed as specified in section 8340(b) of title 5, except that in no case may the annuity payable to such retired judge, as increased under this subsection, exceed 95 per centum of the salary of a United States district judge in regular active service.

History of 28 U.S.C. §373: June 25, 1948, ch. 646, 62 Stat. 904; Oct. 31, 1951, ch. 655, §40, 65 Stat. 724; Feb. 10, 1954, ch. 6, §5, 68 Stat. 13; July 7, 1958, P.L. 85-508, §12(d), 72 Stat. 348; Mar. 18, 1959, P.L. 86-3, §14(d), 73 Stat. 10; Sept. 12, 1966, P.L. 89-571, §2, 80 Stat. 764; Oct. 11, 1976, P.L. 94-470, 90 Stat. 2052; Aug. 27, 1986, P.L. 99-396, §21(a), 100 Stat. 844.

§374. RESIDENCE OF RETIRED JUDGES; OFFICIAL STATION

Retired judges of the United States are not subject to restrictions as to residence. The place where a retired judge maintains the actual abode in which he customarily lives shall be deemed to be his official station for the purposes of section 456 of this title. The place where a judge or magistrate judge recalled under section 155, 375, 636, or 797 of this title maintains the actual abode in which the judge or magistrate judge customarily lives shall be deemed to be the official station of such judge or magistrate judge for purposes of section 604(a)(7) of this title.

History of 28 U.S.C. §374: June 25, 1948, ch. 646, 62 Stat. 904; Sept. 21, 1959, P.L. 86-312, §1, 73 Stat. 587; Nov. 14, 1986, P.L. 99-651, §202(b), 100 Stat. 3648.

§375. RECALL OF CERTAIN JUDGES & MAGISTRATE JUDGES

(a)(1) A bankruptcy judge or a United States magistrate judge appointed under chapter 43 of this title, who has retired under the provisions of section 377 of this title or under the applicable provisions of title 5 upon attaining the age and years of service requirements established in section 371(c) of this title, may agree to be recalled to serve under this section for a period of five years as a bankruptcy judge or magistrate judge, as the case may be, upon certification that substantial service is expected to be performed by such retired judge or magistrate judge during such 5-year period. With the agreement of the judge or magistrate judge involved, a certification under this subsection may be renewed for successive 5-year periods.

(2) For purposes of paragraph (1) of this subsection, a certification may be made, in the case of a bankruptcy judge or a United States magistrate,[1] by the judicial council of the circuit in which the official duty station of the judge or magistrate[1] at the time of retirement was located.

(3) For purposes of this section, the term "bankruptcy judge" means a bankruptcy judge appointed under chapter 6 of this title or serving as a bankruptcy judge on March 31, 1984.

(b) A judge or magistrate judge recalled under this section may exercise all of the powers and duties of the office of judge or magistrate judge held at the time of retirement, including the ability to serve in any other judicial district to the extent applicable, but may not engage in the practice of law or engage in any other business, occupation, or employment inconsistent with the expeditious, proper, and impartial performance of duties as a judicial officer.

(c) During the 5-year period in which a certification under subsection (a) is in effect, the judge or magistrate judge involved shall receive, in addition to the annuity provided under the provisions of section 377 of this title or under the applicable provisions of title 5, an amount equal to the difference between that annuity and the current salary of the office to which the judge or magistrate judge is recalled. The annuity of a bankruptcy judge or magistrate judge who completes that 5-year period of service, whose certification is not renewed, and who retired under section 377 of this title shall be equal to the salary in effect, at the end of that 5-year period, for the office from which he or she retired.

(d) A certification under subsection (a) may be terminated in accordance with chapter 16 of this title, and such a certification shall be terminated upon the death of the recalled judge or magistrate judge involved.

(e) Except as provided in subsection (b), nothing in this section shall affect the right of judges or magistrate judges who retire under the provisions of chapter 83 or chapter 84 of title 5 to serve as reemployed annuitants in accordance with the provisions of title 5. A judge or magistrate judge to whom this section applies may be recalled under section 155, 636(h), or 797 of this title, as the case may be, other than during a 5-year period in which a certification under subsection (a) is in effect with respect to that judge or magistrate judge.

(f) For purposes of determining the years of service requirements in order to be eligible for recall under this section, any service as a bankruptcy judge or a United States magistrate judge, and any prior service as a referee in bankruptcy or a United States commissioner, may be credited.

(g) Except as provided in subsection (c), a judge or magistrate judge recalled under this section who retired under the applicable provisions of title 5 shall be considered to be a reemployed annuitant under chapter 83 or chapter 84, as the case may be, of title 5.

(h) The Judicial Conference of the United States may promulgate regulations to implement this section.

1. **Editor's note:** So in original. "Magistrate" probably should be followed by "judge."

History of 28 U.S.C. §375: Nov. 14, 1986, P.L. 99-651, §201(b)(1), 100 Stat. 3647; Nov. 15, 1988, P.L. 100-659, §4(b), 102 Stat. 3918; Dec. 1, 1990, P.L. 101-650, §325(b)(2), 104 Stat. 5121; Oct. 29, 1992, P.L. 102-572, §904(a), 106 Stat. 4517; Nov. 2, 2002, P.L. 107-273, §11043(d), 116 Stat. 1855.

§376. ANNUITIES FOR SURVIVORS OF CERTAIN JUDICIAL OFFICIALS OF THE UNITED STATES

(a) For the purposes of this section—

(1) "judicial official" means:

(A) a Justice or judge of the United States, as defined by section 451 of this title;

(B) a judge of the District Court of Guam, the District Court of the Northern Mariana Islands, or the District Court of the Virgin Islands;

(C) a Director of the Administrative Office of the United States Courts, after he or she has filed a waiver under subsection (a) of section 611 of this title;

(D) a Director of the Federal Judicial Center, after he or she has filed a waiver under subsection (a) of section 627 of this title;

(E) a Counselor to the Chief Justice of the United States, after he or she has filed a waiver in accordance with both subsection (a) of section 677 and subsection (a) of section 611 of this title;

(F) a full-time bankruptcy judge or a full-time United States magistrate judge; or

(G) a judge of the United States Court of Federal Claims;

who notifies the Director of the Administrative Office of the United States Courts in writing of his or her intention to come within the purview of this section within six months after (i) the date upon which he or she takes office, (ii) the date upon which he or she marries, (iii) January 1, 1977, (iv) October 1, 1986, (v) the date of the enactment of the Retirement and Survivors' Annuities for Bankruptcy Judges and Magistrates Act of 1988, in the case of a full-time bankruptcy judge or United States magistrate judge in active service on that date, (vi) the date of the enactment of the Federal Courts Study Committee Implementation Act of 1990, in the case of a full-time judge of the Court of Federal Claims in active service on that date, or (vii) the date of the enactment of the Federal Courts Administration Act of 1992;

(2) "retirement salary" means:

(A) in the case of a Justice or judge of the United States, as defined by section 451 of this title, salary paid (i) after retirement from regular active service under subsection (b) of section 371 or subsection (a) of section 372 of this title, or (ii) after retirement from office by resignation on salary under subsection (a) of section 371 of this title;

(B) in the case of a judge of the District Court of Guam, the District Court of the Northern Mariana Islands, or the District Court of the Virgin Islands, (i) an annuity paid under subsection (a) of section 373 of this title or (ii) compensation paid under paragraph (4) of subsection (c) of section 373 of this title;

(C) in the case of a Director of the Administrative Office of the United States Courts, an annuity paid under subsection (b) or (c) of section 611 of this title;

(D) in the case of a Director of the Federal Judicial Center, an annuity paid under subsection (b) or (c) of section 627 of this title;

(E) in the case of a Counselor to the Chief Justice of the United States, an annuity paid in accordance with both subsection (a) of section 677 and subsection (a) of section 611 of this title;

(F) in the case of a bankruptcy judge or United States magistrate judge, an annuity paid under section 377 of this title; and

(G) in the case of a judge of the United States Court of Federal Claims, an annuity paid under section 178 of this title;

(3) "widow" means the surviving wife of a "judicial official", who:

(A) has been married to him for at least one year on the day of his death; or

(B) is the mother of issue by that marriage;

(4) "widower" means the surviving husband of a "judicial official", who:

(A) has been married to her for at least one year on the day of her death; or

(B) is the father of issue by that marriage;

(5) "child" means:

(A) an unmarried child under eighteen years of age, including (i) an adopted child and (ii) a stepchild or recognized natural child who lived with the judicial official in a regular parent-child relationship;

(B) such unmarried child between eighteen and twenty-two years of age who is a student regularly pursuing a full-time course of study or training in residence in a high school, trade school, technical or vocational institute, junior college, college, university, or comparable educational institution. A child whose twenty-second birthday occurs before July 1, or after August 31, of a calendar year, and while he or she is regularly pursuing such a course of study or training, is deemed to have become twenty-two years of age on the first day of July immediately following that birthday. A child who is a student is deemed not to have ceased being a student during an interim period between school years, if that interim period lasts no longer than five consecutive months and if that child shows, to the satisfaction of the Director of the Administrative Office of the United States Courts, that he or she has a bona fide intention of continuing to pursue a course of study or training in the same or a different school during the school semester, or other period into which the school year is divided, immediately following that interim period; or

(C) such unmarried child, regardless of age, who is incapable of self-support because of a mental or physical disability incurred either (i) before age eighteen, or (ii) in the case of a child who is receiving an annuity as a full-time student under paragraph (5)(B) of this subsection, before the termination of that annuity;

(6) "former spouse" means a former spouse of a judicial official if the former spouse was married to such judicial official for at least 9 months; and

(7) "assassinated" and "assassination" mean the killing of a judicial official described in paragraph (1)(A), (B), (F), or (G) of this subsection that is motivated by the performance by that judicial official of his or her official duties.

(b)(1) Every judicial official who files a written notification of his or her intention to come within the purview of this section, in accordance with paragraph (1) of subsection (a) of this section, shall be deemed thereby to consent and agree to having deducted and withheld from his or her salary a sum equal to 2.2 percent of that salary, and a sum equal to 3.5 percent of his or her retirement salary. The deduction from any retirement salary—

(A) of a justice or judge of the United States retired from regular active service under section 371(b) or section 372(a) of this title,

(B) of a judge of the United States Court of Federal Claims retired under section 178 of this title, or

(C) of a judicial official on recall under section 155(b), 373(c)(4), 375, or 636(h) of this title,

shall be an amount equal to 2.2 percent of retirement salary.

(2) A judicial official who is not entitled to receive an immediate retirement salary upon leaving office but who is eligible to receive a deferred retirement salary on a later date shall file, within 90 days before leaving office, a written notification of his or her intention to remain within the purview of this section under such conditions and procedures as may be determined by the Director of the Administrative Office of the United States Courts. Every judicial official who files a written notification in accordance with this paragraph shall be deemed to consent to contribute, during the period before such a judicial official begins to receive his or her retirement salary, a sum equal to 3.5 percent of the deferred retirement salary which that judicial official is entitled to receive. Any judicial official who fails to file a written notification under this paragraph shall be deemed to have revoked his or her election under subsection (a) of this section.

(3) The amounts deducted and withheld from the salary of each judicial official under paragraphs (1) and (2) of this subsection shall, in accordance with such procedures as may be prescribed by the Comptroller General of the United States, be covered into the Treasury of the United States and credited to the "Judicial Survivors' Annuities Fund" established by section 3 of the Judicial Survivors' Annuities Reform Act. Such fund shall be used for the payment of annuities, refunds, and allowances as provided by this section. Payment of such salary

less such deductions (and any deductions made under section 178 or 377 of this title or under subchapter III of chapter 83, or chapter 84, of title 5) shall be a full and complete discharge and acquittance of all claims and demands whatsoever for all services rendered by such judicial official during the period covered by such payment, except the rights to those benefits to which such judicial official, or his or her survivors, shall be entitled under the provisions of this section (and under section 178 or 377 of this title or under subchapter III of chapter 83, or chapter 84, of title 5).

(c)(1) There shall also be deposited to the credit of the Judicial Survivors' Annuities Fund, in accordance with such procedures as the Comptroller General of the United States may prescribe, amounts required to reduce to zero the unfunded liability of the Judicial Survivors' Annuities Fund: Provided, That such amounts shall not exceed the equivalent of 9 percent of salary or retirement salary. Such deposits shall, subject to appropriations Acts, be taken from the fund used to pay the compensation of the judicial official, and shall immediately become an integrated part of the Judicial Survivors' Annuities Fund for any use required under this section.

(2) For purposes of paragraph (1), the term "unfunded liability" means the estimated excess, determined on an annual basis in accordance with the provisions of section 9503 of title 31, United States Code, of the present value of all benefits payable from the Judicial Survivors' Annuities Fund, over the sum of—

(A) the present value of deductions to be withheld from the future basic pay of judicial officials; plus

(B) the balance in the Fund as of the date the unfunded liability is determined.

In making any determination under this paragraph, the Comptroller General shall use the applicable information contained in the reports filed pursuant to section 9503 of title 31, United States Code, with respect to the judicial survivors' annuities plan established by this section.

(3) There are authorized to be appropriated such sums as may be necessary to carry out this subsection.

(d) Each judicial official shall deposit, with interest at 4 percent per annum to December 31, 1947, and at 3 percent per annum thereafter, compounded on December 31 of each year, to the credit of the "Judicial Survivors' Annuities Fund":

(1) a sum equal to 3.5 percent of that salary, including "retirement salary", which he or she has received for serving in any of the offices designated in paragraph (1) of subsection (a) of this section prior to the date upon which he or she filed notice of an intention to come within the purview of this section with the Director of the Administrative Office of the United States Courts; and

(2) a sum equal to 3.5 percent of the basic salary, pay, or compensation which he or she has received for serving as a Senator, Representative, Delegate, or Resident Commissioner in Congress, or for serving as an "employee", as that term is defined in subsection (1) of section 8331 of title 5, prior to assuming the responsibilities of any of the offices designated in paragraph (1) of subsection (a) of this section.

The interest otherwise required by this subsection shall not be required for any period during which a judicial official was separated from all such service and was not receiving any retirement salary.

Each such judicial official may elect to make such deposits in installments, during the continuance of his or her service in those offices designated in paragraph (1) of subsection (a) of this section, in such amounts and under such conditions as may be determined in each instance by the Director of the Administrative Office of the United States Courts: Provided, That, in each instance in which a judicial official does elect to make such deposits in installments, the Director shall require (i) that the first installment payment made shall be in an amount no smaller than that amount necessary to cover at least the last eighteen months of prior creditable civilian service, and (ii) that at least one additional installment payment shall be made every eighteen months thereafter until the total of all such deposits have been made.

Notwithstanding the failure of any such judicial official to make all such deposits or installment payments, credit shall be allowed for the service rendered, but the annuity of that judicial official's widow or widower shall be reduced by an amount equal to 10 percent of the amount of such deposits, computed as of the date of the death of such judicial official, unless such widow or widower shall elect to eliminate such service entirely from credit under subsection (k) of this section: Provided, That no deposit shall be required from any such judicial official for any honorable active duty service in the Army, Navy, Air Force, Marine Corps, or Coast Guard of the United States, or for any other creditable service rendered prior to August 1, 1920.

(e) The amounts deducted and withheld in accordance with subsection (b) of this section, and the amounts deposited in accordance with subsection (d) of this section, shall be credited to individual accounts in the name of each judicial official from whom such amounts are received, for credit to the "Judicial Survivors' Annuities Fund".

(f) The Secretary of the Treasury shall invest, from time to time, in interest bearing securities of the United States or Federal farm loan bonds, those portions of the "Judicial Survivors' Annuities Fund" which in his judgment may not be immediately required for the payment of annuities, refunds, and allowances as provided in this section. The income derived from such investments shall constitute a part of such fund for the purposes of paying annuities and carrying out the provisions of subsections (g), (h), (m), (o), (p), and (q) of this section.

(g) If any judicial official leaves office and is ineligible to receive a retirement salary or leaves office and is entitled to a deferred retirement salary but fails to make an election under subsection (b)(2) of this section, all amounts credited

to his or her account established under subsection (e), together with interest at 4 percent per annum to December 31, 1947, and at 3 percent per annum thereafter, compounded on December 31 of each year, to the date of his or her relinquishment of office, minus a sum equal to 2.2 percent of salary for service while deductions were withheld under subsection (b) or for which a deposit was made by the judicial official under subsection (d), shall be returned to that judicial official in a lump-sum payment within a reasonable period of time following the date of his or her relinquishment of office. For the purposes of this section, a "reasonable period of time" shall be presumed to be no longer than 1 year following the date upon which such judicial official relinquishes his or her office.

(h) Annuities payable under this section shall be paid only in accordance with the following provisions:

(1) In any case in which a judicial official dies while in office, while receiving retirement salary, or after filing an election and otherwise complying with the conditions under subsection (b)(2) of this section (A) after having completed at least eighteen months of creditable civilian service, as computed in accordance with subsection (k) of this section, for the last eighteen months of which the salary deductions provided by subsection (b) of this section or, in lieu thereof, the deposits required by subsection (d) of this section have actually been made, or (B) if the death of such judicial official was by assassination, before having satisfied the requirements of clause (A) if, for the period of such service, the deductions provided by subsection (b) or, in lieu thereof, the deposits required by subsection (d) have actually been made—

(i) if such judicial official is survived by a widow or widower, but not by a child, there shall be paid to such widow or widower an annuity, beginning on the day on which such judicial official died, in an amount computed as provided in subsection (*l*) of this section; or

(ii) if such judicial official is survived by a widow or widower and a child or children, there shall be paid to such widow or widower an annuity, beginning on the day on which such judicial official died, in an amount computed as provided in subsection (*l*) of this section, and there shall also be paid to or on behalf of each such child an immediate annuity equal to:

(I) 10 percent of the average annual salary determined under subsection (*l*)(1) of this section; or

(II) 20 percent of such average annual salary, divided by the number of children;

whichever is smallest; or

(iii) if such judicial official leaves no surviving widow or widower, but does leave a surviving child or children, there shall be paid to or on behalf of each such child an immediate annuity equal to:

(I) the amount of the annuity to which the judicial official's widow or widower would have been entitled under clause (i) of this paragraph, had such widow or widower survived the judicial official, divided by the number of children; or

(II) 20 percent of the average annual salary determined under subsection (*l*)(1) of this section; or

(III) 40 percent of such average annual salary amount, divided by the number of children;

whichever is smallest.

(2) An annuity payable to a widow or widower under clause (i) or (ii) of paragraph (1) of this subsection shall be terminated upon his or her death or remarriage before attaining age 55, subject to subsection (x).

(3) An annuity payable to a child under this subsection shall terminate:

(A) if such child is receiving an annuity based upon his or her status under paragraph (5)(A) of subsection (a) of this section, on the last day of the month during which he or she becomes eighteen years of age;

(B) if such child is receiving an annuity based upon his or her status under paragraph (5)(B) of subsection (a) of this section, either (i) on the first day of July immediately following his or her twenty-second birthday or (ii) on the last day of the month during which he or she ceases to be a full-time student in accordance with paragraph (5)(B) of subsection (a) of this section, whichever occurs first: Provided, That if such child is rendered incapable of self-support because of a mental or physical disability incurred while receiving that annuity, that annuity shall not terminate, but shall continue without interruption and shall be deemed to have become, as of the date of disability, an annuity based upon his or her status under clause (ii) of paragraph (5)(C) of subsection (a) of this section;

(C) if such child is receiving an annuity based upon his or her status under paragraph (5)(C) of subsection (a) of this section, on the last day of the month during which he or she ceases to be incapable of self-support because of mental or physical disability; or

(D) on the last day of the month during which such child dies or marries.

(4) An annuity payable to a child or children under paragraph (1)(ii) of this subsection shall be recomputed and paid as provided in paragraph (1)(iii) of this subsection upon the death, but not upon the remarriage, of the widow or widower who is receiving an annuity under paragraph (1)(ii) of this subsection.

(5) In any case in which the annuity of a child is terminated, the annuity of each remaining child which is based upon the service of the same judicial official shall be recomputed and paid as though the child whose annuity has been terminated had not survived that judicial official.

(6) In the case of the survivor or survivors of a judicial official to whom paragraph (1)(B) applies, there shall be deducted from the annuities otherwise payable under this sec-

tion an amount equal to the amount of salary deductions that would have been made if such deductions had been made for 18 months prior to the judicial official's death.

(i)(1) All questions of dependency and disability arising under this section shall be determined by the Director of the Administrative Office of the United States Courts, subject to review only by the Judicial Conference of the United States, and the decision of the Judicial Conference of the United States shall be final and conclusive. The Director may order or direct at any time such medical or other examinations as he deems necessary to determine the facts relative to the nature and degree of disability of any child who is an annuitant, or an applicant for an annuity, under this section, and may suspend or deny any such annuity for failure to submit to any such examination.

(2) The Director of the Administrative Office of the United States Courts shall determine whether the killing of a judicial official was an assassination, subject to review only by the Judicial Conference of the United States. The head of any Federal agency that investigates the killing of a judicial official shall provide information to the Director that would assist the Director in making such determination.

(j) In any case in which a payment under this section is to be made to a minor, or to a person mentally incompetent or under other legal disability, as determined by a court of competent jurisdiction, such payment may be made to the person who is constituted guardian or other fiduciary of such claimant by the laws of the State of residence of such claimant, or to any other person who is otherwise legally vested with the care of the claimant or of the claimant's estate, and need not be made directly to such claimant. The Director of the Administrative Office of the United States Courts may, at his or her discretion, determine whether such payment is made directly to such claimant or to such guardian, fiduciary, or other person legally vested with the care of such claimant or the claimant's estate. Where no guardian or other fiduciary of such minor or such person under legal disability has been appointed under the laws of the State of residence of such claimant, the Director of the Administrative Office of the United States Courts shall determine the person who is otherwise legally vested with the care of the claimant or of the claimant's estate.

(k) The years of service rendered by a judicial official which may be creditable in calculating the amount of an annuity for such judicial official's widow or widower under subsection (*l*) of this section shall include—

(1) those years during which such judicial official served in any of the offices designated in paragraph (1) of subsection (a) of this section, including in the case of a Justice or judge of the United States those years during which he or she continued to hold office following retirement from regular active service under section 371 or subsection (a) of section 372 of this title;

(2) those years during which such judicial official served as a Senator, Representative, Delegate, or Resident Commissioner in Congress, prior to assuming the responsibilities of any of the offices designated in paragraph (1) of subsection (a) of this section;

(3) those years during which such judicial official honorably served on active duty in the Army, Navy, Air Force, Marine Corps, or Coast Guard of the United States, prior to assuming the responsibilities of any of the offices designated in paragraph (1) of subsection (a) of this section: Provided, That those years of such military service for which credit has been allowed for the purposes of retirement or retired pay under any other provision of law shall not be included as allowable years of such service under this section;

(4) those years during which such judicial official served as an "employee", as that term is defined in subsection (1) of section 8331 of title 5, prior to assuming the responsibilities of any of the offices designated in paragraph (1) of subsection (a) of this section,[1] and

(5) those years during which such judicial official had deductions withheld from his or her retirement salary in accordance with subsection (b)(1) or (2) of this section.

For the purposes of this subsection the term "years" shall mean full years and twelfth parts thereof, excluding from the aggregate any fractional part of a month which numbers less than fifteen full days and including, as one full month, any fractional part of a month which numbers fifteen full days or more. Nothing in this subsection shall be interpreted as waiving or canceling that reduction in the annuity of a widow or widower which is required by subsection (d) of this section due to the failure of a judicial official to make those deposits required by subsection (d) of this section.

(*l*) The annuity of a widow or widower of a judicial official shall be an amount equal to the sum of—

(1) 1.5 percent of the average annual salary, including retirement salary, which such judicial official received for serving in any of the offices designated in paragraph (1) of subsection (a) of this section (i) during those three years of such service, or during those three years while receiving a retirement salary, in which his or her annual salary or retirement salary was greatest, or (ii) if such judicial official has so served less than three years, then during the total period of such service prior to his or her death, multiplied by the total of:

(A) the number of years of creditable service tabulated in accordance with paragraph (1) of subsection (k) of this section; plus

(B) the number of years of creditable service tabulated in accordance with paragraph (2) of subsection (k) of this section; plus

(C) the number of years of creditable service tabulated in accordance with paragraph (3) of subsection (k) of this section; plus

(D) the number of years during which the judicial official had deductions withheld from his or her retirement salary under subsection (b)(1) or (2) of this section; plus

(E) the number of years up to, but not exceeding, fifteen of creditable service tabulated in accordance with paragraph (4) of subsection (k) of this section,

plus:

(2) three-fourths of 1 percent of such average annual salary, multiplied by the number of years of any prior creditable service, as tabulated in accordance with subsection (k) of this section, not applied under paragraph (1) of this subsection;

except that such annuity shall not exceed an amount equal to 50 percent of such average annual salary, nor be less than an amount equal to 25 percent of such average annual salary. Any annuity determined in accordance with the provisions of this subsection shall be reduced to the extent required by subsection (d) of this section, and by the amount of any annuity payable to a former spouse under subsection (t).

(m) Each time that an increase is made under section 8340(b) of title 5 in annuities paid under subchapter III of chapter 83 of such title, each annuity payable from the Judicial Survivors' Annuities Fund shall be increased at the same time by the same percentage by which annuities are increased under that section.

(n) Each annuity authorized under this section shall accrue monthly and shall be due and payable in monthly installments on the first business day of the month following the month or other period for which the annuity shall have accrued. No annuity authorized under this section shall be assignable, either in law or in equity, except as provided in subsections (s) and (t), or subject to execution, levy, attachment, garnishment, or other legal process.

(o)(1) In any case in which a judicial official dies while in office, while receiving retirement salary, or after filing an election and otherwise complying with the conditions under subsection (b)(2) of this section, and;

(A) subject to paragraph (2) of this subsection, before having completed eighteen months of civilian service, computed in accordance with subsection (k) of this section, during which the salary deductions provided by subsection (b) of this section or the deposit required by subsection (d) of this section have actually been made; or

(B) after having completed eighteen months of civilian service, computed in accordance with subsection (k) of this section, during which all such deductions or deposits have been made, but without a survivor or survivors who are entitled to receive the annuity benefits provided by subsection (h) or (t) of this section; or

(C) the rights of all persons entitled to receive the annuity benefits provided by subsection (h) or (t) of this section terminate before a valid claim therefor has been established;

the total amount credited to the individual account of that judicial official, established under subsection (e) of this section, with interest at 4 percent per annum to December 31, 1947, and at 3 percent per annum thereafter, compounded on December 31, of each year, to the date of that judicial official's death, shall be paid, upon the establishment of a valid claim therefor, to the person or persons surviving at the date title to the payment arises, in the following order of precedence:

First, to the beneficiary or beneficiaries whom that judicial official may have designated in a writing received by the Administrative Office of the United States Courts prior to his or her death;

Second, if there be no such beneficiary, to the widow or widower of such judicial official;

Third, if none of the above, to the child or children of such judicial official and the descendants of any deceased children by representation;

Fourth, if none of the above, to the parents of such judicial official or the survivor of them;

Fifth, if none of the above, to the duly appointed executor, executrix, administrator, or administratrix of the estate of such judicial official;

Sixth, if none of the above, to such other next of kin of such judicial official, as may be determined by the Director of the Administrative Office of the United States Courts to be entitled to such payment, under the laws of the domicile of such judicial official, at the time of his or her death.

Such payment shall be a bar to recovery by any other person. For the purposes of this subsection only, a determination that an individual is a widow, widower, or child of a judicial official may be made by the Director of the Administrative Office of the United States Courts without regard to the definitions of those terms contained in paragraphs (3), (4), and (5) of subsection (a) of this section.

(2) In cases in which a judicial official dies as a result of assassination and leaves a survivor or survivors who are entitled to receive the annuity benefits provided by subsection (h) or (t) of this section, paragraph (1)(A) of this subsection shall not apply.

(p) In any case in which all the annuities which are authorized by this section and based upon the service of a given official terminate before the aggregate amount of annuity payments received by the annuitant or annuitants equals the total amount credited to the individual account of such judicial official, established under subsection (e) of this section with interest at 4 percent per annum to December 31, 1947, and at 3 percent per annum thereafter, compounded on December 31, of each year, to the date of that judicial official's death, the difference between such total amount, with such interest, and such aggregate amount shall be paid, upon establishment of a valid claim therefor, in the order of precedence prescribed in subsection (o) of this section.

(q) Any accrued annuity benefits remaining unpaid upon the termination of an annuity, other than by the death of

an annuitant, shall be paid to that annuitant. Any accrued annuity benefits remaining unpaid upon the death of an annuitant shall be paid, upon the establishment of a valid claim therefor, in the following order of precedence:

First, to the duly appointed executor, executrix, administrator, or administratrix of the estate of such annuitant;

Second, if there is no such executor, executrix, administrator, or administratrix, payments shall be made, after the expiration of sixty days from the date of death of such annuitant, to such individual or individuals as may appear, in the judgment of the Director of the Administrative Office of the United States Courts, to be legally entitled thereto, and such payment shall be a bar to recovery by any other individual.

(r) Nothing contained in this section shall be interpreted to prevent a widow or widower eligible for an annuity under this section from simultaneously receiving such an annuity while also receiving any other annuity to which such widow or widower may also be entitled under any other law without regard to this section: Provided, That service used in the computation of the annuity conferred by this section shall not also be credited in computing any such other annuity.

(s) A judicial official who has a former spouse may elect, under procedures prescribed by the Director of the Administrative Office of the United States Courts, to provide a survivor annuity for such former spouse under subsection (t). An election under this subsection shall be made at the time of retirement, or, if later, within 2 years after the date on which the marriage of the former spouse to the judicial official is dissolved. An election under this subsection—

(1) shall not be effective to the extent that it—

(A) conflicts with—

(i) any court order or decree referred to in subsection (t)(1), which was issued before the date of such election, or

(ii) any agreement referred to in such subsection which was entered into before such date; or

(B) would cause the total of survivor annuities payable under subsections (h) and (t) based on the service of the judicial official to exceed 55 percent of the average annual salary (as such term is used in subsection (*l*)) of such official; and

(2) shall not be effective, in the case of a judicial official who is then married, unless it is made with the spouse's written consent.

The Director of the Administrative Office of the United States Courts shall provide by regulation that paragraph (2) of this subsection may be waived if the judicial official establishes to the satisfaction of the Director that the spouse's whereabouts cannot be determined, or that, due to exceptional circumstances, requiring the judicial official to seek the spouse's consent would otherwise be inappropriate.

(t)(1) Subject to paragraphs (2) through (4) of this subsection, a former spouse of a deceased judicial official is entitled to a survivor annuity under this section if and to the extent expressly provided for in an election under subsection (s), or in the terms of any decree of divorce or annulment or any court order or court-approved property settlement agreement incident to such decree.

(2) The annuity payable to a former spouse under this subsection may not exceed the difference between—

(A) the maximum amount that would be payable as an annuity to a widow or widower under subsection (*l*), determined without taking into account any reduction of such annuity caused by payment of an annuity to a former spouse; and

(B) the amount of any annuity payable under this subsection to any other former spouse of the judicial official, based on an election previously made under subsection (s), or a court order previously issued.

(3) The commencement and termination of an annuity payable under this subsection shall be governed by the terms of the applicable order, decree, agreement, or election, as the case may be, except that any such annuity—

(A) shall not commence before—

(i) the day after the judicial official dies, or

(ii) the first day of the second month beginning after the date on which the Director of the Administrative Office of the United States Courts receives written notice of the order, decree, agreement, or election, as the case may be, together with such additional information or documentation as the Director may prescribe,

whichever is later, and

(B) shall terminate no later than the last day of the month before the former spouse remarries before becoming 55 years of age or dies.

(4) For purposes of this section, a modification in a decree, order, agreement, or election referred to in paragraph (1) of this subsection shall not be effective—

(A) if such modification is made after the retirement of the judicial official concerned, and

(B) to the extent that such modification involves an annuity under this subsection.

(u) In the case of a judicial official who is assassinated, an annuity shall be paid under this section notwithstanding a survivor's eligibility for or receipt of benefits under chapter 81 of title 5, except that the annuity for which a surviving spouse is eligible under this section shall be reduced to the extent that the total benefits paid under this section and chapter 81 of title 5 for any year would exceed the current salary for that year of the office of the judicial official.

(v) Subject to the terms of a decree, court order, or agreement described in subsection (t)(1), if any judicial official ceases to be married after making the election under subsection (a), he or she may revoke such election in writing by notifying the Director of the Administrative Office of the United States Courts. The judicial official shall also notify any spouse or former spouse of the application for revocation in

accordance with such requirements as the Director of the Administrative Office of the United States Courts shall by regulation prescribe. The Director may provide under such regulations that the notification requirement may be waived with respect to a spouse or former spouse if the judicial official establishes to the satisfaction of the Director that the whereabouts of such spouse or former spouse cannot be determined.

(w) The Comptroller General of the United States shall, at the end of each 3-fiscal year period, determine whether the contributions by judicial officials under subsection (b) during that 3-year period accounted for 50 percent of the costs of the Judicial Survivors' Annuities Fund and if not, then what adjustments in the contribution rates under subsection (b) should be made to achieve that 50 percent figure. The Comptroller General shall report the results of each determination under this subsection to the Congress.

(x) In the case of a widow or widower whose annuity under clause (i) or (ii) of subsection (h)(1) is terminated because of remarriage before attaining 55 years of age, the annuity shall be restored at the same rate commencing on the day the remarriage is dissolved by death, divorce, or annulment, if—

(1) the widow or widower elects to receive this annuity instead of any other survivor annuity to which such widow or widower may be entitled, under this chapter or under another retirement system for Government employees, by reason of the remarriage; and

(2) any payment made to such widow or widower under subsection (o) or (p) on termination of the annuity is returned to the Judicial Survivors' Annuities Fund.

(y) For each year of Federal judicial service completed, judicial officials who are enrolled in the Judicial Survivors' Annuities System on the date of enactment of the Judicial Survivors Protection Act of 2009 may purchase, in 3-month increments, up to an additional year of service credit, under the terms set forth in this section. In the case of judicial officials who elect to enroll in the Judicial Survivors' Annuities System during the statutory open enrollment period authorized under the Judicial Survivors Protection Act of 2009, for each year of Federal judicial service completed, such an official may purchase, in 3-month increments, up to an additional year of service credit for each year of Federal judicial service completed, under the terms set forth in section 4(a) of that Act.

1. **Editor's note:** So in original. The comma probably should be a semicolon.

History of 28 U.S.C. §376: Aug. 3, 1956, ch. 944, §2, 70 Stat. 1021; July 7, 1958, P.L. 85-508, §12(n), 72 Stat. 348; Dec. 20, 1967, P.L. 90-219, §202, 81 Stat. 668; Aug. 8, 1968, P.L. 90-466, §1(a), 82 Stat. 662; Aug. 22, 1972, P.L. 92-397, §§2, 3(c), 86 Stat. 579, 580; Oct. 19, 1976, P.L. 94-554, §2, 90 Stat. 2603; Nov. 6, 1978, P.L. 95-598, §211, 92 Stat. 2661; June 19, 1986, P.L. 99-336, §2(a), (d)(1)-(3), (e), 100 Stat. 633, 635-637; Aug. 27, 1986, P.L. 99-396, §21(b), 100 Stat. 846; Nov. 15, 1988, P.L. 100-659, §3(a), 102 Stat. 3917; Nov. 19, 1988, P.L. 100-702, §1017(a), 102 Stat. 4670; Dec. 1, 1990, P.L. 101-650, §§306(b), 322(a)-(f), (g) [(h)], 104 Stat. 5109, 5117-5120; Oct. 29, 1992, P.L. 102-572, §§201(a)-(i), 902(b), 106 Stat. 4508-4510, 4516; Oct. 19, 1996, P.L. 104-317, §§302, 308, 110 Stat. 3851, 3853; Nov. 13, 2000, P.L. 106-518, §312(b), 114 Stat. 2421; Oct. 13, 2008, P.L. 110-402, §1(b)(2), 122 Stat. 4254; Oct. 15, 2008, P.L. 110-428, §3(a), (b), 122 Stat. 4840; Aug. 12, 2009, P.L. 111-49, §6, 123 Stat. 1977.

§377. RETIREMENT OF BANKRUPTCY JUDGES & MAGISTRATE JUDGES

(a) Retirement based on years of service.—A bankruptcy judge or magistrate judge to whom this section applies and who retires from office after attaining the age of 65 years and serving at least 14 years, whether continuously or otherwise, as such bankruptcy judge or magistrate judge shall, subject to subsection (f), be entitled to receive, during the remainder of the judge's or magistrate judge's lifetime, an annuity equal to the salary being received at the time the judge or magistrate judge leaves office.

(b) Retirement upon failure of reappointment.—A bankruptcy judge or magistrate judge to whom this section applies, who is not reappointed following the expiration of the term of office of such judge or magistrate judge, and who retires upon the completion of the term shall, subject to subsection (f), be entitled to receive, upon attaining the age of 65 years and during the remainder of such bankruptcy judge's or magistrate judge's lifetime, an annuity equal to that portion of the salary being received at the time the judge or magistrate judge leaves office which the aggregate number of years of service, not to exceed 14, bears to 14, if—

(1) such judge or magistrate judge has served at least 1 full term as a bankruptcy judge or magistrate judge, and

(2) not earlier than 9 months before the date on which the term of office of such judge or magistrate judge expires, and not later than 6 months before such date, such judge or magistrate judge notified the appointing authority in writing that such judge or magistrate judge was willing to accept reappointment to the position in which such judge or magistrate judge was serving.

For purposes of this subsection, in the case of a bankruptcy judge, the written notice required by paragraph (2) shall be given to the chief judge of the circuit in which such bankruptcy judge is serving and, in the case of a magistrate judge, such notice shall be given to the chief judge of the district court in which the magistrate judge is serving.

(c) Service of at least 8 years.—A bankruptcy judge or magistrate judge to whom this section applies and who retires after serving at least 8 years, whether continuously or otherwise, as such a bankruptcy judge or magistrate judge shall, subject to subsection (f), be entitled to receive, upon attaining the age of 65 years and during the remainder of the judge's or magistrate judge's lifetime, an annuity equal to that portion of the salary being received at the time the judge or magistrate judge leaves office which the aggregate number of years of service, not to exceed 14, bears to 14. Such annuity shall be reduced by 1/6 of 1 percent for each full month such bankruptcy judge or magistrate judge was under the age of 65 at the time the judge or magistrate judge left office, except that such reduction shall not exceed 20 percent.

(d) Retirement for disability.—A bankruptcy judge or magistrate judge to whom this section applies, who has served at least 5 years, whether continuously or otherwise, as such a bankruptcy judge or magistrate judge, and who retires or is removed from office upon the sole ground of mental or physical disability shall, subject to subsection (f), be entitled to receive, during the remainder of the judge's or magistrate judge's lifetime, an annuity equal to 40 percent of the salary being received at the time of retirement or removal or, in the case of a judge or magistrate judge who has served for at least 10 years, an amount equal to that proportion of the salary being received at the time of retirement or removal which the aggregate number of years of service, not to exceed 14, bears to 14.

(e) Cost-of-living adjustments.—A bankruptcy judge or magistrate judge who is entitled to an annuity under this section is also entitled to a cost-of-living adjustment in such annuity, calculated and payable in the same manner as adjustments under section 8340(b) of title 5, except that any such annuity, as increased under this subsection, may not exceed the salary then payable for the position from which the judge or magistrate judge retired or was removed.

(f) Election; annuity in lieu of other annuities.—A bankruptcy judge or magistrate judge shall be entitled to an annuity under this section if the judge or magistrate judge elects an annuity under this section by notifying the Director of the Administrative Office of the United States Courts. A bankruptcy judge or magistrate judge who elects to receive an annuity under this section shall not be entitled to receive

(1) any annuity to which such judge or magistrate judge would otherwise have been entitled under subchapter III of chapter 83, or under chapter 84 (except for subchapters III and VII), of title 5, for service performed as such a judge or magistrate judge or otherwise;

(2) an annuity or salary in senior status or retirement under section 371 or 372 of this title;

(3) retired pay under section 7447 of the Internal Revenue Code of 1986; or

(4) retired pay under section 7296 of title 38.

(g) Calculation of service.—

(1) For purposes of calculating an annuity under this section—

(A) full-time service as a bankruptcy judge or magistrate judge to whom this section applies may be credited; and

(B) each month of service shall be credited as one-twelfth of a year, and the fractional part of any month shall not be credited.

(2)(A) In the case of an individual who is a bankruptcy judge to whom this section applies and who retires under this section or who is removed from office under subsection (d) upon the sole ground of mental or physical disability, any service of that individual as a United States magistrate judge to whom this section applies, and any service of that individual as a full-time judicial officer who performed the duties of a magistrate judge and a bankruptcy judge at the same time, shall be included for purposes of calculating years of service under subsection (a), (b), (c), or (d), as the case may be.

(B) In the case of an individual who is a magistrate judge to whom this section applies and who retires under this section or who is removed from office under subsection (d) upon the sole ground of mental or physical disability, any service of that individual as a bankruptcy judge to whom this section applies, and any service of that individual as a full-time judicial officer who performed the duties of magistrate judge and a bankruptcy judge at the same time, shall be included for purposes of calculating years of service under subsection (a), (b), (c), or (d), as the case may be.

(h) Covered positions and service.—This section applies to—

(1) any bankruptcy judge appointed under—

(A) section 152 of this title;

(B) section 34 of the Bankruptcy Act before the repeal of that Act by section 401 of the Act of November 6, 1978 (Public Law 95-598; 92 Stat. 2682); or

(C) section 404 of the Act of November 6, 1978 (Public Law 95-598; 92 Stat. 2549); and

(2) any United States magistrate judge appointed under section 631 of this title,

only with respect to service on or after October 1, 1979, as such a bankruptcy judge or magistrate judge.

(i) Payments pursuant to court order.—

(1) Payments under this section which would otherwise be made to a bankruptcy judge or magistrate judge based upon his or her service shall be paid (in whole or in part) by the Director of the Administrative Office of the United States Courts to another person if and to the extent expressly provided for in the terms of any court decree of divorce, annulment, or legal separation, or the terms of any court order or court-approved property settlement agreement incident to any court decree of divorce, annulment, or legal separation. Any payment under this paragraph to a person bars recovery by any other person.

(2) Paragraph (1) shall apply only to payments made by the Director of the Administrative Office of the United States Courts after the date of receipt by the Director of written notice of such decree, order, or agreement, and such additional information as the Director may prescribe.

(3) As used in this subsection, the term "court" means any court of any State, the District of Columbia, the Commonwealth of Puerto Rico, Guam, the Northern Mariana Islands, or the Virgin Islands, and any Indian tribal court or courts of Indian offense.

(j) Deductions, contributions, and deposits.—

(1) Deductions.—Beginning with the next pay period after the Director of the Administrative Office of the United

States Courts receives a notice under subsection (f) that a bankruptcy judge or magistrate judge has elected an annuity under this section, the Director shall deduct and withhold 1 percent of the salary of such bankruptcy judge or magistrate judge. Amounts shall be so deducted and withheld in a manner determined by the Director. Amounts deducted and withheld under this subsection shall be deposited in the Treasury of the United States to the credit of the Judicial Officers' Retirement Fund. Deductions under this subsection from the salary of a bankruptcy judge or magistrate judge shall terminate upon the retirement of the bankruptcy judge or magistrate judge or upon completing 14 years of service for which contributions under this section have been made, whether continuously or otherwise, as calculated under subsection (g), whichever occurs first.

(2) Consent to deductions; discharge of claims.—Each bankruptcy judge or magistrate judge who makes an election under subsection (f) shall be deemed to consent and agree to the deductions from salary which are made under paragraph (1). Payment of such salary less such deductions (and any deductions made under section 376 of this title) is a full and complete discharge and acquittance of all claims and demands for all services rendered by such bankruptcy judge or magistrate judge during the period covered by such payment, except the right to those benefits to which the bankruptcy judge or magistrate judge is entitled under this section (and section 376).

(k) Deposits for prior service.—Each bankruptcy judge or magistrate judge who makes an election under subsection (f) may deposit, for service performed before such election for which contributions may be made under this section, an amount equal to 1 percent of the salary received for that service. Credit for any period covered by that service may not be allowed for purposes of an annuity under this section until a deposit under this subsection has been made for that period.

(*l*) Individual retirement records.—The amounts deducted and withheld under subsection (j), and the amounts deposited under subsection (k), shall be credited to individual accounts in the name of each bankruptcy judge or magistrate judge from whom such amounts are received, for credit to the Judicial Officers' Retirement Fund.

(m) Annuities affected in certain cases.—

(1) Practicing law after retirement.—

(A) Forfeiture of annuity.—Subject to subparagraph (B), any bankruptcy judge or magistrate judge who retires under this section and who thereafter practices law shall forfeit all rights to an annuity under this section for all periods beginning on or after the first day on which he or she so practices law.

(B) Forfeiture not to apply where individual elects to freeze amount of annuity.—

(i) If a bankruptcy judge or magistrate judge makes an election to practice law after retirement under this section—

(I) subparagraph (A) shall not apply to such bankruptcy judge or magistrate judge beginning on the date such election takes effect, and

(II) the annuity payable under this section to such bankruptcy judge or magistrate judge, for periods beginning on or after the date such election takes effect, shall be equal to the annuity to which such bankruptcy judge or magistrate judge is entitled on the day before such effective date.

(ii) An election under clause (i)—

(I) may be made by a bankruptcy judge or magistrate judge eligible for retirement under this section, and

(II) shall be filed with the Director of the Administrative Office of the United States Courts.

Such an election, once it takes effect, shall be irrevocable.

(iii) Any election under this subparagraph shall take effect on the first day of the first month following the month in which the election is made.

(2) Recall not permitted.—Any bankruptcy judge or magistrate judge who retires under this section and who thereafter practices law shall not be eligible for recall under section 155(b), 375, or 636(h) of this title.

(3) Accepting other employment.—Any bankruptcy judge or magistrate judge who retires under this section and thereafter accepts compensation for civil office or employment under the United States Government (other than for the performance of functions as a bankruptcy judge or magistrate judge under section 155(b), 375, or 636(h) of this title) shall forfeit all rights to an annuity under this section for the period for which such compensation is received. For purposes of this paragraph, the term "compensation" includes retired pay or salary received in retired status.

(n) Lump-sum payments.—

(1) Eligibility.—

(A) Subject to paragraph (2), an individual who serves as a bankruptcy judge or magistrate judge and—

(i) who leaves office and is not reappointed as a bankruptcy judge or magistrate judge for at least 31 consecutive days;

(ii) who files an application with the Administrative Office of the United States Courts for payment of the lump-sum credit;

(iii) is not serving as a bankruptcy judge or magistrate judge at the time of filing of the application; and

(iv) will not become eligible to receive an annuity under this section within 31 days after filing the application;

is entitled to be paid the lump-sum credit. Payment of the lump-sum credit voids all rights to an annuity under this section based on the service on which the lump-sum credit is based, until that individual resumes office as a bankruptcy judge or magistrate judge.

(B) Lump-sum benefits authorized by subparagraphs (C), (D), and (E) of this paragraph shall be paid to the person

or persons surviving the bankruptcy judge or magistrate judge and alive on the date title to the payment arises, in the order of precedence set forth in subsection (o) of section 376 of this title, and in accordance with the last two sentences of that subsection. For purposes of the preceding sentence, the term "judicial official" as used in subsection (o) of section 376 shall be deemed to mean "bankruptcy judge or magistrate judge".

(C) If a bankruptcy judge or magistrate judge dies before receiving an annuity under this section, the lump-sum credit shall be paid.

(D) If all annuity rights under this section based on the service of a deceased bankruptcy judge or magistrate judge terminate before the total annuity paid equals the lump-sum credit, the difference shall be paid.

(E) If a bankruptcy judge or magistrate judge who is receiving an annuity under this section dies, annuity accrued and unpaid shall be paid.

(F) Annuity accrued and unpaid on the termination, except by death, of the annuity of a bankruptcy judge or magistrate judge shall be paid to that individual.

(G) Subject to paragraph (2), a bankruptcy judge or magistrate judge who forfeits rights to an annuity under subsection (m)(3) before the total annuity paid equals the lump-sum credit, shall be entitled to be paid the difference if the bankruptcy judge or magistrate judge files an application with the Administrative Office of the United States Courts for payment of that difference. A payment under this subparagraph voids all rights to an annuity on which the payment is based.

(2) Spouses and former spouses.—

(A) Payment of the lump-sum credit under paragraph (1)(A) or a payment under paragraph (1)(G)—

(i) may be made only if any current spouse and any former spouse of the bankruptcy judge or magistrate judge are notified of the bankruptcy judge's or magistrate judge's application; and

(ii) shall be subject to the terms of a court decree of divorce, annulment, or legal separation or any court or court approved property settlement agreement incident to such decree, if—

(I) the decree, order, or agreement expressly relates to any portion of the lump-sum credit or other payment involved; and

(II) payment of the lump-sum credit or other payment would extinguish entitlement of the bankruptcy judge's or magistrate judge's spouse or former spouse to any portion of an annuity under subsection (i).

(B) Notification of a spouse or former spouse under this paragraph shall be made in accordance with such requirements as the Director of the Administrative Office of the United States Courts shall by regulation prescribe. The Director may provide under such regulations that subparagraph (A)(i) may be waived with respect to a spouse or former spouse if the bankruptcy judge or magistrate judge establishes to the satisfaction of the Director that the whereabouts of such spouse or former spouse cannot be determined.

(C) The Director shall prescribe regulations under which this paragraph shall be applied in any case in which the Director receives two or more orders or decrees described in subparagraph (A).

(3) Definition.—For purposes of this subsection, the term "lump-sum credit" means the unrefunded amount consisting of—

(A) retirement deductions made under this section from the salary of a bankruptcy judge or magistrate judge;

(B) amounts deposited under subsection (k) by a bankruptcy judge or magistrate judge covering earlier service; and

(C) interest on the deductions and deposits which, for any calendar year, shall be equal to the overall average yield to the Judicial Officers' Retirement Fund during the preceding fiscal year from all obligations purchased by the Secretary of the Treasury during such fiscal year under subsection (o);

but does not include interest—

(i) if the service covered thereby aggregates 1 year or less; or

(ii) for the fractional part of a month in the total service.

(o) Judicial Officers' Retirement Fund.—

(1) Establishment.—There is established in the Treasury a fund which shall be known as the "Judicial Officers' Retirement Fund". The Fund is appropriated for the payment of annuities, refunds, and other payments under this section.

(2) Investment of fund.—The Secretary of the Treasury shall invest, in interest bearing securities of the United States, such currently available portions of the Judicial Officers' Retirement Fund as are not immediately required for payments from the Fund. The income derived from these investments constitutes a part of the Fund.

(3) Unfunded liability.—

(A) There are authorized to be appropriated to the Judicial Officers' Retirement Fund amounts required to reduce to zero the unfunded liability of the Fund.

(B) For purposes of subparagraph (A), the term "unfunded liability" means the estimated excess, determined on an annual basis in accordance with the provisions of section 9503 of title 31, of the present value of all benefits payable from the Judicial Officers' Retirement Fund over the sum of—

(i) the present value of deductions to be withheld under this section from the future basic pay of bankruptcy judges and magistrate judges; plus

(ii) the balance in the Fund as of the date the unfunded liability is determined.

In making any determination under this subparagraph, the Comptroller General shall use the applicable information

contained in the reports filed pursuant to section 9503 of title 31, with respect to the retirement annuities provided for in this section.

(C) There are authorized to be appropriated such sums as may be necessary to carry out this paragraph.

History of 28 U.S.C. §377: Nov. 15, 1988, P.L. 100-659, §2(a), 102 Stat. 3910; Dec. 1, 1990, P.L. 101-650, §325(b)(3), 104 Stat. 5121; May 7, 1991, P.L. 102-40, §402(d)(2), 105 Stat. 239.

CHAPTER 19. DISTRIBUTION OF REPORTS & DIGESTS

§411. SUPREME COURT REPORTS; PRINTING, BINDING, & DISTRIBUTION

(a) The decisions of the Supreme Court of the United States shall be printed, bound, and distributed in the preliminary prints and bound volumes of the United States Reports as soon as practicable after rendition, to be charged to the proper appropriation for the judiciary. The number and distribution of the copies shall be under the control of the Joint Committee on Printing.

(b) Reports printed prior to June 12, 1926, shall not be furnished the Secretary of the Army, the Secretary of the Navy, or the Secretary of the Air Force.

(c) The Public Printer, or other printer designated by the Supreme Court of the United States, upon request, shall furnish to the Superintendent of Documents the reports required to be distributed under the provisions of this section.

History of 28 U.S.C. §411: June 25, 1948, ch. 646, 62 Stat. 904; May 24, 1949, ch. 139, §68, 63 Stat. 99; Oct. 31, 1951, ch. 655, §41, 65 Stat. 725; July 10, 1952, ch. 632, §4, 66 Stat. 540.

§412. SALE OF SUPREME COURT REPORTS

The Public Printer, or other printer designated by the Supreme Court of the United States shall print such additional bound volumes and preliminary prints of such reports as may be required for sale to the public. Such additional copies shall be sold by the Superintendent of Documents, as provided by law.

History of 28 U.S.C. §412: June 25, 1948, ch. 646, 62 Stat. 906; July 10, 1952, ch. 632, §5, 66 Stat. 541.

§413. PUBLICATIONS; DISTRIBUTION TO COURTS

Distribution of publications to Federal courts in accordance with the provisions of this chapter shall not be made to any place where such court is held in a building not owned or controlled by the United States unless such publications are committed to the custody of an officer of the United States at such building.

The Attorney General and the Director in the procurement of law books, books of reference or periodicals may exchange or sell similar items and apply the allowance or proceeds to payment in whole or in part of the cost of the items procured.

History of 28 U.S.C. §413: June 25, 1948, ch. 646, 62 Stat. 906; May 24, 1949, ch. 139, §69, 63 Stat. 100; July 10, 1952, ch. 632, §6, 66 Stat. 541.

§414. TRANSMITTAL OF BOOKS TO SUCCESSORS

All government publications and law books furnished to justices, judges, clerks of courts, and United States attorneys of the United States and its territories and possessions, and other officers of the United States or an agency thereof shall be transmitted to their successors in office. All permanent or bound books and publications furnished under this chapter except those books furnished to the Library of Congress for international exchange shall remain the property of the United States and shall be marked plainly, "The Property of the United States."

History of 28 U.S.C. §414: June 25, 1948, ch. 646, 62 Stat. 906; Oct. 18, 1962, P.L. 87-845, §7, 76A Stat. 699.

§415. REPEALED

Repealed Apr. 2, 1982, P.L. 97-164, §113, 96 Stat. 29.

CHAPTER 21. GENERAL PROVISIONS APPLICABLE TO COURTS & JUDGES

§451. DEFINITIONS

As used in this title:

The term "court of the United States" includes the Supreme Court of the United States, courts of appeals, district courts constituted by chapter 5 of this title, including the Court of International Trade and any court created by Act of Congress the judges of which are entitled to hold office during good behavior.

The terms "district court" and "district court of the United States" mean the courts constituted by chapter 5 of this title.

The term "judge of the United States" includes judges of the courts of appeals, district courts, Court of International Trade and any court created by Act of Congress, the judges of which are entitled to hold office during good behavior.

The term "justice of the United States" includes the Chief Justice of the United States and the associate justices of the Supreme Court.

The terms "district" and "judicial district" mean the districts enumerated in Chapter 5 of this title.

The term "department" means one of the executive departments enumerated in section 1 of Title 5, unless the context shows that such term was intended to describe the executive, legislative, or judicial branches of the government.

The term "agency" includes any department, independent establishment, commission, administration, authority, board or bureau of the United States or any corporation in which the United States has a proprietary interest, unless the context shows that such term was intended to be used in a more limited sense.

History of 28 U.S.C. §451: June 25, 1948, ch. 646, 62 Stat. 907; Mar. 18, 1959, P.L. 86-3, §10, 73 Stat. 9; Sept. 12, 1966, P.L. 89-571, §3, 80 Stat. 764; Nov. 6, 1978, P.L. 95-598, §213, 92 Stat. 2661; Oct. 10, 1980, P.L. 96-417, §501(10), 94 Stat. 1742; Apr. 2, 1982, P.L. 97-164, §114, 96 Stat. 29.

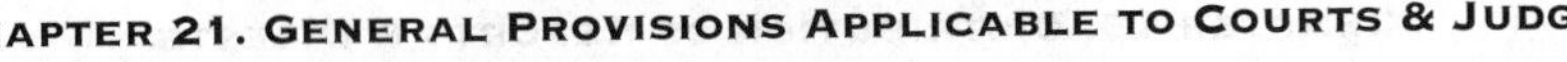

§452. COURTS ALWAYS OPEN; POWERS UNRESTRICTED BY EXPIRATION OF SESSIONS

All courts of the United States shall be deemed always open for the purpose of filing proper papers, issuing and returning process, and making motions and orders.

The continued existence or expiration of a session of a court in no way affects the power of the court to do any act or take any proceeding.

History of 28 U.S.C. §452: June 25, 1948, ch. 646, 62 Stat. 907; Oct. 16, 1963, P.L. 88-139, §2, 77 Stat. 248.

§453. OATHS OF JUSTICES & JUDGES

Each justice or judge of the United States shall take the following oath or affirmation before performing the duties of his office: "I, ______, do solemnly swear (or affirm) that I will administer justice without respect to persons, and do equal right to the poor and to the rich, and that I will faithfully and impartially discharge and perform all the duties incumbent upon me as ______ under the Constitution and laws of the United States. So help me God."

History of 28 U.S.C. §453: June 25, 1948, ch. 646, 62 Stat. 907; Dec. 1, 1990, P.L. 101-650, §404, 104 Stat. 5124.

§454. PRACTICE OF LAW BY JUSTICES & JUDGES

Any justice or judge appointed under the authority of the United States who engages in the practice of law is guilty of a high misdemeanor.

History of 28 U.S.C. §454: June 25, 1948, ch. 646, 62 Stat. 908.

§455. DISQUALIFICATION OF JUSTICE, JUDGE, OR MAGISTRATE JUDGE

(a) Any justice, judge, or magistrate judge of the United States shall disqualify himself in any proceeding in which his impartiality might reasonably be questioned.

(b) He shall also disqualify himself in the following circumstances:

(1) Where he has a personal bias or prejudice concerning a party, or personal knowledge of disputed evidentiary facts concerning the proceeding;

(2) Where in private practice he served as lawyer in the matter in controversy, or a lawyer with whom he previously practiced law served during such association as a lawyer concerning the matter, or the judge or such lawyer has been a material witness concerning it;

(3) Where he has served in governmental employment and in such capacity participated as counsel, adviser or material witness concerning the proceeding or expressed an opinion concerning the merits of the particular case in controversy;

(4) He knows that he, individually or as a fiduciary, or his spouse or minor child residing in his household, has a financial interest in the subject matter in controversy or in a party to the proceeding, or any other interest that could be substantially affected by the outcome of the proceeding;

(5) He or his spouse, or a person within the third degree of relationship to either of them, or the spouse of such a person:

(i) Is a party to the proceeding, or an officer, director, or trustee of a party;

(ii) Is acting as a lawyer in the proceeding;

(iii) Is known by the judge to have an interest that could be substantially affected by the outcome of the proceeding;

(iv) Is to the judge's knowledge likely to be a material witness in the proceeding.

(c) A judge should inform himself about his personal and fiduciary financial interests, and make a reasonable effort to inform himself about the personal financial interests of his spouse and minor children residing in his household.

(d) For the purposes of this section the following words or phrases shall have the meaning indicated:

(1) "proceeding" includes pretrial, trial, appellate review, or other stages of litigation;

(2) the degree of relationship is calculated according to the civil law system;

(3) "fiduciary" includes such relationships as executor, administrator, trustee, and guardian;

(4) "financial interest" means ownership of a legal or equitable interest, however small, or a relationship as director, adviser, or other active participant in the affairs of a party, except that:

(i) Ownership in a mutual or common investment fund that holds securities is not a "financial interest" in such securities unless the judge participates in the management of the fund;

(ii) An office in an educational, religious, charitable, fraternal, or civic organization is not a "financial interest" in securities held by the organization;

(iii) The proprietary interest of a policyholder in a mutual insurance company, of a depositor in a mutual savings association, or a similar proprietary interest, is a "financial interest" in the organization only if the outcome of the proceeding could substantially affect the value of the interest;

(iv) Ownership of government securities is a "financial interest" in the issuer only if the outcome of the proceeding could substantially affect the value of the securities.

(e) No justice, judge, or magistrate judge shall accept from the parties to the proceeding a waiver of any ground for disqualification enumerated in subsection (b). Where the ground for disqualification arises only under subsection (a), waiver may be accepted provided it is preceded by a full disclosure on the record of the basis for disqualification.

(f) Notwithstanding the preceding provisions of this section, if any justice, judge, magistrate judge, or bankruptcy judge to whom a matter has been assigned would be disqualified, after substantial judicial time has been devoted to the

matter, because of the appearance or discovery, after the matter was assigned to him or her, that he or she individually or as a fiduciary, or his or her spouse or minor child residing in his or her household, has a financial interest in a party (other than an interest that could be substantially affected by the outcome), disqualification is not required if the justice, judge, magistrate judge, bankruptcy judge, spouse or minor child, as the case may be, divests himself or herself of the interest that provides the grounds for the disqualification.

History of 28 U.S.C. §455: June 25, 1948, ch. 646, 62 Stat. 908; Dec. 5, 1974, P.L. 93-512, §1, 88 Stat. 1609; Nov. 6, 1978, P.L. 95-598, §214(a), (b), 92 Stat. 2661; Nov. 19, 1988, P.L. 100-702, §1007, 102 Stat. 4667.

See *Commentaries*, "Motion to Recuse," ch. 5-E, p. 321.

§456. TRAVELING EXPENSES OF JUSTICES & JUDGES; OFFICIAL DUTY STATIONS

(a) The Director of the Administrative Office of the United States Courts shall pay each justice or judge of the United States, and each retired justice or judge recalled or designated and assigned to active duty, while attending court or transacting official business at a place other than his official duty station for any continuous period of less than thirty calendar days (1) all necessary transportation expenses certified by the justice or judge; and (2) payments for subsistence expenses at rates or in amounts which the Director establishes, in accordance with regulations which the Director shall prescribe with the approval of the Judicial Conference of the United States and after considering the rates or amounts set by the Administrator of General Services and the President pursuant to section 5702 of title 5. The Director of the Administrative Office of the United States Courts shall also pay each justice or judge of the United States, and each retired justice or judge recalled or designated and assigned to active duty, while attending court or transacting official business under an assignment authorized under chapter 13 of this title which exceeds in duration a continuous period of thirty calendar days, all necessary transportation expenses and actual and necessary expenses of subsistence actually incurred, notwithstanding the provisions of section 5702 of title 5, in accordance with regulations which the Director shall prescribe with the approval of the Judicial Conference of the United States.

(b) The official duty station of the Chief Justice of the United States, the Justices of the Supreme Court of the United States, and the judges of the United States Court of Appeals for the District of Columbia Circuit, the United States Court of Appeals for the Federal Circuit, and the United States District Court for the District of Columbia shall be the District of Columbia.

(c) The official duty station of the judges of the United States Court of International Trade shall be New York City.

(d) The official duty station of each district judge shall be that place where a district court holds regular sessions at or near which the judge performs a substantial portion of his judicial work, which is nearest the place where he maintains his actual abode in which he customarily lives.

(e) The official duty station of a circuit judge shall be that place where a circuit or district court holds regular sessions at or near which the judge performs a substantial portion of his judicial work, or that place where the Director provides chambers to the judge where he performs a substantial portion of his judicial work, which is nearest the place where he maintains his actual abode in which he customarily lives.

(f) The official duty station of a retired judge shall be established in accordance with section 374 of this title.

(g) Each circuit or district judge whose official duty station is not fixed expressly by this section shall notify the Director of the Administrative Office of the United States Courts in writing of his actual abode and official duty station upon his appointment and from time to time thereafter as his official duty station may change.

History of 28 U.S.C. §456: June 25, 1948, ch. 646, 62 Stat. 908; Aug. 8, 1953, ch. 376, 67 Stat. 488; Aug. 7, 1959, P.L. 86-138, 73 Stat. 285; Nov. 6, 1978, P.L. 95-598, §215, 92 Stat. 2661; Oct. 10, 1980, P.L. 96-417, §501(11), 94 Stat. 1742; Apr. 2, 1982, P.L. 97-164, §115(a)(1), 96 Stat. 30; Jan. 2, 1986, P.L. 99-234, §107(d), 99 Stat. 1759.

§457. RECORDS; OBSOLETE PAPERS

The records of district courts and of courts of appeals shall be kept at one or more of the places where court is held. Such places shall be designated by the respective courts except when otherwise directed by the judicial council of the circuit.

Papers of any court established by Act of Congress which have become obsolete and are no longer necessary or useful, may be disposed of with the approval of the court concerned in the manner provided by sections 366-380 of Title 44 and in accordance with the rules of the Judicial Conference of the United States.

History of 28 U.S.C. §457: June 25, 1948, ch. 646, 62 Stat. 908; Nov. 6, 1978, P.L. 95-598, §216, 92 Stat. 2661.

§458. RELATIVE OF JUSTICE OR JUDGE INELIGIBLE TO APPOINTMENT

(a)(1) No person shall be appointed to or employed in any office or duty in any court who is related by affinity or consanguinity within the degree of first cousin to any justice or judge of such court.

(2) With respect to the appointment of a judge of a court exercising judicial power under article III of the United States Constitution (other than the Supreme Court), subsection (b) shall apply in lieu of this subsection.

(b)(1) In this subsection, the term—

(A) "same court" means—

(i) in the case of a district court, the court of a single judicial district; and

(ii) in the case of a court of appeals, the court of appeals of a single circuit; and

(B) "member"—

(i) means an active judge or a judge retired in senior status under section 371(b); and

(ii) shall not include a retired judge, except as described under clause (i).

(2) No person may be appointed to the position of judge of a court exercising judicial power under article III of the United States Constitution (other than the Supreme Court) who is related by affinity or consanguinity within the degree of first cousin to any judge who is a member of the same court.

History of 28 U.S.C. §458: June 25, 1948, ch. 646, 62 Stat. 908; Oct. 27, 1998, P.L. 105-300, §1, 112 Stat. 2836.

§459. ADMINISTRATION OF OATHS & ACKNOWLEDGMENTS

Each justice or judge of the United States may administer oaths and affirmations and take acknowledgments.

History of 28 U.S.C. §459: June 25, 1948, ch. 646, 62 Stat. 908.

§460. APPLICATION TO OTHER COURTS

(a) Sections 452 through 459 and section 462 of this chapter shall also apply to the United States Court of Federal Claims, to each court created by Act of Congress in a territory which is invested with any jurisdiction of a district court of the United States, and to the judges thereof.

(b) The official duty station of each judge referred to in subsection (a) which is not otherwise established by law shall be that place where the court holds regular sessions at or near which the judge performs a substantial portion of his judicial work, which is nearest the place where he maintains his actual abode in which he customarily lives.

History of 28 U.S.C. §460: June 25, 1948, ch. 646, 62 Stat. 908; Oct. 31, 1951, ch. 655, §43(a), 65 Stat. 725; July 7, 1958, P.L. 85-508, §12(e), 72 Stat. 348; Nov. 6, 1978, P.L. 95-598, §217(a), 92 Stat. 2661; Apr. 2, 1982, P.L. 97-164, §115(b)(1), 96 Stat. 31; Oct. 29, 1992, P.L. 102-572, §902(b)(1), 106 Stat. 4516.

§461. ADJUSTMENTS IN CERTAIN SALARIES

(a)(1) Subject to paragraph (2), effective at the beginning of the first applicable pay period commencing on or after the first day of the month in which an adjustment takes effect under section 5303 of title 5 in the rates of pay under the General Schedule (except as provided in subsection (b)), each salary rate which is subject to adjustment under this section shall be adjusted by an amount, rounded to the nearest multiple of $100 (or if midway between multiples of $100, to the next higher multiple of $100) equal to the percentage of such salary rate which corresponds to the most recent percentage change in the ECI (relative to the date described in the next sentence), as determined under section 704(a)(1) of the Ethics Reform Act of 1989. The appropriate date under this sentence is the first day of the fiscal year in which such adjustment in the rates of pay under the General Schedule takes effect.

(2) In no event shall the percentage adjustment taking effect under paragraph (1) in any calendar year (before rounding), in any salary rate, exceed the percentage adjustment taking effect in such calendar year under section 5303 of title 5 in the rates of pay under the General Schedule.

(b) Subsection (a) shall not apply to the extent it would reduce the salary of any individual whose compensation may not, under section 1 of article III of the Constitution of the United States, be diminished during such individual's continuance in office.

History of 28 U.S.C. §461: Aug. 9, 1975, P.L. 94-82, §205(a)(1), 89 Stat. 422; Nov. 30, 1989, P.L. 101-194, §704(a)(2)(A), 103 Stat. 1769; Nov. 5, 1990, P.L. 101-509, §529 [§101(b)(4)(J)], 104 Stat. 1427, 1440; Oct. 13, 1994, P.L. 103-356, §101(4), 108 Stat. 3411.

§462. COURT ACCOMMODATIONS

(a) Sessions of courts of the United States (except the Supreme Court) shall be held only at places where the Director of the Administrative Office of the United States Courts provides accommodations, or where suitable accommodations are furnished without cost to the judicial branch.

(b) The Director of the Administrative Office of the United States Courts shall provide accommodations, including chambers and courtrooms, only at places where regular sessions of court are authorized by law to be held, but only if the judicial council of the appropriate circuit has approved the accommodations as necessary.

(c) The limitations and restrictions contained in subsection (b) of this section shall not prevent the Director from furnishing chambers to circuit judges at places within the circuit other than where regular sessions of court are authorized by law to be held, when the judicial council of the circuit approves.

(d) The Director of the Administrative Office of the United States Courts shall provide permanent accommodations for the United States Court of Appeals for the Federal Circuit and for the United States Court of Federal Claims only at the District of Columbia. However, each such court may hold regular and special sessions at other places utilizing the accommodations which the Director provides to other courts.

(e) The Director of the Administrative Office of the United States Courts shall provide accommodations for probation officers, pretrial service officers, and Federal Public Defender Organizations at such places as may be approved by the judicial council of the appropriate circuit.

(f) Upon the request of the Director, the Administrator of General Services is authorized and directed to provide the accommodations the Director requests, and to close accommodations which the Director recommends for closure with the approval of the Judicial Conference of the United States.

History of 28 U.S.C. §462: Apr. 2, 1982, P.L. 97-164, §115(c)(1), 96 Stat. 31; Nov. 19, 1988, P.L. 100-702, §1015, 102 Stat. 4669; Oct. 29, 1992, P.L. 102-572, §902(b)(1), 106 Stat. 4516.

§463. EXPENSES OF LITIGATION

Whenever a Chief Justice, justice, judge, officer, or employee of any United States court is sued in his official capacity, or is otherwise required to defend acts taken or omissions made in his official capacity, and the services of an attorney for the Government are not reasonably available pursuant to chapter 31 of this title, the Director of the Administrative Of-

fice of the United States Courts may pay the costs of his defense. The Director shall prescribe regulations for such payments subject to the approval of the Judicial Conference of the United States.

History of 28 U.S.C. §463: Apr. 2, 1982, P.L. 97-164, §116(a), 96 Stat. 32.

CHAPTER 23. CIVIL JUSTICE EXPENSE & DELAY REDUCTION PLANS

§471. REQUIREMENT FOR A DISTRICT COURT CIVIL JUSTICE EXPENSE & DELAY REDUCTION PLAN

There shall be implemented by each United States district court, in accordance with this chapter, a civil justice expense and delay reduction plan. The plan may be a plan developed by such district court or a model plan developed by the Judicial Conference of the United States. The purposes of each plan are to facilitate deliberate adjudication of civil cases on the merits, monitor discovery, improve litigation management, and ensure just, speedy, and inexpensive resolutions of civil disputes.

History of 28 U.S.C. §471: Dec. 1, 1990, P.L. 101-650, §103(a), 104 Stat. 5090; Dec. 9, 1991, P.L. 102-198, §2(1), 105 Stat. 1623.

§472. DEVELOPMENT & IMPLEMENTATION OF A CIVIL JUSTICE EXPENSE & DELAY REDUCTION PLAN

(a) The civil justice expense and delay reduction plan implemented by a district court shall be developed or selected, as the case may be, after consideration of the recommendations of an advisory group appointed in accordance with section 478 of this title.

(b) The advisory group of a United States district court shall submit to the court a report, which shall be made available to the public and which shall include—

(1) an assessment of the matters referred to in subsection (c)(1);

(2) the basis for its recommendation that the district court develop a plan or select a model plan;

(3) recommended measures, rules and programs; and

(4) an explanation of the manner in which the recommended plan complies with section 473 of this title.

(c)(1) In developing its recommendations, the advisory group of a district court shall promptly complete a thorough assessment of the state of the court's civil and criminal dockets. In performing the assessment for a district court, the advisory group shall—

(A) determine the condition of the civil and criminal dockets;

(B) identify trends in case filings and in the demands being placed on the court's resources;

(C) identify the principal causes of cost and delay in civil litigation, giving consideration to such potential causes as court procedures and the ways in which litigants and their attorneys approach and conduct litigation; and

(D) examine the extent to which costs and delays could be reduced by a better assessment of the impact of new legislation on the courts.

(2) In developing its recommendations, the advisory group of a district court shall take into account the particular needs and circumstances of the district court, litigants in such court, and the litigants' attorneys.

(3) The advisory group of a district court shall ensure that its recommended actions include significant contributions to be made by the court, the litigants, and the litigants' attorneys toward reducing cost and delay and thereby facilitating access to the courts.

(d) The chief judge of the district court shall transmit a copy of the plan implemented in accordance with subsection (a) and the report prepared in accordance with subsection (b) of this section to—

(1) the Director of the Administrative Office of the United States Courts;

(2) the judicial council of the circuit in which the district court is located; and

(3) the chief judge of each of the other United States district courts located in such circuit.

History of 28 U.S.C. §472: Dec. 1, 1990, P.L. 101-650, §103(a), 104 Stat. 5090.

§473. CONTENT OF CIVIL JUSTICE EXPENSE & DELAY REDUCTION PLANS

(a) In formulating the provisions of its civil justice expense and delay reduction plan, each United States district court, in consultation with an advisory group appointed under section 478 of this title, shall consider and may include the following principles and guidelines of litigation management and cost and delay reduction:

(1) systematic, differential treatment of civil cases that tailors the level of individualized and case specific management to such criteria as case complexity, the amount of time reasonably needed to prepare the case for trial, and the judicial and other resources required and available for the preparation and disposition of the case;

(2) early and ongoing control of the pretrial process through involvement of a judicial officer in—

(A) assessing and planning the progress of a case;

(B) setting early, firm trial dates, such that the trial is scheduled to occur within eighteen months after the filing of the complaint, unless a judicial officer certifies that—

(i) the demands of the case and its complexity make such a trial date incompatible with serving the ends of justice; or

(ii) the trial cannot reasonably be held within such time because of the complexity of the case or the number or complexity of pending criminal cases;

(C) controlling the extent of discovery and the time for completion of discovery, and ensuring compliance with appropriate requested discovery in a timely fashion; and

(D) setting, at the earliest practicable time, deadlines for filing motions and a time framework for their disposition;

(3) for all cases that the court or an individual judicial officer determines are complex and any other appropriate cases, careful and deliberate monitoring through a discovery-case management conference or a series of such conferences at which the presiding judicial officer—

(A) explores the parties' receptivity to, and the propriety of, settlement or proceeding with the litigation;

(B) identifies or formulates the principal issues in contention and, in appropriate cases, provides for the staged resolution or bifurcation of issues for trial consistent with Rule 42(b) of the Federal Rules of Civil Procedure;

(C) prepares a discovery schedule and plan consistent with any presumptive time limits that a district court may set for the completion of discovery and with any procedures a district court may develop to—

(i) identify and limit the volume of discovery available to avoid unnecessary or unduly burdensome or expensive discovery; and

(ii) phase discovery into two or more stages; and

(D) sets, at the earliest practicable time, deadlines for filing motions and a time framework for their disposition;

(4) encouragement of cost-effective discovery through voluntary exchange of information among litigants and their attorneys and through the use of cooperative discovery devices;

(5) conservation of judicial resources by prohibiting the consideration of discovery motions unless accompanied by a certification that the moving party has made a reasonable and good faith effort to reach agreement with opposing counsel on the matters set forth in the motion; and

(6) authorization to refer appropriate cases to alternative dispute resolution programs that—

(A) have been designated for use in a district court; or

(B) the court may make available, including mediation, minitrial, and summary jury trial.

(b) In formulating the provisions of its civil justice expense and delay reduction plan, each United States district court, in consultation with an advisory group appointed under section 478 of this title, shall consider and may include the following litigation management and cost and delay reduction techniques:

(1) a requirement that counsel for each party to a case jointly present a discovery-case management plan for the case at the initial pretrial conference, or explain the reasons for their failure to do so;

(2) a requirement that each party be represented at each pretrial conference by an attorney who has the authority to bind that party regarding all matters previously identified by the court for discussion at the conference and all reasonably related matters;

(3) a requirement that all requests for extensions of deadlines for completion of discovery or for postponement of the trial be signed by the attorney and the party making the request;

(4) a neutral evaluation program for the presentation of the legal and factual basis of a case to a neutral court representative selected by the court at a nonbinding conference conducted early in the litigation;

(5) a requirement that, upon notice by the court, representatives of the parties with authority to bind them in settlement discussions be present or available by telephone during any settlement conference; and

(6) such other features as the district court considers appropriate after considering the recommendations of the advisory group referred to in section 472(a) of this title.

(c) Nothing in a civil justice expense and delay reduction plan relating to the settlement authority provisions of this section shall alter or conflict with the authority of the Attorney General to conduct litigation on behalf of the United States, or any delegation of the Attorney General.

History of 28 U.S.C. §473: Dec. 1, 1990, P.L. 101-650, §103(a), 104 Stat. 5091.

§474. REVIEW OF DISTRICT COURT ACTION

(a)(1) The chief judge of each district court in a circuit and the chief judge of the circuit shall, as a committee—

(A) review each plan and report submitted pursuant to section 472(d) of this title; and

(B) make such suggestions for additional actions or modified actions of that district court as the committee considers appropriate for reducing cost and delay in civil litigation in the district court.

(2) The chief judge of a circuit may designate another judge of the court of appeals of that circuit, and the chief judge of a district court may designate another judge of such court, to perform that chief judge's responsibilities under paragraph (1) of this subsection.

(b) The Judicial Conference of the United States—

(1) shall review each plan and report submitted by a district court pursuant to section 472(d) of this title; and

(2) may request the district court to take additional action if the Judicial Conference determines that such court has not adequately responded to the conditions relevant to the civil and criminal dockets of the court or to the recommendations of the district court's advisory group.

History of 28 U.S.C. §474: Dec. 1, 1990, P.L. 101-650, §103(a), 104 Stat. 5093; Dec. 9, 1991, P.L. 102-198, §2(2), 105 Stat. 1623.

§475. PERIODIC DISTRICT COURT ASSESSMENT

After developing or selecting a civil justice expense and delay reduction plan, each United States district court shall assess annually the condition of the court's civil and criminal

dockets with a view to determining appropriate additional actions that may be taken by the court to reduce cost and delay in civil litigation and to improve the litigation management practices of the court. In performing such assessment, the court shall consult with an advisory group appointed in accordance with section 478 of this title.

History of 28 U.S.C. §475: Dec. 1, 1990, P.L. 101-650, §103(a), 104 Stat. 5093.

§476. ENHANCEMENT OF JUDICIAL INFORMATION DISSEMINATION[1]

(a) The Director of the Administrative Office of the United States Courts shall prepare a semiannual report, available to the public, that discloses for each judicial officer—

(1) the number of motions that have been pending for more than six months and the name of each case in which such motion has been pending;

(2) the number of bench trials that have been submitted for more than six months and the name of each case in which such trials are under submission; and

(3) the number and names of cases that have not been terminated within three years after filing.

(b) To ensure uniformity of reporting, the standards for categorization or characterization of judicial actions to be prescribed in accordance with section 481 of this title shall apply to the semiannual report prepared under subsection (a).

1. **Editor's note:** P.L. 105-53, §2, Oct. 6, 1997, 111 Stat. 1173 amended §103(b)(2) of the Civil Justice Reform Act by stating that the requirements in §476 will remain in effect permanently, while the requirements in §§471-475, 477, and 478 would expire seven years after enactment (i.e., Oct. 6, 2004).

History of 28 U.S.C. §476: Dec. 1, 1990, P.L. 101-650, §103(a), 104 Stat. 5093.

§477. MODEL CIVIL JUSTICE EXPENSE & DELAY REDUCTION PLAN

(a)(1) Based on the plans developed and implemented by the United States district courts designated as Early Implementation District Courts pursuant to section 103(c) of the Civil Justice Reform Act of 1990, the Judicial Conference of the United States may develop one or more model civil justice expense and delay reduction plans. Any such model plan shall be accompanied by a report explaining the manner in which the plan complies with section 473 of this title.

(2) The Director of the Federal Judicial Center and the Director of the Administrative Office of the United States Courts may make recommendations to the Judicial Conference regarding the development of any model civil justice expense and delay reduction plan.

(b) The Director of the Administrative Office of the United States Courts shall transmit to the United States district courts and to the Committees on the Judiciary of the Senate and the House of Representatives copies of any model plan and accompanying report.

History of 28 U.S.C. §477: Dec. 1, 1990, P.L. 101-650, §103(a), 104 Stat. 5094.

§478. ADVISORY GROUPS

(a) Within ninety days after the date of the enactment of this chapter, the advisory group required in each United States district court in accordance with section 472 of this title shall be appointed by the chief judge of each district court, after consultation with the other judges of such court.

(b) The advisory group of a district court shall be balanced and include attorneys and other persons who are representative of major categories of litigants in such court, as determined by the chief judge of such court.

(c) Subject to subsection (d), in no event shall any member of the advisory group serve longer than four years.

(d) Notwithstanding subsection (c), the United States Attorney for a judicial district, or his or her designee, shall be a permanent member of the advisory group for that district court.

(e) The chief judge of a United States district court may designate a reporter for each advisory group, who may be compensated in accordance with guidelines established by the Judicial Conference of the United States.

(f) The members of an advisory group of a United States district court and any person designated as a reporter for such group shall be considered as independent contractors of such court when in the performance of official duties of the advisory group and may not, solely by reason of service on or for the advisory group, be prohibited from practicing law before such court.

History of 28 U.S.C. §478: Dec. 1, 1990, P.L. 101-650, §103(a), 104 Stat. 5094.

§479. INFORMATION ON LITIGATION MANAGEMENT & COST & DELAY REDUCTION

(a) Within four years after the date of the enactment of this chapter, the Judicial Conference of the United States shall prepare a comprehensive report on all plans received pursuant to section 472(d) of this title. The Director of the Federal Judicial Center and the Director of the Administrative Office of the United States Courts may make recommendations regarding such report to the Judicial Conference during the preparation of the report. The Judicial Conference shall transmit copies of the report to the United States district courts and to the Committees on the Judiciary of the Senate and the House of Representatives.

(b) The Judicial Conference of the United States shall, on a continuing basis—

(1) study ways to improve litigation management and dispute resolution services in the district courts; and

(2) make recommendations to the district courts on ways to improve such services.

(c)(1) The Judicial Conference of the United States shall prepare, periodically revise, and transmit to the United States district courts a Manual for Litigation Management

and Cost and Delay Reduction. The Director of the Federal Judicial Center and the Director of the Administrative Office of the United States Courts may make recommendations regarding the preparation of and any subsequent revisions to the Manual.

(2) The Manual shall be developed after careful evaluation of the plans implemented under section 472 of this title, the demonstration program conducted under section 104 of the Civil Justice Reform Act of 1990, and the pilot program conducted under section 105 of the Civil Justice Reform Act of 1990.

(3) The Manual shall contain a description and analysis of the litigation management, cost and delay reduction principles and techniques, and alternative dispute resolution programs considered most effective by the Judicial Conference, the Director of the Federal Judicial Center, and the Director of the Administrative Office of the United States Courts.

History of 28 U.S.C. §479: Dec. 1, 1990, P.L. 101-650, §103(a), 104 Stat. 5095.

§480. TRAINING PROGRAMS

The Director of the Federal Judicial Center and the Director of the Administrative Office of the United States Courts shall develop and conduct comprehensive education and training programs to ensure that all judicial officers, clerks of court, courtroom deputies, and other appropriate court personnel are thoroughly familiar with the most recent available information and analyses about litigation management and other techniques for reducing cost and expediting the resolution of civil litigation. The curriculum of such training programs shall be periodically revised to reflect such information and analyses.

History of 28 U.S.C. §480: Dec. 1, 1990, P.L. 101-650, §103(a), 104 Stat. 5095.

§481. AUTOMATED CASE INFORMATION

(a) The Director of the Administrative Office of the United States Courts shall ensure that each United States district court has the automated capability readily to retrieve information about the status of each case in such court.

(b)(1) In carrying out subsection (a), the Director shall prescribe—

(A) the information to be recorded in district court automated systems; and

(B) standards for uniform categorization or characterization of judicial actions for the purpose of recording information on judicial actions in the district court automated systems.

(2) The uniform standards prescribed under paragraph (1)(B) of this subsection shall include a definition of what constitutes a dismissal of a case and standards for measuring the period for which a motion has been pending.

(c) Each United States district court shall record information as prescribed pursuant to subsection (b) of this section.

History of 28 U.S.C. §481: Dec. 1, 1990, P.L. 101-650, §103(a), 104 Stat. 5095.

§482. DEFINITIONS

As used in this chapter, the term "judicial officer" means a United States district court judge or a United States magistrate judge.

History of 28 U.S.C. §482: Dec. 1, 1990, P.L. 101-650, §103(a), 104 Stat. 5096.

PART II. DEPARTMENT OF JUSTICE

CHAPTER 31. THE ATTORNEY GENERAL

§501. EXECUTIVE DEPARTMENT

The Department of Justice is an executive department of the United States at the seat of Government.

History of 28 U.S.C. §501: Sept. 6, 1966, P.L. 89-554, §4(c), 80 Stat. 611.

§502. SEAL

The Attorney General shall have a seal for the Department of Justice. The design of the seal is subject to the approval of the President.

History of 28 U.S.C. §502: Sept. 6, 1966, P.L. 89-554, §4(c), 80 Stat. 611.

§503. ATTORNEY GENERAL

The President shall appoint, by and with the advice and consent of the Senate, an Attorney General of the United States. The Attorney General is the head of the Department of Justice.

History of 28 U.S.C. §503: Sept. 6, 1966, P.L. 89-554, §4(c), 80 Stat. 612.

§504. DEPUTY ATTORNEY GENERAL

The President may appoint, by and with the advice and consent of the Senate, a Deputy Attorney General.

History of 28 U.S.C. §504: Sept. 6, 1966, P.L. 89-554, §4(c), 80 Stat. 612; Nov. 28, 2001, P.L. 107-77, §612(c), 115 Stat. 800; Nov. 2, 2002, P.L. 107-273, §4004(f), 116 Stat. 1812.

§504A. ASSOCIATE ATTORNEY GENERAL

The President may appoint, by and with the advice and consent of the Senate, an Associate Attorney General.

History of 28 U.S.C. §504A: Oct. 19, 1977, P.L. 95-139, §1(a), 91 Stat. 1171.

§505. SOLICITOR GENERAL

The President shall appoint in the Department of Justice, by and with the advice and consent of the Senate, a Solicitor General, learned in the law, to assist the Attorney General in the performance of his duties.

History of 28 U.S.C. §505: Sept. 6, 1966, P.L. 89-554, §4(c), 80 Stat. 612.

§506. ASSISTANT ATTORNEYS GENERAL

The President shall appoint, by and with the advice and consent of the Senate, 11 Assistant Attorneys General, who shall assist the Attorney General in the performance of his duties.

History of 28 U.S.C. §506: Sept. 6, 1966, P.L. 89-554, §4(c), 80 Stat. 612; Nov. 6, 1978, P.L. 95-598, §218, 92 Stat. 2662; Mar. 9, 2006, P.L. 109-177, §506(a)(2), 120 Stat. 247.

§507. ASSISTANT ATTORNEY GENERAL FOR ADMINISTRATION

(a) The Attorney General shall appoint, with the approval of the President, an Assistant Attorney General for Administration, who shall perform such duties as the Attorney General may prescribe.

(b) The position of Assistant Attorney General for Administration is in the competitive service.

(c) Notwithstanding the provisions of section 901 of title 31, United States Code, the Assistant Attorney General for Administration shall be the Chief Financial Officer of the Department of Justice.

History of 28 U.S.C. §507: Sept. 6, 1966, P.L. 89-554, §4(c), 80 Stat. 612; Nov. 29, 1999, P.L. 106-113-Appx. A, §111, 113 Stat. 1501A-20.

§507A. ASSISTANT ATTORNEY GENERAL FOR NATIONAL SECURITY

(a) Of the Assistant Attorneys General appointed under section 506, one shall serve, upon the designation of the President, as the Assistant Attorney General for National Security.

(b) The Assistant Attorney General for National Security shall—

(1) serve as the head of the National Security Division of the Department of Justice under section 509A of this title;

(2) serve as primary liaison to the Director of National Intelligence for the Department of Justice; and

(3) perform such other duties as the Attorney General may prescribe.

History of 28 U.S.C. §507A: Mar. 9, 2006, P.L. 109-177, §506(a)(1), 120 Stat. 247.

§508. VACANCIES

(a) In case of a vacancy in the office of Attorney General, or of his absence or disability, the Deputy Attorney General may exercise all the duties of that office, and for the purpose of section 3345 of title 5 the Deputy Attorney General is the first assistant to the Attorney General.

(b) When by reason of absence, disability, or vacancy in office, neither the Attorney General nor the Deputy Attorney General is available to exercise the duties of the office of Attorney General, the Associate Attorney General shall act as Attorney General. The Attorney General may designate the Solicitor General and the Assistant Attorneys General, in further order of succession, to act as Attorney General.

History of 28 U.S.C. §508: Sept. 6, 1966, P.L. 89-554, §4(c), 80 Stat. 612; Oct. 19, 1977, P.L. 95-139, §2, 91 Stat. 1171.

§509. FUNCTIONS OF THE ATTORNEY GENERAL

All functions of other officers of the Department of Justice and all functions of agencies and employees of the Department of Justice are vested in the Attorney General except the functions—

(1) vested by subchapter II of chapter 5 of title 5 in administrative law judges employed by the Department of Justice;

(2) of the Federal Prison Industries, Inc.; and

(3) of the Board of Directors and officers of the Federal Prison Industries, Inc.

(4) [Repealed Oct. 12, 1984, P.L. 98-473, §228(A), 98 Stat. 2030.]

History of 28 U.S.C. §509: Sept. 6, 1966, P.L. 89-554, §4(c), 80 Stat. 612; Mar. 27, 1978, P.L. 95-251, §2(a)(6), 92 Stat. 183; Oct. 12, 1984, P.L. 98-473, §228(a), 98 Stat. 2030; Nov. 2, 2002, P.L. 107-273, §§204(d), 4003(b)(1), 116 Stat. 1776, 1811.

§509A. NATIONAL SECURITY DIVISION

(a) There is a National Security Division of the Department of Justice.

(b) The National Security Division shall consist of the elements of the Department of Justice (other than the Federal Bureau of Investigation) engaged primarily in support of the intelligence and intelligence-related activities of the United States Government, including the following:

(1) The Assistant Attorney General designated as the Assistant Attorney General for National Security under section 507A of this title.

(2) The Office of Intelligence Policy and Review (or any successor organization).

(3) The counterterrorism section (or any successor organization).

(4) The counterespionage section (or any successor organization).

(5) Any other element, component, or office designated by the Attorney General.

History of 28 U.S.C. §509A: Mar. 9, 2006, P.L. 109-177, §506(b)(1), 120 Stat. 248.

§509B. SECTION TO ENFORCE HUMAN RIGHTS LAWS

(a) Not later than 90 days after the date of the enactment of the Human Rights Enforcement Act of 2009, the Attorney General shall establish a section within the Criminal Division of the Department of Justice with responsibility for the enforcement of laws against suspected participants in serious human rights offenses.

(b) The section established under subsection (a) is authorized to—

(1) take appropriate legal action against individuals suspected of participating in serious human rights offenses; and

(2) coordinate any such legal action with the United States Attorney for the relevant jurisdiction.

(c) The Attorney General shall, as appropriate, consult with the Secretary of Homeland Security and the Secretary of State.

(d) In determining the appropriate legal action to take against individuals who are suspected of committing serious

human rights offenses under Federal law, the section shall take into consideration the availability of criminal prosecution under the laws of the United States for such offenses or in a foreign jurisdiction that is prepared to undertake a prosecution for the conduct that forms the basis for such offenses.

(e) The term "serious human rights offenses" includes violations of Federal criminal laws relating to genocide, torture, war crimes, and the use or recruitment of child soldiers under sections 1091, 2340, 2340A, 2441, and 2442 of title 18, United States Code.

History of 28 U.S.C. §509B: Dec. 22, 2009, P.L. 111-122, §2(b), 123 Stat. 3480.

§510. Delegation of Authority

The Attorney General may from time to time make such provisions as he considers appropriate authorizing the performance by any other officer, employee, or agency of the Department of Justice of any function of the Attorney General.

History of 28 U.S.C. §510: Sept. 6, 1966, P.L. 89-554, §4(c), 80 Stat. 612.

§511. Attorney General to Advise the President

The Attorney General shall give his advice and opinion on questions of law when required by the President.

History of 28 U.S.C. §511: Sept. 6, 1966, P.L. 89-554, §4(c), 80 Stat. 612.

§512. Attorney General to Advise Heads of Executive Departments

The head of an executive department may require the opinion of the Attorney General on questions of law arising in the administration of his department.

History of 28 U.S.C. §512: Sept. 6, 1966, P.L. 89-554, §4(c), 80 Stat. 613.

§513. Attorney General to Advise Secretaries of Military Departments

When a question of law arises in the administration of the Department of the Army, the Department of the Navy, or the Department of the Air Force, the cognizance of which is not given by statute to some other officer from whom the Secretary of the military department concerned may require advice, the Secretary of the military department shall send it to the Attorney General for disposition.

History of 28 U.S.C. §513: Sept. 6, 1966, P.L. 89-554, §4(c), 80 Stat. 613.

§514. Legal Services on Pending Claims in Departments & Agencies

When the head of an executive department or agency is of the opinion that the interests of the United States require the service of counsel on the examination of any witness concerning any claim, or on the legal investigation of any claim, pending in the department or agency, he shall notify the Attorney General, giving all facts necessary to enable him to furnish proper professional service in attending the examination or making the investigation, and the Attorney General shall provide for the service.

History of 28 U.S.C. §514: Sept. 6, 1966, P.L. 89-554, §4(c), 80 Stat. 613.

§515. Authority for Legal Proceedings; Commission, Oath, & Salary for Special Attorneys

(a) The Attorney General or any other officer of the Department of Justice, or any attorney specially appointed by the Attorney General under law, may, when specifically directed by the Attorney General, conduct any kind of legal proceeding, civil or criminal, including grand jury proceedings and proceedings before committing magistrate judges, which United States attorneys are authorized by law to conduct, whether or not he is a resident of the district in which the proceeding is brought.

(b) Each attorney specially retained under authority of the Department of Justice shall be commissioned as special assistant to the Attorney General or special attorney, and shall take the oath required by law. Foreign counsel employed in special cases are not required to take the oath. The Attorney General shall fix the annual salary of a special assistant or special attorney.

History of 28 U.S.C. §515: Sept. 6, 1966, P.L. 89-554, §4(c), 80 Stat. 613; Nov. 2, 2002, P.L. 107-273, §203(b), 116 Stat. 1775.

§516. Conduct of Litigation Reserved to Department of Justice

Except as otherwise authorized by law, the conduct of litigation in which the United States, an agency, or officer thereof is a party, or is interested, and securing evidence therefor, is reserved to officers of the Department of Justice, under the direction of the Attorney General.

History of 28 U.S.C. §516: Sept. 6, 1966, P.L. 89-554, §4(c), 80 Stat. 613.

§517. Interests of United States in Pending Suits

The Solicitor General, or any officer of the Department of Justice, may be sent by the Attorney General to any State or district in the United States to attend to the interests of the United States in a suit pending in a court of the United States, or in a court of a State, or to attend to any other interest of the United States.

History of 28 U.S.C. §517: Sept. 6, 1966, P.L. 89-554, §4(c), 80 Stat. 613.

§518. Conduct & Argument of Cases

(a) Except when the Attorney General in a particular case directs otherwise, the Attorney General and the Solicitor General shall conduct and argue suits and appeals in the Supreme Court and suits in the United States Court of Federal Claims or in the United States Court of Appeals for the Federal Circuit and in the Court of International Trade in which the United States is interested.

(b) When the Attorney General considers it in the interests of the United States, he may personally conduct and argue any case in a court of the United States in which the United States is interested, or he may direct the Solicitor General or any officer of the Department of Justice to do so.

History of 28 U.S.C. §518: Sept. 6, 1966, P.L. 89-554, §4(c), 80 Stat. 613; Oct. 10, 1980, P.L. 96-417, §503, 94 Stat. 1743; Apr. 2, 1982, P.L. 97-164, §117, 96 Stat. 32; Oct. 29, 1992, P.L. 102-572, §902(b)(1), 106 Stat. 4516.

§519. SUPERVISION OF LITIGATION

Except as otherwise authorized by law, the Attorney General shall supervise all litigation to which the United States, an agency, or officer thereof is a party, and shall direct all United States attorneys, assistant United States attorneys, and special attorneys appointed under section 543 of this title in the discharge of their respective duties.

History of 28 U.S.C. §519: Sept. 6, 1966, P.L. 89-554, §4(c), 80 Stat. 614.

§520. TRANSMISSION OF PETITIONS IN UNITED STATES COURT OF FEDERAL CLAIMS OR IN UNITED STATES COURT OF APPEALS FOR THE FEDERAL CIRCUIT; STATEMENT FURNISHED BY DEPARTMENTS

(a) In suits against the United States in the United States Court of Federal Claims or in the United States Court of Appeals for the Federal Circuit founded on a contract, agreement, or transaction with an executive department or military department, or a bureau, officer, or agent thereof, or when the matter or thing on which the claim is based has been passed on and decided by an executive department, military department, bureau, or officer authorized to adjust it, the Attorney General shall send to the department, bureau, or officer a printed copy of the petition filed by the claimant, with a request that the department, bureau, or officer furnish to the Attorney General all facts, circumstances, and evidence concerning the claim in the possession or knowledge of the department, bureau, or officer.

(b) Within a reasonable time after receipt of the request from the Attorney General, the executive department, military department, bureau, or officer shall furnish the Attorney General with a written statement of all facts, information, and proofs. The statement shall contain a reference to or description of all official documents and papers, if any, as may furnish proof of facts referred to in it, or may be necessary and proper for the defense of the United States against the claim, mentioning the department, office, or place where the same is kept or may be secured. If the claim has been passed on and decided by the department, bureau, or officer, the statement shall briefly state the reasons and principles on which the decision was based. When the decision was founded on an Act of Congress it shall be cited specifically, and if any previous interpretation or construction has been given to the Act, section, or clause by the department, bureau, or officer, it shall be set forth briefly in the statement and a copy of the opinion filed, if any, attached to it. When a decision in the case has been based on a regulation of a department or when a regulation has, in the opinion of the department, bureau, or officer sending the statement, any bearing on the claim, it shall be distinctly quoted at length in the statement. When more than one case or class of cases is pending, the defense of which rests on the same facts, circumstances, and proofs, the department, bureau, or officer may certify and send one statement and it shall be held to apply to all cases as if made out, certified, and sent in each case respectively.

History of 28 U.S.C. §520: Sept. 6, 1966, P.L. 89-554, §4(c), 80 Stat. 614; Apr. 2, 1982, P.L. 97-164, §118(a), 96 Stat. 32; Oct. 29, 1992, P.L. 102-572, §902(b)(1), 106 Stat. 4516.

§521. PUBLICATION & DISTRIBUTION OF OPINIONS

The Attorney General, from time to time—

(1) shall cause to be edited, and printed in the Government Printing Office, such of his opinions as he considers valuable for preservation in volumes; and

(2) may prescribe the manner for the distribution of the volumes.

Each volume shall contain headnotes, an index, and such footnotes as the Attorney General may approve.

History of 28 U.S.C. §521: Sept. 6, 1966, P.L. 89-554, §4(c), 80 Stat. 614.

§522. REPORT OF BUSINESS & STATISTICS

(a) The Attorney General, by April 1 of each year, shall report to Congress on the business of the Department of Justice for the last preceding fiscal year, and on any other matters pertaining to the Department that he considers proper, including—

(1) a statement of the several appropriations which are placed under the control of the Department and the amount appropriated;

(2) the statistics of crime under the laws of the United States; and

(3) a statement of the number of causes involving the United States, civil and criminal, pending during the preceding year in each of the several courts of the United States.

(b) With respect to any data, records, or other information acquired, collected, classified, preserved, or published by the Attorney General for any statistical, research, or other aggregate reporting purpose beginning not later than 1 year after the date of enactment of 21st Century Department of Justice Appropriations Authorization Act and continuing thereafter, and notwithstanding any other provision of law, the same criteria shall be used (and shall be required to be used, as applicable) to classify or categorize offenders and victims (in the criminal context), and to classify or categorize actors and acted upon (in the noncriminal context).

History of 28 U.S.C. §522: Sept. 6, 1966, P.L. 89-554, §4(c), 80 Stat. 615; Apr. 21, 1976, P.L. 94-273, §19, 90 Stat. 379; Nov. 2, 2002, P.L. 107-273, §204(b), 116 Stat. 1776.

§523. REQUISITIONS

The Attorney General shall sign all requisitions for the advance or payment of moneys appropriated for the Department of Justice, out of the Treasury, subject to the same control as is exercised on like estimates or accounts by the Government Accountability Office.

History of 28 U.S.C. §523: Sept. 6, 1966, P.L. 89-554, §4(c), 80 Stat. 615; July 7, 2004, P.L. 108-271, §8(b), 118 Stat. 814.

§524. AVAILABILITY OF APPROPRIATIONS

(a) Appropriations for the Department of Justice are available to the Attorney General for payment of—

(1) notarial fees, including such additional stenographic services as are required in connection therewith in the taking of depositions, and compensation and expenses of witnesses and informants, all at the rates authorized or approved by the Attorney General or the Assistant Attorney General for Administration; and

(2) when ordered by the court, actual expenses of meals and lodging for marshals, deputy marshals, or criers when acting as bailiffs in attendance on juries.

(b) Except as provided in subsection (a) of this section, a claim of not more than $500 for expenses related to litigation that is beyond the control of the Department may be paid out of appropriations currently available to the Department for expenses related to litigation when the Comptroller General settles the payment.

(c)(1) There is established in the United States Treasury a special fund to be known as the Department of Justice Assets Forfeiture Fund (hereafter in this subsection referred to as the "Fund") which shall be available to the Attorney General without fiscal year limitation for the following law enforcement purposes—

(A) the payment, at the discretion of the Attorney General, of any expenses necessary to seize, detain, inventory, safeguard, maintain, advertise, sell, or dispose of property under seizure, detention, or forfeited pursuant to any law enforced or administered by the Department of Justice, or of any other necessary expense incident to the seizure, detention, forfeiture, or disposal of such property including—

(i) payments for—

(I) contract services;

(II) the employment of outside contractors to operate and manage properties or provide other specialized services necessary to dispose of such properties in an effort to maximize the return from such properties; and

(III) reimbursement of any Federal, State, or local agency for any expenditures made to perform the functions described in this clause;

(ii) payments to reimburse any Federal agency participating in the Fund for investigative costs leading to seizures;

(iii) payments for contracting for the services of experts and consultants needed by the Department of Justice to assist in carrying out duties related to asset seizure and forfeiture; and

(iv) payments made pursuant to guidelines promulgated by the Attorney General if such payments are necessary and directly related to seizure and forfeiture program expenses for—

(I) the purchase or lease of automatic data processing systems (not less than a majority of which use will be related to such program);

(II) training;

(III) printing;

(IV) the storage, protection, and destruction of controlled substances; and

(V) contracting for services directly related to the identification of forfeitable assets, and the processing of and accounting for forfeitures;

(B) the payment of awards for information or assistance directly relating to violations of the criminal drug laws of the United States or of sections 1956 and 1957 of title 18, sections 5313 and 5324 of title 31, and section 6050I of the Internal Revenue Code of 1986;

(C) at the discretion of the Attorney General, the payment of awards for information or assistance leading to a civil or criminal forfeiture involving any Federal agency participating in the Fund;

(D) the compromise and payment of valid liens and mortgages against property that has been forfeited pursuant to any law enforced or administered by the Department of Justice, subject to the discretion of the Attorney General to determine the validity of any such lien or mortgage and the amount of payment to be made, and the employment of attorneys and other personnel skilled in State real estate law as necessary;

(E)(i) for disbursements authorized in connection with remission or mitigation procedures relating to property forfeited under any law enforced or administered by the Department of Justice; and

(ii) for payment for—

(I) costs incurred by or on behalf of the Department of Justice in connection with the removal, for purposes of Federal forfeiture and disposition, of any hazardous substance or pollutant or contaminant associated with the illegal manufacture of amphetamine or methamphetamine; and

(II) costs incurred by or on behalf of a State or local government in connection with such removal in any case in which such State or local government has assisted in a Federal prosecution relating to amphetamine or methamphetamine, to the extent such costs exceed equitable sharing payments made to such State or local government in such case;

(F)(i) for equipping for law enforcement functions of any Government-owned or leased vessel, vehicle, or aircraft available for official use by any Federal agency participating in the Fund;

(ii) for equipping any vessel, vehicle, or aircraft available for official use by a State or local law enforcement agency to enable the vessel, vehicle, or aircraft to assist law enforcement functions if the vessel, vehicle, or aircraft will be used in a joint law enforcement operation with a Federal agency participating in the Fund; and

(iii) payments for other equipment directly related to seizure or forfeiture, including laboratory equipment, protective equipment, communications equipment, and the operation and maintenance costs of such equipment;

(G) for purchase of evidence of any violation of the Controlled Substances Act, the Controlled Substances Import and Export Act, chapter 96 of title 18, or sections 1956 and 1957 of title 18;

(H) the payment of State and local property taxes on forfeited real property that accrued between the date of the violation giving rise to the forfeiture and the date of the forfeiture order; and

(I) payment of overtime salaries, travel, fuel, training, equipment, and other similar costs of State or local law enforcement officers that are incurred in a joint law enforcement operation with a Federal law enforcement agency participating in the Fund.

Amounts for paying the expenses authorized by subparagraphs (B), (F), and (G) shall be specified in appropriations Acts and may be used under authorities available to the organization receiving the funds. Amounts for other authorized expenditures and payments from the Fund, including equitable sharing payments, are not required to be specified in appropriations acts. The Attorney General may exempt the procurement of contract services under subparagraph (A) under the Fund from division C (except sections 3302, 3501(b), 3509, 3906, 4710, and 4711) of subtitle I of title 41, section 6101(b) to (d) of title 41, and other provisions of law as may be necessary to maintain the security and confidentiality of related criminal investigations.

(2) Any award paid from the Fund, as provided in paragraph (1) (B) or (C), shall be paid at the discretion of the Attorney General or his delegate, under existing departmental delegation policies for the payment of awards, except that the authority to pay an award of $250,000 or more shall not be delegated to any person other than the Deputy Attorney General, the Associate Attorney General, the Director of the Federal Bureau of Investigation, or the Administrator of the Drug Enforcement Administration. Any award pursuant to paragraph (1)(B) shall not exceed $500,000. Any award pursuant to paragraph (1)(C) shall not exceed the lesser of $500,000 or one-fourth of the amount realized by the United States from the property forfeited, without both the personal approval of the Attorney General and written notice within 30 days thereof to the Chairmen and ranking minority members of the Committees on Appropriations and the Judiciary of the Senate and of the House of Representatives.

(3) Any amount under subparagraph (G) of paragraph (1) shall be paid at the discretion of the Attorney General or his delegate, except that the authority to pay $100,000 or more may be delegated only to the respective head of the agency involved.

(4) There shall be deposited in the Fund—

(A) all amounts from the forfeiture of property under any law enforced or administered by the Department of Justice, except all proceeds of forfeitures available for use by the Secretary of the Treasury or the Secretary of the Interior pursuant to section 11(d) of the Endangered Species Act (16 U.S.C. 1540(d)) or section 6(d) of the Lacey Act Amendments of 1981 (16 U.S.C. 3375(d)), or the Postmaster General of the United States pursuant to 39 U.S.C. 2003(b)(7);

(B) all amounts representing the Federal equitable share from the forfeiture of property under any Federal, State, local, or foreign law, for any Federal agency participating in the Fund;

(C) all amounts transferred by the Secretary of the Treasury pursuant to section 9703(g)(4)(A)(ii) of title 31; and

(D) all amounts collected—

(i) by the United States pursuant to a reimbursement order under paragraph (2) of section 413(q) of the Controlled Substances Act (21 U.S.C. 853(q)); and

(ii) pursuant to a restitution order under paragraph (1) or (3) of section 413(q) of the Controlled Substances Act for injuries to the United States.

(5) Amounts in the Fund, and in any holding accounts associated with the Fund, that are not currently needed for the purpose of this section shall be kept on deposit or invested in obligations of, or guaranteed by, the United States and all earnings on such investments shall be deposited in the Fund.

(6)(A) The Attorney General shall transmit to Congress and make available to the public, not later than 4 months after the end of each fiscal year, detailed reports for the prior fiscal year as follows:

(i) A report on total deposits to the Fund by State of deposit.

(ii) A report on total expenses paid from the Fund, by category of expense and recipient agency, including equitable sharing payments.

(iii) A report describing the number, value, and types of properties placed into official use by Federal agencies, by recipient agency.

(iv) A report describing the number, value, and types of properties transferred to State and local law enforcement agencies, by recipient agency.

(v) A report, by type of disposition, describing the number, value, and types of forfeited property disposed of during the year.

(vi) A report on the year-end inventory of property under seizure, but not yet forfeited, that reflects the type of property, its estimated value, and the estimated value of liens and mortgages outstanding on the property.

(vii) A report listing each property in the year-end inventory, not yet forfeited, with an outstanding equity of not less than $1,000,000.

(B) The Attorney General shall transmit to Congress and make available to the public, not later than 2 months after final issuance, the audited financial statements for each fiscal year for the Fund.

(C) Reports under subparagraph (A) shall include information with respect to all forfeitures under any law enforced or administered by the Department of Justice.

(D) The transmittal and publication requirements in subparagraphs (A) and (B) may be satisfied by—

(i) posting the reports on an Internet website maintained by the Department of Justice for a period of not less than 2 years; and

(ii) notifying the Committees on the Judiciary of the House of Representatives and the Senate when the reports are available electronically.

(7) The provisions of this subsection relating to deposits in the Fund shall apply to all property in the custody of the Department of Justice on or after the effective date of the Comprehensive Forfeiture Act of 1983.

(8)(A) There are authorized to be appropriated such sums as necessary for the purposes described in subparagraphs (B), (F), and (G) of paragraph (1).

(B) Subject to subparagraphs (C) and (D), at the end of each of fiscal years 1994, 1995, and 1996, the Attorney General shall transfer from the Fund not more than $100,000,000 to the Special Forfeiture Fund established by section 6073 of the Anti-Drug Abuse Act of 1988.

(C) Transfers under subparagraph (B) may be made only from the excess unobligated balance and may not exceed one-half of the excess unobligated balance for any year. In addition, transfers under subparagraph (B) may be made only to the extent that the sum of the transfers in a fiscal year and one-half of the unobligated balance at the beginning of that fiscal year for the Special Forfeiture Fund does not exceed $100,000,000.

(D) For the purpose of determining amounts available for distribution at year end for any fiscal year, "excess unobligated balance" means the unobligated balance of the Fund generated by that fiscal year's operations, less any amounts that are required to be retained in the Fund to ensure the availability of amounts in the subsequent fiscal year for purposes authorized under paragraph (1).

(E)[1] Subject to the notification procedures contained in section 605 of Public Law 103-121, and after satisfying the transfer requirement in subparagraph (B) of this paragraph, any excess unobligated balance remaining in the Fund on September 30, 1997 and thereafter shall be available to the Attorney General, without fiscal year limitation, for any Federal law enforcement, litigative/prosecutive, and correctional activities, or any other authorized purpose of the Department of Justice. Any amounts provided pursuant to this subparagraph may be used under authorities available to the organization receiving the funds.

(9)(A) Following the completion of procedures for the forfeiture of property pursuant to any law enforced or administered by the Department, the Attorney General is authorized, in her discretion, to warrant clear title to any subsequent purchaser or transferee of such property.

(B) For fiscal years 2002 and 2003, the Attorney General is authorized to transfer, under such terms and conditions as the Attorney General shall specify, real or personal property of limited or marginal value, to a State or local government agency, or its designated contractor or transferee, for use to support drug abuse treatment, drug and crime prevention and education, housing, job skills, and other community-based public health and safety programs. Each such transfer shall be subject to satisfaction by the recipient involved of any outstanding lien against the property transferred, but no such transfer shall create or confer any private right of action in any person against the United States.

(10) The Attorney General shall transfer from the Fund to the Secretary of the Treasury for deposit in the Department of the Treasury Forfeiture Fund amounts appropriate to reflect the degree of participation of the Department of the Treasury law enforcement organizations (described in section 9703(p) of title 31) in the law enforcement effort resulting in the forfeiture pursuant to laws enforced or administered by the Department of Justice.

(11) For purposes of this subsection and notwithstanding section 9703 of title 31 or any other law, property is forfeited pursuant to a law enforced or administered by the Department of Justice if it is forfeited pursuant to—

(A) a judicial forfeiture proceeding when the underlying seizure was made by an officer of a Federal law enforcement agency participating in the Department of Justice Assets Forfeiture Fund or the property was maintained by the United States Marshals Service; or

(B) a civil administrative forfeiture proceeding conducted by a Department of Justice law enforcement component or pursuant to the authority of the Secretary of Commerce.

(d)(1) The Attorney General may accept, hold, administer, and use gifts, devises, and bequests of any property or services for the purpose of aiding or facilitating the work of the Department of Justice.

(2) Gifts, devises, and bequests of money, the proceeds of sale or liquidation of any other property accepted hereunder, and any income accruing from any property accepted hereunder—

(A) shall be deposited in the Treasury in a separate fund and held in trust by the Secretary of the Treasury for the benefit of the Department of Justice; and

(B) are hereby appropriated, without fiscal year limitation, and shall be disbursed on order of the Attorney General.

(3) Upon request of the Attorney General, the Secretary of the Treasury may invest and reinvest the fund described herein in public debt securities with maturities suitable for the needs of the fund and bearing interest at rates determined by the Secretary of the Treasury, taking into consideration the current average market yield on outstanding marketable obligations of the United States or comparable maturities.

(4) Evidences of any intangible personal property (other than money) accepted hereunder shall be deposited with the Secretary of the Treasury, who may hold or liquidate them, except that they shall be liquidated upon the request of the Attorney General.

(5) For purposes of federal income, estate, and gift taxes, property accepted hereunder shall be considered a gift, devise, or bequest to, or for the use of, the United States.

1. **Editor's note:** P.L. 104-99, §211 amended P.L. 104-91, §101(a), thereby enacting §109 of H.R. 2076, Dec. 6, 1995, into law. Section 109 purports to amend §524(c)(9) by adding subparagraph (E). Probably should add such subparagraph (E) to §524(c)(8), redesignated from §524(c)(9) by P.L. 104-66, §1091(h)(2); P.L. 104-208, Sept. 30, 1996.

History of 28 U.S.C. §524: Sept. 6, 1966, P.L. 89-554, §4(c), 80 Stat. 615; Sept. 13, 1982, P.L. 97-258, §2(g)(1)(B)-(D), 96 Stat. 1060; Oct. 12, 1984, P.L. 98-473, §§310, 2303, 98 Stat. 2052, 2193; Oct. 27, 1986, P.L. 99-570, §1152(a), 100 Stat. 3207-12; Nov. 10, 1986, P.L. 99-646, §27, 100 Stat. 3597; Dec. 22, 1987, P.L. 100-202, §101(a) [§210(a)], 101 Stat. 1329, 1329-18; Nov. 18, 1988, P.L. 100-690, §6072, 102 Stat. 4320; Nov. 5, 1990, P.L. 101-509, §1, 104 Stat. 1403; Nov. 29, 1990, P.L. 101-647, §§1601, 2001(a), 2002, 2005, 2006, 104 Stat. 4842, 4854, 4855; Apr. 10, 1991, P.L. 102-27, §101, 105 Stat. 135; Oct. 28, 1991, P.L. 102-140, §112, 105 Stat. 795; Oct. 6, 1992, P.L. 102-393, §638(f), 106 Stat. 1788; Oct. 6, 1992, P.L. 102-395, §114(b), (c), 106 Stat. 1845; Oct. 28, 1992, P.L. 102-550, §1529, 106 Stat. 4065; Oct. 27, 1993, P.L. 103-121, §109, 107 Stat. 1164; Sept. 13, 1994, P.L. 103-322, §§90205(b), 320301, 320302, 320913(a), 108 Stat. 1994, 2114, 2128; Dec. 21, 1995, P.L. 104-66, §1091(h), 109 Stat. 722; Jan. 26, 1996, P.L. 104-99, §211, 110 Stat. 37; Apr. 26, 1996, P.L. 104-134, §101(a) [§122], 110 Stat. 1321-22; May 2, 1996, P.L. 104-140, §1(a), 110 Stat. 1327; Sept. 30, 1996, P.L. 104-208, §101(a) [§§108, 114, 116, 117], 110 Stat. 3009-18, 3009-22, 3009-23; Nov. 26, 1997, P.L. 105-119, §§108, 124, 211, 111 Stat. 2457, 2471, 2487; Oct. 20, 1998, P.L. 105-272, §605, 112 Stat. 2413; Apr. 25, 2000, P.L. 106-185, §19, 114 Stat. 223; Oct. 17, 2000, P.L. 106-310, §§3613(b), 3621(a), 114 Stat. 1230; Nov. 2, 2002, P.L. 107-273, §204(a), 116 Stat. 1775; Jan. 4, 2011, P.L. 111-350, §5(g)(1), 124 Stat. 3848.

§525. PROCUREMENT OF LAW BOOKS, REFERENCE BOOKS, & PERIODICALS; SALE & EXCHANGE

In the procurement of law books, reference books, and periodicals, the Attorney General may exchange or sell similar items and apply the exchange allowances or proceeds of such sales in whole or in part payment therefor.

History of 28 U.S.C. §525: Sept. 6, 1966, P.L. 89-554, §4(c), 80 Stat. 615.

§526. AUTHORITY OF ATTORNEY GENERAL TO INVESTIGATE UNITED STATES ATTORNEYS, MARSHALS, TRUSTEES, CLERKS OF COURT, & OTHERS

(a) The Attorney General may investigate the official acts, records, and accounts of—

(1) the United States attorneys, marshals, trustees, including trustees in cases under title 11; and

(2) at the request and on behalf of the Director of the Administrative Office of the United States Courts, the clerks of the United States courts and of the district court of the Virgin Islands, probation officers, United States magistrate judges, and court reporters;

for which purpose all the official papers, records, dockets, and accounts of these officers, without exception, may be examined by agents of the Attorney General at any time.

(b) Appropriations for the examination of judicial officers are available for carrying out this section.

History of 28 U.S.C. §526: Sept. 6, 1966, P.L. 89-554, §4(c), 80 Stat. 615; Nov. 6, 1978, P.L. 95-598, §219(a), (b), 220, 92 Stat. 2662; Oct. 27, 1986, P.L. 99-554, §144(c), 100 Stat. 3096; Nov. 2, 2002, P.L. 107-273, §4003(b)(2), 116 Stat. 1811.

§527. ESTABLISHMENT OF WORKING CAPITAL FUND

There is hereby authorized to be established a working capital fund for the Department of Justice, which shall be available, without fiscal year limitation, for expenses and equipment necessary for maintenance and operations of such administrative services as the Attorney General, with the approval of the Office of Management and Budget, determines may be performed more advantageously as central services. The capital of the fund shall consist of the amount of the fair and reasonable value of such inventories, equipment, and other assets and inventories on order pertaining to the services to be carried on by the fund as the Attorney General may transfer to the fund less related liabilities and unpaid obligations together with any appropriations made for the purpose of providing capital. The fund shall be reimbursed or credited with advance payments from applicable appropriations and funds of the Department of Justice, other Federal agencies, and other sources authorized by law for supplies, materials, and services at rates which will recover the expenses of operations including accrual of annual leave and depreciation of plant and equipment of the fund. The fund shall also be credited with other receipts from sale or exchange of property or in payment for loss or damage to property held by the fund. There shall be transferred into the Treasury as miscellaneous receipts, as of the close of each fiscal year, any net income after making provisions for prior year losses, if any.

History of 28 U.S.C. §527: Jan. 2, 1975, P.L. 93-613, §1(1), 88 Stat. 1975.

§528. DISQUALIFICATION OF OFFICERS & EMPLOYEES OF THE DEPARTMENT OF JUSTICE

The Attorney General shall promulgate rules and regulations which require the disqualification of any officer or employee of the Department of Justice, including a United States attorney or a member of such attorney's staff, from participation in a particular investigation or prosecution if such participation may result in a personal, financial, or political conflict of interest, or the appearance thereof. Such rules and regulations may provide that a willful violation of any provision thereof shall result in removal from office.

History of 28 U.S.C. §528: Oct. 26, 1978, P.L. 95-521, §603(a), 92 Stat. 1874.

§529. ANNUAL REPORT OF ATTORNEY GENERAL

(a) Beginning on June 1, 1979, and at the beginning of each regular session of Congress thereafter, the Attorney General shall report to Congress on the activities and operations of the Public Integrity Section or any other unit of the Department of Justice designated to supervise the investigation and prosecution of—

(1) any violation of Federal criminal law by any individual who holds or who at the time of such violation held a position, whether or not elective, as a Federal Government officer, employee, or special employee, if such violation relates directly or indirectly to such individual's Federal Government position, employment, or compensation;

(2) any violation of any Federal criminal law relating to lobbying, conflict of interest, campaigns, and election to public office committed by any person, except insofar as such violation relates to a matter involving discrimination or intimidation on grounds of race, color, religion, or national origin;

(3) any violation of Federal criminal law by any individual who holds or who at the time of such violation held a position, whether or not elective, as a State or local government officer or employee, if such violation relates directly or indirectly to such individual's State or local government position, employment, or compensation; and

(4) such other matters as the Attorney General may deem appropriate.

Such report shall include the number, type, and disposition of all investigations and prosecutions supervised by such Section or such unit, except that such report shall not disclose information which would interfere with any pending investigation or prosecution or which would improperly infringe upon the privacy rights of any individuals.

(b) Notwithstanding any provision of law limiting the amount of management or administrative expenses, the Attorney General shall, not later than May 2, 2003, and of every year thereafter, prepare and provide to the Committees on the Judiciary and Appropriations of each House of the Congress using funds available for the underlying programs—

(1) a report identifying and describing every grant (other than one made to a governmental entity, pursuant to a statutory formula), cooperative agreement, or programmatic services contract that was made, entered into, awarded, or, for which additional or supplemental funds were provided in the immediately preceding fiscal year, by or on behalf of the Office of Justice Programs (including any component or unit thereof, and the Office of Community Oriented Policing Services), and including, without limitation, for each such grant, cooperative agreement, or contract: the term, the dollar amount or value, a description of its specific purpose or purposes, the names of all grantees or parties, the names of each unsuccessful applicant or bidder, and a description of the specific purpose or purposes proposed in each unsuccessful application or bid, and of the reason or reasons for rejection or denial of the same; and

(2) a report identifying and reviewing every grant (other than one made to a governmental entity, pursuant to a statutory formula), cooperative agreement, or programmatic services contract made, entered into, awarded, or for which additional or supplemental funds were provided, after October 1, 2002, by or on behalf of the Office of Justice Programs (including any component or unit thereof, and the Office of Community Oriented Policing Services) that was programmatically and financially closed out or that otherwise ended in the immediately preceding fiscal year (or even if not yet closed out, was terminated or otherwise ended in the fiscal year that ended 2 years before the end of such immediately preceding fiscal year), and including, without limitation, for each such grant, cooperative agreement, or contract: a description of how the appropriated funds involved actually were spent, statistics relating to its performance, its specific purpose or purposes, and its effectiveness, and a written declaration by each non-Federal grantee and each non-Federal party to such agreement or to such contract, that—

(A) the appropriated funds were spent for such purpose or purposes, and only such purpose or purposes;

(B) the terms of the grant, cooperative agreement, or contract were complied with; and

(C) all documentation necessary for conducting a full and proper audit under generally accepted accounting principles, and any (additional) documentation that may have been required under the grant, cooperative agreement, or contract, have been kept in orderly fashion and will be preserved for not less than 3 years from the date of such close out, termination, or end;

except that the requirement of this paragraph shall be deemed satisfied with respect to any such description, statistics, or declaration if such non-Federal grantee or such non-Federal party shall have failed to provide the same to the Attorney General, and the Attorney General notes the fact of such failure and the name of such grantee or such party in the report.

History of 28 U.S.C. §529: Oct. 26, 1978, P.L. 95-521, §603(a), 92 Stat. 1874; Nov. 2, 2002, P.L. 107-273, §§205(a), 4003(b)(3), 116 Stat. 1777, 1811.

§530. PAYMENT OF TRAVEL & TRANSPORTATION EXPENSES OF NEWLY APPOINTED SPECIAL AGENTS

The Attorney General or the Attorney General's designee is authorized to pay the travel expenses of newly appointed special agents and the transportation expenses of their families and household goods and personal effects from place of residence at time of selection to the first duty station, to the extent such payments are authorized by section 5723 of title 5 for new appointees who may receive payments under that section.

History of 28 U.S.C. §530: Aug. 26, 1983, P.L. 98-86, §1, 97 Stat. 492.

§530A. AUTHORIZATION OF APPROPRIATIONS FOR TRAVEL & RELATED EXPENSES & FOR HEALTH CARE OF PERSONNEL SERVING ABROAD

There are authorized to be used from appropriations, for any fiscal year, for the Department of Justice, such sums as may be necessary—

(1) for travel and related expenses of employees of the Department of Justice serving abroad and their families, to be payable in the same manner as applicable with respect to the Foreign Service under paragraphs (2), (3), (5), (6), (8), (9), (11), and (15) of section 901 of the Foreign Service Act of 1980, and under the regulations issued by the Secretary of State; and

(2) for health care for such employees and families, to be provided under section 904 of that Act.

History of 28 U.S.C. §530A: Nov. 18, 1988, P.L. 100-690, §6281(a), 102 Stat. 4368; Nov. 18, 2011, P.L. 112-55, §218, 125 Stat. 621.

§530B. ETHICAL STANDARDS FOR ATTORNEYS FOR THE GOVERNMENT

(a) An attorney for the Government shall be subject to State laws and rules, and local Federal court rules, governing attorneys in each State where such attorney engages in that attorney's duties, to the same extent and in the same manner as other attorneys in that State.

(b) The Attorney General shall make and amend rules of the Department of Justice to assure compliance with this section.

(c) As used in this section, the term "attorney for the Government" includes any attorney described in section 77.2(a) of part 77 of title 28 of the Code of Federal Regulations and also includes any independent counsel, or employee of such a counsel, appointed under chapter 40.

History of 28 U.S.C. §530B: Oct. 21, 1998, P.L. 105-277, §801(a), 1112 Stat. 2681-118. Effective date: The amendments made by this section shall take effect 180 days after the date of the enactment of this Act and shall apply during that portion of fiscal year 1999 that follows that taking effect, and in each succeeding fiscal year.

§530C. AUTHORITY TO USE AVAILABLE FUNDS

(a) In general.—Except to the extent provided otherwise by law, the activities of the Department of Justice (including any bureau, office, board, division, commission, subdivision, unit, or other component thereof) may, in the reasonable discretion of the Attorney General, be carried out through any means, including—

(1) through the Department's own personnel, acting within, from, or through the Department itself;

(2) by sending or receiving details of personnel to other branches or agencies of the Federal Government, on a reimbursable, partially-reimbursable, or nonreimbursable basis;

(3) through reimbursable agreements with other Federal agencies for work, materials, or equipment;

(4) through contracts, grants, or cooperative agreements with non-Federal parties; and

(5) as provided in subsection (b), in section 524, and in any other provision of law consistent herewith, including, without limitation, section 102(b) of Public Law 102-395 (106 Stat. 1838), as incorporated by section 815(d) of Public Law 104-132 (110 Stat.1315).

(b) Permitted uses.—

(1) General permitted uses.—Funds available to the Attorney General (i.e., all funds available to carry out the activities described in subsection (a)) may be used, without limitation, for the following:

(A) The purchase, lease, maintenance, and operation of passenger motor vehicles, or police-type motor vehicles for law enforcement purposes, without regard to general purchase price limitation for the then-current fiscal year.

(B) The purchase of insurance for motor vehicles, boats, and aircraft operated in official Government business in foreign countries.

(C) Services of experts and consultants, including private counsel, as authorized by section 3109 of title 5, and at rates of pay for individuals not to exceed the maximum daily rate payable from time to time under section 5332 of title 5.

(D) Official reception and representation expenses (i.e., official expenses of a social nature intended in whole or in predominant part to promote goodwill toward the Department or its missions, but excluding expenses of public tours of facilities of the Department of Justice), in accordance with distributions and procedures established, and rules issued, by the Attorney General, and expenses of public tours of facilities of the Department of Justice.

(E) Unforeseen emergencies of a confidential character, to be expended under the direction of the Attorney General and accounted for solely on the certificate of the Attorney General.

(F) Miscellaneous and emergency expenses authorized or approved by the Attorney General, the Deputy Attorney General, the Associate Attorney General, or the Assistant Attorney General for Administration.

(G) In accordance with procedures established and rules issued by the Attorney General—

(i) attendance at meetings and seminars;

(ii) conferences and training; and

(iii) advances of public moneys under section 3324 of title 31: Provided, That travel advances of such moneys to law enforcement personnel engaged in undercover activity shall be considered to be public money for purposes of section 3527 of title 31.

(H) Contracting with individuals for personal services abroad, except that such individuals shall not be regarded as employees of the United States for the purpose of any law administered by the Office of Personnel Management.

(I) Payment of interpreters and translators who are not citizens of the United States, in accordance with procedures established and rules issued by the Attorney General.

(J) Expenses or allowances for uniforms as authorized by section 5901 of title 5, but without regard to the general purchase price limitation for the then-current fiscal year.

(K) Expenses of—

(i) primary and secondary schooling for dependents of personnel stationed outside the United States at cost not in excess of those authorized by the Department of Defense for the same area, when it is determined by the Attorney General that schools available in the locality are unable to provide adequately for the education of such dependents; and

(ii) transportation of those dependents between their place of residence and schools serving the area which those dependents would normally attend when the Attorney General, under such regulations as he may prescribe, determines that such schools are not accessible by public means of transportation.

(L) payment of rewards (i.e., payments pursuant to public advertisements for assistance to the Department of Justice), in accordance with procedures and regulations established or issued by the Attorney General: Provided, That—

(i) no such reward shall exceed $2,000,000, unless—

(I) the reward is to combat domestic terrorism or international terrorism (as defined in section 2331 of title 18); or

(II) a statute should authorize a higher amount;

(ii) no such reward of $250,000 or more may be made or offered without the personal approval of either the Attorney General or the President;

(iii) the Attorney General shall give written notice to the Chairmen and ranking minority members of the Committees on Appropriations and the Judiciary of the Senate and of the House of Representatives not later than 30 days after the approval of a reward under clause (ii);

(iv) any executive agency or military department (as defined, respectively, in sections 105 and 102 of title 5) may provide the Attorney General with funds for the payment of rewards; and

(v) neither the failure of the Attorney General to authorize a payment nor the amount authorized shall be subject to judicial review.

(2) Specific permitted uses.—

(A) Aircraft and boats.—Funds available to the Attorney General for United States Attorneys, for the Federal Bureau of Investigation, for the United States Marshals Service, for the Bureau of Alcohol, Tobacco, Firearms and Explosives, for the Drug Enforcement Administration, and for the Immigration and Naturalization Service may be used for the purchase, lease, maintenance, and operation of aircraft and boats, for law enforcement purposes.

(B) Purchase of ammunition and firearms; firearms competitions.—Funds available to the Attorney General for United States Attorneys, for the Federal Bureau of Investigation, for the United States Marshals Service, for the Bureau of Alcohol, Tobacco, Firearms and Explosives, for the Drug Enforcement Administration, for the Federal Prison System, for the Office of the Inspector General, and for the Immigration and Naturalization Service may be used for—

(i) the purchase of ammunition and firearms; and

(ii) participation in firearms competitions.

(C) Construction.—Funds available to the Attorney General for construction may be used for expenses of planning, designing, acquiring, building, constructing, activating, renovating, converting, expanding, extending, remodeling, equipping, repairing, or maintaining buildings or facilities, including the expenses of acquisition of sites therefor, and all necessary expenses incident or related thereto; but the foregoing shall not be construed to mean that funds generally available for salaries and expenses are not also available for certain incidental or minor construction, activation, remodeling, maintenance, and other related construction costs.

(3) Fees and expenses of witnesses.—Funds available to the Attorney General for fees and expenses of witnesses may be used for—

(A) expenses, mileage, compensation, protection, and per diem in lieu of subsistence, of witnesses (including advances of public money) and as authorized by section 1821 or other law, except that no witness may be paid more than 1 attendance fee for any 1 calendar day;

(B) fees and expenses of neutrals in alternative dispute resolution proceedings, where the Department of Justice is a party; and

(C) construction of protected witness safesites.

(4) Federal Bureau of Investigation.—Funds available to the Attorney General for the Federal Bureau of Investigation for the detection, investigation, and prosecution of crimes against the United States may be used for the conduct of all its authorized activities.

(5) Immigration and Naturalization Service.—Funds available to the Attorney General for the Immigration and Naturalization Service may be used for—

(A) acquisition of land as sites for enforcement fences, and construction incident to such fences;

(B) cash advances to aliens for meals and lodging en route;

(C) refunds of maintenance bills, immigration fines, and other items properly returnable, except deposits of aliens who become public charges and deposits to secure payment of fines and passage money; and

(D) expenses and allowances incurred in tracking lost persons, as required by public exigencies, in aid of State or local law enforcement agencies.

(6) Federal Prison System.—Funds available to the Attorney General for the Federal Prison System may be used for—

(A) inmate medical services and inmate legal services, within the Federal prison system;

(B) the purchase and exchange of farm products and livestock;

(C) the acquisition of land as provided in section 4010 of title 18; and

(D) the construction of buildings and facilities for penal and correctional institutions (including prison camps), by contract or force account, including the payment of United States prisoners for their work performed in any such construction;

except that no funds may be used to distribute or make available to a prisoner any commercially published information or material that is sexually explicit or features nudity.

(7) Detention Trustee.—Funds available to the Attorney General for the Detention Trustee may be used for all the activities of such Trustee in the exercise of all power and functions authorized by law relating to the detention of Federal prisoners in non-Federal institutions or otherwise in the custody of the United States Marshals Service and to the detention of aliens in the custody of the Immigration and Naturalization Service, including the overseeing of construction of detention facilities or for housing related to such detention, the management of funds appropriated to the Department for the exercise of detention functions, and the direction of the United States Marshals Service and Immigration Service with respect to the exercise of detention policy setting and operations for the Department of Justice.

(c) Related provisions.—

(1) Limitation of compensation of individuals employed as attorneys.—No funds available to the Attorney General may be used to pay compensation for services provided by an individual employed as an attorney (other than an individual employed to provide services as a foreign attorney in special cases) unless such individual is duly licensed and authorized to practice as an attorney under the law of a State, a territory of the United States, or the District of Columbia.

(2) Reimbursements paid to governmental entities.—Funds available to the Attorney General that are paid as reimbursement to a governmental unit of the Department of Justice, to another Federal entity, or to a unit of State or local government, may be used under authorities available to the unit or entity receiving such reimbursement.

(d) Foreign reimbursements.—Whenever the Department of Justice or any component participates in a cooperative project to improve law enforcement or national security operations or services with a friendly foreign country on a cost-sharing basis, any reimbursements or contributions received from that foreign country to meet its share of the project may be credited to appropriate current appropriations accounts of the Department of Justice or any component. The amount of a reimbursement or contribution credited shall be available only for payment of the share of the project expenses allocated to the participating foreign country.

(e) Railroad police training fees.—The Attorney General is authorized to establish and collect a fee to defray the costs of railroad police officers participating in a Federal Bureau of Investigation law enforcement training program authorized by Public Law 106-110, and to credit such fees to the appropriation account "Federal Bureau of Investigation, Salaries and Expenses", to be available until expended for salaries and expenses incurred in providing such services.

(f) Warranty work.—In instances where the Attorney General determines that law enforcement-, security-, or mission-related considerations mitigate against obtaining maintenance or repair services from private sector entities for equipment under warranty, the Attorney General is authorized to seek reimbursement from such entities for warranty work performed at Department of Justice facilities, and to credit any payment made for such work to any appropriation charged therefor.

History of 28 U.S.C. §530C: Nov. 2, 2002, P.L. 107-273, §201(a), 116 Stat. 1767; Jan. 23, 2004, P.L. 108-199, §3, 118 Stat. 53.

§530D. REPORT ON ENFORCEMENT OF LAWS

(a) Report.—

(1) In general.—The Attorney General shall submit to the Congress a report of any instance in which the Attorney General or any officer of the Department of Justice—

(A) establishes or implements a formal or informal policy to refrain—

(i) from enforcing, applying, or administering any provision of any Federal statute, rule, regulation, program, policy, or other law whose enforcement, application, or administration is within the responsibility of the Attorney General or such officer on the grounds that such provision is unconstitutional; or

(ii) within any judicial jurisdiction of or within the United States, from adhering to, enforcing, applying, or complying with, any standing rule of decision (binding upon courts of, or inferior to those of, that jurisdiction) established by a final decision of any court of, or superior to those of, that jurisdiction, respecting the interpretation, construction, or application of the Constitution, any statute, rule, regulation, program, policy, or other law whose enforcement, application, or administration is within the responsibility of the Attorney General or such officer;

(B) determines—

(i) to contest affirmatively, in any judicial, administrative, or other proceeding, the constitutionality of any provision of any Federal statute, rule, regulation, program, policy, or other law; or

(ii) to refrain (on the grounds that the provision is unconstitutional) from defending or asserting, in any judicial, administrative, or other proceeding, the constitutionality of any provision of any Federal statute, rule, regulation, program, policy, or other law, or not to appeal or request review of any judicial, administrative, or other determination adversely affecting the constitutionality of any such provision; or

(C) approves (other than in circumstances in which a report is submitted to the Joint Committee on Taxation, pursuant to section 6405 of the Internal Revenue Code of 1986) the settlement or compromise (other than in bankruptcy) of any claim, suit, or other action—

(i) against the United States (including any agency or instrumentality thereof) for a sum that exceeds, or is likely to exceed, $2,000,000, excluding prejudgment interest; or

(ii) by the United States (including any agency or instrumentality thereof) pursuant to an agreement, consent decree, or order (or pursuant to any modification of an agreement, consent decree, or order) that provides injunctive or other nonmonetary relief that exceeds, or is likely to exceed, 3 years in duration: Provided, That for purposes of this clause, the term "injunctive or other nonmonetary relief" shall not be understood to include the following, where the same are a matter of public record—

(I) debarments, suspensions, or other exclusions from Government contracts or grants;

(II) mere reporting requirements or agreements (including sanctions for failure to report);

(III) requirements or agreements merely to comply with statutes or regulations;

(IV) requirements or agreements to surrender professional licenses or to cease the practice of professions, occupations, or industries;

(V) any criminal sentence or any requirements or agreements to perform community service, to serve probation, or to participate in supervised release from detention, confinement, or prison; or

(VI) agreements to cooperate with the government in investigations or prosecutions (whether or not the agreement is a matter of public record).

(2) Submission of report to the Congress.—For the purposes of paragraph (1), a report shall be considered to be submitted to the Congress if the report is submitted to—

(A) the majority leader and minority leader of the Senate;

(B) the Speaker, majority leader, and minority leader of the House of Representatives;

(C) the chairman and ranking minority member of the Committee on the Judiciary of the House of Representatives and the chairman and ranking minority member of the Committee on the Judiciary of the Senate; and

(D) the Senate Legal Counsel and the General Counsel of the House of Representatives.

(b) Deadline.—A report shall be submitted—

(1) under subsection (a)(1)(A), not later than 30 days after the establishment or implementation of each policy;

(2) under subsection (a)(1)(B), within such time as will reasonably enable the House of Representatives and the Senate to take action, separately or jointly, to intervene in timely fashion in the proceeding, but in no event later than 30 days after the making of each determination; and

(3) under subsection (a)(1)(C), not later than 30 days after the conclusion of each fiscal-year quarter, with respect to all approvals occurring in such quarter.

(c) Contents.—A report required by subsection (a) shall—

(1) specify the date of the establishment or implementation of the policy described in subsection (a)(1)(A), of the making of the determination described in subsection (a)(1)(B), or of each approval described in subsection (a)(1)(C);

(2) include a complete and detailed statement of the relevant issues and background (including a complete and detailed statement of the reasons for the policy or determination, and the identity of the officer responsible for establishing or implementing such policy, making such determination, or approving such settlement or compromise), except that—

(A) such details may be omitted as may be absolutely necessary to prevent improper disclosure of national-security-or classified information, of any information subject to the deliberative-process-, executive-, attorney-work-product-, or attorney-client privileges, or of any information the disclosure of which is prohibited by section 6103 of the Internal Revenue Code of 1986, or other law or any court order if the fact of each such omission (and the precise ground or grounds therefor) is clearly noted in the statement: Provided, That this subparagraph shall not be construed to deny to the Congress (including any House, Committee, or agency thereof) any such omitted details (or related information) that it lawfully may seek, subsequent to the submission of the report; and

(B) the requirements of this paragraph shall be deemed satisfied—

(i) in the case of an approval described in subsection (a)(1)(C)(i), if an unredacted copy of the entire settlement agreement and consent decree or order (if any) is provided, along with a statement indicating the legal and factual basis or bases for the settlement or compromise (if not apparent on the face of documents provided); and

(ii) in the case of an approval described in subsection (a)(1)(C)(ii), if an unredacted copy of the entire settlement agreement and consent decree or order (if any) is provided,

along with a statement indicating the injunctive or other nonmonetary relief (if not apparent on the face of documents provided); and

(3) in the case of a determination described in subsection (a)(1)(B) or an approval described in subsection (a)(1)(C), indicate the nature, tribunal, identifying information, and status of the proceeding, suit, or action.

(d) Declaration.—In the case of a determination described in subsection (a)(1)(B), the representative of the United States participating in the proceeding shall make a clear declaration in the proceeding that any position expressed as to the constitutionality of the provision involved is the position of the executive branch of the Federal Government (or, as applicable, of the President or of any executive agency or military department).

(e) Applicability to the President and to executive agencies and military departments.—The reporting, declaration, and other provisions of this section relating to the Attorney General and other officers of the Department of Justice shall apply to the President (but only with respect to the promulgation of any unclassified Executive order or similar memorandum or order), to the head of each executive agency or military department (as defined, respectively, in sections 105 and 102 of title 5, United States Code) that establishes or implements a policy described in subsection (a)(1)(A) or is authorized to conduct litigation, and to the officers of such executive agency.

History of 28 U.S.C. §530D: Nov. 2, 2002, P.L. 107-273, §202(a), 116 Stat. 1771.

CHAPTER 33. FEDERAL BUREAU OF INVESTIGATION

§531. FEDERAL BUREAU OF INVESTIGATION

The Federal Bureau of Investigation is in the Department of Justice.

History of 28 U.S.C. §531: Sept. 6, 1966, P.L. 89-554, §4(c), 80 Stat. 616.

§532. DIRECTOR OF THE FEDERAL BUREAU OF INVESTIGATION

The Attorney General may appoint a Director of the Federal Bureau of Investigation. The Director of the Federal Bureau of Investigation is the head of the Federal Bureau of Investigation.

History of 28 U.S.C. §532: Sept. 6, 1966, P.L. 89-554, §4(c), 80 Stat. 616.

§533. INVESTIGATIVE & OTHER OFFICIALS; APPOINTMENT

The Attorney General may appoint officials—

(1) to detect and prosecute crimes against the United States;

(2) to assist in the protection of the person of the President; and

(3) to assist in the protection of the person of the Attorney General.

(4) to conduct such other investigations regarding official matters under the control of the Department of Justice and the Department of State as may be directed by the Attorney General.

This section does not limit the authority of departments and agencies to investigate crimes against the United States when investigative jurisdiction has been assigned by law to such departments and agencies.

History of 28 U.S.C. §533: Sept. 6, 1966, P.L. 89-554, §4(c), 80 Stat. 616; Nov. 2, 2002, P.L. 107-273, §204(e), 116 Stat. 1776.

§534. ACQUISITION, PRESERVATION, & EXCHANGE OF IDENTIFICATION RECORDS & INFORMATION; APPOINTMENT OF OFFICIALS

(a) The Attorney General shall—

(1) acquire, collect, classify, and preserve identification, criminal identification, crime, and other records;

(2) acquire, collect, classify, and preserve any information which would assist in the identification of any deceased individual who has not been identified after the discovery of such deceased individual;

(3) acquire, collect, classify, and preserve any information which would assist in the location of any missing person (including an unemancipated person as defined by the laws of the place of residence of such person) and provide confirmation as to any entry for such a person to the parent, legal guardian, or next of kin of that person (and the Attorney General may acquire, collect, classify, and preserve such information from such parent, guardian, or next of kin); and

(4) exchange such records and information with, and for the official use of, authorized officials of the Federal Government, including the United States Sentencing Commission, the States, including State sentencing commissions, Indian tribes, cities, and penal and other institutions.

(b) The exchange of records and information authorized by subsection (a)(4) of this section is subject to cancellation if dissemination is made outside the receiving departments or related agencies.

(c) The Attorney General may appoint officials to perform the functions authorized by this section.

(d) Indian Law Enforcement Agencies.—The Attorney General shall permit tribal and Bureau of Indian Affairs law enforcement agencies—

(1) to access and enter information into Federal criminal information databases; and

(2) to obtain information from the databases.

(e) For purposes of this section, the term "other institutions" includes—

(1) railroad police departments which perform the administration of criminal justice and have arrest powers pursuant to a State statute, which allocate a substantial part of their annual budget to the administration of criminal justice, and

which meet training requirements established by law or ordinance for law enforcement officers; and

(2) police departments of private colleges or universities which perform the administration of criminal justice and have arrest powers pursuant to a State statute, which allocate a substantial part of their annual budget to the administration of criminal justice, and which meet training requirements established by law or ordinance for law enforcement officers.

(f)(1) Information from national crime information databases consisting of identification records, criminal history records, protection orders, and wanted person records may be disseminated to civil or criminal courts for use in domestic violence or stalking cases. Nothing in this subsection shall be construed to permit access to such records for any other purpose.

(2) Federal, tribal, and State criminal justice agencies authorized to enter information into criminal information databases may include—

(A) arrests, convictions, and arrest warrants for stalking or domestic violence or for violations of protection orders for the protection of parties from stalking or domestic violence; and

(B) protection orders for the protection of persons from stalking or domestic violence, provided such orders are subject to periodic verification.

(3) As used in this subsection—

(A) the term "national crime information databases" means the National Crime Information Center and its incorporated criminal history databases, including the Interstate Identification Index; and

(B) the term "protection order" includes—

(i) any injunction, restraining order, or any other order issued by a civil or criminal court for the purpose of preventing violent or threatening acts or harassment against, sexual violence or contact or communication with or physical proximity to, another person, including any temporary or final orders issued by civil or criminal courts whether obtained by filing an independent action or as a pendente lite order in another proceeding so long as any civil order was issued in response to a complaint, petition, or motion filed by or on behalf of a person seeking protection; and

(ii) any support, child custody or visitation provisions, orders, remedies, or relief issued as part of a protection order, restraining order, or stay away injunction pursuant to State, tribal, territorial, or local law authorizing the issuance of protection orders, restraining orders, or injunctions for the protection of victims of domestic violence, dating violence, sexual assault, or stalking.

History of 28 U.S.C. §534: Sept. 6, 1966, P.L. 89-554, §4(c), 80 Stat. 616; Oct. 12, 1982, P.L. 97-292, §§2, 3(a), 96 Stat. 1259; Nov. 18, 1988, P.L. 100-690, §7333, 102 Stat. 4469; Sept. 13, 1994, P.L. 103-322, §40601(a), 108 Stat. 1950; Nov. 2, 2002, P.L. 107-273, §§4003(b)(4), 11004, 116 Stat. 1811, 1816; Jan. 5, 2006, P.L. 109-162, §§118, 905(a), 119 Stat. 2989, 3079; July 27, 2006, P.L. 109-248, §153(i), 120 Stat. 611; July 29, 2010, P.L. 111-211, §233(a), 124 Stat. 2279; Jan. 4, 2011, P.L. 111-369, §2, 124 Stat. 4068.

§535. INVESTIGATION OF CRIMES INVOLVING GOVERNMENT OFFICERS & EMPLOYEES; LIMITATIONS

(a) The Attorney General and the Federal Bureau of Investigation may investigate any violation of Federal criminal law involving Government officers and employees—

(1) notwithstanding any other provision of law; and

(2) without limiting the authority to investigate any matter which is conferred on them or on a department or agency of the Government.

(b) Any information, allegation, matter, or complaint witnessed, discovered, or received in a department or agency of the executive branch of the Government relating to violations of Federal criminal law involving Government officers and employees shall be expeditiously reported to the Attorney General by the head of the department or agency, or the witness, discoverer, or recipient, as appropriate, unless—

(1) the responsibility to perform an investigation with respect thereto is specifically assigned otherwise by another provision of law; or

(2) as to any department or agency of the Government, the Attorney General directs otherwise with respect to a specified class of information, allegation, or complaint.

(c) This section does not limit—

(1) the authority of the military departments to investigate persons or offenses over which the armed forces have jurisdiction under the Uniform Code of Military Justice (chapter 47 of title 10); or

(2) the primary authority of the Postmaster General to investigate postal offenses.

History of 28 U.S.C. §535: Sept. 6, 1966, P.L. 89-554, §4(c), 80 Stat. 616; Nov. 2, 2002, P.L. 107-273, §206, 116 Stat. 1779.

§536. POSITIONS IN EXCEPTED SERVICE

All positions in the Federal Bureau of Investigation are excepted from the competitive service, and the incumbents of such positions occupy positions in the excepted service.

History of 28 U.S.C. §536: Sept. 6, 1966, P.L. 89-554, §4(c), 80 Stat. 617.

§537. EXPENSES OF UNFORESEEN EMERGENCIES OF A CONFIDENTIAL CHARACTER

Appropriations for the Federal Bureau of Investigation are available for expenses of unforeseen emergencies of a confidential character, when so specified in the appropriation concerned, to be spent under the direction of the Attorney General. The Attorney General shall certify the amount spent that he considers advisable not to specify, and his certification is a sufficient voucher for the amount therein expressed to have been spent.

History of 28 U.S.C. §537: Sept. 6, 1966, P.L. 89-554, §4(c), 80 Stat. 617.

§538. INVESTIGATION OF AIRCRAFT PIRACY & RELATED VIOLATIONS

The Federal Bureau of Investigation shall investigate any violation of section 46314 or chapter 465 of title 49.

History of 28 U.S.C. §538: July 5, 1994, P.L. 103-272, §4(e)(1), 108 Stat. 1361.

§539. COUNTERINTELLIGENCE OFFICIAL RECEPTION & REPRESENTATION EXPENSES

The Director of the Federal Bureau of Investigation may use funds available to the Federal Bureau of Investigation for counterintelligence programs to pay the expenses of hosting foreign officials in the United States under the auspices of the Federal Bureau of Investigation for consultation on counterintelligence matters.

History of 28 U.S.C. §539: Oct. 27, 1986, P.L. 99-569, §401(a), 100 Stat. 3195.

§540. INVESTIGATION OF FELONIOUS KILLINGS OF STATE OR LOCAL LAW ENFORCEMENT OFFICERS

The Attorney General and the Federal Bureau of Investigation may investigate felonious killings of officials and employees of a State or political subdivision thereof while engaged in or on account of the performance of official duties relating to the prevention, detection, investigation, or prosecution of an offense against the criminal laws of a State or political subdivision, when such investigation is requested by the head of the agency employing the official or employee killed, and under such guidelines as the Attorney General or his designee may establish.

History of 28 U.S.C. §540: Nov. 18, 1988, P.L. 100-690, §7331(a), 102 Stat. 4468.

§540A. INVESTIGATION OF VIOLENT CRIMES AGAINST TRAVELERS

(a) In general.—At the request of an appropriate law enforcement official of a State or political subdivision, the Attorney General and Director of the Federal Bureau of Investigation may assist in the investigation of a felony crime of violence in violation of the law of any State in which the victim appears to have been selected because he or she is a traveler.

(b) Foreign travelers.—In a case in which the traveler who is a victim of a crime described in subsection (a) is from a foreign nation, the Attorney General and Director of the Federal Bureau of Investigation, and, when appropriate, the Secretary of State shall assist the prosecuting and law enforcement officials of a State or political subdivision to the fullest extent possible in securing from abroad such evidence or other information as may be needed for the effective investigation and prosecution of the crime.

(c) Definitions.—In this section—

(1) "felony crime of violence" means an offense punishable by more than one year in prison that has as an element the use, attempted use, or threatened use of physical force against the person of another.

(2) "State" means a State, the District of Columbia, and any commonwealth, territory, or possession of the United States.

(3) "traveler" means a victim of a crime of violence who is not a resident of the State in which the crime of violence occurred.

History of 28 U.S.C. §540A: Sept. 13, 1994, P.L. 103-322, §320916(a), 108 Stat. 2129; Oct. 11, 1996, P.L. 104-294, §604(b)(21), 110 Stat. 3507.

§540B. INVESTIGATION OF SERIAL KILLINGS

(a) In general.—The Attorney General and the Director of the Federal Bureau of Investigation may investigate serial killings in violation of the laws of a State or political subdivision, if such investigation is requested by the head of a law enforcement agency with investigative or prosecutorial jurisdiction over the offense.

(b) Definitions.—In this section:

(1) Killing.—The term "killing" means conduct that would constitute an offense under section 1111 of title 18, United States Code, if Federal jurisdiction existed.

(2) Serial killings.—The term "serial killings" means a series of three or more killings, not less than one of which was committed within the United States, having common characteristics such as to suggest the reasonable possibility that the crimes were committed by the same actor or actors.

(3) State.—The term "State" means a State of the United States, the District of Columbia, and any commonwealth, territory, or possession of the United States.

History of 28 U.S.C. §540B: Oct. 30, 1998, P.L. 105-314, §701(a), 112 Stat. 2986.

§540C. FBI POLICE

(a) Definitions.—In this section:

(1) Director.—The term "Director" means the Director of the Federal Bureau of Investigation.

(2) FBI buildings and grounds.—

(A) In general.—The term "FBI buildings and grounds" means—

(i) the whole or any part of any building or structure which is occupied under a lease or otherwise by the Federal Bureau of Investigation and is subject to supervision and control by the Federal Bureau of Investigation;

(ii) the land upon which there is situated any building or structure which is occupied wholly by the Federal Bureau of Investigation; and

(iii) any enclosed passageway connecting 2 or more buildings or structures occupied in whole or in part by the Federal Bureau of Investigation.

(B) Inclusion.—The term "FBI buildings and grounds" includes adjacent streets and sidewalks not to exceed 500 feet from such property.

(3) FBI police.—The term "FBI police" means the permanent police force established under subsection (b).

(b) Establishment of FBI police; duties.—

(1) In general.—Subject to the supervision of the Attorney General, the Director may establish a permanent police force, to be known as the FBI police.

(2) Duties.—The FBI police shall perform such duties as the Director may prescribe in connection with the protection of persons and property within FBI buildings and grounds.

(3) Uniformed representative.—The Director, or designated representative duly authorized by the Attorney General, may appoint uniformed representatives of the Federal Bureau of Investigation as FBI police for duty in connection with the policing of all FBI buildings and grounds.

(4) Authority.—

(A) In general.—In accordance with regulations prescribed by the Director and approved by the Attorney General, the FBI police may—

(i) police the FBI buildings and grounds for the purpose of protecting persons and property;

(ii) in the performance of duties necessary for carrying out subparagraph (A), make arrests and otherwise enforce the laws of the United States, including the laws of the District of Columbia;

(iii) carry firearms as may be required for the performance of duties;

(iv) prevent breaches of the peace and suppress affrays and unlawful assemblies; and

(v) hold the same powers as sheriffs and constables when policing FBI buildings and grounds.

(B) Exception.—The authority and policing powers of FBI police under this paragraph shall not include the service of civil process.

(5) Pay and benefits.—

(A) In general.—The rates of basic pay, salary schedule, pay provisions, and benefits for members of the FBI police shall be equivalent to the rates of basic pay, salary schedule, pay provisions, and benefits applicable to members of the United States Secret Service Uniformed Division.

(B) Application.—Pay and benefits for the FBI police under subparagraph (A)—

(i) shall be established by regulation;

(ii) shall apply with respect to pay periods beginning after January 1, 2003; and

(iii) shall not result in any decrease in the rates of pay or benefits of any individual.

(c) Authority of Metropolitan Police Force.—This section does not affect the authority of the Metropolitan Police Force of the District of Columbia with respect to FBI buildings and grounds.

History of 28 U.S.C. §540C: Nov. 2, 2002, P.L. 107-273, §11024(a), 116 Stat. 1831; Dec. 13, 2003, P.L. 108-177, §361(i), 117 Stat. 2625.

CHAPTER 35. UNITED STATES ATTORNEYS

§541. UNITED STATES ATTORNEYS

(a) The President shall appoint, by and with the advice and consent of the Senate, a United States attorney for each judicial district.

(b) Each United States attorney shall be appointed for a term of four years. On the expiration of his term, a United States attorney shall continue to perform the duties of his office until his successor is appointed and qualifies.

(c) Each United States attorney is subject to removal by the President.

History of 28 U.S.C. §541: Sept. 6, 1966, P.L. 89-554, §4(c), 80 Stat. 617.

§542. ASSISTANT UNITED STATES ATTORNEYS

(a) The Attorney General may appoint one or more assistant United States attorneys in any district when the public interest so requires.

(b) Each assistant United States attorney is subject to removal by the Attorney General.

History of 28 U.S.C. §542: Sept. 6, 1966, P.L. 89-554, §4(c), 80 Stat. 618.

§543. SPECIAL ATTORNEYS

(a) The Attorney General may appoint attorneys to assist United States attorneys when the public interest so requires, including the appointment of qualified tribal prosecutors and other qualified attorneys to assist in prosecuting Federal offenses committed in Indian country.

(b) Each attorney appointed under this section is subject to removal by the Attorney General.

(c) Indian Country.—In this section, the term "Indian country" has the meaning given that term in section 1151 of title 18.

History of 28 U.S.C. §543: Sept. 6, 1966, P.L. 89-554, §4(c), 80 Stat. 618; July 29, 2010, P.L. 111-211, §213(a)(1), 124 Stat. 2268.

§544. OATH OF OFFICE

Each United States attorney, assistant United States attorney, and attorney appointed under section 543 of this title, before taking office, shall take an oath to execute faithfully his duties.

History of 28 U.S.C. §544: Sept. 6, 1966, P.L. 89-554, §4(c), 80 Stat. 618.

§545. RESIDENCE

(a) Each United States attorney shall reside in the district for which he is appointed, except that these officers of the District of Columbia, the Southern District of New York, and the Eastern District of New York may reside within 20 miles thereof. Each assistant United States attorney shall reside in the district for which he or she is appointed or within 25 miles thereof. The provisions of this subsection shall not apply to any United States attorney or assistant United States attorney appointed for the Northern Mariana Islands who at the same time is serving in the same capacity in another district. Pursuant to an order from the Attorney General or his

designee, a United States attorney or an assistant United States attorney may be assigned dual or additional responsibilities that exempt such officer from the residency requirement in this subsection for a specific period as established by the order and subject to renewal.

(b) The Attorney General may determine the official stations of United States attorneys and assistant United States attorneys within the districts for which they are appointed.

History of 28 U.S.C. §545: Sept. 6, 1966, P.L. 89-554, §4(c), 80 Stat. 618; Oct. 27, 1978, P.L. 95-530, §1, 92 Stat. 2028; Oct. 25, 1979, P.L. 96-91, 93 Stat. 700; Sept. 13, 1994, P.L. 103-322, §320932, 108 Stat. 2135; Mar. 9, 2006, P.L. 109-177, §501(a), 120 Stat. 246.

§546. VACANCIES

(a) Except as provided in subsection (b), the Attorney General may appoint a United States attorney for the district in which the office of United States attorney is vacant.

(b) The Attorney General shall not appoint as United States attorney a person to whose appointment by the President to that office the Senate refused to give advice and consent.

(c) A person appointed as United States attorney under this section may serve until the earlier of—

(1) the qualification of a United States attorney for such district appointed by the President under section 541 of this title; or

(2) the expiration of 120 days after appointment by the Attorney General under this section.

(d) If an appointment expires under subsection (c)(2), the district court for such district may appoint a United States attorney to serve until the vacancy is filled. The order of appointment by the court shall be filed with the clerk of the court.

History of 28 U.S.C. §546: Sept. 6, 1966, P.L. 89-554, §4(c), 80 Stat. 618; Nov. 10, 1986, P.L. 99-646, §69, 100 Stat. 3616; Mar. 9, 2006, P.L. 109-177, §502, 120 Stat. 246; June 14, 2007, P.L. 110-34, §2, 121 Stat. 224.

§547. DUTIES

Except as otherwise provided by law, each United States attorney, within his district, shall—

(1) prosecute for all offenses against the United States;

(2) prosecute or defend, for the Government, all civil actions, suits or proceedings in which the United States is concerned;

(3) appear in behalf of the defendants in all civil actions, suits or proceedings pending in his district against collectors, or other officers of the revenue or customs for any act done by them or for the recovery of any money exacted by or paid to these officers, and by them paid into the Treasury;

(4) institute and prosecute proceedings for the collection of fines, penalties, and forfeitures incurred for violation of any revenue law, unless satisfied on investigation that justice does not require the proceedings; and

(5) make such reports as the Attorney General may direct.

History of 28 U.S.C. §547: Sept. 6, 1966, P.L. 89-554, §4(c), 80 Stat. 618.

§548. SALARIES

Subject to sections 5315 through 5317 of title 5, the Attorney General shall fix the annual salaries of United States attorneys, assistant United States attorneys, and attorneys appointed under section 543 of this title at rates of compensation not in excess of the rate of basic compensation provided for Executive Level IV of the Executive Schedule set forth in section 5315 of title 5, United States Code.

History of 28 U.S.C. §548: Sept. 6, 1966, P.L. 89-554, §4(c), 80 Stat. 618; Oct. 12, 1984, P.L. 98-473, §1701(a) 98 Stat. 2184.

§549. EXPENSES

Necessary office expenses of United States attorneys shall be allowed when authorized by the Attorney General.

History of 28 U.S.C. §549: Sept. 6, 1966, P.L. 89-554, §4(c), 80 Stat. 618.

§550. CLERICAL ASSISTANTS, MESSENGERS, & PRIVATE PROCESS SERVERS

The United States attorneys may employ clerical assistants, messengers, and private process servers on approval of the Attorney General.

History of 28 U.S.C. §550: Sept. 6, 1966, P.L. 89-554, §4(c), 80 Stat. 619; Nov. 29, 1990, P.L. 101-647, §3626(a), 104 Stat. 4965.

CHAPTER 37. UNITED STATES MARSHALS SERVICE

§561. UNITED STATES MARSHALS SERVICE

(a) There is hereby established a United States Marshals Service as a bureau within the Department of Justice under the authority and direction of the Attorney General. There shall be at the head of the United States Marshals Service (hereafter in this chapter referred to as the "Service") a Director who shall be appointed by the President, by and with the advice and consent of the Senate.

(b) The Director of the United States Marshals Service (hereafter in this chapter referred to as the "Director") shall, in addition to the powers and duties set forth in this chapter, exercise such other functions as may be delegated by the Attorney General.

(c) The President shall appoint, by and with the advice and consent of the Senate, a United States marshal for each judicial district of the United States and for the Superior Court of the District of Columbia, except that any marshal appointed for the Northern Mariana Islands may at the same time serve as marshal in another judicial district. Each United States marshal shall be an official of the Service and shall serve under the direction of the Director.

(d) Each marshal shall be appointed for a term of four years. A marshal shall, unless that marshal has resigned or been removed by the President, continue to perform the duties of that office after the end of that 4-year term until a successor is appointed and qualifies.

(e) The Director shall designate places within a judicial district for the official station and offices of each marshal.

Each marshal shall reside within the district for which such marshal is appointed, except that—

(1) the marshal for the District of Columbia, for the Superior Court of the District of Columbia, and for the Southern District of New York may reside within 20 miles of the district for which the marshal is appointed; and

(2) any marshal appointed for the Northern Mariana Islands who at the same time is serving as marshal in another district may reside in such other district.

(f) The Director is authorized to appoint and fix the compensation of such employees as are necessary to carry out the powers and duties of the Service and may designate such employees as law enforcement officers in accordance with such policies and procedures as the Director shall establish pursuant to the applicable provisions of title 5 and regulations issued thereunder.

(g) The Director shall supervise and direct the United States Marshals Service in the performance of its duties.

(h) The Director may administer oaths and may take affirmations of officials and employees of the Service, but shall not demand or accept any fee or compensation therefor.

(i) Each marshal appointed under this section should have—

(1) a minimum of 4 years of command-level law enforcement management duties, including personnel, budget, and accountable property issues, in a police department, sheriff's office or Federal law enforcement agency;

(2) experience in coordinating with other law enforcement agencies, particularly at the State and local level;

(3) college-level academic experience; and

(4) experience in or with county, State, and Federal court systems or experience with protection of court personnel, jurors, and witnesses.

History of 28 U.S.C. §561: Nov. 18, 1988, P.L. 100-690, §7608(a)(1), 102 Stat. 4512; Nov. 2, 2002, P.L. 107-273, §301(b), 116 Stat. 1781; Mar. 9, 2006, P.L. 109-177, §505, 120 Stat. 247.

§562. VACANCIES

(a) In the case of a vacancy in the office of a United States marshal, the Attorney General may designate a person to perform the functions of and act as marshal, except that the Attorney General may not designate to act as marshal any person who was appointed by the President to that office but with respect to such appointment the Senate has refused to give its advice and consent.

(b) A person designated by the Attorney General under subsection (a) may serve until the earliest of the following events:

(1) The entry into office of a United States marshal appointed by the President, pursuant to section 561(c).

(2) The expiration of the thirtieth day following the end of the next session of the Senate.

(3) If such designee of the Attorney General is appointed by the President pursuant to section 561(c), but the Senate refuses to give its advice and consent to the appointment, the expiration of the thirtieth day following such refusal.

History of 28 U.S.C. §562: Nov. 18, 1988, P.L. 100-690, §7608(a)(1), 102 Stat. 4513.

§563. OATH OF OFFICE

The Director and each United States marshal and law enforcement officer of the Service, before taking office, shall take an oath or affirmation to faithfully execute the duties of that office.

History of 28 U.S.C. §563: Nov. 18, 1988, P.L. 100-690, §7608(a)(1), 102 Stat. 4513.

§564. POWERS AS SHERIFF

United States marshals, deputy marshals and such other officials of the Service as may be designated by the Director, in executing the laws of the United States within a State, may exercise the same powers which a sheriff of the State may exercise in executing the laws thereof.

History of 28 U.S.C. §564: Nov. 18, 1988, P.L. 100-690, §7608(a)(1), 102 Stat. 4513.

§565. EXPENSES OF THE SERVICE

The Director is authorized to use funds appropriated for the Service to make payments for expenses incurred pursuant to personal services contracts and cooperative agreements, authorized by the Attorney General, for security guards and for the service of summons on complaints, subpoenas, and notices in lieu of services by United States marshals and deputy marshals.

History of 28 U.S.C. §565: Nov. 18, 1988, P.L. 100-690, §7608(a)(1), 102 Stat. 4513.

§566. POWERS & DUTIES

(a) It is the primary role and mission of the United States Marshals Service to provide for the security and to obey, execute, and enforce all orders of the United States District Courts, the United States Courts of Appeals, the Court of International Trade, and the United States Tax Court, as provided by law.

(b) The United States marshal of each district is the marshal of the district court and of the court of appeals when sitting in that district, and of the Court of International Trade holding sessions in that district, and may, in the discretion of the respective courts, be required to attend any session of court.

(c) Except as otherwise provided by law or Rule of Procedure, the United States Marshals Service shall execute all lawful writs, process, and orders issued under the authority of the United States, and shall command all necessary assistance to execute its duties.

(d) Each United States marshal, deputy marshal, and any other official of the Service as may be designated by the Director may carry firearms and make arrests without war-

rant for any offense against the United States committed in his or her presence, or for any felony cognizable under the laws of the United States if he or she has reasonable grounds to believe that the person to be arrested has committed or is committing such felony.

(e)(1) The United States Marshals Service is authorized to—

(A) provide for the personal protection of Federal jurists, court officers, witnesses, and other threatened persons in the interests of justice where criminal intimidation impedes on the functioning of the judicial process or any other official proceeding; and

(B) investigate such fugitive matters, both within and outside the United States, as directed by the Attorney General.

(2) Nothing in paragraph (1)(B) shall be construed to interfere with or supersede the authority of other Federal agencies or bureaus.

(f) In accordance with procedures established by the Director, and except for public money deposited under section 2041 of this title, each United States marshal shall deposit public moneys that the marshal collects into the Treasury, subject to disbursement by the marshal. At the end of each accounting period, the earned part of public moneys accruing to the United States shall be deposited in the Treasury to the credit of the appropriate receipt accounts.

(g) Prior to resignation, retirement, or removal from office—

(1) a United States marshal shall deliver to the marshal's successor all prisoners in his custody and all unserved process; and

(2) a deputy marshal shall deliver to the marshal all process in the custody of the deputy marshal.

(h) The United States marshals shall pay such office expenses of United States Attorneys as may be directed by the Attorney General.

(i) The Director of the United States Marshals Service shall consult with the Judicial Conference of the United States on a continuing basis regarding the security requirements for the judicial branch of the United States Government, to ensure that the views of the Judicial Conference regarding the security requirements for the judicial branch of the Federal Government are taken into account when determining staffing levels, setting priorities for programs regarding judicial security, and allocating judicial security resources. In this paragraph, the term "judicial security" includes the security of buildings housing the judiciary, the personal security of judicial officers, the assessment of threats made to judicial officers, and the protection of all other judicial personnel. The United States Marshals Service retains final authority regarding security requirements for the judicial branch of the Federal Government.

History of 28 U.S.C. §566: Nov. 18, 1988, P.L. 100-690, §7608(a)(1), 102 Stat. 4514; Jan. 7, 2008, P.L. 110-177, §§101(a), 102(a), 121 Stat. 2534, 2535.

§567. COLLECTION OF FEES; ACCOUNTING

(a) Each United States marshal shall collect, as far as possible, his lawful fees and account for the same as public moneys.

(b) The marshal's accounts of fees and costs paid to a witness or juror on certificate of attendance issued as provided by sections 1825 and 1871 of this title may not be reexamined to charge him for an erroneous payment of the fees or costs.

History of 28 U.S.C. §567: Sept. 6, 1966, P.L. 89-554, §4(c), 80 Stat. 621, §572. Renumbered as §567, Nov. 18, 1988, P.L. 100-690, §7608(a)(2)(B), 102 Stat. 4514.

§568. PRACTICE OF LAW PROHIBITED

A United States marshal or deputy marshal may not practice law in any court of the United States.

History of 28 U.S.C. §568: Sept. 6, 1966, P.L. 89-554, §4(c), 80 Stat. 621, §575. Renumbered as §568, Nov. 18, 1988, P.L. 100-690, §7608(a)(2)(B), 102 Stat. 4514.

§569. REEMPLOYMENT RIGHTS

(a) A United States marshal for a judicial district who was appointed from a position in the competitive service (as defined in section 2102 of title 5) in the United States Marshals Service and who, for reasons other than misconduct, neglect of duty, or malfeasance, is removed from such office, is entitled to be reemployed in any vacant position in the competitive service in the United States Marshals Service at the same grade or pay level, or lower, as the individual's former position if—

(1) the individual is qualified for the vacant position; and

(2) the individual has made application for the position not later than ninety days after being removed from office as a United States marshal.

Such individual shall be so reemployed within thirty days after making such application or after being removed from office, whichever is later. An individual denied reemployment under this section in a position because the individual is not qualified for that position may appeal that denial to the Merit Systems Protection Board under section 7701 of title 5.

(b) Any United States marshal serving on the effective date of this section shall continue to serve for the remainder of the term for which such marshal was appointed, unless sooner removed by the President.

History of 28 U.S.C. §569: Oct. 12, 1984, P.L. 98-473, §1211(a), 98 Stat. 2163, §576. Renumbered as §569, Nov. 18, 1988, P.L. 100-690, §7608(a)(2)(B), 102 Stat. 4514.

§§570, 571. REPEALED

Repealed Nov. 18, 1988, P.L. 100-690, §7608(a)(1), 102 Stat. 4512.

§572. RENUMBERED

Renumbered as §567, Nov. 18, 1988, P.L. 100-690, §7608(a)(2)(B), 102 Stat. 4514.

§§572A TO 574. REPEALED

Repealed Nov. 18, 1988, P.L. 100-690, §7608(a)(2)(A), 102 Stat. 4514.

§§575, 576. RENUMBERED

Renumbered as §§568, 569, Nov. 18, 1988, P.L. 100-690, §7608(a)(2)(B), 102 Stat. 4514.

CHAPTER 39. UNITED STATES TRUSTEES

§581. UNITED STATES TRUSTEES

(a) The Attorney General shall appoint one United States trustee for each of the following regions composed of Federal judicial districts (without regard to section 451):

(1) The judicial districts established for the States of Maine, Massachusetts, New Hampshire, and Rhode Island.

(2) The judicial districts established for the States of Connecticut, New York, and Vermont.

(3) The judicial districts established for the States of Delaware, New Jersey, and Pennsylvania.

(4) The judicial districts established for the States of Maryland, North Carolina, South Carolina, Virginia, and West Virginia and for the District of Columbia.

(5) The judicial districts established for the States of Louisiana and Mississippi.

(6) The Northern District of Texas and the Eastern District of Texas.

(7) The Southern District of Texas and the Western District of Texas.

(8) The judicial districts established for the States of Kentucky and Tennessee.

(9) The judicial districts established for the States of Michigan and Ohio.

(10) The Central District of Illinois and the Southern District of Illinois; and the judicial districts established for the State of Indiana.

(11) The Northern District of Illinois; and the judicial districts established for the State of Wisconsin.

(12) The judicial districts established for the States of Minnesota, Iowa, North Dakota, and South Dakota.

(13) The judicial districts established for the States of Arkansas, Nebraska, and Missouri.

(14) The District of Arizona.

(15) The Southern District of California; and the judicial districts established for the State of Hawaii, and for Guam and the Commonwealth of the Northern Mariana Islands.

(16) The Central District of California.

(17) The Eastern District of California and the Northern District of California; and the judicial district established for the State of Nevada.

(18) The judicial districts established for the States of Alaska, Idaho (exclusive of Yellowstone National Park), Montana (exclusive of Yellowstone National Park), Oregon, and Washington.

(19) The judicial districts established for the States of Colorado, Utah, and Wyoming (including those portions of Yellowstone National Park situated in the States of Montana and Idaho).

(20) The judicial districts established for the States of Kansas, New Mexico, and Oklahoma.

(21) The judicial districts established for the States of Alabama, Florida, and Georgia and for the Commonwealth of Puerto Rico and the Virgin Islands of the United States.

(b) Each United States trustee shall be appointed for a term of five years. On the expiration of his term, a United States trustee shall continue to perform the duties of his office until his successor is appointed and qualifies.

(c) Each United States trustee is subject to removal by the Attorney General.

History of 28 U.S.C. §581: Nov. 6, 1978, P.L. 95-598, §224(a), 92 Stat. 2662; Oct. 27, 1986, P.L. 99-554, §111(a)-(c), 100 Stat. 3090, 3091.

§582. ASSISTANT UNITED STATES TRUSTEES

(a) The Attorney General may appoint one or more assistant United States trustees in any region when the public interest so requires.

(b) Each assistant United States trustee is subject to removal by the Attorney General.

History of 28 U.S.C. §582: Nov. 6, 1978, P.L. 95-598, §224(a), 92 Stat. 2663; Oct. 27, 1986, P.L. 99-554, §111(d), 100 Stat. 3091.

§583. OATH OF OFFICE

Each United States trustee and assistant United States trustee, before taking office, shall take an oath to execute faithfully his duties.

History of 28 U.S.C. §583: Nov. 6, 1978, P.L. 95-598, §224(a), 92 Stat. 2663.

§584. OFFICIAL STATIONS

The Attorney General may determine the official stations of the United States trustees and assistant United States trustees within the regions for which they were appointed.

History of 28 U.S.C. §584: Nov. 6, 1978, P.L. 95-598, §224(a), 92 Stat. 2663; Oct. 27, 1986, P.L. 99-554, §144(d), 100 Stat. 3096.

§585. VACANCIES

(a) The Attorney General may appoint an acting United States trustee for a region in which the office of the United States trustee is vacant. The individual so appointed may serve until the date on which the vacancy is filled by appointment under section 581 of this title or by designation under subsection (b) of this section.

(b) The Attorney General may designate a United States trustee to serve in not more than two regions for such time as the public interest requires.

History of 28 U.S.C. §585: Nov. 6, 1978, P.L. 95-598, §224(a), 92 Stat. 2663; Oct. 27, 1986, P.L. 99-554, §112, 100 Stat. 3091.

§586. DUTIES; SUPERVISION BY ATTORNEY GENERAL

(a) Each United States trustee, within the region for which such United States trustee is appointed, shall—

(1) establish, maintain, and supervise a panel of private trustees that are eligible and available to serve as trustees in cases under chapter 7 of title 11;

(2) serve as and perform the duties of a trustee in a case under title 11 when required under title 11 to serve as trustee in such a case;

(3) supervise the administration of cases and trustees in cases under chapter 7, 11, 12, 13, or 15 of title 11 by, whenever the United States trustee considers it to be appropriate—

(A)(i) reviewing, in accordance with procedural guidelines adopted by the Executive Office of the United States Trustee (which guidelines shall be applied uniformly by the United States trustee except when circumstances warrant different treatment), applications filed for compensation and reimbursement under section 330 of title 11; and

(ii) filing with the court comments with respect to such application and, if the United States Trustee considers it to be appropriate, objections to such application;

(B) monitoring plans and disclosure statements filed in cases under chapter 11 of title 11 and filing with the court, in connection with hearings under sections 1125 and 1128 of such title, comments with respect to such plans and disclosure statements;

(C) monitoring plans filed under chapters 12 and 13 of title 11 and filing with the court, in connection with hearings under sections 1224, 1229, 1324, and 1329 of such title, comments with respect to such plans;

(D) taking such action as the United States trustee deems to be appropriate to ensure that all reports, schedules, and fees required to be filed under title 11 and this title by the debtor are properly and timely filed;

(E) monitoring creditors' committees appointed under title 11;

(F) notifying the appropriate United States attorney of matters which relate to the occurrence of any action which may constitute a crime under the laws of the United States and, on the request of the United States attorney, assisting the United States attorney in carrying out prosecutions based on such action;

(G) monitoring the progress of cases under title 11 and taking such actions as the United States trustee deems to be appropriate to prevent undue delay in such progress;

(H) in small business cases (as defined in section 101 of title 11), performing the additional duties specified in title 11 pertaining to such cases; and

(I) monitoring applications filed under section 327 of title 11 and, whenever the United States trustee deems it to be appropriate, filing with the court comments with respect to the approval of such applications;

(4) deposit or invest under section 345 of title 11 money received as trustee in cases under title 11;

(5) perform the duties prescribed for the United States trustee under title 11 and this title, and such duties consistent with title 11 and this title as the Attorney General may prescribe;

(6) make such reports as the Attorney General directs, including the results of audits performed under section 603(a) of the Bankruptcy Abuse Prevention and Consumer Protection Act of 2005;

(7) in each of such small business cases—

(A) conduct an initial debtor interview as soon as practicable after the date of the order for relief but before the first meeting scheduled under section 341(a) of title 11, at which time the United States trustee shall—

(i) begin to investigate the debtor's viability;

(ii) inquire about the debtor's business plan;

(iii) explain the debtor's obligations to file monthly operating reports and other required reports;

(iv) attempt to develop an agreed scheduling order; and

(v) inform the debtor of other obligations;

(B) if determined to be appropriate and advisable, visit the appropriate business premises of the debtor, ascertain the state of the debtor's books and records, and verify that the debtor has filed its tax returns; and

(C) review and monitor diligently the debtor's activities, to determine as promptly as possible whether the debtor will be unable to confirm a plan; and

(8) in any case in which the United States trustee finds material grounds for any relief under section 1112 of title 11, apply promptly after making that finding to the court for relief.

(b) If the number of cases under chapter 12 or 13 of title 11 commenced in a particular region so warrants, the United States trustee for such region may, subject to the approval of the Attorney General, appoint one or more individuals to serve as standing trustee, or designate one or more assistant United States trustees to serve in cases under such chapter. The United States trustee for such region shall supervise any such individual appointed as standing trustee in the performance of the duties of standing trustee.

(c) Each United States trustee shall be under the general supervision of the Attorney General, who shall provide general coordination and assistance to the United States trustees.

(d)(1) The Attorney General shall prescribe by rule qualifications for membership on the panels established by United States trustees under paragraph (a)(1) of this section, and qualifications for appointment under subsection (b) of this section to serve as standing trustee in cases under chapter 12 or 13 of title 11. The Attorney General may not require that an individual be an attorney in order to qualify for appointment under subsection (b) of this section to serve as standing trustee in cases under chapter 12 or 13 of title 11.

(2) A trustee whose appointment under subsection (a)(1) or under subsection (b) is terminated or who ceases to be assigned to cases filed under title 11, United States Code, may obtain judicial review of the final agency decision by commencing an action in the district court of the United States for the district for which the panel to which the trustee is appointed under subsection (a)(1), or in the district court of the United States for the district in which the trustee is appointed under subsection (b) resides, after first exhausting all available administrative remedies, which if the trustee so elects, shall also include an administrative hearing on the record. Unless the trustee elects to have an administrative hearing on the record, the trustee shall be deemed to have exhausted all administrative remedies for purposes of this paragraph if the agency fails to make a final agency decision within 90 days after the trustee requests administrative remedies. The Attorney General shall prescribe procedures to implement this paragraph. The decision of the agency shall be affirmed by the district court unless it is unreasonable and without cause based on the administrative record before the agency.

(e)(1) The Attorney General, after consultation with a United States trustee that has appointed an individual under subsection (b) of this section to serve as standing trustee in cases under chapter 12 or 13 of title 11, shall fix—

(A) a maximum annual compensation for such individual consisting of—

(i) an amount not to exceed the highest annual rate of basic pay in effect for level V of the Executive Schedule; and

(ii) the cash value of employment benefits comparable to the employment benefits provided by the United States to individuals who are employed by the United States at the same rate of basic pay to perform similar services during the same period of time; and

(B) a percentage fee not to exceed—

(i) in the case of a debtor who is not a family farmer, ten percent; or

(ii) in the case of a debtor who is a family farmer, the sum of—

(I) not to exceed ten percent of the payments made under the plan of such debtor, with respect to payments in an aggregate amount not to exceed $450,000; and

(II) three percent of payments made under the plan of such debtor, with respect to payments made after the aggregate amount of payments made under the plan exceeds $450,000;

based on such maximum annual compensation and the actual, necessary expenses incurred by such individual as standing trustee.

(2) Such individual shall collect such percentage fee from all payments received by such individual under plans in the cases under chapter 12 or 13 of title 11 for which such individual serves as standing trustee. Such individual shall pay to the United States trustee, and the United States trustee shall deposit in the United States Trustee System Fund—

(A) any amount by which the actual compensation of such individual exceeds 5 per centum upon all payments received under plans in cases under chapter 12 or 13 of title 11 for which such individual serves as standing trustee; and

(B) any amount by which the percentage for all such cases exceeds—

(i) such individual's actual compensation for such cases, as adjusted under subparagraph (A) of paragraph (1); plus

(ii) the actual, necessary expenses incurred by such individual as standing trustee in such cases. Subject to the approval of the Attorney General, any or all of the interest earned from the deposit of payments under plans by such individual may be utilized to pay actual, necessary expenses without regard to the percentage limitation contained in subparagraph (d)(1)(B) of this section.

(3) After first exhausting all available administrative remedies, an individual appointed under subsection (b) may obtain judicial review of final agency action to deny a claim of actual, necessary expenses under this subsection by commencing an action in the district court of the United States for the district where the individual resides. The decision of the agency shall be affirmed by the district court unless it is unreasonable and without cause based upon the administrative record before the agency.

(4) The Attorney General shall prescribe procedures to implement this subsection.

(f)(1) The United States trustee for each district is authorized to contract with auditors to perform audits in cases designated by the United States trustee, in accordance with the procedures established under section 603(a) of the Bankruptcy Abuse Prevention and Consumer Protection Act of 2005.

(2)(A) The report of each audit referred to in paragraph (1) shall be filed with the court and transmitted to the United States trustee. Each report shall clearly and conspicuously specify any material misstatement of income or expenditures or of assets identified by the person performing the audit. In any case in which a material misstatement of income or expenditures or of assets has been reported, the clerk of the district court (or the clerk of the bankruptcy court if one is certified under section 156(b) of this title) shall give notice of the misstatement to the creditors in the case.

(B) If a material misstatement of income or expenditures or of assets is reported, the United States trustee shall—

(i) report the material misstatement, if appropriate, to the United States Attorney pursuant to section 3057 of title 18; and

(ii) if advisable, take appropriate action, including but not limited to commencing an adversary proceeding to revoke the debtor's discharge pursuant to section 727(d) of title 11.

History of 28 U.S.C. §586: Nov. 6, 1978, P.L. 95-598, §224(a), 92 Stat. 2663; Oct. 27, 1986, P.L. 99-554, §113, 100 Stat. 3091; Nov. 5, 1990, P.L. 101-509, §529 [§110(a)], 104 Stat. 1427, 1452; Oct. 22, 1994, P.L. 103-394, §§224(a), 502, 108 Stat. 4130, 4147; Apr. 20, 2005, P.L. 109-8, §§439, 603(b), 802(c)(3), 1231, 119 Stat. 113, 122, 146, 201; Dec. 22, 2010, P.L. 111-327, §2(c)(3), 124 Stat. 3563.

§587. SALARIES

Subject to sections 5315 through 5317 of title 5, the Attorney General shall fix the annual salaries of United States trustees and assistant United States trustees at rates of compensation not in excess of the rate of basic compensation provided for Executive Level IV of the Executive Schedule set forth in section 5315 of title 5, United States Code.

History of 28 U.S.C. §587: Nov. 6, 1978, P.L. 95-598, §224(a), 92 Stat. 2664; Oct. 27, 1986, P.L. 99-554, §114(a), 100 Stat. 3093.

§588. EXPENSES

Necessary office expenses of the United States trustee shall be allowed when authorized by the Attorney General.

History of 28 U.S.C. §588: Nov. 6, 1978, P.L. 95-598, §224(a), 92 Stat. 2664.

§589. STAFF & OTHER EMPLOYEES

The United States trustee may employ staff and other employees on approval of the Attorney General.

History of 28 U.S.C. §589: Nov. 6, 1978, P.L. 95-598, §224(a), 92 Stat. 2664.

A §589a. UNITED STATES TRUSTEE SYSTEM FUND

(a) There is hereby established in the Treasury of the United States a special fund to be known as the "United States Trustee System Fund" (hereinafter in this section referred to as the "Fund"). Monies in the Fund shall be available to the Attorney General without fiscal year limitation in such amounts as may be specified in appropriations Acts for the following purposes in connection with the operations of United States trustees—

(1) salaries and related employee benefits;

(2) travel and transportation;

(3) rental of space;

(4) communication, utilities, and miscellaneous computer charges;

(5) security investigations and audits;

(6) supplies, books, and other materials for legal research;

(7) furniture and equipment;

(8) miscellaneous services, including those obtained by contract; and

(9) printing.

(b) For the purpose of recovering the cost of services of the United States Trustee System, there shall be deposited as offsetting collections to the appropriation "United States Trustee System Fund", to remain available until expended, the following—

(1)(A) 40.46 percent of the fees collected under section 1930(a)(1)(A); and

(B) 28.33 percent of the fees collected under section 1930(a)(1)(B);

(2) 48.89 percent of the fees collected under section 1930(a)(3) of this title;

(3) one-half of the fees collected under section 1930(a)(4) of this title;

(4) one-half of the fees collected under section 1930(a)(5) of this title;

(5) 100 percent of the fees collected under section 1930(a)(6) of this title;

(6) three-fourths of the fees collected under the last sentence of section 1930(a) of this title;

(7) the compensation of trustees received under section 330(d) of title 11 by the clerks of the bankruptcy courts;

(8) excess fees collected under section 586(e)(2) of this title;

(9) interest earned on Fund investment; and

(10) fines imposed under section 110(*l*) of title 11, United States Code.

(c) Amounts in the Fund which are not currently needed for the purposes specified in subsection (a) shall be kept on deposit or invested in obligations of, or guaranteed by, the United States.

(d) The Attorney General shall transmit to the Congress, not later than 120 days after the end of each fiscal year, a detailed report on the amounts deposited in the Fund and a description of expenditures made under this section.

(e) There are authorized to be appropriated to the Fund for any fiscal year such sums as may be necessary to supplement amounts deposited under subsection (b) for the purposes specified in subsection (a).

History of 28 U.S.C. §589a: Oct. 27, 1986, P.L. 99-554, §115(a), 100 Stat. 3094; Nov. 21, 1989, P.L. 101-162, §406(c), 103 Stat. 1016; Oct. 28, 1991, P.L. 102-140, §111(b), (c), 105 Stat. 795; Oct. 27, 1993, P.L. 103-121, §111(a)(2), (b)(2), (3), 107 Stat. 1164; Sept. 30, 1996, P.L. 104-208, §101(a) [§109(b)], 110 Stat. 3009-18; Nov. 29, 1999, P.L. 106-113-Appx. A, §113, 113 Stat. 1501A-3; Apr. 20, 2005, P.L. 109-8, §325(b), 119 Stat. 99; May 11, 2005, P.L. 109-13, §6058(a), 119 Stat. 297; Dec. 26, 2007, P.L. 110-161, §212(a), 121 Stat. 1914; May 25, 2012, P.L. 112-121, §3(b), 126 Stat. 348.

§589b. BANKRUPTCY DATA

(a) Rules.—The Attorney General shall, within a reasonable time after the effective date of this section, issue rules requiring uniform forms for (and from time to time thereafter to appropriately modify and approve)—

(1) final reports by trustees in cases under chapters 7, 12, and 13 of title 11; and

(2) periodic reports by debtors in possession or trustees in cases under chapter 11 of title 11.

(b) Reports.—Each report referred to in subsection (a) shall be designed (and the requirements as to place and man-

ner of filing shall be established) so as to facilitate compilation of data and maximum possible access of the public, both by physical inspection at one or more central filing locations, and by electronic access through the Internet or other appropriate media.

(c) Required information.—The information required to be filed in the reports referred to in subsection (b) shall be that which is in the best interests of debtors and creditors, and in the public interest in reasonable and adequate information to evaluate the efficiency and practicality of the Federal bankruptcy system. In issuing rules proposing the forms referred to in subsection (a), the Attorney General shall strike the best achievable practical balance between—

(1) the reasonable needs of the public for information about the operational results of the Federal bankruptcy system;

(2) economy, simplicity, and lack of undue burden on persons with a duty to file reports; and

(3) appropriate privacy concerns and safeguards.

(d) Final reports.—The uniform forms for final reports required under subsection (a) for use by trustees under chapters 7, 12, and 13 of title 11 shall, in addition to such other matters as are required by law or as the Attorney General in the discretion of the Attorney General shall propose, include with respect to a case under such title—

(1) information about the length of time the case was pending;

(2) assets abandoned;

(3) assets exempted;

(4) receipts and disbursements of the estate;

(5) expenses of administration, including for use under section 707(b), actual costs of administering cases under chapter 13 of title 11;

(6) claims asserted;

(7) claims allowed; and

(8) distributions to claimants and claims discharged without payment, in each case by appropriate category and, in cases under chapters 12 and 13 of title 11, date of confirmation of the plan, each modification thereto, and defaults by the debtor in performance under the plan.

(e) Periodic reports.—The uniform forms for periodic reports required under subsection (a) for use by trustees or debtors in possession under chapter 11 of title 11 shall, in addition to such other matters as are required by law or as the Attorney General in the discretion of the Attorney General shall propose, include—

(1) information about the industry classification, published by the Department of Commerce, for the businesses conducted by the debtor;

(2) length of time the case has been pending;

(3) number of full-time employees as of the date of the order for relief and at the end of each reporting period since the case was filed;

(4) cash receipts, cash disbursements and profitability of the debtor for the most recent period and cumulatively since the date of the order for relief;

(5) compliance with title 11, whether or not tax returns and tax payments since the date of the order for relief have been timely filed and made;

(6) all professional fees approved by the court in the case for the most recent period and cumulatively since the date of the order for relief (separately reported, for the professional fees incurred by or on behalf of the debtor, between those that would have been incurred absent a bankruptcy case and those not); and

(7) plans of reorganization filed and confirmed and, with respect thereto, by class, the recoveries of the holders, expressed in aggregate dollar values and, in the case of claims, as a percentage of total claims of the class allowed.

History of 28 U.S.C. §589b: Apr. 20, 2005, P.L. 109-8, §602(a), 119 Stat. 120.

§§591 TO 599. EXPIRED

CHAPTER 40A. BUREAU OF ALCOHOL, TOBACCO, FIREARMS, & EXPLOSIVES

§599A. BUREAU OF ALCOHOL, TOBACCO, FIREARMS, & EXPLOSIVES

(a) Establishment.—

(1) In general.—There is established within the Department of Justice under the general authority of the Attorney General the Bureau of Alcohol, Tobacco, Firearms, and Explosives (in this section referred to as the "Bureau").

(2) Director.—There shall be at the head of the Bureau a Director, Bureau of Alcohol, Tobacco, Firearms, and Explosives (in this subtitle referred to as the "Director"). The Director shall be appointed by the President, by and with the advice and consent of the Senate and shall perform such functions as the Attorney General shall direct. The Director shall receive compensation at the rate prescribed by law under section 5314 of title V,[1] United States Code, for positions at level III of the Executive Schedule.

(3) Coordination.—The Attorney General, acting through the Director and such other officials of the Department of Justice as the Attorney General may designate, shall provide for the coordination of all firearms, explosives, tobacco enforcement, and arson enforcement functions vested in the Attorney General so as to assure maximum cooperation between and among any officer, employee, or agency of the Department of Justice involved in the performance of these and related functions.

(4) Performance of transferred functions.—The Attorney General may make such provisions as the Attorney General determines appropriate to authorize the perfor-

mance by any officer, employee, or agency of the Department of Justice of any function transferred to the Attorney General under this section.

(b) Responsibilities.—Subject to the direction of the Attorney General, the Bureau shall be responsible for investigating—

(1) criminal and regulatory violations of the Federal firearms, explosives, arson, alcohol, and tobacco smuggling laws;

(2) the functions transferred by subsection (c) of section 1111 of the Homeland Security Act of 2002 (as enacted on the date of the enactment of such Act); and

(3) any other function related to the investigation of violent crime or domestic terrorism that is delegated to the Bureau by the Attorney General.

(c) Transfer of authorities, functions, personnel, and assets to the Department of Justice.—

(1) In general.—Subject to paragraph (2), but notwithstanding any other provision of law, there are transferred to the Department of Justice the authorities, functions, personnel, and assets of the Bureau of Alcohol, Tobacco and Firearms, which shall be maintained as a distinct entity within the Department of Justice, including the related functions of the Secretary of the Treasury.

(3)[2] Building prospectus.—Prospectus PDC-98W10, giving the General Services Administration the authority for site acquisition, design, and construction of a new headquarters building for the Bureau of Alcohol, Tobacco and Firearms, is transferred, and deemed to apply, to the Bureau of Alcohol, Tobacco, Firearms, and Explosives established in the Department of Justice under subsection (a).

1. **Editor's note:** So in original. Probably should be "title 5."

2. **Editor's note:** So in original. Paragraph (2) of subsection (c) was not transferred to this section from 6 U.S.C. §531.

History of 28 U.S.C. §599A: Nov. 25, 2002, P.L. 107-296, §1111(a), (b), (c)(1), (3), 116 Stat. 2274. Redesignated §599A and amended Jan. 5, 2006, P.L. 109-162, §1187(b), (c)(1), 119 Stat. 3127; Mar. 9, 2006, P.L. 109-177, §504, 120 Stat. 247.

§599B. PERSONNEL MANAGEMENT DEMONSTRATION PROJECT

Notwithstanding any other provision of law, the Personnel Management Demonstration Project established under section 102 of title I of division C of the Omnibus Consolidated and Emergency Supplemental Appropriations Act for Fiscal Year 1999 (Public Law 105-277; 122[1] Stat. 2681-585) shall be transferred to the Attorney General of the United States for continued use by the Bureau of Alcohol, Tobacco, Firearms, and Explosives, Department of Justice, and the Secretary of the Treasury for continued use by the Tax and Trade Bureau.

1. **Editor's note:** So in original. Probably should be "112."

History of 28 U.S.C. §599B: Nov. 25, 2002, P.L. 107-296, §1115, 116 Stat. 2274. Redesignated §599B and amended Jan. 5, 2006, P.L. 109-162, §1187(b), (c)(2), 119 Stat. 3127, 3128.

PART III. COURT OFFICERS & EMPLOYEES

CHAPTER 41. ADMINISTRATIVE OFFICE OF UNITED STATES COURTS

§601. CREATION; DIRECTOR & DEPUTY DIRECTOR

The Administrative Office of the United States Courts shall be maintained at the seat of government. It shall be supervised by a Director and a Deputy Director appointed and subject to removal by the Chief Justice of the United States, after consulting with the Judicial Conference. The Director and Deputy Director shall be deemed to be officers for purposes of title 5, United States Code.

History of 28 U.S.C. §601: June 25, 1948, ch. 646, 62 Stat. 913; Sept. 23, 1959, P.L. 86-370, §5(a)(1), 73 Stat. 652; Dec. 1, 1990, P.L. 101-650, §307, 104 Stat. 5112; Oct. 19, 1996, P.L. 104-317, §602, 110 Stat. 3857.

§602. EMPLOYEES

(a) The Director shall appoint and fix the compensation of necessary employees of the Administrative Office in accordance with the Administrative Office of the United States Courts Personnel Act of 1990.

(b) Notwithstanding any other law, the Director may appoint certified interpreters in accordance with section 604(a)(16)(B) of this title without regard to the provisions of chapter 51 and subchapter III of chapter 53 of title 5, relating to classification and General Schedule pay rates, but the compensation of any person appointed under this subsection shall not exceed the appropriate equivalent of the highest rate of pay payable for the highest grade established in the General Schedule, section 5332 of title 5.

(c) The Director may obtain personal services as authorized by section 3109 of title 5, at rates not to exceed the appropriate equivalent of the highest rate of pay payable for the highest grade established in the General Schedule, section 5332 of title 5.

(d) All functions of other officers and employees of the Administrative Office and all functions of organizational units of the Administrative Office are vested in the Director. The Director may delegate any of the Director's functions, powers, duties, and authority (except the authority to promulgate rules and regulations) to such officers and employees of the judicial branch of Government as the Director may designate, and subject to such terms and conditions as the Director may consider appropriate; and may authorize the successive redelegation of such functions, powers, duties, and authority as the Director may deem desirable. All official acts performed by such officers and employees shall have the same force and effect as though performed by the Director in person.

History of 28 U.S.C. §602: June 25, 1948, ch. 646, 62 Stat. 913; Oct. 28, 1978, P.L. 95-539, §5, 92 Stat. 2044; Oct. 30, 1990, P.L. 101-474, §5(a), (q), 104 Stat. 1099, 1101; Dec. 1, 1990, P.L. 101-650, §325(b)(4), 104 Stat. 5121.

§603. SALARIES

The salary of the Director shall be the same as the salary of a district judge. Notwithstanding any other provision of law,

the Director shall not be deemed to be an "employee" for the purpose of subchapter I of chapter 63 of title 5. The salary of the Deputy Director shall be 92 percent of the salary of the Director. The salaries of six additional positions shall be fixed by the Director at rates not to exceed the annual rate of basic pay for positions at level IV of the Executive Schedule under section 5315 of title 5.

History of 28 U.S.C. §603: June 25, 1948, ch. 646, 62 Stat. 913; Oct. 15, 1949, ch. 695, §§5(b), 6(b), 63 Stat. 881; Oct. 31, 1951, ch. 655, §43(b), 65 Stat. 725; Sept. 23, 1959, P.L. 86-370, §5(a)(1), 73 Stat. 652; Aug. 14, 1964, P.L. 88-426, §403(g), 78 Stat. 434; Dec. 16, 1967, P.L. 90-206, §213(d), 81 Stat. 635; Oct. 28, 1978, P.L. 95-539, §6, 92 Stat. 2044; Dec. 22, 1987, P.L. 100-202, §101(a) [§409], 101 Stat. 1329, 1329-27; Oct. 1, 1988, P.L. 100-459, §406, 102 Stat. 2213; Oct. 30, 1990, P.L. 101-474, §5(b), 104 Stat. 1099.

§604. DUTIES OF DIRECTOR GENERALLY

(a) The Director shall be the administrative officer of the courts, and under the supervision and direction of the Judicial Conference of the United States, shall:

(1) Supervise all administrative matters relating to the offices of clerks and other clerical and administrative personnel of the courts;

(2) Examine the state of the dockets of the courts; secure information as to the courts' need of assistance; prepare and transmit semiannually to the chief judges of the circuits, statistical data and reports as to the business of the courts;

(3) Submit to the annual meeting of the Judicial Conference of the United States, at least two weeks prior thereto, a report of the activities of the Administrative Office and the state of the business of the courts, together with the statistical data submitted to the chief judges of the circuits under paragraph (a)(2) of this section, and the Director's recommendations, which report, data and recommendations shall be public documents.

(4) Submit to Congress and the Attorney General copies of the report, data and recommendations required by paragraph (a)(3) of this section;

(5) Fix the compensation of clerks of court, deputies, librarians, criers, messengers, law clerks, secretaries, stenographers, clerical assistants, and other employees of the courts whose compensation is not otherwise fixed by law, and, notwithstanding any other provision of law, pay on behalf of Justices and judges of the United States appointed to hold office during good behavior, United States magistrate judges, bankruptcy judges appointed under chapter 6 of this title, judges of the District Court of Guam, judges of the District Court for the Northern Mariana Islands, judges of the District Court of the Virgin Islands, bankruptcy judges and magistrate judges retired under section 377 of this title, and judges retired under section 373 of this title, who are aged 65 or over, any increases in the cost of Federal Employees' Group Life Insurance imposed after April 24, 1999, including any expenses generated by such payments, as authorized by the Judicial Conference of the United States;

(6) Determine and pay necessary office expenses of courts, judges, and those court officials whose expenses are by law allowable, and the lawful fees of United States magistrate judges;

(7) Regulate and pay annuities to widows and surviving dependent children of justices and judges of the United States, judges of the United States Court of Federal Claims, bankruptcy judges, United States magistrate judges, Directors of the Federal Judicial Center, and Directors of the Administrative Office, and necessary travel and subsistence expenses incurred by judges, court officers and employees, and officers and employees of the Administrative Office, and the Federal Judicial Center, while absent from their official stations on official business, without regard to the per diem allowances and amounts for reimbursement of actual and necessary expenses established by the Administrator of General Services under section 5702 of title 5, except that the reimbursement of subsistence expenses may not exceed that authorized by the Director for judges of the United States under section 456 of this title;

(8) Disburse appropriations and other funds for the maintenance and operation of the courts;

(9) Establish pretrial services pursuant to section 3152 of title 18, United States Code;

(10)(A) Purchase, exchange, transfer, distribute, and assign the custody of lawbooks, equipment, supplies, and other personal property for the judicial branch of Government (except the Supreme Court unless otherwise provided pursuant to paragraph (17)); (B) provide or make available readily to each court appropriate equipment for the interpretation of proceedings in accordance with section 1828 of this title; and (C) enter into and perform contracts and other transactions upon such terms as the Director may deem appropriate as may be necessary to the conduct of the work of the judicial branch of Government (except the Supreme Court unless otherwise provided pursuant to paragraph (17)), and contracts for nonpersonal services providing pretrial services, agencies, for the interpretation of proceedings, and for the provision of special interpretation services pursuant to section 1828 of this title may be awarded without regard to section 6101(b) to (d) of title 41;

(11) Audit vouchers and accounts of the courts, the Federal Judicial Center, the offices providing pretrial services, and their clerical and administrative personnel;

(12) Provide accommodations for the courts, the Federal Judicial Center, the offices providing pretrial services and their clerical and administrative personnel;

(13) Lay before Congress, annually, statistical tables that will accurately reflect the business transacted by the several bankruptcy courts, and all other pertinent data relating to such courts;

(14) Pursuant to section 1827 of this title, establish a program for the certification and utilization of interpreters in courts of the United States;

(15) Pursuant to section 1828 of this title, establish a program for the provision of special interpretation services in courts of the United States;

(16)(A) In those districts where the Director considers it advisable based on the need for interpreters, authorize the full-time or part-time employment by the court of certified interpreters; (B) where the Director considers it advisable based on the need for interpreters, appoint certified interpreters on a full-time or part-time basis, for services in various courts when he determines that such appointments will result in the economical provision of interpretation services; and (C) pay out of moneys appropriated for the judiciary interpreters' salaries, fees, and expenses, and other costs which may accrue in accordance with the provisions of sections 1827 and 1828 of this title;

(17) In the Director's discretion, (A) accept and utilize voluntary and uncompensated (gratuitous) services, including services as authorized by section 3102(b) of title 5, United States Code; and (B) accept, hold, administer, and utilize gifts and bequests of personal property for the purpose of aiding or facilitating the work of the judicial branch of Government, but gifts or bequests of money shall be covered into the Treasury;

(18) Establish procedures and mechanisms within the judicial branch for processing fines, restitution, forfeitures of bail bonds or collateral, and assessments;

(19) Regulate and pay annuities to bankruptcy judges and United States magistrate judges in accordance with section 377 of this title and paragraphs (1)(B) and (2) of section 2(c) of the Retirement and Survivors' Annuities for Bankruptcy Judges and Magistrates Act of 1988;

(20) Periodically compile—

(A) the rules which are prescribed under section 2071 of this title by courts other than the Supreme Court;

(B) the rules which are prescribed under section 358 of this title; and

(C) the orders which are required to be publicly available under section 360(b) of this title;

so as to provide a current record of such rules and orders;

(21) Establish a program of incentive awards for employees of the judicial branch of the United States Government, other than any judge who is entitled to hold office during good behavior;

(22) Receive and expend, either directly or by transfer to the United States Marshals Service or other Government agency, funds appropriated for the procurement, installation, and maintenance of security equipment and protective services for the United States Courts in courtrooms and adjacent areas, including building ingress/egress control, inspection of packages, directed security patrols, and other similar activities;

(23) Regulate and pay annuities to judges of the United States Court of Federal Claims in accordance with section 178 of this title; and

(24) Perform such other duties as may be assigned to him by the Supreme Court or the Judicial Conference of the United States.

(b) The clerical and administrative personnel of the courts shall comply with all requests by the Director for information or statistical data as to the state of court dockets.

(c) Inspection of court dockets outside the continental United States may be made through United States officials residing within the jurisdiction where the inspection is made.

(d) The Director, under the supervision and direction of the conference, shall:

(1) supervise all administrative matters relating to the offices of the United States magistrate judges;

(2) gather, compile, and evaluate all statistical and other information required for the performance of his duties and the duties of the conference with respect to such officers;

(3) lay before Congress annually statistical tables and other information which will accurately reflect the business which has come before the various United States magistrate judges, including (A) the number of matters in which the parties consented to the exercise of jurisdiction by a magistrate judge, (B) the number of appeals taken pursuant to the decisions of magistrate judges and the disposition of such appeals, and (C) the professional background and qualifications of individuals appointed under section 631 of this title to serve as magistrate judge;

(4) prepare and distribute a manual, with annual supplements and periodic revisions, for the use of such officers, which shall set forth their powers and duties, describe all categories of proceedings that may arise before them, and contain such other information as may be required to enable them to discharge their powers and duties promptly, effectively, and impartially.

(e) The Director may promulgate appropriate rules and regulations approved by the conference and not inconsistent with any provision of law, to assist him in the performance of the duties conferred upon him by subsection (d) of this section. Magistrate judges shall keep such records and make such reports as are specified in such rules and regulations.

(f) The Director may make, promulgate, issue, rescind, and amend rules and regulations (including regulations prescribing standards of conduct for Administrative Office employees) as may be necessary to carry out the Director's functions, powers, duties, and authority. The Director may publish in the Federal Register such rules, regulations, and notices for the judicial branch of Government as the Director determines to be of public interest; and the Director of the Federal Register hereby is authorized to accept and shall publish such materials.

(g)(1) When authorized to exchange personal property, the Director may exchange or sell similar items and may apply the exchange allowance or proceeds of sale in such cases

in whole or in part payment for the property acquired, but any transaction carried out under the authority of this subsection shall be evidenced in writing.

(2) The Director hereby is authorized to enter into contracts for public utility services and related terminal equipment for periods not exceeding ten years.

(3)(A) In order to promote the recycling and reuse of recyclable materials, the Director may provide for the sale or disposal of recyclable scrap materials from paper products and other consumable office supplies held by an entity within the judicial branch.

(B) The sale or disposal of recyclable materials under subparagraph (A) shall be consistent with the procedures provided in sections 541-555 of title 40 for the sale of surplus property.

(C) Proceeds from the sale of recyclable materials under subparagraph (A) shall be deposited as offsetting collections to the fund established under section 1931 of this title and shall remain available until expended to reimburse any appropriations for the operation and maintenance of the judicial branch.

(4) The Director is hereby authorized:

(A) to enter into contracts for the acquisition of severable services for a period that begins in one fiscal year and ends in the next fiscal year to the same extent as the head of an executive agency under the authority of section 2531 of title 41, United States Code;

(B) to enter into contracts for multiple years for the acquisition of property and services to the same extent as executive agencies under the authority of section 254c of title 41, United States Code; and

(C) to make advance, partial, progress or other payments under contracts for property or services to the same extent as executive agencies under the authority of section 255 of title 41, United States Code.

(h)(1) The Director shall, out of funds appropriated for the operation and maintenance of the courts, provide facilities and pay necessary expenses incurred by the judicial councils of the circuits and the Judicial Conference under chapter 16 of this title, including mileage allowance and witness fees, at the same rate as provided in section 1821 of this title. Administrative and professional assistance from the Administrative Office of the United States Courts may be requested by each judicial council and the Judicial Conference for purposes of discharging their duties under chapter 16 of this title.

(2) The Director of the Administrative Office of the United States Courts shall include in his annual report filed with the Congress under this section a summary of the number of complaints filed with each judicial council under chapter 16 of this title, indicating the general nature of such complaints and the disposition of those complaints in which action has been taken.

History of 28 U.S.C. §604: June 25, 1948, ch. 646, 62 Stat. 914; Aug. 3, 1956, ch. 944, §3, 70 Stat. 1026; Dec. 20, 1967, P.L. 90-219, §203(a)-(c), 81 Stat. 669; Oct. 17, 1968, P.L. 90-578, §201, 82 Stat. 1114; Aug. 22, 1972, P.L. 92-397, §4, 86 Stat. 580; Jan. 3, 1975, P.L. 93-619, §204, 88 Stat. 2089; Oct. 28, 1978, P.L. 95-539, §§3, 4, 92 Stat. 2043; Nov. 6, 1978, P.L. 95-598, §225, 92 Stat. 2664; Oct. 10, 1979, P.L. 96-82, §5, 93 Stat. 645; Oct. 15, 1980, P.L. 96-458, §5, 94 Stat. 2040; Dec. 12, 1980, P.L. 96-523, §1(c)(1), 94 Stat. 3040; Sept. 27, 1982, P.L. 97-267, §7, 96 Stat. 1139; Oct. 27, 1986, P.L. 99-554, §116, 100 Stat. 3095; Dec. 11, 1987, P.L. 100-185, §2, 101 Stat. 1279; Nov. 15, 1988, P.L. 100-659, §6(a), 102 Stat. 3918; Nov. 19, 1988, P.L. 100-702, §§402(a), 1008, 1010, 1011, 1020(a)(2), 102 Stat. 4650, 4667, 4668, 4671; Oct. 30, 1990, P.L. 101-474, §5(r), 104 Stat. 1101; Nov. 29, 1990, P.L. 101-647, §2548, 104 Stat. 4888; Dec. 1, 1990, P.L. 101-650, §§306(e)(1), 325(c)(1), 104 Stat. 5111, 5121; Oct. 29, 1992, P.L. 102-572, §§503, 902(b)(1), 106 Stat. 4513, 4516; Nov. 29, 1999, P.L. 106-113-Appx. A, §305, 113 Stat. 1501A-37; Nov. 13, 2000, P.L. 106-518, §§204, 304(d), 114 Stat. 2414, 2418; Aug. 21, 2002, P.L. 107-217, §3(g)(1), 116 Stat. 1299; Nov. 2, 2002, P.L. 107-273, §11043(e), 116 Stat. 1855; Nov. 30, 2005, P.L. 109-115, §407(a), 119 Stat. 2471; Jan. 7, 2008, P.L. 110-177, §502(a), 121 Stat. 2542; Mar. 11, 2009, P.L. 111-8, §307(a), 123 Stat. 648; Jan. 4, 2011, P.L. 111-350, §5(g)(2), 124 Stat. 3848.

§605. BUDGET ESTIMATES

The Director, under the supervision of the Judicial Conference of the United States, shall submit to the Office of Management and Budget annual estimates of the expenditures and appropriations necessary for the maintenance and operation of the courts and the Administrative Office and the operation of the judicial survivors annuity fund, and such supplemental and deficiency estimates as may be required from time to time for the same purposes, according to law. The Director shall cause periodic examinations of the judicial survivors annuity fund to be made by an actuary, who may be an actuary employed by another department of the Government temporarily assigned for the purpose, and whose findings and recommendations shall be transmitted by the Director to the Judicial Conference.

Such estimates shall be approved, before presentation to the Office of Management and Budget, by the Judicial Conference of the United States, except that the estimate with respect to the Court of International Trade shall be approved by such court and the estimate with respect to the United States Court of Appeals for the Federal Circuit shall be approved by such court.

History of 28 U.S.C. §605: June 25, 1948, ch. 646, 62 Stat. 915; July 9, 1956, ch. 517, §1(e), 70 Stat. 497; Aug. 3, 1956, ch. 944, §4, 70 Stat. 1026; Sept. 19, 1961, P.L. 87-253, §3, 75 Stat. 521; Oct. 10, 1980, P.L. 96-417, §501(14), 94 Stat. 1742; Apr. 2, 1982, P.L. 97-164, §119(a), 96 Stat. 33; Sept. 13, 1982, P.L. 97-258, §5(b), 96 Stat. 1068, 1085.

§606. DUTIES OF DEPUTY DIRECTOR

The Deputy Director shall perform the duties assigned to him by the Director, and shall act as Director during the absence or incapacity of the Director or when the Director's office is vacant.

History of 28 U.S.C. §606: June 25, 1948, ch. 646, 62 Stat. 915; Sept. 23, 1959, P.L. 86-370, §5(a)(1), 73 Stat. 652.

§607. PRACTICE OF LAW PROHIBITED

An officer or employee of the Administrative Office shall not engage directly or indirectly in the practice of law in any court of the United States.

History of 28 U.S.C. §607: June 25, 1948, ch. 646, 62 Stat. 915.

§608. SEAL

The Director shall use a seal approved by the Supreme Court. Judicial notice shall be taken of such seal.

History of 28 U.S.C. §608: June 25, 1948, ch. 646, 62 Stat. 915.

§609. COURTS' APPOINTIVE POWER UNAFFECTED

The authority of the courts to appoint their own administrative or clerical personnel shall not be limited by any provisions of this chapter.

History of 28 U.S.C. §609: June 25, 1948, ch. 646, 62 Stat. 915.

§610. COURTS DEFINED

As used in this chapter the word "courts" includes the courts of appeals and district courts of the United States, the United States District Court for the District of the Canal Zone, the District Court of Guam, the District Court of the Virgin Islands, the United States Court of Federal Claims, and the Court of International Trade.

History of 28 U.S.C. §610: June 25, 1948, ch. 646, 62 Stat. 915; Oct. 31, 1951, ch. 655, §44, 65 Stat. 725; July 7, 1958, P.L. 85-508, §12(e), 72 Stat. 348; Nov. 6, 1978, P.L. 95-598, §226, 92 Stat. 2665; Oct. 10, 1980, P.L. 96-417, §501(15), 94 Stat. 1742; Apr. 2, 1982, P.L. 97-164, §120(a), 96 Stat. 33; Oct. 29, 1992, P.L. 102-572, §902(b)(1), 106 Stat. 4516.

§611. RETIREMENT OF DIRECTOR

(a) The Director may, by written election filed with the Chief Justice of the United States within 6 months after the date on which he takes office, waive coverage under chapter 83 of title 5, subchapter III (the Civil Service Retirement System) or chapter 84 of title 5 (the Federal Employees' Retirement System), whichever is applicable, and bring himself within the purview of this section. A Director who elects coverage under this section shall be deemed an "employee" for purposes of chapter 84 of title 5, subchapter III, regardless of whether he has waived the coverage of chapter 83, subchapter III, or chapter 84. Waiver of coverage under chapter 83, subchapter III, and election of this section shall not operate to foreclose to the Director, upon separation from service other than by retirement, such opportunity as the law may provide to secure retirement credit under chapter 83 for service as Director by depositing with interest the amount required by section 8334 of title 5. A Director who waives coverage under chapter 84 and elects this section may secure retirement credit under chapter 84 for service as Director by depositing with interest 1.3 percent of basic pay for service from January 1, 1984, through December 31, 1986, and the amount referred to in section 8422(a) of title 5, for service after December 31, 1986. Interest shall be computed under section 8334(e) of title 5.

(b) Upon the retirement of a Director who has elected coverage under this section and who has at least fifteen years of service and has attained the age of sixty-five years the Administrative Office of the United States Courts shall pay him an annuity for life equal to 80 per centum of the salary of the office at the time of his retirement.

Upon the retirement of a Director who has elected coverage under this section and who has at least ten years of service, but who is not eligible to receive an annuity under the first paragraph of this subsection, the Administrative Office of the United States Courts shall pay him an annuity for life equal to that proportion of 80 per centum of the salary of the office at the time of his retirement that the number of years of his service bears to fifteen, reduced by one-quarter of 1 per centum for each full month, if any, he is under the age of sixty-five at the time of separation from service.

(c) A Director who has elected coverage under this section and who becomes permanently disabled to perform the duties of his office shall be retired and shall receive an annuity for life equal to 80 per centum of the salary of the office at the time of his retirement if he has at least fifteen years of service, or equal to that proportion of 80 per centum of such salary that the aggregate number of years of his service bears to fifteen if he has less than fifteen years of service, but in no event less than 50 per centum of such salary.

(d) For the purpose of this section, "service" means service, whether or not continuous, as Director of the Administrative Office of the United States Courts, and any service, not to exceed five years, as a judge of the United States, a Senator or Representative in Congress, a congressional employee in the capacity of primary administrative assistant to a Member of Congress or in the capacity of staff director or chief counsel for the majority or the minority of a committee or subcommittee of the Senate or House of Representatives, or a civilian official appointed by the President, by and with the advice and consent of the Senate.

(e) Each annuity payable under this section shall be increased by the same percentage amount and effective on the same date as annuities payable under chapter 83 of title 5, are increased as provided by section 8340 of title 5.

History of 28 U.S.C. §611: Dec. 20, 1967, P.L. 90-219, §201(a), 81 Stat. 668; Nov. 19, 1988, P.L. 100-702, §§1004(a), 1006(a)(1), 102 Stat. 4665, 4666; Nov. 13, 2000, P.L. 106-518, §301(a), 114 Stat. 2416.

§612. JUDICIARY INFORMATION TECHNOLOGY FUND

(a) Establishment and availability of Fund.—There is hereby established in the Treasury of the United States a special fund to be known as the "Judiciary Information Technology Fund" (hereafter in this section referred to as the "Fund"). Moneys in the Fund shall be available to the Director without fiscal year limitation for the procurement (by lease, purchase, exchange, transfer, or otherwise) of information technology resources for program activities included in the courts of appeals, district courts, and other judicial services account of the judicial branch of the United States. The Fund shall also be available for expenses, including personal services, support personnel in the courts and in the Administrative Office of the United States Courts, and other costs, for the effective management, coordination, operation, and use of information technology resources purchased by the Fund. In addition, all agencies of the judiciary may make deposits into the Fund to meet their information technology needs in accordance with subsections (b) and (c)(2).

(b) Plan for meeting information technology needs.—

(1) Development of plan.—The Director shall develop and annually revise, with the approval of the Judicial Conference of the United States, a long range plan for meeting the information technology resources needs of the activities funded under subsection (a) and shall include an annual estimate of any fees that may be collected under section 404 of the Judiciary Appropriations Act, 1991 (Public Law 101-515; 104 Stat. 2133). Such plan and revisions shall be submitted to Congress.

(2) Expenditures consistent with plan.—The Director may use amounts in the Fund to procure information technology resources for the activities funded under subsection (a) only in accordance with the plan developed under paragraph (1).

(c) Deposits into Fund.—

(1) Deposits.—There shall be deposited in the Fund—

(A) all proceeds resulting from activities conducted under subsection (a), including net proceeds of disposal of excess or surplus property, all fees collected after the date of the enactment of the Judicial Amendments Act of 1994 by the judiciary under section 404 of the Judiciary Appropriations Act, 1991 (Public Law 101-515; 104 Stat. 2133) and receipts from carriers and others for loss of or damage to property;

(B) amounts available for activities described in subsection (a) from funds appropriated to the judiciary; and

(C) any advances and reimbursements required by paragraph (2).

(2) Advances and reimbursements.—Whenever the Director procures information technology resources for any entity in the judicial branch other than the courts or the Administrative Office, that entity shall advance or reimburse the Fund, whichever the Director considers appropriate, for the costs of the information technology resources, from appropriations available to that entity.

(d) Authorization of appropriations.—There are authorized to be appropriated to the Fund for any fiscal year such sums as are required to supplement amounts deposited under subsection (c) in order to conduct activities under subsection (a).

(e) Contract authority.—

(1) For each fiscal year.—In fiscal year 1990, and in each succeeding fiscal year, the Director may enter into contracts for the procurement of information technology resources in amounts which, in the aggregate, do not exceed amounts estimated to be collected under subsection (c) for that fiscal year in advance of the availability of amounts in the Fund for such contracts.

(2) Multiyear contracts.—In conducting activities under subsection (a), the Director is authorized to enter into multiyear contracts for information technology resources for periods of not more than five years for any contract, if—

(A) funds are available and adequate for payment of the costs of such contract for the first fiscal year and for payment of any costs of cancellation or termination of the contract;

(B) such contract is in accordance with the Director's authority in section 604(g) of 28 U.S.C.; and,[1]

(C) the Director determines that—

(i) the need for the information technology resources being provided will continue over the period of the contract; and

(ii) the use of the multi-year contract will yield substantial cost savings when compared with other methods of providing the necessary resources.

(3) Cancellation costs of multiyear contract.—Any cancellation costs incurred with respect to a contract entered into under paragraph (2) shall be paid from currently available amounts in the Fund.

(f) Authority of Administrator of General Services.—Nothing in this section shall be construed to limit the authority of the Administrator of General Services under sections 501-505 of title 40.

(g) Annual report.—

(1) In general.—The Director shall submit to the Congress an annual report on the operation of the Fund, including on the inventory, use, and acquisition of information technology resources from the Fund and the consistency of such acquisition with the plan prepared under subsection (b). The report shall set forth the amounts deposited into the Fund under subsection (c).

(2) Additional contents of report.—The annual report submitted under this subsection shall include—

(A) the specific actions taken and the progress made to improve the plan developed under subsection (b) and the long range automation plan and strategic business plan developed under subsection (k); and

(B) a comparison of planned Fund expenditures and accomplishments with actual Fund expenditures and accomplishments, and the reasons for any delays in scheduled systems development, or budget overruns.

(3) [Repealed Nov. 13, 2000, P.L. 106-518, §101(3), 114 Stat. 2411.]

(h) Reprogramming.—The Director of the Administrative Office of the United States Courts, under the supervision of the Judicial Conference of the United States, may transfer amounts up to $1,000,000 from the Fund into the account to which the funds were originally appropriated. Any amounts transferred from the Fund in excess of $1,000,000 in any fiscal year may only be transferred by following reprogramming procedures in compliance with section 606 of the Departments of Commerce, Justice, and State, the Judiciary, and Related Agencies Appropriations Act, 1989 (Public Law 100-459; 102 Stat. 2227).

(i) Appropriations into the Fund.—If the budget request of the judiciary is appropriated in full, the amount deposited into the Fund during any fiscal year under the authority of subsection (c)(1)(B) will be the same as the amount of funds requested by the judiciary for activities described in subsection (a). If an amount to be deposited is not specified in statute by Congress and if the full request is not appropriated, the amount to be deposited under subsection (c)(1)(B) will be set by the spending priorities established by the Judicial Conference.

(j) Long range management and business plans.—The Director of the Administrative Office of the United States Court shall—

(1) develop an overall strategic business plan which would identify the judiciary's missions, goals, and objectives;

(2) develop a long range automation plan based on the strategic business plan and user needs assessments;

(3) establish effective Administrative Office oversight of court automation efforts to ensure the effective operation of existing systems and control over developments of future systems;

(4) expedite efforts to complete the development and implementation of life cycle management standards;

(5) utilize the standards in developing the next generation of case management and financial systems; and

(6) assess the current utilization and future user requirements of the data communications network.

1. **Editor's note:** So in original. The comma probably should not appear.

History of 28 U.S.C. §612: Nov. 21, 1989, P.L. 101-162, §404(b)(1), 103 Stat. 1013; Oct. 25, 1994, P.L. 103-420, §2, 108 Stat. 4343; Feb. 10, 1996, P.L. 104-106, §5602, 110 Stat. 699; Sept. 30, 1996, P.L. 104-208, 110 Stat. 3009, 3009-45; Nov. 18, 1997, P.L. 105-85, §1073(h)(2), 111 Stat. 1907; Nov. 26, 1997, P.L. 105-119, §304, 111 Stat. 2491; Nov. 13, 2000, P.L. 106-518, §101, 114 Stat. 2411; Aug. 21, 2002, P.L. 107-217, §3(g)(2), 116 Stat. 1299; Nov. 30, 2005, P.L. 109-115, §407(b), 199 Stat. 2471.

§613. DISBURSING & CERTIFYING OFFICERS

(a) Disbursing officers.—The Director may designate in writing officers and employees of the judicial branch of the Government, including the courts as defined in section 610 other than the Supreme Court, to be disbursing officers in such numbers and locations as the Director considers necessary. Such disbursing officers shall—

(1) disburse moneys appropriated to the judicial branch and other funds only in strict accordance with payment requests certified by the Director or in accordance with subsection (b);

(2) examine payment requests as necessary to ascertain whether they are in proper form, certified, and approved; and

(3) be held accountable for their actions as provided by law, except that such a disbursing officer shall not be held accountable or responsible for any illegal, improper, or incorrect payment resulting from any false, inaccurate, or misleading certificate for which a certifying officer is responsible under subsection (b).

(b) Certifying officers.—

(1) In general.—The Director may designate in writing officers and employees of the judicial branch of the Government, including the courts as defined in section 610 other than the Supreme Court, to certify payment requests payable from appropriations and funds. Such certifying officers shall be responsible and accountable for—

(A) the existence and correctness of the facts recited in the certificate or other request for payment or its supporting papers;

(B) the legality of the proposed payment under the appropriation or fund involved; and

(C) the correctness of the computations of certified payment requests.

(2) Liability.—The liability of a certifying officer shall be enforced in the same manner and to the same extent as provided by law with respect to the enforcement of the liability of disbursing and other accountable officers. A certifying officer shall be required to make restitution to the United States for the amount of any illegal, improper, or incorrect payment resulting from any false, inaccurate, or misleading certificates made by the certifying officer, as well as for any payment prohibited by law or which did not represent a legal obligation under the appropriation or fund involved.

(c) Rights.—A certifying or disbursing officer—

(1) has the right to apply for and obtain a decision by the Comptroller General on any question of law involved in a payment request presented for certification; and

(2) is entitled to relief from liability arising under this section in accordance with title 31.

(d) Other authority not affected.—Nothing in this section affects the authority of the courts with respect to moneys deposited with the courts under chapter 129 of this title.

History of 28 U.S.C. §613: Nov. 13, 2000, P.L. 106-518, §304(a), 114 Stat. 2417.

CHAPTER 42. FEDERAL JUDICIAL CENTER

§620. FEDERAL JUDICIAL CENTER

(a) There is established within the judicial branch of the Government a Federal Judicial Center, whose purpose it shall be to further the development and adoption of improved judicial administration in the courts of the United States.

(b) The Center shall have the following functions:

(1) to conduct research and study of the operation of the courts of the United States, and to stimulate and coordinate such research and study on the part of other public and private persons and agencies;

(2) to develop and present for consideration by the Judicial Conference of the United States recommendations for

improvement of the administration and management of the courts of the United States;

(3) to stimulate, create, develop, and conduct programs of continuing education and training for personnel of the judicial branch of the Government and other persons whose participation in such programs would improve the operation of the judicial branch, including, but not limited to, judges, United States magistrate judges, clerks of court, probation officers, and persons serving as mediators and arbitrators;

(4) insofar as may be consistent with the performance of the other functions set forth in this section, to provide staff, research, and planning assistance to the Judicial Conference of the United States and its committees;

(5) Insofar[1] as may be consistent with the performance of the other functions set forth in this section, to cooperate with the State Justice Institute in the establishment and coordination of research and programs concerning the administration of justice; and

(6) insofar as may be consistent with the performance of the other functions set forth in this section, to cooperate with and assist agencies of the Federal Government and other appropriate organizations in providing information and advice to further improvement in the administration of justice in the courts of foreign countries and to acquire information about judicial administration in foreign countries that may contribute to performing the other functions set forth in this section.

1. **Editor's note:** So in original. Probably should not be capitalized.

History of 28 U.S.C. §620: Dec. 20, 1967, P.L. 90-219, §101, 81 Stat. 664; Nov. 6, 1978, P.L. 95-598, §227, 92 Stat. 2665; Nov. 8, 1984, P.L. 98-620, §214, 98 Stat. 3346; June 19, 1986, P.L. 99-336, §6(b), 100 Stat. 639; Nov. 19, 1988, P.L. 100-702, §303, 102 Stat. 4648; Oct. 29, 1992, P.L. 102-572, §602(a), 106 Stat. 4514.

§621. BOARD; COMPOSITION, TENURE OF MEMBERS, COMPENSATION

(a) The activities of the Center shall be supervised by a Board to be composed of—

(1) the Chief Justice of the United States, who shall be the permanent Chairman of the Board;

(2) two circuit judges, three district judges, one bankruptcy judge, and one magistrate judge, elected by vote of the members of the Judicial Conference of the United States, except that any circuit or district judge so elected may be either a judge in regular active service or a judge retired from regular active service under section 371(b) of this title but shall not be a member of the Judicial Conference of the United States; and

(3) the Director of the Administrative Office of the United States Courts, who shall be a permanent member of the Board.

(b) The term of office of each elected member of the Board shall be four years. A member elected to serve for an unexpired term arising by virtue of the death, disability, retirement pursuant to section 371(a) or section 372(a) of this title, or resignation of a member shall be elected only for such unexpired term.

(c) No member elected for a four-year term shall be eligible for reelection to the Board.

(d) Members of the Board shall serve without additional compensation, but shall be reimbursed for actual and necessary expenses incurred in the performance of their official duties.

History of 28 U.S.C. §621: Dec. 20, 1967, P.L. 90-219, §101, 81 Stat. 664; Nov. 6, 1978, P.L. 95-598, §§228, 229, 92 Stat. 2665; Oct. 19, 1996, P.L. 104-317, §601(b), 110 Stat. 3847.

§622. MEETINGS; CONDUCT OF BUSINESS

(a) Regular meetings of the Board shall be held quarterly. Special meetings shall be held from time to time upon the call of the Chairman, acting at his own discretion or pursuant to the petition of any four members.

(b) Each member of the Board shall be entitled to one vote. A simple majority of the membership shall constitute a quorum for the conduct of business. The Board shall act upon the concurrence of a simple majority of the members present and voting.

History of 28 U.S.C. §622: Dec. 20, 1967, P.L. 90-219, §101, 81 Stat. 665.

§623. DUTIES OF THE BOARD

(a) In its direction and supervision of the activities of the Federal Judicial Center, the Board shall—

(1) establish such policies and develop such programs for the Federal Judicial Center as will further achievement of its purpose and performance of its functions;

(2) formulate recommendations for improvements in the administration of the courts of the United States, in the training of the personnel of those courts, and in the management of their resources;

(3) submit to the Judicial Conference of the United States, at least one month in advance of its annual meeting, a report of the activities of the Center and such recommendations as the Board may propose for the consideration of the Conference;

(4) present to other government departments, agencies, and instrumentalities whose programs or activities relate to the administration of justice in the courts of the United States the recommendations of the Center for the improvement of such programs or activities;

(5) study and determine ways in which automatic data processing and systems procedures may be applied to the administration of the courts of the United States, and include in the annual report required by paragraph (3) of this subsection details of the results of the studies and determinations made pursuant to this paragraph;

(6) consider and recommend to both public and private agencies aspects of the operation of the courts of the United States deemed worthy of special study; and

(7) conduct, coordinate, and encourage programs relating to the history of the judicial branch of the United States Government.

(b) The Board shall transmit to Congress and to the Attorney General of the United States copies of all reports and recommendations submitted to the Judicial Conference of the United States. The Board shall also keep the Committees on the Judiciary of the United States Senate and House of Representatives fully and currently informed with respect to the activities of the Center.

History of 28 U.S.C. §623: Dec. 20, 1967, P.L. 90-219, §101, 81 Stat. 665; Nov. 19, 1988, P.L. 100-702, §302, 102 Stat. 4648.

§624. POWERS OF THE BOARD

The Board is authorized—

(1) to appoint and fix the duties of the Director and the Deputy Director of the Federal Judicial Center, who shall serve at the pleasure of the Board;

(2) to request from any department, agency, or independent instrumentality of the Government any information it deems necessary to the performance of the functions of the Federal Judicial Center set forth in this chapter, and each such department, agency, or instrumentality is directed to cooperate with the Board and, to the extent permitted by law, to furnish such information to the Center upon request of the Chairman or upon request of the Director when the Board has delegated this authority to him;

(3) to contract with and compensate government and private agencies or persons for research projects and other services, without regard to section 6101(b) to (d) of title 41, and to delegate such contract authority to the Director of the Federal Judicial Center, who is hereby empowered to exercise such delegated authority.

History of 28 U.S.C. §624: Dec. 20, 1967, P.L. 90-219, §101, 81 Stat. 666; Nov. 19, 1988, P.L. 100-702, §304(a), 102 Stat. 4648; Jan. 4, 2011, P.L. 111-350, §5(g)(3), 124 Stat. 3848.

§625. DIRECTOR & STAFF

(a) The Director shall supervise the activities of persons employed by the Center and perform other duties assigned to him by the Board.

(b) The Director shall appoint and fix the compensation of such additional professional personnel as the Board may deem necessary, without regard to the provisions of title 5, United States Code, governing appointments in competitive service, or the provisions of chapter 51 and subchapter III of chapter 53 of such title, relating to classification and General Schedule pay rates: Provided, however, That the compensation of any person appointed under this subsection shall not exceed the annual rate of basic pay of level V of the Executive Schedule pay rates, section 5316, title 5, United States Code: And provided further, That the salary of a reemployed annuitant under the Civil Servive[1] Retirement Act shall be adjusted pursuant to the provisions of section 8344, title 5, United States Code.

(c) The Director shall appoint and fix the compensation of such secretarial and clerical personnel as he may deem necessary, subject to the provisions of title 5, United States Code, governing appointments in competitive service without regard to the provisions of chapter 51 and subchapter III of chapter 53 of such title, relating to classification and General Schedule pay rates.

(d) The Director may procure personal services as authorized by section 3109 of title 5, United States Code, at rates not to exceed the daily equivalent of the highest rate payable under General Schedule pay rates, section 5332, title 5, United States Code.

(e) The Director is authorized to incur necessary travel and other miscellaneous expenses incident to the operation of the Center.

1. **Editor's note:** So in original. Probably should be "Service."

History of 28 U.S.C. §625: Dec. 20, 1967, P.L. 90-219, §101, 81 Stat. 666; Oct. 29, 1992, P.L. 102-572, §602(b), 106 Stat. 4514.

§626. COMPENSATION OF THE DIRECTOR & DEPUTY DIRECTOR

The compensation of the Director of the Federal Judicial Center shall be the same as that of the Director of the Administrative Office of the United States Courts, and his appointment and salary shall not be subject to the provisions of title 5, United States Code, governing appointments in competitive service, or the provisions of chapter 51 and subchapter III of chapter 53 of such title, relating to classification and General Schedule pay rates: Provided, however, That any Director who is a justice or judge of the United States in active or retired status shall serve without additional compensation. The compensation of the Deputy Director of the Federal Judicial Center shall be the same as that of the Deputy Director of the Administrative Office of the United States Courts.

History of 28 U.S.C. §626: Dec. 20, 1967, P.L. 90-219, §101, 81 Stat. 666; Nov. 19, 1988, P.L. 100-702, §304(b)(1), 102 Stat. 4648.

§627. RETIREMENT; EMPLOYEE BENEFITS

(a) The Director, Deputy Director, the professional staff, and the clerical and secretarial employees of the Federal Judicial Center shall be deemed to be officers and employees of the judicial branch of the United States Government within the meaning of subchapter III of chapter 83 (relating to civil service retirement), chapter 84 (relating to the Federal Employees' Retirement System), chapter 87 (relating to Federal employees' life insurance program), and chapter 89 (relating to Federal employees' health benefits program) of title 5, United States Code: Provided, however, That the Director, upon written notice filed with the Director of the Administrative Office of the United States Courts within 6 months after the date on which he takes office, may waive coverage under chapter 83 of title 5, subchapter III (the Civil Service Retirement System) or chapter 84 of title 5 (the Federal Employees' Retirement System), whichever is applicable, and elect coverage under the retirement and disability provisions of this section. A Director

who elects coverage under this section shall be deemed an "employee" for purposes of chapter 84 of title 5, subchapter III, regardless of whether he has waived the coverage of chapter 83, subchapter III, or chapter 84: And provided further, That upon his nonretirement separation from the Federal Judicial Center, waiver of coverage under chapter 83, subchapter III, and election of this section shall not operate to foreclose to the Director such opportunity as the law may provide to secure retirement credit under chapter 83 for service as Director by depositing with interest the amount required by section 8334 of title 5. A Director who waives coverage under chapter 84 and elects this section may secure retirement credit under chapter 84 for service as Director by depositing with interest 1.3 percent of basic pay for service from January 1, 1984, through December 31, 1986, and the amount referred to in section 8422(a) of title 5, for service after December 31, 1986. Interest shall be computed under section 8334(e) of title 5.

(b) Upon the retirement of a Director who has elected coverage under this section and who has at least fifteen years of service and has attained the age of sixty-five years the Director of the Administrative Office of the United States Courts shall pay him an annuity for life equal to 80 per centum of the salary of the office at the time of his retirement.

Upon the retirement of a Director who has elected coverage under this section and who has at least ten years of service, but who is not eligible to receive an annuity under the first paragraph of this subsection, the Administrative Office of the United States Courts shall pay him an annuity for life equal to that proportion of 80 per centum of the salary of the office at the time of his retirement that the number of years of his service bears to fifteen, reduced by one-quarter of 1 per centum for each full month, if any, he is under the age of sixty-five at the time of separation from service.

(c) A Director who has elected coverage under this section and who becomes permanently disabled to perform the duties of his office shall be retired and shall receive an annuity for life equal to 80 per centum of the salary of the office at the time of his retirement if he has at least fifteen years of service, or equal to that proportion of 80 per centum of such salary that the aggregate number of years of his service bears to fifteen if he has less than fifteen years of service, but in no event less than 50 per centum of such salary.

(d) For the purpose of this section, "service" means service, whether or not continuous, as Director of the Federal Judicial Center, and any service, not to exceed five years, as a judge of the United States, a Senator or Representative in Congress, a congressional employee in the capacity of primary administrative assistant to a Member of Congress or in the capacity of staff director or chief counsel for the majority or the minority of a committee or subcommittee of the Senate or House of Representatives, or a civilian official appointed by the President, by and with the advice and consent of the Senate.

(e) Each annuity payable under this section shall be increased by the same percentage amount and effective on the same date as annuities payable under chapter 83 of title 5, are increased as provided by section 8340 of title 5.

History of 28 U.S.C. §627: Dec. 20, 1967, P.L. 90-219, §101, 81 Stat. 666; Nov. 19, 1988, P.L. 100-702, §§1004(a), 1006(a)(2), 102 Stat. 4665, 4666; Oct. 19, 1996, P.L. 104-317, §604, 110 Stat. 3857; Nov. 13, 2000, P.L. 106-518, §§301(b), 312(a), 114 Stat. 2416, 2421.

§628. APPROPRIATIONS & ACCOUNTING

There are hereby authorized to be appropriated such sums as may be necessary to carry out the provisions of this chapter. The Administrative Office of the United States Courts shall provide accounting, disbursing, auditing, and other fiscal services for the Federal Judicial Center.

History of 28 U.S.C. §628: Dec. 20, 1967, P.L. 90-219, §101, 81 Stat. 667.

§629. FEDERAL JUDICIAL CENTER FOUNDATION

(a) There is established a private nonprofit corporation which shall be known as the Federal Judicial Center Foundation (hereafter in this section referred to as the "Foundation") and which shall be incorporated in the District of Columbia. The purpose of the Foundation shall be to have sole authority to accept and receive gifts of real and personal property and services made for the purpose of aiding or facilitating the work of the Federal Judicial Center. The Foundation shall not accept conditional or otherwise restricted gifts, except gifts that are designated for the support of specific projects previously approved by the Board of the Center may be accepted. The Foundation shall have no authority to administer or otherwise determine the use of gifts accepted under this section.

(b) The business of the Foundation shall be conducted by a Board that shall have seven members, including a chairman. Three members, including the chairman, shall be appointed by the Chief Justice of the United States, two by the President Pro Tempore of the Senate, and two by the Speaker of the House of Representatives. The term of office of each member of the Board shall be 5 years, except that the initial terms shall be 5 years for the chairman, one member appointed by the President Pro Tempore and one member appointed by the Speaker, 3 years for the other member appointed by the President Pro Tempore and the other member appointed by the Speaker, and two years for the two other members appointed by the Chief Justice. Members of the Board shall serve without compensation but, upon authorization of the Director of the Center, shall be reimbursed by the Federal Judicial Center for actual and necessary expenses incurred in the performance of their official duties. No person who is a Federal or State judge in regular active service or otherwise eligible to perform judicial duties shall be eligible for membership on the Board. The Center shall provide all administrative support and facilities necessary for the operation of the Board.

(c) The Federal Judicial Center is authorized to administer and use gifts received by the Foundation under this sec-

tion. The gifts shall be used to further the goals of the Center as determined by the Board of the Center.

(d) Gifts of money and proceeds from sales of other property received as gifts shall be deposited in a separate fund in the Treasury of the United States and disbursed on the order of the Director of the Center, in accordance with policies established by the Board of the Center.

(e) The Board of the Foundation shall, not later than October 1 of each year, submit to the Committees on the Judiciary of the United States Senate and House of Representatives a report with respect to gifts received under this section during the preceding 12-month period, including the source of each such gift, the amount of each gift of cash or cash equivalent, and a description of any other gift. The Center shall include in its annual report of the activities of the Center under section 623(a)(3) a description of the purposes for which gifts were used during the year covered by the report.

(f) For the purpose of Federal income, estate, and gift taxes, property accepted under this section shall be considered as a gift or bequest to or for the use of the United States.

History of 28 U.S.C. §629: Nov. 19, 1988, P.L. 100-702, §301(a), 102 Stat. 4646.

CHAPTER 43. UNITED STATES MAGISTRATE JUDGES

§631. APPOINTMENT & TENURE

(a) The judges of each United States district court and the district courts of the Virgin Islands, Guam, and the Northern Mariana Islands shall appoint United States magistrate judges in such numbers and to serve at such locations within the judicial districts as the Judicial Conference may determine under this chapter. In the case of a magistrate judge appointed by the district court of the Virgin Islands, Guam, or the Northern Mariana Islands, this chapter shall apply as though the court appointing such a magistrate judge were a United States district court. Where there is more than one judge of a district court, the appointment, whether an original appointment or a reappointment, shall be by the concurrence of a majority of all the judges of such district court, and when there is no such concurrence, then by the chief judge. Where the conference deems it desirable, a magistrate judge may be designated to serve in one or more districts adjoining the district for which he is appointed. Such a designation shall be made by the concurrence of a majority of the judges of each of the district courts involved and shall specify the duties to be performed by the magistrate judge in the adjoining district or districts.

(b) No individual may be appointed or reappointed to serve as a magistrate judge under this chapter unless:

(1) He has been for at least five years a member in good standing of the bar of the highest court of a State, the District of Columbia, the Commonwealth of Puerto Rico, the Territory of Guam, the Commonwealth of the Northern Mariana Islands, or the Virgin Islands of the United States, except that an individual who does not meet the bar membership requirements of this paragraph may be appointed and serve as a part-time magistrate judge if the appointing court or courts and the conference find that no qualified individual who is a member of the bar is available to serve at a specific location;

(2) He is determined by the appointing district court or courts to be competent to perform the duties of the office;

(3) In the case of an individual appointed to serve in a national park, he resides within the exterior boundaries of that park, or at some place reasonably adjacent thereto;

(4) He is not related by blood or marriage to a judge of the appointing court or courts at the time of his initial appointment; and

(5) He is selected pursuant to standards and procedures promulgated by the Judicial Conference of the United States. Such standards and procedures shall contain provision for public notice of all vacancies in magistrate judge positions and for the establishment by the district courts of merit selection panels, composed of residents of the individual judicial districts, to assist the courts in identifying and recommending persons who are best qualified to fill such positions.

(c) A magistrate judge may hold no other civil or military office or employment under the United States: Provided, however, That, with the approval of the conference, a part-time referee in bankruptcy or a clerk or deputy clerk of a court of the United States may be appointed and serve as a part-time United States magistrate judge, but the conference shall fix the aggregate amount of compensation to be received for performing the duties of part-time magistrate judge and part-time referee in bankruptcy, clerk or deputy clerk: And provided further, That retired officers and retired enlisted personnel of the Regular and Reserve components of the Army, Navy, Air Force, Marine Corps, and Coast Guard, members of the Reserve components of the Army, Navy, Air Force, Marine Corps, and Coast Guard, and members of the Army National Guard of the United States, the Air National Guard of the United States, and the Naval Militia and of the National Guard of a State, territory, or the District of Columbia, except the National Guard disbursing officers who are on a full-time salary basis, may be appointed and serve as United States magistrate judges.

(d) Except as otherwise provided in sections 375 and 636(h) of this title, no individual may serve under this chapter after having attained the age of seventy years: Provided, however, That upon a majority vote of all the judges of the appointing court or courts, which is taken upon the magistrate judge's attaining age seventy and upon each subsequent anniversary thereof, a magistrate judge who has attained the age of seventy years may continue to serve and may be reappointed under this chapter.

(e) The appointment of any individual as a full-time magistrate judge shall be for a term of eight years, and the appointment of any individuals as a part-time magistrate judge

28 U.S.C. §631

shall be for a term of four years, except that the term of a full-time or part-time magistrate judge appointed under subsection (k) shall expire upon—

(1) the expiration of the absent magistrate judge's term,

(2) the reinstatement of the absent magistrate judge in regular service in office as a magistrate judge,

(3) the failure of the absent magistrate judge to make timely application under subsection (j) of this section for reinstatement in regular service in office as a magistrate judge after discharge or release from military service,

(4) the death or resignation of the absent magistrate judge, or

(5) the removal from office of the absent magistrate judge pursuant to subsection (i) of this section,

whichever may first occur.

(f) Upon the expiration of his term, a magistrate judge may, by a majority vote of the judges of the appointing district court or courts and with the approval of the judicial council of the circuit, continue to perform the duties of his office until his successor is appointed, or for 180 days after the date of the expiration of the magistrate judge's term, whichever is earlier.

(g) Each individual appointed as a magistrate judge under this section shall take the oath or affirmation prescribed by section 453 of this title before performing the duties of his office.

(h) Each appointment made by a judge or judges of a district court shall be entered of record in such court, and notice of such appointment shall be given at once by the clerk of that court to the Director.

(i) Removal of a magistrate judge during the term for which he is appointed shall be only for incompetency, misconduct, neglect of duty, or physical or mental disability, but a magistrate judge's office shall be terminated if the conference determines that the services performed by his office are no longer needed. Removal shall be by the judges of the district court for the judicial district in which the magistrate judge serves; where there is more than one judge of a district court, removal shall not occur unless a majority of all the judges of such court concur in the order of removal; and when there is a tie vote of the judges of the district court on the question of the removal or retention in office of a magistrate judge, then removal shall be only by a concurrence of a majority of all the judges of the council. In the case of a magistrate judge appointed under the third sentence of subsection (a) of this section, removal shall not occur unless a majority of all the judges of the appointing district courts concur in the order of removal; and where there is a tie vote on the question of the removal or retention in office of a magistrate judge, then removal shall be only by a concurrence of a majority of all the judges of the council or councils. Before any order or removal shall be entered, a full specification of the charges shall be furnished to the magistrate judge, and he shall be accorded by the judge or judges of the removing court, courts, council, or councils an opportunity to be heard on the charges.

(j) Upon the grant by the appropriate district court or courts of a leave of absence to a magistrate judge entitled to such relief under chapter 43 of title 38, such court or courts may proceed to appoint, in the manner specified in subsection (a) of this section, another magistrate judge, qualified for appointment and service under subsections (b), (c), and (d) of this section, who shall serve for the period specified in subsection (e) of this section.

(k) A United States magistrate judge appointed under this chapter shall be exempt from the provisions of subchapter I of chapter 63 of title 5.

(*l*) [Redesignated (k).]

History of 28 U.S.C. §631: June 25, 1948, ch. 646, 62 Stat. 915; May 24, 1949, ch. 139, §73, 63 Stat. 100; July 9, 1952, ch. 609, §1, 66 Stat. 509; July 25, 1956, ch. 722, 70 Stat. 642; Oct. 17, 1968, P.L. 90-578, §101, 82 Stat. 1108; Oct. 17, 1976, P.L. 94-520, §2, 90 Stat. 2458; Nov. 6, 1978, P.L. 95-598, §231, 92 Stat. 2665; Oct. 10, 1979, P.L. 96-82, §3(a)-(d), 93 Stat. 644, 645; Aug. 6, 1982, P.L. 97-230, 96 Stat. 255; Nov. 14, 1986, P.L. 99-651, §201(a)(1), 100 Stat. 3646; Nov. 15, 1988, P.L. 100-659, §5, 102 Stat. 3918; Nov. 19, 1988, P.L. 100-702, §1003(a)(2), 102 Stat. 4665; June 30, 1989, P.L. 101-45, §104, 103 Stat. 122; Dec. 1, 1990, P.L. 101-650, §308(b), 104 Stat. 5112; Oct. 13, 1994, P.L. 103-353, §2(c), 108 Stat. 3169; Nov. 13, 2000, P.L. 106-518, §201, 114 Stat. 2412; Jan. 7, 2008, P.L. 110-177, §504, 121 Stat. 2542; May 27, 2010, P.L. 111-174, §2, 124 Stat. 1216.

See ***Commentaries***, "Magistrate Judges & Special Masters," ch. 5-B, p. 297.

§632. CHARACTER OF SERVICE

(a) Full-time United States magistrate judges may not engage in the practice of law, and may not engage in any other business, occupation, or employment inconsistent with the expeditious, proper, and impartial performance of their duties as judicial officers.

(b) Part-time United States magistrate judges shall render such service as judicial officers as is required by law. While so serving they may engage in the practice of law, but may not serve as counsel in any criminal action in any court of the United States, nor act in any capacity that is, under such regulations as the conference may establish, inconsistent with the proper discharge of their office. Within such restrictions, they may engage in any other business, occupation, or employment which is not inconsistent with the expeditious, proper, and impartial performance of their duties as judicial officers.

History of 28 U.S.C. §632: June 25, 1948, ch. 646, 62 Stat. 916; Oct. 17, 1968, P.L. 90-578, §101, 82 Stat. 1110.

See ***Commentaries***, "Magistrate Judges & Special Masters," ch. 5-B, p. 297.

§633. DETERMINATION OF NUMBER, LOCATIONS, & SALARIES OF MAGISTRATE JUDGES

(a) Surveys by the Director.—

(1) The Director shall, within one year immediately following the date of the enactment of the Federal Magistrates Act, make a careful survey of conditions in judicial districts to determine (A) the number of appointments of full-time mag-

istrates and part-time magistrates required to be made under this chapter to provide for the expeditious and effective administration of justice, (B) the locations at which such officers shall serve, and (C) their respective salaries under section 634 of this title. Thereafter, the Director shall, from time to time, make such surveys, general or local, as the conference shall deem expedient.

(2) In the course of any survey, the Director shall take into account local conditions in each judicial district, including the areas and the populations to be served, the transportation and communications facilities available, the amount and distribution of business of the type expected to arise before officers appointed under this chapter (including such matters as may be assigned under section 636(b) of this chapter), and any other material factors. The Director shall give consideration to suggestions from any interested parties, including district judges, United States magistrate judges or officers appointed under this chapter, United States attorneys, bar associations, and other parties having relevant experience or information.

(3) The surveys shall be made with a view toward creating and maintaining a system of full-time United States magistrate judges. However, should the Director find, as a result of any such surveys, areas in which the employment of a full-time magistrate judge would not be feasible or desirable, he shall recommend the appointment of part-time United States magistrate judges in such numbers and at such locations as may be required to permit prompt and efficient issuance of process and to permit individuals charged with criminal offenses against the United States to be brought before a judicial officer of the United States promptly after arrest.

(b) Determination by the conference.—Upon the completion of the initial surveys required by subsection (a) of this section, the Director shall report to the district courts, the councils, and the conference his recommendations concerning the number of full-time magistrates and part-time magistrates, their respective locations, and the amount of their respective salaries under section 634 of this title. The district courts shall advise their respective councils, stating their recommendations and the reasons therefor; the councils shall advise the conference, stating their recommendations and the reasons therefor, and shall also report to the conference the recommendations of the district courts. The conference shall determine, in the light of the recommendations of the Director, the district courts, and the councils, the number of full-time United States magistrates and part-time United States magistrates, the locations at which they shall serve, and their respective salaries. Such determinations shall take effect in each judicial district at such time as the district court for such judicial district shall determine, but in no event later than one year after they are promulgated.

(c) Changes in number, locations, and salaries.—Except as otherwise provided in this chapter, the conference may, from time to time, in the light of the recommendations of the Director, the district courts, and the councils, change the number, locations, and salaries of full-time and part-time magistrate judges, as the expeditious administration of justice may require.

History of 28 U.S.C. §633: June 25, 1948, ch. 646, 62 Stat. 916; Aug. 13, 1954, ch. 728, §1(a), (b), 68 Stat. 703; Sept. 2, 1957, P.L. 85-276, §§1, 2, 71 Stat. 600; Oct. 17, 1968, P.L. 90-578, §101, 82 Stat. 1111; Oct. 10, 1979, P.L. 96-82, §4, 93 Stat. 645; Nov. 14, 1986, P.L. 99-651, §202(d), 100 Stat. 3648; Dec. 1, 1990, P.L. 101-650, §321, 104 Stat. 5117.

See *Commentaries*, "Magistrate Judges & Special Masters," ch. 5-B, p. 297.

§634. COMPENSATION

(a) Officers appointed under this chapter shall receive, as full compensation for their services, salaries to be fixed by the conference pursuant to section 633, at rates for full-time United States magistrate judges up to an annual rate equal to 92 percent of the salary of a judge of the district court of the United States, as determined pursuant to section 135, and at rates for part-time magistrate judges of not less than an annual salary of $100, nor more than one-half the maximum salary payable to a full-time magistrate judge. In fixing the amount of salary to be paid to any officer appointed under this chapter, consideration shall be given to the average number and the nature of matters that have arisen during the immediately preceding period of five years, and that may be expected thereafter to arise, over which such officer would have jurisdiction and to such other factors as may be material. Disbursement of salaries shall be made by or pursuant to the order of the Director.

(b) Except as provided by section 8344, title 5, relating to reductions of the salaries of reemployed annuitants under subchapter III of chapter 83 of such title and unless the office has been terminated as provided in this chapter, the salary of a full-time United States magistrate judge shall not be reduced, during the term in which he is serving, below the salary fixed for him at the beginning of that term.

(c) All United States magistrate judges, effective upon their taking the oath or affirmation of office, and all necessary legal, clerical, and secretarial assistants employed in the offices of full-time United States magistrate judges shall be deemed to be officers and employees in the judicial branch of the United States Government within the meaning of subchapter III (relating to civil service retirement) of chapter 83, chapter 87 (relating to Federal employees' group life insurance), and chapter 89 (relating to Federal employees' health benefits program) of title 5. Part-time magistrate judges shall not be excluded from coverage under these chapters solely for lack of a prearranged regular tour of duty. A legal assistant appointed under this section shall be exempt from the provisions of subchapter I of chapter 63 of title 5, unless specifically included by the appointing judge or by local rule of court.

History of 28 U.S.C. §634: June 25, 1948, ch. 646, 62 Stat. 917; Oct. 17, 1968, P.L. 90-578, §101, 82 Stat. 1112; Sept. 21, 1972, P.L. 92-428, 86 Stat. 721; Oct. 17, 1976, P.L. 94-520, §1, 90 Stat. 2458; Nov. 6, 1978, P.L. 95-598, §232, 92

Stat. 2665; Oct. 10, 1979, P.L. 96-82, §8(b), 93 Stat. 647; July 10, 1984, P.L. 98-353, §§108(a), 210, 98 Stat. 342, 351; Dec. 22, 1987, P.L. 100-202, §§101(a), 408(b), 101 Stat. 1329, 1329-27; Nov. 19, 1988, P.L. 100-702, §1003(a)(4), 102 Stat. 4665.

See *Commentaries*, "Magistrate Judges & Special Masters," ch. 5-B, p. 297.

§635. EXPENSES

(a) Full-time United States magistrate judges serving under this chapter shall be allowed their actual and necessary expenses incurred in the performance of their duties, including the compensation of such legal assistants as the Judicial Conference, on the basis of the recommendations of the judicial councils of the circuits, considers necessary, and the compensation of necessary clerical and secretarial assistance. Such expenses and compensation shall be determined and paid by the Director under such regulations as the Director shall prescribe with the approval of the conference. The Administrator of General Services shall provide such magistrate judges with necessary courtrooms, office space, furniture and facilities within United States courthouses or office buildings owned or occupied by departments or agencies of the United States, or should suitable courtroom and office space not be available within any such courthouse or office building, the Administrator of General Services, at the request of the Director, shall procure and pay for suitable courtroom and office space, furniture and facilities for such magistrate judge in another building, but only if such request has been approved as necessary by the judicial council of the appropriate circuit.

(b) Under such regulations as the Director shall prescribe with the approval of the conference, the Director shall reimburse part-time magistrate judges for actual expenses necessarily incurred by them in the performance of their duties under this chapter. Such reimbursement may be made, at rates not exceeding those prescribed by such regulations, for expenses incurred by such part-time magistrate judges for clerical and secretarial assistance, stationery, telephone and other communications services, travel, and such other expenses as may be determined to be necessary for the proper performance of the duties of such officers: Provided, however, That no reimbursement shall be made for all or any portion of the expense incurred by such part-time magistrate judges for the procurement of office space.

History of 28 U.S.C. §635: June 25, 1948, ch. 646, 62 Stat. 917; Oct. 17, 1968, P.L. 90-578, §101, 82 Stat. 1112; Oct. 10, 1979, P.L. 96-82, §8(a), 93 Stat. 646.

See *Commentaries*, "Magistrate Judges & Special Masters," ch. 5-B, p. 297.

§636. JURISDICTION, POWERS, & TEMPORARY ASSIGNMENT

(a) Each United States magistrate judge serving under this chapter shall have within the district in which sessions are held by the court that appointed the magistrate judge, at other places where that court may function, and elsewhere as authorized by law—

(1) all powers and duties conferred or imposed upon United States commissioners by law or by the Rules of Criminal Procedure for the United States District Courts;

(2) the power to administer oaths and affirmations, issue orders pursuant to section 3142 of title 18 concerning release or detention of persons pending trial, and take acknowledgements, affidavits, and depositions;

(3) the power to conduct trials under section 3401, title 18, United States Code, in conformity with and subject to the limitations of that section;

(4) the power to enter a sentence for a petty offense; and

(5) the power to enter a sentence for a class A misdemeanor in a case in which the parties have consented.

(b)(1) Notwithstanding any provision of law to the contrary—

(A) a judge may designate a magistrate judge to hear and determine any pretrial matter pending before the court, except a motion for injunctive relief, for judgment on the pleadings, for summary judgment, to dismiss or quash an indictment or information made by the defendant, to suppress evidence in a criminal case, to dismiss or to permit maintenance of a class action, to dismiss for failure to state a claim upon which relief can be granted, and to involuntarily dismiss an action. A judge of the court may reconsider any pretrial matter under this subparagraph (A) where it has been shown that the magistrate judge's order is clearly erroneous or contrary to law.

(B) a judge may also designate a magistrate judge to conduct hearings, including evidentiary hearings, and to submit to a judge of the court proposed findings of fact and recommendations for the disposition, by a judge of the court, of any motion excepted in subparagraph (A), of applications for posttrial relief made by individuals convicted of criminal offenses and of prisoner petitions challenging conditions of confinement.

(C) the magistrate judge shall file his proposed findings and recommendations under subparagraph (B) with the court and a copy shall forthwith be mailed to all parties.

Within fourteen days after being served with a copy, any party may serve and file written objections to such proposed findings and recommendations as provided by rules of court. A judge of the court shall make a de novo determination of those portions of the report or specified proposed findings or recommendations to which objection is made. A judge of the court may accept, reject, or modify, in whole or in part, the findings or recommendations made by the magistrate judge. The judge may also receive further evidence or recommit the matter to the magistrate judge with instructions.

(2) A judge may designate a magistrate judge to serve as a special master pursuant to the applicable provisions of this title and the Federal Rules of Civil Procedure for the United States district courts. A judge may designate a magistrate judge to serve as a special master in any civil case, upon con-

sent of the parties, without regard to the provisions of rule 53(b) of the Federal Rules of Civil Procedure for the United States district courts.

(3) A magistrate judge may be assigned such additional duties as are not inconsistent with the Constitution and laws of the United States.

(4) Each district court shall establish rules pursuant to which the magistrate judges shall discharge their duties.

(c) Notwithstanding any provision of law to the contrary—

(1) Upon the consent of the parties, a full-time United States magistrate judge or a part-time United States magistrate judge who serves as a full-time judicial officer may conduct any or all proceedings in a jury or nonjury civil matter and order the entry of judgment in the case, when specially designated to exercise such jurisdiction by the district court or courts he serves. Upon the consent of the parties, pursuant to their specific written request, any other part-time magistrate judge may exercise such jurisdiction, if such magistrate judge meets the bar membership requirements set forth in section 631(b)(1) and the chief judge of the district court certifies that a full-time magistrate judge is not reasonably available in accordance with guidelines established by the judicial council of the circuit. When there is more than one judge of a district court, designation under this paragraph shall be by the concurrence of a majority of all the judges of such district court, and when there is no such concurrence, then by the chief judge.

(2) If a magistrate judge is designated to exercise civil jurisdiction under paragraph (1) of this subsection, the clerk of court shall, at the time the action is filed, notify the parties of the availability of a magistrate judge to exercise such jurisdiction. The decision of the parties shall be communicated to the clerk of court. Thereafter, either the district court judge or the magistrate judge may again advise the parties of the availability of the magistrate judge, but in so doing, shall also advise the parties that they are free to withhold consent without adverse substantive consequences. Rules of court for the reference of civil matters to magistrate judges shall include procedures to protect the voluntariness of the parties' consent.

(3) Upon entry of judgment in any case referred under paragraph (1) of this subsection, an aggrieved party may appeal directly to the appropriate United States court of appeals from the judgment of the magistrate judge in the same manner as an appeal from any other judgment of a district court. The consent of the parties allows a magistrate judge designated to exercise civil jurisdiction under paragraph (1) of this subsection to direct the entry of a judgment of the district court in accordance with the Federal Rules of Civil Procedure. Nothing in this paragraph shall be construed as a limitation of any party's right to seek review by the Supreme Court of the United States.

(4) The court may, for good cause shown on its own motion, or under extraordinary circumstances shown by any party, vacate a reference of a civil matter to a magistrate judge under this subsection.

(5) The magistrate judge shall, subject to guidelines of the Judicial Conference, determine whether the record taken pursuant to this section shall be taken by electronic sound recording, by a court reporter, or by other means.

(6), (7) [Redesignated (4) and (5).]

(d) The practice and procedure for the trial of cases before officers serving under this chapter shall conform to rules promulgated by the Supreme Court pursuant to section 2072 of this title.

(e) **Contempt authority.—**

(1) **In general.**—A United States magistrate judge serving under this chapter shall have within the territorial jurisdiction prescribed by the appointment of such magistrate judge the power to exercise contempt authority as set forth in this subsection.

(2) **Summary criminal contempt authority.**—A magistrate judge shall have the power to punish summarily by fine or imprisonment, or both, such contempt of the authority of such magistrate judge constituting misbehavior of any person in the magistrate judge's presence so as to obstruct the administration of justice. The order of contempt shall be issued under the Federal Rules of Criminal Procedure.

(3) **Additional criminal contempt authority in civil consent and misdemeanor cases.**—In any case in which a United States magistrate judge presides with the consent of the parties under subsection (c) of this section, and in any misdemeanor case proceeding before a magistrate judge under section 3401 of title 18, the magistrate judge shall have the power to punish, by fine or imprisonment, or both, criminal contempt constituting disobedience or resistance to the magistrate judge's lawful writ, process, order, rule, decree, or command. Disposition of such contempt shall be conducted upon notice and hearing under the Federal Rules of Criminal Procedure.

(4) **Civil contempt authority in civil consent and misdemeanor cases.**—In any case in which a United States magistrate judge presides with the consent of the parties under subsection (c) of this section, and in any misdemeanor case proceeding before a magistrate judge under section 3401 of title 18, the magistrate judge may exercise the civil contempt authority of the district court. This paragraph shall not be construed to limit the authority of a magistrate judge to order sanctions under any other statute, the Federal Rules of Civil Procedure, or the Federal Rules of Criminal Procedure.

(5) **Criminal contempt penalties.**—The sentence imposed by a magistrate judge for any criminal contempt provided for in paragraphs (2) and (3) shall not exceed the penalties for a Class C misdemeanor as set forth in sections 3581(b)(8) and 3571(b)(6) of title 18.

(6) Certification of other contempts to the district court.—Upon the commission of any such act—

(A) in any case in which a United States magistrate judge presides with the consent of the parties under subsection (c) of this section, or in any misdemeanor case proceeding before a magistrate judge under section 3401 of title 18, that may, in the opinion of the magistrate judge, constitute a serious criminal contempt punishable by penalties exceeding those set forth in paragraph (5) of this subsection, or

(B) in any other case or proceeding under subsection (a) or (b) of this section, or any other statute, where—

(i) the act committed in the magistrate judge's presence may, in the opinion of the magistrate judge, constitute a serious criminal contempt punishable by penalties exceeding those set forth in paragraph (5) of this subsection,

(ii) the act that constitutes a criminal contempt occurs outside the presence of the magistrate judge, or

(iii) the act constitutes a civil contempt,

the magistrate judge shall forthwith certify the facts to a district judge and may serve or cause to be served, upon any person whose behavior is brought into question under this paragraph, an order requiring such person to appear before a district judge upon a day certain to show cause why that person should not be adjudged in contempt by reason of the facts so certified. The district judge shall thereupon hear the evidence as to the act or conduct complained of and, if it is such as to warrant punishment, punish such person in the same manner and to the same extent as for a contempt committed before a district judge.

(7) Appeals of magistrate judge contempt orders.—The appeal of an order of contempt under this subsection shall be made to the court of appeals in cases proceeding under subsection (c) of this section. The appeal of any other order of contempt issued under this section shall be made to the district court.

(f) In an emergency and upon the concurrence of the chief judges of the districts involved, a United States magistrate judge may be temporarily assigned to perform any of the duties specified in subsection (a), (b), or (c) of this section in a judicial district other than the judicial district for which he has been appointed. No magistrate judge shall perform any of such duties in a district to which he has been temporarily assigned until an order has been issued by the chief judge of such district specifying (1) the emergency by reason of which he has been transferred, (2) the duration of his assignment, and (3) the duties which he is authorized to perform. A magistrate judge so assigned shall not be entitled to additional compensation but shall be reimbursed for actual and necessary expenses incurred in the performance of his duties in accordance with section 635.

(g) A United States magistrate judge may perform the verification function required by section 4107 of title 18, United States Code. A magistrate judge may be assigned by a judge of any United States district court to perform the verification required by section 4108 and the appointment of counsel authorized by section 4109 of title 18, United States Code, and may perform such functions beyond the territorial limits of the United States. A magistrate judge assigned such functions shall have no authority to perform any other function within the territory of a foreign country.

(h) A United States magistrate judge who has retired may, upon the consent of the chief judge of the district involved, be recalled to serve as a magistrate judge in any judicial district by the judicial council of the circuit within which such district is located. Upon recall, a magistrate judge may receive a salary for such service in accordance with regulations promulgated by the Judicial Conference, subject to the restrictions on the payment of an annuity set forth in section 377 of this title or in subchapter III of chapter 83, and chapter 84, of title 5 which are applicable to such magistrate judge. The requirements set forth in subsections (a), (b)(3), and (d) of section 631, and paragraph (1) of subsection (b) of such section to the extent such paragraph requires membership of the bar of the location in which an individual is to serve as a magistrate judge, shall not apply to the recall of a retired magistrate judge under this subsection or section 375 of this title. Any other requirement set forth in section 631(b) shall apply to the recall of a retired magistrate judge under this subsection or section 375 of this title unless such retired magistrate judge met such requirement upon appointment or reappointment as a magistrate judge under section 631.

History of 28 U.S.C. §636: June 25, 1948, ch. 646, 62 Stat. 917; Oct. 17, 1968, P.L. 90-578, §101, 82 Stat. 1113; Mar. 1, 1972, P.L. 92-239, §§1, 2, 86 Stat. 47; Oct. 21, 1976, P.L. 94-577, §1, 90 Stat. 2729; Oct. 28, 1977, P.L. 95-144, §2, 91 Stat. 1220; Oct. 10, 1979, P.L. 96-82, §2, 93 Stat. 643; Oct. 12, 1984, P.L. 98-473, §208, 98 Stat. 1986; Nov. 8, 1984, P.L. 98-620, §402(29)(B), 98 Stat. 3359; Nov. 14, 1986, P.L. 99-651, §201(a)(2), 100 Stat. 3647; Nov. 15, 1988, P.L. 100-659, §4(c), 102 Stat. 3918; Nov. 18, 1988, P.L. 100-690, §7322, 102 Stat. 4467; Nov. 19, 1988, P.L. 100-702, §§404(b)(1), 1014, 102 Stat. 4651, 4669; Dec. 1, 1990, P.L. 101-650, §308(a), 104 Stat. 5112; Oct. 19, 1996, P.L. 104-317, §§201, 202(b), 207, 110 Stat. 3848-51; Nov. 13, 2000, P.L. 106-518, §§202, 203(b), 114 Stat. 2412, 2414; Nov. 2, 2002, P.L. 107-273, §3002(b), 116 Stat. 1805; Sept. 9, 2005, P.L. 109-63, §2(d), 119 Stat. 1995; May 7, 2009, P.L. 111-16, §6, 123 Stat. 1608.

See ***Commentaries***, "Magistrate Judges & Special Masters," ch. 5-B, p. 297.

§637. TRAINING

The Federal Judicial Center shall conduct periodic training programs and seminars for both full-time and part-time United States magistrate judges, including an introductory training program for new magistrate judges, to be held within one year after initial appointment.

History of 28 U.S.C. §637: June 25, 1948, ch. 646, 62 Stat. 917; Oct. 17, 1968, P.L. 90-578, §101, 82 Stat. 1114.

See ***Commentaries***, "Magistrate Judges & Special Masters," ch. 5-B, p. 297.

§638. DOCKETS & FORMS; UNITED STATES CODE; SEALS

(a) The Director shall furnish to United States magistrate judges adequate docket books and forms prescribed by the Director. The Director shall also furnish to each such officer a copy of the current edition of the United States Code.

(b) All property furnished to any such officer shall remain the property of the United States and, upon the termination of his term of office, shall be transmitted to his successor in office or otherwise disposed of as the Director orders.

(c) The Director shall furnish to each United States magistrate judge appointed under this chapter an official impression seal in a form prescribed by the conference. Each such officer shall affix his seal to every jurat or certificate of his official acts without fee.

History of 28 U.S.C. §638: June 25, 1948, ch. 646, 62 Stat. 917; Oct. 17, 1968, P.L. 90-578, §101, 82 Stat. 1114.

See ***Commentaries***, "Magistrate Judges & Special Masters," ch. 5-B, p. 297.

§639. DEFINITIONS

As used in this chapter—

(1) "Conference" shall mean the Judicial Conference of the United States;

(2) "Council" shall mean the Judicial Council of the Circuit;

(3) "Director" shall mean the Director of the Administrative Office of the United States Courts;

(4) "Full-time magistrate judge" shall mean a full-time United States magistrate judge;

(5) "Part-time magistrate judge" shall mean a part-time United States magistrate judge; and

(6) "United States magistrate judge" and "magistrate judge" shall mean both full-time and part-time United States magistrate judges.

History of 28 U.S.C. §639: June 25, 1948, ch. 646, 62 Stat. 917; Oct. 17, 1968, P.L. 90-578, §101, 82 Stat. 1114.

See ***Commentaries***, "Magistrate Judges & Special Masters," ch. 5-B, p. 297.

CHAPTER 44. ALTERNATIVE DISPUTE RESOLUTION

§651. AUTHORIZATION OF ALTERNATIVE DISPUTE RESOLUTION

(a) Definition.—For purposes of this chapter, an alternative dispute resolution process includes any process or procedure, other than an adjudication by a presiding judge, in which a neutral third party participates to assist in the resolution of issues in controversy, through processes such as early neutral evaluation, mediation, minitrial, and arbitration as provided in sections 654 through 658.

(b) Authority.—Each United States district court shall authorize, by local rule adopted under section 2071(a), the use of alternative dispute resolution processes in all civil actions, including adversary proceedings in bankruptcy, in accordance with this chapter, except that the use of arbitration may be authorized only as provided in section 654. Each United States district court shall devise and implement its own alternative dispute resolution program, by local rule adopted under section 2071(a), to encourage and promote the use of alternative dispute resolution in its district.

(c) Existing alternative dispute resolution programs.—In those courts where an alternative dispute resolution program is in place on the date of the enactment of the Alternative Dispute Resolution Act of 1998, the court shall examine the effectiveness of that program and adopt such improvements to the program as are consistent with the provisions and purposes of this chapter.

(d) Administration of alternative dispute resolution programs.—Each United States district court shall designate an employee, or a judicial officer, who is knowledgeable in alternative dispute resolution practices and processes to implement, administer, oversee, and evaluate the court's alternative dispute resolution program. Such person may also be responsible for recruiting, screening, and training attorneys to serve as neutrals and arbitrators in the court's alternative dispute resolution program.

(e) Title 9 not affected.—This chapter shall not affect title 9, United States Code.

(f) Program support.—The Federal Judicial Center and the Administrative Office of the United States Courts are authorized to assist the district courts in the establishment and improvement of alternative dispute resolution programs by identifying particular practices employed in successful programs and providing additional assistance as needed and appropriate.

History of 28 U.S.C. §651: Nov. 19, 1988, P.L. 100-702, §901(a), 102 Stat. 4659; Oct. 30, 1998, P.L. 105-315, §3, 112 Stat. 2993.

§652. JURISDICTION

(a) Consideration of alternative dispute resolution in appropriate cases.—Notwithstanding any provision of law to the contrary and except as provided in subsections (b) and (c), each district court shall, by local rule adopted under section 2071(a), require that litigants in all civil cases consider the use of an alternative dispute resolution process at an appropriate stage in the litigation. Each district court shall provide litigants in all civil cases with at least one alternative dispute resolution process, including, but not limited to, mediation, early neutral evaluation, minitrial, and arbitration as authorized in sections 654 through 658. Any district court that elects to require the use of alternative dispute resolution in certain cases may do so only with respect to mediation, early neutral evaluation, and, if the parties consent, arbitration.

(b) Actions exempted from consideration of alternative dispute resolution.—Each district court may exempt from the requirements of this section specific cases or categories of cases in which use of alternative dispute resolution would not be appropriate. In defining these exemptions, each district court shall consult with members of the bar, including the United States Attorney for that district.

(c) Authority of the Attorney General.—Nothing in this section shall alter or conflict with the authority of the Attorney General to conduct litigation on behalf of the United States, with the authority of any Federal agency authorized to

conduct litigation in the United States courts, or with any delegation of litigation authority by the Attorney General.

(d) Confidentiality provisions.—Until such time as rules are adopted under chapter 131 of this title providing for the confidentiality of alternative dispute resolution processes under this chapter, each district court shall, by local rule adopted under section 2071(a), provide for the confidentiality of the alternative dispute resolution processes and to prohibit disclosure of confidential dispute resolution communications.

History of 28 U.S.C. §652: Nov. 19, 1988, P.L. 100-702, §901(a), 102 Stat. 4659; Oct. 30, 1998, P.L. 105-315, §4, 112 Stat. 2994.

§653. NEUTRALS

(a) Panel of neutrals.—Each district court that authorizes the use of alternative dispute resolution processes shall adopt appropriate processes for making neutrals available for use by the parties for each category of process offered. Each district court shall promulgate its own procedures and criteria for the selection of neutrals on its panels.

(b) Qualifications and training.—Each person serving as a neutral in an alternative dispute resolution process should be qualified and trained to serve as a neutral in the appropriate alternative dispute resolution process. For this purpose, the district court may use, among others, magistrate judges who have been trained to serve as neutrals in alternative dispute resolution processes, professional neutrals from the private sector, and persons who have been trained to serve as neutrals in alternative dispute resolution processes. Until such time as rules are adopted under chapter 131 of this title relating to the disqualification of neutrals, each district court shall issue rules under section 2071(a) relating to the disqualification of neutrals (including, where appropriate, disqualification under section 455 of this title, other applicable law, and professional responsibility standards).

History of 28 U.S.C. §653: Nov. 19, 1988, P.L. 100-702, §901(a), 102 Stat. 4660; Oct. 30, 1998, P.L. 105-315, §5, 112 Stat. 2995.

§654. ARBITRATION

(a) Referral of actions to arbitration.—Notwithstanding any provision of law to the contrary and except as provided in subsections (a), (b), and (c) of section 652 and subsection (d) of this section, a district court may allow the referral to arbitration of any civil action (including any adversary proceeding in bankruptcy) pending before it when the parties consent, except that referral to arbitration may not be made where—

(1) the action is based on an alleged violation of a right secured by the Constitution of the United States;

(2) jurisdiction is based in whole or in part on section 1343 of this title; or

(3) the relief sought consists of money damages in an amount greater than $150,000.

(b) Safeguards in consent cases.—Until such time as rules are adopted under chapter 131 of this title relating to procedures described in this subsection, the district court shall, by local rule adopted under section 2071(a), establish procedures to ensure that any civil action in which arbitration by consent is allowed under subsection (a)—

(1) consent to arbitration is freely and knowingly obtained; and

(2) no party or attorney is prejudiced for refusing to participate in arbitration.

(c) Presumptions.—For purposes of subsection (a)(3), a district court may presume damages are not in excess of $150,000 unless counsel certifies that damages exceed such amount.

(d) Existing programs.—Nothing in this chapter is deemed to affect any program in which arbitration is conducted pursuant to section[1] title IX of the Judicial Improvements and Access to Justice Act (Public Law 100-702), as amended by section 1 of Public Law 105-53.

1. **Editor's note:** So in original. The word "section" probably should not appear.

History of 28 U.S.C. §654: Nov. 19, 1988, P.L. 100-702, §901(a), 102 Stat. 4660; Oct. 30, 1998, P.L. 105-315, §6, 112 Stat. 2995.

§655. ARBITRATORS

(a) Powers of arbitrators.—An arbitrator to whom an action is referred under section 654 shall have the power, within the judicial district of the district court which referred the action to arbitration—

(1) to conduct arbitration hearings;

(2) to administer oaths and affirmations; and

(3) to make awards.

(b) Standards for certification.—Each district court that authorizes arbitration shall establish standards for the certification of arbitrators and shall certify arbitrators to perform services in accordance with such standards and this chapter. The standards shall include provisions requiring that any arbitrator—

(1) shall take the oath or affirmation described in section 453; and

(2) shall be subject to the disqualification rules under section 455.

(c) Immunity.—All individuals serving as arbitrators in an alternative dispute resolution program under this chapter are performing quasi-judicial functions and are entitled to the immunities and protections that the law accords to persons serving in such capacity.

History of 28 U.S.C. §655: Nov. 19, 1988, P.L. 100-702, §901(a), 102 Stat. 4661; Oct. 30, 1998, P.L. 105-315, §7, 112 Stat. 2996.

§656. SUBPOENAS

Rule 45 of the Federal Rules of Civil Procedure (relating to subpoenas) applies to subpoenas for the attendance of witnesses and the production of documentary evidence at an arbitration hearing under this chapter.

History of 28 U.S.C. §656: Nov. 19, 1988, P.L. 100-702, §901(a), 102 Stat. 4662; Oct. 30, 1998, P.L. 105-315, §8, 112 Stat. 2996.

§657. ARBITRATION AWARD & JUDGMENT

(a) Filing and effect of arbitration award.—An arbitration award made by an arbitrator under this chapter, along with proof of service of such award on the other party by the prevailing party or by the plaintiff, shall be filed promptly after the arbitration hearing is concluded with the clerk of the district court that referred the case to arbitration. Such award shall be entered as the judgment of the court after the time has expired for requesting a trial de novo. The judgment so entered shall be subject to the same provisions of law and shall have the same force and effect as a judgment of the court in a civil action, except that the judgment shall not be subject to review in any other court by appeal or otherwise.

(b) Sealing of arbitration award.—The district court shall provide, by local rule adopted under section 2071(a), that the contents of any arbitration award made under this chapter shall not be made known to any judge who might be assigned to the case until the district court has entered final judgment in the action or the action has otherwise terminated.

(c) Trial de novo of arbitration awards.—

(1) Time for filing demand.—Within 30 days after the filing of an arbitration award with a district court under subsection (a), any party may file a written demand for a trial de novo in the district court.

(2) Action restored to court docket.—Upon a demand for a trial de novo, the action shall be restored to the docket of the court and treated for all purposes as if it had not been referred to arbitration.

(3) Exclusion of evidence of arbitration.—The court shall not admit at the trial de novo any evidence that there has been an arbitration proceeding, the nature or amount of any award, or any other matter concerning the conduct of the arbitration proceeding, unless—

(A) the evidence would otherwise be admissible in the court under the Federal Rules of Evidence; or

(B) the parties have otherwise stipulated.

History of 28 U.S.C. §657: Nov. 19, 1988, P.L. 100-702, §901(a), 102 Stat. 4662; Oct. 30, 1998, P.L. 105-315, §9, 112 Stat. 2997.

§658. COMPENSATION OF ARBITRATORS & NEUTRALS

(a) Compensation.—The district court shall, subject to regulations approved by the Judicial Conference of the United States, establish the amount of compensation, if any, that each arbitrator or neutral shall receive for services rendered in each case under this chapter.

(b) Transportation allowances.—Under regulations prescribed by the Director of the Administrative Office of the United States Courts, a district court may reimburse arbitrators and other neutrals for actual transportation expenses necessarily incurred in the performance of duties under this chapter.

History of 28 U.S.C. §658: Nov. 19, 1988, P.L. 100-702, §901(a), 102 Stat. 4662; Oct. 30, 1998, P.L. 105-315, §10, 112 Stat. 2997.

CHAPTER 45. SUPREME COURT

§671. CLERK

(a) The Supreme Court may appoint and fix the compensation of a clerk and one or more deputy clerks. The clerk shall be subject to removal by the Court. Deputy clerks shall be subject to removal by the clerk with the approval of the Court or the Chief Justice of the United States.

(b) [Repealed June 6, 1972, P.L. 92-310, §206(c), 86 Stat. 203.]

(c) The clerk may appoint and fix the compensation of necessary assistants and messengers with the approval of the Chief Justice of the United States.

(d) The clerk shall pay into the Treasury all fees, costs, and other moneys collected by him. He shall make annual returns thereof to the Court under regulations prescribed by it.

History of 28 U.S.C. §671: June 25, 1948, ch. 646, 62 Stat. 918; Mar. 10, 1964, P.L. 88-279, §1, 78 Stat. 158; June 6, 1972, P.L. 92-310, §206(c), 86 Stat. 203.

§672. MARSHAL

(a) The Supreme Court may appoint a marshal, who shall be subject to removal by the Court, and may fix his compensation.

(b) The marshal may, with the approval of the Chief Justice of the United States, appoint and fix the compensation of necessary assistants and other employees to attend the Court, and necessary custodial employees.

(c) The marshal shall:

(1) Attend the Court at its sessions;

(2) Serve and execute all process and orders issued by the Court or a member thereof;

(3) Take charge of all property of the United States used by the Court or its members;

(4) Disburse funds appropriated for work upon the Supreme Court building and grounds under the jurisdiction of the Architect of the Capitol upon certified vouchers submitted by the Architect;

(5) Disburse funds appropriated for the purchase of books, pamphlets, periodicals and other publications, and for their repair, binding, and rebinding, upon vouchers certified by the librarian of the Court;

(6) Pay the salaries of the Chief Justice, associate justices, and all officers and employees of the Court and disburse other funds appropriated for disbursement, under the direction of the Chief Justice;

(7) Pay the expenses of printing briefs and travel expenses of attorneys in behalf of persons whose motions to appear in forma pauperis in the Supreme Court have been approved and when counsel have been appointed by the Supreme Court, upon vouchers certified by the clerk of the Court;

(8) Oversee the Supreme Court Police.

History of 28 U.S.C. §672: June 25, 1948, ch. 646, 62 Stat. 918; Mar. 10, 1964, P.L. 88-279, §2, 78 Stat. 158; Dec. 29, 1982, P.L. 97-390, §2, 96 Stat. 1958.

§673. REPORTER

(a) The Supreme Court may appoint and fix the compensation of a reporter of its decisions who shall be subject to removal by the Court.

(b) The reporter may appoint and fix the compensation of necessary professional and clerical assistants and other employees, with the approval of the Court or the Chief Justice of the United States.

(c) The reporter shall, under the direction of the Court or the Chief Justice, prepare the decisions of the Court for publication in bound volumes and advance copies in pamphlet installments.

The reporter shall determine the quality and size of the paper, type, format, proofs and binding subject to the approval of the Court or the Chief Justice.

History of 28 U.S.C. §673: June 25, 1948, ch. 646, 62 Stat. 919.

§674. LIBRARIAN

(a) The Supreme Court may appoint a librarian, whose salary it shall fix, and who shall be subject to removal by the Court.

(b) The librarian shall, with the approval of the Chief Justice, appoint necessary assistants and fix their compensation and make rules governing the use of the library.

(c) He shall select and acquire by purchase, gift, bequest, or exchange, such books, pamphlets, periodicals, microfilm and other processed copy as may be required by the Court for its official use and for the reasonable needs of its bar.

(d) The librarian shall certify to the marshal for payment vouchers covering expenditures for the purchase of such books and other material, and for binding, rebinding and repairing the same.

History of 28 U.S.C. §674: June 25, 1948, ch. 646, 62 Stat. 919; June 6, 1972, P.L. 92-310, §206(d), 86 Stat. 203.

§675. LAW CLERKS & SECRETARIES

The Chief Justice of the United States, and the associate justices of the Supreme Court may appoint law clerks and secretaries whose salaries shall be fixed by the Court.

History of 28 U.S.C. §675: June 25, 1948, ch. 646, 62 Stat. 919.

§676. PRINTING & BINDING

(a) The printing and binding for the Supreme Court, including the printing and binding of individual copies, advance pamphlet installments, and bound volumes, of its decisions, whether requisitioned or ordered by the Court or any of its officers or by any other office or agency, and whether paid for by, or charged to the appropriation for, the Court or any other office or agency, shall be done by the printer or printers whom the Court or the Chief Justice of the United States may select, unless it shall otherwise order.

(b) Whenever advance pamphlet installments and bound volumes of the Court's decisions are printed by a private printer, an adequate number of copies for distribution in accordance with the requirements of section 411 of this title and for sale to the public shall be provided and made available for these purposes in such manner and at such prices as may be determined from time to time by the Supreme Court or the Chief Justice of the United States, in lieu of compliance by the Public Printer and the Superintendent of Documents with the requirements of sections 411 and 412 of this title with respect to such copies. Pending distribution or sale, such copies shall be the property of the United States and shall be held in the custody of the marshal or such other person, organization, or agency, as the Supreme Court or the Chief Justice of the United States may designate.

History of 28 U.S.C. §676: June 25, 1948, ch. 646, 62 Stat. 919; May 24, 1949, ch. 139, §74, 63 Stat. 100; Oct. 31, 1951, ch. 655, §45, 65 Stat. 725.

§677. COUNSELOR TO THE CHIEF JUSTICE

(a) The Chief Justice of the United States may appoint a Counselor who shall serve at the pleasure of the Chief Justice and shall perform such duties as may be assigned to him by the Chief Justice. The salary payable to the Counselor shall be fixed by the Chief Justice at a rate which shall not exceed the salary payable to the Director of the Administrative Office of the United States Courts. The Counselor may elect to bring himself within the same retirement program available to the Director of the Administrative Office of the United States Courts, as provided by section 611 of this title, by filing a written election with the Chief Justice within the time and in the manner prescribed by section 611.

(b) The Counselor, with the approval of the Chief Justice, may appoint and fix the compensation of necessary employees. The Counselor and his employees shall be deemed employees of the Supreme Court.

(c)(1) Notwithstanding section 1342 of title 31, the Counselor, with the approval of the Chief Justice, may accept voluntary personal services to assist with public and visitor programs.

(2) No person may volunteer personal services under this subsection unless the person has first agreed, in writing, to waive any claim against the United States arising out of or in connection with such services, other than a claim under chapter 81 of title 5.

(3) No person volunteering personal services under this subsection shall be considered an employee of the United States for any purpose other than for purposes of—

(A) chapter 81 of title 5; or

(B) chapter 171 of this title.

(4) In the administration of this subsection, the Counselor shall ensure that the acceptance of personal services shall not result in the reduction of pay or displacement of any employee of the Supreme Court.

History of 28 U.S.C. §677: Mar. 1, 1972, P.L. 92-238, §1, 86 Stat. 46; Aug. 13, 1998, P.L. 105-233, §1, 112 Stat. 1535; Oct. 13, 2008, P.L. 110-402, §1(b)(3)(A), 122 Stat. 4254.

CHAPTER 47. COURTS OF APPEALS

§711. CLERKS & EMPLOYEES

(a) Each court of appeals may appoint a clerk who shall be subject to removal by the court.

(b) The clerk, with the approval of the court, may appoint necessary deputies, clerical assistants and employees in such number as may be approved by the Director of the Administrative Office of the United States Courts. Such deputies, clerical assistants and employees shall be subject to removal by the clerk with the approval of the court.

(c) The clerk shall pay into the Treasury all fees, costs and other moneys collected by him and make returns thereof to the Director of the Administrative Office of the United States Courts under regulations prescribed by him.

History of 28 U.S.C. §711: June 25, 1948, ch. 646, 62 Stat. 920.

§712. LAW CLERKS & SECRETARIES

Circuit judges may appoint necessary law clerks and secretaries. A law clerk appointed under this section shall be exempt from the provisions of subchapter I of chapter 63 of title 5, unless specifically included by the appointing judge or by local rule of court.

History of 28 U.S.C. §712: June 25, 1948, ch. 646, 62 Stat. 920; Nov. 19, 1988, P.L. 100-702, §1003(a)(3), 102 Stat. 4665.

§713. LIBRARIANS

(a) Each court of appeals may appoint a librarian who shall be subject to removal by the court.

(b) The librarian, with the approval of the court, may appoint necessary library assistants in such numbers as the Director of the Administrative Office of the United States Courts may approve. The librarian may remove such library assistants with the approval of the court.

History of 28 U.S.C. §713: June 25, 1948, ch. 646, 62 Stat. 920; May 24, 1949, ch. 139, §75, 63 Stat. 100; Apr. 2, 1982, P.L. 97-164, §120(b)(1), 96 Stat. 33.

§714. CRIERS & MESSENGERS

(a) Each court of appeals may appoint a crier who shall be subject to removal by the court.

(b) The crier, with the approval of the court, may appoint necessary messengers in such number as the Director of the Administrative Office of the United States Courts may approve. The crier may remove such messengers with the approval of the court. The crier shall also perform the duties of bailiff and messenger.

History of 28 U.S.C. §714: Apr. 2, 1982, P.L. 97-164, §120(c)(1), 96 Stat. 33.

§715. STAFF ATTORNEYS & TECHNICAL ASSISTANTS

(a) The chief judge of each court of appeals, with the approval of the court, may appoint a senior staff attorney, who shall be subject to removal by the chief judge with the approval of the court.

(b) The senior staff attorney, with the approval of the chief judge, may appoint necessary staff attorneys and secretarial and clerical employees in such numbers as the Director of the Administrative Office of the United States Courts may approve, but in no event may the number of staff attorneys exceed the number of positions expressly authorized in an annual appropriation Act. The senior staff attorney may remove such staff attorneys and secretarial and clerical employees with the approval of the chief judge.

(c) The chief judge of the Court of Appeals for the Federal Circuit, with the approval of the court, may appoint a senior technical assistant who shall be subject to removal by the chief judge with the approval of the court.

(d) The senior technical assistant, with the approval of the court, may appoint necessary technical assistants in such number as the Director of the Administrative Office of the United States Courts may approve, but in no event may the number of technical assistants in the Court of Appeals for the Federal Circuit exceed the number of circuit judges in regular active service within such circuit. The senior technical assistant may remove such technical assistants with the approval of the court.

History of 28 U.S.C. §715: Apr. 2, 1982, P.L. 97-164, §120(c)(1), 96 Stat. 34.

CHAPTER 49. DISTRICT COURTS

§751. CLERKS

(a) Each district court may appoint a clerk who shall be subject to removal by the court.

(b) The clerk may appoint, with the approval of the court, necessary deputies, clerical assistants and employees in such number as may be approved by the Director of the Administrative Office of the United States Courts. Such deputies, clerical assistants and employees shall be subject to removal by the clerk with the approval of the court.

(c) The clerk of each district court shall reside in the district for which he is appointed, except that the clerk of the district court for the District of Columbia and the Southern District of New York may reside within twenty miles thereof. The district court may designate places within the district for the offices of the clerk and his deputies, and their official stations.

(d) A clerk of a district court or his deputy or assistant shall not receive any compensation or emoluments through any office or position to which he is appointed by the court, other than that received as such clerk, deputy or assistant, whether from the United States or from private litigants.

This subsection shall not apply to clerks or deputy clerks appointed as United States magistrate judges pursuant to section 631 of this title.

(e) The clerk of each district court shall pay into the Treasury all fees, costs and other moneys collected by him, except naturalization fees listed in section 742 of Title 8 and uncollected fees not required by Act of Congress to be prepaid.

He shall make returns thereof to the Director of the Administrative Office of the United States Courts under regulations prescribed by him.

(f) When the Court of International Trade is sitting in a judicial district, other than the Southern District or Eastern District of New York, the clerk of the district court of such judicial district or an authorized deputy clerk, upon the request of the chief judge of the Court of International Trade and with the approval of such district court, shall act in the district as clerk of the Court of International Trade, as prescribed by the rules and orders of the Court of International Trade for all purposes relating to the civil action then pending before such court.

History of 28 U.S.C. §751: June 25, 1948, ch. 646, 62 Stat. 920; Oct. 17, 1968, P.L. 90-578, §402(b)(2), 82 Stat. 1118; Oct. 10, 1980, P.L. 96-417, §504, 94 Stat. 1743; Dec. 1, 1990, P.L. 101-650, §321, 104 Stat. 5117.

§752. LAW CLERKS & SECRETARIES

District judges may appoint necessary law clerks and secretaries subject to any limitation on the aggregate salaries of such employees which may be imposed by law. A law clerk appointed under this section shall be exempt from the provisions of subchapter I of chapter 63 of title 5, unless specifically included by the appointing judge or by local rule of court.

History of 28 U.S.C. §752: June 25, 1948, ch. 646, 62 Stat. 921; Sept. 1, 1959, P.L. 86-221, 73 Stat. 452; Nov. 19, 1988, P.L. 100-702, §1003(a)(3), 102 Stat. 4665.

§753. REPORTERS

(a) Each district court of the United States, the United States District Court for the District of the Canal Zone, the District Court of Guam, and the District Court of the Virgin Islands shall appoint one or more court reporters.

The number of reporters shall be determined by the Judicial Conference of the United States.

The qualifications of such reporters shall be determined by standards formulated by the Judicial Conference. Each reporter shall take an oath faithfully to perform the duties of his office.

Each such court, with the approval of the Director of the Administrative Office of the United States Courts, may appoint additional reporters for temporary service not exceeding three months, when there is more reporting work in the district than can be performed promptly by the authorized number of reporters and the urgency is so great as to render it impracticable to obtain the approval of the Judicial Conference.

If any such court and the Judicial Conference are of the opinion that it is in the public interest that the duties of reporter should be combined with those of any other employee of the court, the Judicial Conference may authorize such a combination and fix the salary for the performance of the duties combined.

(b) Each session of the court and every other proceeding designated by rule or order of the court or by one of the judges shall be recorded verbatim by shorthand, mechanical means, electronic sound recording, or any other method, subject to regulations promulgated by the Judicial Conference and subject to the discretion and approval of the judge. The regulations promulgated pursuant to the preceding sentence shall prescribe the types of electronic sound recording or other means which may be used. Proceedings to be recorded under this section include (1) all proceedings in criminal cases had in open court; (2) all proceedings in other cases had in open court unless the parties with the approval of the judge shall agree specifically to the contrary; and (3) such other proceedings as a judge of the court may direct or as may be required by rule or order of court as[1] may be requested by any party to the proceeding.

The reporter or other individual designated to produce the record shall attach his official certificate to the original shorthand notes or other original records so taken and promptly file them with the clerk who shall preserve them in the public records of the court for not less than ten years.

The reporter or other individual designated to produce the record shall transcribe and certify such parts of the record of proceedings as may be required by any rule or order of court, including all arraignments, pleas, and proceedings in connection with the imposition of sentence in criminal cases unless they have been recorded by electronic sound recording as provided in this subsection and the original records so taken have been certified by him and filed with the clerk as provided in this subsection. He shall also transcribe and certify such other parts of the record of proceedings as may be required by rule or order of court. Upon the request of any party to any proceeding which has been so recorded who has agreed to pay the fee therefor, or of a judge of the court, the reporter or other individual designated to produce the record shall promptly transcribe the original records of the requested parts of the proceedings and attach to the transcript his official certificate, and deliver the same to the party or judge making the request.

The reporter or other designated individual shall promptly deliver to the clerk for the records of the court a certified copy of any transcript so made.

The transcript in any case certified by the reporter or other individual designated to produce the record shall be deemed prima facie a correct statement of the testimony taken and proceedings had. No transcripts of the proceedings of the court shall be considered as official except those made from the records certified by the reporter or other individual designated to produce the record.

The original notes or other original records and the copy of the transcript in the office of the clerk shall be open during office hours to inspection by any person without charge.

(c) The reporters shall be subject to the supervision of the appointing court and the Judicial Conference in the performance of their duties, including dealings with parties requesting transcripts.

(d) The Judicial Conference shall prescribe records which shall be maintained and reports which shall be filed by the reporters. Such records shall be inspected and audited in the same manner as the records and accounts of clerks of the district courts, and may include records showing:

(1) the quantity of transcripts prepared;

(2) the fees charged and the fees collected for transcripts;

(3) any expenses incurred by the reporters in connection with transcripts;

(4) the amount of time the reporters are in attendance upon the courts for the purpose of recording proceedings; and

(5) such other information as the Judicial Conference may require.

(e) Each reporter shall receive an annual salary to be fixed from time to time by the Judicial Conference of the United States. For the purposes of subchapter III of chapter 83 of title 5 and chapter 84 of such title, a reporter shall be considered a full-time employee during any pay period for which a reporter receives a salary at the annual salary rate fixed for a full-time reporter under the preceding sentence. All supplies shall be furnished by the reporter at his own expense.

(f) Each reporter may charge and collect fees for transcripts requested by the parties, including the United States, at rates prescribed by the court subject to the approval of the Judicial Conference. He shall not charge a fee for any copy of a transcript delivered to the clerk for the records of court. Fees for transcripts furnished in criminal proceedings to persons proceeding under the Criminal Justice Act (18 U.S.C. 3006A), or in habeas corpus proceedings to persons allowed to sue, defend, or appeal in forma pauperis, shall be paid by the United States out of moneys appropriated for those purposes. Fees for transcripts furnished in proceedings brought under section 2255 of this title to persons permitted to sue or appeal in forma pauperis shall be paid by the United States out of money appropriated for that purpose if the trial judge or a circuit judge certifies that the suit or appeal is not frivolous and that the transcript is needed to decide the issue presented by the suit or appeal. Fees for transcripts furnished in other proceedings to persons permitted to appeal in forma pauperis shall also be paid by the United States if the trial judge or a circuit judge certifies that the appeal is not frivolous (but presents a substantial question). The reporter may require any party requesting a transcript to prepay the estimated fee in advance except as to transcripts that are to be paid for by the United States.

(g) If, upon the advice of the chief judge of any district court within the circuit, the judicial council of any circuit determines that the number of court reporters provided such district court pursuant to subsection (a) of this section is insufficient to meet temporary demands and needs and that the services of additional court reporters for such district court should be provided the judges of such district court (including the senior judges thereof when such senior judges are performing substantial judicial services for such court) on a contract basis, rather than by appointment of court reporters as otherwise provided in this section, and such judicial council notifies the Director of the Administrative Office, in writing, of such determination, the Director of the Administrative Office is authorized to and shall contract, without regard to section 6101(b) to (d) of title 41, with any suitable person, firm, association, or corporation for the providing of court reporters to serve such district court under such terms and conditions as the Director of the Administrative Office finds, after consultation with the chief judge of the district court, will best serve the needs of such district court.

1. **Editor's note:** So in original. Probably should be "or as."

History of 28 U.S.C. §753: June 25, 1948, ch. 646, 62 Stat. 921; Oct. 31, 1951, ch. 655, §46, 65 Stat. 726; June 28, 1955, ch. 189, §3(c), 69 Stat. 176; June 20, 1958, P.L. 85-462, §3(c), 72 Stat. 207; July 7, 1958, P.L. 85-508, §12(e), 72 Stat. 348; July 1, 1960, P.L. 86-568, §116(c), 74 Stat. 303; Sept. 2, 1965, P.L. 89-163, 79 Stat. 619; Sept. 2, 1965, P.L. 89-167, 79 Stat. 647; June 2, 1970, P.L. 91-272, §14, 84 Stat. 298; Dec. 11, 1970, P.L. 91-545, 84 Stat. 1412; Apr. 2, 1982, P.L. 97-164, §401(a), 96 Stat. 56; Oct. 19, 1996, P.L. 104-317, §305, 110 Stat. 3852; Jan. 4, 2011, P.L. 111-350, §5(g)(4), 124 Stat. 3848.

§754. RECEIVERS OF PROPERTY IN DIFFERENT DISTRICTS

A receiver appointed in any civil action or proceeding involving property, real, personal or mixed, situated in different districts shall, upon giving bond as required by the court, be vested with complete jurisdiction and control of all such property with the right to take possession thereof.

He shall have capacity to sue in any district without ancillary appointment, and may be sued with respect thereto as provided in section 959 of this title.

Such receiver shall, within ten days after the entry of his order of appointment, file copies of the complaint and such order of appointment in the district court for each district in which property is located. The failure to file such copies in any district shall divest the receiver of jurisdiction and control over all such property in that district.

History of 28 U.S.C. §754: June 25, 1948, ch. 646, 62 Stat. 922.

§755. CRIERS & BAILIFFS

Each district judge may appoint a crier for the court in which he presides who shall perform also the duties of bailiff and messenger. A crier may perform also the duties of law clerk if he is qualified to do so and the district judge who appointed him designates him to serve as a crier-law clerk. A crier designated to serve as a crier-law clerk shall receive the compensation of a law clerk, but only so much of that compensation as is in excess of the compensation to which he would be entitled as a crier shall be deemed the compensation of a law clerk for the purposes of any limitation imposed by law upon the aggregate salaries of law clerks and secretaries appointed by a district judge.

Each United States marshal may employ, with the approval of the judge, not exceeding four bailiffs as the district judge may determine, to attend the court, maintain order,

wait upon the grand and petit juries, and perform such other necessary duties as the judge or marshal may direct.

If the position of crier or bailiff is to be filled by the appointment of a person who has not previously served as either crier or bailiff, preference in the appointment shall be given to a person who has served in the military or naval forces of the United States in time of war and who has been honorably discharged therefrom, if in the opinion of the appointing officer such person is as well qualified as any other available person to perform to the satisfaction of the appointing officer all the duties of the position.

History of 28 U.S.C. §755: June 25, 1948, ch. 646, 62 Stat. 923; Oct. 21, 1965, P.L. 89-281, 79 Stat. 1012; Nov. 18, 1988, P.L. 100-690, §7608(b), 102 Stat. 4515.

§756. POWER TO APPOINT

Whenever a majority of the district judges of any district court cannot agree upon the appointment of any officer of such court, the chief judge shall make such appointment.

History of 28 U.S.C. §756: June 25, 1948, ch. 646, 62 Stat. 923.

CHAPTER 50. [OMITTED]

CHAPTER 51. UNITED STATES COURT OF FEDERAL CLAIMS

§791. CLERK

(a) The United States Court of Federal Claims may appoint a clerk, who shall be subject to removal by the court. The clerk, with the approval of the court, may appoint necessary deputies and employees in such numbers as may be approved by the Director of the Administrative Office of the United States Courts. Such deputies and employees shall be subject to removal by the clerk with the approval of the court.

(b) The clerk shall pay into the Treasury all fees, costs and other moneys collected by him. He shall make returns thereof to the Director of the Administrative Office of the United States Courts under regulations prescribed by him.

(c) On the first day of every regular session of Congress, the clerk shall transmit to Congress a full and complete statement of all the judgments rendered by the court during the previous year, showing the dates and amounts thereof and the parties in whose favor they were rendered, together with a brief synopsis of the nature of the claims upon which they were rendered, and a statement of the costs taxed in each case.

History of 28 U.S.C. §791: June 25, 1948, ch. 646, 62 Stat. 923; Apr. 2, 1982, P.L. 97-164, §121(a), 96 Stat. 34; Oct. 29, 1992, P.L. 102-572, §902(a)(1), 106 Stat. 4516.

§792. REPEALED

Repealed Apr. 2, 1982, P.L. 97-164, §121(b), 96 Stat. 34.

§793. REPEALED

Repealed July 28, 1953, ch. 253, §6, 67 Stat. 226.

§794. LAW CLERKS & SECRETARIES

The judges of the United States Court of Federal Claims may appoint necessary law clerks and secretaries, in such numbers as the Judicial Conference of the United States may approve for district judges, subject to any limitation of the aggregate salaries of such employees which may be imposed by law. A law clerk appointed under this section shall be exempt from the provisions of subchapter I of chapter 63 of title 5, unless specifically included by the appointing judge or by local rule of court.

History of 28 U.S.C. §794: June 25, 1948, ch. 646, 62 Stat. 924; Apr. 2, 1982, P.L. 97-164, §121(c)(1), 96 Stat. 34; Nov. 19, 1988, P.L. 100-702, §1003(a)(3), 102 Stat. 4665; Oct. 29, 1992, P.L. 102-572, §§902(a)(1), 905, 106 Stat. 4516, 4517.

§795. BAILIFFS & MESSENGERS

The chief judge of[1] United States Court of Federal Claims, with the approval of the court, may appoint necessary bailiffs and messengers, in such numbers as the Director of the Administrative Office of the United States Courts may approve, each of whom shall be subject to removal by the chief judge, with the approval of the court.

1. **Editor's note:** So in original. "The" probably should follow "of."

History of 28 U.S.C. §795: June 25, 1948, ch. 646, 62 Stat. 924; Apr. 2, 1982, P.L. 97-164, §121(d)(1), 96 Stat. 35; Oct. 29, 1992, P.L. 102-572, §902(a)(1), 106 Stat. 4516.

§796. REPORTING OF COURT PROCEEDINGS

Subject to the approval of the United States Court of Federal Claims, the Director of the Administrative Office of the United States Courts is authorized to contract for the reporting of all proceedings had in open court, and in such contract to fix the terms and conditions under which such reporting services shall be performed, including the terms and conditions under which transcripts shall be supplied by the contractor to the court and to other persons, departments, and agencies.

History of 28 U.S.C. §796: June 2, 1970, P.L. 91-272, §15(a), 84 Stat. 298; Apr. 2, 1982, P.L. 97-164, §121(e), 96 Stat. 35; Oct. 29, 1992, P.L. 102-572, §902(a)(1), 106 Stat. 4516.

§797. RECALL OF RETIRED JUDGES

(a)(1) Any judge of the United States Court of Federal Claims who has retired from regular active service under subchapter III of chapter 83, or chapter 84, of title 5 shall be known and designated as a senior judge and may perform duties as a judge when recalled pursuant to subsection (b) of this section.

(2) Any judge of the Court of Federal Claims receiving an annuity under section 178(c) of this title (pertaining to disability) who, in the estimation of the chief judge, has recovered sufficiently to render judicial service, shall be known and designated as a senior judge and may perform duties as a judge when recalled under subsection (b) of this section.

(b) The chief judge of the Court of Federal Claims may, whenever he deems it advisable, recall any senior judge, with such judge's consent, to perform such duties as a judge and for such period of time as the chief judge may specify.

(c) Any senior judge performing duties pursuant to this section shall not be counted as a judge for purposes of the number of judgeships authorized by section 171 of this title.

(d) Any senior judge, while performing duties pursuant to this section, shall be paid the same allowances for travel and other expenses as a judge in active service. Such senior judge shall also receive from the Court of Federal Claims supplemental pay in an amount sufficient, when added to his retirement annuity, to equal the salary of a judge in active service for the same period or periods of time. Such supplemental pay shall be paid in the same manner as the salary of a judge.

History of 28 U.S.C. §797: Aug. 10, 1972, P.L. 92-375, §2, 86 Stat. 529; Apr. 2, 1982, P.L. 97-164, §121(f)(1), 96 Stat. 35; Nov. 14, 1986, P.L. 99-651, §202(c), 100 Stat. 3648; Oct. 29, 1992, P.L. 102-572, §§902(a), 904(b), 106 Stat. 4516, 4517; Nov. 13, 2000, P.L. 106-518, §308, 114 Stat. 2419.

§798. PLACES OF HOLDING COURT; APPOINTMENT OF SPECIAL MASTERS

(a) The United States Court of Federal Claims is authorized to use facilities and hold court in Washington, District of Columbia, and throughout the United States (including its territories and possessions) as necessary for compliance with sections 173 and 2503(c) of this title. The facilities of the Federal courts, as well as other comparable facilities administered by the General Services Administration, shall be made available for trials and other proceedings outside of the District of Columbia.

(b) Upon application of a party or upon the judge's own initiative, and upon a showing that the interests of economy, efficiency, and justice will be served, the chief judge of the Court of Federal Claims may issue an order authorizing a judge of the court to conduct proceedings, including evidentiary hearings and trials, in a foreign country whose laws do not prohibit such proceedings, except that an interlocutory appeal may be taken from such an order pursuant to section 1292(d)(2) of this title, and the United States Court of Appeals for the Federal Circuit may, in its discretion, consider the appeal.

(c) The chief judge of the Court of Federal Claims may appoint special masters to assist the court in carrying out its functions. Any special masters so appointed shall carry out their responsibilities and be compensated in accordance with procedures set forth in the rules of the court.

History of 28 U.S.C. §798: Nov. 8, 1984, P.L. 98-620, §416(a), 98 Stat. 3364; Oct. 29, 1992, P.L. 102-572, §§902(a)(2), 906(a), (b), 106 Stat. 4516-4518.

CHAPTER 53. REPEALED

§§831 TO 834. REPEALED

Repealed Apr. 2, 1982, P.L. 97-164, §122(a), 96 Stat. 36.

CHAPTER 55. COURT OF INTERNATIONAL TRADE

§871. CLERK, CHIEF DEPUTY CLERK, ASSISTANT CLERK, DEPUTIES, ASSISTANTS, & OTHER EMPLOYEES

The Court of International Trade may appoint a clerk, a chief deputy clerk, an assistant clerk, deputy clerks, and such deputies, assistants, and other employees as may be necessary for the effective dispatch of the business of the court, who shall be subject to removal by the court.

History of 28 U.S.C. §871: June 25, 1948, ch. 646, 62 Stat. 925; Sept. 9, 1959, P.L. 86-243, §1, 73 Stat. 474; Oct. 10, 1980, P.L. 96-417, §501(17), 94 Stat. 1742.

§872. CRIERS, BAILIFFS, & MESSENGERS

The Court of International Trade may appoint such criers as it may require for said court, which criers shall also perform the duties of bailiffs and messengers and such other duties as the court directs and shall be subject to removal by the court.

History of 28 U.S.C. §872: Sept. 9, 1959, P.L. 86-243, §1, 73 Stat. 474, §873; Oct. 10, 1980, P.L. 96-417, §501(19), 94 Stat. 1742. Renumbered as §872, Oct. 14, 1986, P.L. 99-466, §3(b)(2), 100 Stat. 1191.

CHAPTER 57. GENERAL PROVISIONS APPLICABLE TO COURT OFFICERS & EMPLOYEES

§951. OATH OF OFFICE OF CLERKS & DEPUTIES

Each clerk of court and his deputies shall take the following oath or affirmation before entering upon their duties: "I, ____, having been appointed _____, do solemnly swear (or affirm) that I will truly and faithfully enter and record all orders, decrees, judgments and proceedings of such court, and will faithfully and impartially discharge all other duties of my office according to the best of my abilities and understanding. So help me God."

History of 28 U.S.C. §951: June 25, 1948, ch. 646, 62 Stat. 925.

§952. REPEALED

Repealed June 6, 1972, P.L. 92-310, §206(e)(1), 86 Stat. 203.

§953. ADMINISTRATION OF OATHS & ACKNOWLEDGMENTS

Each clerk of court and his deputies may administer oaths and affirmations and take acknowledgments.

History of 28 U.S.C. §953: June 25, 1948, ch. 646, 62 Stat. 926.

§954. VACANCY IN CLERK POSITION; ABSENCE OF CLERK

When the office of clerk is vacant, the deputy clerks shall perform the duties of the clerk in the name of the last person who held that office. When the clerk is incapacitated, absent, or otherwise unavailable to perform official duties, the deputy clerks shall perform the duties of the clerk in the name of the clerk. The court may designate a deputy clerk to act temporarily as clerk of the court in his or her own name.

History of 28 U.S.C. §954: June 25, 1948, ch. 646, 62 Stat. 926; June 6, 1972, P.L. 92-310, §206(f), 86 Stat. 203; Oct. 19, 1996, P.L. 104-317, §204(a), 110 Stat. 3850.

§955. PRACTICE OF LAW RESTRICTED

The clerk of each court and his deputies and assistants shall not practice law in any court of the United States.

History of 28 U.S.C. §955: June 25, 1948, ch. 646, 62 Stat. 926.

§956. POWERS & DUTIES OF CLERKS & DEPUTIES

The clerk of each court and his deputies and assistants shall exercise the powers and perform the duties assigned to them by the court.

History of 28 U.S.C. §956: June 25, 1948, ch. 646, 62 Stat. 926.

§957. CLERKS INELIGIBLE FOR CERTAIN OFFICES

A clerk of a court or any of his deputies shall not be appointed a commissioner, master, referee or receiver in any case, unless there are special reasons requiring such appointment which are recited in the order of appointment.

History of 28 U.S.C. §957: June 25, 1948, ch. 646, 62 Stat. 926; Nov. 6, 1978, P.L. 95-598, §234, 92 Stat. 2667; Apr. 2, 1982, P.L. 97-164, §122(b), 96 Stat. 36; July 10, 1984, P.L. 98-353, §109, 98 Stat. 342.

§958. PERSONS INELIGIBLE AS RECEIVERS

A person holding any civil or military office or employment under the United States or employed by any justice or judge of the United States shall not at the same time be appointed a receiver in any case in any court of the United States.

History of 28 U.S.C. §958: June 25, 1948, ch. 646, 62 Stat. 926.

§959. TRUSTEES & RECEIVERS SUABLE; MANAGEMENT; STATE LAWS

(a) Trustees, receivers or managers of any property, including debtors in possession, may be sued, without leave of the court appointing them, with respect to any of their acts or transactions in carrying on business connected with such property. Such actions shall be subject to the general equity power of such court so far as the same may be necessary to the ends of justice, but this shall not deprive a litigant of his right to trial by jury.

(b) Except as provided in section 1166 of title 11, a trustee, receiver or manager appointed in any cause pending in any court of the United States, including a debtor in possession, shall manage and operate the property in his possession as such trustee, receiver or manager according to the requirements of the valid laws of the State in which such property is situated, in the same manner that the owner or possessor thereof would be bound to do if in possession thereof.

History of 28 U.S.C. §959: June 25, 1948, ch. 646, 62 Stat. 926; Nov. 6, 1978, P.L. 95-598, §235, 92 Stat. 2667.

§960. TAX LIABILITY

(a) Any officers and agents conducting any business under authority of a United States court shall be subject to all Federal, State and local taxes applicable to such business to the same extent as if it were conducted by an individual or corporation.

(b) A tax under subsection (a) shall be paid on or before the due date of the tax under applicable nonbankruptcy law, unless—

(1) the tax is a property tax secured by a lien against property that is abandoned under section 554 of title 11, within a reasonable period of time after the lien attaches, by the trustee in a case under title 11; or

(2) payment of the tax is excused under a specific provision of title 11.

(c) In a case pending under chapter 7 of title 11, payment of a tax may be deferred until final distribution is made under section 726 of title 11, if—

(1) the tax was not incurred by a trustee duly appointed or elected under chapter 7 of title 11; or

(2) before the due date of the tax, an order of the court makes a finding of probable insufficiency of funds of the estate to pay in full the administrative expenses allowed under section 503(b) of title 11 that have the same priority in distribution under section 726(b) of title 11 as the priority of that tax.

History of 28 U.S.C. §960: June 25, 1948, ch. 646, 62 Stat. 927; Apr. 20, 2005, P.L. 109-8, §712(a), 119 Stat. 127.

§961. OFFICE EXPENSES OF CLERKS

Each clerk of court shall be allowed his necessary office expenses when authorized by the Director of the Administrative Office of the United States Courts.

History of 28 U.S.C. §961: June 25, 1948, ch. 646, 62 Stat. 927.

§962. REPEALED

Repealed Sept. 6, 1966, P.L. 89-554, §8(a), 80 Stat. 663.

§963. COURTS DEFINED

As used in this chapter, unless the context indicates otherwise, the words "court" and "courts" include the Supreme Court of the United States and the courts enumerated in section 610 of this title.

History of 28 U.S.C. §963: June 25, 1948, ch. 646, 62 Stat. 927.

CHAPTER 58. UNITED STATES SENTENCING COMMISSION

§991. UNITED STATES SENTENCING COMMISSION; ESTABLISHMENT & PURPOSES

(a) There is established as an independent commission in the judicial branch of the United States a United States Sentencing Commission which shall consist of seven voting members and one nonvoting member. The President, after consultation with representatives of judges, prosecuting attorneys, defense attorneys, law enforcement officials, senior citizens, victims of crime, and others interested in the criminal justice process, shall appoint the voting members of the Commission, by and with the advice and consent of the Senate, one of whom shall be appointed, by and with the advice and consent of the Senate, as the Chair and three of whom shall be designated by the President as Vice Chairs. At least 3 of the members shall be Federal judges selected after considering a list of six judges recommended to the President by the Judicial Conference of the United States. Not more than four of the members of the Commission shall be members of the same political party, and of the three Vice Chairs, no more than two shall be members of the same political party. The Attorney General, or the Attorney General's designee, shall be an ex officio, nonvoting member of the Commission. The Chair, Vice Chairs, and members of the Commission shall be subject to removal from the Commission by the President only for neglect of duty or malfeasance in office or for other good cause shown.

(b) The purposes of the United States Sentencing Commission are to—

(1) establish sentencing policies and practices for the Federal criminal justice system that—

(A) assure the meeting of the purposes of sentencing as set forth in section 3553(a)(2) of title 18, United States Code;

(B) provide certainty and fairness in meeting the purposes of sentencing, avoiding unwarranted sentencing disparities among defendants with similar records who have been found guilty of similar criminal conduct while maintaining sufficient flexibility to permit individualized sentences when warranted by mitigating or aggravating factors not taken into account in the establishment of general sentencing practices; and

(C) reflect, to the extent practicable, advancement in knowledge of human behavior as it relates to the criminal justice process; and

(2) develop means of measuring the degree to which the sentencing, penal, and correctional practices are effective in meeting the purposes of sentencing as set forth in section 3553(a)(2) of title 18, United States Code.

History of 28 U.S.C. §991: Oct. 12, 1984, P.L. 98-473, §217(a), 98 Stat. 2017; Apr. 15, 1985, P.L. 99-22, §1(1), 99 Stat. 46; Sept. 13, 1994, P.L. 103-322, §280005(a), (c)(1), (2), 108 Stat. 2096, 2097; Apr. 30, 2003, P.L. 108-21, §401(n)(1), 117 Stat. 676; Oct. 13, 2008, P.L. 110-406, §16, 122 Stat. 4295.

§992. TERMS OF OFFICE; COMPENSATION

(a) The voting members of the United States Sentencing Commission shall be appointed for six-year terms, except that the initial terms of the first members of the Commission shall be staggered so that—

(1) two members, including the Chair, serve terms of six years;

(2) three members serve terms of four years; and

(3) two members serve terms of two years.

(b)(1) Subject to paragraph (2)—

(A) no voting member of the Commission may serve more than two full terms; and

(B) a voting member appointed to fill a vacancy that occurs before the expiration of the term for which a predecessor was appointed shall be appointed only for the remainder of such term.

(2) A voting member of the Commission whose term has expired may continue to serve until the earlier of—

(A) the date on which a successor has taken office; or

(B) the date on which the Congress adjourns sine die to end the session of Congress that commences after the date on which the member's term expired.

(c) The Chair and Vice Chairs of the Commission shall hold full-time positions and shall be compensated during their terms of office at the annual rate at which judges of the United States courts of appeals are compensated. The voting members of the Commission, other than the Chair and Vice Chairs, shall hold full-time positions until the end of the first six years after the sentencing guidelines go into effect pursuant to section 235(a)(1)(B)(ii) of the Sentencing Reform Act of 1984, and shall be compensated at the annual rate at which judges of the United States courts of appeals are compensated. Thereafter, the voting members of the Commission, other than the Chair and Vice Chairs,,[1] shall hold part-time positions and shall be paid at the daily rate at which judges of the United States courts of appeals are compensated. A Federal judge may serve as a member of the Commission without resigning the judge's appointment as a Federal judge.

(d) Sections 44(c) and 134(b) of this title (relating to the residence of judges) do not apply to any judge holding a full-time position on the Commission under subsection (c) of this section.

1. **Editor's note:** So in original. The second comma probably should not appear.

History of 28 U.S.C. §992: Oct. 12, 1984, P.L. 98-473, §217(a), 98 Stat. 2018; Nov. 10, 1986, P.L. 99-646, §§4, 6(a), 100 Stat. 3592; Aug. 26, 1992, P.L. 102-349, §1, 106 Stat. 933; Sept. 13, 1994, P.L. 103-322, §280005(b), (c)(1), (3), 108 Stat. 2096, 2097.

§993. POWERS & DUTIES OF CHAIR

The Chair shall—

(a) call and preside at meetings of the Commission, which shall be held for at least two weeks in each quarter after the members of the Commission hold part-time positions; and

(b) direct—

(1) the preparation of requests for appropriations for the Commission; and

(2) the use of funds made available to the Commission.

History of 28 U.S.C. §993: Oct. 12, 1984, P.L. 98-473, §217(a), 98 Stat. 2019; Apr. 15, 1985, P.L. 99-22, §1(2), 99 Stat. 46; Nov. 10, 1986, P.L. 99-646, §5, 100 Stat. 3592; Sept. 13, 1994, P.L. 103-322, §280005(c)(1), 108 Stat. 2097.

§994. DUTIES OF THE COMMISSION

(a) The Commission, by affirmative vote of at least four members of the Commission, and pursuant to its rules and regulations and consistent with all pertinent provisions of any Federal statute, shall promulgate and distribute to all courts of the United States and to the United States Probation System—

(1) guidelines, as described in this section, for use of a sentencing court in determining the sentence to be imposed in a criminal case, including—

(A) a determination whether to impose a sentence to probation, a fine, or a term of imprisonment;

(B) a determination as to the appropriate amount of a fine or the appropriate length of a term of probation or a term of imprisonment;

(C) a determination whether a sentence to a term of imprisonment should include a requirement that the defendant be placed on a term of supervised release after imprisonment, and, if so, the appropriate length of such a term;

(D) a determination whether multiple sentences to terms of imprisonment should be ordered to run concurrently or consecutively; and

(E) a determination under paragraphs (6) and (11)[1] of section 3563(b) of title 18;

(2) general policy statements regarding application of the guidelines or any other aspect of sentencing or sentence implementation that in the view of the Commission would further the purposes set forth in section 3553(a)(2) of title 18, United States Code, including the appropriate use of—

(A) the sanctions set forth in sections 3554, 3555, and 3556 of title 18;

(B) the conditions of probation and supervised release set forth in sections 3563(b) and 3583(d) of title 18;

(C) the sentence modification provisions set forth in sections 3563(c), 3564, 3573, and 3582(c) of title 18;

(D) the fine imposition provisions set forth in section 3572 of title 18;

(E) the authority granted under rule 11(e)(2) of the Federal Rules of Criminal Procedure to accept or reject a plea agreement entered into pursuant to rule 11(e)(1); and

(F) the temporary release provisions set forth in section 3622 of title 18, and the prerelease custody provisions set forth in section 3624(c) of title 18; and

(3) guidelines or general policy statements regarding the appropriate use of the provisions for revocation of probation set forth in section 3565 of title 18, and the provisions for modification of the term or conditions of supervised release and revocation of supervised release set forth in section 3583(e) of title 18.

(b)(1) The Commission, in the guidelines promulgated pursuant to subsection (a)(1), shall, for each category of offense involving each category of defendant, establish a sentencing range that is consistent with all pertinent provisions of title 18, United States Code.

(2) If a sentence specified by the guidelines includes a term of imprisonment, the maximum of the range established for such a term shall not exceed the minimum of that range by more than the greater of 25 percent or 6 months, except that, if the minimum term of the range is 30 years or more, the maximum may be life imprisonment.

(c) The Commission, in establishing categories of offenses for use in the guidelines and policy statements governing the imposition of sentences of probation, a fine, or imprisonment, governing the imposition of other authorized sanctions, governing the size of a fine or the length of a term of probation, imprisonment, or supervised release, and governing the conditions of probation, supervised release, or imprisonment, shall consider whether the following matters, among others, have any relevance to the nature, extent, place of service, or other incidents[2] of an appropriate sentence, and shall take them into account only to the extent that they do have relevance—

(1) the grade of the offense;

(2) the circumstances under which the offense was committed which mitigate or aggravate the seriousness of the offense;

(3) the nature and degree of the harm caused by the offense, including whether it involved property, irreplaceable property, a person, a number of persons, or a breach of public trust;

(4) the community view of the gravity of the offense;

(5) the public concern generated by the offense;

(6) the deterrent effect a particular sentence may have on the commission of the offense by others; and

(7) the current incidence of the offense in the community and in the Nation as a whole.

(d) The Commission in establishing categories of defendants for use in the guidelines and policy statements governing the imposition of sentences of probation, a fine, or imprisonment, governing the imposition of other authorized sanctions, governing the size of a fine or the length of a term of probation, imprisonment, or supervised release, and governing the conditions of probation, supervised release, or imprisonment, shall consider whether the following matters, among others, with respect to a defendant, have any relevance to the nature, extent, place of service, or other incidents[2] of an appropriate sentence, and shall take them into account only to the extent that they do have relevance—

(1) age;

(2) education;

(3) vocational skills;

(4) mental and emotional condition to the extent that such condition mitigates the defendant's culpability or to the extent that such condition is otherwise plainly relevant;

(5) physical condition, including drug dependence;

(6) previous employment record;

(7) family ties and responsibilities;

(8) community ties;

(9) role in the offense;

(10) criminal history; and

(11) degree of dependence upon criminal activity for a livelihood.

The Commission shall assure that the guidelines and policy statements are entirely neutral as to the race, sex, national origin, creed, and socioeconomic status of offenders.

(e) The Commission shall assure that the guidelines and policy statements, in recommending a term of imprisonment or length of a term of imprisonment, reflect the general inappropriateness of considering the education, vocational skills, employment record, family ties and responsibilities, and community ties of the defendant.

(f) The Commission, in promulgating guidelines pursuant to subsection (a)(1), shall promote the purposes set forth

in section 991(b)(1), with particular attention to the requirements of subsection 991(b)(1)(B) for providing certainty and fairness in sentencing and reducing unwarranted sentence disparities.

(g) The Commission, in promulgating guidelines pursuant to subsection (a)(1) to meet the purposes of sentencing as set forth in section 3553(a)(2) of title 18, United States Code, shall take into account the nature and capacity of the penal, correctional, and other facilities and services available, and shall make recommendations concerning any change or expansion in the nature or capacity of such facilities and services that might become necessary as a result of the guidelines promulgated pursuant to the provisions of this chapter. The sentencing guidelines prescribed under this chapter shall be formulated to minimize the likelihood that the Federal prison population will exceed the capacity of the Federal prisons, as determined by the Commission.

(h) The Commission shall assure that the guidelines specify a sentence to a term of imprisonment at or near the maximum term authorized for categories of defendants in which the defendant is eighteen years old or older and—

(1) has been convicted of a felony that is—

(A) a crime of violence; or

(B) an offense described in section 401 of the Controlled Substances Act (21 U.S.C. 841), sections 1002(a), 1005, and 1009 of the Controlled Substances Import and Export Act (21 U.S.C. 952(a), 955, and 959), and chapter 705 of title 46; and

(2) has previously been convicted of two or more prior felonies, each of which is—

(A) a crime of violence; or

(B) an offense described in section 401 of the Controlled Substances Act (21 U.S.C. 841), sections 1002(a), 1005, and 1009 of the Controlled Substances Import and Export Act (21 U.S.C. 952(a), 955, and 959), and chapter 705 of title 46.

(i) The Commission shall assure that the guidelines specify a sentence to a substantial term of imprisonment for categories of defendants in which the defendant—

(1) has a history of two or more prior Federal, State, or local felony convictions for offenses committed on different occasions;

(2) committed the offense as part of a pattern of criminal conduct from which the defendant derived a substantial portion of the defendant's income;

(3) committed the offense in furtherance of a conspiracy with three or more persons engaging in a pattern of racketeering activity in which the defendant participated in a managerial or supervisory capacity;

(4) committed a crime of violence that constitutes a felony while on release pending trial, sentence, or appeal from a Federal, State, or local felony for which he was ultimately convicted; or

(5) committed a felony that is set forth in section 401 or 1010 of the Comprehensive Drug Abuse Prevention and Control Act of 1970 (21 U.S.C. 841 and 960), and that involved trafficking in a substantial quantity of a controlled substance.

(j) The Commission shall insure that the guidelines reflect the general appropriateness of imposing a sentence other than imprisonment in cases in which the defendant is a first offender who has not been convicted of a crime of violence or an otherwise serious offense, and the general appropriateness of imposing a term of imprisonment on a person convicted of a crime of violence that results in serious bodily injury.

(k) The Commission shall insure that the guidelines reflect the inappropriateness of imposing a sentence to a term of imprisonment for the purpose of rehabilitating the defendant or providing the defendant with needed educational or vocational training, medical care, or other correctional treatment.

(*l*) The Commission shall insure that the guidelines promulgated pursuant to subsection (a)(1) reflect—

(1) the appropriateness of imposing an incremental penalty for each offense in a case in which a defendant is convicted of—

(A) multiple offenses committed in the same course of conduct that result in the exercise of ancillary jurisdiction over one or more of the offenses; and

(B) multiple offenses committed at different times, including those cases in which the subsequent offense is a violation of section 3146 (penalty for failure to appear) or is committed while the person is released pursuant to the provisions of section 3147 (penalty for an offense committed while on release) of title 18; and

(2) the general inappropriateness of imposing consecutive terms of imprisonment for an offense of conspiring to commit an offense or soliciting commission of an offense and for an offense that was the sole object of the conspiracy or solicitation.

(m) The Commission shall insure that the guidelines reflect the fact that, in many cases, current sentences do not accurately reflect the seriousness of the offense. This will require that, as a starting point in its development of the initial sets of guidelines for particular categories of cases, the Commission ascertain the average sentences imposed in such categories of cases prior to the creation of the Commission, and in cases involving sentences to terms of imprisonment, the length of such terms actually served. The Commission shall not be bound by such average sentences, and shall independently develop a sentencing range that is consistent with the purposes of sentencing described in section 3553(a)(2) of title 18, United States Code.

(n) The Commission shall assure that the guidelines reflect the general appropriateness of imposing a lower sentence than would otherwise be imposed, including a sentence

that is lower than that established by statute as a minimum sentence, to take into account a defendant's substantial assistance in the investigation or prosecution of another person who has committed an offense.

(o) The Commission periodically shall review and revise, in consideration of comments and data coming to its attention, the guidelines promulgated pursuant to the provisions of this section. In fulfilling its duties and in exercising its powers, the Commission shall consult with authorities on, and individual and institutional representatives of, various aspects of the Federal criminal justice system. The United States Probation System, the Bureau of Prisons, the Judicial Conference of the United States, the Criminal Division of the United States Department of Justice, and a representative of the Federal Public Defenders shall submit to the Commission any observations, comments, or questions pertinent to the work of the Commission whenever they believe such communication would be useful, and shall, at least annually, submit to the Commission a written report commenting on the operation of the Commission's guidelines, suggesting changes in the guidelines that appear to be warranted, and otherwise assessing the Commission's work.

(p) The Commission, at or after the beginning of a regular session of Congress, but not later than the first day of May, may promulgate under subsection (a) of this section and submit to Congress amendments to the guidelines and modifications to previously submitted amendments that have not taken effect, including modifications to the effective dates of such amendments. Such an amendment or modification shall be accompanied by a statement of the reasons therefor and shall take effect on a date specified by the Commission, which shall be no earlier than 180 days after being so submitted and no later than the first day of November of the calendar year in which the amendment or modification is submitted, except to the extent that the effective date is revised or the amendment is otherwise modified or disapproved by Act of Congress.

(q) The Commission and the Bureau of Prisons shall submit to Congress an analysis and recommendations concerning maximum utilization of resources to deal effectively with the Federal prison population. Such report shall be based upon consideration of a variety of alternatives, including—

(1) modernization of existing facilities;

(2) inmate classification and periodic review of such classification for use in placing inmates in the least restrictive facility necessary to ensure adequate security; and

(3) use of existing Federal facilities, such as those currently within military jurisdiction.

(r) The Commission, not later than two years after the initial set of sentencing guidelines promulgated under subsection (a) goes into effect, and thereafter whenever it finds it advisable, shall recommend to the Congress that it raise or lower the grades, or otherwise modify the maximum penalties, of those offenses for which such an adjustment appears appropriate.

(s) The Commission shall give due consideration to any petition filed by a defendant requesting modification of the guidelines utilized in the sentencing of such defendant, on the basis of changed circumstances unrelated to the defendant, including changes in—

(1) the community view of the gravity of the offense;

(2) the public concern generated by the offense; and

(3) the deterrent effect particular sentences may have on the commission of the offense by others.

(t) The Commission, in promulgating general policy statements regarding the sentencing modification provisions in section 3582(c)(1)(A) of title 18, shall describe what should be considered extraordinary and compelling reasons for sentence reduction, including the criteria to be applied and a list of specific examples. Rehabilitation of the defendant alone shall not be considered an extraordinary and compelling reason.

(u) If the Commission reduces the term of imprisonment recommended in the guidelines applicable to a particular offense or category of offenses, it shall specify in what circumstances and by what amount the sentences of prisoners serving terms of imprisonment for the offense may be reduced.

(v) The Commission shall ensure that the general policy statements promulgated pursuant to subsection (a)(2) include a policy limiting consecutive terms of imprisonment for an offense involving a violation of a general prohibition and for an offense involving a violation of a specific prohibition encompassed within the general prohibition.

(w)(1) The Chief Judge of each district court shall ensure that, within 30 days following entry of judgment in every criminal case, the sentencing court submits to the Commission, in a format approved and required by the Commission, a written report of the sentence, the offense for which it is imposed, the age, race, sex of the offender, and information regarding factors made relevant by the guidelines. The report shall also include—

(A) the judgment and commitment order;

(B) the written statement of reasons for the sentence imposed (which shall include the reason for any departure from the otherwise applicable guideline range and which shall be stated on the written statement of reasons form issued by the Judicial Conference and approved by the United States Sentencing Commission);

(C) any plea agreement;

(D) the indictment or other charging document;

(E) the presentence report; and

(F) any other information as the Commission finds appropriate.

The information referred to in subparagraphs (A) through (F) shall be submitted by the sentencing court in a format approved and required by the Commission.

(2) The Commission shall, upon request, make available to the House and Senate Committees on the Judiciary, the written reports and all underlying records accompanying those reports described in this section, as well as other records received from courts.

(3) The Commission shall submit to Congress at least annually an analysis of these documents, any recommendations for legislation that the Commission concludes is warranted by that analysis, and an accounting of those districts that the Commission believes have not submitted the appropriate information and documents required by this section.

(4) The Commission shall make available to the Attorney General, upon request, such data files as the Commission itself may assemble or maintain in electronic form as a result of the information submitted under paragraph (1). Such data files shall be made available in electronic form and shall include all data fields requested, including the identity of the sentencing judge.

(x) The provisions of section 553 of title 5, relating to publication in the Federal Register and public hearing procedure, shall apply to the promulgation of guidelines pursuant to this section.

(y) The Commission, in promulgating guidelines pursuant to subsection (a)(1), may include, as a component of a fine, the expected costs to the Government of any imprisonment, supervised release, or probation sentence that is ordered.

1. **Editor's note:** Paragraphs (6) and (11) were renumbered as paragraphs (5) and (10), respectively. Apr. 24, 1996, P.L. 104-132, §203(2)(B), 110 Stat. 1227.

2. **Editor's note:** So in original. Probably should be "incidence."

History of 28 U.S.C. §994: Oct. 12, 1984, P.L. 98-473, §217(a), 98 Stat. 2019; Dec. 26, 1985, P.L. 99-217, §3, 99 Stat. 1728; July 11, 1986, P.L. 99-363, §2, 100 Stat. 770; Oct. 27, 1986, P.L. 99-570, §§1006(b), 1008, 100 Stat. 3207-7; Nov. 10, 1986, P.L. 99-646, §§6(b), 56, 100 Stat. 3592, 3611; Dec. 7, 1987, P.L. 100-182, §§16(b), 23, 101 Stat. 1269, 1271; Nov. 18, 1988, P.L. 100-690, §§7083, 7103(b), 7109, 102 Stat. 4408, 4417, 4419; Sept. 13, 1994, P.L. 103-322, §§20403(b), 280005(c)(4), 330003(f)(1), 108 Stat. 1825, 2097, 2141; Apr. 30, 2003, P.L. 108-21, §401(h), (k), 117 Stat. 672-674; Mar. 9, 2006, P.L. 109-177, §735, 120 Stat. 271; Oct. 6, 2006, P.L. 109-304, §17(f)(1), 120 Stat. 1708.

§995. POWERS OF THE COMMISSION

(a) The Commission, by vote of a majority of the members present and voting, shall have the power to—

(1) establish general policies and promulgate such rules and regulations for the Commission as are necessary to carry out the purposes of this chapter;

(2) appoint and fix the salary and duties of the Staff Director of the Sentencing Commission, who shall serve at the discretion of the Commission and who shall be compensated at a rate not to exceed the highest rate now or hereafter prescribed for Level 6 of the Senior Executive Service Schedule (5 U.S.C. 5382);

(3) deny, revise, or ratify any request for regular, supplemental, or deficiency appropriations prior to any submission of such request to the Office of Management and Budget by the Chair;

(4) procure for the Commission temporary and intermittent services to the same extent as is authorized by section 3109(b) of title 5, United States Code;

(5) utilize, with their consent, the services, equipment, personnel, information, and facilities of other Federal, State, local, and private agencies and instrumentalities with or without reimbursement therefor;

(6) without regard to 31 U.S.C. 3324, enter into and perform such contracts, leases, cooperative agreements, and other transactions as may be necessary in the conduct of the functions of the Commission, with any public agency, or with any person, firm, association, corporation, educational institution, or nonprofit organization;

(7) accept and employ, in carrying out the provisions of this title, voluntary and uncompensated services, notwithstanding the provisions of 31 U.S.C. 1342, however, individuals providing such services shall not be considered Federal employees except for purposes of chapter 81 of title 5, United States Code, with respect to job-incurred disability and title 28, United States Code, with respect to tort claims;

(8) request such information, data, and reports from any Federal agency or judicial officer as the Commission may from time to time require and as may be produced consistent with other law;

(9) monitor the performance of probation officers with regard to sentencing recommendations, including application of the Sentencing Commission guidelines and policy statements;

(10) issue instructions to probation officers concerning the application of Commission guidelines and policy statements;

(11) arrange with the head of any other Federal agency for the performance by such agency of any function of the Commission, with or without reimbursement;

(12) establish a research and development program within the Commission for the purpose of—

(A) serving as a clearinghouse and information center for the collection, preparation, and dissemination of information on Federal sentencing practices; and

(B) assisting and serving in a consulting capacity to Federal courts, departments, and agencies in the development, maintenance, and coordination of sound sentencing practices;

(13) collect systematically the data obtained from studies, research, and the empirical experience of public and private agencies concerning the sentencing process;

(14) publish data concerning the sentencing process;

(15) collect systematically and disseminate information concerning sentences actually imposed, and the relationship of such sentences to the factors set forth in section 3553(a) of title 18, United States Code;

(16) collect systematically and disseminate information regarding effectiveness of sentences imposed;

(17) devise and conduct, in various geographical locations, seminars and workshops providing continuing studies for persons engaged in the sentencing field;

(18) devise and conduct periodic training programs of instruction in sentencing techniques for judicial and probation personnel and other persons connected with the sentencing process;

(19) study the feasibility of developing guidelines for the disposition of juvenile delinquents;

(20) make recommendations to Congress concerning modification or enactment of statutes relating to sentencing, penal, and correctional matters that the Commission finds to be necessary and advisable to carry out an effective, humane and rational sentencing policy;

(21) hold hearings and call witnesses that might assist the Commission in the exercise of its powers or duties;

(22) perform such other functions as are required to permit Federal courts to meet their responsibilities under section 3553(a) of title 18, United States Code, and to permit others involved in the Federal criminal justice system to meet their related responsibilities;

(23) retain private attorneys to provide legal advice to the Commission in the conduct of its work, or to appear for or represent the Commission in any case in which the Commission is authorized by law to represent itself, or in which the Commission is representing itself with the consent of the Department of Justice; and the Commission may in its discretion pay reasonable attorney's fees to private attorneys employed by it out of its appropriated funds. When serving as officers or employees of the United States, such private attorneys shall be considered special government employees as defined in section 202(a) of title 18; and

(24) grant incentive awards to its employees pursuant to chapter 45 of title 5, United States Code.

(b) The Commission shall have such other powers and duties and shall perform such other functions as may be necessary to carry out the purposes of this chapter, and may delegate to any member or designated person such powers as may be appropriate other than the power to establish general policy statements and guidelines pursuant to section 994(a)(1) and (2), the issuance of general policies and promulgation of rules and regulations pursuant to subsection (a)(1) of this section, and the decisions as to the factors to be considered in establishment of categories of offenses and offenders pursuant to section 994(b). The Commission shall, with respect to its activities under subsections (a)(9), (a)(10), (a)(11), (a)(12), (a)(13), (a)(14), (a)(15), (a)(16), (a)(17), and (a)(18), to the extent practicable, utilize existing resources of the Administrative Office of the United States Courts and the Federal Judicial Center for the purpose of avoiding unnecessary duplication.

(c) Upon the request of the Commission, each Federal agency is authorized and directed to make its services, equipment, personnel, facilities, and information available to the greatest practicable extent to the Commission in the execution of its functions.

(d) A simple majority of the membership then serving shall constitute a quorum for the conduct of business. Other than for the promulgation of guidelines and policy statements pursuant to section 994, the Commission may exercise its powers and fulfill its duties by the vote of a simple majority of the members present.

(e) Except as otherwise provided by law, the Commission shall maintain and make available for public inspection a record of the final vote of each member on any action taken by it.

(f) [Expired.]

History of 28 U.S.C. §995: Oct. 12, 1984, P.L. 98-473, §217(a), 98 Stat. 2024; Nov. 18, 1988, P.L. 100-690, §§7104, 7105, 7106(b), 102 Stat. 4418; Dec. 1, 1990, P.L. 101-650, §325(b)(5), 104 Stat. 5121; Sept. 13, 1994, P.L. 103-322, §280005(c)(1), 108 Stat. 2097; Jan. 7, 2008, P.L. 110-177, §501, 121 Stat. 2541.

§996. DIRECTOR & STAFF

(a) The Staff Director shall supervise the activities of persons employed by the Commission and perform other duties assigned to the Staff Director by the Commission.

(b) The Staff Director shall, subject to the approval of the Commission, appoint such officers and employees as are necessary in the execution of the functions of the Commission. The officers and employees of the Commission shall be exempt from the provisions of part III of title 5, except the following: chapters 45 (Incentive Awards), 63 (Leave), 81 (Compensation for Work Injuries), 83 (Retirement), 85 (Unemployment Compensation), 87 (Life Insurance), and 89 (Health Insurance), and subchapter VI of chapter 55 (Payment for accumulated and accrued leave).

History of 28 U.S.C. §996: Oct. 12, 1984, P.L. 98-473, §217(a), 98 Stat. 2026; Nov. 18, 1988, P.L. 100-690, §7106(c), 102 Stat. 4418; Dec. 1, 1990, P.L. 101-650, §325(b)(6), 104 Stat. 5121; Sept. 13, 1994, P.L. 103-322, §280005(c)(5), 108 Stat. 2097; Nov. 13, 2000, P.L. 106-518, §302(a), 114 Stat. 2416.

§997. ANNUAL REPORT

The Commission shall report annually to the Judicial Conference of the United States, the Congress, and the President of the United States on the activities of the Commission.

History of 28 U.S.C. §997: Oct. 12, 1984, P.L. 98-473, §217(a), 98 Stat. 2026.

§998. DEFINITIONS

As used in this chapter—

(a) "Commission" means the United States Sentencing Commission;

(b) "Commissioner" means a member of the United States Sentencing Commission;

(c) "guidelines" means the guidelines promulgated by the Commission pursuant to section 994(a) of this title; and

(d) "rules and regulations" means rules and regulations promulgated by the Commission pursuant to section 995 of this title.

History of 28 U.S.C. §998: Oct. 12, 1984, P.L. 98-473, §217(a), 98 Stat. 2026.

PART IV. JURISDICTION & VENUE
CHAPTER 81. SUPREME COURT

§1251. ORIGINAL JURISDICTION

(a) The Supreme Court shall have original and exclusive jurisdiction of all controversies between two or more States.

(b) The Supreme Court shall have original but not exclusive jurisdiction of:

(1) All actions or proceedings to which ambassadors, other public ministers, consuls, or vice consuls of foreign states are parties;

(2) All controversies between the United States and a State;

(3) All actions or proceedings by a State against the citizens of another State or against aliens.

History of 28 U.S.C. §1251: June 25, 1948, ch. 646, 62 Stat. 927; Sept. 30, 1978, P.L. 95-393, §8(b), 92 Stat. 810.

§1252. REPEALED

Repealed June 27, 1988, P.L. 100-352, §1, 102 Stat. 662.

§1253. DIRECT APPEALS FROM DECISIONS OF THREE-JUDGE COURTS

Except as otherwise provided by law, any party may appeal to the Supreme Court from an order granting or denying, after notice and hearing, an interlocutory or permanent injunction in any civil action, suit or proceeding required by any Act of Congress to be heard and determined by a district court of three judges.

History of 28 U.S.C. §1253: June 25, 1948, ch. 646, 62 Stat. 928.

§1254. COURTS OF APPEALS; CERTIORARI; CERTIFIED QUESTIONS

Cases in the courts of appeals may be reviewed by the Supreme Court by the following methods:

(1) By writ of certiorari granted upon the petition of any party to any civil or criminal case, before or after rendition of judgment or decree;

(2) By certification at any time by a court of appeals of any question of law in any civil or criminal case as to which instructions are desired, and upon such certification the Supreme Court may give binding instructions or require the entire record to be sent up for decision of the entire matter in controversy.

History of 28 U.S.C. §1254: June 25, 1948, ch. 646, 62 Stat. 928; June 27, 1988, P.L. 100-352, §2(a), (b), 102 Stat. 662.

§§1255, 1256. REPEALED

Repealed Apr. 2, 1982, P.L. 97-164, §123, 96 Stat. 36.

§1257. STATE COURTS; CERTIORARI

(a) Final judgments or decrees rendered by the highest court of a State in which a decision could be had, may be reviewed by the Supreme Court by writ of certiorari where the validity of a treaty or statute of the United States is drawn in question or where the validity of a statute of any State is drawn in question on the ground of its being repugnant to the Constitution, treaties, or laws of the United States, or where any title, right, privilege, or immunity is specially set up or claimed under the Constitution or the treaties or statutes of, or any commission held or authority exercised under, the United States.

(b) For the purposes of this section, the term "highest court of a State" includes the District of Columbia Court of Appeals.

History of 28 U.S.C. §1257: June 25, 1948, ch. 646, 62 Stat. 929; July 29, 1970, P.L. 91-358, §172(a)(1), 84 Stat. 590; June 27, 1988, P.L. 100-352, §3, 102 Stat. 662.

§1258. SUPREME COURT OF PUERTO RICO; CERTIORARI

Final judgments or decrees rendered by the Supreme Court of the Commonwealth of Puerto Rico may be reviewed by the Supreme Court by writ of certiorari where the validity of a treaty or statute of the United States is drawn in question or where the validity of a statute of the Commonwealth of Puerto Rico is drawn in question on the ground of its being repugnant to the Constitution, treaties, or laws of the United States, or where any title, right, privilege, or immunity is specially set up or claimed under the Constitution or the treaties or statutes of, or any commission held or authority exercised under, the United States.

History of 28 U.S.C. §1258: Aug. 30, 1961, P.L. 87-189, §1, 75 Stat. 417; June 27, 1988, P.L. 100-352, §4, 102 Stat. 662.

§1259. COURT OF APPEALS FOR THE ARMED FORCES; CERTIORARI

Decisions of the United States Court of Appeals for the Armed Forces may be reviewed by the Supreme Court by writ of certiorari in the following cases:

(1) Cases reviewed by the Court of Appeals for the Armed Forces under section 867(a)(1) of title 10.

(2) Cases certified to the Court of Appeals for the Armed Forces by the Judge Advocate General under section 867(a)(2) of title 10.

(3) Cases in which the Court of Appeals for the Armed Forces granted a petition for review under section 867(a)(3) of title 10.

(4) Cases, other than those described in paragraphs (1), (2), and (3) of this subsection, in which the Court of Appeals for the Armed Forces granted relief.

History of 28 U.S.C. §1259: Dec. 6, 1983, P.L. 98-209, §10(a)(1), 97 Stat. 1405; Nov. 29, 1989, P.L. 101-189, §1304(b)(3), 103 Stat. 1577; Oct. 5, 1994, P.L. 103-337, §924(d)(1)(C), (2)(A), 108 Stat. 2832.

CHAPTER 83. COURTS OF APPEALS

§1291. FINAL DECISIONS OF DISTRICT COURTS

The courts of appeals (other than the United States Court of Appeals for the Federal Circuit) shall have jurisdiction of appeals from all final decisions of the district courts of the

United States, the United States District Court for the District of the Canal Zone, the District Court of Guam, and the District Court of the Virgin Islands, except where a direct review may be had in the Supreme Court. The jurisdiction of the United States Court of Appeals for the Federal Circuit shall be limited to the jurisdiction described in sections 1292(c) and (d) and 1295 of this title.

History of 28 U.S.C. §1291: June 25, 1948, ch. 646, 62 Stat. 929; Oct. 31, 1951, ch. 655, §48, 65 Stat. 726; July 7, 1958, P.L. 85-508, §12(e), 72 Stat. 348; Apr. 2, 1982, P.L. 97-164, §124, 96 Stat. 36.

§1292. INTERLOCUTORY DECISIONS

(a) Except as provided in subsections (c) and (d) of this section, the courts of appeals shall have jurisdiction of appeals from:

(1) Interlocutory orders of the district courts of the United States, the United States District Court for the District of the Canal Zone, the District Court of Guam, and the District Court of the Virgin Islands, or of the judges thereof, granting, continuing, modifying, refusing or dissolving injunctions, or refusing to dissolve or modify injunctions, except where a direct review may be had in the Supreme Court;

(2) Interlocutory orders appointing receivers, or refusing orders to wind up receiverships or to take steps to accomplish the purposes thereof, such as directing sales or other disposals of property;

(3) Interlocutory decrees of such district courts or the judges thereof determining the rights and liabilities of the parties to admiralty cases in which appeals from final decrees are allowed.

(b) When a district judge, in making in a civil action an order not otherwise appealable under this section, shall be of the opinion that such order involves a controlling question of law as to which there is substantial ground for difference of opinion and that an immediate appeal from the order may materially advance the ultimate termination of the litigation, he shall so state in writing in such order. The Court of Appeals which would have jurisdiction of an appeal of such action may thereupon, in its discretion, permit an appeal to be taken from such order, if application is made to it within ten days after the entry of the order: Provided, however, That application for an appeal hereunder shall not stay proceedings in the district court unless the district judge or the Court of Appeals or a judge thereof shall so order.

(c) The United States Court of Appeals for the Federal Circuit shall have exclusive jurisdiction—

(1) of an appeal from an interlocutory order or decree described in subsection (a) or (b) of this section in any case over which the court would have jurisdiction of an appeal under section 1295 of this title; and

(2) of an appeal from a judgment in a civil action for patent infringement which would otherwise be appealable to the United States Court of Appeals for the Federal Circuit and is final except for an accounting.

(d)(1) When the chief judge of the Court of International Trade issues an order under the provisions of section 256(b) of this title, or when any judge of the Court of International Trade, in issuing any other interlocutory order, includes in the order a statement that a controlling question of law is involved with respect to which there is a substantial ground for difference of opinion and that an immediate appeal from that order may materially advance the ultimate termination of the litigation, the United States Court of Appeals for the Federal Circuit may, in its discretion, permit an appeal to be taken from such order, if application is made to that Court within ten days after the entry of such order.

(2) When the chief judge of the United States Court of Federal Claims issues an order under section 798(b) of this title, or when any judge of the United States Court of Federal Claims, in issuing an interlocutory order, includes in the order a statement that a controlling question of law is involved with respect to which there is a substantial ground for difference of opinion and that an immediate appeal from that order may materially advance the ultimate termination of the litigation, the United States Court of Appeals for the Federal Circuit may, in its discretion, permit an appeal to be taken from such order, if application is made to that Court within ten days after the entry of such order.

(3) Neither the application for nor the granting of an appeal under this subsection shall stay proceedings in the Court of International Trade or in the Court of Federal Claims, as the case may be, unless a stay is ordered by a judge of the Court of International Trade or of the Court of Federal Claims or by the United States Court of Appeals for the Federal Circuit or a judge of that court.

(4)(A) The United States Court of Appeals for the Federal Circuit shall have exclusive jurisdiction of an appeal from an interlocutory order of a district court of the United States, the District Court of Guam, the District Court of the Virgin Islands, or the District Court for the Northern Mariana Islands, granting or denying, in whole or in part, a motion to transfer an action to the United States Court of Federal Claims under section 1631 of this title.

(B) When a motion to transfer an action to the Court of Federal Claims is filed in a district court, no further proceedings shall be taken in the district court until 60 days after the court has ruled upon the motion. If an appeal is taken from the district court's grant or denial of the motion, proceedings shall be further stayed until the appeal has been decided by the Court of Appeals for the Federal Circuit. The stay of proceedings in the district court shall not bar the granting of preliminary or injunctive relief, where appropriate and where expedition is reasonably necessary. However, during the period in which proceedings are stayed as provided in this subparagraph, no transfer to the Court of Federal Claims pursuant to the motion shall be carried out.

(e) The Supreme Court may prescribe rules, in accordance with section 2072 of this title, to provide for an appeal of

an interlocutory decision to the courts of appeals that is not otherwise provided for under subsection (a), (b), (c), or (d).

History of 28 U.S.C. §1292: June 25, 1948, ch. 646, 62 Stat. 929; Oct. 31, 1951, ch. 655, §49, 65 Stat. 726; July 7, 1958, P.L. 85-508, §12(e), 72 Stat. 348; Sept. 2, 1958, P.L. 85-919, 72 Stat. 1770; Apr. 2, 1982, P.L. 97-164, §125, 96 Stat. 36; Nov. 8, 1984, P.L. 98-620, §412, 98 Stat. 3362; Nov. 19, 1988, P.L. 100-702, §501, 102 Stat. 4652; Oct. 29, 1992, P.L. 102-572, §§101, 902(b), 906(c), 106 Stat. 4506, 4516, 4518.

§1293. REPEALED

Repealed Aug. 30, 1961, P.L. 87-189, §3, 75 Stat. 417.

§1294. CIRCUITS IN WHICH DECISIONS REVIEWABLE

Except as provided in sections 1292(c), 1292(d), and 1295 of this title, appeals from reviewable decisions of the district and territorial courts shall be taken to the courts of appeals as follows:

(1) From a district court of the United States to the court of appeals for the circuit embracing the district;

(2) From the United States District Court for the District of the Canal Zone, to the Court of Appeals for the Fifth Circuit;

(3) From the District Court of the Virgin Islands, to the Court of Appeals for the Third Circuit;

(4) From the District Court of Guam, to the Court of Appeals for the Ninth Circuit.

History of 28 U.S.C. §1294: June 25, 1948, ch. 646, 62 Stat. 930; Oct. 31, 1951, ch. 655, §50(a), 65 Stat. 727; July 7, 1958, P.L. 85-508, §12(g), 72 Stat. 348; Mar. 18, 1959, P.L. 86-3, §14(c), 73 Stat. 10; Aug. 30, 1961, P.L. 87-189, §5, 75 Stat. 417; Nov. 6, 1978, P.L. 95-598, §237, 92 Stat. 2667; Apr. 2, 1982, P.L. 97-164, §126, 96 Stat. 37.

§1295. JURISDICTION OF THE UNITED STATES COURT OF APPEALS FOR THE FEDERAL CIRCUIT

(a) The United States Court of Appeals for the Federal Circuit shall have exclusive jurisdiction—

(1) of an appeal from a final decision of a district court of the United States, the District Court of Guam, the District Court of the Virgin Islands, or the District Court of the Northern Mariana Islands, in any civil action arising under, or in any civil action in which a party has asserted a compulsory counterclaim arising under, any Act of Congress relating to patents or plant variety protection;

(2) of an appeal from a final decision of a district court of the United States, the United States District Court for the District of the Canal Zone, the District Court of Guam, the District Court of the Virgin Islands, or the District Court for the Northern Mariana Islands, if the jurisdiction of that court was based, in whole or in part, on section 1346 of this title, except that jurisdiction of an appeal in a case brought in a district court under section 1346(a)(1), 1346(b), 1346(e), or 1346(f) of this title or under section 1346(a)(2) when the claim is founded upon an Act of Congress or a regulation of an executive department providing for internal revenue shall be governed by sections 1291, 1292, and 1294 of this title;

(3) of an appeal from a final decision of the United States Court of Federal Claims;

(4) of an appeal from a decision of—

(A) the Patent Trial and Appeal Board of the United States Patent and Trademark Office with respect to a patent application, derivation proceeding, reexamination, post-grant review, or inter partes review under title 35, at the instance of a party who exercised that party's right to participate in the applicable proceeding before or appeal to the Board, except that an applicant or a party to a derivation proceeding may also have remedy by civil action pursuant to section 145 or 146 of title 35; an appeal under this subparagraph of a decision of the Board with respect to an application or derivation proceeding shall waive the right of such applicant or party to proceed under section 145 or 146 of title 35;

(B) the Under Secretary of Commerce for Intellectual Property and Director of the United States Patent and Trademark Office or the Trademark Trial and Appeal Board with respect to applications for registration of marks and other proceedings as provided in section 21 of the Trademark Act of 1946 (15 U.S.C. 1071); or

(C) a district court to which a case was directed pursuant to section 145, 146, or 154(b) of title 35;

(5) of an appeal from a final decision of the United States Court of International Trade;

(6) to review the final determinations of the United States International Trade Commission relating to unfair practices in import trade, made under section 337 of the Tariff Act of 1930 (19 U.S.C. 1337);

(7) to review, by appeal on questions of law only, findings of the Secretary of Commerce under U.S. note 6 to subchapter X of chapter 98 of the Harmonized Tariff Schedule of the United States (relating to importation of instruments or apparatus);

(8) of an appeal under section 71 of the Plant Variety Protection Act (7 U.S.C. 2461);

(9) of an appeal from a final order or final decision of the Merit Systems Protection Board, pursuant to sections 7703(b)(1) and 7703(d) of title 5;

(10) of an appeal from a final decision of an agency board of contract appeals pursuant to section 7107(a)(1) of title 41;

(11) of an appeal under section 211 of the Economic Stabilization Act of 1970;

(12) of an appeal under section 5 of the Emergency Petroleum Allocation Act of 1973;

(13) of an appeal under section 506(c) of the Natural Gas Policy Act of 1978; and

(14) of an appeal under section 523 of the Energy Policy and Conservation Act.

(b) The head of any executive department or agency may, with the approval of the Attorney General, refer to the Court of Appeals for the Federal Circuit for judicial review any final decision rendered by a board of contract appeals pursuant to the terms of any contract with the United States

awarded by that department or agency which the head of such department or agency has concluded is not entitled to finality pursuant to the review standards specified in section 7107(b) of title 41. The head of each executive department or agency shall make any referral under this section within one hundred and twenty days after the receipt of a copy of the final appeal decision.

(c) The Court of Appeals for the Federal Circuit shall review the matter referred in accordance with the standards specified in section 7107(b) of title 41. The court shall proceed with judicial review on the administrative record made before the board of contract appeals on matters so referred as in other cases pending in such court, shall determine the issue of finality of the appeal decision, and shall, if appropriate, render judgment thereon, or remand the matter to any administrative or executive body or official with such direction as it may deem proper and just.

History of 28 U.S.C. §1295: Apr. 2, 1982, P.L. 97-164, §127(a), 96 Stat. 37; Nov. 8, 1984, P.L. 98-622, §205(a), 98 Stat. 3388; Aug. 23, 1988, P.L. 100-418, §1214(a)(3), 102 Stat. 1156; Nov. 19, 1988, P.L. 100-702, §1020(a)(3), 102 Stat. 4671; Oct. 29, 1992, P.L. 102-572, §§102(c), 902(b)(1), 106 Stat. 4507, 4516; Nov. 29, 1999, P.L. 106-113-Appx. I, §§4402(b)(2), 4732(b)(14), 113 Stat. 1501A-560, 1501A-584; Jan. 4, 2011, P.L. 111-350, §5(g)(5), 124 Stat. 3848; Sept. 16, 2011, P.L. 112-29, §§7(c)(2), 19(b), 125 Stat. 314, 331.

§1296. REVIEW OF CERTAIN AGENCY ACTIONS[1]

(a) Jurisdiction.—Subject to the provisions of chapter 179, the United States Court of Appeals for the Federal Circuit shall have jurisdiction over a petition for review of a final decision under chapter 5 of title 3 of—

(1) an appropriate agency (as determined under section 454 of title 3);

(2) the Federal Labor Relations Authority made under part D of subchapter II of chapter 5 of title 3, notwithstanding section 7123 of title 5; or

(3) the Secretary of Labor or the Occupational Safety and Health Review Commission, made under part C of subchapter II of chapter 5 of title 3.

(b) Filing of petition.—Any petition for review under this section must be filed within 30 days after the date the petitioner receives notice of the final decision.

1. **Editor's note:** Former §1296, "Precedence of cases in the United States Court of Appeals for the Federal Circuit," was repealed Nov. 8, 1984, by P.L. 98-620, §402(29)(C), 98 Stat. 3359.

History of 28 U.S.C. §1296: Oct. 26, 1996, P.L. 104-331, §3(a)(1), 110 Stat. 4069.

CHAPTER 85. DISTRICT COURTS; JURISDICTION

§1330. ACTIONS AGAINST FOREIGN STATES

(a) The district courts shall have original jurisdiction without regard to amount in controversy of any nonjury civil action against a foreign state as defined in section 1603(a) of this title as to any claim for relief in personam with respect to which the foreign state is not entitled to immunity either under sections 1605-1607 of this title or under any applicable international agreement.

(b) Personal jurisdiction over a foreign state shall exist as to every claim for relief over which the district courts have jurisdiction under subsection (a) where service has been made under section 1608 of this title.

(c) For purposes of subsection (b), an appearance by a foreign state does not confer personal jurisdiction with respect to any claim for relief not arising out of any transaction or occurrence enumerated in sections 1605-1607 of this title.

History of 28 U.S.C. §1330: Oct. 21, 1976, P.L. 94-583, §2(a), 90 Stat. 2891.

§1331. FEDERAL QUESTION

The district courts shall have original jurisdiction of all civil actions arising under the Constitution, laws, or treaties of the United States.

History of 28 U.S.C. §1331: June 25, 1948, ch. 646, 62 Stat. 930; July 25, 1958, P.L. 85-554, §1, 72 Stat. 415; Oct. 21, 1976, P.L. 94-574, §2, 90 Stat. 2721; Dec. 1, 1980, P.L. 96-486, §2(a), 94 Stat. 2369.

See *Commentaries*, "Choosing the Court—Jurisdiction," ch. 2-F, p. 112.

§1332. DIVERSITY OF CITIZENSHIP; AMOUNT IN CONTROVERSY; COSTS

(a) The district courts shall have original jurisdiction of all civil actions where the matter in controversy exceeds the sum or value of $75,000, exclusive of interest and costs, and is between—

(1) citizens of different States;

(2) citizens of a State and citizens or subjects of a foreign state, except that the district courts shall not have original jurisdiction under this subsection of an action between citizens of a State and citizens or subjects of a foreign state who are lawfully admitted for permanent residence in the United States and are domiciled in the same State;

(3) citizens of different States and in which citizens or subjects of a foreign state are additional parties; and

(4) a foreign state, defined in section 1603(a) of this title, as plaintiff and citizens of a State or of different States.

(b) Except when express provision therefor is otherwise made in a statute of the United States, where the plaintiff who files the case originally in the Federal courts is finally adjudged to be entitled to recover less than the sum or value of $75,000, computed without regard to any setoff or counterclaim to which the defendant may be adjudged to be entitled, and exclusive of interest and costs, the district court may deny costs to the plaintiff and, in addition, may impose costs on the plaintiff.

(c) For the purposes of this section and section 1441 of this title—

(1) a corporation shall be deemed to be a citizen of every State and foreign state by which it has been incorporated and of the State or foreign state where it has its principal place of business, except that in any direct action against the insurer of a policy or contract of liability insurance, whether incorpo-

rated or unincorporated, to which action the insured is not joined as a party-defendant, such insurer shall be deemed a citizen of—

(A) every State and foreign state of which the insured is a citizen;

(B) every State and foreign state by which the insurer has been incorporated; and

(C) the State or foreign state where the insurer has its principal place of business; and

(2) the legal representative of the estate of a decedent shall be deemed to be a citizen only of the same State as the decedent, and the legal representative of an infant or incompetent shall be deemed to be a citizen only of the same State as the infant or incompetent.

(d)(1) In this subsection—

(A) the term "class" means all of the class members in a class action;

(B) the term "class action" means any civil action filed under rule 23 of the Federal Rules of Civil Procedure or similar State statute or rule of judicial procedure authorizing an action to be brought by 1 or more representative persons as a class action;

(C) the term "class certification order" means an order issued by a court approving the treatment of some or all aspects of a civil action as a class action; and

(D) the term "class members" means the persons (named or unnamed) who fall within the definition of the proposed or certified class in a class action.

(2) The district courts shall have original jurisdiction of any civil action in which the matter in controversy exceeds the sum or value of $5,000,000, exclusive of interest and costs, and is a class action in which—

(A) any member of a class of plaintiffs is a citizen of a State different from any defendant;

(B) any member of a class of plaintiffs is a foreign state or a citizen or subject of a foreign state and any defendant is a citizen of a State; or

(C) any member of a class of plaintiffs is a citizen of a State and any defendant is a foreign state or a citizen or subject of a foreign state.

(3) A district court may, in the interests of justice and looking at the totality of the circumstances, decline to exercise jurisdiction under paragraph (2) over a class action in which greater than one-third but less than two-thirds of the members of all proposed plaintiff classes in the aggregate and the primary defendants are citizens of the State in which the action was originally filed based on consideration of—

(A) whether the claims asserted involve matters of national or interstate interest;

(B) whether the claims asserted will be governed by laws of the State in which the action was originally filed or by the laws of other States;

(C) whether the class action has been pleaded in a manner that seeks to avoid Federal jurisdiction;

(D) whether the action was brought in a forum with a distinct nexus with the class members, the alleged harm, or the defendants;

(E) whether the number of citizens of the State in which the action was originally filed in all proposed plaintiff classes in the aggregate is substantially larger than the number of citizens from any other State, and the citizenship of the other members of the proposed class is dispersed among a substantial number of States; and

(F) whether, during the 3-year period preceding the filing of that class action, 1 or more other class actions asserting the same or similar claims on behalf of the same or other persons have been filed.

(4) A district court shall decline to exercise jurisdiction under paragraph (2)—

(A)(i) over a class action in which—

(I) greater than two-thirds of the members of all proposed plaintiff classes in the aggregate are citizens of the State in which the action was originally filed;

(II) at least 1 defendant is a defendant—

(aa) from whom significant relief is sought by members of the plaintiff class;

(bb) whose alleged conduct forms a significant basis for the claims asserted by the proposed plaintiff class; and

(cc) who is a citizen of the State in which the action was originally filed; and

(III) principal injuries resulting from the alleged conduct or any related conduct of each defendant were incurred in the State in which the action was originally filed; and

(ii) during the 3-year period preceding the filing of that class action, no other class action has been filed asserting the same or similar factual allegations against any of the defendants on behalf of the same or other persons; or

(B) two-thirds or more of the members of all proposed plaintiff classes in the aggregate, and the primary defendants, are citizens of the State in which the action was originally filed.

(5) Paragraphs (2) through (4) shall not apply to any class action in which—

(A) the primary defendants are States, State officials, or other governmental entities against whom the district court may be foreclosed from ordering relief; or

(B) the number of members of all proposed plaintiff classes in the aggregate is less than 100.

(6) In any class action, the claims of the individual class members shall be aggregated to determine whether the matter in controversy exceeds the sum or value of $5,000,000, exclusive of interest and costs.

(7) Citizenship of the members of the proposed plaintiff classes shall be determined for purposes of paragraphs (2) through (6) as of the date of filing of the complaint or amended complaint, or, if the case stated by the initial pleading is not subject to Federal jurisdiction, as of the date of service by plaintiffs of an amended pleading, motion, or other paper, indicating the existence of Federal jurisdiction.

(8) This subsection shall apply to any class action before or after the entry of a class certification order by the court with respect to that action.

(9) Paragraph (2) shall not apply to any class action that solely involves a claim—

(A) concerning a covered security as defined under 16(f)(3)[1] of the Securities Act of 1933 (15 U.S.C. 78p(f)(3)) and section 28(f)(5)(E) of the Securities Exchange Act of 1934 (15 U.S.C. 78bb(f)(5)(E));

(B) that relates to the internal affairs or governance of a corporation or other form of business enterprise and that arises under or by virtue of the laws of the State in which such corporation or business enterprise is incorporated or organized; or

(C) that relates to the rights, duties (including fiduciary duties), and obligations relating to or created by or pursuant to any security (as defined under section 2(a)(1) of the Securities Act of 1933 (15 U.S.C. 77b(a)(1)) and the regulations issued thereunder).

(10) For purposes of this subsection and section 1453, an unincorporated association shall be deemed to be a citizen of the State where it has its principal place of business and the State under whose laws it is organized.

(11)(A) For purposes of this subsection and section 1453, a mass action shall be deemed to be a class action removable under paragraphs (2) through (10) if it otherwise meets the provisions of those paragraphs.

(B)(i) As used in subparagraph (A), the term "mass action" means any civil action (except a civil action within the scope of section 1711(2)) in which monetary relief claims of 100 or more persons are proposed to be tried jointly on the ground that the plaintiffs' claims involve common questions of law or fact, except that jurisdiction shall exist only over those plaintiffs whose claims in a mass action satisfy the jurisdictional amount requirements under subsection (a).

(ii) As used in subparagraph (A), the term "mass action" shall not include any civil action in which—

(I) all of the claims in the action arise from an event or occurrence in the State in which the action was filed, and that allegedly resulted in injuries in that State or in States contiguous to that State;

(II) the claims are joined upon motion of a defendant;

(III) all of the claims in the action are asserted on behalf of the general public (and not on behalf of individual claimants or members of a purported class) pursuant to a State statute specifically authorizing such action; or

(IV) the claims have been consolidated or coordinated solely for pretrial proceedings.

(C)(i) Any action(s) removed to Federal court pursuant to this subsection shall not thereafter be transferred to any other court pursuant to section 1407, or the rules promulgated thereunder, unless a majority of the plaintiffs in the action request transfer pursuant to section 1407.

(ii) This subparagraph will not apply—

(I) to cases certified pursuant to rule 23 of the Federal Rules of Civil Procedure; or

(II) if plaintiffs propose that the action proceed as a class action pursuant to rule 23 of the Federal Rules of Civil Procedure.

(D) The limitations periods on any claims asserted in a mass action that is removed to Federal court pursuant to this subsection shall be deemed tolled during the period that the action is pending in Federal court.

(e) The word "States", as used in this section, includes the Territories, the District of Columbia, and the Commonwealth of Puerto Rico.

1. **Editor's note:** So in original. Probably should be preceded by "section."

History of 28 U.S.C. §1332: June 25, 1948, ch. 646, 62 Stat. 930; July 26, 1956, ch. 740, 70 Stat. 658; July 25, 1958, P.L. 85-554, §2, 72 Stat. 415; Aug. 14, 1964, P.L. 88-439, §1, 78 Stat. 445; Oct. 21, 1976, P.L. 94-583, §3, 90 Stat. 2891; Nov. 19, 1988, P.L. 100-702, §§201(a), 202(a), 203(a), 102 Stat. 4646; Oct. 19, 1996, P.L. 104-317, §205, 110 Stat. 3850; Feb. 18, 2005, P.L. 109-2, §4(a), 119 Stat. 9; Dec. 7, 2011, P.L. 112-63, §§101, 102, 105, 125 Stat. 758, 762.

See *Commentaries*, "Choosing the Court—Jurisdiction," ch. 2-F, p. 112.

§1333. ADMIRALTY, MARITIME & PRIZE CASES

The district courts shall have original jurisdiction, exclusive of the courts of the States, of:

(1) Any civil case of admiralty or maritime jurisdiction, saving to suitors in all cases all other remedies to which they are otherwise entitled.

(2) Any prize brought into the United States and all proceedings for the condemnation of property taken as prize.

History of 28 U.S.C. §1333: June 25, 1948, ch. 646, 62 Stat. 931; May 24, 1949, ch. 139, §79, 63 Stat. 101.

§1334. BANKRUPTCY CASES & PROCEEDINGS

(a) Except as provided in subsection (b) of this section, the district courts shall have original and exclusive jurisdiction of all cases under title 11.

(b) Except as provided in subsection (e)(2), and notwithstanding any Act of Congress that confers exclusive jurisdiction on a court or courts other than the district courts, the district courts shall have original but not exclusive jurisdiction of all civil proceedings arising under title 11, or arising in or related to cases under title 11.

(c)(1) Except with respect to a case under chapter 15 of title 11, nothing in this section prevents a district court in the interest of justice, or in the interest of comity with State courts or respect for State law, from abstaining from hearing a par-

ticular proceeding arising under title 11 or arising in or related to a case under title 11.

(2) Upon timely motion of a party in a proceeding based upon a State law claim or State law cause of action, related to a case under title 11 but not arising under title 11 or arising in a case under title 11, with respect to which an action could not have been commenced in a court of the United States absent jurisdiction under this section, the district court shall abstain from hearing such proceeding if an action is commenced, and can be timely adjudicated, in a State forum of appropriate jurisdiction.

(d) Any decision to abstain or not to abstain made under subsection (c) (other than a decision not to abstain in a proceeding described in subsection (c)(2)) is not reviewable by appeal or otherwise by the court of appeals under section 158(d), 1291, or 1292 of this title or by the Supreme Court of the United States under section 1254 of this title. Subsection (c) and this subsection shall not be construed to limit the applicability of the stay provided for by section 362 of title 11, United States Code, as such section applies to an action affecting the property of the estate in bankruptcy.

(e) The district court in which a case under title 11 is commenced or is pending shall have exclusive jurisdiction—

(1) of all the property, wherever located, of the debtor as of the commencement of such case, and of property of the estate; and

(2) over all claims or causes of action that involve construction of section 327 of title 11, United States Code, or rules relating to disclosure requirements under section 327.

History of 28 U.S.C. §1334: June 25, 1948, ch. 646, 62 Stat. 931; Nov. 6, 1978, P.L. 95-598, §238(a), 92 Stat. 2667; July 10, 1984, P.L. 98-353, §101(a), 98 Stat. 333; Oct. 27, 1986, P.L. 99-554, §144(e), 100 Stat. 3096; Dec. 1, 1990, P.L. 101-650, §309(b), 104 Stat. 5113; Oct. 22, 1994, P.L. 103-394, §104(b), 108 Stat. 4109; Apr. 20, 2005, P.L. 109-8, §§324(a), 802(c)(2), 1219, 119 Stat. 98, 145, 195.

§1335. INTERPLEADER

(a) The district courts shall have original jurisdiction of any civil action of interpleader or in the nature of interpleader filed by any person, firm, or corporation, association, or society having in his or its custody or possession money or property of the value of $500 or more, or having issued a note, bond, certificate, policy of insurance, or other instrument of value or amount of $500 or more, or providing for the delivery or payment or the loan of money or property of such amount or value, or being under any obligation written or unwritten to the amount of $500 or more, if

(1) Two or more adverse claimants, of diverse citizenship as defined in subsection (a) or (d) of section 1332 of this title, are claiming or may claim to be entitled to such money or property, or to any one or more of the benefits arising by virtue of any note, bond, certificate, policy or other instrument, or arising by virtue of any such obligation; and if

(2) the plaintiff has deposited such money or property or has paid the amount of or the loan or other value of such instrument or the amount due under such obligation into the registry of the court, there to abide the judgment of the court, or has given bond payable to the clerk of the court in such amount and with such surety as the court or judge may deem proper, conditioned upon the compliance by the plaintiff with the future order or judgment of the court with respect to the subject matter of the controversy.

(b) Such an action may be entertained although the titles or claims of the conflicting claimants do not have a common origin, or are not identical, but are adverse to and independent of one another.

History of 28 U.S.C. §1335: June 25, 1948, ch. 646, 62 Stat. 931; Feb. 18, 2005, P.L. 109-2, §4(b), 119 Stat. 12.

See *Commentaries*, "Interpleader," ch. 2-C, p. 87.

§1336. SURFACE TRANSPORTATION BOARD'S ORDERS

(a) Except as otherwise provided by Act of Congress, the district courts shall have jurisdiction of any civil action to enforce, in whole or in part, any order of the Surface Transportation Board, and to enjoin or suspend, in whole or in part, any order of the Surface Transportation Board for the payment of money or the collection of fines, penalties, and forfeitures.

(b) When a district court or the United States Court of Federal Claims refers a question or issue to the Surface Transportation Board for determination, the court which referred the question or issue shall have exclusive jurisdiction of a civil action to enforce, enjoin, set aside, annul, or suspend, in whole or in part, any order of the Surface Transportation Board arising out of such referral.

(c) Any action brought under subsection (b) of this section shall be filed within 90 days from the date that the order of the Surface Transportation Board becomes final.

History of 28 U.S.C. §1336: June 25, 1948, ch. 646, 62 Stat. 931; Aug. 30, 1964, P.L. 88-513, §1, 78 Stat. 695; Jan. 2, 1975, P.L. 93-584, §1, 88 Stat. 1917; Apr. 2, 1982, P.L. 97-164, §128, 96 Stat. 39; Oct. 29, 1992, P.L. 102-572, §902(b)(1), 106 Stat. 4516; Dec. 29, 1995, P.L. 104-88, §305(a)(1), (2), 109 Stat. 944.

§1337. COMMERCE & ANTITRUST REGULATIONS; AMOUNT IN CONTROVERSY, COSTS

(a) The district courts shall have original jurisdiction of any civil action or proceeding arising under any Act of Congress regulating commerce or protecting trade and commerce against restraints and monopolies: Provided, however, That the district courts shall have original jurisdiction of an action brought under section 11706 or 14706 of title 49, only if the matter in controversy for each receipt or bill of lading exceeds $10,000, exclusive of interest and costs.

(b) Except when express provision therefor is otherwise made in a statute of the United States, where a plaintiff who files the case under section 11706 or 14706 of title 49, originally in the Federal courts is finally adjudged to be entitled to recover less than the sum or value of $10,000, computed without regard to any setoff or counterclaim to which the defendant may be adjudged to be entitled, and exclusive of any interest and costs, the district court may deny costs to the plaintiff and, in addition, may impose costs on the plaintiff.

(c) The district courts shall not have jurisdiction under this section of any matter within the exclusive jurisdiction of the Court of International Trade under chapter 95 of this title.

History of 28 U.S.C. §1337: June 25, 1948, ch. 646, 62 Stat. 931; Oct. 20, 1978, P.L. 95-486, §9(a), 92 Stat. 1633; Oct. 10, 1980, P.L. 96-417, §505, 94 Stat. 1743; Jan. 12, 1983, P.L. 97-449, §5(f), 96 Stat. 2442; Dec. 29, 1995, P.L. 104-88, §305(a)(3), 109 Stat. 944.

§1338. PATENTS, PLANT VARIETY PROTECTION, COPYRIGHTS, MASK WORKS, DESIGNS, TRADEMARKS, & UNFAIR COMPETITION

(a) The district courts shall have original jurisdiction of any civil action arising under any Act of Congress relating to patents, plant variety protection, copyrights and trademarks. No State court shall have jurisdiction over any claim for relief arising under any Act of Congress relating to patents, plant variety protection, or copyrights. For purposes of this subsection, the term "State" includes any State of the United States, the District of Columbia, the Commonwealth of Puerto Rico, the United States Virgin Islands, American Samoa, Guam, and the Northern Mariana Islands.

(b) The district courts shall have original jurisdiction of any civil action asserting a claim of unfair competition when joined with a substantial and related claim under the copyright, patent, plant variety protection or trademark laws.

(c) Subsections (a) and (b) apply to exclusive rights in mask works under chapter 9 of title 17, and to exclusive rights in designs under chapter 13 of title 17, to the same extent as such subsections apply to copyrights.

History of 28 U.S.C. §1338: June 25, 1948, ch. 646, 62 Stat. 931; Dec. 24, 1970, P.L. 91-577, §143(b), 84 Stat. 1559; Nov. 19, 1988, P.L. 100-702, §1020(a)(4), 102 Stat. 4671; Oct. 28, 1998, P.L. 105-304, §503(b)(1), 2(A), 112 Stat. 2917; Nov. 29, 1999, P.L. 106-113-Appx. I, §3009, 113 Stat. 1501A-551; Sept. 16, 2011, P.L. 112-29, §19(a), 125 Stat. 331.

§1339. POSTAL MATTERS

The district courts shall have original jurisdiction of any civil action arising under any Act of Congress relating to the postal service.

History of 28 U.S.C. §1339: June 25, 1948, ch. 646, 62 Stat. 932.

§1340. INTERNAL REVENUE; CUSTOMS DUTIES

The district courts shall have original jurisdiction of any civil action arising under any Act of Congress providing for internal revenue, or revenue from imports or tonnage except matters within the jurisdiction of the Court of International Trade.

History of 28 U.S.C. §1340: June 25, 1948, ch. 646, 62 Stat. 932; Oct. 10, 1980, P.L. 96-417, §501(21), 94 Stat. 1742.

§1341. TAXES BY STATES

The district courts shall not enjoin, suspend or restrain the assessment, levy or collection of any tax under State law where a plain, speedy and efficient remedy may be had in the courts of such State.

History of 28 U.S.C. §1341: June 25, 1948, ch. 646, 62 Stat. 932.

§1342. RATE ORDERS OF STATE AGENCIES

The district courts shall not enjoin, suspend or restrain the operation of, or compliance with, any order affecting rates chargeable by a public utility and made by a State administrative agency or a rate-making body of a State political subdivision, where:

(1) Jurisdiction is based solely on diversity of citizenship or repugnance of the order to the Federal Constitution; and,

(2) The order does not interfere with interstate commerce; and,

(3) The order has been made after reasonable notice and hearing; and,

(4) A plain, speedy and efficient remedy may be had in the courts of such State.

History of 28 U.S.C. §1342: June 25, 1948, ch. 646, 62 Stat. 932.

§1343. CIVIL RIGHTS & ELECTIVE FRANCHISE

(a) The district courts shall have original jurisdiction of any civil action authorized by law to be commenced by any person:

(1) To recover damages for injury to his person or property, or because of the deprivation of any right or privilege of a citizen of the United States, by any act done in furtherance of any conspiracy mentioned in section 1985 of Title 42;

(2) To recover damages from any person who fails to prevent or to aid in preventing any wrongs mentioned in section 1985 of Title 42 which he had knowledge were about to occur and power to prevent;

(3) To redress the deprivation, under color of any State law, statute, ordinance, regulation, custom or usage, of any right, privilege or immunity secured by the Constitution of the United States or by any Act of Congress providing for equal rights of citizens or of all persons within the jurisdiction of the United States;

(4) To recover damages or to secure equitable or other relief under any Act of Congress providing for the protection of civil rights, including the right to vote.

(b) For purposes of this section—

(1) the District of Columbia shall be considered to be a State; and

(2) any Act of Congress applicable exclusively to the District of Columbia shall be considered to be a statute of the District of Columbia.

History of 28 U.S.C. §1343: June 25, 1948, ch. 646, 62 Stat. 932; Sept. 3, 1954, ch. 1263, §42, 68 Stat. 1241; Sept. 9, 1957, P.L. 85-315, §121, 71 Stat. 637; Dec. 29, 1979, P.L. 96-170, §2, 93 Stat. 1284.

§1344. ELECTION DISPUTES

The district courts shall have original jurisdiction of any civil action to recover possession of any office, except that of

elector of President or Vice President, United States Senator, Representative in or delegate to Congress, or member of a state legislature, authorized by law to be commenced, wherein it appears that the sole question touching the title to office arises out of denial of the right to vote, to any citizen offering to vote, on account of race, color or previous condition of servitude.

The jurisdiction under this section shall extend only so far as to determine the rights of the parties to office by reason of the denial of the right, guaranteed by the Constitution of the United States and secured by any law, to enforce the right of citizens of the United States to vote in all the States.

History of 28 U.S.C. §1344: June 25, 1948, ch. 646, 62 Stat. 932.

§1345. UNITED STATES AS PLAINTIFF

Except as otherwise provided by Act of Congress, the district courts shall have original jurisdiction of all civil actions, suits or proceedings commenced by the United States, or by any agency or officer thereof expressly authorized to sue by Act of Congress.

History of 28 U.S.C. §1345: June 25, 1948, ch. 646, 62 Stat. 933.

§1346. UNITED STATES AS DEFENDANT

(a) The district courts shall have original jurisdiction, concurrent with the United States Court of Federal Claims, of:

(1) Any civil action against the United States for the recovery of any internal-revenue tax alleged to have been erroneously or illegally assessed or collected, or any penalty claimed to have been collected without authority or any sum alleged to have been excessive or in any manner wrongfully collected under the internal-revenue laws;

(2) Any other civil action or claim against the United States, not exceeding $10,000 in amount, founded either upon the Constitution, or any Act of Congress, or any regulation of an executive department, or upon any express or implied contract with the United States, or for liquidated or unliquidated damages in cases not sounding in tort, except that the district courts shall not have jurisdiction of any civil action or claim against the United States founded upon any express or implied contract with the United States or for liquidated or unliquidated damages in cases not sounding in tort which are subject to sections 7104(b)(1) and 7107(a)(1) of title 41. For the purpose of this paragraph, an express or implied contract with the Army and Air Force Exchange Service, Navy Exchanges, Marine Corps Exchanges, Coast Guard Exchanges, or Exchange Councils of the National Aeronautics and Space Administration shall be considered an express or implied contract with the United States.

(b)(1) Subject to the provisions of chapter 171 of this title, the district courts, together with the United States District Court for the District of the Canal Zone and the District Court of the Virgin Islands, shall have exclusive jurisdiction of civil actions on claims against the United States, for money damages, accruing on and after January 1, 1945, for injury or loss of property, or personal injury or death caused by the negligent or wrongful act or omission of any employee of the Government while acting within the scope of his office or employment, under circumstances where the United States, if a private person, would be liable to the claimant in accordance with the law of the place where the act or omission occurred.

(2) No person convicted of a felony who is incarcerated while awaiting sentencing or while serving a sentence may bring a civil action against the United States or an agency, officer, or employee of the Government, for mental or emotional injury suffered while in custody without a prior showing of physical injury.

(c) The jurisdiction conferred by this section includes jurisdiction of any set-off, counterclaim, or other claim or demand whatever on the part of the United States against any plaintiff commencing an action under this section.

(d) The district courts shall not have jurisdiction under this section of any civil action or claim for a pension.

(e) The district courts shall have original jurisdiction of any civil action against the United States provided in section 6226, 6228(a), 7426, or 7428 (in the case of the United States district court for the District of Columbia) or section 7429 of the Internal Revenue Code of 1986.

(f) The district courts shall have exclusive original jurisdiction of civil actions under section 2409a to quiet title to an estate or interest in real property in which an interest is claimed by the United States.

(g) Subject to the provisions of chapter 179, the district courts of the United States shall have exclusive jurisdiction over any civil action commenced under section 453(2) of title 3, by a covered employee under chapter 5 of such title.

History of 28 U.S.C. §1346: June 25, 1948, ch. 646, 62 Stat. 933; Apr. 25, 1949, ch. 92, §2(a), 63 Stat. 62; May 24, 1949, ch. 139, §80(a), (b), 63 Stat. 101; Oct. 31, 1951, ch. 655, §50(b), 65 Stat. 727; July 30, 1954, ch. 648, §1, 68 Stat. 589; July 7, 1958, P.L. 85-508, §12(e), 72 Stat. 348; Aug. 30, 1964, P.L. 88-519, 78 Stat. 699; Nov. 2, 1966, P.L. 89-719, §202(a), 80 Stat. 1148; July 23, 1970, P.L. 91-350, §1(a), 84 Stat. 449; Oct. 25, 1972, P.L. 92-562, §1, 86 Stat. 1176; Oct. 4, 1976, P.L. 94-455, §§1204(c)(1), 1306(b)(7), 90 Stat. 1697, 1719; Nov. 1, 1978, P.L. 95-563, §14(a), 92 Stat. 2389; Apr. 2, 1982, P.L. 97-164, §129, 96 Stat. 39; Sept. 3, 1982, P.L. 97-248, §402(c)(17), 96 Stat. 669; Oct. 22, 1986, P.L. 99-514, §2, 100 Stat. 2095; Oct. 29, 1992, P.L. 102-572, §902(b)(1), 106 Stat. 4516; Apr. 26, 1996, P.L. 104-134, §101(a) [§806], 110 Stat. 1321-75; May 2, 1996, P.L. 104-140, 110 Stat. 1327; Oct. 26, 1996, P.L. 104-331, §3(b)(1), 110 Stat. 4069; Jan. 4, 2011, P.L. 111-350, §5(g)(6), 124 Stat. 3848.

§1347. PARTITION ACTION WHERE UNITED STATES IS JOINT TENANT

The district courts shall have original jurisdiction of any civil action commenced by any tenant in common or joint tenant for the partition of lands where the United States is one of the tenants in common or joint tenants.

History of 28 U.S.C. §1347: June 25, 1948, ch. 646, 62 Stat. 933.

§1348. BANKING ASSOCIATION AS PARTY

The district courts shall have original jurisdiction of any civil action commenced by the United States, or by direction of any officer thereof, against any national banking association, any civil action to wind up the affairs of any such association, and any action by a banking association established in the district for which the court is held, under chapter 2 of Title 12, to enjoin the Comptroller of the Currency, or any receiver acting under his direction, as provided by such chapter.

All national banking associations shall, for the purposes of all other actions by or against them, be deemed citizens of the States in which they are respectively located.

History of 28 U.S.C. §1348: June 25, 1948, ch. 646, 62 Stat. 933.

§1349. CORPORATION ORGANIZED UNDER FEDERAL LAW AS PARTY

The district courts shall not have jurisdiction of any civil action by or against any corporation upon the ground that it was incorporated by or under an Act of Congress, unless the United States is the owner of more than one-half of its capital stock.

History of 28 U.S.C. §1349: June 25, 1948, ch. 646, 62 Stat. 934.

§1350. ALIEN'S ACTION FOR TORT

The district courts shall have original jurisdiction of any civil action by an alien for a tort only, committed in violation of the law of nations or a treaty of the United States.

History of 28 U.S.C. §1350: June 25, 1948, ch. 646, 62 Stat. 934.

§1351. CONSULS, VICE CONSULS, & MEMBERS OF A DIPLOMATIC MISSION AS DEFENDANT

The district courts shall have original jurisdiction, exclusive of the courts of the States, of all civil actions and proceedings against—

(1) consuls or vice consuls of foreign states; or

(2) members of a mission or members of their families (as such terms are defined in section 2 of the Diplomatic Relations Act).

History of 28 U.S.C. §1351: June 25, 1948, ch. 646, 62 Stat. 934; May 24, 1949, ch. 139, §80(c), 63 Stat. 101; Sept. 30, 1978, P.L. 95-393, §8(a)(1), 92 Stat. 810.

§1352. BONDS EXECUTED UNDER FEDERAL LAW

The district courts shall have original jurisdiction, concurrent with State courts, of any action on a bond executed under any law of the United States, except matters within the jurisdiction of the Court of International Trade under section 1582 of this title.

History of 28 U.S.C. §1352: June 25, 1948, ch. 646, 62 Stat. 934; Oct. 10, 1980, P.L. 96-417, §506, 94 Stat. 1743.

§1353. INDIAN ALLOTMENTS

The district courts shall have original jurisdiction of any civil action involving the right of any person, in whole or in part of Indian blood or descent, to any allotment of land under any Act of Congress or treaty.

The judgment in favor of any claimant to an allotment of land shall have the same effect, when properly certified to the Secretary of the Interior, as if such allotment had been allowed and approved by him; but this provision shall not apply to any lands held on or before December 21, 1911, by either of the Five Civilized Tribes, the Osage Nation of Indians, nor to any of the lands within the Quapaw Indian Agency.

History of 28 U.S.C. §1353: June 25, 1948, ch. 646, 62 Stat. 934.

§1354. LAND GRANTS FROM DIFFERENT STATES

The district courts shall have original jurisdiction of actions between citizens of the same state claiming lands under grants from different states.

History of 28 U.S.C. §1354: June 25, 1948, ch. 646, 62 Stat. 934.

§1355. FINE, PENALTY OR FORFEITURE

(a) The district courts shall have original jurisdiction, exclusive of the courts of the States, of any action or proceeding for the recovery or enforcement of any fine, penalty, or forfeiture, pecuniary or otherwise, incurred under any Act of Congress, except matters within the jurisdiction of the Court of International Trade under section 1582 of this title.

(b)(1) A forfeiture action or proceeding may be brought in—

(A) the district court for the district in which any of the acts or omissions giving rise to the forfeiture occurred, or

(B) any other district where venue for the forfeiture action or proceeding is specifically provided for in section 1395 of this title or any other statute.

(2) Whenever property subject to forfeiture under the laws of the United States is located in a foreign country, or has been detained or seized pursuant to legal process or competent authority of a foreign government, an action or proceeding for forfeiture may be brought as provided in paragraph (1), or in the United States District court[1] for the District of Columbia.

(c) In any case in which a final order disposing of property in a civil forfeiture action or proceeding is appealed, removal of the property by the prevailing party shall not deprive the court of jurisdiction. Upon motion of the appealing party, the district court or the court of appeals shall issue any order necessary to preserve the right of the appealing party to the full value of the property at issue, including a stay of the judgment of the district court pending appeal or requiring the prevailing party to post an appeal bond.

(d) Any court with jurisdiction over a forfeiture action pursuant to subsection (b) may issue and cause to be served in any other district such process as may be required to bring before the court the property that is the subject of the forfeiture action.

1. **Editor's note:** So in original. Probably should be capitalized.

History of 28 U.S.C. §1355: June 25, 1948, ch. 646, 62 Stat. 934; Oct. 10, 1980, P.L. 96-417, §507, 94 Stat. 1743; Oct. 28, 1992, P.L. 102-550, §1521, 106 Stat. 4062.

§1356. SEIZURES NOT WITHIN ADMIRALTY & MARITIME JURISDICTION

The district courts shall have original jurisdiction, exclusive of the courts of the States, of any seizure under any law of the United States on land or upon waters not within admiralty and maritime jurisdiction, except matters within the jurisdiction of the Court of International Trade under section 1582 of this title.

History of 28 U.S.C. §1356: June 25, 1948, ch. 646, 62 Stat. 934; Oct. 10, 1980, P.L. 96-417, §508, 94 Stat. 1743.

§1357. INJURIES UNDER FEDERAL LAWS

The district courts shall have original jurisdiction of any civil action commenced by any person to recover damages for any injury to his person or property on account of any act done by him, under any Act of Congress, for the protection or collection of any of the revenues, or to enforce the right of citizens of the United States to vote in any State.

History of 28 U.S.C. §1357: June 25, 1948, ch. 646, 62 Stat. 934.

§1358. EMINENT DOMAIN

The district courts shall have original jurisdiction of all proceedings to condemn real estate for the use of the United States or its departments or agencies.

History of 28 U.S.C. §1358: June 25, 1948, ch. 646, 62 Stat. 935.

§1359. PARTIES COLLUSIVELY JOINED OR MADE

A district court shall not have jurisdiction of a civil action in which any party, by assignment or otherwise, has been improperly or collusively made or joined to invoke the jurisdiction of such court.

History of 28 U.S.C. §1359: June 25, 1948, ch. 646, 62 Stat. 935.

§1360. STATE CIVIL JURISDICTION IN ACTIONS TO WHICH INDIANS ARE PARTIES

(a) Each of the States listed in the following table shall have jurisdiction over civil causes of action between Indians or to which Indians are parties which arise in the areas of Indian country listed opposite the name of the State to the same extent that such State has jurisdiction over other civil causes of action, and those civil laws of such State that are of general application to private persons or private property shall have the same force and effect within such Indian country as they have elsewhere within the State:

State of	*Indian country affected*
Alaska	All Indian country within the State.
California	All Indian country within the State.
Minnesota	All Indian country within the State, except the Red Lake Reservation.
Nebraska	All Indian country within the State.
Oregon	All Indian country within the State, except the Warm Springs Reservation.
Wisconsin	All Indian country within the State.

(b) Nothing in this section shall authorize the alienation, encumbrance, or taxation of any real or personal property, including water rights, belonging to any Indian or any Indian tribe, band, or community that is held in trust by the United States or is subject to a restriction against alienation imposed by the United States; or shall authorize regulation of the use of such property in a manner inconsistent with any Federal treaty, agreement, or statute or with any regulation made pursuant thereto; or shall confer jurisdiction upon the State to adjudicate, in probate proceedings or otherwise, the ownership or right to possession of such property or any interest therein.

(c) Any tribal ordinance or custom heretofore or hereafter adopted by an Indian tribe, band, or community in the exercise of any authority which it may possess shall, if not inconsistent with any applicable civil law of the State, be given full force and effect in the determination of civil causes of action pursuant to this section.

History of 28 U.S.C. §1360: Aug. 15, 1953, ch. 505, §4, 67 Stat. 589; Aug. 24, 1954, ch. 910, §2, 68 Stat. 795; Aug. 8, 1958, P.L. 85-615, §2, 72 Stat. 545; Nov. 6, 1978, P.L. 95-598, §239, 92 Stat. 2668; July 10, 1984, P.L. 98-353, §110, 98 Stat. 342.

§1361. ACTION TO COMPEL AN OFFICER OF THE UNITED STATES TO PERFORM HIS DUTY

The district courts shall have original jurisdiction of any action in the nature of mandamus to compel an officer or employee of the United States or any agency thereof to perform a duty owed to the plaintiff.

History of 28 U.S.C. §1361: Oct. 5, 1962, P.L. 87-748, §1(a), 76 Stat. 744.

§1362. INDIAN TRIBES

The district courts shall have original jurisdiction of all civil actions, brought by any Indian tribe or band with a governing body duly recognized by the Secretary of the Interior, wherein the matter in controversy arises under the Constitution, laws, or treaties of the United States.

History of 28 U.S.C. §1362: Oct. 10, 1966, P.L. 89-635, §1, 80 Stat. 880.

§1363. JURORS' EMPLOYMENT RIGHTS

The district courts shall have original jurisdiction of any civil action brought for the protection of jurors' employment under section 1875 of this title.

History of 28 U.S.C. §1363: Nov. 2, 1978, P.L. 95-572, §6(b)(1), 92 Stat. 2457.

§1364. DIRECT ACTIONS AGAINST INSURERS OF MEMBERS OF DIPLOMATIC MISSIONS & THEIR FAMILIES

(a) The district courts shall have original and exclusive jurisdiction, without regard to the amount in controversy, of

any civil action commenced by any person against an insurer who by contract has insured an individual, who is, or was at the time of the tortious act or omission, a member of a mission (within the meaning of section 2(3) of the Diplomatic Relations Act (22 U.S.C. 254a(3))) or a member of the family of such a member of a mission, or an individual described in section 19 of the Convention on Privileges and Immunities of the United Nations of February 13, 1946, against liability for personal injury, death, or damage to property.

(b) Any direct action brought against an insurer under subsection (a) shall be tried without a jury, but shall not be subject to the defense that the insured is immune from suit, that the insured is an indispensable party, or in the absence of fraud or collusion, that the insured has violated a term of the contract, unless the contract was cancelled before the claim arose.

History of 28 U.S.C. §1364: Sept. 30, 1978, P.L. 95-393, §7(a), 92 Stat. 809; Aug. 24, 1982, P.L. 97-241, §203(b)(4), 96 Stat. 291; Dec. 22, 1987, P.L. 100-204, §138(a), 101 Stat. 1347.

§1365. SENATE ACTIONS

(a) The United States District Court for the District of Columbia shall have original jurisdiction, without regard to the amount in controversy, over any civil action brought by the Senate or any authorized committee or subcommittee of the Senate to enforce, to secure a declaratory judgment concerning the validity of, or to prevent a threatened refusal or failure to comply with, any subpena[1] or order issued by the Senate or committee or subcommittee of the Senate to any entity acting or purporting to act under color or authority of State law or to any natural person to secure the production of documents or other materials of any kind or the answering of any deposition or interrogatory or to secure testimony or any combination thereof. This section shall not apply to an action to enforce, to secure a declaratory judgment concerning the validity of, or to prevent a threatened refusal to comply with, any subpena[1] or order issued to an officer or employee of the executive branch of the Federal Government acting within his or her official capacity, except that this section shall apply if the refusal to comply is based on the assertion of a personal privilege or objection and is not based on a governmental privilege or objection the assertion of which has been authorized by the executive branch of the Federal Government.

(b) Upon application by the Senate or any authorized committee or subcommittee of the Senate, the district court shall issue an order to an entity or person refusing, or failing to comply with, or threatening to refuse or not to comply with, a subpena[1] or order of the Senate or committee or subcommittee of the Senate requiring such entity or person to comply forthwith. Any refusal or failure to obey a lawful order of the district court issued pursuant to this section may be held by such court to be a contempt thereof. A contempt proceeding shall be commenced by an order to show cause before the court why the entity or person refusing or failing to obey the court order should not be held in contempt of court. Such contempt proceeding shall be tried by the court and shall be summary in manner. The purpose of sanctions imposed as a result of such contempt proceeding shall be to compel obedience to the order of the court. Process in any such action or contempt proceeding may be served in any judicial district wherein the entity or party refusing, or failing to comply, or threatening to refuse or not to comply, resides, transacts business, or may be found, and subpenas[2] for witnesses who are required to attend such proceeding may run into any other district. Nothing in this section shall confer upon such court jurisdiction to affect by injunction or otherwise the issuance or effect of any subpena[1] or order of the Senate or any committee or subcommittee of the Senate or to review, modify, suspend, terminate, or set aside any such subpena[1] or order. An action, contempt proceeding, or sanction brought or imposed pursuant to this section shall not abate upon adjournment sine die by the Senate at the end of a Congress if the Senate or the committee or subcommittee of the Senate which issued the subpena[1] or order certifies to the court that it maintains its interest in securing the documents, answers, or testimony during such adjournment.

(c) [Repealed Nov. 8, 1984, P.L. 98-620, title IV, §402(29)(D), 98 Stat. 3359.]

(d) The Senate or any committee or subcommittee of the Senate commencing and prosecuting a civil action or contempt proceeding under this section may be represented in such action by such attorneys as the Senate may designate.

(e) A civil action commenced or prosecuted under this section, may not be authorized pursuant to the Standing Order of the Senate "authorizing suits by Senate Committees" (S. Jour. 572, May 28, 1928).

(f) For the purposes of this section the term "committee" includes standing, select, or special committees of the Senate established by law or resolution.

1. **Editor's note:** So in original. Probably should be "subpoena."
2. **Editor's note:** So in original. Probably should be "subpoenas."

History of 28 U.S.C. §1365: Oct. 26, 1978, P.L. 95-521, §705(f)(1), 92 Stat. 1879; Nov. 8, 1984, P.L. 98-620, §402(29)(D), 98 Stat. 3359. Renumbered as §1365, June 19, 1986, P.L. 99-336, §6(a)(1)(B), 100 Stat. 638; Oct. 11, 1996, P.L. 104-292, §4, 110 Stat. 3460.

§1366. CONSTRUCTION OF REFERENCES TO LAWS OF THE UNITED STATES OR ACTS OF CONGRESS

For the purposes of this chapter, references to laws of the United States or Acts of Congress do not include laws applicable exclusively to the District of Columbia.

History of 28 U.S.C. §1366: July 29, 1970, P.L. 91-358, §172(c)(1), 84 Stat. 590. Renumbered as §1364, Nov. 2, 1978, P.L. 95-572, §6(b)(1), 92 Stat. 2456; renumbered as §1366, June 19, 1986, P.L. 99-336, §6(a)(1)(C), 100 Stat. 639.

§1367. SUPPLEMENTAL JURISDICTION

(a) Except as provided in subsections (b) and (c) or as expressly provided otherwise by Federal statute, in any civil action of which the district courts have original jurisdiction, the district courts shall have supplemental jurisdiction over all other claims that are so related to claims in the action within such original jurisdiction that they form part of the

same case or controversy under Article III of the United States Constitution. Such supplemental jurisdiction shall include claims that involve the joinder or intervention of additional parties.

(b) In any civil action of which the district courts have original jurisdiction founded solely on section 1332 of this title, the district courts shall not have supplemental jurisdiction under subsection (a) over claims by plaintiffs against persons made parties under Rule 14, 19, 20, or 24 of the Federal Rules of Civil Procedure, or over claims by persons proposed to be joined as plaintiffs under Rule 19 of such rules, or seeking to intervene as plaintiffs under Rule 24 of such rules, when exercising supplemental jurisdiction over such claims would be inconsistent with the jurisdictional requirements of section 1332.

(c) The district courts may decline to exercise supplemental jurisdiction over a claim under subsection (a) if—

(1) the claim raises a novel or complex issue of State law,

(2) the claim substantially predominates over the claim or claims over which the district court has original jurisdiction,

(3) the district court has dismissed all claims over which it has original jurisdiction, or

(4) in exceptional circumstances, there are other compelling reasons for declining jurisdiction.

(d) The period of limitations for any claim asserted under subsection (a), and for any other claim in the same action that is voluntarily dismissed at the same time as or after the dismissal of the claim under subsection (a), shall be tolled while the claim is pending and for a period of 30 days after it is dismissed unless State law provides for a longer tolling period.

(e) As used in this section, the term "State" includes the District of Columbia, the Commonwealth of Puerto Rico, and any territory or possession of the United States.

History of 28 U.S.C. §1367: Dec. 1, 1990, P.L. 101-650, §310(a), 104 Stat. 5113.

See *Commentaries*, "Supplemental Jurisdiction," ch. 2-F, §6, p. 134.

§1368. COUNTERCLAIMS IN UNFAIR PRACTICES IN INTERNATIONAL TRADE

The district courts shall have original jurisdiction of any civil action based on a counterclaim raised pursuant to section 337(c) of the Tariff Act of 1930, to the extent that it arises out of the transaction or occurrence that is the subject matter of the opposing party's claim in the proceeding under section 337(a) of that Act.

History of 28 U.S.C. §1368: Dec. 8, 1994, P.L. 103-465, §321(b)(3)(A), 108 Stat. 4946.

§1369. MULTIPARTY, MULTIFORUM JURISDICTION

(a) In general.—The district courts shall have original jurisdiction of any civil action involving minimal diversity between adverse parties that arises from a single accident, where at least 75 natural persons have died in the accident at a discrete location, if—

(1) a defendant resides in a State and a substantial part of the accident took place in another State or other location, regardless of whether that defendant is also a resident of the State where a substantial part of the accident took place;

(2) any two defendants reside in different States, regardless of whether such defendants are also residents of the same State or States; or

(3) substantial parts of the accident took place in different States.

(b) Limitation of jurisdiction of district courts.—The district court shall abstain from hearing any civil action described in subsection (a) in which—

(1) the substantial majority of all plaintiffs are citizens of a single State of which the primary defendants are also citizens; and

(2) the claims asserted will be governed primarily by the laws of that State.

(c) Special rules and definitions.—For purposes of this section—

(1) minimal diversity exists between adverse parties if any party is a citizen of a State and any adverse party is a citizen of another State, a citizen or subject of a foreign state, or a foreign state as defined in section 1603(a) of this title;

(2) a corporation is deemed to be a citizen of any State, and a citizen or subject of any foreign state, in which it is incorporated or has its principal place of business, and is deemed to be a resident of any State in which it is incorporated or licensed to do business or is doing business;

(3) the term "injury" means—

(A) physical harm to a natural person; and

(B) physical damage to or destruction of tangible property, but only if physical harm described in subparagraph (A) exists;

(4) the term "accident" means a sudden accident, or a natural event culminating in an accident, that results in death incurred at a discrete location by at least 75 natural persons; and

(5) the term "State" includes the District of Columbia, the Commonwealth of Puerto Rico, and any territory or possession of the United States.

(d) Intervening parties.—In any action in a district court which is or could have been brought, in whole or in part, under this section, any person with a claim arising from the accident described in subsection (a) shall be permitted to intervene as a party plaintiff in the action, even if that person could not have brought an action in a district court as an original matter.

(e) Notification of judicial panel on multidistrict litigation.—A district court in which an action under this section is pending shall promptly notify the judicial panel on multidistrict litigation of the pendency of the action.

History of 28 U.S.C. §1369: Nov. 2, 2002, P.L. 107-273, §11020(b)(1)(A), 116 Stat. 1826.

See *Commentaries*, "Multiparty Jurisdiction," ch. 2-F, §5, p. 129.

CHAPTER 87. DISTRICT COURTS; VENUE

§1390. SCOPE

(a) Venue defined.—As used in this chapter, the term "venue" refers to the geographic specification of the proper court or courts for the litigation of a civil action that is within the subject-matter jurisdiction of the district courts in general, and does not refer to any grant or restriction of subject-matter jurisdiction providing for a civil action to be adjudicated only by the district court for a particular district or districts.

(b) Exclusion of certain cases.—Except as otherwise provided by law, this chapter shall not govern the venue of a civil action in which the district court exercises the jurisdiction conferred by section 1333, except that such civil actions may be transferred between district courts as provided in this chapter.

(c) Clarification regarding cases removed from State courts.—This chapter shall not determine the district court to which a civil action pending in a State court may be removed, but shall govern the transfer of an action so removed as between districts and divisions of the United States district courts.

History of 28 U.S.C. §1390: Dec. 7, 2011, P.L. 112-63, §§201(a), 205, 125 Stat. 762, 764.

See *Commentaries*, "Choosing the Court—Venue," ch. 2-G, p. 143.

§1391. VENUE GENERALLY

(a) Applicability of section.—Except as otherwise provided by law—

(1) this section shall govern the venue of all civil actions brought in district courts of the United States; and

(2) the proper venue for a civil action shall be determined without regard to whether the action is local or transitory in nature.

(b) Venue in general.—A civil action may be brought in—

(1) a judicial district in which any defendant resides, if all defendants are residents of the State in which the district is located;

(2) a judicial district in which a substantial part of the events or omissions giving rise to the claim occurred, or a substantial part of property that is the subject of the action is situated; or

(3) if there is no district in which an action may otherwise be brought as provided in this section, any judicial district in which any defendant is subject to the court's personal jurisdiction with respect to such action.

(c) Residency.—For all venue purposes—

(1) a natural person, including an alien lawfully admitted for permanent residence in the United States, shall be deemed to reside in the judicial district in which that person is domiciled;

(2) an entity with the capacity to sue and be sued in its common name under applicable law, whether or not incorporated, shall be deemed to reside, if a defendant, in any judicial district in which such defendant is subject to the court's personal jurisdiction with respect to the civil action in question and, if a plaintiff, only in the judicial district in which it maintains its principal place of business; and

(3) a defendant not resident in the United States may be sued in any judicial district, and the joinder of such a defendant shall be disregarded in determining where the action may be brought with respect to other defendants.

(d) Residency of corporations in States with multiple districts.—For purposes of venue under this chapter, in a State which has more than one judicial district and in which a defendant that is a corporation is subject to personal jurisdiction at the time an action is commenced, such corporation shall be deemed to reside in any district in that State within which its contacts would be sufficient to subject it to personal jurisdiction if that district were a separate State, and, if there is no such district, the corporation shall be deemed to reside in the district within which it has the most significant contacts.

(e) Actions where defendant is officer or employee of the United States—

(1) In general.—A civil action in which a defendant is an officer or employee of the United States or any agency thereof acting in his official capacity or under color of legal authority, or an agency of the United States, or the United States, may, except as otherwise provided by law, be brought in any judicial district in which

(A) a defendant in the action resides,

(B) a substantial part of the events or omissions giving rise to the claim occurred, or a substantial part of property that is the subject of the action is situated, or

(C) the plaintiff resides if no real property is involved in the action. Additional persons may be joined as parties to any such action in accordance with the Federal Rules of Civil Procedure and with such other venue requirements as would be applicable if the United States or one of its officers, employees, or agencies were not a party.

(2) Service.—The summons and complaint in such an action shall be served as provided by the Federal Rules of Civil Procedure except that the delivery of the summons and complaint to the officer or agency as required by the rules may be made by certified mail beyond the territorial limits of the district in which the action is brought.

(f) Civil actions against a foreign state.—A civil action against a foreign state as defined in section 1603(a) of this title may be brought—

(1) in any judicial district in which a substantial part of the events or omissions giving rise to the claim occurred, or a substantial part of property that is the subject of the action is situated;

(2) in any judicial district in which the vessel or cargo of a foreign state is situated, if the claim is asserted under section 1605(b) of this title;

(3) in any judicial district in which the agency or instrumentality is licensed to do business or is doing business, if the action is brought against an agency or instrumentality of a foreign state as defined in section 1603(b) of this title; or

(4) in the United States District Court for the District of Columbia if the action is brought against a foreign state or political subdivision thereof.

(g) Multiparty, multiforum litigation.—A civil action in which jurisdiction of the district court is based upon section 1369 of this title may be brought in any district in which any defendant resides or in which a substantial part of the accident giving rise to the action took place.

History of 28 U.S.C. §1391: June 25, 1948, ch. 646, 62 Stat. 935; Oct. 5, 1962, P.L. 87-748, §2, 76 Stat. 744; Dec. 23, 1963, P.L. 88-234, 77 Stat. 473; Nov. 2, 1966, P.L. 89-714, §§1, 2, 80 Stat. 1111; Oct. 21, 1976, P.L. 94-574, §3, 90 Stat. 2721; Oct. 21, 1976, P.L. 94-583, §5, 90 Stat. 2897; Nov. 19, 1988, P.L. 100-702, §1013(a), 102 Stat. 4669; Dec. 1, 1990, P.L. 101-650, §311, 104 Stat. 5114; Dec. 9, 1991, P.L. 102-198, §3, 105 Stat. 1623; Oct. 29, 1992, P.L. 102-572, §504, 106 Stat. 4513; Oct. 3, 1995, P.L. 104-34, §1, 109 Stat. 293; Nov. 2, 2002, P.L. 107-273, §11020(b)(2), 116 Stat. 1827; Dec. 7, 2011, P.L. 112-63, §§202, 205, 125 Stat. 763, 764.

See *Commentaries*, "Choosing the Court—Venue," ch. 2-G, p. 143.

§1392. REPEALED

Repealed Dec. 7, 2011, P.L. 112-63, §§203, 205, 125 Stat. 764.

§1393. REPEALED

Repealed Nov. 19, 1988, P.L. 100-702, §1001(a), 102 Stat. 4664.

§1394. BANKING ASSOCIATION'S ACTION AGAINST COMPTROLLER OF CURRENCY

Any civil action by a national banking association to enjoin the Comptroller of the Currency, under the provisions of any Act of Congress relating to such associations, may be prosecuted in the judicial district where such association is located.

History of 28 U.S.C. §1394: June 25, 1948, ch. 646, 62 Stat. 935.

§1395. FINE, PENALTY OR FORFEITURE

(a) A civil proceeding for the recovery of a pecuniary fine, penalty or forfeiture may be prosecuted in the district where it accrues or the defendant is found.

(b) A civil proceeding for the forfeiture of property may be prosecuted in any district where such property is found.

(c) A civil proceeding for the forfeiture of property seized outside any judicial district may be prosecuted in any district into which the property is brought.

(d) A proceeding in admiralty for the enforcement of fines, penalties and forfeitures against a vessel may be brought in any district in which the vessel is arrested.

(e) Any proceeding for the forfeiture of a vessel or cargo entering a port of entry closed by the President in pursuance of law, or of goods and chattels coming from a State or section declared by proclamation of the President to be in insurrection, or of any vessel or vehicle conveying persons or property to or from such State or section or belonging in whole or in part to a resident thereof, may be prosecuted in any district into which the property is taken and in which the proceeding is instituted.

History of 28 U.S.C. §1395: June 25, 1948, ch. 646, 62 Stat. 936.

§1396. INTERNAL REVENUE TAXES

Any civil action for the collection of internal revenue taxes may be brought in the district where the liability for such tax accrues, in the district of the taxpayer's residence, or in the district where the return was filed.

History of 28 U.S.C. §1396: June 25, 1948, ch. 646, 62 Stat. 936.

§1397. INTERPLEADER

Any civil action of interpleader or in the nature of interpleader under section 1335 of this title may be brought in the judicial district in which one or more of the claimants reside.

History of 28 U.S.C. §1397: June 25, 1948, ch. 646, 62 Stat. 936.

See *Commentaries*, "Interpleader," ch. 2-C, p. 87.

§1398. INTERSTATE COMMERCE COMMISSION'S ORDERS

(a) Except as otherwise provided by law, a civil action brought under section 1336(a) of this title shall be brought only in a judicial district in which any of the parties bringing the action resides or has its principal office.

(b) A civil action to enforce, enjoin, set aside, annul, or suspend, in whole or in part, an order of the Interstate Commerce Commission made pursuant to the referral of a question or issue by a district court or by the United States Court of Federal Claims, shall be brought only in the court which referred the question or issue.

History of 28 U.S.C. §1398: June 25, 1948, ch. 646, 62 Stat. 936; Aug. 30, 1964, P.L. 88-513, §2, 78 Stat. 695; Jan. 2, 1975, P.L. 93-584, §2, 88 Stat. 1917; Apr. 2, 1982, P.L. 97-164, §130, 96 Stat. 39; Oct. 29, 1992, P.L. 102-572, §902(b)(1), 106 Stat. 4516.

§1399. PARTITION ACTION INVOLVING UNITED STATES

Any civil action by any tenant in common or joint tenant for the partition of lands, where the United States is one of the tenants in common or joint tenants, may be brought only in the judicial district where such lands are located or, if located in different districts in the same State, in any of such districts.

History of 28 U.S.C. §1399: June 25, 1948, ch. 646, 62 Stat. 936.

§1400. PATENTS & COPYRIGHTS, MASK WORKS, & DESIGNS

(a) Civil actions, suits, or proceedings arising under any Act of Congress relating to copyrights or exclusive rights in

mask works or designs may be instituted in the district in which the defendant or his agent resides or may be found.

(b) Any civil action for patent infringement may be brought in the judicial district where the defendant resides, or where the defendant has committed acts of infringement and has a regular and established place of business.

History of 28 U.S.C. §1400: June 25, 1948, ch. 646, 62 Stat. 936; Nov. 19, 1988, P.L. 100-702, §1020(a)(5), 102 Stat. 4671; Oct. 28, 1998, P.L. 105-304, §503(b)(2)(B), 112 Stat. 2917; Aug. 5, 1999, P.L. 106-44, §2(a), 113 Stat. 223.

§1401. STOCKHOLDER'S DERIVATIVE ACTION

Any civil action by a stockholder on behalf of his corporation may be prosecuted in any judicial district where the corporation might have sued the same defendants.

History of 28 U.S.C. §1401: June 25, 1948, ch. 646, 62 Stat. 936.

§1402. UNITED STATES AS DEFENDANT

(a) Any civil action in a district court against the United States under subsection (a) of section 1346 of this title may be prosecuted only:

(1) Except as provided in paragraph (2), in the judicial district where the plaintiff resides;

(2) In the case of a civil action by a corporation under paragraph (1) of subsection (a) of section 1346, in the judicial district in which is located the principal place of business or principal office or agency of the corporation; or if it has no principal place of business or principal office or agency in any judicial district (A) in the judicial district in which is located the office to which was made the return of the tax in respect of which the claim is made, or (B) if no return was made, in the judicial district in which lies the District of Columbia. Notwithstanding the foregoing provisions of this paragraph a district court, for the convenience of the parties and witnesses, in the interest of justice, may transfer any such action to any other district or division.

(b) Any civil action on a tort claim against the United States under subsection (b) of section 1346 of this title may be prosecuted only in the judicial district where the plaintiff resides or wherein the act or omission complained of occurred.

(c) Any civil action against the United States under subsection (e) of section 1346 of this title may be prosecuted only in the judicial district where the property is situated at the time of levy, or if no levy is made, in the judicial district in which the event occurred which gave rise to the cause of action.

(d) Any civil action under section 2409a to quiet title to an estate or interest in real property in which an interest is claimed by the United States shall be brought in the district court of the district where the property is located or, if located in different districts, in any of such districts.

History of 28 U.S.C. §1402: June 25, 1948, ch. 646, 62 Stat. 937; Sept. 2, 1958, P.L. 85-920, 72 Stat. 1770; Nov. 2, 1966, P.L. 89-719, §202(b), 80 Stat. 1149; Oct. 25, 1972, P.L. 92-562, §2, 86 Stat. 1176; Apr. 2, 1982, P.L. 97-164, §131, 96 Stat. 39.

§1403. EMINENT DOMAIN

Proceedings to condemn real estate for the use of the United States or its departments or agencies shall be brought in the district court of the district where the land is located or, if located in different districts in the same State, in any of such districts.

History of 28 U.S.C. §1403: June 25, 1948, ch. 646, 62 Stat. 937.

§1404. CHANGE OF VENUE

(a) For the convenience of parties and witnesses, in the interest of justice, a district court may transfer any civil action to any other district or division where it might have been brought or to any district or division to which all parties have consented.

(b) Upon motion, consent or stipulation of all parties, any action, suit or proceeding of a civil nature or any motion or hearing thereof, may be transferred, in the discretion of the court, from the division in which pending to any other division in the same district. Transfer of proceedings in rem brought by or on behalf of the United States may be transferred under this section without the consent of the United States where all other parties request transfer.

(c) A district court may order any civil action to be tried at any place within the division in which it is pending.

(d) Transfers from a district court of the United States to the District Court of Guam, the District Court for the Northern Mariana Islands, or the District Court of the Virgin Islands shall not be permitted under this section. As otherwise used in this section, the term "district court" includes the District Court of Guam, the District Court for the Northern Mariana Islands, and the District Court of the Virgin Islands, and the term "district" includes the territorial jurisdiction of each such court.

History of 28 U.S.C. §1404: June 25, 1948, ch. 646, 62 Stat. 937; Oct. 18, 1962, P.L. 87-845, §9, 76A Stat. 699; Oct. 19, 1996, P.L. 104-317, §610, 110 Stat. 3860; Dec. 7, 2011, P.L. 112-63, §§204, 205, 125 Stat. 764.

See *Commentaries*, "Motion to Transfer Venue—28 U.S.C. §1404," ch. 3-K, p. 221.

§1405. CREATION OR ALTERATION OF DISTRICT OR DIVISION

Actions or proceedings pending at the time of the creation of a new district or division or transfer of a county or territory from one division or district to another may be tried in the district or division as it existed at the institution of the action or proceeding, or in the district or division so created or to which the county or territory is so transferred as the parties shall agree or the court direct.

History of 28 U.S.C. §1405: June 25, 1948, ch. 646, 62 Stat. 937.

§1406. CURE OR WAIVER OF DEFECTS

(a) The district court of a district in which is filed a case laying venue in the wrong division or district shall dismiss, or if it be in the interest of justice, transfer such case to any district or division in which it could have been brought.

(b) Nothing in this chapter shall impair the jurisdiction of a district court of any matter involving a party who does not interpose timely and sufficient objection to the venue.

(c) As used in this section, the term "district court" includes the District Court of Guam, the District Court for the Northern Mariana Islands, and the District Court of the Virgin Islands, and the term "district" includes the territorial jurisdiction of each such court.

History of 28 U.S.C. §1406: June 25, 1948, ch. 646, 62 Stat. 937; May 24, 1949, ch. 139, §81, 63 Stat. 101; Sept. 13, 1960, P.L. 86-770, §1, 74 Stat. 912; Oct. 18, 1962, P.L. 87-845, §10, 76A Stat. 699; Apr. 2, 1982, P.L. 97-164, §132, 96 Stat. 39; Oct. 19, 1996, P.L. 104-317, §601(b), 110 Stat. 3860.

§1407. MULTIDISTRICT LITIGATION

(a) When civil actions involving one or more common questions of fact are pending in different districts, such actions may be transferred to any district for coordinated or consolidated pretrial proceedings. Such transfers shall be made by the judicial panel on multidistrict litigation authorized by this section upon its determination that transfers for such proceedings will be for the convenience of parties and witnesses and will promote the just and efficient conduct of such actions. Each action so transferred shall be remanded by the panel at or before the conclusion of such pretrial proceedings to the district from which it was transferred unless it shall have been previously terminated: Provided, however, That the panel may separate any claim, cross-claim, counter-claim, or third-party claim and remand any of such claims before the remainder of the action is remanded.

(b) Such coordinated or consolidated pretrial proceedings shall be conducted by a judge or judges to whom such actions are assigned by the judicial panel on multidistrict litigation. For this purpose, upon request of the panel, a circuit judge or a district judge may be designated and assigned temporarily for service in the transferee district by the Chief Justice of the United States or the chief judge of the circuit, as may be required, in accordance with the provisions of chapter 13 of this title. With the consent of the transferee district court, such actions may be assigned by the panel to a judge or judges of such district. The judge or judges to whom such actions are assigned, the members of the judicial panel on multidistrict litigation, and other circuit and district judges designated when needed by the panel may exercise the powers of a district judge in any district for the purpose of conducting pretrial depositions in such coordinated or consolidated pretrial proceedings.

(c) Proceedings for the transfer of an action under this section may be initiated by—

(i) the judicial panel on multidistrict litigation upon its own initiative, or

(ii) motion filed with the panel by a party in any action in which transfer for coordinated or consolidated pretrial proceedings under this section may be appropriate. A copy of such motion shall be filed in the district court in which the moving party's action is pending.

The panel shall give notice to the parties in all actions in which transfers for coordinated or consolidated pretrial proceedings are contemplated, and such notice shall specify the time and place of any hearing to determine whether such transfer shall be made. Orders of the panel to set a hearing and other orders of the panel issued prior to the order either directing or denying transfer shall be filed in the office of the clerk of the district court in which a transfer hearing is to be or has been held. The panel's order of transfer shall be based upon a record of such hearing at which material evidence may be offered by any party to an action pending in any district that would be affected by the proceedings under this section, and shall be supported by findings of fact and conclusions of law based upon such record. Orders of transfer and such other orders as the panel may make thereafter shall be filed in the office of the clerk of the district court of the transferee district and shall be effective when thus filed. The clerk of the transferee district court shall forthwith transmit a certified copy of the panel's order to transfer to the clerk of the district court from which the action is being transferred. An order denying transfer shall be filed in each district wherein there is a case pending in which the motion for transfer has been made.

(d) The judicial panel on multidistrict litigation shall consist of seven circuit and district judges designated from time to time by the Chief Justice of the United States, no two of whom shall be from the same circuit. The concurrence of four members shall be necessary to any action by the panel.

(e) No proceedings for review of any order of the panel may be permitted except by extraordinary writ pursuant to the provisions of title 28, section 1651, United States Code. Petitions for an extraordinary writ to review an order of the panel to set a transfer hearing and other orders of the panel issued prior to the order either directing or denying transfer shall be filed only in the court of appeals having jurisdiction over the district in which a hearing is to be or has been held. Petitions for an extraordinary writ to review an order to transfer or orders subsequent to transfer shall be filed only in the court of appeals having jurisdiction over the transferee district. There shall be no appeal or review of an order of the panel denying a motion to transfer for consolidated or coordinated proceedings.

(f) The panel may prescribe rules for the conduct of its business not inconsistent with Acts of Congress and the Federal Rules of Civil Procedure.

(g) Nothing in this section shall apply to any action in which the United States is a complainant arising under the antitrust laws. "Antitrust laws" as used herein include those acts referred to in the Act of October 15, 1914, as amended (38 Stat. 730; 15 U.S.C. 12), and also include the Act of June 19, 1936 (49 Stat. 1526; 15 U.S.C. 13, 13a, and 13b) and the Act of September 26, 1914, as added March 21, 1938 (52 Stat. 116,

117; 15 U.S.C. 56); but shall not include section 4A of the Act of October 15, 1914, as added July 7, 1955 (69 Stat. 282; 15 U.S.C. 15a).

(h) Notwithstanding the provisions of section 1404 or subsection (f) of this section, the judicial panel on multidistrict litigation may consolidate and transfer with or without the consent of the parties, for both pretrial purposes and for trial, any action brought under section 4C of the Clayton Act.

History of 28 U.S.C. §1407: Apr. 29, 1968, P.L. 90-296, §1, 82 Stat. 109; Sept. 30, 1976, P.L. 94-435, §303, 90 Stat. 1396.

See the Rules of Procedure of the Judicial Panel on Multidistrict Litigation, p. 1011.

§1408. VENUE OF CASES UNDER TITLE 11

Except as provided in section 1410 of this title, a case under title 11 may be commenced in the district court for the district—

(1) in which the domicile, residence, principal place of business in the United States, or principal assets in the United States, of the person or entity that is the subject of such case have been located for the one hundred and eighty days immediately preceding such commencement, or for a longer portion of such one-hundred-and-eighty-day period than the domicile, residence, or principal place of business, in the United States, or principal assets in the United States, of such person were located in any other district; or

(2) in which there is pending a case under title 11 concerning such person's affiliate, general partner, or partnership.

History of 28 U.S.C. §1408: July 10, 1984, P.L. 98-353, §102(a), 98 Stat. 334.

§1409. VENUE OF PROCEEDINGS ARISING UNDER TITLE 11 OR ARISING IN OR RELATED TO CASES UNDER TITLE 11

(a) Except as otherwise provided in subsections (b) and (d), a proceeding arising under title 11 or arising in or related to a case under title 11 may be commenced in the district court in which such case is pending.

(b) Except as provided in subsection (d) of this section, a trustee in a case under title 11 may commence a proceeding arising in or related to such case to recover a money judgment of or property worth less than [$1,175][1] or a consumer debt of less than [$17,575],[1] or a debt (excluding a consumer debt) against a noninsider of less than [$11,725],[1] only in the district court for the district in which the defendant resides.

(c) Except as provided in subsection (b) of this section, a trustee in a case under title 11 may commence a proceeding arising in or related to such case as statutory successor to the debtor or creditors under section 541 or 544(b) of title 11 in the district court for the district where the State or Federal court sits in which, under applicable nonbankruptcy venue provisions, the debtor or creditors, as the case may be, may have commenced an action on which such proceeding is based if the case under title 11 had not been commenced.

(d) A trustee may commence a proceeding arising under title 11 or arising in or related to a case under title 11 based on a claim arising after the commencement of such case from the operation of the business of the debtor only in the district court for the district where a State or Federal court sits in which, under applicable nonbankruptcy venue provisions, an action on such claim may have been brought.

(e) A proceeding arising under title 11 or arising in or related to a case under title 11, based on a claim arising after the commencement of such case from the operation of the business of the debtor, may be commenced against the representative of the estate in such case in the district court for the district where the State or Federal court sits in which the party commencing such proceeding may, under applicable nonbankruptcy venue provisions, have brought an action on such claim, or in the district court in which such case is pending.

1. **Editor's note:** Dollar amounts as adjusted by the Judicial Conference of the United States. 75 F.R. 8747; *see* 11 U.S.C. §104(b). The amounts are effective through March 31, 2013. *See* 75 F.R. 8747. Check the Federal Register for the amounts effective after April 1, 2013.

History of 28 U.S.C. §1409: July 10, 1984, P.L. 98-353, §102(a), 98 Stat. 334; Apr. 20, 2005, P.L. 109-8, §410, 119 Stat. 106.

§1410. VENUE OF CASES ANCILLARY TO FOREIGN PROCEEDINGS

A case under chapter 15 of title 11 may be commenced in the district court of the United States for the district—

(1) in which the debtor has its principal place of business or principal assets in the United States;

(2) if the debtor does not have a place of business or assets in the United States, in which there is pending against the debtor an action or proceeding in a Federal or State court; or

(3) in a case other than those specified in paragraph (1) or (2), in which venue will be consistent with the interests of justice and the convenience of the parties, having regard to the relief sought by the foreign representative.

History of 28 U.S.C. §1410: July 10, 1984, P.L. 98-353, §102(a), 98 Stat. 335; Apr. 20, 2005, P.L. 109-8, §802(c)(4), 119 Stat. 146.

§1411. JURY TRIALS

(a) Except as provided in subsection (b) of this section, this chapter and title 11 do not affect any right to trial by jury that an individual has under applicable nonbankruptcy law with regard to a personal injury or wrongful death tort claim.

(b) The district court may order the issues arising under section 303 of title 11 to be tried without a jury.

History of 28 U.S.C. §1411: July 10, 1984, P.L. 98-353, §102(a), 98 Stat. 335.

§1412. CHANGE OF VENUE

A district court may transfer a case or proceeding under title 11 to a district court for another district, in the interest of justice or for the convenience of the parties.

History of 28 U.S.C. §1412: July 10, 1984, P.L. 98-353, §102(a), 98 Stat. 335.

§1413. VENUE OF CASES UNDER CHAPTER 5 OF TITLE 3

Notwithstanding the preceding provisions of this chapter, a civil action under section 1346(g) may be brought in the United States district court for the district in which the employee is employed or in the United States District Court for the District of Columbia.

History of 28 U.S.C. §1413: Oct. 26, 1996, P.L. 104-331, §3, 110 Stat. 4053.

CHAPTER 89. DISTRICT COURTS; REMOVAL OF CASES FROM STATE COURTS

§1441. REMOVAL OF CIVIL ACTIONS

(a) Generally.—Except as otherwise expressly provided by Act of Congress, any civil action brought in a State court of which the district courts of the United States have original jurisdiction, may be removed by the defendant or the defendants, to the district court of the United States for the district and division embracing the place where such action is pending.

(b) Removal based on diversity of citizenship—

(1) In determining whether a civil action is removable on the basis of the jurisdiction under section 1332(a) of this title, the citizenship of defendants sued under fictitious names shall be disregarded.

(2) A civil action otherwise removable solely on the basis of the jurisdiction under section 1332(a) of this title may not be removed if any of the parties in interest properly joined and served as defendants is a citizen of the State in which such action is brought.

(c) Joinder of Federal law claims and State law claims—

(1) If a civil action includes—

(A) a claim arising under the Constitution, laws, or treaties of the United States (within the meaning of section 1331 of this title), and

(B) a claim not within the original or supplemental jurisdiction of the district court or a claim that has been made nonremovable by statute,

the entire action may be removed if the action would be removable without the inclusion of the claim described in subparagraph (B).

(2) Upon removal of an action described in paragraph (1), the district court shall sever from the action all claims described in paragraph (1)(B) and shall remand the severed claims to the State court from which the action was removed. Only defendants against whom a claim described in paragraph (1)(A) has been asserted are required to join in or consent to the removal under paragraph (1).

(d) Actions against foreign states.—Any civil action brought in a State court against a foreign state as defined in section 1603(a) of this title may be removed by the foreign state to the district court of the United States for the district and division embracing the place where such action is pending. Upon removal the action shall be tried by the court without jury. Where removal is based upon this subsection, the time limitations of section 1446(b) of this chapter may be enlarged at any time for cause shown.

(e) Multiparty, multiforum jurisdiction—

(1) Notwithstanding the provisions of subsection (b) of this section, a defendant in a civil action in a State court may remove the action to the district court of the United States for the district and division embracing the place where the action is pending if—

(A) the action could have been brought in a United States district court under section 1369 of this title; or

(B) the defendant is a party to an action which is or could have been brought, in whole or in part, under section 1369 in a United States district court and arises from the same accident as the action in State court, even if the action to be removed could not have been brought in a district court as an original matter.

The removal of an action under this subsection shall be made in accordance with section 1446 of this title, except that a notice of removal may also be filed before trial of the action in State court within 30 days after the date on which the defendant first becomes a party to an action under section 1369 in a United States district court that arises from the same accident as the action in State court, or at a later time with leave of the district court.

(2) Whenever an action is removed under this subsection and the district court to which it is removed or transferred under section 1407(j) has made a liability determination requiring further proceedings as to damages, the district court shall remand the action to the State court from which it had been removed for the determination of damages, unless the court finds that, for the convenience of parties and witnesses and in the interest of justice, the action should be retained for the determination of damages.

(3) Any remand under paragraph (2) shall not be effective until 60 days after the district court has issued an order determining liability and has certified its intention to remand the removed action for the determination of damages. An appeal with respect to the liability determination of the district court may be taken during that 60-day period to the court of appeals with appellate jurisdiction over the district court. In the event a party files such an appeal, the remand shall not be effective until the appeal has been finally disposed of. Once the remand has become effective, the liability determination shall not be subject to further review by appeal or otherwise.

(4) Any decision under this subsection concerning remand for the determination of damages shall not be reviewable by appeal or otherwise.

(5) An action removed under this subsection shall be deemed to be an action under section 1369 and an action in which jurisdiction is based on section 1369 of this title for purposes of this section and sections 1407, 1697, and 1785 of this title.

(6) Nothing in this subsection shall restrict the authority of the district court to transfer or dismiss an action on the ground of inconvenient forum.

(f) Derivative removal jurisdiction.—The court to which a civil action is removed under this section is not precluded from hearing and determining any claim in such civil action because the State court from which such civil action is removed did not have jurisdiction over that claim.

History of 28 U.S.C. §1441: June 25, 1948, ch. 646, 62 Stat. 937; Oct. 21, 1976, P.L. 94-583, §6, 90 Stat. 2898; June 19, 1986, P.L. 99-336, §3(a), 100 Stat. 637; Nov. 19, 1988, P.L. 100-702, §1016(a), 102 Stat. 4669; Dec. 1, 1990, P.L. 101-650, §312, 104 Stat. 5114; Dec. 9, 1991, P.L. 102-198, §4, 105 Stat. 1623; Nov. 2, 2002, P.L. 107-273, §11020(b)(3), 116 Stat. 1827; Dec. 7, 2011, P.L. 112-63, §§103(a), 105, 125 Stat. 759, 762.

See *Commentaries*, "Removal & Remand," ch. 4, p. 239.

§1442. FEDERAL OFFICERS OR AGENCIES SUED OR PROSECUTED

(a) A civil action or criminal prosecution that is commenced in a State court and that is against or directed to any of the following may be removed by them to the district court of the United States for the district and division embracing the place wherein it is pending:

(1) The United States or any agency thereof or any officer (or any person acting under that officer) of the United States or of any agency thereof, in an official or individual capacity, for or relating to any act under color of such office or on account of any right, title or authority claimed under any Act of Congress for the apprehension or punishment of criminals or the collection of the revenue.

(2) A property holder whose title is derived from any such officer, where such action or prosecution affects the validity of any law of the United States.

(3) Any officer of the courts of the United States, for or relating to any act under color of office or in the performance of his duties;

(4) Any officer of either House of Congress, for or relating to any act in the discharge of his official duty under an order of such House.

(b) A personal action commenced in any State court by an alien against any citizen of a State who is, or at the time the alleged action accrued was, a civil officer of the United States and is a nonresident of such State, wherein jurisdiction is obtained by the State court by personal service of process, may be removed by the defendant to the district court of the United States for the district and division in which the defendant was served with process.

(c) As used in subsection (a), the terms "civil action" and "criminal prosecution" include any proceeding (whether or not ancillary to another proceeding) to the extent that in such proceeding a judicial order, including a subpoena for testimony or documents, is sought or issued. If removal is sought for a proceeding described in the previous sentence, and there is no other basis for removal, only that proceeding may be removed to the district court.

History of 28 U.S.C. §1442: June 25, 1948, ch. 646, 62 Stat. 938; Oct. 19, 1996, P.L. 104-317, §206, 110 Stat. 3847; Nov. 9, 2011, P.L. 112-51, §2(a), (b), 125 Stat. 545.

See *Commentaries*, "Removal & Remand," ch. 4, p. 239.

§1442A. MEMBERS OF ARMED FORCES SUED OR PROSECUTED

A civil or criminal prosecution in a court of a State of the United States against a member of the armed forces of the United States on account of an act done under color of his office or status, or in respect to which he claims any right, title, or authority under a law of the United States respecting the armed forces thereof, or under the law of war, may at any time before the trial or final hearing thereof be removed for trial into the district court of the United States for the district where it is pending in the manner prescribed by law, and it shall thereupon be entered on the docket of the district court, which shall proceed as if the cause had been originally commenced therein and shall have full power to hear and determine the cause.

History of 28 U.S.C. §1442a: Aug. 10, 1956, ch. 1041, §19(a), 70A Stat. 626.

§1443. CIVIL RIGHTS CASES

Any of the following civil actions or criminal prosecutions, commenced in a State court may be removed by the defendant to the district court of the United States for the district and division embracing the place wherein it is pending:

(1) Against any person who is denied or cannot enforce in the courts of such State a right under any law providing for the equal civil rights of citizens of the United States, or of all persons within the jurisdiction thereof;

(2) For any act under color of authority derived from any law providing for equal rights, or for refusing to do any act on the ground that it would be inconsistent with such law.

History of 28 U.S.C. §1443: June 25, 1948, ch. 646, 62 Stat. 938.

See *Commentaries*, "Removal & Remand," ch. 4, p. 239.

§1444. FORECLOSURE ACTION AGAINST UNITED STATES

Any action brought under section 2410 of this title against the United States in any State court may be removed by the United States to the district court of the United States for the district and division in which the action is pending.

History of 28 U.S.C. §1444: June 25, 1948, ch. 646, 62 Stat. 938; May 24, 1949, ch. 139, §82, 63 Stat. 101.

See *Commentaries*, "Removal & Remand," ch. 4, p. 239.

§1445. NONREMOVABLE ACTIONS

(a) A civil action in any State court against a railroad or its receivers or trustees, arising under sections 1-4 and 5-10 of the Act of April 22, 1908 (45 U.S.C. 51-54, 55-60), may not be removed to any district court of the United States.

(b) A civil action in any State court against a carrier or its receivers or trustees to recover damages for delay, loss, or injury of shipments, arising under section 11706 or 14706 of title 49, may not be removed to any district court of the United States unless the matter in controversy exceeds $10,000, exclusive of interest and costs.

(c) A civil action in any State court arising under the workmen's compensation laws of such State may not be removed to any district court of the United States.

(d) A civil action in any State court arising under section 40302 of the Violence Against Women Act of 1994 may not be removed to any district court of the United States.

History of 28 U.S.C. §1445: June 25, 1948, ch. 646, 62 Stat. 939; July 25, 1958, P.L. 85-554, §5, 72 Stat. 415; Oct. 17, 1978, P.L. 95-473, §2(a)(3)(A), 92 Stat. 1465; Oct. 20, 1978, P.L. 95-486, §9(b), 92 Stat. 1634; Sept. 13, 1994, P.L. 103-322, §40302(e)(5), 108 Stat. 1942; Dec. 29, 1995, P.L. 104-88, §305(b), 109 Stat. 944; Oct. 11, 1996, P.L. 104-287, §3, 110 Stat. 3388.

See *Commentaries*, "Removal & Remand," ch. 4, p. 239.

§1446. PROCEDURE FOR REMOVAL OF CIVIL ACTIONS

(a) Generally.—A defendant or defendants desiring to remove any civil action from a State court shall file in the district court of the United States for the district and division within which such action is pending a notice of removal signed pursuant to Rule 11 of the Federal Rules of Civil Procedure and containing a short and plain statement of the grounds for removal, together with a copy of all process, pleadings, and orders served upon such defendant or defendants in such action.

(b) Requirements; generally—

(1) The notice of removal of a civil action or proceeding shall be filed within 30 days after the receipt by the defendant, through service or otherwise, of a copy of the initial pleading setting forth the claim for relief upon which such action or proceeding is based, or within 30 days after the service of summons upon the defendant if such initial pleading has then been filed in court and is not required to be served on the defendant, whichever period is shorter.

(2)(A) When a civil action is removed solely under section 1441(a), all defendants who have been properly joined and served must join in or consent to the removal of the action.

(B) Each defendant shall have 30 days after receipt by or service on that defendant of the initial pleading or summons described in paragraph (1) to file the notice of removal.

(C) If defendants are served at different times, and a later-served defendant files a notice of removal, any earlier-served defendant may consent to the removal even though that earlier-served defendant did not previously initiate or consent to removal.

(3) Except as provided in subsection (c), if the case stated by the initial pleading is not removable, a notice of removal may be filed within 30 days after receipt by the defendant, through service or otherwise, of a copy of an amended pleading, motion, order or other paper from which it may first be ascertained that the case is one which is or has become removable.

(c) Requirements; removal based on diversity of citizenship—

(1) A case may not be removed under subsection (b)(3) on the basis of jurisdiction conferred by section 1332 more than 1 year after commencement of the action, unless the district court finds that the plaintiff has acted in bad faith in order to prevent a defendant from removing the action.

(2) If removal of a civil action is sought on the basis of the jurisdiction conferred by section 1332(a), the sum demanded in good faith in the initial pleading shall be deemed to be the amount in controversy, except that—

(A) the notice of removal may assert the amount in controversy if the initial pleading seeks—

(i) nonmonetary relief; or

(ii) a money judgment, but the State practice either does not permit demand for a specific sum or permits recovery of damages in excess of the amount demanded; and

(B) removal of the action is proper on the basis of an amount in controversy asserted under subparagraph (A) if the district court finds, by the preponderance of the evidence, that the amount in controversy exceeds the amount specified in section 1332(a).

(3)(A) If the case stated by the initial pleading is not removable solely because the amount in controversy does not exceed the amount specified in section 1332(a), information relating to the amount in controversy in the record of the State proceeding, or in responses to discovery, shall be treated as an "other paper" under subsection (b)(3).

(B) If the notice of removal is filed more than 1 year after commencement of the action and the district court finds that the plaintiff deliberately failed to disclose the actual amount in controversy to prevent removal, that finding shall be deemed bad faith under paragraph (1).

(d) Notice to adverse parties and State court.—Promptly after the filing of such notice of removal of a civil action the defendant or defendants shall give written notice thereof to all adverse parties and shall file a copy of the notice with the clerk of such State court, which shall effect the removal and the State court shall proceed no further unless and until the case is remanded.

(e) Counterclaim in 337 proceeding.—With respect to any counterclaim removed to a district court pursuant to section 337(c) of the Tariff Act of 1930, the district court shall resolve such counterclaim in the same manner as an original complaint under the Federal Rules of Civil Procedure, except that the payment of a filing fee shall not be required in such cases and the counterclaim shall relate back to the date of the original complaint in the proceeding before the International Trade Commission under section 337 of that Act.

(f) [Blank.]

(g) Where the civil action or criminal prosecution that is removable under section 1442(a) is a proceeding in which a judicial order for testimony or documents is sought or issued or sought to be enforced, the 30-day requirement of subsection (b) of this section and paragraph (1) of section 1455(b) is satisfied if the person or entity desiring to remove the pro-

ceeding files the notice of removal not later than 30 days after receiving, through service, notice of any such proceeding.

History of 28 U.S.C. §1446: June 25, 1948, ch. 646, 62 Stat. 939; May 24, 1949, ch. 139, §83, 63 Stat. 101; Sept. 29, 1965, P.L. 89-215, 79 Stat. 887; July 30, 1977, P.L. 95-78, §3, 91 Stat. 321; Nov. 19, 1988, P.L. 100-702, §1016(b), 102 Stat. 4669; Dec. 9, 1991, P.L. 102-198, §10(a), 105 Stat. 1626; Dec. 8, 1994, P.L. 103-465, §321(b)(2), 108 Stat. 4946; Oct. 19, 1996, P.L. 104-317, §603, 110 Stat. 3857; Nov. 9, 2011, P.L. 112-51, §2(c), 125 Stat. 545; Dec. 7, 2011, P.L. 112-63, §§103(b), 104, 105, 125 Stat. 760, 762.

See *Commentaries*, "Removal & Remand," ch. 4, p. 239.

§1447. PROCEDURE AFTER REMOVAL GENERALLY

(a) In any case removed from a State court, the district court may issue all necessary orders and process to bring before it all proper parties whether served by process issued by the State court or otherwise.

(b) It may require the removing party to file with its clerk copies of all records and proceedings in such State court or may cause the same to be brought before it by writ of certiorari issued to such State court.

(c) A motion to remand the case on the basis of any defect other than lack of subject-matter jurisdiction must be made within 30 days after the filing of the notice of removal under section 1446(a). If at any time before final judgment it appears that the district court lacks subject-matter jurisdiction, the case shall be remanded. An order remanding the case may require payment of just costs and any actual expenses, including attorney fees, incurred as a result of the removal. A certified copy of the order of remand shall be mailed by the clerk to the clerk of the State court. The State court may thereupon proceed with such case.

(d) An order remanding a case to the State court from which it was removed is not reviewable on appeal or otherwise, except that an order remanding a case to the State court from which it was removed pursuant to section 1442 or 1443 of this title shall be reviewable by appeal or otherwise.

(e) If after removal the plaintiff seeks to join additional defendants whose joinder would destroy subject-matter jurisdiction, the court may deny joinder, or permit joinder and remand the action to the State court.

History of 28 U.S.C. §1447: June 25, 1948, ch. 646, 62 Stat. 939; May 24, 1949, ch. 139, §84, 63 Stat. 102; July 2, 1964, P.L. 88-352, §901, 78 Stat. 266; Nov. 19, 1988, P.L. 100-702, §1016(c), 102 Stat. 4670; Dec. 9, 1991, P.L. 102-198, §10(b), 105 Stat. 1626; Oct. 1, 1996, P.L. 104-219, §1, 110 Stat. 3022; Nov. 9, 2011, P.L. 112-51, §2(d), 125 Stat. 546.

See *Commentaries*, "Removal & Remand," ch. 4, p. 239.

§1448. PROCESS AFTER REMOVAL

In all cases removed from any State court to any district court of the United States in which any one or more of the defendants has not been served with process or in which the service has not been perfected prior to removal, or in which process served proves to be defective, such process or service may be completed or new process issued in the same manner as in cases originally filed in such district court.

This section shall not deprive any defendant upon whom process is served after removal of his right to move to remand the case.

History of 28 U.S.C. §1448: June 25, 1948, ch. 646, 62 Stat. 940.

See *Commentaries*, "Removal & Remand," ch. 4, p. 239.

§1449. STATE COURT RECORD SUPPLIED

Where a party is entitled to copies of the records and proceedings in any suit or prosecution in a State court, to be used in any district court of the United States, and the clerk of such State court, upon demand, and the payment or tender of the legal fees, fails to deliver certified copies, the district court may, on affidavit reciting such facts, direct such record to be supplied by affidavit or otherwise. Thereupon such proceedings, trial, and judgment may be had in such district court, and all such process awarded, as if certified copies had been filed in the district court.

History of 28 U.S.C. §1449: June 25, 1948, ch. 646, 62 Stat. 940; May 24, 1949, ch. 139, §85, 63 Stat. 102.

See *Commentaries*, "Removal & Remand," ch. 4, p. 239.

§1450. ATTACHMENT OR SEQUESTRATION; SECURITIES

Whenever any action is removed from a State court to a district court of the United States, any attachment or sequestration of the goods or estate of the defendant in such action in the State court shall hold the goods or estate to answer the final judgment or decree in the same manner as they would have been held to answer final judgment or decree had it been rendered by the State court.

All bonds, undertakings, or security given by either party in such action prior to its removal shall remain valid and effectual notwithstanding such removal.

All injunctions, orders, and other proceedings had in such action prior to its removal shall remain in full force and effect until dissolved or modified by the district court.

History of 28 U.S.C. §1450: June 25, 1948, ch. 646, 62 Stat. 940.

§1451. DEFINITIONS

For purposes of this chapter—

(1) The term "State court" includes the Superior Court of the District of Columbia.

(2) The term "State" includes the District of Columbia.

History of 28 U.S.C. §1451: July 29, 1970, P.L. 91-358, §172(d)(1), 84 Stat. 591.

See *Commentaries*, "Removal & Remand," ch. 4, p. 239.

§1452. REMOVAL OF CLAIMS RELATED TO BANKRUPTCY CASES

(a) A party may remove any claim or cause of action in a civil action other than a proceeding before the United States Tax Court or a civil action by a governmental unit to enforce such governmental unit's police or regulatory power, to the district court for the district where such civil action is pending, if such district court has jurisdiction of such claim or cause of action under section 1334 of this title.

(b) The court to which such claim or cause of action is removed may remand such claim or cause of action on any equitable ground. An order entered under this subsection remanding a claim or cause of action, or a decision to not remand, is not reviewable by appeal or otherwise by the court of appeals under section 158(d), 1291, or 1292 of this title or by the Supreme Court of the United States under section 1254 of this title.

History of 28 U.S.C. §1452: July 10, 1984, P.L. 98-353, §103(a), 98 Stat. 335; Dec. 1, 1990, P.L. 101-650, §309(c), 104 Stat. 5113.

See *Commentaries*, "Removal & Remand," ch. 4, p. 239.

§1453. REMOVAL OF CLASS ACTIONS

(a) Definitions.—In this section, the terms "class", "class action", "class certification order", and "class member" shall have the meanings given such terms under section 1332(d)(1).

(b) In general.—A class action may be removed to a district court of the United States in accordance with section 1446 (except that the 1-year limitation under section 1446(c)(1) shall not apply), without regard to whether any defendant is a citizen of the State in which the action is brought, except that such action may be removed by any defendant without the consent of all defendants.

(c) Review of remand orders—

(1) In general.—Section 1447 shall apply to any removal of a case under this section, except that notwithstanding section 1447(d), a court of appeals may accept an appeal from an order of a district court granting or denying a motion to remand a class action to the State court from which it was removed if application is made to the court of appeals not more than 10 days after entry of the order.

(2) Time period for judgment.—If the court of appeals accepts an appeal under paragraph (1), the court shall complete all action on such appeal, including rendering judgment, not later than 60 days after the date on which such appeal was filed, unless an extension is granted under paragraph (3).

(3) Extension of time period.—The court of appeals may grant an extension of the 60-day period described in paragraph (2) if—

(A) all parties to the proceeding agree to such extension, for any period of time; or

(B) such extension is for good cause shown and in the interests of justice, for a period not to exceed 10 days.

(4) Denial of appeal.—If a final judgment on the appeal under paragraph (1) is not issued before the end of the period described in paragraph (2), including any extension under paragraph (3), the appeal shall be denied.

(d) Exception.—This section shall not apply to any class action that solely involves—

(1) a claim concerning a covered security as defined under section 16(f)(3) of the Securities Act of 1933 (15 U.S.C. 78p(f)(3)) and section 28(f)(5)(E) of the Securities Exchange Act of 1934 (15 U.S.C. 78bb(f)(5)(E));

(2) a claim that relates to the internal affairs or governance of a corporation or other form of business enterprise and arises under or by virtue of the laws of the State in which such corporation or business enterprise is incorporated or organized; or

(3) a claim that relates to the rights, duties (including fiduciary duties), and obligations relating to or created by or pursuant to any security (as defined under section 2(a)(1) of the Securities Act of 1933 (15 U.S.C. 77b(a)(1)) and the regulations issued thereunder).

History of 28 U.S.C. §1453: Feb. 18, 2005, P.L. 109-2, §5(a), 119 Stat. 12; May 7, 2009, P.L. 111-16, §6, 123 Stat. 1608; Dec. 7, 2011, P.L. 112-63, §§103(d)(2), 105, 125 Stat. 762.

See *Commentaries*, "Removal & Remand," ch. 4, p. 239.

§1454. PATENT, PLANT VARIETY PROTECTION, & COPYRIGHT CASES

(a) In general.—A civil action in which any party asserts a claim for relief arising under any Act of Congress relating to patents, plant variety protection, or copyrights may be removed to the district court of the United States for the district and division embracing the place where the action is pending.

(b) Special rules.—The removal of an action under this section shall be made in accordance with section 1446, except that if the removal is based solely on this section—

(1) the action may be removed by any party; and

(2) the time limitations contained in section 1446(b) may be extended at any time for cause shown.

(c) Clarification of jurisdiction in certain cases.—The court to which a civil action is removed under this section is not precluded from hearing and determining any claim in the civil action because the State court from which the civil action is removed did not have jurisdiction over that claim.

(d) Remand.—If a civil action is removed solely under this section, the district court—

(1) shall remand all claims that are neither a basis for removal under subsection (a) nor within the original or supplemental jurisdiction of the district court under any Act of Congress; and

(2) may, under the circumstances specified in section 1367(c), remand any claims within the supplemental jurisdiction of the district court under section 1367.

History of 28 U.S.C. §1454: Sept. 16, 2011, P.L. 112-29, §19(c)(1), 125 Stat. 332.

See *Commentaries*, "Supplemental Jurisdiction," ch. 2-F, §6, p. 134; "Removal & Remand," ch. 4, p. 239.

§1455. PROCEDURE FOR REMOVAL OF CRIMINAL PROSECUTIONS

(a) Notice of removal.—A defendant or defendants desiring to remove any criminal prosecution from a State court shall file in the district court of the United States for the district and division within which such prosecution is pending a notice of removal signed pursuant to Rule 11 of the Fed-

eral Rules of Civil Procedure and containing a short and plain statement of the grounds for removal, together with a copy of all process, pleadings, and orders served upon such defendant or defendants in such action.

(b) Requirements—

(1) A notice of removal of a criminal prosecution shall be filed not later than 30 days after the arraignment in the State court, or at any time before trial, whichever is earlier, except that for good cause shown the United States district court may enter an order granting the defendant or defendants leave to file the notice at a later time.

(2) A notice of removal of a criminal prosecution shall include all grounds for such removal. A failure to state grounds that exist at the time of the filing of the notice shall constitute a waiver of such grounds, and a second notice may be filed only on grounds not existing at the time of the original notice. For good cause shown, the United States district court may grant relief from the limitations of this paragraph.

(3) The filing of a notice of removal of a criminal prosecution shall not prevent the State court in which such prosecution is pending from proceeding further, except that a judgment of conviction shall not be entered unless the prosecution is first remanded.

(4) The United States district court in which such notice is filed shall examine the notice promptly. If it clearly appears on the face of the notice and any exhibits annexed thereto that removal should not be permitted, the court shall make an order for summary remand.

(5) If the United States district court does not order the summary remand of such prosecution, it shall order an evidentiary hearing to be held promptly and, after such hearing, shall make such disposition of the prosecution as justice shall require. If the United States district court determines that removal shall be permitted, it shall so notify the State court in which prosecution is pending, which shall proceed no further.

(c) Writ of habeas corpus.—If the defendant or defendants are in actual custody on process issued by the State court, the district court shall issue its writ of habeas corpus, and the marshal shall thereupon take such defendant or defendants into the marshal's custody and deliver a copy of the writ to the clerk of such State court.

History of 28 U.S.C. §1455: Dec. 7, 2011, P.L. 112-63, §§103(c), 105, 125 Stat. 761, 762.

CHAPTER 90. [OMITTED]

§§1471 TO 1482. [OMITTED]

CHAPTER 91. UNITED STATES COURT OF FEDERAL CLAIMS

A §1491. CLAIMS AGAINST UNITED STATES GENERALLY; ACTIONS INVOLVING TENNESSEE VALLEY AUTHORITY

(a)(1) The United States Court of Federal Claims shall have jurisdiction to render judgment upon any claim against the United States founded either upon the Constitution, or any Act of Congress or any regulation of an executive department, or upon any express or implied contract with the United States, or for liquidated or unliquidated damages in cases not sounding in tort. For the purpose of this paragraph, an express or implied contract with the Army and Air Force Exchange Service, Navy Exchanges, Marine Corps Exchanges, Coast Guard Exchanges, or Exchange Councils of the National Aeronautics and Space Administration shall be considered an express or implied contract with the United States.

(2) To provide an entire remedy and to complete the relief afforded by the judgment, the court may, as an incident of and collateral to any such judgment, issue orders directing restoration to office or position, placement in appropriate duty or retirement status, and correction of applicable records, and such orders may be issued to any appropriate official of the United States. In any case within its jurisdiction, the court shall have the power to remand appropriate matters to any administrative or executive body or official with such direction as it may deem proper and just. The Court of Federal Claims shall have jurisdiction to render judgment upon any claim by or against, or dispute with, a contractor arising under section 7104(b)(1) of title 41, including a dispute concerning termination of a contract, rights in tangible or intangible property, compliance with cost accounting standards, and other nonmonetary disputes on which a decision of the contracting officer has been issued under section 6 of that Act.[1]

(b)(1) Both the Unites[2] States Court of Federal Claims and the district courts of the United States shall have jurisdiction to render judgment on an action by an interested party objecting to a solicitation by a Federal agency for bids or proposals for a proposed contract or to a proposed award or the award of a contract or any alleged violation of statute or regulation in connection with a procurement or a proposed procurement. Both the United States Court of Federal Claims and the district courts of the United States shall have jurisdiction to entertain such an action without regard to whether suit is instituted before or after the contract is awarded.

(2) To afford relief in such an action, the courts may award any relief that the court considers proper, including declaratory and injunctive relief except that any monetary relief shall be limited to bid preparation and proposal costs.

(3) In exercising jurisdiction under this subsection, the courts shall give due regard to the interests of national defense and national security and the need for expeditious resolution of the action.

(4) In any action under this subsection, the courts shall review the agency's decision pursuant to the standards set forth in section 706 of title 5.

(5) If an interested party who is a member of the private sector commences an action described in paragraph (1) with respect to a public-private competition conducted under Office of Management and Budget Circular A-76 regarding the performance of an activity or function of a Federal agency, or

a decision to convert a function performed by Federal employees to private sector performance without a competition under Office of Management and Budget Circular A–76, then an interested party described in section 3551(2)(B) of title 31 shall be entitled to intervene in that action.

(6) Jurisdiction over any action described in paragraph (1) arising out of a maritime contract, or a solicitation for a proposed maritime contract, shall be governed by this section and shall not be subject to the jurisdiction of the district courts of the United States under the Suits in Admiralty Act (chapter 309 of title 46) or the Public Vessels Act (chapter 311 of title 46).

(c) Nothing herein shall be construed to give the United States Court of Federal Claims jurisdiction of any civil action within the exclusive jurisdiction of the Court of International Trade, or of any action against, or founded on conduct of, the Tennessee Valley Authority, or to amend or modify the provisions of the Tennessee Valley Authority Act of 1933 with respect to actions by or against the Authority.

1. **Editor's note:** So in original. "[S]ection 6 of that Act" probably should be "41 U.S.C. §7103." P.L. 111-350, Jan. 4, 2011, 124 Stat. 3677 amended §1491(a)(2) by striking "section 10(a)(1) of Contract Disputes Act of 1978" and substituting "section 7104(b)(1) of title 41," but it did not change "section 6 of that Act."

2. **Editor's note:** So in original. Probably should be "United."

History of 28 U.S.C. §1491: June 25, 1948, ch. 646, 62 Stat. 940; July 28, 1953, ch. 253, §7, 67 Stat. 226; Sept. 3, 1954, ch. 1263, §44(a), (b), 68 Stat. 1241; July 23, 1970, P.L. 91-350, §1(b), 84 Stat. 449; Aug. 29, 1972, P.L. 92-415, §1, 86 Stat. 652; Nov. 1, 1978, P.L. 95-563, §14(i), 92 Stat. 2391; Oct. 10, 1980, P.L. 96-417, §509, 94 Stat. 1743; Apr. 2, 1982, P.L. 97-164, §133(a), 96 Stat. 39; Oct. 29, 1992, P.L. 102-572, §§902(a), 907(b)(1), 106 Stat. 4516, 4519; Oct. 19, 1996, P.L. 104-320, §12(a), 110 Stat. 3874; Dec. 26, 2007, P.L. 110-161, §739(c)(2), 121 Stat. 2031; Jan. 28, 2008, P.L. 110-181, §326(c), 122 Stat. 63; Oct. 14, 2008, P.L. 110-417, §1061(d), 122 Stat. 4613; Jan. 4, 2011, P.L. 111-350, §5(g)(7), 124 Stat. 3848; Dec. 31, 2011, P.L. 112-81, §861(a), 125 Stat. 1521.

§1492. CONGRESSIONAL REFERENCE CASES

Any bill, except a bill for a pension, may be referred by either House of Congress to the chief judge of the United States Court of Federal Claims for a report in conformity with section 2509 of this title.

History of 28 U.S.C. §1492: June 25, 1948, ch. 646, 62 Stat. 941; Oct. 15, 1966, P.L. 89-681, §1, 80 Stat. 958; Apr. 2, 1982, P.L. 97-164, §133(b), 96 Stat. 40; Oct. 29, 1992, P.L. 102-572, §902(a)(1), 106 Stat. 4516.

§1493. REPEALED

Repealed July 28, 1953, ch. 253, §8, 67 Stat. 226.

§1494. ACCOUNTS OF OFFICERS, AGENTS OR CONTRACTORS

The United States Court of Federal Claims shall have jurisdiction to determine the amount, if any, due to or from the United States by reason of any unsettled account of any officer or agent of, or contractor with, the United States, or a guarantor, surety or personal representative of any such officer, agent or contractor, and to render judgment thereof,[1] where—

(1) claimant or the person he represents has applied to the proper department of the Government for settlement of the account;

(2) three years have elapsed from the date of such application without settlement; and

(3) no suit upon the same has been brought by the United States.

1. **Editor's note:** So in original. Probably should be "thereon."

History of 28 U.S.C. §1494: June 25, 1948, ch. 646, 62 Stat. 941; July 28, 1953, ch. 253, §9, 67 Stat. 226; Sept. 3, 1954, ch. 1263, §44(c), 68 Stat. 1242; Apr. 2, 1982, P.L. 97-164, §133(c)(1), 96 Stat. 40; Oct. 29, 1992, P.L. 102-572, §902(a)(1), 106 Stat. 4516.

§1495. DAMAGES FOR UNJUST CONVICTION & IMPRISONMENT; CLAIM AGAINST UNITED STATES

The United States Court of Federal Claims shall have jurisdiction to render judgment upon any claim for damages by any person unjustly convicted of an offense against the United States and imprisoned.

History of 28 U.S.C. §1495: June 25, 1948, ch. 646, 62 Stat. 941; Apr. 2, 1982, P.L. 97-164, §133(c)(1), 96 Stat. 40; Oct. 29, 1992, P.L. 102-572, §902(a)(1), 106 Stat. 4516.

§1496. DISBURSING OFFICERS' CLAIMS

The United States Court of Federal Claims shall have jurisdiction to render judgment upon any claim by a disbursing officer of the United States or by his administrator or executor for relief from responsibility for loss, in line of duty, of Government funds, vouchers, records or other papers in his charge.

History of 28 U.S.C. §1496: June 25, 1948, ch. 646, 62 Stat. 941; Apr. 2, 1982, P.L. 97-164, §133(c)(1), 96 Stat. 40; Oct. 29, 1992, P.L. 102-572, §902(a)(1), 106 Stat. 4516.

§1497. OYSTER GROWERS' DAMAGES FROM DREDGING OPERATIONS

The United States Court of Federal Claims shall have jurisdiction to render judgment upon any claim for damages to oyster growers on private or leased lands or bottoms arising from dredging operations or use of other machinery and equipment in making river and harbor improvements authorized by Act of Congress.

History of 28 U.S.C. §1497: June 25, 1948, ch. 646, 62 Stat. 941; Apr. 2, 1982, P.L. 97-164, §133(c), 96 Stat. 40; Oct. 29, 1992, P.L. 102-572, §902(a)(1), 106 Stat. 4516.

§1498. PATENT & COPYRIGHT CASES

(a) Whenever an invention described in and covered by a patent of the United States is used or manufactured by or for the United States without license of the owner thereof or lawful right to use or manufacture the same, the owner's remedy shall be by action against the United States in the United States Court of Federal Claims for the recovery of his reasonable and entire compensation for such use and manufacture. Reasonable and entire compensation shall include the owner's reasonable costs, including reasonable fees for expert witnesses and attorneys, in pursuing the action if the owner is an independent inventor, a nonprofit organization, or an entity that had no more than 500 employees at any time during the 5-year period preceding the use or manufacture of the patented invention by or for the United States. Nothwith-

standing[1] the preceding sentences, unless the action has been pending for more than 10 years from the time of filing to the time that the owner applies for such costs and fees, reasonable and entire compensation shall not include such costs and fees if the court finds that the position of the United States was substantially justified or that special circumstances make an award unjust.

For the purposes of this section, the use or manufacture of an invention described in and covered by a patent of the United States by a contractor, a subcontractor, or any person, firm, or corporation for the Government and with the authorization or consent of the Government, shall be construed as use or manufacture for the United States.

The court shall not award compensation under this section if the claim is based on the use or manufacture by or for the United States of any article owned, leased, used by, or in the possession of the United States prior to July 1, 1918.

A Government employee shall have the right to bring suit against the Government under this section except where he was in a position to order, influence, or induce use of the invention by the Government. This section shall not confer a right of action on any patentee or any assignee of such patentee with respect to any invention discovered or invented by a person while in the employment or service of the United States, where the invention was related to the official functions of the employee, in cases in which such functions included research and development, or in the making of which Government time, materials or facilities were used.

(b) Hereafter, whenever the copyright in any work protected under the copyright laws of the United States shall be infringed by the United States, by a corporation owned or controlled by the United States, or by a contractor, subcontractor, or any person, firm, or corporation acting for the Government and with the authorization or consent of the Government, the exclusive action which may be brought for such infringement shall be an action by the copyright owner against the United States in the Court of Federal Claims for the recovery of his reasonable and entire compensation as damages for such infringement, including the minimum statutory damages as set forth in section 504(c) of title 17, United States Code: Provided, That a Government employee shall have a right of action against the Government under this subsection except where he was in a position to order, influence, or induce use of the copyrighted work by the Government: Provided, however, That this subsection shall not confer a right of action on any copyright owner or any assignee of such owner with respect to any copyrighted work prepared by a person while in the employment or service of the United States, where the copyrighted work was prepared as a part of the official functions of the employee, or in the preparation of which Government time, material, or facilities were used: And provided further, That before such action against the United States has been instituted the appropriate corporation owned or controlled by the United States or the head of the appropriate department or agency of the Government, as the case may be, is authorized to enter into an agreement with the copyright owner in full settlement and compromise for the damages accruing to him by reason of such infringement and to settle the claim administratively out of available appropriations.

Except as otherwise provided by law, no recovery shall be had for any infringement of a copyright covered by this subsection committed more than three years prior to the filing of the complaint or counterclaim for infringement in the action, except that the period between the date of receipt of a written claim for compensation by the Department or agency of the Government or corporation owned or controlled by the United States, as the case may be, having authority to settle such claim and the date of mailing by the Government of a notice to the claimant that his claim has been denied shall not be counted as a part of the three years, unless suit is brought before the last-mentioned date.

(c) The provisions of this section shall not apply to any claim arising in a foreign country.

(d) Hereafter, whenever a plant variety protected by a certificate of plant variety protection under the laws of the United States shall be infringed by the United States, by a corporation owned or controlled by the United States, or by a contractor, subcontractor, or any person, firm, or corporation acting for the Government and with the authorization and consent of the Government, the exclusive remedy of the owner of such certificate shall be by action against the United States in the Court of Federal Claims for the recovery of his reasonable and entire compensation as damages for such infringement: Provided, That a Government employee shall have a right of action against the Government under this subsection except where he was in a position to order, influence, or induce use of the protected plant variety by the Government: Provided, however, That this subsection shall not confer a right of action on any certificate owner or any assignee of such owner with respect to any protected plant variety made by a person while in the employment or service of the United States, where such variety was prepared as a part of the official functions of the employee, or in the preparation of which Government time, material, or facilities were used: And provided further, That before such action against the United States has been instituted, the appropriate corporation owned or controlled by the United States or the head of the appropriate agency of the Government, as the case may be, is authorized to enter into an agreement with the certificate owner in full settlement and compromise, for the damages accrued to him by reason of such infringement and to settle the claim administratively out of available appropriations.

(e) Subsections (b) and (c) of this section apply to exclusive rights in mask works under chapter 9 of title 17, and to exclusive rights in designs under chapter 13 of title 17, to the same extent as such subsections apply to copyrights.

1. **Editor's note:** So in original. Probably should be "Notwithstanding."

History of 28 U.S.C. §1498: June 25, 1948, ch. 646, 62 Stat. 941; May 24, 1949, ch. 139, §87, 63 Stat. 102; Oct. 31, 1951, ch. 655, §50(c), 65 Stat. 727; July 17, 1952, ch. 930, 66 Stat. 757; Sept. 8, 1960, P.L. 86-726, §§1, 4, 74 Stat. 855,

856; Dec. 24, 1970, P.L. 91-577, §143(d), 84 Stat. 1559; Oct. 19, 1976, P.L. 94-553, §105(c), 90 Stat. 2599; Apr. 2, 1982, P.L. 97-164, §133(d), 96 Stat. 40; Nov. 19, 1988, P.L. 100-702, §1020(a)(6), 102 Stat. 4671; Oct. 29, 1992, P.L. 102-572, §902(a), 106 Stat. 4516; Oct. 19, 1996, P.L. 104-308, §1, 110 Stat. 3814; Dec. 16, 1997, P.L. 105-147, §3, 111 Stat. 2680; Oct. 28, 1998, P.L. 105-304, §503(d), 112 Stat. 2917.

§1499. LIQUIDATED DAMAGES WITHHELD FROM CONTRACTORS UNDER CHAPTER 37 OF TITLE 40

The United States Court of Federal Claims shall have jurisdiction to render judgment upon any claim for liquidated damages withheld from a contractor or subcontractor under section 3703 of title 40.

History of 28 U.S.C. §1499: June 25, 1948, ch. 646, 62 Stat. 942; Aug. 13, 1962, P.L. 87-581, §202(a), 76 Stat. 360; Apr. 2, 1982, P.L. 97-164, §133(e)(1), (2)(A), 96 Stat. 40, 41; Dec. 1, 1990, P.L. 101-650, §325(b)(7), 104 Stat. 5121; Oct. 29, 1992, P.L. 102-572, §902(a)(1), 106 Stat. 4516; Aug. 21, 2002, P.L. 107-217, §3(g)(3), 116 Stat. 1299; Sept. 27, 2006, P.L. 109-284, §4(2), 120 Stat. 1211.

§1500. PENDENCY OF CLAIMS IN OTHER COURTS

The United States Court of Federal Claims shall not have jurisdiction of any claim for or in respect to which the plaintiff or his assignee has pending in any other court any suit or process against the United States or any person who, at the time when the cause of action alleged in such suit or process arose, was, in respect thereto, acting or professing to act, directly or indirectly under the authority of the United States.

History of 28 U.S.C. §1500: June 25, 1948, ch. 646, 62 Stat. 942; Apr. 2, 1982, P.L. 97-164, §133(e)(1), 96 Stat. 40; Oct. 29, 1992, P.L. 102-572, §902(a)(1), 106 Stat. 4516.

§1501. PENSIONS

The United States Court of Federal Claims shall not have jurisdiction of any claim for a pension.

History of 28 U.S.C. §1501: June 25, 1948, ch. 646, 62 Stat. 942; Apr. 2, 1982, P.L. 97-164, §133(e)(1), 96 Stat. 40; Oct. 29, 1992, P.L. 102-572, §902(a)(1), 106 Stat. 4516.

§1502. TREATY CASES

Except as otherwise provided by Act of Congress, the United States Court of Federal Claims shall not have jurisdiction of any claim against the United States growing out of or dependent upon any treaty entered into with foreign nations.

History of 28 U.S.C. §1502: June 25, 1948, ch. 646, 62 Stat. 942; May 24, 1949, ch. 139, §88, 63 Stat. 102; Apr. 2, 1982, P.L. 97-164, §133(e)(1), 96 Stat. 40; Oct. 29, 1992, P.L. 102-572, §902(a)(1), 106 Stat. 4516.

§1503. SET-OFFS

The United States Court of Federal Claims shall have jurisdiction to render judgment upon any set-off or demand by the United States against any plaintiff in such court.

History of 28 U.S.C. §1503: June 25, 1948, ch. 646, 62 Stat. 942; Apr. 2, 1982, P.L. 97-164, §133(e)(1), 96 Stat. 40; Oct. 29, 1992, P.L. 102-572, §902(a)(1), 106 Stat. 4516.

§1504. REPEALED

Repealed Apr. 2, 1982, P.L. 97-164, §133(f), 96 Stat. 41.

§1505. INDIAN CLAIMS

The United States Court of Federal Claims shall have jurisdiction of any claim against the United States accruing after August 13, 1946, in favor of any tribe, band, or other identifiable group of American Indians residing within the territorial limits of the United States or Alaska whenever such claim is one arising under the Constitution, laws or treaties of the United States, or Executive orders of the President, or is one which otherwise would be cognizable in the Court of Federal Claims if the claimant were not an Indian tribe, band or group.

History of 28 U.S.C. §1505: May 24, 1949, ch. 139, §89(a), 63 Stat. 102; Apr. 2, 1982, P.L. 97-164, §133(g), 96 Stat. 41; Oct. 29, 1992, P.L. 102-572, §902(a), 106 Stat. 4516.

§1506. REPEALED

Repealed Apr. 2, 1982, P.L. 97-164, §133(h), 96 Stat. 41.

§1507. JURISDICTION FOR CERTAIN DECLARATORY JUDGMENTS

The United States Court of Federal Claims shall have jurisdiction to hear any suit for and issue a declaratory judgment under section 7428 of the Internal Revenue Code of 1986.

History of 28 U.S.C. §1507: Oct. 4, 1976, P.L. 94-455, §1306(b)(9)(A), 90 Stat. 1720; Apr. 2, 1982, P.L. 97-164, §133(i), 96 Stat. 41; Oct. 22, 1986, P.L. 99-514, §2, 100 Stat. 2095; Oct. 29, 1992, P.L. 102-572, §902(a)(1), 106 Stat. 4516.

§1508. JURISDICTION FOR CERTAIN PARTNERSHIP PROCEEDINGS

The Court of Federal Claims shall have jurisdiction to hear and to render judgment upon any petition under section 6226 or 6228(a) of the Internal Revenue Code of 1986.

History of 28 U.S.C. §1508: Sept. 3, 1982, P.L. 97-248, §402(c)(18)(A), 96 Stat. 669; Oct. 22, 1986, P.L. 99-514, §2, 100 Stat. 2095; Oct. 29, 1992, P.L. 102-572, §902(a)(2), 106 Stat. 4516.

§1509. NO JURISDICTION IN CASES INVOLVING REFUNDS OF TAX SHELTER PROMOTER & UNDERSTATEMENT PENALTIES

The United States Court of Federal Claims shall not have jurisdiction to hear any action or proceeding for any refund or credit of any penalty imposed under section 6700 of the Internal Revenue Code of 1986 (relating to penalty for promoting abusive tax shelters, etc.) or section 6701 of such Code (relating to penalties for aiding and abetting understatement of tax liability).

History of 28 U.S.C. §1509: July 18, 1984, P.L. 98-369, div. A, §714(g)(2), 98 Stat. 962; Oct. 22, 1986, P.L. 99-514, §2, 100 Stat. 2095; Oct. 29, 1992, P.L. 102-572, §902(a)(1), 106 Stat. 4516.

CHAPTER 93. REPEALED

§§1541 TO 1546. REPEALED

Repealed Apr. 2, 1982, P.L. 97-164, §134, 96 Stat. 41.

CHAPTER 95. COURT OF INTERNATIONAL TRADE

§1581. CIVIL ACTIONS AGAINST THE UNITED STATES & AGENCIES & OFFICERS THEREOF

(a) The Court of International Trade shall have exclusive jurisdiction of any civil action commenced to contest the denial of a protest, in whole or in part, under section 515 of the Tariff Act of 1930.

(b) The Court of International Trade shall have exclusive jurisdiction of any civil action commenced under section 516 of the Tariff Act of 1930.

(c) The Court of International Trade shall have exclusive jurisdiction of any civil action commenced under section 516A of the Tariff Act of 1930.

(d) The Court of International Trade shall have exclusive jurisdiction of any civil action commenced to review—

(1) any final determination of the Secretary of Labor under section 223 of the Trade Act of 1974 with respect to the eligibility of workers for adjustment assistance under such Act;

(2) any final determination of the Secretary of Commerce under section 251 of the Trade Act of 1974 with respect to the eligibility of a firm for adjustment assistance under such Act;

(3) any final determination of the Secretary of Commerce under section 273 of the Trade Act of 1974 with respect to the eligibility of a community for adjustment assistance under such Act; and

(4) any final determination of the Secretary of Agriculture under section 293 or 296 of the Trade Act of 1974 (19 U.S.C. 2401b) with respect to the eligibility of a group of agricultural commodity producers for adjustment assistance under such Act.

(e) The Court of International Trade shall have exclusive jurisdiction of any civil action commenced to review any final determination of the Secretary of the Treasury under section 305(b)(1) of the Trade Agreements Act of 1979.

(f) The Court of International Trade shall have exclusive jurisdiction of any civil action involving an application for an order directing the administering authority or the International Trade Commission to make confidential information available under section 777(c)(2) of the Tariff Act of 1930.

(g) The Court of International Trade shall have exclusive jurisdiction of any civil action commenced to review—

(1) any decision of the Secretary of the Treasury to deny a customs broker's license under section 641(b)(2) or (3) of the Tariff Act of 1930, or to deny a customs broker's permit under section 641(c)(1) of such Act, or to revoke a license or permit under section 641(b)(5) or (c)(2) of such Act;

(2) any decision of the Secretary of the Treasury to revoke or suspend a customs broker's license or permit, or impose a monetary penalty in lieu thereof, under section 641(d)(2)(B) of the Tariff Act of 1930; and

(3) any decision or order of the Customs Service to deny, suspend, or revoke accreditation of a private laboratory under section 499(b) of the Tariff Act of 1930.

(h) The Court of International Trade shall have exclusive jurisdiction of any civil action commenced to review, prior to the importation of the goods involved, a ruling issued by the Secretary of the Treasury, or a refusal to issue or change such a ruling, relating to classification, valuation, rate of duty, marking, restricted merchandise, entry requirements, drawbacks, vessel repairs, or similar matters, but only if the party commencing the civil action demonstrates to the court that he would be irreparably harmed unless given an opportunity to obtain judicial review prior to such importation.

(i) In addition to the jurisdiction conferred upon the Court of International Trade by subsections (a)-(h) of this section and subject to the exception set forth in subsection (j) of this section, the Court of International Trade shall have exclusive jurisdiction of any civil action commenced against the United States, its agencies, or its officers, that arises out of any law of the United States providing for—

(1) revenue from imports or tonnage;

(2) tariffs, duties, fees, or other taxes on the importation of merchandise for reasons other than the raising of revenue;

(3) embargoes or other quantitative restrictions on the importation of merchandise for reasons other than the protection of the public health or safety; or

(4) administration and enforcement with respect to the matters referred to in paragraphs (1)-(3) of this subsection and subsections (a)-(h) of this section.

This subsection shall not confer jurisdiction over an antidumping or countervailing duty determination which is reviewable either by the Court of International Trade under section 516A(a) of the Tariff Act of 1930 or by a binational panel under article 1904 of the North American Free Trade Agreement or the United States-Canada Free-Trade Agreement and section 516A(g) of the Tariff Act of 1930.

(j) The Court of International Trade shall not have jurisdiction of any civil action arising under section 305 of the Tariff Act of 1930.

History of 28 U.S.C. §1581: Oct. 10, 1980, P.L. 96-417, §201, 94 Stat. 1728; Oct. 30, 1984, P.L. 98-573, §212(b)(1), 98 Stat. 2983; Oct. 22, 1986, P.L. 99-514, §1891(1), 100 Stat. 2926; Sept. 28, 1988, P.L. 100-449, §402(a), 102 Stat. 1883; Dec. 8, 1993, P.L. 103-182, §§414(a)(1), 684(a)(1), 107 Stat. 2147, 2219; Feb. 17, 2009, P.L. 111-5, §1873(b)(2), 123 Stat. 414.

§1582. CIVIL ACTIONS COMMENCED BY THE UNITED STATES

The Court of International Trade shall have exclusive jurisdiction of any civil action which arises out of an import transaction and which is commenced by the United States—

(1) to recover a civil penalty under section 592, 593A, 641(b)(6), 641(d)(2)(A), 704(i)(2), or 734(i)(2) of the Tariff Act of 1930;

(2) to recover upon a bond relating to the importation of merchandise required by the laws of the United States or by the Secretary of the Treasury; or

(3) to recover customs duties.

History of 28 U.S.C. §1582: Oct. 10, 1980, P.L. 96-417, §201, 94 Stat. 1729; Oct. 30, 1984, P.L. 98-573, §212(b)(2), 98 Stat. 2983; Oct. 22, 1986, P.L. 99-514, §1891(2), 100 Stat. 2926; Dec. 8, 1993, P.L. 103-182, §684(c), 107 Stat. 2219.

§1583. COUNTERCLAIMS, CROSS-CLAIMS, & THIRD-PARTY ACTIONS

In any civil action in the Court of International Trade, the court shall have exclusive jurisdiction to render judgment upon any counterclaim, cross-claim, or third-party action of any party, if (1) such claim or action involves the imported merchandise that is the subject matter of such civil action, or (2) such claim or action is to recover upon a bond or customs duties relating to such merchandise.

History of 28 U.S.C. §1583: Oct. 10, 1980, P.L. 96-417, §201, 94 Stat. 1729.

§1584. CIVIL ACTIONS UNDER THE NORTH AMERICAN FREE TRADE AGREEMENT OR THE UNITED STATES-CANADA FREE-TRADE AGREEMENT

The United States Court of International Trade shall have exclusive jurisdiction of any civil action which arises under section 777(f) of the Tariff Act of 1930 and is commenced by the United States to enforce administrative sanctions levied for violation of a protective order or an undertaking.

EFFECT OF TERMINATION OF NAFTA COUNTRY STATUS

For provisions relating to effect of termination of NAFTA country status on sections 401 to 416 of P.L. 103-182, see section 3451 of Title 19, Customs Duties.

History of 28 U.S.C. §1584: Sept. 28, 1988, P.L. 100-449, §402(d)(1), 102 Stat. 1884; Dec. 8, 1993, P.L. 103-182, §414(a)(2), 107 Stat. 2147.

§1585. POWERS IN LAW & EQUITY

The Court of International Trade shall possess all the powers in law and equity of, or as conferred by statute upon, a district court of the United States.

History of 28 U.S.C. §1585: Oct. 10, 1980, P.L. 96-417, §201, 94 Stat. 1730.

CHAPTER 97. JURISDICTIONAL IMMUNITIES OF FOREIGN STATES

§1602. FINDINGS & DECLARATION OF PURPOSE

The Congress finds that the determination by United States courts of the claims of foreign states to immunity from the jurisdiction of such courts would serve the interests of justice and would protect the rights of both foreign states and litigants in United States courts. Under international law, states are not immune from the jurisdiction of foreign courts insofar as their commercial activities are concerned, and their commercial property may be levied upon for the satisfaction of judgments rendered against them in connection with their commercial activities. Claims of foreign states to immunity should henceforth be decided by courts of the United States and of the States in conformity with the principles set forth in this chapter.

History of 28 U.S.C. §1602: Oct. 21, 1976, P.L. 94-583, §4(a), 90 Stat. 2892.

See *Commentaries*, "Removal & Remand," ch. 4, p. 239.

§1603. DEFINITIONS

For purposes of this chapter—

(a) A "foreign state", except as used in section 1608 of this title, includes a political subdivision of a foreign state or an agency or instrumentality of a foreign state as defined in subsection (b).

(b) An "agency or instrumentality of a foreign state" means any entity—

(1) which is a separate legal person, corporate or otherwise, and

(2) which is an organ of a foreign state or political subdivision thereof, or a majority of whose shares or other ownership interest is owned by a foreign state or political subdivision thereof, and

(3) which is neither a citizen of a State of the United States as defined in section 1332(c) and (e) of this title, nor created under the laws of any third country.

(c) The "United States" includes all territory and waters, continental or insular, subject to the jurisdiction of the United States.

(d) A "commercial activity" means either a regular course of commercial conduct or a particular commercial transaction or act. The commercial character of an activity shall be determined by reference to the nature of the course of conduct or particular transaction or act, rather than by reference to its purpose.

(e) A "commercial activity carried on in the United States by a foreign state" means commercial activity carried on by such state and having substantial contact with the United States.

History of 28 U.S.C. §1603: Oct. 21, 1976, P.L. 94-583, §4(a), 90 Stat. 2892; Feb. 18, 2005, P.L. 109-2, §4(b), 119 Stat. 12.

§1604. IMMUNITY OF A FOREIGN STATE FROM JURISDICTION

Subject to existing international agreements to which the United States is a party at the time of enactment of this Act a foreign state shall be immune from the jurisdiction of the courts of the United States and of the States except as provided in sections 1605 to 1607 of this chapter.

History of 28 U.S.C. §1604: Oct. 21, 1976, P.L. 94-583, §4(a), 90 Stat. 2892.

§1605. GENERAL EXCEPTIONS TO THE JURISDICTIONAL IMMUNITY OF A FOREIGN STATE

(a) Exceptions from immunity.[1] A foreign state shall not be immune from the jurisdiction of courts of the United States or of the States in any case—

(1) in which the foreign state has waived its immunity either explicitly or by implication, notwithstanding any withdrawal of the waiver which the foreign state may purport to effect except in accordance with the terms of the waiver;

(2) in which the action is based upon a commercial activity carried on in the United States by the foreign state; or upon an act performed in the United States in connection with a commercial activity of the foreign state elsewhere; or upon an act outside the territory of the United States in connection with a commercial activity of the foreign state elsewhere and that act causes a direct effect in the United States;

(3) in which rights in property taken in violation of international law are in issue and that property or any property exchanged for such property is present in the United States in connection with a commercial activity carried on in the United States by the foreign state; or that property or any property exchanged for such property is owned or operated by an agency or instrumentality of the foreign state and that agency or instrumentality is engaged in a commercial activity in the United States;

(4) in which rights in property in the United States acquired by succession or gift or rights in immovable property situated in the United States are in issue;

(5) not otherwise encompassed in paragraph (2) above, in which money damages are sought against a foreign state for personal injury or death, or damage to or loss of property, occurring in the United States and caused by the tortious act or omission of that foreign state or of any official or employee of that foreign state while acting within the scope of his office or employment; except this paragraph shall not apply to—

(A) any claim based upon the exercise or performance or the failure to exercise or perform a discretionary function regardless of whether the discretion be abused, or

(B) any claim arising out of malicious prosecution, abuse of process, libel, slander, misrepresentation, deceit, or interference with contract rights; or

(6) in which the action is brought, either to enforce an agreement made by the foreign state with or for the benefit of a private party to submit to arbitration all or any differences which have arisen or which may arise between the parties with respect to a defined legal relationship, whether contractual or not, concerning a subject matter capable of settlement by arbitration under the laws of the United States, or to confirm an award made pursuant to such an agreement to arbitrate, if (A) the arbitration takes place or is intended to take place in the United States, (B) the agreement or award is or may be governed by a treaty or other international agreement in force for the United States calling for the recognition and enforcement of arbitral awards, (C) the underlying claim, save for the agreement to arbitrate, could have been brought in a United States court under this section or section 1607, or (D) paragraph (1) of this subsection is otherwise applicable.

(b) Maritime liens.[1] A foreign state shall not be immune from the jurisdiction of the courts of the United States in any case in which a suit in admiralty is brought to enforce a maritime lien against a vessel or cargo of the foreign state, which maritime lien is based upon a commercial activity of the foreign state: Provided, That—

(1) notice of the suit is given by delivery of a copy of the summons and of the complaint to the person, or his agent, having possession of the vessel or cargo against which the maritime lien is asserted; and if the vessel or cargo is arrested pursuant to process obtained on behalf of the party bringing the suit, the service of process of arrest shall be deemed to constitute valid delivery of such notice, but the party bringing the suit shall be liable for any damages sustained by the foreign state as a result of the arrest if the party bringing the suit had actual or constructive knowledge that the vessel or cargo of a foreign state was involved; and

(2) notice to the foreign state of the commencement of suit as provided in section 1608 of this title is initiated within ten days either of the delivery of notice as provided in paragraph (1) of this subsection or, in the case of a party who was unaware that the vessel or cargo of a foreign state was involved, of the date such party determined the existence of the foreign state's interest.

(c) Notice, hearing, and determination.[1] Whenever notice is delivered under subsection (b)(1), the suit to enforce a maritime lien shall thereafter proceed and shall be heard and determined according to the principles of law and rules of practice of suits in rem whenever it appears that, had the vessel been privately owned and possessed, a suit in rem might have been maintained. A decree against the foreign state may include costs of the suit and, if the decree is for a money judgment, interest as ordered by the court, except that the court may not award judgment against the foreign state in an amount greater than the value of the vessel or cargo upon which the maritime lien arose. Such value shall be determined as of the time notice is served under subsection (b)(1). Decrees shall be subject to appeal and revision as provided in other cases of admiralty and maritime jurisdiction. Nothing shall preclude the plaintiff in any proper case from seeking relief in personam in the same action brought to enforce a maritime lien as provided in this section.

(d) Foreclosure of preferred mortgage.[1] A foreign state shall not be immune from the jurisdiction of the courts of the United States in any action brought to foreclose a preferred mortgage, as defined in section 31301 of title 46. Such action shall be brought, heard, and determined in accordance with the provisions of chapter 313 of title 46 and in accordance with the principles of law and rules of practice of suits in rem, whenever it appears that had the vessel been privately owned and possessed a suit in rem might have been maintained.

(e), (f) [Repealed Jan. 28, 2008, P.L. 110-181, §1083(b)(1)(B), 122 Stat. 341.]

(g) Limitation on discovery—

(1) In general.—(A) Subject to paragraph (2), if an action is filed that would otherwise be barred by section 1604, but for section 1605A, the court, upon request of the Attorney General, shall stay any request, demand, or order for discovery on the United States that the Attorney General certifies would significantly interfere with a criminal investigation or prosecution, or a national security operation, related to the incident that gave rise to the cause of action, until such time as the Attorney General advises the court that such request, demand, or order will no longer so interfere.

(B) A stay under this paragraph shall be in effect during the 12-month period beginning on the date on which the court

issues the order to stay discovery. The court shall renew the order to stay discovery for additional 12-month periods upon motion by the United States if the Attorney General certifies that discovery would significantly interfere with a criminal investigation or prosecution, or a national security operation, related to the incident that gave rise to the cause of action.

(2) Sunset.—(A) Subject to subparagraph (B), no stay shall be granted or continued in effect under paragraph (1) after the date that is 10 years after the date on which the incident that gave rise to the cause of action occurred.

(B) After the period referred to in subparagraph (A), the court, upon request of the Attorney General, may stay any request, demand, or order for discovery on the United States that the court finds a substantial likelihood would—

(i) create a serious threat of death or serious bodily injury to any person;

(ii) adversely affect the ability of the United States to work in cooperation with foreign and international law enforcement agencies in investigating violations of United States law; or

(iii) obstruct the criminal case related to the incident that gave rise to the cause of action or undermine the potential for a conviction in such case.

(3) Evaluation of evidence.—The court's evaluation of any request for a stay under this subsection filed by the Attorney General shall be conducted ex parte and in camera.

(4) Bar on motions to dismiss.—A stay of discovery under this subsection shall constitute a bar to the granting of a motion to dismiss under rules 12(b)(6) and 56 of the Federal Rules of Civil Procedure.

(5) Construction.—Nothing in this subsection shall prevent the United States from seeking protective orders or asserting privileges ordinarily available to the United States.

1. **Editor's note:** Titles supplied by editor.

History of 28 U.S.C. §1605: Oct. 21, 1976, P.L. 94-583, §4(a), 90 Stat. 2892; Nov. 9, 1988, P.L. 100-640, §1, 102 Stat. 3333; Nov. 16, 1988, P.L. 100-669, §2, 102 Stat. 3969; Dec. 1, 1990, P.L. 101-650, §325(b)(8), 104 Stat. 5121; Apr. 24, 1996, P.L. 104-132, §221(a), 110 Stat. 1241; Apr. 25, 1997, P.L. 105-11, 111 Stat. 22; Nov. 28, 2001, P.L. 107-77, §626(c), 115 Stat. 803; Jan. 10, 2002, P.L. 107-217, §208, 115 Stat. 2299; Oct. 6, 2006, P.L. 109-304, §17(f)(2), 120 Stat. 1708; Jan. 28, 2008, P.L. 110-181, §1083(b)(1), 122 Stat. 341.

§1605A. TERRORISM EXCEPTION TO THE JURISDICTIONAL IMMUNITY OF A FOREIGN STATE

(a) In General.—

(1) No immunity.—A foreign state shall not be immune from the jurisdiction of courts of the United States or of the States in any case not otherwise covered by this chapter in which money damages are sought against a foreign state for personal injury or death that was caused by an act of torture, extrajudicial killing, aircraft sabotage, hostage taking, or the provision of material support or resources for such an act if such act or provision of material support or resources is engaged in by an official, employee, or agent of such foreign state while acting within the scope of his or her office, employment, or agency.

(2) Claim heard.—The court shall hear a claim under this section if—

(A)(i)(I) the foreign state was designated as a state sponsor of terrorism at the time the act described in paragraph (1) occurred, or was so designated as a result of such act, and, subject to subclause (II), either remains so designated when the claim is filed under this section or was so designated within the 6-month period before the claim is filed under this section; or

(II) in the case of an action that is refiled under this section by reason of section 1083(c)(2)(A) of the National Defense Authorization Act for Fiscal Year 2008 or is filed under this section by reason of section 1083(c)(3) of that Act, the foreign state was designated as a state sponsor of terrorism when the original action or the related action under section 1605(a)(7) (as in effect before the enactment of this section) or section 589 of the Foreign Operations, Export Financing, and Related Programs Appropriations Act, 1997 (as contained in section 101(c) of division A of Public Law 104-208) was filed;

(ii) the claimant or the victim was, at the time the act described in paragraph (1) occurred—

(I) a national of the United States;

(II) a member of the armed forces; or

(III) otherwise an employee of the Government of the United States, or of an individual performing a contract awarded by the United States Government, acting within the scope of the employee's employment; and

(iii) in a case in which the act occurred in the foreign state against which the claim has been brought, the claimant has afforded the foreign state a reasonable opportunity to arbitrate the claim in accordance with the accepted international rules of arbitration; or

(B) the act described in paragraph (1) is related to Case Number 1:00CV03110 (EGS) in the United States District Court for the District of Columbia.

(b) Limitations.—An action may be brought or maintained under this section if the action is commenced, or a related action was commenced under section 1605(a)(7) (before the date of the enactment of this section) or section 589 of the Foreign Operations, Export Financing, and Related Programs Appropriations Act, 1997 (as contained in section 101(c) of division A of Public Law 104-208) not later than the latter of—

(1) 10 years after April 24, 1996; or

(2) 10 years after the date on which the cause of action arose.

(c) Private Right of Action.—A foreign state that is or was a state sponsor of terrorism as described in subsection

(a)(2)(A)(i), and any official, employee, or agent of that foreign state while acting within the scope of his or her office, employment, or agency, shall be liable to—

(1) a national of the United States,

(2) a member of the armed forces,

(3) an employee of the Government of the United States, or of an individual performing a contract awarded by the United States Government, acting within the scope of the employee's employment, or

(4) the legal representative of a person described in paragraph (1), (2), or (3),

for personal injury or death caused by acts described in subsection (a)(1) of that foreign state, or of an official, employee, or agent of that foreign state, for which the courts of the United States may maintain jurisdiction under this section for money damages. In any such action, damages may include economic damages, solatium, pain and suffering, and punitive damages. In any such action, a foreign state shall be vicariously liable for the acts of its officials, employees, or agents.

(d) Additional Damages.—After an action has been brought under subsection (c), actions may also be brought for reasonably foreseeable property loss, whether insured or uninsured, third party liability, and loss claims under life and property insurance policies, by reason of the same acts on which the action under subsection (c) is based.

(e) Special Masters—

(1) In general.—The courts of the United States may appoint special masters to hear damage claims brought under this section.

(2) Transfer of funds.—The Attorney General shall transfer, from funds available for the program under section 1404C of the Victims of Crime Act of 1984 (42 U.S.C. 10603c), to the Administrator of the United States district court in which any case is pending which has been brought or maintained under this section such funds as may be required to cover the costs of special masters appointed under paragraph (1). Any amount paid in compensation to any such special master shall constitute an item of court costs.

(f) Appeal.—In an action brought under this section, appeals from orders not conclusively ending the litigation may only be taken pursuant to section 1292(b) of this title.

(g) Property Disposition—

(1) In general.—In every action filed in a United States district court in which jurisdiction is alleged under this section, the filing of a notice of pending action pursuant to this section, to which is attached a copy of the complaint filed in the action, shall have the effect of establishing a lien of lis pendens upon any real property or tangible personal property that is—

(A) subject to attachment in aid of execution, or execution, under section 1610;

(B) located within that judicial district; and

(C) titled in the name of any defendant, or titled in the name of any entity controlled by any defendant if such notice contains a statement listing such controlled entity.

(2) Notice.—A notice of pending action pursuant to this section shall be filed by the clerk of the district court in the same manner as any pending action and shall be indexed by listing as defendants all named defendants and all entities listed as controlled by any defendant.

(3) Enforceability.—Liens established by reason of this subsection shall be enforceable as provided in chapter 111 of this title.

(h) Definitions.—For purposes of this section—

(1) the term "aircraft sabotage" has the meaning given that term in Article 1 of the Convention for the Suppression of Unlawful Acts Against the Safety of Civil Aviation;

(2) the term "hostage taking" has the meaning given that term in Article 1 of the International Convention Against the Taking of Hostages;

(3) the term "material support or resources" has the meaning given that term in section 2339A of title 18;

(4) the term "armed forces" has the meaning given that term in section 101 of title 10;

(5) the term "national of the United States" has the meaning given that term in section 101(a)(22) of the Immigration and Nationality Act (8 U.S.C. 1101(a)(22));

(6) the term "state sponsor of terrorism" means a country the government of which the Secretary of State has determined, for purposes of section 6(j) of the Export Administration Act of 1979 (50 U.S.C. App. 2405(j)), section 620A of the Foreign Assistance Act of 1961 (22 U.S.C. 2371), section 40 of the Arms Export Control Act (22 U.S.C. 2780), or any other provision of law, is a government that has repeatedly provided support for acts of international terrorism; and

(7) the terms "torture" and "extrajudicial killing" have the meaning given those terms in section 3 of the Torture Victim Protection Act of 1991 (28 U.S.C. 1350 note).

History of 28 U.S.C. §1605A: Jan. 28, 2008, P.L. 110-181, §1083(a)(1), 122 Stat. 338.

§1606. EXTENT OF LIABILITY

As to any claim for relief with respect to which a foreign state is not entitled to immunity under section 1605 or 1607 of this chapter, the foreign state shall be liable in the same manner and to the same extent as a private individual under like circumstances; but a foreign state except for an agency or instrumentality thereof shall not be liable for punitive damages; if, however, in any case wherein death was caused, the law of the place where the action or omission occurred provides, or has been construed to provide, for damages only punitive in nature, the foreign state shall be liable for actual or compensatory damages measured by the pecuniary injuries resulting from such death which were incurred by the persons for whose benefit the action was brought.

History of 28 U.S.C. §1606: Oct. 21, 1976, P.L. 94-583, §4(a), 90 Stat. 2894; Oct. 21, 1998, P.L. 105-277, §101(h) [§117(b)], 112 Stat. 2681-491; Oct. 28, 2000, P.L. 106-386, §2002(f)(2), 114 Stat. 1543.

§1607. COUNTERCLAIMS

In any action brought by a foreign state, or in which a foreign state intervenes, in a court of the United States or of a State, the foreign state shall not be accorded immunity with respect to any counterclaim—

(a) for which a foreign state would not be entitled to immunity under section 1605 or 1605A of this chapter had such claim been brought in a separate action against the foreign state; or

(b) arising out of the transaction or occurrence that is the subject matter of the claim of the foreign state; or

(c) to the extent that the counterclaim does not seek relief exceeding in amount or differing in kind from that sought by the foreign state.

History of 28 U.S.C. §1607: Oct. 21, 1976, P.L. 94-583, §4(a), 90 Stat. 2894; Jan. 28, 2008, P.L. 110-181, §1083(b)(2), 122 Stat. 341.

§1608. SERVICE; TIME TO ANSWER; DEFAULT

(a) Service in the courts of the United States and of the States shall be made upon a foreign state or political subdivision of a foreign state:

(1) by delivery of a copy of the summons and complaint in accordance with any special arrangement for service between the plaintiff and the foreign state or political subdivision; or

(2) if no special arrangement exists, by delivery of a copy of the summons and complaint in accordance with an applicable international convention on service of judicial documents; or

(3) if service cannot be made under paragraphs (1) or (2), by sending a copy of the summons and complaint and a notice of suit, together with a translation of each into the official language of the foreign state, by any form of mail requiring a signed receipt, to be addressed and dispatched by the clerk of the court to the head of the ministry of foreign affairs of the foreign state concerned, or

(4) if service cannot be made within 30 days under paragraph (3), by sending two copies of the summons and complaint and a notice of suit, together with a translation of each into the official language of the foreign state, by any form of mail requiring a signed receipt, to be addressed and dispatched by the clerk of the court to the Secretary of State in Washington, District of Columbia, to the attention of the Director of Special Consular Services—and the Secretary shall transmit one copy of the papers through diplomatic channels to the foreign state and shall send to the clerk of the court a certified copy of the diplomatic note indicating when the papers were transmitted.

As used in this subsection, a "notice of suit" shall mean a notice addressed to a foreign state and in a form prescribed by the Secretary of State by regulation.

(b) Service in the courts of the United States and of the States shall be made upon an agency or instrumentality of a foreign state:

(1) by delivery of a copy of the summons and complaint in accordance with any special arrangement for service between the plaintiff and the agency or instrumentality; or

(2) if no special arrangement exists, by delivery of a copy of the summons and complaint either to an officer, a managing or general agent, or to any other agent authorized by appointment or by law to receive service of process in the United States; or in accordance with an applicable international convention on service of judicial documents; or

(3) if service cannot be made under paragraphs (1) or (2), and if reasonably calculated to give actual notice, by delivery of a copy of the summons and complaint, together with a translation of each into the official language of the foreign state—

(A) as directed by an authority of the foreign state or political subdivision in response to a letter rogatory or request or

(B) by any form of mail requiring a signed receipt, to be addressed and dispatched by the clerk of the court to the agency or instrumentality to be served, or

(C) as directed by order of the court consistent with the law of the place where service is to be made.

(c) Service shall be deemed to have been made—

(1) in the case of service under subsection (a)(4), as of the date of transmittal indicated in the certified copy of the diplomatic note; and

(2) in any other case under this section, as of the date of receipt indicated in the certification, signed and returned postal receipt, or other proof of service applicable to the method of service employed.

(d) In any action brought in a court of the United States or of a State, a foreign state, a political subdivision thereof, or an agency or instrumentality of a foreign state shall serve an answer or other responsive pleading to the complaint within sixty days after service has been made under this section.

(e) No judgment by default shall be entered by a court of the United States or of a State against a foreign state, a political subdivision thereof, or an agency or instrumentality of a foreign state, unless the claimant establishes his claim or right to relief by evidence satisfactory to the court. A copy of any such default judgment shall be sent to the foreign state or political subdivision in the manner prescribed for service in this section.

History of 28 U.S.C. §1608: Oct. 21, 1976, P.L. 94-583, §4(a), 90 Stat. 2894.

See *Commentaries*, "Serving foreign government," ch. 2-H, §6.6, p. 161; "If defendant is foreign sovereign," ch. 7-A, §6.1.7, p. 594.

§1609. IMMUNITY FROM ATTACHMENT & EXECUTION OF PROPERTY OF A FOREIGN STATE

Subject to existing international agreements to which the United States is a party at the time of enactment of this Act the property in the United States of a foreign state shall be immune from attachment arrest and execution except as provided in sections 1610 and 1611 of this chapter.

History of 28 U.S.C. §1609: Oct. 21, 1976, P.L. 94-583, §4(a), 90 Stat. 2895.

A

§1610. EXCEPTIONS TO THE IMMUNITY FROM ATTACHMENT OR EXECUTION

(a) The property in the United States of a foreign state, as defined in section 1603(a) of this chapter, used for a commercial activity in the United States, shall not be immune from attachment in aid of execution, or from execution, upon a judgment entered by a court of the United States or of a State after the effective date of this Act, if—

(1) the foreign state has waived its immunity from attachment in aid of execution or from execution either explicitly or by implication, notwithstanding any withdrawal of the waiver the foreign state may purport to effect except in accordance with the terms of the waiver, or

(2) the property is or was used for the commercial activity upon which the claim is based, or

(3) the execution relates to a judgment establishing rights in property which has been taken in violation of international law or which has been exchanged for property taken in violation of international law, or

(4) the execution relates to a judgment establishing rights in property—

(A) which is acquired by succession or gift, or

(B) which is immovable and situated in the United States: Provided, That such property is not used for purposes of maintaining a diplomatic or consular mission or the residence of the Chief of such mission, or

(5) the property consists of any contractual obligation or any proceeds from such a contractual obligation to indemnify or hold harmless the foreign state or its employees under a policy of automobile or other liability or casualty insurance covering the claim which merged into the judgment, or

(6) the judgment is based on an order confirming an arbitral award rendered against the foreign state, provided that attachment in aid of execution, or execution, would not be inconsistent with any provision in the arbitral agreement, or

(7) the judgment relates to a claim for which the foreign state is not immune under section 1605A or section 1605(a)(7) (as such section was in effect on January 27, 2008), regardless of whether the property is or was involved with the act upon which the claim is based.

(b) In addition to subsection (a), any property in the United States of an agency or instrumentality of a foreign state engaged in commercial activity in the United States shall not be immune from attachment in aid of execution, or from execution, upon a judgment entered by a court of the United States or of a State after the effective date of this Act, if—

(1) the agency or instrumentality has waived its immunity from attachment in aid of execution or from execution either explicitly or implicitly, notwithstanding any withdrawal of the waiver the agency or instrumentality may purport to effect except in accordance with the terms of the waiver, or

(2) the judgment relates to a claim for which the agency or instrumentality is not immune by virtue of section 1605(a)(2), (3), or (5) or 1605(b) of this chapter, regardless of whether the property is or was involved in the act upon which the claim is based, or

(3) the judgment relates to a claim for which the agency or instrumentality is not immune by virtue of section 1605A of this chapter or section 1605(a)(7) of this chapter (as such section was in effect on January 27, 2008), regardless of whether the property is or was involved in the act upon which the claim is based.

(c) No attachment or execution referred to in subsections (a) and (b) of this section shall be permitted until the court has ordered such attachment and execution after having determined that a reasonable period of time has elapsed following the entry of judgment and the giving of any notice required under section 1608(e) of this chapter.

(d) The property of a foreign state, as defined in section 1603(a) of this chapter, used for a commercial activity in the United States, shall not be immune from attachment prior to the entry of judgment in any action brought in a court of the United States or of a State, or prior to the elapse of the period of time provided in subsection (c) of this section, if—

(1) the foreign state has explicitly waived its immunity from attachment prior to judgment, notwithstanding any withdrawal of the waiver the foreign state may purport to effect except in accordance with the terms of the waiver, and

(2) the purpose of the attachment is to secure satisfaction of a judgment that has been or may ultimately be entered against the foreign state, and not to obtain jurisdiction.

(e) The vessels of a foreign state shall not be immune from arrest in rem, interlocutory sale, and execution in actions brought to foreclose a preferred mortgage as provided in section 1605(d).

(f)(1)(A) Notwithstanding any other provision of law, including but not limited to section 208(f) of the Foreign Missions Act (22 U.S.C. 4308(f)), and except as provided in subparagraph (B), any property with respect to which financial transactions are prohibited or regulated pursuant to section 5(b) of the Trading with the Enemy Act (50 U.S.C. App. 5(b)), section 620(a) of the Foreign Assistance Act of 1961 (22 U.S.C. 2370(a)), sections 202 and 203 of the International Emergency Economic Powers Act (50 U.S.C. 1701-1702), or any other proclamation, order, regulation, or license issued

pursuant thereto, shall be subject to execution or attachment in aid of execution of any judgment relating to a claim for which a foreign state (including any agency or instrumentality or such state) claiming such property is not immune under section 1605(a)(7) (as in effect before the enactment of section 1605A) or section 1605A.

(B) Subparagraph (A) shall not apply if, at the time the property is expropriated or seized by the foreign state, the property has been held in title by a natural person or, if held in trust, has been held for the benefit of a natural person or persons.

(2)(A) At the request of any party in whose favor a judgment has been issued with respect to a claim for which the foreign state is not immune under section 1605(a)(7) (as in effect before the enactment of section 1605A) or section 1605A, the Secretary of the Treasury and the Secretary of State should make every effort to fully, promptly, and effectively assist any judgment creditor or any court that has issued any such judgment in identifying, locating, and executing against the property of that foreign state or any agency or instrumentality of such state.

(B) In providing such assistance, the Secretaries—

(i) may provide such information to the court under seal; and

(ii) should make every effort to provide the information in a manner sufficient to allow the court to direct the United States Marshall's office to promptly and effectively execute against that property.

(3) Waiver.—The President may waive any provision of paragraph (1) in the interest of national security.

(g) Property in Certain Actions—

(1) In general.—Subject to paragraph (3), the property of a foreign state against which a judgment is entered under section 1605A, and the property of an agency or instrumentality of such a state, including property that is a separate juridical entity or is an interest held directly or indirectly in a separate juridical entity, is subject to attachment in aid of execution, and execution, upon that judgment as provided in this section, regardless of—

(A) the level of economic control over the property by the government of the foreign state;

(B) whether the profits of the property go to that government;

(C) the degree to which officials of that government manage the property or otherwise control its daily affairs;

(D) whether that government is the sole beneficiary in interest of the property; or

(E) whether establishing the property as a separate entity would entitle the foreign state to benefits in United States courts while avoiding its obligations.

(2) United States sovereign immunity inapplicable.—Any property of a foreign state, or agency or instrumentality of a foreign state, to which paragraph (1) applies shall not be immune from attachment in aid of execution, or execution, upon a judgment entered under section 1605A because the property is regulated by the United States Government by reason of action taken against that foreign state under the Trading With the Enemy Act or the International Emergency Economic Powers Act.

(3) Third-party joint property holders.—Nothing in this subsection shall be construed to supersede the authority of a court to prevent appropriately the impairment of an interest held by a person who is not liable in the action giving rise to a judgment in property subject to attachment in aid of execution, or execution, upon such judgment.

History of 28 U.S.C. §1610: Oct. 21, 1976, P.L. 94-583, §4(a), 90 Stat. 2896; Nov. 9, 1988, P.L. 100-640, §2, 102 Stat. 3333; Nov. 16, 1988, P.L. 100-669, §3, 102 Stat. 3969; Dec. 1, 1990, P.L. 101-650, §325(b)(9), 104 Stat. 5121; Apr. 24, 1996, P.L. 104-132, §221(b), 110 Stat. 1242; Oct. 21, 1998, P.L. 105-277, §117, 112 Stat. 2681-491; Oct. 28, 2000, P.L. 106-386, §2002(f)(1), 114 Stat. 1543; Nov. 26, 2002, P.L. 107-297, §201(c)(3), 116 Stat. 2337; Jan. 28, 2008, P.L. 110-181, §1083(b)(3), 122 Stat. 341; Aug. 10, 2012, P.L. 112-158, §502(e)(1), 126 Stat. 1260.

§1611. CERTAIN TYPES OF PROPERTY IMMUNE FROM EXECUTION

(a) Notwithstanding the provisions of section 1610 of this chapter, the property of those organizations designated by the President as being entitled to enjoy the privileges, exemptions, and immunities provided by the International Organizations Immunities Act shall not be subject to attachment or any other judicial process impeding the disbursement of funds to, or on the order of, a foreign state as the result of an action brought in the courts of the United States or of the States.

(b) Notwithstanding the provisions of section 1610 of this chapter, the property of a foreign state shall be immune from attachment and from execution, if—

(1) the property is that of a foreign central bank or monetary authority held for its own account, unless such bank or authority, or its parent foreign government, has explicitly waived its immunity from attachment in aid of execution, or from execution, notwithstanding any withdrawal of the waiver which the bank, authority or government may purport to effect except in accordance with the terms of the waiver; or

(2) the property is, or is intended to be, used in connection with a military activity and

(A) is of a military character, or

(B) is under the control of a military authority or defense agency.

(c) Notwithstanding the provisions of section 1610 of this chapter, the property of a foreign state shall be immune from attachment and from execution in an action brought under section 302 of the Cuban Liberty and Democratic Solidarity (LIBERTAD) Act of 1996 to the extent that the property is a facility or installation used by an accredited diplomatic mission for official purposes.

History of 28 U.S.C. §1611: Oct. 21, 1976, P.L. 94-583, §4(a), 90 Stat. 2897; Mar. 12, 1996, P.L. 104-114, §302(e), 110 Stat. 818.

CHAPTER 99. GENERAL PROVISIONS

§1631. TRANSFER TO CURE WANT OF JURISDICTION

Whenever a civil action is filed in a court as defined in section 610 of this title or an appeal, including a petition for review of administrative action, is noticed for or filed with such a court and that court finds that there is a want of jurisdiction, the court shall, if it is in the interest of justice, transfer such action or appeal to any other such court in which the action or appeal could have been brought at the time it was filed or noticed, and the action or appeal shall proceed as if it had been filed in or noticed for the court to which it is transferred on the date upon which it was actually filed in or noticed for the court from which it is transferred.

History of 28 U.S.C. §1631: Apr. 2, 1982, P.L. 97-164, §301(a), 96 Stat. 55.

PART V. PROCEDURE

CHAPTER 111. GENERAL PROVISIONS

§1651. WRITS

(a) The Supreme Court and all courts established by Act of Congress may issue all writs necessary or appropriate in aid of their respective jurisdictions and agreeable to the usages and principles of law.

(b) An alternative writ or rule nisi may be issued by a justice or judge of a court which has jurisdiction.

History of 28 U.S.C. §1651: June 25, 1948, ch. 646, 62 Stat. 944; May 24, 1949, ch. 139, §90, 63 Stat. 102.

§1652. STATE LAWS AS RULES OF DECISION

The laws of the several states, except where the Constitution or treaties of the United States or Acts of Congress otherwise require or provide, shall be regarded as rules of decision in civil actions in the courts of the United States, in cases where they apply.

History of 28 U.S.C. §1652: June 25, 1948, ch. 646, 62 Stat. 944.

§1653. AMENDMENT OF PLEADINGS TO SHOW JURISDICTION

Defective allegations of jurisdiction may be amended, upon terms, in the trial or appellate courts.

History of 28 U.S.C. §1653: June 25, 1948, ch. 646, 62 Stat. 944.

§1654. APPEARANCE PERSONALLY OR BY COUNSEL

In all courts of the United States the parties may plead and conduct their own cases personally or by counsel as, by the rules of such courts, respectively, are permitted to manage and conduct causes therein.

History of 28 U.S.C. §1654: June 25, 1948, ch. 646, 62 Stat. 944; May 24, 1949, ch. 139, §91, 63 Stat. 103.

See *Commentaries*, "The Attorney," ch. 1-I, p. 58.

§1655. LIEN ENFORCEMENT; ABSENT DEFENDANTS

In an action in a district court to enforce any lien upon or claim to, or to remove any incumbrance or lien or cloud upon the title to, real or personal property within the district, where any defendant cannot be served within the State, or does not voluntarily appear, the court may order the absent defendant to appear or plead by a day certain.

Such order shall be served on the absent defendant personally if practicable, wherever found, and also upon the person or persons in possession or charge of such property, if any. Where personal service is not practicable, the order shall be published as the court may direct, not less than once a week for six consecutive weeks.

If an absent defendant does not appear or plead within the time allowed, the court may proceed as if the absent defendant had been served with process within the State, but any adjudication shall, as regards the absent defendant without appearance, affect only the property which is the subject of the action. When a part of the property is within another district, but within the same state, such action may be brought in either district.

Any defendant not so personally notified may, at any time within one year after final judgment, enter his appearance, and thereupon the court shall set aside the judgment and permit such defendant to plead on payment of such costs as the court deems just.

History of 28 U.S.C. §1655: June 25, 1948, ch. 646, 62 Stat. 944.

§1656. CREATION OF NEW DISTRICT OR DIVISION OR TRANSFER OF TERRITORY; LIEN ENFORCEMENT

The creation of a new district or division or the transfer of any territory to another district or division shall not affect or divest any lien theretofore acquired in a district court upon property within such district, division or territory.

To enforce such lien, the clerk of the court in which the same is acquired, upon the request and at the cost of the party desiring the same, shall make a certified copy of the record thereof, which, when filed in the proper court of the district or division in which such property is situated after such creation or transfer shall be evidence in all courts and places equally with the original thereof; and, thereafter like proceedings shall be had thereon, and with the same effect, as though the case or proceeding had been originally instituted in such court.

History of 28 U.S.C. §1656: June 25, 1948, ch. 646, 62 Stat. 944; Nov. 6, 1978, P.L. 95-598, §242, 92 Stat. 2671.

§1657. PRIORITY OF CIVIL ACTIONS

(a) Notwithstanding any other provision of law, each court of the United States shall determine the order in which civil actions are heard and determined, except that the court shall expedite the consideration of any action brought under chapter 153 or section 1826 of this title, any action for temporary or preliminary injunctive relief, or any other action if

good cause therefor is shown. For purposes of this subsection, "good cause" is shown if a right under the Constitution of the United States or a Federal Statute (including rights under section 552 of title 5) would be maintained in a factual context that indicates that a request for expedited consideration has merit.

(b) The Judicial Conference of the United States may modify the rules adopted by the courts to determine the order in which civil actions are heard and determined, in order to establish consistency among the judicial circuits.

History of 28 U.S.C. §1657: Nov. 8, 1984, P.L. 98-620, §401(a), 98 Stat. 3356.

§1658. TIME LIMITATIONS ON THE COMMENCEMENT OF CIVIL ACTIONS ARISING UNDER ACTS OF CONGRESS

(a) Except as otherwise provided by law, a civil action arising under an Act of Congress enacted after the date of the enactment of this section may not be commenced later than 4 years after the cause of action accrues.

(b) Notwithstanding subsection (a), a private right of action that involves a claim of fraud, deceit, manipulation, or contrivance in contravention of a regulatory requirement concerning the securities laws, as defined in section 3(a)(47) of the Securities Exchange Act of 1934 (15 U.S.C. 78c(a)(47)), may be brought not later than the earlier of—

(1) 2 years after the discovery of the facts constituting the violation; or

(2) 5 years after such violation.

History of 28 U.S.C. §1658: Dec. 1, 1990, P.L. 101-650, §313(a), 104 Stat. 5114; July 30, 2002, P.L. 107-204, §804(a), 116 Stat. 801.

§1659. STAY OF CERTAIN ACTIONS PENDING DISPOSITION OF RELATED PROCEEDINGS BEFORE THE UNITED STATES INTERNATIONAL TRADE COMMISSION

(a) Stay.—In a civil action involving parties that are also parties to a proceeding before the United States International Trade Commission under section 337 of the Tariff Act of 1930, at the request of a party to the civil action that is also a respondent in the proceeding before the Commission, the district court shall stay, until the determination of the Commission becomes final, proceedings in the civil action with respect to any claim that involves the same issues involved in the proceeding before the Commission, but only if such request is made within—

(1) 30 days after the party is named as a respondent in the proceeding before the Commission, or

(2) 30 days after the district court action is filed, whichever is later.

(b) Use of Commission record.—Notwithstanding section 337(n)(1) of the Tariff Act of 1930, after dissolution of a stay under subsection (a), the record of the proceeding before the United States International Trade Commission shall be transmitted to the district court and shall be admissible in the civil action, subject to such protective order as the district court determines necessary, to the extent permitted under the Federal Rules of Evidence and the Federal Rules of Civil Procedure.

History of 28 U.S.C. §1659: Dec. 8, 1994, P.L. 103-465, §321(b)(1)(A), 108 Stat. 4945.

CHAPTER 113. PROCESS

§1691. SEAL & TESTE OF PROCESS

All writs and process issuing from a court of the United States shall be under the seal of the court and signed by the clerk thereof.

History of 28 U.S.C. §1691: June 25, 1948, ch. 646, 62 Stat. 945.

§1692. PROCESS & ORDERS AFFECTING PROPERTY IN DIFFERENT DISTRICTS

In proceedings in a district court where a receiver is appointed for property, real, personal, or mixed, situated in different districts, process may issue and be executed in any such district as if the property lay wholly within one district, but orders affecting the property shall be entered of record in each of such districts.

History of 28 U.S.C. §1692: June 25, 1948, ch. 646, 62 Stat. 945.

§1693. PLACE OF ARREST IN CIVIL ACTION

Except as otherwise provided by Act of Congress, no person shall be arrested in one district for trial in another in any civil action in a district court.

History of 28 U.S.C. §1693: June 25, 1948, ch. 646, 62 Stat. 945.

§1694. PATENT INFRINGEMENT ACTION

In a patent infringement action commenced in a district where the defendant is not a resident but has a regular and established place of business, service of process, summons or subpoena upon such defendant may be made upon his agent or agents conducting such business.

History of 28 U.S.C. §1694: June 25, 1948, ch. 646, 62 Stat. 945.

§1695. STOCKHOLDER'S DERIVATIVE ACTION

Process in a stockholder's action in behalf of his corporation may be served upon such corporation in any district where it is organized or licensed to do business or is doing business.

History of 28 U.S.C. §1695: June 25, 1948, ch. 646, 62 Stat. 945.

§1696. SERVICE IN FOREIGN & INTERNATIONAL LITIGATION

(a) The district court of the district in which a person resides or is found may order service upon him of any document issued in connection with a proceeding in a foreign or international tribunal. The order may be made pursuant to a letter rogatory issued, or request made, by a foreign or international tribunal or upon application of any interested person and shall direct the manner of service. Service pursuant to this subsection does not, of itself, require the recognition or

enforcement in the United States of a judgment, decree, or order rendered by a foreign or international tribunal.

(b) This section does not preclude service of such a document without an order of court.

History of 28 U.S.C. §1696: Oct. 3, 1964, P.L. 88-619, §4(a), 78 Stat. 995.

§1697. SERVICE IN MULTIPARTY, MULTIFORUM ACTIONS

When the jurisdiction of the district court is based in whole or in part upon section 1369 of this title, process, other than subpoenas, may be served at any place within the United States, or anywhere outside the United States if otherwise permitted by law.

History of 28 U.S.C. §1697: Nov. 2, 2002, P.L. 107-273, §11020(b)(4)(A)(i), 116 Stat. 1828.

CHAPTER 114. CLASS ACTIONS

§1711. DEFINITIONS

In this chapter:

(1) Class.—The term "class" means all of the class members in a class action.

(2) Class action.—The term "class action" means any civil action filed in a district court of the United States under rule 23 of the Federal Rules of Civil Procedure or any civil action that is removed to a district court of the United States that was originally filed under a State statute or rule of judicial procedure authorizing an action to be brought by 1 or more representatives as a class action.

(3) Class counsel.—The term "class counsel" means the persons who serve as the attorneys for the class members in a proposed or certified class action.

(4) Class members.—The term "class members" means the persons (named or unnamed) who fall within the definition of the proposed or certified class in a class action.

(5) Plaintiff class action.—The term "plaintiff class action" means a class action in which class members are plaintiffs.

(6) Proposed settlement.—The term "proposed settlement" means an agreement regarding a class action that is subject to court approval and that, if approved, would be binding on some or all class members.

History of 28 U.S.C. §1711: Feb. 18, 2005, P.L. 109-2, §3(a), 119 Stat. 5.

§1712. COUPON SETTLEMENTS

(a) Contingent fees in coupon settlements.—If a proposed settlement in a class action provides for a recovery of coupons to a class member, the portion of any attorney's fee award to class counsel that is attributable to the award of the coupons shall be based on the value to class members of the coupons that are redeemed.

(b) Other attorney's fee awards in coupon settlements—

(1) In general.—If a proposed settlement in a class action provides for a recovery of coupons to class members, and a portion of the recovery of the coupons is not used to determine the attorney's fee to be paid to class counsel, any attorney's fee award shall be based upon the amount of time class counsel reasonably expended working on the action.

(2) Court approval.—Any attorney's fee under this subsection shall be subject to approval by the court and shall include an appropriate attorney's fee, if any, for obtaining equitable relief, including an injunction, if applicable. Nothing in this subsection shall be construed to prohibit application of a lodestar with a multiplier method of determining attorney's fees.

(c) Attorney's fee awards calculated on a mixed basis in coupon settlements.—If a proposed settlement in a class action provides for an award of coupons to class members and also provides for equitable relief, including injunctive relief—

(1) that portion of the attorney's fee to be paid to class counsel that is based upon a portion of the recovery of the coupons shall be calculated in accordance with subsection (a); and

(2) that portion of the attorney's fee to be paid to class counsel that is not based upon a portion of the recovery of the coupons shall be calculated in accordance with subsection (b).

(d) Settlement valuation expertise.—In a class action involving the awarding of coupons, the court may, in its discretion upon the motion of a party, receive expert testimony from a witness qualified to provide information on the actual value to the class members of the coupons that are redeemed.

(e) Judicial scrutiny of coupon settlements.—In a proposed settlement under which class members would be awarded coupons, the court may approve the proposed settlement only after a hearing to determine whether, and making a written finding that, the settlement is fair, reasonable, and adequate for class members. The court, in its discretion, may also require that a proposed settlement agreement provide for the distribution of a portion of the value of unclaimed coupons to 1 or more charitable or governmental organizations, as agreed to by the parties. The distribution and redemption of any proceeds under this subsection shall not be used to calculate attorneys' fees under this section.

History of 28 U.S.C. §1712: Feb. 18, 2005, P.L. 109-2, §3(a), 119 Stat. 6.

§1713. PROTECTION AGAINST LOSS BY CLASS MEMBERS

The court may approve a proposed settlement under which any class member is obligated to pay sums to class counsel that would result in a net loss to the class member only if the court makes a written finding that nonmonetary benefits to the class member substantially outweigh the monetary loss.

History of 28 U.S.C. §1713: Feb. 18, 2005, P.L. 109-2, §3(a), 119 Stat. 7.

§1714. PROTECTION AGAINST DISCRIMINATION BASED ON GEOGRAPHIC LOCATION

The court may not approve a proposed settlement that provides for the payment of greater sums to some class members than to others solely on the basis that the class members to whom the greater sums are to be paid are located in closer geographic proximity to the court.

History of 28 U.S.C. §1714: Feb. 18, 2005, P.L. 109-2, §3(a), 119 Stat. 7.

§1715. NOTIFICATIONS TO APPROPRIATE FEDERAL & STATE OFFICIALS

(a) Definitions—

(1) Appropriate Federal official.—In this section, the term "appropriate Federal official" means—

(A) the Attorney General of the United States; or

(B) in any case in which the defendant is a Federal depository institution, a State depository institution, a depository institution holding company, a foreign bank, or a nondepository institution subsidiary of the foregoing (as such terms are defined in section 3 of the Federal Deposit Insurance Act (12 U.S.C. 1813)), the person who has the primary Federal regulatory or supervisory responsibility with respect to the defendant, if some or all of the matters alleged in the class action are subject to regulation or supervision by that person.

(2) Appropriate State official.—In this section, the term "appropriate State official" means the person in the State who has the primary regulatory or supervisory responsibility with respect to the defendant, or who licenses or otherwise authorizes the defendant to conduct business in the State, if some or all of the matters alleged in the class action are subject to regulation by that person. If there is no primary regulator, supervisor, or licensing authority, or the matters alleged in the class action are not subject to regulation or supervision by that person, then the appropriate State official shall be the State attorney general.

(b) In general.—Not later than 10 days after a proposed settlement of a class action is filed in court, each defendant that is participating in the proposed settlement shall serve upon the appropriate State official of each State in which a class member resides and the appropriate Federal official, a notice of the proposed settlement consisting of—

(1) a copy of the complaint and any materials filed with the complaint and any amended complaints (except such materials shall not be required to be served if such materials are made electronically available through the Internet and such service includes notice of how to electronically access such material);

(2) notice of any scheduled judicial hearing in the class action;

(3) any proposed or final notification to class members of—

(A)(i) the members' rights to request exclusion from the class action; or

(ii) if no right to request exclusion exists, a statement that no such right exists; and

(B) a proposed settlement of a class action;

(4) any proposed or final class action settlement;

(5) any settlement or other agreement contemporaneously made between class counsel and counsel for the defendants;

(6) any final judgment or notice of dismissal;

(7)(A) if feasible, the names of class members who reside in each State and the estimated proportionate share of the claims of such members to the entire settlement to that State's appropriate State official; or

(B) if the provision of information under subparagraph (A) is not feasible, a reasonable estimate of the number of class members residing in each State and the estimated proportionate share of the claims of such members to the entire settlement; and

(8) any written judicial opinion relating to the materials described under subparagraphs (3) through (6).

(c) Depository institutions notification—

(1) Federal and other depository institutions.—In any case in which the defendant is a Federal depository institution, a depository institution holding company, a foreign bank, or a non-depository institution subsidiary of the foregoing, the notice requirements of this section are satisfied by serving the notice required under subsection (b) upon the person who has the primary Federal regulatory or supervisory responsibility with respect to the defendant, if some or all of the matters alleged in the class action are subject to regulation or supervision by that person.

(2) State depository institutions.—In any case in which the defendant is a State depository institution (as that term is defined in section 3 of the Federal Deposit Insurance Act (12 U.S.C. 1813)), the notice requirements of this section are satisfied by serving the notice required under subsection (b) upon the State bank supervisor (as that term is defined in section 3 of the Federal Deposit Insurance Act (12 U.S.C. 1813)) of the State in which the defendant is incorporated or chartered, if some or all of the matters alleged in the class action are subject to regulation or supervision by that person, and upon the appropriate Federal official.

(d) Final approval.—An order giving final approval of a proposed settlement may not be issued earlier than 90 days after the later of the dates on which the appropriate Federal official and the appropriate State official are served with the notice required under subsection (b).

(e) Noncompliance if notice not provided—

(1) In general.—A class member may refuse to comply with and may choose not to be bound by a settlement agreement or consent decree in a class action if the class member demonstrates that the notice required under subsection (b) has not been provided.

(2) Limitation.—A class member may not refuse to comply with or to be bound by a settlement agreement or consent decree under paragraph (1) if the notice required under subsection (b) was directed to the appropriate Federal official and to either the State attorney general or the person that has primary regulatory, supervisory, or licensing authority over the defendant.

(3) Application of rights.—The rights created by this subsection shall apply only to class members or any person acting on a class member's behalf, and shall not be construed to limit any other rights affecting a class member's participation in the settlement.

(f) Rule of construction.—Nothing in this section shall be construed to expand the authority of, or impose any obligations, duties, or responsibilities upon, Federal or State officials.

History of 28 U.S.C. §1715: Feb. 18, 2005, P.L. 109-2, §3(a), 119 Stat. 7.

CHAPTER 115. EVIDENCE; DOCUMENTARY

§1731. HANDWRITING

The admitted or proved handwriting of any person shall be admissible, for purposes of comparison, to determine genuineness of other handwriting attributed to such person.

History of 28 U.S.C. §1731: June 25, 1948, ch. 646, 62 Stat. 945.

§1732. RECORD MADE IN REGULAR COURSE OF BUSINESS; PHOTOGRAPHIC COPIES

If any business, institution, member of a profession or calling, or any department or agency of government, in the regular course of business or activity has kept or recorded any memorandum, writing, entry, print, representation or combination thereof, of any act, transaction, occurrence, or event, and in the regular course of business has caused any or all of the same to be recorded, copied, or reproduced by any photographic, photostatic, microfilm, micro-card, miniature photographic, or other process which accurately reproduces or forms a durable medium for so reproducing the original, the original may be destroyed in the regular course of business unless its preservation is required by law. Such reproduction, when satisfactorily identified, is as admissible in evidence as the original itself in any judicial or administrative proceeding whether the original is in existence or not and an enlargement or facsimile of such reproduction is likewise admissible in evidence if the original reproduction is in existence and available for inspection under direction of court. The introduction of a reproduced record, enlargement, or facsimile does not preclude admission of the original. This subsection[1] shall not be construed to exclude from evidence any document or copy thereof which is otherwise admissible under the rules of evidence.

1. **Editor's note:** So in original. Probably should be "section."

History of 28 U.S.C. §1732: June 25, 1948, ch. 646, 62 Stat. 945; Aug. 28, 1951, ch. 351, §§1, 3, 65 Stat. 205, 206; Aug. 30, 1961, P.L. 87-183, 75 Stat. 413; Jan. 2, 1975, P.L. 93-595, §2(b), 88 Stat. 1949.

§1733. GOVERNMENT RECORDS & PAPERS; COPIES

(a) Books or records of account or minutes of proceedings of any department or agency of the United States shall be admissible to prove the act, transaction or occurrence as a memorandum of which the same were made or kept.

(b) Properly authenticated copies or transcripts of any books, records, papers or documents of any department or agency of the United States shall be admitted in evidence equally with the originals thereof.

(c) This section does not apply to cases, actions, and proceedings to which the Federal Rules of Evidence apply.

History of 28 U.S.C. §1733: June 25, 1948, ch. 646, 62 Stat. 946; Jan. 2, 1975, P.L. 93-595, §2(c), 88 Stat. 1949.

§1734. COURT RECORD LOST OR DESTROYED, GENERALLY

(a) A lost or destroyed record of any proceeding in any court of the United States may be supplied on application of any interested party not at fault, by substituting a copy certified by the clerk of any court in which an authentic copy is lodged.

(b) Where a certified copy is not available, any interested person not at fault may file in such court a verified application for an order establishing the lost or destroyed record.

Every other interested person shall be served personally with a copy of the application and with notice of hearing on a day stated, not less than sixty days after service. Service may be made on any nonresident of the district anywhere within the jurisdiction of the United States or in any foreign country.

Proof of service in a foreign country shall be certified by a minister or consul of the United States in such country, under his official seal.

If, after the hearing, the court is satisfied that the statements contained in the application are true, it shall enter an order reciting the substance and effect of the lost or destroyed record. Such order, subject to intervening rights of third persons, shall have the same effect as the original record.

History of 28 U.S.C. §1734: June 25, 1948, ch. 646, 62 Stat. 946.

§1735. COURT RECORD LOST OR DESTROYED WHERE UNITED STATES INTERESTED

(a) When the record of any case or matter in any court of the United States to which the United States is a party, is lost or destroyed, a certified copy of any official paper of a United

States attorney, United States marshal or clerk or other certifying or recording officer of any such court, made pursuant to law, on file in any department or agency of the United States and relating to such case or matter, shall, on being filed in the court to which it relates, have the same effect as an original paper filed in such court. If the copy so filed discloses the date and amount of a judgment or decree and the names of the parties thereto, the court may enforce the judgment or decree as though the original record had not been lost or destroyed.

(b) Whenever the United States is interested in any lost or destroyed records or files of a court of the United States, the clerk of such court and the United States attorney for the district shall take the steps necessary to restore such records or files, under the direction of the judges of such court.

History of 28 U.S.C. §1735: June 25, 1948, ch. 646, 62 Stat. 946.

§1736. CONGRESSIONAL JOURNALS

Extracts from the Journals of the Senate and the House of Representatives, and from the Executive Journal of the Senate when the injunction of secrecy is removed, certified by the Secretary of the Senate or the Clerk of the House of Representatives shall be received in evidence with the same effect as the originals would have.

History of 28 U.S.C. §1736: June 25, 1948, ch. 646, 62 Stat. 947.

§1737. COPY OF OFFICER'S BOND

Any person to whose custody the bond of any officer of the United States has been committed shall, on proper request and payment of the fee allowed by any Act of Congress, furnish certified copies thereof, which shall be prima facie evidence in any court of the execution, filing and contents of the bond.

History of 28 U.S.C. §1737: June 25, 1948, ch. 646, 62 Stat. 947.

§1738. STATE & TERRITORIAL STATUTES & JUDICIAL PROCEEDINGS; FULL FAITH & CREDIT

The Acts of the legislature of any State, Territory, or Possession of the United States, or copies thereof, shall be authenticated by affixing the seal of such State, Territory or Possession thereto.

The records and judicial proceedings of any court of any such State, Territory or Possession, or copies thereof, shall be proved or admitted in other courts within the United States and its Territories and Possessions by the attestation of the clerk and seal of the court annexed, if a seal exists, together with a certificate of a judge of the court that the said attestation is in proper form.

Such Acts, records and judicial proceedings or copies thereof, so authenticated, shall have the same full faith and credit in every court within the United States and its Territories and Possessions as they have by law or usage in the courts of such State, Territory or Possession from which they are taken.

History of 28 U.S.C. §1738: June 25, 1948, ch. 646, 62 Stat. 947.

§1738A. FULL FAITH & CREDIT GIVEN TO CHILD CUSTODY DETERMINATIONS

(a) The appropriate authorities of every State shall enforce according to its terms, and shall not modify except as provided in subsections (f), (g), and (h) of this section, any custody determination or visitation determination made consistently with the provisions of this section by a court of another State.

(b) As used in this section, the term—

(1) "child" means a person under the age of eighteen;

(2) "contestant" means a person, including a parent or grandparent, who claims a right to custody or visitation of a child;

(3) "custody determination" means a judgment, decree, or other order of a court providing for the custody of a child, and includes permanent and temporary orders, and initial orders and modifications;

(4) "home State" means the State in which, immediately preceding the time involved, the child lived with his parents, a parent, or a person acting as parent, for at least six consecutive months, and in the case of a child less than six months old, the State in which the child lived from birth with any of such persons. Periods of temporary absence of any of such persons are counted as part of the six-month or other period;

(5) "modification" and "modify" refer to a custody or visitation determination which modifies, replaces, supersedes, or otherwise is made subsequent to, a prior custody or visitation determination concerning the same child, whether made by the same court or not;

(6) "person acting as a parent" means a person, other than a parent, who has physical custody of a child and who has either been awarded custody by a court or claims a right to custody;

(7) "physical custody" means actual possession and control of a child;

(8) "State" means a State of the United States, the District of Columbia, the Commonwealth of Puerto Rico, or a territory or possession of the United States; and

(9) "visitation determination" means a judgment, decree, or other order of a court providing for the visitation of a child and includes permanent and temporary orders and initial orders and modifications.

(c) A child custody or visitation determination made by a court of a State is consistent with the provisions of this section only if—

(1) such court has jurisdiction under the law of such State; and

(2) one of the following conditions is met:

(A) such State (i) is the home State of the child on the date of the commencement of the proceeding, or (ii) had been the child's home State within six months before the date

of the commencement of the proceeding and the child is absent from such State because of his removal or retention by a contestant or for other reasons, and a contestant continues to live in such State;

(B)(i) it appears that no other State would have jurisdiction under subparagraph (A), and (ii) it is in the best interest of the child that a court of such State assume jurisdiction because (I) the child and his parents, or the child and at least one contestant, have a significant connection with such State other than mere physical presence in such State, and (II) there is available in such State substantial evidence concerning the child's present or future care, protection, training, and personal relationships;

(C) the child is physically present in such State and (i) the child has been abandoned, or (ii) it is necessary in an emergency to protect the child because the child, a sibling, or parent of the child has been subjected to or threatened with mistreatment or abuse;

(D)(i) it appears that no other State would have jurisdiction under subparagraph (A), (B), (C), or (E), or another State has declined to exercise jurisdiction on the ground that the State whose jurisdiction is in issue is the more appropriate forum to determine the custody or visitation of the child, and (ii) it is in the best interest of the child that such court assume jurisdiction; or

(E) the court has continuing jurisdiction pursuant to subsection (d) of this section.

(d) The jurisdiction of a court of a State which has made a child custody or visitation determination consistently with the provisions of this section continues as long as the requirement of subsection (c)(1) of this section continues to be met and such State remains the residence of the child or of any contestant.

(e) Before a child custody or visitation determination is made, reasonable notice and opportunity to be heard shall be given to the contestants, any parent whose parental rights have not been previously terminated and any person who has physical custody of a child.

(f) A court of a State may modify a determination of the custody of the same child made by a court of another State, if—

(1) it has jurisdiction to make such a child custody determination; and

(2) the court of the other State no longer has jurisdiction, or it has declined to exercise such jurisdiction to modify such determination.

(g) A court of a State shall not exercise jurisdiction in any proceeding for a custody or visitation determination commenced during the pendency of a proceeding in a court of another State where such court of that other State is exercising jurisdiction consistently with the provisions of this section to make a custody or visitation determination.

(h) A court of a State may not modify a visitation determination made by a court of another State unless the court of the other State no longer has jurisdiction to modify such determination or has declined to exercise jurisdiction to modify such determination.

History of 28 U.S.C. §1738A: Dec. 28, 1980, P.L. 96-611, §8(a), 94 Stat. 3569; Nov. 12, 1998, P.L. 105-374, §1, 112 Stat. 3383; Oct. 28, 2000, P.L. 106-386, §1303(d), 114 Stat. 1512.

§1738B. FULL FAITH & CREDIT FOR CHILD SUPPORT ORDERS

(a) General rule.—The appropriate authorities of each State—

(1) shall enforce according to its terms a child support order made consistently with this section by a court of another State; and

(2) shall not seek or make a modification of such an order except in accordance with subsections (e), (f), and (i).

(b) Definitions.—In this section:

"child" means—

(A) a person under 18 years of age; and

(B) a person 18 or more years of age with respect to whom a child support order has been issued pursuant to the laws of a State.

"child's State" means the State in which a child resides.

"child's home State" means the State in which a child lived with a parent or a person acting as parent for at least 6 consecutive months immediately preceding the time of filing of a petition or comparable pleading for support and, if a child is less than 6 months old, the State in which the child lived from birth with any of them. A period of temporary absence of any of them is counted as part of the 6-month period.

"child support" means a payment of money, continuing support, or arrearages or the provision of a benefit (including payment of health insurance, child care, and educational expenses) for the support of a child.

"child support order"—

(A) means a judgment, decree, or order of a court requiring the payment of child support in periodic amounts or in a lump sum; and

(B) includes—

(i) a permanent or temporary order; and

(ii) an initial order or a modification of an order.

"contestant" means—

(A) a person (including a parent) who—

(i) claims a right to receive child support;

(ii) is a party to a proceeding that may result in the issuance of a child support order; or

(iii) is under a child support order; and

(B) a State or political subdivision of a State to which the right to obtain child support has been assigned.

"court" means a court or administrative agency of a State that is authorized by State law to establish the amount of child support payable by a contestant or make a modification of a child support order.

"modification" means a change in a child support order that affects the amount, scope, or duration of the order and modifies, replaces, supersedes, or otherwise is made subsequent to the child support order.

"State" means a State of the United States, the District of Columbia, the Commonwealth of Puerto Rico, the territories and possessions of the United States, and Indian country (as defined in section 1151 of title 18).

(c) Requirements of child support orders.—A child support order made by a court of a State is made consistently with this section if—

(1) a court that makes the order, pursuant to the laws of the State in which the court is located and subsections (e), (f), and (g)—

(A) has subject-matter jurisdiction to hear the matter and enter such an order; and

(B) has personal jurisdiction over the contestants; and

(2) reasonable notice and opportunity to be heard is given to the contestants.

(d) Continuing jurisdiction.—A court of a State that has made a child support order consistently with this section has continuing, exclusive jurisdiction over the order if the State is the child's State or the residence of any individual contestant unless the court of another State, acting in accordance with subsections (e) and (f), has made a modification of the order.

(e) Authority to modify orders.—A court of a State may modify a child support order issued by a court of another State if—

(1) the court has jurisdiction to make such a child support order pursuant to subsection (i); and

(2)(A) the court of the other State no longer has continuing, exclusive jurisdiction of the child support order because that State no longer is the child's State or the residence of any individual contestant; or

(B) each individual contestant has filed written consent with the State of continuing, exclusive jurisdiction for a court of another State to modify the order and assume continuing, exclusive jurisdiction over the order.

(f) Recognition of child support orders.—If 1 or more child support orders have been issued with regard to an obligor and a child, a court shall apply the following rules in determining which order to recognize for purposes of continuing, exclusive jurisdiction and enforcement:

(1) If only 1 court has issued a child support order, the order of that court must be recognized.

(2) If 2 or more courts have issued child support orders for the same obligor and child, and only 1 of the courts would have continuing, exclusive jurisdiction under this section, the order of that court must be recognized.

(3) If 2 or more courts have issued child support orders for the same obligor and child, and more than 1 of the courts would have continuing, exclusive jurisdiction under this section, an order issued by a court in the current home State of the child must be recognized, but if an order has not been issued in the current home State of the child, the order most recently issued must be recognized.

(4) If 2 or more courts have issued child support orders for the same obligor and child, and none of the courts would have continuing, exclusive jurisdiction under this section, a court having jurisdiction over the parties shall issue a child support order, which must be recognized.

(5) The court that has issued an order recognized under this subsection is the court having continuing, exclusive jurisdiction under subsection (d).

(g) Enforcement of modified orders.—A court of a State that no longer has continuing, exclusive jurisdiction of a child support order may enforce the order with respect to nonmodifiable obligations and unsatisfied obligations that accrued before the date on which a modification of the order is made under subsections (e) and (f).

(h) Choice of law—

(1) In general.—In a proceeding to establish, modify, or enforce a child support order, the forum State's law shall apply except as provided in paragraphs (2) and (3).

(2) Law of state of issuance of order.—In interpreting a child support order including the duration of current payments and other obligations of support, a court shall apply the law of the State of the court that issued the order.

(3) Period of limitation.—In an action to enforce arrears under a child support order, a court shall apply the statute of limitation of the forum State or the State of the court that issued the order, whichever statute provides the longer period of limitation.

(i) Registration for modification.—If there is no individual contestant or child residing in the issuing State, the party or support enforcement agency seeking to modify, or to modify and enforce, a child support order issued in another State shall register that order in a State with jurisdiction over the nonmovant for the purpose of modification.

History of 28 U.S.C. §1738B: Oct. 22, 1994, P.L. 103-383, §3(a), 108 Stat. 4064; Aug. 22, 1996, P.L. 104-193, §322, 110 Stat. 2221; Aug. 5, 1997, P.L. 105-33, §5554, 111 Stat. 636.

§1738C. CERTAIN ACTS, RECORDS, & PROCEEDINGS & THE EFFECT THEREOF

No State, territory, or possession of the United States, or Indian tribe, shall be required to give effect to any public act, record, or judicial proceeding of any other State, territory, possession, or tribe respecting a relationship between per-

sons of the same sex that is treated as a marriage under the laws of such other State, territory, possession, or tribe, or a right or claim arising from such relationship.

History of 28 U.S.C. §1738C: Sept. 21, 1996, P.L. 104-199, §2(a), 110 Stat. 2419.

§1739. STATE & TERRITORIAL NONJUDICIAL RECORDS; FULL FAITH & CREDIT

All nonjudicial records or books kept in any public office of any State, Territory, or Possession of the United States, or copies thereof, shall be proved or admitted in any court or office in any other State, Territory, or Possession by the attestation of the custodian of such records or books, and the seal of his office annexed, if there be a seal, together with a certificate of a judge of a court of record of the county, parish, or district in which such office may be kept, or of the Governor, or secretary of state, the chancellor or keeper of the great seal, of the State, Territory, or Possession that the said attestation is in due form and by the proper officers.

If the certificate is given by a judge, it shall be further authenticated by the clerk or prothonotary of the court, who shall certify, under his hand and the seal of his office, that such judge is duly commissioned and qualified; or, if given by such Governor, secretary, chancellor, or keeper of the great seal, it shall be under the great seal of the State, Territory, or Possession in which it is made.

Such records or books, or copies thereof, so authenticated, shall have the same full faith and credit in every court and office within the United States and its Territories and Possessions as they have by law or usage in the courts or offices of the State, Territory, or Possession from which they are taken.

History of 28 U.S.C. §1739: June 25, 1948, ch. 646, 62 Stat. 947.

§1740. COPIES OF CONSULAR PAPERS

Copies of all official documents and papers in the office of any consul or vice consul of the United States, and of all official entries in the books or records of any such office, authenticated by the consul or vice consul, shall be admissible equally with the originals.

History of 28 U.S.C. §1740: June 25, 1948, ch. 646, 62 Stat. 947.

§1741. FOREIGN OFFICIAL DOCUMENTS

An official record or document of a foreign country may be evidenced by a copy, summary, or excerpt authenticated as provided in the Federal Rules of Civil Procedure.

History of 28 U.S.C. §1741: June 25, 1948, ch. 646, 62 Stat. 948; May 24, 1949, ch. 139, §92(b), 63 Stat. 103; Oct. 3, 1964, P.L. 88-619, §5(a), 78 Stat. 996.

§1742. REPEALED

Repealed Oct. 3, 1964, P.L. 88-619, §6(a), 78 Stat. 996.

§1743. DEMAND ON POSTMASTER

The certificate of the Postmaster General or the Government Accountability Office of the mailing to a postmaster of a statement of his account and that payment of the balance stated has not been received shall be sufficient evidence of a demand notwithstanding any allowances or credits subsequently made. A copy of such statement shall be attached to the certificate.

History of 28 U.S.C. §1743: June 25, 1948, ch. 646, 62 Stat. 948; July 7, 2004, P.L. 108-271, §8(b), 118 Stat. 814.

§1744. COPIES OF UNITED STATES PATENT & TRADEMARK OFFICE DOCUMENTS, GENERALLY

Copies of letters patent or of any records, books, papers, or drawings belonging to the United States Patent and Trademark Office and relating to patents, authenticated under the seal of the United States Patent and Trademark Office and certified by the Under Secretary of Commerce for Intellectual Property and Director of the United States Patent and Trademark Office, or by another officer of the United States Patent and Trademark Office authorized to do so by the Director, shall be admissible in evidence with the same effect as the originals.

Any person making application and paying the required fee may obtain such certified copies.

History of 28 U.S.C. §1744: June 25, 1948, ch. 646, 62 Stat. 948; May 24, 1949, ch. 139, §92(c), 63 Stat. 103; Nov. 29, 1999, P.L. 106-113-Appx. I, §4732(b)(15), 113 Stat. 1501A-584.

§1745. COPIES OF FOREIGN PATENT DOCUMENTS

Copies of the specifications and drawings of foreign letters patent, or applications for foreign letters patent, and copies of excerpts of the official journals and other official publications of foreign patent offices belonging to the United States Patent and Trademark Office, certified in the manner provided by section 1744 of this title are prima facie evidence of their contents and of the dates indicated on their face.

History of 28 U.S.C. §1745: June 25, 1948, ch. 646, 62 Stat. 948, §1746. Renumbered and amended as §1745, May 24, 1949, ch. 139, §92(e), 63 Stat. 103. Oct. 3, 1964, P.L. 88-619, §7(a), 78 Stat. 996; Nov. 29, 1999, P.L. 106-113-Appx. I, §4732(b)(16), 113 Stat. 1501A-585.

§1746. UNSWORN DECLARATIONS UNDER PENALTY OF PERJURY

Wherever, under any law of the United States or under any rule, regulation, order, or requirement made pursuant to law, any matter is required or permitted to be supported, evidenced, established, or proved by the sworn declaration, verification, certificate, statement, oath, or affidavit, in writing of the person making the same (other than a deposition, or an oath of office, or an oath required to be taken before a specified official other than a notary public), such matter may, with like force and effect, be supported, evidenced, established, or proved by the unsworn declaration, certificate, verification, or statement, in writing of such person which is subscribed by him, as true under penalty of perjury, and dated, in substantially the following form:

(1) If executed without the United States: "I declare (or certify, verify, or state) under penalty of perjury under the

laws of the United States of America that the foregoing is true and correct. Executed on (date).

(Signature)."

(2) If executed within the United States, its territories, possessions, or commonwealths: "I declare (or certify, verify, or state) under penalty of perjury that the foregoing is true and correct. Executed on (date).

(Signature)."

History of 28 U.S.C. §1746: Oct. 18, 1976, P.L. 94-550, §1(a), 90 Stat. 2534.

CHAPTER 117. EVIDENCE; DEPOSITIONS

§1781. TRANSMITTAL OF LETTER ROGATORY OR REQUEST

(a) The Department of State has power, directly, or through suitable channels—

(1) to receive a letter rogatory issued, or request made, by a foreign or international tribunal, to transmit it to the tribunal, officer, or agency in the United States to whom it is addressed, and to receive and return it after execution; and

(2) to receive a letter rogatory issued, or request made, by a tribunal in the United States, to transmit it to the foreign or international tribunal, officer, or agency to whom it is addressed, and to receive and return it after execution.

(b) This section does not preclude—

(1) the transmittal of a letter rogatory or request directly from a foreign or international tribunal to the tribunal, officer, or agency in the United States to whom it is addressed and its return in the same manner; or

(2) the transmittal of a letter rogatory or request directly from a tribunal in the United States to the foreign or international tribunal, officer, or agency to whom it is addressed and its return in the same manner.

History of 28 U.S.C. §1781: June 25, 1948, ch. 646, 62 Stat. 948; Oct. 3, 1964, P.L. 88-619, §8(a), 78 Stat. 996.

See Hague Convention on the Taking of Evidence Abroad in Civil or Commercial Matters, p. 1566.

§1782. ASSISTANCE TO FOREIGN & INTERNATIONAL TRIBUNALS & TO LITIGANTS BEFORE SUCH TRIBUNALS

(a) The district court of the district in which a person resides or is found may order him to give his testimony or statement or to produce a document or other thing for use in a proceeding in a foreign or international tribunal, including criminal investigations conducted before formal accusation. The order may be made pursuant to a letter rogatory issued, or request made, by a foreign or international tribunal or upon the application of any interested person and may direct that the testimony or statement be given, or the document or other thing be produced, before a person appointed by the court. By virtue of his appointment, the person appointed has power to administer any necessary oath and take the testimony or statement. The order may prescribe the practice and procedure, which may be in whole or part the practice and procedure of the foreign country or the international tribunal, for taking the testimony or statement or producing the document or other thing. To the extent that the order does not prescribe otherwise, the testimony or statement shall be taken, and the document or other thing produced, in accordance with the Federal Rules of Civil Procedure.

A person may not be compelled to give his testimony or statement or to produce a document or other thing in violation of any legally applicable privilege.

(b) This chapter does not preclude a person within the United States from voluntarily giving his testimony or statement, or producing a document or other thing, for use in a proceeding in a foreign or international tribunal before any person and in any manner acceptable to him.

History of 28 U.S.C. §1782: June 25, 1948, ch. 646, 62 Stat. 949; May 24, 1949, ch. 139, §93, 63 Stat. 103; Oct. 3, 1964, P.L. 88-619, §9(a), 78 Stat. 997; Feb. 10, 1996, P.L. 104-106, §1342(b), 110 Stat. 486.

See *Commentaries*, "Discovery for proceeding in foreign tribunal," ch. 6-B, §2.2.14, p. 460.

§1783. SUBPOENA OF PERSON IN FOREIGN COUNTRY

(a) A court of the United States may order the issuance of a subpoena requiring the appearance as a witness before it, or before a person or body designated by it, of a national or resident of the United States who is in a foreign country, or requiring the production of a specified document or other thing by him, if the court finds that particular testimony or the production of the document or other thing by him is necessary in the interest of justice, and, in other than a criminal action or proceeding, if the court finds, in addition, that it is not possible to obtain his testimony in admissible form without his personal appearance or to obtain the production of the document or other thing in any other manner.

(b) The subpoena shall designate the time and place for the appearance or for the production of the document or other thing. Service of the subpoena and any order to show cause, rule, judgment, or decree authorized by this section or by section 1784 of this title shall be effected in accordance with the provisions of the Federal Rules of Civil Procedure relating to service of process on a person in a foreign country. The person serving the subpoena shall tender to the person to whom the subpoena is addressed his estimated necessary travel and attendance expenses, the amount of which shall be determined by the court and stated in the order directing the issuance of the subpoena.

History of 28 U.S.C. §1783: June 25, 1948, ch. 646, 62 Stat. 949; Oct. 3, 1964, P.L. 88-619, §10(a), 78 Stat. 997.

§1784. CONTEMPT

(a) The court of the United States which has issued a subpoena served in a foreign country may order the person who has failed to appear or who has failed to produce a docu-

ment or other thing as directed therein to show cause before it at a designated time why he should not be punished for contempt.

(b) The court, in the order to show cause, may direct that any of the person's property within the United States be levied upon or seized, in the manner provided by law or court rules governing levy or seizure under execution, and held to satisfy any judgment that may be rendered against him pursuant to subsection (d) of this section if adequate security, in such amount as the court may direct in the order, be given for any damage that he might suffer should he not be found in contempt. Security under this subsection may not be required of the United States.

(c) A copy of the order to show cause shall be served on the person in accordance with section 1783(b) of this title.

(d) On the return day of the order to show cause or any later day to which the hearing may be continued, proof shall be taken. If the person is found in contempt, the court, notwithstanding any limitation upon its power generally to punish for contempt, may fine him not more than $100,000 and direct that the fine and costs of the proceedings be satisfied by a sale of the property levied upon or seized, conducted upon the notice required and in the manner provided for sales upon execution.

History of 28 U.S.C. §1784: June 25, 1948, ch. 646, 62 Stat. 949; Oct. 3, 1964, P.L. 88-619, §11, 78 Stat. 998.

§1785. SUBPOENAS IN MULTIPARTY, MULTIFORUM ACTIONS

When the jurisdiction of the district court is based in whole or in part upon section 1369 of this title, a subpoena for attendance at a hearing or trial may, if authorized by the court upon motion for good cause shown, and upon such terms and conditions as the court may impose, be served at any place within the United States, or anywhere outside the United States if otherwise permitted by law.

History of 28 U.S.C. §1785: Nov. 2, 2002, P.L. 107-273, §11020(b)(4)(B)(i), 116 Stat. 1829.

History of Former 28 U.S.C. §1785: Repealed Oct. 3, 1964, P.L. 88-619, §12(a), 78 Stat. 998.

CHAPTER 119. EVIDENCE; WITNESSES

§1821. PER DIEM & MILEAGE GENERALLY; SUBSISTENCE

(a)(1) Except as otherwise provided by law, a witness in attendance at any court of the United States, or before a United States Magistrate Judge, or before any person authorized to take his deposition pursuant to any rule or order of a court of the United States, shall be paid the fees and allowances provided by this section.

(2) As used in this section, the term "court of the United States" includes, in addition to the courts listed in section 451 of this title, any court created by Act of Congress in a territory which is invested with any jurisdiction of a district court of the United States.

(b) A witness shall be paid an attendance fee of $40 per day for each day's attendance. A witness shall also be paid the attendance fee for the time necessarily occupied in going to and returning from the place of attendance at the beginning and end of such attendance or at any time during such attendance.

(c)(1) A witness who travels by common carrier shall be paid for the actual expenses of travel on the basis of the means of transportation reasonably utilized and the distance necessarily traveled to and from such witness's residence by the shortest practical route in going to and returning from the place of attendance. Such a witness shall utilize a common carrier at the most economical rate reasonably available. A receipt or other evidence of actual cost shall be furnished.

(2) A travel allowance equal to the mileage allowance which the Administrator of General Services has prescribed, pursuant to section 5704 of title 5, for official travel of employees of the Federal Government shall be paid to each witness who travels by privately owned vehicle. Computation of mileage under this paragraph shall be made on the basis of a uniformed table of distances adopted by the Administrator of General Services.

(3) Toll charges for toll roads, bridges, tunnels, and ferries, taxicab fares between places of lodging and carrier terminals, and parking fees (upon presentation of a valid parking receipt), shall be paid in full to a witness incurring such expenses.

(4) All normal travel expenses within and outside the judicial district shall be taxable as costs pursuant to section 1920 of this title.

(d)(1) A subsistence allowance shall be paid to a witness when an overnight stay is required at the place of attendance because such place is so far removed from the residence of such witness as to prohibit return thereto from day to day.

(2) A subsistence allowance for a witness shall be paid in an amount not to exceed the maximum per diem allowance prescribed by the Administrator of General Services, pursuant to section 5702(a) of title 5, for official travel in the area of attendance by employees of the Federal Government.

(3) A subsistence allowance for a witness attending in an area designated by the Administrator of General Services as a high-cost area shall be paid in an amount not to exceed the maximum actual subsistence allowance prescribed by the Administrator, pursuant to section 5702(c)(B) of title 5, for official travel in such area by employees of the Federal Government.

(4) When a witness is detained pursuant to section 3144 of title 18 for want of security for his appearance, he shall be entitled for each day of detention when not in attendance at court, in addition to his subsistence, to the daily attendance fee provided by subsection (b) of this section.

(e) An alien who has been paroled into the United States for prosecution, pursuant to section 212(d)(5) of the

Immigration and Nationality Act (8 U.S.C. 1182(d)(5)), or an alien who either has admitted belonging to a class of aliens who are deportable or has been determined pursuant to section 240 of such Act (8 U.S.C. 1252(b))[1] to be deportable, shall be ineligible to receive the fees or allowances provided by this section.

(f) Any witness who is incarcerated at the time that his or her testimony is given (except for a witness to whom the provisions of section 3144 of title 18 apply) may not receive fees or allowances under this section, regardless of whether such a witness is incarcerated at the time he or she makes a claim for fees or allowances under this section.

1. **Editor's note:** So in original. Probably should be 8 U.S.C. §1229a.

History of 28 U.S.C. §1821: June 25, 1948, ch. 646, 62 Stat. 950; May 10, 1949, ch. 96, 63 Stat. 65; May 24, 1949, ch. 139, §94, 63 Stat. 103; Oct. 31, 1951, ch. 655, §51(a), 65 Stat. 727; Sept. 3, 1954, ch. 1263, §45, 68 Stat. 1242; Aug. 1, 1956, ch. 826, 70 Stat. 798; Mar. 27, 1968, P.L. 90-274, §102(b), 82 Stat. 62; Oct. 27, 1978, P.L. 95-535, §1, 92 Stat. 2033; Dec. 1, 1990, P.L. 101-650, §314(a), 104 Stat. 5115; Oct. 14, 1992, P.L. 102-417, §2(a)-(c), 106 Stat. 2138; Sept. 30, 1996, P.L. 104-208, §308(g)(5)(E), 110 Stat. 3009-623.

§1822. COMPETENCY OF INTERESTED PERSONS; SHARE OF PENALTIES PAYABLE

Any person interested in a share of any fine, penalty or forfeiture incurred under any Act of Congress, may be examined as a witness in any proceeding for the recovery of such fine, penalty or forfeiture by any party thereto. Such examination shall not deprive the witness of his share.

History of 28 U.S.C. §1822: June 25, 1948, ch. 646, 62 Stat. 950.

§1823. REPEALED

Repealed Dec. 19, 1970, P.L. 91-563, §5(a), 84 Stat. 1478.

§1824. MILEAGE FEES UNDER SUMMONS AS BOTH WITNESS & JUROR

No constructive or double mileage fees shall be allowed by reason of any person being summoned both as a witness and a juror.

History of 28 U.S.C. §1824: June 25, 1948, ch. 646, 62 Stat. 951.

§1825. PAYMENT OF FEES

(a) In any case in which the United States or an officer or agency of the United States is a party, the United States marshal for the district shall pay all fees of witnesses on the certificate of the United States attorney or assistant United States attorney, and in the proceedings before a United States magistrate judge, on the certificate of such magistrate judge, except that any fees of defense witnesses, other than experts, appearing pursuant to subpoenas issued upon approval of the court, shall be paid by the United States marshal for the district—

(1) on the certificate of a Federal public defender or assistant Federal public defender, in a criminal case in which the defendant is represented by such Federal public defender or assistant Federal public defender, and

(2) on the certificate of the clerk of the court upon the affidavit of such witnesses' attendance given by other counsel appointed pursuant to section 3006A of title 18, in a criminal case in which a defendant is represented by such other counsel.

(b) In proceedings in forma pauperis for a writ of habeas corpus, and in proceedings in forma pauperis under section 2255 of this title, the United States marshal for the district shall pay, on the certificate of the district judge, all fees of witnesses for the party authorized to proceed in forma pauperis, except that any fees of witnesses for such party, other than experts, appearing pursuant to subpoenas issued upon approval of the court, shall be paid by the United States marshal for the district—

(1) on the certificate of a Federal public defender or assistant Federal public defender, in any such proceedings in which a party is represented by such Federal public defender or assistant Federal public defender, and

(2) on the certificate of the clerk of the court upon the affidavit of such witnesses' attendance given by other counsel appointed pursuant to section 3006A of title 18, in any such proceedings in which a party is represented by such other counsel.

(c) Fees and mileage need not be tendered to a witness upon service of a subpoena issued on behalf of the United States or an officer or agency of the United States, upon service of a subpoena issued on behalf of a defendant represented by a Federal public defender, assistant Federal public defender, or other attorney appointed pursuant to section 3006A of title 18, or upon service of a subpoena issued on behalf of a party authorized to proceed in forma pauperis, if the payment of such fees and mileage is to be made by the United States marshal under this section.

History of 28 U.S.C. §1825: June 25, 1948, ch. 646, 62 Stat. 951; Sept. 2, 1965, P.L. 89-162, 79 Stat. 618; Nov. 14, 1986, P.L. 99-651, §104, 100 Stat. 3645.

§1826. RECALCITRANT WITNESSES

(a) Whenever a witness in any proceeding before or ancillary to any court or grand jury of the United States refuses without just cause shown to comply with an order of the court to testify or provide other information, including any book, paper, document, record, recording or other material, the court, upon such refusal, or when such refusal is duly brought to its attention, may summarily order his confinement at a suitable place until such time as the witness is willing to give such testimony or provide such information. No period of such confinement shall exceed the life of—

(1) the court proceeding, or

(2) the term of the grand jury, including extensions,

before which such refusal to comply with the court order occurred, but in no event shall such confinement exceed eighteen months.

(b) No person confined pursuant to subsection (a) of this section shall be admitted to bail pending the determination of an appeal taken by him from the order for his confinement if it appears that the appeal is frivolous or taken for de-

lay. Any appeal from an order of confinement under this section shall be disposed of as soon as practicable, but not later than thirty days from the filing of such appeal.

(c) Whoever escapes or attempts to escape from the custody of any facility or from any place in which or to which he is confined pursuant to this section or section 4243 of title 18, or whoever rescues or attempts to rescue or instigates, aids, or assists the escape or attempt to escape of such a person, shall be subject to imprisonment for not more than three years, or a fine of not more than $10,000, or both.

History of 28 U.S.C. §1826: Oct. 15, 1970, P.L. 91-452, §301(a), 84 Stat. 932; Oct. 12, 1984, P.L. 98-473, §1013, 98 Stat. 2142.

§1827. INTERPRETERS IN COURTS OF THE UNITED STATES

(a) The Director of the Administrative Office of the United States Courts shall establish a program to facilitate the use of certified and otherwise qualified interpreters in judicial proceedings instituted by the United States.

(b)(1) The Director shall prescribe, determine, and certify the qualifications of persons who may serve as certified interpreters, when the Director considers certification of interpreters to be merited, for the hearing impaired (whether or not also speech impaired) and persons who speak only or primarily a language other than the English language, in judicial proceedings instituted by the United States. The Director may certify interpreters for any language if the Director determines that there is a need for certified interpreters in that language. Upon the request of the Judicial Conference of the United States for certified interpreters in a language, the Director shall certify interpreters in that language. Upon such a request from the judicial council of a circuit and the approval of the Judicial Conference, the Director shall certify interpreters for that circuit in the language requested. The judicial council of a circuit shall identify and evaluate the needs of the districts within a circuit. The Director shall certify interpreters based on the results of criterion-referenced performance examinations. The Director shall issue regulations to carry out this paragraph within 1 year after the date of the enactment of the Judicial Improvements and Access to Justice Act.

(2) Only in a case in which no certified interpreter is reasonably available as provided in subsection (d) of this section, including a case in which certification of interpreters is not provided under paragraph (1) in a particular language, may the services of otherwise qualified interpreters be used. The Director shall provide guidelines to the courts for the selection of otherwise qualified interpreters, in order to ensure that the highest standards of accuracy are maintained in all judicial proceedings subject to the provisions of this chapter.

(3) The Director shall maintain a current master list of all certified interpreters and otherwise qualified interpreters and shall report periodically on the use and performance of both certified and otherwise qualified interpreters in judicial proceedings instituted by the United States and on the languages for which interpreters have been certified. The Director shall prescribe, subject to periodic review, a schedule of reasonable fees for services rendered by interpreters, certified or otherwise, used in proceedings instituted by the United States, and in doing so shall consider the prevailing rate of compensation for comparable service in other governmental entities.

(c)(1) Each United States district court shall maintain on file in the office of the clerk, and each United States attorney shall maintain on file, a list of all persons who have been certified as interpreters by the Director in accordance with subsection (b) of this section. The clerk shall make the list of certified interpreters for judicial proceeding available upon request.

(2) The clerk of the court, or other court employee designated by the chief judge, shall be responsible for securing the services of certified interpreters and otherwise qualified interpreters required for proceedings initiated by the United States, except that the United States attorney is responsible for securing the services of such interpreters for governmental witnesses.

(d)(1) The presiding judicial officer, with the assistance of the Director of the Administrative Office of the United States Courts, shall utilize the services of the most available certified interpreter, or when no certified interpreter is reasonably available, as determined by the presiding judicial officer, the services of an otherwise qualified interpreter, in judicial proceedings instituted by the United States, if the presiding judicial officer determines on such officer's own motion or on the motion of a party that such party (including a defendant in a criminal case), or a witness who may present testimony in such judicial proceedings—

(A) speaks only or primarily a language other than the English language; or

(B) suffers from a hearing impairment (whether or not suffering also from a speech impairment)

so as to inhibit such party's comprehension of the proceedings or communication with counsel or the presiding judicial officer, or so as to inhibit such witness' comprehension of questions and the presentation of such testimony.

(2) Upon the motion of a party, the presiding judicial officer shall determine whether to require the electronic sound recording of a judicial proceeding in which an interpreter is used under this section. In making this determination, the presiding judicial officer shall consider, among other things, the qualifications of the interpreter and prior experience in interpretation of court proceedings; whether the language to be interpreted is not one of the languages for which the Director has certified interpreters, and the complexity or length of the proceeding. In a grand jury proceeding, upon the motion of the accused, the presiding judicial officer shall require the electronic sound recording of the portion of the proceeding in which an interpreter is used.

(e)(1) If any interpreter is unable to communicate effectively with the presiding judicial officer, the United States

attorney, a party (including a defendant in a criminal case), or a witness, the presiding judicial officer shall dismiss such interpreter and obtain the services of another interpreter in accordance with this section.

(2) In any judicial proceedings instituted by the United States, if the presiding judicial officer does not appoint an interpreter under subsection (d) of this section, an individual requiring the services of an interpreter may seek assistance of the clerk of court or the Director of the Administrative Office of the United States Courts in obtaining the assistance of a certified interpreter.

(f)(1) Any individual other than a witness who is entitled to interpretation under subsection (d) of this section may waive such interpretation in whole or in part. Such a waiver shall be effective only if approved by the presiding judicial officer and made expressly by such individual on the record after opportunity to consult with counsel and after the presiding judicial officer has explained to such individual, utilizing the services of the most available certified interpreter, or when no certified interpreter is reasonably available, as determined by the presiding judicial officer, the services of an otherwise competent interpreter, the nature and effect of the waiver.

(2) An individual who waives under paragraph (1) of this subsection the right to an interpreter may utilize the services of a noncertified interpreter of such individual's choice whose fees, expenses, and costs shall be paid in the manner provided for the payment of such fees, expenses, and costs of an interpreter appointed under subsection (d) of this section.

(g)(1) There are authorized to be appropriated to the Federal judiciary, and to be paid by the Director of the Administrative Office of the United States Courts, such sums as may be necessary to establish a program to facilitate the use of certified and otherwise qualified interpreters, and otherwise fulfill the provisions of this section and the Judicial Improvements and Access to Justice Act, except as provided in paragraph (3).

(2) Implementation of the provisions of this section is contingent upon the availability of appropriated funds to carry out the purposes of this section.

(3) Such salaries, fees, expenses, and costs that are incurred with respect to Government witnesses (including for grand jury proceedings) shall, unless direction is made under paragraph (4), be paid by the Attorney General from sums appropriated to the Department of Justice.

(4) Upon the request of any person in any action for which interpreting services established pursuant to subsection (d) are not otherwise provided, the clerk of the court, or other court employee designated by the chief judge, upon the request of the presiding judicial officer, shall, where possible, make such services available to that person on a cost-reimbursable basis, but the judicial officer may also require the prepayment of the estimated expenses of providing such services.

(5) If the Director of the Administrative Office of the United States Courts finds it necessary to develop and administer criterion-referenced performance examinations for purposes of certification, or other examinations for the selection of otherwise qualified interpreters, the Director may prescribe for each examination a uniform fee for applicants to take such examination. In determining the rate of the fee for each examination, the Director shall consider the fees charged by other organizations for examinations that are similar in scope or nature. Notwithstanding section 3302(b) of title 31, the Director is authorized to provide in any contract or agreement for the development or administration of examinations and the collection of fees that the contractor may retain all or a portion of the fees in payment for the services. Notwithstanding paragraph (6) of this subsection, all fees collected after the effective date of this paragraph and not retained by a contractor shall be deposited in the fund established under section 1931 of this title and shall remain available until expended.

(6) Any moneys collected under this subsection may be used to reimburse the appropriations obligated and disbursed in payment for such services.

(h) The presiding judicial officer shall approve the compensation and expenses payable to interpreters, pursuant to the schedule of fees prescribed by the Director under subsection (b)(3).

(i) The term "presiding judicial officer" as used in this section refers to any judge of a United States district court, including a bankruptcy judge, a United States magistrate judge, and in the case of grand jury proceedings conducted under the auspices of the United States attorney, a United States attorney.

(j) The term "judicial proceedings instituted by the United States" as used in this section refers to all proceedings, whether criminal or civil, including pretrial and grand jury proceedings (as well as proceedings upon a petition for a writ of habeas corpus initiated in the name of the United States by a relator) conducted in, or pursuant to the lawful authority and jurisdiction of a United States district court. The term "United States district court" as used in this subsection includes any court which is created by an Act of Congress in a territory and is invested with any jurisdiction of a district court established by chapter 5 of this title.

(k) The interpretation provided by certified or otherwise qualified interpreters pursuant to this section shall be in the simultaneous mode for any party to a judicial proceeding instituted by the United States and in the consecutive mode for witnesses, except that the presiding judicial officer, sua sponte or on the motion of a party, may authorize a simultaneous, or consecutive interpretation when such officer determines after a hearing on the record that such interpretation will aid in the efficient administration of justice. The presiding judicial officer, on such officer's motion or on the motion of a party, may order that special interpretation services as

authorized in section 1828 of this title be provided if such officer determines that the provision of such services will aid in the efficient administration of justice.

(*l*) Notwithstanding any other provision of this section or section 1828, the presiding judicial officer may appoint a certified or otherwise qualified sign language interpreter to provide services to a party, witness, or other participant in a judicial proceeding, whether or not the proceeding is instituted by the United States, if the presiding judicial officer determines, on such officer's own motion or on the motion of a party or other participant in the proceeding, that such individual suffers from a hearing impairment. The presiding judicial officer shall, subject to the availability of appropriated funds, approve the compensation and expenses payable to sign language interpreters appointed under this section in accordance with the schedule of fees prescribed by the Director under subsection (b)(3) of this section.

History of 28 U.S.C. §1827: Oct. 28, 1978, P.L. 95-539, §2(a), 92 Stat. 2040; Nov. 19, 1988, P.L. 100-702, §§702-710, 102 Stat. 4654-4657; Oct. 19, 1996, P.L. 104-317, §§306, 402(a), 110 Stat. 3852, 3854.

§1828. SPECIAL INTERPRETATION SERVICES

(a) The Director of the Administrative Office of the United States Courts shall establish a program for the provision of special interpretation services in criminal actions and in civil actions initiated by the United States (including petitions for writs of habeas corpus initiated in the name of the United States by relators) in a United States district court. The program shall provide a capacity for simultaneous interpretation services in multidefendant criminal actions and multidefendant civil actions.

(b) Upon the request of any person in any action for which special interpretation services established pursuant to subsection (a) are not otherwise provided, the Director, with the approval of the presiding judicial officer, may make such services available to the person requesting the services on a reimbursable basis at rates established in conformity with section 9701 of title 31, but the Director may require the prepayment of the estimated expenses of providing the services by the person requesting them.

(c) Except as otherwise provided in this subsection, the expenses incident to providing services under subsection (a) of this section shall be paid by the Director from sums appropriated to the Federal judiciary. A presiding judicial officer, in such officer's discretion, may order that all or part of the expenses shall be apportioned between or among the parties or shall be taxed as costs in a civil action, and any moneys collected as a result of such order may be used to reimburse the appropriations obligated and disbursed in payment for such services.

(d) Appropriations available to the Director shall be available to provide services in accordance with subsection (b) of this section, and moneys collected by the Director under that subsection may be used to reimburse the appropriations charged for such services. A presiding judicial officer, in such officer's discretion, may order that all or part of the expenses shall be apportioned between or among the parties or shall be taxed as costs in the action.

History of 28 U.S.C. §1828: Oct. 28, 1978, P.L. 95-539, §2(a), 92 Stat. 2042; Sept. 13, 1982, P.L. 97-258, §3(g), 96 Stat. 1065.

CHAPTER 121. JURIES; TRIAL BY JURY

§1861. DECLARATION OF POLICY

It is the policy of the United States that all litigants in Federal courts entitled to trial by jury shall have the right to grand and petit juries selected at random from a fair cross section of the community in the district or division wherein the court convenes. It is further the policy of the United States that all citizens shall have the opportunity to be considered for service on grand and petit juries in the district courts of the United States, and shall have an obligation to serve as jurors when summoned for that purpose.

History of 28 U.S.C. §1861: June 25, 1948, ch. 646, 62 Stat. 951; Sept. 9, 1957, P.L. 85-315, part V, §152, 71 Stat. 638; Mar. 27, 1968, P.L. 90-274, §101, 82 Stat. 54.

See *Commentaries*, "Jury Selection," ch. 8-A, p. 673.

§1862. DISCRIMINATION PROHIBITED

No citizen shall be excluded from service as a grand or petit juror in the district courts of the United States or in the Court of International Trade on account of race, color, religion, sex, national origin, or economic status.

History of 28 U.S.C. §1862: June 25, 1948, ch. 646, 62 Stat. 952; Mar. 27, 1968, P.L. 90-274, §101, 82 Stat. 54; Oct. 10, 1980, P.L. 96-417, §302(c), 94 Stat. 1739.

See *Commentaries*, "Jury Selection," ch. 8-A, p. 673.

§1863. PLAN FOR RANDOM JURY SELECTION

(a) Each United States district court shall devise and place into operation a written plan for random selection of grand and petit jurors that shall be designed to achieve the objectives of sections 1861 and 1862 of this title, and that shall otherwise comply with the provisions of this title. The plan shall be placed into operation after approval by a reviewing panel consisting of the members of the judicial council of the circuit and either the chief judge of the district whose plan is being reviewed or such other active district judge of that district as the chief judge of the district may designate. The panel shall examine the plan to ascertain that it complies with the provisions of this title. If the reviewing panel finds that the plan does not comply, the panel shall state the particulars in which the plan fails to comply and direct the district court to present within a reasonable time an alternative plan remedying the defect or defects. Separate plans may be adopted for each division or combination of divisions within a judicial district. The district court may modify a plan at any time and it shall modify the plan when so directed by the reviewing panel. The district court shall promptly notify the panel, the Administrative Office of the United States Courts, and the Attorney General of the United States, of the initial

adoption and future modifications of the plan by filing copies therewith. Modifications of the plan made at the instance of the district court shall become effective after approval by the panel. Each district court shall submit a report on the jury selection process within its jurisdiction to the Administrative Office of the United States Courts in such form and at such times as the Judicial Conference of the United States may specify. The Judicial Conference of the United States may, from time to time, adopt rules and regulations governing the provisions and the operation of the plans formulated under this title.

(b) Among other things, such plan shall—

(1) either establish a jury commission, or authorize the clerk of the court, to manage the jury selection process. If the plan establishes a jury commission, the district court shall appoint one citizen to serve with the clerk of the court as the jury commission: Provided, however, That the plan for the District of Columbia may establish a jury commission consisting of three citizens. The citizen jury commissioner shall not belong to the same political party as the clerk serving with him. The clerk or the jury commission, as the case may be, shall act under the supervision and control of the chief judge of the district court or such other judge of the district court as the plan may provide. Each jury commissioner shall, during his tenure in office, reside in the judicial district or division for which he is appointed. Each citizen jury commissioner shall receive compensation to be fixed by the district court plan at a rate not to exceed $50 per day for each day necessarily employed in the performance of his duties, plus reimbursement for travel, subsistence, and other necessary expenses incurred by him in the performance of such duties. The Judicial Conference of the United States may establish standards for allowance of travel, subsistence, and other necessary expenses incurred by jury commissioners.

(2) specify whether the names of prospective jurors shall be selected from the voter registration lists or the lists of actual voters of the political subdivisions within the district or division. The plan shall prescribe some other source or sources of names in addition to voter lists where necessary to foster the policy and protect the rights secured by sections 1861 and 1862 of this title. The plan for the District of Columbia may require the names of prospective jurors to be selected from the city directory rather than from voter lists. The plans for the districts of Puerto Rico and the Canal Zone may prescribe some other source or sources of names of prospective jurors in lieu of voter lists, the use of which shall be consistent with the policies declared and rights secured by sections 1861 and 1862 of this title. The plan for the district of Massachusetts may require the names of prospective jurors to be selected from the resident list provided for in chapter 234A, Massachusetts General Laws, or comparable authority, rather than from voter lists.

(3) specify detailed procedures to be followed by the jury commission or clerk in selecting names from the sources specified in paragraph (2) of this subsection. These procedures shall be designed to ensure the random selection of a fair cross section of the persons residing in the community in the district or division wherein the court convenes. They shall ensure that names of persons residing in each of the counties, parishes, or similar political subdivisions within the judicial district or division are placed in a master jury wheel; and shall ensure that each county, parish, or similar political subdivision within the district or division is substantially proportionally represented in the master jury wheel for that judicial district, division, or combination of divisions. For the purposes of determining proportional representation in the master jury wheel, either the number of actual voters at the last general election in each county, parish, or similar political subdivision, or the number of registered voters if registration of voters is uniformly required throughout the district or division, may be used.

(4) provide for a master jury wheel (or a device similar in purpose and function) into which the names of those randomly selected shall be placed. The plan shall fix a minimum number of names to be placed initially in the master jury wheel, which shall be at least one-half of 1 per centum of the total number of persons on the lists used as a source of names for the district or division; but if this number of names is believed to be cumbersome and unnecessary, the plan may fix a smaller number of names to be placed in the master wheel, but in no event less than one thousand. The chief judge of the district court, or such other district court judge as the plan may provide, may order additional names to be placed in the master jury wheel from time to time as necessary. The plan shall provide for periodic emptying and refilling of the master jury wheel at specified times, the interval for which shall not exceed four years.

(5)(A) except as provided in subparagraph (B), specify those groups of persons or occupational classes whose members shall, on individual request therefor, be excused from jury service. Such groups or classes shall be excused only if the district court finds, and the plan states, that jury service by such class or group would entail undue hardship or extreme inconvenience to the members thereof, and excuse of members thereof would not be inconsistent with sections 1861 and 1862 of this title.

(B) specify that volunteer safety personnel, upon individual request, shall be excused from jury service. For purposes of this subparagraph, the term "volunteer safety personnel" means individuals serving a public agency (as defined in section 1203(6) of title I of the Omnibus Crime Control and Safe Streets Act of 1968) in an official capacity, without compensation, as firefighters or members of a rescue squad or ambulance crew.

(6) specify that the following persons are barred from jury service on the ground that they are exempt: (A) members in active service in the Armed Forces of the United States; (B) members of the fire or police departments of any State,

the District of Columbia, any territory or possession of the United States, or any subdivision of a State, the District of Columbia, or such territory or possession; (C) public officers in the executive, legislative, or judicial branches of the Government of the United States, or of any State, the District of Columbia, any territory or possession of the United States, or any subdivision of a State, the District of Columbia, or such territory or possession, who are actively engaged in the performance of official duties.

(7) fix the time when the names drawn from the qualified jury wheel shall be disclosed to parties and to the public. If the plan permits these names to be made public, it may nevertheless permit the chief judge of the district court, or such other district court judge as the plan may provide, to keep these names confidential in any case where the interests of justice so require.

(8) specify the procedures to be followed by the clerk or jury commission in assigning persons whose names have been drawn from the qualified jury wheel to grand and petit jury panels.

(c) The initial plan shall be devised by each district court and transmitted to the reviewing panel specified in subsection (a) of this section within one hundred and twenty days of the date of enactment of the Jury Selection and Service Act of 1968. The panel shall approve or direct the modification of each plan so submitted within sixty days thereafter. Each plan or modification made at the direction of the panel shall become effective after approval at such time thereafter as the panel directs, in no event to exceed ninety days from the date of approval. Modifications made at the instance of the district court under subsection (a) of this section shall be effective at such time thereafter as the panel directs, in no event to exceed ninety days from the date of modification.

(d) State, local, and Federal officials having custody, possession, or control of voter registration lists, lists of actual voters, or other appropriate records shall make such lists and records available to the jury commission or clerks for inspection, reproduction, and copying at all reasonable times as the commission or clerk may deem necessary and proper for the performance of duties under this title. The district courts shall have jurisdiction upon application by the Attorney General of the United States to compel compliance with this subsection by appropriate process.

History of 28 U.S.C. §1863: June 25, 1948, ch. 646, 62 Stat. 952; Mar. 27, 1968, P.L. 90-274, §101, 82 Stat. 54; Apr. 6, 1972, P.L. 92-269, §2, 86 Stat. 117; Nov. 2, 1978, P.L. 95-572, §2(a), 92 Stat. 2453; Nov. 19, 1988, P.L. 100-702, §802(b), (c), 102 Stat. 4657, 4658; Oct. 29, 1992, P.L. 102-572, §401, 106 Stat. 4511.

See *Commentaries*, "Jury Selection," ch. 8-A, p. 673.

§1864. DRAWING OF NAMES FROM THE MASTER JURY WHEEL; COMPLETION OF JUROR QUALIFICATION FORM

(a) From time to time as directed by the district court, the clerk or a district judge shall draw at random from the master jury wheel the names of as many persons as may be required for jury service. The clerk or jury commission shall post a general notice for public review in the clerk's office and on the court's website explaining the process by which names are periodically and randomly drawn. The clerk or jury commission may, upon order of the court, prepare an alphabetical list of the names drawn from the master jury wheel. Any list so prepared shall not be disclosed to any person except pursuant to the district court plan or pursuant to section 1867 or 1868 of this title. The clerk or jury commission shall mail to every person whose name is drawn from the master wheel a juror qualification form accompanied by instructions to fill out and return the form, duly signed and sworn, to the clerk or jury commission by mail within ten days. If the person is unable to fill out the form, another shall do it for him, and shall indicate that he has done so and the reason therefor. In any case in which it appears that there is an omission, ambiguity, or error in a form, the clerk or jury commission shall return the form with instructions to the person to make such additions or corrections as may be necessary and to return the form to the clerk or jury commission within ten days. Any person who fails to return a completed juror qualification form as instructed may be summoned by the clerk or jury commission forthwith to appear before the clerk or jury commission to fill out a juror qualification form. A person summoned to appear because of failure to return a juror qualification form as instructed who personally appears and executes a juror qualification form before the clerk or jury commission may, at the discretion of the district court, except where his prior failure to execute and mail such form was willful, be entitled to receive for such appearance the same fees and travel allowances paid to jurors under section 1871 of this title. At the time of his appearance for jury service, any person may be required to fill out another juror qualification form in the presence of the jury commission or the clerk or[1] the court, at which time, in such cases as it appears warranted, the person may be questioned, but only with regard to his responses to questions contained on the form. Any information thus acquired by the clerk or jury commission may be noted on the juror qualification form and transmitted to the chief judge or such district court judge as the plan may provide.

(b) Any person summoned pursuant to subsection (a) of this section who fails to appear as directed shall be ordered by the district court forthwith to appear and show cause for his failure to comply with the summons. Any person who fails to appear pursuant to such order or who fails to show good cause for noncompliance with the summons may be fined not more than $1,000, imprisoned not more than three days, ordered to perform community service, or any combination thereof. Any person who willfully misrepresents a material fact on a juror qualification form for the purpose of avoiding or securing service as a juror may be fined not more than $1,000, imprisoned not more than three days, ordered to perform community service, or any combination thereof.

1. **Editor's note:** So in original. Probably should be "of."

History of 28 U.S.C. §1864: June 25, 1948, ch. 646, 62 Stat. 952; Mar. 27, 1968, P.L. 90-274, §101, 82 Stat. 57; Nov. 19, 1988, P.L. 100-702, §803(a), 102 Stat. 4658; Oct. 13, 2008, P.L. 110-406, §§5(a), 17(a), 122 Stat. 4292, 4295.

See *Commentaries*, "Jury Selection," ch. 8-A, p. 673.

§1865. QUALIFICATIONS FOR JURY SERVICE

(a) The chief judge of the district court, or such other district court judge as the plan may provide, on his initiative or upon recommendation of the clerk or jury commission, or the clerk under supervision of the court if the court's jury selection plan so authorizes, shall determine solely on the basis of information provided on the juror qualification form and other competent evidence whether a person is unqualified for, or exempt, or to be excused from jury service. The clerk shall enter such determination in the space provided on the juror qualification form and in any alphabetical list of names drawn from the master jury wheel. If a person did not appear in response to a summons, such fact shall be noted on said list.

(b) In making such determination the chief judge of the district court, or such other district court judge as the plan may provide, or the clerk if the court's jury selection plan so provides, shall deem any person qualified to serve on grand and petit juries in the district court unless he—

(1) is not a citizen of the United States eighteen years old who has resided for a period of one year within the judicial district;

(2) is unable to read, write, and understand the English language with a degree of proficiency sufficient to fill out satisfactorily the juror qualification form;

(3) is unable to speak the English language;

(4) is incapable, by reason of mental or physical infirmity, to render satisfactory jury service; or

(5) has a charge pending against him for the commission of, or has been convicted in a State or Federal court of record of, a crime punishable by imprisonment for more than one year and his civil rights have not been restored.

History of 28 U.S.C. §1865: June 25, 1948, ch. 646, 62 Stat. 952; Mar. 27, 1968, P.L. 90-274, §101, 82 Stat. 58; Apr. 6, 1972, P.L. 92-269, §1, 86 Stat. 117; Nov. 2, 1978, P.L. 95-572, §3(a), 92 Stat. 2453; Nov. 19, 1988, P.L. 100-702, §803(b), 102 Stat. 4658; Nov. 13, 2000, P.L. 106-518, §305, 114 Stat. 2418.

See *Commentaries*, "Jury Selection," ch. 8-A, p. 673.

§1866. SELECTION & SUMMONING OF JURY PANELS

(a) The jury commission, or in the absence thereof the clerk, shall maintain a qualified jury wheel and shall place in such wheel names of all persons drawn from the master jury wheel who are determined to be qualified as jurors and not exempt or excused pursuant to the district court plan. From time to time, the jury commission or the clerk shall draw at random from the qualified jury wheel such number of names of persons as may be required for assignment to grand and petit jury panels. The clerk or jury commission shall post a general notice for public review in the clerk's office and on the court's website explaining the process by which names are periodically and randomly drawn. The jury commission or the clerk shall prepare a separate list of names of persons assigned to each grand and petit jury panel.

(b) When the court orders a grand or petit jury to be drawn, the clerk or jury commission or their duly designated deputies shall issue summonses for the required number of jurors.

Each person drawn for jury service may be served personally, or by registered, certified, or first-class mail addressed to such person at his usual residence or business address.

If such service is made personally, the summons shall be delivered by the clerk or the jury commission or their duly designated deputies to the marshal who shall make such service.

If such service is made by mail, the summons may be served by the marshal or by the clerk, the jury commission or their duly designated deputies, who shall make affidavit of service and shall attach thereto any receipt from the addressee for a registered or certified summons.

(c) Except as provided in section 1865 of this title or in any jury selection plan provision adopted pursuant to paragraph (5) or (6) of section 1863(b) of this title, no person or class of persons shall be disqualified, excluded, excused, or exempt from service as jurors: Provided, That any person summoned for jury service may be (1) excused by the court, or by the clerk under supervision of the court if the court's jury selection plan so authorizes, upon a showing of undue hardship or extreme inconvenience, for such period as the court deems necessary, at the conclusion of which such person either shall be summoned again for jury service under subsections (b) and (c) of this section or, if the court's jury selection plan so provides, the name of such person shall be reinserted into the qualified jury wheel for selection pursuant to subsection (a) of this section, or (2) excluded by the court on the ground that such person may be unable to render impartial jury service or that his service as a juror would be likely to disrupt the proceedings, or (3) excluded upon peremptory challenge as provided by law, or (4) excluded pursuant to the procedure specified by law upon a challenge by any party for good cause shown, or (5) excluded upon determination by the court that his service as a juror would be likely to threaten the secrecy of the proceedings, or otherwise adversely affect the integrity of jury deliberations. No person shall be excluded under clause (5) of this subsection unless the judge, in open court, determines that such is warranted and that exclusion of the person will not be inconsistent with sections 1861 and 1862 of this title. The number of persons excluded under clause (5) of this subsection shall not exceed one per centum of the number of persons who return executed jury qualification forms during the period, specified in the plan, between two consecutive fillings of the master jury wheel. The names of persons excluded under clause (5) of this subsection, together with detailed explanations for the exclusions, shall be forwarded immediately to the judicial council of the circuit, which shall have the power to make any appropriate order, prospective or retroactive, to redress any misapplication of clause (5) of this subsection, but otherwise

exclusions effectuated under such clause shall not be subject to challenge under the provisions of this title. Any person excluded from a particular jury under clause (2), (3), or (4) of this subsection shall be eligible to sit on another jury if the basis for his initial exclusion would not be relevant to his ability to serve on such other jury.

(d) Whenever a person is disqualified, excused, exempt, or excluded from jury service, the jury commission or clerk shall note in the space provided on his juror qualification form or on the juror's card drawn from the qualified jury wheel the specific reason therefor.

(e) In any two-year period, no person shall be required to (1) serve or attend court for prospective service as a petit juror for a total of more than thirty days, except when necessary to complete service in a particular case, or (2) serve on more than one grand jury, or (3) serve as both a grand and petit juror.

(f) When there is an unanticipated shortage of available petit jurors drawn from the qualified jury wheel, the court may require the marshal to summon a sufficient number of petit jurors selected at random from the voter registration lists, lists of actual voters, or other lists specified in the plan, in a manner ordered by the court consistent with sections 1861 and 1862 of this title.

(g) Any person summoned for jury service who fails to appear as directed may be ordered by the district court to appear forthwith and show cause for failure to comply with the summons. Any person who fails to show good cause for noncompliance with a summons may be fined not more than $1,000, imprisoned not more than three days, ordered to perform community service, or any combination thereof.

History of 28 U.S.C. §1866: June 25, 1948, ch. 646, 62 Stat. 952; May 24, 1949, ch. 139, §96, 63 Stat. 103; Mar. 27, 1968, P.L. 90-274, §101, 82 Stat. 58; Dec. 11, 1970, P.L. 91-543, 84 Stat. 1408; Nov. 2, 1978, P.L. 95-572, §2(b), 92 Stat. 2453; Jan. 12, 1983, P.L. 97-463, §2, 96 Stat. 2531; Nov. 19, 1988, P.L. 100-702, §801, 102 Stat. 4657; Oct. 13, 2008, P.L. 110-406, §§4, 5(b), 17(b), 122 Stat. 4292, 4295.

See *Commentaries*, "Jury Selection," ch. 8-A, p. 673.

§1867. CHALLENGING COMPLIANCE WITH SELECTION PROCEDURES

(a) In criminal cases, before the voir dire examination begins, or within seven days after the defendant discovered or could have discovered, by the exercise of diligence, the grounds therefor, whichever is earlier, the defendant may move to dismiss the indictment or stay the proceedings against him on the ground of substantial failure to comply with the provisions of this title in selecting the grand or petit jury.

(b) In criminal cases, before the voir dire examination begins, or within seven days after the Attorney General of the United States discovered or could have discovered, by the exercise of diligence, the grounds therefor, whichever is earlier, the Attorney General may move to dismiss the indictment or stay the proceedings on the ground of substantial failure to comply with the provisions of this title in selecting the grand or petit jury.

(c) In civil cases, before the voir dire examination begins, or within seven days after the party discovered or could have discovered, by the exercise of diligence, the grounds therefor, whichever is earlier, any party may move to stay the proceedings on the ground of substantial failure to comply with the provisions of this title in selecting the petit jury.

(d) Upon motion filed under subsection (a), (b), or (c) of this section, containing a sworn statement of facts which, if true, would constitute a substantial failure to comply with the provisions of this title, the moving party shall be entitled to present in support of such motion the testimony of the jury commission or clerk, if available, any relevant records and papers not public or otherwise available used by the jury commissioner or clerk, and any other relevant evidence. If the court determines that there has been a substantial failure to comply with the provisions of this title in selecting the grand jury, the court shall stay the proceedings pending the selection of a grand jury in conformity with this title or dismiss the indictment, whichever is appropriate. If the court determines that there has been a substantial failure to comply with the provisions of this title in selecting the petit jury, the court shall stay the proceedings pending the selection of a petit jury in conformity with this title.

(e) The procedures prescribed by this section shall be the exclusive means by which a person accused of a Federal crime, the Attorney General of the United States or a party in a civil case may challenge any jury on the ground that such jury was not selected in conformity with the provisions of this title. Nothing in this section shall preclude any person or the United States from pursuing any other remedy, civil or criminal, which may be available for the vindication or enforcement of any law prohibiting discrimination on account of race, color, religion, sex, national origin or economic status in the selection of persons for service on grand or petit juries.

(f) The contents of records or papers used by the jury commission or clerk in connection with the jury selection process shall not be disclosed, except pursuant to the district court plan or as may be necessary in the preparation or presentation of a motion under subsection (a), (b), or (c) of this section, until after the master jury wheel has been emptied and refilled pursuant to section 1863(b)(4) of this title and all persons selected to serve as jurors before the master wheel was emptied have completed such service. The parties in a case shall be allowed to inspect, reproduce, and copy such records or papers at all reasonable times during the preparation and pendency of such a motion. Any person who discloses the contents of any record or paper in violation of this subsection may be fined not more than $1,000 or imprisoned not more than one year, or both.

History of 28 U.S.C. §1867: June 25, 1948, ch. 646, 62 Stat. 953; Sept. 2, 1957, P.L. 85-259, 71 Stat. 583; Mar. 27, 1968, P.L. 90-274, §101, 82 Stat. 59.

See *Commentaries*, "Jury Selection," ch. 8-A, p. 673.

§1868. MAINTENANCE & INSPECTION OF RECORDS

After the master jury wheel is emptied and refilled pursuant to section 1863(b)(4) of this title, and after all persons selected to serve as jurors before the master wheel was emptied have completed such service, all records and papers compiled and maintained by the jury commission or clerk before the master wheel was emptied shall be preserved in the custody of the clerk for four years or for such longer period as may be ordered by a court, and shall be available for public inspection for the purpose of determining the validity of the selection of any jury.

History of 28 U.S.C. §1868: June 25, 1948, ch. 646, 62 Stat. 953; Mar. 27, 1968, P.L. 90-274, §101, 82 Stat. 60.

See *Commentaries*, "Jury Selection," ch. 8-A, p. 673.

§1869. DEFINITIONS

For purposes of this chapter—

(a) "clerk" and "clerk of the court" shall mean the clerk of the district court of the United States, any authorized deputy clerk, and any other person authorized by the court to assist the clerk in the performance of functions under this chapter;

(b) "chief judge" shall mean the chief judge of any district court of the United States;

(c) "voter registration lists" shall mean the official records maintained by State or local election officials of persons registered to vote in either the most recent State or the most recent Federal general election, or, in the case of a State or political subdivision thereof that does not require registration as a prerequisite to voting, other official lists of persons qualified to vote in such election. The term shall also include the list of eligible voters maintained by any Federal examiner pursuant to the Voting Rights Act of 1965 where the names on such list have not been included on the official registration lists or other official lists maintained by the appropriate State or local officials. With respect to the districts of Guam and the Virgin Islands, "voter registration lists" shall mean the official records maintained by territorial election officials of persons registered to vote in the most recent territorial general election;

(d) "lists of actual voters" shall mean the official lists of persons actually voting in either the most recent State or the most recent Federal general election;

(e) "division" shall mean: (1) one or more statutory divisions of a judicial district; or (2) in statutory divisions that contain more than one place of holding court, or in judicial districts where there are no statutory divisions, such counties, parishes, or similar political subdivisions surrounding the places where court is held as the district court plan shall determine: *Provided*, That each county, parish, or similar political subdivision shall be included in some such division;

(f) "district court of the United States", "district court", and "court" shall mean any district court established by chapter 5 of this title, and any court which is created by Act of Congress in a territory and is invested with any jurisdiction of a district court established by chapter 5 of this title;

(g) "jury wheel" shall include any device or system similar in purpose or function, such as a properly programed[1] electronic data processing system or device;

(h) "juror qualification form" shall mean a form prescribed by the Administrative Office of the United States Courts and approved by the Judicial Conference of the United States, which shall elicit the name, address, age, race, occupation, education, length of residence within the judicial district, distance from residence to place of holding court, prior jury service, and citizenship of a potential juror, and whether he should be excused or exempted from jury service, has any physical or mental infirmity impairing his capacity to serve as juror, is able to read, write, speak, and understand the English language, has pending against him any charge for the commission of a State or Federal criminal offense punishable by imprisonment for more than one year, or has been convicted in any State or Federal court of record of a crime punishable by imprisonment for more than one year and has not had his civil rights restored. The form shall request, but not require, any other information not inconsistent with the provisions of this title and required by the district court plan in the interests of the sound administration of justice. The form shall also elicit the sworn statement that his responses are true to the best of his knowledge. Notarization shall not be required. The form shall contain words clearly informing the person that the furnishing of any information with respect to his religion, national origin, or economic status is not a prerequisite to his qualification for jury service, that such information need not be furnished if the person finds it objectionable to do so, and that information concerning race is required solely to enforce nondiscrimination in jury selection and has no bearing on an individual's qualification for jury service.

(i) "public officer" shall mean a person who is either elected to public office or who is directly appointed by a person elected to public office;

(j) "undue hardship or extreme inconvenience", as a basis for excuse from immediate jury service under section 1866(c)(1) of this chapter, shall mean great distance, either in miles or traveltime, from the place of holding court, grave illness in the family or any other emergency which outweighs in immediacy and urgency the obligation to serve as a juror when summoned, or any other factor which the court determines to constitute an undue hardship or to create an extreme inconvenience to the juror; and in addition, in situations where it is anticipated that a trial or grand jury proceeding may require more than thirty days of service, the court may consider, as a further basis for temporary excuse, severe economic hardship to an employer which would result from the absence of a key employee during the period of such service; and

(k) "jury summons" shall mean a summons issued by a clerk of court, jury commission, or their duly designated depu-

ties, containing either a preprinted or stamped seal of court, and containing the name of the issuing clerk imprinted in preprinted, type, or facsimile manner on the summons or the envelopes transmitting the summons.

1. **Editor's note:** So in original. Probably should be "programmed."

History of 28 U.S.C. §1869: June 25, 1948, ch. 646, 62 Stat. 953; Oct. 16, 1963, P.L. 88-139, §2, 77 Stat. 248; Mar. 27, 1968, P.L. 90-274, §101, 82 Stat. 61; July 29, 1970, P.L. 91-358, §172(b), 84 Stat. 590; Sept. 29, 1972, P.L. 92-437, §1, 86 Stat. 740; Nov. 2, 1978, P.L. 95-572, §§3(b), 4, 92 Stat. 2453; Nov. 6, 1978, P.L. 95-598, §243, 92 Stat. 2671; Nov. 14, 1986, P.L. 99-650, §3, 100 Stat. 3641; Nov. 19, 1988, P.L. 100-702, §§802(a), 804, 102 Stat. 4657, 4658; Oct. 13, 2008, P.L. 110-406, §5(c), 122 Stat. 4292.

See *Commentaries*, "Jury Selection," ch. 8-A, p. 673.

§1870. CHALLENGES

In civil cases, each party shall be entitled to three peremptory challenges. Several defendants or several plaintiffs may be considered as a single party for the purposes of making challenges, or the court may allow additional peremptory challenges and permit them to be exercised separately or jointly.

All challenges for cause or favor, whether to the array or panel or to individual jurors, shall be determined by the court.

History of 28 U.S.C. §1870: June 25, 1948, ch. 646, 62 Stat. 953; Sept. 16, 1959, P.L. 86-282, 73 Stat. 565.

See *Commentaries*, "Jury Selection," ch. 8-A, p. 673.

§1871. FEES

(a) Grand and petit jurors in district courts appearing pursuant to this chapter shall be paid the fees and allowances provided by this section. The requisite fees and allowances shall be disbursed on the certificate of the clerk of court in accordance with the procedure established by the Director of the Administrative Office of the United States Courts. Attendance fees for extended service under subsection (b) of this section shall be certified by the clerk only upon the order of a district judge.

(b)(1) A juror shall be paid an attendance fee of $40 per day for actual attendance at the place of trial or hearing. A juror shall also be paid the attendance fee for the time necessarily occupied in going to and returning from such place at the beginning and end of such service or at any time during such service.

(2) A petit juror required to attend more than ten days in hearing one case may be paid, in the discretion of the trial judge, an additional fee, not exceeding $10 more than the attendance fee, for each day in excess of ten days on which he is required to hear such case.

(3) A grand juror required to attend more than forty-five days of actual service may be paid, in the discretion of the district judge in charge of the particular grand jury, an additional fee, not exceeding $10 more than the attendance fee, for each day in excess of forty-five days of actual service.

(4) A grand or petit juror required to attend more than ten days of actual service may be paid, in the discretion of the judge, the appropriate fees at the end of the first ten days and at the end of every ten days of service thereafter.

(5) Certification of additional attendance fees may be ordered by the judge to be made effective commencing on the first day of extended service, without reference to the date of such certification.

(c)(1) A travel allowance not to exceed the maximum rate per mile that the Director of the Administrative Office of the United States Courts has prescribed pursuant to section 604(a)(7) of this title for payment to supporting court personnel in travel status using privately owned automobiles shall be paid to each juror, regardless of the mode of transportation actually employed. The prescribed rate shall be paid for the distance necessarily traveled to and from a juror's residence by the shortest practical route in going to and returning from the place of service. Actual mileage in full at the prescribed rate is payable at the beginning and at the end of a juror's term of service.

(2) The Director shall promulgate rules regulating interim travel allowances to jurors. Distances traveled to and from court should coincide with the shortest practical route.

(3) Toll charges for toll roads, bridges, tunnels, and ferries shall be paid in full to the juror incurring such charges. In the discretion of the court, reasonable parking fees may be paid to the juror incurring such fees upon presentation of a valid parking receipt. Parking fees shall not be included in any tabulation of mileage cost allowances.

(4) Any juror who travels to district court pursuant to summons in an area outside of the contiguous forty-eight States of the United States shall be paid the travel expenses provided under this section, or actual reasonable transportation expenses subject to the discretion of the district judge or clerk of court as circumstances indicate, exercising due regard for the mode of transportation, the availability of alternative modes, and the shortest practical route between residence and court.

(5) A grand juror who travels to district court pursuant to a summons may be paid the travel expenses provided under this section or, under guidelines established by the Judicial Conference, the actual reasonable costs of travel by aircraft when travel by other means is not feasible and when certified by the chief judge of the district court in which the grand juror serves.

(d)(1) A subsistence allowance covering meals and lodging of jurors shall be established from time to time by the Director of the Administrative Office of the United States Courts pursuant to section 604(a)(7) of this title, except that such allowance shall not exceed the allowance for supporting court personnel in travel status in the same geographical area. Claims for such allowance shall not require itemization.

(2) A subsistence allowance shall be paid to a juror when an overnight stay is required at the place of holding court, and for the time necessarily spent in traveling to and from the place of attendance if an overnight stay is required.

(3) A subsistence allowance for jurors serving in district courts outside of the contiguous forty-eight States of the United States shall be allowed at a rate not to exceed that per diem allowance which is paid to supporting court personnel in travel status in those areas where the Director of the Administrative Office of the United States Courts has prescribed an increased per diem fee pursuant to section 604(a)(7) of this title.

(e) During any period in which a jury is ordered to be kept together and not to separate, the actual cost of subsistence shall be paid upon the order of the court in lieu of the subsistence allowances payable under subsection (d) of this section. Such allowance for the jurors ordered to be kept separate or sequestered shall include the cost of meals, lodging, and other expenditures ordered in the discretion of the court for their convenience and comfort.

(f) A juror who must necessarily use public transportation in traveling to and from court, the full cost of which is not met by the transportation expenses allowable under subsection (c) of this section on account of the short distance traveled in miles, may be paid, in the discretion of the court, the actual reasonable expense of such public transportation, pursuant to the methods of payment provided by this section. Jurors who are required to remain at the court beyond the normal business closing hour for deliberation or for any other reason may be transported to their homes, or to temporary lodgings where such lodgings are ordered by the court, in a manner directed by the clerk and paid from funds authorized under this section.

(g) The Director of the Administrative Office of the United States Courts shall promulgate such regulations as may be necessary to carry out his authority under this section.

History of 28 U.S.C. §1871: June 25, 1948, ch. 646, 62 Stat. 953; May 24, 1949, ch. 139, §97, 63 Stat. 103; July 14, 1949, ch. 333, 63 Stat. 411; Sept. 7, 1957, P.L. 85-299, 71 Stat. 618; Sept. 2, 1965, P.L. 89-165, 79 Stat. 645; Mar. 27, 1968, P.L. 90-274, §102(a), 82 Stat. 62; Nov. 2, 1978, P.L. 95-572, §5, 92 Stat. 2454; Dec. 1, 1990, P.L. 101-650, §314(b), 104 Stat. 5115; Oct. 29, 1992, P.L. 102-572, §402, 106 Stat. 4511; Oct. 13, 2008, P.L. 110-406, §3, 122 Stat. 4292.

See *Commentaries*, "Jury Selection," ch. 8-A, p. 673.

§1872. ISSUES OF FACT IN SUPREME COURT

In all original actions at law in the Supreme Court against citizens of the United States, issues of fact shall be tried by a jury.

History of 28 U.S.C. §1872: June 25, 1948, ch. 646, 62 Stat. 953.

See *Commentaries*, "Jury Selection," ch. 8-A, p. 673.

§1873. ADMIRALTY & MARITIME CASES

In any case of admiralty and maritime jurisdiction relating to any matter of contract or tort arising upon or concerning any vessel of twenty tons or upward, enrolled and licensed for the coasting trade, and employed in the business of commerce and navigation between places in different states upon the lakes and navigable waters connecting said lakes, the trial of all issues of fact shall be by jury if either party demands it.

History of 28 U.S.C. §1873: June 25, 1948, ch. 646, 62 Stat. 953.

See *Commentaries*, "Jury Selection," ch. 8-A, p. 673.

§1874. ACTIONS ON BONDS & SPECIALTIES

In all actions to recover the forfeiture annexed to any articles of agreement, covenant, bond, or other specialty, wherein the forfeiture, breach, or nonperformance appears by default or confession of the defendant, the court shall render judgment for the plaintiff for such amount as is due. If the sum is uncertain, it shall, upon request of either party, be assessed by a jury.

History of 28 U.S.C. §1874: June 25, 1948, ch. 646, 62 Stat. 953.

See *Commentaries*, "Jury Selection," ch. 8-A, p. 673.

§1875. PROTECTION OF JURORS' EMPLOYMENT

(a) No employer shall discharge, threaten to discharge, intimidate, or coerce any permanent employee by reason of such employee's jury service, or the attendance or scheduled attendance in connection with such service, in any court of the United States.

(b) Any employer who violates the provisions of this section—

(1) shall be liable for damages for any loss of wages or other benefits suffered by an employee by reason of such violation;

(2) may be enjoined from further violations of this section and ordered to provide other appropriate relief, including but not limited to the reinstatement of any employee discharged by reason of his jury service; and

(3) shall be subject to a civil penalty of not more than $5,000 for each violation as to each employee, and may be ordered to perform community service.

(c) Any individual who is reinstated to a position of employment in accordance with the provisions of this section shall be considered as having been on furlough or leave of absence during his period of jury service, shall be reinstated to his position of employment without loss of seniority, and shall be entitled to participate in insurance or other benefits offered by the employer pursuant to established rules and practices relating to employees on furlough or leave of absence in effect with the employer at the time such individual entered upon jury service.

(d)(1) An individual claiming that his employer has violated the provisions of this section may make application to the district court for the district in which such employer maintains a place of business and the court shall, upon finding probable merit in such claim, appoint counsel to represent such individual in any action in the district court necessary to the resolution of such claim. Such counsel shall be compensated and necessary expenses repaid to the extent provided by section 3006A of title 18, United States Code.

(2) In any action or proceeding under this section, the court may award a prevailing employee who brings such action by retained counsel a reasonable attorney's fee as part of the costs. The court may tax a defendant employer, as costs payable to the court, the attorney fees and expenses incurred on behalf of a prevailing employee, where such costs were expended by the court pursuant to paragraph (1) of this subsection. The court may award a prevailing employer a reasonable attorney's fee as part of the costs only if the court finds that the action is frivolous, vexatious, or brought in bad faith.

History of 28 U.S.C. §1875: Nov. 2, 1978, P.L. 95-572, §6(a)(1), 92 Stat. 2456; Jan. 12, 1983, P.L. 97-463, §1, 96 Stat. 2531; Oct. 13, 2008, P.L. 110-406, §19, 122 Stat. 4295.

See *Commentaries*, "Jury Selection," ch. 8-A, p. 673.

§1876. TRIAL BY JURY IN THE COURT OF INTERNATIONAL TRADE

(a) In any civil action in the Court of International Trade which is to be tried before a jury, the jury shall be selected in accordance with the provisions of this chapter and under the procedures set forth in the jury selection plan of the district court for the judicial district in which the case is to be tried.

(b) Whenever the Court of International Trade conducts a jury trial—

(1) the clerk of the district court for the judicial district in which the Court of International Trade is sitting, or an authorized deputy clerk, shall act as clerk of the Court of International Trade for the purposes of selecting and summoning the jury;

(2) the qualifications for jurors shall be the same as those established by section 1865(b) of this title for jurors in the district courts of the United States;

(3) each party shall be entitled to challenge jurors in accordance with section 1870 of this title; and

(4) jurors shall be compensated in accordance with section 1871 of this title.

History of 28 U.S.C. §1876: Oct. 10, 1980, P.L. 96-417, §302(a), 94 Stat. 1739.

See *Commentaries*, "Jury Selection," ch. 8-A, p. 673.

§1877. PROTECTION OF JURORS

(a) Subject to the provisions of this section and title 5 of the United States Code, subchapter 1 of chapter 81, title 5, United States Code, applies to a Federal grand or petit juror, except that entitlement to disability compensation payments does not commence until the day after the date of termination of service as a juror.

(b) In administering this section with respect to a juror covered by this section—

(1) a juror is deemed to receive monthly pay at the minimum rate for grade GS-2 of the General Schedule unless his actual pay as a Government employee while serving on court leave is higher, in which case monthly pay is determined in accordance with section 8114 of title 5, United States Code, and

(2) performance of duty as a juror includes that time when a juror is (A) in attendance at court pursuant to a summons, (B) in deliberation, (C) sequestered by order of a judge, or (D) at a site, by order of the court, for the taking of a view.

History of 28 U.S.C. §1877: Jan. 12, 1983, P.L. 97-463, §3(1), 96 Stat. 2531.

See *Commentaries*, "Jury Selection," ch. 8-A, p. 673.

§1878. OPTIONAL USE OF A ONE-STEP SUMMONING & QUALIFICATION PROCEDURE

(a) At the option of each district court, jurors may be summoned and qualified in a single procedure, if the court's jury selection plan so authorizes, in lieu of the two separate procedures otherwise provided for by this chapter. Courts shall ensure that a one-step summoning and qualification procedure conducted under this section does not violate the policies and objectives set forth in sections 1861 and 1862 of this title.

(b) Jury selection conducted under this section shall be subject to challenge under section 1867 of this title for substantial failure to comply with the provisions of this title in selecting the jury. However, no challenge under section 1867 of this title shall lie solely on the basis that a jury was selected in accordance with a one-step summoning and qualification procedure authorized by this section.

History of 28 U.S.C. §1878: Nov. 19, 1988, P.L. 100-702, §805(a), 102 Stat. 4658; Oct. 29, 1992, P.L. 102-572, §403(a), 106 Stat. 4512.

See *Commentaries*, "Jury Selection," ch. 8-A, p. 673.

CHAPTER 123. FEES & COSTS

§1911. SUPREME COURT

The Supreme Court may fix the fees to be charged by its clerk.

The fees of the clerk, cost of serving process, and other necessary disbursements incidental to any case before the court, may be taxed against the litigants as the court directs.

History of 28 U.S.C. §1911: June 25, 1948, ch. 646, 62 Stat. 954.

§1912. DAMAGES & COSTS ON AFFIRMANCE

Where a judgment is affirmed by the Supreme Court or a court of appeals, the court in its discretion may adjudge to the prevailing party just damages for his delay, and single or double costs.

History of 28 U.S.C. §1912: June 25, 1948, ch. 646, 62 Stat. 954.

§1913. COURTS OF APPEALS

The fees and costs to be charged and collected in each court of appeals shall be prescribed from time to time by the Judicial Conference of the United States. Such fees and costs shall be reasonable and uniform in all the circuits.

History of 28 U.S.C. §1913: June 25, 1948, ch. 646, 62 Stat. 954.

§1914. DISTRICT COURT; FILING & MISCELLANEOUS FEES; RULES OF COURT

(a) The clerk of each district court shall require the parties instituting any civil action, suit or proceeding in such

court, whether by original process, removal or otherwise, to pay a filing fee of $350, except that on application for a writ of habeas corpus the filing fee shall be $5.

(b) The clerk shall collect from the parties such additional fees only as are prescribed by the Judicial Conference of the United States.

(c) Each district court by rule or standing order may require advance payment of fees.

History of 28 U.S.C. §1914: June 25, 1948, ch. 646, 62 Stat. 954; Nov. 6, 1978, P.L. 95-598, §244, 92 Stat. 2671; June 19, 1986, P.L. 99-336, §4(a), 100 Stat. 637; Oct. 18, 1986, P.L. 99-500, §101(b) [§407(a)], 100 Stat. 1783-39, 1783-64; Oct. 30, 1986, P.L. 99-591, §101(b) [§407(a)], 100 Stat. 3341-39, 3341-64; Oct. 19, 1996, P.L. 104-317, §401(a), 110 Stat. 3853; Dec. 8, 2004, P.L. 108-447, §307(a), 118 Stat. 2895; Feb. 8, 2006, P.L. 109-171, §10001(a), 120 Stat. 183.

§1915. PROCEEDINGS IN FORMA PAUPERIS

(a)(1) Subject to subsection (b), any court of the United States may authorize the commencement, prosecution or defense of any suit, action or proceeding, civil or criminal, or appeal therein, without prepayment of fees or security therefor, by a person who submits an affidavit that includes a statement of all assets such prisoner possesses that the person is unable to pay such fees or give security therefor. Such affidavit shall state the nature of the action, defense or appeal and affiant's belief that the person is entitled to redress.

(2) A prisoner seeking to bring a civil action or appeal a judgment in a civil action or proceeding without prepayment of fees or security therefor, in addition to filing the affidavit filed under paragraph (1), shall submit a certified copy of the trust fund account statement (or institutional equivalent) for the prisoner for the 6-month period immediately preceding the filing of the complaint or notice of appeal, obtained from the appropriate official of each prison at which the prisoner is or was confined.

(3) An appeal may not be taken in forma pauperis if the trial court certifies in writing that it is not taken in good faith.

(b)(1) Notwithstanding subsection (a), if a prisoner brings a civil action or files an appeal in forma pauperis, the prisoner shall be required to pay the full amount of a filing fee. The court shall assess and, when funds exist, collect, as a partial payment of any court fees required by law, an initial partial filing fee of 20 percent of the greater of—

(A) the average monthly deposits to the prisoner's account; or

(B) the average monthly balance in the prisoner's account for the 6-month period immediately preceding the filing of the complaint or notice of appeal.

(2) After payment of the initial partial filing fee, the prisoner shall be required to make monthly payments of 20 percent of the preceding month's income credited to the prisoner's account. The agency having custody of the prisoner shall forward payments from the prisoner's account to the clerk of the court each time the amount in the account exceeds $10 until the filing fees are paid.

(3) In no event shall the filing fee collected exceed the amount of fees permitted by statute for the commencement of a civil action or an appeal of a civil action or criminal judgment.

(4) In no event shall a prisoner be prohibited from bringing a civil action or appealing a civil or criminal judgment for the reason that the prisoner has no assets and no means by which to pay the initial partial filing fee.

(c) Upon the filing of an affidavit in accordance with subsections (a) and (b) and the prepayment of any partial filing fee as may be required under subsection (b), the court may direct payment by the United States of the expenses of (1) printing the record on appeal in any civil or criminal case, if such printing is required by the appellate court; (2) preparing a transcript of proceedings before a United States magistrate judge in any civil or criminal case, if such transcript is required by the district court, in the case of proceedings conducted under section 636(b) of this title or under section 3401(b) of title 18, United States Code; and (3) printing the record on appeal if such printing is required by the appellate court, in the case of proceedings conducted pursuant to section 636(c) of this title. Such expenses shall be paid when authorized by the Director of the Administrative Office of the United States Courts.

(d) The officers of the court shall issue and serve all process, and perform all duties in such cases. Witnesses shall attend as in other cases, and the same remedies shall be available as are provided for by law in other cases.

(e)(1) The court may request an attorney to represent any person unable to afford counsel.

(2) Notwithstanding any filing fee, or any portion thereof, that may have been paid, the court shall dismiss the case at any time if the court determines that—

(A) the allegation of poverty is untrue; or

(B) the action or appeal—

(i) is frivolous or malicious;

(ii) fails to state a claim on which relief may be granted; or

(iii) seeks monetary relief against a defendant who is immune from such relief.

(f)(1) Judgment may be rendered for costs at the conclusion of the suit or action as in other proceedings, but the United States shall not be liable for any of the costs thus incurred. If the United States has paid the cost of a stenographic transcript or printed record for the prevailing party, the same shall be taxed in favor of the United States.

(2)(A) If the judgment against a prisoner includes the payment of costs under this subsection, the prisoner shall be required to pay the full amount of the costs ordered.

(B) The prisoner shall be required to make payments for costs under this subsection in the same manner as is provided for filing fees under subsection (a)(2).

(C) In no event shall the costs collected exceed the amount of the costs ordered by the court.

(g) In no event shall a prisoner bring a civil action or appeal a judgment in a civil action or proceeding under this section if the prisoner has, on 3 or more prior occasions, while incarcerated or detained in any facility, brought an action or appeal in a court of the United States that was dismissed on the grounds that it is frivolous, malicious, or fails to state a claim upon which relief may be granted, unless the prisoner is under imminent danger of serious physical injury.

(h) As used in this section, the term "prisoner" means any person incarcerated or detained in any facility who is accused of, convicted of, sentenced for, or adjudicated delinquent for, violations of criminal law or the terms and conditions of parole, probation, pretrial release, or diversionary program.

History of 28 U.S.C. §1915: June 25, 1948, ch. 646, 62 Stat. 954; May 24, 1949, ch. 139, §98, 63 Stat. 104; Oct. 31, 1951, ch. 655, §51(b), (c), 65 Stat. 727; Sept. 21, 1959, P.L. 86-320, 73 Stat. 590; Oct. 10, 1979, P.L. 96-82, §6, 93 Stat. 645; Apr. 26, 1996, P.L. 104-134, §101(a) [§804(a), (c)-(e)], 110 Stat. 1321-73 to 1321-75; May 2, 1996, P.L. 104-140, §1(a), 110 Stat. 1327.

See *Commentaries*, "Pleading & Motion Practice," ch. 1-B, p. 7.

§1915A. SCREENING

(a) Screening.—The court shall review, before docketing, if feasible or, in any event, as soon as practicable after docketing, a complaint in a civil action in which a prisoner seeks redress from a governmental entity or officer or employee of a governmental entity.

(b) Grounds for dismissal.—On review, the court shall identify cognizable claims or dismiss the complaint, or any portion of the complaint, if the complaint—

(1) is frivolous, malicious, or fails to state a claim upon which relief may be granted; or

(2) seeks monetary relief from a defendant who is immune from such relief.

(c) Definition.—As used in this section, the term "prisoner" means any person incarcerated or detained in any facility who is accused of, convicted of, sentenced for, or adjudicated delinquent for, violations of criminal law or the terms and conditions of parole, probation, pretrial release, or diversionary program.

History of 28 U.S.C. §1915A: Apr. 26, 1996, P.L. 104-134, §101(a) [§805(a)], 110 Stat. 1321-75; May 2, 1996, P.L. 104-140, §1(a), 110 Stat. 1327.

§1916. SEAMEN'S SUITS

In all courts of the United States, seamen may institute and prosecute suits and appeals in their own names and for their own benefit for wages or salvage or the enforcement of laws enacted for their health or safety without prepaying fees or costs or furnishing security therefor.

History of 28 U.S.C. §1916: June 25, 1948, ch. 646, 62 Stat. 955.

§1917. DISTRICT COURTS; FEE ON FILING NOTICE OF OR PETITION FOR APPEAL

Upon the filing of any separate or joint notice of appeal or application for appeal or upon the receipt of any order allowing, or notice of the allowance of, an appeal or of a writ of certiorari $5 shall be paid to the clerk of the district court, by the appellant or petitioner.

History of 28 U.S.C. §1917: June 25, 1948, ch. 646, 62 Stat. 955.

§1918. DISTRICT COURTS; FINES, FORFEITURES & CRIMINAL PROCEEDINGS

(a) Costs shall be included in any judgment, order, or decree rendered against any person for the violation of an Act of Congress in which a civil fine or forfeiture of property is provided for.

(b) Whenever any conviction for any offense not capital is obtained in a district court, the court may order that the defendant pay the costs of prosecution.

History of 28 U.S.C. §1918: June 25, 1948, ch. 646, 62 Stat. 955.

§1919. DISMISSAL FOR LACK OF JURISDICTION

Whenever any action or suit is dismissed in any district court, the Court of International Trade, or the Court of Federal Claims for want of jurisdiction, such court may order the payment of just costs.

History of 28 U.S.C. §1919: June 25, 1948, ch. 646, 62 Stat. 955; Oct. 10, 1980, P.L. 96-417, §510, 94 Stat. 1743; Oct. 29, 1992, P.L. 102-572, §908(a), (b)(1), 106 Stat. 4519.

§1920. TAXATION OF COSTS

A judge or clerk of any court of the United States may tax as costs the following:

(1) Fees of the clerk and marshal;

(2) Fees for printed or electronically recorded transcripts necessarily obtained for use in the case;

(3) Fees and disbursements for printing and witnesses;

(4) Fees for exemplification and the costs of making copies of any materials where the copies are necessarily obtained for use in the case;

(5) Docket fees under section 1923 of this title;

(6) Compensation of court appointed experts, compensation of interpreters, and salaries, fees, expenses, and costs of special interpretation services under section 1828 of this title.

A bill of costs shall be filed in the case and, upon allowance, included in the judgment or decree.

History of 28 U.S.C. §1920: June 25, 1948, ch. 646, 62 Stat. 955; Oct. 28, 1978, P.L. 95-539, §7, 92 Stat. 2044; Oct. 13, 2008, P.L. 110-406, §6, 122 Stat. 4292.

See *Commentaries*, "Taxable Costs," ch. 9-D, p. 761.

§1921. UNITED STATES MARSHAL'S FEES

(a)(1) The United States marshals or deputy marshals shall routinely collect, and a court may tax as costs, fees for the following:

(A) Serving a writ of possession, partition, execution, attachment in rem, or libel in admiralty, warrant, attachment, summons, complaints, or any other writ, order or process in any case or proceeding.

(B) Serving a subpoena or summons for a witness or appraiser.

(C) Forwarding any writ, order, or process to another judicial district for service.

(D) The preparation of any notice of sale, proclamation in admiralty, or other public notice or bill of sale.

(E) The keeping of attached property (including boats, vessels, or other property attached or libeled), actual expenses incurred, such as storage, moving, boat hire, or other special transportation, watchmen's or keepers' fees, insurance, and an hourly rate, including overtime, for each deputy marshal required for special services, such as guarding, inventorying, and moving.

(F) Copies of writs or other papers furnished at the request of any party.

(G) Necessary travel in serving or endeavoring to serve any process, writ, or order, except in the District of Columbia, with mileage to be computed from the place where service is returnable to the place of service or endeavor.

(H) Overtime expenses incurred by deputy marshals in the course of serving or executing civil process.

(2) The marshals shall collect, in advance, a deposit to cover the initial expenses for special services required under paragraph (1)(E), and periodically thereafter such amounts as may be necessary to pay such expenses until the litigation is concluded. This paragraph applies to all private litigants, including seamen proceeding pursuant to section 1916 of this title.

(3) For purposes of paragraph (1)(G), if two or more services or endeavors, or if an endeavor and a service, are made in behalf of the same party in the same case on the same trip, mileage shall be computed to the place of service or endeavor which is most remote from the place where service is returnable, adding thereto any additional mileage traveled in serving or endeavoring to serve in behalf of the party. If two or more writs of any kind, required to be served in behalf of the same party on the same person in the same case or proceeding, may be served at the same time, mileage on only one such writ shall be collected.

(b) The Attorney General shall from time to time prescribe by regulation the fees to be taxed and collected under subsection (a). Such fees shall, to the extent practicable, reflect the actual and reasonable cost of the service provided.

(c)(1) The United States Marshals Service shall collect a commission of 3 percent of the first $1,000 collected and 1 1/2 percent on the excess of any sum over $1,000, for seizing or levying on property (including seizures in admiralty), disposing of such property by sale, setoff, or otherwise, and receiving and paying over money, except that the amount of commission shall be within the range set by the Attorney General. if[1] the property is not disposed of by marshal's sale, the commission shall be in such amount, within the range set by the Attorney General, as may be allowed by the court. In any case in which the vessel or other property is sold by a public auctioneer, or by some party other than a marshal or deputy marshal, the commission authorized under this subsection shall be reduced by the amount paid to such auctioneer or other party. This subsection applies to any judicially ordered sale or execution sale, without regard to whether the judicial order of sale constitutes a seizure or levy within the meaning of State law. This subsection shall not apply to any seizure, forfeiture, sale, or other disposition of property pursuant to the applicable provisions of law amended by the Comprehensive Forfeiture Act of 1984 (98 Stat. 2040).

(2) The Attorney General shall prescribe from time to time regulations which establish a minimum and maximum amount for the commission collected under paragraph (1).

(d) The United States marshals may require a deposit to cover the fees and expenses prescribed under this section.

(e) Notwithstanding section 3302 of title 31, the United States Marshals Service is authorized, to the extent provided in advance in appropriations Acts—

(1) to credit to such Service's appropriation all fees, commissions, and expenses collected by such Service for—

(A) the service of civil process, including complaints, summonses, subpoenas, and similar process; and

(B) seizures, levies, and sales associated with judicial orders of execution; and

(2) to use such credited amounts for the purpose of carrying out such activities.

1. **Editor's note:** So in original. Probably should be capitalized.

History of 28 U.S.C. §1921: June 25, 1948, ch. 646, 62 Stat. 955; Sept. 9, 1950, ch. 937, 64 Stat. 824; Aug. 31, 1962, P.L. 87-621, §1, 76 Stat. 417; Nov. 10, 1986, P.L. 99-646, §39(a), 100 Stat. 3600; Nov. 18, 1988, P.L. 100-690, §7608(c), 102 Stat. 4515; Nov. 29, 1990, P.L. 101-647, §1212, 104 Stat. 4833.

See *Commentaries*, "Taxable Costs," ch. 9-D, p. 761.

§1922. WITNESS FEES BEFORE UNITED STATES MAGISTRATE JUDGES

The fees of more than four witnesses shall not be taxed against the United States, in the examination of any criminal case before a United States magistrate judge, unless their materiality and importance are first approved and certified to by the United States attorney for the district in which the examination is had.

History of 28 U.S.C. §1922: June 25, 1948, ch. 646, 62 Stat. 956; Oct. 17, 1968, P.L. 90-578, §402(b)(2), 82 Stat. 1118; Dec. 1, 1990, P.L. 101-650, §321, 104 Stat. 5117.

See *Commentaries*, "Taxable Costs," ch. 9-D, p. 761.

§1923. DOCKET FEES & COSTS OF BRIEFS

(a) Attorney's and proctor's docket fees in courts of the United States may be taxed as costs as follows:

$20 on trial or final hearing (including a default judgment whether entered by the court or by the clerk) in civil, criminal, or admiralty cases, except that in cases of admiralty and maritime jurisdiction where the libellant recovers less than $50 the proctor's docket fee shall be $10;

$20 in admiralty appeals involving not over $1,000;

$50 in admiralty appeals involving not over $5,000;

$100 in admiralty appeals involving more than $5,000;

$5 on discontinuance of a civil action;

$5 on motion for judgment and other proceedings on recognizances;

$2.50 for each deposition admitted in evidence.

(b) The docket fees of United States attorneys and United States trustees shall be paid to the clerk of court and by him paid into the Treasury.

(c) In admiralty appeals the court may allow as costs for printing the briefs of the successful party not more than:

$25 where the amount involved is not over $1,000;

$50 where the amount involved is not over $5,000;

$75 where the amount involved is over $5,000.

History of 28 U.S.C. §1923: June 25, 1948, ch. 646, 62 Stat. 956; June 18, 1954, ch. 304, 68 Stat. 253; Nov. 6, 1978, P.L. 95-598, §245, 92 Stat. 2671.

See *Commentaries*, "Taxable Costs," ch. 9-D, p. 761.

§1924. VERIFICATION OF BILL OF COSTS

Before any bill of costs is taxed, the party claiming any item of cost or disbursement shall attach thereto an affidavit, made by himself or by his duly authorized attorney or agent having knowledge of the facts, that such item is correct and has been necessarily incurred in the case and that the services for which fees have been charged were actually and necessarily performed.

History of 28 U.S.C. §1924: June 25, 1948, ch. 646, 62 Stat. 957.

See *Commentaries*, "Taxable Costs," ch. 9-D, p. 761.

§1925. ADMIRALTY & MARITIME CASES

Except as otherwise provided by Act of Congress, the allowance and taxation of costs in admiralty and maritime cases shall be prescribed by rules promulgated by the Supreme Court.

History of 28 U.S.C. §1925: June 25, 1948, ch. 646, 62 Stat. 957.

See *Commentaries*, "Taxable Costs," ch. 9-D, p. 761.

§1926. COURT OF FEDERAL CLAIMS

(a) The Judicial Conference of the United States shall prescribe from time to time the fees and costs to be charged and collected in the United States Court of Federal Claims.

(b) The court and its officers shall collect only such fees and costs as the Judicial Conference prescribes. The court may require advance payment of fees by rule.

History of 28 U.S.C. §1926: June 25, 1948, ch. 646, 62 Stat. 957; Apr. 2, 1982, P.L. 97-164, §139(p)(1), 96 Stat. 44; Oct. 29, 1992, P.L. 102-572, §902(b), 106 Stat. 4516.

See *Commentaries*, "Taxable Costs," ch. 9-D, p. 761.

§1927. COUNSEL'S LIABILITY FOR EXCESSIVE COSTS

Any attorney or other person admitted to conduct cases in any court of the United States or any Territory thereof who so multiplies the proceedings in any case unreasonably and vexatiously may be required by the court to satisfy personally the excess costs, expenses, and attorneys' fees reasonably incurred because of such conduct.

History of 28 U.S.C. §1927: June 25, 1948, ch. 646, 62 Stat. 957; Sept. 12, 1980, P.L. 96-349, §3, 94 Stat. 1156.

See *Commentaries*, "Pleading & Motion Practice," ch. 1-B, p. 7; "Motion for Sanctions," ch. 5-O, p. 384; "Taxable Costs," ch. 9-D, p. 761.

§1928. PATENT INFRINGEMENT ACTION; DISCLAIMER NOT FILED

Whenever a judgment is rendered for the plaintiff in any patent infringement action involving a part of a patent and it appears that the patentee, in his specifications, claimed to be, but was not, the original and first inventor or discoverer of any material or substantial part of the thing patented, no costs shall be included in such judgment, unless the proper disclaimer has been filed in the United States Patent and Trademark Office prior to the commencement of the action.

History of 28 U.S.C. §1928: June 25, 1948, ch. 646, 62 Stat. 957; Nov. 29, 1999, P.L. 106-113-Appx. I, §4732(b)(17), 113 Stat. 1501A-585.

See *Commentaries*, "Taxable Costs," ch. 9-D, p. 761.

§1929. EXTRAORDINARY EXPENSES NOT EXPRESSLY AUTHORIZED

Where the ministerial officers of the United States incur extraordinary expense in executing Acts of Congress, the payment of which is not specifically provided for, the Attorney General may allow the payment thereof.

History of 28 U.S.C. §1929: June 25, 1948, ch. 646, 62 Stat. 957.

See *Commentaries*, "Taxable Costs," ch. 9-D, p. 761.

A §1930. BANKRUPTCY FEES

(a) The parties commencing a case under title 11 shall pay to the clerk of the district court or the clerk of the bankruptcy court, if one has been certified pursuant to section 156(b) of this title, the following filing fees:

(1) For a case commenced under—

(A) chapter 7 of title 11, $245, and

(B) chapter 13 of title 11, $235.

(2) For a case commenced under chapter 9 of title 11, equal to the fee specified in paragraph (3) for filing a case under chapter 11 of title 11. The amount by which the fee payable under this paragraph exceeds $300 shall be deposited in the fund established under section 1931 of this title.

(3) For a case commenced under chapter 11 of title 11 that does not concern a railroad, as defined in section 101 of title 11, $1,167.

(4) For a case commenced under chapter 11 of title 11 concerning a railroad, as so defined, $1,000.

(5) For a case commenced under chapter 12 of title 11, $200.

(6) In addition to the filing fee paid to the clerk, a quarterly fee shall be paid to the United States trustee, for deposit in the Treasury, in each case under chapter 11 of title 11 for each quarter (including any fraction thereof) until the case is converted or dismissed, whichever occurs first. The fee shall be $325 for each quarter in which disbursements total less than $15,000; $650 for each quarter in which disbursements total $15,000 or more but less than $75,000; $975 for each quarter in which disbursements total $75,000 or more but less than $150,000; $1,625 for each quarter in which disbursements total $150,000 or more but less than $225,000; $1,950 for each quarter in which disbursements total $225,000 or more but less than $300,000; $4,875 for each quarter in which disbursements total $300,000 or more but less than $1,000,000; $6,500 for each quarter in which disbursements total $1,000,000 or more but less than $2,000,000; $9,750 for each quarter in which disbursements total $2,000,000 or more but less than $3,000,000; $10,400 for each quarter in which disbursements total $3,000,000 or more but less than $5,000,000; $13,000 for each quarter in which disbursements total $5,000,000 or more but less than $15,000,000; $20,000 for each quarter in which disbursements total $15,000,000 or more but less than $30,000,000; $30,000 for each quarter in which disbursements total more than $30,000,000. The fee shall be payable on the last day of the calendar month following the calendar quarter for which the fee is owed.

(7) In districts that are not part of a United States trustee region as defined in section 581 of this title, the Judicial Conference of the United States may require the debtor in a case under chapter 11 of title 11 to pay fees equal to those imposed by paragraph (6) of this subsection. Such fees shall be deposited as offsetting receipts to the fund established under section 1931 of this title and shall remain available until expended.

An individual commencing a voluntary case or a joint case under title 11 may pay such fee in installments. For converting, on request of the debtor, a case under chapter 7, or 13 of title 11, to a case under chapter 11 of title 11, the debtor shall pay to the clerk of the district court or the clerk of the bankruptcy court, if one has been certified pursuant to section 156(b) of this title, a fee of the amount equal to the difference between the fee specified in paragraph (3) and the fee specified in paragraph (1).

(b) The Judicial Conference of the United States may prescribe additional fees in cases under title 11 of the same kind as the Judicial Conference prescribes under section 1914(b) of this title.

(c) Upon the filing of any separate or joint notice of appeal or application for appeal or upon the receipt of any order allowing, or notice of the allowance of, an appeal or a writ of certiorari $5 shall be paid to the clerk of the court, by the appellant or petitioner.

(d) Whenever any case or proceeding is dismissed in any bankruptcy court for want of jurisdiction, such court may order the payment of just costs.

(e) The clerk of the court may collect only the fees prescribed under this section.

(f)(1) Under the procedures prescribed by the Judicial Conference of the United States, the district court or the bankruptcy court may waive the filing fee in a case under chapter 7 of title 11 for an individual if the court determines that such individual has income less than 150 percent of the income official poverty line (as defined by the Office of Management and Budget, and revised annually in accordance with section 673(2) of the Omnibus Budget Reconciliation Act of 1981) applicable to a family of the size involved and is unable to pay that fee in installments. For purposes of this paragraph, the term "filing fee" means the filing fee required by subsection (a), or any other fee prescribed by the Judicial Conference under subsections (b) and (c) that is payable to the clerk upon the commencement of a case under chapter 7.

(2) The district court or the bankruptcy court may waive for such debtors other fees prescribed under subsections (b) and (c).

(3) This subsection does not restrict the district court or the bankruptcy court from waiving, in accordance with Judicial Conference policy, fees prescribed under this section for other debtors and creditors.

History of 28 U.S.C. §1930: Nov. 6, 1978, P.L. 95-598, §246(a), 92 Stat. 2671; July 10, 1984, P.L. 98-353, §111(a), (b), 98 Stat. 342; Oct. 18, 1986, P.L. 99-500, §101(b) [§407(b)], 100 Stat. 1783-64; Oct. 27, 1986, P.L. 99-554, §§117, 144(f), 100 Stat. 3095, 3097; Oct. 30, 1986, P.L. 99-591, §101(b) [§407(b)], 100 Stat. 3341-39, 3341-64; Nov. 21, 1989, P.L. 101-162, §406(a), 103 Stat. 1016; Oct. 28, 1991, P.L. 102-140, §111(a), 105 Stat. 795; Oct. 27, 1993, P.L. 103-121, §111(a)(1), (b)(1), 107 Stat. 1164; Jan. 26, 1996, P.L. 104-99, §211, 110 Stat. 37; Sept. 30, 1996, P.L. 104-208, §109(a), 110 Stat. 3009-18; Nov. 29, 1999, P.L. 106-113-Appx. A, §113, 113 Stat. 1501A-20; Nov. 13, 2000, P.L. 106-518, §§103-105, 114 Stat. 2411, 2412; Apr. 20, 2005, P.L. 109-8, §§325(a), 418, 119 Stat. 98, 108; May 11, 2005, P.L. 109-13, §6058(a), 119 Stat. 297; Feb. 8, 2006, P.L. 109-171, §10101(a), 120 Stat. 184; Dec. 26, 2007, P.L. 110-161, §213(a), 121 Stat. 1914; May 25, 2012, P.L. 112-121, §3(a), 126 Stat. 348.

See *Commentaries*, "Taxable Costs," ch. 9-D, p. 761.

§1931. DISPOSITION OF FILING FEES

(a) Of the amounts paid to the clerk of court as a fee under section 1914(a) or as part of a judgment for costs under section 2412(a)(2) of this title, $190 shall be deposited into a special fund of the Treasury to be available to offset funds appropriated for the operation and maintenance of the courts of the United States.

(b) If the court authorizes a fee under section 1914(a) or an amount included in a judgment for costs under section 2412(a)(2) of this title of less than $250, the entire fee or amount, up to $190, shall be deposited into the special fund provided in this section.

History of 28 U.S.C. §1931: Oct. 18, 1986, P.L. 99-500, §101(b) [§407(c)], 100 Stat. 1783-39, 1783-64; Oct. 30, 1986, P.L. 99-591, §101(b) [§407(c)], 100 Stat. 3341-64; Nov. 21, 1989, P.L. 101-162, §406(d), 103 Stat. 1016; Oct. 29, 1992, P.L. 102-572, §301(b), 106 Stat. 4511; Oct. 19, 1996, P.L. 104-317, §401(b), 110 Stat. 3853; Dec. 8, 2004, P.L. 108-447, §307(b), 118 Stat. 2895.

See *Commentaries*, "Taxable Costs," ch. 9-D, p. 761.

§1932[A*]. JUDICIAL PANEL ON MULTIDISTRICT LITIGATION

In 1996, Congress enacted two sections 1932. Section 1932[A] was enacted by P.L. 104-317, §403(a)(1), on Oct. 19, 1996. The [A*] has been added by the editor to distinguish this §1932 from the other, which is marked with [B*].*

The Judicial Conference of the United States shall prescribe from time to time the fees and costs to be charged and collected by the Judicial Panel on Multidistrict Litigation.

History of 28 U.S.C. §1932[A*]: Oct. 19, 1996, P.L. 104-317, §403(a)(1), 110 Stat. 3854.

§1932[B*]. REVOCATION OF EARNED RELEASE CREDIT

In 1996, Congress enacted two sections 1932. Section 1932[B] was enacted by P.L. 104-134, §101(a)(1), on Apr. 26, 1996. The [B*] has been added by the editor to distinguish this §1932 from the other, which is marked with [A*].*

In any civil action brought by an adult convicted of a crime and confined in a Federal correctional facility, the court may order the revocation of such earned good time credit under section 3624(b) of title 18, United States Code, that has not yet vested, if, on its own motion or the motion of any party, the court finds that—

(1) the claim was filed for a malicious purpose;

(2) the claim was filed solely to harass the party against which it was filed; or

(3) the claimant testifies falsely or otherwise knowingly presents false evidence or information to the court.

History of 28 U.S.C. §1932[B*]: Apr. 26, 1996, P.L. 104-134, §101(a) [§809(a)], 110 Stat. 1321-76; May 2, 1996, P.L. 104-140, §1(a), 110 Stat. 1327.

CHAPTER 125. PENDING ACTIONS & JUDGMENTS

§1961. INTEREST

(a) Interest shall be allowed on any money judgment in a civil case recovered in a district court. Execution therefor may be levied by the marshal, in any case where, by the law of the State in which such court is held, execution may be levied for interest on judgments recovered in the courts of the State. Such interest shall be calculated from the date of the entry of the judgment, at a rate equal to the weekly average 1-year constant maturity Treasury yield, as published by the Board of Governors of the Federal Reserve System, for the calendar week preceding.[1] the date of the judgment. The Director of the Administrative Office of the United States Courts shall distribute notice of that rate and any changes in it to all Federal judges.

(b) Interest shall be computed daily to the date of payment except as provided in section 2516(b) of this title and section 1304(b) of title 31, and shall be compounded annually.

(c)(1) This section shall not apply in any judgment of any court with respect to any internal revenue tax case. Interest shall be allowed in such cases at the underpayment rate or overpayment rate (whichever is appropriate) established under section 6621 of the Internal Revenue Code of 1986.

(2) Except as otherwise provided in paragraph (1) of this subsection, interest shall be allowed on all final judgments against the United States in the United States Court of Appeals for the Federal circuit,[2] at the rate provided in subsection (a) and as provided in subsection (b).

(3) Interest shall be allowed, computed, and paid on judgments of the United States Court of Federal Claims only as provided in paragraph (1) of this subsection or in any other provision of law.

(4) This section shall not be construed to affect the interest on any judgment of any court not specified in this section.

1. **Editor's note:** So in original. The period probably should not appear.
2. **Editor's note:** So in original. Probably should be capitalized.

History of 28 U.S.C. §1961: June 25, 1948, ch. 646, 62 Stat. 957; Apr. 2, 1982, P.L. 97-164, §302(a), 96 Stat. 55; Sept. 13, 1982, P.L. 97-258, §2(m)(1), 96 Stat. 1062; Jan. 12, 1983, P.L. 97-452, §2(d)(1), 96 Stat. 2478; Oct. 22, 1986, P.L. 99-514, §§2, 1511(c)(17), 100 Stat. 2095, 2745; Oct. 29, 1992, P.L. 102-572, §902(b)(1), 106 Stat. 4516; Dec. 21, 2000, P.L. 106-554, §307(d)(1), 114 Stat. 2763A-636.

§1962. LIEN

Every judgment rendered by a district court within a State shall be a lien on the property located in such State in the same manner, to the same extent and under the same conditions as a judgment of a court of general jurisdiction in such State, and shall cease to be a lien in the same manner and time. This section does not apply to judgments entered in favor of the United States. Whenever the law of any State requires a judgment of a State court to be registered, recorded, docketed or indexed, or any other act to be done, in a particular manner, or in a certain office or county or parish before such lien attaches, such requirements shall apply only if the law of such State authorizes the judgment of a court of the United States to be registered, recorded, docketed, indexed or otherwise conformed to rules and requirements relating to judgments of the courts of the State.

History of 28 U.S.C. §1962: June 25, 1948, ch. 646, 62 Stat. 958; Nov. 29, 1990, P.L. 101-647, §3627, 104 Stat. 4965.

§1963. REGISTRATION OF JUDGMENTS FOR ENFORCEMENT IN OTHER DISTRICTS

A judgment in an action for the recovery of money or property entered in any court of appeals, district court, bankruptcy court, or in the Court of International Trade may be registered by filing a certified copy of the judgment in any other district or, with respect to the Court of International Trade, in any judicial district, when the judgment has become final by appeal or expiration of the time for appeal or when ordered by the court that entered the judgment for good cause shown. Such a judgment entered in favor of the United States may be so registered any time after judgment is entered. A judgment so registered shall have the same effect as a judgment of the district court of the district where registered and may be enforced in like manner.

A certified copy of the satisfaction of any judgment in whole or in part may be registered in like manner in any district in which the judgment is a lien.

The procedure prescribed under this section is in addition to other procedures provided by law for the enforcement of judgments.

History of 28 U.S.C. §1963: June 25, 1948, ch. 646, 62 Stat. 958; Aug. 23, 1954, ch. 837, 68 Stat. 772; July 7, 1958, P.L. 85-508, §12(o), 72 Stat. 349; Nov. 19, 1988, P.L. 100-702, §1002(a), (b)(1), 102 Stat. 4664; Nov. 29, 1990, P.L. 101-647, §3628, 104 Stat. 4965; Oct. 19, 1996, P.L. 104-317, §203(a), 110 Stat. 3849.

§1963A. REPEALED

Repealed Nov. 19, 1988, P.L. 100-702, §1002(b)(2), 102 Stat. 4664.

§1964. CONSTRUCTIVE NOTICE OF PENDING ACTIONS

Where the law of a State requires a notice of an action concerning real property pending in a court of the State to be registered, recorded, docketed, or indexed in a particular manner, or in a certain office or county or parish in order to give constructive notice of the action as it relates to the real property, and such law authorizes a notice of an action concerning real property pending in a United States district court to be registered, recorded, docketed, or indexed in the same manner, or in the same place, those requirements of the State law must be complied with in order to give constructive notice of such an action pending in a United States district court as it relates to real property in such State.

History of 28 U.S.C. §1964: Aug. 20, 1958, P.L. 85-689, §1(a), 72 Stat. 683.

CHAPTER 127. EXECUTIONS & JUDICIAL SALES

§2001. SALE OF REALTY GENERALLY

(a) Any realty or interest therein sold under any order or decree of any court of the United States shall be sold as a whole or in separate parcels at public sale at the courthouse of the county, parish, or city in which the greater part of the property is located, or upon the premises or some parcel thereof located therein, as the court directs. Such sale shall be upon such terms and conditions as the court directs.

Property in the possession of a receiver or receivers appointed by one or more district courts shall be sold at public sale in the district wherein any such receiver was first appointed, at the courthouse of the county, parish, or city situated therein in which the greater part of the property in such district is located, or on the premises or some parcel thereof located in such county, parish, or city, as such court directs, unless the court orders the sale of the property or one or more parcels thereof in one or more ancillary districts.

(b) After a hearing, of which notice to all interested parties shall be given by publication or otherwise as the court directs, the court may order the sale of such realty or interest or any part thereof at private sale for cash or other consideration and upon such terms and conditions as the court approves, if it finds that the best interests of the estate will be conserved thereby. Before confirmation of any private sale, the court shall appoint three disinterested persons to appraise such property or different groups of three appraisers each to appraise properties of different classes or situated in different localities. No private sale shall be confirmed at a price less than two-thirds of the appraised value. Before confirmation of any private sale, the terms thereof shall be published in such newspaper or newspapers of general circulation as the court directs at least ten days before confirmation. The private sale shall not be confirmed if a bona fide offer is made, under conditions prescribed by the court, which guarantees at least a 10 per centum increase over the price offered in the private sale.

(c) This section shall not apply to sales and proceedings under Title 11 or by receivers or conservators of banks appointed by the Comptroller of the Currency.

History of 28 U.S.C. §2001: June 25, 1948, ch. 646, 62 Stat. 958; May 24, 1949, ch. 139, §99, 63 Stat. 104.

§2002. NOTICE OF SALE OF REALTY

A public sale of realty or interest therein under any order, judgment or decree of any court of the United States shall not be made without notice published once a week for at least four weeks prior to the sale in at least one newspaper regularly issued and of general circulation in the county, state, or judicial district of the United States wherein the realty is situated.

If such realty is situated in more than one county, state, district or circuit, such notice shall be published in one or more of the counties, states, or districts wherein it is situated, as the court directs. The notice shall be substantially in such form and contain such description of the property by reference or otherwise as the court approves. The court may direct that the publication be made in other newspapers.

This section shall not apply to sales and proceedings under Title 11 or by receivers or conservators of banks appointed by the Comptroller of the Currency.

History of 28 U.S.C. §2002: June 25, 1948, ch. 646, 62 Stat. 959; May 24, 1949, ch. 139, §100, 63 Stat. 104.

§2003. MARSHAL'S INCAPACITY AFTER LEVY ON OR SALE OF REALTY

Whenever a United States marshal dies, is removed from office, or the term of his commission expires, after levying on realty or any interest therein under a writ of execution issued by a court of the United States, and before sale or other final disposition thereof, like process shall issue to the succeeding marshal and the same proceedings shall be had as if such contingency had not occurred.

Whenever any such contingency arises after a marshal has sold any realty or interest therein and before a deed is executed, the court may, on application by the purchaser, or the plaintiff in whose action the sale was made, setting forth the facts of the case and the reason why the title was not perfected by such marshal, order the succeeding marshal to perfect the title and execute a deed to the purchaser, upon payment of the purchase money and unpaid costs.

History of 28 U.S.C. §2003: June 25, 1948, ch. 646, 62 Stat. 959; May 24, 1949, ch. 139, §101, 63 Stat. 104.

§2004. SALE OF PERSONALTY GENERALLY

Any personalty sold under any order or decree of any court of the United States shall be sold in accordance with section 2001 of this title, unless the court orders otherwise.

This section shall not apply to sales and proceedings under Title 11 or by receivers or conservators of banks appointed by the Comptroller of the Currency.

History of 28 U.S.C. §2004: June 25, 1948, ch. 646, 62 Stat. 959.

§2005. APPRAISAL OF GOODS TAKEN ON EXECUTION

Whenever State law requires that goods taken on execution be appraised before sale, goods taken under execution issued from a court of the United States shall be appraised in like manner.

The United States marshal shall summon the appraisers in the same manner as the sheriff is required to summon appraisers under State law.

If the appraisers fail to attend and perform their required duties, the marshal may sell the goods without an appraisal. Appraisers attending and performing their duties, shall receive the fees allowed for appraisals under State law.

History of 28 U.S.C. §2005: June 25, 1948, ch. 646, 62 Stat. 959.

§2006. EXECUTION AGAINST REVENUE OFFICER

Execution shall not issue against a collector or other revenue officer on a final judgment in any proceeding against him for any of his acts, or for the recovery of any money exacted by or paid to him and subsequently paid into the Treasury, in performing his official duties, if the court certifies that:

(1) probable cause existed; or

(2) the officer acted under the directions of the Secretary of the Treasury, the Director, Bureau of Alcohol, Tobacco, Firearms, and Explosives, Department of Justice, or other proper Government officer.

When such certificate has been issued, the amount of the judgment shall be paid out of the proper appropriation by the Treasury.

History of 28 U.S.C. §2006: June 25, 1948, ch. 646, 62 Stat. 960; Nov. 2, 2002, P.L. 107-296 §1112(*l*), 116 Stat. 2277.

§2007. IMPRISONMENT FOR DEBT

(a) A person shall not be imprisoned for debt on a writ of execution or other process issued from a court of the United States in any State wherein imprisonment for debt has been abolished. All modifications, conditions, and restrictions upon such imprisonment provided by State law shall apply to any writ of execution or process issued from a court of the United States in accordance with the procedure applicable in such State.

(b) Any person arrested or imprisoned in any State on a writ of execution or other process issued from any court of the United States in a civil action shall have the same jail privileges and be governed by the same regulations as persons confined in like cases on process issued from the courts of such State. The same requirements governing discharge as are applicable in such State shall apply. Any proceedings for discharge shall be conducted before a United States magistrate judge for the judicial district wherein the defendant is held.

History of 28 U.S.C. §2007: June 25, 1948, ch. 646, 62 Stat. 960; Oct. 17, 1968, P.L. 90-578, §402(b)(2), 82 Stat. 1118; Dec. 1, 1990, P.L. 101-650, §321, 104 Stat. 5117.

CHAPTER 129. MONEYS PAID INTO COURT

§2041. DEPOSIT OF MONEYS IN PENDING OR ADJUDICATED CASES

All moneys paid into any court of the United States, or received by the officers thereof, in any case pending or adjudicated in such court, shall be forthwith deposited with the Treasurer of the United States or a designated depositary, in the name and to the credit of such court.

This section shall not prevent the delivery of any such money to the rightful owners upon security, according to agreement of parties, under the direction of the court.

History of 28 U.S.C. §2041: June 25, 1948, ch. 646, 62 Stat. 960; Sept. 13, 1982, P.L. 97-258, §2(g)(4)(C), 96 Stat. 1061.

§2042. WITHDRAWAL

No money deposited under section 2041 of this title shall be withdrawn except by order of court.

In every case in which the right to withdraw money deposited in court under section 2041 has been adjudicated or is not in dispute and such money has remained so deposited for at least five years unclaimed by the person entitled thereto, such court shall cause such money to be deposited in the Treasury in the name and to the credit of the United States. Any claimant entitled to any such money may, on petition to the court and upon notice to the United States attorney and full proof of the right thereto, obtain an order directing payment to him.

History of 28 U.S.C. §2042: June 25, 1948, ch. 646, 62 Stat. 960; Sept. 13, 1982, P.L. 97-258, §2(g)(4)(D), 96 Stat. 1061.

§2043. DEPOSIT OF OTHER MONEYS

Except for public moneys deposited under section 2041 of this title, each clerk of the United States courts shall deposit public moneys that the clerk collects into a checking account in the Treasury, subject to disbursement by the clerk. At the end of each accounting period, the earned part of public moneys accruing to the United States shall be deposited in the Treasury to the credit of the appropriate receipt accounts.

History of 28 U.S.C. §2043: Sept. 13, 1982, P.L. 97-258, §2(g)(4)(E), 96 Stat. 1061.

§2044. PAYMENT OF FINE WITH BOND MONEY

On motion of the United States attorney, the court shall order any money belonging to and deposited by or on behalf of the defendant with the court for the purposes of a criminal

appearance bail bond (trial or appeal) to be held and paid over to the United States attorney to be applied to the payment of any assessment, fine, restitution, or penalty imposed upon the defendant. The court shall not release any money deposited for bond purposes after a plea or a verdict of the defendant's guilt has been entered and before sentencing except upon a showing that an assessment, fine, restitution or penalty cannot be imposed for the offense the defendant committed or that the defendant would suffer an undue hardship. This section shall not apply to any third party surety.

History of 28 U.S.C. §2044: Nov. 29, 1990, P.L. 101-647, §3629(a), 104 Stat. 4966.

§2045. INVESTMENT OF COURT REGISTRY FUNDS

(a) The Director of the Administrative Office of the United States Courts, or the Director's designee under subsection (b), may request the Secretary of the Treasury to invest funds received under section 2041 in public debt securities with maturities suitable to the needs of the funds, as determined by the Director or the Director's designee, and bearing interest at a rate determined by the Secretary of the Treasury, taking into consideration current market yields on outstanding marketable obligations of the United States of comparable maturity.

(b) The Director may designate the clerk of a court described in section 610 to exercise the authority conferred by subsection (a).

History of 28 U.S.C. §2045: Oct. 13, 2008, P.L. 110-406, §8(a), 122 Stat. 4293.

CHAPTER 131. RULES OF COURTS

§2071. RULE-MAKING POWER GENERALLY

(a) The Supreme Court and all courts established by Act of Congress may from time to time prescribe rules for the conduct of their business. Such rules shall be consistent with Acts of Congress and rules of practice and procedure prescribed under section 2072 of this title.

(b) Any rule prescribed by a court, other than the Supreme Court, under subsection (a) shall be prescribed only after giving appropriate public notice and an opportunity for comment. Such rule shall take effect upon the date specified by the prescribing court and shall have such effect on pending proceedings as the prescribing court may order.

(c)(1) A rule of a district court prescribed under subsection (a) shall remain in effect unless modified or abrogated by the judicial council of the relevant circuit.

(2) Any other rule prescribed by a court other than the Supreme Court under subsection (a) shall remain in effect unless modified or abrogated by the Judicial Conference.

(d) Copies of rules prescribed under subsection (a) by a district court shall be furnished to the judicial council, and copies of all rules prescribed by a court other than the Supreme Court under subsection (a) shall be furnished to the Director of the Administrative Office of the United States Courts and made available to the public.

(e) If the prescribing court determines that there is an immediate need for a rule, such court may proceed under this section without public notice and opportunity for comment, but such court shall promptly thereafter afford such notice and opportunity for comment.

(f) No rule may be prescribed by a district court other than under this section.

History of 28 U.S.C. §2071: June 25, 1948, ch. 646, 62 Stat. 961; May 24, 1949, ch. 139, §102, 63 Stat. 104; Nov. 19, 1988, P.L. 100-702, §403(a)(1), 102 Stat. 4650.

§2072. RULES OF PROCEDURE & EVIDENCE; POWER TO PRESCRIBE

(a) The Supreme Court shall have the power to prescribe general rules of practice and procedure and rules of evidence for cases in the United States district courts (including proceedings before magistrate judges thereof) and courts of appeals.

(b) Such rules shall not abridge, enlarge or modify any substantive right. All laws in conflict with such rules shall be of no further force or effect after such rules have taken effect.

(c) Such rules may define when a ruling of a district court is final for the purposes of appeal under section 1291 of this title.

History of 28 U.S.C. §2072: Nov. 19, 1988, P.L. 100-702, §401(a), 102 Stat. 4648; Dec. 1, 1990, P.L. 101-650, §315, 104 Stat. 5115.

§2073. RULES OF PROCEDURE & EVIDENCE; METHOD OF PRESCRIBING

(a)(1) The Judicial Conference shall prescribe and publish the procedures for the consideration of proposed rules under this section.

(2) The Judicial Conference may authorize the appointment of committees to assist the Conference by recommending rules to be prescribed under sections 2072 and 2075 of this title. Each such committee shall consist of members of the bench and the professional bar, and trial and appellate judges.

(b) The Judicial Conference shall authorize the appointment of a standing committee on rules of practice, procedure, and evidence under subsection (a) of this section. Such standing committee shall review each recommendation of any other committees so appointed and recommend to the Judicial Conference rules of practice, procedure, and evidence and such changes in rules proposed by a committee appointed under subsection (a)(2) of this section as may be necessary to maintain consistency and otherwise promote the interest of justice.

(c)(1) Each meeting for the transaction of business under this chapter by any committee appointed under this section shall be open to the public, except when the committee so meeting, in open session and with a majority present, determines that it is in the public interest that all or part of the

remainder of the meeting on that day shall be closed to the public, and states the reason for so closing the meeting. Minutes of each meeting for the transaction of business under this chapter shall be maintained by the committee and made available to the public, except that any portion of such minutes, relating to a closed meeting and made available to the public, may contain such deletions as may be necessary to avoid frustrating the purposes of closing the meeting.

(2) Any meeting for the transaction of business under this chapter, by a committee appointed under this section, shall be preceded by sufficient notice to enable all interested persons to attend.

(d) In making a recommendation under this section or under section 2072 or 2075, the body making that recommendation shall provide a proposed rule, an explanatory note on the rule, and a written report explaining the body's action, including any minority or other separate views.

(e) Failure to comply with this section does not invalidate a rule prescribed under section 2072 or 2075 of this title.

History of 28 U.S.C. §2073: Nov. 19, 1988, P.L. 100-702, §401(a), 102 Stat. 4649; Oct. 22, 1994, P.L. 103-394, §104(e), 108 Stat. 4110.

§2074. RULES OF PROCEDURE & EVIDENCE; SUBMISSION TO CONGRESS; EFFECTIVE DATE

(a) The Supreme Court shall transmit to the Congress not later than May 1 of the year in which a rule prescribed under section 2072 is to become effective a copy of the proposed rule. Such rule shall take effect no earlier than December 1 of the year in which such rule is so transmitted unless otherwise provided by law. The Supreme Court may fix the extent such rule shall apply to proceedings then pending, except that the Supreme Court shall not require the application of such rule to further proceedings then pending to the extent that, in the opinion of the court in which such proceedings are pending, the application of such rule in such proceedings would not be feasible or would work injustice, in which event the former rule applies.

(b) Any such rule creating, abolishing, or modifying an evidentiary privilege shall have no force or effect unless approved by Act of Congress.

History of 28 U.S.C. §2074: Nov. 19, 1988, P.L. 100-702, §401(a), 102 Stat. 4649.

§2075. BANKRUPTCY RULES

The Supreme Court shall have the power to prescribe by general rules, the forms of process, writs, pleadings, and motions, and the practice and procedure in cases under title 11.

Such rules shall not abridge, enlarge, or modify any substantive right.

The Supreme Court shall transmit to Congress not later than May 1 of the year in which a rule prescribed under this section is to become effective a copy of the proposed rule. The rule shall take effect no earlier than December 1 of the year in which it is transmitted to Congress unless otherwise provided by law.

The bankruptcy rules promulgated under this section shall prescribe a form for the statement required under section 707(b)(2)(C) of title 11 and may provide general rules on the content of such statement.

History of 28 U.S.C. §2075: Oct. 3, 1964, P.L. 88-623, §1, 78 Stat. 1001; Nov. 6, 1978, P.L. 95-598, §247, 92 Stat. 2672; Oct. 22, 1994, P.L. 103-394, §104(f), 108 Stat. 4110; Apr. 20, 2005, P.L. 109-8, §1232, 119 Stat. 202.

§2076. REPEALED

Repealed Nov. 19, 1988, P.L. 100-702, §401(c), 102 Stat. 4650.

§2077. PUBLICATION OF RULES; ADVISORY COMMITTEES

(a) The rules for the conduct of the business of each court of appeals, including the operating procedures of such court, shall be published. Each court of appeals shall print or cause to be printed necessary copies of the rules. The Judicial Conference shall prescribe the fees for sales of copies under section 1913 of this title, but the Judicial Conference may provide for free distribution of copies to members of the bar of each court and to other interested persons.

(b) Each court, except the Supreme Court, that is authorized to prescribe rules of the conduct of such court's business under section 2071 of this title shall appoint an advisory committee for the study of the rules of practice and internal operating procedures of such court and, in the case of an advisory committee appointed by a court of appeals, of the rules of the judicial council of the circuit. The advisory committee shall make recommendations to the court concerning such rules and procedures. Members of the committee shall serve without compensation, but the Director may pay travel and transportation expenses in accordance with section 5703 of title 5.

History of 28 U.S.C. §2077: Apr. 2, 1982, P.L. 97-164, §208(a), 96 Stat. 54; Nov. 19, 1988, P.L. 100-702, §401(b), 102 Stat. 4650; Dec. 1, 1990, P.L. 101-650, §406, 104 Stat. 5124.

CHAPTER 133. REVIEW—MISCELLANEOUS PROVISIONS

§2101. SUPREME COURT; TIME FOR APPEAL OR CERTIORARI; DOCKETING; STAY

(a) A direct appeal to the Supreme Court from any decision under section 1253 of this title, holding unconstitutional in whole or in part, any Act of Congress, shall be taken within thirty days after the entry of the interlocutory or final order, judgment or decree. The record shall be made up and the case docketed within sixty days from the time such appeal is taken under rules prescribed by the Supreme Court.

(b) Any other direct appeal to the Supreme Court which is authorized by law, from a decision of a district court in any civil action, suit or proceeding, shall be taken within thirty days from the judgment, order or decree, appealed from, if interlocutory, and within sixty days if final.

(c) Any other appeal or any writ of certiorari intended to bring any judgment or decree in a civil action, suit or proceeding before the Supreme Court for review shall be taken or applied for within ninety days after the entry of such judgment

or decree. A justice of the Supreme Court, for good cause shown, may extend the time for applying for a writ of certiorari for a period not exceeding sixty days.

(d) The time for appeal or application for a writ of certiorari to review the judgment of a State court in a criminal case shall be as prescribed by rules of the Supreme Court.

(e) An application to the Supreme Court for a writ of certiorari to review a case before judgment has been rendered in the court of appeals may be made at any time before judgment.

(f) In any case in which the final judgment or decree of any court is subject to review by the Supreme Court on writ of certiorari, the execution and enforcement of such judgment or decree may be stayed for a reasonable time to enable the party aggrieved to obtain a writ of certiorari from the Supreme Court. The stay may be granted by a judge of the court rendering the judgment or decree or by a justice of the Supreme Court, and may be conditioned on the giving of security, approved by such judge or justice, that if the aggrieved party fails to make application for such writ within the period allotted therefor, or fails to obtain an order granting his application, or fails to make his plea good in the Supreme Court, he shall answer for all damages and costs which the other party may sustain by reason of the stay.

(g) The time for application for a writ of certiorari to review a decision of the United States Court of Appeals for the Armed Forces shall be as prescribed by rules of the Supreme Court.

History of 28 U.S.C. §2101: June 25, 1948, ch. 646, 62 Stat. 961; May 24, 1949, ch. 139, §106, 63 Stat. 104; Dec. 6, 1983, P.L. 98-209, §10(b), 97 Stat. 1406; June 27, 1988, P.L. 100-352, §5(b), 102 Stat. 663; Oct. 5, 1994, P.L. 103-337, §924(d)(1)(C), 108 Stat. 2832.

§2102. PRIORITY OF CRIMINAL CASE ON APPEAL FROM STATE COURT

Criminal cases on review from State courts shall have priority, on the docket of the Supreme Court, over all cases except cases to which the United States is a party and such other cases as the court may decide to be of public importance.

History of 28 U.S.C. §2102: June 25, 1948, ch. 646, 62 Stat. 962.

§2103. REPEALED

Repealed June 27, 1988, P.L. 100-352, §5(c), 102 Stat. 663.

§2104. REVIEWS OF STATE COURT DECISIONS

A review by the Supreme Court of a judgment or decree of a State court shall be conducted in the same manner and under the same regulations, and shall have the same effect, as if the judgment or decree reviewed had been rendered in a court of the United States.

History of 28 U.S.C. §2104: June 25, 1948, ch. 646, 62 Stat. 962; June 27, 1988, P.L. 100-352, §5(d)(1), 102 Stat. 663.

§2105. SCOPE OF REVIEW; ABATEMENT

There shall be no reversal in the Supreme Court or a court of appeals for error in ruling upon matters in abatement which do not involve jurisdiction.

History of 28 U.S.C. §2105: June 25, 1948, ch. 646, 62 Stat. 963.

§2106. DETERMINATION

The Supreme Court or any other court of appellate jurisdiction may affirm, modify, vacate, set aside or reverse any judgment, decree, or order of a court lawfully brought before it for review, and may remand the cause and direct the entry of such appropriate judgment, decree, or order, or require such further proceedings to be had as may be just under the circumstances.

History of 28 U.S.C. §2106: June 25, 1948, ch. 646, 62 Stat. 963.

§2107. TIME FOR APPEAL TO COURT OF APPEALS

(a) Except as otherwise provided in this section, no appeal shall bring any judgment, order or decree in an action, suit or proceeding of a civil nature before a court of appeals for review unless notice of appeal is filed, within thirty days after the entry of such judgment, order or decree.

(b) In any such action, suit, or proceeding, the time as to all parties shall be 60 days from such entry if one of the parties is—

(1) the United States;

(2) a United States agency;

(3) a United States officer or employee sued in an official capacity; or

(4) a current or former United States officer or employee sued in an individual capacity for an act or omission occurring in connection with duties performed on behalf of the United States, including all instances in which the United States represents that officer or employee when the judgment, order, or decree is entered or files the appeal for that officer or employee.

(c) The district court may, upon motion filed not later than 30 days after the expiration of the time otherwise set for bringing appeal, extend the time for appeal upon a showing of excusable neglect or good cause. In addition, if the district court finds—

(1) that a party entitled to notice of the entry of a judgment or order did not receive such notice from the clerk or any party within 21 days of its entry, and

(2) that no party would be prejudiced,

the district court may, upon motion filed within 180 days after entry of the judgment or order or within 14 days after receipt of such notice, whichever is earlier, reopen the time for appeal for a period of 14 days from the date of entry of the order reopening the time for appeal.

(d) This section shall not apply to bankruptcy matters or other proceedings under Title 11.

History of 28 U.S.C. §2107: June 25, 1948, ch. 646, 62 Stat. 963; May 24, 1949, ch. 139, §§107, 108, 63 Stat. 104; Nov. 6, 1978, P.L. 95-598, §248, 92 Stat. 2672; Dec. 9, 1991, P.L. 102-198, §12, 105 Stat. 1627; May 7, 2009, P.L. 111-16, §6, 123 Stat. 1608; Dec. 1, 2011, P.L. 112-62, §3, 125 Stat. 757.

See *Commentaries*, "Motion to Extend Time to File Notice of Appeal," ch. 10-G, p. 817; "Motion to Reopen Time for Appeal," ch. 10-H, p. 821.

§2108. PROOF OF AMOUNT IN CONTROVERSY

Where the power of any court of appeals to review a case depends upon the amount or value in controversy, such amount or value, if not otherwise satisfactorily disclosed upon the record, may be shown and ascertained by the oath of a party to the case or by other competent evidence.

History of 28 U.S.C. §2108: June 25, 1948, ch. 646, 62 Stat. 963.

§2109. QUORUM OF SUPREME COURT JUSTICES ABSENT

If a case brought to the Supreme Court by direct appeal from a district court cannot be heard and determined because of the absence of a quorum of qualified justices, the Chief Justice of the United States may order it remitted to the court of appeals for the circuit including the district in which the case arose, to be heard and determined by that court either sitting in banc or specially constituted and composed of the three circuit judges senior in commission who are able to sit, as such order may direct. The decision of such court shall be final and conclusive. In the event of the disqualification or disability of one or more of such circuit judges, such court shall be filled as provided in chapter 15 of this title.

In any other case brought to the Supreme Court for review, which cannot be heard and determined because of the absence of a quorum of qualified justices, if a majority of the qualified justices shall be of opinion that the case cannot be heard and determined at the next ensuing term, the court shall enter its order affirming the judgment of the court from which the case was brought for review with the same effect as upon affirmance by an equally divided court.

History of 28 U.S.C. §2109: June 25, 1948, ch. 646, 62 Stat. 963.

§2110. REPEALED

Repealed Apr. 2, 1982, P.L. 97-164, §136, 96 Stat. 41.

§2111. HARMLESS ERROR

On the hearing of any appeal or writ of certiorari in any case, the court shall give judgment after an examination of the record without regard to errors or defects which do not affect the substantial rights of the parties.

History of 28 U.S.C. §2111: May 24, 1949, ch. 139, §110, 63 Stat. 105.

§2112. RECORD ON REVIEW & ENFORCEMENT OF AGENCY ORDERS

(a) The rules prescribed under the authority of section 2072 of this title may provide for the time and manner of filing and the contents of the record in all proceedings instituted in the courts of appeals to enjoin, set aside, suspend, modify, or otherwise review or enforce orders of administrative agencies, boards, commissions, and officers. Such rules may authorize the agency, board, commission, or officer to file in the court a certified list of the materials comprising the record and retain and hold for the court all such materials and transmit the same or any part thereof to the court, when and as required by it, at any time prior to the final determination of the proceeding, and such filing of such certified list of the materials comprising the record and such subsequent transmittal of any such materials when and as required shall be deemed full compliance with any provision of law requiring the filing of the record in the court. The record in such proceedings shall be certified and filed in or held for and transmitted to the court of appeals by the agency, board, commission, or officer concerned within the time and in the manner prescribed by such rules. If proceedings are instituted in two or more courts of appeals with respect to the same order, the following shall apply:

(1) If within ten days after issuance of the order the agency, board, commission, or officer concerned receives, from the persons instituting the proceedings, the petition for review with respect to proceedings in at least two courts of appeals, the agency, board, commission, or officer shall proceed in accordance with paragraph (3) of this subsection. If within ten days after the issuance of the order the agency, board, commission, or officer concerned receives, from the persons instituting the proceedings, the petition for review with respect to proceedings in only one court of appeals, the agency, board, commission, or officer shall file the record in that court notwithstanding the institution in any other court of appeals of proceedings for review of that order. In all other cases in which proceedings have been instituted in two or more courts of appeals with respect to the same order, the agency, board, commission, or officer concerned shall file the record in the court in which proceedings with respect to the order were first instituted.

(2) For purposes of paragraph (1) of this subsection, a copy of the petition or other pleading which institutes proceedings in a court of appeals and which is stamped by the court with the date of filing shall constitute the petition for review. Each agency, board, commission, or officer, as the case may be, shall designate by rule the office and the officer who must receive petitions for review under paragraph (1).

(3) If an agency, board, commission, or officer receives two or more petitions for review of an order in accordance with the first sentence of paragraph (1) of this subsection, the agency, board, commission, or officer shall, promptly after the expiration of the ten-day period specified in that sentence, so notify the judicial panel on multidistrict litigation authorized by section 1407 of this title, in such form as that panel shall prescribe. The judicial panel on multidistrict litigation shall, by means of random selection, designate one court of appeals, from among the courts of appeals in which petitions for review have been filed and received within the ten-day period specified in the first sentence of paragraph (1), in which the record is to be filed, and shall issue an order

consolidating the petitions for review in that court of appeals. The judicial panel on multidistrict litigation shall, after providing notice to the public and an opportunity for the submission of comments, prescribe rules with respect to the consolidation of proceedings under this paragraph. The agency, board, commission, or officer concerned shall file the record in the court of appeals designated pursuant to this paragraph.

(4) Any court of appeals in which proceedings with respect to an order of an agency, board, commission, or officer have been instituted may, to the extent authorized by law, stay the effective date of the order. Any such stay may thereafter be modified, revoked, or extended by a court of appeals designated pursuant to paragraph (3) with respect to that order or by any other court of appeals to which the proceedings are transferred.

(5) All courts in which proceedings are instituted with respect to the same order, other than the court in which the record is filed pursuant to this subsection, shall transfer those proceedings to the court in which the record is so filed. For the convenience of the parties in the interest of justice, the court in which the record is filed may thereafter transfer all the proceedings with respect to that order to any other court of appeals.

(b) The record to be filed in the court of appeals in such a proceeding shall consist of the order sought to be reviewed or enforced, the findings or report upon which it is based, and the pleadings, evidence, and proceedings before the agency, board, commission, or officer concerned, or such portions thereof (1) as the rules prescribed under the authority of section 2072 of this title may require to be included therein, or (2) as the agency, board, commission, or officer concerned, the petitioner for review or respondent in enforcement, as the case may be, and any intervenor in the court proceeding by written stipulation filed with the agency, board, commission, or officer concerned or in the court in any such proceeding may consistently with the rules prescribed under the authority of section 2072 of this title designate to be included therein, or (3) as the court upon motion of a party or, after a prehearing conference, upon its own motion may by order in any such proceeding designate to be included therein. Such a stipulation or order may provide in an appropriate case that no record need be filed in the court of appeals. If, however, the correctness of a finding of fact by the agency, board, commission, or officer is in question all of the evidence before the agency, board, commission, or officer shall be included in the record except such as the agency, board, commission, or officer concerned, the petitioner for review or respondent in enforcement, as the case may be, and any intervenor in the court proceeding by written stipulation filed with the agency, board, commission, or officer concerned or in the court agree to omit as wholly immaterial to the questioned finding. If there is omitted from the record any portion of the proceedings before the agency, board, commission, or officer which the court subsequently determines to be proper for it to consider to enable it to review or enforce the order in question the court may direct that such additional portion of the proceedings be filed as a supplement to the record. The agency, board, commission, or officer concerned may, at its option and without regard to the foregoing provisions of this subsection, and if so requested by the petitioner for review or respondent in enforcement shall, file in the court the entire record of the proceedings before it without abbreviation.

(c) The agency, board, commission, or officer concerned may transmit to the court of appeals the original papers comprising the whole or any part of the record or any supplemental record, otherwise true copies of such papers certified by an authorized officer or deputy of the agency, board, commission, or officer concerned shall be transmitted. Any original papers thus transmitted to the court of appeals shall be returned to the agency, board, commission, or officer concerned upon the final determination of the review or enforcement proceeding. Pending such final determination any such papers may be returned by the court temporarily to the custody of the agency, board, commission, or officer concerned if needed for the transaction of the public business. Certified copies of any papers included in the record or any supplemental record may also be returned to the agency, board, commission, or officer concerned upon the final determination of review or enforcement proceedings.

(d) The provisions of this section are not applicable to proceedings to review decisions of the Tax Court of the United States or to proceedings to review or enforce those orders of administrative agencies, boards, commissions, or officers which are by law reviewable or enforceable by the district courts.

History of 28 U.S.C. §2112: Aug. 28, 1958, P.L. 85-791, §2, 72 Stat. 941; Nov. 6, 1966, P.L. 89-773, §5(a), (b), 80 Stat. 1323; Jan. 8, 1988, P.L. 100-236, §1, 101 Stat. 1731.

§2113. DEFINITION

For purposes of this chapter, the terms "State court," "State courts," and "highest court of a State" include the District of Columbia Court of Appeals.

History of 28 U.S.C. §2113: July 29, 1970, P.L. 91-358, §172(a)(2)(A), 84 Stat. 590.

PART VI. PARTICULAR PROCEEDINGS

CHAPTER 151. DECLARATORY JUDGMENTS

§2201. CREATION OF REMEDY

(a) In a case of actual controversy within its jurisdiction, except with respect to Federal taxes other than actions brought under section 7428 of the Internal Revenue Code of 1986, a proceeding under section 505 or 1146 of title 11, or in any civil action involving an antidumping or countervailing duty proceeding regarding a class or kind of merchandise of a free trade area country (as defined in section 516A(f)(10) of the Tariff Act of 1930), as determined by the administering authority, any court of the United States, upon the filing of an appropriate pleading, may declare the rights and other legal

relations of any interested party seeking such declaration, whether or not further relief is or could be sought. Any such declaration shall have the force and effect of a final judgment or decree and shall be reviewable as such.

(b) For limitations on actions brought with respect to drug patents see section 505 or 512 of the Federal Food, Drug, and Cosmetic Act, or section 351 of the Public Health Service Act.

History of 28 U.S.C. §2201: June 25, 1948, ch. 646, 62 Stat. 964; May 24, 1949, ch. 139, §111, 63 Stat. 105; Aug. 28, 1954, ch. 1033, 68 Stat. 890; July 7, 1958, P.L. 85-508, §12(p), 72 Stat. 349; Oct. 4, 1976, P.L. 94-455, §1306(b)(8), 90 Stat. 1719; Nov. 6, 1978, P.L. 95-598, §249, 92 Stat. 2672; Sept. 24, 1984, P.L. 98-417, §106, 98 Stat. 1597; Sept. 28, 1988, P.L. 100-449, §402(c), 102 Stat. 1884; Nov. 16, 1988, P.L. 100-670, §107(b), 102 Stat. 3984; Dec. 8, 1993, P.L. 103-182, §414(b), 107 Stat. 2147; Mar. 23, 2010, P.L. 111-148, §7002(c)(2), 124 Stat. 816.

See *Commentaries*, "Declaratory Judgment," ch. 2-E, p. 107.

§2202. FURTHER RELIEF

Further necessary or proper relief based on a declaratory judgment or decree may be granted, after reasonable notice and hearing, against any adverse party whose rights have been determined by such judgment.

History of 28 U.S.C. §2202: June 25, 1948, ch. 646, 62 Stat. 964.

See *Commentaries*, "Declaratory Judgment," ch. 2-E, p. 107.

CHAPTER 153. HABEAS CORPUS

§2241. POWER TO GRANT WRIT

(a) Writs of habeas corpus may be granted by the Supreme Court, any justice thereof, the district courts and any circuit judge within their respective jurisdictions. The order of a circuit judge shall be entered in the records of the district court of the district wherein the restraint complained of is had.

(b) The Supreme Court, any justice thereof, and any circuit judge may decline to entertain an application for a writ of habeas corpus and may transfer the application for hearing and determination to the district court having jurisdiction to entertain it.

(c) The writ of habeas corpus shall not extend to a prisoner unless—

(1) He is in custody under or by color of the authority of the United States or is committed for trial before some court thereof; or

(2) He is in custody for an act done or omitted in pursuance of an Act of Congress, or an order, process, judgment or decree of a court or judge of the United States; or

(3) He is in custody in violation of the Constitution or laws or treaties of the United States; or

(4) He, being a citizen of a foreign state and domiciled therein is in custody for an act done or omitted under any alleged right, title, authority, privilege, protection, or exemption claimed under the commission, order or sanction of any foreign state, or under color thereof, the validity and effect of which depend upon the law of nations; or

(5) It is necessary to bring him into court to testify or for trial.

(d) Where an application for a writ of habeas corpus is made by a person in custody under the judgment and sentence of a State court of a State which contains two or more Federal judicial districts, the application may be filed in the district court for the district wherein such person is in custody or in the district court for the district within which the State court was held which convicted and sentenced him and each of such district courts shall have concurrent jurisdiction to entertain the application. The district court for the district wherein such an application is filed in the exercise of its discretion and in furtherance of justice may transfer the application to the other district court for hearing and determination.

(e)(1) No court, justice, or judge shall have jurisdiction to hear or consider an application for a writ of habeas corpus filed by or on behalf of an alien detained by the United States who has been determined by the United States to have been properly detained as an enemy combatant or is awaiting such determination.

(2) Except as provided in paragraphs (2) and (3) of section 1005(e) of the Detainee Treatment Act of 2005 (10 U.S.C. 801 note), no court, justice, or judge shall have jurisdiction to hear or consider any other action against the United States or its agents relating to any aspect of the detention, transfer, treatment, trial, or conditions of confinement of an alien who is or was detained by the United States and has been determined by the United States to have been properly detained as an enemy combatant or is awaiting such determination.

History of 28 U.S.C. §2241: June 25, 1948, ch. 646, 62 Stat. 964; May 24, 1949, ch. 139, §112, 63 Stat. 105; Sept. 19, 1966, P.L. 89-590, 80 Stat. 811; Dec. 30, 2005, P.L. 109-148, §1005(e)(1), 119 Stat. 2742; Jan. 6, 2006, P.L. 109-163, §1405(e)(1), 119 Stat. 3477; Oct. 17, 2006, P.L. 109-366, §7(a), 120 Stat. 2635.

§2242. APPLICATION

Application for a writ of habeas corpus shall be in writing signed and verified by the person for whose relief it is intended or by someone acting in his behalf.

It shall allege the facts concerning the applicant's commitment or detention, the name of the person who has custody over him and by virtue of what claim or authority, if known.

It may be amended or supplemented as provided in the rules of procedure applicable to civil actions.

If addressed to the Supreme Court, a justice thereof or a circuit judge it shall state the reasons for not making application to the district court of the district in which the applicant is held.

History of 28 U.S.C. §2242: June 25, 1948, ch. 646, 62 Stat. 965.

§2243. ISSUANCE OF WRIT; RETURN; HEARING; DECISION

A court, justice or judge entertaining an application for a writ of habeas corpus shall forthwith award the writ or issue an order directing the respondent to show cause why the writ should not be granted, unless it appears from the application that the applicant or person detained is not entitled thereto.

The writ, or order to show cause shall be directed to the person having custody of the person detained. It shall be returned within three days unless for good cause additional time, not exceeding twenty days, is allowed.

The person to whom the writ or order is directed shall make a return certifying the true cause of the detention.

When the writ or order is returned a day shall be set for hearing, not more than five days after the return unless for good cause additional time is allowed.

Unless the application for the writ and the return present only issues of law the person to whom the writ is directed shall be required to produce at the hearing the body of the person detained.

The applicant or the person detained may, under oath, deny any of the facts set forth in the return or allege any other material facts.

The return and all suggestions made against it may be amended, by leave of court, before or after being filed.

The court shall summarily hear and determine the facts, and dispose of the matter as law and justice require.

History of 28 U.S.C. §2243: June 25, 1948, ch. 646, 62 Stat. 965.

§2244. FINALITY OF DETERMINATION

(a) No circuit or district judge shall be required to entertain an application for a writ of habeas corpus to inquire into the detention of a person pursuant to a judgment of a court of the United States if it appears that the legality of such detention has been determined by a judge or court of the United States on a prior application for a writ of habeas corpus, except as provided in section 2255.

(b)(1) A claim presented in a second or successive habeas corpus application under section 2254 that was presented in a prior application shall be dismissed.

(2) A claim presented in a second or successive habeas corpus application under section 2254 that was not presented in a prior application shall be dismissed unless—

(A) the applicant shows that the claim relies on a new rule of constitutional law, made retroactive to cases on collateral review by the Supreme Court, that was previously unavailable; or

(B)(i) the factual predicate for the claim could not have been discovered previously through the exercise of due diligence; and

(ii) the facts underlying the claim, if proven and viewed in light of the evidence as a whole, would be sufficient to establish by clear and convincing evidence that, but for constitutional error, no reasonable factfinder would have found the applicant guilty of the underlying offense.

(3)(A) Before a second or successive application permitted by this section is filed in the district court, the applicant shall move in the appropriate court of appeals for an order authorizing the district court to consider the application.

(B) A motion in the court of appeals for an order authorizing the district court to consider a second or successive application shall be determined by a three-judge panel of the court of appeals.

(C) The court of appeals may authorize the filing of a second or successive application only if it determines that the application makes a prima facie showing that the application satisfies the requirements of this subsection.

(D) The court of appeals shall grant or deny the authorization to file a second or successive application not later than 30 days after the filing of the motion.

(E) The grant or denial of an authorization by a court of appeals to file a second or successive application shall not be appealable and shall not be the subject of a petition for rehearing or for a writ of certiorari.

(4) A district court shall dismiss any claim presented in a second or successive application that the court of appeals has authorized to be filed unless the applicant shows that the claim satisfies the requirements of this section.

(c) In a habeas corpus proceeding brought in behalf of a person in custody pursuant to the judgment of a State court, a prior judgment of the Supreme Court of the United States on an appeal or review by a writ of certiorari at the instance of the prisoner of the decision of such State court, shall be conclusive as to all issues of fact or law with respect to an asserted denial of a Federal right which constitutes ground for discharge in a habeas corpus proceeding, actually adjudicated by the Supreme Court therein, unless the applicant for the writ of habeas corpus shall plead and the court shall find the existence of a material and controlling fact which did not appear in the record of the proceeding in the Supreme Court and the court shall further find that the applicant for the writ of habeas corpus could not have caused such fact to appear in such record by the exercise of reasonable diligence.

(d)(1) A 1-year period of limitation shall apply to an application for a writ of habeas corpus by a person in custody pursuant to the judgment of a State court. The limitation period shall run from the latest of—

(A) the date on which the judgment became final by the conclusion of direct review or the expiration of the time for seeking such review;

(B) the date on which the impediment to filing an application created by State action in violation of the Constitution or laws of the United States is removed, if the applicant was prevented from filing by such State action;

(C) the date on which the constitutional right asserted was initially recognized by the Supreme Court, if the right has been newly recognized by the Supreme Court and made retroactively applicable to cases on collateral review; or

(D) the date on which the factual predicate of the claim or claims presented could have been discovered through the exercise of due diligence.

(2) The time during which a properly filed application for State post-conviction or other collateral review with respect to the pertinent judgment or claim is pending shall not be counted toward any period of limitation under this subsection.

History of 28 U.S.C. §2244: June 25, 1948, ch. 646, 62 Stat. 965; Nov. 2, 1966, P.L. 89-711, §1, 80 Stat. 1104; Apr. 24, 1996, P.L. 104-132, §§101, 106, 110 Stat. 1217, 1220.

§2245. CERTIFICATE OF TRIAL JUDGE ADMISSIBLE IN EVIDENCE

On the hearing of an application for a writ of habeas corpus to inquire into the legality of the detention of a person pursuant to a judgment the certificate of the judge who presided at the trial resulting in the judgment, setting forth the facts occurring at the trial, shall be admissible in evidence. Copies of the certificate shall be filed with the court in which the application is pending and in the court in which the trial took place.

History of 28 U.S.C. §2245: June 25, 1948, ch. 646, 62 Stat. 966.

§2246. EVIDENCE; DEPOSITIONS; AFFIDAVITS

On application for a writ of habeas corpus, evidence may be taken orally or by deposition, or, in the discretion of the judge, by affidavit. If affidavits are admitted any party shall have the right to propound written interrogatories to the affiants, or to file answering affidavits.

History of 28 U.S.C. §2246: June 25, 1948, ch. 646, 62 Stat. 966.

§2247. DOCUMENTARY EVIDENCE

On application for a writ of habeas corpus documentary evidence, transcripts of proceedings upon arraignment, plea and sentence and a transcript of the oral testimony introduced on any previous similar application by or in behalf of the same petitioner, shall be admissible in evidence.

History of 28 U.S.C. §2247: June 25, 1948, ch. 646, 62 Stat. 966.

§2248. RETURN OR ANSWER; CONCLUSIVENESS

The allegations of a return to the writ of habeas corpus or of an answer to an order to show cause in a habeas corpus proceeding, if not traversed, shall be accepted as true except to the extent that the judge finds from the evidence that they are not true.

History of 28 U.S.C. §2248: June 25, 1948, ch. 646, 62 Stat. 966.

§2249. CERTIFIED COPIES OF INDICTMENT, PLEA & JUDGMENT; DUTY OF RESPONDENT

On application for a writ of habeas corpus to inquire into the detention of any person pursuant to a judgment of a court of the United States, the respondent shall promptly file with the court certified copies of the indictment, plea of petitioner and the judgment, or such of them as may be material to the questions raised, if the petitioner fails to attach them to his petition, and same shall be attached to the return to the writ, or to the answer to the order to show cause.

History of 28 U.S.C. §2249: June 25, 1948, ch. 646, 62 Stat. 966.

§2250. INDIGENT PETITIONER ENTITLED TO DOCUMENTS WITHOUT COST

If on any application for a writ of habeas corpus an order has been made permitting the petitioner to prosecute the application in forma pauperis, the clerk of any court of the United States shall furnish to the petitioner without cost certified copies of such documents or parts of the record on file in his office as may be required by order of the judge before whom the application is pending.

History of 28 U.S.C. §2250: June 25, 1948, ch. 646, 62 Stat. 966.

§2251. STAY OF STATE COURT PROCEEDINGS

(a) In general—

(1) Pending matters.—A justice or judge of the United States before whom a habeas corpus proceeding is pending, may, before final judgment or after final judgment of discharge, or pending appeal, stay any proceeding against the person detained in any State court or by or under the authority of any State for any matter involved in the habeas corpus proceeding.

(2) Matter not pending.—For purposes of this section, a habeas corpus proceeding is not pending until the application is filed.

(3) Application for appointment of counsel.—If a State prisoner sentenced to death applies for appointment of counsel pursuant to section 3599(a)(2) of title 18 in a court that would have jurisdiction to entertain a habeas corpus application regarding that sentence, that court may stay execution of the sentence of death, but such stay shall terminate not later than 90 days after counsel is appointed or the application for appointment of counsel is withdrawn or denied.

(b) No further proceedings.—After the granting of such a stay, any such proceeding in any State court or by or under the authority of any State shall be void. If no stay is granted, any such proceeding shall be as valid as if no habeas corpus proceedings or appeal were pending.

History of 28 U.S.C. §2251: June 25, 1948, ch. 646, 62 Stat. 966; Mar. 9, 2006, P.L. 109-177, §507(f), 120 Stat. 251.

§2252. NOTICE

Prior to the hearing of a habeas corpus proceeding in behalf of a person in custody of State officers or by virtue of State laws notice shall be served on the attorney general or other appropriate officer of such State as the justice or judge at the time of issuing the writ shall direct.

History of 28 U.S.C. §2252: June 25, 1948, ch. 646, 62 Stat. 967.

§2253. APPEAL

(a) In a habeas corpus proceeding or a proceeding under section 2255 before a district judge, the final order shall be subject to review, on appeal, by the court of appeals for the circuit in which the proceeding is held.

(b) There shall be no right of appeal from a final order in a proceeding to test the validity of a warrant to remove to an-

other district or place for commitment or trial a person charged with a criminal offense against the United States, or to test the validity of such person's detention pending removal proceedings.

(c)(1) Unless a circuit justice or judge issues a certificate of appealability, an appeal may not be taken to the court of appeals from—

(A) the final order in a habeas corpus proceeding in which the detention complained of arises out of process issued by a State court; or

(B) the final order in a proceeding under section 2255.

(2) A certificate of appealability may issue under paragraph (1) only if the applicant has made a substantial showing of the denial of a constitutional right.

(3) The certificate of appealability under paragraph (1) shall indicate which specific issue or issues satisfy the showing required by paragraph (2).

History of 28 U.S.C. §2253: June 25, 1948, ch. 646, 62 Stat. 967; May 24, 1949, ch. 139, §113, 63 Stat. 105; Oct. 31, 1951, ch. 655, §52, 65 Stat. 727; Apr. 24, 1996, P.L. 104-132, §102, 110 Stat. 1217.

§2254. STATE CUSTODY; REMEDIES IN FEDERAL COURTS

(a) The Supreme Court, a Justice thereof, a circuit judge, or a district court shall entertain an application for a writ of habeas corpus in behalf of a person in custody pursuant to the judgment of a State court only on the ground that he is in custody in violation of the Constitution or laws or treaties of the United States.

(b)(1) An application for a writ of habeas corpus on behalf of a person in custody pursuant to the judgment of a State court shall not be granted unless it appears that—

(A) the applicant has exhausted the remedies available in the courts of the State; or

(B)(i) there is an absence of available State corrective process; or

(ii) circumstances exist that render such process ineffective to protect the rights of the applicant.

(2) An application for a writ of habeas corpus may be denied on the merits, notwithstanding the failure of the applicant to exhaust the remedies available in the courts of the State.

(3) A State shall not be deemed to have waived the exhaustion requirement or be estopped from reliance upon the requirement unless the State, through counsel, expressly waives the requirement.

(c) An applicant shall not be deemed to have exhausted the remedies available in the courts of the State, within the meaning of this section, if he has the right under the law of the State to raise, by any available procedure, the question presented.

(d) An application for a writ of habeas corpus on behalf of a person in custody pursuant to the judgment of a State court shall not be granted with respect to any claim that was adjudicated on the merits in State court proceedings unless the adjudication of the claim—

(1) resulted in a decision that was contrary to, or involved an unreasonable application of, clearly established Federal law, as determined by the Supreme Court of the United States; or

(2) resulted in a decision that was based on an unreasonable determination of the facts in light of the evidence presented in the State court proceeding.

(e)(1) In a proceeding instituted by an application for a writ of habeas corpus by a person in custody pursuant to the judgment of a State court, a determination of a factual issue made by a State court shall be presumed to be correct. The applicant shall have the burden of rebutting the presumption of correctness by clear and convincing evidence.

(2) If the applicant has failed to develop the factual basis of a claim in State court proceedings, the court shall not hold an evidentiary hearing on the claim unless the applicant shows that—

(A) the claim relies on—

(i) a new rule of constitutional law, made retroactive to cases on collateral review by the Supreme Court, that was previously unavailable; or

(ii) a factual predicate that could not have been previously discovered through the exercise of due diligence; and

(B) the facts underlying the claim would be sufficient to establish by clear and convincing evidence that but for constitutional error, no reasonable factfinder would have found the applicant guilty of the underlying offense.

(f) If the applicant challenges the sufficiency of the evidence adduced in such State court proceeding to support the State court's determination of a factual issue made therein, the applicant, if able, shall produce that part of the record pertinent to a determination of the sufficiency of the evidence to support such determination. If the applicant, because of indigency or other reason is unable to produce such part of the record, then the State shall produce such part of the record and the Federal court shall direct the State to do so by order directed to an appropriate State official. If the State cannot provide such pertinent part of the record, then the court shall determine under the existing facts and circumstances what weight shall be given to the State court's factual determination.

(g) A copy of the official records of the State court, duly certified by the clerk of such court to be a true and correct copy of a finding, judicial opinion, or other reliable written indicia showing such a factual determination by the State court shall be admissible in the Federal court proceeding.

(h) Except as provided in section 408 of the Controlled Substances Act, in all proceedings brought under this section, and any subsequent proceedings on review, the court may ap-

point counsel for an applicant who is or becomes financially unable to afford counsel, except as provided by a rule promulgated by the Supreme Court pursuant to statutory authority. Appointment of counsel under this section shall be governed by section 3006A of title 18.

(i) The ineffectiveness or incompetence of counsel during Federal or State collateral post-conviction proceedings shall not be a ground for relief in a proceeding arising under section 2254.

History of 28 U.S.C. §2254: June 25, 1948, ch. 646, 62 Stat. 967; Nov. 2, 1966, P.L. 89-711, §2, 80 Stat. 1105; Apr. 24, 1996, P.L. 104-132, §104, 110 Stat. 1218.

§2255. FEDERAL CUSTODY; REMEDIES ON MOTION ATTACKING SENTENCE

(a) A prisoner in custody under sentence of a court established by Act of Congress claiming the right to be released upon the ground that the sentence was imposed in violation of the Constitution or laws of the United States, or that the court was without jurisdiction to impose such sentence, or that the sentence was in excess of the maximum authorized by law, or is otherwise subject to collateral attack, may move the court which imposed the sentence to vacate, set aside or correct the sentence.

(b) Unless the motion and the files and records of the case conclusively show that the prisoner is entitled to no relief, the court shall cause notice thereof to be served upon the United States attorney, grant a prompt hearing thereon, determine the issues and make findings of fact and conclusions of law with respect thereto. If the court finds that the judgment was rendered without jurisdiction, or that the sentence imposed was not authorized by law or otherwise open to collateral attack, or that there has been such a denial or infringement of the constitutional rights of the prisoner as to render the judgment vulnerable to collateral attack, the court shall vacate and set the judgment aside and shall discharge the prisoner or resentence him or grant a new trial or correct the sentence as may appear appropriate.

(c) A court may entertain and determine such motion without requiring the production of the prisoner at the hearing.

(d) An appeal may be taken to the court of appeals from the order entered on the motion as from a final judgment on application for a writ of habeas corpus.

(e) An application for a writ of habeas corpus in behalf of a prisoner who is authorized to apply for relief by motion pursuant to this section, shall not be entertained if it appears that the applicant has failed to apply for relief, by motion, to the court which sentenced him, or that such court has denied him relief, unless it also appears that the remedy by motion is inadequate or ineffective to test the legality of his detention.

(f) A 1-year period of limitation shall apply to a motion under this section. The limitation period shall run from the latest of—

(1) the date on which the judgment of conviction becomes final;

(2) the date on which the impediment to making a motion created by governmental action in violation of the Constitution or laws of the United States is removed, if the movant was prevented from making a motion by such governmental action;

(3) the date on which the right asserted was initially recognized by the Supreme Court, if that right has been newly recognized by the Supreme Court and made retroactively applicable to cases on collateral review; or

(4) the date on which the facts supporting the claim or claims presented could have been discovered through the exercise of due diligence.

(g) Except as provided in section 408 of the Controlled Substances Act, in all proceedings brought under this section, and any subsequent proceedings on review, the court may appoint counsel, except as provided by a rule promulgated by the Supreme Court pursuant to statutory authority. Appointment of counsel under this section shall be governed by section 3006A of title 18.

(h) A second or successive motion must be certified as provided in section 2244 by a panel of the appropriate court of appeals to contain—

(1) newly discovered evidence that, if proven and viewed in light of the evidence as a whole, would be sufficient to establish by clear and convincing evidence that no reasonable factfinder would have found the movant guilty of the offense; or

(2) a new rule of constitutional law, made retroactive to cases on collateral review by the Supreme Court, that was previously unavailable.

History of 28 U.S.C. §2255: June 25, 1948, ch. 646, 62 Stat. 967; May 24, 1949, ch. 139, §114, 63 Stat. 105; Apr. 24, 1996, P.L. 104-132, §105, 110 Stat. 1220; Jan. 7, 2008, P.L. 110-177, §511, 121 Stat. 2545.

CHAPTER 154. SPECIAL HABEAS CORPUS PROCEDURES IN CAPITAL CASES

§2261. PRISONERS IN STATE CUSTODY SUBJECT TO CAPITAL SENTENCE; APPOINTMENT OF COUNSEL; REQUIREMENT OF RULE OF COURT OR STATUTE; PROCEDURES FOR APPOINTMENT

(a) This chapter shall apply to cases arising under section 2254 brought by prisoners in State custody who are subject to a capital sentence. It shall apply only if the provisions of subsections (b) and (c) are satisfied.

(b) **Counsel.**—This chapter is applicable if—

(1) the Attorney General of the United States certifies that a State has established a mechanism for providing counsel in postconviction proceedings as provided in section 2265; and

(2) counsel was appointed pursuant to that mechanism, petitioner validly waived counsel, petitioner retained counsel, or petitioner was found not to be indigent.

(c) Any mechanism for the appointment, compensation, and reimbursement of counsel as provided in subsection (b) must offer counsel to all State prisoners under capital sentence and must provide for the entry of an order by a court of record—

(1) appointing one or more counsels to represent the prisoner upon a finding that the prisoner is indigent and accepted the offer or is unable competently to decide whether to accept or reject the offer;

(2) finding, after a hearing if necessary, that the prisoner rejected the offer of counsel and made the decision with an understanding of its legal consequences; or

(3) denying the appointment of counsel upon a finding that the prisoner is not indigent.

(d) No counsel appointed pursuant to subsections (b) and (c) to represent a State prisoner under capital sentence shall have previously represented the prisoner at trial in the case for which the appointment is made unless the prisoner and counsel expressly request continued representation.

(e) The ineffectiveness or incompetence of counsel during State or Federal post-conviction proceedings in a capital case shall not be a ground for relief in a proceeding arising under section 2254. This limitation shall not preclude the appointment of different counsel, on the court's own motion or at the request of the prisoner, at any phase of State or Federal post-conviction proceedings on the basis of the ineffectiveness or incompetence of counsel in such proceedings.

History of 28 U.S.C. §2261: Apr. 24, 1996, P.L. 104-132, §107(a), 110 Stat. 1221; Mar. 9, 2006, P.L. 109-177, §507(a), (b), 120 Stat. 250.

§2262. MANDATORY STAY OF EXECUTION; DURATION; LIMITS ON STAYS OF EXECUTION; SUCCESSIVE PETITIONS

(a) Upon the entry in the appropriate State court of record of an order under section 2261(c), a warrant or order setting an execution date for a State prisoner shall be stayed upon application to any court that would have jurisdiction over any proceedings filed under section 2254. The application shall recite that the State has invoked the post-conviction review procedures of this chapter and that the scheduled execution is subject to stay.

(b) A stay of execution granted pursuant to subsection (a) shall expire if—

(1) a State prisoner fails to file a habeas corpus application under section 2254 within the time required in section 2263;

(2) before a court of competent jurisdiction, in the presence of counsel, unless the prisoner has competently and knowingly waived such counsel, and after having been advised of the consequences, a State prisoner under capital sentence waives the right to pursue habeas corpus review under section 2254; or

(3) a State prisoner files a habeas corpus petition under section 2254 within the time required by section 2263 and fails to make a substantial showing of the denial of a Federal right or is denied relief in the district court or at any subsequent stage of review.

(c) If one of the conditions in subsection (b) has occurred, no Federal court thereafter shall have the authority to enter a stay of execution in the case, unless the court of appeals approves the filing of a second or successive application under section 2244(b).

History of 28 U.S.C. §2262: Apr. 24, 1996, P.L. 104-132, §107(a), 110 Stat. 1222.

§2263. FILING OF HABEAS CORPUS APPLICATION; TIME REQUIREMENTS; TOLLING RULES

(a) Any application under this chapter for habeas corpus relief under section 2254 must be filed in the appropriate district court not later than 180 days after final State court affirmance of the conviction and sentence on direct review or the expiration of the time for seeking such review.

(b) The time requirements established by subsection (a) shall be tolled—

(1) from the date that a petition for certiorari is filed in the Supreme Court until the date of final disposition of the petition if a State prisoner files the petition to secure review by the Supreme Court of the affirmance of a capital sentence on direct review by the court of last resort of the State or other final State court decision on direct review;

(2) from the date on which the first petition for post-conviction review or other collateral relief is filed until the final State court disposition of such petition; and

(3) during an additional period not to exceed 30 days, if—

(A) a motion for an extension of time is filed in the Federal district court that would have jurisdiction over the case upon the filing of a habeas corpus application under section 2254; and

(B) a showing of good cause is made for the failure to file the habeas corpus application within the time period established by this section.

History of 28 U.S.C. §2263: Apr. 24, 1996, P.L. 104-132, §107(a), 110 Stat. 1223.

§2264. SCOPE OF FEDERAL REVIEW; DISTRICT COURT ADJUDICATIONS

(a) Whenever a State prisoner under capital sentence files a petition for habeas corpus relief to which this chapter applies, the district court shall only consider a claim or claims that have been raised and decided on the merits in the State courts, unless the failure to raise the claim properly is—

(1) the result of State action in violation of the Constitution or laws of the United States;

(2) the result of the Supreme Court's recognition of a new Federal right that is made retroactively applicable; or

(3) based on a factual predicate that could not have been discovered through the exercise of due diligence in time to present the claim for State or Federal post-conviction review.

(b) Following review subject to subsections (a), (d), and (e) of section 2254, the court shall rule on the claims properly before it.

History of 28 U.S.C. §2264: Apr. 24, 1996, P.L. 104-132, §107(a), 110 Stat. 1223.

§2265. CERTIFICATION & JUDICIAL REVIEW

(a) Certification—

(1) In general.—If requested by an appropriate State official, the Attorney General of the United States shall determine—

(A) whether the State has established a mechanism for the appointment, compensation, and payment of reasonable litigation expenses of competent counsel in State postconviction proceedings brought by indigent prisoners who have been sentenced to death;

(B) the date on which the mechanism described in subparagraph (A) was established; and

(C) whether the State provides standards of competency for the appointment of counsel in proceedings described in subparagraph (A).

(2) Effective date.—The date the mechanism described in paragraph (1)(A) was established shall be the effective date of the certification under this subsection.

(3) Only express requirements.—There are no requirements for certification or for application of this chapter other than those expressly stated in this chapter.

(b) Regulations.—The Attorney General shall promulgate regulations to implement the certification procedure under subsection (a).

(c) Review of certification—

(1) In general.—The determination by the Attorney General regarding whether to certify a State under this section is subject to review exclusively as provided under chapter 158 of this title.

(2) Venue.—The Court of Appeals for the District of Columbia Circuit shall have exclusive jurisdiction over matters under paragraph (1), subject to review by the Supreme Court under section 2350 of this title.

(3) Standard of review.—The determination by the Attorney General regarding whether to certify a State under this section shall be subject to de novo review.

History of 28 U.S.C. §2265: Mar. 9, 2006, P.L. 109-177, §507(c)(1), 120 Stat. 250.

History of Former 28 U.S.C. §2265: Repealed Mar. 9, 2006, P.L. 109-177, §507(c)(1), 120 Stat. 250.

§2266. LIMITATION PERIODS FOR DETERMINING APPLICATIONS & MOTIONS

(a) The adjudication of any application under section 2254 that is subject to this chapter, and the adjudication of any motion under section 2255 by a person under sentence of death, shall be given priority by the district court and by the court of appeals over all noncapital matters.

(b)(1)(A) A district court shall render a final determination and enter a final judgment on any application for a writ of habeas corpus brought under this chapter in a capital case not later than 450 days after the date on which the application is filed, or 60 days after the date on which the case is submitted for decision, whichever is earlier.

(B) A district court shall afford the parties at least 120 days in which to complete all actions, including the preparation of all pleadings and briefs, and if necessary, a hearing, prior to the submission of the case for decision.

(C)(i) A district court may delay for not more than one additional 30-day period beyond the period specified in subparagraph (A), the rendering of a determination of an application for a writ of habeas corpus if the court issues a written order making a finding, and stating the reasons for the finding, that the ends of justice that would be served by allowing the delay outweigh the best interests of the public and the applicant in a speedy disposition of the application.

(ii) The factors, among others, that a court shall consider in determining whether a delay in the disposition of an application is warranted are as follows:

(I) Whether the failure to allow the delay would be likely to result in a miscarriage of justice.

(II) Whether the case is so unusual or so complex, due to the number of defendants, the nature of the prosecution, or the existence of novel questions of fact or law, that it is unreasonable to expect adequate briefing within the time limitations established by subparagraph (A).

(III) Whether the failure to allow a delay in a case that, taken as a whole, is not so unusual or so complex as described in subclause (II), but would otherwise deny the applicant reasonable time to obtain counsel, would unreasonably deny the applicant or the government continuity of counsel, or would deny counsel for the applicant or the government the reasonable time necessary for effective preparation, taking into account the exercise of due diligence.

(iii) No delay in disposition shall be permissible because of general congestion of the court's calendar.

(iv) The court shall transmit a copy of any order issued under clause (i) to the Director of the Administrative Office of the United States Courts for inclusion in the report under paragraph (5).

(2) The time limitations under paragraph (1) shall apply to—

(A) an initial application for a writ of habeas corpus;

(B) any second or successive application for a writ of habeas corpus; and

(C) any redetermination of an application for a writ of habeas corpus following a remand by the court of appeals or the Supreme Court for further proceedings, in which case the limitation period shall run from the date the remand is ordered.

(3)(A) The time limitations under this section shall not be construed to entitle an applicant to a stay of execution, to which the applicant would otherwise not be entitled, for the purpose of litigating any application or appeal.

(B) No amendment to an application for a writ of habeas corpus under this chapter shall be permitted after the filing of the answer to the application, except on the grounds specified in section 2244(b).

(4)(A) The failure of a court to meet or comply with a time limitation under this section shall not be a ground for granting relief from a judgment of conviction or sentence.

(B) The State may enforce a time limitation under this section by petitioning for a writ of mandamus to the court of appeals. The court of appeals shall act on the petition for a writ of mandamus not later than 30 days after the filing of the petition.

(5)(A) The Administrative Office of the United States Courts shall submit to Congress an annual report on the compliance by the district courts with the time limitations under this section.

(B) The report described in subparagraph (A) shall include copies of the orders submitted by the district courts under paragraph (1)(B)(iv).

(c)(1)(A) A court of appeals shall hear and render a final determination of any appeal of an order granting or denying, in whole or in part, an application brought under this chapter in a capital case not later than 120 days after the date on which the reply brief is filed, or if no reply brief is filed, not later than 120 days after the date on which the answering brief is filed.

(B)(i) A court of appeals shall decide whether to grant a petition for rehearing or other request for rehearing en banc not later than 30 days after the date on which the petition for rehearing is filed unless a responsive pleading is required, in which case the court shall decide whether to grant the petition not later than 30 days after the date on which the responsive pleading is filed.

(ii) If a petition for rehearing or rehearing en banc is granted, the court of appeals shall hear and render a final determination of the appeal not later than 120 days after the date on which the order granting rehearing or rehearing en banc is entered.

(2) The time limitations under paragraph (1) shall apply to—

(A) an initial application for a writ of habeas corpus;

(B) any second or successive application for a writ of habeas corpus; and

(C) any redetermination of an application for a writ of habeas corpus or related appeal following a remand by the court of appeals en banc or the Supreme Court for further proceedings, in which case the limitation period shall run from the date the remand is ordered.

(3) The time limitations under this section shall not be construed to entitle an applicant to a stay of execution, to which the applicant would otherwise not be entitled, for the purpose of litigating any application or appeal.

(4)(A) The failure of a court to meet or comply with a time limitation under this section shall not be a ground for granting relief from a judgment of conviction or sentence.

(B) The State may enforce a time limitation under this section by applying for a writ of mandamus to the Supreme Court.

(5) The Administrative Office of the United States Courts shall submit to Congress an annual report on the compliance by the courts of appeals with the time limitations under this section.

History of 28 U.S.C. §2266: Apr. 24, 1996, P.L. 104-132, §107(a), 110 Stat. 1224; Mar. 9, 2006, P.L. 109-177, §507(e), 120 Stat. 251.

CHAPTER 155. INJUNCTIONS; THREE-JUDGE COURTS

§§2281, 2282. REPEALED

Repealed Aug. 12, 1976, P.L. 94-381, §§1, 2, 90 Stat. 1119.

§2283. STAY OF STATE COURT PROCEEDINGS

A court of the United States may not grant an injunction to stay proceedings in a State court except as expressly authorized by Act of Congress, or where necessary in aid of its jurisdiction, or to protect or effectuate its judgments.

History of 28 U.S.C. §2283: June 25, 1948, ch. 646, 62 Stat. 968.

§2284. THREE-JUDGE COURT; WHEN REQUIRED; COMPOSITION; PROCEDURE

(a) A district court of three judges shall be convened when otherwise required by Act of Congress, or when an action is filed challenging the constitutionality of the apportionment of congressional districts or the apportionment of any statewide legislative body.

(b) In any action required to be heard and determined by a district court of three judges under subsection (a) of this section, the composition and procedure of the court shall be as follows:

(1) Upon the filing of a request for three judges, the judge to whom the request is presented shall, unless he determines that three judges are not required, immediately notify

the chief judge of the circuit, who shall designate two other judges, at least one of whom shall be a circuit judge. The judges so designated, and the judge to whom the request was presented, shall serve as members of the court to hear and determine the action or proceeding.

(2) If the action is against a State, or officer or agency thereof, at least five days' notice of hearing of the action shall be given by registered or certified mail to the Governor and attorney general of the State.

(3) A single judge may conduct all proceedings except the trial, and enter all orders permitted by the rules of civil procedure except as provided in this subsection. He may grant a temporary restraining order on a specific finding, based on evidence submitted, that specified irreparable damage will result if the order is not granted, which order, unless previously revoked by the district judge, shall remain in force only until the hearing and determination by the district court of three judges of an application for a preliminary injunction. A single judge shall not appoint a master, or order a reference, or hear and determine any application for a preliminary or permanent injunction or motion to vacate such an injunction, or enter judgment on the merits. Any action of a single judge may be reviewed by the full court at any time before final judgment.

History of 28 U.S.C. §2284: June 25, 1948, ch. 646, 62 Stat. 968; June 11, 1960, P.L. 86-507, §1(19), 74 Stat. 201; Aug. 12, 1976, P.L. 94-381, §3, 90 Stat. 1119; Nov. 8, 1984, P.L. 98-620, §402(29)(E), 98 Stat. 3359.

CHAPTER 157. SURFACE TRANSPORTATION BOARD ORDERS; ENFORCEMENT & REVIEW

§2321. JUDICIAL REVIEW OF BOARD'S ORDERS & DECISIONS; PROCEDURE GENERALLY; PROCESS

(a) Except as otherwise provided by an Act of Congress, a proceeding to enjoin or suspend, in whole or in part, a rule, regulation, or order of the Surface Transportation Board shall be brought in the court of appeals as provided by and in the manner prescribed in chapter 158 of this title.

(b) The procedure in the district courts in actions to enforce, in whole or in part, any order of the Surface Transportation Board other than for payment of money or the collection of fines, penalties, and forfeitures, shall be as provided in this chapter.

(c) The orders, writs, and process of the district courts may, in the cases specified in subsection (b) and in enforcement actions and actions to collect civil penalties under subtitle IV of title 49, run, be served and be returnable anywhere in the United States.

History of 28 U.S.C. §2321: June 25, 1948, ch. 646, 62 Stat. 969; May 24, 1949, ch. 139, §115, 63 Stat. 105; Jan. 2, 1975, P.L. 93-584, §5, 88 Stat. 1917; Oct. 17, 1978, P.L. 95-473, §2(a)(3)(B), 92 Stat. 1465; Dec. 29, 1995, P.L. 104-88, §305(c)(1)(B), (C), 109 Stat. 945.

§2322. UNITED STATES AS PARTY

All actions specified in section 2321 of this title shall be brought by or against the United States.

History of 28 U.S.C. §2322: June 25, 1948, ch. 646, 62 Stat. 969.

§2323. DUTIES OF ATTORNEY GENERAL; INTERVENORS

The Attorney General shall represent the Government in the actions specified in section 2321 of this title and in enforcement actions and actions to collect civil penalties under subtitle IV of title 49.

The Surface Transportation Board and any party or parties in interest to the proceeding before the Board, in which an order or requirement is made, may appear as parties of their own motion and as of right, and be represented by their counsel, in any action involving the validity of such order or requirement or any part thereof, and the interest of such party.

Communities, associations, corporations, firms, and individuals interested in the controversy or question before the Board, or in any action commenced under the aforesaid sections may intervene in said action at any time after commencement thereof.

The Attorney General shall not dispose of or discontinue said action or proceeding over the objection of such party or intervenor, who may prosecute, defend, or continue said action or proceeding unaffected by the action or nonaction of the Attorney General therein.

History of 28 U.S.C. §2323: June 25, 1948, ch. 646, 62 Stat. 970; May 24, 1949, ch. 139, §116, 63 Stat. 105; Jan. 2, 1975, P.L. 93-584, §6, 88 Stat. 1917; Oct. 17, 1978, P.L. 95-473, §2(a)(3)(C), 92 Stat. 1465; Dec. 29, 1995, P.L. 104-88, §305(c)(1)(C), (D), 109 Stat. 945.

§§2324, 2325. REPEALED

Repealed Jan. 2, 1975, P.L. 93-584, §7, 88 Stat. 1918.

CHAPTER 158. ORDERS OF FEDERAL AGENCIES; REVIEW

§2341. DEFINITIONS

As used in this chapter—

(1) "clerk" means the clerk of the court in which the petition for the review of an order, reviewable under this chapter, is filed;

(2) "petitioner" means the party or parties by whom a petition to review an order, reviewable under this chapter, is filed; and

(3) "agency" means—

(A) the Commission, when the order sought to be reviewed was entered by the Federal Communications Commission, the Federal Maritime Commission, or the Atomic Energy Commission, as the case may be;

(B) the Secretary, when the order was entered by the Secretary of Agriculture or the Secretary of Transportation;

(C) the Administration, when the order was entered by the Maritime Administration;

(D) the Secretary, when the order is under section 812 of the Fair Housing Act; and

(E) the Board, when the order was entered by the Surface Transportation Board.

History of 28 U.S.C. §2341: Sept. 6, 1966, P.L. 89-554, §4(e), 80 Stat. 622; Jan. 2, 1975, P.L. 93-584, §3, 88 Stat. 1917; Sept. 13, 1988, P.L. 100-430, §11(b), 102 Stat. 1635; Sept. 3, 1992, P.L. 102-365, §5(c)(1), 106 Stat. 975; Dec. 29, 1995, P.L. 104-88, §305(d)(1)-(4), 109 Stat. 945.

§2342. JURISDICTION OF COURT OF APPEALS

The court of appeals (other than the United States Court of Appeals for the Federal Circuit) has exclusive jurisdiction to enjoin, set aside, suspend (in whole or in part), or to determine the validity of—

(1) all final orders of the Federal Communications Commission made reviewable by section 402(a) of title 47;

(2) all final orders of the Secretary of Agriculture made under chapters 9 and 20A of title 7, except orders issued under sections 210(e), 217a, and 499g(a) of title 7;

(3) all rules, regulations, or final orders of—

(A) the Secretary of Transportation issued pursuant to section 50501, 50502, 56101-56104, or 57109 of title 46 or pursuant to part B or C of subtitle IV, subchapter III of chapter 311, chapter 313, or chapter 315 of title 49; and

(B) the Federal Maritime Commission issued pursuant to section 305, 41304, 41308, or 41309 or chapter 421 or 441 of title 46;

(4) all final orders of the Atomic Energy Commission made reviewable by section 2239 of title 42;

(5) all rules, regulations, or final orders of the Surface Transportation Board made reviewable by section 2321 of this title;

(6) all final orders under section 812 of the Fair Housing Act; and

(7) all final agency actions described in section 20114(c) of title 49.

Jurisdiction is invoked by filing a petition as provided by section 2344 of this title.

History of 28 U.S.C. §2342: Sept. 6, 1966, P.L. 89-554, §4(e), 80 Stat. 622; Jan. 2, 1975, P.L. 93-584, §4, 88 Stat. 1917; Oct. 13, 1978, P.L. 95-454, §206, 92 Stat. 1144; Oct. 15, 1980, P.L. 96-454, §8(b)(2), 94 Stat. 2021; Apr. 2, 1982, P.L. 97-164, §137, 96 Stat. 41; Oct. 30, 1984, P.L. 98-554, §227(a)(4), 98 Stat. 2852; June 19, 1986, P.L. 99-336, §5(a), 100 Stat. 638; Sept. 13, 1988, P.L. 100-430, §11(a), 102 Stat. 1635; Sept. 3, 1992, P.L. 102-365, §5(c)(2), 106 Stat. 975; July 5, 1994, P.L. 103-272, §5(h), 108 Stat. 1375; Dec. 29, 1995, P.L. 104-88, §305(d)(5)-(8), 109 Stat. 945; Oct. 11, 1996, P.L. 104-287, §6(f)(2), 110 Stat. 3399; Aug. 10, 2005, P.L. 109-59, §4125(a), 109 Stat. 1738; Oct. 6, 2006, P.L. 109-304, §17(f)(3), 120 Stat. 1708.

§2343. VENUE

The venue of a proceeding under this chapter is in the judicial circuit in which the petitioner resides or has its principal office, or in the United States Court of Appeals for the District of Columbia Circuit.

History of 28 U.S.C. §2343: Sept. 6, 1966, P.L. 89-554, §4(e), 80 Stat. 622.

§2344. REVIEW OF ORDERS; TIME; NOTICE; CONTENTS OF PETITION; SERVICE

On the entry of a final order reviewable under this chapter, the agency shall promptly give notice thereof by service or publication in accordance with its rules. Any party aggrieved by the final order may, within 60 days after its entry, file a petition to review the order in the court of appeals wherein venue lies. The action shall be against the United States. The petition shall contain a concise statement of—

(1) the nature of the proceedings as to which review is sought;

(2) the facts on which venue is based;

(3) the grounds on which relief is sought; and

(4) the relief prayed.

The petitioner shall attach to the petition, as exhibits, copies of the order, report, or decision of the agency. The clerk shall serve a true copy of the petition on the agency and on the Attorney General by registered mail, with request for a return receipt.

History of 28 U.S.C. §2344: Sept. 6, 1966, P.L. 89-554, §4(e), 80 Stat. 622.

§2345. PREHEARING CONFERENCE

The court of appeals may hold a prehearing conference or direct a judge of the court to hold a prehearing conference.

History of 28 U.S.C. §2345: Sept. 6, 1966, P.L. 89-554, §4(e), 80 Stat. 622.

§2346. CERTIFICATION OF RECORD ON REVIEW

Unless the proceeding has been terminated on a motion to dismiss the petition, the agency shall file in the office of the clerk the record on review as provided by section 2112 of this title.

History of 28 U.S.C. §2346: Sept. 6, 1966, P.L. 89-554, §4(e), 80 Stat. 623.

§2347. PETITIONS TO REVIEW; PROCEEDINGS

(a) Unless determined on a motion to dismiss, petitions to review orders reviewable under this chapter are heard in the court of appeals on the record of the pleadings, evidence adduced, and proceedings before the agency, when the agency has held a hearing whether or not required to do so by law.

(b) When the agency has not held a hearing before taking the action of which review is sought by the petition, the court of appeals shall determine whether a hearing is required by law. After that determination, the court shall—

(1) remand the proceedings to the agency to hold a hearing, when a hearing is required by law;

(2) pass on the issues presented, when a hearing is not required by law and it appears from the pleadings and affidavits filed by the parties that no genuine issue of material fact is presented; or

(3) transfer the proceedings to a district court for the district in which the petitioner resides or has its principal office for a hearing and determination as if the proceedings were originally initiated in the district court, when a hearing is not required by law and a genuine issue of material fact is presented. The procedure in these cases in the district court is governed by the Federal Rules of Civil Procedure.

(c) If a party to a proceeding to review applies to the court of appeals in which the proceeding is pending for leave to adduce additional evidence and shows to the satisfaction of the court that—

(1) the additional evidence is material; and

(2) there were reasonable grounds for failure to adduce the evidence before the agency;

the court may order the additional evidence and any counterevidence the opposite party desires to offer to be taken by the agency. The agency may modify its findings of fact, or make new findings, by reason of the additional evidence so taken, and may modify or set aside its order, and shall file in the court the additional evidence, the modified findings or new findings, and the modified order or the order setting aside the original order.

History of 28 U.S.C. §2347: Sept. 6, 1966, P.L. 89-554, §4(e), 80 Stat. 623.

§2348. REPRESENTATION IN PROCEEDING; INTERVENTION

The Attorney General is responsible for and has control of the interests of the Government in all court proceedings under this chapter. The agency, and any party in interest in the proceeding before the agency whose interests will be affected if an order of the agency is or is not enjoined, set aside, or suspended, may appear as parties thereto of their own motion and as of right, and be represented by counsel in any proceeding to review the order. Communities, associations, corporations, firms, and individuals, whose interests are affected by the order of the agency, may intervene in any proceeding to review the order. The Attorney General may not dispose of or discontinue the proceeding to review over the objection of any party or intervenor, but any intervenor may prosecute, defend, or continue the proceeding unaffected by the action or inaction of the Attorney General.

History of 28 U.S.C. §2348: Sept. 6, 1966, P.L. 89-554, §4(e), 80 Stat. 623.

§2349. JURISDICTION OF THE PROCEEDING

(a) The court of appeals has jurisdiction of the proceeding on the filing and service of a petition to review. The court of appeals in which the record on review is filed, on the filing, has jurisdiction to vacate stay orders or interlocutory injunctions previously granted by any court, and has exclusive jurisdiction to make and enter, on the petition, evidence, and proceedings set forth in the record on review, a judgment determining the validity of, and enjoining, setting aside, or suspending, in whole or in part, the order of the agency.

(b) The filing of the petition to review does not of itself stay or suspend the operation of the order of the agency, but the court of appeals in its discretion may restrain or suspend, in whole or in part, the operation of the order pending the final hearing and determination of the petition. When the petitioner makes application for an interlocutory injunction restraining or suspending the enforcement, operation, or execution of, or setting aside, in whole or in part, any order reviewable under this chapter, at least 5 days' notice of the hearing thereon shall be given to the agency and to the Attorney General. In a case in which irreparable damage would otherwise result to the petitioner, the court of appeals may, on hearing, after reasonable notice to the agency and to the Attorney General, order a temporary stay or suspension, in whole or in part, of the operation of the order of the agency for not more than 60 days from the date of the order pending the hearing on the application for the interlocutory injunction, in which case the order of the court of appeals shall contain a specific finding, based on evidence submitted to the court of appeals, and identified by reference thereto, that irreparable damage would result to the petitioner and specifying the nature of the damage. The court of appeals, at the time of hearing the application for an interlocutory injunction, on a like finding, may continue the temporary stay or suspension, in whole or in part, until decision on the application.

History of 28 U.S.C. §2349: Sept. 6, 1966, P.L. 89-554, §4(e), 80 Stat. 624; Nov. 8, 1984, P.L. 98-620, §402(29)(F), 98 Stat. 3359.

§2350. REVIEW IN SUPREME COURT ON CERTIORARI OR CERTIFICATION

(a) An order granting or denying an interlocutory injunction under section 2349(b) of this title and a final judgment of the court of appeals in a proceeding to review under this chapter are subject to review by the Supreme Court on a writ of certiorari as provided by section 1254(1) of this title. Application for the writ shall be made within 45 days after entry of the order and within 90 days after entry of the judgment, as the case may be. The United States, the agency, or an aggrieved party may file a petition for a writ of certiorari.

(b) The provisions of section 1254(2) of this title, regarding certification, and of section 2101(f) of this title, regarding stays, also apply to proceedings under this chapter.

History of 28 U.S.C. §2350: Sept. 6, 1966, P.L. 89-554, §4(e), 80 Stat. 624; June 27, 1988, P.L. 100-352, §5(e), 102 Stat. 663.

§2351. ENFORCEMENT OF ORDERS BY DISTRICT COURTS

The several district courts have jurisdiction specifically to enforce, and to enjoin and restrain any person from violating any order issued under section 193 of title 7.

History of 28 U.S.C. §2351: Sept. 6, 1966, P.L. 89-554, §4(e), 80 Stat. 624.

§2352. REPEALED

Repealed Nov. 6, 1966, P.L. 89-773, §4, 80 Stat. 1323.

§2353. REPEALED

Repealed Apr. 2, 1982, P.L. 97-164, §138, 96 Stat. 42.

CHAPTER 159. INTERPLEADER

§2361. PROCESS & PROCEDURE

In any civil action of interpleader or in the nature of interpleader under section 1335 of this title, a district court may issue its process for all claimants and enter its order restraining them from instituting or prosecuting any proceeding in any State or United States court affecting the property, instru-

ment or obligation involved in the interpleader action until further order of the court. Such process and order shall be returnable at such time as the court or judge thereof directs, and shall be addressed to and served by the United States marshals for the respective districts where the claimants reside or may be found.

Such district court shall hear and determine the case, and may discharge the plaintiff from further liability, make the injunction permanent, and make all appropriate orders to enforce its judgment.

History of 28 U.S.C. §2361: June 25, 1948, ch. 646, 62 Stat. 970; May 24, 1949, ch. 139, §117, 63 Stat. 105.

See *Commentaries*, "Interpleader," ch. 2-C, p. 87.

CHAPTER 161. UNITED STATES AS PARTY GENERALLY

§2401. TIME FOR COMMENCING ACTION AGAINST UNITED STATES

(a) Except as provided by chapter 71 of title 41, every civil action commenced against the United States shall be barred unless the complaint is filed within six years after the right of action first accrues. The action of any person under legal disability or beyond the seas at the time the claim accrues may be commenced within three years after the disability ceases.

(b) A tort claim against the United States shall be forever barred unless it is presented in writing to the appropriate Federal agency within two years after such claim accrues or unless action is begun within six months after the date of mailing, by certified or registered mail, of notice of final denial of the claim by the agency to which it was presented.

History of 28 U.S.C. §2401: June 25, 1948, ch. 646, 62 Stat. 971; Apr. 25, 1949, ch. 92, §1, 63 Stat. 62; Sept. 8, 1959, P.L. 86-238, §1(3), 73 Stat. 472; July 18, 1966, P.L. 89-506, §7, 80 Stat. 307; Nov. 1, 1978, P.L. 95-563, §14(b), 92 Stat. 2389; Jan. 4, 2011, P.L. 111-350, §5(g)(8), 124 Stat. 3848.

§2402. JURY TRIAL IN ACTIONS AGAINST UNITED STATES

Subject to chapter 179 of this title, any action against the United States under section 1346 shall be tried by the court without a jury, except that any action against the United States under section 1346(a)(1) shall, at the request of either party to such action, be tried by the court with a jury.

History of 28 U.S.C. §2402: June 25, 1948, ch. 646, 62 Stat. 971; July 30, 1954, ch. 648, §2(a), 68 Stat. 589; Oct. 26, 1996, P.L. 104-331, §3(b)(3), 110 Stat. 4069.

§2403. INTERVENTION BY UNITED STATES OR A STATE; CONSTITUTIONAL QUESTION

(a) In any action, suit or proceeding in a court of the United States to which the United States or any agency, officer or employee thereof is not a party, wherein the constitutionality of any Act of Congress affecting the public interest is drawn in question, the court shall certify such fact to the Attorney General, and shall permit the United States to intervene for presentation of evidence, if evidence is otherwise admissible in the case, and for argument on the question of constitutionality. The United States shall, subject to the applicable provisions of law, have all the rights of a party and be subject to all liabilities of a party as to court costs to the extent necessary for a proper presentation of the facts and law relating to the question of constitutionality.

(b) In any action, suit, or proceeding in a court of the United States to which a State or any agency, officer, or employee thereof is not a party, wherein the constitutionality of any statute of that State affecting the public interest is drawn in question, the court shall certify such fact to the attorney general of the State, and shall permit the State to intervene for presentation of evidence, if evidence is otherwise admissible in the case, and for argument on the question of constitutionality. The State shall, subject to the applicable provisions of law, have all the rights of a party and be subject to all liabilities of a party as to court costs to the extent necessary for a proper presentation of the facts and law relating to the question of constitutionality.

History of 28 U.S.C. §2403: June 25, 1948, ch. 646, 62 Stat. 971; Aug. 12, 1976, P.L. 94-381, §5, 90 Stat. 1120.

§2404. DEATH OF DEFENDANT IN DAMAGE ACTION

A civil action for damages commenced by or on behalf of the United States or in which it is interested shall not abate on the death of a defendant but shall survive and be enforceable against his estate as well as against surviving defendants.

History of 28 U.S.C. §2404: June 25, 1948, ch. 646, 62 Stat. 971.

§2405. GARNISHMENT

In any action or suit commenced by the United States against a corporation for the recovery of money upon a bill, note, or other security, the debtors of the corporation may be summoned as garnishees. Any person so summoned shall appear in open court and depose in writing to the amount of his indebtedness to the corporation at the time of the service of the summons and at the time of making the deposition, and judgment may be entered in favor of the United States for the sum admitted by the garnishee to be due the corporation as if it had been due the United States. A judgment shall not be entered against any garnishee until after judgment has been rendered against the corporation, nor until the sum in which the garnishee is indebted is actually due.

When any garnishee deposes in open court that he is not and was not at the time of the service of the summons indebted to the corporation, an issue may be tendered by the United States upon such deposition. If, upon the trial of that issue, a verdict is rendered against the garnishee, judgment shall be entered in favor of the United States, pursuant to such verdict, with costs.

Any garnishee who fails to appear at the term to which he is summoned shall be subject to attachment for contempt.

History of 28 U.S.C. §2405: June 25, 1948, ch. 646, 62 Stat. 971.

§2406. CREDITS IN ACTIONS BY UNITED STATES; PRIOR DISALLOWANCE

In an action by the United States against an individual, evidence supporting the defendant's claim for a credit shall not be admitted unless he first proves that such claim has been disallowed, in whole or in part, by the Government Accountability Office, or that he has, at the time of the trial, obtained possession of vouchers not previously procurable and has been prevented from presenting such claim to the Government Accountability Office by absence from the United States or unavoidable accident.

History of 28 U.S.C. §2406: June 25, 1948, ch. 646, 62 Stat. 972; July 7, 2004, P.L. 108-271, §8(b), 118 Stat. 814.

§2407. DELINQUENTS FOR PUBLIC MONEY; JUDGMENT AT RETURN TERM; CONTINUANCE

In an action by the United States against any person accountable for public money who fails to pay into the Treasury the sum reported due the United States, upon the adjustment of his account the court shall grant judgment upon motion unless a continuance is granted as specified in this section.

A continuance may be granted if the defendant, in open court and in the presence of the United States attorney, states under oath that he is equitably entitled to credits which have been disallowed by the Government Accountability Office prior to the commencement of the action, specifying each particular claim so rejected, and stating that he cannot safely come to trial.

A continuance may also be granted if such an action is commenced on a bond or other sealed instrument and the court requires the original instrument to be produced.

History of 28 U.S.C. §2407: June 25, 1948, ch. 646, 62 Stat. 972; July 7, 2004, P.L. 108-271, §8(b), 118 Stat. 814.

§2408. SECURITY NOT REQUIRED OF UNITED STATES

Security for damages or costs shall not be required of the United States, any department or agency thereof or any party acting under the direction of any such department or agency on the issuance of process or the institution or prosecution of any proceeding.

Costs taxable, under other Acts of Congress, against the United States or any such department, agency or party shall be paid out of the contingent fund of the department or agency which directed the proceedings to be instituted.

History of 28 U.S.C. §2408: June 25, 1948, ch. 646, 62 Stat. 972.

§2409. PARTITION ACTIONS INVOLVING UNITED STATES

Any civil action by any tenant in common or joint tenant owning an undivided interest in lands, where the United States is one of such tenants in common or joint tenants, against the United States alone or against the United States and any other of such owners, shall proceed, and be determined, in the same manner as would a similar action between private persons.

Whenever in such action the court orders a sale of the property or any part thereof the Attorney General may bid for the same in behalf of the United States. If the United States is the purchaser, the amount of the purchase money shall be paid from the Treasury upon a warrant drawn by the Secretary of the Treasury on the requisition of the Attorney General.

History of 28 U.S.C. §2409: June 25, 1948, ch. 646, 62 Stat. 972.

§2409a. REAL PROPERTY QUIET TITLE ACTIONS

(a) The United States may be named as a party defendant in a civil action under this section to adjudicate a disputed title to real property in which the United States claims an interest, other than a security interest or water rights. This section does not apply to trust or restricted Indian lands, nor does it apply to or affect actions which may be or could have been brought under sections 1346, 1347, 1491, or 2410 of this title, sections 7424, 7425, or 7426 of the Internal Revenue Code of 1986, as amended (26 U.S.C. 7424, 7425, and 7426), or section 208 of the Act of July 10, 1952 (43 U.S.C. 666).

(b) The United States shall not be disturbed in possession or control of any real property involved in any action under this section pending a final judgment or decree, the conclusion of any appeal therefrom, and sixty days; and if the final determination shall be adverse to the United States, the United States nevertheless may retain such possession or control of the real property or of any part thereof as it may elect, upon payment to the person determined to be entitled thereto of an amount which upon such election the district court in the same action shall determine to be just compensation for such possession or control.

(c) No preliminary injunction shall issue in any action brought under this section.

(d) The complaint shall set forth with particularity the nature of the right, title, or interest which the plaintiff claims in the real property, the circumstances under which it was acquired, and the right, title, or interest claimed by the United States.

(e) If the United States disclaims all interest in the real property or interest therein adverse to the plaintiff at any time prior to the actual commencement of the trial, which disclaimer is confirmed by order of the court, the jurisdiction of the district court shall cease unless it has jurisdiction of the civil action or suit on ground other than and independent of the authority conferred by section 1346(f) of this title.

(f) A civil action against the United States under this section shall be tried by the court without a jury.

(g) Any civil action under this section, except for an action brought by a State, shall be barred unless it is commenced within twelve years of the date upon which it accrued. Such action shall be deemed to have accrued on the date the plaintiff or his predecessor in interest knew or should have known of the claim of the United States.

(h) No civil action may be maintained under this section by a State with respect to defense facilities (including land) of the United States so long as the lands at issue are being used or required by the United States for national defense purposes as determined by the head of the Federal agency with jurisdiction over the lands involved, if it is determined that the State action was brought more than twelve years after the State knew or should have known of the claims of the United States. Upon cessation of such use or requirement, the State may dispute title to such lands pursuant to the provisions of this section. The decision of the head of the Federal agency is not subject to judicial review.

(i) Any civil action brought by a State under this section with respect to lands, other than tide or submerged lands, on which the United States or its lessee or right-of-way or easement grantee has made substantial improvements or substantial investments or on which the United States has conducted substantial activities pursuant to a management plan such as range improvement, timber harvest, tree planting, mineral activities, farming, wildlife habitat improvement, or other similar activities, shall be barred unless the action is commenced within twelve years after the date the State received notice of the Federal claims to the lands.

(j) If a final determination in an action brought by a State under this section involving submerged or tide lands on which the United States or its lessee or right-of-way or easement grantee has made substantial improvements or substantial investments is adverse to the United States and it is determined that the State's action was brought more than twelve years after the State received notice of the Federal claim to the lands, the State shall take title to the lands subject to any existing lease, easement, or right-of-way. Any compensation due with respect to such lease, easement, or right-of-way shall be determined under existing law.

(k) Notice for the purposes of the accrual of an action brought by a State under this section shall be—

(1) by public communications with respect to the claimed lands which are sufficiently specific as to be reasonably calculated to put the claimant on notice of the Federal claim to the lands, or

(2) by the use, occupancy, or improvement of the claimed lands which, in the circumstances, is open and notorious.

(l) For purposes of this section, the term "tide or submerged lands" means "lands beneath navigable waters" as defined in section 2 of the Submerged Lands Act (43 U.S.C. 1301).

(m) Not less than one hundred and eighty days before bringing any action under this section, a State shall notify the head of the Federal agency with jurisdiction over the lands in question of the State's intention to file suit, the basis therefor, and a description of the lands included in the suit.

(n) Nothing in this section shall be construed to permit suits against the United States based upon adverse possession.

History of 28 U.S.C. §2409a: Oct. 25, 1972, P.L. 92-562, §3(a), 86 Stat. 1176; Oct. 22, 1986, P.L. 99-514, §2, 100 Stat. 2095; Nov. 4, 1986, P.L. 99-598, 100 Stat. 3351.

§2410. ACTIONS AFFECTING PROPERTY ON WHICH UNITED STATES HAS LIEN

(a) Under the conditions prescribed in this section and section 1444 of this title for the protection of the United States, the United States may be named a party in any civil action or suit in any district court, or in any State court having jurisdiction of the subject matter—

(1) to quiet title to,

(2) to foreclose a mortgage or other lien upon,

(3) to partition,

(4) to condemn, or

(5) of interpleader or in the nature of interpleader with respect to,

real or personal property on which the United States has or claims a mortgage or other lien.

(b) The complaint or pleading shall set forth with particularity the nature of the interest or lien of the United States. In actions or suits involving liens arising under the internal revenue laws, the complaint or pleading shall include the name and address of the taxpayer whose liability created the lien and, if a notice of the tax lien was filed, the identity of the internal revenue office which filed the notice, and the date and place such notice of lien was filed. In actions in the State courts service upon the United States shall be made by serving the process of the court with a copy of the complaint upon the United States attorney for the district in which the action is brought or upon an assistant United States attorney or clerical employee designated by the United States attorney in writing filed with the clerk of the court in which the action is brought and by sending copies of the process and complaint, by registered mail, or by certified mail, to the Attorney General of the United States at Washington, District of Columbia. In such actions the United States may appear and answer, plead or demur within sixty days after such service or such further time as the court may allow.

(c) A judgment or decree in such action or suit shall have the same effect respecting the discharge of the property from the mortgage or other lien held by the United States as may be provided with respect to such matters by the local law of the place where the court is situated. However, an action to foreclose a mortgage or other lien, naming the United States as a party under this section, must seek judicial sale. A sale to satisfy a lien inferior to one of the United States shall be made subject to and without disturbing the lien of the United States, unless the United States consents that the property may be sold free of its lien and the proceeds divided

as the parties may be entitled. Where a sale of real estate is made to satisfy a lien prior to that of the United States, the United States shall have one year from the date of sale within which to redeem, except that with respect to a lien arising under the internal revenue laws the period shall be 120 days or the period allowable for redemption under State law, whichever is longer, and in any case in which, under the provisions of section 505 of the Housing Act of 1950, as amended (12 U.S.C. 1701k), and subsection (d) of section 3720 of title 38 of the United States Code, the right to redeem does not arise, there shall be no right of redemption. In any case where the debt owing the United States is due, the United States may ask, by way of affirmative relief, for the foreclosure of its own lien and where property is sold to satisfy a first lien held by the United States, the United States may bid at the sale such sum, not exceeding the amount of its claim with expenses of sale, as may be directed by the head (or his delegate) of the department or agency of the United States which has charge of the administration of the laws in respect to which the claim of the United States arises. In any case where the United States is a bidder at the judicial sale, it may credit the amount determined to be due it against the amount it bids at such sales.

(d) In any case in which the United States redeems real property under this section or section 7425 of the Internal Revenue Code of 1986, the amount to be paid for such property shall be the sum of—

(1) the actual amount paid by the purchaser at such sale (which, in the case of a purchaser who is the holder of the lien being foreclosed, shall include the amount of the obligation secured by such lien to the extent satisfied by reason of such sale),

(2) interest on the amount paid (as determined under paragraph (1)) at 6 percent per annum from the date of such sale, and

(3) the amount (if any) equal to the excess of (A) the expenses necessarily incurred in connection with such property, over (B) the income from such property plus (to the extent such property is used by the purchaser) a reasonable rental value of such property.

(e) Whenever any person has a lien upon any real or personal property, duly recorded in the jurisdiction in which the property is located, and a junior lien, other than a tax lien, in favor of the United States attaches to such property, such person may make a written request to the officer charged with the administration of the laws in respect of which the lien of the United States arises, to have the same extinguished. If after appropriate investigation, it appears to such officer that the proceeds from the sale of the property would be insufficient to wholly or partly satisfy the lien of the United States, or that the claim of the United States has been satisfied or by lapse of time or otherwise has become unenforceable, such officer may issue a certificate releasing the property from such lien.

History of 28 U.S.C. §2410: June 25, 1948, ch. 646, 62 Stat. 972; May 24, 1949, ch. 139, §119, 63 Stat. 105; July 7, 1958, P.L. 85-508, §12(h), 72 Stat. 348; June 11, 1960, P.L. 86-507, §1(20), 74 Stat. 201; Nov. 2, 1966, P.L. 89-719, §201, 80 Stat. 1147; Oct. 22, 1986, P.L. 99-514, §2, 100 Stat. 2095; Nov. 29, 1990, P.L. 101-647, §3630, 104 Stat. 4966; Aug. 6, 1991, P.L. 102-83, §5(c)(2), 105 Stat. 406; Oct. 19, 1996, P.L. 104-316, §114, 110 Stat. 3834.

§2411. INTEREST

In any judgment of any court rendered (whether against the United States, a collector or deputy collector of internal revenue, a former collector or deputy collector, or the personal representative in case of death) for any overpayment in respect of any internal-revenue tax, interest shall be allowed at the overpayment rate established under section 6621 of the Internal Revenue Code of 1986 upon the amount of the overpayment, from the date of the payment or collection thereof to a date preceding the date of the refund check by not more than thirty days, such date to be determined by the Commissioner of Internal Revenue. The Commissioner is authorized to tender by check payment of any such judgment, with interest as herein provided, at any time after such judgment becomes final, whether or not a claim for such payment has been duly filed, and such tender shall stop the running of interest, whether or not such refund check is accepted by the judgment creditor.

History of 28 U.S.C. §2411: June 25, 1948, ch. 646, 62 Stat. 973; May 24, 1949, ch. 139, §120, 63 Stat. 106; Jan. 3, 1975, P.L. 93-625, §7(a)(2), 88 Stat. 2115; Apr. 2, 1982, P.L. 97-164, §302(b), 96 Stat. 56; Oct. 22, 1986, P.L. 99-514, §§2, 1511(c)(18), 100 Stat. 2095, 2746.

§2412. COSTS & FEES

(a)(1) Except as otherwise specifically provided by statute, a judgment for costs, as enumerated in section 1920 of this title, but not including the fees and expenses of attorneys, may be awarded to the prevailing party in any civil action brought by or against the United States or any agency or any official of the United States acting in his or her official capacity in any court having jurisdiction of such action. A judgment for costs when taxed against the United States shall, in an amount established by statute, court rule, or order, be limited to reimbursing in whole or in part the prevailing party for the costs incurred by such party in the litigation.

(2) A judgment for costs, when awarded in favor of the United States in an action brought by the United States, may include an amount equal to the filing fee prescribed under section 1914(a) of this title. The preceding sentence shall not be construed as requiring the United States to pay any filing fee.

(b) Unless expressly prohibited by statute, a court may award reasonable fees and expenses of attorneys, in addition to the costs which may be awarded pursuant to subsection (a), to the prevailing party in any civil action brought by or against the United States or any agency or any official of the United States acting in his or her official capacity in any court having jurisdiction of such action. The United States shall be liable for such fees and expenses to the same extent

that any other party would be liable under the common law or under the terms of any statute which specifically provides for such an award.

(c)(1) Any judgment against the United States or any agency and any official of the United States acting in his or her official capacity for costs pursuant to subsection (a) shall be paid as provided in sections 2414 and 2517 of this title and shall be in addition to any relief provided in the judgment.

(2) Any judgment against the United States or any agency and any official of the United States acting in his or her official capacity for fees and expenses of attorneys pursuant to subsection (b) shall be paid as provided in sections 2414 and 2517 of this title, except that if the basis for the award is a finding that the United States acted in bad faith, then the award shall be paid by any agency found to have acted in bad faith and shall be in addition to any relief provided in the judgment.

(d)(1)(A) Except as otherwise specifically provided by statute, a court shall award to a prevailing party other than the United States fees and other expenses, in addition to any costs awarded pursuant to subsection (a), incurred by that party in any civil action (other than cases sounding in tort), including proceedings for judicial review of agency action, brought by or against the United States in any court having jurisdiction of that action, unless the court finds that the position of the United States was substantially justified or that special circumstances make an award unjust.

(B) A party seeking an award of fees and other expenses shall, within thirty days of final judgment in the action, submit to the court an application for fees and other expenses which shows that the party is a prevailing party and is eligible to receive an award under this subsection, and the amount sought, including an itemized statement from any attorney or expert witness representing or appearing in behalf of the party stating the actual time expended and the rate at which fees and other expenses were computed. The party shall also allege that the position of the United States was not substantially justified. Whether or not the position of the United States was substantially justified shall be determined on the basis of the record (including the record with respect to the action or failure to act by the agency upon which the civil action is based) which is made in the civil action for which fees and other expenses are sought.

(C) The court, in its discretion, may reduce the amount to be awarded pursuant to this subsection, or deny an award, to the extent that the prevailing party during the course of the proceedings engaged in conduct which unduly and unreasonably protracted the final resolution of the matter in controversy.

(D) If, in a civil action brought by the United States or a proceeding for judicial review of an adversary adjudication described in section 504(a)(4) of title 5, the demand by the United States is substantially in excess of the judgment finally obtained by the United States and is unreasonable when compared with such judgment, under the facts and circumstances of the case, the court shall award to the party the fees and other expenses related to defending against the excessive demand, unless the party has committed a willful violation of law or otherwise acted in bad faith, or special circumstances make an award unjust. Fees and expenses awarded under this subparagraph shall be paid only as a consequence of appropriations provided in advance.

(2) For the purposes of this subsection—

(A) "fees and other expenses" includes the reasonable expenses of expert witnesses, the reasonable cost of any study, analysis, engineering report, test, or project which is found by the court to be necessary for the preparation of the party's case, and reasonable attorney fees (The amount of fees awarded under this subsection shall be based upon prevailing market rates for the kind and quality of the services furnished, except that (i) no expert witness shall be compensated at a rate in excess of the highest rate of compensation for expert witnesses paid by the United States; and (ii) attorney fees shall not be awarded in excess of $125 per hour unless the court determines that an increase in the cost of living or a special factor, such as the limited availability of qualified attorneys for the proceedings involved, justifies a higher fee.);

(B) "party" means (i) an individual whose net worth did not exceed $2,000,000 at the time the civil action was filed, or (ii) any owner of an unincorporated business, or any partnership, corporation, association, unit of local government, or organization, the net worth of which did not exceed $7,000,000 at the time the civil action was filed, and which had not more than 500 employees at the time the civil action was filed; except that an organization described in section 501(c)(3) of the Internal Revenue Code of 1986 (26 U.S.C. 501(c)(3)) exempt from taxation under section 501(a) of such Code, or a cooperative association as defined in section 15(a) of the Agricultural Marketing Act (12 U.S.C. 1141j(a)), may be a party regardless of the net worth of such organization or cooperative association or for purposes of subsection (d)(1)(D), a small entity as defined in section 601 of title 5;

(C) "United States" includes any agency and any official of the United States acting in his or her official capacity;

(D) "position of the United States" means, in addition to the position taken by the United States in the civil action, the action or failure to act by the agency upon which the civil action is based; except that fees and expenses may not be awarded to a party for any portion of the litigation in which the party has unreasonably protracted the proceedings;

(E) "civil action brought by or against the United States" includes an appeal by a party, other than the United States, from a decision of a contracting officer rendered pursuant to a disputes clause in a contract with the Government or pursuant to chapter 71 of title 41;

(F) "court" includes the United States Court of Federal Claims and the United States Court of Appeals for Veterans Claims;

(G) "final judgment" means a judgment that is final and not appealable, and includes an order of settlement;

(H) "prevailing party", in the case of eminent domain proceedings, means a party who obtains a final judgment (other than by settlement), exclusive of interest, the amount of which is at least as close to the highest valuation of the property involved that is attested to at trial on behalf of the property owner as it is to the highest valuation of the property involved that is attested to at trial on behalf of the Government; and

(I) "demand" means the express demand of the United States which led to the adversary adjudication, but shall not include a recitation of the maximum statutory penalty (i) in the complaint, or (ii) elsewhere when accompanied by an express demand for a lesser amount.

(3) In awarding fees and other expenses under this subsection to a prevailing party in any action for judicial review of an adversary adjudication, as defined in subsection (b)(1)(C) of section 504 of title 5, United States Code, or an adversary adjudication subject to chapter 71 of title 41, the court shall include in that award fees and other expenses to the same extent authorized in subsection (a) of such section, unless the court finds that during such adversary adjudication the position of the United States was substantially justified, or that special circumstances make an award unjust.

(4) Fees and other expenses awarded under this subsection to a party shall be paid by any agency over which the party prevails from any funds made available to the agency by appropriation or otherwise.

(e) The provisions of this section shall not apply to any costs, fees, and other expenses in connection with any proceeding to which section 7430 of the Internal Revenue Code of 1986 applies (determined without regard to subsections (b) and (f) of such section). Nothing in the preceding sentence shall prevent the awarding under subsection (a) of section 2412 of title 28, United States Code, of costs enumerated in section 1920 of such title (as in effect on October 1, 1981).

(f) If the United States appeals an award of costs or fees and other expenses made against the United States under this section and the award is affirmed in whole or in part, interest shall be paid on the amount of the award as affirmed. Such interest shall be computed at the rate determined under section 1961(a) of this title, and shall run from the date of the award through the day before the date of the mandate of affirmance.

History of 28 U.S.C. §2412: June 25, 1948, ch. 646, 62 Stat. 973; July 18, 1966, P.L. 89-507, §1, 80 Stat. 308; Oct. 21, 1980, P.L. 96-481, §204(a), (c), 94 Stat. 2327, 2329; Sept. 3, 1982, P.L. 97-248, §292(c), 96 Stat. 574; Aug. 5, 1985, P.L. 99-80, §§2, 6, 99 Stat. 184, 186; Oct. 22, 1986, P.L. 99-514, §2, 100 Stat. 2095; Oct. 29, 1992, P.L. 102-572, §§301(a), 502(b), 506(a), 902(b)(1), 106 Stat. 4511-4513, 4516; Dec. 21, 1995, P.L. 104-66, §1091(b), 109 Stat. 722; Mar. 29, 1996, P.L. 104-121, §232, 110 Stat. 863; Nov. 11, 1998, P.L. 105-368, §512(b)(1)(B), 112 Stat. 3342; Jan. 4, 2011, P.L. 111-350, §5(g)(9), 124 Stat. 3848.

See *Commentaries*, "Motion for Attorney Fees," ch. 9-C, p. 745.

§2413. EXECUTIONS IN FAVOR OF UNITED STATES

A writ of execution on a judgment obtained for the use of the United States in any court thereof shall be issued from and made returnable to the court which rendered the judgment, but may be executed in any other State, in any Territory, or in the District of Columbia.

History of 28 U.S.C. §2413: June 25, 1948, ch. 646, 62 Stat. 974.

§2414. PAYMENT OF JUDGMENTS & COMPROMISE SETTLEMENTS

Except as provided by chapter 71 of title 41, payment of final judgments rendered by a district court or the Court of International Trade against the United States shall be made on settlements by the Secretary of the Treasury. Payment of final judgments rendered by a State or foreign court or tribunal against the United States, or against its agencies or officials upon obligations or liabilities of the United States, shall be made on settlements by the Secretary of the Treasury after certification by the Attorney General that it is in the interest of the United States to pay the same.

Whenever the Attorney General determines that no appeal shall be taken from a judgment or that no further review will be sought from a decision affirming the same, he shall so certify and the judgment shall be deemed final.

Except as otherwise provided by law, compromise settlements of claims referred to the Attorney General for defense of imminent litigation or suits against the United States, or against its agencies or officials upon obligations or liabilities of the United States, made by the Attorney General or any person authorized by him, shall be settled and paid in a manner similar to judgments in like causes and appropriations or funds available for the payment of such judgments are hereby made available for the payment of such compromise settlements.

History of 28 U.S.C. §2414: June 25, 1948, ch. 646, 62 Stat. 974; Aug. 30, 1961, P.L. 87-187, §1, 75 Stat. 415; Nov. 1, 1978, P.L. 95-563, §14(d), 92 Stat. 2390; Oct. 10, 1980, P.L. 96-417, §512, 94 Stat. 1744; Oct. 19, 1996, P.L. 104-316, §202(k), 110 Stat. 3843; Jan. 4, 2011, P.L. 111-350, §5(g)(10), 124 Stat. 3848.

§2415. TIME FOR COMMENCING ACTIONS BROUGHT BY THE UNITED STATES

(a) Subject to the provisions of section 2416 of this title, and except as otherwise provided by Congress, every action for money damages brought by the United States or an officer or agency thereof which is founded upon any contract express or implied in law or fact, shall be barred unless the complaint is filed within six years after the right of action accrues or within one year after final decisions have been rendered in applicable administrative proceedings required by contract or by law, whichever is later: Provided, That in the event of later partial payment or written acknowledgment of debt, the right of action shall be deemed to accrue again at the time of each such payment or acknowledgment: Provided further, That an

action for money damages brought by the United States for or on behalf of a recognized tribe, band or group of American Indians shall not be barred unless the complaint is filed more than six years and ninety days after the right of action accrued: Provided further, That an action for money damages which accrued on the date of enactment of this Act in accordance with subsection (g) brought by the United States for or on behalf of a recognized tribe, band, or group of American Indians, or on behalf of an individual Indian whose land is held in trust or restricted status, shall not be barred unless the complaint is filed sixty days after the date of publication of the list required by section 4(c) of the Indian Claims Limitation Act of 1982: Provided, That, for those claims that are on either of the two lists published pursuant to the Indian Claims Limitation Act of 1982, any right of action shall be barred unless the complaint is filed within (1) one year after the Secretary of the Interior has published in the Federal Register a notice rejecting such claim or (2) three years after the date the Secretary of the Interior has submitted legislation or legislative report to Congress to resolve such claim or more than two years after a final decision has been rendered in applicable administrative proceedings required by contract or by law, whichever is later.

(b) Subject to the provisions of section 2416 of this title, and except as otherwise provided by Congress, every action for money damages brought by the United States or an officer or agency thereof which is founded upon a tort shall be barred unless the complaint is filed within three years after the right of action first accrues: Provided, That an action to recover damages resulting from a trespass on lands of the United States; an action to recover damages resulting from fire to such lands; an action to recover for diversion of money paid under a grant program; and an action for conversion of property of the United States may be brought within six years after the right of action accrues, except that such actions for or on behalf of a recognized tribe, band or group of American Indians, including actions relating to allotted trust or restricted Indian lands, may be brought within six years and ninety days after the right of action accrues, except that such actions for or on behalf of a recognized tribe, band, or group of American Indians, including actions relating to allotted trust or restricted Indian lands, or on behalf of an individual Indian whose land is held in trust or restricted status which accrued on the date of enactment of this Act in accordance with subsection (g) may be brought on or before sixty days after the date of the publication of the list required by section 4(c) of the Indian Claims Limitation Act of 1982: Provided, That, for those claims that are on either of the two lists published pursuant to the Indian Claims Limitation Act of 1982, any right of action shall be barred unless the complaint is filed within (1) one year after the Secretary of the Interior has published in the Federal Register a notice rejecting such claim or (2) three years after the Secretary of the Interior has submitted legislation or legislative report to Congress to resolve such claim.

(c) Nothing herein shall be deemed to limit the time for bringing an action to establish the title to, or right of possession of, real or personal property.

(d) Subject to the provisions of section 2416 of this title and except as otherwise provided by Congress, every action for the recovery of money erroneously paid to or on behalf of any civilian employee of any agency of the United States or to or on behalf of any member or dependent of any member of the uniformed services of the United States, incident to the employment or services of such employee or member, shall be barred unless the complaint is filed within six years after the right of action accrues: Provided, That in the event of later partial payment or written acknowledgment of debt, the right of action shall be deemed to accrue again at the time of each such payment or acknowledgment.

(e) In the event that any action to which this section applies is timely brought and is thereafter dismissed without prejudice, the action may be recommenced within one year after such dismissal, regardless of whether the action would otherwise then be barred by this section. In any action so recommenced the defendant shall not be barred from interposing any claim which would not have been barred in the original action.

(f) The provisions of this section shall not prevent the assertion, in an action against the United States or an officer or agency thereof, of any claim of the United States or an officer or agency thereof against an opposing party, a co-party, or a third party that arises out of the transaction or occurrence that is the subject matter of the opposing party's claim. A claim of the United States or an officer or agency thereof that does not arise out of the transaction or occurrence that is the subject matter of the opposing party's claim may, if time-barred, be asserted only by way of offset and may be allowed in an amount not to exceed the amount of the opposing party's recovery.

(g) Any right of action subject to the provisions of this section which accrued prior to the date of enactment of this Act shall, for purposes of this section, be deemed to have accrued on the date of enactment of this Act.

(h) Nothing in this Act shall apply to actions brought under the Internal Revenue Code or incidental to the collection of taxes imposed by the United States.

(i) The provisions of this section shall not prevent the United States or an officer or agency thereof from collecting any claim of the United States by means of administrative offset, in accordance with section 3716 of title 31.

History of 28 U.S.C. §2415: July 18, 1966, P.L. 89-505, §1, 80 Stat. 304; July 18, 1972, P.L. 92-353, 86 Stat. 499; Oct. 13, 1972, P.L. 92-485, 86 Stat. 803; July 11, 1977, P.L. 95-64, 91 Stat. 268; Aug. 15, 1977, P.L. 95-103, 91 Stat. 842; Mar. 27, 1980, P.L. 96-217, §1, 94 Stat. 126; Oct. 25, 1982, P.L. 97-365, §9, 96 Stat. 1754; Dec. 30, 1982, P.L. 97-394, §2, 96 Stat. 1976; Jan. 12, 1983, P.L. 97-452, §2(d)(2), 96 Stat. 2478; Apr. 3, 1984, P.L. 98-250, §4(a), 98 Stat. 118.

§2416. TIME FOR COMMENCING ACTIONS BROUGHT BY THE UNITED STATES—EXCLUSIONS

For the purpose of computing the limitations periods established in section 2415, there shall be excluded all periods during which—

(a) the defendant or the res is outside the United States, its territories and possessions, the District of Columbia, or the Commonwealth of Puerto Rico; or

(b) the defendant is exempt from legal process because of infancy, mental incompetence, diplomatic immunity, or for any other reason; or

(c) facts material to the right of action are not known and reasonably could not be known by an official of the United States charged with the responsibility to act in the circumstances; or

(d) the United States is in a state of war declared pursuant to article I, section 8, of the Constitution of the United States.

History of 28 U.S.C. §2416: July 18, 1966, P.L. 89-505, §1, 80 Stat. 305.

CHAPTER 163. FINES, PENALTIES & FORFEITURES

§2461. MODE OF RECOVERY

(a) Whenever a civil fine, penalty or pecuniary forfeiture is prescribed for the violation of an Act of Congress without specifying the mode of recovery or enforcement thereof, it may be recovered in a civil action.

(b) Unless otherwise provided by Act of Congress, whenever a forfeiture of property is prescribed as a penalty for violation of an Act of Congress and the seizure takes place on the high seas or on navigable waters within the admiralty and maritime jurisdiction of the United States, such forfeiture may be enforced by libel in admiralty but in cases of seizures on land the forfeiture may be enforced by a proceeding by libel which shall conform as near as may be to proceedings in admiralty.

(c) If a person is charged in a criminal case with a violation of an Act of Congress for which the civil or criminal forfeiture of property is authorized, the Government may include notice of the forfeiture in the indictment or information pursuant to the Federal Rules of Criminal Procedure. If the defendant is convicted of the offense giving rise to the forfeiture, the court shall order the forfeiture of the property as part of the sentence in the criminal case pursuant to to[1] the Federal Rules of Criminal Procedure and section 3554 of title 18, United States Code. The procedures in section 413 of the Controlled Substances Act (21 U.S.C. 853) apply to all stages of a criminal forfeiture proceeding, except that subsection (d) of such section applies only in cases in which the defendant is convicted of a violation of such Act.

1. **Editor's note:** So in original. The second "to" probably should not appear.

History of 28 U.S.C. §2461: June 25, 1948, ch. 646, 62 Stat. 974; Apr. 25, 2000, P.L. 106-185, §16, 114 Stat. 221; Mar. 9, 2006, P.L. 109-177, §410, 120 Stat. 246.

§2462. TIME FOR COMMENCING PROCEEDINGS

Except as otherwise provided by Act of Congress, an action, suit or proceeding for the enforcement of any civil fine, penalty, or forfeiture, pecuniary or otherwise, shall not be entertained unless commenced within five years from the date when the claim first accrued if, within the same period, the offender or the property is found within the United States in order that proper service may be made thereon.

History of 28 U.S.C. §2462: June 25, 1948, ch. 646, 62 Stat. 974.

§2463. PROPERTY TAKEN UNDER REVENUE LAW NOT REPLEVIABLE

All property taken or detained under any revenue law of the United States shall not be repleviable, but shall be deemed to be in the custody of the law and subject only to the orders and decrees of the courts of the United States having jurisdiction thereof.

History of 28 U.S.C. §2463: June 25, 1948, ch. 646, 62 Stat. 974.

§2464. SECURITY; SPECIAL BOND

(a) Except in cases of seizures for forfeiture under any law of the United States, whenever a warrant of arrest or other process in rem is issued in any admiralty case, the United States marshal shall stay the execution of such process, or discharge the property arrested if the process has been levied, on receiving from the respondent or claimant of the property a bond or stipulation in double the amount claimed by the libellant, with sufficient surety, to be approved by the judge of the district court where the case is pending, or, in his absence, by the collector of the port, conditioned to answer the decree of the court in such case. Such bond or stipulation shall be returned to the court, and judgment or decree thereon, against both the principal and sureties, may be secured at the time of rendering the decree in the original case. The owner of any vessel may deliver to the marshal a bond or stipulation, with sufficient surety, to be approved by the judge of the district court, conditioned to answer the decree of such court in all or any cases that are brought thereafter in such court against the vessel. Thereupon the execution of all such process against such vessel shall be stayed so long as the amount secured by such bond or stipulation is at least double the aggregate amount claimed by libellants in such suits which are begun and pending against such vessel. Similar judgments or decrees and remedies may be had on such bond or stipulation as if a special bond or stipulation had been filed in each of such suits.

(b) The court may make necessary orders to carry this section into effect, particularly in giving proper notice of any such suit. Such bond or stipulation shall be indorsed by the clerk with a minute of the suits wherein process is so stayed. Further security may be required by the court at any time.

(c) If a special bond or stipulation in the particular case is given under this section, the liability as to said case on the general bond or stipulation shall cease. The parties may

stipulate the amount of the bond or stipulation for the release of a vessel or other property to be not more than the amount claimed in the libel, with interest, plus an allowance for libellant's costs. In the event of the inability or refusal of the parties to so stipulate, the court shall fix the amount, but if not so fixed then a bond shall be required in the amount prescribed in this section.

History of 28 U.S.C. §2464: June 25, 1948, ch. 646, 62 Stat. 974.

§2465. RETURN OF PROPERTY TO CLAIMANT; LIABILITY FOR WRONGFUL SEIZURE; ATTORNEY FEES, COSTS & INTEREST

(a) Upon the entry of a judgment for the claimant in any proceeding to condemn or forfeit property seized or arrested under any provision of Federal law—

(1) such property shall be returned forthwith to the claimant or his agent; and

(2) if it appears that there was reasonable cause for the seizure or arrest, the court shall cause a proper certificate thereof to be entered and, in such case, neither the person who made the seizure or arrest nor the prosecutor shall be liable to suit or judgment on account of such suit or prosecution, nor shall the claimant be entitled to costs, except as provided in subsection (b).

(b)(1) Except as provided in paragraph (2), in any civil proceeding to forfeit property under any provision of Federal law in which the claimant substantially prevails, the United States shall be liable for—

(A) reasonable attorney fees and other litigation costs reasonably incurred by the claimant;

(B) post-judgment interest, as set forth in section 1961 of this title; and

(C) in cases involving currency, other negotiable instruments, or the proceeds of an interlocutory sale—

(i) interest actually paid to the United States from the date of seizure or arrest of the property that resulted from the investment of the property in an interest-bearing account or instrument; and

(ii) an imputed amount of interest that such currency, instruments, or proceeds would have earned at the rate applicable to the 30-day Treasury Bill, for any period during which no interest was paid (not including any period when the property reasonably was in use as evidence in an official proceeding or in conducting scientific tests for the purpose of collecting evidence), commencing 15 days after the property was seized by a Federal law enforcement agency, or was turned over to a Federal law enforcement agency by a State or local law enforcement agency.

(2)(A) The United States shall not be required to disgorge the value of any intangible benefits nor make any other payments to the claimant not specifically authorized by this subsection.

(B) The provisions of paragraph (1) shall not apply if the claimant is convicted of a crime for which the interest of the claimant in the property was subject to forfeiture under a Federal criminal forfeiture law.

(C) If there are multiple claims to the same property, the United States shall not be liable for costs and attorneys fees associated with any such claim if the United States—

(i) promptly recognizes such claim;

(ii) promptly returns the interest of the claimant in the property to the claimant, if the property can be divided without difficulty and there are no competing claims to that portion of the property;

(iii) does not cause the claimant to incur additional, reasonable costs or fees; and

(iv) prevails in obtaining forfeiture with respect to one or more of the other claims.

(D) If the court enters judgment in part for the claimant and in part for the Government, the court shall reduce the award of costs and attorney fees accordingly.

History of 28 U.S.C. §2465: June 25, 1948, ch. 646, 62 Stat. 975; Apr. 25, 2000, P.L. 106-185, §4(a), 114 Stat. 212.

§2466. FUGITIVE DISENTITLEMENT

(a) A judicial officer may disallow a person from using the resources of the courts of the United States in furtherance of a claim in any related civil forfeiture action or a claim in third party proceedings in any related criminal forfeiture action upon a finding that such person—

(1) after notice or knowledge of the fact that a warrant or process has been issued for his apprehension, in order to avoid criminal prosecution—

(A) purposely leaves the jurisdiction of the United States;

(B) declines to enter or reenter the United States to submit to its jurisdiction; or

(C) otherwise evades the jurisdiction of the court in which a criminal case is pending against the person; and

(2) is not confined or held in custody in any other jurisdiction for commission of criminal conduct in that jurisdiction.

(b) Subsection (a) may be applied to a claim filed by a corporation if any majority shareholder, or individual filing the claim on behalf of the corporation is a person to whom subsection (a) applies.

History of 28 U.S.C. §2466: Apr. 25, 2000, P.L. 106-185, §14(a), 114 Stat. 219; Oct. 26, 2001, P.L. 107-56, §322, 115 Stat. 315.

§2467. ENFORCEMENT OF FOREIGN JUDGMENT

(a) Definitions.—In this section—

(1) the term "foreign nation" means a country that has become a party to the United Nations Convention Against Illicit Traffic in Narcotic Drugs and Psychotropic Substances (referred to in this section as the "United Nations Convention") or a foreign jurisdiction with which the United States

has a treaty or other formal international agreement in effect providing for mutual forfeiture assistance; and

(2) the term "forfeiture or confiscation judgment" means a final order of a foreign nation compelling a person or entity—

(A) to pay a sum of money representing the proceeds of an offense described in Article 3, Paragraph 1, of the United Nations Convention, any violation of foreign law that would constitute a violation or an offense for which property could be forfeited under Federal law if the offense were committed in the United States, or any foreign offense described in section 1956(c)(7)(B) of title 18, or property the value of which corresponds to such proceeds; or

(B) to forfeit property involved in or traceable to the commission of such offense.

(b) Review by Attorney General—

(1) In general.—A foreign nation seeking to have a forfeiture or confiscation judgment registered and enforced by a district court of the United States under this section shall first submit a request to the Attorney General or the designee of the Attorney General, which request shall include—

(A) a summary of the facts of the case and a description of the proceedings that resulted in the forfeiture or confiscation judgment;

(B) certified[1] copy of the forfeiture or confiscation judgment;

(C) an affidavit or sworn declaration establishing that the foreign nation took steps, in accordance with the principles of due process, to give notice of the proceedings to all persons with an interest in the property in sufficient time to enable such persons to defend against the charges and that the judgment rendered is in force and is not subject to appeal; and

(D) such additional information and evidence as may be required by the Attorney General or the designee of the Attorney General.

(2) Certification of request.—The Attorney General or the designee of the Attorney General shall determine whether, in the interest of justice, to certify the request, and such decision shall be final and not subject to either judicial review or review under subchapter II of chapter 5, or chapter 7, of title 5 (commonly known as the "Administrative Procedure Act").

(c) Jurisdiction and venue—

(1) In general.—If the Attorney General or the designee of the Attorney General certifies a request under subsection (b), the United States may file an application on behalf of a foreign nation in district court of the United States seeking to enforce the foreign forfeiture or confiscation judgment as if the judgment had been entered by a court in the United States.

(2) Proceedings.—In a proceeding filed under paragraph (1)—

(A) the United States shall be the applicant and the defendant or another person or entity affected by the forfeiture or confiscation judgment shall be the respondent;

(B) venue shall lie in the district court for the District of Columbia or in any other district in which the defendant or the property that may be the basis for satisfaction of a judgment under this section may be found; and

(C) the district court shall have personal jurisdiction over a defendant residing outside of the United States if the defendant is served with process in accordance with rule 4 of the Federal Rules of Civil Procedure.

(d) Entry and enforcement of judgment—

(1) In general.—The district court shall enter such orders as may be necessary to enforce the judgment on behalf of the foreign nation unless the court finds that—

(A) the judgment was rendered under a system that provides tribunals or procedures incompatible with the requirements of due process of law;

(B) the foreign court lacked personal jurisdiction over the defendant;

(C) the foreign court lacked jurisdiction over the subject matter;

(D) the foreign nation did not take steps, in accordance with the principles of due process, to give notice of the proceedings to a person with an interest in the property of the proceedings[2] in sufficient time to enable him or her to defend; or

(E) the judgment was obtained by fraud.

(2) Process.—Process to enforce a judgment under this section shall be in accordance with rule 69(a) of the Federal Rules of Civil Procedure.

(3) Preservation of property—

(A) Restraining orders—

(i) In general.—To preserve the availability of property subject to civil or criminal forfeiture under foreign law, the Government may apply for, and the court may issue, a restraining order at any time before or after the initiation of forfeiture proceedings by a foreign nation.

(ii) Procedures—

(I) In general.—A restraining order under this subparagraph shall be issued in a manner consistent with subparagraphs (A), (C), and (E) of paragraph (1) and the procedural due process protections for a restraining order under section 983(j) of title 18.

(II) Application.—For purposes of applying such section 983(j)—

(aa) references in such section 983(j) to civil forfeiture or the filing of a complaint shall be deemed to refer to the applicable foreign criminal or forfeiture proceedings; and

(bb) the reference in paragraph (1)(B)(i) of such section 983(j) to the United States shall be deemed to refer to the foreign nation.

(B) Evidence.—The court, in issuing a restraining order under subparagraph (A)—

(i) may rely on information set forth in an affidavit describing the nature of the proceeding or investigation underway in the foreign country, and setting forth a reasonable basis to believe that the property to be restrained will be named in a judgment of forfeiture at the conclusion of such proceeding; or

(ii) may register and enforce a restraining order that has been issued by a court of competent jurisdiction in the foreign country and certified by the Attorney General pursuant to subsection (b)(2).

(C) Limit on grounds for objection.—No person may object to a restraining order under subparagraph (A) on any ground that is the subject of parallel litigation involving the same property that is pending in a foreign court.

(e) Finality of foreign findings.—In entering orders to enforce the judgment, the court shall be bound by the findings of fact to the extent that they are stated in the foreign forfeiture or confiscation judgment.

(f) Currency conversion.—The rate of exchange in effect at the time the suit to enforce is filed by the foreign nation shall be used in calculating the amount stated in any forfeiture or confiscation judgment requiring the payment of a sum of money submitted for registration.

1. **Editor's note:** So in original. Probably should be preceded by "a."

2. **Editor's note:** So in original. The words "of the proceedings" probably should not appear.

History of 28 U.S.C. §2467: Apr. 25, 2000, P.L. 106-185, §15(a), 114 Stat. 219; Oct. 26, 2001, P.L. 107-56, §323, 115 Stat. 315-16; Dec. 22, 2010, P.L. 111-342, §2, 124 Stat. 3607.

CHAPTER 165. UNITED STATES COURT OF FEDERAL CLAIMS PROCEDURE

§2501. TIME FOR FILING SUIT

Every claim of which the United States Court of Federal Claims has jurisdiction shall be barred unless the petition thereon is filed within six years after such claim first accrues.

Every claim under section 1497 of this title shall be barred unless the petition thereon is filed within two years after the termination of the river and harbor improvements operations on which the claim is based.

A petition on the claim of a person under legal disability or beyond the seas at the time the claim accrues may be filed within three years after the disability ceases.

A suit for the fees of an officer of the United States shall not be filed until his account for such fees has been finally acted upon, unless the Government Accountability Office fails to act within six months after receiving the account.

History of 28 U.S.C. §2501: June 25, 1948, ch. 646, 62 Stat. 976; Sept. 3, 1954, ch. 1263, §52, 68 Stat. 1246; Apr. 2, 1982, P.L. 97-164, §139(a), 96 Stat. 42; Oct. 29, 1992, P.L. 102-572, §902(a)(1), 106 Stat. 4516; July 7, 2004, P.L. 108-271, §8(b), 118 Stat. 814.

§2502. ALIENS' PRIVILEGE TO SUE

(a) Citizens or subjects of any foreign government which accords to citizens of the United States the right to prosecute claims against their government in its courts may sue the United States in the United States Court of Federal Claims if the subject matter of the suit is otherwise within such court's jurisdiction.

(b) See section 7422(f) of the Internal Revenue Code of 1986 for exception with respect to suits involving internal revenue taxes.

History of 28 U.S.C. §2502: June 25, 1948, ch. 646, 62 Stat. 976; Nov. 2, 1966, P.L. 89-713, §3(b), 80 Stat. 1108; Apr. 2, 1982, P.L. 97-164, §139(a), 96 Stat. 42; Oct. 22, 1986, P.L. 99-514, §2, 100 Stat. 2095; Oct. 29, 1992, P.L. 102-572, §902(a)(1), 106 Stat. 4516.

§2503. PROCEEDINGS GENERALLY

(a) Parties to any suit in the United States Court of Federal Claims may appear before a judge of that court in person or by attorney, produce evidence, and examine witnesses.

(b) The proceedings of the Court of Federal Claims shall be in accordance with such rules of practice and procedure (other than the rules of evidence) as the Court of Federal Claims may prescribe and in accordance with the Federal Rules of Evidence.

(c) The judges of the Court of Federal Claims shall fix times for trials, administer oaths or affirmations, examine witnesses, receive evidence, and enter dispositive judgments. Hearings shall, if convenient, be held in the counties where the witnesses reside.

(d) For the purpose of construing sections 1821, 1915, 1920, and 1927 of this title, the United States Court of Federal Claims shall be deemed to be a court of the United States.

History of 28 U.S.C. §2503: June 25, 1948, ch. 646, 62 Stat. 976; Sept. 3, 1954, ch. 1263, §53, 68 Stat. 1246; Apr. 2, 1982, P.L. 97-164, §139(b)(1), 96 Stat. 42; Oct. 29, 1992, P.L. 102-572, §§902(a), 909, 106 Stat. 4516, 4519.

§2504. PLAINTIFF'S TESTIMONY

The United States Court of Federal Claims may, at the instance of the Attorney General, order any plaintiff to appear, upon reasonable notice, before any judge of the court and be examined on oath as to all matters pertaining to his claim. Such examination shall be reduced to writing by the judge, and shall be returned to and filed in the court, and may, at the discretion of the attorneys for the United States, be read and used as evidence on the trial. If any plaintiff, after such order is made and due and reasonable notice thereof is given to him, fails to appear, or refuses to testify or answer fully as to all material matters within his knowledge, the court may order that the case shall not be tried until he fully complies with such order.

History of 28 U.S.C. §2504: June 25, 1948, ch. 646, 62 Stat. 976; Apr. 2, 1982, P.L. 97-164, §139(c), 96 Stat. 42; Oct. 29, 1992, P.L. 102-572, §902(a)(1), 106 Stat. 4516.

§2505. TRIAL BEFORE JUDGES

Any judge of the United States Court of Federal Claims may sit at any place within the United States to take evidence and enter judgment.

History of 28 U.S.C. §2505: June 25, 1948, ch. 646, 62 Stat. 976; Sept. 3, 1954, ch. 1263, §54(a), (b), 68 Stat. 1246; Apr. 2, 1982, P.L. 97-164, §139(d), 96 Stat. 42; Oct. 29, 1992, P.L. 102-572, §902(a)(1), 106 Stat. 4516.

§2506. INTEREST OF WITNESS

A witness in a suit in the United States Court of Federal Claims shall not be exempt or disqualified because he is a party to or interested in such suit.

History of 28 U.S.C. §2506: June 25, 1948, ch. 646, 62 Stat. 977; Apr. 2, 1982, P.L. 97-164, §139(e), 96 Stat. 42; Oct. 29, 1992, P.L. 102-572, §902(a)(1), 106 Stat. 4516.

§2507. CALLS & DISCOVERY

(a) The United States Court of Federal Claims may call upon any department or agency of the United States or upon any party for any information or papers, not privileged, for purposes of discovery or for use as evidence. The head of any department or agency may refuse to comply with a call issued pursuant to this subsection when, in his opinion, compliance will be injurious to the public interest.

(b) Without limitation on account of anything contained in subsection (a) of this section, the court may, in accordance with its rules, provide additional means for the discovery of any relevant facts, books, papers, documents or tangible things, not privileged.

(c) The Court of Federal Claims may use all recorded and printed reports made by the committees of the Senate or House of Representatives.

History of 28 U.S.C. §2507: June 25, 1948, ch. 646, 62 Stat. 977; Sept. 3, 1954, ch. 1263, §55(a)-(c), 68 Stat. 1247; Apr. 2, 1982, P.L. 97-164, §139(f), 96 Stat. 42; Oct. 29, 1992, P.L. 102-572, §902(a)(1), 106 Stat. 4516.

§2508. COUNTERCLAIM OR SET-OFF; REGISTRATION OF JUDGMENT

Upon the trial of any suit in the United States Court of Federal Claims in which any setoff, counterclaim, claim for damages, or other demand is set up on the part of the United States against any plaintiff making claim against the United States in said court, the court shall hear and determine such claim or demand both for and against the United States and plaintiff.

If upon the whole case it finds that the plaintiff is indebted to the United States it shall render judgment to that effect, and such judgment shall be final and reviewable.

The transcript of such judgment, filed in the clerk's office of any district court, shall be entered upon the records and shall be enforceable as other judgments.

History of 28 U.S.C. §2508: June 25, 1948, ch. 646, 62 Stat. 977; July 28, 1953, ch. 253, §10, 67 Stat. 227; Sept. 3, 1954, ch. 1263, §47(a), 68 Stat. 1243; Apr. 2, 1982, P.L. 97-164, §139(g), 96 Stat. 42; Oct. 29, 1992, P.L. 102-572, §902(a)(1), 106 Stat. 4516.

§2509. CONGRESSIONAL REFERENCE CASES

(a) Whenever a bill, except a bill for a pension, is referred by either House of Congress to the chief judge of the United States Court of Federal Claims pursuant to section 1492 of this title, the chief judge shall designate a judge as hearing officer for the case and a panel of three judges of the court to serve as a reviewing body. One member of the review panel shall be designated as presiding officer of the panel.

(b) Proceedings in a congressional reference case shall be under rules and regulations prescribed for the purpose by the chief judge who is hereby authorized and directed to require the application of the pertinent rules of practice of the Court of Federal Claims insofar as feasible. Each hearing officer and each review panel shall have authority to do and perform any acts which may be necessary or proper for the efficient performance of their duties, including the power of subpena[1] and the power to administer oaths and affirmations. None of the rules, rulings, findings, or conclusions authorized by this section shall be subject to judicial review.

(c) The hearing officer to whom a congressional reference case is assigned by the chief judge shall proceed in accordance with the applicable rules to determine the facts, including facts relating to delay or laches, facts bearing upon the question whether the bar of any statute of limitation should be removed, or facts claimed to excuse the claimant for not having resorted to any established legal remedy. He shall append to his findings of fact conclusions sufficient to inform Congress whether the demand is a legal or equitable claim or a gratuity, and the amount, if any, legally or equitably due from the United States to the claimant.

(d) The findings and conclusions of the hearing officer shall be submitted by him, together with the record in the case, to the review panel for review by it pursuant to such rules as may be provided for the purpose, which shall include provision for submitting the report of the hearing officer to the parties for consideration, exception, and argument before the panel. The panel, by majority vote, shall adopt or modify the findings or the conclusions of the hearing officer.

(e) The panel shall submit its report to the chief judge for transmission to the appropriate House of Congress.

(f) Any act or failure to act or other conduct by a party, a witness, or an attorney which would call for the imposition of sanctions under the rules of practice of the Court of Federal Claims shall be noted by the panel or the hearing officer at the time of occurrence thereof and upon failure of the delinquent or offending party, witness, or attorney to make prompt compliance with the order of the panel or the hearing officer a full statement of the circumstances shall be incorporated in the report of the panel.

(g) The Court of Federal Claims is hereby authorized and directed, under such regulations as it may prescribe, to provide the facilities and services of the office of the clerk of the court for the filing, processing, hearing, and dispatch of congressional reference cases and to include within its annual appropriations the costs thereof and other costs of administration, including (but without limitation to the items herein listed) the salaries and traveling expenses of the judges serving as hearing officers and panel members, mail-

ing and service of process, necessary physical facilities, equipment, and supplies, and personnel (including secretaries and law clerks).

1. **Editor's note:** So in original. Probably should be "subpoena."

History of 28 U.S.C. §2509: June 25, 1948, ch. 646, 62 Stat. 977; Oct. 15, 1966, P.L. 89-681, §2, 80 Stat. 958; Apr. 2, 1982, P.L. 97-164, §139(h), 96 Stat. 42; Oct. 29, 1992, P.L. 102-572, §902(a), 106 Stat. 4516.

§2510. REFERRAL OF CASES BY COMPTROLLER GENERAL

(a) The Comptroller General may transmit to the United States Court of Federal Claims for trial and adjudication any claim or matter of which the Court of Federal Claims might take jurisdiction on the voluntary action of the claimant, together with all vouchers, papers, documents, and proofs pertaining thereto.

(b) The Court of Federal Claims shall proceed with the claims or matters so referred as in other cases pending in such Court and shall render judgment thereon.

History of 28 U.S.C. §2510: June 25, 1948, ch. 646, 62 Stat. 977; July 28, 1953, ch. 253, §11, 67 Stat. 227; Sept. 3, 1954, ch. 1263, §47(b), 68 Stat. 1243; Nov. 1, 1978, P.L. 95-563, §14(h)(1), (2)(A), 92 Stat. 2390; Apr. 2, 1982, P.L. 97-164, §139(i)(1), 96 Stat. 43; Oct. 29, 1992, P.L. 102-572, §902(a), 106 Stat. 4516.

§2511. ACCOUNTS OF OFFICERS, AGENTS OR CONTRACTORS

Notice of suit under section 1494 of this title shall be given to the Attorney General, to the Comptroller General, and to the head of the department requested to settle the account in question.

The judgment of the United States Court of Federal Claims in such suit shall be conclusive upon the parties, and payment of the amount found due shall discharge the obligation.

The transcript of such judgment, filed in the clerk's office of any district court, shall be entered upon the records, and shall be enforceable as other judgments.

History of 28 U.S.C. §2511: June 25, 1948, ch. 646, 62 Stat. 977; July 28, 1953, ch. 253, §12, 67 Stat. 227; Apr. 2, 1982, P.L. 97-164, §139(j), 96 Stat. 43; Oct. 29, 1992, P.L. 102-572, §902(a)(1), 106 Stat. 4516.

§2512. DISBURSING OFFICERS; RELIEF

Whenever the United States Court of Federal Claims finds that any loss by a disbursing officer of the United States was without his fault or negligence, it shall render a judgment setting forth the amount thereof, and the Government Accountability Office shall allow the officer such amount as a credit in the settlement of his accounts.

History of 28 U.S.C. §2512: June 25, 1948, ch. 646, 62 Stat. 978; Apr. 2, 1982, P.L. 97-164, §139(j)(2), 96 Stat. 43; Oct. 29, 1992, P.L. 102-572, §902(a)(1), 106 Stat. 4516; July 7, 2004, P.L. 108-271, §8(b), 118 Stat. 814.

§2513. UNJUST CONVICTION & IMPRISONMENT

(a) Any person suing under section 1495 of this title must allege and prove that:

(1) His conviction has been reversed or set aside on the ground that he is not guilty of the offense of which he was convicted, or on new trial or rehearing he was found not guilty of such offense, as appears from the record or certificate of the court setting aside or reversing such conviction, or that he has been pardoned upon the stated ground of innocence and unjust conviction and

(2) He did not commit any of the acts charged or his acts, deeds, or omissions in connection with such charge constituted no offense against the United States, or any State, Territory or the District of Columbia, and he did not by misconduct or neglect cause or bring about his own prosecution.

(b) Proof of the requisite facts shall be by a certificate of the court or pardon wherein such facts are alleged to appear, and other evidence thereof shall not be received.

(c) No pardon or certified copy of a pardon shall be considered by the United States Court of Federal Claims unless it contains recitals that the pardon was granted after applicant had exhausted all recourse to the courts and that the time for any court to exercise its jurisdiction had expired.

(d) The Court may permit the plaintiff to prosecute such action in forma pauperis.

(e) The amount of damages awarded shall not exceed $100,000 for each 12-month period of incarceration for any plaintiff who was unjustly sentenced to death and $50,000 for each 12-month period of incarceration for any other plaintiff.

History of 28 U.S.C. §2513: June 25, 1948, ch. 646, 62 Stat. 978; Sept. 3, 1954, ch. 1263, §56, 68 Stat. 1247; Apr. 2, 1982, P.L. 97-164, §139(j)(2), 96 Stat. 43; Oct. 29, 1992, P.L. 102-572, §902(a)(1), 106 Stat. 4516; Oct. 30, 2004, P.L. 108-405, §431, 118 Stat. 2293.

§2514. FORFEITURE OF FRAUDULENT CLAIMS

A claim against the United States shall be forfeited to the United States by any person who corruptly practices or attempts to practice any fraud against the United States in the proof, statement, establishment, or allowance thereof.

In such cases the United States Court of Federal Claims shall specifically find such fraud or attempt and render judgment of forfeiture.

History of 28 U.S.C. §2514: June 25, 1948, ch. 646, 62 Stat. 978; Apr. 2, 1982, P.L. 97-164, §139(j)(2), 96 Stat. 43; Oct. 29, 1992, P.L. 102-572, §902(a)(1), 106 Stat. 4516.

§2515. NEW TRIAL; STAY OF JUDGMENT

(a) The United States Court of Federal Claims may grant a plaintiff a new trial on any ground established by rules of common law or equity applicable as between private parties.

(b) Such court, at any time while any suit is pending before it, or after proceedings for review have been instituted, or within two years after the final disposition of the suit, may grant the United States a new trial and stay the payment of any judgment upon satisfactory evidence, cumulative or otherwise, that any fraud, wrong, or injustice has been done the United States.

History of 28 U.S.C. §2515: June 25, 1948, ch. 646, 62 Stat. 978; Apr. 2, 1982, P.L. 97-164, §139(j)(2), 96 Stat. 43; Oct. 29, 1992, P.L. 102-572, §902(a)(1), 106 Stat. 4516.

§2516. INTEREST ON CLAIMS & JUDGMENTS

(a) Interest on a claim against the United States shall be allowed in a judgment of the United States Court of Federal Claims only under a contract or Act of Congress expressly providing for payment thereof.

(b) Interest on a judgment against the United States affirmed by the Supreme Court after review on petition of the United States is paid at a rate equal to the weekly average 1-year constant maturity Treasury yield, as published by the Board of Governors of the Federal Reserve System, for the calendar week preceding the date of the judgment.

History of 28 U.S.C. §2516: June 25, 1948, ch. 646, 62 Stat. 978; Sept. 3, 1954, ch. 1263, §57, 68 Stat. 1248; Apr. 2, 1982, P.L. 97-164, §§139(j)(2), 302(d), 96 Stat. 43, 56; Sept. 13, 1982, P.L. 97-258, §2(g)(5), (m)(3), 96 Stat. 1061, 1062; Oct. 29, 1992, P.L. 102-572, §902(a)(1), 106 Stat. 4516; Dec. 21, 2000, P.L. 106-554, §307(d)(2), 114 Stat. 2763A-636.

§2517. PAYMENT OF JUDGMENTS

(a) Except as provided by chapter 71 of title 41, every final judgment rendered by the United States Court of Federal Claims against the United States shall be paid out of any general appropriation therefor, on presentation to the Secretary of the Treasury of a certification of the judgment by the clerk and chief judge of the court.

(b) Payment of any such judgment and of interest thereon shall be a full discharge to the United States of all claims and demands arising out of the matters involved in the case or controversy, unless the judgment is designated a partial judgment, in which event only the matters described therein shall be discharged.

History of 28 U.S.C. §2517: June 25, 1948, ch. 646, 62 Stat. 979; Nov. 1, 1978, P.L. 95-563, §14(e), (f), 92 Stat. 2390; Apr. 2, 1982, P.L. 97-164, §139(k), 96 Stat. 43; Oct. 29, 1992, P.L. 102-572, §902(a)(1), 106 Stat. 4516; Oct. 19, 1996, P.L. 104-316, §202(*l*), 110 Stat. 3843; Jan. 4, 2011, P.L. 111-350, §5(g)(11), 124 Stat. 3848.

§2518. REPEALED

Repealed Apr. 2, 1982, P.L. 97-164, §139(*l*), 96 Stat. 43.

§2519. CONCLUSIVENESS OF JUDGMENT

A final judgment of the United States Court of Federal Claims against any plaintiff shall forever bar any further claim, suit, or demand against the United States arising out of the matters involved in the case or controversy.

History of 28 U.S.C. §2519: June 25, 1948, ch. 646, 62 Stat. 979; Apr. 2, 1982, P.L. 97-164, §139(m), 96 Stat. 43; Oct. 29, 1992, P.L. 102-572, §902(a)(1), 106 Stat. 4516.

§2520. REPEALED

Repealed Nov. 13, 2000, P.L. 106-518, §207, 114 Stat. 2414.

§2521. SUBPOENAS & INCIDENTAL POWERS

(a) Subpoenas requiring the attendance of parties or witnesses and subpoenas requiring the production of books, papers, documents or tangible things by any party or witness having custody or control thereof, may be issued for purposes of discovery or for use of the things produced as evidence in accordance with the rules and orders of the court. Such subpoenas shall be issued and served and compliance therewith shall be compelled as provided in the rules and orders of the court.

(b) The United States Court of Federal Claims shall have power to punish by fine or imprisonment, at its discretion, such contempt of its authority as—

(1) misbehavior of any person in its presence or so near thereto as to obstruct the administration of justice;

(2) misbehavior of any of its officers in their official transactions; or

(3) disobedience or resistance to its lawful writ, process, order, rule, decree, or command.

(c) The United States Court of Federal Claims shall have such assistance in the carrying out of its lawful writ, process, order, rule, decree, or command as is available to a court of the United States. The United States marshal for any district in which the Court of Federal Claims is sitting shall, when requested by the chief judge of the Court of Federal Claims, attend any session of the Court of Federal Claims in such district.

History of 28 U.S.C. §2521: Sept. 3, 1954, ch. 1263, §59(a), 68 Stat. 1248; Oct. 29, 1992, P.L. 102-572, §910(a), 106 Stat. 4519.

§2522. NOTICE OF APPEAL

Review of a decision of the United States Court of Federal Claims shall be obtained by filing a notice of appeal with the clerk of the Court of Federal Claims within the time and in the manner prescribed for appeals to United States courts of appeals from the United States district courts.

History of 28 U.S.C. §2522: Apr. 2, 1982, P.L. 97-164, §139(q)(1), 96 Stat. 44; Oct. 29, 1992, P.L. 102-572, §902(a), 106 Stat. 4516.

CHAPTER 167. REPEALED

§§2601 TO 2604. REPEALED

Repealed Apr. 2, 1982, P.L. 97-164, §140, 96 Stat. 44.

CHAPTER 169. COURT OF INTERNATIONAL TRADE PROCEDURE

§2631. PERSONS ENTITLED TO COMMENCE A CIVIL ACTION

(a) A civil action contesting the denial of a protest, in whole or in part, under section 515 of the Tariff Act of 1930 may be commenced in the Court of International Trade by the person who filed the protest pursuant to section 514 of such Act, or by a surety on the transaction which is the subject of the protest.

(b) A civil action contesting the denial of a petition under section 516 of the Tariff Act of 1930 may be commenced in the Court of International Trade by the person who filed such petition.

(c) A civil action contesting a determination listed in section 516A of the Tariff Act of 1930 may be commenced in

the Court of International Trade by any interested party who was a party to the proceeding in connection with which the matter arose.

(d)(1) A civil action to review any final determination of the Secretary of Labor under section 223 of the Trade Act of 1974 with respect to the eligibility of workers for adjustment assistance under such Act may be commenced in the Court of International Trade by a worker, group of workers, certified or recognized union, or authorized representative of such worker or group that applies for assistance under such Act and is aggrieved by such final determination.

(2) A civil action to review any final determination of the Secretary of Commerce under section 251 of the Trade Act of 1974 with respect to the eligibility of a firm for adjustment assistance under such Act may be commenced in the Court of International Trade by a firm or its representative that applies for assistance under such Act and is aggrieved by such final determination, or by any other interested domestic party that is aggrieved by such final determination.

(3) A civil action to review any final determination of the Secretary of Commerce under section 271 of the Trade Act of 1974 with respect to the eligibility of a community for adjustment assistance under such Act may be commenced in the Court of International Trade by a community that applies for assistance under such Act and is aggrieved by such final determination, or by any other interested domestic party that is aggrieved by such final determination.

(e) A civil action to review a final determination made under section 305(b)(1) of the Trade Agreements Act of 1979 may be commenced in the Court of International Trade by any person who was a party-at-interest with respect to such determination.

(f) A civil action involving an application for the issuance of an order directing the administering authority or the International Trade Commission to make confidential information available under section 777(c)(2) of the Tariff Act of 1930 may be commenced in the Court of International Trade by any interested party whose application for disclosure of such confidential information was denied under section 777(c)(1) of such Act.

(g)(1) A civil action to review any decision of the Secretary of the Treasury to deny a customs broker's license under section 641(b)(2) or (3) of the Tariff Act of 1930, or to deny a customs broker's permit under section 641(c)(1) of such Act, or to revoke such license or permit under section 641(b)(5) or (c)(2) of such Act, may be commenced in the Court of International Trade by the person whose license or permit was denied or revoked.

(2) A civil action to review any decision of the Secretary of the Treasury to revoke or suspend a customs broker's license or permit or impose a monetary penalty in lieu thereof under section 641(d)(2)(B) of the Tariff Act of 1930 may be commenced in the Court of International Trade by the person against whom the decision was issued.

(3) A civil action to review any decision or order of the Customs Service to deny, suspend, or revoke accreditation of a private laboratory under section 499(b) of the Tariff Act of 1930 may be commenced in the Court of International Trade by the person whose accreditation was denied, suspended, or revoked.

(h) A civil action described in section 1581(h) of this title may be commenced in the Court of International Trade by the person who would have standing to bring a civil action under section 1581(a) of this title if he imported the goods involved and filed a protest which was denied, in whole or in part, under section 515 of the Tariff Act of 1930.

(i) Any civil action of which the Court of International Trade has jurisdiction, other than an action specified in subsections (a)-(h) of this section, may be commenced in the court by any person adversely affected or aggrieved by agency action within the meaning of section 702 of title 5.

(j)(1) Any person who would be adversely affected or aggrieved by a decision in a civil action pending in the Court of International Trade may, by leave of court, intervene in such action, except that—

(A) no person may intervene in a civil action under section 515 or 516 of the Tariff Act of 1930;

(B) in a civil action under section 516A of the Tariff Act of 1930, only an interested party who was a party to the proceeding in connection with which the matter arose may intervene, and such person may intervene as a matter of right; and

(C) in a civil action under section 777(c)(2) of the Tariff Act of 1930, only a person who was a party to the investigation may intervene, and such person may intervene as a matter of right.

(2) In those civil actions in which intervention is by leave of court, the Court of International Trade shall consider whether the intervention will unduly delay or prejudice the adjudication of the rights of the original parties.

(k) In this section—

(1) "interested party" has the meaning given such term in section 771(9) of the Tariff Act of 1930; and

(2) "party-at-interest" means—

(A) a foreign manufacturer, producer, or exporter, or a United States importer, of merchandise which is the subject of a final determination under section 305(b)(1) of the Trade Agreements Act of 1979;

(B) a manufacturer, producer, or wholesaler in the United States of a like product;

(C) United States members of a labor organization or other association of workers whose members are employed in the manufacture, production, or wholesale in the United States of a like product;

(D) a trade or business association a majority of whose members manufacture, produce, or wholesale a like product in the United States,[1] and

(E) an association composed of members who represent parties-at-interest described in subparagraph (B), (C), or (D).

1. **Editor's note:** So in original. The comma probably should be a semicolon.

History of 28 U.S.C. §2631: Oct. 10, 1980, P.L. 96-417, §301, 94 Stat. 1730; Oct. 30, 1984, P.L. 98-573, §§212(b)(3), 612(b)(3), 98 Stat. 2983, 3034; Dec. 8, 1993, P.L. 103-182, §684(a)(2), 107 Stat. 2219.

§2632. COMMENCEMENT OF A CIVIL ACTION

(a) Except for civil actions specified in subsections (b) and (c) of this section, a civil action in the Court of International Trade shall be commenced by filing concurrently with the clerk of the court a summons and complaint, with the content and in the form, manner, and style prescribed by the rules of the court.

(b) A civil action in the Court of International Trade under section 515 or section 516 of the Tariff Act of 1930 shall be commenced by filing with the clerk of the court a summons, with the content and in the form, manner, and style prescribed by the rules of the court.

(c) A civil action in the Court of International Trade under section 516A of the Tariff Act of 1930 shall be commenced by filing with the clerk of the court a summons or a summons and a complaint, as prescribed in such section, with the content and in the form, manner, and style prescribed by the rules of the court.

(d) The Court of International Trade may prescribe by rule that any summons, pleading, or other paper mailed by registered or certified mail properly addressed to the clerk of the court with the proper postage affixed and return receipt requested shall be deemed filed as of the date of mailing.

History of 28 U.S.C. §2632: Oct. 10, 1980, P.L. 96-417, §301, 94 Stat. 1732.

§2633. PROCEDURE & FEES

(a) A filing fee shall be payable to the clerk of the Court of International Trade upon the commencement of a civil action in such court. The amount of the fee shall be prescribed by the rules of the court, but shall be not less than $5 nor more than the filing fee for commencing a civil action in a district court of the United States. The court may fix all other fees to be charged by the clerk of the court.

(b) The Court of International Trade shall prescribe rules governing the summons, pleadings, and other papers, for their amendment, service, and filing, for consolidations, severances, suspensions of cases, and for other procedural matters.

(c) All summons, pleadings, and other papers filed in the Court of International Trade shall be served on all parties in accordance with rules prescribed by the court. When the United States, its agencies, or its officers are adverse parties, service of the summons shall be made upon the Attorney General and the head of the Government agency whose action is being contested. When injunctive relief is sought, the summons, pleadings, and other papers shall also be served upon the named officials sought to be enjoined.

History of 28 U.S.C. §2633: Oct. 10, 1980, P.L. 96-417, §301, 94 Stat. 1732.

§2634. NOTICE

Reasonable notice of the time and place of trial or hearing before the Court of International Trade shall be given to all parties to any civil action, as prescribed by the rules of the court.

History of 28 U.S.C. §2634: Oct. 10, 1980, P.L. 96-417, §301, 94 Stat. 1733.

§2635. FILING OF OFFICIAL DOCUMENTS

(a) In any action commenced in the Court of International Trade contesting the denial of a protest under section 515 of the Tariff Act of 1930 or the denial of a petition under section 516 of such Act, the Customs Service, as prescribed by the rules of the court, shall file with the clerk of the court, as part of the official record, any document, paper, information or data relating to the entry of merchandise and the administrative determination that is the subject of the protest or petition.

(b)(1) In any civil action commenced in the Court of International Trade under section 516A of the Tariff Act of 1930, within forty days or within such other period of time as the court may specify, after the date of service of a complaint on the administering authority established to administer title VII of the Tariff Act of 1930 or the United States International Trade Commission, the administering authority or the Commission shall transmit to the clerk of the court the record of such action, as prescribed by the rules of the court. The record shall, unless otherwise stipulated by the parties, consist of—

(A) a copy of all information presented to or obtained by the administering authority or the Commission during the course of the administrative proceedings, including all governmental memoranda pertaining to the case and the record of ex parte meetings required to be maintained by section 777(a)(3) of the Tariff Act of 1930; and

(B)(i) a copy of the determination and the facts and conclusions of law upon which such determination was based, **(ii)** all transcripts or records of conferences or hearings, and **(iii)** all notices published in the Federal Register.

(2) The administering authority or the Commission shall identify and transmit under seal to the clerk of the court any document, comment, or information that is accorded confidential or privileged status by the Government agency whose action is being contested and that is required to be transmitted to the clerk under paragraph (1) of this subsection. Any such document, comment, or information shall be accompanied by a nonconfidential description of the nature of the material being transmitted. The confidential or privileged status of such material shall be preserved in the civil action, but the court may examine the confidential or privileged material in camera and may make such material available under such terms and conditions as the court may order.

(c) Within fifteen days, or within such other period of time as the Court of International Trade may specify, after service of a summons and complaint in a civil action involving an application for an order directing the administering authority or the International Trade Commission to make confidential information available under section 777(c)(2) of the Tariff Act of 1930, the administering authority or the Commission shall transmit under seal to the clerk of the Court of International Trade, as prescribed by its rules, the confidential information involved, together with pertinent parts of the record. Such information shall be accompanied by a nonconfidential description of the nature of the information being transmitted. The confidential status of such information shall be preserved in the civil action, but the court may examine the confidential information in camera and may make such information available under a protective order consistent with section 777(c)(2) of the Tariff Act of 1930.

(d)(1) In any other civil action in the Court of International Trade in which judicial review is to proceed upon the basis of the record made before an agency, the agency shall, within forty days or within such other period of time as the court may specify, after the date of service of the summons and complaint upon the agency, transmit to the clerk of the court, as prescribed by its rules—

(A) a copy of the contested determination and the findings or report upon which such determination was based;

(B) a copy of any reported hearings or conferences conducted by the agency; and

(C) any documents, comments, or other papers filed by the public, interested parties, or governments with respect to the agency's action.

(2) The agency shall identify and transmit under seal to the clerk of the court any document, comment, or other information that was obtained on a confidential basis and that is required to be transmitted to the clerk under paragraph (1) of this subsection. Any such document, comment, or information shall include a nonconfidential description of the nature of the material being transmitted. The confidential or privileged status of such material shall be preserved in the civil action, but the court may examine such material in camera and may make such material available under such terms and conditions as the court may order.

(3) The parties may stipulate that fewer documents, comments, or other information than those specified in paragraph (1) of this subsection shall be transmitted to the clerk of the court.

History of 28 U.S.C. §2635: Oct. 10, 1980, P.L. 96-417, §301, 94 Stat. 1733; Dec. 8, 1993, P.L. 103-182, §684(d), 107 Stat. 2219.

§2636. TIME FOR COMMENCEMENT OF ACTION

(a) A civil action contesting the denial, in whole or in part, of a protest under section 515 of the Tariff Act of 1930 is barred unless commenced in accordance with the rules of the Court of International Trade—

(1) within one hundred and eighty days after the date of mailing of notice of denial of a protest under section 515(a) of such Act; or

(2) within one hundred and eighty days after the date of denial of a protest by operation of law under the provisions of section 515(b) of such Act.

(b) A civil action contesting the denial of a petition under section 516 of the Tariff Act of 1930 is barred unless commenced in accordance with the rules of the Court of International Trade within thirty days after the date of mailing of a notice pursuant to section 516(c) of such Act.

(c) A civil action contesting a reviewable determination listed in section 516A of the Tariff Act of 1930 is barred unless commenced in accordance with the rules of the Court of International Trade within the time specified in such section.

(d) A civil action contesting a final determination of the Secretary of Labor under section 223 of the Trade Act of 1974 or a final determination of the Secretary of Commerce under section 251 or section 271 of such Act is barred unless commenced in accordance with the rules of the Court of International Trade within sixty days after the date of notice of such determination.

(e) A civil action contesting a final determination made under section 305(b)(1) of the Trade Agreements Act of 1979 is barred unless commenced in accordance with the rules of the Court of International Trade within thirty days after the date of the publication of such determination in the Federal Register.

(f) A civil action involving an application for the issuance of an order making confidential information available under section 777(c)(2) of the Tariff Act of 1930 is barred unless commenced in accordance with the rules of the Court of International Trade within ten days after the date of the denial of the request for such confidential information.

(g) A civil action contesting the denial or revocation by the Secretary of the Treasury of a customs broker's license or permit under subsection (b) or (c) of section 641 of the Tariff Act of 1930, or the revocation or suspension of such license or permit or the imposition of a monetary penalty in lieu thereof by such Secretary under section 641(d) of such Act, is barred unless commenced in accordance with the rules of the Court of International Trade within sixty days after the date of the entry of the decision or order of such Secretary.

(h) A civil action contesting the denial, suspension, or revocation by the Customs Service of a private laboratory's accreditation under section 499(b) of the Tariff Act of 1930 is barred unless commenced in accordance with the rules of the Court of International Trade within 60 days after the date of the decision or order of the Customs Service.

(i) A civil action of which the Court of International Trade has jurisdiction under section 1581 of this title, other than an action specified in subsections (a)-(h) of this sec-

tion, is barred unless commenced in accordance with the rules of the court within two years after the cause of action first accrues.

History of 28 U.S.C. §2636: Oct. 10, 1980, P.L. 96-417, §301, 94 Stat. 1734; Oct. 30, 1984, P.L. 98-573, §§212(b)(4), 623(b)(1), 98 Stat. 2984, 3041; Dec. 8, 1993, P.L. 103-182, §684(a)(3), 107 Stat. 2219.

§2637. EXHAUSTION OF ADMINISTRATIVE REMEDIES

(a) A civil action contesting the denial of a protest under section 515 of the Tariff Act of 1930 may be commenced in the Court of International Trade only if all liquidated duties, charges, or exactions have been paid at the time the action is commenced, except that a surety's obligation to pay such liquidated duties, charges, or exactions is limited to the sum of any bond related to each entry included in the denied protest.

(b) A civil action contesting the denial of a petition under section 516 of the Tariff Act of 1930 may be commenced in the Court of International Trade only by a person who has first exhausted the procedures set forth in such section.

(c) A civil action described in section 1581(h) of this title may be commenced in the Court of International Trade prior to the exhaustion of administrative remedies if the person commencing the action makes the demonstration required by such section.

(d) In any civil action not specified in this section, the Court of International Trade shall, where appropriate, require the exhaustion of administrative remedies.

History of 28 U.S.C. §2637: Oct. 10, 1980, P.L. 96-417, §301, 94 Stat. 1735.

§2638. NEW GROUNDS IN SUPPORT OF A CIVIL ACTION

In any civil action under section 515 of the Tariff Act of 1930 in which the denial, in whole or in part, of a protest is a precondition to the commencement of a civil action in the Court of International Trade, the court, by rule, may consider any new ground in support of the civil action if such new ground—

(1) applies to the same merchandise that was the subject of the protest; and

(2) is related to the same administrative decision listed in section 514 of the Tariff Act of 1930 that was contested in the protest.

History of 28 U.S.C. §2638: Oct. 10, 1980, P.L. 96-417, §301, 94 Stat. 1736.

§2639. BURDEN OF PROOF; EVIDENCE OF VALUE

(a)(1) Except as provided in paragraph (2) of this subsection, in any civil action commenced in the Court of International Trade under section 515, 516, or 516A of the Tariff Act of 1930, the decision of the Secretary of the Treasury, the administering authority, or the International Trade Commission is presumed to be correct. The burden of proving otherwise shall rest upon the party challenging such decision.

(2) The provisions of paragraph (1) of this subsection shall not apply to any civil action commenced in the Court of International Trade under section 1582 of this title.

(b) In any civil action described in section 1581(h) of this title, the person commencing the action shall have the burden of making the demonstration required by such section by clear and convincing evidence.

(c) Where the value of merchandise or any of its components is in issue in any civil action in the Court of International Trade—

(1) reports or depositions of consuls, customs officers, and other officers of the United States, and depositions and affidavits of other persons whose attendance cannot reasonably be had, may be admitted into evidence when served upon the opposing party as prescribed by the rules of the court; and

(2) price lists and catalogs may be admitted in evidence when duly authenticated, relevant, and material.

History of 28 U.S.C. §2639: Oct. 10, 1980, P.L. 96-417, §301, 94 Stat. 1736.

§2640. SCOPE & STANDARD OF REVIEW

(a) The Court of International Trade shall make its determinations upon the basis of the record made before the court in the following categories of civil actions:

(1) Civil actions contesting the denial of a protest under section 515 of the Tariff Act of 1930.

(2) Civil actions commenced under section 516 of the Tariff Act of 1930.

(3) Civil actions commenced to review a final determination made under section 305(b)(1) of the Trade Agreements Act of 1979.

(4) Civil actions commenced under section 777(c)(2) of the Tariff Act of 1930.

(5) Civil actions commenced to review any decision of the Secretary of the Treasury under section 641 of the Tariff Act of 1930, with the exception of decisions under section 641(d)(2)(B), which shall be governed by subdivision (d) of this section.

(6) Civil actions commenced under section 1582 of this title.

(b) In any civil action commenced in the Court of International Trade under section 516A of the Tariff Act of 1930, the court shall review the matter as specified in subsection (b) of such section.

(c) In any civil action commenced in the Court of International Trade to review any final determination of the Secretary of Labor under section 223 of the Trade Act of 1974 or any final determination of the Secretary of Commerce under section 251 or section 271 of such Act, the court shall review the matter as specified in section 284 of such Act.

(d) In any civil action commenced to review any order or decision of the Customs Service under section 499(b) of the Tariff Act of 1930, the court shall review the action on the basis of the record before the Customs Service at the time of issuing such decision or order.

(e) In any civil action not specified in this section, the Court of International Trade shall review the matter as provided in section 706 of title 5.

History of 28 U.S.C. §2640: Oct. 10, 1980, P.L. 96-417, §301, 94 Stat. 1736; Oct. 30, 1984, P.L. 98-573, §212(b)(5), 98 Stat. 2984; Dec. 8, 1993, P.L. 103-182, §684(a)(4), 107 Stat. 2219.

§2641. WITNESSES; INSPECTION OF DOCUMENTS

(a) Except as otherwise provided by law, in any civil action in the Court of International Trade, each party and its counsel shall have an opportunity to introduce evidence, to hear and cross-examine the witnesses of the other party, and to inspect all samples and papers admitted or offered as evidence, as prescribed by the rules of the court. Except as provided in section 2639 of this title, subsection (b) of this section, or the rules of the court, the Federal Rules of Evidence shall apply to all civil actions in the Court of International Trade.

(b) The Court of International Trade may order that trade secrets and commercial or financial information which is privileged and confidential, or any information provided to the United States by any foreign government or foreign person, may be disclosed to a party, its counsel, or any other person under such terms and conditions as the court may order.

History of 28 U.S.C. §2641: Oct. 10, 1980, P.L. 96-417, §301, 94 Stat. 1737.

§2642. ANALYSIS OF IMPORTED MERCHANDISE

The Court of International Trade may order an analysis of imported merchandise and reports thereon by laboratories or agencies of the United States or laboratories accredited by the Customs Service under section 499(b) of the Tariff Act of 1930.

History of 28 U.S.C. §2642: Oct. 10, 1980, P.L. 96-417, §301, 94 Stat. 1737; Dec. 8, 1993, P.L. 103-182, §684(a)(5), 107 Stat. 2219.

§2643. RELIEF

(a) The Court of International Trade may enter a money judgment—

(1) for or against the United States in any civil action commenced under section 1581 or 1582 of this title; and

(2) for or against the United States or any other party in any counterclaim, cross-claim, or third-party action under section 1583 of this title.

(b) If the Court of International Trade is unable to determine the correct decision on the basis of the evidence presented in any civil action, the court may order a retrial or rehearing for all purposes, or may order such further administrative or adjudicative procedures as the court considers necessary to enable it to reach the correct decision.

(c)(1) Except as provided in paragraphs (2), (3), (4), and (5) of this subsection, the Court of International Trade may, in addition to the orders specified in subsections (a) and (b) of this section, order any other form of relief that is appropriate in a civil action, including, but not limited to, declaratory judgments, orders of remand, injunctions, and writs of mandamus and prohibition.

(2) The Court of International Trade may not grant an injunction or issue a writ of mandamus in any civil action commenced to review any final determination of the Secretary of Labor under section 223 of the Trade Act of 1974, or any final determination of the Secretary of Commerce under section 251 or section 271 of such Act.

(3) In any civil action involving an application for the issuance of an order directing the administering authority or the International Trade Commission to make confidential information available under section 777(c)(2) of the Tariff Act of 1930, the Court of International Trade may issue an order of disclosure only with respect to the information specified in such section.

(4) In any civil action described in section 1581(h) of this title, the Court of International Trade may only order the appropriate declaratory relief.

(5) In any civil action involving an antidumping or countervailing duty proceeding regarding a class or kind of merchandise of a free trade area country (as defined in section 516A(f)(10) of the Tariff Act of 1930), as determined by the administering authority, the Court of International Trade may not order declaratory relief.

(d) If a surety commences a civil action in the Court of International Trade, such surety shall recover only the amount of the liquidated duties, charges, or exactions paid on the entries included in such action. The excess amount of any recovery shall be paid to the importer of record.

(e) In any proceeding involving assessment or collection of a monetary penalty under section 641(b)(6) or 641(d)(2)(A) of the Tariff Act of 1930, the court may not render judgment in an amount greater than that sought in the initial pleading of the United States, and may render judgment in such lesser amount as shall seem proper and just to the court.

History of 28 U.S.C. §2643: Oct. 10, 1980, P.L. 96-417, §301, 94 Stat. 1737; Oct. 30, 1984, P.L. 98-573, §212(b)(6), 98 Stat. 2984; Sept. 28, 1988, P.L. 100-449, §402(b), 102 Stat. 1884; Dec. 8, 1993, P.L. 103-182, §414(b), 107 Stat. 2147.

§2644. INTEREST

If, in a civil action in the Court of International Trade under section 515 of the Tariff Act of 1930, the plaintiff obtains monetary relief by a judgment or under a stipulation agreement, interest shall be allowed at an annual rate established under section 6621 of the Internal Revenue Code of 1986. Such interest shall be calculated from the date of the filing of the summons in such action to the date of the refund.

History of 28 U.S.C. §2644: Oct. 10, 1980, P.L. 96-417, §301, 94 Stat. 1738; Oct. 22, 1986, P.L. 99-514, §2, 100 Stat. 2095.

§2645. DECISIONS

(a) A final decision of the Court of International Trade in a contested civil action or a decision granting or refusing a preliminary injunction shall be supported by—

(1) a statement of findings of fact and conclusions of law; or

(2) an opinion stating the reasons and facts upon which the decision is based.

(b) After the Court of International Trade has rendered a judgment, the court may, upon the motion of a party or upon its own motion, amend its findings or make additional findings and may amend the decision and judgment accordingly. A motion of a party or the court shall be made not later than thirty days after the date of entry of the judgment.

(c) A decision of the Court of International Trade is final and conclusive, unless a retrial or rehearing is granted pursuant to section 2646 of this title or an appeal is taken to the Court of Appeals for the Federal Circuit by filing a notice of appeal with the clerk of the Court of International Trade within the time and in the manner prescribed for appeals to United States courts of appeals from the United States district courts.

History of 28 U.S.C. §2645: Oct. 10, 1980, P.L. 96-417, §301, 94 Stat. 1738; Apr. 2, 1982, P.L. 97-164, §141, 96 Stat. 45.

§2646. RETRIAL OR REHEARING

After the Court of International Trade has rendered a judgment or order, the court may, upon the motion of a party or upon its own motion, grant a retrial or rehearing, as the case may be. A motion of a party or the court shall be made not later than thirty days after the date of entry of the judgment or order.

History of 28 U.S.C. §2646: Oct. 10, 1980, P.L. 96-417, §301, 94 Stat. 1739.

§2647. REPEALED

Repealed Nov. 8, 1984, P.L. 98-620, §402(29)(G), 98 Stat. 3359.

CHAPTER 171. TORT CLAIMS PROCEDURE

§2671. DEFINITIONS

As used in this chapter and sections 1346(b) and 2401(b) of this title, the term—

"Federal agency" includes the executive departments, the judicial and legislative branches, the military departments, independent establishments of the United States, and corporations primarily acting as instrumentalities or agencies of the United States, but does not include any contractor with the United States.

"Employee of the government" includes (1) officers or employees of any federal agency, members of the military or naval forces of the United States, members of the National Guard while engaged in training or duty under section 115, 316, 502, 503, 504, or 505 of title 32, and persons acting on behalf of a federal agency in an official capacity, temporarily or permanently in the service of the United States, whether with or without compensation, and (2) any officer or employee of a Federal public defender organization, except when such officer or employee performs professional services in the course of providing representation under section 3006A of title 18.

"Acting within the scope of his office or employment", in the case of a member of the military or naval forces of the United States or a member of the National Guard as defined in section 101(3) of title 32, means acting in line of duty.

History of 28 U.S.C. §2671: June 25, 1948, ch. 646, 62 Stat. 982; May 24, 1949, ch. 139, §124, 63 Stat. 106; July 18, 1966, P.L. 89-506, §8, 80 Stat. 307; Dec. 29, 1981, P.L. 97-124, §1, 95 Stat. 1666; Nov. 18, 1988, P.L. 100-694, §3, 102 Stat. 4564; Oct. 30, 2000, P.L. 106-398, §665(b), 114 Stat. 1645A-169; Nov. 13, 2000, P.L. 106-518, §401, 114 Stat. 2421.

§2672. ADMINISTRATIVE ADJUSTMENT OF CLAIMS

The head of each Federal agency or his designee, in accordance with regulations prescribed by the Attorney General, may consider, ascertain, adjust, determine, compromise, and settle any claim for money damages against the United States for injury or loss of property or personal injury or death caused by the negligent or wrongful act or omission of any employee of the agency while acting within the scope of his office or employment, under circumstances where the United States, if a private person, would be liable to the claimant in accordance with the law of the place where the act or omission occurred: Provided, That any award, compromise, or settlement in excess of $25,000 shall be effected only with the prior written approval of the Attorney General or his designee. Notwithstanding the proviso contained in the preceding sentence, any award, compromise, or settlement may be effected without the prior written approval of the Attorney General or his or her designee, to the extent that the Attorney General delegates to the head of the agency the authority to make such award, compromise, or settlement. Such delegations may not exceed the authority delegated by the Attorney General to the United States attorneys to settle claims for money damages against the United States. Each Federal agency may use arbitration, or other alternative means of dispute resolution under the provisions of subchapter IV of chapter 5 of title 5, to settle any tort claim against the United States, to the extent of the agency's authority to award, compromise, or settle such claim without the prior written approval of the Attorney General or his or her designee.

Subject to the provisions of this title relating to civil actions on tort claims against the United States, any such award, compromise, settlement, or determination shall be final and conclusive on all officers of the Government, except when procured by means of fraud.

Any award, compromise, or settlement in an amount of $2,500 or less made pursuant to this section shall be paid by the head of the Federal agency concerned out of appropriations available to that agency. Payment of any award, compromise, or settlement in an amount in excess of $2,500 made pursuant to this section or made by the Attorney General in any amount pursuant to section 2677 of this title shall be paid in a manner similar to judgments and compromises in like causes and appropriations or funds available for the payment of such judgments and compromises are hereby made available for the payment of awards, compromises, or settlements under this chapter.

The acceptance by the claimant of any such award, compromise, or settlement shall be final and conclusive on the claimant, and shall constitute a complete release of any claim against the United States and against the employee of the government whose act or omission gave rise to the claim, by reason of the same subject matter.

History of 28 U.S.C. §2672: June 25, 1948, ch. 646, 62 Stat. 983; Apr. 25, 1949, ch. 92, §2(b), 63 Stat. 62; May 24, 1949, ch. 139, §125, 63 Stat. 106; Sept. 23, 1950, ch. 1010, §9, 64 Stat. 987; Sept. 8, 1959, P.L. 86-238, §1(1), 73 Stat. 471; July 18, 1966, P.L. 89-506, §§1, 9(a), 80 Stat. 306, 308; Nov. 15, 1990, P.L. 101-552, §8(a), 104 Stat. 2746.

§2673. REPORTS TO CONGRESS

The head of each federal agency shall report annually to Congress all claims paid by it under section 2672 of this title, stating the name of each claimant, the amount claimed, the amount awarded, and a brief description of the claim.[1]

1. **Editor's note:** P.L. 89-348, §1(1), Nov. 8, 1965, 79 Stat. 1310 repealed the requirement that an annual report to Congress be made of the administrative adjustment of tort claims of $2,500 or less, stating the name of each claimant, the amount claimed, the amount awarded, and a brief description of the claim.

History of 28 U.S.C. §2673: June 25, 1948, ch. 646, 62 Stat. 983; Nov. 8, 1965, P.L. 89-348, §1(1), 79 Stat. 1310.

§2674. LIABILITY OF UNITED STATES

The United States shall be liable, respecting the provisions of this title relating to tort claims, in the same manner and to the same extent as a private individual under like circumstances, but shall not be liable for interest prior to judgment or for punitive damages.

If, however, in any case wherein death was caused, the law of the place where the act or omission complained of occurred provides, or has been construed to provide, for damages only punitive in nature, the United States shall be liable for actual or compensatory damages, measured by the pecuniary injuries resulting from such death to the persons respectively, for whose benefit the action was brought, in lieu thereof.

With respect to any claim under this chapter, the United States shall be entitled to assert any defense based upon judicial or legislative immunity which otherwise would have been available to the employee of the United States whose act or omission gave rise to the claim, as well as any other defenses to which the United States is entitled.

With respect to any claim to which this section applies, the Tennessee Valley Authority shall be entitled to assert any defense which otherwise would have been available to the employee based upon judicial or legislative immunity, which otherwise would have been available to the employee of the Tennessee Valley Authority whose act or omission gave rise to the claim as well as any other defenses to which the Tennessee Valley Authority is entitled under this chapter.

History of 28 U.S.C. §2674: June 25, 1948, ch. 646, 62 Stat. 983; Nov. 18, 1988, P.L. 100-694, §§4, 9(c), 102 Stat. 4564, 4567.

§2675. DISPOSITION BY FEDERAL AGENCY AS PREREQUISITE; EVIDENCE

(a) An action shall not be instituted upon a claim against the United States for money damages for injury or loss of property or personal injury or death caused by the negligent or wrongful act or omission of any employee of the Government while acting within the scope of his office or employment, unless the claimant shall have first presented the claim to the appropriate Federal agency and his claim shall have been finally denied by the agency in writing and sent by certified or registered mail. The failure of an agency to make final disposition of a claim within six months after it is filed shall, at the option of the claimant any time thereafter, be deemed a final denial of the claim for purposes of this section. The provisions of this subsection shall not apply to such claims as may be asserted under the Federal Rules of Civil Procedure by third party complaint, cross-claim, or counterclaim.

(b) Action under this section shall not be instituted for any sum in excess of the amount of the claim presented to the federal agency, except where the increased amount is based upon newly discovered evidence not reasonably discoverable at the time of presenting the claim to the federal agency, or upon allegation and proof of intervening facts, relating to the amount of the claim.

(c) Disposition of any claim by the Attorney General or other head of a federal agency shall not be competent evidence of liability or amount of damages.

History of 28 U.S.C. §2675: June 25, 1948, ch. 646, 62 Stat. 983; May 24, 1949, ch. 139, §126, 63 Stat. 107; July 18, 1966, P.L. 89-506, §2, 80 Stat. 306.

§2676. JUDGMENT AS BAR

The judgment in an action under section 1346(b) of this title shall constitute a complete bar to any action by the claimant, by reason of the same subject matter, against the employee of the government whose act or omission gave rise to the claim.

History of 28 U.S.C. §2676: June 25, 1948, ch. 646, 62 Stat. 984.

§2677. COMPROMISE

The Attorney General or his designee may arbitrate, compromise, or settle any claim cognizable under section 1346(b) of this title, after the commencement of an action thereon.

History of 28 U.S.C. §2677: June 25, 1948, ch. 646, 62 Stat. 984; July 18, 1966, P.L. 89-506, §3, 80 Stat. 307.

§2678. ATTORNEY FEES; PENALTY

No attorney shall charge, demand, receive, or collect for services rendered, fees in excess of 25 per centum of any judgment rendered pursuant to section 1346(b) of this title or any settlement made pursuant to section 2677 of this title, or in excess of 20 per centum of any award, compromise, or settlement made pursuant to section 2672 of this title.

Any attorney who charges, demands, receives, or collects for services rendered in connection with such claim any

amount in excess of that allowed under this section, if recovery be had, shall be fined not more than $2,000 or imprisoned not more than one year, or both.

History of 28 U.S.C. §2678: June 25, 1948, ch. 646, 62 Stat. 984; July 18, 1966, P.L. 89-506, §4, 80 Stat. 307.

§2679. EXCLUSIVENESS OF REMEDY

(a) The authority of any federal agency to sue and be sued in its own name shall not be construed to authorize suits against such federal agency on claims which are cognizable under section 1346(b) of this title, and the remedies provided by this title in such cases shall be exclusive.

(b)(1) The remedy against the United States provided by sections 1346(b) and 2672 of this title for injury or loss of property, or personal injury or death arising or resulting from the negligent or wrongful act or omission of any employee of the Government while acting within the scope of his office or employment is exclusive of any other civil action or proceeding for money damages by reason of the same subject matter against the employee whose act or omission gave rise to the claim or against the estate of such employee. Any other civil action or proceeding for money damages arising out of or relating to the same subject matter against the employee or the employee's estate is precluded without regard to when the act or omission occurred.

(2) Paragraph (1) does not extend or apply to a civil action against an employee of the Government—

(A) which is brought for a violation of the Constitution of the United States, or

(B) which is brought for a violation of a statute of the United States under which such action against an individual is otherwise authorized.

(c) The Attorney General shall defend any civil action or proceeding brought in any court against any employee of the Government or his estate for any such damage or injury. The employee against whom such civil action or proceeding is brought shall deliver within such time after date of service or knowledge of service as determined by the Attorney General, all process served upon him or an attested true copy thereof to his immediate superior or to whomever was designated by the head of his department to receive such papers and such person shall promptly furnish copies of the pleadings and process therein to the United States attorney for the district embracing the place wherein the proceeding is brought, to the Attorney General, and to the head of his employing Federal agency.

(d)(1) Upon certification by the Attorney General that the defendant employee was acting within the scope of his office or employment at the time of the incident out of which the claim arose, any civil action or proceeding commenced upon such claim in a United States district court shall be deemed an action against the United States under the provisions of this title and all references thereto, and the United States shall be substituted as the party defendant.

(2) Upon certification by the Attorney General that the defendant employee was acting within the scope of his office or employment at the time of the incident out of which the claim arose, any civil action or proceeding commenced upon such claim in a State court shall be removed without bond at any time before trial by the Attorney General to the district court of the United States for the district and division embracing the place in which the action or proceeding is pending. Such action or proceeding shall be deemed to be an action or proceeding brought against the United States under the provisions of this title and all references thereto, and the United States shall be substituted as the party defendant. This certification of the Attorney General shall conclusively establish scope of office or employment for purposes of removal.

(3) In the event that the Attorney General has refused to certify scope of office or employment under this section, the employee may at any time before trial petition the court to find and certify that the employee was acting within the scope of his office or employment. Upon such certification by the court, such action or proceeding shall be deemed to be an action or proceeding brought against the United States under the provisions of this title and all references thereto, and the United States shall be substituted as the party defendant. A copy of the petition shall be served upon the United States in accordance with the provisions of Rule 4(d)(4) of the Federal Rules of Civil Procedure. In the event the petition is filed in a civil action or proceeding pending in a State court, the action or proceeding may be removed without bond by the Attorney General to the district court of the United States for the district and division embracing the place in which it is pending. If, in considering the petition, the district court determines that the employee was not acting within the scope of his office or employment, the action or proceeding shall be remanded to the State court.

(4) Upon certification, any action or proceeding subject to paragraph (1), (2), or (3) shall proceed in the same manner as any action against the United States filed pursuant to section 1346(b) of this title and shall be subject to the limitations and exceptions applicable to those actions.

(5) Whenever an action or proceeding in which the United States is substituted as the party defendant under this subsection is dismissed for failure first to present a claim pursuant to section 2675(a) of this title, such a claim shall be deemed to be timely presented under section 2401(b) of this title if—

(A) the claim would have been timely had it been filed on the date the underlying civil action was commenced, and

(B) the claim is presented to the appropriate Federal agency within 60 days after dismissal of the civil action.

(e) The Attorney General may compromise or settle any claim asserted in such civil action or proceeding in the manner provided in section 2677, and with the same effect.

History of 28 U.S.C. §2679: June 25, 1948, ch. 646, 62 Stat. 984; Sept. 21, 1961, P.L. 87-258, §1, 75 Stat. 539; July 18, 1966, P.L. 89-506, §5(a), 80 Stat. 307; Nov. 18, 1988, P.L. 100-694, §§5, 6, 102 Stat. 4564.

See *Commentaries*, "Removal & Remand," ch. 4, p. 239.

§2680. EXCEPTIONS

The provisions of this chapter and section 1346(b) of this title shall not apply to—

(a) Any claim based upon an act or omission of an employee of the Government, exercising due care, in the execution of a statute or regulation, whether or not such statute or regulation be valid, or based upon the exercise or performance or the failure to exercise or perform a discretionary function or duty on the part of a federal agency or an employee of the Government, whether or not the discretion involved be abused.

(b) Any claim arising out of the loss, miscarriage, or negligent transmission of letters or postal matter.

(c) Any claim arising in respect of the assessment or collection of any tax or customs duty, or the detention of any goods, merchandise, or other property by any officer of customs or excise or any other law enforcement officer, except that the provisions of this chapter and section 1346(b) of this title apply to any claim based on injury or loss of goods, merchandise, or other property, while in the possession of any officer of customs or excise or any other law enforcement officer, if—

(1) the property was seized for the purpose of forfeiture under any provision of Federal law providing for the forfeiture of property other than as a sentence imposed upon conviction of a criminal offense;

(2) the interest of the claimant was not forfeited;

(3) the interest of the claimant was not remitted or mitigated (if the property was subject to forfeiture); and

(4) the claimant was not convicted of a crime for which the interest of the claimant in the property was subject to forfeiture under a Federal criminal forfeiture law..[1]

(d) Any claim for which a remedy is provided by chapter 309 or 311 of title 46 relating to claims or suits in admiralty against the United States.

(e) Any claim arising out of an act or omission of any employee of the Government in administering the provisions of sections 1-31 of Title 50, Appendix.

(f) Any claim for damages caused by the imposition or establishment of a quarantine by the United States.

(g) [Repealed Sept. 26, 1950, ch. 1049, §13(5), 64 Stat. 1043.]

(h) Any claim arising out of assault, battery, false imprisonment, false arrest, malicious prosecution, abuse of process, libel, slander, misrepresentation, deceit, or interference with contract rights: Provided, That, with regard to acts or omissions of investigative or law enforcement officers of the United States Government, the provisions of this chapter and section 1346(b) of this title shall apply to any claim arising, on or after the date of the enactment of this proviso, out of assault, battery, false imprisonment, false arrest, abuse of process, or malicious prosecution. For the purpose of this subsection, "investigative or law enforcement officer" means any officer of the United States who is empowered by law to execute searches, to seize evidence, or to make arrests for violations of Federal law.

(i) Any claim for damages caused by the fiscal operations of the Treasury or by the regulation of the monetary system.

(j) Any claim arising out of the combatant activities of the military or naval forces, or the Coast Guard, during time of war.

(k) Any claim arising in a foreign country.

(*l*) Any claim arising from the activities of the Tennessee Valley Authority.

(m) Any claim arising from the activities of the Panama Canal Company.

(n) Any claim arising from the activities of a Federal land bank, a Federal intermediate credit bank, or a bank for cooperatives.

1. **Editor's note:** So in original. The second period probably should not appear.

History of 28 U.S.C. §2680: June 25, 1948, ch. 646, 62 Stat. 984; July 16, 1949, ch. 340, 63 Stat. 444; Sept. 26, 1950, ch. 1049, §§2(a)(2), 13(5), 64 Stat. 1038, 1043; Aug. 18, 1959, P.L. 86-168, §202(b), 73 Stat. 389; Mar. 16, 1974, P.L. 93-253, §2, 88 Stat. 50; Apr. 25, 2000, P.L. 106-185, §3(a), 114 Stat. 211; Oct. 6, 2006, P.L. 109-304, §17(f)(4), 120 Stat. 1708.

CHAPTER 173. ATTACHMENT IN POSTAL SUITS

§2710. RIGHT OF ATTACHMENT

(a) Where debts are due from a defaulting or delinquent postmaster, contractor, or other officer, agent or employee of the Post Office Department, a warrant of attachment may issue against all property and legal and equitable rights belonging to him, and his sureties, or either of them, where he—

(1) is a nonresident of the district where he was appointed, or has departed from that district for the purpose of permanently residing outside thereof, or of avoiding the service of civil process; and

(2) has conveyed away, or is about to convey away any of his property, or has removed or is about to remove the same from the district wherein it is situated, with intent to defraud the United States.

(b) When the property has been removed, the marshal of the district into which it has been removed, upon receipt of certified copies of the warrant, may seize the property and convey it to a convenient place within the jurisdiction of the court which issued the warrant. Alias warrants may be issued upon due application. The warrant first issued remains valid until the return day thereof.

History of 28 U.S.C. §2710: Sept. 2, 1960, P.L. 86-682, §9, 74 Stat. 706.

§2711. APPLICATION FOR WARRANT

A United States attorney or assistant United States attorney or a person authorized by the Attorney General—

(1) upon his own affidavit or that of another credible person, stating the existence of either of the grounds of attachments enumerated in section 2710 of this title and

(2) upon production of legal evidence of the debt

may apply for a warrant of attachment to a judge, or, in his absence, to the clerk of any court of the United States having original jurisdiction of the cause of action.

History of 28 U.S.C. §2711: Sept. 2, 1960, P.L. 86-682, §9, 74 Stat. 707.

§2712. ISSUE OF WARRANT

Upon an order of a judge of a court, or, in his absence and upon the clerk's own initiative, the clerk shall issue a warrant for the attachment of the property belonging to the person specified in the affidavit. The marshal shall execute the warrant forthwith and take the property attached, if personal, in his custody, subject to the interlocutory or final orders of the court.

History of 28 U.S.C. §2712: Sept. 2, 1960, P.L. 86-682, §9, 74 Stat. 707.

§2713. TRIAL OF OWNERSHIP OF PROPERTY

Not later than twenty days before the return day of a warrant issued under section 2712 of this title, the party whose property is attached, on notice to the United States Attorney, may file a plea in abatement, denying the allegations of the affidavit, or denying ownership in the defendant of the property attached. The court, upon application of either party, shall order a trial by jury of the issues. Where the parties, by consent, waive a trial by jury, the court shall decide the issues. A party claiming ownership of the property attached and seeking its return is limited to the remedy afforded by this section, but his right to an action of trespass, or other action for damages, is not impaired.

History of 28 U.S.C. §2713: Sept. 2, 1960, P.L. 86-682, §9, 74 Stat. 707.

§2714. INVESTMENT OF PROCEEDS OF ATTACHED PROPERTY

When the property attached is sold on an interlocutory order or is producing revenue, the money arising from the sale or revenue shall be invested, under the order of the court, in securities of the United States. The accretions therefrom are subject to the order of the court.

History of 28 U.S.C. §2714: Sept. 2, 1960, P.L. 86-682, §9, 74 Stat. 707.

§2715. PUBLICATION

The marshal shall cause publication of an executed warrant of attachment—

(1) for two months in case of an absconding debtor, and

(2) for four months in case of a nonresident debtor

in a newspaper published in the district where the property is situated pursuant to the details of the order under which the warrant is issued.

History of 28 U.S.C. §2715: Sept. 2, 1960, P.L. 86-682, §9, 74 Stat. 707.

§2716. PERSONAL NOTICE

After the first publication of the notice of attachment, a person indebted to, or having possession of property of a defendant and having knowledge of the notice, shall answer for the amount of his debt or the value of the property. Any disposal or attempted disposal of the property, to the injury of the United States, is unlawful. When the person indebted to, or having possession of the property of a defendant, is known to the United States attorney or marshal, the officer shall cause a personal notice of the attachment to be served upon him, but the lack of the notice does not invalidate the attachment.

History of 28 U.S.C. §2716: Sept. 2, 1960, P.L. 86-682, §9, 74 Stat. 707.

§2717. DISCHARGE

The court, or a judge thereof, upon—

(1) application of the party when property has been attached and

(2) execution to the United States of a penal bond, approved by a judge, in double the value of the property attached and conditioned upon the return of the property or the payment of any judgment rendered by the court

may discharge the warrant of attachment as to the property of the applicant.

History of 28 U.S.C. §2717: Sept. 2, 1960, P.L. 86-682, §9, 74 Stat. 708.

§2718. INTEREST ON BALANCES DUE DEPARTMENT

In suits for balances due the Post Office Department may recover interest at the rate of 6 per centum per year from the time of default.

History of 28 U.S.C. §2718: Sept. 2, 1960, P.L. 86-682, §9, 74 Stat. 708.

CHAPTER 175. REPEALED

Repealed Oct. 17, 2000, P.L. 106-310, §3405(c)(1), 114 Stat. 1221.

CHAPTER 176. FEDERAL DEBT COLLECTION PROCEDURE

SUBCHAPTER A. DEFINITIONS & GENERAL PROVISIONS

§3001. APPLICABILITY OF CHAPTER

(a) In general.—Except as provided in subsection (b), the[1] chapter provides the exclusive civil procedures for the United States—

(1) to recover a judgment on a debt; or

(2) to obtain, before judgment on a claim for a debt, a remedy in connection with such claim.

(b) Limitation.—To the extent that another Federal law specifies procedures for recovering on a claim or a judgment for a debt arising under such law, those procedures shall apply to such claim or judgment to the extent those procedures are inconsistent with this chapter.

(c) Amounts owing other than debts.—This chapter shall not apply with respect to an amount owing that is not a debt or to a claim for an amount owing that is not a debt.

1. **Editor's note:** So in original. Probably should be "this."

History of 28 U.S.C. §3001: Nov. 29, 1990, P.L. 101-647, §3611, 104 Stat. 4933.

§3002. DEFINITIONS

As used in this chapter:

(1) "Counsel for the United States" means—

(A) a United States attorney, an assistant United States attorney designated to act on behalf of the United States attorney, or an attorney with the United States Department of Justice or with a Federal agency who has litigation authority; and

(B) any private attorney authorized by contract made in accordance with section 3718 of title 31 to conduct litigation for collection of debts on behalf of the United States.

(2) "Court" means any court created by the Congress of the United States, excluding the United States Tax Court.

(3) "Debt" means—

(A) an amount that is owing to the United States on account of a direct loan, or loan insured or guaranteed, by the United States; or

(B) an amount that is owing to the United States on account of a fee, duty, lease, rent, service, sale of real or personal property, overpayment, fine, assessment, penalty, restitution, damages, interest, tax, bail bond forfeiture, reimbursement, recovery of a cost incurred by the United States, or other source of indebtedness to the United States, but that is not owing under the terms of a contract originally entered into by only persons other than the United States;

and includes any amount owing to the United States for the benefit of an Indian tribe or individual Indian, but excludes any amount to which the United States is entitled under section 3011(a).

(4) "Debtor" means a person who is liable for a debt or against whom there is a claim for a debt.

(5) "Disposable earnings" means that part of earnings remaining after all deductions required by law have been withheld.

(6) "Earnings" means compensation paid or payable for personal services, whether denominated as wages, salary, commission, bonus, or otherwise, and includes periodic payments pursuant to a pension or retirement program.

(7) "Garnishee" means a person (other than the debtor) who has, or is reasonably thought to have, possession, custody, or control of any property in which the debtor has a substantial nonexempt interest, including any obligation due the debtor or to become due the debtor, and against whom a garnishment under section 3104 or 3205 is issued by a court.

(8) "Judgment" means a judgment, order, or decree entered in favor of the United States in a court and arising from a civil or criminal proceeding regarding a debt.

(9) "Nonexempt disposable earnings" means 25 percent of disposable earnings, subject to section 303 of the Consumer Credit Protection Act.

(10) "Person" includes a natural person (including an individual Indian), a corporation, a partnership, an unincorporated association, a trust, or an estate, or any other public or private entity, including a State or local government or an Indian tribe.

(11) "Prejudgment remedy" means the remedy of attachment, receivership, garnishment, or sequestration authorized by this chapter to be granted before judgment on the merits of a claim for a debt.

(12) "Property" includes any present or future interest, whether legal or equitable, in real, personal (including choses in action), or mixed property, tangible or intangible, vested or contingent, wherever located and however held (including community property and property held in trust (including spendthrift and pension trusts)), but excludes—

(A) property held in trust by the United States for the benefit of an Indian tribe or individual Indian; and

(B) Indian lands subject to restrictions against alienation imposed by the United States.

(13) "Security agreement" means an agreement that creates or provides for a lien.

(14) "State" means any of the several States, the District of Columbia, the Commonwealth of Puerto Rico, the Commonwealth of the Northern Marianas, or any territory or possession of the United States.

(15) "United States" means—

(A) a Federal corporation;

(B) an agency, department, commission, board, or other entity of the United States; or

(C) an instrumentality of the United States.

(16) "United States marshal" means a United States marshal, a deputy marshal, or an official of the United States Marshals Service designated under section 564.

History of 28 U.S.C. §3002: Nov. 29, 1990, P.L. 101-647, §3611, 104 Stat. 4933.

§3003. RULES OF CONSTRUCTION

(a) Terms.—For purposes of this chapter—

(1) the terms "includes" and "including" are not limiting;

(2) the term "or" is not exclusive; and

(3) the singular includes the plural.

(b) Effect on rights of the United States.—This chapter shall not be construed to curtail or limit the right of the United States under any other Federal law or any State law—

(1) to collect taxes or to collect any other amount collectible in the same manner as a tax;

(2) to collect any fine, penalty, assessment, restitution, or forfeiture arising in a criminal case;

(3) to appoint or seek the appointment of a receiver; or

(4) to enforce a security agreement.

(c) Effect on other laws.—This chapter shall not be construed to supersede or modify the operation of—

(1) title 11;

(2) admiralty law;

(3) section 3713 of title 31;

(4) section 303 of the Consumer Credit Protection Act (15 U.S.C. 1673);

(5) a statute of limitation applicable to a criminal proceeding;

(6) the common law or statutory rights to set-off or recoupment;

(7) any Federal law authorizing, or any inherent authority of a court to provide, injunctive relief;

(8) the authority of a court—

(A) to impose a sanction under the Federal Rules of Civil Procedure;

(B) to appoint a receiver to effectuate its order; or

(C) to exercise the power of contempt under any Federal law;

(9) any law authorizing the United States to obtain partition, or to recover possession, of property in which the United States holds title; or

(10) any provision of any other chapter of this title, except to the extent such provision is inconsistent with this chapter.

(d) Preemption.—This chapter shall preempt State law to the extent such law is inconsistent with a provision of this chapter.

(e) Effect on rights of the United States under foreign and international law.—This chapter shall not be construed to curtail or limit the rights of the United States under foreign law, under a treaty or an international agreement, or otherwise under international law.

(f) Applicability of Federal Rules of Civil Procedure.—Except as provided otherwise in this chapter, the Federal Rules of Civil Procedure shall apply with respect to actions and proceedings under this chapter.

History of 28 U.S.C. §3003: Nov. 29, 1990, P.L. 101-647, §3611, 104 Stat. 4935.

§3004. SERVICE OF PROCESS; ENFORCEMENT; NOTICE

(a) Manner of service.—A complaint, notice, writ, or other process required to be served in an action or proceeding under this chapter shall be served in accordance with the Federal Rules of Civil Procedure unless otherwise provided in this chapter.

(b) Nationwide enforcement.—**(1)** Except as provided in paragraph (2)—

(A) any writ, order, judgment, or other process, including a summons and complaint, filed under this chapter may be served in any State; and

(B) such writ, order, or judgment may be enforced by the court issuing the writ, order, or process, regardless of where the person is served with the writ, order, or process.

(2) If the debtor so requests, within 20 days after receiving the notice described in section 3101(d) or 3202(b), the action or proceeding in which the writ, order, or judgment was issued shall be transferred to the district court for the district in which the debtor resides.

(c) Notice and other process.—At such time as counsel for the United States considers appropriate, but not later than the time a prejudgment or postjudgment remedy is put into effect under this chapter, counsel for the United States shall exercise reasonable diligence to serve on the debtor and any person who the United States believes, after exercising due diligence, has possession, custody, or control of the property, a copy of the application for such remedy, the order granting such remedy, and the notice required by section 3101(d) or 3202(b).

History of 28 U.S.C. §3004: Nov. 29, 1990, P.L. 101-647, §3611, 104 Stat. 4936.

§3005. APPLICATION OF CHAPTER TO JUDGMENTS

This chapter shall not apply with respect to a judgment on a debt if such judgment is entered more than 10 years before the effective date of this chapter.

History of 28 U.S.C. §3005: Nov. 29, 1990, P.L. 101-647, §3611, 104 Stat. 4936.

§3006. AFFIDAVIT REQUIREMENTS

Any affidavit required of the United States by this chapter may be made on information and belief, if reliable and reasonably necessary, establishing with particularity, to the court's satisfaction, facts supporting the claim of the United States.

History of 28 U.S.C. §3006: Nov. 29, 1990, P.L. 101-647, §3611, 104 Stat. 4936.

§3007. PERISHABLE PERSONAL PROPERTY

(a) Authority to sell.—If at any time during any action or proceeding under this chapter the court determines on its own initiative or upon motion of any party, that any seized or detained personal property is likely to perish, waste, or be destroyed, or otherwise substantially depreciate in value during the pendency of the proceeding, the court shall order a commercially reasonable sale of such property.

(b) Deposit of sale proceeds.—Within 5 days after such sale, the proceeds shall be deposited with the clerk of the court, accompanied by a statement in writing and signed by the United States marshal, to be filed in the action or proceeding, stating the time and place of sale, the name of the purchaser, the amount received, and an itemized account of expenses.

(c) Presumption.—For purposes of liability on the part of the United States, there shall be a presumption that the price paid at a sale under subsection (a) is the fair market value of the property or portion.

History of 28 U.S.C. §3007: Nov. 29, 1990, P.L. 101-647, §3611, 104 Stat. 4937.

§3008. PROCEEDINGS BEFORE UNITED STATES MAGISTRATE JUDGES

A district court of the United States may assign its duties in proceedings under this chapter to a United States magistrate judge to the extent not inconsistent with the Constitution and laws of the United States.

History of 28 U.S.C. §3008: Nov. 29, 1990, P.L. 101-647, §3611, 104 Stat. 4937; Dec. 1, 1990, P.L. 101-650, §321, 104 Stat. 5117.

§3009. UNITED STATES MARSHALS' AUTHORITY TO DESIGNATE KEEPER

Whenever a United States marshal is authorized to seize property pursuant to this chapter, the United States marshal may designate another person or Federal agency to hold for safekeeping such property seized.

History of 28 U.S.C. §3009: Nov. 29, 1990, P.L. 101-647, §3611, 104 Stat. 4937.

§3010. CO-OWNED PROPERTY

(a) Limitation.—The remedies available to the United States under this chapter may be enforced against property which is co-owned by a debtor and any other person only to the extent allowed by the law of the State where the property is located. This section shall not be construed to limit any right or interest of a debtor or co-owner in a retirement system for Federal military or civilian personnel established by the United States or any agency thereof or in a qualified retirement arrangement.

(b) Definitions.—For purposes of subsection (a)—

(1) the term "retirement system for Federal military or civilian personnel" means a pension or annuity system for Federal military or civilian personnel of more than one agency, or for some or all of such personnel of a single agency, established by statute or by regulation pursuant to statutory authority; and

(2) the term "qualified retirement arrangement" means a plan qualified under section 401(a), 403(a), or 409 of the Internal Revenue Code of 1986 or a plan that is subject to the requirements of section 205 of the Employee Retirement Income Security Act of 1974.

History of 28 U.S.C. §3010: Nov. 29, 1990, P.L. 101-647, §3611, 104 Stat. 4937.

§3011. ASSESSMENT OF SURCHARGE ON A DEBT

(a) Surcharge authorized.—In an action or proceeding under subchapter B or C, and subject to subsection (b), the United States is entitled to recover a surcharge of 10 percent of the amount of the debt in connection with the recovery of the debt, to cover the cost of processing and handling the litigation and enforcement under this chapter of the claim for such debt.

(b) Limitation.—Subsection (a) shall not apply if—

(1) the United States receives an attorney's fee in connection with the enforcement of the claim; or

(2) the law pursuant to which the action on the claim is based provides any other amount to cover such costs.

History of 28 U.S.C. §3011: Nov. 29, 1990, P.L. 101-647, §3611, 104 Stat. 4937.

§3012. JOINDER OF ADDITIONAL DEFENDANT

The United States or the debtor may join as an additional defendant in an action or proceeding under this chapter any person reasonably believed to owe money (including money owed on account of a requirement to provide goods or services pursuant to a loan or loan guarantee extended under Federal law) to the debtor arising out of the transaction or occurrence giving rise to a debt.

History of 28 U.S.C. §3012: Nov. 29, 1990, P.L. 101-647, §3611, 104 Stat. 4938.

§3013. MODIFICATION OR PROTECTIVE ORDER; SUPERVISION OF ENFORCEMENT

The court may at any time on its own initiative or the motion of any interested person, and after such notice as it may require, make an order denying, limiting, conditioning, regulating, extending, or modifying the use of any enforcement procedure under this chapter.

History of 28 U.S.C. §3013: Nov. 29, 1990, P.L. 101-647, §3611, 104 Stat. 4938.

§3014. EXEMPT PROPERTY

(a) Election to exempt property.—An individual debtor may, in an action or proceeding under this chapter, elect to exempt property listed in either paragraph (1) or, in the alternative, paragraph (2). If such action or proceeding is against debtors who are husband and wife, one debtor may not elect to exempt property listed in paragraph (1) and the other debtor elect to exempt property listed in paragraph (2). If the debtors cannot agree on the alternative to be elected, they shall be deemed to elect paragraph (1). Such property is either—

(1) property that is specified in section 522(d) of title 11, as amended from time to time; or

(2)(A) any property that is exempt under Federal law, other than paragraph (1), or State or local law that is applicable on the date of the filing of the application for a remedy under this chapter at the place in which the debtor's domicile has been located for the 180 days immediately preceding the date of the filing of such application, or for a longer portion of such 180-day period than in any other place; and

(B) any interest in property in which the debtor had, immediately before the filing of such application, an interest as a tenant by the entirety or joint tenant, or an interest in a community estate, to the extent that such interest is exempt from process under applicable nonbankruptcy law.

(b) Effect on assertion and manner of determination—

(1) Statement.—A court may order the debtor to file a statement with regard to any claimed exemption. A copy of

such statement shall be served on counsel for the United States. Such statement shall be under oath and shall describe each item of property for which exemption is claimed, the value and the basis for such valuation, and the nature of the debtor's ownership interest.

(2) Hearing.—The United States or the debtor, by application to the court in which an action or proceeding under this chapter is pending, may request a hearing on the applicability of any exemption claimed by the debtor. The court shall determine the extent (if any) to which the exemption applies. Unless it is reasonably evident that the exemption applies, the debtor shall bear the burden of persuasion.

(3) Stay of disposition.—Assertion of an exemption shall prevent the United States from selling or otherwise disposing of the property for which such exemption is claimed until the court determines whether the debtor has a substantial nonexempt interest in such property. The United States may not take possession of, dispose of, sell, or otherwise interfere with the debtor's normal use and enjoyment of an interest in property the United States knows or has reason to know is exempt.

(c) Debtors in joint cases.—Subject to the limitation in subsection (a), this section shall apply separately with respect to each debtor in a joint case.

History of 28 U.S.C. §3014: Nov. 29, 1990, P.L. 101-647, §3611, 104 Stat. 4938.

§3015. DISCOVERY AS TO DEBTOR'S FINANCIAL CONDITION

(a) In general.—Except as provided in subsection (b), in an action or proceeding under subchapter B or C, the United States may have discovery regarding the financial condition of the debtor in the manner in which discovery is authorized by the Federal Rules of Civil Procedure in an action on a claim for a debt.

(b) Limitation.—Subsection (a) shall not apply with respect to an action or proceeding under subchapter B unless there is a reasonable likelihood that the debt involved exceeds $50,000.

History of 28 U.S.C. §3015: Nov. 29, 1990, P.L. 101-647, §3611, 104 Stat. 4939.

SUBCHAPTER B. PREJUDGMENT REMEDIES

§3101. PREJUDGMENT REMEDIES

(a) Application.—**(1)** The United States may, in a proceeding in conjunction with the complaint or at any time after the filing of a civil action on a claim for a debt, make application under oath to a court to issue any prejudgment remedy.

(2) Such application shall be filed with the court and shall set forth the factual and legal basis for each prejudgment remedy sought.

(3) Such application shall—

(A) state that the debtor against whom the prejudgment remedy is sought shall be afforded an opportunity for a hearing; and

(B) set forth with particularity that all statutory requirements under this chapter for the issuance of the prejudgment remedy sought have been satisfied.

(b) Grounds.—Subject to section 3102, 3103, 3104, or 3105, a prejudgment remedy may be granted by any court if the United States shows reasonable cause to believe that—

(1) the debtor—

(A) is about to leave the jurisdiction of the United States with the effect of hindering, delaying, or defrauding the United States in its effort to recover a debt;

(B) has or is about to assign, dispose, remove, conceal, ill treat, waste, or destroy property with the effect of hindering, delaying, or defrauding the United States;

(C) has or is about to convert the debtor's property into money, securities, or evidence of debt in a manner prejudicial to the United States with the effect of hindering, delaying, or defrauding the United States; or

(D) has evaded service of process by concealing himself or has temporarily withdrawn from the jurisdiction of the United States with the effect of hindering, delaying, or defrauding the United States; or

(2) a prejudgment remedy is required to obtain jurisdiction within the United States and the prejudgment remedy sought will result in obtaining such jurisdiction.

(c) Affidavit.—**(1)** The application under subsection (a) shall include an affidavit establishing with particularity to the court's satisfaction facts supporting the probable validity of the claim for a debt and the right of the United States to recover what is demanded in the application.

(2) The affidavit shall state—

(A) specifically the amount of the debt claimed by the United States and any interest or costs attributable to such debt;

(B) one or more of the grounds specified in subsection (b); and

(C) the requirements of section 3102(b), 3103(a), 3104(a), or 3105(b), as the case may be.

(3) No bond is required of the United States.

(d) Notice and Hearing.—**(1)** On filing an application by the United States as provided in this section, the counsel for the United States shall prepare, and the clerk shall issue, a notice for service on the debtor against whom the prejudgment remedy is sought and on any other person whom the United States reasonably believes, after exercising due diligence, has possession, custody, or control of property affected by such remedy. Three copies of the notice shall be served on each such person. The form and content of such notice shall be approved jointly by a majority of the chief judges of the Federal districts in the State in which the court is located and shall be in substantially the following form:

"NOTICE

"You are hereby notified that this [property] is being taken by the United States Government ('the Government'), which says that [name of debtor] owes it a debt of $[amount] for [reason for debt] and has filed a lawsuit to collect this debt. The Government says it must take this property at this time because [recite the pertinent ground or grounds from section 3101(b)]. The Government wants to make sure [name of debtor] will pay if the court determines that this money is owed.

"In addition, you are hereby notified that there are exemptions under the law which may protect some of this property from being taken by the Government if [name of debtor] can show that the exemptions apply. Below is a summary of the major exemptions which apply in most situations in the State of [State where property is located]:

"[A statement summarizing in plain and understandable English the election available with respect to such State under section 3014 and the types of property that may be exempted under each of the alternatives specified in paragraphs (1) and (2) of section 3014(a), and a statement that different property may be so exempted with respect to the State in which the debtor resides.]

"If you are [name of debtor] and you disagree with the reason the Government gives for taking your property now, or if you think you do not owe the money to the Government that it says you do, or if you think the property the Government is taking qualifies under one of the above exemptions, you have a right to ask the court to return your property to you.

"If you want a hearing, you must promptly notify the court. You must make your request in writing, and either mail it or deliver it in person to the clerk of the court at [address]. If you wish, you may use this notice to request the hearing by checking the box below and mailing this notice to the court clerk. You must also send a copy of your request to the Government at [address], so the Government will know you want a hearing. The hearing will take place within 5 days after the clerk receives your request, if you ask for it to take place that quickly, or as soon after that as possible.

"At the hearing you may explain to the judge why you think you do not owe the money to the Government, why you disagree with the reason the Government says it must take your property at this time, or why you believe the property the Government has taken is exempt or belongs to someone else. You may make any or all of these explanations as you see fit.

"If you think you live outside the Federal judicial district in which the court is located, you may request, not later than 20 days after you receive this notice, that this proceeding to take your property be transferred by the court to the Federal judicial district in which you reside. You must make your request in writing, and either mail it or deliver it in person to the clerk of the court at [address]. You must also send a copy of your request to the Government at [address], so the Government will know you want the proceeding to be transferred.

"Be sure to keep a copy of this notice for your own records. If you have any questions about your rights or about this procedure, you should contact a lawyer, an office of public legal assistance, or the clerk of the court. The clerk is not permitted to give legal advice, but can refer you to other sources of information."

(2) By requesting, at any time before judgment on the claim for a debt, the court to hold a hearing, the debtor may move to quash the order granting such remedy. The court shall hold a hearing on such motion as soon as practicable, or, if requested by the debtor, within 5 days after receiving the request for a hearing or as soon thereafter as possible. The issues at such hearing shall be limited to—

(A) the probable validity of the claim for the debt for which such remedy was granted and of any defense or claim of exemption asserted by such person;

(B) compliance with any statutory requirement for the issuance of the prejudgment remedy granted;

(C) the existence of any ground set forth in subsection (b); and

(D) the inadequacy of alternative remedies (if any) to protect the interests of the United States.

(e) Issuance of writ.—On the court's determination that the requirements of subsections (a), (b), and (c) have been met, the court shall issue all process sufficient to put into effect the prejudgment remedy sought.

History of 28 U.S.C. §3101: Nov. 29, 1990, P.L. 101-647, §3611, 104 Stat. 4939.

§3102. ATTACHMENT

(a) Property subject to attachment.—(1) Any property in the possession, custody, or control of the debtor and in which the debtor has a substantial nonexempt interest, except earnings, may be attached pursuant to a writ of attachment in an action or proceeding against a debtor on a claim for a debt and may be held as security to satisfy such judgment, and interest and costs, as the United States may recover on such claim.

(2) The value of property attached shall not exceed the amount by which the sum of the amount of the debt claimed by the United States and the amount of interest and costs reasonably likely to be assessed against the debtor by the court exceeds the aggregate value of the nonexempt interest of the debtor in any—

(A) property securing the debt; and

(B) property garnished or in receivership, or income sequestered, under this subchapter.

(b) Availability of attachment.—If the requirements of section 3101 are satisfied, a court shall issue a writ authorizing the United States to attach property in which the debtor has a substantial nonexempt interest, as security for such judgment (and interest and costs) as the United States may recover on a claim for a debt—

(1) in an action on a contract, express or implied, against the debtor for payment of money, only if the United States shows reasonable cause to believe that—

(A) the contract is not fully secured by real or personal property; or

(B) the value of the original security is substantially diminished, without any act of the United States or the person to whom the security was given, below the amount of the debt;

(2) in an action against the debtor for damages in tort;

(3) if the debtor resides outside the jurisdiction of the United States; or

(4) in an action to recover a fine, penalty, or tax.

(c) Issuance of writ; contents.—(1) Subject to subsections (a) and (b), a writ of attachment shall be issued by the court directing the United States marshal of the district where property described in subsection (a) is located to attach the property.

(2) Several writs of attachment may be issued at the same time, or in succession, and sent to different judicial districts until sufficient property is attached.

(3) The writ of attachment shall contain—

(A) the date of the issuance of the writ;

(B) the identity of the court, the docket number of the action, and the identity of the cause of action;

(C) the name and last known address of the debtor;

(D) the amount to be secured by the attachment; and

(E) a reasonable description of the property to be attached.

(d) Levy of attachment.—(1) The United States marshal receiving the writ shall proceed without delay to levy upon the property specified for attachment if found within the district. The marshal may not sell property unless ordered by the court.

(2) In performing the levy, the United States marshal may enter any property owned, occupied, or controlled by the debtor, except that the marshal may not enter a residence or other building unless the writ expressly authorizes the marshal to do so or upon specific order of the court.

(3) Levy on real property is made by entering the property and posting the writ and notice of levy in a conspicuous place upon the property.

(4) Levy on personal property is made by taking possession of it. Levy on personal property not easily taken into possession or which cannot be taken into possession without great inconvenience or expense may be made by affixing a copy of the writ and notice of levy on it or in a conspicuous place in the vicinity of it describing in the notice of levy the property by quantity and with sufficient detail to identify the property levied on.

(5) The United States marshal shall file a copy of the notice of levy in the same manner as provided for judgments in section 3201(a)(1). The United States marshal shall serve a copy of the writ and notice of levy on—

(A) the debtor against whom the writ is issued; and

(B) the person who has possession of the property subject to the writ;

in the same manner that a summons is served in a civil action and make the return thereof.

(e) Return of writ; duties of marshal; further return.—(1) A United States marshal executing a writ of attachment shall return the writ with the marshal's action endorsed thereon or attached thereto and signed by the marshal, to the court from which it was issued, within 5 days after the date of the levy.

(2) The return shall describe the property attached with sufficient certainty to identify it and shall state the location where it was attached, the date and time it was attached, and the disposition made of the property. If no property was attached, the return shall so state.

(3) If the property levied on is claimed, replevied under subsection (j)(2), or sold under section 3007 after the return, the United States marshal shall immediately make a further return to the clerk of the court showing the disposition of the property.

(4) If personal property is replevied, the United States marshal shall deliver the replevin bond to the clerk of the court to be filed in the action.

(f) Levy of attachment as lien on property; satisfaction of lien.—(1) A levy on property under a writ of attachment under this section creates a lien in favor of the United States on the property or, in the case of perishable property sold under section 3007, on the proceeds of the sale.

(2) Such lien shall be ranked ahead of any other security interests perfected after the later of the time of levy and the time a copy of the notice of levy is filed under subsection (d)(5).

(3) Such lien shall arise from the time of levy and shall continue until a judgment in the action is obtained or denied, or the action is otherwise dismissed. The death of the debtor whose property is attached does not terminate the attachment lien. Upon issuance of a judgment in the action and registration under this chapter, the judgment lien so created relates back to the time of levy.

(g) Reduction or dissolution of attachment.—(1) If an excessive or unreasonable attachment is made, the debtor may submit a motion to the court for a reduction of the amount of the attachment or its dissolution. Notice of such motion shall be served on the United States.

(2) The court shall order a part of the property to be released, if after a hearing the court finds that the amount of the attachment is excessive or unreasonable or if the attach-

ment is for an amount larger than the sum of the liquidated or ascertainable amount of the debt and the amount of interest and costs likely to be taxed.

(3) The court shall dissolve the attachment if the amount of the debt is unliquidated and unascertainable by calculation.

(4) If any property claimed to be exempt is levied on, the debtor may, at any time after such levy, request that the court vacate such levy. If it appears to the court that the property so levied upon is exempt, the court shall order the levy vacated and the property returned to the debtor.

(h) Replevin of attached property by debtor; bond.—If attached property is not sold before judgment, the debtor may replevy such property or any part thereof by giving a bond approved by counsel for the United States or the court and payable to the United States in double the reasonable value of the property to be replevied or double the value of the claim, whichever is less.

(i) Preservation of personal property under attachment.—If personal property in custody of the United States marshal under a writ of attachment is not replevied, claimed, or sold, the court may make such order for its preservation or use as appears to be in the interest of the parties.

(j) Judgment and disposition of attached property—

(1) Judgment for the United States.—On entry of judgment for the United States, the court shall order the proceeds of personal property sold pursuant to section 3007 to be applied to the satisfaction of the judgment, and shall order the sale of any remaining personal property and any real property levied on to the extent necessary to satisfy the judgment.

(2) Judgment for the United States when personal property replevied.—With respect to personal property under attachment that is replevied, the judgment which may be entered shall be against the debtor against whom the writ of attachment is issued and also against the sureties on the debtor's replevin bond for the value of the property.

(3) Restoration of property and exoneration of replevin bond.—If the attachment is vacated or if the judgment on the claim for the debt is for the person against whom the writ attachment is issued, the court shall order the property, or proceeds of perishable property sold under section 3007, restored to the debtor and shall exonerate any replevin bond.

History of 28 U.S.C. §3102: Nov. 29, 1990, P.L. 101-647, §3611, 104 Stat. 4942.

§3103. RECEIVERSHIP

(a) Appointment of a receiver.—If the requirements of section 3101 are satisfied, a court may appoint a receiver for property in which the debtor has a substantial nonexempt interest if the United States shows reasonable cause to believe that there is a substantial danger that the property will be removed from the jurisdiction of the court, lost, concealed, materially injured or damaged, or mismanaged.

(b) Powers of receiver.—**(1)** The appointing court may authorize a receiver—

(A) to take possession of real and personal property and sue for, collect, and sell obligations upon such conditions and for such purposes as the court shall direct; and

(B) to administer, collect, improve, lease, repair or sell pursuant to section 3007 such real and personal property as the court shall direct.

A receiver appointed to manage residential or commercial property shall have demonstrable expertise in the management of these types of property.

(2) Unless expressly authorized by order of the court, a receiver shall have no power to employ attorneys, accountants, appraisers, auctioneers, or other professional persons.

(c) Duration of receivership.—A receivership shall not continue past the entry of judgment, or the conclusion of an appeal of such judgment, unless the court orders it continued under section 3203(e) or unless the court otherwise directs its continuation.

(d) Accounts; requirement to report.—A receiver shall keep written accounts itemizing receipts and expenditures, describing the property and naming the depository of receivership funds. The receiver's accounts shall be open to inspection by any person having an apparent interest in the property. The receiver shall file reports at regular intervals as directed by the court and shall serve the debtor and the United States with a copy thereof.

(e) Modification of powers; removal.—On motion of the receiver or on its own initiative, the court which appointed the receiver may remove the receiver or modify the receiver's powers at any time.

(f) Priority.—If more than one court appoints a receiver for particular property, the receiver first qualifying under law shall be entitled to take possession, control, or custody of the property.

(g) Compensation of receivers.—**(1)** A receiver is entitled to such commissions, not exceeding 5 percent of the sums received and disbursed by him, as the court allows unless the court otherwise directs.

(2) If, at the termination of a receivership, there are no funds in the hands of a receiver, the court may fix the compensation of the receiver in accordance with the services rendered and may direct the party who moved for the appointment of the receiver to pay such compensation in addition to the necessary expenditures incurred by the receiver which remain unpaid.

(3) At the termination of a receivership, the receiver shall file a final accounting of the receipts and disbursements

and apply for compensation setting forth the amount sought and the services rendered by the receiver.

History of 28 U.S.C. §3103: Nov. 29, 1990, P.L. 101-647, §3611, 104 Stat. 4944.

§3104. GARNISHMENT

(a) In general.—If the requirements of section 3101 are satisfied, a court may issue a writ of garnishment against property (excluding earnings) in which the debtor has a substantial nonexempt interest and which is in the possession, custody, or control of a person other than the debtor in order to satisfy a claim for a debt. Co-owned property shall be subject to garnishment to the same extent as co-owned property is subject to garnishment under the law of the State in which such property is located. A court may issue simultaneous separate writs of garnishment to several garnishees. A writ of garnishment issued under this subsection shall be continuing and shall terminate only as provided in section 3205(c)(10).

(b) Writ.—**(1)** Subsections (b)(2) and (c) of section 3205 shall apply with respect to garnishment under this section, except that for purposes of this section—

(A) earnings of the debtor shall not be subject to garnishment; and

(B) a reference in such subsections to a judgment debtor shall be deemed to be a reference to a debtor.

(2) The United States shall include in its application for a writ of garnishment—

(A) the amount of the claim asserted by the United States for a debt; and

(B) the date the writ is issued.

(c) Limitation.—The value of property garnished shall not exceed the amount by which the sum of the amount of the debt claimed by the United States and the amount of interest and costs reasonably likely to be assessed against the debtor by the court exceeds the aggregate value of the nonexempt interest of the debtor in any—

(1) property securing the debt; and

(2) property attached or in receivership, or income sequestered, under this subchapter.

History of 28 U.S.C. §3104: Nov. 29, 1990, P.L. 101-647, §3611, 104 Stat. 4945.

§3105. SEQUESTRATION

(a) Property subject to sequestration.—**(1)** Any income from property in which the debtor has a substantial nonexempt interest may be sequestered pursuant to a writ of sequestration in an action or proceeding against a debtor on a claim for a debt and may be held as security to satisfy such judgment, and interest and costs, as the United States may recover on such claim.

(2) The amount of income sequestered shall not exceed the amount by which the sum of the amount of the debt claimed by the United States and the amount of interest and costs reasonably likely to be assessed against the debtor by the court exceeds the aggregate value of the nonexempt interest of the debtor in any—

(A) property securing the debt; and

(B) property attached, garnished, or in receivership under this subchapter.

(b) Availability of sequestration.—If the requirements of section 3101 are satisfied, a court shall issue a writ authorizing the United States to sequester income from property in which the debtor has a substantial nonexempt interest, as security for such judgment (and interest and costs) as the United States may recover on a claim for a debt—

(1) in an action on a contract, express or implied, against the debtor for payment of money, only if the United States shows reasonable cause to believe that—

(A) the contract is not fully secured by real or personal property; or

(B) the value of the original security is substantially diminished, without any act of the United States or the person to whom the security was given, below the amount of the debt;

(2) in an action against the debtor for damages in tort;

(3) if the debtor resides outside the jurisdiction of the United States; or

(4) in an action to recover a fine, penalty, or tax.

(c) Issuance of writ; contents.—**(1)** Subject to subsections (a) and (b), a writ of sequestration shall be issued by the court directing the United States marshal of the district where income described in subsection (a) is located to sequester the income.

(2) Several writs of sequestration may be issued at the same time, or in succession, and sent to different judicial districts until sufficient income is sequestered.

(3) The writ of sequestration shall contain—

(A) the date of the issuance of the writ;

(B) the identity of the court, the docket number of the action, and the identity of the cause of action;

(C) the name and last known address of the debtor;

(D) the amount to be secured by the sequestration; and

(E) a reasonable description of the income to be sequestered.

(d) Execution of writ.—**(1)** The United States marshal receiving the writ shall proceed without delay to execute the writ.

(2) The United States marshal shall file a copy of the notice of sequestration in the same manner as provided for judgments in section 3201(a)(1). The United States marshal shall serve a copy of the writ and notice of sequestration on—

(A) the debtor against whom the writ is issued; and

(B) the person who has possession of the income subject to the writ;

in the same manner that a summons is served in a civil action and make the return thereof.

(e) Deposit of sequestered income.—A person who has possession of the income subject to a writ of sequestration shall deposit such income with the clerk of the court, accompanied by a statement in writing stating the person's name, the name of the debtor, the amount of such income, the property from which such income is produced, and the period during which such income is produced.

(f) Return of writ; duties of marshal; further return.—

(1) A United States marshal executing a writ of sequestration shall return the writ with the marshal's action endorsed thereon or attached thereto and signed by the marshal, to the court from which it was issued, within 5 days after the date of the execution.

(2) The return shall describe the income sequestered with sufficient certainty to identify it and shall state the location where it was sequestered, and the date and time it was sequestered. If no income was sequestered, the return shall so state.

(3) If sequestered income is claimed after the return, the United States marshal shall immediately make a further return to the clerk of the court showing the disposition of the income.

(g) Reduction or dissolution of sequestration.—**(1)** If an excessive or unreasonable sequestration is made, the debtor may submit a motion to the court for a reduction of the amount of the sequestration or its dissolution. Notice of such motion shall be served on the United States.

(2) The court shall order a part of the income to be released, if after a hearing the court finds that the amount of the sequestration is excessive or unreasonable or if the sequestration is for an amount larger than the sum of the liquidated or ascertainable amount of the debt and the amount of interest and costs likely to be taxed.

(3) The court shall dissolve the sequestration if the amount of the debt is unliquidated and unascertainable by calculation.

(h) Preservation of income under sequester.—If personal property in custody of the United States marshal under a writ of sequestration is not claimed, the court may make such order for its preservation or use as appears to be in the interest of the parties.

(i) Judgment and disposition of sequestered income—

(1) Judgment for the United States.—On entry of judgment for the United States, the court shall order the sequestered income to be applied to the satisfaction of the judgment.

(2) Restoration of income.—If the sequestration is vacated or if the judgment on the claim for the debt is for the person against whom the writ of sequestration is issued, the court shall order the income restored to the debtor.

History of 28 U.S.C. §3105: Nov. 29, 1990, P.L. 101-647, §3611, 104 Stat. 4946.

SUBCHAPTER C. POSTJUDGMENT REMEDIES

§3201. JUDGMENT LIENS

(a) Creation.—A judgment in a civil action shall create a lien on all real property of a judgment debtor on filing a certified copy of the abstract of the judgment in the manner in which a notice of tax lien would be filed under paragraphs (1) and (2) of section 6323(f) of the Internal Revenue Code of 1986. A lien created under this paragraph is for the amount necessary to satisfy the judgment, including costs and interest.

(b) Priority of lien.—A lien created under subsection (a) shall have priority over any other lien or encumbrance which is perfected later in time.

(c) Duration of lien; renewal.—**(1)** Except as provided in paragraph (2), a lien created under subsection (a) is effective, unless satisfied, for a period of 20 years.

(2) Such lien may be renewed for one additional period of 20 years upon filing a notice of renewal in the same manner as the judgment is filed and shall relate back to the date the judgment is filed if—

(A) the notice of renewal is filed before the expiration of the 20-year period to prevent the expiration of the lien; and

(B) the court approves the renewal of such lien under this paragraph.

(d) Release of judgment lien.—A judgment lien shall be released on the filing of a satisfaction of judgment or release of lien in the same manner as the judgment is filed to obtain the lien.

(e) Effect of lien on eligibility for Federal grants, loans or programs.—A debtor who has a judgment lien against the debtor's property for a debt to the United States shall not be eligible to receive any grant or loan which is made, insured, guaranteed, or financed directly or indirectly by the United States or to receive funds directly from the Federal Government in any program, except funds to which the debtor is entitled as beneficiary, until the judgment is paid in full or otherwise satisfied. The agency of the United States that is responsible for such grants and loans may promulgate regulations to allow for waiver of this restriction on eligibility for such grants, loans, and funds.

(f) Sale of property subject to judgment lien.—**(1)** On proper application to a court, the court may order the United States to sell, in accordance with sections 2001 and 2002, any real property subject to a judgment lien in effect under this section.

(2) This subsection shall not preclude the United States from using an execution sale pursuant to section 3203(g) to sell real property subject to a judgment lien.

History of 28 U.S.C. §3201: Nov. 29, 1990, P.L. 101-647, §3611, 104 Stat. 4948.

§3202. ENFORCEMENT OF JUDGMENTS

(a) Enforcement Remedies.—A judgment may be enforced by any of the remedies set forth in this subchapter. A court may issue other writs pursuant to section 1651 of title 28, United States Code, as necessary to support such remedies, subject to rule 81(b) of the Federal Rules of Civil Procedure.

(b) Notice.—On the commencement by the United States of an action or proceeding under this subchapter to obtain a remedy, the counsel for the United States shall prepare, and clerk of the court shall issue, a notice in substantially the following form:

"NOTICE

"You are hereby notified that this [property] is being taken by the United States Government, which has a court judgment in [case docket number and jurisdiction of court] of $[amount] for [reason of debt].

"In addition, you are hereby notified that there are exemptions under the law which may protect some of this property from being taken by the United States Government if [name of judgment debtor] can show that the exemptions apply. Below is a summary of the major exemptions which apply in most situations in the State of [State where property is located]:

"[A statement summarizing in plain and understandable English the election available with respect to such State under section 3014 and the types of property that may be exempted under each of the alternatives specified in paragraphs (1) and (2) of section 3014(a) and a statement that different property may be so exempted with respect to the State in which the debtor resides.]

"If you are [name of judgment debtor], you have a right to ask the court to return your property to you if you think the property the Government is taking qualifies under one of the above exemptions [For a default judgment:] or if you think you do not owe the money to the United States Government that it says you do.

"If you want a hearing, you must notify the court within 20 days after you receive this notice. You must make your request in writing, and either mail it or deliver it in person to the clerk of the court at [address]. If you wish, you may use this notice to request the hearing by checking the box below and mailing this notice to the court clerk. You must also send a copy of your request to the Government at [address], so the Government will know you want a hearing. The hearing will take place within 5 days after the clerk receives your request, if you ask for it to take place that quickly, or as soon after that as possible.

"At the hearing you may explain to the judge why you believe the property the Government has taken is exempt [For a default judgment:] or why you think you do not owe the money to the Government. [For a writ of execution:] If you do not request a hearing within 20 days of receiving this notice, your [property] may be sold at public auction and the payment used toward the money you owe the Government.

"If you think you live outside the Federal judicial district in which the court is located, you may request, not later than 20 days after your[1] receive this notice, that this proceeding to take your property be transferred by the court to the Federal judicial district in which you reside. You must make your request in writing, and either mail it or deliver it in person to the clerk of the court at [address]. You must also send a copy of your request to the Government at [address], so the Government will know you want the proceeding to be transferred.

"Be sure to keep a copy of this notice for your own records. If you have any questions about your rights or about this procedure, you should contact a lawyer, an office of public legal assistance, or the clerk of the court. The clerk is not permitted to give legal advice, but can refer you to other sources of information."

(c) Service.—A copy of the notice and a copy of the application for granting a remedy under this subchapter shall be served by counsel for the United States on the judgment debtor against whom such remedy is sought and on each person whom the United States, after diligent inquiry, has reasonable cause to believe has an interest in property to which the remedy is directed.

(d) Hearing.—By requesting, within 20 days after receiving the notice described in section 3202(b), the court to hold a hearing, the judgment debtor may move to quash the order granting such remedy. The court that issued such order shall hold a hearing on such motion as soon as practicable, or, if so requested by the judgment debtor, within 5 days after receiving the request or as soon thereafter as possible. The issues at such hearing shall be limited—

(1) to the probable validity of any claim of exemption by the judgment debtor;

(2) to compliance with any statutory requirement for the issuance of the postjudgment remedy granted; and

(3) if the judgment is by default and only to the extent that the Constitution or another law of the United States provides a right to a hearing on the issue, to—

(A) the probable validity of the claim for the debt which is merged in the judgment; and

(B) the existence of good cause for setting aside such judgment.

This subparagraph shall not be construed to afford the judgment debtor the right to more than one such hearing except to the extent that the Constitution or another law of the United States provides a right to more than one such hearing.

(e) Sale of property.—The property of a judgment debtor which is subject to sale to satisfy the judgment may be sold by judicial sale, pursuant to sections 2001, 2002, and 2004 or by execution sale pursuant to section 3203(g). If a hearing is requested pursuant to subsection (d), property with respect to which the request relates shall not be sold before such hearing.

1. **Editor's note:** So in original. Probably should be "you."

History of 28 U.S.C. §3202: Nov. 29, 1990, P.L. 101-647, §3611, 104 Stat. 4949.

§3203. EXECUTION

(a) Property subject to execution.—All property in which the judgment debtor has a substantial nonexempt interest shall be subject to levy pursuant to a writ of execution. The debtor's earnings shall not be subject to execution while in the possession, custody, or control of the debtor's employer. Co-owned property shall be subject to execution to the extent such property is subject to execution under the law of the State in which it is located.

(b) Creation of execution lien.—A lien shall be created in favor of the United States on all property levied on under a writ of execution and shall date from the time of the levy. Such lien shall have priority over all subsequent liens and shall be for the aggregate amount of the judgment, costs, and interest. The execution lien on any real property as to which the United States has a judgment lien shall relate back to the judgment lien date.

(c) Writ of execution—

(1) Issuance.—On written application of counsel for the United States, the court may issue a writ of execution. Multiple writs may issue simultaneously, and successive writs may issue before the return date of a writ previously issued.

(2) Form of writ—

(A) General contents.—A writ of execution shall specify the date that the judgment is entered, the court in which it is entered, the amount of the judgment if for money, the amount of the costs, the amount of interest due, the sum due as of the date the writ is issued, the rate of postjudgment interest, the name of the judgment debtor, and the judgment debtor's last known address.

(B) Additional contents.—**(i)** Except as provided in clauses (ii) and (iii), the writ shall direct the United States marshal to satisfy the judgment by levying on and selling property in which the judgment debtor has a substantial nonexempt interest, but not to exceed property reasonably equivalent in value to the aggregate amount of the judgment, costs, and interest.

(ii) A writ of execution issued on a judgment for the delivery to the United States of the possession of personal property, or for the delivery of the possession of real property, shall particularly describe the property, and shall require the marshal to deliver the possession of the property to the United States.

(iii) A writ of execution on a judgment for the recovery of personal property or its value shall direct the marshal, in case a delivery of the specific property cannot be had, to levy and collect such value out of any property in which the judgment debtor has a substantial nonexempt interest.

(d) Levy of execution—

(1) In general.—Levy on property pursuant to a writ of execution issued under this section shall be made in the same manner as levy on property is made pursuant to a writ of attachment issued under section 3102(d).

(2) Death of judgment debtor.—The death of the judgment debtor after a writ of execution is issued stays the execution proceedings, but any lien acquired by levy of the writ shall be recognized and enforced by the court for the district in which the estate of the deceased is located. The execution lien may be enforced—

(A) against the executor, administrator, or personal representative of the estate of the deceased; or

(B) if there be none, against the deceased's property coming to the heirs or devisees or at their option against cash in their possession, but only to the extent of the value of the property coming to them.

(3) Records of United States marshal.—**(A)** A United States marshal receiving a writ of execution shall endorse thereon the exact hour and date of receipt.

(B) The United States marshal shall make a written record of every levy, specify the property on which levy is made, the date on which levy is made, and the marshal's costs, expenses, and fees.

(C) The United States marshal shall make a written return to the court on each writ of execution stating concisely what is done pursuant to the writ and shall deliver a copy to counsel for the United States who requests the writ. The writ shall be returned not more than—

(i) 90 days after the date of issuance if levy is not made; or

(ii) 10 days after the date of sale of property on which levy is made.

(e) Appointment of receiver.—Pending the levy of execution, the court may appoint a receiver to manage property described in such writ if there is a substantial danger that the property will be removed from the jurisdiction of the court, lost, materially injured or damaged, or mismanaged.

(f) Replevy; redemption—

(1) Before execution sale—

(A) Before execution sale, the United States marshal may return property[1] to the judgment debtor any personal property taken in execution, on—

(i) satisfaction of the judgment, interest, and costs, and any costs incurred in connection with scheduling the sale; or

(ii) receipt from the judgment debtor of a bond—

(I) payable to the United States, with 2 or more good and sufficient sureties to be approved by the marshal, conditioned on the delivery of the property to the marshal at the time and place named in the bond to be sold under subsection (g); or

(II) for the payment to the marshal of a fair value thereof which shall be stated in the bond.

(B) A judgment debtor who sells or disposes of property replevied under subparagraph (A) shall pay the United States marshal the stipulated value of such property.

(C) If the judgment debtor fails to deliver such property to the United States marshal pursuant to the terms of the delivery described in subparagraph (A)(ii)(I) and fails to pay the United States marshal the stipulated value of such property, the United States marshal shall endorse the bond "forfeited" and return it to the court from which the writ of execution issued. If the judgment is not fully satisfied, the court shall issue a writ of execution against the judgment debtor and the sureties on the bond for the amount due, not exceeding the stipulated value of the property, on which execution no delivery bond shall be taken, which instruction shall be endorsed on the writ.

(2) After execution sale.—The judgment debtor shall not be entitled to redeem the property after the execution sale.

(g) Execution sale—

(1) General procedures.—An execution sale under this section shall be conducted in a commercially reasonable manner—

(A) Sale of real property—

(i) In general.—**(I)** Except as provided in clause (ii), real property, or any interest therein, shall be sold, after the expiration of the 90-day period beginning on the date of levy under subsection (d), for cash at public auction at the courthouse of the county, parish, or city in which the greater part of the property is located or on the premises or some parcel thereof.

(II) The court may order the sale of any real property after the expiration of the 30-day period beginning on the date of levy under subsection (d) if the court determines that such property is likely to perish, waste, be destroyed, or otherwise substantially depreciate in value during the 90-day period beginning on the date of levy.

(III) The time and place of sale of real property, or any interest therein, under execution shall be advertised by the United States marshal, by publication of notice, once a week for at least 3 weeks prior to the sale, in at least one newspaper of general circulation in the county or parish where the property is located. The first publication shall appear not less than 25 days preceding the day of sale. The notice shall contain a statement of the authority by which the sale is to be made, the time of levy, the time and place of sale, and a brief description of the property to be sold, sufficient to identify the property (such as a street address for urban property and the survey identification and location for rural property), but it shall not be necessary for the notice to contain field notes. Such property shall be open for inspection and appraisal, subject to the judgment debtor's reasonable objections, for a reasonable period before the day of sale.

(IV) The United States marshal shall serve written notice of public sale by personal delivery, or certified or registered mail, to each person whom the marshal has reasonable cause to believe, after a title search is conducted by the United States, has an interest in property under execution, including lienholders, co-owners, and tenants, at least 25 days before the day of sale, to the last known address of each such person.

(ii) Sale of city lots.—If the real property consists of several lots, tracts, or parcels in a city or town, each lot, tract, or parcel shall be offered for sale separately, unless not susceptible to separate sale because of the character of improvements.

(iii) Sale of rural property.—If the real property is not located in a city or town, the judgment debtor may—

(I) divide the property into lots of not less than 50 acres or in such greater or lesser amounts as ordered by the court;

(II) furnish a survey of such prepared by a registered surveyor; and

(III) designate the order in which those lots shall be sold.

When a sufficient number of lots are sold to satisfy the amount of the execution and costs of sale, the marshal shall stop the sale.

(B) Sale of personal property.—**(i)** Personal property levied on shall be offered for sale on the premises where it is located at the time of levy, at the courthouse of the county, parish or city wherein it is located, or at another location if ordered by the court. Personal property susceptible of being exhibited shall not be sold unless it is present and subject to the view of those attending the sale unless—

(I) the property consists of shares of stock in corporations;

(II) by reason of the nature of the property, it is impractical to exhibit it; or

(III) the debtor's interest in the property does not include the right to the exclusive possession.

(ii)(I) Except as provided in subclause (II), personal property, or any interest therein, shall be sold after the expiration of the 30-day period beginning on the date of levy under subsection (d).

(II) The court may order the sale of any personal property before the expiration of such 30-day period if the court determines that such property is likely to perish, waste, be destroyed, or otherwise substantially depreciate in value during such 30-day period.

(iii) Notice of the time and place of the sale of personal property shall be given by the United States marshal by posting notice thereof for not less than 10 days successively immediately before the day of sale at the courthouse of any county, parish, or city, and at the place where the sale is to be made.

(iv) The United States marshal shall serve written notice of public sale by personal delivery, or registered or certified mail at their last known addresses, on the judgment debtor and other persons who the marshal has reasonable cause to believe, after diligent inquiry, have a substantial interest in the property.

(2) Postponement of sale.—The United States marshal may postpone an execution sale from time to time by continuing the required posting or publication of notice until the date to which the sale is postponed, and appending, at the foot of each such notice of a current copy of the following:

"The above sale is postponed until the ___ day of ___, 19__, at __ o'clock __.M., ___, United States Marshal for the District of___, by ___, Deputy, dated ___."

(3) Sale procedures—

(A) Bidding requirements.—A bidder at an execution sale of property, may be required by the United States marshal to make a cash deposit of as much as 20 percent of the sale price proposed before the bid is accepted.

(B) Resale of property.—If the terms of the sale are not complied with by the successful bidder, the United States marshal shall proceed to sell the property again on the same day if there is sufficient time. If there is insufficient time, the marshal shall schedule and notice a subsequent sale of the property as provided in paragraphs (1) and (2).

(4) Rights and liabilities of purchasers—

(A) Transfer of title after sale—

(i) If property is sold under this subsection and the successful bidder complies with the terms of the sale, the United States marshal shall execute and deliver all documents necessary to transfer to the successful bidder, without warranty, all the rights, titles, interests, and claims of the judgment debtor in the property.

(ii) If the successful bidder dies before execution and delivery of the documents needed to transfer ownership, the United States marshal shall execute and deliver them to the successful bidder's estate. Such delivery to the estate shall have the same effect as if accomplished during the lifetime of the purchaser.

(B) Purchaser considered innocent purchaser without notice.—The purchaser of property sold under execution shall be deemed to be an innocent purchaser without notice if the purchaser would have been considered an innocent purchaser without notice had the sale been made voluntarily and in person by the judgment debtor.

(C) Liability of successful bidder who fails to comply.—A successful bidder at an execution sale who fails to comply with the terms of the sale shall forfeit to the United States the cash deposit or, at the election of the United States, shall be liable to the United States, on a subsequent sale of the property, for all net losses incurred by the United States as a result of such failure.

(h) Disposition of proceeds; further levy—

(1) Distribution of sale proceeds.—**(A)** The United States marshal shall first deliver to the judgment debtor such amounts to which the judgment debtor is entitled from the sale of partially exempt property.

(B) The United States marshal shall next deduct from the proceeds of an execution sale of property an amount equal to the reasonable expenses incurred in making the levy of execution and in keeping and maintaining the property.

(C) Except as provided in subparagraph (D), the United States marshal shall deliver the balance of the proceeds to the counsel for the United States as soon as practicable.

(D) If more proceeds are received from the execution sale than is necessary to satisfy the executions held by the United States marshal, the marshal shall pay the surplus to the judgment debtor.

(2) Further levy if execution not satisfied.—If the proceeds of the execution sale of the property levied on are insufficient to satisfy the execution, the United States marshal shall proceed on the same writ of execution to levy other property of the judgment debtor.

1. **Editor's note:** So in original. The word "property" probably should not appear.

History of 28 U.S.C. §3203: Nov. 29, 1990, P.L. 101-647, §3611, 104 Stat. 4950.

§3204. INSTALLMENT PAYMENT ORDER

(a) Authority to issue order.—Subject to subsection (c), if it is shown that the judgment debtor—

(1) is receiving or will receive substantial nonexempt disposable earnings from self employment that are not subject to garnishment; or

(2) is diverting or concealing substantial earnings from any source, or property received in lieu of earnings;

then upon motion of the United States and notice to the judgment debtor, the court may, if appropriate, order that the judgment debtor make specified installment payments to the United States. Notice of the motion shall be served on the judgment debtor in the same manner as a summons or by registered or certified mail, return receipt requested. In fixing the amount of the payments, the court shall take into consideration after a hearing, the income, resources, and reasonable requirements of the judgment debtor and the judgment debtor's dependents, any other payments to be made in satisfaction of judgments against the judgment debtor, and the amount due on the judgment in favor of the United States.

(b) Modification of order.—On motion of the United States or the judgment debtor, and upon a showing that the judgment debtor's financial circumstances have changed or that assets not previously disclosed by the judgment debtor have been discovered, the court may modify the amount of payments, alter their frequency, or require full payment.

(c) Limitation.—**(1)** An order may not be issued under subsection (a), and if so issued shall have no force or effect, against a judgment debtor with respect to whom there is in effect a writ of garnishment of earnings issued under this chapter and based on the same debt.

(2) An order may not be issued under subsection (a) with respect to any earnings of the debtor except nonexempt disposable earnings.

History of 28 U.S.C. §3204: Nov. 29, 1990, P.L. 101-647, §3611, 104 Stat. 4955.

§3205. GARNISHMENT

(a) In general.—A court may issue a writ of garnishment against property (including nonexempt disposable earnings) in which the debtor has a substantial nonexempt interest and which is in the possession, custody, or control of a person other than the debtor, in order to satisfy the judgment against the debtor. Co-owned property shall be subject to garnishment to the same extent as co-owned property is subject to garnishment under the law of the State in which such property is located. A court may issue simultaneous separate writs of garnishment to several garnishees. A writ of garnishment issued under this subsection shall be continuing and shall terminate only as provided in subsection (c)(10).

(b) Writ—

(1) General requirements.—The United States shall include in its application for a writ of garnishment—

(A) the judgment debtor's name, social security number (if known), and last known address;

(B) the nature and amount of the debt owed and the facts that not less than 30 days has elapsed since demand on the debtor for payment of the debt was made and the judgment debtor has not paid the amount due; and

(C) that the garnishee is believed to have possession of property (including nonexempt disposable earnings) in which the debtor has a substantial nonexempt interest.

(2) Proper garnishee for particular property—

(A) If the property consists of a right to or share in the stock of an association or corporation, or interests or profits therein, for which a certificate of stock or other negotiable instrument is not outstanding, the corporation, or the president or treasurer of the association shall be the garnishee.

(B) If the property consists of an interest in a partnership interest, any partner other than the debtor shall be the garnishee on behalf of the partnership.

(C) If the property or a debt is evidenced by a negotiable instrument for the payment of money, a negotiable document of title or a certificate of stock of an association or corporation, the instrument, document, or certificate shall be treated as property capable of delivery and the person holding it shall be the garnishee, except that—

(i) subject to clause (ii), in the case of a security which is transferable in the manner set forth in State law, the entity that carries on its books an account in the name of the debtor in which is reflected such security shall be the garnishee; and

(ii) notwithstanding clause (i), the pledgee shall be the garnishee if such security is pledged.

(c) Procedures applicable to writ—

(1) Court determination.—If the court determines that the requirements of this section are satisfied, the court shall issue an appropriate writ of garnishment.

(2) Form of writ.—The writ shall state—

(A) The nature and amount of the debt, and any cost and interest owed with respect to the debt.

(B) The name and address of the garnishee.

(C) The name and address of counsel for the United States.

(D) The last known address of the judgment debtor.

(E) That the garnishee shall answer the writ within 10 days of service of the writ.

(F) That the garnishee shall withhold and retain any property in which the debtor has a substantial nonexempt interest and for which the garnishee is or may become indebted to the judgment debtor pending further order of the court.

(3) Service of writ.—The United States shall serve the garnishee and the judgment debtor with a copy of the writ of garnishment and shall certify to the court that this service was made. The writ shall be accompanied by—

(A) an instruction explaining the requirement that the garnishee submit a written answer to the writ; and

(B) instructions to the judgment debtor for objecting to the answer of the garnishee and for obtaining a hearing on the objections.

(4) Answer of the garnishee.—In its written answer to the writ of garnishment, the garnishee shall state under oath—

(A) whether the garnishee has custody, control or possession of such property;

(B) a description of such property and the value of such interest;

(C) a description of any previous garnishments to which such property is subject and the extent to which any remaining property is not exempt; and

(D) the amount of the debt the garnishee anticipates owing to the judgment debtor in the future and whether the period for payment will be weekly or another specified period.

The garnishee shall file the original answer with the court issuing the writ and serve a copy on the debtor and counsel for the United States.

(5) Objections to answer.—Within 20 days after receipt of the answer, the judgment debtor or the United States may file a written objection to the answer and request a hearing. The party objecting shall state the grounds for the objection and bear the burden of proving such grounds. A copy of the objection and request for a hearing shall be served on the garnishee and all other parties. The court shall hold a hearing within 10 days after the date the request is received by the court, or as soon thereafter as is practicable, and give notice of the hearing date to all the parties.

(6) Garnishee's failure to answer or pay.—If a garnishee fails to answer the writ of garnishment or to withhold property in accordance with the writ, the United States may petition the court for an order requiring the garnishee to appear before the court to answer the writ and to so withhold property before the appearance date. If the garnishee fails to appear, or appears and fails to show good cause why the garnishee failed to comply with the writ, the court shall enter judgment against the garnishee for the value of the judgment debtor's nonexempt interest in such property (including nonexempt disposable earnings). The court may award a reasonable attorney's fee to the United States and against the garnishee if the writ is not answered within the time specified therein and a petition requiring the garnishee to appear is filed as provided in this section.

(7) Disposition order.—After the garnishee files an answer and if no hearing is requested within the required time period, the court shall promptly enter an order directing the garnishee as to the disposition of the judgment debtor's nonexempt interest in such property. If a hearing is timely requested, the order shall be entered within 5 days after the hearing, or as soon thereafter as is practicable.

(8) Priorities.—Judicial orders and garnishments for the support of a person shall have priority over a writ of garnishment issued under this section. As to any other writ of garnishment or levy, a garnishment issued under this section shall have priority over writs which are issued later in time.

(9) Accounting.—**(A)** While a writ of garnishment is in effect under this section, the United States shall give an annual accounting on the garnishment to the judgment debtor and the garnishee.

(B) Within 10 days after the garnishment terminates, the United States shall give a cumulative written accounting to the judgment debtor and garnishee of all property it receives under a writ of garnishment. Within 10 days after such accounting is received, the judgment debtor or garnishee may file a written objection to the accounting and a request for hearing. The party objecting shall state grounds for the objection. The court shall hold a hearing on the objection within 10 days after the court receives the request for a hearing, or as soon thereafter as is practicable.

(10) Termination of garnishment.—A garnishment under this chapter is terminated only by—

(A) a court order quashing the writ of garnishment;

(B) exhaustion of property in the possesion,[1] custody, or control of the garnishee in which the debtor has a substantial nonexempt interest (including nonexempt disposable earnings), unless the garnishee reinstates or reemploys the judgment debtor within 90 days after the judgment debtor's dismissal or resignation; or

(C) satisfaction of the debt with respect to which the writ is issued.

1. **Editor's note:** So in original. Probably should be "possession."

History of 28 U.S.C. §3205: Nov. 29, 1990, P.L. 101-647, §3611, 104 Stat. 4956.

§3206. DISCHARGE

A person who pursuant to an execution or order issued under this chapter by a court pays or delivers to the United States, a United States marshal, or a receiver, money or other personal property in which a judgment debtor has or will have an interest, or so pays a debt such person owes the judgment debtor, is discharged from such debt to the judgment debtor to the extent of the payment or delivery.

History of 28 U.S.C. §3206: Nov. 29, 1990, P.L. 101-647, §3611, 104 Stat. 4959.

SUBCHAPTER D. FRAUDULENT TRANSFERS INVOLVING DEBTS

§3301. DEFINITIONS

As used in this subchapter:

(1) "Affiliate" means—

(A) a person who directly or indirectly owns, controls, or holds with power to vote, 20 percent or more of the outstanding voting securities of the debtor, other than a person who holds the securities—

(i) as a fiduciary or agent without sole discretionary power to vote the securities; or

(ii) solely to secure a debt, if the person has not exercised the power to vote;

(B) a corporation 20 percent or more of whose outstanding voting securities are directly or indirectly owned, controlled, or held with power to vote, by the debtor or a person who directly or indirectly owns, controls, or holds with power to vote, 20 percent or more of the outstanding voting securities of the debtor, other than the person who holds securities—

(i) as a fiduciary or agent without sole power to vote the securities; or

(ii) solely to secure a debt, if the person has not in fact exercised the power to vote;

(C) a person whose business is operated by the debtor under a lease or other agreement, or a person substantially all of whose assets are controlled by the debtor; or

(D) a person who operates the debtor's business under a lease or other agreement or controls substantially all of the debtor's assets.

(2) "Asset" means property of a debtor, but does not include—

(A) property to the extent it is encumbered by a valid lien;

(B) property to the extent it is generally exempt under nonbankruptcy law; or

(C) an interest in real property held in tenancy by the entirety, or as part of a community estate, to extent such interest is not subject to process by the United States holding a claim against only one tenant or co-owner.

(3) "Claim" means a right to payment, whether or not the right is reduced to judgment, liquidated, unliquidated, fixed, contingent, matured, unmatured, disputed, undisputed, legal, equitable, secured, or unsecured.

(4) "Creditor" means a person who has a claim.

(5) "Insider" includes—

(A) if the debtor is an individual—

(i) a relative of the debtor or of a general partner of the debtor;

(ii) a partnership in which the debtor is a general partner;

(iii) a general partner in a partnership described in clause (ii); or

(iv) a corporation of which the debtor is a director, officer, or person in control;

(B) if the debtor is a corporation—

(i) a director of the debtor;

(ii) an officer of the debtor;

(iii) a person in control of the debtor;

(iv) a partnership in which the debtor is a general partner;

(v) a general partner in a partnership described in clause (iv); or

(vi) a relative of a general partner, director, officer, or person in control of the debtor;

(C) if the debtor is a partnership—

(i) a general partner in the debtor;

(ii) a relative of a general partner in, a general partner of, or a person in control of the debtor;

(iii) another partnership in which the debtor is a general partner;

(iv) a general partner in a partnership described in clause (iii); or

(v) a person in control of the debtor.[1]

(D) an affiliate, or an insider of an affiliate as if the affiliate were the debtor; and

(E) a managing agent of the debtor.

(4)[2] "Lien" means a charge against or an interest in property to secure payment of a debt and includes a security interest created by agreement, a judicial lien obtained by legal or equitable process or proceedings, a common law lien, or a statutory lien.

(5)[3] "Relative" means an individual related, by consanguinity or adoption, within the third degree as determined by the common law, a spouse, or an individual so related to a spouse within the third degree as so determined.

(6)[4] "Transfer" means every mode, direct or indirect, absolute or conditional, voluntary or involuntary, of disposing of or parting with an asset or an interest in an asset, and includes payment of money, release, lease, and creation of a lien or other encumbrance.

(7)[5] "Valid lien" means a lien that is effective against the holder of a judicial lien subsequently obtained in legal or equitable proceeding.

1. **Editor's note:** So in original. The period probably should be a semicolon.
2. **Editor's note:** So in original. Probably should be "(6)."
3. **Editor's note:** So in original. Probably should be "(7)."
4. **Editor's note:** So in original. Probably should be "(8)."
5. **Editor's note:** So in original. Probably should be "(9)."

History of 28 U.S.C. §3301: Nov. 29, 1990, P.L. 101-647, §3611, 104 Stat. 4959.

§3302. INSOLVENCY

(a) In general.—Except as provided in subsection (c), a debtor is insolvent if the sum of the debtor's debts is greater than all of the debtor's assets at a fair valuation.

(b) Presumption.—A debtor who is generally not paying debts as they become due is presumed to be insolvent.

(c) Calculation.—A partnership is insolvent under subsection (a) if the sum of the partnership's debts is greater than the aggregate, at a fair valuation, of—

(1) all of the partnership's assets; and

(2) the sum of the excess of the value of each general partner's non-partnership assets over the partner's non-partnership debts.

(d) Assets.—For purposes of this section, assets do not include property that is transferred, concealed, or removed with intent to hinder, delay, or defraud creditors or that has been transferred in a manner making the transfer voidable under this subchapter.

(e) Debts.—For purposes of this section, debts do not include an obligation to the extent such obligation is secured by a valid lien on property of the debtor not included as an asset.

History of 28 U.S.C. §3302: Nov. 29, 1990, P.L. 101-647, §3611, 104 Stat. 4961.

§3303. VALUE FOR TRANSFER OR OBLIGATION

(a) Transaction.—Value is given for a transfer or an obligation if, in exchange for the transfer or obligation, prop-

erty is transferred or an antecedent debt is secured or satisfied, but value does not include an unperformed promise made otherwise than in the ordinary course of the promisor's business to furnish support to the debtor or another person.

(b) Reasonably equivalent value.—For the purposes of sections 3304 and 3307, a person gives a reasonably equivalent value if the person acquires an interest of the debtor in an asset pursuant to a regularly conducted, noncollusive foreclosure sale or execution of a power of sale for the acquisition or disposition of such interest upon default under a mortgage, deed of trust, or security agreement.

(c) Present value.—A transfer is made for present value if the exchange between the debtor and the transferee is intended by them to be contemporaneous and is in fact substantially contemporaneous.

History of 28 U.S.C. §3303: Nov. 29, 1990, P.L. 101-647, §3611, 104 Stat. 4961.

§3304. TRANSFER FRAUDULENT AS TO A DEBT TO THE UNITED STATES

(a) Debt arising before transfer.—Except as provided in section 3307, a transfer made or obligation incurred by a debtor is fraudulent as to a debt to the United States which arises before the transfer is made or the obligation is incurred if—

(1)(A) the debtor makes the transfer or incurs the obligation without receiving a reasonably equivalent value in exchange for the transfer or obligation; and

(B) the debtor is insolvent at that time or the debtor becomes insolvent as a result of the transfer or obligation; or

(2)(A) the transfer was made to an insider for an antecedent debt, the debtor was insolvent at the time; and

(B) the insider had reasonable cause to believe that the debtor was insolvent.

(b) Transfers without regard to date of judgment—

(1) Except as provided in section 3307, a transfer made or obligation incurred by a debtor is fraudulent as to a debt to the United States, whether such debt arises before or after the transfer is made or the obligation is incurred, if the debtor makes the transfer or incurs the obligation—

(A) with actual intent to hinder, delay, or defraud a creditor; or

(B) without receiving a reasonably equivalent value in exchange for the transfer or obligation if the debtor—

(i) was engaged or was about to engage in a business or a transaction for which the remaining assets of the debtor were unreasonably small in relation to the business or transaction; or

(ii) intended to incur, or believed or reasonably should have believed that he would incur, debts beyond his ability to pay as they became due.

(2) In determining actual intent under paragraph (1), consideration may be given, among other factors, to whether—

(A) the transfer or obligation was to an insider;

(B) the debtor retained possession or control of the property transferred after the transfer;

(C) the transfer or obligation was disclosed or concealed;

(D) before the transfer was made or obligation was incurred, the debtor had been sued or threatened with suit;

(E) the transfer was of substantially all the debtor's assets;

(F) the debtor absconded;

(G) the debtor removed or concealed assets;

(H) the value of the consideration received by the debtor was reasonably equivalent to the value of the asset transferred or the amount of the obligation incurred;

(I) the debtor was insolvent or became insolvent shortly after the transfer was made or the obligation was incurred;

(J) the transfer occurred shortly before or shortly after a substantial debt was incurred; and

(K) the debtor transferred the essential assets of the business to a lienor who transferred the assets to an insider of the debtor.

History of 28 U.S.C. §3304: Nov. 29, 1990, P.L. 101-647, §3611, 104 Stat. 4961.

§3305. WHEN TRANSFER IS MADE OR OBLIGATION IS INCURRED

For the purposes of this subchapter:

(1) A transfer is made—

(A) with respect to an asset that is real property (other than a fixture, but including the interest of a seller or purchaser under a contract for the sale of the asset), when the transfer is so far perfected that a good-faith purchaser of the asset from the debtor against whom applicable law permits the transfer to be perfected cannot acquire an interest in the asset that is superior to the interest of the transferee; and

(B) with respect to an asset that is not real property or that is a fixture, when the transfer is so far perfected that a creditor on a simple contract cannot acquire, otherwise than under this subchapter, a judicial lien that is superior to the interest of the transferee.

(2) If applicable law permits the transfer to be perfected as approved in paragraph (1) and the transfer is not so perfected before the commencement of an action or proceeding for relief under this subchapter, the transfer is deemed made immediately before the commencement of the action or proceeding.

(3) If applicable law does not permit the transfer to be perfected as provided in paragraph (1), the transfer is made when it becomes effective between the debtor and the transferee.

(4) A transfer is not made until the debtor has acquired rights in the asset transferred.

(5) An obligation is incurred—

(A) if oral, when it becomes effective between the parties; or

(B) if evidenced by a writing executed by the obligor, when such writing is delivered to or for the benefit of the obligee.

History of 28 U.S.C. §3305: Nov. 29, 1990, P.L. 101-647, §3611, 104 Stat. 4962.

§3306. REMEDIES OF THE UNITED STATES

(a) In general.—In an action or proceeding under this subchapter for relief against a transfer or obligation, the United States, subject to section 3307 and to applicable principles of equity and in accordance with the Federal Rules of Civil Procedure, may obtain—

(1) avoidance of the transfer or obligation to the extent necessary to satisfy the debt to the United States;

(2) a remedy under this chapter against the asset transferred or other property of the transferee; or

(3) any other relief the circumstances may require.

(b) Limitation.—A claim for relief with respect to a fraudulent transfer or obligation under this subchapter is extinguished unless action is brought—

(1) under section 3304(b)(1)(A) within 6 years after the transfer was made or the obligation was incurred or, if later, within 2 years after the transfer or obligation was or could reasonably have been discovered by the claimant;

(2) under subsection (a)(1) or (b)(1)(B) of section 3304 within 6 years after the transfer was made or the obligation was incurred; or

(3) under section 3304(a)(2) within 2 years after the transfer was made or the obligation was incurred.

History of 28 U.S.C. §3306: Nov. 29, 1990, P.L. 101-647, §3611, 104 Stat. 4963.

§3307. DEFENSES, LIABILITY, & PROTECTION OF TRANSFEREE

(a) Good faith transfer.—A transfer or obligation is not voidable under section 3304(b) with respect to a person who took in good faith and for a reasonably equivalent value or against any transferee or obligee subsequent to such person.

(b) Limitation.—Except as provided in subsection (d), to the extent a transfer is voidable in an action or proceeding by the United States under section 3306(a)(1), the United States may recover judgment for the value of the asset transferred, but not to exceed the judgment on a debt. The judgment may be entered against—

(1) the first transferee of the asset or the person for whose benefit the transfer was made; or

(2) any subsequent transferee, other than a good faith transferee who took for value or any subsequent transferee of such good-faith transferee.

(c) Value of asset.—For purposes of subsection (b), the value of the asset is the value of the asset at the time of the transfer, subject to adjustment as the equities may require.

(d) Rights of good faith transferees and obligees.—Notwithstanding voidability of a transfer or an obligation under this subchapter, a good-faith transferee or obligee is entitled, to the extent of the value given the debtor for the transfer or obligation, to—

(1) a lien on or a right to retain any interest in the asset transferred;

(2) enforcement of any obligation incurred; or

(3) a reduction in the amount of the liability on the judgment.

(e) Exceptions.—A transfer is not voidable under section 3304(a) or section 3304(b)(2) if the transfer results from—

(1) termination of a lease upon default by the debtor when the termination is pursuant to the lease and applicable law; or

(2) enforcement of a security interest in compliance with article 9 of the Uniform Commercial Code or its equivalent in effect in the State where the property is located.

(f) Limitation of voidability.—A transfer is not voidable under section 3304(a)(2)—

(1) to the extent the insider gives new value to or for the benefit of the debtor after the transfer is made unless the new value is secured by a valid lien;

(2) if made in the ordinary course of business or financial affairs of the debtor and the insider; or

(3) if made pursuant to a good-faith effort to rehabilitate the debtor and the transfer secured both present value given for that purpose and an antecedent debt of the debtor.

History of 28 U.S.C. §3307: Nov. 29, 1990, P.L. 101-647, §3611, 104 Stat. 4963.

§3308. SUPPLEMENTARY PROVISION

Except as provided in this subchapter, the principles of law and equity, including the law merchant and the law relating to principal and agent, estoppel, laches, fraud, misrepresentation, duress, coercion, mistake, insolvency, or other validating or invalidating cause shall apply to actions and proceedings under this subchapter.

History of 28 U.S.C. §3308: Nov. 29, 1990, P.L. 101-647, §3611, 104 Stat. 4964.

CHAPTER 178. PROFESSIONAL & AMATEUR SPORTS PROTECTION

§3701. DEFINITIONS

For purposes of this chapter—

(1) the term "amateur sports organization" means—

(A) a person or governmental entity that sponsors, organizes, schedules, or conducts a competitive game in which one or more amateur athletes participate, or

(B) a league or association of persons or governmental entities described in subparagraph (A),

(2) the term "governmental entity" means a State, a political subdivision of a State, or an entity or organization, including an entity or organization described in section 4(5) of the Indian Gaming Regulatory Act (25 U.S.C. 2703(5)), that has governmental authority within the territorial boundaries of the United States, including on lands described in section 4(4) of such Act (25 U.S.C. 2703(4)),

(3) the term "professional sports organization" means—

(A) a person or governmental entity that sponsors, organizes, schedules, or conducts a competitive game in which one or more professional athletes participate, or

(B) a league or association of persons or governmental entities described in subparagraph (A),

(4) the term "person" has the meaning given such term in section 1 of title 1, and

(5) the term "State" means any of the several States, the District of Columbia, the Commonwealth of Puerto Rico, the Commonwealth of the Northern Mariana Islands, Palau, or any territory or possession of the United States.

History of 28 U.S.C. §3701: Oct. 28, 1992, P.L. 102-559, §2(a), 106 Stat. 4227.

§3702. UNLAWFUL SPORTS GAMBLING

It shall be unlawful for—

(1) a governmental entity to sponsor, operate, advertise, promote, license, or authorize by law or compact, or

(2) a person to sponsor, operate, advertise, or promote, pursuant to the law or compact of a governmental entity,

a lottery, sweepstakes, or other betting, gambling, or wagering scheme based, directly or indirectly (through the use of geographical references or otherwise), on one or more competitive games in which amateur or professional athletes participate, or are intended to participate, or on one or more performances of such athletes in such games.

History of 28 U.S.C. §3702: Oct. 28, 1992, P.L. 102-559, §2(a), 106 Stat. 4228.

§3703. INJUNCTIONS

A civil action to enjoin a violation of section 3702 may be commenced in an appropriate district court of the United States by the Attorney General of the United States, or by a professional sports organization or amateur sports organization whose competitive game is alleged to be the basis of such violation.

History of 28 U.S.C. §3703: Oct. 28, 1992, P.L. 102-559, §2(a), 106 Stat. 4228.

§3704. APPLICABILITY

(a) Section 3702 shall not apply to—

(1) a lottery, sweepstakes, or other betting, gambling, or wagering scheme in operation in a State or other governmental entity, to the extent that the scheme was conducted by that State or other governmental entity at any time during the period beginning January 1, 1976, and ending August 31, 1990;

(2) a lottery, sweepstakes, or other betting, gambling, or wagering scheme in operation in a State or other governmental entity where both—

(A) such scheme was authorized by a statute as in effect on October 2, 1991; and

(B) a scheme described in section 3702 (other than one based on parimutuel animal racing or jai-alai games) actually was conducted in that State or other governmental entity at any time during the period beginning September 1, 1989, and ending October 2, 1991, pursuant to the law of that State or other governmental entity;

(3) a betting, gambling, or wagering scheme, other than a lottery described in paragraph (1), conducted exclusively in casinos located in a municipality, but only to the extent that—

(A) such scheme or a similar scheme was authorized, not later than one year after the effective date of this chapter, to be operated in that municipality; and

(B) any commercial casino gaming scheme was in operation in such municipality throughout the 10-year period ending on such effective date pursuant to a comprehensive system of State regulation authorized by that State's constitution and applicable solely to such municipality; or

(4) parimutuel animal racing or jai-alai games.

(b) Except as provided in subsection (a), section 3702 shall apply on lands described in section 4(4) of the Indian Gaming Regulatory Act (25 U.S.C. 2703(4)).

History of 28 U.S.C. §3704: Oct. 28, 1992, P.L. 102-559, §2(a), 106 Stat. 4228.

CHAPTER 179. JUDICIAL REVIEW OF CERTAIN ACTIONS BY PRESIDENTIAL OFFICES

§3901. CIVIL ACTIONS

(a) **Parties.**—In an action under section 1346(g) of this title, the defendant shall be the employing office alleged to have committed the violation involved.

(b) **Jury trial.**—In an action described in subsection (a), any party may demand a jury trial where a jury trial would be available in an action against a private defendant under the relevant law made applicable by chapter 5 of title 3. In any case in which a violation of section 411 of title 3 is alleged, the court shall not inform the jury of the maximum amount of compensatory damages available under section 411(b)(1) or 411(b)(3) of title 3.

History of 28 U.S.C. §3901: Oct. 26, 1996, P.L. 104-331, §3(c), 110 Stat. 4070.

§3902. JUDICIAL REVIEW OF REGULATIONS

In any proceeding under section 1296 or 1346(g) of this title in which the application of a regulation issued under chapter 5 of title 3 is at issue, the court may review the valid-

ity of the regulation in accordance with the provisions of subparagraphs (A) through (D) of section 706(2) of title 5. If the court determines that the regulation is invalid, the court shall apply, to the extent necessary and appropriate, the most relevant substantive executive agency regulation promulgated to implement the statutory provisions with respect to which the invalid regulation was issued. Except as provided in this section, the validity of regulations issued under this chapter is not subject to judicial review.

History of 28 U.S.C. §3902: Oct. 26, 1996, P.L. 104-331, §3(c), 110 Stat. 4070.

§3903. EFFECT OF FAILURE TO ISSUE REGULATIONS

In any proceeding under section 1296 or 1346(g) of this title, if the President, the designee of the President, or the Federal Labor Relations Authority has not issued a regulation on a matter for which chapter 5 of title 3 requires a regulation to be issued, the court shall apply, to the extent necessary and appropriate, the most relevant substantive executive agency regulation promulgated to implement the statutory provision at issue in the proceeding.

History of 28 U.S.C. §3903: Oct. 26, 1996, P.L. 104-331, §3(c), 110 Stat. 4070.

§3904. EXPEDITED REVIEW OF CERTAIN APPEALS

(a) In general.—An appeal may be taken directly to the Supreme Court of the United States from any interlocutory or final judgment, decree, or order of a court upon the constitutionality of any provision of chapter 5 of title 3.

(b) Jurisdiction.—The Supreme Court shall, if it has not previously ruled on the question, accept jurisdiction over the appeal referred to in subsection (a), advance the appeal on the docket, and expedite the appeal to the greatest extent possible.

History of 28 U.S.C. §3904: Oct. 26, 1996, P.L. 104-331, §3(c), 110 Stat. 4070.

§3905. ATTORNEY'S FEES & INTEREST

(a) Attorney's fees.—If a covered employee, with respect to any claim under chapter 5 of title 3, or a qualified person with a disability, with respect to any claim under section 421 of title 3, is a prevailing party in any proceeding under section 1296 or section 1346(g), the court may award attorney's fees, expert fees, and any other costs as would be appropriate if awarded under section 706(k) of the Civil Rights Act of 1964.

(b) Interest.—In any proceeding under section 1296 or section 1346(g), the same interest to compensate for delay in payment shall be made available as would be appropriate if awarded under section 717(d) of the Civil Rights Act of 1964.

(c) Punitive damages.—Except as otherwise provided in chapter 5 of title 3, no punitive damages may be awarded with respect to any claim under chapter 5 of title 3.

History of 28 U.S.C. §3905: Oct. 26, 1996, P.L. 104-331, §3(c), 110 Stat. 4070.

§3906. PAYMENTS

A judgment, award, or compromise settlement against the United States under this chapter (including any interest and costs) shall be paid—

(1) under section 1304 of title 31, if it arises out of an action commenced in a district court of the United States (or any appeal therefrom); or

(2) out of amounts otherwise appropriated or available to the office involved, if it arises out of an appeal from an administrative proceeding under chapter 5 of title 3.

History of 28 U.S.C. §3906: Oct. 26, 1996, P.L. 104-331, §3(c), 110 Stat. 4071.

§3907. OTHER JUDICIAL REVIEW PROHIBITED

Except as expressly authorized by this chapter and chapter 5 of title 3, the compliance or noncompliance with the provisions of chapter 5 of title 3, and any action taken pursuant to chapter 5 of title 3, shall not be subject to judicial review.

History of 28 U.S.C. §3907: Oct. 26, 1996, P.L. 104-331, §3(c), 110 Stat. 4071.

§3908. DEFINITIONS

For purposes of applying this chapter, the terms "employing office" and "covered employee" have the meanings given those terms in section 401 of title 3.

History of 28 U.S.C. §3908: Oct. 26, 1996, P.L. 104-331, §3(c), 110 Stat. 4071.

CHAPTER 180. ASSUMPTION OF CERTAIN CONTRACTUAL OBLIGATIONS

§4001. ASSUMPTION OF CONTRACTUAL OBLIGATIONS RELATED TO TRANSFERS OF RIGHTS IN MOTION PICTURES

(a) Assumption of obligations.—**(1)** In the case of a transfer of copyright ownership under United States law in a motion picture (as the terms "transfer of copyright ownership" and "motion picture" are defined in section 101 of title 17) that is produced subject to 1 or more collective bargaining agreements negotiated under the laws of the United States, if the transfer is executed on or after the effective date of this chapter and is not limited to public performance rights, the transfer instrument shall be deemed to incorporate the assumption agreements applicable to the copyright ownership being transferred that are required by the applicable collective bargaining agreement, and the transferee shall be subject to the obligations under each such assumption agreement to make residual payments and provide related notices, accruing after the effective date of the transfer and applicable to the exploitation of the rights transferred, and any remedies under each such assumption agreement for breach of those obligations, as those obligations and remedies are set forth in the applicable collective bargaining agreement, if—

(A) the transferee knows or has reason to know at the time of the transfer that such collective bargaining agreement was or will be applicable to the motion picture; or

(B) in the event of a court order confirming an arbitration award against the transferor under the collective bargaining agreement, the transferor does not have the financial ability to satisfy the award within 90 days after the order is issued.

(2) For purposes of paragraph (1)(A), "knows or has reason to know" means any of the following:

(A) Actual knowledge that the collective bargaining agreement was or will be applicable to the motion picture.

(B)(i) Constructive knowledge that the collective bargaining agreement was or will be applicable to the motion picture, arising from recordation of a document pertaining to copyright in the motion picture under section 205 of title 17 or from publication, at a site available to the public on-line that is operated by the relevant union, of information that identifies the motion picture as subject to a collective bargaining agreement with that union, if the site permits commercially reasonable verification of the date on which the information was available for access.

(ii) Clause (i) applies only if the transfer referred to in subsection (a)(1) occurs—

(I) after the motion picture is completed, or

(II) before the motion picture is completed and—

(aa) within 18 months before the filing of an application for copyright registration for the motion picture under section 408 of title 17, or

(bb) if no such application is filed, within 18 months before the first publication of the motion picture in the United States.

(C) Awareness of other facts and circumstances pertaining to a particular transfer from which it is apparent that the collective bargaining agreement was or will be applicable to the motion picture.

(b) Scope of exclusion of transfers of public performance rights.—For purposes of this section, the exclusion under subsection (a) of transfers of copyright ownership in a motion picture that are limited to public performance rights includes transfers to a terrestrial broadcast station, cable system, or programmer to the extent that the station, system, or programmer is functioning as an exhibitor of the motion picture, either by exhibiting the motion picture on its own network, system, service, or station, or by initiating the transmission of an exhibition that is carried on another network, system, service, or station. When a terrestrial broadcast station, cable system, or programmer, or other transferee, is also functioning otherwise as a distributor or as a producer of the motion picture, the public performance exclusion does not affect any obligations imposed on the transferee to the extent that it is engaging in such functions.

(c) Exclusion for grants of security interests.—Subsection (a) shall not apply to—

(1) a transfer of copyright ownership consisting solely of a mortgage, hypothecation, or other security interest; or

(2) a subsequent transfer of the copyright ownership secured by the security interest described in paragraph (1) by or under the authority of the secured party, including a transfer through the exercise of the secured party's rights or remedies as a secured party, or by a subsequent transferee.

The exclusion under this subsection shall not affect any rights or remedies under law or contract.

(d) Deferral pending resolution of bona fide dispute.—A transferee on which obligations are imposed under subsection (a) by virtue of paragraph (1) of that subsection may elect to defer performance of such obligations that are subject to a bona fide dispute between a union and a prior transferor until that dispute is resolved, except that such deferral shall not stay accrual of any union claims due under an applicable collective bargaining agreement.

(e) Scope of obligations determined by private agreement.—Nothing in this section shall expand or diminish the rights, obligations, or remedies of any person under the collective bargaining agreements or assumption agreements referred to in this section.

(f) Failure to notify.—If the transferor under subsection (a) fails to notify the transferee under subsection (a) of applicable collective bargaining obligations before the execution of the transfer instrument, and subsection (a) is made applicable to the transferee solely by virtue of subsection (a)(1)(B), the transferor shall be liable to the transferee for any damages suffered by the transferee as a result of the failure to notify.

(g) Determination of disputes and claims.—Any dispute concerning the application of subsections (a) through (f) shall be determined by an action in United States district court, and the court in its discretion may allow the recovery of full costs by or against any party and may also award a reasonable attorney's fee to the prevailing party as part of the costs.

(h) Study.—The Comptroller General, in consultation with the Register of Copyrights, shall conduct a study of the conditions in the motion picture industry that gave rise to this section, and the impact of this section on the motion picture industry. The Comptroller General shall report the findings of the study to the Congress within 2 years after the effective date of this chapter.

History of 28 U.S.C. §4001: Oct. 28, 1998, P.L. 105-304, §406, 112 Stat. 2902.

CHAPTER 181. FOREIGN JUDGMENTS

§4101. DEFINITIONS

In this chapter:

(1) Defamation.—The term "defamation" means any action or other proceeding for defamation, libel, slander, or similar claim alleging that forms of speech are false, have caused damage to reputation or emotional distress, have presented any person in a false light, or have resulted in criticism, dishonor, or condemnation of any person.

(2) Domestic court.—The term "domestic court" means a Federal court or a court of any State.

(3) Foreign court.—The term "foreign court" means a court, administrative body, or other tribunal of a foreign country.

(4) Foreign judgment.—The term "foreign judgment" means a final judgment rendered by a foreign court.

(5) State.—The term "State" means each of the several States, the District of Columbia, and any commonwealth, territory, or possession of the United States.

(6) United states person.—The term "United States person" means—

(A) a United States citizen;

(B) an alien lawfully admitted for permanent residence to the United States;

(C) an alien lawfully residing in the United States at the time that the speech that is the subject of the foreign defamation action was researched, prepared, or disseminated; or

(D) a business entity incorporated in, or with its primary location or place of operation in, the United States.

History of 28 U.S.C. §4101: Aug. 10, 2010, P.L. 111-223, §3(a), 124 Stat. 2381.

§4102. RECOGNITION OF FOREIGN DEFAMATION JUDGMENTS

(a) First Amendment Considerations—

(1) In general.—Notwithstanding any other provision of Federal or State law, a domestic court shall not recognize or enforce a foreign judgment for defamation unless the domestic court determines that—

(A) the defamation law applied in the foreign court's adjudication provided at least as much protection for freedom of speech and press in that case as would be provided by the first amendment to the Constitution of the United States and by the constitution and law of the State in which the domestic court is located; or

(B) even if the defamation law applied in the foreign court's adjudication did not provide as much protection for freedom of speech and press as the first amendment to the Constitution of the United States and the constitution and law of the State, the party opposing recognition or enforcement of that foreign judgment would have been found liable for defamation by a domestic court applying the first amendment to the Constitution of the United States and the constitution and law of the State in which the domestic court is located.

(2) Burden of establishing application of defamation laws.—The party seeking recognition or enforcement of the foreign judgment shall bear the burden of making the showings required under subparagraph (A) or (B).

(b) Jurisdictional Considerations—

(1) In general.—Notwithstanding any other provision of Federal or State law, a domestic court shall not recognize or enforce a foreign judgment for defamation unless the domestic court determines that the exercise of personal jurisdiction by the foreign court comported with the due process requirements that are imposed on domestic courts by the Constitution of the United States.

(2) Burden of establishing exercise of jurisdiction.—The party seeking recognition or enforcement of the foreign judgment shall bear the burden of making the showing that the foreign court's exercise of personal jurisdiction comported with the due process requirements that are imposed on domestic courts by the Constitution of the United States.

(c) Judgment Against Provider of Interactive Computer Service—

(1) In general.—Notwithstanding any other provision of Federal or State law, a domestic court shall not recognize or enforce a foreign judgment for defamation against the provider of an interactive computer service, as defined in section 230 of the Communications Act of 1934 (47 U.S.C. 230) unless the domestic court determines that the judgment would be consistent with section 230 if the information that is the subject of such judgment had been provided in the United States.

(2) Burden of establishing consistency of judgment.—The party seeking recognition or enforcement of the foreign judgment shall bear the burden of establishing that the judgment is consistent with section 230.

(d) Appearances Not a Bar.—An appearance by a party in a foreign court rendering a foreign judgment to which this section applies shall not deprive such party of the right to oppose the recognition or enforcement of the judgment under this section, or represent a waiver of any jurisdictional claims.

(e) Rule of Construction.—Nothing in this section shall be construed to—

(1) affect the enforceability of any foreign judgment other than a foreign judgment for defamation; or

(2) limit the applicability of section 230 of the Communications Act of 1934 (47 U.S.C. 230) to causes of action for defamation.

History of 28 U.S.C. §4102: Aug. 10, 2010, P.L. 111-223, §3(a), 124 Stat. 2381.

§4103. REMOVAL

In addition to removal allowed under section 1441, any action brought in a State domestic court to enforce a foreign judgment for defamation in which—

(1) any plaintiff is a citizen of a State different from any defendant;

(2) any plaintiff is a foreign state or a citizen or subject of a foreign state and any defendant is a citizen of a State; or

(3) any plaintiff is a citizen of a State and any defendant is a foreign state or citizen or subject of a foreign state,

may be removed by any defendant to the district court of the

United States for the district and division embracing the place where such action is pending without regard to the amount in controversy between the parties.

History of 28 U.S.C. §4103: Aug. 10, 2010, P.L. 111-223, §3(a), 124 Stat. 2383.

See *Commentaries*, "Removal & Remand," ch. 4, p. 239.

§4104. DECLARATORY JUDGMENTS

(a) Cause of Action—

(1) In general.—Any United States person against whom a foreign judgment is entered on the basis of the content of any writing, utterance, or other speech by that person that has been published, may bring an action in district court, under section 2201(a), for a declaration that the foreign judgment is repugnant to the Constitution or laws of the United States. For the purposes of this paragraph, a judgment is repugnant to the Constitution or laws of the United States if it would not be enforceable under section 4102 (a), (b), or (c).

(2) Burden of establishing unenforceability of judgment.—The party bringing an action under paragraph (1) shall bear the burden of establishing that the foreign judgment would not be enforceable under section 4102 (a), (b), or (c).

(b) Nationwide Service of Process.—Where an action under this section is brought in a district court of the United States, process may be served in the judicial district where the case is brought or any other judicial district of the United States where the defendant may be found, resides, has an agent, or transacts business.

History of 28 U.S.C. §4104: Aug. 10, 2010, P.L. 111-223, §3(a), 124 Stat. 2383.

See *Commentaries*, "Declaratory Judgment," ch. 2-E, p. 107.

§4105. ATTORNEYS' FEES

In any action brought in a domestic court to enforce a foreign judgment for defamation, including any such action removed from State court to Federal court, the domestic court shall, absent exceptional circumstances, allow the party opposing recognition or enforcement of the judgment a reasonable attorney's fee if such party prevails in the action on a ground specified in section 4102 (a), (b), or (c).

History of 28 U.S.C. §4105: Aug. 10, 2010, P.L. 111-223, §3(a), 124 Stat. 2383.

See *Commentaries*, "Motion for Attorney Fees," ch. 9-C, p. 745.

42 U.S.C.

CHAPTER 21. CIVIL RIGHTS

SUBCHAPTER I. GENERALLY

42 U.S.C. §1981. EQUAL RIGHTS UNDER THE LAW

(a) Statement of equal rights.—All persons within the jurisdiction of the United States shall have the same right in every State and Territory to make and enforce contracts, to sue, be parties, give evidence, and to the full and equal benefit of all laws and proceedings for the security of persons and property as is enjoyed by white citizens, and shall be subject to like punishment, pains, penalties, taxes, licenses, and exactions of every kind, and to no other.

(b) "Make and enforce contracts" defined.—For purposes of this section, the term "make and enforce contracts" includes the making, performance, modification, and termination of contracts, and the enjoyment of all benefits, privileges, terms, and conditions of the contractual relationship.

(c) Protection against impairment.—The rights protected by this section are protected against impairment by nongovernmental discrimination and impairment under color of State law.

History of 42 U.S.C. §1981: R.S. §1977; Nov. 21, 1991, P.L. 102-166, §101, 105 Stat. 1071.

42 U.S.C. §1982. PROPERTY RIGHTS OF CITIZENS

All citizens of the United States shall have the same right, in every State and Territory, as is enjoyed by white citizens thereof to inherit, purchase, lease, sell, hold, and convey real and personal property.

History of 42 U.S.C. §1982: R.S. §1978.

42 U.S.C. §1983. CIVIL ACTION FOR DEPRIVATION OF RIGHTS

Every person who, under color of any statute, ordinance, regulation, custom, or usage, of any State or Territory or the District of Columbia, subjects, or causes to be subjected, any citizen of the United States or other person within the jurisdiction thereof to the deprivation of any rights, privileges, or immunities secured by the Constitution and laws, shall be liable to the party injured in an action at law, suit in equity, or other proper proceeding for redress, except that in any action brought against a judicial officer for an act or omission taken in such officer's judicial capacity, injunctive relief shall not be granted unless a declaratory decree was violated or declaratory relief was unavailable. For the purposes of this section, any Act of Congress applicable exclusively to the District of Columbia shall be considered to be a statute of the District of Columbia.

History of 42 U.S.C. §1983: R.S. §1979; Dec. 29, 1979, P.L. 96-170, §1, 93 Stat. 1284; Oct. 19, 1996, P.L. 104-317, §309(c), 110 Stat. 3853.

See *O'Connor's Federal Civil Forms* (2012), FORMS 2B:18, 19, 3L:20, 21, 6G:27-30, 6H:27-30, 6I:27-30.

42 U.S.C. §1988. PROCEEDINGS IN VINDICATION OF CIVIL RIGHTS

(a) Applicability of statutory and common law—

The jurisdiction in civil and criminal matters conferred on the district courts by the provisions of titles 13, 24, and 70 of the Revised Statutes for the protection of all persons in the United States in their civil rights, and for their vindication, shall be exercised and enforced in conformity with the laws of the United States, so far as such laws are suitable to carry the same into effect; but in all cases where they are not adapted to the object, or are deficient in the provisions necessary to

furnish suitable remedies and punish offenses against law, the common law, as modified and changed by the constitution and statutes of the State wherein the court having jurisdiction of such civil or criminal cause is held, so far as the same is not inconsistent with the Constitution and laws of the United States, shall be extended to and govern the said courts in the trial and disposition of the cause, and, if it is of a criminal nature, in the infliction of punishment on the party found guilty.

(b) Attorney's fees—

In any action or proceeding to enforce a provision of sections 1981, 1981a, 1982, 1983, 1985, and 1986 of this title, title IX of Public Law 92-318 [20 U.S.C. 1681 et seq.], the Religious Freedom Restoration Act of 1993 [42 U.S.C. 2000bb et seq.], the Religious Land Use and Institutionalized Persons Act of 2000 [42 U.S.C. 2000cc et seq.], title VI of the Civil Rights Act of 1964 [42 U.S.C. 2000d et seq.], or section 13981 of this title, the court, in its discretion, may allow the prevailing party, other than the United States, a reasonable attorney's fee as part of the costs, except that in any action brought against a judicial officer for an act or omission taken in such officer's judicial capacity such officer shall not be held liable for any costs, including attorney's fees, unless such action was clearly in excess of such officer's jurisdiction.

(c) Expert fees—

In awarding an attorney's fee under subsection (b) of this section in any action or proceeding to enforce a provision of section 1981 or 1981a of this title, the court, in its discretion, may include expert fees as part of the attorney's fee.

History of 42 U.S.C. §1988: R.S. §722; Oct. 19, 1976, P.L. 94-559, §2, 90 Stat. 2641; Oct. 21, 1980, P.L. 96-481, §205(c), 94 Stat. 2330; Nov. 21, 1991, P.L. 102-166, §§103, 113(a), 105 Stat. 1074, 1079; Nov. 16, 1993, P.L. 103-141, §4(a), 107 Stat. 1489; Sept. 13, 1994, P.L. 103-322, §40303, 108 Stat. 1942; Oct. 19, 1996, P.L. 104-317, §309(b), 110 Stat. 3853; Sept. 22, 2000, P.L. 106-274, §4(d), 114 Stat. 804.

50 U.S.C. APP.

SERVICEMEMBERS CIVIL RELIEF ACT

50 U.S.C. APP. §521. PROTECTION OF SERVICEMEMBERS AGAINST DEFAULT JUDGMENTS

(a) Applicability of section.—This section applies to any civil action or proceeding, including any child custody proceeding, in which the defendant does not make an appearance.

(b) Affidavit requirement—

(1) Plaintiff to file affidavit.—In any action or proceeding covered by this section, the court, before entering judgment for the plaintiff, shall require the plaintiff to file with the court an affidavit—

(A) stating whether or not the defendant is in military service and showing necessary facts to support the affidavit; or

(B) if the plaintiff is unable to determine whether or not the defendant is in military service, stating that the plaintiff is unable to determine whether or not the defendant is in military service.

(2) Appointment of attorney to represent defendant in military service.—If in an action covered by this section it appears that the defendant is in military service, the court may not enter a judgment until after the court appoints an attorney to represent the defendant. If an attorney appointed under this section to represent a servicemember cannot locate the servicemember, actions by the attorney in the case shall not waive any defense of the servicemember or otherwise bind the servicemember.

(3) Defendant's military status not ascertained by affidavit.—If based upon the affidavits filed in such an action, the court is unable to determine whether the defendant is in military service, the court, before entering judgment, may require the plaintiff to file a bond in an amount approved by the court. If the defendant is later found to be in military service, the bond shall be available to indemnify the defendant against any loss or damage the defendant may suffer by reason of any judgment for the plaintiff against the defendant, should the judgment be set aside in whole or in part. The bond shall remain in effect until expiration of the time for appeal and setting aside of a judgment under applicable Federal or State law or regulation or under any applicable ordinance of a political subdivision of a State. The court may issue such orders or enter such judgments as the court determines necessary to protect the rights of the defendant under this Act.[1]

(4) Satisfaction of requirement for affidavit.—The requirement for an affidavit under paragraph (1) may be satisfied by a statement, declaration, verification, or certificate, in writing, subscribed and certified or declared to be true under penalty of perjury.

(c) Penalty for making or using false affidavit.—A person who makes or uses an affidavit permitted under subsection (b) (or a statement, declaration, verification, or certificate as authorized under subsection (b)(4)) knowing it to be false, shall be fined as provided in title 18, United States Code, or imprisoned for not more than one year, or both.

(d) Stay of proceedings.—In an action covered by this section in which the defendant is in military service, the court shall grant a stay of proceedings for a minimum period of 90 days under this subsection upon application of counsel, or on the court's own motion, if the court determines that—

(1) there may be a defense to the action and a defense cannot be presented without the presence of the defendant; or

(2) after due diligence, counsel has been unable to contact the defendant or otherwise determine if a meritorious defense exists.

(e) Inapplicability of section 202 procedures.—A stay of proceedings under subsection (d) shall not be controlled by procedures or requirements under section 202.[2]

(f) Section 202 protection.—If a servicemember who is a defendant in an action covered by this section receives actual notice of the action, the servicemember may request a stay of proceeding under section 202.[2]

(g) Vacation or setting aside of default judgments—

(1) Authority for court to vacate or set aside judgment.—If a default judgment is entered in an action covered by this section against a servicemember during the servicemember's period of military service (or within 60 days after termination of or release from such military service), the court entering the judgment shall, upon application by or on behalf of the servicemember, reopen the judgment for the purpose of allowing the servicemember to defend the action if it appears that—

(A) the servicemember was materially affected by reason of that military service in making a defense to the action; and

(B) the servicemember has a meritorious or legal defense to the action or some part of it.

(2) Time for filing application.—An application under this subsection must be filed not later than 90 days after the date of the termination of or release from military service.

(h) Protection of bona fide purchaser.—If a court vacates, sets aside, or reverses a default judgment against a servicemember and the vacating, setting aside, or reversing is because of a provision of this Act,[1] that action shall not impair a right or title acquired by a bona fide purchaser for value under the default judgment.

1. **Editor's note:** 50 U.S.C. App. §§501-597b.

2. **Editor's note:** 50 U.S.C. App. §522.

History of 50 U.S.C. App. §521: Oct. 17, 1940, ch. 888, §201; Dec. 19, 2003, P.L. 108-189, §1, 117 Stat. 2840; Jan. 28, 2008, P.L. 110-181, §584(a), 122 Stat. 128.

See *Commentaries*, "Default Judgment," ch. 7-A, p. 583.

50 U.S.C. APP. §522. STAY OF PROCEEDINGS WHEN SERVICEMEMBER HAS NOTICE

(a) Applicability of section.—This section applies to any civil action or proceeding, including any child custody proceeding, in which the plaintiff or defendant at the time of filing an application under this section—

(1) is in military service or is within 90 days after termination of or release from military service; and

(2) has received notice of the action or proceeding.

(b) Stay of proceedings—

(1) Authority for stay—

At any stage before final judgment in a civil action or proceeding in which a servicemember described in subsection (a) is a party, the court may on its own motion and shall, upon application by the servicemember, stay the action for a period of not less than 90 days, if the conditions in paragraph (2) are met.

(2) Conditions for stay—

An application for a stay under paragraph (1) shall include the following:

(A) A letter or other communication setting forth facts stating the manner in which current military duty requirements materially affect the servicemember's ability to appear and stating a date when the servicemember will be available to appear.

(B) A letter or other communication from the servicemember's commanding officer stating that the servicemember's current military duty prevents appearance and that military leave is not authorized for the servicemember at the time of the letter.

(c) Application not a waiver of defenses—

An application for a stay under this section does not constitute an appearance for jurisdictional purposes and does not constitute a waiver of any substantive or procedural defense (including a defense relating to lack of personal jurisdiction).

(d) Additional stay—

(1) Application—

A servicemember who is granted a stay of a civil action or proceeding under subsection (b) may apply for an additional stay based on continuing material affect of military duty on the servicemember's ability to appear. Such an application may be made by the servicemember at the time of the initial application under subsection (b) or when it appears that the servicemember is unavailable to prosecute or defend the action. The same information required under subsection (b)(2) shall be included in an application under this subsection.

(2) Appointment of counsel when additional stay refused—

If the court refuses to grant an additional stay of proceedings under paragraph (1), the court shall appoint counsel to represent the servicemember in the action or proceeding.

(e) Coordination with section 201—

A servicemember who applies for a stay under this section and is unsuccessful may not seek the protections afforded by section 201.[1]

(f) Inapplicability to section 301—

The protections of this section do not apply to section 301.[2]

1. **Editor's note:** 50 U.S.C. App. §521.

2. **Editor's note:** 50 U.S.C. App. §531.

History of 50 U.S.C. App. §522: Oct. 17, 1940, ch. 888, §202; Dec. 19, 2003, P.L. 108-189, §1, 117 Stat. 2842; Dec. 10, 2004, P.L. 108-454, §703, 118 Stat. 3624; Jan. 28, 2008, P.L. 110-181, §584(b), 122 Stat. 128.

(g) Vacation or setting aside of default judgments—

(1) Authority for court to vacate or set aside judgment—If a default judgment is entered in an action covered by this section against a servicemember during the servicemember's period of military service (or within 60 days after termination of or release from such military service), the court entering the judgment shall, upon application by or on behalf of the servicemember, reopen the judgment for the purpose of allowing the servicemember to defend the action if it appears that—

(A) the servicemember was materially affected by reason of that military service in making a defense to the action; and

(B) the servicemember has a meritorious or legal defense to the action or some part of it.

(2) Time for filing application.—An application under this subsection must be filed not later than 90 days after the date of the termination of or release from military service.

(h) Protection of bona fide purchaser.—If a court vacates, sets aside, or reverses a default judgment against a servicemember and the vacating, setting aside, or reversing is because of a provision of this Act,[1] that action shall not impair a right or title acquired by a bona fide purchaser for value under the default judgment.

1. Editor's note: 50 U.S.C. App. §§501-597b.

2. Editor's note: 50 U.S.C. App. §522.

History: 50 U.S.C. App. §521; Oct. 17, 1940, ch. 888, §201; Dec. 19, 2003, P.L. 108-189, §1, 117 Stat. 2840; Jan. 28, 2008, P.L. 110-181, §584(a), 122 Stat. 128.

See Commentaries, "Default Judgment," ch. 7-B, [illegible].

50 U.S.C. APP. §522. STAY OF PROCEEDINGS WHEN SERVICEMEMBER HAS NOTICE

(a) Applicability of section.—This section applies to any civil action or proceeding, including any child custody proceeding, in which the plaintiff or defendant at the time of filing an application under this section—

(1) is in military service or is within 90 days after termination of or release from military service; and

(2) has received notice of the action or proceeding.

(b) Stay of proceedings.—

(1) Authority for stay—

At any stage before final judgment in a civil action or proceeding in which a servicemember described in subsection (a) is a party, the court may on its own motion and shall, upon application by the servicemember, stay the action for a period of not less than 90 days, if the conditions in paragraph (2) are met.

(2) Conditions for stay—

An application for a stay under paragraph (1) shall include the following:

(A) A letter or other communication setting forth facts stating the manner in which current military duty requirements materially affect the servicemember's ability to appear and stating a date when the servicemember will be available to appear.

(B) A letter or other communication from the servicemember's commanding officer stating that the servicemember's current military duty prevents appearance and that military leave is not authorized for the servicemember at the time of the letter.

(c) Application not a waiver of defenses—

An application for a stay under this section does not constitute an appearance for jurisdictional purposes and does not constitute a waiver of any substantive or procedural defense (including a defense relating to lack of personal jurisdiction).

(d) Additional stay—

(1) Application—

A servicemember who is granted a stay of a civil action or proceeding under subsection (b) may apply for an additional stay based on continuing material affect of military duty on the servicemember's ability to appear. Such an application may be made by the servicemember at the time of the initial application under subsection (b) or when it appears that the servicemember is unavailable to prosecute or defend the action. The same information required under subsection (b)(2) shall be included in an application under this subsection.

(2) Appointment of counsel when additional stay refused—

If the court refuses to grant an additional stay of proceedings under paragraph (1), the court shall appoint counsel to represent the servicemember in the action or proceeding.

(e) Coordination with section 201—

A servicemember who applies for a stay under this section and is unsuccessful may not seek the protections afforded by section 201.[1]

(f) Inapplicability to section 301—

The protections of this section do not apply to section 301.[2]

1. Editor's note: 50 U.S.C. App. §521.

2. Editor's note: 50 U.S.C. App. §531.

History: 50 U.S.C. App. §522; Oct. 17, 1940, ch. 888, §202; Dec. 19, 2003, P.L. 108-189, §1, 117 Stat. 2841; Dec. 10, 2004, P.L. 108-454, §701(a), 118 Stat. 3624; Jan. 28, 2008, P.L. 110-181, §584(b), 122 Stat. 129.

U.S. CONSTITUTION

THE CONSTITUTION OF THE UNITED STATES OF AMERICA

PREAMBLE

We the People of the United States, in Order to form a more perfect Union, establish Justice, insure domestic Tranquility, provide for the common defence, promote the general Welfare, and secure the Blessings of Liberty to ourselves and our Posterity, do ordain and establish this Constitution for the United States of America.

ARTICLE I.

Section 1. All legislative Powers herein granted shall be vested in a Congress of the United States, which shall consist of a Senate and House of Representatives.

Section 2. The House of Representatives shall be composed of Members chosen every second Year by the People of the several States, and the Electors in each State shall have the Qualifications requisite for Electors of the most numerous Branch of the State Legislature.

No Person shall be a Representative who shall not have attained to the Age of twenty five Years, and been seven Years a Citizen of the United States, and who shall not, when elected, be an Inhabitant of that State in which he shall be chosen.

Representatives and direct Taxes shall be apportioned among the several States which may be included within this Union, according to their respective Numbers, which shall be determined by adding to the whole Number of free Persons, including those bound to Service for a Term of Years, and excluding Indians not taxed, three fifths of all other Persons. The actual Enumeration shall be made within three Years after the first Meeting of the Congress of the United States, and within every subsequent Term of ten Years, in such Manner as they shall by Law direct. The Number of Representatives shall not exceed one for every thirty Thousand, but each State shall have at Least one Representative; and until such enumeration shall be made, the State of New Hampshire shall be entitled to chuse three, Massachusetts eight, Rhode-Island and Providence Plantations one, Connecticut five, New-York six, New Jersey four, Pennsylvania eight, Delaware one, Maryland six, Virginia ten, North Carolina five, South Carolina five, and Georgia three.

When vacancies happen in the Representation from any State, the Executive Authority thereof shall issue Writs of Election to fill such Vacancies.

The House of Representatives shall chuse their Speaker and other Officers; and shall have the sole Power of Impeachment.

Section 3. The Senate of the United States shall be composed of two Senators from each State, chosen by the Legislature thereof, for six Years; and each Senator shall have one Vote.

Immediately after they shall be assembled in Consequence of the first Election, they shall be divided as equally as may be into three Classes. The Seats of the Senators of the first Class shall be vacated at the Expiration of the second Year, of the second Class at the Expiration of the fourth Year, and of the third Class at the Expiration of the sixth Year, so that one third may be chosen every second Year; and if Vacancies happen by Resignation, or otherwise, during the Recess of the Legislature of any State, the Executive thereof may make temporary Appointments until the next Meeting of the Legislature, which shall then fill such Vacancies.

No Person shall be a Senator who shall not have attained to the Age of thirty Years, and been nine Years a Citizen of the United States, and who shall not, when elected, be an Inhabitant of that State for which he shall be chosen.

The Vice President of the United States shall be President of the Senate, but shall have no Vote, unless they be equally divided.

The Senate shall chuse their other Officers, and also a President pro tempore, in the Absence of the Vice President, or when he shall exercise the Office of President of the United States.

The Senate shall have the sole Power to try all Impeachments. When sitting for that Purpose, they shall be on Oath or Affirmation. When the President of the United States is tried, the Chief Justice shall preside: And no Person shall be convicted without the Concurrence of two thirds of the Members present.

Judgment in Cases of Impeachment shall not extend further than to removal from Office, and disqualification to hold and enjoy any Office of honor, Trust or Profit under the United States: but the Party convicted shall nevertheless be liable and subject to Indictment, Trial, Judgment and Punishment, according to Law.

Section 4. The Times, Places and Manner of holding Elections for Senators and Representatives, shall be prescribed in each State by the Legislature thereof; but the Congress may at any time by Law make or alter such Regulations, except as to the Places of chusing Senators.

The Congress shall assemble at least once in every Year, and such Meeting shall be on the first Monday in December, unless they shall by Law appoint a different Day.

Section 5. Each House shall be the Judge of the Elections, Returns and Qualifications of its own Members, and a Majority of each shall constitute a Quorum to do Business; but a smaller Number may adjourn from day to day, and may be authorized to compel the Attendance of absent Members, in such Manner, and under such Penalties as each House may provide.

Each House may determine the Rules of its Proceedings, punish its Members for disorderly Behaviour, and, with the Concurrence of two thirds, expel a Member.

Each House shall keep a Journal of its Proceedings, and from time to time publish the same, excepting such Parts as may in their Judgment require Secrecy; and the Yeas and

Nays of the Members of either House on any question shall, at the Desire of one fifth of those Present, be entered on the Journal.

Neither House, during the Session of Congress, shall, without the Consent of the other, adjourn for more than three days, nor to any other Place than that in which the two Houses shall be sitting.

Section 6. The Senators and Representatives shall receive a Compensation for their Services, to be ascertained by Law, and paid out of the Treasury of the United States. They shall in all Cases, except Treason, Felony and Breach of the Peace, be privileged from Arrest during their Attendance at the Session of their respective Houses, and in going to and returning from the same; and for any Speech or Debate in either House, they shall not be questioned in any other Place.

No Senator or Representative shall, during the Time for which he was elected, be appointed to any civil Office under the Authority of the United States, which shall have been created, or the Emoluments whereof shall have been encreased during such time; and no Person holding any Office under the United States, shall be a Member of either House during his Continuance in Office.

Section 7. All Bills for raising Revenue shall originate in the House of Representatives; but the Senate may propose or concur with Amendments as on other Bills.

Every Bill which shall have passed the House of Representatives and the Senate, shall, before it become a Law, be presented to the President of the United States: If he approve he shall sign it, but if not he shall return it, with his Objections to that House in which it shall have originated, who shall enter the Objections at large on their Journal, and proceed to reconsider it. If after such Reconsideration two thirds of that House shall agree to pass the Bill, it shall be sent, together with the Objections, to the other House, by which it shall likewise be reconsidered, and if approved by two thirds of that House, it shall become a Law. But in all such Cases the Votes of both Houses shall be determined by yeas and Nays, and the Names of the Persons voting for and against the Bill shall be entered on the Journal of each House respectively. If any Bill shall not be returned by the President within ten Days (Sundays excepted) after it shall have been presented to him, the Same shall be a Law, in like Manner as if he had signed it, unless the Congress by their Adjournment prevent its Return, in which Case it shall not be a Law.

Every Order, Resolution, or Vote to which the Concurrence of the Senate and House of Representatives may be necessary (except on a question of Adjournment) shall be presented to the President of the United States; and before the Same shall take Effect, shall be approved by him, or being disapproved by him, shall be repassed by two thirds of the Senate and House of Representatives, according to the Rules and Limitations prescribed in the Case of a Bill.

Section 8. The Congress shall have Power To lay and collect Taxes, Duties, Imposts and Excises, to pay the Debts and provide for the common Defence and general Welfare of the United States; but all Duties, Imposts and Excises shall be uniform throughout the United States;

To borrow Money on the credit of the United States;

To regulate Commerce with foreign Nations, and among the several States, and with the Indian Tribes;

To establish an uniform Rule of Naturalization, and uniform Laws on the subject of Bankruptcies throughout the United States;

To coin Money, regulate the Value thereof, and of foreign Coin, and fix the Standard of Weights and Measures;

To provide for the Punishment of counterfeiting the Securities and current Coin of the United States;

To establish Post Offices and post Roads;

To promote the Progress of Science and useful Arts, by securing for limited Times to Authors and Inventors the exclusive Right to their respective Writings and Discoveries;

To constitute Tribunals inferior to the supreme Court;

To define and punish Piracies and Felonies committed on the high Seas, and Offences against the Law of Nations;

To declare War, grant Letters of Marque and Reprisal, and make Rules concerning Captures on Land and Water;

To raise and support Armies, but no Appropriation of Money to that Use shall be for a longer Term than two Years;

To provide and maintain a Navy;

To make Rules for the Government and Regulation of the land and naval Forces;

To provide for calling forth the Militia to execute the Laws of the Union, suppress Insurrections and repel Invasions;

To provide for organizing, arming, and disciplining, the Militia, and for governing such Part of them as may be employed in the Service of the United States, reserving to the States respectively, the Appointment of the Officers, and the Authority of training the Militia according to the discipline prescribed by Congress;

To exercise exclusive Legislation in all Cases whatsoever, over such District (not exceeding ten Miles square) as may, by Cession of particular States, and the Acceptance of Congress, become the Seat of the Government of the United States, and to exercise like Authority over all Places purchased by the Consent of the Legislature of the State in which the Same shall be, for the Erection of Forts, Magazines, Arsenals, dock-Yards, and other needful Buildings;—And

To make all Laws which shall be necessary and proper for carrying into Execution the foregoing Powers, and all other Powers vested by this Constitution in the Government of the United States, or in any Department or Officer thereof.

Section 9. The Migration or Importation of such Persons as any of the States now existing shall think proper to admit, shall not be prohibited by the Congress prior to the Year one thousand eight hundred and eight, but a Tax or duty may be imposed on such Importation, not exceeding ten dollars for each Person.

The Privilege of the Writ of Habeas Corpus shall not be suspended, unless when in Cases of Rebellion or Invasion the public Safety may require it.

No Bill of Attainder or ex post facto Law shall be passed.

No Capitation, or other direct, Tax shall be laid, unless in Proportion to the Census or enumeration herein before directed to be taken.

No Tax or Duty shall be laid on Articles exported from any State.

No Preference shall be given by any Regulation of Commerce or Revenue to the Ports of one State over those of another; nor shall Vessels bound to, or from, one State, be obliged to enter, clear, or pay Duties in another.

No Money shall be drawn from the Treasury, but in Consequence of Appropriations made by Law; and a regular Statement and Account of the Receipts and Expenditures of all public Money shall be published from time to time.

No Title of Nobility shall be granted by the United States: And no Person holding any Office of Profit or Trust under them, shall, without the Consent of the Congress, accept of any present, Emolument, Office, or Title, of any kind whatever, from any King, Prince, or foreign State.

Section 10. No State shall enter into any Treaty, Alliance, or Confederation; grant Letters of Marque and Reprisal; coin Money; emit Bills of Credit; make any Thing but gold and silver Coin a Tender in Payment of Debts; pass any Bill of Attainder, ex post facto Law, or Law impairing the Obligation of Contracts, or grant any Title of Nobility.

No State shall, without the Consent of the Congress, lay any Imposts or Duties on Imports or Exports, except what may be absolutely necessary for executing it's inspection Laws: and the net Produce of all Duties and Imposts, laid by any State on Imports or Exports, shall be for the Use of the Treasury of the United States; and all such Laws shall be subject to the Revision and Controul of the Congress.

No State shall, without the Consent of Congress, lay any Duty of Tonnage, keep Troops, or Ships of War in time of Peace, enter into any Agreement or Compact with another State, or with a foreign Power, or engage in War, unless actually invaded, or in such imminent Danger as will not admit of delay.

ARTICLE II.

Section 1. The executive Power shall be vested in a President of the United States of America. He shall hold his Office during the Term of four Years, and, together with the Vice President, chosen for the same Term, be elected, as follows:

Each State shall appoint, in such Manner as the Legislature thereof may direct, a Number of Electors, equal to the whole Number of Senators and Representatives to which the State may be entitled in the Congress: but no Senator or Representative, or Person holding an Office of Trust or Profit under the United States, shall be appointed an Elector.

The Electors shall meet in their respective States, and vote by Ballot for two Persons, of whom one at least shall not be an Inhabitant of the same State with themselves. And they shall make a List of all the Persons voted for, and of the Number of Votes for each; which List they shall sign and certify, and transmit sealed to the Seat of the Government of the United States, directed to the President of the Senate. The President of the Senate shall, in the Presence of the Senate and House of Representatives, open all the Certificates, and the Votes shall then be counted. The Person having the greatest Number of Votes shall be the President, if such Number be a Majority of the whole Number of Electors appointed; and if there be more than one who have such Majority, and have an equal Number of Votes, then the House of Representatives shall immediately chuse by Ballot one of them for President; and if no Person have a Majority, then from the five highest on the List the said House shall in like Manner chuse the President. But in chusing the President, the Votes shall be taken by States, the Representation from each State having one Vote; A quorum for this purpose shall consist of a Member or Members from two thirds of the States, and a Majority of all the States shall be necessary to a Choice. In every Case, after the Choice of the President, the Person having the greatest Number of Votes of the Electors shall be the Vice President. But if there should remain two or more who have equal Votes, the Senate shall chuse from them by Ballot the Vice President.[1]

The Congress may determine the Time of chusing the Electors, and the Day on which they shall give their Votes; which Day shall be the same throughout the United States.

No Person except a natural born Citizen, or a Citizen of the United States, at the time of the Adoption of this Constitution, shall be eligible to the Office of President; neither shall any Person be eligible to that Office who shall not have attained to the Age of thirty five Years, and been fourteen Years a Resident within the United States.

In Case of the Removal of the President from Office, or of his Death, Resignation, or Inability to discharge the Powers and Duties of the said Office, the Same shall devolve on the Vice President, and the Congress may by Law provide for the Case of Removal, Death, Resignation or Inability, both of the President and Vice President, declaring what Officer shall then act as President, and such Officer shall act accordingly, until the Disability be removed, or a President shall be elected.

The President shall, at stated Times, receive for his Services, a Compensation, which shall neither be increased nor diminished during the Period for which he shall have been elected, and he shall not receive within that Period any other Emolument from the United States, or any of them.

Before he enter on the Execution of his Office, he shall take the following Oath or Affirmation:—"I do solemnly swear (or affirm) that I will faithfully execute the Office of

President of the United States, and will to the best of my Ability, preserve, protect and defend the Constitution of the United States."

Section 2. The President shall be Commander in Chief of the Army and Navy of the United States, and of the Militia of the several States, when called into the actual Service of the United States; he may require the Opinion, in writing, of the principal Officer in each of the executive Departments, upon any Subject relating to the Duties of their respective Offices, and he shall have Power to grant Reprieves and Pardons for Offences against the United States, except in Cases of Impeachment.

He shall have Power, by and with the Advice and Consent of the Senate, to make Treaties, provided two thirds of the Senators present concur; and he shall nominate, and by and with the Advice and Consent of the Senate, shall appoint Ambassadors, other public Ministers and Consuls, Judges of the supreme Court, and all other Officers of the United States, whose Appointments are not herein otherwise provided for, and which shall be established by Law: but the Congress may by Law vest the Appointment of such inferior Officers, as they think proper, in the President alone, in the Courts of Law, or in the Heads of Departments.

The President shall have Power to fill up all Vacancies that may happen during the Recess of the Senate, by granting Commissions which shall expire at the End of their next Session.

Section 3. He shall from time to time give to the Congress Information of the State of the Union, and recommend to their Consideration such Measures as he shall judge necessary and expedient; he may, on extraordinary Occasions, convene both Houses, or either of them, and in Case of Disagreement between them, with Respect to the Time of Adjournment, he may adjourn them to such Time as he shall think proper; he shall receive Ambassadors and other public Ministers; he shall take Care that the Laws be faithfully executed, and shall Commission all the Officers of the United States.

Section 4. The President, Vice President and all civil Officers of the United States, shall be removed from Office on Impeachment for, and Conviction of, Treason, Bribery, or other high Crimes and Misdemeanors.

1. **Editor's note:** This paragraph has been superseded by Amendment XII.

ARTICLE III.

Section 1. The judicial Power of the United States shall be vested in one supreme Court, and in such inferior Courts as the Congress may from time to time ordain and establish. The Judges, both of the supreme and inferior Courts, shall hold their Offices during good Behaviour, and shall, at stated Times, receive for their Services a Compensation, which shall not be diminished during their Continuance in Office.

Section 2. The judicial Power shall extend to all Cases, in Law and Equity, arising under this Constitution, the Laws of the United States, and Treaties made, or which shall be made, under their Authority;—to all Cases affecting Ambassadors, other public Ministers and Consuls;—to all Cases of admiralty and maritime Jurisdiction;—to Controversies to which the United States shall be a Party;—to Controversies between two or more States,—between a State and Citizens of another State,—between Citizens of different States,—between Citizens of the same State claiming Lands under Grants of different States, and between a State, or the Citizens thereof, and foreign States, Citizens or Subjects.[1]

In all Cases affecting Ambassadors, other public Ministers and Consuls, and those in which a State shall be Party, the supreme Court shall have original Jurisdiction. In all the other Cases before mentioned, the supreme Court shall have appellate Jurisdiction, both as to Law and Fact, with such Exceptions, and under such Regulations as the Congress shall make.

The Trial of all Crimes, except in Cases of Impeachment, shall be by Jury; and such Trial shall be held in the State where the said Crimes shall have been committed; but when not committed within any State, the Trial shall be at such Place or Places as the Congress may by Law have directed.

Section 3. Treason against the United States, shall consist only in levying War against them, or in adhering to their Enemies, giving them Aid and Comfort. No Person shall be convicted of Treason unless on the Testimony of two Witnesses to the same overt Act, or on Confession in open Court.

The Congress shall have Power to declare the Punishment of Treason, but no Attainder of Treason shall work Corruption of Blood, or Forfeiture except during the Life of the Person attainted.

1. **Editor's note:** Sections of this paragraph have been superseded by Amendment XI.

ARTICLE IV.

Section 1. Full Faith and Credit shall be given in each State to the public Acts, Records, and judicial Proceedings of every other State. And the Congress may by general Laws prescribe the Manner in which such Acts, Records and Proceedings shall be proved, and the Effect thereof.

Section 2. The Citizens of each State shall be entitled to all Privileges and Immunities of Citizens in the several States.

A Person charged in any State with Treason, Felony, or other Crime, who shall flee from Justice, and be found in another State, shall on Demand of the executive Authority of the State from which he fled, be delivered up, to be removed to the State having Jurisdiction of the Crime.

No Person held to Service or Labour in one State, under the Laws thereof, escaping into another, shall, in Consequence of any Law or Regulation therein, be discharged from such Service or Labour, but shall be delivered up on Claim of the Party to whom such Service or Labour may be due.[1]

Section 3. New States may be admitted by the Congress into this Union; but no new State shall be formed or erected

within the Jurisdiction of any other State; nor any State be formed by the Junction of two or more States, or Parts of States, without the Consent of the Legislatures of the States concerned as well as of the Congress.

The Congress shall have Power to dispose of and make all needful Rules and Regulations respecting the Territory or other Property belonging to the United States; and nothing in this Constitution shall be so construed as to Prejudice any Claims of the United States, or of any particular State.

Section 4. The United States shall guarantee to every State in this Union a Republican Form of Government, and shall protect each of them against Invasion; and on Application of the Legislature, or of the Executive (when the Legislature cannot be convened), against domestic Violence.

1. **Editor's note:** This paragraph has been superseded by Amendment XIII.

ARTICLE V.

The Congress, whenever two thirds of both Houses shall deem it necessary, shall propose Amendments to this Constitution, or, on the Application of the Legislatures of two thirds of the several States, shall call a Convention for proposing Amendments, which, in either Case, shall be valid to all Intents and Purposes, as Part of this Constitution, when ratified by the Legislatures of three fourths of the several States, or by Conventions in three fourths thereof, as the one or the other Mode of Ratification may be proposed by the Congress; Provided that no Amendment which may be made prior to the Year One thousand eight hundred and eight shall in any Manner affect the first and fourth Clauses in the Ninth Section of the first Article; and that no State, without its Consent, shall be deprived of its equal Suffrage in the Senate.

ARTICLE VI.

All Debts contracted and Engagements entered into, before the Adoption of this Constitution, shall be as valid against the United States under this Constitution, as under the Confederation.

This Constitution, and the Laws of the United States which shall be made in Pursuance thereof; and all Treaties made, or which shall be made, under the Authority of the United States, shall be the supreme Law of the Land; and the Judges in every State shall be bound thereby, any Thing in the Constitution or Laws of any State to the Contrary notwithstanding.

The Senators and Representatives before mentioned, and the Members of the several State Legislatures, and all executive and judicial Officers, both of the United States and of the several States, shall be bound by Oath or Affirmation, to support this Constitution; but no religious Test shall ever be required as a Qualification to any Office or public Trust under the United States.

ARTICLE VII.

The Ratification of the Conventions of nine States, shall be sufficient for the Establishment of this Constitution between the States so ratifying the Same.

done in Convention by the Unanimous Consent of the States present the Seventeenth Day of September in the Year of our Lord one thousand seven hundred and Eighty seven and of the Independance of the United States of America the Twelfth In witness whereof We have hereunto subscribed our Names,[1]

Go. Washington—Presidt. and deputy from Virginia

[Signed also by the deputies of twelve States.]

New Hampshire—John Langdon, Nicholas Gilman

Massachusetts—Nathaniel Gorham, Rufus King

Connecticut—Wm Saml Johnson, Roger Sherman

New York—Alexander Hamilton

New Jersey—Wil: Livingston, David Brearley, Wm Patterson, Jona: Dayton

Pennsylvania—B Franklin, Thomas Mifflin, Robt Morris, Geo. Clymer, Thos. FitzSimons, Jared Ingersol, James Wilson, Gouv Morris

Delaware—Geo: Read, Gunning Bedford jun, John Dickinson, Richard Bassett, Jaco: Broom

Maryland—James McHenry, Dan of St Thos Jenifer, Danl Carroll

Virginia—John Blair, James Madison Jr.

North Carolina—Wm Blount, Richd Dobbs Spaight, Hu Williamson

South Carolina—J. Rutledge, Charles Cotesworth Pinckney, Charles Pinckney, Pierce Butler

Georgia—William Few, Abr Baldwin

Attest William Jackson Secretary

1. **Editor's note:** The signatories' names are spelled as provided by the Government Printing Office, www.gpo.gov/fdsys/pkg/GPO-CONAN-2002/pdf/GPO-CONAN-2002-5.pdf (literal print).

AMENDMENTS TO THE CONSTITUTION

***Editor's note:** Brackets indicate editorially supplied headings. Many of the amendments were ratified without either a title or a number. Dates of completed ratification are in parentheses.*

[AMENDMENT 1.] (1791)

Congress shall make no law respecting an establishment of religion, or prohibiting the free exercise thereof; or abridging the freedom of speech, or of the press; or the right of the people peaceably to assemble, and to petition the Government for a redress of grievances.

[AMENDMENT 2.] (1791)

A well regulated Militia, being necessary to the security of a free State, the right of the people to keep and bear Arms, shall not be infringed.

[AMENDMENT 3.] (1791)

No Soldier shall, in time of peace be quartered in any house, without the consent of the Owner, nor in time of war, but in a manner to be prescribed by law.

[AMENDMENT 4.] (1791)

The right of the people to be secure in their persons, houses, papers, and effects, against unreasonable searches and seizures, shall not be violated, and no Warrants shall issue, but upon probable cause, supported by Oath or affirmation, and particularly describing the place to be searched, and the persons or things to be seized.

[AMENDMENT 5.] (1791)

No person shall be held to answer for a capital, or otherwise infamous crime, unless on a presentment or indictment of a Grand Jury, except in cases arising in the land or naval forces, or in the Militia, when in actual service in time of War or public danger; nor shall any person be subject for the same offence to be twice put in jeopardy of life or limb; nor shall be compelled in any criminal case to be a witness against himself, nor be deprived of life, liberty, or property, without due process of law; nor shall private property be taken for public use, without just compensation.

[AMENDMENT 6.] (1791)

In all criminal prosecutions, the accused shall enjoy the right to a speedy and public trial, by an impartial jury of the State and district wherein the crime shall have been committed, which district shall have been previously ascertained by law, and to be informed of the nature and cause of the accusation; to be confronted with the witnesses against him; to have compulsory process for obtaining witnesses in his favor, and to have the Assistance of Counsel for his defence.

[AMENDMENT 7.] (1791)

In Suits at common law, where the value in controversy shall exceed twenty dollars, the right of trial by jury shall be preserved, and no fact tried by a jury, shall be otherwise reexamined in any Court of the United States, than according to the rules of the common law.

[AMENDMENT 8.] (1791)

Excessive bail shall not be required, nor excessive fines imposed, nor cruel and unusual punishments inflicted.

[AMENDMENT 9.] (1791)

The enumeration in the Constitution, of certain rights, shall not be construed to deny or disparage others retained by the people.

[AMENDMENT 10.] (1791)

The powers not delegated to the United States by the Constitution, nor prohibited by it to the States, are reserved to the States respectively, or to the people.

[AMENDMENT 11.] (1795)

The Judicial power of the United States shall not be construed to extend to any suit in law or equity, commenced or prosecuted against one of the United States by Citizens of another State, or by Citizens or Subjects of any Foreign State.

[AMENDMENT 12.] (1804)

The Electors shall meet in their respective states and vote by ballot for President and Vice-President, one of whom, at least, shall not be an inhabitant of the same state with themselves; they shall name in their ballots the person voted for as President, and in distinct ballots the person voted for as Vice-President, and they shall make distinct lists of all persons voted for as President, and of all persons voted for as Vice-President, and of the number of votes for each, which lists they shall sign and certify, and transmit sealed to the seat of the government of the United States, directed to the President of the Senate;—the President of the Senate shall, in the presence of the Senate and House of Representatives, open all the certificates and the votes shall then be counted;—The person having the greatest number of votes for President, shall be the President, if such number be a majority of the whole number of Electors appointed; and if no person have such majority, then from the persons having the highest numbers not exceeding three on the list of those voted for as President, the House of Representatives shall choose immediately, by ballot, the President. But in choosing the President, the votes shall be taken by states, the representation from each state having one vote; a quorum for this purpose shall consist of a member or members from two-thirds of the states, and a majority of all the states shall be necessary to a choice. And if the House of Representatives shall not choose a President whenever the right of choice shall devolve upon them, before the fourth day of March next following, then the Vice-President shall act as President, as in case of the death or other constitutional disability of the President.[1] The person having the greatest number of votes as Vice-President, shall be the Vice-President, if such number be a majority of the whole number of Electors appointed, and if no person have a majority, then from the two highest numbers on the list, the Senate shall choose the Vice-President; a quorum for the purpose shall consist of two-thirds of the whole number of Senators, and a majority of the whole number shall be necessary to a choice. But no person constitutionally ineligible to the office of President shall be eligible to that of Vice-President of the United States.

1. **Editor's note:** This sentence has been superseded by Amendment XX, Section 3.

[AMENDMENT 13.] (1865)

Section 1. Neither slavery nor involuntary servitude, except as a punishment for crime whereof the party shall have been duly convicted, shall exist within the United States, or any place subject to their jurisdiction.

Section 2. Congress shall have power to enforce this article by appropriate legislation.

[AMENDMENT 14.] (1868)

Section 1. All persons born or naturalized in the United States, and subject to the jurisdiction thereof, are citizens of the United States and of the State wherein they reside. No State shall make or enforce any law which shall abridge the

privileges or immunities of citizens of the United States; nor shall any State deprive any person of life, liberty, or property, without due process of law; nor deny to any person within its jurisdiction the equal protection of the laws.

Section 2. Representatives shall be apportioned among the several States according to their respective numbers, counting the whole number of persons in each State, excluding Indians not taxed. But when the right to vote at any election for the choice of electors for President and Vice-President of the United States, Representatives in Congress, the Executive and Judicial officers of a State, or the members of the Legislature thereof, is denied to any of the male inhabitants of such State, being twenty-one years of age, and citizens of the United States, or in any way abridged, except for participation in rebellion, or other crime, the basis of representation therein shall be reduced in the proportion which the number of such male citizens shall bear to the whole number of male citizens twenty-one years of age in such State.

Section 3. No person shall be a Senator or Representative in Congress, or elector of President and Vice-President, or hold any office, civil or military, under the United States, or under any State, who, having previously taken an oath, as a member of Congress, or as an officer of the United States, or as a member of any State legislature, or as an executive or judicial officer of any State, to support the Constitution of the United States, shall have engaged in insurrection or rebellion against the same, or given aid or comfort to the enemies thereof. But Congress may by a vote of two-thirds of each House, remove such disability.

Section 4. The validity of the public debt of the United States, authorized by law, including debts incurred for payment of pensions and bounties for services in suppressing insurrection or rebellion, shall not be questioned. But neither the United States nor any State shall assume or pay any debt or obligation incurred in aid of insurrection or rebellion against the United States, or any claim for the loss or emancipation of any slave; but all such debts, obligations and claims shall be held illegal and void.

Section 5. The Congress shall have the power to enforce, by appropriate legislation, the provisions of this article.

[AMENDMENT 15.] (1870)

Section 1. The right of citizens of the United States to vote shall not be denied or abridged by the United States or by any State on account of race, color, or previous condition of servitude.

Section 2. The Congress shall have the power to enforce this article by appropriate legislation.

[AMENDMENT 16.] (1913)

The Congress shall have power to lay and collect taxes on incomes, from whatever source derived, without apportionment among the several States, and without regard to any census or enumeration.

[AMENDMENT 17.] (1913)

The Senate of the United States shall be composed of two Senators from each State, elected by the people thereof, for six years; and each Senator shall have one vote. The electors in each State shall have the qualifications requisite for electors of the most numerous branch of the State legislatures.

When vacancies happen in the representation of any State in the Senate, the executive authority of such State shall issue writs of election to fill such vacancies: Provided, That the legislature of any State may empower the executive thereof to make temporary appointments until the people fill the vacancies by election as the legislature may direct.

This amendment shall not be so construed as to affect the election or term of any Senator chosen before it becomes valid as part of the Constitution.

[AMENDMENT 18.][1] (1919)

Section 1. After one year from the ratification of this article the manufacture, sale, or transportation of intoxicating liquors within, the importation thereof into, or the exportation thereof from the United States and all territory subject to the jurisdiction thereof for beverage purposes is hereby prohibited.

Section 2. The Congress and the several States shall have concurrent power to enforce this article by appropriate legislation.

Section 3. This article shall be inoperative unless it shall have been ratified as an amendment to the Constitution by the legislatures of the several States, as provided in the Constitution, within seven years from the date of the submission hereof to the States by the Congress.

1. **Editor's note:** This Amendment was repealed by Amendment XXI, Section 1.

[AMENDMENT 19.] (1920)

The right of citizens of the United States to vote shall not be denied or abridged by the United States or by any State on account of sex.

Congress shall have power to enforce this article by appropriate legislation.

[AMENDMENT 20.] (1933)

Section 1. The terms of the President and the Vice President shall end at noon on the 20th day of January, and the terms of Senators and Representatives at noon on the 3d day of January, of the years in which such terms would have ended if this article had not been ratified; and the terms of their successors shall then begin.

Section 2. The Congress shall assemble at least once in every year, and such meeting shall begin at noon on the 3d day of January, unless they shall by law appoint a different day.

Section 3. If, at the time fixed for the beginning of the term of the President, the President elect shall have died, the Vice President elect shall become President. If a President shall not have been chosen before the time fixed for the be-

ginning of his term, or if the President elect shall have failed to qualify, then the Vice President elect shall act as President until a President shall have qualified; and the Congress may by law provide for the case wherein neither a President elect nor a Vice President shall have qualified, declaring who shall then act as President, or the manner in which one who is to act shall be selected, and such person shall act accordingly until a President or Vice President shall have qualified.

Section 4. The Congress may by law provide for the case of the death of any of the persons from whom the House of Representatives may choose a President whenever the right of choice shall have devolved upon them, and for the case of the death of any of the persons from whom the Senate may choose a Vice President whenever the right of choice shall have devolved upon them.

Section 5. Sections 1 and 2 shall take effect on the 15th day of October following the ratification of this article.

Section 6. This article shall be inoperative unless it shall have been ratified as an amendment to the Constitution by the legislatures of three-fourths of the several States within seven years from the date of its submission.

[AMENDMENT 21.] (1933)

Section 1. The eighteenth article of amendment to the Constitution of the United States is hereby repealed.

Section 2. The transportation or importation into any State, Territory, or Possession of the United States for delivery or use therein of intoxicating liquors, in violation of the laws thereof, is hereby prohibited.

Section 3. This article shall be inoperative unless it shall have been ratified as an amendment to the Constitution by conventions in the several States, as provided in the Constitution, within seven years from the date of the submission hereof to the States by the Congress.

[AMENDMENT 22.] (1951)

Section 1. No person shall be elected to the office of the President more than twice, and no person who has held the office of President, or acted as President, for more than two years of a term to which some other person was elected President shall be elected to the office of President more than once. But this Article shall not apply to any person holding the office of President when this Article was proposed by Congress, and shall not prevent any person who may be holding the office of President, or acting as President, during the term within which this Article becomes operative from holding the office of President or acting as President during the remainder of such term.

Section 2. This article shall be inoperative unless it shall have been ratified as an amendment to the Constitution by the legislatures of three-fourths of the several States within seven years from the date of its submission to the States by the Congress.

[AMENDMENT 23.] (1961)

Section 1. The District constituting the seat of Government of the United States shall appoint in such manner as Congress may direct:

A number of electors of President and Vice President equal to the whole number of Senators and Representatives in Congress to which the District would be entitled if it were a State, but in no event more than the least populous State; they shall be in addition to those appointed by the States, but they shall be considered, for the purposes of the election of President and Vice President, to be electors appointed by a State; and they shall meet in the District and perform such duties as provided by the twelfth article of amendment.

Section 2. The Congress shall have power to enforce this article by appropriate legislation.

[AMENDMENT 24.] (1964)

Section 1. The right of citizens of the United States to vote in any primary or other election for President or Vice President, for electors for President or Vice President, or for Senator or Representative in Congress, shall not be denied or abridged by the United States or any State by reason of failure to pay poll tax or other tax.

Section 2. The Congress shall have power to enforce this article by appropriate legislation.

[AMENDMENT 25.] (1967)

Section 1. In case of the removal of the President from office or of his death or resignation, the Vice President shall become President.

Section 2. Whenever there is a vacancy in the office of the Vice President, the President shall nominate a Vice President who shall take office upon confirmation by a majority vote of both Houses of Congress.

Section 3. Whenever the President transmits to the President pro tempore of the Senate and the Speaker of the House of Representatives his written declaration that he is unable to discharge the powers and duties of his office, and until he transmits to them a written declaration to the contrary, such powers and duties shall be discharged by the Vice President as Acting President.

Section 4. Whenever the Vice President and a majority of either the principal officers of the executive departments or of such other body as Congress may by law provide, transmit to the President pro tempore of the Senate and the Speaker of the House of Representatives their written declaration that the President is unable to discharge the powers and duties of his office, the Vice President shall immediately assume the powers and duties of the office as Acting President.

Thereafter, when the President transmits to the President pro tempore of the Senate and the Speaker of the House of Representatives his written declaration that no inability exists, he shall resume the powers and duties of his office unless the Vice President and a majority of either the principal

officers of the executive department[1] or of such other body as Congress may by law provide, transmit within four days to the President pro tempore of the Senate and the Speaker of the House of Representatives their written declaration that the President is unable to discharge the powers and duties of his office. Thereupon Congress shall decide the issue, assembling within forty-eight hours for that purpose if not in session. If the Congress, within twenty-one days after receipt of the latter written declaration, or, if Congress is not in session, within twenty-one days after Congress is required to assemble, determines by two-thirds vote of both Houses that the President is unable to discharge the powers and duties of his office, the Vice President shall continue to discharge the same as Acting President; otherwise, the President shall resume the powers and duties of his office.

1. **Editor's note:** So in original. Probably should be "departments."

[AMENDMENT 26.] (1971)

Section 1. The right of citizens of the United States, who are eighteen years of age or older, to vote shall not be denied or abridged by the United States or by any State on account of age.

Section 2. The Congress shall have power to enforce this article by appropriate legislation.

[AMENDMENT 27.] (1992)

No law, varying the compensation for the services of the Senators and Representatives, shall take effect, until an election of representatives shall have intervened.

CONVENTION ON THE SERVICE ABROAD OF JUDICIAL & EXTRAJUDICIAL DOCUMENTS IN CIVIL OR COMMERCIAL MATTERS

(Concluded 15 November 1965)

The States signatory to the present Convention,

Desiring to create appropriate means to ensure that judicial and extrajudicial documents to be served abroad shall be brought to the notice of the addressee in sufficient time,

Desiring to improve the organisation of mutual judicial assistance for that purpose by simplifying and expediting the procedure,

Have resolved to conclude a Convention to this effect and have agreed upon the following provisions:

ARTICLE 1

The present Convention shall apply in all cases, in civil or commercial matters, where there is occasion to transmit a judicial or extrajudicial document for service abroad.

This Convention shall not apply where the address of the person to be served with the document is not known.

CHAPTER I. JUDICIAL DOCUMENTS

ARTICLE 2

Each Contracting State shall designate a Central Authority which will undertake to receive requests for service coming from other Contracting States and to proceed in conformity with the provisions of Articles 3 to 6.

Each State shall organise the Central Authority in conformity with its own law.

ARTICLE 3

The authority or judicial officer competent under the law of the State in which the documents originate shall forward to the Central Authority of the State addressed a request conforming to the model annexed to the present Convention, without any requirement of legalisation or other equivalent formality.

The document to be served or a copy thereof shall be annexed to the request. The request and the document shall both be furnished in duplicate.

ARTICLE 4

If the Central Authority considers that the request does not comply with the provisions of the present Convention it shall promptly inform the applicant and specify its objections to the request.

ARTICLE 5

The Central Authority of the State addressed shall itself serve the document or shall arrange to have it served by an appropriate agency, either—

(a) by a method prescribed by its internal law for the service of documents in domestic actions upon persons who are within its territory, or

(b) by a particular method requested by the applicant, unless such a method is incompatible with the law of the State addressed.

Subject to sub-paragraph (b) of the first paragraph of this Article, the document may always be served by delivery to an addressee who accepts it voluntarily.

If the document is to be served under the first paragraph above, the Central Authority may require the document to be written in, or translated into, the official language or one of the official languages of the State addressed.

That part of the request, in the form attached to the present Convention, which contains a summary of the document to be served, shall be served with the document.

ARTICLE 6

The Central Authority of the State addressed or any authority which it may have designated for that purpose, shall complete a certificate in the form of the model annexed to the present Convention.

The certificate shall state that the document has been served and shall include the method, the place and the date of service and the person to whom the document was delivered. If the document has not been served, the certificate shall set out the reasons which have prevented service.

The applicant may require that a certificate not completed by a Central Authority or by a judicial authority shall be countersigned by one of these authorities.

The certificate shall be forwarded directly to the applicant.

ARTICLE 7

The standard terms in the model annexed to the present Convention shall in all cases be written either in French or in English. They may also be written in the official language, or in one of the official languages, of the State in which the documents originate.

The corresponding blanks shall be completed either in the language of the State addressed or in French or in English.

ARTICLE 8

Each Contracting State shall be free to effect service of judicial documents upon persons abroad, without application of any compulsion, directly through its diplomatic or consular agents.

Any State may declare that it is opposed to such service within its territory, unless the document is to be served upon a national of the State in which the documents originate.

ARTICLE 9

Each Contracting State shall be free, in addition, to use consular channels to forward documents, for the purpose of service, to those authorities of another Contracting State which are designated by the latter for this purpose.

Each Contracting State may, if exceptional circumstances so require, use diplomatic channels for the same purpose.

ARTICLE 10

Provided the State of destination does not object, the present Convention shall not interfere with—

(a) the freedom to send judicial documents, by postal channels, directly to persons abroad,

(b) the freedom of judicial officers, officials or other competent persons of the State of origin to effect service of judicial documents directly through the judicial officers, officials or other competent persons of the State of destination,

(c) the freedom of any person interested in a judicial proceeding to effect service of judicial documents directly through the judicial officers, officials or other competent persons of the State of destination.

ARTICLE 11

The present Convention shall not prevent two or more Contracting States from agreeing to permit, for the purpose of service of judicial documents, channels of transmission other than those provided for in the preceding Articles and, in particular, direct communication between their respective authorities.

ARTICLE 12

The service of judicial documents coming from a Contracting State shall not give rise to any payment or reimbursement of taxes or costs for the services rendered by the State addressed.

The applicant shall pay or reimburse the costs occasioned by—

(a) the employment of a judicial officer or of a person competent under the law of the State of destination,

(b) the use of a particular method of service.

ARTICLE 13

Where a request for service complies with the terms of the present Convention, the State addressed may refuse to comply therewith only if it deems that compliance would infringe its sovereignty or security.

It may not refuse to comply solely on the ground that, under its internal law, it claims exclusive jurisdiction over the subject-matter of the action or that its internal law would not permit the action upon which the application is based.

The Central Authority shall, in case of refusal, promptly inform the applicant and state the reasons for the refusal.

ARTICLE 14

Difficulties which may arise in connection with the transmission of judicial documents for service shall be settled through diplomatic channels.

ARTICLE 15

Where a writ of summons or an equivalent document had to be transmitted abroad for the purpose of service, under the provisions of the present Convention, and the defendant has not appeared, judgment shall not be given until it is established that—

(a) the document was served by a method prescribed by the internal law of the State addressed for the service of documents in domestic actions upon persons who are within its territory, or

(b) the document was actually delivered to the defendant or to his residence by another method provided for by this Convention,

and that in either of these cases the service or the delivery was effected in sufficient time to enable the defendant to defend.

Each Contracting State shall be free to declare that the judge, notwithstanding the provisions of the first paragraph of this Article, may give judgment even if no certificate of service or delivery has been received, if all the following conditions are fulfilled—

(a) the document was transmitted by one of the methods provided for in this Convention,

(b) a period of time of not less than six months, considered adequate by the judge in the particular case, has elapsed since the date of the transmission of the document,

(c) no certificate of any kind has been received, even though every reasonable effort has been made to obtain it through the competent authorities of the State addressed.

Notwithstanding the provisions of the preceding paragraphs the judge may order, in case of urgency, any provisional or protective measures.

ARTICLE 16

When a writ of summons or an equivalent document had to be transmitted abroad for the purpose of service, under the provisions of the present Convention, and a judgment has been entered against a defendant who has not appeared, the judge shall have the power to relieve the defendant from the effects of the expiration of the time for appeal from the judgment if the following conditions are fulfilled—

(a) the defendant, without any fault on his part, did not have knowledge of the document in sufficient time to defend, or knowledge of the judgment in sufficient time to appeal, and

(b) the defendant has disclosed a prima facie defence to the action on the merits.

An application for relief may be filed only within a reasonable time after the defendant has knowledge of the judgment.

Each Contracting State may declare that the application will not be entertained if it is filed after the expiration of a time to be stated in the declaration, but which shall in no case be less than one year following the date of the judgment.

This Article shall not apply to judgments concerning status or capacity of persons.

CHAPTER II. EXTRAJUDICIAL DOCUMENTS

ARTICLE 17

Extrajudicial documents emanating from authorities and judicial officers of a Contracting State may be transmitted for the purpose of service in another Contracting State by the methods and under the provisions of the present Convention.

CHAPTER III. GENERAL CLAUSES

Article 18

Each Contracting State may designate other authorities in addition to the Central Authority and shall determine the extent of their competence.

The applicant shall, however, in all cases, have the right to address a request directly to the Central Authority.

Federal States shall be free to designate more than one Central Authority.

Article 19

To the extent that the internal law of a Contracting State permits methods of transmission, other than those provided for in the preceding Articles, of documents coming from abroad, for service within its territory, the present Convention shall not affect such provisions.

Article 20

The present Convention shall not prevent an agreement between any two or more Contracting States to dispense with—

(a) the necessity for duplicate copies of transmitted documents as required by the second paragraph of Article 3,

(b) the language requirements of the third paragraph of Article 5 and Article 7,

(c) the provisions of the fourth paragraph of Article 5,

(d) the provisions of the second paragraph of Article 12.

Article 21

Each Contracting State shall, at the time of the deposit of its instrument of ratification or accession, or at a later date, inform the Ministry of Foreign Affairs of the Netherlands of the following—

(a) the designation of authorities, pursuant to Articles 2 and 18,

(b) the designation of the authority competent to complete the certificate pursuant to Article 6,

(c) the designation of the authority competent to receive documents transmitted by consular channels, pursuant to Article 9.

Each Contracting State shall similarly inform the Ministry, where appropriate, of—

(a) opposition to the use of methods of transmission pursuant to Articles 8 and 10,

(b) declarations pursuant to the second paragraph of Article 15 and the third paragraph of Article 16,

(c) all modifications of the above designations, oppositions and declarations.

Article 22

Where Parties to the present Convention are also Parties to one or both of the Conventions on civil procedure signed at The Hague on 17th July 1905 [99 BFSP 990], and on 1st March 1954 [286 UNTS 265], this Convention shall replace as between them Articles 1 to 7 of the earlier Conventions.

Article 23

The present Convention shall not affect the application of Article 23 of the Convention on civil procedure signed at The Hague on 17th July 1905, or of Article 24 of the Convention on civil procedure signed at The Hague on 1st March 1954.

These Articles shall, however, apply only if methods of communication, identical to those provided for in these Conventions, are used.

Article 24

Supplementary agreements between Parties to the Conventions of 1905 and 1954 shall be considered as equally applicable to the present Convention, unless the Parties have otherwise agreed.

Article 25

Without prejudice to the provisions of Articles 22 and 24, the present Convention shall not derogate from Conventions containing provisions on the matters governed by this Convention to which the Contracting States are, or shall become, Parties.

Article 26

The present Convention shall be open for signature by the States represented at the Tenth Session of the Hague Conference on Private International Law.

It shall be ratified, and the instruments of ratification shall be deposited with the Ministry of Foreign Affairs of the Netherlands.

Article 27

The present Convention shall enter into force on the sixtieth day after the deposit of the third instrument of ratification referred to in the second paragraph of Article 26.

The Convention shall enter into force for each signatory State which ratifies subsequently on the sixtieth day after the deposit of its instrument of ratification.

Article 28

Any State not represented at the Tenth Session of the Hague Conference on Private International Law may accede to the present Convention after it has entered into force in accordance with the first paragraph of Article 27. The instrument of accession shall be deposited with the Ministry of Foreign Affairs of the Netherlands.

The Convention shall enter into force for such a State in the absence of any objection from a State, which has ratified the Convention before such deposit, notified to the Ministry of Foreign Affairs of the Netherlands within a period of six months after the date on which the said Ministry has notified it of such accession.

In the absence of any such objection, the Convention shall enter into force for the acceding State on the first day of the month following the expiration of the last of the periods referred to in the preceding paragraph.

ARTICLE 29

Any State may, at the time of signature, ratification or accession, declare that the present Convention shall extend to all the territories for the international relations of which it is responsible, or to one or more of them. Such a declaration shall take effect on the date of entry into force of the Convention for the State concerned.

At any time thereafter, such extensions shall be notified to the Ministry of Foreign Affairs of the Netherlands.

The Convention shall enter into force for the territories mentioned in such an extension on the sixtieth day after the notification referred to in the preceding paragraph.

ARTICLE 30

The present Convention shall remain in force for five years from the date of its entry into force in accordance with the first paragraph of Article 27, even for States which have ratified it or acceded to it subsequently.

If there has been no denunciation, it shall be renewed tacitly every five years.

Any denunciation shall be notified to the Ministry of Foreign Affairs of the Netherlands at least six months before the end of the five year period.

It may be limited to certain of the territories to which the Convention applies.

The denunciation shall have effect only as regards the State which has notified it. The Convention shall remain in force for the other Contracting States.

ARTICLE 31

The Ministry of Foreign Affairs of the Netherlands shall give notice to the States referred to in Article 26, and to the States which have acceded in accordance with Article 28, of the following—

(a) the signatures and ratifications referred to in Article 26;

(b) the date on which the present Convention enters into force in accordance with the first paragraph of Article 27;

(c) the accessions referred to in Article 28 and the dates on which they take effect;

(d) the extensions referred to in Article 29 and the dates on which they take effect;

(e) the designations, oppositions and declarations referred to in Article 21;

(f) the denunciations referred to in the third paragraph of Article 30.

IN WITNESS WHEREOF the undersigned, being duly authorised thereto, have signed the present Convention.

DONE at The Hague, on the 15th day of November, 1965, in the English and French languages, both texts being equally authentic, in a single copy which shall be deposited in the archives of the Government of the Netherlands, and of which a certified copy shall be sent, through the diplomatic channel, to each of the States represented at the Tenth Session of the Hague Conference on Private International Law.

[SIGNATURES OMITTED.]

Entered into force for the United States February 10, 1969, 20 UST 361; TIAS 6638; 658 UNTS 163.

Editor's note: *The following are contracting states to the Hague Convention on Service Abroad as of November 1, 2012. Because the Hague Convention allows a contracting state to modify or object to articles of the Convention, a party seeking to enforce service in that state should consult the website of the Hague Conference on Private International Law, www.hcch.net, to determine how that state applies the Convention.*

Albania, Antigua & Barbuda, Argentina, Armenia,[1] Australia, Bahamas, Barbados, Belarus, Belgium, Belize, Bosnia and Herzegovina, Botswana, Bulgaria, Canada, China (People's Republic of), Croatia, Cyprus, Czech Republic, Denmark, Egypt, Estonia, Finland, France, Germany, Greece, Hungary, Iceland, India, Ireland, Israel, Italy, Japan, Korea (Republic of), Kuwait, Latvia, Lithuania, Luxembourg, Malawi, Malta, Mexico, Monaco, Moldova (Republic of),[2] Montenegro, Morocco, Netherlands, Norway, Pakistan, Poland, Portugal, Romania, Russian Federation, Saint Vincent & the Grenadines, San Marino, Serbia, Seychelles, Slovakia, Slovenia, Spain, Sri Lanka, Sweden, Switzerland, the former Yugoslav Republic of Macedonia, Turkey, Ukraine, United Kingdom of Great Britain & Northern Ireland, United States of America, and Venezuela.

Editor's note: *The Annex to the Convention: Active Model Forms (Request, Certificate, Summary) are available on the website of the Hague Conference on Private International Law, www.hcch.net.*

1. **Editor's note:** This state acceded to the Convention on June 27, 2012, and it is scheduled to enter the Convention into force on February 1, 2013.

2. **Editor's note:** This state acceded to the Convention on July 4, 2012, and it is scheduled to enter the Convention into force on February 1, 2013.

See *Commentaries*, "Serving Process Abroad," ch. 2-H, §6, p. 156.
See also FRCP 4(f) (foreign process generally).

CONVENTION ON THE TAKING OF EVIDENCE ABROAD IN CIVIL OR COMMERCIAL MATTERS

(Concluded 18 March 1970)

The States signatory to the present Convention,

Desiring to facilitate the transmission and execution of Letters of Request and to further the accommodation of the different methods which they use for this purpose,

Desiring to improve mutual judicial co-operation in civil or commercial matters,

Have resolved to conclude a Convention to this effect and have agreed upon the following provisions:

CHAPTER I. LETTERS OF REQUEST

ARTICLE 1

In civil or commercial matters a judicial authority of a Contracting State may, in accordance with the provisions of the law of that State, request the competent authority of another Contracting State, by means of a Letter of Request, to obtain evidence, or to perform some other judicial act.

A Letter shall not be used to obtain evidence which is not intended for use in judicial proceedings, commenced or contemplated.

The expression "other judicial act" does not cover the service of judicial documents or the issuance of any process by which judgments or orders are executed or enforced, or orders for provisional or protective measures.

ARTICLE 2

A Contracting State shall designate a Central Authority which will undertake to receive Letters of Request coming from a judicial authority of another Contracting State and to transmit them to the authority competent to execute them. Each State shall organise the Central Authority in accordance with its own law.

Letters shall be sent to the Central Authority of the State of execution without being transmitted through any other authority of that State.

ARTICLE 3

A Letter of Request shall specify—

(a) the authority requesting its execution and the authority requested to execute it, if known to the requesting authority;

(b) the names and addresses of the parties to the proceedings and their representatives, if any;

(c) the nature of the proceedings for which the evidence is required, giving all necessary information in regard thereto;

(d) the evidence to be obtained or other judicial act to be performed.

Where appropriate, the Letter shall specify, inter alia—

(e) the names and addresses of the persons to be examined;

(f) the questions to be put to the persons to be examined or a statement of the subject-matter about which they are to be examined;

(g) the documents or other property, real or personal, to be inspected;

(h) any requirement that the evidence is to be given on oath or affirmation, and any special form to be used;

(i) any special method or procedure to be followed under Article 9.

A Letter may also mention any information necessary for the application of Article 11.

No legalisation or other like formality may be required.

ARTICLE 4

A Letter of Request shall be in the language of the authority requested to execute it or be accompanied by a translation into that language.

Nevertheless, a Contracting State shall accept a Letter in either English or French, or a translation into one of these languages, unless it has made the reservation authorised by Article 33.

A Contracting State which has more than one official language and cannot, for reasons of internal law, accept Letters in one of these languages for the whole of its territory, shall, by declaration, specify the language in which the Letter or translation thereof shall be expressed for execution in the specified parts of its territory. In case of failure to comply with this declaration, without justifiable excuse, the costs of translation into the required language shall be borne by the State of origin.

A Contracting State may, by declaration, specify the language or languages other than those referred to in the preceding paragraphs, in which a Letter may be sent to its Central Authority.

Any translation accompanying a Letter shall be certified as correct, either by a diplomatic officer or consular agent or by a sworn translator or by any other person so authorised in either State.

ARTICLE 5

If the Central Authority considers that the request does not comply with the provisions of the present Convention, it shall promptly inform the authority of the State of origin which transmitted the Letter of Request, specifying the objections to the Letter.

ARTICLE 6

If the authority to whom a Letter of Request has been transmitted is not competent to execute it, the Letter shall be sent forthwith to the authority in the same State which is competent to execute it in accordance with the provisions of its own law.

ARTICLE 7

The requesting authority shall, if it so desires, be informed of the time when, and the place where, the proceedings will take place, in order that the parties concerned, and their representatives, if any, may be present. This information shall be sent directly to the parties or their representatives when the authority of the State of origin so requests.

ARTICLE 8

A Contracting State may declare that members of the judicial personnel of the requesting authority of another Contracting State may be present at the execution of a Letter of Request. Prior authorisation by the competent authority designated by the declaring State may be required.

ARTICLE 9

The judicial authority which executes a Letter of Request shall apply its own law as to the methods and procedures to be followed.

However, it will follow a request of the requesting authority that a special method or procedure be followed, unless this is incompatible with the internal law of the State of execution or is impossible of performance by reason of its internal practice and procedure or by reason of practical difficulties.

A Letter of Request shall be executed expeditiously.

ARTICLE 10

In executing a Letter of Request the requested authority shall apply the appropriate measures of compulsion in the instances and to the same extent as are provided by its internal law for the execution of orders issued by the authorities of its own country or of requests made by parties in internal proceedings.

ARTICLE 11

In the execution of a Letter of Request the person concerned may refuse to give evidence in so far as he has a privilege or duty to refuse to give the evidence—

(a) under the law of the State of execution; or

(b) under the law of the State of origin, and the privilege or duty has been specified in the Letter, or, at the instance of the requested authority, has been otherwise confirmed to that authority by the requesting authority.

A Contracting State may declare that, in addition, it will respect privileges and duties existing under the law of States other than the State of origin and the State of execution, to the extent specified in that declaration.

ARTICLE 12

The execution of a Letter of Request may be refused only to the extent that—

(a) in the State of execution the execution of the Letter does not fall within the functions of the judiciary; or

(b) the State addressed considers that its sovereignty or security would be prejudiced thereby.

Execution may not be refused solely on the ground that under its internal law the State of execution claims exclusive jurisdiction over the subject-matter of the action or that its internal law would not admit a right of action on it.

ARTICLE 13

The documents establishing the execution of the Letter of Request shall be sent by the requested authority to the requesting authority by the same channel which was used by the latter.

In every instance where the Letter is not executed in whole or in part, the requesting authority shall be informed immediately through the same channel and advised of the reasons.

ARTICLE 14

The execution of the Letter of Request shall not give rise to any reimbursement of taxes or costs of any nature.

Nevertheless, the State of execution has the right to require the State of origin to reimburse the fees paid to experts and interpreters and the costs occasioned by the use of a special procedure requested by the State of origin under Article 9, paragraph 2.

The requested authority whose law obliges the parties themselves to secure evidence, and which is not able itself to execute the Letter, may, after having obtained the consent of the requesting authority, appoint a suitable person to do so. When seeking this consent the requested authority shall indicate the approximate costs which would result from this procedure. If the requesting authority gives its consent it shall reimburse any costs incurred; without such consent the requesting authority shall not be liable for the costs.

CHAPTER II. TAKING OF EVIDENCE BY DIPLOMATIC OFFICERS, CONSULAR AGENTS & COMMISSIONERS

ARTICLE 15

In a civil or commercial matter, a diplomatic officer or consular agent of a Contracting State may, in the territory of another Contracting State and within the area where he exercises his functions, take the evidence without compulsion of nationals of a State which he represents in aid of proceedings commenced in the courts of a State which he represents.

A Contracting State may declare that evidence may be taken by a diplomatic officer or consular agent only if permission to that effect is given upon application made by him or on his behalf to the appropriate authority designated by the declaring State.

ARTICLE 16

A diplomatic officer or consular agent of a Contracting State may, in the territory of another Contracting State and within the area where he exercises his functions, also take the evidence, without compulsion, of nationals of the State in which he exercises his functions or of a third State, in aid of proceedings commenced in the courts of a State which he represents, if—

(a) a competent authority designated by the State in which he exercises his functions has given its permission either generally or in the particular case, and

(b) he complies with the conditions which the competent authority has specified in the permission.

A Contracting State may declare that evidence may be taken under this Article without its prior permission.

ARTICLE 17

In a civil or commercial matter, a person duly appointed as a commissioner for the purpose may, without compulsion, take evidence in the territory of a Contracting State in aid of proceedings commenced in the courts of another Contracting State if—

(a) a competent authority designated by the State where the evidence is to be taken has given its permission either generally or in the particular case; and

(b) he complies with the conditions which the competent authority has specified in the permission.

A Contracting State may declare that evidence may be taken under this Article without its prior permission.

ARTICLE 18

A Contracting State may declare that a diplomatic officer, consular agent or commissioner authorised to take evidence under Articles 15, 16 or 17, may apply to the competent authority designated by the declaring State for appropriate assistance to obtain the evidence by compulsion. The declaration may contain such conditions as the declaring State may see fit to impose.

If the authority grants the application it shall apply any measures of compulsion which are appropriate and are prescribed by its law for use in internal proceedings.

ARTICLE 19

The competent authority, in giving the permission referred to in Articles 15, 16 or 17, or in granting the application referred to in Article 18, may lay down such conditions as it deems fit, inter alia, as to the time and place of the taking of the evidence. Similarly it may require that it be given reasonable advance notice of the time, date and place of the taking of the evidence; in such a case a representative of the authority shall be entitled to be present at the taking of the evidence.

ARTICLE 20

In the taking of evidence under any Article of this Chapter persons concerned may be legally represented.

ARTICLE 21

Where a diplomatic officer, consular agent or commissioner is authorised under Articles 15, 16 or 17 to take evidence—

(a) he may take all kinds of evidence which are not incompatible with the law of the State where the evidence is taken or contrary to any permission granted pursuant to the above Articles, and shall have power within such limits to administer an oath or take an affirmation;

(b) a request to a person to appear or to give evidence shall, unless the recipient is a national of the State where the action is pending, be drawn up in the language of the place where the evidence is taken or be accompanied by a translation into such language;

(c) the request shall inform the person that he may be legally represented and, in any State that has not filed a declaration under Article 18, shall also inform him that he is not compelled to appear or to give evidence;

(d) the evidence may be taken in the manner provided by the law applicable to the court in which the action is pending provided that such manner is not forbidden by the law of the State where the evidence is taken;

(e) a person requested to give evidence may invoke the privileges and duties to refuse to give the evidence contained in Article 11.

ARTICLE 22

The fact that an attempt to take evidence under the procedure laid down in this Chapter has failed, owing to the refusal of a person to give evidence, shall not prevent an application being subsequently made to take the evidence in accordance with Chapter I.

CHAPTER III. GENERAL CLAUSES

ARTICLE 23

A Contracting State may at the time of signature, ratification or accession, declare that it will not execute Letters of Request issued for the purpose of obtaining pre-trial discovery of documents as known in Common Law countries.

ARTICLE 24

A Contracting State may designate other authorities in addition to the Central Authority and shall determine the extent of their competence. However, Letters of Request may in all cases be sent to the Central Authority.

Federal States shall be free to designate more than one Central Authority.

ARTICLE 25

A Contracting State which has more than one legal system may designate the authorities of one of such systems, which shall have exclusive competence to execute Letters of Request pursuant to this Convention.

ARTICLE 26

A Contracting State, if required to do so because of constitutional limitations, may request the reimbursement by the State of origin of fees and costs, in connection with the execution of Letters of Request, for the service of process necessary to compel the appearance of a person to give evidence, the costs of attendance of such persons, and the cost of any transcript of the evidence.

Where a State has made a request pursuant to the above paragraph, any other Contracting State may request from that State the reimbursement of similar fees and costs.

ARTICLE 27

The provisions of the present Convention shall not prevent a Contracting State from—

(a) declaring that Letters of Request may be transmitted to its judicial authorities through channels other than those provided for in Article 2;

(b) permitting, by internal law or practice, any act provided for in this Convention to be performed upon less restrictive conditions;

(c) permitting, by internal law or practice, methods of taking evidence other than those provided for in this Convention.

ARTICLE 28

The present Convention shall not prevent an agreement between any two or more Contracting States to derogate from—

(a) the provisions of Article 2 with respect to methods of transmitting Letters of Request;

(b) the provisions of Article 4 with respect to the languages which may be used;

(c) the provisions of Article 8 with respect to the presence of judicial personnel at the execution of Letters;

(d) the provisions of Article 11 with respect to the privileges and duties of witnesses to refuse to give evidence;

(e) the provisions of Article 13 with respect to the methods of returning executed Letters to the requesting authority;

(f) the provisions of Article 14 with respect to fees and costs;

(g) the provisions of Chapter II.

ARTICLE 29

Between Parties to the present Convention who are also Parties to one or both of the Conventions on Civil Procedure signed at The Hague on the 17th of July 1905 and the 1st of March 1954, this Convention shall replace Articles 8-16 of the earlier Conventions.

ARTICLE 30

The present Convention shall not affect the application of Article 23 of the Convention of 1905, or of Article 24 of the Convention of 1954.

ARTICLE 31

Supplementary Agreements between Parties to the Conventions of 1905 and 1954 shall be considered as equally applicable to the present Convention unless the Parties have otherwise agreed.

ARTICLE 32

Without prejudice to the provisions of Articles 29 and 31, the present Convention shall not derogate from conventions containing provisions on the matters covered by this Convention to which the Contracting States are, or shall become Parties.

ARTICLE 33

A State may, at the time of signature, ratification or accession exclude, in whole or in part, the application of the provisions of paragraph 2 of Article 4 and of Chapter II. No other reservation shall be permitted.

Each Contracting State may at any time withdraw a reservation it has made; the reservation shall cease to have effect on the sixtieth day after notification of the withdrawal.

When a State has made a reservation, any other State affected thereby may apply the same rule against the reserving State.

ARTICLE 34

A State may at any time withdraw or modify a declaration.

ARTICLE 35

A Contracting State shall, at the time of the deposit of its instrument of ratification or accession, or at a later date, inform the Ministry of Foreign Affairs of the Netherlands of the designation of authorities, pursuant to Articles 2, 8, 24 and 25.

A Contracting State shall likewise inform the Ministry, where appropriate, of the following—

(a) the designation of the authorities to whom notice must be given, whose permission may be required, and whose assistance may be invoked in the taking of evidence by diplomatic officers and consular agents, pursuant to Articles 15, 16 and 18 respectively;

(b) the designation of the authorities whose permission may be required in the taking of evidence by commissioners pursuant to Article 17 and of those who may grant the assistance provided for in Article 18;

(c) declarations pursuant to Articles 4, 8, 11, 15, 16, 17, 18, 23 and 27;

(d) any withdrawal or modification of the above designations and declarations;

(e) the withdrawal of any reservation.

ARTICLE 36

Any difficulties which may arise between Contracting States in connection with the operation of this Convention shall be settled through diplomatic channels.

ARTICLE 37

The present Convention shall be open for signature by the States represented at the Eleventh Session of the Hague Conference on Private International Law.

It shall be ratified, and the instruments of ratification shall be deposited with the Ministry of Foreign Affairs of the Netherlands.

ARTICLE 38

The present Convention shall enter into force on the sixtieth day after the deposit of the third instrument of ratification referred to in the second paragraph of Article 37.

The Convention shall enter into force for each signatory State which ratifies subsequently on the sixtieth day after the deposit of its instrument of ratification.

ARTICLE 39

Any State not represented at the Eleventh Session of the Hague Conference on Private International Law which is a Member of this Conference or of the United Nations or of a specialised agency of that Organisation, or a Party to the Statute of the International Court of Justice may accede to the present Convention after it has entered into force in accordance with the first paragraph of Article 38.

The instrument of accession shall be deposited with the Ministry of Foreign Affairs of the Netherlands.

The Convention shall enter into force for a State acceding to it on the sixtieth day after the deposit of its instrument of accession.

The accession will have effect only as regards the relations between the acceding State and such Contracting States as will have declared their acceptance of the accession. Such declaration shall be deposited at the Ministry of Foreign Affairs of the Netherlands; this Ministry shall forward, through diplomatic channels, a certified copy to each of the Contracting States.

The Convention will enter into force as between the acceding State and the State that has declared its acceptance of the accession on the sixtieth day after the deposit of the declaration of acceptance.

ARTICLE 40

Any State may, at the time of signature, ratification or accession, declare that the present Convention shall extend to all the territories for the international relations of which it is responsible, or to one or more of them. Such a declaration shall take effect on the date of entry into force of the Convention for the State concerned.

At any time thereafter, such extensions shall be notified to the Ministry of Foreign Affairs of the Netherlands.

The Convention shall enter into force for the territories mentioned in such an extension on the sixtieth day after the notification indicated in the preceding paragraph.

ARTICLE 41

The present Convention shall remain in force for five years from the date of its entry into force in accordance with the first paragraph of Article 38, even for States which have ratified it or acceded to it subsequently.

If there has been no denunciation, it shall be renewed tacitly every five years.

Any denunciation shall be notified to the Ministry of Foreign Affairs of the Netherlands at least six months before the end of the five year period.

It may be limited to certain of the territories to which the Convention applies.

The denunciation shall have effect only as regards the State which has notified it. The Convention shall remain in force for the other Contracting States.

ARTICLE 42

The Ministry of Foreign Affairs of the Netherlands shall give notice to the States referred to in Article 37, and to the States which have acceded in accordance with Article 39, of the following—

(a) the signatures and ratifications referred to in Article 37;

(b) the date on which the present Convention enters into force in accordance with the first paragraph of Article 38;

(c) the accessions referred to in Article 39 and the dates on which they take effect;

(d) the extensions referred to in Article 40 and the dates on which they take effect;

(e) the designations, reservations and declarations referred to in Articles 33 and 35;

(f) the denunciations referred to in the third paragraph of Article 41.

IN WITNESS WHEREOF the undersigned, being duly authorised thereto, have signed the present Convention.

DONE at The Hague, on the 18th day of March, 1970, in the English and French languages, both texts being equally authentic, in a single copy which shall be deposited in the archives of the Government of the Netherlands, and of which a certified copy shall be sent, through the diplomatic channel, to each of the States represented at the Eleventh Session of the Hague Conference on Private International Law.

[SIGNATURES OMITTED.]

Entered into force for the United States October 7, 1972, 23 UST 2555; TIAS 7444; 847 UNTS 231.

Editor's note: *The following are contracting states to the Hague Convention on the Taking of Evidence Abroad as of November 1, 2012. Because the Hague Convention allows a contracting state to modify or object to articles of the Convention, a party seeking to take evidence in that state should consult the website of the Hague Conference on Private International Law, www.hcch.net, to determine how that state applies the Convention.*

Albania, Argentina, Armenia, Australia, Barbados, Belarus, Bosnia and Herzegovina, Bulgaria, China (People's Republic of), Colombia, Croatia, Cyprus, Czech Republic, Denmark, Estonia, Finland, France, Germany, Greece, Hungary, Iceland, India, Israel, Italy, Korea (Republic of), Kuwait, Latvia, Liechtenstein, Lithuania, Luxembourg, Malta, Mexico, Monaco, Montenegro, Morocco, Netherlands, Norway, Poland, Portugal, Romania, Russian Federation, Serbia, Seychelles, Singapore, Slovakia, Slovenia, South Africa, Spain, Sri Lanka, Sweden, Switzerland, the former Yugoslav Republic of Macedonia, Turkey, Ukraine, United Kingdom of Great Britain and Northern Ireland, United States of America, and Venezuela.

See ***Commentaries***, "In foreign country," ch. 6-F, §3.3.2(1), p. 544.

See also 28 U.S.C. §1781 (transmittal of letter rogatory or request).

TIMETABLES

TABLE OF CONTENTS

1. **PLEADINGS & PRETRIAL-MOTIONS SCHEDULE 1574**
2. **PRETRIAL DISCLOSURES & CONFERENCES 1577**
3. **DISCOVERY STATUS SHEET 1579**
4. **REMOVAL & REMAND 1581**
5. **TEMPORARY RESTRAINING ORDER & INJUNCTION 1583**
6. **REQUEST TO CLERK FOR DEFAULT JUDGMENT 1586**
7. **MOTION TO COURT FOR DEFAULT JUDGMENT 1587**
8. **SUMMARY JUDGMENT 1589**
9. **APPEAL OF CIVIL TRIAL 1591**

TIMETABLES

1. PLEADINGS & PRETRIAL-MOTIONS SCHEDULE

STEP	ACTION	RULE	DEADLINE	DUE	FILED
1	Plaintiff files complaint (if requesting TRO, see "TRO & Injunction," timetable 5). FORMS 2B	FRCP 3	Before statute of limitations expires		
2	Jury demand by either party. FORM 5C:1	FRCP 38(b)	Anytime after Step 1, but no later than 14 days after service of last pleading directed to issue that is triable by jury		
3	Plaintiff notifies defendant of lawsuit and requests that defendant waive service. FORM 2H:1	FRCP 4(d)(1)	Immediately after Step 1		
4	Defendant returns waiver of service. FORM 2H:2	FRCP 4(d)(1)(F)	If defendant is in U.S., at least 30 days after Step 3; If defendant is outside U.S., at least 60 days after Step 3		
5	Defendant refuses to waive service	FRCP 4(d)(1)(F)	After Step 3		
6	Plaintiff presents summons to clerk. FFCiv 3	FRCP 4(b)	As soon as possible after Step 1; or after Step 5		
7	Plaintiff furnishes summons and complaint to person who makes service. FFCiv 3	FRCP 4(c)	After Step 6		
8	Defendant is served with summons and complaint	FRCP 4(c), (f), (j)(1), (m)	If defendant is in U.S., Step 1 + 120 days ❶; If defendant is outside U.S., Step 1 + time limit provided in international agreement		
9	Plaintiff files motion to collect expenses of service if defendant is in U.S. (if necessary)	FRCP 4(d)(2)	After Step 8		
10	Plaintiff files proof of service and affidavit (if necessary) with court	FRCP 4(*l*)(1)	As soon as possible after Step 8		
11	Defendant files answer or FRCP 12(b) motion. FORMS 3B-3D, 3F, 3G, 3I, 3L	FRCP 4(d)(3), 12(a)	Step 8 + 21 days; If U.S. is a defendant, Step 8 + 60 days; If defendant is in U.S. and waives service, Step 3 + 60 days; If defendant is outside U.S. and waives service, Step 3 + 90 days; If FRCP 12(b) motion is filed, answer due 14 days after FRCP 12(b) motion is denied or postponed		

❶ If the plaintiff needs additional time to complete service of the complaint and summons on a defendant that is in the United States, FRCP 4(m) requires the court to extend the time if the plaintiff shows good cause and permits the court to extend the time even if the plaintiff does not show good cause. See "Motion to extend time to serve party," ch. 5-F, §4.3, p. 334.

1. PLEADINGS & PRETRIAL-MOTIONS SCHEDULE (CONT'D)

STEP	ACTION	RULE	DEADLINE	DUE	FILED
12	Plaintiff files request for entry of default (see timetable 6 or 7). FORMS 7A	FRCP 55(a)	Immediately after Step 11 if defendant has not filed answer or otherwise defended		
13	Either party adds or drops a party. FORMS 5L	FRCP 21	No deadline		
14	Plaintiff amends proof of service	FRCP 4(*l*)(3)	No deadline—at court's discretion		
15	Motion to intervene. FORMS 5J	FRCP 24(a), (b)	On timely motion		
16	Motion to substitute party	FRCP 25(a)(1)	90 days after service of statement noting death of party		
17	Motion for leave to file supplemental pleadings	FRCP 15(d)	On reasonable notice		
18	Amend pleadings. FORMS 5I	FRCP 15(a)(1), (2)	Once as a matter of course (1) 21 days after serving the pleading or (2) if the pleading requires a responsive pleading, whichever is earlier: 21 days after service of the responsive pleading or a motion under FRCP 12(b), (e), or (f); otherwise, with opposing party's written consent or court's leave		
19	Response to amended pleadings. FORM 5I:2	FRCP 15(a)(3)	Whichever is later: within the time remaining to respond to original pleading or 14 days after service of amended pleading ❷		
20	Movant files and serves MSJ (see "Summary Judgment," timetable 8). FORMS 7B	FRCP 56(b)	Anytime until 30 days after the close of all discovery ❸		
21	Trial setting	*See* FRCP 40	As set by local rules		
22	Motion in limine. FORMS 5H	Determined by local rule	Filed before pretrial conference; presented for ruling at pretrial conference but no later than voir dire		
23	Plaintiff's voluntary dismissal. FORMS 7C	FRCP 41(a)	Anytime before Step 11 or 20, whichever is first; by stipulation signed by all parties who have appeared; or by court order		
24	Offer of proof. FORMS 8E	FRE 103	Immediately after evidence excluded		
25	Trial	FRCP 39			

❷ The court may order a deadline for the response that is different from the deadlines provided by the rule. FRCP 15(a)(3).

❸ The deadline for an MSJ may be different under court order or local rule. FRCP 56(b).

1. PLEADINGS & PRETRIAL-MOTIONS SCHEDULE (CONT'D)

Legend:

FRCP	Federal Rules of Civil Procedure
FRE	Federal Rules of Evidence
MSJ	Motion for summary judgment
TRO	Temporary restraining order
FORM	***O'Connor's Federal Civil Forms***
FFCiv	FRCP Forms, pp. 991-1000, this book

Note:
Always check local rules.

2. PRETRIAL DISCLOSURES & CONFERENCES

STEP	ACTION	RULE	DEADLINE	DUE	FILED
1	Plaintiff files complaint. FORMS 2B	FRCP 3	Before statute of limitations expires		
2	Defendant is served with summons and complaint, or if waiver of service is requested, notice of commencement of suit and request for waiver of service. FORM 2H:1; FFCiv 3, 5, 6	FRCP 4(c), (d), (f), (j)(1), (m)	If defendant is in U.S., Step 1 + 120 days ❶; If defendant is outside U.S., Step 1 + time limit provided in international agreement		
3	Defendant files answer or FRCP 12(b) motion. FORMS 3B-3D, 3F, 3G, 3I, 3L	FRCP 4(d)(3), 12(a)	Step 2 + 21 days; If U.S. is a defendant, Step 2 + 60 days; If defendant is in U.S. and waives service, Step 2 + 60 days; If defendant is outside U.S. and waives service, Step 2 + 90 days; If FRCP 12(b) motion is filed, answer due 14 days after FRCP 12(b) motion is denied or postponed		
4	Parties hold discovery conference	FRCP 26(f)(1)	As soon as practical after Step 3, but no later than 21 days before Step 7 ❷		
5	Parties file discovery plan. FORM 6A:1	FRCP 26(f)(2)	Step 4 + 14 days ❷		
6	Parties make initial disclosures. FORM 6E:2	FRCP 26(a)(1)(C)	Step 4 + 14 days, or by court order or parties' stipulation		
7	Court issues scheduling order	FRCP 16(b)(2)	As soon as practical after Step 5, but no later than Step 2 + 120 days or Step 3 + 90 days, whichever is earlier		
8	Court conducts pretrial conference and issues pretrial order	FRCP 16(c), (d)	Anytime after Step 7		
9	Parties make expert disclosures. FORM 6E:3	FRCP 26(a)(2)(D)	*Experts:* As set by court order or parties' stipulation, or no later than 90 days before Step 13; *Rebuttal experts:* As set by court order or parties' stipulation, or no later than 30 days after other party's disclosure on same subject matter		
10	Parties make final pretrial disclosures. FORM 6E:4	FRCP 26(a)(3)(B)	As set by court order, or no later than 30 days before Step 13		

❶ If the plaintiff needs additional time to complete service of the complaint and summons on a defendant that is in the United States, FRCP 4(m) requires the court to extend the time if the plaintiff shows good cause and permits the court to extend the time even if the plaintiff does not show good cause. See "Motion to extend time to serve party," ch. 5-F, §4.3, p. 334.

❷ This deadline may be shortened by local rule. FRCP 26(f)(4).

2. PRETRIAL DISCLOSURES & CONFERENCES (CONT'D)

STEP	ACTION	RULE	DEADLINE	DUE	FILED
11	Parties make objections to other party's deposition designations and exhibit lists	FRCP 26(a)(3)(B)	Step 10 + 14 days, or by court order		
12	Court conducts final pretrial conference	FRCP 16(e)	As close to Step 13 as is reasonable		
13	Trial	FRCP 39			

Legend:
FRCP Federal Rules of Civil Procedure
FORM *O'Connor's Federal Civil Forms*
FFCiv FRCP Forms, pp. 991-1000, this book

Note:
Always check local rules.

3. DISCOVERY STATUS SHEET

DISCOVERY IN ____________________ V. ____________________

SCHEDULING CONFERENCE OR ORDER DUE ______________, 20__

THIS CASE IS SET FOR TRIAL ON ______________

JURY/NONJURY

CUTOFF DATES FOR DISCOVERY	DISCOVERY REQUESTS, MOTIONS & RESPONSES	DEADLINE TO SERVE/ ANSWER	SERVED/ ANSWERED
	FRCP 26(f) conference. FORMS 6A:1-8		
Initial disclosure			
	By plaintiff. FORM 6E:2		
	By defendant. FORM 6E:2		
Interrogatories			
	Plaintiff's interrogatories to defendant. FORMS 6G		
	Defendant serves answers/objections. FORMS 6G		
	Defendant's interrogatories to plaintiff. FORMS 6G		
	Plaintiff serves answers/objections. FORMS 6G		
	Request for hearing on objections		
	Date for hearing on objections		
Requests for admissions			
	Plaintiff's request for admissions to defendant. FORMS 6H		
	Defendant serves answers/objections. FORMS 6H		
	Defendant's request for admissions to plaintiff. FORMS 6H		
	Plaintiff serves answers/objections. FORMS 6H		
	Request for hearing on objections		
	Date for hearing on objections		
Requests for production			
	Plaintiff's request for production to defendant. FORMS 6I		
	Defendant serves production and/or objections. FORMS 6I		
	Defendant's request for production to plaintiff. FORMS 6I		
	Plaintiff serves production and/or objections. FORMS 6I		
	Request for hearing on objections		
	Date for hearing on objections		

3. Discovery Status Sheet (cont'd)

Cutoff Dates for Discovery	Discovery Requests, Motions & Responses	Deadline to Serve/ Answer	Served/ Answered
Expert disclosures			
	Plaintiff serves expert disclosure, which (1) identifies experts it may use to provide expert testimony and (2) includes expert reports or FRCP 26(a)(2)(C) disclosures. FORM 6E:3		
	Defendant serves expert disclosure, which (1) identifies experts it may use to provide expert testimony and (2) includes expert reports or FRCP 26(a)(2)(C) disclosures. FORM 6E:3		
Depositions of expert witnesses			
	Plaintiff completes all depositions of expert witnesses		
	Defendant completes all depositions of expert witnesses		
Lists of fact witnesses			
	Plaintiff serves list of all fact witnesses (other than for rebuttal or impeachment) it may call to testify: names, addresses, and telephone numbers. FORM 6E:2		
	Defendant serves list of all fact witnesses (other than for rebuttal or impeachment) it may call to testify: names, addresses, and telephone numbers. FORM 6E:2		
Depositions of fact witnesses			
	Plaintiff completes all depositions of fact witnesses. FORMS 6F		
	Defendant completes all depositions of fact witnesses. FORMS 6F		
Documentary & other exhibits			
	Plaintiff serves list of all documentary and other tangible exhibits that may be introduced at trial. FORMS 6A, 6E		
	Defendant serves list of all documentary and other tangible exhibits that may be introduced at trial. FORMS 6A, 6E		
Medical examinations			
	Plaintiff files motions for mental or physical examinations. FORMS 6J		
	Defendant files motions for mental or physical examinations. FORMS 6J		

Legend:

FRCP Federal Rules of Civil Procedure
FORM *O'Connor's Federal Civil Forms*

4. REMOVAL & REMAND

STEP	ACTION	RULE	DEADLINE	DUE	FILED
1	Plaintiff files suit in state court		Before statute of limitations expires		
2	Defendant is served the complaint and summons with state-court suit		According to state law		
3	Defendant's answer due in state court		According to state law		
4	Defendant files notice of removal in federal court. ❶ FORM 4A:1	28 USC §1446(b), (c)	If suit is removable as initially filed, Step 2 + 30 days; If suit is not removable as initially filed, on receipt of pleading or other paper that makes suit removable + 30 days, but no later than Step 1 + one year (unless court finds that plaintiff acted in bad faith to prevent removal)		
5	Defendant files copy of notice of removal in state court. FORM 4A:2	28 USC §1446(d)	Promptly after Step 4		
6	Removal effective in federal court	*Anthony*, 76 F.3d 210, 214 (8th 1996)	Immediately at Step 5		
7	Defendant gives all adverse parties written notice of removal	28 USC §1446(d)	Promptly after Step 4		
8	Action in state court automatically stayed	28 USC §1446(d)	Immediately at Step 5		
9	Defendant amends notice of removal (optional)	*See Energy Catering*, 911 F.Supp. 221, 222-23 (E.D.La. 1995)	Step 2 + 30 days		
10	Defendant files answer in federal court if it did not answer before removal. FORMS 3L	FRCP 81(c)(2)	Whichever is later: receipt of copy of state-court suit + 21 days; Step 2 + 21 days; or Step 4 + seven days		
11	Jury demand by defendant. FORM 5C:1	FRCP 38(b), 81(c)(3)(B)	Step 4 + 14 days		
	Jury demand by plaintiff. FORM 5C:1		Step 7 + 14 days		

❶ The Federal Courts Jurisdiction and Venue Clarification Act of 2011 made significant changes to 28 U.S.C. §1446(b). For a discussion of these changes and of removal deadlines when there are multiple defendants or when certain entities (e.g., the Federal Deposit Insurance Corporation) are a party, see "Deadlines for Removal," ch. 4-A, §4, p. 242.

4. REMOVAL & REMAND (CONT'D)

STEP	ACTION	RULE	DEADLINE	DUE	FILED
12	Plaintiff files motion to remand to state court. FORM 4B:1	28 USC §1447(c)	If motion based on defect in removal procedure, Step 4 + 30 days; If court lacks subject-matter jurisdiction, at any time		
13	Plaintiff files amended pleading, or motion for leave to amend, to join additional parties to destroy jurisdiction	*See* FRCP 15(a); 28 USC §1447(e)	For amended pleading, once as a matter of course (1) 21 days after serving the pleading or (2) if the pleading requires a responsive pleading, whichever is earlier: 21 days after service of the responsive pleading or a motion under FRCP 12(b), (e), or (f); otherwise, with opposing party's written consent or court's leave; For motion for leave, promptly after Step 7		
14	If federal court remands to state court, suit returned to state court	28 USC §1447(c)			
15	If federal court denies motion to remand to state court, suit proceeds in federal court	*See* 28 USC §1447(c)			

Legend:

FRCP	Federal Rules of Civil Procedure
USC	United States Code
FORM	***O'Connor's Federal Civil Forms***

5. TEMPORARY RESTRAINING ORDER & INJUNCTION

STEP	ACTION	RULE	DEADLINE	DUE	FILED
1	Plaintiff files motion for TRO. FORM 2D:3	*See* FRCP 65(b)	Before or with complaint at Step 3		
2	Plaintiff files motion for preliminary injunction. FORMS 2D	*See* FRCP 65(a)	With TRO at Step 1, or before or with complaint at Step 3		
3	Plaintiff files complaint. FORMS 2B, 2D:1	FRCP 3	Before statute of limitations expires		
4	Plaintiff files request for permanent injunction	*See* FRCP 8(a), 65(a)	With complaint at Step 3		
5	Hearing on TRO	*See* FRCP 65(b)(1)	At earliest possible time, generally before Step 13		
6	Court orders TRO	FRCP 65(b)(1), (d)	After Step 5		
7	Plaintiff files bond	FRCP 65(c), 65.1	After Step 6		
8	Clerk enters TRO	*See* FRCP 65(b)(2)	After Steps 6 and 7		
9	Motion to extend TRO for good cause or by party agreement	FRCP 65(b)(2)	After Step 6		
10	Motion to modify or dissolve TRO	FRCP 65(b)(4)	After Step 6 on two days' notice to party who obtained TRO without notice, or on shorter notice at court's discretion		
11	Hearing on motion to modify or dissolve TRO	FRCP 65(b)(4)	As promptly as justice requires		
12	TRO expires	FRCP 65(b)(2)	On court order but no later than Step 8 + 14 days; If TRO extended for good cause, Step 9 + 14 days; If TRO extended by party agreement, Step 9 + agreed time		
13	Defendant is served with summons and complaint, or if waiver of service is requested, notice of commencement of suit and request for waiver of service. FORM 2H:1; FFCiv 3, 5, 6	FRCP 4(c), (d), (f), (j)(1), (m)	If defendant is in U.S., Step 3 + 120 days ❶; If defendant is outside U.S., Step 3 + time limit provided in international agreement		
14	Plaintiff files proof of service and affidavit (if necessary) with court	FRCP 4(*l*)(1)	As soon as possible after Step 13		

❶ If the plaintiff needs additional time to complete service of the complaint and summons on a defendant that is in the United States, FRCP 4(m) requires the court to extend the time if the plaintiff shows good cause and permits the court to extend the time even if the plaintiff does not show good cause.

5. TEMPORARY RESTRAINING ORDER & INJUNCTION (CONT'D)

STEP	ACTION	RULE	DEADLINE	DUE	FILED
15	Defendant files answer or FRCP 12(b) motion. FORMS 3B-3D, 3F, 3G, 3I, 3L	FRCP 4(d)(3), 12(a)	Step 13 + 21 days; If U.S. is a defendant, Step 13 + 60 days; If defendant is in U.S. and waives service, Step 13 + 60 days; If defendant is outside U.S. and waives service, Step 13 + 90 days; If FRCP 12(b) motion is filed, answer due 14 days after FRCP 12(b) motion is denied or postponed		
16	Hearing on preliminary injunction	FRCP 65(b)(3)	At earliest possible time if TRO issued without notice, or after Step 13		
17	Court makes findings of fact and conclusions of law	FRCP 52(a)(2)	After Step 16		
18	Court orders preliminary injunction and gives notice to defendant. FORM 2D:2	*See* FRCP 65(a)(1), (d)	After Step 17		
19	Plaintiff files bond	FRCP 65(c), 65.1	After Step 18		
20	Clerk issues preliminary injunction		After Steps 18 and 19		
21	Motion for reconsideration	*See* FRCP 52(b), 59(e)	Step 20 + 28 days		
22	Court denies motion for reconsideration		After Step 21		
23	Notice of appeal filed for order on preliminary injunction. FFApp 1	FRAP 4(a)(1), (4); 28 USC §1292(a)(1)	Step 20 + 30 days; If motion for reconsideration filed, Step 22 + 30 days; If U.S. is a party, Step 20 + 60 days ❷		
24	Motion to extend time to file notice of appeal. FORM 10G:1	FRAP 4(a)(5)	Step 23 + 30 days		
25	Motion to stay injunction pending appeal	FRCP 62(a), (c)	Immediately after Step 23		
26	Court consolidates hearing on preliminary injunction with trial on merits	FRCP 65(a)(2)	Before or at Step 16		
27	Court advances trial on merits for permanent injunction, fully adjudicating parties' rights	*See* FRCP 65	After Step 16 or 17		

❷ The 60-day deadline applies if one of the parties is (1) the United States, (2) a U.S. agency, (3) a U.S. officer or employee sued in an official capacity, or (4) a current or former U.S. officer or employee sued in an individual capacity for an act or omission occurring in connection with duties performed on behalf of the United States. FRAP 4(a)(1)(B).

5. TEMPORARY RESTRAINING ORDER & INJUNCTION (CONT'D)

Legend:

FRAP	Federal Rules of Appellate Procedure
FRCP	Federal Rules of Civil Procedure
TRO	Temporary restraining order
USC	United States Code
FORM	***O'Connor's Federal Civil Forms***
FFApp	FRAP Forms, pp. 1125-32, this book
FFCiv	FRCP Forms, pp. 991-1000, this book

Note:
Always check local rules.

6. Request to Clerk for Default Judgment

Step	Action	Rule	Deadline	Due	Filed
1	Plaintiff files complaint. FORMS 2B	FRCP 3	Before statute of limitations expires		
2	Defendant is served with summons and complaint, or if waiver of service is requested, notice of commencement of suit and request for waiver of service. FORM 2H:1; FFCiv 3, 5, 6	FRCP 4(c), (d), (f), (j)(1), (m)	If defendant is in U.S., Step 1 + 120 days ❶; If defendant is outside U.S., Step 1 + time limit provided in international agreement		
3	Defendant files response	FRCP 4(d)(3), 12(a)	Step 2 + 21 days; If U.S. is a defendant, Step 2 + 60 days; If defendant is in U.S. and waives service, Step 2 + 60 days; If defendant is outside U.S. and waives service, Step 2 + 90 days		
4	Plaintiff files request for entry of default with clerk. FORM 7A:1	FRCP 55(a)	After Step 3		
5	Clerk enters default. FORM 7A:2	FRCP 55(a)	After Step 4		
6	Defendant files motion to set aside entry of default. FORM 7A:3	FRCP 55(c)	After Step 4; after Step 5 if filed		
7	Plaintiff files request for default judgment with clerk. FORM 7A:8	FRCP 55(b)(1)	After Step 5		
8	Clerk enters default judgment. FORM 7A:9	FRCP 55(b)(1)	After Step 7		
9	Defendant files motion to vacate default judgment. FORM 7A:14	*See* FRCP 60(b), (c)(1)	A motion based on FRCP 60(b)(1)-(3) must be made within a reasonable time after Step 8, but no later than one year after Step 8 or one year of the date of the proceeding; A motion based on FRCP 60(b)(4)-(6) must be made within a reasonable time after Step 8		
10	Court denies motion to vacate. FORM 7A:16		After Step 9		
BEGIN THE APPEAL, see "Appeal of Civil Trial," timetable 9					

❶ If the plaintiff needs additional time to complete service of the complaint and summons on a defendant that is in the United States, FRCP 4(m) requires the court to extend the time if the plaintiff shows good cause and permits the court to extend the time even if the plaintiff does not show good cause.

Legend:

FRCP Federal Rules of Civil Procedure
FORM *O'Connor's Federal Civil Forms*
FFCiv FRCP Forms, pp. 991-1000, this book

Note:
Always check local rules.

7. MOTION TO COURT FOR DEFAULT JUDGMENT

STEP	ACTION	RULE	DEADLINE	DUE	FILED
1	Plaintiff files complaint. FORMS 2B	FRCP 3	Before statute of limitations expires		
2	Defendant is served with summons and complaint, or if waiver of service is requested, notice of commencement of suit and request for waiver of service. FORM 2H:1; FFCiv 3, 5, 6	FRCP 4(c), (d), (f), (j)(1), (m)	If defendant is in U.S., Step 1 + 120 days ❶; If defendant is outside U.S., Step 1 + time limit provided in international agreement		
3	Defendant files response	FRCP 4(d)(3), 12(a)	Step 2 + 21 days; If U.S. is a defendant, Step 2 + 60 days; If defendant is in U.S. and waives service, Step 2 + 60 days; If defendant is outside U.S. and waives service, Step 2 + 90 days		
4	Plaintiff files request for entry of default with clerk. FORM 7A:1	FRCP 55(a)	After Step 3		
5	Clerk enters default. FORM 7A:2	FRCP 55(a)	After Step 4		
6	Defendant files motion to set aside entry of default. FORM 7A:3	FRCP 55(c)	After Step 4; after Step 5 if filed		
7	Plaintiff files motion for default judgment with court. FORM 7A:10	FRCP 55(b)(2)	After Step 5		
8	If defendant has not appeared, court enters default judgment	FRCP 55(b)(2)	After Step 7		
9	If defendant has appeared, notice of hearing is served on defendant. FORM 1E:1	FRCP 55(b)(2)	After Step 7		
10	If defendant has appeared, a hearing is held	FRCP 55(b)(2)	When set, at least seven days after notice is served under Step 9		
11	Court enters default judgment. FORM 7A:12	FRCP 55(b)(2)	After Step 10		
12	Clerk enters default judgment	FRCP 58(b)	After Step 11		
13	Defendant files motion to vacate default judgment. FORM 7A:14	*See* FRCP 60(b), (c)(1)	A motion based on FRCP 60(b)(1)-(3) must be made within a reasonable time after Step 8, but no later than one year after Step 8 or 11 or one year of the date of the proceeding; A motion based on FRCP 60(b)(4)-(6) must be made within a reasonable time after Step 8 or 11		

❶ If the plaintiff needs additional time to complete service of the complaint and summons on a defendant that is in the United States, FRCP 4(m) requires the court to extend the time if the plaintiff shows good cause and permits the court to extend the time even if the plaintiff does not show good cause.

7. Motion to Court for Default Judgment (cont'd)

Step	Action	Rule	Deadline	Due	Filed
14	Court denies motion to vacate. FORM 7A:16		After Step 13		
BEGIN THE APPEAL, see "Appeal of Civil Trial," timetable 9					

Legend:

FRCP Federal Rules of Civil Procedure
FORM *O'Connor's Federal Civil Forms*
FFCiv FRCP Forms, pp. 991-1000, this book

Note:
Always check local rules.

8. SUMMARY JUDGMENT

STEP	ACTION	RULE	DEADLINE	DUE	FILED
1	Plaintiff files complaint. FORMS 2B	FRCP 3	Before statute of limitations expires		
2	Defendant is served with summons and complaint, or if waiver of service is requested, notice of commencement of suit and request for waiver of service. FORM 2H:1; FFCiv 3, 5, 6	FRCP 4(c), (d), (f), (j)(1), (m)	If defendant is in U.S., Step 1 + 120 days ❶; If defendant is outside U.S., Step 1 + time limit provided in international agreement		
3	Defendant files answer or FRCP 12(b) motion. FORMS 3B-3D, 3F, 3G, 3I, 3L	FRCP 4(d)(3), 12(a)	Step 2 + 21 days; If U.S. is a defendant, Step 2 + 60 days; If defendant is in U.S. and waives service, Step 2 + 60 days; If defendant is outside U.S. and waives service, Step 2 + 90 days; If FRCP 12(b) motion is filed, answer due 14 days after FRCP 12(b) motion is denied or postponed		
4	Movant files and serves MSJ. FORMS 7B	FRCP 56(b)	Anytime until 30 days after the close of discovery ❷		
5	Nonmovant files motion for continuance requesting time to obtain affidavits or conduct discovery. FORM 7B:9	FRCP 56(d)(2)	As soon as possible, but before or with Step 6; check local rules		
6	Nonmovant files response to MSJ. FORMS 7B		After Step 4; check local rules and court order for deadline to file response		
7	Movant files reply to MSJ response		After Step 6; check local rules and court order for deadline to file reply		
8	Hearing on MSJ ❸	*See* FRCP 6(c)	When set, but no earlier than 14 days after motion is served under Step 4		
9	Court signs SJ or order denying SJ. FORM 7B:8	FRCP 54, 56(a)	As soon as practical after Step 8		

❶ If the plaintiff needs additional time to complete service of the complaint and summons on a defendant that is in the United States, FRCP 4(m) requires the court to extend the time if the plaintiff shows good cause and permits the court to extend the time even if the plaintiff does not show good cause.

❷ The deadline for a motion for summary judgment may be different under court order or local rule. FRCP 56(b).

❸ If either party wants an oral hearing on the motion for summary judgment, it should make a timely request in writing. *See* FRCP 6(c)(1). The form of the request for a hearing is generally governed by local rule. The court is more likely to grant a hearing if the case involves numerous or complex issues, or if the arguments supporting the motion and response need clarification.

8. SUMMARY JUDGMENT (CONT'D)

STEP	ACTION	RULE	DEADLINE	DUE	FILED
10	If MSJ granted and no additional claims remain, court may enter final judgment	*See* FRCP 54(b), 56(a)	As soon as practical after Step 8		
	If partial MSJ granted and additional claims remain, trial begins on additional claims, and final judgment signed	*See* FRCP 54(b), 56(a)	After trial of remaining issues		
11	If MSJ granted, clerk prepares and enters judgment	FRCP 54(b), 58, 79(a)(2)(C)	Promptly after Step 9		
12	If SJ entered, party files motion for new trial. FORMS 10C:1, 2	FRCP 59(b)	Step 11 + 28 days		
13	Nonmovant files opposing affidavits to motion for new trial based on affidavits. FORM 1B:4	FRCP 59(c)	Step 12 + 14 days		
14	Response to motion for new trial filed. FORM 10C:3	*See* FRCP 59(c)	Check local rules for deadline to file response ❹		
15	Reply affidavits filed in support of motion for new trial based on affidavits. FORM 1B:4	FRCP 59(c)	No deadline—at court's discretion		
16	Court denies motion for new trial. FORM 10C:4	FRCP 59	After Step 13, 14, or 15		
BEGIN THE APPEAL, see "Appeal of Civil Trial," timetable 9					

❹ FRCP 59 does not contain a deadline for the response, but it should be filed within any limits set by local rules for responses. FRCP 59(c) does, however, contain a deadline for filing opposing affidavits.

Legend:

FRCP	Federal Rules of Civil Procedure
MSJ	Motion for summary judgment
SJ	Summary judgment
FORM	***O'Connor's Federal Civil Forms***
FFCiv	FRCP Forms, pp. 991-1000, this book

Note:
Always check local rules.

9. APPEAL OF CIVIL TRIAL

STEP	ACTION	RULE	DEADLINE	DUE	FILED
1	Judgment entered by clerk	FRAP 4(a)(7); FRCP 58, 79(a)(2)(C)	Immediately after jury's verdict, decision of court in nonjury case, or court denies all relief		
2	Losing party files motion for new trial or to modify or correct the judgment, or other motion requesting relief from judgment. FORMS 10C, 10D, 10F	FRAP 4(a)(4); FRCP 55(c), 59(b), (e), 60(b), (c)(1)	For most postjudgment motions, Step 1 + 28 days; For motions based on FRCP 60(b)(1)-(3), a reasonable time after Step 1, but no later than Step 1 + one year or the date of the proceeding + one year; For motions based on FRCP 60(b)(4)-(6), a reasonable time after Step 1		
3	Motion denied		By entry of written order		
4	Judgment is final when entered, subject to court's action on postjudgment motions listed in FRAP 4(a)(4)	FRAP 4(a)(7); FRCP 58, 79(a)(2)(C)	If separate document is not required, at Step 1; If separate document is required, whichever is earlier: after Step 1 + when judgment set in separate document, or Step 1 + 150 days		
5	Perfect the appeal—appellant files notice of appeal and filing fee with district clerk. FFApp 1	FRAP 3, 4(a); 28 USC §2107	Step 1 + 30 days, or Step 4 + 30 days; If U.S. is a party, Step 1 + 60 days, or Step 4 + 60 days ❶		
6	Cross-appeal—appellee files notice of appeal. FFApp 1	FRAP 4(a)(3)	Whichever is later: Step 5 + 14 days or the deadlines in Step 5		
7	Appellant files motion to post supersedeas bond to stay execution of judgment in district court (optional)	FRAP 8(a); FRCP 62(d)	At or after Step 5		
8	Appellant sends transcript order form to court reporter	FRAP 10(b)(1)	Whichever is later: Step 3 + 14 days or Step 5 + 14 days; If cross-appeal, whichever is later: Step 3 + 14 days or Step 6 + 14 days		
9	If ordering partial transcript, appellant files and serves statement of issues	FRAP 10(b)(3)(A)	Whichever is later: Step 3 + 14 days; Step 5 + 14 days; or Step 6 + 14 days		
10	Appellee files and serves designation of additional parts to be included in transcript	FRAP 10(b)(3)(B)	Step 9 + 14 days		
11	Appellant orders additional parts to be included in transcript	FRAP 10(b)(3)(C)	Step 10 + 14 days		

❶ The 60-day deadline applies if one of the parties is (1) the United States, (2) a U.S. agency, (3) a U.S. officer or employee sued in an official capacity, or (4) a current or former U.S. officer or employee sued in an individual capacity for an act or omission occurring in connection with duties performed on behalf of the United States. FRAP 4(a)(1)(B); 28 U.S.C. §2107(b).

9. APPEAL OF CIVIL TRIAL (CONT'D)

STEP	ACTION	RULE	DEADLINE	DUE	FILED
12	Appellee includes request or order for additional parts with transcript	FRAP 10(b)(3)(C)	Step 11 + 14 days only if appellant has not ordered all parts		
13	Court reporter files transcript with clerk of district court	FRAP 11(b)(1)	30 days after order received or as soon as complete		
14	Court reporter files motion for extension of time to file transcript with clerk of CA	FRAP 11(b)(1)(B)	Before Step 13		
15	District clerk files record in CA	FRAP 11(b)(2)	As soon as record is complete		
16	Appellant files brief in CA (25 copies or by local rule or court order) and serves it on opponent (two copies or by local rule or court order)	FRAP 31(a), (b)	Step 15 + 40 days ❷		
17	Appellee files brief in CA (25 copies or by local rule or court order) and serves it on opponent (two copies or by local rule or court order)	FRAP 31(a), (b)	Step 16 + 30 days ❷		
18	Appellant files reply brief in CA (25 copies or by local rule or court order) and serves it on opponent (two copies or by local rule or court order)	FRAP 31(a), (b)	Step 17 + 14 days, but at least seven days before Step 19 ❷		
19	Oral argument, if requested and granted	FRAP 34	Set by clerk		
20	CA issues opinion and judgment entered	FRAP 36	By act of the clerk or court		
21	Losing party files petition for rehearing in CA (25 copies or by local rule or court order) and serves it on opponent (two copies or by local rule or court order)	FRAP 31(b), 40(a)(1), (b)	Step 20 + 14 days; If U.S. is a party, Step 20 + 45 days ❸		
22	If requested by court, winning party files answer to petition for rehearing (25 copies or by local rule or court order) and serves it on opponent (two copies or by local rule or court order)	FRAP 31(b), 40(a)(3), (b)	After Step 21		
23	CA denies petition for rehearing	FRAP 40(a)	By written order		

❷ This deadline may be shortened by local rule or court order. FRAP 31(a)(2).

❸ This deadline may be modified by local rule or court order. FRAP 40(a)(1). The 45-day deadline applies if one of the parties is (1) the United States, (2) a U.S. agency, (3) a U.S. officer or employee sued in an official capacity, or (4) a current or former U.S. officer or employee sued in an individual capacity for an act or omission occurring in connection with duties performed on behalf of the United States. *Id.*

9. APPEAL OF CIVIL TRIAL (CONT'D)

STEP	ACTION	RULE	DEADLINE	DUE	FILED
24	Petitioner files petition for writ of certiorari in SCt (40 copies) and serves it on opponent	28 USC §2101(c); SCR 12.1, 13.1, 13.3, 29	If no rehearing, Step 20 + 90 days; If motion for rehearing, Step 23 + 90 days		
25	Petitioner enters notice of appearance and pays docket fee	SCR 9, 38(a)	At Step 24		
26	Clerk places petition on the docket	SCR 12.3, 29	After Step 24 + filing of proof of service		
27	Other party may file cross-petition for writ of certiorari (40 copies)	SCR 12.5, 29	Step 26 + 30 days		
28	Respondent files answer to petition (40 copies)	SCR 15.3, 29	Step 26 + 30 days		
29	Petitioner files reply brief (40 copies)	*See* SCR 15.6, 29	As soon as possible		
30	Petitioner-respondent files answer to cross-petition (if necessary) (40 copies)	SCR 15.3, 29	Step 26 + 30 days		
31	SCt grants or denies writ	SCR 16	After Step 30		
32	If certiorari denied, petitioner files petition for rehearing (40 copies)	SCR 44.2	Step 31 + 25 days		
33	If certiorari granted, petitioner serves designation of parts of record to be included in joint appendix	SCR 26.2	In absence of agreement, Step 31 + 10 days		
34	Respondent serves designation of additional parts of record to be included in joint appendix	SCR 26.2	Step 33 + 10 days		
35	If certiorari granted, petitioner files brief on merits (40 copies)	SCR 25.1	Step 31 + 45 days		
36	Respondent files brief on merits (40 copies)	SCR 25.2	Step 35 + 30 days		
37	Petitioner files reply brief (40 copies)	SCR 25.3	Step 36 + 30 days, but no later than 2 p.m. one week before Step 38		
38	Oral argument	SCR 27, 28	Set by court		
39	SCt issues opinion and judgment	SCR 41	After Step 38		
40	Petition for rehearing filed in SCt (40 copies)	SCR 44.1	Step 39 + 25 days		
41	SCt denied motion for rehearing		After Step 40		
42	Mandate issued	*See* SCR 45.3	If specifically directed		

9. APPEAL OF CIVIL TRIAL (CONT'D)

Legend:

CA	Court of Appeals
FRAP	Federal Rules of Appellate Procedure
FRCP	Federal Rules of Civil Procedure
SCR	Supreme Court Rules
SCt	United States Supreme Court
USC	United States Code
FORM	***O'Connor's Federal Civil Forms***
FFApp	FRAP Forms, pp. 1125-32, this book

Note:
Always check local rules.

INDEX

INDEX

Page numbers in ***boldface italic***

ABATEMENT, MOTION
Action by or against U.S. for death of defendant, 28 U.S.C. 2404
Scope of review, Supreme Court, 28 U.S.C. 2105
Substitution of public officers, FRCP 25
Suggestion of death, FRCP 25

ABSTENTION
Generally, ***138***
Anti-Injunction Act, *see* Jurisdiction, this index
Appellate review, ***143***
Brillhart, ***139***
Burford, ***138***
Colorado River
  Generally, ***139***
  Parallel federal proceedings, ***140***
  Parallel state proceedings, ***139***
Pullman, ***138***
Stay, related proceedings, ***139***
Thibodaux, ***138***
Younger, ***138***

ACCORD & SATISFACTION
Pleading, as affirmative defense, FRCP 8; ***233***

ACCOUNTING
Federal Judicial Center, 28 U.S.C. 628
U.S. Marshals Service, 28 U.S.C. 567

ACCOUNTS
Court of Federal Claims, accounts of
  Agents or contractors, 28 U.S.C. 1494, 2511
  Officers, 28 U.S.C. 1494, 2511
Deposits with court, FRCP 67

ACKNOWLEDGMENT
Administration of, 28 U.S.C. 459
Clerks of court, 28 U.S.C. 953
Service, proof of, FRAP 25

AD LITEM
Appointment, ***75***

ADJOURNMENT
District courts, 28 U.S.C. 140

ADMINISTRATIVE OFFICE OF U.S. COURTS
Generally, 28 U.S.C. 601-613

ADMIRALTY & MARITIME CLAIMS
Generally, FRCP ADM-A-F
Amendment, pleading, FRCP 9
Answer, FRCP ADM-B
Appearance, FRCP ADM-E
Application of rules, FRCP 1; FRE 1101
Attachment, FRCP ADM-A, B, E
Bonds, FRCP 65.1
Contribution, third-party practice, FRCP 14
Costs
  Docket fees, 28 U.S.C. 1923
  Taxation, 28 U.S.C. 1925
  U.S. marshal's fees, 28 U.S.C. 1921
District courts, appeals as of right, FRAP 4
Fines, 28 U.S.C. 1395
Foreign countries, 28 U.S.C. 1391

ADMIRALTY & MARITIME CLAIMS (continued)
Forfeiture, FRCP 26, ADM-A, G; 28 U.S.C. 1395
Garnishment, FRCP 9, ADM-A, B, E
In rem actions, FRCP 9, ADM-C, E, G
Interlocutory appeals, 28 U.S.C. 1292
Interpleader, FRCP 22
Joinder
  Claims & remedies, FRCP 18
  Parties, FRCP 20
Judgments & decrees
  Attachment, FRCP ADM-E
  Bond, 28 U.S.C. 2464
  Foreign countries, actions against, 28 U.S.C. 1605
Jurisdiction, 28 U.S.C. 1333
Jurisdictional grounds, FRCP 9
Jury trial, right to, ***312***
Liability, limitation of, FRCP ADM-A, F
Money damages, FRCP 9
Notice
  Attachment, FRCP ADM-B
  Garnishment, FRCP ADM-E
  Possession of vessel, FRCP ADM-D
Partition actions, FRCP 9, ADM-A, D, E
Penalties, venue, 28 U.S.C. 1395
Pleadings, FRCP 9, ADM-E
Privileges & immunities, foreign countries, exceptions, 28 U.S.C. 1605
Process
  Fees, 28 U.S.C. 1921
  Jury trial, right to, FRCP 38; 28 U.S.C. 1873
  Separate trials, FRCP 42
Removal, ***260***
Tort Claims Act, exceptions, 28 U.S.C. 2680
Undertakings, FRCP 65.1
Venue
  Generally, FRCP 9, 82; 28 U.S.C. 1395; ***144***
  Change, limitation of liability, FRCP ADM-F
  Penalties, 28 U.S.C. 1395

ADMISSIBILITY, LIMITED
Generally, FRE 105
Request, ***704***

ADMISSIONS
Generally, FRCP 36; ***563***
Appellate review, ***569***
Challenging, ***565***
Deemed, ***566***
Refusal to admit, FRCP 37
Request
  Generally, ***564***
  Number, FRCP 26; ***564***
  Service, FRCP 36; ***564***
Response, ***564***
Sanctions, ***567***
Set aside, deemed admissions, ***566***
Using, ***568***
Withdrawal, ***567***

ADOPTION
Hearsay exception, FRE 803, 804

ADOPTION BY REFERENCE
Pleading, FRCP 10; ***9***, ***13***

ADR
See Alternative Dispute Resolution, this index

ADVERSE OR PECUNIARY INTEREST
Disqualification of judge, 28 U.S.C. 455
Witnesses, 28 U.S.C. 2506

ADVISORY JURY
Generally, FRCP 39
Motion, ***315***

AFFIDAVIT
Amend substance of judgment, motion to, ***796***
Attorney fees, ***754***
Continuance, ***337***
Debt collection, 28 U.S.C. 3006
Habeas, evidence, 28 U.S.C. 2246
In forma pauperis, *see* this index
Nonreceipt of document, proof of, ***37***
Proving service, ***36***
Summary-judgment proof, FRCP 56; ***610***
Verification of pleadings, ***11***

AFFIDAVIT OF INDIGENCE
See In Forma Pauperis, this index

AFFINITY
See Relatives, this index

AFFIRMATIVE DEFENSES
Generally, FRCP 8; ***231***
Accord & satisfaction, FRCP 8; ***233***
Affirmative defense vs. counterclaim, ***232***
Answer, defendant's, FRCP 8; ***231***
Arbitration award, FRCP 8; ***233***
Assumption of risk, FRCP 8; ***233***
Avoidance, FRCP 8
Catchall provision, ***233***
Consideration, failure of, FRCP 8; ***233***
Contributory negligence, FRCP 8; ***233***
Duress, ***233***
Estoppel, FRCP 8; ***233***
Failure to plead, effect of, ***232***
Fraud, ***233***
Illegality, ***233***
Inconsistent, ***235***
Injury by fellow servant, FRCP 8; ***233***
Laches, FRCP 8; ***233***
License, FRCP 8; ***233***
Payment, FRCP 8; ***233***
Pleadings, asserting in, FRCP 8; ***231***
Release, FRCP 8; ***233***
Res judicata, FRCP 8; ***233***
Statute of frauds, FRCP 8; ***233***
Statute of limitations, FRCP 8; ***233***
Sufficiency, ***234***
Summary judgment, FRCP 56; ***617***, ***618***
Vs. counterclaim, ***232***
Waiver, FRCP 8; ***233***

AGENCY ORDERS, REVIEW
Generally, 28 U.S.C. 2341-51

INDEX

Page numbers in ***boldface italic***

AGENTS
Court of Federal Claims, accounts of, 8 U.S.C. 1494, 2511
Hearsay, statements by, FRE 801
Service of process, FRCP 4; ***152***

ALIENS
See Jurisdiction, this index

ALLEGATIONS
Pleadings, contents, ***9***

ALTER JUDGMENT, MOTION TO
See Postjudgment Motions, this index

ALTERNATIVE DISPUTE RESOLUTION
Generally, 28 U.S.C. 651-658; ***74***
Arbitration, *see* this index
Binding arbitration, ***74***, ***650***
Compromise, Federal Tort Claims, 28 U.S.C. 2672
Settlement, Federal Tort Claims, 28 U.S.C. 2672
U.S., claims against, 28 U.S.C. 2672

ALTERNATIVE RELIEF
Claims, FRCP 8; ***10***
Defenses, FRCP 8; ***10***

AMEND JUDGMENT, MOTION TO
See Postjudgment Motions, this index

AMENDMENTS, PLEADINGS
Deadline, pretrial, ***345***
Incorporation by reference, FRCP 10; ***9***, ***13***
Matter of course, ***345***
Post-trial, motion
  Generally, FRCP 15; ***710***
  Appellate review, ***714***
  Attachments, ***711***
  Continuance, ***713***
  Deadline, ***712***
  Grounds, ***710***
  Response, ***712***
  Ruling, ***713***
  Trial by consent, express, ***711***
  Trial by consent, implied, ***711***
Pretrial, motion
  Generally, FRCP 15; ***345***, ***350***, ***351***
  Appellate review, ***355***
  Deadline, ***345***, ***351***
  Relation back, ***347***, ***350***
  Response, ***351***
  Ruling, ***353***
Relation back, FRCP 15
Trial, motion
  Generally, FRCP 15; ***710***
  Appellate review, ***714***
  Attachments, ***711***
  Continuance, ***713***
  Deadline, ***712***
  Grounds, ***710***
  Response, ***712***
  Ruling, ***713***
  Trial by consent, express, ***711***
  Trial by consent, implied, ***711***

AMICUS CURIAE
Appeal, FRAP 29

AMOUNT IN CONTROVERSY
Generally, ***123***
Alienage jurisdiction, ***129***
Courts of appeals, proof of, 28 U.S.C. 2108
Diversity jurisdiction
  Generally, 28 U.S.C. 1332; ***123***
  Notice of removal, ***262***
Interpleader, 28 U.S.C. 1335; ***89***
U.S. as defendant, 28 U.S.C. 1346

ANCIENT DOCUMENTS
Authentication, FRE 901
Hearsay exception, FRE 803

ANSWER
Affirmative defenses, FRCP 8; ***231***
Counterclaims, FRCP 13; ***235***
Cross-claims, FRCP 13; ***236***
Deadline to serve, FRCP 12; ***175***
Denials, types, FRCP 8, 9, 12-15; ***230***
Third-party suit, FRCP 14; ***236***

ANTI-INJUNCTION ACT
See Jurisdiction, this index

APPEALS
Agency orders, review of, FRAP 15-20
Agreed statement of case, FRAP 10
Appellant, duty to file transcript, FRAP 11
Applicability of rules, FRAP 1
As of right, FRAP 3, 4
Attorneys
  Generally, FRAP 46
  Representation statement, FRAP 12
Bankruptcy appeals, FRAP 6
Bond, FRAP 7
Briefs, *see* Briefs, Appeal, this index
By permission, FRAP 5
Collateral orders, ***741***
Computation of time, FRAP 26
Conference, prehearing, FRAP 33
Consolidated appeals, FRAP 3
Constitutional questions, FRAP 44
Courts of appeals, FRAP 12
Death of party, substitution of parties, FRAP 43
Delay, damages, FRAP 38
Disclosure statement, corporate, FRAP 26.1
Disposition, judicial, citing of, FRAP 32.1
District court, FRAP 12
Docketing, FRAP 12
Document, redacted, FRAP 25
Duties of clerks, FRAP 45
En banc determination, FRAP 35
Enforcement of administrative orders, FRAP 15
Entry of judgments, FRAP 36
Error
  Manifest, ***43***
  Plain, ***42***
  Preserving for appeal, ***42***
  Types, ***42***

APPEALS (continued)
Extension of time, FRAP 4, 26; 28 U.S.C. 2107; ***815***, ***817***
Failure to docket, FRAP 11, 12
Failure to file transcript of, FRAP 11, 12
Filing & service, FRAP 25
Forwarding the record, FRAP 11
Immediate appeal, FRAP 5; 28 U.S.C. 1292
Injunction or stay, FRAP 8
Issuance of mandate, FRAP 41
Joint appeals, FRAP 3
Judgment of magistrate, district court's review of, FRAP 3
Judgments, ***737***
Judicial disposition, citing of, FRAP 32.1
Jurisdiction, rules not to affect, FRAP 1
Leave, magistrate, FRAP 3
Mandate
  Issuance, FRAP 41
  Magistrate, appeal from judgment of, FRAP 3
  Stay pending application for certiorari, FRAP 41
Motions
  Contents, FRAP 27
  Extend time to file notice, *see* Postjudgment Motions, this index
  Form, FRAP 27
  Power of judge to entertain, FRAP 27
  Procedural orders, disposition of motions for, FRAP 27
  Reopen time to file appeal, *see* Postjudgment Motions, this index
  Response, FRAP 27
NLRB proceedings, FRAP 15.1
Notice
  Generally, FRAP 3
  After extension, ***820***
  Contents, FRAP 3
  Deadline, ***817***
  Premature motion, ***818***
Oral argument, FRAP 34
Orders, ***739***
Partial transcript, notice, FRAP 10
Prehearing conference, FRAP 33
Preliminary injunction, FRAP 8
Preliminary motion, FRAP 11
Process, service, FRAP 25
Record on, FRAP 10-11
Rehearing, FRAP 40
Reopen time to file
  Deadline, FRAP 4; ***822***
  Hearing, ***823***, ***824***
  Motion, FRAP 4; 28 U.S.C. 2107; ***821***
  Notice of judgment, ***819***, ***821***
  Time, FRAP 4; ***821***
Representation statement, filing of, FRAP 12
Sanctions, increasing costs of litigation, FRAP 38
Scope of rules, FRAP 1
Separate trials, ***370***

Page numbers in ***boldface italic***

APPEALS (continued)
Service
Generally, FRAP 25
Notice of appeal, FRAP 3
Process, FRAP 25
Statement of evidence, FRAP 10
Stay of mandate, FRAP 41
Stay pending appeal, FRAP 8
Substitution of parties, FRAP 43
Tax-court decisions
Applicability of other rules, FRAP 14
Review, FRAP 13
Temporary injunctions, FRAP 8
Transcript, payment for, FRAP 10
Unsupported finding or conclusion, FRAP 10
Voluntary dismissal, FRAP 42

APPEARANCE
Condemnation, FRCP 71A
Default judgment, FRCP 55; ***590***
Deposition, failure to appear, FRCP 37; ***447***

ARBITRATION
Generally, ***650***
Appellate review
Final order, ***650***
Interlocutory order, ***651***
Standard of review, ***667***
Waiver, ***668***
Award, pleading as affirmative defense, FRCP 8; ***233***
Motion to compel
Generally, ***650***
Grounds, ***651***
Request stay, ***653***
Response, ***653***
Ruling, ***658***
Motion to confirm domestic award
Generally, ***663***
Deadline, ***663***
Jurisdiction, ***663***
Response, ***664***
Ruling, ***664***
Venue, ***663***
Motion to confirm foreign award
Generally, ***664***
Deadline, ***665***
Jurisdiction, ***665***
Response, ***665***
Ruling, ***666***
Venue, ***665***
Motion to modify award
Generally, ***659***
Grounds, ***660***
Jurisdiction, ***659***
Limitations period, ***660***
Venue, ***659***
Motion to vacate award
Generally, ***659***
Grounds, ***661***
Jurisdiction, ***659***
Limitations period, ***660***
Venue, ***659***
Review by district court, ***663***

ARBITRATION (continued)
Ruling, ***658***
Waiver, ***657***

ARTFUL-PLEADING DOCTRINE
See Jurisdiction, this index

ASSIGNMENTS
Cases for trial, FRCP 40

ASSUMPTION OF RISK
Pleading, as affirmative defense, FRCP 8; ***233***

ATTACHMENT, POSTAL SUITS
Generally, 28 U.S.C. 2710-2718

ATTORNEY-CLIENT PRIVILEGE
See Privileges, this index

ATTORNEY FEES
Generally, ***67***
American rule, ***67***
Amount of claim, ***753***
Appellate review, ***69, 629, 760***
As costs, FRCP 54; 28 U.S.C. 2412; ***746***
As damages, ***746***
Bad-faith litigation, ***753***
Calculating
Common-fund cases, ***758***
Lodestar, ***754***
Public-interest litigation, ***759***
Substantial-benefit cases, ***759***
Common-fund doctrine, ***68***
Costs vs. damages, ***746***
Diversity jurisdiction, amount in controversy, ***124***
Grounds, statutory, ***749***
Hearing, ***759***
Judgment, FRCP 54; ***747***
Lodestar, ***754***
Motion for fees
Generally, ***745***
As costs, ***746***
As damages, ***745, 746***
Deadline, ***747***
Grounds, ***749***
Response, ***759***
Order, as costs, ***759***
Pretrial conference, sanctions, FRCP 16; ***294***
Prevailing plaintiff, ***750***
Reasonable, ***754***
Request
Hearing, ***759***
Response, ***759***
Ruling, ***760***
Substantial-benefit doctrine, ***753***
Summary judgment, ***605***
Time records, evidence of, ***755***
Tort-claims procedures, 28 U.S.C. 2678
Waiver, ***746***

ATTORNEY GENERAL
Generally, 28 U.S.C. 503
Administration, assistant for, 28 U.S.C. 507
Adviser, 28 U.S.C. 511-513
Annual report, 28 U.S.C. 529

ATTORNEY GENERAL (continued)
Appropriations
Authorization, 28 U.S.C. 530A
Availability, 28 U.S.C. 524
Assistant, 28 U.S.C. 506, 507A
Associate, 28 U.S.C. 504a
Authority, delegation, 28 U.S.C. 510
Authority to investigate
Clerks of court, 28 U.S.C. 526
Marshals, 28 U.S.C. 526
Others, 28 U.S.C. 526
Trustees, 28 U.S.C. 526
U.S. attorneys, 28 U.S.C. 526
Constitutional challenge, notice of, FRCP 5.1; ***12***
Court of Federal Claims, petitions transmitted to, 28 U.S.C. 520
Department of Justice
Executive department, 28 U.S.C. 501
Head of, 28 U.S.C. 503
Seal, 28 U.S.C. 502
Deputy, 28 U.S.C. 504
Disqualification of
Employees, 28 U.S.C. 528
Officers, 28 U.S.C. 528
Executive departments, adviser to heads of, 28 U.S.C. 512
Expenses, payment of travel, 28 U.S.C. 530
Functions, 28 U.S.C. 509
Intervention, notice of constitutional question, FRCP 4; 28 U.S.C. 2403; ***12, 360***
Law books, procurement of, 28 U.S.C. 525
Legal proceedings
Authority to conduct, 28 U.S.C. 515
Conduct & argument of, 28 U.S.C. 516, 518
Supervision, 28 U.S.C. 519
Legal services, 28 U.S.C. 514
Military departments, adviser to secretaries of, 28 U.S.C. 513
National security, 28 U.S.C. 507A, 509A
Oath, special attorneys, 28 U.S.C. 515
Opinions, 28 U.S.C. 521
President, adviser to, 28 U.S.C. 511
Reference books, procurement of, 28 U.S.C. 525
Requisitions, 28 U.S.C. 523
Service of process, FRCP 4; ***155***
Solicitor, 28 U.S.C. 505
Statistics, report of, 28 U.S.C. 522
U.S., interest in suit, 28 U.S.C. 517
Vacancies, 28 U.S.C. 508
Working capital fund, establishment of, 28 U.S.C. 527

ATTORNEYS
Generally, ***58***
Ad litem, appointment of, ***75***
Agreements, ***67***
Appeals, FRAP 46
Appearance of impropriety, ***66***
Appearing
Generally, ***59***
Pro se, ***60***

Page numbers in ***boldface italic***

ATTORNEYS (continued)
Application
General admission, ***59***
Limited admission, ***59***
Communications, ***61***
Disqualification, ***62***
Fees, *see* Attorney Fees, this index
In charge, ***30***, ***61***
Privilege, attorney-client, ***432***, ***463***
Pro hac vice, ***59***
Serving, ***30***
Substitute, ***62***
Termination by client, ***62***
U.S., 28 U.S.C. 541-550
Withdrawal, ***62***

AUTHENTICATION
Generally, FRCP 44; FRE 901, 902; ***694***
Self-authenticating documents, FRE 902; ***697***

AVOIDANCE
Pleading, as affirmative defense, FRCP 8

BANKRUPTCY
Appeals, FRAP 6
Fees, 28 U.S.C. 1930
Judges, *see* this index
Jurisdiction, district courts, 28 U.S.C. 1334; ***114***
Motions, 28 U.S.C. 2075
Removal, 28 U.S.C. 1452; ***258***
Venue, 28 U.S.C. 1408, 1409; ***146***

BIAS & PREJUDICE
Disqualification, judges, 28 U.S.C. 144, 455; ***322***

BIFURCATED TRIAL
See Separate Trials, Motion for, this index

BILL OF COSTS
Generally, ***766***
Deadline, ***766***
Objections, ***767***

BILL OF EXCEPTIONS
Exceptions unnecessary, FRCP 46; ***41***

BONDS
Actions on, jury, 28 U.S.C. 1874; ***588***
Appeal, FRAP 7
Copy of officer's, 28 U.S.C. 1737
Fine paid with, deposits, 28 U.S.C. 2044
Injunction, ***105***
Jurisdiction, district courts, 28 U.S.C. 1352
TRO, ***100***

BOUNDARIES
Hearsay exception, FRE 803

BRIEFS
Reply, summary judgment, ***609***

BRIEFS, APPEAL
Generally, FRAP 28
Amicus curiae, FRAP 29
Appendixes, FRAP 30
Costs, 28 U.S.C. 1923

BRIEFS, APPEAL (continued)
Filing, FRAP 31
Form, FRAP 32

BRILLHART
See Abstention, this index

BURFORD
See Abstention, this index

CALCULATION OF TIME
See also Deadline, this index
Generally, FRAP 26; FRCP 6; ***23***, ***33***
Responses, ***33***

CAPACITY
Complaint, ***78***
Parties, FRCP 17; ***78***

CASE MANAGEMENT/ELECTRONIC CASE FILES (CM/ECF)
See Electronic Filing, this index

CERTIFICATE
Attorney's, motion to recuse, ***322***
Conference
Motion to compel, ***445***
Protective order, ***442***
Retax costs, ***769***
Sanctions, ***448***
Probable cause, habeas corpus, FRAP 22
Service, FRCP 5; ***12***, ***33***
Trial judge's, habeas corpus, 28 U.S.C. 2245

CERTIFIED QUESTIONS, APPEAL
Supreme Court, 28 U.S.C. 1254

CERTIORARI
Courts of appeals, 28 U.S.C. 1254
Harmless error, 28 U.S.C. 2111
Mandate, stay, FRAP 41
State courts, 28 U.S.C. 1257
Stay to obtain writ, 28 U.S.C. 2101
Time, 28 U.S.C. 2101

CHALLENGES FOR CAUSE
See Jury Selection, this index

CHARACTER EVIDENCE
Generally, FRE 404, 405; ***691***
Opinion evidence, FRE 405, 608
Personal or family history, FRE 803
Reputation evidence, FRE 608; ***692***

CHARGE
See Jury Charge, this index

CHARTS
Computing deadlines to respond, chart 1-2, ***36***
Deadline, filing vs. service, chart 1-1, ***22***
Defendant's responses, chart 3-1, ***177***
Diversity jurisdiction, ***111***, ***233***
General jurisdiction, chart 3-3, ***182***
Methods of discovery, chart 6-1, ***414***
Modifying discovery procedures, chart 6-2, ***419***
Postjudgment motions, chart 10-1, ***775***
Pursuing adverse ruling, chart 8-1, ***705***

CHARTS (continued)
Relationships, degree of, chart 5-1, ***328***
Removal, diversity jurisdiction, ***250***
Rule vs. statutory interpleader, chart 2-1, ***90***
Specific jurisdiction, chart 3-2, ***181***

CIVIL FORFEITURE
See Admiralty & Maritime Claims, this index

CLASS ACTIONS
See also Jurisdiction, this index
Generally, FRCP 23
Class Action Fairness Act, ***129***

CLASS CERTIFICATION, MOTION
See Motions, this index

CLAWBACK AGREEMENT
Generally, ***418***

CLERGY
Privilege, ***474***

CLERKS OF COURTS
Generally, FRCP 79
Costs taxed by, ***767***
Court of appeals, 28 U.S.C. 711
Court of Federal Claims, 28 U.S.C. 791
Court of International Trade, 28 U.S.C. 871
Court officers, *see* this index
Death of, 28 U.S.C. 954
Deputy
Duties, 28 U.S.C. 954, 956
Oath, 28 U.S.C. 951
District court, FRCP 77; 28 U.S.C. 751
Duties, 28 U.S.C. 956
Entry of default by, FRCP 55; ***587***
Entry of default judgment by, ***590***
Filing
Duties, ***28***
Hours open, ***18***
Receipt of documents, ***18***
Notice
Entry of judgment, ***741***
Reopen time for appeal, ***821***
Ruling, ***46***
Oath of office
Administration of, 28 U.S.C. 953
Clerks, 28 U.S.C. 951
Deputies, 28 U.S.C. 951
Office, ineligibility for, 28 U.S.C. 957
Office expenses, clerks, 28 U.S.C. 961
Summons, clerk's duty, ***152***
U.S. Supreme Court, 28 U.S.C. 671

CLIENTS
Disqualification of attorney, ***62***
Litigation adverse to, ***63***, ***66***

CLOSING ARGUMENT
Generally, ***727***
Appellate review, ***731***
Error, ***730***
Limits, ***727***
Permitted argument, ***727***
Preserving error, ***729***
Prohibited argument, ***728***

INDEX

Page numbers in ***boldface italic***

CM/ECF
See Electronic Filing, this index

COLORADO RIVER
See Abstention, this index

COMMENCEMENT OF ACTION
Generally, FRCP 3

COMMUNICATIONS
Ex parte, ***61***

COMPEL, MOTION TO
Generally, FRCP 37; ***444***
Certificate of conference, ***445***

COMPLAINT
Generally, FRCP 3-5, 7-11, 15, 17-20, 38; ***75***
Alienage jurisdiction, ***80***
Allegations
  Civil-rights suits, ***83***
  Conclusory, ***81***
  Damages, ***84***
  Facts, ***81***
  Fraud, ***83***
  Jurisdiction, ***78***
  Mistake, ***83***
  Theories of recovery, ***84***
  Time & place, ***83***
  Venue, ***80***
Amend, pretrial, after dismissal, ***347***
Attorney fees, ***85***
Capacity, ***78***
Conditions precedent, ***85***
Constitutional question, ***86***
Costs, ***85***
Cover sheet, ***86***
Damages
  Generally, ***84***
  General, ***84***
  Punitive, ***84***
  Special, ***84***
Diversity jurisdiction, ***79***
Exhibits
  Generally, ***86***
  Excessive, ***86***
  Incorporation by attachment, ***86***
Factual allegations, ***81***
Fair-notice pleading, ***81***
Federal-question jurisdiction, ***79***
Fees, ***86***
Filing, ***86***
Interest, ***85***
John Doe parties, ***76***
Jurisdiction, allegations, ***78***
Jury demand, ***85***
Misidentification, ***75***
Misnomer, ***75***
Misspelled name, ***75***
Multiparty jurisdiction, ***80***
Notice pleading, ***81***
Omitted parties, ***78***
Parties, ***75***
Plausibility, ***81***
Relief, ***85***
Requirements, ***75***

COMPLAINT (continued)
Short & plain statement, ***80***
Signature, ***85***
Standing, ***77***
Statement of claim, ***80***
Supplemental jurisdiction, ***80***
Venue, ***80***
Verification, ***86***

COMPROMISE & SETTLEMENT
Admissibility, FRE 408; ***342***
Award for negligence, tort claims, 28 U.S.C. 2672
Class action, FRCP 23
Derivative actions, FRCP 23.1
Dismissal, voluntary, FRAP 42
Judgments against U.S., 28 U.S.C. 2414
Pretrial conference, FRCP 16
Tort claims against U.S., 28 U.S.C. 2672, 2677, 2679

COMPULSORY COUNTERCLAIM
Pleading, FRCP 13; ***235***

COMPUTATION OF TIME
See also Deadline, this index
Generally, FRAP 26; FRCP 6; ***23, 33***
Responses, ***33***

CONCLUSIONS OF LAW
Generally, FRCP 52
Attorney fees, ***760***
New trial, amendment, FRCP 59; ***788***

CONDEMNATION
Generally, FRCP 71A

CONDITIONS, MENTAL, EMOTIONAL, OR PHYSICAL
Hearsay exception, FRE 803

CONDITIONS PRECEDENT
Class actions, FRCP 23
Pleading, FRCP 9; ***231***

CONDUCT
Character & reputation evidence, FRE 404, 405, 608; ***692***
Compromise & settlement evidence, FRE 408; ***342***

CONFIDENTIAL INFORMATION
See Privileges, this index

CONFLICT OF INTEREST
Disqualification
  Attorney, ***63***
  Judge, 28 U.S.C. 455; ***322, 323***
Witnesses, 28 U.S.C. 2506

CONFUSION
Exclusion of evidence because of, FRE 403

CONSANGUINITY
See Relatives, this index

CONSENT
Hearing, outside district, FRCP 77
Magistrate judges, trial, FRCP 73; ***301***

CONSENT (continued)
Pleading, FRCP 15
Removal, ***263***
Trial by
  Defective pleading, ***13***
  Express consent, ***711***
  Implied consent, ***711***
  Jury, FRCP 39; ***310***
Withdrawal, demand for jury trial, FRCP 38; ***310***

CONSIDERATION
Pleading failure of, as affirmative defense, FRCP 8; ***233***

CONSOLIDATION OF ACTIONS
Generally, FRCP 42; ***362***
Appellate review, ***365***
Deadline, ***364***
Effect, ***365***
Grounds, ***363***
Motion, ***362***
Order, ***364***
Response
  Generally, ***364***
  Waiver, ***364***

CONSTITUTION, U.S.
Generally, ***1553***

CONTEMPT
Commitment for civil, FRCP 4.1
Discovery, refusal to comply, FRCP 37; ***450***
Judgment directing performance of specific acts, FRCP 70
Production of documents, national in foreign country, 28 U.S.C. 1784
Recalcitrant witnesses, 28 U.S.C. 1826
Service of, order, FRCP 4.1
Subpoena, FRCP 45; ***58, 450***
Summary judgment, affidavit in bad faith, FRCP 56; ***612***
Witnesses, failing to
  Appear, masters, FRCP 53
  Respond to subpoena, foreign country, 28 U.S.C. 1784

CONTINUANCE, MOTION FOR
Generally, FRCP 15, 56; ***337***
Affidavits, ***337***
Agreed, ***337***
Appellate review, ***340***
Deadline, ***337***
Grounds, ***337***
Notice, ***337***
Response, ***340***
Surprise evidence, ***340***
Surprise testimony, ***340***
Unavailable for trial
  Attorney, ***340***
  Witness or party, ***339***

CONTRIBUTORY NEGLIGENCE
Pleading, as affirmative defense, FRCP 8; ***233***

Page numbers in ***boldface italic***

CONVICTION OF CRIME
Hearsay exception, FRE 803
Witness's credibility, FRE 609; ***693***

COPARTIES
Cross-claims, FRCP 13; ***236***

COPIES
Generally, FRE 1001-1004; ***695***
Books & records of states, 28 U.S.C. 1738, 1739
Business records, 28 U.S.C. 1732
Consular papers, 28 U.S.C. 1740
Costs, 28 U.S.C. §1920; ***763***
Court record lost or destroyed, 28 U.S.C. 1734; ***29***
Filing, FRAP 25, 14
Foreign documents, 28 U.S.C. 1741
Full faith & credit
  Books & records, 28 U.S.C. 1738, 1739
  State judicial proceedings, 28 U.S.C. 1738
  State laws, 28 U.S.C. 1738
Laws & judicial proceedings of states, 28 U.S.C. 1738
Opinions, mailing, FRAP 36
Order of reference, FRCP 53
Production, FRCP 34
Public record, authentication, FRCP 44; ***698***
Served with admissions, FRCP 36
Service, FRAP 25
State books & records, 28 U.S.C. 1739
State laws & judicial proceedings, 28 U.S.C. 1738
Summons, FRCP 4
Taxable costs, 28 U.S.C. §1920; ***763***
Written instruments as exhibits, FRCP 10; ***11***

CORPORATIONS
Derivative actions, FRCP 23.1
Disclosure statement
  Defendant, FRCP 7.1; ***237***
  Plaintiff, FRCP 7.1; ***86***
Jurisdiction, generally, 28 U.S.C. 1332; ***119***, ***128***
Jurisdiction, organized under federal law, 28 U.S.C. 1349
Pro se appearance, ***60***
Venue, 28 U.S.C. 1391; ***144***, ***147***, ***193***

CORRECTIONS
Record, appeal, FRAP 10

COST BOND, APPEAL
Generally, FRAP 7

COSTS
Generally, FRCP 54; 28 U.S.C. §1920; ***761***
Admiralty & maritime cases, 28 U.S.C. 1925
Against attorney, ***765***
Against U.S., ***765***
Appellate review, ***769***
Attorney fees, ***68***
Award
  Appellate review, ***769***
  District-court review, ***767***
  Error, ***770***

COSTS (continued)
Award (continued)
  Grounds, ***767***
  Prevailing party, ***765***
  Reducing, invalid grounds, ***768***
Bankruptcy fees, 28 U.S.C. 1930
Bill of costs, ***766***
Clerk, fees of, ***761***
Clerk's award, ***767***
Copies, ***763***
  Electronic, ***763***
  Paper, ***763***
Court of Federal Claims, 28 U.S.C. 1926
Court-reporter fees, ***761***
Court's award, FRCP 54; ***765***
Courts of appeals, 28 U.S.C. 1913
Depositions, videotaped, ***761***
Determining, offer of judgment, FRCP 68; 28 U.S.C. 1918; ***320***
Dismissal, lack of jurisdiction, 28 U.S.C. 1919
District court
  Generally, 28 U.S.C. 1914; ***86***
  Notice of appeal, fee for filing, 28 U.S.C. 1917
Docket fees, 28 U.S.C. 1920, 1923; ***761***
Excessive costs, attorney liability, 28 U.S.C. 1927; ***388***, ***396***
Exemplification, ***763***
Extraordinary expenses, 28 U.S.C. 1929
Filing fees, where deposited, 28 U.S.C. 1931
In forma pauperis, *see* this index
Judgment, ***765***
Marshal's fees, 28 U.S.C. 1921; ***761***
Patent infringement, 28 U.S.C. 1928
Printing fees, 28 U.S.C. 1920; ***761***
Retax, motion to, ***767***
Review of clerk's award by district court, ***767***
Seamen's suits, 28 U.S.C. 1916
Stenographic transcription, ***761***
Supreme Court, 28 U.S.C. 1911, 1912
Taxable, 28 U.S.C. 1920; ***761***
Witness fees, 28 U.S.C. 1920, 1922; ***761***

COUNTERCLAIMS
Generally, FRCP 13; ***235***
Compulsory, ***235***
Permissive, FRCP 13; ***236***

COURT OF FEDERAL CLAIMS
Accounts
  Agents, 28 U.S.C. 1494, 2511
  Contractors, 28 U.S.C. 1494, 2511
  Officers, 28 U.S.C. 1494, 2511
Alien, privilege to sue, 28 U.S.C. 2502
Attorney General, petitions transmitted by, 28 U.S.C. 520
Bailiffs, 28 U.S.C. 795
Claims
  Against U.S., 28 U.S.C. 1491
  Congressional-reference cases, 28 U.S.C. 1492
  Disbursing officer's, 28 U.S.C. 1496

COURT OF FEDERAL CLAIMS (continued)
Claims (continued)
  Forfeiture of fraudulent, 28 U.S.C. 2514
  Indian, 28 U.S.C. 1505
  Pending in other courts, 28 U.S.C. 1500
Clerk, 28 U.S.C. 791
Comptroller General, cases referred by, 28 U.S.C. 2510
Congressional-reference cases, 28 U.S.C. 2509
Costs, 28 U.S.C. 1926
Counterclaim, 28 U.S.C. 2508
Court
  Place of holding, 28 U.S.C. 798
  Places & times, 28 U.S.C. 173
  Proceedings, reporting, 28 U.S.C. 796
Damages, 28 U.S.C. 1495-1499
Discovery, 28 U.S.C. 2507
Filing suit, time for, 28 U.S.C. 2501
Interest, 28 U.S.C. 2516
Judges, 28 U.S.C. 171-179
Judgment
  Conclusiveness, 28 U.S.C. 2519
  Payment, 28 U.S.C. 2517
  Registration, 28 U.S.C. 2508
  Stay, 28 U.S.C. 2515
Jurisdiction
  Declaratory judgments, certain, 28 U.S.C. 1507
  Indian suits, 28 U.S.C. 1505
  Partnership proceedings, certain, 28 U.S.C. 1508
  Pension claims, 28 U.S.C. 1501
  Set-off, 28 U.S.C. 1503
  Tax refunds, 28 U.S.C. 1509
  Treaty cases, 28 U.S.C. 1502
Law clerks, 28 U.S.C. 794
Messengers, 28 U.S.C. 795
New trial, 28 U.S.C. 2515
Notice of appeal, 28 U.S.C. 2522
Pensions, jurisdiction, 28 U.S.C. 1501
Powers, incidental, 28 U.S.C. 2521
Proceedings, 28 U.S.C. 2503
Retired judges, recall, 28 U.S.C. 797
Secretaries, 28 U.S.C. 794
Set-off
  Generally, 28 U.S.C. 2508
  Jurisdiction, 28 U.S.C. 1503
Subpoenas, 28 U.S.C. 2521
Testimony, by plaintiff, 28 U.S.C. 2504
Time for filing suit, 28 U.S.C. 2501
Treaty cases, 28 U.S.C. 1502
Trial before judges, 28 U.S.C. 2505
Witness, interested, 28 U.S.C. 2506

COURT OF INTERNATIONAL TRADE
Bailiffs, 28 U.S.C. 872
Civil actions
  Analysis, imported merchandise, 28 U.S.C. 2642
  Burden of proof, 28 U.S.C. 2639
  Commence, persons entitled to, 28 U.S.C. 2631

Page numbers in ***boldface italic***

COURT OF INTERNATIONAL TRADE (continued)
Civil actions (continued)
Commencement, 28 U.S.C. 2632
Commencement, time for, 28 U.S.C. 2636
Counterclaims, 28 U.S.C. 1583
Cross-claims, 28 U.S.C. 1583
Decisions, 28 U.S.C. 2645
Documents, inspection, 28 U.S.C. 2641
Evidence of value, 28 U.S.C. 2639
Exhaustion of administrative remedies, 28 U.S.C. 2637
Fees, 28 U.S.C. 2633
Filing, official documents, 28 U.S.C. 2635
Imported merchandise, analysis, 28 U.S.C. 2642
Inspection, documents, 28 U.S.C. 2641
Interest, 28 U.S.C. 2644
NAFTA, brought under, 28 U.S.C. 1584
New grounds supporting, 28 U.S.C. 2638
Notice, 28 U.S.C. 2634
Official documents, filing, 28 U.S.C. 2635
Powers in law & equity, 28 U.S.C. 1585
Procedure, 28 U.S.C. 2633
Rehearing, 28 U.S.C. 2646
Relief, 28 U.S.C. 2643
Retrial, 28 U.S.C. 2646
Scope, 28 U.S.C. 2640
Standard of review, 28 U.S.C. 2640
Third-party actions, 28 U.S.C. 1583
U.S., against, 28 U.S.C. 1581
U.S., commenced by, 28 U.S.C. 1582
Witnesses, 28 U.S.C. 2641
Clerk, 28 U.S.C. 871
Criers, 28 U.S.C. 872
Judges
Chief judge, duties, 28 U.S.C. 253
Number, 28 U.S.C. 251
Offices, 28 U.S.C. 251
Precedence, 28 U.S.C. 253
Salaries, 28 U.S.C. 252
Tenure, 28 U.S.C. 252
Messengers, 28 U.S.C. 872
Trials
At ports other than New York, 28 U.S.C. 256
Decisions, publication, 28 U.S.C. 257
Single-judge, 28 U.S.C. 254
Three-judge, 28 U.S.C. 255

COURT OFFICERS
Clerks of courts, *see* this index
Courts, defined, 28 U.S.C. 963
Receivers, persons ineligible as, 28 U.S.C. 958
Receivers, suable, 28 U.S.C. 959
Restrictions, practice of law, 28 U.S.C. 955
Tax liability, 28 U.S.C. 960
Trustees, suable, 28 U.S.C. 959

COURTS OF APPEALS
Assignment, judges to division, 28 U.S.C. 49
Assignments, 28 U.S.C. 46
Clerks, 28 U.S.C. 711
Composition, 28 U.S.C. 41, 43
Criers, 28 U.S.C. 714

COURTS OF APPEALS (continued)
Disqualification of trial judge to hear appeal, 28 U.S.C. 47
Employees, 28 U.S.C. 711
Hearings, 28 U.S.C. 46
Justices, 28 U.S.C. 42, 44, 45
Law clerks, 28 U.S.C. 712
Librarians, 28 U.S.C. 713
Messengers, 28 U.S.C. 714
Number, 28 U.S.C. 41
Quorum, 28 U.S.C. 46
Rules of practice, FRAP 47
Secretaries, 28 U.S.C. 712
Staff attorneys, 28 U.S.C. 715
Technical assistants, 28 U.S.C. 715
Terms of court, 28 U.S.C. 48

CREDIBILITY
Witness, impeachment, FRE 607-615; ***692***

CROSS-CLAIMS
Generally, FRCP 13; ***236***

CROSS-EXAMINATION
Character & reputation, FRE 405
Deposition, ***546***
Evidence, introducing, ***689***
Witnesses, FRE 611; ***689***

DAMAGES
Generally, ***84***
Action against U.S. for death of defendant, 28 U.S.C. 2404
Appeal, delay, FRAP 38
Discovery, ***459***
Excessive, motion for new trial, ***788***
Pleading, FRCP 9; ***84***

DAUBERT HEARING
Generally, FRCP 16, 26; FRE 104, 401-403, 702-706; ***376***

DEADLINE
See also each particular pleading or motion, this index
Backward-looking deadline, ***24***
Computing
Generally, ***23***
Responses, ***33***
Counting
Days, ***24***
Hours, ***27***
Months, ***27***
Years, ***27***
Extending
Generally, ***25***
Agreement, ***28***, ***333***
Holidays, ***25***
Inaccessibility, clerk's office, ***26***
Motion for continuance, ***28***, ***337***
Motion to extend, ***28***, ***332***
Three-day extension, ***34***
Filing
Generally, ***22***
Electronic, ***21***, ***22***
Fax, ***19***, ***22***

DEADLINE (continued)
Filing vs. service, chart, ***22***
Forward-looking deadline, ***24***
Holidays, ***25***
Inaccessibility, clerk's office, ***26***
Motions, *see* this index
Responses, after service by
Clerk's office, ***34***
Electronic means, ***34***
Fax, ***34***
FedEx or UPS, ***34***
Mail, ***33***
Personal delivery, ***33***
Service
Generally, ***22***, ***33***
Affidavits, ***33***
Motion for hearing, ***33***
Time limits
Calculating, ***23***
Extending, ***28***, ***29***

DEATH
Abatement, motion, *see* this index
Hearsay, *see* this index
Judge, during term, FRCP 63; ***40***
Party, substitution of, FRCP 25; ***332***, ***336***
Witness, use of deposition, FRCP 32; ***551***

DEBT COLLECTION
Affidavit, 28 U.S.C. 3006
Attachment, remedies, 28 U.S.C. 3102
Defendant, joined, 28 U.S.C. 3012
Definitions, 28 U.S.C. 3002
Discharge, remedies, 28 U.S.C. 3206
Discovery, debtor's financial condition, 28 U.S.C. 3015
Enforcement, supervision of, 28 U.S.C. 3013
Enforcement of judgments, remedies, 28 U.S.C. 3202
Execution, remedies, 28 U.S.C. 3203
Fraudulent transfers, 28 U.S.C. 3301-3308
Garnishment, remedies, 28 U.S.C. 3104, 3205
Installment-payment order, remedies, 28 U.S.C. 3204
Joinder, additional defendant, 28 U.S.C. 3012
Judgment liens, remedies, 28 U.S.C. 3201
Judgments, application of chapter to, 28 U.S.C. 3005
Keeper, marshal's authority to designate, 28 U.S.C. 3009
Magistrates, proceedings before, 28 U.S.C. 3008
Postjudgment remedies, 28 U.S.C. 3201-3206
Prejudgment remedies, 28 U.S.C. 3101-3105
Property
Co-owned, 28 U.S.C. 3010
Exempt, 28 U.S.C. 3014
Perishable, 28 U.S.C. 3007
Protective order, modification of, 28 U.S.C. 3013
Receivership, remedies, 28 U.S.C. 3103
Sequestration, remedies, 28 U.S.C. 3105
Service of process, 28 U.S.C. 3004

Page numbers in ***boldface italic***

DEBT COLLECTION (continued)
Sports protection
  Applicability, 28 U.S.C. 3704
  Definitions, 28 U.S.C. 3701
  Gambling, unlawful, 28 U.S.C. 3702
  Injunctions, 28 U.S.C. 3703
Surcharge, assessment of, 28 U.S.C. 3011

DECLARATION
Summary-judgment proof, FRCP 56; ***610***
Verification of pleading, ***12***

DECLARATORY JUDGMENT
Generally, FRCP 57; 28 U.S.C. 2201, 2202; ***107***
Appellate review, ***112***
Attorney fees, ***111***
Availability, ***108***
Burden of proof, ***110***
Damages, ***111***
Declaratory Judgment Act, ***108***
Diversity jurisdiction, amount in controversy, ***124***
Hearing, ***110***
Judgment
  Amending, ***111***
  Discretionary, ***110***
  Dismissal, ***111***
  Exercising jurisdiction, ***110***
  Stay, ***111***
Jurisdiction
  Case-or-controversy requirement, ***108***
  Future controversy, ***108***
  Subject-matter, ***108***
Jury trial, FRCP 38, 39, 57; ***110***
Pending, other actions
  Federal court, ***109***
  State court, ***109***
Procedure
  Generally, 28 U.S.C. 2201; ***110***
  Complaint, ***110***
Relief, additional, 28 U.S.C. 2202; ***111***
Remedy, creation of, 28 U.S.C. 2201; ***111***
Trial, ***110***
Unavailability
  Generally, ***108***
  Criminal matters, ***109***
  Injunction barred, ***110***
  Personal-injury litigation, ***109***
  Tax matters, ***109***

DEFAULT
See Entry of Default, this index

DEFAULT JUDGMENT
See also Entry of Default, this index
Generally, FRCP 55; ***583***
Affidavits, ***586***, ***592***, ***594***
Against U.S., FRCP 55; ***585***
Appellate review, ***602***
Attachment, ***592***, ***594***
By clerk, ***590***
By court
  Generally, ***593***
  Affidavits, ***594***
  Hearing, ***596***

DEFAULT JUDGMENT (continued)
By court (continued)
  Notice of hearing, ***594***
  Objections to entry, ***595***
  Ruling, ***597***
Compared to entry of default, ***583***
Counterclaimants, FRCP 55; ***584***
Cross-claimants, FRCP 55; ***584***
Motion to vacate
  Generally, FRCP 60; ***598***
  Deadline to file, ***601***
  Form, ***598***
  Grounds, ***598***
  Ruling, ***602***
Notice, ***598***
Objections, ***592***, ***595***
Plaintiffs, FRCP 55; ***584***
Request to clerk
  Generally, ***590***
  Objections to entry, ***586***
Set aside entry of default, motion to, FRCP 55; ***588***
Sum certain, ***591***

DEFECTS
Cure, venue, 28 U.S.C. 1406; ***198***
Pleadings, waiver, ***13***
Remand, ***271***
Trial by consent, ***13***

DEFENDANT
Counterclaims, ***235***
Cross-claim, ***236***
Denying liability, ***230***
Pre-answer motion, ***171***
Responses, chart, ***177***
Serving, ***149***
Summons, securing, ***151***
Third-party suit, ***236***
Waiver of service, ***149***

DEFENSES
See also Affirmative Defenses, this index
Generally, FRCP 8; ***230***
Consolidation, ***219***
Failure to join required party, ***214***
Failure to plead claim properly, ***218***
Failure to state claim, ***204***
Improper venue, ***192***
Insufficient service of process, ***209***
Personal jurisdiction, lack of, ***172***, ***178***
Subject-matter jurisdiction, lack of, ***187***
Summary, ***177***

DEFINITIONS, JURY
See Jury Charge, this index

DELIVERY
Filing by, ***19***
Serving documents by, ***31***

DEMAND FOR JURY TRIAL
Generally, FRCP 38, 39; ***309***
Appellate review, ***316***
Deadlines, ***310***
Jury trial, right to, ***311***

DEMAND FOR JURY TRIAL (continued)
Partial, ***309***
Reliance on other party's, ***310***
Scope, ***309***
Strike, motion to, ***314***
Trial by advisory jury, motion for, ***315***
Trial by jury, motion for, ***314***
Withdrawal, ***310***
Writing, ***309***

DEPARTMENT OF JUSTICE
Attorney General, *see* this index
Bureau of Alcohol, Tobacco, Firearms & Explosives, 28 U.S.C. 599A, 599B
Federal Bureau of Investigation, *see* this index
Independent counsel, *see* Attorneys, this index
U.S. attorneys, *see* Attorneys, this index
U.S. Marshals Service, *see* this index
U.S. trustees, *see* Trustees, U.S., this index

DEPOSITIONS
Generally, FRCP 27, 28, 30-32; ***538***
Admissibility, objections to, ***554***
Agreements, FRCP 29; ***546***
Attend, failure to, FRCP 37; ***447***
Attendance, ***545***
Certification, officer's, FRCP 30; ***548***
Cross-examination, ***546***
Discovery, method of, ***415***
Examination, ***546***
Exhibits, FRCP 30; ***548***
Leave of court, ***539***
Making changes, FRCP 30; ***550***
Notice, FRCP 30; ***540***, ***554***
Objections, FRCP 26; ***546***
Oral, FRCP 30; ***538***
Pending appeal, FRCP 27; ***538***
Perpetuating testimony, FRCP 27; ***555***
Procedure
  Generally, ***538***
  Modifying, ***546***
Recording method, FRCP 30; ***543***
Reviewing, ***549***
Taking, before authorized officer, FRCP 28; ***544***
Telephone, FRCP 30; ***543***
Using
  Generally, ***551***
  Presentation, FRCP 32; ***553***
  Restrictions, FRCP 32; ***552***
  Waiver of errors, FRCP 32; ***553***
Video, FRCP 30; ***543***
Written questions
  Generally, FRCP 31; ***538***, ***554***
  Notice, when completed, ***555***
  Notice, when filed, ***554***

DEPOSITS
Bond money, fine paid with, 28 U.S.C. 2044
Money
  Other than public, 28 U.S.C. 2043
  Public, 28 U.S.C. 2041
Withdrawal, 28 U.S.C. 2042

Page numbers in ***boldface italic***

DERIVATIVE ACTIONS
Generally, FRCP 23.1
Process, 28 U.S.C. 1695
Venue, 28 U.S.C. 1401

DESTROYED DOCUMENTS
Generally, FRE 1004; ***695***

DIRECT EXAMINATION
Generally, ***688***

DIRECTED VERDICT
See Judgment as a Matter of Law, Motion for, this index

DIRECTORIES
Hearsay exception, FRE 803

DISCLOSURES
Compel, motion for order to, FRCP 37; ***444***
Deadline
- Expert, ***535***
- Initial, ***533***
- Pretrial, final, ***536***

Expert, ***534***
Failure to disclose, FRCP 37; ***444***, ***448***, ***451***
False, FRCP 37
Forms of, FRCP 26
Initial, ***533***
Mandatory
- Generally, FRCP 26; ***415***, ***532***
- Exempt proceedings, ***534***
- Expert, FRCP 26; ***534***
- Initial, ***532***
- Objections, ***537***
- Pretrial, final, FRCP 26; ***532***, ***536***
- Sanctions, ***537***
- Stages, ***532***

Misleading, FRCP 37
Pretrial, final, ***536***
Privileged information, ***430***
Protected information, ***432***, ***518***, ***523***
Redacted, FRCP 5.2, ***17***
Signing, FRCP 26; ***532***
Statement
- Defendant, FRCP 7.1; ***237***
- Plaintiff, FRCP 7.1; ***86***

Supplemental, FRCP 26; ***439***

DISCOVERY
Generally, FRCP 26-37, 45; ***413***
Additional matter, methods to discover, FRCP 26
Appellate review
- Appeal, ***454***
- Mandamus, ***455***

Case-management conference, FRCP 26; ***289***
Certificates, ***420***
Compel, motion to, *see* Motions, this index
Conference
- Generally, FRCP 26
- Certificate, ***442***, ***445***
- Deadline, ***416***
- Objectives, ***416***

DISCOVERY (continued)
Conference (continued)
- Pretrial, ***416***
- Requirement, ***416***
- Scheduling, ***416***

Deadline to respond, ***422***
Depositions, *see* this index
Disclosures, *see* this index
Electronically stored information, *see* this index
Examination
- Mental, FRCP 35; ***574***
- Order for, FRCP 35
- Physical, FRCP 35; ***574***

Examiner, report of, FRCP 35; ***577***
Expert witnesses, *see* this index
Failure to participate, FRCP 37; ***444***
False disclosure, FRCP 37
Filing
- Generally, FRCP 5, 26; ***438***
- Redacted, FRCP 5.2, ***17***

Forms
- Generally, ***413***
- Admissions, request for, FRCP 36; ***415***, ***563***
- Deposition, oral, FRCP 30; ***415***
- Deposition, written questions, FRCP 31; ***415***
- Disclosures, *see* this index
- Entry on land, request for, FRCP 34; ***416***
- Examination, mental, FRCP 35; ***416***
- Examination, physical, FRCP 35; ***416***
- Interrogatories, FRCP 33; ***415***
- Production, request for, FRCP 34; ***415***

Inspection, request for, FRCP 34; ***579***
International conventions, effect of, ***460***
Mandatory disclosures, *see* Disclosures, this index
Medical records, ***570***
Meeting, parties, FRCP 26; ***416***
Mental examination, FRCP 35; ***574***
Misleading disclosure, FRCP 37
Modifying, ***419***
Objections
- Generally, ***424***
- Invalid, ***426***
- Waiver, ***429***

Obtaining, ***421***
Order compelling, FRCP 37
Parties, meeting, FRCP 26; ***416***
Persons not parties, FRCP 34; ***50***, ***458***
Physical examination, FRCP 35; ***574***
Plan, FRCP 26; ***417***
Preservation of evidence, ***416***, ***486***
Preservation plan, FRCP 26; ***73***, ***417***
Presuit, ***75***
Privilege log, ***426***
Privileges, asserting after production
- Generally, FRCP 26; ***430***
- Clawback agreement, ***418***
- Quick-peek agreement, ***418***

Privileges, types, *see* Privileges, this index
Protective order, *see* Motions, this index
Purpose, ***413***
Refusal to admit, FRCP 37; ***448***

DISCOVERY (continued)
Report, FRCP 26; ***418***
Request for inspection, FRCP 34; ***579***
Resisting
- Generally, FRCP 26; ***424***
- Asserting privileges, ***426***
- Burden to partially comply, ***428***
- Burden to resolve dispute, ***427***
- Hearing, ***428***
- Objections, ***424***

Response, extending time
- After deadline, ***422***
- Agreement, ***422***
- Before deadline, ***422***
- Court order, ***422***

Sanctions, motion for
- Generally, ***446***
- Discovery, not certifying, ***448***
- Discovery, not obeying, FRCP 37; ***446***
- Discovery, not responding, ***447***
- Discovery, not supplementing, ***448***
- Discovery plan, not participating, ***448***
- Due process, ***446***
- Grounds, ***446***
- Types available, ***448***

Scheduling conference, FRCP 26; ***289***
Scheduling order, *see* this index
Scope
- Generally, FRCP 26; ***456***
- Damages information, ***459***
- Discoverable, ***457***
- Documents, FRCP 34; ***458***
- Electronically stored information, ***458***
- Entry on land, FRCP 34; ***460***
- Expert witnesses, *see* this index
- Fact witnesses, ***458***
- Financial information, ***459***
- Insurance, ***459***
- International conventions, ***460***
- Limitations, FRCP 26; ***460***
- Medical condition, ***460***
- Nonparty statement, ***458***
- Not discoverable, ***460***
- Party contentions, ***458***
- Party opinions, ***458***
- Party statement, ***458***
- Privileged information, *see* Privileges, this index
- Protected information, *see* Privileges, this index
- Tangible things, ***458***
- Trial-preparation materials, FRCP 26; ***459***
- Waiver, ***429***

Securing
- Order, ***421***
- Request, ***421***
- Stipulation, ***421***

Sequence, FRCP 26
Signing requirement
- Generally, ***420***
- Disclosures, FRCP 26; ***420***
- Objections, FRCP 26; ***420***

Page numbers in ***boldface italic***

DISCOVERY (continued)
Signing requirement (continued)
Requests, FRCP 26; ***420***
Responses, FRCP 26; ***420***
Supplementation, ***439***
Stipulations, FRCP 29; ***419***
Subpoenas, *see* this index
Supplement
Generally, ***438***
Disclose, failure to, ***439***
Disclosures, FRCP 26; ***439***
Respond, failure to, ***440***
Responses, FRCP 26; ***438***
Signing requirement, ***439***
Timing, ***439***
When not required, ***439***
When required, ***438***
Timing, FRCP 26
Waiver, ***429***
Written, producing
Generally, ***423***
Discovery not required, ***423***
Discovery required, ***423***
Form, ***423***
Service, ***423***

DISMISSAL
Costs, FRCP 41
Counterclaim, FRCP 41; ***737***
Cross-claim, FRCP 41; ***737***
Involuntary, FRCP 41; ***642***
Voluntary, FRCP 41; ***629***

DISQUALIFICATION
See also Recuse, Motion to, this index
Attorney
Adverse to current client, ***66***
Adverse to former client, ***63***
Appellate review, ***68***
Grounds, ***63***
Mediator, serving as, ***67***
Presumptions, imputed knowledge, ***65***
Presumptions, shared confidences, ***64***
Standards governing, ***62***
Witness, serving as, ***63***
Challenge to order, ***67***

DISTRICT COURTS
Adjournment, 28 U.S.C. 140
Always open, FRCP 77; ***18***
Appoint, power to, 28 U.S.C. 756
Bailiffs, 28 U.S.C. 755
Chambers, orders in, FRCP 77
Clerks, 28 U.S.C. 751
Clerk's office, FRCP 77; ***18***
Composition of, 28 U.S.C. 132
Creation of, 28 U.S.C. 132
Criers, 28 U.S.C. 755
Disqualification
Bias, 28 U.S.C. 144, 455
Prejudice, 28 U.S.C. 144, 455
Districts, generally, 28 U.S.C. 81-131
Hearings, FRCP 77; ***38***

DISTRICT COURTS (continued)
Judges
Appointment, 28 U.S.C. 133
Chief judges, 28 U.S.C. 136
Division of business among, 28 U.S.C. 137
Number, 28 U.S.C. 133
Precedence, 28 U.S.C. 136
Residence, 28 U.S.C. 134
Salaries, 28 U.S.C. 135
Tenure, 28 U.S.C. 134
Terms abolished, 28 U.S.C. 138
Law, procedures when no controlling, FRCP 83
Law clerks, 28 U.S.C. 752
Local rules, FRCP 83; ***5***
Notice
Judgments, FRCP 77; ***46, 741***
Orders, FRCP 77; ***46***
Orders by clerk, FRCP 77
Receivers, 28 U.S.C. 754
Reporters, 28 U.S.C. 753; ***40***
Secretaries, 28 U.S.C. 752
Sessions, times for holding regular, 28 U.S.C. 139
Special masters, power to appoint, ***302***
Special sessions
Notice, 28 U.S.C. 141
Places, 28 U.S.C. 141
Trials, FRCP 77
Vacant judgeship, 28 U.S.C. 143

DIVERSITY JURISDICTION
See Jurisdiction, this index

DOCKET
Clerks to keep, FRCP 79
District courts, appeals, FRAP 12
Entries, FRCP 79; ***45***
Entry of judgment, FRAP 36
Fees & costs of briefs, 28 U.S.C. 1923; ***761***
File number of action, FRCP 79
Indices, FRCP 79
Jury trial, designation, FRCP 39
Record service of notice of order or judgment, FRCP 77

DOCTORS
Examination, motion for mental or physical, ***575***
Medical condition, ***460***
Psychotherapist-client privilege, ***472***

DOCUMENTS
Admissions, FRCP 36; ***564***
Ancient documents, hearsay exception, FRE 803
Authentication, FRE 901; ***694***
Copies, *see* this index
Filing, ***17***
Foreign public documents, FRCP 44; ***697***
Introducing at trial, ***694***
Lost, ***29***
Original, ***694***
Pleading official document, FRCP 9
Redacted, FRCP 5.2, 25; ***17, 23***

DOCUMENTS (continued)
Refusal to file, FRCP 5; ***28***
Request, FRCP 34; ***569***
Serving
Generally, ***29***
Methods, ***30***
Withdrawing, ***29***

DOMICILE & RESIDENCE
Attorneys, *see* this index
Clerks of courts, *see* this index
Judges, *see* this index
Parties, capacity to sue or be sued, FRCP 17; ***78***
Removal, residence of party, 28 U.S.C. 1441; ***250***
Venue, *see* this index

DROP BOX
Filing documents, ***18***

DURESS
Pleading, as affirmative defense, FRCP 8; ***233***

DYING DECLARATIONS
Hearsay exception, FRE 804; ***691***

ECF
See Electronic Filing, this index

E-DISCOVERY
See Electronically Stored Information, this index

E-FILING
See Electronic Filing, this index

ELECTRONIC DATA
Authenticating, ***696***

ELECTRONIC FILING
Generally, FRAP 25; FRCP 6; ***20***
CM/ECF, ***20***
Exceptions, FRAP 25; FRCP 5, 16
Fees, ***21***
Procedure, ***20***
Retention of documents, ***22***
Timing, ***21***

ELECTRONIC SERVICE
Generally, ***31***
Consent, ***31, 32***
Proof of service, ***37***
Response, ***34***

ELECTRONICALLY STORED INFORMATION
Generally, FRCP 26; ***481***
Compel, motion to, FRCP 26; ***510***
Conference, FRCP 26(f); ***495***
Costs, ***490***
Defined, FRCP 34; ***482***
Definitions, ***483***
Discovery
Depositions, ***499***
Disclosures, ***498***
Interrogatories, ***499***

Page numbers in ***boldface italic***

ELECTRONICALLY STORED INFORMATION (continued)
Discovery (continued)
Requests for admissions, ***499***
Requests for production, ***500***
Scope, ***493***
Discovery plan, FRCP 26; ***417***
Failure to produce, FRCP 37; ***445***
Form of production, FRCP 26, 34; ***497, 500***
Keyword searches, ***491***
Lost or destroyed, sanctions
Generally, FRCP 37; ***513***
Good-faith defense, ***514***
Routine operation, ***497, 514***
Metadata, ***485, 500***
Not reasonably accessible, ***494***
Objecting to, FRCP 34; ***503***
Predictive coding, ***491***
Preservation, ***486***
Preservation plan, FRCP 26; ***417, 486***
Protective order, FRCP 26; ***442, 505***
Reasonably accessible, FRCP 26; ***493***
Resisting discovery, FRCP 26; ***503***
Sanctions, FRCP 37; ***513***
Scope of discovery, ***493***
Search techniques, ***490***
Social-networking sites, ***459***
Subpoena, FRCP 45; ***48, 53***
Waiver of privilege, ***490***

E-MAIL
Filing, *see* Electronic Filing, this index
Service, *see* Electronic Service, this index

EN BANC PROCEEDINGS
When proceeding may be ordered, FRAP 35

ENFORCEMENT
Administrative orders, on appeal, FRAP 15
Agency orders, 28 U.S.C. 2351
Judgment, 28 U.S.C. 3202
Service of process, Federal Debt Collection Procedure, 28 U.S.C. 3004
Supervision of, procedure, 28 U.S.C. 3013

ENTRY OF DEFAULT
Generally, FRCP 55; ***583***
Affidavits, ***586***
Attachments, ***586***
By clerk, ***587***
Compared to default judgment, ***583***
Defenses, ***586***
Effect of entry by clerk, ***587***
Motion to set aside
Generally, ***588***
Deadline, ***589***
Form, ***588***
Grounds, ***588***
Motion for leave, ***590***
Proposed pleading, ***590***
Notice, ***586***
Objections, ***586***
Order, not appealable, ***588***
Request to clerk, ***584***

ENTRY OF JUDGMENT
See Judgment, this index

ENTRY ON LAND, REQUEST FOR
Generally, FRCP 34; ***579***
Appellate review, ***580***
Nonparty, subpoena, ***579***
Response, ***579***

ERROR
Generally, ***41***
Appealable, ***42***
Clerical, *see* Postjudgment Motions, this index
Deposition, errors in, FRCP 32; ***553***
Final argument, error in, ***730***
Harmless
Generally, FRCP 61
Certiorari, 28 U.S.C. 2111
Plain
Generally, FRCP 51; FRE 103; ***42***
Offer of proof, ***709***
Preserving
Excluded evidence, ***705***
Failure to preserve, ***43***
Final argument, ***729***
Jury charge, ***726***
Jury selection, ***678***
New trial, ***784***
Objections, ***42***
Opening statement, ***687***
Raised on appeal, ***43***
Types, ***41***

ESTOPPEL
Pleading, as affirmative defense, FRCP 8; ***233***

EVIDENCE
Admissibility
Irrelevant evidence, FRE 402; ***688***
Pleas, FRE 410
Relevant evidence, FRE 402; ***688***
State law, FRE 302
Appellate review
Admissibility, ***706***
Standard of review, ***706***
Applicability of rules, FRE 1101; ***3***
Business record, 28 U.S.C. 1732; ***695***
Character, FRE 404, 405
Child-custody determinations, full faith & credit, 28 U.S.C. 1738A
Child-support orders, full faith & credit, 28 U.S.C. 1738B
Congressional journals, 28 U.S.C. 1736
Consular papers, copies of, 28 U.S.C. 1740
Contempt, 28 U.S.C. 1784
Court, function of, FRE 1008
Declarations, unsworn, 28 U.S.C. 1746; ***12***
Documents
Authentication, ***694***
Domestic official records, introducing, FRCP 44; ***698***
Foreign official records, introducing, FRCP 44; ***698***
Self-authentication, ***697***
Electronic data, ***696***

EVIDENCE (continued)
Excluded, preserving error, ***705***
Exclusion of relevant evidence, FRE 405
Federal Rules of Evidence, *see* this index
Fees, payment of, 28 U.S.C. 1825
Foreign
Official documents, 28 U.S.C. 1741
Patent documents, 28 U.S.C. 1745
Tribunals, assistance to, 28 U.S.C. 1782; ***460***
Foreign country, subpoena of person in, 28 U.S.C. 1783
Full faith & credit
Books & records, 28 U.S.C. 1739
State judicial proceedings, 28 U.S.C. 1738
State laws, 28 U.S.C 1738
Government records, 28 U.S.C. 1733
Habit, FRE 406
Handwriting, 28 U.S.C. 1731
Impeaching witness
Bias, FRE 613; ***693***
Conviction, FRE 609; ***693***
Prior inconsistent statement, FRE 613; ***693***
Reputation, FRE 405, 608; ***692***
Insurance, FRE 411; ***341***
International tribunals, assistance to, 28 U.S.C. 1782; ***460***
Interpreters
Generally, 28 U.S.C. 1827
Special services, 28 U.S.C. 1828
Introducing
Generally, ***688***
Audio recording, ***692***
Cross-examination, FRE 611; ***689***
Demonstrative evidence, ***692***
Direct examination, FRE 402, 403; ***688***
Documents, ***694***
Dying declaration, proving, FRE 804; ***691***
Expert, FRE 702; ***690***
Lay witness, ***690***
Learned treatise, FRE 803; ***690***
Opening, trial, ***688***
Prior bad acts, proving, FRE 403, 404, 607-609; ***691***
Questions by jurors, ***689***
Rebuttal, ***689***
Video recording, ***692***
Journals, congressional, 28 U.S.C. 1736
Juror summoned as witness, mileage fees, 28 U.S.C. 1824
Jury, function of, FRE 1008
Letter rogatory, transmittal of, 28 U.S.C. 1781
Liability insurance, FRE 411; ***341***
Limited admissibility, FRE 105; ***704***
Medical expenses, payment, FRE 409
Newly discovered, grounds for new trial, ***791***
Nonjudicial books & records, full faith & credit, 28 U.S.C. 1739
Objection
Generally, FRE 103, 403; ***700***
Nonruling on, ***705***
Ruling on, ***704***
Officer's bond, copy of, 28 U.S.C. 1737
Official foreign documents, 28 U.S.C. 1741

Page numbers in ***boldface italic***

EVIDENCE (continued)
Papers, government, 28 U.S.C. 1733
Party
Testimony, FRE 1007
Written admissions, FRE 1007
Patent Office documents, 28 U.S.C. 1744
Payment, medical expenses, FRE 409
Photographs
Generally, ***695***
Admissibility of duplicates, FRE 1003; ***695***
Contents, other evidence of, FRE 1004
Defined, FRE 1001
Public records, FRE 1005
Requirement of original, FRE 1002
Summaries, FRE 1006
Postmaster, demand on, 28 U.S.C. 1743
Preliminary questions
Admissibility, FRE 104
Jury, FRE 104
Relevancy, conditioned, FRE 104
Presumptions, FRE 301
Privileges, *see* this index
Recordings
Admissibility of duplicates, FRE 1003
Contents, other evidence of, FRE 1004
Defined, FRE 1001
Public records, FRE 1005
Requirement of original, FRE 1002
Summaries, FRE 1006
Records
Business, 28 U.S.C. 1732
Government, 28 U.S.C. 1733
Lost or destroyed, generally, 28 U.S.C. 1734
Lost or destroyed, U.S. as interested party, 28 U.S.C. 1735
Nonjudicial, state, 28 U.S.C. 1739
Nonjudicial, territorial, 28 U.S.C. 1739
Rehabilitating witness
Generally, ***694***
Character for truthfulness, proving, FRE 608; ***694***
Improper influence, rebutting charge of, ***694***
Reputation for truthfulness, proving, FRE 608; ***694***
Relevancy, FRE 401
Request, transmittal of, 28 U.S.C. 1781
Rulings
Generally, FRE 103
Appellate review, ***699***
Sex-offense cases
Generally, FRE 412
Victim's past behavior, FRE 412
State laws & judicial proceedings, 28 U.S.C. 1738
Strike, motion to, ***705***
Subpoena, person in foreign country, 28 U.S.C. 1783
Subsequent remedial measures, FRE 407
Territorial laws & judicial proceedings, 28 U.S.C. 1738
Testimony of party, FRE 1007
Transfer venue, motion to, ***225***

EVIDENCE (continued)
Witness
Recalcitrant, 28 U.S.C. 1826
Summoned as juror, mileage fees, 28 U.S.C. 1824
Writings
Contents, other evidence of, FRE 1004
Defined, FRE 1001
Duplicates, admissibility, FRE 1003
Public records, FRE 1005
Requirement of original, FRE 1002
Summaries, FRE 1006
Written admissions of party, FRE 1007

EX PARTE
Allowed, ***61***
Challenging, ***58***
Court, ***61***
Defined, ***61***
Jury, ***61***
Nonparties, ***61***
Parties, ***61***
Witnesses, ***61***

EXAMINATION, MOTION FOR
See Mental Examination, this index

EXCITED UTTERANCE
Hearsay exception, FRE 803

EXECUTION
Generally, FRCP 69
Against public officers, FRCP 69
Against revenue officer, 28 U.S.C. 2006
Appraisal of goods taken on, 28 U.S.C. 2005
Imprisonment for debt, 28 U.S.C. 2007
Public officers, against, FRCP 69
Realty, levy on
Marshal's incapacity after, 28 U.S.C. 2003
Personalty, sale of, 28 U.S.C. 2004
Realty, sale of
Generally, 28 U.S.C. 2001
Marshal's incapacity after, 28 U.S.C. 2003
Notice, 28 U.S.C. 2002
Revenue officer, against, 28 U.S.C. 2006

EXEMPTIONS FOR JURORS
Mandatory, ***676***
Permissive, ***676***

EXHAUSTION OF ADMINISTRATIVE REMEDIES
Generally, ***73***

EXHIBITS
Excessive, complaint, ***86***
Incorporated by attachment, ***86***
Learned treatises, hearsay exception, FRE 803
Motions, ***15***
Pleading
Discrepancy with, ***11***
Incorporation, FRCP 10; ***11***, ***86***
Recorded recollection, hearsay exception, FRE 803
Written instrument, ***11***

EXPERT WITNESSES
Consulting
Generally, ***525***
Consulting & testifying, ***521***, ***522***
Nonretained, ***527***
Retained, ***525***
With facts, ***527***
Court-appointed, FRE 706
Disclosures, *see* this index
Discovery, ***515***
Discovery, scope of
Consulting, nonretained, ***527***
Consulting, with facts, ***527***
Consulting, work reviewed, ***526***
Consulting-only, ***525***
Testifying, consultant, ***521***, ***522***
Testifying, de-designated, ***521***
Testifying, nonretained, ***522***
Testifying, with facts, ***520***
Testifying-only, ***516***
FRCP 26(a)(2)(C) disclosure, ***523***, ***528***, ***536***
Motion to exclude
Generally, FRE 104, 401-403, 702-706; ***285***
Affidavits, ***379***, ***382***
Appellate review, ***384***
Deadline, ***379***
Disclosures, pretrial order, ***285***
Grounds, ***376***
Hearing, ***379***, ***382***
Response, ***379***
Ruling, ***383***
Opinion, ultimate issue, FRE 704
Opinions, bases for, FRE 703, 705
Payment, ***530***
Pretrial disclosure, ***296***
Protection, work product, ***518***, ***523***
Report, ***516***, ***528***, ***529***, ***535***
Supplementing, ***527***
Testifying
Generally, ***516***
Consulting & testifying, ***521***, ***522***
Nonretained, ***522***
Retained, ***516***
With facts, ***520***
Work-product protection, ***518***, ***523***

EXTEND TIME, MOTION TO
Generally, ***332***
Agreement, ***332***
Appellate review, ***336***
Deadline, ***332***
Discovery, ***336***
Grounds, ***333***, ***335***
Serve party, ***334***
Substitute party, ***336***

EXTENSION OF TIME
See Time, this index

EXTRAORDINARY WRITS
Generally, FRAP 21
All Writs Act, 28 U.S.C. 1651-1659

FAILURE OF CONSIDERATION
Pleading, as affirmative defense, FRCP 8; ***233***

Page numbers in ***boldface italic***

FAMILY RECORDS
Hearsay exception, FRE 803

FAX
Filing, FRCP 5; ***19***
Proof of service, ***37***
Service, ***31***

FEDERAL BUREAU OF INVESTIGATION
Generally, 28 U.S.C. 531
Appropriations, unforeseen emergencies, 28 U.S.C. 537
Competitive service, positions excepted, 28 U.S.C. 536
Counterintelligence, expenses, 28 U.S.C. 539
Crimes, investigation of
- Aircraft piracy, 28 U.S.C. 538
- Felonious killings, 28 U.S.C. 540
- Government employees or officers, crimes involving, 28 U.S.C. 535
- Limitations, 28 U.S.C. 535
- Serial killers, 28 U.S.C. 540B
- Violent crimes, 28 U.S.C. 540A

Director, 28 U.S.C. 532
Identification records
- Acquisition, 28 U.S.C. 534
- Exchange, 28 U.S.C. 534
- Indian law-enforcement agency, 28 U.S.C. 534
- Preservation, 28 U.S.C. 534
- Protective order, 28 U.S.C. 534

Officials, appointment, 28 U.S.C. 533

FEDERAL CLAIMS COURT
See Court of Federal Claims, this index

FEDERAL JUDICIAL CENTER
Generally, 28 U.S.C. 620-629

FEDERAL RULES OF APPELLATE PROCEDURE
Generally, ***3***
Amending, ***4***
Forms, ***1125***

FEDERAL RULES OF CIVIL PROCEDURE
Generally, ***3***
Amending, ***4***
Forms, ***3***

FEDERAL RULES OF EVIDENCE
Generally, ***3***
Amending, ***4***
Waiver of privilege, ***417***, ***430***

FEES
As costs, ***746***
Attorney fees, ***67***
Bankruptcy, 28 U.S.C. 1930
Collection of, U.S. marshal, 28 U.S.C. 567
Costs, judgment, FRAP 39; FRCP 54
Declaratory judgment, ***111***
Docket, 28 U.S.C. 1923
Filing, ***86***
In forma pauperis, *see* this index
Jury, 28 U.S.C. 1871

FEES (continued)
Mileage, summons as juror & witness, 28 U.S.C. 1824
Sanctions, pretrial, attorney fees, FRCP 16
Summary judgment, affidavit in bad faith, FRCP 56; ***605***
Tort claims, 28 U.S.C. 2678
U.S. as party, 28 U.S.C. 2412
U.S. marshal's fees, 28 U.S.C. 1921
Witness, before U.S. commissioners, 28 U.S.C. 1922

FICTITIOUS NAMES
Pleading, real party in interest, FRCP 17

FILING
Generally, FRCP 5, 6; ***17***
After service, reasonable time, ***22***
Appeals, FRAP 25
Briefs, appeal, FRAP 31
Completing, ***23***
Considerations, ***74***
Courtesy copies, ***19***
Deadlines
- Generally, ***22***
- Computing time, FRCP 6; ***23***
- Filing vs. service, chart, ***22***
- Motion to extend time, FRCP 6; ***28***

Discovery, ***17***
Documents
- Delivery, ***19***
- Drop box, ***18***
- Electronically, *see* Electronic Filing, this index
- Fax, FRCP 5; ***19***
- Mail, ***17***
- Personal delivery, ***18***

Redacted, FRCP 5.2; ***17***

FILMS
Generally, FRE 1001; ***695***

FINAL ARGUMENT
See Closing Argument, this index

FINAL JUDGMENT
See Judgment, this index

FINDINGS OF FACT
Generally, FRCP 52; ***799***
Add or amend, motion to
- Generally, FRCP 52; ***799***
- Affidavits, ***802***
- Appellate review, ***803***
- Deadline, ***800***
- Grounds, ***801***
- Hearing, ***802***
- Inadequate finding, appellate procedure, ***803***
- New trial, motion filed with, FRCP 52, 59; ***802***
- Response, ***802***
- Ruling, ***802***

Attorney fees, ***760***
Extending time, FRCP 6

FINDINGS OF FACT (continued)
Objections, findings by magistrate, 28 U.S.C. 636; ***299***, ***300***
When necessary, ***799***

FOREIGN COUNTRIES
Answer, time to, 28 U.S.C. 1608; ***163***
Authentication, official records, FRCP 44; ***699***
Civil actions, 28 U.S.C. 1330
Counterclaims, 28 U.S.C. 1607
Damages, liabilities, 28 U.S.C. 1606
Default, 28 U.S.C. 1608
Definitions, 28 U.S.C. 1603
District courts, jurisdiction, 28 U.S.C. 1330
Diversity of citizenship, jurisdiction, 28 U.S.C. 1332
Foreign law, determination, FRCP 44.1
Immunity
- Attachment, 28 U.S.C. 1609
- Executions, 28 U.S.C. 1609, 1611
- Foreign property, banks, 28 U.S.C. 1611
- From district-court jurisdiction, 28 U.S.C. 1330

Immunity, exceptions
- Attachment, 28 U.S.C. 1610
- Counterclaims, 28 U.S.C. 1607
- Executions, 28 U.S.C. 1610
- Fraud by officers & employees, 28 U.S.C. 1605
- Jurisdictional immunity, 28 U.S.C. 1605
- Libel by officers & employees, 28 U.S.C. 1605
- Malicious prosecution by officers & employees, 28 U.S.C. 1605
- Military property, 28 U.S.C. 1611
- Negligence of officers & employees, 28 U.S.C. 1605
- Personal injury caused by officers & employees, 28 U.S.C. 1605
- Tort Claims Act, 28 U.S.C. 2680
- Tortious acts of officers & employees, 28 U.S.C. 1605

Jurisdictional immunity, 28 U.S.C. 1605
Letters rogatory, 28 U.S.C. 1781, 1782
Liability, extent of, 28 U.S.C. 1606
Limitation of actions, 28 U.S.C. 2416, 2501
Personal jurisdiction of district courts, 28 U.S.C. 1330
Pleadings, service, 28 U.S.C. 1608
Proof, official records, FRCP 44
Removal of cases, actions against, 28 U.S.C. 1441
Service, 28 U.S.C. 1608
Service of foreign process, FRCP 4; 28 U.S.C. 1696; ***156***
Subpoena, persons in foreign country, FRCP 45; 28 U.S.C. 1783, 1784
Time to answer, 28 U.S.C. 1608
Venue, actions against, 28 U.S.C. 1391
Waiver, 28 U.S.C. 1605, 1610

FORFEITURE ACTIONS
See Admiralty & Maritime Claims, this index

INDEX

Page numbers in ***boldface italic***

FORUM
See Venue, this index

FORUM NON CONVENIENS
See Motions to Dismiss, this index

FORUM-SELECTION CLAUSE
Appellate review, ***199***
Asserting, ***173***
Enforceability, ***194***
Venue, motion to transfer, ***224***

FRAP
See Federal Rules of Appellate Procedure, this index

FRAUD
Pleading, as affirmative defense, FRCP 8; ***233***

FRAUDS, STATUTE OF
Pleading, as affirmative defense, FRCP 8; ***233***

FRCP
See Federal Rules of Civil Procedure, this index

FRE
See Federal Rules of Evidence, this index

GROUNDS
See each particular motion, this index

GUARDIAN AD LITEM
Appointment, ***75***

HABEAS CORPUS
Generally, FRAP 22
Answer, 28 U.S.C. 2248
Appeal, FRAP 22; 28 U.S.C. 2253
Application, FRAP 22; 28 U.S.C. 2242
Certificate, probable cause, FRAP 22
Decision, 28 U.S.C. 2243
Determination, finality of, 28 U.S.C. 2244
Evidence
  Affidavits, 28 U.S.C. 2246
  Certificate of trial judge admissible, 28 U.S.C. 2245
  Depositions, 28 U.S.C. 2246
  Documentary, 28 U.S.C. 2247
  Judgment, certified copies, 28 U.S.C. 2249
  Plea, certified copies, 28 U.S.C. 2249
Federal custody, remedies, 28 U.S.C. 2255
Hearing, 28 U.S.C. 2243
Indigent petitioner, 28 U.S.C. 2250
Issuance of writ, 28 U.S.C. 2243
Notice, 28 U.S.C. 2252
Power to grant writ, 28 U.S.C. 2241
Respondent's duty, 28 U.S.C. 2249
Return, 28 U.S.C. 2243, 2248
State custody, remedies, 28 U.S.C. 2254
Stay, 28 U.S.C. 2251

HABIT
Evidence of, FRE 406

HAGUE CONVENTION ON SERVICE ABROAD
Generally, ***156***

HAGUE CONVENTION ON TAKING OF EVIDENCE ABROAD
Generally,

HANDWRITING
Generally, FRE 1001

HARMLESS ERROR
Generally, FRCP 61

HEARINGS
Generally, FRCP 6, 43, 77, 78; ***38***
Add or amend findings, motion to, ***802***
Amend substance of judgment, motion to, ***797***
Appeal, preliminary conference, FRAP 33
Arbitration, 28 U.S.C. 655
Attorney fees as costs, request for, ***759***
Challenging venue, ***197***
Conducting
  Methods, ***39***
  Who conducts, ***40***
Consent to, outside district, FRCP 77
Court of International Trade, rehearing in civil actions, 28 U.S.C. 2646
Courts of appeals, 28 U.S.C. 46
Daubert hearing, ***382***
Declaratory-judgment action, ***110***
Default judgment, ***596***
District courts, FRCP 77
Failure to state claim, motion to dismiss, ***206***
Forum non conveniens, ***206***
Habeas corpus, 28 U.S.C. 2243
Indispensable party, ***217***
Injunction
  Consolidated with trial, FRCP 65
  Permanent, ***104***
  Preliminary, ***104***
  TRO, ***97***
Insufficient process, motion to dismiss, ***210***
Interpleader, ***91***
Judgment nunc pro tunc, *see* Postjudgment Motions, this index
Judicial notice, request for, ***374***
Limine, motion in, ***343***
Mental examination, request for, ***577***
More definite statement, motion for, ***213***
Motions, ***38***
New trial, motion for, ***786***
Notice, ***38***
Notice of appeal, extend time to file, ***820***
Personal jurisdiction, motion to dismiss, ***185***
Relief from judgment, motion for, ***812***
Remand, motion for, ***275***
Renewed motion for JMOL, ***779***
Reopen time for appeal, motion to, ***823***, ***824***
Request
  Generally, ***38***
  Court reporter, ***40***
Submission, ***39***
Summary judgment, motion for, ***623***
Telephone, ***39***
Types, ***39***
Video teleconferencing, ***40***
Witnesses, compelling attendance, ***40***

HEARSAY
Generally, FRE 801
Admissibility, FRE 802
Admission by party-opponent, FRE 801
Credibility, FRE 806
Definitions, FRE 801
Exceptions
  Business records, FRE 803
  Community reputation, FRE 803
  Dying declaration, FRE 804
  Excited utterances, FRE 803
  Family records, FRE 803
  Former testimony, FRE 804
  Impending death, FRE 804
  Interest, statement against, FRE 804
  Learned treatises, FRE 803
  Market reports & commercial publications, FRE 803
  Medical diagnosis or treatment, FRE 803
  Personal or family history, statement of, FRE 804
  Property interests, FRE 803
  Public records, FRE 803
  Recorded recollection, FRE 803
  Reputation, FRE 803
  Unavailability of declarant, FRE 804
  Vital statistics, FRE 803
Prior statements by witness, FRE 801
Within hearsay, FRE 805

HOLIDAYS
Computation of time, FRCP 6
Recognized, ***25***

ILLEGALITY
Pleading, as affirmative defense, FRCP 8; ***233***

IMPEACHMENT
Character, witness
  Opinion evidence, FRE 405
  Reputation evidence, FRE 405
  Specific instances of conduct, FRE 405
Conviction of crime, witness, FRE 609
Depositions, use of, ***551***
Prior statements, witness, FRE 613
Who may impeach, FRE 607

IN FORMA PAUPERIS
Affidavits, 28 U.S.C. 1915
Attorney, 28 U.S.C. 1915
Courts of appeals, FRAP 24
Dismiss, frivolous action, 28 U.S.C. 1915
Fees, 28 U.S.C. 1915
Filing, FRAP 24
Form, FRAP 24, FRAP Form 4
Leave to proceed, FRAP 24
Proceedings, FRAP 24
Process, FRCP 4; 28 U.S.C. 1915
Record on appeal, 28 U.S.C. 1915
Service of process, FRCP 4; 28 U.S.C. 1915
Summons, service, FRCP 4
Witness, 28 U.S.C. 1915

INDICATIVE RULING
Generally, FRAP 12.1; FRCP 62.1; ***813***
Appellate court ruling, ***815***

Page numbers in ***boldface italic***

INDICATIVE RULING (continued)
District court ruling, ***815***
Notice, ***814, 815***

INDIGENT PERSONS
See In Forma Pauperis, this index

INDISPENSABLE PARTIES
See Motions to Dismiss, this index

INFORMANTS
Government privileges, ***479***

INJUNCTIONS
Generally, FRCP 65; ***93***
Adequate remedy at law, ***95***
Answer, filing, ***105***
Anti-Injunction Act, ***141***
Appellate review, ***106***
Authority
  Equity, ***94***
  Federal, ***96***
  State, ***96***
Challenging request, ***105***
Diversity jurisdiction, amount in controversy, ***124***
Effect on
  Nonparties, ***96***
  Parties, ***96***
  Successor companies, ***99***
Grounds, ***94***
Hardship, ***96***
Irreparable harm, ***95***
Likelihood of success, ***96***
Notice
  Preliminary injunction, ***102***
  TRO, ex parte, ***97***
Permanent
  Generally, ***104***
  Application, ***104***
  Bond, ***105***
  Hearing, ***104***
  Modifying, ***105***
  Order, ***104***
Preliminary
  Generally, ***101***
  Application, ***101***
  Bond, ***101***
  Consolidation with trial, ***103***
  Defenses, ***105***
  Effect, ***104***
  Elements of relief, ***101***
  Findings, ***104***
  Hearing, ***102***
  Modifying, ***104***
  Order, ***103***
Public interest, ***96***
Response, ***105***
Show-cause order, ***101***
TRO
  Application, ***97***
  Bond, ***100***
  Effect, ***98***
  Ex parte, ***97***
  Extending, ***99***

INJUNCTIONS (continued)
TRO (continued)
  Findings, ***101***
  Form, ***97***
  Hearing, ***97***
  Order, ***97***

INJURY BY FELLOW SERVANT
Pleading, as affirmative defense, FRCP 8; ***233***

INSTRUCTED VERDICT
See Judgment as a Matter of Law, Motion for, this index

INSUFFICIENCY OF BOND
See Appeals, this index

INSURANCE
Evidence of, FRE 411

INTEREST
Attachment in postal suit, interest on balances, 28 U.S.C. 2718
Court of Federal Claims, on claims or judgments, 28 U.S.C. 2516
Court of International Trade, 28 U.S.C. 2644
Damages, ***85***
In judgment, appeal, FRAP 37
On judgment, 28 U.S.C. 1961

INTERLOCUTORY ORDERS, JUDGMENTS, OR DECREES
Class actions, certification, FRCP 23
Judgments, FRCP 62
Motions, open court, FRCP 77
Orders, 28 U.S.C. 1292
Summary judgment, FRCP 56

INTERNATIONAL CONVENTIONS
Hague Convention on Service Abroad, ***1563***
Hague Convention on Taking of Evidence Abroad, ***1566***

INTERPLEADER
Generally, FRCP 22; 28 U.S.C. 1335, 1397, 2361; ***87***
Appellate review, ***93***
Attorney fees, ***92***
Bad-faith, ***91***
Binding effect, nonparties, ***93***
Claim
  Adverse, ***88***
  Multiple, ***88***
Complaint, ***87***
Costs, ***92***
Deposit
  Rule, ***89***
  Statutory, 28 U.S.C. 1335, ***89***
Fund, existence of, ***87***
Hearing, ***91***
Interest, ***93***
Joinder, FRCP 18
Jurisdiction
  Rule, FRCP 22; ***88***
  Statutory, 28 U.S.C. 1335; ***89***
Jury, request, ***91***
Multiple claimants, ***88***

INTERPLEADER (continued)
Order
  Discharge, ***92***
  Injunction, ***92***
Parties
  Claimant, ***87***
  Stakeholder, ***87***
Procedure, 28 U.S.C. 2361
Relief
  Attorney fees, ***90***
  Costs, ***90***
  Discharge, ***90***
  Injunction, ***90***
Response, ***90***
Rule, FRCP 22; ***88***
Service of process, ***90***
Stake, ***87***
Stakeholder
  Disinterested, ***87***
  Interested, ***87***
Statutory, 28 U.S.C. 1335; ***89***
Trial, ***92***
Types, ***88***
Venue
  Rule, 28 U.S.C. 1391, ***89***
  Statutory, 28 U.S.C. 1397, ***89***

INTERPRETERS
Generally, FRE 604

INTERROGATORIES
Generally, FRCP 26, 33; ***557***
Answers, FRCP 33; ***559***
Availability, FRCP 33
Business records, producing, FRCP 33; ***561***
Compel answers, motion to, ***562***
Electronically stored information, producing, FRCP 33; ***561***
Failure to serve, FRCP 37
Filing, ***561***
Form, answers
  Generally, ***560***
  Separate, ***560***
  Sufficiency of, ***560***
  Verified, ***560***
  Writing, ***560***
Number, FRCP 33; ***558***
Objections, FRCP 33; ***562***
Opinion, ***559***
Person answering, ***560***
Responding to, ***559***
Sanctions, motion for, ***562***
Scope, FRCP 33; ***558***
Serving, ***557***
Standard questions, ***558***
Supplement, time, ***561***
Using
  Summary judgment, ***563***
  Trial, FRCP 33; ***563***
Who must answer, ***560***

INTERVENE, MOTION TO
Generally, FRCP 24; ***356***
Appeal, ***361***
Appellate review, ***361***

INDEX

Page numbers in ***boldface italic***

INTERVENE, MOTION TO (continued)
Constitutional challenge, notice of, FRCP 5.1; ***360***
Deadline, ***360***
Grounds, ***356***
Of right, FRCP 24; ***356***
Order, ***361***
Permissive, FRCP 24; ***359***
Pleadings, applicant, ***360***
Procedure, FRCP 24
Standing, ***356, 359***

INVOLUNTARY DISMISSAL
Generally, FRCP 16, 37, 41; ***642***
Appellate review, ***649***
Grounds, ***643***
Motion, ***642***
Notice
Generally, ***647***
Intent to dismiss indigent suit, ***647***
Sanctions, ***647***
Order
Generally, ***647***
Findings, ***647***
Scope, ***648***
Response, ***646***
Sanctions, ***645***
Sua sponte, ***643***

JOINDER
Claims, FRCP 18
Fraudulent, removal, ***247, 252***
Remedies, FRCP 18

JUDGES
Accommodations, court, 28 U.S.C. 462
Acknowledgments, administration of, 28 U.S.C. 459
Appointment, relative of judge ineligible, 28 U.S.C. 458
Assignment
Circuit judges, 28 U.S.C. 291
Conditions, 28 U.S.C. 295
Court of International Trade, 28 U.S.C. 293
District judges, 28 U.S.C. 292
Powers, 28 U.S.C. 296
Retired justices or judges, active duty, 28 U.S.C. 294
To courts of freely associated compact states, 28 U.S.C. 297
Bankruptcy
Appeals, 28 U.S.C. 158
Appointment, 28 U.S.C. 152
Businesses, division of, 28 U.S.C. 154
Chief judge, 28 U.S.C. 154
Courts, designation, 28 U.S.C. 151
Expenses, 28 U.S.C. 156
Procedures, 28 U.S.C. 157
Retirement, 28 U.S.C. 377
Salaries, 28 U.S.C. 153
Service, 28 U.S.C. 153
Staff, 28 U.S.C. 156
Transfer, temporary, 28 U.S.C. 155

JUDGES (continued)
Circuits
Judicial conferences, 28 U.S.C. 333
Judicial councils, 28 U.S.C. 332
Complaints against, 28 U.S.C. 351-364
Court of International Trade, Judicial Conference, 28 U.S.C. 335
Courts always open, 28 U.S.C. 452
Designation
Conditions, 28 U.S.C. 295
Powers, 28 U.S.C. 296
Disqualification, 28 U.S.C. 144, 455; ***322***
Ex parte communications, ***61***
Expenses
Litigation, 28 U.S.C. 463
Traveling, 28 U.S.C. 456
Judicial conference, 28 U.S.C. 331
Magistrates, retirement, 28 U.S.C. 377
Oaths
Generally, 28 U.S.C. 453
Administration of, 28 U.S.C. 459
Obsolete papers, 28 U.S.C. 457
Official station, retired judges, 28 U.S.C. 374
Possessions, 28 U.S.C. 373
Practice of law by, 28 U.S.C. 454
Recall
Judges, 28 U.S.C. 375
Magistrates, 28 U.S.C. 375
Records, 28 U.S.C. 457
Recusal, ***321***
Residence, retired judges, 28 U.S.C. 374
Retirement
Disability, 28 U.S.C. 372
Salary, 28 U.S.C. 371
Senior status, 28 U.S.C. 371
Salaries, adjustments, 28 U.S.C. 461
Sentencing
Institutes on, 28 U.S.C. 334
Joint councils on, 28 U.S.C. 334
Substitute judge, failure to retire, 28 U.S.C. 372
Survivors, annuities for, 28 U.S.C. 376
Territories, 28 U.S.C. 373
Traveling expenses, 28 U.S.C. 456

JUDGMENT
Appealable
Generally, ***737***
Collateral orders, ***741***
Consolidated cases, ***739***
Final judgment, ***737***
Judgments covering fewer than all claims or parties, ***738***
Automatic stay, FRCP 62
Changing, ***742***
Clerical error, motion to correct, *see* Postjudgment Motions, this index
Costs & attorney fees, FRAP 39; FRCP 54
Declaratory judgment, *see* this index
Default judgment, *see* this index
Defined, FRCP 54
Delays on appeal, damages, FRAP 38
Demand, FRCP 54

JUDGMENT (continued)
Entry of judgment
Generally, FRCP 54-63, 77, 79; 28 U.S.C. 1291, 1292; ***735***
Accepting, ***743***
Grounds, ***745***
Hearing, ***745***
Motion, FRCP 54-63, 77-79; ***743***
Request, ***744***
When to file motion, ***744***
Final
Generally, ***735***
Effective, ***737***
Exceptions, ***739***
Preparing, ***736***
Requirements, ***735***
Inadvertent, relief from, FRCP 60; ***807***
Interest, FRAP 37
Judgment as a matter of law, motion for, *see* this index
Lien, 28 U.S.C. 1962
Mistake, relief from, FRCP 60; ***807***
Motion for relief from judgment
Generally, FRCP 60; ***804***
Appellate review, ***815***
Deadline, ***804***
Grounds, ***806***
Indicative ruling, ***813***
Motion to alter or amend
Generally, FRCP 59; ***793***
Appellate review, ***797***
Deadline, ***793***
Motion to correct clerical error in, *see* Postjudgment Motions, this index
Multiple claims, FRCP 54
Multiple parties, FRCP 54
Notice, ***741***
Nunc pro tunc, *see* Postjudgment Motions, this index
Offer of judgment, *see* this index
Registration of, 28 U.S.C. 1963
Relief from mistake, inadvertence, surprise, or neglect, FRCP 60; ***806***
Specific acts, FRCP 70
Summary judgment, *see* this index
Vesting title, FRCP 70

JUDGMENT AS A MATTER OF LAW (JMOL), MOTION FOR
Generally, FRCP 50; ***714***
Appellate review, ***718***
Burden, ***716***
Diversity cases, ***714***
Grounds, ***715***
Nonjury case, ***718***
Renewed, *see* Renewed Motion for Judgment as a Matter of Law, this index
Response, ***716***
Reurging, ***717***
Ruling, ***717***
Time to make, ***715***

Page numbers in ***boldface italic***

JUDGMENT NOTWITHSTANDING THE VERDICT
See Judgment as a Matter of Law, Motion for, this index

JUDGMENT NUNC PRO TUNC
See Postjudgment Motions, this index

JUDGMENT ON THE PLEADINGS
See Motions, this index

JUDICIAL NOTICE, MOTION FOR
Generally, FRCP 44, 44.1; FRE 201; ***370***
Adjudicative facts, FRE 201; ***370***
Appellate review, ***375***
Deadline, FRE 201; ***373***
Discretionary, FRE 201
Foreign law, ***372***
Hearing, ***374***
Jury instructions, FRE 201
Mandatory, FRE 201
Motion, ***372***
Notice, ***373***
Opportunity to be heard, FRE 201
Response, ***374***
Ruling, ***374***
Time of taking, FRE 201

JURISDICTION
Generally, 28 U.S.C. 1331, 1332, 1367; ***112***
Abstention, *see* this index
Aggregation of claims, ***124***
Alienage
- Generally, ***127***
- Amount in controversy, ***129***
- Citizenship, ***127***
- Removal, ***260***

Aliens, diversity, ***117, 118, 123, 127***
Allegations, ***78, 113***
Amount in controversy
- Generally, ***123, 130***
- Aggregation of claims, ***124***
- Attorney fees, ***124***
- Declaratory judgment, ***124***
- Injunctive relief, ***124***

Anti-Injunction Act
- Generally, ***141***
- Exceptions, ***141***
- In-aid-of-jurisdiction exception, ***141***
- Purpose, ***141***
- Relitigation exception, ***141***
- State administrative proceedings, ***142***
- U.S. as party to litigation, ***142***

Appellate review, ***142***
Artful-pleading doctrine, ***113***
Causes of action
- Exclusive to state, ***115***
- Implied, ***115***
- Preemption, ***116***

Challenging subject-matter jurisdiction
- Generally, ***188***
- Grounds, ***188***

Citizenship, for diversity jurisdiction
- Aliens, ***117, 118, 123, 127***
- Banks, ***121***

JURISDICTION (continued)
Citizenship, for diversity jurisdiction (continued)
- Business associations, ***121***
- Class actions, ***119, 129***
- Collusive joinder, ***123***
- Corporations, ***119***
- Decedent, ***119***
- Dual nationals, ***119, 127***
- Fictitious, ***122***
- Incompetent, ***119***
- Infant, ***119***
- Insurance company, ***121***
- Natural, ***118***
- Nominal party, ***122***
- Real party in interest, ***122***
- Representatives, ***119***
- Stateless, ***123***
- States, ***123***
- Subsidiary corporation, ***121***
- Substituted defendant, ***122***
- Trustees, ***119***
- Unnamed party, ***122***
- U.S. citizens domiciled abroad, ***123***
- U.S. government, ***123***
- U.S. nationals living abroad, ***119***

Class actions
- Amount in controversy, ***130***
- Citizenship requirement, ***131***
- Class Action Fairness Act, ***129***
- Defined, ***130***
- Interstate, ***129***
- Jurisdiction, ***129, 132***
- Mass action, ***131***
- Minimal diversity, ***131***

Courts of appeals
- Circuits in which decisions reviewable, 28 U.S.C. 1294
- Federal Circuit, 28 U.S.C. 1295
- Final decisions of district courts, 28 U.S.C. 1291
- Interlocutory decisions, 28 U.S.C. 1292

District courts
- Admiralty, 28 U.S.C. 1333
- Agencies, state, 28 U.S.C. 1342
- Amount in controversy, 28 U.S.C. 1332
- Antitrust regulations, 28 U.S.C. 1337
- Banking association, 28 U.S.C. 1348
- Bankruptcy, 28 U.S.C. 1334
- Bonds, 28 U.S.C. 1352
- Civil rights, 28 U.S.C. 1343
- Collusive joinder, parties, 28 U.S.C. 1359
- Commerce regulations, 28 U.S.C. 1337
- Consuls, 28 U.S.C. 1351
- Copyrights, 28 U.S.C. 1338
- Corporation, 28 U.S.C. 1349
- Diplomatic mission, insurers of members, 28 U.S.C. 1364
- Diplomatic mission, members of, 28 U.S.C. 1351
- Diversity, 28 U.S.C. 1332; ***116***
- Election disputes, 28 U.S.C. 1344
- Elective franchise, 28 U.S.C. 1343
- Eminent domain, 28 U.S.C. 1358

JURISDICTION (continued)
District courts (continued)
- Federal-question, 28 U.S.C. 1331; ***113***
- Final decisions, 28 U.S.C. 1291
- Fine, 28 U.S.C. 1355
- Foreign states, actions against, 28 U.S.C. 1330
- Forfeiture, 28 U.S.C. 1355
- General, ***182***
- Indian allotments, 28 U.S.C. 1353
- Indian tribes, 28 U.S.C. 1362
- Injuries, 28 U.S.C. 1357
- Internal revenue, 28 U.S.C. 1340
- Internet contacts, based on, ***180, 182***
- Interpleader, 28 U.S.C. 1335
- Interstate Commerce Commission, 28 U.S.C. 1336
- Jurors' employment rights, 28 U.S.C. 1363
- Land grants, 28 U.S.C. 1354
- Maritime, 28 U.S.C. 1333
- Partition action, 28 U.S.C. 1347
- Patents, 28 U.S.C. 1338
- Penalty, 28 U.S.C. 1355
- Postal matters, 28 U.S.C. 1339
- Seizures, 28 U.S.C. 1356
- Senate actions, 28 U.S.C. 1365
- Specific, ***179***
- Stream of commerce, based on, ***179***
- Supplemental jurisdiction, 28 U.S.C. 1367; ***134***
- Taxes, state, 28 U.S.C. 1341
- Tort action, alien's, 28 U.S.C. 1350
- U.S. as defendant, 28 U.S.C. 1346
- U.S. as plaintiff, 28 U.S.C. 1345
- U.S. officer, action to compel, 28 U.S.C. 1361
- Vice consuls, 28 U.S.C. 1351

Diversity
- Generally, ***116***
- Aggregation of claims, ***124***
- Amount in controversy, ***123***
- Citizenship of parties, ***118***
- Collusive assignments, ***123***
- Complete, ***116***
- Declining to exercise, ***126***
- Domestic relations, exception, ***126***
- Exceptions to exercising, ***126***
- Exempt from suit, ***122***
- Impairing, ***125***
- JMOL, motion for, ***714***
- Minimal, class actions, ***131***
- Minimal, mass accidents, ***133***
- Parties, ***118, 122***
- Probate, ***126***
- Removal, ***249***
- Time-of-filing rule, ***125***
- Time-of-filing rule, exceptions to, ***126***

Federal-question
- Generally, ***113***
- Arising under federal law, ***113***
- Exclusive jurisdiction, ***114***
- Federal causes of action, ***114***
- Grounds, ***113***
- Nonexclusive jurisdiction, ***114***

Page numbers in ***boldface italic***

JURISDICTION (continued)
Federal-question (continued)
Preemption, ***116***
Removal, ***249***
Scope, ***113***
State claims, ***115***
General, ***182***
Impairing diversity, ***125***
Mass accidents
Generally, ***133***
Multiparty, Multiforum Trial Jurisdiction Act, ***133***
Single events, ***133***
Minimal diversity
Class actions, ***131***
Mass accidents, ***134***
Nerve-center test, corporations, ***120***
Personal, *see* Motions to Dismiss, this index
Pleading, ***78***
Specific, ***179***
Supplemental
Generally, ***134***
Ancillary, ***136***
Declining, ***136***
Losing, ***137***
Pendent claims, ***135***
Pendent parties, ***135***
Reach, ***135***
Restrictions, ***136***
When required, ***136***
Supreme Court
Certified questions, 28 U.S.C. 1254
Certiorari, 28 U.S.C. 1254, 1257-1259
Courts of appeals, 28 U.S.C. 1254
Direct appeals, 28 U.S.C. 1253
Military Appeals, Court of, 28 U.S.C. 1259
Original, 28 U.S.C. 1251
Puerto Rico, 28 U.S.C. 1258
State courts, 28 U.S.C. 1257
Well-pleaded-complaint rule, ***113***

JURY
Generally, FRCP 38, 39; 28 U.S.C. 1861; ***309***
Admiralty, 28 U.S.C. 1873
Advisory jury, *see* this index
Bonds, actions on, 28 U.S.C. 1874
Challenges, 28 U.S.C. 1870
Court of International Trade, trial by jury, 28 U.S.C. 1876
Definitions, 28 U.S.C. 1869
Demand for jury trial, *see* this index
Discrimination, prohibited, 28 U.S.C. 1862
Ex parte communications with, ***61***
Exemptions, ***675***
Fees, 28 U.S.C. 1871
General verdict, FRCP 49
Inspection, records, 28 U.S.C. 1868
Interrogatories, general verdict accompanied, FRCP 49
Jurors, protection of, 28 U.S.C. 1877
Jurors' employment, protection of, 28 U.S.C. 1875
Limitations on, ***313***
Maintenance, records, 28 U.S.C. 1868

JURY (continued)
Maritime, 28 U.S.C. 1873
Master jury wheel, drawing names from, 28 U.S.C. 1864
Misconduct, ***685***
Motion, ***314***
Note-taking, ***684***
Number of jurors, FRCP 48
One-step summoning, 28 U.S.C. 1878
Panels, selecting, 28 U.S.C. 1866
Panels, summoning, 28 U.S.C. 1866
Participation of jurors, FRCP 48
Polling, FRCP 48; ***725***
Qualifications, 28 U.S.C. 1865
Records, inspection, 28 U.S.C. 1868
Records, maintenance, 28 U.S.C. 1868
Right to, ***311***
Selection, plan for, 28 U.S.C. 1863
Selection procedures, challenging compliance with, 28 U.S.C. 1867
Special verdict, FRCP 49
Specialties, actions on, 28 U.S.C. 1874
Supreme Court, issues of fact in, 28 U.S.C. 1872

JURY CHARGE
Generally, FRCP 49, 51; ***720***
Allen charge, ***724***
Appellate review, ***725***
Charge conference, ***722***
Drafting, ***722***
Final charge, ***723***
General verdict accompanied by answers to interrogatories, FRCP 49; ***721***
Objections
Generally, FRCP 51; ***722***
Preserving error, ***723***
Timing, ***723***
Omissions, FRCP 49
Polling jury, ***725***
Preparing instructions
Generally, ***721***
Deadline, ***721***
Procedure, FRCP 51
Requests, filing written, FRCP 51
Special verdict, FRCP 49; ***720***
Types of verdicts, ***720***
Verdict-urging instructions, ***724***

JURY SELECTION
Generally, FRCP 38, 39, 47, 48; 28 U.S.C. 1861-1873; ***673***
Appellate review, ***685***
Batson challenge, ***681***
Challenges, peremptory, ***681***
Challenges for cause
Generally, ***679***
Grounds, ***679***
Timing, ***681***
Challenging selection process, ***674***
Disqualifications, statutory, ***675***
Exclusions, ***676***

JURY SELECTION (continued)
Jurors
Mandatory exemptions, ***676***
Number, ***674***
Permissive exemptions, ***676***
Qualifications, ***675***
Questionnaire form, ***677***
Seating or excusing, ***685***
Jury
Jury Selection & Service Act, ***673***
Panel, assembling, ***673***
Plan, district, ***674***
Qualification form, ***674***
Trial, ***673***
Wheel, ***674***
Preserving error, ***678***
Voir dire
Generally, ***677***
Improper questions & comments, ***679***
Proper subjects, ***678***

JURY TRIAL
Generally, FRCP 38, 39
Advisory jury, FRCP 39; ***315***
Bench trial, conversion to, ***310***
Constitutional authority, ***311***, ***673***
Demand for jury trial, *see* this index
Motion, ***314***
Polling, FRCP 48; ***725***
Right preserved, FRCP 38
Specification of issues, FRCP 38
Statutory authority, ***312***, ***673***
Waiver, FRCP 38; ***310***

LACHES
Pleading, as affirmative defense, FRCP 8; ***233***

LAND
See Entry on Land, Request for, this index

LAW-ENFORCEMENT PRIVILEGE
See Privileges, this index

LAW FIRM
Signature on pleading, ***11***

LAWYER
See Attorneys, this index

LEARNED TREATISES
Hearsay exception, FRE 803(18)

LEGAL CAPACITY
Generally, FRCP 17; ***78***

LEGAL HOLIDAYS
Computation of time, FRCP 6; ***25***
Office hours, clerks of court, FRCP 77

LETTERS ROGATORY
Depositions in foreign countries, FRCP 28; 28 U.S.C. 1781
Foreign countries, service of process, 28 U.S.C. 1608
Privileges of witness, 28 U.S.C. 1782

Page numbers in ***boldface italic***

LETTERS ROGATORY (continued)
Service of process
Foreign countries, actions against, 28 U.S.C. 1608
Summons, FRCP 4
Subpoena of witness, 28 U.S.C. 1783, 1784

LICENSE
Pleading, as affirmative defense, FRCP 8; ***233***

LIMINE, MOTION IN
Generally, FRE 103; ***341***
Agreed, ***343***
Appellate review, ***344***
Deadline, ***343***
Grounds, ***341***
Hearing, ***343***
Offer at trial, ***344***
Response, ***343***
Ruling, ***343***

LIS PENDENS
Notice, 28 U.S.C. 1964

LOCAL RULES
Generally, FRCP 83; 28 U.S.C. 471; ***5***
Adoption, ***5***
Amending, ***5***
Authority, ***5***
Construction, ***6***
Effective date, ***5***
Force of law, ***5***
Notice, ***6***
Standing orders, generally, ***6***

LOST OR DESTROYED INSTRUMENTS
Generally, FRE 1004
Notice for order, 28 U.S.C. 1734

LUNATICS
See Mentally Deficient Persons, this index

MAGISTRATE JUDGE
Generally, FRCP 72, 73; 28 U.S.C. 631-639; ***297***
Appeal options, FRCP 73
Appellate review, ***307***
Appointment, 28 U.S.C. 631
Character of service, 28 U.S.C. 632
Compensation, 28 U.S.C. 634
Consent for referral of trial to, FRCP 73; ***301***
Definitions, 28 U.S.C. 639
Dispositive pretrial matters, ***299***
Dockets, 28 U.S.C. 638
Expenses, 28 U.S.C. 635
Forms, 28 U.S.C. 638
Jurisdiction, 28 U.S.C. 636
Locations of, determining, 28 U.S.C. 633
Nondispositive pretrial matters, ***298***
Number of, determining, 28 U.S.C. 633
Order
Appeal to court of appeals, ***308***
Objection to magistrate's, ***299***, ***300***
Review by district court of magistrate's, ***299***, ***301***
Powers, 28 U.S.C. 636
Pretrial matters, FRCP 72; ***298***

MAGISTRATE JUDGE (continued)
Referral of trial, FRCP 73; ***301***
Salaries of, determining, 28 U.S.C. 633
Seals, 28 U.S.C. 638
Temporary assignment, 28 U.S.C. 636
Tenure, 28 U.S.C. 631
Training, 28 U.S.C. 637
Transfer of pretrial matters, ***298***

MAILBOX RULE
Additional time after certain methods of service, FRCP 6; ***34***

MAILING
Additional time after, FRCP 6; ***34***
Attorneys, service, FRCP 5
Documents, ***30***
Entry of order or judgment, FRCP 77
Filing, FRAP 25; ***19***
Findings, magistrates, 28 U.S.C. 636
Grand jury, service of summons, 28 U.S.C. 1866
Judgments & decrees, copies, FRAP 36
Masters, filing report, FRCP 53
Notice of appeal, FRAP 3
Opinions, copies, FRAP 36
Service of process
Generally, FRCP 4
Additional time, FRCP 6
Attorney representing party, FRCP 5
Notice of appeal, FRAP 3
Serving documents
Date of mailing, ***31***
Mail, defined, ***30***
When complete, ***30***

MANDAMUS
Generally, FRAP 21

MANDATE
Certiorari, FRAP 41
Costs, FRAP 39
Interest on judgments, FRAP 37
Issuance & stay, FRAP 41
Petition for rehearing en banc, FRAP 35
Supersedeas or stay, FRAP 41

MARKET REPORTS
Hearsay exception, FRE 803

MARSHAL
See U.S. Marshals Service, this index

MASTERS
Generally, FRCP 53; ***302***
Appointment
Generally, ***302***
Appeal, ***308***
Disqualification, ***304***
Grounds, ***303***
Hearing, ***304***
Notice, ***304***
Order, ***305***
Scope, ***303***

MASTERS (continued)
Order
Generally, ***306***
Adopt or modify, motion to, ***306***
Court action, ***306***
Objection, ***306***
Payment, ***306***
Recommendation
Generally, ***306***
Adopt or modify, motion to, ***306***
Court action, ***306***
Objection, ***306***
Report
Generally, ***306***
Adopt or modify, motion to, ***306***
Court action, ***306***
Objection, ***306***
Types
Generally, ***303***
Consent, ***303***
Post-trial, ***304***
Pretrial, ***303***
Trial, ***303***

MEDICAL EXPENSES
Payments, FRE 409

MEDICAL RECORDS
See Discovery, this index

MENTAL EXAMINATION
Generally, FRCP 35; ***574***
Examiner's report, ***577***
Hearing, ***577***
Motion, FRCP 35; ***574***
Recording device, ***577***
Response, ***576***
Sanctions, ***577***
Waiver of privilege, ***578***

MENTALLY DEFICIENT PERSONS
Competency as witnesses, FRE 601
Confidential or privileged information, *see* Privileges, this index
Witnesses, FRE 601

MINORS
Competency to testify, FRE 601

MISJOINDER
Generally, FRCP 21

MODIFICATION
Pretrial order, ***295***

MOTION DAY
Generally, FRCP 78

MOTIONS
Generally, ***14***
Add or amend findings, *see* Findings of Fact, this index
Advisory jury, FRCP 39; ***315***
Affidavits, ***16***
Allegations, ***15***
Alter or amend judgment, *see* Postjudgment Motions, this index

Page numbers in ***boldface italic***

MOTIONS (continued)
Amendments
Evidence, conform to, FRCP 15
Findings by court, FRCP 52
Judgment, substance of, FRCP 59; ***793***
Pleadings, *see* Amendments, Pleadings, this index
Substance of judgment, FRCP 59; ***793***
Arbitration, *see* this index
Attorney fees, *see* this index
Bankruptcy, 28 U.S.C. 2075
Captions, FRCP 7; ***15***
Certificates
Conference, ***16***
Service, ***16***
Challenging venue, FRCP 12; 28 U.S.C. 1391, 1404, 1406; ***192, 221***
Class certification
Generally, FRCP 23; ***398***
Appellate review, ***406***
Counsel, interim, ***403***
Deadline, ruling, ***404***
Discovery, precertification, ***403***
Grounds, ***399***
Order, ***404***
Response, ***402***
Ruling, ***403***
Clerical errors, correcting, *see* Postjudgment Motions, this index
Close, *see* Closing Argument, this index
Compel, motion to, *see* this index
Consolidation of actions, *see* this index
Continuance, motion for, *see* this index
Courts of appeals, FRAP 27
Default judgment, motion to vacate, FRCP 60; ***598***
Defenses, FRCP 12
Discovery
Motion to compel, FRCP 37; ***444***
Proceedings, FRCP 26
Dismiss, *see* Motions to Dismiss, this index
Entry of default, motion to set aside, FRCP 55; ***588***
Entry of judgment, *see* Judgment, this index
Entry on land, request for, *see* this index
Evidence on, FRCP 43
Exclude expert witness, *see* Expert Witnesses, this index
Excusable neglect, FRCP 60
Exhibits, ***15***
Extend time for party to act, *see* Extend Time, Motion to, this index
Extend time to file notice of appeal, *see* Postjudgment Motions, this index
Extension of time, FRCP 6
Failure to join parties, FRCP 12, 19; ***214***
Failure to state claim for relief, FRCP 12; ***204***
Findings of fact, *see* this index
Form, ***14***
Fraud, FRCP 60
Hearings, ***16, 38***
Impleader, FRCP 14
Improper venue, FRCP 12; ***193***
Inadvertence, FRCP 60

MOTIONS (continued)
Injunctions, FRCP 65; 28 U.S.C. 636
Insufficiency of process, FRCP 12
Interlocutory, FRCP 77
Interpleader, FRCP 22
Intervene, motion to, *see* this index
Judgment, alter or amend, *see* Postjudgment Motions, this index
Judgment as a matter of law, motion for, *see* this index
Judgment on the pleadings
Generally, FRCP 12, ***603***
Summary judgment, compared to, ***603***
Judicial notice, motion for, *see* this index
Lack of jurisdiction, FRCP 12
Limine, motion in, *see* this index
Mental examination, *see* this index
Misconduct, FRCP 60
Mistrial, ***705***
More definite statement
Generally, FRCP 12; ***212***
Appellate review, ***214***
Deadline, ***213***
Grounds, ***212***
Hearing, ***213***
Response, ***213***
Ruling, ***214***
New trial, motion for, *see* this index
Newly discovered evidence, FRCP 60
Nunc pro tunc, *see* Postjudgment Motions, this index
Open, *see* Opening Statement, this index
Permanent injunction, FRCP 65
Perpetuation of testimony pending appeal, FRCP 27
Physical exam, FRCP 35
Postjudgment, *see* this index
Preanswer
Generally, FRCP 12; ***171***
Consolidation of defenses, FRCP 12
Deadlines, ***174***
Defenses available, ***171***
Preliminary injunction, FRCP 65
Process, insufficiency, FRCP 12
Protective orders
Generally, FRCP 26
Grounds, ***441***
Order, ***442***
Relief, motion for, ***440***
Timing, ***441***
Quash or modify subpoenas, *see* Subpoenas, this index
Recuse, motion to, *see* this index
Relief from judgment, *see* Postjudgment Motions, this index
Remand, motion to, *see* this index
Removal, *see* this index
Reopen for additional evidence
Generally, ***718***
Appellate review, ***720***
Deadline, ***719***
Grounds, ***719***
Ruling, ***719***

MOTIONS (continued)
Reopen time for appeal, *see* Postjudgment Motions, this index
Retax costs, FRCP 54, 58; 28 U.S.C. 1920-1931; ***767***
Sanctions, motion for, *see* this index
Separate trials, motion for, *see* this index
Severance of trials, *see* Severance, Motion for, this index
Signing, FRCP 7, 11; ***15***
Strike, claims, FRCP 14
Strike, pleading, FRCP 12
Subpoenas, *see* this index
Substitution of parties, FRCP 25
Summary judgment, *see* this index
Surprise, FRCP 60
Transfer venue
Generally, 28 U.S.C. 1404; ***221***
Forum-selection clause, ***224***
Grounds, ***222***
Trial by consent, FRCP 39
Venue, *see* this index
Verifications, ***16***
Waiver, defenses, FRCP 12; ***172***
Writing, FRCP 7; ***15***

MOTIONS, POSTJUDGMENT
See Postjudgment Motions, this index

MOTIONS TO DISMISS
Conversion to summary-judgment motion, FRCP 12; ***603***
Failure to plead properly
Generally, ***218***
Appellate review, ***221***
Consolidation, ***219***
Grounds, ***219***
Hearing, ***220***
Response, ***220***
Ruling, ***220***
Failure to state claim
Generally, FRCP 12; ***204***
Appellate review, ***208***
Grounds, ***204***
Hearing, ***206***
Plausibility, ***207***
Response, ***206***
Ruling, ***207***
Waiver, ***205***
Forum non conveniens
Generally, ***199***
Adequate alternative forum, ***200***
Appellate review, ***203***
Burden of persuasion, ***201***
Filing deadline, ***202***
Grounds, ***199***
Gulf Oil factors, ***200***
Hearing, ***203***
Response, ***202***
Ruling, ***203***
Improper venue
Generally, ***193***
Appellate review, ***198***
Discovery, ***196***

Page numbers in ***boldface italic***

MOTIONS TO DISMISS (continued)
Improper venue (continued)
 Forum-selection clause, ***194***
 Grounds, ***193***
 Hearing, ***197***
 Response, ***197***
 Ruling, ***198***
 Substantial connection, lack of, ***194***
 Waiver, ***196***
Insufficient process, quashing
 Generally, FRCP 12; ***209***
 Appellate review, ***211***
 Burden of proof, defendant, ***210***
 Burden of proof, plaintiff, ***210***
 Filing deadline, ***209***
 Grounds, ***209***
 Hearing, ***210***
 Response, ***210***
 Ruling, ***210***
 Waiver, ***209***
Interpleader, ***90***
Personal jurisdiction
 Generally, FRCP 12; ***178***
 Appellate review, ***186***
 Discovery, ***185***
 Due process, challenging, ***178***
 General jurisdiction, ***182***
 Grounds, ***178***
 Hearing, ***185***
 Internet contacts, ***180***, ***182***
 Minimum-contacts analysis, ***179***
 Purposeful availment, ***179***
 Response, ***184***
 Ruling, ***186***
 Specific jurisdiction, ***179***
 Statutory authorization, challenging, ***178***
 Stream of commerce, ***179***
 Waiver of motion, ***183***
Required party
 Generally, FRCP 12, 19; ***214***
 Appellate review, ***218***
 Burden of proof, ***216***
 Filing deadline, ***216***
 Grounds, ***215***
 Hearing, ***217***
 Response, ***216***
 Ruling, ***217***
 Waiver, ***216***
Subject-matter jurisdiction
 Generally, FRCP 12; ***187***
 Appellate review, ***192***
 Grounds, ***188***
 Hearing, ***190***
 Response, ***189***
 Ruling, ***191***
 Standing, ***188***

MULTIDISTRICT LITIGATION
Generally, ***1011***

MULTIPARTY, MULTIFORUM JURISDICTION
Generally, 28 U.S.C. 1369; ***129***
Establishing, 28 U.S.C. 1369; ***129***

MULTIPARTY, MULTIFORUM JURISDICTION (continued)
Limitations, 28 U.S.C. 1369; ***134***
Removal, 28 U.S.C. 1441; ***259***
Venue, 28 U.S.C. 1391; ***145***

NAMES
Assumed, FRCP 17
Officers, suit in official capacity, FRCP 25
Omitted parties, FRCP 19
Parties, amended pleadings, FRCP 15
Pleading, FRCP 10
Summons, FRCP 4

NECESSARY PARTIES
Joinder, FRCP 19

NEW TRIAL, MOTION FOR
Generally, FRAP 4; FRCP 6, 59; ***783***
Affidavit, ***785***
Appellate review, ***791***
Damages, ***788***
Deadline, ***783***
Denied, ***787***, ***791***
Error, ***789***
Granted, ***787***, ***792***
Grounds, ***784***
Hearing, ***785***, ***786***
New evidence, ***791***
Preserving error, ***784***
Response, ***786***
Ruling, ***786***
Standard, ***786***, ***788***
Surprise, ***791***

NEWSPAPERS
Self-authentication, FRE 902

NEXT FRIEND
Appointment, FRCP 17

NOLO CONTENDERE
Admissibility, FRE 410

NONJOINDER OF PARTIES
Generally, FRCP 19, 21
Joinder not feasible, FRCP 19
Pleading, FRCP 19

NOTICE
Constitutional challenge, FRCP 5.1; ***12***
Demand letters, ***73***
Prefiling considerations, ***73***
Removal, ***261***
Rulings, ***46***

NOTICE OF APPEAL
See Appeals, this index

NUNC PRO TUNC
See Postjudgment Motions, this index

OBJECTIONS
Generally, ***41***
Discovery, ***424***
Evidence, ***692***, ***700***
Grounds, ***41***
Improper argument, ***729***

OBJECTIONS (continued)
Motion, FRCP 12
Pleading, FRCP 12
Preserving error, ***42***
Question, ***703***
Repeating, ***703***
Ruling, ***704***
Running, ***693***, ***704***
Specificity, ***701***
Time to make, ***700***
Types, ***41***
Waiver, discovery, ***429***
Witness, ***701***

OFFER OF JUDGMENT
Generally, FRCP 68; ***317***
Accepting, ***319***
Appellate review, ***321***
Contents, ***318***
Costs, determining, FRCP 68; 28 U.S.C. 1821, 1920; ***320***
Deadline, ***317***
Rejection, ***319***
Response, ***319***
Revoking, ***319***
Service, ***317***

OFFER OF PROOF
Generally, FRE 103; ***707***
Appellate review, ***709***
Response, ***709***
Ruling, ***709***
Time to make, ***707***

OFFICIAL BONDS
See Bonds, this index

OFFICIAL PUBLICATIONS
Self-authentication, FRE 902

OPENING STATEMENT
Generally, ***686***
Appellate review, ***687***
Limits, ***687***
Motion to open, ***686***
Preserving error, ***687***

OPINIONS
Character & reputation, FRE 405
Expert witnesses
 Generally, FRE 702
 Bases of testimony, FRE 703
 Disclosure of underlying facts or data, FRE 705; ***529***
 Ultimate issue, FRE 704
Handwriting, FRE 901
Lay witnesses, FRE 701

OPTIONAL COMPLETENESS
Generally, FRE 106

ORDERS
Appealable
 Generally, ***739***
 Collateral orders, ***741***
 Intervention, ***361***
 Statutory provisions, ***739***

INDEX

Page numbers in ***boldface italic***

ORDERS (continued)
Appeals, *see* this index
Docket entry, ***45***
Minute entry, ***45***
Oral, ***45***
Pretrial, FRCP 16
Written, ***45***

ORGANIZATIONS
See also Jurisdiction, this index
See also Venue, this index
Routine practice, FRE 406

ORIGINAL DOCUMENTS
Generally, FRE 1001, 1002
In possession of opponent, FRE 1004
Lost or destroyed, FRE 1004
Not obtainable, FRE 1004

OWNERSHIP
Liability insurance, FRE 411
Subsequent remedial measures, FRE 407

PARTIES
Generally, ***75***
Capacity, FRCP 17; ***78***
Designation
Generally, ***8***
Considered for diversity jurisdiction, ***118***
Not considered for diversity jurisdiction, ***122***
Diversity, ***116, 249***
Fictitious, ***76***
Incompetent persons, FRCP 17; ***78***
Infants, FRCP 17; ***78***
John Doe, ***76***
Joinder, FRCP 19-21
Misidentification, ***75***
Misnomer, ***75***
Multiple, service, ***30***
Omitted, ***78***
Real party in interest, FRCP 17
Stakeholder, ***87***
Unincorporated associations, FRCP 23.2
U.S.
Actions affecting property, 28 U.S.C. 2410
Commencing action against, time for, 28 U.S.C. 2401
Commencing action by, time for, 28 U.S.C. 2415, 2416
Costs, 28 U.S.C. 2412
Credits, actions by, 28 U.S.C. 2406
Death of defendant, damages action, 28 U.S.C. 2404
Delinquents for public money, judgment at return, 28 U.S.C. 2407
Executions in favor of, 28 U.S.C. 2413
Fees, 28 U.S.C. 2412
Garnishment, 28 U.S.C. 2405
Interest, 28 U.S.C. 2411
Intervention by, 28 U.S.C. 2403; ***12, 360***
Jury trial, 28 U.S.C. 2402
Partition actions involving, 28 U.S.C. 2409
Payment, compromise settlements, 28 U.S.C. 2414

PARTIES (continued)
U.S. (continued)
Payment, judgments, 28 U.S.C. 2414
Real-property quiet-title actions, 28 U.S.C. 2409A
Security not required of, 28 U.S.C. 2408
Time for commencing action against, 28 U.S.C. 2401
Time for commencing actions brought by, 28 U.S.C. 2415
Venue, *see* this index

PAYMENT
Pleading, as affirmative defense, FRCP 8; ***233***

PEREMPTORY CHALLENGE
Generally, FRCP 47; ***681***

PERMISSIVE COUNTERCLAIM
Pleading, FRCP 13; ***236***

PERSONAL INJURIES
Medical & hospital expenses, payment, FRE 409

PHOTOCOPIES
Self-authentication, FRE 902

PHOTOGRAPHS
Generally, FRE 1001

PHYSICAL EXAMINATION
See Mental Examination, this index

PLAUSIBILITY
See also Pleadings, this index
Standard, ***80, 207***

PLEA
Generally, FRE 410

PLEADINGS
Generally, FRCP 7-15; ***7***
Affidavits, ***11***
Affirmative defenses, *see* this index
Allegations
Generally, ***9***
Adopting by reference, FRCP 10; ***9, 13***
Alternative, ***9***
Form, ***9***
Amendments, *see* Amendments, Pleadings, this index
Appellate review, ***14***
Attorney fees
As costs, ***68***
As damages, ***68***
Attorney in charge, ***11***
Caption, FRCP 10; ***8, 75***
Certificate of service, ***12***
Certification, ***10***
Civil cover sheet, ***8***
Claims, FRCP 10; ***80***
Conforming to evidence, FRCP 15
Counts, ***10***
Damages, ***84***

PLEADINGS (continued)
Defective pleadings
Generally, ***13***
Effect, ***13***
Trial by consent, ***13***
Waiver, ***13***
Defendant's
Generally, ***171***
Answer, ***173, 230***
Defenses, FRCP 10; ***10***
Exhibits
Generally, ***11***
Discrepancy with pleading, ***11***
Incorporation, ***11***
Fair notice, ***9***
Filing, ***14, 17***
Form, ***7***
Groundless, ***385***
Incorporation by reference, FRCP 10; ***9, 13***
Notice, ***9, 80***
Numbered paragraphs, ***8***
Plausibility, ***80, 207***
Prayer, ***10***
Pretrial conference, FRCP 16
Redacted, FRCP 5.2, ***17***
Relation back, amendment, FRCP 15
Response, ***14***
Serving, ***14, 30, 149***
Signature, FRCP 11; ***10***
Special matters, ***82***
Strike, motion to, FRCP 12
Supplemental, FRCP 15; ***13, 350***
Verification, ***11***
Written instrument, ***11***

POSTJUDGMENT MOTIONS
Generally, ***775***
Add or amend findings of fact, *see* Findings of Fact, this index
Appeal, extend time to file notice
Generally, FRAP 4; 28 U.S.C. 2107; ***817***
Affidavits, ***819***
Certificate of service, ***819***
Deadline, ***818***
Grounds, ***818***
Hearing, ***819, 820***
Notice of judgment, ***817***
Objections, ***820***
Response, ***820***
Review, ***820***
Ruling, ***820***
Appeal, reopen time
Generally, FRAP 4; 28 U.S.C. 2107; ***821***
Affidavits, ***824***
Deadline, ***822***
Grounds, ***823***
Hearing, ***823, 824***
Notice of judgment, ***821***
Objections, ***823***
Response, ***823***
Review, ***825***
Ruling, ***824***
Chart, ***775***

INDEX

Page numbers in ***boldface italic***

POSTJUDGMENT MOTIONS (continued)
Clerical errors, correcting
  Generally, FRCP 60; ***825***
  Appellate review, ***828***
  Clerical vs. substantive errors, ***826***
  Deadline, ***826***
  Grounds, ***827***
  Hearing, ***828***
  Objections, ***828***
  Response, ***828***
  Ruling, ***828***
Findings of fact, add or amend, *see* Findings of Fact, this index
Judgment, alter or amend
  Generally, FRCP 59; ***793***
  Appellate review, ***797***
  Deadline, ***793***
  Grounds, ***795***
  Hearing, ***797***
  Misnomer, ***796***
  Objections, ***796***
  Response, ***796***
  Ruling, ***797***
Judgment, relief from
  Generally, FRCP 60; ***804***
  Affidavit, ***811***
  Appellate review, ***815***
  Deadline, ***804***
  Grounds, ***806***
  Hearing, ***811***, ***812***
  Indicative ruling, ***813***
  Mistake, ***807***
  Neglect, ***807***
  Objections, ***811***
  Other relief, ***812***
  Response, ***811***
  Ruling, ***812***
  Surprise, ***807***
  Who can seek, ***810***
New trial, motion for, *see* this index
Nunc pro tunc, *see* Clerical errors, correcting, this entry
Renewed motion for judgment as a matter of law, *see* this index

PREJUDICE
Disqualification judges, 28 U.S.C. 144, 455; ***322***

PREMATURE APPEALS
See Appeals, this index

PRESENT SENSE IMPRESSION
Hearsay exception, FRE 803

PRESERVING ERROR
See Error, this index
See Objections, this index

PRETRIAL CONFERENCE
Generally, FRCP 16, 26; ***290***
Attendance, ***291***
Attorney fees, sanctions, FRCP 16
Final, FRCP 16; ***296***
Sanctions, attorney fees, FRCP 16

PRETRIAL CONFERENCE (continued)
Scheduling, ***290***
Scope, ***291***

PRETRIAL ORDER
Appellate review, ***297***
Enforceability, ***294***
Modification, ***295***, ***296***
Waiver, ***293***

PRIOR CONSISTENT & INCONSISTENT STATEMENTS
Witnesses, FRE 613

PRIVILEGES
Generally, FRE 501, 502; ***430***, ***460***
Attorney-client, ***432***, ***463***
Attorney-expert, ***518***
Bank examination, ***480***
Clergy, ***474***
Confidential information, FRE 501; ***440***, ***464***, ***473***, ***475***
Deliberative process, ***476***
Disclosure, inadvertent, ***431***, ***434***
Executive, ***479***
Government, ***476***
Journalists', ***475***
Judicial, ***480***
Law-enforcement, ***479***
Legislative, ***480***
Litigation, ***480***
New, recognizing, ***461***
Not recognized, ***462***
Preserving after disclosure
  Generally, ***55***, ***430***
  Clawback agreement, ***418***
  Quick-peek agreement, ***418***
Psychotherapist-patient, ***472***
Self-incrimination, ***471***
Settlement negotiations, ***481***
Spousal, ***481***
State secret, ***478***
Statutory, ***480***
Trade-secret, ***480***
Waiver, ***429***
Work-product, ***432***, ***467***, ***518***, ***523***

PRO HAC VICE
Application, ***59***
Hearing, ***60***
Implied, ***59***
Permission to appear, ***60***
Review of status, ***68***
Standards, ***60***

PRO SE
Appearance, ***60***
Corporations, ***60***
Right to represent self, ***60***

PROBATIVE VALUE
Prejudice outweighs, FRE 403

PROCESS, SERVICE OF
See Service of Process, this index

PRODUCT LIABILITY
Defect, manufacturer's notification of, FRE 407
Subsequent remedial measures, FRE 407

PRODUCTION, REQUEST FOR
Generally, FRCP 34; ***569***
Compel, motion to, ***574***
Electronically stored information, ***500***
Manner, ***573***
Nonparties, subpoena, ***569***
Parties, ***570***
Response, ***572***
Sanctions, ***574***

PROOF OF SERVICE
See Service of Documents, this index

PROTECTIVE ORDER
See Motions, this index

PUBLIC DOCUMENTS
Self-authentication, FRE 902; ***697***

PULLMAN
See Abstention, this index

PUNITIVE DAMAGES
Excessive, motion for new trial, ***788***

QUASHING SERVICE
See Motions to Dismiss, this index

RECEIVERS
Generally, FRCP 66

RECORDED RECOLLECTION
Hearsay exception, FRE 803

RECORDS
Business
  Generally, FRE 902
  Photocopies, admissibility, FRE 1001
  Self-authentication, FRE 902
Documents affecting interest in property, hearsay exception, FRE 803
Family, hearsay exception, FRE 803
Public
  Authentication, FRE 901
  Hearsay exception, FRE 803
Regularly conducted activity
  Absence of entry in, FRE 803
  Hearsay exception, FRE 803
Religious organizations, hearsay exception, FRE 803
Vital statistics, hearsay exception, FRE 803

RECUSE, MOTION TO
Generally, 28 U.S.C. 144, 455; ***321***
Appellate review, ***330***
Attorney's certificate, ***322***
Deadline, ***328***
Financial interest, ***326***
Grounds, ***322***
Relation to party, ***327***
Response, ***329***
Ruling, ***329***
Statutes, ***322***

INDEX

Page numbers in ***boldface italic***

RECUSE, MOTION TO (continued)
Voluntary, inability to proceed, FRCP 63
Waiver, ***329***

REFRESHING MEMORY
Writings, FRE 612

REHABILITATION
Witness, FRE 608

RELATIVES
Affinity, ***327, 328***
Consanguinity, ***327***
Counting degrees, ***327***
Motion to recuse, ***327***
Relationships, degree of, chart 5-1, ***328***

RELEASE
Pleading, as affirmative defense, FRCP 8; ***233***

RELEVANCY
Generally, FRE 401 et seq.
Admissibility, FRE 402
Conditioned on fact, FRE 104
Defined, FRE 401
Exclusion, special grounds, FRE 403
Inadmissibility, FRE 402

RELIGIOUS BELIEFS OR OPINIONS
Witnesses, FRE 610

RELIGIOUS ORGANIZATIONS
Hearsay exception, FRE 803

REMAND, MOTION TO
Generally, ***268***
Abstention, ***277***
Amending complaint, ***268***
Appellate review, ***279***
Attorney fees, award, ***277***
Bankruptcy cases, ***277***
Class actions
  Appellate review, ***281***
  Remand discretionary, ***277***
  Remand mandatory, ***277***
Costs, award, ***277***
Court's motion, ***276***
De novo review, ***279***
Deadline, ***273***
Discretionary remand, ***277***
Diversity jurisdiction, lack of
  Deadline to remand, ***273***
  Ground, ***272***
  Remand mandatory, ***276***
Expenses, award, ***277***
Federal-question jurisdiction, lack of
  Deadline to remand, ***273***
  Ground, ***271***
  Nonremovable claims brought with, ***272***
  Remand mandatory, ***276***
Findings of fact, ***279***
Forum-selection clause
  Appellate review, ***280***
  Deadline to remand, ***274***
  Ground, ***272***
  Review of remand, ***280***

REMAND, MOTION TO (continued)
Grounds
  Jurisdictional, ***271***
  Procedural, ***272***
Hearing, ***273, 275***
Mandamus, ***283***
Mandatory remand
  Denying remand, ***277***
  Granting remand, ***276***
Nonremovable claims, ***272***
Order
  Generally, ***276***
  Delivery to state court, ***279***
Procedural defect
  Appellate review, ***280***
  Curable, ***276***
  Deadline to remand, ***274***
  Ground, ***272***
  Remand mandatory, ***276***
Ruling, ***276***
Subject-matter jurisdiction, lack of
  Appellate review, ***280, 281***
  Court's motion, ***276***
  Deadline to remand, ***273***
  Ground, ***271***
  Remand mandatory, ***276***
Supplemental jurisdiction
  Discretionary remand, ***277***
Waiver
  Defendant's actions, ***272***
  Plaintiff's actions, ***271, 274***

REMOVAL
Generally, ***241***
Actions removable, generally, ***249***
Admiralty & maritime cases, ***260***
Alienage jurisdiction, ***260***
Amended complaint, reviving deadline to file, ***248***
Amending notice, ***263***
Amount in controversy
  Discovery of, ***256***
  Diversity jurisdiction, ***254***
  Not specified, ***255***
  Notice of removal, ***262***
Arbitration, effect on removal, ***267***
Armed forces, suit against members of, ***258***
Attachment, 28 U.S.C. 1450
Automatic stay, ***266***
Award of costs, ***277***
Bad faith, deadline to file notice, ***247***
Bankruptcy cases, ***258***
Checklist, ***242***
Citizenship of parties, ***250***
Civil-rights cases, ***258***
Class actions
  Consent of defendants, ***264***
  Deadline to file notice, ***247***
  Ground, ***257, 259***
Common carriers, suits against, ***260***
Congress, actions against members of, ***258***

REMOVAL (continued)
Consent
  Generally, ***263***
  Deadline, ***244***
  Form, ***264***
Copyright cases
  Deadline to file notice, ***248***
  Ground, ***259***
Counterclaim defendants, authority to remove, ***261***
Cross-claim defendants, authority to remove, ***261***
Deadline to file notice, ***242***
Defendants, authority to remove, ***261***
Discovery
  Amount in controversy, ***256***
  Effect on removal, ***267***
Diversity jurisdiction
  Amount in controversy, ***254***
  Deadline to file notice, ***246***
  Diversity of citizenship, ***250***
  Ground, ***249***
Extending deadline to file, ***248***
FDIC
  Deadline to file notice, ***248***
  Ground, ***258***
Federal agency, action against, ***257***
Federal officers & employees, actions against, ***257***
Federal question jurisdiction
  Consent of defendants, ***264***
  Ground, ***249***
  Nonremovable claims brought with, ***249***
Fictitious defendant, ***252***
Filing notice, ***263***
Foreclosure actions against U.S., ***258***
Foreign states
  Consent of defendants, ***264***
  Deadline to file notice, ***248***
  Ground, ***259***
Forum defendant, ***251***
Fraudulent joinder, ***247, 252***
FTCA
  Deadline to file notice, ***248***
  Ground, ***258***
Grounds, ***249***
Injunctive relief, effect on removal, ***267***
Jones Act, ***260***
Local defendant, ***251***
Military, suits against members of, ***258***
Motion for new trial, effect on removal, ***267***
Multiparty, multiforum actions, ***259***
Multiple defendants
  Consent, requirements for, ***263***
  Deadline to file notice or consent, ***244***
Nominal defendant, ***264***
Nonremovable actions
  Generally, ***260***
  Brought with federal question, ***249***
Notice, ***261***
Order, ***265***
Other papers
  Insufficient to support removal, ***246***
  Sufficient to support removal, ***245***

Page numbers in ***boldface italic***

REMOVAL (continued)
Patent cases
Deadline to file notice, ***248***
Ground, ***259***
Plaintiffs, authority to remove, ***261***
Plant variety protection cases
Deadline to file notice, ***248***
Ground, ***259***
Prohibitions against, ***260***
Railroads, suits against, ***260***
Reasons for, ***241***
Reviving deadline to file, ***248***
Securities Act, ***259***, ***260***
Sequestration, 28 U.S.C. 1450
Serving notice, ***263***
State-court record, 28 U.S.C. 1449
Stay, automatic, ***266***
Subpoena for testimony or documents
Deadline to file notice, ***248***
Ground, ***258***
Supplemental jurisdiction, ***249***, ***260***
Third party defendants, authority to remove, ***261***
Waiver, ***266***
When effective, ***266***
When prohibited, ***260***
Workers' compensation, ***260***

RENEWED MOTION FOR JUDGMENT AS A MATTER OF LAW
Generally, FRCP 50; ***775***
Appellate review, ***781***
Deadline, ***776***
Grounds, ***778***
Hearing, ***779***
Motion for new trial, post-JMOL, ***781***
Procedural prerequisites, ***776***
Relief, ***780***
Response, ***779***
Ruling, ***779***

REPUTATION EVIDENCE
Boundaries, FRE 803
Character, hearsay exception, FRE 803
Family history, hearsay exception, FRE 803
General history, FRE 803
Personal history, hearsay exception, FRE 803
Witness, FRE 608

REQUIRED PARTY
See Motions to Dismiss, this index

RES JUDICATA
Pleading, as affirmative defense, FRCP 8; ***233***

RESPONSES
See also each particular pleading or motion, this index
After service, ***33***
Defendant's, chart 3-1, ***177***

REVIEW
See each particular pleading or motion, this index

ROUTINE
Evidence of, FRE 406

RULINGS
Generally, FRCP 54, 55, 58, 60, 77, 79; ***44***
Appellate review, ***46***
Docket entry, ***45***
Form, ***46***
Minute entry, ***45***
Notice, ***46***
Order, ***45***
Record, ***45***
Requesting, ***45***
Securing, ***45***

SANCTIONS, MOTION FOR
Generally, FRCP 11, 16, 26, 37, 56; ***384***
Appellate review, ***397***
Conduct
Does not justify sanctions, ***391***
Justifies sanctions, ***385***
Cost of litigation, increasing, FRAP 30
Court's inherent power, ***389***
Deadline, ***392***
Disclosure, failure to comply, FRCP 37; ***448***
Discovery abuse, ***446***, ***562***
Dismissal, ***645***
Failure to obey order, ***446***
Failure to respond, ***447***
Failure to serve, ***38***
Local rules, ***390***
Notice, ***394***
On court's initiative, ***392***
Order, ***396***
Persons to sanction, ***384***
Pleadings, signing, FRCP 11; ***385***
Pretrial order, FRCP 16
Purpose, ***446***
Refusing to disclose, ***448***
Response, ***393***
Types, ***395***, ***448***
Unauthorized, ***396***

SCHEDULING CONFERENCE
Purpose, FRCP 26; ***289***

SCHEDULING ORDER
Generally, FRCP 16; ***289***
Contents
Generally, ***289***
Mandatory items, ***289***
Permissive items, ***290***
Deadline, ***289***
Modification, ***290***

SELF-AUTHENTICATION
Documents, FRE 902; ***697***, ***698***

SEPARATE TRIALS, MOTION FOR
Generally, FRCP 13, 20, 21, 42; ***366***
Appeal, ***370***
Appellate review, ***370***
Counterclaim, FRCP 13, 42
Cross-claim, FRCP 13, 42
Deadline, ***367***
Grounds, FRCP 20, 42; ***367***, ***368***
Joinder, parties, FRCP 20
Judgment, counterclaim, FRCP 13
Judgment, cross-claim, FRCP 13

SEPARATE TRIALS, MOTION FOR (continued)
Order, FRCP 42; ***368***
Response, ***368***, ***369***
Ruling, ***369***

SERVICE OF DOCUMENTS
Generally, FRCP 5; ***29***
Clerk, ***31***
Deadlines
Generally, ***33***
Affidavits, ***33***
Filing vs. service, chart, ***22***
Motions for hearing, ***33***
Delivery, ***31***
Electronic delivery
Generally, ***31***
Consent, ***32***
Delivery date, ***32***
E-mail, ***32***
Fax, ***31***
Through court, ***31***
Extend time, motion to, ***334***
Extension, three-day, ***34***
FedEx, ***30***
Mail, ***30***
Notice of ruling, ***46***
Proving
Generally, ***36***
Affidavit, ***36***
E-mail, ***37***
Fax, ***37***
Mail, ***36***
Nonreceipt, ***37***
Personal delivery, ***37***
Return receipt, ***36***
Sanctions, ***38***
UPS, ***30***

SERVICE OF PROCESS
Generally, FRCP 4, 4.1; ***149***
Abroad
Alternative service, ***159***
Central authority, service through, ***158***
Court order, service by, ***160***
Extension of time, waiver, ***157***
Federal long-arm service, FRCP 4, ***160***
Hague Convention, ***156***, ***1563***
International agreements, ***157***
Limitations on service, ***156***
State long-arm service, ***160***
Time limit, ***161***
Treaty, absence of, ***159***
Waiver of service, ***156***
Agent, service on, ***153***
Appeals
Manner, FRAP 25
Proof, FRAP 25
Service of all papers, FRAP 25
Civil action, place of arrest, 28 U.S.C. 1693
Court order, service by, ***153***
Deadlines, ***152***
Default judgment, foreign government, ***163***
Defendants, multiple, ***152***

INDEX

Page numbers in ***boldface italic***

SERVICE OF PROCESS (continued)
Extend time, ***153, 155***
Foreign litigation, 28 U.S.C. 1696
Foreign service, ***156***
Hague Convention, effect of, ***158***
Insufficient, ***209***
International litigation, 28 U.S.C. 1696
Long-arm statute, service under, ***153***
Mail, service by, ***153***
Patent-infringement action, 28 U.S.C. 1694
Personal delivery, service by, ***153***
Process servers
  Central authority, ***164***
  Court appointee, ***163***
  Nonparty, ***163***
  U.S. marshal, ***163***
Property, process affecting, 28 U.S.C. 1692
Proving
  Generally, ***36, 165***
  Affidavit, ***165***
  Marshal's signature, ***165***
  Waiver of service, ***165***
Publication, service by, ***153***
Seal, 28 U.S.C. 1691
Serving abroad
  Foreign businesses, ***161***
  Foreign government, ***161***
  Incompetents, ***161***
  Individuals, ***157***
  Minors, ***161***
Serving in U.S.
  Agency, ***155***
  Businesses, ***154***
  Incompetents, ***154***
  Individuals, ***153***
  Minors, ***154***
  Nonresidents, ***156***
  State governments, ***154***
  U.S. employee, ***155***
  U.S. government, ***154***
  U.S. officer, ***155***
Stockholder's derivative action, 28 U.S.C. 1695
Summons
  Amending, ***152***
  Caption, ***151***
  Clerk, duty of, ***152***
  Court information, ***151***
  Deadline, ***152***
  Defendant's identity, ***152***
  Plaintiff's duty, ***152***
  Plaintiff's identity, ***151***
  Requirements, ***151***
  Securing, ***151***
Territorial limits
  Generally, ***164***
  100-mile rule, ***164***
  Federal Interpleader Act, ***164***
  Federal long-arm, FRCP 4, ***165***
  Federal statute, ***164***
  State long-arm, ***164***
Teste, 28 U.S.C. 1691

SERVICE OF PROCESS (continued)
Waiver
  Generally, ***149, 156***
  Deadline to return, ***150***
  Filing, ***150***
  Foreign service, ***156***
  No summons, ***150***
  Notice, ***150***
  Refusal to waive, ***151***
  Request, ***150***
Who can serve, ***163***

SETTLEMENT
See Compromise & Settlement, this index

SEVERANCE, MOTION FOR
Generally, FRCP 13, 20, 21, 42; ***366***
Appellate review, ***369***
Grounds, ***366***
Response, ***368***
Ruling, ***369***

SIGNATURE
Motion, ***15***
Pleading, ***10***

SPECIAL MASTERS
See Masters, this index

STAKEHOLDER
See Interpleader, this index

STANDING
Complaint, ***77***

STANDING ORDERS
Generally, ***6***

STATUTE OF FRAUDS
Pleading, as affirmative defense, FRCP 8; ***233***

STATUTE OF LIMITATIONS
Diversity cases, ***74***
Federal-question cases, ***74***
Pleading, as affirmative defense, FRCP 8; ***233***

STOCK & STOCKHOLDERS
Derivative actions, FRCP 23.1

SUBJECT-MATTER JURISDICTION
Generally, ***112***
Challenging, ***188***
Determining, ***112***

SUBPOENAS
Generally, FRCP 45; ***47, 689***
Alternative dispute resolution, use of subpoena, 28 U.S.C. 656
Attorney, issuing, ***50***
Challenging, ***55***
Clerk, issuing, ***50***
Compel, motion to
  Generally, FRCP 45; ***55***
  Grounds, ***55, 444***
  Where to file, ***55***
Documents, ***52***
Duces tecum, ***47, 48, 50***
Electronically stored information, FRCP 45; ***48, 52***

SUBPOENAS (continued)
Enforcing, ***58***
Entry on land, ***48, 579, 580***
Inspection, ***52***
Issuing, ***50***
Mileage allowance, ***52***
Nonparty, ***49***
Notice, ***50***
Objection to, production or inspection, ***54***
Party, ***49***
Production, ***52***
Quash or modify, motion to
  Generally, FRCP 45; ***55***
  Deadline, ***56***
  Grounds, discretionary, ***57***
  Grounds, mandatory, ***56***
  Where to file, ***56***
  Who can file, ***55***
Range, ***49***
Requirements, ***48***
Service
  Deadline, ***52***
  Manner, ***51***
  Proof, ***52***
Tangible things, ***52***
Types
  Generally, ***47***
  Deposition, ***47***
  Discovery, ***47***
  Hearing, ***40, 47***
  Production, ***47***
  Trial, ***47***
Witness fee, ***52***

SUBSEQUENT REMEDIAL MEASURES
Evidence of, FRE 407

SUBSTITUTION OF PARTIES
Generally, FRCP 25

SUMMARIES
As evidence, FRE 1006

SUMMARY JUDGMENT
Generally, FRCP 56; ***603***
Affidavits, FRCP 56; ***610***
Affirmative defense, ***617, 618***
Amend pleading, ***609***
Appellate review, ***628***
Attorney fees, ***605***
Bad faith, affidavit, FRCP 56
Brief, ***606, 609***
Burden of proof, ***615***
Citation, ***604, 608, 610, 614***
Contempt, FRCP 56
Continuance
  Generally, ***620***
  Further discovery, FRCP 56
  Grounds, ***620***
Conversion from motion to dismiss, FRCP 12; ***603***
Counterclaim, ***617***
Deadlines, ***619***
Declaration, FRCP 56; ***610***
Declaratory judgment, FRCP 56

INDEX

Page numbers in ***boldface italic***

SUMMARY JUDGMENT (continued)
Defending party, FRCP 56
Defer ruling, ***609***
Delay, affidavit presented, FRCP 56
Deposition, FRCP 56
Discovery, continuance for further, FRCP 56
Expenses, bad-faith affidavit, FRCP 56
Extension of time, ***609***
Fact disputes, ***604***, ***608***, ***610***
Facts, statement of, ***606***, ***609***
Findings, FRCP 52
Form, affidavit, FRCP 56
Grounds, ***604***
Hearing, ***623***
Interrogatories, FRCP 56
Memorandum, ***606***, ***609***
Motion for reconsideration, ***627***
Motion to strike, evidence, ***607***
Objections
  Reply, ***610***
  Response, ***607***
Order, ***627***
Organization, ***614***
Partial, ***605***
Point-counterpoint statement, ***606***, ***609***
Pretrial conference, FRCP 16
Proof
  Generally, FRCP 56; ***604***, ***608***, ***610***
  Citation, ***604***, ***608***, ***610***, ***614***
  Organization of, ***614***
  Placing in record, ***614***
  Reference, ***604***, ***608***, ***614***
  Sham affidavit, ***611***
  Types, ***610***
  Verification, FRCP 56
Response, ***606***
Ruling
  Generally, ***623***
  On party's motion, ***625***
  Order, ***627***
  Review proof, ***623***, ***624***
  Sua sponte, ***626***
Sua sponte, ***626***

SUPERSEDEAS & STAY
Generally, FRCP 62
District court
  Appeals, FRAP 7
  Cost bonds, FRAP 7
  Record for preliminary motion in court of appeals, FRAP 11
  Stay or injunction pending appeal, FRAP 8
Stay on appeal, FRCP 62
Time for giving, FRCP 62
U.S., FRCP 62

SUPPLEMENTAL JURISDICTION
See Jurisdiction, this index

SUPPLEMENTING
Generally, FRCP 15; ***13***, ***350***
Discovery, ***438***
Pleadings, ***350***
Pretrial, ***350***

SUPREME COURT
Administrative assistant, 28 U.S.C. 677
Associate justices, precedence of, 28 U.S.C. 4
Binding, 28 U.S.C. 676
Clerk, 28 U.S.C. 671
Justices, number of, 28 U.S.C. 1
Law clerks, 28 U.S.C. 675
Librarian, 28 U.S.C. 674
Marshal, 28 U.S.C. 672
Printing, 28 U.S.C. 676
Quorum, 28 U.S.C. 1
Records, 28 U.S.C. 6
Reporter, 28 U.S.C. 673
Rule-making authority, 28 U.S.C. 2071, 2072
Salaries, 28 U.S.C. 5
Secretaries, 28 U.S.C. 675
Terms, 28 U.S.C. 2
Vacancy, Chief Justice, 28 U.S.C. 3

SURPRISE
Motion for relief, FRCP 60
Orders of court, FRCP 60

TAXABLE COSTS
See Costs, this index

TELEPHONE
Conversations, authentication or identification, FRE 901
Depositions, FRCP 30

TEMPORARY RESTRAINING ORDER (TRO)
Generally, ***97***

TESTIMONY
Affirmation in lieu of oath, FRCP 43
Evidence on motions, FRCP 43
Interpreters, FRCP 43
Introducing, ***689***
Taking of, FRCP 43

THIBODAUX
See Abstention, this index

THIRD-PARTY PRACTICE
Generally, FRCP 14; ***236***
Impleader, FRCP 14

TIME
Backward-looking deadline, ***24***
Computing deadlines, ***23***
Continuance, additional time for discovery, ***337***
Counting
  Days, ***24***
  Hours, ***27***
  Months, ***27***
  Years, ***27***
Extend, motion to, FRCP 6; ***332***
Extension of, appeals, FRAP 4; ***816***, ***817***
Forward-looking deadline, ***24***
Holidays, ***25***
Inaccessibility, clerk's office, ***26***
Reopen time for appeal, FRAP 4; ***821***
Weekends, ***25***

TIMETABLES
Appeal of civil trial, ***1591***
Discovery status sheet, ***1579***
Motion to court for default judgment, ***1587***
Pleadings schedule, ***1574***
Pretrial disclosures & conferences, ***1577***
Removal to federal court, ***1581***
Request to clerk for default judgment, ***1586***
Summary judgment, ***1589***
Temporary restraining order & injunction, ***1583***

TORT CLAIMS ACT
Administrative adjustment of claims, 28 U.S.C. 2672
Attorney fees, 28 U.S.C. 2678
Compromise, 28 U.S.C. 2677
Definitions, 28 U.S.C. 2671
Evidence, 28 U.S.C. 2675
Exceptions, 28 U.S.C. 2680
Exclusiveness of remedy, 28 U.S.C. 2679
Judgment as bar, 28 U.S.C. 2676
Liability of U.S., 28 U.S.C. 2674
Penalties, 28 U.S.C. 2678
Prerequisites, 28 U.S.C. 2675
Reports to Congress, 28 U.S.C. 2673
Venue, ***146***

TRANSCRIPT, APPEAL
See Appeals, this index

TREATISES
Learned, hearsay exception, FRE 803

TRIAL
Advisory jury, FRCP 39
Assignment of cases for, FRCP 40
By consent, FRCP 39
By jury, FRCP 39
Order, ***45***
Separate, appeal, ***370***

TRUSTEES, U.S.
Generally, 28 U.S.C. 581
Assistant U.S. trustees, 28 U.S.C. 582
Attorney General, supervision by, 28 U.S.C. 586
Duties, 28 U.S.C. 586
Expenses, 28 U.S.C. 588
Oath, 28 U.S.C. 583
Official stations, 28 U.S.C. 584
Other employees, 28 U.S.C. 589
Salaries, 28 U.S.C. 587
Staff, 28 U.S.C. 589
U.S. Trustee System Fund, 28 U.S.C. 589a
Vacancies, 28 U.S.C. 585

U.S. MARSHALS SERVICE
Generally, 28 U.S.C. 561
Accounting, 28 U.S.C. 567
Duties, 28 U.S.C. 566
Expenses, 28 U.S.C. 565
Fees, collecting, 28 U.S.C. 567
Oath of office, 28 U.S.C. 563
Powers, 28 U.S.C. 566
Powers as sheriff, 28 U.S.C. 564

Page numbers in ***boldface italic***

U.S. MARSHALS SERVICE (continued)
Practice of law prohibited, 28 U.S.C. 568
Qualifications, 28 U.S.C. 561
Reemployment rights, 28 U.S.C. 569
Vacancies, 28 U.S.C. 562

VENIRE
See Jury, this index

VENUE
Generally, FRCP 12; 28 U.S.C. 1390, 1391, 1404, 1406; ***143***
Admiralty & maritime, ***146***
Alteration
  District, 28 U.S.C. 1405
  Division, 28 U.S.C. 1405
Appellate review, ***198***, ***229***
Arbitration, ***147***
Banking association, civil action, 28 U.S.C. 1394
Bankruptcy, ***146***
Change
  Generally, 28 U.S.C. 1404
  Consent, ***227***
  Title 11, 28 U.S.C. 1412
Consent, ***227***
Consideration, ***193***
Copyrights, 28 U.S.C. 1400
Creation
  District, 28 U.S.C. 1405
  Division, 28 U.S.C. 1405
Cure, defects, 28 U.S.C. 1406
Defined, ***144***
Diversity suits, ***144***
EEOC, ***147***
Eminent domain, 28 U.S.C. 1403
ERISA, ***147***
Federal officers, ***145***
Federal question suits, ***144***
Fine, civil action for recovery of, 28 U.S.C. 1395
Foreign proceedings, cases ancillary to, 28 U.S.C. 1410
Foreign state as defendant, ***146***
Forfeiture, civil action for recovery, 28 U.S.C. 1395
Forum-selection clauses
  Generally, ***156***
  Appellate review, ***199***
  Asserting, ***173***
General venue statute, ***144***
Improper, FRCP 12; 28 U.S.C. 1406; ***192***
Internal revenue taxes, 28 U.S.C. 1396
Interpleader, 28 U.S.C. 1397; ***146***
Interstate Commerce Commission, orders, 28 U.S.C. 1398
Jury trials, unaffected, 28 U.S.C. 1411
Multidistrict litigation, 28 U.S.C. 1407; ***146***
Multiple parties & claims, ***148***
NLRB, ***147***
Partition action involving U.S., 28 U.S.C. 1399
Patents, 28 U.S.C. 1400; ***146***
Penalty, civil action for recovery of, 28 U.S.C. 1395

VENUE (continued)
Pendent, ***148***
Place of event or property, 28 U.S.C. 1391; ***144***
Residence
  Generally, 28 U.S.C. 1391; ***147***
  Aliens, ***147***, ***148***
  Corporation, ***147***, ***148***
  Individual, ***147***, ***148***
  Partnership, ***147***
  State officials, ***147***
  Unincorporated associations, ***147***
RICO, ***147***
Securities, ***146***
Statute, not general, ***146***
Stockholder's derivative action, 28 U.S.C. 1401
Time to determine, ***148***
Title 11, proceedings arising under, 28 U.S.C. 1409
Title 11 cases, 28 U.S.C. 1408
Tort Claims Act, 28 U.S.C. 1402; ***146***
Transfer, motion to
  Generally, 28 U.S.C. 1404; ***221***
  Agreed, ***227***
  Appellate review, ***229***
  Burden, ***225***
  Choice-of-law rules, ***229***
  Deadline, ***227***
  Discovery, ***225***
  Evidence, ***225***
  Grounds, ***222***
  Hearing, ***228***
  Response, ***225***
  Ruling, ***228***
  Stay of transfer, ***229***
U.S. as defendant, 28 U.S.C. 1402; ***145***
Waiver of defects, 28 U.S.C. 1406, ***196***

VERDICT
Generally, FRCP 48, 49; ***720***
Directed or instructed, *see* Judgment as a Matter of Law, Motion for, this index

VERIFICATION
Generally, ***11***
Bill of costs, FRAP 39; 28 U.S.C. 1924

VICTIMS
Character & reputation, FRE 404

VIDEOTAPE
Generally, FRE 1001

VITAL STATISTICS
Hearsay exception, FRE 803

VOICE IDENTIFICATION
Generally, FRE 901

VOIR DIRE
See Jury, this index

VOLUNTARY DISMISSAL
Generally, FRCP 23, 41; ***629***
Appeal, ***640***
Appellate review, ***640***
Challenging, ***639***

VOLUNTARY DISMISSAL (continued)
Court-ordered, motion for
  Generally, ***632***
  Deadline, ***633***
  Form, ***633***
  Grounds, ***633***
Effect, ***631***, ***638***
Notice
  Generally, ***630***
  Deadline, ***631***
  Form, ***630***
  Grounds, ***630***
Order, ***635***
Response, ***631***, ***633***
Stipulation
  Generally, ***631***
  Deadline, ***632***
  Form, ***631***
Types, ***629***

WAIVER
Defenses, FRCP 12; ***172***
Discovery, ***429***
Indispensable party, ***216***
Jurisdictional immunity, foreign state, 28 U.S.C. 1605, 1610
Jury trial, FRCP 38
Mental examination, ***578***
Personal jurisdiction, ***183***
Pleading, as affirmative defense, FRCP 8; ***233***
Pretrial order, ***293***
Privileges, FRE 502; ***430***
Protection, FRE 502; ***432***
Recusal, ***329***
Remand, ***272***
Removal, ***266***
Service, ***149***
Subject-matter jurisdiction, ***189***
Summons, ***150***
Venue defects, 28 U.S.C. 1406; ***196***

WANT OF PROSECUTION
See Involuntary Dismissal, this index

WELL-PLEADED COMPLAINT
Generally, ***113***

WITHDRAWAL
Admissions, FRCP 36; ***567***
Attorney, ***62***
Jury-trial demand, FRCP 38
Offer of judgment, FRCP 68
Pleas of guilty & related statements, admissibility, FRE 410

WITNESSES
Calling, FRE 614
Character, evidence of
  Generally, FRE 608
  Opinion testimony, FRE 608
  Reputation testimony, FRE 608
Conduct, evidence of, FRE 608
Ex parte communications with, ***61***
Expert witnesses, *see* this index

Page numbers in ***boldface italic***

WITNESSES (continued)
Fact
- Generally, ***458***
- Cost, ***458***
- Discovery, ***458***
- Potential, ***458***
- Trial, ***458***

Impeaching, ***692***
Incompetency, FRE 601
Insanity, FRE 601
Interested, ***613***
Interpreters, FRE 604
Interrogating, FRE 614
Judge, competency as, FRE 605
Lay witness, FRE 701; ***690***
Objection, ***701***
Order of interrogation
- Generally, FRE 611
- Control, FRE 611
- Cross-examination, FRE 611
- Leading questions, FRE 611
- Scope, FRE 611

Prior statements, FRE 613
Religious beliefs, FRE 610
Sequestering, FRE 615
Subpoenaed, FRCP 45; ***40***, ***47***, ***689***
Testimony, ***689***
Writings used to refresh memory, FRE 612

WORK-PRODUCT PROTECTION
Generally, FRCP 26, ***467***
Experts, ***518***, ***523***
Waiver, FRE 502; ***432***

WRITTEN INSTRUMENTS
Authentication, FRE 901 et seq.
Definitions, FRE 1001

YOUNGER
See Abstention, this index

Notes

Notes

GRADE 5

Math

Table of Contents

Roman Numerals 4
Place Value 5
Powers of 10 6
Addition 7
Subtraction 8
Addition and Subtraction 9
Rounding 10
Rounding and Estimating 11
Prime Numbers 12
Multiples 13
Factor Trees 14
Add Integers 15
Multiplication (One-Digit Multiplier) 16
Multiplication (Two-Digit Multiplier) 17
One-Digit Multiplication With Regrouping 18
Multiplication 19
Problem Solving 20
Multiplication's Opposite 21
Division 22
Checking Division 23
Check It Out 24
Adding Money 25
At the Science Store 26
Multiplying Money 27
What Do You Mean? 28
Adding and Subtracting Like Fractions 29
Adding and Subtracting Unlike Fractions 30
Improper Fractions 31

Send all inquiries to:
School Specialty Publishing
8720 Orion Place
Columbus, OH 43240-2111

ISBN 0-7696-7615-4

1 2 3 4 5 6 7 8 9 10 WAL 09 08 07 06 05

Conversion 32
Mixed Numbers 33
Subtracting Mixed Numbers 34
Fractions: Mixed to Improper 35
Multiplying Fractions 36
Multiplying Mixed Numbers 37
Dividing Fractions 38
Fractions: Multiplication and Division 39
Decimals 40
That's the Point 41
Missing Train 42
Adding and Subtracting Decimals 43
Multiplying Decimals 44
Dividing With Decimals 45
Working With Decimals 46
Giving 100% 47
Percent 48
Finding Percents 49
Ratios 50
What Are the Chances? 51
Lines 52
Polygons 53
Three-Dimensional Objects 54
Geometric Patterns 55
Similar, Congruent, and Symmetrical Figures 56
Volume 57
Perimeter, Area, and Volume 58
Triangle Angles 59
Length 60
Weight 61
Length: Metric 62
Capacity: Metric 63
Weights and Measures 64
Renaming Lengths 65
Temperature: Fahrenheit 66
Graphs 67
Circle Graph 68
Locating Points on a Grid 69
Answer Key 70-80

Name ___________________________

Roman Numerals

STAR GAMES PART VI

Example:

Roman Numeral	Value
I	1
V	5
X	10
L	50
C	100
D	500
M	1,000

Rules for Roman Numerals

- When a series of letters goes from a greater to a lesser value, add.
- When a series of letters goes from a lesser to a greater value, subtract.
- No letter repeats more than 3 times.

VII = 5 + 1 + 1 = 7
CXV = 100 + 10 + 5 = 115
IV = 5 − 1 = 4
CD = 500 − 100 = 400
XIV = 10 + (5 − 1) = 10 + 4 = 14
MMCXL = 1,000 + 1,000 + 100 + (50 − 10) = 2,140

Directions: Match each Roman numeral in **Column A** with the correct number in **Column B.** Write the letter on the line.

Column A		Column B
1. _______	VII	**a.** 331
2. _______	CXX	**b.** 165
3. _______	IX	**c.** 26
4. _______	MC	**d.** 120
5. _______	DLIII	**e.** 1,100
6. _______	CLXV	**f.** 98
7. _______	MCMXI	**g.** 7
8. _______	XXVI	**h.** 104
9. _______	CIV	**i.** 642
10. _______	DCXLII	**j.** 9
11. _______	CCCXXXI	**k.** 1,911
12. _______	XCVIII	**l.** 553

Name ______________________________

Place Value

The **place value** of a digit or numeral is shown by where it is in the number. In the number 1,234, 1 has the place value of thousands, 2 is hundreds, 3 is tens and 4 is ones.

Example: 1,250,000,000

Read: One billion, two hundred fifty million

Write: 1,250,000,000

Billions			Millions			Thousands			Ones		
h	t	o	h	t	o	h	t	o	h	t	o
		1,	**2**	**5**	**0,**	**0**	**0**	**0,**	**0**	**0**	**0**

Directions: Read the words. Then write the numbers.

twenty million, three hundred four thousand ______________________

five thousand, four hundred twenty-three ______________________

one hundred fifty billion, eight million, one thousand, five hundred ______________________

sixty billion, seven hundred million, one hundred thousand, three hundred twelve ______________________

four hundred million, fifteen thousand, seven hundred one ______________________

six hundred ninety-nine million, four thousand, nine hundred forty-two ______________________

Here's a game to play with a partner.

Write a ten-digit number using each digit, 0 to 9, only once. Do not show the number to your partner. Give clues like: "There is a five in the hundreds place." The clues can be given in any order. See if your partner can write the same number you have written.

Name ____________________

Powers of 10

Example:

A power of 10 equals the number 10 multiplied by itself a given number of times.

100,000 = 10 x 10 x 10 x 10 x 10.

There are 5 zeros in 100,000, so 10 is multiplied by itself 5 times.

Directions: Write the missing number or numbers.

Example: 1,000 = 10 x 10 x 10

100,000 =

10 x 10 =

10,000 =

10 x 10 x 10 x 10 =

10 =

10 x 10 x 10 =

1,000,000 =

10 x 10 x 10 x 10 x 10 =

100 =

10 x 10 x 10 x 10 x 10 x 10 =

10,000,000 =

Name ____________________

Addition

Teachers of an Earth Science class planned to take 50 students on an overnight hiking and camping experience. After planning the menu, they went to the grocery store for supplies.

Breakfast	Lunch	Dinner	Snacks
bacon	hot dogs/buns	pasta	crackers
eggs	apples	sauce	marshmallows
bread	chips	garlic bread	chocolate bars
cereal	juice	salad	cocoa mix
juice	granola bars	cookies	
$34.50	$ 52.15	$ 47.25	$ 23.40

Directions: Answer the questions. Write the total amount spent on food for the tri

What information do you need to answer the question? ____________________

____

What is the total? ____________________

Directions: Add.

462 + 574	918 + 359	527 + 582	386 + 745	295 + 764
397 + 448	524 + 725	906 + 337	750 + 643	891 + 419
1,568 + 2,341	3,214 + 2,896	5,147 + 4,285	7,259 + 2,451	9,317 + 3,583

Name ______________________

Subtraction

When working with larger numbers, it is important to keep the numbers lined up according to place value.

Directions: Subtract.

398 – 149	543 – 287	491 – 311	
786 – 597	1,825 – 495	4,172 – 2,785	
8,391 – 5,492	63,852 – 34,765	24,107 – 19,350	52,900 – 43,081

Eagle Peak is the highest mountain peak at Yellowstone National Park. It is 11,353 feet high. The next highest point at the park is Mount Washburn. It is 10,243 feet tall. How much higher is Eagle Peak?

____

The highest mountain peak in North America is Mount McKinley, which stretches 20,320 feet toward the sky. Two other mountain ranges in North America have peaks at 10,302 feet and 8,194 feet. What is the greatest difference between the peaks?

____

Name ______________________

Addition and Subtraction

Directions: Check the answers. Write **T** if the answer is true and **F** if it is false.

Example:

$$\begin{array}{r} 48{,}973 \\ -\ 35{,}856 \\ \hline 13{,}118 \end{array} \quad \text{Check: } \underline{\ F\ } \quad \begin{array}{r} 35{,}856 \\ +\ 13{,}118 \\ \hline 48{,}974 \end{array}$$

$$\begin{array}{r} 18{,}264 \\ +\ 17{,}893 \\ \hline 36{,}157 \end{array} \quad \text{Check: } \underline{\qquad}$$

$$\begin{array}{r} 458{,}342 \\ -\ 297{,}652 \\ \hline 160{,}680 \end{array} \quad \text{Check: } \underline{\qquad}$$

$$\begin{array}{r} 39{,}854 \\ +\ 52{,}713 \\ \hline 92{,}577 \end{array} \quad \text{Check: } \underline{\qquad}$$

$$\begin{array}{r} 631{,}928 \\ -\ 457{,}615 \\ \hline 174{,}313 \end{array} \quad \text{Check: } \underline{\qquad}$$

$$\begin{array}{r} 14{,}389 \\ +\ 93{,}587 \\ \hline 107{,}976 \end{array} \quad \text{Check: } \underline{\qquad}$$

$$\begin{array}{r} 554{,}974 \\ -\ 376{,}585 \\ \hline 178{,}389 \end{array} \quad \text{Check: } \underline{\qquad}$$

$$\begin{array}{r} 87{,}321 \\ -\ 62{,}348 \\ \hline 24{,}973 \end{array} \quad \text{Check: } \underline{\qquad}$$

$$\begin{array}{r} 109{,}568 \\ +\ 97{,}373 \\ \hline 206{,}941 \end{array} \quad \text{Check: } \underline{\qquad}$$

Directions: Read the story problem. Write the equation and check the answer.

A camper hikes 53,741 feet out into the wilderness. On his return trip he takes a shortcut, walking 36,752 feet back to his cabin. The shortcut saves him 16,998 feet of hiking. True or False?

Name ____________________

Rounding

Follow these steps to round numbers to a given place.

Example: Round 35,634 to the nearest thousand.

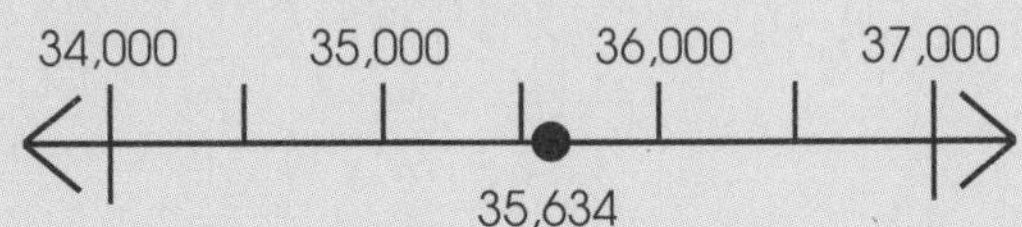

a. Locate and highlight the place to which the number is to be rounded.
► Highlight the digit in the thousands place: 3**5**,634

b. Look at the digit to the right of the designated place. If the number is 5 or greater, round the highlighted number up. If the number is 4 or less, round the highlighted number down by keeping the digit the same.
► Six is greater than 5, so round the highlighted number up.

c. Rewrite the original number with the amended digit in the highlighted place and change all of the digits to the right to zeros.
► The rounded number is 36,000.

Example: Round 782 to the nearest 10.

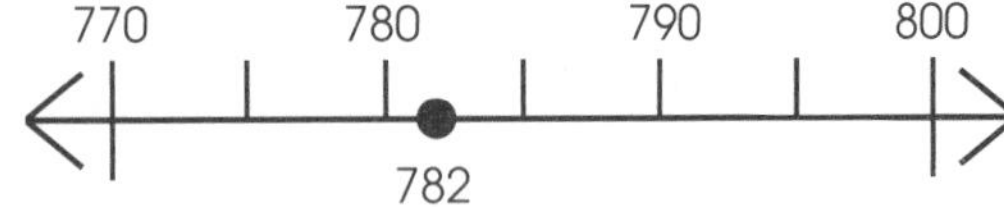

► Highlight the digit in the tens place: 7**8**2

► Two is four or less, so round down by keeping the tens digit the same. 782

► The rounded number is 780.

Directions: Round each number to the given place.

nearest 10:	**1.** 855 ________	**2.** 333 ________
nearest 100:	**3.** 725 ________	**4.** 2,348 ________
nearest 1,000:	**5.** 4,317 ________	**6.** 8,650 ________
nearest 10,000:	**7.** 25,199 ________	**8.** 529,740________
nearest 100,000:	**9.** 496,225________	**10.** 97,008 ________

Name ______________________

Rounding and Estimating

Rounding numbers and estimating answers is an easy way of finding the approximate answer without writing out the problem or using a calculator.

Directions: Circle the correct answer.

Round to the nearest **ten:**

73 → 70 / 80

48 → 40 / 50

65 → 60 / 70

85 → 80 / 90

92 → 90 / 100

37 → 30 / 40

Round to the nearest **hundred:**

139 → 100 / 200

782 → 700 / 800

390 → 300 / 400

640 → 600 / 700

525 → 500 / 600

457 → 400 / 500

Round to the nearest **thousand:**

1,375 → 1,000 / 2,000

21,800 → 21,000 / 22,000

36,240 → 36,000 / 37,000

Sam wanted to buy a new computer. He knew he had only about $1,200 to spend. Which of the following ones could he afford to buy?

$1,165

$1,279

$1,249

If Sam spent $39 on software for his new computer, $265 for a printer, and $38 for a cordless mouse, about how much money did he need?

____

Name ______________________

Prime Numbers

Example: 3 is a **prime number.** $3 \div 1 = 3$ and $3 \div 3 = 1$

A prime number
is a positive whole number
that can be divided evenly
only by itself or one.

Any other divisor will result in a mixed number or fraction.

Example:

11 can be divided only by 1 and 11.
It is a prime number.

Directions: Write the first 15 prime numbers.

Prime Numbers:

_______ _______ _______ _______ _______

_______ _______ _______ _______ _______

_______ _______ _______ _______ _______

How many prime numbers are there between 0 and 100? ____

Name ____________________

Multiples

A **multiple** is the product of a specific number and any other number. When you multiply two numbers, the answer is called the **product**.

Example:

The multiples of 2 are 2 (2 x 1), 4 (2 x 2), 6, 8, 10, 12, and so on.
The **least common multiple** (LCM) of two or more numbers is the smallest number other than 0 that is a multiple of each number.

LCM

Example:

Multiples of 3 are 3, 6, 9, 12, 15, 18, 21, 24, etc.
Multiples of 6 are 6, 12, 18, 24, 30, 36, 42, etc.
Multiples that 3 and 6 have in common are 6, 12, 18, 24.
The LCM of 3 and 6 is 6.

Directions: Write the first nine multiples of 3, 4, and 6. Write the LCM.

3: ______, ______, ______, ______, ______, ______, ______, ______, ______
4: ______, ______, ______, ______, ______, ______, ______, ______, ______
6: ______, ______, ______, ______, ______, ______, ______, ______, ______

LCM = ______

Directions: Write the first nine multiples of 2 and 5. Write the LCM.

2: ______, ______, ______, ______, ______, ______, ______, ______, ______
5: ______, ______, ______, ______, ______, ______, ______ ______, ______

LCM = ______

Directions: Find the LCM for each pair of numbers.

7 and 3 ________ 4 and 6 ________ 6 and 9 ________
5 and 15 ________ 5 and 4 ________ 3 and 18 ________

Directions: Fill in the missing numbers.

30 has multiples of 5 and ____, of 2 and _____, of 3 and _____.

Name ______________________________

Factor Trees

A **factor tree** shows the prime factors of a number. A prime number, such as 7, has for its factors only itself and 1.

Example:

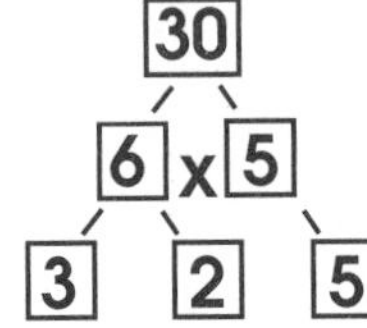

30 = 3 x 2 x 5.
3, 2, and 5 are prime numbers.

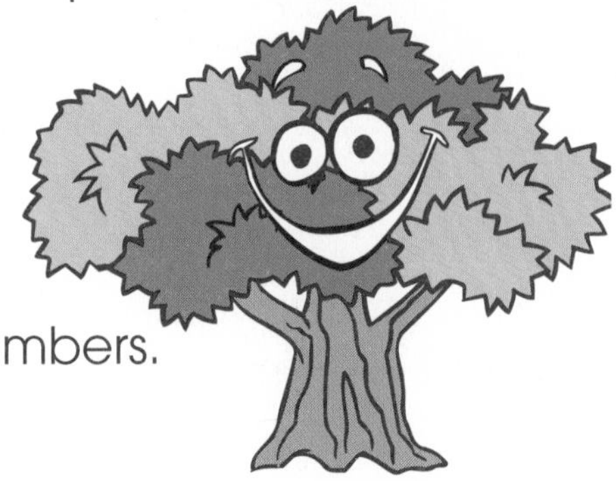

Directions: Fill in the numbers in the factor trees.

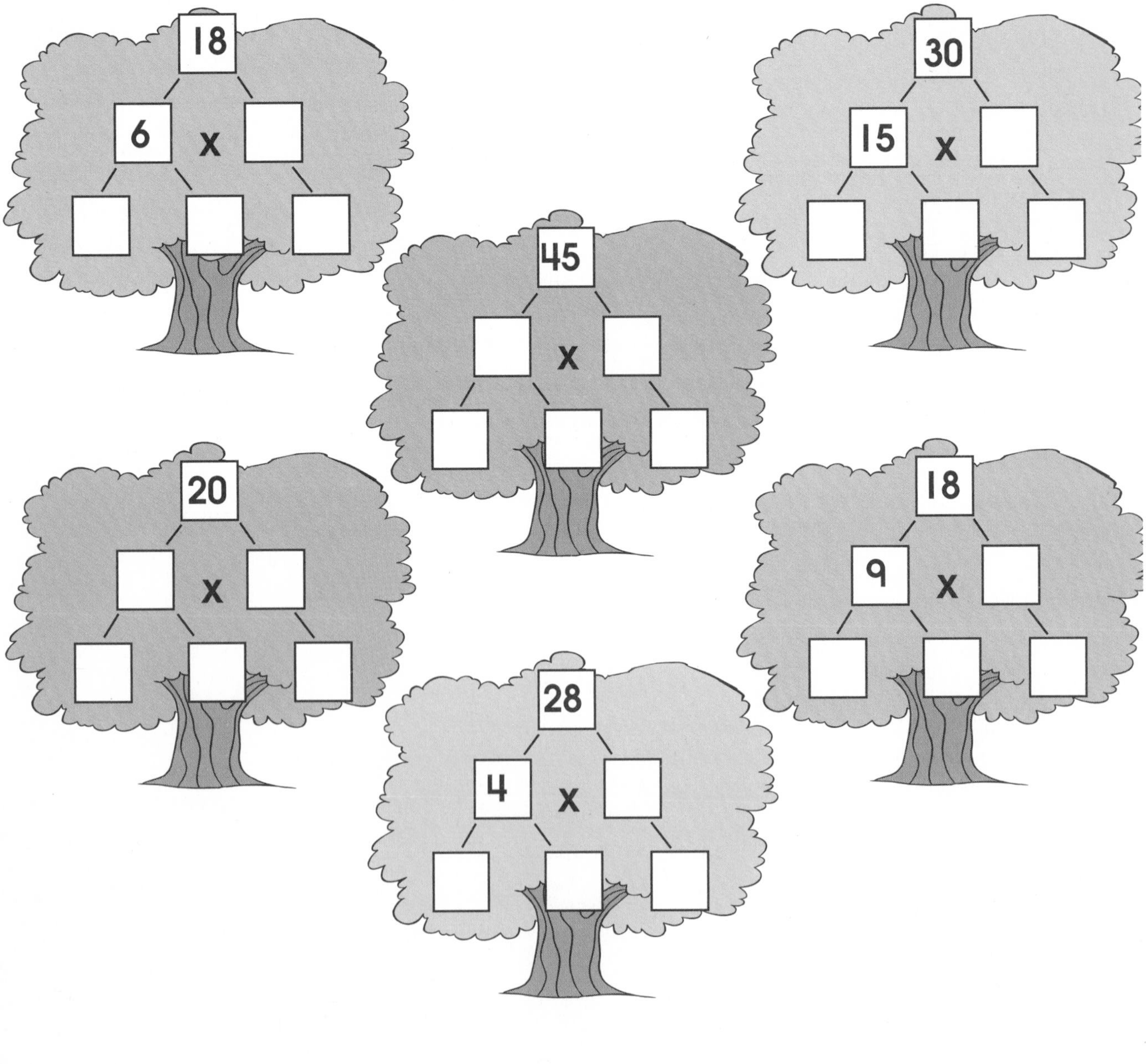

18 = 6 x ☐ ; ☐ ☐ ☐

30 = 15 x ☐ ; ☐ ☐ ☐

45 = ☐ x ☐ ; ☐ ☐ ☐

20 = ☐ x ☐ ; ☐ ☐ ☐

18 = 9 x ☐ ; ☐ ☐ ☐

28 = 4 x ☐ ; ☐ ☐ ☐

Name ______________________

Add Integers

Example:

A number line can be used to add integers. To add positive integers, move to the right. To add negative integers, move to the left.

4 + (–5) = (–1)
Find 4 on the number line. Move 5 spaces to the left.

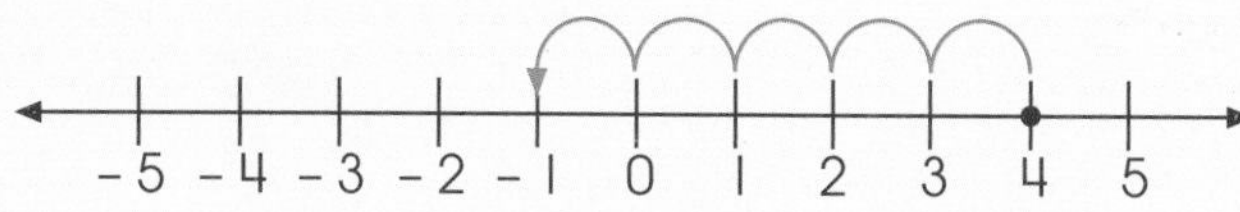

(–3) + 4 = 1

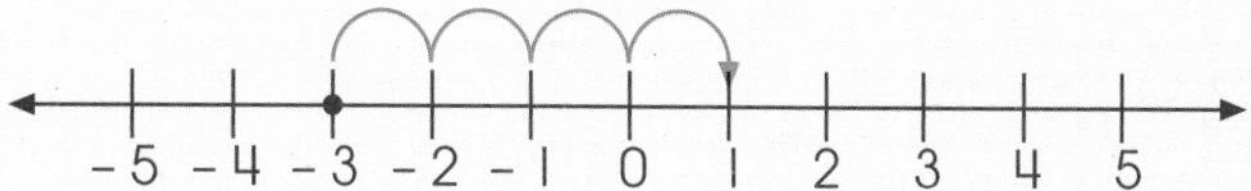

(–2) + (–1) = (–3)

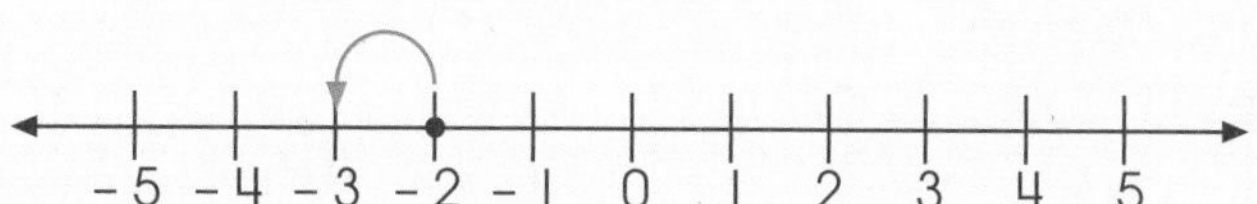

Directions: Add. Use the number lines to help you.

2 + (–4) = ____________ –5 –4 –3 –2 –1 0 1 2 3 4 5

(–3) + (–1) = ____________ –5 –4 –3 –2 –1 0 1 2 3 4 5

(–1) + 4 = ____________ –5 –4 –3 –2 –1 0 1 2 3 4 5

(–2) + 2 = ____________ –5 –4 –3 –2 –1 0 1 2 3 4 5

4 + (–7) = ____________ –5 –4 –3 –2 –1 0 1 2 3 4 5

0 + (–4) = ____________ –5 –4 –3 –2 –1 0 1 2 3 4 5

Name ____________________

Multiplication (One-Digit Multiplier)

Example A (no regrouping)

```
  234
x   2
  468
```

Step 1 Multiply ones. 2 x 4 = 8
Step 2 Multiply tens. 2 x 3 = 6
Step 3 Multiply hundreds. 2 x 2 = 4

Example B (regrouping)

```
  2 1
  563
x   4
2,252
```

Step 1 Multiply ones. 4 x 3 = 12 ones = 1 ten 2 ones. Carry the 1.
Step 2 Multiply tens. 4 x 6 + 1 = 25 tens = 2 hundreds 5 tens. Carry the 2.
Step 3 Multiply hundreds. 4 x 5 + 2 = 22 hundreds = 2 thousands 2 hundrec

Example C (regrouping and zeros)

```
   7 5
 7,086
x    9
63,774
```

Step 1 Multiply ones. 9 x 6 = 54 ones = 5 tens 4 ones. Carry the 5.
Step 2 Multiply tens. 9 x 8 + 5 = 77 tens = 7 hundreds 7 tens. Carry the 7.
Step 3 Multiply hundreds. 9 x 0 + 7 = 7 hundreds.
Step 4 Multiply thousands. 9 x 7 = 63 thousands = 6 ten-thousands 3 thousands.

Directions: Multiply.

1. 323 x 8
2. 1,132 x 2
3. 789 x 5
4. 4,008 x 7
5. 2,580 x 3
6. 888 x 6
7. 4,234 x 4
8. 589 x 9
9. 3,211 x 3

Name ______________________________

Multiplication (Two-Digit Multiplier)

Example A
(no regrouping)

```
   21
x  44
-----
   84
+ 840
-----
  924
```

Step 1 Multiply by ones.
4 x 1 = 4
4 x 2 = 8

Step 2 Multiply by tens.
Add zero in the ones column.
4 x 1 = 4
4 x 2 = 8

Step 3 Add.
84 + 840 = 924

Example B
(regrouping)

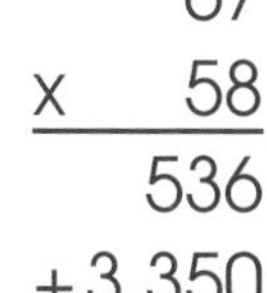
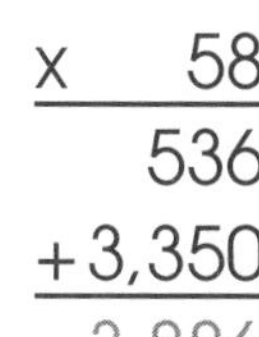

```
    67
x   58
------
   536
+3,350
------
 3,886
```

Step 1 Multiply by ones.
8 x 7 = 56 (Carry the 5.)
8 x 6 + 5 = 53

Step 2 Multiply by tens.
Add zero in the ones column.
5 x 7 = 35 (Carry the 3.)
5 x 6 + 3 = 33

Step 3 Add.
536 + 3,350 = 3,886

Directions: Multiply.

```
1.    43        2.    55        3.    78
    x 33            x 46            x 68

4.    39        5.    21        6.    77
    x 27            x 87            x 24

7.    44        8.    80        9.    65
    x 16            x 71            x 49
```

Name ____________________

One-Digit Multiplication With Regrouping

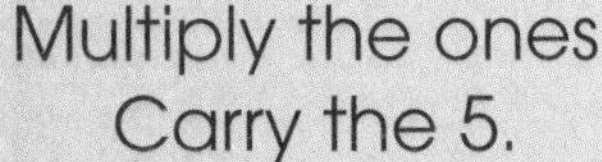

Example:

Here's how to do 1-digit multiplication with regrouping.

Multiply the ones. Carry the 5.	Multiply the tens. Add the 5. Carry the 2.	Multiply the hundreds and thousands.
5	2 5	1 2 5
4, 1 3 7	4, 1 3 7	4, 1 3 7
x 8	x 8	x 8
6	9 6	3 3, 0 9 6

Directions: Multiply.

216	415	311	738	129	561
x 6	x 8	x 5	x 4	x 3	x 9

1,857	4,286	8,134	3,629	6,295	14,526
x 2	x 7	x 6	x 3	x 4	x 7

Directions: Write a numeral in each box to make the multiplication problem true.

□□□	□□□	□□□	□□□
x □	x □	x □	x □
1, 2 5 4	1, 2 8 8	1, 9 0 2	3, 2 4 4

□□□	□,□□□	□,□□□	□,□□□
x □	x □	x □	x □
2, 3 1 6	8, 1 8 4	3 4, 8 8 8	1 0, 2 4 8

Name ____________________

Multiplication

Be certain to keep the proper place value when multiplying by tens and hundreds.

Examples:

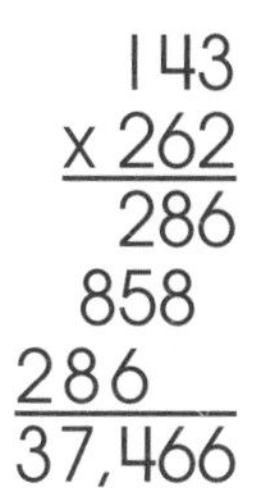

143
x 262
286
858
286
37,466

250
x 150
000
1250
250
37,500

Directions: Multiply.

701 x 308	621 x 538	348 x 200	597 x 424
537 x 189	416 x 727	682 x 472	180 x 340
878 x 638	267 x 196	893 x 214	907 x 428

An airplane flies 720 trips a year between the cities of Chicago and Columbus. Each trip is 375 miles. How many miles does the airplane fly each year?

____

Name ______________________________

Problem Solving

Directions: Solve each problem.

1. There are 6 rows of desks in the office. Each row has 8 desks. How many desks are in the office?

   There are ______ rows of desks.
   There are ______ desks in each row.
   There are ______ desks in all.

2. There are 9 rows of trees. There are 7 trees in each row. How many trees are there in all?

   There are ______ rows of trees.
   There are ______ trees in each row.
   There are ______ trees in all.

3. The people at the park were separated into teams of 8 people each. Nine teams were formed. How many people were in the park?

   Each team had ______ people.
   There were ______ teams formed.
   There were ______ people in the park.

4. There were 6 people in each car. There were 7 cars. How many people were there in all?

   There were ______ people in each car.
   There were ______ cars.
   There were ______ people in all.

5. How many cents would you need to buy eight 8-cent pencils?

   You would need ______ cents.

1.
2.
3.
4.
5.

Name ______________________

Multiplication's Opposite

Directions: Use the multiplication problem to help solve the division problems.

Example:
6 x 7 = 42
42 ÷ 7 = 6
42 ÷ 6 = 7

1. 4 x 8 = 32
32 ÷ _____ = 4
32 ÷ _____ = 8

2. 9 x 9 = 81
81 ÷ 9 = _____

3. 7 x 8 = 56
_____ ÷ 8 = 7
56 ÷ _____ = 8

4. 22 x 12 = 264
_____ ÷ 12 = 22
264 ÷ 22 = _____

5. 37 x 19 = 703
_____ ÷ 37 = 19
703 ÷ 19 = _____

Directions: Solve the following problems and write two related division problems for each.

6. 22 x 17 = _____

7. 45 x 29 = _____

8. 19 x 82 = _____

9. 671 x 63 = _____

10. 663 x 54 = _____

11. 719 x 73 = _____

Name ____________________

Division

Division is the reverse of multiplication. It is the process of dividing a number into equal groups of smaller numbers.

Directions: Divide.

Greg had 936 marbles to share with his two brothers. If the boys divided them evenly, how many will each one get? ____________________

The marbles Greg kept were four different colors: blue, green, red, and orange. He had the same number of each color. He divided them into two groups. One group had only orange marbles. The rest of the marbles were in the other group. How many marbles did he have in each group?

orange __________ others __________

The **dividend** is the number to be divided by another number. In the problem 28 ÷ 7 = 4, 28 is the dividend.

The **divisor** is the number by which another number is divided. In the problem 28 ÷ 7 = 4, 7 is the divisor.

The **quotient** is the answer in a division problem. In the problem 28 ÷ 7 = 4, 4 is the quotient.

The **remainder** is the number left over in the quotient of a division problem. In the problem 29 ÷ 7 = 4 r1, 1 is the remainder.

Directions: Write the answers.

In the problem 25 ÷ 8 = 3 r1 . . .

What is the divisor? __________ What is the remainder? __________

What is the quotient? __________ What is the dividend? __________

Directions: Divide.

$9\overline{)2,025}$ $6\overline{)2,508}$ $3\overline{)225}$ $5\overline{)400}$ $2\overline{)1,156}$

Name ______________________

Checking Division

Answers in division problems can be checked by multiplying.

Example:

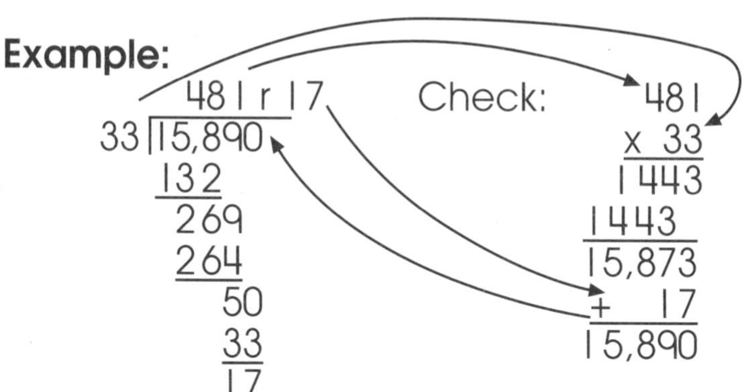

Directions: Divide and check your answers.

61 ⟌ 2,736 Check:	73 ⟌ 86,143 Check:
59 ⟌ 9,390 Check:	43 ⟌ 77,141 Check:
33 ⟌ 82,050 Check:	93 ⟌ 84,039 Check:

Denny has a baseball card collection. He has 13,789 cards. He wants to put the cards in a scrapbook that holds 15 cards on a page. How many pages does Denny need in his scrapbook? _______

Name ____________________

Check It Out

Check the answer to a division problem using multiplication and addition.

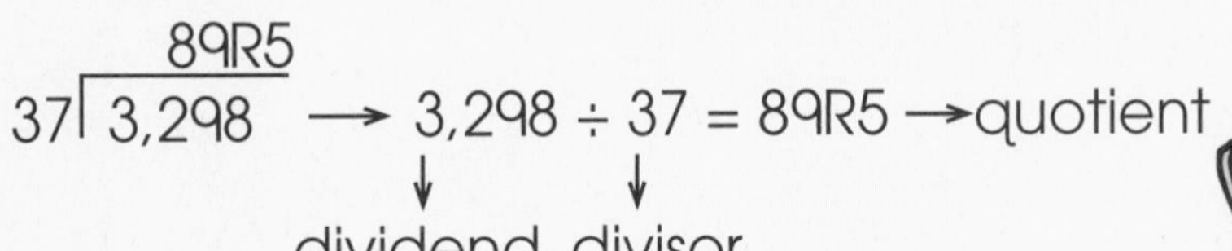

Steps:

1. Multiply the quotient by the divisor: 89 x 37 = 3,293
2. Add the remainder: 3,293 + 5 = 3,298
3. The total should equal the dividend: 3,298 = 3,298

Directions: Check these division problems using multiplication and addition. Circle the four incorrect answers on this page. Then, find the correct answers.

48⟌1,730 = 36R2	121⟌8,954 = 74	104⟌8,543 = 81R5
85⟌2,572 = 30R22	253⟌10,373 = 42	56⟌3,136 = 56
12,726 ÷ 202 = 64R3	2,701 ÷ 73 = 37	8,009 ÷ 9 = 889R8
7,684 ÷ 44 = 174R28	5,459 ÷ 483 = 10R97	15,853 ÷ 8 = 1,981R5

Name ______________________

Adding Money

Example:

Steps:

1. Align the decimal points.
2. Add.

```
  $4.32       $10.43
+ $2.19       $ 4.25
  $6.51     + $12.04
              $26.72
```

Directions: Rewrite the problems and align the decimal points. Then, add.

$1.15 + $2.25 =

$2.09 + $1.46 =

$1.11 + $5.35 =

$3.87 + $2.95 =

$10.42 + $2.54 =

$8.12 + $3.29 =

$11.13 + $10.26 =

$4.03 + $2.99 =

$42.80 + $103.25 + $32.54 =

$3.64 + $49.39 + $1.00 =

Name ______________________

At the Science Store

Directions: Solve. Remember to align the decimal points.

Telescope	$75.15
Geode	$13.50
Rock set	$ 5.95
Book	$ 9.99
Chemistry set	$26.59
Fossils small	$ 8.79
large	$12.89
Star chart	$21.47
Pendulum	$18.64

Tax included in prices!

1. Mr. Fargas buys 2 books. How much does he spend?

   $19.98

   $\begin{array}{r} \$\ 9.99 \\ +\ \$\ 9.99 \\ \hline \$19.98 \end{array}$

2. Janice buys a star chart and a pendulum. How much does she spend?

   ______

3. Can Troy buy a chemistry set and a rock set for less than $30?

   ______

4. Jack buys a rock set and pendulum. He pays with a $20 bill and a $10 bill. How much change does he receive?

   ______

5. Oliver buys ***Dinosaurs, The Great Ice Age***, and ***Rocks of Hawaii***. How much will his books cost?

   ______

6. Find the price of a large fossil, the chemistry set, and a telescope.

   ______

Name ______________________

Multiplying Money

Example:

Joey buys 14 paperback books for $1.95 each. How much does he spend?

```
  $1.95
x    14
    780
+  1950
 $27.30  ←— set decimal point two numbers in from the right
```

Directions: Rewrite the problems and multiply.

$1.55 x 7 =

$10.85 x 19 =

$ 3.06 x 9 =

$5.35 x 12 =

$10.00 x 15 =

$1.25 x 105 =

$9.87 x 13 =

$4.95 x 22 =

1. Lauren buys wood for bookshelves at a cost of $0.58 per foot. If she buys 27 feet, how much does she spend?

   ____

2. Which costs more: 5 new books for $5.97 each or 12 used books for $2.50 each?

   ____

Name ___________________________

What Do You Mean?

Probably the most common average is the **mean.** To find the mean, add all the numbers in the list, then divide the sum by the total number of addends.

Suppose a hurdler completes his trials in the following times. Find the mean.

Trial	Time in Seconds
1	35
2	29
3	34
4	30
5	31
6	33

Mean
The sum of all the numbers divided by the number of addends

Add the numbers: 35 + 29 + 34 + 30 + 31 + 33 = 192
Divide 192 by 6 because there are 6 numbers in the list: 192 ÷ 6 = 32.
The mean is 32 seconds.

The mean may or may not be a number in the list. The mean may also be different from the median and/or the mode.

Directions: Find the mean.

3, 6, 9, 5, 12 ___________

11, 5, 9, 11, 3, 7, 9, 9 ___________

3, 1, 0, 2, 0, 0 ___________

4, 6, −1, −1 ___________

−3, −2, −3, −1, −1 ___________

2, −1, 1, −2 ___________

3, 3, 3, 3, 3, 3, 3, 3, 3, 3 ___________

5, 9, 6, 2, 7, 9, 12, 4, 8, 8 ___________

9, 4, 5, 2, 6, 0, 3, 4, 3 ___________

6, 7, 3, 6, 4, 2, 7, 5 ___________

Name ______________________

Adding and Subtracting Like Fractions

A **fraction** is a number that names part of a whole. Examples of fractions are $\frac{1}{2}$ and $\frac{1}{3}$. **Like fractions** have the same **denominator**, or bottom number. Examples of like fractions are $\frac{1}{4}$ and $\frac{3}{4}$.

To add or subtract fractions, the denominators must be the same. Add or subtract only the **numerators,** the numbers above the line in fractions.

Example:

numerators / denominators $\frac{5}{8} - \frac{1}{8} = \frac{4}{8}$

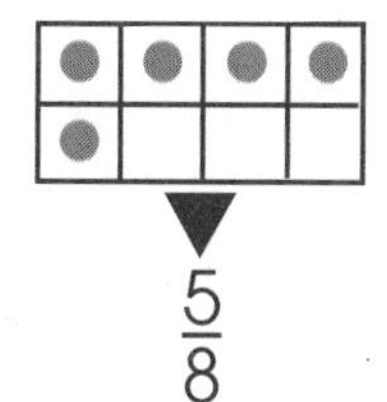 – ● = 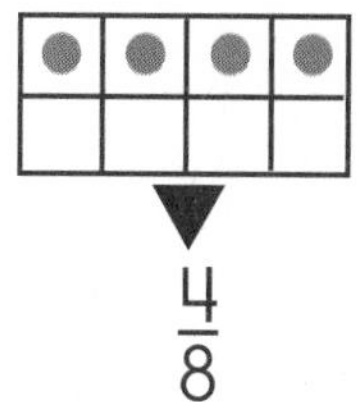

$\frac{5}{8}$ $\frac{1}{8}$ $\frac{4}{8}$

Directions: Add or subtract these fractions.

$\frac{6}{12} - \frac{3}{12} =$	$\frac{4}{9} + \frac{1}{9} =$	$\frac{1}{3} + \frac{1}{3} =$	$\frac{5}{11} + \frac{4}{11} =$
$\frac{3}{5} - \frac{1}{5} =$	$\frac{5}{6} - \frac{2}{6} =$	$\frac{3}{4} - \frac{2}{4} =$	$\frac{5}{10} + \frac{3}{10} =$
$\frac{3}{8} + \frac{2}{8} =$	$\frac{1}{7} + \frac{4}{7} =$	$\frac{2}{20} + \frac{15}{20} =$	$\frac{11}{15} - \frac{9}{15} =$

Directions: Color the part of each pizza that equals the given fraction.

$\frac{2}{4}$ + $\frac{1}{4}$ =

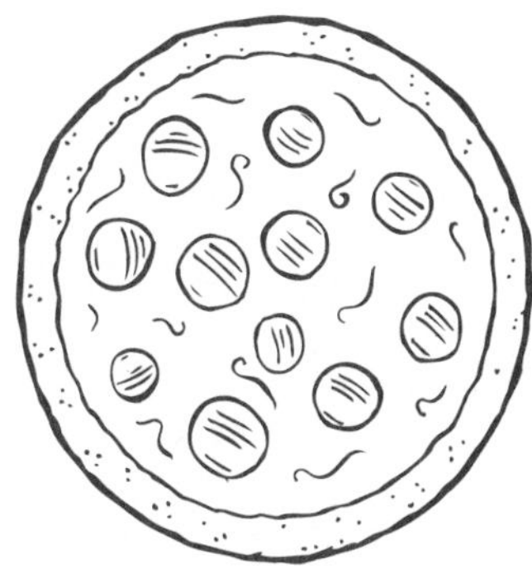

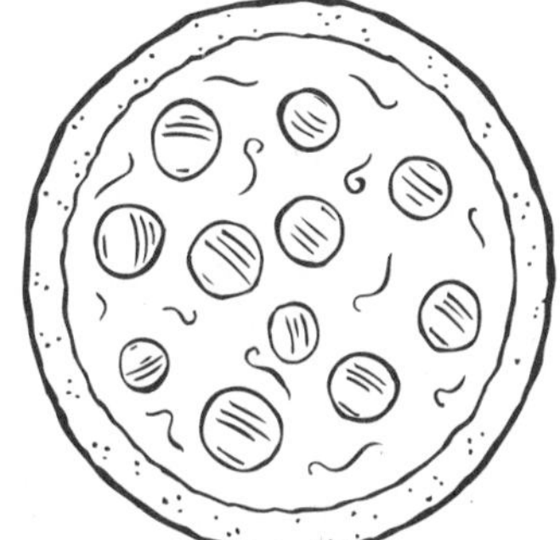

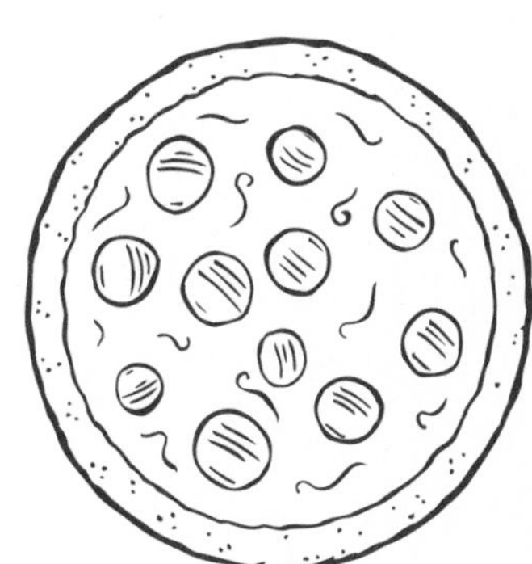

Name ____________________

Adding and Subtracting Unlike Fractions

Unlike fractions have different denominators. Examples of unlike fractions are $\frac{1}{4}$ and $\frac{2}{5}$. To add or subtract fractions, the denominators must be the same.

Example:

Step 1: Make the denominators the same by finding the least common denominator. The LCD of a pair of fractions is the same as the least common multiple (LCM) of their denominators.

$\frac{1}{3} + \frac{1}{4} =$

Multiples of 3 are 3, 6, 9, 12, 15.
Multiples of 4 are 4, 8, 12, 16.
LCM (and LCD) = 12

Step 2: Multiply by a number that will give the LCD. The numerator and denominator must be multiplied by the same number.

A. $\frac{1}{3} \times \frac{4}{4} = \frac{4}{12}$ **B.** $\frac{1}{4} \times \frac{3}{3} = \frac{3}{12}$

Step 3: Add the fractions. $\frac{1}{3} + \frac{1}{4} = \frac{4}{12} + \frac{3}{12} = \frac{7}{12}$

Directions: Follow the above steps to add or subtract unlike fractions. Write the LCM.

$\frac{2}{4} + \frac{3}{8} =$ LCM = ________	$\frac{3}{6} + \frac{1}{3} =$ LCM = ________	$\frac{4}{5} - \frac{1}{4} =$ LCM = ________
$\frac{2}{3} + \frac{2}{9} =$ LCM = ________	$\frac{4}{7} - \frac{2}{14} =$ LCM = ________	$\frac{7}{12} - \frac{2}{4} =$ LCM = ________

The basketball team ordered two pizzas.
They left $\frac{1}{3}$ of one $\frac{1}{4}$ and of the other.
How much pizza was left?

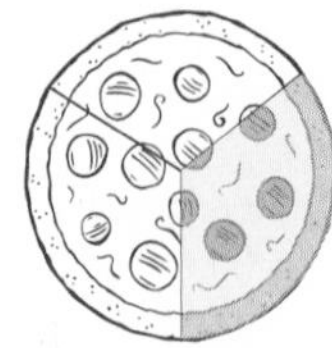

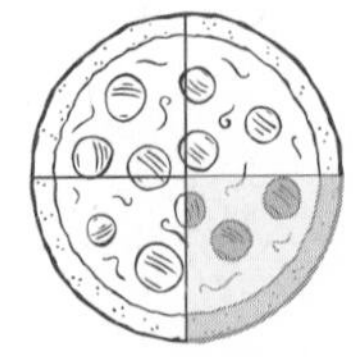

____

Name ______________________________

Improper Fractions

An improper fraction has a numerator that is greater than its denominator. An example of an improper fraction is $\frac{7}{6}$. An improper fraction should be reduced to its lowest terms.

Example: $\frac{5}{4}$ is an improper fraction because its numerator is greater than its denominator.

Step 1: Divide the numerator by the denominator: $5 \div 4 = 1$, r 1

Step 2: Write the remainder as a fraction: $\frac{1}{4}$

$\frac{5}{4} = 1\frac{1}{4}$ $1\frac{1}{4}$ is a mixed number—a whole number and a fraction.

Directions: Follow the steps above to change the improper fractions to mixed numbers.

$\frac{9}{8} =$	$\frac{11}{5} =$	$\frac{5}{3} =$	$\frac{7}{6} =$	$\frac{8}{7} =$	$\frac{4}{3} =$
$\frac{21}{5} =$	$\frac{9}{4} =$	$\frac{3}{2} =$	$\frac{9}{6} =$	$\frac{25}{4} =$	$\frac{8}{3} =$

Sara had 29 duplicate stamps in her stamp collection. She decided to give them to four of her friends. If she gave each of them the same number of stamps, how many duplicates will she have left? ____________________

Name the improper fraction in this problem. ____________________

What step must you do next to solve the problem? ______________

____

Write your answer as a mixed number.______________________________

____

How many stamps could she give each of her friends?____________________

Name ______________________

Conversion

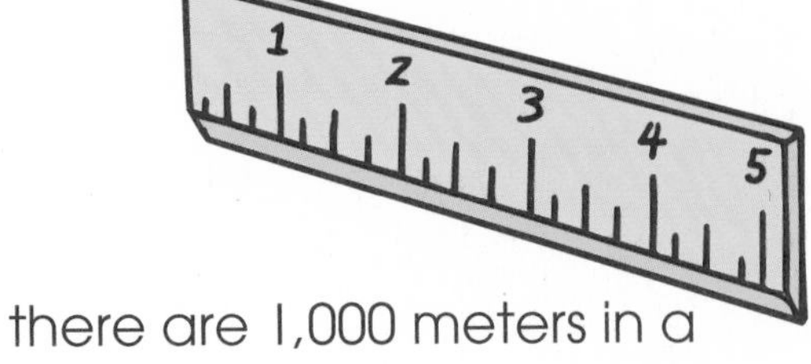

Directions: Find the number of units in each fraction described.

1. If there are 12 eggs in a dozen, how many eggs are in . . .
   $\frac{1}{2}$ dozen? ______________
   $\frac{1}{4}$ dozen? ______________
   $\frac{1}{3}$ dozen? ______________

2. If there are 100 centimeters (cm) in a meter, how many cm are in . . .
   $\frac{1}{2}$ meter? ______________
   $\frac{1}{4}$ meter? ______________
   $\frac{1}{10}$ meter? ______________

3. If there are 16 ounces in a pound, how many ounces are in . . .
   $\frac{1}{2}$ pound? ______________
   $\frac{1}{4}$ pound? ______________
   $\frac{3}{8}$ pound? ______________

4. If there are 4 quarts in a gallon, how many quarts are in . . .
   $\frac{1}{2}$ gallon? ______________
   $\frac{1}{4}$ gallon? ______________
   $\frac{3}{4}$ gallon? ______________

5. If there are 60 seconds in a minute, how many seconds are in . . .
   $\frac{1}{2}$ minute? ______________
   $\frac{1}{4}$ minute? ______________
   $\frac{3}{4}$ minute? ______________

6. If there are 1,000 meters in a kilometer, how many meters are in . . .
   $\frac{1}{10}$ kilometer? ______________
   $\frac{1}{2}$ kilometer? ______________
   $\frac{1}{4}$ kilometer? ______________

7. If there are 30 days in most months, how many days are in . . .
   $\frac{1}{3}$ month? ______________
   $\frac{1}{6}$ month? ______________
   $\frac{1}{10}$ month? ______________

8. If there are 24 hours in a day, how many hours are in . . .
   $\frac{1}{3}$ day? ______________
   $\frac{2}{3}$ day? ______________
   $\frac{1}{4}$ day? ______________

9. If there are 36 inches in a yard, how many inches are in . . .
   $\frac{2}{3}$ yard? ______________
   $\frac{1}{4}$ yard? ______________
   $\frac{1}{2}$ yard? ______________

10. If there are 2,000 pounds in a ton, how many pounds are in . . .
    $\frac{1}{2}$ ton? ______________
    $\frac{1}{4}$ ton? ______________
    $\frac{1}{20}$ ton? ______________

Name ____________________

Mixed Numbers

A **mixed number** is a whole number and a fraction together. An example of a mixed number is $2\frac{3}{4}$. A mixed number can be changed to an improper fraction.

Example: $2\frac{3}{4}$

Step 1: Multiply the denominator by the whole number: $4 \times 2 = 8$

Step 2: Add the numerator: $8 + 3 = 11$

Step 3: Write the sum over the denominator: $\frac{11}{4}$

Directions: Follow the steps above to change the mixed numbers to improper fractions.

$3\frac{2}{3} =$	$6\frac{1}{5} =$	$4\frac{7}{8} =$	$2\frac{1}{2} =$
$1\frac{4}{5} =$	$5\frac{3}{4} =$	$7\frac{1}{8} =$	$9\frac{1}{9} =$
$8\frac{1}{2} =$	$7\frac{1}{6} =$	$5\frac{3}{5} =$	$9\frac{3}{8} =$
$12\frac{1}{5} =$	$25\frac{1}{2} =$	$10\frac{2}{3} =$	$14\frac{3}{8} =$

Name ______________________________

Subtracting Mixed Numbers

Directions: To subtract mixed numbers, first find the least common denominator. Reduce the answer to its lowest terms.

Directions: Subtract. Reduce to lowest terms.

Example:

$$6\frac{5}{8} \rightarrow 6\frac{10}{16}$$
$$-3\frac{4}{16} \rightarrow -3\frac{4}{16}$$
$$3\frac{6}{16} = 3\frac{3}{8}$$

$2\frac{3}{7} - 1\frac{1}{14}$ ______

$7\frac{2}{3} - 5\frac{1}{8}$ ______

$6\frac{3}{4} - 2\frac{3}{12}$ ______

$9\frac{5}{12} - 5\frac{9}{24}$ ______

$5\frac{1}{2} - 3\frac{1}{3}$ ______

$7\frac{3}{8} - 5\frac{1}{6}$ ______

$8\frac{3}{8} - 6\frac{5}{12}$ ______

$11\frac{5}{6} - 7\frac{1}{12}$ ______

$9\frac{3}{5} - 7\frac{1}{15}$ ______

$4\frac{4}{5} - 2\frac{1}{4}$ ______

$9\frac{2}{3} - 4\frac{1}{6}$ ______

$13\frac{3}{8} - 9\frac{3}{16}$ ______

The Rodriguez Farm has $9\frac{1}{2}$ acres of corn. The Johnson Farm has $7\frac{1}{3}$ acres of corn. How many more acres of corn does the Rodriguez Farm have? ______________________

Name ______________________________

Fractions: Mixed to Improper

Directions: Change the fractions to mixed numbers. Shade in each answer to find the path to the pot of gold.

1. $\frac{11}{9}$ =	2. $\frac{8}{3}$ =	3. $\frac{8}{7}$ =	4. $\frac{11}{6}$ =
5. $\frac{7}{3}$ =	6. $\frac{7}{6}$ =	7. $\frac{9}{4}$ =	8. $\frac{8}{5}$ =
9. $\frac{4}{3}$ =	10. $\frac{7}{2}$ =	11. $\frac{3}{2}$ =	12. $\frac{6}{5}$ =
13. $\frac{7}{4}$ =	14. $\frac{9}{2}$ =	15. $\frac{11}{8}$ =	16. $\frac{5}{2}$ =
17. $\frac{9}{7}$ =	18. $\frac{11}{4}$ =	19. $\frac{17}{12}$ =	20. $\frac{13}{12}$ =

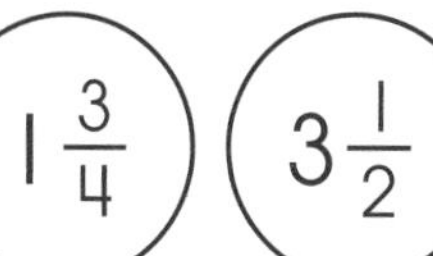

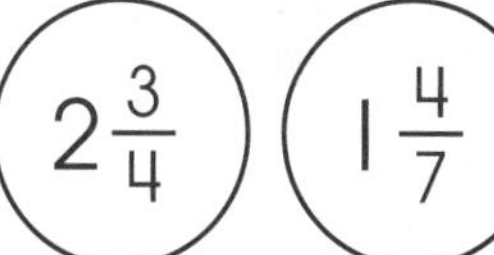

		$1\frac{3}{5}$	$1\frac{1}{7}$	$1\frac{3}{4}$	$3\frac{1}{2}$	$1\frac{3}{8}$	$2\frac{3}{4}$	$1\frac{4}{7}$
$1\frac{5}{8}$	$2\frac{1}{3}$	$7\frac{3}{8}$	$2\frac{11}{12}$	$3\frac{7}{8}$	$2\frac{5}{6}$	$1\frac{4}{5}$	$2\frac{2}{3}$	$2\frac{1}{6}$
$1\frac{7}{12}$	$2\frac{1}{2}$	$1\frac{5}{6}$	$1\frac{2}{7}$	$2\frac{1}{4}$	$1\frac{1}{12}$	$1\frac{1}{2}$	$1\frac{11}{12}$	$1\frac{5}{7}$
$1\frac{1}{5}$	$4\frac{2}{3}$	$3\frac{1}{6}$	$1\frac{3}{7}$	$1\frac{4}{9}$	$2\frac{1}{5}$	$3\frac{1}{3}$	$4\frac{1}{3}$	$2\frac{6}{7}$
$2\frac{3}{11}$	$1\frac{2}{9}$	$1\frac{1}{3}$	$1\frac{5}{12}$	$2\frac{1}{3}$	$4\frac{1}{2}$	$1\frac{1}{6}$		

Name ______________________________

Multiplying Fractions

To multiply fractions, follow these steps:

$\frac{1}{2} \times \frac{3}{4} =$

Step 1: Multiply the numerators. $1 \times 3 = \underline{3}$

Step 2: Multiply the denominators. $2 \times 4 = 8$

When multiplying a fraction by a whole number, first change the whole number to a fraction.

Example:

$$\frac{1}{2} \times 8 = \frac{1}{2} \times \frac{8}{1} = \frac{8}{2} = 4$$ reduced to lowest terms

Directions: Multiply. Reduce your answers to lowest terms.

$\frac{3}{4} \times \frac{1}{6} =$	$\frac{1}{2} \times \frac{5}{8} =$	$\frac{2}{3} \times \frac{1}{6} =$	$\frac{2}{3} \times \frac{1}{2} =$
$\frac{5}{6} \times 4 =$	$\frac{3}{8} \times \frac{1}{16} =$	$\frac{1}{5} \times 5 =$	$\frac{7}{8} \times \frac{3}{4} =$
$\frac{7}{11} \times \frac{1}{3} =$	$\frac{2}{9} \times \frac{9}{4} =$	$\frac{1}{3} \times \frac{1}{3} \times \frac{1}{3} =$	$\frac{1}{8} \times \frac{1}{4} \times \frac{1}{2} =$

Jennifer has 10 pets. Two-fifths of the pets are cats, one-half are fish and one-tenth are dogs. How many of each pet does she have?

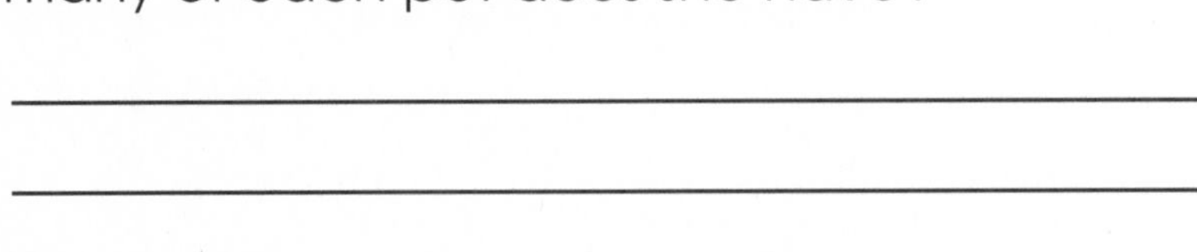

Name ______________________________

Multiplying Mixed Numbers

Multiply mixed numbers by first changing them to improper fractions. Always reduce your answers to lowest terms.

Example:

$$2\frac{1}{3} \times 1\frac{1}{8} = \frac{7}{3} \times \frac{9}{8} = \frac{63}{24} = 2\frac{15}{24} = 2\frac{5}{8}$$

Directions: Multiply. Reduce to lowest terms.

$4\frac{1}{4} \times 2\frac{1}{5} =$	$1\frac{1}{3} \times 3\frac{1}{4} =$	$1\frac{1}{9} \times 3\frac{3}{5} =$
$1\frac{6}{7} \times 4\frac{1}{2} =$	$2\frac{3}{4} \times 2\frac{3}{5} =$	$4\frac{2}{3} \times 3\frac{1}{7} =$
$6\frac{2}{5} \times 2\frac{1}{8} =$	$3\frac{1}{7} \times 4\frac{5}{8} =$	$7\frac{3}{8} \times 2\frac{1}{9} =$

Sunnyside Farm has two barns with 25 stalls in each barn. Cows use $\frac{3}{5}$ of the stalls, and horses use the rest.

How many stalls are for cows? ________

How many are for horses? ____________

(Hint: First, find how many total stalls are in the two barns.)

Name ______________________

Dividing Fractions

To divide fractions, follow these steps:

$$\frac{3}{4} \div \frac{1}{4} =$$

Step 1: "Invert" the divisor. That means to turn it upside down.

$$\frac{3}{4} \div \frac{4}{1}$$

Step 2: Multiply the two fractions:

$$\frac{3}{4} \times \frac{4}{1} = \frac{12}{4}$$

Step 3: Reduce the fraction to lowest terms by dividing the denominator into the numerator.

$$12 \div 4 = 3$$

$$\frac{3}{4} \div \frac{1}{4} = 3$$

Directions: Follow the above steps to divide fractions.

$\frac{1}{4} \div \frac{1}{5} =$	$\frac{1}{3} \div \frac{1}{12} =$	$\frac{3}{4} \div \frac{1}{3} =$
$\frac{5}{12} \div \frac{1}{3} =$	$\frac{3}{4} \div \frac{1}{6} =$	$\frac{2}{9} \div \frac{2}{3} =$
$\frac{3}{7} \div \frac{1}{4} =$	$\frac{2}{3} \div \frac{4}{6} =$	$\frac{1}{8} \div \frac{2}{3} =$
$\frac{4}{5} \div \frac{1}{3} =$	$\frac{4}{8} \div \frac{1}{2} =$	$\frac{5}{12} \div \frac{6}{8} =$

Name ______________________________

Fractions: Multiplication and Division

Directions: Solve.

1. $\frac{7}{9} \times \frac{1}{4} =$ ____

2. $\frac{5}{6} \times \frac{1}{10} =$ ____

3. $\frac{9}{10} \times \frac{2}{3} =$ ____

4. $8 \times \frac{1}{4} =$ ____

5. $\frac{1}{3} \times 15 =$ ____

6. Jaime sat in his chair for $\frac{5}{6}$ of an hour. For $\frac{1}{3}$ of this time, he worked on this assignment. What fraction of an hour did he work on this assignment?

7. $\frac{1}{2} \div \frac{1}{5} =$ ____

8. $\frac{1}{5} \div \frac{1}{2} =$ ____

9. $\frac{3}{4} \div \frac{3}{8} =$ ____

10. $\frac{7}{16} \div \frac{4}{7} =$ ____

Name ____________________

Decimals

A **decimal** is a number with one or more places to the right of a decimal point.

Examples: 6.5 and 2.25

Fractions with denominators of 10 or 100 can be written as decimals.

1/2

0.50

Examples:

$\frac{7}{10} = 0.7$ 0 (ones) . 7 (tenths) 0 (hundredths)

$1\frac{52}{100} = 1.52$ 1 (ones) . 5 (tenths) 2 (hundredths)

Directions: Write the fractions as decimals.

$\frac{1}{2} = \frac{}{10} =$ 0. ____

$\frac{2}{5} = \frac{}{10} =$ 0. ____

$\frac{1}{5} = \frac{}{10} =$ 0. ____

$\frac{3}{5} = \frac{}{10} =$ 0. ____

$\frac{1}{2}$	$\frac{1}{4}$	$\frac{1}{5}$	1/10
			1/10
	$\frac{1}{4}$	$\frac{1}{5}$	1/10
			1/10
		$\frac{1}{5}$	1/10
$\frac{1}{2}$	$\frac{1}{4}$		1/10
		$\frac{1}{5}$	1/10
	$\frac{1}{4}$		1/10
		$\frac{1}{5}$	1/10
			1/10

$\frac{63}{100} =$	$2\frac{8}{10} =$	$38\frac{4}{100} =$	$6\frac{13}{100} =$
$\frac{1}{4} =$	$\frac{2}{5} =$	$\frac{1}{50} =$	$\frac{100}{200} =$
$5\frac{2}{100} =$	$\frac{4}{25} =$	$15\ \frac{3}{5} =$	$\frac{3}{100} =$

Name ____________________

That's the Point

When writing a decimal, place the decimal point between the ones column and the tenths column. Here are some place values to the right and left of the decimal point:

hundreds | tens | ones . tenths | hundredths | thousandths

Steps:

1. Read the whole number.
2. Say the word "and" or "point."
3. Read the number after the decimal point.
4. Say the decimal place of the last digit to the right.

and
or
point

Examples:

45.91 is read "forty-five and ninety-one hundredths"
222.1 is read "two hundred twenty-two point one"
10.004 is read "ten and four thousandths"

Directions: Fill in the numbers or write the names to complete the place-value chart.

Hundreds	Tens	Ones	.	Tenths	Hundredths	Thousandths	
	1	☐	.	8			eleven and eight tenths
		3	.	☐	☐	1	three and one hundred forty-one thousandths
		☐	.	☐	☐		two and fifteen hundredths
4	0	5	.	☐	☐	☐	four hundred five and fifty-six thousandths
		☐	.	☐	☐		forty-eight hundredths
	5	6	.	1	1	1	____________________
	☐	☐	.	☐	☐		ninety-eight and three hundredths

Name ____________________

Missing Train

Directions: Circle the . . .

1.	smallest number	0.31 (A)	0.05 (F)	0.20 (R)
2.	greatest number	0.001 (R)	0.137 (O)	0.100 (A)
3.	greatest number	9.910 (L)	9.010 (C)	9.909 (T)
4.	smallest number	0.110 (A)	0.09 (L)	0.3 (R)
5.	greatest number	0.090 (S)	0.10 (P)	0.12 (O)
6.	smallest number	0.131 (H)	0.2 (T)	0.08 (W)
7.	greatest number	1.310 (E)	1.03 (H)	1.33 (T)
8.	smallest number	2.001 (H)	2.9 (F)	2.010 (A)
9.	greatest number	0.3 (E)	0.03 (A)	0.003 (R)
10.	greatest number	1.01 (U)	1.001 (R)	1.1 (T)
11.	greatest number	3.04 (R)	3.009 (U)	3.039 (N)
12.	smallest number	6.01 (A)	6.11 (C)	6.030 (O)
13.	greatest number	0.001 (T)	0.100 (C)	0.090 (N)
14.	smallest number	1.027 (K)	1.270 (R)	1.207 (P)
15.	smallest number	9.909 (N)	9.09 (G)	9.009 (S)

Directions: Fill in the circled letters to solve the riddle below.

How do you search for a missing train?

__ __ __ __ __ __   __ __ __   __ __ __ __ __ __
1 2 3 4 5 6   7 8 9   10 11 12 13 14 15

Name ______________________

Adding and Subtracting Decimals

Add and subtract with decimals the same way you do with whole numbers. Keep the decimal points lined up so that you work with hundredths, then tenths, then ones, and so on.

Directions: Add or subtract. Remember to keep the decimal point in the proper place.

0.5 + 0.8	0.35 + 0.25	47.5 − 32.7	85.7 − 9.8
13.90 + 4.23	9.53 − 8.16	72.8 − 63.9	6.43 + 4.58
638.07 − 19.34	811.060 + 78.430	521.09 − 148.75	
916.635 + 172.136	287.768 − 63.951	467.05 − 398.19	

Sean ran a 1-mile race in 5.58 minutes. Carlos ran it in 6.38 minutes. How much less time did Sean need?

____

Name ______________________________

Multiplying Decimals

Directions: Multiply with decimals the same way you do with whole numbers. The decimal point moves in multiplication. Count the number of decimal places in the problem and use the same number of decimal places in your answer.

Example:

```
  3.5
x 1.5
 175
 35
 5.25
```

Directions: Multiply.

2.5 × .9	67.4 × 2.3	83.7 × 9.8	13.35 × 3.06
9.06 × 2.38	28.97 × 5.16	33.41 × .93	28.7 × 11.9

The jet flies 1.5 times faster than the plane with a propeller. The propeller plane flies 165.7 miles per hour. How fast does the jet fly?

____

Name ______________________

Dividing With Decimals

Directions: When the dividend has a decimal, place the decimal point for the answer directly above the decimal point in the dividend. The first one has been done for you.

```
   12.5
3 )37.5
  - 3
    07
   - 6
    15
   -15
     0
```

4) 34.4

2) 31.6

3) 131.4

5) 187.5

7) 181.3

6) 340.8

9) 294.3

3) 135.6

5) 264.5

2) 134.6

8) 754.4

5) 35.25

7) 79.45

9) 28.71

36) 199.44

Name ____________________

Working With Decimals

Directions: Solve.

1. Write 207.426 in words.

   ____

2. Write forty-seven and thirteen thousandths in numerals. ____________

3. Use > or < to indicate which decimal fraction is greater.
   17.35 ______ 17.295

Directions: Fill in the blanks.

4. Round 12.836 to the nearest whole number. ____________
5. Round 12.836 to the nearest tenth. ____________
6. Round 12.836 to the nearest hundredth. ____________
7. Write 0.36 as a fraction in lowest terms. ____________
8. Write 0.25 as a fraction in lowest terms. ____________
9. Write $\frac{3}{4}$ as a decimal number. ____________

Directions: Solve.

10. 36.2 + 27.325 = ________
11. 87.36 – 84.95 = ________
12. 4.6 x 1.2 = ________
13. 3.46 x 10 = ________
14. 11.55 ÷ 7 = ________
15. 39 ÷ 12 = ________
16. 367.52 ÷ 10 = ________

Name ____________________

Giving 100%

Example:

The word **percent** means "for each hundred." A test score of 95% means that 95 out of 100 answers are correct.

There are 100 squares in this grid. Each square represents one hundredth. Since 63 squares are shaded, 63% is shaded.

Directions: Write the percent of squares shaded.

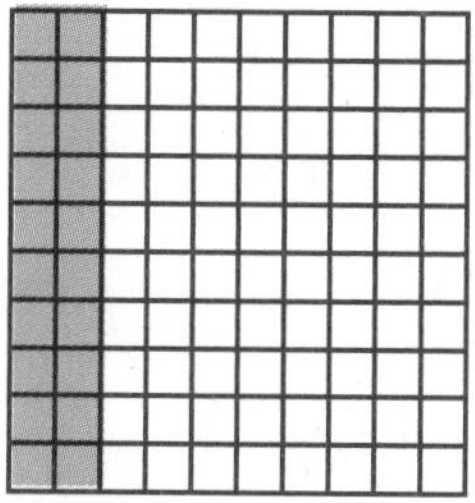

____

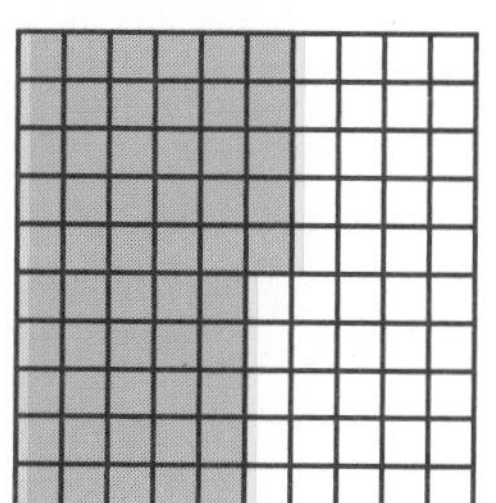

____

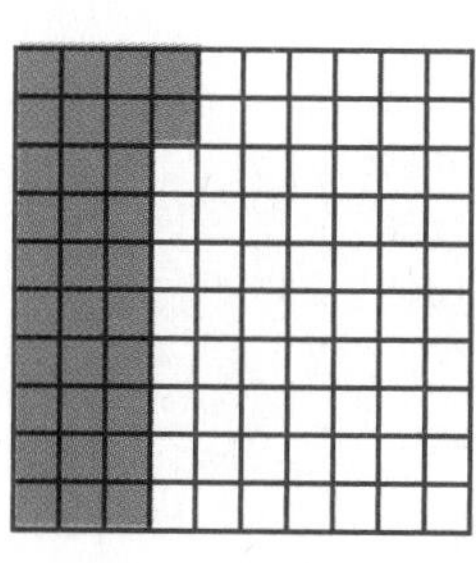

____

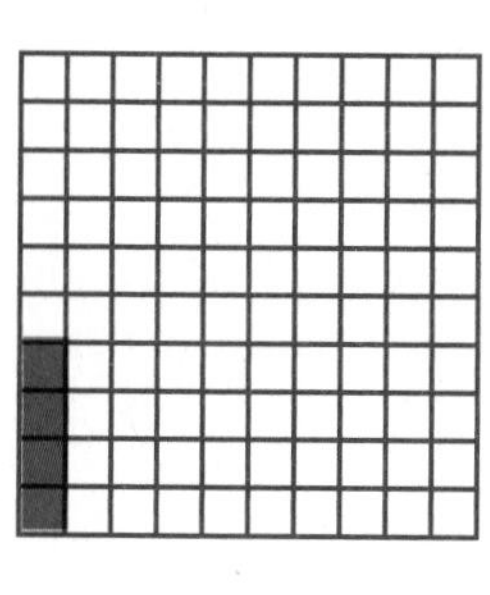

____

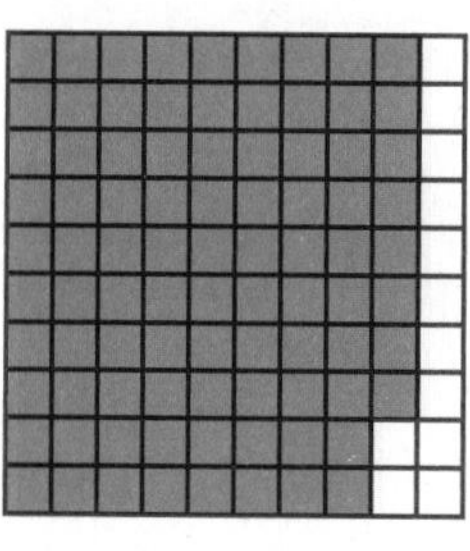

____

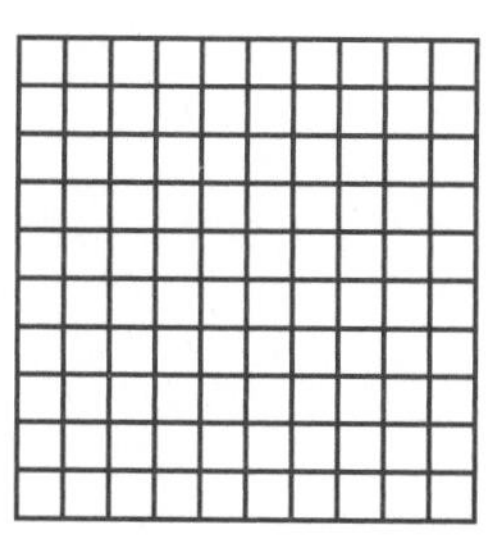

____

Shade each grid to show the percent.

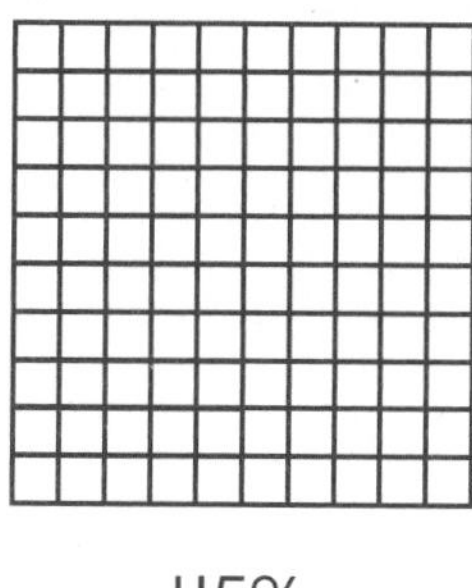

45%

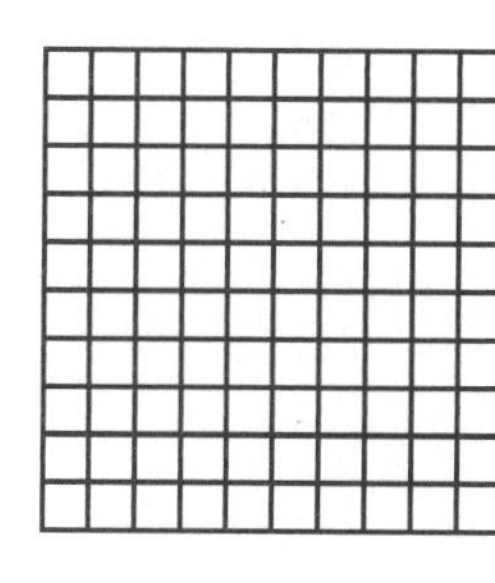

10%

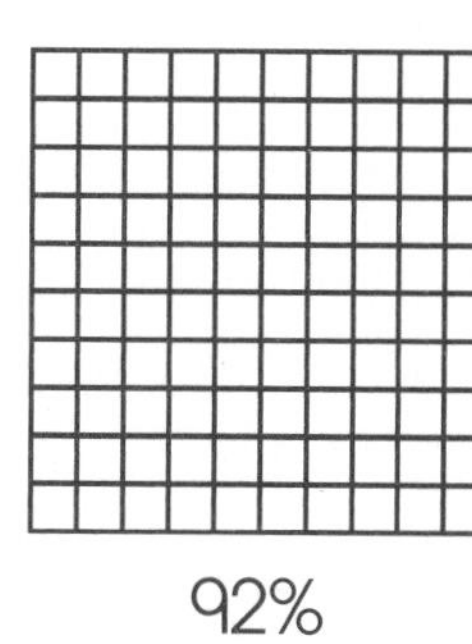

92%

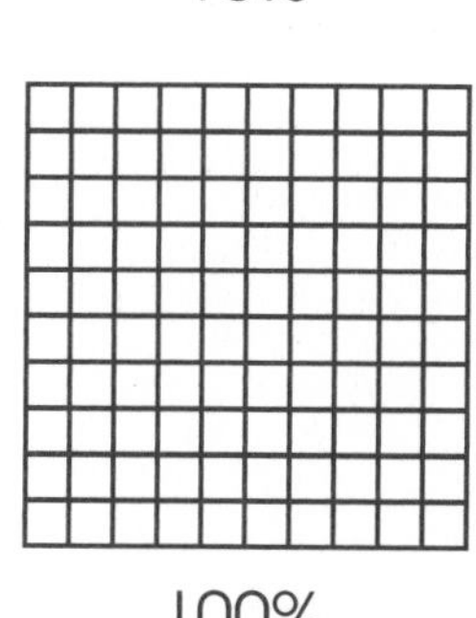

100%

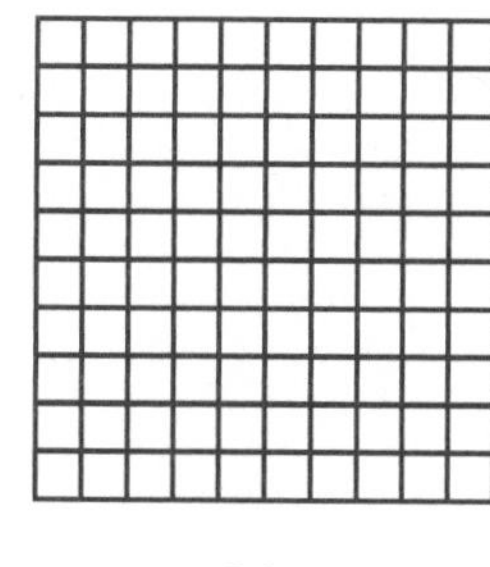

8%

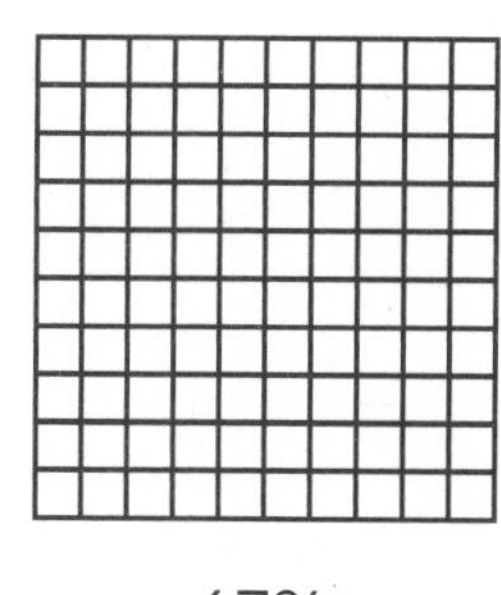

67%

Name ______________________________

Percent

Directions: Percent is a ratio meaning "per hundred." It is written with a % sign. 20% means 20 percent or 20 per hundred.

Example:

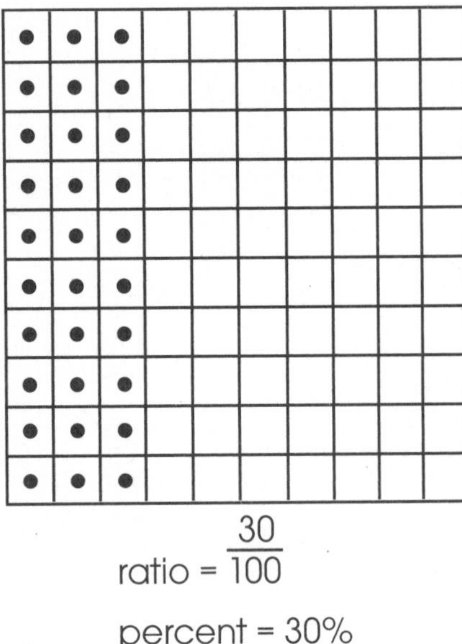

ratio = $\frac{30}{100}$

percent = 30%

ratio = ____________

percent = __________

Directions: Write the percent for each ratio.

$\frac{7}{100}$ =	$\frac{38}{100}$ =
$\frac{63}{100}$ =	$\frac{3}{100}$ =
$\frac{40}{100}$ =	$\frac{1}{5}$ =

The school received 100 books for the Book Fair. It sold 43 books.

What is the percent of books sold to books received? ________________

Name ______________________

Finding Percents

Find percent by dividing the number you have by the number possible.

Example:

15 out of 20 possible: $20\overline{)15.00} = 0.75 = 75\%$

```
   0.75
20)15.00
 -140
   100
   100
```

Annie has been keeping track of the scores she earned on each spelling test during the grading period.

Directions: Find out each percentage grade she earned. The first one has been done for you.

Week	Number Correct		Total Number of Words	Score in Percent
1	14	(out of)	20	70%
2	16		20	______
3	18		20	______
4	12		15	______
5	16		16	______
6	17		18	______
Review Test	51		60	______

If Susan scored 5% higher than Annie on the review test, how many words did she get right? ______________

Carrie scored 10% lower than Susan on the review test. How many words did she spell correctly? ______________

Of the 24 students in Annie's class, 25% had the same score as Annie. Only 10% had a higher score. What percent had a lower score? ______________

Is that answer possible? ______________________________

Why? ______________________________

Name ______________________________

Ratios

A ratio compares two numbers.

Example:

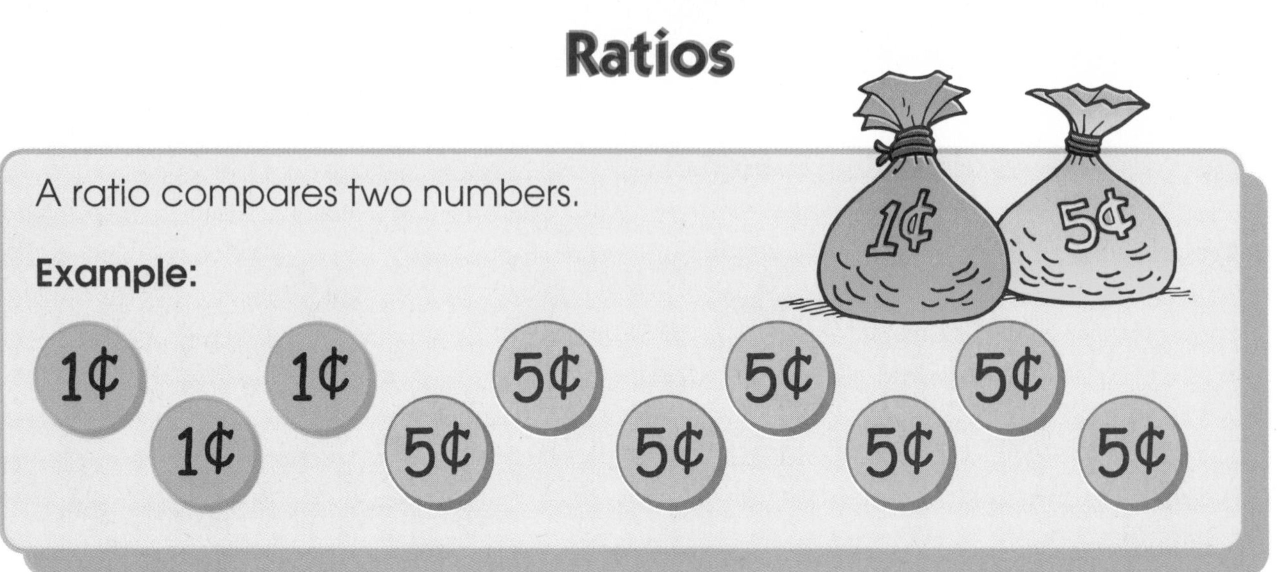

Directions: Put 10 pennies and 10 nickels in a bag. Without looking, pull out a small handful of coins. Draw the coins in a box below. Write each ratio. Return the coins to the bag and repeat 4 more times. The first example is shown.

1¢ 1¢ 1¢ 5¢ 5¢ 5¢ 5¢ 5¢

pennies to nickels **3:5** coins to pennies **8:3**
nickels to pennies **5:3** nickels to coins **5:8**
pennies to coins **3:8** coins to nickels **8:5**

pennies to nickels ____ coins to pennies ____
nickels to pennies ____ nickels to coins ____
pennies to coins ____ coins to nickels ____

pennies to nickels ____ coins to pennies ____
nickels to pennies ____ nickels to coins ____
pennies to coins ____ coins to nickels ____

pennies to nickels ____ coins to pennies ____
nickels to pennies ____ nickels to coins ____
pennies to coins ____ coins to nickels ____

pennies to nickels ____ coins to pennies ____
nickels to pennies ____ nickels to coins ____
pennies to coins ____ coins to nickels ____

pennies to nickels ____ coins to pennies ____
nickels to pennies ____ nickels to coins ____
pennies to coins ____ coins to nickels ____

Name ____________________

What Are the Chances?

Probability is the chance that something will happen.

Example:

This spinner has 8 equal-sized spaces. What is the probability, or chance, that a person would spin:

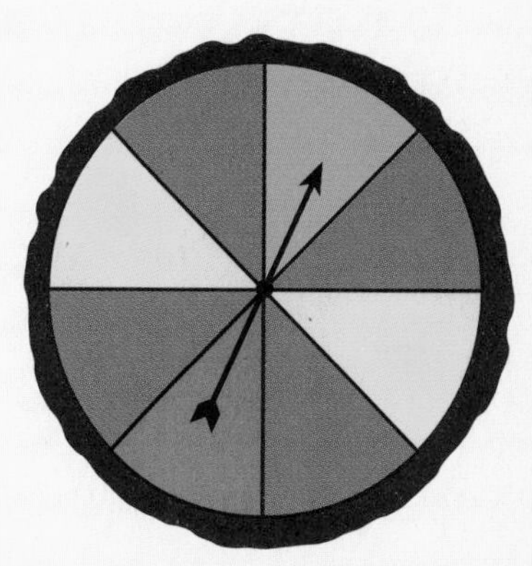

Blue? $\frac{4}{8}$ or 4:8, because 4 of 8 sections are blue.
Red? $\frac{1}{8}$ or 1:8, because 1 of 8 sections is red.
Yellow? $\frac{2}{8}$ or 2:8, because 2 of 8 sections are yellow.
Green? $\frac{1}{8}$ or 1:8, because 1 of 8 sections is green.

Directions: Use the spinner to the right to answer the questions.

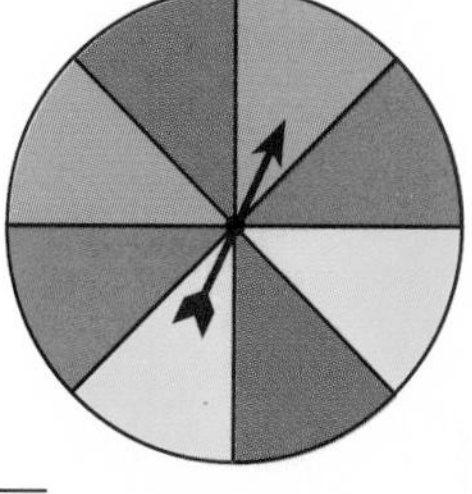

1. What is the probability of spinning blue? __________
2. What is the probability of spinning yellow? __________
3. What is the probability of spinning green? __________
4. What is the probability of spinning yellow or red? __________

Directions: Use the spinner to the right to answer the questions.

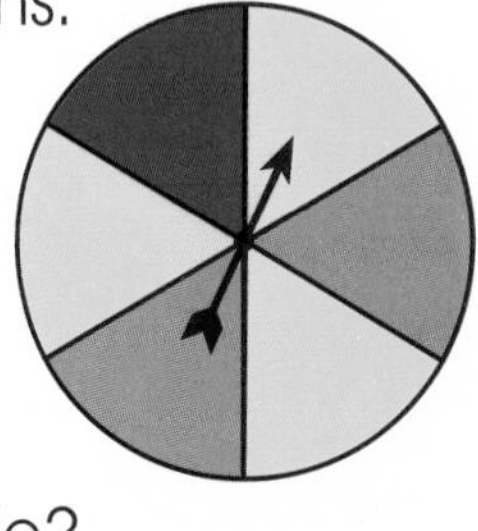

1. What is the probability of spinning purple? __________
2. What is the probability of spinning orange? __________
3. What is the probability of spinning yellow? __________
4. What is the probability of spinning yellow, orange or purple? __________

Directions: Use the spinner to the right to answer the questions.

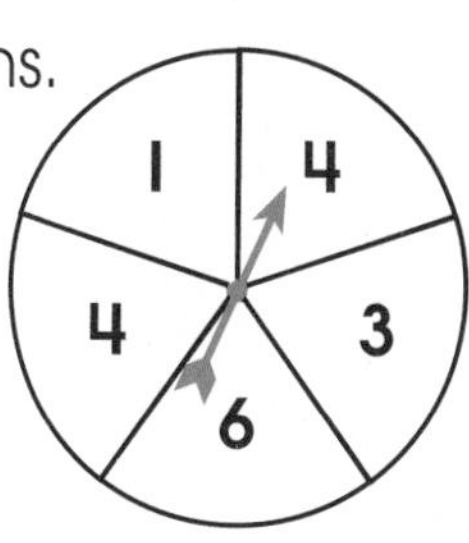

1. What is the probability of spinning a 4? __________
2. What is the probability of spinning a 1? __________
3. What is the probability of spinning a 3? __________
4. What is the probability of spinning 3, 4, or 6? __________

Name ______________________

Lines

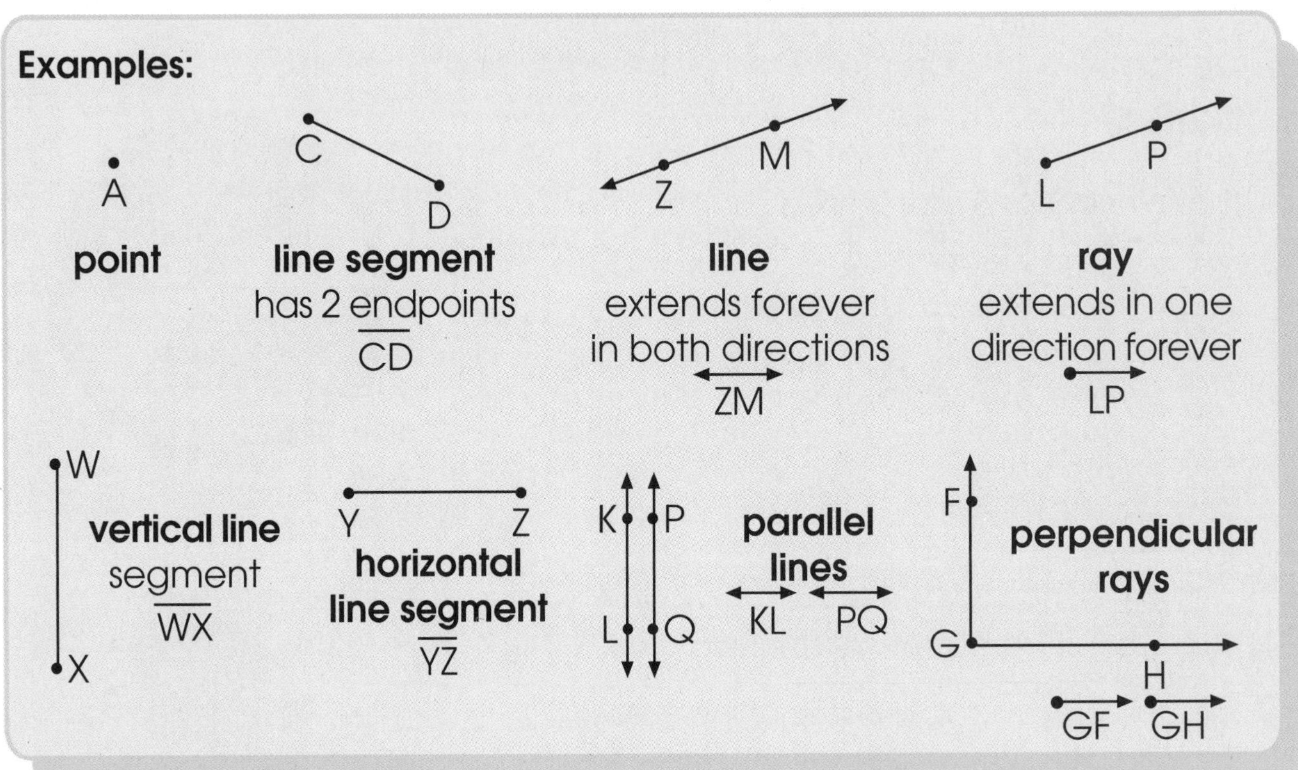

Directions: Describe each object using words and symbols.

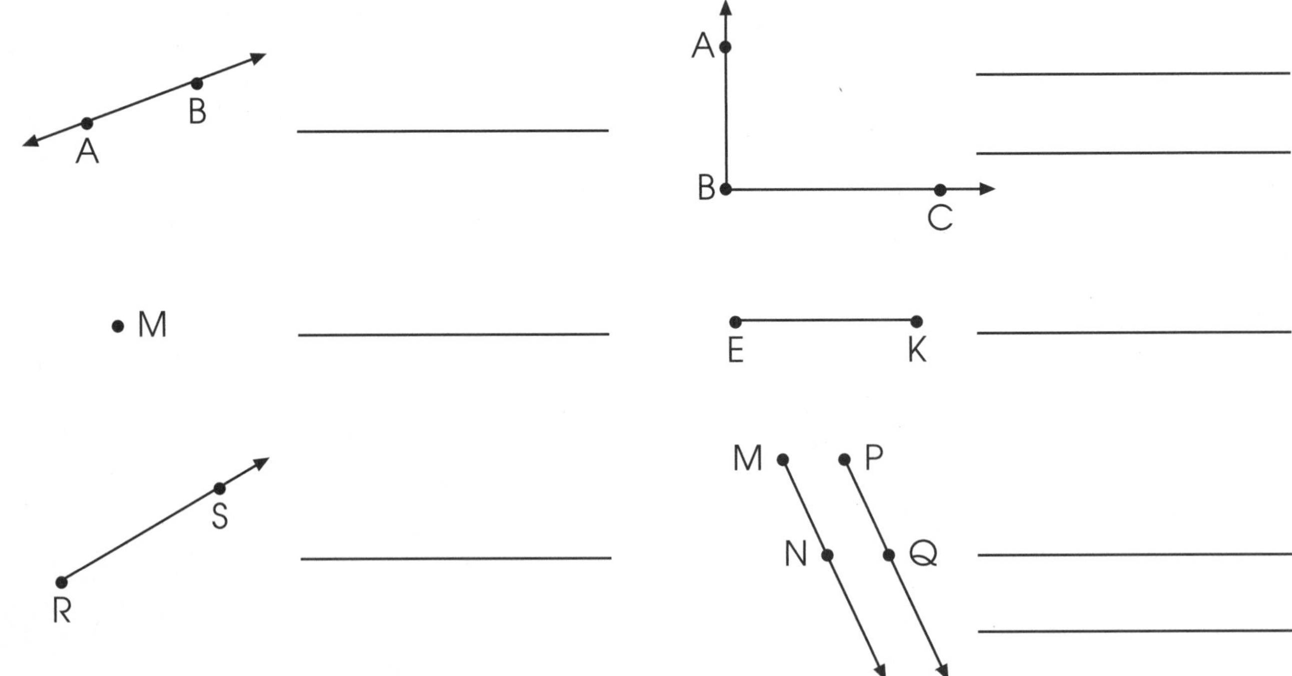

Name ____________________

Polygons

Polygons are named for the number of sides they have.

Triangle	Quadrilateral	Pentagon	Hexagon	Heptagon	Octagon
3 sides	___ sides	___ sides	___ sides	___ sides	___ sides

Look at the hexagon at the right.
All of the sides are the same length.
All of the angles have the same measure.
This is a regular hexagon.

Directions: On the line after each name, write the letter(s) of the figure(s) it describes. Some names will have more than one letter. Some figures have more than one name.

1. pentagon b.,h.
2. hexagon ____________
3. octagon ____________
4. triangle ____________
5. heptagon ____________
6. quadrilateral ____________
7. regular triangle ____________
8. regular hexagon ____________
9. regular pentagon ____________

a. b. c. d. e. f. g. h. i.

Directions: Answer the following questions.

10. What is another name for a regular quadrilateral? ____________

11. What of the triangles show below are regular triangles? ____________

a. b. c. d. e. f.

Name ______________________________

Three-Dimensional Objects

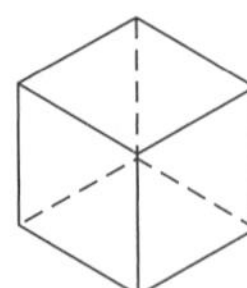

Cube

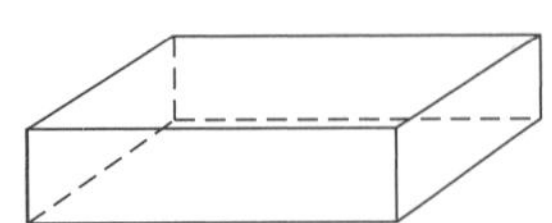

Rectangular Prism

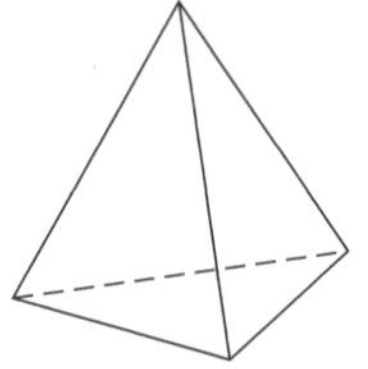

Triangular Pyramid

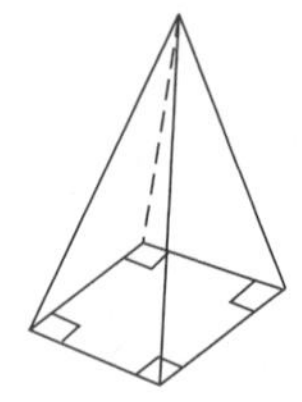

Square Pyramid

Each of these objects has faces, edges, and vertices.
Each of the faces of these objects is a polygon.

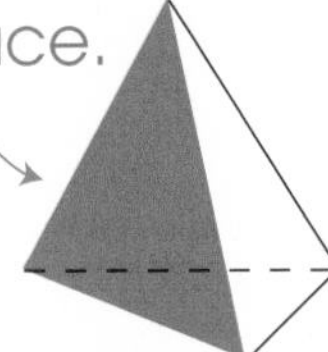
This is a face.

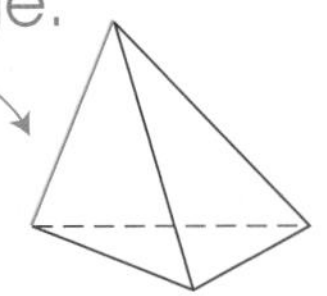
This is an edge.

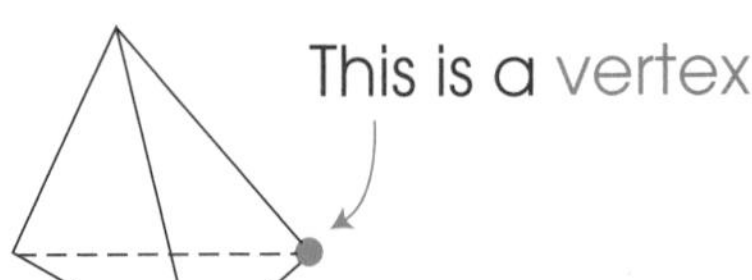
This is a vertex.

---

edge	face	rectangle	square	triangle	vertex
edges	faces	rectangles	squares	triangles	vertices

Directions: Choose from the list above to complete each sentence. You might use some words more than once. You might not use all the words.

1. All of the faces of a cube are ____________.

2. All of the faces of a retangular prism are ____________ .

3. The bottom face of a triangular pyramid is a ____________ .

4. The colored part of object A below is a(n) ____________ .

5. The colored part of object B below is a(n) ____________ .

6. The colored part of object C below is a(n) ____________ .

A 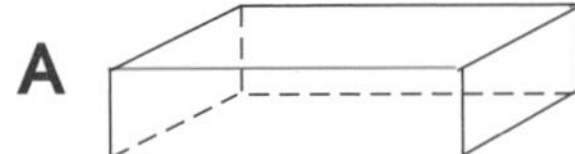

B 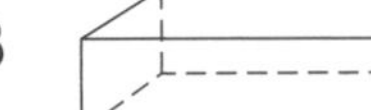

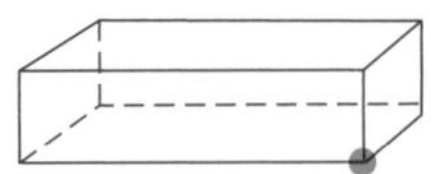

C 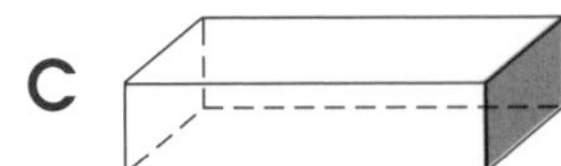

Directions: Answer each question with **yes** or **no.**

7. Are all squares rectangles? __________

8. Are all faces of a cube rectangles? __________

9. Is a cube a rectangular prism? __________

Name ____________________

Geometric Patterns

Directions: Draw the next three shapes in the pattern.

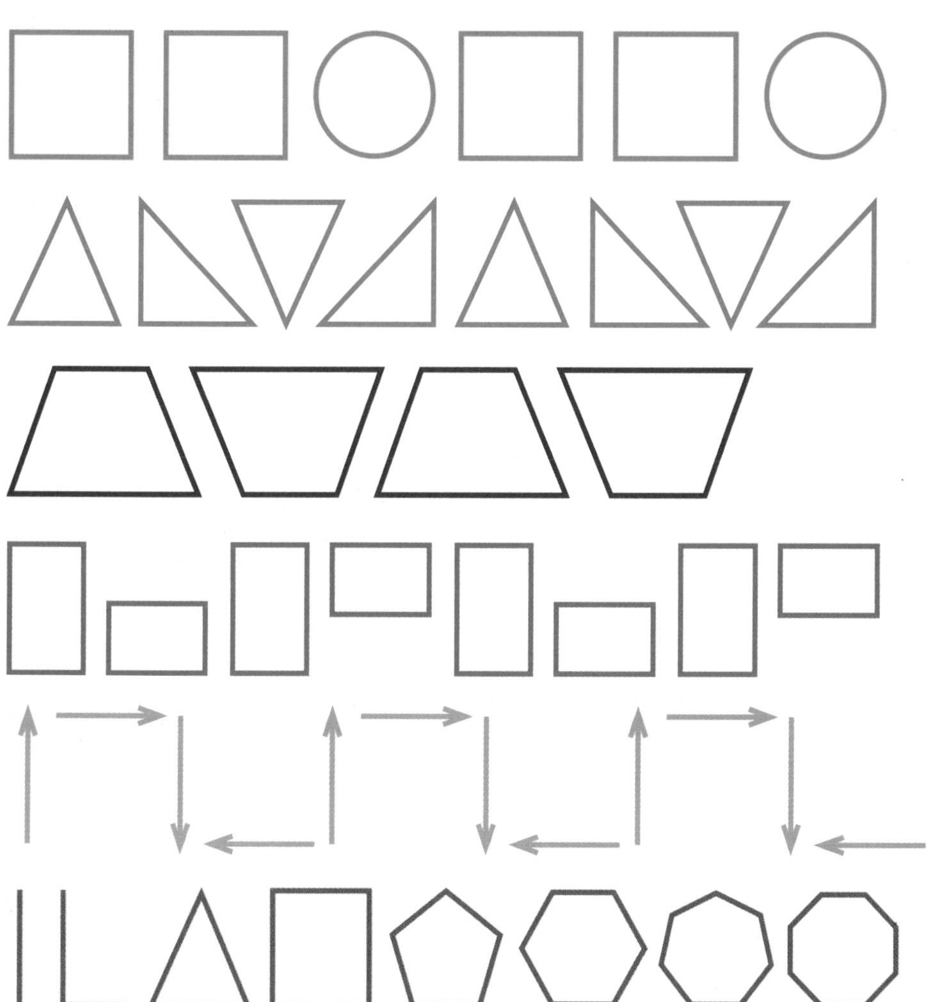

Directions: Draw a pattern that uses shapes. Have another person draw the next three shapes in the pattern.

_______ _______ _______ _______ _______ _______

_______ _______ _______ _______ _______ _______

Name ____________________

Similar, Congruent, and Symmetrical Figures

Similar figures have the same shape but have varying sizes.

Figures that are **congruent** have identical shapes but different orientations. That means they face in different directions.

Symmetrical figures can be divided equally into two identical parts.

Directions: Cross out the shape that does not belong in each group. Label the two remaining shapes as similiar, congruent, or symmetrical.

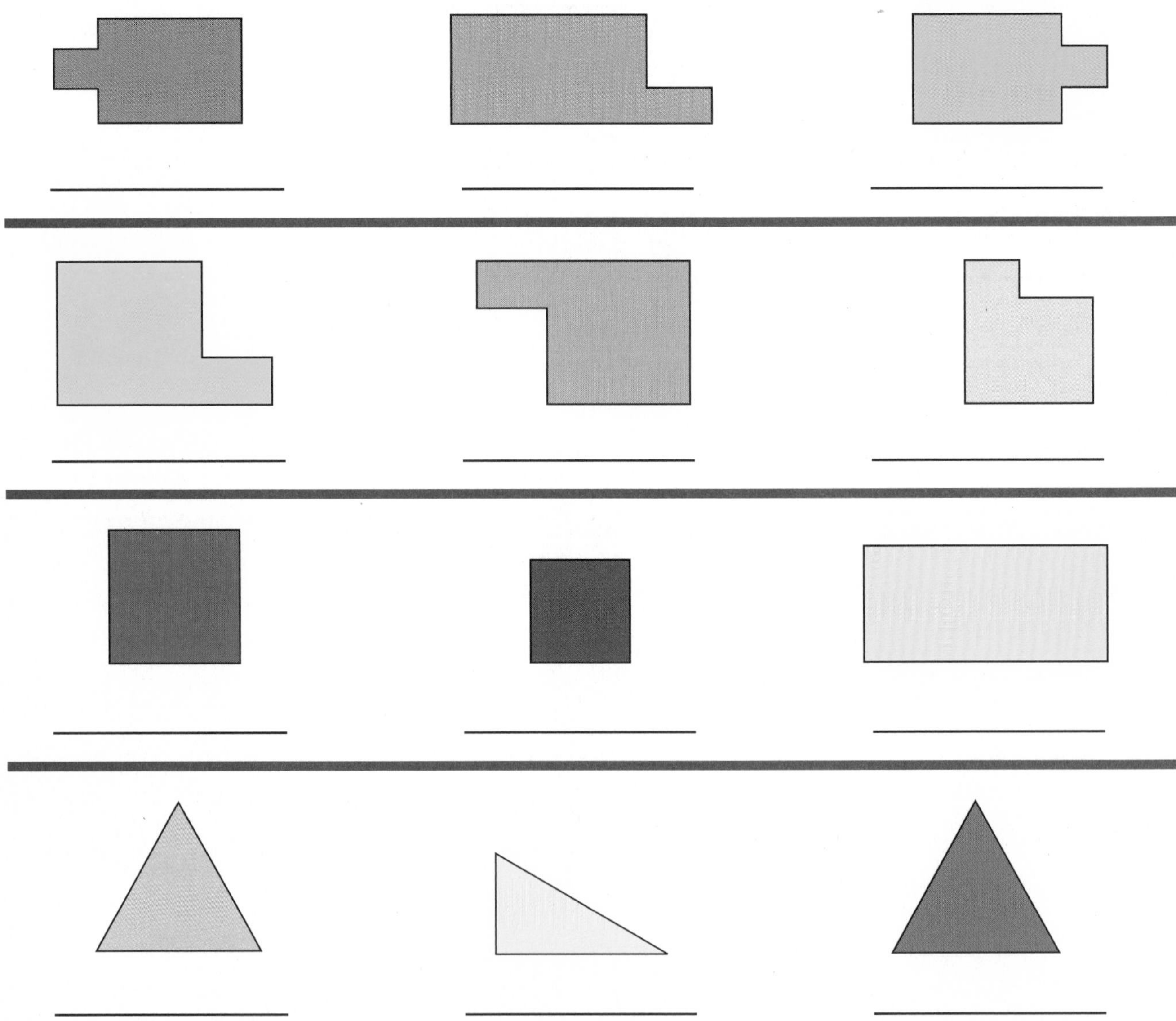

Name ______________________________

Volume

The formula for finding the **volume** (depth) of a box is length times width times height **(L x W x H).** The answer is given in cubic units.

Directions: Solve the problems.

Example:

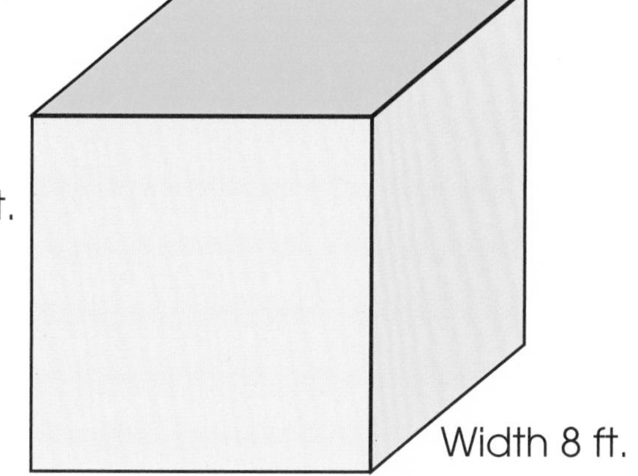

Height 8 ft.
Length 8 ft.
Width 8 ft. **L** x **W** x **H** = volume
8' x 8' x 8' = 512 cubic ft. or 512 ft.^{3}

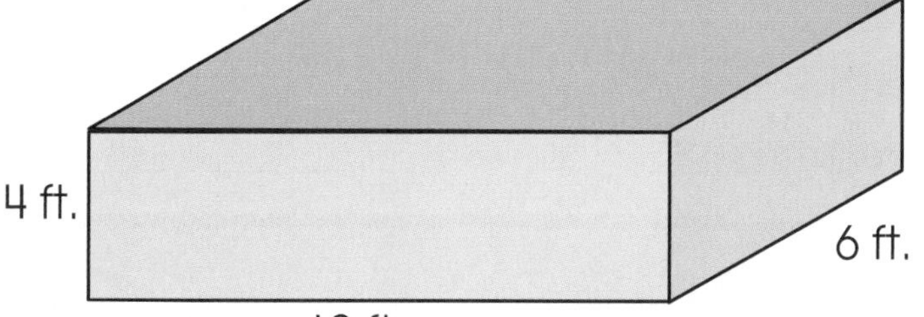

V = ________

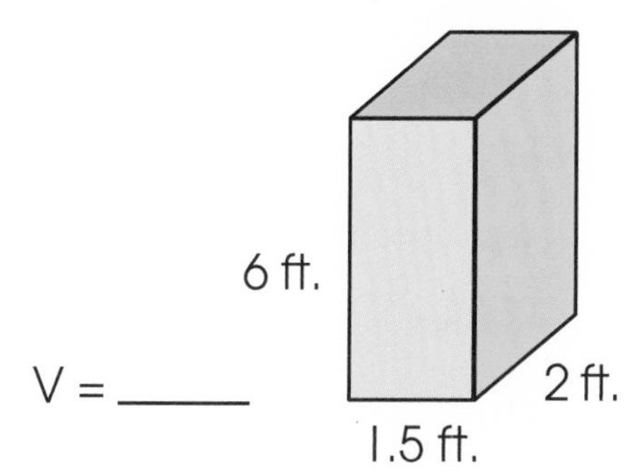

V = ______

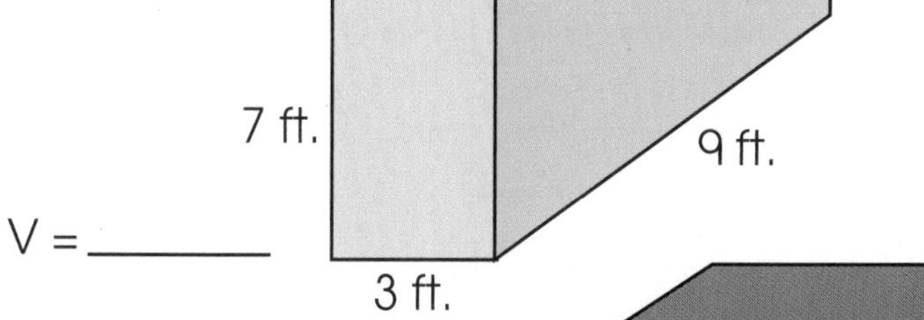

V = ________

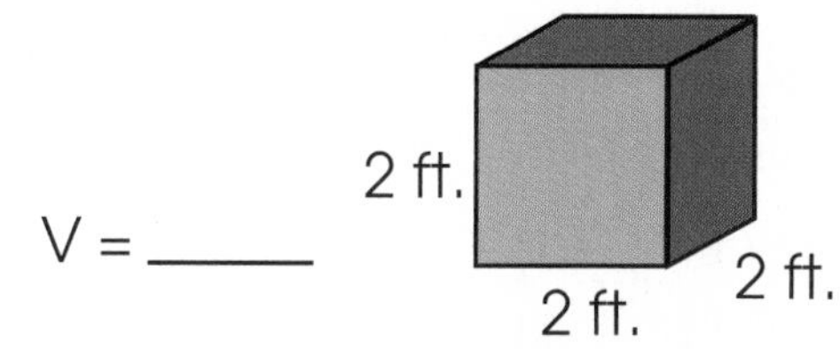

V = ______

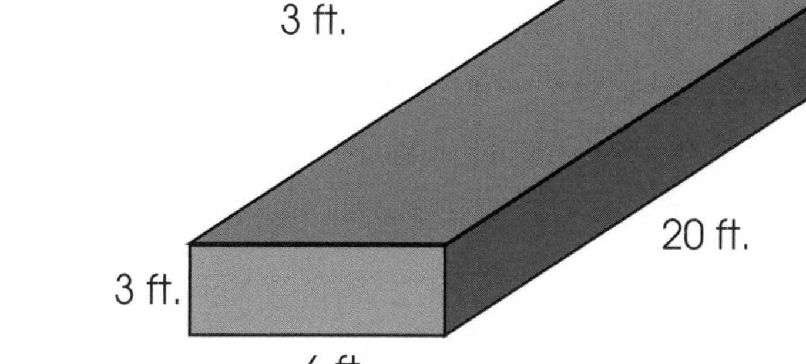

V = ________

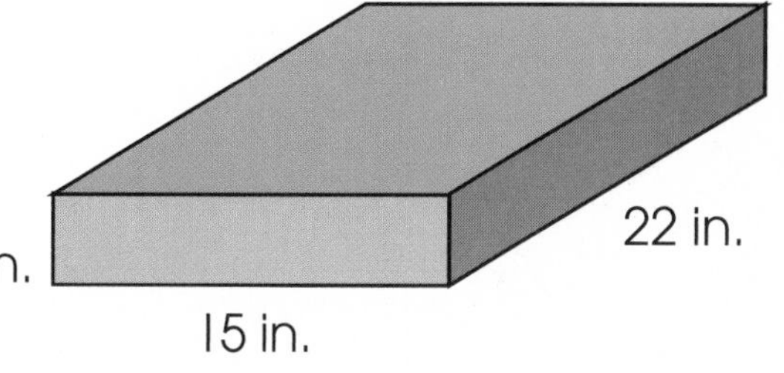

V = ________ in.^{3} V = ________ ft.^{3}

Name ____________________

Perimeter, Area, and Volume

Directions: Find the perimeter and area.

1. Length = 8 ft.
   Width = 11 ft.
   P = ________ A = ________

2. Length = 12 ft.
   Width = 10 ft.
   P = ________ A = ________

3. Length = 121 ft.
   Width = 16 ft.
   P = ________ A = ________

4. Length = 72 in.
   Width = 5 ft.
   P = ________ A = ________

Directions: Find the perimeter, area, and volume.

5. Length = 7 ft.
   Width = 12 ft.
   Height = 10 ft.
   P = ________
   A = ________
   V = ________

6. Length = 48 in.
   Width = 7 ft.
   Height = 12 in.
   P = ________
   A = ________
   V = ________

7. Length = 12 in.
   Width = 15 in.
   Height = 20 in.
   P = ________
   A = ________
   V = ________

8. Length = 22 ft.
   Width = 40 ft.
   Height = 10 ft.
   P = ________
   A = ________
   V = ________

Name ____________________

Triangle Angles

A triangle is a figure with three corners and three sides. Every triangle contains three angles. The sum of the angles is always 180°, regardless of the size or shape of the triangle.

If you know two of the angles, you can add them together, then subtract the total from 180 to find the number of degrees in the third angle.

Directions: Find the number of degrees in the third angle of each triangle.

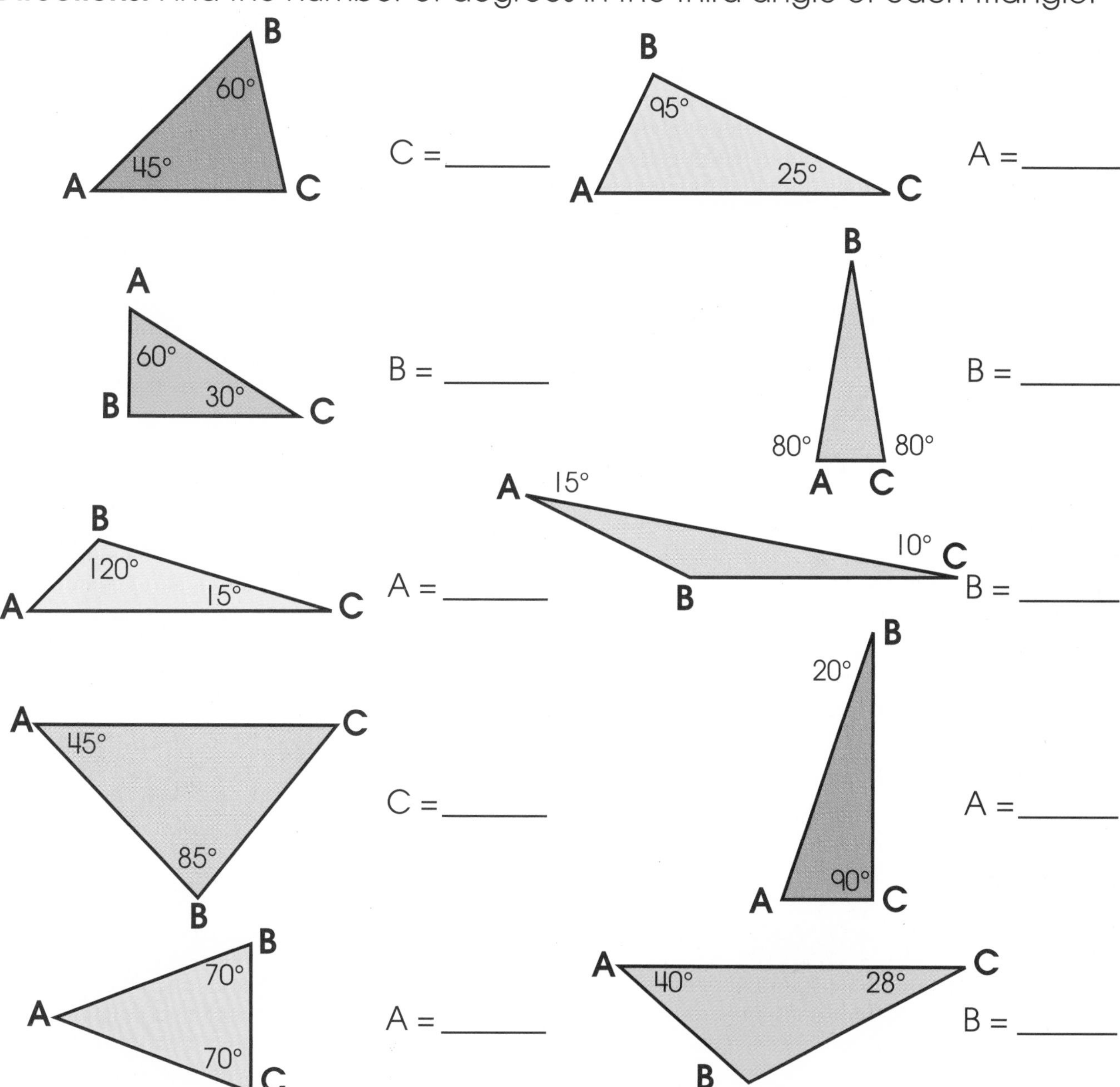

Name ______________________________

Length

Inches, feet, yards, and miles are used to measure length in the United States.

12 inches = 1 foot (ft.)
3 feet = 1 yard (yd.)
36 inches = 1 yard
1,760 yards = 1 mile (mi.)

Directions: Circle the best unit to measure each object. The first one has been done for you.

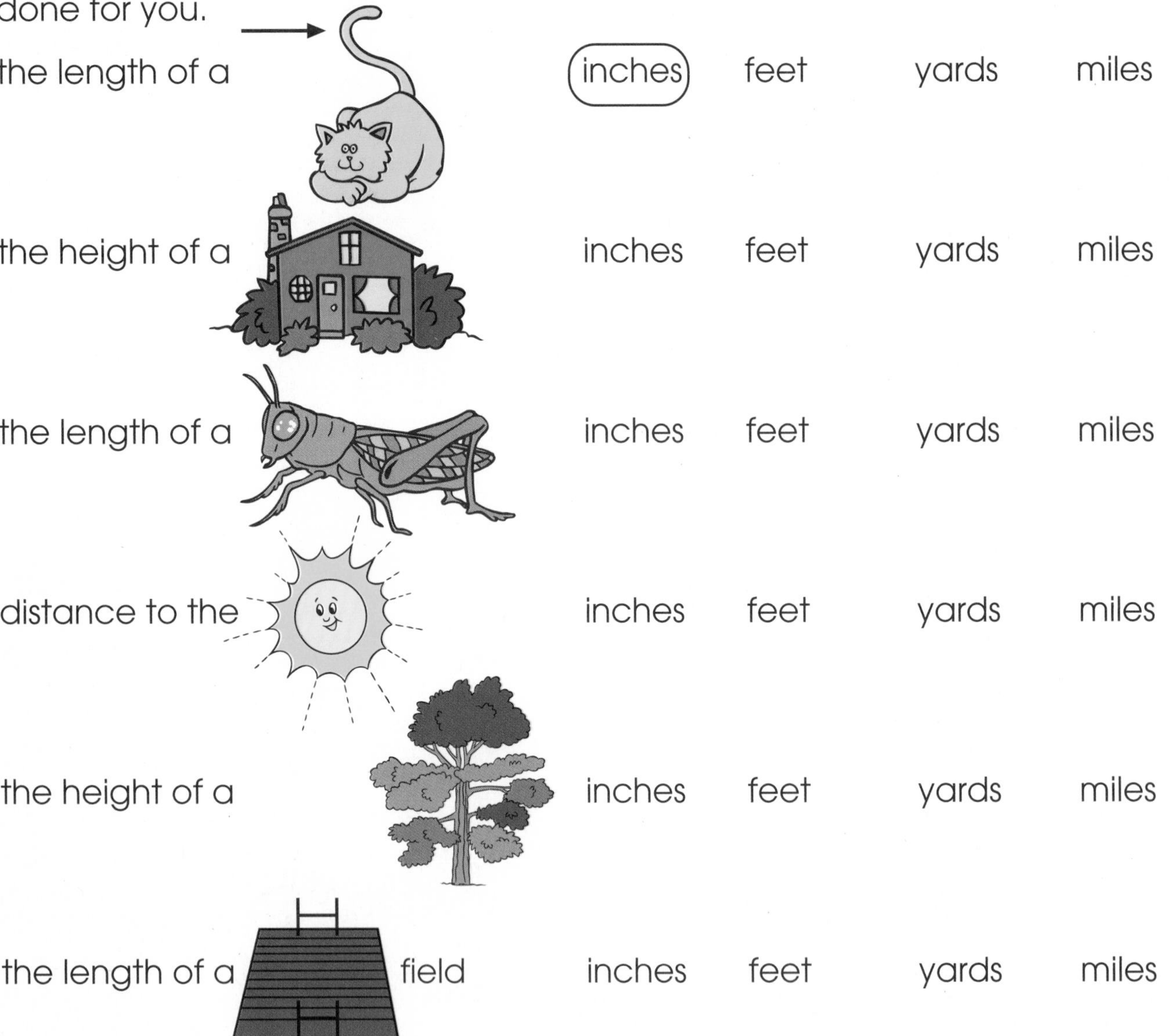

the length of a (cat)	(inches)	feet	yards	miles
the height of a (house)	inches	feet	yards	miles
the length of a (grasshopper)	inches	feet	yards	miles
distance to the (sun)	inches	feet	yards	miles
the height of a (tree)	inches	feet	yards	miles
the length of a (football) field	inches	feet	yards	miles

Name ______________________________

Weight

Ounces, pounds, and **tons** are used to measure weight in the United States.

16 ounces = 1 pound (lb.)

2,000 pounds = 1 ton (tn.)

Directions: Circle the most reasonable estimate for the weight of each object. The first one has been done for you.

10 ounces	(10 pounds)	10 tons
6 ounces	6 pounds	6 tons
2 ounces	2 pounds	2 tons
3 ounces	3 pounds	3 tons
1,800 ounces	1,800 pounds	1,800 tons
20 ounces	20 pounds	20 tons
1 ounce	1 pound	1 ton

Name ______________________________

Length: Metric

Millimeters, centimeters, meters, and **kilometers** are used to measure length in the metric system.

1 meter = 39.37 inches
1 kilometer = about $\frac{5}{8}$ mile
10 millimeters = 1 centimeter (cm)
100 centimeters = 1 meter (m)
1,000 meters = 1 kilometer (km)

Directions: Circle the best unit to measure each object. The first one has been done for you.

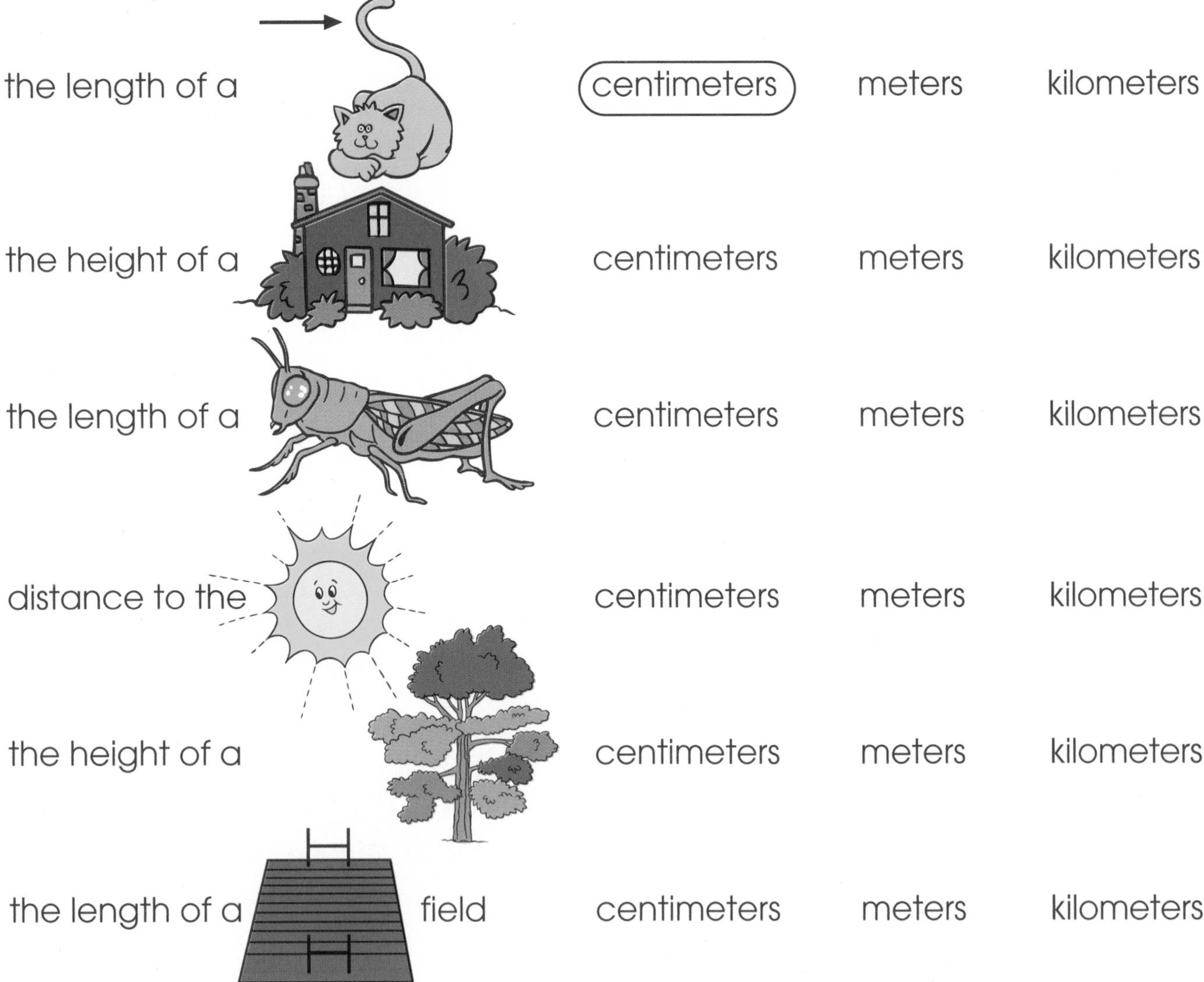

Name ___________________________

Capacity: Metric

Milliliters and **liters** are units of capacity in the metric system. A can of soda contains about 350 milliliters of liquid. A large plastic bottle contains 1 liter of liquid. A liter is about a quart.

1,000 milliliters (mL) = 1 liter (L)

Directions: Circle the best unit to measure each liquid.

Name ____________________

Weights and Measures

Example:

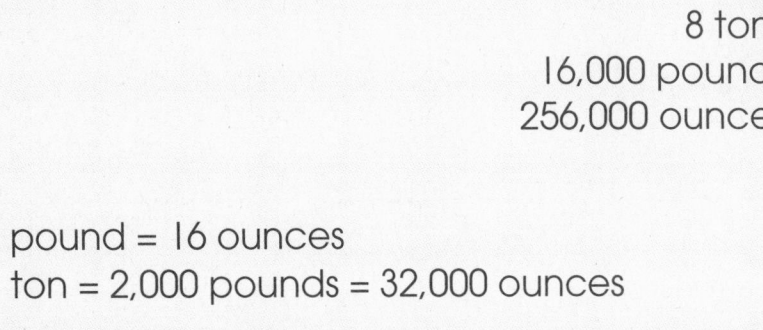

8 tons
16,000 pounds
256,000 ounces

1 pound = 16 ounces
1 ton = 2,000 pounds = 32,000 ounces

Steps to convert one customary unit of weight to another:

Multiply to change a larger unit to a smaller one.

3 pounds = ________ ounces
3 pounds x 16 = 48 ounces

Divide to change a smaller unit to a larger one.

10,000 pounds = ________ tons
10,000 pounds ÷ 2000 = 5 tons

Directions: Change each measurement to tons.

6,000 pounds ________ 192,000 ounces ________ 14,000 pounds ________

9,000 pounds ________ 128,000 ounces ________ 1,000 pounds ________

Directions: Change each measurement to pounds.

5 tons ________ 160 ounces ________ $3\frac{1}{2}$ tons ________

192 ounces ________ 2,160 ounces ________ 92 ounces ________

Directions: Change each measurement to ounces.

8 pounds ________ 4.5 pounds ________ 2 tons ________

43 pounds ________ 0.6 tons ________ 101 pounds ________

Name ______________________________

Renaming Lengths

Example:

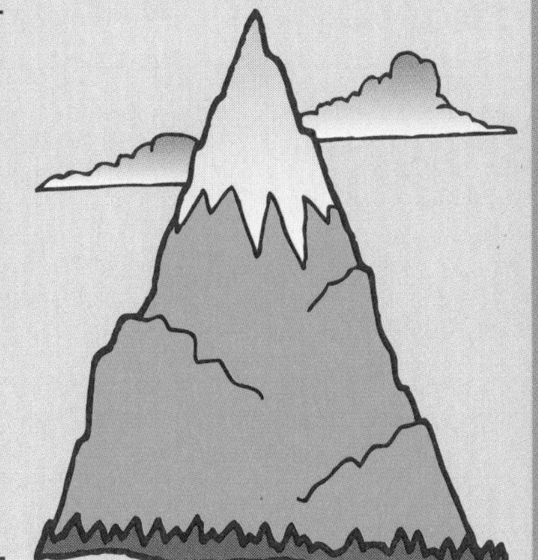

I foot = 12 inches
I yard = 3 feet = 36 inches
I mile = 5,280 feet = 1,760 yards = 63,360 inches

Steps to convert, or change, one customary unit of length to another:

Multiply to change a larger unit to a smaller one. 8 yards = ______ feet
8 yards x 3 = 24 feet

Divide to change a smaller unit to a larger one. 36 inches = ______ feet
36 inches ÷ 12 = 3 feet

Directions: Find the missing number in each problem.

4 feet = _______ inches
144 inches = _______ feet
237 yards = _______ inches

78 yards = _______ feet
3 miles = _______ yards
180 inches = _______ yards

2 miles = _______ yards
6 yards = _______ inches
10,560 feet = _______ miles

10 yards = _______ inches
8,800 yards = _______ miles
30 feet = _______ yards

72 feet = _______ yards
360 inches = _______ yards
5,280 yards = _______ miles

7 miles = _______ feet
18 inches = _______ feet
45 yards = _______ feet

Name ____________________

Temperature: Fahrenheit

Degrees **Fahrenheit** (°F) is a unit for measuring temperature.

Directions: Write the temperature in degrees Fahrenheit (°F).

Example:

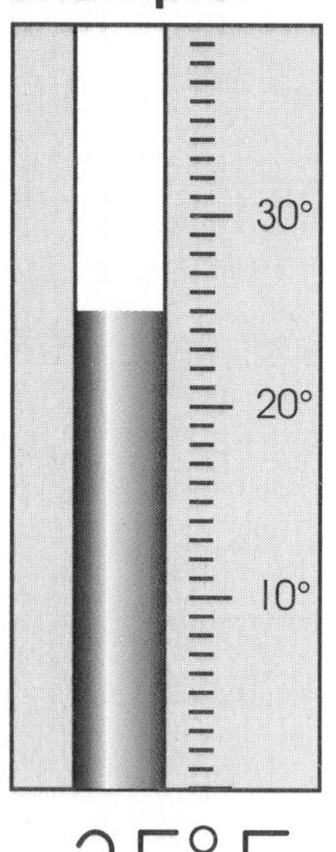

25°F

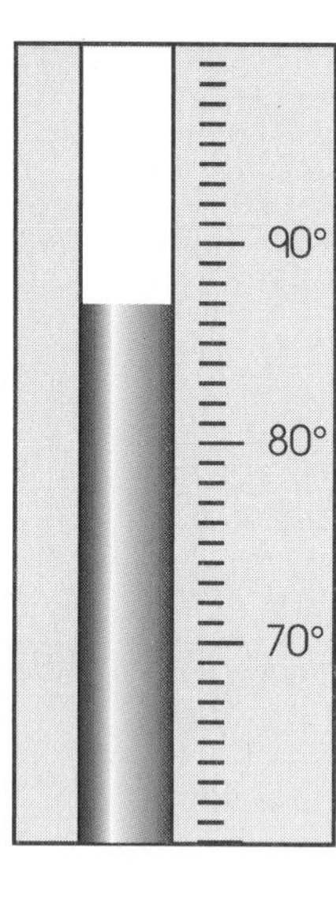

______

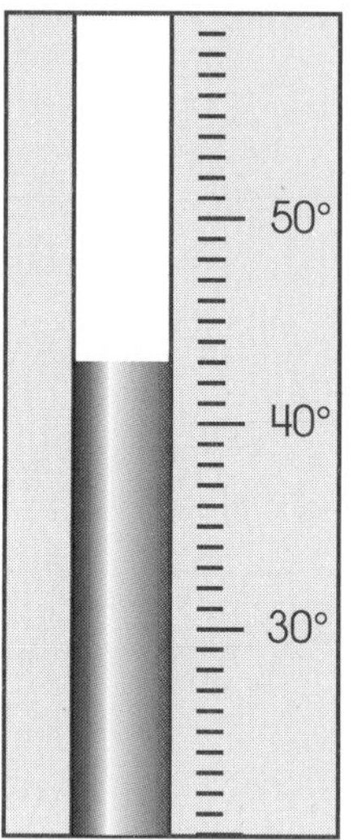

______

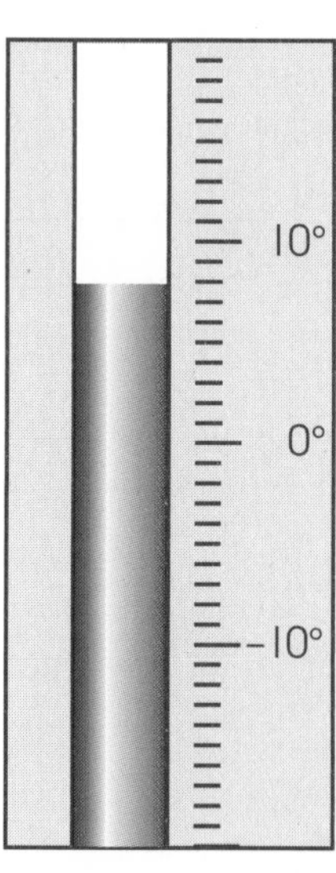

______

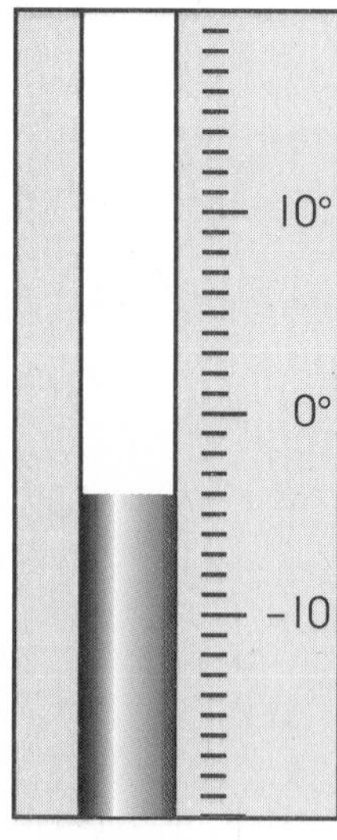

______

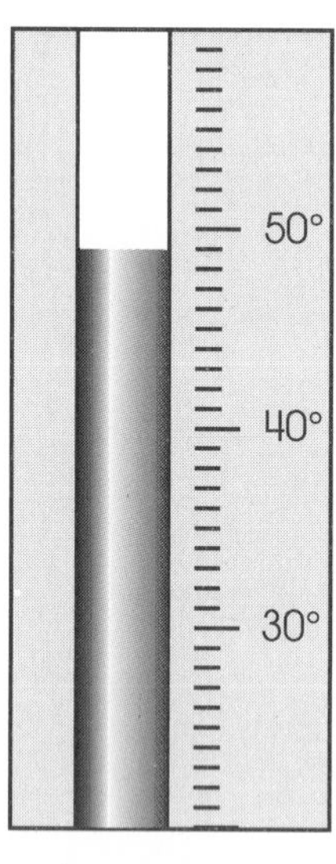

______

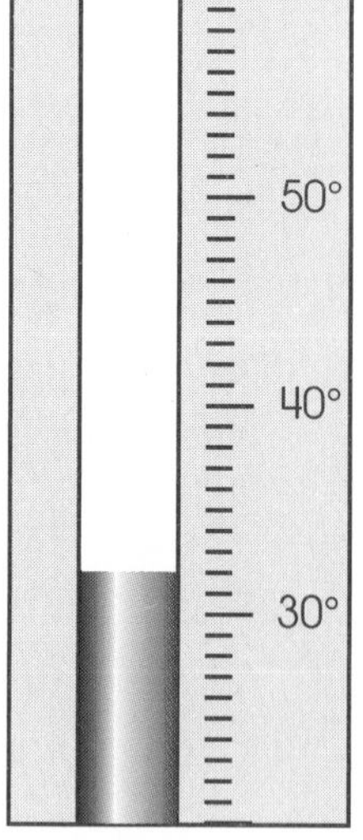

______

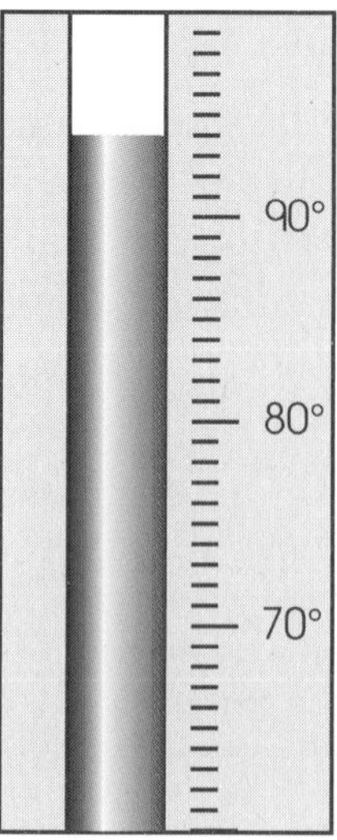

______

Name ____________________

Graphs

Directions: Read each graph and follow the directions.

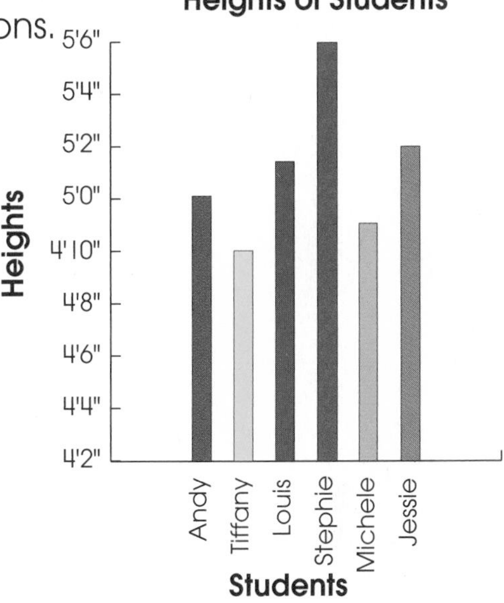

List the names of the students from the shortest to the tallest.

1. ____________ 4. ____________

2. ____________ 5. ____________

3. ____________ 6. ____________

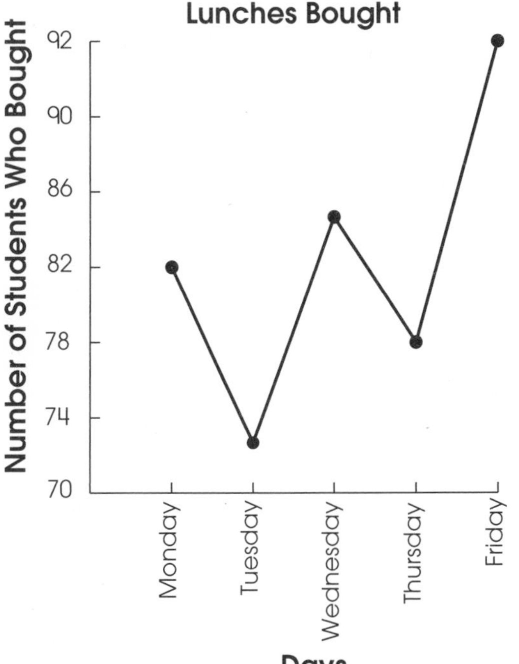

List how many lunches the students bought each day, from the day the most were bought to the least.

1. ____________ 4. ____________

2. ____________ 5. ____________

3. ____________

Days of Outside Recess

Number of Days: 20, 18, 16, 14, 12, 10, 8, 6, 4, 2, 0

Months: September, October, November, December, January, February, March, April, May, June

List the months in the order of the most number of outside recesses to the least number.

1. ____________ 6. ____________

2. ____________ 7. ____________

3. ____________ 8. ____________

4. ____________ 9. ____________

5. ____________ 10. ____________

Name ______________________

Circle Graph

Ned earns an allowance of $10.00 each week. He created this circle graph on his computer to show his parents how he spends the money.

Directions: Refer to the graph to answer each question below.

Ned's Allowance

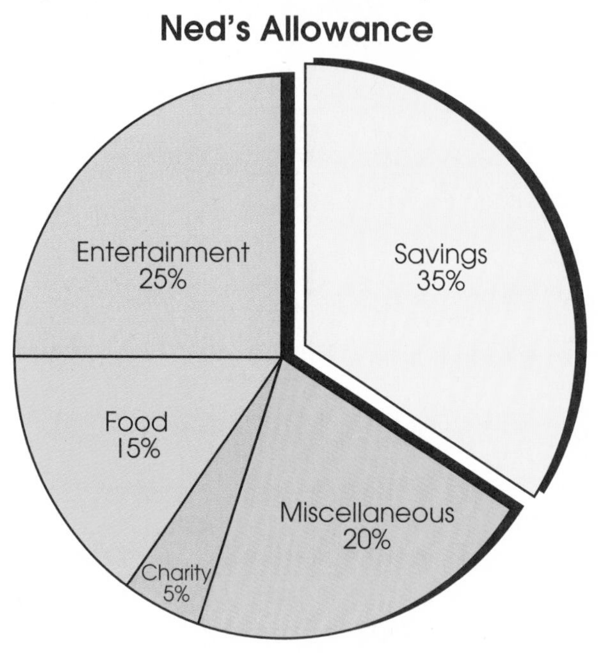

1. Ned highlighted the savings segment of the circle graph because his family believes that having a savings account is very important. If Ned saves $3.50 each week, how much will he have left for other things?

   ____

2. Ned spends all of his entertainment allowance on movies. How much does he spend each week on movies?

   ____

3. How much does Ned spend each week on miscellaneous expenses? Name some things he might buy which would fall into this category.

   ____

4. If you have an allowance, create your own circle graph detailing your spending habits. If you don't have an allowance, write two sentences describing how you would spend $10.00 differently than Ned.

   ____

   ____

Name ______________________________

Locating Points on a Grid

To locate points on a grid, read the first coordinate and follow it to the second coordinate.

Example: C, 3

Directions: Maya is new in town. Help her learn the way around her new neighborhood. Place the following locations on the grid below.

Grocery	C, 10
Home	B, 2
School	A, 12
Playground	B, 13
Library	D, 6
Bank	G, 1
Post Office	E, 7
Ice-Cream Shop	D, 3

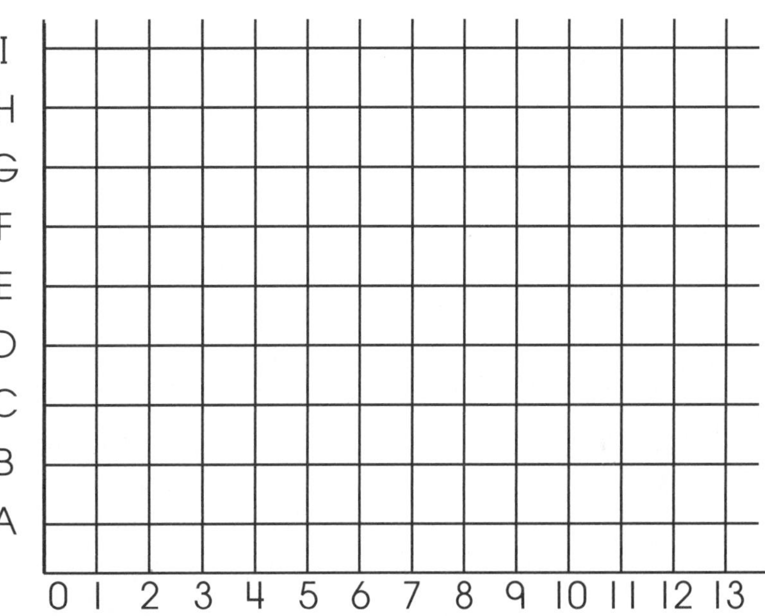

Is her home closer to the bank or the grocery? ______________________________

Does she pass the playground on her way to school? ______________________________

If she needs to stop at the library after school, will she be closer to home or farther away? ______________________________

Answer Key

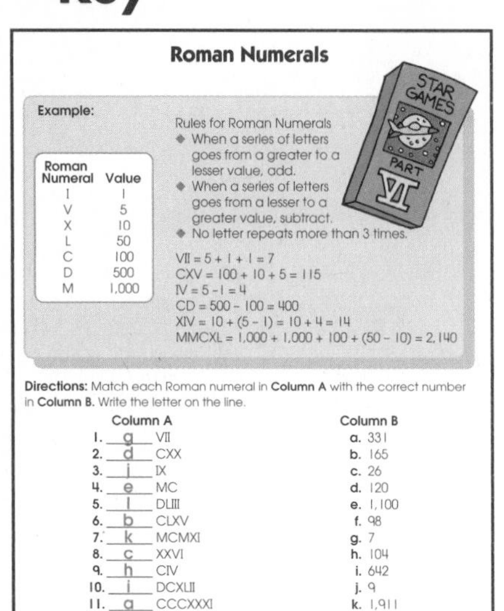

Roman Numerals

Example:

Roman Numeral	Value
I	1
V	5
X	10
L	50
C	100
D	500
M	1,000

Rules for Roman Numerals
- When a series of letters goes from a greater to a lesser value, add.
- When a series of letters goes from a lesser to a greater value, subtract.
- No letter repeats more than 3 times.

VII = 5 + 1 + 1 = 7
CXV = 100 + 10 + 5 = 115
IV = 5 - 1 = 4
CD = 500 - 100 = 400
XIV = 10 + (5 - 1) = 10 + 4 = 14
MMCXL = 1,000 + 1,000 + 100 + (50 - 10) = 2,140

Directions: Match each Roman numeral in **Column A** with the correct number in **Column B.** Write the letter on the line.

	Column A		Column B
1.	g VII	a.	331
2.	d CXX	b.	165
3.	j IX	c.	26
4.	e MC	d.	120
5.	l DLIII	e.	1,100
6.	b CLXV	f.	98
7.	k MCMXI	g.	7
8.	c XXVI	h.	104
9.	h CIV	i.	642
10.	i DCXLII	j.	9
11.	a CCCXXXI	k.	1,911
12.	f XCVIII	l.	553

4

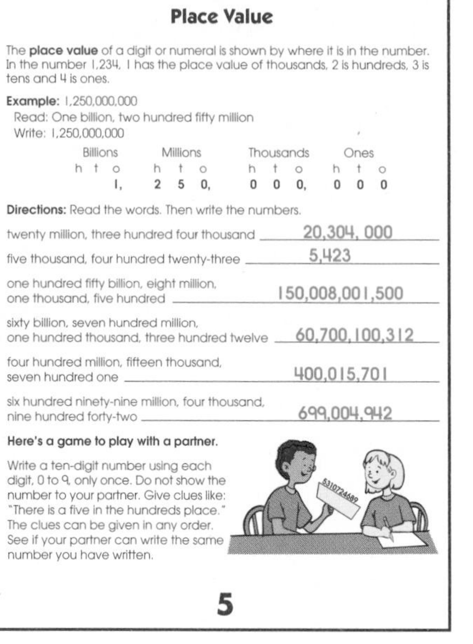

Place Value

The **place value** of a digit or numeral is shown by where it is in the number. In the number 1,234, 1 has the place value of thousands, 2 is hundreds, 3 is tens and 4 is ones.

Example: 1,250,000,000
Read: One billion, two hundred fifty million
Write: 1,250,000,000

Billions			Millions			Thousands			Ones		
h	t	o	h	t	o	h	t	o	h	t	o
		1,	2	5	0,	0	0	0,	0	0	0

Directions: Read the words. Then write the numbers.

twenty million, three hundred four thousand 20,304,000

five thousand, four hundred twenty-three 5,423

one hundred fifty billion, eight million, one thousand, five hundred 150,008,001,500

sixty billion, seven hundred million, one hundred thousand, three hundred twelve 60,700,100,312

four hundred million, fifteen thousand, seven hundred one 400,015,701

six hundred ninety-nine million, four thousand, nine hundred forty-two 699,004,942

Here's a game to play with a partner.

Write a ten-digit number using each digit, 0 to 9, only once. Do not show the number to your partner. Give clues like: "There is a five in the hundreds place." The clues can be given in any order. See if your partner can write the same number you have written.

5

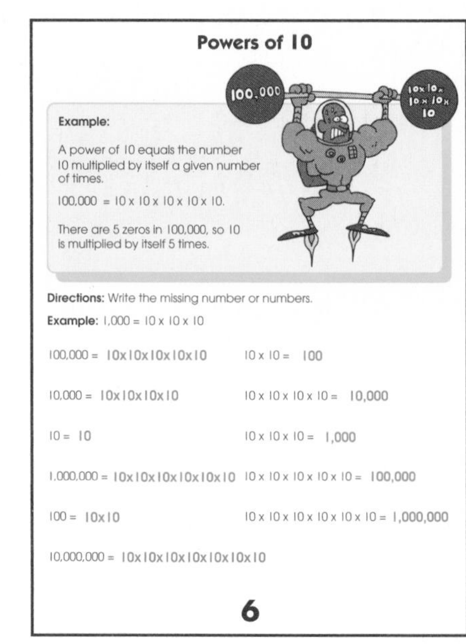

Powers of 10

Example:

A power of 10 equals the number 10 multiplied by itself a given number of times.

100,000 = 10 x 10 x 10 x 10 x 10.

There are 5 zeros in 100,000, so 10 is multiplied by itself 5 times.

Directions: Write the missing number or numbers.

Example: 1,000 = 10 x 10 x 10

100,000 = 10x10x10x10x10 | 10 x 10 = 100

10,000 = 10x10x10x10 | 10 x 10 x 10 x 10 = 10,000

10 = 10 | 10 x 10 x 10 = 1,000

1,000,000 = 10x10x10x10x10x10 | 10 x 10 x 10 x 10 x 10 = 100,000

100 = 10x10 | 10 x 10 x 10 x 10 x 10 x 10 = 1,000,000

10,000,000 = 10x10x10x10x10x10x10

6

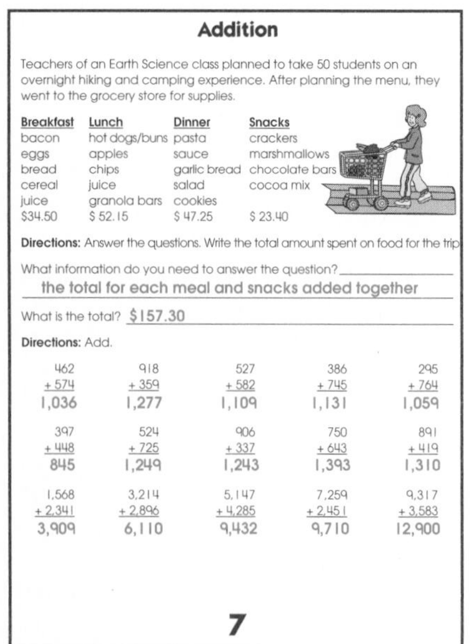

Addition

Teachers of an Earth Science class planned to take 50 students on an overnight hiking and camping experience. After planning the menu, they went to the grocery store for supplies.

Breakfast	Lunch	Dinner	Snacks
bacon	hot dogs/buns	pasta	crackers
eggs	apples	sauce	marshmallows
bread	chips	garlic bread	chocolate bars
cereal	juice	salad	cocoa mix
juice	granola bars	cookies	
$34.50	$ 52.15	$ 47.25	$ 23.40

Directions: Answer the questions. Write the total amount spent on food for the trip.

What information do you need to answer the question? the total for each meal and snacks added together

What is the total? $157.30

Directions: Add.

462 + 574 = 1,036	918 + 359 = 1,277	527 + 582 = 1,109	386 + 745 = 1,131	295 + 764 = 1,059
397 + 448 = 845	524 + 725 = 1,249	906 + 337 = 1,243	750 + 643 = 1,393	891 + 419 = 1,310
1,568 + 2,341 = 3,909	3,214 + 2,896 = 6,110	5,147 + 4,285 = 9,432	7,259 + 2,451 = 9,710	9,317 + 3,583 = 12,900

7

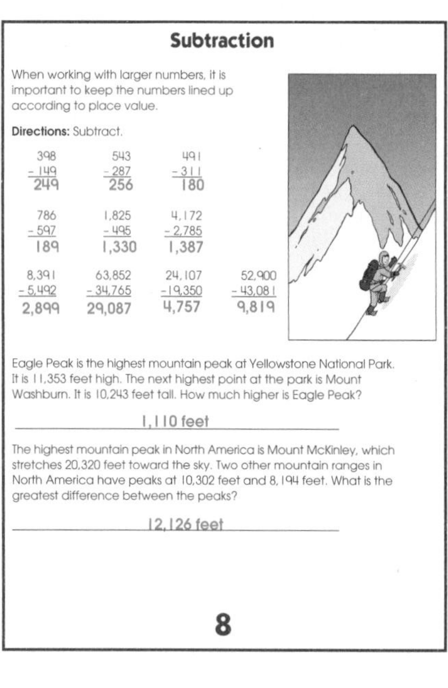

Subtraction

When working with larger numbers, it is important to keep the numbers lined up according to place value.

Directions: Subtract.

398 - 149 = 249	543 - 287 = 256	491 - 311 = 180	
786 - 597 = 189	1,825 - 495 = 1,330	4,172 - 2,785 = 1,387	
8,391 - 5,492 = 2,899	63,852 - 34,765 = 29,087	24,107 - 19,350 = 4,757	52,900 - 43,081 = 9,819

Eagle Peak is the highest mountain peak at Yellowstone National Park. It is 11,353 feet high. The next highest point at the park is Mount Washburn. It is 10,243 feet tall. How much higher is Eagle Peak?

1,110 feet

The highest mountain peak in North America is Mount McKinley, which stretches 20,320 feet toward the sky. Two other mountain ranges in North America have peaks at 10,302 feet and 8,194 feet. What is the greatest difference between the peaks?

12,126 feet

8

Addition and Subtraction

Directions: Check the answers. Write **T** if the answer is true and **F** if it is false.

Example: 48,973 - 35,856 = 13,118 Check: F 35,856 + 13,118 = 48,974

18,264 + 17,893 = 36,157 Check: T 36,157 - 17,893 = 18,264

458,342 - 297,652 = 160,680 Check: F 160,680 + 297,652 = 458,332

39,854 + 52,713 = 92,577 Check: F 92,577 - 52,713 = 39,864

631,928 - 457,615 = 174,313 Check: T 174,313 + 457,615 = 631,928

14,389 + 93,587 = 107,976 Check: T 107,976 - 93,587 = 14,389

554,974 - 376,585 = 178,389 Check: T 178,389 + 376,585 = 554,974

87,321 - 62,348 = 24,973 Check: T 24,973 + 62,348 = 87,321

109,568 + 97,373 = 206,941 Check: T 206,941 - 97,373 = 109,568

Directions: Read the story problem. Write the equation and check the answer.

A camper hikes 53,741 feet out into the wilderness. On his return trip he takes a shortcut, walking 36,752 feet back to his cabin. The shortcut saves him 16,998 feet of hiking. True or (False)?

53,741 - 36,752 = 16,989 16,989 + 36,752 = 53,741

9

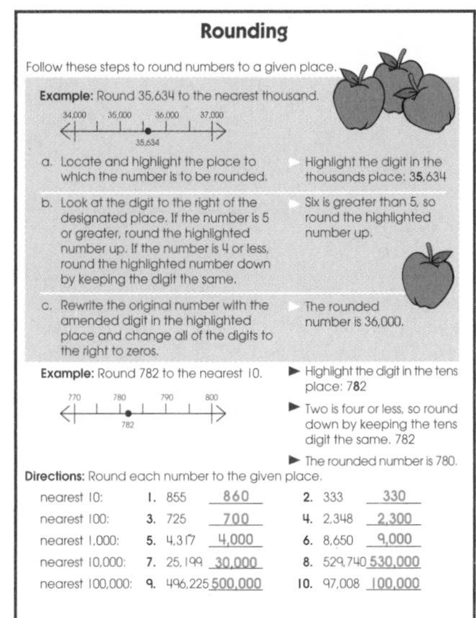

Rounding

Follow these steps to round numbers to a given place.

Example: Round 35,634 to the nearest thousand.

34,000 35,000 36,000 37,000
35,634

a. Locate and highlight the place to which the number is to be rounded. ▶ Highlight the digit in the thousands place: 35,634

b. Look at the digit to the right of the designated place. If the number is 5 or greater, round the highlighted number up. If the number is 4 or less, round the highlighted number down by keeping the digit the same. ▶ Six is greater than 5, so round the highlighted number up.

c. Rewrite the original number with the amended digit in the highlighted place and change all of the digits to the right to zeros. ▶ The rounded number is 36,000.

Example: Round 782 to the nearest 10.

770 780 790 800
782

▶ Highlight the digit in the tens place: 782

▶ Two is four or less, so round down by keeping the tens digit the same. 782

▶ The rounded number is 780.

Directions: Round each number to the given place.

nearest 10:	1. 855	860	2. 333	330
nearest 100:	3. 725	700	4. 2,348	2,300
nearest 1,000:	5. 4,317	4,000	6. 8,650	9,000
nearest 10,000:	7. 25,199	30,000	8. 529,740	530,000
nearest 100,000:	9. 496,225	500,000	10. 97,008	100,000

10

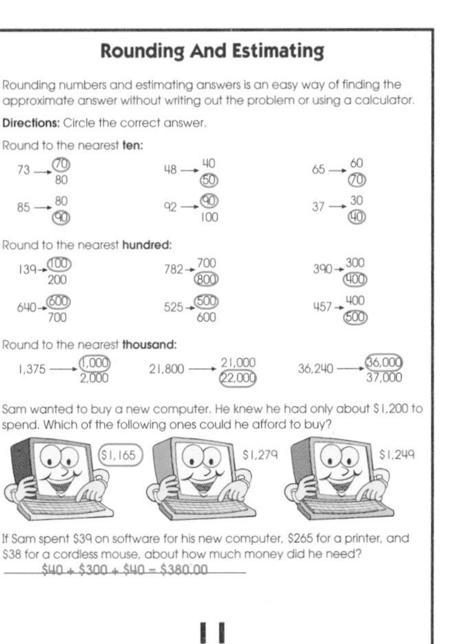

Rounding And Estimating

Rounding numbers and estimating answers is an easy way of finding the approximate answer without writing out the problem or using a calculator.

Directions: Circle the correct answer.

Round to the nearest **ten:**

73 → (70) 80 | 48 → 40 (50) | 65 → 60 (70)

85 → 80 (90) | 92 → (90) 100 | 37 → 30 (40)

Round to the nearest **hundred:**

139 → (100) 200 | 782 → 700 (800) | 390 → 300 (400)

640 → (600) 700 | 525 → (500) 600 | 457 → 400 (500)

Round to the nearest **thousand:**

1,375 → (1,000) 2,000 | 21,800 → 21,000 (22,000) | 36,240 → (36,000) 37,000

Sam wanted to buy a new computer. He knew he had only about $1,200 to spend. Which of the following ones could he afford to buy?

If Sam spent $39 on software for his new computer, $265 for a printer, and $38 for a cordless mouse, about how much money did he need?

$40 + $300 + $40 = $380.00

11

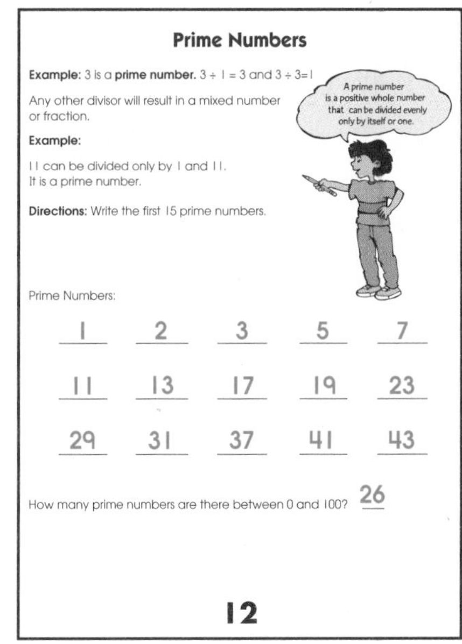

Prime Numbers

Example: 3 is a **prime number.** 3 ÷ 1 = 3 and 3 ÷ 3 = 1

Any other divisor will result in a mixed number or fraction.

A prime number is a positive whole number that can be divided evenly only by itself or one.

Example:

11 can be divided only by 1 and 11.
It is a prime number.

Directions: Write the first 15 prime numbers.

Prime Numbers:

1	2	3	5	7
11	13	17	19	23
29	31	37	41	43

How many prime numbers are there between 0 and 100? 26

12

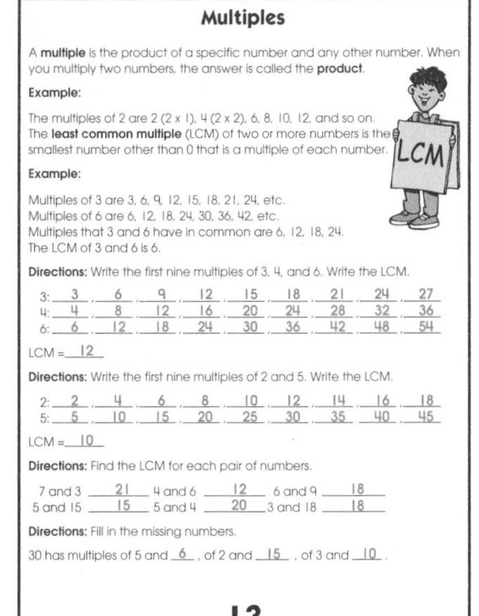

Multiples

A **multiple** is the product of a specific number and any other number. When you multiply two numbers, the answer is called the **product.**

Example:

The multiples of 2 are 2 (2 x 1), 4 (2 x 2), 6, 8, 10, 12, and so on.
The **least common multiple** (LCM) of two or more numbers is the smallest number other than 0 that is a multiple of each number.

Example:

Multiples of 3 are 3, 6, 9, 12, 15, 18, 21, 24, etc.
Multiples of 6 are 6, 12, 18, 24, 30, 36, 42, etc.
Multiples that 3 and 6 have in common are 6, 12, 18, 24.
The LCM of 3 and 6 is 6.

Directions: Write the first nine multiples of 3, 4, and 6. Write the LCM.

3:	3	6	9	12	15	18	21	24	27
4:	4	8	12	16	20	24	28	32	36
6:	6	12	18	24	30	36	42	48	54

LCM = 12

Directions: Write the first nine multiples of 2 and 5. Write the LCM.

2:	2	4	6	8	10	12	14	16	18
5:	5	10	15	20	25	30	35	40	45

LCM = 10

Directions: Find the LCM for each pair of numbers.

7 and 3 21 | 4 and 6 12 | 6 and 9 18
5 and 15 15 | 5 and 4 20 | 3 and 18 18

Directions: Fill in the missing numbers.

30 has multiples of 5 and 6, of 2 and 15, of 3 and 10.

13

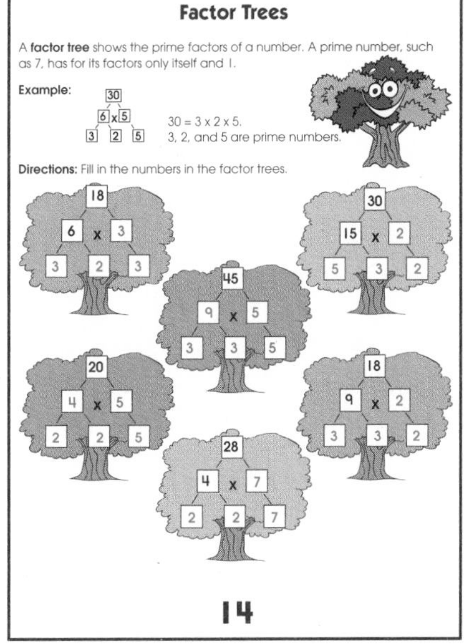

Factor Trees

A **factor tree** shows the prime factors of a number. A prime number, such as 7, has for its factors only itself and 1.

Example:

30
6 x 5
3 2 5

30 = 3 x 2 x 5.
3, 2, and 5 are prime numbers.

Directions: Fill in the numbers in the factor trees.

14

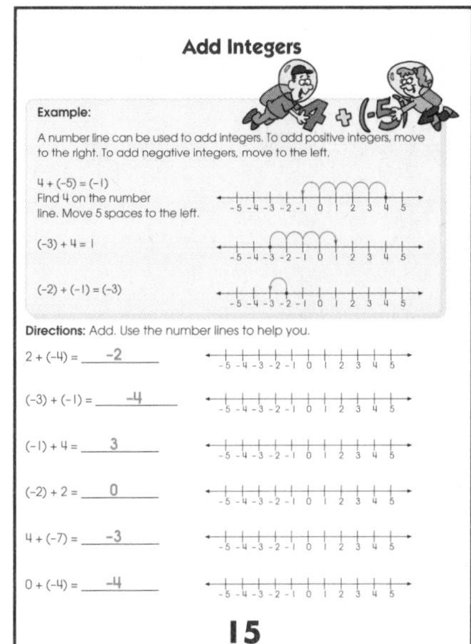

Add Integers

Example:

A number line can be used to add integers. To add positive integers, move to the right. To add negative integers, move to the left.

4 + (-5) = (-1)
Find 4 on the number line. Move 5 spaces to the left.

(-3) + 4 = 1

(-2) + (-1) = (-3)

Directions: Add. Use the number lines to help you.

2 + (-4) = -2

(-3) + (-1) = -4

(-1) + 4 = 3

(-2) + 2 = 0

4 + (-7) = -3

0 + (-4) = -4

15

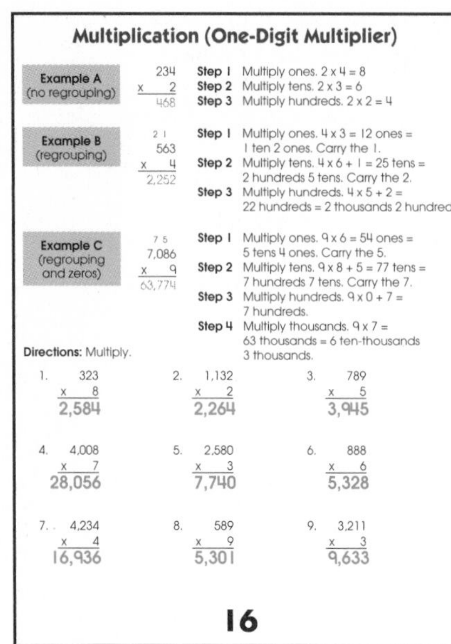

Multiplication (One-Digit Multiplier)

Example A (no regrouping)

234
x 2
468

Step 1 Multiply ones. 2 x 4 = 8
Step 2 Multiply tens. 2 x 3 = 6
Step 3 Multiply hundreds. 2 x 2 = 4

Example B (regrouping)

2 1
563
x 4
2,252

Step 1 Multiply ones. 4 x 3 = 12 ones = 1 ten 2 ones. Carry the 1.
Step 2 Multiply tens. 4 x 6 + 1 = 25 tens = 2 hundreds 5 tens. Carry the 2.
Step 3 Multiply hundreds. 4 x 5 + 2 = 22 hundreds = 2 thousands 2 hundreds

Example C (regrouping and zeros)

7 5
7,086
x 9
63,774

Step 1 Multiply ones. 9 x 6 = 54 ones = 5 tens 4 ones. Carry the 5.
Step 2 Multiply tens. 9 x 8 + 5 = 77 tens = 7 hundreds 7 tens. Carry the 7.
Step 3 Multiply hundreds. 9 x 0 + 7 = 7 hundreds.
Step 4 Multiply thousands. 9 x 7 = 63 thousands = 6 ten-thousands 3 thousands.

Directions: Multiply.

1. 323 x 8 = 2,584
2. 1,132 x 2 = 2,264
3. 789 x 5 = 3,945
4. 4,008 x 7 = 28,056
5. 2,580 x 3 = 7,740
6. 888 x 6 = 5,328
7. 4,234 x 4 = 16,936
8. 589 x 9 = 5,301
9. 3,211 x 3 = 9,633

16

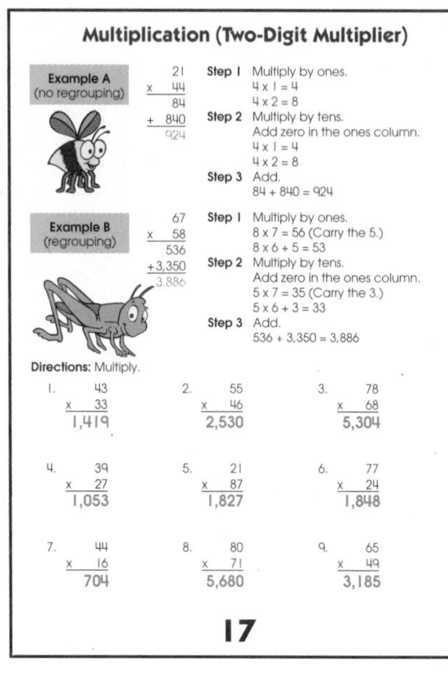

Multiplication (Two-Digit Multiplier)

Example A (no regrouping)

21
x 44
84
+ 840
924

Step 1 Multiply by ones.
4 x 1 = 4
4 x 2 = 8
Step 2 Multiply by tens.
Add zero in the ones column.
4 x 1 = 4
4 x 2 = 8
Step 3 Add.
84 + 840 = 924

Example B (regrouping)

67
x 58
536
+3,350
3,886

Step 1 Multiply by ones.
8 x 7 = 56 (Carry the 5.)
8 x 6 + 5 = 53
Step 2 Multiply by tens.
Add zero in the ones column.
5 x 7 = 35 (Carry the 3.)
5 x 6 + 3 = 33
Step 3 Add.
536 + 3,350 = 3,886

Directions: Multiply.

1. 43 x 33 = 1,419
2. 55 x 46 = 2,530
3. 78 x 68 = 5,304
4. 39 x 27 = 1,053
5. 21 x 87 = 1,827
6. 77 x 24 = 1,848
7. 44 x 16 = 704
8. 80 x 71 = 5,680
9. 65 x 49 = 3,185

17

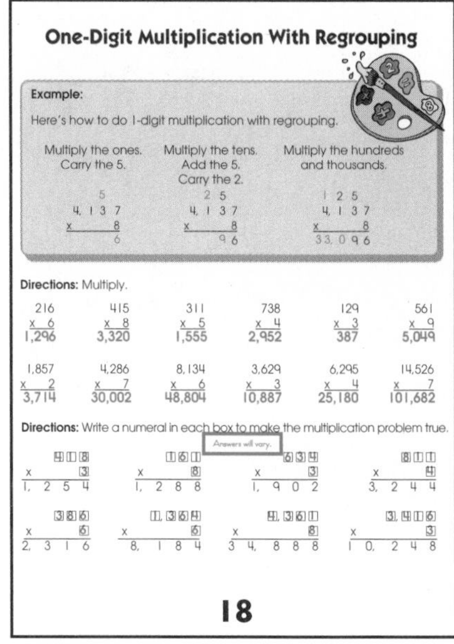

One-Digit Multiplication With Regrouping

Example:

Here's how to do 1-digit multiplication with regrouping.

Multiply the ones. Carry the 5.	Multiply the tens. Add the 5. Carry the 2.	Multiply the hundreds and thousands.
5 4,137 x 8 6	2 5 4,137 x 8 96	1 2 5 4,137 x 8 33,096

Directions: Multiply.

216 x 6 = 1,296
415 x 8 = 3,320
311 x 5 = 1,555
738 x 4 = 2,952
129 x 3 = 387
561 x 9 = 5,049

1,857 x 2 = 3,714
4,286 x 7 = 30,002
8,134 x 6 = 48,804
3,629 x 3 = 10,887
6,295 x 4 = 25,180
14,526 x 7 = 101,682

Directions: Write a numeral in each box to make the multiplication problem true.

Answers will vary.

418 x 3 = 1,254
136 x 8 = 1,288
634 x 3 = 1,902
811 x 4 = 3,244

386 x 6 = 2,316
1,364 x 6 = 8,184
4,361 x 8 = 34,888
3,416 x 3 = 10,248

18

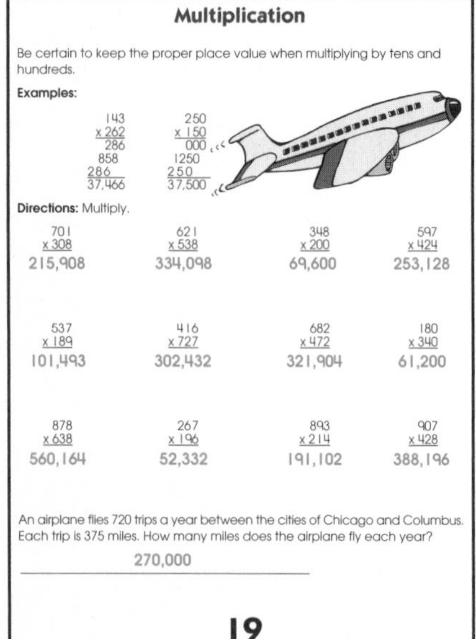

Multiplication

Be certain to keep the proper place value when multiplying by tens and hundreds.

Examples:

143
x 262
286
858
286
37,466

250
x 150
000
1250
250
37,500

Directions: Multiply.

701 x 308 = 215,908
621 x 538 = 334,098
348 x 200 = 69,600
597 x 424 = 253,128

537 x 189 = 101,493
416 x 727 = 302,432
682 x 472 = 321,904
180 x 340 = 61,200

878 x 638 = 560,164
267 x 196 = 52,332
893 x 214 = 191,102
907 x 428 = 388,196

An airplane flies 720 trips a year between the cities of Chicago and Columbus. Each trip is 375 miles. How many miles does the airplane fly each year?

270,000

19

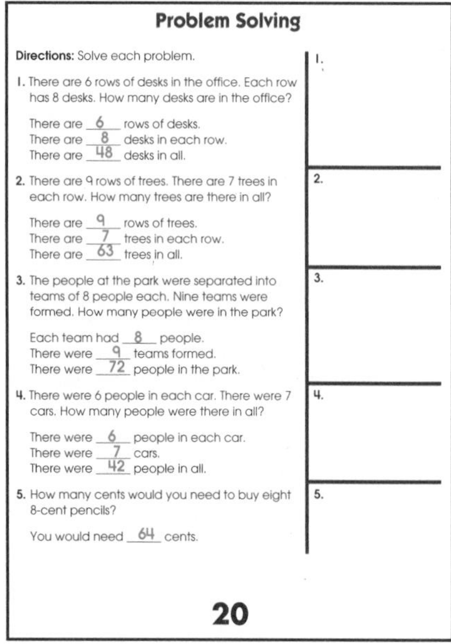

Problem Solving

Directions: Solve each problem.

1. There are 6 rows of desks in the office. Each row has 8 desks. How many desks are in the office?

There are 6 rows of desks.
There are 8 desks in each row.
There are 48 desks in all.

2. There are 9 rows of trees. There are 7 trees in each row. How many trees are there in all?

There are 9 rows of trees.
There are 7 trees in each row.
There are 63 trees in all.

3. The people at the park were separated into teams of 8 people each. Nine teams were formed. How many people were in the park?

Each team had 8 people.
There were 9 teams formed.
There were 72 people in the park.

4. There were 6 people in each car. There were 7 cars. How many people were there in all?

There were 6 people in each car.
There were 7 cars.
There were 42 people in all.

5. How many cents would you need to buy eight 8-cent pencils?

You would need 64 cents.

20

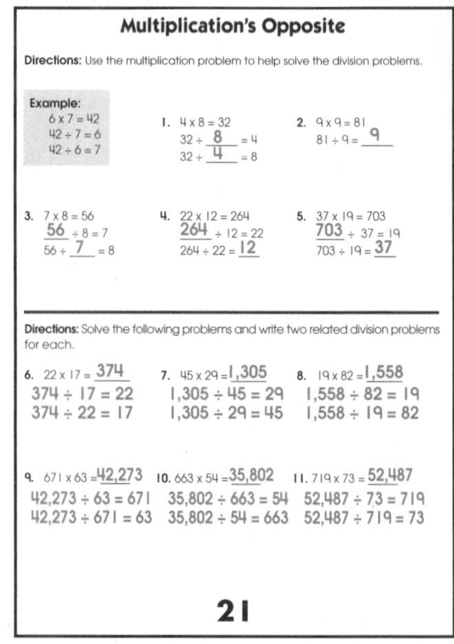

Multiplication's Opposite

Directions: Use the multiplication problem to help solve the division problems.

Example:
6 x 7 = 42
42 ÷ 7 = 6
42 ÷ 6 = 7

1. 4 x 8 = 32
32 ÷ 8 = 4
32 ÷ 4 = 8

2. 9 x 9 = 81
81 ÷ 9 = 9

3. 7 x 8 = 56
56 ÷ 8 = 7
56 ÷ 7 = 8

4. 22 x 12 = 264
264 ÷ 12 = 22
264 ÷ 22 = 12

5. 37 x 19 = 703
703 ÷ 37 = 19
703 ÷ 19 = 37

Directions: Solve the following problems and write two related division problems for each.

6. 22 x 17 = 374
374 ÷ 17 = 22
374 ÷ 22 = 17

7. 45 x 29 = 1,305
1,305 ÷ 45 = 29
1,305 ÷ 29 = 45

8. 19 x 82 = 1,558
1,558 ÷ 82 = 19
1,558 ÷ 19 = 82

9. 671 x 63 = 42,273
42,273 ÷ 63 = 671
42,273 ÷ 671 = 63

10. 663 x 54 = 35,802
35,802 ÷ 663 = 54
35,802 ÷ 54 = 663

11. 719 x 73 = 52,487
52,487 ÷ 73 = 719
52,487 ÷ 719 = 73

21

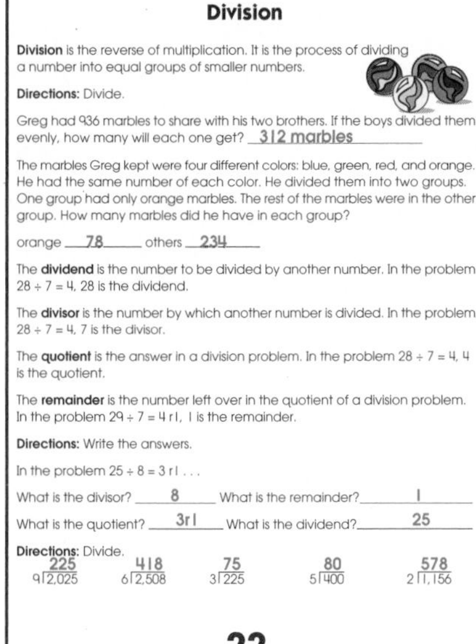

Division

Division is the reverse of multiplication. It is the process of dividing a number into equal groups of smaller numbers.

Directions: Divide.

Greg had 936 marbles to share with his two brothers. If the boys divided them evenly, how many will each one get? 312 marbles

The marbles Greg kept were four different colors: blue, green, red, and orange. He had the same number of each color. He divided them into two groups. One group had only orange marbles. The rest of the marbles were in the other group. How many marbles did he have in each group?

orange 78 others 234

The **dividend** is the number to be divided by another number. In the problem 28 ÷ 7 = 4, 28 is the dividend.

The **divisor** is the number by which another number is divided. In the problem 28 ÷ 7 = 4, 7 is the divisor.

The **quotient** is the answer in a division problem. In the problem 28 ÷ 7 = 4, 4 is the quotient.

The **remainder** is the number left over in the quotient of a division problem. In the problem 29 ÷ 7 = 4 r1, 1 is the remainder.

Directions: Write the answers.

In the problem 25 ÷ 8 = 3 r1 . . .

What is the divisor? 8 What is the remainder? 1

What is the quotient? 3r1 What is the dividend? 25

Directions: Divide.

9⟌2,025 = 225 6⟌2,508 = 418 3⟌225 = 75 5⟌400 = 80 2⟌1,156 = 578

22

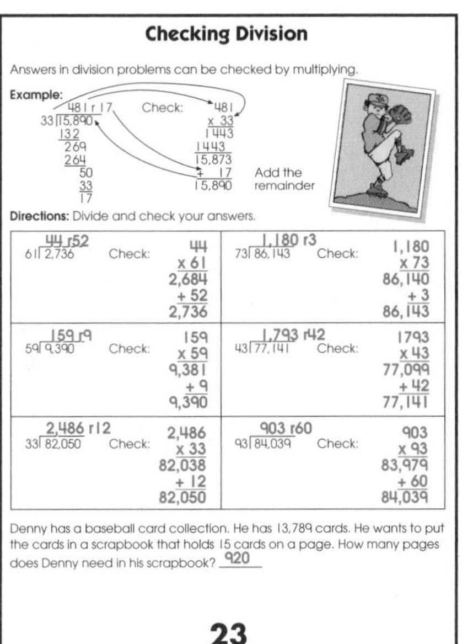

Checking Division

Answers in division problems can be checked by multiplying.

Example:

33⟌15,890 = 481 r17 Check: 481 x 33 = 15,873 + 17 = 15,890 Add the remainder

Directions: Divide and check your answers.

61⟌2,736 = 44 r52 Check: 44 x 61 = 2,684 + 52 = 2,736	73⟌86,143 = 1,180 r3 Check: 1,180 x 73 = 86,140 + 3 = 86,143
59⟌9,390 = 159 r9 Check: 159 x 59 = 9,381 + 9 = 9,390	43⟌77,141 = 1,793 r42 Check: 1793 x 43 = 77,099 + 42 = 77,141
33⟌82,050 = 2,486 r12 Check: 2,486 x 33 = 82,038 + 12 = 82,050	93⟌84,039 = 903 r60 Check: 903 x 93 = 83,979 + 60 = 84,039

Denny has a baseball card collection. He has 13,789 cards. He wants to put the cards in a scrapbook that holds 15 cards on a page. How many pages does Denny need in his scrapbook? 920

23

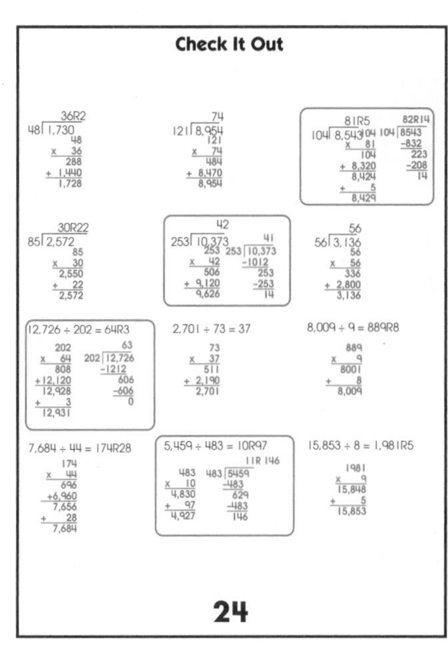

Check It Out

48⟌1,730 = 36R2; 48 x 36 = 288 + 1,440 = 1,728

121⟌8,954 = 74; 121 x 74 = 484 + 8,470 = 8,954

104⟌8,543 = 81R5 / 82R14; 104 x 81 = 104 + 8,320 = 8,424 + 5 = 8,429; 104⟌8543 −832 = 223 −208 = 14

85⟌2,572 = 30R22; 85 x 30 = 2,550 + 22 = 2,572

253⟌10,373 = 42 / 41; 253 x 42 = 506 + 9,120 = 9,626; 253⟌10,373 −1012 = 253 −253 = 14

56⟌3,136 = 56; 56 x 56 = 336 + 2,800 = 3,136

12,726 ÷ 202 = 64R3; 202 x 64 = 808 + 12,120 = 12,928 + 3 = 12,931; 202⟌12,726 = 63, −1212 = 606, −606 = 0

2,701 ÷ 73 = 37; 73 x 37 = 511 + 2,190 = 2,701

8,009 ÷ 9 = 889R8; 889 x 9 = 8001 + 8 = 8,009

7,684 ÷ 44 = 174R28; 174 x 44 = 696 + 6,960 = 7,656 + 28 = 7,684

5,459 ÷ 483 = 10R97; 483 x 10 = 4,830 + 97 = 4,927; 483⟌5459 = 11R 146, −483 = 629, −483 = 146

15,853 ÷ 8 = 1,981R5; 1981 x 8 = 15,848 + 5 = 15,853

24

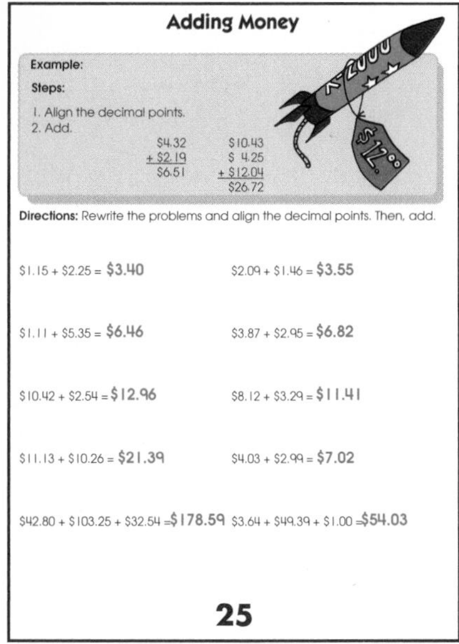

Adding Money

Example:

Steps:

1. Align the decimal points.
2. Add.

$4.32 + $2.19 = $6.51 $10.43 + $4.25 + $12.04 = $26.72

Directions: Rewrite the problems and align the decimal points. Then, add.

$1.15 + $2.25 = $3.40 $2.09 + $1.46 = $3.55

$1.11 + $5.35 = $6.46 $3.87 + $2.95 = $6.82

$10.42 + $2.54 = $12.96 $8.12 + $3.29 = $11.41

$11.13 + $10.26 = $21.39 $4.03 + $2.99 = $7.02

$42.80 + $103.25 + $32.54 = $178.59 $3.64 + $49.39 + $1.00 = $54.03

25

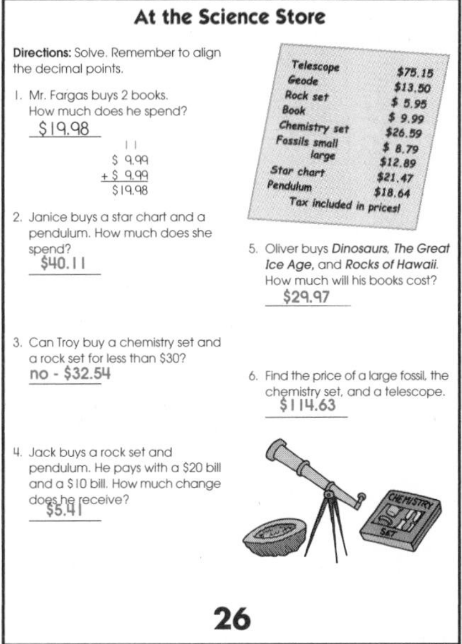

At the Science Store

Directions: Solve. Remember to align the decimal points.

Telescope	$75.15
Geode	$13.50
Rock set	$ 5.95
Book	$ 9.99
Chemistry set	$26.59
Fossils small	$ 8.79
large	$12.89
Star chart	$21.47
Pendulum	$18.64

Tax included in prices!

1. Mr. Fargas buys 2 books. How much does he spend? $19.98 ($ 9.99 + $ 9.99 = $19.98)
2. Janice buys a star chart and a pendulum. How much does she spend? $40.11
3. Can Troy buy a chemistry set and a rock set for less than $30? no - $32.54
4. Jack buys a rock set and pendulum. He pays with a $20 bill and a $10 bill. How much change does he receive? $5.41
5. Oliver buys *Dinosaurs, The Great Ice Age,* and *Rocks of Hawaii.* How much will his books cost? $29.97
6. Find the price of a large fossil, the chemistry set, and a telescope. $114.63

26

Multiplying Money

Example:

Joey buys 14 paperback books for $1.95 each. How much does he spend?

$1.95 x 14 = 780 + 1950 = $27.30 ← set decimal point two numbers in from the right

Directions: Rewrite the problems and multiply.

$1.55 x 7 = $10.85 $10.85 x 19 = $206.15

$3.06 x 9 = $27.54 $5.35 x 12 = $64.20

$10.00 x 15 = $150.00 $1.25 x 105 = $131.25

$9.87 x 13 = $128.31 $4.95 x 22 = $108.90

1. Lauren buys wood for bookshelves at a cost of $0.58 per foot. If she buys 27 feet, how much does she spend? $15.66
2. Which costs more: 5 new books for $5.97 each or 12 used books for $2.50 each? the used books

27

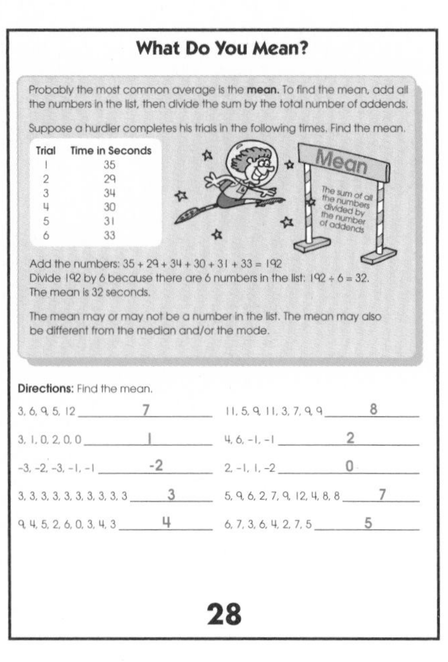

What Do You Mean?

Probably the most common average is the **mean.** To find the mean, add all the numbers in the list, then divide the sum by the total number of addends.

Suppose a hurdler completes his trials in the following times. Find the mean.

Trial	Time in Seconds
1	35
2	29
3	34
4	30
5	31
6	33

Mean
The sum of all the numbers divided by the number of addends

Add the numbers: 35 + 29 + 34 + 30 + 31 + 33 = 192
Divide 192 by 6 because there are 6 numbers in the list: 192 ÷ 6 = 32.
The mean is 32 seconds.

The mean may or may not be a number in the list. The mean may also be different from the median and/or the mode.

Directions: Find the mean.

3, 6, 9, 5, 12 ___7___ 11, 5, 9, 11, 3, 7, 9, 9 ___8___
3, 1, 0, 2, 0, 0 ___1___ 4, 6, -1, -1 ___2___
-3, -2, -3, -1, -1 ___-2___ 2, -1, 1, -2 ___0___
3, 3, 3, 3, 3, 3, 3, 3, 3 ___3___ 5, 9, 6, 2, 7, 9, 12, 4, 8, 8 ___7___
9, 4, 5, 2, 6, 0, 3, 4, 3 ___4___ 6, 7, 3, 6, 4, 2, 7, 5 ___5___

28

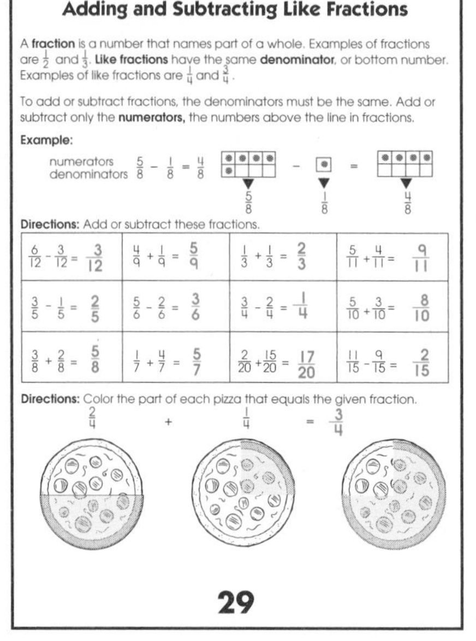

Adding and Subtracting Like Fractions

A **fraction** is a number that names part of a whole. Examples of fractions are $\frac{1}{2}$ and $\frac{1}{3}$. **Like fractions** have the same **denominator**, or bottom number. Examples of like fractions are $\frac{1}{4}$ and $\frac{3}{4}$.

To add or subtract fractions, the denominators must be the same. Add or subtract only the **numerators,** the numbers above the line in fractions.

Example:

numerators / denominators $\frac{5}{8} - \frac{1}{8} = \frac{4}{8}$

Directions: Add or subtract these fractions.

$\frac{6}{12} - \frac{3}{12} = \frac{3}{12}$	$\frac{4}{9} + \frac{1}{9} = \frac{5}{9}$	$\frac{1}{3} + \frac{1}{3} = \frac{2}{3}$	$\frac{5}{11} + \frac{4}{11} = \frac{9}{11}$
$\frac{3}{5} - \frac{1}{5} = \frac{2}{5}$	$\frac{5}{6} - \frac{2}{6} = \frac{3}{6}$	$\frac{3}{4} - \frac{2}{4} = \frac{1}{4}$	$\frac{5}{10} + \frac{3}{10} = \frac{8}{10}$
$\frac{3}{8} + \frac{2}{8} = \frac{5}{8}$	$\frac{1}{7} + \frac{4}{7} = \frac{5}{7}$	$\frac{2}{20} + \frac{15}{20} = \frac{17}{20}$	$\frac{11}{15} - \frac{9}{15} = \frac{2}{15}$

Directions: Color the part of each pizza that equals the given fraction.

$\frac{2}{4}$ + $\frac{1}{4}$ = $\frac{3}{4}$

29

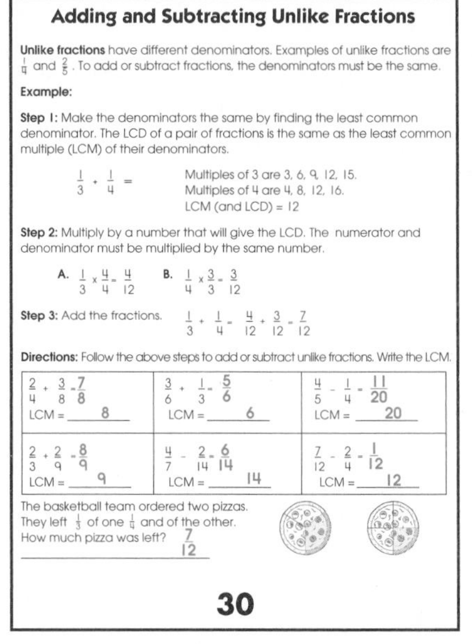

Adding and Subtracting Unlike Fractions

Unlike fractions have different denominators. Examples of unlike fractions are $\frac{1}{4}$ and $\frac{2}{5}$. To add or subtract fractions, the denominators must be the same.

Example:

Step 1: Make the denominators the same by finding the least common denominator. The LCD of a pair of fractions is the same as the least common multiple (LCM) of their denominators.

$\frac{1}{3} + \frac{1}{4} =$ Multiples of 3 are 3, 6, 9, 12, 15. Multiples of 4 are 4, 8, 12, 16. LCM (and LCD) = 12

Step 2: Multiply by a number that will give the LCD. The numerator and denominator must be multiplied by the same number.

A. $\frac{1}{3} \times \frac{4}{4} = \frac{4}{12}$ **B.** $\frac{1}{4} \times \frac{3}{3} = \frac{3}{12}$

Step 3: Add the fractions. $\frac{1}{3} + \frac{1}{4} = \frac{4}{12} + \frac{3}{12} = \frac{7}{12}$

Directions: Follow the above steps to add or subtract unlike fractions. Write the LCM.

$\frac{2}{4} + \frac{3}{8} = \frac{7}{8}$ LCM = 8	$\frac{3}{6} + \frac{1}{3} = \frac{5}{6}$ LCM = 6	$\frac{4}{5} - \frac{1}{4} = \frac{11}{20}$ LCM = 20
$\frac{2}{3} + \frac{2}{9} = \frac{8}{9}$ LCM = 9	$\frac{4}{7} - \frac{2}{14} = \frac{6}{14}$ LCM = 14	$\frac{7}{12} - \frac{2}{4} = \frac{1}{12}$ LCM = 12

The basketball team ordered two pizzas. They left $\frac{1}{3}$ of one $\frac{1}{4}$ and of the other. How much pizza was left? $\frac{7}{12}$

30

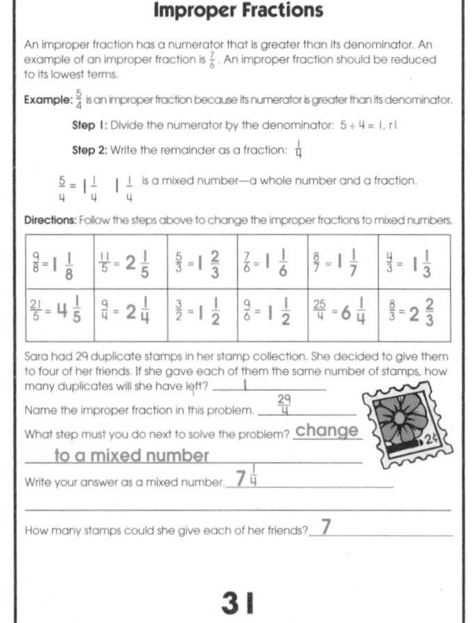

Improper Fractions

An improper fraction has a numerator that is greater than its denominator. An example of an improper fraction is $\frac{7}{6}$. An improper fraction should be reduced to its lowest terms.

Example: $\frac{5}{4}$ is an improper fraction because its numerator is greater than its denominator.

Step 1: Divide the numerator by the denominator: 5 ÷ 4 = 1, r1

Step 2: Write the remainder as a fraction: $\frac{1}{4}$

$\frac{5}{4} = 1\frac{1}{4}$ $1\frac{1}{4}$ is a mixed number—a whole number and a fraction.

Directions: Follow the steps above to change the improper fractions to mixed numbers.

$\frac{9}{8} = 1\frac{1}{8}$	$\frac{11}{5} = 2\frac{1}{5}$	$\frac{5}{3} = 1\frac{2}{3}$	$\frac{7}{6} = 1\frac{1}{6}$	$\frac{8}{7} = 1\frac{1}{7}$	$\frac{4}{3} = 1\frac{1}{3}$
$\frac{21}{5} = 4\frac{1}{5}$	$\frac{9}{4} = 2\frac{1}{4}$	$\frac{3}{2} = 1\frac{1}{2}$	$\frac{9}{6} = 1\frac{1}{2}$	$\frac{25}{4} = 6\frac{1}{4}$	$\frac{8}{3} = 2\frac{2}{3}$

Sara had 29 duplicate stamps in her stamp collection. She decided to give them to four of her friends. If she gave each of them the same number of stamps, how many duplicates will she have left? ___1___

Name the improper fraction in this problem. $\frac{29}{4}$

What step must you do next to solve the problem? change to a mixed number

Write your answer as a mixed number. $7\frac{1}{4}$

How many stamps could she give each of her friends? ___7___

31

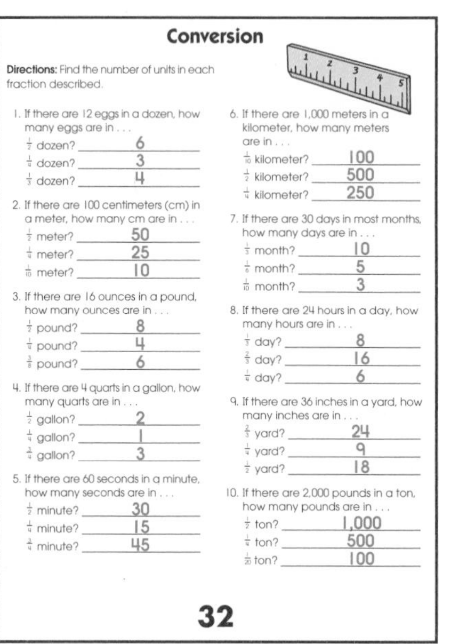

Conversion

Directions: Find the number of units in each fraction described.

1. If there are 12 eggs in a dozen, how many eggs are in . . .
   $\frac{1}{2}$ dozen? 6
   $\frac{1}{4}$ dozen? 3
   $\frac{1}{3}$ dozen? 4
2. If there are 100 centimeters (cm) in a meter, how many cm are in . . .
   $\frac{1}{2}$ meter? 50
   $\frac{1}{4}$ meter? 25
   $\frac{1}{10}$ meter? 10
3. If there are 16 ounces in a pound, how many ounces are in . . .
   $\frac{1}{2}$ pound? 8
   $\frac{1}{4}$ pound? 4
   $\frac{3}{8}$ pound? 6
4. If there are 4 quarts in a gallon, how many quarts are in . . .
   $\frac{1}{2}$ gallon? 2
   $\frac{1}{4}$ gallon? 1
   $\frac{3}{4}$ gallon? 3
5. If there are 60 seconds in a minute, how many seconds are in . . .
   $\frac{1}{2}$ minute? 30
   $\frac{1}{4}$ minute? 15
   $\frac{3}{4}$ minute? 45
6. If there are 1,000 meters in a kilometer, how many meters are in . . .
   $\frac{1}{10}$ kilometer? 100
   $\frac{1}{2}$ kilometer? 500
   $\frac{1}{4}$ kilometer? 250
7. If there are 30 days in most months, how many days are in . . .
   $\frac{1}{3}$ month? 10
   $\frac{1}{6}$ month? 5
   $\frac{1}{10}$ month? 3
8. If there are 24 hours in a day, how many hours are in . . .
   $\frac{1}{3}$ day? 8
   $\frac{2}{3}$ day? 16
   $\frac{1}{4}$ day? 6
9. If there are 36 inches in a yard, how many inches are in . . .
   $\frac{2}{3}$ yard? 24
   $\frac{1}{4}$ yard? 9
   $\frac{1}{2}$ yard? 18
10. If there are 2,000 pounds in a ton, how many pounds are in . . .
    $\frac{1}{2}$ ton? 1,000
    $\frac{1}{4}$ ton? 500
    $\frac{1}{20}$ ton? 100

32

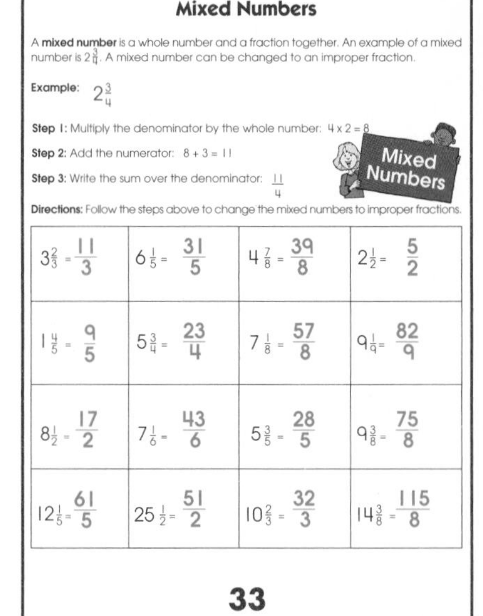

Mixed Numbers

A **mixed number** is a whole number and a fraction together. An example of a mixed number is $2\frac{3}{4}$. A mixed number can be changed to an improper fraction.

Example: $2\frac{3}{4}$

Step 1: Multiply the denominator by the whole number: 4 x 2 = 8

Step 2: Add the numerator: 8 + 3 = 11

Step 3: Write the sum over the denominator: $\frac{11}{4}$

Mixed Numbers

Directions: Follow the steps above to change the mixed numbers to improper fractions.

$3\frac{2}{3} = \frac{11}{3}$	$6\frac{1}{5} = \frac{31}{5}$	$4\frac{7}{8} = \frac{39}{8}$	$2\frac{1}{2} = \frac{5}{2}$
$1\frac{4}{5} = \frac{9}{5}$	$5\frac{3}{4} = \frac{23}{4}$	$7\frac{1}{8} = \frac{57}{8}$	$9\frac{1}{9} = \frac{82}{9}$
$8\frac{1}{2} = \frac{17}{2}$	$7\frac{1}{6} = \frac{43}{6}$	$5\frac{3}{5} = \frac{28}{5}$	$9\frac{3}{8} = \frac{75}{8}$
$12\frac{1}{5} = \frac{61}{5}$	$25\frac{1}{2} = \frac{51}{2}$	$10\frac{2}{3} = \frac{32}{3}$	$14\frac{3}{8} = \frac{115}{8}$

33

Subtracting Mixed Numbers

Directions: To subtract mixed numbers, first find the least common denominator. Reduce the answer to its lowest terms.

Directions: Subtract. Reduce to lowest terms.

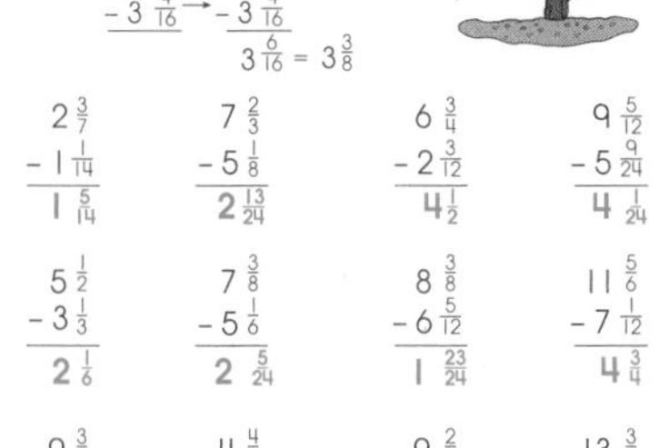

Example:

$$\begin{array}{r} 6\frac{5}{8} \\ -\,3\frac{4}{16} \\ \hline \end{array} \rightarrow \begin{array}{r} 6\frac{10}{16} \\ -\,3\frac{4}{16} \\ \hline 3\frac{6}{16} \end{array} = 3\frac{3}{8}$$

$$\begin{array}{r} 2\frac{3}{7} \\ -\,1\frac{1}{14} \\ \hline 1\frac{5}{14} \end{array} \qquad \begin{array}{r} 7\frac{2}{3} \\ -\,5\frac{1}{8} \\ \hline 2\frac{13}{24} \end{array} \qquad \begin{array}{r} 6\frac{3}{4} \\ -\,2\frac{3}{12} \\ \hline 4\frac{1}{2} \end{array} \qquad \begin{array}{r} 9\frac{5}{12} \\ -\,5\frac{9}{24} \\ \hline 4\frac{1}{24} \end{array}$$

$$\begin{array}{r} 5\frac{1}{2} \\ -\,3\frac{1}{3} \\ \hline 2\frac{1}{6} \end{array} \qquad \begin{array}{r} 7\frac{3}{8} \\ -\,5\frac{1}{6} \\ \hline 2\frac{5}{24} \end{array} \qquad \begin{array}{r} 8\frac{3}{8} \\ -\,6\frac{5}{12} \\ \hline 1\frac{23}{24} \end{array} \qquad \begin{array}{r} 11\frac{5}{6} \\ -\,7\frac{1}{12} \\ \hline 4\frac{3}{4} \end{array}$$

$$\begin{array}{r} 9\frac{3}{5} \\ -\,7\frac{1}{15} \\ \hline 2\frac{8}{15} \end{array} \qquad \begin{array}{r} 4\frac{4}{5} \\ -\,2\frac{1}{4} \\ \hline 2\frac{11}{20} \end{array} \qquad \begin{array}{r} 9\frac{2}{3} \\ -\,4\frac{1}{6} \\ \hline 5\frac{1}{2} \end{array} \qquad \begin{array}{r} 13\frac{3}{8} \\ -\,9\frac{3}{16} \\ \hline 4\frac{3}{16} \end{array}$$

The Rodriguez Farm has $9\frac{1}{2}$ acres of corn. The Johnson Farm has $7\frac{1}{3}$ acres of corn. How many more acres of corn does the Rodriguez Farm have? $2\frac{1}{6}$

34

Fractions: Mixed to Improper

Directions: Change the fractions to mixed numbers. Shade in each answer to find the path to the pot of gold.

1. $\frac{11}{9} = 1\frac{2}{9}$ 2. $\frac{8}{3} = 2\frac{2}{3}$ 3. $\frac{8}{7} = 1\frac{1}{7}$ 4. $\frac{11}{6} = 1\frac{5}{6}$
5. $\frac{7}{3} = 2\frac{1}{3}$ 6. $\frac{7}{6} = 1\frac{1}{6}$ 7. $\frac{9}{4} = 2\frac{1}{4}$ 8. $\frac{8}{5} = 1\frac{3}{5}$
9. $\frac{4}{3} = 1\frac{1}{3}$ 10. $\frac{7}{2} = 3\frac{1}{2}$ 11. $\frac{3}{2} = 1\frac{1}{2}$ 12. $\frac{6}{5} = 1\frac{1}{5}$
13. $\frac{7}{4} = 1\frac{3}{4}$ 14. $\frac{9}{2} = 4\frac{1}{2}$ 15. $\frac{11}{8} = 1\frac{3}{8}$ 16. $\frac{5}{2} = 2\frac{1}{2}$
17. $\frac{9}{7} = 1\frac{2}{7}$ 18. $\frac{11}{4} = 2\frac{3}{4}$ 19. $\frac{17}{12} = 1\frac{5}{12}$ 20. $\frac{13}{12} = 1\frac{1}{12}$

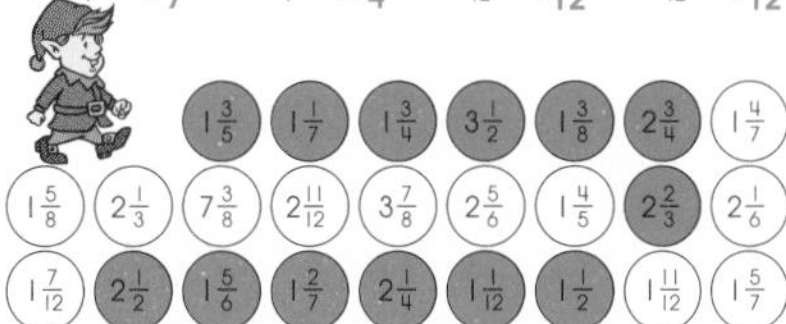

		$1\frac{3}{5}$	$1\frac{1}{7}$	$1\frac{3}{4}$	$3\frac{1}{2}$	$1\frac{3}{8}$	$2\frac{3}{4}$	$1\frac{4}{7}$
$1\frac{5}{8}$	$2\frac{1}{3}$	$7\frac{3}{8}$	$2\frac{11}{12}$	$3\frac{7}{8}$	$2\frac{5}{6}$	$1\frac{4}{5}$	$2\frac{2}{3}$	$2\frac{1}{6}$
$1\frac{7}{12}$	$2\frac{1}{2}$	$1\frac{5}{6}$	$1\frac{2}{7}$	$2\frac{1}{4}$	$1\frac{1}{12}$	$1\frac{1}{2}$	$1\frac{11}{12}$	$1\frac{5}{7}$
$1\frac{1}{5}$	$4\frac{2}{3}$	$3\frac{1}{6}$	$1\frac{3}{7}$	$1\frac{4}{9}$	$2\frac{1}{5}$	$3\frac{1}{3}$	$4\frac{1}{3}$	$2\frac{6}{7}$
$2\frac{3}{11}$	$1\frac{2}{9}$	$1\frac{1}{3}$	$1\frac{5}{12}$	$2\frac{1}{3}$	$4\frac{1}{2}$	$1\frac{1}{6}$		

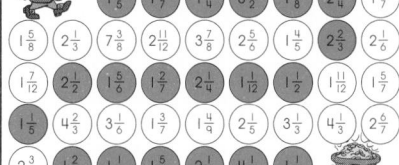

35

Multiplying Fractions

To multiply fractions, follow these steps:

$\frac{1}{2} \times \frac{3}{4} =$ **Step 1:** Multiply the numerators. $1 \times 3 = 3$
Step 2: Multiply the denominators. $2 \times 4 = 8$

When multiplying a fraction by a whole number, first change the whole number to a fraction.

Example:

$\frac{1}{2} \times 8 = \frac{1}{2} \times \frac{8}{1} = \frac{8}{2} = 4$ reduced to lowest terms

Directions: Multiply. Reduce your answers to lowest terms.

$\frac{3}{4} \times \frac{1}{6} = \frac{1}{8}$	$\frac{1}{2} \times \frac{5}{8} = \frac{5}{16}$	$\frac{2}{3} \times \frac{1}{6} = \frac{1}{9}$	$\frac{2}{3} \times \frac{1}{2} = \frac{1}{3}$
$\frac{5}{6} \times 4 = 3\frac{1}{3}$	$\frac{3}{8} \times \frac{1}{16} = \frac{3}{128}$	$\frac{1}{5} \times 5 = 1$	$\frac{7}{8} \times \frac{3}{4} = \frac{21}{32}$
$\frac{7}{11} \times \frac{1}{3} = \frac{7}{33}$	$\frac{2}{9} \times \frac{9}{4} = \frac{1}{2}$	$\frac{1}{3} \times \frac{1}{3} \times \frac{1}{3} = \frac{1}{27}$	$\frac{1}{8} \times \frac{1}{4} \times \frac{1}{2} = \frac{1}{64}$

Jennifer has 10 pets. Two-fifths of the pets are cats, one-half are fish and one-tenth are dogs. How many of each pet does she have?

Cats = 4
Fish = 5
Dogs = 1

36

Multiplying Mixed Numbers

Multiply mixed numbers by first changing them to improper fractions. Always reduce your answers to lowest terms.

Example:

$2\frac{1}{3} \times 1\frac{1}{8} = \frac{7}{3} \times \frac{9}{8} = \frac{63}{24} = 2\frac{15}{24} = 2\frac{5}{8}$

Directions: Multiply. Reduce to lowest terms.

$4\frac{1}{4} \times 2\frac{1}{5} = 9\frac{7}{20}$	$1\frac{1}{3} \times 3\frac{1}{4} = 4\frac{1}{3}$	$1\frac{1}{9} \times 3\frac{3}{5} = 4$
$1\frac{6}{7} \times 4\frac{1}{2} = 8\frac{5}{14}$	$2\frac{3}{4} \times 2\frac{3}{5} = 7\frac{3}{20}$	$4\frac{2}{3} \times 3\frac{1}{7} = 14\frac{2}{3}$
$6\frac{2}{5} \times 2\frac{1}{8} = 13\frac{3}{5}$	$3\frac{1}{7} \times 4\frac{5}{8} = 14\frac{15}{28}$	$7\frac{3}{8} \times 2\frac{1}{9} = 15\frac{41}{72}$

Sunnyside Farm has two barns with 25 stalls in each barn. Cows use $\frac{3}{5}$ of the stalls, and horses use the rest.

How many stalls are for cows? 30

How many are for horses? 20

(Hint: First, find how many total stalls are in the two barns.)

37

Dividing Fractions

To divide fractions, follow these steps:

$\frac{3}{4} \div \frac{1}{4} =$

Step 1: "Invert" the divisor. That means to turn it upside down.

$\frac{3}{4} \div \frac{4}{1}$

Step 2: Multiply the two fractions:

$\frac{3}{4} \times \frac{4}{1} = \frac{12}{4}$

Step 3: Reduce the fraction to lowest terms by dividing the denominator into the numerator.

$12 \div 4 = 3$
$\frac{3}{4} \div \frac{1}{4} = 3$

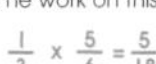

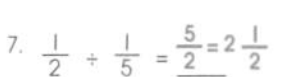

Directions: Follow the above steps to divide fractions.

$\frac{1}{4} \div \frac{1}{5} = 1\frac{1}{4}$	$\frac{1}{3} \div \frac{1}{12} = 4$	$\frac{3}{4} \div \frac{1}{3} = 2\frac{1}{4}$
$\frac{5}{12} \div \frac{1}{3} = 1\frac{1}{4}$	$\frac{3}{4} \div \frac{1}{6} = 4\frac{1}{2}$	$\frac{2}{9} \div \frac{2}{3} = \frac{1}{3}$
$\frac{3}{7} \div \frac{1}{4} = 1\frac{5}{7}$	$\frac{2}{3} \div \frac{4}{6} = 1$	$\frac{1}{8} \div \frac{2}{3} = \frac{3}{16}$
$\frac{4}{5} \div \frac{1}{3} = 2\frac{2}{5}$	$\frac{4}{8} \div \frac{1}{2} = 1$	$\frac{5}{12} \div \frac{6}{8} = \frac{5}{9}$

38

Fractions: Multiplication and Division

Directions: Solve.

1. $\frac{7}{9} \times \frac{1}{4} = \frac{7}{36}$
2. $\frac{5}{6} \times \frac{1}{10} = \frac{5}{60} = \frac{1}{12}$
3. $\frac{9}{10} \times \frac{2}{3} = \frac{18}{30} = \frac{3}{5}$
4. $8 \times \frac{1}{4} = \frac{8}{4} = 2$
5. $\frac{1}{3} \times 15 = \frac{15}{3} = 5$
6. Jaime sat in his chair for $\frac{5}{6}$ of an hour. For $\frac{1}{3}$ of this time, he worked on this assignment. What fraction of an hour did he work on this assignment?
$\frac{1}{3} \times \frac{5}{6} = \frac{5}{18}$
7. $\frac{1}{2} \div \frac{1}{5} = \frac{5}{2} = 2\frac{1}{2}$
8. $\frac{1}{5} \div \frac{1}{2} = \frac{2}{5}$
9. $\frac{3}{4} \div \frac{3}{8} = \frac{24}{12} = 2$
10. $\frac{7}{16} \div \frac{4}{7} = \frac{49}{64}$

39

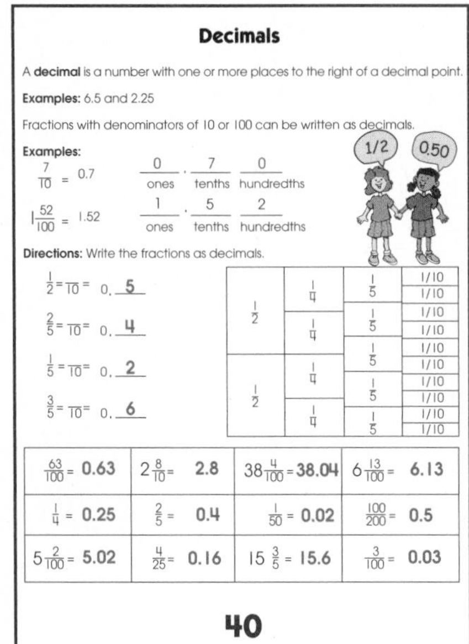

Decimals

A **decimal** is a number with one or more places to the right of a decimal point.

Examples: 6.5 and 2.25

Fractions with denominators of 10 or 100 can be written as decimals.

Examples:

$\frac{7}{10}$ = 0.7 — 0 (ones) . 7 (tenths) 0 (hundredths)

$1\frac{52}{100}$ = 1.52 — 1 (ones) . 5 (tenths) 2 (hundredths)

Directions: Write the fractions as decimals.

$\frac{1}{2} = \frac{}{10} =$ 0. 5

$\frac{2}{5} = \frac{}{10} =$ 0. 4

$\frac{1}{5} = \frac{}{10} =$ 0. 2

$\frac{3}{5} = \frac{}{10} =$ 0. 6

$\frac{63}{100}$ = 0.63	$2\frac{8}{10}$ = 2.8	$38\frac{4}{100}$ = 38.04	$6\frac{13}{100}$ = 6.13
$\frac{1}{4}$ = 0.25	$\frac{2}{5}$ = 0.4	$\frac{1}{50}$ = 0.02	$\frac{100}{200}$ = 0.5
$5\frac{2}{100}$ = 5.02	$\frac{4}{25}$ = 0.16	$15\frac{3}{5}$ = 15.6	$\frac{3}{100}$ = 0.03

40

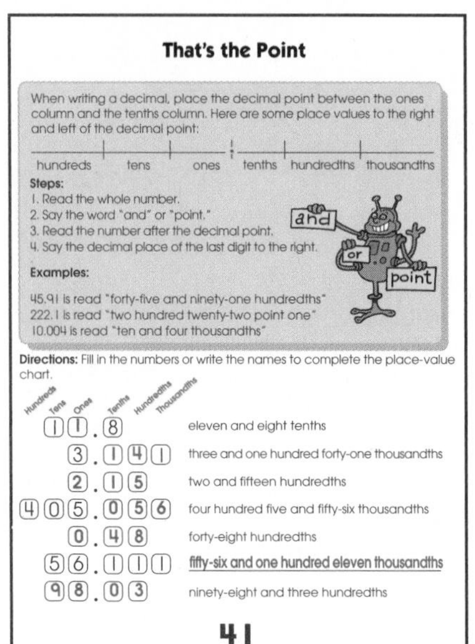

That's the Point

When writing a decimal, place the decimal point between the ones column and the tenths column. Here are some place values to the right and left of the decimal point:

hundreds tens ones . tenths hundredths thousandths

Steps:
1. Read the whole number.
2. Say the word "and" or "point."
3. Read the number after the decimal point.
4. Say the decimal place of the last digit to the right.

Examples:

45.91 is read "forty-five and ninety-one hundredths"
222.1 is read "two hundred twenty-two point one"
10.004 is read "ten and four thousandths"

Directions: Fill in the numbers or write the names to complete the place-value chart.

Hundreds Tens Ones Tenths Hundredths Thousandths

11.8 — eleven and eight tenths
3.141 — three and one hundred forty-one thousandths
2.15 — two and fifteen hundredths
405.056 — four hundred five and fifty-six thousandths
0.48 — forty-eight hundredths
56.111 — fifty-six and one hundred eleven thousandths
98.03 — ninety-eight and three hundredths

41

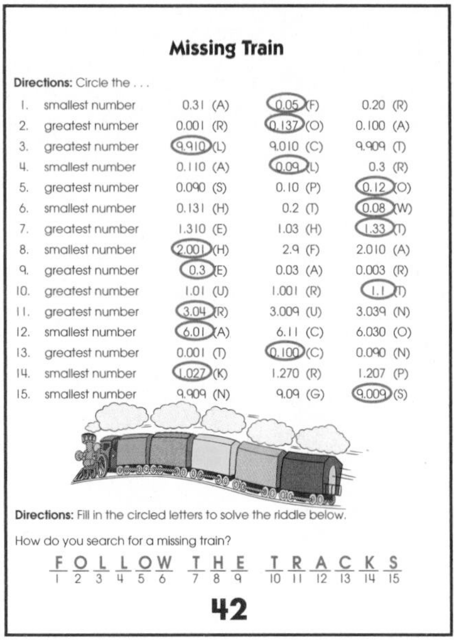

Missing Train

Directions: Circle the . . .

1. smallest number 0.31 (A) **0.05 (F)** 0.20 (R)
2. greatest number 0.001 (R) **0.137 (O)** 0.100 (A)
3. greatest number **9.910 (L)** 9.010 (C) 9.909 (T)
4. smallest number 0.110 (A) **0.09 (L)** 0.3 (R)
5. greatest number 0.090 (S) 0.10 (P) **0.12 (O)**
6. smallest number 0.131 (H) 0.2 (T) **0.08 (W)**
7. greatest number 1.310 (E) 1.03 (H) **1.33 (T)**
8. smallest number **2.001 (H)** 2.9 (F) 2.010 (A)
9. greatest number **0.3 (E)** 0.03 (A) 0.003 (R)
10. greatest number 1.01 (U) 1.001 (R) **1.1 (T)**
11. greatest number **3.04 (R)** 3.009 (U) 3.039 (N)
12. smallest number **6.01 (A)** 6.11 (C) 6.030 (O)
13. greatest number 0.001 (T) **0.100 (C)** 0.090 (N)
14. smallest number **1.027 (K)** 1.270 (R) 1.207 (P)
15. smallest number 9.909 (N) 9.09 (G) **9.009 (S)**

Directions: Fill in the circled letters to solve the riddle below.

How do you search for a missing train?

F O L L O W   T H E   T R A C K S
1 2 3 4 5 6   7 8 9   10 11 12 13 14 15

42

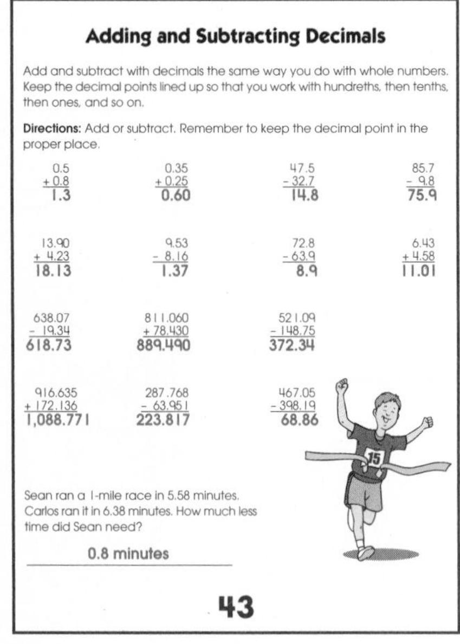

Adding and Subtracting Decimals

Add and subtract with decimals the same way you do with whole numbers. Keep the decimal points lined up so that you work with hundreths, then tenths, then ones, and so on.

Directions: Add or subtract. Remember to keep the decimal point in the proper place.

0.5 + 0.8 = 1.3 | 0.35 + 0.25 = 0.60 | 47.5 − 32.7 = 14.8 | 85.7 − 9.8 = 75.9

13.90 + 4.23 = 18.13 | 9.53 − 8.16 = 1.37 | 72.8 − 63.9 = 8.9 | 6.43 + 4.58 = 11.01

638.07 − 19.34 = 618.73 | 811.060 + 78.430 = 889.490 | 521.09 − 148.75 = 372.34

916.635 + 172.136 = 1,088.771 | 287.768 − 63.951 = 223.817 | 467.05 − 398.19 = 68.86

Sean ran a 1-mile race in 5.58 minutes. Carlos ran it in 6.38 minutes. How much less time did Sean need?

0.8 minutes

43

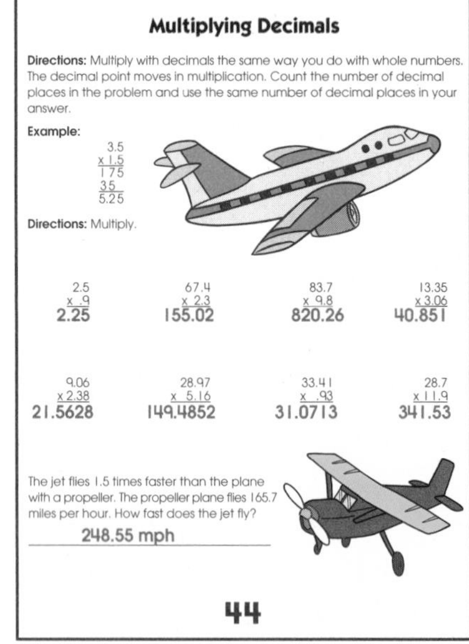

Multiplying Decimals

Directions: Multiply with decimals the same way you do with whole numbers. The decimal point moves in multiplication. Count the number of decimal places in the problem and use the same number of decimal places in your answer.

Example:

3.5 × 1.5: 175 + 35 = 5.25

Directions: Multiply.

2.5 × .9 = 2.25 | 67.4 × 2.3 = 155.02 | 83.7 × 9.8 = 820.26 | 13.35 × 3.06 = 40.851

9.06 × 2.38 = 21.5628 | 28.97 × 5.16 = 149.4852 | 33.41 × .93 = 31.0713 | 28.7 × 11.9 = 341.53

The jet flies 1.5 times faster than the plane with a propeller. The propeller plane flies 165.7 miles per hour. How fast does the jet fly?

248.55 mph

44

Dividing With Decimals

Directions: When the dividend has a decimal, place the decimal point for the answer directly above the decimal point in the dividend. The first one has been done for you.

37.5 ÷ 3 = 12.5 | 34.4 ÷ 4 = 8.6 | 31.6 ÷ 2 = 15.8 | 131.4 ÷ 3 = 43.8

187.5 ÷ 5 = 37.5 | 181.3 ÷ 7 = 25.9 | 340.8 ÷ 6 = 56.8 | 294.3 ÷ 9 = 32.7

135.6 ÷ 3 = 45.2 | 264.5 ÷ 5 = 52.9 | 134.6 ÷ 2 = 67.3 | 754.4 ÷ 8 = 94.3

35.25 ÷ 5 = 7.05 | 79.45 ÷ 7 = 11.35 | 28.71 ÷ 9 = 3.19 | 199.44 ÷ 36 = 5.54

45

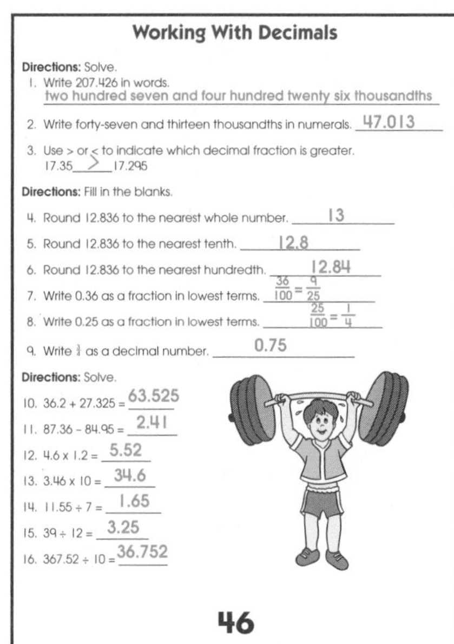

Working With Decimals

Directions: Solve.

1. Write 207.426 in words. two hundred seven and four hundred twenty six thousandths
2. Write forty-seven and thirteen thousandths in numerals. 47.013
3. Use > or < to indicate which decimal fraction is greater. 17.35 > 17.295

Directions: Fill in the blanks.

4. Round 12.836 to the nearest whole number. 13
5. Round 12.836 to the nearest tenth. 12.8
6. Round 12.836 to the nearest hundredth. 12.84
7. Write 0.36 as a fraction in lowest terms. $\frac{36}{100} = \frac{9}{25}$
8. Write 0.25 as a fraction in lowest terms. $\frac{25}{100} = \frac{1}{4}$
9. Write $\frac{3}{4}$ as a decimal number. 0.75

Directions: Solve.

10. 36.2 + 27.325 = 63.525
11. 87.36 – 84.95 = 2.41
12. 4.6 x 1.2 = 5.52
13. 3.46 x 10 = 34.6
14. 11.55 ÷ 7 = 1.65
15. 39 ÷ 12 = 3.25
16. 367.52 ÷ 10 = 36.752

46

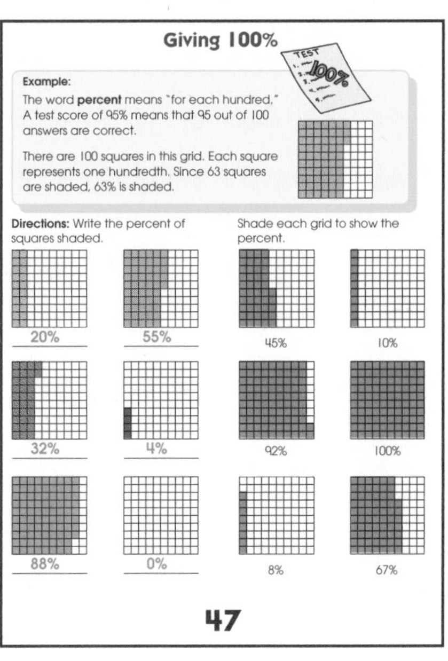

Giving 100%

Example:

The word **percent** means "for each hundred." A test score of 95% means that 95 out of 100 answers are correct.

There are 100 squares in this grid. Each square represents one hundredth. Since 63 squares are shaded, 63% is shaded.

Directions: Write the percent of squares shaded.

20% 55%

32% 4%

88% 0%

Shade each grid to show the percent.

45% 10%

92% 100%

8% 67%

47

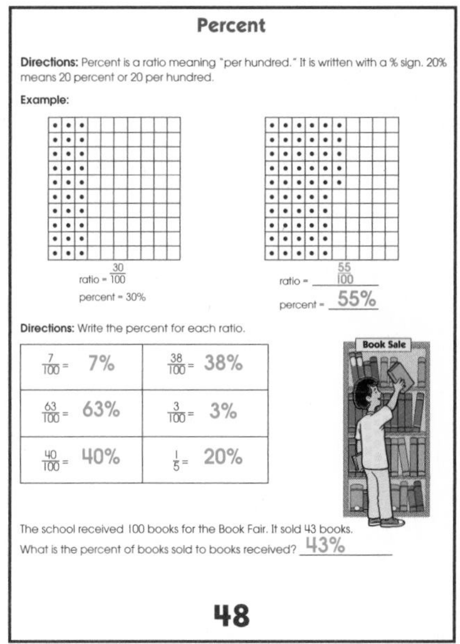

Percent

Directions: Percent is a ratio meaning "per hundred." It is written with a % sign. 20% means 20 percent or 20 per hundred.

Example:

ratio = $\frac{30}{100}$
percent = 30%

ratio = $\frac{55}{100}$
percent = 55%

Directions: Write the percent for each ratio.

$\frac{7}{100}$ = 7%	$\frac{38}{100}$ = 38%
$\frac{63}{100}$ = 63%	$\frac{3}{100}$ = 3%
$\frac{40}{100}$ = 40%	$\frac{1}{5}$ = 20%

The school received 100 books for the Book Fair. It sold 43 books. What is the percent of books sold to books received? 43%

48

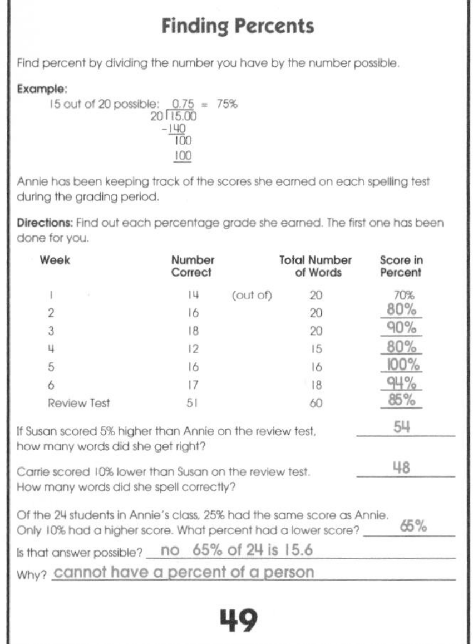

Finding Percents

Find percent by dividing the number you have by the number possible.

Example:

15 out of 20 possible: $20\overline{)15.00}$ = 0.75 = 75%
–140
100
100

Annie has been keeping track of the scores she earned on each spelling test during the grading period.

Directions: Find out each percentage grade she earned. The first one has been done for you.

Week	Number Correct		Total Number of Words	Score in Percent
1	14	(out of)	20	70%
2	16		20	80%
3	18		20	90%
4	12		15	80%
5	16		16	100%
6	17		18	94%
Review Test	51		60	85%

If Susan scored 5% higher than Annie on the review test, how many words did she get right? 54

Carrie scored 10% lower than Susan on the review test. How many words did she spell correctly? 48

Of the 24 students in Annie's class, 25% had the same score as Annie. Only 10% had a higher score. What percent had a lower score? 65%

Is that answer possible? no 65% of 24 is 15.6

Why? cannot have a percent of a person

49

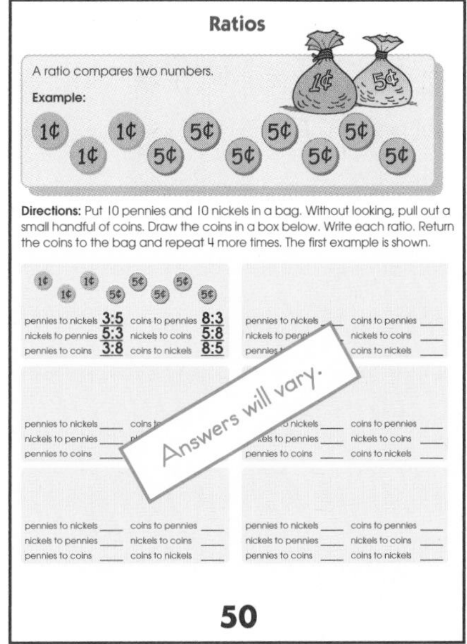

Ratios

A ratio compares two numbers.

Example:

1¢ 1¢ 1¢ 5¢ 5¢ 5¢ 5¢ 5¢ 5¢ 5¢

Directions: Put 10 pennies and 10 nickels in a bag. Without looking, pull out a small handful of coins. Draw the coins in a box below. Write each ratio. Return the coins to the bag and repeat 4 more times. The first example is shown.

pennies to nickels 3:5 coins to pennies 8:3
nickels to pennies 5:3 nickels to coins 5:8
pennies to coins 3:8 coins to nickels 8:5

pennies to nickels ___ coins to pennies ___
nickels to pennies ___ nickels to coins ___
pennies to coins ___ coins to nickels ___

Answers will vary.

50

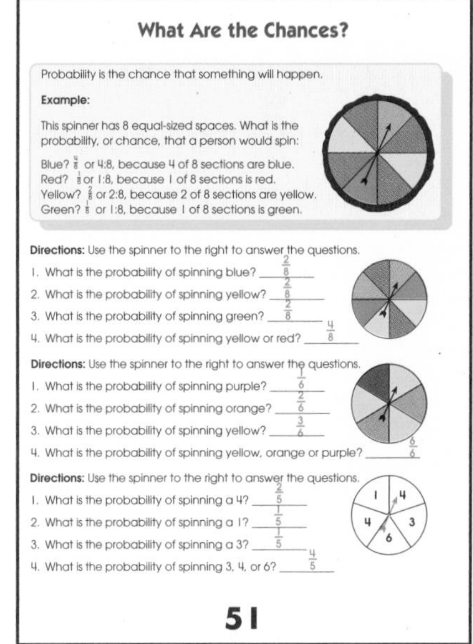

What Are the Chances?

Probability is the chance that something will happen.

Example:

This spinner has 8 equal-sized spaces. What is the probability, or chance, that a person would spin:

Blue? $\frac{4}{8}$ or 4:8, because 4 of 8 sections are blue.
Red? $\frac{1}{8}$ or 1:8, because 1 of 8 sections is red.
Yellow? $\frac{2}{8}$ or 2:8, because 2 of 8 sections are yellow.
Green? $\frac{1}{8}$ or 1:8, because 1 of 8 sections is green.

Directions: Use the spinner to the right to answer the questions.

1. What is the probability of spinning blue? $\frac{2}{8}$
2. What is the probability of spinning yellow? $\frac{2}{8}$
3. What is the probability of spinning green? $\frac{2}{8}$
4. What is the probability of spinning yellow or red? $\frac{4}{8}$

Directions: Use the spinner to the right to answer the questions.

1. What is the probability of spinning purple? $\frac{1}{6}$
2. What is the probability of spinning orange? $\frac{2}{6}$
3. What is the probability of spinning yellow? $\frac{3}{6}$
4. What is the probability of spinning yellow, orange or purple? $\frac{6}{6}$

Directions: Use the spinner to the right to answer the questions.

1. What is the probability of spinning a 4? $\frac{2}{5}$
2. What is the probability of spinning a 1? $\frac{1}{5}$
3. What is the probability of spinning a 3? $\frac{1}{5}$
4. What is the probability of spinning 3, 4, or 6? $\frac{4}{5}$

51

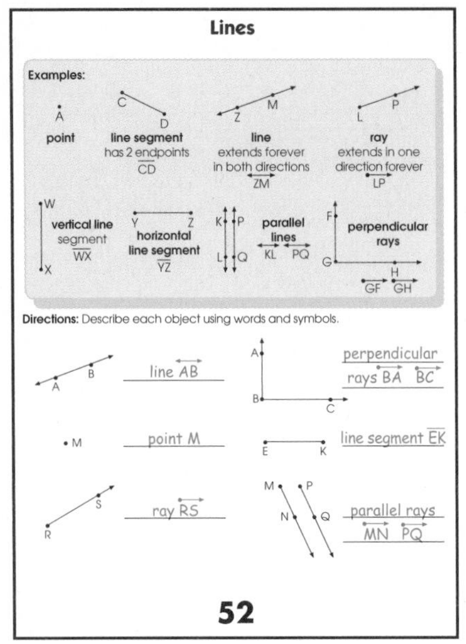

Lines

Examples:

point: A
line segment: has 2 endpoints, $\overline{CD}$
line: extends forever in both directions, $\overleftrightarrow{ZM}$
ray: extends in one direction forever, $\overrightarrow{LP}$
vertical line segment: $\overline{WX}$
horizontal line segment: $\overline{YZ}$
parallel lines: $\overleftrightarrow{KL}$ $\overleftrightarrow{PQ}$
perpendicular rays: $\overrightarrow{GF}$ $\overrightarrow{GH}$

Directions: Describe each object using words and symbols.

line $\overleftrightarrow{AB}$

perpendicular rays $\overrightarrow{BA}$ $\overrightarrow{BC}$

point M

line segment $\overline{EK}$

ray $\overrightarrow{RS}$

parallel rays $\overrightarrow{MN}$ $\overrightarrow{PQ}$

52

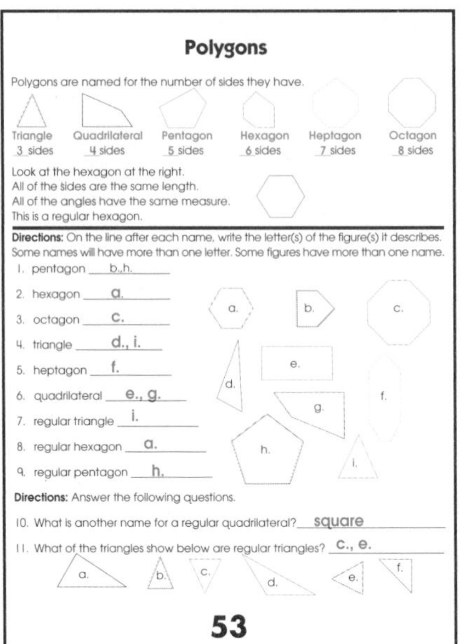

Polygons

Polygons are named for the number of sides they have.

Triangle 3 sides; Quadrilateral 4 sides; Pentagon 5 sides; Hexagon 6 sides; Heptagon 7 sides; Octagon 8 sides

Look at the hexagon at the right.
All of the sides are the same length.
All of the angles have the same measure.
This is a regular hexagon.

Directions: On the line after each name, write the letter(s) of the figure(s) it describes. Some names will have more than one letter. Some figures have more than one name.

1. pentagon b.,h.
2. hexagon a.
3. octagon c.
4. triangle d., i.
5. heptagon f.
6. quadrilateral e., g.
7. regular triangle i.
8. regular hexagon a.
9. regular pentagon h.

Directions: Answer the following questions.

10. What is another name for a regular quadrilateral? square
11. What of the triangles show below are regular triangles? c., e.

53

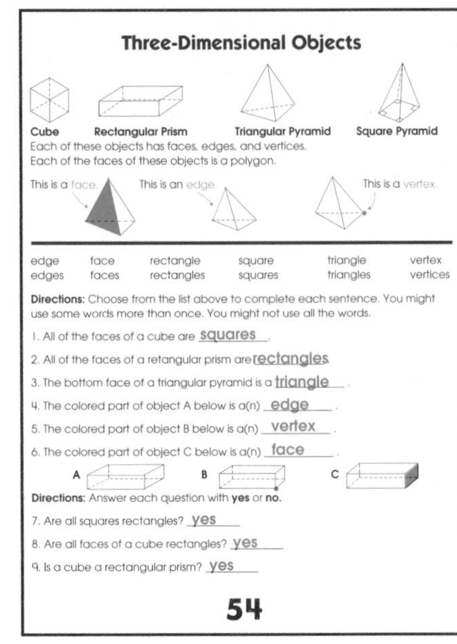

Three-Dimensional Objects

Cube; Rectangular Prism; Triangular Pyramid; Square Pyramid

Each of these objects has faces, edges, and vertices.
Each of the faces of these objects is a polygon.

This is a face. This is an edge. This is a vertex.

edge / edges; face / faces; rectangle / rectangles; square / squares; triangle / triangles; vertex / vertices

Directions: Choose from the list above to complete each sentence. You might use some words more than once. You might not use all the words.

1. All of the faces of a cube are squares.
2. All of the faces of a retangular prism are rectangles.
3. The bottom face of a triangular pyramid is a triangle.
4. The colored part of object A below is a(n) edge.
5. The colored part of object B below is a(n) vertex.
6. The colored part of object C below is a(n) face.

Directions: Answer each question with **yes** or **no.**

7. Are all squares rectangles? yes
8. Are all faces of a cube rectangles? yes
9. Is a cube a rectangular prism? yes

54

Geometric Patterns

Directions: Draw the next three shapes in the pattern.

Directions: Draw a pattern that uses shapes. Have another person draw the next three shapes in the pattern.

Answers will vary.

55

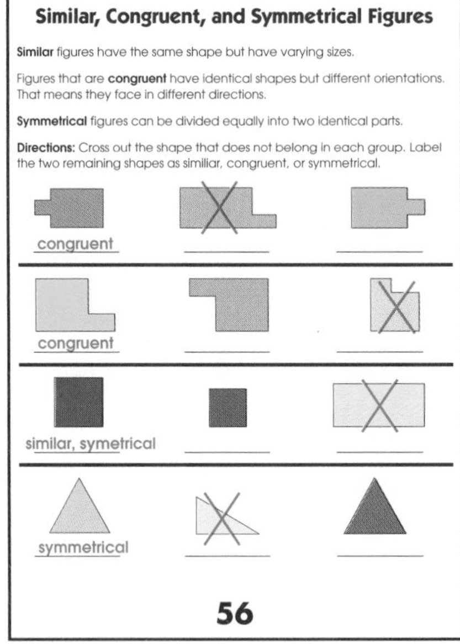

Similar, Congruent, and Symmetrical Figures

Similar figures have the same shape but have varying sizes.

Figures that are **congruent** have identical shapes but different orientations. That means they face in different directions.

Symmetrical figures can be divided equally into two identical parts.

Directions: Cross out the shape that does not belong in each group. Label the two remaining shapes as similiar, congruent, or symmetrical.

congruent

congruent

similar, symetrical

symmetrical

56

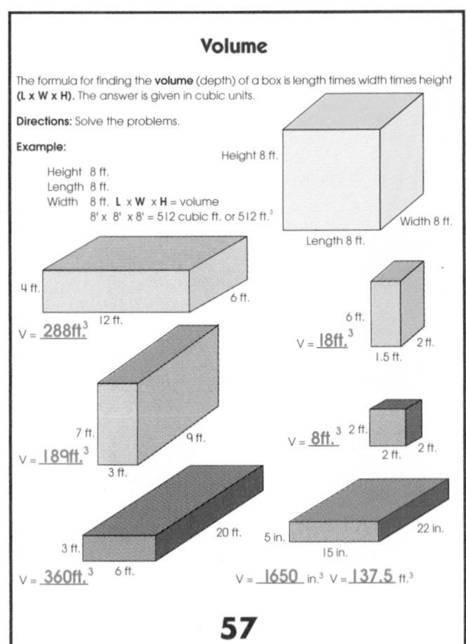

Volume

The formula for finding the **volume** (depth) of a box is length times width times height (**L x W x H**). The answer is given in cubic units.

Directions: Solve the problems.

Example:

Height 8 ft.
Length 8 ft.
Width 8 ft. **L** x **W** x **H** = volume
8' x 8' x 8' = 512 cubic ft. or 512 ft.^{3}

V = 288ft.^{3} (4 ft., 12 ft., 6 ft.)

V = 18ft.^{3} (6 ft., 2 ft., 1.5 ft.)

V = 189ft.^{3} (7 ft., 9 ft., 3 ft.)

V = 8ft.^{3} (2 ft., 2 ft., 2 ft.)

V = 360ft.^{3} (3 ft., 20 ft., 6 ft.)

V = 1650 in.^{3} V = 137.5 ft.^{3} (5 in., 22 in., 15 in.)

57

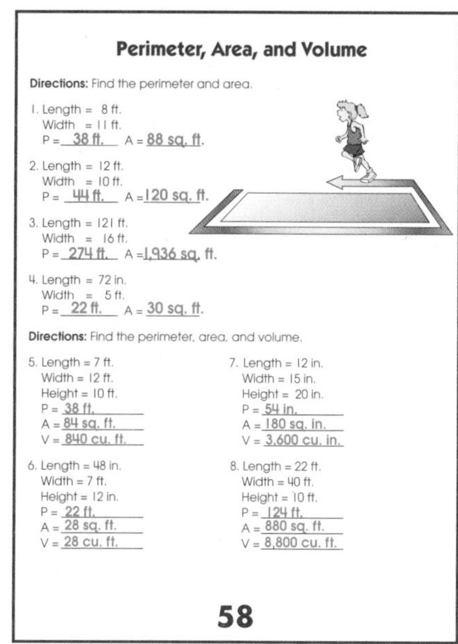

Perimeter, Area, and Volume

Directions: Find the perimeter and area.

1. Length = 8 ft.
   Width = 11 ft.
   P = 38 ft. A = 88 sq. ft.
2. Length = 12 ft.
   Width = 10 ft.
   P = 44 ft. A = 120 sq. ft.
3. Length = 121 ft.
   Width = 16 ft.
   P = 274 ft. A = 1,936 sq. ft.
4. Length = 72 in.
   Width = 5 ft.
   P = 22 ft. A = 30 sq. ft.

Directions: Find the perimeter, area, and volume.

5. Length = 7 ft.
   Width = 12 ft.
   Height = 10 ft.
   P = 38 ft.
   A = 84 sq. ft.
   V = 840 cu. ft.
6. Length = 48 in.
   Width = 7 ft.
   Height = 12 in.
   P = 22 ft.
   A = 28 sq. ft.
   V = 28 cu. ft.
7. Length = 12 in.
   Width = 15 in.
   Height = 20 in.
   P = 54 in.
   A = 180 sq. in.
   V = 3,600 cu. in.
8. Length = 22 ft.
   Width = 40 ft.
   Height = 10 ft.
   P = 124 ft.
   A = 880 sq. ft.
   V = 8,800 cu. ft.

58

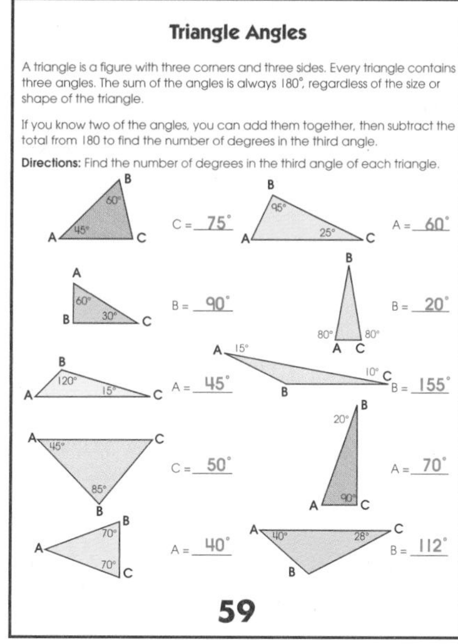

Triangle Angles

A triangle is a figure with three corners and three sides. Every triangle contains three angles. The sum of the angles is always 180°, regardless of the size or shape of the triangle.

If you know two of the angles, you can add them together, then subtract the total from 180 to find the number of degrees in the third angle.

Directions: Find the number of degrees in the third angle of each triangle.

C = 75° A = 60°
B = 90° B = 20°
A = 45° B = 155°
C = 50° A = 70°
A = 40° B = 112°

59

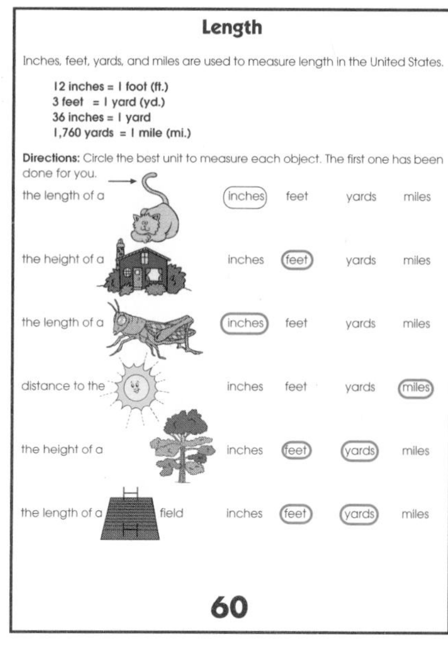

Length

Inches, feet, yards, and miles are used to measure length in the United States.

12 inches = 1 foot (ft.)
3 feet = 1 yard (yd.)
36 inches = 1 yard
1,760 yards = 1 mile (mi.)

Directions: Circle the best unit to measure each object. The first one has been done for you.

the length of a	**inches**	feet	yards	miles
the height of a	inches	**feet**	yards	miles
the length of a	**inches**	feet	yards	miles
distance to the	inches	feet	yards	**miles**
the height of a	inches	**feet**	**yards**	miles
the length of a field	inches	**feet**	**yards**	miles

60

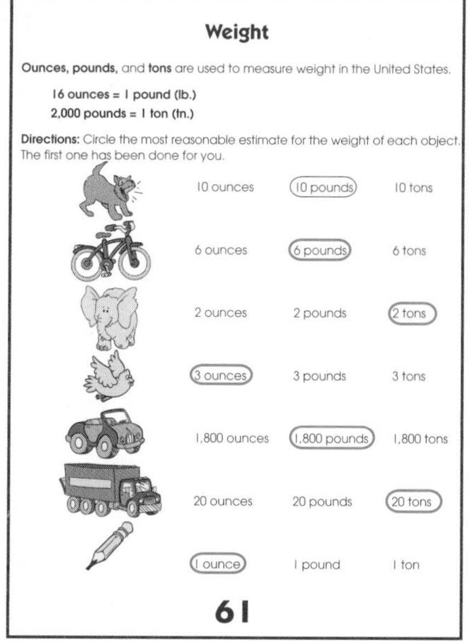

Weight

Ounces, pounds, and **tons** are used to measure weight in the United States.

16 ounces = 1 pound (lb.)
2,000 pounds = 1 ton (tn.)

Directions: Circle the most reasonable estimate for the weight of each object. The first one has been done for you.

10 ounces	**10 pounds**	10 tons
6 ounces	**6 pounds**	6 tons
2 ounces	2 pounds	**2 tons**
3 ounces	3 pounds	3 tons
1,800 ounces	**1,800 pounds**	1,800 tons
20 ounces	20 pounds	**20 tons**
1 ounce	1 pound	1 ton

61

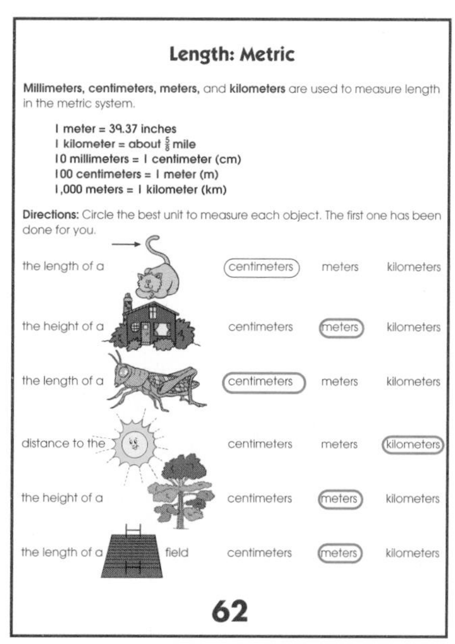

Length: Metric

Millimeters, centimeters, meters, and **kilometers** are used to measure length in the metric system.

1 meter = 39.37 inches
1 kilometer = about $\frac{5}{8}$ mile
10 millimeters = 1 centimeter (cm)
100 centimeters = 1 meter (m)
1,000 meters = 1 kilometer (km)

Directions: Circle the best unit to measure each object. The first one has been done for you.

the length of a	**centimeters**	meters	kilometers
the height of a	centimeters	**meters**	kilometers
the length of a	**centimeters**	meters	kilometers
distance to the	centimeters	meters	**kilometers**
the height of a	centimeters	**meters**	kilometers
the length of a field	centimeters	**meters**	kilometers

62

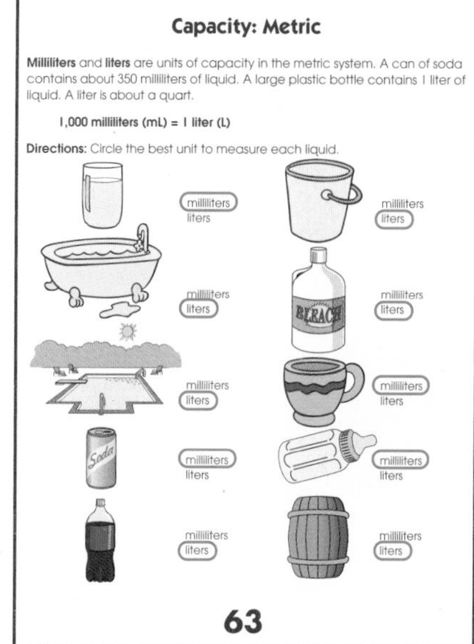

Capacity: Metric

Milliliters and **liters** are units of capacity in the metric system. A can of soda contains about 350 milliliters of liquid. A large plastic bottle contains 1 liter of liquid. A liter is about a quart.

1,000 milliliters (mL) = 1 liter (L)

Directions: Circle the best unit to measure each liquid.

milliliters / liters	milliliters / **liters**
milliliters / **liters**	milliliters / **liters**
milliliters / **liters**	**milliliters** / liters
milliliters / liters	**milliliters** / liters
milliliters / **liters**	milliliters / **liters**

63

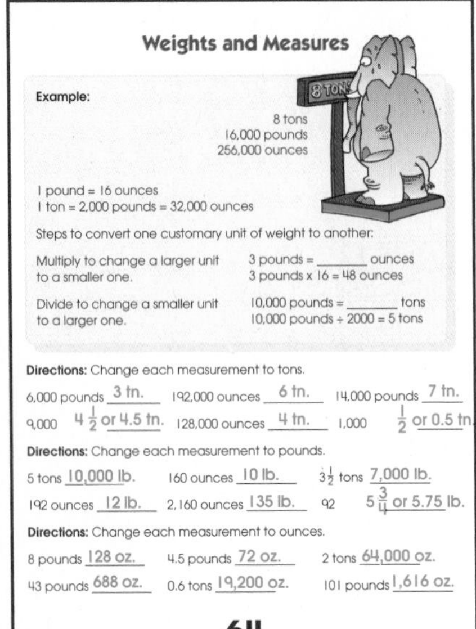
Weights and Measures

Example:

8 tons
16,000 pounds
256,000 ounces

1 pound = 16 ounces
1 ton = 2,000 pounds = 32,000 ounces

Steps to convert one customary unit of weight to another:

Multiply to change a larger unit to a smaller one. 3 pounds = ______ ounces
3 pounds x 16 = 48 ounces

Divide to change a smaller unit to a larger one. 10,000 pounds = ______ tons
10,000 pounds ÷ 2000 = 5 tons

Directions: Change each measurement to tons.

6,000 pounds 3 tn. 192,000 ounces 6 tn. 14,000 pounds 7 tn.
9,000 $4\frac{1}{2}$ or 4.5 tn. 128,000 ounces 4 tn. 1,000 $\frac{1}{2}$ or 0.5 tn.

Directions: Change each measurement to pounds.

5 tons 10,000 lb. 160 ounces 10 lb. $3\frac{1}{2}$ tons 7,000 lb.
192 ounces 12 lb. 2,160 ounces 135 lb. 92 $5\frac{3}{4}$ or 5.75 lb.

Directions: Change each measurement to ounces.

8 pounds 128 oz. 4.5 pounds 72 oz. 2 tons 64,000 oz.
43 pounds 688 oz. 0.6 tons 19,200 oz. 101 pounds 1,616 oz.

64

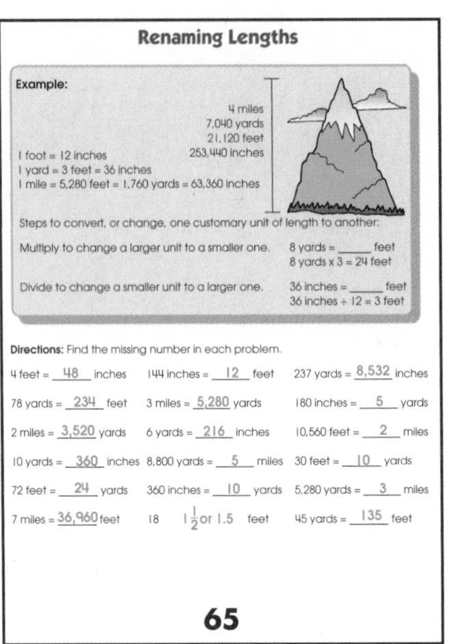
Renaming Lengths

Example:

4 miles
7,040 yards
21,120 feet
253,440 inches

1 foot = 12 inches
1 yard = 3 feet = 36 inches
1 mile = 5,280 feet = 1,760 yards = 63,360 inches

Steps to convert, or change, one customary unit of length to another:

Multiply to change a larger unit to a smaller one. 8 yards = ______ feet
8 yards x 3 = 24 feet

Divide to change a smaller unit to a larger one. 36 inches = ______ feet
36 inches ÷ 12 = 3 feet

Directions: Find the missing number in each problem.

4 feet = 48 inches 144 inches = 12 feet 237 yards = 8,532 inches
78 yards = 234 feet 3 miles = 5,280 yards 180 inches = 5 yards
2 miles = 3,520 yards 6 yards = 216 inches 10,560 feet = 2 miles
10 yards = 360 inches 8,800 yards = 5 miles 30 feet = 10 yards
72 feet = 24 yards 360 inches = 10 yards 5,280 yards = 3 miles
7 miles = 36,960 feet 18 $1\frac{1}{2}$ or 1.5 feet 45 yards = 135 feet

65

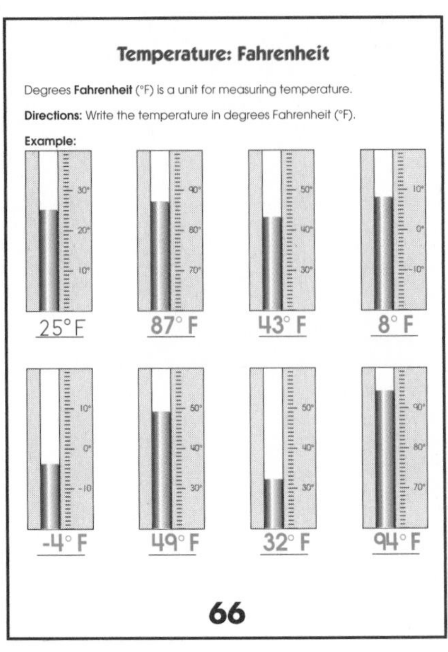
Temperature: Fahrenheit

Degrees **Fahrenheit** (°F) is a unit for measuring temperature.

Directions: Write the temperature in degrees Fahrenheit (°F).

Example:

25° F 87° F 43° F 8° F
-4° F 49° F 32° F 94° F

66

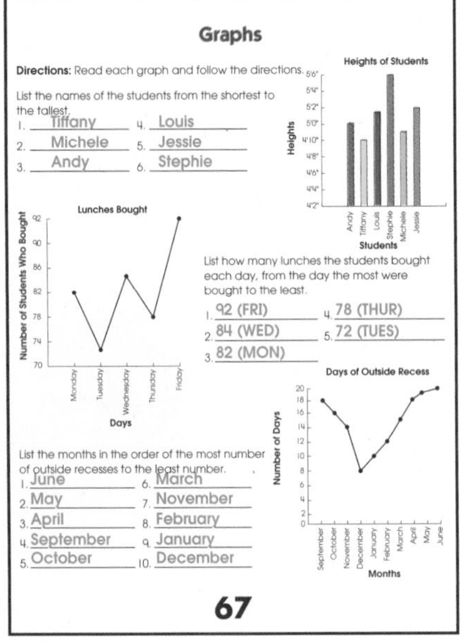
Graphs

Directions: Read each graph and follow the directions.

List the names of the students from the shortest to the tallest.

1. Tiffany 4. Louis
2. Michele 5. Jessie
3. Andy 6. Stephie

List how many lunches the students bought each day, from the day the most were bought to the least.

1. 92 (FRI) 4. 78 (THUR)
2. 84 (WED) 5. 72 (TUES)
3. 82 (MON)

List the months in the order of the most number of outside recesses to the least number.

1. June 6. March
2. May 7. November
3. April 8. February
4. September 9. January
5. October 10. December

67

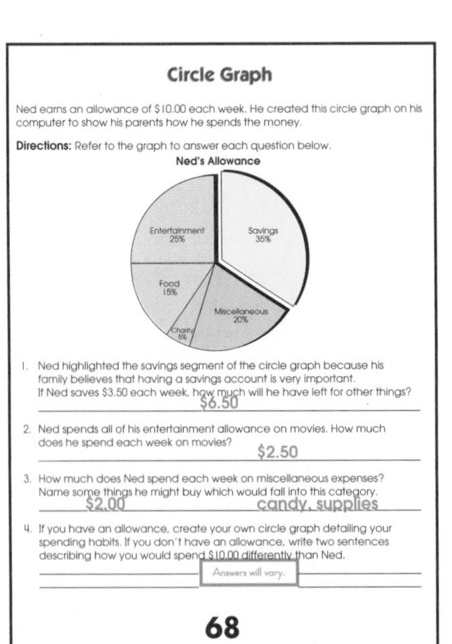
Circle Graph

Ned earns an allowance of $10.00 each week. He created this circle graph on his computer to show his parents how he spends the money.

Directions: Refer to the graph to answer each question below.

1. Ned highlighted the savings segment of the circle graph because his family believes that having a savings account is very important. If Ned saves $3.50 each week, how much will he have left for other things? $6.50
2. Ned spends all of his entertainment allowance on movies. How much does he spend each week on movies? $2.50
3. How much does Ned spend each week on miscellaneous expenses? Name some things he might buy which would fall into this category. $2.00 candy, supplies
4. If you have an allowance, create your own circle graph detailing your spending habits. If you don't have an allowance, write two sentences describing how you would spend $10.00 differently than Ned. Answers will vary.

68

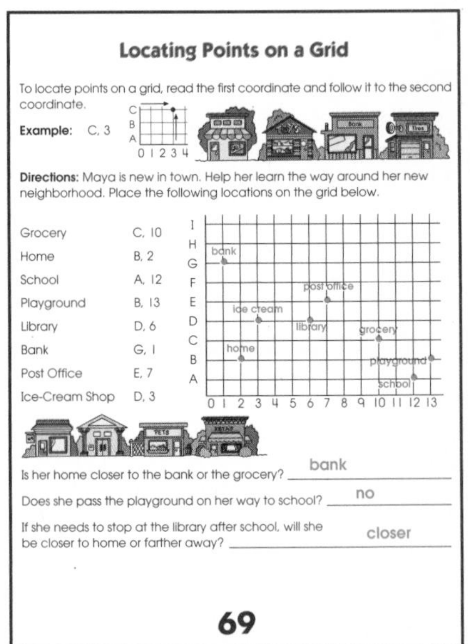
Locating Points on a Grid

To locate points on a grid, read the first coordinate and follow it to the second coordinate.

Example: C, 3

Directions: Maya is new in town. Help her learn the way around her new neighborhood. Place the following locations on the grid below.

Grocery	C, 10
Home	B, 2
School	A, 12
Playground	B, 13
Library	D, 6
Bank	G, 1
Post Office	E, 7
Ice-Cream Shop	D, 3

Is her home closer to the bank or the grocery? bank

Does she pass the playground on her way to school? no

If she needs to stop at the library after school, will she be closer to home or farther away? closer

69